D1322707

Halsbury's Statutes

Consolidated Index
2009–2010

Including alphabetical and chronological lists of statutes printed in the volumes

Editor
MATTHEW YORE, LLB

Compiled by the editorial staff of
Halsbury's Statutes and Statutory Instruments

Important
This volume supersedes the Consolidated Index for 2008–2009 which
should now be discarded

Members of the LexisNexis Group worldwide

United Kingdom	LexisNexis, a Division of Reed Elsevier (UK) Ltd, Halsbury House, 35 Chancery Lane, London, WC2A 1EL, and London House, 20–22 East London Street, Edinburgh, EH7 4BQ
Australia	LexisNexis Butterworths, Chatswood, New South Wales
Austria	LexisNexis Verlag ARD Orac GmbH & Co KG, Vienna
Benelux	LexisNexis Benelux, Amsterdam
Canada	LexisNexis Canada, Markham, Ontario
China	LexisNexis China, Beijing and Shanghai
France	LexisNexis SA, Paris
Germany	LexisNexis Deutschland GmbH, Munster
Hong Kong	LexisNexis Hong Kong, Hong Kong
India	LexisNexis India, New Delhi
Italy	Giuffrè Editore, Milan
Japan	LexisNexis Japan, Tokyo
Malaysia	Malayan Law Journal Sdn Bhd, Kuala Lumpur
New Zealand	LexisNexis NZ Ltd, Wellington
Poland	Wydawnictwo Prawnicze LexisNexis Sp, Warsaw
Singapore	LexisNexis Singapore, Singapore
South Africa	LexisNexis Butterworths, Durban
USA	LexisNexis, Dayton, Ohio

© Reed Elsevier (UK) Ltd 2009
Published by LexisNexis

This is a Butterworths title

A CIP Catalogue record for this book is available from the British Library

ISBN 13: 978 1 405 742 382

Typeset by Letterpart Ltd, Reigate, Surrey

Printed and bound in the UK by CPI William Clowes, Beccles NR34 7TL

Visit LexisNexis at www.lexisnexis.co.uk

Table of Contents

Introduction

Tables of Statutes   The first part of this volume contains alphabetical and chronological lists of all statutes printed in the current volumes of Halsbury's Statutes of England and Wales published as at 1 November 2009, and in the Current Statutes Service binders up to and including Issue 141. Statutes printed in the Service rather than a bound volume are indicated by the letter **(S)** following their volume number.

Consolidated Index   The second part of this volume contains the consolidated index to the current volumes of Halsbury's Statutes of England and Wales published as at 1 November 2009, and to the Current Statutes Service binders up to and including Issue 141. A complete list of the volumes to which this index refers is set out in the **Halsbury's Statutes Title Scheme** printed overleaf.

Entries in this index differ depending on whether the information can be found in a bound volume (indicated by the volume number in bold) or a Service binder (indicated by the volume number in bold followed by the letter **(S)**), for example:

> **land drainage—**
>   byelaws, **32(S)**, Open Spaces 109
>   Coal Authority, powers, **29**, 160–3
>   town development, works during, **46**, [14]

The numbers given are either page numbers or, for the more recently reissued volumes, paragraph numbers which appear in square brackets.

Volumes published after 1 November 2009 will be covered by their own indexes which will supersede the relevant entries in this index.

November 2009

Halsbury's Statutes Title Scheme

Volumes 1(1), 1(2) (2008 Reissue)
Agency
Agriculture, Fisheries and Food

Volume 2 (2007 Reissue)
Allotments (See Agriculture, Fisheries and Food)
Animals
Arbitration
Architects

Volume 3 (2005 Reissue)
Armed Forces

Volume 4(1) (2008 Reissue)
Aviation

Volume 4(2) (2008 Reissue)
Bankruptcy and Insolvency

Volume 5(1) (2007 Reissue)
Betting, Gaming and Lotteries

Volume 5(2) (2007 Reissue)
Bills of Exchange; Building Societies (see Financial Services and Institutions)
Bills of Sale (see Sale of Goods and Consumer Law)
Burial and Cremation
Carriers
Charities

Volume 6 (2006 Reissue)
Children

Volume 7(1) (2008 Reissue)
Civil Liberties and Human Rights

Volume 7(2) (2008 Reissue)
Commons (see Land, Tenancies and Housing)
Commonwealth and Other Territories

Volumes 8 (1999 Reissue), 8(1) (2007 Reissue)
Companies

Volume 9 (2004 Reissue)
Compulsory Acquisition

Volume 10 (2007 Reissue)
Constitutional Law

Volume 11(1) (2006 Reissue)
Consumer Credit (see Sale of Goods and Consumer Law)
Contract
Copyright, Patents and Designs
Coroners

Volumes 11(2), 11(3) (2006 Reissue), 11(4) (2008 Reissue)
Courts and Legal Services

Volumes 12(1), 12(2), 12(3), 12(4) (2008 Reissue)
Criminal Law

Volume 13 (2008 Reissue)
Crown Proceedings
Culture, Entertainment and Sport
Customs and Excise
Damages
Distress
Easements and Profits à Prendre (see Land, Tenancies and Housing)

Volume 14 (2003 Reissue)
Ecclesiastical Law

Volumes 15(1), 15(2) (2007 Reissue)
Education

Volume 15(3) (2006 Reissue)
Elections

Volume 16 (2009 Reissue)
Employment

Volumes 17(1), 17(2) (2009 Reissue)
Energy and Mining

Volume 18 (2009 Reissue)
European Community
Evidence
Executors and Administrators
Explosives
Extradition
Fire and Rescue Services
Forestry
Health and Safety at Work

Volumes 19(1), 19(2) (2008 Reissue)
Financial Services and Institutions

Enquiry Bureau   hsieb@lexisnexis.co.uk

Volume 19(3) (2009 Reissue)
Judgments and Enforcement
Juries
Land Drainage
Libel and Slander
Licensing and Liquor Duties
Limitation of Actions

Volumes 20, 21, 22, 23, 24 (2009 Reissue)
Land, Tenancies and Housing

Volumes 25(1), 25(2), 26(1), 26(2) (2009 Reissue)
Local Government

Volume 27 (2006 Reissue)
Markets and Fairs
Matrimonial Law and Civil Partnerships

Volume 28 (2008 Reissue)
Medicine and Pharmacy

Volume 29 (2009 Reissue)
Mental Health

Volume 30 (2007 Reissue)
Money (see Financial Services and Institutions)
National Health Service

Volume 31 (2006 Reissue)
Nationality and Immigration
Negligence
Northern Ireland

Volume 32 (2007 Reissue)
Open Spaces and National Heritage
Parliament
Partnership

Volume 33(1) (2007 Reissue)
Peerages and Dignities
Pensions and Superannuation

Volume 33(2) (2007 Reissue)
Perpetuities
Police

Volume 34 (2004 Reissue)
Ports and Harbours (See Shipping and Ports)
Postal Services
Prisons and Prisoners (See Criminal Law)

Volumes 35(1), 35(2) (2007 Reissue)
Public Health and Environmental
   Protection

Volumes 36, 37, 38(1), 38(2) (2009 Reissue)
Registration Concerning the Individual
Roads, Railways and Transport

Volume 39(1) (2008 Reissue)
Sale of Goods and Consumer Law
Sheriffs and Bailiffs

Volume 39(2) (2008 Reissue)
Shipping and Ports

Volumes 40(1), 40(2) (2006 Reissue)
Social Security

Volume 41 (2008 Reissue)
Stamp Duties
Statutes

Volumes 42, 43(1), 43(2), 44(1) (2005 Reissue), 44(2), 44(3), 44(4) (2007 Reissue)
Taxation

Volume 45 (2008 Reissue)
Telecommunications and Broadcasting
Time
Tort

Volume 46 (2004 Reissue)
Town and Country Planning

Volume 47 (2004 Reissue)
Trade and Industry

Volume 48 (2001 Reissue)
Trade Marks and Trade Names
Trusts and Settlements

Volume 49 (2004 Reissue)
Water

Volume 50 (2006 Reissue)
Value Added Tax
War and Emergency
*Weights and Measures (see Sale of Goods and
   Consumer Law)*
Wills

Alphabetical List of Statutes

The following is an alphabetical list of all Statutes printed in the Volumes as at 1 November 2009, and all Statutes printed in the Service up to and including those in Issue 141 (published in September 2009).

A

Abortion Act 1967	**12(1)**, 484
Access to Health Records Act 1990	**7(1)**, 308
Access to Justice Act 1999	**11(3)**, 391
Access to Medical Reports Act 1988	**28**, 655
Access to Neighbouring Land Act 1992	**23**, 91
Accession Declaration Act 1910	**10**, 132
Accessories and Abettors Act 1861	**12(1)**, 120
Accommodation Agencies Act 1953	**21**, 133
Acquisition of Land Act 1981	**9**, 404
Acquisition of Land (Authorisation Procedure) Act 1946	**9**, 124
Act of Settlement (1700)	**10**, 50
Act of Supremacy (1558)	**14**, 46
Act of Uniformity 1662	**14**, 52
Activity Centres (Young Persons' Safety) Act 1995	**6**, 841
Acts of Parliament (Commencement) Act 1793	**41**, 701
Acts of Parliament (Expiration) Act 1808	**41**, 703
Acts of Parliament Numbering and Citation Act 1962	**41**, 767
Aden, Perim and Kuria Muria Islands Act 1967	**7(2)**, 488
Administration of Estates Act 1925	**18**, 538
Administration of Estates Act 1971	**18**, 617
Administration of Estates (Small Payments) Act 1965	**18**, 602
Administration of Justice Act 1920	**19(3)**, 11
Administration of Justice Act 1925—	
ss 22, 29	**4(2)**, 33
ss 23, 29	**39(1)**, 48
Administration of Justice Act 1956—	
ss 40, 51, 55, 57, Sch 1, Pt II	**19(3)**, 32
ss 55, 57, Sch 1	**31**, 839
Administration of Justice Act 1960—	
ss 1, 2, 4–6, 9, 17–20, Sch 2, Pt I	**12(1)**, 365
ss 12, 13, 17, 18, 20, Sch 2	**11(2)**, 149
ss 14, 15, 17(1)(c), (2), (6), 18, 20, Sch 2	**7(1)**, 39
Administration of Justice Act 1964	**25(1)**, 722
Administration of Justice Act 1965	**11(2)**, 159
Administration of Justice Act 1968	**11(2)**, 166
Administration of Justice Act 1969—	
ss 12–16, 34–36	**11(2)**, 173
ss 20, 21, 34, 36	**31**, 851
Administration of Justice Act 1970—	
ss 1, 41, 52, 54, Schs 9, 11	**11(2)**, 181
ss 10, 54	**11(1)**, 734
ss 11, 28, 54, Schs 4, 8	**4(2)**, 40
ss 31–35, 54	**31**, 855
ss 36, 38A, 39, 54	**21**, 440
ss 40, 54	**12(1)**, 682
ss 44, 44A, 54	**19(3)**, 38
Administration of Justice Act 1973—	
ss 8, 21	**21**, 482
ss 5, 9, 12, 21	**11(2)**, 253
ss 18, 21	**12(1)**, 711
Administration of Justice Act 1977—	
ss 2, 3, 23, 31, 32, Schs 4, 5	**11(2)**, 370

Administration of Justice Act 1977—*contd*
  ss 4, 32, Sch 5, Pt I .... **19(3)**, 93
  ss 7, 32(1), (5) **8**, 86
Administration of Justice Act 1982—
  ss 1, 5, 73(1), (3), (4)(a), 76–78 .... **13**, 1268
  ss 2, 73, 76–78 .... **45**, 1582
  ss 15, 37–47, 55, 73, 75–78, Sch 9 .... **11(2)**, 1012
  ss 20–25, 27, 28, 73, 76–78, Sch 2 .... **50**, 787
  ss 68, 69, 72, 73, 76–78, Schs 6, 7 .... **31**, 1160
Administration of Justice Act 1985—
  ss 8–43, 47, 48, 53, 56, 67–69, Schs 2–9 .... **11(3)**, 2
  ss 49, 50, 56, 68, 69 .... **18**, 686
  ss 64, 68, 69 .... **31**, 1168
Administration of Justice (Appeals) Act 1934 .... **11(2)**, 131
Administration of Justice (Miscellaneous Provisions) Act 1933—
  ss 2, 10, Sch 2 .... **12(1)**, 250
  ss 7, 9, 10 .... **13**, 7
Admiralty Offences (Colonial) Act 1849 .... **7(2)**, 297
Admiralty Offences (Colonial) Act 1860 .... **7(2)**, 300
Admiralty Pensions Act 1921 .... **3**, 223
Admission to Holy Communion Measure 1972 .... **14**, 773
Adoption Act 1976 .... **6**, 231
Adoption and Children Act 2002 .... **6**, 1092
Adoption (Intercountry Aspects) Act 1999 .... **6**, 950
Age-Related Payments Act 2004 .... **40(2)**, 716
Aggravated Vehicle-Taking Act 1992 .... **12(2)**, 174
Agricultural Credits Act 1923 .... **1(1)**, 284
Agricultural Credits Act 1928 .... **1(1)**, 313
Agricultural Credits Act 1932 .... **1(1)**, 331
Agricultural Holdings Act 1986 .... **22**, 636
Agricultural Holdings (Amendment) Act 1990 .... **23**, 81
Agricultural Land (Removal of Surface Soil) Act 1953 .... **1(1)**, 458
Agricultural Land (Utilisation) Act 1931 .... **1(1)**, 327
Agricultural Marketing Act 1958 .... **1(1)**, 491
Agricultural Marketing Act 1983 .... **1(2)**, 219
Agricultural Mortgage Corporation Act 1956 .... **1(1)**, 476
Agricultural Produce (Grading and Marking) Act 1928 .... **1(1)**, 304
Agricultural Produce (Grading and Marking) Amendment Act 1931 ... **1(1)**, 324
Agricultural Research etc (Pensions) Act 1961 .... **1(1)**, 561
Agricultural Statistics Act 1979 .... **1(2)**, 168
Agricultural Tenancies Act 1995 .... **23**, 388
Agricultural Wages Act 1948 .... **1(1)**, 414
Agriculture Act 1947 .... **1(1)**, 388
Agriculture Act 1957 .... **1(1)**, 483
Agriculture Act 1958 .... **1(1)**, 547
Agriculture Act 1967 .... **1(1)**, 639
Agriculture Act 1970—
  ss 28–30, 32, 33, 37–56, 58–87, 110, 111, 113, Sch 3 .... **1(1)**, 829
  ss 92, 98, 113 .... **49**, 383
  ss 106, 110, 111, 113(1), (2) **2**, 297
Agriculture Act 1986 .... **1(2)**, 449
Agriculture Act 1993 .... **1(2)**, 581
Agriculture (Amendment) Act 1984 .... **1(2)**, 253
Agriculture and Forestry (Financial Provisions) Act 1991 .... **1(2)**, 569
Agriculture and Horticulture Act 1964 .... **1(1)**, 596
Agriculture (Artificial Insemination) Act 1946 .... **2**, 232
Agriculture (Miscellaneous Provisions) Act 1949 .... **1(1)**, 443
Agriculture (Miscellaneous Provisions) Act 1954 .... **1(1)**, 463
Agriculture (Miscellaneous Provisions) Act 1963 .... **1(1)**, 562
Agriculture (Miscellaneous Provisions) Act 1968—
  ss 2, 3, 6–8, 50, 51, 53, 54 .... **2**, 283
  ss 12, 13, 15, 17, 46, 50–54, Schs 3, 8 .... **1(1)**, 782
  ss 48, 54 .... **32**, 243
Agriculture (Miscellaneous Provisions) Act 1972—
  ss 9, 10, 12, 17, 20, 25–27, Sch 6 .... **1(1)**, 900

Agriculture (Miscellaneous Provisions) Act 1972—*contd*
ss 19, 26(1), (2), 27(1) **2**, 311
Agriculture (Miscellaneous Provisions) Act 1976 .... **1(2)**, 60
Agriculture (Safety, Health and Welfare Provisions) Act 1956 .... **1(1)**, 478
AIDS (Control) Act 1987 .... **30**, 513
Air Force Act 1955 .... **3**, 673
Air Force (Constitution) Act 1917 .... **3**, 206
Aircraft and Shipbuilding Industries Act 1977 .... **47**, 320
Airports Act 1986 .... **4(1)**, 390
Alcoholic Liquor Duties Act 1979 .... **19(3)**, 453
Alderney (Transfer of Property, etc) Act 1923 .... **7(2)**, 338
Aliens' Employment Act 1955 .... **31**, 53
Aliens Restriction (Amendment) Act 1919 .... **31**, 20
Allotments Act 1922 .... **1(1)**, 270
Allotments Act 1925 .... **1(1)**, 286
Allotments Act 1950 .... **1(1)**, 445
Ancient Monuments and Archaeological Areas Act 1979 .... **32**, 321
Anglo-Portuguese Commercial Treaty Act 1914 .... **48**, 37
Anglo-Portuguese Commercial Treaty Act 1916 .... **48**, 43
Anguilla Act 1980 .... **7(2)**, 586
Animal Boarding Establishments Act 1963 .... **2**, 261
Animal Health Act 1981 .... **2**, 377
Animal Health Act 2002 .... **2**, 671
Animal Health (Amendment) Act 1998 .... **2**, 658
Animal Health and Welfare Act 1984 .... **2**, 548
Animal Welfare Act 2006 .... **2**, 705
Animals Act 1971 .... **2**, 301
Animals (Cruel Poisons) Act 1962 .... **2**, 259
Animals (Scientific Procedures) Act 1986 .... **2**, 555
Antarctic Act 1994 .... **10**, 1110
Antarctic Minerals Act 1989 .... **17(1)**, 973
Antarctic Treaty Act 1967 .... **2**, 278
Anti-social Behaviour Act 2003—
ss 1–11, 11A–11L, 17, 30–32, 34–36, 39, 85, 88, 91–97, Sch 3 .... **12(3)**, 702
ss 19–29, 93, 94, 96, 97 .... **6**, 1261
ss 40–45, 47–52, 54–56, 93, 94, 96, 97 .... **35(2)**, 712
ss 65–84, 93, 94, 96, 97 .... **24**, 190
Anti-terrorism, Crime and Security Act 2001 .... **12(3)**, 114
"Anzac" (Restriction on Trade Use of Word) Act 1916 .... **48**, 44
Appellate Jurisdiction Act 1876 .... **11(2)**, 84
Appellate Jurisdiction Act 1887 .... **11(2)**, 95
Appellate Jurisdiction Act 1908 .... **11(2)**, 115
Appellate Jurisdiction Act 1947 .... **11(2)**, 141
Appointment of Bishops Act 1533 .... **14**, 23
Apportionment Act 1870 .... **20**, 307
Arbitration Act 1950 .... **2**, 782
Arbitration Act 1996 .... **2**, 812
Arbitration (International Investment Disputes) Act 1966 .... **2**, 792
Architects Act 1997 .... **2**, 912
Armed Forces Act 1966 .... **3**, 1206
Armed Forces Act 1971 .... **3**, 1289
Armed Forces Act 1976 .... **3**, 1301
Armed Forces Act 1981 .... **3**, 1384
Armed Forces Act 1986 .... **3**, 1423
Armed Forces Act 1991 .... **3**, 1461
Armed Forces Act 1996 .... **3**, 1631
Armed Forces Act 2001 .... **3**, 1660
Armed Forces Act 2006 .... **3(S)**, Armed Forces, 1
Armed Forces Discipline Act 2000 .... **3**, 1655
Armed Forces (Housing Loans) Act 1949 .... **3**, 275
Armed Forces (Housing Loans) Act 1958 .... **3**, 1183
Armed Forces (Housing Loans) Act 1965 .... **3**, 1205
Armed Forces (Pensions and Compensation) Act 2004 .... **3**, 1723
Arms Control and Disarmament (Inspections) Act 1991 .... **10**, 1096
Arms Control and Disarmament (Inspections) Act 2003 .... **10**, 1245

Arms Control and Disarmament (Privileges and Immunities) Act 1988 .... **10**, 1094
Army Act 1955 .... **3**, 386
Army Act 1992 .... **3**, 1487
Army and Air Force Act 1961 .... **3**, 1196
Army and Air Force (Women's Service) Act 1948 .... **3**, 272
Army (Artillery, etc) Pensions Act 1833 .... **3**, 45
Army Chaplains Act 1868 .... **14**, 210
Army Pensions Act 1914 .... **3**, 195
Army Schools Act 1891 .... **15(1)**, 103
Asylum and Immigration Act 1996 .... **31**, 281
Asylum and Immigration Appeals Act 1993 .... **31**, 276
Asylum and Immigration (Treatment of Claimants, etc) Act 2004 .... **31**, 654
Atomic Energy Act 1946 .... **17(1)**, 59
Atomic Energy Act 1989 .... **17(1)**, 969
Atomic Energy Authority Act 1954 .... **17(1)**, 105
Atomic Energy Authority Act 1959 .... **17(1)**, 325
Atomic Energy Authority Act 1971 .... **17(1)**, 586
Atomic Energy Authority Act 1986 .... **17(1)**, 744
Atomic Energy Authority Act 1995 .... **17(2)**, 344
Atomic Energy Authority (Weapons Group) Act 1973 .... **17(1)**, 617
Atomic Energy (Miscellaneous Provisions) Act 1981 .... **17(1)**, 680
Atomic Weapons Establishment Act 1991 .... **10**, 568
Attachment of Earnings Act 1971 .... **19(3)**, 41
Attendance of Witnesses Act 1854 .... **18**, 147
Auctioneers Act 1845 .... **39(1)**, 17
Auctions (Bidding Agreements) Act 1927 .... **39(1)**, 49
Auctions (Bidding Agreements) Act 1969 .... **39(1)**, 110
Audit Commission Act 1998 .... **26(1)**, 425
Australia Act 1986 .... **7(2)**, 601
Australian Constitution (Public Record Copy) Act 1990 .... **18**, 303
Austrian State Treaty Act 1955 .... **10**, 820
Aviation and Maritime Security Act 1990—
    ss 1, 48, 50–52, 54, Sch 4 .... **4(1)**, 511
    ss 9–46, 50–54, Sch 2 .... **39(2)**, 574
Aviation (Offences) Act 2003 .... **4(1)**, 703
Aviation Security Act 1982 .... **4(1)**, 307

B

Bahamas Independence Act 1973 .... **7(2)**, 513
Bail Act 1976 .... **12(1)**, 749
Bail (Amendment) Act 1993 .... **12(2)**, 220
Bangladesh Act 1973 .... **7(2)**, 520
Bank Act 1892 .... **19(1)**, 120
Bank Charter Act 1844 .... **19(1)**, 37
Bank Notes Act 1852 .... **19(1)**, 40
Bank of England Act 1694 .... **19(1)**, 30
Bank of England Act 1946 .... **19(1)**, 205
Bank of England Act 1998 .... **19(1)**, 1222
Bankers' Books Evidence Act 1879 .... **18**, 165
Banking Act 1979 .... **19(1)**, 518
Banking Act 2009 .... **19(S)**, Financial, 41
Banking and Financial Dealings Act 1971—
    entire Act .... **19(1)**, 369
    ss 1, 4, 5, Schs 1, 2 .... **45**, 1538
Banking (Special Provisions) Act 2008 .... **19(2)**, 611
Bankruptcy (Scotland) Act 1985 .... **4(2)**, 51
Baptismal Fees Abolition Act 1872 .... **14**, 239
Baptismal Registers Measure 1961 .... **14**, 526
Barbados Independence Act 1966 .... **7(2)**, 478
Barracks Act 1890 .... **3**, 145
Bearing of Armour (1313) **32**, 1034
Bees Act 1980 .... **2**, 372
Behring Sea Award Act 1894 .... **1(1)**, 203

Belize Act 1981 .... **7(2)**, 587
Benefices Act 1898 .... **14**, 250
Benefices Measure 1972 .... **14**, 801
Benefices (Sequestrations) Measure 1933 .... **14**, 353
Benefices (Transfer of Rights of Patronage) Measure 1930 .... **14**, 338
Bermuda Constitution Act 1967 .... **7(2)**, 487
Betting and Gaming Duties Act 1981 .... **5(1)**, 46
Betting, Gaming and Lotteries Act 1963 .... **5(1)**, 13
Bill of Rights (1688) **10**, 42
Bills of Exchange Act 1882 .... **19(1)**, 48
Bills of Exchange (Time of Noting) Act 1917 .... **19(1)**, 177
Bills of Sale Act 1878 .... **39(1)**, 21
Bills of Sale Act (1878) Amendment Act 1882 .... **39(1)**, 36
Bills of Sale Act 1890 .... **39(1)**, 46
Bills of Sale Act 1891 .... **39(1)**, 47
Biological Standards Act 1975 .... **28**, 356
Biological Weapons Act 1974 .... **12(1)**, 713
Birds (Registration Charges) Act 1997 .... **32**, 775
Births and Deaths Registration Act 1874 .... **36**, 14
Births and Deaths Registration Act 1926 .... **36**, 29
Births and Deaths Registration Act 1953 .... **36**, 59
Bishops in Foreign Countries Act 1841 .... **14**, 147
Bishops (Retirement) Measure 1986 .... **14**, 1111
Bishops Trusts Substitution Act 1858 .... **5(2)**, 517
Board of Agriculture Act 1889 .... **10**, 318
Board of Agriculture and Fisheries Act 1903 .... **10**, 324
Board of Trade Arbitrations, &c Act 1874 .... **36**, 482
Bodies Corporate (Joint Tenancy) Act 1899 .... **20**, 353
Borders, Citizenship and Immigration Act 2009—
    ss 1–23, 25–38, 53, 56–59, Sch .... **13(S)**, Customs 15
    ss 39–52, 54–59, Sch .... **31(S)**, Nationality 77
Botswana Independence Act 1966 .... **7(2)**, 467
Boundary Commissions Act 1992 .... **15(3)**, 412
Breeding and Sale of Dogs (Welfare) Act 1999 .... **2**, 659
Breeding of Dogs Act 1973 .... **2**, 315
Breeding of Dogs Act 1991 .... **2**, 624
British Aerospace Act 1980 .... **47**, 395
British Council and Commonwealth Institute Superannuation Act 1986 .... **33(1)**, 274
British Film Institute Act 1949 .... **13**, 99
British Fishing Boats Act 1983 .... **1(2)**, 236
British Law Ascertainment Act 1859 .... **18**, 150
British Library Act 1972 .... **13**, 160
British Museum Act 1963 .... **13**, 106
British Nationality Act 1948 .... **31**, 23
British Nationality Act 1958 .... **31**, 56
British Nationality Act 1964 .... **31**, 60
British Nationality Act 1965 .... **31**, 67
British Nationality Act 1981 .... **31**, 180
British Nationality (Falkland Islands) Act 1983 .... **31**, 261
British Nationality (Hong Kong) Act 1990 .... **31**, 270
British Nationality (Hong Kong) Act 1997 .... **31**, 289
British Nationality (No 2) Act 1964 .... **31**, 62
British Overseas Territories Act 2002 .... **31**, 506
British Railways Board (Finance) Act 1991 .... **38(1)**, 412
British Railways (Pension Schemes) Act 1981 .... **37**, 133
British Settlements Act 1887 .... **7(2)**, 321
British Settlements Act 1945 .... **7(2)**, 346
British Shipbuilders Act 1983 .... **47**, 449
British Shipbuilders (Borrowing Powers) Act 1983 .... **47**, 455
British Shipbuilders (Borrowing Powers) Act 1987 .... **47**, 462
British Steel Act 1988 .... **47**, 462
British Technology Group Act 1991 .... **47**, 486
British Telecommunications Act 1981—
    entire Act **45**, 48
    ss 78, 81–86, 89, 90 .... **34**, 579

British Waterways Act 1995 .... **38(1)**, 915
Broadcasting Act 1990—
  ss 3–5, 13–19, 21, 22–24, 28, 29, 37, 40–42B, 48–56, 58, 60–61A, 63, 64, 66–67, 71,
    85–89, 97–106ZA, 109–111B, 114–121, 126–133, 135–141, 177, 178, 180,
    183–185, 188, 193, 194A–196, 198–204, Sch 2, Pts I, II, Schs 3, 6, 7, 9, 10, 11,
    19–22 .... **45**, 139
  ss 162, 167, 195, 201, 202, 204, Sch 15 .... **12(2)**, 58
  ss 166, 201, 202(1), (5), 204 .... **19(3)**, 393
  ss 176, 201, 202(1), (5), 204(1)–(3), Sch 17 .... **11(1)**, 1341
Broadcasting Act 1996 .... **45**, 349
Brunei and Maldives Act 1985 .... **7(2)**, 596
Brunei (Appeals) Act 1989 .... **7(2)**, 609
Building Act 1984 .... **35(1)**, 546
Building Societies Act 1986 .... **19(1)**, 535
Building Societies Act 1997 .... **19(1)**, 1204
Building Societies (Distributions) Act 1997 .... **19(1)**, 1221
Building Societies (Funding and Mutual Societies (Transfers) Act 2007 .... **19(2)**, 605
Building Societies (Joint Account Holders) Act 1995 .... **19(1)**, 1203
Burial Act 1852 .... **5(2)**, 444
Burial Act 1853 .... **5(2)**, 448
Burial Act 1855 .... **5(2)**, 451
Burial Act 1857 .... **5(2)**, 455
Burial Act 1859 .... **5(2)**, 459
Burial Ground Act 1816 .... **14**, 66
Burial Laws Amendment Act 1880 .... **5(2)**, 463
Business Names Act 1985 .... **48**, 94
Business Rate Supplements Act 2009 .... **25(S)**, **26(S)**, Local Govt 1

C

Cable and Wireless Act 1946 .... **45**, 28
Caldey Island Act 1990 .... **25(2)**, 1180
Calendar Act 1751 .... **45**, 1532
Calendar (New Style) Act 1750 .... **45**, 1507
Cambridge University Act 1856 .... **15(1)**, 65
Canada Act 1982 .... **7(2)**, 595
Canal Carriers Act 1845 .... **36**, 362
Canal (Carriers) Act 1847 .... **36**, 398
Canals Protection (London) Act 1898 .... **36**, 500
Cancer Act 1939 .... **28**, 14
Capital Allowances Act 2001 .... **43(1)**, 947
Caravan Sites Act 1968 .... **21**, 412
Caravan Sites and Control of Development Act 1960 .... **32**, 212
Caravans (Standard Community Charge and Rating) Act 1991 .... **25(2)**, 1232
Care of Cathedrals (Amendment) Measure 2005 .... **14(S)**, Ecclesiastical Law 47
Care of Cathedrals Measure 1990 .... **14**, 1193
Care of Cathedrals (Supplementary Provisions) Measure 1994 .... **14**, 1291
Care of Churches and Ecclesiastical Jurisdiction Measure 1991 .... **14**, 1215
Care of Places of Worship Measure 1999 .... **14**, 1366
Care Standards Act 2000—
  ss 1–5, 5A, 5B, 8, 10–38, 42, 54–71, 80–93, 111, 113–115, 117–123, Sch 1, Sch 5,
    paras 1, 2, Sch 6 .... **35(2)**, 430
  ss 43, 45, 48–50, 52, 53, 72–79, 103, 114–123, Schs 2, 2A, 2B, 4–6 .... **6**, 968
Carers and Disabled Children Act 2000 .... **40(2)**, 420
Carers (Equal Opportunities) Act 2004 .... **40(2)**, 723
Carers (Recognition and Services) Act 1995 .... **40(2)**, 59
Carriage by Air Act 1961 .... **4(1)**, 10
Carriage by Air and Road Act 1979 .... **4(1)**, 85
Carriage by Air (Supplementary Provisions) Act 1962 .... **4(1)**, 74
Carriage of Goods by Road Act 1965 .... **36**, 733
Carriage of Goods by Sea Act 1971 .... **39(2)**, 392
Carriage of Goods by Sea Act 1992 .... **39(2)**, 686
Carriers Act 1830 .... **5(2)**, 504
Cathedrals Measure 1963 .... **14**, 619

Cathedrals Measure 1976 .... **14**, 824
Cathedrals Measure 1999 .... **14**, 1337
Celluloid and Cinematograph Film Act 1922 .... **35(1)**, 104
Cemeteries Clauses Act 1847 .... **5(2)**, 417
Census Act 1920 .... **36**, 19
Census (Amendment) Act 2000 .... **36**, 138
Census (Confidentiality) Act 1991 .... **36**, 136
Cestui que Vie Act 1666 .... **20**, 61
Cestui que Vie Act 1707 .... **20**, 63
Ceylon Independence Act 1947 .... **7(2)**, 353
Chancel Repairs Act 1932 .... **14**, 350
Channel Islands (Church Legislation) Measure 1931 .... **14**, 343
Channel Islands (Church Legislation) Measure 1931 (Amendment) Measure 1957 .... **14**, 494
Channel Islands (Representation) Measure 1931 .... **14**, 346
Channel Tunnel Act 1987 .... **37**, 618
Channel Tunnel Rail Link Act 1996 .... **38(1)**, 956
Channel Tunnel Rail Link (Supplementary Provisions) Act 2008 .... **38(2)**, 801
Charging Orders Act 1979 .... **19(3)**, 96
Charitable Trusts (Validation) Act 1954 .... **5(2)**, 529
Charities Act 1960 .... **5(2)**, 539
Charities Act 1992 .... **5(2)**, 544
Charities Act 1993 .... **5(2)**, 580
Charities Act 2006 .... **5(2)**, 836
Charities (Amendment) Act 1995 .... **5(2)**, 836
Charlwood and Horley Act 1974 .... **25(2)**, 477
Charter Trustees Act 1985 .... **25(2)**, 702
Chartered Associations (Protection of Names and Uniforms) Act 1926 .... **48**, 45
Chelsea and Kilmainham Hospitals Act 1826 .... **3**, 31
Chelsea Hospital Act 1876 .... **3**, 133
Chemical Weapons Act 1996 .... **12(2)**, 508
Chequers Estate Act 1917 .... **10**, 326
Chequers Estate Act 1958 .... **10**, 357
Cheques Act 1957 .... **19(1)**, 236
Cheques Act 1992 .... **19(1)**, 907
Chevening Estate Act 1959 .... **10**, 360
Chevening Estate Act 1987 .... **10**, 546
Child Abduction Act 1984 .... **12(1)**, 955
Child Abduction and Custody Act 1985 .... **6**, 260
Child Benefit Act 2005 .... **40(2)**, 726
Child Maintenance and Other Payments Act 2008—
    ss 1–45, 55–63, Schs 1–8 .... **6(S)**, Children 311
    ss 46–50, 52, 53, 61–63 .... **40(2)**, 844
Child Support Act 1991 .... **6**, 679
Child Support Act 1995 .... **6**, 846
Child Support, Pensions and Social Security Act 2000—
    ss 26–29, 83–87, Schs 3, 8, Sch 9, Pts I, IX **6**, 1024
    ss 30, 33, 36, 38, 42, 62–65, 69, 70, 74, 75, 78, 79, 84–87, Sch 7, Sch 9, Pts II,
    V–VIII .... **40(2)**, 430
    ss 52, 56, 58, 84–87, Sch 5, Pt II, Sch 9, Pts III, IV .... **33(1)**, 805
Child Trust Funds Act 2004 .... **6**, 1278
Childcare Act 2006 .... **6(S)**, Children 39
Children Act 1972 .... **6**, 206
Children Act 1989 .... **6**, 365
Children Act 2004 .... **6**, 1307
Children and Adoption Act 2006 .... **6(S)**, Children 1
Children and Young Persons Act 1933 .... **6**, 37
Children and Young Persons Act 1963 .... **6**, 113
Children and Young Persons Act 1969 .... **6**, 153
Children and Young Persons Act 2008 .... **6(S)**, Children 427
Children and Young Persons (Harmful Publications) Act 1955 .... **12(1)**, 331
Children and Young Persons (Protection from Tobacco) Act 1991 .... **6**, 673
Children (Leaving Care) Act 2000 .... **6**, 1044
Children (Scotland) Act 1995 .... **6**, 857
Children's Commissioner for Wales Act 2001 .... **6**, 1091
China Indemnity (Application) Act 1931 .... **19(2)**, 776

Chiropractors Act 1994 .... **28**, 913
Christmas Day (Trading) Act 2004 .... **18**, 1407
Chronically Sick and Disabled Persons Act 1970—
  ss 1, 2, 12, 18, 28, 28A, 29 .... **40(1)**, 91
  ss 3, 28, 29 .... **21**, 443
  ss 4–7, 8A, 8B, 28, 29 .... **35(1)**, 282
  ss 8, 28, 29 .... **15(1)**, 185
  ss 9, 29 .... **3**, 1287
  ss 13, 14, 16, 28, 29 .... **16**, 62
  ss 15, 28, 29 .... **25(1)**, 966
  ss 17, 22, 24, 28, 29 .... **30**, 425
  ss 20, 21, 21A–21C, 28, 29 .... **36**, 930
Chronically Sick and Disabled Persons (Amendment) Act 1976 .... **18**, 1378
Church Building Act 1822 .... **14**, 68
Church Commissioners (Assistance for Priority Areas) Measure 1988 .... **14**, 1181
Church Commissioners (Loans for Theological Colleges and Training Houses)
  Measure 1964 .... **14**, 629
Church Commissioners Measure 1947 .... **14**, 417
Church Commissioners Measure 1964 .... **14**, 647
Church Commissioners Measure 1970 .... **14**, 772
Church Commissioners (Miscellaneous Provisions) Measure 1975 .... **14**, 819
Church Dignitaries (Retirement) Measure 1949 .... **14**, 433
Church Funds Investment Measure 1958 .... **14**, 495
Church of England Assembly (Powers) Act 1919 .... **14**, 294
Church of England Convocations Act 1966 .... **14**, 650
Church of England (Ecumenical Relations) Measure 1988 .... **14**, 1183
Church of England (Legal Aid and Miscellaneous Provisions) Measure 1988 .... **14**, 1178
Church of England (Legal Aid) Measure 1994 .... **14**, 1298
Church of England Marriage Measure 2008 .... **14(S)**, Ecclesiastical Law 211
Church of England (Miscellaneous Provisions) Measure 1976 .... **14**, 831
Church of England (Miscellaneous Provisions) Measure 1978 .... **14**, 954
Church of England (Miscellaneous Provisions) Measure 1983 .... **14**, 1108
Church of England (Miscellaneous Provisions) Measure 1992 .... **14**, 1255
Church of England (Miscellaneous Provisions) Measure 1995 .... **14**, 1308
Church of England (Miscellaneous Provisions) Measure 2000 .... **14**, 1373
Church of England (Miscellaneous Provisions) Measure 2005 .... **14(S)**, Ecclesiastical Law 73
Church of England (Miscellaneous Provisions) Measure 2006 .... **14(S)**, Ecclesiastical Law 91
Church of England Pensions (Amendment) Measure 2009 .... **14(S)**, Ecclesiastical Law 217
Church of England (Pensions) Measure 1988 .... **14**, 1187
Church of England (Pensions) Measure 2003 .... **14**, 1397
Church of England (Worship and Doctrine) Measure 1974 .... **14**, 811
Church Property (Miscellaneous Provisions) Measure 1960 .... **14**, 515
Church Seats Act 1872 .... **14**, 240
Churchwardens Measure 2001 .... **14**, 1381
Cinemas Act 1985 .... **13**, 312
Cinematograph Films (Animals) Act 1937 .... **2**, 229
Cinque Ports Act 1821 .... **11(2)**, 26
Cinque Ports Act 1855 .... **11(2)**, 63
City of London (Courts) Act 1964 .... **11(2)**, 157
City of London (Guild Churches) Act 1952 .... **14**, 448
City of London (Guild Churches) Act 1960 .... **14**, 510
City of London Militia Act 1662 .... **25(1)**, 46
City of London (Union of Parishes) Act 1907 .... **25(1)**, 123
City of London (Various Powers) Act 1933 .... **25(1)**, 204
City of London (Various Powers) Act 1952 .... **25(1)**, 464
City of London (Various Powers) Act 1957 .... **25(1)**, 506
City of London (Various Powers) Act 1958 .... **25(1)**, 554
City of London (Various Powers) Act 1959 .... **25(1)**, 572
City of London (Various Powers) Act 1960 .... **25(1)**, 603
City of London (Various Powers) Act 1961 .... **25(1)**, 609
City of London (Various Powers) Act 1962 .... **25(1)**, 631
City of London (Various Powers) Act 1963 .... **25(1)**, 719
City of London (Various Powers) Act 1965 .... **25(1)**, 730
City of London (Various Powers) Act 1967 .... **25(1)**, 803
City of London (Various Powers) Act 1968 .... **25(1)**, 831

City of London (Various Powers) Act 1969 .... **25(1)**, 870
City of London (Various Powers) Act 1970 .... **25(1)**, 968
City of London (Various Powers) Act 1971 .... **25(1)**, 984
City of London (Various Powers) Act 1973 .... **25(2)**, 391
City of London (Various Powers) Act 1977 .... **25(2)**, 534
City of London (Various Powers) Act 1987 .... **25(2)**, 837
City of London (Various Powers) Act 1990 .... **25(2)**, 1223
City of London (Ward Elections) Act 2002 .... **26(2)**, 247
Civic Amenities Act 1967 .... **46**, 30
Civic Restaurants Act 1947 .... **25(1)**, 364
Civil Aviation Act 1980 .... **4(1)**, 111
Civil Aviation Act 1982 .... **4(1)**, 126
Civil Aviation Act 2006 .... **4(1)**, 722
Civil Aviation (Amendment) Act 1996 .... **4(1)**, 552
Civil Aviation Authority (Borrowing Powers) Act 1990 .... **4(1)**, 510
Civil Aviation (Eurocontrol) Act 1983 .... **4(1)**, 389
Civil Contingencies Act 2004 .... **50**, 535
Civil Evidence Act 1968 .... **18**, 227
Civil Evidence Act 1972 .... **18**, 246
Civil Evidence Act 1995 .... **18**, 326
Civil Jurisdiction and Judgments Act 1982—
  entire Act .... **11(2)**, 861
  ss 36, 52, 53, 55, Sch 13 .... **27**, 553
Civil Jurisdiction and Judgments Act 1991 .... **11(3)**, 243
Civil Liability (Contribution) Act 1978 .... **13**, 1259
Civil List Act 1837 .... **10**, 103
Civil List Act 1937 .... **10**, 151
Civil List Act 1952 .... **10**, 155
Civil List Act 1972 .... **10**, 182
Civil List Act 1975 .... **10**, 188
Civil List Audit Act 1816 .... **10**, 99
Civil Partnership Act 2004 .... **27**, 769
Civil Procedure Act 1997 .... **11(3)**, 335
Civil Service (Management Functions) Act 1992 .... **10**, 612
Clean Air Act 1993 .... **35(2)**, 2
Clean Neighbourhoods and Environment Act 2005—
  ss 1, 33, 34, 41, 46, 49, 54, 69–81, 96–98, 100, 104–111, Schs 4, 5 ...... **35(2)**, 811
  ss 3–9, 108–111 .... **38(2)**, 663
  ss 55–61, 63–68, 107–111, Sch 5, Pts 5, 6 .... **2**, 686
  ss 87–95, 107–111, Schs 2, 3, Sch 5, Pt 8 .... **2**, 945
Clergy Discipline Measure 2003 .... **14(S)**, Ecclesiastical Law 1
Clergy Ordination Act 1804 .... **14**, 63
Clergy (Ordination and Miscellaneous Provisions) Measure 1964 .... **14**, 643
Clergy (Ordination) Measure 1990 .... **14**, 1192
Clergy Pensions (Amendment) Measure 1967 .... **14**, 651
Clergy Pensions (Amendment) Measure 1972 .... **14**, 805
Clergy Pensions (Amendment) Measure 1982 .... **14**, 962
Clergy Pensions Measure 1961 .... **14**, 529
Clergy Residences Repair Act 1776 .... **14**, 62
Clerical Disabilities Act 1870 .... **14**, 220
Clerical Disabilities Act 1870 (Amendment) Measure 1934 .... **14**, 355
Clerical Subscription Act 1865 .... **14**, 200
Clerk of the Council Act 1859 .... **10**, 291
Clerk of the Parliaments Act 1824 .... **32**, 1050
Climate Change Act 2008 .... **35(S)**, Public Health 45
Climate Change and Sustainable Energy Act 2006 .... **17(2)**, 885
Coal Industry Act 1949 .... **17(1)**, 78
Coal Industry Act 1975 .... **17(1)**, 626
Coal Industry Act 1977 .... **17(1)**, 660
Coal Industry Act 1980 .... **17(1)**, 679
Coal Industry Act 1983 .... **17(1)**, 715
Coal Industry Act 1985 .... **17(1)**, 727
Coal Industry Act 1987 .... **17(1)**, 949
Coal Industry Act 1994 .... **17(2)**, 157
Coal Industry Nationalisation Act 1946 .... **17(1)**, 45

Coal Mining Subsidence Act 1991 .... **17(2)**, 1
Coast Protection Act 1949 .... **49**, 271
Coastguard Act 1925 .... **3**, 228
Coinage Act 1971 .... **10**, 206
College Charter Act 1871 .... **15(1)**, 99
Collegiate Churches (Capital Endowments) Measure 1970 .... **14**, 769
Colonial Affidavits Act 1859 .... **7(2)**, 299
Colonial Bishops Act 1853 .... **14**, 178
Colonial Boundaries Act 1895 .... **7(2)**, 335
Colonial Clergy Act 1874 .... **14**, 244
Colonial Courts of Admiralty Act 1890 .... **11(2)**, 97
Colonial Laws Validity Act 1865 .... **7(2)**, 301
Colonial Marriages Act 1865 .... **7(2)**, 305
Colonial Naval Defence Act 1931 .... **3**, 232
Colonial Naval Defence Act 1949 .... **3**, 273
Colonial Prisoners Removal Act 1869 .... **7(2)**, 306
Colonial Prisoners Removal Act 1884 .... **7(2)**, 311
Colonial Probates Act 1892 .... **18**, 533
Colonial Probates (Protected States and Mandated Territories) Act 1927 .... **18**, 593
Commissioner for Older People (Wales) Act 2006 .... **35(2)**, 897
Commissioners Clauses Act 1847 .... **10**, 234
Commissioners for Oaths Act 1889 .... **18**, 173
Commissioners for Oaths Act 1891 .... **18**, 178
Commissioners for Revenue and Customs Act 2005 .... **43(2)**, 1016
Commissioners of Works Act 1852 .... **10**, 109
Commissioners of Works Act 1894 .... **10**, 124
Common Informers Act 1951 .... **12(1)**, 283
Common Law Procedure Act 1852 .... **20**, 209
Common Law Procedure Act 1854 .... **19(1)**, 42
Commonable Rights Compensation Act 1882 .... **20**, 342
Commonhold and Leasehold Reform Act 2002 .... **24**, 1
Commons Act 1876 .... **20**, 315
Commons Act 1879 .... **20**, 335
Commons Act 1899 .... **20**, 354
Commons Act 1908 .... **20**, 370
Commons Act 2006 .... **24**, 572
Commons (Expenses) Act 1878 .... **20**, 332
Commons Registration Act 1965 .... **21**, 268
Commonwealth Act 2002 .... **7(2)**, 660
Commonwealth Development Corporation Act 1978 .... **7(2)**, 531
Commonwealth Development Corporation Act 1999 .... **7(2)**, 618
Commonwealth Secretariat Act 1966 .... **7(2)**, 457
Commonwealth Telecommunications Act 1968 .... **45**, 47
Commonwealth Telegraphs Act 1949 .... **45**, 31
Communications Act 2003 .... **45**, 714
Community Care (Delayed Discharges etc) Act 2003 .... **40(2)**, 689
Community Care (Direct Payments) Act 1996 .... **40(2)**, 153
Community Care (Residential Accommodation) Act 1992 .... **40(2)**, 33
Community Care (Residential Accommodation) Act 1998 .... **40(2)**, 343
Community Health Councils (Access to Information) Act 1988 .... **30**, 518
Companies Act 1985 .... **8**, 88
Companies Act 1989—
   ss 1, 23–54, 92–107, 117, 118, 120, 130, 133–135, 139–142, 144, 145, 152, 153,
     212–216, Schs 11–14, 16, 18, 19, 24 .... **8**, 872
   ss 82–91, 154, 155, 157–167, 169, 170, 172–191, 213, 215, 216 .... **19(1)**, 826
Companies Act 2006 .... **8(1)**, 216
Companies (Audit, Investigations and Community Enterprise) Act 2004 .... **8(1)**, 107
Companies Clauses Act 1863 .... **8**, 69
Companies Clauses Act 1869 .... **8**, 81
Companies Clauses Consolidation Act 1845 .... **8**, 10
Companies Clauses Consolidation Act 1888 .... **8**, 83
Companies Consolidation (Consequential Provisions) Act 1985 .... **8**, 817
Company and Business Names (Chamber of Commerce, Etc) Act 1999 .... **48**, 212
Company Directors Disqualification Act 1986 .... **8**, 837

Compensation Act 2006—
  ss 1–3, 16–18 .... **31(S)**, Negligence 1
  ss 4–18, Schedule .... **11(3)**, 1057
Compensation (Defence) Act 1939 .... **9**, 81
Competition Act 1980 .... **47**, 381
Competition Act 1998 .... **47**, 531
Competition and Service (Utilities) Act 1992 .... **17(2)**, 84
Compulsory Church Rate Abolition Act 1868 .... **14**, 214
Compulsory Purchase Act 1965 .... **9**, 236
Compulsory Purchase (Vesting Declarations) Act 1981 .... **9**, 386
Computer Misuse Act 1990 .... **12(2)**, 40
Concessionary Bus Travel Act 2007 .... **38(2)**, 789
Confirmation and Probate Amendment Act 1859 .... **18**, 522
Confirmation of Charters and Statutes (1415–16) **10**, 29
Confirmation of Liberties (1423) **10**, 30
Confirmation of the Charters (1297) **10**, 22
Confiscation of Alcohol (Young Persons) Act 1997 .... **6**, 886
Congenital Disabilities (Civil Liability) Act 1976 .... **45**, 1556
Consecration of Churchyards Act 1867 .... **14**, 205
Consecration of Churchyards Act 1868 .... **14**, 209
Conservation of Seals Act 1970 .... **1(1)**, 818
Consolidated Fund Act 1816 .... **19(2)**, 644
Consolidated Fund (Civil List Provisions) Act 1951 .... **10**, 155
Consolidation of Enactments (Procedure) Act 1949 .... **41**, 756
Constables Protection Act 1750 .... **33(2)**, 30
Constitutional Reform Act 2005 .... **11(3)**, 752
Consular Conventions Act 1949 .... **10**, 807
Consular Fees Act 1980 .... **10**, 1079
Consular Relations Act 1968 .... **10**, 1001
Consumer Credit Act 1974 .... **39(1)**, 125
Consumer Credit Act 2006 .... **39(1)**, 686
Consumer Protection Act 1987 .... **39(1)**, 618
Consumers, Estate Agents and Redress Act 2007 .... **39(1)**, 719
Contempt of Court Act 1981 .... **11(2)**, 688
Continental Shelf Act 1964 .... **17(1)**, 405
Continental Shelf Act 1989 .... **17(1)**, 1267
Contingencies Fund Act 1970 .... **19(2)**, 891
Contingencies Fund Act 1974 .... **19(2)**, 927
Contracts (Applicable Law) Act 1990 .... **11(1)**, 379
Contracts (Rights of Third Parties) Act 1999 .... **11(1)**, 462
Control of Pollution Act 1974 .... **35(1)**, 304
Control of Pollution (Amendment) Act 1989 .... **35(1)**, 728
Controlled Drugs (Penalties) Act 1985 .... **28**, 655
Convention (Ireland) Act Repeal Act 1879 .... **32**, 1062
Convention Parliament (1688) **32**, 1042
Conveyancing Act 1881 .... **20**, 336
Convocations of the Clergy Measure 1920 .... **14**, 301
Co-operative Development Agency and Industrial Development Act 1984 ...... **47**, 456
Co-operatives and Community Benefit Societies Act 2003 .... **19(2)**, 598
Copyright Act 1956 .... **11(1)**, 635
Copyright (Computer Software) Amendment Act 1985 .... **11(1)**, 928
Copyright, Designs and Patents Act 1988—
  entire Act .... **11(1)**, 930
  ss 302, 304(1), (2), (4)(e), (6), 305(3), 306 .... **48**, 103
Copyright, etc and Trade Marks (Offences and Enforcement) Act 2002 ...... **11(1)**, 1349
Copyright (Visually Impaired Persons) Act 2002 .... **11(1)**, 1352
Corn Rents Act 1963 .... **14**, 550
Corn Sales Act 1921 .... **1(1)**, 268
Coronation Oath Act 1688 .... **10**, 37
Coroners Act 1988 .... **11(1)**, 1370
Corporate Bodies' Contracts Act 1960 .... **11(1)**, 359
Corporate Manslaughter and Corporate Homicide Act 2007 .... **12(4)**, 416
Costs of Leases Act 1958 .... **21**, 255
Council Tax (New Valuation Lists for England) Act 2006 .... **26(2)**, 544
Counter-Inflation Act 1973 .... **47**, 148

Counter-Terrorism Act 2008 .... **12(S)**, Criminal 1
Countryside Act 1968—
 ss 1, 2, 4, 6–13, 15, 15A, 16, 18, 20, 21, 37, 38, 41–50, Schs 1, 2, 5 .... **32**, 245
 ss 23, 24, 24A, 49(1), (2), 50 .... **18**, 1173
 ss 27, 30, 49, 50 .... **36**, 759
Countryside and Rights of Way Act 2000—
 ss 1–12, 14–46, 75, 76, 82–95, 99–104, Schs 1–3, 11, 13, 14, 15, Pt II, 16 .... **32**, 781
 ss 47–50, 52–62, 71, 72, 99, 100, 103, 104, Sch 6, Pt I .... **38(2)**, 51
County Courts Act 1984 .... **11(2)**, 1035
County Courts (Penalties for Contempt) Act 1983 .... **11(2)**, 1034
Courts Act 1971 .... **11(2)**, 192
Courts Act 2003 .... **11(3)**, 503
Courts and Legal Services Act 1990—
 ss 1, 8–11, 13, 15, 17, 18, 18A, 21–29, 31, 31A–31C, 34–46, 46A, 46B, 47–53,
  57–58B, 60, 61, 63, 66, 69–76, 78, 79, 81, 89, 104–107, 115, 116, 119–125,
  Schs 3–8, 11, 14, 17–20 .... **11(3)**, 93
 ss 5, 113, 119(1), 120(1)–(3), (6), 123, 124, 125(1), (6), Sch 19, para 17 .... **18**, 304
 ss 54–56, 120, 124, 125, Sch 9 .... **18**, 696
Courts (Colonial) Jurisdiction Act 1874 .... **7(2)**, 309
Courts-Martial (Appeals) Act 1951 .... **3**, 277
Courts-Martial (Appeals) Act 1968 .... **3**, 1232
Credit Unions Act 1979 .... **19(1)**, 491
Cremation Act 1902 .... **5(2)**, 472
Cremation Act 1952 .... **5(2)**, 478
Crime and Disorder Act 1998—
 ss 1, 1A–1K, 4–7, 17, 17A, 18, 28–32, 34, 37–42, 57A–57E, 94, 106, 109, 111,
  114–121, Schs 2, 8–10 .... **12(2)**, 816
 ss 8–16, 18, 47, 65, 66, 98, 114, 117, 121 .... **6**, 889
 ss 49, 50, 50A, 51, 51A–51E, 52, 52A, 52B, 114, 117, 121, Sch 3 .... **11(3)**, 352
Crime and Punishment (Scotland) Act 1997 .... **12(2)**, 761
Crime (International Co-operation) Act 2003—
 ss 1–36, 42–51, 82, 84, 90, 91, 93–96, Schs 1, 2, 4–6 .... **12(3)**, 631
 ss 54–75, 92–94, 96, Sch 3 .... **38(2)**, 377
Crime (Sentences) Act 1997—
 ss 28, 30–32, 34, 35, 40–42, 53–57, Schs 1, 2, 4–6 .... **12(2)**, 712
 ss 47, 48, 54, 57 .... **29**, 293
Criminal Appeal Act 1968 .... **12(1)**, 490
Criminal Appeal Act 1995 .... **12(2)**, 374
Criminal Appeal (Northern Ireland) Act 1980 .... **31**, 1106
Criminal Attempts Act 1981 .... **12(1)**, 882
Criminal Cases Review (Insanity) Act 1999 .... **12(2)**, 923
Criminal Damage Act 1971 .... **12(1)**, 687
Criminal Defence Service Act 2006 .... **11(3)**, 1051
Criminal Defence Service (Advice and Assistance) Act 2001 .... **11(3)**, 502
Criminal Evidence Act 1898 .... **18**, 180
Criminal Evidence (Amendment) Act 1997 .... **12(2)**, 671
Criminal Evidence (Witness Anonymity) Act 2008 .... **18**, 486
Criminal Injuries Compensation Act 1995 .... **12(2)**, 492
Criminal Jurisdiction Act 1802 .... **12(1)**, 84
Criminal Jurisdiction Act 1975 .... **31**, 925
Criminal Justice Act 1925 .... **11(2)**, 125
Criminal Justice Act 1948 .... **12(1)**, 268
Criminal Justice Act 1961—
 ss 18, 19, 36, 39(3), (4), 41–45 .... **6**, 107
 ss 22–24, 35–45 .... **12(1)**, 377
Criminal Justice Act 1967—
 ss 8–10, 12, 17, 22, 25, 32, 36, 65, 66, 69–72, 89, 91, 92, 98, 100–106, Schs 5,
  7 .... **12(1)**, 451
 ss 20, 36, 106 .... **11(2)**, 162
Criminal Justice Act 1972—
 ss 34, 36, 46, 60, 63–66, Sch 6 .... **12(1)**, 698
 ss 46, 51, 66 .... **11(2)**, 249
 ss 51, 66 .... **6**, 207
Criminal Justice Act 1982—
 ss 1, 32, 68, 70, 72, 76–81, Sch 1, Sch 13, Pt III, Schs 16, 17 .... **12(1)**, 906

Criminal Justice Act 1982—*contd*
  ss 35–40, 46, 47, 59, 80, 81, Sch 2 .... **11(2)**, 996
Criminal Justice Act 1987 .... **12(1)**, 1261
Criminal Justice Act 1988—
  ss 30–32, 168, 171–173 .... **18**, 291
  ss 34, 171(1), (2), (5), 172, 173 .... **6**, 360
  ss 35, 36, 39–41, 96, 97, 123, 133–135, 138, 139, 139A, 139B, 141, 141A, 142, 150,
    151, 159, 160, 160A, 167–173, Schs 3, 8, 12, 15, 16 .... **12(1)**, 1298
  ss 50, 146, 171–173, Sch 13 .... **3**, 1442
  ss 51–53, 55, 57, 59, 67, 152, 171–173 .... **11(3)**, 76
  ss 118, 122, 171–173 .... **19(3)**, 204
Criminal Justice Act 1991—
  ss 16, 17, 20A, 26, 30, 33, 33A, 34A, 35–39, 40A, 41–47, 49–51, 53, 80–92, 95,
    98–102, Schs 3, 6, 10–13 .... **12(2)**, 76
  ss 24, 30, 99, 102 .... **11(3)**, 246
  ss 60, 61, 61A, 65, 68, 70, 71, 99, 101(1), 102, Sch 8, Sch 12, paras 15, 18, 19,
    22–24 .... **6**, 827
Criminal Justice Act 1993—
  ss 1–6, 23, 65, 70, 71, 73, 77, 78, 79, Sch 6 .... **12(2)**, 224
  ss 52–64, 78(2)–(4), (10), 79(1), (2), (9)–(11), Schs 1, 2 .... **8**, 960
Criminal Justice Act 2003—
  ss 12, 14–17, 21–25, 27, 28, 33, 39, 43–50, 57–68, 71–80, 82–97, 142–153, 156–174,
    176–235, 237–270, 273, 274, 276–286, 291, 293–295, 298, 299, 302–305, 307, 321,
    324–339, Schs 4, 5, 8–17, 19, 21, 22, 25–27, 32, 34A, Sch 36, Pts 1, 4, 6, Schs 37,
    38 .... **12(3)**, 937
  ss 29, 30, 41, 154, 155, 300, 301, 305, 330–333, 335–339, Sch 3, Pts 1, 2, Sch 31,
    Sch 36, Pt 2, Sch 37, Pt 4 .... **11(3)**, 693
  ss 51–56, 98–129, 132–141, 330–339, Schs 6, 7, Sch 37, Pts 5, 6 .... **18**, 427
Criminal Justice Administration Act 1851 .... **12(1)**, 115
Criminal Justice Administration Act 1914 .... **11(2)**, 118
Criminal Justice (Amendment) Act 1981 .... **11(2)**, 687
Criminal Justice and Court Services Act 2000—
  ss 1–8, 10, 18, 20–23, 25, 43–45, 59–62, 64, 70, 71, 74–82, Schs 1, 1A, 6–8 .... **12(2)**, 1395
  ss 11–16, 18–21, 23–38, 42, 76–82, Schs 2–4 .... **6**, 1048
Criminal Justice and Immigration Act 2008—
  ss 1–9, 11, 13, 19–23, 26, 27, 32–36, 43, 46, 47, 49, 51, 52, 60–68, 71, 73–79,
    96–124, 138, 140, 144, 147–154, Schs 1–4, 6, 8, 10, 11, 14–17, 21, 26, 27, 28 ...... **12(4)**, 649
  ss 39–41, 53, 54, 56–58, 80–92, 147, 148, 150, 152–154, Schs 7, 13, 18, 19 .... **11(S)**, Courts 1
  ss 48, 125, 143, 147, 148, 150, 152–154, Sch 9 .... **6(S)**, Children 289
  ss 50, 126–129, 147, 148, 150, 152–154, Schs 22, 23 .... **33(S)**, Police 1
  ss 130–137, 146–148, 150, 152–154 .... **31(S)**, Nationality 59
  ss 145, 147, 148, 150–154, Sch 25 .... **3(S)**, Armed Forces 491
Criminal Justice and Police Act 2001—
  ss 1–16, 33–37, 39–42A, 45–47, 50–70, 78, 80, 82, 86, 102, 128, 130, 135–138,
    Schs 1, 2, 7 .... **12(3)**, 1
  ss 19–28, 138 .... **19(3)**, 575
  ss 97, 98, 100, 101, 103, 127, 136, 138 .... **33(2)**, 379
Criminal Justice and Public Order Act 1994—
  ss 7–15, 25, 51, 60, 60AA, 60A, 61–69, 75–79, 100, 102, 104–106, 112, 114,
    117–128, 136–140, 146, 147, 157, 163, 166–172, Schs 1, 2, 7, 9, 11 .... **12(2)**, 245
  ss 32, 34–39, 172 .... **18**, 312
  ss 80, 172 .... **32**, 702
Criminal Justice (International Co-operation) Act 1990—
  ss 5, 6, 9, 10, 18, 20, 21, 24, 30–32, Schs 3–5 .... **12(2)**, 24
  ss 12, 13, 19–21, 24, 32, Schs 2, 3 .... **28**, 760
Criminal Justice (International Co-operation) (Amendment) Act 1998 .... **28**, 981
Criminal Justice (Scotland) Act 1963 .... **12(1)**, 393
Criminal Justice (Terrorism and Conspiracy) Act 1998 .... **12(2)**, 920
Criminal Law Act 1826 .... **12(1)**, 100
Criminal Law Act 1967—
  ss 1, 3–6, 9–13, 15, Schs 2–4 .... **12(1)**, 424
  ss 14, 15 .... **45**, 1553
Criminal Law Act 1977—
  ss 1–10, 12, 12A, 13, 32, 33, 37, 51, 64, 65, Sch 13, Sch 14, paras 1, 5 .... **12(1)**, 797
  ss 15, 28, 30, 31, 38A, 38B, 39, 40, 48, 64, 65, Sch 14 .... **11(2)**, 386

Criminal Law Amendment Act 1867 .... **12(1)**, 157
Criminal Law (Consolidation) (Scotland) Act 1995 .... **12(2)**, 408
Criminal Libel Act 1819 .... **19(3)**, 357
Criminal Procedure Act 1853 .... **12(1)**, 116
Criminal Procedure Act 1865 .... **18**, 153
Criminal Procedure and Investigations Act 1996—
 ss 1–6, 6A–6E, 7A, 8, 10–43, 45, 47, 54–61, 71, 72, 74–81, Schs 1, 4, 5 .... **12(2)**, 549
 ss 68, 77, 79, 81, Sch 2 .... **11(3)**, 330
Criminal Procedure (Attendance of Witnesses) Act 1965 .... **12(1)**, 413
Criminal Procedure (Consequential Provisions) (Scotland) Act 1995 .... **12(2)**, 413
Criminal Procedure (Insanity) Act 1964 .... **12(1)**, 399
Criminal Procedure (Insanity and Unfitness to Plead) Act 1991 .... **12(2)**, 72
Criminal Procedure (Right of Reply) Act 1964 .... **18**, 225
Criminal Procedure (Scotland) Act 1995 .... **12(2)**, 458
Crossbows Act 1987 .... **12(1)**, 1258
Crossrail Act 2008 .... **38(2)**, 802
Crown Agents Act 1979 .... **10**, 484
Crown Agents Act 1995 .... **10**, 651
Crown and Parliament Recognition Act 1689 .... **10**, 48
Crown Debts Act 1801 .... **41**, 702
Crown Estate Act 1961 .... **10**, 166
Crown Lands Act 1623 .... **10**, 32
Crown Lands Act 1702 .... **10**, 83
Crown Lands Act 1823 .... **10**, 102
Crown Lands Act 1851 .... **10**, 105
Crown Lands Act 1894 .... **10**, 126
Crown Lands Act 1906 .... **10**, 129
Crown Lands Act 1927 .... **10**, 135
Crown Lands Act 1936 .... **10**, 136
Crown Office Act 1877 .... **10**, 312
Crown Office Act 1890 .... **10**, 323
Crown Private Estate Act 1800 .... **10**, 90
Crown Private Estates Act 1862 .... **10**, 113
Crown Private Estates Act 1873 .... **10**, 118
Crown Proceedings Act 1947 .... **13**, 9
Crown Proceedings (Armed Forces) Act 1987 .... **13**, 39
Crown Prosecution Service Inspectorate Act 2000 .... **12(2)**, 1215
Currency Act 1982 .... **10**, 221
Currency Act 1983—
 ss 1, 4 .... **10**, 222
 ss 2–4, Schedule .... **19(1)**, 530
Currency and Bank Notes Act 1928 .... **19(1)**, 196
Currency and Bank Notes Act 1954 .... **19(1)**, 232
Customs and Excise Duties (General Reliefs) Act 1979 .... **13**, 844
Customs and Excise Management Act 1979 .... **13**, 612
Customs and Inland Revenue Act 1879 .... **13**, 563
Customs and Inland Revenue Act 1883 .... **2**, 196
Customs Buildings Act 1879 .... **13**, 564
Customs Consolidation Act 1876 .... **13**, 559
Cycle Tracks Act 1984 .... **37**, 430
Cyprus Act 1960 .... **7(2)**, 374

D

Damages Act 1996 .... **13**, 1273
Dangerous Dogs Act 1989 .... **2**, 594
Dangerous Dogs Act 1991 .... **2**, 627
Dangerous Dogs (Amendment) Act 1997 .... **2**, 656
Dangerous Vessels Act 1985 .... **39(2)**, 516
Dangerous Wild Animals Act 1976 .... **2**, 354
Data Protection Act 1998 .... **7(1)**, 608
Deaconesses and Lay Ministry Measure 1972 .... **14**, 803
Deaconesses and Lay Workers (Pensions) Measure 1980 .... **14**, 957
Deacons (Ordination of Women) Measure 1986 .... **14**, 1175

Dealing in Cultural Objects (Offences) Act 2003 .... **13**, 451
Debtors Act 1869 .... **4(2)**, 9
Debtors Act 1878 .... **4(2)**, 16
Decimal Currency Act 1969 .... **10**, 189
Deeds of Arrangement Act 1914 .... **4(2)**, 17
Deep Sea Mining (Temporary Provisions) Act 1981 .... **17(1)**, 683
Deer Act 1991 .... **2**, 605
Defamation Act 1952 .... **19(3)**, 385
Defamation Act 1996 .... **19(3)**, 398
Defective Premises Act 1972 .... **21**, 446
Defence Act 1842 .... **3**, 49
Defence Act 1854 .... **3**, 71
Defence Act 1859 .... **3**, 73
Defence Act 1860 .... **3**, 76
Defence Act 1865 .... **3**, 103
Defence Act Amendment Act 1864 .... **3**, 101
Defence Acts Amendment Act 1873 .... **3**, 131
Defence Contracts Act 1958 .... **11(1)**, 724
Defence of the Realm (Acquisition of Land) Act 1916 .... **9**, 68
Defence of the Realm (Acquisition of Land) Act 1920 .... **9**, 77
Defence (Transfer of Functions) Act 1964 .... **10**, 373
Demise of the Crown Act 1702 .... **10**, 86
Demise of the Crown Act 1727 .... **10**, 87
Demise of the Crown Act 1901 .... **10**, 126
Dentists Act 1984 .... **28**, 495
Deputy Speaker Act 1855 .... **32**, 1051
Deregulation and Contracting Out Act 1994—
    ss 1, 6, 40, 80–82, Sch 17 .... **41**, 992
    ss 31, 40, 82, Sch 9 .... **1(2)**, 649
    ss 33, 40(1), (4), (6), 82 .... **35(2)**, 89
    ss 34, 40, 58, 82 .... **38(1)**, 794
    ss 37, 40, 82 .... **18**, 1402
    ss 69, 71–80, 82, Schs 15, 16 .... **10**, 632
    ss 70–73, 75, 77, 79, 79A–79C, 82, Sch 15 .... **26(1)**, 305
Derelict Land Act 1982 .... **32**, 578
Deserted Tenements Act 1817 .... **13**, 1311
Destructive Imported Animals Act 1932 .... **2**, 218
Development of Inventions Act 1967 .... **47**, 118
Development of Rural Wales Act 1976 .... **46**, 42
Development of Tourism Act 1969 .... **47**, 120
Digital Switchover (Disclosure of Information) Act 2007 .... **45**, 1494
Diocesan Boards of Education Measure 1991 .... **14**, 1245
Diocesan Boards of Finance Measure 1925 .... **14**, 332
Diocesan Stipends Funds Measure 1953 .... **14**, 472
Diocese in Europe Measure 1980 .... **14**, 959
Dioceses Measure 1978 .... **14**, 905
Dioceses, Pastoral and Mission Measure 2007 .... **14(S)**, Ecclesiastical Law 123
Diplomatic and Consular Premises Act 1987 .... **10**, 1085
Diplomatic and other Privileges Act 1971 .... **10**, 1052
Diplomatic Privileges Act 1964 .... **10**, 990
Disability Discrimination Act 1995 .... **7(1)**, 348
Disability Discrimination Act 2005 .... **7(1)**, 962
Disability Grants Act 1993 .... **40(2)**, 38
Disability Living Allowance and Disability Working Allowance Act 1991 .... **40(1)**, 342
Disabled Persons Act 1981 .... **35(1)**, 459
Disabled Persons (Employment) Act 1944 .... **16**, 19
Disabled Persons (Employment) Act 1958 .... **16**, 24
Disabled Persons (Services, Consultation and Representation) Act 1986 .... **40(1)**, 231
Diseases of Fish Act 1937 .... **1(1)**, 350
Diseases of Fish Act 1983 .... **1(2)**, 246
Disqualifications Act 2000 .... **32**, 1159
Distress for Rent Act 1689 .... **13**, 1293
Distress for Rent Act 1737 .... **13**, 1296
Distribution of German Enemy Property Act 1949 .... **50**, 469
Distribution of German Enemy Property Act 1952 .... **50**, 479

District Councils (Water Supply Facilities) Act 1897 .... **20**, 348
Disused Burial Grounds Act 1884 .... **5(2)**, 470
Disused Burial Grounds (Amendment) Act 1981 .... **5(2)**, 491
Divorce (Religious Marriages) Act 2002 .... **27**, 768
Dock Work Act 1989 .... **16**, 184
Docking and Nicking of Horses Act 1949 .... **2**, 234
Docks and Harbours Act 1966 .... **39(2)**, 201
Dockyard Ports Regulation Act 1865 .... **39(2)**, 100
Dockyard Services Act 1986 .... **39(2)**, 524
Documentary Evidence Act 1868 .... **18**, 159
Documentary Evidence Act 1882 .... **18**, 171
Documentary Evidence Act 1895 .... **18**, 179
Dogs Act 1871 .... **2**, 189
Dogs Act 1906 .... **2**, 200
Dogs (Amendment) Act 1928 .... **2**, 217
Dogs (Protection of Livestock) Act 1953 .... **2**, 243
Domestic and Appellate Proceedings (Restriction of Publicity) Act 1968—
   ss 1, 4, 5 .... **11(2)**, 168
   ss 2, 4(4), 5 .... **27**, 314
Domestic Proceedings and Magistrates' Courts Act 1978 .... **27**, 509
Domestic Violence, Crime and Victims Act 2004 .... **12(4)**, 1
Domicile Act 1861 .... **18**, 526
Domicile and Matrimonial Proceedings Act 1973—
   ss 1, 5, 6, 17, Schs 1, 6 .... **27**, 498
   ss 3, 4, 17(1), (4), (5) **6**, 218
Dormant Bank and Building Society Accounts Act 2008 .... **19(S)**, Financial 1
Dower Act 1833 .... **18**, 510
Drouly Fund Act 1838 .... **3**, 46
Drug Trafficking Act 1994 .... **12(2)**, 350
Drug Trafficking Offences Act 1986 .... **12(1)**, 1207
Drugs Act 2005—
   ss 2, 22, 24 .... **28**, 1125
   ss 7, 9–19, 22–24, Sch 2 .... **12(4)**, 209
Duchy of Lancaster Act 1920 .... **10**, 342
Duchy of Lancaster Act 1988 .... **10**, 553
Durham County Palatine Act 1858 .... **10**, 111

E

Easter Act 1928 .... **45**, 1535
Ecclesiastical Commissioners Act 1836 .... **14**, 89
Ecclesiastical Commissioners Act 1840 .... **14**, 131
Ecclesiastical Commissioners Act 1841 .... **14**, 141
Ecclesiastical Commissioners Act 1850 .... **14**, 175
Ecclesiastical Commissioners Act 1860 .... **14**, 194
Ecclesiastical Commissioners Act 1866 .... **14**, 203
Ecclesiastical Commissioners (Curate Grants) Measure 1946 .... **14**, 416
Ecclesiastical Commissioners (Loans for Church Training Colleges) Measure 1931 .... **14**, 341
Ecclesiastical Commissioners Measure 1926 .... **14**, 336
Ecclesiastical Commissioners (Powers) Measure 1936 .... **14**, 374
Ecclesiastical Commissioners (Powers) Measure 1938 .... **14**, 394
Ecclesiastical Commissioners (Sodor and Man) Measure 1930 .... **14**, 337
Ecclesiastical Corporations Act 1832 .... **14**, 73
Ecclesiastical Courts Jurisdiction Act 1860 .... **14**, 191
Ecclesiastical Dilapidations (Amendment) Measure 1929 .... **14**, 337
Ecclesiastical Dilapidations Measure 1923 .... **14**, 326
Ecclesiastical Fees Measure 1986 .... **14**, 1119
Ecclesiastical Houses of Residence Act 1842 .... **14**, 148
Ecclesiastical Judges and Legal Officers Measure 1976 .... **14**, 825
Ecclesiastical Jurisdiction (Amendment) Measure 1974 .... **14**, 810
Ecclesiastical Jurisdiction Measure 1963 .... **14**, 554
Ecclesiastical Leases Act 1836 .... **14**, 80
Ecclesiastical Leases Act 1865 .... **14**, 198
Ecclesiastical Leases (Amendment) Act 1836 .... **14**, 84

Enquiry Bureau   hsieb@lexisnexis.co.uk

Ecclesiastical Leasing Act 1842 .... **14**, 153
Ecclesiastical Leasing Act 1858 .... **14**, 185
Ecclesiastical Licences Act 1533 .... **14**, 27
Ecclesiastical Offices (Age Limit) Measure 1975 .... **14**, 820
Ecclesiastical Offices (Terms of Service) Measure 2009 .... **14(S)**, Ecclesiastical Law 219
Ecclesiastical Titles Act 1871 .... **14**, 238
Education Act 1918 .... **15(1)**, 119
Education Act 1962 .... **15(1)**, 172
Education Act 1967 .... **15(1)**, 183
Education Act 1973 .... **15(1)**, 189
Education Act 1980 .... **15(1)**, 196
Education Act 1986 .... **15(1)**, 211
Education Act 1994 .... **15(1)**, 444
Education Act 1996 .... **15(1)**, 470
Education Act 1997 .... **15(1)**, 780
Education Act 2002 .... **15(2)**, 549
Education Act 2005 .... **15(2)**, 866
Education and Inspections Act 2006 .... **15(2)**, 1036
Education and Skills Act 2008 .... **15(S)**, Education 101
Education (Fees and Awards) Act 1983 .... **15(1)**, 199
Education (No 2) Act 1986 .... **15(1)**, 213
Education Reform Act 1988 .... **15(1)**, 220
Education (Schools) Act 1997 .... **15(1)**, 834
Education (Student Loans) Act 1990 .... **15(1)**, 338
Education (Student Loans) Act 1996 .... **15(1)**, 459
Education (Student Loans) Act 1998 .... **15(1)**, 841
Elected Authorities (Northern Ireland) Act 1989 .... **31**, 1172
Election Publications Act 2001 .... **15(3)**, 812
Elections Act 2001 .... **15(3)**, 814
Elections (Northern Ireland) Act 1985 .... **15(3)**, 357
Electoral Administration Act 2006 .... **15(3)**, 882
Electoral Fraud (Northern Ireland) Act 2002 .... **15(3)**, 817
Electricity Act 1989 .... **17(1)**, 975
Electricity (Miscellaneous Provisions) Act 2003 .... **17(2)**, 569
Electronic Communications Act 2000 .... **45**, 525
Elementary School Teachers (Superannuation) Act 1898 .... **15(1)**, 108
Elementary School Teachers (Superannuation) Act 1912 .... **15(1)**, 117
Elementary School Teachers Superannuation (Jersey) Act 1900 .... **15(1)**, 115
Emergency Laws (Miscellaneous Provisions) Act 1947—
   entire Act **50**, 466
   ss 2(1), 12(1), Sch 2, para 1 .... **33(2)**, 82
Emergency Laws (Miscellaneous Provisions) Act 1953—
   ss 1, 2, 13, 14, Schs 1, 2 .... **50**, 480
   ss 5, 13, 14 .... **1(1)**, 461
   ss 10, 13, 14 .... **3**, 384
Emergency Laws (Re-enactments and Repeals) Act 1964 .... **50**, 506
Emergency Laws (Repeal) Act 1959 .... **50**, 502
Emergency Powers Act 1964 .... **50**, 505
Emergency Workers (Obstruction) Act 2006 .... **50(S)**, War 1
Employer's Liability (Defective Equipment) Act 1969 .... **16**, 28
Employers' Liability (Compulsory Insurance) Act 1969 .... **16**, 29
Employment Act 1988 .... **16**, 177
Employment Act 1989—
   ss 1, 2, 4–6, 8, 11, 12, 27, 28(1)–(3), (4)(a), (5), 29(1), (2), (6), 30, Sch 1, Sch 9,
    para 1 .... **7(1)**, 294
   ss 9, 10, 22, 25, 27–30, Sch 2, Pt II, Schs 5, 7–9 .... **16**, 190
Employment Act 1990 .... **16**, 212
Employment Act 2002—
   ss 7, 8, 10–16, 48, 51, 52, 55, Sch 1 .... **40(2)**, 671
   ss 28, 38, 40, 44–46, 51–55, Schs 5, 7, 8 .... **16**, 1189
Employment Act 2008 .... **16**, 1252
Employment Agencies Act 1973 .... **16**, 65
Employment and Training Act 1973 .... **16**, 85
Employment and Training Act 1981 .... **16**, 138
Employment (Continental Shelf) Act 1978 .... **16**, 136

Employment Medical Advisory Service Act 1972 .... **18**, 1284
Employment of Children Act 1973 .... **6**, 210
Employment of Women, Young Persons, and Children Act 1920 .... **16**, 14
Employment Protection Act 1975 .... **16**, 117
Employment Protection (Consolidation) Act 1978 .... **16**, 131
Employment Relations Act 1999 .... **16**, 1156
Employment Relations Act 2004 .... **16**, 1215
Employment Rights Act 1996 .... **16**, 732
Employment Rights (Dispute Resolution) Act 1998 .... **16**, 1081
Employment Tribunals Act 1996 .... **16**, 655
Endangered Species (Import and Export) Act 1976 .... **13**, 586
Endowments and Glebe Measure 1976 .... **14**, 836
Enemy Property Act 1953 .... **50**, 489
Energy Act 1976 .... **17(1)**, 629
Energy Act 1983 .... **17(1)**, 707
Energy Act 2004—
   ss 1–50, 76–80, 82, 84–91, 93, 95–100, 104–119, 121–122, 124–134, 137–144, 146,
     148, 150, 152, 154–177, 179, 180, 184, 185, 188–198, Schs 1–9, 16–23 .... **17(2)**, 581
   ss 51–56, 58–71, 192, 196, 198, Schs 10–14 .... **33(2)**, 618
Energy Act 2008 .... **17(2)**, 906
Energy Conservation Act 1996 .... **17(2)**, 377
Enterprise Act 2002—
   ss 1–247, 273–281, Schs 1–15, 24–26 .... **47**, 803
   ss 248, 249, 254–257, 261, 264, 266, 268, 270, 276, 277, 279–281, Schs 17, 19,
     21 .... **4(2)**, 688
Environment Act 1995—
   ss 1–19, 37–56, 80–95, 107–125, Schs 1–5, 11, 18, 20–24 .... **35(2)**, 92
   ss 61–66, 68–72, 74–79, 97–99, 115, 123–125, Schs 7–10 .... **32**, 706
   ss 96, 122, 125, Schs 13, 14 .... **46**, 1140
   ss 105, 124, 125, Sch 15 .... **1(2)**, 697
Environment and Safety Information Act 1988 .... **35(1)**, 723
Environmental Protection Act 1990—
   ss 1–4, 6–15, 19–30, 33–40, 42–48, 51, 52, 52A, 55, 57, 59, 59ZA, 59A, 60, 62A,
     63A, 64–66, 71, 73–82, 84, 106–127, 140–142, 144, 152–154, 156–164, Schs 1, 2A,
     2B, 3, 12, 15, 16 .... **35(1)**, 749
   ss 86–89, 91–99, 128–132, 134, 139, 157–164, Schs 3A, 4, 6, 11 .... **32**, 635
   ss 149, 150, 159(1)–(6), 160, 161(1)–(4), 163, 164(1) **2**, 596
Episcopal Church (Scotland) Act 1864 .... **14**, 196
Episcopal Church (Scotland) Act 1964 .... **14**, 628
Episcopal Endowments and Stipends Measure 1943 .... **14**, 409
Equal Pay Act 1970 .... **16**, 36
Equality Act 2006 .... **7(1)**, 979
Essential Commodities Reserves Act 1938 .... **47**, 38
Estate Agents Act 1979 .... **21**, 818
European Communities Act 1972 .... **18**, 5
European Communities (Amendment) Act 1986 .... **18**, 80
European Communities (Amendment) Act 1993 .... **18**, 83
European Communities (Amendment) Act 1998 .... **18**, 93
European Communities (Amendment) Act 2002 .... **18**, 94
European Communities (Finance) Act 2008 .... **18**, 107
European Communities (Greek Accession) Act 1979 .... **18**, 79
European Communities (Spanish and Portuguese Accession) Act 1985 .... **18**, 79
European Economic Area Act 1993 .... **18**, 86
European Parliament (Pay and Pensions) Act 1979 .... **18**, 69
European Parliament (Representation) Act 2003 .... **15(3)**, 852
European Parliamentary and Local Elections (Pilots) Act 2004 .... **15(3)**, 872
European Parliamentary Elections Act 2002 .... **15(3)**, 821
European Union (Accessions) Act 1994 .... **18**, 92
European Union (Accessions) Act 2003 .... **18**, 96
European Union (Accessions) Act 2006 .... **18**, 99
European Union (Amendment) Act 2008 .... **18**, 108
Evidence Act 1845 .... **18**, 136
Evidence Act 1851 .... **18**, 139
Evidence Act 1938 .... **18**, 187
Evidence Amendment Act 1853 .... **18**, 146

Evidence and Powers of Attorney Act 1940 .... **18**, 189
Evidence and Powers of Attorney Act 1943 .... **18**, 190
Evidence (Colonial Statutes) Act 1907 .... **18**, 183
Evidence (Foreign, Dominion and Colonial Documents) Act 1933 .... **18**, 185
Evidence (Proceedings in Other Jurisdictions) Act 1975 .... **18**, 251
Exchange Equalisation Account Act 1979 .... **19(2)**, 943
Exchequer and Audit Act (Northern Ireland) 1921 .... **31**, 1699
Exchequer and Audit Departments Act 1866 .... **19(2)**, 654
Exchequer and Audit Departments Act 1921 .... **19(2)**, 743
Exchequer and Audit Departments Act 1957 .... **19(2)**, 816
Exchequer and Financial Provisions Act (Northern Ireland) 1950 .... **31**, 1718
Exchequer Extra Receipts Act 1868 .... **19(2)**, 665
Excise Duties (Surcharges or Rebates) Act 1979 .... **13**, 962
Execution Act 1844 .... **19(3)**, 10
Explosive Substances Act 1883 .... **12(1)**, 191
Explosives Act 1875 .... **18**, 720
Explosives (Age of Purchase &c) Act 1976 .... **18**, 756
Export and Investment Guarantees Act 1991 .... **47**, 500
Export Control Act 2002 .... **50**, 519
Extradition Act 2003 .... **18**, 789
Extra-Parochial Ministry Measure 1967 .... **14**, 654

F

Factories Act 1961 .... **18**, 1188
Factors Act 1889 .... **1(1)**, 6
Faculty Jurisdiction Measure 1964 .... **14**, 636
Fair Trading Act 1973 .... **47**, 154
Fairs Act 1871 .... **27**, 36
Fairs Act 1873 .... **27**, 49
Family Law Act 1986—
    ss 1, 2, 2A, 3, 5–7, 19, 19A, 20, 22–25, 27–43, 55A, 56–60, 68, 69, Sch 2 .... **6**, 294
    ss 44–52, 54, 55, 58–62, 68(3), 69 .... **27**, 608
Family Law Act 1996 .... **27**, 645
Family Law Reform Act 1969—
    ss 1, 8, 9, 12, 28, Schs 2, 3 .... **6**, 145
    ss 2, 19, 28 .... **27**, 316
    ss 3, 28 .... **50**, 785
    ss 14, 28 .... **18**, 614
    ss 20–26, 28 .... **18**, 238
Family Law Reform Act 1987—
    ss 1, 2, 17, 19, 27, 30–34, Schs 3, 4 .... **6**, 343
    ss 1, 18, 21, 33, 34, Sch 3, paras 8, 10 .... **18**, 691
Family Provision Act 1966 .... **18**, 612
Farm and Garden Chemicals Act 1967 .... **1(1)**, 708
Farm Land and Rural Development Act 1988 .... **1(2)**, 480
Farriers (Registration) Act 1975 .... **2**, 325
Farriers (Registration) (Amendment) Act 1977 .... **2**, 371
Fatal Accidents Act 1976 .... **31**, 776
Federation of Malaya Independence Act 1957 .... **7(2)**, 368
Female Genital Mutilation Act 2003 .... **12(3)**, 627
Ferries (Acquisition by Local Authorities) Act 1919 .... **36**, 512
Fiji Independence Act 1970 .... **7(2)**, 506
Films Act 1985 .... **13**, 317
Finance Act 1895 .... **41**, 51
Finance Act 1898 .... **41**, 54
Finance Act 1899 .... **41**, 59
Finance Act 1900 .... **41**, 61
Finance Act 1901 .... **13**, 570
Finance Act 1902 .... **13**, 572
Finance Act 1907 .... **41**, 63
Finance Act 1916—
    ss 63, 65, 69 .... **42**, 32
    ss 65–67, 69 .... **19(2)**, 735

Finance Act 1969—
  ss 1, 59, 61, Sch 7 .... **13**, 581
  ss 58, 61, Sch 21 .... **42**, 121
Finance Act 1970—
  ss 33, 36 .... **41**, 149
  s 36, Sch 8 .... **42**, 362
Finance Act 1971—
  ss 21, 37, 38, 69, Schs 3, 14 .... **42**, 373
  ss 67, 69, Sch 13 .... **30**, 429
Finance Act 1972 .... **42**, 392
Finance Act 1973—
  ss 32, 38, 41, 59, Schs 15, 22 .... **42**, 404
  ss 50, 54, 59 .... **41**, 153
  ss 56, 59 .... **10**, 430
  ss 58, 59(1), (4) **48**, 594
Finance Act 1974 .... **42**, 419
Finance Act 1975 .... **42**, 425
Finance Act 1976—
  ss 72, 131, 132, Schs 9, 15 .... **42**, 523
  ss 127, 131, 132 .... **41**, 158
Finance Act 1977—
  ss 7, 10, 59, Sch 3 .... **13**, 605
  ss 56, 59 .... **14**, 879
  s 59, Sch 9 .... **42**, 534
Finance Act 1978—
  ss 6, 80 .... **13**, 609
  s 80, Sch 13 .... **42**, 541
Finance Act 1980—
  ss 97, 98, 102, 122 .... **41**, 161
  ss 106–109, 118, 122, Schs 17, 20 .... **42**, 565
  ss 120, 122, Sch 19 .... **19(2)**, 946
Finance Act 1981—
  ss 6, 11, 139 .... **13**, 967
  ss 107, 108, 139 .... **41**, 165
  ss 111–113, 115, 117, 118, 121, 139, Sch 19 .... **42**, 593
  ss 137, 139 .... **31**, 1158
Finance Act 1982—
  ss 11, 157 .... **13**, 969
  ss 27, 134, 135, 145, 157, Schs 18, 22 .... **42**, 613
  ss 129, 157 .... **41**, 170
Finance Act 1983—
  ss 9, 36, 37, 46, 48, Schs 8, 10 .... **42**, 637
  ss 43, 45, 48 .... **19(2)**, 951
Finance Act 1984—
  ss 73, 113–116, 126–128, Sch 23 .... **42**, 699
  ss 110, 111, 128 .... **41**, 174
  ss 117, 128 .... **40(1)**, 209
Finance Act 1985—
  ss 8, 98, Sch 5, Pt II, Sch 27, Pt III .... **5(1)**, 125
  ss 10, 98 .... **13**, 971
  ss 81–85, 87–89, 98, Sch 24 .... **41**, 178
  ss 93–96, 98, Schs 25, 27 .... **42**, 981
Finance Act 1986—
  ss 6, 114, Sch 4, Pt III, Sch 23, Pt III .... **5(1)**, 129
  s 8 .... **19(3)**, 559
  ss 8, 114 .... **13**, 975
  ss 24, 100–104, 106–109, 114, Schs 18–21, 23 .... **42**, 1002
  ss 66–72, 72A, 75–79, 80A–80C, 84–88, 88A, 88B, 89A, 89AA, 90–99, 114 .... **41**, 188
Finance Act 1987—
  ss 50, 54, 55, 72 .... **41**, 259
  ss 57–59, 61–66, 72, Schs 10, 12–14, 16 .... **42**, 1042
  ss 68, 72 .... **19(2)**, 989
Finance Act 1988—
  ss 8, 149 .... **13**, 980

Finance Act 1988—*contd*
  ss 35, 36, 38, 40, 65, 66, 66A, 73, 127, 130–132, 134, 138, 145–149, Schs 3, 6,
    7 .... **42**, 1090
  ss 143, 149 .... **41**, 264
Finance Act 1989—
  ss 29, 188 .... **50**, 5
  ss 43, 44, 67–77, 82–88, 89–90A, 102, 103, 107, 110, 111, 115, 151, 178, 182, 182A,
    186–188, Schs 5–7, 8A, 12, 17 .... **42**, 1136
  ss 175–177, 188 .... **41**, 267
  ss 185, 188 .... **14**, 1191
Finance Act 1990—
  ss 25, 30, 41, 42, 48, 52, 53, 69, 80, 88, 89, 114, 125–127, 131, 133, Schs 6, 7, 12,
    19 .... **42**, 1246
  ss 107–111, 133 .... **41**, 270
  ss 128, 133 .... **19(2)**, 1003
Finance Act 1991—
  s 7 .... **19(3)**, 564
  ss 27, 48, 50–54, 58, 62–65, 71–73, 76, 78, 104–106, 108, 121–124, Schs 7, 9, 11,
    19 .... **42**, 1283
  ss 110–114, 116, 117, 122, 124 .... **41**, 275
Finance Act 1992 .... **42**, 1920
Finance Act 1993—
  ss 10, 12, 214 .... **13**, 989
  ss 24–29, 31–35, 37, 38, 40, 41, 214 .... **5(1)**, 133
  ss 72, 79, 80, 86–88, 91–92E, 97, 98, 101, 102, 112, 118–120, 122, 170–176,
    178–180, 182, 184–187, 189–195, 212–214, Schs 9, 19–21, 23 .... **43(1)**, 2
  ss 202, 204, 214 .... **41**, 282
Finance Act 1994—
  ss 7–27, 259, Sch 5 .... **13**, 993
  ss 28–44, 259, Sch 6 .... **4(1)**, 523
  ss 48–56, 59–74, 257, 259, Schs 6A, 7, 7A .... **19(1)**, 1128
  ss 77, 81, 101–103, 108, 112, 113, 118, 119, 133, 137, 138, 142, 146, 196, 199, 209,
    211, 215, 218–223, 225–234, 236–238, 248–253, 257–259, Schs 20, 22, 24–26 .... **43(1)**, 80
  ss 240–245, 257, 259 .... **41**, 285
Finance Act 1995—
  ss 4, 5, 163 .... **19(3)**, 566
  ss 14, 163 .... **5(1)**, 223
  ss 19, 163, Sch 4 .... **13**, 1174
  ss 26, 163 .... **50**, 398
  ss 42, 48, 51, 53–55, 58, 60, 67, 70–75, 79, 86, 87, 90, 103, 107, 109, 110, 113, 116,
    123, 125–128, 130, 133, 135, 137, 139, 152–154, 161–163, Schs 6, 8, 10, 18,
    21–23, 25, 29 .... **43(1)**, 181
  ss 151, 152(1), (2)(b), (3)(c), (d), (j), (4)–(6), (7)(b), 161, 163 .... **41**, 293
  ss 157, 163 .... **19(2)**, 1008
Finance Act 1996—
  ss 17, 197, 206 .... **13**, 1181
  ss 25, 26, 206 .... **50**, 401
  ss 39–71, 204, 206, Sch 5 .... **35(2)**, 295
  ss 72, 73, 79–84A, 85A, 85B, 87–88A, 90A, 91A–91G, 94–101, 103–105, 116,
    132–138, 148, 151, 153, 154, 156, 160, 163–166, 168, 175, 182, 198–206,
    Schs 7–11, 14, 15, 18, 31, 37, 41 .... **43(1)**, 262
  ss 186, 206 .... **41**, 300
  ss 197(1), (2)(a), (3)–(5), (7), 206 .... **4(1)**, 550
Finance Act 1997—
  s 3 .... **19(3)**, 571
  ss 10–15, 113, 114, Sch 1, Sch 18, Pt II .... **5(1)**, 225
  ss 24, 29, 61, 69, 74–76, 79, 80, 82, 83, 85, 87, 89, 110, 112–114, Schs 10, 12, 13,
    18 .... **43(1)**, 444
  ss 47, 49, 114 .... **50**, 403
  ss 50, 51, 110, 114, Sch 5, Pts I, V **13**, 1185
  ss 95, 96, 100, 101, 112, 114 .... **41**, 302
Finance Act 1998—
  ss 5, 165, 166, Sch 27, Pt 1 .... **19(3)**, 572
  ss 6, 20, 166, Sch 2 .... **13**, 1198

Finance Act 1998—*contd*
 ss 30–32, 35, 36, 38, 41, 42, 46, 48, 56, 57, 62, 70, 72, 74, 76, 86, 90, 92, 108, 110,
  111, 113, 117, 118, 121–125, 130–132, 137, 140, 142, 146, 155–158, 160, 161,
  163–166, Sch 3, Sch 5, Pt 4, Schs, 8, 11, 14, 15, 17, 18, 22, 23, 25–27 .... **43(1)**, 549
 ss 150, 166 .... **41**, 310
 ss 153, 165, 166, Sch 27, Pt V(3) .... **17(2)**, 481
Finance Act 1999—
 ss 9, 11, 126–129, 131, 140, Sch 1 .... **13**, 1202
 ss 13, 140, Sch 2 .... **50**, 407
 ss 28, 31, 32, 34, 36, 38, 41, 46, 52–54, 56, 63, 65, 66, 68, 72–74, 79, 81–83, 85–87,
  93–98, 125, 131–133, 138–140, Schs 5, 6, 10, 20 .... **43(1)**, 689
 ss 110, 112–115, 119, 121–123, 138, 140, Schs 13–19 .... **41**, 312
 ss 135, 136, 140 .... **19(2)**, 1011
Finance Act 2000—
 ss 20, 23, 157, Sch 4 .... **13**, 1211
 ss 30, 155, 157, Sch 6 .... **35(2)**, 574
 ss 38–41, 44, 46, 48–50, 54, 61, 63–65, 68, 69, 74, 82, 91, 92, 97, 98, 102–105, 107,
  108, 143, 144, 146–149, 152, 155–157, Sch 12, Pt 3, Schs 13, 15, Sch 17, Pts 2, 3,
  Sch 19, Pt 2, Schs 20, 22, Sch 27, Pt 1, Schs 28–31, 38, 40 .... **43(1)**, 752
 ss 118–122, 128–131, 155, 157, Schs 32–34 .... **41**, 352
 ss 153, 157 .... **19(2)**, 1013
Finance Act 2001—
 ss 8, 12, 13, 15, 111, Sch 3 .... **13**, 1218
 ss 16–48, 51, 57, 59, 63–71, 76, 78, 81, 83, 87, 88, 95, 101, 102, 109–111,
  Schs 4–10, Sch 15, Pt 3, Schs 16, 17, 20, 22, 27, 32, 33 .... **43(2)**, 2
 ss 92, 92A, 92B, 94, 109, 111, Sch 30 .... **41**, 373
 ss 99, 111 .... **50**, 411
 ss 107, 111 .... **10**, 669
Finance Act 2002—
 ss 5, 6, 19, 20, 143, Sch 2 .... **13**, 1229
 ss 12, 141, 143, Sch 4, Pt 2, Sch 40, Pt 1 .... **5(1)**, 266
 ss 26–32, 40, 43–45, 47, 48, 50, 51, 53–59, 61, 63–66, 71, 79–86, 93, 98, 99, 109,
  134–143, Sch 9, Pt 3, Schs 10–13, 16, 18, 22, Sch 23, Pt 3, Sch 25, Pt 3, Schs 26,
  28, 29, 33, 39, 40 .... **43(2)**, 135
 ss 110–113, 115, 116, 142, 143, Schs 34–37 .... **41**, 381
Finance Act 2003—
 ss 22, 217 .... **50**, 413
 ss 24–41, 217 .... **13**, 1235
 ss 42–58C, 60–64, 65–71A, 73–130, 215, 217, Schs 3–10, Sch 11, Pt 2,
  Schs 11A–17A, 19, 20 .... **41**, 404
 ss 132, 136, 139–143, 147, 148, 150–153, 155, 156, 159–164, 167–174, 177, 178,
  181–184, 195–200, 204, 205, 215–217, Schs 22–24, 26, Sch 28, Pt 3, Schs 30, 32,
  33, Sch 34, Pts 1, 4, Sch 37, Pt 1, Sch 43 .... **43(2)**, 400
Finance Act 2004—
 entire Act .... **43(2)**, 492
 ss 323, 328 .... **13**, 1252
Finance Act 2005 .... **43(2)**, 895
Finance Act 2006—
 ss 16–22, 178–180, Sch 26, Pt 2 .... **50(S)**, VAT 1
 ss 23–64, 69–161, 173–176, 178–180, Schs 1–23, 26 .... **43(S)**, Taxation 1
 ss 65–68, 179, 180 .... **13**, 537
 ss 166, 178–180 .... **41**, 667
 ss 172, 179, 180 .... **35(2)**, 866
Finance Act 2007—
 ss 1–4, 14, 17, 18, 21, 22, 25–55, 57–61, 66, 68–70, 82, 84–97, 102–104, 107–110,
  112–115, Sch 3, Pt 2, Schs 4–15, Sch 16, Pts 1–14, Schs 17–20, 22–27 ...... **43(S)**, Taxation 505
 ss 8, 113–115, Sch 27, Pt 6 .... **5(1)**, 726
 ss 13, 15, 16, 23, 113–115, Schs 2, 27 .... **35(2)**, 936
 ss 71–73, 79, 113–115 .... **41**, 671
 ss 98–100, 113–115, Sch 27, Pt 6 .... **50(S)**, VAT 17
Finance Act 2008 .... **43(S)**, Taxation 829
Finance Act 2009—
 ss 1–8, 11, 23–75, 84–111, 122–127, Schs 1, 2, 6–35, 38–58, 61 .... **43(S)**, Taxation 1357
 ss 9, 76–79, 113, Schs 3, 36 .... **50(S)**, VAT 25
 ss 10, 80–83, 126, 127, Sch 37 .... **41(S)**, Stamp Duties 1

Finance Act 2009—*contd*
   ss 12–16, 112, 120, 121, 126, 127, Sch 4 .... **13(S)**, Customs 1
   ss 17, 126, 127, Sch 5 .... **4(S)**, Aviation 1
   ss 18, 117–119, 126, 127, Schs 59, 60 .... **35(S)**, Public Health 173
   ss 19–22, 114–116, 126, 127 .... **5(S)**, Betting 1
Finance (No 2) Act 1915 .... **19(2)**, 733
Finance (No 2) Act 1931 .... **42**, 36
Finance (No 2) Act 1945 .... **42**, 54
Finance (No 2) Act 1975—
   ss 72, 75 .... **41**, 156
   ss 73, 75 .... **19(2)**, 928
   s 75, Sch 14 .... **42**, 515
Finance (No 2) Act 1979 .... **42**, 549
Finance (No 2) Act 1983—
   ss 15, 16 .... **41**, 173
   s 16, Sch 2 .... **42**, 645
Finance (No 2) Act 1987—
   ss 86, 95, 97, 101, 104, Schs 8, 9 .... **42**, 1081
   ss 102, 104 .... **19(2)**, 991
   ss 103, 104 .... **13**, 978
Finance (No 2) Act 1992—
   ss 1, 2, 4, 83, Sch 1 .... **13**, 981
   ss 20, 24, 28, 34, 40A–43, 55, 56, 62–66, 73–77, 81–83, Schs 6, 9, 12, 14, 17,
     18 .... **42**, 1921
Finance (No 2) Act 1997 .... **43(1)**, 496
Finance (No 2) Act 2005—
   ss 2, 71, 72 .... **50**, 415
   ss 7–46, 61, 67–72, Schs 2–9, 11 .... **43(2)**, 1087
   ss 47–49, 70–72, Sch 10 .... **41**, 660
Financial Services Act 1986 .... **8**, 860
Financial Services and Markets Act 2000 .... **19(2)**, 3
Fines and Recoveries Act 1833 .... **20**, 97
Fire and Rescue Services Act 2004 .... **18**, 1033
Fire Safety and Safety of Places of Sport Act 1987 .... **13**, 334
Fire Services Act 1947 .... **18**, 1014
Fire Services Act 1951 .... **18**, 1023
Fire Services Act 1959 .... **18**, 1024
Fire Services Act 2003 .... **18**, 1029
Firearms Act 1968 .... **12(1)**, 550
Firearms Act 1982 .... **12(1)**, 897
Firearms (Amendment) Act 1988 .... **12(1)**, 1356
Firearms (Amendment) Act 1992 .... **12(2)**, 177
Firearms (Amendment) Act 1994 .... **12(2)**, 244
Firearms (Amendment) Act 1997 .... **12(2)**, 649
Firearms (Amendment) (No 2) Act 1997 .... **12(2)**, 773
Fires Prevention (Metropolis) Act 1774 .... **19(1)**, 35
Fireworks Act 1951 .... **18**, 748
Fireworks Act 1964 .... **18**, 756
Fireworks Act 2003 .... **18**, 758
Fisheries Act 1891 .... **1(1)**, 189
Fisheries Act 1955 .... **39(2)**, 123
Fisheries Act 1981 .... **1(2)**, 179
Fishery Limits Act 1964 .... **1(1)**, 608
Fishery Limits Act 1976 .... **1(2)**, 153
Food Act 1984—
   ss 50–57, 57A, 59–61, 93–95, 110, 121, 132, 136 .... **27**, 69
   ss 69, 69A, 95, 132, 136 .... **1(2)**, 254
Food and Environment Protection Act 1985—
   ss 1–4, 16–25, 27, 28, Schs 1, 2, 5 .... **1(2)**, 264
   ss 5–7, 7A, 8–15, 20(2), (3), (4)(c), (5), 21(2A), (3)–(8), 22–24, 25(1), (3), (4), (5),
     26–28, Sch 2, paras 1(c), 2, 3, 4(1), 5–10, Schs 3, 4 .... **49**, 564
Food Safety Act 1990 .... **1(2)**, 488
Food Standards Act 1999 .... **1(2)**, 755
Football (Disorder) Act 2000 .... **13**, 445
Football (Offences) Act 1991 .... **13**, 407

Football (Offences and Disorder) Act 1999 .... **13**, 443
Football Spectators Act 1989 .... **13**, 362
Forced Marriage (Civil Protection) Act 2007 .... **27(S)**, Matrimonial 1
Foreign Compensation Act 1950 .... **10**, 811
Foreign Compensation Act 1962 .... **10**, 983
Foreign Compensation Act 1969 .... **10**, 1049
Foreign Compensation (Amendment) Act 1993 .... **10**, 1109
Foreign Corporations Act 1991 .... **8**, 959
Foreign Enlistment Act 1870 .... **12(1)**, 160
Foreign Judgments (Reciprocal Enforcement) Act 1933 .... **19(3)**, 18
Foreign Jurisdiction Act 1890 .... **7(2)**, 325
Foreign Jurisdiction Act 1913 .... **7(2)**, 337
Foreign Limitation Periods Act 1984 .... **19(3)**, 940
Foreign Marriage Act 1892 .... **27**, 112
Foreign Marriage Act 1947 .... **27**, 162
Foreign Marriage (Amendment) Act 1988 .... **27**, 627
Foreign Prison-made Goods Act 1897 .... **13**, 566
Forestry Act 1967 .... **18**, 1095
Forestry Act 1979 .... **18**, 1179
Forestry Act 1981 .... **18**, 1181
Forestry Act 1986 .... **18**, 1182
Forestry Act 1991 .... **18**, 1183
Forfeiture Act 1870 .... **12(1)**, 158
Forfeiture Act 1982 .... **12(1)**, 900
Forged Transfers Act 1891 .... **19(1)**, 116
Forged Transfers Act 1892 .... **19(1)**, 119
Forgery Act 1861 .... **12(1)**, 125
Forgery and Counterfeiting Act 1981 .... **12(1)**, 857
Fraud Act 2006 .... **12(4)**, 267
Free and Voluntary Present to His Majesty (1661) **10**, 37
Freedom of Information Act 2000 .... **7(1)**, 793
Friendly and Industrial and Provident Societies Act 1968 .... **19(1)**, 339
Friendly Societies Act 1955 .... **19(1)**, 234
Friendly Societies Act 1971 .... **19(1)**, 369
Friendly Societies Act 1974 .... **19(1)**, 377
Friendly Societies Act 1984 .... **19(1)**, 533
Friendly Societies Act 1992 .... **19(1)**, 907
Fur Farming (Prohibition) Act 2000 .... **2**, 665
Further and Higher Education Act 1992 .... **15(1)**, 347
Further Education Act 1985 .... **15(1)**, 204
Further Education and Training Act 2007 .... **15(S)**, Education 1

G

Gambia Independence Act 1964 .... **7(2)**, 450
Gambling Act 2005 .... **5(1)**, 320
Game Act 1831 .... **2**, 147
Game Act 1970 .... **2**, 294
Game Laws (Amendment) Act 1960 .... **2**, 254
Game Licences Act 1860 .... **2**, 174
Gangmasters (Licensing) Act 2004 .... **1(2)**, 815
Gas Act 1965 .... **17(1)**, 410
Gas Act 1972 .... **17(1)**, 616
Gas Act 1986 .... **17(1)**, 751
Gas Act 1995 .... **17(2)**, 345
Gas (Exempt Supplies) Act 1993 .... **17(2)**, 90
Gender Recognition Act 2004 .... **7(1)**, 922
Geneva Conventions Act 1957 .... **10**, 825
Geneva Conventions (Amendment) Act 1995 .... **10**, 1137
Geneva Conventions and United Nations Personnel (Protocols) Act 2009 ... **10(S)**, Constitutional 123
Geological Survey Act 1845 .... **10**, 232
German Conventions Act 1955 .... **10**, 822
Ghana (Consequential Provision) Act 1960 .... **7(2)**, 373
Ghana Independence Act 1957 .... **7(2)**, 364

Gifts for Churches Act 1811 .... **14**, 64
Goods Vehicles (Licensing of Operators) Act 1995 .... **38(1)**, 821
Government and other Stocks (Emergency Provisions) Act 1939 .... **19(2)**, 787
Government Annuities Act 1929 .... **19(2)**, 746
Government of Wales Act 1998 .... **10**, 1291
Government of Wales Act 2006 .... **10**, 1542
Government Resources and Accounts Act 2000 .... **19(2)**, 1015
Government Trading Act 1990—
   ss 2(5), 5, Sch 2, Pt II **10**, 564
   ss 4, 5, Sch 2, Pt I .... **19(2)**, 1005
Government Trading Funds Act 1973 .... **10**, 434
Great Seal Act 1688 .... **10**, 40
Great Seal Act 1884 .... **10**, 317
Great Seal (Offices) Act 1874 .... **10**, 305
Greater London Authority Act 1999 .... **26(1)**, 576
Greater London Authority Act 2007 .... **26(2)**, 556
Greater London Authority (Referendum) Act 1998 .... **26(1)**, 416
Greater London Council (General Powers) Act 1966 .... **25(1)**, 757
Greater London Council (General Powers) Act 1967 .... **25(1)**, 772
Greater London Council (General Powers) Act 1968 .... **25(1)**, 835
Greater London Council (General Powers) Act 1969 .... **25(1)**, 873
Greater London Council (General Powers) Act 1970 .... **25(1)**, 971
Greater London Council (General Powers) Act 1971 .... **25(1)**, 980
Greater London Council (General Powers) Act 1972 .... **25(2)**, 381
Greater London Council (General Powers) Act 1973 .... **25(2)**, 393
Greater London Council (General Powers) Act 1974 .... **25(2)**, 480
Greater London Council (General Powers) Act 1975 .... **25(2)**, 498
Greater London Council (General Powers) Act 1976 .... **25(2)**, 526
Greater London Council (General Powers) Act 1978 .... **25(2)**, 540
Greater London Council (General Powers) Act 1979 .... **25(2)**, 562
Greater London Council (General Powers) Act 1981 .... **25(2)**, 600
Greater London Council (General Powers) Act 1982 .... **25(2)**, 647
Greater London Council (General Powers) Act 1983 .... **25(2)**, 663
Greater London Council (General Powers) Act 1984 .... **25(2)**, 671
Greater London Council (General Powers) Act 1986 .... **25(2)**, 820
Greater London Council (General Powers) (No 2) Act 1978 .... **25(2)**, 553
Green Belt (London and Home Counties) Act 1938 .... **32**, 77
Greenwich Hospital Act 1865 .... **3**, 107
Greenwich Hospital Act 1869 .... **3**, 125
Greenwich Hospital Act 1872 .... **3**, 128
Greenwich Hospital Act 1883 .... **3**, 134
Greenwich Hospital Act 1885 .... **3**, 142
Greenwich Hospital Act 1942 .... **3**, 260
Greenwich Hospital Act 1947 .... **3**, 262
Greenwich Hospital Act 1967 .... **3**, 1231
Greenwich Hospital Act 1990 .... **3**, 1460
Ground Game Act 1880 .... **2**, 191
Ground Game (Amendment) Act 1906 .... **2**, 199
Guard Dogs Act 1975 .... **2**, 348
Gun Barrel Proof Act 1868 .... **48**, 15
Gun Barrel Proof Act 1950 .... **48**, 48
Gun Barrel Proof Act 1978 .... **48**, 88
Guyana Independence Act 1966 .... **7(2)**, 462
Guyana Republic Act 1970 .... **7(2)**, 500

H

Habeas Corpus Act 1679 .... **7(1)**, 23
Habeas Corpus Act 1803 .... **7(1)**, 32
Habeas Corpus Act 1804 .... **7(1)**, 33
Habeas Corpus Act 1816 .... **7(1)**, 34
Habeas Corpus Act 1862 .... **7(1)**, 38
Habeas Corpus Act (Ireland) 1781 .... **31**, 810
Hairdressers (Registration) Act 1964 .... **47**, 105

Hallmarking Act 1973 .... **48**, 51
Harbours Act 1964 .... **39(2)**, 126
Harbours and Passing Tolls, &c Act 1861 .... **39(2)**, 82
Harbours, Docks, and Piers Clauses Act 1847 .... **39(2)**, 21
Harbours (Loans) Act 1972 .... **39(2)**, 404
Harbours Transfer Act 1862 .... **39(2)**, 90
Hares Act 1848 .... **2**, 171
Hares Preservation Act 1892 .... **2**, 197
Health Act 1999—
  ss 13, 16, 44, 61–69, Sch 5 .... **30**, 642
  ss 60, 62, 64, 67–69, Sch 3 .... **28**, 982
Health Act 2006—
  ss 1–13, 76, 77, 79, 82–84, Schs 1, 2 .... **35(2)**, 869
  ss 17–25, 27–31, 76–79, 82–84 .... **28**, 1129
  ss 43, 57–71, 75–84, Schs 4–9 .... **30**, 909
Health and Medicines Act 1988—
  ss 1, 4–7, 9, 17–19, 24–28, Schs 1, 3 .... **30**, 521
  ss 21–23, 26–28 .... **28**, 662
Health and Safety at Work etc Act 1974—
  ss 1–4, 6–28, 33–54, 80–82, 84, 85, Schs 1–3A **18**, 1288
  ss 55–60, 81, 82, 84, 85 .... **16**, 107
Health and Safety (Offences) Act 2008 .... **18**, 1411
Health and Social Care Act 2001—
  ss 14, 39, 63–70, Sch 5, Pt 1, Sch 6, Pts 1, 2 .... **30**, 676
  ss 49–52, 54–57, 59, 64–70, Sch 5, Pt 2, Sch 6, Pt 3 .... **40(2)**, 506
Health and Social Care Act 2008—
  ss 1–97, 130–144, 149–158, 160–173, Schs 1–5, 12 14, 15 .... **30(S)**, NHS 1
  ss 52, 161–163, 169–173, Sch 3 .... **29**, 526
  ss 98–128, 161–166, 169–173, Schs 6–10, Sch 15, Pt 2 .... **28(S)**, Medicine 1
  ss 129, 130, 159, 166, 169–173, Sch 11, Sch 15, Pts 3, 7 .... **35(S)**, Public Health 1
  ss 132, 137, 138, 145–148, 161–164, 169–173, Sch 13 .... **40(2)**, 855
Health and Social Care (Community Health and Standards) Act 2003—
  ss 34, 41, 43–75, 102(1), (2), 113–115, 120–124, 126, 128, 130, 132, 134, 136–138,
    140, 142–169, 173, 176, 184, 186, 187, 189, 190, 193–203, Schs 4, 6, 8–12,
    14 .... **30**, 743
  ss 42–44, 76–102, 120–123, 125, 127, 129, 131, 133, 135, 139, 141, 148, 194, 195,
    199, 202, 203, Schs 7, 8 .... **35(2)**, 734
Health and Social Security Act 1984—
  entire Act .... **40(1)**, 211
  ss 5, 21, 23–29, Sch 8, Pt I **30**, 496
Health and Social Services and Social Security Adjudications Act 1983—
  entire Act .... **40(1)**, 186
  ss 4, 9, 11, 28, 31–34 .... **6**, 252
Health Authorities Act 1995 .... **30**, 599
Health Protection Agency Act 2004 .... **35(2)**, 782
Health Service Commissioners Act 1993 .... **30**, 561
Health Service Commissioners (Amendment) Act 1996 .... **30**, 623
Health Service Commissioners (Amendment) Act 2000 .... **30**, 675
Health Services Act 1980 .... **30**, 486
Health Services and Public Health Act 1968—
  ss 45, 46, 79 .... **40(1)**, 87
  ss 59, 79 .... **11(1)**, 731
  ss 62, 79 .... **35(1)**, 279
  ss 63–65, 77–79, Schs 3, 4 .... **30**, 406
  ss 66, 79 .... **29**, 19
Health (Wales) Act 2003 .... **30**, 730
Hearing Aid Council Act 1968 .... **28**, 68
Hearing Aid Council (Amendment) Act 1989 .... **28**, 668
Hearing Aid Council (Extension) Act 1975 .... **28**, 361
Higher Education Act 2004 .... **15(2)**, 808
Highway Act 1835 .... **36**, 255
Highway (Railway Crossings) Act 1839 .... **36**, 260
Highways Act 1980 .... **36**, 1070
Highways (Amendment) Act 1986 .... **37**, 613
Highways (Obstruction by Body Corporate) Act 2004 .... **38(2)**, 512

Hill Farming Act 1946 .... **1(1)**, 372
Hill Farming Act 1985 .... **1(2)**, 264
Hire-Purchase Act 1964 .... **39(1)**, 51
His Majesty's Declaration of Abdication Act 1936 .... **10**, 144
Historic Buildings and Ancient Monuments Act 1953 .... **32**, 194
Home Energy Conservation Act 1995 .... **17(2)**, 337
Home Safety Act 1961 .... **25(1)**, 608
Homelessness Act 2002 .... **23**, 857
Homicide Act 1957 .... **12(1)**, 348
Hong Kong Act 1985 .... **7(2)**, 598
Hong Kong Economic and Trade Office Act 1996 .... **10**, 1138
Hong Kong (Overseas Public Servants) Act 1996 .... **33(1)**, 720
Hong Kong (War Wives and Widows) Act 1996 .... **31**, 280
Honours (Prevention of Abuses) Act 1925 .... **33(1)**, 9
Horserace Betting and Olympic Lottery Act 2004 .... **5(1)**, 272
Horserace Betting Levy Act 1969 .... **5(1)**, 29
Horserace Betting Levy Act 1981 .... **5(1)**, 40
Horserace Totalisator and Betting Levy Boards Act 1972 .... **5(1)**, 36
Horserace Totalisator Board Act 1997 .... **5(1)**, 224
Horses (Protective Headgear for Young Riders) Act 1990 .... **6**, 670
Horticultural Produce Act 1986 .... **1(2)**, 444
Horticultural Produce (Sales on Commission) Act 1926 .... **1(1)**, 289
Horticulture Act 1960 .... **1(1)**, 560
Hospital Complaints Procedure Act 1985 .... **30**, 506
Hotel Proprietors Act 1956 .... **19(3)**, 448
House of Commons (Administration) Act 1978 .... **32**, 1131
House of Commons Disqualification Act 1975 .... **32**, 1083
House of Commons (Disqualifications) Act 1801 .... **32**, 1048
House of Commons Members' Fund Act 1939 .... **32**, 1067
House of Commons Members' Fund Act 1948 .... **32**, 1075
House of Commons Members' Fund Act 1957 .... **32**, 1079
House of Commons Members' Fund Act 1962 .... **32**, 1081
House of Commons Members' Fund and Parliamentary Pensions Act 1981 .... **32**, 1138
House of Commons Offices Act 1856 .... **32**, 1052
House of Commons (Removal of Clergy Disqualification) Act 2001 .... **32**, 1160
House of Lords Act 1999 .... **32**, 1154
House of Lords Precedence Act 1539 .... **33(1)**, 3
House to House Collections Act 1939 .... **5(2)**, 519
Household Waste Recycling Act 2003 .... **35(2)**, 673
Housing Act 1969 .... **21**, 422
Housing Act 1974 .... **21**, 498
Housing Act 1980 .... **21**, 877
Housing Act 1985 .... **22**, 1
Housing Act 1988 .... **22**, 903
Housing Act 1996 .... **23**, 513
Housing Act 2004—
    entire Act **24**, 215
    ss 217, 268–270 .... **17(2)**, 881
Housing and Building Control Act 1984 .... **35(1)**, 543
Housing and Planning Act 1986—
    ss 2, 4, 6, 8, 15, 18, 24, 39, 40, 48, 49, 56–59, Schs 4, 5, 12 .... **46**, 276
    ss 42, 57–59 .... **25(2)**, 816
Housing and Regeneration Act 2008 .... **24**, 687
Housing Associations Act 1985 .... **22**, 501
Housing (Consequential Provisions) Act 1985 .... **22**, 616
Housing Corporation (Delegation) etc Act 2006 .... **24**, 663
Housing Grants, Construction and Regeneration Act 1996—
    ss 1–3, 19–24, 29–31, 33–44, 51, 52, 55–59, 92–95, 98–103, 146–151, Sch 3 .... **23**, 802
    ss 104–117, 146, 148–151 .... **11(1)**, 431
    ss 126–128, 147, 148, 150, 151, Sch 3, Pt III **46**, 1178
Housing Repairs and Rents Act 1954 .... **21**, 135
Hovercraft Act 1968 .... **39(2)**, 380
Human Fertilisation and Embryology Act 1990 .... **28**, 773
Human Fertilisation and Embryology Act 2008 .... **28(S)**, Medicine 85
Human Fertilisation and Embryology (Deceased Fathers) Act 2003 .... **28**, 1034

Human Fertilisation and Embryology (Disclosure of Information) Act 1992 .... **28**, 847
Human Reproductive Cloning Act 2001 .... **28**, 994
Human Rights Act 1998 .... **7(1)**, 743
Human Tissue Act 2004 .... **28**, 1038
Hunting Act 2004 .... **2**, 673
Hydrocarbon Oil Duties Act 1979 .... **13**, 870
Hypnotism Act 1952 .... **13**, 100

I

Identity Cards Act 2006 .... **36**, 139
Immigration Act 1971 .... **31**, 71
Immigration Act 1988 .... **31**, 264
Immigration and Asylum Act 1999 .... **31**, 304
Immigration, Asylum and Nationality Act 2006 .... **31**, 706
Imperial Telegraphs Act 1938 .... **45**, 26
Imperial War Graves Endowment Fund Act 1926 .... **3**, 231
Imperial War Museum Act 1920 .... **13**, 78
Imperial War Museum Act 1955 .... **13**, 104
Import and Export Control Act 1990 .... **50**, 519
Import, Export and Customs Powers (Defence) Act 1939 .... **50**, 427
Import of Live Fish (England and Wales) Act 1980 .... **1(2)**, 175
Imprisonment (Temporary Provisions) Act 1980 .... **12(1)**, 849
Improvement of Land Act 1864 .... **20**, 244
Improvement of Land Act 1899 .... **20**, 367
Incitement to Disaffection Act 1934 .... **12(1)**, 255
Inclosure Act 1773 .... **20**, 72
Inclosure Act 1845 .... **20**, 140
Inclosure Act 1846 .... **20**, 189
Inclosure Act 1847 .... **20**, 193
Inclosure Act 1848 .... **20**, 197
Inclosure Act 1849 .... **20**, 204
Inclosure Act 1852 .... **20**, 216
Inclosure Act 1854 .... **20**, 222
Inclosure Act 1857 .... **20**, 234
Inclosure Act 1859 .... **20**, 240
Inclosure and Drainage (Rates) Act 1833 .... **20**, 93
Inclosure, etc, Expenses Act 1868 .... **20**, 305
Income and Corporation Taxes Act 1988 .... **44(1)**, 1
Income Tax Act 2007 .... **44(4)**, 2
Income Tax (Earnings and Pensions) Act 2003 .... **44(2)**, 2
Income Tax (Repayment of Post-War Credits) Act 1959 .... **42**, 73
Income Tax (Trading and Other Income) Act 2005 .... **44(3)**, 2
Incumbents and Churchwardens (Trusts) Measure 1964 .... **14**, 630
Incumbents (Vacation of Benefices) (Amendment) Measure 1993 .... **14**, 1266
Incumbents (Vacation of Benefices) Measure 1977 .... **14**, 880
Indecent Displays (Control) Act 1981 .... **12(1)**, 852
India (Consequential Provision) Act 1949 .... **7(2)**, 363
Indian Independence Act 1947 .... **7(2)**, 347
Indictable Offences Act 1848 .... **12(1)**, 111
Indictments Act 1915 .... **12(1)**, 232
Industrial and Provident Societies Act 1965 .... **19(1)**, 253
Industrial and Provident Societies Act 1967 .... **19(1)**, 335
Industrial and Provident Societies Act 1975 .... **19(1)**, 486
Industrial and Provident Societies Act 1978 .... **19(1)**, 488
Industrial and Provident Societies Act 2002 .... **19(2)**, 595
Industrial Assurance Act 1923 .... **19(1)**, 177
Industrial Assurance and Friendly Societies Act 1948 .... **19(1)**, 211
Industrial Common Ownership Act 1976 .... **47**, 318
Industrial Development Act 1982 .... **47**, 430
Industrial Development Act 1985 .... **47**, 460
Industrial Development (Financial Assistance) Act 2003 .... **47**, 1200
Industrial Diseases (Notification) Act 1981 .... **36**, 135
Industrial Organisation and Development Act 1947 .... **47**, 58

Industrial Training Act 1982 .... **16**, 141
Industrial Training Act 1986 .... **16**, 176
Industry Act 1972 .... **39(2)**, 407
Industry Act 1975 .... **47**, 241
Industry Act 1979 .... **47**, 372
Industry Act 1980 .... **47**, 403
Industry Act 1981 .... **47**, 411
Industry and Exports (Financial Support) Act 2009 .... **47(S)**, Trade 13
Inebriates Act 1898 .... **19(3)**, 440
Infant Life (Preservation) Act 1929 .... **12(1)**, 248
Infanticide Act 1938 .... **12(1)**, 265
Inheritance Act 1833 .... **18**, 515
Inheritance (Provision for Family and Dependants) Act 1975 .... **18**, 628
Inheritance Tax Act 1984 .... **42**, 720
Injuries in War (Compensation) Act 1914 .... **3**, 193
Injuries in War (Compensation) Act 1914 (Session 2) **3**, 196
Inland Revenue Buildings Act 1881 .... **10**, 122
Inner Urban Areas Act 1978 .... **46**, 44
Innkeepers Act 1878 .... **19(3)**, 439
Inquiries Act 2005 .... **10**, 746
Insolvency Act 1985 .... **4(2)**, 47
Insolvency Act 1986 .... **4(2)**, 68
Insolvency Act 1994 .... **4(2)**, 670
Insolvency Act 2000 .... **4(2)**, 673
Insolvency (No 2) Act 1994 .... **4(2)**, 672
Inspection of Churches Measure 1955 .... **14**, 479
Insurance Companies Act 1980 .... **19(1)**, 521
Insurance Companies Amendment Act 1973 .... **19(1)**, 375
Intelligence Services Act 1994 .... **10**, 615
International Carriage of Perishable Foodstuffs Act 1976 .... **1(2)**, 70
International Cocoa Agreement Act 1973 .... **13**, 585
International Criminal Court Act 2001 .... **10**, 1148
International Development Act 2002—
    ss 1–10, 16–20, Schs 1, 3–5 .... **7(2)**, 646
    ss 5–7, 11, 12, 16–18, 20, Sch 5 .... **19(2)**, 1042
    ss 5–7, 13, 14, 16–18, 20, Sch 2 .... **15(2)**, 541
International Development (Reporting and Transparency) Act 2006 .... **7(2)**, 665
International Headquarters and Defence Organisations Act 1964 .... **10**, 985
International Monetary Arrangements Act 1983 .... **19(2)**, 969
International Monetary Fund Act 1979 .... **19(2)**, 937
International Organisations Act 1968 .... **10**, 1027
International Organisations Act 1981 .... **10**, 1081
International Organisations Act 2005 .... **10**, 1249
International Parliamentary Organisations (Registration) Act 1989 .... **32**, 1146
International Road Haulage Permits Act 1975 .... **36**, 968
International Sugar Organisation Act 1973 .... **10**, 1054
International Transport Conventions Act 1983 .... **37**, 183
International Tribunals (Sierra Leone) Act 2007 .... **10**, 1254
Internationally Protected Persons Act 1978 .... **10**, 1054
Interpretation Act 1978 .... **41**, 796
Interpretation Measure 1925 .... **14**, 329
Intestates Estates Act 1884 .... **18**, 529
Intestates' Estates Act 1890 .... **18**, 531
Intestates' Estates Act 1952 .... **18**, 597
Intoxicating Substances (Supply) Act 1985 .... **12(1)**, 1189
Investment Exchanges and Clearing Houses Act 2006 .... **19(2)**, 604
Ireland Act 1949 .... **7(2)**, 358
Irish Free State (Consequential Provisions) Act 1922 (Session 2) **31**, 827
Iron and Steel Act 1982 .... **47**, 414
Island of Rockall Act 1972 .... **10**, 82
Isle of Man Act 1979 .... **7(2)**, 555

Isle of Man (Church Building and New Parishes) Act 1897 .... **14**, 248

J

Jamaica Independence Act 1962 .... **7(2)**, 403
Japanese Treaty of Peace Act 1951 .... **10**, 818
Jersey and Guernsey (Financial Provisions) Act 1947 .... **7(2)**, 352
Jews Relief Act 1858 .... **14**, 185
Jobseekers Act 1995 .... **40(2)**, 63
John F Kennedy Memorial Act 1964 .... **32**, 241
Judges Salaries Act 1872 .... **11(2)**, 83
Judgments Act 1838 .... **19(3)**, 6
Judicature (Northern Ireland) Act 1978 .... **31**, 954
Judicial Committee Act 1833 .... **11(2)**, 32
Judicial Committee Act 1843 .... **11(2)**, 48
Judicial Committee Act 1844 .... **11(2)**, 56
Judicial Committee Act 1881 .... **11(2)**, 90
Judicial Committee Act 1915 .... **11(2)**, 123
Judicial Committee Amendment Act 1895 .... **11(2)**, 110
Judicial Pensions Act 1959 .... **11(2)**, 147
Judicial Pensions Act 1981 .... **11(2)**, 616
Judicial Pensions and Retirement Act 1993 .... **11(3)**, 253
Judicial Proceedings (Regulation of Reports) Act 1926 .... **12(1)**, 246
Judicial Trustees Act 1896 .... **48**, 227
Juries Act 1825 .... **19(3)**, 179
Juries Act 1974 .... **19(3)**, 180
Jurisdiction in Rating Act 1877 .... **25(1)**, 58
Justice and Security (Northern Ireland) Act 2007 .... **31(S)**, N Ireland 77
Justice (Northern Ireland) Act 2002 .... **31**, 1526
Justice (Northern Ireland) Act 2004 .... **31**, 1663
Justices of the Peace Act 1361 .... **11(2)**, 23
Justices of the Peace Act 1949 .... **11(2)**, 142
Justices of the Peace Act 1968 .... **11(2)**, 171

K

Kenya Independence Act 1963 .... **7(2)**, 425
Kenya Republic Act 1965 .... **7(2)**, 455
Kiribati Act 1979 .... **7(2)**, 547
Knives Act 1997 .... **12(2)**, 677

L

Land Charges Act 1972 .... **21**, 452
Land Compensation Act 1961 .... **9**, 185
Land Compensation Act 1973—
  ss 1–13, 15–19, 26, 27, 29, 29A, 30, 32–38, 44–48, 50–59, 61, 63, 84–89,
    Sch 3 .... **9**, 282
  ss 20, 20A, 84, 87, 89 .... **35(1)**, 298
  ss 28, 39–43, 84, 85, 87, 89 .... **21**, 484
Land Drainage Act 1976 .... **19(3)**, 217
Land Drainage Act 1991 .... **19(3)**, 230
Land Drainage Act 1994 .... **19(3)**, 346
Land Powers (Defence) Act 1958—
  ss 1, 12–18, 18A, 18B, 21–27, Schs 2, 4 .... **9**, 157
  ss 6, 7, 10, 11, 27 .... **3**, 1176
  ss 8, 9, 25–27, Sch 3 .... **36**, 604
Land Registration Act 1986 .... **22**, 779
Land Registration Act 1997 .... **23**, 854
Land Registration Act 2002 .... **23**, 869
Land Settlement (Facilities) Act 1919 .... **1(1)**, 254
Land Transfer Act 1897 .... **20**, 350
Landlord and Tenant Act 1709 .... **20**, 67

Landlord and Tenant Act 1730 .... **20**, 70
Landlord and Tenant Act 1851 .... **20**, 207
Landlord and Tenant Act 1927 .... **21**, 42
Landlord and Tenant Act 1954 .... **21**, 138
Landlord and Tenant Act 1985 .... **22**, 558
Landlord and Tenant Act 1987 .... **22**, 793
Landlord and Tenant Act 1988 .... **22**, 897
Landlord and Tenant (Covenants) Act 1995 .... **23**, 431
Landlord and Tenant (Licensed Premises) Act 1990 .... **23**, 82
Landlord and Tenant (Requisitioned Land) Act 1942 .... **21**, 110
Landlord and Tenant (Requisitioned Land) Act 1944 .... **21**, 129
Landlord and Tenant (War Damage) Act 1939 .... **21**, 73
Landlord and Tenant (War Damage) (Amendment) Act 1941 .... **21**, 101
Landmines Act 1998 .... **12(2)**, 788
Lands Clauses Consolidation Act 1845 .... **9**, 7
Lands Clauses Consolidation Acts Amendment Act 1860 .... **9**, 65
Lands Tribunal Act 1949 .... **9**, 140
Late Payment of Commercial Debts (Interest) Act 1998 .... **11(1)**, 448
Latent Damage Act 1986 .... **19(3)**, 944
Law Commissions Act 1965 .... **41**, 767
Law of Distress Amendment Act 1888 .... **13**, 1312
Law of Distress Amendment Act 1895 .... **13**, 1315
Law of Distress Amendment Act 1908 .... **13**, 1317
Law of Libel Amendment Act 1888 .... **19(3)**, 380
Law of Property Act 1922—
    entire Act **20**, 375
    ss 43, 191 .... **14**, 303
Law of Property Act 1925 .... **20**, 582
Law of Property Act 1969 .... **21**, 426
Law of Property Amendment Act 1859 .... **18**, 523
Law of Property (Amendment) Act 1924 .... **20**, 393
Law of Property (Amendment) Act 1926 .... **21**, 39
Law of Property (Amendment) Act 1929 .... **21**, 67
Law of Property (Entailed Interests) Act 1932 .... **21**, 68
Law of Property (Joint Tenants) Act 1964 .... **21**, 266
Law of Property (Miscellaneous Provisions) Act 1989 .... **23**, 2
Law of Property (Miscellaneous Provisions) Act 1994—
    ss 1–13, 20–24, Sch 2 .... **23**, 372
    ss 14, 17–20, 22–24 .... **18**, 708
Law Officers Act 1944 .... **10**, 347
Law Officers Act 1997 .... **10**, 666
Law Officers Fees Act 1872 .... **10**, 304
Law presentment (1351–2) **10**, 25
Law Reform (Contributory Negligence) Act 1945 .... **31**, 760
Law Reform (Frustrated Contracts) Act 1943 .... **11(1)**, 355
Law Reform (Husband and Wife) Act 1962 .... **27**, 309
Law Reform (Married Women and Tortfeasors) Act 1935 .... **27**, 157
Law Reform (Miscellaneous Provisions) Act 1934—
    ss 1, 4 .... **18**, 594
    ss 3, 4 .... **11(2)**, 133
Law Reform (Miscellaneous Provisions) Act 1970—
    ss 1–3, 7, Schedule **27**, 319
    ss 5, 7 .... **45**, 1554
Law Reform (Personal Injuries) Act 1948 .... **45**, 1550
Law Reform (Succession) Act 1995 .... **18**, 714
Law Reform (Year and a Day Rule) Act 1996 .... **12(2)**, 546
Laying of Documents before Parliament (Interpretation) Act 1948 .... **41**, 753
Learner Travel (Wales) Measure 2008 .... **15(S)**, Education 63
Learning and Skills Act 2000 .... **15(2)**, 389
Learning and Skills (Wales) Measure 2009 .... **15(S)**, Education 327
Leasehold Property (Repairs) Act 1938 .... **21**, 69
Leasehold Reform Act 1967 .... **21**, 289
Leasehold Reform Act 1979 .... **21**, 876
Leasehold Reform, Housing and Urban Development Act 1993 .... **23**, 102
Lecturers and Parish Clerks Act 1844 .... **14**, 171

Legal Aid Act 1988 .... **11(3)**, 91
Legal Deposit Libraries Act 2003 .... **13**, 455
Legal Services Act 2007 .... **11(4)**, 251
Legislative and Regulatory Reform Act 2006—
  ss 1–20, 27, 30–35, Schedule **41**, 1158
  ss 21–24, 32–35 .... **10**, 794
  ss 27, 32–35 .... **18**, 102
Legislative Procedure Act (Northern Ireland) 1968 .... **31**, 1743
Legitimacy Act 1976 .... **6**, 221
Lesotho Independence Act 1966 .... **7(2)**, 471
Letters Patent Act 1571 .... **10**, 31
Level Crossings Act 1983 .... **37**, 185
Liability for War Damage (Miscellaneous Provisions) Act 1939 .... **50**, 452
Libel Act 1792 .... **19(3)**, 355
Libel Act 1843 .... **19(3)**, 362
Libel Act 1845 .... **19(3)**, 366
Liberties, Charters and Statutes Confirmed (1405–6) **10**, 28
Liberty of Subject (1354) **10**, 26
Libraries Offences Act 1898 .... **13**, 76
Licensed Premises (Exclusion of Certain Persons) Act 1980 .... **19(3)**, 541
Licensing Act 1872 .... **19(3)**, 436
Licensing Act 1902 .... **19(3)**, 443
Licensing Act 2003 .... **19(3)**, 589
Licensing (Alcohol Education and Research) Act 1981 .... **19(3)**, 545
Lieutenancies Act 1997 .... **26(1)**, 383
Life Annuities Act 1808 .... **19(2)**, 643
Life Assurance Act 1774 .... **19(1)**, 32
Life Assurance Companies (Payment into Court) Act 1896 .... **19(1)**, 121
Life Peerages Act 1958 .... **33(1)**, 11
Limitation Act 1980 .... **19(3)**, 875
Limitation Amendment Act 1980 .... **18**, 663
Limitation (Enemies and War Prisoners) Act 1945 .... **19(3)**, 871
Limitations of Actions and Costs Act 1842 .... **11(2)**, 46
Limited Liability Partnerships Act 2000 .... **32**, 1227
Limited Owners Residences Act 1870 .... **20**, 310
Limited Owners Residences Act (1870) Amendment Act 1871 .... **20**, 313
Limited Partnerships Act 1907 .... **32**, 1219
Literary and Scientific Institutions Act 1854 .... **13**, 60
Litigants in Person (Costs and Expenses) Act 1975 .... **11(2)**, 367
Litter Act 1983 .... **32**, 604
Livestock Rearing Act 1951 .... **1(1)**, 453
Local Authorities (Goods and Services) Act 1970 .... **25(1)**, 936
Local Authorities (Land) Act 1963 .... **25(1)**, 641
Local Authorities Loans Act 1945 .... **19(2)**, 799
Local Authorities' Mutual Investment Trust Act 1968 .... **48**, 592
Local Authorities (Restoration of Works Powers) Act 1977 .... **25(2)**, 532
Local Authority Social Services Act 1970 .... **25(1)**, 944
Local Employment Act 1970 .... **47**, 136
Local Employment Act 1972 .... **47**, 142
Local Government (Access to Information) Act 1985 .... **25(2)**, 700
Local Government Act 1888 .... **25(1)**, 85
Local Government Act 1894 .... **25(1)**, 102
Local Government Act 1929 .... **25(1)**, 164
Local Government Act 1948 .... **25(1)**, 394
Local Government Act 1958 .... **25(1)**, 537
Local Government Act 1966 .... **25(1)**, 751
Local Government Act 1972—
  ss 1–16A, 17A, 18–35, 37, 38, 53–61, 65, 67–76, 78–92, 94–109, 111–117,
   119–146A, 148, 150–152, 168, 172–179, 186, 187, 189, 191, 195, 202, 210, 211,
   216, 219, 222–256, 259, 260, 262, 263, 265–267, 269–274, Schs 1–5, 8, 11–12B,
   29–30 .... **25(2)**, 2
  ss 180, 181, 274, Sch 14 .... **35(1)**, 288
  ss 182, 185, 274, Sch 16 .... **46**, 33
  ss 184, 274, Sch 17, Pt III **32**, 310
  ss 206, 208, 274 .... **13**, 169

Local Government Act 1972—*contd*
  ss 214, 215, 274, Sch 26 .... **5(2)**, 482
Local Government Act 1974 .... **25(2)**, 419
Local Government Act 1978 .... **25(2)**, 539
Local Government Act 1985 .... **25(2)**, 703
Local Government Act 1986 .... **25(2)**, 807
Local Government Act 1988—
  ss 17–23, 29, 31, 34, 40–42, Schs 2, 3, 5, 7 .... **25(2)**, 856
  ss 24–26, 40, 42 .... **22**, 889
  ss 37, 39–42, Sch 7, Pt IV **2**, 588
Local Government Act 1992 .... **26(1)**, 168
Local Government Act 1999 .... **26(1)**, 525
Local Government Act 2000 .... **26(2)**, 2
Local Government Act 2003—
  ss 1–29, 31–33, 36–36B, 38–59, 68, 69, 73, 75, 83, 90, 93–106, 110, 114, 116, 117,
  123–129, Schs 1, 4–8 .... **26(2)**, 281
  ss 87, 88, 92, 124, 128, 129 .... **24**, 183
Local Government (Amendment) Act 1993 .... **26(1)**, 203
Local Government and Housing Act 1989—
  ss 1–13, 15–21, 24, 25, 31, 67–73, 139, 149–152, 154, 155, 157, 190–195, Schs 1, 5,
  11, 12 .... **25(2)**, 1075
  ss 74–80B, 82–89, 91–100, 165, 166, 168, 169, 171, 186, 190–193, 195, Schs 4, 7,
  10 .... **23**, 11
  ss 172, 173, 175, 190, 191, 195 .... **46**, 305
  ss 187, 192, 195 .... **47**, 482
Local Government and Public Involvement in Health Act 2007 .... **26(2)**, 582
Local Government and Rating Act 1997 .... **26(1)**, 395
Local Government (Contracts) Act 1997 .... **26(1)**, 405
Local Government (Emergency Provisions) Act 1916 .... **25(1)**, 141
Local Government Finance Act 1982 .... **25(2)**, 637
Local Government Finance Act 1988 .... **25(2)**, 877
Local Government Finance Act 1992 .... **26(1)**, 2
Local Government (Financial Provisions) Act 1963 .... **25(1)**, 700
Local Government Grants (Social Need) Act 1969 .... **25(1)**, 862
Local Government (Miscellaneous Provisions) Act 1953—
  ss 4–7, 18, 19 .... **36**, 591
  ss 8, 18, 19 .... **35(1)**, 245
Local Government (Miscellaneous Provisions) Act 1976—
  ss 7, 44–80, 83 .... **36**, 975
  ss 11, 12, 16, 30–33, 38, 40, 41, 44, 83 .... **25(2)**, 508
  ss 13–15, 29, 44, 83, Sch 1 .... **9**, 361
  ss 17, 19–27, 35, 39, 44, 81–83, Sch 2 .... **35(1)**, 398
  ss 36, 44(1), (1ZA), (6), 83 .... **27**, 63
  ss 42, 44(6), 83 .... **46**, 40
Local Government (Miscellaneous Provisions) Act 1982—
  ss 2, 49, Sch 3 .... **13**, 226
  ss 3, 49, Sch 4 .... **47**, 419
  ss 13–17, 29–32, 49 .... **35(1)**, 461
  ss 12, 41, 45, 47–49, Sch 7 .... **25(2)**, 619
  ss 33, 49 .... **21**, 923
  ss 37, 49 .... **27**, 66
Local Government (Overseas Assistance) Act 1993 .... **26(1)**, 200
Local Government, Planning and Land Act 1980—
  ss 1–4, 93–100, 116, 185, 192, 193, 196, 197, Schs 1, 7, 16, 33 .... **25(2)**, 570
  ss 47, 86, 91, 101, 124, 134–144, 146, 148, 149, 151–154, 157, 157A, 157B,
  159–172, 179, 194, 196, 197, Schs 17, 26–29, 31, 32, 34 .... **46**, 57
  ss 112, 113, 115, 121–123, 196, 197 .... **9**, 376
Local Government (Records) Act 1962 .... **25(1)**, 624
Local Government (Wales) Act 1994 .... **26(1)**, 207
Local Government (Wales) Measure 2009 .... **25(S)**, **26(S)**, Local Govt 45
Local Land Charges Act 1975 .... **21**, 509
Local Transport Act 2008 .... **38(2)**, 1023
Locomotive Act 1861 .... **36**, 407
London Building Act 1930 .... **25(1)**, 184
London Building Act (Amendment) Act 1935 .... **25(1)**, 239

London Passenger Transport Act 1933 .... **36**, 546
London Transport Act 1982 .... **25(2)**, 657
Lord Chancellor (Tenure of Office and Discharge of Ecclesiastical Functions)
  Act 1974 .... **10**, 450
Lord Chancellor's Pension Act 1832 .... **10**, 224

M

Magistrates' Courts Act 1980 .... **11(2)**, 401
Magistrates' Courts (Appeals from Binding Over Orders) Act 1956 .... **11(2)**, 146
Magistrates' Courts (Procedure) Act 1998 .... **11(3)**, 350
Magna Carta (1297) **10**, 18
Maintenance Enforcement Act 1991 .... **27**, 630
Maintenance Orders Act 1950—
  ss 4, 9, 12, 27, 28, 32 .... **6**, 101
  ss 15–28, 31, 32, Sch 2 .... **27**, 250
Maintenance Orders Act 1958 .... **27**, 283
Maintenance Orders Act 1968 .... **6**, 131
Maintenance Orders (Facilities for Enforcement) Act 1920 .... **27**, 141
Maintenance Orders (Reciprocal Enforcement) Act 1972 .... **27**, 337
Maintenance Orders (Reciprocal Enforcement) Act 1992 .... **27**, 636
Malawi Independence Act 1964 .... **7(2)**, 436
Malawi Republic Act 1966 .... **7(2)**, 466
Malaysia Act 1963 .... **7(2)**, 421
Malicious Communications Act 1988 .... **12(1)**, 1295
Malicious Damage Act 1861 .... **12(1)**, 121
Malta Independence Act 1964 .... **7(2)**, 446
Malta Republic Act 1975 .... **7(2)**, 523
Mandated and Trust Territories Act 1947 .... **7(2)**, 356
Manoeuvres Act 1958 .... **3**, 1184
Marine and Aviation Insurance (War Risks) Act 1952 .... **19(1)**, 223
Marine Insurance Act 1906 .... **19(1)**, 123
Marine Insurance (Gambling Policies) Act 1909 .... **19(1)**, 174
Marine Safety Act 2003 .... **39(2)**, 1150
Markets and Fairs Clauses Act 1847 .... **27**, 9
Markets and Fairs (Weighing of Cattle) Act 1887 .... **27**, 52
Markets and Fairs (Weighing of Cattle) Act 1891 .... **27**, 56
Markets and Fairs (Weighing of Cattle) Act 1926 .... **27**, 59
Marriage Act 1939 .... **27**, 160
Marriage Act 1949—
  ss 1–52, 68–75, 77–80, Schs 1, 4–6 .... **27**, 163
  ss 43, 53–67, 74, 76, 78, 80 .... **36**, 38
Marriage Act 1983 .... **27**, 562
Marriage Act 1994 .... **27**, 639
Marriage Act 1949 (Amendment) Act 1954 .... **27**, 276
Marriage Acts Amendment Act 1958 .... **27**, 279
Marriage Ceremony (Prescribed Words) Act 1996 .... **27**, 767
Marriage Confirmation Act 1830 .... **27**, 106
Marriage (Enabling) Act 1960 .... **27**, 306
Marriage of British Subjects (Facilities) Act 1915 .... **27**, 137
Marriage of British Subjects (Facilities) Amendment Act 1916 .... **27**, 140
Marriage (Prohibited Degrees of Relationship) Act 1986 .... **27**, 606
Marriage (Registrar General's Licence) Act 1970 .... **27**, 322
Marriage (Registration of Buildings) Act 1990 .... **27**, 629
Marriage (Scotland) Act 1956 .... **27**, 277
Marriage (Secretaries of Synagogues) Act 1959 .... **27**, 305
Marriage (Wales) Act 1986 .... **27**, 605
Marriage (Wales and Monmouthshire) Act 1962 .... **27**, 307
Marriage with Foreigners Act 1906 .... **27**, 131
Marriages Confirmation Act 1825 .... **27**, 105
Marriages Validity (Provisional Orders) Act 1924 .... **27**, 156
Married Women (Restraint upon Anticipation) Act 1949 .... **27**, 249
Married Women's Property Act 1882 .... **27**, 107
Married Women's Property Act 1893 .... **27**, 128

Married Women's Property Act 1907 .... **27**, 136
Married Women's Property Act 1964 .... **27**, 310
Marshall Aid Commemoration Act 1953 .... **15(1)**, 169
Marshall Scholarships Act 1959 .... **15(1)**, 171
Matrimonial and Family Proceedings Act 1984 .... **27**, 565
Matrimonial Causes Act 1965 .... **27**, 311
Matrimonial Causes Act 1973 .... **27**, 408
Matrimonial Causes (Property and Maintenance) Act 1958 .... **27**, 279
Matrimonial Homes and Property Act 1981 .... **27**, 551
Matrimonial Proceedings and Property Act 1970 .... **27**, 333
Matrimonial Proceedings (Children) Act 1958 .... **27**, 304
Matrimonial Proceedings (Transfers) Act 1988 .... **27**, 625
Mauritius Independence Act 1968 .... **7(2)**, 488
Mauritius Republic Act 1992 .... **7(2)**, 615
Medical Act (1858) **28**, 10
Medical Act 1860 .... **28**, 12
Medical Act 1983 .... **28**, 363
Medical (Professional Performance) Act 1995 .... **28**, 977
Medical Qualifications (Amendment) Act 1991 .... **28**, 846
Medicinal Products: Prescription by Nurses etc Act 1992 .... **30**, 559
Medicines Act 1968 .... **28**, 84
Medicines Act 1971 .... **28**, 336
Meeting of Parliament Act 1694 .... **32**, 1042
Meeting of Parliament Act 1797 .... **32**, 1046
Meeting of Parliament Act 1799 .... **32**, 1047
Meeting of Parliament Act 1870 .... **32**, 1059
Mental Capacity Act 2005 .... **29**, 298
Mental Health Act 1959 .... **29**, 10
Mental Health Act 1983 .... **29**, 28
Mental Health Act 2007 .... **29**, 479
Mental Health (Amendment) Act 1982 .... **29**, 21
Mental Health (Patients in the Community) Act 1995 .... **29**, 291
Mental Health (Scotland) Act 1984 .... **29**, 282
Mercantile Law Amendment Act 1856 .... **11(1)**, 353
Merchant Shipping Act 1988 .... **39(2)**, 567
Merchant Shipping Act 1995 .... **39(2)**, 693
Merchant Shipping and Maritime Security Act 1997 .... **39(2)**, 1135
Merchant Shipping Law Amendment Act 1853 .... **39(2)**, 78
Merchant Shipping (Liner Conferences) Act 1982 .... **39(2)**, 475
Merchant Shipping (Pollution) Act 2006 .... **39(2)**, 1170
Merchant Shipping Repeal Act 1854 .... **39(2)**, 79
Metropolis Management Act 1855 .... **25(1)**, 55
Metropolis Management (Thames River Prevention of Floods) Amendment
  Act 1879 .... **49**, 99
Metropolis Water Act 1852 .... **49**, 62
Metropolis Water Act 1871 .... **49**, 81
Metropolis Water Act 1897 .... **49**, 127
Metropolis Water Act 1902 .... **49**, 129
Metropolitan Board of Works (Various Powers) Act 1882 .... **49**, 121
Metropolitan Board of Works (Various Powers) Act 1885 .... **25(1)**, 83
Metropolitan Commons Act 1866 .... **20**, 289
Metropolitan Commons Act 1878 .... **20**, 333
Metropolitan Commons Amendment Act 1869 .... **20**, 306
Metropolitan Fairs Act 1868 .... **27**, 34
Metropolitan Fire Brigade Act 1865 .... **18**, 1010
Metropolitan Magistrates' Courts Act 1959 .... **33(2)**, 84
Metropolitan Police Act 1829 .... **33(2)**, 31
Metropolitan Police Act 1839—
  ss 33, 78, 79 .... **12(1)**, 103
  ss 38–40 .... **27**, 6
  s 44 .... **19(3)**, 434
  ss 52–55, 58, 60, 61, 68, 75, 76, 78, 79 .... **36**, 261
  ss 68, 75, 76, 78, 79 .... **33(2)**, 35
Metropolitan Police Act 1860 .... **33(2)**, 37
Metropolitan Police Act 1864 .... **36**, 420

Metropolitan Police Act 1886 .... **33(2)**, 42
Metropolitan Police Act 1887 .... **33(2)**, 51
Metropolitan Police Act 1899 .... **33(2)**, 58
Metropolitan Police Courts Act 1839 .... **12(1)**, 104
Metropolitan Police Courts Act 1840 .... **11(2)**, 45
Metropolitan Police Courts Act 1897 .... **11(2)**, 114
Metropolitan Police (Receiver) Act 1861 .... **33(2)**, 40
Metropolitan Police (Receiver) Act 1867 .... **33(2)**, 41
Metropolitan Police (Receiver) Act 1895 .... **33(2)**, 52
Metropolitan Police (Staff Superannuation and Police Fund) Act 1931 .... **33(2)**, 64
Metropolitan Public Carriage Act 1869 .... **36**, 435
Metropolitan Streets Act 1867 .... **36**, 424
Metropolitan Streets Act Amendment Act 1867 .... **36**, 429
Metropolitan Water Board Act 1927 .... **49**, 192
Metropolitan Water Board Act 1929 .... **49**, 198
Metropolitan Water Board Act 1932 .... **49**, 206
Metropolitan Water Board Act 1935 .... **49**, 216
Metropolitan Water Board Act 1939 .... **49**, 219
Metropolitan Water Board Act 1946 .... **49**, 264
Metropolitan Water Board (Charges) Act 1907 .... **49**, 163
Metropolitan Water Board (Charges) Act 1921 .... **49**, 184
Middlesex Deeds Act 1940 .... **21**, 97
Military Lands Act 1892 .... **3**, 146
Military Lands Act 1897 .... **3**, 180
Military Lands Act 1900 .... **3**, 181
Military Lands Act 1903 .... **3**, 190
Militia (City of London) Act 1820 .... **25(1)**, 47
Militia (Lands and Buildings) Act 1873 .... **3**, 130
Milk (Cessation of Production) Act 1985 .... **1(2)**, 259
Millbank Prison Act 1892 .... **12(1)**, 205
Mineral Exploration and Investment Grants Act 1972 .... **17(1)**, 614
Mineral Workings Act 1951 .... **17(1)**, 82
Mineral Workings Act 1985 .... **17(1)**, 717
Mineral Workings (Offshore Installations) Act 1971 .... **17(1)**, 604
Miners' Welfare Act 1952 .... **17(1)**, 85
Mines and Quarries Act 1954 .... **17(1)**, 120
Mines and Quarries (Tips) Act 1969 .... **17(1)**, 535
Mines (Working Facilities and Support) Act 1923 .... **36**, 516
Mines (Working Facilities and Support) Act 1966 .... **17(1)**, 515
Mines (Working Facilities and Support) Act 1974 .... **17(1)**, 625
Mining Industry Act 1920 .... **17(1)**, 37
Mining Industry Act 1926 .... **17(1)**, 42
Minister of Food (Financial Powers) Act 1949 .... **10**, 356
Minister of Works Act 1942 .... **10**, 345
Ministerial and other Pensions and Salaries Act 1991—
    ss 1, 2, 4, 6, 8, 9 .... **33(1)**, 291
    ss 5, 8(2), (3), 9 .... **10**, 566
Ministerial and other Salaries Act 1975 .... **10**, 474
Ministerial and other Salaries Act 1997 .... **10**, 669
Ministers of the Crown Act 1975 .... **10**, 460
Ministries Act (Northern Ireland) 1944 .... **31**, 1716
Ministry of Agriculture and Fisheries Act 1919 .... **10**, 341
Ministry of Defence Police Act 1987 .... **33(2)**, 133
Ministry of Fuel and Power Act 1945 .... **10**, 348
Ministry of Housing and Local Government Provisional Order Confirmation (Greater
    London Parks and Open Spaces) Act 1967 .... **25(1)**, 786
Ministry of Transport Act 1919 .... **10**, 337
Minors' Contracts Act 1987 .... **6**, 340
Miscellaneous Financial Provisions Act 1946 .... **19(2)**, 803
Miscellaneous Financial Provisions Act 1955—
    ss 4, 6 .... **36**, 603
    ss 5, 6 .... **19(2)**, 812
Miscellaneous Financial Provisions Act 1968 .... **17(1)**, 533
Miscellaneous Financial Provisions Act 1983 .... **47**, 451
Misrepresentation Act 1967 .... **39(1)**, 57

Misuse of Drugs Act 1971 .... **28**, 270
Mobile Homes Act 1975 .... **32**, 319
Mobile Homes Act 1983 .... **21**, 929
Mobile Telephones (Re-programming) Act 2002 .... **12(3)**, 624
Motor Cycle Noise Act 1987 .... **37**, 615
Motor Vehicles (International Circulation) Act 1952 .... **36**, 587
Motor Vehicles (Safety Equipment for Children) Act 1991 .... **38(1)**, 249
Motor Vehicles (Wearing of Rear Seat Belts by Children) Act 1988 .... **37**, 746
Multilateral Investment Guarantee Agency Act 1988 .... **19(2)**, 994
Municipal Corporations Act 1882 .... **25(1)**, 59
Municipal Corporations Act 1883 .... **25(1)**, 79
Murder (Abolition of Death Penalty) Act 1965 .... **12(1)**, 422
Museum of London Act 1965 .... **13**, 136
Museum of London Act 1986 .... **13**, 331
Museums and Galleries Act 1992 .... **13**, 410
Museums and Galleries Admission Charges Act 1972 .... **13**, 172

N

Namibia Act 1991 .... **7(2)**, 613
National Assistance Act 1948 .... **40(1)**, 26
National Assistance (Amendment) Act 1951 .... **40(1)**, 68
National Assistance (Amendment) Act 1959 .... **40(1)**, 70
National Audit Act 1983 .... **19(2)**, 953
National Debt Act 1870 .... **19(2)**, 665
National Debt Act 1889 .... **19(2)**, 722
National Debt Act 1972 .... **19(2)**, 911
National Debt Commissioners Act 1818 .... **19(2)**, 649
National Debt (Conversion) Act 1888 .... **19(2)**, 720
National Debt (Conversion of Stock) Act 1884 .... **19(2)**, 713
National Debt Reduction Act 1786 .... **19(2)**, 641
National Debt Reduction Act 1823 .... **19(2)**, 649
National Debt Reduction Act 1866 .... **19(2)**, 653
National Debt (Stockholders Relief) Act 1892 .... **19(2)**, 725
National Health Service Act 1946 .... **30**, 396
National Health Service Act 1977 .... **30**, 433
National Health Service Act 2006 .... **30**, 959
National Health Service (Amendment) Act 1986 .... **30**, 509
National Health Service (Amendment) Act 1995 .... **30**, 620
National Health Service and Community Care Act 1990—
    ss 18, 60, 61, 63–67, Schs 8–10 .... **30**, 538
    ss 46–49, 64(1)(d), (e), 65, 67 .... **40(1)**, 316
National Health Service (Consequential Provisions) Act 2006 .... **30**, 1840
National Health Service (Primary Care) Act 1997 .... **30**, 627
National Health Service (Private Finance) Act 1997 .... **30**, 641
NHS Redress Act 2006 .... **30**, 1886
NHS Redress (Wales) Measure 2008 .... **30(S)**, NHS 207
National Health Service Reform and Health Care Professions Act 2002—
    entire Act **28**, 996
    ss 2, 4, 19, 22, 37–42, Sch 2, Pt 2, Schs 8, 9 .... **30**, 703
National Health Service (Residual Liabilities) Act 1996 .... **30**, 626
National Health Service (Wales) Act 2006 .... **30**, 1477
National Heritage Act 1980—
    ss 1–7, 16–18, Schs 1, 2 .... **13**, 211
    ss 8–14, 17, 18, Sch 2 .... **42**, 557
National Heritage Act 1983—
    ss 1–7, 9–15, 17–31A, 40–43, Schs 1, 2, 6 .... **13**, 241
    ss 32–38, 41–43, Sch 3 .... **32**, 615
National Heritage Act 1997 .... **13**, 442
National Heritage Act 2002 .... **32**, 892
National Institutions Measure 1998 .... **14**, 1322
National Insurance Act 1965 .... **40(1)**, 71
National Insurance Act 1974 .... **40(1)**, 118
National Insurance Contributions Act 2002 .... **40(2)**, 570

National Insurance Contributions Act 2006 .... **40(2)**, 733
National Insurance Contributions Act 2008 .... **40(2)**, 876
National Insurance Contributions and Statutory Payments Act 2004 .... **40(2)**, 709
National Loans Act 1939 .... **19(2)**, 789
National Loans Act 1968 .... **19(2)**, 832
National Lottery Act 1998 .... **5(1)**, 245
National Lottery Act 2006 .... **5(1)**, 707
National Lottery etc Act 1993 .... **5(1)**, 146
National Lottery (Funding of Endowments) Act 2003 .... **5(1)**, 271
National Maritime Museum Act 1934 .... **13**, 84
National Maritime Museum Act 1989 .... **13**, 359
National Minimum Wage Act 1998 .... **16**, 1090
National Parks and Access to the Countryside Act 1949—
    ss 1, 3, 4A–7, 9, 11A–22, 59, 60, 64–78, 80–82, 85–86A, 89–92, 99–101, 103, 104,
      106–115, Schs 1, 2 .... **32**, 114
    ss 50A–55, 57, 99–101, 109–111A, 114, 115 .... **36**, 569
National Savings Bank Act 1971 .... **19(2)**, 892
National Theatre Act 1949 .... **13**, 98
National Theatre Act 1974 .... **13**, 173
National Trust Act 1907 .... **32**, 48
National Trust Act 1937 .... **32**, 70
National Trust Act 1939 .... **32**, 104
National Trust Act 1953 .... **32**, 209
National Trust Act 1971 .... **32**, 297
National Trust Charity Scheme Confirmation Act 1919 .... **32**, 65
Nationality, Immigration and Asylum Act 2002 .... **31**, 511
Natural Environment and Rural Communities Act 2006—
    ss 1–46, 52, 53, 64, 65, 78–86, 98–100, 102–109, Schs 1–7, 11, 12 .... **32**, 924
    ss 66, 67, 71, 73, 107–109 .... **38(2)**, 687
    ss 87–97, 101, 107–109, Schs 8–10 .... **1(2)**, 844
Nature Conservancy Council Act 1973 .... **32**, 315
Nautical Almanack Act 1828 .... **39(2)**, 20
Naval Agency and Distribution Act 1864 .... **3**, 90
Naval and Marine Pay and Pensions Act 1865 .... **3**, 103
Naval and Military War Pensions, &c, Act 1915 .... **3**, 199
Naval and Military War Pensions, &c (Administrative Expenses) Act 1917 .... **3**, 204
Naval Discipline Act 1957 .... **3**, 958
Naval Forces (Enforcement of Maintenance Liabilities) Act 1947 .... **3**, 268
Naval Knights of Windsor (Dissolution) Act 1892 .... **3**, 145
Naval Medical Compassionate Fund Act 1915 .... **3**, 198
Naval Pensions Act 1884 .... **3**, 137
Naval Prize Act 1864 .... **11(2)**, 64
Naval Prize (Procedure) Act 1916 .... **11(2)**, 124
Navy and Marines (Property of Deceased) Act 1865 .... **3**, 117
Navy and Marines (Wills) Act 1865 .... **50**, 771
Navy and Marines (Wills) Act 1930 .... **50**, 776
Navy and Marines (Wills) Act 1939 .... **50**, 777
Navy and Marines (Wills) Act 1953 .... **50**, 778
New Hebrides Act 1980 .... **7(2)**, 583
New Housing Areas (Church Buildings) Measure 1954 .... **14**, 477
New Parishes Act 1843 .... **14**, 170
New Parishes Acts and Church Building Acts Amendment Act 1869 .... **14**, 217
New Parishes Measure 1943 .... **14**, 396
New Roads and Street Works Act 1991 .... **38(1)**, 249
New Towns Act 1981 .... **46**, 168
New Towns (Amendment) Act 1994 .... **46**, 1140
New Towns and Urban Development Corporations Act 1985 .... **46**, 272
Newspaper Libel and Registration Act 1881 .... **19(3)**, 372
Newspapers, Printers, and Reading Rooms Repeal Act 1869 .... **19(3)**, 367
Nigeria Independence Act 1960 .... **7(2)**, 380
Nigeria Republic Act 1963 .... **7(2)**, 433
Night Poaching Act 1828 .... **2**, 144
Night Poaching Act 1844 .... **2**, 170
Noise Act 1996 .... **35(2)**, 367
Noise and Statutory Nuisance Act 1993 .... **35(2)**, 80

Non-Domestic Rating Act 1992 .... **26(1)**, 191
Non-Domestic Rating Act 1993 .... **26(1)**, 197
Non-Domestic Rating Act 1994 .... **26(1)**, 204
Non-Domestic Rating (Information) Act 1996 .... **26(1)**, 358
Non-parochial Registers Act 1840 .... **36**, 7
None put to answere without due Process (1368) .... **12(1)**, 77
North Sea Fisheries Act 1893 .... **1(1)**, 194
Northern Ireland Act 1947 .... **31**, 835
Northern Ireland Act 1962 .... **31**, 847
Northern Ireland Act 1974 .... **31**, 899
Northern Ireland Act 1998 .... **31**, 1247
Northern Ireland Act 2000 .... **31**, 1431
Northern Ireland Act 2006 .... **31**, 1689
Northern Ireland Act 2009 .... **31(S)**, N Ireland 123
Northern Ireland Arms Decommissioning Act 1997 .... **31**, 1177
Northern Ireland Arms Decommissioning (Amendment) Act 2002 .... **31**, 1525
Northern Ireland Assembly Disqualification Act 1975 .... **31**, 907
Northern Ireland Assembly Elections Act 2003 .... **31**, 1652
Northern Ireland Assembly (Elections and Periods of Suspension) Act 2003 .... **31**, 1653
Northern Ireland Constitution Act 1973 .... **31**, 862
Northern Ireland (Emergency Provisions) Act 1973 .... **31**, 894
Northern Ireland (Emergency Provisions) (Amendment) Act 1975 .... **31**, 947
Northern Ireland (Loans) Act 1975 .... **31**, 951
Northern Ireland (Loans) Act 1985 .... **31**, 1171
Northern Ireland (Location of Victims' Remains) Act 1999 .... **31**, 1427
Northern Ireland (Miscellaneous Provisions) Act 1928 .... **31**, 831
Northern Ireland (Miscellaneous Provisions) Act 1932 .... **31**, 831
Northern Ireland (Miscellaneous Provisions) Act 1945 .... **31**, 833
Northern Ireland (Miscellaneous Provisions) Act 2006—
    ss 1, 6, 8–11, 13–15, 29–33, Sch 1, Sch 4, Pt 1, Sch 5 .... **15(3)**, 993
    ss 16–22, 26, 28, 30–33, Schs 2, 3, Sch 4, Pt 3, Sch 5 .... **31(S)**, N Ireland 1
Northern Ireland (Monitoring Commission etc) Act 2003 .... **31**, 1659
Northern Ireland (Sentences) Act 1998 .... **31**, 1227
Northern Ireland (St Andrews Agreement) Act 2006 .... **31(S)**, N Ireland 27
Northern Ireland (St Andrews Agreement) Act 2007 .... **31(S)**, N Ireland 75
Northern Ireland (Temporary Provisions) Act 1972 .... **31**, 860
Nuclear Explosions (Prohibition and Inspections) Act 1998 .... **12(2)**, 775
Nuclear Industry (Finance) Act 1977 .... **17(1)**, 657
Nuclear Installations Act 1965 .... **17(1)**, 470
Nuclear Installations Act 1969 .... **17(1)**, 585
Nuclear Material (Offences) Act 1983 .... **12(1)**, 943
Nuclear Safeguards Act 2000 .... **17(2)**, 484
Nuclear Safeguards and Electricity (Finance) Act 1978 .... **17(1)**, 665
Nursery Education and Grant-Maintained Schools Act 1996 .... **15(1)**, 461

O

Oaths Act 1775 .... **11(2)**, 24
Oaths Act 1978 .... **18**, 261
Oaths and Evidence (Overseas Authorities and Countries) Act 1963 .... **18**, 221
Obscene Publications Act 1959 .... **12(1)**, 357
Obscene Publications Act 1964 .... **12(1)**, 397
Occupiers' Liability Act 1957 .... **21**, 249
Occupiers' Liability Act 1984 .... **21**, 948
OECD Support Fund Act 1975 .... **19(2)**, 935
Offences against the Person Act 1861 .... **12(1)**, 128
Offences at Sea Act 1799 .... **12(1)**, 83
Offender Management Act 2007 .... **12(4)**, 447
Offensive Weapons Act 1996 .... **12(2)**, 638
Office of Communications Act 2002 .... **45**, 703
Officers Commissions Act 1862 .... **3**, 89
Offices, Shops and Railway Premises Act 1963 .... **18**, 1242
Official Secrets Act 1911 .... **12(1)**, 224
Official Secrets Act 1920 .... **12(1)**, 239

Official Secrets Act 1939 .... **12(1)**, 267
Official Secrets Act 1989 .... **12(2)**, 2
Offshore Safety Act 1992—
  ss 1–3, 6, 7, Schs 1, 2 .... **18**, 1379
  ss 5–7 .... **17(2)**, 81
Oil and Gas (Enterprise) Act 1982 .... **17(1)**, 700
Oil and Pipelines Act 1985 .... **17(1)**, 729
Oil Taxation Act 1975 .... **42**, 443
Oil Taxation Act 1983 .... **42**, 647
Olympic Symbol etc (Protection) Act 1995 .... **48**, 199
Open Spaces Act 1906 .... **32**, 30
Opencast Coal Act 1958 .... **17(1)**, 204
Opticians Act 1989 .... **28**, 669
Ordination of Women (Financial Provisions) Measure 1993 .... **14**, 1279
Ordnance Board Transfer Act 1855 .... **10**, 288
Ordnance Factories and Military Services Act 1984 .... **10**, 528
Ordnance Survey Act 1841 .... **10**, 227
Osborne Estate Act 1902 .... **10**, 127
Osborne Estate Act 1914 .... **10**, 133
Osteopaths Act 1993 .... **28**, 848
Outer Space Act 1986 .... **4(1)**, 498
Oversea Superannuation Act 1991 .... **33(1)**, 296
Overseas and Other Clergy (Ministry and Ordination) Measure 1967 .... **14**, 656
Overseas Pensions Act 1973 .... **33(1)**, 238
Oxford and Cambridge Act 1571 .... **15(1)**, 31
Oxford University Act 1854 .... **15(1)**, 54
Oxford University Act 1857 .... **15(1)**, 75
Oxford University Act 1860 .... **15(1)**, 77
Oxford University Act 1862 .... **15(1)**, 78
Oxford University, Vinerian Foundation, Act 1865 .... **15(1)**, 83

P

Pakistan Act 1990 .... **7(2)**, 611
Papua New Guinea, Western Samoa and Nauru (Miscellaneous Provisions)
  Act 1980 .... **7(2)**, 580
Parish Councils Act 1957 .... **25(1)**, 498
Parish Councils and Burial Authorities (Miscellaneous Provisions) Act 1970 .... **5(2)**, 480
Parish Notices Act 1837 .... **14**, 93
Parking Act 1989 .... **38(1)**, 226
Parks Regulation Act 1872 .... **32**, 25
Parks Regulation (Amendment) Act 1926 .... **32**, 67
Parks Regulation (Amendment) Act 1974 .... **32**, 318
Parliament Act 1911 .... **32**, 1063
Parliament Act 1949 .... **32**, 1078
Parliament (Elections and Meeting) Act 1943 .... **32**, 1073
Parliament (Joint Departments) Act 2007 .... **32**, 1178
Parliament (Qualification of Women) Act 1918 .... **32**, 1067
Parliamentary and Health Service Commissioners Act 1987 .... **10**, 550
Parliamentary and other Pensions Act 1972 .... **33(1)**, 233
Parliamentary and other Pensions Act 1987 .... **33(1)**, 275
Parliamentary and other Pensions and Salaries Act 1976 .... **33(1)**, 268
Parliamentary Commissioner Act 1967 .... **10**, 388
Parliamentary Commissioner Act 1994 .... **10**, 631
Parliamentary Commissioner (Consular Complaints) Act 1981 .... **10**, 527
Parliamentary Constituencies Act 1986 .... **15(3)**, 393
Parliamentary Corporate Bodies Act 1992 .... **32**, 1148
Parliamentary Costs Act 2006 .... **32**, 1162
Parliamentary Oaths Act 1866 .... **32**, 1054
Parliamentary Papers Act 1840 .... **19(3)**, 359
Parliamentary Pensions etc Act 1984 .... **33(1)**, 272
Parliamentary Privilege Act 1737 .... **13**, 3
Parliamentary Privilege Act 1770 .... **32**, 1044
Parliamentary Returns Act 1869 .... **32**, 1058

Parliamentary Standards Act 2009 .... **32(S)**, Parliament 1
Parliamentary Witnesses Act 1858 .... **32**, 1053
Parliamentary Witnesses Oaths Act 1871 .... **32**, 1060
Parochial Church Councils (Powers) Measure 1956 .... **14**, 485
Parochial Libraries Act 1708 .... **14**, 55
Parochial Registers and Records Measure 1978 .... **14**, 929
Parsonages Act 1838 .... **14**, 97
Parsonages Act 1865 .... **14**, 198
Parsonages (Amendment) Measure 1947 .... **14**, 431
Parsonages Measure 1938 .... **14**, 379
Partnership Act 1890 .... **32**, 1191
Party Wall etc Act 1996 .... **35(2)**, 387
Pastoral (Amendment) Measure 1994 .... **14**, 1289
Pastoral (Amendment) Measure 2006 .... **14(S)**, Ecclesiastical Law 119
Pastoral Measure 1983 .... **14**, 963
Patents Act 1949 .... **11(1)**, 492
Patents Act 1957 .... **11(1)**, 721
Patents Act 1977 .... **11(1)**, 737
Patents Act 2004 .... **11(1)**, 1353
Patents and Designs Act 1907 .... **11(1)**, 489
Patents, Designs and Marks Act 1986 .... **48**, 100
Patents, Designs, Copyright and Trade Marks (Emergency) Act 1939 .... **50**, 456
Patriotic Fund Reorganisation Act 1903 .... **3**, 185
Patronage (Benefices) Measure 1986 .... **14**, 1130
Paymaster General Act 1835 .... **10**, 225
Paymaster General Act 1848 .... **10**, 286
Pedlars Act 1871 .... **27**, 37
Pedlars Act 1881 .... **27**, 51
Peerage Act 1963 .... **33(1)**, 12
Penal Servitude Act 1857 .... **12(1)**, 118
Penal Servitude Act 1891 .... **12(1)**, 204
Penalties for Drunkenness Act 1962 .... **19(3)**, 451
Pension Schemes Act 1993 .... **33(1)**, 297
Pensioners' Payments and National Insurance Act 1973 .... **40(1)**, 117
Pensions Act 1995—
   ss 3, 4, 6–12, 14, 15, 22, 23, 25, 26, 27–30, 32–41, 47, 49–54, 62–76, 87–89, 91–94,
     115–126, 135, 137, 145, 149, 151, 162, 163, 166, 168, 170, 172–181, Sch 4, Pt 1,
     Sch 5, Sch 7, Pts I, III, IV .... **33(1)**, 568
   ss 126, 128, 148, 177–181, Sch 4, Sch 7, Pt II .... **40(2)**, 137
Pensions Act 2004 .... **33(1)**, 819
Pensions Act 2007—
   ss 2, 4–7, 12, 13, 24–31, Sch 1, Pts 2, 4, 5, 7, 8, Sch 2, Pt 3, Sch 7, Pts 1–5 .... **40(2)**, 820
   ss 14–31, Schs 4–7 .... **33(S)**, Pensions 1
Pensions Act 2008 .... **33(S)**, Pensions 71
Pensions and Yeomanry Pay Act 1884 .... **3**, 138
Pensions Appeal Tribunals Act 1943 .... **33(1)**, 62
Pensions Appeal Tribunals Act 1949 .... **33(1)**, 97
Pensions Commutation Act 1871 .... **33(1)**, 44
Pensions Commutation Act 1882 .... **33(1)**, 50
Pensions Commutation Act 1984 .... **33(1)**, 269
Pensions (Increase) Act 1971 .... **33(1)**, 115
Pensions (Increase) Act 1974 .... **33(1)**, 246
Pensions Measure 1997 .... **14**, 1312
Pensions (Mercantile Marine) Act 1942 .... **3**, 253
Pensions (Miscellaneous Provisions) Act 1990 .... **33(1)**, 289
Pensions (Navy, Army, Air Force and Mercantile Marine) Act 1939 .... **3**, 243
Performing Animals (Regulation) Act 1925 .... **2**, 210
Perjury Act 1911 .... **12(1)**, 213
Perpetuities and Accumulations Act 1964 .... **33(2)**, 3
Personal Injuries (Emergency Provisions) Act 1939 .... **33(1)**, 54
Pesticides Act 1998 .... **1(2)**, 754
Pesticides (Fees and Enforcement) Act 1989 .... **1(2)**, 486
Pests Act 1954—
   ss 1–4, 7, 13–15 .... **1(1)**, 470
   ss 6, 13–15 .... **35(1)**, 248

Pests Act 1954—*contd*
ss 8, 9, 12–15 .... **2**, 249
Pet Animals Act 1951 .... **2**, 237
Pet Animals Act 1951 (Amendment) Act 1983 .... **2**, 547
Petition of Right (1627) **10**, 34
Petroleum Act 1987 .... **17(1)**, 956
Petroleum Act 1998 .... **17(2)**, 378
Petroleum (Consolidation) Act 1928 .... **35(1)**, 124
Petroleum Revenue Tax Act 1980 .... **42**, 553
Petroleum Royalties (Relief) Act 1983 .... **17(1)**, 714
Petroleum Royalties (Relief) and Continental Shelf Act 1989 .... **17(1)**, 964
Petroleum (Transfer of Licences) Act 1936 .... **35(1)**, 137
Physical Training and Recreation Act 1937 .... **35(1)**, 224
Pig Industry Levy Act 1983 .... **1(2)**, 230
Pilotage Act 1987 .... **39(2)**, 530
Pipe-lines Act 1962 .... **17(1)**, 326
Piracy Act 1837 .... **12(1)**, 102
Piracy Act 1850 .... **12(1)**, 114
Places of Worship (Enfranchisement) Act 1920 .... **14**, 298
Places of Worship Registration Act 1855 .... **14**, 178
Places of Worship Sites Act 1873 .... **14**, 240
Places of Worship Sites Amendment Act 1882 .... **14**, 245
Planning Act 2008 .... **46(S)**, Planning 5
Planning and Compensation Act 1991—
ss 4, 10, 21, 22, 25, 27, 28, 31, 32, 66, 70, 81, 84, Schs 2, 4, 19 .... **46**, 1048
ss 80, 82, 84, Sch 18 .... **9**, 463
Planning and Compulsory Purchase Act 2004—
entire Act **46**, 1289
ss 106, 107, 110, 111, 121, 122, 124, 125 .... **9**, 474
Planning and Energy Act 2008 .... **46(S)**, Planning 1
Planning (Consequential Provisions) Act 1990 .... **46**, 1029
Planning (Consequential Provisions) (Scotland) Act 1997 .... **46**, 1197
Planning-gain Supplement (Preparations) Act 2007 .... **43(S)**, Taxation 503
Planning (Hazardous Substances) Act 1990 .... **46**, 969
Planning (Listed Buildings and Conservation Areas) Act 1990 .... **46**, 838
Plant Health Act 1967 .... **1(1)**, 629
Plant Varieties Act 1997 .... **1(2)**, 706
Plant Varieties and Seeds Act 1964 .... **1(1)**, 571
Plate Assay (Sheffield and Birmingham) Act 1772 .... **48**, 13
Pluralities Act 1838 .... **14**, 98
Pluralities Acts Amendment Act 1885 .... **14**, 246
Pneumoconiosis etc (Workers' Compensation) Act 1979 .... **40(1)**, 151
Poaching Prevention Act 1862 .... **2**, 186
Poisons Act 1972 .... **28**, 339
Police Act 1964 .... **33(2)**, 87
Police Act 1976 .... **33(2)**, 125
Police Act 1996 .... **33(2)**, 168
Police Act 1997 .... **33(2)**, 309
Police and Criminal Evidence Act 1984—
ss 1–24, 24A, 26–32, 34–47, 47A, 50, 51, 53–56, 58, 60–67, 113–115, 117–122,
Schs 1, 2, Sch 7, Pt I .... **12(1)**, 993
ss 71–82, 113(12), (13), 118(1), 119(2), (3), 120–122, Sch 7, Pts II–V **18**, 267
ss 107, 108, 115, 119–122, Sch 7, Pt VI .... **33(2)**, 127
Police and Firemen (War Service) Act 1939 .... **33(2)**, 65
Police and Firemen (War Service) Act 1944 .... **33(2)**, 75
Police and Firemen's Pensions Act 1997 .... **18**, 1028
Police and Justice Act 2006—
ss 1–7, 9, 13, 41, 49, 52–55, Schs 1–5, 15, Pt 1 .... **33(2)**, 817
ss 12, 14, 17–21, 26, 27, 32–36, 38, 39, 47, 49–55, Schs 8, 10, 14, 15 ...... **12(4)**, 348
ss 23–25, 49, 53–55 .... **6(S)**, Children 275
ss 42, 43, 49, 53–55, Sch 13 .... **18**, 994
Police and Magistrates' Courts Act 1994 .... **33(2)**, 150
Police, Factories, etc (Miscellaneous Provisions) Act 1916 .... **33(2)**, 59
Police (Health and Safety) Act 1997 .... **33(2)**, 305
Police (Insurance of Voluntary Assistants) Act 1997 .... **33(2)**, 308

Police (Northern Ireland) Act 1998 .... **31**, 1217
Police (Northern Ireland) Act 2000 .... **31**, 1519
Police Officers (Central Service) Act 1989 .... **33(2)**, 150
Police (Overseas Service) Act 1945 .... **33(2)**, 80
Police Pensions Act 1961 .... **33(2)**, 86
Police Pensions Act 1976 .... **33(2)**, 102
Police (Property) Act 1897 .... **33(2)**, 53
Police (Property) Act 1997 .... **33(2)**, 304
Police Reform Act 2002 .... **33(2)**, 386
Police (Scotland) Act 1967 .... **33(2)**, 97
Policies of Assurance Act 1867 .... **19(1)**, 44
Polish Resettlement Act 1947—
    ss 1, 7, 10, 12, 13 .... **3**, 263
    ss 2, 3, 10, 13, Schedule .... **40(1)**, 20
    ss 4, 10, 12, 13 .... **30**, 400
Political Parties and Elections Act 2009 .... **15(S)**, Elections 1
Political Parties, Elections and Referendums Act 2000 .... **15(3)**, 445
Pollution Prevention and Control Act 1999 .... **35(2)**, 412
Poor Rates Recovery Act 1862 .... **25(1)**, 57
Population (Statistics) Act 1938 .... **36**, 34
Population (Statistics) Act 1960 .... **36**, 133
Port of London Act 1968 .... **39(2)**, 212
Port of London Act 1970 .... **39(2)**, 389
Port of London Act 1982 .... **39(2)**, 468
Ports Act 1991 .... **39(2)**, 634
Ports (Finance) Act 1985 .... **39(2)**, 521
Ports (Financial Assistance) Act 1981 .... **39(2)**, 423
Ports (Reduction of Debt) Act 1983 .... **39(2)**, 515
Post Office Act 1969—
    ss 2–6, 22, 49, 74–76, 80, 86–88, 136, 138–140, 142, Schs 1, 4, 9 .... **34**, 541
    ss 94, 108, 109, 114, 132, 139, 140, 142 .... **19(2)**, 886
    ss 134, 135, 142 .... **2**, 292
Post Office Works Act 1959 .... **34**, 537
Postal Services Act 2000 .... **34**, 589
Powers of Attorney Act 1971 .... **1(1)**, 17
Powers of Criminal Courts (Sentencing) Act 2000 .... **12(2)**, 926
Poynings' Law 1495 .... **31**, 809
Prayer Book (Further Provisions) Measure 1968 .... **14**, 661
Prayer Book (Tables of Lessons) Act 1871 .... **14**, 224
Prayer Book (Versions of the Bible) Measure 1965 .... **14**, 648
Prerogativa Regis (temp incert) **10**, 23
Prescription Act 1832 .... **20**, 86
Prevention of Corruption Act 1906 .... **12(1)**, 208
Prevention of Corruption Act 1916 .... **12(1)**, 237
Prevention of Crime Act 1953 .... **12(1)**, 329
Prevention of Crimes Act 1871 .... **12(1)**, 178
Prevention of Damage by Pests Act 1949 .... **35(1)**, 227
Prevention of Damage by Rabbits Act 1939 .... **2**, 231
Prevention of Oil Pollution Act 1971 .... **49**, 387
Prevention of Terrorism Act 2005 .... **12(4)**, 87
Price Commission Act 1977 .... **47**, 370
Prices Act 1974 .... **47**, 233
Priests (Ordination of Women) Measure 1993 .... **14**, 1269
Princess Sophia's Precedence Act 1711 .... **10**, 72
Printer's Imprint Act 1961 .... **19(3)**, 392
Prison Act 1952 .... **12(1)**, 285
Prison Security Act 1992 .... **12(2)**, 175
Prisoners and Criminal Proceedings (Scotland) Act 1993 .... **12(2)**, 192
Prisoners' Earnings Act 1996 .... **12(2)**, 644
Prisoners (Return to Custody) Act 1995 .... **12(2)**, 372
Prisons (Alcohol Testing) Act 1997 .... **12(2)**, 686
Prisons (Scotland) Act 1989 .... **12(2)**, 22
Private Hire Vehicles (Carriage of Guide Dogs etc) Act 2002 .... **7(1)**, 920
Private Hire Vehicles (London) Act 1998 .... **38(2)**, 8

Private International Law (Miscellaneous Provisions) Act 1995—
  ss 5, 6, 8, 16–19 .... **27**, 640
  ss 9–16, 18, 19 .... **45**, 1587
Private Security Industry Act 2001 .... **47**, 742
Privilege of Parliament Act 1512 .... **32**, 1038
Privilege of Parliament Act 1603 .... **32**, 1041
Privy Council Registrar Act 1853 .... **11(2)**, 60
Prize Act 1939 .... **11(2)**, 135
Prize Courts Act 1894 .... **11(2)**, 108
Prize Courts Act 1915 .... **11(2)**, 121
Prize Courts (Procedure) Act 1914 .... **11(2)**, 117
Prize Salvage Act 1944 .... **11(2)**, 139
Proceeds of Crime Act 1995 .... **12(2)**, 370
Proceeds of Crime Act 2002 .... **12(3)**, 217
Proceeds of Crime (Scotland) Act 1995 .... **12(2)**, 422
Promissory Oaths Act 1868 .... **10**, 292
Promissory Oaths Act 1871 .... **10**, 302
Property Misdescriptions Act 1991 .... **23**, 83
Property Services Agency and Crown Suppliers Act 1990 .... **10**, 559
Prorogation Act 1867 .... **32**, 1056
Prosecution of Offences Act 1985 .... **12(1)**, 1141
Protection from Eviction Act 1977 .... **21**, 799
Protection from Harassment Act 1997 .... **12(2)**, 700
Protection of Animals Act 1911 .... **2**, 204
Protection of Animals (Amendment) Act 1927 .... **2**, 216
Protection of Animals (Amendment) Act 1954 .... **2**, 248
Protection of Animals (Amendment) Act 1988 .... **2**, 592
Protection of Badgers Act 1992 .... **2**, 640
Protection of Children Act 1978 .... **12(1)**, 834
Protection of Children Act 1999 .... **6**, 924
Protection of Children (Tobacco) Act 1986 .... **6**, 294
Protection of Military Remains Act 1986 .... **3**, 1431
Protection of Trading Interests Act 1980—
  ss 1–3, 5–8 .... **47**, 373
  ss 4, 8 .... **18**, 266
Protection of Wrecks Act 1973 .... **39(2)**, 418
Provisional Collection of Taxes Act 1968 .... **42**, 110
Provisional Order (Marriages) Act 1905 .... **27**, 129
Public Audit (Wales) Act 2004 .... **26(2)**, 446
Public Bodies (Admission to Meetings) Act 1960 .... **25(1)**, 591
Public Bodies Corrupt Practices Act 1889 .... **12(1)**, 200
Public Expenditure and Receipts Act 1968 .... **19(2)**, 877
Public Health Act 1875 .... **35(1)**, 51
Public Health Act 1925 .... **35(1)**, 113
Public Health Act 1936 .... **35(1)**, 139
Public Health Act 1961 .... **35(1)**, 250
Public Health Acts Amendment Act 1890 .... **35(1)**, 80
Public Health Acts Amendment Act 1907 .... **35(1)**, 88
Public Health (Control of Disease) Act 1984 .... **35(1)**, 473
Public Health (Drainage of Trade Premises) Act 1937 .... **35(1)**, 222
Public Interest Disclosure Act 1998 .... **16**, 1089
Public Lavatories (Turnstiles) Act 1963 .... **35(1)**, 278
Public Lending Right Act 1979 .... **13**, 203
Public Libraries and Museums Act 1964 .... **13**, 116
Public Meeting Act 1908 .... **12(1)**, 212
Public Notaries Act 1801 .... **11(2)**, 24
Public Notaries Act 1843 .... **11(2)**, 53
Public Offices Fees Act 1879 .... **19(2)**, 707
Public Offices (Site) Act 1947 .... **10**, 349
Public Order Act 1936 .... **12(1)**, 260
Public Order Act 1963 .... **12(1)**, 396
Public Order Act 1986 .... **12(1)**, 1209
Public Passenger Vehicles Act 1981 .... **37**, 1
Public Processions (Northern Ireland) Act 1998 .... **31**, 1187
Public Records Act 1958 .... **18**, 191

Public Records Act 1967 .... **18**, 226
Public Revenue and Consolidated Fund Charges Act 1854 .... **19(2)**, 651
Public Schools Act 1868 .... **15(1)**, 84
Public Services Ombudsman (Wales) Act 2005 .... **10**, 671
Public Statues (Metropolis) Act 1854 .... **25(1)**, 51
Public Stores Act 1875 .... **12(1)**, 181
Public Trustee Act 1906 .... **48**, 230
Public Trustee and Administration of Funds Act 1986—
   ss 1, 3, 6 .... **48**, 597
   ss 1, 6 .... **11(3)**, 74
   ss 3, 6 .... **29**, 289
Public Trustee (Fees) Act 1957 .... **48**, 558
Public Trustee (General Deposit Fund) Act 1939 .... **48**, 554
Public Trustee (Liability and Fees) Act 2002 .... **48(S)**, Trusts 1
Public Utility Transfers and Water Charges Act 1988 .... **49**, 599
Public Works and Fisheries Acts Amendment Act 1863 .... **39(2)**, 98
Public Works Loans Act 1875 .... **19(2)**, 677
Public Works Loans Act 1911 .... **19(2)**, 732
Public Works Loans Act 1944 .... **19(2)**, 798
Public Works Loans Act 1946 .... **19(2)**, 805
Public Works Loans Act 1964 .... **19(2)**, 825
Public Works Loans Act 1965 .... **19(2)**, 827
Public Works Loans Act 1967 .... **19(2)**, 831
Public Works Loans (Money) Act 1876 .... **19(2)**, 703

Q

Queen Anne's Bounty Act 1714 .... **14**, 59
Queen Anne's Bounty Act 1838 .... **14**, 95
Queen's Remembrancer Act 1859 .... **13**, 4
Quia Emptores (1289–90) **20**, 53

R

Race Relations Act 1976 .... **7(1)**, 160
Race Relations (Amendment) Act 2000 .... **7(1)**, 789
Race Relations (Remedies) Act 1994 .... **7(1)**, 347
Racial and Religious Hatred Act 2006 .... **12(4)**, 226
Radioactive Material (Road Transport) Act 1991 .... **38(1)**, 389
Radioactive Substances Act 1993 .... **17(2)**, 91
Ragwort Control Act 2003 .... **1(2)**, 814
Railway and Canal Commission (Abolition) Act 1949 .... **36**, 566
Railway and Canal Traffic Act 1888 .... **36**, 484
Railway Companies Act 1867 .... **36**, 421
Railway Fires Act 1905 .... **36**, 504
Railway Fires Act (1905) Amendment Act 1923 .... **36**, 537
Railway Heritage Act 1996 .... **38(1)**, 950
Railway Regulation Act 1840 .... **36**, 271
Railway Regulation Act 1842 .... **36**, 274
Railway Rolling Stock Protection Act 1872 .... **36**, 477
Railways Act 1974 .... **36**, 961
Railways Act 1993 .... **38(1)**, 485
Railways Act 2005 .... **38(2)**, 513
Railways and Transport Safety Act 2003—
   ss 1–17, 103, 114–122, Sch 1, Sch 2, Pt 2, Schs 3, 6, 8 .... **38(2)**, 344
   ss 18–68, 70–77, 116–122, Schs 4, 5, 8 .... **33(2)**, 556
   ss 78–86, 88–91, 112, 117, 119–122 .... **39(2)**, 1153
   ss 92–102, 117, 119–122 .... **4(1)**, 705
Railways Clauses Act 1863 .... **36**, 408
Railways Clauses Consolidation Act 1845 .... **36**, 292
Rating and Valuation Act 1925 .... **25(1)**, 157
Rating (Caravan Sites) Act 1976 .... **25(2)**, 504
Rating (Caravans and Boats) Act 1996 .... **26(1)**, 356
Rating (Empty Properties) Act 2007 .... **26(2)**, 545

Rating (Former Agricultural Premises and Rural Shops) Act 2001 .... **26(2)**, 245
Rating (Valuation) Act 1999 .... **26(1)**, 523
Recess Elections Act 1975 .... **32**, 1127
Recognition of Trusts Act 1987 .... **48**, 599
Recorded Delivery Service Act 1962 .... **41**, 763
Recreational Charities Act 1958 .... **5(2)**, 534
Redundant Churches and Other Religious Buildings Act 1969 .... **14**, 663
Referendums (Scotland and Wales) Act 1997 .... **10**, 1256
Refreshment Houses Act 1860 .... **19(3)**, 435
Refuse Disposal (Amenity) Act 1978 .... **35(1)**, 423
Regency Act 1937 .... **10**, 146
Regency Act 1943 .... **10**, 154
Regency Act 1953 .... **10**, 163
Regimental Charitable Funds Act 1935 .... **3**, 241
Regimental Debts Act 1893 .... **3**, 162
Regional Assemblies (Preparations) Act 2003 .... **26(2)**, 254
Regional Development Agencies Act 1998 .... **46**, 1210
Registered Designs Act 1949 .... **11(1)**, 567
Registration of Births, Deaths, and Marriages (Army) Act 1879 .... **36**, 17
Registration of Births, Deaths and Marriages (Special Provisions) Act 1957 .... **36**, 125
Registration of Burials Act 1864 .... **5(2)**, 460
Registration of Political Parties Act 1998 .... **15(3)**, 415
Registration Service Act 1953 .... **36**, 110
Regulation of Financial Services (Land Transactions) Act 2005 .... **19(2)**, 603
Regulation of Investigatory Powers Act 2000 .... **45**, 540
Regulation of Railways Act 1868 .... **36**, 430
Regulation of Railways Act 1873 .... **36**, 479
Regulation of Railways Act 1889 .... **36**, 495
Regulatory Enforcement and Sanctions Act 2008—
    ss 1–35, 74–77, Schs 1–4 .... **26(2)**, 853
    ss 36–77, Schs 5–7 .... **10(S)**, Constitutional 73
Regulatory Reform Act 2001 .... **41**, 1088
Rehabilitation of Offenders Act 1974 .... **12(1)**, 719
Reinsurance (Acts of Terrorism) Act 1993 .... **19(1)**, 1126
Remission of Penalties Act 1859 .... **12(1)**, 119
Rent Act 1974 .... **21**, 506
Rent Act 1977 .... **21**, 613
Rent (Agriculture) Act 1976 .... **21**, 532
Rent (Agriculture) Amendment Act 1977 .... **21**, 594
Rent (Amendment) Act 1985 .... **21**, 952
Rentcharges Act 1977 .... **21**, 594
Repair of Benefice Buildings Measure 1972 .... **14**, 773
Repatriation of Prisoners Act 1984 .... **12(1)**, 964
Representation of the People Act 1867 .... **32**, 1057
Representation of the People Act 1981 .... **32**, 1141
Representation of the People Act 1983 .... **15(3)**, 20
Representation of the People Act 1985—
    ss 1–3, 10–12, 15, 16, 18, 19, 21–24, 26–29, Schs 1, 5 .... **15(3)**, 364
    ss 20, 27, 29 .... **32**, 1143
Representation of the People Act 1989 .... **15(3)**, 409
Representation of the People Act 1991 .... **15(3)**, 410
Representation of the People Act 1993 .... **15(3)**, 414
Representation of the People Act 2000 .... **15(3)**, 417
Republic of The Gambia Act 1970 .... **7(2)**, 504
Requisitioned Land and War Works Act 1945 .... **9**, 100
Requisitioned Land and War Works Act 1948 .... **9**, 125
Reserve and Auxiliary Forces (Protection of Civil Interests) Act 1951 .... **3**, 283
Reserve Forces Act 1980 .... **3**, 1327
Reserve Forces Act 1996 .... **3**, 1490
Reserve Forces (Safeguard of Employment) Act 1985 .... **3**, 1400
Reservoirs Act 1975 .... **49**, 509
Residence of Incumbents Act 1869 .... **14**, 219
Restriction of Advertisement (War Risks Insurance) Act 1939 .... **19(1)**, 200
Restriction of Offensive Weapons Act 1959 .... **12(1)**, 352
Restriction of Offensive Weapons Act 1961 .... **12(1)**, 376

Restrictive Practices Court Act 1976 .... **47**, 309
Revenue Act 1884—
  ss 1, 11 .... **18**, 527
  ss 1, 14 .... **19(2)**, 715
Revenue Act 1889—
  ss 30, 37 .... **3**, 143
  ss 31, 32, 37 .... **19(2)**, 724
Revenue Act 1898—
  ss 1, 20 .... **13**, 568
  ss 7, 10, 12, 20 .... **41**, 56
  ss 9, 20 .... **19(2)**, 729
Revenue Act 1903 .... **19(2)**, 730
Revenue Act 1909 .... **41**, 65
Revenue, Friendly Societies, and National Debt Act 1882—
  ss 1, 18, 19 .... **19(2)**, 711
  ss 1, 24 .... **10**, 315
Revenue Solicitors' Act 1828 .... **11(2)**, 31
Reverter of Sites Act 1987 .... **22**, 781
Review of Justices Decisions Act 1872 .... **11(2)**, 81
Revised Tables of Lessons Measure 1922 .... **14**, 305
Revision of the Army and Air Force Acts (Transitional Provisions) Act 1955 .... **3**, 953
Revocatio Novarum Ordinationum (1322) **32**, 1035
Rhodesia and Nyasaland Act 1963 .... **7(2)**, 419
Riding Establishments Act 1964 .... **2**, 267
Riding Establishments Act 1970 .... **2**, 295
Rights of Entry (Gas and Electricity Boards) Act 1954 .... **17(1)**, 100
Rights of Light Act 1959 .... **21**, 256
Rights of Way Act 1990 .... **38(1)**, 247
Riot (Damages) Act 1886 .... **33(2)**, 45
Rivers (Prevention of Pollution) Act 1951 .... **49**, 344
Rivers (Prevention of Pollution) Act 1961 .... **49**, 360
Road and Rail Traffic Act 1933 .... **36**, 563
Road Safety Act 2006 .... **38(2)**, 696
Road Traffic Act 1930 .... **36**, 538
Road Traffic Act 1960 .... **36**, 613
Road Traffic Act 1974 .... **36**, 964
Road Traffic Act 1988 .... **37**, 747
Road Traffic Act 1991 .... **38(1)**, 397
Road Traffic (Amendment) Act 1967 .... **36**, 755
Road Traffic (Consequential Provisions) Act 1988 .... **38(1)**, 211
Road Traffic (Driver Licensing and Information Systems) Act 1989 .... **38(1)**, 228
Road Traffic (Drivers' Ages and Hours of Work) Act 1976 .... **36**, 973
Road Traffic (Driving Instruction by Disabled Persons) Act 1993 .... **38(1)**, 484
Road Traffic (Foreign Vehicles) Act 1972 .... **36**, 946
Road Traffic (New Drivers) Act 1995 .... **38(1)**, 799
Road Traffic Offenders Act 1988 .... **38(1)**, 2
Road Traffic Reduction Act 1997 .... **38(2)**, 2
Road Traffic Reduction (National Targets) Act 1998 .... **38(2)**, 5
Road Traffic Regulation Act 1984 .... **37**, 189
Road Traffic Regulation (Parking) Act 1986 .... **37**, 614
Road Traffic Regulation (Special Events) Act 1994 .... **38(1)**, 793
Road Traffic (Temporary Restrictions) Act 1991 .... **38(1)**, 387
Road Traffic (Vehicle Testing) Act 1999 .... **38(2)**, 48
Roman Catholic Relief Act 1829 .... **14**, 70
Roosevelt Memorial Act 1946 .... **25(1)**, 360
Royal and Parliamentary Titles Act 1927 .... **10**, 134
Royal Assent Act 1967 .... **32**, 1082
Royal Marriages Act 1772 .... **10**, 89
Royal Mines Act 1688 .... **10**, 41
Royal Mines Act 1693 .... **10**, 49
Royal Parks (Trading) Act 2000 .... **32**, 777
Royal Patriotic Fund Corporation Act 1950 .... **3**, 276

Royal Titles Act 1953 .... **10**, 162

S

Sacrament Act 1547 .... **14**, 44
Safeguarding Vulnerable Groups Act 2006 .... **6(S)**, Children 173
Safety of Sports Grounds Act 1975 .... **13**, 174
Sailors and Soldiers (Gifts for Land Settlement) Act 1916 .... **3**, 202
Saint Helena Act 1833 .... **7(2)**, 296
Sale and Supply of Goods Act 1994 .... **39(1)**, 682
Sale of Farming Stock Act 1816 .... **13**, 1306
Sale of Goods Act 1979 .... **39(1)**, 395
Sale of Goods (Amendment) Act 1994 .... **39(1)**, 681
Sale of Goods (Amendment) Act 1995 .... **39(1)**, 685
Sale of Land by Auction Act 1867 .... **39(1)**, 18
Sale of Offices Act 1551 .... **12(1)**, 79
Sale of Offices Act 1809 .... **12(1)**, 85
Sale of Student Loans Act 2008 .... **15(S)**, Education 45
Salmon Act 1986 .... **1(2)**, 471
Salmon and Freshwater Fisheries Act 1975 .... **1(2)**, 2
Saving Gateway Accounts Act 2009 .... **40(S)**, Social Security 1
Savings Banks Act 1887 .... **19(2)**, 716
Savings Banks Act 1949 .... **19(2)**, 806
School Grants Act 1855 .... **20**, 232
School Sites Act 1841 .... **20**, 128
School Sites Act 1844 .... **20**, 137
School Sites Act 1849 .... **20**, 201
School Sites Act 1851 .... **20**, 206
School Sites Act 1852 .... **20**, 208
School Standards and Framework Act 1998 .... **15(2)**, 2
Science and Technology Act 1965 .... **10**, 378
Scotch Whisky Act 1988 .... **19(3)**, 561
Scotland Act 1998 .... **10**, 1360
Scottish Parliament (Constituencies) Act 2004 .... **10**, 1538
Scrap Metal Dealers Act 1964 .... **47**, 78
Sea Fish (Conservation) Act 1967 .... **1(1)**, 739
Sea Fish (Conservation) Act 1992 .... **1(2)**, 578
Sea Fish Industry Act 1938 .... **1(1)**, 370
Sea Fish Industry Act 1951—
  ss 21, 29, Sch 4 .... **39(2)**, 110
  ss 25, 29 .... **1(1)**, 456
Sea Fish Industry Act 1962 .... **1(1)**, 567
Sea Fish Industry Act 1970 .... **1(1)**, 815
Sea Fisheries Act 1868 .... **1(1)**, 170
Sea Fisheries Act 1883 .... **1(1)**, 179
Sea Fisheries Act 1968 .... **1(1)**, 793
Sea Fisheries Regulation Act 1966 .... **1(1)**, 610
Sea Fisheries (Shellfish) Act 1967 .... **1(1)**, 713
Sea Fisheries (Shellfish) Act 1973 .... **1(1)**, 911
Sea Fisheries (Shellfish) (Amendment) Act 1997 .... **1(2)**, 706
Sea Fisheries (Wildlife Conservation) Act 1992 .... **1(2)**, 576
Sea Fishing Grants (Charges) Act 2000 .... **1(2)**, 812
Seal Fisheries (North Pacific) Act 1895 .... **1(1)**, 215
Seal Fisheries (North Pacific) Act 1912 .... **1(1)**, 250
Seal Fishery Act 1875 .... **1(1)**, 176
Seamen's and Soldiers' False Characters Act 1906 .... **3**, 191
Sea-Sand (Devon and Cornwall) (1609) **49**, 19
Secretaries of State Act 1926 .... **10**, 344
Security Service Act 1989 .... **10**, 554
Security Service Act 1996 .... **10**, 665
Septennial Act 1715 .... **32**, 1043
Sequestration Act 1849 .... **14**, 174
Sequestration Act 1871 .... **14**, 236
Serious Crime Act 2007 .... **12(4)**, 490

Serious Organised Crime and Police Act 2005—
    ss 1–59, 123, 139, 141, 150, 151, 153, 155, 156, 158–163, 168, 170, 172–174,
       176–179, Schs 1, 3, 4, 13, 17 .... **33(2)**, 662
    ss 60–67, 69–76, 78–94, 96, 97, 111, 112, 114, 117, 120, 121, 124, 128–138,
       145–149, 172, 174, 175, 177–179, Schs 5, 7, 16 .... **12(4)**, 123
    ss 144, 172, 177–179, Sch 10 .... **6**, 1384
    ss 171, 172, 177–179, Sch 15 .... **47(S)**, Trade 1
Settled Land Act 1882 .... **20**, 347
Settled Land Act 1925 .... **20**, 396
Settled Land and Trustee Acts (Court's General Powers) Act 1943 .... **21**, 127; **48**, 556
Sex Discrimination Act 1975 .... **7(1)**, 44
Sex Discrimination Act 1986 .... **7(1)**, 286
Sex Discrimination (Election Candidates) Act 2002 .... **7(1)**, 918
Sex Disqualification (Removal) Act 1919—
    ss 1, 4 .... **16**, 13
    ss 3, 4 .... **15(1)**, 120
Sexual Offences Act 1956 .... **12(1)**, 335
Sexual Offences Act 1967 .... **12(1)**, 450
Sexual Offences Act 1985 .... **12(1)**, 1190
Sexual Offences Act 1993 .... **12(2)**, 223
Sexual Offences Act 2003 .... **12(3)**, 746
Sexual Offences (Amendment) Act 1976 .... **12(1)**, 795
Sexual Offences (Amendment) Act 1992 .... **12(2)**, 178
Sexual Offences (Amendment) Act 2000 .... **12(2)**, 1469
Sexual Offences (Conspiracy and Incitement) Act 1996 .... **12(2)**, 639
Sexual Offences (Protected Material) Act 1997 .... **12(2)**, 686
Seychelles Act 1976 .... **7(2)**, 525
Sharing of Church Buildings Act 1969 .... **14**, 668
Sharing of Church Buildings Measure 1970 .... **14**, 770
Sheriff Courts (Scotland) Act 1971 .... **41**, 776
Sheriffs Act 1887 .... **39(1)**, 811
Shipbuilding Act 1979 .... **39(2)**, 422
Shipping and Trading Interests (Protection) Act 1995 .... **39(2)**, 1124
Short Titles Act 1896 .... **41**, 705
Sierra Leone Independence Act 1961 .... **7(2)**, 385
Sierra Leone Republic Act 1972 .... **7(2)**, 510
Simony Act 1588 .... **14**, 47
Simony Act 1688 .... **14**, 54
Singapore Act 1966 .... **7(2)**, 474
Slander of Women Act 1891 .... **19(3)**, 384
Slaughter of Poultry Act 1967 .... **1(1)**, 700
Slaughterhouses Act 1974 .... **1(1)**, 911
Slave Trade Act 1824 .... **47**, 30
Slave Trade Act 1843 .... **47**, 33
Slave Trade Act 1873 .... **47**, 34
Small Holdings and Allotments Act 1908 .... **1(1)**, 220
Small Holdings and Allotments Act 1926 .... **1(1)**, 292
Social Security Act 1973 .... **40(1)**, 98
Social Security Act 1979 .... **40(1)**, 148
Social Security Act 1980 .... **40(1)**, 162
Social Security Act 1981 .... **40(1)**, 174
Social Security Act 1985 .... **40(1)**, 224
Social Security Act 1986 .... **40(1)**, 257
Social Security Act 1988 .... **40(1)**, 284
Social Security Act 1989—
    ss 4, 6, 28–31, 33, Sch 5, Pt I, Sch 9 .... **40(1)**, 294
    ss 25, 28–31, 33 .... **3**, 1454
Social Security Act 1990 .... **40(1)**, 326
Social Security Act 1993 .... **40(2)**, 34
Social Security Act 1998 .... **40(2)**, 199
Social Security Administration Act 1992 .... **40(1)**, 796
Social Security Administration (Fraud) Act 1997 .... **40(2)**, 193
Social Security and Housing Benefits Act 1982 .... **40(1)**, 176
Social Security (Consequential Provisions) Act 1975 .... **40(1)**, 120
Social Security (Consequential Provisions) Act 1992 .... **40(2)**, 2

Social Security (Contributions) Act 1994 .... **40(2)**, 40
Social Security Contributions and Benefits Act 1992 .... **40(1)**, 347
Social Security Contributions (Share Options) Act 2001 .... **40(2)**, 531
Social Security Contributions (Transfer of Functions, etc) Act 1999 .... **40(2)**, 344
Social Security Fraud Act 2001 .... **40(2)**, 489
Social Security (Incapacity for Work) Act 1994 .... **40(2)**, 44
Social Security (Miscellaneous Provisions) Act 1977—
    ss 12, 24(1), (3), 25 .... **3**, 1324
    ss 23–25, Sch 2 .... **40(1)**, 143
Social Security (Mortgage Interest Payments) Act 1992 .... **40(2)**, 31
Social Security (Overpayments) Act 1996 .... **40(2)**, 154
Social Security Pensions Act 1975 .... **33(1)**, 252
Social Security (Recovery of Benefits) Act 1997 .... **40(2)**, 156
Social Work (Scotland) Act 1968 .... **6**, 132
Solicitors Act 1974 .... **11(2)**, 258
Solomon Islands Act 1978 .... **7(2)**, 535
South Africa Act 1962 .... **7(2)**, 400
South Africa Act 1995 .... **7(2)**, 617
Southern Rhodesia Act 1979 .... **7(2)**, 552
Special Constables Act 1923 .... **33(2)**, 62
Special Educational Needs and Disability Act 2001 .... **15(2)**, 528
Special Educational Needs (Information) Act 2008 .... **15(S)**, Education 59
Special Immigration Appeals Commission Act 1997 .... **31**, 293
Sporting Events (Control of Alcohol etc) Act 1985 .... **12(1)**, 1199
Sri Lanka Republic Act 1972 .... **7(2)**, 511
Stamp Act 1815 .... **18**, 508
Stamp Act 1853 .... **19(1)**, 41
Stamp Act 1891 .... **41**, 23
Stamp Duties Management Act 1891 .... **41**, 11
Stannaries Act 1836 .... **11(2)**, 42
Stannaries Act 1855 .... **11(2)**, 61
Stannaries Court (Abolition) Act 1896 .... **11(2)**, 112
State Immunity Act 1978 .... **10**, 1060
State Pension Credit Act 2002 .... **40(2)**, 541
Statement of Rates Act 1919 .... **20**, 373
Statistics and Registration Service Act 2007—
    ss 1–47, 49–51, 53–67, 73–76, Schs 1–3, Sch 4, Pt 1 .... **10(S)**, Constitutional 1
    ss 68, 69, 73–76, Sch 4, Pt 2 .... **36**, 201
Statistics of Trade Act 1947 .... **47**, 43
Status of Aliens Act 1914 .... **31**, 18
Status of Children Born Abroad (1350–1) **10**, 25
Statute Concerning Tallage (1297) **10**, 23
Statute concerning Tenants by the Curtesy of England (temp incert) **20**, 55
Statute Law (Repeals) Act 1969 .... **41**, 773
Statute Law (Repeals) Act 1973 .... **41**, 780
Statute Law (Repeals) Act 1974 .... **41**, 785
Statute Law (Repeals) Act 1975 .... **41**, 791
Statute Law (Repeals) Act 1976 .... **41**, 792
Statute Law (Repeals) Act 1977 .... **41**, 794
Statute Law (Repeals) Act 1978 .... **41**, 835
Statute Law (Repeals) Act 1981 .... **41**, 837
Statute Law (Repeals) Act 1986 .... **41**, 862
Statute Law (Repeals) Act 1989 .... **41**, 891
Statute Law (Repeals) Act 1993 .... **41**, 936
Statute Law (Repeals) Act 1995 .... **41**, 1007
Statute Law (Repeals) Act 1998 .... **41**, 1050
Statute Law (Repeals) Act 2004 .... **41**, 1103
Statute Law (Repeals) Act 2008 .... **41**, 1186
Statute Law Revision Act 1893 .... **41**, 704
Statute Law Revision Act 1948 .... **41**, 755
Statute Law Revision Act 1950 .... **41**, 759
Statute Law Revision Act 1958 .... **41**, 761
Statute Law Revision (Isle of Man) Act 1991 .... **41**, 933
Statute Law Revision (Northern Ireland) Act 1973 .... **31**, 898
Statute of Distribution (1670) **18**, 506

Statute of Frauds (1677) .... **11(1)**, 351
Statute of Frauds Amendment Act 1828 .... **11(1)**, 352
Statute of Marlborough (1267)—
   cc 1, 4, 15 .... **13**, 1289
   c 23 .... **20**, 48
Statute of Monopolies (1623) .... **11(1)**, 487
Statute of Uses (1535) **20**, 56
Statute of Westminster 1931 .... **7(2)**, 339
Statute of Westminster the First (1275)—
   c 5 .... **15(3)**, 20
   c 50 .... **10**, 16
Statute of Westminster the Second (1285)—
   c 1 .... **20**, 49
Statutes of the Exchequer (temp incert) **13**, 1292
Statutory Companies (Redeemable Stock) Act 1915 .... **8**, 85
Statutory Corporations (Financial Provisions) Act 1974 .... **36**, 959
Statutory Corporations (Financial Provisions) Act 1975 .... **19(2)**, 931
Statutory Declarations Act 1835 .... **18**, 129
Statutory Instruments Act 1946 .... **41**, 740
Statutory Instruments (Production and Sale) Act 1996 .... **41**, 1049
Statutory Orders (Special Procedure) Act 1945 .... **41**, 728
Statutory Orders (Special Procedure) Act 1965 .... **41**, 772
Statutory Sick Pay Act 1991 .... **40(1)**, 339
Statutory Sick Pay Act 1994 .... **40(2)**, 42
Statutory Water Companies Act 1991 .... **49**, 1587
Still-Birth (Definition) Act 1992 .... **36**, 137
Stipends (Cessation of Special Payments) Measure 2005 .... **14(S)**, Ecclesiastical Law 43
Stock Exchange (Completion of Bargains) Act 1976 .... **48**, 595
Stock Transfer Act 1963 .... **19(1)**, 241
Stock Transfer Act 1982 .... **19(1)**, 523
Stock Transfer Act 1982 .... **30**, 283
Street Offences Act 1959 .... **12(1)**, 354
Submarine Telegraph Act 1885 .... **45**, 17
Submission of the Clergy Act 1533 .... **14**, 21
Succession to the Crown Act 1707 .... **10**, 69
Suffragan Bishops Act 1534 .... **14**, 38
Suffragan Bishops Act 1898 .... **14**, 249
Suffragans Nomination Act 1888 .... **14**, 247
Suicide Act 1961 .... **12(1)**, 390
Summary Jurisdiction (Process) Act 1881 .... **11(2)**, 91
Summer Time Act 1972 .... **45**, 1542
Summons to Parliament (1382) **32**, 1037
Sunday Observance Act 1833 .... **45**, 1534
Sunday Trading Act 1994 .... **18**, 1387
Sunday Working (Scotland) Act 2003 .... **16**, 1213
Superannuation Act 1965 .... **33(1)**, 98
Superannuation Act 1972 .... **33(1)**, 163
Superannuation and other Trust Funds (Validation) Act 1927 .... **48**, 546
Superannuation (Miscellaneous Provisions) Act 1948 .... **33(1)**, 89
Superannuation (Miscellaneous Provisions) Act 1967—
   ss 7, 18 .... **30**, 403
   ss 11, 13, 15, 17, 18 .... **33(2)**, 91
   ss 11, 17, 18 .... **33(1)**, 112
Superannuation Schemes (War Service) Act 1940 .... **33(1)**, 59
Superannuation (Various Services) Act 1938 .... **33(1)**, 51
Supplementary Benefits Act 1976 .... **40(1)**, 136
Supply of Goods and Services Act 1982 .... **39(1)**, 466
Supply of Goods (Implied Terms) Act 1973 .... **39(1)**, 115
Supply Powers Act 1975 .... **10**, 451
Suppression of Terrorism Act 1978 .... **18**, 779
Supreme Court Act 1981—
   ss 1–46, 46A, 48–56, 56B, 57–82, 84, 86–93, 95–102, 104, 129, 131–137, 139, 140,
     142, 150–153, Schs 1, 2, 4, 6, 7 .... **11(2)**, 711
   ss 105–128, 151–153, Sch 6, paras 7–11, 13 .... **18**, 664
Supreme Court of Judicature Act 1891 .... **11(2)**, 107

Surrogacy Arrangements Act 1985 .... **12(1)**, 1193
Sustainable and Secure Buildings Act 2004 .... **35(2)**, 806
Sustainable Communities Act 2007 .... **26(2)**, 548
Sustainable Energy Act 2003 .... **17(2)**, 572
Swaziland Independence Act 1968 .... **7(2)**, 492
Synodical Government (Amendment) Measure 1974 .... **14**, 809
Synodical Government (Amendment) Measure 2003 .... **14**, 1393
Synodical Government Measure 1969 .... **14**, 684
Synodical Government (Special Majorities) Measure 1971 .... **14**, 772

T

Taking of Hostages Act 1982 .... **12(1)**, 893
Tanganyika Independence Act 1961 .... **7(2)**, 389
Tanganyika Republic Act 1962 .... **7(2)**, 417
Tanzania Act 1969 .... **7(2)**, 496
Tattooing of Minors Act 1969 .... **6**, 144
Tax Credits Act 2002 .... **40(2)**, 575
Taxation of Chargeable Gains Act 1992 .... **42**, 1320
Taxes Management Act 1970 .... **42**, 145
Teaching and Higher Education Act 1998 .... **15(1)**, 845
Team and Group Ministries Measure 1995 .... **14**, 1305
Technical and Industrial Institutions Act 1892 .... **15(1)**, 104
Telecommunications Act 1984 .... **45**, 71
Telegraph Act 1868 .... **45**, 15
Telegraph Act 1870 .... **45**, 16
Television Licences (Disclosure of Information) Act 2000 .... **45**, 536
Tenures Abolition Act 1660 .... **20**, 60
Territorial Sea Act 1987 .... **49**, 593
Territorial Waters Jurisdiction Act 1878 .... **12(1)**, 186
Terrorism Act 2000—
   entire Act.. **12(2)**, 1221
   ss 2, 60, 65–75, 77–96, 98, 99, 101–113, 117, 118, 120A, 121, 123, 125, 127–131,
     Schs 1, 9–13, 16 .... **31**, 1447
Terrorism Act 2006 .... **12(4)**, 227
Terrorism (Northern Ireland) Act 2006 .... **31**, 1683
Thames Barrier and Flood Prevention Act 1972 .... **49**, 405
Theatres Act 1968 .... **13**, 148
Theatres Trust Act 1976 .... **13**, 198
Theft Act 1968 .... **12(1)**, 641
Theft Act 1978 .... **12(1)**, 831
Theft (Amendment) Act 1996 .... **12(2)**, 648
Third Parties (Rights Against Insurers) Act 1930 .... **4(2)**, 36
Timeshare Act 1992 .... **11(1)**, 402
Tithe Act 1536 .... **14**, 41
Tithe Act 1832 .... **14**, 77
Tithe Act 1836 .... **14**, 86
Tithe Act 1839 .... **14**, 130
Tithe Act 1860 .... **14**, 194
Tithe Act 1936 .... **14**, 357
Tithe Act 1951 .... **14**, 440
Tithe Annuities Apportionment Act 1921 .... **14**, 302
Tithes and Offerings (1548) **14**, 45
Titles Deprivation Act 1917 .... **33(1)**, 7
Tobacco Advertising and Promotion Act 2002 .... **47**, 783
Tobacco Products Duty Act 1979 .... **13**, 940
Tokyo Convention Act 1967 .... **4(1)**, 84
Tonga Act 1970 .... **7(2)**, 501
Torts (Interference with Goods) Act 1977 .... **45**, 1562
Tourism (Overseas Promotion) (Scotland) Act 1984 .... **47**, 455
Tourism (Overseas Promotion) (Wales) Act 1992 .... **47**, 512
Town and Country Amenities Act 1974 .... **46**, 38
Town and Country Planning Act 1954 .... **9**, 154

Town and Country Planning Act 1959—
  ss 22–24, 26, 29, 30, 57, 59, Sch 4 .... **25(1)**, 559
  ss 45, 57, 59 .... **9**, 182
Town and Country Planning Act 1990 .... **46**, 314
Town and Country Planning (Costs of Inquiries etc) Act 1995 .... **46**, 1172
Town and Country Planning (Scotland) Act 1997 .... **46**, 1183
Town Development Act 1952 .... **46**, 16
Town Gardens Protection Act 1863 .... **32**, 20
Town Police Clauses Act 1847—
  ss 1–4, 21, 23–29, 37, 38, 40–66, 68 .... **36**, 368
  ss 1–4, 31 .... **35(1)**, 47
Town Police Clauses Act 1889 .... **36**, 491
Towns Improvement Clauses Act 1847 .... **35(1)**, 40
Trade Descriptions Act 1968 .... **39(1)**, 86
Trade Marks Act 1994 .... **48**, 105
Trade Union and Labour Relations (Consolidation) Act 1992 .... **16**, 214
Trade Union Reform and Employment Rights Act 1993 .... **16**, 640
Trading Representations (Disabled Persons) Act 1958 .... **47**, 75
Trading Representations (Disabled Persons) Amendment Act 1972 .... **47**, 147
Trading Schemes Act 1996 .... **47**, 529
Trading Stamps Act 1964 .... **47**, 95
Trading with the Enemy Act 1939 .... **50**, 432
Traffic Calming Act 1992 .... **38(1)**, 413
Traffic Management Act 2004 .... **38(2)**, 406
Tramways Act 1870 .... **36**, 445
Transport Act 1962 .... **36**, 625
Transport Act 1968 .... **36**, 764
Transport Act 1978 .... **36**, 1014
Transport Act 1980 .... **36**, 1022
Transport Act 1981—
  ss 5–18, 40–43, Schs 2–5, Sch 12, Pts I, II .... **39(2)**, 425
  ss 35, 41–43 .... **37**, 96
Transport Act 1982—
  ss 8–15, 17, 20–26, 70–76, Schs 5, 6 .... **37**, 145
  ss 66, 76 .... **39(2)**, 511
Transport Act 1983—
  ss 1, 2, 6–9, 12, Schedule **37**, 178
  ss 11, 12 .... **16**, 175
Transport Act 1985 .... **37**, 437
Transport Act 2000—
  ss 1–107, 273–280, Schs 1, 2, 5–7, 9, Sch 31, Pt I .... **4(1)**, 553
  ss 108–109C, 112–141, 143, 144, 145A–150, 153–155, 157, 160–199, 215, 227, 240,
    241, 244, 247, 248, 250, 253, 254, 260, 263, 268, 272–280, Schs 10, 12, 25, 26, 28,
    29, 31 .... **38(2)**, 91
Transport and Works Act 1992 .... **38(1)**, 414
Transport Charges &c (Miscellaneous Provisions) Act 1954—
  ss 6, 8, 12–15 .... **39(2)**, 115
  ss 8, 10, 12–15 .... **36**, 597
Transport (Finance) Act 1982 .... **37**, 142
Transport for London Act 2008 .... **26(2)**, 898
Transport Holding Company Act 1972 .... **36**, 941
Transport (London) Act 1969 .... **25(1)**, 864
Transport Police (Jurisdiction) Act 1994 .... **38(1)**, 792
Transport (Wales) Act 2006—
  ss 1–10, 12–17 .... **38(2)**, 676
  ss 11–17 .... **4(1)**, 719
Travel Concessions (Eligibility) Act 2002 .... **38(2)**, 342
Treason (1495) .... **12(1)**, 78
Treason Act 1351 .... **12(1)**, 75
Treason Act 1695 .... **12(1)**, 82
Treason Act 1702 .... **10**, 55
Treason Act 1814 .... **12(1)**, 92
Treason Act 1842 .... **12(1)**, 107
Treason Felony Act 1848 .... **12(1)**, 109
Treasure Act 1996 .... **32**, 764

Treasury Bills Act 1877 .... **19(2)**, 704
Treasury Instruments (Signature) Act 1849 .... **10**, 288
Treasury Solicitor Act 1876 .... **10**, 308
Treaties of Peace (Italy, Roumania, Bulgaria, Hungary and Finland) Act 1947 .... **10**, 805
Trees Act 1970 .... **18**, 1178
Trial of Lunatics Act 1883 .... **12(1)**, 198
Tribunals and Inquiries Act 1992 .... **10**, 574
Tribunals, Courts and Enforcement Act 2007—
   ss 1–61, 106, 107, 139–149, Schs 1–11, 16, 22, 23 .... **11(4)**, 20
   ss 62–70, 88–93, 95–105, 146–149, Schs 12, 13, 15, Sch 23, Pt 3 .... **19(3)**, 105
   ss 71–87, 89, 90, 147–149, Sch 14 .... **24**, 664
   ss 109–133, 147–149, Schs 20, 21 .... **4(2)**, 711
   ss 134–138, 147–149 .... **13**, 544
Trinidad and Tobago Independence Act 1962 .... **7(2)**, 408
Trinidad and Tobago Republic Act 1976 .... **7(2)**, 529
Trustee Act 1925 .... **48**, 453
Trustee Act 2000 .... **48**, 619
Trustee Delegation Act 1999 .... **48**, 610
Trustee Investments Act 1961 .... **48**, 567
Trustee Savings Banks Act 1985 .... **19(2)**, 970
Trusts of Land and Appointment of Trustees Act 1996—
   ss 1–18, 22–27, Schs 1, 2, 4 .... **23**, 478
   ss 19–24, 26, 27 .... **48**, 604
Tuvalu Act 1978 .... **7(2)**, 543

U

Uganda Act 1964 .... **7(2)**, 435
Uganda Independence Act 1962 .... **7(2)**, 412
UK Borders Act 2007 .... **31(S)**, Nationality 1
Underground Works (London) Act 1956 .... **50**, 491
Unfair Contract Terms Act 1977 .... **11(1)**, 360
Uniform Laws on International Sales Act 1967 .... **39(1)**, 60
Uniforms Act 1894 .... **3**, 178
Union with Ireland Act 1800 .... **31**, 820
Union with Scotland Act 1706 .... **10**, 56
Union with Scotland (Amendment) Act 1707 .... **10**, 68
United Nations Act 1946 .... **10**, 801
United Nations Personnel Act 1997 .... **10**, 1142
Universities Act 1825 .... **12(1)**, 99
Universities and College Estates Act 1925 .... **21**, 2
Universities and College Estates Act 1964 .... **21**, 262
Universities and Colleges (Trusts) Act 1943 .... **15(1)**, 166
Universities of Oxford and Cambridge Act 1877 .... **15(1)**, 100
Universities of Oxford and Cambridge Act 1923 .... **15(1)**, 121
Universities Tests Act 1871 .... **15(1)**, 96
Unsolicited Goods and Services Act 1971—
   ss 2, 5–7 .... **39(1)**, 113
   ss 3, 3A, 5, 6(2), 7 .... **47**, 138
   ss 4, 6, 7 .... **12(1)**, 684
Unsolicited Goods and Services (Amendment) Act 1975 .... **47**, 240
Urban Development Corporations (Financial Limits) Act 1987 .... **46**, 304
Utilities Act 2000 .... **17(2)**, 501

V

Vacancies in Sees Measure 1959 .... **14**, 509
Vaccine Damage Payments Act 1979 .... **35(1)**, 445
Vagrancy Act 1824 .... **12(1)**, 93
Vagrancy Act 1935 .... **12(1)**, 259
Value Added Tax Act 1994 .... **50**, 6
Variation of Trusts Act 1958 .... **48**, 561
Vehicle and Driving Licences Act 1969 .... **36**, 927
Vehicle Excise and Registration Act 1994 .... **13**, 1034

Vehicle Registration Marks Act 2007 .... **13**, 1254
Vehicles (Crime) Act 2001 .... **47**, 690
Veterinary Surgeons Act 1966 .... **28**, 17
Video Recordings Act 1984 .... **13**, 286
Video Recordings Act 1993 .... **13**, 441
Violent Crime Reduction Act 2006—
   ss 1–14, 28, 29, 32, 35–41, 43, 47, 49–51, 54–57, 60, 61, 63–66, Schs 1–3, 5 .... **12(4)**, 286
   ss 15–20, 27, 64, 66 .... **19(3)**, 853
Visiting Forces Act 1952 .... **3**, 356
Visiting Forces (British Commonwealth) Act 1933 .... **3**, 235
Voluntary Hospitals (Paying Patients) Act 1936 .... **30**, 391

W

War Crimes Act 1991 .... **12(2)**, 69
War Damage Act 1965 .... **50**, 518
War Memorials (Local Authorities' Powers) Act 1923 .... **25(1)**, 155
War Orphans Act 1942 .... **3**, 252
War Pensions Act 1920 .... **3**, 219
War Pensions Act 1921 .... **3**, 225
War Pensions (Administrative Provisions) Act 1918 .... **3**, 211
War Pensions (Administrative Provisions) Act 1919 .... **3**, 213
Warm Homes and Energy Conservation Act 2000 .... **17(2)**, 565
Waste and Emissions Trading Act 2003 .... **35(2)**, 674
Waste Minimisation Act 1998 .... **35(2)**, 411
Water Act 1945 .... **49**, 224
Water Act 1973 .... **49**, 485
Water Act 1981 .... **49**, 548
Water Act 1983 .... **49**, 549
Water Act 1989 .... **49**, 604
Water Act 2003 .... **49**, 1637
Water Consolidation (Consequential Provisions) Act 1991 .... **49**, 1604
Water Industry Act 1991 .... **49**, 699
Water Industry Act 1999 .... **49**, 1631
Water Officers Compensation Act 1960 .... **49**, 358
Water Rate Definition Act 1885 .... **49**, 126
Water Resources Act 1963 .... **49**, 369
Water Resources Act 1971 .... **49**, 386
Water Resources Act 1991 .... **49**, 1233
Waterworks Clauses Act 1847 .... **49**, 20
Waterworks Clauses Act 1863 .... **49**, 72
Weeds Act 1959 .... **1(1)**, 553
Weights and Measures Act 1824 .... **39(1)**, 16
Weights and Measures Act 1985 .... **39(1)**, 491
Weights and Measures &c Act 1976 .... **39(1)**, 388
Welfare of Animals at Slaughter Act 1991 .... **1(2)**, 568
Welfare Reform Act 2007 .... **40(2)**, 735
Welfare Reform and Pensions Act 1999—
   ss 1–3, 6–8, 11, 12, 18, 19, 21, 23–31, 33–35, 38, 40–46, 83–91, Schs 1, 5, 13 .... **33(1)**, 722
   ss 47–52, 60, 68, 72, 79, 81, 82, 83(1), (2), (4)–(11), 84(2)–(4), 85(6), (7), 86, 87,
   89–91, Sch 8, Pt VIII, Sch 11 .... **40(2)**, 389
Wellington Museum Act 1947 .... **13**, 90
Welsh Church Act 1914 .... **14**, 254
Welsh Church (Amendment) Act 1938 .... **14**, 378
Welsh Church (Burial Grounds) Act 1945 .... **14**, 413
Welsh Church (Temporalities) Act 1919 .... **14**, 290
Welsh Development Agency Act 1975 .... **47**, 262
Welsh Development Agency Act 1997 .... **47**, 530
Welsh Language Act 1993 .... **7(1)**, 319
West Indies Act 1962 .... **7(2)**, 393
West Indies Act 1967 .... **7(2)**, 482
Whaling Industry (Regulation) Act 1934 .... **1(1)**, 333
White Herring Fisheries Act 1771 .... **1(1)**, 167
Wild Creatures and Forest Laws Act 1971 .... **10**, 73

Wild Mammals (Protection) Act 1996 .... **2**, 653
Wildlife and Countryside Act 1981—
   ss 1–28S, 31–37A, 39, 41–45, 47, 49–52, 66A–74, Schs ZA1–9, 10A–12, 17 .... **32**, 423
   ss 53–53B, 54A–59, 62, 63, 66, 67–70A, 71–74, Schs 14–16 .... **37**, 99
Wildlife and Countryside (Amendment) Act 1985 .... **32**, 633
Wildlife and Countryside (Amendment) Act 1991 .... **32**, 701
Wildlife and Countryside (Service of Notices) Act 1985 .... **32**, 634
Wills Act 1837 .... **50**, 744
Wills Act 1963 .... **50**, 780
Wills Act 1968 .... **50**, 784
Wills (Soldiers and Sailors) Act 1918 .... **50**, 774
Wireless Telegraphy Act 1967 .... **45**, 38
Wireless Telegraphy Act 2006 .... **45**, 1313
Witnesses Act 1806 .... **18**, 128
Witnesses (Public Inquiries) Protection Act 1892 .... **12(1)**, 206
Work and Families Act 2006 .... **16**, 1235
Works and Public Buildings Act 1874 .... **10**, 120
Writ of Subpoena Act 1805 .... **18**, 126

Y

Yelverton's Act (Ireland) 1781 .... **31**, 817
Youth Justice and Criminal Evidence Act 1999 .... **18**, 340

Z

Zambia Independence Act 1964 .... **7(2)**, 441
Zanzibar Act 1963 .... **7(2)**, 429
Zimbabwe Act 1979 .... **7(2)**, 572
Zoo Licensing Act 1981 .... **2**, 506

Chronological List of Statutes

The following is a chronological list of all Statutes printed in the Volumes as at 1 November 2009, and all Statutes printed in the Service up to and including those in Issue 141 (published in September 2009).

Temp incert................	Statutes of the Exchequer (temp incert)	**13**, 1292
	Statute concerning Tenants by the Curtesy of England	**20**, 55
52 Hen 3...................	Statute of Marlborough (1267)—	
	cc 1, 4, 15	**13**, 1289
	c 23	**20**, 48
3 Edw 1...................	Statute of Westminster the First (1275)—	
	c 5	**15(3)**, 20
	c 50	**10**, 16
13 Edw 1...................	Statute of Westminster the Second (1285), c 1	**20**, 49
18 Edw 1...................	Quia Emptores (1289–90)	**20**, 53
25 Edw 1...................	Statute Concerning Tallage (1297)	**10**, 23
	Confirmation of the Charters (1297)	**10**, 22
	Magna Carta (1297)	**10**, 18
	Prerogativa Regis (temp incert)	**10**, 23
7 Edw 2...................	Bearing of Armour (1313)	**32**, 1034
15 Edw 2...................	Revocatio Novarum Ordinationum (1322)	**32**, 1035
25 Edw 3 Stat 1...........	Status of Children Born Abroad (1350–1)	**10**, 25
25 Edw 3 Stat 5...........	Law presentment (1351–2)	**10**, 25
c 2...........	Treason Act 1351	**12(1)**, 75
28 Edw 3...................	Liberty of Subject (1354)	**10**, 26
34 Edw 3 c 1..............	Justices of the Peace Act 1361	**11(2)**, 23
42 Edw 3 (1368)..........	None put to answere without due Process (1368)	**12(1)**, 77
5 Ric 2 Stat 2 c 4........	Summons to Parliament (1382)	**32**, 1037
7 Hen 4...................	Liberties, Charters and Statutes Confirmed (1405–6)	**10**, 28
4 Hen 5 Stat 2............	Confirmation of Charters and Statutes (1415–16)	**10**, 29
2 Hen 6...................	Confirmation of Liberties (1423)	**10**, 30
10 Hen 7 c 22 (Ir)........	Poynings' Law 1495	**31**, 809
11 Hen 7 c 1..............	Treason (1495)	**12(1)**, 78
4 Hen 8 c 8...............	Privilege of Parliament Act 1512	**32**, 1038
25 Hen 8		
c 19.............	Submission of the Clergy Act 1533	**14**, 21
c 20.............	Appointment of Bishops Act 1533	**14**, 23
c 21.............	Ecclesiastical Licences Act 1533	**14**, 27
26 Hen 8 c 14.............	Suffragan Bishops Act 1534	**14**, 38
27 Hen 8 c 10.............	Statute of Uses (1535)	**20**, 56
28 Hen 8 c 11.............	Tithe Act 1536	**14**, 41
31 Hen 8 c 10.............	House of Lords Precedence Act 1539	**33(1)**, 3
1 Edw 6 c 1...............	Sacrament Act 1547	**14**, 44
2 & 3 Edw 6 c 13.........	Tithes and Offerings (1548)	**14**, 45
5 & 6 Edw 6 c 16.........	Sale of Offices Act 1551	**12(1)**, 79
1 Eliz c 1................	Act of Supremacy (1558)	**14**, 46
13 Eliz 1 c 6.............	Letters Patent Act 1571	**10**, 31
13 Eliz 1 c 29............	Oxford and Cambridge Act 1571	**15(1)**, 31
31 Eliz 1 c 6.............	Simony Act 1588	**14**, 47
1 Ja 1 c 13...............	Privilege of Parliament Act 1603	**32**, 1041
7 Ja 1 c 18...............	Sea-Sand (Devon and Cornwall) (1609)	**49**, 19
21 Ja 1		
c 3..............	Statute of Monopolies (1623)	**11(1)**, 487
c 25.............	Crown Lands Act 1623	**10**, 32
3 Cha 1 c 1...............	Petition of Right (1627)	**10**, 34
12 Car 2 c 24.............	Tenures Abolition Act 1660	**20**, 60
13 Cha 2 Stat 1 c 4.......	Free and Voluntary Present to His Majesty (1661)	**10**, 37
14 Cha 2		
c 3..............	City of London Militia Act 1662	**25(1)**, 46

14 Cha 2—*contd*
    c 4.............. Act of Uniformity 1662 .... **14**, 52
18 & 19 Car 2 c 11........ Cestui que Vie Act 1666 .... **20**, 61
22 & 23 Cha 2 c 10...... Statute of Distribution (1670) **18**, 506
29 Cha 2 c 3.............. Statute of Frauds (1677) .... **11(1)**, 351
31 Cha 2 c 2.............. Habeas Corpus Act 1679 .... **7(1)**, 23
1 Will & Mar
    c 1.............. Convention Parliament (1688) **32**, 1042
    c 6.............. Coronation Oath Act 1688 .... **10**, 37
    c 16.............. Simony Act 1688 .... **14**, 54
    c 21.............. Great Seal Act 1688 .... **10**, 40
    c 30.............. Royal Mines Act 1688 .... **10**, 41
1 Will & Mar Sess 2 c 2... Bill of Rights (1688) **10**, 42
2 Will & Mar
    c 1.............. Crown and Parliament Recognition Act 1689 .... **10**, 48
    c 5.............. Distress for Rent Act 1689 .... **13**, 1293
5 Will & Mar c 6.......... Royal Mines Act 1693 .... **10**, 49
5 & 6 Will & Mar c 20.... Bank of England Act 1694 .... **19(1)**, 30
6 & 7 Will & Mar c 2..... Meeting of Parliament Act 1694 .... **32**, 1042
7 & 8 Will 3 c 3.......... Treason Act 1695 .... **12(1)**, 82
12 & 13 Will 3 c 2........ Act of Settlement (1700) **10**, 50
1 Anne
    c 1.............. Crown Lands Act 1702 .... **10**, 83
    c 2.............. Demise of the Crown Act 1702 .... **10**, 86
1 Anne Stat 2 c 21........ Treason Act 1702 .... **10**, 55
6 Anne
    c 11.............. Union with Scotland Act 1706 .... **10**, 56
    c 40.............. Union with Scotland (Amendment) Act 1707 .... **10**, 68
    c 41.............. Succession to the Crown Act 1707 .... **10**, 69
    c 72.............. Cestui que Vie Act 1707 .... **20**, 63
7 Anne c 14.................. Parochial Libraries Act 1708 .... **14**, 55
8 Anne c 18................. Landlord and Tenant Act 1709 .... **20**, 67
10 Anne c 8................. Princess Sophia's Precedence Act 1711 .... **10**, 72
1 Geo 1 Stat 2
    c 10.............. Queen Anne's Bounty Act 1714 .... **14**, 59
    c 38.............. Septennial Act 1715 .... **32**, 1043
1 Geo 2 Stat 1 c 5........ Demise of the Crown Act 1727 .... **10**, 87
4 Geo 2 c 28............... Landlord and Tenant Act 1730 .... **20**, 70
11 Geo 2
    c 19.............. Distress for Rent Act 1737 .... **13**, 1296
    c 24.............. Parliamentary Privilege Act 1737 .... **13**, 3
24 Geo 2
    c 23.............. Calendar (New Style) Act 1750 .... **45**, 1507
    c 44.............. Constables Protection Act 1750 .... **33(2)**, 30
25 Geo 2
    c 30.............. Calendar Act 1751 .... **45**, 1532
10 Geo 3 c 50............. Parliamentary Privilege Act 1770 .... **32**, 1044
11 Geo 3 c 31.............. White Herring Fisheries Act 1771 .... **1(1)**, 167
12 Geo 3 c 11.............. Royal Marriages Act 1772 .... **10**, 89
13 Geo 3
    c 52.............. Plate Assay (Sheffield and Birmingham) Act 1772 .... **48**, 13
    c 81.............. Inclosure Act 1773 .... **20**, 72
14 Geo 3
    c 48.............. Life Assurance Act 1774 .... **19(1)**, 32
    c 78.............. Fires Prevention (Metropolis) Act 1774 .... **19(1)**, 35
15 Geo 3 c 39.............. Oaths Act 1775 .... **11(2)**, 24
17 Geo 3 c 53.............. Clergy Residences Repair Act 1776 .... **14**, 62
21 & 22 Geo 3
    c 11 (Ir)........ Habeas Corpus Act (Ireland) 1781 .... **31**, 810
    c 48 (Ir)........ Yelverton's Act (Ireland) 1781 .... **31**, 817
26 Geo 3 c 31.............. National Debt Reduction Act 1786 .... **19(2)**, 641
32 Geo 3
    c 60.............. Libel Act 1792 .... **19(3)**, 355
33 Geo 3 c 13.............. Acts of Parliament (Commencement) Act 1793 .... **41**, 701
37 Geo 3 c 127............ Meeting of Parliament Act 1797 .... **32**, 1046

39 Geo 3 c 37................ Offences at Sea Act 1799 .... **12(1)**, 83
39 & 40 Geo 3
    c 14.............. Meeting of Parliament Act 1799 .... **32**, 1047
    c 67.............. Union with Ireland Act 1800 .... **31**, 820
    c 88.............. Crown Private Estate Act 1800 .... **10**, 90
41 Geo 3
    c 52.............. House of Commons (Disqualifications) Act 1801 .... **32**, 1048
    c 79.............. Public Notaries Act 1801 .... **11(2)**, 24
    c 90.............. Crown Debts Act 1801 .... **41**, 702
42 Geo 3 c 85.............. Criminal Jurisdiction Act 1802 .... **12(1)**, 84
43 Geo 3 c 140............. Habeas Corpus Act 1803 .... **7(1)**, 32
44 Geo 3
    c 43.............. Clergy Ordination Act 1804 .... **14**, 63
    c 102............ Habeas Corpus Act 1804 .... **7(1)**, 33
45 Geo 3 c 92.............. Writ of Subpoena Act 1805 .... **18**, 126
46 Geo 3 c 37.............. Witnesses Act 1806 .... **18**, 128
48 Geo 3
    c 106............ Acts of Parliament (Expiration) Act 1808 .... **41**, 708
    c 142............ Life Annuities Act 1808 .... **19(2)**, 643
49 Geo 3 c 126............. Sale of Offices Act 1809 .... **12(1)**, 85
51 Geo 3 c 115............. Gifts for Churches Act 1811 .... **14**, 64
54 Geo 3 c 146............. Treason Act 1814 .... **12(1)**, 92
55 Geo 3 c 184............. Stamp Act 1815 .... **18**, 508
56 Geo 3
    c 46.............. Civil List Audit Act 1816 .... **10**, 99
    c 50.............. Sale of Farming Stock Act 1816 .... **13**, 1306
    c 98.............. Consolidated Fund Act 1816 .... **19(2)**, 644
    c 100............ Habeas Corpus Act 1816 .... **7(1)**, 34
    c 141............ Burial Ground Act 1816 .... **14**, 66
57 Geo 3 c 52.............. Deserted Tenements Act 1817 .... **13**, 1311
58 Geo 3 c 66.............. National Debt Commissioners Act 1818 .... **19(2)**, 649
60 Geo 3 & 1 Geo 4
    c 8.............. Criminal Libel Act 1819 .... **19(3)**, 357
1 Geo 4 c 100............. Militia (City of London) Act 1820 .... **25(1)**, 47
1 & 2 Geo 4 c 76.......... Cinque Ports Act 1821 .... **11(2)**, 26
3 Geo 4 c 72.............. Church Building Act 1822 .... **14**, 68
4 Geo 4
    c 18.............. Crown Lands Act 1823 .... **10**, 102
    c 19.............. National Debt Reduction Act 1823 .... **19(2)**, 649
5 Geo 4
    c 74.............. Weights and Measures Act 1824 .... **39(1)**, 16
    c 82.............. Clerk of the Parliaments Act 1824 .... **32**, 1050
    c 83.............. Vagrancy Act 1824 .... **12(1)**, 93
    c 113............ Slave Trade Act 1824 .... **47**, 30
6 Geo 4
    c 50.............. Juries Act 1825 .... **19(3)**, 179
    c 92.............. Marriages Confirmation Act 1825 .... **27**, 105
    c 97.............. Universities Act 1825 .... **12(1)**, 99
7 Geo 4
    c 16.............. Chelsea and Kilmainham Hospitals Act 1826 .... **3**, 31
    c 64.............. Criminal Law Act 1826 .... **12(1)**, 100
9 Geo 4
    c 14.............. Statute of Frauds Amendment Act 1828 .... **11(1)**, 352
    c 25.............. Revenue Solicitors' Act 1828 .... **11(2)**, 31
    c 66.............. Nautical Almanack Act 1828 .... **39(2)**, 20
    c 69.............. Night Poaching Act 1828 .... **2**, 144
10 Geo 4
    c 7.............. Roman Catholic Relief Act 1829 .... **14**, 70
    c 44.............. Metropolitan Police Act 1829 .... **33(2)**, 31
11 Geo 4 & 1 Will 4
    c 18.............. Marriage Confirmation Act 1830 .... **27**, 106
    c 68.............. Carriers Act 1830 .... **5(2)**, 504
1 & 2 Will 4
    c 22.............. London Hackney Carriage Act 1831 .... **36**, 249
    c 32.............. Game Act 1831 .... **2**, 147

2 & 3 Will 4
    c 71 .... Prescription Act 1832 .... **20**, 86
    c 80 .... Ecclesiastical Corporations Act 1832 .... **14**, 73
    c 100 .... Tithe Act 1832 .... **14**, 77
    c 111 .... Lord Chancellor's Pension Act 1832 .... **10**, 224
3 & 4 Will 4
    c 29 .... Army (Artillery, etc) Pensions Act 1833 .... **3**, 45
    c 31 .... Sunday Observance Act 1833 .... **45**, 1534
    c 35 .... Inclosure and Drainage (Rates) Act 1833 .... **20**, 93
    c 41 .... Judicial Committee Act 1833 .... **11(2)**, 32
    c 74 .... Fines and Recoveries Act 1833 .... **20**, 97
    c 85 .... Saint Helena Act 1833 .... **7(2)**, 296
    c 105 .... Dower Act 1833 .... **18**, 510
    c 106 .... Inheritance Act 1833 .... **18**, 515
5 & 6 Will 4
    c 35 .... Paymaster General Act 1835 .... **10**, 225
    c 50 .... Highway Act 1835 .... **36**, 255
    c 62 .... Statutory Declarations Act 1835 .... **18**, 129
6 & 7 Will 4
    c 20 .... Ecclesiastical Leases Act 1836 .... **14**, 80
    c 64 .... Ecclesiastical Leases (Amendment) Act 1836 .... **14**, 84
    c 71 .... Tithe Act 1836 .... **14**, 86
    c 77 .... Ecclesiastical Commissioners Act 1836 .... **14**, 89
    c 106 .... Stannaries Act 1836 .... **11(2)**, 42
1 & 2 Vict c 2 .... Civil List Act 1837 .... **10**, 103
7 Will 4 & 1 Vict
    c 26 .... Wills Act 1837 .... **50**, 744
    c 45 .... Parish Notices Act 1837 .... **14**, 93
    c 88 .... Piracy Act 1837 .... **12(1)**, 102
1 & 2 Vict
    c 20 .... Queen Anne's Bounty Act 1838 .... **14**, 95
    c 23 .... Parsonages Act 1838 .... **14**, 97
    c 89 .... Drouly Fund Act 1838 .... **3**, 46
    c 106 .... Pluralities Act 1838 .... **14**, 98
    c 110 .... Judgments Act 1838 .... **19(3)**, 6
2 & 3 Vict
    c 45 .... Highway (Railway Crossings) Act 1839 .... **36**, 260
    c 47 .... Metropolitan Police Act 1839—
                    ss 33, 78, 79 .... **12(1)**, 103
                    ss 38–40 .... **27**, 6
                    s 44 .... **19(3)**, 434
                    ss 52–55, 58, 60, 61, 68, 75, 76, 78, 79 .... **36**, 261
                    ss 68, 75, 76, 78, 79 .... **33(2)**, 35
    c 62 .... Tithe Act 1839 .... **14**, 130
    c 71 .... Metropolitan Police Courts Act 1839 .... **12(1)**, 104
3 & 4 Vict
    c 9 .... Parliamentary Papers Act 1840 .... **19(3)**, 359
    c 84 .... Metropolitan Police Courts Act 1840 .... **11(2)**, 45
    c 92 .... Non-Parochial Registers Act 1840 .... **36**, 7
    c 97 .... Railway Regulation Act 1840 .... **36**, 271
    c 113 .... Ecclesiastical Commissioners Act 1840 .... **14**, 131
4 & 5 Vict
    c 30 .... Ordnance Survey Act 1841 .... **10**, 227
    c 38 .... School Sites Act 1841 .... **20**, 128
    c 39 .... Ecclesiastical Commissioners Act 1841 .... **14**, 141
5 Vict c 6 .... Bishops in Foreign Countries Act 1841 .... **14**, 147
5 & 6 Vict
    c 26 .... Ecclesiastical Houses of Residence Act 1842 .... **14**, 148
    c 51 .... Treason Act 1842 .... **12(1)**, 107
    c 55 .... Railway Regulation Act 1842 .... **36**, 274
    c 94 .... Defence Act 1842 .... **3**, 49
    c 97 .... Limitations of Actions and Costs Act 1842 .... **11(2)**, 46
    c 108 .... Ecclesiastical Leasing Act 1842 .... **14**, 153
6 & 7 Vict
    c 37 .... New Parishes Act 1843 .... **14**, 170

Enquiry Bureau   hsieb@lexisnexis.co.uk

6 & 7 Vict—*contd*

 c 38 .... Judicial Committee Act 1843 .... **11(2)**, 48
 c 86 .... London Hackney Carriages Act 1843 .... **36**, 279
 c 90 .... Public Notaries Act 1843 .... **11(2)**, 53
 c 96 .... Libel Act 1843 .... **19(3)**, 362
 c 98 .... Slave Trade Act 1843 .... **47**, 33

7 & 8 Vict

 c 29 .... Night Poaching Act 1844 .... **2**, 170
 c 32 .... Bank Charter Act 1844 .... **19(1)**, 37
 c 37 .... School Sites Act 1844 .... **20**, 137
 c 59 .... Lecturers and Parish Clerks Act 1844 .... **14**, 171
 c 69 .... Judicial Committee Act 1844 .... **11(2)**, 56
 c 96 .... Execution Act 1844 .... **19(3)**, 10

8 & 9 Vict

 c 15 .... Auctioneers Act 1845 .... **39(1)**, 17
 c 16 .... Companies Clauses Consolidation Act 1845 .... **8**, 10
 c 18 .... Lands Clauses Consolidation Act 1845 .... **9**, 7
 c 20 .... Railways Clauses Consolidation Act 1845 .... **36**, 292
 c 42 .... Canal Carriers Act 1845 .... **36**, 362
 c 63 .... Geological Survey Act 1845 .... **10**, 232
 c 75 .... Libel Act 1845 .... **19(3)**, 366
 c 113 .... Evidence Act 1845 .... **18**, 136
 c 118 .... Inclosure Act 1845 .... **20**, 140

9 & 10 Vict

 c 70 .... Inclosure Act 1846 .... **20**, 189

10 & 11 Vict

 c 14 .... Markets and Fairs Clauses Act 1847 .... **27**, 9
 c 16 .... Commissioners Clauses Act 1847 .... **10**, 234
 c 17 .... Waterworks Clauses Act 1847 .... **49**, 20
 c 27 .... Harbours, Docks, and Piers Clauses Act 1847 .... **39(2)**, 21
 c 34 .... Towns Improvement Clauses Act 1847 .... **35(1)**, 40
 c 65 .... Cemeteries Clauses Act 1847 .... **5(2)**, 417
 c 89 .... Town Police Clauses Act 1847—
        ss 1–4, 21, 23–29, 37, 38, 40–66, 68 .... **36**, 368
        ss 1–4, 31 .... **35(1)**, 47
 c 94 .... Canal (Carriers) Act 1847 .... **36**, 398
 c 111 .... Inclosure Act 1847 .... **20**, 193

11 & 12 Vict

 c 12 .... Treason Felony Act 1848 .... **12(1)**, 109
 c 29 .... Hares Act 1848 .... **2**, 171
 c 42 .... Indictable Offences Act 1848 .... **12(1)**, 111
 c 55 .... Paymaster General Act 1848 .... **10**, 286
 c 99 .... Inclosure Act 1848 .... **20**, 197

12 & 13 Vict

 c 49 .... School Sites Act 1849 .... **20**, 201
 c 67 .... Sequestration Act 1849 .... **14**, 174
 c 83 .... Inclosure Act 1849 .... **20**, 204
 c 89 .... Treasury Instruments (Signature) Act 1849 .... **10**, 288
 c 96 .... Admiralty Offences (Colonial) Act 1849 .... **7(2)**, 297

13 & 14 Vict

 c 7 .... London Hackney Carriages Act 1850 .... **36**, 400
 c 26 .... Piracy Act 1850 .... **12(1)**, 114
 c 94 .... Ecclesiastical Commissioners Act 1850 .... **14**, 175

14 & 15 Vict

 c 24 .... School Sites Act 1851 .... **20**, 206
 c 25 .... Landlord and Tenant Act 1851 .... **20**, 207
 c 42 .... Crown Lands Act 1851 .... **10**, 105
 c 55 .... Criminal Justice Administration Act 1851 .... **12(1)**, 115
 c 99 .... Evidence Act 1851 .... **18**, 139

15 & 16 Vict

 c 28 .... Commissioners of Works Act 1852 .... **10**, 109
 c 49 .... School Sites Act 1852 .... **20**, 208
 c 76 .... Common Law Procedure Act 1852 .... **20**, 209
 c 79 .... Inclosure Act 1852 .... **20**, 216
 c 84 .... Metropolis Water Act 1852 .... **49**, 62

15 & 16 Vict—*contd*
    c 85 .... Burial Act 1852 .... **5(2)**, 444
16 & 17 Vict
    c 2 .... Bank Notes Act 1852 .... **19(1)**, 40
    c 30 .... Criminal Procedure Act 1853 .... **12(1)**, 116
    c 33 .... London Hackney Carriage Act 1853 .... **36**, 402
    c 49 .... Colonial Bishops Act 1853 .... **14**, 178
    c 59 .... Stamp Act 1853 .... **19(1)**, 41
    c 83 .... Evidence Amendment Act 1853 .... **18**, 146
    c 85 .... Privy Council Registrar Act 1853 .... **11(2)**, 60
    c 131 .... Merchant Shipping Law Amendment Act 1853 .... **39(2)**, 78
    c 134 .... Burial Act 1853 .... **5(2)**, 448
17 & 18 Vict
    c 33 .... Public Statues (Metropolis) Act 1854 .... **25(1)**, 51
    c 34 .... Attendance of Witnesses Act 1854 .... **18**, 147
    c 67 .... Defence Act 1854 .... **3**, 71
    c 81 .... Oxford University Act 1854 .... **15(1)**, 54
    c 94 .... Public Revenue and Consolidated Fund Charges Act
                       1854 .... **19(2)**, 651
    c 97 .... Inclosure Act 1854 .... **20**, 222
    c 112 .... Literary and Scientific Institutions Act 1854 .... **13**, 60
    c 120 .... Merchant Shipping Repeal Act 1854 .... **39(2)**, 79
    c 125 .... Common Law Procedure Act 1854 .... **19(1)**, 42
18 & 19 Vict
    c 32 .... Stannaries Act 1855 .... **11(2)**, 61
    c 48 .... Cinque Ports Act 1855 .... **11(2)**, 63
    c 81 .... Places of Worship Registration Act 1855 .... **14**, 178
    c 84 .... Deputy Speaker Act 1855 .... **32**, 1051
    c 117 .... Ordnance Board Transfer Act 1855 .... **10**, 288
    c 120 .... Metropolis Management Act 1855 .... **25(1)**, 55
    c 128 .... Burial Act 1855 .... **5(2)**, 451
    c 131 .... School Grants Act 1855 .... **20**, 232
19 & 20 Vict
    c 1 .... House of Commons Offices Act 1856 .... **32**, 1052
    c 88 .... Cambridge University Act 1856 .... **15(1)**, 65
    c 97 .... Mercantile Law Amendment Act 1856 .... **11(1)**, 353
20 & 21 Vict
    c 3 .... Penal Servitude Act 1857 .... **12(1)**, 118
    c 25 .... Oxford University Act 1857 .... **15(1)**, 75
    c 31 .... Inclosure Act 1857 .... **20**, 234
    c 81 .... Burial Act 1857 .... **5(2)**, 455
21 & 22 Vict
    c 45 .... Durham County Palatine Act 1858 .... **10**, 111
    c 49 .... Jews Relief Act 1858 .... **14**, 185
    c 57 .... Ecclesiastical Leasing Act 1858 .... **14**, 185
    c 71 .... Bishops Trusts Substitution Act 1858 .... **5(2)**, 517
    c 78 .... Parliamentary Witnesses Act 1858 .... **32**, 1053
    c 90 .... Medical Act (1858) **28**, 10
22 Vict
    c 1 .... Burial Act 1859 .... **5(2)**, 459
    c 12 .... Defence Act 1859 .... **3**, 73
    c 30 .... Confirmation and Probate Amendment Act 1859 .... **18**, 522
    c 32 .... Remission of Penalties Act 1859 .... **12(1)**, 119
22 & 23 Vict
    c 1 .... Clerk of the Council Act 1859 .... **10**, 291
    c 12 .... Colonial Affidavits Act 1859 .... **7(2)**, 299
    c 21 .... Queen's Remembrancer Act 1859 .... **13**, 4
    c 35 .... Law of Property Amendment Act 1859 .... **18**, 523
    c 43 .... Inclosure Act 1859 .... **20**, 240
    c 63 .... British Law Ascertainment Act 1859 .... **18**, 150
23 & 24 Vict
    c 27 .... Refreshment Houses Act 1860 .... **19(3)**, 435
    c 32 .... Ecclesiastical Courts Jurisdiction Act 1860 .... **14**, 191
    c 66 .... Medical Act 1860 .... **28**, 12
    c 90 .... Game Licences Act 1860 .... **2**, 174

23 & 24 Vict—*contd*

 c 91.............. Oxford University Act 1860 .... **15(1)**, 77
 c 93.............. Tithe Act 1860 .... **14**, 194
 c 106........... Lands Clauses Consolidation Acts Amendment
        Act 1860 .... **9**, 65
 c 112........... Defence Act 1860 .... **3**, 76
 c 122........... Admiralty Offences (Colonial) Act 1860 .... **7(2)**, 300
 c 124........... Ecclesiastical Commissioners Act 1860 .... **14**, 194
 c 135........... Metropolitan Police Act 1860 .... **33(2)**, 37

24 & 25 Vict

 c 47.............. Harbours and Passing Tolls, &c Act 1861 .... **39(2)**, 82
 c 70.............. Locomotive Act 1861 .... **36**, 407
 c 94.............. Accessories and Abettors Act 1861 .... **12(1)**, 120
 c 97.............. Malicious Damage Act 1861 .... **12(1)**, 121
 c 98.............. Forgery Act 1861 .... **12(1)**, 125
 c 100........... Offences against the Person Act 1861 .... **12(1)**, 128
 c 121........... Domicile Act 1861 .... **18**, 526
 c 124........... Metropolitan Police (Receiver) Act 1861 .... **33(2)**, 40

25 & 26 Vict

 c 4............... Officers Commissions Act 1862 .... **3**, 89
 c 20.............. Habeas Corpus Act 1862 .... **7(1)**, 38
 c 26.............. Oxford University Act 1862 .... **15(1)**, 78
 c 37.............. Crown Private Estates Act 1862 .... **10**, 113
 c 69.............. Harbours Transfer Act 1862 .... **39(2)**, 90
 c 82.............. Poor Rates Recovery Act 1862 .... **25(1)**, 57
 c 114........... Poaching Prevention Act 1862 .... **2**, 186

26 & 27 Vict

 c 13.............. Town Gardens Protection Act 1863 .... **32**, 20
 c 81.............. Public Works and Fisheries Acts Amendment Act
        1863 .... **39(2)**, 98
 c 92.............. Railways Clauses Act 1863 .... **36**, 408
 c 93.............. Waterworks Clauses Act 1863 .... **49**, 72
 c 118........... Companies Clauses Act 1863 .... **8**, 69

27 & 28 Vict

 c 24.............. Naval Agency and Distribution Act 1864 .... **3**, 90
 c 25.............. Naval Prize Act 1864 .... **11(2)**, 64
 c 55.............. Metropolitan Police Act 1864 .... **36**, 420
 c 89.............. Defence Act Amendment Act 1864 .... **3**, 101
 c 94.............. Episcopal Church (Scotland) Act 1864 .... **14**, 196
 c 97.............. Registration of Burials Act 1864 .... **5(2)**, 460
 c 114........... Improvement of Land Act 1864 .... **20**, 244

28 & 29 Vict

 c 18.............. Criminal Procedure Act 1865 .... **18**, 153
 c 55.............. Oxford University, Vinerian Foundation, Act 1865 .... **15(1)**, 83
 c 57.............. Ecclesiastical Leases Act 1865 .... **14**, 198
 c 63.............. Colonial Laws Validity Act 1865 .... **7(2)**, 301
 c 64.............. Colonial Marriages Act 1865 .... **7(2)**, 305
 c 65.............. Defence Act 1865 .... **3**, 103
 c 69.............. Parsonages Act 1865 .... **14**, 198
 c 72.............. Navy and Marines (Wills) Act 1865 .... **50**, 771
 c 73.............. Naval and Marine Pay and Pensions Act 1865 .... **3**, 103
 c 89.............. Greenwich Hospital Act 1865 .... **3**, 107
 c 90.............. Metropolitan Fire Brigade Act 1865 .... **18**, 1010
 c 111........... Navy and Marines (Property of Deceased) Act 1865 .... **3**, 117
 c 122........... Clerical Subscription Act 1865 .... **14**, 200
 c 125........... Dockyard Ports Regulation Act 1865 .... **39(2)**, 100

29 & 30 Vict

 c 11.............. National Debt Reduction Act 1866 .... **19(2)**, 653
 c 19.............. Parliamentary Oaths Act 1866 .... **32**, 1054
 c 39.............. Exchequer and Audit Departments Act 1866 .... **19(2)**, 654
 c 111........... Ecclesiastical Commissioners Act 1866 .... **14**, 203
 c 122........... Metropolitan Commons Act 1866 .... **20**, 289

30 & 31 Vict

 c 35.............. Criminal Law Amendment Act 1867 .... **12(1)**, 157
 c 39.............. Metropolitan Police (Receiver) Act 1867 .... **33(2)**, 41

30 & 31 Vict—*contd*

c 48	Sale of Land by Auction Act 1867	**39(1)**, 18
c 81	Prorogation Act 1867	**32**, 1056
c 102	Representation of the People Act 1867	**32**, 1057
c 127	Railway Companies Act 1867	**36**, 421
c 133	Consecration of Churchyards Act 1867	**14**, 205
c 134	Metropolitan Streets Act 1867	**36**, 424
c 144	Policies of Assurance Act 1867	**19(1)**, 44

31 & 32 Vict

c 5	Metropolitan Streets Act Amendment Act 1867	**36**, 429
c 9	Exchequer Extra Receipts Act 1868	**19(2)**, 665
c 37	Documentary Evidence Act 1868	**18**, 159
c 45	Sea Fisheries Act 1868	**1(1)**, 170
c 47	Consecration of Churchyards Act 1868	**14**, 209
c 72	Promissory Oaths Act 1868	**10**, 292
c 83	Army Chaplains Act 1868	**14**, 210
c 89	Inclosure, etc, Expenses Act 1868	**20**, 305
c 106	Metropolitan Fairs Act 1868	**27**, 34
c 109	Compulsory Church Rate Abolition Act 1868	**14**, 214
c 110	Telegraph Act 1868	**45**, 15
c 118	Public Schools Act 1868	**15(1)**, 84
c 119	Regulation of Railways Act 1868	**36**, 430
c cxiii	Gun Barrel Proof Act 1868	**48**, 15

32 & 33 Vict

c 10	Colonial Prisoners Removal Act 1869	**7(2)**, 306
c 24	Newspapers, Printers, and Reading Rooms Repeal Act 1869	**19(3)**, 367
c 44	Greenwich Hospital Act 1869	**3**, 125
c 48	Companies Clauses Act 1869	**8**, 81
c 62	Debtors Act 1869	**4(2)**, 9
c 86	Parliamentary Returns Act 1869	**32**, 1058
c 94	New Parishes Acts and Church Building Acts Amendment Act 1869	**14**, 217
c 107	Metropolitan Commons Amendment Act 1869	**20**, 306
c 109	Residence of Incumbents Act 1869	**14**, 219
c 115	Metropolitan Public Carriage Act 1869	**36**, 435

33 & 34 Vict

c 23	Forfeiture Act 1870	**12(1)**, 158
c 35	Apportionment Act 1870	**20**, 307
c 56	Limited Owners Residences Act 1870	**20**, 310
c 71	National Debt Act 1870	**19(2)**, 665
c 78	Tramways Act 1870	**36**, 445
c 81	Meeting of Parliament Act 1870	**32**, 1059
c 88	Telegraph Act 1870	**45**, 16
c 90	Foreign Enlistment Act 1870	**12(1)**, 160
c 91	Clerical Disabilities Act 1870	**14**, 220

34 & 35 Vict

c 12	Fairs Act 1871	**27**, 36
c 26	Universities Tests Act 1871	**15(1)**, 96
c 36	Pensions Commutation Act 1871	**33(1)**, 44
c 37	Prayer Book (Tables of Lessons) Act 1871	**14**, 224
c 45	Sequestration Act 1871	**14**, 236
c 48	Promissory Oaths Act 1871	**10**, 302
c 53	Ecclesiastical Titles Act 1871	**14**, 238
c 56	Dogs Act 1871	**2**, 189
c 63	College Charter Act 1871	**15(1)**, 99
c 83	Parliamentary Witnesses Oaths Act 1871	**32**, 1060
c 84	Limited Owners Residences Act (1870) Amendment Act 1871	**20**, 313
c 96	Pedlars Act 1871	**27**, 37
c 112	Prevention of Crimes Act 1871	**12(1)**, 178
c 113	Metropolis Water Act 1871	**49**, 81

35 & 36 Vict

c 15	Parks Regulation Act 1872	**32**, 25
c 26	Review of Justices Decisions Act 1872	**11(2)**, 81

35 & 36 Vict—*contd*

c 36.............. Baptismal Fees Abolition Act 1872 .... **14**, 239
c 49.............. Church Seats Act 1872 .... **14**, 240
c 50.............. Railway Rolling Stock Protection Act 1872 .... **36**, 477
c 51.............. Judges Salaries Act 1872 .... **11(2)**, 83
c 67.............. Greenwich Hospital Act 1872 .... **3**, 128
c 70.............. Law Officers Fees Act 1872 .... **10**, 304
c 94.............. Licensing Act 1872 .... **19(3)**, 436

36 & 37 Vict

c 37.............. Fairs Act 1873 .... **27**, 49
c 48.............. Regulation of Railways Act 1873 .... **36**, 479
c 50.............. Places of Worship Sites Act 1873 .... **14**, 240
c 61.............. Crown Private Estates Act 1873 .... **10**, 118
c 68.............. Militia (Lands and Buildings) Act 1873 .... **3**, 130
c 72.............. Defence Acts Amendment Act 1873 .... **3**, 131
c 88.............. Slave Trade Act 1873 .... **47**, 34

37 & 38 Vict

c 27.............. Courts (Colonial) Jurisdiction Act 1874 .... **7(2)**, 309
c 40.............. Board of Trade Arbitrations, &c Act 1874 .... **36**, 482
c 77.............. Colonial Clergy Act 1874 .... **14**, 244
c 81.............. Great Seal (Offices) Act 1874 .... **10**, 305
c 84.............. Works and Public Buildings Act 1874 .... **10**, 120
c 88.............. Births and Deaths Registration Act 1874 .... **36**, 14

38 & 39 Vict

c 17.............. Explosives Act 1875 .... **18**, 720
c 18.............. Seal Fishery Act 1875 .... **1(1)**, 176
c 25.............. Public Stores Act 1875 .... **12(1)**, 181
c 55.............. Public Health Act 1875 .... **35(1)**, 51
c 89.............. Public Works Loans Act 1875 .... **19(2)**, 677

39 & 40 Vict

c 14.............. Chelsea Hospital Act 1876 .... **3**, 133
c 18.............. Treasury Solicitor Act 1876 .... **10**, 308
c 31.............. Public Works Loans (Money) Act 1876 .... **19(2)**, 703
c 36.............. Customs Consolidation Act 1876 .... **13**, 559
c 56.............. Commons Act 1876 .... **20**, 315
c 59.............. Appellate Jurisdiction Act 1876 .... **11(2)**, 84

40 & 41 Vict

c 2............... Treasury Bills Act 1877 .... **19(2)**, 704
c 11.............. Jurisdiction in Rating Act 1877 .... **25(1)**, 58
c 41.............. Crown Office Act 1877 .... **10**, 312
c 48.............. Universities of Oxford and Cambridge Act 1877 .... **15(1)**, 100

41 & 42 Vict

c 31.............. Bills of Sale Act 1878 .... **39(1)**, 21
c 38.............. Innkeepers Act 1878 .... **19(3)**, 439
c 54.............. Debtors Act 1878 .... **4(2)**, 16
c 56.............. Commons (Expenses) Act 1878 .... **20**, 332
c 71.............. Metropolitan Commons Act 1878 .... **20**, 333
c 73.............. Territorial Waters Jurisdiction Act 1878 .... **12(1)**, 186

42 & 43 Vict

c 8............... Registration of Births, Deaths and Marriages (Army) Act
                    1879 .... **36**, 17
c 11.............. Bankers' Books Evidence Act 1879 .... **18**, 165
c 21.............. Customs and Inland Revenue Act 1879 .... **13**, 563
c 28.............. Convention (Ireland) Act Repeal Act 1879 .... **32**, 1062
c 36.............. Customs Buildings Act 1879 .... **13**, 564
c 37.............. Commons Act 1879 .... **20**, 335
c 58.............. Public Offices Fees Act 1879 .... **19(2)**, 707
c cxcviii........ Metropolis Management (Thames River Prevention of
                    Floods) Amendment Act 1879 .... **49**, 99

43 & 44 Vict

c 41.............. Burial Laws Amendment Act 1880 .... **5(2)**, 463
c 47.............. Ground Game Act 1880 .... **2**, 191

44 & 45 Vict

c 3............... Judicial Committee Act 1881 .... **11(2)**, 90
c 10.............. Inland Revenue Buildings Act 1881 .... **10**, 122

44 & 45 Vict—*contd*
    c 24.............. Summary Jurisdiction (Process) Act 1881 .... **11(2)**, 91
    c 41.............. Conveyancing Act 1881 .... **20**, 336
    c 45.............. Pedlars Act 1881 .... **27**, 51
    c 60.............. Newspaper Libel and Registration Act 1881 .... **19(3)**, 372
45 & 46 Vict
    c 9.............. Documentary Evidence Act 1882 .... **18**, 171
    c 15.............. Commonable Rights Compensation Act 1882 .... **20**, 342
    c 21.............. Places of Worship Sites Amendment Act 1882 .... **14**, 245
    c 38.............. Settled Land Act 1882 .... **20**, 347
    c 43.............. Bills of Sale Act (1878) Amendment Act 1882 .... **39(1)**, 36
    c 44.............. Pensions Commutation Act 1882 .... **33(1)**, 50
    c 50.............. Municipal Corporations Act 1882 .... **25(1)**, 59
    c 61.............. Bills of Exchange Act 1882 .... **19(1)**, 48
    c 72.............. Revenue, Friendly Societies and National Debt Act 1882—
                        ss 1, 18, 19 .... **19(2)**, 711
                        ss 1, 24 .... **10**, 315
    c 75.............. Married Women's Property Act 1882 .... **27**, 107
    c lvi.............. Metropolitan Board of Works (Various Powers) Act
                        1882 .... **49**, 121
46 & 47 Vict
    c 3.............. Explosive Substances Act 1883 .... **12(1)**, 191
    c 10.............. Customs and Inland Revenue Act 1883 .... **2**, 196
    c 18.............. Municipal Corporations Act 1883 .... **25(1)**, 79
    c 22.............. Sea Fisheries Act 1883 .... **1(1)**, 179
    c 32.............. Greenwich Hospital Act 1883 .... **3**, 134
    c 38.............. Trial of Lunatics Act 1883 .... **12(1)**, 198
47 & 48 Vict
    c 23.............. National Debt (Conversion of Stock) Act 1884 .... **19(2)**, 713
    c 30.............. Great Seal Act 1884 .... **10**, 317
    c 31.............. Colonial Prisoners Removal Act 1884 .... **7(2)**, 311
    c 44.............. Naval Pensions Act 1884 .... **3**, 137
    c 55.............. Pensions and Yeomanry Pay Act 1884 .... **3**, 138
    c 62.............. Revenue Act 1884—
                        ss 1, 11 .... **18**, 527
                        ss 1, 14 .... **19(2)**, 715
    c 71.............. Intestates Estates Act 1884 .... **18**, 529
    c 72.............. Disused Burial Grounds Act 1884 .... **5(2)**, 470
48 & 49 Vict
    c 34.............. Water Rate Definition Act 1885 .... **49**, 126
    c 42.............. Greenwich Hospital Act 1885 .... **3**, 142
    c 49.............. Submarine Telegraph Act 1885 .... **45**, 17
    c 54.............. Pluralities Acts Amendment Act 1885 .... **14**, 246
    c clxvii.......... Metropolitan Board of Works (Various Powers) Act
                        1885 .... **25(1)**, 83
49 & 50 Vict
    c 22.............. Metropolitan Police Act 1886 .... **33(2)**, 42
    c 38.............. Riot (Damages) Act 1886 .... **33(2)**, 45
50 & 51 Vict
    c 27.............. Markets and Fairs (Weighing of Cattle) Act 1887 .... **27**, 52
    c 40.............. Savings Banks Act 1887 .... **19(2)**, 716
    c 45.............. Metropolitan Police Act 1887 .... **33(2)**, 51
    c 54.............. British Settlements Act 1887 .... **7(2)**, 321
    c 55.............. Sheriffs Act 1887 .... **39(1)**, 811
    c 70.............. Appellate Jurisdiction Act 1887 .... **11(2)**, 95
51 & 52 Vict
    c 2.............. National Debt (Conversion) Act 1888 .... **19(2)**, 720
    c 21.............. Law of Distress Amendment Act 1888 .... **13**, 1312
    c 25.............. Railway and Canal Traffic Act 1888 .... **36**, 484
    c 41.............. Local Government Act 1888 .... **25(1)**, 85
    c 48.............. Companies Clauses Consolidation Act 1888 .... **8**, 83
    c 56.............. Suffragans Nomination Act 1888 .... **14**, 247
    c 64.............. Law of Libel Amendment Act 1888 .... **19(3)**, 380
52 & 53 Vict
    c 6.............. National Debt Act 1889 .... **19(2)**, 722

Enquiry Bureau   hsieb@lexisnexis.co.uk

52 & 53 Vict—*contd*

c 10..............	Commissioners for Oaths Act 1889	**18**, 173
c 14..............	Town Police Clauses Act 1889	**36**, 491
c 30..............	Board of Agriculture Act 1889	**10**, 318
c 42..............	Revenue Act 1889—	
	ss 30, 37	**3**, 143
	ss 31, 32, 37	**19(2)**, 724
c 45..............	Factors Act 1889	**1(1)**, 6
c 57..............	Regulation of Railways Act 1889	**36**, 495
c 69..............	Public Bodies Corrupt Practices Act 1889	**12(1)**, 200

53 & 54 Vict

c 2..............	Crown Office Act 1890	**10**, 323
c 25..............	Barracks Act 1890	**3**, 145
c 27..............	Colonial Courts of Admiralty Act 1890	**11(2)**, 97
c 29..............	Intestates' Estates Act 1890	**18**, 531
c 37..............	Foreign Jurisdiction Act 1890	**7(2)**, 325
c 39..............	Partnership Act 1890	**32**, 1191
c 53..............	Bills of Sale Act 1890	**39(1)**, 46
c 59..............	Public Health Acts Amendment Act 1890	**35(1)**, 80
c ccxliii.........	London Council (General Powers) Act 1890	**25(1)**, 99

54 & 55 Vict

c 16..............	Army Schools Act 1891	**15(1)**, 103
c 35..............	Bills of Sale Act 1891	**39(1)**, 47
c 37..............	Fisheries Act 1891	**1(1)**, 189
c 38..............	Stamp Duties Management Act 1891	**41**, 11
c 39..............	Stamp Act 1891	**41**, 23
c 43..............	Forged Transfers Act 1891	**19(1)**, 116
c 50..............	Commissioners for Oaths Act 1891	**18**, 178
c 51..............	Slander of Women Act 1891	**19(3)**, 384
c 53..............	Supreme Court of Judicature Act 1891	**11(2)**, 107
c 69..............	Penal Servitude Act 1891	**12(1)**, 204
c 70..............	Markets and Fairs (Weighing of Cattle) Act 1891	**27**, 56

55 & 56 Vict

c 1..............	Millbank Prison Act 1892	**12(1)**, 205
c 6..............	Colonial Probates Act 1892	**18**, 533
c 8..............	Hares Preservation Act 1892	**2**, 197
c 23..............	Foreign Marriage Act 1892	**27**, 112
c 29..............	Technical and Industrial Institutions Act 1892	**15(1)**, 104
c 34..............	Naval Knights of Windsor (Dissolution) Act 1892	**3**, 145
c 36..............	Forged Transfers Act 1892	**19(1)**, 119
c 39..............	National Debt (Stockholders Relief) Act 1892	**19(2)**, 725
c 43..............	Military Lands Act 1892	**3**, 146
c 48..............	Bank Act 1892	**19(1)**, 120
c 64..............	Witnesses (Public Inquiries) Protection Act 1892	**12(1)**, 206
c ccxxxviii......	London County Council (General Powers) Act 1892	**25(1)**, 100

56 & 57 Vict

c 5..............	Regimental Debts Act 1893	**3**, 162
c 14..............	Statute Law Revision Act 1893	**41**, 704
c 17..............	North Sea Fisheries Act 1893	**1(1)**, 194
c 63..............	Married Women's Property Act 1893	**27**, 128
c 73..............	Local Government Act 1894	**25(1)**, 102

57 & 58 Vict

c 2..............	Behring Sea Award Act 1894	**1(1)**, 203
c 23..............	Commissioners of Works Act 1894	**10**, 124
c 39..............	Prize Courts Act 1894	**11(2)**, 108
c 43..............	Crown Lands Act 1894	**10**, 126
c 45..............	Uniforms Act 1894	**3**, 178
c ccxii..........	London County Council (General Powers) Act 1894	**25(1)**, 115

58 & 59 Vict

c 9..............	Documentary Evidence Act 1895	**18**, 179
c 12..............	Metropolitan Police (Receiver) Act 1895	**33(2)**, 52
c 16..............	Finance Act 1895	**41**, 51
c 21..............	Seal Fisheries (North Pacific) Act 1895	**1(1)**, 215
c 24..............	Law of Distress Amendment Act 1895	**13**, 1315
c 34..............	Colonial Boundaries Act 1895	**7(2)**, 335

58 & 59 Vict—*contd*
    c 44 .... Judicial Committee Amendment Act 1895 .... **11(2)**, 110
59 & 60 Vict
    c 8 .... Life Assurance Companies (Payment into Court) Act
                      1896 .... **19(1)**, 121
    c 14 .... Short Titles Act 1896 .... **41**, 705
    c 27 .... London Cab Act 1896 .... **36**, 499
    c 35 .... Judicial Trustees Act 1896 .... **48**, 227
    c 45 .... Stannaries Court (Abolition) Act 1896 .... **11(2)**, 112
60 & 61 Vict
    c 6 .... Military Lands Act 1897 .... **3**, 180
    c 26 .... Metropolitan Police Courts Act 1897 .... **11(2)**, 114
    c 30 .... Police (Property) Act 1897 .... **33(2)**, 53
    c 33 .... Isle of Man (Church Building and New Parishes) Act
                      1897 .... **14**, 248
    c 44 .... District Councils (Water Supply Facilities) Act 1897 .... **20**, 348
    c 56 .... Metropolis Water Act 1897 .... **49**, 127
    c 63 .... Foreign Prison-made Goods Act 1897 .... **13**, 566
    c 65 .... Land Transfer Act 1897 .... **20**, 350
61 & 62 Vict
    c 10 .... Finance Act 1898 .... **41**, 54
    c 11 .... Suffragan Bishops Act 1898 .... **14**, 249
    c 16 .... Canals Protection (London) Act 1898 .... **36**, 500
    c 36 .... Criminal Evidence Act 1898 .... **18**, 180
    c 46 .... Revenue Act 1898—
                      ss 1, 20 .... **13**, 568
                      ss 7, 10, 12, 20 .... **41**, 56
                      ss 9, 20 .... **19(2)**, 729
    c 48 .... Benefices Act 1898 .... **14**, 250
    c 53 .... Libraries Offences Act 1898 .... **13**, 76
    c 57 .... Elementary School Teachers (Superannuation) Act
                      1898 .... **15(1)**, 108
    c 60 .... Inebriates Act 1898 .... **19(3)**, 440
62 & 63 Vict
    c 9 .... Finance Act 1899 .... **41**, 59
    c 20 .... Bodies Corporate (Joint Tenancy) Act 1899 .... **20**, 353
    c 26 .... Metropolitan Police Act 1899 .... **33(2)**, 58
    c 30 .... Commons Act 1899 .... **20**, 354
    c 46 .... Improvement of Land Act 1899 .... **20**, 367
63 & 64 Vict
    c 7 .... Finance Act 1900 .... **41**, 61
    c 40 .... Elementary School Teachers Superannuation (Jersey)
                      Act 1900 .... **15(1)**, 115
    c 56 .... Military Lands Act 1900 .... **3**, 181
    c cclxviii .... London County Council (General Powers) Act 1900 .... **25(1)**, 118
1 Edw 7
    c 5 .... Demise of the Crown Act 1901 .... **10**, 126
    c 7 .... Finance Act 1901 .... **13**, 570
2 Edw 7
    c 7 .... Finance Act 1902 .... **13**, 572
    c 8 .... Cremation Act 1902 .... **5(2)**, 472
    c 28 .... Licensing Act 1902 .... **19(3)**, 443
    c 37 .... Osborne Estate Act 1902 .... **10**, 127
    c 41 .... Metropolis Water Act 1902 .... **49**, 129
3 Edw 7
    c 20 .... Patriotic Fund Reorganisation Act 1903 .... **3**, 185
    c 31 .... Board of Agriculture and Fisheries Act 1903 .... **10**, 324
    c 46 .... Revenue Act 1903 .... **19(2)**, 730
    c 47 .... Military Lands Act 1903 .... **3**, 190
    c clxxxvii .... London County Council (General Powers) Act 1903 .... **25(1)**, 121
5 Edw 7
    c 11 .... Railway Fires Act 1905 .... **36**, 504
    c 23 .... Provisional Order (Marriages) Act 1905 .... **27**, 129
6 Edw 7
    c 5 .... Seamen's and Soldiers' False Characters Act 1906 .... **3**, 191

Enquiry Bureau   hsieb@lexisnexis.co.uk

6 Edw 7—*contd*

c 21.............. Ground Game (Amendment) Act 1906 .... **2**, 199
c 25.............. Open Spaces Act 1906 .... **32**, 30
c 28.............. Crown Lands Act 1906 .... **10**, 129
c 32.............. Dogs Act 1906 .... **2**, 200
c 34.............. Prevention of Corruption Act 1906 .... **12(1)**, 208
c 40.............. Marriage with Foreigners Act 1906 .... **27**, 131
c 41.............. Marine Insurance Act 1906 .... **19(1)**, 123
c 55.............. Public Trustee Act 1906 .... **48**, 230

7 Edw 7

c 10.............. Evidence (Colonial Statutes) Act 1907 .... **18**, 183
c 13.............. Finance Act 1907 .... **41**, 63
c 18.............. Married Women's Property Act 1907 .... **27**, 136
c 24.............. Limited Partnerships Act 1907 .... **32**, 1219
c 29.............. Patents and Designs Act 1907 .... **11(1)**, 489
c 53.............. Public Health Acts Amendment Act 1907 .... **35(1)**, 88
c 55.............. London Cab and Stage Carriage Act 1907 .... **36**, 508
c cxxxvi........ National Trust Act 1907 .... **32**, 48
c lxxi........... Metropolitan Water Board (Charges) Act 1907 .... **49**, 163
c lxxv.......... London County Council (General Powers) Act 1907 .... **49**, 177
c cxl............ City of London (Union of Parishes) Act 1907 .... **25(1)**, 123

8 Edw 7

c 36.............. Small Holdings and Allotments Act 1908 .... **1(1)**, 220
c 44.............. Commons Act 1908 .... **20**, 370
c 51.............. Appellate Jurisdiction Act 1908 .... **11(2)**, 115
c 53.............. Law of Distress Amendment Act 1908 .... **13**, 1317
c 66.............. Public Meeting Act 1908 .... **12(1)**, 212

9 Edw 7

c 12.............. Marine Insurance (Gambling Policies) Act 1909 .... **19(1)**, 174
c 43.............. Revenue Act 1909 .... **41**, 65

10 Edw 7 & 1 Geo 5

c 29................... Accession Declaration Act 1910 .... **10**, 132

1 & 2 Geo 5

c 6................ Perjury Act 1911 .... **12(1)**, 213
c 13.............. Parliament Act 1911 .... **32**, 1063
c 17.............. Public Works Loans Act 1911 .... **19(2)**, 732
c 27.............. Protection of Animals Act 1911 .... **2**, 204
c 28.............. Official Secrets Act 1911 .... **12(1)**, 224

2 & 3 Geo 5

c 10.............. Seal Fisheries (North Pacific) Act 1912 .... **1(1)**, 250
c 12.............. Elementary School Teachers (Superannuation) Act
                       1912 .... **15(1)**, 117
c civ............ London County Council (General Powers) Act 1912 .... **25(1)**, 134

3 & 4 Geo 5 c 16.......... Foreign Jurisdiction Act 1913 .... **7(2)**, 337

4 & 5 Geo 5

c 13.............. Prize Courts (Procedure) Act 1914 .... **11(2)**, 117
c 17.............. Status of Aliens Act 1914 .... **31**, 18
c 30.............. Injuries in War (Compensation) Act 1914 .... **3**, 193
c 36.............. Osborne Estate Act 1914 .... **10**, 133
c 47.............. Deeds of Arrangement Act 1914 .... **4(2)**, 17
c 58.............. Criminal Justice Administration Act 1914 .... **11(2)**, 118
c 83.............. Army Pensions Act 1914 .... **3**, 195
c 91.............. Welsh Church Act 1914 .... **14**, 254

5 & 6 Geo 5

c 1................ Anglo-Portuguese Commercial Treaty Act 1914 .... **48**, 37
c 18.............. Injuries in War (Compensation) Act 1914 (Session 2) **3**, 196
c 28.............. Naval Medical Compassionate Fund Act 1915 .... **3**, 198
c 40.............. Marriage of British Subjects (Facilities) Act 1915 .... **27**, 137
c 44.............. Statutory Companies (Redeemable Stock) Act 1915 .... **8**, 85
c 57.............. Prize Courts Act 1915 .... **11(2)**, 121
c 83.............. Naval and Military War Pensions, &c, Act 1915 .... **3**, 199
c 89.............. Finance (No 2) Act 1915 .... **19(2)**, 733
c 90.............. Indictments Act 1915 .... **12(1)**, 232
c 92.............. Judicial Committee Act 1915 .... **11(2)**, 123

6 & 7 Geo 5

c 2.............. Naval Prize (Procedure) Act 1916 .... **11(2)**, 124
c 12.............. Local Government (Emergency Provisions) Act 1916 .... **25(1)**, 141
c 21.............. Marriage of British Subjects (Facilities) Amendment Act
1916 .... **27**, 140
c 24.............. Finance Act 1916—
ss 63, 65, 69 .... **42**, 32
ss 65–67, 69 .... **19(2)**, 735
c 31.............. Police, Factories, etc (Miscellaneous Provisions) Act
1916 .... **33(2)**, 59
c 39.............. Anglo-Portuguese Commercial Treaty Act 1916 .... **48**, 43
c 51.............. "Anzac" (Restriction on Trade Use of Word) Act
1916 .... **48**, 44
c 60.............. Sailors and Soldiers (Gifts for Land Settlement) Act
1916 .... **3**, 202
c 63.............. Defence of the Realm (Acquisition of Land) Act
1916 .... **9**, 68
c 64.............. Prevention of Corruption Act 1916 .... **12(1)**, 237

7 & 8 Geo 5

c 14.............. Naval and Military War Pensions, &c (Administrative
Expenses) Act 1917 .... **3**, 204
c 31.............. Finance Act 1917 .... **19(2)**, 738
c 47.............. Titles Deprivation Act 1917 .... **33(1)**, 7
c 48.............. Bills of Exchange (Time of Noting) Act 1917 .... **19(1)**, 177
c 51.............. Air Force (Constitution) Act 1917 .... **3**, 206
c 55.............. Chequers Estate Act 1917 .... **10**, 326
c 58.............. Wills (Soldiers and Sailors) Act 1918 .... **50**, 774

8 & 9 Geo 5

c 39.............. Education Act 1918 .... **15(1)**, 119
c 47.............. Parliament (Qualification of Women) Act 1918 .... **32**, 1067
c 57.............. War Pensions (Administrative Provisions) Act 1918 .... **3**, 211

9 & 10 Geo 5

c 31.............. Statement of Rates Act 1919 .... **20**, 373
c 50.............. Ministry of Transport Act 1919 .... **10**, 337
c 53.............. War Pensions (Administrative Provisions) Act 1919 .... **3**, 213
c 59.............. Land Settlement (Facilities) Act 1919 .... **1(1)**, 254
c 65.............. Welsh Church (Temporalities) Act 1919 .... **14**, 290
c 71.............. Sex Disqualification (Removal) Act 1919—
ss 1, 4 .... **16**, 13
ss 3, 4 .... **15(1)**, 120
c 75.............. Ferries (Acquisition by Local Authorities) Act 1919 .... **36**, 512
c 76.............. Church of England Assembly (Powers) Act 1919 .... **14**, 294
c 91.............. Ministry of Agriculture and Fisheries Act 1919 .... **10**, 341
c 92.............. Aliens Restriction (Amendment) Act 1919 .... **31**, 20
c lxxxiv.......... National Trust Charity Scheme Confirmation Act
1919 .... **32**, 65

10 & 11 Geo 5

c 16.............. Imperial War Museum Act 1920 .... **13**, 78
c 23.............. War Pensions Act 1920 .... **3**, 219
c 33.............. Maintenance Orders (Facilities for Enforcement) Act
1920 .... **27**, 141
c 41.............. Census Act 1920 .... **36**, 19
c 50.............. Mining Industry Act 1920 .... **17(1)**, 37
c 51.............. Duchy of Lancaster Act 1920 .... **10**, 342
c 56.............. Places of Worship (Enfranchisement) Act 1920 .... **14**, 298
c 65.............. Employment of Women, Young Persons, and Children Act
1920 .... **16**, 14
c 75.............. Official Secrets Act 1920 .... **12(1)**, 239
c 79.............. Defence of the Realm (Acquisition of Land) Act
1920 .... **9**, 77
c 81.............. Administration of Justice Act 1920 .... **19(3)**, 11
c lxxxix.......... London County Council (General Powers) Act 1920 .... **25(1)**, 145
No 1.............. Convocations of the Clergy Measure 1920 .... **14**, 301

11 & 12 Geo 5

c 20.............. Tithe Annuities Apportionment Act 1921 .... **14**, 302

11 & 12 Geo 5—*contd*

c 32	Finance Act 1921	**19(2)**, 740
c 35	Corn Sales Act 1921	**1(1)**, 268
c 39	Admiralty Pensions Act 1921	**3**, 223
c 49	War Pensions Act 1921	**3**, 225
c 52	Exchequer and Audit Departments Act 1921	**19(2)**, 743
c l	London County Council (General Powers) Act 1921	**25(1)**, 153
c xciv	Metropolitan Water Board (Charges) Act 1921	**49**, 184

12 Geo 5 c 2 (NI) .... Exchequer and Audit Act (Northern Ireland) 1921 .... **31**, 1699

12 & 13 Geo 5

c 16	Law of Property Act 1922—	
	entire Act	**20**, 375
	ss 43, 191	**14**, 303
c 35	Celluloid and Cinematograph Film Act 1922	**35(1)**, 104
c 51	Allotments Act 1922	**1(1)**, 270
No 3	Revised Tables of Lessons Measure 1922	**14**, 305

13 Geo 5 c 2 .... Irish Free State (Consequential Provisions) Act 1922
(Session 2) **31**, 827

13 & 14 Geo 5

c 8	Industrial Assurance Act 1923	**19(1)**, 177
c 11	Special Constables Act 1923	**33(2)**, 62
c 15	Alderney (Transfer of Property, etc) Act 1923	**7(2)**, 338
c 18	War Memorials (Local Authorities' Powers) Act 1923	**25(1)**, 155
c 20	Mines (Working Facilities and Support) Act 1923	**36**, 516
c 27	Railway Fires Act (1905) Amendment Act 1923	**36**, 537
c 33	Universities of Oxford and Cambridge Act 1923	**15(1)**, 121
c 34	Agricultural Credits Act 1923	**1(1)**, 284

14 & 15 Geo 5

No 3	Ecclesiastical Dilapidations Measure 1923	**14**, 326
c 20	Marriages Validity (Provisional Orders) Act 1924	**27**, 156
c 21	Finance Act 1924	**2**, 208

15 & 16 Geo 5

c 5	Law of Property (Amendment) Act 1924	**20**, 393
c 18	Settled Land Act 1925	**20**, 396
c 19	Trustee Act 1925	**48**, 453
c 20	Law of Property Act 1925	**20**, 582
c 23	Administration of Estates Act 1925	**18**, 538
c 24	Universities and College Estates Act 1925	**21**, 2
c 28	Administration of Justice Act 1925—	
	ss 22, 29	**4(2)**, 33
	ss 23, 29	**39(1)**, 48
c 36	Finance Act 1925	**42**, 34
c 38	Performing Animals (Regulation) Act 1925	**2**, 210
c 61	Allotments Act 1925	**1(1)**, 286
c 71	Public Health Act 1925	**35(1)**, 113
c 72	Honours (Prevention of Abuses) Act 1925	**33(1)**, 9
c 86	Criminal Justice Act 1925	**11(2)**, 125
c 88	Coastguard Act 1925	**3**, 228
c 90	Rating and Valuation Act 1925	**25(1)**, 157
c cxix	London County Council (General Powers) Act 1925	**25(1)**, 161
No 1	Interpretation Measure 1925	**14**, 329
No 3	Diocesan Boards of Finance Measure 1925	**14**, 332

16 & 17 Geo 5

c 11	Law of Property (Amendment) Act 1926	**21**, 39
c 14	Imperial War Graves Endowment Fund Act 1926	**3**, 231
c 18	Secretaries of State Act 1926	**10**, 344
c 21	Markets and Fairs (Weighing of Cattle) Act 1926	**27**, 59
c 26	Chartered Associations (Protection of Names and Uniforms) Act 1926	**48**, 45
c 28	Mining Industry Act 1926	**17(1)**, 42
c 36	Parks Regulation (Amendment) Act 1926	**32**, 67
c 39	Horticultural Produce (Sales on Commission) Act 1926	**1(1)**, 289
c 48	Births and Deaths Registration Act 1926	**36**, 29
c 52	Small Holdings and Allotments Act 1926	**1(1)**, 292

16 & 17 Geo 5—*contd*
  c 61 .... Judicial Proceedings (Regulation of Reports) Act
                      1926 .... **12(1)**, 246
  No 4 .... Ecclesiastical Commissioners Measure 1926 .... **14**, 336
17 & 18 Geo 5
  c 4 .... Royal and Parliamentary Titles Act 1927 .... **10**, 134
  c 12 .... Auctions (Bidding Agreements) Act 1927 .... **39(1)**, 49
  c 27 .... Protection of Animals (Amendment) Act 1927 .... **2**, 216
  c 23 .... Crown Lands Act 1927 .... **10**, 135
  c 36 .... Landlord and Tenant Act 1927 .... **21**, 42
  c 41 .... Superannuation and other Trust Funds (Validation) Act
                      1927 .... **48**, 546
  c 43 .... Colonial Probates (Protected States and Mandated
                      Territories) Act 1927 .... **18**, 593
  c lxxi .... Metropolitan Water Board Act 1927 .... **49**, 192
18 & 19 Geo 5
  c 13 .... Currency and Bank Notes Act 1928 .... **19(1)**, 196
  c 17 .... Finance Act 1928 .... **41**, 67
  c 19 .... Agricultural Produce (Grading and Marking) Act
                      1928 .... **1(1)**, 304
  c 21 .... Dogs (Amendment) Act 1928 .... **2**, 217
  c 24 .... Northern Ireland (Miscellaneous Provisions) Act 1928 .... **31**, 831
  c 32 .... Petroleum (Consolidation) Act 1928 .... **35(1)**, 124
  c 35 .... Easter Act 1928 .... **45**, 1535
  c 43 .... Agricultural Credits Act 1928 .... **1(1)**, 313
19 & 20 Geo 5
  c 9 .... Law of Property (Amendment) Act 1929 .... **21**, 67
  c 17 .... Local Government Act 1929 .... **25(1)**, 164
  c 29 .... Government Annuities Act 1929 .... **19(2)**, 746
  c 34 .... Infant Life (Preservation) Act 1929 .... **12(1)**, 248
  c xl .... Metropolitan Water Board Act 1929 .... **49**, 198
  c lxxxvii .... London County Council (General Powers) Act 1929—
                      ss 1, 4, 51, 52 .... **49**, 201
                      ss 1, 4(1), 53, 69 .... **25(1)**, 181
  No 3 .... Ecclesiastical Dilapidations (Amendment) Measure
                      1929 .... **14**, 337
20 & 21 Geo 5
  c 25 .... Third Parties (Rights Against Insurers) Act 1930 .... **4(2)**, 36
  c 28 .... Finance Act 1930—
                      ss 42, 53 .... **41**, 69
                      ss 49, 51, 53 .... **19(2)**, 774
  c 38 .... Navy and Marines (Wills) Act 1930 .... **50**, 776
  c 43 .... Road Traffic Act 1930 .... **36**, 538
  c clviii .... London Building Act 1930 .... **25(1)**, 184
  c clix .... London County Council (General Powers) Act 1930 .... **25(1)**, 199
  No 5 .... Ecclesiastical Commissioners (Sodor and Man) Measure
                      1930 .... **14**, 337
  No 8 .... Benefices (Transfer of Rights of Patronage) Measure
                      1930 .... **14**, 338
21 & 22 Geo 5
  c 7 .... China Indemnity (Application) Act 1931 .... **19(2)**, 776
  c 9 .... Colonial Naval Defence Act 1931 .... **3**, 232
  c 12 .... Metropolitan Police (Staff Superannuation and Police Fund)
                      Act 1931 .... **33(2)**, 64
  c 28 .... Finance Act 1931 .... **41**, 74
  c 40 .... Agricultural Produce (Grading and Marking) Amendment
                      Act 1931 .... **1(1)**, 324
  c 41 .... Agricultural Land (Utilisation) Act 1931 .... **1(1)**, 327
  c 49 .... Finance (No 2) Act 1931 .... **42**, 36
  c lix .... London County Council (General Powers) Act 1931 .... **25(1)**, 202
  No 2 .... Ecclesiastical Commissioners (Loans for Church Training
                      Colleges) Measure 1931 .... **14**, 341
  No 4 .... Channel Islands (Church Legislation) Measure 1931 .... **14**, 343
  No 5 .... Channel Islands (Representation) Measure 1931 .... **14**, 346

22 & 23 Geo 5
    c 4 .... Statute of Westminster 1931 .... **7(2)**, 339
    c 11 .... Northern Ireland (Miscellaneous Provisions) Act 1932 .... **31**, 831
    c 12 .... Destructive Imported Animals Act 1932 .... **2**, 218
    c 20 .... Chancel Repairs Act 1932 .... **14**, 350
    c 25 .... Finance Act 1932—
             ss 25, 31 .... **30**, 121
             ss 29, 31 .... **42**, 38
    c 27 .... Law of Property (Entailed Interests) Act 1932 .... **21**, 68
    c 35 .... Agricultural Credits Act 1932 .... **1(1)**, 331
    c lxx .... London County Council (General Powers) Act 1932 .... **49**, 204
    c lxxxv .... Metropolitan Water Board Act 1932 .... **49**, 206
23 & 24 Geo 5
    c 4 .... Evidence (Foreign, Dominion and Colonial Documents)
             Act 1933 .... **18**, 185
    c 6 .... Visiting Forces (British Commonwealth) Act 1933 .... **3**, 235
    c 12 .... Children and Young Persons Act 1933 .... **6**, 37
    c 13 .... Foreign Judgments (Reciprocal Enforcement) Act
             1933 .... **19(3)**, 18
    c 14 .... London Passenger Transport Act 1933 .... **36**, 546
    c 19 .... Finance Act 1933 .... **41**, 79
    c 36 .... Administration of Justice (Miscellaneous Provisions) Act
             1933—
             ss 2, 10, Sch 2 .... **12(1)**, 250
             ss 7, 9, 10 .... **13**, 7
    c 53 .... Road and Rail Traffic Act 1933 .... **36**, 563
    c xxiii .... City of London (Various Powers) Act 1933 .... **25(1)**, 204
    c xxviii .... London County Council (General Powers) Act 1933 .... **25(1)**, 209
    c xliv .... London Overground Wires, etc Act 1933 .... **25(1)**, 214
    No 4 .... Benefices (Sequestrations) Measure 1933 .... **14**, 353
24 & 25 Geo 5
    c 32 .... Finance Act 1934 .... **19(2)**, 779
    c 40 .... Administration of Justice (Appeals) Act 1934 .... **11(2)**, 131
    c 41 .... Law Reform (Miscellaneous Provisions) Act 1934—
             ss 1, 4 .... **18**, 594
             ss 3, 4 .... **11(2)**, 133
    c 43 .... National Maritime Museum Act 1934 .... **13**, 84
    c 49 .... Whaling Industry (Regulation) Act 1934 .... **1(1)**, 333
    c 56 .... Incitement to Disaffection Act 1934 .... **12(1)**, 255
    c xl .... London County Council (General Powers) Act 1934 .... **25(1)**, 231
    No 1 .... Clerical Disabilities Act 1870 (Amendment) Measure
             1934 .... **14**, 355
25 & 26 Geo 5
    c 11 .... Regimental Charitable Funds Act 1935 .... **3**, 241
    c 20 .... Vagrancy Act 1935 .... **12(1)**, 259
    c 23 .... Law Reform (Married Women and Tortfeasors) Act
             1935 .... **27**, 157
    c 24 .... Finance Act 1935 .... **42**, 40
    c xxxiii .... London County Council (General Powers) Act 1935 .... **25(1)**, 235
    c lxxxiv .... Metropolitan Water Board Act 1935 .... **49**, 216
    c xcii .... London Building Act (Amendment) Act 1935 .... **25(1)**, 239
26 Geo 5 & 1 Edw 8
    c 17 .... Voluntary Hospitals (Paying Patients) Act 1936 .... **30**, 391
    c 27 .... Petroleum (Transfer of Licences) Act 1936 .... **35(1)**, 137
    c 43 .... Tithe Act 1936 .... **14**, 357
    c 47 .... Crown Lands Act 1936 .... **10**, 136
    c 49 .... Public Health Act 1936 .... **35(1)**, 139
    c lx .... London County Council (General Powers) Act 1936 .... **25(1)**, 244
    No 5 .... Ecclesiastical Commissioners (Powers) Measure 1936 .... **14**, 374
1 Edw 8 & 1 Geo 6
    c 3 .... His Majesty's Declaration of Abdication Act 1936 .... **10**, 144
    c 6 .... Public Order Act 1936 .... **12(1)**, 260
    c 16 .... Regency Act 1937 .... **10**, 146
    c 32 .... Civil List Act 1937 .... **10**, 151
    c 33 .... Diseases of Fish Act 1937 .... **1(1)**, 350

1 Edw 8 & 1 Geo 6—*contd*
     c 40.............. Public Health (Drainage of Trade Premises) Act 1937 .... **35(1)**, 222
     c 46.............. Physical Training and Recreation Act 1937 .... **35(1)**, 224
     c 54.............. Finance Act 1937 .... **19(2)**, 782
     c 59.............. Cinematograph Films (Animals) Act 1937 .... **2**, 229
     c lvii............ National Trust Act 1937 .... **32**, 70
     c xci............. London County Council (General Powers) Act 1937 .... **25(1)**, 248
1 & 2 Geo 6
     c 12.............. Population (Statistics) Act 1938 .... **36**, 34
     c 13.............. Superannuation (Various Services) Act 1938 .... **33(1)**, 51
     c 28.............. Evidence Act 1938 .... **18**, 187
     c 30.............. Sea Fish Industry Act 1938 .... **1(1)**, 370
     c 34.............. Leasehold Property (Repairs) Act 1938 .... **21**, 69
     c 36.............. Infanticide Act 1938 .... **12(1)**, 265
     c 39.............. Welsh Church (Amendment) Act 1938 .... **14**, 378
     c 46.............. Finance Act 1938 .... **42**, 42
     c 51.............. Essential Commodities Reserves Act 1938 .... **47**, 38
     c 57.............. Imperial Telegraphs Act 1938 .... **45**, 26
     c xxxviii........ London County Council (General Powers) Act 1938 .... **25(1)**, 255
     c xciii........... Green Belt (London and Home Counties) Act 1938 .... **32**, 77
     No 3............. Parsonages Measure 1938 .... **14**, 379
     No 4............. Ecclesiastical Commissioners (Powers) Measure 1938 .... **14**, 394
2 & 3 Geo 6
     c 13.............. Cancer Act 1939 .... **28**, 14
     c 33.............. Marriage Act 1939 .... **27**, 160
     c 41.............. Finance Act 1939 .... **19(2)**, 784
     c 43.............. Prevention of Damage by Rabbits Act 1939 .... **2**, 231
     c 44.............. House to House Collections Act 1939 .... **5(2)**, 519
     c 49.............. House of Commons Members' Fund Act 1939 .... **32**, 1067
     c 51.............. Public Trustee (General Deposit Fund) Act 1939 .... **48**, 554
     c 65.............. Prize Act 1939 .... **11(2)**, 135
     c 69.............. Import, Export and Customs Powers (Defence) Act
                      1939 .... **50**, 427
     c 72.............. Landlord and Tenant (War Damage) Act 1939 .... **21**, 73
     c 75.............. Compensation (Defence) Act 1939 .... **9**, 81
     c 82.............. Personal Injuries (Emergency Provisions) Act 1939 .... **33(1)**, 54
     c 83.............. Pensions (Navy, Army, Air Force and Mercantile Marine)
                      Act 1939 .... **3**, 243
     c 87.............. Navy and Marines (Wills) Act 1939 .... **50**, 777
     c 89.............. Trading with the Enemy Act 1939 .... **50**, 432
     c 100........... Government and other Stocks (Emergency Provisions) Act
                      1939 .... **19(2)**, 787
     c 102........... Liability for War Damage (Miscellaneous Provisions) Act
                      1939 .... **50**, 452
     c 103........... Police and Firemen (War Service) Act 1939 .... **33(2)**, 65
     c 107........... Patents, Designs, Copyright and Trade Marks (Emergency)
                      Act 1939 .... **50**, 456
     c 117........... National Loans Act 1939 .... **19(2)**, 789
     c 120........... Restriction of Advertisement (War Risks Insurance) Act
                      1939 .... **19(1)**, 200
     c 121........... Official Secrets Act 1939 .... **12(1)**, 267
     c lxxxvi.......... National Trust Act 1939 .... **32**, 104
     c xcvi........... Metropolitan Water Board Act 1939 .... **49**, 219
     c xcvii.......... London Building Acts (Amendment) Act 1939 .... **25(1)**, 258
3 & 4 Geo 6
     c 26.............. Superannuation Schemes (War Service) Act 1940 .... **33(1)**, 59
     c 28.............. Evidence and Powers of Attorney Act 1940 .... **18**, 189
     c 29.............. Finance Act 1940 .... **42**, 46
     c 34.............. Middlesex Deeds Act 1940 .... **21**, 97
4 & 5 Geo 6 c 41......... Landlord and Tenant (War Damage) (Amendment) Act
                      1941 .... **21**, 101
5 & 6 Geo 6
     c 8............... War Orphans Act 1942 .... **3**, 252
     c 13.............. Landlord and Tenant (Requisitioned Land) Act 1942 .... **21**, 110
     c 21.............. Finance Act 1942 .... **19(2)**, 792

5 & 6 Geo 6—*contd*

c 23.............. Minister of Works Act 1942 .... **10**, 345
c 26.............. Pensions (Mercantile Marine) Act 1942 .... **3**, 253
c 35.............. Greenwich Hospital Act 1942 .... **3**, 260

6 & 7 Geo 6

c 9................ Universities and Colleges (Trusts) Act 1943 .... **15(1)**, 166
c 18.............. Evidence and Powers of Attorney Act 1943 .... **18**, 190
c 25.............. Settled Land and Trustee Acts (Court's General Powers) Act
                      1943 .... **21**, 127; **48**, 556
c 39.............. Pensions Appeal Tribunals Act 1943 .... **33(1)**, 62
c 40.............. Law Reform (Frustrated Contracts) Act 1943 .... **11(1)**, 355
c 42.............. Regency Act 1943 .... **10**, 154
c 48.............. Parliament (Elections and Meeting) Act 1943 .... **32**, 1073
No 1............. New Parishes Measure 1943 .... **14**, 396
No 2............. Episcopal Endowments and Stipends Measure 1943 .... **14**, 409
1944 c 14 (NI). Ministries Act (Northern Ireland) 1944 .... **31**, 1716

7 & 8 Geo 6

c 5................ Landlord and Tenant (Requisitioned Land) Act 1944 .... **21**, 129
c 7................ Prize Salvage Act 1944 .... **11(2)**, 139
c 10.............. Disabled Persons (Employment) Act 1944 .... **16**, 19
c 16.............. Public Works Loans Act 1944 .... **19(2)**, 798
c 22.............. Police and Firemen (War Service) Act 1944 .... **33(2)**, 75
c 23.............. Finance Act 1944—
                      ss 42, 49, Sch 4 .... **42**, 48
                      ss 45, 49 .... **41**, 82
c 25.............. Law Officers Act 1944 .... **10**, 347

8 & 9 Geo 6

c 12.............. Northern Ireland (Miscellaneous Provisions) Act 1945 .... **31**, 833
c 16.............. Limitation (Enemies and War Prisoners) Act 1945 .... **19(3)**, 871
c 18.............. Local Authorities Loans Act 1945 .... **19(2)**, 799
c 19.............. Ministry of Fuel and Power Act 1945 .... **10**, 348
c 27.............. Welsh Church (Burial Grounds) Act 1945 .... **14**, 413
c 28.............. Law Reform (Contributory Negligence) Act 1945 .... **31**, 760
c 42.............. Water Act 1945 .... **49**, 224
c 43.............. Requisitioned Land and War Works Act 1945 .... **9**, 100

9 & 10 Geo 6

c 7................ British Settlements Act 1945 .... **7(2)**, 346
c 13.............. Finance (No 2) Act 1945 .... **42**, 54
c 17.............. Police (Overseas Service) Act 1945 .... **33(2)**, 80
c 18.............. Statutory Orders (Special Procedure) Act 1945 .... **41**, 728
c 27.............. Bank of England Act 1946 .... **19(1)**, 205
c 29.............. Agriculture (Artificial Insemination) Act 1946 .... **2**, 232
c 36.............. Statutory Instruments Act 1946 .... **41**, 740
c 40.............. Miscellaneous Financial Provisions Act 1946 .... **19(2)**, 803
c 41.............. Public Works Loans Act 1946 .... **19(2)**, 805
c 45.............. United Nations Act 1946 .... **10**, 801
c 49.............. Acquisition of Land (Authorisation Procedure) Act
                      1946 .... **9**, 124
c 59.............. Coal Industry Nationalisation Act 1946 .... **17(1)**, 45
c 64.............. Finance Act 1946—
                      ss 52, 67 .... **41**, 84
                      ss 62, 67 .... **42**, 57
c 73.............. Hill Farming Act 1946 .... **1(1)**, 372
c 80.............. Atomic Energy Act 1946 .... **17(1)**, 59
c 81.............. National Health Service Act 1946 .... **30**, 396
c 82.............. Cable and Wireless Act 1946 .... **45**, 28
c 83.............. Roosevelt Memorial Act 1946 .... **25(1)**, 360
c xvii........... Metropolitan Water Board Act 1946 .... **49**, 264
No 1............. Ecclesiastical Commissioners (Curate Grants) Measure
                      1946 .... **14**, 416

10 & 11 Geo 6

c 5................ Greenwich Hospital Act 1947 .... **3**, 262
c 11.............. Appellate Jurisdiction Act 1947 .... **11(2)**, 141
c 19.............. Polish Resettlement Act 1947—
                      ss 1, 7, 10, 12, 13 .... **3**, 263

10 & 11 Geo 6—*contd*

c 19.............. Polish Resettlement Act 1947—*contd*
    ss 2, 3, 10, 13, Schedule .... **40(1)**, 20
    ss 4, 10, 12, 13 .... **30**, 400
c 22.............. Civic Restaurants Act 1947 .... **25(1)**, 364
c 23.............. Treaties of Peace (Italy, Roumania, Bulgaria, Hungary and
    Finland) Act 1947 .... **10**, 805
c 24.............. Naval Forces (Enforcement of Maintenance Liabilities) Act
    1947 .... **3**, 268
c 30.............. Indian Independence Act 1947 .... **7(2)**, 347
c 33.............. Foreign Marriage Act 1947 .... **27**, 162
c 35.............. Finance Act 1947 .... **41**, 86
c 37.............. Northern Ireland Act 1947 .... **31**, 835
c 39.............. Statistics of Trade Act 1947 .... **47**, 43
c 40.............. Industrial Organisation and Development Act 1947 .... **47**, 58
c 41.............. Fire Services Act 1947 .... **18**, 1014
c 44.............. Crown Proceedings Act 1947 .... **13**, 9
c 45.............. Public Offices (Site) Act 1947 .... **10**, 349
c 46.............. Wellington Museum Act 1947 .... **13**, 90
c 48.............. Agriculture Act 1947 .... **1(1)**, 388
c xlvi.......... London County Council (General Powers) Act 1947 .... **25(1)**, 366
No 2............. Church Commissioners Measure 1947 .... **14**, 417
No 3............. Parsonages (Amendment) Measure 1947 .... **14**, 431

11 & 12 Geo 6

c 2.............. Jersey and Guernsey (Financial Provisions) Act 1947 .... **7(2)**, 352
c 7.............. Ceylon Independence Act 1947 .... **7(2)**, 353
c 8.............. Mandated and Trust Territories Act 1947 .... **7(2)**, 356
c 10.............. Emergency Laws (Miscellaneous Provisions) Act 1947—
    entire Act **50**, 466
    ss 2(1), 12(1), Sch 2, para 1 .... **33(2)**, 82
c 17.............. Requisitioned Land and War Works Act 1948 .... **9**, 125
c 21.............. Army and Air Force (Women's Service) Act 1948 .... **3**, 272
c 26.............. Local Government Act 1948 .... **25(1)**, 394
c 29.............. National Assistance Act 1948 .... **40(1)**, 26
c 33.............. Superannuation (Miscellaneous Provisions) Act 1948 .... **33(1)**, 89
c 36.............. House of Commons Members' Fund Act 1948 .... **32**, 1075
c 39.............. Industrial Assurance and Friendly Societies Act 1948 .... **19(1)**, 211
c 41.............. Law Reform (Personal Injuries) Act 1948 .... **45**, 1550
c 47.............. Agricultural Wages Act 1948 .... **1(1)**, 414
c 49.............. Finance Act 1948 .... **41**, 90
c 56.............. British Nationality Act 1948 .... **31**, 23
c 58.............. Criminal Justice Act 1948 .... **12(1)**, 268
c 59.............. Laying of Documents before Parliament (Interpretation) Act
    1948 .... **41**, 753
c 62.............. Statute Law Revision Act 1948 .... **41**, 755
c liii............ London County Council (General Powers) Act 1948 .... **25(1)**, 404

12, 13 & 14 Geo 6

c 11.............. Railway and Canal Commission (Abolition) Act 1949 .... **36**, 566
c 12.............. Pensions Appeal Tribunals Act 1949 .... **33(1)**, 97
c 13.............. Savings Banks Act 1949 .... **19(2)**, 806
c 15.............. Minister of Food (Financial Powers) Act 1949 .... **10**, 356
c 16.............. National Theatre Act 1949 .... **13**, 98
c 18.............. Colonial Naval Defence Act 1949 .... **3**, 273
c 29.............. Consular Conventions Act 1949 .... **10**, 807
c 33.............. Consolidation of Enactments (Procedure) Act 1949 .... **41**, 756
c 35.............. British Film Institute Act 1949 .... **13**, 99
c 37.............. Agriculture (Miscellaneous Provisions) Act 1949 .... **1(1)**, 443
c 39.............. Commonwealth Telegraphs Act 1949 .... **45**, 31
c 41.............. Ireland Act 1949 .... **7(2)**, 358
c 42.............. Lands Tribunal Act 1949 .... **9**, 140
c 47.............. Finance Act 1949—
    ss 36, 52 .... **41**, 93
    ss 48, 52 .... **19(2)**, 808
c 53.............. Coal Industry Act 1949 .... **17(1)**, 78
c 55.............. Prevention of Damage by Pests Act 1949 .... **35(1)**, 227

12, 13 & 14 Geo 6—*contd*

c 70	Docking and Nicking of Horses Act 1949	**2**, 234
c 74	Coast Protection Act 1949	**49**, 271
c 76	Marriage Act 1949—	
	ss 1–52, 68–75, 77–80, Schs 1, 4–6	**27**, 163
	ss 43, 53–67, 74, 76, 78(1), (2), 80	**36**, 38
c 77	Armed Forces (Housing Loans) Act 1949	**3**, 275
c 78	Married Women (Restraint upon Anticipation) Act 1949	**27**, 249
c 85	Distribution of German Enemy Property Act 1949	**50**, 469
c 87	Patents Act 1949	**11(1)**, 492
c 88	Registered Designs Act 1949	**11(1)**, 567
c 92	India (Consequential Provision) Act 1949	**7(2)**, 363
c 97	National Parks and Access to the Countryside Act 1949—	
	ss 1, 3, 4A–7, 9, 11A–22, 59, 60, 64–78, 80–82, 85–86A, 89–92, 99–101, 103, 104, 106–115, Schs 1, 2	**32**, 114
	ss 50A–55, 57, 99–101, 109–111A, 114, 115	**36**, 569
c 101	Justices of the Peace Act 1949	**11(2)**, 142
c 103	Parliament Act 1949	**32**, 1078
c lv	London County Council (General Powers) Act 1949	**25(1)**, 412
No 1	Church Dignitaries (Retirement) Measure 1949	**14**, 433

14 Geo 6

c 6	Statute Law Revision Act 1950	**41**, 759
c 10	Royal Patriotic Fund Corporation Act 1950	**3**, 276
c 12	Foreign Compensation Act 1950	**10**, 811
c 15	Finance Act 1950	**42**, 61
c 27	Arbitration Act 1950	**2**, 782
c 31	Allotments Act 1950	**1(1)**, 445
c 37	Maintenance Orders Act 1950—	
	ss 4, 9, 12, 27, 28, 32	**6**, 101
	ss 15–28, 31, 32, Sch 2	**27**, 250
c iii	Gun Barrel Proof Act 1950	**48**, 48
c xlii	London County Council (General Powers) Act 1950	**25(1)**, 455

14 & 15 Geo 6

c 3 (NI)	Exchequer and Financial Provisions Act (Northern Ireland) 1950	**31**, 1718
c 18	Livestock Rearing Act 1951	**1(1)**, 453
c 27	Fire Services Act 1951	**18**, 1023
c 30	Sea Fish Industry Act 1951—	
	ss 21, 29, Sch 4	**39(2)**, 110
	ss 25, 29	**1(1)**, 456
c 35	Pet Animals Act 1951	**2**, 237
c 39	Common Informers Act 1951	**12(1)**, 283
c 43	Finance Act 1951	**41**, 97
c 46	Courts-Martial (Appeals) Act 1951	**3**, 277
c 50	Consolidated Fund (Civil List Provisions) Act 1951	**10**, 155
c 57	National Assistance (Amendment) Act 1951	**40(1)**, 68
c 58	Fireworks Act 1951	**18**, 748
c 60	Mineral Workings Act 1951	**17(1)**, 82
c 62	Tithe Act 1951	**14**, 440
c 64	Rivers (Prevention of Pollution) Act 1951	**49**, 344
c 65	Reserve and Auxiliary Forces (Protection of Civil Interests) Act 1951	**3**, 283
c xli	London County Council (General Powers) Act 1951	**25(1)**, 458

15 & 16 Geo 6 c 6 .... Japanese Treaty of Peace Act 1951 | **10**, 818

15 & 16 Geo 6 & 1 Eliz 2

c 23	Miners' Welfare Act 1952	**17(1)**, 85
c 30	Distribution of German Enemy Property Act 1952	**50**, 479
c 31	Cremation Act 1952	**5(2)**, 478
c 33	Finance Act 1952	**41**, 100
c 37	Civil List Act 1952	**10**, 155
c 39	Motor Vehicles (International Circulation) Act 1952	**36**, 587
c 46	Hypnotism Act 1952	**13**, 100
c 52	Prison Act 1952	**12(1)**, 285
c 54	Town Development Act 1952	**46**, 16

15 & 16 Geo 6 & 1 Eliz 2—*contd*
    c 57.............. Marine and Aviation Insurance (War Risks) Act 1952 .... **19(1)**, 223
    c 64.............. Intestates' Estates Act 1952 .... **18**, 597
    c 66.............. Defamation Act 1952 .... **19(3)**, 385
    c 67.............. Visiting Forces Act 1952 .... **3**, 356
    c vi.............. City of London (Various Powers) Act 1952 .... **25(1)**, 464
    c xxxviii........ City of London (Guild Churches) Act 1952 .... **14**, 448
1 & 2 Eliz 2
    c 9.............. Royal Titles Act 1953 .... **10**, 162
    c 10.............. Agricultural Land (Removal of Surface Soil) Act 1953 .... **1(1)**, 458
    c 14.............. Prevention of Crime Act 1953 .... **12(1)**, 329
    c 20.............. Births and Deaths Registration Act 1953 .... **36**, 59
    c 23.............. Accommodation Agencies Act 1953 .... **21**, 133
    c 24.............. Navy and Marines (Wills) Act 1953 .... **50**, 778
    c 26.............. Local Government (Miscellaneous Provisions) Act 1953—
                ss 4–7, 18, 19 .... **36**, 591
                ss 8, 18, 19 .... **35(1)**, 245
    c 28.............. Dogs (Protection of Livestock) Act 1953 .... **2**, 243
    c 34.............. Finance Act 1953 .... **41**, 105
    c 37.............. Registration Service Act 1953 .... **36**, 110
    c 39.............. Marshall Aid Commemoration Act 1953 .... **15(1)**, 169
    c 47.............. Emergency Laws (Miscellaneous Provisions) Act 1953—
                ss 1, 2, 13, 14, Schs 1, 2 .... **50**, 480
                ss 5, 13, 14 .... **1(1)**, 461
                ss 10, 13, 14 .... **3**, 384
    c 49.............. Historic Buildings and Ancient Monuments Act 1953 .... **32**, 194
    c 52.............. Enemy Property Act 1953 .... **50**, 489
    c vii.............. National Trust Act 1953 .... **32**, 209
    c xliii........... London County Council (General Powers) Act 1953 .... **25(1)**, 468
    No 2............. Diocesan Stipends Funds Measure 1953 .... **14**, 472
2 & 3 Eliz 2
    c 1.............. Regency Act 1953 .... **10**, 163
    c 12.............. Currency and Bank Notes Act 1954 .... **19(1)**, 232
    c 21.............. Rights of Entry (Gas and Electricity Boards) Act 1954 .... **17(1)**, 100
    c 32.............. Atomic Energy Authority Act 1954 .... **17(1)**, 105
    c 39.............. Agriculture (Miscellaneous Provisions) Act 1954 .... **1(1)**, 463
    c 40.............. Protection of Animals (Amendment) Act 1954 .... **2**, 248
    c 44.............. Finance Act 1954—
                ss 15, 35 .... **42**, 68
                ss 34, 35 .... **19(2)**, 810
    c 47.............. Marriage Act 1949 (Amendment) Act 1954 .... **27**, 276
    c 53.............. Housing Repairs and Rents Act 1954 .... **21**, 135
    c 56.............. Landlord and Tenant Act 1954 .... **21**, 138
    c 58.............. Charitable Trusts (Validation) Act 1954 .... **5(2)**, 529
    c 64.............. Transport Charges &c (Miscellaneous Provisions) Act
                1954—
                ss 6, 8, 12–15 .... **39(2)**, 115
                ss 8, 10, 12–15 .... **36**, 597
    c 68.............. Pests Act 1954—
                ss 1–4, 7, 13–15 .... **1(1)**, 470
                ss 6, 13–15 .... **35(1)**, 248
                ss 8, 9, 12–15 .... **2**, 249
    c 70.............. Mines and Quarries Act 1954 .... **17(1)**, 120
    c 72.............. Town and Country Planning Act 1954 .... **9**, 154
    c xxiv........... London County Council (General Powers) Act 1954 .... **25(1)**, 473
    No 1............. New Housing Areas (Church Buildings) Measure
                1954 .... **14**, 477
3 & 4 Eliz 2
    c 7.............. Fisheries Act 1955 .... **39(2)**, 123
    c 14.............. Imperial War Museum Act 1955 .... **13**, 104
    c 18.............. Army Act 1955 .... **3**, 386
    c 19.............. Air Force Act 1955 .... **3**, 673
    c 20.............. Revision of the Army and Air Force Acts (Transitional
                Provisions) Act 1955 .... **3**, 953

3 & 4 Eliz 2—*contd*

c 28.............. Children and Young Persons (Harmful Publications) Act 1955 .... **12(1)**, 331

No 1............ Inspection of Churches Measure 1955 .... **14**, 479

4 & 5 Eliz 2

c 1.............. Austrian State Treaty Act 1955 .... **10**, 820

c 2.............. German Conventions Act 1955 .... **10**, 822

c 6.............. Miscellaneous Financial Provisions Act 1955—

    ss 4, 6 .... **36**, 603

    ss 5, 6 .... **19(2)**, 812

c 18.............. Aliens' Employment Act 1955 .... **31**, 53

c 19.............. Friendly Societies Act 1955 .... **19(1)**, 234

c xxix............ London County Council (General Powers) Act 1955 .... **25(1)**, 476

c 38.............. Agricultural Mortgage Corporation Act 1956 .... **1(1)**, 476

c 44.............. Magistrates' Courts (Appeals from Binding Over Orders) Act 1956 .... **11(2)**, 146

c 46.............. Administration of Justice Act 1956—

    ss 40, 51, 55, 57, Sch 1, Pt II .... **19(3)**, 32

    ss 55, 57, Sch 1 .... **31**, 839

c 49.............. Agriculture (Safety, Health and Welfare Provisions) Act 1956 .... **1(1)**, 478

c 54.............. Finance Act 1956—

    ss 26, 44 .... **42**, 71

    ss 43, 44 .... **19(2)**, 814

c 59.............. Underground Works (London) Act 1956 .... **50**, 491

c 62.............. Hotel Proprietors Act 1956 .... **19(3)**, 448

c 69.............. Sexual Offences Act 1956 .... **12(1)**, 335

c 70.............. Marriage (Scotland) Act 1956 .... **27**, 277

c 74.............. Copyright Act 1956 .... **11(1)**, 635

c lxxvii.......... London County Council (General Powers) Act 1956 .... **25(1)**, 495

No 3............ Parochial Church Councils (Powers) Measure 1956 .... **14**, 485

5 & 6 Eliz 2

c 6.............. Ghana Independence Act 1957 .... **7(2)**, 364

c 11.............. Homicide Act 1957 .... **12(1)**, 348

c 12.............. Public Trustee (Fees) Act 1957 .... **48**, 558

c 13.............. Patents Act 1957 .... **11(1)**, 721

c 24.............. House of Commons Members' Fund Act 1957 .... **32**, 1079

c 31.............. Occupiers' Liability Act 1957 .... **21**, 249

c 36.............. Cheques Act 1957 .... **19(1)**, 236

c 42.............. Parish Councils Act 1957 .... **25(1)**, 498

c 45.............. Exchequer and Audit Departments Act 1957 .... **19(2)**, 816

c 52.............. Geneva Conventions Act 1957 .... **10**, 825

c 53.............. Naval Discipline Act 1957 .... **3**, 958

c 57.............. Agriculture Act 1957 .... **1(1)**, 483

c 58.............. Registration of Births, Deaths and Marriages (Special Provisions) Act 1957 .... **36**, 125

c 60.............. Federation of Malaya Independence Act 1957 .... **7(2)**, 368

c x.............. City of London (Various Powers) Act 1957 .... **25(1)**, 506

c xxxv.......... London County Council (General Powers) Act 1957—

    ss 1–3, 48, 62–68, 70–78, 81, 88, 89 .... **25(1)**, 519

    ss 1–3, 53–61 .... **49**, 347

No 1............ Channel Islands (Church Legislation) Measure 1931 (Amendment) Measure 1957 .... **14**, 494

6 & 7 Eliz 2

c 10.............. British Nationality Act 1958 .... **31**, 56

c 17.............. Recreational Charities Act 1958 .... **5(2)**, 534

c 21.............. Life Peerages Act 1958 .... **33(1)**, 11

c 29.............. Marriage Acts Amendment Act 1958 .... **27**, 279

c 30.............. Land Powers (Defence) Act 1958—

    ss 1, 12–18, 18A, 18B, 21–27, Schs 2, 4 .... **9**, 157

    ss 6, 7, 10, 11, 27 .... **3**, 1176

    ss 8, 9, 25–27, Sch 3 .... **36**, 604

c 33.............. Disabled Persons (Employment) Act 1958 .... **16**, 24

c 35.............. Matrimonial Causes (Property and Maintenance) Act 1958 .... **27**, 279

Enquiry Bureau   020 7400 2518

6 & 7 Eliz 2—*contd*

c 38 .... Defence Contracts Act 1958 .... **11(1)**, 724
c 39 .... Maintenance Orders Act 1958 .... **27**, 283
c 40 .... Matrimonial Proceedings (Children) Act 1958 .... **27**, 304
c 46 .... Statute Law Revision Act 1958 .... **41**, 761
c 47 .... Agricultural Marketing Act 1958 .... **1(1)**, 491
c 49 .... Trading Representations (Disabled Persons) Act 1958 .... **47**, 75
c 51 .... Public Records Act 1958 .... **18**, 191
c 52 .... Costs of Leases Act 1958 .... **21**, 255
c 53 .... Variation of Trusts Act 1958 .... **48**, 561
c 55 .... Local Government Act 1958 .... **25(1)**, 537
c 60 .... Chequers Estate Act 1958 .... **10**, 357
c 69 .... Opencast Coal Act 1958 .... **17(1)**, 204
c 71 .... Agriculture Act 1958 .... **1(1)**, 547
c xxi .... London County Council (General Powers) Act 1958 .... **25(1)**, 543
c xlvii .... City of London (Various Powers) Act 1958 .... **25(1)**, 554
No 1 .... Church Funds Investment Measure 1958 .... **14**, 495

7 & 8 Eliz 2

c 1 .... Armed Forces (Housing Loans) Act 1958 .... **3**, 1183
c 7 .... Manoeuvres Act 1958 .... **3**, 1184
c 13 .... Marriage (Secretaries of Synagogues) Act 1959 .... **27**, 305
c 19 .... Emergency Laws (Repeal) Act 1959 .... **50**, 502
c 28 .... Income Tax (Repayment of Post-War Credits) Act
                    1959 .... **42**, 73
c 30 .... National Assistance (Amendment) Act 1959 .... **40(1)**, 70
c 37 .... Restriction of Offensive Weapons Act 1959 .... **12(1)**, 352
c 43 .... Post Office Works Act 1959 .... **34**, 537
c 44 .... Fire Services Act 1959 .... **18**, 1024
c 45 .... Metropolitan Magistrates' Courts Act 1959 .... **33(2)**, 84
c 49 .... Chevening Estate Act 1959 .... **10**, 360
c 53 .... Town and Country Planning Act 1959—
                    ss 22–24, 26, 29, 30, 57, 59, Sch 4 .... **25(1)**, 559
                    ss 45, 57, 59 .... **9**, 182
c 54 .... Weeds Act 1959 .... **1(1)**, 553
c 56 .... Rights of Light Act 1959 .... **21**, 256
c 57 .... Street Offences Act 1959 .... **12(1)**, 354
c 58 .... Finance Act 1959 .... **41**, 107
c 66 .... Obscene Publications Act 1959 .... **12(1)**, 357
c 72 .... Mental Health Act 1959 .... **29**, 10
c xlix .... City of London (Various Powers) Act 1959 .... **25(1)**, 572
c lii .... London County Council (General Powers) Act 1959 .... **25(1)**, 578
No 2 .... Vacancies in Sees Measure 1959 .... **14**, 509

8 & 9 Eliz 2

c 3 .... Marshall Scholarships Act 1959 .... **15(1)**, 171
c 5 .... Atomic Energy Authority Act 1959 .... **17(1)**, 325
c 9 .... Judicial Pensions Act 1959 .... **11(2)**, 147
c 15 .... Water Officers Compensation Act 1960 .... **49**, 358
c 16 .... Road Traffic Act 1960 .... **36**, 613
c 22 .... Horticulture Act 1960 .... **1(1)**, 560
c 29 .... Marriage (Enabling) Act 1960 .... **27**, 306
c 32 .... Population (Statistics) Act 1960 .... **36**, 133
c 36 .... Game Laws (Amendment) Act 1960 .... **2**, 254
c 41 .... Ghana (Consequential Provision) Act 1960 .... **7(2)**, 373
c 44 .... Finance Act 1960—
                    ss 74, 74A, 79 .... **41**, 114
                    ss 77, 79 .... **19(2)**, 818
c 46 .... Corporate Bodies' Contracts Act 1960 .... **11(1)**, 359
c 52 .... Cyprus Act 1960 .... **7(2)**, 374
c 55 .... Nigeria Independence Act 1960 .... **7(2)**, 380
c 58 .... Charities Act 1960 .... **5(2)**, 539
c 62 .... Caravan Sites and Control of Development Act 1960 .... **32**, 212
c 65 .... Administration of Justice Act 1960—
                    ss 1, 2, 4–6, 9, 17–20, Sch 2, Pt I .... **12(1)**, 365
                    ss 12, 13, 17, 18, 20, Sch 2 .... **11(2)**, 149
                    ss 14, 15, 17(1)(c), (2), (6), 18, 20, Sch 2 .... **7(1)**, 39

8 & 9 Eliz 2—*contd*

c 67.............. Public Bodies (Admission to Meetings) Act 1960 .... **25(1)**, 591
c xxix............ London County Council (General Powers) Act 1960 .... **25(1)**, 597
c xxx............. City of London (Guild Churches) Act 1960 .... **14**, 510
c xxxvi.......... City of London (Various Powers) Act 1960 .... **25(1)**, 603
No 1.............. Church Property (Miscellaneous Provisions) Measure
          1960 .... **14**, 515

9 & 10 Eliz 2

c 9............... Agricultural Research etc (Pensions) Act 1961 .... **1(1)**, 561
c 16............. Sierra Leone Independence Act 1961 .... **7(2)**, 385
c 20............. Home Safety Act 1961 .... **25(1)**, 608
c 22............. Restriction of Offensive Weapons Act 1961 .... **12(1)**, 376
c 27............. Carriage by Air Act 1961 .... **4(1)**, 10
c 31............. Printer's Imprint Act 1961 .... **19(3)**, 392
c 33............. Land Compensation Act 1961 .... **9**, 185
c 34............. Factories Act 1961 .... **18**, 1188
c 35............. Police Pensions Act 1961 .... **33(2)**, 86
c 36............. Finance Act 1961 .... **42**, 78
c 39............. Criminal Justice Act 1961—
          ss 18, 19, 36, 39(3), (4), 41–45 .... **6**, 107
          ss 22–24, 35–45 .... **12(1)**, 377
c 50............. Rivers (Prevention of Pollution) Act 1961 .... **49**, 360
c 52............. Army and Air Force Act 1961 .... **3**, 1196
c 55............. Crown Estate Act 1961 .... **10**, 166
c 60............. Suicide Act 1961 .... **12(1)**, 390
c 62............. Trustee Investments Act 1961 .... **48**, 567
c 64............. Public Health Act 1961 .... **35(1)**, 250
c xxviii......... City of London (Various Powers) Act 1961 .... **25(1)**, 609
c xliii........... London County Council (General Powers) Act 1961 .... **49**, 363
No 2............. Baptismal Registers Measure 1961 .... **14**, 526
No 3............. Clergy Pensions Measure 1961 .... **14**, 529

10 & 11 Eliz 2

c 1............... Tanganyika Independence Act 1961 .... **7(2)**, 389
c 12............. Education Act 1962 .... **15(1)**, 172
c 19............. West Indies Act 1962 .... **7(2)**, 393
c 23............. South Africa Act 1962 .... **7(2)**, 400
c 26............. Animals (Cruel Poisons) Act 1962 .... **2**, 259
c 27............. Recorded Delivery Service Act 1962 .... **41**, 763
c 30............. Northern Ireland Act 1962 .... **31**, 847
c 31............. Sea Fish Industry Act 1962 .... **1(1)**, 567
c 32............. Marriage (Wales and Monmouthshire) Act 1962 .... **27**, 307
c 34............. Acts of Parliament Numbering and Citation Act 1962 .... **41**, 767
c 40............. Jamaica Independence Act 1962 .... **7(2)**, 403
c 43............. Carriage by Air (Supplementary Provisions) Act 1962 .... **4(1)**, 74
c 44............. Finance Act 1962—
          ss 33, 34 .... **19(2)**, 820
          s 34, Sch 11 .... **41**, 119
c 46............. Transport Act 1962 .... **36**, 625
c 48............. Law Reform (Husband and Wife) Act 1962 .... **27**, 309
c 52............. Penalties for Drunkenness Act 1962 .... **19(3)**, 451
c 53............. House of Commons Members' Fund Act 1962 .... **32**, 1081
c 54............. Trinidad and Tobago Independence Act 1962 .... **7(2)**, 408
c 56............. Local Government (Records) Act 1962 .... **25(1)**, 624
c 57............. Uganda Independence Act 1962 .... **7(2)**, 412
c 58............. Pipe-lines Act 1962 .... **17(1)**, 326
c xliii........... City of London (Various Powers) Act 1962 .... **25(1)**, 631
c xlv............ London County Council (General Powers) Act 1962—
          ss 1–3, 22–24 .... **25(1)**, 634
          ss 1, 3, 29 .... **49**, 367

11 & 12 Eliz 2

c 1............... Tanganyika Republic Act 1962 .... **7(2)**, 417
c 4............... Foreign Compensation Act 1962 .... **10**, 983

1963

c 2............... Betting, Gaming and Lotteries Act 1963 .... **5(1)**, 13
c 11............. Agriculture (Miscellaneous Provisions) Act 1963 .... **1(1)**, 562

1963—*contd*

c 14	Corn Rents Act 1963	**14**, 550
c 18	Stock Transfer Act 1963	**19(1)**, 241
c 24	British Museum Act 1963	**13**, 106
c 25	Finance Act 1963—	
	ss 67, 73	**41**, 128
	ss 71, 73	**19(2)**, 822
	s 73, Schs 13, 14	**42**, 80
c 27	Oaths and Evidence (Overseas Authorities and Countries) Act 1963	**18**, 221
c 29	Local Authorities (Land) Act 1963	**25(1)**, 641
c 32	Public Lavatories (Turnstiles) Act 1963	**35(1)**, 278
c 33	London Government Act 1963	**25(1)**, 648
c 34	Rhodesia and Nyasaland Act 1963	**7(2)**, 419
c 35	Malaysia Act 1963	**7(2)**, 421
c 37	Children and Young Persons Act 1963	**6**, 113
c 38	Water Resources Act 1963	**49**, 369
c 39	Criminal Justice (Scotland) Act 1963	**12(1)**, 393
c 41	Offices, Shops and Railway Premises Act 1963	**18**, 1242
c 43	Animal Boarding Establishments Act 1963	**2**, 261
c 44	Wills Act 1963	**50**, 780
c 46	Local Government (Financial Provisions) Act 1963	**25(1)**, 700
c 48	Peerage Act 1963	**33(1)**, 12
c 52	Public Order Act 1963	**12(1)**, 396
c 54	Kenya Independence Act 1963	**7(2)**, 425
c 55	Zanzibar Act 1963	**7(2)**, 429
c 57	Nigeria Republic Act 1963	**7(2)**, 433
c xvii	London County Council (General Powers) Act 1963	**25(1)**, 704
c xxxiv	City of London (Various Powers) Act 1963	**25(1)**, 719
No 1	Ecclesiastical Jurisdiction Measure 1963	**14**, 554
No 2	Cathedrals Measure 1963	**14**, 619

1964

c 5	International Headquarters and Defence Organisations Act 1964	**10**, 985
c 9	Public Works Loans Act 1964	**19(2)**, 825
c 12	Episcopal Church (Scotland) Act 1964	**14**, 628
c 14	Plant Varieties and Seeds Act 1964	**1(1)**, 571
c 15	Defence (Transfer of Functions) Act 1964	**10**, 373
c 19	Married Women's Property Act 1964	**27**, 310
c 20	Uganda Act 1964	**7(2)**, 435
c 22	British Nationality Act 1964	**31**, 60
c 23	Fireworks Act 1964	**18**, 756
c 28	Agriculture and Horticulture Act 1964	**1(1)**, 596
c 29	Continental Shelf Act 1964	**17(1)**, 405
c 34	Criminal Procedure (Right of Reply) Act 1964	**18**, 225
c 38	Emergency Powers Act 1964	**50**, 505
c 40	Harbours Act 1964	**39(2)**, 126
c 42	Administration of Justice Act 1964	**25(1)**, 722
c 46	Malawi Independence Act 1964	**7(2)**, 436
c 48	Police Act 1964	**33(2)**, 87
c 51	Universities and College Estates Act 1964	**21**, 262
c 53	Hire-Purchase Act 1964	**39(1)**, 51
c 54	British Nationality (No 2) Act 1964	**31**, 62
c 55	Perpetuities and Accumulations Act 1964	**33(2)**, 3
c 60	Emergency Laws (Re-enactments and Repeals) Act 1964	**50**, 506
c 63	Law of Property (Joint Tenants) Act 1964	**21**, 266
c 65	Zambia Independence Act 1964	**7(2)**, 441
c 69	Scrap Metal Dealers Act 1964	**47**, 78
c 70	Riding Establishments Act 1964	**2**, 267
c 71	Trading Stamps Act 1964	**47**, 95
c 72	Fishery Limits Act 1964	**1(1)**, 608
c 74	Obscene Publications Act 1964	**12(1)**, 397
c 75	Public Libraries and Museums Act 1964	**13**, 116
c 81	Diplomatic Privileges Act 1964	**10**, 990

1964—*contd*

  c 84.............. Criminal Procedure (Insanity) Act 1964 .... **12(1)**, 399
  c 85.............. John F Kennedy Memorial Act 1964 .... **32**, 241
  c 86.............. Malta Independence Act 1964 .... **7(2)**, 446
  c 89.............. Hairdressers (Registration) Act 1964 .... **47**, 105
  c 93.............. Gambia Independence Act 1964 .... **7(2)**, 450
  c iv.............. City of London (Courts) Act 1964 .... **11(2)**, 157
  No 1............. Church Commissioners (Loans for Theological Colleges
        and Training Houses) Measure 1964 .... **14**, 629
  No 2............. Incumbents and Churchwardens (Trusts) Measure
        1964 .... **14**, 630
  No 5............. Faculty Jurisdiction Measure 1964 .... **14**, 636
  No 6............. Clergy (Ordination and Miscellaneous Provisions) Measure
        1964 .... **14**, 643
  No 8............. Church Commissioners Measure 1964 .... **14**, 647

1965

  c 2.............. Administration of Justice Act 1965 .... **11(2)**, 159
  c 4.............. Science and Technology Act 1965 .... **10**, 378
  c 5.............. Kenya Republic Act 1965 .... **7(2)**, 455
  c 9.............. Armed Forces (Housing Loans) Act 1965 .... **3**, 1205
  c 12.............. Industrial and Provident Societies Act 1965 .... **19(1)**, 253
  c 17.............. Museum of London Act 1965 .... **13**, 136
  c 18.............. War Damage Act 1965 .... **50**, 518
  c 22.............. Law Commissions Act 1965 .... **41**, 767
  c 25.............. Finance Act 1965—
        ss 90, 97 .... **41**, 131
        s 97, Sch 22 .... **42**, 92
  c 32.............. Administration of Estates (Small Payments) Act 1965 .... **18**, 602
  c 34.............. British Nationality Act 1965 .... **31**, 67
  c 36.............. Gas Act 1965 .... **17(1)**, 410
  c 37.............. Carriage of Goods by Road Act 1965 .... **36**, 733
  c 43.............. Statutory Orders (Special Procedure) Act 1965 .... **41**, 772
  c 51.............. National Insurance Act 1965 .... **40(1)**, 71
  c 56.............. Compulsory Purchase Act 1965 .... **9**, 236
  c 57.............. Nuclear Installations Act 1965 .... **17(1)**, 470
  c 63.............. Public Works Loans Act 1965 .... **19(2)**, 827
  c 64.............. Commons Registration Act 1965 .... **21**, 268
  c 69.............. Criminal Procedure (Attendance of Witnesses) Act
        1965 .... **12(1)**, 413
  c 71.............. Murder (Abolition of Death Penalty) Act 1965 .... **12(1)**, 422
  c 72.............. Matrimonial Causes Act 1965 .... **27**, 311
  c 74.............. Superannuation Act 1965 .... **33(1)**, 98
  c xxxix.......... City of London (Various Powers) Act 1965 .... **25(1)**, 730
  No 4............. Prayer Book (Versions of the Bible) Measure 1965 .... **14**, 648

1966

  c 2.............. Church of England Convocations Act 1966 .... **14**, 650
  c 4.............. Mines (Working Facilities and Support) Act 1966 .... **17(1)**, 515
  c 10.............. Commonwealth Secretariat Act 1966 .... **7(2)**, 457
  c 14.............. Guyana Independence Act 1966 .... **7(2)**, 462
  c 18.............. Finance Act 1966—
        ss 2, 53, Sch 1 .... **13**, 573
        ss 45, 53 .... **41**, 134
        s 53, Sch 13 .... **42**, 103
  c 22.............. Malawi Republic Act 1966 .... **7(2)**, 466
  c 23.............. Botswana Independence Act 1966 .... **7(2)**, 467
  c 24.............. Lesotho Independence Act 1966 .... **7(2)**, 471
  c 28.............. Docks and Harbours Act 1966 .... **39(2)**, 201
  c 29.............. Singapore Act 1966 .... **7(2)**, 474
  c 35.............. Family Provision Act 1966 .... **18**, 612
  c 36.............. Veterinary Surgeons Act 1966 .... **28**, 17
  c 37.............. Barbados Independence Act 1966 .... **7(2)**, 478
  c 38.............. Sea Fisheries Regulation Act 1966 .... **1(1)**, 610
  c 41.............. Arbitration (International Investment Disputes) Act
        1966 .... **2**, 792
  c 42.............. Local Government Act 1966 .... **25(1)**, 751

1966—*contd*

    c 45 .... Armed Forces Act 1966 .... **3**, 1206
    c xxviii .... Greater London Council (General Powers) Act 1966 .... **25(1)**, 757

1967

    c 3 .... Education Act 1967 .... **15(1)**, 183
    c 4 .... West Indies Act 1967 .... **7(2)**, 482
    c 7 .... Misrepresentation Act 1967 .... **39(1)**, 57
    c 8 .... Plant Health Act 1967 .... **1(1)**, 629
    c 10 .... Forestry Act 1967 .... **18**, 1095
    c 13 .... Parliamentary Commissioner Act 1967 .... **10**, 388
    c 22 .... Agriculture Act 1967 .... **1(1)**, 639
    c 23 .... Royal Assent Act 1967 .... **32**, 1082
    c 24 .... Slaughter of Poultry Act 1967 .... **1(1)**, 700
    c 28 .... Superannuation (Miscellaneous Provisions) Act 1967—
                         ss 7, 18 .... **30**, 403
                         ss 11, 13, 15, 17, 18 .... **33(2)**, 91
                         ss 11, 17, 18 .... **33(1)**, 112
    c 32 .... Development of Inventions Act 1967 .... **47**, 118
    c 44 .... Public Records Act 1967 .... **18**, 226
    c 45 .... Uniform Laws on International Sales Act 1967 .... **39(1)**, 60
    c 48 .... Industrial and Provident Societies Act 1967 .... **19(1)**, 335
    c 50 .... Farm and Garden Chemicals Act 1967 .... **1(1)**, 708
    c 52 .... Tokyo Convention Act 1967 .... **4(1)**, 84
    c 54 .... Finance Act 1967 .... **41**, 136
    c 58 .... Criminal Law Act 1967—
                         ss 1, 3–6, 9–13, 15, Schs 2–4 .... **12(1)**, 424
                         ss 14, 15 .... **45**, 1553
    c 60 .... Sexual Offences Act 1967 .... **12(1)**, 450
    c 61 .... Public Works Loans Act 1967 .... **19(2)**, 831
    c 63 .... Bermuda Constitution Act 1967 .... **7(2)**, 487
    c 65 .... Antarctic Treaty Act 1967 .... **2**, 278
    c 69 .... Civic Amenities Act 1967 .... **46**, 30
    c 70 .... Road Traffic (Amendment) Act 1967 .... **36**, 755
    c 71 .... Aden, Perim and Kuria Muria Islands Act 1967 .... **7(2)**, 488
    c 72 .... Wireless Telegraphy Act 1967 .... **45**, 38
    c 74 .... Greenwich Hospital Act 1967 .... **3**, 1231
    c 77 .... Police (Scotland) Act 1967 .... **33(2)**, 97
    c 80 .... Criminal Justice Act 1967—
                         ss 8–10, 12, 17, 22, 25, 32, 36, 65, 66, 69–72, 89, 91,
                             92, 98, 100–106, Schs 5, 7 .... **12(1)**, 451
                         ss 20, 36, 106 .... **11(2)**, 162
    c 83 .... Sea Fisheries (Shellfish) Act 1967 .... **1(1)**, 713
    c 84 .... Sea Fish (Conservation) Act 1967 .... **1(1)**, 739
    c 87 .... Abortion Act 1967 .... **12(1)**, 484
    c 88 .... Leasehold Reform Act 1967 .... **21**, 289
    c xx .... Greater London Council (General Powers) Act 1967 .... **25(1)**, 772
    c xxix .... Ministry of Housing and Local Government Provisional
                      Order Confirmation (Greater London Parks and Open
                      Spaces) Act 1967 .... **25(1)**, 786
    c xlii .... City of London (Various Powers) Act 1967 .... **25(1)**, 803
    No 1 .... Clergy Pensions (Amendment) Measure 1967 .... **14**, 651
    No 2 .... Extra-Parochial Ministry Measure 1967 .... **14**, 654
    No 3 .... Overseas and Other Clergy (Ministry and Ordination)
                      Measure 1967 .... **14**, 656

1968

    c 2 .... Provisional Collection of Taxes Act 1968 .... **42**, 110
    c 5 .... Administration of Justice Act 1968 .... **11(2)**, 166
    c 7 .... London Cab Act 1968 .... **36**, 756
    c 8 .... Mauritius Independence Act 1968 .... **7(2)**, 488
    c 13 .... National Loans Act 1968 .... **19(2)**, 832
    c 14 .... Public Expenditure and Receipts Act 1968 .... **19(2)**, 877
    c 18 .... Consular Relations Act 1968 .... **10**, 1001
    c 19 .... Criminal Appeal Act 1968 .... **12(1)**, 490
    c 20 .... Courts-Martial (Appeals) Act 1968 .... **3**, 1232
    c 24 .... Commonwealth Telecommunications Act 1968 .... **45**, 47

Enquiry Bureau   hsieb@lexisnexis.co.uk

1968—*contd*

c 25 .... Local Authorities' Mutual Investment Trust Act 1968 .... **48**, 592
c 27 .... Firearms Act 1968 .... **12(1)**, 550
c 28 .... Wills Act 1968 .... **50**, 784
c 29 .... Trade Descriptions Act 1968 .... **39(1)**, 86
c 34 .... Agriculture (Miscellaneous Provisions) Act 1968—
     ss 2, 3, 6–8, 50, 51, 53, 54 .... **2**, 283
     ss 12, 13, 15, 17, 46, 50–54, Schs 3, 8 .... **1(1)**, 782
     ss 48, 54 .... **32**, 243
c 36 .... Maintenance Orders Act 1968 .... **6**, 131
c 41 .... Countryside Act 1968—
     ss 1, 2, 4, 6–13, 15, 15A, 16, 18, 20, 21, 37, 38, 41–50,
     Schs 1, 2, 5 .... **32**, 245
     ss 23, 24, 24A, 49(1), (2), 50 .... **18**, 1173
     ss 27, 30, 49, 50 .... **36**, 759
c 44 .... Finance Act 1968—
     ss 54, 61, Sch 18 .... **19(2)**, 881
     s 61, Sch 20 .... **42**, 115
c 46 .... Health Services and Public Health Act 1968—
     ss 45, 46, 79 .... **40(1)**, 87
     ss 59, 79 .... **11(1)**, 731
     ss 62, 79 .... **35(1)**, 279
     ss 63–65, 77–79, Schs 3, 4 .... **30**, 406
     ss 66, 79 .... **29**, 19
c 48 .... International Organisations Act 1968 .... **10**, 1027
c 49 .... Social Work (Scotland) Act 1968 .... **6**, 132
c 50 .... Hearing Aid Council Act 1968 .... **28**, 68
c 52 .... Caravan Sites Act 1968 .... **21**, 412
c 54 .... Theatres Act 1968 .... **13**, 148
c 55 .... Friendly and Industrial and Provident Societies Act
     1968 .... **19(1)**, 339
c 56 .... Swaziland Independence Act 1968 .... **7(2)**, 492
c 59 .... Hovercraft Act 1968 .... **39(2)**, 380
c 60 .... Theft Act 1968 .... **12(1)**, 641
c 63 .... Domestic and Appellate Proceedings (Restriction of
     Publicity) Act 1968—
     ss 1, 4, 5 .... **11(2)**, 168
     ss 2, 4(4), 5 .... **27**, 314
c 64 .... Civil Evidence Act 1968 .... **18**, 227
c 67 .... Medicines Act 1968 .... **28**, 84
c 69 .... Justices of the Peace Act 1968 .... **11(2)**, 171
c 73 .... Transport Act 1968 .... **36**, 764
c 75 .... Miscellaneous Financial Provisions Act 1968 .... **17(1)**, 533
c 77 .... Sea Fisheries Act 1968 .... **1(1)**, 793
c xxxii .... Port of London Act 1968 .... **39(2)**, 212
c xxxvii .... City of London (Various Powers) Act 1968 .... **25(1)**, 831
c xxxix .... Greater London Council (General Powers) Act 1968 .... **25(1)**, 835
c 24 (NI) .... Legislative Procedure Act (Northern Ireland) 1968 .... **31**, 1743
No 2 .... Prayer Book (Further Provisions) Measure 1968 .... **14**, 661

1969

c 2 .... Local Government Grants (Social Need) Act 1969 .... **25(1)**, 862
c 10 .... Mines and Quarries (Tips) Act 1969 .... **17(1)**, 535
c 14 .... Horserace Betting Levy Act 1969 .... **5(1)**, 29
c 18 .... Nuclear Installations Act 1969 .... **17(1)**, 585
c 19 .... Decimal Currency Act 1969 .... **10**, 189
c 20 .... Foreign Compensation Act 1969 .... **10**, 1049
c 22 .... Redundant Churches and Other Religious Buildings Act
     1969 .... **14**, 663
c 24 .... Tattooing of Minors Act 1969 .... **6**, 144
c 27 .... Vehicle and Driving Licences Act 1969 .... **36**, 927
c 29 .... Tanzania Act 1969 .... **7(2)**, 496
c 32 .... Finance Act 1969—
     ss 1, 59, 61, Sch 7 .... **13**, 581
     ss 58, 61, Sch 21 .... **42**, 121
c 33 .... Housing Act 1969 .... **21**, 422

1969—*contd*

c 35	Transport (London) Act 1969	**25(1)**, 864
c 37	Employers' Liability (Defective Equipment) Act 1969	**16**, 28
c 38	Sharing of Church Buildings Act 1969	**14**, 668
c 46	Family Law Reform Act 1969—	
	ss 1, 8, 9, 12, 28, Schs 2, 3	**6**, 145
	ss 2, 19, 28	**27**, 316
	ss 3, 28	**50**, 785
	ss 14, 28	**18**, 614
	ss 20–26, 28	**18**, 238
c 48	Post Office Act 1969—	
	ss 2–6, 22, 49, 74–76, 80, 86–88, 136, 138–140, 142,	
	Schs 1, 4, 9	**34**, 541
	ss 94, 108, 109, 114, 132, 139, 140, 142	**19(2)**, 886
	ss 134, 135, 142	**2**, 292
c 51	Development of Tourism Act 1969	**47**, 120
c 52	Statute Law (Repeals) Act 1969	**41**, 773
c 54	Children and Young Persons Act 1969	**6**, 153
c 56	Auctions (Bidding Agreements) Act 1969	**39(1)**, 110
c 57	Employer's Liability (Compulsory Insurance) Act 1969	**16**, 29
c 58	Administration of Justice Act 1969—	
	ss 12–16, 34–36	**11(2)**, 173
	ss 20, 21, 34, 36	**31**, 851
c 59	Law of Property Act 1969	**21**, 426
c xxxix	City of London (Various Powers) Act 1969	**25(1)**, 870
c lii	Greater London Council (General Powers) Act 1969	**25(1)**, 873
No 2	Synodical Government Measure 1969	**14**, 684

1970

c 7	Local Employment Act 1970	**47**, 136
c 9	Taxes Management Act 1970	**42**, 145
c 11	Sea Fish Industry Act 1970	**1(1)**, 815
c 13	Game Act 1970	**2**, 294
c 18	Guyana Republic Act 1970	**7(2)**, 500
c 22	Tonga Act 1970	**7(2)**, 501
c 24	Finance Act 1970—	
	ss 33, 36	**41**, 149
	s 36, Sch 8	**42**, 362
c 29	Parish Councils and Burial Authorities (Miscellaneous	
	Provisions) Act 1970	**5(2)**, 480
c 30	Conservation of Seals Act 1970	**1(1)**, 818
c 31	Administration of Justice Act 1970—	
	ss 1, 41, 52, 54, Schs 9, 11	**11(2)**, 181
	ss 10, 54	**11(1)**, 734
	ss 11, 28, 54, Schs 4, 8	**4(2)**, 40
	ss 31–35, 54	**31**, 855
	ss 36, 38A, 39, 54	**21**, 440
	ss 40, 54	**12(1)**, 682
	ss 44, 44A, 54	**19(3)**, 38
c 32	Riding Establishments Act 1970	**2**, 295
c 33	Law Reform (Miscellaneous Provisions) Act 1970—	
	ss 1–3, 7, Schedule	**27**, 319
	ss 5, 7	**45**, 1554
c 34	Marriage (Registrar General's Licence) Act 1970	**27**, 322
c 37	Republic of The Gambia Act 1970	**7(2)**, 504
c 39	Local Authorities (Goods and Services) Act 1970	**25(1)**, 936
c 40	Agriculture Act 1970—	
	ss 28–30, 32, 33, 37–56, 58–87, 110, 111, 113,	
	Sch 3	**1(1)**, 829
	ss 92, 98, 113	**49**, 383
	ss 106, 110, 111, 113(1), (2)	**2**, 297
c 41	Equal Pay Act 1970	**16**, 36
c 42	Local Authority Social Services Act 1970	**25(1)**, 944
c 43	Trees Act 1970	**18**, 1178
c 44	Chronically Sick and Disabled Persons Act 1970—	
	ss 1, 2, 12, 18, 28, 28A, 29	**40(1)**, 91

1970—contd

c 44	Chronically Sick and Disabled Persons Act 1970—contd		
	ss 3, 28, 29	**21**, 443	
	ss 4–7, 8A, 8B, 28, 29	**35(1)**, 282	
	ss 8, 28, 29	**15(1)**, 185	
	ss 9, 29	**3**, 1287	
	ss 13, 14, 16, 28, 29	**16**, 62	
	ss 15, 28, 29	**25(1)**, 966	
	ss 17, 22, 24, 28, 29	**30**, 425	
	ss 20, 21, 21A–21C, 28, 29	**36**, 930	
c 45	Matrimonial Proceedings and Property Act 1970	**27**, 333	
c 50	Fiji Independence Act 1970	**7(2)**, 506	
c 56	Contingencies Fund Act 1970	**19(2)**, 891	
c lxix	City of London (Various Powers) Act 1970	**25(1)**, 968	
c lxxvi	Greater London Council (General Powers) Act 1970	**25(1)**, 971	
c lxxviii	Port of London Act 1970	**39(2)**, 389	
No 1	Collegiate Churches (Capital Endowments) Measure 1970	**14**, 769	
No 2	Sharing of Church Buildings Measure 1970	**14**, 770	
No 3	Church Commissioners Measure 1970	**14**, 772	

1971

c 11	Atomic Energy Authority Act 1971	**17(1)**, 586	
c 19	Carriage of Goods by Sea Act 1971	**39(2)**, 392	
c 22	Animals Act 1971	**2**, 301	
c 23	Courts Act 1971	**11(2)**, 192	
c 24	Coinage Act 1971	**10**, 206	
c 25	Administration of Estates Act 1971	**18**, 617	
c 27	Powers of Attorney Act 1971	**1(1)**, 17	
c 29	National Savings Bank Act 1971	**19(2)**, 892	
c 30	Unsolicited Goods and Services Act 1971—		
	ss 2, 5–7	**39(1)**, 113	
	ss 3, 3A, 5, 6(2), 7	**47**, 138	
	ss 4, 6, 7	**12(1)**, 684	
c 32	Attachment of Earnings Act 1971	**19(3)**, 41	
c 33	Armed Forces Act 1971	**3**, 1289	
c 34	Water Resources Act 1971	**49**, 386	
c 38	Misuse of Drugs Act 1971	**28**, 270	
c 47	Wild Creatures and Forest Laws Act 1971	**10**, 73	
c 48	Criminal Damage Act 1971	**12(1)**, 687	
c 56	Pensions (Increase) Act 1971	**33(1)**, 115	
c 58	Sheriff Courts (Scotland) Act 1971	**41**, 776	
c 60	Prevention of Oil Pollution Act 1971	**49**, 387	
c 61	Mineral Workings (Offshore Installations) Act 1971	**17(1)**, 604	
c 64	Diplomatic and other Privileges Act 1971	**10**, 1052	
c 66	Friendly Societies Act 1971	**19(1)**, 369	
c 68	Finance Act 1971—		
	ss 21, 37, 38, 69, Schs 3, 14	**42**, 373	
	ss 67, 69, Sch 13	**30**, 429	
c 69	Medicines Act 1971	**28**, 336	
c 77	Immigration Act 1971	**31**, 71	
c 80	Banking and Financial Dealings Act 1971—		
	entire Act	**19(1)**, 369	
	ss 1, 4, 5, Schs 1, 2	**45**, 1538	
c vi	National Trust Act 1971	**32**, 297	
c xxviii	Greater London Council (General Powers) Act 1971	**25(1)**, 980	
c lxi	City of London (Various Powers) Act 1971	**25(1)**, 984	
No 1	Synodical Government (Special Majorities) Measure 1971	**14**, 772	

1972

c 1	Sierra Leone Republic Act 1972	**7(2)**, 510	
c 2	Island of Rockall Act 1972	**10**, 82	
c 5	Local Employment Act 1972	**47**, 142	
c 6	Summer Time Act 1972	**45**, 1542	
c 7	Civil List Act 1972	**10**, 182	
c 9	Mineral Exploration and Investment Grants Act 1972	**17(1)**, 614	

1972—*contd*

c 11 .... Superannuation Act 1972 .... **33(1)**, 163
c 14 .... Transport Holding Company Act 1972 .... **36**, 941
c 16 .... Harbours (Loans) Act 1972 .... **39(2)**, 404
c 18 .... Maintenance Orders (Reciprocal Enforcement) Act
         1972 .... **27**, 337
c 22 .... Northern Ireland (Temporary Provisions) Act 1972 .... **31**, 860
c 27 .... Road Traffic (Foreign Vehicles) Act 1972 .... **36**, 946
c 28 .... Employment Medical Advisory Service Act 1972 .... **18**, 1284
c 30 .... Civil Evidence Act 1972 .... **18**, 246
c 35 .... Defective Premises Act 1972 .... **21**, 446
c 41 .... Finance Act 1972 .... **42**, 392
c 44 .... Children Act 1972 .... **6**, 206
c 45 .... Trading Representations (Disabled Persons) Amendment
         Act 1972 .... **47**, 147
c 48 .... Parliamentary and other Pensions Act 1972 .... **33(1)**, 233
c 54 .... British Library Act 1972 .... **13**, 160
c 55 .... Sri Lanka Republic Act 1972 .... **7(2)**, 511
c 60 .... Gas Act 1972 .... **17(1)**, 616
c 61 .... Land Charges Act 1972 .... **21**, 452
c 62 .... Agriculture (Miscellaneous Provisions) Act 1972—
         ss 9, 10, 12, 17, 20, 25–27, Sch 6 .... **1(1)**, 900
         ss 19, 26(1), (2), 27(1) **2**, 311
c 63 .... Industry Act 1972 .... **39(2)**, 407
c 65 .... National Debt Act 1972 .... **19(2)**, 911
c 66 .... Poisons Act 1972 .... **28**, 339
c 68 .... European Communities Act 1972 .... **18**, 5
c 69 .... Horserace Totalisator and Betting Levy Boards Act
         1972 .... **5(1)**, 36
c 70 .... Local Government Act 1972—
         ss 1–16A, 17A, 18–35, 37, 38, 53–61, 65, 67–76, 78–92,
           94–109, 111–117, 119–146A, 148, 150–152, 168,
           172–179, 186, 187, 189, 191, 195, 202, 210, 211,
           216, 219, 222–256, 259, 260, 262, 263, 265–267,
           269–274, Schs 1–5, 8, 11–12B, 29–30 .... **25(2)**, 2
         ss 180, 181, 274, Sch 14 .... **35(1)**, 288
         ss 182, 185, 274, Sch 16 .... **46**, 33
         ss 184, 274, Sch 17, Pt III **32**, 310
         ss 206, 208, 274 .... **13**, 169
         ss 214, 215, 274, Sch 26 .... **5(2)**, 482
c 71 .... Criminal Justice Act 1972—
         ss 34, 36, 46, 60, 63–66, Sch 6 .... **12(1)**, 698
         ss 46, 51, 66 .... **11(2)**, 249
         ss 51(2), 66 .... **6**, 207
c 73 .... Museums and Galleries Admission Charges Act 1972 .... **13**, 172
c xl .... Greater London Council (General Powers) Act 1972 .... **25(2)**, 381
c xlv .... Thames Barrier and Flood Prevention Act 1972 .... **49**, 405
No 1 .... Admission to Holy Communion Measure 1972 .... **14**, 773
No 2 .... Repair of Benefice Buildings Measure 1972 .... **14**, 773
No 3 .... Benefices Measure 1972 .... **14**, 801
No 4 .... Deaconesses and Lay Ministry Measure 1972 .... **14**, 803
No 5 .... Clergy Pensions (Amendment) Measure 1972 .... **14**, 805

1973

c 4 .... Atomic Energy Authority (Weapons Group) Act 1973 .... **17(1)**, 617
c 9 .... Counter-Inflation Act 1973 .... **47**, 148
c 13 .... Supply of Goods (Implied Terms) Act 1973 .... **39(1)**, 115
c 15 .... Administration of Justice Act 1973—
         ss 5, 9, 12, 21 .... **11(2)**, 253
         ss 8, 21 .... **21**, 482
         ss 18, 21 .... **12(1)**, 711
c 16 .... Education Act 1973 .... **15(1)**, 189
c 18 .... Matrimonial Causes Act 1973 .... **27**, 408
c 21 .... Overseas Pensions Act 1973 .... **33(1)**, 238
c 24 .... Employment of Children Act 1973 .... **6**, 210

1973—*contd*

c 26.............. Land Compensation Act 1973—
ss 1–13, 15–19, 26, 27, 29, 29A, 30, 32–38, 44–48,
50–59, 61, 63, 84–89, Sch 3 .... **9**, 282
ss 20, 20A, 84, 87, 89 .... **35(1)**, 298
ss 28, 39–43, 84, 85, 87, 89 .... **21**, 484
c 27............. Bahamas Independence Act 1973 .... **7(2)**, 513
c 30............. Sea Fisheries (Shellfish) Act 1973 .... **1(1)**, 911
c 33............. Protection of Wrecks Act 1973 .... **39(2)**, 418
c 35............. Employment Agencies Act 1973 .... **16**, 65
c 36............. Northern Ireland Constitution Act 1973 .... **31**, 862
c 37............. Water Act 1973 .... **49**, 485
c 38............. Social Security Act 1973 .... **40(1)**, 98
c 39............. Statute Law (Repeals) Act 1973 .... **41**, 780
c 41............. Fair Trading Act 1973 .... **47**, 154
c 43............. Hallmarking Act 1973 .... **48**, 51
c 45............. Domicile and Matrimonial Proceedings Act 1973—
ss 1, 5, 6, 17, Schs 1, 6 .... **27**, 498
ss 3, 4, 17(1), (4), (5) **6**, 218
c 46............. International Cocoa Agreement Act 1973 .... **13**, 585
c 49............. Bangladesh Act 1973 .... **7(2)**, 520
c 50............. Employment and Training Act 1973 .... **16**, 85
c 51............. Finance Act 1973—
ss 32, 38, 41, 59, Schs 15, 22 .... **42**, 404
ss 50, 54, 59 .... **41**, 153
ss 56, 59 .... **10**, 430
ss 58, 59(1), (4) **48**, 594
c 53............. Northern Ireland (Emergency Provisions) Act 1973 .... **31**, 894
c 54............. Nature Conservancy Council Act 1973 .... **32**, 315
c 55............. Statute Law Revision (Northern Ireland) Act 1973 .... **31**, 898
c 58............. Insurance Companies Amendment Act 1973 .... **19(1)**, 375
c 60............. Breeding of Dogs Act 1973 .... **2**, 315
c 61............. Pensioners' Payments and National Insurance Act
1973 .... **40(1)**, 117
c 63............. Government Trading Funds Act 1973 .... **10**, 434
c 68............. International Sugar Organisation Act 1973 .... **10**, 1054
c xx............. City of London (Various Powers) Act 1973 .... **25(2)**, 391
c xxx............ Greater London Council (General Powers) Act 1973 .... **25(2)**, 393

1974

c 3............. Slaughterhouses Act 1974 .... **1(1)**, 911
c 6............. Biological Weapons Act 1974 .... **12(1)**, 713
c 7............. Local Government Act 1974 .... **25(2)**, 419
c 8............. Statutory Corporations (Financial Provisions) Act
1974 .... **36**, 959
c 9............. Pensions (Increase) Act 1974 .... **33(1)**, 246
c 11............. Charlwood and Horley Act 1974 .... **25(2)**, 477
c 14............. National Insurance Act 1974 .... **40(1)**, 118
c 18............. Contingencies Fund Act 1974 .... **19(2)**, 927
c 22............. Statute Law (Repeals) Act 1974 .... **41**, 785
c 23............. Juries Act 1974 .... **19(3)**, 180
c 24............. Prices Act 1974 .... **47**, 233
c 25............. Lord Chancellor (Tenure of Office and Discharge of
Ecclesiastical Functions) Act 1974 .... **10**, 450
c 28............. Northern Ireland Act 1974 .... **31**, 899
c 29............. Parks Regulation (Amendment) Act 1974 .... **32**, 318
c 30............. Finance Act 1974 .... **42**, 419
c 32............. Town and Country Amenities Act 1974 .... **46**, 38
c 36............. Mines (Working Facilities and Support) Act 1974 .... **17(1)**, 625
c 37............. Health and Safety at Work etc Act 1974—
ss 1–4, 6–28, 33–54, 80–82, 84, 85, Schs 1–3A **18**, 1288
ss 55–60, 81, 82, 84, 85 .... **16**, 107
c 39............. Consumer Credit Act 1974 .... **39(1)**, 125
c 40............. Control of Pollution Act 1974 .... **35(1)**, 304
c 44............. Housing Act 1974 .... **21**, 498
c 46............. Friendly Societies Act 1974 .... **19(1)**, 377

1974—*contd*

c 47.............. Solicitors Act 1974 .... **11(2)**, 258
c 48.............. Railways Act 1974 .... **36**, 961
c 50.............. Road Traffic Act 1974 .... **36**, 964
c 51.............. Rent Act 1974 .... **21**, 506
c 53.............. Rehabilitation of Offenders Act 1974 .... **12(1)**, 719
c 55.............. National Theatre Act 1974 .... **13**, 173
c xxiv........... Greater London Council (General Powers) Act 1974 .... **25(2)**, 480
No 1............. Synodical Government (Amendment) Measure 1974 .... **14**, 809
No 2............. Ecclesiastical Jurisdiction (Amendment) Measure 1974 .... **14**, 810
No 3............. Church of England (Worship and Doctrine) Measure
                   1974 .... **14**, 811

1975

c 4.............. Biological Standards Act 1975 .... **28**, 356
c 7.............. Finance Act 1975 .... **42**, 425
c 9.............. Supply Powers Act 1975 .... **10**, 451
c 10............. Statute Law (Repeals) Act 1975 .... **41**, 791
c 13............. Unsolicited Goods and Services (Amendment) Act
                   1975 .... **47**, 240
c 18............. Social Security (Consequential Provisions) Act 1975 .... **40(1)**, 120
c 22............. Oil Taxation Act 1975 .... **42**, 443
c 23............. Reservoirs Act 1975 .... **49**, 509
c 24............. House of Commons Disqualification Act 1975 .... **32**, 1083
c 25............. Northern Ireland Assembly Disqualification Act 1975 .... **31**, 907
c 26............. Ministers of the Crown Act 1975 .... **10**, 460
c 27............. Ministerial and other Salaries Act 1975 .... **10**, 474
c 31............. Malta Republic Act 1975 .... **7(2)**, 523
c 34............. Evidence (Proceedings in Other Jurisdictions) Act
                   1975 .... **18**, 251
c 35............. Farriers (Registration) Act 1975 .... **2**, 325
c 39............. Hearing Aid Council (Extension) Act 1975 .... **28**, 361
c 41............. Industrial and Provident Societies Act 1975 .... **19(1)**, 486
c 45............. Finance (No 2) Act 1975—
                   ss 72, 75 .... **41**, 156
                   ss 73, 75 .... **19(2)**, 928
                   s 75, Sch 14 .... **42**, 515
c 46............. International Road Haulage Permits Act 1975 .... **36**, 968
c 47............. Litigants in Person (Costs and Expenses) Act 1975 .... **11(2)**, 367
c 49............. Mobile Homes Act 1975 .... **32**, 319
c 50............. Guard Dogs Act 1975 .... **2**, 348
c 51............. Salmon and Freshwater Fisheries Act 1975 .... **1(2)**, 2
c 52............. Safety of Sports Grounds Act 1975 .... **13**, 174
c 55............. Statutory Corporations (Financial Provisions) Act
                   1975 .... **19(2)**, 931
c 56............. Coal Industry Act 1975 .... **17(1)**, 626
c 59............. Criminal Jurisdiction Act 1975 .... **31**, 925
c 60............. Social Security Pensions Act 1975 .... **33(1)**, 252
c 62............. Northern Ireland (Emergency Provisions) (Amendment)
                   Act 1975 .... **31**, 947
c 63............. Inheritance (Provision for Family and Dependants) Act
                   1975 .... **18**, 628
c 65............. Sex Discrimination Act 1975 .... **7(1)**, 44
c 66............. Recess Elections Act 1975 .... **32**, 1127
c 68............. Industry Act 1975 .... **47**, 241
c 70............. Welsh Development Agency Act 1975 .... **47**, 262
c 71............. Employment Protection Act 1975 .... **16**, 117
c 76............. Local Land Charges Act 1975 .... **21**, 509
c 80............. OECD Support Fund Act 1975 .... **19(2)**, 935
c 82............. Civil List Act 1975 .... **10**, 188
c 83............. Northern Ireland (Loans) Act 1975 .... **31**, 951
c xxx........... Greater London Council (General Powers) Act 1975 .... **25(2)**, 498
No 1............. Church Commissioners (Miscellaneous Provisions) Measure
                   1975 .... **14**, 819
No 2............. Ecclesiastical Offices (Age Limit) Measure 1975 .... **14**, 820

1976

c 3............... Road Traffic (Drivers' Ages and Hours of Work) Act
1976 .... **36**, 973
c 15.............. Rating (Caravan Sites) Act 1976 .... **25(2)**, 504
c 16.............. Statute Law (Repeals) Act 1976 .... **41**, 792
c 19.............. Seychelles Act 1976 .... **7(2)**, 525
c 26.............. Explosives (Age of Purchase &c) Act 1976 .... **18**, 756
c 27.............. Theatres Trust Act 1976 .... **13**, 198
c 28.............. Congenital Disabilities (Civil Liability) Act 1976 .... **45**, 1556
c 30.............. Fatal Accidents Act 1976 .... **31**, 776
c 31.............. Legitimacy Act 1976 .... **6**, 221
c 33.............. Restrictive Practices Court Act 1976 .... **47**, 309
c 35.............. Police Pensions Act 1976 .... **33(2)**, 102
c 36.............. Adoption Act 1976 .... **6**, 231
c 38.............. Dangerous Wild Animals Act 1976 .... **2**, 354
c 40.............. Finance Act 1976—
ss 72, 131, 132, Schs 9, 15 .... **42**, 523
ss 127, 131, 132 .... **41**, 158
c 46.............. Police Act 1976 .... **33(2)**, 125
c 47.............. Stock Exchange (Completion of Bargains) Act 1976 .... **48**, 595
c 48.............. Parliamentary and other Pensions and Salaries Act
1976 .... **33(1)**, 268
c 49.............. Chronically Sick and Disabled Persons (Amendment) Act
1976 .... **18**, 1378
c 52.............. Armed Forces Act 1976 .... **3**, 1301
c 54.............. Trinidad and Tobago Republic Act 1976 .... **7(2)**, 529
c 55.............. Agriculture (Miscellaneous Provisions) Act 1976 .... **1(2)**, 60
c 57.............. Local Government (Miscellaneous Provisions) Act 1976—
ss 7, 44–80, 83 .... **36**, 975
ss 11, 12, 16, 30–33, 38, 40, 41, 44, 83 .... **25(2)**, 508
ss 13–15, 29, 44, 83, Sch 1 .... **9**, 361
ss 17, 19–27, 35, 39, 44, 81–83, Sch 2 .... **35(1)**, 398
ss 36, 44(1), (1ZA), (6), 83 .... **27**, 63
ss 42, 44(6), 83 .... **46**, 40
c 58.............. International Carriage of Perishable Foodstuffs Act
1976 .... **1(2)**, 70
c 63.............. Bail Act 1976 .... **12(1)**, 749
c 70.............. Land Drainage Act 1976 .... **19(3)**, 217
c 71.............. Supplementary Benefits Act 1976 .... **40(1)**, 136
c 72.............. Endangered Species (Import and Export) Act 1976 .... **13**, 586
c 74.............. Race Relations Act 1976 .... **7(1)**, 160
c 75.............. Development of Rural Wales Act 1976 .... **46**, 42
c 76.............. Energy Act 1976 .... **17(1)**, 629
c 77.............. Weights and Measures &c Act 1976 .... **39(1)**, 388
c 78.............. Industrial Common Ownership Act 1976 .... **47**, 318
c 80.............. Rent (Agriculture) Act 1976 .... **21**, 532
c 82.............. Sexual Offences (Amendment) Act 1976 .... **12(1)**, 795
c 86.............. Fishery Limits Act 1976 .... **1(2)**, 153
c xxvi........... Greater London Council (General Powers) Act 1976 .... **25(2)**, 526
No 1............. Cathedrals Measure 1976 .... **14**, 824
No 2............. Ecclesiastical Judges and Legal Officers Measure 1976 .... **14**, 825
No 3............. Church of England (Miscellaneous Provisions) Measure
1976 .... **14**, 831
No 4............. Endowments and Glebe Measure 1976 .... **14**, 836

1977

c 3............... Aircraft and Shipbuilding Industries Act 1977 .... **47**, 320
c 5............... Social Security (Miscellaneous Provisions) Act 1977—
ss 12, 24(1), (3), 25 .... **3**, 1324
ss 23–25, Sch 2 .... **40(1)**, 143
c 7............... Nuclear Industry (Finance) Act 1977 .... **17(1)**, 657
c 17.............. Rent (Agriculture) Amendment Act 1977 .... **21**, 594
c 18.............. Statute Law (Repeals) Act 1977 .... **41**, 794
c 30.............. Rentcharges Act 1977 .... **21**, 594
c 31.............. Farriers (Registration) (Amendment) Act 1977 .... **2**, 371
c 32.............. Torts (Interference with Goods) Act 1977 .... **45**, 1562

1977—*contd*

c 33	Price Commission Act 1977	**47**, 370
c 36	Finance Act 1977—	
	ss 7, 10, 59, Sch 3	**13**, 605
	ss 56, 59	**14**, 879
	s 59, Sch 9	**42**, 534
c 37	Patents Act 1977	**11(1)**, 737
c 38	Administration of Justice Act 1977—	
	ss 2, 3, 23, 31, 32, Schs 4, 5	**11(2)**, 370
	ss 4, 32, Sch 5, Pt I	**19(3)**, 93
	ss 7, 32(1), (5)	**8**, 86
c 39	Coal Industry Act 1977	**17(1)**, 660
c 42	Rent Act 1977	**21**, 613
c 43	Protection from Eviction Act 1977	**21**, 799
c 45	Criminal Law Act 1977—	
	ss 1–10, 12, 12A, 13, 32, 33, 37, 51, 64, 65, Sch 13, Sch 14, paras 1, 5	**12(1)**, 797
	ss 15, 28, 30, 31, 38A, 38B, 39, 40, 48, 64, 65, Sch 14	**11(2)**, 386
c 47	Local Authorities (Restoration of Works Powers) Act 1977	**25(2)**, 532
c 49	National Health Service Act 1977	**30**, 433
c 50	Unfair Contract Terms Act 1977	**11(1)**, 360
c xv	City of London (Various Powers) Act 1977	**25(2)**, 534
No 1	Incumbents (Vacation of Benefices) Measure 1977	**14**, 880

1978

c 2	Commonwealth Development Corporation Act 1978	**7(2)**, 531
c 3	Refuse Disposal (Amenity) Act 1978	**35(1)**, 423
c 9	Gun Barrel Proof Act 1978	**48**, 88
c 15	Solomon Islands Act 1978	**7(2)**, 535
c 17	Internationally Protected Persons Act 1978	**10**, 1054
c 19	Oaths Act 1978	**18**, 261
c 20	Tuvalu Act 1978	**7(2)**, 543
c 22	Domestic Proceedings and Magistrates' Courts Act 1978	**27**, 509
c 23	Judicature (Northern Ireland) Act 1978	**31**, 954
c 25	Nuclear Safeguards and Electricity (Finance) Act 1978	**17(1)**, 665
c 26	Suppression of Terrorism Act 1978	**18**, 779
c 30	Interpretation Act 1978	**41**, 796
c 31	Theft Act 1978	**12(1)**, 831
c 33	State Immunity Act 1978	**10**, 1060
c 34	Industrial and Provident Societies Act 1978	**19(1)**, 488
c 36	House of Commons (Administration) Act 1978	**32**, 1131
c 37	Protection of Children Act 1978	**12(1)**, 834
c 39	Local Government Act 1978	**25(2)**, 539
c 42	Finance Act 1978—	
	ss 6, 80	**13**, 609
	s 80, Sch 13	**42**, 541
c 44	Employment Protection (Consolidation) Act 1978	**16**, 131
c 45	Statute Law (Repeals) Act 1978	**41**, 835
c 46	Employment (Continental Shelf) Act 1978	**16**, 136
c 47	Civil Liability (Contribution) Act 1978	**13**, 1259
c 50	Inner Urban Areas Act 1978	**46**, 44
c 55	Transport Act 1978	**36**, 1014
c xiii	Greater London Council (General Powers) Act 1978	**25(2)**, 540
c xvi	Greater London Council (General Powers) (No 2) Act 1978	**25(2)**, 553
No 1	Dioceses Measure 1978	**14**, 905
No 2	Parochial Registers and Records Measure 1978	**14**, 929
No 3	Church of England (Miscellaneous Provisions) Measure 1978	**14**, 954

1979

c 2	Customs and Excise Management Act 1979	**13**, 612
c 3	Customs and Excise Duties (General Reliefs) Act 1979	**13**, 844

1979—*contd*

c 4	Alcoholic Liquor Duties Act 1979	**19(3)**, 453
c 5	Hydrocarbon Oil Duties Act 1979	**13**, 870
c 7	Tobacco Products Duty Act 1979	**13**, 940
c 8	Excise Duties (Surcharges or Rebates) Act 1979	**13**, 962
c 10	Public Lending Right Act 1979	**13**, 203
c 13	Agricultural Statistics Act 1979	**1(2)**, 168
c 17	Vaccine Damage Payments Act 1979	**35(1)**, 445
c 18	Social Security Act 1979	**40(1)**, 148
c 21	Forestry Act 1979	**18**, 1179
c 27	Kiribati Act 1979	**7(2)**, 547
c 28	Carriage by Air and Road Act 1979	**4(1)**, 85
c 29	International Monetary Fund Act 1979	**19(2)**, 937
c 30	Exchange Equalisation Account Act 1979	**19(2)**, 943
c 32	Industry Act 1979	**47**, 372
c 34	Credit Unions Act 1979	**19(1)**, 491
c 37	Banking Act 1979	**19(1)**, 518
c 38	Estate Agents Act 1979	**21**, 818
c 41	Pneumoconiosis etc (Workers' Compensation) Act 1979	**40(1)**, 151
c 43	Crown Agents Act 1979	**10**, 484
c 44	Leasehold Reform Act 1979	**21**, 876
c 46	Ancient Monuments and Archaeological Areas Act 1979	**32**, 321
c 47	Finance (No 2) Act 1979	**42**, 549
c 50	European Parliament (Pay and Pensions) Act 1979	**18**, 69
c 52	Southern Rhodesia Act 1979	**7(2)**, 552
c 53	Charging Orders Act 1979	**19(3)**, 96
c 54	Sale of Goods Act 1979	**39(1)**, 395
c 57	European Communities (Greek Accession) Act 1979	**18**, 79
c 58	Isle of Man Act 1979	**7(2)**, 555
c 59	Shipbuilding Act 1979	**39(2)**, 422
c 60	Zimbabwe Act 1979	**7(2)**, 572
c xxiii	Greater London Council (General Powers) Act 1979	**25(2)**, 562

1980

c 1	Petroleum Revenue Tax Act 1980	**42**, 553
c 2	Papua New Guinea, Western Samoa and Nauru (Miscellaneous Provisions) Act 1980	**7(2)**, 580
c 9	Reserve Forces Act 1980	**3**, 1327
c 11	Protection of Trading Interests Act 1980—	
	ss 1–3, 5–8	**47**, 373
	ss 4, 8	**18**, 266
c 12	Bees Act 1980	**2**, 372
c 16	New Hebrides Act 1980	**7(2)**, 583
c 17	National Heritage Act 1980—	
	ss 1–7, 16–18, Schs 1, 2	**13**, 211
	ss 8–14, 17, 18, Sch 2	**42**, 557
c 20	Education Act 1980	**15(1)**, 196
c 21	Competition Act 1980	**47**, 381
c 23	Consular Fees Act 1980	**10**, 1079
c 24	Limitation Amendment Act 1980	**18**, 663
c 25	Insurance Companies Act 1980	**19(1)**, 521
c 26	British Aerospace Act 1980	**47**, 395
c 27	Import of Live Fish (England and Wales) Act 1980	**1(2)**, 175
c 30	Social Security Act 1980	**40(1)**, 162
c 32	Licensed Premises (Exclusion of Certain Persons) Act 1980	**19(3)**, 541
c 33	Industry Act 1980	**47**, 403
c 34	Transport Act 1980	**36**, 1022
c 43	Magistrates' Courts Act 1980	**11(2)**, 401
c 47	Criminal Appeal (Northern Ireland) Act 1980	**31**, 1106
c 48	Finance Act 1980—	
	ss 97, 98, 102, 122	**41**, 161
	ss 106–109, 118, 122, Schs 17, 20	**42**, 565
	ss 120, 122, Sch 19	**19(2)**, 946

1980—*contd*

c 50............. Coal Industry Act 1980 .... **17(1)**, 679
c 51............. Housing Act 1980 .... **21**, 877
c 53............. Health Services Act 1980 ....**30**, 486
c 57............. Imprisonment (Temporary Provisions) Act 1980 .... **12(1)**, 849
c 58............. Limitation Act 1980 .... **19(3)**, 875
c 60............. Civil Aviation Act 1980 .... **4(1)**, 111
c 65............. Local Government, Planning and Land Act 1980—
    ss 1–4, 93–100, 116, 185, 192, 193, 196, 197, Schs 1, 7,
    16, 33 ....**25(2)**, 570
    ss 47, 86, 91, 101, 124, 134–144, 146, 148, 149,
    151–154, 157, 157A, 157B, 159–172, 179, 194, 196,
    197, Schs 17, 26–29, 31, 32, 34 .... **46**, 57
    ss 112, 113, 115, 121–123, 196, 197 .... **9**, 376
c 66............. Highways Act 1980 ....**36**, 1070
c 67............. Anguilla Act 1980 ....**7(2)**, 586
No 1............. Deaconesses and Lay Workers (Pensions) Measure
    1980 .... **14**, 957
No 2............. Diocese in Europe Measure 1980 .... **14**, 959

1981

c 6............... Industry Act 1981 .... **47**, 411
c 7............... House of Commons Members' Fund and Parliamentary
    Pensions Act 1981 .... **32**, 1138
c 9............... International Organisations Act 1981 .... **10**, 1081
c 11............. Parliamentary Commissioner (Consular Complaints) Act
    1981 .... **10**, 527
c 12............. Water Act 1981 .... **49**, 548
c 14............. Public Passenger Vehicles Act 1981 .... **37**, 1
c 18............. Disused Burial Grounds (Amendment) Act 1981 .... **5(2)**, 491
c 19............. Statute Law (Repeals) Act 1981 .... **41**, 837
c 20............. Judicial Pensions Act 1981 .... **11(2)**, 616
c 21............. Ports (Financial Assistance) Act 1981 .... **39(2)**, 423
c 22............. Animal Health Act 1981 .... **2**, 377
c 24............. Matrimonial Homes and Property Act 1981 .... **27**, 551
c 25............. Industrial Diseases (Notification) Act 1981 .... **36**, 135
c 27............. Criminal Justice (Amendment) Act 1981 .... **11(2)**, 687
c 28............. Licensing (Alcohol Education and Research) Act
    1981 .... **19(3)**, 545
c 29............. Fisheries Act 1981 .... **1(2)**, 179
c 30............. Horserace Betting Levy Act 1981 .... **5(1)**, 40
c 33............. Social Security Act 1981 .... **40(1)**, 174
c 34............. Representation of the People Act 1981 .... **32**, 1141
c 35............. Finance Act 1981—
    ss 6, 11, 139 .... **13**, 967
    ss 107, 108, 139 .... **41**, 165
    ss 111–113, 115, 117, 118, 121, 139, Sch 19 .... **42**, 593
    ss 137, 139 .... **31**, 1158
c 37............. Zoo Licensing Act 1981 .... **2**, 506
c 38............. British Telecommunications Act 1981—
    entire Act **45**, 48
    ss 78, 81–86, 89, 90 .... **34**, 579
c 39............. Forestry Act 1981 .... **18**, 1181
c 42............. Indecent Displays (Control) Act 1981 .... **12(1)**, 852
c 43............. Disabled Persons Act 1981 .... **35(1)**, 459
c 45............. Forgery and Counterfeiting Act 1981 .... **12(1)**, 857
c 47............. Criminal Attempts Act 1981 .... **12(1)**, 882
c 48............. Atomic Energy (Miscellaneous Provisions) Act 1981 .... **17(1)**, 680
c 49............. Contempt of Court Act 1981 .... **11(2)**, 688
c 52............. Belize Act 1981 .... **7(2)**, 587
c 53............. Deep Sea Mining (Temporary Provisions) Act 1981 .... **17(1)**, 683
c 54............. Supreme Court Act 1981—
    ss 1–46, 46A, 48–56, 56B, 57–82, 84, 86–93, 95–102,
    104, 129, 131–137, 139, 140, 142, 150–153, Schs 1,
    2, 4, 6, 7 .... **11(2)**, 711
    ss 105–128, 151–153, Sch 6, paras 7–11, 13 .... **18**, 664

1981—*contd*
      c 55 .... Armed Forces Act 1981 .... **3**, 1384
      c 56 .... Transport Act 1981—
          ss 5–18, 40–43, Schs 2–5, Sch 12, Pts I, II .... **39(2)**, 425
          ss 35, 41–43 .... **37**, 96
      c 57 .... Employment and Training Act 1981 .... **16**, 138
      c 61 .... British Nationality Act 1981 .... **31**, 180
      c 63 .... Betting and Gaming Duties Act 1981 .... **5(1)**, 46
      c 64 .... New Towns Act 1981 .... **46**, 168
      c 66 .... Compulsory Purchase (Vesting Declarations) Act 1981 .... **9**, 386
      c 67 .... Acquisition of Land Act 1981 .... **9**, 404
      c 69 .... Wildlife and Countryside Act 1981—
          ss 1–28S, 31–37A, 39, 41–45, 47, 49–52, 66A–74,
            Schs ZA1–9, 10A–12, 17 .... **32**, 423
          ss 53–53B, 54A–59, 62, 63, 66, 67–70A, 71–74,
            Schs 14–16 .... **37**, 99
      c xv............. British Railways (Pension Schemes) Act 1981 .... **37**, 133
      c xvii........... Greater London Council (General Powers) Act 1981 .... **25(2)**, 600

1982
      c 3 .... Currency Act 1982 .... **10**, 221
      c 6 .... Transport (Finance) Act 1982 .... **37**, 142
      c 10 .... Industrial Training Act 1982 .... **16**, 141
      c 11 .... Canada Act 1982 .... **7(2)**, 595
      c 16 .... Civil Aviation Act 1982 .... **4(1)**, 126
      c 23 .... Oil and Gas (Enterprise) Act 1982 .... **17(1)**, 700
      c 24 .... Social Security and Housing Benefits Act 1982 .... **40(1)**, 176
      c 25 .... Iron and Steel Act 1982 .... **47**, 414
      c 27 .... Civil Jurisdiction and Judgments Act 1982—
          entire Act .... **11(2)**, 861
          ss 36, 52, 53, 55, Sch 13 .... **27**, 553
      c 28 .... Taking of Hostages Act 1982 .... **12(1)**, 893
      c 29 .... Supply of Goods and Services Act 1982 .... **39(1)**, 466
      c 30 .... Local Government (Miscellaneous Provisions) Act 1982—
          ss 2, 49, Sch 3 .... **13**, 226
          ss 3, 49, Sch 4 .... **47**, 419
          ss 13–17, 29–32, 49 .... **35(1)**, 461
          ss 12, 41, 45, 47–49, Sch 7 .... **25(2)**, 619
          ss 33, 49 .... **21**, 923
          ss 37, 49 .... **27**, 66
      c 31 .... Firearms Act 1982 .... **12(1)**, 897
      c 32 .... Local Government Finance Act 1982 .... **25(2)**, 637
      c 34 .... Forfeiture Act 1982 .... **12(1)**, 900
      c 36 .... Aviation Security Act 1982 .... **4(1)**, 307
      c 37 .... Merchant Shipping (Liner Conferences) Act 1982 .... **39(2)**, 475
      c 39 .... Finance Act 1982—
          ss 11, 157 .... **13**, 969
          ss 27, 134, 135, 145, 157, Schs 18, 22 .... **42**, 613
          ss 129, 157 .... **41**, 170
      c 41 .... Stock Transfer Act 1982 .... **19(1)**, 523
      c 42 .... Derelict Land Act 1982 .... **32**, 578
      c 48 .... Criminal Justice Act 1982—
          ss 1, 32, 68, 70, 72, 76–81, Sch 1, Sch 13, Pt III,
            Schs 16, 17 .... **12(1)**, 906
          ss 35–40, 46, 47, 59, 80, 81, Sch 2 .... **11(2)**, 996
      c 49 .... Transport Act 1982—
          ss 8–15, 17, 20–26, 70–76, Schs 5, 6 .... **37**, 145
          ss 66, 76 .... **39(2)**, 511
      c 51 .... Mental Health (Amendment) Act 1982 .... **29**, 21
      c 52 .... Industrial Development Act 1982 .... **47**, 430
      c 53 .... Administration of Justice Act 1982—
          ss 1, 5, 73(1), (3), (4)(a), 76–78 .... **13**, 1268
          ss 2, 73, 76–78 .... **45**, 1582
          ss 15, 37–47, 55, 73, 75–78, Sch 9 .... **11(2)**, 1012
          ss 20–25, 27, 28, 73, 76–78, Sch 2 .... **50**, 787
          ss 68, 69, 72, 73, 76–78, Schs 6, 7 .... **31**, 1160

1982—*contd*

c i	Greater London Council (General Powers) Act 1982	**25(2)**, 647
c v	London Transport Act 1982	**25(2)**, 657
c ix	Port of London Act 1982	**39(2)**, 468
No 2	Clergy Pensions (Amendment) Measure 1982	**14**, 962

1983

c 2	Representation of the People Act 1983	**15(3)**, 20
c 3	Agricultural Marketing Act 1983	**1(2)**, 219
c 4	Pig Industry Levy Act 1983	**1(2)**, 230
c 6	British Nationality (Falkland Islands) Act 1983	**31**, 261
c 8	British Fishing Boats Act 1983	**1(2)**, 236
c 9	Currency Act 1983—	
	ss 1, 4	**10**, 222
	ss 2–4, Schedule	**19(1)**, 530
c 10	Transport Act 1983—	
	ss 1, 2, 6–9, 12, Schedule	**37**, 178
	ss 11, 12	**16**, 175
c 11	Civil Aviation (Eurocontrol) Act 1983	**4(1)**, 389
c 14	International Transport Conventions Act 1983	**37**, 183
c 15	British Shipbuilders Act 1983	**47**, 449
c 16	Level Crossings Act 1983	**37**, 185
c 18	Nuclear Material (Offences) Act 1983	**12(1)**, 943
c 20	Mental Health Act 1983	**29**, 28
c 22	Ports (Reduction of Debt) Act 1983	**39(2)**, 515
c 23	Water Act 1983	**49**, 549
c 25	Energy Act 1983	**17(1)**, 707
c 26	Pet Animals Act 1951 (Amendment) Act 1983	**2**, 547
c 28	Finance Act 1983—	
	ss 9, 36, 37, 46, 48, Schs 8, 10	**42**, 637
	ss 43, 45, 48	**19(2)**, 951
c 29	Miscellaneous Financial Provisions Act 1983	**47**, 451
c 30	Diseases of Fish Act 1983	**1(2)**, 246
c 32	Marriage Act 1983	**27**, 562
c 34	Mobile Homes Act 1983	**21**, 929
c 35	Litter Act 1983	**32**, 604
c 40	Education (Fees and Awards) Act 1983	**15(1)**, 199
c 41	Health and Social Services and Social Security Adjudications Act 1983—	
	whole Act	**40(1)**, 186
	ss 4, 9, 11, 28, 31–34	**6**, 252
c 44	National Audit Act 1983	**19(2)**, 953
c 45	County Courts (Penalties for Contempt) Act 1983	**11(2)**, 1034
c 47	National Heritage Act 1983—	
	ss 1–7, 9–15, 17–31A, 40–43, Schs 1, 2, 6	**13**, 241
	ss 32–38, 41–43, Sch 3	**32**, 615
c 49	Finance (No 2) Act 1983—	
	ss 15, 16	**41**, 173
	s 16, Sch 2	**42**, 645
c 51	International Monetary Arrangements Act 1983	**19(2)**, 969
c 54	Medical Act 1983	**28**, 363
c 56	Oil Taxation Act 1983	**42**, 647
c 58	British Shipbuilders (Borrowing Powers) Act 1983	**47**, 455
c 59	Petroleum Royalties (Relief) Act 1983	**17(1)**, 714
c 60	Coal Industry Act 1983	**17(1)**, 715
c iii	Greater London Council (General Powers) Act 1983	**25(2)**, 663
No 1	Pastoral Measure 1983	**14**, 963
No 2	Church of England (Miscellaneous Provisions) Measure 1983	**14**, 1108

1984

c 3	Occupiers' Liability Act 1984	**21**, 948
c 4	Tourism (Overseas Promotion) (Scotland) Act 1984	**47**, 455
c 7	Pensions Commutation Act 1984	**33(1)**, 269
c 12	Telecommunications Act 1984	**45**, 71
c 16	Foreign Limitation Periods Act 1984	**19(3)**, 940
c 20	Agriculture (Amendment) Act 1984	**1(2)**, 253

Enquiry Bureau   hsieb@lexisnexis.co.uk

1984—*contd*

c 22.............. Public Health (Control of Disease) Act 1984 .... **35(1)**, 473
c 24.............. Dentists Act 1984 .... **28**, 495
c 27.............. Road Traffic Regulation Act 1984 .... **37**, 189
c 28.............. County Courts Act 1984 .... **11(2)**, 1035
c 29.............. Housing and Building Control Act 1984 .... **35(1)**, 543
c 30.............. Food Act 1984—
         ss 50–57, 57A, 59–61, 93–95, 110, 121, 132, 136 .... **27**, 69
         ss 69, 69A, 95, 132, 136 .... **1(2)**, 254
c 36.............. Mental Health (Scotland) Act 1984 .... **29**, 282
c 37.............. Child Abduction Act 1984 .... **12(1)**, 955
c 38.............. Cycle Tracks Act 1984 .... **37**, 430
c 39.............. Video Recordings Act 1984 .... **13**, 286
c 40.............. Animal Health and Welfare Act 1984 .... **2**, 548
c 42.............. Matrimonial and Family Proceedings Act 1984 .... **27**, 565
c 43.............. Finance Act 1984—
         ss 73, 113–116, 126–128, Sch 23 .... **42**, 699
         ss 110, 111, 128 .... **41**, 174
         ss 117, 128 .... **40(1)**, 209
c 47.............. Repatriation of Prisoners Act 1984 .... **12(1)**, 964
c 48.............. Health and Social Security Act 1984—
         whole Act .... **40(1)**, 211
         ss 5, 21, 23–29, Sch 8, Pt I **30**, 496
c 51.............. Inheritance Tax Act 1984 .... **42**, 720
c 52.............. Parliamentary Pensions etc Act 1984 .... **33(1)**, 272
c 55.............. Building Act 1984 .... **35(1)**, 546
c 57.............. Co-operative Development Agency and Industrial
         Development Act 1984 .... **47**, 456
c 59.............. Ordnance Factories and Military Services Act 1984 .... **10**, 528
c 60.............. Police and Criminal Evidence Act 1984—
         ss 1–24, 24A, 26–32, 34–47, 47A, 50, 51, 53–56, 58,
           60–67, 113–115, 117–122, Schs 1, 2, Sch 7,
           Pt I .... **12(1)**, 993
         ss 71–82, 113(12), (13), 118(1), 119(2), (3), 120–122,
           Sch 7, Pts II–V **18**, 267
         ss 107, 108, 115, 119–122, Sch 7, Pt VI .... **33(2)**, 127
c 62.............. Friendly Societies Act 1984 .... **19(1)**, 533
c xxvii.......... Greater London Council (General Powers) Act 1984 .... **25(2)**, 671

1985

c 2.............. Elections (Northern Ireland) Act 1985 .... **15(3)**, 357
c 3.............. Brunei and Maldives Act 1985 .... **7(2)**, 596
c 4.............. Milk (Cessation of Production) Act 1985 .... **1(2)**, 259
c 5.............. New Towns and Urban Development Corporations Act
         1985 .... **46**, 272
c 6.............. Companies Act 1985 .... **8**, 88
c 7.............. Business Names Act 1985 .... **48**, 94
c 9.............. Companies Consolidation (Consequential Provisions) Act
         1985 .... **8**, 817
c 12.............. Mineral Workings Act 1985 .... **17(1)**, 717
c 13.............. Cinemas Act 1985 .... **13**, 312
c 15.............. Hong Kong Act 1985 .... **7(2)**, 598
c 17.............. Reserve Forces (Safeguard of Employment) Act 1985 .... **3**, 1400
c 21.............. Films Act 1985 .... **13**, 317
c 22.............. Dangerous Vessels Act 1985 .... **39(2)**, 516
c 23.............. Prosecution of Offences Act 1985 .... **12(1)**, 1141
c 24.............. Rent (Amendment) Act 1985 .... **21**, 952
c 25.............. Industrial Development Act 1985 .... **47**, 460
c 26.............. Intoxicating Substances (Supply) Act 1985 .... **12(1)**, 1189
c 27.............. Coal Industry Act 1985 .... **17(1)**, 727
c 30.............. Ports (Finance) Act 1985 .... **39(2)**, 521
c 31.............. Wildlife and Countryside (Amendment) Act 1985 .... **32**, 633
c 32.............. Hill Farming Act 1985 .... **1(2)**, 264
c 39.............. Controlled Drugs (Penalties) Act 1985 .... **28**, 655
c 41.............. Copyright (Computer Software) Amendment Act
         1985 .... **11(1)**, 928

1985—*contd*

c 42.............. Hospital Complaints Procedure Act 1985 .... **30**, 506
c 43.............. Local Government (Access to Information) Act 1985 .... **25(2)**, 700
c 44.............. Sexual Offences Act 1985 .... **12(1)**, 1190
c 45.............. Charter Trustees Act 1985 .... **25(2)**, 702
c 47.............. Further Education Act 1985 .... **15(1)**, 204
c 48.............. Food and Environment Protection Act 1985—
           ss 1–4, 16–25, 27, 28, Schs 1, 2, 5 .... **1(2)**, 264
           ss 5–7, 7A, 8–15, 20(2), (3), (4)(c), (5), 21(2A), (3)–(8),
           22–24, 25(1), (3), (4), (5), 26–28, Sch 2, paras 1(c), 2,
           3, 4(1), 5–10, Schs 3, 4 .... **49**, 564
c 49.............. Surrogacy Arrangements Act 1985 .... **12(1)**, 1193
c 50.............. Representation of the People Act 1985—
           ss 1–3, 10–12, 15, 16, 18, 19, 21–24, 26–29, Schs 1,
           5 .... **15(3)**, 364
           ss 20, 27, 29 .... **32**, 1143
c 51.............. Local Government Act 1985 .... **25(2)**, 703
c 53.............. Social Security Act 1985 .... **40(1)**, 224
c 54.............. Finance Act 1985—
           ss 8, 98, Sch 5, Pt II, Sch 27, Pt III .... **5(1)**, 125
           ss 10, 98 .... **13**, 971
           ss 81–85, 87–89, 98, Sch 24 .... **41**, 178
           ss 93–96, 98, Schs 25, 27 .... **42**, 981
c 57.............. Sporting Events (Control of Alcohol etc) Act 1985 .... **12(1)**, 1199
c 58.............. Trustee Savings Banks Act 1985 .... **19(2)**, 970
c 59.............. Wildlife and Countryside (Service of Notices) Act
           1985 .... **32**, 634
c 60.............. Child Abduction and Custody Act 1985 .... **6**, 260
c 61.............. Administration of Justice Act 1985—
           ss 8–43, 47, 48, 53, 56, 67–69, Schs 2–9 .... **11(3)**, 2
           ss 49, 50, 56, 68, 69 .... **18**, 686
           ss 64, 68, 69 .... **31**, 1168
c 62.............. Oil and Pipelines Act 1985 .... **17(1)**, 729
c 65.............. Insolvency Act 1985 .... **4(2)**, 47
c 66.............. Bankruptcy (Scotland) Act 1985 .... **4(2)**, 51
c 67.............. Transport Act 1985 .... **37**, 437
c 68.............. Housing Act 1985 .... **22**, 1
c 69.............. Housing Associations Act 1985 .... **22**, 501
c 70.............. Landlord and Tenant Act 1985 .... **22**, 558
c 71.............. Housing (Consequential Provisions) Act 1985 .... **22**, 616
c 72.............. Weights and Measures Act 1985 .... **39(1)**, 491
c 75.............. European Communities (Spanish and Portuguese Accession)
           Act 1985 .... **18**, 79
c 76.............. Northern Ireland (Loans) Act 1985 .... **31**, 1171

1986

c 2.............. Australia Act 1986 .... **7(2)**, 601
c 3.............. Atomic Energy Authority Act 1986 .... **17(1)**, 744
c 5.............. Agricultural Holdings Act 1986 .... **22**, 636
c 7.............. Marriage (Wales) Act 1986 .... **27**, 605
c 8.............. Museum of London Act 1986 .... **13**, 331
c 10.............. Local Government Act 1986 .... **25(2)**, 807
c 12.............. Statute Law (Repeals) Act 1986 .... **41**, 862
c 13.............. Highways (Amendment) Act 1986 .... **37**, 613
c 14.............. Animals (Scientific Procedures) Act 1986 .... **2**, 555
c 15.............. Industrial Training Act 1986 .... **16**, 176
c 16.............. Marriage (Prohibited Degrees of Relationship) Act
           1986 .... **27**, 606
c 20.............. Horticultural Produce Act 1986 .... **1(2)**, 444
c 21.............. Armed Forces Act 1986 .... **3**, 1423
c 26.............. Land Registration Act 1986 .... **22**, 779
c 27.............. Road Traffic Regulation (Parking) Act 1986 .... **37**, 614
c 30.............. Forestry Act 1986 .... **18**, 1182
c 31.............. Airports Act 1986 .... **4(1)**, 390
c 32.............. Drug Trafficking Offences Act 1986 .... **12(1)**, 1207

1986—*contd*

c 33 .... Disabled Persons (Services, Consultation and
Representation) Act 1986 .... **40(1)**, 231
c 34 .... Protection of Children (Tobacco) Act 1986 .... **6**, 294
c 35 .... Protection of Military Remains Act 1986 .... **3**, 1431
c 37 .... Latent Damage Act 1986 .... **19(3)**, 944
c 38 .... Outer Space Act 1986 .... **4(1)**, 498
c 39 .... Patents, Designs and Marks Act 1986 .... **48**, 100
c 40 .... Education Act 1986 .... **15(1)**, 211
c 41 .... Finance Act 1986—
ss 6, 114, Sch 4, Pt III, Sch 23, Pt III .... **5(1)**, 129
s 8 .... **19(3)**, 559
ss 8, 114 .... **13**, 975
ss 24, 100–104, 106–109, 114, Schs 18–21, 23 .... **42**, 1002
ss 66–72, 72A, 75–79, 80A–80C, 84–88, 88A, 88B, 89A,
89AA, 90–99, 114 .... **41**, 188
c 44 .... Gas Act 1986 .... **17(1)**, 751
c 45 .... Insolvency Act 1986 .... **4(2)**, 68
c 46 .... Company Directors Disqualification Act 1986 .... **8**, 837
c 49 .... Agriculture Act 1986 .... **1(2)**, 449
c 50 .... Social Security Act 1986 .... **40(1)**, 257
c 51 .... British Council and Commonwealth Institute
Superannuation Act 1986 .... **33(1)**, 274
c 52 .... Dockyard Services Act 1986 .... **39(2)**, 524
c 53 .... Building Societies Act 1986 .... **19(1)**, 535
c 55 .... Family Law Act 1986—
ss 1, 2, 2A, 3, 5–7, 19, 19A, 20, 22–25, 27–43, 55A,
56–60, 68, 69, Sch 2 .... **6**, 294
ss 44–52, 54, 55, 58–62, 68(3), 69 .... **27**, 608
c 56 .... Parliamentary Constituencies Act 1986 .... **15(3)**, 393
c 57 .... Public Trustee and Administration of Funds Act 1986—
ss 1, 3, 6 .... **48**, 597
ss 1, 6 .... **11(3)**, 74
ss 3, 6 .... **29**, 289
c 58 .... European Communities (Amendment) Act 1986 .... **18**, 80
c 59 .... Sex Discrimination Act 1986 .... **7(1)**, 286
c 60 .... Financial Services Act 1986 .... **8**, 860
c 61 .... Education (No 2) Act 1986 .... **15(1)**, 213
c 62 .... Salmon Act 1986 .... **1(2)**, 471
c 63 .... Housing and Planning Act 1986—
ss 2, 4, 6, 8, 15, 18, 24, 39, 40, 48, 49, 56–59, Schs 4, 5,
12 .... **46**, 276
ss 42, 57–59 .... **25(2)**, 816
c 64 .... Public Order Act 1986 .... **12(1)**, 1209
c 66 .... National Health Service (Amendment) Act 1986 .... **30**, 509
c iv .... Greater London Council (General Powers) Act 1986 .... **25(2)**, 820
No 1 .... Bishops (Retirement) Measure 1986 .... **14**, 1111
No 2 .... Ecclesiastical Fees Measure 1986 .... **14**, 1119
No 3 .... Patronage (Benefices) Measure 1986 .... **14**, 1130
No 4 .... Deacons (Ordination of Women) Measure 1986 .... **14**, 1175

1987

c 3 .... Coal Industry Act 1987 .... **17(1)**, 949
c 4 .... Ministry of Defence Police Act 1987 .... **33(2)**, 133
c 12 .... Petroleum Act 1987 .... **17(1)**, 956
c 13 .... Minors' Contracts Act 1987 .... **6**, 340
c 14 .... Recognition of Trusts Act 1987 .... **48**, 599
c 15 .... Reverter of Sites Act 1987 .... **22**, 781
c 16 .... Finance Act 1987—
ss 50, 54, 55, 72 .... **41**, 259
ss 57–59, 61–66, 72, Schs 10, 12–14, 16 .... **42**, 1042
ss 68, 72 .... **19(2)**, 989
c 20 .... Chevening Estate Act 1987 .... **10**, 546
c 21 .... Pilotage Act 1987 .... **39(2)**, 530
c 25 .... Crown Proceedings (Armed Forces) Act 1987 .... **13**, 39
c 27 .... Fire Safety and Safety of Places of Sport Act 1987 .... **13**, 334

Enquiry Bureau 020 7400 2518

1987—*contd*

c 31 .... Landlord and Tenant Act 1987 .... **22**, 793
c 32 .... Crossbows Act 1987 .... **12(1)**, 1258
c 33 .... AIDS (Control) Act 1987 .... **30**, 513
c 34 .... Motor Cycle Noise Act 1987 .... **37**, 615
c 38 .... Criminal Justice Act 1987 .... **12(1)**, 1261
c 39 .... Parliamentary and Health Service Commissioners Act
                    1987 .... **10**, 550
c 42 .... Family Law Reform Act 1987—
                    ss 1, 2, 17, 19, 27, 30–34, Schs 3, 4 .... **6**, 343
                    ss 1, 18, 21, 33, 34, Sch 3, paras 8, 10 .... **18**, 691
c 43 .... Consumer Protection Act 1987 .... **39(1)**, 618
c 45 .... Parliamentary and other Pensions Act 1987 .... **33(1)**, 275
c 46 .... Diplomatic and Consular Premises Act 1987 .... **10**, 1085
c 49 .... Territorial Sea Act 1987 .... **49**, 593
c 51 .... Finance (No 2) Act 1987—
                    ss 86, 95, 97, 101, 104, Schs 8, 9 .... **42**, 1081
                    ss 102, 104 .... **19(2)**, 991
                    ss 103, 104 .... **13**, 978
c 52 .... British Shipbuilders (Borrowing Powers) Act 1987 .... **47**, 462
c 53 .... Channel Tunnel Act 1987 .... **37**, 618
c 57 .... Urban Development Corporations (Financial Limits) Act
                    1987 .... **46**, 304
c xv .... City of London (Various Powers) Act 1987 .... **25(2)**, 837

1988

c 1 .... Income and Corporation Taxes Act 1988 .... **44(1)**, 1
c 2 .... Arms Control and Disarmament (Privileges and
                    Immunities) Act 1988 .... **10**, 1094
c 7 .... Social Security Act 1988 .... **40(1)**, 284
c 8 .... Multilateral Investment Guarantee Agency Act 1988 .... **19(2)**, 994
c 9 .... Local Government Act 1988—
                    ss 17–23, 29, 31, 34, 40–42, Schs 2, 3, 5, 7 .... **25(2)**, 856
                    ss 24–26, 40, 42 .... **22**, 889
                    ss 37, 39–42, Sch 7, Pt IV **2**, 588
c 10 .... Duchy of Lancaster Act 1988 .... **10**, 553
c 12 .... Merchant Shipping Act 1988 .... **39(2)**, 567
c 13 .... Coroners Act 1988 .... **11(1)**, 1370
c 14 .... Immigration Act 1988 .... **31**, 264
c 15 .... Public Utility Transfers and Water Charges Act 1988 .... **49**, 599
c 16 .... Farm Land and Rural Development Act 1988 .... **1(2)**, 480
c 18 .... Matrimonial Proceedings (Transfers) Act 1988 .... **27**, 625
c 19 .... Employment Act 1988 .... **16**, 177
c 22 .... Scotch Whisky Act 1988 .... **19(3)**, 561
c 23 .... Motor Vehicles (Wearing of Rear Seat Belts by Children)
                    Act 1988 .... **37**, 746
c 24 .... Community Health Councils (Access to Information) Act
                    1988 .... **30**, 518
c 26 .... Landlord and Tenant Act 1988 .... **22**, 897
c 27 .... Malicious Communications Act 1988 .... **12(1)**, 1295
c 28 .... Access to Medical Reports Act 1988 .... **28**, 655
c 29 .... Protection of Animals (Amendment) Act 1988 .... **2**, 592
c 30 .... Environment and Safety Information Act 1988 .... **35(1)**, 723
c 33 .... Criminal Justice Act 1988—
                    ss 30–32, 168, 171–173 .... **18**, 291
                    ss 34, 171(1), (2), (5), 172, 173 .... **6**, 360
                    ss 35, 36, 39–41, 96, 97, 123, 133–135, 138, 139, 139A,
                        139B, 141, 141A, 142, 150, 151, 159, 160, 160A,
                        167–173, Schs 3, 8, 12, 15, 16 .... **12(1)**, 1298
                    ss 50, 146, 171–173, Sch 13 .... **3**, 1442
                    ss 51–53, 55, 57, 59, 67, 152, 171–173 .... **11(3)**, 76
                    ss 118, 122, 171–173 .... **19(3)**, 204
c 34 .... Legal Aid Act 1988 .... **11(3)**, 91
c 35 .... British Steel Act 1988 .... **47**, 462
c 39 .... Finance Act 1988—
                    ss 8, 149 .... **13**, 980

1988—*contd*

c 39.............. Finance Act 1988—*contd*
ss 35, 36, 38, 40, 65, 66, 66A, 73, 127, 130–132, 134,
138, 145–149, Schs 3, 6, 7 .... **42**, 1090
ss 143, 149 .... **41**, 264
c 40.............. Education Reform Act 1988 .... **15(1)**, 220
c 41.............. Local Government Finance Act 1988 .... **25(2)**, 877
c 44.............. Foreign Marriage (Amendment) Act 1988 .... **27**, 627
c 45.............. Firearms (Amendment) Act 1988 .... **12(1)**, 1356
c 48.............. Copyright, Designs and Patents Act 1988—
entire Act .... **11(1)**, 930
ss 302, 304(1), (2), (4)(e), (6), 305(3), 306 .... **48**, 103
c 49.............. Health and Medicines Act 1988—
ss 1, 4–7, 9, 17–19, 24–28, Schs 1, 3 .... **30**, 521
ss 21–23, 26–28 .... **28**, 662
c 50.............. Housing Act 1988 .... **22**, 903
c 52.............. Road Traffic Act 1988 .... **37**, 747
c 53.............. Road Traffic Offenders Act 1988 .... **38(1)**, 2
c 54.............. Road Traffic (Consequential Provisions) Act 1988 .... **38(1)**, 211
No 1............. Church of England (Legal Aid and Miscellaneous
Provisions) Measure 1988 .... **14**, 1178
No 2............. Church Commissioners (Assistance for Priority Areas)
Measure 1988 .... **14**, 1181
No 3............. Church of England (Ecumenical Relations) Measure
1988 .... **14**, 1183
No 4............. Church of England (Pensions) Measure 1988 .... **14**, 1187

1989

c 1.............. Petroleum Royalties (Relief) and Continental Shelf Act
1989 .... **17(1)**, 964
c 3.............. Elected Authorities (Northern Ireland) Act 1989 .... **31**, 1172
c 5.............. Security Service Act 1989 .... **10**, 554
c 6.............. Official Secrets Act 1989 .... **12(2)**, 2
c 7.............. Atomic Energy Act 1989 .... **17(1)**, 969
c 8.............. National Maritime Museum Act 1989 .... **13**, 359
c 11............. Police Officers (Central Service) Act 1989 .... **33(2)**, 150
c 12............. Hearing Aid Council (Amendment) Act 1989 .... **28**, 668
c 13............. Dock Work Act 1989 .... **16**, 184
c 14............. Control of Pollution (Amendment) Act 1989 .... **35(1)**, 728
c 15............. Water Act 1989 .... **49**, 604
c 16............. Parking Act 1989 .... **38(1)**, 226
c 19............. International Parliamentary Organisations (Registration) Act
1989 .... **32**, 1146
c 21............. Antarctic Minerals Act 1989 .... **17(1)**, 973
c 22............. Road Traffic (Driver Licensing and Information Systems)
Act 1989 .... **38(1)**, 228
c 24............. Social Security Act 1989—
ss 4, 6, 28–31, 33, Sch 5, Pt I, Sch 9 .... **40(1)**, 294
ss 25, 28–31, 33 .... **3**, 1454
c 26............. Finance Act 1989—
ss 27, 29, 188 .... **50**, 5
ss 43, 44, 67–77, 82–88, 89–90A, 102, 103, 107, 110,
111, 115, 151, 178, 182, 182A, 186–188, Schs 5–7,
8A, 12, 17 .... **42**, 1136
ss 175–177, 188 .... **41**, 267
ss 185, 188 .... **14**, 1191
c 27............. Pesticides (Fees and Enforcement) Act 1989 .... **1(2)**, 486
c 28............. Representation of the People Act 1989 .... **15(3)**, 409
c 29............. Electricity Act 1989 .... **17(1)**, 975
c 30............. Dangerous Dogs Act 1989 .... **2**, 594
c 34............. Law of Property (Miscellaneous Provisions) Act 1989 .... **23**, 2
c 35............. Continental Shelf Act 1989 .... **17(1)**, 1267
c 36............. Brunei (Appeals) Act 1989 .... **7(2)**, 609
c 37............. Football Spectators Act 1989 .... **13**, 362

1989—*contd*

c 38 .... Employment Act 1989—
           ss 1, 2, 4–6, 8, 11, 12, 27, 28(1)–(3), (4)(a), (5),
            29(1), (2), (6), 30, Sch 1, Sch 9, para 1 .... **7(1)**, 294
           ss 9, 10, 22, 25, 27–30, Sch 2, Pt II, Schs 5, 7–9 .... **16**, 190
c 40 .... Companies Act 1989—
           ss 1, 23–54, 92–107, 117, 118, 120, 130, 133–135,
            139–142, 144, 145, 152, 153, 212–216, Schs 11–14,
            16, 18, 19, 24 .... **8**, 872
           ss 82–91, 154, 155, 157–167, 169, 170, 172–191, 213,
            215, 216 .... **19(1)**, 826
c 41 .... Children Act 1989 .... **6**, 365
c 42 .... Local Government and Housing Act 1989—
           ss 1–13, 15–21, 24, 25, 31, 67–73, 139, 149–152, 154,
            155, 157, 190–195, Schs 1, 5, 11, 12 .... **25(2)**, 1075
           ss 74–80B, 82–89, 91–100, 165, 166, 168, 169, 171, 186,
            190–193, 195, Schs 4, 7, 10 .... **23**, 11
           ss 172, 173, 175, 190, 191, 195 .... **46**, 305
           ss 187, 192, 195 .... **47**, 482
c 43 .... Statute Law (Repeals) Act 1989 .... **41**, 891
c 44 .... Opticians Act 1989 .... **28**, 669
c 45 .... Prisons (Scotland) Act 1989 .... **12(2)**, 22

1990

c 2 .... Civil Aviation Authority (Borrowing Powers) Act
           1990 .... **4(1)**, 510
c 5 .... Criminal Justice (International Co-operation) Act 1990—
           ss 5, 6, 9, 10, 18, 20, 21, 24, 30–32, Schs 3–5 .... **12(2)**, 24
           ss 12, 13, 19–21, 24, 32, Schs 2, 3 .... **28**, 760
c 6 .... Education (Student Loans) Act 1990 .... **15(1)**, 338
c 7 .... Pensions (Miscellaneous Provisions) Act 1990 .... **33(1)**, 289
c 8 .... Town and Country Planning Act 1990 .... **46**, 314
c 9 .... Planning (Listed Buildings and Conservation Areas) Act
           1990 .... **46**, 838
c 10 .... Planning (Hazardous Substances) Act 1990 .... **46**, 969
c 11 .... Planning (Consequential Provisions) Act 1990 .... **46**, 1029
c 12 .... Property Services Agency and Crown Suppliers Act
           1990 .... **10**, 559
c 13 .... Greenwich Hospital Act 1990 .... **3**, 1460
c 14 .... Pakistan Act 1990 .... **7(2)**, 611
c 15 .... Agricultural Holdings (Amendment) Act 1990 .... **23**, 81
c 16 .... Food Safety Act 1990 .... **1(2)**, 488
c 17 .... Australian Constitution (Public Record Copy) Act
           1990 .... **18**, 303
c 18 .... Computer Misuse Act 1990 .... **12(2)**, 40
c 19 .... National Health Service and Community Care Act 1990—
           ss 18, 60, 61, 63–67, Schs 8–10 .... **30**, 538
           ss 46–49, 64(1)(d), (e), 65, 67 .... **40(1)**, 316
c 23 .... Access to Health Records Act 1990 .... **7(1)**, 308
c 24 .... Rights of Way Act 1990 .... **38(1)**, 247
c 25 .... Horses (Protective Headgear for Young Riders) Act
           1990 .... **6**, 670
c 27 .... Social Security Act 1990 .... **40(1)**, 326
c 29 .... Finance Act 1990—
           ss 25, 30, 41, 42, 48, 52, 53, 69, 80, 88, 89, 114,
            125–127, 131, 133, Schs 6, 7, 12, 19 .... **42**, 1246
           ss 107–111, 133 .... **41**, 270
           ss 128, 133 .... **19(2)**, 1003
c 30 .... Government Trading Act 1990—
           ss 2, 5, Sch 2, Pt II **10**, 564
           ss 4, 5, Sch 2, Pt I .... **19(2)**, 1005
c 31 .... Aviation and Maritime Security Act 1990—
           ss 1, 48, 50–52, 54, Sch 4 .... **4(1)**, 511
           ss 9–46, 50–54, Sch 2 .... **39(2)**, 574
c 33 .... Marriage (Registration of Buildings) Act 1990 .... **27**, 629
c 34 .... British Nationality (Hong Kong) Act 1990 .... **31**, 270

1990—*contd*

c 36 .... Contracts (Applicable Law) Act 1990 .... **11(1)**, 379
c 37 .... Human Fertilisation and Embryology Act 1990 .... **28**, 773
c 38 .... Employment Act 1990 .... **16**, 212
c 39 .... Landlord and Tenant (Licensed Premises) Act 1990 .... **23**, 83
c 41 .... Courts and Legal Services Act 1990—
             ss 1, 8–11, 13, 15, 17, 18, 18A, 21–29, 31, 31A–31C,
             34–46, 46A, 46B, 47–53, 57–58B, 60, 61, 63, 66,
             69–76, 78, 79, 81, 89, 104–107, 115, 116, 119–125,
             Schs 3–8, 11, 14, 17–20 .... **11(3)**, 93
             ss 5, 113, 119(1), 120(1)–(3), (6), 123, 124, 125(1), (6),
             Sch 19, para 17 .... **18**, 304
             ss 54–56, 120, 124, 125, Sch 9 .... **18**, 696
c 42 .... Broadcasting Act 1990—
             ss 3–5, 13–19, 21, 22–24, 28, 29, 37, 40–42B, 48–56, 58,
             60–61A, 63, 64, 66–67, 71, 85–89, 97–106ZA,
             109–111B, 114–121, 126–133, 135–141, 177, 178,
             180, 183–185, 188, 193, 194A–196, 198–204, Sch 2,
             Pts I, II, Schs 3, 6, 7, 9, 10, 11, 19–22 .... **45**, 139
             ss 162, 167, 195, 201, 202, 204, Sch 15 .... **12(2)**, 58
             ss 166, 201, 202(1), (5), 204 .... **19(3)**, 393
             ss 176, 201, 202(1), (5), 204(1)–(3), Sch 17 .... **11(1)**, 1341
c 43 .... Environmental Protection Act 1990—
             ss 1–4, 6–15, 19–30, 33–40, 42–48, 51, 52, 52A, 55, 57,
             59, 59ZA, 59A, 60, 62A, 63A, 64–66, 71, 73–82, 84,
             106–127, 140–142, 144, 152–154, 156–164, Schs 1,
             2A, 2B, 3, 12, 15, 16 .... **35(1)**, 749
             ss 86–89, 91–99, 128–132, 134, 139, 157–164, Schs 3A,
             4, 6, 11 .... **32**, 635
             ss 149, 150, 159(1)–(6), 160, 161(1)–(4), 163,
             164(1) **2**, 596
c 44 .... Caldey Island Act 1990 .... **25(2)**, 1180
c 45 .... Import and Export Control Act 1990 .... **50**, 519
c vii .... London Local Authorities Act 1990 .... **25(2)**, 1182
c xxiv .... City of London (Various Powers) Act 1990 .... **25(2)**, 1223
c xxx .... London Local Authorities (No 2) Act 1990 .... **25(2)**, 1226
No 1 .... Clergy (Ordination) Measure 1990 .... **14**, 1192
No 2 .... Care of Cathedrals Measure 1990 .... **14**, 1193

1991

c 2 .... Caravans (Standard Community Charge and Rating) Act
             1991 .... **25(2)**, 1232
c 3 .... Statutory Sick Pay Act 1991 .... **40(1)**, 339
c 4 .... Namibia Act 1991 .... **7(2)**, 613
c 5 .... Ministerial and other Pensions and Salaries Act 1991—
             ss 1, 2, 4, 6, 8, 9 .... **33(1)**, 291
             ss 5, 8(2), (3), 9 .... **10**, 566
c 6 .... Census (Confidentiality) Act 1991 .... **36**, 136
c 11 .... Representation of the People Act 1991 .... **15(3)**, 410
c 12 .... Civil Jurisdiction and Judgments Act 1991 .... **11(3)**, 243
c 13 .... War Crimes Act 1991 .... **12(2)**, 69
c 14 .... Motor Vehicles (Safety Equipment for Children) Act
             1991 .... **38(1)**, 249
c 16 .... Oversea Superannuation Act 1991 .... **33(1)**, 296
c 17 .... Maintenance Enforcement Act 1991 .... **27**, 630
c 19 .... Football (Offences) Act 1991 .... **13**, 407
c 21 .... Disability Living Allowance and Disability Working
             Allowance Act 1991 .... **40(1)**, 342
c 22 .... New Roads and Street Works Act 1991 .... **38(1)**, 249
c 23 .... Children and Young Persons (Protection from Tobacco) Act
             1991 .... **6**, 673
c 25 .... Criminal Procedure (Insanity and Unfitness to Plead) Act
             1991 .... **12(2)**, 72
c 26 .... Road Traffic (Temporary Restrictions) Act 1991 .... **38(1)**, 387
c 27 .... Radioactive Material (Road Transport) Act 1991 .... **38(1)**, 389
c 29 .... Property Misdescriptions Act 1991 .... **23**, 84

1991—*contd*

c 30 .... Welfare of Animals at Slaughter Act 1991 .... **1(2)**, 568
c 31 .... Finance Act 1991—
               s 7 .... **19(3)**, 564
               ss 27, 48, 50–54, 58, 62–65, 71–73, 76, 78, 104–106,
               108, 121–124, Schs 7, 9, 11, 19 .... **42**, 1283
               ss 110–114, 116, 117, 122, 124 .... **41**, 275
c 33 .... Agriculture and Forestry (Financial Provisions) Act
               1991 .... **1(2)**, 569
c 34 .... Planning and Compensation Act 1991—
               ss 4, 10, 21, 22, 25, 27, 28, 31, 32, 66, 70, 81, 84,
               Schs 2, 4, 19 .... **46**, 1048
               ss 80, 82, 84, Sch 18 .... **9**, 463
c 38 .... Medical Qualifications (Amendment) Act 1991 .... **28**, 846
c 39 .... Wildlife and Countryside (Amendment) Act 1991 .... **32**, 701
c 40 .... Road Traffic Act 1991 .... **38(1)**, 397
c 41 .... Arms Control and Disarmament (Inspections) Act
               1991 .... **10**, 1096
c 43 .... Forestry Act 1991 .... **18**, 1183
c 44 .... Foreign Corporations Act 1991 .... **8**, 959
c 45 .... Coal Mining Subsidence Act 1991 .... **17(2)**, 1
c 46 .... Atomic Weapons Establishment Act 1991 .... **10**, 568
c 48 .... Child Support Act 1991 .... **6**, 679
c 52 .... Ports Act 1991 .... **39(2)**, 634
c 53 .... Criminal Justice Act 1991—
               ss 16, 17, 20A, 26, 30, 33, 33A, 34A, 35–39, 40A,
               41–47, 49–51, 53, 80–92, 95, 98–102, Schs 3, 6,
               10–13 .... **12(2)**, 76
               ss 24, 30, 99, 102 .... **11(3)**, 246
               ss 60, 61, 61A, 65, 68, 70, 71, 99, 101(1), 102, Sch 8,
               Sch 12, paras 15, 18, 19, 22–24 .... **6**, 827
c 54 .... Deer Act 1991 .... **2**, 605
c 56 .... Water Industry Act 1991 .... **49**, 699
c 57 .... Water Resources Act 1991 .... **49**, 1233
c 58 .... Statutory Water Companies Act 1991 .... **49**, 1587
c 59 .... Land Drainage Act 1991 .... **19(3)**, 230
c 60 .... Water Consolidation (Consequential Provisions) Act
               1991 .... **49**, 1604
c 61 .... Statute Law Revision (Isle of Man) Act 1991 .... **41**, 933
c 62 .... Armed Forces Act 1991 .... **3**, 1461
c 63 .... British Railways Board (Finance) Act 1991 .... **38(1)**, 412
c 64 .... Breeding of Dogs Act 1991 .... **2**, 624
c 65 .... Dangerous Dogs Act 1991 .... **2**, 627
c 66 .... British Technology Group Act 1991 .... **47**, 486
c 67 .... Export and Investment Guarantees Act 1991 .... **47**, 500
c xiii .... London Local Authorities Act 1991 .... **25(2)**, 1233
No 1 .... Care of Churches and Ecclesiastical Jurisdiction Measure
               1991 .... **14**, 1215
No 2 .... Diocesan Boards of Education Measure 1991 .... **14**, 1245

1992

c 4 .... Social Security Contributions and Benefits Act 1992 .... **40(1)**, 347
c 5 .... Social Security Administration Act 1992 .... **40(1)**, 796
c 6 .... Social Security (Consequential Provisions) Act 1992 .... **40(2)**, 2
c 11 .... Aggravated Vehicle-Taking Act 1992 .... **12(2)**, 174
c 12 .... Taxation of Chargeable Gains Act 1992 .... **42**, 1320
c 13 .... Further and Higher Education Act 1992 .... **15(1)**, 347
c 14 .... Local Government Finance Act 1992 .... **26(1)**, 2
c 15 .... Offshore Safety Act 1992—
               ss 1–3, 6, 7, Schs 1, 2 .... **18**, 1379
               ss 5–7 .... **17(2)**, 81
c 19 .... Local Government Act 1992 .... **26(1)**, 168
c 20 .... Finance Act 1992 .... **42**, 1920
c 23 .... Access to Neighbouring Land Act 1992 .... **23**, 91
c 25 .... Prison Security Act 1992 .... **12(2)**, 175
c 26 .... Tourism (Overseas Promotion) (Wales) Act 1992 .... **47**, 512

1992—*contd*

c 27.............. Parliamentary Corporate Bodies Act 1992 .... **32**, 1148
c 28.............. Medicinal Products: Prescription by Nurses etc Act
                  1992 .... **30**, 559
c 29.............. Still-Birth (Definition) Act 1992 .... **36**, 137
c 30.............. Traffic Calming Act 1992 .... **38(1)**, 413
c 31.............. Firearms (Amendment) Act 1992 .... **12(2)**, 177
c 32.............. Cheques Act 1992 .... **19(1)**, 907
c 33.............. Social Security (Mortgage Interest Payments) Act
                  1992 .... **40(2)**, 31
c 34.............. Sexual Offences (Amendment) Act 1992 .... **12(2)**, 178
c 35.............. Timeshare Act 1992 .... **11(1)**, 402
c 36.............. Sea Fisheries (Wildlife Conservation) Act 1992 .... **1(2)**, 576
c 39.............. Army Act 1992 .... **3**, 1487
c 40.............. Friendly Societies Act 1992 .... **19(1)**, 907
c 41.............. Charities Act 1992 .... **5(2)**, 544
c 42.............. Transport and Works Act 1992 .... **38(1)**, 414
c 43.............. Competition and Service (Utilities) Act 1992 .... **17(2)**, 84
c 44.............. Museums and Galleries Act 1992 .... **13**, 410
c 45.............. Mauritius Republic Act 1992 .... **7(2)**, 615
c 46.............. Non-Domestic Rating Act 1992 .... **26(1)**, 191
c 48.............. Finance (No 2) Act 1992—
                  ss 1, 2, 4, 83, Sch 1 .... **13**, 981
                  ss 20, 24, 28, 34, 40A–43, 55, 56, 62–66, 73–77, 81–83,
                  Schs 6, 9, 12, 14, 17, 18 .... **42**, 1921
c 49.............. Community Care (Residential Accommodation) Act
                  1992 .... **40(2)**, 33
c 50.............. Carriage of Goods by Sea Act 1992 .... **39(2)**, 686
c 51.............. Protection of Badgers Act 1992 .... **2**, 640
c 52.............. Trade Union and Labour Relations (Consolidation) Act
                  1992 .... **16**, 214
c 53.............. Tribunals and Inquiries Act 1992 .... **10**, 574
c 54.............. Human Fertilisation and Embryology (Disclosure of
                  Information) Act 1992 .... **28**, 847
c 55.............. Boundary Commissions Act 1992 .... **15(3)**, 412
c 56.............. Maintenance Orders (Reciprocal Enforcement) Act
                  1992 .... **27**, 636
c 60.............. Sea Fish (Conservation) Act 1992 .... **1(2)**, 578
c 61.............. Civil Service (Management Functions) Act 1992 .... **10**, 612
No 1.............. Church of England (Miscellaneous Provisions) Measure
                  1992 .... **14**, 1255

1993

c 1 .... Gas (Exempt Supplies) Act 1993 .... **17(2)**, 90
c 3 .... Social Security Act 1993 .... **40(2)**, 34
c 8 .... Judicial Pensions and Retirement Act 1993 .... **11(3)**, 253
c 9 .... Prisoners and Criminal Proceedings (Scotland) Act
                  1993 .... **12(2)**, 192
c 10.............. Charities Act 1993 .... **5(2)**, 580
c 11.............. Clean Air Act 1993 .... **35(2)**, 2
c 12.............. Radioactive Substances Act 1993 .... **17(2)**, 91
c 14.............. Disability Grants Act 1993 .... **40(2)**, 38
c 16.............. Foreign Compensation (Amendment) Act 1993 .... **10**, 1109
c 17.............. Non-Domestic Rating Act 1993 .... **26(1)**, 197
c 18.............. Reinsurance (Acts of Terrorism) Act 1993 .... **19(1)**, 1126
c 19.............. Trade Union Reform and Employment Rights Act
                  1993 .... **16**, 640
c 21.............. Osteopaths Act 1993 .... **28**, 848
c 23.............. Asylum and Immigration Appeals Act 1993 .... **31**, 276
c 24.............. Video Recordings Act 1993 .... **13**, 441
c 25.............. Local Government (Overseas Assistance) Act 1993 .... **26(1)**, 200
c 26.............. Bail (Amendment) Act 1993 .... **12(2)**, 220
c 27.............. Local Government (Amendment) Act 1993 .... **26(1)**, 203
c 28.............. Leasehold Reform, Housing and Urban Development Act
                  1993 .... **23**, 102
c 29.............. Representation of the People Act 1993 .... **15(3)**, 414

1993—*contd*

c 30.............. Sexual Offences Act 1993 .... **12(2)**, 223
c 31.............. Road Traffic (Driving Instruction by Disabled Persons) Act
                   1993 .... **38(1)**, 484
c 32.............. European Communities (Amendment) Act 1993 .... **18**, 83
c 34.............. Finance Act 1993—
                   ss 10, 12, 214 .... **13**, 989
                   ss 24–29, 31–35, 37, 38, 40, 41, 214 .... **5(1)**, 133
                   ss 72, 79, 80, 86–88, 91–92E, 97, 98, 101, 102, 112,
                      118–120, 122, 170–176, 178–180, 182, 184–187,
                      189–195, 212–214, Schs 9, 19–21, 23 .... **43(1)**, 2
                   ss 202, 204, 214 .... **41**, 282
c 36.............. Criminal Justice Act 1993—
                   ss 1–6, 23, 65, 70, 71, 73, 77, 78, 79, Sch 6 .... **12(2)**, 224
                   ss 52–64, 78(2)–(4), (10), 79(1), (2), (9)–(11), Schs 1,
                     2 .... **8**, 960
c 37.............. Agriculture Act 1993 .... **1(2)**, 581
c 38.............. Welsh Language Act 1993 .... **7(1)**, 319
c 39.............. National Lottery etc Act 1993 .... **5(1)**, 146
c 40.............. Noise and Statutory Nuisance Act 1993 .... **35(2)**, 80
c 43.............. Railways Act 1993 .... **38(1)**, 485
c 46.............. Health Service Commissioners Act 1993 .... **30**, 561
c 48.............. Pension Schemes Act 1993 .... **33(1)**, 297
c 50.............. Statute Law (Repeals) Act 1993 .... **41**, 936
c 51.............. European Economic Area Act 1993 .... **18**, 86
No 1............. Incumbents (Vacation of Benefices) (Amendment) Measure
                 1993 .... **14**, 1266
No 2............. Priests (Ordination of Women) Measure 1993 .... **14**, 1269
No 3............. Ordination of Women (Financial Provisions) Measure
                 1993 .... **14**, 1279

1994

c 1.............. Social Security (Contributions) Act 1994 .... **40(2)**, 40
c 2.............. Statutory Sick Pay Act 1994 .... **40(2)**, 42
c 3.............. Non-Domestic Rating Act 1994 .... **26(1)**, 204
c 5.............. New Towns (Amendment) Act 1994 .... **46**, 1140
c 7.............. Insolvency Act 1994 .... **4(2)**, 670
c 8.............. Transport Police (Jurisdiction) Act 1994 .... **38(1)**, 792
c 9.............. Finance Act 1994—
                   ss 7–27, 259, Sch 5 .... **13**, 993
                   ss 28–44, 259, Sch 6 .... **4(1)**, 523
                   ss 48–56, 59–74, 257, 259, Schs 6A, 7, 7A .... **19(1)**, 1128
                   ss 77, 81, 101–103, 108, 112, 113, 118, 119, 133, 137,
                      138, 142, 146, 196, 199, 209, 211, 215, 218–223,
                      225–234, 236–238, 248–253, 257–259, Schs 20, 22,
                      24–26 .... **43(1)**, 80
                   ss 240–245, 257, 259 .... **41**, 285
c 10.............. Race Relations (Remedies) Act 1994 .... **7(1)**, 347
c 11.............. Road Traffic Regulation (Special Events) Act 1994 .... **38(1)**, 793
c 12.............. Insolvency (No 2) Act 1994 .... **4(2)**, 672
c 13.............. Intelligence Services Act 1994 .... **10**, 615
c 14.............. Parliamentary Commissioner Act 1994 .... **10**, 631
c 15.............. Antarctic Act 1994 .... **10**, 1110
c 17.............. Chiropractors Act 1994 .... **28**, 913
c 18.............. Social Security (Incapacity for Work) Act 1994 .... **40(2)**, 44
c 19.............. Local Government (Wales) Act 1994 .... **26(1)**, 207
c 20.............. Sunday Trading Act 1994 .... **18**, 1387
c 21.............. Coal Industry Act 1994 .... **17(2)**, 157
c 22.............. Vehicle Excise and Registration Act 1994 .... **13**, 1034
c 23.............. Value Added Tax Act 1994 .... **50**, 6
c 25.............. Land Drainage Act 1994 .... **19(3)**, 346
c 26.............. Trade Marks Act 1994 .... **48**, 105
c 29.............. Police and Magistrates' Courts Act 1994 .... **33(2)**, 150
c 30.............. Education Act 1994 .... **15(1)**, 444
c 31.............. Firearms (Amendment) Act 1994 .... **12(2)**, 244
c 32.............. Sale of Goods (Amendment) Act 1994 .... **39(1)**, 681

        Enquiry Bureau   hsieb@lexisnexis.co.uk

1994—*contd*

c 33.............. Criminal Justice and Public Order Act 1994—
   ss 7–15, 25, 51, 60, 60AA, 60A, 61–69, 75–79, 100, 102,
    104–106, 112, 114, 117–128, 136–140, 146, 147,
    157, 163, 166–172, Schs 1, 2, 7, 9, 11 .... **12(2)**, 245
   ss 32, 34–39, 172 .... **18**, 312
   ss 80, 172 .... **32**, 702
c 34.............. Marriage Act 1994 .... **27**, 639
c 35.............. Sale and Supply of Goods Act 1994 .... **39(1)**, 682
c 36.............. Law of Property (Miscellaneous Provisions) Act 1994—
   ss 1–13, 20–24, Sch 2 .... **23**, 372
   ss 14, 17–20, 22–24 .... **18**, 708
c 37.............. Drug Trafficking Act 1994 .... **12(2)**, 350
c 38.............. European Union (Accessions) Act 1994 .... **18**, 92
c 40.............. Deregulation and Contracting Out Act 1994—
   ss 1, 6, 40, 80–82, Sch 17 .... **41**, 992
   ss 31, 40, 82, Sch 9 .... **1(2)**, 649
   ss 33, 40(1), (4), (6), 82 .... **35(2)**, 89
   ss 34, 40, 58, 82 .... **38(1)**, 794
   ss 37, 40, 82 .... **18**, 1402
   ss 69, 71–80, 82, Schs 15, 16 .... **10**, 632
   ss 70–73, 75, 77, 79, 79A–79C, 82, Sch 15 .... **26(1)**, 305
c xii.............. London Local Authorities Act 1994 .... **26(1)**, 323
No 1.............. Pastoral (Amendment) Measure 1994 .... **14**, 1289
No 2.............. Care of Cathedrals (Supplementary Provisions) Measure
   1994 .... **14**, 1291
No 3.............. Church of England (Legal Aid) Measure 1994 .... **14**, 1298

1995

c 3.............. South Africa Act 1995 .... **7(2)**, 617
c 4.............. Finance Act 1995—
   ss 4, 5, 163 .... **19(3)**, 566
   ss 14, 163 .... **5(1)**, 223
   ss 19, 163, Sch 4 .... **13**, 1174
   ss 26, 163 .... **50**, 398
   ss 42, 48, 51, 53–55, 58, 60, 67, 70–75, 79, 86, 87, 90,
    103, 107, 109, 110, 113, 116, 123, 125–128, 130,
    133, 135, 137, 139, 152–154, 161–163, Schs 6, 8, 10,
    18, 21–23, 25, 29 .... **43(1)**, 181
   ss 151, 152(1), (2)(b), (3)(c), (d), (j), (4)–(6), (7)(b), 161,
    163 .... **41**, 293
   ss 157, 163 .... **19(2)**, 1008
c 5.............. Building Societies (Joint Account Holders) Act 1995 .... **19(1)**, 1203
c 8.............. Agricultural Tenancies Act 1995 .... **23**, 388
c 10.............. Home Energy Conservation Act 1995 .... **17(2)**, 337
c 11.............. Proceeds of Crime Act 1995 .... **12(2)**, 370
c 12.............. Carers (Recognition and Services) Act 1995 .... **40(2)**, 59
c 13.............. Road Traffic (New Drivers) Act 1995 .... **38(1)**, 799
c 15.............. Activity Centres (Young Persons' Safety) Act 1995 .... **6**, 841
c 16.............. Prisoners (Return to Custody) Act 1995 .... **12(2)**, 372
c 17.............. Health Authorities Act 1995 .... **30**, 599
c 18.............. Jobseekers Act 1995 .... **40(2)**, 63
c 21.............. Merchant Shipping Act 1995 .... **39(2)**, 693
c 22.............. Shipping and Trading Interests (Protection) Act 1995 .... **39(2)**, 1124
c 23.............. Goods Vehicles (Licensing of Operators) Act 1995 .... **38(1)**, 821
c 24.............. Crown Agents Act 1995 .... **10**, 651
c 25.............. Environment Act 1995—
   ss 1–19, 37–56, 80–95, 107–125, Schs 1–5, 11, 18,
    20–24 .... **35(2)**, 92
   ss 61–66, 68–72, 74–79, 97–99, 115, 123–125,
    Schs 7–10 .... **32**, 706
   ss 96, 122, 125, Schs 13, 14 .... **46**, 1140
   ss 105, 124, 125, Sch 15 .... **1(2)**, 697

1995—*contd*

c 26 .... Pensions Act 1995—
                 ss 3, 4, 6–12, 14, 15, 22, 23, 25, 26, 27–30, 32–41, 47,
                     49–54, 62–76, 87–89, 91–94, 115–126, 135, 137,
                     145, 149, 151, 162, 163, 166, 168, 170, 172–181,
                     Sch 4, Pt 1, Sch 5, Sch 7, Pts I, III, IV .... **33(1)**, 568
                 ss 126, 128, 148, 177–181, Sch 4, Sch 7, Pt II .... **40(2)**, 137
c 27 .... Geneva Conventions (Amendment) Act 1995 .... **10**, 1137
c 28 .... Sale of Goods (Amendment) Act 1995 .... **39(1)**, 685
c 30 .... Landlord and Tenant (Covenants) Act 1995 .... **23**, 431
c 31 .... National Health Service (Amendment) Act 1995 .... **30**, 620
c 32 .... Olympic Symbol etc (Protection) Act 1995 .... **48**, 199
c 34 .... Child Support Act 1995 .... **6**, 846
c 35 .... Criminal Appeal Act 1995 .... **12(2)**, 374
c 36 .... Children (Scotland) Act 1995 .... **6**, 857
c 37 .... Atomic Energy Authority Act 1995 .... **17(2)**, 344
c 38 .... Civil Evidence Act 1995 .... **18**, 326
c 39 .... Criminal Law (Consolidation) (Scotland) Act 1995 .... **12(2)**, 408
c 40 .... Criminal Procedure (Consequential Provisions) (Scotland)
                 Act 1995 .... **12(2)**, 413
c 41 .... Law Reform (Succession) Act 1995 .... **18**, 714
c 42 .... Private International Law (Miscellaneous Provisions) Act
                 1995—
                 ss 5, 6, 8, 16–19 .... **27**, 640
                 ss 9–16, 18, 19 .... **45**, 1587
c 43 .... Proceeds of Crime (Scotland) Act 1995 .... **12(2)**, 422
c 44 .... Statute Law (Repeals) Act 1995 .... **41**, 1007
c 45 .... Gas Act 1995 .... **17(2)**, 345
c 46 .... Criminal Procedure (Scotland) Act 1995 .... **12(2)**, 458
c 48 .... Charities (Amendment) Act 1995 .... **5(2)**, 836
c 49 .... Town and Country Planning (Costs of Inquiries etc) Act
                 1995 .... **46**, 1172
c 50 .... Disability Discrimination Act 1995 .... **7(1)**, 348
c 51 .... Medical (Professional Performance) Act 1995 .... **28**, 977
c 52 .... Mental Health (Patients in the Community) Act 1995 .... **29**, 291
c 53 .... Criminal Injuries Compensation Act 1995 .... **12(2)**, 492
c i .... British Waterways Act 1995 .... **38(1)**, 915
c x .... London Local Authorities Act 1995 .... **26(1)**, 327
No 1 .... Team and Group Ministries Measure 1995 .... **14**, 1305
No 2 .... Church of England (Miscellaneous Provisions) Measure
                 1995 .... **14**, 1308

1996

c 2 .... Hong Kong (Overseas Public Servants) Act 1996 .... **33(1)**, 720
c 3 .... Wild Mammals (Protection) Act 1996 .... **2**, 653
c 5 .... Health Service Commissioners (Amendment) Act
                 1996 .... **30**, 623
c 6 .... Chemical Weapons Act 1996 .... **12(2)**, 508
c 8 .... Finance Act 1996—
                 ss 17, 197, 206 .... **13**, 1181
                 ss 25, 26, 197, 206 .... **50**, 401
                 ss 39–71, 204, 206, Sch 5 .... **35(2)**, 295
                 ss 72, 73, 79–84A, 85A, 85B, 87–88A, 90A, 91A–91G,
                     94–101, 103–105, 116, 132–138, 148, 151, 153, 154,
                     156, 160, 163–166, 168, 175, 182, 198–206,
                     Schs 7–11, 14, 15, 18, 31, 37, 41 .... **43(1)**, 262
                 ss 186, 206 .... **41**, 300
                 ss 197(1), (2)(a), (3)–(5), (7), 206 .... **4(1)**, 550
c 9 .... Education (Student Loans) Act 1996 .... **15(1)**, 459
c 12 .... Rating (Caravans and Boats) Act 1996 .... **26(1)**, 356
c 13 .... Non-Domestic Rating (Information) Act 1996 .... **26(1)**, 358
c 14 .... Reserve Forces Act 1996 .... **3**, 1490
c 15 .... National Health Service (Residual Liabilities) Act
                 1996 .... **30**, 626
c 16 .... Police Act 1996 .... **33(2)**, 168
c 17 .... Employment Tribunals Act 1996 .... **16**, 655

1996—*contd*

c 18 .... Employment Rights Act 1996 .... **16**, 732
c 19 .... Law Reform (Year and a Day Rule) Act 1996 .... **12(2)**, 546
c 23 .... Arbitration Act 1996 .... **2**, 812
c 24 .... Treasure Act 1996 .... **32**, 764
c 25 .... Criminal Procedure and Investigations Act 1996—
         ss 1–6, 6A–6E, 7A, 8, 10–43, 45, 47, 54–61, 71, 72,
          74–81, Schs 1, 4, 5 .... **12(2)**, 549
         ss 68, 77, 79, 81, Sch 2 .... **11(3)**, 330
c 26 .... Offensive Weapons Act 1996 .... **12(2)**, 638
c 27 .... Family Law Act 1996 .... **27**, 645
c 29 .... Sexual Offences (Conspiracy and Incitement) Act
         1996 .... **12(2)**, 639
c 30 .... Community Care (Direct Payments) Act 1996 .... **40(2)**, 153
c 31 .... Defamation Act 1996 .... **19(3)**, 398
c 32 .... Trading Schemes Act 1996 .... **47**, 529
c 33 .... Prisoners' Earnings Act 1996 .... **12(2)**, 644
c 34 .... Marriage Ceremony (Prescribed Words) Act 1996 .... **27**, 767
c 35 .... Security Service Act 1996 .... **10**, 665
c 37 .... Noise Act 1996 .... **35(2)**, 367
c 38 .... Energy Conservation Act 1996 .... **17(2)**, 377
c 39 .... Civil Aviation (Amendment) Act 1996 .... **4(1)**, 552
c 40 .... Party Wall etc Act 1996 .... **35(2)**, 387
c 41 .... Hong Kong (War Wives and Widows) Act 1996 .... **31**, 280
c 42 .... Railway Heritage Act 1996 .... **38(1)**, 950
c 46 .... Armed Forces Act 1996 .... **3**, 1631
c 47 .... Trusts of Land and Appointment of Trustees Act 1996—
         ss 1–18, 22–27, Schs 1, 2, 4 .... **23**, 478
         ss 19–24, 26, 27 .... **48**, 604
c 48 .... Damages Act 1996 .... **13**, 1273
c 49 .... Asylum and Immigration Act 1996 .... **31**, 281
c 50 .... Nursery Education and Grant-Maintained Schools Act
         1996 .... **15(1)**, 461
c 51 .... Social Security (Overpayments) Act 1996 .... **40(2)**, 154
c 52 .... Housing Act 1996 .... **23**, 513
c 53 .... Housing Grants, Construction and Regeneration Act
         1996—
         ss 1–3, 19–24, 29–31, 33–44, 51, 52, 55–59, 92–95,
          98–103, 146–151, Sch 3 .... **23**, 802
         ss 104–117, 146, 148–151 .... **11(1)**, 431
         ss 126–128, 147, 148, 150, 151, Sch 3, Pt III **46**, 1178
c 54 .... Statutory Instruments (Production and Sale) Act 1996 .... **41**, 1049
c 55 .... Broadcasting Act 1996 .... **45**, 349
c 56 .... Education Act 1996 .... **15(1)**, 470
c 61 .... Channel Tunnel Rail Link Act 1996 .... **38(1)**, 956
c 62 .... Theft (Amendment) Act 1996 .... **12(2)**, 648
c 63 .... Hong Kong Economic and Trade Office Act 1996 .... **10**, 1138
c ix .... London Local Authorities Act 1996 .... **26(1)**, 359

1997

c 1 .... Horserace Totalisator Board Act 1997 .... **5(1)**, 224
c 2 .... Land Registration Act 1997 .... **23**, 854
c 3 .... Sea Fisheries (Shellfish) (Amendment) Act 1997 .... **1(2)**, 706
c 5 .... Firearms (Amendment) Act 1997 .... **12(2)**, 649
c 7 .... Northern Ireland Arms Decommissioning Act 1997 .... **31**, 1177
c 8 .... Town and Country Planning (Scotland) Act 1997 .... **46**, 1183
c 11 .... Planning (Consequential Provisions) (Scotland) Act
         1997 .... **46**, 1197
c 12 .... Civil Procedure Act 1997 .... **11(3)**, 335
c 13 .... United Nations Personnel Act 1997 .... **10**, 1142
c 14 .... National Heritage Act 1997 .... **13**, 442
c 16 .... Finance Act 1997—
         s 3 .... **19(3)**, 571
         ss 10–15, 113, 114, Sch 1, Sch 18, Pt II .... **5(1)**, 225
         ss 24, 29, 61, 69, 74–76, 79, 80, 82, 83, 85, 87, 89, 110,
          112–114, Schs 10, 12, 13, 18 .... **43(1)**, 444

1997—*contd*

    c 16 .... Finance Act 1997—*contd*
                      ss 47, 49, 114 .... **50**, 403
                      ss 50, 51, 110, 114, Sch 5, Pts I, V **13**, 1185
                      ss 95, 96, 100, 101, 112, 114 .... **41**, 302
    c 17 .... Criminal Evidence (Amendment) Act 1997 .... **12(2)**, 671
    c 20 .... British Nationality (Hong Kong) Act 1997 .... **31**, 289
    c 21 .... Knives Act 1997 .... **12(2)**, 677
    c 22 .... Architects Act 1997 .... **2**, 912
    c 23 .... Lieutenancies Act 1997 .... **26(1)**, 383
    c 27 .... Social Security (Recovery of Benefits) Act 1997 .... **40(2)**, 156
    c 28 .... Merchant Shipping and Maritime Security Act 1997 .... **39(2)**, 1135
    c 29 .... Local Government and Rating Act 1997 .... **26(1)**, 395
    c 30 .... Police (Property) Act 1997 .... **33(2)**, 304
    c 32 .... Building Societies Act 1997 .... **19(1)**, 1204
    c 33 .... Confiscation of Alcohol (Young Persons) Act 1997 .... **6**, 886
    c 37 .... Welsh Development Agency Act 1997 .... **47**, 530
    c 38 .... Prisons (Alcohol Testing) Act 1997 .... **12(2)**, 686
    c 39 .... Sexual Offences (Protected Material) Act 1997 .... **12(2)**, 686
    c 40 .... Protection from Harassment Act 1997 .... **12(2)**, 700
    c 41 .... Building Societies (Distributions) Act 1997 .... **19(1)**, 1221
    c 42 .... Police (Health and Safety) Act 1997 .... **33(2)**, 305
    c 43 .... Crime (Sentences) Act 1997—
                      ss 28, 30–32, 34, 35, 40–42, 53–57, Schs 1, 2, 4–6 .... **12(2)**, 712
                      ss 47, 48, 54, 57 .... **29**, 293
    c 44 .... Education Act 1997 .... **15(1)**, 780
    c 45 .... Police (Insurance of Voluntary Assistants) Act 1997 .... **33(2)**, 308
    c 46 .... National Health Service (Primary Care) Act 1997 .... **30**, 627
    c 47 .... Social Security Administration (Fraud) Act 1997 .... **40(2)**, 193
    c 48 .... Crime and Punishment (Scotland) Act 1997 .... **12(2)**, 761
    c 50 .... Police Act 1997 .... **33(2)**, 309
    c 52 .... Police and Firemen's Pensions Act 1997 .... **18**, 1028
    c 53 .... Dangerous Dogs (Amendment) Act 1997 .... **2**, 656
    c 54 .... Road Traffic Reduction Act 1997 .... **38(2)**, 2
    c 55 .... Birds (Registration Charges) Act 1997 .... **32**, 775
    c 56 .... National Health Service (Private Finance) Act 1997 .... **30**, 641
    c 58 .... Finance (No 2) Act 1997 .... **43(1)**, 496
    c 59 .... Education (Schools) Act 1997 .... **15(1)**, 834
    c 60 .... Law Officers Act 1997 .... **10**, 666
    c 61 .... Referendums (Scotland and Wales) Act 1997 .... **10**, 1256
    c 62 .... Ministerial and other Salaries Act 1997 .... **10**, 669
    c 64 .... Firearms (Amendment) (No 2) Act 1997 .... **12(2)**, 773
    c 65 .... Local Government (Contracts) Act 1997 .... **26(1)**, 405
    c 66 .... Plant Varieties Act 1997 .... **1(2)**, 706
    c 68 .... Special Immigration Appeals Commission Act 1997 .... **31**, 293
    No 1 .... Pensions Measure 1997 .... **14**, 1312

1998

    c 1 .... Education (Student Loans) Act 1998 .... **15(1)**, 841
    c 2 .... Public Processions (Northern Ireland) Act 1998 .... **31**, 1187
    c 3 .... Greater London Authority (Referendum) Act 1998 .... **26(1)**, 416
    c 7 .... Nuclear Explosions (Prohibition and Inspections) Act
                      1998 .... **12(2)**, 775
    c 8 .... Employment Rights (Dispute Resolution) Act 1998 .... **16**, 1081
    c 11 .... Bank of England Act 1998 .... **19(1)**, 1222
    c 13 .... Animal Health (Amendment) Act 1998 .... **2**, 658
    c 14 .... Social Security Act 1998 .... **40(2)**, 199
    c 15 .... Magistrates' Courts (Procedure) Act 1998 .... **11(3)**, 350
    c 17 .... Petroleum Act 1998 .... **17(2)**, 378
    c 18 .... Audit Commission Act 1998 .... **26(1)**, 425
    c 19 .... Community Care (Residential Accommodation) Act
                      1998 .... **40(2)**, 343
    c 20 .... Late Payment of Commercial Debts (Interest) Act
                      1998 .... **11(1)**, 448
    c 21 .... European Communities (Amendment) Act 1998 .... **18**, 93
    c 22 .... National Lottery Act 1998 .... **5(1)**, 245

1998—*contd*

c 23 . . . . Public Interest Disclosure Act 1998 . . . . **16**, 1089
c 24 . . . . Road Traffic Reduction (National Targets) Act 1998 . . . . **38(2)**, 5
c 26 . . . . Pesticides Act 1998 . . . . **1(2)**, 754
c 27 . . . . Criminal Justice (International Co-operation) (Amendment)
                      Act 1998 . . . . **28**, 981
c 29 . . . . Data Protection Act 1998 . . . . **7(1)**, 608
c 30 . . . . Teaching and Higher Education Act 1998 . . . . **15(1)**, 845
c 31 . . . . School Standards and Framework Act 1998 . . . . **15(2)**, 2
c 32 . . . . Police (Northern Ireland) Act 1998 . . . . **31**, 1217
c 33 . . . . Landmines Act 1998 . . . . **12(2)**, 788
c 34 . . . . Private Hire Vehicles (London) Act 1998 . . . . **38(2)**, 8
c 35 . . . . Northern Ireland (Sentences) Act 1998 . . . . **31**, 1227
c 36 . . . . Finance Act 1998—
                      ss 5, 165, 166, Sch 27, Pt 1 . . . . **19(3)**, 572
                      ss 6, 20, 166, Sch 2 . . . . **13**, 1198
                      ss 30–32, 35, 36, 38, 41, 42, 46, 48, 56, 57, 62, 70, 72,
                        74, 76, 86, 90, 92, 108, 110, 111, 113, 117, 118,
                        121–125, 130–132, 137, 140, 142, 146, 155–158,
                        160, 161, 163–166, Sch 3, Sch 5, Pt 4, Schs, 8, 11,
                        14, 15, 17, 18, 22, 23, 25–27 . . . . **43(1)**, 549
                      ss 150, 166 . . . . **41**, 310
                      ss 153, 165, 166, Sch 27, Pt V(3) . . . . **17(2)**, 481
c 37 . . . . Crime and Disorder Act 1998—
                      ss 1, 1A–1K, 4–7, 17, 17A, 18, 28–32, 34, 37–42,
                        57A–57E, 94, 106, 109, 111, 114–121, Schs 2,
                        8–10 . . . . **12(2)**, 816
                      ss 8–16, 18, 47, 65, 66, 98, 114, 117, 121 . . . . **6**, 889
                      ss 49, 50, 50A, 51, 51A–51E, 52, 52A, 52B, 114, 117,
                        121, Sch 3 . . . . **11(3)**, 352
c 38 . . . . Government of Wales Act 1998 . . . . **10**, 1291
c 39 . . . . National Minimum Wage Act 1998 . . . . **16**, 1090
c 40 . . . . Criminal Justice (Terrorism and Conspiracy) Act 1998 . . . . **12(2)**, 920
c 41 . . . . Competition Act 1998 . . . . **47**, 531
c 42 . . . . Human Rights Act 1998 . . . . **7(1)**, 743
c 43 . . . . Statute Law (Repeals) Act 1998 . . . . **41**, 1050
c 44 . . . . Waste Minimisation Act 1998 . . . . **35(2)**, 411
c 45 . . . . Regional Development Agencies Act 1998 . . . . **46**, 1210
c 46 . . . . Scotland Act 1998 . . . . **10**, 1360
c 47 . . . . Northern Ireland Act 1998 . . . . **31**, 1248
c 48 . . . . Registration of Political Parties Act 1998 . . . . **15(3)**, 415
No 1 . . . . National Institutions Measure 1998 . . . . **14**, 1322

1999

c 2 . . . . Social Security Contributions (Transfer of Functions, etc)
                      Act 1999 . . . . **40(2)**, 344
c 6 . . . . Rating (Valuation) Act 1999 . . . . **26(1)**, 523
c 7 . . . . Northern Ireland (Location of Victims' Remains) Act
                      1999 . . . . **31**, 1427
c 8 . . . . Health Act 1999
                      ss 13, 16, 44, 61–69, Sch 5 . . . . **30**, 642
                      ss 60, 62, 64, 67–69, Sch 3 . . . . **28**, 982
c 9 . . . . Water Industry Act 1999 . . . . **49**, 1631
c 11 . . . . Breeding and Sale of Dogs (Welfare) Act 1999 . . . . **2**, 659
c 12 . . . . Road Traffic (Vehicle Testing) Act 1999 . . . . **38(2)**, 48
c 14 . . . . Protection of Children Act 1999 . . . . **6**, 924
c 15 . . . . Trustee Delegation Act 1999 . . . . **48**, 610
c 16 . . . . Finance Act 1999—
                      ss 9, 11, 126–129, 131, 140, Sch 1 . . . . **13**, 1202
                      ss 13, 140, Sch 2 . . . . **50**, 407
                      ss 28, 31, 32, 34, 36, 38, 41, 46, 52–54, 56, 63, 65, 66,
                        68, 72–74, 79, 81–83, 85–87, 93–98, 125, 131–133,
                        138–140, Schs 5, 6, 10, 20 . . . . **43(1)**, 689
                      ss 110, 112–115, 119, 121–123, 138, 140,
                        Schs 13–19 . . . . **41**, 312
                      ss 135, 136, 140 . . . . **19(2)**, 1011

1999—*contd*

c 18............. Adoption (Intercountry Aspects) Act 1999 .... **6**, 950
c 19............. Company and Business Names (Chamber of Commerce,
                  Etc) Act 1999 .... **48**, 212
c 20............. Commonwealth Development Corporation Act 1999 .... **7**(2), 618
c 21............. Football (Offences and Disorder) Act 1999 .... **13**, 443
c 22............. Access to Justice Act 1999 .... **11**(3), 391
c 23............. Youth Justice and Criminal Evidence Act 1999 .... **18**, 340
c 24............. Pollution Prevention and Control Act 1999 .... **35**(2), 412
c 25............. Criminal Cases Review (Insanity) Act 1999 .... **12**(2), 923
c 26............. Employment Relations Act 1999 .... **16**, 1156
c 27............. Local Government Act 1999 .... **26**(1), 525
c 28............. Food Standards Act 1999 .... **1**(2), 755
c 29............. Greater London Authority Act 1999 .... **26**(1), 576
c 30............. Welfare Reform and Pensions Act 1999—
                  ss 1–3, 6–8, 11, 12, 18, 19, 21, 23–31, 33–35, 38, 40–46,
                  83–91, Schs 1, 5, 13 .... **33**(1), 722
                  ss 47–52, 60, 68, 72, 79, 81, 82, 83(1), (2), (4)–(11),
                  84(2)–(4), 85(6), (7), 86, 87, 89–91, Sch 8, Pt VIII,
                  Sch 11 .... **40**(2), 389
c 31............. Contracts (Rights of Third Parties) Act 1999 .... **11**(1), 462
c 33............. Immigration and Asylum Act 1999 .... **31**, 304
c 34............. House of Lords Act 1999 .... **32**, 1154
No 1............. Cathedrals Measure 1999 .... **14**, 1337
No 2............. Care of Places of Worship Measure 1999 .... **14**, 1366

2000

c 1............. Northern Ireland Act 2000 .... **31**, 1431
c 2............. Representation of the People Act 2000 .... **15**(3), 417
c 4............. Armed Forces Discipline Act 2000 .... **3**, 1655
c 5............. Nuclear Safeguards Act 2000 .... **17**(2), 484
c 6............. Powers of Criminal Courts (Sentencing) Act 2000 .... **12**(2), 926
c 7............. Electronic Communications Act 2000 .... **45**, 525
c 8............. Financial Services and Markets Act 2000 .... **19**(2), 3
c 10............. Crown Prosecution Service Inspectorate Act 2000 .... **12**(2), 1215
c 11............. Terrorism Act 2000—
                  entire Act .... **12**(2), 1221
                  ss 2, 60, 65–75, 77–96, 98, 99, 101–113, 117, 118,
                  120A, 121, 123, 125, 127–131, Schs 1, 9–13,
                  16 .... **31**, 1447
c 12............. Limited Liability Partnerships Act 2000 .... **32**, 1227
c 13............. Royal Parks (Trading) Act 2000 .... **32**, 777
c 14............. Care Standards Act 2000—
                  ss 1–5, 5A, 5B, 8, 10–38, 42, 54–71, 80–93, 111,
                  113–115, 117–123, Sch 1, Sch 5, paras 1, 2,
                  Sch 6 .... **35**(2), 430
                  ss 43, 45, 48–50, 52, 53, 72–79, 103, 114–123, Schs 2,
                  2A, 2B, 4–6 .... **6**, 968
c 15............. Television Licences (Disclosure of Information) Act
                  2000 .... **45**, 536
c 16............. Carers and Disabled Children Act 2000 .... **40**(2), 420
c 17............. Finance Act 2000—
                  ss 20, 23, 157, Sch 4 .... **13**, 1211
                  ss 30, 155, 157, Sch 6 .... **35**(2), 574
                  ss 38–41, 44, 46, 48–50, 54, 61, 63–65, 68, 69, 74, 82,
                  91, 92, 97, 98, 102–105, 107, 108, 143, 144,
                  146–149, 152, 155–157, Sch 12, Pt 3, Schs 13, 15,
                  Sch 17, Pts 2, 3, Sch 19, Pt 2, Schs 20, 22, Sch 27,
                  Pt 1, Schs 28–31, 38, 40 .... **43**(1), 752
                  ss 118–122, 128–131, 155, 157, Schs 32–34 .... **41**, 352
                  ss 153, 157 .... **19**(2), 1013
c 18............. Sea Fishing Grants (Charges) Act 2000 .... **1**(2), 812
c 19............. Child Support, Pensions and Social Security Act 2000—
                  ss 26–29, 83–87, Schs 3, 8, Sch 9, Pts I, IX **6**, 1024
                  ss 30, 33, 36, 38, 42, 62–65, 69, 70, 74, 75, 78, 79,
                  84–87, Sch 7, Sch 9, Pts II, V–VIII .... **40**(2), 430

2000—*contd*

c 19............. Child Support, Pensions and Social Security Act
                  2000—*contd*
                  ss 52, 56, 58, 84–87, Sch 5, Pt II, Sch 9, Pts III, IV .... **33(1)**, 805
c 20............. Government Resources and Accounts Act 2000 .... **19(2)**, 1015
c 21............. Learning and Skills Act 2000 .... **15(2)**, 389
c 22............. Local Government Act 2000 .... **26(2)**, 2
c 23............. Regulation of Investigatory Powers Act 2000 .... **45**, 540
c 24............. Census (Amendment) Act 2000 .... **36**, 138
c 25............. Football (Disorder) Act 2000 .... **13**, 445
c 26............. Postal Services Act 2000 .... **34**, 589
c 27............. Utilities Act 2000 .... **17(2)**, 501
c 28............. Health Service Commissioners (Amendment) Act
                  2000 .... **30**, 675
c 29............. Trustee Act 2000 .... **48**, 619
c 31............. Warm Homes and Energy Conservation Act 2000 .... **17(2)**, 565
c 32............. Police (Northern Ireland) Act 2000 .... **31**, 1519
c 33............. Fur Farming (Prohibition) Act 2000 .... **2**, 665
c 34............. Race Relations (Amendment) Act 2000 .... **7(1)**, 789
c 35............. Children (Leaving Care) Act 2000 .... **6**, 1044
c 36............. Freedom of Information Act 2000 .... **7(1)**, 793
c 37............. Countryside and Rights of Way Act 2000—
                  ss 1–12, 14–46, 75, 76, 82–95, 99–104, Schs 1–3, 11, 13,
                  14, 15, Pt II, 16 .... **32**, 781
                  ss 47–50, 52–62, 71, 72, 99, 100, 103, 104, Sch 6,
                  Pt I .... **38(2)**, 51
c 38............. Transport Act 2000—
                  ss 1–107, 273–280, Schs 1, 2, 5–7, 9, Sch 31, Pt I .... **4(1)**, 553
                  ss 108–109C, 112–141, 143, 144, 145A–150, 153–155,
                  157, 160–199, 215, 227, 240, 241, 244, 247, 248,
                  250, 253, 254, 260, 263, 268, 272–280, Schs 10, 12,
                  25, 26, 28, 29, 31 .... **38(2)**, 91
c 39............. Insolvency Act 2000 .... **4(2)**, 673
c 41............. Political Parties, Elections and Referendums Act 2000 .... **15(3)**, 445
c 42............. Disqualifications Act 2000 .... **32**, 1159
c 43............. Criminal Justice and Court Services Act 2000—
                  ss 1–8, 10, 18, 20–23, 25, 43–45, 59–62, 64, 70, 71,
                  74–82, Schs 1, 1A, 6–8 .... **12(2)**, 1395
                  ss 11–16, 18–21, 23–38, 42, 76–82, Schs 2–4 .... **6**, 1048
c 44............. Sexual Offences (Amendment) Act 2000 .... **12(2)**, 1469
c vii............. London Local Authorities Act 2000 .... **26(2)**, 210
No 1............. Church of England (Miscellaneous Provisions) Measure
                  2000 .... **14**, 1373

2001

c 2............. Capital Allowances Act 2001 .... **43(1)**, 947
c 3............. Vehicles (Crime) Act 2001 .... **47**, 690
c 4............. Criminal Defence Service (Advice and Assistance) Act
                  2001 .... **11(3)**, 502
c 5............. Election Publications Act 2001 .... **15(3)**, 812
c 6............. Regulatory Reform Act 2001 .... **41**, 1088
c 7............. Elections Act 2001 .... **15(3)**, 814
c 9............. Finance Act 2001—
                  ss 8, 12, 13, 15, 111, Sch 3 .... **13**, 1218
                  ss 16–48, 51, 57, 59, 63–71, 76, 78, 81, 83, 87, 88, 95,
                  101, 102, 109–111, Schs 4–10, Sch 15, Pt 3, Schs 16,
                  17, 20, 22, 27, 32, 33 .... **43(2)**, 2
                  ss 92, 92A, 92B, 94, 109, 111, Sch 30 .... **41**, 373
                  ss 99, 111 .... **50**, 411
                  ss 107, 111 .... **10**, 669
c 10............. Special Educational Needs and Disability Act 2001 .... **15(2)**, 528
c 11............. Social Security Fraud Act 2001 .... **40(2)**, 489
c 12............. Private Security Industry Act 2001 .... **47**, 742
c 13............. House of Commons (Removal of Clergy Disqualification)
                  Act 2001 .... **32**, 1160

2001—*contd*

c 14.............. Rating (Former Agricultural Premises and Rural Shops) Act
2001 .... **26(2)**, 245
c 15.............. Health and Social Care Act 2001—
ss 14, 39, 63–70, Sch 5, Pt 1, Sch 6, Pts 1, 2 .... **30**, 676
ss 49–52, 54–57, 59, 64–70, Sch 5, Pt 2, Sch 6,
Pt 3 .... **40(2)**, 506
c 16.............. Criminal Justice and Police Act 2001—
ss 1–16, 33–37, 39–42A, 45–47, 50–70, 78, 80, 82, 86,
130, 135–138, Schs 1, 2, 7 .... **12(3)**, 1
ss 19–28, 138 .... **19(3)**, 575
ss 97, 98, 100, 101, 103, 127, 136, 138 .... **33(2)**, 379
c 17.............. International Criminal Court Act 2001 .... **10**, 1148
c 18.............. Children's Commissioner for Wales Act 2001 .... **6**, 1091
c 19.............. Armed Forces Act 2001 .... **3**, 1660
c 20.............. Social Security Contributions (Share Options) Act
2001 .... **40(2)**, 531
c 23.............. Human Reproductive Cloning Act 2001 .... **28**, 994
c 24.............. Anti-terrorism, Crime and Security Act 2001 .... **12(3)**, 114
No 1............. Churchwardens Measure 2001 .... **14**, 1381

2002

c 1............... International Development Act 2002—
ss 1–10, 16–20, Schs 1, 3–5 .... **7(2)**, 646
ss 5–7, 11, 12, 16–18, 20, Sch 5 .... **19(2)**, 1042
ss 5–7, 13, 14, 16–18, 20, Sch 2 .... **15(2)**, 541
c 2............... Sex Discrimination (Election Candidates) Act 2002 .... **7(1)**, 918
c 3............... European Communities (Amendment) Act 2002 .... **18**, 94
c 4............... Travel Concessions (Eligibility) Act 2002 .... **38(2)**, 342
c 6............... Northern Ireland Arms Decommissioning (Amendment)
Act 2002 .... **31**, 1525
c 7............... Homelessness Act 2002 .... **23**, 857
c 8............... British Overseas Territories Act 2002 .... **31**, 506
c 9............... Land Registration Act 2002 .... **23**, 869
c 11.............. Office of Communications Act 2002 .... **45**, 703
c 13.............. Electoral Fraud (Northern Ireland) Act 2002 .... **15(3)**, 817
c 14.............. National Heritage Act 2002 .... **32**, 892
c 15.............. Commonhold and Leasehold Reform Act 2002 .... **24**, 1
c 16.............. State Pension Credit Act 2002 .... **40(2)**, 541
c 17.............. National Health Service Reform and Health Care
Professions Act 2002—
entire Act **28**, 996
ss 2, 4, 19, 22, 37–42, Sch 2, Pt 2, Schs 8, 9 .... **30**, 703
c 19.............. National Insurance Contributions Act 2002 .... **40(2)**, 570
c 20.............. Industrial and Provident Societies Act 2002 .... **19(2)**, 595
c 21.............. Tax Credits 2002 .... **40(2)**, 575
c 22.............. Employment Act 2002—
ss 7, 8, 10–16, 48, 51, 52, 55, Sch 1 .... **40(2)**, 671
ss 28, 38, 40, 44–46, 51–55, Schs 5, 7, 8 .... **16**, 1189
c 23.............. Finance Act 2002—
ss 5, 6, 19, 20, 143, Sch 2 .... **13**, 1229
ss 12, 141, 143, Sch 4, Pt 2, Sch 40, Pt 1 .... **5(1)**, 266
ss 26–32, 40, 43–45, 47, 48, 50, 51, 53–59, 61, 63–66,
71, 79–86, 93, 98, 99, 109, 134–143, Sch 9, Pt 3,
Schs 10–13, 16, 18, 22, Sch 23, Pt 3, Sch 25, Pt 3,
Schs 26, 28, 29, 33, 39, 40 .... **43(2)**, 135
ss 110–113, 115, 116, 142, 143, Schs 34–37 .... **41**, 381
c 24.............. European Parliamentary Elections Act 2002 .... **15(3)**, 821
c 25.............. Copyright etc, and Trade Marks (Offences and
Enforcement) Act 2002 .... **11(1)**, 1349
c 26.............. Justice (Northern Ireland) Act 2002 .... **31**, 1526
c 27.............. Divorce (Religious Marriages) Act 2002 .... **27**, 768
c 28.............. Export Control Act 2002 .... **50**, 519
c 29.............. Proceeds of Crime Act 2002 .... **12(3)**, 217
c 30.............. Police Reform Act 2002 .... **33(2)**, 386
c 31.............. Mobile Telephones (Re-programming) Act 2002 .... **12(3)**, 624

2002—*contd*

c 32............. Education Act 2002 .... **15(2)**, 549
c 33............. Copyright (Visually Impaired Persons) Act 2002 .... **11(1)**, 1352
c 35............. Public Trustee (Liability and Fees) Act 2002 .... **48(S)**, Trusts 1
c 36............. Tobacco Advertising and Promotion Act 2002 .... **47**, 783
c 37............. Private Hire Vehicles (Carriage of Guide Dogs etc) Act
                  2002 .... **7(1)**, 920
c 38............. Adoption and Children Act 2002 .... **6**, 1092
c 39............. Commonwealth Act 2002 .... **7(2)**, 660
c 40............. Enterprise Act 2002—
                  ss 1–247, 273–281, Schs 1–15, 24–26 .... **47**, 803
                  ss 248, 249, 254–257, 261, 264, 266, 268, 270, 276, 277,
                  279–281, Schs 17, 19, 21 .... **4(2)**, 688
c 41............. Nationality, Immigration and Asylum Act 2002 .... **31**, 511
c 42............. Animal Health Act 2002 .... **2**, 671
c vi............. City of London (Ward Elections) Act 2002 .... **26(2)**, 247

2003

c 1............. Income Tax (Earnings and Pensions) Act 2003 .... **44(2)**, 2
c 3............. Northern Ireland Assembly Elections Act 2003 .... **31**, 1652
c 4............. Health (Wales) Act 2003 .... **30**, 730
c 5............. Community Care (Delayed Discharges etc) Act 2003 .... **40(2)**, 689
c 7............. European Parliament (Representation) Act 2003 .... **15(3)**, 852
c 9............. Electricity (Miscellaneous Provisions) Act 2003 .... **17(2)**, 569
c 10............. Regional Assemblies (Preparations) Act 2003 .... **26(2)**, 254
c 11............. Industrial Development (Financial Assistance) Act
                  2003 .... **47**, 1200
c 12............. Northern Ireland Assembly (Elections and Periods of
                  Suspension) Act 2003 .... **31**, 1653
c 14............. Finance Act 2003—
                  ss 22, 217 .... **50**, 413
                  ss 24–41, 217 .... **13**, 1235
                  ss 42–58C, 60–64, 65–71A, 73–130, 215, 217,
                  Schs 3–10, Sch 11, Pt 2, Schs 11A–17A, 19, 20 .... **41**, 404
                  ss 132, 136, 139–143, 147, 148, 150–153, 155, 156,
                  159–164, 167–174, 177, 178, 181–184, 195–200,
                  204, 205, 215–217, Schs 22–24, 26, Sch 28, Pt 3,
                  Schs 30, 32, 33, Sch 34, Pts 1, 4, Sch 37, Pt 1,
                  Sch 43 .... **43(2)**, 400
c 15............. Co-operatives and Community Benefit Societies Act
                  2003 .... **19(2)**, 598
c 16............. Marine Safety Act 2003 .... **39(2)**, 1150
c 17............. Licensing Act 2003 .... **19(3)**, 589
c 18............. Sunday Working (Scotland) Act 2003 .... **16**, 1213
c 19............. Aviation (Offences) Act 2003 .... **4(1)**, 703
c 20............. Railways and Transport Safety Act 2003—
                  ss 1–17, 103, 114–122, Sch 1, Sch 2, Pt 2, Schs 3, 6,
                  8 .... **38(2)**, 344
                  ss 18–68, 70–77, 116–122, Schs 4, 5, 8 .... **33(2)**, 556
                  ss 78–86, 88–91, 112, 117, 119–122 .... **39(2)**, 1153
                  ss 92–102, 117, 119–122 .... **4(1)**, 705
c 21............. Communications Act 2003 .... **45**, 714
c 22............. Fireworks Act 2003 .... **18**, 758
c 23............. National Lottery (Funding of Endowments) Act 2003 .... **5(1)**, 271
c 24............. Human Fertilisation and Embryology (Deceased Fathers)
                  Act 2003 .... **28**, 1034
c 25............. Northern Ireland (Monitoring Commission etc) Act
                  2003 .... **31**, 1659
c 26............. Local Government Act 2003—
                  ss 1–29, 31–33, 36–36B, 38–59, 68, 69, 73, 75, 83, 90,
                  93–106, 110, 114, 116, 117, 123–129, Schs 1,
                  4–8 .... **26(2)**, 281
                  ss 87, 88, 92, 124, 128, 129 .... **24**, 183
c 27............. Dealing in Cultural Objects (Offences) Act 2003 .... **13**, 451
c 28............. Legal Deposit Libraries Act 2003 .... **13**, 455
c 29............. Household Waste Recycling Act 2003 .... **35(2)**, 673

2003—*contd*

c 30 .... Sustainable Energy Act 2003 .... **17(2)**, 572
c 31 .... Female Genital Mutilation Act 2003 .... **12(3)**, 627
c 32 .... Crime (International Co-operation) Act 2003—
    ss 1–36, 42–51, 82, 84, 90, 91, 93–96, Schs 1, 2,
    4–6 .... **12(3)**, 631
    ss 54–75, 92–94, 96, Sch 3 .... **38(2)**, 377
c 33 .... Waste and Emissions Trading Act 2003 .... **35(2)**, 674
c 34 .... Arms Control and Disarmament (Inspections) Act
    2003 .... **10**, 1245
c 35 .... European Union (Accessions) Act 2003 .... **18**, 96
c 36 .... Fire Services Act 2003 .... **18**, 1029
c 37 .... Water Act 2003 .... **49**, 1637
c 38 .... Anti-social Behaviour Act 2003—
    ss 1–11, 11A–11L, 17, 30–32, 34–36, 39, 85, 88, 91–97,
    Sch 3 .... **12(3)**, 702
    ss 19–29, 93, 94, 96, 97 .... **6**, 1261
    ss 40–45, 47–52, 54–56, 93, 94, 96, 97 .... **35(2)**, 712
    ss 65–84, 93, 94, 96, 97 .... **24**, 190
c 39 .... Courts Act 2003 .... **11(3)**, 503
c 40 .... Ragwort Control Act 2003 .... **1(2)**, 814
c 41 .... Extradition Act 2003 .... **18**, 789
c 42 .... Sexual Offences Act 2003 .... **12(3)**, 746
c 43 .... Health and Social Care (Community Health and Standards)
    Act 2003—
    ss 34, 41, 43–75, 102(1), (2), 113–115, 120–124, 126,
    128, 130, 132, 134, 136–138, 140, 142–169, 173,
    176, 184, 186, 187, 189, 190, 193–203, Schs 4, 6,
    8–12, 14 .... **30**, 743
    ss 42–44, 76–102, 120–123, 125, 127, 129, 131, 133,
    135, 139, 141, 148, 194, 195, 199, 202, 203, Schs 7,
    8 .... **35(2)**, 734
c 44 .... Criminal Justice Act 2003—
    ss 12, 14–17, 21–25, 27, 28, 33, 39, 43–50, 57–68,
    71–80, 82–97, 142–153, 156–174, 176–235, 237–270,
    273, 274, 276–286, 291, 293–295, 298, 299,
    302–305, 307, 321, 324–339, Schs 4, 5, 8–17, 19, 21,
    22, 25–27, 32, 34A, Sch 36, Pts 1, 4, 6, Schs 37,
    38 .... **12(3)**, 937
    ss 29, 30, 41, 154, 155, 300, 301, 305, 330–333,
    335–339, Sch 3, Pts 1, 2, Sch 31, Sch 36, Pt 2,
    Sch 37, Pt 4 .... **11(3)**, 693
    ss 51–56, 98–129, 132–141, 330–339, Schs 6, 7, Sch 37,
    Pts 5, 6 .... **18**, 427
c i .... London Development Agency Act 2003 .... **26(2)**, 406
c iii .... London Local Authorities and Transport for London Act
    2003 .... **26(2)**, 407
No 1 .... Synodical Government (Amendment) Measure 2003 .... **14**, 1393
No 2 .... Church of England (Pensions) Measure 2003 .... **14**, 1397
No 3 .... Clergy Discipline Measure 2003 .... **14(S)**, Ecclesiastical Law 1

2004

c 2 .... European Parliamentary and Local Elections (Pilots) Act
    2004 .... **15(3)**, 872
c 3 .... National Insurance Contributions and Statutory Payments
    Act 2004 .... **40(2)**, 709
c 4 .... Justice (Northern Ireland) Act 2004 .... **31**, 1663
c 5 .... Planning and Compulsory Purchase Act 2004—
    entire Act **46**, 1289
    ss 106, 107, 110, 111, 121, 122, 124, 125 .... **9**, 474
c 6 .... Child Trust Funds Act 2004 .... **6**, 1278
c 7 .... Gender Recognition Act 2004 .... **7(1)**, 922
c 8 .... Higher Education Act 2004 .... **15(2)**, 808
c 10 .... Age-Related Payments Act 2004 .... **40(2)**, 716
c 11 .... Gangmasters (Licensing) Act 2004 .... **1(2)**, 815

2004—*contd*

c 12.............. Finance Act 2004—
                        entire Act .... **43(2)**, 492
                        ss 323, 328 .... **13**, 1252
c 13.............. Scottish Parliament (Constituencies) Act 2004 .... **10**, 1538
c 14.............. Statute Law (Repeals) Act 2004 .... **41**, 1103
c 15.............. Carers (Equal Opportunities) Act 2004 .... **40(2)**, 723
c 16.............. Patents Act 2004 .... **11(1)**, 1353
c 17.............. Health Protection Agency Act 2004 .... **35(2)**, 782
c 18.............. Traffic Management Act 2004 .... **38(2)**, 406
c 19.............. Asylum and Immigration (Treatment of Claimants, etc) Act
                        2004 .... **31**, 654
c 20.............. Energy Act 2004—
                        ss 1–50, 76–80, 82, 84–91, 93, 95–100, 104–119,
                            121–122, 124–134, 137–144, 146, 148, 150, 152,
                            154–177, 179, 180, 184, 185, 188–198, Schs 1–9,
                            16–23 .... **17(2)**, 581
                        ss 51–56, 58–71, 192, 196, 198, Schs 10–14 .... **33(2)**, 618
c 21.............. Fire and Rescue Services Act 2004 .... **18**, 1033
c 22.............. Sustainable and Secure Buildings Act 2004 .... **35(2)**, 806
c 23.............. Public Audit (Wales) Act 2004 .... **26(2)**, 446
c 24.............. Employment Relations Act 2004 .... **16**, 1215
c 25.............. Horserace Betting and Olympic Lottery Act 2004 .... **5(1)**, 272
c 26.............. Christmas Day (Trading) Act 2004 .... **18**, 1407
c 27.............. Companies (Audit, Investigations and Community
                        Enterprise) Act 2004 .... **8(1)**, 107
c 28.............. Domestic Violence, Crime and Victims Act 2004 .... **12(4)**, 1
c 29.............. Highways (Obstruction by Body Corporate) Act 2004 .... **38(2)**, 512
c 30.............. Human Tissue Act 2004 .... **28**, 1038
c 31.............. Children Act 2004 .... **6**, 1307
c 32.............. Armed Forces (Pensions and Compensation) Act 2004 .... **3**, 1723
c 33.............. Civil Partnership Act 2004 .... **27**, 769
c 34.............. Housing Act 2004—
                        entire Act **24**, 215
                        ss 217, 268–270 .... **17(2)**, 881
c 35.............. Pensions Act 2004 .... **33(1)**, 819
c 36.............. Civil Contingencies Act 2004 .... **50**, 535
c 37.............. Hunting Act 2004 .... **2**, 673
c i................ London Local Authorities Act 2004 .... **26(2)**, 520

2005

c 2................ Prevention of Terrorism Act 2005 .... **12(4)**, 87
c 4................ Constitutional Reform Act 2005 .... **11(3)**, 752
c 5................ Income Tax (Trading and Other Income) Act 2005 .... **44(3)**, 2
c 6................ Child Benefit Act 2005 .... **40(2)**, 726
c 7................ Finance Act 2005 .... **43(2)**, 895
c 9................ Mental Capacity Act 2005 .... **29**, 298
c 10.............. Public Services Ombudsman (Wales) Act 2005 .... **10**, 671
c 11.............. Commissioners for Revenue and Customs Act 2005 .... **43(2)**, 1016
c 12.............. Inquiries Act 2005 .... **10**, 746
c 13.............. Disability Discrimination Act 2005 .... **7(1)**, 962
c 14.............. Railways Act 2005 .... **38(2)**, 513
c 15.............. Serious Organised Crime and Police Act 2005—
                        ss 1–59, 123, 139, 141, 150, 151, 153, 155, 156,
                            158–163, 168, 170, 172–174, 176–179, Schs 1, 3, 4,
                            13, 17 .... **33(2)**, 662
                        ss 60–67, 69–76, 78–94, 96, 97, 111, 112, 114, 117, 120,
                            121, 124, 128–138, 145–149, 172, 174, 175,
                            177–179, Schs 5, 7, 16 .... **12(4)**, 123
                        ss 144, 172, 177–179, Sch 10 .... **6**, 1384
                        ss 171, 172, 177–179, Sch 15 .... **47(S)**, Trade 1
c 16.............. Clean Neighbourhoods and Environment Act 2005—
                        ss 1, 33, 34, 41, 46, 49, 54, 69–81, 96–98, 100, 104–111,
                            Schs 4, 5 .... **35(2)**, 811
                        ss 3–9, 108–111 .... **38(2)**, 663
                        ss 55–61, 63–68, 107–111, Sch 5, Pts 5, 6 .... **2**, 686

2005—*contd*

c 16 .... Clean Neighbourhoods and Environment Act 2005—*contd*
    ss 87–95, 107–111, Schs 2, 3, Sch 5, Pt 8 .... **2**, 945
c 17 .... Drugs Act 2005—
    ss 2, 22, 24 .... **28**, 1125
    ss 7, 9–19, 22–24, Sch 2 .... **12(4)**, 209
c 18 .... Education Act 2005 .... **15(2)**, 866
c 19 .... Gambling Act 2005 .... **5(1)**, 320
c 20 .... International Organisations Act 2005 .... **10**, 1249
c 22 .... Finance (No 2) Act 2005—
    ss 2, 71, 72 .... **50**, 415
    ss 7–46, 61, 67–72, Schs 2–9, 11 .... **43(2)**, 1087
    ss 47–49, 70–72, Sch 10 .... **41**, 660
c 24 .... Regulation of Financial Services (Land Transactions) Act
    2005 .... **19(2)**, 603
No 1 .... Stipends (Cessation of Special Payments) Measure
    2005 .... **14(S)**, Ecclesiastical Law 43
No 2 .... Care of Cathedrals (Amendment) Measure 2005 .... **14(S)**,
    Ecclesiastical Law 47
No 3 .... Church of England (Miscellaneous Provisions) Measure
    2005 .... **14(S)**, Ecclesiastical Law 73

2006

c 1 .... Racial and Religious Hatred Act 2006 .... **12(4)**, 226
c 2 .... European Union (Accessions) Act 2006 .... **18**, 99
c 3 .... Equality Act 2006 .... **7(1)**, 979
c 4 .... Terrorism (Northern Ireland) Act 2006 .... **31**, 1683
c 5 .... Transport (Wales) Act 2006—
    ss 1–10, 12–17 .... **38(2)**, 676
    ss 11–17 .... **4(1)**, 719
c 7 .... Council Tax (New Valuation Lists for England) Act
    2006 .... **26(2)**, 544
c 8 .... Merchant Shipping (Pollution) Act 2006 .... **39(2)**, 1170
c 9 .... Criminal Defence Service Act 2006 .... **11(3)**, 1051
c 10 .... National Insurance Contributions Act 2006 .... **40(2)**, 733
c 11 .... Terrorism Act 2006 .... **12(4)**, 227
c 12 .... London Olympic Games and Paralympic Games Act
    2006 .... **13**, 470
c 13 .... Immigration, Asylum and Nationality Act 2006 .... **31**, 706
c 14 .... Consumer Credit Act 2006 .... **39(1)**, 686
c 15 .... Identity Cards Act 2006 .... **36**, 139
c 16 .... Natural Environment and Rural Communities Act 2006—
    ss 1–46, 52, 53, 64, 65, 78–86, 98–100, 102–109,
      Schs 1–7, 11, 12 .... **32**, 924
    ss 66, 67, 71, 73, 107–109 .... **38(2)**, 687
    ss 87–97, 101, 107–109, Schs 8–10 .... **1(2)**, 844
c 17 .... Northern Ireland Act 2006 .... **31**, 1689
c 18 .... Work and Families Act 2006 .... **16**, 1235
c 19 .... Climate Change and Sustainable Energy Act 2006 .... **17(2)**, 885
c 20 .... Children and Adoption Act 2006 .... **6(S)**, Children 1
c 21 .... Childcare Act 2006 .... **6(S)**, Children 39
c 22 .... Electoral Administration Act 2006 .... **15(3)**, 882
c 23 .... National Lottery Act 2006 .... **5(1)**, 707
c 25 .... Finance Act 2006—
    ss 16–22, 178–180, Sch 26, Pt 2 .... **50(S)**, VAT 1
    ss 23–64, 69–161, 173–176, 178–180, Schs 1–23,
      26 .... **43(S)**, Taxation 1
    ss 65–68, 179, 180 .... **13**, 537
    ss 166, 178–180 .... **41**, 667
    ss 172, 179, 180 .... **35(2)**, 866
c 26 .... Commons Act 2006 .... **24**, 572
c 27 .... Housing Corporation (Delegation) etc Act 2006 .... **24**, 663
c 28 .... Health Act 2006—
    ss 1–13, 76, 77, 79, 82–84, Schs 1, 2 .... **35(2)**, 869
    ss 43, 57–71, 75–84, Schs 4–9 .... **30**, 909
    ss 17–25, 27–31, 76–79, 82–84 .... **28**, 1129

Enquiry Bureau hsieb@lexisnexis.co.uk

2006—*contd*
c 29 .... Compensation Act 2006—
              ss 1–3, 16–18 .... **31(S)**, Negligence 1
              ss 4–18, Schedule .... **11(3)**, 1057
c 30 .... Commissioner for Older People (Wales) Act 2006 .... **35(2)**, 897
c 31 .... International Development (Reporting and Transparency)
              Act 2006 .... **7(2)**, 665
c 32 .... Government of Wales Act 2006 .... **10**, 1542
c 33 .... Northern Ireland (Miscellaneous Provisions) Act 2006—
              ss 1, 6, 8–11, 13–15, 29–33, Sch 1, Sch 4, Pt 1,
              Sch 5 .... **15(3)**, 993
              ss 16–22, 26, 28, 30–33, Schs 2, 3, Sch 4, Pt 3,
              Sch 5 .... **31(S)**, N Ireland 1
c 34 .... Civil Aviation Act 2006 .... **4(1)**, 722
c 35 .... Fraud Act 2006 .... **12(4)**, 267
c 36 .... Wireless Telegraphy Act 2006 .... **45**, 1313
c 37 .... Parliamentary Costs Act 2006 .... **32**, 1162
c 38 .... Violent Crime Reduction Act 2006—
              ss 1–14, 28, 29, 32, 35–41, 43, 47, 49–51, 54–57, 60, 61,
              63–66, Schs 1–3, 5 .... **12(4)**, 286
              ss 15–20, 27, 64, 66 .... **19(3)**, 853
c 39 .... Emergency Workers (Obstruction) Act 2006 .... **50(S)**, War 1
c 40 .... Education and Inspections Act 2006 .... **15(2)**, 1036
c 41 .... National Health Service Act 2006 .... **30**, 959
c 42 .... National Health Service (Wales) Act 2006 .... **30**, 1477
c 43 .... National Health Service (Consequential Provisions) Act
              2006 .... **30**, 1840
c 44 .... NHS Redress Act 2006 .... **30**, 1886
c 45 .... Animal Welfare Act 2006 .... **2**, 705
c 46 .... Companies Act 2006 .... **8(1)**, 216
c 47 .... Safeguarding Vulnerable Groups Act 2006 .... **6(S)**, Children 173
c 48 .... Police and Justice Act 2006—
              ss 1–7, 9, 13, 41, 49, 52–55, Schs 1–5, 15, Pt 1 .... **33(2)**, 817
              ss 12, 14, 17–21, 26, 27, 32–36, 38, 39, 47, 49–55,
              Schs 8, 10, 14, 15 .... **12(4)**, 348
              ss 23–25, 49, 53–55 .... **6(S)**, Children 275
              ss 42, 43, 49, 53–55, Sch 13 .... **18**, 994
c 49 .... Road Safety Act 2006 .... **38(2)**, 696
c 50 .... Charities Act 2006 .... **5(2)**, 836
c 51 .... Legislative and Regulatory Reform Act 2006—
              ss 1–20, 27, 30–35, Schedule **41**, 1158
              ss 21–24, 32–35 .... **10**, 794
              ss 27, 32–35 .... **18**, 102
c 52 .... Armed Forces Act 2006 .... **3(S)**, Armed Forces, 1
c 53 .... Northern Ireland (St Andrews Agreement) Act 2006 .... **31(S)**,
                                                            N Ireland 27
c 55 .... Investment Exchanges and Clearing Houses Act 2006 .... **19(2)**, 604
No 1 .... Church of England (Miscellaneous Provisions) Measure
              2006 .... **14(S)**, Ecclesiastical Law 91
No 2 .... Pastoral (Amendment) Measure 2006 .... **14(S)**, Ecclesiastical Law 119
2007
c 2 .... Planning-gain Supplement (Preparations) Act 2007 ... **43(S)**, Taxation 503
c 3 .... Income Tax Act 2007 .... **44(4)**, 2
c 4 .... Northern Ireland (St Andrews Agreement) Act 2007 .... **31(S)**,
                                                            N Ireland 75
c 5 .... Welfare Reform Act 2007 .... **40(2)**, 735
c 6 .... Justice and Security (Northern Ireland) Act 2007 ..... **31(S)**, N Ireland 77
c 7 .... International Tribunals (Sierra Leone) Act 2007 .... **10**, 1254
c 8 .... Digital Switchover (Disclosure of Information) Act
              2007 .... **45**, 1494
c 9 .... Rating (Empty Properties) Act 2007 .... **26(2)**, 545

2007—*contd*

c 11 .... Finance Act 2007—
                    ss 1–4, 14, 17, 18, 21, 22, 25–55, 57–61, 66, 68–70, 82,
                        84–97, 102–104, 107–110, 112–115, Sch 3, Pt 2,
                        Schs 4–15, Sch 16, Pts 1–14, Schs 17–20,
                        Schs 22–27 .... **43(S)**, Taxation 505
                    ss 8, 113–115, Sch 27, Pt 6 .... **5(1)**, 726
                    ss 13, 15, 16, 23, 113–115, Schs 2, 27 .... **35(2)**, 936
                    ss 71–73, 79, 113–115 .... **41**, 671
                    ss 98–100, 113–115, Sch 27, Pt 6 .... **50(S)**, VAT 17
c 12 .... Mental Health Act 2007 .... **29**, 479
c 13 .... Concessionary Bus Travel Act 2007 .... **38(2)**, 789
c 14 .... Vehicle Registration Marks Act 2007 .... **13**, 1254
c 15 .... Tribunals, Courts and Enforcement Act 2007—
                    ss 1–61, 106, 107, 139–149, Schs 1–11, 16, 22, 23 .... **11(4)**, 20
                    ss 62–70, 88–93, 95–105, 146–149, Schs 12, 13, 15,
                        Sch 23, Pt 3 .... **19(3)**, 105
                    ss 71–87, 89, 90, 147–149, Sch 14 .... **24**, 664
                    ss 109–133, 147–149, Schs 20, 21 .... **4(2)**, 711
                    ss 134–138, 147–149 .... **13**, 544
c 16 .... Parliament (Joint Departments) Act 2007 .... **32**, 1178
c 17 .... Consumers, Estate Agents and Redress Act 2007 .... **39(1)**, 719
c 18 .... Statistics and Registration Service Act 2007—
                    ss 1–47, 49–51, 53–67, 73–76, Schs 1–3, Sch 4,
                        Pt 1 .... **10(S)**, Constitutional 1
                    ss 68, 69, 73–76, Sch 4, Pt 2 .... **36**, 201
c 19 .... Corporate Manslaughter and Corporate Homicide Act
                    2007 .... **12(4)**, 416
c 20 .... Forced Marriage (Civil Protection) Act 2007 .... **27(S)**, Matrimonial 1
c 21 .... Offender Management Act 2007 .... **12(4)**, 447
c 22 .... Pensions Act 2007—
                    ss 2, 4–7, 12, 13, 24–31, Sch 1, Pts 2, 4, 5, 7, 8, Sch 2,
                        Pt 3, Sch 7, Pts 1–5 .... **40(2)**, 820
                    ss 14–31, Schs 4–7 .... **33(S)**, Pensions 1
c 23 .... Sustainable Communities Act 2007 .... **26(2)**, 548
c 24 .... Greater London Authority Act 2007 .... **26(2)**, 556
c 25 .... Further Education and Training Act 2007 .... **15(S)**, Education 1
c 26 .... Building Societies (Funding) and Mutual Societies
                    (Transfers) Act 2007 .... **19(2)**, 605
c 27 .... Serious Crime Act 2007 .... **12(4)**, 490
c 28 .... Local Government and Public Involvement in Health Act
                    2007 .... **26(2)**, 582
c 29 .... Legal Services Act 2007 .... **11(4)**, 251
c 30 .... UK Borders Act 2007 .... **31(S)**, Nationality 1
c ii .... London Local Authorities Act 2007 .... **26(2)**, 789
No 1 .... Dioceses, Pastoral and Mission Measure 2007 .... **14(S)**,
                                                                    Ecclesiastical Law 123

2008

c 1 .... European Communities (Finance) Act 2008 .... **18**, 107
c 2 .... Banking (Special Provisions) Act 2008 .... **19(2)**, 611
c 4 .... Criminal Justice and Immigration Act 2008—
                    ss 1–9, 11, 13, 19–23, 26, 27, 32–36, 43, 46, 47, 49, 51,
                        52, 60–68, 71, 73–79, 96–124, 138, 140, 144,
                        147–154, Schs 1–4, 6, 8, 10, 11, 14–17, 21, 26, 27,
                        28 .... **12(4)**, 649
                    ss 39–41, 53, 54, 56–58, 80–92, 147, 148, 150, 152–154,
                        Schs 7, 13, 18, 19 .... **11(S)**, Courts 1
                    ss 48, 125, 143, 147, 148, 150, 152–154, Sch 9 ... **6(S)**, Children 289
                    ss 50, 126–129, 147, 148, 150, 152–154, Schs 22,
                        23 .... **33(S)**, Police 1
                    ss 130–137, 146–148, 150, 152–154 .... **31(S)**, Nationality 59
                    ss 145, 147, 148, 150–154, Sch 25 .... **3(S)**, Armed Forces 491
c 5 .... Channel Tunnel Rail Link (Supplementary Provisions) Act
                    2008 .... **38(2)**, 801

2008—*contd*

c 6 .... Child Maintenance and Other Payments Act 2008—
  ss 1–45, 55–63, Schs 1–8 .... **6(S)**, Children 311
  ss 46–50, 52, 53, 61–63 .... **40(2)**, 844
c 7 .... European Union (Amendment) Act 2008 .... **18**, 108
c 9 .... Finance Act 2008 .... **43(S)**, Taxation 829
c 10 .... Sale of Student Loans Act 2008 .... **15(S)**, Education 45
c 11 .... Special Educational Needs (Information) Act 2008 .... **15(S)**,
  Education 59
c 12 .... Statute Law (Repeals) Act 2008 .... **41**, 1186
c 13 .... Regulatory Enforcement and Sanctions Act 2008—
  ss 1–35, 74–77, Schs 1–4 .... **26(2)**, 853
  ss 36–77, Schs 5–7 .... **10(S)**, Constitutional 73
c 14 .... Health and Social Care Act 2008—
  ss 1–97, 130–144, 149–158, 160–173, Schs 1–5, 12 14,
  15 .... **30(S)**, NHS 1
  ss 52, 161–163, 169–173, Sch 3 .... **29**, 526
  ss 98–128, 161–166, 169–173, Schs 6–10, Sch 15,
  Pt 2 .... **28(S)**, Medicine 1
  ss 129, 130, 159, 166, 169–173, Sch 11, Sch 15, Pts 3,
  7 .... **35(S)**, Public Health 1
  ss 132, 137, 138, 145–148, 161–164, 169–173,
  Sch 13 .... **40(2)**, 855
c 15 .... Criminal Evidence (Witness Anonymity) Act 2008 .... **18**, 486
c 16 .... National Insurance Contributions Act 2008 .... **40(2)**, 876
c 17 .... Housing and Regeneration Act 2008 .... **24**, 687
c 18 .... Crossrail Act 2008 .... **38(2)**, 802
c 20 .... Health and Safety (Offences) Act 2008 .... **18**, 1411
c 21 .... Planning and Energy Act 2008 .... **46(S)**, Planning 1
c 22 .... Human Fertilisation and Embryology Act 2008 .... **28(S)**, Medicine 85
c 23 .... Children and Young Persons Act 2008 .... **6(S)**, Children 427
c 24 .... Employment Act 2008 .... **16**, 1252
c 25 .... Employment Act 2008 .... **15(S)**, Education 101
c 26 .... Local Transport Act 2008 .... **38(2)**, 1023
c 27 .... Climate Change Act 2008 .... **35(S)**, Public Health 45
c 28 .... Counter-Terrorism Act 2008 .... **12(S)**, Criminal 1
c 29 .... Planning Act 2008 .... **46(S)**, Planning 5
c 30 .... Pensions Act 2008 .... **33(S)**, Pensions 71
c 31 .... Dormant Bank and Building Society Accounts Act
  2008 .... **19(S)**, Financial 1
c 32 .... Energy Act 2008 .... **17(2)**, 906
nawm 1 .... NHS Redress (Wales) Measure 2008 .... **30(S)**, NHS 207
nawm 2 .... Learner Travel (Wales) Measure 2008 .... **15(S)**, Education 63
c i .... Transport for London Act 2008 .... **26(2)**, 898
c iii .... London Local Authorities and Transport for London Act
  2008 .... **26(2)**, 938
No 1 .... Church of England Marriage Measure 2008 .... **14(S)**,
  Ecclesiastical Law 211

2009

c 1 .... Banking Act 2009 .... **19(S)**, Financial 41
c 3 .... Northern Ireland Act 2009 .... **31(S)**, N Ireland 123
c 5 .... Industry and Exports (Financial Support) Act 2009 .... **47(S)**, Trade 13
c 6 .... Geneva Conventions and United Nations Personnel
  (Protocols) Act 2009 .... **10(S)**, Constitutional 123
c 7 .... Business Rate Supplements Act 2009 .... **25(S), 26(S)**, Local Govt 1
c 8 .... Saving Gateway Accounts Act 2009 .... **40(S)**, Social Security 1
c 10 .... Finance Act 2009—
  ss 1–8, 11, 23–75, 84–111, 122–127, Schs 1, 2, 6–35,
  38–58, 61 .... **43(S)**, Taxation 1357
  ss 9, 76–79, 113, Schs 3, 36 .... **50(S)**, VAT 25
  ss 10, 80–83, 126, 127, Sch 37 .... **41(S)**, Stamp Duties 1
  ss 12–16, 112, 120, 121, 126, 127, Sch 4 .... **13(S)**, Customs 1
  ss 17, 126, 127, Sch 5 .... **4(S)**, Aviation 1
  ss 18, 117–119, 126, 127, Schs 59, 60 .... **35(S)**, Public Health 173
  ss 19–22, 114–116, 126, 127 .... **5(S)**, Betting 1

2009—*contd*

c 11.............. Borders, Citizenship and Immigration Act 2009—
                          ss 1–23, 25–38, 53, 56–59, Sch .... **13(S)**, Customs 15
                          ss 39–52, 54–59, Sch .... **31(S)**, Nationality 77
c 12.............. Political Parties and Elections Act 2009 .... **15(S)**, Elections 1
c 13.............. Parliamentary Standards Act 2009 .... **32(S)**, Parliament 1
nawm 1 .... Learning and Skills (Wales) Measure 2009 .... **15(S)**, Education 327
nawm 2 .... Local Government (Wales) Measure 2009 .... **25(S)**, **26(S)**, Local Govt 45
No 1 .... Ecclesiastical Offices (Terms of Service) Measure 2009 .... **14(S)**,
                          Ecclesiastical–
                          Law 219
No 2 .... Church of England Pensions (Amendment) Measure
                          2009 .... **14(S)**, Ecclesiastical Law 217

Consolidated Index

The following consolidated index contains references to both paragraph numbers (with square brackets) and page numbers (without). Bold numbers indicate the Volume in which the reference may be found.

A

A2 improvement works
acquisition of land for, **38(1)**, [675], [708]
  blight, compensation for pre-enactment
    acquisition, **38(1)**, [676]
authorised, **38(1)**, [674]
  description of, **38(1)**, [705]
  new roads, regulation of traffic on,
    38(1), [707]
  operation and works, status of, **38(1)**, [707]
  status of new highways, **38(1)**, [707]
  stopping up of highways and private
    access, **38(1)**, [706]
  temporary interference with highways,
    38(1), [706]

A20 improvement works
ancillary, status of, **37**, [540]
construction, regulation of, **37**, [540]
description of, **37**, [538]
deviation, limits of, **37**, [538]
generally, **37**, [516]
meaning, **37**, [516]
status of new highways, **37**, [540]
stopping up of highways, **37**, [539]
temporary interference with highways,
  37, [539]
traffic on new road, regulation of, **37**, [540]

abandoned children
registration of birth, **36**, [73]

abatement
overcrowding, notice requiring, **22**, [291]

abdication
declaration of, **10**, [189]–[192]

abduction
child in care—
  offence of, **6**, [366]
  recovery, **6**, [367]
  recovery order—
    application for, **6**, [367]
    making of, **6**, [367]
    offences under, **6**, [367]
    powers under, **6**, [367]

abduction—*contd*
child in care—*contd*
  report on, **6**, [201]
child in police protection, **6**, [366]
child, of. *See* **child**
emergency protection order, child under,
  6, [366]
firearms, possessing during, **12(1)**, [545]
International Child Abduction, Hague
  Convention—
  access to child, rights of, **6**, [226]
  applications to court—
    cost of, **6**, [206], [226]
    interim powers as to, **6**, [200]
    outside UK, from, **6**, [198]
British Islands and Colonies, application of
  provisions, **6**, [224]
central authorities, **6**, [198], [226]
Convention—
  application to United Kingdom, **6**, [196]
  contracting states, **6**, [197]
  text, **6**, [226]
costs and expenses, administrative, **6**, [222],
  [226]
courts—
  declaration by, **6**, [203]
  jurisdiction, **6**, [199]
  rules, **6**, [205]
  suspension of powers, **6**, [204]
documents, proof of, **6**, [202], [226]
evidence, **6**, [202], [226]
generally, **6**, [1]
information, provision of, **6**, [201], [226]
judicial authorities, **6**, [199]
legal aid, **6**, [206]
Northern Ireland, **6**, [199], [230]
Orders in Council, **6**, [197]
removal of child, wrongful, **6**, [1], [226]
reports, **6**, [201]
reservation by UK, **6**, [206]
retention of child—
  outside UK, **6**, [203]
  wrongful, **6**, [203], [226]
return of child, **6**, [221], [226]
rules of court, power to make, **6**, [205]
Scotland, orders made in, **6**, [229]

abduction—*contd*
International Child Abduction, Hague
  Convention—*contd*
    whereabouts of child, disclosure, **6**, [220]
  search after, **6**, [367]

abortion
drugs, procuring for, **12(1)**, [100]
generally, **12(1)**, [1]
instruments, use to procure, **12(1)**, [99]
medical termination of pregnancy—
  conscientious objection to treatment,
    12(1), [412]
  information on, **12(1)**, [410]
  international headquarters, members of,
    12(1), [411]
  legal, conditions, **12(1)**, [409]
  limit on length of pregnancy, **12(1)**, [409]
  medicine used in, approval, **12(1)**, [409]
  more than one foetus, **12(1)**, [413]
  necessity for, **12(1)**, [409]
  notification, **12(1)**, [410]
  place of, approval of, **12(1)**, [409]
  risk in continuance, **12(1)**, [409]
  visiting forces, members of, **12(1)**, [411]
procuring, **12(1)**, [100]
unlawful, **12(1)**, [413]

abroad
companies. *See* **oversea company**
execution of deed on behalf of company,
  8, 138
official seal, use of, **8**, 139
transaction of business, **8**, 138

absence without leave
air force, from—
  arrest, **3**, [957], [960]
  board of inquiry, **3**, [906]
  certificate of arrest or surrender, **3**, [960],
    [1253]
  civil court, proceedings before, **3**, [958]
  failure to report or apprehend, **3**, [768]
  generally, **3**, [767]
  governor of civil prison, duties of, **3**, [961]
  police, surrendering to, **3**, [959]
army, from—
  arrest, **3**, [684]
  certificate of arrest or surrender, **3**, [687],
    [1253]
  civil court, proceedings before, **3**, [685]
  failure to report or apprehend, **3**, [495]
  generally, **3**, [494]
  police, surrender to, **3**, [686]
  prison, reception into, **3**, [688]
colonial naval force, from, **3**, [1193]
commonwealth forces, from, **3**, [1193]
navy, from—
  arrest, **3**, [1182]
  assisting, **3**, [1174]
  certificate of arrest, **3**, [1281]
  failure to report, **3**, [1032]
  false pretence, **3**, [1173]
  forfeiture of pay and effects, **3**, [1152]
  generally, **3**, [1031]

absence without leave—*contd*
navy, from—*contd*
  police, surrender to, **3**, [1185]
  procuring, **3**, [1174]
reserve forces, from—
  arrest, **3**, [1676]
  certificates of arrest or surrender, **3**, [1676]
  false pretence of illegal absence, **3**, [1641],
    [1642]
  inducing a person to absent himself,
    3, [1644]
  prison governors' duties to receive
    absentees, **3**, [1676]
  proceedings before civil court where
    persons suspected of, **3**, [1676]
  record of illegal absence, **3**, [1645]
  service, failure to attend for, **3**, [1639]
  surrender to police, **3**, [1676]
Ulster Defence Regiment, from, **3**, [1440]
visiting force, member of, **3**, [452]

absent and untraced owner
compensation, **9**, [23], [27]
notice to treat, in case of, **9**, [296]

absolute discharge
conviction, not, **12(2)**, [729]
order for, **12(2)**, [727]
rehabilitation of offenders, effect on,
  12(1), [630], [634]

abstract of title
commencement of title, **20**, [662]
expense of obtaining evidence, **20**, [663]
over-reachable interests, exclusion from,
  20, [634]
property sold in lots, **20**, [663]
purchaser, expenses borne by, **20**, [663]

Academy
agreement for establishment, **15(1)**, [608]
financial provisions, **15(1)**, [609]
governing body, exemption order from
  education legislation requirements—
    application for, **15(2)**, [342]
    generally, **15(2)**, [340]
    revocation of, **15(2)**, [341]
    variation of, **15(2)**, [341]
land—
  appropriation, restrictions on, **15(1)**, [719]
  disposal of, restrictions on, **15(1)**, [719]
  former academies, of, **15(1)**, [719]
  transfer schemes relating to, **15(1)**, [719]
new—
  establishment of—
    consultation on, **15(2)**, [745]
    notices as to, **15(2)**, [745]
    proposals for, **15(2)**, [897]
      adjudicator, consideration by,
        15(2), [898]
      implementation of, **15(2)**, [899]
      local authority, consideration by,
        15(2), [898]
    proposals, invitations for, **15(2)**, [743],
      [897]

Academy—*contd*
new—*contd*
establishment of—*contd*
relevant LEA, outside area of,
15(2), [749]
special educational needs, **15(1)**, [610]

access
disabled persons, for—
factories, to, **35(1)**, [289]
improvement of means of, **35(1)**, [290]
office, etc premises, to, **35(1)**, [289]
public buildings or premises, to,
35(1), [285]
information, to. *See* **local authority**
neighbouring land, to. *See* **land**
telecommunications works, obstruction by,
45, [72]

accident. *See also* **industrial injuries benefit**
aircraft. *See* **aircraft**
gas underground storage, arising from,
17(1), [310], [329]
industrial. *See* **industrial accident**
road. *See* **road accident**

accommodation. *See also* **dwelling-house;
housing**
alternative—
availability, **22**, [429]
duty to provide, **22**, [371]
suitable—
meaning, **22**, [295]
requirement to be, **22**, [371], [431]
asylum-seekers, tenancy of, **22**, [427]
buildings for, acquisition of, **22**, [19]
charges, power to make, **22**, [24]
chronically sick persons for, **21**, [381]
county council staff, for, **22**, [32]
crew, for. *See* **crew**
director or officer of company, provided for
outside UK, **43(S)**, 873–4
disabled persons, for, **21**, [381]
facilities, provision of—
board and refreshments, **22**, [12]
furniture and fittings, **22**, [11]
laundry services, **22**, [12]
meals and refreshments, **22**, [12]
open spaces, **22**, [15]
outside authority's district, **22**, [16]
recreation grounds, **22**, [14]
roads and streets, **22**, [15]
shops, **22**, [14]
welfare services, **22**, [13]
gypsies and travellers, for, duties of local
housing authorities, **24**, [373], [374]
heating charges, **22**, [98]
homeless, for. *See* **homeless persons**
housing action area, in, **22**, [217]
housing conditions. *See* **housing conditions**
land for. *See* **land**
living—
annual value—
disputes as to, **44(2)**, [122]
meaning, **44(2)**, [121]

accommodation—*contd*
living—*contd*
application of provisions to, **44(2)**, [108]
cash equivalent, calculating, **44(2)**, [114]
Chevening House, exception for
occupation of, **44(2)**, [112]
cost, calculation of, **44(2)**, [115]–[118]
not over £75,000, **44(2)**, [116]
over £75,000, **44(2)**, [117]
special rule for, **44(2)**, [118]
council tax paid for, **44(2)**, [318]
duties of employment, used in performance
of, **44(2)**, [110], [320]
earnings, benefit treated as, **44(2)**, [113],
[375]
expenses exempt from tax, **44(2)**, [319]
local authority, provided by, **44(2)**, [109]
more than one employee, provided for,
44(2), [119]
person involved in providing, meaning,
44(2), [123]
priority of rules applying to, **44(2)**, [120]
property, meaning, **44(2)**, [124]
repairs and alterations, expenses of,
44(2), [317]
scope of provisions, **44(2)**, [108]
security threat, provided as result of,
44(2), [111]
local housing authority tenants, payments
for, **22**, [906]
London. *See* **Greater London**
meaning, **22**, [62]
mobility, payment towards costs, **23**, [41]
needs, reviews of, **22**, [9]
overseas employments, expenses of,
44(2), [387]
privately let, financial assistance for—
consent for, **22**, [780], [781]
power to provide, **22**, [779]
provision of—
county council, by. *See* **county council**
environmental considerations, **22**, [407]
methods of, **22**, [10]
outside authority's district, **22**, [16]
removal expenses, assistance with, **22**, [26]
rent. *See* **rent**
service charge. *See* **service charge**
ship or aircraft, in, requisitioning, **9**, [120]
compensation, **9**, [124]
summary of provisions, **20**, [1]
temporary—
condemned houses, use of, **22**, [258]
persons taking employment, for, **22**, [427]

accommodation agency
commissions and advertisements, illegal,
21, [149]
summary of provisions, **20**, [1]

accommodation centre
accommodation in—
provisional assistance, **31**, [379]
residence restriction, requirement in,
31, [378]
Advisory Group, **31**, [388]

accommodation centre—*contd*
conditions of residence, **31**, [385]
destitute asylum-seeker, support for,
31, [372], [377]
establishment of, **31**, [371]
length of stay in, **31**, [380]
local authority, provision by, **31**, [393]
manager of, **31**, [383]
Monitor, **31**, [389]
Northern Ireland, in, **31**, [396]
orders and regulations, **31**, [394]
resident of—
breach of condition by, **31**, [385]
educational provisions, **31**, [391]–[392]
facilities for, **31**, [384]
financial contribution by, **31**, [386]
meaning, **31**, [382]
tenure, **31**, [387]
Scotland, in, **31**, [395]
summary of provisions, **31**, [1]
Wales, in, **31**, [397]

account
action for, limitation of time, **19(3)**, [751]

accountancy
change in, spreading of adjustment—
corporation tax, **43(S)**, 349–51
income tax, **43(S)**, 346–8

Accountant-General. *See* **Supreme Court**

accountants
partnership, number of partners, **8**, 578–81

accounting
false, **12(1)**, [568]

accounting period
company, of, **44(1)**, [7]
controlled foreign company, of, **44(1)**, [467]
meaning, **44(4)**, [956]
payments in, **44(4)**, [957]
payments otherwise than in, **44(4)**, [958]

accounting practice
enactments operating by reference to,
amendment, **43(2)**, [535]–[536]
foreign currency accounting, **43(2)**, [536]
generally accepted, meaning, **43(2)**, [287]
group of companies, use of differing practices
in, **43(2)**, [288]
international standards, **43(2)**, [287]
loan relationships, for, **43(2)**, [535]
provisions operating by reference to,
amendment, **43(2)**, [289]
regulations with retrospective effect, power to
make, **43(2)**, [654]
securitisation companies, application of
accounting standards to, **43(2)**, [636];
43(S), 101
spreading of adjustment, **43(S)**, 102
trade profits, calculating, **44(3)**, [25]
traditional adjustments, deferment on change
of, **43(2)**, [635]

accounting records
accounting reference date—
alteration of, **8(1)**, [470]
meaning, **8(1)**, [469]
accounting reference period, **8(1)**, [469]
adequate, **8(1)**, [464]
contents of, **8(1)**, [464]
duty to keep, **8(1)**, [464]
offences—
failure to keep records, **8(1)**, [465]
place and duration of holding, as to,
8(1), [467]
place of keeping, **8(1)**, [466]
preservation, duration of, **8(1)**, [466]
trade unions, of—
duty to keep, **16**, [202]
duty to keep available for inspection,
16, [203]
right of access to, **16**, [204]
failure to comply with request, **16**, [205]

accounting standards
annual accounts, in relation to, **8(1)**, [542]
bodies concerned with—
exemption from liability, **8(1)**, [19]
expenses, levy to pay, **8(1)**, [18]
grants to, **8(1)**, [17]
meaning, **8**, 339; **8(1)**, [542]
references to, **8**, 339
requirements, power to alter, **8**, 339–40

accounts
abbreviated—
approval and singing, **8(1)**, [528]
special auditors' report on, **8(1)**, [527]
accounting standards, **8(1)**, [542]
annual, meaning, **8(1)**, [549]
approval and signing, **8(1)**, [492]
audit. *See* **audit; auditor**
banking partnership, application of provisions
to, **8(1)**, [548]
circulation of—
default in, offence of, **8(1)**, [503]
duty of, **8(1)**, [501]
time allowed for, **8(1)**, [502]
company—
accounting policies, disclosure of, **8**, 627,
683, 690, 709
accounting principles—
departure from, **8**, 622, 678, 703, 735
generally, **8**, 622, 678, 703, 734
accounting reference date—
alteration of, **8**, 286–7
specification of, **8**, 284
accounting reference periods—
alteration of, **8**, 286–7
determination of, **8**, 284–5
first, **8**, 285
notices respecting, **8**, 286
oversea company, **8**, 552
accounting rules, **8**, 623–5, 678–81, 703–6,
735–43
alternative, **8**, 681–3, 706–8
annual—
duty to prepare, **8**, 287–8

accounts—*contd*
company—*contd*
annual—*contd*
meaning, **8**, 343
approval of, **8**, 296–7
assets. *See* **companies**
auditors. *See* **auditors**
balance sheet. *See* **balance sheet**
banking company. *See* **banking company**
Companies Clauses Acts. *See* **Companies Clauses Acts**
copies—
persons entitled to, **8**, 302
registrar, to be sent to, **8**, 306
shareholders' rights to, **8**, 302–3
court, persons authorised to apply, **8**, 315
default order, **8**, 306
defective, **8**, 313–14
definitions, **8**, 343–8
dormant company, **8**, 329–30
financial year, meaning, **8**, 284
fixed assets, treatment of, **8**, 623–4, 679, 703–5
form of, **8**, 615–22, 671–8, 688–9, 702, 723–34
general rules, **8**, 613–15, 670–1, 692–3, 721–3
group. *See* **companies**
holding company. *See* **holding company**
individual company, duty to prepare, **8**, 287–8
insurance company. *See* **insurance company**
investment company, **8**, 633–4
laying and delivering—
default order, **8**, 306
defective accounts, **8**, 313–14
directors' duty, **8**, 305
ECUs, in, **8**, 308
non-compliance with requirements, **8**, 307–8
period allowed for, **8**, 310–11
private company, elective resolution to dispense with, **8**, 332–3
unlimited companies, exemption of, **8**, 334–5
loans etc to be shown, directors, to, **8**, 660–3
medium-sized company—
cases where special provisions not applicable, **8**, 319
qualification as, **8**, 318–19
special auditors' report, **8**, 320
special provisions for, **8**, 317–18
non-statutory, publication of, **8**, 304
notes to—
generally, **8**, 627–33, 683–6, 690–1, 709–16, 743–9
information in, **8**, 343
matters to be disclosed in—
chairman's emoluments, **8**, 654–7
compensation payments, **8**, 657–8
directors' emoluments and benefits, **8**, 295–6, 654–7
excess retirement benefits, **8**, 657

accounts—*contd*
company—*contd*
notes to—*contd*
matters to be disclosed in—*contd*
identification of ultimate parent company, **8**, 653
related undertakings, **8**, 294–5
shareholdings, **8**, 648–52
subsidiaries, information as to, **8**, 649
third parties, sums paid to, **8**, 658
transactions and arrangements, **8**, 664
oversea company. *See* **oversea company**
parent undertaking, meaning, **8**, 340
private company—
elective resolution, **8**, 332–3
shareholder requiring, **8**, 333
profit and loss. *See* **companies**
publication in ECUs, **8**, 308
publication of, **8**, 304
records—
auditors' duty as to, **8**, 301–2
contents, **8**, 281
default as to, penalties, **8**, 282
duty to keep, **8**, 281–2
place of keeping, **8**, 282–3
preservation, period of, **8**, 283
registrar, delivery to—
duty of, **8**, 306
failure to comply, penalty for, **8**, 307–8
Secretary of State, notice of, **8**, 313
share premium. *See* **companies**
signing, **8**, 296–7
small company—
cases where special provisions not applicable, **8**, 319
qualification as, **8**, 318–19
special auditors' report, **8**, 320
special provisions for, **8**, 315–17
subsidiary undertakings, of—
appending, **8**, 309–10
meaning, **8**, 340
summary financial statement, provision of, **8**, 331
transactions favouring directors, disclosure of, **8**, 664
voluntary revision of, **8**, 311–12
defective—
application to court—
applicant, **8(1)**, [11], [534]
authorisation order, **8(1)**, [535]
revision, order for, **8(1)**, [534]
tax authorities, disclosure of, **8(1)**, [536]
disclosure of information obtained under compulsory powers—
amendment of categories, **8(1)**, [540]
permitted, **8(1)**, [539]
restrictions on, **8(1)**, [538]
documents, information and explanations, power of authorised person to require, **8(1)**, [537]
Secretary of State's notice, **8(1)**, [533]
tax information, disclosure by Inland Revenue, **8(1)**, [12]
voluntary revision of, **8(1)**, [532]
definitions, **8(1)**, [552]

accounts—*contd*
Directive disclosure requirements, subject to, **8(1)**, [1156]
distributions, justification of. *See* **distributions**
documents, information and explanations, power of authorised person to require, **8(1)**, [13], [69], [72]
euros, preparation and filing in, **8(1)**, [547]
filing—
  default in—
    civil penalty for, **8(1)**, [531]
    court order, **8(1)**, [530]
    offence, **8(1)**, [529]
  euros, in, **8(1)**, [547]
  medium-sized companies, obligations of, **8(1)**, [523]
  period allowed for, **8(1)**, [520]
    calculation of, **8(1)**, [521]
  quoted companies, obligations of, **8(1)**, [525]
  registrar, with, **8(1)**, [519]
  small companies regime, companies subject to, **8(1)**, [522]
  unlimited companies, exempt, **8(1)**, [526]
  unquoted companies, obligations of, **8(1)**, [524]
further provision, power to make, **8(1)**, [546]
group—
  applicable accounting framework, **8(1)**, [481]
  Companies Act—
    contents of, **8(1)**, [482]
    subsidiary undertakings included in consolidation, **8(1)**, [483]
    true and fair view, **8(1)**, [482]
  consistency of financial reporting within group, **8(1)**, [485]
  duty to prepare, **8(1)**, [477]
  EEA group accounts of larger group, exemption for company included in, **8(1)**, [478]
  exemption where no subsidiary undertakings need by included in consolidation, **8(1)**, [480]
  IAS, statement of, **8(1)**, [484]
  individual profit and loss account, **8(1)**, [486]
  non-EEA group accounts of larger group, exemption for company included in, **8(1)**, [479]
  small companies' option to prepare, **8(1)**, [476]
individual—
  applicable accounting framework, **8(1)**, [473]
  Companies Act, contents of, **8(1)**, [474]
  duty to prepare, **8(1)**, [472]
  IAS, statement of, **8(1)**, [475]
  meaning, **8(1)**, [472]
issuers of listed securities, supervision of, **8(1)**, [15]
name of signatory to be stated in, **8(1)**, [511]

accounts—*contd*
notes, information in—
  directors' benefits—
    advances, credit and guarantees, **8(1)**, [491]
    remuneration, **8(1)**, [490]
  employee numbers and costs, **8(1)**, [489]
  presentation of, **8(1)**, [550]
  related undertakings, as to, **8(1)**, [487]
    alternative compliance, **8(1)**, [488]
overseas company, of, **8(1)**, [1127]
periodic, supervision of, **8(1)**, [15]
public company, laying before general meeting, **8(1)**, [515]
  failure, offence of, **8(1)**, [516]
publication—
  auditor's report accompanying, **8(1)**, [512]
  meaning, **8(1)**, [514]
  non-statutory, requirements, **8(1)**, [513]
  statutory, requirements, **8(1)**, [512]
quoted and unquoted companies, definition, **8(1)**, [463]
quoted company, of, publication on website, **8(1)**, [508]
regulations, procedure for, **8(1)**, [551]
right of member or debenture holder to demand copies of—
  quoted companies, **8(1)**, [510]
  unquoted companies, **8(1)**, [509]
scheme of provisions, **8(1)**, [458]
small companies regime, companies subject to, **8(1)**, [459]
summary financial statement—
  defective—
    application to court, **8(1)**, [534]–[536]
    disclosure of information obtained under compulsory powers, **8(1)**, [538]–[540]
    documents, information and explanations, power of authorised person to require, **8(1)**, [537]
    revision, order for, **8(1)**, [534]
    Secretary of State's notice, **8(1)**, [533]
    tax authorities, disclosure of information by, **8(1)**, [536]
    voluntary revision of, **8(1)**, [532]
  false or misleading statements in, liability for, **8(1)**, [541]
  form and content of—
    quoted companies, **8(1)**, [506]
    unquoted companies, **8(1)**, [505]
  offences, **8(1)**, [507]
  option to provide, **8(1)**, [504]
  true and fair view, to give, **8(1)**, [471]

accrued income losses
calculating, general rule, **44(4)**, [636]–[637]
excluded persons: disregard of certain payments and transfers, **44(4)**, [646]
next interest period, treated as payments in, **44(4)**, [645]
relief for, **44(4)**, [645]
transfer of securities—
  interest on—
    foreign trustees, **44(4)**, [688]
    generally, **44(4)**, [687]

accrued income losses—*contd*
 transfer of securities—*contd*
  interest on—*contd*
   unrealised, received by transferee after,
    44(4), [689]

accrued income profits
 calculating—
  general rule, **44(4)**, [636]–[637]
  settlement day outside interest period,
   44(4), [638]
   amount where, **44(4)**, [639]
 charge to tax, **44(4)**, [624]
 excluded securities, **44(4)**, [627]
 included securities, **44(4)**, [627]
 income charged, **44(4)**, [625]
 person liable, **44(4)**, [626]
 transfer of securities—
  accrued interest—
   with, **44(4)**, [631]
    calculation of, **44(4)**, [667]
    default, interest in, **44(4)**, [667]
    excluded transferors and transferees,
     44(4), [647]–[649]
    payment, treatment of, **44(4)**, [640]
   without, **44(4)**, [632]
    calculation of, **44(4)**, [667]
    default, interest in, **44(4)**, [667]
    excluded transferors and transferees,
     44(4), [647]–[649]
    payment, treatment of, **44(4)**, [641]
  applicable transactions, **44(4)**, [628]
  charitable trusts, securities ceasing to be
   held on, **44(4)**, [660]
  different kinds, **44(4)**, [630]
  excluded transferors and transferees—
   charitable trusts, **44(4)**, [653]
   disregard of certain payments and
    transfers, **44(4)**, [646]
   individuals to whom remittance basis
    applies, **44(4)**, [652]
   manufactured payments, makers of,
    44(4), [655], [671]
   non-residents, **44(4)**, [651]
   pension scheme trustees, **44(4)**, [654]
   small holdings—
    individuals, **44(4)**, [647]
    trustees of disabled person's trusts,
     44(4), [649]
   traders, **44(4)**, [650]
  excluded transfers—
   sale and repurchase agreements,
    44(4), [662]
    non-standard, power to modify
     regulations for, **44(4)**, [664], [666]
    redemption arrangements, power to
     modify regulations for,
     44(4), [665]–[666]
    transfer under, **44(4)**, [663]
   stock lending, **44(4)**, [661]
  foreign currency securities—
   sterling equivalents of payments on
    transfers, **44(4)**, [672]
   unrealised interest payable in foreign
    currency, **44(4)**, [673]

accrued income profits—*contd*
 transfer of securities—*contd*
  legatee, exception where transfer to,
   44(4), [644]
  new securities with extra return,
   44(4), [657], [670]
  nominees and trustees, **44(4)**, [674]–[675]
  owner becoming entitled to securities as
   trustee, **44(4)**, [659]
  relief where transfer proceeds
   unremittable, **44(4)**, [676]–[678]
  "settlement day", meaning, **44(4)**, [682]
  small holdings, personal representatives,
   44(4), [648]
  strips of gilt-edge securities, **44(4)**, [656]
  trading stock appropriations, **44(4)**, [658]
  transferees, **44(4)**, [629]
  transferors, **44(4)**, [629]
  unrealised interest, with, **44(4)**, [633]
   calculation of, **44(4)**, [668]
   default, interest in, **44(4)**, [668]
  unremittable transfer proceeds, relief
   where, **44(4)**, [676]–[678]
  variable rate securities, **44(4)**, [634]
   meaning, **44(4)**, [635]
   payment, treatment of, **44(4)**, [643]
 transitional provisions and savings,
  44(4), [1058]
 unrealised interest, with—
  calculation of, **44(4)**, [668]–[669]
  default, interest in, **44(4)**, [668]–[669]
  payment, treatment of, **44(4)**, [642]

accumulations. *See also* **conveyancing and
law of property**
 amendment of Law of Property Act,
  33(2), [14]
 capital money, held as, **20**, [775]
 payment of debts, for, saving, **20**, [773]
 permitted periods, **33(2)**, [14]
 perpetuities. *See under* **conveyancing and
  law of property**
 portions, for raising, **20**, [773]
 restrictions on—
  general, **20**, [773]
  purchase of land, for, **20**, [775]
  qualification of, **20**, [774]
 right to stop, **33(2)**, [15]
 timber or wood, for purchase of, **20**, [773]

acknowledgment
 effect on third parties, **19(3)**, [761]
 formal provisions on, **19(3)**, [760]
 fresh accrual of action on, **19(3)**, [759]

acquisition
 company, stamp duty relief, **41**, [166], [167]

acquisition of land
 advances by local authority for, **25(1)**, [684]
 agreement, by, **46**, [491]
  application of compulsory purchase
   provisions to, **9**, [292]
  compulsory purchase, land subject to,
   9, [261]

acquisition of land—*contd*
  agreement, by—*contd*
    Crown, application of provisions, **9**, [247]
    Defence Acts, under, for exchange, **9**, [156]
    extraordinary purposes, for, **9**, [11]
    home loss payment, to person displaced
      from dwelling by, **9**, [328]
    incapacitated persons, from, **9**, [13]
    Lands Clauses Acts, under, **9**, [6]
    municipal corporation, from, **9**, [14]
    oil installations, for, **9**, [195]
    parties under disability—
      compensation where, **9**, [9], [295]
      entitlement to sell and convey, **9**, [7]
      powers, **9**, [8], [97], [295]
      powers generally, **9**, [7]
      purchase money, ascertainment, **9**, [9],
        [295]
      release and apportionment of
        rentcharge, **9**, [8], [295]
    persons entitled to sell, **9**, [7], [262], [295]
    public works, to mitigate adverse effects
      of, **9**, [323]
    rentcharge—
      apportionment, **9**, [8], [295]
      purchase by way of, reduction of
        borrowing powers where, **9**, [99]
      purchase money, ascertainment of
        amount, **9**, [9]
      recovery of rent, **9**, [10], [97]
      release, **9**, [8], [295]
      sale and repurchase after, **9**, [12]
      sale in consideration of, **9**, [295]
      tolls, charge on, **9**, [10], [98]
    urban development corporation, by,
      46, [106]
    valuation, **9**, [295]
  agricultural. *See* **agricultural land**
  airfields, obstruction of, **3**, [1235]
  airport, for. *See* **civil aviation**
  amalgamation of agricultural units, for,
    1(1), [642]
  bodies empowered as to, **25(1)**, [599]
  Chelsea Hospital, purchase by. *See* **Chelsea**
    Hospital
  City of London, in. *See* **London, City of**
  clearance area, in, **22**, [249]
  coastguard, held in connection with, **3**, [320]
  compulsory. *See* **compulsory acquisition**
  Corporation, by, **22**, [487]
  county council, by, **22**, [32]
  Crossrail, for. *See* **Crossrail**
  Defence Act, purchase under, **3**, [58]
  defence purposes, for—
    agreement in restraint of building, **3**, [71]
    brooks etc, power to alter course of, **3**, [82]
    buildings, keeping free from—
      exercise of powers, **3**, [77]
      generally, **3**, [76], [119]
    compensation—
      application of, **3**, [72]
      determining, **3**, [67]
      expenses, addition of, **3**, [73]
      failure to deduce title, **3**, [74]
      interests not purchased, for, **3**, [78]

acquisition of land—*contd*
  defence purposes, for—*contd*
    compensation—*contd*
      money paid into court, **3**, [74]
      payment, **3**, [72]
    corporations etc, agreement of, **3**, [68]
    damage done by works, **3**, [69]–[70]
    definitions, **3**, [85]
    highways etc, diverting, **3**, [81]
    notices, **3**, [66]
      service of, **3**, [83]
    sale of, **3**, [179]
    summary of provisions, **3**, [1]
    See also military purposes *below*
  discontinuance of proceedings for, **22**, [251]
  disposal, **46**, [497]–[498]
  Duchy of Lancaster, dealing with, **3**, [178]
  duties respecting, **22**, [19]
  electrical apparatus, interference with,
    3, [1236]
  emergency acquisition powers, **3**, [1]
  exchange, for, **46**, [494]
  house, possession of, **46**, [506]
  Inclosure Act, valuer under, **3**, [59]
  limited training purposes, use for, **3**, [1233]
  local authority, by. *See* **local authority**
  London borough council, by, **25(1)**, [575],
    [832]
  manoeuvres area, in, **3**, [1240]
  military manoeuvres, use for, **3**, [1]
  military purposes, for—
    alignment marks, entry to fix, **3**, [214]
    byelaws—
      highways on, **3**, [211]
      leased land, **3**, [213]
      notice and enforcement, **3**, [212]
      power to make, **3**, [209]
      private rights, affecting, **3**, [210]
      sea or tidal water, abutting on, **3**, [255]
    cessation of use, **3**, [207]
    compulsory purchase, time for, **3**, [257]
    council hiring land, **3**, [264]
    council leasing, **3**, [254]
    Crown land, **3**, [205]
    footpaths, stopping or diverting, **3**, [208]
    generally, **3**, [1]
    letting, **3**, [202]
    local inquiry, **3**, [201]
    meaning, **3**, [216], [256]
    New Forest, saving for, **3**, [217]
    other Acts, saving for, **3**, [215]
    powers to purchase, **3**, [200]
    procedure, **3**, [201]
    public purposes, held for, **3**, [206]
    summary of provisions, **3**, [1]
    volunteer corps, by, **3**, [200]
      borrowing, **3**, [203], [252]
        security of lease, on, **3**, [254]
      disbandment of, **3**, [204]
      hiring land, **3**, [264]
  military remains. *See* **military remains**
  ordnance, land purchased for—
    body politic etc—
      power to treat, **3**, [34]
      selling, **3**, [41]

acquisition of land—*contd*
  ordnance, land purchased for—*contd*
    compensation, rights, for, **3**, [38]
    consent of owner, **3**, [43]
    Duchy of Cornwall, property of, **3**, [57]
    enrolment of deeds, **3**, [51]
    entitlement of persons in possession, **3**, [50]
    entries and claims by principal officers,
      3, [54]
    footpaths and bridle-roads, **3**, [40]
    generally, **3**, [30]–[31]
    principal officers—
      exemption from liability, **3**, [55]
      purchase by, **3**, [33]
    property belonging to Her Majesty, **3**, [56]
    purchase money, **3**, [36]
      application for, **3**, [45]
      application of, **3**, [47]–[48]
      investment of, **3**, [46]
    purchaser, rights of, **3**, [37]
    removal of buildings on, **3**, [44]
    selling, exchanging and letting, **3**, [35]
    surveying and marking out, **3**, [39]
    trustees, vesting in, **3**, [32], [115]
    valuation of premises, **3**, [42]
    vesting of stock, **3**, [49]
  parish council, for, **25(2)**, [123]
  planning purposes, for, **46**, [511]
  powers of, **22**, [18]
  purposes of, **22**, [18]
  residuary bodies, by, **25(2)**, [647]
  Rural Development Board, by, **1(1)**, [648]
  sea areas, byelaws over, **3**, [1234]
  Secretary of State for Defence—
    conveyance to, **3**, [61], [64]
    recovery of possession by, **3**, [62]
  Secretary of State, power of to require,
    46, [495]
  transactions requiring consent, **25(1)**, [595],
    [596]
  Transport for London, by, **26(1)**, [777]
  urban development corporation, by, **46**, [66]
  walkways, for, **25(1)**, [874], [947]

acquittal
  proof of, **18**, [248]
  tainted—
    effect of provisions, **12(2)**, [473]
    intimidation, etc, by, **12(2)**, [470]
    order, conditions for, **12(2)**, [471]
    time limit for proceedings, **12(2)**, [472]

Act of Parliament. *See also* **statutes**
  copies printed by authority as evidence,
    18, [151]
  Crown, whether bound by, **10**, [2]
  meaning, **41**, [480], [596]
  property vested by, stamp duty on
    acquisition, **41**, [49], [84]

Act of Uniformity
  meaning, **14**, 330

action
  admiralty. *See* **Admiralty jurisdiction**
  cause of, surviving after death, **18**, [566]
  costs of company in, **8**, 588

action plan order
  amendment, **12(2)**, [850]
  appeals, **12(2)**, [850]
  appropriate court, meaning, **12(2)**, [850]
  breach of requirement, **12(2)**, [850]
  directions, **12(2)**, [768]
  electronic monitoring of requirements,
    12(2), [751]
  further hearing, power to fix, **12(2)**, [769]
  power to make, **12(2)**, [767]
  presence of offender in court, **12(2)**, [850]
  reports, **12(2)**, [767]
  requirements included in, **12(2)**, [768]
  revocation, **12(2)**, [850]

activity centre
  adventure activities—
    facilities for, meaning, **6**, [557]
    licensing, **6**, [557]
    offences, **6**, [558]
    orders and regulations, **6**, [559]
    generally, **6**, [1]

Acts and Measures
  copyright in, **11(1)**, [991]

actuary
  books, access to, **19(2)**, [416]
  disqualification, **19(2)**, [420]
  false or misleading information provided to,
    19(2), [421]
  Financial Services Authority, information to,
    19(2), [417], [418]
  requirement to appoint, **19(2)**, [415]
  resignation, notice of, **19(2)**, [419]
  standards bodies, levy to pay expenses of,
    8(1), [1352]

acupuncture
  practice of—
    byelaws as to—
      display of copy on premises, **35(1)**, [435]
      making, **35(1)**, [433]
      scope of, **35(1)**, [433]
    entry on premises, power of, **35(1)**, [436]
    local application of provisions as to,
      35(1), [432]
    medical practitioner or dentist, under
      supervision of, **35(1)**, [433]
    person carrying on—
      offences by, **35(1)**, [436]
      registration of—
        certificate of—
          display on premises, **35(1)**, [435]
          issue, **35(1)**, [433]
        charge for, **35(1)**, [433]
        requirement of, **35(1)**, [433]
        suspension or cancellation,
          35(1), [435]

acupuncture—*contd*
practice of—*contd*
premises for carrying on—
registration of—
certificate of—
display on premises, **35(1)**, [435]
issue of, **35(1)**, [433]
charge for, **35(1)**, [433]
requirement of, **35(1)**, [433]
suspension or cancellation,
35(1), [435]

acupuncturists
amendment of enactments, **26(2)**, [163]
application of provisions, **26(2)**, [164]
entry, powers of, **25(2)**, [969]
existing, application of provisions to,
25(2), [970]
licence—
appeals, **25(2)**, [967]; **26(2)**, [163]
application for, **25(2)**, [961]
cancellation, **25(2)**, [963]
conditions, **25(2)**, [960]
enforcement, **25(2)**, [968]
provisional grant, **25(2)**, [965]
refusal of, **25(2)**, [962]
renewal and transfer, **26(2)**, [163]
requirement of, **25(2)**, [960]
standard terms, conditions and restrictions,
25(2), [964]
transmission, **25(2)**, [963]
variation, **25(2)**, [966]
registration of, **25(2)**, [466]
special treatment premises, as, **25(2)**, [958]
termination of registration, **26(1)**, [238]

ad valorem duty
calculation of, **41**, [20], [35], [154]
foreign currency, expressed in, **41**, [20], [154]

administration
bank. *See* **bank administration**
company in, tax on, **44(1)**, [175]
Financial Services Authority, participation in
proceedings. *See* **Financial Services
Authority**
market charges, modification of provisions
for, **19(1)**, [794]
public-private partnership (PPP), order
relating to. *See* **public-private partnership
(PPP) agreement**

administration of estates. *See also* **executor;
probate**
absolute interest—
benefits received, meaning, **44(1)**, [439]
foreign estate, **44(1)**, [438]
meaning, **44(1)**, [443]
residuary income. *See* residuary income
below
residue, in, **44(1)**, [438]
successive, **44(1)**, [440]
adjustments, **44(1)**, [442]
administration period, meaning, **44(1)**, [437]

administration of estates—*contd*
administrator. *See* **administrator**
advancement, powers as to, **18**, [550]
aggregate income, **44(1)**, [437], [438], [443]
amounts disposable without representation,
18, [573], [579]–[581]
appropriation, powers of, **18**, [544]
assets—
administration—
estate solvent, where, **18**, [563]
intestacy, on, **18**, [537]
charges on property, payment of, **18**, [538]
order of application, **18**, [563]
payment of debts, for, **18**, [535]
solvent estates, **18**, [537]
title to, representation to constitute,
18, [491]
trusts for sale, **18**, [536]
beneficiary—
meaning, **18**, [627], [660]
minor, where, **18**, [641]
caveats, **18**, [635]
charges on property, payment of, **18**, [538]
charges on residue, meaning, **44(1)**, [443]
conveyance—
meaning, **18**, [559]
revocation of representation, effect,
18, [540]
validity of, **18**, [540]
Crown nominee, to, **18**, [533]
cum testament annexo, **18**, [452]
curtesy, abolition of, **18**, [548]
dating back to death, **19(3)**, [753]
deaths before 1925, **20**, [455]
debts, payment of, **18**, [535]
deemed income, **44(1)**, [437], [438]
descent. *See* **inheritance**
devolution on personal representative,
18, [513]
differing residuary dispositions, **44(1)**, [443]
discretionary payments, **44(1)**, [440]
dispositions—
avoidance of family provision, for,
18, [609]
intended to defeat certain applications,
18, [609]
nomination by, **18**, [574], [582]
without representation, **18**, [573],
[579]–[581]
distribution—
intestate estate, **18**, [448], [686]
no descendants, where, **18**, [450]
one year delay in, **18**, [451]
power to postpone, **18**, [547]
surplus, of, **18**, [449]
table of succession, **18**, [549]
wife and children, to, **18**, [448]
documents—
construction of, **18**, [554]
delivery to IR Commissioners, **18**, [637]
examination of persons as to, **18**, [649]
place for deposit of, **18**, [651]
subpoena to bring in, **18**, [650]
dower. *See* **dower**
entailed interests, disposal of, **18**, [539], [548]

administration of estates—*contd*
escheat—
　abolition of, **18**, [548]
　real estate, of, **18**, [493]
estate income—
　absolute interests in residue, **44(3)**, [664]
　absolute, limited and discretionary interests
　　in, **44(3)**, [662]
　administration period, assessments,
　　adjustments and claims after, **44(3)**, [695]
　administration period, meaning,
　　44(3), [665]
　aggregate income, **44(3)**, [676]
　assumed entitlement, **44(3)**, [677]
　　absolute interest following limited
　　　interest, holder of, **44(3)**, [684]
　　applicable rate for determining,
　　　44(3), [682]
　basic amount—
　　absolute interests, **44(3)**, [672]
　　discretionary interests, **44(3)**, [674]
　　grossing up, **44(3)**, [675]
　　income from which treated as paid,
　　　44(3), [691]
　　limited interests, **44(3)**, [673]
　　successive limited interests, **44(3)**, [687]
　charge to tax, **44(3)**, [661]
　discretionary interests in residue,
　　44(3), [667]
　final tax year, meaning, **44(3)**, [665]
　foreign estate—
　　income charged, **44(3)**, [669]
　　income, special rules for, **44(3)**, [670]
　　meaning, **44(3)**, [663]
　　UK income tax borne by,
　　　44(3), [689]–[690]
　income charged, **44(3)**, [668]–[669]
　income treated as—
　　dividend income, **44(3)**, [693]
　　income tax, bearing, **44(3)**, [692]
　　savings income, **44(3)**, [693]
　limited interests in residue, **44(3)**, [666]
　person liable for tax, **44(3)**, [671]
　residuary, **44(3)**, [678]
　　accrued income, inheritance tax on,
　　　44(3), [681]
　　reduction in share, **44(3)**, [680]
　　shares of, **44(3)**, [679]
　successive interests—
　　absolute, **44(3)**, [683]
　　apportionments, **44(3)**, [688]
　　assumed income entitlement,
　　　44(3), [684]
　　basic amount of estate income,
　　　44(3), [687]
　　limited interests followed by absolute
　　　interests, **44(3)**, [685]
　　limited interests, holders of, **44(3)**, [686]
　transfers of assets treated as payments,
　　44(3), [694]
　UK estate—
　　income charged, **44(3)**, [668]
　　meaning, **44(3)**, [663]
expenses of, **18**, [537]

administration of estates—*contd*
family provision. *See* **family provision**
foreign consul, by, **10**, [919]–[922]
foreign estate—
　absolute interest, **44(1)**, [438]
　limited interest, **44(1)**, [437]
　meaning, **44(1)**, [443]
　untaxed sums comprised in income,
　　44(1), [441]
foreign nationals, **18**, [489]
fraud in connection with, **18**, [531]
funeral expenses, payment of, **18**, [537]
grant of—
　beneficiary a minor, where, **18**, [641]
　false statement in application, **18**, [671]
　limited, **18**, [640], [643]
　more than one executor, to, **18**, [641]
　nominee of Crown, to, **18**, [533]
　non-marital birth, provisions as to,
　　18, [665]–[667]
　probate. *See* **probate**
　recall or revocation, **18**, [521]
　refused where tax unpaid, **18**, [636]
　revocation of, **18**, [521], [648]
　　legal proceedings pending on, **18**, [521]
　severance, **18**, [640]
　trust corporation, to, **18**, [642]
　vesting of intestate's estate in Public Trustee,
　　until, **18**, [520]
　will annexed with, **18**, [646]
heir—
　abolition of descent to, **18**, [548]
　right to take beneficially, **18**, [555]
　taking as devisee, **18**, [469]
information, power to obtain, **44(1)**, [442]
inheritance. *See* **inheritance**
inheritance tax. *See* **inheritance tax**
intestacy—
　enactments applied to, **18**, [568]
　escheat of real estate, **18**, [493]
　illegitimate children—
　　construction of documents, **18**, [666]
　　property rights, **18**, [666], [667]
　　right to succeed, **18**, [549], [665]–[667]
　　succession by parents, **18**, [585]
　meaning, **18**, [494], [559]
　partial, provisions applied, **18**, [553]
　provisions extended where will left,
　　18, [575]
　Public Trustee, vesting of estate in,
　　18, [520], [678]
　residue, widow's share, **18**, [500]
　statutory trusts, **18**, [550]
　succession on, table of, **18**, [549]
　summary of provisions, **18**, [447]
　variation, identification of settlor,
　　43(S), 311–12, 331–2
　widows, provision for, **18**, [497]
legal estate, meaning, **18**, [559]
letters. *See* **letters of administration**
limited interest—
　foreign estate, **44(1)**, [437]
　meaning, **44(1)**, [443]
　residue, in, **44(1)**, [437]
management, powers of, **18**, [542]

administration of estates—*contd*
    meaning, **18**, [559], [655]
    meaning of administration, **10**, [455]
    minor—
        management during minority, **18**, [542]
        trustees, appointment, **18**, [545]
    nomination, disposition by, **18**, [574], [582]
    notices affecting land—
        absence of knowledge of intended
            recipient's death, **18**, [679]
        Public Trustee, functions in relation to,
            18, [681]
        service of, **18**, [680]
    pecuniary legacy, meaning, **18**, [559]
    personal chattels, meaning, **18**, [559]
    personal estate—
        meaning, **18**, [556]
        succession to on intestacy, **18**, [549]
        valuation, **18**, [502]
    personal representatives, right in another
        estate, **44(1)**, [440]
    persons acting on, protection of, **18**, [530]
    pre-1925 legislation, use of, **18**, [447]
    property, meaning, **18**, [559]
    Public Trustee—
        notices affecting land, functions in relation
            to, **18**, [681]
        vesting of estate in, where intestacy or lack
            of executors, **18**, [678]
    purchaser, meaning, **18**, [559]
    real estate. *See* **real estate**
    repealed statutes, preservation of law,
        18, [447]
    representation. *See* **executor**
    residuary estate—
        descent to heir, abolition of, **18**, [548]
        succession to, order of, **18**, [549]
    residuary income—
        ascertainment of, **44(1)**, [439]
        charge to tax, **44(1)**, [438]
        company, of, **44(1)**, [438]
        foreign estate, **44(1)**, [438]
    retainer etc, abolition of, **18**, [594]
    rules of court, **18**, [534]
    small payments without representation—
        amount of, **18**, [573]
        disposal without, **18**, [579]–[581]
        power to increase limit, **18**, [576], [577]
    specific disposition, meaning, **44(1)**, [443]
    Statutes of Distribution, construction of
        references to, **18**, [447], [554]
    statutory limit—
        advancement, powers as to, **18**, [550]
        failure of, **18**, [550]
        relatives of intestate, in favour of, **18**, [550]
    sums payable, references to, **44(1)**, [443]
    surviving spouse—
        life interest, redemption of, **18**, [551]
        matrimonial home, rights as to, **18**, [569],
            [572]
        personal representative's powers as to,
            18, [552]
    temporary, grant of, **18**, [522]
    tenancy by the curtesy, abolition, **18**, [548]

administration of estates—*contd*
    Treasury Solicitor—
        disposal of property by, **10**, [453]
        grant to, **10**, [451]
        powers of, **10**, [452]
    trust for sale, intestacy, arising on, **18**, [536]
    UK estate, meaning, **44(1)**, [443]
    untaxed sums comprised in income,
        44(1), [441]
    valuation—
        personalty, **18**, [502]
        realty, **18**, [501]
    waste, liability for, **18**, [532]

administration of justice
    London. *See* **Greater London**

Administration of Justice Act 1985
    amendments to, **11(4)**, [358], [360]

administration order
    application for, **11(4)**, [63]
    attachment of earnings to secure payment,
        19(3), [41]
    bankruptcy—
        exclusion, **11(4)**, [63]
        petition during currency of, **11(4)**, [63]
    consequential amendments, **11(4)**, [107]
    county court, in. *See* **county court**
    debt management arrangements, effect on,
        11(S), Courts 82–3
    debt—
        discharge from, **11(4)**, [63]
        due, becoming, **11(4)**, [63]
        expressions relating to, **11(4)**, [63]
        inability to pay, **11(4)**, [63]
        management arrangements, effect on,
            11(4), [63]
        qualifying—
            calculating, **11(4)**, [63]
            total amount, failure to take account of,
                11(4), [63]
        scheduled—
            declared, **11(4)**, [63]
            descheduling, **11(4)**, [63]
            interest on, **11(4)**, [63]
            new, **11(4)**, [63]
        scheduling and descheduling, **11(4)**, [63]
    debtor's surplus income, calculating,
        11(4), [63]
    duration, **11(4)**, [63]
        variation of, **11(4)**, [63]
        application for, **11(4)**, [64]
        bankruptcy exclusion, **11(4)**, [64]
        charges, restriction on, **11(4)**, [64]
        debt—
            expressions relating to, **11(4)**, [64]
            inability to pay, **11(4)**, [64]
            management arrangements, effect on,
                11(4), [64]
        duration, **11(4)**, [64]
            variation of, **11(4)**, [99]
        exclusion, debtor excluded under,
            11(4), [64]

administration order—*contd*

duration—*contd*

existing county court proceedings, stay of, **11(4)**, [64]

failure to comply, offence of, **11(4)**, [64]

nature of, **11(4)**, [64]

property, disposal of, **11(4)**, [64]

interpretation, **11(4)**, [64]

meaning, **11(4)**, [64]

notification of events, **11(4)**, [64]

power to make, **11(4)**, [64]

regulations, **11(4)**, [64]

requirements imposed by—

bankruptcy petition, presentation of, **11(4)**, [64]

gas or electricity supplies, stopping, **11(4)**, [64]

remedies other than bankruptcy, **11(4)**, [64]

repayment, **11(4)**, [64]

revocation—

duty of, **11(4)**, [64]

effect of, **11(4)**, [64]

notification, **11(4)**, [64]

power of, **11(4)**, [64]

variation—

duration, of, **11(4)**, [64]

notification, **11(4)**, [64]

voluntary arrangement exclusion, **11(4)**, [64]

exclusion, debtor excluded under, **11(4)**, [63]

existing county court proceedings, stay of, **11(4)**, [63]

extension of power to make, **19(3)**, [40]

failure to pay under, **8**, 848

information, duty of debtor to provide—

failure to comply, offence of, **11(4)**, [63]

nature of, **11(4)**, [63]

property, disposal of, **11(4)**, [63]

interpretation, **11(4)**, [63]

market charge, enforcement of, **19(1)**, [794]

meaning, **11(4)**, [63]

money paid into court, appropriation of, **11(4)**, [63]

notification of events, **11(4)**, [63]

power to make, **11(4)**, [63]

regulations, **11(4)**, [63]

remedies other than bankruptcy, restriction, **11(4)**, [63]

repayment requirement, **11(4)**, [63]

repeals, **11(4)**, [113]

revocation—

duty of, **11(4)**, [63]

effect of, **11(4)**, [63]

notification, **11(4)**, [63]

power of, **11(4)**, [63]

stopping of gas or electricity during currency of, restriction, **11(4)**, [63]

variation—

duration, of, **11(4)**, [63]

notification, **11(4)**, [63]

power of court, **11(4)**, [63]

voluntary arrangement exclusion, **11(4)**, [63]

Administrative Justice and Tribunals Council

annual reports, **11(4)**, [96]

Chairman, **11(4)**, [95]

establishment of, **11(4)**, [44]

functions, **11(4)**, [96]

interpretation, **11(4)**, [98]

listed tribunal, meaning, **11(4)**, [98]

membership, **11(4)**, [95]

programme of work, **11(4)**, [96]

remuneration of members, **11(4)**, [95]

reports, **11(4)**, [96]

responsible authorities, **11(4)**, [98]

rules for listed tribunals, consultation on, **11(4)**, [97]

Scottish Committee, **11(4)**, [95]

status, **11(4)**, [95]

term of office of members, **11(4)**, [95]

Welsh Committee, **11(4)**, [95]

administrator. *See also* **executor**

accounting by, **18**, [448]

appointment—

court, by, **18**, [643]

pending suit, **18**, [644]

debtor as, of creditor, **18**, [524]

duties generally, **18**, [528]

meaning, **18**, [559]

protection of, acting on probate, **18**, [530]

revocation of grant, proceedings pending on, **18**, [521]

rights and liabilities, **18**, [523]

summary of provisions, **18**, [447]

sureties, requirement to produce, **18**, [647]

trust corporation as, **18**, [642]

Admiralty

county court proceedings. *See* **county court**

Court of, dominion parliament, powers of, **7(2)**, [428]

droits of, **11(2)**, [130]

pre-emption, right of, **11(2)**, [83]

prize as, **11(2)**, [84]

Jurisdiction, International Oil Pollution Compensation Fund, claim on, **39(2)**, [851]

offences—

admiral, jurisdiction of, **7(2)**, [353]

colony—

meaning of, **7(2)**, [355]

trial in, **7(2)**, [353]

jurisdiction, **7(2)**, [352]

legislation of overseas possessions, **7(2)**, [357]

New South Wales, jurisdiction in, **7(2)**, [354]

Van Diemen's Land, jurisdiction in, **7(2)**, [354]

pre-emption, right of, **34**, [1062]

Receiver General of Droits—

directions to, **39(2)**, [98]

receivers appointed by, **39(2)**, [99]

fees, application of, **39(2)**, [101]

payments to, **39(2)**, [100]

Admiralty Board
Defence Council functions, carrying out,
10, [528]
establishment of, **10**, [528]
Royal Navy, administrating, **3**, [1]

Admiralty Court
business of, **11(2)**, [736]
Colonial. *See* **Colonial Courts of
Admiralty**
High Court, part of, **11(2)**, [673]
privy council, contempt on appeal to,
11(2), [62]
prize appeals, **11(2)**, [33]
registry, sums transmitted to, **11(2)**, [46]

Admiralty jurisdiction
actions in personam, restrictions on,
11(2), [689]
aircraft—
application to, **11(2)**, [918]
claims in respect of, **4(1)**, [141]
Channel Islands, **11(2)**, [787]
claims relating to, **11(2)**, [689]
colonies, as to, **11(2)**, [787]
county court. *See* **county court**
exercise, mode of, **11(2)**, [688]
generally, **11(2)**, [1]
High Court, part of, **11(2)**, [687]
International Oil Pollution Compensation
Fund, claim on, **39(2)**, [638]
Isle of Man, **11(2)**, [787]
Rhine Convention—
exclusion of cases within, **11(2)**, [690]
meaning, **11(2)**, [691]
seamen's wages, **11(2)**, [917]
security requirement, **11(2)**, [821]
stay of proceedings, **11(2)**, [821]

Admiralty Marshal
vessel or aircraft in possession of, **11(2)**, [918]

admission
deemed, where, **14**, 1087
ordination before, **14**, 52

adoption
Adopted Children Register—
cancellation on legitimation, **6**, [864]
copy of entry, right to have, **6**, [805]
entry in, **6**, [804], [864]
foreign adoptions, **6**, [864]
maintenance of, **6**, [804]
rectification of, **6**, [864]
Register of Births, connection with,
6, [806], [865]
searches, **6**, [805]
adopters, exempt payments to,
44(3), [758]–[761]
Adoption and Children Act Register—
closed to public inspection or search,
6, [841]
disclosure of information, **6**, [845]
establishment of, **6**, [841]
maintenance of, **6**, [841]

adoption—*contd*
Adoption and Children Act Register—*contd*
supplementary provisions, **6**, [847]
supply of information for, **6**, [844]
territorial application, **6**, [846]
use of organisation—
agency for payments, as, **6**, [843]
establish register, to, **6**, [842]
adoptive relatives, **6**, [173], [795]
agency—
advertisements, restriction on, **6**, [839]
amended provisions, **6(S)**, 430
counselling, requirement to give
information about, **6**, [790]
determinations relating to, independent
review of, **6(S)**, 471–2
fees, **6**, [739]
general power to regulate, **6**, [737]
independent review of determinations,
6, [740]
management of, **6**, [738]
meaning, **6**, [184]
persons carrying on or managing,
notification of matters relating to,
6(S), 466–7
placement of children for adoption by,
6, [745]
advanced consent to adoption, **6**, [747]
contact, **6**, [753]–[754]
further consequences of, **6**, [755]
parental consent, with, **6**, [746]
parental responsibility, **6**, [752]
recovery by parent—
where child not placed or is a baby,
6, [758]
where child placed and consent
withdrawn, **6**, [759]
where child placed and placement
order refused, **6**, [760]
removal of children, prohibition on,
6, [757]
reports where, **6**, [770]
premises, inspection of, **6**, [743]
recovery by parent—
where child not placed or is a baby,
6, [758]
where child placed and consent
withdrawn, **6**, [759]
where child placed and placement order
refused, **6**, [760]
regulation of, **6**, [170], [791]
return of child, **6**, [762]
applications for, **6**, [764], [776]
arrangements, meaning of, **6**, [184]
arranging—
offences, **6**, [820]
restrictions on, **6**, [819]
care order, effect of, **6**, [346]
Channel Islands, in—
registration, **6**, [864]
regulations, **6**, [834]
child to live with adopters before application,
6, [769]

adoption—*contd*
Children and Family Court Advisory and
Support Service. *See* **Children and Family
Court Advisory and Support Service**
citizenship by. *See* **citizenship**
consent to, evidence of, **6**, [830]
contact register—
closed to public inspection and search,
6, [808]
entries in, **6**, [807]
maintenance of, **6**, [807]
Convention—
1965 Convention orders, saving for,
6, [632]
meaning, **6**, [184]
order. *See* order *below*
status conferred by, **6**, [172]
counselling service for adopted persons,
6, [790]
couple, by, **6**, [777]
default power of appropriate Minister,
6, [742]
delay, avoiding, **6**, [835]
devolution provisions, **6**, [631]
dispositions of property, effect on—
date of birth, depending on, **6**, [160],
[175], [797]
generally, **6**, [174]
meaning, **6**, [178], [800]
peerages, devolving with, **6**, [798]
personal representative, protection of,
6, [177], [799]
rules of interpretation for instruments
concerning, **6**, [796]
trustees, protection of, **6**, [177], [799]
effect on denial of parentage, **6**, [488]
evidence of—
Northern Ireland, in, **6**, [833]
Scotland, in, **6**, [833]
foreign—
bringing children into UK, restriction on,
6, [810], [813]
parental responsibility prior to adoption
abroad, giving, **6**, [811]
registration, **6**, [864]
taking children out of UK, restriction on,
6, [812]–[813]
foreign element, with—
amended provisions, **6(S)**, 26
charges, **6(S)**, 25
extra conditions, imposition of, **6(S)**, 23–4
restricted countries, review, **6(S)**, 21
special restrictions—
declaration of, **6(S)**, 20–1
nature of, **6(S)**, 22
summary of provisions, **6(S)**, 1
generally, **6**, [1]
glossary, **6**, [869]
Hague Convention, **6**, [815]–[817], [850]
information—
disclosure of—
adopted adult, to, **6**, [787]
during adoption process, **6**, [781]
offence, **6**, [786]
other information, **6**, [785]

adoption—*contd*
information—*contd*
disclosure of—*contd*
protected information—
adults, about, **6**, [788]
children, about, **6**, [789]
restrictions on, **6**, [784]
to be kept about a person's, **6**, [783]
information concerning, **6**, [741]
inspection of premises, **6**, [638]
insurance on child, effect on, **6**, [181], [803]
intercountry Convention, under—
Central Authority, **6**, [629], [634]
generally, **6**, [1]
procedural requirements, **6**, [634]
recognition and effects of, **6**, [634]
regulations giving effect to, **6**, [628]
requirements, **6**, [634]
text of Convention, **6**, [634]
Isle of Man, in—
registration, **6**, [864]
regulations, **6**, [834]
kindred and affinity, effect on, **6**, [179]
leave, unfair employment-related benefit
scheme provisions, **40(1)**, [205]
legitimation, effect of, **6**, [1], [160]
meaning, **6**, [171], [793]
natural parent, by, **6**, [172]
Northern Ireland, in—
effect of certain Northern Irish orders and
provisions, **6**, [832]
evidence of, **6**, [833]
registration, **6**, [864]
notices—
intention to adopt, of, **6**, [771]
service of, **6**, [836]
offences—
body corporate, by, **6**, [856]
proceedings for, **6**, [826]
unincorporated bodies, by, **6**, [856]
one person, by, **6**, [778]
order—
application for. *See* applications *above*
British, **6**, [184]
Convention—
1965 orders, saving for, **6**, [632]
meaning, **6**, [184]
freeing child for, **6**, [184]
generally, **6**, [1]
making of, **6**, [773]
conditions, **6**, [774]
restrictions on, **6**, [775]
meaning, **6**, [184]
person over eighteen, **6**, [116]
revocation, legitimation, on, **6**, [159]
rules and regulations, power to make,
6, [183], [853]
overseas—
annulment, **6**, [816]–[817]
declaration of—
application for, **6**, [265]
Attorney-General, powers, **6**, [267]
effect, **6**, [266]
making of, **6**, [266]
supplementary provisions, **6**, [268]

adoption—*contd*
  overseas—*contd*
    determinations, **6**, [818]
    meaning, **6**, [184], [814]
    orders, **6**, [818]
  parental consent, **6**, [779]
  parental responsibility, **6**, [752]
  pay. *See* **statutory adoption pay**
  payments—
    excepted, **6**, [823]
    meaning, **6**, [824]
    prohibition of certain, **6**, [822]
  peerage, etc, effect on, **6**, [176]
  pension payable at time of, **6**, [180], [802]
  personal representatives, protection of,
    6, [177]
  placement orders, **6**, [748]
    application for, **6**, [749]
    further consequences of, **6**, [756]
    refused, recovery by parent of child
      where, **6**, [760]
    removal of children, prohibition on,
      6, [761]
    revocation, **6**, [751]
    variation, **6**, [750]
  pre-commencement, information for, **6**, [825]
  privacy of proceedings, **6**, [827]
  property, disposition etc. *See* disposition *above*
  protected child. *See* **child**
  recovery orders, **6**, [768]
  relative, adoptive, **6**, [173], [795]
  removal of children in non-agency cases,
    restriction on, **6**, [763]–[767]
  reports, restrictions on, **6**, [821]
  research into, **6**, [411]
  revocation, legitimation, on, **6**, [159], [782]
  rules and regulations, **6**, [183]
  rules of procedure, **6**, [182], [854]
  Scotland, in—
    effect of certain Scottish orders and
      provisions, **6**, [1831]
    evidence of, **6**, [833]
    registration, **6**, [864]
  Service—
    local authority plans for, **6**, [733]
    maintenance of, **6**, [731]
    meaning, **6**, [730]
  society—
    cancellation of registration, arrangements
      on, **6**, [734]
    disclosure of protected information, offence
      of, **6**, [786]
    inactive or defunct, **6**, [735]
    meaning, **6**, [184], [730]
    regulations, **6**, [170]
  status conferred by, **6**, [172], [794]
  suitability of adopters, **6**, [772]
  summary of provisions, **6**, [1]
  support agency—
    meaning, **6**, [736]
    persons carrying on or managing,
      notification of matters relating to,
      6(S), 466–7
  support services—
    assessments for, **6**, [732]

adoption—*contd*
  support services—*contd*
    meaning, **6**, [730]
  titles of honour, effect on, **6**, [176]
  trustees, protection of, **6**, [177]
  unmarried father, parental responsibility of,
    6, [837]
  voluntary adoption agency—
    distribution of functions, **6**, [744]
    management of, **6**, [738]
  voluntary agency—
    functions, distribution of, **35(2)**, [315]
    meaning, **35(2)**, [283]
    transitional provisions, **35(2)**, [364]
  welfare of child, **6**, [1], [729]
  wills, effect on, **6**, [174]

adoption leave
  additional, **16**, [706]
  ordinary, **16**, [705]
  redundancy and dismissal during, **16**, [707]
  regulations, **16**, [708]
  unfair dismissal relating to, **16**, [746]

Adult Learning Inspectorate
  abolished, **15(2)**, [848]

adultery
  finding of, admissible as evidence, **18**, [205]

adults
  Convention on International Protection of,
    giving effect to, **29**, [294], [321]–[326]
  vulnerable. *See* **vulnerable adult**

advance decision
  alteration of, **29**, [250]
  applicability of, **29**, [251]
  effect of, **29**, [252]
  meaning, **29**, [250]
  treatment, to refuse, **29**, [250]
  validity of, **29**, [251]
  withdrawal, **29**, [250]
  withholding treatment, no liability arising
    from, **29**, [252]

advertisement
  accommodation agency, illegal, **21**, [149]
  adoption agency, for, **6**, [839]
  aerial advertising, prohibition, **4(1)**, [133]
  cancer, relating to treatment for, **28**, [10]
  closing transfer register, of, **8**, 20
  control of, **46**, [484]
  decisions, validity of, **46**, [549]
  deemed planning permission, **46**, [486]
  disability discrimination in, **7(1)**, [318]
  display, deemed, **46**, [488]
  enforcement of control, **46**, [488]
  estate agency work, **21**, [678]
  experimental areas, **46**, [485]
  food, for. *See* **food and food safety**
  fostering, related to, **6**, [452]
  gambling. *See* **gambling**
  general meeting, of, **8**, 40
  hackney carriage, exhibition on, **36**, [428]

advertisement—*contd*
housing provisions, under—
dispensing with, **22**, [415]
forms etc, **22**, [414]
innocent publication of, **39(1)**, [100]
investment. *See* **investment**
London, in. *See* **London**
London streets, carriage etc through,
36, [463]
meaning, **7(1)**, [116], [207]; **38(2)**, [40];
39(1), [112]; **46**, [612]
medicinal products, of. *See* **medicinal products**
notices given by, **8**, 63
offences, **46**, [488]
operational land, display on, **46**, [548]
placard, removal or obliteration of,
35(2), [521]
pool betting, **5(1)**, [56]
poster, removal or obliteration of,
35(2), [521]
private hire-car, display on, **38(2)**, [40]
prohibited, expense of removing, **46**, [487]
prostitution, relating to, **12(3)**, [28], [29]
pyramid selling scheme, as to, **47**, [186]
racial discrimination in, **7(1)**, [165]
regulations—
control by, **46**, [484]
different areas, for, **46**, [485]
removal, power of, **46**, [487]
sex discrimination in, **7(1)**, [82]
special control, areas of, **46**, [485]
surrogacy arrangements, of, **12(1)**, [977]
tobacco products. *See* **tobacco products**
trade description, used in, **39(1)**, [91]
trading stamps, respecting, **47**, [74]
trustee, by, **48**, 483
unauthorised hoardings, removal of,
26(1), [218]
operational land, entry on, **26(1)**, [221]
unlawful display, defence, **35(2)**, [520]
validity of orders, **46**, [549], [553]
war risks insurance—
Advisory Committee on, **19(1)**, [268]
exceptions from restrictions, **19(1)**, [266]
offences and penalties, **19(1)**, [269]
permitted, requirements where,
19(1), [267]
restriction on, **19(1)**, [266]
Welsh television, on, **45**, [112]

advertising
gambling. *See* **gambling**

Advisory Committee on Legal Education and Conduct
abolition of, **11(3)**, [311]
generally, **11(2)**, [1]

Advisory, Conciliation and Arbitration Service
advice by, **16**, [416]
annual report and accounts, **16**, [467]
arbitration—
reference to, **16**, [413]

Advisory, Conciliation and Arbitration Service—*contd*
arbitration—*contd*
unfair dismissal, scheme for, **16**, [414]
See also Central Arbitration Committee
below
body corporate, as, **16**, [460]
Central Arbitration Committee—
annual report and accounts, **16**, [483]
armed forces, service pay, reference of
matters to, **16**, [37]
arrears date, **16**, [39]
qualifying date, **16**, [38]
Scotland, determination of period in,
16, [40]
awards, **16**, [482]
collective bargaining. *See* **collective bargaining**
deputy chairmen, appointment of,
16, [477]
equal pay, matters arising—
agricultural wages, **16**, [35]
reference to, **16**, [35]
functions of, **16**, [476]
members—
appointment of, **16**, [477]
remuneration, **16**, [479]
resignation, **16**, [478]
terms of appointment, **16**, [478]
vacancy, **16**, [477]
proceedings, **16**, [480], [481]
staff, **16**, [476]
Certification Officer. *See* **Certification Officer**
Codes of Practice—
failure to comply with, **16**, [406]
later Code superseding, **16**, [408]
power to issue, **16**, [398]
procedure for issue, **16**, [399]
revision, **16**, [398], [400]
revocation, **16**, [401]
subject-matter of, **16**, [398]
common seal, **16**, [464]
conciliation—
offer of, **16**, [410]
officers, **16**, [412]
continuation of, **16**, [460]
Council—
constitution, **16**, [461]
deputy chairmen—
appointment of, **16**, [461]
resignation, **16**, [462]
members—
appointment of, **16**, [461], [462]
remuneration, **16**, [463]
resignation, **16**, [462]
terms of appointment, **16**, [462]
vacancy, **16**, [462]
dismissal procedures agreements, **16**, [415], [997]
equal pay, duty as to panel of experts, **16**, [34]
fees for exercise of functions, **16**, [465]
financial provisions, **16**, [93], [466]
functions of, **16**, [460]

Advisory, Conciliation and Arbitration Service—*contd*
industrial relations, promoting improvement of, **16**, [409]
inquiry by, **16**, [417]
officers and staff, **16**, [464]
offices, **16**, [460]
receipts by, disposal, **16**, [110]
recognition disputes, information required for settling, **16**, [411]
secretary, **16**, [464]

advocate
adjustment income, spreading, **44(3)**, [238]–[239]
disability discrimination and harassment by, **7(1)**, [306]
adjustments, duty to make, **7(1)**, [307]
duties of, **11(4)**, [303]
employed, **11(4)**, [304]
trade profits, **44(3)**, [159]

advowson
grant by Crown, **10**, [9]
in gross, becoming, **14**, 1155
Law of Property Act, application, **20**, [800]
parochial church councils, **14**, 1260
quare impedit proceedings, **41**, [544]
registration, abolition, **14**, 1136
settled land, comprised in, **14**, 1155–6
transfer of certain, **14**, 1155–6
trust for sale, held on, **14**, 1155–6
university or college—
gratuitous transfer of, **21**, [37]
power to sell, **21**, [33]
purchase of, **21**, [34]

aerodrome. *See also* **airport**
abandoned vehicles, disposal, **4(1)**, [305]
air navigation installations. *See* **air navigation**
authority. *See* **Airports Authority; Civil Aviation Authority**
British Airports Authority. *See* **Airports Authority**
byelaws as to. *See* **airports**
cables etc, restriction on installation, **4(1)**, [97]
charges, noise and emissions, charge by reference to, **4(1)**, [86]
See also **airport**
Civil Aviation Authority. *See* **Civil Aviation Authority**
consultation in matters concerning, **4(1)**, [79], [84]
customs and excise—
flight from, prevention, **13**, [616], [919]
inspection, **13**, [615]
patrolling by customs officer, **13**, [678]
dangerous articles, possession, **4(1)**, [181]
depreciation in land value through use of, **9**, [304], [312], [318]
designated airport, becoming or ceasing to be, supplementary orders, **4(1)**, [231]
designated, meaning, **4(1)**, [131]
financial assistance, **4(1)**, [83]

aerodrome—*contd*
government department, in occupation of, exemption for, **9**, [364]
grants, **4(1)**, [83]
health control, **4(1)**, [85]
hostilities or emergency, order for possession in time of, **4(1)**, [470]
interpretation, **4(1)**, [471]
infectious diseases at, **35(1)**, [455]
land, acquisition. *See* **civil aviation**
licence-holder, information required by CAA, **4(1)**, [135]
licensed, meaning, **4(1)**, [98]
licensing of, consideration of environmental factors, **4(1)**, [58]
loans in respect of, **4(1)**, [83]
local authorities—
ancillary business by, **4(1)**, [82]
powers of, **4(1)**, [81]
See also **airport**
local authority aerodrome, meaning, **4(1)**, [82]
management—
Civil Aviation Authority, by, **4(1)**, [80]
Secretary of State's aerodromes, **4(1)**, [78]
meaning, **4(1)**, [153], [236]; **9**, [367]; **13**, [590]
noise—
control schemes—
amendment or revocation of, **4(1)**, [87]
breach of, **4(1)**, [89]
establishment and maintenance of, **4(1)**, [87]
requirements imposed, **4(1)**, [87]–[88]
vibration or pollution—
charges, fixing by reference to, **4(1)**, [86]
minimisation, **4(1)**, [58], [302]
nuisance caused by, **4(1)**, [126]
regulation of, **4(1)**, [127]
sound-proofing buildings near, **4(1)**, [130]
See also under **aircraft**
nuisance by aircraft on, **4(1)**, [126]
obstructions—
control over, **4(1)**, [97]
removal, **4(1)**, [98]
warning of presence, **4(1)**, [98]
orders—
exercise of powers, parliamentary control, **4(1)**, [173]–[175]
power to make, **4(1)**, [151]
planning decision, compensation, **4(1)**, [104]
police—
disputes with managers of aerodromes—
independent experts—
appointment of, **4(1)**, [228]
removal of, **4(1)**, [229]
replacement of, **4(1)**, [229]
Secretary of State, referral to, **4(1)**, [227]
tribunal dealing with, **4(1)**, [230]
functions, exercise of, **4(1)**, [223]
provisions as to, **4(1)**, [526]
services agreement—
consultation before entering into, **4(1)**, [221]

aerodrome—*contd*
police—*contd*
services agreement—*contd*
disputes arising—
referral to Secretary of State,
4(1), [227]
tribunal dealing with, **4(1)**, [230]
duration of, **4(1)**, [222]
meaning, **4(1)**, [222]
special constables, appointment, **4(1)**, [108]
stop and search powers, **4(1)**, [219]
See also **airports**
powers, exercise of, **4(1)**, [175]
proprietor, meaning, **4(1)**, [98]
provision—
Civil Aviation Authority, restriction on,
4(1), [80]
local authorities, by, **4(1)**, [81]
Secretary of State, by, **4(1)**, [78]
restricted zones, designation of, **4(1)**, [188]
road traffic control, **4(1)**, [302], [304]
roads, provision of, **4(1)**, [78], [81]
runway or apron alterations, **9**, [312], [318]
safety of—
endangering, **4(1)**, [345]
land use restriction, **4(1)**, [96], [166]
See also security *below*
search, security, **4(1)**, [190], [191]
Secretary of State, provision by—
byelaws, **4(1)**, [302]
consultation as to management etc,
4(1), [79]
powers, **4(1)**, [78]
security—
air cargo agents—
documents, offences, **4(1)**, [213]
provision for, **4(1)**, [212]
aircraft, unauthorised persons on,
4(1), [210]
annual report on, **4(1)**, [216]
authorised persons, offences, **4(1)**, [211]
dangerous articles, possession, **4(1)**, [181]
directions by Secretary of State, **4(1)**, [189]
enforcement notice—
contents, **4(1)**, [198]
objections to, **4(1)**, [200]
offences, **4(1)**, [199]
proceedings relating to, **4(1)**, [201]
revocation or variation, **4(1)**, [201]
service of, **4(1)**, [197]
inspection as to compliance, **4(1)**, [203]
limitations on scope, **4(1)**, [194]
matters included in, **4(1)**, [193]
objections to, **4(1)**, [196]
operation of, **4(1)**, [202]
urgent or general, **4(1)**, [195]
false statements—
baggage, cargo or stores, relating to,
4(1), [207]
identity documents, in connection
with, **4(1)**, [208]
fund. *See* **aviation security**
information required as to, **4(1)**, [187]
inspections, **4(1)**, [203]

aerodrome—*contd*
security—*contd*
measures to be taken—
compensation, **4(1)**, [215], [240]
directions as to, **4(1)**, [192]
meaning, **4(1)**, [236]
objection to directions, **4(1)**, [196]
Northern Ireland, application to,
4(1), [232]
occurrences, duty to report, **4(1)**, [214]
restricted zone—
meaning, **4(1)**, [218]
unauthorised persons in, **4(1)**, [209]
searches, **4(1)**, [190], [191]
service of documents, **4(1)**, [217]
suspicion of intended offence, **4(1)**, [184]
unauthorised persons—
aircraft, on board, **4(1)**, [210]
restricted zone, in, **4(1)**, [209]
urgent directions, **4(1)**, [195]
services and facilities, provision—
air navigation services, meaning,
4(1), [153]
Secretary of State's aerodromes, **4(1)**, [78]
statutory undertakers, obstruction caused by,
4(1), [98]
stop and search powers at, **12(4)**, [258]
transfer to—
Airports Authority. *See* **Airports
Authority**
Civil Aviation Authority, **4(1)**, [75], [161]
trees, control over height of, **4(1)**, [97]
trespass on, **4(1)**, [90]
violence, protection against acts of,
4(1), [186]

aerosol paint
children, sale to, **35(2)**, [437]

affidavit. *See also* **oath**
armed forces officer taking, **3**, [459], [705],
[978]
authorised person—
meaning, **18**, [280]
taking by, **18**, [75], [280], [673]
commissioners, taking before, **18**, [161], [280]
declaration substituted for—
acceptance by courts, **18**, [84], [86]
Bank of England, by, **18**, [85]
Crown debts, to prove, **18**, [88]
execution of will, to prove, **18**, [87]
fees payable, **18**, [90]
form of, **18**, [91], [92]
Treasury, by, **18**, [79]
interest in proceedings, person having, bar on
taking, **18**, [280]
meaning, **18**, [159]
persons authorised to take, **18**, [75], [280],
[673]
place and date, statement as to, **18**, [280]
prize proceedings, for, **18**, [156]
probate or letters of administration, required
for, **18**, [673]
procedure for making, **41**, [13], [53]
statement of affairs, to verify, **4(2)**, [100]

affidavit—*contd*
taking of—
fee, **11(2)**, [363]
powers, **11(2)**, [362]
solicitor, by, **11(2)**, [362]
winding up, swearing in, **4(2)**, [237]

affiliation order
deduction from pay—
air force, **3**, [920]
army, **3**, [647]
summons, service of, **3**, [1178]

affiliation proceedings
abolition of, **6**, [279]

affirmation. *See also* **oath**
administration without jurisdiction, **18**, [84]
declaration substituted for—
Bank of England, by, **18**, [85]
generally, **18**, [79]–[91]
universities, by, **18**, [83]
force and effect of, **18**, [238]
form of, **18**, [239]
oath, in lieu of, **18**, [75], [238]
permission to make, **18**, [238]
right to affirm, **18**, [75]
Welsh language, in, **18**, [75]

affray
offence of, **12(1)**, [993], [997]

after-care. *See* **probation**

age
attained, when, **45**, [918]
birth certificate, registrar supplying,
15(1), [698]
compulsory school, **15(1)**, [502]
criminal responsibility, of, **6**, [38]
determination of, **12(2)**, [834]
employment of children, relevant to, **6**, [149]
evidence of, **3**, [699], [972], [1216];
15(1), [699]
independent domicile, of acquiring, **6**, [153]
magistrates' court, determining, **11(2)**, [574]
majority—
of, **6**, [110]
when attained, **45**, [918]
parliamentary candidate, minimum for,
15(3), [608]
presumption and determination, **6**, [48]
presumption of, **15(1)**, [590], [699]
parties to conveyance, **20**, [638]
social security, for purposes of, **40(1)**, [456]
time of attaining, **6**, [112]

agency
contract, meaning, **44(2)**, [47]
profit share, entitlement to profits, **43(S)**, 552
worker—
arrangements with agency, **44(2)**, [45]
excluded services, **44(2)**, [47]
income tax treatment, **44(2)**, [44]
PAYE payments, **44(2)**, [688]

agency—*contd*
worker—*contd*
remuneration, meaning, **44(2)**, [47]
unincorporated bodies, **44(2)**, [46]

agency worker
remuneration, return of, **42**, [121]

agent
accommodation. *See* **accommodation
agency**
bill of exchange, liability as to, **19(1)**, [55],
[56]
bookmaker's. *See* **bookmaker**
carrier by air, of. *See* **carrier (air)**
collecting. *See* **dividend**
common law powers, **1(1)**, [14]
corruption in transaction with—
penalty, **12(1)**, [173]
prosecution of offences, **12(1)**, [175]
Crown—
liability for torts of, **13**, [11]
meaning, **13**, [38]
estate. *See* **estate agent**
liability, not exempt from, **1(1)**, [13]
libel, publication by, **19(3)**, [277]
mercantile. *See* **mercantile agent**
paying. *See* **dividend**
protection of, **42**, [214]
trustee or personal representative, of,
48, 475–6
underwriter. *See* **underwriter**

Agent-General
capital gains tax, residence for purposes of,
42, [1093]

aggregate
agreement to supply, subject to, **43(2)**, [4]
construction, use for purposes of, **43(2)**, [34]
contract to supply, adjustment of, **43(2)**, [29]
exempt, **43(2)**, [2]
exploitation—
commercial, **43(2)**, [4]
responsibility for, **43(2)**, [7]
subject to, **43(2)**, [2], [4]
meaning, **43(2)**, [2]
quantity of, **43(2)**, [2]
references to, **43(2)**, [3]
relevant substances, **43(2)**, [3]
sites—
operators, **43(2)**, [6]
originating, **43(2)**, [5]
meaning, **43(2)**, [5]
mixing of aggregate on, **43(2)**, [5]
removal of aggregate from, **43(2)**, [4]
taxable, meaning, **43(2)**, [2]
weight of, **43(2)**, [8]

aggregates levy
aggregate removed from railway, etc,
exemption for, **43(S)**, 523
appeals—
determinations on, **43(2)**, [28]
reduction of penalties on, **43(2)**, [32]

aggregates levy—*contd*
  appeals—*contd*
    reviewed decisions, against, **43(2)**, [27]
  business—
    death or incapacity of person carrying on, **43(2)**, [24]
    transfer as going concern, **43(2)**, [25]
  charge to, **43(2)**, [1]
  Commissioners for Her Majesty's Revenue and Customs—
    appeal against reviewed decisions, **43(2)**, [27]
    certificate of, **43(2)**, [64]
    determinations on, **43(2)**, [28]
    interest payable by, **43(2)**, [67]
    penalties, reduction of, **43(2)**, [32]
    powers of, **43(2)**, [31]
    review of decisions, **43(2)**, [26]
  connected activities, meaning, **43(2)**, [64]
  credits, **43(2)**, [15]
    Northern Ireland, transitional, **43(2)**, [16]
  definitions, **43(2)**, [34]
  directors, liability for civil penalties, **43(2)**, [62]
  entry on premises—
    inspection, for, **43(2)**, [64]
    search, for, **43(2)**, [64]
  evasion of, **43(2)**, [13]
  evidence by certificate, **43(2)**, [64]
  exempt processes, meaning, **43(2)**, [3]
  group treatment—
    application for, **43(2)**, [66]
    applications relating to, **43(2)**, [66]
    eligibility for, **43(2)**, [66]
    modification, **43(2)**, [66]
    notifications, **43(2)**, [66]
    termination, **43(2)**, [66]
  groups of companies—
    representative member, charge to levy, **43(2)**, [21]
    same control, bodies under, **43(2)**, [66]
  information—
    disclosure of, **43(2)**, [64]
    inducements to provide, **43(2)**, [64]
    order for access to, **43(2)**, [64]
    production of documents, **43(2)**, [64]
      powers relating to, **43(2)**, [64]
    provision of, **43(2)**, [64]
    removal of documents, **43(2)**, [64]
  information and inspection powers, **43(S)**, 1412–13, 1692–8
  insolvency, application of procedure, **43(2)**, [23]
  interest—
    amounts assessed, on, **43(2)**, [65]
    assessments, **43(2)**, [60]
    Commissioners, payable by, **43(2)**, [65]
    overdue levy paid before assessment, on, **43(2)**, [60]
    overpayments of, **43(2)**, [65]
    payment without deduction of income tax, **43(2)**, [60]
    penalty—
      assessments, **43(2)**, [60]
      nature of, **43(2)**, [60]

aggregates levy—*contd*
  interest—*contd*
    penalty—*contd*
      no return made, where, **43(2)**, [60]
      under-declared levy on, **43(2)**, [60]
      unpaid levy on, **43(2)**, [60]
      unpaid ordinary interests on, **43(2)**, [60]
      unpaid penalties, on, **43(2)**, [67]
  non-resident taxpayer—
    meaning, **43(2)**, [34]
    tax representative, requirement to have. *See* tax representatives *below*
  Northern Ireland, transitional tax credit scheme, new, **43(2)**, [509]
  notices, service of, **43(2)**, [33]
  offences—
    arrest, **43(2)**, [61]
    evasion, **43(2)**, [61]
      preparations for, **43(2)**, [61]
    misstatements, **43(2)**, [61]
    proceedings, **43(2)**, [61]
  overpayments—
    interest, of, **43(2)**, [65]
    repayment of, **43(2)**, [17]
  partnership, responsibility for levy, **43(2)**, [22]
  payment, requirement of, **43(2)**, [10]
  penalties—
    assessment to, **43(2)**, [67]
      time limit, **43(2)**, [67]
    civil, **43(2)**, [32], [62], [67]
    daily, assessment to, **43(2)**, [67]
    directors, liability of, **43(2)**, [62]
    evasion, for, **43(2)**, [62]
    incorrect records evidence claim to tax credits, for, **43(2)**, [62]
    liability to, **43(2)**, [67]
    misdeclaration or neglect, for, **43(2)**, [62]
    reduction on appeal, **43(2)**, [32]
    unpaid, penalty interest on, **43(2)**, [67]
  rates of, **43(S)**, 518, 850
  receipts, destination of, **43(2)**, [30]
  record-keeping, **43(S)**, 1705
  records—
    evidence of, **43(2)**, [64]
    obligations as to, **43(2)**, [64]
  recovery—
    assessments, **43(2)**, [60]
      notification, **43(2)**, [60]
      supplementary, **43(2)**, [60]
      time limits, **43(2)**, [60]
    debt due, as, **43(2)**, [60]
    walking possession agreements, **43(2)**, [60]
  register—
    correction of, **43(2)**, [59]
    establishment and maintenance of, **43(2)**, [9]
    information in, **43(2)**, [9]
    publication of, **43(2)**, [59]
  registration—
    cancellation, **43(2)**, [59]
    form of, **43(2)**, [59]
    notifications, regulations, **43(2)**, [59]
    registrability—
      loss or prospective loss, notification of, **43(2)**, [59]

aggregates levy—*contd*
registration—*contd*
registrability—*contd*
notification of, **43(2)**, [59]
requirement of, **43(2)**, [9]
regulations, **43(2)**, [31]
repayments—
excessive, assessment for, **43(2)**, [65]
obtaining, **43(2)**, [63]
overpaid levy, of, **43(2)**, [17]
reference to, **43(2)**, [34]
reimbursement arrangements, **43(2)**, [65]
time limit, **43(2)**, [18]
unjust enrichment, **43(2)**, [18]
returns—
failure to comply, **43(2)**, [10]
none made, penalty interest on, **43(2)**, [60]
requirement to make, **43(2)**, [10]
samples, power to take, **43(2)**, [64]
security, **43(2)**, [11]
set-off—
amounts due, of, **43(2)**, [65]
other taxes and duties, of or against,
43(2), [65]
restrictions, **43(2)**, [65]
tax credits, **43(2)**, [15]–[16]
Northern Ireland, transitional, **43(2)**, [16]
tax representatives—
effect of appointment, **43(2)**, [20]
incorrect records evidencing claim,
43(2), [62]
liability of, **43(2)**, [20]
meaning, **43(2)**, [34]
offences, **43(2)**, [20]
requirement to appoint, **43(2)**, [19]
time limits for assessments, claims, etc,
amendment, **43(S)**, 1713–14
unincorporated body, responsibility for levy,
43(2), [22]
unpaid, penalty interest, **43(2)**, [60]
wrongdoing, penalties,
43(S), 1328–39. *See also* **tax penalty**

agreement
acquisition of land—
by. *See* **acquisition of land**
otherwise than by, under Lands
Clauses Acts, **9**, [15]–[31]
mercantile agent's clerk, with, **1(1)**, [7]
stamp duty. *See* **stamp duty**

agricultural boards
appropriate authority, meaning, **1(2)**, [739]
areas of, **1(2)**, [730]
charging by, **1(2)**, [747]
directions to, **1(2)**, [736], [738]
exercise of functions, approval of, **1(2)**, [747]
functions assigned to, **1(2)**, [746]
grants to, **1(2)**, [737]
incidental powers, **1(2)**, [747]
investigative powers, **1(2)**, [747]
levies, **1(2)**, [747]
members—
appointment, **1(2)**, [745]
remuneration and pensions, **1(2)**, [745]

agricultural boards—*contd*
members—*contd*
term of office, **1(2)**, [745]
offences, **1(2)**, [747]
orders, procedure for, **1(2)**, [740]
permissible functions, **1(2)**, [732]
permissible purposes, **1(2)**, [731]
power to dissolve, **1(2)**, [735]
power to establish, **1(2)**, [730]
registers, returns and information, **1(2)**, [747]
report and accounts, **1(2)**, [745]
reserve funds, **1(2)**, [747]
staff, **1(2)**, [745]
status, **1(2)**, [745]
subsidiaries, acting through, **1(2)**, [747]

agricultural bodies
reform—
boards, power to establish. *See* **agricultural
boards**
levy bodies, power to dissolve,
1(2), [734]–[736]

agricultural building
allowance. *See* **capital allowances**
construction, expenditure on, **43(1)**, [972]
husbandry, meaning, **43(1)**, [971]
meaning, **43(1)**, [970]
non-domestic rates, exemption from,
25(2), [835]
related agricultural land—
different relevant interests in, **43(1)**, [980]
meaning, **43(1)**, [970]
relevant interest—
different, in different parts of land,
43(1), [980]
ending of lease, provisions applying on,
43(1), [977]
general rule, **43(1)**, [973]
leasehold, merger of, **43(1)**, [976]
security, conveyed or assigned by way of,
43(1), [975]
subordinate lease, effect of creating,
43(1), [974]

agricultural buildings allowance
abolition from 2011, **43(S)**, 911
consequential amendments, **43(S)**, 1237–40
savings, **43(S)**, 1241
availability of, **43(1)**, [970]
balancing adjustments—
balancing charge, overall limit on,
43(1), [996]
balancing events—
avoidance affecting proceeds of,
43(1), [1209]
proceeds from, **43(1)**, [992]–[993]
calculation, **43(1)**, [994]
chargeable period when made, **43(1)**, [986]
definitions, **43(1)**, [999]
qualifying expenditure, **43(S)**, 535–6
relevant interest in part of land, acquisition
of, **43(1)**, [997]
residue of qualifying expenditure,
43(1), [995]

agricultural buildings allowance—*contd*
balancing adjustments—*contd*
subordinate interest, sale subject to,
43(1), [998]
when made, **43(1)**, [989]
contribution allowances, **43(1)**, [1177]
definitions, **43(1)**, [1002]
phasing out before abolition, **43(S)**, 911–13
qualifying expenditure—
construction, capital expenditure on,
43(1), [978]
different parts of land, different relevant
interests in, **43(1)**, [980]
first use of building, purchase of relevant
interest before, **43(1)**, [979]
trades, giving effect to for, **43(1)**, [1000]
transitional charging period, **43(S)**, 911–13
transitional provisions, **43(1)**, [1227]
UK property and Schedule A business, for,
43(1), [1001]
writing-down—
calculation of—
acquisition, after, **43(1)**, [985]
basic rule, **43(1)**, [982]
chargeable period when balancing
adjustment made, **43(1)**, [986]
entitlement to, **43(1)**, [981]
final, **43(1)**, [988]
first use of building not for purposes of
husbandry, where, **43(1)**, [983]
relevant interest, acquisition after first use of
building, **43(1)**, [984]
residue of qualifying expenditure, limited
to, **43(1)**, [987]

agricultural charge
validity and rights of parties, **19(1)**, [600]

agricultural crafts
grants in connection with, **1(2)**, [50]
proficiency tests, devising, **1(2)**, [50]

agricultural credits. *See also* **Agricultural
Mortgage Corporation**
assets, charges on, **1(1)**, [302]
charges—
agricultural society debenture, created by,
1(1), [310]
bankruptcy, effect of, **1(1)**, [304]
distress, whether protected from,
1(1), [305]
farming stock and assets, on, **1(1)**, [302]
fixed, effect of, **1(1)**, [303]
floating—
effect of, **1(1)**, [304]
property effected by, **1(1)**, [302]
forms, **1(1)**, [302]
fraudulent creation, **1(1)**, [308]
growing crops, inclusion of, **1(1)**, [305]
interest payable under, **1(1)**, [266]
priorities, **1(1)**, [305]
publication, restriction on, **1(1)**, [307]
register, official searches in, **1(1)**, [312]
registration, **1(1)**, [306]
sanction, application for, **1(1)**, [266]

agricultural credits—*contd*
charges—*contd*
stamp duty exemption, **1(1)**, [305]
farmer, meaning, **1(1)**, [302]
farming stock, meaning, **1(1)**, [302]
ministerial expenses and receipts, **1(1)**, [669]
mortgages—
improvement, for defraying expenses of,
1(1), [323]
land held in trust, where, **1(1)**, [323]
provisions applicable, **1(1)**, [321]
repayment by instalments, **1(1)**, [322]
summary of provisions, **1(1)**, [124]
tenant farmer, rights of, **1(1)**, [309]

agricultural development councils
levies by, **1(2)**, [528]

agricultural holding. *See also* **agricultural
land**
acquisition of land. *See* **agricultural land**
amalgamation of units. *See* **agricultural land**
arable land—
grassland excluded, **22**, [580]
system of cropping, **22**, [580]
arbitration, **22**, [649]
arbitration for rent, effect of VAT changes,
50(S), VAT 29
assured tenancy, exclusion of, **22**, [913]
business—
capital grants, **1(1)**, [798], [799]
falsely obtaining, **1(2)**, [53]
charges on, **22**, [651]
commercial rent arrears recovery (CRAR),
24, [526]
compulsorily acquired, compensation on,
9, [347]
compulsory purchase. *See* **agricultural land**
condition of, record of—
person to make, appointment, **22**, [587]
right to require, **22**, [587]
corporations, offences by, **1(1)**, [752]
Crown land, provisions as to, **22**, [660]
displacement after compulsory purchase,
allowances for, **1(1)**, [556], [757]
distress for rent. *See under* **agricultural
tenancy**
disturbance—
additional payments for, **1(1)**, [747], [757]
compensation to tenant for, **22**, [625]
early resumption clause, effect of,
1(1), [749]
possession, tenant not in, **1(1)**, [748]
entry on—
landlord's right of, **22**, [588]
minister's powers, **1(1)**, [396]
obstructing, **1(1)**, [396]
fertilisers. *See* **fertilisers and feeding stuffs**
improvements—
capital monies, application for, **1(1)**, [664]
grants, livestock rearing land. *See* **livestock**
land, grants for, **1(1)**, [367], [799]
mortgage, defraying expenses by,
1(1), [323]

agricultural holding—*contd*
  improvements—*contd*
    See also under **agricultural tenancy**
  Landlord and Tenant Act 1954, exclusion from
    Part II, **21**, [207]
  leasehold enfranchisement or extension,
    exclusion from, **21**, [292]
  market gardens. *See* **market garden**
  meaning, **9**, [367]; **22**, [566]
  notice to quit—
    breach of tenancy, in case of, **22**, [670]
    compensation, **22**, [627]
    consent by Tribunal to—
      breach of conditions, penalty, **22**, [592]
      condition attaching, **22**, [592]
      notice to do work, non-compliance
        with, **22**, [593]
      requirement, **22**, [591]
    counter-notice by tenant, **22**, [591]
    death of tenant—
      after, **22**, [670], [671]
      consent to operation of, application for,
        22, [609]
      effect on succession, **22**, [603]
      restriction on operation of notice,
        22, [608]
    good husbandry, tenant not farming in
      accordance with, **22**, [670], [671]
    insolvency of tenant, **22**, [670]
    land required for—
      public undertaking, **22**, [683]
      purpose other than agriculture,
        22, [670], [671]
    length, **22**, [590]
    Minister, by, **22**, [670]
    notice to do work, failure to comply,
      22, [593]
    old tenancy, **22**, [683]
    part, of—
      compensation for remainder, option for,
        9, [362]
      compensation, right to opt for, **9**, [361]
      counter-notice to—
        effect of, **9**, [358]
        reference to Lands Tribunal, **9**, [360]
        service, **9**, [357]
      service, **9**, [357]
    part of holding—
      length of, **22**, [590]
      reduction of rent on, **22**, [598]
      treatment as notice to quit entire
        holding, **22**, [597]
      validity, **22**, [596]
    procedure for taking possession, **9**, [359]
    public undertaking, by, **22**, [683]
    rent, failure to pay, **22**, [670]
    restriction on operation, **22**, [591], [593]
    retirement notice, effect on, **22**, [617]
    retirement of tenant, on—
      effect of, **22**, [617]
      restriction on operation of, **22**, [619]
    savings, **23**, [56]
    serviceman, tenant being, **22**, [673]

agricultural holding—*contd*
  notice to quit—*contd*
    small-holding, holding let as—
      alternative accommodation, **22**, [670],
        [671]
      in case of, **22**, [670]
    repairing obligations, **22**, [518]
    requisitioned land. *See* **requisitioned land**
    secure tenancy, exclusion of, **22**, [427]
    security of tenure, **20**, [1]
    servicemen, interests of, **3**, [405]
    special system of farming, compensation on
      termination, **22**, [635]
    succession to tenancy. *See* **agricultural
      tenancy**
    surface soil, removal of. *See* **agricultural
      land**
    tenancy. *See also* **agricultural tenancy**
      legislation on, **20**, [1]
      protection, exclusion from, **21**, [530]
    tenancy not a secure tenancy, **22**, [427]
    transitional provisions, **22**, [684]
    war damage. *See* **war damage**

agricultural housing
  exchequer contributions, abolition, **23**, [557]

agricultural land. *See also* **agricultural
  holding; agriculture**
  acquisition of—
    acquired land, powers as to, **1(1)**, [389]
    agreement, by, **1(1)**, [388]
    compulsory—
      additional payments to tenant,
        1(1), [747], [757]
      displacement allowance, **1(1)**, [556]
      research, experiment and demonstrations,
        for, **1(1)**, [748]
  agricultural units—
    amalgamation—
      acquisition of land to assist, **1(1)**, [642]
      amendments relating to, **1(1)**, [801]
      breach of conditions, **1(1)**, [671]
      co-ordinated scheme, **1(1)**, [653]
      conditions applying to, **1(1)**, [671]
      grants—
        amended provisions, **1(1)**, [801]
        conditions applying to, **1(1)**, [859]
        falsely obtaining, **1(1)**, [665]
        generally, **1(1)**, [643]
        recovery, **1(1)**, [644]
        transactions qualifying for, **1(1)**, [639]
      loans to assist, **1(1)**, [641], [859]
      non-compliance with conditions,
        1(1), [644]
      promotion of, **1(1)**, [642], [650]
      schemes—
        general provisions, **1(1)**, [643]
        revocation of approval, effect,
          1(1), [644]
      tenancies affected by, **1(1)**, [650]
      transfer of land, restriction, **1(1)**, [671]
    boundaries. *See* boundary adjustments *below*
    commercial unit, meaning, **1(1)**, [646]
    meaning, **1(1)**, [399]

agricultural land—*contd*
  agricultural units—*contd*
    rural areas, in. *See* **Rural Development Boards**
    uncommercial—
      dwelling house, occupation of, **1(1)**, [642]
      grants, recovery of, **1(1)**, [644]
      meaning, **1(1)**, [646]
      relinquishing, grants for, **1(1)**, [640]
      schemes as to, general provisions, **1(1)**, [643]
  assured tenancy, exclusion of, **22**, [913]
  boundary adjustments—
    approval of schemes for, **1(1)**, [639]
    duration of scheme, **1(1)**, [639]
    grants or loans for—
      amended provisions, **1(1)**, [858]
      conditions for, **1(1)**, [859]
      false statements to obtain, **1(1)**, [665]
      generally, **1(1)**, [643]
      procedure, **1(1)**, [641]
      recovery of, **1(1)**, [644]
      transactions qualifying for, **1(1)**, [639]
    promotion of, **1(1)**, [642], [650]
    schemes for—
      general provisions for, **1(1)**, [643]
      power to make, **1(1)**, [639]
      revocation of approval, effect, **1(1)**, [644]
    transfer of land, for, **1(1)**, [639]
  capital allowances. *See* **capital allowances**
  change of use, **1(1)**, [389]
  commonhold, exclusion from, **24**, [144]
  compulsory purchase. *See* acquisition *above*
  emergency powers, compensation when taken under, **9**, [121]
  entry on—
    minister's powers, **1(1)**, [396]
    obstructing, **1(1)**, [396]
    proposed, notice of, **1(1)**, [396]
  environmentally sensitive areas, **1(2)**, [396]
  false statements to obtain grants, **1(1)**, [665]
  farm structure. *See* agricultural units *above*
  fertilisers. *See* **fertilisers and feeding stuffs**
  footpaths, bridleways and restricted byways passing over, ploughing and works on, **36**, [1191]
  good estate management, **1(1)**, [382]
  good husbandry, **1(1)**, [383]
  grants for giving up, **42**, [1394]
  highway, encroachment by crops, **36**, [1197]
  improvements. *See* **agricultural holding; agricultural tenancy**
  interest in, power to require information, **1(1)**, [467]
  ironstone workings, **17(1)**, [546]
  lease, surrender of, **9**, [356]
  letting. *See* **agricultural tenancy**
  meaning, **9**, [136], [367]; **21**, [547]; **22**, [566]
  mortgage of, **1(1)**, [323]
  non-domestic rates, exemption from, **25(2)**, [835]

agricultural land—*contd*
  notice to treat—
    part of land, for—
      counter-notice to—
        effect of, **9**, [356]
        lease, acquiring authority becoming entitled to, **9**, [356]
        reference to Lands Tribunal, **9**, [356]
        service of, **9**, [355]
        withdrawal, **9**, [356]
      service, **9**, [355]
      withdrawal, **9**, [356]
  occupier's loss payment, **9**, [331]
    dual entitlement, **9**, [337]
  opencast coal working in. *See* **opencast coal** (compensation)
  restoration after construction of pipe-line, **17(1)**, [261]
  severance, **9**, [355]
  subsidence, damage caused by. *See under* **coal mining subsidence**
  surface soil, removal—
    offences, **1(1)**, [451]
    peat cutting, saving for, **1(1)**, [451]
    penalties, **1(1)**, [452]
    planning permission, without, **1(1)**, [451]
    prosecution, consent to, **1(1)**, [453]
  tenancies. *See* **agricultural tenancy**
  uncommercial units—
    dwelling house, occupation of, **1(1)**, [642]
    grants, recovery of, **1(1)**, [644]
    meaning, **1(1)**, [646]
    relinquishing, grants for, **1(1)**, [640]
    schemes as to, general provisions, **1(1)**, [643]
  weeds. *See* **weeds**

Agricultural Land Tribunal
  applications to, **1(1)**, [385]
  areas for establishment of, **1(1)**, [385]
  assessors, appointment, **1(1)**, [402]
  chairman, **1(1)**, [402]
  composition, **19(3)**, [200]
  constitution, **1(1)**, [402]
  costs, power to award, **1(1)**, [458]
  ditches, order to cleanse, **19(3)**, [197]
  divisions, sitting in, **1(1)**, [385]
  documents, proof of, **1(1)**, [402]
  duty of, **1(1)**, [385]
  establishment, **1(1)**, [385]
  hearings, **1(1)**, [402]
  High Court, references to, **1(1)**, [459]
  incidental powers, **19(3)**, [200]
  Lord Chancellor, functions, **1(1)**, [534], [539], [540]
  market garden, powers as to, **22**, [645]
  members—
    disqualification, **1(1)**, [402]
    panels for appointment, **1(1)**, [402]
    remuneration, **1(1)**, [402]
  notice to quit, consent to—
    breach of conditions, penalty, **22**, [592]
    condition attaching, **22**, [592]
    notice to do work, non-compliance with, **22**, [593]

Agricultural Land Tribunal—*contd*
  notice to quit, consent to—*contd*
    requirement, **22**, [591]
  officers and servants, **1(1)**, [402]
  procedure, **1(1)**, [385], [459]
  questions of law, reference to High Court, **1(1)**, [459]
  references to—
    generally, **1(1)**, [385]
    land in two areas, where, **1(1)**, [387]
    matters to be determined, **1(1)**, [386]
    power to require, **1(1)**, [386]
    reports to minister on, **1(1)**, [386]
  succession to tenancy. *See* **agricultural tenancy**
  validity of proceedings, **1(1)**, [402]

agricultural levies
  evasion, **13**, [658]
  goods not in free circulation in member states of European Communities, **13**, [585]
  member States of EEC, recovery of amounts due in other, **13**, [585]
  Northern Ireland, provisions as to, **13**, [659]
  proceedings for theft relating to, **13**, [907]

agricultural marketing
  boards. *See* **agricultural marketing schemes**
  body corporate, offences by, **1(2)**, [529]
  cereals. *See* **cereals**
  corporate bodies, offences by, **1(1)**, [520]
  Faculties Committee, abolition of, **1(1)**, [860]
  Fund—
    accounts, **1(1)**, [500], [510]
    administration and control, **1(1)**, [510]
    compensation payable from, **1(1)**, [500]
    continuation in existence, **1(1)**, [510]
    contributions to, **1(1)**, [500]
    establishment, **1(1)**, [500]
    expenses payable from, **1(1)**, [515]
    loans made from, **1(1)**, [510]
    payments to or from, **1(1)**, [510]–[512], [860]
  grants—
    co-operation, for promotion of, **1(1)**, [555]
    false statements to obtain, **1(2)**, [520]
      offence of, **1(2)**, [520]
      time limit for prosecution, **1(2)**, [521]
    Northern Ireland, extension of provisions to, **1(2)**, [531]
    provision for, **1(2)**, [519]
  guaranteed prices. *See* **agricultural produce**
  hops. *See* **hops**
  horticultural produce. *See* **horticultural produce**
  metrication, adaptation, **1(1)**, [248]; **1(2)**, [52]
  orders, procedure for making, **1(1)**, [521]
  Reorganisation Commissions—
    constitution, **1(1)**, [513]
    expenses of, defrayment, **1(1)**, [514]
    functions, **1(1)**, [513]
    inquiries, power to hold, **1(1)**, [513]
    investigations by, **1(1)**, [513]
    officers of, **1(1)**, [518]

agricultural marketing—*contd*
  rules, etc, power to make, **1(1)**, [521]
  schemes. *See* **agricultural marketing scheme**

Agricultural Marketing Board
  diseases of animals, information as to, **2**, [541]

agricultural marketing scheme. *See also* **agricultural marketing**
  amendment—
    approval by minister, **1(1)**, [527]
    effect of, **1(1)**, [527]
  approval by minister, **1(1)**, [489]
  arbitration, provision for, **1(1)**, [495], [499]
  boards—
    acts contrary to public interests, **1(1)**, [506]
    borrowing by, **1(1)**, [502]
    co-operation, promotion of, **1(1)**, [494]
    composition of, **1(1)**, [528]
    constitution, **1(1)**, [490], [528]
    consultations by, **1(1)**, [517]
    debentures, issue of, **1(1)**, [502]
    directions by minister to, **1(1)**, [508]
    disciplinary committee—
      chairman's casting vote, **1(1)**, [496]
      constitution, **1(1)**, [496]
      enforcement of decisions, **1(1)**, [499]
      evidence before, **1(1)**, [496]
      losses, power to recover, **1(1)**, [496]
      penalties, recovery of, **1(1)**, [496]
      sittings and hearings, **1(1)**, [496]
    dissolution, **1(1)**, [528]
    education, promotion of, **1(1)**, [494]
    executive committees, appointment, **1(1)**, [490]
    expenses payable by, **1(1)**, [514]
    financial powers, **1(1)**, [500]–[502]
    fines payable to, **1(1)**, [493]
    grants by, **1(1)**, [501]
    grants to, **1(1)**, [502]
    guarantees by, **1(1)**, [501]
    inspection powers, **1(1)**, [495]
    investments by, **1(1)**, [503]
    loans by, **1(1)**, [501]
    loans to—
      generally, **1(1)**, [502]
      long-term, **1(1)**, [512]
      short-term, **1(1)**, [511]
    losses, recovery of, **1(1)**, [497]
    members, number of, **1(1)**, [528]
    penalties—
      power to postpone, **1(1)**, [498]
      recovery of, **1(1)**, [496]
    powers and duties, **1(1)**, [494]
    relations with ministers, **1(1)**, [508]
    research, promotion of, **1(1)**, [494]
    services, rendering, **1(1)**, [494]
    status of, **1(1)**, [528]
    surplus fund, investment, **1(1)**, [503]
    temporary directions to, **1(1)**, [509]
    winding up, **1(1)**, [528]
  bodies corporate, offences by, **1(1)**, [520]

agricultural marketing scheme—*contd*
  cereals, for. *See* **cereals**
  consumers' committee—
    officers of, **1(1)**, [518]
    report by, for investigation, **1(1)**, [508]
  contracts—
    effect of, **1(1)**, [504]
    registration, **1(1)**, [505]
      appeal from refusal of, **1(1)**, [505]
  corresponding schemes—
    co-operation with, **1(1)**, [494]
    meaning, **1(1)**, [495]
  draft, laying before Parliament, **1(1)**, [489]
  exemptions from, **1(1)**, [495]
  hops, for. *See* **hops**
  incidental contents, **1(1)**, [496]
  information—
    disclosure, restrictions on, **1(1)**, [519]
    producers, to be given to, **1(1)**, [492]
  investigation committees—
    officers of, **1(1)**, [518]
    reference of questions to, **1(1)**, [508]
    reports by, **1(1)**, [506]
  market investigation references, remedying
    adverse effects after, **1(1)**, [507]
  matters provided for in, **1(1)**, [493], [494]
  milk. *See* **milk**
  ministers for purposes of, **1(1)**, [523],
    [529]–[533]
  Northern Ireland, application to, **1(1)**, [524]
  objections to, **1(1)**, [489]
  poll on—
    amendment of scheme, **1(1)**, [527]
    initial, meaning, **1(1)**, [523]
    procedure, **1(1)**, [491]
    purposes of holding, **1(1)**, [491]
    requisite majority, meaning, **1(1)**, [523]
  producers—
    disciplinary procedure, **1(1)**, [496]
    information to be given to, **1(1)**, [492]
    list to be prepared, **1(1)**, [492]
    meaning, **1(1)**, [523]
    register—
      inspection, **1(1)**, [495]
      removal from, **1(1)**, [495]
    registered—
      compensation to, **1(1)**, [500]
      contributions to scheme fund,
        1(1), [500]
      death, incapacity, etc, **1(1)**, [496]
      information required of, **1(1)**, [495]
    See also **agricultural marketing**
  loans to, **1(1)**, [501]
  penalties on—
    imposition of, **1(1)**, [496]
    postponement, **1(1)**, [498]
    recovery of, **1(1)**, [496]
  publication of, **1(1)**, [489]
  registration—
    application for, **1(1)**, [492]
    partnership, **1(1)**, [492]
    provision for, **1(1)**, [491]
  regulated products—
    buying by boards, **1(1)**, [493]
    consumers of, meaning, **1(1)**, [528]

agricultural marketing scheme—*contd*
  regulated products—*contd*
    directions by minister as to, **1(1)**, [508]
    grading and marking, **1(1)**, [494]
    marketing, consultations as to, **1(1)**, [517]
    meaning, **1(1)**, [523]
    offences and penalties, **1(1)**, [493]
    products manufactured from, **1(1)**, [493]
  reports to Parliament on, **1(1)**, [516]
  revocation, **1(1)**, [527]
  sales by, restrictions on, **1(1)**, [504]
  submission by producers, **1(1)**, [488]
  substitutional scheme—
    meaning, **1(1)**, [523]
    submission for approval, **1(1)**, [488]

Agricultural Mortgage Corporation. *See also*
agricultural credits
  advances to, further, **1(1)**, [472]
  debentures, validating, **1(1)**, [472]
  repeals, **1(2)**, [479], [483]

agricultural produce. *See also* **horticultural**
produce
  animals, prevention of damage by, **1(1)**, [391]
  bank loans, grants respecting, **1(1)**, [662]
  body corporate, offences by, **1(1)**, [667]
  cereals. *See* **cereals**
  consumable, meaning, **21**, [453]
  corn. *See* **corn**
  eggs. *See* **eggs**
  grade designations—
    applied, when deemed to be, **1(1)**, [293]
    contract, implied terms of, **1(1)**, [293]
    enforcement of provisions, **1(1)**, [297]
    marks—
      conditions attaching to, **1(1)**, [314]
      conditions, **1(1)**, [294]
      expenses in connection with, **1(1)**, [314]
      false belief as to, **1(1)**, [315]
      forgery, **1(1)**, [294]
      prescription of, **1(1)**, [294]
      proceedings for offences, **1(1)**, [315]
      protection of, **1(1)**, [315]
    prescription of, **1(1)**, [293]
    regulations and orders, **1(1)**, [298]
  guaranteed prices—
    marking of produce, **1(1)**, [480]
    offences and penalties, **1(1)**, [482]
    orders—
      procedure, **1(1)**, [483]
      provisions of, **1(1)**, [480]
    protection of, **1(1)**, [480]
  hops. *See* **hops**
  marketing. *See* **agricultural marketing**
  meaning, **1(1)**, [299], [399], [484], [523],
    [661]
  metrication, adoption of, **1(1)**, [248];
    1(2), [52]
  notices, service of, **1(1)**, [397]
  pest control. *See* **pests**
  potatoes. *See* **potatoes**
  producers. *See* **agricultural marketing**
    scheme
  quality, meaning, **1(1)**, [299]

agricultural produce—*contd*
  regulated. *See* **agricultural marketing schemes**
  statistics. *See* **agriculture**
  weights for sale of, **1(1)**, [248]

agricultural property
  farm cottages, valuation of, **42**, [704]
  gift—
    capital gains tax relief, **42**, [1466]
    subject to reservation, **42**, [865], [879]
  inheritance tax provisions. *See* **inheritance tax**
  Scottish lease, accounting for, **42**, [712]

agricultural society
  debenture of—
    floating charge, creation of, **1(1)**, [310]
    registration, **1(1)**, [310]
  rules, registration of, **19(1)**, [336]
  tax exemption, **44(1)**, [369]

agricultural statistics. *See* **agriculture**

agricultural tenancy
  agreements, **22**, [668]
    restrictions on, **22**, [570]
  amalgamation of units affecting, **1(1)**, [650]
  arable land—
    grassland excluded, **22**, [580]
    method of cropping, **22**, [580]
  arbitration—
    milk quotas, effect of, **1(2)**, [394]
    model clause terms, as to, **22**, [572]
    new tenancy granted on death of former tenant, terms of, **22**, [612]
    orders—
      power to make, **22**, [649]
      provision by, **22**, [672]
    permanent pasture, variation of terms as to, **22**, [579]
    procedure, **22**, [649]
    reference of terms to, **22**, [571]
    rent, of, **22**, [577]
    terms of tenancy as to rent, **22**, [669]
    time limit in making award, **22**, [672]
    written agreements, **22**, [571]
  breach of contract, restriction on landlord's remedies, **22**, [589]
  charge—
    compensation, for repayment, **22**, [651]
    general provisions, **22**, [652]
    landlord's power to obtain, **22**, [651]
  compensation—
    agreements, recoverable under, **22**, [643]
    charge on holding for, **22**, [651]
    custom, under, **22**, [642]
    deterioration, for—
      general, **22**, [637]
      part of holding, **22**, [636]
      series of tenancies, during, **22**, [638]
    displacement, after compulsory purchase, **1(1)**, [556], [757]
    disturbance—
      additional payments, **22**, [625]

agricultural tenancy—*contd*
  compensation—*contd*
    disturbance—*contd*
      not payable, where, **22**, [626]
      part of holding, **22**, [628]
      payment for, **22**, [625]
      sub-tenant, **22**, [628]
    improvements, for—
      after March 1948, schedules, **22**, [676]–[681]
      consent of landlord, **22**, [632], [634], [676], [677]
      grants taken into account, **22**, [631], [633]
      hill farming scheme, **22**, [633]
      improvement notice, carried out under, **22**, [633]
      long-term, **22**, [632]
      measure of, **22**, [631]
      notice of carrying out, **22**, [633]
      old tenancy, **22**, [683]
      old, right to, **22**, [680], [681]
      outgoing tenant, paid by incoming tenant, **22**, [634]
      power to vary provisions, **22**, [656]
      right to, **22**, [629]
      series of tenancies, during, **22**, [634]
      short-term, **22**, [678]
    market garden, rights for, **22**, [644], [682]
    milk quota, in respect of. *See* **milk**
    recovery—
      county court order, **22**, [650]
      trustee landlord, from, **22**, [650]
    rent, set off against, **22**, [582]
    reversionary estate severed, where, **22**, [640]
    special system of farming, in case of, **22**, [635]
    tenant-right matters, for, **22**, [630], [679]
      exclusion, **22**, [642]
      old tenancy, **22**, [683]
    termination, on, **22**, [628]
    things done in compliance with Act, for, **22**, [641]
  continuation—
    agreement, by, exclusion, **22**, [570]
    death of tenant before term date, **22**, [569]
    year to year, **22**, [568]
  corporation, offences by, **1(1)**, [752]
  cropping of arable land, system of, **22**, [580]
  crops and produce, tenant's rights of disposal, **22**, [580]
  Crown lands, provisions as to, **22**, [660]
  distress for rent—
    agisted livestock, **22**, [583]
    compensation, set off, **22**, [582]
    disputes, settlement, **22**, [584]
    livestock, on, **22**, [583]
    more than one year previously, due, **22**, [581]
    property of third party, protection, **22**, [583]
  disturbance, compensation—
    additional payments, **22**, [625]
    not payable, where, **22**, [626]

agricultural tenancy—*contd*
  disturbance, compensation—*contd*
    part of holding, **22**, [628]
    payment for, **22**, [625]
    sub-tenant, **22**, [628]
  Duchy land, **22**, [660]
  emblements, extension in lieu of, **22**, [586]
  family succession. *See* succession *below*
  farm business tenancy. *See* **farm business tenancy**
  fixed equipment—
    meaning, **22**, [661]
    model clauses, **22**, [572]
    provision, direction to landlord, **22**, [576]
    statutory requirement, compliance with, **22**, [576]
    transfer of liability, transitional arrangements, **22**, [574]
  fixtures—
    old tenancy, **22**, [683]
    purchase by landlord, **22**, [575]
    record of, **22**, [587]
    removal by tenant, **22**, [575]
  game, damage by, **22**, [585]
  improvements—
    compensation. *See* compensation *above*
    landlord's, rent increase for, **22**, [578]
    limited owners, application of capital moneys, **22**, [653]
    record of, **22**, [587]
    valuation, advisory committee, **22**, [657]
  landlord—
    condition of holding, record of, **22**, [587]
    entry, power of, **22**, [588]
    fixed equipment, provision of, **22**, [576]
    improvements by. *See* improvements *above*
    injunction by in restraint of cropping, **22**, [580]
    remedies for breach, restriction on, **22**, [589]
  less than one year, restriction, **22**, [567]
  limited owner—
    capital moneys, application of, **22**, [654]
    consents by, **22**, [653]
    powers of, **1(2)**, [401]
  market gardens. *See* **market garden**
  model clauses—
    incorporation, deemed, **22**, [572]
    regulations, **22**, [572]
    written agreement, inconsistency with, **22**, [573]
  notice to quit. *See* **agricultural holding**
  notices, service of, **22**, [658]
  old, application of provisions, **22**, [663], [683]
  opencast coal compulsory rights order, effect of, on, **17(1)**, [173]
  orders and regulations, power to make, **22**, [659]
  part of holding—
    disturbance allowance, **22**, [628]
    termination, **22**, [639]
  permanent pasture, variation of terms as to, **22**, [579]
  produce, disposal of, **22**, [580]
  record of condition of holding, **22**, [587]

agricultural tenancy—*contd*
  rent—
    arbitration on terms of, **22**, [577], [669]
    milk quotas, effect of, **1(2)**, [394]
    best, estimate of, **22**, [655]
    distress for. *See* distress for rent *above*
    landlord's improvements, increase for, **22**, [578]
  savings generally, **22**, [662]
  statutory succession. *See* succession *below*
  sub-tenant, compensation for disturbance, **22**, [628]
  succession on death of tenant—
    application for tenancy—
      determination, **22**, [604]
      directions by tribunal, **22**, [605], [610]
      eligible person, by, **22**, [601]
      two or more applicants, by, **22**, [604]
    application of provisions, **22**, [599], [600]
    close relative, meaning, **22**, [600]
    commercial units, effect of occupation, **22**, [674]
    company, land occupied by, **22**, [674]
    definitions, **22**, [600], [624]
    determination by minister, **22**, [674]
    eligible person—
      application for tenancy, **22**, [601]
      further education, period undergoing, **22**, [674]
      livelihood condition, **22**, [674]
      meaning, **22**, [601]
      not fully eligible, treatment as eligible, **22**, [606]
      supplementary provisions, **22**, [674]
    milk quota, transfer of, **1(2)**, [399]
    more than one holding, **22**, [607]
    net annual value of land, determining, **22**, [674]
    new tenancy—
      arbitration on matters arising, **22**, [613]
      grant of, **22**, [604]
      terms unless varied by arbitration, **22**, [612]
    notice to quit—
      consent to operation of, application for, **22**, [609]
      restriction on operation, **22**, [608]
      tenancy subject to, **22**, [603]
    occupation of land for purposes of, **22**, [674]
    relevant time, meaning, **22**, [611]
    spouse or civil partner, land occupied by, **22**, [674]
    two already having occurred, where, **22**, [602]
    will, person designated by, **22**, [604]
  succession on retirement of tenant—
    application of provisions, **22**, [599], [614], [675]
    close relative, meaning, **22**, [614]
    commercial units, occupation of, **22**, [674]
    company, land occupied by, **22**, [674]
    directions, **22**, [620], [623]
    eligible person—
      livelihood condition, **22**, [674]

agricultural tenancy—*contd*
　succession on retirement of tenant—*contd*
　　eligible person—*contd*
　　　meaning, **22**, [615]
　　　right to apply, **22**, [615]
　　excluded applications, **22**, [616]
　　incapacity of tenant, **22**, [616]
　　milk quota, transfer of, **1(2)**, [399]
　　net annual value of land, determining,
　　　22, [674]
　　new tenancy, terms of, **22**, [621]
　　nominated successor—
　　　application by, **22**, [618]
　　　grant of tenancy to, **22**, [618]
　　　meaning, **22**, [614]
　　notice to quit—
　　　effect of, **22**, [617]
　　　restriction on operation of, **22**, [619]
　　occupation of land for purposes of,
　　　22, [674]
　　related holding, meaning, **22**, [614]
　　relevant time, meaning, **22**, [620]
　　retiring tenant, death of, **22**, [622]
　　spouse or civil partner, land occupied by,
　　　22, [674]
　summary of provisions, **1(1)**, [124]
　tenant—
　　arable land, cropping of, **22**, [580]
　　counter-notice to notice to quit, **22**, [591],
　　　[593]
　　crops and produce, disposal, **22**, [580]
　　death—
　　　before term date, restriction on
　　　　continuation, **22**, [569]
　　　succession. *See* succession *above*
　　displacement, allowance for, **1(1)**, [556]
　　good husbandry, responsibility as to,
　　　1(1), [383]
　　improvements by. *See* improvements *above*
　　record of condition of holding, right to
　　　require, **22**, [587]
　　recovery of compensation by, **22**, [650]
　　retirement, nomination of successor on,
　　　22, [616]
　　serviceman as, notice to quit, **22**, [673]
　tenant-right matters, advisory committee,
　　22, [657]
　term date—
　　death of tenant before, **22**, [569]
　　meaning, **22**, [569]
　termination—
　　early resumption clause, on,
　　　compensation, **22**, [627]
　　notice to quit. *See* **agricultural holding**
　　part of holding, **22**, [639]
　　settlement of claims, **22**, [648]
　terms. *See* contract *above*
　transitional provisions, **22**, [684]
　two years or more, continuation as year to
　　year, **22**, [568]
　written agreements—
　　contents, **22**, [668]
　　model clauses, inconsistency with,
　　　22, [573]
　　right to, **22**, [571]

agricultural tenancy—*contd*
　year to year, **22**, [566]

agricultural unit
　depreciation in value through use of public
　　works, **9**, [305]

agricultural wages
　agreements as to, avoidance of, **1(1)**, [413]
　agriculture, meaning, **1(1)**, [420]
　application to committee as to, **1(1)**, [411]
　arrears, **16**, [96]
　benefit in kind as, **1(1)**, [409]
　Board. *See* **Agricultural Wages Board**
　committees. *See* **agricultural wages
　　committees**
　employer—
　　agent of, criminal liability, **1(1)**, [412]
　　defences open to, **1(1)**, [412]
　enforcement officers, **16**, [1013]
　equal pay, involving, **16**, [35]
　holidays with pay—
　　agreements contravening provisions,
　　　1(1), [413]
　　modification of provisions, **1(1)**, [419]
　　orders fixing, **1(1)**, [405]
　injury pay, **1(1)**, [663]
　learners—
　　certification of, **1(1)**, [408]
　　premiums payable by, **1(1)**, [408]
　minimum rates—
　　fixing, **1(1)**, [405]
　　learners, for, **1(1)**, [408]
　　modification of provisions, **1(1)**, [419]
　　sick pay, **1(1)**, [663]
　　time and piece work, **1(1)**, [405]
　Minister—
　　annual report to Parliament, **1(1)**, [415]
　　expenses, defrayment, **1(1)**, [416]
　national minimum, **1(1)**, [405]
　　enforcement, **1(1)**, [406]
　　meaning, **1(1)**, [420]
　　officers, information obtained by,
　　　1(1), [418]
　　regulations, **1(1)**, [420]
　　relationship of provisions, **1(1)**, [421]
　national minimum wage, effect of legislation,
　　16, [956]
　offences, institution of proceedings,
　　1(1), [412]
　officers—
　　appointment, **1(1)**, [414]
　　information obtained by, **1(1)**, [419];
　　　16, [921]
　　powers of, **1(1)**, [415]
　orders—
　　effective date of, **1(1)**, [405]
　　enforcement, **1(1)**, [406]
　piece work—
　　additional wages for, **1(1)**, [410]
　　minimum rates, **1(1)**, [405]
　sick pay, **1(1)**, [663]
　transitional provisions, **16**, [97]

Agricultural Wages Board
amendment of provisions, **16**, [89]
annual report, **1(1)**, [415]
benefits and advantages, valuation of,
  1(1), [409]
committees, **1(1)**, [427]
constitution, **1(1)**, [427]
establishment, **1(1)**, [403]
equal pay, amendment of orders, **16**, [35]
functions, **1(1)**, [403]
members—
  allowances to, **1(1)**, [427]
  appointment or election, **1(1)**, [427]
orders—
  application of, **1(1)**, [429]
  effect to be given to, **1(1)**, [753]
  enforcement, **1(1)**, [406]
  evidence of, **1(1)**, [417]
  notice of, **1(1)**, [429]
  objections to, **1(1)**, [429]
  procedure for making, **1(1)**, [429]
  subject-matter of. *See* **agricultural wages**
  variation or revocation, **1(1)**, [429]
power to fix wages, holidays, etc, **1(1)**, [405]
proceedings of, **1(1)**, [427]

agricultural wages committees
annual reports, **1(1)**, [415]
applications to, **1(1)**, [411]
attendance before, compensation, **1(1)**, [411]
combined counties, for, **1(1)**, [404]
complaints to, **1(1)**, [410]
constitution, **1(1)**, [428]
establishment, **1(1)**, [404]
functions of, **1(1)**, [751]
  additional, **1(1)**, [751]
Greater London, in, **1(1)**, [422]
learners, issue of certificates for, **1(1)**, [408]
members—
  election, **1(1)**, [428]
  remuneration, **1(1)**, [427]
procedure of, **1(1)**, [428]
resolution etc—
  evidence of, **1(1)**, [417]
  passing of, **1(1)**, [428]
sub-committees, **1(1)**, [428]
workers' housing, valuation of, **1(1)**, [409]

agricultural workers
accident, inquest on death by, **1(1)**, [475]
dwelling houses for. *See* housing *below*
holidays—
  agreements as to, **1(1)**, [413]
  allowance, fixing, **1(1)**, [405]
  enforcement of orders, **1(1)**, [407]
  weekly half-holiday, **1(1)**, [405]
houses for, fitness of, **22**, [513]
housing—
  access by landlord and tenant, **21**, [498]
  accommodation information, minister's
    powers, **21**, [481], [482]
  advisory committees—
    constitution, **21**, [480]
    hearings and procedure, **21**, [480]
    information, supply to, **21**, [481]

agricultural workers—*contd*
housing—*contd*
  alternative accommodation—
    not provided, **21**, [496]
    provision, **21**, [478], [479], [496]
  body corporate, offences by, **21**, [487]
  condition as to occupation, suspension,
    21, [483]
  Crown interest—
    provisions applicable, **21**, [486];
    22, [660]
    statutory tenancy excluded, **21**, [457]
  death of original occupier, **21**, [455]
  definitions, index of, **21**, [491]
  distress for rent, restriction on levy,
    21, [460]
  Duchies of Cornwall and Lancaster,
    application of provisions, **21**, [486];
    22, [660]
  employment, meaning, **21**, [495]
  fitness of, **22**, [513]
  hours of employment—
    absence from work, effect, **21**, [493]
    standard, **21**, [495]
  incapable of whole time work,
    determination of person being, **21**, [493]
  information—
    kinds available, **21**, [482]
    non-disclosure, **21**, [481]
    power to obtain, **21**, [481]
    service of notice, **21**, [482]
  Isles of Scilly, application of provisions,
    21, [485]
  landlord—
    meaning, **21**, [484]
    obligations, **21**, [498]
  landlord's agent, service of notice on,
    21, [476]
  licence—
    meaning, **21**, [484]
    terms derived from, **21**, [498]
  living accommodation, meaning, **21**, [474]
  long tenancy—
    low rent, at, **21**, [461]
    meaning, **21**, [461]
  low rent tenancy—
    meaning, **21**, [484]
    treated as statutorily protected, **21**, [461]
  ministerial expenses, **21**, [489]
  notice to quit, service on landlord,
    21, [498]
  offences—
    body corporate, by, **21**, [487]
    prosecution, **21**, [488]
  operative date of provisions—
    order, **21**, [453]
    transitional provisions, **21**, [499]
  permit worker—
    absence from work, **21**, [493]
    meaning, **21**, [493]
  planning permission, suspension of
    condition attaching, **21**, [483]
  possession—
    assignment of sub-tenancy, unlawful,
      21, [496]

agricultural workers—*contd*
  housing—*contd*
    possession—*contd*
      discretion of court, **21**, [459], [496]
      family occupation, required by landlord
        for, **21**, [496]
      furniture, ill-treatment of, **21**, [496]
      grounds for, **21**, [458], [496], [497]
      misconduct or default of tenant, on,
        21, [496]
      assignment of sub-tenancy, unlawful,
        21, [496]
      discretion of court, **21**, [459], [496]
      family occupation, required by landlord
        for, **21**, [496]
      furniture, ill-treatment of, **21**, [496]
      grounds for, **21**, [458], [496], [497]
      misconduct or default of tenant, on,
        21, [496]
      schedule of cases, **21**, [458], [496], [497]
      sub-letting, in case of, **21**, [496], [497]
      sub-tenant, protection, **21**, [461]
    proceedings, jurisdiction and procedure,
      21, [477]
    protected occupancies—
      generally, **21**, [454]
      possession. *See* possession *above*
      shared accommodation, **21**, [474]
      succession, occupiers by, **21**, [455]
    qualifying ownership, **21**, [454], [493]
    qualifying worker, meaning, **21**, [454],
      [493]
    quiet enjoyment, **21**, [498]
    rateable value, **21**, [464]
    rates, liability for, **21**, [498]
    re-housing—
      application for, **21**, [478], [479]
      housing authority, duty of, **21**, [479]
    regulations, power to make, **21**, [469]
    relevant licence—
      meaning, **21**, [453], [492]
      protected occupancy under, **21**, [454],
        [455]
    relevant tenancy—
      meaning, **21**, [453], [492]
      protected occupancy under, **21**, [453],
        [455]
    rent—
      advance payment, avoidance, **21**, [471]
      agreed, **21**, [463]
      arrear, payment in, **21**, [462]
      books, rectification, **21**, [473]
      excess, recovery, **21**, [472]
      increases, notice of, **21**, [467]
      low, long tenancy at, **21**, [461]
      provisional, **21**, [464]
      recoverable, **21**, [471]
      registered—
        amount payable, **21**, [463], [464]
        generally, **21**, [466]
      registration, application for, **21**, [465]
      weekly, paid, **21**, [462]
    rental periods, adjustment for differences,
      21, [468]
    security of tenure, **21**, [458]

agricultural workers—*contd*
  housing—*contd*
    services or facilities, provision, **21**, [498]
    shared accommodation, **21**, [474]
    statutory tenancies—
      Crown interest, none in case of,
        21, [457]
      generally, **21**, [456]
      local authority, interest belonging to,
        21, [457]
      possession. *See* possession *above*
      re-housing of tenant, **21**, [479]
      shared accommodation, **21**, [474]
      terms and conditions, **21**, [462], [498]
      variation, **21**, [498]
    sub-tenant, protection, **21**, [461], [475]
    succession, occupiers by, **21**, [455]
    superior tenancy, determination, **21**, [461]
    tenant—
      meaning, **21**, [484]
      obligations, **21**, [498]
    whole-time worker, absence from work,
      21, [493]
  housing authorities, duties, **21**, [479]
  learners—
    premiums paid by, **1(1)**, [408]
    terms of employment, **1(1)**, [408]
  meaning, **1(1)**, [478]
  premises, order for possession of, **21**, [599],
    [652], [656], [666]
  qualifying, **21**, [761]
  safety and health—
    Crown, application to, **1(1)**, [477]
    offences—
      defences, **1(1)**, [476]
      regulations, under, **1(1)**, [474]
  sick or injury pay, **1(1)**, [663]
  statistical information, requirement for,
    1(2), [142]
  terms of employment, **1(1)**, [405]
  training, arrangements for, **1(1)**, [430]
  wages. *See* **agricultural wages**
  young persons, meaning, **1(1)**, [478]

agriculture
  accident, death by, **1(1)**, [475]
  acquisition of land. *See* **agricultural land**
  Act, 1993—
    Northern Ireland, extension to, **1(2)**, [531]
    orders and regulations, **1(2)**, [530]
  advisory committees, abolition, **1(2)**, [741]
  agricultural business—
    grants, **1(2)**, [410]
    meaning, **1(2)**, [410]
  agricultural credits. *See* **agricultural credits**
  agricultural holdings. *See* **agricultural
    holdings**
  agricultural institutions, staff pensions,
    1(1), [553]
  agricultural marketing. *See* **agricultural
    marketing**
  agricultural produce. *See* **agricultural
    produce**
  animals, prevention of damage on escape,
    1(1), [391]

agriculture—*contd*
boundary adjustments. *See* **agricultural land**
business—
bank loans, grants in respect of, **1(1)**, [662]
grants, **1(2)**, [410]
meaning, **1(1)**, [797]; **1(2)**, [410]
capital grants, **1(1)**, [798], [799]
falsely obtaining, **1(2)**, [53]
chemicals used in—
analysis, evidence of, **1(1)**, [686]
classes of, **1(1)**, [684]
container, meaning, **1(1)**, [687]
labelling, general provisions, **1(1)**, [683]
marking, **1(1)**, [683]
offences—
penalties, **1(1)**, [685]
proceedings, **1(1)**, [685]
unlabelled, selling etc, **1(1)**, [685]
common policy. *See* **common agricultural policy**
co-operation. *See* **Central Council for Agricultural and Horticultural Co-operation**
crafts, grants and promotion of proficiency, **1(2)**, [50]
EC provisions. *See* **European Communities**
equipment, compensation for requisition, **9**, [123]
ex-servicemen, gifts for settlement of, **3**, [281]
farm—
business—
bank loans, grants in respect of, **1(1)**, [662]
grants, **1(2)**, [410]
meaning, **1(2)**, [410]
capital grants, **1(1)**, [798], [799]
falsely obtaining, **1(2)**, [53]
structure, grants, **1(1)**, [800], [858]
See also **agricultural land** (agricultural units)
fertilisers. *See* **fertilisers and feeding stuffs**
fixed equipment, meaning, **1(1)**, [399]
Food from Britain. *See* **Food from Britain**
gangmasters—
acting as, meaning, **1(2)**, [702]
annual report as to, **1(2)**, [721]
compliance officers—
appointment, **1(2)**, [713]
obstruction of, **1(2)**, [716]
powers of, **1(2)**, [714]
employment agencies and businesses, exclusion of provisions relating to, **1(2)**, [725]
enforcement officers—
appointment, **1(2)**, [713]
obstruction of, **1(2)**, [716]
powers of, **1(2)**, [712], [714]
relevant authorities, arrangements with, **1(2)**, [713]
warrant, entry on premises by, **1(2)**, [715]
information relating to, supply of, **1(2)**, [717]

agriculture—*contd*
gangmasters—*contd*
Licensing Authority. *See* Gangmasters Licensing Authority *below*
Northern Ireland, application of provisions, **1(2)**, [726], [729]
offences—
body corporate, by, **1(2)**, [718]
enforcement officer, powers of, **1(2)**, [712]
entering into arrangements, **1(2)**, [711]
false documents, possession of, **1(2)**, [710]
partnership, by, **1(2)**, [720]
partnership, grant to, **1(2)**, [720]
unincorporated authority, by, **1(2)**, [719]
unlicensed activities, **1(2)**, [710]
regulations, rules and orders, **1(2)**, [723]
scope of provisions, **1(2)**, [701]
territorial scope of provisions, **1(2)**, [703]
unlicensed activities, prohibition, **1(2)**, [704], [710]
worker, meaning, **1(2)**, [724]
Gangmasters Licensing Authority—
establishment of, **1(2)**, [699]
financial provisions, **1(2)**, [722]
functions of, **1(2)**, [699]
licence—
activities authorised by, **1(2)**, [705]
appeals, **1(2)**, [708]
body corporate, granted to, **1(2)**, [718]
grant of, **1(2)**, [705]
holder, **1(2)**, [705]
modification, **1(2)**, [707]
register of, **1(2)**, [709]
revocation, **1(2)**, [707]
transfer, **1(2)**, [707]
unincorporated authority, grant to, **1(2)**, [719]
rules, power to make, **1(2)**, [706]
Secretary of State, directions by, **1(2)**, [700]
general note, **1(1)**, [124]
good estate management, **1(1)**, [382]
good husbandry—
meaning, **1(1)**, [383]
notices, service of, **1(1)**, [397]
goods and services connected with, provision of, **1(2)**, [391]
grants—
bodies promoting co-operation, to, **1(1)**, [555]
business capital, **1(1)**, [798], [799]
crafts, in connection with, **1(2)**, [50]
false statement to obtain, **1(1)**, [665]
livestock rearing. *See* **livestock**
woodlands, in respect of, **1(2)**, [411]
grass and heather burning—
covenants against, relaxation of, **1(1)**, [373]
orders and regulations, **1(1)**, [372]
regulation of, **1(1)**, [372]
hill farming. *See* **hill farming**
interests, balance of, **1(2)**, [395]
land. *See* **agricultural land**
liming, etc, materials, sale by quantity, **39(1)**, [580]

agriculture—*contd*
  livestock rearing. *See* **livestock**
  meaning, **1(2)**, [701]; **21**, [453]; **36**, [1381]
  Northern Ireland, provisions applying,
    1(1), [668]
  notices, service of, **1(1)**, [397]
  pest control. *See* **pests**
  pesticides. *See* **pesticides**
  public paths orders, protection under,
    36, [1033], [1160]
  regulations and orders, procedure, **1(1)**, [398]
  research, promotion of, **1(1)**, [494]
  rural development. *See* **Rural Development**
    Boards
  special drainage charge, **49**, [1191]
  statistics—
    information—
      categories of, required, **1(2)**, [142]
      disclosure, restrictions on, **1(2)**, [143]
      falsification, etc, **1(2)**, [144]
      notices, service of, **1(2)**, [145]
      obtaining, powers of, **1(2)**, [142]
      offences relating to, **1(2)**, [144]
  surface soil, removal of—
    offences, **1(1)**, [451]
    peat cutting, saving for, **1(1)**, [451]
    penalties, **1(1)**, [452]
    planning permission, without, **1(1)**, [451]
    prosecution, consent to, **1(1)**, [453]
  training in, facilities for, **1(1)**, [430]
  vehicles used, drivers' hours, when provisions
    inapplicable, **36**, [812]
  weeds. *See* **weeds**
  woodlands, grants in respect of, **1(2)**, [411]
  work, meaning, **1(2)**, [701]

Agriculture and Fisheries, Board of
  Acts and documents, construction of,
    10, [471]
  expenses, **10**, [470]
  government departments, transfers to,
    10, [469]
  ministry, substitution of, **10**, [491]
    See also **Agriculture, Fisheries and**
      Food, Minister of
  powers and duties, **10**, [468], [474]
  staff, **10**, [470]
  superintendence of fisheries transferred to,
    10, [477]

Agriculture, Fisheries and Food, Minister
of
  acquired land, **1(1)**, [389]
  acquisition of land by—
    agreement, by, **1(1)**, [388]
    land subject to, **1(1)**, [388]
    notices, service of, **1(1)**, [397]
  agricultural wages—
    administration expenses, **1(1)**, [416]
    annual report, **1(1)**, [415]
  allotments powers. *See* **allotments**
  animal diseases. *See* **diseases of animals**
  appointment, **10**, [491]
  balance of interests, **1(2)**, [395]
  board, transfer from, **10**, [491]

Agriculture, Fisheries and Food, Minister
of—*contd*
  contracts, payment for, **10**, [515]
  directions to—
    Central Council for Agricultural and
      Horticultural Co-operation, **1(1)**, [660]
    Rural Development Board, **1(1)**, [656]
  entry, powers of, **1(1)**, [396]
  interest in land, power to require information
    on, **1(1)**, [467]
  notices, service of, **1(1)**, [397]
  regulations and orders, procedure, **1(1)**, [398]
  representations to, procedure, **1(1)**, [394]
  salary, **10**, [612]
  smallholding powers. *See* **smallholding**
  weeds, default powers as to, **1(1)**, [544]

aiding and abetting
  criminal conduct by member of services,
    3(S), 62
  desertion or absence without leave, **3(S)**, 314
  explosives offences, **12(1)**, [164]
  false statement, making of, **12(1)**, [201]
  malingering, **3(S)**, 315–16
  offence, trial of, **11(2)**, [462]
  offences, in commission of, **12(1)**, [59]
  official secrets offences, **12(1)**, [233]
  perjury, **12(1)**, [201]
  principal offender, treatment as, **12(1)**, [59]
  service offences, **3(S)**, 57
  suicide, **12(1)**, [330], [332], [333]

AIDS
  periodical reports, **30**, [505], [509]

Air Force. *See* **Royal Air Force**

Air Force, Auxiliary. *See* **Royal Auxiliary Air**
Force

Air Force Board
  Defence Council functions, carrying out,
    10, [528]
  establishment of, **10**, [528]

Air Force Reserve. *See also* **reserve forces**
  absence without leave. *See* **absence without**
    leave
  call out—
    permanent service, for, **3**, [1394], [1450]
      notices, **3**, [1401]
      special reservist, **3**, [1427]
      training, for, **3**, [1450]
  desertion. *See* **desertion**
  enlistment. *See* **enlistment**
  generally. *See also* **reserve forces**, **3**, [15],
    [749]
  office holder, powers of, **3**, [1426], [1430]
  permanent services—
    call out for, **3**, [1394]
      notices, **3**, [1401]
      postponement of discharge of members
        during, **3**, [1396]
      duration of, **3**, [1395]

Air Force Reserve—*contd*
  special reservist—
    permanent service, call out for, **3**, [1427]
    training, call out for, **3**, [1428]
  training—
    call out, **3**, [1450]
    generally, **3**, [1412]–[1413]

Air Force stores
  unlawful purchase of, **3**, [968]

air navigation. *See also* **carriage by air; civil aviation**
  accidents. *See under* **aircraft**
  Chicago Convention—
    expenses incurred, **4(1)**, [111]
    functions under, performance, **4(1)**, [73]
    orders giving effect to, **4(1)**, [110]
  Civil Aviation Authority. *See* **Civil Aviation Authority**
  dangerous articles, possession endangering installation, **4(1)**, [181]
  directions, **4(1)**, [442]
  Eurocontrol—
    application of provisions, **4(1)**, [106], [162]
    body corporate, as, **4(1)**, [162]
    immunities and privileges, **4(1)**, [162]
    jurisdiction of the courts, **4(1)**, [162]
    meaning, **4(1)**, [77]
    payments to, **4(1)**, [162]
    route charges, enforcement of foreign judgments, **4(1)**, [123]
  European Organisation for Safety of Air Navigation, **4(1)**, [77]
  installations—
    dangerous articles, possession endangering, **4(1)**, [181]
    inspection as to security, **4(1)**, [203]
    meaning, **4(1)**, [236]
    not part of UK aerodrome, security, **4(1)**, [206]
    security directions, application of provisions, **4(1)**, [206]
  national security nominee, **4(1)**, [443]
  obstructions—
    control over, **4(1)**, [97]
    warning of presence, **4(1)**, [98]
  offences, general provisions, **4(1)**, [148]
  orders—
    Chicago Convention, giving effect to, **4(1)**, [110]
    exercise of powers, parliamentary control, **4(1)**, [173]–[175]
    functions under, performance, **4(1)**, [73]
    matters to be provided for, **4(1)**, [110]
    offences against, **4(1)**, [111]
    power to make, **4(1)**, [151], [153], [173]–[175]
    supplemental provisions, **4(1)**, [111]
  powers, exercise of, **4(1)**, [110]
  regulation of—
    matters to be provided for, **4(1)**, [110]
    orders for, **4(1)**, [110], [173]–[175]
  route charges, enforcement of foreign judgments, **4(1)**, [123]

air navigation—*contd*
  safety of, Eurocontrol. *See* Eurocontrol *above*
  security. *See* **aviation security**
  services, meaning, **4(1)**, [153]
  summary of provisions, **4(1)**, [1]

air passenger duty
  accounting for, **4(1)**, [363]
  administration and enforcement, **4(1)**, [365], [371]
  aircraft operators, liability of—
    administrative representatives, **4(1)**, [359]
    fiscal representatives, **4(1)**, [358]–[360]
    handling agents, **4(1)**, [362]
    registration, **4(1)**, [357]
  amended provisions, **4(S)**, Aviation 4–5
  change of circumstances after issue of ticket, **4(1)**, [356]
  charge of, **4(1)**, [352]
  chargeable aircraft, **4(1)**, [353]
  customs and excise, setting of rates of interest, **13**, [1062]
  definitions, **4(1)**, [368]
  evidence by certificate, **4(1)**, [371]
  excise enactments, application of, **4(1)**, [371]
  exempted passengers, **4(1)**, [355]
  information, provision of, **4(1)**, [371]
  interest—
    assessment, **4(1)**, [371]
    Commissioners of Customs and Excise, payable by or to, **4(1)**, [371]
    rates of, **4(1)**, [372]
  introduction of, **4(1)**, [1]
  offences, **4(1)**, [366]
  payment of, **4(1)**, [363]
  rate of, **4(1)**, [354]; **4(S)**, Aviation 1–2; **43(S)**, 987
  regulations and orders, **4(1)**, [367]
  reliefs, simplification of operation of, **4(1)**, [364]
  security for payment of, **4(1)**, [361]
  simplified operation, schemes for, **4(S)**, Aviation 4–5
  standard class travel, pitch of seats, **43(S)**, 987
  territories, **4(S)**, Aviation 5–7

air pollution
  building, authorisation of works, **35(2)**, [54]
  cable, burning insulation from, offence of, **35(2)**, [32]
  default powers, **35(2)**, [60]
  emission limits, **35(1)**, [711]
  emission of pollutants—
    Crown premises, from, **35(2)**, [46]
    information about—
      kinds of, **35(2)**, [39]
      notice requiring—
        appeal against, **35(2)**, [36]
        regulations as to, **35(2)**, [37]
        service by local authority, **35(2)**, [35]
      obtaining, **35(2)**, [34]
      provision by local authority, **35(2)**, [38]
      trade secrets, disclosure, **35(2)**, [49]
    research and publicity, regulations as to, **35(2)**, [33]

air pollution—*contd*
enforcement of provisions, **35(2)**, [55]
entry and inspection, rights of, **35(2)**, [56], [57]
fuel oil—
regulations as to—
Crown, application to, **35(2)**, [31]
enforcement, **35(2)**, [29]
exemptions, **35(2)**, [31]
limiting sulphur content, **35(2)**, [30]
offences and penalties, **35(2)**, [31]
information, local authorities obtaining, **35(2)**, [58]
inquiries, **35(2)**, [59]
international agreements, giving effect to, **35(2)**, [48]
local authority functions, joint exercise of, **35(2)**, [61]
motor fuel, regulations as to, **35(2)**, [29]
offences—
act or default of another, due to, **35(2)**, [53]
bodies corporate, by, **35(2)**, [52]
cumulative penalties, **35(2)**, [50]
occupiers, notification of, **35(2)**, [51]
Public Health Acts, application of, **35(1)**, [1]
regulations and orders, **35(2)**, [63]

air quality
consultation requirements, **35(2)**, [173]
county councils for areas for which there are district councils, functions of, **35(2)**, [135]
Environment Agency, functions of, **35(2)**, [130]
exchange of information with county councils in England, **35(2)**, [173]
information about, public access to, **35(2)**, [173]
interpretation provisions, **35(2)**, [141]
Isles of Scilly, application of provisions to, **35(2)**, [139]
joint exercise of local authority functions, **35(2)**, [173]
local authority reviews, **35(2)**, [131]
management areas—
designation of, **35(2)**, [132]
duties of local authorities in relation to, **35(2)**, [133]
Mayor of London—
functions exercisable by, **35(2)**, [136]
strategy of—
consultations, **26(1)**, [710]
contents of, **26(1)**, [710]
directions to local authorities, **26(1)**, [713]
information, advice and assistance, provision of, **26(1)**, [713]
local authorities taking account of, **26(1)**, [712]
preparation and publication of, **26(1)**, [710]
Secretary of State, directions by, **26(1)**, [711]
national strategy, **35(2)**, [129]
offences, fixed penalty, **35(2)**, [173]

air quality—*contd*
public access to information about, **35(2)**, [173]
regulations, **35(2)**, [137]
Scottish Environment Protection Agency, reserve powers of, **35(2)**, [134]
Secretary of State—
guidance by, **35(2)**, [138]
reserve powers of, **35(2)**, [134]

air signal
false, **3**, [479], [752], [1015]
meaning, **3**, [723], [1223]

air traffic services
air traffic administration order—
administrator, **4(1)**, [492]
conditions for, **4(1)**, [404]
government financial help during, **4(1)**, [407]
guarantees, **4(1)**, [408]
manager, appointment, **4(1)**, [403]
meaning, **4(1)**, [405]
modification of provisions, **4(1)**, [492], [493]
petition for, **4(1)**, [404]
effect of, **4(1)**, [406]
withdrawal, **4(1)**, [406]
power to make, **4(1)**, [404]
purpose of, **4(1)**, [405]
schemes, **4(1)**, [494]
authorisation of, **4(1)**, [378]
body corporate, offences by, **4(1)**, [484]
Civil Aviation Authority—
Competition Commission, reference to, **4(1)**, [386]
compliance with duty or condition, order for securing, **4(1)**, [396]
effect of, **4(1)**, [400]
exceptions, **4(1)**, [397]
procedural requirements, **4(1)**, [398]
validity, **4(1)**, [399]
directions to, **4(1)**, [468], [469]
general duty of, **4(1)**, [376]
information, power to obtain, **4(1)**, [401], [467]
investigations by, **4(1)**, [410]
licence, grant of, **4(1)**, [380]
register, maintenance of, **4(1)**, [411]
review by, **4(1)**, [467]
Competition Commission—
direction—
position following, **4(1)**, [392]
power to give, **4(1)**, [391]
safety, priority of duty of, **4(1)**, [393]
Enterprise Act, application of provisions of, **4(1)**, [394]
privilege attaching, **4(1)**, [394]
reference to, **4(1)**, [386]
Enterprise Act, application of provisions of, **4(1)**, [388]
modifications to licence following report, **4(1)**, [390]
reports, **4(1)**, [389]
time limits, **4(1)**, [387]

air traffic services—*contd*
competition functions—
Competition Act, under, **4(1)**, [464]
concurrent, CAA and OFT, **4(1)**, [462], [465]
Enterprise Act, under, **4(1)**, [463]
exercise of, **4(1)**, [465]
interpretation, **4(1)**, [461]
Crown, provisions binding, **4(1)**, [481], [482]
drainage works affecting, protection, **19(3)**, [259]
exemptions, **4(1)**, [378]
extension of provisions outside UK, **4(1)**, [483]
false statements, making, **4(1)**, [471]
hostilities, directions in time of, **4(1)**, [469]
interpretation, **4(1)**, [471]
information, disclosure of, **4(1)**, [498]
interpretation, **4(1)**, [416]
licence—
application for, **4(1)**, [380]
excluded services, **4(1)**, [383]
grant of, **4(1)**, [379], [380]
modification, **4(1)**, [381], [385]
Competition Commission report, following, **4(1)**, [390]
order, by, **4(1)**, [395]
provisions in, **4(1)**, [381]
register, maintenance of, **4(1)**, [411]
requirement, **4(1)**, [377]
validity, requirements for, **4(1)**, [379]
licence holders—
acquisition of land by, **4(1)**, [93]
authorised services, provision of, **4(1)**, [382]
breach of duties or conditions by, **4(1)**, [384]
company, protection from winding up or administration, **4(1)**, [402]
compliance, order for securing, **4(1)**, [396]
effect of, **4(1)**, [400]
exceptions, **4(1)**, [397]
procedural requirements, **4(1)**, [398]
validity, **4(1)**, [399]
duties of, **4(1)**, [382]
security, protection from enforcement of, **4(1)**, [402]
See also air traffic administration order *above*
statutory undertakers, as, **4(1)**, [495]
meaning, **4(1)**, [474]
national security, directions in interests of, **4(1)**, [414]
restrictions on providing, **4(1)**, [377]
review of, **4(1)**, [467]
safety, high standard of, **4(1)**, [375], [376], [393]
Secretary of State—
authorisation, grant of, **4(1)**, [378]
environment, directions relating to, **4(1)**, [415]
general duty of, **4(1)**, [375]
licence, grant of, **4(1)**, [380]
national security, directions in interests of, **4(1)**, [414]
service of documents, **4(1)**, [476]

air traffic services—*contd*
transfer schemes. *See* **Civil Aviation Authority**
Wales, financial assistance in, **4(1)**, [519]

air weapon
firing beyond premises, **12(1)**, [496]
loaded—
carrying in public place, **12(1)**, [493]
deemed to be, **12(1)**, [541]
meaning, **12(1)**, [474]
person under fourteen—
having, **12(1)**, [497]
supplying to, **12(1)**, [499]
public place, person under seventeen having in, **12(1)**, [497]
registration of particulars, **12(1)**, [548]
rifle club, use at, **12(1)**, [498]
sale of—
registered dealer, to be made by, **12(4)**, [230]
trade of business, by, requirement to be face to face, **12(4)**, [230]
shooting gallery, use at, **12(1)**, [498]
transfer, registered dealer, to be made by, **12(4)**, [230]

aircraft
access to, gaining, **4(1)**, [346]
accidents—
inquiry into, proceedings arising, **4(1)**, [111]
investigation—
Chicago Convention, **4(1)**, [124]
regulations, power to make, **4(1)**, [124]
meaning, **4(1)**, [111], [124]
proceedings, institution of, **4(1)**, [111]
accommodation, regulation of provision of, **4(1)**, [120]
admiralty jurisdiction, **4(1)**, [141]; **11(2)**, [918]
aerial advertising, prohibition, **4(1)**, [133]
air force requisitioning, **3**, [945]
annoyance by flying, **3**, [510], [783]
Antarctica, entering, **10**, [1093]
aviation duty, preparation for introduction of, **43(S)**, 987
birth or death in, registration, **36**, [143]
births occurring in, registration, **4(1)**, [134]
British controlled, meaning, **4(1)**, [142]
British, meaning, **10**, [1211]
broadcasting from, prohibition. *See under* **broadcasting**
civil, meaning, **4(1)**, [180]
claims in respect of, jurisdiction, **4(1)**, [141]
commander—
constable, delivery of restrained persons to, **4(1)**, [143]
disembarkation of persons endangering aircraft, **4(1)**, [143]
meaning, **4(1)**, [143]
powers, **4(1)**, [143]
crimes during flight—
jurisdiction, **4(1)**, [142]
summary of provisions, **4(1)**, [1]

aircraft—*contd*
  crimes during flight—*contd*
    suspicion of intended, **4(1)**, [184]
  criminal law, application, **4(1)**, [142], [183]
  Crown, provisions applicable to, **4(1)**, [150]
  customs and excise—
    access, powers of, **13**, [611], [919]
    boarding, powers of, **13**, [610], [615]
    cargo, missing, inability to account for,
      13, [684]
    clearance outwards. *See* **exportation**
    commander, duties, **13**, [602], [615]
    concealed goods, **13**, [611], [633], [682]
    control of movement, **13**, [602]
    Crown aircraft, application of provisions
      to, **13**, [593]
    detention, powers of, **13**, [612], [616],
      [919]
    documents, inspection, **13**, [615]
    entry and search, **13**, [709]
    explosives, carriage in, **13**, [666]
    exportation. *See* **exportation**
    importation. *See* **importation**
    inspection, **13**, [615]
    report inwards, **13**, [617]
    smuggling. *See* **smuggling**
    stores—
      failure to reach destination, **13**, [650]
      landing or unloading in UK, **13**, [60]
      quantity, control of, **13**, [650]
    unauthorised unloading, **13**, [656]
  damage to, **3**, [500], [773], [1043]
  damaging, offence of, **4(1)**, [179]
  dangerous articles, possession, **4(1)**, [181]
  dangerous flying, **3**, [507], [780]; **4(1)**, [132]
  deaths occurring in, registration, **4(1)**, [134]
  depreciation in value of land interests due to,
    9, [304]
  destroying, offence of, **4(1)**, [179]
  detention—
    airport charges, unpaid, **4(1)**, [138]
    direction for, **4(1)**, [205]
    patent infringement, exemption,
      4(1), [139]
  discipline on board, commander's powers,
    4(1), [143]
  distress, in, duty of ship to assist, **39(2)**, [757]
  dumping at sea by. *See* **pollution** (sea)
  endangering, offence of, **4(1)**, [179], [180]
  evidence in connection with offences on—
    documentary, **4(1)**, [145]
    provisions as to, **4(1)**, [144]
  false information, endangering by, **4(1)**, [180]
  flight, meaning, **4(1)**, [153]
  flying over or landing in territory, prevention
    of, **4(1)**, [346]
  food safety, entry to inspect, **1(2)**, [245],
    [261], [475]
    transitional provisions, **1(2)**, [475]
  foreign, civil jurisdiction, **10**, [994]
  fuel used in, duty on, **43(S)**, 1045–7
  hazarding, **3**, [1033]
  Her Majesty's, meaning of, **3**, [1220]
  hijacking, **4(1)**, [178], [183]

aircraft—*contd*
  HM—
    arrest, etc, exclusion of proceedings for,
      13, [32]
    customs provisions, application of,
      13, [593]
    meaning, **13**, [38]
  importation and exportation, control of,
    50, [181]
  inaccurate certification, **3**, [781], [1039]
  infectious diseases in—
    detention, powers of, **35(1)**, [454]
    entry, powers of, **35(1)**, [454]
    passengers, **35(1)**, [454]
    regulations as to, **35(1)**, [454]
    signals as to, **35(1)**, [454]
  loss of, **3**, [500], [773], [1043]
  low flying, **3**, [509], [782]
  mail, carriage by. *See* **Post Office**
  maintenance, consultation on, **4(1)**, [167]
  manufacture of, stopping up of highway for
    use of, **36**, [666]
  material, meaning, **3**, [723], [995], [1223]
  meaning, **3**, [723], [995], [1223]; **4(1)**, [142];
    9, [136]
  military—
    loans for, **3**, [1261]
    offence under Air Navigation Order,
      3(S), 64
  mortgage of, **4(1)**, [136]
  movements. *See* **airport**
  noise—
    byelaws as to, **4(1)**, [302]
    caused by, **35(1)**, [332]
    measurement, **4(1)**, [127]
    minimisation, **4(1)**, [58]
    nuisance by, **4(1)**, [126]
    order to operators, **4(1)**, [127]
    penalties for offences, **4(1)**, [127]
    penalty schemes, **4(1)**, [128]
      amendment of, **4(1)**, [129]
      establishment of, **4(1)**, [129]
      revocation of, **4(1)**, [129]
    prevention by authorised persons,
      4(1), [127]
    regulation of, **4(1)**, [127]
    sound-proofing, grants towards costs,
      4(1), [130]
  nuisance by—
    aerodrome, when on, **4(1)**, [126]
    liability, **4(1)**, [126]
  offences—
    body corporate, by, **4(1)**, [347]
    general provisions, **4(1)**, [148]
    on board—
      ancillary, **4(1)**, [183]
      evidence in proceedings, **4(1)**, [144],
        [145]
      powers of commander, **4(1)**, [143]
      suspicion of intended, **4(1)**, [184]
      See also crimes *above*
    prosecution and proceedings, **4(1)**, [185]
    search of persons and aircraft, **4(1)**, [190],
      [191]
  operator, meaning, **4(1)**, [153]

aircraft—*contd*
  order for possession of—
    hostilities, in time of, **4(1)**, [470]
    international tension, in time of,
      4(1), [470]
    national emergency, in time of, **4(1)**, [470]
  passengers—
    Air Force Act applying to, **3**, [984]
    Army Act applying to, **3**, [711]
  patent claims against, **4(1)**, [139], [172]
  petroleum-spirit, keeping and use for,
    regulations as to, **35(1)**, [107]
  pilot in command—
    meaning, **4(1)**, [143]
    powers, **4(1)**, [143]
  pilotage—
    claims, jurisdiction, **11(2)**, [918]
    meaning, **11(2)**, [920]
  piracy by or against, **4(1)**, [182]
  pollution caused by—
    byelaws, **4(1)**, [302]
    minimisation, **4(1)**, [58]
  powers as to, exercise of, **4(1)**, [175]
  prize, as. *See* **prize**
  propaganda, aerial, prohibition, **4(1)**, [133]
  protection, orders under 1973 Act, **4(1)**, [241]
    See also security *below*
  recognition of rights in, international
    convention, **4(1)**, [140]
  requisition of—
    compensation for, **9**, [123]
    space and accommodation in, compensation
      for, **9**, [121], [124]
  restraint of persons on board, **4(1)**, [143]
  safety of, endangering, **4(1)**, [179], [180]
    See also security *below*
  sale of, for unpaid charges, **4(1)**, [138]
  salvage, **4(1)**, [137]
  seaplanes, provisions applicable, **4(1)**, [146]
  search by immigration officers, **31**, [128]
  search, security, **4(1)**, [190], [191]
  security—
    air cargo agents—
      documents, offences, **4(1)**, [213]
      provision for, **4(1)**, [212]
    annual report on, **4(1)**, [216]
    dangerous articles, possession, **4(1)**, [181]
    directions by Secretary of State,
      4(1), [189]–[191]
      enforcement notice—
        contents, **4(1)**, [198]
        objections to, **4(1)**, [200]
        offences, **4(1)**, [199]
        proceedings relating to, **4(1)**, [201]
        revocation or variation, **4(1)**, [201]
        service of, **4(1)**, [197]
      inspection as to compliance, **4(1)**, [203]
      limitation on scope of, **4(1)**, [194]
      matters included in, **4(1)**, [193]
      objection to, **4(1)**, [196]
      operation of, **4(1)**, [202]
      urgent or general, **4(1)**, [195]
    endangering safety, **4(1)**, [179], [180]
    fund, **4(1)**, [233]
    information required as to, **4(1)**, [187]

aircraft—*contd*
  security—*contd*
    inspections, **4(1)**, [203]
    measures to be taken—
      compensation, **4(1)**, [215]
      directions as to, **4(1)**, [192]
      meaning, **4(1)**, [236]
    Northern Ireland, application to,
      4(1), [232]
    occurrences, duty to report, **4(1)**, [214]
    restrictions in relation to aircraft,
      4(1), [189]
    service of documents, **4(1)**, [217]
    summary of provisions, **4(1)**, [1]
    suspicion of intended offence, **4(1)**, [184]
    unauthorised persons on board, **4(1)**, [210]
    urgent directions, **4(1)**, [195]
  seizure on patent claims, exemption from,
    4(1), [139]
  service offences—
    flying—
      annoyance by, **3(S)**, 52
      dangerous, **3(S)**, 49–50
      low, **3(S)**, 51
    prize—
      officer in command, by, **3(S)**, 53–4
      person subject to service law, by,
        3(S), 54–5
    stop and search powers, **3(S)**, 92
  short-term overseas leasing, **43(1)**, [683]
  surface damage by, liability, **4(1)**, [125]
  take-off and landing, periods prescribed,
    4(1), [127]
  terrorism offences, **18**, [752], [757]
  towage—
    claims, jurisdiction, **11(2)**, [918]
    meaning, **11(2)**, [920]
  trespass by, liability, **4(1)**, [125]
  value added tax, **50**, [151]
  vibration—
    byelaws relating to, **4(1)**, [302]
    minimisation, **4(1)**, [58]
    penalty schemes, **4(1)**, [128]
      amendment of, **4(1)**, [129]
      establishment of, **4(1)**, [129]
      revocation of, **4(1)**, [129]
    regulation of, **4(1)**, [127]
  violence, acts of—
    against, offence of, **4(1)**, [179]
    meaning, **4(1)**, [179], [186]
  war risks. *See* **war risks insurance**
  will executed on, **50**, [534]
  wireless telegraphy, offences, **45**, [879]
  wreck, application of law, **4(1)**, [137]

**Aircraft and Shipbuilding Industries
Arbitration Tribunal**
  constitution, **47**, [301]
  enforcement of orders, **47**, [320]
  establishment, **47**, [301]
  expenses of, **47**, [303]
  members—
    appointment, **47**, [301]
    terms of office, **47**, [301]
  procedure of, **47**, [318]

**Aircraft and Shipbuilding Industries
Arbitration Tribunal**—*contd*
proceedings—
constitution for hearing, **47**, [301]
general provisions, **47**, [318]
Scottish proceedings, **47**, [302], [319]
staff of, **47**, [303]

airforce
wills. *See* **will**

airport. *See also* **aerodrome**
abandoned vehicles, disposal of, **4(1)**, [305]
accommodation, special—
grants in respect of, **4(1)**, [306]
provision of, **4(1)**, [306]
acquisition of land. *See* **civil aviation**
activities not licensable, **19(3)**, [665]
advertising in, regulation of, **4(1)**, [302]
air transport licensing—
functions, meaning, **4(1)**, [266]
movements, power to limit, **4(1)**, [269]
aircraft movements—
availability of airports for, **4(1)**, [272]
limitation of, **4(1)**, [269]
meaning, **4(1)**, [266]
monitoring, **4(1)**, [307]
reports to Minister, **4(1)**, [307]
See also operational activities *below*
authority. *See* **Airports Authority**
availability, regulation of, **4(1)**, [272]
byelaws—
body corporate, by, **4(1)**, [325]
noise etc, as to, **4(1)**, [302]
other than Minister, by, **4(1)**, [325]
penalties under, **4(1)**, [303]
power to make, **4(1)**, [302]
proposed, notice of, **4(1)**, [302]
revocation, variation etc, **4(1)**, [303]
subject-matter of, **4(1)**, [302]
capacity—
allocation of, **4(1)**, [270]
recommendations as to—
duties respecting, **4(1)**, [308]
implementation, **4(1)**, [308]
scheme for allocating, **4(1)**, [270]
charges—
associated companies—
complaints as to, **4(1)**, [323]
monopoly references, **4(1)**, [323]
Competition Commission, references to—
associated companies, in respect of,
4(1), [323]
authority to make, **4(1)**, [278]
conditions imposed following,
4(1), [285]
expenses of, **4(1)**, [286]
information—
disclosed by, **4(1)**, [310]
to be given, **4(1)**, [281]
investigations—
powers of, **4(1)**, [283]
requirement for, **4(1)**, [280]
public interest, **4(1)**, [280]
questions to be referred, **4(1)**, [280]

airport—*contd*
charges—*contd*
Competition Commission, references
to—*contd*
reports on, **4(1)**, [284]
specified matters, **4(1)**, [302]
supplementary provisions, **4(1)**, [281]
time limits, **4(1)**, [282]
complaints as to—
associated companies, in case of,
4(1), [323]
investigation of, **4(1)**, [287]
making, **4(1)**, [287]
conditions—
accounts, as to—
breach of, **4(1)**, [289]
imposition of, **4(1)**, [277]
offences and penalties, **4(1)**, [289]
associated companies, in case of,
4(1), [323]
breach of, **4(1)**, [287]
loss or damage by, **4(1)**, [288]
CAA functions, **4(1)**, [292]
compliance orders—
application to quash, **4(1)**, [288]
associated companies, **4(1)**, [323]
contents of, **4(1)**, [287]
contravention of, **4(1)**, [288]
making, **4(1)**, [287]
obligations under, **4(1)**, [288]
validity of, **4(1)**, [288]
discretionary, **4(1)**, [278]
associated companies, **4(1)**, [323]
enforcement, **4(1)**, [287]
groups of airports, **4(1)**, [291]
imposition of, **4(1)**, [276]
mandatory, **4(1)**, [277]
modification of, **4(1)**, [290], [293]
non-compliance with, **4(1)**, [287]
period of duration, **4(1)**, [277], [290]
revocation of, **4(1)**, [293]
designated airports, for, **4(1)**, [277]
exceptions from provisions, **4(1)**, [274]
fixing of, **4(1)**, [278]
functions of CAA, **4(1)**, [276]
groups of airports, in case of, **4(1)**, [291]
international obligations, **4(1)**, [276]
levels of, **4(1)**, [278]
levy of, **4(1)**, [274]
unauthorised, **4(1)**, [274]
limitation of, **4(1)**, [277], [279]
maximum amount, regulating, **4(1)**, [277]
meaning, **4(1)**, [138], [273]
permission to levy—
application for, **4(1)**, [275]
conditions for. *See* conditions *above*
date of coming into force, **4(1)**, [275]
fee for, **4(1)**, [275]
grant or refusal of, **4(1)**, [275]
levying without, **4(1)**, [274]
ministerial functions, **4(1)**, [292]
requirement for, **4(1)**, [274]
revocation, **4(1)**, [288]
relevant activities for, **4(1)**, [273]
special, provision for, **4(1)**, [270]

airport—*contd*
  charges—*contd*
    summary of provisions, **4(1)**, [1]
    unpaid, detention etc of aircraft for,
      4(1), [138]
  constabulary—
    functions, **4(1)**, [304]
    meaning, **4(1)**, [304]
    See also policing *below*
  customs and excise—
    enforcement powers, **13**, [919]
    examination stations—
      approval, **13**, [603]
      meaning, **13**, [604]
    flight from—
      before clearance, prevention, **13**, [616]
      other than, prevention, **13**, [616]
    hovercraft proceedings to or from, control
      of movement of, **13**, [605]
    imported goods to be brought to, **13**, [602]
    landing at, **13**, [602]
    meaning, **13**, [602]
    procedure on arrival at, **13**, [626]
    uncleared goods—
      control of movement, **13**, [613]
      licence to move, **13**, [613]
  designated—
    aerodrome becoming or ceasing to be,
      4(1), [231]
    byelaws, **4(1)**, [225]
    charges at, **4(1)**, [277]
      See also charges *above*
    meaning, **4(1)**, [232]
    policing. *See* policing *below*
    road traffic control, **4(1)**, [226]
    theft at, prevention, **4(1)**, [224]
  economic regulation—
    airports subject to, **4(1)**, [274]
    levy of charges, **4(1)**, [274]
  international, sale of intoxicating liquor,
    19(3), [665]
  licence, meaning, **4(1)**, [135]
  local authority undertakings—
    activities associated with, **4(1)**, [250]
    airport land, meaning, **4(1)**, [250]
    companies to operate—
      activities included, **4(1)**, [250]
      directions to form, **4(1)**, [250]
      formation of, **4(1)**, [250]
      stamp duty exemption, **4(1)**, [312]
      status of, **4(1)**, [250]
      transfer to. *See* transfer *below*
    control of, **4(1)**, [249]
    meaning, **4(1)**, [249]
    pension rights—
      diminution, compensation for,
        4(1), [265]
      meaning, **4(1)**, [265]
      payments without probate etc,
        4(1), [265]
      regulations, **4(1)**, [265]
    road traffic—
      control of, **4(1)**, [226]
      regulation of, **4(1)**, [302]
    summary of provisions, **4(1)**, [1]

airport—*contd*
  local authority undertakings—*contd*
    transfer of, to companies—
      airports subject to, **4(1)**, [251]
      directions as to, **4(1)**, [250]
      See also companies *above*
    transfer scheme—
      approval required, **4(1)**, [252]
      construction of, **4(1)**, [252]
      functions under, **4(1)**, [311]
      preparation, **4(1)**, [252]
      property etc defined in, **4(1)**, [311]
      provisions made by, **4(1)**, [311]
      stamp duty provisions, **4(1)**, [312]
      submission to Minister, **4(1)**, [252]
      substitution by Minister, **4(1)**, [252]
  lost property, custody etc of, **4(1)**, [302]
  meaning, **4(1)**, [319]
  metropolitan county undertakings, **4(1)**, [250]
  national security, interests of, **4(1)**, [267]
  nationally significant infrastructure projects,
    46(S), 43–4. *See also* **nationally**
  significant infrastructure projects
  noise, mitigation etc, **4(1)**, [58], [302]
  offences by bodies corporate, **4(1)**, [315]
  operational activities—
    associated companies, by, **4(1)**, [323]
    availability for, **4(1)**, [272]
    byelaws affecting, **4(1)**, [302]
    meaning, **4(1)**, [267]
    Ministerial control of, **4(1)**, [267]
  operator—
    accounts, **4(1)**, [277]
    associated companies—
      accounts, **4(1)**, [323]
      conditions imposed on, **4(1)**, [323]
      meaning, **4(1)**, [319]
      provisions applied to, **4(1)**, [323]
    byelaws, power to make, **4(1)**, [302]
    charges by. *See* charges *above*
    compensation payable by, **4(1)**, [300]
    directions by Minister—
      consultation prior to giving, **4(1)**, [267]
      disclosure, restriction on, **4(1)**, [267]
      duty to comply with, **4(1)**, [317]
      generally, **4(1)**, [267]
      national security, as to, **4(1)**, [267]
    land—
      acquisition of, **4(1)**, [298]
      disposal, power of, **4(1)**, [299]
      rights over, power as to, **4(1)**, [298]
      meaning, **4(1)**, [319]
    special accommodation, duty to provide,
      4(1), [306]
    statutory undertakers, **4(1)**, [297], [324]
  orders and regulations—
    aircraft movements, as to, **4(1)**, [269]
    procedure for making, **4(1)**, [316]
  overseas territory, provisions applied,
    4(1), [321]
  planning decisions affecting, **4(1)**, [300]
  policing, **4(1)**, [526], [530]
    byelaws, **4(1)**, [225]
    chief officer, constables under, **4(1)**, [220]
    constables' powers, **4(1)**, [223]

airport—*contd*
  policing—*contd*
    consultation about, **4(1)**, [221]
    disputes between managers and police—
      independent experts—
        appointment of, **4(1)**, [228]
        removal of, **4(1)**, [229]
        replacement of, **4(1)**, [229]
      Secretary of State, referral to, **4(1)**, [227]
      tribunal dealing with, **4(1)**, [230]
    functions, exercise of, **4(1)**, [223]
    police services agreements, **4(1)**, [222]
      disputes arising—
        referral to Secretary of State,
          4(1), [227]
        tribunal dealing with, **4(1)**, [230]
    special constables, appointment, **4(1)**, [108]
    stop and search powers, **4(1)**, [219]
    thefts, prevention of, **4(1)**, [224]
  privatisation, summary of provisions, **4(1)**, [1]
  public airport company—
    activities—
      additional, **4(1)**, [255]
      control of, **4(1)**, [254]
    auditors, appointment, **4(1)**, [260]
    consents under Act, **4(1)**, [264]
    constitution of, **4(1)**, [254]
    control of, **4(1)**, [254]
    controlling authority—
      capital controls by, **4(1)**, [260]
      investment by, **4(1)**, [258]
      officers, prohibition on employment of,
        4(1), [257]
      references to, **4(1)**, [253]
      services provided by, **4(1)**, [261]
    directions by Minister, **4(1)**, [254]
    directors—
      disabilities of, **4(1)**, [256]
      interest in contracts, **4(1)**, [256]
      requirement as to, **4(1)**, [254]
    employees' share schemes, **4(1)**, [258]
    employment by, restriction on, **4(1)**, [257]
    financial backing for, **4(1)**, [262]
    investment in, **4(1)**, [258]
    loans to, **4(1)**, [262]
    meaning, **4(1)**, [253]
    pension rights—
      diminution, compensation for,
        4(1), [265]
      payments without probate etc,
        4(1), [265]
      regulations, **4(1)**, [265]
    references to, **4(1)**, [249], [253]
    securities—
      disposal of, by holder, **4(1)**, [263]
      transfer of, restrictions on, **4(1)**, [263]
      See also shares *below*
    services for—
      agreements as to, **4(1)**, [261]
      payment for, **4(1)**, [261]
    shares—
      acquisition of, **4(1)**, [258]
      disposal of, **4(1)**, [258]
    winding up, meeting liabilities, **4(1)**, [262]

airport—*contd*
  road traffic—
    control of, **4(1)**, [304]
    designated airports, control at, **4(1)**, [226]
    enactments applied, **4(1)**, [304]
    regulation of, **4(1)**, [302]
    transitional provisions, **4(1)**, [326]
  roads in, treatment of, **4(1)**, [304]
  safety—
    byelaws, **4(1)**, [302]
    compensation, provision for, **4(1)**, [300]
    planning decisions relating to, **4(1)**, [300]
  security. *See* **aerodrome**
  summary of provisions, **4(1)**, [1]
  taxis, standings for, **4(1)**, [302]
  telecommunications apparatus—
    alteration etc of, **4(1)**, [301]
    code, application of, **4(1)**, [301]
  traffic distribution rules—
    consultations on making, **4(1)**, [268]
    power to make, **4(1)**, [268]
    subject-matter of, **4(1)**, [268]
  transfer of functions as to, **25(2)**, [600]
  transitional provisions, **4(1)**, [326]
  works, telecommunications code applied,
    4(1), [301]

Airports Authority
  dissolution, vesting of property. *See* successor
    company *below*
  financial structure, **4(1)**, [247]
  Government holding—
    group relief, claims for, **4(1)**, [314]
    initial, **4(1)**, [244]
    nominees—
      acquisition of securities by, **4(1)**, [245]
      appointment, **4(1)**, [245]
      target investment limit, **4(1)**, [246]
    securities—
      flotation—
        invitations or advertisements,
          4(1), [248]
        statements in connection with,
          4(1), [248]
      issue of, **4(1)**, [244]
      nominees, to, **4(1)**, [245]
    shares—
      issue of, **4(1)**, [244]
      offer to public, **4(1)**, [248]
      See also securities *above*
    status of, **4(1)**, [314]
    statutory reserve of, **4(1)**, [247]
    summary of provisions, **4(1)**, [1]
  local Acts, power to amend, **4(1)**, [320]
  property, rights etc, transfer of. *See* transfer
    schemes *below*
  reorganisation, **4(1)**, [1]
  stamp duty land tax, **4(1)**, [313]
  successor company—
    accounts—
      statutory, **4(1)**, [247]
      valuation of assets etc for, **4(1)**, [247]
    corporation tax, **4(1)**, [312]
  transfer schemes—
    property etc defined in, **4(1)**, [311]

Airports Authority—*contd*
transfer schemes—*contd*
provisions made by, **4(1)**, [311]
stamp duty provisions, **4(1)**, [312]

air-raid precautions
generally, **50**, [180]

air-raid shelter
deep tube—
British Transport Commission, provisions
relating to, **50**, [251]
compensation, **50**, [246]
drains, **50**, [248], [256]
land and works, vesting of, **50**, [245]
Lendal Terrace subway, building work by,
50, [250]
London Electricity Board, provisions
relating to, **50**, [252]
roads and streets, **50**, [247], [255]
superjacent strata, support of, **50**, [249]
water-pipes, **50**, [248], [256]

alarm
causing, offence of, **12(1)**, [995], [996]

alcohol. *See also* **beer; cider; intoxicating
liquor; spirits; wine**
denatured, **19(3)**, [469]
account taken, excess or deficiency on,
19(3), [428]
authorised denaturer, meaning, **19(3)**, [426]
beverage, prohibition of use as,
19(3), [430]
defaults, **19(3)**, [428]
denaturer—
authorised, **19(3)**, [426]
licence requirements, **19(3)**, [426]
licence, denaturing under, **19(3)**, [426]
manufacture, licence to, **19(3)**, [426]
meaning, **19(3)**, [375]
medicine, use as, **19(3)**, [430]
offences and penalties, **19(3)**, [427]
premises, inspection, **19(3)**, [429]
prohibited uses, **19(3)**, [430]
regulations, power to make, **19(3)**, [427]
samples, power to take, **19(3)**, [429]
wholesale dealing—
licence requirements, **19(3)**, [426]
meaning, **19(3)**, [426]
designated public place, consumption in—
byelaws, effect of provisions on, **12(3)**, [15]
definitions, **12(3)**, [16]
meaning, **12(3)**, [13]
places not being, **12(3)**, [14]
police powers, **12(3)**, [12]
disorder related to, individuals, directions to,
19(3), [715]
driving above limit. *See* **road traffic
offences**
liquors, blending, **19(3)**, [425]
meaning, **19(3)**, [373]
misuse of, **19(3)**, [349]
proof system, replacement in customs and
excise Acts, **13**, [584]

alcohol—*contd*
spirits contained in, computation,
19(3), [373]

alcohol dependence
not considered as mental disorder, **29**, [23]

alcohol disorder zone
designation—
guidance, **19(3)**, [713]
local authority procedure, **19(3)**, [710]
local chief officer of police, functions of,
19(3), [712]
order for, **19(3)**, [711]
review of, **19(3)**, [711]
licence holders in, power to impose charges
on, **19(3)**, [709]
meaning, **19(3)**, [714]

Alcohol Education and Research Council
accounts and audit, **19(3)**, [454]
annual report, **19(3)**, [458]
chairman, **19(3)**, [450], [458]
charitable purposes, **19(3)**, [452]
dissolution, powers, **19(3)**, [458]
establishment, **19(3)**, [450]
expenses, **19(3)**, [458]
Fund—
application, **19(3)**, [451]
compensation authorities' fund, transfer
of, **19(3)**, [449]
establishment, **19(3)**, [450]
members—
number of, **19(3)**, [450]
tenure of office, **19(3)**, [458]
transfers to, **19(3)**, [451]
repayment schemes, **19(3)**, [453]
status, **19(3)**, [458]

alcohol related disorder
individuals representing risk of, directions to,
19(3), [715]

alcoholic liquor duties
definitions, **19(3)**, [375]
denatured alcohol, **19(3)**, [469]
directions as to, **19(3)**, [432]
dutiable and duty, meanings, **19(3)**, [372]
dutiable liquors, **19(3)**, [372]
See further **beer; cider; spirits; wine**
excise licence duty, abolition, **19(3)**, [461]
ingredients, liquor used as, **19(3)**, [468]
liquor to which applicable, **19(3)**, [372]
rates of, **43(S)**, 842, 1370–2
regulations, procedure, **19(3)**, [431]
repayment, **19(3)**, [468]
review and appeal, decisions subject to,
43(S), 1341–3
summary of provisions, **19(3)**, [349]
vinegar, liquor converted to, **19(3)**, [468]
wrongdoing, penalties,
43(S), 1328–39. *See also* **tax penalty**

aldermen
honorary, rights etc, **25(2)**, [212]

Alderney
transfer of property, **7(2)**, [421]

alibi
notice of, **12(1)**, [383]; **12(2)**, [480]

alien
armed forces. *See also* **Army, reserve forces**, etc
capacity to hold property, **31**, [2]
deportation. *See* **deportation**
disaffection amongst forces, incitement to cause, **31**, [6]
employment—
certificate of, **31**, [50]
civil service, in, **31**, [7], [50]
immigration. *See* **immigration**
incitement to sedition or disaffection, **31**, [6]
jury service, disqualification from, **31**, [8]
marriage, citizenship by. *See* **citizenship**
meaning, **31**, [4], [13], [42], [180]
obstruction in execution of duty, **3**, [693]
offences and penalties, **31**, [9]
office, disqualification to hold, **31**, [2]
office, holding, **3**, [1]
property, right to hold, **31**, [2]
regular forces, service in, **3**, [474], [747]
sedition, acts likely to cause, **31**, [6]
ship, British, disqualification from ownership of, **31**, [2]
summary of provisions, **31**, [1]
title to property, derivation through, **31**, [2]
trial of, **31**, [3]

allied headquarters
meaning, **41**, [99], [100]
stamp duty exemption, **41**, [99]

allotment (agricultural). *See also* **allotment garden; smallholding**
arbitration and valuation—
compensation, for, **1(1)**, [222]
generally, **1(1)**, [219]
associations—
formation etc, **1(1)**, [215]
letting to, **1(1)**, [242]
common pasture, provision of, **1(1)**, [203]
commons—
acquisition of land of, **1(1)**, [244]
restriction on acquisition, **1(1)**, [208]
compensation—
assessment, **1(1)**, [256]
compulsory acquisition, on, **1(1)**, [206]
improvements, for, **1(1)**, [214], [255]
land let, in respect of, **1(1)**, [242]
loss of employment, for, **1(1)**, [210]
Minister, payable by, **1(1)**, [442]
recovery of, **1(1)**, [256]
tenant, by, to outgoing tenant, **1(1)**, [255]
compulsory hiring of land—
orders for, **1(1)**, [223]
possession, power to resume, **1(1)**, [213]
procedure, **1(1)**, [206]
provisions applied to, **1(1)**, [233]
tenancy, renewal, **1(1)**, [211]

allotment (agricultural)—*contd*
co-operative societies, **1(1)**, [215]
Crown lands, provisions as to, **1(1)**, [207], [257]
cultivation, provision of equipment for, **1(1)**, [240]
emergency provisions, under, **1(1)**, [124]
field gardens, **1(1)**, [124]
fuel allotments, **1(1)**, [124]
functions of local authorities, **25(2)**, [262]
grazing rights, **1(1)**, [209]
hens, right to keep, on, **1(1)**, [441]
implements etc, provision of, **1(1)**, [240]
improvements—
compensation, **1(1)**, [214]
local authority, by, **1(1)**, [196]
matters treated as, **1(1)**, [224], [225]
removal on quitting, **1(1)**, [214]
kinds of, **1(1)**, [124]
land—
acquired—
appropriation of, **1(1)**, [241]
powers as to, extension of, **1(1)**, [234]
acquisition—
agreement, by, **1(1)**, [195], [205]
annuity, for, **1(1)**, [233]
commons, **1(1)**, [244]
entry, powers of, **1(1)**, [232]
extension of powers, **1(1)**, [234]
future requirements, for, **1(1)**, [269]
local authority, by, **1(1)**, [269]
local inquiry as to, **1(1)**, [222]
loss of employment by, **1(1)**, [210]
Minister's approval not required, **1(1)**, [235]
power of, **1(1)**, [195]
restrictions on, **1(1)**, [208]
adaptation of, for, **1(1)**, [196]
annuity, sale and acquisition for, **1(1)**, [233], [247]
appropriated, sale of, **1(1)**, [271]
appropriation—
purposes of, **1(1)**, [241]
restrictions on, **1(1)**, [244]
compulsory hiring. *See* compulsory hiring *above*
compulsory purchase—
amendments as to, **1(1)**, [237], [258]
notice to treat, **1(1)**, [261]
orders for, **1(1)**, [222]
power of, **1(1)**, [195]
procedure, **1(1)**, [206]
entry to inspect, **1(1)**, [239]
hiring. *See* compulsory hiring *above*
improvement by local authority, **1(1)**, [196]
interchange of, **1(1)**, [212]
leasing, **1(1)**, [195], [234]
letting—
local authority, by, **1(1)**, [262]
parish council, to, **1(1)**, [238]
limited owners, sale by, **1(1)**, [207]
purchase by agreement, **1(1)**, [205]
sale by local authority, **1(1)**, [271], [280], [281]
superfluous, sale of, **1(1)**, [201]

allotment (agricultural)—*contd*
  land—*contd*
    unsuitable, sale of, **1(1)**, [201]
  letting—
    general provisions for, **1(1)**, [197]
    rules as to, **1(1)**, [198]
  local authority—
    borrowing powers, **1(1)**, [216], [217]
    expenses of, **1(1)**, [217]
    loans to, **1(1)**, [236]
    obligations, restriction of, **1(1)**, [439]
    provision by, **1(1)**, [124]
    rents chargeable by, **1(1)**, [440]
    transfer to, **1(1)**, [202]
  local inquiries, **1(1)**, [218]
  London, in, **1(1)**, [124]
  management, **1(1)**, [199]
    transfer of, **1(1)**, [124]
  managers, appointment etc, **1(1)**, [199]
  meaning, **1(1)**, [124], [253], [268]
  meetings, use of schoolroom for, **1(1)**, [204]
  modern legislation, **1(1)**, [124]
  opencast mining, **17(1)**, [203], [226]
  parochial charity lands, **1(1)**, [124]
  Poor Laws, under, **1(1)**, [124]
  possession—
    recovery, **1(1)**, [200]
    resumption, **1(1)**, [260], [272]
  provision of, **1(1)**, [124], [194]
  rabbits, right to keep, on, **1(1)**, [441]
  rent—
    arrears—
      eviction for, **1(1)**, [200]
      recovery of, **1(1)**, [200]
    charging, **1(1)**, [440]
    payment, **1(1)**, [440]
  societies—
    formation etc, **1(1)**, [215]
    grants and loans to, **1(1)**, [215]
  summary of provisions, **1(1)**, [124]
  tenancy—
    renewal, **1(1)**, [211]
    termination—
      compensation, **1(1)**, [242], [252], [434]
      trees etc, removal of, **1(1)**, [214]
  transfer to local authorities, **1(1)**, [202]
  valuation—
    compensation purposes, for, **1(1)**, [256]
    compulsory hiring, for, **1(1)**, [223]
    costs of, **1(1)**, [256]

allotment garden. *See also* **allotment;**
smallholding
  compensation—
    Crown lands, **1(1)**, [438]
    deterioration of land, for, **1(1)**, [435]
    determination and recovery of, **1(1)**, [438]
    disturbance, for, **1(1)**, [434]
    landlord, to, **1(1)**, [435]
    Minister, payable by, **1(1)**, [442]
    quitting, on, **1(1)**, [252]
    recovery of, **1(1)**, [256]
    set-off against rent, **1(1)**, [436]
  compulsory acquisition of land for—
    amendments as to, **1(1)**, [258]

allotment garden—*contd*
  compulsory acquisition of land for—*contd*
    notice to treat, **1(1)**, [261]
  compulsory hiring of land—
    amendments as to, **1(1)**, [258]
    restrictions on, **1(1)**, [208]
  Defence Regulations, under, **1(1)**, [455]
  land—
    compulsory hire or purchase, **1(1)**, [208],
      [258]
    deterioration, compensation for,
      1(1), [435]
    letting of, **1(1)**, [455]
    resumption of possession, **1(1)**, [260]
    unoccupied, entry on, **1(1)**, [259]
    used by tenant as, **1(1)**, [264]
  meaning, **1(1)**, [124], [399]
  New Forest, in, **1(1)**, [263]
  notice to quit, **1(1)**, [251]
  provision of, duties as to, **1(1)**, [194]
  provisions applicable to, **1(1)**, [253]
  re-entry, power of, **1(1)**, [251]
  rent, set-off of compensation against,
    1(1), [436]
  summary of provisions, **1(1)**, [124]
  termination of tenancy—
    compensation—
      mortgagee, from, **1(1)**, [254], [436]
      quitting, on, **1(1)**, [252]
      recovery of, **1(1)**, [256]
    improvements removable on, **1(1)**, [255]
    restriction on, **1(1)**, [251]
  valuation, **1(1)**, [256]

allotment (shares and debentures)
  applications for, **8**, 161
  arrangement providing for, **8**, 177
  authority of company required, **8**, 158–9
    private company election, **8**, 160
  class rights. *See* **shares in company**
  consideration for, non-cash—
    public company, transfer to, **8**, 178–81
    registrar, matters communicated to,
      8, 184–5
    valuation—
      full disclosure to valuer, **8**, 184
      person qualified for, **8**, 181
      report on, contents, **8**, 181–3
      requirement for, **8**, 177–8
    work, undertaking to do, **8**, 188
  contravention of requirements, **8**, 160, 188
  damages and compensation, right to, **8**, 185
  discount, at—
    authority for, **8**, 173
    prohibition of, **8**, 175
  extension of authority for, **8**, 158–9
  general provisions, **8**, 158–9
  interest, appropriate rate of, **8**, 181
  irregular, effect of, **8**, 164
  issue not fully subscribed, where, **8**, 163
  letter of, abolition of stamp duty, **41**, [148],
    [157]
  liabilities—
    relief in respect of, **8**, 186–7
    subsequent holder, of, **8**, 185–6

allotment (shares and debentures)—*contd*
long-term undertaking, payment by, **8**, 176–7
meaning, **8**, 600
minimum subscription required, **8**, 162
payment for shares on, general rules, **8**, 208
See further under **shares in company**
pre-emption basis, on—
communication of, to shareholders, **8**, 168
contravention of provisions, **8**, 169
definitions respecting, **8**, 170
disapplication of rights, **8**, 171
generally, **8**, 167
joint shareholders, in case of, **8**, 168
offers to be in writing, **8**, 168
other restrictions, saving for, **8**, 170
private company, by, **8**, 169
procedure, saving for, **8**, 172
prospectus offering shares for sale, **8**, 165
quarter paid-up, to be, **8**, 176
renounceable letters etc of, stamp duty
exemption, **41**, [148]
returns as to, **8**, 165–6
shareholders, to, **8**, 167
special cases, **8**, 188
stock exchange, to be dealt in on, **8**, 164–5
subscribers to memorandum, to, **8**, 181
subsequent holders, liability of, **8**, 185–6
time for, **8**, 161

alms
soliciting, **12(1)**, [26]

almshouse
contribution towards maintenance of,
5(2), [517]
licence to occupy, **22**, [427]
meaning, **5(2)**, [517]

Alnwick
corporation of, status of, **25(1)**, [53]

alternative finance arrangements
application of provisions, **43(2)**, [614]
companies, treatment of, **43(2)**, [608]
diminishing shared ownership, **43(S)**, 94–5
employees, beneficial loans to, **43(S)**, 96
financial institution, meaning, **43(2)**, [604]
foreign currency payments, **43(2)**, [606]
Government borrowing, **43(S)**, 992
ancillary arrangements, **43(S)**, 1353
decision to raise money, **43(S)**, 1353
interpretation, **43(S)**, 1355
liabilities, **43(S)**, 1354
money raised, treatment of, **43(S)**, 1354
other legislation, modification, **43(S)**, 1355
persons other than Treasury, involvement
of, **43(S)**, 1353
powers and duties, **43(S)**, 1354
property, **43(S)**, 1354
regulations, **43(S)**, 1352, 1355
terms, conditions and procedures,
43(S), 1353
things to be done other than in
regulations, **43(S)**, 1355
interest, references to, **43(2)**, [650]

alternative finance arrangements—*contd*
investment bonds—
amended provisions, **43(S)**, 550–1
arrangements for, **43(S)**, 547–9
discount, **43(S)**, 550
effects, **43(S)**, 547–9
stamp duty and stamp duty reserve tax on,
43(S), 988–9
meaning, **43(2)**, [604]
money placed at interest, **43(2)**, [650]
non-residents, payments to, **43(2)**, [606]
persons other than companies, treatment of,
43(2), [609]
power to vary provisions, **43(S)**, 991
profit share agency, **43(S)**, 91–3
profit share return, **43(2)**, [607]
distribution, not to be treated as,
43(2), [612]
property, anti-avoidance, **43(S)**, 990
provisions not at arm's length, **43(2)**, [610]
regulations, **43(S)**, 97
relevant arrangements, meaning, **43(2)**, [650]
return, giving rise to, **43(2)**, [605]
sale and purchase of assets, **43(2)**, [611]
Saving Gateway accounts, **40(S)**, 14

alternative finance investment bonds
issue, transfer and redemption of rights,
43(S), 1758–9
meaning, **43(S)**, 1758
underlying assets consisting of land,
transactions relating to—
bond-holder acquiring control of
underlying asset, **43(S)**, 1766
capital allowances, **43(S)**, 1763–5
capital gains taxation relief, **43(S)**, 1762
commencement, **43(S)**, 1769
consequential amendments, **43(S)**, 1768
discharge of charge, notification,
43(S), 1765
general conditions, **43(S)**, 1759–60
improper arrangements, effect of,
43(S), 1766
regulations, **43(S)**, 1767
stamp duty land tax relief, **43(S)**, 1761–2
substitution of asset, **43(S)**, 1765

alum
mines or works, charge to tax, **44(1)**, [34]

ambassador
oath, administration by, **18**, [158], [196]

ambulance
false calls for, **25(1)**, [247]
speed limit exemption, **37**, [261]
vehicle excise duty, exemption from,
13, [1049]

amenity
preservation, **37**, [165]

amenity—*contd*
proper maintenance of land affecting. *See* **land**

ammunition. *See* **explosives; firearms**

amphibians
importation and exportation, restriction on.
  See **animals**
sale, etc, restriction on. *See* **animals**

amusement machine
categories of, **5(1)**, [67]
charitable entertainments etc, at, **5(1)**, [97]
licence—
    application for, **5(1)**, [98]
    duration, **5(1)**, [98]
    exemptions from requirements, **5(1)**, [97]
    holder, requirements to be observed,
      5(1), [98]
    issue, evidence of, **5(1)**, [87]
    number of machines authorised by,
      5(1), [68]
    operating without, **5(1)**, [68]
    part-year, **5(1)**, [65]
    production of, **5(1)**, [98]
    requirement to hold, **5(1)**, [65]
    seasonal, **5(1)**, [97]
    special, grant of, **5(1)**, [65]
    surrender of, **5(1)**, [98]
    transfer, **5(1)**, [98]
    types of, **5(1)**, [65]
licence duty—
    administration, **5(1)**, [98]
    amount of, **5(1)**, [67]; **43(S)**, 853
    amount, provisions affecting,
      5(S), Betting 3–4
    charge of, **5(1)**, [66]
    determination of amount, **5(1)**, [329]
    enforcement, **5(1)**, [98]
    instalments, payment by, **5(1)**, [98]
    rates of, **5(1)**, [67]
    summary of provisions, **5(1)**, [1]
    supplementary provisions, **5(1)**, [71]
    table of, **5(S)**, Betting 2–3
    unlicensed machine, chargeable on,
      5(1), [99]
restrictions on provision of, **5(1)**, [68]
meaning, **5(1)**, [70]
pool betting duty, extension of, **5(1)**, [195]

amusements with prizes
bingo. *See* **bingo**
competitions. *See* **prize competitions**
gaming machines. *See* **gaming machine**

analyst
public—
    certificate by as evidence, **28**, [257]
    medicinal products, analysis of—
        analysis by, **28**, [171], [194]
        certificate of, **28**, [171], [194]
        fee of, **28**, [171]
        meaning, **28**, [171], [194]

ancient monument
acquisition for provision of housing, **22**, [408]
advice on, **32**, [347]
agreement or gift, acquisition by, **32**, [335]
agreements concerning, **32**, [341]
Broads, in area of, **32**, [374]
coal mining subsidence, damage due to,
  17(2), [19]
coast protection work, savings, **49**, [421]
compensation—
    assessment of, **32**, [349]
    claim for, **32**, [369]
    exercise of powers, damage caused by,
      32, [368]
compulsory acquisition of, **32**, [334]
Crown land, on, **32**, [371]
damaging—
    compensation order, **32**, [351]
    offence of, **32**, [350]
destroying, **32**, [350]
disposal of land, **32**, [352]
ecclesiastical property, **32**, [372]
entry, powers of—
    objects found, custody of, **32**, [376]
    provisions on, **32**, [365]–[366]
    survey and valuation, for, **32**, [365]
exclusion from listed building provision,
  46, [703]
expenditure on, **32**, [346]
functions relating to, **25(2)**, [581]
generally, **32**, [1]
guardianship—
    effect of, **32**, [337]
    local land charge, deed as, **32**, [336]
    power to place under, **32**, [336]
    qualifying interests for, **32**, [336]
    termination of, **32**, [338]
information on interests in land, **32**, [379]
interim preservation order on, **32**, [388]
investigations, expenditure on, **32**, [367]
land believed to contain, entry on, **32**, [341]
land in vicinity of—
    acquisition of, **32**, [339]
    agreements concerning, **32**, [341]
    easements, acquisition of, **32**, [340]
    guardianship of, **32**, [339]
    rights over, acquisition of, **32**, [340]
limited owner, powers of, **32**, [342]
meaning, **32**, [382], [734]
offences—
    body corporate, by, **32**, [380]
    compensation order, **32**, [351]
    damaging or destroying, **32**, [350]
protection of, generally, **32**, [1]
public access to—
    charges for, **32**, [343]
    exclusion of, **32**, [343]
    facilities, provision of, **32**, [344]
    information, provision of, **32**, [344]
    regulation of, **32**, [343]
    times of, **32**, [343]
regulations and orders, **32**, [381]
saving for law as to, **35(1)**, [275]

ancient monument—*contd*
  scheduled—
    Commission, information given by,
      32, [324]
    compensation—
      recovery on grant of consent, **32**, [332]
      refusal of consent, for, **32**, [331]
      works ceasing to be authorised, where,
        32, [333]
    consent—
      application for, **32**, [385]
      duration, **32**, [327]
      grant of, **32**, [326]
      inquiries, **32**, [385]
      meaning, **32**, [325]
      modification of, **32**, [327], [386]
      refusal, compensation for, **32**, [331]
        recovery of, **32**, [332]
      revocation, **32**, [327], [386]
    dwelling house, not to be, **32**, [323]
    entry for inspection, power of, **32**, [329]
    list of, **32**, [323]
    meaning, **32**, [323]
    owner and occupier, notifying, **32**, [323]
    Schedule, **32**, [323]
    urgent works, execution of, **32**, [328]
    works, control of, **32**, [325]
  service of documents, **32**, [378]
  site of, **32**, [382]
  superintendence of work, **32**, [347]
  territorial waters, in, **32**, [375]
  transfer between authorities, **32**, [345]
  transitional provisions, **32**, [388]

Anglo–Portuguese Commercial Treaty
  text of, **48**, 38–43

angostura bitters
  duty, power to exempt, **19(3)**, [378]
  nature of, **19(3)**, [372]
  spirit, deemed not, **19(3)**, [372]

Anguilla
  administration of, **7(2)**, [745]
  court, powers of, **7(2)**, [613]
  status of, **7(2)**, [745]

Animal Procedures Committee
  consultation with, **2**, [609]
  establishment of, **2**, [619]
  functions of, **2**, [620]
  information, consultation as to, **2**, [621]
  members, **2**, [619]

animals
  accidents involving, **37**, [788]
  Antarctic, in. *See* **Antarctica**
  arrest of offenders, **2**, [510]
  artificial insemination, **2**, [274], [597]
  badgers. *See* **badgers**
  boarding establishment—
    disqualification for keeping, **2**, [311]
    inspection, **2**, [310]
    licences, **2**, [309]
    meaning of animal, **2**, [313]

animals—*contd*
  boarding establishment—*contd*
    offences, **2**, [311]
    prosecutions, **2**, [312]
  brucellosis—
    control of, **2**, [431]
    eradication, **2**, [346]
    offences respecting, **2**, [347]
  captive, prevention of escape, **1(1)**, [391]
  carcase—
    meaning, **2**, [548]
    offences respecting, **2**, [472]
    seizure and disposal, **2**, [472]
    treatment of, **2**, [454]
    washed ashore, burial, **2**, [507]
  cattle. *See* **cattle**
  coypus, use of poison against, **2**, [363]
  cruelty. *See* **cruelty to animals**
  damage by—
    common law rules replaced, **2**, [350]
    dangerous animal, liability, **2**, [351]
    exceptions from liability, **2**, [354]
    meaning, **2**, [360]
    straying on highway, **2**, [357]
  dangerous—
    damage by, liability, **2**, [351]
    meaning, **2**, [355]
    order for destruction, **2**, [210], [643], [678]
    wild. *See* **wild animals**
    zoos, kept in, **2**, [412]
  deer. *See* **deer**
  destructive—
    extension of provisions to, **2**, [264]
    summary of provisions, **2**, [140]
      See also **pests**
  detention and sale of, **2**, [356]
  diseases. *See* **diseases of animals**
  distress, in—
    orders in relation to, **2**, [791], [792]
    powers in relation to, **2**, [789], [790]
  dogs. *See* **dogs**
  domestic, meaning, **2**, [241]
  endangered species, enforcement of
    regulations implementing Community
    legislation, **12(3)**, [1032]
  enforcement of provisions—
    default of local authority in, **2**, [509]
    police powers and duties, **2**, [510]
  export. *See* **export**
  farriers. *See* **farriers**
  feeding and watering, **2**, [488], [560]
  feeding stuffs. *See* **fertilisers and feeding
    stuffs**
  films, in, protection of, **2**, [265]
  game. *See* **game**
  grey squirrels, use of poison against, **2**, [363]
  health and welfare—
    summary of provisions, **2**, [140]
    territorial zones, powers in, **2**, [595]
  highway, straying on, **36**, [1220]
  hill. *See* **hill farming**
  horses. *See* **horses**
  humane killing, appropriate methods of,
    2, [631]

animals—*contd*
  hunting. *See* **hunting**
  importation—
    control of, **1(1)**, [481]
    offences and penalties, **1(1)**, [482]
    See also **importation**
  intercourse with, **12(3)**, [733]
  keeper—
    liability for damage, **2**, [353]
    meaning, **2**, [355]
  keeping and breeding, regulation of, **2**, [140]
  lairs and sheds—
    cleansing and disinfecting, **2**, [434]
    provision of, **2**, [504]
  leading or driving in streets, **35(1)**, [70]
  licences—
    false statements to obtain, **2**, [528]
    falsification, **2**, [526]
    inspections in connection with, **2**, [796], [797]
    issue of, in blank, **2**, [527]
    orders with respect to, **2**, [813]
  licensing of activities involving, **2**, [784], [836], [838]
  live or dead—
    importation and exportation of certain—
      body corporate, offences by, **13**, [573]
      entry of premises, **13**, [566]
      forfeiture, **13**, [566]
      licence for—
        charge for, **13**, [566]
        conditions of issue, **13**, [566]
        derivatives, **13**, [566]
        issue, **13**, [566]
        offences as to, **13**, [566]
        scientific authorities—
          advice on issue, **13**, [566]
          establishment and duties, **13**, [567]
        voidance on commission of offence, **13**, [566]
      movement after—
        offences, **13**, [571], [572]
        restriction on, **13**, [571], [572]
        scientific authorities, consultation with, **13**, [571], [572]
        specified premises, to or from, **13**, [571], [572]
      place of, restriction on, **13**, [570]
      restrictions on, **13**, [566], [568], [569]
    imported illegally—
      body corporate, offences by, **13**, [573]
      sale, etc, or display to public—
        derivatives, **13**, [569]
        licence for, **13**, [569]
        offences, **13**, [569]
        restricted articles, **13**, [569]
        restriction on, **13**, [569]
  livestock. *See* **livestock**
  local authority—
    charges, power to make, **2**, [504]
    default powers of Minister, **2**, [509]
    land acquisition, **2**, [505]
    regulations, proof of, **2**, [508]
  markets—
    cleansing and disinfecting, **2**, [434]

animals—*contd*
  markets—*contd*
    regulating or prohibiting, **2**, [436]
    meaning, **1(1)**, [830]]; **2**, [546]; **37**, [788]
    medicinal tests. *See* **medicinal products**
    mischievous propensities, **2**, [350]
    movement of—
      feeding and watering, **2**, [488], [560]
      suffering, prevention, **2**, [487]
    musk rats. *See* **musk rats**
    notices, form and service, **2**, [542]
    offences—
      appeals respecting, **2**, [537]
      evidence and procedure, **2**, [538]
      generally, **2**, [532]
      licences, as to, **2**, [526]–[529]
      local authority's power to prosecute, **2**, [801]
      post-conviction—
        deprivation, **2**, [804]
        destruction in interests of animal, **2**, [808]
        disqualification, **2**, [805]–[807], [814]
        fine, **2**, [803]
        forfeiture of equipment used in offences, **2**, [811]
        imprisonment, **2**, [803]
        orders, **2**, [812]
      prosecution, time limit, **2**, [530], [802]
      summary, penalty, **2**, [534]
      triable either way, **2**, [535]
      See also **cruelty to animals**
    performing—
      exhibition and training—
        exceptions from restrictions, **2**, [251]
        meaning, **2**, [250]
        military etc, animals, **2**, [251]
        offences and proceedings, **2**, [249]
        premises, power to enter, **2**, [248]
        prohibition by court, **2**, [247]
        registration for, **2**, [246]
        restriction on, **2**, [246]
      meaning of animal, **2**, [250]
    pests, deemed to be, **1(1)**, [390]. *See also* **pests**
    pets. *See* **pet animals**
    poisoned grain etc, providing, **2**, [239]
    poisons, use of, **2**, [305], [306]
    ponies. *See* **pony**
    prejudicial to health, keeping of, byelaws for prevention of, **35(1)**, [133]
    production, expenditure on, **43(1)**, [589]
    protected, **2**, [773]
      birth or hatching, procedures for, **2**, [602]
      killing, **2**, [602], [615]
      meaning, **2**, [601]
      use of, **2**, [601]
    protection—
      cruelty, from. *See* **cruelty to animals**
      performances, in. *See* performing *above*
      summary of provisions, **2**, [140]
    rabbits. *See* **rabbits**
    rabid state, in, destruction of, **36**, [230]
    rams. *See* **sheep**
    research organisations—
      extension of provisions, **12(4)**, [138]

animals—*contd*
  research organisations—*contd*
    interference with contractual relationships
      so as to harm, **12(4)**, [134]
    intimidation of persons connected with,
      12(4), [135]
    meaning, **12(4)**, [137]
    offences, penalty for, **12(4)**, [136]
  responsibility for, **2**, [774]
  sale of restricted, **13**, [582]
  scientific procedures—
    Animal Procedures Committee. *See*
      Animal Procedures Committee
    breeding and supplying establishments—
      animals to be obtained from, **2**, [632]
      designation, **2**, [607]
    codes of practice, **2**, [621]
    designation certificates—
      application for, **2**, [606]
      breeding and supplying establishments,
        for, **2**, [607]
      conditions, **2**, [610]
      consultation, **2**, [609]
      fees, **2**, [608]
      issue of, **2**, [606]
      representations, right to make, **2**, [612]
      revocation, **2**, [611]
      scientific procedure establishments, for,
        2, [606]
      suspension in cases of urgency, **2**, [613]
      variation, **2**, [611]
    establishments, **2**, [606]
    fees, **2**, [608]
    guidance, **2**, [621]
    inspectors—
      appointment of, **2**, [618]
      duties of, **2**, [618]
    licences—
      conditions, **2**, [610]
      consultation, **2**, [609]
      fees, **2**, [608]
      personal, **2**, [604]
      project, **2**, [605]
      representations, right to make, **2**, [612]
      revocation, **2**, [611]
      suspension in cases of urgency, **2**, [613]
      variation, **2**, [611]
    neuromuscular blocking agents, prohibition
      of use, **2**, [617]
    Northern Ireland, provisions applying to,
      2, [629]
    offences—
      confidential information, protection of,
        2, [624]
      false statements, **2**, [623]
      penalties, **2**, [622]
      powers of entry, **2**, [625]
      prosecutions, **2**, [626]
    orders, **2**, [628]
    protected animals, **2**, [601]
      killing at end of, **2**, [615]
      re-use of, **2**, [614]
    public displays, prohibition of, **2**, [616]
    regulated procedures—
      breeding for, **2**, [607]

animals—*contd*
  scientific procedures—*contd*
    regulated procedures—*contd*
      meaning, **2**, [602]
      tagging, ringing or marking, **2**, [602]
      transitional provisions, **2**, [634]
      unlicensed, prohibition of, **2**, [603]
  sheep. *See* **sheep**
  sheep dipping facilities, **2**, [506]
  slaughter of. *See* **knacker's yard;**
    slaughterhouse
  straying on highway, **2**, [357]
  street offences involving. *See* **street offences**
  summary of provisions, **2**, [140]
  tagging, ringing or marking, **2**, [602]
  trading stock, **44(3)**, [30]
  transit, in—
    feeding and watering, **2**, [488]
    suffering, prevention, **2**, [487]
  trespassing—
    damage by, **2**, [353]
    detention and sale of, **2**, [356]
  welfare—
    aircraft, power to detain, **2**, [821]
    codes of practice—
      generally, **2**, [785]
      making and approval of, **2**, [786], [787]
      revocation of, **2**, [788]
    Crown application, **2**, [826]
    duty of person responsible for animal to
      ensure, **2**, [780]
      improvement notices, **2**, [781]
    entry, powers of, **2**, [819], [839]
    hovercraft, power to detain, **2**, [821]
    inspection, powers of, **2**, [819], [839]
    inspectors, **2**, [817]
    orders and regulations, **2**, [827]
    registration of activities involving, **2**, [784],
      [798], [837], [838]
    regulations to promote, **2**, [783]
      Community obligations, inspection
        relating to, **2**, [800]
      farm premises, inspection of, **2**, [799]
    scientific research, **2**, [824]
    search, powers of, **2**, [819], [839]
    transfer of animals by way of sale or prize
      to persons under 16, **2**, [782]
    vehicles, power to stop and detain, **2**, [820]
    vessels, power to detain, **2**, [821]
    warrant, conditions for grant of, **2**, [818]
    See also **cruelty to animals**
  wild. *See* **wild animals**
  zoos, in. *See* **zoo**

annual general meeting
  public company—
    circulation of resolution—
      duty of company, **8(1)**, [417]
      expenses of, **8(1)**, [418]
      members' power to require, **8(1)**, [416]
    notice of, **8(1)**, [415]
    requirement to hold, **8(1)**, [414]
    time for, **8(1)**, [414]

annual leave
right to, **16**, [1022]
summary of provisions, **16**, [1]

annual payment
charge to tax, **44(3)**, [696]
charity, covenanted donation to. *See* **charity**
commercial, **44(3)**, [742]
company payments not distributions,
collection of tax on. *See* **collection of tax**
deduction of tax—
"applicable rate", meaning, **44(4)**, [910]
commercial payments made by individuals,
44(4), [908]
dividends or non-taxable consideration,
for, **44(4)**, [912]
overview, **44(4)**, [906]
payments made by other persons,
44(4), [909]
qualifying, meaning, **44(4)**, [907]
dividends, for, **44(1)**, [102]
exempt, **44(3)**, [741]
adopters, payments to, **44(3)**, [758]–[761]
compensation awards, **44(3)**, [746]
foreign maintenance, **44(3)**, [744]
health and employment insurance
payments—
aggregation of, **44(3)**, [755]
conditions, **44(3)**, [749], [753]–[754]
insured, meaning, **44(3)**, [756]
others who contribute to payments, for
benefit of, **44(3)**, [757]
period for which made, **44(3)**, [751]
risks and benefits, **44(3)**, [750]
significant loss, risk of, **44(3)**, [752]
personal injury damages, periodical
payments of, **44(3)**, [745]–[748]
persons liable to pool betting duty, by,
44(3), [762]
trusts for injured persons, payment from,
44(3), [748]
gross amount of payment, meaning,
44(4), [460]
income charged, **44(3)**, [697]
non-taxable consideration, for, **44(1)**, [102]
person liable for tax, **44(3)**, [698]
received after deduction of tax, **44(3)**, [700]
relief for—
individuals, for, **44(4)**, [456]
other persons, for, **44(4)**, [457]
overview, **44(4)**, [455]
payments ineligible for, **44(4)**, [458]
s 733 ICTA, special rule for persons
affected by, **44(4)**, [459]
right to receive, transfer of, **44(1)**, [519]
Schedule A, under, **44(1)**, [12]
Schedule D Case III, under, **44(1)**, [13]
settlor-interested settlements, **44(3)**, [699]

annual return
contents of—
general, **8(1)**, [933]
regulations, power to make further
provision by, **8(1)**, [935]

annual return—*contd*
contents of—*contd*
share capital and shareholders, information
as to, **8(1)**, [934]
duty to deliver, **8(1)**, [932]
failure to deliver, **8(1)**, [936]
return date, **8(1)**, [932]
shadow directors, provisions applied to,
8(1), [937]

annuity
bond securing, **41**, [39]
business. *See* **insurance company**
capital element, **42**, [1060]
charge on land, register of, **21**, [391], [410]
deferred, payments securing, **44(1)**, [165],
[166]
employment-related—
another's services, in recognition of,
44(2), [611]
dependants, for benefit of, **44(2)**, [609]
non-registered occupational pension
schemes, under, **44(2)**, [610]
person liable or tax, **44(2)**, [614]
taxable pension income, **44(2)**, [612]
foreign, taxable pension income, **44(2)**, [613]
Government. *See* **Government annuity**
land transaction, consideration for, **41**, [323]
Law of Property Act, provisions inapplicable,
20, [626]
life—
amended provisions, **43(2)**, [657]
contract—
insurers, information given by,
44(1), [385], [386]
overseas insurers, tax representatives for,
44(1), [387], [388]
loan to buy, interest relief, **44(1)**, [181]
purchased. *See* **purchased life annuity**
lifetime and dependants' purchased together,
43(2), [657]
losses from life contracts, no loss relief for,
43(S), 1398
meaning, **21**, [407]
PAYE, application of, **43(2)**, [657]
payment, natural days and times for, **45**, [924]
purchased life. *See* **purchased life annuity**
register of, **21**, [391], [410]
retirement. *See* **retirement annuity**
sale etc, of allotments land for, **1(1)**, [233],
[247], [278]
savings bank. *See* **savings bank**
Schedule D Case III, under, **44(1)**, [13]
stamp duties, **41**, [36], [39]
steep-reduction, meaning, **44(1)**, [265]
transaction providing for, **44(1)**, [537]

antarctic minerals
British Antarctic Territory, law of, jurisdiction
and proceedings, **17(1)**, [726]
courts in the United Kingdom—
jurisdiction, **17(1)**, [726]
proceedings in, **17(1)**, [726]

Antarctica
  Convention—
    further provision, power to make,
      10, [1113]
    meaning, **10**, [1090]
    places protected under, **10**, [1099]
    United Kingdom nationals working under,
      10, [1111]
  Convergence, **10**, [1119]
  environmental protection—
    extension of application, **10**, [1114]
    offences—
      bodies corporate, by, **10**, [1107]
      defences, **10**, [1106]
      penalties, **10**, [1108]
      proceedings, **10**, [1105]
  fauna and flora, conservation of, **10**, [1095]
    agreed measures, giving effect to, **2**, [323],
      [324]
    extension of provisions, **2**, [326]
    interpretation of provisions, **2**, [327]
    offences, **2**, [325]
  general note, **10**, [1]
  Historic Sites and Monuments, **10**, [1098]
  meaning, **10**, [1089]
  mineral resource activities, **10**, [1094]
  offences—
    environmental protection—
      bodies corporate, by, **10**, [1106]
      defences, **10**, [1107]
      penalties, **10**, [1108]
      proceedings, **10**, [1105]
    evidence, **10**, [1118]
    institution of proceedings, **10**, [1116]
    power of arrest, **10**, [1117]
    proceedings in United Kingdom,
      10, [1112]
    under the Act, meaning, **10**, [1115]
  permits—
    application for, **10**, [1102]
    British expeditions, for, **10**, [1091]
    British stations, for, **10**, [1092]
    British vessels and aircraft, for, **10**, [1093]
    conditions, **10**, [1101]
    delegation of powers, **10**, [1104]
    grant of, **10**, [1100]
    non-native animals and plants, for
      introducing, **10**, [1096]
    production of, **10**, [1102]
    revocation, **10**, [1102]
    suspension, **10**, [1102]
  Protocol—
    areas restricted under, **10**, [1097]
    duty to have regard to, **10**, [1103]
    further provision, power to make,
      10, [1113]
    meaning, **10**, [1090]
  Treaty—
    further provision, power to make,
      10, [1113]
    meaning, **10**, [1090]
    Orders in Council as to, **2**, [324]
    United Kingdom nationals working under,
      10, [1110]

Antarctica—*contd*
  unclaimed sector, United Kingdom nationals
    in, **10**, [1109]

ante-natal care
  time of work for—
    employment tribunal, complaints to,
      16, [681]
    remuneration, **16**, [680]
    right to, **16**, [679]

anthozoans
  importation and exportation, restrictions on.
  See **animals**

anti-social behaviour
  conduct, meaning, **12(4)**, [265]
  crime and disorder reduction strategies,
    35(2), [519]
  generally, **6**, [1]
  groups, dispersal of—
    authorisation, **12(3)**, [648]–[650]
    British Transport Police, authorisations by,
      12(3), [652]
    code of practice, **12(3)**, [651]
    directions, **12(3)**, [648], [650]
  housing benefit, loss of. *See* **housing benefit**
  housing-related, meaning, **12(4)**, [265]
  injunction—
    local authority proceedings, in—
      power of arrest and remand, **12(4)**, [266]
      powers to remand, **12(4)**, [283]
    meaning, **12(4)**, [265]
    medical report, court requiring,
      12(4), [266]
    power to grant, **12(4)**, [265]
  injunctions against—
    arrest, power of, **23**, [468], [471], [472],
      [474], [555]
    breach of tenancy agreement, **23**, [469]
    conditions, **23**, [466]
    discharge, **23**, [470]
    ex parte applications, **23**, [471]
    exclusion order, **23**, [468]
    medical examination and report, remand
      for, **23**, [473]
    remand, **23**, [472], [473], [555]
    unlawful use of premises, **23**, [467]
    variation, **23**, [470]
  landlord's policies and procedures, **23**, [531]
  meaning, **6**, [880]; **12(3)**, [646], [653]
  orders, **33(2)**, [578]
    amendment of provisions, **12(3)**, [655]
    disclosure of information as to, **24**, [362]
  parenting contract in respect of,
    6, [876]. *See also* **parenting contract**
  parenting order in respect of,
    6, [877]. *See also* **parenting order**
  persons under 16, removal to place of
    residence—
    authorisation, **12(3)**, [648]–[650]
    British Transport Police, authorisations by,
      12(3), [652]
    code of practice, **12(3)**, [651]
    directions, **12(3)**, [648], [650]

anti-social behaviour—*contd*
  premises associated with persistent disorder or
  nuisance—
    closure notice—
      exemption from liability, **12(3)**, [643]
      financial loss, compensation for,
        12(3), [644]
      guidance, **12(3)**, [645]
      interpretation, **12(3)**, [646]
      making, **12(3)**, [635]
      offences, **12(3)**, [638]
      service of, **12(3)**, [635]
    closure order—
      appeals, **12(3)**, [640]
      complaint, **12(3)**, [639]
      costs, reimbursement of, **12(3)**, [642]
      enforcement, **12(3)**, [637]
      exemption from liability, **12(3)**, [643]
      extension and discharge, **12(3)**, [639]
      financial loss, compensation for,
        12(3), [644]
      guidance, **12(3)**, [645]
      interpretation, **12(3)**, [646]
      local authority, meaning, **12(3)**, [646]
      making, **12(3)**, [636]
      other premises, access to, **12(3)**, [641]
      Part 1A, meaning, **12(3)**, [646]
      police Part 1A, meaning, **12(3)**, [646]
  reporting restrictions, **33(2)**, [579]
  right to buy, suspended in case of, **22**, [114];
    24, [361]
  tenancy—
    possession, **22**, [73]
    secure, demotion, **22**, [68]

anti-social behaviour order
  appeals, **12(2)**, [661]
  application for, **12(2)**, [646]
  breach of, **12(2)**, [646]
  consultation requirements, **12(2)**, [654]
  county court proceedings, in, **12(2)**, [650]
  criminal proceedings, on conviction in,
    12(2), [651]
    variation or discharge, **12(2)**, [652]
  duration of, **12(2)**, [646]
  individual support orders, **12(4)**, [528], [584]
    breach, **12(2)**, [649]
    effect of, **12(2)**, [648]
    explanation to defendant, **12(2)**, [649]
    power to make, **12(2)**, [648]
    variation or discharge, **12(2)**, [649]
  interim, **12(2)**, [653]
  intervention orders—
    breach, **12(2)**, [657]
    effect of, **12(2)**, [656]
    explanation to defendant, **12(2)**, [657]
    power to make, **12(2)**, [656]
    relevant conditions for, **12(2)**, [656]
    variation, **12(2)**, [657]
  local authority functions, contracting out of,
    12(2), [655]
  making of, **12(2)**, [646]
  prohibitions imposed by, **12(2)**, [646]
  relevant authority, **12(2)**, [646], [647]

anti-social behaviour order—*contd*
  review of orders, **12(2)**, [659], [660];
    12(4), [537], [584]
  Transport for London, application by,
    26(2), [819]
  witnesses, special measures for, **12(2)**, [658]

Antigua and Barbuda
  Commonwealth citizenship, **31**, [186]

antiques
  customs and excise duties, relief from,
    13, [797]

Anzac
  use of term, **48**, 13, 45

apothecaries
  licensed, in Northern Ireland, saving for
    business of, **28**, [347]
  Society of, Licentiate in Medicine and
    Surgery, **28**, [278]

appeal. *See also subjects of appeal*
  alternative destination of, power to prescribe,
    11(3), [290]
  amenity of neighbourhood, notices as to,
    46, [481]–[482]
  Cathedrals Fabric Commission, to,
    14, 1200–1
  certificate of lawfulness of existing or
    proposed use or development, decisions as
    to, **46**, [452]–[453]
  compensation order, **12(2)**, [809]
  contempt of court, as to, **12(1)**, [437]
  Conveyancing Appeal Tribunal, **11(3)**, [100]
  corporation tax—
    amount discovered to be incorrect,
      determination of, **43(1)**, [397]
    appeal against, **43(1)**, [398]
    discovery, **43(1)**, [397]
    double, **43(1)**, [398]
    excessive, **43(1)**, [398]
    fraudulent or negligent conduct, finding
      of, **43(1)**, [397]
    loss of tax, discovery of, **43(1)**, [397]
    notice of, **43(1)**, [406]
    procedure, **43(1)**, [397]
    Special Commissioners, to, **43(1)**, [406]
    time limit for, **43(1)**, [397]
  costs. *See* **costs**
  Court of Appeal, assignment to, **11(3)**, [291]
  criminal cases, in. *See* **criminal appeal**
  Crown Court, to, against forfeiture of sum for
    unauthorised entry, **9**, [272]
  Crown proceedings, in, **13**, [25]
  default of planning decision, in, **46**, [342]
  demolition, against, **22**, [399]
  determination—
    appointed person, by, **46**, [626]
    second person, appointment of, **46**, [626]
    Secretary of State, by, **46**, [626]
  emergency measures, as to, **24**, [231]
  Employment Appeal Tribunal, to. *See*
    Employment Appeal Tribunal

appeal—*contd*
empty dwelling management orders, **24**, [436]
enforcement notice, against. *See* **enforcement notice**
groundless, disposal of, **12(1)**, [439]
hazardous substance consent, as to. *See* **hazardous substances**
hearing, **46**, [626]
High Court, on validity of order, **9**, [435]
house in multiple occupation—
    licensing, as to, **24**, [252], [429]
    overcrowding notice, against, **24**, [324]
House of Laity elections, concerning, **14**, 742–4
improvement notices, as to, **24**, [204], [419]
industrial and provident society, as to registration of, **19(1)**, [342]
Inland Revenue Board, determinations requiring sanction of, **43(1)**, [359]
Lands Tribunal, from, **9**, [126], [183]
listed building consent. *See* **listed building**
listed building enforcement notice, against. *See* **listed building**
local inquiry in relation to, **46**, [626]
local planning authority, functions of, **46**, [343]
management orders, as to, **24**, [432]
permission to, **11(3)**, [288]
planning decision, against, **46**, [342]–[344]
planning obligations, as to, **46**, [370]
procedure, **46**, [597]
prohibition orders, as to, **24**, [213], [422]
prosecution, by—
    evidentiary rulings, in respect of—
        Court of Appeal, determined by, **12(3)**, [842]
        expedited and non-expedited, **12(3)**, [840]
        meaning, **12(3)**, [838]
        offences not affected, continuation of proceedings, **12(3)**, [841]
        prosecution case, significantly weakening, **12(3)**, [839]
        qualifying offences, **12(3)**, [1052], [1053]
        reversal of, conditions for, **12(3)**, [843]
        right of, **12(3)**, [838]
    House of Lords, to, **12(3)**, [844]
    interpretation, **12(3)**, [848]
    reporting restrictions, **12(3)**, [845]
        offences, **12(3)**, [846]
    rights, extent of, **12(3)**, [833]
    rules of court, **12(3)**, [847]
    rulings, right in respect of—
        Court of Appeal, determined by, **12(3)**, [837]
        expedited and non-expedited, **12(3)**, [835]
        general, **12(3)**, [834]
        offences not affected, continuation of proceedings, **12(3)**, [836]
registered providers, as to—
    compensation for failure by, against, **24**, [784]
    appeals, **24**, [660]
    enforcement notice, against, **24**, [762]

appeal—*contd*
registered providers, as to—*contd*
    penalty notice, against, **24**, [774]
    registration, **24**, [660]
    removal or suspension of officers, against, **24**, [807]
    removal from register of social landlords, against, **23**, [345]
    repeals and revocations, **11(3)**, [316]
    replacement of tree, as to, **46**, [468]
    residential property tribunal, from, **24**, [440]
    roll of parish, concerning, **14**, 741–5
    second, **11(3)**, [289]
    Secretary of State, directions of, **46**, [626]
    self-assessment. *See* **self-assessment**
    social security appeal tribunals. *See* **social security appeal tribunals**
    stopping, **46**, [626]
    supervision order, as to, **12(2)**, [849]
    windfall tax, of, **43(1)**, [329]

Apple and Pear Development Council
Food from Britain, contributions to, **1(2)**, [197]

application programme interface
meaning, **45**, [492]

appointment
stamp duty, abolition, **41**, [152], [157]

Appointments Committee of the Church of England
membership of, **14**, 1330

apportionment
rentcharge. *See* **rentcharge**

apprentice
bankruptcy of employer, **4(2)**, [432]
harm, doing to, **12(1)**, [82]

apprenticeship
child in care, of, **6**, [441]
Learning and Skills Council for England, functions of, **15(S)**, Education 194

appropriation
personal representative—
    by, stamp duty, **41**, [151]
    powers of, **18**, [544]

appropriation of land. *See* **land**

approved enforcement agency
meaning, **11(2)**, [548]
powers of, **11(2)**, [549], [583]
warrant, execution of, **11(2)**, [548]

approved institution
discontinuance of, **6**, [130]
financial provisions, **6**, [139]
grants, **6**, [131]
home for children in care, use as, **6**, [139]

approved institution—*contd*
  meaning, **6**, [130]
  staff, provisions as to, **6**, [139]
  transitional provisions, **6**, [140]
  voluntary, grants to, **6**, [131]

approved school
  administration of, **6**, [44], [59]
  approval of, **6**, [42]
  buildings and grounds, altering, **6**, [59]
  classification of, **6**, [44]
  discontinuance of, **6**, [42], [130]
  documents, provisions as to, **6**, [54]
  expenses, payment of, **6**, [52], [73]
  financial provisions, **6**, [139]
  home for children in care, use as, **6**, [139]
  management of, **6**, [44]
  managers of, regulation—
    constitution of, **6**, [68]
    Secretary of State, directions by,
      6, [67]–[68]
  order sending person to, **6**, [118], [124]
  power to send offender to, **6**, [39]
  provision of, by local authority, **6**, [43]
  religious instruction, **6**, [59]
  rules for, **6**, [59]
  staff, provisions as to, **6**, [139]
  superannuation of officers, **6**, [59]
  surrender of approval, **6**, [42]
  use of premises, **6**, [139]
  withdrawal of approval, **6**, [42]

approved share incentive plan
  corporation tax deductions, **44(1)**, [635]
  exemptions, **43(2)**, [53]
  trustees of—
    "applicable period" in relation to shares,
      determining, **44(4)**, [497]
    income from, special rates for, **44(4)**, [496]

Apsley House. *See* **Wellington Museum.**

aqueducts
  open, restriction of, **49**, [86]

arbitration. *See also* **Companies Clauses Acts**
  agreement—
    bankrupt as party to, **4(2)**, [434]
    consumer—
      legal person, regulations applicable where
        consumer is, **2**, [952]
      unfair terms regulations, application to,
        2, [951]
      unfair where modest amount sought,
        2, [953]
    death of a party, **2**, [870]
    definition, **2**, [868]
    domestic—
      effectiveness of, to exclude court's
        jurisdiction, **2**, [949]
      meaning, **2**, [947]
      modification of provisions, **2**, [947]
      staying of legal proceedings, **2**, [948]
    separability of, **2**, [869]
    writing, to be in, **2**, [867]

arbitration—*contd*
  agricultural holdings, matters arising. *See*
    **agriculture holding; agricultural
    tenancy**
  agricultural marketing scheme, provision in,
    1(1), [495], [499]
  allotments, as to, **2**, [27], [30]
  alteration of sewers, etc, **35(1)**, [207]
  application of provisions, **2**, [864]
  awards—
    additional, **2**, [919]
    appeal against—
      order of the court, effect of, **2**, [933]
      point of law, on, **2**, [931]
      supplementary provisions, **2**, [932]
    challenging—
      order of the court, effect of, **2**, [933]
      serious irregularity, **2**, [930]
      substantive jurisdiction, **2**, [929]
      supplementary provisions, **2**, [932]
    correction of, **2**, [919]
    costs, of, **2**, [923]
    date of, **2**, [916]
    different issues, on, **2**, [909]
    effect of, **2**, [920]
    enforcement of, **2**, [928]
    extension of time for making, **2**, [912]
    foreign—
      application of provisions, **2**, [844]
      Convention, **2**, [843], [853]
      effect, **2**, [845]
      enforcement—
        conditions for, **2**, [846]
        evidence required, **2**, [847]
        Northern Ireland, in, **2**, [850]
        resistance to, **2**, [846]
        saving for other rights, **2**, [849]
      final, meaning, **2**, [848]
      Orders in Council, **2**, [844]
      protocol, **2**, [852]
      summary of provisions, **2**, [843]
      unenforceable, when, **2**, [846]
    foreign currency, expressed in, **19(3)**, [78]
    form of, **2**, [914]
    Geneva Convention, enforcement of,
      2, [961]
    interest, **2**, [911]
    New York Convention—
      enforcement of—
        evidence to be produced by party
          seeking, **2**, [964]
        generally, **2**, [965]
        refusal of, **2**, [965]
        saving for other bases of, **2**, [966]
      meaning, **2**, [962]
    reciprocal enforcement, **19(3)**, [24]
    recognition of—
      evidence to be produced by party
        seeking, **2**, [964]
      generally, **2**, [963]
      refusal of, **2**, [965]
      saving for other bases of, **2**, [966]
    non-payment, power to withhold in case
      of, **2**, [918]
    notification of, **2**, [917]

arbitration—*contd*
  awards—*contd*
    place where treated as made, **2**, [915]
    provisional, **2**, [901]
    remedies, **2**, [910]
    settlement, **2**, [913]
    substance of dispute, rules applicable to,
      2, [908]
  Behring Sea. *See under* **seal fisheries**
  building society disputes, **19(1)**, [748]
  carriage of goods by road (Convention),
    36, [757]
  common law savings, **2**, [943]
  companies clauses. *See* **Companies
    Clauses Acts**
  compensation, absent or untraced owner,
    9, [23], [27]
  consequential amendments, **2**, [969]
  costs—
    agreement or award about, effect of,
      2, [924]
    agreement to pay in any event, **2**, [922]
    award of, **2**, [923]
    definition of, **2**, [921]
    recoverable, **2**, [925]
      power to limit, **2**, [927]
  county court, jurisdiction of, **2**, [967]
  Crown a party, costs where, **13**, [7]
  Crown application, **2**, [968]
  damage by local authority, settlement of
    compensation for, **35(1)**, [41], [44]
  defined expressions, index of, **2**, [945]
  documents, powers of court in relation to
    service of, **2**, [939]
  drainage rate disputes, **19(3)**, [220]
  effect of, **35(1)**, [45]
  employment. *See* **Advisory**, **Conciliation
    and Arbitration Service**
  finality of, **35(1)**, [45]
  friendly societies, disputes concerning,
    19(1), [881]
  general principles, **2**, [863]
  health and safety at work, extent of
    application, **18**, [1195]
  High Court, jurisdiction of, **2**, [967]
  immunity of arbitral institutions, **2**, [936]
  injurious affection of water rights,
    35(1), [209]
  international investment disputes—
    Arbitral Tribunal—
      award by, **2**, [862]
      constitution, **2**, [862]
      powers and functions, **2**, [864]
    arbitrators—
      appointment, **2**, [862]
      panels, **2**, [862]
      replacement and disqualification, **2**, [862]
    awards—
      annulment, **2**, [862]
      generally, **2**, [862]
      interpretation, **2**, [862]
      meaning, **2**, [854]
      recognition and enforcement, **2**, [862]
      registration, **2**, [854], [855]
      revision, **2**, [862]

arbitration—*contd*
  international investment disputes—*contd*
    British possessions, application to, **2**, [859]
    conciliation—
      Commission, **2**, [862]
      proceedings, **2**, [862]
      request for, **2**, [862]
    conciliators, appointment etc, **2**, [862]
    Convention—
      administrative provisions, **2**, [862]
      amendment, **2**, [862]
      awards, registration, **2**, [854], [855]
      disputes between contracting States,
        2, [862]
      expenses incurred under, **2**, [858]
      immunities conferred, **2**, [857], [862]
      privileges conferred, **2**, [857], [862]
      status conferred, **2**, [857], [862]
      text, **2**, [862]
    Crown, provisions binding on, **2**, [854]
    International Centre for Settlement—
      administrative council, **2**, [862]
      establishment and organisation, **2**, [862]
      financial provisions, **2**, [862]
      jurisdiction, **2**, [862]
      secretariat, **2**, [862]
      status, immunities and privileges,
        2, [857], [862]
    Northern Ireland, provisions applicable,
      2, [860]
    proceedings—
      costs, **2**, [862]
      place of, **2**, [862]
      request for arbitration, **2**, [862]
  mandatory provisions, **2**, [866], [973]
  mining disputes, reference to, **17(1)**, [18];
    17(2), [171]
  minor definitions, **2**, [944]
  non-mandatory provisions, **2**, [866]
  Northern Ireland, provisions applicable,
    2, [860]
  notices, service of, **2**, [938]
  Plant Varieties and Seeds Tribunal, jurisdiction
    of, **1(2)**, [628]
  proceedings—
    beginning, power of court to extend time
      for, **2**, [874]
    commencement, **2**, [876]
    concurrent hearings, **2**, [897]
    consolidation of, **2**, [897]
    court powers exercisable in support of,
      2, [906]
    legal or other representation, **2**, [898]
    Limitation Acts, application of, **2**, [875]
    notice and other requirements in
      connection with legal proceedings,
      2, [942]
    object, loss of right to, **2**, [935]
    parties, general duties of, **2**, [902]
    peremptory orders of tribunal, enforcement
      of, **2**, [904]
    preliminary point of law, determination by
      court of, **2**, [907]
    saving for rights of person who takes no
      part in, **2**, [934]

arbitration—*contd*
  proceedings—*contd*
    time limits, powers of court to extend,
      2, [941]
    witnesses, securing attendance of, **2**, [905]
  reckoning periods of time, **2**, [940]
  reference to, mode of, **35(1)**, [193]
  scope of provisions, **2**, [864]
  seat of, **2**, [865]
  single arbitrator, by, **35(1)**, [633]
  small claims in county court, provisions not
    applicable to, **2**, [954]
  solicitors' costs, charge to secure, **2**, [937]
  state immunity, and, **10**, [1048]
  statutory, **2**, [956]–[959]
  stay of legal proceedings—
    domestic arbitration agreement, **2**, [947]
    generally, **2**, [871]
    interpleader issue to arbitration, reference
      of, **2**, [872]
    retention of security where Admiralty
      proceedings stayed, **2**, [873]
  summary of provisions, **2**, [843]
  transitional provisions, **2**, [946]
  tribunal—
    arbitrators—
      appointment—
        agreed qualifications, court to have
          regard to, **2**, [881]
        failure of procedure, **2**, [880]
        judges, of, **2**, [955], [974]
        procedure for, **2**, [878]
      chairman, **2**, [882]
      death of, **2**, [888]
      decision-making where no chairman or
        umpire, **2**, [882]–[884]
      fees and expenses recoverable, **2**, [926]
      immunity of, **2**, [891]
      joint and several liability of parties to, for
        fees and expenses, **2**, [890]
      judges, appointment of, as, **2**, [955],
        [974]
      number of, agreement, as to, **2**, [877]
      removal of, **2**, [886]
      resignation of, **2**, [887]
      revocation of authority of, **2**, [885]
      sole, power in case of default to
        appoint, **2**, [879]
      umpire, **2**, [883]
      vacancy, filling of, **2**, [889]
    assessors, power to appoint, **2**, [899]
    evidential matters, **2**, [896]
    experts, power to appoint, **2**, [899]
    general duty, **2**, [895]
    general powers exercisable by, **2**, [900]
    jurisdiction—
      competence to rule on its own, **2**, [892]
      preliminary point of, determination of,
        2, [894]
      substantive, objection to, **2**, [893]
    legal advisors, power to appoint, **2**, [899]
    party's default, powers in case of, **2**, [903]
    peremptory orders, enforcement of,
      2, [904]
    procedural matters, **2**, [896]

arbitration—*contd*
  tribunal—*contd*
    provisional awards, power to make, **2**, [901]
  works of dock undertakers and railway
    companies, protection of, **35(1)**, [210]

arbitrator. *See also* **umpire**
  appointment—
    agreed qualifications, court to have regard
      to, **2**, [881]
    failure of procedure, **2**, [880]
    judges, of, **2**, [955], [974]
    procedure for, **2**, [878]
  chairman, **2**, [882]
  costs, determination of, **9**, [30]
  death of, **2**, [888]
  decision-making where no chairman or
    umpire, **2**, [884]
  fees and expenses recoverable, **2**, [926]
  High Court, powers exercisable by,
    11(2), [716]
  immunity of, **2**, [891]
  international investment disputes—
    appointment, **2**, [862]
    panels, **2**, [862]
    replacement and disqualification, **2**, [862]
  joint and several liability of parties to, for fees
    and expenses, **2**, [890]
  judges, appointment of, as, **2**, [955], [974]
  Lands Tribunal—
    acting as, **9**, [181], [183]
    appointment by, **9**, [181]
  number of, agreement as to, **2**, [877]
  panel of, appointment of, **9**, [181]
  questions, submission of, to, **9**, [28], [181]
  removal of, **2**, [886]
  resignation of, **2**, [887]
  revocation of authority of, **2**, [885]
  sole, power in case of default to appoint,
    2, [879]
  umpire, **2**, [883]
  vacancy, filling of, **2**, [889]

archaeological area
  Broads, in area of, **32**, [374]
  compensation—
    claim for, **32**, [369]
    exercise of powers, damage caused by,
      32, [368]
  Crown land, **32**, [371]
  designation order—
    coming into operation, **32**, [387]
    Historic Buildings and Ancient Monuments
      Commission, by, **32**, [387]
    local authority, by, **32**, [387]
    local land charge, as, **32**, [355]
    power to make, **32**, [355]
    revocation of, **32**, [355], [387]
    Secretary of State, by, **32**, [387]
    validity, questioning, **32**, [377]
    variation of, **32**, [355], [387]
  ecclesiastical property, **32**, [372]
  entry, powers of—
    investigation, for, **32**, [348]
    objects found, custody of, **32**, [376]

archaeological area—*contd*
  entry, powers of—*contd*
    provisions on, **32**, [365]–[366]
    site of operations, on, **32**, [362]
    survey and valuation, for, **32**, [365]
  examination, meaning, **32**, [382]
  information on interests in land, **32**, [379]
  investigating authorities—
    appointment, **32**, [356]
    excavations by, **32**, [360]
    Historic Buildings and Ancient Monuments
      Commission as, **32**, [356]
    investigation in advance of operations,
      32, [361]
    operations, consent to, **32**, [358]
    Secretary of State as, **32**, [356]
  investigations—
    expenditure on, **32**, [367]
    meaning, **32**, [382]
    operations notice, in advance of, **32**, [361]
    power of entry for, **32**, [348]
    results, publication of, **32**, [367]
  minerals, boring for, **32**, [365]
  offences—
    body corporate, by, **32**, [380]
    defences, **32**, [359]
    obstruction, **32**, [366]
    operations notice, failure to give, **32**, [357]
    removal of articles, **32**, [364]
  operations—
    entry on site, powers of, **32**, [362]
    excavations by investigating authority,
      32, [360]
    injunction against, **32**, [357]
    investigating authority, with consent of,
      32, [358]
    notice—
      certificate accompanying, **32**, [358]
      clearance of site, work after, **32**, [357]
      contents of, **32**, [357]
      Crown land, concerning, **32**, [371]
      excavations following, **32**, [360]
      exemptions, **32**, [359]
      investigations in advance of, **32**, [361]
      offences, **32**, [357]
      requirement of, **32**, [357]
      service of, **32**, [357]
  protection of, generally, **32**, [1]
  regulations and orders, **32**, [381]
  service of documents, **32**, [378]
  treasure. *See* **treasure**

archaeological consultant. *See* **cathedral**

archbishop
  absence or illness, exercise of power during,
    14, 822
  appeal to—
    licence of non-residence, against revocation
      of, **14**, 109
    procedure, **14**, 121
    refusal to institute, against, **14**, 250
    sequestration for non-residence, against,
      14, 110–11
  appointment by Crown, **14**, 23–4

archbishop—*contd*
  Archbishops' Council. *See* **Archbishops'
    Council**
  boundaries, agreements to ascertain, **14**, 74
  clerks subject to discipline, keeping list of,
    14(S), 30–1
  complaint against—
    articles, content of, **14**, 582
    commission of convocation—
      appointment of, **14**, 583
      conduct of trial by, **14**, 583–4
    episcopal committee, inquiry by, **14**, 581–2
    finding, action or, **14**, 584
    inquiry, referral on, **14**, 586
  complaint against bishop, dealing with,
    14, 585–6
  consecration of, **14**, 25–6
  declaration by, recording, **14**, 609
  deposition from Holy Orders, **14**, 594
  deprivation—
    censure of, **14**, 594
    offence, after conviction of, **14**, 597–8
  disciplinary proceedings—
    institution of, **14(S)**, 8–9
    jurisdiction, **14(S)**, 5–6
    misconduct, for, **14(S)**, 7
    suspension during, **14(S)**, 29–30
  election of, **14**, 23–4
  evidence, verifying, **14**, 126
  exempt or peculiar benefice, powers as to,
    14, 120
  fees paid by, reimbursement of, **14**, 1126
  inhibition, performance of duties during,
    14, 605–6
  legal secretary, abolition of office, **14**, 829
  medical examination, **14**, 1115, 1117
  precedence of, **33(1)**, [4]
  proceedings for offences by, **14**, 573
  provisions on bishops extending to, **14**, 120
  resignation of, **14**, 1114
  retirement of—
    age-limit, on reaching, **14**, 1115
    disability, in case of, **14**, 1115
      medical examination of, **14**, 1115
    pensions, provisions as to, **14**, 1116
  retiring age, continuing in office after,
    14, 821
  sentences of imprisonment and matrimonial
    orders, effect of, **14(S)**, 25–6
  suspension, performance of duties during,
    14, 605–6
  trial of, **14**, 557
  vacant see, exercising powers in, **14**, 1109

Archbishop of Canterbury
  Board of Governors, chairman of, **14**, 420
  Church Commissioners, chairman of, **14**, 419
  dispensations, etc, granting, **14**, 28
  licences, granting, **14**, 28–9
  refusal to grant licence, appeal, **14**, 34–5

archbishopric
  vacancy, effect of declaration of, **14**, 1116

Archbishops' Council
accounts and audit, **14**, 1325
committees, **14**, 1334
constitution, **14**, 1332–3
documents, **14**, 1334
establishment, **14**, 1323
funds, application of, **14**, 1324
membership, **14**, 1332–3
officers transferred to, **14**, 1328, 1335–6
procedure, **14**, 1334
report and budgets, **14**, 1325–6
status of, **14**, 1333
transfer of functions to, **14**, 1326–7, 1334

archdeacon
cathedral preferment, holder of, **14**, 135
emeritus, designation of, **14**, 1309
enquiry into pastoral situation, action on,
14, 884–5
faculty, grant of, **14**, 1224
functions, discharge during absence, **14**, 1110
inspection of church, ensuring, **14**, 482
jurisdiction of, **14**, 93
official principal, abolition of office, **14**, 830
powers of bishop, exercising, **14**, 509
qualifications of, **14**, 133
registrar, abolition of office, **14**, 830
resignation of, **14**, 1310
stipend, Church Commissioners paying sums
towards, **14**, 841
visitations, **14**, 1261

archdeaconry
canonry, annexation to, **14**, 135
creation of scheme for, **14**, 925
dissolution—
compensation, **14**, 999, 1095
pastoral scheme, by, **14**, 997–8
pastoral scheme dealing with, **14**, 985

Arches Court of Canterbury
appeal to, **14**, 590
judges—
generally, **14**, 561–2
oath of, **14**, 614
jurisdiction of, **14**, 557–8, 565–6
original jurisdiction, abolition of, **14**, 611
vacation of see, effect of, **14**, 570

architects
cathedral. *See* **cathedral**
Commission for Architecture and the Built
Environment. *See* **Commission for
Architecture and the Built Environment**
financial assistance, **2**, [1019]
summary of provisions, **2**, [976]
title, use of, **2**, [996], [997]

Architects Registration Board
appointed members, **2**, [1006]
casual vacancies, **2**, [1006]
chairman, **2**, [1006]
code of practice, **2**, [989]
committees—
establishment of, **2**, [1007], [1008]

Architects Registration Board—*contd*
committees—*contd*
general, **2**, [1009]
other, **2**, [1008]
professional conduct committee, **2**, [1007]
consequential amendments, **2**, [1003]
continuation of, **2**, [977]
disciplinary orders, **2**, [991]
elected members, **2**, [1006]
erasure orders, **2**, [994]
interpretation provisions, **2**, [1002]
membership, **2**, [1006]
penalty orders, **2**, [992]
procedure, **2**, [1006]
professional misconduct and incompetence,
2, [990]
register—
maintenance of, **2**, [979]
removal from—
appeals against, **2**, [998], [999]
change of address, failure to notify,
2, [987]
competence to practise, **2**, [985]
disqualification in an EEA state, **2**, [986]
retention of name in, **2**, [984]
registrar—
appointment of, **2**, [978]
list of visiting EEA architects, to maintain,
2, [988]
registration—
EEA qualifications, **2**, [981]
false representation, penalty for obtaining
by, **2**, [983]
further procedural requirements, **2**, [982]
general, **2**, [980]
rules, **2**, [1000]
seal, **2**, [1006]
service of documents, **2**, [1001]
staff, **2**, [1006]
suspension orders, **2**, [993]
term of office, **2**, [1006]
transitional provisions and savings, **2**, [1010]
visiting EEA architects—
discipline provisions, application of, to,
2, [995]
list of, to be maintained, **2**, [988]

architectural etc interest, works of
acquisition for housing purposes, **22**, [408]
historic building. *See* **historic building**
listed buildings. *See* **listed building**
preserving in housing proposals, **22**, [407]

Architectural Heritage Fund
grants to, **32**, [370]

architectural interest, buildings of
acquisition of, London, **25(1)**, [402], [674]
demolition under London Building Acts,
25(1), [336]

architecture
Commission for Architecture and the Built
Environment. *See* **Commission for
Architecture and the Built Environment**

architecture—*contd*
financial assistance, **2**, [1019]

area
units of measurement, **39(1)**, [554]

area of outstanding natural beauty
advice on questions relating to, **32**, [180]
appropriate planning authority, **32**, [183]
appropriation of land, **32**, [191]
byelaws, **32**, [184], [192]
conservation boards for—
   chairman, **32**, [725]
   constitution, **32**, [725]
   deputy chairman, **32**, [725]
   establishment of, **32**, [704]
   grants to, **32**, [709]
   land, acquisition and disposal of, **32**, [726]
   local authority members, **32**, [725]
   management plans, **32**, [707]–[708]
   orders establishing, **32**, [706]
   parish members, **32**, [725]
   powers of, **32**, [705]
   purposes of, **32**, [705]
   Secretary of State, members appointed by,
     32, [725]
   status, **32**, [725]
   supplemental powers, **32**, [725]
derelict land in, grant for, **32**, [512]
designation of—
   generally, **32**, [1], [700]
   orders, procedure for, **32**, [701]
disposal of houses in, restriction on, **22**, [44],
   [169]; **23**, [356]
disposal of land, **32**, [191]
local authority—
   compulsory acquisition of land by,
     32, [183]
   financial contributions by, **32**, [187]
   works, carrying out, **32**, [183]
local planning authority—
   byelaws, making, **32**, [184]
   functions of, relating to, **32**, [702]
   trees, planting, **32**, [183]
public bodies, duties regarding, **32**, [703]
undertakings, holding by, **49**, [965]

area synod
constituting, **14**, 918–19

armed conflict
international, protection of victims,
   10, [966]–[971]
non-international, protection of victims,
   10, [972]–[976]

armed forces. *See also particular branches*
absence without leave—
   aiding and abetting, **3(S)**, 314
   arrest, warrant for, **3(S)**, 288–9
   civilian police, surrender to, **3(S)**, 286–7
   forfeiture of service, **3(S)**, 299
   proceedings before civilian court,
     3(S), 287–8
active service, **3**, [722]

armed forces—*contd*
Acts—
   continuance of, **3**, [1709]
   correction of deficiencies, **3**, [1495]
additional duties commitment, **3(S)**, 339
administrative reduction in rank or rate,
   restriction on, **3(S)**, 300–1
affidavits and declarations, power of authorised
   officer to take, **3(S)**, 320
age, determination of, **3(S)**, 339
agricultural work, temporarily employed in,
   50, [260]
alcohol testing—
   definitions, **3(S)**, 279
   obtaining and analysis of samples,
     3(S), 279–80
   powers regarding, **3**, [1734], [1744]
   sample—
     failure to provide, **3**, [1744]
     meaning, **3**, [1735]
     provision of, for, **3**, [1734]
   serious incident, after, **3**, [1734];
     3(S), 277–8
   summary of provisions, **3**, [1]
aliens in, restrictions on, **3(S)**, 308–9
See also **aliens**
alignment of enactments, **3(S)**, 342–3
amended provisions, **3(S)**, 500–11
arrest—
   anticipation of commission of offence, in,
     3(S), 81–2
   charge, after, by order of commanding
     officer, **3(S)**, 117
   civil authorities, by—
     absence without leave, for, **3(S)**, 285–9
     desertion, for, **3(S)**, 285–9
     judge advocate, under warrant of,
       3(S), 285
     persons unlawfully at large, of, **3(S)**, 289
     reasonable force, use of, **3(S)**, 290
     service custody, transfer to, **3(S)**, 290
     service offences, for, **3(S)**, 285
   custody proceedings rules, **3(S)**, 119
   direction of court for, **3(S)**, 118
   entry, search and seizure powers—
     person other than service policeman,
       by, **3(S)**, 100–1
     service policeman, by, **3(S)**, 99–100
   former member of forces, of, **3(S)**, 81
   mutiny, involvement in, **3(S)**, 81
   powers of entry and search, provision by
     Secretary of State, **3(S)**, 102
   proceedings, during, by order of
     commanding officer, **3(S)**, 117
   search on—
     clothing, removal of, **3(S)**, 84
     mouth, of, **3(S)**, 84
     person other than policeman, by,
       3(S), 83
     premises, of, **3(S)**, 85
     reasonable extent of, **3(S)**, 84
     seizure and retention of articles on,
       3(S), 85
     service policeman, by, **3(S)**, 82
   service offence, for, **3(S)**, 79–80

armed forces—*contd*

assignment or charge on pay and pensions, avoidance of, **3(S)**, 322

aviation offences, application of provisions, **4(1)**, [512]

bad character, evidence of, **18**, [428]

billeting. *See* **billeting**

births, deaths and marriages, overseas, registration, **36**, [142]

British overseas territory—
    civilian court, service matters punishable by, **3(S)**, 317
        maximum penalties, reference to, **3(S)**, 318
    forces serving with UK forces, provisions applying, **3(S)**, 330
    power to apply provisions, **3(S)**, 323

cadet force adult volunteers, national minimum wage, exclusion from provisions, **16**, [944]

certificates etc, forgery of, **3**, [266]

Channel Islands, application of provisions to, **3**, [1738]

children at risk overseas, protection of, **3**, [1]

children of service families, protection of, **3(S)**, 390–5

civil court. *See* **civil court**

civil defence training, **50**, [242]–[243]

civil interests. *See* **civil interests of servicemen**

civil offence. *See* **civil offence**

civil prison. *See* **civil prison**

civil trial. *See* **civil trial**

civilian—
    criminal justice enactments—
        areas of legislation subject to, **3**, [1733]
        provisions equivalent to, power to make, **3**, [1733]
    limitation of action against, **3**, [1491]

civilian court, service matters punishable by—
    British overseas territory, in, **3(S)**, 317
        maximum penalties, reference to, **3(S)**, 318
    desertion or absence without leave, aiding and abetting, **3(S)**, 314
    evidence in proceedings, **3(S)**, 332
    malingering, aiding and abetting, **3(S)**, 315–16
    offences committed abroad, **3(S)**, 317
    persons subject to service law, obstructing, **3(S)**, 316

civilian employed in. *See* **civilian**

colonial forces. *See* **colonial forces**

colonial naval force. *See* **colonial naval force**

colonies. *See* **colonies**

command. *See* **command**

commanding officer, meaning, **3(S)**, 325

Commonwealth force. *See* **commonwealth force**

compulsory service, **50**, [180]

contempt of court—
    civil courts, certification to, **3(S)**, 283
    decisions of court, **3(S)**, 283–4
    fine, imposition of, **3(S)**, 284
    misbehaviour in court, **3(S)**, 280–1

armed forces—*contd*

contempt of court—*contd*
    power to detain offender, **3(S)**, 282
    qualifying service courts, **3(S)**, 281

corporate manslaughter and homicide provisions, application of, **12(4)**, [300]

council tax relief, **43(S)**, 879

court-martial. *See* **court-martial**

Criminal Cases Review Commission, powers of, **3(S)**, 379–84

criminal evidence provisions, **18**, [260]

criminal justice enactments—
    definitions, **3(S)**, 293
    power to make provision in consequence of, **3(S)**, 292

criminal justice provisions, effect of amendments, **12(4)**, [546]

death on active service, inheritance tax relief, **42**, [689]

death or disablement, benefits for, **3**, [1383]

death or injury, liability of Crown where, **13**, [14]

definitions, **3(S)**, 334–6

deserters—
    aiding and abetting, **3(S)**, 314
    arrest, warrant for, **3(S)**, 288–9
    civilian police, surrender to, **3(S)**, 286–7
    forfeiture of service, **3(S)**, 299
    proceedings before civilian court, **3(S)**, 287–8
    summary of provisions, **3(S)**, 1–5

desertion. *See* **desertion**

disaffection. *See* **incitement to disaffection**

drink or drugs, application of provisions as to, **37**, [800]; **38(1)**, [114]

driving licences, exercise of functions as to, **37**, [799]

drugs—
    meaning, **3**, [1735]
    summary of provisions, **3**, [1]
    testing—
        definitions, **3(S)**, 279
        obtaining and analysis of samples, **3(S)**, 279–80
        power of, **3(S)**, 276–7
        powers regarding, **3**, [1734], [1744]
        sample—
            failure to provide, **3**, [1744]
            meaning, **3**, [1735]
            provision of, for, **3**, [1734]
            serious incident, after, **3**, [1734]; **3(S)**, 277–8

duration of enactments, **3(S)**, 343–4

early departure scheme, lump sums under, **44(2)**, [637]

eliciting, publishing or communicating evidence as to members of, **12(S)**, 80–1, 142–4

employment and support allowance, entitlement to, **40(2)**, [551]

employment, provisions applying to, **16**, [486], [842]

enlistment—
    mode of making regulations relating to, **3**, [1689]

armed forces—*contd*
  enlistment—*contd*
    regulations, **3(S)**, 296
    summary of provisions, **3(S)**, 5
    terms and conditions of, **3(S)**, 297–8
  entry, search and seizure powers—
    arrest, for purpose of—
      person other than service policeman,
        by, **3(S)**, 100–1
      service policeman, by, **3(S)**, 99–100
    evidence, for purpose of obtaining—
      excluded material, access to, **3(S)**, 96
      interpretation, **3(S)**, 94
      judge advocate, authorisation by,
        3(S), 93
      officer, authorisation by, **3(S)**, 97–8
      person other than service policeman,
        by, **3(S)**, 98
      review by judge advocate, **3(S)**, 99
      service policeman, by, **3(S)**, 97
      special procedure material, access to,
        3(S), 96
      supplementary provisions, power to
        make, **3(S)**, 95
    Secretary of State, powers conferred by,
      3(S), 102
  exemptions from income tax liability—
    food, drink and mess allowances, for,
      44(2), [299]
    leave travel facilities, for, **44(2)**, [298]
    Operational Allowance, for, **44(2)**, [300]
  financial penalty enforcement order,
    regulations, **3(S)**, 291
  First World War, pardons for servicemen
    executed for disciplinary offences in,
    3(S), 324
  foreign marriage, solemnised by forces
    chaplain serving abroad, **27**, [155], [203]
  friendly society members, protection,
    19(1), [545]
  Geneva Conventions, provisions of,
    10, [954]–[976]
  hearsay evidence, provisions applying,
    18, [429]
  higher authority, meaning, **3(S)**, 325
  homosexual acts, **12(2)**, [239], [240]
  individual grievances, redress of—
    Defence Council, role of, **3(S)**, 304
    Her Majesty, reference to, **3(S)**, 306
    service complaint panel—
      composition and procedure, **3(S)**, 305
      role of, **3(S)**, 304
    service complaints, **3(S)**, 302–3
  instruments, execution of, **3**, [722]
  insubordinate behaviour. *See* **insubordinate**
  behaviour
  interim hospital orders, effect of, **3(S)**, 501
  Isle of Man, application of provisions to,
    3, [1738]
  jobseeker's allowance, **40(2)**, [72]
  judge advocate, definition, **3(S)**, 326
  jury service, excusal from, **19(3)**, [135]
  local probation boards, activities of,
    12(2), [980]

armed forces—*contd*
  members, assistance in enforcement of
    customs and excise matters, **13**, [598]
  miscarriages of justice, compensation for,
    3(S), 255
    assessors, **3(S)**, 377–8
  motor vehicle driver's hours, exemption,
    36, [835]
  national minimum wage, exclusion from
    provisions, **16**, [943]
  naval chaplains, reference to, **3(S)**, 331
  nuclear material, activities relating to,
    12(1), [805]
  offences—
    abrogation of common law corroboration
      rules, **3**, [1691]
    absence without leave, **3(S)**, 29–30
    aiding, abetting, counselling or procuring,
      3(S), 57
    Air Navigation Order, under, **3(S)**, 64
    alcohol or drugs, unfitness or misconduct
      through, **3(S)**, 38–9
    arrest, resistance to, **3(S)**, 45
    arrest. *See* arrest *above*
    attempts, **3(S)**, 55–6
    charge—
      allocated for summary hearing, CO
        hearing, **3(S)**, 128
      commanding officer, by, **3(S)**, 124–5
      Director of Service Prosecutions,
        direction by, **3(S)**, 126
      powers of commanding officer after,
        3(S), 127
    charges capable of being heard summarily,
      3(S), 67–8
      permission of senior officer, with,
        3(S), 70, 347
    charging and mode of trial, regulations,
      3(S), 131
    circumstances, service police to be aware
      of, **3(S)**, 120
    civil court costs, **3**, [1728]
    civilian courts dealing with, **3(S)**, 251
    code of practice for enquiries, **12(1)**, [919],
      [920]
    commanding officer, charge by—
      circumstances for, **3(S)**, 124
      power of, **3(S)**, 125
    community punishments, **3(S)**, 506
    confirmation of findings of courts-martial,
      abolition of, **3**, [1696]
    consent of Attorney general or DPP,
      exclusion of enactments requiring,
      3(S), 295
    conviction, meaning, **3(S)**, 338
    criminal conduct—
      aiding, abetting, counselling or
        procuring, **3(S)**, 62
      attempt, trial of, **3(S)**, 61
      attempting, **3(S)**, 60
      conspiracy to commit, **3(S)**, 61
      incitement, **3(S)**, 62
      offence under law of England and
        Wales, **3(S)**, 63
      punishable, **3(S)**, 58

armed forces—*contd*
offences—*contd*
custody after charge—
conditions for, **3(S)**, 114
judge advocate, accused brought before, **3(S)**, 112–13
period of, **3(S)**, 113
proceedings, during, **3(S)**, 116
release from, **3(S)**, 114–15
review of, **3(S)**, 115–16
custody without charge—
civil authorities, transfer from, **3(S)**, 111
commanding officer, authorisation by, **3(S)**, 107
delegation of functions, **3(S)**, 112
judge advocate, extension by, **3(S)**, 109–11
limitations on, **3(S)**, 106
records, keeping, **3(S)**, 112
representations, **3(S)**, 112
review by commanding officer, **3(S)**, 108
desertion, **3(S)**, 28
Director of Service Prosecutions. *See*
Director of Service Prosecutions
disgraceful conduct of cruel or indecent kind, **3(S)**, 41
double jeopardy—
civilian proceedings barring subsequent service proceedings, **3(S)**, 78–9
directions, effect of, **3(S)**, 78
sentence quashed, where, **3(S)**, 78
service proceedings barring subsequent civilian proceedings, **3(S)**, 77
service proceedings barring subsequent service proceedings, **3(S)**, 76
enactment, meaning, **3(S)**, 105
enemy, assisting, **3(S)**, 22
entry, search and seizure. *See* entry, search and seizure powers *above*
evidence of, **3**, [1512]
excuses, evidential burden, **3(S)**, 294
failing to escape when captured by enemy, **3(S)**, 26
failure to attend for of perform duty, **3(S)**, 34
failure to cause apprehension of deserters or absentees, **3(S)**, 30
false air signals, giving, **3(S)**, 49
false records, making, **3(S)**, 37
fighting or threatening behaviour, **3(S)**, 39–40
fingerprinting of certain offenders, **3**, [1693]
flying—
causing annoyance by, **3(S)**, 52
dangerous, **3(S)**, 49–50
low, **3(S)**, 51
good order and discipline, conduct prejudicial to, **3(S)**, 38
inaccurate certification, **3(S)**, 52–3
incitement, **3(S)**, 57
information useful to enemy, disclosure of, **3(S)**, 36

armed forces—*contd*
offences—*contd*
investigation—
commanding officer, duty of, **3(S)**, 121
multiple offences or offenders, of, **3(S)**, 122
referral of case following, **3(S)**, 121–2
lawful commands, disobedience to, **3(S)**, 32
limitation of action—
civilians, in respect of, **3**, [1491]
generally, **3**, [1490]
local probation boards, provision as to, **3(S)**, 295
looting, **3(S)**, 25
low flying, **3(S)**, 51
malingering, **3(S)**, 35
aiding and abetting, **3(S)**, 315–16
miscarriages of justice, **3(S)**, 508–9, 511
misconduct on operations, **3(S)**, 23
mutiny—
failure to suppress, **3(S)**, 28
taking part in, **3(S)**, 27
obstructing operations, **3(S)**, 24
official documents, tampering with or suppressing, **3(S)**, 37
premises, meaning, **3(S)**, 105
prisoners, allowing escape or unlawful release of, **3(S)**, 47
prize—
officer in command, by, **3(S)**, 53–4
person subject to service law, by, **3(S)**, 54–5
proceedings, time for commencing, **3**, [1490]
property in possession of service police or CO, disposal of, **3(S)**, 103
public or service property—
damage to, **3(S)**, 42
definitions, **3(S)**, 43–4
loss of, **3(S)**, 42
misapplying, **3(S)**, 43
wasting, **3(S)**, 43
punishable with imprisonment, interpretation, **3(S)**, 339
reasonable force, power to use, **3(S)**, 106
rehabilitation of offenders, **3**, [1695]
samples, taking of, from certain offenders, **3**, [1694]
savings, **3(S)**, 104
Schedule 2, **3(S)**, 120, 347–50
sentences, required custodial, **3**, [1726], [1742]
sentry, etc, using force against, **3(S)**, 34
serious, police to be aware of possibility of, **3(S)**, 120
seriousness, deciding, **3(S)**, 223–4
Service Civilian Court. *See* **Service Civilian Court**
service custody, relating to, **3(S)**, 46
service living accommodation, meaning, **3(S)**, 105
service parent or guardian, recognizance and fines by—
amount of, **3(S)**, 219

armed forces—*contd*
  offences—*contd*
    service parent or guardian, recognizance
      and fines by—*contd*
      appeals, **3(S)**, 220
      duration, **3(S)**, 219
      forfeiture of recognizance, **3(S)**, 221–2
      order for, **3(S)**, 219
      variation and revocation, **3(S)**, 220
    service policeman, obstructing or failing to
      assist, **3(S)**, 44
    ship, hazarding, **3(S)**, 48
    standing civilian court, custody in case of
      trial by, amendments to, **3**, [1743]
    standing orders, contravention of, **3(S)**, 33
    stop and search. *See* stop and search powers
      below
    subordinates, ill-treatment of, **3(S)**, 40
    summary appeal court—
      appeal from decision of, **3(S)**, 148
      constitution, **3(S)**, 143
      costs, **3**, [1728]–[1730]
      court administration officer, **3(S)**, 326
      establishment of, **3(S)**, 142
      hearings by, **3(S)**, 146
      membership—
        eligibility of warrant officers for,
          3, [1725]
        officers and warrant officers ineligible
          for in particular circumstances,
          3(S), 145
        officers and warrant officers qualified
          for, **3(S)**, 143–5
      open court, sitting in, **3(S)**, 146
      powers of, **3(S)**, 146–7
      right of appeal to, **3(S)**, 142
      rules, **3(S)**, 149
      sitting, place of, **3(S)**, 142
      substituted punishment by, **3(S)**, 147
      summary of provisions, **3**, [1]
      suspended sentence, powers as to,
        3(S), 190
      witnesses and persons attending,
        privileges and immunities of, **3(S)**, 148
    summary hearing—
      combinations of punishments,
        prohibited, **3(S)**, 140
      commanding officer, by, **3(S)**, 133
      dealt with at, **3(S)**, 69, 346
      detention, maximum term of, **3(S)**, 136
      dismissal of charge, **3(S)**, 133
      findings, review of, **3(S)**, 150–1
      fines, maximum amount of, **3(S)**, 138
      maximum penalties, savings for,
        3(S), 141
      punishments on, **3(S)**, 134–5
      punishments, review of, **3(S)**, 150–1
      reduction in rank, limits on powers,
        3(S), 137–8
      rules, **3(S)**, 151
      seniority, forfeiture of, **3(S)**, 137
      service compensation orders, **3(S)**, 139
    summary of provisions, **3(S)**, 1
    superior officer, misconduct towards,
      3(S), 31

armed forces—*contd*
  offences—*contd*
    time limits for commencing proceedings—
      civilians formerly subject to service
        discipline, **3(S)**, 72–3
      exceptions, **3(S)**, 74
      financial statement order, failure to
        comply with, **3(S)**, 74
      former members of regular or reserve
        forces, **3(S)**, 70
      members or former members of
        ex-regular reserve forces subject to
        additional commitments, **3(S)**, 71
      person released from custody, breach of
        requirement, **3(S)**, 73
      persons formerly subject to service law,
        3(S), 71–2
      reserve force officers, **3(S)**, 75
    summary of provisions, **3(S)**, 5
  orders, rules and regulations, **3(S)**, 332–3
  overseas service hospitals, detention of persons
    in, **3(S)**, 385–90
  pay and conditions, reference of complaints,
    16, [37]
    arrears date, **16**, [39]
    qualifying date, **16**, [38]
    Scotland, determination of period in,
      16, [40]
  pay and pensions—
    Admiralty pension—
      commutation of, **3**, [310]
      forfeited, restoration of, **3**, [311]
      meaning, **3**, [312]
    air force—
      assignment of, **3**, [977]
      charges, **3**, [977]
      documents, illegal dealings in, **3**, [969]
      forfeitures and deductions—
        absence from duty, for, **3**, [915]
        barrack damage, for, **3**, [918]
        civil penalties, for, **3**, [916]
        generally, **3**, [914]
        judgment debt, for, **3**, [924]
        limit of, **3**, [925]
        pension, from, **3**, [1378]
        remission of, **3**, [919]
        wife or child, maintenance of,
          3, [923]
      generally, **3**, [287]
      maintenance. *See* **maintenance**
      negligence, loss occasioned by, **3**, [917]
      wrongful act, loss occasioned by,
        3, [917]
    apprentice pilot, **3**, [350]
    army—
      assignment of, **3**, [704]
      charge on, **3**, [704]
      documents, illegal dealings in, **3**, [696]
      forfeitures and deductions—
        absence from duty, **3**, [642]
        barrack damage, for, **3**, [645]
        civil penalties, for, **3**, [643]
        generally, **3**, [641]
        judgment debt, for, **3**, [651]
        limit of, **3**, [652]

armed forces—*contd*
pay and pensions—*contd*
army—*contd*
forfeitures and deductions—*contd*
maintenance and affiliation orders,
3, [647]
remission of, **3**, [646]
maintenance. *See* **maintenance**
military pensions, paying, **3**, [1456]
mode of payment, **3**, [271]
negligence, loss for, **3**, [644]
stoppages, **3**, [644]
wrongful act, loss for, **3**, [644]
compensation schemes—
deceased persons, payments due from
scheme administrator in respect of,
3, [1755]
establishment of, **3**, [1754]
injuries and damage, compensation for,
3, [348]
injuries in war. *See* **injuries in war**
mariners, awards to—
detention, suffering, **3**, [339]
generally, **3**, [349]
war injuries, **3**, [339]
naval and marine—
assignment of, avoidance of, **3**, [1210]
charge on, avoidance of, **3**, [1210]
deductions, limit on, **3**, [1495]
financial penalty enforcement orders,
3, [1209]
forfeitures and deductions—
civil penalties, **3**, [1205]
generally, **3**, [1204]
judgment debt, **3**, [1208]
maintenance, liability for, **3**, [366]
negligence, compensation for,
3, [1206]
remission of, **3**, [1207]
wrongful act, compensation for,
3, [1206]
Greenwich Hospital pension, including,
3, [189]
London Gazette, publication in,
3, [1457]
Order in Council, payment directed by,
3, [123]
stamp duty on instruments, **3**, [124]
pension schemes—
accrued rights, **3**, [1756]
deceased persons, payments due from
scheme administrator in respect of,
3, [1755]
establishment of, **3**, [1754]
reserve forces, **3**, [1557]
persons serving on ships, to, **3**, [341]
physical injury, meaning of, **3**, [351]
pilot, award to, **3**, [340], [350]
probate, distribution without, **3**, [192]
salvage operations, persons engaged in,
3, [350A]
schemes—
expenses of, **3**, [354]
generally, **3**, [343], [353]
soldiers, Royal order on, **3**, [191]

armed forces—*contd*
pay and pensions—*contd*
stamp duty, exemptions from, **3**, [193]
summary of provisions, **3**, [1]
war damage to effects, award for, **3**, [342]
war pensions—
central advisory committee, **3**, [314],
[1363]
children, care of, **3**, [294], [346]
disablement, claim for, **3**, [315]
forfeited, restoration of, **3**, [305]
generally, **3**, [303]
power to commute, **3**, [317]
regulations, **3**, [318]
stamp duty, exemption from, **3**, [307]
voluntary funds, **3**, [283]
widow or dependant, right to, **3**, [306]
pay, bounty and allowances, provision for,
3(S), 301
pay, forfeiture and reductions—
permitted, **3(S)**, 310–10
provision for, **3(S)**, 309
restrictions on, **3(S)**, 309
Pensions Appeal Tribunal—
appeal to, **3**, [299], [1757], [1765]
constitution of, **3**, [302]
jurisdiction of, **3**, [302]
procedure of, **3**, [302]
person subject to military law, persons ceasing
to be, offences by, **3**, [1491]
person unlawfully at large, arrest of—
civilian police, by, **3(S)**, 289
service policeman, power of, **3(S)**, 275
personnel, registration of civil partnership,
27, [841]
amended provisions, **27**, [971]
commanding officers' certificates, **27**, [866]
Commonwealth forces, **27**, [869]
police. *See* **Ministry of Defence Police**
Police and Criminal Evidence Act, application
to, **12(1)**, [920]
possession, order for, **21**, [652], [655]
powers of command dependent on rank or
rate, extension of, **3(S)**, 321
process, service of, **3(S)**, 322
prohibited place, interfering with near,
12(1), [231]
property used for service purposes, exemption
from execution, **3(S)**, 319
provisions applying to, **12(2)**, [485]
racial discrimination, application of
provisions, **7(1)**, [199]
regular forces—
members of, references to, **3(S)**, 329–30
reserve, comparison of rank, **3(S)**, 339
regular, discharge from and transfer to
reserve, **3(S)**, 299–399
reserve—
amended provisions, **3(S)**, 396–404
regular, comparison of rank, **3(S)**, 339
reserve and auxiliary forces, training
allowances, **44(2)**, [301]
sentences—
absolute discharge—
effect of, **3(S)**, 183

armed forces—*contd*
  sentences—*contd*
    absolute discharge—*contd*
      meaning, **3(S)**, 182
    civilian courts, passed by, **3(S)**, 276
    community punishments, general
      restriction, **3(S)**, 250
    conditional discharge—
      commission of further offence, powers
        on, **3(S)**, 182
      effect of, **3(S)**, 183
      meaning, **3(S)**, 181
      period of, **3(S)**, 181
    consecutive sentences—
      custodial, **3(S)**, 184
      service detention, of, **3(S)**, 185
    custodial—
      discretionary, **3(S)**, 242–3
      duty to pass, effect on other powers of
        punishment, **3(S)**, 245
      England and Wales, removal to,
        3(S), 271
      licence conditions, power to
        recommend, **3(S)**, 244
      prison governor, duty to receive
        prisoners, **3(S)**, 272
      rank or rate, effect of, **3(S)**, 268
      remission of sentences on passing of,
        3(S), 274–5
      service custody, detention in,
        3(S), 270–1
      unrepresented offender, restriction on
        imposing on, **3(S)**, 244
      WO or MCO in custody, effect on rank
        or rate of, **3(S)**, 268–9
    custody plus order—
      imposition of, **3(S)**, 192
      meaning, **3(S)**, 199
      revocation and amendment, **3(S)**, 193
      Scotland or Northern Ireland, transfer
        to, **3(S)**, 193
    detention and training order—
      appeal against, **3(S)**, 206
      civilian, application of provisions
        applying to, **3(S)**, 204
      offences during currency of, **3(S)**, 204–6
      offenders under 18, imposed on,
        3(S), 202
      term of, **3(S)**, 203
    disability, increase for aggravation related
      to, **3(S)**, 226
    discretionary custodial—
      general restriction, **3(S)**, 242
      length of, **3(S)**, 243
    dismissal, of—
      effect of, **3(S)**, 269
      general restriction, **3(S)**, 246
    explanation, duty to give, **3(S)**, 235–7
    financial statement order—
      failure to comply with, **3(S)**, 74
      meaning, **3(S)**, 247
      power to make, **3(S)**, 246–7
    fines—
      fixing of, **3(S)**, 233

armed forces—*contd*
  sentences—*contd*
    fines—*contd*
      fixing where payable by parent or
        guardian, **3(S)**, 249
      order for parent or guardian to pay,
        3(S), 248
      payment by instalments, **3(S)**, 234
      remission, power of, **3(S)**, 247
    guidelines, **3(S)**, 241–2
    guilty plea, reduction for, **3(S)**, 224
    imprisonment for term under 12 months—
      custody plus order, with or without,
        3(S), 192–3
      relevant service court, meaning,
        3(S), 191
    individual, for each offence, **3(S)**, 238
    interpretation, **3(S)**, 338
    mandatory life imprisonment, **3(S)**, 207
    mentally disordered offenders, requirement
      for medical report, **3(S)**, 240–1
    mitigation, power of, **3(S)**, 237–8
    offenders under 18, mandatory detention
      for life at Her Majesty's pleasure,
      3(S), 207–8
    overseas community order—
      breach, revocation and amendment of,
        3(S), 357–60
      meaning, **3(S)**, 179
      provisions not applying to, **3(S)**, 180
      requirements, **3(S)**, 179
      young offenders, **3(S)**, 361–2
    persons under 18, restrictions on imposing
      imprisonment on, **3(S)**, 199
    pre-sentence reports, **3(S)**, 238–40
    purposes of sentencing, duty to have regard
      to, **3(S)**, 222–3
    racial or religious aggravation, increase for,
      3(S), 225
    reasons, duty to give, **3(S)**, 235–7
    reduction in rank—
      general restriction, **3(S)**, 232
      limits on powers, **3(S)**, 137–8
    required—
      appeals where previous convictions set
        aside, **3(S)**, 215
      dangerous offenders over 18,
        3(S), 208–9
      dangerous offenders under 18, **3(S)**, 210
      firearms offences, for, **3(S)**, 214–15
      place of detention, **3(S)**, 213
      required opinion, **3(S)**, 212
      third domestic burglary, for, **3(S)**, 214
      third drug trafficking offence, for,
        3(S), 213
      violent or sexual offenders over 18,
        3(S), 209–10
      violent or sexual offenders under 18,
        3(S), 211
    seniority, forfeiture of—
      general restriction, **3(S)**, 232
      summary hearing, at, **3(S)**, 137
    serious offences, detention for—
      place of detention, **3(S)**, 201
      specified period, for, **3(S)**, 200

armed forces—*contd*
sentences—*contd*
seriousness of offence, deciding,
3(S), 223–4
service community order—
breach, revocation and amendment of,
3(S), 356–7
meaning, 3(S), 175–6
periodic review of, 3(S), 177
requirements, 3(S), 175–6
Scotland or Northern Ireland, transfer
to, 3(S), 178
service compensation order—
appeals, 3(S), 173
determination of, 3(S), 234
fixing where payable by parent or
guardian, 3(S), 249
imposition of, 3(S), 172–3
meaning, 3(S), 171
order for parent or guardian to pay,
3(S), 248
payment by instalments, 3(S), 234
review of, 3(S), 174–5
summary hearing, at, 3(S), 139
service custody rules, 3(S), 272–3
service detention—
commencement of, 3(S), 265
combined term, limit on, 3(S), 228–9
consecutive terms, commencement,
3(S), 266
duration of, periods disregarded,
3(S), 273–4
general restriction on, 3(S), 227
rank or rate, effect of, 3(S), 268
service of, 3(S), 270
suspended. *See* suspended sentence of
service detention *below*
term of, 3(S), 227–9
time, crediting, 3(S), 230–2
unrepresented offender, restriction on
imposing on, 3(S), 244
WO or MCO in custody, effect on rank
or rate of, 3(S), 268–9
service supervision and punishment order—
meaning, 3(S), 170
period of, 3(S), 170
requirements, 3(S), 170–1
review of, 3(S), 171
sexual orientation, increase for aggravation
related to, 3(S), 226
suspended. *See* suspended sentence of
imprisonment, suspended sentence of
service detention *below*
service—
desertion and absence without leave,
forfeiture on, 3(S), 299
summary of provisions, 3(S), 5
terms and conditions of, 3(S), 297–8
service chapels, marriages in, 3, [1746]
service complaint panel—
composition and procedure, 3(S), 305
role of, 3(S), 304
Service Complaints Commissioner. *See*
Service Complaints Commissioner
service court, meaning, 12(S), 95

armed forces—*contd*
service discipline, civilians subject to,
3(S), 331, 405–9
service inquiries—
offences, 3(S), 313
regulations, 3(S), 312–13
service law—
criminal justice provisions, effect of
amendments to, 3(S), 496
persons subject to, 3(S), 329
service living accommodation, meaning,
3, [1723]
service offence, meaning, 12(S), 95
service restraining order—
appeals, 3(S), 218
power to make, 3(S), 216
provisions applying to, 3(S), 217
variation and revocation, 3(S), 218
sex discrimination, 7(1), [119]
sheriff, member not to serve as, 3, [681]
social security benefits, 40(1), [359], [360]
standing civilian court—
evidence before, 3, [1512]
suspended sentences by, 3, [1507]
stop and search powers—
clothing, removal of, 3(S), 91
further provision for, 3(S), 92
garden or yard, limitations relating to,
3(S), 90–1
interpretation, 3(S), 89
person other than policeman, of,
3(S), 87–8
places in which exercised, 3(S), 90
service policeman, of, 3(S), 86
ships and aircraft, provisions applying,
3(S), 92
time of detention, 3(S), 91
suspended sentence of imprisonment—
breach of requirement, effect of,
3(S), 363–5
commencement of, 3(S), 271
community requirements, with—
amendment, 3(S), 198
meaning, 3(S), 194
provisions not applying to, 3(S), 195
review of, 3(S), 196
Scotland or Northern Ireland, transfer
to, 3(S), 197
community requirements, without—
meaning, 3(S), 194
provisions not applying to, 3(S), 195
further conviction, effect of, 3(S), 363–5
suspended sentence of service detention—
CO, activation by—
maximum term, 3(S), 189
order for, 3(S), 188–8
commencement of, 3(S), 267
Court Martial, activation by—
appeals, 3(S), 187–8
order for, 3(S), 186–7
meaning, 3(S), 185–6
Summary Appeal Court, powers of,
3(S), 190
taking effect, 3(S), 185–6

armed forces—*contd*
    termination of service, payments on,
        44(2), [417]
    tolls and charges, vehicles exempt from,
        3(S), 319
    tolls, exemption from, **3**, [682]
    transitory provisions, **16**, [894]
    war pensions committees—
        establishment, **3**, [1513]
        financial provisions, **3**, [1514]
        functions, **3**, [1513]
        orders, **3**, [1515]
        regulations, **3**, [1515]
        war pension, meaning, **3**, [1513]
        war pensioner, meaning, **3**, [1513]
    wills. *See* **will**
    young offenders, custodial sentences,
        12(1), [1114]
    See also **young offenders**

Armed Forces Museums
    designated institutions—
        conditions, **13**, [291]
        governing body—
            offers of employment by, **13**, [301]
            superannuation, **13**, [301]
            terms of employment by, **13**, [301]
        grants to, **13**, [290]
    grants to, **13**, [290]
    summary of provisions, **13**, [49]

armorial bearings
    local authority, of, **25(2)**, [210]

Armouries
    admission, powers as to payment for,
        13, [277]
    arms and armour, preservation and
        recording, **13**, [277]
    Board of Trustees—
        accounts and audit, **13**, [299]
        allowances, **13**, [299]
        appointment, **13**, [299]
        committees, **13**, [299]
        companies, power to form, **13**, [278]
        establishment, **13**, [276]
        general functions, **13**, [277]
        incorporation, **13**, [299]
        information, supply of, **13**, [299]
        land, acquisition and disposal, **13**, [277]
        membership, **13**, [299]
        proceedings, **13**, [299]
        reports by, **13**, [299]
        research and services, **13**, [277]
        sealing of documents, **13**, [299]
        status, **13**, [299]
        vesting of property, **13**, [279]
    collections, care and preservation, **13**, [277]
    finances, **13**, [282]
    loans from, **13**, [281]
    Master, appointment, **13**, [299]
    objects—
        acquisition and disposal of, **13**, [280]
        lending and borrowing, **13**, [281]
    premises, **13**, [277]

Armouries—*contd*
    staff, **13**, [299]
    summary of provisions, **13**, [49]
    Tower of London, premises in, **13**, [277]

arms control and disarmament
    CFE Treaty—
        further implementation, **10**, [1234]
        future revisions, implementation of,
            10, [1235], [1237]
    challenge inspection—
        meaning, **10**, [1080]
        obstruction, offences, **10**, [1082]
        rights of entry, **10**, [1081]
    Crown land, powers in relation to, **10**, [1083]
    escort team—
        obstruction, offences, **10**, [1082]
        references to, **10**, [1080]
    general note, **10**, [1]
    inspection team—
        conduct of inspections, **10**, [1086]
        meaning, **10**, [1080]
        obstruction, offences, **10**, [1082]
    inspectors and transport crew members,
        privileges and immunities, **10**, [1084]
    observers and inspectors, privileges and
        immunities, **10**, [1078]
    Protocol, **10**, [1080], [1086]

Army
    absence without leave. *See* **absence without
        leave**
    Act, continuation of, **3**, [1004]–[1011]
    acting rank, **3**, [723]
    active service—
        meaning, **3**, [722]
        on, **3**, [1278]
    air force, attachment to, **3**, [679]
    alcohol, testing for—
        generally, **3**, [1]
        sample, failure to provide, **3**, [1024]–[1025]
    annoyance by flying, **3**, [510]
    arrest—
        commanding officer's warrant, **3**, [689]
        deserter, of, **3**, [684], [687]
        entry to premises for, **3**, [1717]
        offenders, of, **3**, [1]
        person unlawfully at large, **3**, [690]
        power of, **3**, [534]
        proceedings, during, **3**, [545], [1084]
        resistance to, **3**, [512]
        search upon, **3**, [1718]
    assisting the enemy, **3**, [478]
    award, review of, **3**, [602]
    barrack damage, **3**, [645]
    billeting, **10**, [28]
    charges—
        amendment or substitution of, **3**, [549]
        court-martial trial, right to opt for,
            3, [551]
        higher authority, reference to, **3**, [550],
            [552]
        investigation by commanding officer,
            3, [549]

Army—*contd*
  charges—*contd*
    sentence. *See* **sentence**
    summary dealing—
      generally, **3**, [552]
      punishments available on, **3**, [553]
      regulations as to, **3**, [556]
      summary appeal court. *See* summary
        appeal court *below*
    summary finding, review of, **3**, [602]
    superior authority, meaning of, **3**, [555]
    See also offences *below*
  children of personnel, caring for, **3**, [294]
  civil court, trial by, **3**, [1279]
  civil offences—
    committing, **3**, [526]
    guilty plea, reduction in minimum sentence
      for, **3**, [527]
    life sentence, not passing, **3**, [528]
  commanding officer—
    charge by, **3**, [555]
    meaning, **3**, [723]
  complaints, procedure for, **3**, [680]
  confinement, escape from, **3**, [513]
  corps—
    meaning of, **3**, [723]
    transfer between, **3**, [464]
  court-martial. *See* **court-martial**
  custody—
    after charge—
      generally, **3**, [541], [1080]
      release from, **3**, [544], [1083]
      review of, **3**, [542], [1081]
    court-martial proceedings, during, **3**, [543],
      [1082]
    release from, **3**, [544], [1083]
    review of, **3**, [537], [1076]
    rules, **3**, [548], [1086]
    Standing Civilian Court, in case of trial
      by, **3**, [547]
    without charge—
      authorisation of, **3**, [536], [1075]
      extension of, **3**, [538], [1077]
      illegal absence, in case of, **3**, [539],
        [1078]
      limitations on, **3**, [535], [1074]
      supplementary provisions, **3**, [540],
        [1079]
  dangerous flying, **3**, [507]
  desertion. *See* **desertion**
  disabled—
    gifts for assisting, **3**, [284]
    provision for, **3**, [278]
  discharge—
    authorisation of, **3**, [467]
    certificate of, **3**, [467]
    entitlement, **3**, [467]
    postponement—
      generally, **3**, [465]
      pending proceedings, **3**, [469]
    retention in state of war, **3**, [465]
    sentence, during, **3**, [469]
    transfer to reserve, **3**, [465]
    UK, outside at time of, **3**, [467]

Army—*contd*
  discharge—*contd*
    warrant officer, on reduction to ranks,
      3, [470]
  discipline—
    conduct to prejudices of, **3**, [525]
    generally, **3**, [1]
  disgraceful conduct, **3**, [522]
  disobedience to lawful commands, **3**, [488]
  disorderly conduct, **3**, [497]
  drugs, testing for—
    generally, **3**, [1]
    sample, failure to provide, **3**, [489]–[490]
    serious incident, following, **3**, [490]
  drunkenness, **3**, [497]
  duty—
    failure to attend for, **3**, [483]
    neglect of, **3**, [483]
  enemy—
    assisting, **3**, [478]
    meaning, **3**, [723]
  enlistment. *See* **enlistment**
  equipment, interference with, **3**, [501]
  false air signal, giving, **3**, [479]
  false document, making, **3**, [517]
  fighting unlawfully, **3**, [498]
  forces, meaning, **3**, [1280]
  forfeiture of service, **3**, [471]
  ill-treatment, **3**, [521]
  inaccurate certification, **3**, [508]
  information, unauthorised disclosure, **3**, [515]
  insubordinate behaviour, **3**, [487]
  issues, offences relating to, **3**, [503]
  judicial officers, appointment of, **3**, [546],
    [1085]
  lance-bombardier, **3**, [1255]
  lance-corporal, **3**, [1255]
  looting, **3**, [484]
  low flying, **3**, [509]
  malingering, **3**, [496]
  mental disorder, treatment for, **3**, [1452]
  messages and signals, interference with,
    3, [501]
  military law. *See* **military law**
  misconduct in action, **3**, [477]
  mutiny—
    failure to suppress, **3**, [486]
    generally, **3**, [485]
  naval force, attachment to, **3**, [679]
  negligence, loss occasioned by, **3**, [644]
  non-commissioned officer, reduction in rank,
    3, [702]
  obstructing operations, **3**, [479]
  offences—
    action, in, **3**, [477]
    aiding and abetting, **3**, [524]
    attempts to commit, **3**, [523]
    charge of. *See* charges *above*
    civil, **3**, [526]
    civil court, trial by, **3**, [631]
    civil custody, reception in, **3**, [703]
    civilian population, against, **3**, [518]
    condoned, **3**, [631]
    court-martial, relating to, **3**, [514]
    decorations, relating to, **3**, [503]

Army—*contd*
  offences—*contd*
    equipment, interference with, **3**, [501]
    generally, **3**, [1]
    inciting, **3**, [524]
    juveniles, **3**, [530]
    limitation of time for trial, **3**, [628]
    messages and signals, interference with,
      3, [501]
    morale, against, **3**, [519]
    persons in custody, relating to, **3**, [511]
    persons on watch, by, **3**, [482]
    property, relating to, **3**, [499]
    prosecuting authority. *See* prosecuting
      authority *below*
    punishments. *See* **court-martial**
    required custodial sentences, **3**, [1726],
      [1742]
    sentence. *See* **sentence**
    sentries, **3**, [482]
    standing civilian court, custody in case of
      trial by, **3**, [1743]
    summary appeal court, eligibility of warrant
      officers for membership, **3**, [1725]
    young offenders, **3**, [531]–[532]
  officer—
    complaint to, **3**, [680]
    ill-treatment by, **3**, [521]
    scandalous conduct by, **3**, [520]
    sheriff, not to be, **3**, [681]
  officers' commissions, form of, **3**, [87]
  overseas authority, person arrested by,
    3, [1274]
  pay and pensions. *See* **armed forces**
  peace, keeping in time of, **3**, [1]
  pensioner—
    meaning, **3**, [1406]
    recall, **3**, [1406]
      exemption, **3**, [1449]
      occasion for, **3**, [1407]
      period of, **3**, [1407]
  persons on watch, offences by, **3**, [482]
  powers of command, **3**, [677]
  prisoner—
    assisting escape or harbouring after,
      12(1), [328A]
    permitting to escape, **3**, [511]
    releasing, **3**, [511]
  prisoner or young offender unlawfully at
    large, **12(1)**, [275AO]
  prize offences, **3**, [480]
  prosecuting authority—
    appointment of, **3**, [568]
    commanding officer, power to refer cases
      back to, **3**, [570]
    functions of, **3**, [569]
    police forces, advising, **3**, [571]
    prosecuting officers, **3**, [572]
    qualification as, **3**, [568]
  provost officer—
    meaning, **3**, [723]
    obstructing, **3**, [491]
  punishments, review of, **3**, [602]
  recall of former soldier—
    generally, **3**, [1408]

Army—*contd*
  recall of former soldier—*contd*
    notice of, **3**, [1409]
  sentence. *See* **sentence**
  sentries, offences by, **3**, [482]
  Service Acts, continuation of, **3**, [1709]
  service property—
    equipment, interference with, **3**, [501]
    loss or damage, **3**, [500]
    misapplication and waste, **3**, [502]
  ship, loss or hazarding, **3**, [506]
  soldier, complaint by, **3**, [680]
  standing, keeping, **10**, [40]
  standing orders, disobedience to, **3**, [492]
  summary appeal court—
    appeals—
      constitution for, **3**, [560]
      hearings, **3**, [562]
      right of, **3**, [561]
    decisions from, **3**, [564]
    generally, **3**, [1]
    judge advocates, appointment of, **3**, [558]
    members—
      generally, **3**, [557]
      oaths administered to, **3**, [566]
      officers qualifying as, **3**, [559]
    powers, **3**, [563]
    rules of, **3**, [565]
    witnesses, privileges of, **3**, [567]
  threatening words, using, **3**, [498]
  transfer to reserve—
    entitlement, **3**, [468]
    national danger, in, **3**, [466]
    postponement pending proceedings,
      3, [469]
    sentence, during, **3**, [469]
    state of war, during, **3**, [465]
    UK, serving outside at time of, **3**, [468]
  transfer to reserve or discharge from,
    postponement of, **3**, [1683]
  warrant officer—
    reduction in rank, **3**, [702]
    reduction to ranks, **3**, [470]
  women, including, **3**, [368]
  wrongful act, loss occasioned by, **3**, [644]
  young offenders, amendment of law as to,
    6, [551]

Army Board
  Defence Council functions, carrying out,
    10, [528]
  establishment of, **10**, [528]

army chaplain
  archbishop or bishop, under jurisdiction of,
    14, 213
  Church of Scotland, connected with, **14**, 213
  declaration of, **14**, 211
  extra-parochial district—
    appointment in, **14**, 212
    chapel in, **14**, 212
  functions, performing in, **14**, 212
  meaning, **14**, 210
  station—
    meaning, **14**, 210

army chaplain—*contd*
  station—*contd*
    metes and bounds, map of, **14**, 212
    precinct, setting out, **14**, 211

Army Reserve. *See also* **reserve forces**
  absence without leave. *See* **absence without leave**
  call out—
    permanent service, for, **3**, [1391], [1450]
    notices, **3**, [1401]
    training, for, **3**, [1450]
  desertion. *See* **desertion**
  enlistment in. *See* **enlistment**
  military office holder, powers of, **3**, [1425], [1430]
  permanent service—
    call out, **3**, [1391]
    duration of, **3**, [1392]
    postponement of discharge of members during call out, **3**, [1393]
  training—
    call out, **3**, [1450]
    generally, **3**, [1412]–[1413]

army school
  educational endowments, schemes for, **15(1)**, [150]
  meaning, **15(1)**, [150]

arrest. *See also* **Air Force; Army; Navy,** etc
  acts of terrorism, in connection with, **12(2)**, [908]
  anti-social behaviour proceedings, power attached to injunction, **12(4)**, [266]
  arrestable offences, amended provisions, **12(4)**, [148]
  assault preventing, **12(1)**, [94]
  Auxiliary Reserve. *See* **reserve associations**
  aviation offences, **4(1)**, [508]
  aviation security, in relation to, **12(3)**, [127]
  bail after, **12(1)**, [895]
  bail, failure to surrender when on, **12(1)**, [657]
  children, of. *See* **child**
  civilian, of, **3**, [1172]
  conditional caution, failure to comply with provisions of, **12(3)**, [818]; **12(4)**, [261]
  cross-border powers of, **12(2)**, [235]
    detention under, **12(2)**, [236]
    search, powers of, **12(2)**, [237]
  Customs and Excise officer, power of, **12(1)**, [1102]
  debtor about to quit England, **4(2)**, [8]
  delay in notifying, **12(1)**, [904], [989]
  derogating control order, pending, **12(4)**, [67]
  designated site, trespass on, **12(4)**, [125]
  detention after. *See* **police**
  entry and search after, **12(1)**, [852]
  entry without search warrant, **12(1)**, [960]
  extradition proceedings. *See* **extradition**
  fingerprints, to take, **12(1)**, [861]
  firearms—
    powers, **12(1)**, [542]
    using to resist, **12(1)**, [491]

arrest—*contd*
  force, use of, **12(1)**, [361]
  further offence, for, **12(1)**, [871]
  imitation firearm, using to resist, **12(1)**, [491]
  immigration offences, in case of. *See* **immigration**
  immigration officers, powers of, **31**, [501]
  information to be given on, **12(1)**, [862]
  legal advice, person entitled to, **12(1)**, [905]
  meaning, **3**, [723]
  Northern Ireland. *See under* **Northern Ireland**
  parliamentary privilege from, **13**, [2]
  police bail, failure to answer to, **12(1)**, [894]
  police station, person to be taken to, **12(1)**, [864]
  preserved powers of, **12(1)**, [931]
  prostitution, for, loitering or soliciting, **12(1)**, [306]
  reciprocal powers, **12(2)**, [238]
  repealed provisions, **12(4)**, [146], [147]
  retrial after acquittal, in case of, **12(3)**, [861]
  reward for, **12(1)**, [34]
  right to have someone informed of, **12(1)**, [904]
  search on, **12(1)**, [872]
  terrorists, suspected, **12(2)**, [908]
  trespassory assembly, in relation to, **12(1)**, [1007]
  visiting force, member of, **3**, [445]
  warrant of. *See* **warrant**
  warrant, without—
    constables, by, **12(1)**, [858]
    driving offences, **37**, [571]
    persons other than constables, by, **12(1)**, [859]
    powers, **12(1)**, [858], [859], [960]
    statutory powers, repeal of, **12(1)**, [860]
  witness, of, **12(1)**, [355]
  wounding while resisting, **12(1)**, [75]
  young person, of, **6**, [126]

arrest of judgment
  criminal libel, restriction of seized copies, **19(3)**, [266]
  libel prosecution, defendant's right, **19(3)**, [265]

arson
  imprisonment, **12(1)**, [599]
  property, damaging or destroying by fire, **12(1)**, [596]

art galleries
  loans by, indemnity for loss or damage, **13**, [253], [254]
  local authority—
    admission charges, **13**, [153]
    agreement with another authority, **13**, [152]
    byelaws, **13**, [158]
    exhibits—
      amalgamation of funds for, **13**, [155], [205]
      funds for purchase of, **13**, [155]

art galleries—*contd*
  local authority—*contd*
    exhibits—*contd*
      management of funds for, **13**, [165]
    expenses incurred by another body,
      contribution to, **13**, [154], [205]
    premises, use for educational or cultural
      events, **13**, [159]
    provision and maintenance of, **13**, [49],
      [152]
    transfer to another authority, **13**, [152],
      [205]
  summary of provisions, **13**, [49]
  transfer of objects between. *See under names of*
    galleries

articles of association
  alteration—
    members, effect on, **8**, 118
    registration of, **8**, 119
    special resolution for, **8**, 112
  amendment—
    members, effect on, **8(1)**, [103]
    registrar, sent to, **8(1)**, [104]
      notice to comply, **8(1)**, [105]
    restriction on—
      company exempt from requirement to
        use "limited", **8(1)**, [141]
      notification to registrar, **8(1)**, [101]
      statement of compliance, **8(1)**, [102]
    special resolution, by, **8(1)**, [99]
  application of profits, as to, **8**, 360
  change of company name, provision for,
    8(1), [157]
  commissions, authority to pay, **8**, 173
  commonhold association, of, amendment,
    8(1), [1359]
  company limited by guarantee, **8**, 111, 118
  copies issued by company, documents
    incorporated in or accompanying,
    8(1), [114]
  copies, provision to members, **8**, 120
  corresponding right of pre-emption in,
    8(1), [646]
  distributions, provisions as to, **8(1)**, [926]
  effect of, **8**, 117
  enjoyment or exercise of members' rights,
    effect of provisions, **8(1)**, [223]
  entitlement to vote, provisions determining,
    8(1), [365]
  entrenched provisions, **8(1)**, [100]
  existing companies, provisions of
    memorandum treated as provisions of,
    8(1), [106]
  form of, **8**, 111–12
  meaning, **8**, 602
  members, provided to, **8(1)**, [110]
  model—
    default application of, **8(1)**, [98]
    power of Secretary of State to prescribe,
      8(1), [97]
  new transferee company on division, approval
    of, **8(1)**, [1006]
  new transferee company on merger, approval
    of, **8(1)**, [990]

articles of association—*contd*
  objects, statement of, **8(1)**, [109]
  order sanctioning compromise or
    arrangement, obligations relating to,
    8(1), [979]
  order sanctioning reconstruction or
    amalgamation, obligations relating to,
    8(1), [979]
  registration of, requirement for, **8**, 111,
    113–14
  requirement for, **8(1)**, [96]
  rights as to general meetings, saving for,
    8(1), [409]
  signatures to, **8**, 111
  Table A, adoption of, **8**, 111
  Table G, **8**, 112
  Tables C, D, E, to accord with, **8**, 111
  written resolutions, relationship of provisions
    on, **8(1)**, [378]

articulated vehicle
  enactments applicable, **37**, [803]
  meaning, **37**, [311], [705]

artificial lighting
  public works, from, compensation for,
    9, [304]
    See also **public works**

Arts and Humanities Research Council
  accounts and records of, **15(2)**, [540]
  activities outside United Kingdom,
    15(2), [541]
  Arts and Humanities Research Board, transfer
    of property, rights and liabilities of,
    15(2), [536]
  Charter, **15(2)**, [535], [542]
  employees, pensions, **15(2)**, [539]
  establishment of, **15(2)**, [535]
  expenses of, **15(2)**, [537]
  objects, **15(2)**, [535]
  returns and reports of, **15(2)**, [538]

Arts Council
  properties to vest in, **25(2)**, [606]

ashpits
  room over, prohibition on use as living
    sleeping or work room, **35(1)**, [126]

Asian Development Bank
  establishment of, **19(1)**, [1]

assault
  actual bodily harm, occasioning,
    imprisonment, **12(1)**, [97]
  arrest, to prevent, **12(1)**, [94]
  burial, preventing, **12(1)**, [92]
  clergyman, on, **12(1)**, [92]
  common—
    imprisonment, **12(1)**, [97]
    summary offence, as, **12(1)**, [1083]
  court security officer, of, **11(3)**, [372]
  dismissal of complaint, **12(1)**, [95]
    bar to proceedings, **12(1)**, [96]

assault—*contd*

divine service, preventing, **12(1)**, [92]

foreign officer, on, **12(3)**, [611]

indictment, proceedings brought on, **12(1)**, [97]

intent to rob, with, **12(1)**, [560]

magistrate preserving wreck, on, **12(1)**, [93]

penetration, by, **12(3)**, [666]

child under 13, of, **12(3)**, [670]

racially or religiously aggravated, **12(2)**, [669]

sexual, **12(3)**, [667]

child under 13, of, **12(3)**, [671]

traffic officer, of, **38(2)**, [304]

assay office

Birmingham, **48**, 14

British Hallmarking Council, compliance with directions of, **48**, 64

charges, **48**, 63

closure of, **48**, 65–6

constitution of, **48**, 65–6

delivery of article after conviction to, **48**, 62

functions of, **48**, 65

hallmark, striking. *See* **hallmark**

inspection of, **48**, 82–3

meaning, **48**, 69

orders relating to—

power to make, **48**, 65–6

procedure for, **48**, 84–6

powers and duties of, **48**, 82–4

refusal to hallmark by, **48**, 56

Sheffield, **48**, 14

sponsors' marks, register of, **48**, 54–5

unauthorised mark, treatment of, **48**, 60

assembly. *See also* **public assembly**

trespassory—

arrest, **12(1)**, [1007]

offences, **12(1)**, [1007]

police powers, delegation, **12(1)**, [1009]

proceeding to, stopping, **12(1)**, [1008]

prohibition, **12(1)**, [1006]

assessment

appeal against—

General Commissioners, to, **42**, [157]

notice of, **42**, [156]

right of, **42**, [155]

Special Commissioners, to, **42**, [158], [159], [175]

company, **43(1)**, [362]

corporation tax. *See* **corporation tax**

double, **42**, [160]

error in, **42**, [161]

excessive, relief for, **42**, [161]

final determination of, **42**, [258]

form of, **42**, [253]

further, **42**, [170]

limits on, **42**, [171]

generally, **42**, [1]

income tax, of, **42**, [153]

Inland Revenue Board, determinations requiring sanction of, **43(1)**, [359]

loss of tax discovered, where, **42**, [151]

loss or destruction of, **42**, [252]

assessment—*contd*

mistake in, **42**, [161]

notice of, **42**, [153]

officer, by, **42**, [151]

overpayment, recovery of, **42**, [152]

petroleum revenue tax, to, **42**, [346]

procedure, **42**, [153]

remittance basis—

amended provisions, **43(S)**, 1608–12

amount remitted, **43(S)**, 1060–1

anti-avoidance, **43(S)**, 1063

application without claim, **43(S)**, 1053–4

claims, **43(S)**, 1052–3, 1084

commencement, **43(S)**, 1085

Commissioners, money paid to, **43(S)**, 1064

connected operation, dealings in case of, **43(S)**, 1060

consideration for services, **43(S)**, 1064

deemed income or gains, **43(S)**, 1064

effect of, **43(S)**, 1054–6

employment income, **43(S)**, 1069–78

employment-related securities, taxable specific income from, **43(S)**, 1072–5, 1077

exempt property, **43(S)**, 1064–5, 68

foreign chargeable gains, **43(S)**, 1063

foreign securities income, **43(S)**, 1074–5

gift recipients, **43(S)**, 1059

income and gains treated as remitted, **43(S)**, 1055

interpretation, **43(S)**, 1069

minor amendments, **43(S)**, 1083–5

mixed funds, transfers from, **43(S)**, 1061–3

non-resident company. *See* **non-resident**

notional remitted amount, **43(S)**, 1068

order of remittances, **43(S)**, 1055–6

overview, **43(S)**, 1052

personal use rule, **43(S)**, 1067

public access rule, **43(S)**, 1065–7

qualifying property, **43(S)**, 1059

relevant foreign income, **43(S)**, 1078–80

relevant person, meaning, **43(S)**, 1058

remitted to UK, meaning, **43(S)**, 1057–8

repair rule, **43(S)**, 1067

temporary importation rule, **43(S)**, 1067–8

temporary non-residents, **43(S)**, 1079

transitional provision, **43(S)**, 1085–7

self-assessment. *See* **self-assessment**

stamp duty, **41**, [23]

time limits, **43(S)**, 1314–20

fraudulent or negligent conduct, **42**, [165]

income received after year of assessment, **42**, [164]

ordinary, **42**, [163]

personal representative, on, **42**, [167]

transfer of allowances, effect of, **42**, [166]

want of form, effect of, **42**, [254]

assessment order. *See* **child**

assessors

Lands Tribunal, assistance to, **9**, [183], [184]

asset
  leased—
    hire-purchase agreements, subject to,
      44(1), [528]
    special cases, **44(1)**, [526]
    supplemental, **44(1)**, [527]
    traders and others, to, **44(1)**, [525]
  meaning, **44(1)**, [529]
  transfer abroad, amended provisions,
    43(S), 214–18
  See also **tax avoidance**

Assets Recovery Agency
  abolition, **12(4)**, [431]
  redistribution of functions, **12(4)**, [431], [458]

assignment
  assured tenancy of, **22**, [810]
  breach of duty, **22**, [787]
  charge in respect of land drainage, **20**, [307],
    [339]
  consent to—
    another, of, approval of, **22**, [786]
    application, passing on, **22**, [785]
    county court jurisdiction, **21**, [216]
    unreasonably withholding, **21**, [65];
      22, [784]
  covenant against, **21**, [65]
  exchange, by way of, **22**, [80]
  ground for possession, as, **21**, [651]
  insurable interest, of, **19(1)**, [160]
  landlord's interest, of, notice of, **22**, [506]
  life assurance policy, **19(1)**, [23], [25]
  marine insurance policy, **19(1)**, [195], [196]
  protected shorthold tenancy, of, **21**, [725]
  rentcharge, **20**, [339]
  seamen, by, stamp duty exemption, **41**, [77]
  secure tenancy—
    exceptions from prohibition, **22**, [79]
    prohibition of, **22**, [79]
    tenant condition not satisfied, **22**, [83]
    withholding consent, grounds for,
      22, [433]
  summary of provisions, **20**, [1]

Associated British Ports
  accounts and annual reports, **39(2)**, [490]
  agricultural land, notice to quit, **22**, [683]
  amenities and facilities, **39(2)**, [488]
  auditors, appointment, **39(2)**, [487]
  bills, promotion or opposition, **39(2)**, [488]
  borrowing powers, **39(2)**, [488]
  British Transport Commission, vesting of
    property etc of—
    assets, **36**, [707]
    staff, transfer of, **36**, [709]
    statutory functions, **36**, [708], [739]–[741]
    undertakings, distribution of, **36**, [710],
      [742]
  British Transport Docks Board reconstituted
    as, **39(2)**, [469]
  chairman and deputy, **39(2)**, [487], [490]
  chairman, appointment of, **36**, [682]
  charges, **39(2)**, [488], [490]
    power to make, **36**, [715], [747], [748]

Associated British Ports—*contd*
  commencing capital debt, **36**, [712], [877]
  common carrier, not being, **36**, [714]
  Companies Acts, provisions applicable,
    39(2), [474]
  constitution, **39(2)**, [471]
  definitions, **39(2)**, [478]
  directors—
    executive, **39(2)**, [487]
    members as, **39(2)**, [471]
    proceedings, **39(2)**, [487]
    remuneration and allowances, **39(2)**, [487]
    resignation and vacation of office,
      39(2), [487]
    transitional provisions, **39(2)**, [490]
  disposal and discontinuance of undertakings,
    39(2), [488]
  documents, keeping and inspection,
    39(2), [476]
  duties generally, **39(2)**, [473]
  education, powers as to, **39(2)**, [488]
  employees, accommodation for, **39(2)**, [488]
  establishment of, **36**, [682]
  financial structure, **39(2)**, [470]
  generally, **36**, [210]
  goods—
    consignment and carriage, **39(2)**, [488]
    storage of, **39(2)**, [488]
  Harbour Acts, provisions applicable,
    39(2), [471]
  harbours—
    operation of, **39(2)**, [488]
    undertakings, acquisition of, **39(2)**, [488]
  holding company—
    Board as subsidiary, **39(2)**, [469]
    formation, **39(2)**, [469]
    meaning, **39(2)**, [469], [478]
    payments to, **39(2)**, [475]
    restrictions by, on certain financial
      arrangements, **39(2)**, [488]
    securities, **39(2)**, [489]
    shares and securities, issue of, **39(2)**, [470]
    transfer of functions to other company,
      39(2), [477]
  housing, provision or loans, **39(2)**, [488]
  instruments, transitional provisions as to,
    39(2), [490]
  land, powers, **39(2)**, [488]
  local boards, **39(2)**, [489]
  members, appointment of, **36**, [682]
  Northern Ireland, provisions applicable,
    39(2), [484]
  operations, **39(2)**, [488]
  pension orders, existing, **39(2)**, [489]
  pension scheme—
    orders, **36**, [725]
    transitional provisions, **36**, [745]
  pensions—
    meaning, **39(2)**, [478]
    provisions as to, **39(2)**, [488]
  pipelines, construction and operation of,
    39(2), [488]
  port facilities, provision, **39(2)**, [488]
  powers—
    generally, **39(2)**, [472]

Associated British Ports—*contd*
  powers—*contd*
    schedule of, **39(2)**, [488]
    research, powers as to, **39(2)**, [488]
    secretary, **39(2)**, [487]
    ship's agent, activities as, **39(2)**, [488]
    staff, terms and conditions of employment,
      36, [723]
    stamp duty, exemption from, **36**, [713]
    subsidiaries, statutory undertakers, as,
      39(2), [489]
    summary of provisions, **39(2)**, [1]
    taxation, **39(2)**, [489]
    training, powers as to, **39(2)**, [488]
    Transport Acts, provisions applicable,
      39(2), [488]
    working agreements with other persons,
      39(2), [488]

associated persons
  leasing, for purposes of, **44(1)**, [527]
  meaning, **44(1)**, [131]
  transactions between. *See* **tax avoidance**

association
  false statement by member, **12(1)**, [570]
  seat, place of—
    domicile provisions, **11(2)**, [834], [848]
    exclusive jurisdiction provisions,
      11(2), [835]

Association of Chief Police Officers
  consultation with, **33(2)**, [615], [634]
  pensions for staff, **33(2)**, [345]
  president, **33(2)**, [389]

assurance
  defective disentailing, cure of, **19(3)**, [754]
  industrial. *See* **industrial assurance**

assured agricultural occupancy
  agricultural worker conditions, **22**, [921]
  meaning, **22**, [822]
  provisions applying to, **22**, [822]
  security of tenure, **22**, [823]
  succession to, **22**, [832]
  tenancies and licences being, **22**, [822]

assured shorthold tenancy
  demoted, **22**, [818]
  expiry or termination of, recovery of
    possession on, **22**, [819]
  meaning, **22**, [815]
  possession, recovery of, **22**, [819]
  post-Housing Act 1996 tenancies—
    general, **22**, [815]
    statement as to terms of, duty of landlord
      to provide, **22**, [817]
  pre-Housing Act 1996 tenancies, **22**, [816]
  rent—
    determination by rent assessment
      committee, **22**, [820]
    reference of excessive, to rent assessment
      committee, **22**, [820]
  tenancy being, **22**, [827]

assured shorthold tenancy—*contd*
  tenancy deposit scheme. *See* **tenancy deposit**

assured tenancy
  allowances. *See* **assured tenancy allowances**
  alternative accommodation—
    availability of, **22**, [917]
    suitability of, **22**, [918]
  anti-social behaviour—
    demotion because of, **22**, [797]
    possession proceedings, effect on, **22**, [802]
  approved body—
    landlord ceasing to belong to, **21**, [732]
    meaning, **21**, [727]
  assured agricultural occupancies, being,
    22, [822]
  certificate of fitness, **21**, [730]
  conditions for—
    building to which works carried out,
      21, [729]
    newly erected buildings, **21**, [728]
  dwelling-house let with other land, of,
    22, [792]
  exclusions—
    agricultural holdings, **22**, [913]
    agricultural land, tenancy of, **22**, [913]
    asylum-seekers, accommodation for,
      22, [913]
    business tenancies, **22**, [913]
    Crown tenancy, **22**, [913]
    high rateable value, dwelling-houses with,
      22, [913]
    holiday lettings, **22**, [913]
    housing action trust tenancy, **22**, [913]
    housing association tenancy, **22**, [913]
    law rent, tenancy at, **22**, [913]
    licensed premises, **22**, [913]
    local authority tenancy, **22**, [913]
    protected tenancy, **22**, [913]
    resident landlord, where, **22**, [913]
    secure tenancy, **22**, [913]
    student lettings, **22**, [913]
  fixed term—
    periodic tenancy following, **22**, [795]
    possession, order for, **22**, [798]
  Housing Act 1980, under, restriction of,
    22, [830]
  human habitation, fitness for, **21**, [731]
  Landlord and Tenant Act 1954, application
    of, **21**, [733], [758]
  landlord, housing association as, **22**, [791]
  meaning, **21**, [727]; **22**, [791]; **43(1)**, [1127]
  periodic—
    fixed term, following, **22**, [795]
    notice to quit, **22**, [795]
    parting with possession, **22**, [810]
    protected long tenancy at low rent,
      following, **23**, [55]
  rent—
    increases of, **22**, [806]
    interim increases of, where landlord
      liable for council tax, **22**, [808]
  statutory—
    meaning, **22**, [795]

assured tenancy—*contd*
  periodic—*contd*
    statutory—*contd*
      rent assessment committee,
        determination of terms by, **22**, [796]
      terms, fixing, **22**, [796]
    succession by spouse to, **22**, [812]
    succession to, **22**, [832]
  possession of—
    court, discretion of, **22**, [801]
    grounds for—
      alternative accommodation, availability
        of, **22**, [917]
      arrears of rent, **22**, [917]
      breach of obligations, **22**, [917]
      death of previous tenant, proceedings
        before, **22**, [916]
      delay in payment of rent, **22**, [917]
      demolition or reconstruction of
        premises, **22**, [916]
      discretionary, **22**, [917]
      employment, tenant ceasing to be in,
        22, [917]
      furniture, ill-treatment of, **22**, [917]
      general, **22**, [798]
      holiday letting, **22**, [916]
      illegal or immoral purposes, premises
        used for, **22**, [917]
      landlord, required for occupation by,
        22, [916]
      mandatory, **22**, [916]
      minister of religion, required for,
        22, [916]
      mortgagee, sale by, **22**, [916]
      neglect of property, **22**, [917]
      non-shortholds, **22**, [920]
      nuisance or annoyance, conduct
        causing, **22**, [917]
      partner leaving where dwelling-house
        occupied by married couple or couple
        living as husband and wife, **22**, [917]
      rent, failure to pay, **22**, [917]
      student letting, **22**, [916]
    misrepresentation or concealment by
      landlord, **22**, [805]
    notices, **22**, [919]
    proceedings—
      additional notice requirements where
        ground of domestic violence, **22**, [800]
      anti-social behaviour, effect of, **22**, [802]
      notice of, **22**, [799]
    removal expenses, payment of, **22**, [804]
    shared accommodation, provisions
      applicable to, **22**, [803]
  protected tenancy, not being, **21**, [537]
  provisions applying to, **22**, [791]
  registered social landlord, landlord as,
    22, [797]
  rent—
    disregarded matters, **22**, [807]
    distress for, **22**, [814]
    factors taken into account, **22**, [807]
    improvements, relevant, **22**, [807]
    increase in, **22**, [806]
    meaning, **22**, [807]

assured tenancy—*contd*
  rent—*contd*
    periodic tenancies, increase under,
      22, [806]
    rates, disregarding, **22**, [807]
  rent assessment committee—
    determination by, **22**, [807]
    interim determination where landlord liable
      to council tax, **22**, [809]
  repairs, access for, **22**, [811]
  restricted contract, not, **21**, [540]
  reversions, provisions as to, **22**, [813]
  security of tenure, **22**, [795]
  shorthold. *See* **assured shorthold tenancy**
  subletting, effect of, **22**, [794]
  succession to, **22**, [922]
  tenancy, meaning, **22**, [791]
  tenant sharing accommodation, **22**, [793]

assured tenancy allowances
  approved body, meaning, **43(1)**, [1129]
  availability of, **43(1)**, [1127]
  balancing adjustments—
    adjusted net cost, **43(1)**, [1159]
    balancing events—
      meaning, **43(1)**, [1151]
      proceeds from, **43(1)**, [1152]
    charge, overall limit on, **43(1)**, [1155]
    dwelling-house—
      not qualifying throughout, where,
        43(1), [1154]
      qualifying throughout, where,
        43(1), [1153]
    old initial allowance made on incorrect
      assumption, recovery of, **43(1)**, [1156]
    relevant period of ownership, **43(1)**, [1157]
    starting expenditure, **43(1)**, [1158]
    when made, **43(1)**, [1150]
  balancing events, avoidance affecting proceeds
    of, **43(1)**, [1209]
  construction of building, expenditure on,
    43(1), [1130]
  demolition costs, treatment of, **43(1)**, [1165]
  dwelling-house—
    landlord of, **43(1)**, [1141]
    meaning, **43(1)**, [1168]
    purchase of—
      sold unused by developer, **43(1)**, [1140]
      unused, developer not involved,
        43(1), [1139]
    qualifying—
      ceasing to be, **43(1)**, [1143]
      exclusions, **43(1)**, [1142]
      landlord of, **43(1)**, [1141]
    qualifying expenditure attributable to,
      43(1), [1147]
      residue, **43(1)**, [1149]
    relevant interest in, **43(1)**, [1137]
  giving effect to, **43(1)**, [1166]
  lease, meaning, **43(1)**, [1168]
  non-qualifying assets, apportionment of sums
    partly referable to, **43(1)**, [1167]
  old expenditure, for, **43(1)**, [1128]
  qualifying expenditure—
    construction, on, **43(1)**, [1138]

assured tenancy allowances—*contd*
  qualifying expenditure—*contd*
    dwelling-house, attributable to,
      43(1), [1147]
      residue, **43(1)**, [1149]
    dwelling-house, purchase of—
      sold unused by developer, **43(1)**, [1140]
      unused, developer not involved,
        43(1), [1139]
    relevant interest—
      building, in—
        completion of construction, acquired
          on, **43(1)**, [1133]
        general rule, **43(1)**, [1132]
        leasehold interest, merger of,
          43(1), [1135]
        subordinate interest, creation of,
          43(1), [1134]
        termination of lease, **43(1)**, [1136]
      dwelling-house, in, **43(1)**, [1137]
      meaning, **43(1)**, [1132]
    sale, calculation of allowance after,
      43(1), [1146]
    writing-down—
      amount, calculation of, **43(1)**, [1146]
      entitlement to, **43(1)**, [1144]
      residue of qualifying expenditure, limited
        to, **43(1)**, [1147]
      sale of relevant interest, after sale of,
        43(1), [1146]
      writing-off, **43(1)**, [1162]
  writing-off expenditure—
    building not used as qualifying
      dwelling-house, periods of, **43(1)**, [1163]
    demolition costs, treatment of,
      43(1), [1165]
    extent and time of, **43(1)**, [1161]
    increase of expenditure where balancing
      adjustment made, **43(1)**, [1164]
    initial allowances, **43(1)**, [1161]
    writing-down allowances, **43(1)**, [1162]

asylum
  appeals, Asylum and Immigration Tribunal. *See*
    Asylum and Immigration Tribunal
  claim—
    appeals—
      determination of, **31**, [428]
      limited leave, variation of, **31**, [425]
      matters to be considered, **31**, [427]
      national security decisions, **31**, [439]
      right of, **31**, [424]
      successful, direction on, **31**, [429]
      unification of system, **31**, [509]
    Asylum and Immigration Tribunal. *See*
      Asylum and Immigration Tribunal
    claimants, behaviour damaging credibility,
      31, [495]
    determining, **31**, [376]
    late, **31**, [407]
    meaning, **31**, [209], [270], [284], [339],
      [456], [495], [538]
    pending, no removal during, **31**, [419]
  Convention—
    meaning, **31**, [209]

asylum—*contd*
  Convention—*contd*
    primacy of, **31**, [210]
  immigration document, failure to have,
    31, [492]
  seeker. *See* **asylum-seeker**

Asylum and Immigration Tribunal
  decision, review of, **31**, [443]
  delegation, **31**, [487]
  direction by, **31**, [429]
  establishment of, **31**, [422]
  members, **31**, [487]
  payments to, **31**, [487]
  practice directions, **31**, [451]
  President, **31**, [487]
  proceedings, **31**, [487]
  reconsideration of appeal—
    appeal on point of law following, **31**, [444]
    appellate court, appeal to, **31**, [445]
    legal aid, **31**, [446], [535]
    remittal to, **31**, [448]
  right of appeal to, **31**, [423]
    asylum claim, **31**, [424]
    limited leave, variation of, **31**, [425]
  rules, **31**, [450]
  sitting as panel, appeal from, **31**, [447]
  staff, **31**, [487]
  transitional provisions, **31**, [521]

asylum-seeker
  accommodation for, local connection,
    31, [498]
  accommodation centre. *See* **accommodation
    centre**
  accommodation, tenancy of, **22**, [427]
  age of, **31**, [376]
  definition, **31**, [373]
  dependent, definition, **31**, [375], [399]
  deportation—
    proof of identity of persons, **31**, [242]
  destitute—
    definition, **31**, [374], [399]
    support for, **31**, [372], [376]
    withdrawal of support, **31**, [381]
  failed—
    accommodation of, **31**, [497]–[498]
    withdrawal of support, **31**, [496], [569]
  family with children as, **31**, [401]
  fingerprinting, **31**, [315], [554]
    attendance for, **31**, [316], [555]
    destruction of fingerprints, **31**, [317]
    summary of provisions, **31**, [1]
  helping to enter UK, offence, **31**, [94]
  meaning, **31**, [486]
  physical characteristics, other methods of
    collecting data about, **31**, [318]
  redirection of post, requirement to supply
    information about, **31**, [314]
  reporting restriction—
    imposition of, **31**, [415]
    meaning, **31**, [415]
    travelling expenses, payment of, **31**, [414]
  restrictions imposed on, **31**, [416]

asylum-seeker—*contd*
  safe country, removal to—
    amendment of lists, **31**, [527]
    definitions, **31**, [522]
    individuals, countries safe for, **31**, [526]
    lists of countries, **31**, [523]–[525]
  serious criminal, removal of, **31**, [417]
  summary of provisions, **31**, [1]
  support for—
    ancillary provisions, **31**, [390]
    appeals—
      adjudicators, **31**, [292], [350]
      generally, **31**, [293]
      Secretary of State's rules, **31**, [294]
      summary of provisions, **31**, [1]
    back-dating of benefits where person
      recorded as refugee, **31**, [310]
    choice of form of, **31**, [403]
    corporation sole, Secretary of State as,
      31, [311]
    destitute, **31**, [372]
    eligibility, **31**, [285]
    exclusions—
      accommodation by housing authority,
        31, [307]
      benefits, from, **31**, [305]
      children, support for, **31**, [309]
      homelessness in Scotland and Northern
        Ireland, **31**, [308]
      summary of provisions, **31**, [1]
    form of, **31**, [398]
    ineligibility for, **31**, [486]
    interim provisions, **31**, [349]
    late claim, refusal on, **31**, [407]
    local authorities—
      payments to, **31**, [300]
      provision by, **31**, [289]
      summary of provisions, **31**, [1]
    offences, **31**, [486]
      delay, **31**, [297]
      dishonest representations, **31**, [296]
      failure of sponsor to maintain, **31**, [298]
      false representations, **31**, [295]
      obstruction, **31**, [297]
      summary of provisions, **31**, [1]
      supplemental, **31**, [299]
    premises, provided—
      entry of, **31**, [312]
      information from property owners,
        31, [313]
    provision of, **31**, [400], [486]
    reception zones, **31**, [291]
    recovery of expenditure on—
      misrepresentation, **31**, [302]
      overpayments, **31**, [304]
      sponsor, from, **31**, [303]
      summary of provisions, **31**, [1]
    refusal, appeal against, **31**, [405]
    regulations, **31**, [348]
    Secretary of State, local authority and other
      assistance for, **31**, [290]
    summary of provisions, **31**, [1]
    supplemental, **31**, [287]
    temporary, **31**, [288]
    types of, **31**, [486]

asylum-seeker—*contd*
  support for—*contd*
    voluntary organisations, grants to, **31**, [301]
    ways in which may be provided, **31**, [286]
    withdrawal, **31**, [381]
  voluntary departure from United Kingdom,
    31, [408]
  young, **31**, [402]

atomic energy. *See also* **nuclear installations;
radioactive substances**
  acquisition for purposes of, **17(1)**, [42]
    compensation, **17(1)**, [42], [44]
    minerals. *See* minerals *below*
    prescribed substances, of, **17(1)**, [29]
    procedure, **17(1)**, [43]
    rights under contract, **17(1)**, [30]
  authority. *See* **United Kingdom Atomic
    Energy Authority**
  contract rights, acquisition of, **17(1)**, [30]
  development, promotion and control,
    17(1), [23], [75]
  information—
    improper disclosure, **17(1)**, [32], [34]
    power to obtain, **17(1)**, [25], [32]
  inventions, special provisions, **17(1)**, [33]
  meaning, **17(1)**, [39]
  minerals—
    compulsory acquisition of—
      compensation, **17(1)**, [29]
      powers, **17(1)**, [29]
      procedure for, **17(1)**, [43]
    discovery of, power as to, **17(1)**, [27]
    information, requirement for, **17(1)**, [25]
    meaning, **17(1)**, [39]
    production and use, control of, **17(1)**, [31]
    rights to work—
      compensation, provision for, **17(1)**, [28]
      compulsory acquisition of, **17(1)**, [28]
      generally, **17(1)**, [28]
    search for—
      compensation respecting, **17(1)**, [28],
        [42]
      powers, **17(1)**, [27]
  Minister's functions and powers, **17(1)**, [23],
    [24]
  Mutual Assistance Convention, **17(1)**, [723],
    [725]
  notices, service of, **17(1)**, [38]
  offences and penalties, **17(1)**, [35]
  orders—
    making of, **17(1)**, [36]
    procedure for making, **17(1)**, [28]
  plant—
    information as to—
      disclosure, restriction on, **17(1)**, [32],
        [34]
      power to obtain, **17(1)**, [25]
    meaning, **17(1)**, [39]
  premises, entry and inspection, **17(1)**, [26]
  production and use, control of, **17(1)**, [31]
  research, **17(1)**, [579]
  Safeguards Agreement. *See* **nuclear
    installations**

atomic energy—*contd*
    substances, prescribed—
        compulsory acquisition, **17(1)**, [29]
        information, power to obtain, **17(1)**, [25]
        inspection, powers of, **17(1)**, [26]
        meaning, **17(1)**, [39]
        minerals containing, search for, **17(1)**, [27]
        See also **radioactive substances**
    summary of provisions, **17(1)**, [1]
    use, control and licensing, **17(1)**, [31]

Atomic Energy Authority. *See* **United Kingdom Atomic Energy Authority**

Atomic Weapons Establishment
    activities carried on, arrangements for,
        10, [710]
    application of enactments, **10**, [716]
    privileges and immunities, **10**, [712]
    transfer of employees, **10**, [711]

attachment
    moneys payable by Crown, **13**, [30]

attachment of debts
    county court jurisdiction, **11(2)**, [988]
    creditor's rights, restriction, **4(2)**, [221]
    discretion of court, **4(2)**, [12]
    High Court jurisdiction, **11(2)**, [710]

attachment of earnings
    administration order—
        application of provisions, **19(3)**, [37]
        power to make, **19(3)**, [40]
        to secure payment under, **19(3)**, [41]
    alternative remedies, effect on, **19(3)**, [45]
    collecting officer—
        action on request only, **19(3)**, [60]
        application of sums received by, **19(3)**, [51]
        court fees, deduction of, **19(3)**, [51]
        officers to act as, **19(3)**, [42]
    consolidated order, **19(3)**, [59]
    county court, by, **19(3)**, [36]
    court fees, deduction of, **19(3)**, [51]
    Crown employees, of, **19(3)**, [64]
    debtor—
        appearance, order requiring, **19(3)**, [52]
        change of employment, **19(3)**, [44], [53]
        costs, order to pay, **19(3)**, [63]
        current employer of, finding, **19(3)**, [54]
        failure to appear, **19(3)**, [62]
        falsification by, **19(3)**, [65]
        identification of, **19(3)**, [42]
        imprisonment, liability to, **19(3)**, [65]
        information disclosure and use regulations,
            19(3), [55]
            making of, **19(3)**, [56]
            offences against, **19(3)**, [57]
        information to be given by, **19(3)**, [52]
    debtor's current employer, finding,
        19(3), [102]
    deduction rate—
        fixed, amended provisions, **19(3)**, [101],
            [122], [123]
        normal, reduction of, **19(3)**, [48]

attachment of earnings—*contd*
    deduction rate—*contd*
        specification in order, **19(3)**, [42]
    deductions—
        fixed deductions scheme—
            amended provisions, **19(3)**, [101], [122],
                [123]
            changing from, **19(3)**, [76]
            changing to, **19(3)**, [75]
            making of, **19(3)**, [43]
        fixed, suspension of orders for, **19(3)**, [47]
        liability for, termination of, **19(3)**, [50]
        scheme of, **19(3)**, [73]
        statement of, to debtor, **19(3)**, [42]
    earnings—
        attachable, meaning, **19(3)**, [73]
        determining whether payments are,
            19(3), [58]
        meaning, **19(3)**, [66]
        particulars to be given of, **19(3)**, [52]
        payments excluded from, **19(3)**, [66]
    employer—
        duty to comply with order, **19(3)**, [44]
        expenses, power to deduct, **19(3)**, [44]
        provisions for deductions by, **19(3)**, [73]
        termination of liability to deduct,
            19(3), [50]
    employment, change of, notice of,
        19(3), [44], [53]
    enforcement provisions, **19(3)**, [1], [65]
    fixed deductions scheme—
        amended provisions, **19(3)**, [101], [122],
            [123]
        changing from, **19(3)**, [76]
        changing to, **19(3)**, [75]
        making of, **19(3)**, [43]
    High Court, by, **19(3)**, [36]
    income tax, deduction of, **19(3)**, [51]
    judgment, enforcement of, **19(3)**, [1]
    magistrates' court—
        application to, for order—
            complaint, by, **19(3)**, [61]
            designated officer for magistrates' court,
                by, **19(3)**, [60]
            procedure, **19(3)**, [61]
        costs of proceedings, **19(3)**, [63]
        designated officer, powers and duties,
            19(3), [60]
        jurisdiction, extent of, **19(3)**, [62]
        order, power to make, **19(3)**, [36]
        special provisions respecting,
            19(3), [60]–[63]
    maintenance order—
        application for, **19(3)**, [39]
        meaning, **19(3)**, [38]
        orders applicable, **19(3)**, [71]
    offences in respect of, **19(3)**, [65]
    order—
        application for—
            grounds for, **19(3)**, [39]
            magistrates' court, to, **19(3)**, [61]
            who may make, **19(3)**, [39]
        ceasing to have effect, **19(3)**, [49]
        committal, in place of, **19(3)**, [39]
        consolidated orders, **19(3)**, [59]

attachment of earnings—*contd*
order—*contd*
contents, **19(3)**, [42]
costs of proceedings, **19(3)**, [63]
courts with power to make, **19(3)**, [28]
discharge, power to order, **19(3)**, [46]
effect of, **19(3)**, [42]
fixed deductions, suspension of, **19(3)**, [47]
interrelation with other remedies,
19(3), [45]
lapse of, **19(3)**, [46]
priority as between orders, **19(3)**, [44],
[74]
taxes and social security contributions,
relevant, **19(3)**, [72]
transfer between courts, **19(3)**, [59]
variation of, **19(3)**, [46]
penalties for offences, **19(3)**, [65]
protected earnings rate, **19(3)**, [42]
residents outside UK, **19(3)**, [62]
rules of court, **19(3)**, [46], [68]
summary of provisions, **19(3)**, [1]
transitional provisions, **19(3)**, [68]

attempt
act in view, nature of, **12(1)**, [752]
common law, at, abolition, **12(1)**, [756]
completed offence, finding of guilt on,
12(1), [364]
computer misuse, to commit, **12(1)**, [751]
criminal conduct, by member of services,
3(S), 60
trial of, **3(S)**, 61
jurisdiction in relation to, **12(1)**, [752]
offence, to commit—
meaning, **12(1)**, [751]
provisions, application of, **12(1)**, [753];
12(2), [166]
special statutory provision, under,
12(1), [754]
penalties, **12(1)**, [755]
place of act, relevance, **12(1)**, [752]
service offence, to commit, **3(S)**, 55–6
summary of provisions, **12(1)**, [1]
trial of, **12(1)**, [755]

attendance allowance
accommodation, exclusion on provision of,
40(1), [316]
adjudication. *See* **social security
adjudication**
Christmas bonus, for purposes of,
40(1), [402]
claim for, **40(1)**, [314]
daily entitlement, **40(1)**, [145]
day attendance condition, **40(1)**, [313]
entitlement to, **40(1)**, [313]
exclusions, **40(1)**, [316]
in-patient, not allowable for, **40(1)**, [316]
medical examination and report, reference of
claim for, **40(1)**, [556]
night attendance condition, **40(1)**, [313]
non-contributory benefit, as, **40(1)**, [312]
period of, **40(1)**, [314]
period preceding claim, for, **40(1)**, [314]

attendance allowance—*contd*
persons awarded, medical examination,
40(1), [560]
rate of, **40(1)**, [314], [467]
terminally ill, for, **40(1)**, [315]
transitional provisions and savings, **40(2)**, [10]

Attendance Allowance Board
dissolution of, **40(1)**, [225]

attendance centre
meaning, **12(3)**, [952]
power to search persons in for weapons,
12(4), [239]
provision of, **12(3)**, [952]

attendance centre order
amendment, **12(2)**, [847]
appeal, made on, **12(2)**, [847]
breach of action plan or reparation order,
imposed for, **12(2)**, [850]
breach of community order, imposed for,
12(2), [844]
breach of order or rules, **12(2)**, [847]
breach of supervision order, imposed for,
12(2), [849]
copies, provision of, **12(2)**, [758]
defaulters, for, **12(2)**, [847]
hours of attendance, **12(2)**, [758]
power to make, **12(2)**, [758]
revocation, **12(2)**, [847]

attorney
person practising as, **11(2)**, [13]

Attorney General
Charity Tribunal proceedings, intervention
in, **5(2)**, [543]
civil proceedings by or against, **13**, [21]
corruption in office, institution of
proceedings, **12(1)**, [175]
Director of Public Prosecutions, appointment
of, **12(1)**, [934]
explosives—
inquiry as to, **12(1)**, [165]
prosecutions by leave of, **12(1)**, [166]
fees, **10**, [440]
landmines, institution of proceedings,
12(2), [636]
Northern Ireland, for, **10**, [792]
See also **Northern Ireland**
nuclear industry, institution of proceedings
concerning, **12(3)**, [126]
nuclear matter, institution of proceedings,
12(2), [604]
nuclear weapons, consent to prosecution,
12(3), [101]
proceedings by, or relation of other person,
13, [26]
review of sentence on reference by,
12(4), [488]
review of sentences, reference of cases to
Court of Appeal, **12(1)**, [1082]
salary, **10**, [614]

Attorney General—*contd*
  Serious Fraud Office, superintendence of,
    12(1), [1056]
  Solicitor General, functions exercised by,
    10, [791]

auction
  Acts, exhibition of copies, **39(1)**, [64], [119]
  bidding—
    abstention from, **39(1)**, [63], [118]
    agreements—
      Acts, exhibition of copies, **39(1)**, [64],
        [119]
      deposit of copy, **39(1)**, [63]
      illegal, where, **39(1)**, [63]
      offences, **39(1)**, [63]
      rights of seller, **39(1)**, [118]
      trial of offences, **39(1)**, [116]
    puffer, by, **39(1)**, [6]
    seller of land, by, **39(1)**, [8]
  dealer—
    illegal agreement by, **39(1)**, [63]
    meaning, **39(1)**, [63]
  puffer—
    bidding by, **39(1)**, [6]
    meaning, **39(1)**, [5]
  sale of goods by, **39(1)**, [438]
  sale of land by—
    bidding—
      opening of, discontinuance, **39(1)**, [9]
      seller, by, **39(1)**, [8]
    puffer, employment of, **39(1)**, [6]
    reserve price, **39(1)**, [7]
  seller—
    land, of, bidding by, **39(1)**, [8]
    rights of, **39(1)**, [118]
  trustee, power of sale at, **48**, 464

auctioneer
  chargeable gains, return of, **42**, [139]
  firearms, safety precautions, **12(1)**, [483],
    [1126]
    possession of, **12(1)**, [483], [1126]
  meaning, **39(1)**, [5]
  name and address, exhibition of notice of,
    39(1), [3]

audible intruder alarms
  alarm notification area—
    designation of, **35(2)**, [526]
    fixed penalty—
      amount of, **35(2)**, [531]
      notices, **35(2)**, [530], [533]
      receipts, use of, **35(2)**, [532]
    key-holders—
      nominated, notification of, **35(2)**, [528]
      nomination of, **35(2)**, [529]
    withdrawal of designation, **35(2)**, [527]
  orders and regulations, **35(2)**, [537]
  powers of entry, **35(2)**, [534], [536]
  warrant to enter premises by force,
    35(2), [535], [536]

audit
  concerns, right of members to raise at
    accounts meeting—
    quoted company, meaning, **8(1)**, [609]
    website publication—
      availability requirement, **8(1)**, [606]
      offences, **8(1)**, [608]
      requirement of, **8(1)**, [605]
      supplementary duty of company,
        8(1), [607]
  exemption from—
    dormant companies—
      conditions for, **8(1)**, [558]
      exclusions, **8(1)**, [559]
    small companies—
      conditions for, **8(1)**, [555]
      exclusions, **8(1)**, [556]
      group company, availability to,
        8(1), [557]
  major, meaning, **8(1)**, [603]
  power to amend provisions, **8(1)**, [562]
  public sector—
    non-profit-making companies subject to,
      8(1), [560]
    Scottish public sector companies, of,
      8(1), [561]
  requirement of, **8(1)**, [553]
  right of members to require, **8(1)**, [554]
  second—
    costs of, **8(1)**, [1327]
    power of Secretary of State to require,
      8(1), [1326]
    statutory provisions applying, **8(1)**, [1327]

Audit Commission
  Care Quality Commission, role as to studies
    by, **30(S)**, NHS 64–5
  data matching, **12(4)**, [454]

Audit Commission for Local Authorities
  agreed audit of accounts by, **26(1)**, [346]
  annual report, **26(1)**, [382]
  Auditor-General for Wales—
    co-operation with, **26(1)**, [376];
      26(2), [388], [408]
    information provided to, **26(1)**, [377]
    provision of information by, **26(2)**, [403]
  benefit information supplied to, **26(1)**, [374]
  claims and returns, certification of,
    26(1), [345]
  continuation in being, **26(1)**, [318]
  data matching—
    code of practice, **26(1)**, [356]
    exercises, power to conduct, **26(1)**, [350]
    fees, **26(1)**, [355]
    mandatory provision of data, **26(1)**, [351]
    publication of reports, **26(1)**, [354]
    results, disclosure of, **26(1)**, [353]
    Secretary of State, powers of, **26(1)**, [357]
    use of, **26(1)**, [350]
    voluntary provision of data, **26(1)**, [352]
  disclosure of information, restriction on,
    26(1), [372], [373]
  financial provisions, **26(1)**, [382]
  financial year, **26(2)**, [309]

Audit Commission for Local Authorities—*contd*
information and documents provided to, **26(1)**, [371]
inspection of local education authority, collaboration in, **15(1)**, [752]
members, **26(1)**, [318]
  remuneration, **26(1)**, [382]
  tenure of office, **26(1)**, [382]
name, change of, **26(2)**, [608], [664]
other authorities, interaction with—
  exercise of functions, **26(1)**, [385]
  interpretation, **26(1)**, [384]
performance, categorisation of local authorities by reference to, **26(2)**, [301]
performance standards, reports relating to, **26(1)**, [369]
proceedings, **26(1)**, [382]
public bodies, accounts and audit. *See* **public bodies**
publication of information by, **26(1)**, [375]
registered social landlords—
  advice and assistance for, **26(1)**, [367]
  information, provision of, **26(1)**, [364]
  inspections, **26(1)**, [365], [366]
  meaning, **26(1)**, [368]
  studies relating to, **26(1)**, [363]
Secretary of State—
  functions of, **26(1)**, [382]
  references and reports to, **26(1)**, [362]
social security references, **26(1)**, [362]
staff, **26(1)**, [382]
status, **26(1)**, [382]
studies by—
  benefit administration, **26(1)**, [361]
  economy, efficiency and effectiveness, studies for improving, **26(1)**, [358]
  educational bodies, at request of, **26(1)**, [360]
  impact of statutory provisions, reports on, **26(1)**, [359]
  registered social landlords, relating to, **26(1)**, [363]
transitional provisions, **26(1)**, [386]

Audit Commission for Local Authorities and the National Health Service in England
Benefits, Benefit Fraud Inspectorate, transfers from, **26(2)**, [609], [665]
change of name to, **26(2)**, [608], [664]

Auditor General
statutory auditor, as. *See* **statutory auditor**

Auditor General for Wales
access to documents, **10**, [1645]
accounting officer, as, **10**, [1645]
accounts, **10**, [1645]
  audit of, **10**, [1263]
ancillary powers, **10**, [1645]
appointment, **10**, [1645]
Audit Commission—
  co-operation with, **26(1)**, [376];
  26(2), [388], [408]

Auditor General for Wales—*contd*
Audit Commission—*contd*
  provision of information to, **26(2)**, [403]
audit of accounts, **10**, [1645]
auditor of, **10**, [1645]
benefit information, supply to, **26(2)**, [401]
best practice functions, code of practice and fees, **26(1)**, [400], [401]
best value inspections, **26(1)**, [404]
  fees, **26(1)**, [407]
  reports, **26(1)**, [409]
borrowing, **10**, [1645]
Care Quality Commission
  co-operation with, **26(2)**, [408]
  provision of information to, **30(S)**, NHS 77
claims and returns, certification of, **10**, [1645]
co-operation with, **10**, [1610]
corporation sole, as, **10**, [1645]
data matching, **12(4)**, [455]
  code of practice, **26(2)**, [417]
  fees, **26(2)**, [416]
  information, disclosure of, **26(2)**, [414]
  mandatory provision of data, **26(2)**, [412]
  power to conduct, **26(2)**, [411]
  publication of report, **26(2)**, [415]
  results, disclosure of, **26(2)**, [414]
  Secretary of State, powers of, **26(2)**, [418]
  voluntary provision of data, **26(2)**, [413]
disclosure of information—
  consent for, **26(2)**, [400]
  restriction on, **26(2)**, [399]
documents and information, rights to, **26(2)**, [397]
  offences, **26(2)**, [398]
documents of, **10**, [1645]
duties of CHAI relating to, **30**, [720]
educational bodies, studies at request of, **10**, [1283]
Environment Agency functions, transfer of, **10**, [1287]
estimates by, **10**, [1645]
examination of accounts by, **10**, [1264]
extraordinary audit, direction for, **26(2)**, [382]
fees, charging, **10**, [1645]
finance, **10**, [1645]
functions of, **10**, [1607]
improvement of economy in services, studies for, **10**, [1282]
independence and status, **10**, [1645]
information, provided to, **26(1)**, [377]
inspection of local education authority, collaboration in, **15(1)**, [753]
inspectorates, provision of assistance to, **26(2)**, [421]
local government bodies, auditors for—
  appointment, **26(2)**, [359]
  code of audit practice, **26(2)**, [361]
  fees, scale of, **26(2)**, [365]
  persons assisting, arrangements for, **26(2)**, [360]
local government improvement—
  annual improvement reports, **25(S)**, 70
  audit and assessment reports, **25(S)**, 64–6

Auditor General for Wales—*contd*
　local government improvement—*contd*
　　co-ordination of regulatory functions,
　　25(S), 69–70
　　improvement assessments, **25(S)**, 64
　　information and planning audit, **25(S)**, 63
　　information sharing, **25(S)**, 79
　　scales of fees, prescription of, **25(S)**, 73–4
　　special inspections, **25(S)**, 67–9
　　statement of practice, **25(S)**, 71
　office of, **10**, [1610]
　performance standards, publication of
　　information as to, **26(2)**, [391]–[394]
　police authorities, receipt of documents
　　relating to, **26(2)**, [385]
　powers of, **10**, [1645]
　preparation of accounts, **10**, [1262]
　property, rights and liabilities, transfer schemes
　　for, **26(2)**, [422], [431]
　provision of information to CHAI by,
　　30, [691]
　public interest reports, **10**, [1645]
　publication of information by, **26(2)**, [402]
　registered social landlords—
　　advice and assistance for, **26(2)**, [610]
　　studies relating to, **10**, [1284]
　remuneration, **10**, [1645]
　social security references and reports,
　　26(2), [396]
　staff, **10**, [1645]
　studies by—
　　benefit administration, as to, **26(2)**, [390]
　　economy, efficiency and effectiveness in
　　　services, for improving, **26(2)**, [386]
　　impact of statutory provisions, as to,
　　　26(2), [387]
　　local government bodies, at request of,
　　　26(2), [389]
　tenure, **10**, [1645]
　transitional provisions, **10**, [1652]
　use of resources by public body, examination
　　into, **10**, [1281]
　Welsh NHS bodies, audit of, **26(2)**, [407]
　　Care Quality Commission, provision of
　　　information by, **26(2)**, [410]
　　officers, of, **26(2)**, [409]

auditors
　adequate accounting records, opinion on,
　　8(1), [576]
　casual vacancies in office, **8(1)**, [604]
　ceasing to hold office—
　　accounting authorities, information to,
　　　8(1), [602]
　　appropriate audit authority, meaning,
　　　8(1), [603]
　　audit authority, duty of company to
　　　notify, **8(1)**, [601]
　　audit authority, duty to notify, **8(1)**, [600]
　　major audit, meaning, **8(1)**, [603]
　　statement on—
　　　company, duties of, **8(1)**, [598]
　　　deposit of, **8(1)**, [597]
　　　registrar, copy sent to, **8(1)**, [599]
　community interest company, of, **8(1)**, [44]

auditors—*contd*
　company—
　　access to company's books, **8**, 301
　　accountancy bodies, provision for changes
　　　affecting, **8**, 896
　　appointment of—
　　　certain small companies, exemption of,
　　　　8, 445
　　　dormant company, exemption of, **8**, 445
　　　duty to, **8**, 441
　　　general meeting at which accounts laid,
　　　　at, **8**, 442
　　　private company not obliged to lay
　　　　accounts, by, **8**, 442–3
　　　Secretary of State, default powers, **8**, 444
　　appropriate qualification, meaning,
　　　8, 881–2
　　associate, meaning, **8**, 897
　　audience, right of, **8**, 447
　　casual vacancy, filling, **8**, 444–5
　　ceasing to hold office, statement on, **8**, 453
　　Companies Clauses Acts. *See* **Companies
　　　Clauses Acts**
　　consequential amendments, **8**, 895–6
　　definitions, **8**, 897–99
　　eligibility for appointment, **8**, 876–7
　　　authorisation under 1967 Act, **8**, 884
　　failure to comply, **8**, 454
　　fees, **8**, 891–2
　　independence, effect of lack of, **8**, 877–8
　　ineligibility for appointment—
　　　effect of, **8**, 878–9
　　　lack of independence, on ground of,
　　　　8, 877–8
　　meaning, **8**, 876
　　notices, service of, **8**, 894–5
　　partnership as, **8**, 877
　　restrictive practices, **8**, 893–4
　　second audit, power to require, **8**, 879–80
　　vacation of office, **8**, 878
　definitions, **8(1)**, [617]
　delegation order, **8**, 892–3
　　body established by, **8**, 940–3
　disclosure of services provided and
　　remuneration, **8(1)**, [8]
　disclosure to, statement in directors' report,
　　8(1), [496]
　dormant company's resolution not to
　　appoint, **8**, 329–30
　duties of, **8(1)**, [576]
　failure to re-appoint—
　　special notice of resolution for general
　　　meeting, **8(1)**, [593]
　　written resolution, special procedure for,
　　　8(1), [592]
　first, appointment, **8**, 442
　friendly societies. *See* **friendly society**
　independent monitoring, **8(1)**, [2]
　information, disclosure to—
　　directors' report, statement in, **8(1)**, [10]
　　offences relating to, **8(1)**, [9]
　　rights to, **8(1)**, [9]
　information etc—
　　failure to obtain, **8**, 301
　　rights to, **8**, 446

auditors—*contd*
investigations by, **8**, 301
liability—
  costs of successfully defending proceedings, indemnity for, **8(1)**, [611]
  limitation agreements—
    authorisation by members, **8(1)**, [614]
    disclosure by company, **8(1)**, [616]
    effect of, **8(1)**, [615]
    meaning, **8(1)**, [612]
    terms of, **8(1)**, [613]
    validity, **8(1)**, [612]
  protection from, voidness of provisions, **8(1)**, [610]
  provisions relieving, avoidance of, **8**, 375
meetings, right to attend, **8**, 447
non-audit work, remuneration for, **8**, 448
not re-appointed, rights of, **8**, 449–50
offences—
  body corporate, by, **8**, 889
  false and misleading statements, **8**, 889
  jurisdiction, **8**, 891
  partnerships, by, **8**, 890
  procedure, **8**, 891
  time limits for prosecution, **8**, 890
  unincorporated associations, by, **8**, 890
overseas qualifications, approval of, **8**, 883–4; **8(1)**, [7]
private company, of—
  appointment—
    directors, by, **8(1)**, [563]
    each financial year, for, **8(1)**, [563]
    members, by, **8(1)**, [563]
    Secretary of State, default power of, **8(1)**, [564]
  deemed re-appointment, prevention by members, **8(1)**, [566]
  term of office, **8(1)**, [565]
proceedings against, relief in, **8**, 589
public company, of—
  appointment—
    directors, by, **8(1)**, [567]
    each financial year, for, **8(1)**, [567]
    members, by, **8(1)**, [567]
    Secretary of State, default power of, **8(1)**, [568]
  term of office, **8(1)**, [569]
qualifying body—
  competition law, exemptions, **8**, 946–7
  compliance orders, **8**, 887–8
  guidance issued by, references to, **8**, 881
  information, Secretary of State calling for, **8**, 887
  international obligations, directions to comply with, **8**, 888
  meaning, **8**, 882
  recognition—
    application for, **8**, 936–7
    grant and refusal of, **8**, 937
    requirements for, **8**, 938–40
    revocation of, **8**, 937–8
  restrictive practices, **8**, 943–6
  rules, references to, **8**, 882
  Secretary of State, matters to be notified to, **8**, 886–7

auditors—*contd*
recognised supervisory bodies—
  arrangements in which required to participate, **8(1)**, [3]
  independent monitoring, **8(1)**, [3]
  professional integrity and independence, standards for, **8(1)**, [3]
  public interest cases, independent investigation, **8(1)**, [3]
  recognition, additional requirements—
    amended provisions, **8(1)**, [2]
    arrangements to which relating, **8(1)**, [3]
  Secretary of State, delegation of functions by—
    circumstances for, **8(1)**, [5]
    new or existing body, to, **8(1)**, [4]
    orders, **8(1)**, [6]
  technical standards, setting, **8(1)**, [3]
register, regulations as to, **8**, 884–5
removal from office—
  representations, **8(1)**, [589]
  resolution for, **8(1)**, [588]
    notice to registrar, **8(1)**, [590]
    special notice, **8(1)**, [589]
  rights on, **8(1)**, [591]
removal of, **8**, 449
removed, rights of, **8**, 449–50
remuneration, **8**, 447–8
  disclosure, **8(1)**, [572]
  fixing, **8(1)**, [570]
report of—
  abbreviated accounts, as to, **8(1)**, [527]
  annual accounts, on, **8(1)**, [573]
  circulation of—
    default in, offence of, **8(1)**, [503]
    duty of, **8(1)**, [501]
    time allowed for, **8(1)**, [502]
  contents, **8**, 299–300; **8(1)**, [573]
  Directive disclosure requirements, subject to, **8(1)**, [1156]
  directors' remuneration report, on auditable parts of, **8(1)**, [575]
  directors' report, on, **8(1)**, [574]
  filing—
    default in, **8(1)**, [529]–[531]
    medium-sized companies, obligations of, **8(1)**, [523]
    period allowed for, **8(1)**, [520]–[521]
    quoted companies, obligations of, **8(1)**, [525]
    registrar, with, **8(1)**, [519]
    unlimited companies, exempt, **8(1)**, [526]
    unquoted companies, obligations of, **8(1)**, [524]
  further provision, power to make, **8(1)**, [546]
  inspection by members, **8**, 304–5
  investigations for, **8**, 301
  name of signatory to be stated in, **8(1)**, [511]
  names to be omitted from, **8(1)**, [584]
  names to be stated in, **8(1)**, [583]
  offences, **8(1)**, [585]
  overseas company, of, **8(1)**, [1127]

auditors—*contd*
report of—*contd*
persons entitled to receive, **8**, 302
public company, laying before general
meeting, **8(1)**, [515]
failure, offence of, **8(1)**, [516]
publication, meaning, **8(1)**, [514]
purchase of own shares by private company,
as to—
availability for inspection, **8(1)**, [798]
disclosure of, **8(1)**, [796]
requirement of, **8(1)**, [792]
quoted company, publication on website
of, **8(1)**, [508]
reading in general meeting, **8**, 305
registrar, delivery to, **8**, 306–8
regulatory and prosecuting authorities,
guidance for, **8(1)**, [586]
requirement to make, **8**, 299–300
right of member or debenture holder to
demand copies of—
quoted companies, **8(1)**, [510]
unquoted companies, **8(1)**, [509]
signature, **8(1)**, [581]
signing, **8**, 300–1
small companies regime, companies subject
to, **8(1)**, [522]
statutory accounts, accompanying,
8(1), [512]
true and fair view, opinion on, **8(1)**, [573]
resignation—
notice of, contents, **8**, 450; **8(1)**, [594]
registrar, notice to, **8(1)**, [595]
requisitioning meeting after, right of,
8, 451
rights on, **8(1)**, [596]
rights of—
information, to—
books, accounts and vouchers, access
to, **8(1)**, [577]
offences, **8(1)**, [579]
overseas subsidiaries, from, **8(1)**, [578]
provision to, **8(1)**, [577]
meetings, to attend and be heard at,
8(1), [580]
notices, receipt of, **8(1)**, [580]
removal from office, on, **8(1)**, [591]
resignation, on, **8(1)**, [596]
resolutions, receipt of, **8(1)**, [580]
services provided and related remuneration,
disclosure of, **8(1)**, [572]
statutory. *See* **statutory auditor**
terms of appointment, disclosure of,
8(1), [571]
Secretary of State, delegation of functions
by—
circumstances for, **8(1)**, [5]
new or existing body, to, **8(1)**, [4]
orders, **8(1)**, [6]
supervisory body—
competition law, exemptions, **8**, 946–7
compliance orders, **8**, 887–8
guidance issued by, references to, **8**, 881
information about firms, making available,
8, 885–6

auditors—*contd*
supervisory body—*contd*
information, Secretary of State calling for,
8, 887
international obligations, directions to
comply with, **8**, 888
liability for damages, exemption, **8**, 894
meaning, **8**, 880
members, meaning, **8**, 881
recognition—
application for, **8**, 932
grant and refusal of, **8**, 932
requirements for, **8**, 934–6
revocation of, **8**, 932–3
restrictive practices, **8**, 943–6
rules, reference to, **8**, 880–1
Secretary of State, matters notified to,
8, 886–7
summary of provisions, **8(1)**, [1]
termination of appointment where not
appointed annually, **8**, 452
trade union. of. *See* **trade unions**
Welsh local government bodies, for. *See*
Wales
written resolutions, rights as to, **8**, 437–8

Australia
appeals to Privy Council, ending of,
7(2), [777]
Commonwealth citizenship, **31**, [186]
Commonwealth Constitution—
meaning, **7(2)**, [782]
saving for, **7(2)**, [771]
Constitution Act 1900, cessation as a public
record, **18**, [277]
constitution of, **7(2)**, [430]
federal state of, **7(2)**, [350]
Queensland Constitution, amendment,
7(2), [779]
States—
Governors, **7(2)**, [773]
laws—
assent to, **7(2)**, [775]
disallowance, not subject to, **7(2)**, [774]
form of, **7(2)**, [772]
manner of making, **7(2)**, [772]
suspension of operation, **7(2)**, [774]
Parliaments, legislative powers, **7(2)**, [769]
termination of restrictions on,
7(2), [770]
presence of Her Majesty in, **7(2)**, [773]
reservation of acts, **7(2)**, [775]
UK responsibility, termination of,
7(2), [776]
States, laws made under authority of,
7(2), [431]
Statute of Westminster—
adopting, **7(2)**, [432]
amendment of, **7(2)**, [778]
effect of, **7(2)**, [771]
method of repealing etc, **7(2)**, [781]
preamble, **7(2)**, [423]
territories of, **7(2)**, [350]
UK Parliament powers ended, **7(2)**, [768]

Australia—*contd*
Western Australia Constitution, amendment,
7(2), [780]

Austria
accession to European Union, **18**, [47]
State Treaty, **10**, [937]

**Authorised Conveyancing Practitioners
Board**
accounts and audit, **11(3)**, [153]
annual report, **11(3)**, [153]
authorisation of practitioners. *See*
conveyancing services
compensation scheme, **11(3)**, [103]
constitution of, **11(3)**, [93]
defective appointment to, **11(3)**, [153]
delegation of powers, **11(3)**, [153]
disclosure of information, restrictions on—
exceptions from, **11(3)**, [111]
generally, **11(3)**, [110]
documents—
requiring production of, **11(3)**, [108]
served by, **11(3)**, [153]
financial provisions, **11(3)**, [94]
functions of, **11(3)**, [94]
information, power to obtain, **11(3)**, [108]
intervention powers, **11(3)**, [112]–[113]
investigations on behalf of, **11(3)**, [109]
members, appointment of, **11(3)**, [93], [153]
proceedings of, **11(3)**, [153]
remuneration, **11(3)**, [153]
seal, authentication of, **11(3)**, [153]
staff, **11(3)**, [153]
status of, **11(3)**, [93]
vacancies, **11(3)**, [153]

authorised investment fund
authorised unit trust, as, **43(2)**, [733]
derivative contracts, **43(2)**, [734]
distribution, methods of, **43(2)**, [734]
information regarding, provision of,
43(2), [734]
loan relationships, **43(2)**, [734]
meaning, **43(2)**, [733]
open-ended investment company, as,
43(2), [733]
regulations as to, **43(2)**, [733]–[735]

authorities. *See* **water authorities**

automatic machines
medicinal products, for sale of—
construction, location and use, **28**, [123]
information, display on, **28**, [148]
restriction on, **28**, [109]
section, general sale list, **28**, [109]

autrefois acquit
plea, decision on, without jury, **19(3)**, [157]

autrefois convict
plea, decision on, without jury, **19(3)**, [157]

Auxiliary Air Force. *See* **Royal Auxiliary Air
Force**

aviation. *See* **air navigation; aircraft;
Airports Authority; carriage by air; civil
aviation**

Aviation Authority
Treasury guarantee of loans to, **4(1)**, [67]

aviation duty
preparation for introduction of, **43(S)**, 987

aviation insurance. *See* **war risks insurance**

aviation security
See also **aerodrome** (security); **aircraft**
(security)
aerodromes, trespass on, **12(3)**, [127]
arrest without warrant, **12(3)**, [127]
definitions, **4(1)**, [236]
extension of Act outside UK, **4(1)**, [237]
extraterritorial application of provisions,
12(3), [128]
fund—
reimbursement from, **4(1)**, [233]
winding up, powers, **4(1)**, [234]
offences by bodies corporate, **4(1)**, [235]
past offences, **4(1)**, [241]
services, approved providers, **4(1)**, [204]

B

badgers
cruelty to, **2**, [690]
licences, grant of, **2**, [698]
live, selling and possession of, **2**, [692]
  defence to, **2**, [697]
marking and ringing, **2**, [693]
meaning, **2**, [703]
offences—
  constables, powers of, **2**, [699]
  dog used or present at commission of,
    2, [702]
  forfeiture, **2**, [700]
  general exceptions, **2**, [694]
  penalties, **2**, [700]
  summary proceedings, time limit for
    bringing, **2**, [701]
setts, interfering with, **2**, [691]
  defence to, **2**, [696]
taking, injuring or killing, **2**, [689]
  defence to, **2**, [695]

Bahamas
British ships registered in, **7(2)**, [665]
citizens of, **7(2)**, [659]
Commonwealth citizenship, **31**, [186]
fully responsible status of, **7(2)**, [658]
legislative powers, **7(2)**, [664]
meaning, **7(2)**, [662]
United Kingdom citizenship, persons
  retaining, **7(2)**, [660]
visiting forces in, **7(2)**, [665]

bail
absconding—
  amended provisions, **12(3)**, [809]
  arrest, **12(1)**, [657]
  offence, **12(1)**, [656]
acknowledging in another's name, **12(1)**, [65]
amended provisions, **12(3)**, [1099]
appeal against—
  hearing of, **12(2)**, [158]
  prosecution right of, **12(2)**, [158]
appeal, pending, **11(2)**, [534]
  Court of Appeal, to, **12(1)**, [438]
  House of Lords, to, **12(1)**, [317], [318],
    [455]
applications for, **31**, [269]
arrest—
  after, **12(1)**, [895]
  on, **11(2)**, [459]
case stated—
  on, **12(1)**, [262]
  pending, **11(2)**, [534]
certiorari, on application for, **12(1)**, [262]
committal for trial on, **11(2)**, [416]

bail—*contd*
conditions—
  appeal—
    Crown Court, to, **12(3)**, [810]
    High Court, to, **12(3)**, [811]
  breaking, **12(1)**, [657]
  electronic monitoring of compliance,
    12(1), [648]–[650]
  police bail, **12(1)**, [651], [654]
  restrictions on, **12(1)**, [663]
  variation by court, **12(1)**, [869]
  variation by police, **12(1)**, [868]
  varying or imposing, **12(1)**, [647], [653]
continuous, **11(2)**, [157]
conviction, meaning, **12(1)**, [646]
criminal appeal provisions, **12(1)**, [438]
Crown Court, granted by, **11(2)**, [755]
custody officer, release by, **12(1)**, [876]
  breach, **12(1)**, [879], [880]
  consultations with Director of Public
    Prosecutions, **12(1)**, [878]
  guidance, **12(1)**, [877]
  police station, attendance at, **12(1)**, [881]
customs detention, persons in, **12(1)**, [1101]
definitions, **12(1)**, [645], [646], [667]
drug assessments, relationship with
  provisions, **12(4)**, [160]
elsewhere than at police station, **12(1)**, [865]
  failure to answer to, **12(1)**, [870]
  notices, **12(1)**, [866]
excessive, **10**, [40]
extradition proceedings—
  decisions by magistrates' courts, powers of
    High Court, **18**, [996]
  restrictions where undertaking given,
    18, [920]
full argument on, hearing, **12(1)**, [653]
general right to, **12(1)**, [652]
High Court granting or varying, **12(1)**, [385]
homicide, persons charged with after previous
  conviction, **12(2)**, [190]
hostel, requirement of residence in,
  12(1), [647]
House of Lords, appeal to, on, **3**, [1338]
immigration appeals, **31**, [129]
imprisonable offences, **12(1)**, [664]
incidents of, **12(1)**, [647]
incorrigible rogue, committal of, **11(2)**, [214]
justice dealing with, sitting after, **11(2)**, [458]
live link, grant of, **12(1)**, [893]
magistrates' court, grant by, where police bail
  has been granted, **11(2)**, [461]
magistrates' court withholding, **12(1)**, [653]
meaning, **12(1)**, [645]
murder, on charge of, **12(1)**, [647]
non-imprisonable offences, **12(1)**, [665]

bail—*contd*
Northern Ireland. *See under* **Northern Ireland**
offences committed on, **12(3)**, [808]
offences, imprisonment for, **12(4)**, [269]
person in custody, **3**, [1]
persons entitled to, exceptions, **12(1)**, [663]
persons on, disqualification from jury service, **19(3)**, [154]
persons under 18, decisions relating to, **12(1)**, [660]
police—
     conditions of, **12(1)**, [651], [654]
     failure to answer to, power of arrest, **12(1)**, [894]
     record of decision, **12(1)**, [654]
police station, requirement to attend, **12(1)**, [865]
     cessation, notice of, **12(1)**, [867]
     designated, **12(1)**, [867]
rape, persons charged with after previous conviction, **12(2)**, [190]
reconsideration of decisions, **12(1)**, [655]
record of decision on, **12(1)**, [653], [654]
refusal, on subsequent hearings, **12(1)**, [666]
release on, electronic monitoring, **12(4)**, [568]
remand on, **11(2)**, [556]–[557]
requirements of, **12(1)**, [647]
retrial after acquittal, in case of—
     application, before, **12(3)**, [862]
     before hearing, **12(3)**, [863]
     during and after hearing, **12(3)**, [864]
     revocation of, **12(3)**, [865]
right to, generally, **12(1)**, [652]
security—
     forfeiture, **12(1)**, [653]
     requirement of, **12(1)**, [647]
     serious offence, in, court reasons for, **12(1)**, [663]
summary of provisions, **12(1)**, [1]
summary offences and offences tried summarily, for, **12(4)**, [402]
surety—
     amount of, **12(1)**, [658]
     child or young person, for, **12(1)**, [647]
     forfeited—
         enforcement, **12(2)**, [817]
         periods of imprisonment or detention, **12(2)**, [816]
         powers of court, **12(2)**, [816]
     indemnifying, offence of, **12(1)**, [659]
     recognisance, entering, **12(1)**, [658]
     requirement of, **12(1)**, [647], [658]
     suitability of, **12(1)**, [658]
surety requirements, altering, **11(2)**, [539]
surrender to custody—
     duty, **12(1)**, [647]
     failure, **12(1)**, [656]
     meaning, **12(1)**, [646]
total time in custody, **12(1)**, [663]
transitional provisions, **12(1)**, [669]
treason, person charged with, **11(2)**, [457]
variation of conditions, court's powers, **12(1)**, [385]

bail—*contd*
warrant for arrest endorsed for, **11(2)**, [538]
withholding, reasons for, **12(1)**, [653]
young person, **6**, [34]

bailee
breach of duty to bailor, **45**, [964]
meaning, **45**, [974]
sale, power of, **45**, [974]

bailiff
certificated, levy of distress by. *See* **distress**
declaration of office, **39(1)**, [759], [769]
misconduct by, **39(1)**, [762]
sale of offices, **39(1)**, [761]

bailment
collection of goods, obligation, **45**, [980]
conversion, action for, **45**, [964]
storage, warehousing etc, **45**, [980]
uncollected goods, disposal of—
     accounting for, bailee's liability, **45**, [974]
     collection, notice to bailor requiring, **45**, [980]
     delivery, bailor's obligation to take, **45**, [974], [980]
     repair or treatment, goods accepted for, **45**, [980]
     sale—
         authorised by court, **45**, [975]
         bailee's power of, **45**, [974]
         costs deductible, **45**, [974]
         notice of intention, **45**, [974], [981]
         owner other than bailor, where, **45**, [974]
         terms, **45**, [974]
         title given to purchaser, **45**, [974]
     valuation or appraisal, goods accepted for, **45**, [980]
war damage, provisions on, **50**, [202]

balance sheet
delivery to auditors, **8**, 53
formats—
     detailed, **8**, 615–18, 671–4, 688–9, 694–5, 723–5
     examples, **8**, 615–18, 671–4, 688–9, 694–5, 723–5
     general rules, **8**, 613–15, 670–1, 688–9, 692–3, 721–3
     notes on, **8**, 618–19, 674–5, 689, 695–8, 725–9
information supplementing—
     fixed assets, as to, **8**, 628–9, 683–4, 690–1, 710–11
     guarantees and commitments, **8**, 630–1, 685–6, 712–13, 746–7
     indebtedness, details of, **8**, 630, 685, 691, 746
     investments, as to, **8**, 629, 684, 745
     miscellaneous matters, **8**, 631, 686, 715–16, 747
     reserves and provisions, **8**, 629–30, 684–5, 711, 745–6

balance sheet—*contd*
  information supplementing—*contd*
    share capital and debentures, **8**, 628, 683,
      690, 709–10, 744
    tax, provision for, **8**, 630, 711, 746

balcony
  public occasion, used on, safety of,
    35(1), [53]

ballast
  carriage by road, **39(1)**, [573]
  meaning, **39(1)**, [572]
  measures for, **39(1)**, [572]
  volume, to be sold by, **39(1)**, [572]
    exceptions, **39(1)**, [572]

ballots. *See* **trade unions**

Bangladesh
  adaptation of Acts of Parliament, **7(2)**, [669]
  British ship registered in, **7(2)**, [669]
  Commonwealth citizenship, **31**, [186]
  existing law, operation of, **7(2)**, [666]
  register of companies kept in, **7(2)**, [669]
  veterinary qualification granted in, **7(2)**, [669]
  visiting forces in, **7(2)**, [669]

bank administration
  administration. *See* **bank administration**
  administration order—
    application for, **19(S)**, Financial 193
      grounds for, **19(S)**, Financial 194
      grounds for making, **19(S)**, Financial 195
      meaning, **19(S)**, Financial 193
  administrator—
    eligibility for appointment,
      19(S), Financial 193
    information, sharing,
      19(S), Financial 207–8
    nomination of, **19(S)**, Financial 194
    officer of the court, as,
      19(S), Financial 206
    powers and duties of,
      19(S), Financial 195–206
    proposals, **19(S)**, Financial 207
  applied provisions, table of,
    19(S), Financial 194–206
  bridge bank—
    information, sharing,
      19(S), Financial 207–8
    private purchaser, transfer to,
      19(S), Financial 209–10
    property transfer from,
      19(S), Financial 210–11
    supporting, objective of,
      19(S), Financial 190
      duration, **19(S)**, Financial 191
  building societies, provisions applying to,
    19(S), Financial 216
  courts, co-operation between,
    19(S), Financial 220
  credit unions, provisions applying to,
    19(S), Financial 217
  directors, disqualification, **19(S)**, Financial 214

bank administration—*contd*
  effect of, **19(S)**, Financial 195
  evidence, **19(S)**, Financial 219
  features of, **19(S)**, Financial 186–8
  fees, **19(S)**, Financial 218
  general note, **19(S)**, Financial 49–51
  insolvency. *See* **bank insolvency**
  insolvency or administration law, application
    of, **19(S)**, Financial 215
  inter-bank payment systems. *See* **inter-bank payment systems**
  interpretation, **19(S)**, Financial 221
  multiple transfers—
    application of provisions,
      19(S), Financial 209
    bridge bank to private purchaser,
      19(S), Financial 209–10
    property transfer—
      bridge bank, from,
        19(S), Financial 210–11
      temporary public ownership, from,
        19(S), Financial 211–12
  objectives—
    bridge bank, supporting,
      19(S), Financial 190
      duration, **19(S)**, Financial 191
    generally, **19(S)**, Financial 186–9
    normal administration, **19(S)**, Financial 192
    private sector purchaser, supporting,
      19(S), Financial 186–90
      duration, **19(S)**, Financial 191
  other processes, participation in,
    19(S), Financial 215
  overview, **19(S)**, Financial 186–8
  partnerships, provisions applying to,
    19(S), Financial 219
  private sector purchaser—
    bridge bank, transfer from,
      19(S), Financial 209–10
    supporting, objective of,
      19(S), Financial 190
      duration, **19(S)**, Financial 190
  procedure, **19(S)**, Financial 186–8
  rules, **19(S)**, Financial 218
  Scottish partnerships, provisions applying to,
    19(S), Financial 220
  special resolution regime. *See* **special resolution regime**
  temporary public ownership, property transfer
    from, **19(S)**, Financial 211–12
  termination—
    successful rescue, on, **19(S)**, Financial 212
    voluntary arrangement, on,
      19(S), Financial 213
    winding-up, on, **19(S)**, Financial 213

bank and banking
  Treasury support—
    Consolidated Fund, payment from,
      19(S), Financial 264
    National Loans Fund, payments from,
      19(S), Financial 265
    reports, **19(S)**, Financial 266

bank and banking. *See also* **deposit-taker**
Bank of England. *See* **Bank of England**
bank account, requests for information for use
in UK—
    power to make, **12(3)**, [601]
    sending, **12(3)**, [603]
    transactions, monitoring, **12(3)**, [602]
banker—
    authority to pay, revocation, **19(1)**, [108]
    books—
        copy of entries, verification, **18**, [143]
        entries, proof of, **18**, [141]
        inspection—
            costs, **18**, [146]
            court may order, **18**, [145]
        legal proceedings, meaning, **18**, [148]
        meaning, **18**, [147]
        production not compellable, where,
            18, [144]
        proof of, **18**, [142]
    meaning, **18**, [147]
    protection of, collecting payment,
        19(1), [306]
    rights of, collecting unindorsed cheque,
        19(1), [304]
cheque. *See* **cheque**
circulating capital, conversion of, **44(1)**, [321]
compulsory liquidation, in—
    application of provisions, **42**, [1519]
    carry-back, election for, **42**, [1519]
    rights to payments transferred, application
        of charge, **42**, [1519]
    Schedule D, Case VI, taxation of receipts
        under, **42**, [1519]
    tax relief, **42**, [1519]
dividend warrant, crossed, **19(1)**, [128]
dormant account money—
    apportionment, **19(S)**, Financial 17
    Big Lottery Fund, distribution to. *See*
        National Lottery
    English expenditure, distribution for
        meeting, **19(S)**, Financial 18
    meaning, **19(S)**, Financial 16
    Northern Ireland expenditure, distribution
        for meeting, **19(S)**, Financial 20
    power to add or remove distributors,
        19(S), Financial 23
    power to prohibit distribution,
        19(S), Financial 22
    Scottish expenditure, distribution for
        meeting, **19(S)**, Financial 19
    Welsh expenditure, distribution for
        meeting, **19(S)**, Financial 19
dormant accounts—
    account, meaning, **19(S)**, Financial 12
    assets-limit condition, **19(S)**, Financial 7
    balance, meaning, **19(S)**, Financial 11–12
    bank, meaning, **19(S)**, Financial 11
    charities, transfer of balances to with
        proportion to reclaim fund,
        19(S), Financial 5–6
    directors' report, information in,
        19(S), Financial 14
    dormant, meaning, **19(S)**, Financial 12–13

bank and banking—*contd*
    dormant accounts—*contd*
        information, disclosure of,
            19(S), Financial 14
        insolvency, customer's rights preserved on,
            19(S), Financial 13
        interest on, **43(S)**, 866
        interpretation, **19(S)**, Financial 10
        reclaim fund—
            articles of association, provision to be
                made in, **19(S)**, Financial 28
            business transfer schemes,
                19(S), Financial 30
            functions of, **19(S)**, Financial 8–9
            regulated activities, **19(S)**, Financial 29
            transfer of balances to,
                19(S), Financial 4–6
        review and report to Parliament,
            19(S), Financial 15
        summary of provisions,
            19(S), Financial 1–2
        transfer of, **43(S)**, 867
    drafts—
        authority for payment, **19(1)**, [17]
        indorsement, **19(1)**, [17]
    financial dealings, power to suspend,
        19(1), [440]
    interpretation of terms, **4**, [585]
    manager, meaning, **4**, [584]
    meaning, **44(1)**, [624]
    migration of companies, information on,
        44(1), [495]
    non-resident, provisions applicable to,
        44(1), [634]
    note. *See* **bank note**
    payment on demand, forged indorsement,
        19(1), [90]
    supervisory board. *See under* **Financial
        Services Authority**
    transactions in England and Wales and
        Northern Ireland, requests for information
        for use abroad—
        account information, obtaining,
            12(3), [598]
        account monitoring order—
            discharge, **12(3)**, [599]
            making of, **12(3)**, [599]
            meaning, **12(3)**, [598]
            power to make, **12(3)**, [598]
            variation, **12(3)**, [599]
        customer information order—
            discharge, **12(3)**, [596]
            making of, **12(3)**, [596]
            meaning, **12(3)**, [595]
            offences, **12(3)**, [597]
            power to make, **12(3)**, [595]
            variation, **12(3)**, [596]
        disclosure of information, offence of,
            12(3), [600]
        offences, **12(3)**, [597]

Bank for International Settlements
    taxation, exempt from, **19(2)**, [788]

bank holiday
financial dealings, suspension of, **19(1)**, [440]
historical note on, **45**, [934]
list of, **45**, [937]
payments due on, **45**, [934]
specification of, **19(1)**, [439], [443]

bank insolvency
administration order—
  application, conditions for determining,
    19(S), Financial 177–8
  liquidator, application by,
    19(S), Financial 173
administrator, conditions for appointment,
  19(S), Financial 177–8
applied provisions, table of,
  19(S), Financial 159–67
bank, meaning, **19(S)**, Financial 148
building societies, provisions applying to,
  19(S), Financial 184
company voluntary arrangements, proposal
  for, **19(S)**, Financial 172
court, meaning, **19(S)**, Financial 149
courts, co-operation between,
  19(S), Financial 183
credit unions, provisions applying to,
  19(S), Financial 184–5
directors, disqualification, **19(S)**, Financial 178
dissolution—
  date, deferment of, **19(S)**, Financial 175
  liquidator, application by,
    19(S), Financial 174
effect, **19(S)**, Financial 158–9
evidence, **19(S)**, Financial 183
features of, **19(S)**, Financial 147
fees, **19(S)**, Financial 182
Financial Services Compensation Scheme, role
  of, **19(S)**, Financial 180
general note, **19(S)**, Financial 47–9
insolvency law, application of,
  19(S), Financial 179
Insolvency Services Account, payments into,
  19(S), Financial 183
interpretation, **19(S)**, Financial 149–50
liquidation committee—
  ceasing to exit, **19(S)**, Financial 156
  establishment of, **19(S)**, Financial 155
  final meeting, **19(S)**, Financial 174
  functions of, **19(S)**, Financial 155
  meetings, **19(S)**, Financial 156
  members of, **19(S)**, Financial 155
  objectives, recommendation of,
    19(S), Financial 156–7
liquidation, objectives, **19(S)**, Financial 154
liquidator—
  administration order, application for,
    19(S), Financial 173
  company voluntary arrangements, proposal
    for, **19(S)**, Financial 172
  court, removal by, **19(S)**, Financial 169
  creditors, removal by, **19(S)**, Financial 170
  disqualification, **19(S)**, Financial 170
  eligibility for appointment,
    19(S), Financial 150
  objectives, **19(S)**, Financial 154

bank insolvency—*contd*
liquidator—*contd*
  officer of the court, as,
    19(S), Financial 168
  powers and duties, **19(S)**, Financial 158–67
  release, **19(S)**, Financial 171
  replacement, **19(S)**, Financial 171
  resignation, **19(S)**, Financial 168
  term of appointment, **19(S)**, Financial 168
  winding up, application for,
    19(S), Financial 174
Northern Ireland, provisions applying,
  19(S), Financial 186–7
order—
  alternative to winding up or administration,
    as, **19(S)**, Financial 176
  application for—
    grounds for, **19(S)**, Financial 152
    person making, **19(S)**, Financial 151
  commencement, **19(S)**, Financial 153
  grounds for making, **19(S)**, Financial 153
  meaning, **19(S)**, Financial 150
  other procedures, exclusion of,
    19(S), Financial 176
overview, **19(S)**, Financial 147
partnerships, provisions applying to,
  19(S), Financial 185
procedure, **19(S)**, Financial 147
rules, **19(S)**, Financial 181–2
Scottish partnerships, provisions applying to,
  19(S), Financial 186
transfer of accounts, **19(S)**, Financial 181
voluntary winding up, resolution for—
  approval of court for, **19(S)**, Financial 176
  conditions for, **19(S)**, Financial 177–8
winding up—
  liquidator, application by,
    19(S), Financial 174
  petition, conditions for determining,
    19(S), Financial 177–8
Northern Ireland, provisions applying,
  19(S), Financial 221–2

bank note
account of issues, weekly, **19(1)**, [12], [15],
  [263]
cashier's name, impressment by machine,
  19(1), [16]
counterfeiting. *See* **counterfeiting**
currency, deemed to be, **12(1)**, [742]
currency note, transfer of issue, **19(1)**, [260]
defacing, penalty, **19(1)**, [264]
exchange of, **19(1)**, [298]
issue—
  Bank of England—
    by, **19(S)**, Financial 263
    powers, **19(1)**, [298]
  fiduciary, limit on amount, **19(1)**, [608]
  meaning, **19(S)**, Financial 252
  profits, transfer to Treasury, **19(1)**, [261]
  restriction on, **19(1)**, [13], [608]
  Scotland and Northern Ireland, banks in,
    19(1), [262]

bank note—*contd*
  issue—*contd*
    Scotland and Northern Ireland, in—
      application to court,
        19(S), Financial 262
      authorised bank, meaning,
        19(S), Financial 252
      backing assets, **19(S)**, Financial 256–7
      bank insolvency, provision for,
        19(S), Financial 259
      Bank of England, expenses incurred and
        sums received by, **19(S)**, Financial 263
      ceasing business of, **19(S)**, Financial 258
      commencement of provisions,
        19(S), Financial 253
      discretionary functions,
        19(S), Financial 263
      existing issuers, saving for,
        19(S), Financial 253
      financial penalties, **19(S)**, Financial 261
      general note, **19(S)**, Financial 53–5
      information, provision of,
        19(S), Financial 257
      old authorising enactments, repeal of,
        19(S), Financial 253
      overview, **19(S)**, Financial 251
      regulations, **19(S)**, Financial 255
      repeals and amendments,
        19(S), Financial 254
      rules, **19(S)**, Financial 255
      termination of right,
        19(S), Financial 261
      unlawful, **19(S)**, Financial 260
    security for, **19(1)**, [259]
    weekly accounts, **19(1)**, [12], [15], [263]
  issue of, **10**, [1]
  legal tender, as, **19(1)**, [298]
  meaning, **19(1)**, [14], [299], [610];
    19(S), Financial 251
  recall, powers of, **19(1)**, [298]
  reproducing—
    directors' liability, **12(1)**, [741]
    offence of, **12(1)**, [735]
  unpresented, writing off on ceasing to be legal
    tender, **19(1)**, [609]
  zero-rating, **50**, [151]

Bank of England
  account of issues, weekly, **19(1)**, [12], [15],
    [263]
  accounts—
    consolidation of, **19(2)**, [617]
    Exchequer. *See* **Exchequer**
    government stock and annuities of,
      19(2), [618]
    public moneys, for, **19(2)**, [618]
  accounts and records, **19(1)**, [1008]
  annual report, **19(1)**, [1005]
  bank notes, issue of. *See* **bank note**
  Bank of Ireland, discharge of functions in
    place of, **43(2)**, [128]
  building societies, financial assistance to,
    19(2), [578]; **19(S)**, Financial 279–80
  capital stock, enactments to which subject,
    19(1), [139]

Bank of England—*contd*
  cash ratio deposits, **19(1)**, [1036]
  cashier's name on notes, **19(1)**, [16]
  charges, registration of, **19(S)**, Financial 280
  charter, **19(1)**, [1]
  constitution, **19(1)**, [273]
  court of directors—
    chair, **19(S)**, Financial 274
    continuation of, **19(1)**, [1002]
    functions of, **19(1)**, [1003]
    meetings, **19(1)**, [1035];
      19(S), Financial 274
    membership, **19(1)**, [1002]
    Monetary Policy Committee procedures,
      review of, **19(1)**, [1014]
    non-executive members, functions of,
      19(1), [1004]
    number of, **19(S)**, Financial 274
    powers, **19(1)**, [1035]
    proceedings, **19(1)**, [1035]
    qualifications for appointment,
      19(1), [1035]
    quorum, **19(S)**, Financial 275
    removal from office, **19(1)**, [1035]
    remuneration, **19(1)**, [1035]
    terms of office, **19(1)**, [1035]
  currency note issue, transfer of, **19(1)**, [260]
  dealing, permitted, **19(1)**, [4]
  Exchequer Account, payments into,
    19(2), [864]
  Financial Services Authority, transfer of
    functions to, **19(1)**, [1019], [1038]
    See also **Financial Services Authority**
  Financial Stability Committee,
    19(S), Financial 272–3
  financial stability objective,
    19(S), Financial 272
  gold bullion, weekly accounts, **19(1)**, [12],
    [15]
  government stock—
    incidental provisions on transfer of stock,
      19(1), [277]
    interest on, **19(1)**, [272], [277]
    issue, **19(1)**, [272], [277]
    redemption, **19(1)**, [272], [277]
    registration of, **19(2)**, [807]
  Governor, tenure, **19(S)**, Financial 275
  history, **19(1)**, [1]
  immunity as monetary authority,
    19(S), Financial 276
  incorporation, **19(1)**, [2]
  indemnity to, **48**, 540
  information—
    disclosure of, **19(S)**, Financial 277
    disclosure, restrictions on, **19(1)**, [1039]
    offences relating to supply of,
      19(1), [1026], [1027]
    power to obtain, **19(1)**, [1015]
  issue department—
    establishment, **19(1)**, [11]
    profits, payment of, **19(2)**, [856]
    redemption of securities held in,
      19(2), [860]
    security for note issue, **19(1)**, [259]
  issues, regulations as to balances, **4**, [554]

Bank of England—*contd*
  meaning, **41**, [605]
  Monetary Policy Committee—
    court of directors—
      report to, **19(1)**, [1037]
      review of procedures by, **19(1)**, [1014]
    decisions, publication of statements about,
      19(1), [1012]
    meetings, **19(1)**, [1037]
    members of, **19(1)**, [1011]
      qualifications for appointment,
        19(1), [1037]
      removal, **19(1)**, [1037]
      terms of office, **19(1)**, [1037]
    minutes of meetings, publication of,
      19(1), [1013]
    proceedings, **19(1)**, [1037]
    responsibility of, **19(1)**, [1011]
  monetary policy objectives, **19(1)**, [1009]
    specification of relevant matters,
      19(1), [1010]
  national debt, interest on, **4**, [555]
  notes. *See* **bank note**
  powers and duties, **19(1)**, [1]
  powers, consequential provisions as to,
    19(1), [273]
  promissory notes, issue, **19(1)**, [11]
  public control, transfer to, **19(1)**, [272]
  repeals, **41**, [699]
  reports, **19(1)**, [1016]
  reserve powers, **19(1)**, [1017]
  seal, custody and use of, **19(1)**, [1006]
  settlement arrangements provided by,
    19(1), [791]
  silver bullion, weekly accounts, **19(1)**, [12],
    [15]
  stock, transfer to Treasury, **19(1)**, [272]
  summary of provisions, **19(1)**, [1]
  trading prohibition, **19(1)**, [3]
  Treasury—
    directions by, **19(1)**, [274]
    lending to, **19(2)**, [857]
    reserve powers, **19(1)**, [1017]
    transfer of stock to, **19(1)**, [272]

Bank of Ireland
  accounts—
    consolidation of, **19(2)**, [31]
    Exchequer. *See* **Exchequer**
    government stock and annuities, for,
      19(2), [618]
    public moneys for, **19(2)**, [618]
  meaning, **41**, [605]
  national debt, interest on, **4**, [555]

banking
  business transfer scheme. *See* **business
    transfer scheme**
  company, meaning, **8(1)**, [1242]
  group, meaning, **8(1)**, [1242]
  partnership—
    accounts and reports provisions, application
      of, **8(1)**, [548]
    meaning, **8(1)**, [548]

banking company
  accounts—
    accounting policies, disclosure of, **8**, 709
    accounting principles—
      departure from, **8**, 703
      generally, **8**, 703
    accounting rules, **8**, 703–6
      alternative, **8**, 706–8
    assets denominated in foreign currencies,
      8, 708, 713–14
    disclosure requirements, modification of,
      8, 336
    fixed assets, treatment of, **8**, 703–5
    general rules, **8**, 692–3
    generally, **8**, 335
    group accounts, **8**, 336
    liabilities denominated in foreign
      currencies, **8**, 708, 713–14
    modification of provisions, **8**, 755–6
    notes to, generally, **8**, 709–16
    partnerships, application of provisions to,
      8, 338
  assets—
    current, valuation, **8**, 705
    depreciation rules, **8**, 707
    fixed, treatment of, **8**, 703–5
    foreign currencies, denominated in, **8**, 708,
      713–14
  balance sheet—
    formats—
      detailed, **8**, 694–5
      examples, **8**, 694–5
      general rules, **8**, 692–3
      notes on, **8**, 695–8
    information supplementing—
      debt and other fixed income securities,
        8, 712
      details of assets charged, **8**, 712
      fixed assets, as to, **8**, 710–11
      fixed cumulative dividends, **8**, 712
      guarantees and commitments, **8**, 712–13
      leasing transactions, **8**, 713
      maturity analysis, **8**, 711
      memorandum items, **8**, 713
      miscellaneous matters, **8**, 714
      reserves and provisions, **8**, 711
      share capital and debentures, **8**, 709–10
      subordinated liabilities, **8**, 712
      tax, particulars of, **8**, 714
      transferable securities, **8**, 713
  consolidated accounts—
    additional disclosure—
      emoluments and other benefits of
        directors and others, **8**, 719–20
      related undertakings, **8**, 719
    foreign currency translation, **8**, 718
    minority interests and associated
      undertakings, **8**, 717–8
    undertakings to be included in, **8**, 717
  distributions by, **8**, 360
  loans, meaning, **8**, 716
  materiality, meaning, **8**, 716
  meaning, **8**, 602; **8(1)**, [1242]

banking company—*contd*
profit and loss account—
formats—
detailed, **8**, 699–701
notes on, **8**, 701–2
information supplementing—
income, particulars of, **8**, 714–15
management and agency services, **8**, 715
miscellaneous matters, **8**, 715–16
staff, particulars of, **8**, 715
tax, particulars of, **8**, 714
Scots land tenure, meaning, **8**, 717

bankrupt. *See also* **bankruptcy**
absconding—
arrest of, **4(2)**, [8], [447]
offence of, **4(2)**, [443]
arbitration agreement, party to, **4(2)**, [434]
business—
engaging in, **4(2)**, [445]
permission to carry on, **4(2)**, [391]
civil partner, dwelling house, right of
occupation, **4(2)**, [414]
concealment by—
books, papers, etc, **4(2)**, [440]
property, **4(2)**, [439]
contracts, party to, **4(2)**, [429]
correspondence, re-direction of, **4(2)**, [454]
credit—
fraudulently obtaining, **4(2)**, [11]
offence of obtaining, **4(2)**, [445]
discharge. *See* **bankruptcy**
disqualification—
devolved assemblies, **4(2)**, [515]
Northern Ireland or Scotland, order in,
4(2), [517], [595]
parliamentary, **4(2)**, [514]–[517]
provision, **4(2)**, [596]
duties, trustee, in relation to, **4(2)**, [410]
estate of. *See* **bankruptcy**
false statement by, **4(2)**, [441]
falsification of papers etc, **4(2)**, [440]
imprisonment. *See* **bankruptcy** (debtor)
inability to pay debts, meaning, **4(2)**, [337]
investigation of affairs, **4(2)**, [360]
justice of the peace, as, **4**, [1191]
local authority, member of, **4**, [1193]
meaning, **4(2)**, [464]
offences by. *See* **bankruptcy**
official receiver—
duties in relation to, **4(2)**, [362]
See further **official receiver**
parliamentary disqualification,
4(2), [514]–[517]
Northern Ireland or Scotland, order in,
4(2), [517], [595]
preferences given by—
relevant time for purposes of, **4(2)**, [419]
remedy for, **4(2)**, [418]
premises occupied by, payment for,
4(2), [416]
property of. *See* **bankruptcy** (bankrupt's
estate)
public examination of, **4(2)**, [361], [450]

bankrupt—*contd*
spouse—
debts due to, **4(2)**, [406]
dwelling house, right of occupation,
4(2), [414]
statement of affairs, **4(2)**, [359]
wrongdoing by, **4(2)**, [438]–[445]

bankruptcy. *See also* **company insolvency;
individual insolvency**
absconding debtor—
arrest, **4**, [634], [1046]
meaning, **4**, [1042]
agricultural credit, effect on, **1(1)**, [304]
annual report for Parliament, **4(2)**, [462]
apprenticeship, effect on, **4(2)**, [432]
arbitration agreement, bankrupt as party to,
4(2), [434]
assignment of book debts, **4(2)**, [428]
associate of person, meaning, **4(2)**, [528]
attachment, discretion of court, **4(2)**, [12]
bankrupt. *See* **bankrupt**
bankrupt's estate—
actions as to, stay of, **4(2)**, [356]
administration of—
completion, final meeting, **4(2)**, [408]
duties as to, **4(2)**, [376]
trustee's report on, **4(2)**, [408]
administration order, subject to, **4(2)**, [379]
after-acquired property, **4(2)**, [381], [411]
concealment of property, **4(2)**, [439]
confiscation order discharged or quashed,
where, **4(2)**, [380]
control over—
acquisition of, **4(2)**, [387]
surrender of, **4(2)**, [388]
delivery to official receiver, **4(2)**, [362]
disclaimer of property—
dwelling house, **4(2)**, [395]
land subject to rentcharge, **4(2)**, [396]
notice of, **4(2)**, [393]
onerous property. *See* onerous property
below
disposal of—
associate of bankrupt, to, **4(2)**, [391]
restrictions on, **4(2)**, [355]
distress, treatment of, **4(2)**, [431]
distribution—
claims by unsatisfied creditors,
4(2), [402]
criminal bankruptcy, in, **4(2)**, [404]
dividend, by means of, **4(2)**, [401]
final, **4(2)**, [407]
priority payments, **4(2)**, [405]
specie, in, **4(2)**, [403]
stay in case of second bankruptcy,
4(2), [411]
dwelling house—
charge on, **4(2)**, [389]
disclaimer of, **4(2)**, [395]
home, exclusion of, **4(2)**, [354], [593]
low value home, **4(2)**, [390]
occupation—
bankrupt, by, **4(2)**, [415]
civil partner, by, **4(2)**, [414]

bankruptcy—*contd*
  bankrupt's estate—*contd*
    dwelling house—*contd*
      occupation—*contd*
        payments in respect of, **4(2)**, [416]
        spouse, by, **4(2)**, [414]
      saving in respect of, **4(2)**, [409]
      tenancy, vesting of, **4(2)**, [383]
      vesting of, **4(2)**, [397]
    exceptions from, **4(2)**, [353]
    excessive pension contributions, recovery
      of—
      application for, **4(2)**, [421]
      calculation and verification of value,
        4(2), [423]
      estate, part of, **4(2)**, [423]
      information, provision of, **4(2)**, [423]
      orders, **4(2)**, [422]
      pension-sharing, in cases of,
        4(2), [424]–[426]
      regulations, **4(2)**, [423]
    interim receiver, appointment, **4(2)**, [357]
    leasehold—
      disclaimer of, **4(2)**, [394]
      vesting of, **4(2)**, [398]
    manager for, **4(2)**, [358]
    meaning, **4(2)**, [353]
    notices, time-limit for, **4(2)**, [384]
    onerous property, disclaimer—
      dwelling house, **4(2)**, [395]
      effect of, **4(2)**, [392]
      general power, **4(2)**, [392]
      land subject to rentcharge, **4(2)**, [396]
      leaseholds, **4(2)**, [394]
      meaning, **4(2)**, [392]
      notice of, **4(2)**, [393]
      vesting disclaimed property, **4(2)**, [397]
    property—
      comprising, **4(2)**, [353]
      meaning, **4(2)**, [529]
      proceedings under EC Regulation,
        modified definition, **4(2)**, [530]
    protection of, **4(2)**, [357]
    receivership—
      interim receiver, appointment,
        4(2), [357]
      order, subject to, **4(2)**, [379]
      pending appointment of trustee,
        4(2), [358]
    reference to, **4(2)**, [436]
    restraint order, subject to, **4(2)**, [378]
    sequestration, **4(2)**, [9]
    stay of proceedings respecting, **4(2)**, [356]
    surplus, application of, **4(2)**, [407]
    trustee. *See* trustee in *below*
    vesting of—
      items of excess value, **4(2)**, [382]
      time of, **4(2)**, [377]
  book debts, assignment of, **4(2)**, [428]
  books, papers etc—
    acquisition by trustee, **4(2)**, [387]
    concealment of, **4(2)**, [440]
    delivery up of, **4(2)**, [388]
    falsification of, **4(2)**, [440]
    lien on, unenforceable, **4(2)**, [433]

bankruptcy—*contd*
  books, papers etc—*contd*
    seizure, warrant for, **4(2)**, [448]
  charity trustee, of, **5(2)**, [563]
  commencement of, time of, **4(2)**, [347]
  contracts—
    bankrupt as party to, **4(2)**, [429]
    discharge of obligations under, **4(2)**, [429]
  contributory in winding up, of, **4(2)**, [123]
  copyright, effect on, **4(2)**, [563]
  court—
    arrest, warrant for, **4(2)**, [447]
    bankrupt's letters, powers as to, **4(2)**, [454]
    co-operation between courts, **4(2)**, [513]
    enforcement powers, **4(2)**, [450]
    examination of bankrupt, **4(2)**, [450]
    general control by, **4(2)**, [446]
    inland revenue documents, production of,
      4(2), [452]
    inquiry into bankrupt's dealings,
      4(2), [449]–[451]
    meaning, **4(2)**, [468]
    powers, **4(2)**, [446]
    priorities decided by, **4(2)**, [446]
  county court plaintiff, of, **11(2)**, [933]
  creditors—
    committee—
      functions, exercise by Minister,
        4(2), [373]
      power to establish, **4(2)**, [372]
    defrauding, **4(2)**, [11]
    meaning, **4(2)**, [466]
    meeting—
      corporate representatives at, **4(2)**, [526]
      final, summoning, **4(2)**, [407]
      requisition, power to, **4(2)**, [365]
    security, with, **4(2)**, [338]
    transactions defrauding, **4(2)**, [510]–[512]
    unsatisfied, claims by, **4(2)**, [402]
  criminal bankruptcy order—
    distribution under, **4(2)**, [404]
    Official Petitioner for, **4(2)**, [487]
    pending, effect on petition, **4(2)**, [335]
    petition based on, **4(2)**, [346]
  debt management scheme. *See* **debts**
  debt relief order. *See* **debts**
  debt repayment plan. *See* **debts**
  debtor—
    absconding, **4(2)**, [8], [447]
    arrest of, **4(2)**, [8], [447]
    imprisonment—
      abolition, exceptions from, **4(2)**, [6]
      jurisdiction as to, **4(2)**, [48]
      maximum period, **4(2)**, [6]
      restriction on, **4(2)**, [6], [48]
      small debts, for, **4(2)**, [7]
    meaning, **4(2)**, [468]
    property of. *See* bankrupt's estate *above*
    statutory demand to be made to,
      4(2), [337]
    writ of attachment, court's discretion,
      4(2), [12]
  debts—
    inability to pay, meaning, **4(2)**, [337]
    incurred after commencement, **4(2)**, [355]

bankruptcy—*contd*
  debts—*contd*
    interest provable as part of, **4(2)**, [399]
    meaning, **4(2)**, [465]
    mutual credits etc, **4(2)**, [400]
    priority of, **4(2)**, [405]
    proof of, **4(2)**, [399]
    ranking of, **4(2)**, [405]
    reasonable prospect of paying, **4(2)**, [340]
    set off, **4(2)**, [400]
    spouse, to, **4(2)**, [406]
  discharge—
    application for, **4(2)**, [349]
    effect of, **4(2)**, [350]
    liabilities after, **4(2)**, [350]
    order of court, by, **4(2)**, [349]
    postponement, **4(2)**, [349]
    report by receiver as to, **4(2)**, [360]
    restrictions after, **4(2)**, [351]
    time for, **4(2)**, [349]
  disqualification by—
    devolved assemblies, **4(2)**, [515]
    parliamentary, **4(2)**, [514]–[517]
      Northern Ireland or Scotland, order in,
        4(2), [517], [595]
      provision, **4(2)**, [596]
  documents—
    inland revenue, production of, **4(2)**, [452]
    stamp duty exemption, **4(2)**, [461]
  duration, **4(2)**, [604]
  earlier and later, adjustment between,
    4(2), [412]
  employer, of. *See* **employer**
  enforcement provisions, **4(2)**, [430]
  estate agent, of, **21**, [700]
  excessive pension contributions, recovery of—
    application for, **4(2)**, [421]
    calculation and verification of value,
      4(2), [423]
    estate, part of, **4(2)**, [423]
    information, provision of, **4(2)**, [423]
    orders, **4(2)**, [422]
    pension-sharing, in cases of,
      4(2), [424]–[426]
    regulations, **4(2)**, [423]
  execution, provisions as to, **4(2)**, [430]
  expenses, defrayment of, **4(2)**, [407]
  extortionate credit transactions, **4(2)**, [427]
  fees orders, **4(2)**, [498]–[500]
  Financial Services Authority—
    participation by, **19(2)**, [449]
    petition by, **19(2)**, [447]
    report to, **19(2)**, [448]
  financial services compensation scheme, rights
    of, **19(2)**, [267]
  friendly society officer, of, priority on,
    19(1), [503]
  inability to pay debts, meaning, **4(2)**, [337]
  income payments—
    agreement, **4(2)**, [386]
    orders, **4(2)**, [385]
  individual insolvency. *See* **individual
    insolvency**
  interpretation of provisions, **4(2)**, [463]–[468]
  investigatory duties, **4(2)**, [174], [360]

bankruptcy—*contd*
  legal professional privilege, and, **4(2)**, [527]
  lessee, forfeiture of lease on, **20**, [756]
  liens, unenforceability, **4(2)**, [433]
  meaning, **20**, [436], [804]
  monetary limits, **4(2)**, [336]
    prescription of, **4(2)**, [504]
  mortgagor, of, effect, **20**, [728]
  N. Ireland, provisions applied, **4(2)**, [534]
  offences—
    absconding, **4(2)**, [443]
    application of provisions, **4(2)**, [435]
    bodies corporate, by, **4(2)**, [522]
    business, engaging in, **4(2)**, [445]
    concealment, **4(2)**, [439]
    credit, obtaining, **4(2)**, [445]
    definitions as to, **4(2)**, [436]
    false statements, making, **4(2)**, [441]
    falsification of papers etc, **4(2)**, [440]
    fraudulent dealing with property,
      4(2), [444]
    fraudulent disposal, **4(2)**, [442]
    general provisions, **4(2)**, [435]
    innocent intention, defence of, **4(2)**, [437]
    non-disclosure, **4(2)**, [438]
    penalties, **4(2)**, [520], [561]
    proceedings, consent required, **4(2)**, [435]
    schedule of, **4(2)**, [520], [561]
    summary proceedings, **4(2)**, [521]
    transitional provisions, **4(2)**, [563]
  Official Petitioner, functions, **4(2)**, [487]
  official receiver. *See* **official receiver**
  order—
    actions stayed by, **4(2)**, [356]
    annulment of, **4(2)**, [320], [352]
    conditions in respect of debtor, **4(2)**, [334]
    debtor's petition, on, **4(2)**, [343]
    default of voluntary arrangement, for,
      4(2), [345]
    meaning, **4(2)**, [464]
    period of, **4(2)**, [348]
    property acquired after, **4(2)**, [381]
    registration as land charge, **21**, [396]
  period of, **4(2)**, [348]
  petition—
    administration order, presentation during
      currency of, **11(4)**, [63]
    creditors'—
      amendment of, **4(2)**, [340]
      amount of debt for, **4(2)**, [336]
      bankruptcy level, meaning, **4(2)**, [336]
      creditor with security, **4(2)**, [338]
      dismissal of, grounds for, **4(2)**, [340]
      expedited petition, **4(2)**, [339]
      grounds for, **4(2)**, [336]
      order, time for making, **4(2)**, [339]
      proceedings on, **4(2)**, [340]
    criminal bankruptcy order, based on,
      4(2), [346]
    debtor, conditions to be satisfied,
      4(2), [334]
    debtor's—
      grounds for, **4(2)**, [341]
      inability to pay, for, **4(2)**, [341]

bankruptcy—*contd*
  petition—*contd*
    debtor's—*contd*
      insolvency practitioner—
        court may appoint, **4(2)**, [342]
        report on debtor, **4(2)**, [343]
        See also **insolvency practitioner**
      minimum debt for, **4(2)**, [342]
      order made on, **4(2)**, [343]
      statement to accompany, **4(2)**, [341]
    dismissal by court, **4(2)**, [335]
    expedited, **4(2)**, [339]
    meaning, **4(2)**, [468]; **19(2)**, [267]
    presentation, conditions for, **4(2)**, [334], [335]
    proceedings pending, effect, **4(2)**, [356]
    registration as land charge, **21**, [395]
    who may present, **4(2)**, [333]
    withdrawal, leave required, **4(2)**, [335]
  preferences given by bankrupt, **4(2)**, [418], [419]
  prior transactions—
    excessive pension contributions, **4(2)**, [421]–[426]
    extortionate credit transactions, **4(2)**, [427]
    gifts, **4(2)**, [417]
    orders by court as to, **4(2)**, [420]
    preferences given, **4(2)**, [418], [419]
    relevant time for purposes of, **4(2)**, [419]
    undervalue, at, **4(2)**, [417]
  priority of debts, **4(2)**, [405]
  proceeds of crime, restriction of powers, **12(3)**, [495]
    Northern Ireland, **12(3)**, [499]
  proof of debts in, **8**, 63
  property—
    credit, obtained on, **4(2)**, [444]
    fraudulent dealing with, **4(2)**, [442]
    inquiries in respect of, **4(2)**, [449]–[451]
    public examination of bankrupt, **4(2)**, [361], [450]
    rent, distress for, **4(2)**, [431]
    restrictions order, **4(2)**, [553], [596]
    Scotland. *See* **Scotland**
    second, effect of, **4(2)**, [411]
    seizure of, warrant for, **4(2)**, [448]
    transitional provisions, **4(2)**, [563]
    See also bankrupt's estate *above*
  property excluded from estate, **12(3)**, [495]
    Northern Ireland, **12(3)**, [498]
  receiving or sequestration order, registration as land charge, **21**, [396]
  security, meaning, **4(2)**, [466]
  sequestration, debtor's property, **4(2)**, [9]
  servicemen, stay of proceedings against, **3**, [388]
  special manager—
    defects in appointment, **4(2)**, [460]
    duties etc, **4(2)**, [453]
    power to appoint, **4(2)**, [453]
  statement of affairs, **4(2)**, [359]
  summary of provisions, **4(2)**, [1]
  tainted gifts, **12(3)**, [497]
    Northern Ireland, **12(3)**, [500]

bankruptcy—*contd*
  tenant in tail. *See* **entail**
  third party insurance—
    information for purposes of, **4(2)**, [44]
    limited liability partnerships, **4(2)**, [46]
    rights of third parties, **4(2)**, [43]
    settlement between parties, **4(2)**, [45]
  transitional provisions, **4(2)**, [531], [562]
  trust of land, powers relating to rights under, **4(2)**, [413]
  trustee in—
    acquisition of control by, **4(2)**, [387]
    application to court for directions, **4(2)**, [374]
    appointment—
      failure to make, **4(2)**, [366]
      formal defects in, **4(2)**, [460]
      notice of, **4(2)**, [367]
      power to make, **4(2)**, [363]
      receivership pending, **4(2)**, [358]
      Secretary of State, by, **4(2)**, [367]
      special cases, **4(2)**, [368]
    books, papers etc—
      acquisition of, **4(2)**, [387]
      delivery up of, **4(2)**, [388]
    contributory in winding up, as, **4(2)**, [123]
    control over, **4**, [973]–[974]
    decision of, as to disclaimer, **4(2)**, [393]
    distribution by. *See* bankrupt's estate *above*
    dividend—
      notice of declaring, **4(2)**, [401]
      order by court to pay, **4(2)**, [402]
    duty of bankrupt in relation to, **4(2)**, [410]
    expenses, defrayment of, **4(2)**, [407]
    final dividend, declaration of, **4(2)**, [407]
    first, meeting to appoint, **4(2)**, [363]
    functions, general, **4(2)**, [376]
    income payments—
      agreement, **4(2)**, [386]
      order, **4(2)**, [385]
    joint trustees, **4(2)**, [363]
    liability of, **4(2)**, [375]
    meeting to appoint—
      failure of appointment, **4(2)**, [366]
      requisition by creditor for, **4(2)**, [365]
      summoning, **4(2)**, [364]
    misfeasance etc by, **4(2)**, [375]
    money received by, interest on, **4(2)**, [490]
    official name of, **4(2)**, [376]
    payment to, **3**, [704], [977]
    powers of—
      ancillary, **4(2)**, [556]
      exercisable with sanction, **4(2)**, [554]
      generally, **4(2)**, [391], [555]
    property, powers as to, **4(2)**, [555], [556]
    qualification to act, **4(2)**, [363]
    release of, **4(2)**, [370]
    removal of, **4(2)**, [369]
    replacement of, **4(2)**, [369]
    transitional provisions, **4(2)**, [563]
    vacancy in office, filling, **4(2)**, [371]
    vacation of office, **4(2)**, [369]
    validity of acts, **4(2)**, [460]

bankruptcy—*contd*
  trustee in—*contd*
    vesting of estate in—
      confiscation order discharged or quashed, where, **4(2)**, [380]
      items of excess value, **4(2)**, [382]
      notice requiring, **4(2)**, [381]
        time-limit for, **4(2)**, [384]
      receivership or administration order, subject to, **4(2)**, [379]
      restraint order, property subject to, **4(2)**, [378]
      tenancy, **4(2)**, [383]
      time of, **4(2)**, [377]
  undischarged bankrupt as director, **8**, 847–8

banns of marriage
  completion of publication in another church, **14**, 1092
  not published, where, **27**, [128]
  parish church, published in, **14**, 1000
  publication of—
    authorisation following, **27**, [209]
    certificates of, **27**, [217]
    chapel, in—
      extra-parochial place, in, **27**, [227]
      licensing, **27**, [226]
      public, meaning, **27**, [226]
    extra-parochial place, in, **27**, [212], [227]
    HM ships, on board, **27**, [220]
    layman, by, **27**, [215]
    manner of, **27**, [213]
    naval, military and air force chapels, in, **27**, [266]
    Northern Ireland, in, **27**, [219]
    notice to clergyman before, **27**, [214]
    person effecting, **27**, [215]
    place of, **27**, [212]
    repair and rebuilding of church, during, **27**, [224]
    Republic of Ireland, in, **27**, [219]
    Scotland, in, **27**, [219]
    second church, completion in, **27**, [216]
    solemnisation following, **27**, [218]
    time of, **27**, [213]
    Wales and Monmouthshire, provisions extending to, **27**, [331]
    war damage, church injured by, **27**, [225]
  register book, **27**, [213]
  register, custody of, **14**, 934
  residence, proof of not necessary, **27**, [230]

baptism
  certificate, falsification, **36**, [6]
  fee for, abolition of, **14**, 239
  guild church, in, **14**, 465
  registers—
    annotation in, **14**, 528–9, 529
    cathedrals, in, **14**, 933–4
    custody of, **14**, 934
    entry, making, **14**, 931, 952
    errors, correction of, **14**, 933
    evidence, as, **36**, [4], [11]
    forgery, **36**, [6]
    provision of book, **14**, 930

baptism—*contd*
  registers—*contd*
    search and inspection, **36**, [3]
    search in, **14**, 946–8
    summary of provisions, **36**, [1]
    wilful damage to, **36**, [6]
    See also **parochial registers and records**
  short certificate of, **14**, 527–8

Barbados
  British ship registered in, **7(2)**, [611]
  Commonwealth citizenship, **31**, [186]
  Constitution Order, **7(2)**, [608]
  fully responsible status of, **7(2)**, [606]
  legislative powers of, **7(2)**, [610]
  visiting forces in, **7(2)**, [611]

barber
  byelaws as to, **35(1)**, [272]
  London—
    offences, increased fines, **25(2)**, [527]
    registration of, **25(1)**, [834]

Barbican Arts Centre
  catering facilities at, **25(1)**, [887]

barge
  unsafe, use of, **39(2)**, [763]

barley. *See also* **cereals**
  weights for basis of payment, **1(1)**, [248]

Barnet Gas and Water Company
  saving for, **49**, [227]

Barotseland
  Northern Rhodesia, agreements with, **7(2)**, [558]

barracks
  damage to, **3**, [645], [918]

barrator
  common, abolition of offence, **12(1)**, [369]

barratry
  justice of the peace, jurisdiction of, **11(2)**, [1A]

barrister
  adjustment income, spreading, **44(3)**, [238]–[239]
  appointments open to, **4**, [1206A]
  bar practising certificates, **11(3)**, [282]
  call to the bar, **4**, [1206A]
  clerk, discrimination by—
    disability, **7(1)**, [304]
    racial, **7(1)**, [161]
    relationships having come to an end, **7(1)**, [79]
    sexual, **7(1)**, [78]
  contract, right to enter into, **11(4)**, [545]

barrister—*contd*
discrimination by or in relation to—
  disability, **7(1)**, [304]
    adjustments, duty to make, **7(1)**, [305]
  racial, **7(1)**, [161]
  relationships having come to an end,
    7(1), [79]
  sexual, **7(1)**, [78]
general note, **4**, [1206A]
immunities, **4**, [1206A], [1208]
law report by person other than,
  11(3), [1358]; **11(4)**, [561]
legal aid work—
  complaints, **11(3)**, [33]; **11(4)**, [507]
    disciplinary provisions, application of,
    11(3), [34]; **11(4)**, [508]
  exclusion from, **11(3)**, [35]; **11(4)**, [509]
magistrates' court, representing party before,
  11(2), [543]
meaning, **11(4)**, [321]
pretending to be, offence of, **11(4)**, [296]
pupil or tenant, discrimination in relation
  to—
  disability, **7(1)**, [304]
  racial, **7(1)**, [161]
  relationships having come to an end,
    7(1), [79]
  sexual, **7(1)**, [78]
Queen's Counsel, fees on application for
  appointment as, **11(3)**, [281]
regulations and rules, **11(3)**, [311]
right of audience, **11(3)**, [86], [89]
solicitors, employed by, **11(3)**, [280]
trade profits, **44(3)**, [159]
unincorporated association, prohibition from
  entering into, **4**, [1209]

basic loss payment
amounts, **9**, [330]
claims, **9**, [334]
death before claim made, **9**, [336]
disputes as to, determined by Lands Tribunal,
  9, [338]
exclusions, **9**, [333]
insolvency proceedings instituted before claim
  made, **9**, [335]
interest in land, acquired by agreement,
  9, [339]
payment of, **9**, [338]
pre-commencement acquisition of interest in
  land, **9**, [463]
regulations, **9**, [340]

bat
dwelling-house, in, **32**, [411]

bathing
public—
  bathing huts, etc, provision by local
    authority, **35(1)**, [158]
  byelaws as to, **35(1)**, [157], [380]
  pools, byelaws as to, **35(1)**, [159]

bathing place
closure during winter months, **35(1)**, [153]

bathing place—*contd*
life-saving appliances at, **35(1)**, [160]
provision of, **35(1)**, [148]
public place, deemed, **35(1)**, [151]
regulation of, byelaws for, **35(1)**, [150]
sale etc, by trustees to local authority,
  35(1), [155]
sports, etc, use by school or club for,
  35(1), [152]
swimming contests, etc, use by school or club
  for, **35(1)**, [152]
use for other purposes during winter
  months, **35(1)**, [153]
water or electricity, supply on favourable
  terms to, **35(1)**, [156]
water to or from, laying of pipes for
  conducting, **35(1)**, [154]

bathing pools
byelaws as to, **35(1)**, [159]

bathroom
requirement to provide, **22**, [58]

baths. *See* **washhouses**

battery
child, punishment of, **6**, [966]
dismissal of complaint, **12(1)**, [95]
  bar to proceedings, **12(1)**, [96]
indictment, proceedings brought on,
  12(1), [97]
punishment, **12(1)**, [97]
summary offence, as, **12(1)**, [1083]

beacon
expenses, payment of, **39(2)**, [890]
injury to, **39(2)**, [896]
inspection of, **39(2)**, [876]
local—
  inspection of, **39(2)**, [876]
  surrender of, **39(2)**, [881]
management of, **39(2)**, [873]
meaning, **39(2)**, [901]
rates, etc, exemption from, **39(2)**, [898]

bearer instrument
meaning, **41**, [265]
stamp duty, **41**, [251], [265]–[267]
  abolition in part, **41**, [208]
  charging provisions, **41**, [265]–[267]
  exemptions, **41**, [266]
  false statement, penalty for, **41**, [267]
  interest, **41**, [267]
  issue, on, **41**, [267]
  transfer of stock, on, **41**, [267]

Bechuanaland Protectorate
Botswana, becoming, **7(2)**, [591]

Bedfordshire
statutes repealed, **41**, [694]

beef. *See* **cattle**

beer. *See also* **intoxicating liquor**
domestic use, brewing for, **19(3)**, [404]
excise duty—
  amount, **19(3)**, [395]
  charge of, **19(3)**, [395], [467]
  drawback, provisions ceasing to have
    effect, **19(3)**, [472]
  private consumption, exemption of brewing
    for, **19(3)**, [404]
  rate, **19(3)**, [395]
  remission or repayment—
    research, etc, used for, **19(3)**, [407]
    spoilt beer, **19(3)**, [408]
  small breweries. *See* small breweries *below*
  summary of provisions, **19(3)**, [349]
  suspension, registration of persons and
    premises, **19(3)**, [405]
excise duty, surcharges or rebates,
  13, [898]–[900]
exportation, drawback on, **19(3)**, [406]
gravity—
  meaning, **19(3)**, [374]
  method of ascertaining, **19(3)**, [374]
licence, use of premises for adding solutions,
  19(3), [461]
meaning, **19(3)**, [372]
private consumption, duty exemption of
  brewing for, **19(3)**, [404]
registered brewer, drawback, **19(3)**, [411]
registration of producers, **19(3)**, [409]
regulations, **19(3)**, [410]
research or experiment, remission of duty on
  use for, **19(3)**, [407]
retailer, meaning, **19(3)**, [375]
sale by retail, meaning, **19(3)**, [375]
small breweries, from—
  brewery, meaning, **19(3)**, [397]
  co-operated—
    beer from, meaning, **19(3)**, [400]
    conditions, **19(3)**, [400]
    meaning, **19(3)**, [397]
    rate of duty, **19(3)**, [401]
  exclusions, **19(3)**, [396]
  incorrectly low rate applied, assessments,
    19(3), [402]
  meaning, **19(3)**, [397]
  rate of, **19(3)**, [399]
  reduced rates of duty, power to vary
    provisions, **19(3)**, [403]
  singleton—
    beer from, meaning, **19(3)**, [398]
    conditions, **19(3)**, [398]
    meaning, **19(3)**, [397]
    rate of duty, **19(3)**, [399]
spoilt or destroyed, remission of duty on,
  19(3), [408]
stores, drawback on shipment as, **19(3)**, [406]
warehouse, drawback on removal to,
  19(3), [406]
wholesale, meaning, **19(3)**, [375]
wholesaler, meaning, **19(3)**, [375]
worts, quantity and gravity, **19(3)**, [374]

bees
bee product—
  importation control, **2**, [420]
  meaning, **2**, [422]
importation—
  contravention of order, **2**, [420]
  control orders, **2**, [420]
  exemption from prohibition, **2**, [425]
  offences and penalties, **2**, [421]
meaning, **2**, [422]
pests and diseases, control—
  entry of premises for, **2**, [421]
  examination for, **2**, [420]
  infected bees, destruction, **2**, [420]
  orders for, **2**, [420], [425]

begging
child under sixteen used for, **6**, [4]
offences, **12(1)**, [26]–[27]

Behring Sea Arbitration Award. *See under*
seal fisheries

Belfast Gazette
diplomatic agreements, publication of,
  10, [988]

Belize
British ship registered in, **7(2)**, [755]
citizens of, **7(2)**, [750]
Commonwealth citizenship, **31**, [186]
Constitution Order, **7(2)**, [748]
existing law, operation of, **7(2)**, [749]
fully responsible status of, **7(2)**, [747]
legislative powers of, **7(2)**, [754]
United Kingdom citizenship, and, **7(2)**, [751]
visiting forces in, **7(2)**, [755]

benefice. *See also* **incumbent**
advowson. *See* **advowson**
area of—
  alteration, **14**, 982–3, 1012–13
  meaning, **14**, 1073
augmentation of—
  conveyance, form of, **14**, 95
  grants for, meaning, **14**, 96
  lapse, **14**, 61
  mortgage of, **14**, 152
  perpetual benefice, creation by, **14**, 59–60
  Queen Anne's Bounty, by, **14**, 59–60
  sale of lands for, **14**, 199
avoidance—
  breakdown of pastoral relationship, on,
    14, 892–3
  sequestration, by, **14**, 112
buildings, repair of, **14(S)**, 80–1
Church Commissioners determining questions
  on, **14**, 1073
college headship, severance from, **21**, [36[
corruptly instituting, **14**, 50
creation of, **14**, 982–3
dissolution—
  compensation of incumbent, **14**, 1095
  income, application of, **14**, 1008–9
  pastoral scheme, **14**, 982–3, 997–8

benefice—*contd*

dissolution—*contd*

patronage, rights of, **14**, 1006–7

trusts of property, **14**, 1089–90

endowment—

diocesan stipends fund, paid to, **14**, 867, 871

income—

constitution, **14**, 841–2

pastoral scheme, **14**, 1008–9, 1014

meaning, **14**, 1074

exchange of, **14**, 1150

exempt or peculiar, powers of archbishops and bishops, **14**, 120

incumbents, resignation of, **14**, 1260, 1264

institution to, notice of, **14**, 1148

joint parochial church council, having, **14**, 1170

lease, faculty for, **14(S)**, 119–21

meaning, **14**, 97, 126, 253, 330, 899, 1073, 1162

mortgage of, **14**, 152

name, altering by pastoral order, **14**, 982–3, 1013

new—

incumbent of, **14**, 996–7

deemed admission of, **14**, 1087

patronage, vesting of, **14**, 1006

property, vesting of, **14**, 1088

rectory, to be, **14**, 995–6

status and duties, **14**, 995–6

union of two—

annual personal grant to incumbent, **14**, 838

annuity for stipend, provisions, **14**, 837–8

vicarage, to be, **14**, 995–6

non-residence. *See* **house of residence; incumbent**

oath before institution, **14**, 201

parsonage. *See* **parsonage**

patronage. *See* **patronage**

perpetual, creation of, **14**, 59–60

plurality, held in, **14**, 1170

presentation. *See* **presentation**

profits, receipt of during vacancy, **14**, 42

property, sale of, application of money, **14**, 1009

rentcharge belonging to, power to sell, **14**, 376

residence in—

cathedral duties as, **14**, 105–6

house of. *See* **house of residence**

monition, enforced by, **14**, 110–11

costs, **14**, 112

sequestration on second absence, **14**, 112

proceedings for enforcing, **14**, 220

resignation, corrupt, **14**, 50–1

sales, application of money derived from, **14(S)**, 100

sequestration—

curate, appointment of, **14**, 220

generally, **14**, 1256

incumbent seeking other during, **14**, 237

inhibition during, **14**, 237

benefice—*contd*

sequestration—*contd*

monition, not issuing after, **14**, 123

non-residence, on, **14**, 110–11, 112

payments—

duties, for, **14**, 353

profits, of, **14**, 175

property, dealing with, **14**, 1104–5

regulations, **14**, 122

sequestrator, powers of, **14**, 174

void, becoming, **14**, 113

simoniacal presentation, **14**, 49

sinecure rectory, merging with, **14**, 1010

special provisions applied, **14**, 1151

suspension period. *See* **presentation**

team council, having, **14**, 1170

two or more parishes, comprising, **14**, 1168–9

union of—

rectory, to be, **14**, 995

two or more, **14**, 983

vesting of property, **14**, 1088

university or college—

augmentation by, **21**, [33]

endowment, substitution of lands, **21**, [35]

vacancy of—

advertising, **14**, 1141

collate, right to, **14**, 917

nine months, for—

calculating period, **14**, 1146–7

presentation by archbishop, **14**, 1146–7

notification, **14**, 1136–7

occasional duties in, remuneration for, **14**, 353

profits during, reception of, **14**, 42

selection of incumbent, **14**, 1144

sequestrators, powers of, **14**, 354

suspension of presentation, **14**, 1057–8

temporary provision for, **14**, 1163

tithes and profits, rights to, **14**, 42

trustee of charities during, **14**, 1063

void, presentation to, **14**, 1152

beneficiary

breach of trust, indemnity for, **48**, 534

estates in administration, income from. *See* **administration of estates**

family provision order, **18**, [601], [604]

meaning, **18**, [627], [660]

minor, administration of estate where, **18**, [641]

safeguards, **48**, 223

trust accounts, right to, **48**, 244

Benefit Fraud Inspectorate

Audit Commission, transfers to, **26(2)**, [609], [665]

benefit society

statements to be published by, **8**, 584

form of, **8**, 794–5

benefits in kind
beneficial loan arrangements. *See* **loan**
car. *See* **car**
car fuel. *See* **car**
childcare,
  44(2), [323]–[327]. *See also* **childcare**
code—
  deductions from earnings. *See* **earnings**
  definitions, **44(2)**, [76]
  earnings, relationship with, **44(2)**, [74]
  meaning, **44(2)**, [73]
control, meaning, **44(2)**, [79]
credit-token. *See* **credit-token**
director, meaning, **44(2)**, [77]
dispensations, **44(2)**, [75]
earnings rate, calculation of, **44(2)**, [219]
emergency vehicle, private use of,
  44(2), [249]
employment duties, accommodation, supplies
  and services used in, **44(2)**, [320]
employment, meaning, **44(2)**, [76]
employment-related—
  annual rental value, meaning, **44(2)**, [208]
  application of provisions, **44(2)**, [202]
  cash equivalent, treatment as earnings,
    44(2), [204]
  cost, determination of, **44(2)**, [205]–[207]
  excluded, **44(2)**, [203]
  market value, meaning, **44(2)**, [209]
  meaning, **44(2)**, [202]
  minor benefits, exemption, **44(2)**, [211]
  person providing benefit, meaning,
    44(2), [210]
  used or depreciated assets, transfer of,
    44(2), [207]
health and employment insurance payments,
  44(2), [335]
health-screening, **43(S)**, 1389–90
homeworker, additional household expenses
  of, **44(2)**, [321]
living accommodation. *See* **living
accommodation**
loans. *See* **loans**
long service awards, **44(2)**, [332]
lower-paid employment—
  meaning, **44(2)**, [218]
  provisions not applicable to, **44(2)**, [217]
material interest in company, meaning,
  44(2), [78]
meals or canteen provided for all staff,
  44(2), [322]
medical check-up, **43(S)**, 1389–90
minister of religion, **44(2)**, [292]
mobile telephones, **44(2)**, [328]
overseas medical treatment, **44(2)**, [334]
provisions not applicable to lower-paid
  employment, within, **44(2)**, [75], [217]
related employments, **44(2)**, [221]
removal expenses and benefits—
  exemption from liability to tax—
    acquisition benefits and expenses,
      44(2), [279]
      abortive, **44(2)**, [280]
    amendment of provisions, **44(2)**, [288]
    applicable benefits, **44(2)**, [274]

benefits in kind—*contd*
removal expenses and benefits—*contd*
  exemption from liability to tax—*contd*
    bridging loan expenses, **44(2)**, [286],
      [290]–[291]
    change of residence, conditions
      applicable to, **44(2)**, [275]
    disposal benefits and expenses,
      44(2), [281]
    domestic goods, replacement of,
      44(2), [287]
    employment change, meaning,
      44(2), [277]
    limit on, **44(2)**, [289]
    limitation day, meaning, **44(2)**, [276]
    main residence, reference to,
      44(2), [278]
    scope of, **44(2)**, [273]
    transporting belongings, expenses of,
      44(2), [282]
    travelling and subsistence, **44(2)**, [283]
      deduction allowed, effect of,
        44(2), [284]
      taxable car and van facilities,
        exclusion, **44(2)**, [285]
sale of assets, incidental expenses, **44(2)**, [336]
scholarships—
  arrangements entered into by employer or
    connected person, under, **44(2)**, [213]
  cost of, **44(2)**, [215]
  exemption of income, limitation of,
    44(2), [216]
  special rules for, **44(2)**, [212]
  trusts or schemes, under, **44(2)**, [214]
small gift from third party, **44(2)**, [333]
suggestion awards, **44(2)**, [330]–[331]
van fuel—
  cash equivalent, **44(2)**, [172]
  earnings, benefit treated as, **44(2)**, [171]
  proportionate reduction of cash
    equivalent, **44(2)**, [174]
  reduction of cash equivalent, **44(2)**, [175]
vouchers. *See* **voucher**

benevolent society. *See also* **friendly society**

Bermuda
government of, provisions for, **7(2)**, [618]

betterment levy
generally, **42**, [1]

betting. *See also* **gaming; lottery**
agency permit. *See* **bookmaker**
bet—
  avoidance of, **5(1)**, [616]
  appeal, **5(1)**, [617]
  interim moratorium, **5(1)**, [618]
  financial services, regulated for, **5(1)**, [291]
  spread, **5(1)**, [291]
bet-brokers, **5(1)**, [40]
bookmaker. *See* **bookmaker**
cross-category activities—
  gaming, **5(1)**, [297]
  lotteries, **5(1)**, [299]

betting—*contd*

definitions, **16**, [880]

general betting business—

accounts and records, **5(1)**, [94]

meaning, **5(1)**, [94]

notification of carrying on, **5(1)**, [94]

general betting duty—

accounting period, **5(1)**, [42]

administration of, **5(1)**, [94]

bet-brokers, business of, **5(1)**, [41]

bets with bookmaker, on—

general, **5(1)**, [34]

spread bets, **5(1)**, [35]

betting exchanges, bets on, **5(1)**, [39]

charge of, **5(1)**, [33]

enforcement, **5(1)**, [94]

intended bet, no transmission of, **5(1)**, [57]

liability to pay, **5(1)**, [40]

meaning, **5(1)**, [94]

net stake receipts—

amount of, **5(1)**, [37]

losses, relief for, **5(1)**, [38]

non-payment, evidence of, **5(1)**, [87]

Northern Ireland, in, **5(1)**, [106], [108]

officers, protection of, **5(1)**, [88]

pool betting on horse and dog races, on,
5(1), [36]

intermediary, meaning, **5(1)**, [294]

levy board. *See* **Horserace Betting Levy
Board**

licensed betting office, application for licence
by Totalisator Board, **5(1)**, [22]

meaning, **5(1)**, [290]

minor, by, former provisions as to, **6**, [272]

National Lottery, on, **5(1)**, [376]

non-commercial, **5(1)**, [582]

operating licence, requirement, **5(1)**, [346]

See also **gambling**

payment to enter, definition, **5(1)**, [642]

pool. *See* **pool betting**

premises licence—

children, exclusion of, **5(1)**, [463]

machines, number of, **5(1)**, [462]

pool betting—

children, exclusion of, **5(1)**, [463]

dog racing, **5(1)**, [461]

track, on, **5(1)**, [460]

See also **gambling**

premises, powers of entry, **5(1)**, [94]

private—

conditions for, **5(1)**, [666]

facilities for, provision of, **5(1)**, [576]

prize competition, participation in,
5(1), [292]

summary of provisions, **5(1)**, [1]

totalisator. *See* **totalisator**

track—

bookmaker. *See* **bookmaker**

entry, powers of, **5(1)**, [94]

value added tax, exemption from, **50**, [153]

winnings, status for capital gains tax,
42, [1135]

betting office

provision of sanitary appliances at. *See*
sanitary appliances

betting workers

meaning, **16**, [880]

protected—

meaning, **16**, [639]

reduction of pay, **16**, [642]

Sunday working, as to, **16**, [639]

Sunday working—

contractual requirements, **16**, [640], [646]

detriment, right to not suffer, **16**, [661]

explanatory statement, **16**, [645]

guaranteed hours, contracts with, **16**, [641]

notice of objection to, **16**, [643]

opting-in notice, **16**, [640]

opting-out of, **16**, [644]

protection against, **16**, [639]

refusing, unfair dismissal on, **16**, [748]

transitional provisions, **16**, [893]

Bible

versions, use of, **14**, 648–9

bicycle

brakes, bells etc, fitting of, **37**, [666]

bridleway, riding on, **36**, [774]

carriage of persons on, restrictions, **37**, [595]

cycle track. *See* **cycle track**

cyclist. *See* **cyclist**

inspection of, **37**, [666]

interference with, causing danger, **37**, [593]

long-distance routes, on, **36**, [633]

meaning, **37**, [808]

parking, stands and racks for, **37**, [229], [235]

pedal, electrically assisted—

not treated as motor vehicle, **37**, [805]

under age limit of user, **37**, [603]

racing on public ways, regulation of, **37**, [602]

regulations for, **25(1)**, [63]

taking without authority, **12(1)**, [564]

track—

driving or parking motor vehicle on,
37, [591]

meaning, **37**, [178]

temporary prohibition or restriction on
use, **37**, [178]

bigamy

offence, **12(1)**, [98]

bill of exchange

acceptance—

delay in presentment, **19(1)**, [70]

excuses for non-presentment, **19(1)**, [71]

general, **19(1)**, [49]

honour supra protest for, **19(1)**, [95]

meaning, **19(1)**, [32]

presentment—

rules, **19(1)**, [71]

when necessary, **19(1)**, [69]

qualified, **19(1)**, [49], [74], [82], [107]

requisites, **19(1)**, [47]

time for, **19(1)**, [48]

bill of exchange—*contd*
  acceptance—*contd*
    validity, **19(1)**, [47]
  acceptor—
    holder at maturity, **19(1)**, [91]
    liability of, **19(1)**, [84]
  acceptor for honour—
    dishonour by, **19(1)**, [95]
    liability of, **19(1)**, [95]
    presentment to, **19(1)**, [97]
  accommodation party—
    discharge of, **19(1)**, [89]
    liability of, **19(1)**, [58]
    meaning, **19(1)**, [58]
  action—
    lost instrument, on, **19(1)**, [18]
    meaning, **19(1)**, [32]
  agent—
    personal liability, **19(1)**, [56]
    principal's liability, **19(1)**, [55]
  alteration of, **19(1)**, [94]
  ante-dated, **19(1)**, [43]
  banker—
    authority, revocation of, **19(1)**, [108]
    discharge of, **19(1)**, [90]
    duties as to crossed cheque, **19(1)**, [112]
    liability of, **19(1)**, [113]
    meaning, **19(1)**, [32]
    protection of, **19(1)**, [113], [306]
    rights of, collecting unindorsed cheque, **19(1)**, [304]
  bankrupt, meaning, **19(1)**, [32]
  bankruptcy, rules relating to, **19(1)**, [129]
  bearer, meaning, **19(1)**, [32]
  bill, meaning, **19(1)**, [32]
  British Islands, meaning, **19(1)**, [34]
  cancellation, **19(1)**, [93]
  cheque. *See* **cheque**
  common law, applicability of, **19(1)**, [129]
  company, made, accepted or endorsed by, **8(1)**, [130]
  company name in, **8**, 407
  conflict of laws, **19(1)**, [102]
  consideration, valuable, constitution of, **19(1)**, [57]
  damages, measure on dishonoured bill, **19(1)**, [87]
  delivery—
    generally, **19(1)**, [51]
    meaning, **19(1)**, [32]
    transferor by, **19(1)**, [88]
  discharge of, **19(1)**, [89]–[94]
  dishonour—
    case of need, resort to referee, **19(1)**, [45]
    damages, measure of, **19(1)**, [87]
    delay in giving notice, **19(1)**, [80]
    non-acceptance, by, **19(1)**, [73]
    non-notice of—
      effect, **19(1)**, [78]
      excuses for, **19(1)**, [80]
    non-payment, by, **19(1)**, [77]
    notice, **19(1)**, [78], [79]
    noting of, **19(1)**, [81]
    protest of, **19(1)**, [81]
  dividend warrant, crossed, **19(1)**, [128]

bill of exchange—*contd*
  drawee—
    address to, **19(1)**, [36]
    bankrupt, presentment to, **19(1)**, [71]
    dead, presentment to representative, **19(1)**, [71], [75]
    fictitious persons, **19(1)**, [71]
    liability of, **19(1)**, [83]
    named, **19(1)**, [36]
  drawer and drawee same person, effect, **19(1)**, [35]
  drawer, liability of, **19(1)**, [46], [85]
  foreign bill, meaning, **19(1)**, [34]
  foreign country, bill indorsed in, **19(1)**, [102]
  forged—
    indorsement, banker paying demand draft on, **19(1)**, [90]
    signature, **19(1)**, [54]
  good faith—
    meaning, **19(1)**, [97], [123]
    presumption of, **19(1)**, [60]
  holder—
    duties—
      drawee or acceptor, as to, **19(1)**, [82], [107]
      waiver of, by drawer or indorser, **19(1)**, [46]
    fraudulent, **19(1)**, [59]
    in due course, **19(1)**, [59]
    lost bill, right to duplicate, **19(1)**, [99]
    meaning, **19(1)**, [32]
    presentment for payment by, **19(1)**, [75]
    rights, **19(1)**, [48], [68]
    sets, rules as to, **19(1)**, [101]
    undated bill, rights, **19(1)**, [42]
    value, for, **19(1)**, [57]
  inchoate instrument, **19(1)**, [50]
  indorsee, rights of, **19(1)**, [65]
  indorsement—
    blank, in, **19(1)**, [38], [64]
    conditional, **19(1)**, [63]
    irregular, protection of banker paying, **19(1)**, [303]
    meaning, **19(1)**, [32]
    partial, **19(1)**, [62]
    payees, two or more, by, **19(1)**, [62]
    restrictive, **19(1)**, [65]
    special, **19(1)**, [64]
    valid, requisites of, **19(1)**, [62]
  indorser, liability of, **19(1)**, [46], [85]
  inland bill, meaning, **19(1)**, [34]
  issue, meaning, **19(1)**, [32]
  liability—
    acceptor, of, **19(1)**, [84]
    capacity to incur, **19(1)**, [52]
    corporations, of, **19(1)**, [52]
    infants, of, **19(1)**, [52]
    partners of firm, of, **19(1)**, [53]
    personal, of agent, **19(1)**, [56]
    signature essential to, **19(1)**, [53]
    stranger, of, **19(1)**, [86]
  lien, person having, **19(1)**, [57]
  lost bill—
    action on, **19(1)**, [100]
    holder's right to duplicate, **19(1)**, [99]

bill of exchange—*contd*
lost bill—*contd*
protest, **19(1)**, [81]
making, accepting or endorsing, **8**, 138
making etc, by industrial and provident
society, **19(1)**, [352]
meaning, **19(1)**, [33]
month, meaning, **19(1)**, [44]
name mis-spelt, of payee or indorsee,
19(1), [62]
negotiability, **19(1)**, [38]
negotiation—
dishonoured bill, **19(1)**, [66]
drawer, back to, **19(1)**, [67]
methods of, **19(1)**, [61]
overdue bill, of, **19(1)**, [66]
prior indorser, to, **19(1)**, [67]
non-acceptance, **19(1)**, [72]
non-compliance with stamp laws, **41**, [75]
non-presentment for payment, excuses,
19(1), [76]
note, meaning, **19(1)**, [32]
noting of, **19(1)**, [81], [126]
overdue, negotiation of, **19(1)**, [66]
payable—
after sight, time for presenting, **19(1)**, [70]
future, in, **19(1)**, [41]
on demand, **19(1)**, [40]
to order, **19(1)**, [38]
payee—
certainty as to, **19(1)**, [37]
fictitious or non-existent, **19(1)**, [37]
payment—
computation of time of, **19(1)**, [44]
honour, for, supra protest, **19(1)**, [98]
in due course—
discharge by, **19(1)**, [89]
meaning, **19(1)**, [89]
person, meaning, **19(1)**, [32]
post-dated, **19(1)**, [43]
presentment—
acceptance, rules, **19(1)**, [71]
payment—
delay, excuses for, **19(1)**, [76]
rules, **19(1)**, [75]
postal operator, through, **19(1)**, [71], [75]
promissory note. *See* **promissory note**
protest—
notary not accessible, **19(1)**, [127], [131]
noting equivalent to, **19(1)**, [126]
requirements, **19(1)**, [81]
referee in case of need, **19(1)**, [45], [97]
representative, by, negation of personal
liability, **19(1)**, [56]
sets, rules as to, **19(1)**, [101]
signature—
agent, of, **19(1)**, [124]
blank paper, on, **19(1)**, [50]
corporation, of, **19(1)**, [124]
forged, **19(1)**, [54]
liability, essential to, **19(1)**, [53]
procuration, **19(1)**, [55]
requirements, **19(1)**, [124]
unauthorised, **19(1)**, [54]
value, presumption of, **19(1)**, [60]

bill of exchange—*contd*
sum payable, **19(1)**, [39]
summary of provisions, **19(1)**, [1]
time, computation of, **19(1)**, [125]
transfer, **19(1)**, [38]
transfer for value—
indorsement, without, **19(1)**, [61]
liability on, **19(1)**, [88]
undated, **19(1)**, [33], [42]
unindorsed cheque, protection of banker,
19(1), [303]
validity, **19(1)**, [33]
valuable consideration, constitution of,
19(1), [57]
value—
holder for, **19(1)**, [57]
meaning, **19(1)**, [32]
not specified, **19(1)**, [33]
waiver, **19(1)**, [92]
words and figures, discrepancy, **19(1)**, [39]
written, meaning, **19(1)**, [32]

bill of lading
holder of, **39(2)**, [667]
liabilities under, **39(2)**, [665]
representations in, **39(2)**, [666]
rights under, **39(2)**, [664]

Bill of Rights
enactment of, **10**, [1]
text of, **10**, [40]–[42]

bill of sale
affidavit—
execution of, **39(1)**, [21]
renewal of registration, on, **39(1)**, [22]
swearing of, **39(1)**, [28]
attestation, **39(1)**, [19], [47]
consideration, statement of, **39(1)**, [19], [45]
consumer credit agreement, default under,
39(1), [44]
copies, **39(1)**, [27]
crops, growing—
not separately assigned, **39(1)**, [18]
separately assigned, **39(1)**, [42]
debentures, **39(1)**, [54]
distress, powers of, **39(1)**, [17]
duplicate bill, avoidance, **39(1)**, [20]
entry of satisfaction, **39(1)**, [26]
factory, meaning, **39(1)**, [16]
fees, collection of, **39(1)**, [29]
fixtures—
not separately assigned, **39(1)**, [18]
separately assigned, **39(1)**, [42]
form of, **39(1)**, [46], [56]
goods in, restriction on privilege from distress
for rent, **13**, [1203]
grantors—
index to names of, **39(1)**, [23]
personal chattels, not true owner of,
39(1), [30]
rights following siezure, **39(1)**, [43]
imported goods, exemption of letters of
hypothecation, **39(1)**, [57]
local registration, **39(1)**, [48], [61]

bill of sale—*contd*
  meaning, **39(1)**, [15], [39]
  personal chattels, **39(1)**, [15]
    after acquired, **39(1)**, [41]
    "apparent possession", meaning, **39(1)**, [15]
    distress for rates, **39(1)**, [51]
    inventory of, **39(1)**, [40]
    protection of, against rates, **39(1)**, [51]
    seizure—
      liability to, **39(1)**, [43]
      removal after, **39(1)**, [50]
  property, schedule of, **39(1)**, [40]
  register—
    extracts, power to make, **39(1)**, [53]
    form of, **39(1)**, [23]
    rectification of, **39(1)**, [25]
  registrar—
    entry of satisfaction ordered by, **39(1)**, [26]
    person being, **39(1)**, [24]
  registration—
    filing, time for, **39(1)**, [21], [32], [45]
    local, **39(1)**, [48], [61]
    mode of, **39(1)**, [21]
    renewal, **39(1)**, [22]
    requirements, **39(1)**, [19], [45]
    void without, **39(1)**, [19]
  repealed Acts, under, **39(1)**, [33]
  rules, **39(1)**, [31]
  seizure—
    grantor, rights following, **39(1)**, [43]
    personal chattels, removal after, **39(1)**, [50]
    power of, **39(1)**, [43]
  stamp duty on, **41**, [134]
  trade machinery—
    application of provisions to, **39(1)**, [16]
    meaning, **39(1)**, [16]
  transfer, **39(1)**, [21]
  trust, declaration of, subject to, **39(1)**, [21]
  unregistered bill, avoidance, **39(1)**, [19]
  validity—
    exceptions to avoidance, **39(1)**, [42]
    power of seizure, affected by, **39(1)**, [43]
    void under £30, **39(1)**, [49]
  workshop, meaning, **39(1)**, [16]

bill posting
  offences as to, **36**, [226]

billeting
  air force—
    accommodation provided, **3**, [931]
    appeals, **3**, [932]
    bringing into operation, **3**, [947]
    civilians, application to, **3**, [935]
    compensation for damage, **3**, [933]
    offences, **3**, [777]
    payment for, **3**, [931]
    premises, **3**, [928]
    provision of, **3**, [929]
    refusal, **3**, [934]
    requisitions, **3**, [927]
    schemes, **3**, [930]
    suspension of laws against, **3**, [937]
    vehicles, for, **3**, [928]

billeting—*contd*
  army—
    accommodation provided, **3**, [658]
    appeals against, **3**, [659]
    civilians employed with forces, **3**, [662]
    compensation for damage, **3**, [660]
    local authority, **3**, [663]
    offences, **3**, [504], [661]
    operation of, **3**, [674]
    payment for, **3**, [658]
    premises, **3**, [655]
    provision of, **3**, [656]
    refusal, **3**, [661]
    requisitions, **3**, [654]
    schemes, **3**, [657]
    suspension of laws, **3**, [664]
  legality of, **10**, [28]
  navy—
    generally, **3**, [1366]
    offences, **3**, [1047]
  requisitions, issuing, **3**, [1]

Bills in Parliament
  promoting—
    local authority powers, **25(2)**, [199]
    restriction on, **25(2)**, [60]

bingo. *See also* **amusements with prizes**
  child, employment on premises, **5(1)**, [334]
  club, in course of activities of,
    5(1), [555]. *See also* **club; miners'**
    welfare institute
  combined, **5(1)**, [62]
  duty—
    accounting period, **5(1)**, [59]
    administration, **5(1)**, [96]
    amount, **5(1)**, [58]
    charge of, **5(1)**, [58]
    enforcement, **5(1)**, [96]
    exemptions from, **5(1)**, [95]
    Northern Ireland, application of
      provisions, **5(1)**, [106], [108]
    rates of, **5(S)**, Betting 2
    remote bingo, on, **5(S)**, Betting 6–7
    summary of provisions, **5(1)**, [1]
  hall, prize gaming in, **5(1)**, [571]
  high turnover, **5(1)**, [555]
    pubs, in, **5(1)**, [561]
  licence. *See* **gaming**
  meaning, **5(1)**, [64]
  miners' welfare institute. *See* **miners' welfare**
    institute
  operating licence, **5(1)**, [346], [372]
  premises, powers of entry, **5(1)**, [96]
  premises licence, **5(1)**, [453]
    credit, licensee not to give, **5(1)**, [458]
    See also **gambling**
  Prizes, value of, **5(1)**, [622]
  promoter—
    combined bingo, of, **5(1)**, [62]
    losses, carrying forward, **5(1)**, [63]
    registration, **5(1)**, [96]
  receipts, **5(1)**, [60]
  winnings, expenditure on, **5(1)**, [61]

bioblends
application of hydrocarbon oil provisions to,
13, [825]
excise duty on, **13**, [824]
fuel duty, **43(S)**, 1039–44
minor and consequential amendments,
13, [1101]
rebated, restriction on use of, **43(S)**, 1041–2
used other than as fuel for road vehicles,
rebate for, **43(S)**, 1040–1

biodiesel
application of hydrocarbon oil provisions to,
13, [825]
excise duty on, **13**, [823], [1096]
fuel duty, **43(S)**, 1039–44
meaning, **13**, [817]
minor and consequential amendments,
13, [1101]
rebated, restriction on use of, **43(S)**, 1041–2
road fuel, used otherwise than as, repayment
of duty on, **13**, [842]
used other than as fuel for road vehicles,
rebate for, **43(S)**, 1040–1
warehousing, **13**, [856]

bioethanol
application of hydrocarbon oil provisions to,
13, [828]
blends—
application of hydrocarbon oil provisions
to, **13**, [828]
excise duty on, **13**, [827]
excise duty on, **13**, [826]
meaning, **13**, [818]

biological standards. *See* **National Biological
Standards Board**

biological weapons
body corporate, offences by, **12(1)**, [626]
evidence, obtaining, **12(1)**, [627]
extraterritorial application of provisions,
12(1), [623]
prosecution of offences, **12(1)**, [625]
restriction on development, **12(1)**, [622]
Revenue and Customs prosecutions,
12(1), [624]
search warrant for, **12(1)**, [627]

birds
importation and exportation, restriction on.
See **animals**
sale, etc, restriction on. *See* **animals**

Birmingham
assay office, **48**, 14
assay town, as, **48**, 13
wrought plate—
assaying and marking of, **48**, 13
guardians of standard, **48**, 14

birth
certificate, Factories Acts, application under,
and fee, **18**, [1201]

birth—*contd*
citizenship by. *See* **citizenship**
concealing, **12(1)**, [101]
false statement of particulars, **12(1)**, [198]
notification of, **30**, [1075], [1316]
register, forgery of, **12(1)**, [724]
Registrar General, provision of information
by, **30**, [1076], [1317]

birth, registration of
abandoned child, of, **36**, [73]
aircraft—
commercial, birth in, **4(1)**, [134]
service, birth in, **36**, [143]
armed forces overseas, **36**, [142]
army abroad, evidence of records, **36**, [23],
[24]
birth, meaning, **36**, [116]
certificate—
falsification, **36**, [6]
forgery, **36**, [6], [112]
issue by registrar, **36**, [84]
short form, **36**, [108]
still-birth, **36**, [83]
charges, freedom from, **36**, [75]
delayed, **36**, [76], [77]
district register offices, provision and
maintenance, **36**, [129]
districts, organisation into, **36**, [125]
documents, transmission of, **36**, [64], [115]
fertility treatment, man treated as father
following, **36**, [81]
illegitimate child—
father, registration of, **36**, [80]
re-registration, **36**, [82]
second female parent not in civil
partnership, registration of, **36**, [80]
See also unmarried parents *below*
improper, penalty, **36**, [78]
information—
failure to give, penalty, **36**, [111]
prescribed officer, to, **36**, [79]
requisition by registrar, **36**, [74]
still-births, **36**, [70], [72]
time for giving, **36**, [71], [72]
legitimated persons—
re-registration of, **36**, [86]
service departments, **36**, [147]
live birth, meaning, **36**, [116]
local schemes—
matters to be contained, **36**, [132]
preparation, **36**, [1], [133]
submission and approval, **36**, [133]
marines serving overseas, **36**, [146]
name of child, alteration, **36**, [85]
non-parochial registers—
extracts, **36**, [7]–[11]
searches, **36**, [3]
offences, **36**, [6], [112]
prosecution of, **36**, [113]
offices, **36**, [129], [130]
officials, employment status of, **36**, [204]
parentage, declaration of, re-registration after,
36, [87]

birth, registration of—*contd*
parents not in civil partnership, child of—
  re-registration, **36**, [82]
  second female parent, **36**, [80]
particulars required, **36**, [70]
period of time for—
  expired—
    after twelve months, **36**, [77]
    between three and twelve months,
      36, [76]
registers—
  army and air force, validation of entries,
    36, [146]
  certified copies, **36**, [109]
  compilation, **36**, [1]
  custody, **36**, [102]
  deposit of, **36**, [16]
  errors, correction of, **36**, [103], [104]
  evidence, as, **36**, [4], [11], [109]
  filled, **36**, [102]
  fire-resisting boxes, provision, **36**, [131]
  forgery, **36**, [6]
  form, **36**, [99]
  non-parochial. *See* non-parochial *above*
  offences relating to, **36**, [6], [110], [111]
  preservation, **36**, [1]
  provision, **36**, [99]
  search and inspection, **36**, [3], [107]
  wilful damage to, **36**, [6]
registrars—
  appointment, **36**, [126]
  delivery up of books etc on termination of
    office, **36**, [134]
  deputies, **36**, [127]
  employment status of, **36**, [204]
  fees, **36**, [135]
  interim, **36**, [128]
  meaning, **36**, [116]
  offences by, **36**, [110]
  qualifications, **36**, [126]
  quarterly returns by, **36**, [100]
registration offices, **36**, [129], [130]
regulations, power to make, **36**, [114], [137]
re-registration—
  declaration of parentage, after, **36**, [87]
  legitimated persons, **36**, [86]
  where parents unmarried, **36**, [82]
registration offices, **36**, [129], [130]
regulations, power to make, **36**, [114], [137]
re-registration—
  declaration of parentage, after, **36**, [87]
  legitimated persons, **36**, [86]
  where parents unmarried, **36**, [82]
ships, H.M., birth on board, **36**, [143]
still-birth—
  certificate as to, **36**, [83]
  exposed still-born child, **36**, [70], [72]
  meaning of still-born child, **36**, [116]
  quarterly returns, **36**, [100], [101]
  registers, **36**, [1], [102]
  registration, **36**, [70], [72]
  special provisions, **36**, [83]
sub-district register offices, **36**, [130]
sub-districts, organisation into, **36**, [125]
summary of provisions, **36**, [1]

birth, registration of—*contd*
superintendent registrars—
  appointment, **36**, [126]
  delivery up of books etc on ceasing to hold
    office, **36**, [134]
  deputies, **36**, [127]
  employment status of, **36**, [204]
  fees, **36**, [135]
  indexes kept by, search and copies,
    36, [106]
  interim, **36**, [128]
  meaning, **36**, [116]
  prosecutions by, **36**, [113]
  qualifications, **36**, [126]
  returns—
    by, **36**, [101]
    to, **36**, [100]
time for, **36**, [71], [72], [76], [77]
unmarried parents, child of—
  father, **36**, [80]
  re-registration, **36**, [82]

bishop
absence of, exercise of powers, **14**, 898
assistant, delegation of function to,
  14(S), 136–8
authorisation of office after retiring age,
  14, 822
cathedral, as Visitor of, **14**, 1343
chaplain to, stipend of, **14**, 411
charity trustee, substitution of, **5(2)**, [478]
church representation rules, powers under,
  14, 751–2
colonial, **14**, 178
commendam not to be held by, **14**, 93
complaint against—
  articles, content of, **14**, 582
  commission of convocation—
    appointment of, **14**, 583
    conduct of trial by, **14**, 583–4
  episcopal committee, inquiry by, **14**, 581–2
  finding, action on, **14**, 584
  institution of proceedings, **14**, 573–4
complaint of offence, dealing with, **14**, 576,
  585
conference of diocese, summoning, **14**, 688
consecration of, **14**, 25–6
consent of, signifying, **14**, 388
Crown, appointed by, **14**, 23–4
curate, appointing, **14**, 115–16
declaration by, recording, **14**, 609
delegation of functions, **14**, 913–14
deposition from Holy Orders, **14**, 594
deprivation—
  effect of, **14**, 594
  offence, after conviction of, **14**, 597–8
diocesan—
  Acts conferring functions on, **14(S)**, 140
  deputy performing functions of, **14**, 949
  retiring age, service after, **14**, 821–2
  seniority, determining, **14**, 604
  statutory functions, **14**, 918
suffragan, temporary delegation to,
  14, 913–14
vacation of see, powers during, **14**, 604

bishop—*contd*

diocesan board of finance, member of, **14**, 332–3

diocesan synod, consulting, **14**, 688

Diocese in Europe, of. *See* **Europe, Diocese in**

dioceses commission advising, **14**, 906

disability—
    medical examination of, **14**, 1113
    retirement in case of, **14**, 1113–114

disciplinary proceedings—
    institution of, **14(S)**, 8–9
    jurisdiction, **14(S)**, 5–6
    misconduct, for, **14(S)**, 7
    suspension during, **14(S)**, 29–30
    institution of, **14(S)**, 8–9
    jurisdiction, **14(S)**, 5–6
    misconduct, for, **14(S)**, 7
    suspension during, **14(S)**, 29–30

discipline, role in, **14(S)**, 2

election of—
    default in, **14**, 23–4
    validation, **14**, 26

episcopal functions, scheme for discharge of—
    making, **14**, 915–16
    provision for, **14**, 914–15
    variation of, **14**, 916–17

episcopal ministry, keeping under review, **14(S)**, 136

evidence, verifying, **14**, 126

exchange of benefices, agreement to, **14**, 1150

exempt or peculiar benefices, powers on, **14**, 120

fees paid by, reimbursement of, **14**, 1126

foreign country, in—
    consecration, **14**, 147–8
    spiritual jurisdiction, **14**, 147

house of. *See* **General Synod**

house of residence, certification of, **14**, 389

inhibition, performance of duties during, **14**, 605–6

installation of, **14**, 25–6

jurisdiction of, concurrent jurisdiction ceasing, **14**, 121

jus patronatus, proceedings by, **14**, 564

legal effects of consecration, removal of, **14**, 1231–2
    Crown land, **14**, 1232–3

letters patent, presentation by, **14**, 23–4

medical examination, **14**, 1113, 1117

mission—
    church buildings closed for regular public worship, functions concerning, **14(S)**, 157
    Code of Practice, **14(S)**, 170
    committee. *See* **mission and pastoral committee**
    initiative, **14(S)**, 162–4
        review of duration, **14(S)**, 168
    local ecumenical project, participation in, **14(S)**, 169
    order, provisions in, **14(S)**, 166–8
    visitor, designation of, **14(S)**, 165

new—
    provisions on, **14**, 924

bishop—*contd*

new—*contd*
    residence for, **14**, 922
    stipend of, **14**, 922

office expenses, **14**, 411

orders of, **14**, 1237

overseas—
    episcopal functions, performing, **14**, 658–9
    meaning, **14**, 660

parochial church council—
    making representations to, **14**, 492
    powers, bringing into effect, **14**, 493

pastoral committee, chairman of, **14**, 1081

pastoral proposals, submitting, **14**, 981

patronage, transfer of right of, **14**, 338–9, 925

precedence of, **33(1)**, [4]

proceedings for offences by, **14**, 572

proposals, power to formulate and submit, **14(S)**, 151

refusal to institute presentee, effect of, **14**, 1148

reorganisation scheme, submitting proposal for, **14**, 908

resignation—
    archbishop's acceptance of, **14**, 1112
    delegation of functions, **14**, 1108
    discharge of functions on, **14(S)**, 138–9
    written form, in, **14**, 1112

retirement—
    age-limit, on reaching, **14**, 1113
    church dignitaries, of, powers, **14**, 434
    incapacity, in case of, **14**, 1113
        medical examination, **14**, 1113
    pensions, provisions as to, **14**, 1116

retiring age, continuing in office after, **14**, 821–2

senior, **14**, 1109

sentences of imprisonment and matrimonial orders, effect of, **14(S)**, 25–6

stipend—
    Church Commissioners paying, **14**, 411
    common fund of Commissioners, secured on, **14**, 409
    power of Commissioners to pay, **14(S)**, 145

suffragan—
    collation, rights of, **14**, 917; **14(S)**, 140
    commission, not exceeding, **14**, 41
    consecration—
        costs of, **14**, 41
        time for, **14**, 40
    delegation of functions to, **14**, 913–14; **14(S)**, 136–8
    functions discharged by, **14**, 917–18
    person already consecrated as, **14**, 249
    petition for, **14**, 919–20
    power to commission, abolition, **14**, 917–18
    powers of, **14**, 40
    reorganisation scheme affecting, **14**, 925
    residence of, **14**, 41
    sees of, **14**, 38–9, 248
    vacating office, scheme for, **14**, 925

suspension, performance of duties during, **14**, 605–6

bishop—*contd*
  trial of, **14**, 557
  verification of statements to, **14**, 126

bishopric
  new, scheme for, **14**, 907, 924
  re-endowment, scheme for, **14**, 375
  vacancy—
    archbishop exercising powers, **14**, 1109
    declaration of, effect of, **14**, 1116

black lead
  metallic mineral, as, **11(2)**, [66]

Blackfriars Bridge
  trunk road, not being, **36**, [1013]

blackmail
  offence, **12(1)**, [572]; **12(2)**, [162]

blasphemous libel
  common law offence, abolition, **12(4)**, [509]

blasphemy
  common law offence, abolition, **12(4)**, [509]

blight notice
  agricultural unit—
    meaning, **46**, [417]
    owner-occupier, **46**, [414]
    protection of interests, **46**, [395]
    right to sell, **46**, [412]
    whole, requiring purchase of—
      effect of, **46**, [406]
      objection to, **46**, [405]
      service of, **46**, [404]
  appropriate authority, meaning, **46**, [415]
  appropriate enactment, meaning, **46**, [416]
  boundary, land on, **46**, [417]
  claimant—
    compulsory acquisition of interest of,
      46, [400]
    death of, **46**, [407]
    meaning, **46**, [396]
    sale of hereditament, etc, right of,
      46, [412]
  compensation for acquisitions, **46**, [403]
  compulsory acquisition following, **46**, [400]
  counter-notice—
    compulsory acquisition powers, effect on,
      46, [401]
    further, **46**, [398]
    objections in, **46**, [397]
  Crown land, and, **46**, [562]
  hereditament—
    meaning, **46**, [417]
    owner-occupier, **46**, [414]
    protection of interests, **46**, [395]
    right to sell, **46**, [412]
  meaning, **46**, [395]
  mortgagee, service by, **46**, [408]
  new street order, land affected by, **46**, [632]
  new town order, land affected by, **46**, [632]
  notice to treat, withdrawal of, **46**, [413]

blight notice—*contd*
  objection—
    acquisition, assistance for, **46**, [579]
    compulsory acquisition powers, effect on,
      46, [401]
    Lands Tribunal, reference to, **46**, [399]
    mortgagee, notice served by, **46**, [408]
    service of, **46**, [397]
  owner-occupier—
    meaning, **46**, [414]
    partnership as, **46**, [410]
    resident, **46**, [414]
  partnership, hereditament etc occupied by,
    46, [410]
  personal representative, service by, **46**, [407]
  power to serve, **46**, [396]
  proposed compulsory purchase order, land
    affected by, **46**, [632]
  proposed structure plan, in relation to,
    46, [632]
  scope of provisions, **46**, [395]
  Secretary of State, purchase of land by,
    46, [411]
  simultaneous, prohibition of service of,
    46, [409]
  urban development area, in, **46**, [632]
  valid, effect of, **46**, [400]
  withdrawal of, **46**, [402]

blind person
  aids for, zero-rating, **50**, [151]
  goods sold as made by—
    control of, **47**, [53]
      bodies exempt from, **47**, [53]
    house to house or post, by, **47**, [53]
    offences, **47**, [53]
  highway, regards to needs on, **36**, [1241]
  reference to, **47**, [54]
  relief for, **44(1)**, [156]
  television services, code for—
    duty to draw up, **45**, [672]
    issue and revision, procedure for, **45**, [673]
    observance of, **45**, [676]
    relevant date, meaning, **45**, [674]
    targets, power to modify, **45**, [675]
  travel concession for, **37**, [430]

blood sample
  taking as evidence. *See* **search** (intimate)

blood tests. *See* **parentage**

Board of Audit
  audit by, **19(2)**, [621]

Board of Guardians
  adaptation of references to, **25(1)**, [163]

board of inquiry
  air force—
    absence, into, **3**, [906]
    generally, **3**, [905]
  army—
    absence, into, **3**, [633]
    evidence, **3**, [632]

board of inquiry—*contd*
  army—*contd*
    investigations by, **3**, [632]
    members, **3**, [632]
    rules, **3**, [631]

Board of Trade. *See also* **Secretary of State for Transport**
  title, **39(2)**, [109]

boarding school
  inspections, annual fee for, **6**, [419]
  inspectors—
    appointment of, **6**, [416]
    duties of, **6**, [417]
  welfare of children in—
    generally, **6**, [415]
    national minimum standards for
      safeguarding, **6**, [418]

boat. *See also* **pleasure boat**
  council tax, liability to, **26(1)**, [7]
  non-domestic rating, **26(1)**, [240], [241]
  private pleasure craft, fuel used in,
    43(S), 1047–9
  public health provisions applicable to certain,
    35(1), [169]

Bodleian Library
  legal deposit library, as, **13**, [467]

body corporate. *See also* **companies**;
  corporation
  associate, meaning, **8(1)**, [1338]
  associated, meaning, **8(1)**, [334]
  contract, making, **11(1)**, [303]
  control, meaning, **44(1)**, [622]
  director connected with, meaning, **8(1)**, [332]
  director controlling, meaning, **8(1)**, [333]
  false statements by member, **12(1)**, [570]
  financial year, meaning, **8**, 284
  housing action trust as, **22**, [849]
  meaning, **8**, 600
  migration, **44(1)**, [495]
  mutual business, distribution of assets,
    44(1), [330]
  offences by, **8**, 595–6, 849, 890; **22**, [413];
    23, [536]; **24**, [397]
  officer in default, application of provisions,
    8(1), [1201]
  sale etc of land for housing, **22**, [34]
  statutory auditor, offences relating to,
    8(1), [1333]
  subsidiaries, definitions, **44(1)**, [620]

bollards on roads
  authority for use, **37**, [264]
  grants and loans, **37**, [264]
  Greater London, **37**, [266]
  local traffic authority, powers and duties,
    37, [265]
  outside Greater London, **37**, [264]
  powers of Secretary of State, **37**, [265]
  traffic authority, powers, **37**, [265]

bomb
  hoax, **12(1)**, [688]

bona vacantia
  Crown disclaimer of property vesting as—
    effect of, **8(1)**, [1092]
      England and Wales, in,
        8(1), [1093]–[1097]
      Northern Ireland, **8(1)**, [1093]–[1097]
    leaseholds, **8(1)**, [1094]
    notice of, **8(1)**, [1091]
    persons holding under lease, protection of,
      8(1), [1096]
    rentcharge, land subject to, **8(1)**, [1097]
    time for, **8(1)**, [1091]
    vesting order, power of court to make,
      8(1), [1095]
  disclaimer by Crown, **8**, 521–2
  dissolution of company, on, **8**, 523
  property being, **8(1)**, [1090]
  restoration to register, effect on property,
    8(1), [1112]
  revival of company, effect of, **8**, 522–3

bond
  entry on land on giving, **9**, [48], [297]
  securing annuity, **41**, [39]
  security by, **13**, [762]

bonfire
  street offence, **36**, [226], [385]

book debts
  assignment, avoidance on bankruptcy,
    4(2), [428]
  charge on, registration, **8**, 455–6

Book of Common Prayer
  amendments, **14**, 15
  Bible, use of versions of, **14**, 648–9
  burial service for suicides, **14**, 661
  Holy Commission, admission to, **14**, 773
  Holy Scripture, order of, **14**, 225–6
  meaning, **14**, 648–9
  Tables of Lessons, substitution of, **14**, 225,
    227–36, 305–25

bookmaker. *See also* **betting**
  bet-brokers, **5(1)**, [40]
  Bookmakers Committee—
    constitution of, **5(1)**, [7]
    members, remuneration, **5(1)**, [7]
    schemes for, **5(1)**, [8]
  general betting duty. *See* **betting**
  levy—
    appeal tribunals—
      constitution of, **5(1)**, [10]
      general provisions, **5(1)**, [10]
    assessment of—
      appeal from, **5(1)**, [9], [16]
      declaration for purposes of, **5(1)**, [15]
      generally, **5(1)**, [9]
      individuals, of, **5(1)**, [15]
      notice of, **5(1)**, [9]
    certificate of payment, **5(1)**, [9]

bookmaker—*contd*
  levy—*contd*
    contributions by Totalisator Board—
      determination of, **5(1)**, [17]
      provision for, **5(1)**, [11]
      remission of, **5(1)**, [26]
    default, non-renewal of permit on,
      5(1), [17]
    exemption from, **5(1)**, [9]
    payment on account—
      amount, determination of, **5(1)**, [28]
      appeals in respect of, **5(1)**, [29]
      excess, repayment, **5(1)**, [31]
      notices, service of, **5(1)**, [31]
      relief from, **5(1)**, [30]
      scheme providing for, **5(1)**, [28]
    schemes—
      annual, determination of, **5(1)**, [14]
      provisions made in, **5(1)**, [8]
      recommendations by Committee as to,
        5(1), [8]
  licensed betting office. *See* **betting**
  meaning, **5(1)**, [12]
  renewal of permit, refusal for non-payment of
    levy, **5(1)**, [17]

books
  infected, use of, **13**, [49]
  inspection of, for stamp duty purposes,
    41, [32]
  printer's name and address on—
    duty to print, **19(3)**, [283]
    failure to print, penalty for, **19(3)**, [283]
    relaxation of requirements, **19(3)**, [322]
    university presses, **19(3)**, [283]
  zero-rating, **50**, [151]

Border and Immigration Agency
  Chief Inspector—
    appointment, **31(S)**, Nationality 48
    efficiency and effectiveness of Agency,
      report on, **31(S)**, Nationality 48
    plans by, **31(S)**, Nationality 50–1
    remuneration and allowances,
      31(S), Nationality 49
    reports, **31(S)**, Nationality 50
  establishment of, **31(S)**, Nationality 48
  other bodies, relationship with—
    generally, **31(S)**, Nationality 51
    non-interference notices,
      31(S), Nationality 52
  prescribed matters, **31(S)**, Nationality 53

borehole
  mining operations affecting water
    conservation, notice of, **49**, [1248]
  sinking of, notice required, **49**, [1247]

borough
  charter of incorporation—
    effect of, **25(2)**, [209]
    petition for, **25(2)**, [206]
  corporation as charitable trustee, **25(1)**, [28];
    25(2), [170]
  county, accounting to, **25(1)**, [36]

borough—*contd*
  creation of, **25(1)**, [1]
  existing, preservation of rights etc,
    25(2), [209]
  freedom of trading in, **25(1)**, [40]
  freemen, rights etc, **25(2)**, [211]
  fund—
    application of, **25(1)**, [33]
    payments out of, **25(1)**, [47]
  honorary recorder, **11(2)**, [255]
  incorporation. *See* **municipal corporation**
  rate, application of, **25(1)**, [34]
  status of, **25(2)**, [206]

borough council. *See also* **local authority**
  borrowing powers, **25(1)**, [687]
  general rate fund, use of, **25(1)**, [687]
  lighting, local Acts provisions, **25(1)**, [31]
  London. *See* **London borough council**

borrowing
  government, repeal of provisions,
    19(2), [1019]

Borstal training
  references to, change in, **12(1)**, [1114]

Botswana, Republic of
  Commonwealth citizenship, **31**, [186]
  establishment of, **7(2)**, [591]
  existing law, operation of, **7(2)**, [592]
  visiting forces in, **7(2)**, [594]

bottomry
  insurable interest of lender, **19(1)**, [155]

boundaries
  ecclesiastical—
    Church Commissioners determining,
      14, 1067–8
    disputed, adjudication on, **14**, 74
  road, powers of local authorities, **37**, [299]

Boundary Commission for England
  local government review—
    conduct of, **26(2)**, [506]
    consultation, **26(2)**, [507]
    direction for, **26(2)**, [212]
    information, provision of, **26(2)**, [213]
    Isles of Scilly, provision for, **26(2)**, [219]
    Local Government Act 1992, application
      of, **26(2)**, [217]
    meaning, **26(2)**, [213]
    number of people in area, determining,
      26(2), [213]
    procedure for, **26(2)**, [214]
    recommendations, **26(2)**, [215]
      implementation, **26(2)**, [216]
    referendum, in relation to, **26(2)**, [212],
      [507], [508]
  single tier local government—
    powers of, **26(2)**, [503]
    procedure, **26(2)**, [504]
    request for advice on proposals,
      26(2), [502]

Boundary Commissions
assistant Commissioners, **15(3)**, [264]
chairman, **15(3)**, [264]
constitution of, **15(3)**, [255], [264]
continuation of, **15(3)**, [255]
deputy chairman, **15(3)**, [264]
Electoral Commission—
functions, transfer to, **15(3)**, [316],
[484]–[485]
property, transfer to, **15(3)**, [317]
electoral quota—
meaning, **15(3)**, [265]
observing, **15(3)**, [265]
expenses, **15(3)**, [264]
local inquiry, holding, **15(3)**, [260]
members, **15(3)**, [264]
remuneration, **15(3)**, [271]
officers, **15(3)**, [264]
Orders in Council, provisions on,
15(3), [258]
procedure, **15(3)**, [264]
recommendations by—
generally, **15(3)**, [257]
notices regarding, publication of,
15(3), [259]
redistribution of seats—
periodical reports, **15(3)**, [256]
rules, **15(3)**, [265]
report—
general provisions, **15(3)**, [256]
intervals between, **15(3)**, [256]
local government boundaries to be taken
into account, **15(3)**, [273]
notices regarding, publication of,
15(3), [259]
time limits for submission of, **15(3)**, [272]
reviews by, **15(3)**, [257]

bracken
burning, regulation of, **1(1)**, [372]

branch or agency
replacement of references to, **43(2)**, [219]

brawling
jurisdiction over, **14**, 192–3

breach of duty
deep sea mining, arising from, **17(1)**, [526]
limitation of liability for, **19(3)**, [735]
offshore installations, civil liability,
17(1), [449]
servant, by, liability of mine or quarry
owner, **17(1)**, [138]

breach of promise
abolition of action, **27**, [346]

breach of statutory duty
apology, effect of, **31(S)**, Negligence 2
offer of treatment or other redress, effect of,
31(S), Negligence 2
potential liability, deterrent effect,
31(S), Negligence 1

breach of the peace
plays, provocation by, **13**, [185]

breath tests. *See under* **road traffic offences**

Bretton Woods Agreements
continuation of orders, **19(2)**, [958]
passing of, **19(1)**, [1]

bribery
acts amounting to, **15(3)**, [115]
committed outside UK, **12(3)**, [138]
Director of Serious Fraud Office, powers,
12(1), [1058]
foreign officials, of, **12(3)**, [137]
harbour master or officers, of, **39(2)**, [52]
licensed premises, on, **15(3)**, [159]
Port of London Authority, **39(2)**, [401]

brickfield
charge to tax, **44(1)**, [34]
rent payable in respect of, **44(1)**, [98]

bridge
accommodation works, **36**, [319]
acquisition of land for, **36**, [1288], [1301]
acquisition of rights over land for, **36**, [1288],
[1294]
alteration of, authority requiring, **36**, [1242]
apparatus in and attached to structure,
placing, **38(1)**, [231]
approach to—
highway authority for, **36**, [1007]
materials for repair, **36**, [1049], [1050]
meaning, **36**, [1109], [1381]
privately maintainable, **36**, [1053]
reconstruction and improvement,
36, [1107], [1109]
authority—
meaning, **10**, [169]; **38(1)**, [231]
notice of works to, **38(1)**, [231]
breaking up, gas supplier's powers,
17(1), [696]
canal, over—
Manchester Ship Canal, exclusion of
provisions on, **36**, [1109]
reconstruction interfering with traffic,
36, [1109]
cattle-grid, consent for work on, **36**, [1093]
charge to tax, **44(1)**, [34]
Commissioner of Works, conveyance by,
10, [169]
construction of—
expenses of, **36**, [1302]
highway authority, by, **36**, [1105]
licence for, **36**, [1242]
restriction on, **36**, [1242]
highway—
footbridge over, **36**, [1073]
part of, being, **36**, [1380]
restriction on construction, **36**, [1242]
highway authority for, **36**, [1007]
improvement of—
arbitration, reference to, **36**, [1414]
contribution to costs, **36**, [1108]

bridge—*contd*
improvement of—*contd*
  expenses, apportionment of, **36**, [633]
  orders—
    commencement of, postponement,
      36, [1414]
    limitation on matters dealt with,
      36, [1414]
    power to make, **36**, [1107]
    procedure for making, **36**, [1414]
  powers, exercise of, **36**, [1109]
  public utility undertakers, provisions as to,
    36, [1414]
inland waterway, over—
  highway, responsibility for maintenance,
    36, [855]
  load-bearing capacity, **36**, [856]
  owner, duties of, **36**, [856]
  trunk or special road, carrying, **36**, [858]
  undertakers, provisions applying to,
    36, [859]
  Waterways Board—
    duties of, **36**, [856]
    works by, **36**, [857]
level crossing, substituted for, **36**, [1302]
London—
  byelaws, enforcement, **25(1)**, [75]
  heat supply works affecting, **25(1)**, [452]
maintenance and repair—
  agreement for, **36**, [1043]
  contribution to, **36**, [1325]
  expenses of, **36**, [1302]
  extinguishment of liability, **36**, [1058]
  materials for repair, **36**, [1049], [1050]
  power of entry, **36**, [1341]
major works—
  affecting undertakers' apparatus,
    38(1), [227]
  meaning, **38(1)**, [231]
meaning, **36**, [1381]; **38(1)**, [231]
modification of construction, **36**, [317]
navigable waters, over—
  construction, order or scheme for,
    36, [1125]
  diversion of watercourse, order for,
    36, [1127]
  navigation, reasonable needs of, **36**, [1126]
  objections to, **36**, [1126]
  plans and specifications of, **36**, [1126]
  schemes, **36**, [1398]
offences on, **36**, [221], [222]
opening span, with user of, **36**, [445]
owners, meaning, **36**, [1109]
pipe-line in or on, etc, **17(1)**, [250]
privately maintainable—
  approaches to, **36**, [1053]
  improvement of, **36**, [1107]
  liability, extinguishment of, **36**, [1058]
  reconstruction of, **36**, [1107]
railway, carrying over road—
  dimensions, **36**, [302]
  gradient, **36**, [302], [305]
  level crossing, required instead of, **36**, [441]
  provision of, **36**, [299]
  width of, **36**, [304]

bridge—*contd*
railway company, maintenance by, **36**, [316]
railway, over—
  highway, responsibility for maintenance,
    36, [855]
  load-bearing capacity, **36**, [856]
  London Regional Transport—
    duties of, **36**, [856]
    works by, **36**, [857]
  owner, duties of, **36**, [857]
  Railway Board—
    duties of, **36**, [856]
    works by, **36**, [857]
  trunk or special road, carrying, **36**, [858]
  undertakers, provisions applied to,
    36, [859]
reconstruction of—
  arbitration, reference to, **36**, [1414]
  contributions to costs, **36**, [1108]
  expenses, apportionment of, **36**, [1414]
  highway authority, by, **36**, [1106]
  meaning, **36**, [1381]
  orders—
    commencement, postponement of,
      36, [1414]
    limitation on matters dealt with,
      36, [1414]
    power to make, **36**, [1107]
    procedure for making, **36**, [1414]
  powers, exercise of, **36**, [1109]
  public utility undertakers, provisions as to,
    36, [1414]
refuse bin placed on, **36**, [1248]
removal of, authority requiring, **36**, [1242]
rent payable in respect of, **44(1)**, [98]
repair, enforcement of obligations,
  19(3), [190]
road, carrying over railway—
  construction, regulations on, **36**, [303]
  gradient, **36**, [303], [305]
  level crossing, required instead of, **36**, [441]
  provision of, **36**, [299]
  width of, **36**, [304]
road, interference with. *See* **road**
special road, carrying—
  liability to maintain, extinguishment,
    36, [1058]
  transfer of, **36**, [1315]
storage bin placed on, **36**, [1248]
street works on. *See* **street works**
swing—
  meaning, **36**, [1381]
  operation of, **36**, [1107]
  orders relating to, **36**, [1414]
tidal water, across, **36**, [444]
traffic on, controls removed, **25(2)**, [449]
trailer, excess weight carried by, **37**, [188]
tramway, construction of, **36**, [499]
transfer of liability for, **36**, [1108]
trunk road bridge—
  meaning, **36**, [1109]
  reconstruction or improvement, **36**, [1107],
    [1109]

bridge—*contd*

trunk road, carrying—
liability to maintain, extinguishment,
36, [1058]
transfer of, 36, [1312]
undertaking carried on by owners, over,
36, [1312]
water or ravine, over, 36, [1312]
two areas, situated in, 36, [1109]
two districts, in, 25(2), [637]
water, carrying railway over, 36, [444]
widening of highway on, 36, [1078]
works—
acquisition of land for, 36, [1288]
affecting street works undertakers'
apparatus, 38(1), [227]
consents for, 36, [1411]
notice of, 38(1), [231]

bridleway

agricultural land, passing over—
ploughing, 36, [1190]
works on, authorisation, 36, [1191]
amenities, provision. *See* **highway (services
etc)**
bicycle, riding on, 36, [774]
creation of. *See* **public path**
dedication of, 36, [1029]
district council maintaining, 36, [1046],
[1054], [1409]
disturbance—
authorisation of works, 36, [1191]
surface, of, 36, [1190], [1419]
unlawful, 36, [1187]
diversion of. *See* **public path**
evidence of, 37, [89]
excepted highways, 38(2), [60]
expenses, contributions to, 36, [1323]
extinguishment of. *See* **public path**
field-edge path, meaning, 36, [1381]
gates across, 36, [1208]
local authority using vehicles on, 36, [1350]
maintenance and repair—
highway authority, default powers of,
36, [1061]
liability, enforcement of, 36, [1060]
proceedings for order, at, 36, [1060]
public expense, at, 36, [1041]
surface, making good—
entry on land, 36, [1419]
expenses, 36, [1419]
requirement, 36, [1419]
making up, 36, [1031]
meaning, 36, [1381]; 37, [96], [315], [808]
motor vehicle—
driving on, 37, [301], [605]
trials on, 37, [604]
open to all traffic, 37, [301]
order—
confirmation of, 46, [633]
publicity, 46, [634]
orders—
notice of, 36, [1407]
procedure for making, 36, [1407]
validity and operation, 36, [1408]

bridleway—*contd*

parish or community council maintaining,
36, [1047]
ploughing—
enforcement provisions, 36, [1190]
expenses, 38(1), [156]
making good, 36, [1190], [1419]
other works, authorisation, 36, [1191]
period allowed for, 36, [1190]
right to, 36, [1190]
temporary diversion, 36, [1191]
power of entry on, 36, [1343]
privately maintainable, 36, [1054]
public right of way, extinguishment of,
46, [523]
rail crossing diversion orders, 36, [1154]
railway—
crossing—
stopping up, 36, [1149]
See further **rail crossing; railway**
railway or tramway, over, 38(1), [327]
recreation or refreshment facilities on,
36, [1137]
repairs. *See* maintenance and repair *above*
right of way orders affecting, 37, [95]
services and amenities on. *See* **highway**
signposting, 36, [773]
stile or gate on—
erection, authorisation of, 36, [1210]
maintenance of, 36, [1209]
stopping up, 36, [1147]
stopping up or diversion, 46, [522]
survey of, 36, [1031]
temporary prohibition or restriction on
traffic, 37, [178]
tramway, crossing, 38(1), [327]
wardens, appointment of, 37, [94]
ways shown as, bridleway rights over,
38(2), [61]
extinguishment date, 38(2), [62]
widening, power of, 36, [1075]
works, carrying out, 36, [1031]
young riders using, 6, [458]

British Aerospace

acquired companies—
assets, vesting of, 47, [317]
associated privately owned companies—
meaning, 47, [299]
property etc, vesting of, 47, [299]
meaning, 47, [311]
securities—
conditions for vesting, 47, [314]
meaning, 47, [298], [311]
vesting of, 47, [298], [313]
vesting of assets in, 47, [317]
arbitration tribunal. *See* **Aircraft and
Shipbuilding Industries Arbitration
Tribunal**
compensation stock, 47, [300]
dissolution of—
appointed day, agreements etc in force on,
47, [344], [352]
employment contracts, effect on, 47, [352]
provisions for, 47, [347]
employees, pensions, 47, [306]

British Aerospace—*contd*
information, disclosure, restriction on,
47, [307]
liabilities etc of, **47**, [308]
nominated company, appointed day, **47**, [350]
notices, service of, **47**, [309]
pensions, **47**, [306]
Secretary of State, liability for obligations,
47, [346]
successor company—
appointed day. *See* dissolution *above*
corporation tax liability of, **47**, [348]
development land tax liability, **47**, [348]
dissolution duties of, **47**, [347]
financial structure of, **47**, [345]
meaning, **47**, [344]
nomination of, **47**, [344]
obligations vesting in, Secretary of State's
liability as to, **47**, [346]
regional development grants, **47**, [352]
statutory reserve of, **47**, [345]
vesting of property etc in, **47**, [344]
works, meaning, **47**, [311]

British Airports Authority. *See* **Airports
Authority**

British Airways Board
assets and liabilities, vesting, **4(1)**, [41], [51]
dissolution, **4(1)**, [46]
foreign currency borrowing, **4**, [81]
pension schemes, provisions as to, **4(1)**, [51]
property, vesting, **4(1)**, [41]
public dividend capital, reduction, **4(1)**, [40]
regional development grants, **4(1)**, [51]
successor company—
agreements, modification, **4(1)**, [51]
British Airways plc as, **4(1)**, [1]
financial structure, **4(1)**, [43]
nomination of, **4(1)**, [41]
Secretary of State, administrative expenses,
4(1), [48]
shareholding in, initial, **4(1)**, [42]
shares and securities—
government investment in, **4(1)**, [44],
[45]
initial government holding, **4(1)**, [42]
target investment limit, **4(1)**, [45]
Trustee Investment Act, application,
4, [70]
vesting of property in, **4(1)**, [41]
transfer of assets, **44(1)**, [372]
transitional provisions, **4(1)**, [46], [52]

British Airways plc
establishment, **4(1)**, [1]

British Antarctic Territory
law of, jurisdiction and proceedings under,
17(1), [726]
minerals, exploration etc for. *See* **antarctic
minerals**

British Broadcasting Company
former, **45**, [1]

British Broadcasting Corporation. *See also*
digital broadcasting (sound)
Charter and Agreement, meaning, **45**, [724]
dealers, television sets—
information, call for, **45**, [29]
transactions, requirements as to, **45**, [29]
establishment, **45**, [1]
independent productions, programme quotas
for, **45**, [648], [764]
international obligations, directions by
Secretary of State as to, **45**, [176]
land, provisions applied, **25(2)**, [450]
licence fees, statement of charging principles,
45, [711]
news and current affairs programmes,
45, [650]
OFCOM's functions in relation to, **45**, [582]
original productions, programming quotas
for, **45**, [649]
party political broadcasts, **45**, [699]
programme commissioning, code relating to,
45, [656]
programme quotas for—
independent productions, **45**, [648], [764]
original productions, **45**, [649]
public service remit, OFCOM to report on
fulfilment of, **45**, [635]
services provided by BBC companies,
45, [295]
television licensing powers, transfer to,
45, [171]
transmission network transfer schemes—
agreements with respect to, **45**, [292]
compensation, **45**, [308]
consideration for, **45**, [308]
contents of, **45**, [308]
division of BBC's undertaking by scheme,
45, [308]
effects of, **45**, [308]
modification of, by agreement, **45**, [308]
notice to persons affected by, **45**, [308]
power to make, **45**, [290]
property to which may relate, **45**, [308]
Secretary of State's powers in relation to,
45, [291]
successor companies, **45**, [309]
supplemental provisions of, **45**, [308]
taxation provisions, **45**, [310]
vesting of property, certificate of Secretary
of State as to, **45**, [308]

British Coal Corporation
arbitration, provisions as to, **17(1)**, [18]
borrowing by, loans, extinguishment,
17(2), [146]
Coal Industry Social Welfare Organisation. *See*
**Coal Industry Social Welfare
Organisation**
compulsory acquisition of land, protection of
interests, **17(2)**, [136]
copyhold land, former. *See under* **mines and
mining**
dissolution, **17(2)**, [149]
employees—
redundancy payments, **17(1)**, [500], [557]

British Coal Corporation—*contd*
employees—*contd*
  superannuation—
    provisions, **17(1)**, [12], [45]
    scheme—
      amendment, **17(1)**, [703]
      validity of orders, questioning,
        17(1), [704]
    See also restructuring (pensions) *below*
employment, protection in restructuring,
  17(2), [198]
exploitation rights—
  continental shelf, **17(2)**, [134]
  general, **17(2)**, [133]
  oil and gas, **17(2)**, [135]
  territorial waters, in, **17(2)**, [134]
interests in coal and coal mines—
  protection, **17(2)**, [136]
  vesting in Coal Authority, **17(2)**, [133]
    provisions to which subject,
      17(2), [134], [135]
licences to work coal—
  continuation of, **17(2)**, [150]
  restructuring, after. *See* **coal mining**
    operations
  savings, **17(2)**, [150]
loans to. *See* borrowing *above*
meaning, **17(2)**, [189]
members—
  pensions or compensation, **17(1)**, [365]
  reduction in membership, **17(2)**, [149]
  See also employees *above*
mining operations, powers, restructuring of,
  17(2), [137]
mining subsidence, liabilities and duties. *See*
  under **coal mining subsidence**
National Coal Board, powers of, loss by
  Corporation on restructuring date,
  17(2), [137]
opencast coal mining. *See* **opencast coal**
pension schemes. *See* employees *above*
petroleum, powers as to, loss of, **17(2)**, [137]
plans of. *See* **mines and mining**
powers and duties, restructuring of,
  17(2), [137]
property and interests—
  functions as to, restructuring of,
    17(2), [137]
  restructuring schemes. *See* restructuring
    below
redundant workers, payments to, **17(1)**, [500],
  [557]
restructuring of coal industry—
  compensation, **17(2)**, [198]
  concessionary coal, payments in lieu,
    17(2), [145]
  date, **17(2)**, [133]
  experience and expertise, persons having,
    need for, **17(2)**, [125]
  financial provisions, **17(2)**, [186]
  functions of, **17(2)**, [137]
  grant-making powers, Secretary of State,
    17(2), [143]
  licensing. *See* **coal mining operations**
  payments, **17(2)**, [143]

British Coal Corporation—*contd*
restructuring of coal industry—*contd*
  pensions—
    application of provisions, **17(2)**, [148]
    employees, transfer to private sector,
      17(2), [202]
    general provisions, **17(2)**, [202]
    modification of schemes, **17(2)**, [202]
    private sector—
      protection of rights under schemes,
        17(2), [202]
      transfer, **17(2)**, [202]
  schemes—
    agreements with, **17(2)**, [139]
    contents and effect, **17(2)**, [198]
    modification, **17(2)**, [198], [200]
    notice to persons affected, **17(2)**, [198]
    preparation, **17(2)**, [140]
    property—
      division of, **17(2)**, [198]
      foreign, **17(2)**, [198]
      in relation to, **17(2)**, [138], [198]
    protection of employment, **17(2)**, [198]
    supplemental provisions, **17(2)**, [198]
    third parties, interests etc of,
      17(2), [198]
  taxation provisions—
    chargeable gains—
      capital allowances, **17(2)**, [200]
      disposal of debts, **17(2)**, [200]
      options, **17(2)**, [200]
      roll-over relief, **17(2)**, [200]
      transfers, **17(2)**, [200]
    corporation tax, **17(2)**, [200]
    effects, **17(2)**, [147]
    stamp duties, **17(2)**, [201]
  See also successor companies *below*
rights of, registration of, **17(2)**, [180]
social welfare bodies, validity of orders,
  questioning, **17(1)**, [704]
  See also **Coal Industry Social Welfare**
    Organisation; miners' welfare
staff. *See* employees *above*
subsidence, liabilities and duties. *See under*
  coal mining subsidence
successor companies—
  financial structure—
    borrowing and loans, **17(2)**, [199]
    distributable reserves, **17(2)**, [199]
    dividends, **17(2)**, [199]
    Government assistance, limitation,
      17(2), [142], [199]
    Government holding and investment,
      17(2), [142], [199]
    nominees, Government function
      through, **17(2)**, [142], [199]
    provisions applicable, **17(2)**, [141]
  grants and payments to, **17(2)**, [143], [144]
  meaning, **17(2)**, [189]
  taxable special provision, **17(2)**, [200]
support, rights as to, **17(2)**, [163], [164]
  See further under **mines and mining**
undertaking—
  meaning, **17(2)**, [189]

British Coal Corporation—*contd*
undertaking—*contd*
  restructuring of, **17(2)**, [137]
    protection of employment, **17(2)**, [198]
    shadow directors, **17(2)**, [190]
  unworked coal, interests, vesting in Coal
    Authority, **17(2)**, [133]

British Council
staff superannuation, **33(1)**, [190]

British Electricity Stock. *See* **electricity**

British Energy plc
expenditure, **17(2)**, [366]
grants not subject to tax, **17(2)**, [368]
securities, removal of restrictions on
  acquisition of, **17(2)**, [367]

British European Airways
dissolution, **4(1)**, [1]

British Film Institute
Treasury grants, **13**, [114]

British films. *See under* **cinematograph films**

British Gas Corporation. *See also* **British
Gas plc; gas**
property, rights and liabilities, transfer of,
  17(1), [675]
successor company—
  transfer of property etc to, **17(1)**, [675]
  See now **British Gas plc**
tax provisions, **17(1)**, [684]
transfer date, **17(1)**, [675]
See now **British Gas plc**

British Gas plc. *See also* **gas supplier**
borrowing, temporary restrictions on,
  17(1), [682]
British Gas Corporation, transfer of property,
  rights etc to, **17(1)**, [675]
financial structure, **17(1)**, [681]
Government holding—
  initial, **17(1)**, [677]
  investment in securities, **17(1)**, [678]
  target investment limit, **17(1)**, [680]
levy, payment of. *See under* **gas**
powers and duties. *See* **gas; gas transporter**
securities—
  Government investment in, **17(1)**, [678]
  issue of, **17(1)**, [677]
  shares, issue of, **17(1)**, [677]
statutory reserve, **17(1)**, [681]
tax provisions, **17(1)**, [684]
Treasury—
  issue of securities to, **17(1)**, [677]
  nominees, exercise of functions through,
    17(1), [679]
  stock, holding of, **17(1)**, [676]
Trustee Investments Act 1961, application of
  provisions, **17(1)**, [683]
vesting of property etc in, **17(1)**, [675]
voting rights, **17(1)**, [680]

British Gas Stock
creation and issue, **17(1)**, [676]
Treasury, becoming rights and liabilities of,
  17(1), [676]

British Guiana. *See also* **Guyana**
Guyana, becoming, **7(2)**, [582]

British Hallmarking Council
accounts, **48**, 67, 82
committees, **48**, 81
constitution, **48**, 63–5, 80–1
expenses of, **48**, 82
functions, **48**, 63–4
incorporation of, **48**, 81
officers and servants, **48**, 82
report and accounts, **48**, 67
standing orders, **48**, 81

British Islands
meaning, **41**, [605], [606]

British Library
Board—
  accounts, **13**, [200]
  Advisory Councils, **13**, [197], [203]
  chairman, **13**, [197]
  constitution, **13**, [203]
  incidental powers, **13**, [203]
  members—
    appointment, **13**, [197]
    remuneration, allowances and pensions,
      13, [203]
  membership, **13**, [203]
  proceedings, **13**, [203]
  public library expenses, contributions to,
    13, [196]
  reports by, **13**, [199]
  research, sponsorship of, **13**, [196]
  staff, **13**, [203]
British Museum library, transfer of, **13**, [198]
control and management, **13**, [196]
deposit of publications in, **13**, [457]
establishment, **13**, [49], [196]
financial provisions, **13**, [200]
functions, **13**, [196]
land, transfer of, **13**, [430]
loans by, **13**, [196]
services, availability, **13**, [196]
staff, **13**, [201], [203]
summary of provisions, **13**, [49]
transfer of collections to, **13**, [198]
trust, property subject to, **13**, [198]

British Museum
admission charges, power to make, **13**, [207]
byelaws, ordinances, statutes or rules,
  validity, **13**, [137]
capital gains tax exemption, **42**, [1420]
collections, keeping and inspection, **13**, [129]
Director, **13**, [132]
exempt charity, as, **5(2)**, [691]
history, **13**, [49]
Imperial War Museum, transfers to, **13**, [87]

British Museum—*contd*
land—
  acquired, **13**, [49]
  transfer of, **13**, [430]
  trustees' powers, **13**, [128]
library *See* **British Library**
loans by, **13**, [130]
Natural History Museum—
  separation, **13**, [134]
  transfer of objects to and from, **13**, [135]
  See also **Natural History Museum**
objects—
  disposal of, **13**, [131]
  loan of, **13**, [130]
  powers generally, **13**, [49]
  storage of, **13**, [129]
  temporary removal, **13**, [129]
officers and servants, **13**, [132]
plays, delivery of scripts to, **13**, [190]
repositories—
  access by public to, **13**, [129]
  authorised, **13**, [136]
  sites, **13**, [136], [140]
  storage of objects in, **13**, [129]
staff, **13**, [132]
statutes, summary, **13**, [49]
storage of objects—
  powers, **13**, [129]
  repositories for, **13**, [129], [136]
summary of provisions, **13**, [49]
tax exemption, **44(1)**, [366]
trustees—
  appointment, **13**, [127]
  composition, **13**, [127]
  powers, generally, **13**, [49], [128]
  proceedings, **13**, [138]
  reports, **13**, [133]
  tenure of office, **13**, [138]

British National Formulary
specified publication, as, **28**, [160]

British National Oil Corporation
dissolution of, **17(1)**, [1]
property, rights and liabilities, transfer of, **17(1)**, [562], [569]

British National (Overseas)
Commonwealth citizen, as, **31**, [164]
Hong Kong, persons in, **31**, [180]
meaning, **31**, [180]

British nationality. *See* **nationality**

British Nuclear Fuels Ltd. *See* **Nuclear Fuels Company**

British Overseas Airways Corporation
dissolution, **4(1)**, [1]

British overseas territory
meaning, **41**, [605]

British Pharmaceutical Codex
specified publication, as, **28**, [160]

British Pharmaceutical Codex—*contd*
standards in monograph, compliance with, **28**, [122]

British Pharmacopoeia
amendments, **28**, [159]
compendia—
  amendments, **28**, [159]
  new editions of, **28**, [156]
  substances and articles, lists of names of, **28**, [158]
compliance with standards in monograph, **28**, [122]
new edition, **28**, [156]
publication, **28**, [159]
publications other than, **28**, [156]–[160]
specified publication, as, **28**, [160]
substances and articles—
  information as to, **28**, [156]
  names of, lists of, **28**, [157]

British possession. *See also* **colony**
carriage of goods by road Convention, application, **36**, [760]
meaning, **7(2)**, [391], [398]; **41**, [605]
probate granted in, **18**, [508], [510]
proof of statutes etc in, **18**, [170]

British Potato Council
power to dissolve, **1(2)**, [734]

British Railways Board. *See also* **Strategic Rail Authority**
abolition, **38(2)**, [192]
accounts, **36**, [702]
agricultural land, notice to quit, **22**, [683]
Bills, promoting or opposing, **36**, [694]
borrowing powers—
  Exchequer loans, **36**, [697]
  limits, **36**, [696]
  Treasury guarantees, **36**, [698]
British Transport Commission, vesting of property etc of—
  assets, **36**, [707]
  construction of documents, **36**, [742]
  other Board, works carried out by, **36**, [742]
  property, distribution of, **36**, [742]
  Secretary of State, powers of, **36**, [742]
  staff, transfer of, **36**, [709]
  statutory functions, **36**, [708], [739]–[741]
  third party, effect on, **36**, [742]
bus service—
  conditions—
    imposition of, **37**, [447]
    revocation or variation, **37**, [448], [450]
  substitution—
    provision of, **37**, [447]
    reimbursement of costs, **37**, [452]
  withdrawal of—
    employees affected, **37**, [450]
    information on, **37**, [451]
    notice of, **37**, [448]
    objections to, **37**, [449], [451]
byelaws, making, **36**, [721], [885]

British Railways Board—*contd*
  channel tunnel. *See* **channel tunnel**
  charges—
    harbours, at, **36**, [715], [747], [748]
    power to make, **36**, [747]
  closures by—
    substitution bus services. *See* bus service
     above
    See also **railway passenger services**
  commercial enterprise, duty to act as body
    engaged in, **36**, [862]
  companies, power to form, **38(1)**, [431]
  company for carrying out activities, forming,
    36, [803]
  competent authority for. *See* **London**
    Regional Transport
  constitution of, **36**, [738]
  delegation of functions, **36**, [693]
  deputy chairmen, appointment of, **36**, [794]
  directions, compliance with, **38(1)**, [475]
  disposal, power of, **38(1)**, [436]
  duties of, **36**, [683]
  employees—
    assignment to particular parts of
     undertaking, **38(1)**, [440]
    bus service, effect of withdrawal of,
     37, [450]
    negotiation and consultation machinery,
     36, [865]
    pensions. *See* pension schemes *below*
    terms and conditions of employment,
     36, [723]
  employment, compensation for loss of,
    36, [863]
  establishment of, **36**, [682]
  financial provisions—
    commencing capital debt—
     amount of, **36**, [712]
     amount outstanding, **36**, [796]
     assumption of, **36**, [712], [877]
     deductions, **36**, [712]
     extinguishment of, **36**, [796]
     provisional payments, **36**, [712]
     reduction of, **36**, [912]
    duties, **36**, [695], [795], [796]
    excess reserve, dealing with, **36**, [796]
    sums issued to, account of, **36**, [798]
  Freightliners Limited, transfer of controlling
    interest in, **36**, [967]
  generally, **36**, [210]
  goods—
    carriage of, **36**, [683]
    consignment of, **36**, [683]
    storage of, **36**, [683], [803]
  grants to, **36**, [700]
  harbours, operation of, **36**, [683]
  historical records, transfer and disposal of,
    36, [867]
  holdings in companies, directions on exercise
    of rights, **38(1)**, [437]
  hotels, powers to manage, **36**, [803]
  land—
    acquisition, powers of, **36**, [802]
    compulsory purchase of, **36**, [691]

British Railways Board—*contd*
  land—*contd*
    development, powers of, **36**, [687], [730],
     [802]
    disposal, powers of, **36**, [802]
    level crossings. *See* **level crossing**
    London rail services. *See* **London passenger**
     transport services
  manufacture, powers of, **36**, [689], [801]
  members, appointment of, **36**, [794]
  new authorities, extension of functions to,
    36, [800]
  operational land, entry on, **26(1)**, [221]
  other Board, works carried out by, **36**, [742]
  parking places, provision for vehicles,
    36, [770]
  pension schemes—
    amendment of, **36**, [993]
    continuing validity of orders, **38(1)**, [469]
    debt, cancellation of, **36**, [992]
    definitions, **38(1)**, [495]
    existing schemes, amendment of,
     38(1), [495]
    joint industry scheme, participation in,
     38(1), [495]
    meaning, **36**, [994], [1000]; **37**, [120]
    new, establishment of, **38(1)**, [495]
    orders, powers to make, **36**, [725], [864]
    parliamentary procedure, **38(1)**, [495]
    protection of rights, **38(1)**, [495]
    relevant obligations—
     meaning, **36**, [980], [987]
     proportion corresponding to, **36**, [989]
     supplementation scheme, in respect of,
      36, [990]
     unfunded, **36**, [988]
    rights, assets and liabilities, transfer of,
     38(1), [495]
    transfer, order as to, **36**, [725], [864]
    transfer values, exclusion of payments in
     respect of, **36**, [991]
    transitional provisions, **36**, [745];
     38(1), [495]
    Transport Act 1980, application of
     provisions, **38(1)**, [495]
    trust company—
     appointed day, **37**, [111]
     capital taxes, exemption from, **37**, [116]
     establishment of, **37**, [112]
     interpretation, **37**, [110]
     investment, powers of, **37**, [115]
     nominees, appointment of, **37**, [117]
     rights of Board, saving of, **37**, [114]
     stamp duty, exemption from, **37**, [116]
     transfer of assets, evidence of, **37**, [118]
     vesting of rights, etc, in, **37**, [113]
    trustees of new schemes, Government
     guarantees to, **38(1)**, [495]
  pipe-lines, construction and operation of,
    36, [730]
  plans and policies, duties relating to, **36**, [913]
  Port of London Act, protection under,
    39(2), [436]
  Port of London Authority, arrangements
    with, **39(2)**, [239]

British Railways Board—*contd*
powers of, **36**, [683], [803]–[805]
private street works, exemption from
provisions, **36**, [1265]
production, power of, **36**, [689]
property—
rating, **36**, [873]
rights and liabilities, transfer of, **36**, [878]
railway companies, not regarded as shadow
directors of, **38(1)**, [458]
repair, power of, **36**, [801]
research and development, promotion of,
36, [799]
revenue deficits, grants towards, **36**, [701]
road passenger transport services, providing,
36, [685]
road services, providing, **36**, [684]
Secretary of State—
consent of, powers subject to, **36**, [705]
directions of, **36**, [731]
pensions, orders about, **36**, [725], [864]
powers of, **36**, [704]
report to, **36**, [913]
staff. *See* employees *above*
stamp duty, exemption from, **36**, [713], [872]
status of, **36**, [706]
subsidiaries—
control over, **36**, [703]
disposal, power of, **38(1)**, [436]
functions carried out by, **36**, [804]
joint, **36**, [804]
provisions applying to, **36**, [885];
38(1), [456]
transfer of interests in, **38(1)**, [435]
successor companies—
borrowings, temporary restrictions on,
38(1), [449]
flotation—
listing particulars, responsibility for,
38(1), [454]
Trustee Investments Act, application of,
38(1), [455]
Government investment in, **38(1)**, [446]
target limit, **38(1)**, [448]
Government lending to, **38(1)**, [450]
grants to, **38(1)**, [452]
initial share holding in, **38(1)**, [445]
liabilities, extinguishment of, **38(1)**, [453]
loans, Treasury guarantees, **38(1)**, [451]
nominees, exercise of functions through,
38(1), [447]
supply, power of, **36**, [801]
technical advice, etc, providing, **36**, [803]
Town and Country Planning Acts, application
of, **36**, [730], [866]
transfer of property to Secretary of State,
38(2), [214]
transfer schemes—
accounting provisions, **38(1)**, [441]
agreements, etc, construction of,
38(1), [493]
compensation, **38(1)**, [438]
documents of title, production of,
38(1), [493]
employees, assignment of, **38(1)**, [440]

British Railways Board—*contd*
transfer schemes—*contd*
foreign property, rights and liabilities,
vesting, **38(1)**, [493]
information, Secretary of State or
Franchising Director requiring,
38(1), [442]
interests in companies, as to, **38(1)**, [435]
land, restrictions on dealing with,
38(1), [493]
local or private legislation, functions
under, **38(1)**, [439]
power to make, **38(1)**, [432]
proof of title by certificate, **38(1)**, [493]
property, rights and liabilities, allocation
of, **38(1)**, [493]
provisions of, **38(1)**, [438]
Secretary of State—
functions of, **38(1)**, [443]
transfer of function to, **38(1)**, [434]
stamp duty and stamp duty reserve tax
provisions, **38(1)**, [494]
variation by agreement, **38(1)**, [493]
vesting provisions, third parties affected
by, **38(1)**, [493]
transport police—
constables, provisions relating to, **36**, [722]
jurisdiction, **38(1)**, [498]
transport systems, application or objection to
orders for, **38(1)**, [306]
Treasury guarantee of liabilities, **36**, [698];
37, [121]
unoccupied building on land of, protection
of, **35(1)**, [438]
vice chairmen, appointment of, **36**, [794]
winding down, **38(2)**, [192]

British settlement. *See also* **colony**
courts—
establishment of, **7(2)**, [394]
jurisdiction conferred on, **7(2)**, [396]
delegation of power to, **7(2)**, [395], [434]
government, provision for, **7(2)**, [392]
laws, establishment of, **7(2)**, [394]
meaning, **7(2)**, [398]
Orders in Council, **7(2)**, [397]

British Shipbuilders
accounts—
additional. *See* companies *below*
audit of, **47**, [296]
duty to keep, **47**, [296]
statement of, **47**, [296]
activities—
discontinuance, order for, **47**, [284]
formulation of plans, **47**, [286]
organisation of, **47**, [283]
practices, objection to, **47**, [304]
restriction of, **47**, [284]
annual report of, **47**, [297]
arbitration tribunal. *See* **Aircraft and
Shipbuilding Industries Arbitration
Tribunal**
associated privately owned companies—
meaning, **47**, [299]

British Shipbuilders—*contd*
associated privately owned companies—*contd*
property etc, vesting of, **47**, [299]
Bills, power to promote, **47**, [281]
borrowing—
aggregate amount permitted, **47**, [290]
capital debt—
commencing, **47**, [294]
rate of interest on, **47**, [294]
government loans, obligations as to,
47, [293]
loans by Secretary of State, **47**, [291]
powers, general, **47**, [290]–[291]
subsidiaries, from, **47**, [291]
Treasury guarantees, **47**, [292]
capital—
commencing, **47**, [294]
public dividend, **47**, [295]
companies—
direction to form, **47**, [284]
disposal of interest in, **47**, [284]
compensation stock, **47**, [300]
complaints as to practices of, **47**, [304]
constitution of, **47**, [280]
directions by Minister—
discontinue activities, to, **47**, [284]
effect to be given to, **47**, [282]
Parliamentary control, **47**, [282]
procedure for giving, **47**, [282]
property etc, to dispose of, **47**, [284]
employees—
pensions. **47**, [306]
terms of employment, **47**, [285]
financial provisions—
borrowing powers. *See* borrowing *above*
duties under, **47**, [290]
reports under, **47**, [290]
information—
disclosure, restriction on, **47**, [307]
furnishing and publication, **47**, [287]
interpretation of terms, **47**, [311]
land, provisions applied, **25(2)**, [450]
liabilities etc of, **47**, [308]
members—
financial interests, register of, **47**, [280]
remuneration and allowances, **47**, [280]
name, power to change, **47**, [280]
Northern Ireland bodies, consultation with,
47, [305]
notices, service of, **47**, [309]
overseas technical assistance, **47**, [281]
pensions, **47**, [306]
policies, formulation of, **47**, [286]
powers, summary of, **47**, [281]
public dividend capital, **47**, [295]
regulations, subject matter, **47**, [280]
Secretary of State—
accounts to be prepared by, **47**, [291]
directions by. *See* directions *above*
furnishing information to, **47**, [287]
loans by, **47**, [291]
securities—
conditions for vesting, **47**, [316]
eligible companies, **47**, [315]
meaning, **47**, [298], [311]

British Shipbuilders—*contd*
securities—*contd*
vesting of, **47**, [298]
vesting of assets in, **47**, [317]
status of, **47**, [280]
subsidiaries—
borrowing from or by, **47**, [290]
control of, **47**, [288]
duties as to, **47**, [281]
restrictions on, **47**, [288]
summary of provisions, **47**, [1]
trade disputes, resolution of, **47**, [285]
works, meaning, **47**, [311]

British Steel Corporation. *See also* **iron and steel**
chairman and deputy, **47**, [369]
constitution, **47**, [365], [432]
dissolution, **47**, [422]
establishment, **47**, [365]
final report and accounts, **47**, [432]
ironstone workings—
restoration expenses, payments—
agricultural land, **17(1)**, [547]
Forestry Commission, to, **17(1)**, [548]
meetings and proceedings, **47**, [369]
members—
appointment, **47**, [365]
financial or other interests, **47**, [369]
pension and compensation payments,
47, [432]
terms of office, **47**, [369]
officers, appointment, **47**, [369]
orders, **47**, [429]
Secretary of State, accounts of, **47**, [432]
status of, **47**, [365]
successor company—
borrowings, temporary restrictions on,
47, [421]
corporation tax treatment, **47**, [423]
dividend, payment of, **47**, [432]
financial structure, **47**, [419]
Government investment—
initial holding, **47**, [415]
securities, in, **47**, [416]
target investment limit, **47**, [418]
Treasury nominees, exercise of functions
through, **47**, [417]
property, vesting of, **47**, [414], [429]
foreign, **47**, [432]
Secretary of State, loans by, **47**, [420]
transitional provisions, **47**, [432]

British subject. *See also* **citizenship; nationality; naturalisation**
alien, non-entitlement to rights and
privileges, **31**, [2]
cessation as, former provisions, **31**, [26]
citizens of Eire as, **31**, [12]
citizenship, without, former provisions,
31, [24], [47]
continuance as—
existing subjects of certain descriptions,
31, [158]

British subject—*contd*
continuance as—*contd*
Ireland, certain former citizens of,
31, [159]
deprivation of status—
appeal, **31**, [168]
grounds for, **31**, [167]
former provisions, **31**, [69]
powers, **31**, [162]
Ireland. *See* **Ireland**
loss of status, **31**, [162]
meanings, **31**, [181]
natural-born and other, assimilation of status,
former, **31**, [41]
oath and pledge by person becoming,
31, [170], [187]
registration, minors, **31**, [160]
renunciation by, **31**, [161]
without citizenship—
subjects of certain descriptions, **31**, [158]
wife of, former provisions, **31**, [67]–[69]

British Telecommunications (Corporation).
See also **telecommunications**
Post Office, transfer of property, rights and
liabilities of to, **45**, [40]
property, rights and liabilities, vesting and
transfer—
allocation, **45**, [52]
Channel Islands, application of provisions,
45, [46], [49], [50]
consequential amendments of enactments,
45, [48]
construction of documents, **45**, [52]
contracts of employment, **45**, [52]
financial provisions, **45**, [44]
generally, **45**, [40]
Isle of Man, application of provisions,
45, [46], [49], [50]
land dealings, certain restrictions on,
45, [52]
Northern Ireland, application of
provisions, **45**, [47]
Post Office, from, **45**, [40]
Secretary of State's liability in respect of
liabilities, **45**, [59]
stamp duty, exemption, **45**, [42]
tax provisions, **45**, [43]
third parties, **45**, [52]
title, documents and proof, **45**, [52]
transitional provisions, **45**, [49], [54]
welfare funds, preservation, **45**, [45]
successor company. *See* **British
Telecommunications (plc)**

British Telecommunications (plc). *See also*
telecommunications
corporation tax, **45**, [60]
post office functions, transfer, **34**, [568], [576]
property, rights etc, transfer. *See under* **British
Telecommunications (Corporation)**
successor company, as—
liabilities vested in, Secretary of State's
liability, **45**, [59]
tax provisions, **45**, [60]

British Telecommunications (plc)—*contd*
taxation provisions, **45**, [60]
winding up, Secretary of State's liability on,
45, [59]

British Transport Commission
agreements, construction of, **36**, [742]
charges schemes, cessation of, **36**, [714]
coast protection board, representation on,
49, [381]
commercial enterprise, duty to act as body
engaged in, **36**, [862]
deep tube shelters, provisions relating to,
50, [251]
members, payments on termination of
employment, **36**, [727]
officers and servants, compensation to,
36, [728]
pension schemes, transitional provisions,
36, [745]
pensions, payment of, **36**, [746]
property and functions, distribution of—
assets, **36**, [707]
Secretary of State, alteration by, **36**, [742]
staff, transfer of, **36**, [709]
statutory functions, **36**, [708], [739]–[741]
Treasury Stock, liability for, **36**, [711]
stamp duty, exemption from, **36**, [713]
statutory provisions, construction of, **36**, [742]
undertaking, distribution of, **36**, [742]
vesting provisions, effect on third parties,
36, [742]

British Transport Docks Board
reconstitution. *See* **Associated British Ports**

British Transport Police Authority
annual report, **33(2)**, [451]
body corporate, as, **33(2)**, [412]
British Transport Police Force, maintenance
of, **33(2)**, [414]
British Transport Police Fund, establishment
of, **33(2)**, [480]
budget, **33(2)**, [480]
chairman, **33(2)**, [478]
code of practice, **33(2)**, [441]
committee, **33(2)**, [479]
deputy chairman, **33(2)**, [478]
efficient and effective policing, ensuring,
33(2), [413]
exercise of functions, **33(2)**, [413]
financial year, **33(2)**, [480]
income, **33(2)**, [480]
international assistance by, **33(2)**, [463]
members—
appointment, **33(2)**, [478]
disqualification from appointment,
33(2), [478]
ineligibility for appointment, **33(2)**, [471],
[478]
remuneration and allowances, **33(2)**, [480]
standards of conduct, **33(2)**, [479]
tenure, **33(2)**, [478]
pension schemes, **33(2)**, [480]
performance directions, **33(2)**, [448]

British Transport Police Authority—*contd*
performance targets, **33(2)**, [447]
police services agreement—
compulsory, **33(2)**, [428]
disputes, arbitration, **33(2)**, [429]
entry into, **33(2)**, [427]
payment terms, **33(2)**, [427]
provisions of, **33(2)**, [427]
Secretary of state, approval by, **33(2)**, [427]
policing objectives, setting, **33(2)**, [444]
procedure, **33(2)**, [479]
property, dealing with, **33(2)**, [480]
public consultation by, **33(2)**, [456]
railways policing plan, issue of, **33(2)**, [446]
Secretary of State—
exercise of functions of, **33(2)**, [464]
reports to, **33(2)**, [452]
staff, **33(2)**, [479]
remuneration and allowances, **33(2)**, [480]
status, **33(2)**, [481]
three-year strategy plan, issue of, **33(2)**, [449]
validity of proceedings, **33(2)**, [479]

British Transport Police Federation
function of, **33(2)**, [433]
regulations—
approval in draft, **33(2)**, [434]
Authority, directions to, **33(2)**, [435]
making of, **33(2)**, [433]
scope of, **33(2)**, [433]
Transport Police Conference to discuss, **33(2)**, [440]

British Transport Police Force. *See also*
British Railways Board
assistant Chief Constables **33(2)**, [417]
cadets—
appointment, **33(2)**, [420]
direction and control of, **33(2)**, [420]
regulations, **33(2)**, [432]
trade union membership, prohibited, **33(2)**, [424]
Chief Constable—
appointment, **33(2)**, [415]
cadets, direction and control of, **33(2)**, [420]
code of practice, **33(2)**, [442]
constables, direction and control of, **33(2)**, [418]
criminal proceedings, institution of, **33(2)**, [426]
functions, performance of, **33(2)**, [415]
reports by, **33(2)**, [450]
special constables, direction and control of, **33(2)**, [419]
statistics, supply of, **33(2)**, [453]
suspension and removal, regulations, **33(2)**, [415]
civilian employees—
employment of, **33(2)**, [421]
exercise of powers by, **33(2)**, [422]
terms of employment, **33(2)**, [423], [430]
collaboration agreements, **33(2)**, [198]
constables—
appointment, **33(2)**, [418]

British Transport Police Force—*contd*
constables—*contd*
assault on, **33(2)**, [462]
direction and control of, **33(2)**, [418]
impersonation, **33(2)**, [462]
jurisdiction, **33(2)**, [425]
offences, **33(2)**, [462]
registration documents for vehicle, power to require, **33(2)**, [581]
remuneration and allowances, **33(2)**, [480]
terms of employment, **33(2)**, [423], [430]
trade union membership, prohibited, **33(2)**, [424]
criminal proceedings, institution of, **33(2)**, [426]
Crown property, application of provisions to, **33(2)**, [465]
deficiencies, action plan to remedy, **33(2)**, [460]
deputy Chief Constable, **33(2)**, [416]
establishment, **33(2)**, [414]
expenses of, **33(2)**, [414]
HM Inspectors of Constabulary, inspection by—
adverse report, action after, **33(2)**, [458]
delegation of functions, **33(2)**, [461]
payments for, **33(2)**, [457]
remedial directions, **33(2)**, [459]
report, **33(2)**, [457]
requirement, **33(2)**, [457]
independent police authority. *See* **British Transport Police Authority**
inquiries, **33(2)**, [454]–[455]
interpretation, **33(2)**, [468]
jurisdiction, **12(3)**, [129]; **38(1)**, [498]
maintenance of, **33(2)**, [414]
meaning, **12(3)**, [129]
Ministry of Defence Police—
assistance from, **33(2)**, [132]
having powers of, **33(2)**, [131]
other forces, aid to, **33(2)**, [199]
policing objectives—
Authority, set by, **33(2)**, [444]
Secretary of State, set by, **33(2)**, [445]
railway, meaning, **33(2)**, [468]
railway property, meaning, **33(2)**, [468]
railway safety accreditation scheme, **33(2)**, [380]
railway services, meaning, **33(2)**, [468]
regulations—
appeals, **33(2)**, [437]
approval in draft, **33(2)**, [434]
Authority, directions to, **33(2)**, [435]
cadets, relating to, **33(2)**, [432]
conditions of service, as to, **33(2)**, [440]
making of, **33(2)**, [430], [467]
practice and procedure, as to, **33(2)**, [439]
Secretary of State, by, **33(2)**, [436]
services outside force, as to, **33(2)**, [443]
special constables, relating to, **33(2)**, [431]
standard of equipment, as to, **33(2)**, [438]
Transport Police Conference to discuss, **33(2)**, [440]
Scottish Transport Group, availability to, **36**, [885]

British Transport Police Force—*contd*
special constables—
appointment, **33(2)**, [419]
direction and control of, **33(2)**, [419]
regulations, **33(2)**, [431]
summary of provisions, **33(2)**, [17]
tramway, meaning, **33(2)**, [468]

British Waterways Board. *See also* **inland waterways**
abstraction of water, charges, **49**, [1187]
accounts, **36**, [702]
agricultural land, notice to quit, **22**, [683]
annual report, **36**, [704]
arbitration, **38(1)**, [615]
Bills, promoting or opposing, **36**, [694]
borrowing powers—
Exchequer loans, **36**, [697]
limits, **36**, [696]
Treasury guarantees, **36**, [698]
British Transport Commission, vesting of property etc of—
assets, **36**, [707]
construction of documents, **36**, [742]
other Board, works carried out by, **36**, [742]
property, distribution of, **36**, [742]
Secretary of State, powers of, **36**, [742]
staff, transfer of, **36**, [709]
statutory functions, **36**, [708], [739]–[741]
third party, effect on, **36**, [742]
canal—
access to, **36**, [850]
supply of water for, **36**, [719]
See also **canal**
certificates and licences, conditions as to, **38(1)**, [607]
chairman, appointment of, **36**, [682]
channel tunnel, protection from works, **38(1)**, [715]
charges—
harbours, at, **36**, [715], [747], [748]
power to make, **36**, [714], [747]
common carrier, not being, **36**, [714]
company for carrying on activities, forming, **36**, [803]
constitution of, **36**, [682], [738]
Crossrail, protective provisions, **38(2)**, [643]
Crown rights, **38(1)**, [617]
delegation of functions, **36**, [693]
duties of—
economic, **36**, [686], [843]
enforcement, **36**, [842]
maintenance of waterways, of, **36**, [841], [884]
services and facilities, to provide, **36**, [686], [843]
employees—
negotiation and consultation machinery, **36**, [865]
pensions. *See* pension schemes *below*
terms and conditions of employment, **36**, [723]
employment, compensation for loss of, **36**, [863]

British Waterways Board—*contd*
entry on land, **36**, [210]
compensation for loss or damage caused by, **38(1)**, [601]
emergency operations—
generally, **38(1)**, [595]
meaning, **38(1)**, [594]
savings in cases of, **38(1)**, [598]
further provisions as to, **38(1)**, [599]
interpretation, **38(1)**, [594]
notice of, **38(1)**, [596]
offences, **38(1)**, [603]
payment for, **38(1)**, [600], [602]
Port of London Authority, protection of, **38(1)**, [605]
powers of, **38(1)**, [597]
relevant undertakers—
meaning, **38(1)**, [594]
protection of, **38(1)**, [604]
environmental duties, **38(1)**, [612]
establishment of, **36**, [682]
financial provisions—
commencing capital debt—
amount of, **36**, [712]
assumption of, **36**, [712], [877]
deductions, **36**, [712]
extinguishment of, **36**, [797]
provisional payments, **36**, [712]
duties, **36**, [695], [797]
excess revenue, dealing with, **36**, [797]
sums issued to, account of, **36**, [798]
flood works, approval of, **49**, [176]
generally, **36**, [210]
goods—
carriage of, **36**, [686]
consignment of, **36**, [686]
storage of, **36**, [686], [803]
grants to, **36**, [797]
hotels, management of, **36**, [803]
inland waters owned by, application of provisions, **49**, [1125]
land—
acquisition, power of, **36**, [690], [802]
compulsory purchase of, **36**, [691]
Scotland, **36**, [692]
development, power of, **36**, [687], [730], [802]
disposal, power of, **36**, [802]
legal proceedings, **38(1)**, [616]
manufacture, powers of, **36**, [689], [801]
members, appointment of, **36**, [682]
moorings, control of, **38(1)**, [611]
new authorities, extension of functions to, **36**, [800]
notices, **38(1)**, [614]
operational land, entry on, **26(1)**, [221]
other Board, works carried out by, **36**, [742]
pension schemes—
orders, **36**, [725]
Secretary of State, powers of, **36**, [725]
transitional provisions, **36**, [745]
pipe-lines, construction and operation of, **36**, [688]
powers of, **36**, [686], [690], [803]–[805]

British Waterways Board—*contd*
private street works, exemption from
   provisions, **36**, [1265]
production, powers of, **36**, [689]
recreational duties, **38(1)**, [612]
regulation and management of inland
   waterways, **38(1)**, [606]–[611]
removal of vessels by, to permit works,
   38(1), [609]
repair, power of, **36**, [801]
research and development, promotion of,
   36, [799]
road transport services, provision of,
   36, [686], [803]
saving rights of, **49**, [174]
Scotland, application of provisions to,
   38(1), [620]
Secretary of State—
   consent of, powers subject to, **36**, [705]
   directions of, **36**, [731]
   pensions, orders about, **36**, [725]
   powers of, **36**, [704]
staff. *See* employees *above*
stamp duty, exemption from, **36**, [713], [872]
status of, **36**, [706]
subsidiaries—
   control over, **36**, [703]
   functions carried out by, **36**, [804]
   joint, **36**, [804]
   provisions applying to, **36**, [885]
summary of provisions, **36**, [210]
supply, power of, **36**, [801]
technical advice, etc, providing, **36**, [803]
Town and Country Planning Acts, application
   of, **36**, [730], [866]
transfer of waterways by, **36**, [845]
transport systems, application or objection to
   orders for, **38(1)**, [306]
Trinity House, saving for, **38(1)**, [618]
undertakings, power to establish, on request,
   38(1), [613]
waterways and reservoirs, provision of facilities
   on, **36**, [803]
waterways of. *See* **inland waterways**

broadcasting. *See also* **British Broadcasting
Corporation; independent television;
Independent Television Commission;
Office of Communications**
aircraft, from—
   facilitating, **45**, [856]
      enforcement powers, **45**, [864]
      territorial scope, **45**, [860]
   prohibition, **45**, [851]
Cable Authority, transfer of undertakings,
   42, [1036]
channels. *See* **independent television**
committal proceedings, restriction on report,
   11(2), [418]
competition legislation, application, **45**, [177]
complaints. *See* **Broadcasting Complaints
   Commission; Broadcasting Standards
   Commission**
defamatory material, **19(3)**, [324]
   extension of certain defences, **19(3)**, [314]

broadcasting—*contd*
digital broadcasting. *See* **digital broadcasting**
during election, **15(3)**, [102]
employment—
   equality of opportunity, **45**, [445]
   training, **45**, [445]
financial provisions generally, **45**, [181]
fraudulent reception of programmes—
   apparatus for, rights and remedies in respect
      of, **11(1)**, [1167]
   offence of, **11(1)**, [1163]
   rights and remedies in respect of apparatus
      for, **11(1)**, [1167]
   supplementary provisions, **11(1)**, [1168]
   unauthorised decoders, **11(1)**, [1164]
      forfeiture of, **11(1)**, [1166]
      search warrants for, **11(1)**, [1165]
frequencies, television, additional services by.
   See **independent television** (additional
   services)
Independent Broadcasting Authority, transfer
   of undertakings, **42**, [1036]
listed events—
   categorisation of, **45**, [669]
      code relating to, **45**, [671]
      effects of, **45**, [670]
      programme service for, **45**, [267]
   contract for televising to specify category of
      service, **45**, [269]
   coverage of, **45**, [672]
   EEA States, designated by—
      meaning, **45**, [271]
      restriction on televising, **45**, [272]
   exclusive right, contract for, to be void,
      45, [268]
   meaning, **45**, [266]
   regulations as to coverage of, **45**, [276]
   restriction on televising—
      code of guidance, **45**, [275]
      EEA States, in, **45**, [272]
      general provisions, **45**, [270]
      penalties, **45**, [273]
      report to Secretary of State, **45**, [274]
local items during election period,
   15(3), [102]
meaning of broadcast, **13**, [186]
news reporting of visual images from
   broadcast or cable programmes, avoidance of
   certain terms, **45**, [296]
obscene matter, publication of, **12(1)**, [310]
obscene publication by—
   common law proceedings, exclusion,
      12(2), [58]
   defences, **12(2)**, [58]
   inclusion of matter in, **12(1)**, [310]
   liability, **12(2)**, [58]
   recordings, power to make copies,
      12(2), [53]
   suspected, **12(2)**, [53]
OFCOM's functions, **45**, [441]
offences by bodies corporate, **12(2)**, [54],
   [139]
outside UK, from, **15(3)**, [101]
plays, performance, exceptions under Theatres
   Acts, **13**, [186]

broadcasting—*contd*
  programme and programme service,
    meaning, **12(2)**, [55]
  programme services, **19(3)**, [325]
  programmes, fraudulent reception of. *See
    further* fraudulent reception of transmissions
    above
  racial hatred, stirring up, **12(1)**, [1016]
  religious hatred, stirring up, **12(1)**, [1030]
  satellite. *See* **satellite television services**
  sexual offences, anonymity of victims,
    contravention of provisions, **12(2)**, [139]
  ships, from, unauthorised. *See* marine *above*
  sound broadcasting. *See* **digital broadcasting**
    (sound)
  studio, powers of entry in, **6**, [19]
  summary of provisions, **45**, [1]
  transmission facilities, sharing of, **42**, [1061]
    capital gains tax relief, **42**, [1416]
  video recordings. *See* **video recordings**
  Welsh. *See* **Welsh Authority**
  young persons taking part in, **6**, [81]

Broadcasting Complaints Commission
  IBA, transitional arrangements, provisions,
    45, [197], [199]

Broadcasting Standards Commission
  OFCOM, functions transferred to, **45**, [755]

Broadcasting Standards Council
  IBA transitional arrangements, provisions,
    45, [197], [199]
  international obligations, directions by
    Secretary of State as to, **45**, [176]

Broads
  local planning authority, **46**, [255]

Broads Authority. *See also* **Norfolk and
Suffolk Broads**
  alternative development, authority as to,
    9, [232]
  ancient monuments and archaeological sites in
    area of, **32**, [374]
  capital expenditure. *See* **local authority**
  compulsory purchase, application of
    provisions, **9**, [375]
  Countryside Act, application of, **32**, [280]
  district planning authority, as, **46**, [255]
  emergency financial assistance, **32**, [815]
  employment arrangements with, **25(2)**, [476]
  functions of, **32**, [814]
  Local Government Act, application of,
    25(2), [225]
  provisions applying to, **32**, [198]
  site of special interest, notification as to,
    19(3), [233]

broker
  documents, making available, **42**, [135]
  meaning, **42**, [135]

Brompton Cemetery
  sale, **5(2)**, [382]

Brompton Cemetery—*contd*
  vesting, **5(2)**, [381]

brothel
  child under sixteen in, **6**, [3]
  keeping—
    offence, **12(1)**, [283]
    prosecution and punishment, **12(1)**, [297]
    prostitution, used for, **12(1)**, [284]
  premises let for—
    offence, **12(1)**, [285]
    prosecution and punishment, **12(1)**, [297]
  tenant permitting premises to be used as—
    landlord, rights of, **12(1)**, [296]
    offence, **12(1)**, [286]
    prosecution and punishment, **12(1)**, [297]

brucellosis
  control of, **2**, [431]
  eradication, **2**, [346]
  offences and penalties, **2**, [347]

Brunei
  Commonwealth citizenship, **31**, [186]

Brunei and Maldives
  appeals from Supreme Court of Brunei
    Darussalam, **7(2)**, [784]
  British ship registered in, **7(2)**, [763]
  Commonwealth membership, amendments
    consequent on, **7(2)**, [761]
  visiting forces in, **7(2)**, [763]

**Brussels Convention on jurisdiction and
the enforcement of judgments**. *See* **civil
jurisdiction; civil jurisdiction Conventions;
judgments**

buggery
  anonymity rule, when inapplicable,
    12(2), [138]

builder
  defective premises, liability in case of,
    21, [384]

builders' skip
  conditions for, **36**, [1199]
  control of, **36**, [1199]
  defences, **36**, [1199]
  disposal of, **36**, [1200]
  lighting, **36**, [1199]
  meaning, **36**, [1199]
  occupation of highway, charge for, **36**, [1201];
    38(2), [347]
    double, prevention of imposition of,
      36, [1203]
    duration, determined by reference to,
      36, [1202]
  owner of, **36**, [1199]
  permission for deposit, **36**, [1199]
  regulations as to charges, **36**, [1201]–[1203]
  removal of, **36**, [1200]
  repositioning, offence due to, **36**, [1200]

building

acquisition of, for housing, **22**, [19]

agricultural. *See* **agricultural buildings;
agricultural buildings allowance**

alteration, condition applicable to, **46**, [631]

alteration or removal order—

compensation in respect of, **46**, [377]

confirmation of, **46**, [366]

contravention of, **46**, [446]

enforcement, **46**, [447]

power to make, **46**, [365]

Secretary of State, by, **46**, [367]

angles, rounding off, **36**, [1336]

architectural or historical interest, of,
acquisition by agreement, **46**, [694]

byelaws, references to, construction of,
35(1), [611]

classification, **35(1)**, [554]

closet in, notice by local authority requiring,
35(1), [587]

construction or erection, references to,
35(1), [645]

construction, zero-rating, **50**, [151]

conversion of, **22**, [19]

flats, to, **22**, [410]

Crown property, application of provisions of
Building Act to, **35(1)**, [609]

dangerous, application of provisions,
26(2), [178]

dangerous state, in—

demolition, **35(1)**, [599]

emergency measures where, **35(1)**, [600]

overloading, restriction on use where,
35(1), [599]

powers of local authority as to,
35(1), [599]

demolition—

dangerous state, in, **35(1)**, [599]

notice—

appeal against, **35(1)**, [605], [608]

intended, of, **35(1)**, [602]

local authority, by, **35(1)**, [603], [604]

ruinous or dilapidated state, in,
35(1), [601]

See also **demolition**

door opening outwards on street, prohibition
of, **36**, [1218]

drainage. *See* **drainage; plans**

ecclesiastical—

building preservation notice not to be
served on, **46**, [702]

exemption, restricting, **46**, [702]

works on, **46**, [702]

entertainment, used for, safety of child, **6**, [8]

erection of, operations deemed to be,
35(1), [643]

exits, etc, **35(1)**, [549]

expenses, recovery of, **35(1)**, [630]

fire, notice requiring means of escape from,
35(1), [594]

food storage accommodation in—

notice requiring—

appeal against, **35(1)**, [593], [625]

local authority, given by, **35(1)**, [592]

building—*contd*

frontager—

adoption of street, requiring, **36**, [1274]

consent of—

object or structure, for placing,
36, [1135], [1139]

recreation or refreshment facilities, for
provision of, **36**, [1137]

meaning, **36**, [1135]

highway, constructed over—

demolition notice, **36**, [1243]

licence for, **36**, [1243]

restriction on construction, **36**, [1243]

terms and conditions, **36**, [1243]

industrial. *See* **industrial buildings;
industrial buildings allowance**

Inner London, in. *See* **Inner London**

listed. *See* **listed building**

local Acts as to construction, etc, facilities for
inspection of, **35(1)**, [612]

London—

dangerous—

occupants, priority housing, **25(2)**, [558]

removal of occupants, **25(2)**, [556]

See also **London Building Acts**

material change of use, meaning, **46**, [315]

materials unsuitable for permanent, use of,
plans, passing, conditions on use,
35(1), [545]

meaning, **9**, [253]; **35(1)**, [437], [643];
36, [1076]

name of street, painting on, **35(1)**, [6], [22],
[66], [97]

new, chimney or flue, overreaching that of
adjoining building, **35(1)**, [595]

numbering, **35(1)**, [6], [22]

obstructive. *See* **demolition order**

operations—

Factories Acts, provisions applicable,
18, [1180]

meaning, **18**, [1200]; **46**, [315]

part of—

acquiring authority, required to purchase
whole, **9**, [403]

no requirement to sell, **9**, [53]

paving and drainage of yards and passages,
35(1), [606]

pipe-line, imperilling. *See* **pipe-line**

planning permission. *See* **planning
permission**

plans. *See* **plans**

preservation notice—

affixing to property, **46**, [644]

coming into force, **46**, [643]

compensation for loss, **46**, [669]

effect of, **46**, [643]

lapse of, **46**, [645], [748]

listed, not to be, **46**, [643], [646]

service of, **46**, [643]

urgent cases, in, **46**, [644]

projections on, removal, **36**, [1217]

protected, zero-rating, **50**, [151]

public—

lighting, provision for, **35(1)**, [23]

building—*contd*
 public—*contd*
  works, affected by, sound-proofing of,
   35(1), [298]
 purposes, meaning, **20**, [436], [804]
 rebuilding, **46**, [631]
 removal of refuse from, access for,
  35(1), [548]
 ruinous or dilapidated, powers of local
  authority as to, **35(1)**, [601]
 stock, report on, **35(2)**, [515]
 street lamps attached to, **36**, [1112]
 summary of provisions as to, **35(1)**, [1]
 supervision of own work, public body, by—
  final certificate—
   acceptance, **35(1)**, [578], [663]
   giving to local authority, **35(1)**, [578],
    [663]
   register of information as to,
    35(1), [580]
   rejection, **35(1)**, [578], [663]
    appeal against, **35(1)**, [579]
  notice—
   acceptance, **35(1)**, [578]
   ceasing to be in force, effect of,
    35(1), [578], [663]
   consultation provisions, **35(1)**, [578],
    [683]
   duration, **35(1)**, [578], [663], [683]
   effect, **35(1)**, [578]
   form, **35(1)**, [578]
   giving to local authority, **35(1)**, [578]
   offences, **35(1)**, [581]
   plans certificate—
    acceptance, **35(1)**, [578], [663]
    giving to local authority, **35(1)**, [578],
     [663]
    notice, combined with, **35(1)**, [578],
     [663]
    register of information as to,
     35(1), [580]
    rejection, **35(1)**, [578], [663]
     appeal against, **35(1)**, [579]
    scope of, **35(1)**, [578], [663]
   plans to accompany, **35(1)**, [578]
   registration of information as to,
    35(1), [580]
   rejection, **35(1)**, [578]
    appeal against, **35(1)**, [579]
 supervision of work and inspection of plans—
  amendment notice, effect of, **35(1)**, [574]
  approved inspector—
   approval of, **35(1)**, [570]
   by, **35(1)**, [568]
   certificate by, **35(1)**, [568]
   final certificate, on completion of work,
    35(1), [572]
    register of information as to,
     35(1), [580]
   functions, **35(1)**, [568]
   initial notice by. *See* initial notice as to
    below
   limitations on scope of, **35(1)**, [570]
   meaning, **35(1)**, [570]
   offences, **35(1)**, [581]

building—*contd*
 supervision of work and inspection of
  plans—*contd*
  approved inspector—*contd*
   plans certificate—
    acceptance, **35(1)**, [571]
    appeal on—
     Court of Appeal, to, **35(1)**, [563]
     High Court, to, **35(1)**, [563]
     stated where, **35(1)**, [563]
    extent of, **35(1)**, [571]
    giving by, **35(1)**, [568], [571]
    initial notice combined with,
     35(1), [571]
    reference of questions to Secretary of
     State, **35(1)**, [571]
    register of information as to,
     35(1), [580]
    rejection, **35(1)**, [571]
     appeal against, **35(1)**, [579]
    taking effect, **35(1)**, [571]
   plans, inspection by, **35(1)**, [568]
  initial notice as to—
   acceptance, **35(1)**, [568]
   approved inspector, by, **35(1)**, [568]
   builder, by, **35(1)**, [568]
   cancellation, **35(1)**, [568], [576]
   ceasing to be in force, **35(1)**, [568],
    [572]
    effect of, **35(1)**, [577]
    new notice where, **35(1)**, [577]
   change of person intending to carry out
    work, **35(1)**, [575]
   coming into force, time of, **35(1)**, [568]
   duration, **35(1)**, [568]
   effect of, **35(1)**, [569]
   form of, **35(1)**, [568]
   giving, **35(1)**, [568]
   insurance cover, provision of,
    35(1), [568]
   joint, **35(1)**, [582]
   plans accompanying, **35(1)**, [568], [569]
   plans certificate combined with,
    35(1), [571]
   register of information as to,
    35(1), [580]
   rejection of, **35(1)**, [568]
    appeal against, **35(1)**, [579]
   variation of work to which relates,
    35(1), [573]
  local authorities, other than, by,
   35(1), [568]–[582]
 town scheme, in, grants for repair of,
  46, [721]–[722]
 unlawful erection of, **36**, [1198]
 unoccupied or occupier temporarily absent—
  unauthorised entry—
   works to prevent—
    British Railways Board, on operational
     land of, **35(1)**, [438]
    electricity and water undertakers, on
     operational land of, **35(1)**, [438]
    entry powers in connection with,
     35(1), [437]
    expenses of, **35(1)**, [437], [440]

building—*contd*

unoccupied or occupier temporarily
absent—*contd*
unauthorised entry—*contd*
works to prevent—*contd*
notice of proposal to undertake—
appeal against, **35(1)**, [439]
local authority, by, **35(1)**, [437]
power of local authority to
undertake, **35(1)**, [437]
urban development area, loans in, **46**, [80]
urgent works to preserve—
carrying out, **46**, [696]
expenses, recovery of, **46**, [697]
value added tax—
non-residential, developers of, **50**, [155]
residential and charitable—
alterations, **50**, [149]
change of use, **50**, [155]
conversion, **50**, [149]
election to waiver exemption, **50**, [155]
renovations, **50**, [149]
VAT provisions, **50(S)**, VAT 1, 3–4
workplace, used as, sanitary conveniences in,
35(1), [589]

building line. *See under* **highway**

building regulations

appeal to—
Court of Appeal, **35(1)**, [563]
Crown Court, **35(1)**, [562]
High Court, **35(1)**, [563]
statement of case on, **35(1)**, [563]
magistrates' court, **35(1)**, [561]
Building Regulations Advisory Committee—
appointment, **35(1)**, [540]
consultation with, **35(1)**, [540]
civil liability for breach of, **35(1)**, [559]
classification of buildings for purposes of,
35(1), [554]
consultation with—
Building Regulations Advisory
Committee, **35(1)**, [540]
fire authority, **35(1)**, [541]
contents of, **35(2)**, [512]
continuing requirements of, **35(1)**, [527];
35(2), [513]
contravention of, **35(1)**, [527]
emissions, in relation to, **35(1)**, [528]
fuel, in relation to, **35(1)**, [528]
power, in relation to, **35(1)**, [528]
tests to ascertain whether contravention
of, **35(1)**, [553]
contravention of—
penalty for, **35(1)**, [529], [555]
prosecution for, time limit for, **35(1)**, [556]
removal or alteration of works in—
injunction for, **35(1)**, [557]
notice requiring—
appeal against, **35(1)**, [561]
existing works, in case of,
35(1), [659]
local authority, by, **35(1)**, [532],
[557], [659]

building regulations—*contd*

contravention of—*contd*
removal or alteration of works in—*contd*
notice requiring—*contd*
report on works where, **35(1)**, [558]
withdrawal, **35(1)**, [557]
Crown, application to, **35(1)**, [565]
dispensing with requirement of, **35(1)**, [534]
documents—
approval for purposes of, **35(1)**, [532]
approved, compliance or non-compliance
with, **35(1)**, [533]
registers, kept by local authority,
35(1), [614]
emissions, relating to, compliance report,
17(2), [582]
enforcement by local authorities, **35(1)**, [531],
[613]
entry powers in connection with, **35(1)**, [618]
exemption from—
Civil Aviation Authority, buildings of,
35(1), [530]
educational establishment, **35(1)**, [530]
particular classes of buildings, etc,
35(1), [529]
public bodies, from procedural
requirements, **35(1)**, [531]
school, **35(1)**, [530]
statutory undertakers, buildings of,
35(1), [530]
UK Atomic Energy Authority, buildings
of, **35(1)**, [530]
exemptions, removal of, **35(2)**, [514]
information and documents, registers, kept by
local authority, **35(1)**, [614]
inner London, application to, **35(1)**, [567]
making—
consultation by Secretary of State with
Building Regulations Advisory
Committee before, **35(1)**, [540]
power of, **35(1)**, [525]
materials unsuitable for permanent building,
specification of, **35(1)**, [545]
meaning, **35(1)**, [644]
obstruction in execution of, penalty for,
35(1), [634]
particular type of building matter—
approval—
certificate of, **35(1)**, [538]
delegation of power of, **35(1)**, [539]
Secretary of State, by, **35(1)**, [538]
relaxation in relation to, **35(1)**, [537]
plans, passing of. *See* **plans**
procedural requirements of, exemption of
public bodies from, **35(1)**, [531]
prosecutions relating to, time limits for,
35(1), [556]
prosecutions, time limits, **24**, [843]
provision which may be made by,
35(1), [525], [658]
relaxation—
advertisement of proposal for, **35(1)**, [536]
application for, **35(1)**, [535]
direction for—
appeal against, **35(1)**, [562]

building regulations—*contd*
relaxation—*contd*
  direction for—*contd*
    Secretary of State, by, **35(1)**, [534]
    existing work, for, **35(1)**, [659]
    fire precautions, consultation with fire
      authority, **35(1)**, [541]
    notices as to, **35(1)**, [536]
    particular type of building matter, in
      relation to, **35(1)**, [537], [538]
    provision for, **35(1)**, [534]
    refusal—
      appeal against—
        High Court, to, **35(1)**, [563]
        Secretary of State, to, **35(1)**, [560],
          [564]
  requirements of, **35(1)**, [525], [658]
  scope of, **35(1)**, [525], [658]
  short-lived materials, specification of,
    35(1), [544]
  special historical or architectural interest, for
    buildings of, **35(1)**, [526]
  summary of provisions, **35(1)**, [1]
  supervision of plans and work by approved
    inspectors, **35(1)**, [663]
  tests for conformity with, **35(1)**, [553]
  UK Atomic Energy Authority, application to,
    35(1), [566]
  use of fuel and power, relating to, compliance
    report, **17(2)**, [582]

Building Societies Commission
transfer of functions, **19(2)**, [411], [414]

**Building Societies Investor Protection
Board**
transfer of functions, **19(2)**, [412]

building society
accounts and audit—
  annual accounts, meaning, **19(1)**, [681]
  auditor remuneration, disclosures relating
    to, **19(1)**, [666], [745]
  auditors. *See* auditors *below*
  auditors' report accompanying, **19(1)**, [680]
  consistency, **19(1)**, [662]
  directors, officers and employees, disclosures
    relating to, **19(1)**, [663], [741], [742]
  group accounts—
    Building Societies Act, **19(1)**, [659],
      [660]
    duty to prepare, **19(1)**, [658]
    IAS, **19(1)**, [661]
  individual accounts—
    Building Societies Act, **19(1)**, [655],
      [656]
    duty to prepare, **19(1)**, [654]
    IAS, **19(1)**, [657]
  laying before members, **19(1)**, [679]
  off balance sheet arrangements, disclosures
    relating to, **19(1)**, [665]
  publication of, requirements, **19(1)**, [680]
  records, keeping, **19(1)**, [653]
  related undertakings, disclosures relating
    to, **19(1)**, [664], [743], [744]

building society—*contd*
accounts and audit—*contd*
  true and fair view, meaning, **19(1)**, [681]
  accounting period—
    meaning, **44(4)**, [956]
    payments in, **44(4)**, [957]
    payments otherwise than in, **44(4)**, [958]
  administration orders, **19(1)**, [688], [754],
    [755]
  advertising of meetings, **19(1)**, [732]
  amalgamation—
    agreements required, **19(1)**, [693]
    bonuses to members, **19(1)**, [696]
    compensation, directors and officers,
      19(1), [696]
    confirmation by Authority, **19(1)**, [693],
      [695], [758]
    memorandum, requirements as to,
      19(1), [693], [730]
    proposals—
      merger, interpretation, **19(1)**, [757]
      notifications, duty as to, **19(1)**, [757]
    resolution for, **19(1)**, [693]
    statement to members, **19(1)**, [695], [756]
    successor society, **19(1)**, [693]
    See also transfer of engagements *below*
  amended return, payer's duty to deliver,
    44(4), [966]
  annual general meeting, holding of,
    19(1), [732]
  appeal against cancellation of registration,
    19(1), [708]
  assessments, **44(4)**, [964]–[965], [968]
    time limits, **44(4)**, [967]
  associated undertakings, meaning, **19(1)**, [724]
  audit. *See* accounts and audit *above*
  auditors—
    appointment, **19(1)**, [671], [746]
    appropriate audit authority, duty to notify,
      19(1), [746]
    duties and powers, **19(1)**, [677]
    false or misleading statements to,
      19(1), [677]
    investigations by, **19(1)**, [677]
    liability of, **19(1)**, [715]
    meetings, attendance at, **19(1)**, [677]
    names—
      given in report, **19(1)**, [675]
      omitted from report, **19(1)**, [676]
    removal, **19(1)**, [746]
    report of, **19(1)**, [672]
      accounts, accompanying on publication,
        19(1), [680]
      names—
        omitted from, **19(1)**, [676]
        required to be stated in, **19(1)**, [675]
      signature, **19(1)**, [673]
    resignation, **19(1)**, [746]
    senior statutory auditor, **19(1)**, [674]
    tenure of office, **19(1)**, [746]
  authorisations, transitional provisions,
    19(1), [765]
  balance sheet—
    documents, annexation of, **19(1)**, [678]
    group accounts, **19(1)**, [659]

building society—*contd*
  balance sheet—*contd*
    individual accounts, **19(1)**, [655]
    signing of, **19(1)**, [678]
  bank administration provisions applying,
    19(S), Financial 216
  bank insolvency provisions applying,
    19(S), Financial 184
  Bank of England, assistance from, **19(2)**, [578]
  banker, acting as, **19(1)**, [995]
  borrowers, joint, **19(1)**, [730]
  borrowing powers, **19(1)**, [622]
  Building Societies Act 1986, modification of,
    19(2), [578]
  business associates. *See* directors *below*
  business—
    acquisition or establishment of,
      19(1), [692]
    annual statement, **19(1)**, [667]
    systems of control, **19(1)**, [653]
    transfer to company—
      bonus distribution, **19(1)**, [701]
      compensation for loss of office,
        19(1), [699]
      confirmation by Authority, **19(1)**, [697],
        [698], [761]
      directions, **19(1)**, [629], [735], [736]
      distributions, **19(1)**, [701]
      increased remuneration, **19(1)**, [700]
      meaning of company, **19(1)**, [697]
      members and officers, rights,
        19(1), [697]
      notices, **19(1)**, [760]
      notices, hearings and appeals,
        19(1), [631]
        variation and revocation, **19(1)**, [630]
      powers, **19(1)**, [697]
      procedure, **19(1)**, [697]
      proposals, notification of, **19(1)**, [760]
      protective provisions, **19(1)**, [702]
      regulated terms, **19(1)**, [699]
      regulations, **19(1)**, [703]
      resolution for, **19(1)**, [697], [732]
      second-named joint shareholders, rights
        of, **19(1)**, [704], [707]
      share rights, **19(1)**, [701]
      specially formed successors, **19(1)**, [702]
      statement to members, **19(1)**, [698],
        [759]
      supplementary provisions, **19(1)**, [698]
      terms of, **19(1)**, [701]
      transitional provisions, **19(1)**, [999]
      trustee account holders—
        interests of beneficiaries, **19(1)**, [705],
          [706]
        meaning, **19(1)**, [707]
        supplementary provisions, **19(1)**, [707]
  capacity, **19(1)**, [731]
  capital gains tax—
    amalgamation of, **42**, [1348]
    company, assets transferred to, **42**, [1349]
    qualifying shares, right to acquire,
      42, [1263]
    successor company, shares in, **42**, [1350]
    taper relief, ineligibility for, **42**, [1347]

building society—*contd*
  certified SAYE savings arrangement,
    44(1), [323]
  chairman, appointment, **19(1)**, [639]
  charges, registration of, **19(1)**, [710]
  chief executive—
    appointment, **19(1)**, [640]
    commission, bar on acceptance of,
      19(1), [649]
  collection and payment of tax, **44(4)**, [959]
  collective investment scheme—
    management of, **19(1)**, [623]
    meaning, **19(1)**, [623]
  commodities, restriction on trading in,
    19(1), [623]
  company—
    charges, registration, **19(1)**, [710]
    law, assimilation, **19(1)**, [709]
    transfer of business to. *See* business *above*
  company, transfer of business to—
    capital allowance provisions, **42**, [939]
    certified SAYE savings arrangements,
      42, [939]
    distributions, **42**, [939]
  connected undertakings, investigation by
    Authority, **19(1)**, [636]
  constitution, **19(1)**, [616], [730]
  conveyancing services—
    disclosure by officers as to, **19(1)**, [651]
    meaning, **19(1)**, [651]
  credit agreements, exemption of, **39(1)**, [149]
  currencies, restriction on trading in,
    19(1), [623]
  demutualisation, stamp duty land tax relief,
    41, [337]
  "deposit", meaning, **44(4)**, [863]
  depositions. *See* investors *below*
  derivative investments—
    meaning, **19(1)**, [623]
    restrictions on transactions involving,
      19(1), [623]
  description, restrictions, **19(1)**, [712]
  Directives, reference to, **19(1)**, [723]
  directors—
    accounts, duties as to. *See* accounts and
      audit *above*
    additional, **19(1)**, [641]
    annual business statement, preparation,
      19(1), [667]
    business associates—
      disclosures as to, **19(1)**, [651]
      meaning, **19(1)**, [651]
    business review, **19(1)**, [669]
    chairman, **19(1)**, [639]
    commissions, prohibition in acceptance,
      19(1), [649]
    connected persons—
      meaning, **19(1)**, [652]
      transactions with, **19(1)**, [648]
    co-opted, **19(1)**, [641]
    dealings with, **19(1)**, [643]–[650]
    disclosures in notes to accounts,
      19(1), [663], [741]
    election—
      address by, **19(1)**, [642]

building society—*contd*
  directors—*contd*
    election—*contd*
      provisions as to, **19(1)**, [641]
    eligibility of, **19(1)**, [641]
    interests, disclosure of, **19(1)**, [644]
    leases to, **19(1)**, [646]
    loans to—
      breach of provisions, **19(1)**, [647]
      commissions in connection with,
        prohibition, **19(1)**, [649]
      particulars required, **19(1)**, [737]
      permitted, **19(1)**, [646]
      record of, **19(1)**, [650]
      restriction on, **19(1)**, [646]
    nomination, **19(1)**, [641]
    notifications to Authority, **19(1)**, [642]
    number, **19(1)**, [639]
    power to bind society, **19(1)**, [731]
    property transactions involving,
      19(1), [645]
    related business—
      accountants, **19(1)**, [738]
      conveyancers, **19(1)**, [738]
      income from, disclosure and record of,
        19(1), [651]
      insurance agents etc, **19(1)**, [738]
      particulars required, **19(1)**, [651],
        [738]–[740]
      relevant services, **19(1)**, [651]
      valuers and surveyors, **19(1)**, [738]
    reports, **19(1)**, [668]
    retirement, **19(1)**, [641]
    retirement age, **19(1)**, [641]
    rules as to, **19(1)**, [641]
    shares held by, **19(1)**, [641], [642]
    summary financial statement, preparation,
      19(1), [670]
    supplementary provisions, **19(1)**, [642]
    tax-free payments to, prohibition,
      19(1), [643]
    term of office, **19(1)**, [641]
    transactions by—
      property, substantial, **19(1)**, [645]
      record of, **19(1)**, [650]
      restricted, particulars required,
        19(1), [737]
      voidable, **19(1)**, [648]
  discretionary or accumulation settlements,
    44(4), [881]
  disputes—
    arbitration, **19(1)**, [748]
    courts, jurisdiction of, **19(1)**, [747]
    generally, **19(1)**, [682]
    right of Authority to be heard, **19(1)**, [747]
  disqualification orders, **8**, 854–5
  dissolution—
    borrowing member, liability of,
      19(1), [691]
    cancellation of registration, **19(1)**, [708]
    consent, by, **19(1)**, [684]
      priorities, power to alter, **19(1)**, [689]
    instrument of, **19(1)**, [684]
    modes of, **19(1)**, [683]
    notice to Authority, **19(1)**, [684]

building society—*contd*
  dissolution—*contd*
    void, declaration by court, **19(1)**, [690]
    winding up, on, **19(1)**, [752]
    See also winding up *below*
  dividends, taxation, **44(3)**, [372]
  documents—
    duties to send, exception, **19(1)**, [730]
    evidence, as, **19(1)**, [718]
    form of, **19(1)**, [721]
    production to Authority, **19(1)**, [632]
    service of, **19(1)**, [720]
  dormant account money—
    apportionment, **19(S)**, Financial 17
    Big Lottery Fund, distribution to. *See*
      National Lottery
    English expenditure, distribution for
      meeting, **19(S)**, Financial 18
    meaning, **19(S)**, Financial 16
    Northern Ireland expenditure, distribution
      for meeting, **19(S)**, Financial 20
    power to add or remove distributors,
      19(S), Financial 23
    power to prohibit distribution,
      19(S), Financial 22
    Scottish expenditure, distribution for
      meeting, **19(S)**, Financial 19
    Welsh expenditure, distribution for
      meeting, **19(S)**, Financial 19
  dormant accounts—
    account, meaning, **19(S)**, Financial 12
    assets-limit condition, **19(S)**, Financial 7
    balance, meaning, **19(S)**, Financial 11–12
    charities, transfer of balances to with
      proportion to reclaim fund,
      19(S), Financial 5–6
    dormant, meaning, **19(S)**, Financial 12–13
    information, disclosure of,
      19(S), Financial 14
    insolvency, customer's rights preserved on,
      19(S), Financial 13
    interest on, **43(S)**, 866
    interpretation, **19(S)**, Financial 10
    membership rights, effect of balance
      transfer on, **19(S)**, Financial 8
    reclaim fund—
      articles of association, provision to be
        made in, **19(S)**, Financial 28
      business transfer schemes,
        19(S), Financial 30
      functions of, **19(S)**, Financial 8–9
      regulated activities, **19(S)**, Financial 29
      transfer of balances to,
        19(S), Financial 4–6
    review and report to Parliament,
      19(S), Financial 15
    summary of provisions,
      19(S), Financial 1–2
    transfer of, **43(S)**, 867
  duty to deduct sums, **44(4)**, [859]
    power to disapply, **44(4)**, [860]
  engagements, transfer. *See* transfer of
    engagements *below*
  establishment—
    generally, **19(1)**, [616]

building society—*contd*
  establishment—*contd*
    memorandum, **19(1)**, [730]
    requirements for, **19(1)**, [730]
  financial assistance to, **19(S)**, Financial 279–80
  financial year, **19(1)**, [722]
  first, **19(1)**, [1]
  floating charges, restriction on creation of,
    19(1), [624]
  funding limit, **19(1)**, [621]; **19(2)**, [563]
  funds, power to raise, **19(1)**, [622]
  general client account deposits, **44(4)**, [871]
  heritable security, meaning, **19(1)**, [723]
  incorporation, **19(1)**, [616]
  information, disclosure of, **19(1)**, [634]
  insolvent, application of insolvency
    legislation, **19(1)**, [688], [753]–[755]
  inspection of—
    appointment of inspector, **19(1)**, [637]
    circumstances requiring, **19(1)**, [637]
    reports, **19(1)**, [638]
    special meetings, **19(1)**, [637]
    supplementary provisions, **19(1)**, [638]
    See also investigation *below*
  investigation by auditors, **19(1)**, [677]
  investigation by Authority—
    appointment of investigator, **19(1)**, [636]
    connected undertakings, **19(1)**, [636]
    expenses of, **19(1)**, [637]
    offences arising, **19(1)**, [636]
    supplementary provisions, **19(1)**, [638]
  investments—
    held outside UK, **44(4)**, [876]
    meaning, **44(4)**, [863]
    other, **44(4)**, [878]
  investors—
    death of, **19(1)**, [734]
    special provisions, **19(1)**, [734]
    under age, receipts by, **19(1)**, [734]
  land—
    loan secured on—
      European Economic Area, outside,
        19(1), [618]
      fully, **19(1)**, [619]
      meaning, **19(1)**, [618]
    meaning, **19(1)**, [618]
    services relating to, provision of. *See*
    services *below*
  limitation of actions, **19(1)**, [716]
  Lloyd's premium trust funds, **44(4)**, [875]
  loan relationships, **44(1)**, [323]
  loans—
    directors, to, **19(1)**, [646], [650]
    land, secured on—
      European Economic Area, outside,
        19(1), [618]
      fully, **19(1)**, [619]
      meaning, **19(1)**, [618]
    lending limit, **19(1)**, [617]
    lending syndicate, owed to, **19(1)**, [617]
    transitional provisions, **19(1)**, [999]
    See also advances *above*
  market maker—
    meaning, **19(1)**, [623]
    restriction on acting as, **19(1)**, [623]

building society—*contd*
  marketable securities, **42**, [1072]
  meaning, **19(1)**, [723]; **22**, [490]
  meetings—
    annual general, **19(1)**, [732]
    notice of, **19(1)**, [732]
    rules as to, **19(1)**, [730]
    special, requisition of, **19(1)**, [732]
    voting at, **19(1)**, [732]
  members—
    accounts, laying before, **19(1)**, [679]
    death of, **19(1)**, [734]
    liability, **19(1)**, [730]
    meaning, **19(1)**, [723]
    minors as, **19(1)**, [730]
    register of, **19(1)**, [730]
    resolutions by. *See* resolutions *below*
    rules as to, **19(1)**, [730]
    special meeting, requisition of, **19(1)**, [732]
    transitional provisions, **19(1)**, [999]
    voting rights, **19(1)**, [732]
  memorandum—
    binding nature of, **19(1)**, [730]
    capacity not limited by, **19(1)**, [731]
    contents, **19(1)**, [730]
  merger. *See* amalgamation *above*
  mortgage—
    discharge of, **19(1)**, [620], [733]
    meaning, **19(1)**, [723]
    proper price, mortgagee obtaining,
      19(1), [995]
  mortgage interest. *See* **mortgage interest
  relief**
  mortgagee, agreement to indemnify, **22**, [319]
  name—
    approval of, **19(1)**, [712]
    change of, **19(1)**, [730]
    distinguishing features, **19(1)**, [712]
    offences relating to, **19(1)**, [730]
    required disclosure, **19(1)**, [730]
    restrictions on, **19(1)**, [712], [730]
    transitional provisions, **19(1)**, [765]
    use of, **19(1)**, [730]
  non-UK residence, declarations of—
    individuals, **44(4)**, [866]
    inspection of, **44(4)**, [870]
    personal representatives, **44(4)**, [868]
    Scottish partnerships, **44(4)**, [867]
    settlements, **44(4)**, [869]
  Northern Ireland, application of provisions,
    19(1), [727]
  notices, service of, **19(1)**, [720]
  offences—
    defence of due diligence, **19(1)**, [717]
    officer, liability of, **19(1)**, [717]
    proceedings, time limit, **19(1)**, [716]
  officers—
    appointment, **19(1)**, [640]
    chief executive, **19(1)**, [640]
    disclosures in notes to accounts,
      19(1), [663], [741]
    executive, meaning, **19(1)**, [723]
    liability of, **19(1)**, [715]
    manager, meaning, **19(1)**, [723]
    meaning, **19(1)**, [723]

building society—*contd*
  officers—*contd*
    offences, defence to, **19(1)**, [717]
    secretary, appointment, **19(1)**, [640]
    vacancy in office, **19(1)**, [641]
  persons connected with—
    loans etc to, **19(1)**, [646]
    meaning, **19(1)**, [652]
    property transactions involving,
      19(1), [645]
  post-war credit, repayment to, **42**, [35]
  powers—
    borrowing, **19(1)**, [622]
    exercise of, requirements, **19(1)**, [616]
    generally, **19(1)**, [616]
    raise funds, to, **19(1)**, [622]
    restrictions on, **19(1)**, [616]
    transitional provisions, **19(1)**, [999]
  principal office, change of, **19(1)**, [730]
  proceedings—
    evidence in, **19(1)**, [718]
    limitation of time, **19(1)**, [716]
  prohibition order against, **19(1)**, [627]
  public file, maintenance, **19(1)**, [711]
  qualifying—
    certificates of deposit, **44(4)**, [873]
    shares, incidental costs of issuing,
      44(1), [324]
    time deposits, **44(4)**, [874]
    uncertificated eligible debt security units,
      44(4), [872]
  receivers and managers of, **19(1)**, [688], [754], [755]
  records, mode of keeping, **19(1)**, [719]
  registration—
    cancellation, **19(1)**, [70]
    requirements, **19(1)**, [730]
    transitional provisions, **19(1)**, [765]
    when deemed, **19(1)**, [616]
  regulations, **42**, 1050
  relevant investments, **44(4)**, [864]–[865]
  resolutions—
    amalgamation, on, **19(1)**, [693]
    borrowing members, by, **19(1)**, [732]
    members', **19(1)**, [732]
    special, **19(1)**, [732]
    transfer of business, **19(1)**, [697], [732]
    transfer of engagements, for, **19(1)**, [694]
    voting on, entitlement, **19(1)**, [732]
    winding up, on, **19(1)**, [684]
  restructuring plan, **19(1)**, [626]
    directions, notices, hearings and appeals,
      19(1), [631]
  return periods, **44(4)**, [955]
  rules—
    alteration, **19(1)**, [730]
    binding nature of, **19(1)**, [730]
    copies, supply of, **19(1)**, [730]
    matters provided for in, **19(1)**, [730]
    membership, as to, **19(1)**, [730]
  secretary—
    appointment, **19(1)**, [640]
    commission, prohibition of accepting,
      19(1), [649]

building society—*contd*
  securities—
    payments in respect of, **44(4)**, [897]
    sale and repurchase of, **44(4)**, [877]
  set-off claim—
    conditions for, **44(4)**, [960]
    how it works, **44(4)**, [961]
    proceedings begun after, **44(4)**, [962]
    proceedings begun before, **44(4)**, [963]
  shareholders—
    joint, **19(1)**, [730]
    special provisions, **19(1)**, [734]
    transitional provisions, **19(1)**, [999]
  shares—
    deferred, meaning, **19(1)**, [723]
    directors, held by, **19(1)**, [641], [642]
    holding, value of, **19(1)**, [723]
    issue of, **19(1)**, [622]
    trustees, held by, **19(1)**, [622]
  solicitor's account, keeping in, **11(2)**, [366]; **11(4)**, [460]
  special resolution regime—
    consequential provisions,
      19(S), Financial 145
    dissolution or winding up, distribution of
      assets on, **19(S)**, Financial 144–5
    interpretation, **19(S)**, Financial 145
    provisions applied, **19(S)**, Financial 141–3
    temporary public ownership,
      19(S), Financial 143–4
  stamp duty exemption, **19(1)**, [713]
  stamp duty land tax exemption, **19(1)**, [714]
  summary financial statement, preparation and
    distribution, **19(1)**, [670]
  summary of provisions, **19(1)**, [1]
  supplementary provisions, **44(4)**, [879]–[881]
  transactions, restrictions on, **19(1)**, [623]
  transfer of business to company. *See* business
    above
  transfer of engagements—
    bonuses to members, **19(1)**, [696]
    certificate of registration, **19(1)**, [694]
    compensation, directors and officers,
      19(1), [696]
    confirmation by Authority, **19(1)**, [694], [761]
    directions, **19(1)**, [629], [735], [736]
      notices, hearings and appeals,
        19(1), [631]
      variation and revocation of, **19(1)**, [630]
    registration by Authority, **19(1)**, [694]
    resolutions for, **19(1)**, [694]
    statement to members, **19(1)**, [759]
    supplementary provisions, **19(1)**, [695]
  transitional provisions, **19(1)**, [725], [765], [999]; **44(1)**, [691]
  transitional provisions and savings,
    44(4), [1060]
  voluntary arrangements, **19(1)**, [688], [754], [755]
  voting, **19(1)**, [732]
  winding up—
    borrowing member, liability of,
      19(1), [691]
    contributories in, **19(1)**, [750], [751]

building society—*contd*
winding up—*contd*
court, by—
during voluntary winding up,
19(1), [683]
grounds for, **19(1)**, [686]
legislation applied, **19(1)**, [687],
[749]–[752]
petition for, **19(1)**, [686]
legislation, application of, **19(1)**, [687],
[749]–[752]
modes of, **19(1)**, [683]
priorities, power to alter, **19(1)**, [689]
voluntary—
as mode of, **19(1)**, [683]
court, by, during, **19(1)**, [683]
generally, **19(1)**, [685]
legislation, application of, **19(1)**, [687],
[749]–[752]
liquidator, status, **19(1)**, [685]
resolution for, **19(1)**, [685]
See also dissolution *above*
yearly interest payments excepted from
deductions, **44(4)**, [883]

Bulgaria
accession to European Union, **18**, [57]
peace treaty, **10**, [916]

bunker oil
pollution by, liability for, **39(2)**, [823], [827]
compulsory insurance against, **39(2)**, [835]

buoy
expenses, payment of, **39(2)**, [890]
harbour etc undertakers, laying down by,
39(2), [74]
injury to, **39(2)**, [896]
inspection of, **39(2)**, [876]
local—
inspection of, **39(2)**, [876]
surrender of, **39(2)**, [881]
management of, **39(2)**, [873]
meaning, **39(2)**, [901]
rates, etc, exemption from, **39(2)**, [898]
Thames river, in, **39(2)**, [284], [393]

burglary
aggravated, **12(1)**, [562]
building, entering, **12(1)**, [561]
firearm, having during, **12(1)**, [562]
going equipped for, **12(1)**, [577]
imprisonment, **12(1)**, [561]
meaning, **12(1)**, [561]
third offence, minimum sentence for,
12(2), [802]
appeal, previous conviction set aside on,
12(2), [803]
certificate of conviction, **12(2)**, [804]
day of offence, determination of,
12(2), [806]
service law, conviction under, **12(2)**, [805]
vehicles or vessels, inhabited, **12(1)**, [561]

burial
authority. *See* **burial authority**
boards, replacement, **5(2)**, [452]
body—
disposal of—
certificate before, **36**, [35]
Coroner's order, **36**, [35]
meaning, **36**, [42]
notification to registrar, **36**, [36]
removal from England, **36**, [37]
certificate of, falsification, **36**, [6]
chapel, under or near, **5(2)**, [355]
Church of England—
service in unconsecrated ground,
5(2), [418]
without rites of, **5(2)**, [413]
clergy, relief from certain penalties,
5(2), [419]
coffin containing more than one body,
36, [19]
cremated remains, burial of, **14**, 1258
cremation. *See* **cremation**
discontinuance, order for, **5(2)**, [385]
disorder at, prevention, **5(2)**, [415]
Established Church, persons not members of,
5(2), [351]
exclusive rights—
assignment, **5(2)**, [360], [380]
form of, **5(2)**, [361]
registration, **5(2)**, [362]
burials in place of, **5(2)**, [364]
form of grant, **5(2)**, [358]
giver of land, of, **14**, 208–10
grant of, **5(2)**, [357]
limitation on grant, **5(2)**, [365]
register of grants, **5(2)**, [359]
wills disposing of, **5(2)**, [363]
fees for burial without Church rites,
5(2), [413]
ground. *See* **burial ground; cemetery**
indecent etc behaviour at, **5(2)**, [414]
local authority, duty of, **35(1)**, [487]
notice of—
form, **5(2)**, [423]
generally, **5(2)**, [408]
time of burial, stating, **5(2)**, [410]–[411]
obstruction, **5(2)**, [414]
orderly manner, conduct in, **5(2)**, [414]
penalties, **36**, [41]
poor persons, **5(2)**, [409]
preventing by assault, **12(1)**, [92]
register—
cathedrals, in, **14**, 933–4
cemetery company, keeping by, **5(2)**, [348]
custody of, **14**, 934
default as to, penalty, **5(2)**, [403]
entries in, **5(2)**, [417]; **14**, 932, 952
errors, correction of, **14**, 933
evidence, as, **5(2)**, [404]
falsification etc, **5(2)**, [435]
persons responsible for keeping, **5(2)**, [402]
provision of, **5(2)**, [401]
searches, **5(2)**, [405]; **14**, 946–8

burial—*contd*

register—*contd*

See also **parochial registers and records**

registers—

deposit of, **36**, [16]

evidence, as, **36**, [4], [11]

forgery, **36**, [6]

searches, **36**, [3]

wilful damage to, **36**, [6]

registration, requirement, **5(2)**, [401]

regulation of, **5(2)**, [395], [412]

regulations by cemetery company, **5(2)**, [354]

regulations, power to make, **36**, [39]

religious service, with or without, **5(2)**, [413]

rights as to—

compensation for loss of, **14**, 1046

exclusive. *See* exclusive rights *above*

grant of, form, **5(2)**, [447]

new or altered parish, in, **14**, 1092

restriction on, **5(2)**, [416]

service—

chaplain, by, **5(2)**, [345]

other clergymen, by, **5(2)**, [346]

religious, with or without, **5(2)**, [413]

unconsecrated part of ground, **5(2)**, [352]

still-born child, **36**, [18], [38]

summary of provisions, **5(2)**, [319]; **36**, [1]

value added tax, exemption from, **50**, [153]

vaults—

health dangers, prevention, **5(2)**, [396]

rights as to, grant, **5(2)**, [447]

Wales, in, **14**, 415

war graves, **3**, [323]–[325]

burial authority

authorities deemed to be, **5(2)**, [452]

cemetery—

contributions to persons providing, **5(2)**, [452]

fees for, **5(2)**, [436], [438]

management and control, **5(2)**, [452], [455]

provision for, **5(2)**, [431]

crematorium—

certification, **5(2)**, [442]

transfer to, maintenance after, **5(2)**, [446]

See also **crematorium**

functions, discharge of, **5(2)**, [455]

London—

crematoria, powers as to, **25(1)**, [1008]

meaning, **25(2)**, [377]

references to, construction of, **25(1)**, [705]

rights of interment, power to extinguish, **25(2)**, [377]

maintenance of graves etc, by, **5(2)**, [446]

burial board

officers, transfer of, **25(2)**, [218]

burial ground. *See also* **cemetery**

acquisition of land for, **14**, 397

addition to, form of conveyance, **14**, 207

additional, use of buildings on, **14**, 405

adverse title, discharge from, **14**, 67

bishop, licence or faculty of, **32**, [30]

body, removal of, faculty required, **5(2)**, [398]

burial ground—*contd*

byelaws, **32**, [34]

byelaws for regulation of, **35(1)**, [48]

chapel on, use of, **14**, 405

civil aviation, acquisition for, **4(1)**, [105]

closed—

care and maintenance, **5(2)**, [394]

unconsecrated parts, sale etc, **5(2)**, [397]

compensation, provision for, **32**, [32]

consecrated land—

disused ground, in, **5(2)**, [460]

meaning, **5(2)**, [464]

transfer of body to, **5(2)**, [398]

conveyance of land for—

life tenant, by, **14**, 245–6

person under disability, by, **14**, 242

powers, **14**, 240–1

public body, by, **14**, 245

purchase money, payment of, **14**, 241–2

desecration of, prevention of, **35(1)**, [48]

discontinuance of use—

cities and towns, in, **5(2)**, [385]

disobeying order, penalty, **5(2)**, [392]

exempted grounds, **5(2)**, [386]

postponement, **5(2)**, [391]

prohibition after order for, **5(2)**, [387]

saving of certain rights, **5(2)**, [388]–[389]

disorderly behaviour, prevention, **5(2)**, [415]

district, outside, **14**, 405

disused—

building on, when permitted, **5(2)**, [456]

buildings—

meaning, **5(2)**, [426]

restrictions, **5(2)**, [427]

Charity Commission, saving for jurisdiction of, **5(2)**, [461]

closed churchyard, maintenance, **5(2)**, [453]

High Court charitable jurisdiction, saving for, **5(2)**, [461]

human remains, disposal of, **5(2)**, [457], [466]

local authority, transfer to, **32**, [25]

meaning, **5(2)**, [426]

planning permission for use, **5(2)**, [462]

questions, determination, **5(2)**, [463]

subsequent owners, rights etc, **5(2)**, [458]

tombstones etc, removal, **5(2)**, [457], [466]

tombstones or monuments, removal of, **32**, [30]

trusts and restrictions, discharge of, **5(2)**, [459]

fences surrounding, repair of, **35(1)**, [48]

games or sports played in, **32**, [30]

gravediggers, appointment, **5(2)**, [353]

graves, private, agreement as to, **5(2)**, [446]

highway authority, use by, **46**, [107]

Homes and Communities Agency, powers of, **24**, [857]

housing action trust, acquired by, **22**, [930]

inspection of, **5(2)**, [393]

Jewish, discontinuance of use orders, **5(2)**, [386]

land, prohibition on use for other purposes, **5(2)**, [327]

burial ground—*contd*
  local authority—
    acquisition by, **32**, [1], [28]
    borrowing by, **32**, [37]
    expenses of, **32**, [36]
    jointly, acting, **32**, [35]
    powers already vested in, **32**, [31]
    powers of management, exercising, **32**, [30]
  London—
    closed ground—
      chapel in, **5(2)**, [383]
      maintenance, **5(2)**, [394]
    disused, responsibility for, **25(1)**, [58]
    exclusive rights of burial—
      extinguishment, **25(2)**, [377]
      grant of, **25(1)**, [967]
    graves—
      levelling, **25(1)**, [508]
      maintenance, **25(1)**, [231]
    maintenance—
      expenses, **25(1)**, [231]
      extended powers, **25(1)**, [508];
        25(2), [270]
    monuments—
      maintenance, **25(1)**, [231]
      meaning, **25(1)**, [231]
      power to remove, **25(1)**, [508]
  maintenance, transfer of liability for,
    5(2), [446]
  management and control, **5(2)**, [452], [455]
  meaning, **5(2)**, [406]
    (Pastoral Measure), **14**, 1005
  monuments—
    agreement for maintenance, **5(2)**, [446]
    inscriptions, objection to, **5(2)**, [367]
    removal, **5(2)**, [457], [466]
    right to erect, grant of, **5(2)**, [447]
    unauthorised, removal, **5(2)**, [366]
  neglected, powers as to, **5(2)**, [399]
  new benefice, vesting in, **14**, 1088
  new town, in, use of, **46**, [152]
  Northern Ireland, application of provisions
    to, **32**, [40]
  ordinary, power of over, **14**, 193
  parish, right of burial in, **14**, 833
  pastoral scheme for, **14**, 1004
  private graves, agreement as to, **5(2)**, [446]
  provision by burial authority, **5(2)**, [452],
    [455]
  public health, protection, **5(2)**, [396]
  Quaker, discontinuance of use orders,
    5(2), [386]
  redundancy scheme, included in, **14**, 1034–5
  regional development agencies, vesting of land
    in, **46**, [952]
  registers. *See* **burial**
  regulation of, **5(2)**, [395]
  removal of bodies, faculty required,
    5(2), [398]
  rights for sepulture, **14**, 641
  sale of land for enlarging, **14**, 66
  summary of provisions, **5(2)**, [319]
  transfer of, maintenance after, **5(2)**, [446]
  two or more districts, common to, **14**, 405

burial ground—*contd*
  unconsecrated—
    burial service in, **5(2)**, [352]
    Church of England service in, **5(2)**, [418]
  union house, belonging to, **14**, 210
  urban development corporation, use by,
    46, [107]
  Urban Regeneration Agency, use by,
    46, [859]
  use and development of, **46**, [503]–[504]
  vaults. *See* **burial**
  Wales, in. *See* **Wales, Church in**

Burma
  judges' pensions, increase of, **33(1)**, [102],
    [112], [116]

Burnham Beeches
  access to, provisions relating to, **32**, [199]
  Countryside Act, application to, **32**, [278]

burning
  child exposed to risk of, **6**, [7]

Burnley
  incumbent, provisions on, **14**, 834

bus lanes
  contraventions, civil penalties, **38(2)**, [133]

bus services. *See also* **omnibus; passenger
  transport services; public service vehicles**
  bus, meaning, **37**, [369]
  community permits, **38(2)**, [677]
  competition test for exercise of functions,
    38(2), [141]
    local authorities, by, **38(2)**, [211]
    voluntary multilateral and bilateral
      agreements, **38(2)**, [212]
  concessionary travel. *See* **passenger
    transport services**
  council undertakings—
    companies to run—
      formation, **37**, [405]
      orders as to joint undertakings,
        37, [407], [408]
      schemes, **37**, [406], [460]
    division of undertakings, **37**, [399]
    grants for, **37**, [443]
    information—
      provision of—
        consultations, **38(2)**, [129]
        co-operation, **38(2)**, [131]
        duty of authority, **38(2)**, [130]
        economy, efficiency and effectiveness,
          having regard to, **38(2)**, [131]
        non-discrimination, **38(2)**, [131]
        requirements, **38(2)**, [129]
      requirement to display, **38(2)**, [681]
    interpretation, **36**, [871]
    Isles of Scilly, assistance for, **36**, [792]
    local authorities—
      agreements by, **37**, [405]
      control over, abolition of, **36**, [791]
      co-operation between, **37**, [425]

bus services—*contd*
　local authorities—*contd*
　　exclusion of powers, **37**, [404]
　　joint undertakings, **37**, [405], [407], [408]
　　small services, running of, **37**, [409]
　local services, power to obtain information about, **38(2)**, [132]
　London. *See also* **passenger transport service**
　London local service, **37**, [381]
　meaning, **37**, [381]
　National Bus Company. *See* **National Bus Company**
　operators, grants to, **38(2)**, [142]
　operator's licence requirements, **37**, [368]
　Passenger Transport Executive—
　　transfer of bus undertakings from—
　　　company formation for, **37**, [397]
　　　division of undertakings, **37**, [399]
　　　employee benefits, protection on, **37**, [400]
　　　supplementary provisions, **37**, [459]
　permits—
　　community bus—
　　　conditions, **37**, [373]
　　　contravention of conditions, **37**, [373]
　　　driver's licence, **37**, [373]
　　　forgery and misuse of, **37**, [458]
　　　grant of, **37**, [372]
　　　licence, requirement, **37**, [368]
　　　meaning, **37**, [372]
　　　regulations, **37**, [373], [465], [466]
　　　time limits on, **37**, [374]
　　forgery and misuse of, **37**, [458]
　　limitations on, **38(2)**, [677]
　　　community bus, **38(2)**, [677]
　public service vehicle, licensing requirements exemption, **37**, [368]
　quality contracts schemes—
　　ancillary provisions, **38(2)**, [103]
　　appeals against, **38(2)**, [104]
　　　Transport Tribunal, powers regarding, **38(2)**, [105]
　　boards for—
　　　advice from, **38(2)**, [99]
　　　Commissioner, **38(2)**, [98]
　　　consideration of schemes—
　　　　recommendations from, **38(2)**, [101]
　　　　requests to begin, **38(2)**, [100]
　　　members, **38(2)**, [98]
　　　practice and procedure of, **38(2)**, [102]
　　　reports from, **38(2)**, [102]
　　continuation of, **38(2)**, [110]
　　　appeals, **38(2)**, [114], [115]
　　　consultation document, **38(2)**, [110]
　　　England, areas in, **38(2)**, [112]
　　　exempt continuation proposal—
　　　　deemed as, appeals, **38(2)**, [114]
　　　　meaning, **38(2)**, [111]
　　　　not deemed to be, appeals, **38(2)**, [115]
　　　Wales, areas in, **38(2)**, [113]
　　continuation, exempt proposals, **38(2)**, [667]

bus services—*contd*
　quality contracts schemes—*contd*
　　effect of, **38(2)**, [107]
　　　different operational dates, **38(2)**, [665]
　　　excepted services, **38(2)**, [665]
　　exceptional circumstances, power of authorities to provide services in, **38(2)**, [669]
　　expiry date, **38(2)**, [110]
　　guidance, **38(2)**, [123]
　　interim services—
　　　exceptional circumstances, provided in, **38(2)**, [119]
　　　period for which may be provided, **38(2)**, [120]
　　joint, **38(2)**, [658]
　　local services, registration of, **38(2)**, [674]
　　making, **38(2)**, [103], [658], [662]
　　　appeals against, **38(2)**, [663]
　　maximum period, extension of, **38(2)**, [666]
　　notice and consultation requirements, **38(2)**, [96], [659]
　　　compliance with, **38(2)**, [658]
　　notice of, **38(2)**, [103]
　　postponement, **38(2)**, [106]
　　power to make, **38(2)**, [95]
　　proposed, approval of, **38(2)**, [97], [660]
　　quality contract—
　　　emergency, in, **38(2)**, [109]
　　　exceptions from requirements, **38(2)**, [109]
　　　meaning, **38(2)**, [95]
　　　review, **38(2)**, [95]
　　　tendering for, **38(2)**, [108]
　　regulations, **38(2)**, [121], [670]
　　revocation, **38(2)**, [116], [668]
　　traffic regulation orders, **38(2)**, [673]
　　transitional provisions, **38(2)**, [122], [671]
　　TUPE, application of, **38(2)**, [124], [671]
　　variation, **38(2)**, [668]
　　　exempt, appeals when considered to be, **38(2)**, [117]
　　　procedure for, **38(2)**, [116]
　　　exemptions, **38(2)**, [118]
　　　Transport Tribunal, directed by, **38(2)**, [118]
　quality partnership schemes—
　　appropriate national authority, meaning, **38(2)**, [147]
　　authorities, reference to, **38(2)**, [92]
　　contents of, **38(2)**, [85], [87]
　　effect of, **38(2)**, [89]
　　　different dates for different facilities, **38(2)**, [656]
　　existing facilities, involving, **38(2)**, [90]
　　facilities, dates for provision of, **38(2)**, [87]
　　fares, specifying, **38(2)**, [657]
　　frequencies, specifying, **38(2)**, [657]
　　guidance concerning, **38(2)**, [94]
　　making, **38(2)**, [85]–[87]
　　　different dates for different facilities, **38(2)**, [654]
　　meaning, **38(2)**, [85]

bus services—*contd*
  quality partnership schemes—*contd*
    notice and consultation requirements,
    38(2), [86], [653]
    postponement, **38(2)**, [88]
      particular facilities, **38(2)**, [655]
      particular services, **38(2)**, [655]
    publicity, **38(2)**, [87]
    quality of services, improving, **38(2)**, [652]
    registration restrictions, **38(2)**, [652]
    regulations, **38(2)**, [93]
    revocation, **38(2)**, [91]
    timings, specifying, **38(2)**, [657]
    variation, **38(2)**, [91], [92]
  rural, assistance for, **36**, [792]
  school bus—
    fare-paying passengers on, **37**, [32]
    meaning, **37**, [32]
  small bus services, **37**, [368], [409]
  special control over, abolition, **36**, [791]
  stations—
    discriminatory practices, restrictions on,
    37, [419], [420]
    meaning, **37**, [420]
    parking place, use of, as, **37**, [212]
    provision and maintenance, **37**, [418]
    restrictive practices, **37**, [419], [420]
    supplementary provisions, **37**, [420]
  stopping place, meaning, **37**, [468]
  ticketing schemes—
    effect of, **38(2)**, [128]
    joint and through, **38(2)**, [125]
    making of, **38(2)**, [127]
    notice and consultation requirements,
    38(2), [126]
  Transport for London—
    co-operation, **37**, [403]
    excursions or tours, **37**, [385]

bus shelters. *See* **omnibus**

buses
  vehicle excise duty, **13**, [1043]

business
  carried on by person over sixty, compensation
    for disturbance, **9**, [345]
  defective equipment, employers' liability,
    16, [19]
  disturbance of, damage by, **9**, [217]
  entertainment—
    charge to tax, **44(1)**, [411]
    meaning, **44(1)**, [411]
  meaning, **16**, [19]
  names. *See* **business names**
  premises. *See* **business premises**
  tenancy, compensation on compulsory
    acquisition, **9**, [346]

business expansion scheme
  capital gains tax relief, **42**, [1269]
  proceedings, jurisdiction for, **42**, [180]

business names
  Act, application of, **48**, 94–5

business names—*contd*
  approval of Secretary of State, requiring,
    48, 96
  "chamber of commerce", including,
    48, 212–13
  civil legal proceedings relating to, **48**, 98
  disclosure of, **48**, 97
  generally, **48**, 12–13
  inappropriate indication of company type or
    legal form, containing, **8(1)**, [1275]
  individual or partnership, disclosure in case
    of—
    application of provisions, **8(1)**, [1278]
    business documents, **8(1)**, [1280]
    business premises, **8(1)**, [1282]
    failure to make, consequences of—
      civil, **8(1)**, [1284]
      criminal, **8(1)**, [1283]
    information requiring, **8(1)**, [1279]
    large partnerships, conditions for
      exemption, **8(1)**, [1281]
  interpretation, **8(1)**, [1286]
  lawful, **48**, 100
  saving for, **8(1)**, [1277]
  misleading—
    inappropriate indication of company type
      or legal form, containing, **8(1)**, [1275]
    indication of activities, as to, **8(1)**, [1276]
  Northern Ireland, provisions extended to,
    8(1), [1363]
  offences, **48**, 99
    application of general provisions,
    8(1), [1285]
  prohibited, **48**, 95
  regulations, **48**, 98
  restricted or prohibited—
    application of provisions, **8(1)**, [1270]
    approval of Secretary of State for—
      obtaining, **8(1)**, [1272]
      withdrawal of, **8(1)**, [1274]
    comments of government department or
      other specified body, duty to seek,
      8(1), [1273]
    government or public authority, suggesting
      connection with, **8(1)**, [1271]
    misleading, **8(1)**, [1275]–[1276]
    sensitive words or expressions,
      8(1), [1271]–[1273]

business premises
  improvements—
    compensation for—
      amount of, **21**, [51]
      charges, **21**, [58], [72]
      claims, time for making, **21**, [211]
      conditions, **21**, [53]
      consideration for, effect of, **21**, [52]
      contracting out, **21**, [55], [213]
      Crown and Duchy lands, payable by,
      21, [69], [73]
      deductions, **21**, [57]
      disputes, determination of, **21**, [51]
      holdings to which provisions applied,
      21, [63]
      limitation on right to, **21**, [52], [212]

business premises—*contd*
improvements—*contd*
compensation for—*contd*
mesne landlord, to, **21**, [54]
payment from capital money, **21**, [59]
relief from liability, **21**, [60]
reversionary lease, provisions as to,
21, [61]
right to, **21**, [51]
service of notices, **21**, [68]
tribunal, **21**, [67]
increase in rates, etc, reimbursement of,
21, [62]
landlord's right of entry, **21**, [56]
objections to, **21**, [53]
renewal of tenancy, effect on, **21**, [52]
jurisdiction of court, **21**, [216]
reversions, provisions as to, **21**, [226]
security of tenure—
agreements excluding provisions, **21**, [198],
[199]
agricultural holdings, exclusion of,
21, [207]
business, meaning, **21**, [175]
compensation—
agreement excluding or reducing,
21, [198], [199]
amount of, **21**, [196]
compulsory acquisition, saving for,
21, [200]
special powers, on exercise of, **21**, [221]
competent landlord, acts of, **21**, [240]
compulsory acquisition, effect of, **21**, [200]
contracting out, **21**, [198], [199]
county court—
declarations, jurisdiction to make,
21, [208]
jurisdiction of, **21**, [224]
Crown and Duchy lands, application of
provisions to, **21**, [218], [241]
employment, exclusion of tenancy arising
from, **21**, [207]
exclusions, **21**, [207]
farm business tenancy, exclusion of,
21, [207]
Government departments, provisions
applying to, **21**, [218]
groups of companies, provisions applying
to, **21**, [206]
information, duty of parties to give,
21, [201]
breach of duty, **21**, [203]
transfer cases, in, **21**, [202]
landlord, meaning, **21**, [209]
mesne landlord, provisions as to, **21**, [209],
[240]
mining lease, exclusion of, **21**, [207]
mortgagee in possession, provisions as to,
21, [228]
National Trust, interests of, **21**, [219]
new tenancy—
application for—
court order, **21**, [185]
dismissal of, **21**, [189]
tenant, by, **21**, [176]

business premises—*contd*
security of tenure—*contd*
new tenancy—*contd*
application for—*contd*
time limits, **21**, [186], [187]
compensation where precluded,
21, [196]
Distribution of Industry Acts, special
provisions under, **21**, [222]
duration of, **21**, [192]
grant of economically separable part,
21, [190]
interim rent—
application for determination of,
21, [177]
date from which payable, **21**, [178]
new tenancy of whole premises
granted, where, **21**, [179]
reasonable, **21**, [180]
misrepresentation, refusal induced by,
21, [197]
opposition to application—
demolition, etc, proposed, **21**, [188],
[190]
grounds for, **21**, [188]
notice of, **21**, [182]
successful, being, **21**, [189]
order for—
carrying out, **21**, [195]
court making, **21**, [185]
part only, for, **21**, [190]
partnership, to, **21**, [205]
revocation of, **21**, [195]
property comprised in, **21**, [191]
rent—
amount payable, **21**, [193]
interim, determination of,
21, [177]–[180]
request for—
notice of, **21**, [182]
opposition by landlord, **21**, [182]
time for making, **21**, [182]
reversionary tenancy, power to order,
21, [240]
terms, determination of, **21**, [194]
Welsh Development Agency premises,
21, [223]
notices, provisions as to, **21**, [227]
office holder using premises, exclusion of,
21, [207]
partnerships, provisions applying to,
21, [205]
prohibition, business carried out in breach
of, **21**, [175]
public interest, modification of rights on
ground of, **21**, [219]
rateable value, determining, **21**, [196]
reversions, provisions as to, **21**, [226]
superior landlord—
meaning, **21**, [240]
provisions as to, **21**, [240]
tenancy—
agreement, renewal by, **21**, [184]
assured tenancy, not being, **22**, [913]

business premises—*contd*
security of tenure—*contd*
tenancy—*contd*
continuation of, **21**, [176]
agreement by, **21**, [184]
interim, **21**, [225]
rent during, **21**, [177]–[180]
time limits, **21**, [186], [187]
holding, meaning, **21**, [175]
inferior extending beyond term of
superior, **21**, [226]
meaning, **21**, [230]
new. *See* new tenancy *above*
qualifying, **21**, [175]
termination of—
court order for, **21**, [185]
Distribution of Industry Acts, under,
21, [222]
fixed term, **21**, [183]
forfeiture, by, **21**, [176]
landlord, by, **21**, [181]
notice by tenant, **21**, [176]
notice, contents of, **21**, [181]
notice to quit, meaning, **21**, [230]
special grounds, on, **21**, [220]
surrender, by, **21**, [176]
Welsh Development Agency
premises, **21**, [223]
trust, held on, **21**, [204]
term not exceeding six months, exclusion
of, **21**, [207]
transitional provisions, **21**, [242]
vehicle testing business, exclusion of,
37, [132]
summary of provisions, **20**, [1]

business premises renovation allowances
additional VAT liabilities and rebates,
43(1), [959]–[964]
availability of, **43(1)**, [940]
balancing adjustments, **43(1)**, [952]–[955]
calculation of, **43(1)**, [955]
balancing events, **43(1)**, [953]
proceeds from, **43(1)**, [954]
demolition costs, treatment of, **43(1)**, [958]
giving effect to—
lessors and licensees, **43(1)**, [966]
trades, **43(1)**, [965]
initial, **43(1)**, [946]
writing off, **43(1)**, [957]
lease, etc, meaning, **43(1)**, [969]
non-qualifying trades, sums partly referable
to, **43(1)**, [967]
qualifying building—
completion of conversion, interest acquired
on, **43(1)**, [945]
meaning, **43(1)**, [942]
relevant interest in, **43(1)**, [944]–[945]
qualifying business premises, meaning,
43(1), [943]
qualifying expenditure—
grants in respect of, **43(1)**, [951]
meaning, **43(1)**, [941]
writing off, **43(1)**, [956]–[958]

business premises renovation allowances—*contd*
termination of lease, provisions applying on,
43(1), [968]
writing-down, **43(1)**, [948]–[950]
writing off, **43(1)**, [957]

business tenancy
compensation provisions, **23**, [54]

business transfer scheme
banking—
certificates, **19(2)**, [533]
conditions, **19(2)**, [149]
meaning, **19(2)**, [149]
terminate, rights to, **19(2)**, [156]
insurance—
certificates, **19(2)**, [532]
conditions, **19(2)**, [148]
effected outside UK, **19(2)**, [534]
excluded, **19(2)**, [148]
Lloyd's business, **19(2)**, [398]
meaning, **19(2)**, [148]
order sanctioning, effect of, **19(2)**, [155]
other EEA States, authorised in,
19(2), [161]
policyholders, rights of, **19(2)**, [158]
reinsurance contracts, notice of transfer of,
19(2), [159]
scheme reports, **19(2)**, [152]
termination, rights of, **19(2)**, [156]
transfers overseas, certificates for,
19(2), [160], [534]
modification of provisions, **19(2)**, [162]
order sanctioning—
actuary, appointment of, **19(2)**, [157]
application for, **19(2)**, [150]
conditions for, **19(2)**, [154]
effect of, **19(2)**, [155]
property or liabilities, transfer of,
19(2), [155]
requirement of, **19(2)**, [147]
requirements on applicants, **19(2)**, [151]
right to participate in proceedings,
19(2), [153]

businesses
credit or hire agreements, exemption of,
39(1), [151]

busking
application of provisions, **26(2)**, [166]
licence—
appeals, **26(2)**, [174]
applicants, **26(2)**, [169]
cancellation, **26(2)**, [171]
enforcement, **26(2)**, [175]
power of licensing, **26(2)**, [168]
refusal of, **26(2)**, [170]
revocation, **26(2)**, [172]
standard terms, conditions and restrictions,
power to prescribe, **26(2)**, [173]
streets, designation of, **26(2)**, [167]
meaning, **26(2)**, [165]
police powers, **26(2)**, [176]

busking—*contd*
resolutions, **26(2)**, [177]
seizure of apparatus and equipment,
26(2), [176]

byelaws. *See also* **local authority** *and under*
appropriate subject headings
abolished councils, of, **25(2)**, [627]
acupuncture, **35(1)**, [433], [435]
application of provisions, **35(1)**, [62]
barbers and hairdressers, **35(1)**, [272]
baths, etc, for regulation of, **35(1)**, [150],
[159]
breach of, penalties for, **35(1)**, [27]
building, now building regulations,
35(1), [611]
burial grounds, **35(1)**, [48]
cabmen's shelters, **35(1)**, [54]
confirmation, **35(1)**, [28], [50], [62]
cosmetic piercing, **35(1)**, [434]
country parks, **25(2)**, [636]
dust nuisances, **35(1)**, [133]
electrolysis, **35(1)**, [434]
enforcement of, appointment of officers for,
35(1), [69]
esplanades and promenades, **35(1)**, [73]
explosives. *See* **explosives**
fairs, etc, **35(1)**, [384]
hairdressers and barbers, **35(1)**, [272]
hop-pickers, etc, **35(1)**, [172]
land drainage—
application for, **19(3)**, [258]
commencement, date for, **19(3)**, [258]
confirmation—
application for, **19(3)**, [258]
Minister, by, **19(3)**, [258]
requirement, **19(3)**, [241], [258]
contravention, **19(3)**, [241]
exercise of powers under, **19(3)**, [241]
power to make, **19(3)**, [241]
proof, **19(3)**, [258]
purposes of, **19(3)**, [241]
revocation, **19(3)**, [258]
liquid, as to removal from streets, **35(1)**, [134]
London. *See* **London government**
nuisances, for prevention of certain,
35(1), [133]
offensive matter, as to removal from streets,
35(1), [134]
persons waiting to enter public vehicles,
35(1), [100]
pleasure boats, **35(1)**, [56], [271], [380]
pleasure fairs, **35(1)**, [270]
pleasure grounds, **35(1)**, [24]
power to make, **22**, [23]
public bathing, for regulating, **35(1)**, [157],
[380]
public walks, **35(1)**, [24]
regulations, exclusion in relation to,
35(1), [29]
roller skating rinks, **35(1)**, [270]
savings as to, **35(1)**, [217]
seashore, for regulating use of, **35(1)**, [72]
seaside pleasure boats, **35(1)**, [271], [380]
semi-permanent skin colouring, **35(1)**, [434]

byelaws—*contd*
snow, nuisance from, **35(1)**, [133]
spread of infectious disease from tents, etc, for
preventing, **35(1)**, [497]
swimming baths and bathing pools,
35(1), [159]
tattooing, **35(1)**, [434]
tents, vans and sheds, **35(1)**, [170]
washhouses, **35(1)**, [150]
watercourses, protection of, **19(3)**, [241]
wireless installations, as to wires, etc,
connected with, **35(1)**, [98]

by-pass
cattle grid, in relation to. *See under* **cattle**
grid

byssinosis
disablement payments—
conditions of entitlement, **40(1)**, [90]
dependants, to, **40(1)**, [91]
determination of claims, **40(1)**, [92]
fraudulent statements, **40(1)**, [96]
lump sum, **40(1)**, [1], [89]
minors, for benefit of, **40(1)**, [94]
reconsideration of determinations,
40(1), [93]
regulations, **40(1)**, [95]
relevant employer, definition, **40(1)**, [99]
industrial injuries benefits, **40(1)**, [354], [488]

byway
evidence of, **37**, [89]
meaning, **36**, [773]
open to all traffic, **37**, [178], [301]
definitive map, not to be added to, **37**, [87]
meaning, **37**, [96]
traffic regulation on, in National Parks,
37, [192]
restricted—
agricultural land, passing over, works on,
authorisation, **36**, [1191]
dedication of, **36**, [1029]
district council maintaining, **36**, [1046]
disturbance, authorisation of works,
36, [1191]
existing legislation, power to amend,
38(2), [58]
extinguishment of liabilities, **38(2)**, [56]
highway maintainable at public expense,
as, **38(2)**, [56]
making up, **36**, [1031]
meaning, **37**, [96]
orders—
notice of, **36**, [1407]
validity and operation, **36**, [1408]
parish or community council maintaining,
36, [1047]
ploughing—
other works, authorisation, **36**, [1191]
temporary diversion, **36**, [1191]
private rights over, **38(2)**, [57]
procedure for making, **36**, [1407]
rail crossing diversion orders, **36**, [1154]
railway, crossing, stopping up, **36**, [1149]

byway—*contd*
  restricted—*contd*
    rights, **38(2)**, [55]
    road used as public path, now shown as, **38(2)**, [817]
    survey of, **36**, [1031]
    traffic regulation on, in National Parks, **37**, [192]
    Wales, in, **38(2)**, [58]

byway—*contd*
  restricted—*contd*
    works, carrying out, **36**, [1031]
  restricted rights over, **38(2)**, [55]
  signposting, **36**, [773]
  temporary prohibition or restriction on traffic, **37**, [178]
  wardens, appointment of, **37**, [94]

C

cab. *See* **hackney carriage; taxis and taxicabs**

cable
insulation from, burning, offence of, **35(2)**, [32]
overground. *See* **overground wires**
submarine. *See* **submarine cables**

Cable and Wireless Ltd. *See under* **telecommunications**

Cable Authority
chairman and members, cessation of office, **45**, [155]
dissolution, **45**, [156]
employees, transfer of, **45**, [195]
property, rights and liabilities, transfer to ITC, **45**, [156], [195]

cable services. *See* **Cable Authority**

cables
submarine. *See* **submarine cables**

café
night. *See* **night cafés**

Caldey Island
Pembrokeshire coroner, in district of, **25(2)**, [904]
Tenby, part of, **25(2)**, [903]

calendar. *See also* **time**
bank holidays. *See* **bank holidays**
Gregorian, **45**, [918]
historical note, **45**, [918]
Julian, rectification, **45**, [918]
new style—
abstinence, days of, **45**, [925]
annuities, natural days and times of payment, **45**, [924]
common of pasture, opening and inclosing, **45**, [923], [926]
common year, **45**, [920]
Dominical letter, finding, **45**, [925]
Easter—
provisions as to, **45**, [921]
rule, **45**, [925]
Easter day—
application of Act, extent of, **45**, [931]–[933]
date of, **45**, [930]
table to find, **45**, [925]
fairs, days for holding, **45**, [922]
fasting, days of, **45**, [925]
feasts, table of, **45**, [925]

calendar—*contd*
new style—*contd*
Golden Numbers, **45**, [925]
holy days, rules for, **45**, [925]
interest, natural days and times for payment, **45**, [924]
lands, title to, **45**, [927]
leap year, **45**, [920]
London, Lord Mayor, annual admission and swearing, **45**, [928]
markets, days for holding, **45**, [922]
moveable feasts—
provisions as to, **45**, [921], [930]
table, **45**, [925]
tables and rules, **45**, [925]
Prayer Book, provisions as to moveable feasts, **45**, [921]
reckoning days of the year, **45**, [919]
rents, natural days and time for payment of, **45**, [924], [926]
solemn days, **45**, [925]
Sunday letter, finding, **45**, [925]
supposition of year, old, abolition, **45**, [919]
tables and rules, **45**, [925]
vigils, table of, **45**, [925]

Cambridge
mayor of, liberties of, **15(1)**, [9]

Cambridge, University of. *See also* **universities and colleges**
annual list of members of Senate, **15(1)**, [68]
appointment of constables in, **12(1)**, [32], [33]
Chancellor's Court, ceasing jurisdiction, **11(2)**, [381]
commissioners—
duties of, **15(1)**, [185]
election of, **15(1)**, [191]
establishment of, **15(1)**, [184]
meetings, notice of, **15(1)**, [191]
statute applying to, **15(1)**, [186]
statutes of—
alteration of, **15(1)**, [186]
assessment of college contributions, on, **15(1)**, [187]
trust, altering, **15(1)**, [187]
validity of acts, **15(1)**, [191]
Council of the Senate—
absence from meetings, **15(1)**, [73]
casual vacancies, **15(1)**, [71]
committees, appointing, **15(1)**, [76]
composition of, **15(1)**, [68]
election to, **15(1)**, [70]
establishment of, **15(1)**, [66]
offices, nomination for, **15(1)**, [79]
president of, **15(1)**, [77]

Cambridge, University of—*contd*
  Council of the Senate—*contd*
    professors, eligibility of, **15(1)**, [75]
    quorum, **15(1)**, [78]
    re-election of members, **15(1)**, [70]
    rules of procedure, making, **15(1)**, [76]
    Vice-Chancellor, member becoming, **15(1)**, [74]
    voting for, **15(1)**, [75]
    voting in, **15(1)**, [78]
  deeds and obligations, validity of, **15(1)**, [6]
  electoral roll—
    notice of objection, **15(1)**, [149]
    objections to, **15(1)**, [69]
    promulgation of, **15(1)**, [69]
  hostels, **15(1)**, [82]
  illegal oaths, **15(1)**, [80]
  incorporation, **15(1)**, [3]
  interpretation of terms, **15(1)**, [90], [146]
  land, acquisition of, **15(1)**, [81]
  legal deposit library, as, **13**, [467]
  letters patent, **15(1)**, [4]
  licence to receive students, **15(1)**, [81]
  matriculation, no oath on, **15(1)**, [87]
  patents and liberties granted to, **15(1)**, [7]
  possessions and privileges, **15(1)**, [5]
  powers and privileges, continuation of, **15(1)**, [89]
  principals, **15(1)**, [82]
  privileges and exemptions, removal of, **19(3)**, [688]
  proxy voting, **15(1)**, [83], [92]
  religious belief, no declarations on, **15(1)**, [88]
  statutes—
    doubt as to, settling, **15(1)**, [85], [191]
    Privy Council, submission to, **15(1)**, [147]
    repeal and amendment, **15(1)**, [86]
  substitution of declaration for oath by, **18**, [83]
  superannuation fund, establishing, **15(1)**, [189]
  titles of strangers, etc, saving for, **15(1)**, [8]
  Trinity College, Westminster exhibitions at, **15(1)**, [84]
  trusts. *See* **trusts, university and college**

Cameroon
  Commonwealth—
    admission to, **7(2)**, [854]
    citizenship, **31**, [186]

camping site
  financial aid for, **1(1)**, [649]
  local authority, provision by, **32**, [261]
  National Park, in, **32**, [148]

Canada
  Commonwealth citizenship, **31**, [186]
  constitution of, **7(2)**, [757]
  French version of provisions, **7(2)**, [759]
  Parliament, powers of, **7(2)**, [429]
  United Kingdom legislation in, **7(2)**, [758]

canal. *See also* **inland waterway**
  British Waterways Board—
    not comprised in undertaking of, **36**, [851]
    owned or managed by. *See* **British Waterways Board**
  charge to tax, **44(1)**, [34]
  company. *See* **canal company**
  goods, carriage of, **36**, [364]
  inspection of, **36**, [555]
  land drainage works—
    interference by, **20**, [300]
    protection as to, **20**, [326]
  local authority, expenses of, **36**, [559]
  London, in—
    dangerous places on—
      cost of works, **36**, [576]
      local authority, execution of works by, **36**, [575]
      protection of, **36**, [573]
      requisition, appeals, **36**, [574]
  meaning, **35(1)**, [112], [494]
  nationalisation, **36**, [210]
  navigation, right of, **36**, [854]
  owner, limitation of liability of, **39(2)**, [868]
  protection for, **35(1)**, [208]
  railway company, maintenance by, **36**, [546]
  rent payable in respect of, **44(1)**, [98]
  steam boats, use of, **36**, [365]
  street works near, display of lights, **38(1)**, [235]
  supply of water for, **36**, [719]
  tolls. *See* **toll**
  towing path etc, street works involving, **38(1)**, [234]

canal boat
  detention, **35(1)**, [491]
  entry to, **35(1)**, [491], [503]
  infectious disease—
    duties of local and port health authorities, **35(1)**, [492]
    entry and inspection, powers of, **35(1)**, [491], [503]
    offences, prosecution of, **35(1)**, [493]
    prevention of spread by, **35(1)**, [490]
    regulations as to, **35(1)**, [490]
  inspection, **35(1)**, [491], [503]
  local authority, duties of, **35(1)**, [492]
  meaning, **35(1)**, [494]
  port health authority, duties of, **35(1)**, [492]
  regulations as to, **35(1)**, [490]

canal company
  borrowing powers, **36**, [418]
  byelaws, **36**, [554]
  common carrier, as—
    lawfully acting as, **36**, [364]
    power to sue, **36**, [367]
    provisions applying to, **36**, [368]
  explosives, carriage etc. *See* **explosives**
  general Act, bound by, **36**, [374]
  hauling and tracking vessels, provision of, **36**, [366]
  meaning, **36**, [557]

canal company—*contd*
  other companies—
    contracts between, **36**, [369], [556]
    steam boat, using on canal of, **36**, [365]
  tolls—
    determination of lease, **36**, [373]
    leasing, **36**, [370]
    lessee—
      collectors, deemed, **36**, [371]
      default by, **36**, [372]
    reletting, **36**, [373]
  works, apportionment of expenses of,
    36, [552]

canal undertakers
  meaning, **36**, [1381]
  private street works expenses, exemption
    from, **36**, [1262]
  property of, reference to, **36**, [1381]
  saving for works of, **36**, [1390]

canal undertakings
  British Transport Commission, vesting in,
    36, [210]

cancer
  advertisements offering to treat, restriction
    on, **28**, [10]

candidate
  donations to—
    acceptance of, **15(3)**, [210]
    control of, **15(3)**, [74], [209]–[211]
    election agent, transfer to, **15(3)**, [210]
    general rules regarding, **15(3)**, [209]
    impermissible donors, from, prohibitions on
      accepting, **15(3)**, [210]
    payments not to be regarded as,
      15(3), [209]
    reporting of, **15(3)**, [211]
    restrictions on, evasion of, **15(3)**, [210]
    return of, **15(3)**, [210]
    sponsorship, **15(3)**, [209]
    value of, **15(3)**, [209]
  election agent, as, **15(3)**, [68], [71]
  false statement as to, **15(3)**, [109]
  local government. *See* **local government
    election**
  meaning, **15(3)**, [121]
  minimum age, **15(3)**, [608]
  nomination procedure, **15(3)**, [610]
  parliamentary. *See* **parliamentary election**
  sex discrimination in selection of, **7(1)**, [87],
    [698]
  withdrawal, corrupt inducement of,
    15(3), [110]

cannabis
  cultivation, restriction on, **28**, [204]
  use of premises for smoking, offence of
    permitting, **28**, [206]

canon
  deacon, appointment of, **14**, 1262

canon—*contd*
  incapacity. *See* **diocese**
  meaning, **14**, 141, 624
  qualifications of, **14**, 133
  resignation of, **14**, 1310

canonry
  Christ Church, Oxford, at, **14**, 132
  right of patronage of, transferring, **14**, 925
  St. Pauls, in, patronage, **14**, 133
  Westminster, annexation of rectories to,
    14, 134

canons (canon law)
  constitutions, Royal Assent to, **14**, 21–2
  Crown prerogative, contrary to, **14**, 22
  doctrine of Church of England—
    assent to, providing for, **14**, 814
    safeguarding, **14**, 814–15
  enforcement of, **14**, 22
  General Synod, making, promulging and
    executing, **14**, 685
  majority required for approval, **14**, 814
  promulgation by convocations, **14**, 22
  worship in Church of England, providing
    for, **14**, 812–13

Canterbury
  archbishop. *See* **Archbishop of Canterbury**
  Arches Court. *See* **Arches Court of
    Canterbury**
  commissary court. *See* **commissary court**
  commissary general, **14**, 558
  registrar, office of, **14**, 826–7
  senior bishops, **14**, 1109

capias ad respondendum
  writ of, abolition, **13**, [43]

capital
  international movement of—
    commencement, **43(S)**, 1551
    existing regime, abolition, **43(S)**, 1547
    reporting requirement, **43(S)**, 1547–50
    transitional provisions, **43(S)**, 1551

capital allowances
  abbreviations, list of, **43(1)**, [1220]
  additional VAT liabilities. *See* **value added
    tax**
  additional VAT rebates. *See* **value added tax**
  agricultural buildings, for. *See* **agricultural
    buildings allowance**
  annual investment allowance—
    amended provisions, **43(S)**, 1219
    double relief, prevention of, **43(S)**, 1217
    entitlement to, **43(S)**, 1211–12
    long chargeable periods, **43(S)**, 1215–16
    qualifying activities, **43(S)**, 1215
    qualifying expenditure, **43(S)**, 1210–11
    restrictions, **43(S)**, 1212–15, 1218
    short chargeable periods, **43(S)**, 1216
  assets, part, application of provisions to,
    43(1), [1210]

capital allowances—*contd*
assured tenancy, dwelling-house let on. *See*
assured tenancy allowances
balancing event, avoidance affecting proceeds
of, **43(2)**, [227]
business asset—
replacement of—
group of companies, treatment of,
43(1), [128]
roll-over relief, **43(1)**, [4]
business premises—
conversion to flats, for. *See* **flat conversion
allowances**
renovation, for. *See* **business premises
renovation allowances**
renovation in disadvantaged areas,
43(2), [640], [655]
capital expenditure—
meaning, **43(1)**, [555], [561]
time of incurring, **43(1)**, [556]
capital sums, meaning, **43(1)**, [555]
cars. *See* **motor car**
cars and motor cycles, business expenditure
on, **43(S)**, 1460–8
changes in law, transitional provisions,
43(1), [1223]
chargeable gains, finance lease, disposal of
interest in or asset, **43(1)**, [295]
chargeable period, meaning, **43(1)**, [557]
claims, **43(1)**, [554]
company, share exchanges on reconstruction
of, **43(2)**, [134]
compensation, expenditure met by,
43(1), [1172]
connected persons—
meaning, **43(1)**, [1214]
transactions between, **43(1)**, [76]
consequential and transitional provision,
power to make, **43(S)**, 916
continuity of law, **43(1)**, [1222]
contributions—
allowances—
conditions for, **43(1)**, [1174]
transfer of trade of relevant activity, effect
of, **43(1)**, [1179]
exclusion—
dredging, in case of, **43(1)**, [1170]
general rule, **43(1)**, [1169]
insurance or compensation money,
43(1), [1172]
Northern Ireland regional development
grants, **43(1)**, [1171]
public bodies, not made by, **43(1)**, [1173]
tax relief, not eligible for, **43(1)**, [1173]
transitional provisions, **43(1)**, [1232]
controlled foreign company, **44(1)**, [671]
corporation tax purposes, claims for,
43(1), [401]
definitions, **43(1)**, [1215]
degrouping charge, roll-over of, **43(2)**, [92]
disadvantaged areas, renovation of business
premises in, **43(2)**, [640], [655]
double relief—
exclusion of, **43(1)**, [558]

capital allowances—*contd*
double relief—*contd*
fixtures claims and other claims, interaction
between, **43(1)**, [560]
pooling, not permitted through,
43(1), [559]
double taxation relief, **42**, [1429]
earn-out rights, **43(1)**, [288]
employees' vehicles, withdrawal for,
43(2), [37]
environmentally beneficial plant or machinery,
first-year allowances, **43(2)**, [264]
excess, amounts eligible for group relief,
44(1), [209]
films, expenditure on. *See* **cinematograph
films**
finance lease, lump sum paid on, **43(1)**, [295]
first-year allowances for small enterprises,
temporary increase in, **43(2)**, [355];
43(S), 536–7
first-year, expenditure in 2009–10,
43(S), 1372–3
first-year tax credits—
amended provisions, **43(S)**, 1220–32
claw-back, **43(S)**, 1227–9
entitlement to, **43(S)**, 1221–5
giving effect to, **43(S)**, 1226–7
flat conversion, for. *See* **flat conversion
allowances**
foster-care relief. *See* **foster parents and
fostering**
gains treated as accruing to settlor, deduction
of personal losses from, **43(2)**, [136]
group of companies, restriction on set-off of
pre-entry losses, **43(1)**, [6]
income tax agreements, **43(1)**, [1203]
indexation allowance, freezing, **43(1)**, [365]
industrial buildings. *See* **industrial building
allowance**
insurance company, transfer of business,
43(1), [1197]
interpretation, **43(1)**, [1215], [1220]–[1221]
know-how, on, **44(1)**, [382]
See also **know-how allowance**
leased assets, pooling, **43(1)**, [482]
lessors of ships, restrictions on allowances for,
43(2), [265]
liability, questions affecting two or more
persons, determining, **43(1)**, [1201]
low carbon dioxide emissions, cars with,
43(S), 904–5
machinery and plant, for. *See* **machinery
and plant allowances**
meaning, **44(1)**, [615]
means of giving effect to, **43(1)**, [553]
mineral exploration and access, **44(1)**, [72]
mineral extraction. *See* **mineral extraction
allowance**
mines. *See* **mining and oil industries**
motor vehicles. *See* **motor cars**
Northern Ireland Airports Limited. *See*
Northern Ireland Airports Limited
oil assets put to other uses, **43(S)**, 1664–5
oil decommissioning expenditure, amended
provisions, **43(S)**, 1648–51

capital allowances—*contd*

oil extraction activities, **44(1)**, [331]

oil, in relation to—

abandonment expenditure after ceasing ring fence trade, **43(S)**, 942–4

general decommissioning expenditure, **43(S)**, 941–2

partnership changes, effect of, **43(1)**, [1195]

patent rights, for. *See* **patent; patent allowance**

period of account, meaning, **43(1)**, [557]

property—

sale, references to, **43(1)**, [1211]

sold together, apportionment, **43(1)**, [1200]

provision for, **43(1)**, [552]

qualifying enterprise zone expenditure, transitional provision, **43(S)**, 914

railways. *See* **railways**

research and development. *See* **research and development allowance**

retirement relief, phasing out, **43(1)**, [373]

ring fence trade, expenditure wholly for, **43(2)**, [107]

sale—

alternative amount, treated as being, **43(1)**, [1205]

election for, **43(1)**, [1207]

market value, treated as, **43(1)**, [1206]

property, of, references to, **43(1)**, [1211]

transfers treated as, **43(1)**, [1212]

scientific research, for. *See* **scientific research**

securities—

identification, rules for, **43(1)**, [367]

pooling, abolition, **43(1)**, [366]

shares acquired on same day, alternative treatment of, **43(2)**, [97]

small enterprises, first-year allowances for, **43(S)**, 18–19

special rate expenditure—

amended provisions, **43(S)**, 1234

commencement of provisions, **43(S)**, 1235

connected persons, sale between, **43(S)**, 1235–6

interpretation, **43(S)**, 1237

intra-group transfers, saving for, **43(S)**, 1236

meaning, **43(S)**, 1232

rules for, **43(S)**, 1233

special rate pool, **43(S)**, 1233

succession, effect of, **43(1)**, [1196]

successor water companies, provisions applying to, **49**, [678]

taper relief, minor amendments, **43(2)**, [135]

trading losses, use against chargeable gains, **43(2)**, [96]

transfer of building society business, on, **42**, [939]

transfers of trade, balancing allowances on, **43(S)**, 916–17

transitional provisions, **44(1)**, [691]

types of, **43(1)**, [552]

wasting assets qualifying for, **42**, [1131]

capital gains

transactions in land, on, **44(1)**, [520], [521]

capital gains tax

accrued income scheme, transfer of securities by, **42**, [1217]

allowable capital losses, extension of restrictions on, **43(S)**, 524–5

allowable losses, **43(1)**, [150]

amendment of provisions, **43(S)**, 1008–18

annual exempt amount, **43(2)**, [222]

annual exemption, **42**, [1084]

reporting limits, **42**, [1085]

approved CSOP schemes, **42**, [1480A]

approved profit sharing scheme, and, **42**, [1379]

approved SAYE option schemes, **42**, [1480]

approved share incentive plans, **42**, [1479]

approved share plans, transfers to, **42**, [1478]

approved share schemes, **42**, [1479]

asset—

bare trustee, held by, **42**, [1145]

business, replacement of. *See* business assets *below*

capital sums derived from, **42**, [1104]

compensation and insurance money deriving from, **42**, [1105]

disposal—

consideration due after time of, **42**, [1132]

contract, under, **42**, [1110]

death, on, **42**, [1147]

deemed, on company migration. *See* company migration *below*

donee, emigration of, **42**, [1295]

gift, as, **42**, [1152]

hire-purchase transactions, **42**, [1109]

husband and wife, between, **42**, [1142]

indexation allowance—

assets owned on 31 March 1982, **42**, [1139]

calculation of, **42**, [1138]

calls on shares, **42**, [1212]

no gain/no loss basis, **42**, [1139]

part disposals, **42**, [1140]

provision of, **42**, [1137]

receipts affecting allowable expenditure, **42**, [1141]

reorganisations, **42**, [1231]

rolled-up, **42**, [1139]

know-how, **42**, [1405]

meaning, **42**, [1103]

non-resident, by, **42**, [1107]

part, **42**, [1126]

retirement, associated with. *See* relief *below*

series of transactions, in, **42**, [1101]

insolvent, of, **42**, [1151]

location of, **42**, [1424]; **43(2)**, [744]

co-owners' interest, **42**, [1427]

intangible assets, **42**, [1425], [1426]

lost or destroyed, **42**, [1106]

market value—

aggregate, **42**, [1102]

disposals and acquisitions treated as at, **42**, [1099]

priority share allocation, exception for, **42**, [1268]

capital gains tax—*contd*
asset—*contd*
  market value—*contd*
    estimating, **42**, [1421]
    meaning, **42**, [1421]
    original, **42**, [1102]
    priority share allocation, exception for,
      42, [1268]
    shares or securities, of, **42**, [1421]
  mortgages and charges, **42**, [1108]
  negligible value, of, **42**, [1106]
  nominee, held by, **42**, [1145]
  other asset, derived from, **42**, [1127]
  predictable life of, **42**, [1130]
  property being, **42**, [1103]
  taper relief. *See* taper relief *below*
  wasting—
    allowable expenditure, straightline
      restriction of, **42**, [1130]
    capital allowances, qualifying for,
      42, [1131]
    exemption for, **42**, [1129]
    meaning, **42**, [1128]
    movable property being, **42**, [1129]
    residual or scrap value, **42**, [1130]
bed and breakfasting rules, **43(S)**, 66–7
building societies—
  amalgamation of, **42**, [1348]
  company, assets transferred to, **42**, [1349]
  qualifying shares, right to acquire,
    42, [1263]
  successor company, shares in, **42**, [1350]
  taper relief, gains ineligible for, **42**, [1347]
business asset—
  gift of—
    agricultural property, **42**, [1466]
    donee, emigration of, **42**, [1295]
    dual resident trust, into, **42**, [1296]
    foreign controlled company, to,
      42, [1294]
    held-over gain, reductions in, **42**, [1467]
    limited liability partnership, cessation of
      trade by, **42**, [1297]
    non-resident, to, **42**, [1293]
    relief for, **42**, [1292]
    settled property, **42**, [1466]
  replacement of—
    activities other than trades, **42**, [1287]
    Class I assets, **42**, [1284]
    depreciating, new assets being,
      42, [1282]
    individual, dealt with by, **42**, [1286]
    limited liability partnership, cessation of
      trade by, **42**, [1285]
    non-residents, relief for, **42**, [1288]
    oil field, use in connection with,
      42, [1328]
    partial, **42**, [1280]
    personal company, trade carried on by,
      42, [1286]
    provisional application of provisions,
      42, [1281]
    relevant classes, **42**, [1283]
    roll-over relief, **42**, [1279], [1280]

capital gains tax—*contd*
business, transfer of—
  company, to, **42**, [1290], [1349]
  election for relief not to apply, **42**, [1291]
  harbour authorities, **42**, [1357]
  roll-over relief, **42**, [1290]
charge of, **42**, [1081]
chargeable gains—
  allowable loss, meaning, **42**, [1088]
  allowable losses, restrictions on, **43(S)**, 52
  assets held on 31 March 1982—
    assets derived from other assets,
      42, [1456]
    capital allowance provisions, **42**, [1456]
    disposal of, **42**, [1119]
    election, excluded disposals, **42**, [1456]
    groups of companies, **42**, [1456]
    part disposals, **42**, [1456]
    pre-1965 gains and losses, apportionment
      of, **42**, [1456]
    previous no gain/no loss disposals,
      42, [1456]
  assets held on 6 April 1965, on—
    apportionment over period of
      ownership, **42**, [1454]
    capital allowances, and, **42**, [1455]
    close companies, transferred to,
      42, [1455]
    commodities, **42**, [1454]
    compensation and insurance money,
      42, [1455]
    conversion of securities, **42**, [1454]
    husband and wife, **42**, [1455]
    land reflecting development value,
      42, [1453]
    quoted securities, **42**, [1452]
    share capital, reorganisation of,
      42, [1454]
    unquoted shares, **42**, [1454]
    valuation at, **42**, [1454]
  balancing charge, amount taken as,
    42, [1121]
  buying losses and gains, restrictions on,
    43(S), 53–9
  capital distribution, recovery of tax,
    42, [1320]
  computation, **42**, [1097]
  contingent liabilities, **42**, [1133]
  deductions—
    allowable sums, **42**, [1122]
    costs of disposal or acquisition,
      42, [1122]
    estates and trusts, expenses in
      administration of, **42**, [1149]
    rules for, **42**, [1136]
    tax on income, expenditure by reference
      to, **42**, [1123]
  expenditure reimbursed out of public
    money, exclusion of, **42**, [1134]
  foreign assets, from, delayed remittances,
    42, [1431]
  foreign domicile, person with, **42**, [1094]
  husband and wife, **42**, [1142]
  income tax, consideration chargeable to,
    42, [1121]

capital gains tax—*contd*
  chargeable gains—*contd*
    information, giving, **42**, [107]
    losses accruing, avoidance involving,
      43(S), 60–4
    non-resident company, accruing to,
      42, [1095]
    non-resident group of companies, accruing
      to, **42**, [1096]
    part disposal, on, **42**, [1126]
    pre-31 March 1982, deferred charge on—
      assets derived from other assets,
        42, [1457]
      claims, **42**, [1457]
      deduction or gain, reduction of,
        42, [1457]
      held-over charge, **42**, [1457]
      postponed, **42**, [1457]
      previous no gain/no loss disposals,
        42, [1457]
      rolled-over charge, **42**, [1457]
    pre-change assets, **43(S)**, 55–9
    prescribed period of acquisition, disposal of
      shares and securities within, **43(S)**, 64
    rentcharge, etc, capitalised value of,
      42, [1121]
    total profits including, **42**, [1088]
    wasting assets, disposal of, **42**, [1129]
    woodlands, **42**, [1395]
  chattel exemption, **42**, [1406]
  close company—
    assets, transferring at undervalue,
      42, [1224]
    income tax, relief in respect of, **42**, [1223]
    shortfall in distributions, **42**, [1223]
  collective investment scheme—
    arrangements being, **42**, [1199]
    group, within, **42**, [1196]–[1198]
    investment trust, transfer of assets to,
      42, [1195]
    venture capital trust, transfer of assets to,
      42, [1197]
  commodity futures, and, **42**, [1249]
  companies buying gains or losses, tax
    avoidance scheme, **43(S)**, 530–1
  company merger—
    securities issued, **42**, [1247]
    UK tax charge—
      assets not within, **42**, [1246]
      assets within, **42**, [1245]
  company migration, on, deemed disposal of
    assets—
    ceasing to be resident, on, **42**, [1318]
    postponement of charge on, **42**, [1319]
  company, no liability on, **44(1)**, [1]
  company, reconstruction of—
    bona fide commercial reasons, for,
      42, [1235], [1236]
    clearance in advance, **42**, [1237]
    earn-out rights, use for exchange,
      42, [1238]
    issue of securities, **42**, [1215], [1235]
    non-resident company, transfer of assets to,
      42, [1240]

capital gains tax—*contd*
  company, reconstruction of—*contd*
    non-UK trade, transfer of—
      anti-avoidance, **42**, [1244]
      other member State, to, **42**, [1243]
    scheme, meaning, **42**, [1463]
    transfer of business, **42**, [1239]
    UK trade, transfer of—
      anti-avoidance, **42**, [1242]
      other member state, to, **42**, [1241]
  compensation stock, **42**, [1233]
  concessions deferring charge, **42**, [1441],
    [1442]
  connected persons, transactions between,
    42, [1100], [1444]
  consideration payable by instalments,
    42, [1436]
  corporate bond—
    meaning, **42**, [1216]
    qualifying—
      exemption for, **42**, [1214]
      meaning, **42**, [1216]
    transitional provisions, **42**, [1486]
  damages, on, **42**, [1135]
  death, on—
    allowable losses, **42**, [1147]
    assets, disposal of, **42**, [1147]
    legatee, acquisition of asset as, **42**, [1147]
    personal representatives, **42**, [1147]
    Scotland, application of law in, **42**, [1148]
    variation or disclaimer, effect of, **42**, [1147]
  debts, on, **42**, [1396]
  deferred unascertainable consideration,
    election for treatment of loss, **42**, [1432],
      [1433]; **43(2)**, [225]
    effect of, **42**, [1434], [1435]
    irrevocable, **42**, [1435]
    notice, **42**, [1435]
  definitions, **42**, [1446]
  dependent relative's residence, disposal of,
    42, [1363]
  disposal of assets acquired on no gain/no loss
    disposal, **43(S)**, 1014
  donee, recovery from, **42**, [1438]
  double taxation relief, **42**, [1429]
  earn-out rights, treatment as securities,
    43(2), [224]
  employee share ownership trusts—
    chargeable events—
      bonds, ownership of, **42**, [1373]
      replacement assets, ownership of,
        42, [1371]
      replacement property, ownership of,
        42, [1372]
    double charge, prevention of, **42**, [1375]
    dwelling-house, asset being, **42**, [1369]
    information, requirement of, **42**, [1374]
    relief, claim for, **42**, [1368]
    roll-over relief, conditions for, **42**, [1366],
      [1367]
    shares in, **42**, [1370]
  employee trusts, disposal relating to,
    42, [1381]
  enterprise management incentives, **42**, [1481]

capital gains tax—*contd*
  entrepreneur's relief. *See* **entrepreneur's relief**
  exempt amount, annual, **42**, [1084]
    reporting limits, **42**, [1085]
  exemption—
    annuity, disposal of rights to, **42**, [1335]
    British Museum trustees, **42**, [1420]
    certain pension funds, **42**, [1420]
    certified SAYE savings arrangements, sums under, **42**, [1420]
    chattel, **42**, [1406]
    Chevening Estate, **42**, [1419]
    consular officer or employee, **42**, [1420]
    decorations, **42**, [1417]
    designated international organisations, **42**, [1414]
    employment-related liabilities, **42**, [1408]
    foreign currency for personal expenditure, **42**, [1418]
    gilt-edged securities, **42**, [1214]
    government non-marketable securities, **42**, [1220]
    Historic Buildings and Monuments Commission, **42**, [1420]
    INMARSAT signatory, **42**, [1420]
    Inter-American Development Bank, **42**, [1415]
    local authority and associations, **42**, [1420]
    local constituency associations, **42**, [1413]
    National Endowment for Science, Technology and the Arts, **42**, [1420]
    National Heritage Memorial Fund, **42**, [1420]
    Natural History Museum trustees, **42**, [1420]
    Parliamentary pension funds, **42**, [1420]
    passenger vehicles, **42**, [1407]
    qualifying corporate bonds, **42**, [1214]
    Reserve Bank of India, **42**, [1420]
    sale and repurchase of securities, agreements for, **42**, [1409]
    savings arrangement, sums under, **42**, [1420]
    State Bank of Pakistan, **42**, [1420]
    stock lending arrangements, **42**, [1410], [1411]
    stock, transfer by Treasury, etc, **42**, [1420]
    superannuation fund, disposal of rights in, **42**, [1377]
    transmission facilities, sharing, **42**, [1416]
    trust funds for reduction of National Debt, **42**, [1420]
    unit trust, gains accruing to, **42**, [1420]
    works of art, for, **42**, [1401]
  exploration or exploitation rights, disposal of, **42**, [1428]
  financial futures, and, **42**, [1249]
  foreign currency—
    bank account, debt on, **42**, [1397]
    personal expenditure, for, **42**, [1418]
  foreign tax, allowance for, **42**, [1430]
  forfeited deposit, and, **42**, [1250]
  friendly societies—
    subsequent disposal of assets, **42**, [1353]

capital gains tax—*contd*
  friendly societies—*contd*
    transfer of assets on incorporation, **42**, [1351]
  funds in court, **42**, [1146]
  furnished holiday lettings, **42**, [1385]
  gift—
    business assets of—
      donee, emigration of, **42**, [1295]
      dual resident trust, into, **42**, [1296]
      foreign controlled company, to, **42**, [1294]
      limited liability partnership, cessation of trade by, **42**, [1297]
      non-resident, to, **42**, [1293]
      relief for, **42**, [1292]
    charity, to, **42**, [1399]
    housing associations, to, **42**, [1402]
  gifts relief, restriction of, **43(2)**, [549]
  group of companies, restriction on set-off of pre-entry gains, **42**, [1469]
  group of companies, restriction on set-off of pre-entry losses—
    application and construction of provisions, **42**, [1468]
    company changing group on transfers of shares, **42**, [1468]
    company's nature, change of, **42**, [1468]
    continuity provisions, **42**, [1468]
    deduction, restrictions on, **42**, [1468]
    gains from which deductible, **42**, [1468]
    market value, calculation by reference to, **42**, [1468]
    pooled assets, disposal of, **42**, [1468]
    pre-entry losses not to be treated as post-entry losses, **42**, [1468]
    proportion of losses on assets, **42**, [1468]
    relevant group, identification of, **42**, [1468]
    stock in trade, appropriation to, **42**, [1468]
  halving relief, abolition of, **43(S)**, 1016
  indexation allowance—
    application for corporation tax purposes, **43(S)**, 1017
    freezing, **43(1)**, [365]
  income tax decisions, conclusive nature of, **42**, [1440]
  inheritance tax chargeable on, **42**, [1403]
    payment of tax by instalments, **42**, [1437]
  inheritance tax valuation, use of, **42**, [1423]
  insurance—
    allowable losses, **42**, [1336]
    deferred annuity, **42**, [1335]
    life assurance policy, **42**, [1335]
    losses, ringing fencing of, **42**, [1336]
    policies, rights under, **42**, [1333]
    premiums, disallowance as expenses, **42**, [1334]
    securities, disposal and acquisition, **42**, [1337]
    transfers of business, **42**, [1338]
      unused losses, transfer of, **42**, [1339]
    transitional provisions, **42**, [1343], [1344]
    venture capital investment partnership, gains from, **42**, [1476]
  introduction of, **42**, [1]

capital gains tax—*contd*

kink test, abolition, **43(S)**, 1013–16

know-how, disposal of, **42**, [1405]

land—

agricultural, grants for giving up,
42, [1394]

compulsory acquisition—

compensation paid on, **42**, [1389]

disposal and acquisition, time of,
42, [1390]

roll-over relief, **42**, [1391]–[1393]

part disposal—

allowable expenditure, consideration
exceeding, **42**, [1388]

authority exercising compulsory powers,
to, **42**, [1387]

small, **42**, [1386]

lease—

duration of, **42**, [1482]

income tax charged, where, **42**, [1482]

meaning, **42**, [1482]

premiums, **42**, [1482]

property other than land, of, **42**, [1482]

short, sub-lease out of, **42**, [1482]

wasting asset, as, **42**, [1482]

liability for—

personal representative, of, **42**, [1150]

settlement, trustees of, **42**, [1154]

trustee, of, **42**, [1150]

limited liability partnership, on, **42**, [1144]

loss relief, restrictions for non-active traders,
43(S), 1191–4

losses—

allowable, **42**, [1082]

capital allowances and renewals allowances,
restriction by, **42**, [1125]

computation of, **42**, [1098]

managed payment plans, **43(S)**, 1423–5

manufactured dividends, gains accruing,
42, [1412]

mineral lease—

capital losses, **42**, [1331]

claims, **42**, [1332]

royalties, **42**, [1330]

non-resident—

company with UK permanent
establishment, **42**, [1092]

deemed disposals, **42**, [1107]

temporary, **42**, [1091]; **43(2)**, [743]

UK branch or agency, charge on,
42, [1090]

Northern Ireland Airports Limited. *See*
Northern Ireland Airports Limited

oil field—

business assets, replacement of, **42**, [1328]

disposal of interests in, **42**, [1327]

exploration or exploitation assets, deemed
disposals, **42**, [1329]

oil licence, disposal of—

drilling expenditure, allowance of,
42, [1325]

undeveloped area, relating to, **42**, [1324],
[1326]

option—

abandonment of, **42**, [1250]

capital gains tax—*contd*

option—*contd*

cash-settled, **42**, [1255]

definitions, **42**, [1250]

employment-related securities, **42**, [1264]

exercise of, **42**, [1250]

market value rule, application of,
42, [1251]

market value rule, exception to,
42, [1252]

alteration of to obtain tax advantage,
42, [1254]

non-commercial, **42**, [1253]

grant of, **42**, [1250]

guaranteed return involving,
42, [1260]–[1262]

indexation allowance, **42**, [1256]

quoted—

abandonment, **42**, [1250]

new holdings, part of, **42**, [1258]

traded—

closing purchases, **42**, [1259]

gains arising on, **42**, [1249]

wasting assets, rules on, **42**, [1257]

orders and regulations, **42**, [1445]

overdue, interest on, **42**, [216]; **43(1)**, [149]

overpaid, recovery of—

application of provisions, **43(S)**, 1414

claims, **43(S)**, 1717–23

overseas life insurance companies, application
of provisions to, **42**, [1477]

partners, limit on relief by, **43(S)**, 595–6

contributions, exclusion of amounts by way
of, **43(S)**, 596–7

partnership, on, **42**, [1143]

limited liability, **42**, [1144]

payment of, **42**, [195]

personal pension scheme, withdrawal of
approval, **42**, [1383]

personal representative—

liability for tax, **42**, [1150]

private residence, held by, **42**, [1362]

persons chargeable, **42**, [1082]

pooling, simplification, **43(S)**, 1017–19

policies of insurance and non-deferred
annuities, gains on, **43(S)**, 65–6

private residence, **43(2)**, [550]

amount of relief, **42**, [1359]

dependent relative, occupied by, **42**, [1363]

husband and wife, of, **42**, [1358]

job-related accommodation, **42**, [1358]

main, determining, **42**, [1358]

period of absence from, **42**, [1359]

period of ownership, **42**, [1358]

permitted area of, **42**, [1358]

personal representative, held by, **42**, [1362]

relief on disposal of, **42**, [1358], [1364]

later disposal, **42**, [1365]

settlement, occupied under terms of,
42, [1361]

trade or business, etc, part used for,
42, [1360]

transitional provisions, **42**, [1486]

provisions applied to, **42**, [215]

capital gains tax—*contd*
  railways. *See* **railways**
  rates of, **42**, [1086]; **43(S)**, 841
    special cases, **42**, [1087]
  rebasing to 1982. *See* chargeable gains *above*
  recognised investment exchanges, and,
    42, [1443]
  record-keeping requirements, **43(S)**, 1305–8
  reform, **43(S)**, 1006–19
  relief—
    approved share plans, transfers to,
      42, [1478]
    business expansion scheme, under,
      42, [1269]
    employment-related liabilities, **42**, [1408]
    enterprise investment scheme, under,
      42, [1270]
      reduction of, **42**, [1271]
    reinvestment—
      application of provisions, **42**, [1464]
      chargeable events, **42**, [1464]
        gains accruing on, **42**, [1464]
      claims, **42**, [1464]
      conditions of application, failure of,
        42, [1464]
      disregarded receipts, **42**, [1464]
      information, **42**, [1464]
      insignificant repayments, **42**, [1464]
      interpretation, **42**, [1464]
      investment-linked loans, **42**, [1464]
      investor, value received by, **42**, [1464]
      new company, acquisition of share
        capital by, **42**, [1464]
      options, **42**, [1464]
      original gain, postponement of,
        42, [1464]
      other persons, value received by,
        42, [1464]
      person to whom gain accrued,
        42, [1464]
      pre-arranged exits, **42**, [1464]
      reconstructions and amalgamations,
        42, [1464]
      reorganisation, **42**, [1464]
      replacement value, receipt of,
        42, [1464]
      same company, in, **42**, [1464]
      trustees, **42**, [1464]
    personal equity plans, **42**, [1274]
    private residence, **42**, [1358], [1364]
      later disposal, **42**, [1365]
    roll-over. *See* business assets *above*
    trader, loan to, **42**, [1398]
    venture capital trusts, **42**, [1275]
  remittance basis—
    chargeable gains, **43(S)**, 1080–3
    commencement, **43(S)**, 1085
    non-domiciled individuals, application to,
      43(S), 1080–3
    non-resident company. *See* **non-resident**
    transitional provision, **43(S)**, 1085–7
  repayment supplement, **42**, [1439]
  reporting limits, **42**, [1085]; **43(2)**, [222]
  residence, meaning, **42**, [1089]
  retirement relief, phasing out, **43(1)**, [373]

capital gains tax—*contd*
  securities—
    6 April 1965, held on—
      actual cost, restriction of gain or loss
        by, **42**, [1452]
      deemed acquisition, **42**, [1452]
      pooling—
        election for, **42**, [1452]
        exclusion of, **42**, [1452]
        group, election by, **42**, [1452]
        premiums trust fund, **42**, [1452]
      value, at, **42**, [1452]
    acquired on same day, election for
      alternative treatment, **42**, [1201], [1202]
    conversion of—
      meaning, **42**, [1231]
      premium on, **42**, [1232]
      provisions applicable to, **42**, [1231]
      transitional provisions, **42**, [1486]
    disposal of—
      by company within prescribed period of
        acquisition, **42**, [1204]
      day of acquisition, on or before,
        42, [1201]
      employment-related, **42**, [1264]
        restricted and convertible interest in,
          42, [1265]
        tax charged to, increase in expenditure,
          42, [1218]
      exchange with another company,
        42, [1234]
    gilt-edged—
      compensation stock, **42**, [1233]
      exemptions, **42**, [1214]
      existing, **42**, [1484]
      meaning, **42**, [1483]
      redemption date, past, **42**, [1486]
    government non-marketable—
      exemption, **42**, [1220]
      meaning, **42**, [1220]
    identification, general rule, **42**, [1205]
    market value, **42**, [1421]
    pooling—
      abolition, **43(1)**, [366]
      identification of securities—
        relevant securities, **42**, [1207]
        rules for, **42**, [1206]
      indexation allowance, **42**, [1209], [1210]
      interpretation, **42**, [1200]
      options, **42**, [1213]
      parallel, **42**, [1211]
      pre-April 1982 share pools, **42**, [1208]
      relevant, identification of, **42**, [1207]
    sale and repurchase, exemption of gain on
      agreements for, **42**, [1409]
    unquoted, value of, **42**, [1422]
  settled property—
    amendments, **43(S)**, 402–3
    absolute entitlement, disposal on,
      42, [1156]
    disposal of interest in, deemed disposal of
      underlying assets, **42**, [1458]
    exempt amounts, application of, **42**, [1451]
    held-over gain, **42**, [1159]
    information, provision of, **42**, [1189]

capital gains tax—*contd*
  settled property—*contd*
    interests in, disposal of, **42**, [1160]
    life interest, termination of, **42**, [1157]
    life tenant, death of, **42**, [1158]
    maintenance fund for historic building,
      treatment of, **42**, [1165]
    meaning, **42**, [1153]
    references to, **42**, [1165]
    reporting limits, **42**, [1451]
    right of recovery of tax, **42**, [1164]
    settlor—
      income originating from, **42**, [1165]
      interest in settlement, with, **42**, [1163]
      meaning, **42**, [1165], [1301]
      property originating from, **42**, [1165]
  settlement. *See also* **settlements**
    amendments, **43(S)**, 402–3
    beneficiaries, attribution of gains to,
      42, [1178], [1460]
    capital payment—
      meaning, **42**, [1188]
      provisions on, **42**, [1188]
    companies, payments by and from,
      42, [1187]
    dual resident—
      gains of, **42**, [1179]
      settlor, attribution of gains to,
        42, [1176], [1461]
    foreign element, with, **42**, [1462]
    increases in amounts payable, **42**, [1182]
    losses, restriction on set-off, **42**, [1166]
    migrant, **42**, [1180]
    non-resident—
      beneficiaries, attribution of gain to,
        42, [1178]
      disposal of interests in, **42**, [1174]
      gains of non-resident companies,
        attribution of, **42**, [1167]
      past trustees, liability for tax, **42**, [1170]
      settlor, attribution of gains to,
        42, [1176], [1177], [1461]
    payment, references to, **42**, [1188]
    qualifying amounts, matching—
      application, **42**, [1183]
      special cases, **42**, [1184]
      transfer, matching after, **42**, [1186]
    settlor interested settlements—
      "arrangement", meaning, **42**, [1303]
      exception to application of provisions,
        42, [1300]
      gifts to, **42**, [1298]
      information, power to require,
        42, [1303]
      "interest in a settlement", meaning of,
        42, [1302]
      relief, clawback of, **42**, [1299]
      settlor, meaning, **42**, [1301]
    transfers between, **42**, [1181]
    transfers into, **42**, [1155]
    transfers of property, **42**, [1185]
    trustees—
      borrowing, transfers of value linked
        with, **42**, [1459]
      ceasing to be resident in UK, **42**, [1168]

capital gains tax—*contd*
  settlement—*contd*
    trustees—*contd*
      death of, **42**, [1169], [1170]
      dual resident, acquisition by, **42**, [1173]
      non-resident, **42**, [1154]
      past, liability for tax, **42**, [1170]
      single body, as, **42**, [1154]
      tax assessed on, **42**, [1154]
      UK tax, ceasing to be liable to,
        42, [1171]
      year of assessment, being resident and
        non-resident, **42**, [1172]
  share capital, reorganisation of—
    composite new holdings, **42**, [1229]
    consideration given or received, **42**, [1227]
    equation of holdings, **42**, [1226]
    indexation allowance, **42**, [1230]
    meaning, **42**, [1225]
    new holding, part disposal of, **42**, [1228]
    references to, **42**, [1225]
    transitional provisions, **42**, [1486]
  share option scheme, and, **42**, [1378]
  shares—
    acquired on same day, alternative treatment
      of, **43(2)**, [97]
    approved CSOP schemes, **42**, [1480A]
    approved SAYE option schemes, **42**, [1480]
    approved share incentive plans, **42**, [1479]
    calls on, indexation allowance, **42**, [1212]
    close company, in—
      assets, transferring at undervalue,
        42, [1224]
      income tax, relief for, **42**, [1223]
    conditional interests in, **42**, [1267]
    distributions, not new holding, **42**, [1221]
    market value, **42**, [1421]
      priority share allocation, **42**, [1268]
    research institution spin-out companies,
      42, [1266]
    right to acquire, disposal of, **42**, [1222]
    tax charged to, increase in expenditure,
      42, [1219]
    unquoted, value of, **42**, [1422]
  sideways relief, general restrictions on,
    43(S), 1191–3
  stock dividends, capital gains, **42**, [1248]
  stock in trade, appropriations to and from,
    42, [1289]
  strips—
    corporate, **42**, [1278]
    manipulation of price, **42**, [1277]
    payment giving rise to loss, **42**, [1277]
  subordinate legislation, validity of, **42**, [1486]
  substantial shareholding requirement,
    42, [1472]
  substantial shareholdings, exemption for
    disposals—
    application of, **42**, [1471]
    consequential provisions, **42**, [1475]
    interpretation, **42**, [1474]
    investing company and company invested
      in, requirements, **42**, [1473]
    main exemption, **42**, [1471]
    not applying, **42**, [1471]

capital gains tax—*contd*
substantial shareholdings, exemption for
disposals—*contd*
subsidiary exemption, **42**, [1471]
taper relief—
amendment on provisions on abolition of,
43(S), 1008–13
amount of, **42**, [1083]
ancillary trust funds, rules for, **42**, [1450]
application of, **42**, [1083], [1450]
qualifying holding period, **42**, [1083]
apportionment, rule for, **42**, [1450]
assets—
derived from other assets, **42**, [1450]
qualifying as business asset, **42**, [1450];
43(2), [223]
spouses, transfer between, **42**, [1450]
business or non-business asset, gain on
disposal of, **42**, [1450]
definitions, **42**, [1450]
different purposes, asset used for,
42, [1450]
eligible beneficiaries, **42**, [1450]
enterprise investment scheme, **42**, [1465]
fluctuations in value, limited exposure to,
42, [1450]
joint enterprise companies, relevant
connection, **42**, [1450]
joint venture companies, qualifying
shareholdings in, **42**, [1450]
material interest, meaning, **42**, [1450]
mutual business—
reconstruction, **42**, [1450]
reorganisations, **42**, [1347]
non-qualifying beneficiaries, **42**, [1450]
options, rules for, **42**, [1450]
period for which asset held, **42**, [1450]
postponed gains, **42**, [1450]
property settled by company, **42**, [1450]
qualifying companies, **42**, [1450]
settlements, rules for, **42**, [1450]
share ownership in inactive company,
42, [1450]
shares, qualification as business asset,
42, [1450]
trading company, meaning, **42**, [1450]
trading group, meaning, **42**, [1450]
value shifting, **42**, [1450]
tax year, meaning, **43(S)**, 1019
territorial extension of charge, **42**, [305],
[308]
territorial sea, area of, **42**, [1428]
total income, computing, **42**, [1088]
trader, loan to, **42**, [1398]
trading losses, use against chargeable gains,
43(2), [96]
transfers of value, attribution of gains to
beneficiaries, **43(2)**, [226]
transitional provisions—
assets acquired before commencement,
42, [1487]
betterment levy, allowance for, **42**, [1486]
Case VII—
disposal chargeable under, **42**, [1486]
losses, unrelieved, **42**, [1486]

capital gains tax—*contd*
transitional provisions—*contd*
conversion of securities, **42**, [1486]
disposal before acquisition, **42**, [1486]
estate duty, **42**, [1486]
foreign insurance funds, **42**, [1486]
private residences, **42**, [1486]
qualifying corporate bonds, **42**, [1486]
redemption date, gilt-edged securities past,
42, [1486]
share capital, reorganisation of, **42**, [1486]
sterling devaluation, **42**, [1486]
valuation, **42**, [1485]
value-shifting, **42**, [1486]
works of art, **42**, [1486]
trustee—
non-resident, beneficiary's liability for tax,
42, [1486]
payment of tax by, **42**, [1150]
unit trust scheme—
annual deemed disposal of holdings,
42, [1341]
application of provisions, **42**, [1191]
company's assets, transfer to investment
trust, **42**, [1195]
exempt unit holders, **42**, [1194]
gains and losses, spreading, **42**, [1342]
gains—
calculation of on disposal of units,
42, [1193]
exemption of, **42**, [1194]
market value, **42**, [1421]
umbrella schemes, treatment of, **42**, [1192]
umbrella schemes, treatment of, **42**, [1192]
unpaid, surcharges on, **42**, [196], [206];
43(1), [148]
value-shifting—
chargeable intangible assets, modification of
provisions for, **42**, [1117]
disposals, **42**, [1111]
group—
asset-holding company leaving,
42, [1114]
disposals within followed by disposal of
shares, **42**, [1115]
distributions within followed by disposal
of shares, **42**, [1113]
interpretation, **42**, [1116]
reorganisation of share capital, transactions
treated as, **42**, [1118]
tax-free benefits, **42**, [1112]
transitional provisions, **42**, [1486]
venture capital trust. *See* **venture capital
trust**
winnings, on, **42**, [1135]

capital punishment. *See also* **death sentence**
mutiny, for, **3**, [1365]

capital redemption policy
insurers—
information given by, **44(1)**, [385], [386]
overseas, tax representatives for,
44(1), [387], [388]

capital redemption policy—*contd*
  losses from contracts, no loss relief for,
    43(S), 1398

capital transfer tax. *See also* **inheritance tax**
  generally, **42**, [1]
  inheritance tax, to be known as, **42**, [850]
  National Heritage Memorial Fund, transfer of
    functions to, **42**, [397]
  property accepted in lieu of—
    approval of, **42**, [395]
    disposal of, **42**, [391]
    expenses, **42**, [392]
    interest—
      not carrying, **42**, [907]
      satisfaction of, **42**, [396]
    payment to Commissioners, **42**, [390]
    receipts, **42**, [392]
    stamp duty exemption, **42**, [393]
    stamp duty land tax, exemption, **42**, [394]
  transfer of Treasury functions relating to,
    42, [834]

car (company). *See also* **motor vehicle**
  accessories—
    amount taken into account in respect of,
      44(2), [137]
    list price, **44(2)**, [138]
    meaning, **44(2)**, [136]
    non-standard, meaning, **44(2)**, [136]
    notional price, **44(2)**, [141]
    published price, **44(2)**, [139]–[140]
    qualifying, meaning, **44(2)**, [136]
    replacement, **44(2)**, [142]
    standard, meaning, **44(2)**, [136]
  appropriate percentage—
    car with CO_2 emissions figure,
      44(2), [150]
    car without CO_2 emissions figure,
      44(2), [151]
    determining, **44(2)**, [144]
    diesel car, **44(2)**, [152]
    first registered before 1st January 1998,
      44(2), [153]
    meaning, **44(2)**, [144]
  benefit in kind—
    alternative, offer of, **44(2)**, [130]
    amounts added to earnings for,
      44(2), [220]
    application of provisions to, **44(2)**, [125]
    cash equivalent of benefit, taking—
      calculation, **44(2)**, [132]
      classic cars, **44(2)**, [158]
      shared car, reduction for, **44(2)**, [159]
    earnings, benefit treated as, **44(2)**, [131]
    fuel—
      cash equivalent—
        calculating, **44(2)**, [161]
        nil, **44(2)**, [162]
        proportionate reduction in,
          44(2), [163]
        reduction of, **44(2)**, [164]
      earnings, benefit treated as, **44(2)**, [160]
    capital contribution by employee to,
      44(2), [143]

car (company)—*contd*
  classic, cash equivalent, **44(2)**, [158]
  CO_2 emissions figure, with—
    appropriate percentage, **44(2)**, [150]
    bi-fuel cars, **44(2)**, [148]
    disabled employee, automatic car for,
      44(2), [149]
    meaning, **44(2)**, [145]
    post-September 1999 registration,
      44(2), [147]
    pre-October 1999 registration, **44(2)**, [146]
  CO_2 emissions figure, without, **44(2)**, [145],
    [151]
  CO_2 emissions, threshold for, **43(S)**, 876
  definitions, **44(2)**, [181]–[182]
  disabled person—
    equipment for, **44(2)**, [182]
    vehicle for, **44(2)**, [247]
  emergency vehicle, private use of,
    44(2), [249]
  employee, available to, **44(2)**, [127]
  expenses, payment of, **44(2)**, [240]
  hire, expenditure on, **44(1)**, [414], [415]
  liability of employee, discharge of,
    44(2), [239]
  made available by reason of employment,
    44(2), [128]
  meaning, **44(2)**, [126]
  mileage allowance—
    definitions, **44(2)**, [235]–[236]
    payments, **44(2)**, [229]
      approved amounts, **44(2)**, [230]
      relevant vehicles, **44(2)**, [235]
    relief, **44(2)**, [231]
      giving effect to, **44(2)**, [232]
  more than one member of family or
    household employed by same employer,
    available to, **44(2)**, [178]
  orders relating to, **44(2)**, [180]
  parking provision and expenses, **44(2)**, [237]
  passenger payments—
    approved, **44(2)**, [234]
    approved amount, **44(2)**, [234]
    definitions, **44(2)**, [235]–[236]
    meaning, **44(2)**, [233]
    no liability for, **44(2)**, [233]
    relevant vehicles, **44(2)**, [235]
  pooled, **44(2)**, [176]
  price—
    list, meaning, **44(2)**, [134]
    meaning, **44(2)**, [133]
    notional, **44(2)**, [135]
  private use, available for, **44(2)**, [129]
    payments, deduction for, **44(2)**, [155]
  road fuel gas, running on, reduction in price,
    44(2), [157]
  temporary replacement, **44(2)**, [156]
  unavailability, deductions for, **44(2)**, [154]
  vans. *See* **van**

car fuel
  benefit, 1994–5 onwards, **43(1)**, [1]

car parks. *See* **parking**

car tax
immunities and privileges, relief for persons enjoying, **13**, [803]–[805]
overpaid, recovery of, **50**, [2]

caravan
commons, use on, **20**, [793]
council tax, liability to, **26(1)**, [7]
dweller, displaced, home loss payment to, **9**, [329]
meaning, **44(3)**, [892]
non-domestic rating, **26(1)**, [240], [241]
right to use, **44(1)**, [12]
zero-rating, **50**, [151]

caravan site
agreement—
    duration of, **21**, [777]
    gift of home, effect of, **21**, [777]
    implied terms, **21**, [777]–[779]
        court, implied by, **21**, [778]
        power to amend, **21**, [772]
    interpretation, **21**, [775]
    jurisdiction, **21**, [774]
    overpayments, recovery of, **21**, [777]
    re-siting of mobile home on, **21**, [777]
    sale of mobile home, effect of, **21**, [777]
    successors in title, binding, **21**, [773]
    termination of, **21**, [777]
    terms of, **21**, [771], [777], [778]
    written statement of, particulars, **21**, [770]
agricultural workers, use by, **32**, [245]
building sites, **32**, [245]
caravan, meaning, **32**, [241]
commons, on—
    conservators, consultation with, **32**, [246]
    Crown land, **32**, [240]
    district council prohibiting, **32**, [236]
    lord of the manor, notice to, **32**, [246]
    prohibitions, orders imposing, **32**, [246]
compulsory acquisition of land for, **32**, [237]
court, powers of, **21**, [355]
Crown land, provisions applying to, **32**, [240], [246]
displaced persons, rehousing, **21**, [417]
dwelling-house, use within curtilage of, **32**, [245]
engineering sites, **32**, [245]
eviction orders, suspension of, **21**, [354]
exempted organisations, **32**, [245]
financial aid for, **1(1)**, [649]
financial provisions, **32**, [243], [294]
fire precautions, **32**, [228], [237]
five acres or more, holding of, **32**, [245]
forestry workers, use by, **32**, [245]
gipsies, accommodation for, **32**, [245]
licensing, **32**, [1]
local authority—
    land occupied by, **32**, [245]
    powers of entry, **32**, [239]
    provision by, **32**, [237]
    site licence, granting. *See* site licence *below*
London, in, **25(1)**, [735]

caravan site—*contd*
meaning, **9**, [329]; **25(2)**, [361]; **32**, [224]
model standards for, **32**, [228]
occupier—
    meaning, **32**, [224]
    new, transfer of licence to, **32**, [233]
    responsibility of, **32**, [235]
offences—
    common, stationing caravan on, **32**, [236]
    condition attached to site licence, breaching, **32**, [232]
    failure to surrender licence, **32**, [234]
    licence, use without, **32**, [224]
    officer of local authority, obstructing, **32**, [239]
one or two nights, use for, **32**, [245]
planning permission for, **46**, [331]
protected, minimum standards, **32**, [320]
rating—
    caravanners, information for, **25(2)**, [360]
    single hereditament, pitches as, **25(2)**, [359]
residential contract, protection of, **32**, [1]
residential occupiers, protection of—
    application of provisions, **21**, [351]
    court, powers of, **21**, [355]
    eviction and harassment, against, **21**, [353]
    offences, **21**, [357]
    protected site, meaning, **21**, [351]
    residential contract, minimum length of notice, **21**, [352]
site licence—
    alteration, surrender for, **32**, [234]
    application for, **32**, [226]
    display of, **32**, [228]
    duration of, **32**, [227]
    exemptions, **32**, [225], [245]
    local authority—
        conditions, attaching, **32**, [228]
            alteration of, **32**, [231]
            appeal against, **32**, [230]
            breaches of, **32**, [232]
        failure to issue, **32**, [229]
        issue by, **32**, [226]
        transfer, consent to, **32**, [233]
        works, carrying out, **32**, [232]
    permission for use, requirement of, **32**, [224]
    register of, **32**, [238]
    revocation, **32**, [232]
    transfer of, **32**, [233]
    transmission on death, **32**, [233]
    use of land without, **32**, [224]
standard community charge, repeal of provisions, **25(2)**, [953]
summary of provisions, **20**, [1]
trading income, **44(3)**, [20]
travelling showmen, land used by, **32**, [245]
twin-unit caravans on, **21**, [356]

carbon dioxide
storage of—
    criminal proceedings, **17(2)**, [621]
    enhanced petroleum recovery, for purpose ancillary to, **17(2)**, [626]

carbon dioxide—*contd*
  storage of—*contd*
    inspectors—
      appointment of, **17(2)**, [620]
      powers and duties, **17(2)**, [620]
    installations, abandonment of, **17(2)**, [623]
    licences—
      applications for, **17(2)**, [612]
      conditions of, **17(2)**, [613]
        regulations about, **17(2)**, [614]
      directions—
        licensing authority's powers of,
          17(2), [617]
        non-compliance with, **17(2)**, [618]
      grant of, **17(2)**, [611]
        requirements relating to, **17(2)**, [612]
      offences, **17(2)**, [615], [616]
      register of information relating to,
        17(2), [622]
      termination of, **17(2)**, [624]
      terms of, **17(2)**, [613]
        regulations about, **17(2)**, [614]
    safety zones, **17(2)**, [625]
    Secretary of State's functions as to, power
      to transfer, **17(2)**, [627]
    summary of provisions, **17(1)**, [1]
    unlicensed activities, carrying on—
      injunctions to prevent, **17(2)**, [619]
      offence of, **17(2)**, [615]
      prohibition on, **17(2)**, [610]

carbon reduction trading scheme
  allocations, charges for, **43(S)**, 850–1

carcases. *See* **animals**

care
  duty of—
    builder, by, **21**, [384], [386]
    landlord, of, **21**, [387]
    occupier of premises—
      persons other than visitors, to, **21**, [781]
      visitors, to, **21**, [244]
  establishments and agencies. *See* **care
    establishments and agencies**
  National Care Standards Commission—
    abolition of, **30**, [660]; **35(2)**, [447]
    Commission for Healthcare Audit and
      Inspection—
      functions, transfer to, **35(2)**, [474]
      property and staff, transfer to,
        35(2), [494]
    Commission for Social Care Inspection—
      functions, transfer to, **35(2)**, [474]
      property and staff, transfer to,
        35(2), [494]
  vulnerable adults, work with, access to,
    temporary provision for, **6**, [655]

Care Council for Wales
  accounts, **35(2)**, [363]
  chief officer, **35(2)**, [363]
  codes of practice, **35(2)**, [327]
  delegation of functions, **35(2)**, [363]
  directions to, **35(2)**, [319]

Care Council for Wales—*contd*
  duties of, **35(2)**, [319]
  establishment of, **35(2)**, [319]
  execution of documents, **35(2)**, [363]
  general duty of, **35(2)**, [363]
  general powers of, **35(2)**, [363]
  members—
    appointment, **35(2)**, [363]
    remuneration and allowances, **35(2)**, [363]
  membership, **35(2)**, [363]
  payments to, **35(2)**, [363]
  procedure, **35(2)**, [363]
  reports and information, **35(2)**, [363]
  rules, power to make, **35(2)**, [337]
  seal, application of, **35(2)**, [363]
  social care workers, registers of,
    35(2), [321]. *See also* **social care workers**
  staff, **35(2)**, [363]
  status, **35(2)**, [363]
  training—
    courses, approval of, **35(2)**, [328]
    examinations, conduct of, **35(2)**, [328]
    Minister, functions of, **35(2)**, [332]
    post-registration, **35(2)**, [330]
    qualifications gained outside area,
      35(2), [329]
    Tribunal, appeals to, **35(2)**, [334]
    visitors, appointment of, **35(2)**, [331]
  use of staff, arrangements for, **35(2)**, [363]

care establishments and agencies
  adoption agencies. *See* **adoption**
  annual return, **35(2)**, [311]
  extension of provisions, power of,
    35(2), [318]
  false description, **35(2)**, [304]
  inspections—
    records, of, **35(2)**, [310]
    registration authority—
      persons authorised by, **35(2)**, [309]
      reports, **35(2)**, [310]
    seizure and removal of articles and
      documents, **35(2)**, [310]
  liquidator, appointment of, **35(2)**, [312]
  national minimum standards, **35(2)**, [301]
  offences—
    applications, false statements in,
      35(2), [305]
    bodies corporate, by, **35(2)**, [308]
    contravention of regulations, **35(2)**, [303]
    failure to comply with conditions,
      35(2), [302]
    false description, **35(2)**, [304]
    proceedings, **35(2)**, [307]
    registration certificate, failure to display,
      35(2), [306]
  receiver or manager of, **35(2)**, [312]
  registration—
    appeals, **35(2)**, [297], [299]
    applications, **35(2)**, [290]
      false statements in, **35(2)**, [305]
    authority—
      inspections by persons authorised by,
        35(2), [309]
      reference of worker by, **35(2)**, [342]

care establishments and agencies—*contd*
registration—*contd*
cancellation, **35(2)**, [292]
urgent procedure for, **35(2)**, [298]
certificate, failure to display, **35(2)**, [306]
conditions, proposals for—
decision, notice of, **35(2)**, [297]
notice of, **35(2)**, [295]
representations, right to make,
35(2), [296]
conditions, variation or removal of,
35(2), [293]
copies of registers, provision of,
35(2), [314]
grant of, **35(2)**, [291]
offences, **35(2)**, [289]
refusal, **35(2)**, [291]
registered person—
applications by, **35(2)**, [293]
death of, **35(2)**, [313]
registers, keeping, **35(2)**, [289]
regulations, **35(2)**, [294]
requirement, **35(2)**, [289]
regulation—
conduct, of, **35(2)**, [300]
contents of regulations, **35(2)**, [300]
contravention, **35(2)**, [303]
service of documents, **35(2)**, [316]
staff, transfers of, **35(2)**, [317]

care home
children's accommodation—
notification, **6**, [414]
research and returns of information,
6, [411]
entry by authorised person, **6**, [414]
meaning, **35(2)**, [282]
registration and regulation. *See* **care
establishments and agencies**

care order
accommodation, provision etc. *See* **local
authority**
adoption, effect on, **6**, [346]
age limitation, **6**, [343]
appeals, **6**, [355]
application for—
attendance of child at, **6**, [426]
authorised person, by, **6**, [343]
evidence, giving of, **6**, [429]
generally, **6**, [343]
local authority, by, **6**, [343]
National Society for the Prevention of
Cruelty to Children, **6**, [343]
period for disposal of, **6**, [345]
self-incrimination in evidence, **6**, [429]
authorised person—
application by, **6**, [343]
meaning, **6**, [343]
care plan, **6**, [344], [838]
contact with parents and others, **6**, [347]
discharge of, **6**, [354], [422]
duration of, **6**, [422]
effect of, **6**, [346], [422]

care order—*contd*
emergency protection order, subject to,
6, [422]
generally, **6**, [1], [343]
harm—
child suffering from, **6**, [343]
meaning, **6**, [343]
interim—
examination or assessment of child,
6, [351]
exclusion requirement in, **6**, [352]
making, **6**, [351]
period of, **6**, [351]
residence order with, **6**, [351]
undertakings, **6**, [353]
investigation into child's circumstances,
6, [350]
local authority, powers and duties of, **6**, [343],
[346]
making of, **6**, [343]
meaning, **6**, [343], [435]
name, protection of surname, **6**, [346]
National Society for the Prevention of
Cruelty to Children, application by, **6**, [343]
parental contact, **6**, [347]
parental responsibility, determination of extent
of, **6**, [346]
powers of court, **6**, [350]
abolition of certain, **6**, [421]
refusal of, **6**, [346]
religious persuasion, protection, **6**, [346]
removal from UK, prohibition, **6**, [346]
residence outside England and Wales, **6**, [346]
substitution order, **6**, [354]
variation of, **6**, [354]

Care Quality Commission
accounts, **30(S)**, NHS 131
additional functions, Secretary of State
providing, **30(S)**, NHS 66–7
annual reports, **30(S)**, NHS 86–7
annual reports by, **29**, [168]
assistance to, **30(S)**, NHS 131
Auditor-General for Wales—
co-operating with, **26(2)**, [408]
provision of information by,
30(S), NHS 77
care standards provisions, amendment of,
30(S), NHS 144–53
Comptroller and Auditor General, provision
of material to, **30(S)**, NHS 78
Crown, provisions binding, **30(S)**, NHS 97–8
data, studies and research, reviews of,
30(S), NHS 65
discharge of functions, failure in,
30(S), NHS 86
documents and information, power to
require, **30(S)**, NHS 72
documents, service of, **30(S)**, NHS 95
economy and efficiency studies—
Audit Commission, role of,
30(S), NHS 64–5
promotion of, **30(S)**, NHS 63
results, publication of, **30(S)**, NHS 64
undertaking, **30(S)**, NHS 63

Care Quality Commission—*contd*
electronic communications, **30(S)**, NHS 96
employees, **30(S)**, NHS 130
enforcement action—
    bodies corporate, offences by,
      30(S), NHS 94
    guidance as to, **30(S)**, NHS 91
    information, publication of,
      30(S), NHS 92
    penalty notice, issue of, **30(S)**, NHS 89–91
    proceedings for offence, **30(S)**, NHS 93
    unincorporated associations, offences by,
      30(S), NHS 94
entry and inspection, powers of,
    30(S), NHS 69–71
establishment of, **30(S)**, NHS 12
exercise of functions, **30(S)**, NHS 131
    enquiries, **30(S)**, NHS 80
explanations, power to require,
    30(S), NHS 73
fees, **30(S)**, NHS 88
functions of, **30(S)**, NHS 13
general powers and duties, **30(S)**, NHS 129
health care associated infections—
    code of practice—
      consultation, **30(S)**, NHS 31
      effect of, **30(S)**, NHS 34
      issue of, **30(S)**, NHS 30
      meaning, **30(S)**, NHS 29
health care standards—
    periodic reviews—
      conduct of, **30(S)**, NHS 54
      English local authorities, failings by,
        30(S), NHS 58
      extension of functions, **30(S)**, NHS 57
      frequency and period of, **30(S)**, NHS 55
      Welsh NHS bodies, failings by,
        30(S), NHS 59
    Secretary of State, set by, **30(S)**, NHS 53
    special reviews and investigations,
      30(S), NHS 56
Independent Regulator of NHS Foundation
    Trusts, co-operation with, **30(S)**, NHS 77
information—
    confidential personal, offence of
      disclosing, **30(S)**, NHS 81
    code of practice, **30(S)**, NHS 84
    defence, **30(S)**, NHS 82
    permitted disclosure, **30(S)**, NHS 83
    publication of, **30(S)**, NHS 66
    use of, **30(S)**, NHS 83
information and advice, giving,
    30(S), NHS 62
inspections by—
    registration purposes, for, **30(S)**, NHS 68
    regulatory functions, for purposes of,
      30(S), NHS 67
interpretation, **30(S)**, NHS 98–100
matters to which having regard,
    30(S), NHS 15
members, **30(S)**, NHS 129–30
mental health functions, transfer and
    amendment of, **30(S)**, NHS 60
ministers, arrangements with,
    30(S), NHS 78–9

Care Quality Commission—*contd*
Northern Ireland ministers, arrangements
    with, **30(S)**, NHS 79
objectives, **30(S)**, NHS 14
other authorities, interaction with,
    30(S), NHS 139–43
payments and loans to, **30(S)**, NHS 131
procedure, **30(S)**, NHS 130
programme of reviews, publication of,
    30(S), NHS 85
property and staff transferred to,
    30(S), NHS 133–4
provision of health or social care,
    registration—
      appeals, **30(S)**, NHS 41–2
      applications, false statements in,
        30(S), NHS 46
      bodies required to be notified of certain
        matters, **30(S)**, NHS 48
      cancellation—
        grounds for, **30(S)**, NHS 25
        offences, **30(S)**, NHS 43
        power of, **30(S)**, NHS 25
        urgent procedure for, **30(S)**, NHS 39
      compliance with requirements, guidance as
       to—
        consultation, **30(S)**, NHS 33
        effect of, **30(S)**, NHS 34
        issue of, **30(S)**, NHS 32
      concerns, premises etc, false description
       of, **30(S)**, NHS 45
      conditions, failure to comply with,
        30(S), NHS 41–2
      decisions, notice of, **30(S)**, NHS 36–7
      health or social care, meaning,
        30(S), NHS 18
      inspections, **30(S)**, NHS 68
      liquidators, regulations applying,
        30(S), NHS 50
      periodic returns, **30(S)**, NHS 49
      proposals, notice of, **30(S)**, NHS 35
      registered person, death of,
        30(S), NHS 50–1
      registered persons, applications by,
        30(S), NHS 27–8
      registers, provision of copies of,
        30(S), NHS 47
      regulated activity—
        conditions, failure to comply with,
          30(S), NHS 41–2
        meaning, **30(S)**, NHS 17
        newly regulated, power to modify
          provisions, **30(S)**, NHS 51–2
        regulation of, **30(S)**, NHS 29
      regulated manager—
        application for, **30(S)**, NHS 23
        grant or refusal of, **30(S)**, NHS 23
        service provider registration requiring,
          30(S), NHS 22
      regulations, **30(S)**, NHS 24
        contravention of, **30(S)**, NHS 44
      representations, right to make,
        30(S), NHS 36
      service provider, as—
        application for, **30(S)**, NHS 20

Care Quality Commission—*contd*
provision of health or social care,
registration—*contd*
service provider, as—*contd*
grant or refusal of, **30(S)**, NHS 21
regulated manager condition,
30(S), NHS 22
requirement **30(S)**, NHS 19
suspension—
offences, **30(S)**, NHS 43
power of, **30(S)**, NHS 26
urgent procedure for, **30(S)**, NHS 40
variation, urgent procedure for,
30(S), NHS 40
warning notice, issue of, **30(S)**, NHS 37–8
provision of information by, **26(2)**, [410]
reports, availability of, **30(S)**, NHS 87
reviews or assessments, co-ordination of,
30(S), NHS 75
Secretary of State, consultation with,
29, [165]
status, **30(S)**, NHS 129
summary of provisions, **30(S)**, NHS 1–5
transfer of functions to, **29**, [373]
unreasonable burdens in exercise of regulatory
power, avoidance of, **30(S)**, NHS 75
user involvement, statement on,
30(S), NHS 16
Welsh Ministers, co-operation with,
30(S), NHS 76

care standards
Commission. *See* **National Care Standards
Commission**

careers
grants for promoting, **47**, [379]

careers education
advisers, co-operation of schools and other
institutions with, **15(1)**, [755]
extension or modification of provisions,
15(1), [757]
provision of, in schools, **15(1)**, [754], [756]

careers services
See also under **local education authorities**

careless driving. *See* **road traffic offences**

carer's allowance
entitlement to, **40(1)**, [317]
increase in, **40(1)**, [335]
rate of, **40(1)**, [317], [467]
severely disabled person, meaning,
40(1), [317]

carpets and mats
street offences as to, **36**, [229], [385]

carriage. *See also* **hackney carriage; stage
carriage**
furious driving, **12(1)**, [91]; **36**, [222]
routes, regulations as to, Police
Commissioners' powers, **36**, [224]

carriage by air. *See also* **air navigation;
carrier** (air)**; civil aviation**
air transport licensing. *See* **Civil Aviation
Authority**
baggage, **4(1)**, [17], [19], [21], [37]
Carriage by Air Conventions—
application of provisions, **4(1)**, [2]
carriage not governed by, application of
provisions, **4(1)**, [13]
contracting parties—
actions against, **4(1)**, [10]
designation, **4(1)**, [3]
revision, statutory amendments
consequential on, **4(1)**, [11]
carrier's liability. *See under* **carrier**
functions, Secretary of State, of, **4(1)**, [54]
international—
agents and servants. *See under* **carrier** (air)
air waybill, **4(1)**, [17], [19], [21], [37]
baggage check, **4(1)**, [17], [19], [21], [37]
British possessions, application of
provisions, **4(1)**, [12], [26]
carriage by State, application of provisions,
4(1), [19], [21]
combined carriage, **4(1)**, [17], [19], [21],
[37]
complaint on discovery of damage,
4(1), [17], [19], [21], [37]
Crown, application to, **4(1)**, [15], [27]
damage, liability for—
contributory negligence, **4(1)**, [8], [17],
[19], [21], [37]
death of person liable, **4(1)**, [17], [19],
[21], [37]
limitation, **4(1)**, [5], [19], [21], [37]
partial loss, notice, **4(1)**, [6]
proceedings, time for bringing, **4(1)**, [7],
[17]
See also under **carrier** (air)
extraordinary circumstances, carriage in,
4(1), [19], [21], [37]
fatal accidents, liability, **4(1)**, [4], [17]
infringement of rules, **4(1)**, [19], [21], [37]
military aircraft, exclusion, **4(1)**, [9]
Northern Ireland, application of
provisions, **4(1)**, [14]
Orders in Council, power to make,
4(1), [12], [35]
passenger ticket, **4(1)**, [17], [19], [37]
person other than carrier, by, **4(1)**, [21]
successive carriers, by, **4(1)**, [17], [19],
[21], [37]
supplementary compensation by states,
4(1), [19], [37]
territory in which action commenced,
4(1), [17], [19], [21], [37]
route licences—
foreign judgments, enforcement of,
4(1), [123]
meaning, **4(1)**, [118]
regulation by, **4(1)**, [118]
summary of provisions, **4(1)**, [1]
unlicensed, restriction of, **4(1)**, [112]
Wales, financial assistance in, **4(1)**, [519]

carriage by air—*contd*
Warsaw Convention—
  additional protocol, **4(1)**, [17], [19], [37]
  application of provisions, **4(1)**, [17]
  as amended—
    French text, **4(1)**, [20], [38]
    text, **4(1)**, [19], [37]
  carriage not governed by, application of
    provisions, **4(1)**, [26]
  French text, **4(1)**, [18]
  general provisions, **4(1)**, [17]
  Montreal protocols—
    amendments by, **4(1)**, [32]
    French text, **4(1)**, [20], [38]
    text, **4(1)**, [19], [37]
  substituted provisions, **4(1)**, [19], [37]
  supplementary convention—
    amendments consequential on revision
      of, **4(1)**, [25]
    force of law, having, **4(1)**, [22]
    French text, **4(1)**, [30]
    interpretation, **4(1)**, [23]
    provisions, application, **4(1)**, [24]
    text of, **4(1)**, [29]
  unification of rules, **4(1)**, [21]

carriage of goods by road (Convention)
  actions arising, **36**, [756], [765]
  ADR convention, inspection in connection
    with, **37**, [130]
  application of—
    British possessions etc, **36**, [760]
    Crown, to, **36**, [763]
    Northern Ireland, to, **36**, [761]
    scope of, **36**, [765]
  arbitration, **36**, [757]
  British possession, application to, **36**, [760]
  carriers—
    application of provisions, **36**, [765]
    checks by, **36**, [765]
    contribution between, **36**, [755]
    liability of, **36**, [765]
    non-availability of provisions, **36**, [765]
    persons for whom responsible, **36**, [765]
    successive, **36**, [765]
    wilful misconduct or default, **36**, [765]
  cash on delivery charge, **36**, [765]
  claims, **36**, [765]
  compensation for loss etc—
    calculation, **36**, [765]
    interest, entitlement to, **36**, [765]
    recovery of, **36**, [765]
  conflicts between Conventions, **36**, [758]
  consignee, application of provisions, **36**, [765]
  consignment note, **36**, [765]
  contract of carriage—
    conclusion and performance, **36**, [765]
    contribution between carriers, **36**, [755]
    evidence of, **36**, [765]
    impossibility of performance, **36**, [765]
  court, powers as to other proceedings,
    36, [753]
  Crown, application to, **36**, [763]
  customs or other formalities, **36**, [765]
  dangerous goods, **36**, [765]; **37**, [130]

**carriage of goods by road
(Convention)**—*contd*
  delivery—
    delay in, **36**, [765]
    prevention of, **36**, [765]
    requirements, **36**, [765]
  disposal, right of, **36**, [765]
  extra-contractual claims, **36**, [765]
  force of law, having, **36**, [751]
  foreign judgments, registration, **36**, [754]
  gold francs, replacement by
  High Contracting Parties—
    actions against, **36**, [756]
    designation of, **36**, [752]
  inspection of vehicles, **37**, [130]
  legal proceedings, **36**, [756], [765]
  limitation of actions, **36**, [765]
  loss or damage—
    compensation, **36**, [765]
    contribution between carriers, **36**, [755]
    liability of carrier, **36**, [765]
  Northern Ireland, application to, **36**, [761]
  Orders in Council, **36**, [752], [762]
  persons—
    carrier's responsibility, **36**, [765]
    concerned, **36**, [764]
  revision, **36**, [759]
  sender—
    application of provisions, **36**, [765]
    responsibilities, **36**, [765]
    rights of, **36**, [765]
  signature, protocol of, **36**, [765]
  special drawing right, **36**, [765]
  stipulations contrary to, nullity of, **36**, [765]
  surcharge, **36**, [765]
  TIR Convention, inspections, **37**, [130]

carriage of goods by road (generally). *See*
goods vehicles

carriage of goods by sea
  dangerous, **39(2)**, [753]
  generally, **39(2)**, [1]
  Hague Rules—
    application of, **39(2)**, [439]
    British possessions, etc, application to,
      39(2), [443]
    Contracting States, **39(2)**, [441]
    ports in British possessions, application to
      carriage from, **39(2)**, [444]
    seaworthiness, warranty not to be implied,
      39(2), [442]
    text of, **39(2)**, [446]
  hazardous and noxious substances, *See*
    **hazardous and noxious substances,
    carriage of; ship**
  shipping documents—
    application of provisions to, **39(2)**, [663]
    bills of lading, representations in,
      39(2), [666]
    liabilities under, **39(2)**, [665]
    rights under, **39(2)**, [664]
  shipping interests, protection of,
    39(2), [1012]–[1018]

carriage of goods by sea—*contd*
special drawing rights, substitution of,
39(2), [440]
trading interests, protection of,
39(2), [1012]–[1018]

carriage of passengers and luggage by sea
Convention—
extension of, **39(2)**, [861]
force of law, to have, **39(2)**, [860]
provisions having effect with, **39(2)**, [1001]
text of, **39(2)**, [1000]

carriage of passengers by road (generally).
See **bus services; hackney carriage; motor**
vehicle; omnibus; passenger transport
services; public service vehicle; stage
carriage; taxis

carriageway. *See under* **highway**

carrier
air, by—
action for damages against, **4(1)**, [17], [29],
[37]
agents or servants of—
acts or omissions by, **4(1)**, [29]
liability, limitation of, **4(1)**, [17], [29]
proceedings against, time for, **4(1)**, [7]
protection of, **4(1)**, [7], [29], [37]
cargo, documents relating to, **4(1)**, [19],
[21], [37]
consignor, rights and liabilities, **4(1)**, [19],
[37]
contractual provisions, when void,
4(1), [29]
liability—
amount, **4(1)**, [17], [33]
contributory negligence, **4(1)**, [8], [17],
[19], [21], [37]
death or injury, for, **4(1)**, [19], [21], [37]
delay, for, **4(1)**, [19], [21], [37]
limitation, **4(1)**, [5], [19], [21], [37]
omission or recklessness, **4(1)**, [17]
partial loss, notice, **4(1)**, [6]
special drawing rights, **4(1)**, [33]
amount, **4(1)**, [37]
conversion into sterling, **4(1)**, [34]
successive carriers, **4(1)**, [17], [19], [21],
[37]
See also **carriage by air**
waybill requirements, **4(1)**, [17], [19], [21],
[37]
charges, increased—
damages, included in, **5(2)**, [474]
notice to be displayed, **5(2)**, [469]
receipts to be given, **5(2)**, [470]
valuable parcels, on delivery of, **5(2)**, [469]
coach proprietors' liability—
damages proved, **5(2)**, [476]
felonious acts, **5(2)**, [475]
not limited by public notice, **5(2)**, [471]
restriction of, **5(2)**, [468]
special contracts, **5(2)**, [473]
sued, to be, **5(2)**, [471]

carrier—*contd*
common—
damages to be proved, **5(2)**, [476]
felonious acts, **5(2)**, [475]
liability—
public notice limiting, **5(2)**, [471]
restriction of, **5(2)**, [468]
sued, to be, **5(2)**, [471]
meaning, **5(2)**, [467]
special contracts, **5(2)**, [473]
common law, at, **5(2)**, [467]
Conventions, liability and duties under. *See*
carriage of goods by road
damages for loss—
proof required, **5(2)**, [476]
recovery of charges, **5(2)**, [474]
felonious acts, **5(2)**, [475]
firearms, possession of, **12(1)**, [483], [1126]
liability—
public notice of limitation, **5(2)**, [471]
restriction of, **5(2)**, [468]
sued, to be, **5(2)**, [471]
mail contractors' liability—
damages proved, **5(2)**, [476]
felonious acts, **5(2)**, [473]
not limited by public notice, **5(2)**, [471]
restriction of, **5(2)**, [468]
special contracts, **5(2)**, [473]
sued, to be, **5(2)**, [471]
meaning, **5(2)**, [467]
receiving office, offices deemed to be,
5(2), [472]
road, carriage by. *See* **carriage of goods by**
road (Convention); goods vehicles
special contracts, **5(2)**, [473]
summary of provisions, **5(2)**, [467]

carrier bags
single use—
charges for, **35(S)**, 111, 156–8
civil sanctions, **35(S)**, 158–66
meaning, **35(S)**, 157
regulations, procedures applying,
35(S), 166–7

cart
highway, driven on, **36**, [222]

case stated
application for, **11(2)**, [532]
bail, on, **12(1)**, [262]
bail pending, **11(2)**, [534]
distress warrant, as to, **11(2)**, [575]
High Court decision, enforcement of,
11(2), [533]
mandamus, order of, **11(2)**, [532]
recognizances and fees on, **11(2)**, [535]

casino. *See* **gaming**

cathedral
administrative body, **14**, 624
approval required for alteration to—
application for—
body to which made, **14**, 1197–8

cathedral—*contd*
approval required for alteration to—*contd*
application for—*contd*
Cathedrals Fabric Commission, approval
of, **14**, 1199–200
fabric advisory committee, approval of,
14, 1198–9
contravention of—
approval of proposals already
implemented, **14**, 1295–6
bishop—
directions, power to give, **14**, 1293
preliminary interview by, **14**, 1292
special visitation, power to order,
14, 1292
injunction or restoration order, **14**, 1294
summary of provisions, **14**, 1291
Vicar-General's court—
jurisdiction and composition of,
14, 1295
powers of, **14**, 1295–6
generally, **14**, 1194–5
archaeological consultant, **14**, 1203–4
archaeologist—
appointment of, **14(S)**, 59
records, maintenance of, **14(S)**, 63
reports by, **14(S)**, 62
architect—
appointment of, **14(S)**, 59
meaning, **14**, 1208
provisions as to, **14**, 1203–4
records—
kept by, **14**, 1205
maintenance of, **14(S)**, 63
reports to be made by, **14**, 1205; **14(S)**, 61
Birmingham, charge on revenues, **14**, 620
brawling in, **14**, 192–3
canon, meaning, **14**, 624
capitular body, meaning, **14**, 624
care of—
archaeological consultants, **14**, 1203–4
cathedral architects—
provisions as to, **14**, 1203–4
records kept by, **14**, 1205
reports to be made by, **14**, 1205
general provisions, **14**, 17
inventories, etc, **14**, 1204
listed building consent, application for,
14, 1205–6
notices, **14**, 1208
parish church cathedral, power to exclude,
14, 1206–7
scheduled monument consent, application
for, **14**, 1205–6
summary of provisions, **14(S)**, 47
works, approval of, **14(S)**, 48
approval bodies, general duties of,
14(S), 58
body to which application made,
14(S), 51
conditions applying to, **14(S)**, 56
register of applications, **14(S)**, 57
tenant, right of appeal by, **14(S)**, 57
cathedral duties, two residentiary canons
engaged in, **14**, 1345

cathedral—*contd*
Cathedrals Fabric Commission for England—
appeal to, **14**, 1200–1
application for approval of, **14**, 1199–200
establishment of, **14**, 1195–6, 1210–12
functions, **14**, 1195–6
further powers, **14**, 1203
generally, **14**, 17
Chapter—
accounts, **14**, 1355
bishop, consultation with, **14**, 1343
borrowing powers, **14**, 1355
dean, as chairman of, **14**, 1344
duties, **14**, 1341
establishment of, **14**, 1338
investment powers, **14**, 1351–2
membership, **14**, 1340
powers, **14**, 1341
property, increase in value, **14**, 161–2
retirement of dignitary, meeting to
consider, **14**, 374
See also dean and chapter *below*
College of Canons—
establishment of, **14**, 1338
functions, **14**, 1342
membership, **14**, 1342
Commission of Review, **14**, 1201–2
constitution, **14**, 1345–7
Council's revision of, **14**, 1356–7
Council—
constitution and statutes, revision of,
14, 1356–8
duties, **14**, 1339–40
establishment of, **14**, 1338
meetings, number of, **14**, 1340
membership, **14**, 1339
dean and chapter—
archbishop, electing, **14**, 23–4
bishop, electing, **14**, 23–4
commissary, appointing, **14**, 604
duties, **14**, 1344
meaning, **14**, 624
newly appointed, payment towards expenses
of, **14**, 1354
parochial church council, transfer of
functions from, **14**, 1348–9
stipends of, **14**, 1354
deanery, patronage of, **14**, 133
fabric advisory committee—
application for approval of, **14**, 1198–9;
14(S), 54
application for approval of works, powers as
to, **14(S)**, 50
establishment of, **14**, 1196, 1213–14
functions of, **14(S)**, 50
powers, **14**, 1197
houses—
allocation of,
14, 1353. *See also* **house of residence**
grants for, **14**, 1355
inventories, **14(S)**, 59–60
land, acquisition and disposal of, **14**, 1350–1
meaning, **14**, 624

cathedral—*contd*
moneys—
  Church Commissioners holding on behalf
    of, **14**, 1352
  investment powers, **14**, 1351–2
Newcastle Chapter Endowment fund, **14**, 620
Norwich, severance of canonry from
  archdeaconry, **14**, 620–1
Oxford—
  additional canonry, creation of, **14**, 621
  non-residentiary canons, appointment of,
    14, 622
  provisions applying to, **14**, 626
parish church—
  meaning, **14**, 624
  power to exclude, **14**, 1206–7
precinct plans, **14(S)**, 59–60
preferment—
  archdeacon as holder of, **14**, 135
  authorisation of, **14**, 1072
  meaning, **14**, 126
property—
  endowment, disposal of proceeds, **14**, 1352
  houses, allocation for residentiary use,
    14, 1353
  inspection of, **14**, 1353
  schemes for transfer of, **14**, 1350
  vesting of, **14**, 1349
property within precinct of, exclusion from
  rights—
  acquisition of new lease, of, **23**, [173]
  collective enfranchisement, **23**, [173]
purpose of, duty to have regard to, **14**, 1194,
  1338
residentiary canons of—
  cathedral duties, solely engaged in,
    14, 1345
  newly appointed, payment towards expenses
    of, **14**, 1354
  stipend of, **14**, 1354
sharing agreement not applying to, **14**, 678
Southwark, scheme for, **14**, 623
statutes, **14**, 1347
  Council's revision of, **14**, 1356, 1358
surveyor of fabrics—
  appointment of, **14(S)**, 59
  records, maintenance of, **14(S)**, 63
  reports by, **14(S)**, 61
transitional council, **14**, 1364–5
treasure found within precinct of, **14(S)**, 53
Wales, in, dissolution, **14**, 256

Cathedrals Fabric Commission for England
application for approval of, **14(S)**, 55
functions of, **14(S)**, 49

cats
pets. *See* **pet animal**

cattle. *See also* **livestock**
brucellosis—
  control of, **2**, [431]
  eradication, **2**, [346]
  offences and penalties, **2**, [347]
carcase, burying of, **2**, [507]

cattle—*contd*
Community suckler cow premiums—
  additional grants for person entitled to,
    1(2), [481]
  meaning, **1(2)**, [481]
diseases. *See* **diseases of animals**
distraining. *See* **distress**
dogs injuring, liability, **2**, [234]
drinking fountains for, **35(1)**, [93]
driving through streets, restriction, **36**, [463]
fat, disclosure of weight of, **27**, [98]
hill farming. *See* **hill farming**
impounded—
  release of, unlawful, **36**, [383]
  sale of, **36**, [382]
Local Government Board—
  powers of, **27**, [90]
  transfer of powers, **27**, [93]
meaning, **2**, [237], [548]; **27**, [7], [86];
  36, [377], [461]
plague—
  meaning, **2**, [548]
  slaughter in case of, **2**, [464], [559]
rearing land. *See* **livestock**
slaughter other than in slaughter-house,
  27, [21]
slaughter-house. *See* **slaughter-house**
straying, impounding of, **36**, [381]
street offences involving, **36**, [226], [381]
street, passing along, to or from market,
  35(1), [70]
tolls in respect of, **27**, [29]
weighing—
  accommodation for, **27**, [87], [94]
  auction marts, facilities at, **27**, [95]
  buyer or seller, at option of, **27**, [88]
  exemption from requirements, **27**, [90],
    [99]
  tolls for, **27**, [89], [100]

cattle-grid
acquisition of land for, **36**, [1289]
alteration of, **36**, [1085]
bridge, protection of, **36**, [1093]
by-pass—
  acquisition of land for, **36**, [1289]
  alteration of, **36**, [1085]
  determination of questions, **36**, [1413]
  discontinuance, **36**, [1086]
  improvement of, **36**, [1085]
  land, agreement for use of, **36**, [1090]
  maintenance of, **36**, [1087]
  meaning, **36**, [1085]
  provision of, **36**, [1085], [1413]
contributions towards expenses of, **36**, [1091]
determination of questions, **36**, [1413]
gate, superseding of, **36**, [1089]
improvement of, **36**, [1085]
land, agreement for use of, **36**, [1090]
maintenance of, **36**, [1087]
meaning, **36**, [1085]
Minister, delegation of powers of, **36**, [1092]
neighbouring authorities, agreement
  between, **36**, [1088]
provision of, **36**, [1085], [1413]

cattle-grid—*contd*
railway, protection of, **36**, [1093]
removal of, **36**, [1086]
right of way over, **36**, [1086]
transitional provisions, **36**, [1433]

caveat
probate registry, entry in, **18**, [635]

CDFI. *See* **community development finance institutions**

cellars
construction below subsoil water level—
consent of local authority to, **35(1)**, [596]
exceptions to prohibition on, **35(1)**, [596]
notice requiring alteration or filling in where, **35(1)**, [596]
prohibition, **35(1)**, [596]
street offences as to, **36**, [229], [385]

celluloid
raw. *See* **raw celluloid**

Celsius
replacement of Fahrenheit by, in customs and excise Acts, **13**, [584]

cement and lime
weights and measures for, **39(1)**, [579], [580]

cemetery. *See also* **burial ground**
Acts—
incorporation, **5(2)**, [320]
interpretation, **5(2)**, [321]–[322]
special. *See* special Act *below*
annual accounts of company, **5(2)**, [375]
Brompton Cemetery, **5(2)**, [381]–[382]
burial. *See* **burial**
chapel—
Established Church purposes, for, **5(2)**, [342]
power to build, **5(2)**, [328]
services permitted in, **5(2)**, [352]
chaplain—
appointment and licensing, **5(2)**, [343]
burial service, performance by, **5(2)**, [345]
stipend, **5(2)**, [347]
clerk—
appointment etc, **5(2)**, [350]
parish, payments to, **5(2)**, [373]
closed. *See* **burial ground**
consecrated part—
register of burials, **5(2)**, [348]
removal of bodies from, **5(2)**, [343]
unconsecrated parts and, marking, **5(2)**, [341]
damage, compensation by company, **5(2)**, [334]
deductible payments, **44(1)**, [68]
discontinuance of use. *See* **burial ground**
disorderly behaviour in, prevention, **5(2)**, [415]
disturbances in, penalty, **5(2)**, [374]

cemetery—*contd*
Established Church—
chapels for services of, **5(2)**, [342]
consecration of part for, **5(2)**, [342]
meaning, **5(2)**, [322]
exclusive rights of burial—
assignment, **5(2)**, [360], [380]
form of, **5(2)**, [361]
registration, **5(2)**, [362]
burials in place of, **5(2)**, [364]
form of grant, **5(2)**, [358]
grant of, **5(2)**, [357]
limitation on grant, **5(2)**, [365]
register of grants, **5(2)**, [359]
wills disposing of, **5(2)**, [363]
fencing and inclosure, **5(2)**, [332]
fouling of water, penalty, **5(2)**, [337]–[339]
grave diggers, appointment, **5(2)**, [353]
grounds, laying out, **5(2)**, [328]
incumbents, payments to, **5(2)**, [368]
accounts, **5(2)**, [370]
apportioned, **5(2)**, [372]
half-yearly, made, **5(2)**, [371]
inspection of, **5(2)**, [393]
interments, accounts respecting, **5(2)**, [369]
justices, power of, **5(2)**, [376]
land—
taken for, compensation, **5(2)**, [324]
use for other purposes, prohibition, **5(2)**, [327]
wrong descriptions etc, correction, **5(2)**, [325]
London—
chapels, **5(2)**, [383]
City, in, performance of services in, **25(1)**, [996]
maintenance, **5(2)**, [394]
meaning, **25(2)**, [377]
rights of interment—
extinguishment, **25(2)**, [377]
grant of, **25(1)**, [967]
tombstones, removal of, **25(2)**, [377]
management and control, **5(2)**, [452], [455]
monuments—
inscriptions, objection to, **5(2)**, [367]
maintenance agreements, **5(2)**, [446]
removal of, **5(2)**, [366], [457], [466]
right to erect, grant of, **5(2)**, [447]
nuisances, prevention of, **5(2)**, [336]
protection of, **5(2)**, [374]
provision by burial authority, **5(2)**, [452], [455]
public health, protection, **5(2)**, [396]
register of burials, **5(2)**, [348]–[349]
regulation of, **5(2)**, [354], [395]
removal of bodies from, faculty required, **5(2)**, [398]
repair and maintenance, **5(2)**, [333]
roads—
improvement, **5(2)**, [331]
power to make etc, **5(2)**, [329]
widening, consent for, **5(2)**, [330]
sewers and drains, construction, **5(2)**, [335]
special Act—
certified copies as evidence, **5(2)**, [326]

cemetery—*contd*
special Act—*contd*
copies, inspection of, **5(2)**, [377]–[378]
errors or omissions, correction, **5(2)**, [325]
incorporation with, **5(2)**, [320]
interpretation, **5(2)**, [322]
summary of provisions, **5(2)**, [319]
trade profits—
application of provisions, **44(3)**, [169]
capital expenditure—
ancillary, allocation of, **44(3)**, [171]
deduction for, **44(3)**, [170]
definitions, **44(3)**, [169]
subsidies, met by, **44(3)**, [172]
sale of land, references to, **44(3)**, [169]
unconsecrated part, Church service in,
5(2), [418]
vaults. *See* **burial**

censorship
theatre, abolition, **13**, [181]

censure
appeal, suspension pending, **14**, 607
disobedience to, **14**, 595
number of, limit on, **14**, 592
recording of, **14**, 609
severity of, **14**, 592
types of, **14**, 591–2

census. *See also* **population**
expenses, defrayment, **36**, [31]
false declaration, **36**, [32]
general note, **36**, [1]
improper disclosure of information, **36**, [32]
local authorities, expenses of, **36**, [31]
local, provision for, **36**, [30]
minimum period between, **36**, [25]
Northern Ireland, **36**, [154]
offences and penalties, **36**, [32]
particulars required, **36**, [34]
Registrar-General, duties, **36**, [1]
Registrar General for Scotland, duties,
36, [26]
regulation governing taking of, **36**, [27]
reports and abstracts, **36**, [28]
Statistics Board, duties, **36**, [1], [26]
statistics, preparation, **36**, [1], [29]
taking of, power to direct, **36**, [25]

census of production. *See also* **trade statistics**
advisory committees, **47**, [26]
expenses in respect of, **47**, [33]
functions as to, delegation of, **47**, [24]
information—
false, giving, **47**, [24]
Gazette notice requiring, **47**, [24]
improper disclosure, **47**, [27]
persons entering or leaving UK, by,
47, [29]
restrictions on disclosing, **47**, [27]
Secretary of States, authorised disclosure
by, **47**, [28]
subjects of, **47**, [20], [36]
additional, prescription of, **47**, [23]

census of production—*contd*
notices, service of, **47**, [31]
orders, powers as to, **47**, [30]
report to Parliament, **47**, [25]
returns for—
exemption from making, **47**, [20]
false statements in, **47**, [22]
forms for, **47**, [21]
notice requiring, **47**, [21]
offences relating to, **47**, [22]
bodies corporate, by, **47**, [32]
requirement for, **47**, [19]
times for taking, **47**, [20]

Central Arbitration Committee. *See under*
**Advisory, Conciliation and Arbitration
Service**

**Central Board of Finance of Church of
England**
deposit funds. *See* **Church of England**
investment fund. *See* **Church of England**
jurisdiction of, **14**, 496
Prevention of Fraud (Investments) Act not
applying to, **14**, 497

**Central Council for Agricultural and
Horticultural Co-operation**
directions by minister, **1(1)**, [660]
dissolution, time of, **1(2)**, [196]
functions, **1(1)**, [659]
transfer from Food from Britain,
1(2), [195], [204]
ministers responsible for, **1(1)**, [661]

**Central Council for Education and
Training in Social Work**
abolition, **35(2)**, [336]
transfer of functions, **35(2)**, [336]

Central Criminal Court
accommodation of, **11(2)**, [249]
accommodation, temporary, cost of,
25(1), [879]
catering facilities at, **25(1)**, [887]
Crown Court as, **11(2)**, [675]
judge—
additional, **11(2)**, [262]
remuneration and pensions, **11(2)**, [208]

Central Fire Brigades Advisory Council
abolition of, **18**, [1072]

**Central Police Training and Development
Authority**
abolition, **33(2)**, [610]
establishment, **33(2)**, [344]

**Central Rail Users' Consultative
Committee.** *See now* **Rail Passengers'
Council**

cereals
corn. *See* **corn**
Home-grown Cereals Authority—
Food from Britain, contributions to,
1(2), [197]
levy. *See* levy *below*

certificate (compulsory acquisition)
common land, open spaces, etc, issue of,
9, [432], [453]
rights over land, acquisition, **9**, [452]–[453]
special kinds of land, as to acquisition of—
date of operation, **9**, [438]
giving, **9**, [432], [453]
intention to give, notice of, **9**, [434]
notice of giving, **9**, [434], [453]
quashing, **9**, [436]
suspension, **9**, [436]
validity, **9**, [435]–[439]
statutory undertakers' land—
acquisition without, **9**, [443]
exclusion, **9**, [429]

certificate of tax deposit
interest period, extension of, **42**, [448]

certification
instruments, of, regulations for, **41**, [153]

certification marks
authorised users, rights of, **48**, 189
character or significance, not to be misleading
as to, **48**, 188
geographical origin, indication of, **48**, 188
infringement, **48**, 189
meaning, **48**, 149
proprietor's business, nature of, **48**, 188
registered, consent to assignment, **48**, 189
registration—
invalidity, grounds for, **48**, 190
regulations governing use, **48**, 188–9
revocation, grounds for, **48**, 189
regulations governing use of, **48**, 188–9
signs of which consisting, **48**, 188
transitional provisions, **48**, 195

Certification Officer
annual report and accounts, **16**, [475]
appointment, **16**, [468]
assistants, **16**, [468]
custody of documents, **16**, [474]
payment, **16**, [468]
procedure before, **16**, [470]
remuneration, **16**, [469]
staff, **16**, [468]
striking out of proceedings, **16**, [471]
trade unions, functions relating to. *See* **trade
unions**
vexatious litigants before, **16**, [472], [473]

certiorari
bail on application for, **12(1)**, [262]

cesspools
duty to empty, **35(1)**, [304], [306]

cesspools—*contd*
examination and testing of suspected
defective, **35(1)**, [125]
insufficiency of, **35(1)**, [583]
meaning, **35(1)**, [140], [648], [756]
overflow from, prevention of, **35(1)**, [127]
room over, prohibition on use as living,
sleeping or work room, **35(1)**, [126]
soakage from, prevention of, **35(1)**, [127]
waste collection authority, emptying by,
35(1), [756]

cestui que vie
appearance of beneficiary, endeavour to
procure, **20**, [23]
concealment of death, **20**, [20]
guardians etc, holding over by, **20**, [24]
presumption of death, **20**, [16]–[18]
reversion, of, **20**, [20]
revesting of title after presumed death,
20, [18]

Ceylon. *See* **Sri Lanka**

challenging to fight
abolition of offence, **12(1)**, [369]

champerty
civil rights in respect of, abolition, **45**, [945],
[952]

chancel
insurance of, **14**, 328
liability to repair—
apportionment of, **14**, 373–4
county court, proceedings in, **14**, 351–2
ecclesiastical court, abolition of
jurisdiction, **14**, 350
incumbent, of, abolition, **14**, 328
investment of sum for, **14**, 328–9
notice of, **14**, 350–1
parochial church council, transfer to,
14, 864
payment of sums for, **14**, 328
proceedings, **14**, 350–1
rector, of, **14**, 17
tithe rentcharge, arising from, **14**, 362–3
Wales, in, **14**, 19
meaning, **14**, 352
responsible authority, **14**, 352

Chancellor of the Exchequer
master of the mint, as, **10**, [278]
salary, **10**, [612]

Chancery Court of York
appeal to, **14**, 590
judges of—
Dean of Arches and Auditor, **14**, 561–2
oath of, **14**, 614
persons being, **14**, 561–2
jurisdiction of, **14**, 557–8, 565–6
original jurisdiction, abolition of, **14**, 611
vacation of see, effect of, **14**, 570

Channel Islands

air traffic provisions applied, **4(1)**, [483]
application to—
    Air Force Act, **3**, [989]
    Army Act, **3**, [717]
    Carriage of Goods by Road Act 1965,
    36, [760]
    Naval Discipline Act, **3**, [1201]
arbitration, international investment disputes,
    application, **2**, [859]
British Colony, as, **18**, [109]
British Telecommunications, application of
    provisions, **45**, [4], [46], [49], [50], [68]
children—
    orders affecting, made in, **6**, [431]
    provisions, application of, **6**, [437]
church electoral roll—
    application for enrolment, **14**, 349–50
    persons on, **14**, 348
Church of England, part of, **14**, 5
citizenship, application of provisions, **31**, [43]
civil jurisdiction, **11(2)**, [832], [844]
Commission for Social Care Inspection,
    arrangements with, **35(2)**, [480]
companies incorporated in, **8**, 549
convention country, as, **11(1)**, [525], [734]
Copyright Act, extension of, **11(1)**, [592]
Customs Buildings Act, registration of,
    13, [545]
deanery synod—
    draft scheme before, **14**, 345
    duties, **14**, 347
    lay representatives on, **14**, 348
    rules and procedure, **14**, 349
deportation from, **31**, [131]
disqualification while disqualified in, **37**, [699]
EEC, position as to, **18**, [3], [5]
English warrant backed in, **12(1)**, [48], [50]
evidence in criminal proceedings, provisions as
    to, **18**, [422]
execution of warrant in, **11(2)**, [554]
fishery limits, provisions extending to,
    1(2), [136]
food safety, application of provisions to,
    1(2), [469]
freedom of travel to and from, **31**, [72]
friendly societies, **19(1)**, [550], [921]
goods from, relief from customs duty for,
    13, [794]
house of laity, representation in, **14**, 347
industrial and provident societies,
    19(1), [400], [436]
infectious diseases, regulations as to,
    35(1), [516]
Jersey, international carriage of perishable
    foodstuffs in, **1(2)**, [76]
livestock imported from, **1(1)**, [481]
measures applying to, **14**, 5, 343–4
mentally disordered patients—
    absence from hospital in, **29**, [153]
    community patients—
        removed or transferred to, **29**, [144]
        responsibility for, transfer to England and
        Wales from, **29**, [148]

Channel Islands—*contd*

mentally disordered patients—*contd*
    conditionally discharged—
      responsibilities for—
        transfer from, **29**, [149]
        transfer to, **29**, [145]
    removal of patients to or from, **29**, [143]
nuclear installations, **17(1)**, [361]
offenders found to be insane in, England and
    Wales, transferred to, **29**, [146]
oil pollution, provisions as to, **49**, [480]
Panel on Takeovers and Mergers, power to
    extend provisions as to, **8(1)**, [1043]
Police Act 1997, extension to, **33(2)**, [47]
Post Office Acts, application of provisions,
    34, [588], [598]
post office privileges, surrender of, **34**, [587]
prize, extension of Acts to, **11(2)**, [185], [189]
provisions on opting-in and opting-out
    resolutions, power to extend to, **8(1)**, [1051]
sea fisheries, regulations on, **1(1)**, [743],
    [772]; **1(2)**, [220]
sentencing, provisions applying, **12(3)**, [1050]
serious fraud, request for investigation,
    12(1), [1057]
Services Acts, application of, **3**, [1532]
settlement. *See* **settlements**
shellfish, provisions applying to, **1(1)**, [711]
statutes, when applicable to, **41**, [628], [645],
    [692], [731], [780]
telecommunications, application of
    provisions, **45**, [4], [68]
terrorism provisions extended to, **18**, [754]
torture provisions, application of,
    12(1), [1094]
tourism, assistance as to, **47**, [106]
Uniform Laws on Sale of Goods, application
    of, **39(1)**, [78]
unrecognised degrees, **15(1)**, [356]
visiting forces in, **3**, [454]
warrant, indorsement of, **12(1)**, [53]
weighing equipment, stamping of,
    39(1), [485]

channel tunnel

A2 improvement works—
    authorised, **38(1)**, [674]
    description of, **38(1)**, [705]
    new roads, regulation of traffic on,
      38(1), [707]
    operation and works, status of,
      38(1), [707]
    status of new highways, **38(1)**, [707]
    stopping up of highways and private
      access, **38(1)**, [706]
    temporary interference with highways,
      38(1), [706]
A20 improvement works—
    acquisition of land for, **37**, [517]
    ancillary, status of, **37**, [540]
    construction, regulation of, **37**, [540]
    description of, **37**, [538]
    deviation, limits of, **37**, [538]
    generally, **37**, [516]
    status of new highways, **37**, [540]

channel tunnel—*contd*

A20 improvement works—*contd*
stopping up of highways, **37**, [539]
temporary interference with highways, **37**, [539]
traffic on new road, regulation of, **37**, [540]
arbitration, determination of questions referred to, **37**, [525]
authorised works, operation and use of, **38(1)**, [648]
bodies corporate, offences by, **37**, [526]
British Railway Board—
byelaws, application of, **37**, [504]
highways, **37**, [536]
protection of, **37**, [546]
scheduled works by, **37**, [532]
through services, extension of powers in connection with, **37**, [520]
British Waterways Board, protection of, **38(1)**, [715]
building regulations, **37**, [512]
byelaws—
British Railway Board's, application of, **37**, [504]
concessionaires, of, **37**, [502]
confirmation by Secretary of State, **37**, [503]
coast protection, modification of provisions relating to, **37**, [523]
concession—
agreements—
arbitration law, application of, **37**, [497]
contract law, application of, **37**, [497]
landlord and tenant law, application of, **37**, [498]
expiry, notice of, **37**, [486]
new, application of provisions to, **37**, [485]
operation, notice of, **37**, [486]
termination, notice of, **37**, [486]
concessionaires—
byelaws, **37**, [502]
competition, **37**, [514]
highways, **37**, [536]
operation by, **37**, [501]
railway regulation provisions, application of, **37**, [522]
scheduled works by, **37**, [530], [535]
termination of construction by—
limitation on exercise of Secretary of State's powers, **37**, [509]
maintenance of tunnel system on, **37**, [507]
operation of tunnel system on temporary basis where practicable, **37**, [508]
supplementary provisions, **37**, [510]
construction of tunnel rail link, **37**, [483]; **38(1)**, [635]
controls disapplied and modified, **38(1)**, [703]
county councils—
highways, **37**, [536]
scheduled works by, **37**, [530]
Dover Harbour Board, protection of, **37**, [548]

channel tunnel—*contd*

electronic communications code networks operators, protection of, **37**, [554]; **38(1)**, [713]
financial provisions, **37**, [527]
fisheries, protection of, **38(1)**, [712]
flood defence, protection of, **38(1)**, [712]
Folkestone and District Water Company, further protection of, **37**, [553]
general note, **10**, [1]
heritage, **38(1)**, [699]
ancient monuments, **38(1)**, [699]
conservation areas, **38(1)**, [699]
entry, rights of, **38(1)**, [700]
listed buildings, **38(1)**, [699]
Intergovernmental Commission and Safety Authority—
supervision by, **37**, [499]
supplementary provisions, **37**, [500]
land—
acquisition of, **37**, [490]
A2 improvement works, for. *See* A2 improvement works *above*
A20 improvement works, for, **37**, [517]
combined effect of works, by reference to, **38(1)**, [678]
compulsory, time within which to exercise, **37**, [519]; **38(1)**, [677]
M2 improvement works, for. *See* M2 improvement works *below*
outside limits shown on deposited plans, **38(1)**, [639]
supplementary provisions, **37**, [518], [541]–[543]
within limits shown on deposited plans, **38(1)**, [638]
deposited plans, correction of, **38(1)**, [683]
drainage, protection of, **37**, [551]
private rights of way, extinguishment of, **38(1)**, [641]
scheme for, on abandonment of construction or operation, **37**, [511]
statutory undertakers, extinguishment of, **38(1)**, [642]
temporary possession and use, **38(1)**, [694]
land drainage, protection of, **38(1)**, [712]
M2 improvement works—
authorised—
statutory undertakers, extinguishment of, **38(1)**, [642]
temporary possession and use, **38(1)**, [694]
land drainage, protection of, **38(1)**, [712]
navigation, protection of, **37**, [547]
no government funds or guarantees for, **37**, [484]
offences by bodies corporate, **37**, [526]
operation of tunnel rail link, **37**, [483]
orders, power to make, **37**, [515]
planning permission—
appeals, **38(1)**, [698]
applications, fees for, **38(1)**, [645]
authorised development, **37**, [537]
consultation, **38(1)**, [698]
countryside, **37**, [537]

channel tunnel—*contd*
  planning permission—*contd*
    county council development, consultation
      regarding, **37**, [537]
    Essex, development in, **38(1)**, [697]
    generally, **37**, [491]; **38(1)**, [643]
    Greater London, development in,
      38(1), [696]
    historic sites, **37**, [537]
    Holywell Coombe, protection of site at,
      37, [537]
    interpretation, **38(1)**, [698]
    Kent, development in, **38(1)**, [697]
    nature, **37**, [537]
    permitted development, time limits,
      38(1), [644]
    planning approvals, programming of
      requests for, **38(1)**, [698]
    qualifying authorities, **38(1)**, [695]
    Secretary of State, intervention by,
      38(1), [698]
    spoil, deposit of surplus, **37**, [537]
    supplementary provisions, **37**, [537]
    working sites, **37**, [537]
  policing of, **37**, [496]
  Port of London Authority, protection of,
    38(1), [716]
  Port of Sheerness Limited, protection of,
    38(1), [714]
  powers of harbour authorities, modification of
    provisions relating to, **37**, [523]
  protection of interests—
    British Railways Board, **37**, [546]
    British Waterways Board, **38(1)**, [715]
    certain statutory undertakers, **37**, [550]
    Dover Harbour Board, **37**, [548]
    electricity undertakers, **38(1)**, [711]
    electronic communications code networks
      operators, **37**, [554]; **38(1)**, [713]
    fisheries, **38(1)**, [712]
    flood defence, **38(1)**, [712]
    Folkestone and District Water Company,
      37, [553]
    gas undertakers, **38(1)**, [711]
    highway and traffic, **37**, [545]; **38(1)**, [710]
    land drainage, **37**, [551]; **38(1)**, [712]
    navigation, **37**, [547]
    Port of London Authority, **38(1)**, [716]
    Port of Sheerness Limited, **38(1)**, [714]
    sewerage undertakers, **38(1)**, [711]
    sewers, **37**, [549]
    Southern Water Authority, **37**, [552]
    telecommunications operators, **37**, [554]
    water resources, **38(1)**, [712]
    water undertakers, **38(1)**, [711]
  rail link—
    access agreements, **38(1)**, [651]
    arbitration, **38(1)**, [673]
    burial grounds, removal of human remains
      and monuments from—
        generally, **38(1)**, [669]
        notice, **38(1)**, [704]
        procedure, **38(1)**, [704]
        records, **38(1)**, [704]
    closures, **38(1)**, [652]

channel tunnel—*contd*
  rail link—*contd*
    construction of works, expenditure in
      securing, **38(1)**, [661]
    financial assistance, undertakings with
      respect to, **38(1)**, [663]
    interpretation, **38(1)**, [686]
    landlord and tenant law, application of,
      38(1), [670]
    licensing, **38(1)**, [650]
    noise—
      construction sites, control of,
        38(1), [659]
      insulation regulations, **38(1)**, [679]
      statutory nuisance, defence in respect
        of, **38(1)**, [660]
    nominated undertaker—
      authorised works, operation and use of,
        38(1), [648]
      buildings, underpinning of, **38(1)**, [689]
      co-operate, duty to, **38(1)**, [667]
      Euston Road and York Way improvement
        works, **38(1)**, [689]
      highway accesses, **38(1)**, [689]
      highways, **38(1)**, [690]
      holder of functions of, **38(1)**, [664]
      injurious affection, compensation for,
        38(1), [666]
      land, entry on, for preparatory
        purposes, **38(1)**, [689]
      land, temporary possession and use,
        38(1), [694]
      mitigation and protection works,
        38(1), [689]
      overhead line diversions, **38(1)**, [689]
      scheduled works. *See* scheduled works
        below
      subsidiary works, **38(1)**, [689]
      transfer of functions relating to works,
        38(1), [665]
      trees on neighbouring land, power to
        deal with, **38(1)**, [657]
      water, discharge of, **38(1)**, [689]
      waterways, temporary interference with,
        38(1), [689]
    Office of Rail Regulation—
      duties of, **38(1)**, [655]
      fees required by, **38(1)**, [656]
    operators, unauthorised, **38(1)**, [650]
    overhead lines, consent for, **38(1)**, [680],
      [709]
    railway administration orders, **38(1)**, [653]
    railway operator, transfer of functions
      relating to works, **38(1)**, [665]
    reserved capacity, expenditure, **38(1)**, [662]
    St Pancras, replacement concrete batching
      facilities at, **38(1)**, [681]
    scheduled works. *See* scheduled works *below*
    reserved capacity, expenditure, **38(1)**, [662]
    St Pancras, replacement concrete batching
      facilities at, **38(1)**, [681]
    trees—
      disapplication of controls, **38(1)**, [658]
      on neighbouring land, power to deal
        with, **38(1)**, [657]

channel tunnel—*contd*
  railway legislation, application of,
    38(1), [701], [702]
  railway regulation provisions, application of,
    37, [522], [544]
  regulation of, **37**, [493], [495]
  safety of navigation, modification of provisions
    relating to, **37**, [523]
  scheduled works—
    acquisition of land for, **37**, [490]
      outside limits shown on deposited
        plans, **38(1)**, [639]
      within limits shown on deposited plans,
        38(1), [638], [691]–[693]
    British Railways Board, by, **37**, [532],
      [535]
    concessionaires, by, **37**, [530], [535]
    construction of, **38(1)**, [635]
    county councils, by, **37**, [531], [535]
    description of, **38(1)**, [688]
    generally, **37**, [487]
    maintenance of, **38(1)**, [635]
    supplementary provisions, **37**, [488],
      [534]–[536]
  seaward section, vesting of, in Secretary of
    State subject to concession lease, **37**, [489]
  sewerage undertakers, protection of,
    38(1), [711]
  sewers, protection of, **37**, [549]
  Southern Water Authority, further protection
    of, **37**, [552]
  status, **37**, [492]
  statutory undertakers, protection of certain,
    37, [550]
  telecommunications code, exclusion of rights
    under, **37**, [513]
  telecommunications operators, protection of,
    37, [554]
  terrorism offences, **18**, [757]
  traffic, control of, **37**, [505]
  trains, approval of, **37**, [506]
  trains engaged on international services,
    controls on, **37**, [494], [495]
  water resources, protection of, **38(1)**, [712]

chapel
  burial ground, on, use of, **14**, 405
  cessation of rights to, **14**, 219
  extra-parochial district, in, **14**, 212
  faculty jurisdiction, subject to, **14**, 639–40
  public school, of, **15(1)**, [132]
  redundant, belonging to charity, **14**, 1040–1
  smoke control area, in, adaptation of fireplaces
    in, grants towards, **35(2)**, [25]

chaplain
  army. *See* **army chaplain**
  bishop's, stipend, **14**, 411

charge
  agriculture. *See* **agricultural credits;**
    agricultural holdings; agricultural
    tenancies
  building society, created by, **5(2)**, [258]

charge—*contd*
  company. *See* **company charges**
  investment by trustee in, **48**, 457
  money secured by, limitation of action for,
    19(3), [748]
  part payment for land, as security for,
    20, [578]
  settled land, over, **20**, [519]
  trust property, on sale of, **48**, 461

chargeable gain
  company, of. *See* **company**
  generally. *See* **capital gains tax**

chargeable securities. *See under* **clearance**
  services; depository receipts

charging authorities
  internal drainage board, appointment of
    members, **19(3)**, [253]

charging order
  absolute, **19(3)**, [83]
  application for—
    discharge of order, **19(3)**, [83]
    High Court, to, **19(3)**, [81]
  assets chargeable, **19(3)**, [82]
  conditions, subject to, **19(3)**, [83]
  considerations in making, **19(3)**, [81]
  discharge of, **19(3)**, [83]
  enforcement, **19(3)**, [103]
  financial thresholds, power to set, **19(3)**, [84]
  government stock, on, **19(3)**, [82]
  judgment, enforcement by, **19(3)**, [1]
  jurisdiction to make, **19(3)**, [81]
  meaning, **19(3)**, [86]
  payment by instalments, **19(3)**, [103]
  power to make, **19(3)**, [81]
  property chargeable, **19(3)**, [82]
  rules of court, **19(3)**, [85]
  securities, on, **19(3)**, [82]
  stop notice or order—
    meaning, **19(3)**, [85]
    service of, rules as to, **19(3)**, [85]
  summary of provisions, **19(3)**, [1]
  unit trust units, on, **19(3)**, [82]
  variation of, **19(3)**, [83]

charitable companies
  accounts—
    annual audit or examination, **5(2)**, [716]
    investigation of by Commissioners,
      5(2), [628]
  accounts and audit, repeal of special
    provisions, **8(1)**, [1253], [1395]–[1396]
  auditors, report to Commission, **5(2)**, [627]
  capacity, constitutional limitations, **8(1)**, [120]
  charitable expenditure, **44(1)**, [362]
  charitable incorporated organisation,
    conversion to—
    application for, **5(2)**, [635]
    consideration of application, **5(2)**, [636]
    refusal of, **5(2)**, [636]
    registration, **5(2)**, [637]

charitable companies—*contd*

community interest company, becoming. *See*
community interest company

consent of Commission—
acts of company, to, **5(2)**, [624]
approval by members of transactions, to,
5(2), [623]

correspondence—
name to appear on, **5(2)**, [625]
status to appear on, **5(2)**, [626]

directors, general duties of, **8(1)**, [259]

donors, transactions with substantial,
44(1), [363]–[365]

exemption, **44(1)**, [361]

invalidity of certain transactions, **5(2)**, [622]

meaning, **44(1)**, [362]

memorandum, alteration of, **5(2)**, [715]

non-charitable expenditure—
meaning, **44(1)**, [362]
treatment of, **44(1)**, [362]

objects clause, alteration of, **5(2)**, [621], [715]

offshore income gain, **44(1)**, [489]

qualifying investments, **44(1)**, [665]

qualifying loans, **44(1)**, [666]

relevant income and gains, **44(1)**, [361]

relief from tax, **44(1)**, [361]

tax avoidance by, **44(1)**, [361]

transactions requiring approval of members,
consent of Charity Commissioners to,
8(1), [304]

winding up, **5(2)**, [620]

charitable contributions

meaning, **5(2)**, [518]

charitable incorporated organisations

amalgamation, **5(2)**, [639]–[640]

annual report and returns, **5(2)**, [758]

body corporate, as, **5(2)**, [629]

charitable company, conversion of—
application for, **5(2)**, [635]
consideration of application, **5(2)**, [636]
refusal of, **5(2)**, [636]
registration, **5(2)**, [637]

community interest company, conversion of,
5(2), [638]

constitution, **5(2)**, [630], [696]

duties, **5(2)**, [696]

name and status—
correspondence and business papers,
appearing on, **5(2)**, [631]
offences, **5(2)**, [632]

powers, **5(2)**, [696]

principal office, **5(2)**, [629]

procedure, **5(2)**, [696]

registered industrial and provident society,
conversion of—
application for, **5(2)**, [635]
consideration of application, **5(2)**, [636]
refusal of, **5(2)**, [636]
registration, **5(2)**, [637]

registration—
application for, **5(2)**, [633]
effect of, **5(2)**, [634]

regulations, **5(2)**, [645]

charitable incorporated organisations—*contd*

transfer of undertaking, **5(2)**, [641]

unincorporated charity, power to transfer
property of, **5(2)**, [643]

winding up, insolvency and dissolution,
regulations, **5(2)**, [642]

charitable institutions

Factories Acts, extent of application,
18, [1177]

charitable purposes

amusement machines at entertainments for,
5(1), [97]

meaning, **5(2)**, [684], [700]

public benefit—
guidance as to operation of requirement,
5(2), [702]
test, **5(2)**, [701]

charitable trust

accounting records, **5(2)**, [594]

administration of, **25(1)**, [27]

annual statement of accounts, **5(2)**, [595]

audit, annual, **5(2)**, [596], [599]

breach of trust or duty, power to relieve from
liability, **5(2)**, [651]

carry back of excess non-charitable
expenditure, **44(4)**, [570]–[572]

charitable trade—
exemptions from charges, **44(4)**, [535]
income tax exemption for profits of,
44(4), [532]
meaning, **44(4)**, [533]
small-scale, exemption for profits of,
44(4), [534]

deposits, income tax exemption for
transactions in, **44(4)**, [542]

ecclesiastical. *See* **ecclesiastical trust**

estates in administration, income tax
exemption for income from, **44(4)**, [545]

Eton College, **5(2)**, [481]

fund-raising events, income tax exemption for
profits from, **44(4)**, [537]

gift aid relief, gifts entitling donor to—
income tax—
liability and exemption, **44(4)**, [529]
treated as paid, **44(4)**, [528]

gifts of money from companies, income tax
liability and exemption, **44(4)**, [530]

imperfect trust—
instruments, validation, **5(2)**, [495]
provisions, meaning, **5(2)**, [495]

income tax—
exemption from—
charitable trade, **44(4)**, [532]
claim, requirement to make, **44(4)**, [546]
deposits, transactions in, **44(4)**, [542]
estates in administration, income from,
44(4), [545]
fund-raising events, profits from,
44(4), [537]
gift aid relief, gifts entitling donor to,
44(4), [529]

charitable trust—*contd*
 income tax—*contd*
  exemption from—*contd*
   gifts of money from companies,
    44(4), [530]
   investment income, **44(4)**, [540]
   lotteries, profits from, **44(4)**, [538]
   miscellaneous income, **44(4)**, [544]
   non-exempt amount, **44(4)**, [548]–[550]
   offshore income gains, **44(4)**, [543]
   payments from other charities,
    44(4), [531]
   property income, **44(4)**, [539]
   public revenue dividends, **44(4)**, [541]
   restrictions on, **44(4)**, [547]
   savings income, **44(4)**, [540]
  liability to—
   gift aid relief, gifts entitling donor to,
    44(4), [529]
   gifts of money from companies,
    44(4), [530]
   payments from other charities,
    44(4), [531]
 investment income, income tax exemption
  for, **44(4)**, [540]
 leisure-time occupation. *See* recreational *below*
 lotteries, income tax exemption for profits
  from, **44(4)**, [538]
 meaning, **44(4)**, [527]
 miners' welfare trusts, **5(2)**, [502]
 miscellaneous incoming resources, condition
  as to, **44(4)**, [536]
 non-charitable expenditure—
  approved charitable investments,
   44(4), [566]–[568]
  approved charitable loans, **44(4)**, [569]
  carry back of excess, **44(4)**, [570]–[572]
  investments and loans, **44(4)**, [556]
  meaning, **44(4)**, [551]–[553]
  payment to body outside UK, **44(4)**, [555]
  substantial donor transactions, in,
   44(4), [559]–[561]
  tax year in which incurred, **44(4)**, [554]
 offshore income gains, income tax exemption
  for, **44(4)**, [543]
 payments from other charities, income tax
  liability and exemption, **44(4)**, [531]
 property income, income tax exemption for,
  44(4), [539]
 public revenue dividends, income tax
  exemption for, **44(4)**, [541]
 recreational—
  amended provisions, **5(2)**, [703]
  facilities to be provided, **5(2)**, [501]
  general provisions, **5(2)**, [501]
  past transactions, saving for, **5(2)**, [503]
 savings income, income tax exemption for,
  44(4), [540]
 special rules—
  overview of, **44(4)**, [526]
  transitional provisions and savings,
   44(4), [1055]
 substantial donor transactions—
  connected charities, **44(4)**, [564]
  excepted donors, **44(4)**, [563]

charitable trust—*contd*
 substantial donor transactions—*contd*
  excepted transactions, **44(4)**, [562]
  meaning, **44(4)**, [557]
  non-charitable expenditure in,
   44(4), [559]–[561]
  relievable gift, meaning, **44(4)**, [558]
  supplementary, **44(4)**, [565]
 trading incoming resources, condition as to,
  44(4), [536]
 transfer of securities—
  ceasing to be held on, **44(4)**, [660]
  excluded transferors and transferees,
   44(4), [653]
 trust corporations, applications of provisions
  to, **5(2)**, [588]
 trustees—
  accounting records, **5(2)**, [594]
  acting while disqualified, **5(2)**, [647]
  annual report—
   public inspection of, **5(2)**, [603]
   requirement for, **5(2)**, [601]
  annual statement of accounts, **5(2)**, [595]
  audit, annual, **5(2)**, [596], [599]
  bankruptcy of, **5(2)**, [563]
  Bishop as, substitution of, **5(2)**, [478]
   application, order made on, **5(2)**, [479]
   costs, defraying, **5(2)**, [480]
   endowments not affected, **5(2)**, [482]
   universities and colleges, trusts not
    affected, **5(2)**, [481]
  breach of trust or duty, power to relieve
   from liability, **5(2)**, [651]
  incapacity of, **5(2)**, [563]
  incorporated body—
   dissolution, **5(2)**, [618]
   execution of documents by, **5(2)**, [617]
  incorporation—
   applications for, **5(2)**, [609]
   gifts made before have same effect after,
    5(2), [616]
   nominations of trustees, **5(2)**, [610]
   vacancies, filling up of, **5(2)**, [610]
  incorporation certificate—
   application for, **5(2)**, [607]
   evidence, as, **5(2)**, [612]
   grant of, **5(2)**, [607]
   liability of trustees, **5(2)**, [611]
   orders and directions in, enforcement
    of, **5(2)**, [615]
   power of Commission to amend,
    5(2), [613]
   records of, **5(2)**, [614]
   vesting of estate in body corporate,
    5(2), [608]
  indemnity insurance, **5(2)**, [653]
  local authority as, **25(2)**, [170]
  membership of charity, removal from,
   5(2), [564]
  mismanagement by, **5(2)**, [563]
  municipal corporation as, **25(1)**, [28]
  orders relating to, publicity, **5(2)**, [570]
  persons disqualified, **5(2)**, [646]
  power of Commission to advise,
   5(2), [580]

charitable trust—*contd*
  trustees—*contd*
    property vesting in, **5(2)**, [507]
    registration, duties as to, **5(2)**, [706]
    removal of, **5(2)**, [563]
    remuneration—
      agreement, **5(2)**, [648]–[649]
      conditions for, **5(2)**, [648]
      connected persons, **5(2)**, [649]
      disqualification from acting, **5(2)**, [650]
      guidance, **5(2)**, [649]
    replacement, **5(2)**, [563]
    suspension of, **5(2)**, [563]–[564]
    transfer and evidence of title to property vested in, **5(2)**, [669]
    transfer of property to, **5(2)**, [507]
  universities, **5(2)**, [481]
  validation—
    adverse claims, saving for, **5(2)**, [497]
    Crown, application to, **5(2)**, [499]
    imperfect trust instruments, **5(2)**, [495]
    proceedings pending, **5(2)**, [498]
    provisions—
      dispositions etc subject to, **5(2)**, [496]
      meaning, **5(2)**, [495]
    tax payments liability, **5(2)**, [498]
  Westminster School, **5(2)**, [481]
  Winchester College, **5(2)**, [481]

charity
  abolition of GLC, position on, **25(2)**, [625]
  accounting records, **5(2)**, [594]
  almshouses, contribution towards maintenance of, **5(2)**, [517]
  annual report—
    offences, **5(2)**, [605]
    public inspection of, **5(2)**, [603]
    requirement for, **5(2)**, [601]
  annual returns by registered, **5(2)**, [604]
  annual statement of accounts, **5(2)**, [595]
  audit, annual, **5(2)**, [596], [599]
    company law provisions, amendments reflecting changes in, **5(2)**, [750]
    National Health Service accounts—
      English, **5(2)**, [597]
      Welsh, **5(2)**, [598]
  auditors—
    duty to report to Commission, **5(2)**, [600], [714]
    relief from liability, grant by court, **5(2)**, [652]
  charitable, benevolent or philanthropic institutions, power to give financial assistance to—
    minister, of, **5(2)**, [743]
    National Assembly for Wales, of, **5(2)**, [744]
  charter, governed by, **5(2)**, [560]
  close companies, gift aid payments by, **43(S)**, 43
  commercial participator, meaning, **5(2)**, [518]
  commission. *See* **Charity Commission**
  company, dispensation with "limited", **8**, 130
  control of fund-raising, reserve power, **5(2)**, [527]

charity—*contd*
  covenanted payments to, **43(1)**, [469]
  cy-près application—
    conditions requisite for, **5(2)**, [556]
    current circumstances, by reference to, **5(2)**, [711]
    disclaimer, in case of, **5(2)**, [557], [712]
    donor unknown, **5(2)**, [557], [712]
    occasions for, **5(2)**, [556]
    property subject to, **5(2)**, [556]
    schemes in respect of, **5(2)**, [559]
    solicitations, gifts made in response to, **5(2)**, [558]
  disability discrimination by, **7(1)**, [324]
  distribution to, transitional relief, **43(1)**, [3]
  documents—
    enrolment, **5(2)**, [582]
    preservation of, **5(2)**, [582]
  donations to—
    agent's expenses, contributions to, **44(1)**, [61]
    charges on income, **44(1)**, [173]
  employee seconded to, **44(1)**, [60]
    tax deduction for, **44(3)**, [69]
  exempt—
    amended provisions, **5(2)**, [708]
    exercise of powers by Commission, consultation, **5(2)**, [673]
    increased regulation of, **5(2)**, [709], [757]
    list of, **5(2)**, [691]
    meaning, **5(2)**, [683]
    principal regulator—
      disclosure of information to and by, **5(2)**, [553]
      general duty of, **5(2)**, [710]
    registration, not requiring, **5(2)**, [544]
    special provision relating to accounts and annual reports of, **5(2)**, [602]
  exempt bodies, including, **44(4)**, [438], [454]
  financial year, meaning, **5(2)**, [512]
  functional land, meaning, **22**, [773]
  fund-raising—
    cancellation of payments and agreement, **5(2)**, [523]
    event, exemption from value added tax, **50**, [153]
    institutions not registered charities, false statements relating to, **5(2)**, [525]
    interpretation, **5(2)**, [518]
    regulations, **5(2)**, [526]
    unauthorised, prevention of, **5(2)**, [524]
  fund-raising—
    benefits, statements indicating, **5(2)**, [742]
    business, meaning, **5(2)**, [518]
  gain accruing to, **42**, [1399]
  "gift aid declaration", meaning, **44(4)**, [436]
  gift aid limits, **43(S)**, 557
  gift aid payments—
    benefits associated with a gift—
      admission rights—
        disregard of certain, **44(4)**, [428]–[429]
        meaning, **44(4)**, [428]
      meaning, **44(4)**, [425]

charity—*contd*
    gift aid payments—*contd*
        benefits associated with a gift—*contd*
            periods of less than 12 months, linked
                to, **44(4)**, [427]
            restrictions on, **44(4)**, [426]
        carry back relief, election to, **44(4)**, [434]
        charged amount, meaning, **44(4)**, [435]
        companies, by, **43(1)**, [468]
        donor's liability not less than tax treated as
            deducted—
                measures to ensure—
                    charge to tax, **44(4)**, [432]
                    income tax, total amount to which
                        charged, **44(4)**, [433]
                    restriction of reliefs, **44(4)**, [431]
        election to treat as if gift made in previous
            year, **43(2)**, [121]
        entitlement to, **44(4)**, [422]
        grossed up amount, meaning, **44(4)**, [423]
        individuals, by, **43(1)**, [467]; **43(2)**, [728]
        overseas gifts, disqualified, **44(4)**, [430]
        overview, **44(4)**, [421]
        qualifying donations, **43(2)**, [728]
            meaning, **44(4)**, [424]
        self-assessment return, through,
            43(2), [316]; **44(4)**, [437]
    gift of shares, securities and real property to,
        44(1), [422]
        double relief for, prohibited, **44(4)**, [453]
        net benefit, value of, **44(4)**, [445]
        relief for—
            amount of—
                consideration for disposal,
                    44(4), [444]
                incidental costs of making disposal,
                    44(4), [443]
                relievable amount, **44(4)**, [442]
            double, prohibited, **44(4)**, [453]
            entitlement to, **44(4)**, [439]
            qualifying interests in land—
                certificate required, **44(4)**, [449]
                disqualifying events, **44(4)**, [452]
                held jointly, **44(4)**, [450]
                joint disposal, calculation of relievable
                    amount, **44(4)**, [451]
                meaning, **44(4)**, [441]
            qualifying investment—
                "disposal-related liability", meaning,
                    44(4), [448]
                "disposal-related obligation",
                    meaning, **44(4)**, [447]
                market value of, **44(4)**, [446]
                meaning, **44(4)**, [440]
    gifts from trade profits. *See* **trade profits**
    gifts in kind to, deductions for, **44(1)**, [54]
    gifts to—
        disclosure in directors' report, **8**, 666
        inheritance tax exemption, **42**, [544]
        trade profits, from. *See* **trade profits**
    group accounts, **5(2)**, [695]
    house to house collections. *See* **house to
        house collection**
    housing grants, **23**, [608]
    individuals, donations by, **42**, [1016]

charity—*contd*
    inquiries into—
        Commission, by, **5(2)**, [549]
        report as evidence in proceedings,
            5(2), [587]
    inspection, powers of, **42**, [1493]
    institution of proceedings, **5(2)**, [681]
    instruments, execution of, **5(2)**, [668]
    interim manager appointed for, supplementary
        provisions relating to, **5(2)**, [565]
    jurisdiction over, **5(2)**, [693]
    land—
        consent to dealings with, removal of
            requirements, **5(2)**, [515]
        dispositions—
            connected persons, meaning, **5(2)**, [694]
            restrictions on, **5(2)**, [589]
            supplementary provisions, **5(2)**, [590]
        divestment, **5(2)**, [573]
        mortgaging—
            restrictions on, **5(2)**, [591]
            supplementary provisions, **5(2)**, [592]
    legal proceedings, **5(2)**, [585]–[586]
    legislation—
        early statutes, **5(2)**, [477]
        obsolete, repeal, **5(2)**, [509]
        summary of, **5(2)**, [477]
    local—
        areas, enlargement of, **5(2)**, [692]
        co-operation with local authority,
            5(2), [664]
        index of, **5(2)**, [662]
        reviews of, by local authority, **5(2)**, [663]
    meaning, **5(2)**, [683], [699]; **22**, [773];
        23, [405]; **44(1)**, [173]
    meetings, mode of notice, **5(2)**, [667]
    membership, power of Commission to
        determine, **5(2)**, [581]
    mergers—
        gifts to transferor, effect of registering on,
            5(2), [661]
        pre-merger vesting declarations, **5(2)**, [660]
        register of, **5(2)**, [658]–[659]
    mortgaging—
        restrictions on, **5(2)**, [589]
        supplementary provisions, **5(2)**, [592]
    mortmain law, repeal, **5(2)**, [508]
    name, power of Commission to require
        change of, **5(2)**, [547]–[548]
    National Health Service, annual audit or
        examination of accounts—
            English, **5(2)**, [597]
            Welsh, **5(2)**, [598]
    non-charitable expenditure, **43(S)**, 40–1
    Northern Ireland regulator, disclosure of
        information to and by, **5(2)**, [745]
    offences by bodies corporate, **5(2)**, [528],
        [682]
    official custodian—
        accounts, **5(2)**, [539]
        functions, **5(2)**, [539]
        property—
            held by, **5(2)**, [513]–[515]
            vested in—
                divestment of land, **5(2)**, [573]

charity—*contd*
  official custodian—*contd*
    property—*contd*
      vested in—*contd*
        supplementary provisions as to,
          5(2), [572]
        vesting of, in, **5(2)**, [571]
  operation of 2006 Act, report on, **5(2)**, [746]
  parochial charities—
    general provisions, **5(2)**, [665]
    meaning, **5(2)**, [683]
  payroll deduction scheme, **43(1)**, [466]
    approval of, **44(2)**, [715]
    donations, meaning, **44(2)**, [714]
    operation of scheme, **44(2)**, [713]
  persons making appeals, requirement to
    indicate institutions benefiting and
    arrangements for remuneration, **5(2)**, [521]
    lower-paid collectors, exclusion of,
      5(2), [522]
  poor countries, gifts of money for relief in,
    43(1), [347]
  premises, power of entry, **5(2)**, [584], [713]
  proceedings—
    evidence, provisions as to, **5(2)**, [507]
    who may take, **5(2)**, [506]
  professional fund-raiser—
    agreement in prescribed form, to have,
      5(2), [519]
    arrangements for remuneration, indicating,
      5(2), [520]
    institutions benefiting, indication of,
      5(2), [520]
    meaning, **5(2)**, [518]
  property—
    application, power to direct, **5(2)**, [567]
    cy-près application, **5(2)**, [556]
    dealings with, power to authorise,
      5(2), [577]
    official custodian, held by,
      5(2), [513]–[514]
    protection of, **5(2)**, [563]
    title, evidence of, **5(2)**, [507], [669]
    trust, termination of, **5(2)**, [571]
    vested in trustees, **5(2)**, [507]
    vesting in official custodian,
      5(2), [571]–[573]
    vesting orders of, **48**, 524
  protection—
    copies of orders, Commission sending to
      charity, **5(2)**, [568]
    powers as to, **5(2)**, [563]
    schemes, publicity for, **5(2)**, [569]
    specific directions as to, **5(2)**, [566]
  public assistance, meaning of receipt of,
    24, [813]
  public charitable collection. *See* **public
    charitable collection**
  public collections, **26(1)**, [264]
  qualifying distributions, transitional relief,
    43(1), [318], [331]
  racial discrimination by, **7(1)**, [170]
  recreational. *See* **charitable trust**
  redundant chapel belonging to, **14**, 1040–1

charity—*contd*
  refugee poverty, gifts of money to relieve,
    43(1), [428]
  register—
    Commission, kept by, **5(2)**, [544], [706]
    contents, **5(2)**, [544], [706]
    inspection, open to, **5(2)**, [544]
    meaning, **5(2)**, [684]
    removal from, **5(2)**, [544], [706]
  registered—
    annual returns by, **5(2)**, [604]
    meaning, **23**, [405]
  registered provider of social housing, as—
    accounts—
      accountant's report, **24**, [677]
      audit, **24**, [675]
      auditor's powers, **24**, [679]
      auditor's report, **24**, [676]
      balance sheet, **24**, [674]
      disclosure of information, **24**, [682]
      extraordinary audit, **24**, [678]
      failure to comply with direction,
        provision or requirement, **24**, [681]
      offences, **24**, [680]
      revenue, **24**, [674]
    change of objects, **24**, [752]
    inquiries, **24**, [748]
  registration—
    application for, **5(2)**, [544]
    charities not requiring, **5(2)**, [544]
    claims to, **5(2)**, [545]
    effect of, **5(2)**, [545]
    objections to, **5(2)**, [545]
    requirement, **5(2)**, [706]
    small charities, threshold for, **5(2)**, [707]
    trustees, duties of, **5(2)**, [706]
  regulations and orders, **5(2)**, [530], [672],
    [747]
  rentcharges—
    miscellaneous provisions as to evidence,
      5(2), [680]
    release of, **5(2)**, [593]
  schemes for administration—
    common deposit funds, **5(2)**, [575]
    common investment schemes, **5(2)**, [574]
    jurisdiction to make, **5(2)**, [561]
    publicity for, **5(2)**, [569]
    statutory provisions, altering, **5(2)**, [562]
  Scottish, supervision by Commission,
    5(2), [666]
  service of documents, **5(2)**, [529]
  sex discrimination by, **7(1)**, [88]
  small—
    capital, power to spend, **5(2)**, [657]
    objects, modification of, **5(2)**, [654]
    property, transfer of, **5(2)**, [654]
    registration threshold, **5(2)**, [707]
    trades, exemption from tax, **43(1)**, [471]
  solicitor's bill, taxation, **5(2)**, [583]
  stamp duty exemptions, **41**, [141], [183]
  stamp duty land tax—
    exemptions, **41**, [341]
    relief, **41**, [427]
  status as registered to appear on official
    publications, **5(2)**, [546]

charity—*contd*

statutory, schemes relating to, **5(2)**, [560]

substantial donors, transactions with—

connected charities, **43(S)**, 38

exceptions from provisions, **43(S)**, 37

nature of, **43(S)**, 36

relievable gifts, **43(S)**, 38

summary of provisions, **5(2)**, [477]

supplies by, zero-rating, **50**, [151]

supplies to, exemption from climate change levy, **35(2)**, [370]

trade profits, **43(S)**, 42

tribunal. *See* **Charity Tribunal**

trustees. *See* **charitable trust**

trusts, gifts from, **43(1)**, [470]

unincorporated—

capital, power to spend, **5(2)**, [719]

powers or procedures, modification of, **5(2)**, [656]

property, power to transfer, **5(2)**, [718]

replacement of purposes of, **5(2)**, [655]

Welsh authorities, property held by, **26(1)**, [171]

wholly-owned companies, gift aid relief, **43(S)**, 42

winding up, **5(2)**, [620]

Charity Commission

annual public meeting, **5(2)**, [687]

annual report, **5(2)**, [687]

appeal from, **5(2)**, [679]

auditors, reports from, **5(2)**, [600], [714]

breach of trust or duty, power to relieve from liability, **5(2)**, [651]

charitable company—

accounts, investigation of, **5(2)**, [628]

acts, consent to, **5(2)**, [624]

approval by members of transactions, consent to, **5(2)**, [623]

auditors, report by, **5(2)**, [627]

Charity Commissioners, transfer of functions of, **5(2)**, [704]

Charity Tribunal, references to, **5(2)**, [690]

coal industry trusts, applications concerning, to, **17(1)**, [702]

committees, **5(2)**, [687]

common deposit schemes, **5(2)**, [575]

Scottish and Northern Ireland institutions, definitions, **5(2)**, [576]

common investment schemes, **5(2)**, [574]

Scottish and Northern Ireland institutions, definitions, **5(2)**, [576]

directions, **5(2)**, [677]

documents—

execution of, **5(2)**, [687]

power to call for, **5(2)**, [550]

powers for preservation of, **5(2)**, [582]

supply of copies where open to public inspection, **5(2)**, [670]

dormant bank accounts, power to give directions about, **5(2)**, [579]

duties, general, **5(2)**, [537]

establishment of, **5(2)**, [534], [704]

ex gratia payments, power to authorise, **5(2)**, [578]

Charity Commission—*contd*

exempt charity, consultation before exercise of powers relating to, **5(2)**, [673]

fees, **5(2)**, [671]

functions, general, **5(2)**, [536], [687]

information—

disclosure by, **5(2)**, [552]

disclosure to, **5(2)**, [551]

false or misleading, supply to, **5(2)**, [555]

principal regulators of exempt charities, disclosure to and by, **5(2)**, [553]

relevant public authority, meaning, **5(2)**, [554]

inquiries into charities, **5(2)**, [549]

interim manager, appointed for charity, **5(2)**, [565]

jurisdiction, concurrent with High Court, **5(2)**, [561]

legal proceedings by, **5(2)**, [585]

meaning, **41**, [605]

membership, **5(2)**, [687], [755]

membership of charity, power to determine, **5(2)**, [581]

mergers, register of, **5(2)**, [658]–[659]

objectives, **5(2)**, [535]

official custodian. *See under* **charities**

orders—

contents of, **5(2)**, [676]

enforcement, **5(2)**, [675]

enforcement of requirements by, **5(2)**, [674]

service of, **5(2)**, [678]

substitution of trustee, for, **5(2)**, [478]

application, made on, **5(2)**, [479]

costs, defraying, **5(2)**, [480]

endowments not affected, **5(2)**, [482]

universities and colleges, trusts not affected, **5(2)**, [481]

powers, incidental, **5(2)**, [538]

premises, power of entry, **5(2)**, [584]

property dealings, power to authorise, **5(2)**, [577]

protection of charities—

application of property, power to direct, **5(2)**, [567]

copies of orders, sending to charity, **5(2)**, [568]

powers as to, **5(2)**, [563]

specific directions as to, **5(2)**, [566]

public collections certificate. *See* **public charitable collection**

records, power to search, **5(2)**, [550]

register, keeping, **5(2)**, [544], [706]

report of inquiry as evidence in proceedings, **5(2)**, [587]

requirements, enforcement of, **5(2)**, [674]

resource accounts, **5(2)**, [755]

reverter of land, schemes as to. *See* **land (reverter)**

service of directions of, **5(2)**, [678]

solicitor's bill, order for taxation, **5(2)**, [583]

staff, **5(2)**, [687]

trustees—

orders relating to, publicity, **5(2)**, [570]

power to advise, **5(2)**, [580]

Charity Commissioners
proceedings by or against, **13**, [26]

charity lands
landlord, exercise of powers of, **21**, [74]

Charity Tribunal
appeal from, **5(2)**, [542]
appeal to, **5(2)**, [689]
applications to, **5(2)**, [689]
disqualification provisions, **5(2)**, [756]
establishment of, **5(2)**, [540]
jurisdiction, **5(2)**, [540]
membership, **5(2)**, [688]
panels, **5(2)**, [688]
practice and procedure, **5(2)**, [541], [688]
proceedings, intervention by Attorney
General, **5(2)**, [543]
references to, **5(2)**, [690]
staff and facilities, **5(2)**, [688]

Charlwood
general provisions, **25(2)**, [339]
parish council, **25(2)**, [338]
part transferred to Surrey, **25(2)**, [338]

charter
borough—
effect of, **25(2)**, [209]
petition for, **25(2)**, [206]
London boroughs, to, **25(1)**, [694]
resignation, of, abolition of stamp duty,
41, [152], [157]

charter trustees
accounts, audit. *See* **Audit Commission**
capital finance, **26(2)**, [320]
continuation of, **25(2)**, [577]
expenses, defrayment, **25(2)**, [209]
powers and duties, **25(2)**, [209]
provisions applied to, **26(2)**, [250]

chartered association
names and uniform, protection of, **48**, 12,
46–8

chartered company
general note, **8**, 8–9
summary of provisions, **8**, 8–9

Charterhouse School. *See* public school

chattels
individual shares, division by court, **20**, [789]
loss, damage or disturbance in enjoyment,
compensation, **9**, [212]

cheating. *See also* deception
going equipped for, **12(1)**, [577]
offences involving, **12(2)**, [162]

Chelsea borough council
studio accommodation, provision of,
25(1), [464]

Chelsea Hospital
accounts, **3**, [181]
commissioners, acts done by, **3**, [13]
land—
conveyance to, **3**, [15]
purchase of, **3**, [14]
application of money, **3**, [16]
disputed title, **3**, [19]
expenses, payment of, **3**, [20]
vesting of, **3**, [21]
marking of goods, **3**, [11]
pensioner—
change of abode, notifying, **3**, [7]
expulsion of, **3**, [6]
oath, administration of, **3**, [9]
out-pension, cessation of rights to, **3**, [8]
statement of, **3**, [10]
pensions—
board of ordnance, transfer from, **3**, [22]
entitlement to, **3**, [3]
estimates, **3**, [4]
fraud or misconduct, **3**, [5]
management of, **3**, [2]
out-pensioner receiving, **3**, [24]
regulations, **3**, [4]
removal or refusal, **3**, [5]
treasurer, actions in name of, **3**, [12]

chemical weapons
acts within or outside United Kingdom,
12(2), [379]
amendment of provisions, **12(2)**, [412]
annual reports, **12(2)**, [410]
body corporate, offences by, **12(2)**, [408]
Crown, provisions binding, **12(2)**, [413]
destruction—
compensation, **12(2)**, [384]
entry on premises, **12(2)**, [383]
offences, **12(2)**, [385]
permitted purposes, objects for,
12(2), [386]
removed objects, of, **12(2)**, [382]
evidence, power to obtain, **12(2)**, [405]
forfeiture, **12(2)**, [406]
information—
Convention, for purposes of, **12(2)**, [398]
disclosure of, **12(2)**, [409]
persons having, identification of,
12(2), [399]
Secretary of State requiring, **12(2)**, [397]
inspections—
definitions, **12(2)**, [400]
offences, **12(2)**, [402]
privileges and immunities, **12(2)**, [403]
reimbursement of expenditure, **12(2)**, [404]
rights of entry for, **12(2)**, [401]
meaning, **12(2)**, [377]
permitted purposes, chemicals for,
12(2), [377], [386]
licences, **12(2)**, [396]
restriction on use, **12(2)**, [395]
premises or equipment for producing—
destruction or alteration, notice requiring—
compensation, **12(2)**, [392]
failure to comply with, **12(2)**, [390]

chemical weapons—*contd*
premises or equipment for producing—*contd*
destruction or alteration, notice
requiring—*contd*
impossibility of serving, **12(2)**, [391]
meaning, **12(2)**, [389]
offences, **12(2)**, [393]
service of, **12(2)**, [389]
prohibitions, **12(2)**, [387]
suspicious, **12(2)**, [388]
proceedings, institution of, **12(2)**, [408]
production facility, meaning, **12(2)**, [394]
removal or immobilisation of objects,
12(2), [381]
Revenue and Customs prosecutions,
12(2), [407]
scheduled toxic chemicals and precursors,
12(2), [416]
Scottish partnership, offences by, **12(2)**, [408]
search warrants, **12(2)**, [405]
service of notices, **12(2)**, [411]
suspicious objects, **12(2)**, [380]
transfer of, **12(2)**, [378]
use of, **12(2)**, [378]

chemicals
agriculture, used in. *See* **agriculture**

chemists. *See also* **pharmaceutical chemist**
saving for, **28**, [347]
titles and emblems, restrictions on use,
28, [137], [138]

cheque. *See also* **bill of exchange**
banker's authority, revocation of, **19(1)**, [108]
crossed—
application of provisions to other
instruments, **19(1)**, [307]
drawer, protection of, **19(1)**, [113]
duties of banker as to, **19(1)**, [112], [307]
general and special crossings, **19(1)**, [109]
material part, of, **19(1)**, [111]
"not negotiable", effect of, **19(1)**, [114]
crossing after issue, **19(1)**, [110]
definition, **19(1)**, [103]
delay in presentment, **19(1)**, [104]
meaning, **19(1)**, [103]
non-transferable, **19(1)**, [115]
payment of tax by, **43(S)**, 576–7
presentation for payment—
alternative means of, **19(1)**, [106]
alternative place of, **19(1)**, [105]
generally, **19(1)**, [104]
protection of banker—
collecting payment, **19(1)**, [306]
paying, **19(1)**, [113], [303]
unindorsed, as evidence of payment,
19(1), [305]

Chequers Estate
administrative trustees—
exchequer grants to, **10**, [518]
legal proceedings, **10**, [519]
chattels, assignment of, **10**, [485]
conveyance of, **10**, [485]

Chequers Estate—*contd*
covenants for upkeep, **10**, [485]
custodian trustee—
legal proceedings, **10**, [519]
property etc vesting in, **10**, [519]
deed of settlement—
amendment, **10**, [517], [521]
confirmation of, **10**, [481]
text of, **10**, [485]–[486]
failure of trust, **10**, [485]
name, **10**, [485]
objects of gift, **10**, [485]
stamp duty land tax, **10**, [483]
taxes and duties, **10**, [482]
trusts, **10**, [485]
trustees, **10**, [485]

Chevening Estate
administrative provisions, **10**, [527]
Board of Trustees—
assets and liabilities transferred to, **10**, [682]
functions, **10**, [681]
incorporation, **10**, [681]
instruments, **10**, [685]
meaning, **10**, [527]
members, **10**, [685]
payments to members, **10**, [685]
proceedings, **10**, [685]
proof of documents, **10**, [685]
status, **10**, [685]
capital gains tax exemption, **42**, [1419]
inheritance tax relief, **42**, [691]
occupation of, exemption from income tax
on, **44(2)**, [112]
tax and duty, exemptions from,
10, [524]–[525]
trust instrument—
amendment of, **10**, [683]
confirmation of, **10**, [523]
text of, **10**, [527]
trustees, **10**, [527]
trusts of, **10**, [527]
vesting deed, confirmation of, **10**, [523]

Chicago Convention
Civil Aviation Authority, duties of under,
4(1), [73]
expenses incurred, **4(1)**, [111]
orders relating to—
performance of functions as to, **4(1)**, [73]
power to make, **4(1)**, [110]

**Chief Inspector of Education, Children's
Services and Skills**
fees payable to, **35(2)**, [353]

child. *See also* **local authority; minor; young
offenders; young person**
abandoned—
local authority duty towards, **6**, [320]
registration of birth, **36**, [73]
abduction. *See* **abduction**
abduction of—
adoption order, subject to, **12(1)**, [810],
[818]

child—*contd*
  abduction of—*contd*
    appropriate consent, without, **12(1)**, [810], [818]
    connected person, by—
      institution of proceedings, **12(1)**, [813]
      offence, **12(1)**, [810]
      penalties, **12(1)**, [813]
    custodianship, pending, **12(1)**, [818]
    custody, child subject to, **12(1)**, [810]
    detaining, meaning, **12(1)**, [812]
    guardian, by, **12(1)**, [810]
    local authority, in care of, **12(1)**, [810], [818]
    Northern Ireland, **12(1)**, [816]
    offence, when not committed, **12(1)**, [810]
    parent, by—
      institution of proceedings, **12(1)**, [813]
      meaning, **12(1)**, [812]
      not married to the other, by, **12(1)**, [811]
      offence, **12(1)**, [810]
      penalties, **12(1)**, [813]
    person not being parent, by, **12(1)**, [811]
    place of safety, child in, **12(1)**, [818]
    residence order, child subject to, **12(1)**, [810]
    sending, meaning, **12(1)**, [812]
    taking, meaning, **12(1)**, [812]
    unconnected person, by—
      offence, **12(1)**, [811]
      penalties, **12(1)**, [813]
    voluntary organisation, in care of, **12(1)**, [818]
  absentees from homes, centres, etc, **6**, [128]
  abuse of position of trust as to—
    causing or inciting engagement in sexual activity, **12(3)**, [681]
    engaging in sexual activity in presence of, **12(3)**, [682]
    marriage or civil partnership exception, **12(3)**, [687]
    position of trust—
      interpretation, **12(3)**, [686]
      meaning, **12(3)**, [685]
      relationships pre-dating, **12(3)**, [688]
    Scotland, acts in, **12(3)**, [684]
    sexual act, causing to watch, **12(3)**, [683]
    sexual activity, engaging in, **12(3)**, [680]
  abuse of, prevention, **6**, [440]
  access, right of—
    compulsory care, child in, **6**, [454]
    generally, **6**, [226]
    meaning, **6**, [226]
  accommodation, provision etc. *See* **local authority**
  adoption of. *See* **adoption**
  age—
    criminal responsibility, of, **6**, [38]
    presumption and determination, **6**, [48]
    presumption of, **15(1)**, [590], [699]
    tender years, evidence by child of, **6**, [27]

child—*contd*
  alcohol—
    allowing sale to, **19(3)**, [636]
      persistently, **19(3)**, [637], [638]
        closure notices, **19(3)**, [660], [661]
        premises licence, suspension of, **19(3)**, [638]
    consumption by, **19(3)**, [641]
    delivery to, **19(3)**, [642]
    prohibition of sale, **19(3)**, [635]
    purchase by or on behalf of, **19(3)**, [640]
    sale to, **19(3)**, [635]
    sending to obtain, **19(3)**, [643]
    unsupervised sales by, **19(3)**, [644]
    weights and measures authorities, enforcement role of, **19(3)**, [645]
  alive, capable of being born, **12(1)**, [239]
  approved school. *See* **approved school**
  arrest of—
    absentees from home, centre, etc, **6**, [128]
    execution of process, **6**, [145]
    persons to be informed of, **6**, [23]
    recognisance on release, **6**, [126]
    release, **6**, [126]
  assessment order—
    application for—
      attendance of child at, **6**, [426]
      grounds for, **6**, [358]
      self-incrimination in evidence, **6**, [429]
    powers under, **6**, [358]
    refusal to submit to examination, **6**, [358]
    requirements, **6**, [358]
    rules of court, **6**, [358]
    service families, in relation to—
      content of, **3**, [1528]
      discharge of, **3**, [1530]
      duration of, **3**, [1529]
      effect of, **3**, [1528]
      power to make, **3**, [1527]
      review of, **3**, [1530]
    service family—
      content of, **3**, [1526]
      discharge of, **3**, [1526]
      effect of, **3**, [1526]
      power to make, **3**, [1525]
      summary of provisions, **3**, [1]
      variation of, **3**, [1526]
  at risk, refuges for, **6**, [368]
  bail, applying for, **6**, [34]
  battery as punishment, **6**, [966]
  begging, used for, **6**, [4]
  benefit. *See* **child benefit**
  beyond parental control, **6**, [343]
  birth, time beginning with, **6**, [277]
  boarded out children, transitional provision, **6**, [454]
  brothel, allowing to be in, **6**, [3]
  burning, risk of, **6**, [7]
  care—
    amendments to system, **6(S)**, 427–30
    discharge of functions, arrangements for—
      effect of, **6(S)**, 437
      power to enter into, **6(S)**, 434
      restrictions on, **6(S)**, 436

child—*contd*
  care—*contd*
    long-term, in—
      appropriate officer, notification to,
        6(S), 453
      visits to, **6(S)**, 454
  care, committal to. *See* **local authority**
  care of—
    compulsory. *See* compulsory *below*
    generally, **6**, [1]
    orders. *See* **care order**
    voluntary organisations. *See* **voluntary**
      organisation
  care standards—
    definitions, **6**, [633]
    minor and consequential amendments,
      6, [669]
    orders and regulations, **6**, [660]
    staff transfers, **6**, [656]–[657]
    transitional provisions and savings, **6**, [670]
  care training—
    fees or expenses, **6**, [410]
    meaning, **6**, [410]
    provision of, reviews of, **6**, [411]
  care, committal to. *See* **local authority**
  Children and Family Court Advisory and
    Support Service. *See* **Children and Family**
    Court Advisory and Support Service
  children or young persons, sex offences
    committed by, **12(3)**, [677]
  Children's Commissioner. *See* **Children's**
    Commissioner
  Children's Commissioner for Wales. *See*
    Children's Commissioner for Wales
  children's home. *See* **children's home**
  children's services. *See* **children's services**
  chorister, not employed as, **6**, [21]
  cigarettes and cigarette papers, sale to, **6**, [6]
  civil partnership, of. *See* **civil partnership**
  community home. *See* **community home**
  compulsory care, in—
    access to children, **6**, [454]
    transitional provisions and savings, **6**, [454]
  concealing birth of, **12(1)**, [101]
  congenital injury. *See* **congenital disabilities**
  contact activity conditions—
    conditions for making, **6(S)**, 7–8
    financial assistance, **6(S)**, 8–9
    monitoring, **6(S)**, 10
    parent, on, **6(S)**, 7
    power to make, **6(S)**, 6
  contact activity directions—
    conditions for making, **6(S)**, 7–8
    excepted contract order, **6(S)**, 5
    financial assistance, **6(S)**, 8–9
    making of, **6(S)**, 3–4
    monitoring, **6(S)**, 10
    no power to make, where, **6(S)**, 4
  contact order—
    care, in respect of child under, **6**, [347]
    conditions contained in, **6**, [304]
    discharge of, **6**, [302]
    duration of, **6**, [422]
    enforcement, **6**, [248]

child—*contd*
  contact order—*contd*
    enforcement orders—
      amendment, **6(S)**, 31–4
      breach, **6(S)**, 31–4
      making of, **6(S)**, 12–14
      monitoring, **6(S)**, 14
      revocation, **6(S)**, 31–4
      unpaid work requirement, **6(S)**, 12,
        29–30
      warning notice, **6(S)**, 15
    financial loss, compensation for,
      6(S), 15–17
    general principles, **6**, [304]
    jurisdiction, general, **6**, [233]
    making—
      court's powers, **6**, [232]–[234], [303]
      restriction on, **6**, [302]
    meaning, **6**, [301]
    monitoring, **6(S)**, 10–11
    parents living together, **6**, [304]
    police protection, child under, **6**, [363]
    recognition and registration, **6**, [245]–[246]
    removal of child from jurisdiction, **6**, [254]
    stay of proceedings, **6**, [236]
    supplementary provisions, **6**, [304]
    timetable regarding, **6**, [304]
    transitional provisions, **6(S)**, 19
    variation, **6**, [302]
    warning notice, **6(S)**, 12
    See also **family proceedings**
  contact with family, regulations, **6**, [323],
    [441]
  contribution for care—
    orders for—
      England, **6**, [61]
      Northern Ireland, **6**, [63]
      Scotland, **6**, [62]
  control, beyond, **6**, [343]
  controlled activity relating to—
    health care, treatment or therapy,
      6(S), 194–5
    reference to, **6(S)**, 193–5
    regulations, **6(S)**, 197–8
  court proceedings—
    commencement, **6**, [453A]
    generally, **6**, [453A]
    jurisdiction, **6**, [423]
    medical evidence, **6**, [77]
    presence in, **6**, [25]
    prohibition on publication of particulars,
      6, [428]
    transfer, **6**, [453A]
    welfare, consideration of, **6**, [32]
  criminal capacity, **12(2)**, [673]
  criminal care orders—
    Northern Ireland, provisions, **6**, [124]
    transitional provisions, **6**, [454]
  criminal proceedings against, **11(2)**, [444]
  criminal proceedings, in—
    abolition of certain powers, **6**, [421]
    adults, segregation from, **6**, [22]
    generally, **6**, [1]
    girl, care of, **6**, [22]

child—*contd*
  criminal proceedings, in—*contd*
    parent or guardian, attendance of,
      6, [23]–[24], [126]
    police station, separation from adults in,
      6, [22]
    prohibition on newspaper report, **6**, [28]
    restrictions on, **6**, [117]
  criminal responsibility, age of, **6**, [1], [38]
  cruelty to—
    generally, **6**, [1]
    ill-treatment, **6**, [343]
    penalties, **6**, [2]
    prevention of, **6**, [2]
    See also harm *below*
  custody, International Convention. *See*
    Custody (Luxembourg Convention)
  custody order—
    existing, discharge of, **6**, [454]
    making, variation and revocation of,
      6, [215]
    transitional provisions, **6**, [454]
    See now contact order *above*; Part I order;
      prohibited steps order; residence order;
      specific issue order *below. See also* **family**
      proceedings
  custody, International Convention. *See*
    Custody (Luxembourg Convention)
  dangerous performance—
    taking part in, **6**, [14], [85]
    training for, **6**, [15]
  day care—
    cost of, recoupment, **6**, [341]
    exemptions, **6**, [453]
    generally, **6**, [1]
    inspection of premises or records of,
      6, [409]
    meaning, **6**, [319], [388]
    providers—
      inspection—
        Chief Inspector, functions of, **6**, [400]
        England, in, **6**, [401]
        local authorities, functions of, **6**, [406]
        reports of, **6**, [402]
        rights of entry, **6**, [405]
        seizure of material, **6**, [405]
        Wales, in, **6**, [404]
      protection of children in emergency,
        6, [397]
      registration—
        appeals, **6**, [399]
        application for, **6**, [392]
        cancellation of, **6**, [394]
        grant of, **6**, [393]
        notices regarding, **6**, [398]
        protection of children in emergency,
          6, [397]
        refusal of, **6**, [393]
        requirements, **6**, [391]
        resignation of, **6**, [523]
        suspension of, **6**, [395]
    provision, **6**, [319]
    racial groups, for children in need, **6**, [440]
    registration—
      certificates of, **6**, [453]

child—*contd*
  day care—*contd*
    registration—*contd*
      disqualification for, **6**, [453]
      regulations, **6**, [390]
  dealer in rags and old clothes, prohibition of
    inducement by, **35(1)**, [496]
  death of—
    by suffocation, **6**, [2]
    Local Safeguarding Children Board, supply
      of information to, **6(S)**, 468–9
  death of, causing or allowing—
    evidence and procedure, **12(4)**, [3]
      court-martial, **12(4)**, [5]
      Northern Ireland, **12(4)**, [4]
    offence of, **12(4)**, [2]
  destruction—
    mother's life, preserving, **12(1)**, [239]
    prosecution, **12(1)**, [240]
    punishment, **12(1)**, [239]
  detention of, **12(2)**, [318], [346]
    absentees, from homes, centres, etc,
      6, [128]
    community home, in, **6**, [127]
    persons to be informed, **6**, [23]
    release, **6**, [126]
  development—
    meaning, **6**, [316], [343]
    standard of, unlikely to achieve, **6**, [316]
  disabled—
    accommodation for, **6**, [323]
    direct payments from State for, **6**, [317]
      vouchers, in form of, **6**, [318]
    meaning, **6**, [316]
    register of disabled children, **6**, [440]
    services for, **6**, [316], [440]
    See also **disabled person; school**
  divorce, etc, provision on. *See* **matrimonial**
    causes
  domicile. *See* **domicile**
  drunkenness while in charge of, **19(3)**, [361]
  early years provision, meaning, **6(S)**, 68
  education. *See* **education supervision order**
  emergency protection order—
    abduction of child subject to, **6**, [366]
    alternative orders, **6**, [364]
    application for—
      attendance of child at, **6**, [426]
      generally, **6**, [359]
      self-incrimination in evidence, **6**, [429]
    care order, effect on, **6**, [422]
    contact with other persons allowed,
      6, [359]
    directions by court, **6**, [359]
    discharge of, **6**, [362]
    discharge, removal of restriction on
      hearing, **6(S)**, 468
    disclosure of information, **6**, [365]
    discovery of children, **6**, [365]
    duration, **6**, [362]
    enquiries, **6**, [364]
    exclusion requirement in, **6**, [360]
    extension of period, **6**, [362]
    investigation by local authority, **6**, [364]
    obstruction of officer, **6**, [364], [365]

child—*contd*
  emergency protection order—*contd*
    offences under, **6**, [359], [365]
    people entitled to apply, **6**, [362]
    persons to be notified of, rules as to,
      6, [369]
    power to make, **6**, [359]
    powers under, **6**, [359]
    removal of child under, **6**, [359]
    rules and regulations, provisions generally,
      6, [369]
    supplementary provisions, **6**, [362]
    undertakings, **6**, [361]
    warrant, issue of, **6**, [365]
    whereabouts of child, discovery of, **6**, [365]
    See also police protection *below*
  emigration, when in care, **6**, [454]
  employment of—
    prohibition or restriction, **15(1)**, [693]
    work experience, as, **15(1)**, [694]
    See also **employment**
  endangering life of, **12(1)**, [83]
  engaging in sexual activity in presence of,
    12(3), [675]
  abuse of position of trust, **12(3)**, [682]
  evidence of—
    corroboration requirement, abolition,
      6, [289]
    court, power to clear, **6**, [26]
    deposition, by, **6**, [30]
      admission of, **6**, [31]
    false evidence, **6**, [27]
    hearing and admissibility, **6**, [427]
    medical practitioner, **6**, [77]
    offence against decency or morality, **6**, [26]
  familial sex offences—
    family relationships, interpretation,
      12(3), [691]
    inciting engagement in sexual activity,
      12(3), [690]
    marriage or civil partnership exception,
      12(3), [692]
    relationships pre-dating family relationship,
      12(3), [693]
    sexual activity with child, **12(3)**, [689]
  family assistance—
    officer for, availability of, **6**, [315]
    order—
      amended provisions, **6(S)**, 17–18
      cessation of, **6**, [237]
      making of, **6**, [315]
      other orders deemed included, when,
        6, [237]
  family centres, provision of, **6**, [440]
  family home, maintenance of, **6**, [440]
  family, of, meaning, **27**, [487]
  family of, services for. *See* **local authority**
  family proceedings. *See* **family proceedings;
    family proceedings order**
  financial relief in respect of—
    instrument, settlement by conveyancing
      counsel, **6**, [439]
    maintenance order, alteration of, **6**, [439]
    order for—
      duration, **6**, [439]

child—*contd*
  financial relief in respect of—*contd*
    order for—*contd*
      guardian, against, **6**, [439]
      interim, **6**, [439]
      lump sums, **6**, [439]
      making, **6**, [314]
      matters to be regarded in making,
        6, [439]
      parents—
        after death payments, **6**, [439]
        against, **6**, [439]
      periodical payments, **6**, [439]
      secured, **6**, [439]
      variation, **6**, [439]
    residence order, application to, **6**, [439]
    residence of child outside England and
      Wales, **6**, [439]
    See also family assistance *above*, maintenance
    below
  fit person order, **6**, [124]
  foster and fostering. *See* **foster parents and
    fostering**
  gambling, protection from. *See* **gambling**
  grave offence by, community home, detention
    in, **6**, [127]
  guardian. *See* **guardian**
  gunpowder, sale of, to, **18**, [695]
  harbouring, **6**, [580]
  harm—
    assessment order, in case of, **6**, [358]
    emergency protection order in case of,
      6, [359]
    meaning, **6**, [343]
  health—
    assessment of, order, **6**, [358]
    meaning, **6**, [316], [343]
    standard of, unlikely to achieve, **6**, [316]
  health authority, accommodated by, **6**, [321]
  hearings (Scotland)—
    disposal of referral by, **6**, [577]
    publication of proceedings, prohibition,
      6, [576]
    supervision requirement, making, **6**, [577]
  horse-riding, protective headgear
    requirements, **6**, [456]
  ill-treatment of, **6**, [343]
  illegitimacy, removal of, **18**, [447]
  illegitimate—
    birth, registration. *See* **birth, registration
      of**
    family provision for, **18**, [585], [665]–[667]
    intestacy of, parents succeed on, **18**, [447],
      [585]
    parents, succession by, **18**, [585]
    presumption as to, rebuttal of, **18**, [218]
    statutory references to relationship,
      18, [665]
    succession on intestacy, **18**, [549], [666]
  imprisonment. *See* arrest, detention *above*
  indecency with, protection of anonymity of
    victim, **12(2)**, [136]
  indecent photographs of—
    child aged 16 or over, proof of,
      12(1), [699], [1105]

child—*contd*
  indecent photographs of—*contd*
    child, person taken to be, **12(1)**, [701]
    corporation, offences by, **12(1)**, [702]
    criminal proceedings, for, **12(1)**, [700]
    entry, seizure and search, **12(1)**, [703]
    forfeiture, **12(1)**, [704], [709]; **12(4)**, [273]
    marriage or enduring family relationship,
      defendant and child in, **12(1)**, [699],
      [1105]
    meaning, **12(1)**, [706]
    Northern Ireland, **12(1)**, [707]
    offences, **12(1)**, [698], [1104]
    punishments, **12(1)**, [705]
    transitory and transitional provisions,
      12(4), [577]
  infanticide, **12(1)**, [240], [256]
  information about, provision of, summary of
    provisions, **6(S)**, 45
  Inland Revenue, disclosure of information
    relating to welfare by, **6**, [970]
  inspectors appointed under Acts, **6**, [51]
  intoxicating liquor—
    confiscation, **6**, [586]
    giving to, **6**, [5]
  juvenile court, before. *See* **youth court**
  kidnapping, institution of proceedings,
    12(1), [814]
  learning difficulty, with—
    language, provision on, **15(1)**, [519]
    meaning, **15(1)**, [519]
  legal capacity of, **6**, [1]
  legal proceedings, publication of material
    relating to, **6**, [969]
  legitimacy of. *See* **legitimation**
  legitimacy, presumption of, rebuttal, **18**, [218]
  liability of parent to maintain, **40(1)**, [19]
  licensed premises, prohibited from when
    unaccompanied, **19(3)**, [634]
  liqueur confectionery, sale to, **19(3)**, [639]
  local authority, powers and duties in general.
    See **local authority**
  local authority services—
    annual returns, **6**, [641]
    contravention of regulations, **6**, [642]
    national minimum standards, **6**, [640]
    relevant functions, **6**, [637]
  local authority, powers and duties in general.
    See **local authority**
  local education authority, accommodated by,
    6, [329]
  Local Safeguarding Children Boards—
    children's services authority, functions of,
      6, [929], [947]
    death of child, supply of information as
      to, **6(S)**, 468–9
    establishment of, **6**, [926], [944]
    functions of, **6**, [927], [945]
    funding, **6**, [928], [946]
    members of, **6**, [926]
    objective, **6**, [927], [945]
    partners, **6**, [926]
    procedure, **6**, [927], [945]
    research and returns of information,
      6(S), 470–1

child—*contd*
  magistrates' court, appeal to Crown Court
    from, **6**, [50]
  maintenance—
    agreement or order—
      alteration of, **6**, [439]
      death of one party, provisions, **6**, [439]
    assessment, deferral of right to apply for,
      6, [564]
    bonus, **6**, [563]
    Child Maintenance and Enforcement
      Commission. *See* **Child Maintenance**
      and Enforcement Commission
    collection of, with child support
      payments, **6**, [506]
    contributions, when in care, **6**, [454]
    deductions from pay for, **3**, [650], [923]
    enforcement, **6**, [439], [506]
    generally. *See* **child support**
    instrument, settlement by conveyancing
      counsel, **6**, [439]
    local authority, by. *See* **local authority**
    meaning, **12(2)**, [100]; **15(1)**, [692]
    1933 Act, **6**, [21], [55]
    1969 Act, **6**, [135]
    1973 Act, **6**, [149]
    1986 Act, **6**, [238], [244]
    1989 Act, **6**, [435], [439]
    1991 Act, **6**, [534]
    child of the family, **6**, [435]
    generally, **6**, [1]
  medical examination, order for, **15(1)**, [628]
  minder and minding—
    exemptions, **6**, [453]
    generally, **6**, [1]
    inspection—
      Chief Inspector, functions of, **6**, [400]
      England, in, **6**, [401]
      local authorities, functions of, **6**, [406]
      reports of, **6**, [402]
      rights of entry, **6**, [405]
      seizure of material, **6**, [405]
      Wales, in, **6**, [404]
    inspection of premises or records of,
      6, [409]
    meaning, **6**, [388]
    person not regarded as, **6**, [388]
    protection of children in emergency,
      6, [397]
    registration—
      appeals, **6**, [399]
      application for, **6**, [392]
      authorities, meaning, **6**, [389]
      cancellation of, **6**, [394]
      certificates of, **6**, [453]
      disqualification for, **6**, [453]
      grant of, **6**, [393]
      notices regarding, **6**, [398]
      protection of children in emergency,
        6, [397]
      qualification for, **6**, [389]
      refusal of, **6**, [393]
      requirements, **6**, [391]
      resignation of, **6**, [396]
      suspension of, **6**, [395]

child—*contd*

minder and minding—*contd*

regulations dealing with, **6**, [390]

transitional provisions, **6**, [454]

missing, recovery of, **6**, [367]

name, change of, consents required, **6**, [306]

national authorities, supply of information to for research purposes, **6(S)**, 470

National Health Service Trust, accommodated by, **6**, [329]

neglect of, **6**, [2], [440]

notifiable disease—

liable to convey, exclusion from school, **35(1)**, [462]

prevention of spread, exclusion from places of entertainment for, **35(1)**, [464]

nursing home, accommodated by, **6**, [329]

nutrition—

benefits under schemes for improving, **30**, [748]

schemes for improving, **40(1)**, [190]

oath by, form of, **6**, [78]

offences against—

charges, **6**, [9]

continuing, **6**, [9]

deposition of child, **6**, [30]

admission in evidence, **6**, [31]

generally, **6**, [1]

limitation of time, **6**, [9]

proceedings—

in absence of child, **6**, [29]

instituting, **6**, [88]

special provisions applying to, **6**, [58]

offences committed by—

aiding and abetting offence, **6**, [76]

bodies corporate, by, **6**, [433]

committal, local authority accommodation, **6**, [120], [546]

criminal proceedings. *See* criminal proceedings *above*

detention pending trial, **6**, [545]

execution of process, **6**, [145]

grave, **6**, [127]

information, laying, **6**, [117]

person over seventeen, charged with, **6**, [76]

remand to care of local authority, **6**, [120], [545]

restrictions on proceedings, **6**, [117]

treatment, alteration in, **6**, [118]

See also **young offenders**

offences involving, **12(1)**, [1]

open fire grate, in room with, **6**, [7]

orders and regulations, **6**, [134]

orders in general—

appeals, **6**, [425]

Channel Islands, made in, effect, **6**, [431]

duration, **6**, [422]

England and Wales, as between, effect, **6**, [431]

further application, restriction in, **6**, [422]

Isle of Man, made in, effect, **6**, [431]

Northern Ireland, taken to live in, effect, **6**, [431]

child—*contd*

parent and parental responsibility. *See* **parent**

parent, meaning, **35(2)**, [283]

Parliament, annual abstract of information, laying before, **6**, [411]

Part I order—

delivery up of child, ordering, **6**, [253]

duration of, **6**, [237]

enforcement, **6**, [248]

stay or sist of proceedings, **6**, [249]

generally, **6**, [1]

Northern Ireland, duration of, **6**, [243]

Northern Ireland, variation of, **6**, [243]

recognition of, **6**, [245]

registration of—

application for, **6**, [246]

cancellation and variation of, **6**, [247]

removal of child from jurisdiction, **6**, [254]

variation of, **6**, [237]

periodical payments made to, **11(2)**, [482]

persons unsuitable to work with—

Department of Health list—

duty to keep, **6**, [610]

general note, **6**, [1]

inclusion on—

appeals against, **6**, [617], [622], [627]

Consultancy Service Index, on transfer from, **6**, [616]

effect of, **6**, [621]

individuals named in findings of certain enquiries, **6**, [613]

Part VII of Care Standards Act 2000, on reference under, **6**, [614]

power of certain authorities to refer individuals for, **6**, [612]

reference to Secretary of State, **6**, [611]

removal from, applications for, **6**, [618]–[619]

local authorities proposing to make direct payments in respect of services, **6**, [615]

restoration to, **6**, [620]

general note, **6**, [1]

transitional provisions, **6**, [625]

Tribunal, **6**, [622], [627]

attendance allowances, **6**, [627]

chairmen's panel, members of—

appointment of, **6**, [627]

tenure of office, **6**, [627]

constitution, **6**, [627]

expenses, **6**, [627]

meetings, **6**, [627]

President—

appointment of, **6**, [627]

tenure of office, **6**, [627]

remuneration, **6**, [627]

staff, **6**, [627]

training, **6**, [627]

place of safety—

abscondment, **6**, [579]

absence from, **6**, [128]

meaning, **6**, [55], [581]

orders, **6**, [454]

child—*contd*

police protection, under—
abduction of child, **6**, [366]
accommodation for, **6**, [321], [363]
constables' powers and duties, **6**, [363]
contact with other persons, **6**, [363]
enquiry into, **6**, [364]
investigation by local authority, **6**, [364]
meaning, **6**, [363]
period of, **6**, [363]
persons to be informed, **6**, [363]
removal of child, **6**, [363]
probation order, meaning, **6**, [100]
prohibited steps order—
application for, **6**, [303]
discharge of, **6**, [302]
duration of, **6**, [422]
enforcement, **6**, [248]
general principles, **6**, [304]
jurisdiction, general, **6**, [233]
making of—
court's powers, **6**, [232]–[234], [303]
restrictions on, **6**, [302]
meaning, **6**, [301]
recognition and registration, **6**, [245]–[246]
stay of proceedings, **6**, [236]
supplementary provisions, **6**, [304]
variation of, **6**, [302]
See also **family proceedings; family proceedings order**
prostitution and pornography, abuse through—
arranging or facilitating, **12(3)**, [712]
causing or inciting, **12(3)**, [710]
controlling, **12(3)**, [711]
interpretation, **12(3)**, [713]
sexual services, paying for, **12(3)**, [709]
protection of, generally, **6**, [1]
See also emergency protection order *above*
provision for. *See* **family provision**
public performance—
broadcasting, **6**, [81]
dangerous nature, of, **6**, [15], [85]
meaning, **6**, [21]
fourteen, under, **6**, [82]
generally, **6**, [81], [83]
going abroad for, **6**, [86]
licence, **6**, [16]
proceedings relating to, **6**, [17]
licences, **6**, [81]–[82]
offences, **6**, [84]
prosecution of, **6**, [88]
powers of entry, **6**, [19]
reasonable punishment, **6**, [966]
regulated activity relating to—
appropriate verification—
default provision, **6(S)**, 255–6
definitions, **6(S)**, 259
prescribed, **6(S)**, 256–8
barred person engaging in—
monitoring, subject to, **6(S)**, 181–2
offences, **6(S)**, 180
use of person not subject to monitoring, offence, **6(S)**, 183–4
use of, offence, **6(S)**, 182–3

child—*contd*

regulated activity relating to—*contd*
code of practice, **6(S)**, 203
companies or partnerships, offences by, **6(S)**, 191
Crown, provisions applying to, **6(S)**, 222
damages, claim for, **6(S)**, 227
devolution, alignment of provisions, **6(S)**, 224
educational establishments—
checks, making, **6(S)**, 187–8
members of governing body, check on, **6(S)**, 186
establishments providing, **6(S)**, 250
exceptions, **6(S)**, 251
family and personal relationships, in course of, **6(S)**, 227
fostering, **6(S)**, 223–4
meaning, **6(S)**, 178
meaning, **6(S)**, 247–9
monitoring—
application, **6(S)**, 198–9
ceasing, **6(S)**, 200
cessation of registration, **6(S)**, 206
false declaration, offence of making, **6(S)**, 206
fees, **6(S)**, 200
identification requirements, **6(S)**, 199
independent monitor, **6(S)**, 201–2
individual subject to, **6(S)**, 198
notification of cessation of, **6(S)**, 205
register, **6(S)**, 205
Northern Ireland, provisions applying, **6(S)**, 225
offences, **6(S)**, 191–2
exclusions and defences, **6(S)**, 192–3
office holders—
checks, making, **6(S)**, 187–8
offences, **6(S)**, 187
orders and regulations, **6(S)**, 231
period condition, **6(S)**, 255
personnel suppliers—
barred person, supply of, **6(S)**, 182–3
employment business, failure to check, **6(S)**, 260–1
exclusions and defences, **6(S)**, 192–3
failure to check on person engaging in, **6(S)**, 186
offences, **6(S)**, 191–2
prescribed information, duty to refer, **6(S)**, 208
persons exercising functions, **6(S)**, 250–1
providers—
duty to provide information on request, **6(S)**, 209
failure to check on person engaging in, **6(S)**, 185
meaning, **6(S)**, 179
NHS employment, **6(S)**, 190
prescribed information, duty to refer, **6(S)**, 207
private arrangements, **6(S)**, 179
use of person not subject to monitoring, offence, **6(S)**, 183–4

child—*contd*
  regulated activity relating to—*contd*
    registers—
      barring and cessation of monitoring,
        notice of, **6(S)**, 214–15
      cessation of registration, **6(S)**, 206
      duty to provide information on request,
        6(S), 214
      establishment and maintenance of,
        6(S), 205
      prescribed information, duty of keeper
        to refer, **6(S)**, 212–13
      vetting information, power to apply for,
        6(S), 215–16
    relevant records, prohibition of requirement
      to produce, **6(S)**, 201
    requirement to make monitoring check,
      exceptions to, **6(S)**, 188–9
    supervisory authorities—
      barring, notification of, **6(S)**, 220
      duty to provide information on request,
        6(S), 218
      meaning, **6(S)**, 217
      prescribed information, duty to refer,
        6(S), 216–18
      provision of information to, **6(S)**, 222
      vetting information, power to apply for,
        6(S), 218–19
    transitional provisions, **6(S)**, 264–5
    types of activities, **6(S)**, 249
    vetting information—
      provision of, **6(S)**, 203–4
      relevant, meaning, **6(S)**, 204
      table of, **6(S)**, 261–3
    Wales, provisions applying, **6(S)**, 225–6
  regulations and orders, power to make,
    6, [134], [434]
  relationship, construction of reference to,
    6, [277]
  research, conduct of, **6**, [411]
  residence—
    change of child's name, **6**, [306]
    general principles, **6**, [304]
    habitual, **6**, [135], [235], [260]
    ordinary, meaning, **6**, [435]
    relevance of, **6**, [235]
  residence order—
    amended provisions, **6(S)**, 430
    application for, **6**, [1], [303]
    cessation of effect by custody order,
      6, [237]
    discharge of, **6**, [302]
    duration of, **6**, [422]; **6(S)**, 473
    enforcement, **6**, [248], [307]
    entitlement of relative to apply for,
      6(S), 472
    financial relief under, **6**, [439]
    former, contact with child under care,
      6, [359]
    guardianship, in connection with, **6**, [298]
    interim supervision order with, **6**, [351]
    jurisdiction, **6**, [233]
    making of, **6**, [302]
      court's powers, **6**, [232]–[234], [303]
    meaning, **6**, [301]

child—*contd*
  residence order—*contd*
    parental responsibility order, **6**, [305]
    periods spent in each household,
      specification of, **6**, [304]
    person who is not parent or guardian, in
      favour of, **6**, [305]
    recognition and registration, **6**, [245]–[246]
    removal of child from jurisdiction, **6**, [254],
      [306]
    stay of proceedings, **6**, [236]
    supplementary provisions, **6**, [304]
    variation, **6**, [302]
    See also **family proceedings**
  residential care home, accommodated by,
    6, [329]
  returns of information, requirement
    generally, **6**, [411]
  run away, recovery, **6**, [367]
  safety of, at entertainments, **6**, [8]
  sale of aerosol paint to, **35(2)**, [437], [438]
  school attendance order, discharge of, **6**, [422]
  Scottish legislation, extension to England and
    Wales, **6**, [97], [102]
  search for. *See* **search; search warrant**
  seat-belts, wearing in motor vehicles. *See* **seat
    belts**
  sending to obtain alcohol, **19(3)**, [643]
  separate representation in family proceedings,
    provision for, **27**, [679]
  service families, of, protection of, **3(S)**, 390–5
  settlement on. *See* **settlement**
  sex offenders—
    disclosure of information relating to,
      12(3), [1038]
    interpretation, **12(3)**, [1039]
  sexual abuse of, **6**, [343]
  sexual act, causing to watch, **12(3)**, [676]
    abuse of position of trust, **12(3)**, [683]
  sexual activity, causing or inciting engagement
    in, **12(3)**, [674]
    abuse of position of trust, **12(3)**, [681]
    family member, **12(3)**, [690]
  sexual activity with, **12(3)**, [673]
    abuse of position of trust, **12(3)**, [680]
    family member, **12(3)**, [689]
  sexual grooming, meeting following,
    12(3), [679]
  sexual offences against. *See* indecency *above*;
    See also **sexual intercourse; sexual
    offences**
  sexual offences, witness in proceedings,
    11(2), [525]
  sexual or violent offences against, transfer of
    place of trial—
    delay, avoidance, **12(2)**, [124]
    generally, **12(2)**, [100]
    notice of, **12(2)**, [100], [124]
    procedure in lieu of committal,
      12(2), [124]
    regulations, power to make, **12(2)**, [124]
    remand, person on, **12(2)**, [124]
    reporting restriction, **12(2)**, [124]
  social security benefits, **40(1)**, [677]
  social services functions, **6(S)**, 439

child—*contd*
  Social Work (Scotland) Act, extension to
    England and Wales, **6**, [97], [102]
  social work services, provision of—
    discharge of care functions, arrangements
      for—
        effect of, **6(S)**, 437
        piloting and expiry of, **6(S)**, 439
        power to enter into, **6(S)**, 434
        restrictions on, **6(S)**, 436
    piloting and expiry of arrangements,
      6(S), 439
    providers, regulation of, **6(S)**, 438
    summary of provisions, **6(S)**, 427
  soliciting alms, by, procuring or encouraging,
    12(1), [26]
  solicitor, appointment on behalf of, **6**, [356]
  special allowance for—
    contribution conditions, **40(1)**, [260], [463]
    existing beneficiaries, **40(1)**, [306]
    rate of, **40(1)**, [465]
  special educational needs, with—
    Academy, attending, **15(1)**, [610]
    assessment of, **15(1)**, [532]
      examinations, **15(1)**, [716]
      local education authority, by,
        15(1), [532]
      manner of making, **15(1)**, [716]
      meaning, **15(1)**, [716]
      medical and other advice, **15(1)**, [716]
      offences, **15(1)**, [716]
      parent, at request of, **15(1)**, [539]
      responsible body, at request of,
        15(1), [540]
      timing, **15(1)**, [716]
      two years, under age of, **15(1)**, [541]
    city college, attending, **15(1)**, [610]
    Code of Practice—
      having regard to, **15(1)**, [520]
      issue and revision of, **15(1)**, [520]
      making and approval of, **15(1)**, [521]
    duty to inform parent where provision
      made to child without statement,
      15(1), [526]
    establishment outside England and Wales,
      provision at, **15(1)**, [529]
    general note, **15(1)**, [1]
    goods and services, provision of,
      15(1), [527]
    governing body, duties of, **15(1)**, [525]
    Health Authority—
      local education authority, assisting,
        15(1), [531]
      parent, duty to notify, **15(1)**, [542]
    independent school, education at,
      15(1), [553]
    information—
      provision of, **15(S)**, Education 59
      publication of, **15(S)**, Education 59
    interpretation, **15(S)**, Education 60
    local education authority—
      advice and information for parents,
        provision of, **15(1)**, [543]
      assessment by, **15(1)**, [532]
      certain schools, access to, **15(1)**, [537]

child—*contd*
  special educational needs, with—*contd*
    local education authority—*contd*
      disputes, resolution of, **15(1)**, [544]
      general duty of, **15(1)**, [525], [530]
      Health Authority, assistance of,
        15(1), [531]
      local authority, assistance of, **15(1)**, [531]
      Primary Care Trust, assistance of,
        15(1), [531]
    mainstream schools—
      not in, **15(1)**, [524]
      securing education in, **15(1)**, [523]
    meaning, **15(1)**, [519]
    National Health Service trust, parent, duty
      to notify, **15(1)**, [542]
    NHS foundation trust, parent, duty to
      notify, **15(1)**, [542]
    non-maintained schools, provision of
      education at, **15(1)**, [554]
    nursery education, **15(1)**, [488]
    Primary Care Trust—
      local education authority, assisting,
        15(1), [531]
      parent, duty to notify, **15(1)**, [542]
    provision of education. *See* **education**
    review of, **15(1)**, [538]
    special schools. *See* **special school**
    statement of—
      additional information, provision of,
        15(1), [717]
      amendment of, **15(1)**, [535], [717]
      appeal against, **15(1)**, [535]
      ceasing to maintain, **15(1)**, [717]
      choice of school, **15(1)**, [583], [717]
      content of, **15(1)**, [533]
      decision not to make, appeal against,
        15(1), [534]
      form of, **15(1)**, [533]
      keeping and disclosing, **15(1)**, [717]
      making, **15(1)**, [533], [717]
      named school—
        change of, **15(1)**, [717]
        consultation on specifying,
          15(1), [717]
      representations, **15(1)**, [717]
      review of, **15(1)**, [538]
      service of, **15(1)**, [717]
      service on parents, **15(1)**, [717]
      transfer of, **15(1)**, [717]
      unopposed appeals, **15(1)**, [536]
    Tribunal. *See* **Special Educational Needs
      and Disability Tribunal**
    Wales. *See* **Wales**
  specific issue order—
    application for, **6**, [303]
    discharge of, **6**, [302]
    duration of, **6**, [422]
    enforcement, **6**, [248]
    general principles, **6**, [304]
    jurisdiction, **6**, [233]
    making of—
      court's powers, **6**, [303]
      restrictions on, **6**, [302]
      variation, **6**, [302]

child—*contd*
specific issue order—*contd*
meaning, **6**, [301]
recognition and registration, **6**, [245]–[246]
removal of child from jurisdiction, **6**, [254]
stay of proceedings, **6**, [236]
supplementary principles, **6**, [304]
specified proceedings—
meaning, **6**, [356]
representation at, **6**, [356]
statement made without oath, **12(1)**, [207]
status, declarations of, **6**, [263]–[268]
street trading, involvement in, **6**, [12]
suicide by, aiding and abetting, **12(1)**, [332]
summary proceedings, "conviction" and
"sentence", use of, **6**, [40]
supervision order. *See* **supervision order**
supervision requirement—
making of, **6**, [577]
meaning, **6**, [577]
orders made in different parts of UK,
6, [575]
regulations, **6**, [578]
review, **6**, [577]
support. *See* **child support**
tattooing, **6**, [106]
tobacco, sale of to. *See* **tobacco**
training school. *See* **training school**
trial of other persons, presence during, **6**, [25]
trust funds. *See* **child trust funds**
under 13—
assault by penetration, **12(3)**, [670]
causing to engage in sexual activity,
12(3), [672]
rape of, **12(3)**, [669]
sexual assault, **12(3)**, [671]
upbringing, meaning, **6**, [435]
vetting and barring scheme—
Independent Barring Board. *See*
Independent Barring Board
summary of provisions, **6(S)**, 173
voluntary home, in. *See* **voluntary home**
ward of court, as. *See* **ward of court**
warrant for apprehension of, **6**, [145]
weighing and measuring—
England, **30(S)**, NHS 106–7
Wales, **30(S)**, NHS 108–9
welfare—
court to consider, **6**, [32]
local authorities duties, **6**, [316]
LEA's duties, **15(2)**, [489]
maintained school governing body's duties,
15(2), [489]
paramount importance of, **6**, [293]
regard to be paid to, **6**, [467]
reports on, call for, **6**, [300]
well-being of, **6(S)**, 440
witness as, **6**, [427]; **12(2)**, [100],
[124]. *See also* **witness**
working with—
certificate of suitability for, **6**, [407]
disqualification from, **6**, [1]
unsuitable persons, lists of, **6**, [1]
young, meaning, **6(S)**, 68

child benefit
alteration of rate, effect of, **40(1)**, [681]
annual review of, **40(1)**, [676]
appeals, matters arising, **40(2)**, [165]
application for payments, **40(1)**, [514]
child—
meaning, **40(1)**, [393]
person responsible for, meaning,
40(1), [394]
present in Great Britain, required to be,
40(1), [398]
death of child or qualifying young person,
entitlement after, **40(1)**, [397]
definitions, **40(1)**, [399]
entitlement to, **40(1)**, [392]
death of child or qualifying young person,
after, **40(1)**, [397]
excess, treatment of, **40(1)**, [682]
exclusion of, **40(1)**, [395], [491]
functions of Secretary of State transferred to
Treasury, **40(2)**, [409]
general note, **40(1)**, [1]
HM Revenue and Customs—
functions of Secretary of State transferred
to, **40(2)**, [410]
information regarding, provision of,
40(2), [429]
payment and management by, **40(2)**, [413]
transfer of property, rights and liabilities
to, **40(2)**, [412]
transitional provisions, **40(2)**, [414]
information—
administrative arrangements, **40(2)**, [415]
exchange of, **40(2)**, [429]
powers to use, **40(2)**, [429]
provision by HM Revenue and Customs,
40(2), [429]
legislation of other member States, overlap
with, **40(1)**, [584]
lone parents, power to reduce in case of,
40(2), [193]
qualifying young person—
meaning, **40(1)**, [393]
person responsible for, meaning,
40(1), [394]
presence in Great Britain, requirement of,
40(1), [398]
rate of, **40(1)**, [396]
two or more people entitled to, **40(1)**, [395],
[492]
voluntary organisation, meaning, **40(1)**, [399]

child care
body corporate, offences by, **6(S)**, 134
Chief Inspector of Schools—
annual reports, information in, **6(S)**, 130
authorised person, entry on premises by—
consent to entry, requirements for,
6(S), 128
power of constable to assist, **6(S)**, 129
powers of, **6(S)**, 127
co-operation with authorities, **6(S)**, 137
combined reports, **6(S)**, 130
consent to disclosure, withholding,
6(S), 136

child care—*contd*
  Chief Inspector of Schools—*contd*
    disclosure of information, **6(S)**, 132
    general functions, **6(S)**, 76–7
    information provided by, **6(S)**, 131–2
    inspections—
      early years providers, **6(S)**, 94–5
      later years providers, **6(S)**, 106–8
    registers, maintenance of, **6(S)**, 77
    supply of information to, **6(S)**, 131
  Early Years Foundation Stage—
    duty to implement, **6(S)**, 87
    instruments specifying requirements,
      6(S), 91
    learning and development requirements,
      6(S), 88
    requirements, **6(S)**, 86
    welfare requirements, **6(S)**, 90
  early years providers—
    assessment arrangements, **6(S)**, 89
    exemptions from requirements, **6(S)**, 92
    inspections, **6(S)**, 94
      report of, **6(S)**, 95
    instruments specifying requirements,
      6(S), 91
    learning and development requirements,
      6(S), 88
    meaning, **6(S)**, 140
    provision of information by, **6(S)**, 142–3
    transitory provision, **6(S)**, 144
    Wales, in, **6(S)**, 145–6
    registration—
      appeals, **6(S)**, 123
      applications, **6(S)**, 83
      cancellation, **6(S)**, 116
      certificates, **6(S)**, 84
      combined certificates, **6(S)**, 138
      conditions, **6(S)**, 85
      consent to disclosure, withholding,
        6(S), 136
      disqualification from, **6(S)**, 123–6
      early years childminders. *See* **child
        minding and day care**
      emergency, protection of child in,
        6(S), 120
      entries on register, **6(S)**, 84
      false or misleading statement, offence of
        making, **6(S)**, 133
      procedural safeguards, **6(S)**, 121–2
      requirement, **6(S)**, 80
      suspension, **6(S)**, 117–18
      voluntary removal from register,
        6(S), 119
    welfare requirements, **6(S)**, 90
  early years provision, meaning, **6(S)**, 140
  employees not regarded as providing,
    6(S), 141
  exclusions, **6(S)**, 66–7
  fees, **6(S)**, 135
  later years providers—
    activities, regulations governing,
      6(S), 105–6
    inspections, **6(S)**, 106–7
      report of, **6(S)**, 107–8
    meaning, **6(S)**, 140

child care—*contd*
  later years providers—*contd*
    registration—
      appeals, **6(S)**, 123
      applications, **6(S)**, 101–2
      cancellation, **6(S)**, 116
      certificates, **6(S)**, 103
      combined certificates, **6(S)**, 138
      conditions, **6(S)**, 104–5
      consent to disclosure, withholding,
        6(S), 136
      disqualification from, **6(S)**, 123–6
      emergency, protection of child in,
        6(S), 120
      entries on register, **6(S)**, 103
      false or misleading statement, offence of
        making, **6(S)**, 133
      later years childminders. *See* **child
        minding and day care**
      procedural safeguards, **6(S)**, 121–2
      requirement, **6(S)**, 98–9
      suspension, **6(S)**, 117–18
      voluntary removal from register,
        6(S), 119
  later years provision, meaning, **6(S)**, 140
  local authority, provision by—
    England, in—
      assessment of, **6(S)**, 60
      charges, **6(S)**, 59
      childcare providers, arrangements with,
        6(S), 58–9
      information, advice and assistance, duty
        to provide, **6(S)**, 61
      powers as to, **6(S)**, 57–8
      prescribed early years provision free of
        charge, provision of, **6(S)**, 56
      working parents, duty to secure for,
        6(S), 55
    Wales, in—
      assessment of, **6(S)**, 72
      charges, **6(S)**, 72
      childcare providers, arrangements with,
        6(S), 71
      information, advice and assistance, duty
        to provide, **6(S)**, 73
      powers as to, **6(S)**, 70–1
      working parents, duty to secure for,
        6(S), 69–70
  LEA's duties in respect of, **15(2)**, [117]
  meaning, **6(S)**, 66–7, 76
  notices, **6(S)**, 138
  partnerships, establishment of, **15(2)**, [118]
  proceedings, time limit for, **6(S)**, 134
  providers—
    information, advice and training, duty of
      local authority to provide, **6(S)**, 62–3
    local authority, arrangements with—
      England, in, **6(S)**, 58–9
      Wales, in, **6(S)**, 71
    registration, voluntary, **6(S)**, 43
    regulation, summary of provisions, **6(S)**, 43
  provision, regulation of, summary of
    provisions, **6(S)**, 41–4
  registers, maintenance of, **6(S)**, 77

child care—*contd*
unincorporated association, offences by,
   6(S), 134–5
voluntary registration—
   activities, regulations governing, **6(S)**, 115
   appeals, **6(S)**, 123
   cancellation, **6(S)**, 116
   certificates, **6(S)**, 112
   child care providers, by, **6(S)**, 110
   childminders, applications by, **6(S)**, 108–9
   combined certificates, **6(S)**, 138
   conditions, **6(S)**, 114
   consent to disclosure, withholding,
      6(S), 136
   disqualification from, **6(S)**, 123–6
   emergency, protection of child in,
      6(S), 120
   entries on register, **6(S)**, 112
   false or misleading statement, offence of
      making, **6(S)**, 133
   persons already registered, special procedure
      for, **6(S)**, 113–14
   procedural safeguards, **6(S)**, 121–2
   suspension, **6(S)**, 117–18
   termination on expiry of prescribed
      period, **6(S)**, 119
   voluntary removal from register, **6(S)**, 119

**Child Maintenance and Enforcement
Commission**
accounts and audit, **6(S)**, 388
agency arrangements, **6(S)**, 323
annual report, **6(S)**, 325
chairman, **6(S)**, 385
child support functions, transfer to, **6(S)**, 328,
   393–401
committees, **6(S)**, 387
constitution, **6(S)**, 385
credit reference agency, disclosure of
   information to, **6(S)**, 375
deputy chairman, **6(S)**, 386
directions and guidance to, **6(S)**, 326
directors, **6(S)**, 385
establishment of, **6(S)**, 319
family proceedings, disclosure of information
   relating to, **6(S)**, 372–4
fees, charging, **6(S)**, 322
finance, **6(S)**, 388
functions—
   child maintenance, promotion of, **6(S)**, 321
   contracting out, **6(S)**, 324
   delegation, **6(S)**, 387
   general, **6(S)**, 320
   information and guidance, provision of,
      6(S), 322
instruments of, **6(S)**, 388
members, **6(S)**, 385–6
non-executive functions committee, **6(S)**, 389
objectives, **6(S)**, 320
procedure, **6(S)**, 387
property, rights and liabilities transferred to,
   6(S), 328–9
services, provision of, **6(S)**, 323
staff, **6(S)**, 387
status, review of, **6(S)**, 326–7

**Child Maintenance and Enforcement
Commission**—*contd*
summary of provisions, **6(S)**, 311–12
use of information, **6(S)**, 406–7

child minding and day care
early years childminder, registration—
   appeals, **6(S)**, 123
   applications, **6(S)**, 82
   cancellation, **6(S)**, 116
   certificates, **6(S)**, 84
   combined certificates, **6(S)**, 138
   conditions, **6(S)**, 85
   consent to disclosure, withholding,
      6(S), 136
   disqualification from, **6(S)**, 123–6
   emergency, protection of child in,
      6(S), 120
   entries on register, **6(S)**, 84
   false or misleading statement, offence of
      making, **6(S)**, 133
   procedural safeguards, **6(S)**, 121–2
   requirement, **6(S)**, 78
   summary of provisions, **6(S)**, 41–2
   suspension, **6(S)**, 117–18
   voluntary removal from register, **6(S)**, 119
inspection, **15(2)**, [719]
later years childminder, registration—
   appeals, **6(S)**, 123
   applications, **6(S)**, 100
   cancellation, **6(S)**, 116
   certificates, **6(S)**, 103
   combined certificates, **6(S)**, 138
   conditions, **6(S)**, 104–5
   consent to disclosure, withholding,
      6(S), 136
   disqualification from, **6(S)**, 123–6
   early years providers, special procedure
      for, **6(S)**, 103–4
   emergency, protection of child in,
      6(S), 120
   entries on register, **6(S)**, 103
   false or misleading statement, offence of
      making, **6(S)**, 133
   procedural safeguards, **6(S)**, 121–2
   requirement, **6(S)**, 97
   summary of provisions, **6(S)**, 42
   suspension, **6(S)**, 117–18
   voluntary removal from register, **6(S)**, 119
voluntary registration, applications for,
   6(S), 108–9

child safety order
appeals, **6**, [593]
directions under, **6**, [602]
discharge, **6**, [592]
failure to comply with, **6**, [592]
generally, **6**, [1]
implementation, arrangements for, **6**, [591]
making, **6**, [591]
meaning, **6**, [591]
variation, **6**, [592]

child support
agency, **6**, [1]

child support—*contd*
alleged parent, denial by, **6**, [488]
amendment of enactments, **6**, [681]
appeal tribunal—
   appeal to, **40(2)**, [210]
   appeal to court instead of, **6**, [523]
   decisions, matters arising, **6**, [526]
   officer of, unauthorised disclosure of
     information by, **6**, [529]
appeals—
   Child Support Commissioner, to, **6**, [486]
   Commissioners, from, on question of law,
     6, [487]
   decisions—
      erroneous in law, **6**, [493]
      on matters pending, **6**, [491]
   issues arising in other cases, involving,
     6, [492]
   jurisdiction of courts as to, **6**, [523]
   redetermination of, **6**, [485]
   reduced benefit directions, **6**, [544]
changes to system, summary of provisions,
   6(S), 312–16
Child Maintenance and Enforcement
   Commission. *See* **Child Maintenance and**
   Enforcement Commission
child, meaning, **6(S)**, 376
civil partnership, relationship arising through,
   27, [880]
Commissioners—
   appeal from, on question of law, **6**, [487]
   appeal to, **6**, [486]
   appointment, **6**, [483]
   Chief, appointment, **6**, [483]
   consultation by Lord Chancellor as to,
     6, [483], [541]
   decisions, matters arising, **6**, [526]
   finality of decisions, **6**, [541]
   hearings before, **6**, [483]
   legal practice by, bar on, **6**, [541]
   Northern Ireland, **6**, [484], [541]
   pensions, **6**, [541]
   proceedings before, **6**, [483]
   remuneration, **6**, [541]
   tenure of office, **6**, [541]
   tribunals of, **6**, [541]
Crown, application of certain provisions,
   6, [536]
errors—
   correction, **6**, [494]
   decisions, setting aside, **6**, [494]
   determinations, in, **6**, [493]
   liability, restrictions on, **6**, [493]
generally, **6**, [1]
income-based jobseeker's allowance, receipt
   of, effect of, **6**, [471]
information—
   Crown, application of provisions, **6**, [536]
   Secretary of State—
     provision to, **6**, [540]
     required by, **6**, [477]
   unauthorised disclosure of, **6**, [529]
   use of, **40(2)**, [152]
inspectors—
   appointment, **6**, [479]

child support—*contd*
inspectors—*contd*
   Crown premises, entry on, **6**, [536]
   entry, power of, **6**, [479]
   powers, **6**, [470]
interest and fees, extinction of liability for,
   6(S), 377
interpretation of terms, **6**, [468], [533]
Isles of Scilly, application of provisions,
   6, [537]
magistrates' court, right of audience in,
   6, [528]
maintenance—
   administrative liability orders, **6(S)**, 347–8
   agreement—
     alteration of, **6**, [439]
     existence of, effect, **6**, [473]
     meaning, **6**, [473]
     registered, Scotland, **6(S)**, 369
   arrears—
     deceased's estate, recovery from,
      6(S), 371
     part payment, acceptance in full and final
      satisfaction, **6(S)**, 365
     penalty payments, **6**, [518]
     power to write off, **6(S)**, 366–7
     recovery, **6**, [517]
     transfer of, **6(S)**, 367–8
basic principles, **6**, [466]–[474]
calculation—
   alleged parent, denial by, **6**, [488]
   application for—
     benefit, persons claiming or receiving,
      by, **6**, [471]
     decisions—
      appeals against, **6**, [482]
      decisions superceding earlier,
       6, [481]
      default, **6**, [476]
      interim, **6**, [476]
      review of, **6**, [480]
     determination by Secretary of State,
      6, [475]
     information required, **6**, [469], [477]
     making of, **6**, [469]
     more than one, **6**, [470]
     supplemental provisions, **6**, [470]
   apportionment, **6**, [538]
   basic rate, **6**, [538]
     changes to, **6(S)**, 402
   benefits, persons claiming or receiving,
     application by, **6**, [471]
   consolidated, **6**, [539]
   court order, relationship between,
     6, [474]
   effective date, **6**, [539]
   fees, **6**, [527]
   flat rate, **6**, [538]
     increase, **6(S)**, 402
   form, **6**, [539]
   general rule, **6**, [538]
   gross weekly income, reference to,
     6(S), 401
   income, regulations about, **6**, [538]

child support—*contd*
maintenance—*contd*
calculation—*contd*
jurisdiction—
courts', **6**, [523]
Secretary of State's, **6**, [522]
minimum amount, increase to, **6(S)**, 402
net weekly income, **6**, [538]
nil rate, **6**, [538]
non-resident parent party to other
maintenance agreement, **6(S)**, 402
reduced benefit decisions, **6**, [524]
reduced rate, **6**, [538]
Secretary of State, by, **6**, [472], [475]
Secretary of State's jurisdiction, **6**, [522]
separate, for different periods, **6**, [539]
shared care, **6(S)**, 403
shared case—
basic rate, **6**, [538]
flat rate, **6**, [538]
reduced rate, **6**, [538]
regulations, **6**, [538]
termination of, **6**, [539]
transfer of cases to new rules,
6(S), 404–6
variation, application for, **6(S)**, 331
variation of usual rules—
agreement to, **6**, [500]
application for, **6**, [495], [542]
cases, **6**, [543]
determinations, **6**, [498]
information, use of, **6**, [542]
matters taken into account, **6**, [499]
preliminary consideration, **6**, [496],
[542]
property or capital transfers, **6**, [543]
regular payments condition,
imposition of, **6**, [497]
regulatory controls, **6**, 543A
revisions, **6**, [501]
special expenses, **6**, [543]
supersession, **6**, [501]
transitional provisions, **6**, [503]
voluntary payments, **6**, [504]
weekly income, **6(S)**, 403
change of address, offence of filing to
notify, **6(S)**, 370
collection of—
arrangements for, **6**, [469], [505]
methods, **6**, [505]
other forms of maintenance with,
6, [506]
county court, enforcement in, **6(S)**, 349
courts, role of, **6**, [472]
decisions—
appeals against, **6**, [482]
decisions superceding earlier, **6**, [481]
decisions superseding other decisions,
6(S), 330–1
default, **6**, [476]
interim, **6**, [476]
review of, **6**, [480]
deduction from earnings order—
basic method of payment, as,
6(S), 332–3

child support—*contd*
maintenance—*contd*
deduction from earnings order—*contd*
instructions to employer, **6**, [507]
liable person's earnings, **6(S)**, 334
making of, **6**, [507]
regulations, **6**, [508]
defaulter—
commitment to prison, **6(S)**, 360–2
driving licence, disqualification for
holding or obtaining, **6(S)**, 363
enforcement, **6**, [505]
enforcement action, curfew orders—
amount due, **6(S)**, 355
application for, **6(S)**, 353–4
breach of, **6(S)**, 356–7
costs, recovery of, **6(S)**, 355
custody, effect of, **6(S)**, 357
duration, **6(S)**, 354
monitoring, **6(S)**, 356
supplementary provisions, **6(S)**, 357–9
family proceedings, disclosure of
information relating to, **6(S)**, 372–4
information—
offences, **6**, [478]
provision of, **6**, [469], [477]
liability order—
enforcement—
committal to prison, by,
6, [514]–[515]
county courts, in, **6**, [512]
disqualification from driving, **6**, [514],
[516]
distress, by, **6**, [511]
garnishee proceedings, by, **6**, [512]
imprisonment, **6**, [514]–[515]
throughout the United Kingdom,
6, [513]
making of, **6**, [509]
regulations, **6**, [510]
liable person, disqualification for holding or
obtaining travel authorisation—
duration, **6(S)**, 351
order for, **6(S)**, 349–50
Scotland, application to, **6(S)**, 352
search, power to order, **6(S)**, 351
supplementary provisions, **6(S)**, 352
variation and revocation following
payment, **6(S)**, 351
liable relative provisions, **6(S)**, 378
lump sum deduction orders—
deductions and payments, **6(S)**, 342
final, **6(S)**, 340–1
freezing of accounts, **6(S)**, 341
interim, **6(S)**, 339–40
offences, **6(S)**, 344
power to disapply provisions,
6(S), 342–3
regulations, **6(S)**, 343–4
non-resident parent, recovery from,
6, [471]
obligation, enforcement, **6**, [469], [505]
order—
calculation, relationship between,
6, [474]

child support—*contd*
  maintenance—*contd*
    order—*contd*
      court's powers, **6**, [472]
      meaning, **6**, [472], [474]
      person with care, against, **6**, [472]
    orders preventing avoidance, **6(S)**, 346
    overpaid, repayment of, **6**, [519]
    periodical payments, **6**, [473]
    power to treat liability as satisfied,
      6(S), 364
    recovery—
      authorisation of Secretary of State,
        6, [471]
      deduction from benefit, by, **6**, [521]
    regular deduction from accounts, order
      for—
        joint accounts, **6(S)**, 336
        offences, **6(S)**, 337
        power to make, **6(S)**, 334–6
        regulations, **6(S)**, 336–7
    role of the courts with respect to, **6**, [472]
    special cases, **6**, [520]; **6(S)**, 370
    voluntary payments, **6**, [504]
  meaning of "child", **6**, [534]
  non-resident parent—
    meaning, **6**, [468]
    recovery of maintenance from, **6**, [470]
  Northern Ireland—
    arrangements for, **31**, [1121]
    corresponding provision and co-ordination
      with, **6**, [535], [537], [568]
  parentage—
    declaration of—
      application for, **6**, [489]
      cases, within, **6**, [488]
    denial by alleged parent, **6**, [488]
    disputes about, **6**, [488]
    person with care—
      maintenance order against, **6**, [472]
      meaning, **6**, [468]
    scientific tests, fee for, **6**, [490]
  pilot schemes, **6**, [674]; **6(S)**, 376
  proceedings generally, right of audience,
    6, [528]
  qualifying child, meaning, **6**, [468]
  regulations, power to make, **6**, [530], [565]
  repealed provisions, **6(S)**, 329
  Scotland, provisions applicable, **6**, [537]
  Secretary of State, assessment by, **6**, [472]
  temporary compensation payment scheme,
    6, [673]
  voluntary payments, **6**, [504]

child tax credit
  entitlement, **40(2)**, [368]
  immigration control, persons subject to,
    40(2), [402]
  introduction of, **40(2)**, [361]
  maximum rate, **40(2)**, [369]

child-minder. *See under* **child**

child trust funds
  account provider, **6**, [887]
    information from, **6**, [899]
  accounts, opening, responsible person or
    child, by, **6**, [889]
  appeals—
    exercise of right of, **6**, [906]
    penalty, against, **6**, [904]
    rights of, **6**, [905]
  business, meaning, **43(S)**, 611
  children in care of authority, information
    about, **6**, [900]
  death of child, payments after, **6**, [902]
  eligible children, **6**, [886]
  friendly societies, involvement of, **6**, [898]
  generally, **6**, [1]
  inalienability, **6**, [888]
  Inland Revenue contributions—
    further, **6**, [894]
    initial, **6**, [892]
    recouping, **6**, [895]
    supplementary, **6**, [893]
  insurance companies, involvement of, **6**, [898]
  meaning, **6**, [885]
  opening by Inland Revenue, **6**, [890]
  penalties, imposition of, **6**, [903]
  regulations and orders, **6**, [911]
  requirements, **6**, [887]
  responsible person, management by, **6**, [887]
  subscription limits, **6**, [896]
  tax relief, **6**, [897]
  temporary modification of provisions, **6**, [907]
  terms of, **6**, [887]
  transfers, **6**, [891]
  use of information, **6**, [901]
  vouchers, issue of, **6**, [889]

childcare
  care, meaning, **44(2)**, [325]
  child, meaning, **44(2)**, [325]
  disabled child, for, **44(2)**, [325]
  employer-provided, exemption for,
    44(2), [323]
  exempt amount, power to vary, **44(2)**, [327]
  financial assistance, power to give, **6**, [967]
  provision other than by employer,
    44(2), [324]
  qualifying, **44(2)**, [326]
  qualifying conditions, power to vary,
    44(2), [327]
  qualifying vouchers, **44(2)**, [272]

children
  financial assistance—
    Secretary of State, from—
      delegation of arrangements, **15(2)**, [355]
      forms of, **15(2)**, [353]
      power to give, **15(2)**, [352]
      terms, **15(2)**, [354]
  seat-belts, wearing in motor vehicles. *See* **seat
    belts**

Children and Family Court Advisory and Support Service
accounts, **6**, [724]
ancillary powers, **6**, [724]
audience, right of, **6**, [692]
complaints, **6**, [724]
constitution, **6**, [724]
delegation, **6**, [724]
directions, **6**, [724]
establishment of, **6**, [688]
functions, **11(3)**, [373]
generally, **6**, [1]
inspection of, by Chief Inspector,
15(2), [857]
documents, **15(2)**, [859]
powers of entry, **15(2)**, [858]
litigation, right to conduct, **6**, [692]
meaning, **11(3)**, [373]
members, remuneration of, **6**, [724]
officers—
adoption agency records, right of access
to, **6**, [829]
appointment of, **6**, [356], [724]
cross-examination of, **6**, [693]
family assistance orders, for, **6**, [315]
local authority records, access to, **6**, [357]
rules of appointment, **6**, [828]
rules of court, **6**, [356]
terms and conditions, **6**, [724]
other powers, **6**, [690]
payments to, **6**, [724]
principal functions, **6**, [689]
procedure, **6**, [724]
property, transfer of, **6**, [695], [725]
protection of children—
disqualification from working with
children—
adults, **6**, [703], [705]–[707]
appeals against, **6**, [708]
court, at discretion of, **6**, [705], [707]
juveniles, **6**, [704]–[707]
Northern Ireland, in, **6**, [714]
offences, **6**, [712]
regulated position, meaning of, **6**, [713]
rehabilitation of offenders, **6**, [715]
restoration of disqualification order,
6, [711]
review of, **6**, [709]–[710]
Scotland, in, **6**, [714]
offence against a child—
equivalent armed forces offences,
6, [702]
meaning, **6**, [701], [726]
provision for, **6**, [699]
reports, **6**, [724]
services provision of, to other organisations,
6, [691]
staff—
appointment of, **6**, [724]
definitions, **6**, [694]
provision of, to other organisations,
6, [691]
terms and conditions, **6**, [724]
transfer of, **6**, [696]–[698]
status, **6**, [724]

Children and Family Court Advisory and Support Service—*contd*
supervision, **6**, [724]

children and young persons
congenital injury. *See* **congenital disabilities**
enticement actions, abolition, **45**, [954]
services of, abolition of action for loss of,
45, [983]
sex establishments, admission to or
employment in, penalties, **13**, [261]
video recordings, viewing of, advice as to,
13, [311]

children's car seats
reduced rate VAT, **50**, [149]

Children's Commissioner
accounts, **6**, [977]
annual reports, **6**, [921]
appointment, **6**, [977]
defamation action, protection from, **6**, [977]
establishment, **6**, [915]
evidence of documents, **6**, [977]
functions of, **6**, [916]
Northern Ireland, in, **6**, [920]
Wales, in, **6**, [919], [968]
funding, **6**, [977]
general powers, **6**, [977]
generally, **6**, [1]
inquiries—
holding, **6**, [917]–[918]
initiating, **6**, [917]
pensions, **6**, [977]
remuneration, **6**, [977]
reports, **6**, [916]
staff, **6**, [977]
status, **6**, [977]
tenure, **6**, [977]

Children's Commissioner for Wales
accounting officer, **6**, [666]
accounts, **6**, [666]
appointment, **6**, [666]
Assembly functions, review by, **6**, [646]
audit, **6**, [666]
care arrangements, review and monitoring
of, **6**, [647], [668]
Commissioner for Older People in Wales,
working with, **35(2)**, [602]
consideration and representation, additional
powers of, **6**, [650]
evidence, **6**, [666]
examination of cases by, **6**, [648]
functions of, **6**, [651], [919]
general powers, **6**, [666]
generally, **6**, [1]
obstruction of, **6**, [649]
office of, **6**, [644]
persons subject to review by, **6**, [668]
powers of entry, **6**, [968]
principal aim of, **6**, [645]
remuneration, **6**, [666]
reports, **6**, [666]
restrictions, **6**, [652]

Children's Commissioner for Wales—*contd*
review by—
Assembly functions, of, **6**, [646]
persons subject to, **6**, [668]
staff, **6**, [666]
status, **6**, [666]
tenure of office, **6**, [666]
use of resources, examinations into, **6**, [666]

children's home
accommodation in—
child requiring advice and assistance,
6, [329]
provision, **6**, [331]
boarding school as—
entry by authorised person, **6**, [415]
suspension of duty, **6**, [416]
inspection—
authorised inspectors—
appointment, **6**, [416]
duties, **6**, [417]
welfare of children, **6**, [415]
disqualified persons, carrying on or employed
in, **6**, [381]
appeals, **6**, [382]
employment in, disqualification from, **6**, [381]
appeals, **6**, [382]
establishments not being, **35(2)**, [280]
failure to comply with requirement, power of
Chief Inspector, **6(S)**, 462–3
inspection—
regulations as to, **6**, [450]
Secretary of State's powers, **6**, [409]
meaning, **35(2)**, [280]
notice restricting accommodation at,
6(S), 464
appeals, **6(S)**, 465
persons carrying on or managing, notification
of matters relating to, **6(S)**, 466–7
private, **6**, [1]
registered—
maintenance in, **6**, [375]
refuge for child at risk, as, **6**, [368]
registration and regulation. *See* **care
establishments and agencies**
school, status of, **35(2)**, [280]
welfare of children in, duty as to—
local authority, **6**, [378]
person carrying on home, **6**, [380]

children's services
assessment of, **6**, [935]
authorities—
children and young people's plans, **6**, [930],
[939]
information databases, **6**, [925], [942]
lead members, **6**, [932]
Local Safeguarding Children Boards,
functions relating to, **6**, [929], [947]
proper performance of functions, power to
secure, **6**, [962]
welfare, arrangements to safeguard and
promote, **6**, [924], [941]
well-being, co-operation to improve,
6, [923], [938]

children's services—*contd*
director—
appointment of, **6**, [931]
consequential amendments, **6**, [978]
functions, **6**, [931]
Framework for Inspection of Children's
Services, **6**, [934]
joint area reviews, **6**, [933]
meaning, **6**, [936]
Wales, in. *See* **Wales**

chimney
accidentally allowing to catch fire, **35(1)**, [15]
dark smoke, emission from. *See* **smoke**
furnace of, height of, **35(2)**, [14]–[16]
height of, **35(2)**, [14]–[16]
meaning, **35(2)**, [64]
raising, to that of adjoining taller building,
35(1), [595]
smoke from. *See* **smoke**

China Indemnity Fund
payments made from, **19(2)**, [790], [793]

**Chinese Government Purchasing
Commission**
constitution, **19(2)**, [791], [794]

chiropractors. *See also* **General Chiropractic
Council**
anti-competitive practices, **28**, [717]
appeals—
appeal tribunals, against decisions of,
28, [715]
General Council, against decisions of,
28, [713]
Health Committee, against decisions of,
28, [714]
Professional Conduct Committee, against
decisions of, **28**, [715]
Registrar, against decisions of, **28**, [712]
Code of Practice, **28**, [702]
competition, **28**, [717]
fitness to practise, **28**, [703]
general note, **28**, [1]
interpretation provisions, **28**, [725]
offences, **28**, [716]
post registration training, **28**, [700]
professional conduct, **28**, [703]
professional indemnity insurance, **28**, [721]
proficiency, standards of, **28**, [696]
qualifications—
recognition of, **28**, [697], [698]
withdrawal of recognition, **28**, [699]
register, access to, **28**, [692]
Registrar—
appeals against decisions of, **28**, [712]
appointment, **28**, [684]
duties, **28**, [684]
legal assessors, advice from, **28**, [710]
medical assessors, advice from, **28**, [711]
terms and conditions, **28**, [684]
registration—
conditional, **28**, [686]
error in relation to, **28**, [693]

chiropractors—*contd*
registration—*contd*
fraud in relation to, **28**, [693]
full, **28**, [685]
provisional, **28**, [687]
restoration to register, **28**, [691]
supplemental provisions, **28**, [689]
suspension of, **28**, [690]
temporary, for visiting chiropractors from
relevant European States, **28**, [688]
rehabilitation of offenders, exemption from
provisions about, **28**, [722]
transitional provisions, **28**, [726]

chloroform
using in offence, **12(1)**, [78]

cholera
notifiable disease. *See* **notifiable disease**

chorister
employed, child not deemed to be, **6**, [21]

chose in action. *See* **equitable interest and
chose in action**

Christ Church, Oxford
canon—
additional, **14**, 621
lay, appointment of, **14**, 1309
non-residentiary, **14**, 622
canonry, annexation of, **14**, 132
capitular reserves, charges on, **14**, 161–2
College of University, as, **15(1)**, [59]

chronically sick and disabled persons. *See*
disabled persons
invalid carriages. *See* **invalid carriages**

church
annual fabric report, **14**, 1218–19
Assembly. *See* **Church Assembly**
brawling in, **14**, 192–3
buildings, sharing—
agreements, **14**, 668–9
appropriate authorities, **14**, 679, 683
bishop, consent of, **14**, 669
cathedrals, **14**, 678
Charities Act, provisions of, **14**, 676
Church Commissioners, powers of,
14, 770–1
Church of England—
consecrated church, **14**, 673–4
extra-diocesan, **14**, 678
extra-parochial, **14**, 678
parish church, **14**, 673–4
peculiars, **14**, 678
churches applying to, **14**, 679
financial provisions, **14**, 671–2
management provisions, **14**, 671–2
marriage—
registration of, **14**, 674–5, 682
solemnization of, **14**, 674–5
pastoral committee, consent of, **14**, 669
residential, **14**, 676

church—*contd*
buildings, sharing—*contd*
seal, agreement under, **14**, 669
temporary loan of, **14**, 681
termination of, **14**, 677
trust, held on, **14**, 669–71
Wales, Church in, **14**, 674–5
worship, for purposes of, **14**, 673
centre for worship and mission, as, **14**, 1216
cessation of rights to, **14**, 219
closing, legality of, **14**, 1042
collegiate—
capital endowments, provision of, **14**, 769
meaning, **14**, 769
patronage, **14**, 133
Commissioners. *See* **Church
Commissioners**
communicants, **14(S)**, 98
conveyance of land for—
grant, form of, **14**, 243
life tenant, by, **14**, 245–6
person under disability, by, **14**, 242
powers, **14**, 240–1
public body, by, **14**, 245
purchase money, payment of, **14**, 241–2
corporation giving land for, **14**, 398
Council for the Care of Churches—
duties, **14**, 1366
list—
compilation of, **14**, 1366
effect of inclusion in, **14**, 1368–9
removal from, **14**, 1367–8
curtilage, unconsecrated land in, **14**, 640
demolition—
emergency, **14**, 1229
faculty for, **14**, 1226–8
deposit of articles in place of safety,
14, 1230–1
disposing of, legality of, **14**, 1042
exits, etc, **35(1)**, [549]
fabric, power of ordinary over, **14**, 193
fee simple, vesting of, **14**, 956
housing development, in, area of, **14**, 478
inspection—
archdeacon ensuring, **14**, 482
costs of, **14**, 482
parochial church council, where parish
without, **14**, 483
scheme for—
bishop's duty to establish, **14**, 481
generally, **14**, 479–80
service of notices, **14**, 483
valuable articles, **14**, 481
interment within, prohibition of, **35(1)**, [48]
inventory of articles, **14**, 1218
land granted for—
bodies having power of, **14**, 398
charge, subject to, **14**, 399–400
exercise of powers, **14**, 517–18
manor, common or waste of, **14**, 65, 399
sale of, **14**, 517–18
stamp duty, exemption from, **14**, 404
lands acquired for—
building or repairing, for, vesting of, **14**, 64
no longer required, when, **14**, 402–3

church—*contd*
  lands acquired for—*contd*
    powers, **14**, 397
    proceeds of sale of, **14**, 402
    stamp duty, exemption from, **14**, 404
  lands, drainage proposals affecting, **20**, [301]
  leasehold enfranchisement, **14**, 298–301
  loans for buildings, **14**, 478
  log-book, **14**, 1218
  meaning, **14**, 330, 1074, 1229
  new—
    church buildings closed for regular public
      worship, replacement of, **14(S)**, 158
    grant of land for, **14**, 1064
  parish. *See* **parish church**
  pews. *See* **pews**
  private and local Acts, affected by, **14**, 1078–9
  privately owned, vesting, **14**, 637–8
  redundancy scheme—
    amendment of, **14**, 1043–4
    appropriation, providing for, **14**, 1029
    consecration, removal of effects of,
      14, 1048
    contents of, **14**, 1033–6, 1050–1
    covenants in, **14**, 1049–50
    demolition, providing for, **14**, 1029, 1034
    draft, **14**, 1031–2
    easements, conferring, **14**, 1047
    land, providing for appropriation of,
      14, 1033–4
    procedure for making, **14**, 1031–2
    proceeds of sale, **14**, 1034
    right of way in, **14**, 1047
    site, use for, **14**, 1034
    transitional provisions, **14**, 1105–7
    trusts for repair, **14**, 1050–1
    unused since April 1964, where,
      14, 1039–40
    vesting of property, **14**, 1045–6
    waiting period, **14**, 1029–30
  redundant—
    Advisory Board for Redundant Churches—
      appointing, **14**, 1017–18
      body replacing, **14**, 1023–4
      members, **14**, 1100
    appropriation of, **14**, 1025–6, 1027
    Churches Conservation Trust, re-naming
      from Redundant Churches Fund,
      14, 1289
    Committee of Board of Governors of
      Church Commissioners on, **14**, 1020
    communion table and plate, disposal of,
      14, 1051–2
    compulsory purchase of, **14**, 1042
    contents, disposal of, **14**, 1051–2
    declaration of, **14**, 1001–2
    demolition of, **14**, 1025–6
    diocese, uses committee for, **14**, 1019
      members, **14**, 1100–1
    execution of works, **46**, [702]
    font, removal of, **14**, 1051–2
    fund. *See* **Redundant Churches Fund**
    guild church, **14**, 1077–8
    Historic Buildings and Monuments
      Commission, vesting in, **14**, 1054–6

church—*contd*
  redundant—*contd*
    human remains, disposal of, **14**, 1052–3,
      1102–3
    pastoral scheme, **14**, 1025–8
    proceeds of sale, **14**, 1034
    replacement of, **14**, 1026
    scheme. *See* redundancy scheme *above*
    Secretary of State, transfer to, **14**, 1054–6
    temporary maintenance account, **14**, 1067
    transfer of contents, **14**, 1030
  redundant, execution of works, **46**, [702]
  restoration of redundant building as, **14**, 1044
  reversionary interests, acquisition of,
    14, 299–300
  riot damage compensation, **33(2)**, [47]
  smoke control area, in, adaptation of fireplaces
    in, grants towards, **35(2)**, [25]
  terrier of lands, **14**, 1217–18
  Wales, in. *See* **Wales, Church in**

Church Assembly. *See also* **General Synod**
  constitution of, **14**, 295, 330
  Ecclesiastical Committee—
    meaning, **14**, 295
    measures to be submitted to, **14**, 296–7
    members, appointment of, **14**, 295–6
    procedure, **14**, 295–6
    quorum, **14**, 296
  Ecclesiastical Committee report of, **14**, 297
  establishment of, **14**, 295
  General Synod, reconstituted as, **14**, 686, 768
  Legislative Committee—
    meaning, **14**, 295
    measures, powers on, **14**, 296
  meaning, **14**, 295
  measures—
    Ecclesiastical Committee, submitted to,
      14, 296–7
    interpretation, **14**, 330–1
    Legislative Committee powers, **14**, 296
    meaning, **14**, 295
    Parliament dealing with, **14**, 297
    passing, date of, **14**, 332
    proof of, **14**, 332
    Royal Assent to, **14**, 297
    subject, matter of, **14**, 296

Church Buildings Council
  committees, **14(S)**, 198
  establishment of, **14(S)**, 173
  functions of—
    churches in use, as to, **14(S)**, 174–5
    churches proposed for closure, as to,
      14(S), 176–7
    general, **14(S)**, 177–8
  membership, **14(S)**, 196–8
  proceedings, **14(S)**, 198

Church Commissioners
  accounts, **14**, 425
    certain functions transferred, **14**, 1374
  amended provisions, **14(S)**, 101–2
  annual general meeting, **14**, 419
  annual personal grants, making, **14**, 838

Church Commissioners—*contd*
annual report and accounts, **14**, 425–6
archdeacon, sum towards stipend of, **14**, 841
Assets Committee—
   composition of—
      constitution, **14**, 421
      Estates and Finance Committee,
        replacing, **14**, 647
   procedure, **14**, 423
   management of, **14**, 1329
audit, **14**, 425
Audit Committee, **14**, 421
benefice, determining questions on, **14**, 1073
board of governors—
   chairman, **14**, 420
   constitution, **14**, 420
   functions, **14**, 420
   powers, **14**, 420
boundaries, determining, **14**, 1067–8
business, transacting, **14**, 419
capital, power to spend, **14**, 1400
casual vacancies, **14**, 430–1
cathedral—
   houses, grants for, **14**, 1355
   salaries, grant for, **14**, 1354–5
   stipends, paying, **14**, 1354–5
chairman of, **14**, 419
charitable trusts, dealing with, **14**, 407
church building, grant or loan for, **14**, 478,
   1182
Church in Wales, appointment of property
   of, **14**, 258–9
Church of England Pensions Board—
   directing, **14**, 535
   payments to, **14**, 957
Church of England pension schemes. *See*
   pension schemes
constitution, **14**, 429–30
contracts, taking over, **14**, 426
costs in ecclesiastical cases, paying, **14**, 599
curate, sum towards stipend of, **14**, 843
diocesan board of finance—
   loans to, **14**, 862–3
   substitution of in enactments, **14(S)**, 97,
     105–12
diocesan glebe land, approval of scheme for,
   14, 851–2
diocesan pastoral account, keeping. *See*
   diocesan pastoral account
diocesan stipend fund, keeping. *See* **diocesan
   stipends fund**
disqualification from being, **14**, 429
draft scheme or order by, **14(S)**, 104
ecclesiastical property, fee simple vesting in,
   14, 956
establishment of, **14**, 418
Estates and Finance Committee, replacement
   of, **14**, 647
Farnham Castle, powers relating to, **14(S)**, 94
financial year, **14**, 424, 955
functions, transfer to, **14**, 418–19
general fund—
   charges, extinguishing, **14**, 844
   Church in Wales, grant for, **14**, 286–7
   transfers to, **14**, 424

Church Commissioners—*contd*
general meetings, **14**, 420
glebe, information on given to, **14**, 858
grants or loans from—
   church buildings, for provision of, **14**, 1182
   Church Urban Fund, to, **14**, 1182
guaranteed annuities paid by, cessation,
   14(S), 43
Lambeth library, maintaining, **14**, 203
Lambeth Palace, preserving, **14**, 203, 336
land acquired by—
   churches, for, **14**, 397
   conveyance, sealing, **14**, 404
   disposal, power of, **14**, 402–3, 956
   vesting, **14**, 400–1
lands of new parish, rights of ownership
   over, **14**, 170
lay worker, sum towards stipend of, **14**, 843
loan by, repaying, **14**, 432
meaning, **41**, [605]
meetings, **14**, 423
mining districts, grants for cure of souls in,
   14, 196
mining subsidence, damage to property by,
   payments, **17(2)**, [20]
minutes of proceedings, **14**, 431
oath, administering, **14**, 90
officers, transfer to, **14**, 426
Order in Council confirming scheme of,
   14, 524
parsonages board, advising, **14**, 791
Pastoral Measure, amendment of, **14(S)**, 83–8
patronage, determining questions on,
   14, 1068
payments, enforcing, **14**, 136
pending proceedings, taking over, **14**, 426
pensions—
   capital, application of, **14**, 1317
   funded schemes, transitional grants from,
     14, 1317
   increasing, **14**, 521–2
   liability of, **14**, 1316
   payments for, **14**, 531
   rates of interest, altering, **14**, 544
persons being, **14**, 429
pews or sittings, surrender to, **14**, 217–19
procedure, **14**, 423
property—
   gift of, transfer of, **14**, 847–8
   holding, **14**, 398
   transfer to, **14**, 418–19
publication of notices, expenses of, **14**, 205
redundant churches temporary maintenance
   account, **14**, 1067
rentcharge, holding, **14**, 846
residence—
   consent to sale of, **14**, 379–81
   power to purchase, **14**, 431
   purchase of, powers regarding, **14**, 382–3
   sale of, interim income, accumulating,
     14, 387–8
retirement, notification of, **14**, 430
revenue exceeding statutory income,
   applying, **14**, 195
revenues of, applying, **14**, 137, 176

Church Commissioners—*contd*
sale of investments, authorising, **14**, 138
scheme—
  amending, **14**, 411
  endowments of see, for vesting, **14**, 409
  making, **14**, 139
  preparing, **14**, 90–1
  re-endowment of bishopric, for, **14**, 375
  stock transferred, registration of, **14**, 377
seal of, **14**, 424
sealing and execution of documents,
  14(S), 101
sealing of deeds by, **14**, 525
secretary, **14**, 424
securities held by, **14**, 395
sinecure rectories, vesting of endowments of,
  14, 136
Sodor and Man, stipend of bishop,
  augmenting, **14**, 819
solicitor to, savings for privileges,
  11(2), [369]; **11(4)**, [463]
standing orders, **14**, 423
statistical information, notice requiring,
  1(2), [145]
stipends—
  annuity towards, paying, **14**, 837–8
  paying, **14**, 411
  superannuation provisions, **14**, 427
sums available to, application of, **14(S)**, 44–5
superannuation benefits, **14(S)**, 75
Supreme Court funds transferred to,
  11(2), [880]
theological college, making loans for,
  14, 629–30
tithe, holding, **14**, 846
trusts—
  acceptance of, **14**, 243
  extinguishing of, **14**, 845
voting, **14**, 432
water resources, provisions as to, **49**, [1126]
witnesses, calling, **14**, 90

church electoral roll
addresses on, **14**, 699
alteration of parish boundaries, effect of,
  14, 701
enrolment—
  appeals on, **14**, 741–2
  application for, **14**, 755
formation of, **14**, 698–9
new parish, of, **14**, 699
new, preparation of, **14**, 700–1
  notice of, **14**, 757
number of names on, certifying, **14**, 702
officer of, **14**, 699
omission to make, **14**, 751
other parish, removal of name from, **14**, 701
parochial church council keeping, **14**, 699
persons entered on, **14**, 698
postal vote, application for, **14**, 759
publication of, **14**, 701
removal of name from, **14**, 699
revision of—
  annual, **14**, 700
  form of notice of, **14**, 756

Church Estate Commissioners
appointment of, **14**, 175–6
Audit Committee, on, **14**, 421
declaration, making, **14**, 176
first—
  appointment of, **14**, 175–6
  Assets Committee, on, **14**, 421
  salary, **14**, 176, 395
  transfer of land vested in, **14**, 522
pensions, **14**, 523
salary, **14**, 176, 395
second, **14**, 175–6
third, **14**, 522
transfer of stock, **14**, 522

Church of England. *See also* **church**
actual communicant member of, **14**, 753
Central Board of Finance. *See* **Central Board
  of Finance of Church of England**
deposit fund—
  accounts, **14**, 507
  Charity Commissioners, dealings not
    requiring consent of, **14**, 496
  constitution of, **14**, 506
  contributions to, **14**, 496
  income, application of, **14**, 507
  investment of sums, **14**, 506–7
  refusal or return of deposit, **14**, 507
  separate accounts, **14**, 507
  terms of deposit, **14**, 506
  winding up, **14**, 507
doctrine of—
  assent or subscription to, **14**, 814
  canon safeguarding, **14**, 814–15
furtherance of mission of, **14(S)**, 126
investment fund—
  accounts, **14**, 505
  Archbishops' Council, corporate funds of,
    14(S), 93
  borrowing, power of, **14**, 505
  Central Board—
    held in name of, **14**, 505–6
    jurisdiction of, **14**, 496
    replacement of, **14**, 505–6
  certificates as to value, **14**, 503
  certification of, **14**, 505
  Charity Commissioners, dealings not
    requiring consent of, **14**, 496
  common fund, administration as, **14**, 500
  constitution of, **14**, 499–500
  contributions to, **14**, 496, 500–1
  costs and expenses, **14**, 504–5
  distribution of income, **14**, 503–4
  income and capital apportionment of,
    14, 503–4
  investment of money, **14**, 500
  land, interests in, **14**, 496
  shares in, **14**, 500–2
  valuation of, **14**, 502–3
  winding up, **14**, 506
  withdrawals, **14**, 501–2
lay workers. *See* **lay workers**
legal aid. *See* **legal aid and advice**
liberties, confirmation of, **10**, [4], [18], [21]

Church of England—*contd*
Measures. *See* **General Synod**
monarch to belong to, **10**, [50]
National Assembly. *See* **Church Assembly;**
General Synod
Pastoral Measure, amendment of, **14(S)**, 83–8
Redemption Annuities Account, winding up
of, **14**, 1192
redundant buildings. *See under* **church**
securing, **10**, [50], [69]
training college, loans for, **14**, 341–2
worship in, provision by canon for,
14, 812–13

Church of England Pensions Board. *See*
pensions (ecclesiastical) church rate
audit of accounts, **14**, 214–15
compulsory, abolition, **14**, 214
default in paying, provisions on, **14**, 216
local Acts, made or levied under, **14**, 215
money due on security of, **14**, 214–15
parochial church council, powers of, **14**, 492
secular purposes, applicable to, **14**, 214
vestry, voting at, **14**, 215
voluntary, subscription to, **14**, 216

Church of Ireland
ministers of, **14**, 1308

Church Representation Rules
amendment of, **14**, 690, 1395–6
bishop, powers of, **14**, 751–2
commencement of, **14**, 768
effect of, **14**, 690
notices, **14**, 750
powers, **14**, 751
text of, **14**, 698–767

Church Urban Fund
grants or loans to, **14**, 1182

churchwarden
admission to office, **14**, 1387
annual fabric report, **14**, 1218–19
annually, chosen, **14**, 1385
bishop, powers of, **14**, 1389–90
choosing, **14**, 1385
disqualifications from being—
generally, **14**, 1383–4
six periods of office, after, **14**, 1384
existing customs regarding—
abolition of, **14**, 1390
meaning, **14**, 1391
fabric of church, duties as to, **14**, 1218–19
guild church, in, **14**, 462, 1389
information, recording, **14**, 1217–18
interest in trust, holding, **14**, 633
meeting of parishioners—
chosen in, **14**, 1385
convening of, **14**, 1386
meaning, **14**, 1386
number of, **14**, 1382
parish library, duty as to, **14**, 57
parochial church council—
acting for, **14**, 1071

churchwarden—*contd*
parochial church council—*contd*
member of, **14**, 711
parochial church meeting, elected at, **14**, 710
powers and duties, generally, **14**, 17
qualifications of, **14**, 1382–3
references to, construction of, **25(1)**, [76]
resignation of, **14**, 1388
term of office, **14**, 1387
transfer of powers of, **25(1)**, [77]
vacation of office, **14**, 1388

churchyard
addition to—
consecration of, **14**, 206
conveyance, **14**, 206
exclusive right of burial in, **14**, 208–10
vesting of, **14**, 207
closed, maintenance of, London, **25(1)**, [481]
exclusive right of burial, **14**, 208–10
new benefice, vesting in, **14**, 1088
ordinary, power of over, **14**, 193
pastoral scheme providing for, **14**, 1004
rights for sepulture, **14**, 641
sale of land for enlarging, **14**, 66
stamp duty, gift of not subject to, **14**, 207
timber in, felling, **14**, 789
trees, in, **14**, 219

cider
excise duty—
charge of, **19(3)**, [420]
rate, **19(3)**, [420]
repayment or remission on spoilt cider,
19(3), [423]
summary of provisions, **19(3)**, [349]
surcharges or rebates, **13**, [898]–[900]
importation, duty on, **19(3)**, [420]
made-wine, labelled as, **19(3)**, [414]
maker, registration of premises, **19(3)**, [420]
making of, regulation, **19(3)**, [420]
meaning, **19(3)**, [372]
perry, inclusion in meaning, **19(3)**, [372]
sale by retail, meaning, **19(3)**, [375]
sparkling, **19(3)**, [421], [471]
spoilt, remission of duty, **19(3)**, [423]
strong, labelled as, **19(3)**, [422]

cigarettes
sale to child under sixteen. *See* **tobacco**

cinema
dwelling houses, exhibitions in, **13**, [331]
exhibitions—
dwelling houses, in, **13**, [331]
exempted, **13**, [331]
licensing. *See* licences *below*
meaning, **13**, [334]
non-commercial, **13**, [332]
exhibitors. *See under* **cinematograph films**
private gain—
exhibitions not promoted for, **13**, [331]
promotion for, meaning, **13**, [333]
regulations, **13**, [331]

cinema—*contd*
sex cinemas. *See* **sex establishments**

cinematograph films. *See also* **obscene publications**
British company or partnership—
meanings, **13**, [336]
transfer of rights to, **13**, [336]
British Film Institute, Treasury, grants by, **13**, [114]
British films—
Certification, powers of Secretary of State, **13**, [338]
certification for film tax relief—
application for, **13**, [341]
disputes, determination of, **13**, [341]
grant, **13**, [341]
interim certificate, **13**, [341]
refusal or revocation, **13**, [341]
excluded films, **13**, [341]
makers, payments to, **13**, [337]
meanings, **13**, [336]
production, financial assistance, **13**, [337]
qualification as, **13**, [341]
regulations and orders, power to make, **13**, [341]
what constitutes, **13**, [341]
Cinematograph Films Council—
abolition, **13**, [335]
validity of acts, **13**, [335]
cruelty to animals, involving, **2**, [265]
educational, relief from customs duty for, **13**, [790]
exhibition. *See* **cinemas**
financial provisions. *See* **National Film Finance Corporation**
loans for production etc. *See* **National Film Finance Corporation**
master versions, expenditure on, **42**, [1495]
meaning, **35(1)**, [81]
National Film Finance. *See* **National Film Finance Corporation**
obscene, publication of, **12(1)**, [310], [311]
periods, allocation of expenditure to, **42**, [1496]
election against, **42**, [1498]
not applying, where, **42**, [1497]
preliminary expenditure, relief for, **42**, [1499]
premises where kept or stored—
alterations to, **35(1)**, [80]
fire in, prevention of, **35(1)**, [76]–[86]
fire resisting store-rooms, regulations as to, **35(1)**, [76], [85], [86]
general safety provisions at, **35(1)**, [76]
local authorities, duties as regards, **35(1)**, [79]
offences connected with, **35(1)**, [78]
production or acquisition expenditure, relief for, **42**, [1500]
properly intended for theatrical release, restriction of relief, **43(2)**, [122]
tax relief—
companies benefited by, exit charges—
chargeable event—
consequences of, **43(2)**, [624], [626]

cinematograph films—*contd*
tax relief—*contd*
companies benefited by, exit charges—*contd*
chargeable event—*contd*
occurrence of, **43(2)**, [623]
disposed rights, valuation, **43(2)**, [627]
exit event, meaning, **43(2)**, [623]
film rights company, meaning, **43(2)**, [623]
group, members of, **43(2)**, [628]
guaranteed income, **43(2)**, [623]
rights to, valuation, **43(2)**, [627]
income received on exit event, **43(2)**, [624]
relevant disposal at undervalue, **43(2)**, [625]
companies in partnership—
applicable provisions, **43(2)**, [348]
capital, **43(2)**, [349]
change in membership, **43(2)**, [349]
chargeable amount, **43(2)**, [348]
chargeable gains, relationship with, **43(2)**, [350]
definitions, **43(2)**, [348]
non-income amount, **43(2)**, [348]
total capital contributed, **43(2)**, [348]
deferred income agreement in respect of film, **43(2)**, [618]
entry into after relief claimed, **43(2)**, [620]
excess relief, **43(2)**, [620]
meaning, **43(2)**, [619]
transitional provision, **43(2)**, [622]
unconditional obligation to enter into, **43(2)**, [621]
individuals benefited by—
applicable provisions, **43(2)**, [337]
capital contribution to trade, **43(2)**, [339]
chargeable amount, **43(2)**, [337], [340]
exit event, **43(2)**, [337]
film-related losses, **43(2)**, [342]
losses claimed, **43(2)**, [339]
non-taxable consideration, **43(2)**, [342]
individuals in partnership—
capital contribution to trade, **43(2)**, [341]
losses derived from exploiting licence—
applicable disposals, **43(2)**, [346]
application of provisions, **43(2)**, [343]
definitions, **43(2)**, [345]
income tax charge, **43(2)**, [344]
meaning, **43(2)**, [343]
significant amount of time, meaning, **43(2)**, [347]
production and acquisition expenditure, relief for—
amount, restriction on, **43(2)**, [652]
circumstances, restrictions on, **43(2)**, [651]
disqualifying deduction, **43(2)**, [651]
film in production, meaning, **43(2)**, [653]
limited-budget, **43(2)**, [616]

cinematograph films—*contd*
　tax relief—*contd*
　　production and acquisition expenditure,
　　　relief for—*contd*
　　　　pre-announcement expenditure,
　　　　　meaning, **43(2)**, [653]
　　　　restrictions on, **43(2)**, [617], [651]
　　　　transitional provision, **43(2)**, [651]

Cinque Ports
　jurisdiction respecting, **25(1)**, [50]
　liberties and customs, confirmation of, **10**, [5]
　Lord Warden—
　　deputy, powers, **11(2)**, [10]
　　jurisdiction, **25(1)**, [44]
　　　boundaries of, **11(2)**, [12]
　　　salvage, as to, **11(2)**, [68]
　　powers of, **11(2)**, [11]
　Salvage Commissioners—
　　appeal from, **11(2)**, [8]
　　appointment, **11(2)**, [5]
　　oath to be taken by, **11(2)**, [7]
　　payment of, **11(2)**, [7]
　　pilots' claims, settling, **11(2)**, [6]
　　register, keeping, **11(2)**, [5]
　Winchelsea, status of, **25(1)**, [51]
　writs and judgments, execution of,
　　11(2), [67]

circus
　wild animals kept in, **2**, [412]

cistern
　insanitary, **35(1)**, [144]
　vesting in local authority, **35(1)**, [141]

citizenship. *See also* **British subject**
　abode, right of, **31**, [73]
　　deprivation of, **31**, [74]
　adoption, by—
　　British citizenship, **31**, [133]
　　British Overseas territories, **31**, [147]
　age, construction of references to, **31**, [180]
　armed forces, reference to members of,
　　31(S), Nationality 96
　birth, by—
　　additional grounds, former provisions,
　　　31, [61]
　　British citizenship, **31**, [133]
　　British Overseas territories, **31**, [147]
　　former provisions, **31**, [14]
　　late registration, former provisions,
　　　31, [28], [62]
　　members of armed forces, children born in
　　　UK to, **31(S)**, Nationality 87
　　ship or aircraft, abroad, **31**, [180]
　births, registration, application of provisions,
　　31, [169]
　British—
　　abandoned new-born infant, **31**, [133]
　　absence from UK or dependent territory,
　　　effect of, **31**, [184]
　　acquisition by Hong Kong resident. *See*
　　　Hong Kong
　　adoption, by, **31**, [133]

citizenship—*contd*
　British—*contd*
　　birth, by, **31**, [133]
　　British Indian Ocean Territory, mother
　　　born in, **31**, [361]
　　British overseas territories citizens,
　　　conferral on, **31**, [359]
　　ceremony, **31**, [170]
　　deprivation of—
　　　appeal, **31**, [168]
　　　former provisions, **31**, [31]
　　　grounds for, **31**, [167]
　　　powers, **31**, [167]
　　descent, by, **31**, [134]
　　　meaning, **31**, [146]
　　Falkland Islands. *See* Falkland Islands *below*
　　fees, **31**, [171], [179]
　　full capacity, waiver of requirement for,
　　　31, [174]
　　Hong Kong nationals—
　　　acquisition by, **31**, [201], [223]
　　　connection with, acquisition through,
　　　　31, [226]
　　　Governor, annual report of, **31**, [204]
　　　nationality provisions, **31**, [202]
　　　procedure, **31**, [203]
　　　requirements for, **31**, [223]
　　　selection schemes, **31**, [207]
　　　spouses and minor children, **31**, [208]
　　　treatment of, **31**, [224]
　　　war wives and widows—
　　　　acquisition by, **31**, [215]
　　　　descent, otherwise than by, **31**, [216]
　　　　UK settlement letter—
　　　　　meaning, **31**, [215]
　　　　　recipient of, as, **31**, [215]
　　naturalisation, by—
　　　generally, **31**, [141]
　　　requirements for, **31**, [184]
　　　timing, **31**, [172]
　　oath of allegiance, requirement and form
　　　of, **31**, [45], [170], [187], [485]
　　proof of, for entry into UK, **31**, [75]
　　registration, by—
　　　birth or adoption, acquisition by,
　　　　31, [133]
　　　British Overseas territories citizens,
　　　　31, [136]–[137]
　　　Community treaties, nationals for
　　　　purposes of, **31**, [140]
　　　Crown service, persons in, **31**, [127]
　　　deportation recommendation, effect of,
　　　　31, [127]
　　　effect of, **31**, [20], [127]
　　　minors, **31**, [135]
　　　outside UK, **31**, [19], [127]
　　　persons born between 1961 and 1983,
　　　　31, [139]
　　　persons without other citizenship,
　　　　31, [138]
　　　renunciation of UK etc citizenship,
　　　　following, **31**, [142]
　　　residence in UK, by virtue of, **31**, [127]
　　　timing, **31**, [172]
　　renunciation of, **31**, [144]

citizenship—*contd*
British—*contd*
resumption of, **31**, [145]
UK and colonies—
citizens of, at commencement of Act,
31, [143]
renunciation, following, **31**, [142]
British nationality by virtue of, generally,
31, [11]
British Overseas—
meaning, **31**, [180]
oath of allegiance, requirement and form
of, **31**, [170], [187]
registration, by, minors, **31**, [156]
renunciation, **31**, [157]
UK and Colonies citizens, as, **31**, [155]
British Overseas Territories—
acquisition, by connection with Hong
Kong, **31**, [226]
adoption, by, **31**, [147]
birth, by, **31**, [147]
citizens—
British citizenship, conferral of,
31, [359]
British Dependent Territories citizens
as, **31**, [358]
Hong Kong, connection with, **31**, [369]
deprivation of, **31**, [167]–[168]
descent, by, **31**, [148]
meaning, **31**, [154]
list of, **31**, [188]
meaning of dependent territory, **31**, [180]
naturalisation, by—
generally, **31**, [150]
requirements, **31**, [184]
oath of allegiance, requirement and form
of, **31**, [170], [187]
references to, **31**, [357]
registration, by—
list of rights to, **31**, [151]
minors, **31**, [149]
resumption of UK etc citizenship,
replacement, **31**, [151]
renunciation, **31**, [153]
resumption of, **31**, [153]
UK and Colonies citizens as, **31**, [152]
British protected persons. *See under*
nationality
ceremony, **31**, [187], [485]
certificate of, former provisions, **31**, [35]
Channel Islands, application of provisions,
31, [43]
child, relationship of parents and, **31**, [180]
children, welfare, duty as to,
31(S), Nationality 100
Commonwealth status—
countries to which applicable, **31**, [186]
former list, **31**, [11]
persons qualifying, **31**, [164]
criminal liability, limitation, **31**, [13]
former provisions, **31**, [13]
Cyprus, declaration by citizens as to,
31, [189]
deaths, registration, application of provisions,
31, [169]

citizenship—*contd*
deprivation of, **31**, [366]
colonies and territories, former provisions,
31, [32]
former provisions, **31**, [31]
restrictions on, former provisions, **31**, [63]
descent, by—
British citizen, meaning, **31**, [146]
British citizenship, **31**, [134]
British Overseas territories, **31**, [148]
British Overseas territories citizen,
meaning, **31**, [154]
Falkland Islands, **31**, [192]
former provisions, **31**, [15]
dual, renunciation by reason of, former
provisions, **31**, [29]
evidence of, **31**, [176]
former provisions, **31**, [37]
Falkland Islands—
acquisition of British citizenship—
birth or adoption, by, **31**, [191]
descent, by, **31**, [192]
effect etc of legislation, **31**, [193]–[194]
generally, **31**, [191]–[194]
false statements, penalty, **31**, [177]
fees, regulations as to, **31**, [169]
Ghana, cesser of application of provisions to,
31, [53]
Ilois, acquisition of British citizenship,
31, [361]
incorporation of territory, by, former
provisions, **31**, [22]
Isle of Man, application of provisions, **31**, [43]
kinds of, **31**, [1]
legitimated children, former provisions,
31, [33]
marriage—
British citizen, to, **31**, [67]
effect of, former provisions, **31**, [25],
[67]–[69]
minors, registration of—
British citizenship, **31**, [135]
British Overseas citizenship, **31**, [155]
British Overseas territories, **31**, [149]
former provisions, **31**, [18]
naturalisation, by—
application requirements—
family members, **31(S)**, Nationality 82–5
general, **31(S)**, Nationality 80–2
fee, **31**, [171]
former provisions, **31**, [21]
qualifications for—
ceremony, oath and pledge, **31**, [170],
[187]
former provisions, **31**, [21], [46]
qualifying period, **31(S)**, Nationality 85–7
summary of provisions,
31(S), Nationality 77
See also British; British Overseas territories
above
Northern Ireland, application of provisions,
31, [169]
oath, **31**, [187], [485]
offences and proceedings, **31**, [177]
former provisions, **31**, [38]

citizenship—*contd*
Orders in Council, power to make, **31**, [169]
orders, regulations and rules, former
provisions, **31**, [39]
pledge, **31**, [187], [170], [187], [485]
posthumous children, **31**, [178]
former provisions, **31**, [34]
qualifications for, former provisions, **31**, [21],
[46], [60]–[61]
registration, by—
additional grounds for, former provisions,
31, [60]
applications pending at commencement of
Act, **31**, [189]
British Nationals (Overseas) without other
citizenship, **31(S)**, Nationality 88
ceremony, oath and pledge, **31**, [170],
[187]
effect of, former provisions, **31**, [20], [179]
fee, **31**, [171]
female line, descent through,
31(S), Nationality 89–90
former provisions, **31**, [16]–[17], [54]
general provisions, **31**, [19]
good character requirement,
31(S), Nationality 91–3
Governors etc—
exercise of functions by, **31**, [173]
former provisions as to powers, **31**, [36]
High Commissioners—
exercise of functions by, **31**, [173]
former provisions as to powers, **31**, [36],
[55]
members of armed forces, children born
outside UK to, **31(S)**, Nationality 90–1
minors, **31(S)**, Nationality 88
See also British; British Overseas *above*
regulations, power to make, **31**, [169]
renunciation of, former provisions, **31**, [29],
[58]
residence—
in breach of immigration laws, **31**, [180]
registration by reason of, **31**, [127]
resumption of, former provisions, **31**, [57]
settlement in the UK, children of parents
having settled, **31**, [133]
summary of provisions, **31**, [1]
transitional provisions, **31**, [189]
UK and Colonies—
British citizens, **31**, [143]
British Overseas citizens, as, **31**, [155]
British Overseas territory citizens, as,
31, [152]
citizens of, at commencement of Act,
31, [143], [152], [155]
Cyprus citizens, declarations by, **31**, [189]
former provisions, **31**, [16]
Ghana, cesser of application to, **31**, [53]
meaning of citizen, **31**, [181]
renunciation, citizenship following,
31, [142]
replacement, **31**, [1]
resumption by British Overseas territory
citizen, replacement, **31**, [151]
transitional provisions, former, **31**, [23]

citizenship—*contd*
women—
marriage, former provisions—
British subject without citizenship, to,
31, [67]–[69]
effect of, **31**, [25]
See also marriage *above*

city
charter trustees, continuation of, **25(2)**, [577]
existing, preservation of rights etc,
25(2), [209]
freemen, rights etc, **25(2)**, [211]
inhabitants, rights etc, **25(2)**, [211]

city academy. *See also* **Academy**
Academies, conversion into,
15(2), [387]–[388]

city college. *See also* **Academy**
Academies, conversion into, **15(2)**, [389]
Academy. *See* **Academy**
financial provisions, **15(1)**, [609]
home-school agreements, **15(2)**, [111]
special educational needs, **15(1)**, [610]

City of London. *See* **London, City of**

city technical college
governing body—
exemption order from education legislation
requirements—
application for, **15(2)**, [342]
generally, **15(2)**, [340]
revocation of, **15(2)**, [341]
variation of, **15(2)**, [341]

civic restaurant
authority, meaning, **25(1)**, [371]
financial provisions, **25(1)**, [372]
provision of, **25(1)**, [371]

civil aviation. *See also* **air navigation;**
Airports Authority; carriage by air
accidents. *See under* **aircraft**
Act, extension of provisions outside United
Kingdom, **4(1)**, [156]
air traffic services. *See* **air traffic services**
air transport licensing. *See* **Civil Aviation**
Authority
Air Travel Trust—
contributions to, **4(1)**, [121], [122]
meaning, **4(1)**, [528]
reports, **4(1)**, [528]
variation of deed establishing, **4(1)**, [528]
airport capacity—
allocation of, **4(1)**, [270]
recommendations as to, **4(1)**, [308]
airport charges. *See* **airport**
authority. *See* **Civil Aviation Authority**
British airline, meaning, **4(1)**, [57]
byelaws, transitional provisions, **4(1)**, [176]
cargo, mail included in meaning of,
4(1), [153]
documents etc, production of, to, **4(1)**, [309]

civil aviation—*contd*
  extra-territorial provisions, **4(1)**, [175], [176]
  functions—
    advisory, **4(1)**, [271]
    airport capacity, as to, **4(1)**, [308]
    airport charges, **4(1)**, [276], [292]
    co-ordination with Office of Fair Trading,
      4(1), [295]
    generally. *See* **Civil Aviation Authority**
    matters to be regarded, **4(1)**, [271]
  highways—
    acquisition of land, **4(1)**, [100]
    stopping up or diversion, **4(1)**, [99]
  information to—
    default in giving, **4(1)**, [309]
    disclosure—
      restriction on, **4(1)**, [310]
      unauthorised, **4(1)**, [76]
    falsification, **4(1)**, [309]
    power to require, **4(1)**, [309]
  land—
    acquisition—
      aggrieved persons, **4(1)**, [164]
      air traffic services licence holders, by,
        4(1), [93]
      Civil Aviation Authority, by, **4(1)**, [92]
      compensation, **4(1)**, [165]
      compulsory, **4(1)**, [81], [91]–[93]
      local authorities, by, **4(1)**, [81]
      ownership, effect on, **4(1)**, [95]
      Secretary of State, by, **4(1)**, [91], [100]
      statutory undertakers, **4(1)**, [102]
        adjustment of functions, **4(1)**, [170],
          [171]
    apparatus on etc, restriction on, **4(1)**, [97],
      [99]
    cables, mains, pipes, etc, powers as to,
      4(1), [99]
    consecrated land and burial grounds,
      4(1), [105]
    control over, **4(1)**, [97], [167], [168]
    damage to, compensation, **4(1)**, [95]
    displacements from, **4(1)**, [103]
    easements or servitudes, creation of,
      4(1), [95], [165]
    entry upon, **4(1)**, [95], [101]
    local land charges, **4(1)**, [106]
    notices, service of, **4(1)**, [107]
    obstructions, control over, **4(1)**, [97]
    provisions relating to, construction,
      4(1), [152]
    right of way over, extinguishment,
      4(1), [97]
    rights over—
      acquisition of, **4(1)**, [95]
      Eurocontrol as authority, **4(1)**, [95]
      grantor's successors, effect on, **4(1)**, [94]
      proceedings for offences, **4(1)**, [95]
      Secretary of State, powers of, **4(1)**, [91],
        [163]
      stamp duty on conveyances, exemption,
        4(1), [109]
      survey, power of entry for, **4(1)**, [101]
      transfer to Civil Aviation Authority,
        4(1), [161]

civil aviation—*contd*
  land—*contd*
    rights over—*contd*
      use of, restriction on, **4(1)**, [96]
  lost property, provisions as to, **4(1)**, [302]
  Northern Ireland, application of provisions,
    4(1), [153], [155]
  notices arising, service, **4(1)**, [107]
  offences—
    alcohol and drugs, relating to—
      arrest without warrant, **4(1)**, [508]
      aviation functions, meaning, **4(1)**, [505]
      Crown, application of provisions to,
        4(1), [511]
      military application, **4(1)**, [512]
      penalties, **4(1)**, [506]
      prescribed limit, **4(1)**, [504]
      regulations, **4(1)**, [510]
      right of entry, **4(1)**, [509]
      specimen, provision of, **4(1)**, [507]
      territorial application, **4(1)**, [513]
      unfitness for duty, **4(1)**, [503]
    general provisions, **4(1)**, [148]
  Orders in Council, power to make,
    4(1), [151], [173]–[175]
  orders, power to make, **4(1)**, [151],
    [173]–[175]
  powers, exercise of, **4(1)**, [175]
  property, construction of provisions relating
    to, **4(1)**, [152]
  records and documentary evidence,
    4(1), [527]
  regulations, power to make, **4(1)**, [151],
    [173]–[175]
  Secretary of State—
    functions, **4(1)**, [54]
    information required by, **4(1)**, [135]
    land, powers as to. *See* land *above*
  security. *See* **aerodromes; aircraft**
  summary of provisions, **4(1)**, [1]
  territorial waters, application of provisions,
    4(1), [154]
  tidal waters, limitation on restrictions on use,
    4(1), [96]
  transitional provisions and savings, **4(1)**, [176]
  water, restriction on use of, **4(1)**, [96]

Civil Aviation Authority
  accounts and audit, **4(1)**, [68]
  advice, publication of, **4(1)**, [466]
  aerodromes—
    powers and duties as to. *See* **aerodromes**
    transfer to, **4(1)**, [161]
  air navigation functions—
    directions as to, **4(1)**, [444], [445]
    duty as to exercise of, **4(1)**, [446]
    information, obtaining, **4(1)**, [447]
    meaning, **4(1)**, [448]
  air services, charges for—
    amendment, **4(1)**, [450]
    amounts for recovery, **4(1)**, [454]
    chargeable services, **4(1)**, [453]
    commencement, **4(1)**, [450]
    detention and sale of aircraft, **4(1)**, [459]
    duties as to, **4(1)**, [455]

Civil Aviation Authority—*contd*
air services, charges for—*contd*
interpretation, **4(1)**, [460]
liability to pay, **4(1)**, [452]
offences, **4(1)**, [458]
publication, **4(1)**, [450]
records, **4(1)**, [457]
recovery of, **4(1)**, [452]
revocation, **4(1)**, [450]
Secretary of State, duties of, **4(1)**, [456]
specification, **4(1)**, [449], [451]
air traffic services. *See* **air traffic services**
air transport licensing—
functions, meaning, **4(1)**, [266]
general duties, **4(1)**, [116]
licences—
decisions, publication of, **4(1)**, [115]
grant and refusal of, **4(1)**, [113]
revocation, suspension and variation,
4(1), [114]
transfer, **4(1)**, [115]
movements, power to limit, **4(1)**, [269]
policies, periodical publication of,
4(1), [117]
regulations, **4(1)**, [115]
rules to be complied with, **4(1)**, [268]
statement of reasons, **4(1)**, [115]
unlicensed carriage, restriction of,
4(1), [112]
air transport services, modification of duties
with respect to British airlines, **4(1)**, [119]
annual reports by, **4(1)**, [74]
assets, transfer to, **4(1)**, [161]
assistance and advice, provision of, by,
4(1), [69]
borrowing powers, **4(1)**, [63]
chairman and deputy, **4(1)**, [55], [159]
charges by, scheme for, **4(1)**, [64]
Chicago Convention, duties as to, **4(1)**, [73]
competition functions—
Competition Act, under, **4(1)**, [464]
concurrent with Office of Fair Trading,
4(1), [462], [465]
Enterprise Act, under, **4(1)**, [463]
exercise of, **4(1)**, [465]
interpretation, **4(1)**, [461]
constitution, **4(1)**, [55]
corruption prevention, application of Acts,
4(1), [72]
debt assumed by, interest on, **4(1)**, [62]
directions to, **4(1)**, [468], [469], [480]
drainage of building of, **35(1)**, [583]
enactments applicable, **4(1)**, [72], [160]
environmental factors, consideration,
4(1), [58]
Eurocontrol—
application of provisions, **4(1)**, [77]
route changes, enforcement of foreign
judgments, **4(1)**, [123]
exemption from building regulations for
buildings of, **35(1)**, [530]
financial duties, **4(1)**, [61]
functions—
Crown, performance on behalf of,
4(1), [73]

Civil Aviation Authority—*contd*
functions—*contd*
generally, **4(1)**, [56]
performance of, **4(1)**, [159]
regulation, **4(1)**, [57]–[60]
Secretary of State, directions by, **4(1)**, [59]
special provisions as to, **4(1)**, [60]
supplementary provisions, **4(1)**, [73]
general note, **4(1)**, [1]
grants to, **4(1)**, [65]
information—
particulars required, **4(1)**, [135]
power to withhold, **4(1)**, [60]
provision of—
by, **4(1)**, [70]
for, **4(1)**, [135]
publication of, **4(1)**, [466]
land drainage affecting, **19(3)**, [259]
land—
powers as to. *See* **civil aviation**
provisions applied, **25(2)**, [450]
liabilities, transfer to, **4(1)**, [161]
loans to—
consent to borrowing, **4(1)**, [63]
Secretary of State, by, **4(1)**, [65]
Treasury guarantee, **4(1)**, [67]
meetings, quorum, **4(1)**, [159]
members—
appointment, **4(1)**, [55], [159]
declaration of interests, **4(1)**, [159]
number, **4(1)**, [55]
remuneration, **4(1)**, [159]
resignation, **4(1)**, [159]
tenure of office, **4(1)**, [159]
national interests, Minister's directions in,
4(1), [59]
national security nominee, **4(1)**, [443]
objectives in general, **4(1)**, [57]
officers and servants, appointment, **4(1)**, [159]
official secrets, application of Act, **4(1)**, [71]
orders and regulations, **4(1)**, [479]
Pension Scheme, **4(1)**, [472]
powers in general, **4(1)**, [73]
proceedings, **4(1)**, [159]
property, original transfer to, **4(1)**, [75], [161]
restrictions as to works by, **9**, [373]
revenue—
excess, application of, **4(1)**, [66]
obligation as to, **4(1)**, [61]
seal, use of, **4(1)**, [159]
staff—
appointment, **4(1)**, [159]
contracts of service, **4(1)**, [161]
matters affecting, **4(1)**, [161]
status, **4(1)**, [55]
statutory undertaker, as,
9, [417]. *See also* **statutory undertakers**
statutory undertakers, enactment relating to,
application, **4(1)**, [160]
transfer schemes—
accounting provisions, **4(1)**, [423], [424]
agreement, transfer by, **4(1)**, [496]
allocation, **4(1)**, [29]
certificates, **4(1)**, [496]
direction to make, **4(1)**, [419]

Civil Aviation Authority—*contd*
  transfer schemes—*contd*
    discharge of functions, **4(1)**, [496]
    division of property, rights or liabilities by,
      4(1), [418]
    documents of title, **4(1)**, [496]
    effect of, **4(1)**, [420]
    foreign property, rights and liabilities,
      4(1), [496]
    identification, **4(1)**, [496]
    interpretation, **4(1)**, [441]
    land, provisions concerning, **4(1)**, [437],
      [496]
    liabilities, extinguishment of,
      4(1), [433]–[435]
    matters transferred by, **4(1)**, [418]
    meaning, **4(1)**, [417]
    nominees, exercise of functions through,
      4(1), [438]
    obligations—
      enforcement, **4(1)**, [436]
      imposition of, **4(1)**, [418]
    proceedings, **4(1)**, [496]
    provisions, **4(1)**, [417]
    Secretary of State, by, **4(1)**, [421]
      information for purposes of, **4(1)**, [422]
    tax provisions, **4(1)**, [497]
    transferee companies—
      Crown shareholding, **4(1)**, [427]
      government investment in, **4(1)**, [426]
      grants to, **4(1)**, [430]
      guarantees, **4(1)**, [429]
      loans to, **4(1)**, [428]
      securities, issue of, **4(1)**, [425]
      shadow directors, **4(1)**, [432]
      trustee investments, **4(1)**, [431]

Civil Contingencies Fund
  Contingencies Fund, to be known as,
    19(2), [891]
  temporary increase of, **19(2)**, [819]

civil court
  armed force personnel in, **3**, [1]
  disposal of offences by, **3**, [904]
  financial penalty, enforcing, **3**, [1377]
  illegal absence, proceedings for—
    air force, **3**, [958]
    army, **3**, [685]
  jurisdiction of—
    air force offences, **3**, [902], [991], [1279]
    army offences, **3**, [719]
    naval offences, **3**, [1211]
    visiting forces, over, **3**, [442]–[443]
  meaning, **3**, [723], [995], [1223]

civil defence. *See also* **civil protection**
  emergency, meaning, **50**, [295]
  emergency powers. *See* **emergency powers**
  generally, **50**, [180]
  single framework for, **50**, [180]
  training, **50**, [242]–[243]
  volunteers—
    meaning, **33(1)**, [45]
    pension claim appeals, **33(1)**, [52]

civil defence—*contd*
  volunteers—*contd*
    personal injuries payments, **33(1)**, [42]

civil interests of servicemen
  agricultural holding, **3**, [405]
  business premises, security of tenure of—
    appeals, **3**, [412]
    compensation, claim for, **3**, [411]
    Crown property, application to, **3**, [413]
    further renewal, **3**, [409]
    Landlord and Tenant Act 1927, effect of,
      3, [411]
    landlord, meaning of, **3**, [414]
    mortgage, meaning of, **3**, [414]
    new tenancy—
      application for grant, **3**, [407]
      court, powers to grant, **3**, [408]
      premises comprised in, **3**, [406]
    partnership, **3**, [405]
    reversion itself a tenancy, **3**, [410]
    tenancy—
      expiring during service, **3**, [405]
      meaning of, **3**, [414]
  civil remuneration, making up—
    assimilation of, **3**, [422]
    capacity in which made, **3**, [438]
    civil occupation in forces, **3**, [420]
    coroner, **3**, [420]
    determining authorities, **3**, [419]
    generally, **3**, [418]
    paying authorities, **3**, [419], [438]
    probation committee, by, **3**, [421]
    remuneration, meaning of, **3**, [424]
    service pay, meaning of, **3**, [424]
    widow's benefit, **3**, [418]
  constable, resumption of service as, **3**, [433]
  employment, reinstatement. *See under*
    employment
  friendly societies, non-payment of
    contributions, **3**, [429]
  housing. *See* residence *below*
  legal remedies, protection against—
    application to exercise remedy, **3**, [388]
    appropriate courts, **3**, [391]
    conditional sale agreement—
      meaning, **3**, [434]
      provisions for, **3**, [390]
    enforcement, restrictions on, **3**, [388]–[389]
    exceptions, **3**, [388]
    execution of judgment, **3**, [388]
    failure to observe restrictions, **3**, [393]
    hire-purchase agreement—
      meaning, **3**, [434]
      provision for, **3**, [390]
    lease, provisions for, **3**, [390]
    liabilities, court to consider, **3**, [388]
    procedure, **3**, [391]
    property, relating to, **3**, [382], [388]
    relevant date, meaning of, **3**, [389]
    scope of, **3**, [389]
  licensed premises, tenancy expiring during
    service, **3**, [405]
  life policy, protection of—
    adjustment of rights, **3**, [427]

civil interests of servicemen—*contd*
life policy, protection of—*contd*
collecting societies, **3**, [425], [428]
endowment policy, **3**, [427]
friendly societies, **3**, [426], [428]
industrial assurance, **3**, [425], [428]
relevant premium, meaning of, **3**, [425]
writing-off time, **3**, [427]
Northern Ireland, provisions as to, **3**, [435]
relevant service, **3**, [437]
reserve forces, **3**, [1442]
residence, security of tenure of—
agricultural tenancy, **3**, [398]
board, letting with, **3**, [394]
employee, occupation as, **3**, [400]
end of tenancy, **3**, [396]
furnished premises, **3**, [395]
generally, **3**, [1]
Housing Act extending to, **3**, [396]
licence to occupy, **3**, [398]
men serving abroad, proceedings by,
3, [401]
period of protection, **3**, [394]
police serviceman, **3**, [398]
rent-free letting, **3**, [398]
rent payable, **3**, [399]
rented family home, **3**, [394]
shared accommodation, **3**, [397]
short period of training, during, **3**, [403]
statutory tenancy, meaning of, **3**, [402]
statutory undertaker as landlord, **3**, [400]
tenancy—
meaning of, **3**, [402]
qualifying for protection, **3**, [394]
service—
evidence of performance of, **3**, [431]
meaning of, **3**, [434]
serviceman, meaning of, **3**, [434]
short period of training, meaning of, **3**, [434]

civil jurisdiction Conventions
Note. The following entries relate to the
provisions implementing the Brussels
Convention on Jurisdiction. For entries
relating specifically to judgments, *See the*
main heading **judgments (Convention)**
allocation of courts—
company, proceedings involving,
11(2), [855]
consumer contracts, **11(2)**, [809], [855]
determination of, **11(2)**, [815]
examination as to, **11(2)**, [855]
excluded proceedings, **11(2)**, [816], [856]
exclusive jurisdiction, **11(2)**, [855]
general provisions, **11(2)**, [855]
legal person as defendant, **11(2)**, [855]
prorogation of jurisdiction, **11(2)**, [855]
protective measures, **11(2)**, [855]
provisional measures, **11(2)**, [855]
ship, matters relating to, **11(2)**, [855]
special jurisdiction, **11(2)**, [855]
trusts, **11(2)**, [809]

civil jurisdiction Conventions—*contd*
Brussels Conventions—
1968 Convention—
consumer contracts—
proceedings, **11(2)**, [848]
transitional provisions, **11(2)**, [848]
Denmark, ship's crew dispute,
11(2), [848]
duration, **11(2)**, [848]
EEC members required to accept,
11(2), [848]
entry into force, **11(2)**, [848]
examination as to, **11(2)**, [848]
excluded proceedings, **11(2)**, [848]
exclusive, courts having, **11(2)**, [848]
general provisions, **11(2)**, [848]
insurance, matters relating to,
11(2), [848]
Ireland, ship's crew dispute, **11(2)**, [848]
lis pendens, **11(2)**, [848]
maritime matters, in, **11(2)**, [848]
other conventions, relation to,
11(2), [848]
patent, on, **11(2)**, [848]
prorogation of, **11(2)**, [848]
protective measures, application for,
11(2), [848]
Protocol—
duration, **11(2)**, [849]
EEC members required to accept,
11(2), [849]
entry into force, **11(2)**, [849]
interpretation, rulings on, **11(2)**, [849]
ratification, **11(2)**, [849]
revision, **11(2)**, [849]
provisional measures, application for,
11(2), [848]
ratification, **11(2)**, [848]
related actions, **11(2)**, [848]
revision, requesting, **11(2)**, [848]
scope, **11(2)**, [848]
ship, matters relating to, **11(2)**, [848]
special jurisdiction, **11(2)**, [848]
Accession Conventions—
1989—
ratification, **11(2)**, [852]
text of, **11(2)**, [852]
1996—
ratification, **11(2)**, [853]
text of, **11(2)**, [853]
entry into force, **11(2)**, [850]
ratification, **11(2)**, [850]–[851]
scope, **11(2)**, [850]
Channel Islands, application of provisions,
11(2), [832], [843]
colony, application of provisions,
11(2), [832]
excluded proceedings, **11(2)**, [856]
force of law, having, **11(2)**, [799]
interpretation of, **11(2)**, [800]
Isle of Man, application of provisions,
11(2), [832], [844]
proceedings, staying etc, **11(2)**, [841]
reports on, **11(2)**, [800]
staying of proceedings, **11(2)**, [841]

civil jurisdiction Conventions—*contd*
consumer contracts—
appropriate court, **11(2)**, [809]
proceedings, **11(2)**, [848], [855]
Contracting States—
meaning, **11(2)**, [798]
persons domiciled in, suing, **11(2)**, [848]
domicile, determining. *See* **judgments
(Conventions)**
enforcement of judgments. *See* **judgments
(Conventions)**
examination as to, **11(2)**, [855]
exclusive, courts having, **11(2)**, [854], [855]
insurance, matters relating to, **11(2)**, [854]
interim relief—
arbitration proceedings, in, **11(2)**, [819]
doubtful jurisdiction, in case of,
11(2), [819]
meaning, **11(2)**, [820]
Order in Council, **11(2)**, [820], [822]
substantive proceedings, in absence of,
11(2), [820]
lis pendens, **11(2)**, [854]
Lugano Convention—
accession to, **11(2)**, [854]
admissibility, examination as to,
11(2), [854]
arrangement of provisions, **11(2)**, [854]
Brussels and other Conventions,
relationship to, **11(2)**, [854]
Channel Islands, application of provisions,
11(2), [844]
consumer contracts, proceedings,
11(2), [854]
domicile, law applying to, **11(2)**, [854]
duration of, **11(2)**, [854]
force of law, having, **11(2)**, [801]
implementation of, **11(3)**, [165]
interpretation of, **11(2)**, [802]
Isle of Man, application of provisions,
11(2), [844]
jurisdiction—
consumer contracts, over, **11(2)**, [854]
examination as to, **11(2)**, [854]
exclusive, **11(2)**, [854]
general provisions, **11(2)**, [854]
insurance, relating to, **11(2)**, [854]
prorogation of, **11(2)**, [854]
special, **11(2)**, [854]
lis pendens, **11(2)**, [854]
maritime matters, **11(2)**, [854]
parties to, **11(2)**, [854]
proceedings, staying etc, **11(2)**, [841]
provisional and protected measures,
11(2), [854]
related actions, **11(2)**, [854]
revision, requesting, **11(2)**, [854]
scope, **11(2)**, [854]
staying of proceedings, **11(2)**, [841]
text of, **11(2)**, [854]
transitional provisions, **11(2)**, [854]
uniform interpretation of, **11(2)**, [854]
prorogation of, **11(2)**, [854], [855]
protective measures—
application for, **11(2)**, [854]

civil jurisdiction Conventions—*contd*
protective measures—*contd*
doubtful jurisdiction, **11(2)**, [819]
Scotland, in, **11(2)**, [822]
United Kingdom, in, **11(2)**, [855]
provisional measures—
application for, **11(2)**, [854]
Scotland, in, **11(2)**, [822]
United Kingdom, in, **11(2)**, [855]
related actions, **11(2)**, [854]
torts to immoveable property, proceedings
for, **11(2)**, [824]
United Kingdom, persons sued in,
11(2), [855]

Civil Justice Council
establishment, **11(3)**, [225]
expenses, reimbursement of, **11(3)**, [225]
functions, **11(3)**, [225]
membership, **11(3)**, [225]

civil list
accounts, audit of—
examination on oath, **10**, [113]
instructions for guidance, **10**, [112]
officer to be appointed, **10**, [111]
statement, **10**, [114]
annual payment, **10**, [247]
charge of payments, **10**, [206], [220], [252]
children of George VI, provision for,
10, [203]
consolidated fund—
charge on, **10**, [210]
hereditary revenues, payment to, **10**, [213]
Duchess of Gloucester, provision for,
10, [248]
Duchy of Cornwall, **10**, [212]–[214]
Duke of Cornwall, provision for widow of,
10, [218]
Duke of Edinburgh, payment to, **10**, [215]
excess expenditure, **10**, [247]
expenditure, **10**, [247]
increase, power to, **10**, [249], [251]
parts of years, adjustment for, **10**, [207], [223]
pensions—
restrictions on grant, **10**, [117]
sum for, **10**, [116]
Princess Margaret, provision for, **10**, [217]
Queen Mother, provision for, **10**, [202]
retired allowances, **10**, [205], [219]
Royal Highnesses not provided for, **10**, [248]
royal trustees—
constitution of, **10**, [204], [221]
reports by, **10**, [250]
sums provided, **10**, [1]
supplements, **10**, [255]
tax, payments to be free from, **10**, [118]
widow of Queen's younger sons, provision
for, **10**, [248]
younger children of Elizabeth II, provision
for, **10**, [216]

Civil Nuclear Constabulary
chief constable—
annual report, **33(2)**, [515]

Civil Nuclear Constabulary—*contd*
chief constable—*contd*
appointment of, **33(2)**, [486]
assistant—
appointment of, **33(2)**, [486]
functions of, **33(2)**, [487]
deputy—
appointment of, **33(2)**, [486]
functions of, **33(2)**, [487]
functions of, **33(2)**, [487]
removal of, **33(2)**, [513]
suspension, **33(2)**, [513]
collaboration agreements, **33(2)**, [198]
Federation. *See* **Civil Nuclear Police Federation**
government, administration and conditions of service, **33(2)**, [490]
inspection of, **33(2)**, [495]
interpretation, **33(2)**, [506]
jurisdiction, **33(2)**, [489]
maintenance of, **33(2)**, [485]
members—
appointment of, **33(2)**, [488]
associations from which excluded, **33(2)**, [498]
attestation, **33(2)**, [488]
declaration, **33(2)**, [488]
disciplinary proceedings, representation at, **33(2)**, [499]
other forces, service with—
arrangements for, **33(2)**, [491]
charges for, **33(2)**, [493]
powers and privileges, **33(2)**, [491]
Serious Organised Crime Agency, **33(2)**, [492]
powers and privileges, **33(2)**, [489]
trade union, not to be member of, **33(2)**, [500]
offences relating to constables, application of, **33(2)**, [501]
planning, **33(2)**, [514]
primary function of, **33(2)**, [485]
rank-related organisations, **33(2)**, [498]
reports, **33(2)**, [515]
Secretary of State, directions by, **33(2)**, [516]
senior officers—
removal of, **33(2)**, [513]
suspension, **33(2)**, [513]
summary of provisions, **33(2)**, [17]

Civil Nuclear Police Authority
annual policing plan, **33(2)**, [514]
annual report, **33(2)**, [515]
Civil Nuclear Constabulary, allocation of functions to, **33(2)**, [485]
See also **Civil Nuclear Constabulary**
employees, **33(2)**, [510]
establishment of, **33(2)**, [484]
finances, **33(2)**, [511]
members, **33(2)**, [508]
orders and regulations, **33(2)**, [505]
proceedings, **33(2)**, [509]
seal, **33(2)**, [512]
Secretary of State—
directions by, **33(2)**, [516]

Civil Nuclear Police Authority—*contd*
Secretary of State—*contd*
supervision by, **33(2)**, [496]
status, **33(2)**, [512]
summary of provisions, **33(2)**, [17]
United Kingdom Atomic Energy Authority Constabulary, transfer scheme, **33(2)**, [503]

Civil Nuclear Police Federation
approval of, **33(2)**, [497]
function of, **33(2)**, [497]
representation of Civil Nuclear Constabulary, **33(2)**, [497]

civil offence
air force personnel committing, **3**, [799]
army personnel committing, **3**, [526]
guilty plea, reduction in minimum sentence for, **3**, [527], [1065]
life sentence, not passing, **3**, [528], [1066]
meaning, **3**, [723]
naval personnel committing, **3**, [1064]

civil partner's benefits
bereavement allowance—
application of provisions, **40(1)**, [274]
contributions credits, **40(1)**, [263]
entitlement to, **40(1)**, [279]
rate of, **40(1)**, [280]
bereavement payment, **40(1)**, [273]
retirement pension. *See* **retirement pension**
widowed parent's allowance, **40(1)**, [278]

civil partnership. *See also* **personal reliefs**
administration of estates, amended provisions, **27**, [899]
agreements—
generally, **27**, [127]
meaning, **27**, [769]
termination, effect on property, **27**, [770]
unenforceable, **27**, [769]
children—
ancillary relief for, **27**, [909]
financial relief for, **27**, [768]
orders affecting, restriction on making, **27**, [759]
Community obligations, **27**, [886]
connected persons, as, **44(1)**, [621]
declarations—
application for, **27**, [754]
Attorney General, papers sent to, **27**, [756]
before registration, **27**, [704]
form of, **27**, [757]
hearings, **27**, [757]
making and effect of, **27**, [755]
overseas relationships, **27**, [854]
proceedings for, **27**, [756]
rules of court, **27**, [757]
types of, **27**, [754]
definitions, **18**, [627]; **27**, [696]
dissolution—
absence of financial relief on, **18**, [614]
agreements as to, consideration by court, **27**, [563]
court, meaning, **27**, [850]

civil partnership.—*contd*
  dissolution—*contd*
    court powers available in, **18**, [622]
    desertion, period of, **27**, [742]
    financial relief. *See* financial relief *below*
    generally, **27**, [127]
    grounds for, **27**, [741]
    irretrievable breakdown, on, **27**, [740]
    non-recognition of, **27**, [865]
    order—
      agreements or arrangements,
        consideration by court, **27**, [739]
      applications, time bar on, **27**, [737]
      conditional, period before making final,
        27, [734]
      effect of, **27**, [733]
      power to make, **27**, [733]
      previous separation order, effect of,
        27, [742]
      proceedings before making final,
        27, [736], [744]
      Queen's Proctor, intervention of,
        27, [735]
      reconciliation, attempt at, **27**, [738]
    orders affecting children, restriction on
      making, **27**, [759]
    overseas relationship, proceedings for,
      27, [851]–[853]
    pension sharing order, **27**, [903]
    presumption of breakdown, facts raising,
      27, [741]
    proceedings, relief for respondent in,
      27, [758]
    property adjustment, **27**, [901]
    property involved, stamp duty on
      instruments, **41**, [150]
    recognition of—
      domicile, meaning, **27**, [864]
      grounds for, **27**, [862]
      other part of UK, obtained in, **27**, [860]
      overseas, obtained, **27**, [861]
      refusal of, **27**, [863]
      regulations, **27**, [864]
    refusal in 5 year separation cases on grounds
      of grave hardship, **27**, [743]
    restrictions in proceedings, **18**, [616], [618]
    rules of court, **27**, [760]
    sale of property order, **27**, [902]
    separation cases, protection for respondent
      in, **27**, [744]
    transfer of certain tenancies on, date when
      order made between partners to take
      effect, **27**, [690]
  dissolution or annulment, matters arising in,
    6, [234]
    Northern Ireland, in, **6**, [240]
  document—
    delivery to registrar, **27**, [703]
    meaning, **27**, [703]
    signature, **27**, [697]
  ending, **27**, [696]
  failure to maintain, financial provision on,
    27, [908]
  false statements, **27**, [771]

civil partnership.—*contd*
  family provision, amended provisions,
    27, [899]
  fees, **27**, [730]
  financial relief—
    arrears and repayments, **27**, [911]
    avoidance of transactions intended to
      prevent or reduce, **27**, [913]
    children, for, **27**, [909]
    consent orders, **27**, [912]
    magistrates' courts, in—
      agreed provision, orders for, **27**, [915]
      arrears and repayments, **27**, [920]
      commencement and duration of orders,
        27, [918]
      failure to maintain, **27**, [914]
      interim orders, **27**, [917]
      partners living apart by agreement,
        where, **27**, [916]
      supplementary provisions, **27**, [921]
      variation of orders, **27**, [919]
    maintenance agreements, **27**, [912]
    maintenance pending outcome of
      proceedings, **27**, [907]
    matters to which court has regard,
      27, [904]
    obtaining, **27**, [900]
    overseas dissolution, after, **27**, [922]–[924]
    pensions—
      benefits, orders relating to, **27**, [905]
      Pension Protection Fund compensation,
        27, [906]
    periodical and secured periodical payments,
      duration of, **27**, [909]
    proceedings, commencement of, **27**, [909]
    subsequent civil partnership or marriage,
      effect of, **27**, [909]
    supplementary provisions, **27**, [913]
    variation or discharge of orders, **27**, [910]
  formation of, generally, **27**, [127]
  further provision, power to make, **27**, [885]
  housing and tenancies, amendment of
    provisions, **27**, [925]
  immigration control provisions,
    27, [960]–[963]
  income tax liability, reductions for,
    44(4), [26]
  information on, obtaining, **40(1)**, [631]
  information, publicising, **27**, [706]
  life assurance premiums, **44(1)**, [642]
  nullity—
    court, meaning, **27**, [850]
    financial relief. *See* financial relief *above*
    non-recognition of, **27**, [865]
    order—
      affecting children, restriction on
        making, **27**, [759]
      conditional, period before making final,
        27, [734]
      effect of, **27**, [733]
      power to make, **27**, [733]
      proceedings before finality of, **27**, [736]
      Queen's Proctor, intervention of,
        27, [735]

civil partnership.—*contd*
  nullity—*contd*
    overseas relationship, proceedings for,
      27, [851]–[853]
    partnerships registered outside England and
      Wales, **27**, [750]
    pension sharing order, **27**, [903]
    property adjustment, **27**, [901]
    recognition of—
      domicile, meaning, **27**, [864]
      grounds for, **27**, [862]
      other part of UK, obtained in, **27**, [860]
      overseas, obtained, **27**, [861]
      refusal of, **27**, [863]
      regulations, **27**, [864]
    rules of court, **27**, [760]
    sale of property order, **27**, [902]
    void—
      grounds of, **27**, [745]
      Scotland, **27**, [776]
    voidable—
      bars to relief, **27**, [747]
      grounds of, **27**, [746]
  objection to, notice of, **27**, [709]
  overseas relationships treated as—
    certificate of no impediment, **27**, [867]
    dissolution, proceedings for,
      27, [851]–[853]
    fees, **27**, [870]
    general conditions, **27**, [127], [844]
    general rule, **27**, [845]
    meaning, **27**, [842]
    Northern Ireland jurisdiction. *See*
      Northern Ireland
    nullity, proceedings for, **27**, [851]–[853]
    Orders in Council, **27**, [871]
    person domiciled in UK, registered by,
      27, [847]
    presumption of death order, proceedings
      for, **27**, [852]
    public policy exception, **27**, [848]
    reference to, **27**, [696]
    registration certificate, transmission of,
      27, [868]
    same sex requirement, **27**, [846]
    separation order, proceedings for,
      27, [851]–[853]
    specified, **27**, [843], [957]
    validity, application for directions as to,
      27, [854]
  partners—
    actions in tort between, **27**, [765]
    assurance policy for benefit of, **27**, [766]
    employment field, discrimination in,
      27, [878]
    evidence, rules applying, **27**, [774]
    financial relief for, **27**, [768]
    gender recognition, **27**, [877]
    insurable interest in each other, **27**, [879]
    termination of agreement, effect of,
      27, [770]
  pre-registration procedure, **27**, [700]
  presumption of death order—
    conditional, period before making final,
      27, [734]

civil partnership.—*contd*
  presumption of death order—*contd*
    overseas relationship, proceedings for,
      27, [852]
    power to make, **27**, [733], [751]
    proceedings before finality of, **27**, [736]
    Queen's Proctor, intervention of, **27**, [735]
  proceedings—
    circuit judge, assigned to, **27**, [564]
    meaning, **6**, [238]
    principal registry of Family Division,
      commencement in, **27**, [571]
  property—
    disputes—
      applications in, **27**, [762]
      former partner, application by, **27**, [764]
      property not in possession, where,
        27, [763]
    improvement, contributions to, **27**, [761]
    property adjustment, **27**, [901]
    sale of property order, **27**, [902]
  property transfers in connection with, stamp
    duty exemption, **41**, [150]
  proposed, notice of, **27**, [704]
  recording, offences, **27**, [729]
  references to civil partners, **44(4)**, [1018]
  register of, **27**, [726]
  registered outside England and Wales, validity
    of, **27**, [750]
  Registrar General—
    licence, issue of—
      frivolous objection or representation,
        liability for costs, **27**, [722]
      objection to, **27**, [720]
      offences, **27**, [728]
      power of, **27**, [721]
    meaning, **27**, [726]
    special procedure, report under, **27**, [719]
  registrars, **27**, [725]
  registration—
    applicable period for, **27**, [713]
    armed forces personnel, by, **27**, [841]
      amended provisions, **27**, [971]
      commanding officers' certificates,
        27, [866]
      Commonwealth forces, **27**, [869]
    authority—
      evidence of name, etc, power to
        require, **27**, [705]
      meaning, **27**, [724]
      notice to, **27**, [704]
      relevant, meaning, **27**, [697]
    British consulates, etc, at, **27**, [840]
    certificates of no impediment, Scotland,
      27, [775]
    civil, assimilation of provisions, **27**, [731]
    detained persons, procedure for, **27**, [715]
    eligibility, **27**, [698]
    formation by, **27**, [697]
    former spouses, one of whom has changed
      sex, by, **27**, [897]
    generally, **27**, [127]
    house-bound persons, procedure for,
      27, [714]

civil partnership.—*contd*
registration—*contd*
  non-residents, modified procedure for,
    27, [716]
  Northern Ireland, in. *See* **Northern**
    Ireland
  place of, **27**, [701]–[702]
  prohibited degrees of relationship,
    27, [698], [891]–[892]
  proposed civil partner under 18, parental
    etc consent to—
    appropriate persons, determining,
      27, [699], [893]
    court, provisions relating to, **27**, [896]
    obtaining, **27**, [894]
    requirement of, **27**, [699]
    special procedure, **27**, [895]
  recording, **27**, [697]
  regulations and orders, **27**, [732]
  religious premises, not to be in, **27**, [701]
  special procedure. *See* special procedure
    below
regulations and orders, **27**, [884]
relationships arising through—
  child support, **27**, [880]
  pensions provisions, power to amend,
    27, [881], [970]
  social security provisions, **27**, [880],
    [964]–[966]
  stepchildren, references to, **27**, [873]–[874],
    [958]–[959]
  tax credits, **27**, [880], [969]
schedule, issue of—
  duty of, **27**, [710]
  frivolous objection or representation,
    liability for costs, **27**, [712]
  objection to, **27**, [711]
  offences, **27**, [727]
  refusal, appeal against, **27**, [711]
separation order—
  agreements or arrangements, consideration
    by court, **27**, [739]
  application for, **27**, [752]
  court, meaning, **27**, [850]
  effect of, **27**, [753]
  maintenance pending outcome of
    proceedings, **27**, [907]
  orders affecting children, restriction on
    making, **27**, [759]
  overseas relationship, proceedings for,
    27, [851]–[853]
  power to make, **27**, [733]
  recognition of—
    domicile, meaning, **27**, [864]
    grounds for, **27**, [862]
    other part of UK, obtained in, **27**, [860]
    overseas, obtained, **27**, [861]
    refusal of, **27**, [863]
    regulations, **27**, [864]
  reconciliation, attempt at, **27**, [738]
  rules of court, **27**, [760]
  subsequent dissolution order, not
    precluding, **27**, [742]
sex change of one party, marriage following,
  27, [249]

civil partnership.—*contd*
special procedure—
  evidence to be produced, **27**, [718]
  licence, issue of—
    frivolous objection or representation,
      liability for costs, **27**, [722]
    objection to, **27**, [720]
    offences, **27**, [728]
    power of, **27**, [721]
  notice of proposed partnership, **27**, [717]
  one partner seriously ill and not expected
    to recover, where, **27**, [718]
  Registrar General, report to, **27**, [719]
  registration, period for, **27**, [723]
suspicious, duty to report, **31**, [250]
validation, power of, **27**, [749]
validity—
  declarations, **27**, [754]–[757]
  partnerships registered outside England and
    Wales, **27**, [750]
  proof of matters not necessary to, **27**, [748]
void—
  grounds of, **27**, [745]
  partnerships registered outside England and
    Wales, **27**, [750]
  Scotland, **27**, [776]
voidable—
  bars to relief, **27**, [747]
  grounds of, **27**, [746]
  partnerships registered outside England and
    Wales, **27**, [750]
waiting period—
  information, publicising, **27**, [706]
  meaning, **27**, [707]
  power to shorten, **27**, [708]
wills, **27**, [898]
  dissolution or annulment, effect of,
    50, [499]
  revoked by, **50**, [498]

civil partnership causes
child, county court jurisdiction, **27**, [562]
circuit judge, jurisdiction of, **27**, [564]
county court, jurisdiction of, **27**, [561]
financial provision order, county court's
  jurisdiction, **27**, [562]

civil partnership home
occupation orders—
  agreement to form, evidence of, **27**, [659]
  ex parte orders, **27**, [660]

civil prison
absentee, receiving—
  air force, **3**, [961]
  army, **3**, [688]
deserter, receiving—
  air force, **3**, [961]
  army, **3**, [688]
governor's duties, **3**, [625], [898], [1184]
meaning, **3**, [640], [913], [1223]
sentence served in—
  air force, **3**, [894]
  army, **3**, [621]
  navy, **3**, [1158]

civil procedure
Civil Justice Council. *See* **Civil Justice Council**
court orders—
disclosure of documents before action begun, **11(3)**, [227]
preserving evidence, power to make orders for, **11(3)**, [226]
interpretation provisions, **11(3)**, [228]
Rules—
Committee, **11(3)**, [220]–[221]
different cases, different provision for, **11(3)**, [231]
evidence, **11(3)**, [231]
former rules, matters dealt with by, **11(3)**, [231]
generally, **11(3)**, [219]
jurisdiction, exercise of, **11(3)**, [231]
made on request of Lord Chancellor, **11(3)**, [222A]
orders, power to make, **11(3)**, [221]
other rules, application of, **11(3)**, [231]
power to make, **11(3)**, [398]
practice directions, **11(3)**, [224], [231]
proceedings, removal of, **11(3)**, [231]
process for making, **11(3)**, [399]
statutory instrument, contained in, **11(3)**, [222]

civil proceedings
Crown, by or against. *See* **Crown**
evidence in. *See* **evidence**
meaning, **13**, [26], [38]

civil protection. *See also* **civil defence**
contingency planning—
duties as to, **50**, [296]
guidance, issue of, **50**, [296]–[297]
public, advice and assistance to, **50**, [298]
emergency—
guidance regarding, **50**, [296]–[297]
public, to, **50**, [298]
plans to prevent, **50**, [296]
risk of, assessing, **50**, [296]
enforcement of provisions, **50**, [303]
general measures, **50**, [299]
information, disclosure of, **50**, [300], [304]
list of responders—
amendment of, **50**, [305]
category 1—
functions provided, **50**, [329]
meaning, **50**, [329]
monitoring of, **50**, [302]
category 2—
meaning, **50**, [330]
monitoring of, **50**, [302]
emergency powers. *See* **emergency powers**
National Assembly for Wales, consultation with, **50**, [308]
regulations and orders, **50**, [309]
repeals, **50**, [331], [333]
Scotland—
consultation with ministers, **50**, [306]
cross-border collaboration, **50**, [307]
urgency, directions made in, **50**, [301]

civil rights
armed force personnel having, **3**, [1]

civil servant
disclosure of information by, unauthorised, **6**, [529]

civil service
aliens, employment of, **31**, [7], [50]
home—
delegation of functions, **10**, [740]
exercise of functions without approval, authorisation of, **10**, [741]
Northern Ireland, legislation, **10**, [742]
Scottish, **10**, [1362]

civil service pension
administrative expenses, **33(1)**, [140]
bankruptcy, payment to trustee in, **33(1)**, [126]
benefits not assignable, **33(1)**, [126]
deceased persons, payments due to, **33(1)**, [125]
probate, dispensing with, **33(1)**, [125]
employment—
approved, **33(1)**, [83]
kinds of, **33(1)**, [89]
more than one public office, in—
bodies to which provisions apply, **33(1)**, [81]
meaning of public office, **33(1)**, [81]
rules as to pensions, **33(1)**, [80]
enactments, power to amend, **33(1)**, [127]
existing provisions, **33(1)**, [144]–[145]
incapacity, for, **33(1)**, [123]
increase. *See* **pension**
injury allowance—
damages, award of, effect, **33(1)**, [124]
provisions as to, **33(1)**, [124]
recovery, circumstances for, **33(1)**, [124]
judicial offices, **33(1)**, [82]
loss of office, in respect of, **33(1)**, [123]
meaning of civil service, **33(1)**, [86]
ministerial functions, **33(1)**, [122]
scheme—
additional provisions of, **33(1)**, [123]
administration etc, **33(1)**, [122]
authorised provider, meaning, **33(1)**, [122]
consultations on making, **33(1)**, [122]
employments covered by, **33(1)**, [122], [143]
power to add to, **33(1)**, [122]
incapacitation or death, **33(1)**, [123]
injury etc, providing for, **33(1)**, [124]
laying before parliament, **33(1)**, [123]
questions as to, determining, **33(1)**, [123]
regulations, **33(1)**, [104]
retrospective effect, **33(1)**, [123]
summary of provisions, **33(1)**, [25]
Scottish Parliamentary Corporate Body, delegation of ministerial functions to, **33(1)**, [122]
transitional provisions, **33(1)**, [149]

civil trial
  court-martial, and, **3**, [629]
  proof of outcome—
    air force, **3**, [973]
    army, **3**, [700]
    navy, **3**, [1213]

civilian
  Army Act, application to, **3**, [712], [729]
  court martial—
    appeal, **3**, [1296]
    navy
      community supervision orders, **3**, [1232]
      compensation orders, **3**, [1232]
      custodial orders, **3**, [1232]
      discharge, **3**, [1232]
      jurisdiction, **3**, [1172]
      parents and guardians, orders against,
        3, [1232]
      powers, **3**, [1232]
      punishments and orders, **3**, [1232]
      seduction from duty, for, **3**, [1171]
      spying, for, **3**, [1170]
    reference to Appeal Court, **3**, [1328]
    right to elect, **3**, [1381]
  injury in warlike operations, **3**, [269]
  Naval Discipline Act, application to, **3**, [1231]
  naval law, subject to, **3**, [1195]
  Standing Civilian Court—
    appeal, **3**, [1381]
    assessors, **3**, [1381]
    custody in connection with trial by,
      3, [547], [726], [820], [998]
    decisions of, **3**, [1381]
    definitions, **3**, [1381]
    evidence, rules of, **3**, [1381]
    generally, **3**, [1371], [1381]
    jurisdiction, **3**, [1372]
    powers of, **3**, [1373]
    public, to be in, **3**, [1381]
    punishments, **3**, [1373]
    re-trial, **3**, [1381]
    rules of procedure, **3**, [1381]
    sentence—
      commencement, **3**, [1381]
      duration, **3**, [1381]
      review, **3**, [1381]
      suspending, **3**, [1381], [1507]
    sittings, **3**, [1381]
    unfit to stand trial, **3**, [1381]
    witness, privilege of, **3**, [1381]
  summary fines, level of, **3**, [1276]
  trial of—
    community supervision order, **3**, [730],
      [1002]
    compensation orders, **3**, [730], [1002]
    custodial orders, **3**, [730], [1002]
    discharge, **3**, [730], [1002]
    fines, **3**, [730]
      parents, on, **3**, [1002]
    generally, **3**, [730], [1002]
    punishments and orders, **3**, [730], [1002]
    recognisance of parent or guardian,
      3, [730], [1002]
    sentence, deferment of award of, **3**, [1002]

civilian—*contd*
  visiting force, component of, **3**, [449]

civilian enforcement officer
  meaning, **11(2)**, [547]
  powers of, **11(2)**, [549], [583]
  warrant, execution of, **11(2)**, [547]

claims management services
  regulated services—
    exemption from, **11(3)**, [636]
    offences, **11(3)**, [637], [641]
    provision of, **11(3)**, [634]
    the Regulator, **11(3)**, [635], [638]–[640],
      [649]

Claims Management Services Tribunal
  appeals and references to, **11(3)**, [643]
  establishment, **11(3)**, [642]

class rights. *See* **shares**

clean air. *See* **dust; furnace; smoke**

cleansing station
  provision for cleansing verminous persons
    etc, **35(1)**, [138]

clearance area
  acquired houses—
    repair and management, **22**, [260]
    retention of, **22**, [259]
  acquisition of land in, **22**, [249]
    discontinuance of proceedings for,
      22, [251]
  compensation for loss of rights, **22**, [254]
  condemned houses—
    capable of being made fit, **22**, [260]
    reconstruction, **22**, [245]
    repair and management, **22**, [260]
    use for temporary accommodation,
      22, [258]
  declaration of—
    conditions for, **22**, [248]
    notices, service of, **22**, [248]
    resolution for, **22**, [248]
  definition on map, **22**, [248]
  demolition in, time for, **22**, [250]
  distinct areas in, **22**, [248]
  easements etc, extinguishment, **22**, [254]
  land—
    acquired, dealing with, **22**, [250]
    adjoining, purchase of, **22**, [249]
    housing authority, of, inclusion in,
      22, [252]
  listed buildings in, **22**, [263], [264]
  meaning, **22**, [248]
  methods of clearing, **22**, [250]
  re-development by owner—
    consideration of proposals for, **22**, [268]
    proposals for, approval of, **22**, [266]
    recovery of possession for, **22**, [267]
  rights of way, extinguishment, **22**, [253]
  shop-keepers in, compensation to, **22**, [400]

clearance area—*contd*
  statutory undertakers—
    apparatus—
      meaning, **22**, [255]
      notice of intent to remove etc, **22**, [256]
      removal or alteration, **22**, [255]
      requirements by undertakers, **22**, [256]
    meaning, **22**, [255]
    rights of, saving for, **22**, [255]
    telecommunications apparatus in, **22**, [257]

clearance services
  chargeable securities—
    instalments, payment by, **41**, [190]
    interpretation, **41**, [196]
    meaning, **41**, [196]
    meanings excluded, **41**, [196]
    stamp duty reserve tax, **41**, [190]
      alternative system of charge, election
        for, **41**, [193]
      depositary receipt system, transfer with,
        41, [194]
      exclusions, **41**, [191], [192]
    value of, **41**, [190]
  depositary receipt systems, transfers with,
    41, [165]
  provision of, notification of, **41**, [163], [210]
  relevant securities—
    instalments, payment by, **41**, [162]
    meaning, **41**, [163]
    notification requirements, **41**, [164]
    stamp duty as to, **41**, [162]
    value of, **41**, [162], [164]
  stamp duty abolition, when applicable,
    41, [210]

clearing house
  recognised, composition by, transfer duty,
    41, [124]
  transfer to—
    stamp duty exemption, **41**, [174], [219]
    stamp duty reserve tax exemption,
      41, [220]

clergy. *See also* **deacon**, *etc*
  assault on, **12(1)**, [92]
  bishop. *See* **bishop**
  clergyman, meaning, **36**, [68]
  compensation—
    amended provisions, **14(S)**, 180–1
    amount of, **14**, 1095–6
    appeal tribunal, **14**, 1097–8
    entitlement, **14**, 1095–6
    office, disclosure of, **14**, 1096
    payment of, **14**, 1098
    retiring age, effect of, **14**, 1096–7
    right to, **14**, 999
    sums comprising, **14**, 1096
    suspension of, **14**, 1096
  criminal convictions and arrests, duty to
    disclose, **14(S)**, 26
  disciplinary proceedings—
    appeal, right of, **14(S)**, 16
    complaint—
      bishop, courses available to, **14(S)**, 11

clergy—*contd*
  disciplinary proceedings—*contd*
    complaint—*contd*
      formal investigations, **14(S)**, 14
      institution by, **14(S)**, 8–9
      no further action on, **14(S)**, 11
      preliminary scrutiny of, **14(S)**, 10
    conciliation, **14(S)**, 12–13
    conditional deferment, **14(S)**, 12
    conduct of, **14(S)**, 14–15
    criminal convictions and arrests, duty to
      disclose, **14(S)**, 26
    institution—
      complaint, by, **14(S)**, 8–9
      limitation of time for, **14(S)**, 8
    misconduct, **14(S)**, 7
    provisions of 1963 Measure, application
      of, **14(S)**, 27–8
    regulation of, **14(S)**, 6
    secular courts, in—
      imprisonment and matrimonial orders,
        effect of, **14(S)**, 23–4, 26
      penalties, consequences of, **14(S)**, 26
    standard of proof, **14(S)**, 15
    suspension during, **14(S)**, 28–9
  disciplinary tribunals—
    composition, **14(S)**, 18
    constitution, **14(S)**, 2
    jurisdiction, **14(S)**, 5–6
    members of, **14(S)**, 18
    president, **14(S)**, 4
    provincial panels, **14(S)**, 17
    registrar, **14(S)**, 4
    Vicar-General's court, **14(S)**, 5, 19
  discipline—
    amended Measures, **14(S)**, 36, 39–40
    bishop, role of, **14(S)**, 2
    Clergy Discipline Commission. *See* **Clergy
      Discipline Commission**
    Code of Practice, formulation of, **14(S)**, 31
    conclusive, convictions etc deemed to be,
      14(S), 32
    deposition, removal of, **14(S)**, 21
    interpretation, **14(S)**, 34–5
    limited prohibition—
      imposition of, **14(S)**, 20
      removal of, **14(S)**, 22
    list, archbishop keeping, **14(S)**, 30–1
    misconduct, **14(S)**, 7
    pardon, restoration of position on,
      14(S), 22
    penalties—
      conditional discharge, **14(S)**, 21
      consent, by, **14(S)**, 13
      disobedience to, **14(S)**, 23
      imposition of, **14(S)**, 15
      prohibition for life, **14(S)**, 13
      revoked, compensation for, **14(S)**, 33
      types of, **14(S)**, 20
    proceedings. *See* disciplinary proceedings
      above
    prohibition for life—
      imposition of, **14(S)**, 13, 20
      removal of, **14(S)**, 21
    rules, **14(S)**, 36–7

clergy—*contd*
  discipline—*contd*
    special cases, **14(S)**, 33
    transitional provisions, **14(S)**, 37
    tribunals. *See* disciplinary tribunals *above*
  divorce and separation orders, duty to
    disclose, **14(S)**, 27
  doctrine of Church of England, assent to,
    14, 814
  farm, taking for occupation, **14**, 99–100
  fees, etc, recovery of, **14**, 124
  group ministry. *See under* **incumbent**
  house not belonging to benefice, residing in,
    14, 102–3
  house of. *See* **General Synod**
  House of Commons, removal of
    disqualification from, **32**, [986]
  illegal trading by, **14**, 101–2
  ministry overseas, for, **14**, 659
  offences by. *See* **ecclesiastical offences**
  other churches, of, officiating, **14**, 658
  overseas—
    exercise of ministry by, **14**, 1185–6
    meaning, **14**, 660
    oath of allegiance, dispensing with, **14**, 658
    permission to officiate, **14**, 657
  penalties, recovery of, **14**, 123
  pensions. *See* **pensions (ecclesiastical)**
  permitted occupations, **14**, 101
  residence—
    building or repairing, vesting of lands for,
      14, 64
    house of. *See* **house of residence**
    loan of money for, **14**, 62
    stamp duty, free from, **14**, 62
  school, keeping, **14**, 101
  stipend. *See* **stipend (ecclesiastical)**
  trade, not engaging in, **14**, 101
  unbeneficed, recovery of penalties, **14**, 124

Clergy Discipline Commission
  Code of Practice, formulation of, **14(S)**, 31
  functions, **14(S)**, 2–3

clerk
  person in holy orders becoming, **14**, 172

clerk of the peace
  abolition of office, **11(2)**, [252]
  superannuation provisions, **11(2)**, [265]

cliff
  public access to, **32**, [1]

climate change
  adaptation to—
    programme for, **35(S)**, 98
      Northern Ireland, **35(S)**, 98
    progress reports, **35(S)**, 97
    reporting authorities—
      directions to—
        compliance with, **35(S)**, 101
        consent or consultation with devolved
          authorities, **35(S)**, 101–2
        issue of, **35(S)**, 100

climate change—*contd*
  adaptation to—*contd*
    reporting authorities—*contd*
      directions to—*contd*
        reports on exercise of power,
          35(S), 102
      guidance by Secretary of State to,
        35(S), 99–100
      interpretation, **35(S)**, 105–7
      meaning, **35(S)**, 105
      Welsh Ministers—
        directions by, **35(S)**, 103–5
        guidance by, **35(S)**, 103
    summary of provisions, **35(S)**, 48–9
  adaptation to climate change to London
    strategy—
    directions to revise, **26(1)**, [709]
    preparation and publication of, **26(1)**, [708]
  carbon budgets—
    alteration of—
      consultation on, **35(S)**, 72–3
      power of, **35(S)**, 72
    annual equivalent, **35(S)**, 59
    budgetary period—
      alteration of, **35(S)**, 73
      amounts carried from one to another,
        35(S), 69
      final statement for, **35(S)**, 69–70
      setting for, **35(S)**, 61
    Committee on Climate Change, advice
      of, **35(S)**, 82–3
    consultation on, **35(S)**, 62
    duty to set, **35(S)**, 58
    excess, proposals and policies for
      compensating for, **35(S)**, 70
    final statement for 2050, **35(S)**, 71
    level of, **35(S)**, 58–9
    matters taken into account, **35(S)**, 62–3
    proposals and policies for meeting—
      duty to prepare, **35(S)**, 65
      duty to report on, **35(S)**, 66
    summary of provisions, **35(S)**, 45–7
    target percentages—
      amendment of, **35(S)**, 59–60
      consultation on order amending,
        35(S), 60–1
  carbon emissions, targets for reducing,
    17(2), [346]
  carbon target—
    summary of provisions, **35(S)**, 45–7
    1990 baseline—
      consultation on order amending,
        35(S), 57
      meaning, **35(S)**, 55
      power to amend, **35(S)**, 56
    2050, for, **35(S)**, 55
      Committee on Climate Change, advice
        of, **35(S)**, 82
      consultation on order amending,
        35(S), 57
      power to amend, **35(S)**, 56
  carbon units—
    limit on use of, **35(S)**, 64
    meaning, **35(S)**, 76
    net amount, **35(S)**, 64

climate change—*contd*
  combating, United Kingdom's contribution to, **17(2)**, [574]
  Committee. *See* **Committee on Climate Change**
  development plan documents, **46(S)**, 172
  greenhouse gas emissions—
    meaning, **17(2)**, [590]
    reduction, dynamic demand technologies, **17(2)**, [584]
  impact of—
    report on—
      Committee on Climate Change, advice of, **35(S)**, 97
      making of, **35(S)**, 96–7
    reporting authorities—
      directions to—
        compliance with, **35(S)**, 101
        consent or consultation with devolved authorities, **35(S)**, 101–2
        issue of, **35(S)**, 100
        reports on exercise of power, **35(S)**, 102
      guidance by Secretary of State to, **35(S)**, 99–100
      interpretation, **35(S)**, 105–7
      meaning, **35(S)**, 105
      Welsh Ministers—
        directions by, **35(S)**, 103–5
        guidance by, **35(S)**, 103
    summary of provisions, **35(S)**, 48–9
  international carbon reporting practice, meaning, **35(S)**, 120
  interpretation, **35(S)**, 121–4
  London climate change mitigation and energy strategy—
    directions to revise, **26(1)**, [707]
    preparation and publication of, **26(1)**, [706]
  Mayor and London Assembly, duties with respect to, **26(1)**, [705]
  measures report, Welsh local authorities to have regard to, **17(2)**, [576]
  national authority, meaning, **35(S)**, 120
  net UK carbon account—
    indicative annual ranges for, provision of, **35(S)**, 65
    meaning, **35(S)**, 77
    regulations, **35(S)**, 77–8
    units credited to, **35(S)**, 77
  orders and regulations, **35(S)**, 118
  regional spatial strategies, **46(S)**, 172
  removals of, **35(S)**, 79
  reporting on—
    civil estate, on, **35(S)**, 115–16
    companies, by, **35(S)**, 115
    contribution to objectives, report on, **35(S)**, 114
  summary of provisions, **17(1)**, [1]
  UK domestic action on, duty to have regard to, **35(S)**, 67
  Welsh Ministers, report by, **35(S)**, 113–14

climate change agreement
  circumstances for applying, **35(2)**, [372]
  facilities to which applying, **35(2)**, [372]

climate change agreement—*contd*
  first certification period, **35(2)**, [372]
  meaning, **35(2)**, [372]
  Secretary of State, with, **35(2)**, [372]
  supplies covered by, reduced-rate for, **35(2)**, [372]
  targets, progress towards, **35(2)**, [372]
  umbrella and underlying, combination of, **35(2)**, [372]

climate change levy
  accounting document—
    abolition of self-identification, **43(S)**, 986
    actual supply not followed by, **35(2)**, [371]
    duty to issue, **35(2)**, [371]
    issue of, **35(2)**, [371]
    meaning, **35(2)**, [381]
    provision of, **35(2)**, [381]
  accounting period, due for, **35(2)**, [382]
  amount of, **35(2)**, [372]
  assessment—
    amounts of levy, of, **35(2)**, [375]
    defaults, **35(2)**, [375]
    supplementary, **35(2)**, [374]
    time limits, **35(2)**, [375]
  auto-generator, meaning, **35(2)**, [382]
  business—
    in course or furtherance of, meaning, **35(2)**, [382]
    person carrying on, on behalf of dead or incapacitated individual, **35(2)**, [378]
    transfer as going concern, **35(2)**, [378]
  charge of, **35(2)**, [355]
  civil penalties—
    assessment to, **35(2)**, [377]
      time limit, **35(2)**, [377]
    directors, liability of, **35(2)**, [376]
    evasion, for, **35(2)**, [376]
    meaning, **35(2)**, [377]
    misdeclaration, for, **35(2)**, [376]
    neglect, for, **35(2)**, [376]
    penalty interest on, **35(2)**, [377]
      assessment, **35(2)**, [377]
    reasonable excuse, matters not amounting to, **35(2)**, [377]
    reduction, **35(2)**, [377]
    up-rating, **35(2)**, [377]
  Commissioners of Customs and Excise—
    directions, variation and withdrawal of, **35(2)**, [381]
    disclosure of information, **35(2)**, [380]
    inducements to provide information, **35(2)**, [380]
    information provided to, **35(2)**, [380]
    records, obligation to keep, **35(2)**, [380]
    review of decisions, **35(2)**, [379]
      appeals, **35(2)**, [379]
      determinations on, **35(2)**, [379]
    utility direction, **35(2)**, [382]
  debt due to Crown, recovery as, **35(2)**, [375]
  definitions, **35(2)**, [382]
  distress, levy of, **35(2)**, [375]
  documents—
    powers in relation to, **35(2)**, [380]
    production of, **35(2)**, [380]

climate change levy—*contd*

documents—*contd*

removal of, **35(2)**, [380]

double charges, regulations to avoid, **35(2)**, [370]

electricity—

auto-generator, meaning, **35(2)**, [382]

exempt unlicensed supplier, meaning, **35(2)**, [370]

producers—

self-supplies by, **35(2)**, [370]

supplies other than self-supplies to, **35(2)**, [370]

renewable sources, from, **35(2)**, [370]

supplies of, **35(2)**, [370]

unregulated supplier, meaning, **35(2)**, [382]

utility, meaning, **35(2)**, [382]

energy-intensive installations, **35(2)**, [372]

entry on premises, power of, **35(2)**, [380]

evidence, by certificate, **35(2)**, [380]

gas—

supplies of, **35(2)**, [370]

Northern Ireland, **35(2)**, [370]

unregulated supplier, meaning, **35(2)**, [382]

utility, meaning, **35(2)**, [382]

group of companies, regulations concerning, **35(2)**, [378]

half-rate supplies, abolition, **35(2)**, [562]

heat and power station—

combined—

efficiency percentages, determination of, **35(2)**, [382]

meaning, **35(2)**, [382]

partly exempt, supplies of electricity from, **35(2)**, [370]

supplies other than self-supplies to, **35(2)**, [370]

information and inspection powers, **43(S)**, 1412–13, 1692–8

insolvency—

application of procedures—

deceased individual's estate, **35(2)**, [378]

regulations, **35(2)**, [378]

set-off, **35(2)**, [374]

interest—

adjustments, **35(2)**, [375]

assessments, **35(2)**, [375]

interpretation, **35(2)**, [375]

overpaid levy paid before assessment, on, **35(2)**, [375]

payment without deduction of tax, **35(2)**, [375]

penalty—

assessments, **35(2)**, [375]

liability for, **35(2)**, [375]

no return made, where, **35(2)**, [375]

unpaid penalties, on, **35(2)**, [377]

rate of, **35(2)**, [375]

repayments, on, **35(2)**, [374]

interest on, **35(2)**, [374]

overpayments of, **35(2)**, [374]

under-declared levy, on, **35(2)**, [375]

unpaid levy, on, **35(2)**, [375]

unpaid ordinary interest, on, **35(2)**, [375]

invoices incorrectly showing due, **35(2)**, [381]

climate change levy—*contd*

meters, examination of, **35(2)**, [380]

notices, service of, **35(2)**, [381]

offences—

arrest, **35(2)**, [376]

evasion, **35(2)**, [376]

conduct involving, **35(2)**, [376]

preparations for, **35(2)**, [376]

misstatements, **35(2)**, [376]

conduct involving, **35(2)**, [376]

statutory provisions, applying, **35(2)**, [376]

overpaid, repayments of, **35(2)**, [374]

partnerships, provisions for, **35(2)**, [378]

payment of levy—

accounting periods, **35(2)**, [372]

amount, **35(2)**, [372]

liability to account, **35(2)**, [372]

provision for, **35(2)**, [372]

reimbursement arrangements, **35(2)**, [374]

producers of commodities, supplies to, **43(2)**, [508]

provision for charge of, **35(2)**, [366]

rates of, **35(2)**, [620]; **43(S)**, 849

record-keeping, **43(S)**, 1705

recorded information, order or access to, **35(2)**, [380]

reduced rate—

removal where targets not met, **35(S)**, 176, 178–80

supplies, **35(2)**, [623], [627], [628]

supply, taxable commodities ineligible for, **35(S)**, 175

registration—

cancellation, **35(2)**, [373]

form, **35(2)**, [373]

interpretation, **35(2)**, [373]

notifications, supplemental regulations, **35(2)**, [373]

register—

correction, **35(2)**, [373]

publication of information on, **35(2)**, [373]

registrability—

loss or prospective loss, notification, **35(2)**, [373]

notification, **35(2)**, [373]

requirement, **35(2)**, [373]

regulations and orders, **35(2)**, [381]

renewable source, coal mine methane no longer being, **43(S)**, 985

repayments—

interest, **35(2)**, [374]

interest on, **35(2)**, [374]

overpayments of, **35(2)**, [374]

supplementary assessments, **35(2)**, [374]

meaning, **35(2)**, [382]

overpaid levy, of, **35(2)**, [374]

excessive, **35(2)**, [374]

interest on, **35(2)**, [374]

supplementary assessments, **35(2)**, [374]

reimbursement arrangements, **35(2)**, [374]

representative, notification, **35(2)**, [374]

set-off, **35(2)**, [374]

climate change levy—*contd*
returns—
none made, penalty interest on levy,
35(2), [375]
payment of levy, for, **35(2)**, [372]
samples, power to take, **35(2)**, [380]
security for, **35(2)**, [381]
summary of provisions, **35(1)**, [1]
tax credits, **35(2)**, [374]
obtaining, **35(2)**, [376]
tax representative—
appointment for non-resident taxpayers,
35(2), [378]
climate change levy—
tax representative—
meaning, **35(2)**, [382]
offences by, **35(2)**, [378]
taxable commodity—
commodities being, **35(2)**, [369]
supply, adjustment of contracts for,
35(2), [381]
taxable supplies—
charge to levy, **35(2)**, [370]
course or furtherance of business, in,
35(2), [370]
deemed—
change of circumstances or intentions,
35(2), [370]
utilities and producers, use of
commodities by, **35(2)**, [370]
electricity, of, **35(2)**, [370]
excluded—
domestic or charity use, for, **35(2)**, [370]
for domestic use, meaning, **35(2)**, [370]
supply before 1 April 2001, **35(2)**, [370]
exemption—
averaging periods, **35(2)**, [370]
combined heat and power stations,
supplies other than self-supplies to,
35(2), [370]
electricity producers—
self-supplies by, **35(2)**, [370]
supplies other than self supplies to,
35(2), [370]
fuel, supplies not used as, **35(2)**, [370]
partly exempt combined heat and power
stations, supplies other than self-supplies
from, **35(2)**, [370]
producers of commodities other than
electricity, to, **35(2)**, [370]
recycling processes, supplies used in,
35(2), [370]
regulations giving effect to, **35(2)**, [370]
renewable resources, electricity from,
35(2), [370]
supply not for burning in UK,
35(2), [370]
transport, supply used in, **35(2)**, [370]
gas, of, **35(2)**, [370]
horticultural producers, half-rate to,
35(2), [372]
meaning, **35(2)**, [370]
reduced-rate—
climate change agreement, supplies
covered by, **35(2)**, [372]

climate change levy—*contd*
taxable supplies—*contd*
reduced-rate—*contd*
variation of notices, **35(2)**, [372]
time limits for assessments, claims, etc,
amendment, **43(S)**, 1714
time of supply—
change of rate, spanning, **35(2)**, [371]
deemed supplies, **35(2)**, [371]
directions by Commissioners, **35(2)**, [371]
earlier invoice, **35(2)**, [371]
electricity or gas—
change of rate, spanning, **35(2)**, [371]
climate change levy accounting
document—
actual supply not followed by,
35(2), [371]
duty to issue, **35(2)**, [371]
issue of, **35(2)**, [371]
special utility schemes, **35(2)**, [371]
general rules for, **35(2)**, [371]
later invoice, **35(2)**, [371]
non-UK residents, supply by, **35(2)**, [371]
regulations, **35(2)**, [371]
supplies invoiced or paid for before 1 April
2001, **35(2)**, [371]
unincorporated associations, provisions for,
35(2), [378]
utility—
meaning, **35(2)**, [382]
persons treated as being, **35(2)**, [382]
wrongdoing, penalties,
43(S), 1328–39. *See also* **tax penalty**

clocks, public
consents and access to provide, **25(1)**, [519]
expenses relating to, **25(1)**, [520]
power to provide, **25(1)**, [517]
provision, etc, of, **35(1)**, [25]

cloning
human reproductive, offence of, **28**, [742]

close company
apportionment of income, repeal of
provisions, **42**, [984]
associated, company treated as, **44(1)**, [230]
bearer securities, information about,
42, [1002]
capital gains tax. *See* **capital gains tax**
company not treated as, **44(1)**, [228]
control of, meaning, **44(1)**, [230]
director—
aggregation of loans to, **44(2)**, [197]
meaning, **44(1)**, [231]
distribution, expenses, including, **44(1)**, [232]
exempt approved scheme, shares held on
trust, **44(1)**, [228]
gift aid payments, extension of restrictions
on, **43(S)**, 43
goods and services, debt for supply of,
44(1), [234]
information, provision of, **42**, [1002]
inheritance tax. *See* **inheritance tax**
interest in possession, **43(S)**, 400

close company—*contd*
  investment-holding—
    corporation tax, **44(1)**, [10]
    meaning, **44(1)**, [10]
  loan creditor, meaning, **44(1)**, [231]
  loan to participator—
    release of—
      borrowers liable as settlors, relief for,
        44(3), [418]
      charge to tax, **44(3)**, [415]
      income charged, **44(3)**, [416]
      income tax treated as paid, **44(3)**, [421]
      person liable, **44(3)**, [417]
      persons who die, loans and advances to,
        44(3), [419]
      settlements having ended, loans and
        advances to trustees of, **44(3)**, [420]
      settlor, amounts treated as income of,
        44(3), [650]
  meaning, **44(1)**, [228]
  participator—
    associate, **44(1)**, [231]
    holding shares as trustee, **43(S)**, 399
    loan to—
      charge to tax, **44(1)**, [233]
      controlled company, by, **44(1)**, [236]
      exceptions, **44(1)**, [234]
      release of, **44(1)**, [235]
      repayment of, **44(1)**, [233]
      meaning, **44(1)**, [231]
  quoted companies not treated as, **44(1)**, [229]

closets. *See also* **water-closet**
  defective, repair of, **35(1)**, [124]
  meaning, **35(1)**, [140], [648]
  room over, prohibition on use as living,
    sleeping or work room, **35(1)**, [126]

clothes
  old, prohibition of inducements offered by
    dealer in, **35(1)**, [496]

clothing
  verminous, cleansing, **35(1)**, [137]
  zero-rating, **50**, [151]

club
  associate members, **19(3)**, [556]
    prohibited conditions, **19(3)**, [564]
  authorised persons, meaning, **19(3)**, [558]
  bingo—
    activities, as part of, **5(1)**, [555]
    high turnover period, **5(1)**, [555]
  change of name or alteration of rules,
    notification of, **19(3)**, [571]
  child, employment of, **5(1)**, [334]
  club premises certificate—
    appeals, **19(3)**, [701]
    application for—
      advertising, **19(3)**, [560]
      determination of, **19(3)**, [561]
      documents accompanying, **19(3)**, [560]
      grant or rejection of, **19(3)**, [566]
      making, **19(3)**, [560]
      operating schedule, **19(3)**, [560]

club—*contd*
  club premises certificate—*contd*
    applications and notices, form of,
      19(3), [580]
    certified copy of, **19(3)**, [584]
    duty to keep and produce, **19(3)**, [583]
    false statements for purposes of,
      19(3), [648]
    fees, **19(3)**, [581]
    form of, **19(3)**, [567]
    inspection of premises before grant of,
      19(3), [585]
    mandatory conditions for exhibition of
      films, **19(3)**, [563]
    meaning, **19(3)**, [549]
    period of validity, **19(3)**, [569]
    prohibited conditions—
      associate members and guests,
        19(3), [564]
      plays, performance of, **19(3)**, [565]
    review—
      application for, **19(3)**, [576]
      determination of application,
        19(3), [577]
      relevant representations, **19(3)**, [577]
      supplementary provisions, **19(3)**, [578]
    summary, **19(3)**, [567]
    supply of alcohol for consumption off
      premises, certificate authorising,
        19(3), [562]
    surrender, **19(3)**, [570]
    theft or loss of, **19(3)**, [568]
    transitional provisions, **19(3)**, [706]
    updating, **19(3)**, [582]
    variation—
      application for, **19(3)**, [573]
      determination of application,
        19(3), [574]
      notices, **19(3)**, [575]
      rejection of application, **19(3)**, [575]
      relevant representations, **19(3)**, [574]
      supplementary provisions, **19(3)**, [575]
    withdrawal, **19(3)**, [579]
  commercial—
    exempt gaming in, **5(1)**, [549]–[550]
    meaning, **5(1)**, [547]
  enforcement, entry on premises for,
    5(1), [592]
  entry and search, powers of, **19(3)**, [586]
  exempt gaming in, **5(1)**, [549]–[550]
  exits, etc, **35(1)**, [549]
  gaming. *See* **gaming**
  gaming permit—
    appeals, **5(1)**, [662]
    application for, **5(1)**, [662]
    area for gaming, **5(1)**, [552]
    cancellation and forfeiture, **5(1)**, [662]
    conditions, **5(1)**, [551]
    duration, **5(1)**, [662]
    form of, **5(1)**, [662]
    licensing authority, functions of, **5(1)**, [662]
    maintenance, **5(1)**, [662]
    meaning, **5(1)**, [551]
    procedure, **5(1)**, [554]
    register of, **5(1)**, [662]

club—*contd*
  gaming permit—*contd*
    renewal, **5(1)**, [662]
    Scotland, provision for, **5(1)**, [565]
    vehicles and vessels, not applying to,
      5(1), [662]
  guests, **19(3)**, [556]
    prohibited conditions, **19(3)**, [564]
  interested party, meaning, **19(3)**, [558]
  intoxicating liquor, sale and supply—
    membership rules, **19(3)**, [551]
    summary of provisions, **19(3)**, [349]
  licensing authority—
    club premises certificate, updating,
      19(3), [582]
    relevant, **19(3)**, [557]
  machine permit—
    appeals, **5(1)**, [662]
    application for, **5(1)**, [662]
    cancellation and forfeiture, **5(1)**, [662]
    conditions, **5(1)**, [553]
    duration, **5(1)**, [662]
    form of, **5(1)**, [662]
    licensing authority, functions of, **5(1)**, [662]
    maintenance, **5(1)**, [662]
    meaning, **5(1)**, [553]
    register of, **5(1)**, [662]
    renewal, **5(1)**, [662]
    Scotland, provision for, **5(1)**, [565]
    vehicles and vessels, not applying to,
      5(1), [662]
  members'—
    exempt gaming in, **5(1)**, [549]–[550]
    meaning, **5(1)**, [546]
  premises certificate. *See* club premises
    certificate *above*
  provision of facilities by, **5(1)**, [550]
  qualifying—
    ceasing to be, **19(3)**, [579]
    establishment and conduct in good faith,
      19(3), [552]
    friendly societies, **19(3)**, [554]
    general conditions, **19(3)**, [551]
    industrial and provident societies,
      19(3), [554]
    meaning, **19(3)**, [550]
    miners' welfare institutes, **19(3)**, [555]
    supply of alcohol, additional conditions
      for, **19(3)**, [553]
  qualifying activities—
    authorisation, **19(3)**, [488]
    meaning, **19(3)**, [487]
  registration. *See* intoxicating liquor, sale and
    supply *above*
  relevant registered address, change of,
    19(3), [572]
  responsible authority, meaning, **19(3)**, [558]
  rules. *See* intoxicating liquor, sale and supply
    above
  secretary, **19(3)**, [559]
  sports grounds. *See further under* **intoxicating
    liquor**
  supply of alcohol, meaning, **19(3)**, [559]
  swimming baths and bathing places, use of
    by, **35(1)**, [152]

coach station
  parking places, use as, **37**, [212]

coal. *See also* **coal mining operation; mines
  and mining; solid fuel**
  Authority. *See* **Coal Authority**
  fee simple in, vesting, **17(1)**, [1]
  information held by Authority, public access
    to, **17(2)**, [181]
  meaning, **17(1)**, [20], [211], [368];
    17(2), [189]
  opencast. *See* **opencast coal**
  production—
    corporate venturing scheme, exclusion for,
      43(S), 1123
    enterprise investment scheme, exclusion
      for, **43(S)**, 1123
    enterprise management incentives,
      exclusion from, **43(S)**, 861
    venture capital trusts, exclusion for,
      43(S), 1124
  renewable source, coal mine methane no
    longer being, **43(S)**, 985

Coal Authority
  accounts, **17(2)**, [195]
  annual report by, **17(2)**, [184]
  British Coal Corporation, interests of—
    protection, **17(2)**, [136]
    vesting, **17(2)**, [133]
  chairman, **17(2)**, [124]
  conservation, duty as to, **17(2)**, [126]
  Crown, relationship with, **17(2)**, [124]
  deputy chairman, **17(2)**, [124]
  drainage, acquisition of rights for purposes
    of, **17(1)**, [177]
  drainage work affecting, protection,
    19(3), [259]
  duties, summary of provisions, **17(1)**, [1]
  entry on land of, by highway authority,
    36, [1340]
  establishment, **17(2)**, [124]
  experience and expertise, persons having,
    appointments in coal industry, **17(2)**, [125]
  exploration, powers, **17(2)**, [131]
  finances—
    duties, **17(2)**, [195]
    generally, **17(2)**, [195]
  functions, **17(2)**, [124]
  Health and Safety Executive, co-operation,
    17(2), [127]
  information held by—
    confidentiality of, **17(2)**, [183]
    inaccurate, furnished to, liability for,
      17(2), [182]
    public access to, **17(2)**, [181]
  land—
    powers as to, **17(2)**, [131]
    use, duty as to, **17(2)**, [126]
  liabilities in coal industry, **17(2)**, [125]
  licensing duties—
    generally, **17(2)**, [125], [151]
    issue of licences. *See* **coal mining
      operations; mines and mining**

Coal Authority—*contd*
members—
appointment, **17(2)**, [124], [194]
interests, declaration of, **17(2)**, [194]
number, **17(2)**, [124]
removal of, **17(2)**, [194]
remuneration, allowances and pensions,
17(2), [194]
minutes, **17(2)**, [194]
oil and gas, transfer of interests to,
17(2), [135]
opencast coal mining, rights, orders and other
powers. *See* **opencast coal**
powers, **17(2)**, [124]
delegation of, **17(2)**, [194]
general, **17(2)**, [131]
limitation, **17(2)**, [131]
proceedings, **17(2)**, [194]
property, duty with respect to, **17(2)**, [126]
purposes, **17(2)**, [124]
registration of rights—
duty as to, **17(2)**, [180]
public access to register, **17(2)**, [181]
restructuring schemes, participation in,
17(2), [140]
See further under **British Coal
Corporation**
safety, duty with respect to, **17(2)**, [127]
seal, **17(2)**, [194]
Secretary of State, directions by, **17(2)**, [132]
staff provisions as to, **17(2)**, [194]
status, **17(2)**, [124]
water supply, acquisition of rights for purposes
of, **17(1)**, [177]

coal industry nationalisation. *See also*
National Coal Board
arbitration, provisions as to, **17(1)**, [18]
corporations, offences by, **17(1)**, [16]
dock etc. undertakings, provisions as to,
17(1), [14]
documents, meaning, **17(1)**, [20]
Doncaster Drainage district, provisions as to,
17(1), [14]
information, restriction on disclosure,
17(1), [15]
interpretation of words and phrases,
17(1), [20]
offences—
corporations, by, **17(1)**, [16]
regulations, under, **17(1)**, [19]
prosecutions, provisions as to, **17(1)**, [16]
regulations, provisions as to, **17(1)**, [19]
savings as to certain coal, **17(2)**, [165]
service of notices, **17(1)**, [17]
summary of provisions, **17(1)**, [1]
superannuation rights—
persons eligible, table, **17(1)**, [22]
provisions as to, **17(1)**, [12], [22], [45]

coal industry privatisation
restructuring date, meaning, **17(2)**, [133]
restructuring schemes. *See under* **British Coal
Corporation**
summary of provisions, **17(1)**, [1]

Coal Industry Social Welfare Organisation
cessation, **17(2)**, [148]
Charity Commission, application by
employees organisation to, **17(1)**, [702]
colliery welfare property—
accountability for, **17(1)**, [56]
excepted from transfer, **17(1)**, [55]
meaning, **17(1)**, [53]
Miners' Welfare Commission and Fund,
dissolution etc, **17(1)**, [51]
other purposes, **17(1)**, [69]
purposes, **17(1)**, [53], [68]
records relating to, **17(1)**, [59]
transfer, **17(1)**, [55], [58]
vesting of, **17(1)**, [60]
colliery welfare trusts and agreements,
transfer, **17(1)**, [54], [55]
delegation and transfer of functions,
17(1), [62]; **17(2)**, [148]
determination of questions, **17(1)**, [55]
employee organisations, participation by,
17(1), [702]
grants by British Coal Corporation to,
17(1), [63]
miner's welfare fund—
property trusts, variation, **17(1)**, [13]
winding up and transfer of assets to,
17(1), [52]
orders and regulations, Minister's powers,
17(1), [65]
provisions relating to, **17(1)**, [62]
records of, **17(1)**, [59]
social welfare activities, meaning, **17(1)**, [66]
trusts, participation in, by representative
organisations, **17(1)**, [702]
vocational education trusts, transfer of
interests, liabilities etc, **17(1)**, [57]
winding up, **17(2)**, [148]

coal mines. *See* **mines and mining**

coal mining operations. *See also* **mines and
mining**
information held by Authority—
confidentiality, **17(2)**, [183]
inaccurate, furnished to, liability for,
17(2), [182]
public access to, **17(2)**, [181]
liabilities arising, **17(2)**, [125]
licensed operators—
additional rights, underground land,
17(2), [175]
experience and expertise, persons with
appropriate, **17(2)**, [125]
information disclosed to Authority,
accuracy of, **17(2)**, [182]
insolvency of, **17(2)**, [161]
meaning, **17(2)**, [189]
support—
right to withdraw, **17(2)**, [163]
notice, **17(2)**, [164]
See also **mines and mining** (support)
winding up, **17(2)**, [161]
licensing—
application for licence, **17(2)**, [151]

coal mining operations—*contd*
  licensing—*contd*
    areas of responsibility, **17(2)**, [162]
    arrangements, publication of, **17(2)**, [155]
    authorisation contained in licence,
      17(2), [152]
    conditions of licence—
      general, **17(2)**, [153]
      security, provision of, **17(2)**, [154]
    enforcement orders—
      copies, service of, **17(2)**, [157]
      effect, **17(2)**, [158]
      final, **17(2)**, [156]
      information for purposes of,
        requirement, **17(2)**, [159]
      notices, **17(2)**, [157]
      powers to make, **17(2)**, [156]
      procedural requirements, **17(2)**, [157]
      provisional, **17(2)**, [156]
      revocation, power of, **17(2)**, [156]
      validity, **17(2)**, [158]
    grant, **17(2)**, [151]
    licences issued before restructuring,
      continuation, **17(2)**, [150]
    operations to which applicable,
      17(2), [150]
    register of licences and orders, **17(2)**, [160]
      public access to, **17(2)**, [181]
    requirement, **17(2)**, [150]
  meaning, **17(2)**, [189]
  responsibility, designation of areas of,
    17(2), [162]

coal mining subsidence
  adviser—
    appointment, **17(2)**, [170]
    functions of, **17(2)**, [170]
    regulations as to, **17(2)**, [170]
  agricultural losses—
    crop loss payments, **17(2)**, [27], [55]
    farm loss payments, **17(2)**, [26], [54], [55]
    tenant farmers, payments for, **17(2)**, [28]
  ancient monuments, damage to, **17(2)**, [19]
  blight, property affected by, **17(2)**, [29], [206]
  British Coal Corporation—
    duty of, **17(2)**, [2]
    obligations, **17(2)**, [2]
    references to, interpretation, **17(2)**, [167]
  business, small firms, losses, **17(2)**, [30]
  claims—
    double, avoidance of, **17(2)**, [35]
    meaning, **17(2)**, [46]
  Coal Authority, duties, **17(2)**, [125]
  crop loss payments, **17(2)**, [27], [55]
  damage due to—
    Act applicable, **17(2)**, [1]
    buildings, structures or works, **17(2)**, [1]
    Coal Authority, duties, **17(2)**, [125]
    dwelling house. *See* dwelling house *below*
    further—
      Corporation's obligation, **17(2)**, [16]
      effect of, **17(2)**, [18]
      stop notice after, **17(2)**, [16]
        effect of, **17(2)**, [16]
        period, effective, **17(2)**, [16]

coal mining subsidence—*contd*
  damage due to—*contd*
    further—*contd*
      stop notice after—*contd*
        revocation and review, **17(2)**, [17]
    land, **17(2)**, [1]
    land and property, character and use,
      protection, **17(2)**, [125]
    notice of, **17(2)**, [3]
      action on receipt of, **17(2)**, [203]
      forwarding of, to Coal Authority,
        17(2), [203]
      initial response to, **17(2)**, [4], [203]
      period allowed, **17(2)**, [3]
    obligations arising, **17(2)**, [125]
    responsible person—
      information to be provided by,
        17(2), [169]
      more than one, **17(2)**, [168]
      obligations and liabilities, **17(2)**, [167],
        [168]
      provisions applicable, **17(2)**, [167]
    subsidence damage, meaning, **17(2)**, [1]
    when provisions inapplicable, **17(2)**, [1]
  death, compensation in respect of, **17(2)**, [32]
  depreciation payments—
    amount, **17(2)**, [49]
    basis of valuation, **17(2)**, [49]
    discretionary, **17(2)**, [10]
    general, **17(2)**, [14]
    interest on, **17(2)**, [49]
    obligatory, **17(2)**, [11]
    recipients, **17(2)**, [15]
      special cases, **17(2)**, [50]
    to whom made, **17(2)**, [15]
    units of property, **17(2)**, [14], [49]
  disablement, compensation for, **17(2)**, [32]
  disagreements. *See* disputes and complaints
    below
  discretionary depreciation payments,
    17(2), [10]
  disputes and complaints—
    access etc to premises, **17(2)**, [39]
    agreement or consent, withholding of,
      17(2), [38]
    arbitration, reference to, **17(2)**, [171]
    general, **17(2)**, [37], [171]
    land drainage works, questions arising,
      17(2), [34]
    Lands Tribunal, reference to, **17(2)**, [6],
      [37], [171]
    powers of Lands Tribunal or arbitrator,
      17(2), [171]
    questions to be referred, **17(2)**, [37], [171]
    schedule of remedial works, **17(2)**, [6]
    time limits for certain disputes, **17(2)**, [40]
  disrepair, property in, **17(2)**, [8]
  documents, service of, **17(2)**, [45]
  double claims, avoidance, **17(2)**, [35]
  drainage systems. *See* land drainage systems
    below
  dwelling house—
    compulsory purchase where damage due
      to, **17(2)**, [11]

coal mining subsidence—*contd*
  dwelling house—*contd*
    consultation with local authority, payment after, **17(2)**, [14]
    demolition or closing order, under, **17(2)**, [11]
    depreciation payments, **17(2)**, [11]
    home loss payments, **17(2)**, [22]
    inconvenience or disturbance, compensation, **17(2)**, [25]
    meaning, **17(2)**, [46]
    preventative measures, failure to take, **17(2)**, [33]
    temporary dispossession, relief for—
      alternative accommodation, **17(2)**, [53]
      obligation of Corporation, **17(2)**, [53]
        cessation of, **17(2)**, [53]
      period of, **17(2)**, [53], [55]
      procedural requirements, **17(2)**, [53]
      requirements, **17(2)**, [23]
    vacant, care of, **17(2)**, [24]
  ecclesiastical property—
    damage to, **17(2)**, [20], [33]
    meaning, **17(2)**, [20]
  emergency works, **17(2)**, [2]
    payments in respect of, **17(2)**, [11]
  expenses, claimant's, reimbursement, **17(2)**, [36]
  farm loss payments, **17(2)**, [26], [54], [55]
  fault, meaning, **17(2)**, [31]
  firms losses, compensation, **17(2)**, [30]
  further damage. *See* damage *above*
  home loss payments, **17(2)**, [22], [55]
    amount, **17(2)**, [52]
    right to, **17(2)**, [52]
  information—
    held by Authority—
      confidentiality, **17(2)**, [183]
      inaccurate, furnished to, liability for, **17(2)**, [182]
      public access to, **17(2)**, [181]
    offences with respect to, **17(2)**, [172]
    to accompany notices, regulations as to, **17(2)**, [41], [42]
  injury, personal, compensation for, **17(2)**, [32]
  land drainage systems—
    area, **17(2)**, [34]
    Corporation—
      measures by, **17(2)**, [34]
      powers, **17(2)**, [34]
    determination of questions arising, regulations, **17(2)**, [34]
    main river—
      meaning, **17(2)**, [34]
      property comprised in, **17(2)**, [34]
    procedure, regulations as to, **17(2)**, [34]
    remedial works, **17(2)**, [34]
    stop notice, **17(2)**, [34]
  lawful coal-mining operations, meaning, **17(2)**, [1]
  level or gradient of land, alteration of, when disregarded, **17(2)**, [1]
  local authorities, notices, **17(2)**, [42]
  moveable property—
    compensation for damage, **17(2)**, [31]

coal mining subsidence—*contd*
  moveable property—*contd*
    meaning, **17(2)**, [31]
  notice—
    claimant, by, **17(2)**, [3]
      response to, **17(2)**, [4]
    contents and form, regulations, **17(2)**, [41], [42]
    Corporation, by, **17(2)**, [4]
    local authorities, to, **17(2)**, [14], [42]
    owners and occupiers, to, **17(2)**, [41]
    references to, construction of, **17(2)**, [46]
    service, **17(2)**, [45]
  obligatory payment, **17(2)**, [9]
  owner—
    meaning, **17(2)**, [46]
    notices, **17(2)**, [41]
  payments—
    crop loss, **17(2)**, [27], [55]
    emergency works, **17(2)**, [11]
    farm loss, **17(2)**, [26], [54], [55]
    home loss, **17(2)**, [22], [52], [55]
    in lieu of works—
      advance, **17(2)**, [13]
      apportionment, **17(2)**, [13]
      depreciation—
        amount, **17(2)**, [49]
        basis of valuation, **17(2)**, [49]
        general, **17(2)**, [14]
        interest on, **17(2)**, [49]
        mortgage, property subject to, **17(2)**, [50]
        recipients, **17(2)**, [15]
        rentcharge, property subject to, **17(2)**, [50]
        special cases, **17(2)**, [50]
        to whom made, **17(2)**, [15]
        units of property, **17(2)**, [14], [49]
      discretionary, **17(2)**, [8]
      discretionary depreciation, **17(2)**, [10]
      generally, **17(2)**, [13]
      obligatory, **17(2)**, [9]
      obligatory depreciation, **17(2)**, [11]
      proposal by Corporation, **17(2)**, [5]
      requirements before making of, **17(2)**, [12]
  preventative measures—
    execution of works, **17(2)**, [33]
    failure to take, **17(2)**, [33]
    generally, **17(2)**, [33], [55]
  protected tenants, damage to property of, **17(2)**, [21], [51]
  redevelopment instead of works, **17(2)**, [8]
  regulations and orders, powers to make, generally, **17(2)**, [44]
  remedial action—
    appropriate, determination, **17(2)**, [5]
    duty to take, **17(2)**, [2]
    further damage, after, **17(2)**, [16]
      Corporation proposals, **17(2)**, [18]
    kinds available—
      election by Corporation, **17(2)**, [4], [5]
        revocation, **17(2)**, [5], [8]
    nature of, **17(2)**, [2]
    substituted, **17(2)**, [5]

coal mining subsidence—*contd*
  remedial action—*contd*
    transitional provisions, **17(2)**, [55]
  remedial works—
    disagreement as to, **17(2)**, [6]
    execution of, **17(2)**, [7]
    further damage before completion,
      17(2), [18]
    land drainage systems, **17(2)**, [34]
    restriction, removal of, **17(2)**, [206]
    schedule of, **17(2)**, [6]
      further damage—
        effect, **17(2)**, [16]
        fresh schedule, **17(2)**, [18]
    works, meaning, **17(2)**, [46]
  reports to Secretary of State, **17(2)**, [43]
  responsibility for, **17(2)**, [167]
    See also under damage *above*
  rights and liabilities, transfer, **17(2)**, [167]
  small firms—
    losses, compensation, **17(2)**, [30]
    meaning, **17(2)**, [30], [31]
    moveable property, damage to, **17(2)**, [31]
  tenant farmers, payments to, **17(2)**, [28]
  transitional provisions, **17(2)**, [47], [55]

coast protection
  Continental Shelf Act, 1964, provisions
    applicable, **17(1)**, [291]
  excavation or removal of material
    prohibition, **36**, [1388]
  sea bed in designated area, application of
    provisions, **17(1)**, [291]

Coast Protection Authorities
  agreements, power to enter into, **49**, [382]
  coast protection boards, as, **49**, [381]
  compensation, liability for, **49**, [397]
  compulsory purchase of land, powers,
    49, [384], [392]
  consent to works, requirement, **49**, [394]
  damage or depreciation, compensation for,
    49, [397]
  default powers of Minister, **49**, [407]
  dissolution, officers, matters affecting,
    49, [408]
  entry, powers of, **49**, [403]
  establishment, **49**, [380]
  expenses of works, contribution towards,
    49, [398]
  failure to carry out works, **49**, [407]
  inspection, powers of, **49**, [403]
  land—
    acquired by, use for other purposes,
      49, [400]
    compulsory purchase, **49**, [384], [392]
    dealings in, **49**, [382]
    owner, meaning, **49**, [422]
    ownership, power to require information as
      to, **49**, [404]
  maintenance—
    costs, **49**, [391]
    general powers, **49**, [390]
  maritime districts—
    as, **49**, [380]

Coast Protection Authorities—*contd*
  maritime districts—*contd*
    meaning, **49**, [422]
  materials, sale of, by, **49**, [401]
  notification of works to, **49**, [395]
  officers, matters affecting, **49**, [408]
  parks, recreation grounds, etc, power to
    provide, **49**, [400]
  passage, right of, **49**, [405]
    meaning, **49**, [405]
  powers and duties, **49**, [380], [382]
  repairs—
    costs, **49**, [391]
    general powers, **49**, [390]
  works schemes. *See under* **coast protection
  work**

Coast Protection Board
  coast protection authority, as, **49**, [381]
  constituent authority—
    meaning, **49**, [422]
    representation, order as to, **49**, [381]
  constitution—
    generally, **49**, [381]
    orders relating to—
      dissolution, **49**, [381]
      draft and objections thereto, **49**, [424]
      power to make, **49**, [381]
      procedure, **49**, [424]
      revocation, **49**, [381]
      special Parliamentary procedure,
        49, [425]
      validity when not confirmed, **49**, [426]
  dissolution, order as to, **49**, [381]
  orders. *See* constitution *above*
  representation on, **49**, [381]

coast protection work
  alteration of—
    consent to, **49**, [394]
    navigation, detrimental to, **49**, [412]
  ancient monuments protection, **49**, [421]
  arbitration, provisions as to, **49**, [402]
  charges—
    amount, **49**, [385]
    appeal against, **49**, [385]
    Crown, payable by, **49**, [389], [410]
    dispute as to, **49**, [385]
    Duchy land, payable by, **49**, [389], [410]
    incidence of, **49**, [389]
    instalments, payment by, **49**, [388]
    levy of, **49**, [384], [386]
    meaning, **49**, [384]
    mortgage, payment by, **49**, [389]
    recovery, **49**, [388]
    settled land, in connection with, **49**, [389]
    university and college land, in connection
      with, **49**, [389]
  compensation, provisions as, **49**, [397]
  consent to, **49**, [394], [421]
  county council, contribution towards costs,
    49, [398]
  covenants, restrictive, on land, **49**, [406]
  Crown, application to, **49**, [410]
  Crown land, meaning, **49**, [410]

coast protection work—*contd*
damage or depreciation, compensation,
   49, [397]
district councils, contribution towards costs,
   49, [398]
documents, service of, **49**, [419]
drainage authority, saving for rights of,
   49, [421]
ecclesiastical corporations, provisions as to,
   49, [411]
emergency, in, **49**, [428]
entry, powers of, **49**, [403]
excavation or removal of material
   prohibition, **36**, [1388]
excavation, seashore. *See* seashore *below*
Exchequer grants, **49**, [399]
execution of—
   coast protection authority, by, **49**, [382]
   emergency, in, **49**, [428]
   notice of intention, **49**, [395]
   owner of land, by, **49**, [387]
   restrictions on, **49**, [406]
   without consent, **49**, [395]
expenses—
   contributions towards, **49**, [398]
   Exchequer grants, **49**, [399]
Government—
   grants, **49**, [399]
   incurred by, **49**, [414]
improvement of—
   navigation, detrimental to, **49**, [412]
   without consent, **49**, [395]
inquiries, local, power to hold, **49**, [420]
inspection, powers of, **49**, [403]
local Acts—
   meaning, **49**, [422]
   orders in case—
      procedure, **49**, [424]–[425]
      validity, **49**, [426]
   repeal or amendment, **49**, [409]
maintenance—
   costs—
      complaints as to, **49**, [391]
      recovery, **49**, [391]
   general powers, **49**, [390]
   notice requiring, **49**, [391]
   works scheme for, **49**, [391]
materials—
   meaning, **49**, [422]
   removal from or deposit on seashore,
      49, [412]
   sale of, **49**, [401]
      meaning, **49**, [422]
navigation—
   detention of, emergency restrictions,
      49, [415]
   detrimental to—
      restrictions on—
         enforcement, **49**, [414]
         generally, **49**, [412]
         operations excepted, **49**, [413]
notice of proposals, **49**, [383]
notices, service of, **49**, [419]
notification of, to authority, **49**, [395]
objections to, **49**, [383], [386]

coast protection work—*contd*
obligation to carry out, subsisting, **49**, [393]
offences generally, penalties, **49**, [417]
orders, generally, provisions as to, **49**, [418]
owner of land, by, **49**, [387]
passage, right of, to facilitate work, **49**, [405]
proposals, **49**, [383]
protection, meaning, **49**, [422]
regulations, provisions as to, **49**, [418]
repair work—
   costs—
      complaints as to, **49**, [391]
      recovery, **49**, [391]
   works scheme, for, **49**, [391]
restrictions on land, removal of, **49**, [405]
schemes. *See* works schemes *below*
sea defence commissioners—
   failure to carry out work, **49**, [393]
   meaning, **49**, [422]
sea, meaning, **49**, [422], [429]
seashore—
   excavation—
      licence for—
         grant, **49**, [396]
         without, penalty, **49**, [396]
      materials—
         meaning, **49**, [422]
         removal or deposit of, **49**, [412]
   meaning, **49**, [422]
      waters and rivers excluded, **49**, [429]
   order restricting—
      area, **49**, [396]
      confirmation, **49**, [427]
      interim, **49**, [396], [428]
      objection to, **49**, [427]
      power to make, **49**, [396]
      prohibition on, **49**, [396]
      provisions as to, **49**, [427]
   penalty, **49**, [417]
summary of provisions, **49**, [1]
urgent, **49**, [395]
works schemes—
   approval of, **49**, [383]
   carrying out of work, **49**, [386], [387]
   charges. *See* charges *above*
   compulsory powers, **49**, [384], [392]
   confirmation—
      generally, **49**, [386]
      orders as to, **49**, [386], [424]–[425]
      requirement, **49**, [384]
      validity of orders, **49**, [386], [426]
   local inquiries, **49**, [386]
   local land charge, registration, **49**, [386]
   maintenance work, for, **49**, [391]
   meaning, **49**, [384]
   modification, **49**, [383], [386]
   notice of, **49**, [383]
   objections to, **49**, [383], [386]
   power to make, **49**, [384]
   quashing of, **49**, [386]
   repairs, for, **49**, [391]

coastal waters
Environment Agency's promotion of
   conservation and enhancement, **35(2)**, [92]

coastal waters—*contd*
pollution. *See* **pollution**
vessels lying in, public health provisions
applicable to, **35(1)**, [169]

coastguard
Admiralty, transfer to, **3**, [321]
Board of Trade, transfer to, **3**, [320]
control of, **3**, [1]
emergency, transfer during, **3**, [321]
land held in connection with, **3**, [320]

cocoa
beans, licence to import, **13**, [564]
International Cocoa Agreement, legislation to
implement, **13**, [564]
products, licence to import, **13**, [564]

coinage. *See also* **decimal currency**
Act of Union, after, **10**, [60]
authority, issued without, **10**, [282]
breaking, restrictions on, **10**, [283]
counterfeiting. *See* **counterfeiting**
Crown rights, **10**, [1]
imitation, making—
directors' liability, **12(1)**, [741]
offence, **12(1)**, [736]
impurities, **10**, [277], [293]
legal tender—
bronze coins, **10**, [276]
cupro-nickel coins, **10**, [276]
gold coins, **10**, [276]
silver coins, **10**, [276]
Maundy money, standard of, **10**, [277]
melting, restrictions on, **10**, [283]
mint, the. *See* **mint, the**
offences, **10**, [1]
payments for, **10**, [574]
proclamation, regulation by, **10**, [277]
protected, meaning, **12(1)**, [742]
silver, references to, **10**, [285]
specifications, **10**, [288], [293]
standard trial plates, **10**, [279]
standard weights, **10**, [280]
standards of, **10**, [275]; **39(1)**, [477]
trial of the pyx, **10**, [281]

collection (exhibition)
removal of articles from, **12(1)**, [563]

collection of tax
surrender of life policy on, **44(1)**, [164]

collective agreements
contents of, **16**, [376]
equal pay, matters involving, **16**, [35]
legally enforceable, whether intended to be,
16, [377]
meaning, **16**, [376]
provisions restricting right to take industrial
action, effect of, **16**, [378]
redundancy provisions, power to adapt,
16, [397]

collective bargaining
Central Arbitration Committee—
declarations, **16**, [520]
directions, **16**, [520]
general duty, **16**, [520]
guidance, **16**, [520]
proceedings before, **16**, [481]
recognition. *See* **trade unions**
supply of information to, **16**, [520]
conduct of—
employment tribunal, complaint to,
16, [260]
method of, **16**, [520]
training, **16**, [259]
disclosure of information—
consideration of complaint, **16**, [343]
employers, general duty of, **16**, [379]
restrictions on, **16**, [380]
failure, complaint of, **16**, [381], [382]
determination of claim and award,
16, [383]
inducements relating to, **16**, [341]
interpretation of terms, **16**, [345]
remedies, **16**, [344]
time limit for proceedings, **16**, [342]
meaning, **16**, [376], [514]
method of, **16**, [514]
pay, meaning, **16**, [520]
power to amend provisions, **16**, [520]
recognition for purposes of. *See* **trade unions**
unit, changes affecting, **16**, [514]

collective enfranchisement (leasehold reform)
cathedral precinct, saving for property
within, **23**, [173]
contracting out of right to, prohibition of,
23, [169]
costs of, **23**, [111]
county court—
enforcement of obligations, **23**, [168]
jurisdiction of, **23**, [166]
Crown land, application of provisions to,
23, [171]
estate management schemes. *See* **estate management schemes**
flats—
amendment of rights, **24**, [113]
invitation to participate, **24**, [115]
RTE company, exercisable by, **24**, [114]
stamp duty land tax on,
41(S), Stamp Duties 2–3
ineffective claims, landlord's right to
compensation for, **23**, [116], [117], [423]
initial notice—
application for approval of estate
management scheme, priority, **23**, [152]
compulsory acquisition procedures, effect
on, **23**, [108]
copies of, procedure, **23**, [194]
currency of claim, definition of, **23**, [193]
details of, **23**, [91]
giving of—
procedure following, **23**, [95]–[99]
provision for, **23**, [176]

collective enfranchisement (leasehold reform)—*contd*
  initial notice—*contd*
    inaccuracies or misdescription in, **23**, [195]
    inheritance tax, effect on designation for, **23**, [109]
    registration of, **23**, [174]
    restrictions on participation by tenant, **23**, [193]
    termination of lease prevented during currency of claim, **23**, [193]
    validity of, proceedings relating to, **23**, [100]
    withdrawal of, deemed, **23**, [107]
  Isles of Scilly, application of provisions to, **23**, [180]
  landlords—
    absent, application to court for vesting order by qualifying tenants when, **23**, [104], [105]
    compensation, right to, in relation to ineffective claims, **23**, [116], [117], [423]
    disability, under, **23**, [192]
    ecclesiastical, **23**, [192]
    interest of—
      custodian trustee, vested in, **23**, [192]
      mortgagee in possession of, **23**, [192]
      settlement, subject to, **23**, [192]
      trust, held in, **23**, [192]
    relevant—
      access by, for valuation purposes, **23**, [95]
      acting independently, **23**, [191]
      counter-notice, duty to furnish copies of to reversioner, **23**, [196]
      definition, **23**, [86]
      initial notice—
        duty to furnish copies to reversioner, **23**, [196]
        effect on subsequent transactions by, **23**, [97]
      obligations of, to reversioner, **23**, [191]
      redevelopment, intention to, failure of tenants claim where, **23**, [101]
    resident, **23**, [87]
    reversioner—
      access by, for valuation purposes, **23**, [95]
      acts of, binding on other landlords, **23**, [191]
      agreements with non-participating tenants, duty of nominee purchaser to disclose to, **23**, [96]
      continuing duty to furnish information, **23**, [196]
      contract, failure to enter, application to court over, **23**, [102], [197]
      counter-notice—
        details of, **23**, [99]
        failure to give, **23**, [103]
        information to accompany, **23**, [196]
      definition, **23**, [86]
      evidence of tenant's right to participate, right to, **23**, [98]

collective enfranchisement (leasehold reform)—*contd*
  landlords—*contd*
    reversioner—*contd*
      freeholder—
        replacement by other relevant landlord, **23**, [189]
        to be reversioner, **23**, [189]
      leasehold valuation tribunal, application to over dispute relating to terms of acquisition, **23**, [102]
      obligations of other landlords to, **23**, [191]
      premises with multiple freeholders, **23**, [190]
    service charges, contributions to, **24**, [103]
    university or college, **23**, [192]
  lease—
    long—
      approvals, functions relating to, **24**, [98], [99]
      continued, **24**, [77]
      death or marriage, terminable by notice after, **24**, [77]
      meaning, **24**, [76]
      option for renewal, **24**, [77]
    meaning, **23**, [85]
    shared ownership, meaning of, **23**, [85]
    term date, **23**, [179]
  leasehold interests, acquisition of, **23**, [78]
  leasehold valuation tribunal—
    application to—
      nominee purchaser over dispute relating to terms of acquisition, by, **23**, [102]
      reversioner over disputes relating to terms of acquisition, by, **23**, [102]
    jurisdiction of, **23**, [167]
  local authorities, acquisition of interests from, **23**, [115], [210]
  low rent test, alternative for, **23**, [421]
  National Trust, saving for, **23**, [172]
  nominee purchaser—
    access by, for valuation purposes, **23**, [95]
    application to court for declaration of participating tenants' right to collective enfranchisement, **23**, [100]
    appointment of, **23**, [93]
    contract, failure to enter, by reversioner—
      application to court over, **23**, [102]
      vesting order by court, **23**, [102], [197]
    conveyance to, **23**, [112], [204]
    counter-notice—
      from reversioner, **23**, [99]
      reversioner's failure to give—
        application to court, **23**, [103]
        vesting order by court, **23**, [103], [197]
    death of, **23**, [94]
    discharge of existing mortgages on transfer to, **23**, [113], [205]
    leaseback to former freeholder in certain circumstances—
      certain units, of, **23**, [208]
      general, **23**, [114], [206]
      mandatory, **23**, [207]

collective enfranchisement (leasehold reform)—*contd*
nominee purchaser—*contd*
leaseback to former freeholder in certain circumstances—*contd*
terms of lease granted to freeholder, **23**, [209]
leasehold valuation tribunal, application to over dispute relating to terms of acquisition, **23**, [102]
price payable by—
determination of, **23**, [110]
freeholder's interest in specified premises—
general, **23**, [199]
negative value, with, **23**, [202]
value of, **23**, [199]
general, **23**, [198]
intermediate leasehold interests, **23**, [200]
negative value, specified premises with, **23**, [202]
value of, **23**, [200]
marriage value, freeholder's share of, **23**, [199]
other interests, **23**, [201]
negative value, with, **23**, [203]
part of specified premises, for freehold of, **23**, [199]
replacement of, **23**, [93]
retirement of, **23**, [94]
orders and regulations, power of Secretary of State to make, **23**, [177]
premises—
access to, rights of, **23**, [95]
applicable to, **23**, [79]
excluded, **23**, [80]
resident landlord, **23**, [87]
procedure for, power of Secretary of State to prescribe, **23**, [175]
reversioner. *See* landlords *above*
right to, **23**, [77]
right to manage—
access to premises, right of, **24**, [83]
counter-notice, **24**, [84]
Crown having interest in premises, where, **24**, [107]
definitions, **24**, [111], [112]
enforcement of obligations, **24**, [106]
excluded premises, **24**, [149]
landlord not traceable, where, **24**, [85]
long lease, meaning, **24**, [76], [77]
notice of claim to acquire, **24**, [79]
notices, service of, **24**, [110]
premises to which applying, **24**, [72]
procedure, power to prescribe, **24**, [109]
provision for, **24**, [71]
qualifying tenants, **24**, [75]
RTM company. *See* RTM company *below*
shared ownership lease, meaning, **24**, [76]
statutory provisions applying to, **24**, [150]
trustees, powers of, **24**, [108]
uncommitted service charges, duty to pay, **24**, [94]

collective enfranchisement (leasehold reform)—*contd*
RTE company—
exclusions, **23**, [81]
meaning, **23**, [81]
membership of, **23**, [82]
notice inviting participation by, **23**, [90]
regulations, **23**, [83]
RTM company—
acquisition date, **24**, [90]
cessation of management by, **24**, [104]
claim notice, **24**, [79]
contents of, **24**, [80]
continuation in force, **24**, [81]
counter-notice, **24**, [84]
deemed withdrawal, **24**, [87]
inaccuracy in, **24**, [81]
premises specified in, **24**, [81]
qualifying tenant, naming, **24**, [81]
withdrawal, **24**, [86]
contract notice, **24**, [92]
contractor notice, **24**, [92]
costs, liability for, **24**, [88]
claim ceasing, where, **24**, [89]
duty to give notice of contracts, **24**, [92]
duty to provide information to, **24**, [93]
exercise of right to manage, provisions applying, **24**, [95]
information, right to obtain, **24**, [82]
landlord not traceable, where, **24**, [85]
long leases, grant of approvals under, **24**, [98], [99]
management contract—
existing, **24**, [91]
meaning, **24**, [91]
management functions, **24**, [96], [97]
meaning, **24**, [73]
membership, **24**, [74]
agreements excluding or modifying right of, **24**, [105]
notice inviting participation by, **24**, [78]
participating tenant, amendment of provisions, **24**, [151]
regulations, **24**, [74]
service charges, landlord contributions to, **24**, [103]
statutory functions, **24**, [102]
tenant covenants—
enforcement of, **24**, [100]
monitoring and reporting, **24**, [101]
tenant, obligations owed to, **24**, [97]
shared ownership lease, meaning, **24**, [76]
stamp duty land tax, **41**, [350]
summary of provisions, **20**, [1]
tenants, qualifying—
absent landlord, applications to court for vesting order when, **23**, [104], [105]
company, **24**, [151]
general, **23**, [84]
initial notice. *See* initial notice *above*
nominee purchaser. *See* nominee purchaser *above*
participating—
definition, **23**, [92]
election, by, **23**, [92], [193]

collective enfranchisement (leasehold reform)—*contd*

tenants, qualifying—*contd*

participating—*contd*

failure of claim where landlord intends to redevelop, **23**, [101]

ineffective claims by, landlord's right to compensation for, **23**, [116], [117], [423]

personal representative in event of death of, **23**, [92]

withdrawal from acquisition by, **23**, [106]

right to manage, for, **24**, [75]

right to obtain information about—

existing claims for collective enfranchisement, **23**, [89]

right to collective enfranchisement unable to be exercised, **23**, [89]

superior interests, **23**, [88]

trustees, powers of, **23**, [170]

collective investment scheme

loan relationships, amended provisions, **43(2)**, [535]

meaning, **19(2)**, [288]

overseas—

designated countries of territories, authorised in, **19(2)**, [322]

scheme particulars, **19(2)**, [330]

disapplication of rules, **19(2)**, [318]

facilities and information in UK, **19(2)**, [335]

individually recognised—

alteration of scheme, **19(2)**, [329]

application for recognition, **19(2)**, [326]

comparable authorised schemes, **19(2)**, [324]

determination of applications, **19(2)**, [327]

directions, **19(2)**, [332]–[334]

matters taken into account, **19(2)**, [325]

name, **19(2)**, [324]

operator, trustee or depositary, changes of, **19(2)**, [329]

order as to, **19(2)**, [324]

participants, protection of, **19(2)**, [324]

purposes of, **19(2)**, [324]

refusal of application, **19(2)**, [328]

revocation of recognition, **19(2)**, [331]

scheme particulars, **19(2)**, [330]

other EEA States, constituted in, **19(2)**, [316]

promotion, power to suspend, **19(2)**, [319]–[321]

recognition, refusal of, **19(2)**, [323]

representations and references to Tribunal, **19(2)**, [317]

persons concerned in, **19(2)**, [523]

promotion of—

approval, restrictions on, **19(2)**, [293]

contravention of requirements, **19(2)**, [294]

restrictions on, **19(2)**, [291]

single property schemes, **19(2)**, [292]

summary of provisions, **19(1)**, [1]

collective investment scheme—*contd*

unit trust scheme. *See* **unit trust scheme**

collective marks

authorised users, rights of, **48**, 186

character or significance, not to be misleading as to, **48**, 185

geographical origin, indication of, **48**, 185

infringement, **48**, 186

meaning, **48**, 149

registration—

invalidity, grounds for, **48**, 187

regulations governing use, **48**, 185–6

revocation, grounds for, **48**, 186

regulations governing use of, **48**, 185–6

signs of which consisting, **48**, 185

college

capital moneys, application of, **46**, [602]

charter, laying before Parliament, **15(1)**, [143]

disabled persons, access of to, **15(1)**, [265]

estates. *See* **estates, university and college**

fees, regulations on, **15(1)**, [279]

freedom of speech, **15(1)**, [292]

meaning, **15(1)**, [144]

teacher training, loans for, **15(1)**, [262]

college (ecclesiastical)

Church of England, loans for, **14**, 341–2

corrupt election to, **14**, 47–8

extra-parochial services at, **14**, 654

loans by, **14**, 62, 97

marriage at, **14**, 654–5

theological, loans for, **14**, 629–30

colliery. *See also* **coal mines; mines and mining**

spoilbanks—

combustion of refuse, prevention of, **35(2)**, [42]

emission of smoke or fumes from refuse, prevention of, **35(2)**, [42]

colliery welfare property. *See under* **Coal Industry Social Welfare Organisation**

collision (sea)

action in personam, county court, **11(2)**, [919]

Admiralty jurisdiction, **11(2)**, [917]

duty to assist, **39(2)**, [756]

Colne Valley Water Company

quashing of, **49**, [386]

repairs, for, **49**, [391]

Colonial Courts of Admiralty. *See also* **prize**

appeal—

local, **11(2)**, [127]

meaning, **11(2)**, [136]

Privy Council, to, **11(2)**, [128]

Channel Islands, exclusion, **11(2)**, [133]

declaration of court as, **11(2)**, [124]

droits of Admiralty and Crown, **11(2)**, [130]

Colonial Courts of Admiralty—*contd*
Foreign Jurisdiction Act, extension of
provisions to courts under, **11(2)**, [134]
generally, **11(2)**, [1]
international law, regard to be had to,
11(2), [124]
jurisdiction—
colonial legislature, power of, **11(2)**, [125]
generally, **11(2)**, [124]
limitation, **11(2)**, [125]
rules of court, **11(2)**, [129]
Orders in Council, power to make,
11(2), [135]
possessions excluded, **11(2)**, [133]
practice and procedure, rules, **11(2)**, [129]
prize court—
authorisation to act as, **11(2)**, [140]
fees, application, **11(2)**, [141]
power to act as, **11(2)**, [124]
rules of court, **11(2)**, [129]
Vice-Admiral, appointment, **11(2)**, [132]
Vice-Admiralty court, **11(2)**, [131]

colonial forces
air force law, subject to, **3**, [982]
employment of British protected persons,
3, [1254]
military law, persons subject to, **3**, [709]

colonial legislature
meaning, **41**, [605]

colonial naval force
absence from, **3**, [1193]
desertion from, **3**, [1193]
expenses of, **3**, [328]
joint with other colonies, **3**, [372]
naval law, subject to, **3**, [1192]
navy, acting with, **3**, [1]
provision for, **3**, [327], [372]

colonial naval vessels
expenses of, **3**, [328]
provisions for, **3**, [326], [372]

colonies
British, meaning, **18**, [109]
documentary evidence provisions, **18**, [136]
documents, proof of, **18**, [103], [172]
judgments etc, proof of, **18**, [100]
law of, **3**, [720]
Naval Discipline Act, application to, **3**, [1202]
probates and letters of administration—
cancellation of resealing, **18**, [648]
recognition of, **18**, [505]
sealing of, **18**, [507], [595]
statutes etc, proof of, **18**, [136]
summary fines in, **3**, [720]
terrorism provisions applied, **18**, [754]
Visiting Forces Act, extension to, **3**, [454]

colony
boundary, alteration of, **7(2)**, [416]
colonial law, validation of, **7(2)**, [360]

colony—*contd*
colonial stock *See* **colonial stock**
courts—
establishment of, **7(2)**, [362]
sentences in, **7(2)**, [374]
laws of—
assent to, **7(2)**, [363]
constitutions, altering, **7(2)**, [362]
disallowance of, **7(2)**, [363]
governors' instructions, inconsistency
with, **7(2)**, [361]
marriage, establishing validity of,
7(2), [364]
meaning, **11(2)**, [136]
passing, evidence of, **7(2)**, [363]
repugnancy, void for, **7(2)**, [359]
Royal Assent, **11(2)**, [126]
validity, **7(2)**, [360]
legislation, powers over, **7(2)**, [356]
legislature, meaning, **7(2)**, [365]
legislation, Admiralty jurisdiction,
11(2), [125]
meaning, **7(2)**, [355], [358], [367], [373];
41, [605], [606]
prisoner, removal of—
British possession—
evidence of act of, **7(2)**, [380]
meaning, **7(2)**, [391]
removal from, **7(2)**, [376]
Channel Islands, **7(2)**, [388]
cost of, **7(2)**, [385]
criminal lunatic, **7(2)**, [384], [391]
dealing with, **7(2)**, [382]
definitions, **7(2)**, [367], [391]
escape from custody, **7(2)**, [383]
foreign jurisdiction, application to,
7(2), [389]
Isle of Man, **7(2)**, [388]
laws for carrying Act into effect,
7(2), [386]
legal custody, to be in, **7(2)**, [370]
liability in second colony, **7(2)**, [371]
Orders in Council, **7(2)**, [387]
prison, reception into, **7(2)**, [382]
punishment, for, **7(2)**, [368]
reasons for, **7(2)**, [376]
regulations, **7(2)**, [378]
removing authority, **7(2)**, [379]
return of, **7(2)**, [377]
warrant, **7(2)**, [381]
warrant, **7(2)**, [369], [381]
torture, application of provisions,
12(1), [1094]

Colorado beetle
spread of, orders as to, **1(1)**, [630]
land improvement affecting, **1(1)**, [369]

Comataidh Telebhisien Gaidhlig. *See* **Gaelic
television**

combination order
community punishment and rehabilitation
order, renamed as, **12(2)**, [993]

command
  lawful, disobedience to, **3**, [488]
  powers of—
    armed forces acting together, **3**, [1]
    forces, over, **3**, [1275]
    naval, **3**, [1199]

Commercial Court
  business of, **11(2)**, [736]
  High Court, part of, **11(2)**, [673]

commissary court. *See also* **consistory court**
  judge of, **14**, 558–9
  jurisdiction of, **14**, 557–8

Commission for Architecture and the Built Environment
  accounts, **2**, [1026]
  annual report, **2**, [1026]
  built environment, meaning, **2**, [1013]
  committees, **2**, [1026]
  establishment of, **2**, [976], [1012]
  functions of—
    changes to, **2**, [1014]
    delegation of, **2**, [1026]
    general, **2**, [1013]
  instruments and authentication, **2**, [1026]
  members—
    appointment, **2**, [1026]
    remuneration, **2**, [1026]
    tenure, **2**, [1026]
  old, dissolution of, **2**, [1016]
  power to dissolve, **2**, [1015]
  proceedings, **2**, [1026]
  staff, **2**, [1026]
  staff, property, rights and liabilities, transfer of, **2**, [1027]
  status, **2**, [1026]
  tax provisions, **2**, [1018]
  transitional provisions, **2**, [1026]

Commission for Equality and Human Rights
  accounts, **7(1)**, [833]
  action plans, requirement of, **7(1)**, [767]
  advice and guidance by, **7(1)**, [758]
  annual report, **7(1)**, [832]
  assessments, **7(1)**, [836]
  chairman, **7(1)**, [831]
  changes in society, monitoring, **7(1)**, [756]
  charging, **7(1)**, [833]
  codes of practice—
    contents of, **7(1)**, [759]
    drafts, **7(1)**, [759]
    failure to comply with, **7(1)**, [760]
    proposals, **7(1)**, [759]
    publication of, **7(1)**, [759]
    revision, **7(1)**, [760]
  Commissioners—
    investigating, **7(1)**, [832]
    remuneration, **7(1)**, [833]
    tenure, **7(1)**, [831]
    Transition, **7(1)**, [786]
  Committees, **7(1)**, [832]

Commission for Equality and Human Rights—*contd*
  conciliation services, promotion of, **7(1)**, [772]
  Disability Committee, **7(1)**, [835]
  disabled persons, promotion of equality of opportunity, **7(1)**, [753]
  disclosure of information, **7(1)**, [751]
  education or training, provision of, **7(1)**, [758]
  effectiveness of law, monitoring, **7(1)**, [756]
  equality and diversity, functions as to, **7(1)**, [753]
  establishment of, **7(1)**, [746]
  financial year, **7(1)**, [833]
  functions of, **7(1)**, [754]
  funding, **7(1)**, [833]
  general duty of, **7(1)**, [748]
  general note, **7(1)**, [1], [80]
  grants, **7(1)**, [762]
  groups—
    activities involving, arrangements for, **7(1)**, [764]
    crime affecting, monitoring, **7(1)**, [764]
    meaning, **7(1)**, [755]
    relations between, functions relating to, **7(1)**, [755]
  human rights—
    co-operation with persons interested in, **7(1)**, [763]
    functions as to, **7(1)**, [754]
  information and advice, publication of, **7(1)**, [758]
  inquiries by, **7(1)**, [761], [836]
  investigations by—
    conduct of, **7(1)**, [765], [836]
    evidence, **7(1)**, [836]
    report of, **7(1)**, [765], [836]
    representations, **7(1)**, [836]
    terms of reference, **7(1)**, [836]
  judicial review proceedings, **7(1)**, [775]
  legal proceedings—
    institution or intervention in, **7(1)**, [775]
    party to, assisting—
      conditions, **7(1)**, [773]
      costs, **7(1)**, [774]
  members, **7(1)**, [831]
  pressure to discriminate, application to restrain, **7(1)**, [770], [771]
  proceedings, **7(1)**, [832]
  progress, monitoring, **7(1)**, [757]
  public sector duties—
    compliance, assessment of, **7(1)**, [776]
    compliance notice, **7(1)**, [777]
  research by, **7(1)**, [758]
  Scotland Committee, **7(1)**, [832]
  Scotland, human rights action in, **7(1)**, [752]
  staff, **7(1)**, [832]
  status, **7(1)**, [834]
  strategic plan—
    consultation, **7(1)**, [751]
    preparation of, **7(1)**, [749]
    publication, **7(1)**, [749]
    review and revision, **7(1)**, [749]

Commission for Equality and Human Rights—*contd*
transfer of property of former Commissions, power of, **7(1)**, [782]
transitional provisions, **7(1)**, [787]
unlawful act notice—
  action plan, requiring, **7(1)**, [767]
  appeals, **7(1)**, [766]
  issue of, **7(1)**, [766]
unlawful acts—
  agreements as to, **7(1)**, [768]
  applications to court, **7(1)**, [769]
unlawful advertising, application to restrain, **7(1)**, [770], [771]
Wales Committee, **7(1)**, [832]

Commission for Health Improvement
abolition of, **30**, [660]; **35(2)**, [447]

Commission for Healthcare Audit and Inspection. *See now* **Care Quality Commission**
accounts, **30**, [764]
additional functions, **30**, [679]
advisory functions, **35(2)**, [285]
annual reports, **30**, [708]
assisting other public authorities, power of, **30**, [705]
assistance, **30**, [764]
Audit Commission, co-operation with, **30**, [686]
Auditor-General for Wales—
  duties relating to, **30**, [720]
  provision of information by, **30**, [691]
chairman and other members, **30**, [764]
Channel Islands, arrangements with, **30**, [707]
code of practice, **30**, [715]
Commission for Social Care Inspection, co-operation with—
  exercise of functions, in, **35(2)**, [475]
  joint annual reviews, **35(2)**, [477]
  reviews and investigations, in, **35(2)**, [476]
criteria, **30**, [680]
discharge of functions, **30**, [764]
  failure in, **30**, [710]
documents and information, power to require, **30**, [689]
  explanation of, **30**, [690]
economy and efficiency, studies as to, **30**, [678]
employees, **30**, [764]
entry, right of, **30**, [687]–[688]
establishment of, **30**, [658]
failings—
  code of practice, **30**, [674]
  improvement notices, **30**, [673]
  reports, **30**, [672]
fees charged by, **30**, [683], [684]
fees payable to, **35(2)**, [353]
general duties, **35(2)**, [285]
general function, **30**, [667]
general powers and duties, **30**, [764]
government policy, duty to have regard to., **30**, [709]

Commission for Healthcare Audit and Inspection—*contd*
improvement in quality of services, encouragement of, **35(2)**, [285]
Independent Regulator, co-operation with, **30**, [682]
information obtained by, disclosure of, **30**, [712]–[714]
inquiries, **30**, [711]
interpretation, **30**, [723]
investigations, **30**, [671]
Isle of Man, arrangements with, **30**, [707]
joint working Commission for Social Care Inspection—
  generally, **30**, [702]
  joint annual reviews, **30**, [704]
  reviews and investigations, **30**, [703]
loans, **30**, [764]
Ministers, arrangements with, **30**, [706]
National Assembly, co-operation with, **30**, [719]
National Care Standards Commission—
  functions, transfer of, **35(2)**, [474]
  property and staff, transfer of, **35(2)**, [494]
national performance data, **30**, [668]
payments, **30**, [764]
procedure, **30**, [764]
provision of health care, references to, **30**, [724]
public authority, assisting, **35(2)**, [478]
registration authority, as, **35(2)**, [284]
reports and information, **30**, [685]
reviews, **30**, [670], [671]
  annual, **30**, [669]
  co-ordination of, **30**, [677]
  data, of, **30**, [676]
  material, provision of, **30**, [681]
seal and evidence, **30**, [764]
Secretary of State and Assembly, functions relating to, **30**, [675]
status, **30**, [764]
transfer of functions to, **30**, [698]
transfer of property rights and liabilities to, **30**, [659], [765]

Commission for Patient and Public Involvement in Health
abolition, **26(2)**, [643]
accounts and audit, **30**, [1107]
appointment procedure, **30**, [1107]
assistance, **30**, [1107]
continuation of, **30**, [1049]
delegation of functions, **30**, [1107]
functions, **30**, [1049]
loans to, **30**, [1107]
membership, **30**, [1107]
payments to, **30**, [1107]
powers, **30**, [1107]
remuneration and allowances, **30**, [1107]
reports, **30**, [1107]
seal and evidence, application of, **30**, [1107]
staff, **30**, [1107]
status, **30**, [1107]

Commission for Racial Equality
dissolution, power of, **7(1)**, [781]
replaced. *See now* **Commission for Equality and Human Rights**
transfer of property of, **7(1)**, [782], [783]
transitional provisions, **7(1)**, [787]

Commission for Rural Communities
committees and sub-committees, **32**, [837]
discharge of functions, **32**, [837]
establishment of, **32**, [782]
general purpose of, **32**, [783]
incidental powers, **32**, [788]
information services, **32**, [786]
members—
    appointment, **32**, [837]
    remuneration and pensions, **32**, [837]
    term of office, **32**, [837]
power to charge for services, **32**, [787]
procedure, **32**, [837]
proof of documents, **32**, [837]
reports and accounts, **32**, [839]
representation, advice and monitoring by, **32**, [784]
research by, **32**, [785]
seal, application of, **32**, [837]
Secretary of State—
    directions by, **32**, [790]
    grants by, **32**, [789]
staff, **32**, [837]
status, **32**, [837]

Commission for Social Care Inspection
accounts, **35(2)**, [493]
advisory functions, **35(2)**, [286]
annual reviews, **35(2)**, [451]
assist other public authorities, power to, **30**, [705]
assistance to, **35(2)**, [493]
Audit Commission, joint working with, **35(2)**, [455]
authorised persons—
    obstruction, **35(2)**, [461]
    right of entry, **35(2)**, [460], [461]
chairman, **35(2)**, [493]
Commission for Healthcare Audit and Inspection, co-operation with—
    exercise of functions, in, **35(2)**, [475]
    joint annual reviews, **35(2)**, [477]
    reviews and investigations, in, **35(2)**, [476]
committees, **35(2)**, [493]
confidential personal information, Code of Practice, **35(2)**, [486]
discharge of functions, **35(2)**, [493]
economy, efficiency, etc, studies as to, **35(2)**, [454]
employees, **35(2)**, [493]
establishment, **35(2)**, [445]
evidence of documents, **35(2)**, [493]
explanation, power to require, **35(2)**, [463]
failings, reports on, **35(2)**, [453]
failure in discharge of functions, **35(2)**, [483]
fees payable to, **35(2)**, [353]
functions and powers of—
    additional, **35(2)**, [456]

Commission for Social Care Inspection—*contd*
functions and powers of—*contd*
    criteria for, **35(2)**, [457]
    exercise of, **35(2)**, [448]
    improvement in social services, encouragement of, **35(2)**, [448]
    information and advice, provision of, **35(2)**, [449]
general powers and duties, **35(2)**, [286], [493]
government policy, duty to have regard to, **35(2)**, [482]
improvement in quality of services, encouragement of, **35(2)**, [286]
information—
    making available, **35(2)**, [459]
    obtained by, use of, **35(2)**, [485]
    power to require, **35(2)**, [462]
inquiries, **35(2)**, [288], [484]
Isle of Man and Channel islands, arrangements with, **35(2)**, [480]
joint working with Commission for Healthcare Audit—
    generally, **30**, [702]
    joint annual reviews, **30**, [704]
    reviews and investigations, **30**, [703]
loans, **35(2)**, [493]
members, **35(2)**, [493]
ministers, arrangements with, **35(2)**, [479]
National Care Standards Commission—
    functions, transfer of, **35(2)**, [474]
    property and staff, transfer of, **35(2)**, [494]
payments to, **35(2)**, [493]
procedure, **35(2)**, [493]
public authority, assisting, **35(2)**, [478]
registration authority, as, **35(2)**, [284]
reports, **35(2)**, [459], [481]
representations made to local authorities, consideration of, **6**, [336]
reviews and investigations by, **35(2)**, [452]
seal, **35(2)**, [493]
status, **35(2)**, [493]
studies and research, review of, **35(2)**, [450]
transfer of certain functions to Chief Inspector of Office for Standards in Education, Children's Services and Skills, **15(2)**, [862]
transfer of property rights and liabilities to, **30**, [765]

Commission for the New Towns. *See* **New Towns Commission**

Commission of Review
appointment of, **14**, 569
composition of, **14**, 569
persons advising, **14**, 591
petition for, **14**, 569
precedent, **14**, 591
proceedings before, **14**, 591

Commission on Human Medicines
establishment, **28**, [69]
functions, **28**, [70]
members, **28**, [69]

Commissioner for Older People in Wales
accounting officer, **35(2)**, [616]
appointment, **35(2)**, [616]
arrangements, review of—
  adverse information, **35(2)**, [590]
  advocacy, **35(2)**, [590]
  amendment of provisions, power of,
    35(2), [592]
  complaints, **35(2)**, [590]
  persons subject to, **35(2)**, [618]
  relevant older people, **35(2)**, [591]
  relevant services, **35(2)**, [591]
  whistle-blowing, **35(2)**, [590]
assistance, giving, **35(2)**, [593]
audit, **35(2)**, [616]
care standards, cases relating to, **35(2)**, [619]
complaints procedure, **35(2)**, [605]
Comptroller and Auditor General,
  examinations by, **35(2)**, [616]
defamation, protection against, **35(2)**, [604]
Deputy, **35(2)**, [616]
entry, power of, **35(2)**, [598]
establishment of, **35(2)**, [586]
estimates, **35(2)**, [616]
evidence of documents, **35(2)**, [616]
examination of cases by, **35(2)**, [595]
functions—
  delegation, **35(2)**, [616]
  discharge of—
    reports following, **35(2)**, [600]
    restrictions on, **35(2)**, [606]
    review of, **35(2)**, [588]
  general, **35(2)**, [587]
  supplementary, **35(2)**, [599]
guidance, issue of, **35(2)**, [597]
information, disclosure of, **35(2)**, [603]
Ministers, reports to, **35(2)**, [616]
obstruction of, **35(2)**, [596]
older person—
  interviewing, **35(2)**, [598]
  meaning, **35(2)**, [609]
other ombudsmen, working with,
  35(2), [601]
payments to, **35(2)**, [616]
Public Services Ombudsman for Wales—
  working collaboratively with, **10**, [824]
  working jointly with, **10**, [823];
    35(2), [601]
remuneration, **35(2)**, [616]
research and educational activities,
  35(2), [594]
review of functions by, **35(2)**, [588]
  persons subject to, **35(2)**, [589], [617]
staff, **35(2)**, [616]
status, **35(2)**, [616]
summary of provisions, **35(1)**, [1]
superannuation, **35(2)**, [616]
term of office, **35(2)**, [616]
United Nations Principles for Older People,
  having regard to, **35(2)**, [610]
use of resources, examinations into,
  35(2), [616]

**Commissioners for HM Revenue and
Customs.** *See also* **HM Revenue and
Customs**
assigned matters, **13**, [590], [598]
Community obligations, implementing,
  13, [596]
computer records, production etc of,
  13, [909]
duties—
  Community obligations, implementing,
    13, [596]
  performance of, **13**, [595]
economic and monetary union, expenditure
  incurred by, under, **13**, [1080]
imported goods, disclosure of certain
  information as to, **13**, [597]
information as to imports, disclosure of,
  13, [915]
information to Horserace Betting Levy Board,
  disclosures of, **13**, [561]
Gambling Commission, consultation with,
  5(1), [312]
Immigration, information—
  disclosure of, **31**, [467]
  duty to share, **31**, [561]
    code of practice, **31**, [562]
  power to require, **31**, [560]
Minister of the Crown, treatment as,
  10, [599]
officers—
  access, powers of, **13**, [611]
  detention, powers of, **13**, [612], [919]
  documents—
    order for production of, **13**, [946]
    removal by, **13**, [947]
  duties, performance of, **13**, [595]
  entry, powers of, **13**, [945]
  meaning, **13**, [590]
  members of armed forces to assist,
    13, [598]
  police to assist, **13**, [598]
  powers, exercise of, **13**, [595]
  protection as to seizure and detention of
    goods, **13**, [749]
orders and regulations, **44(1)**, [612]
powers, exercise of, **13**, [595]
prohibited goods, infringing articles treated
  as, **11(1)**, [925]–[926]
recovery of overpayments—
  assessment for excessive repayment,
    13, [1069]
  interest on overpayments assessed,
    13, [1069]
  review of decisions and appeals, **13**, [1069]
supply of information to, by social security
  authorities, **13**, [1066]
transfer of functions, **10**, [599]
wrongful disclosure of information by,
  5(1), [632]

commissioner for oaths
affidavits before, **18**, [161]
fees chargeable, **11(2)**, [363]
powers, **18**, [75], [153]
solicitor as, **11(2)**, [362]

Commissioner for Victims and Witnesses
accounts, **12(4)**, [58]
advice, giving, **12(4)**, [42]
annual plan **12(4)**, [58]
annual report, **12(4)**, [58]
appointment of, **12(4)**, [40]
authorities within remit, **12(4)**, [45], [59]
delegation by, **12(4)**, [58]
deputy, **12(4)**, [58]
functions of—
  general, **12(4)**, [41]
  restrictions on exercise of, **12(4)**, [43]
pensions, **12(4)**, [58]
relevant authority, disclosure of information
  to, **12(4)**, [46]
staff, **12(4)**, [58]
status of, **12(4)**, [40]
terms of appointment, **12(4)**, [58]
victim, meaning, **12(4)**, [44]
witness, meaning, **12(4)**, [44]

Commissioners of Customs and Excise
drug trafficking offences—
  prosecutions, **12(2)**, [168], [264]
  ships, involving, **12(2)**, [25], [26]
stamp duty adjudication. *See* **stamp duty**

Commissioners of Inland Revenue
General. *See* **General Commissioners**
health and safety information, disclosure,
  18, [1283]
meaning, **42**, [181]
probate documents to be sent to, **18**, [637]
special. *See* **Special Commissioners**

Commissioners of Sewers
saving rights of, **20**, [322]

Commissioners of Works
copyholds in trust for, **13**, [543]
customs land vesting in, **13**, [542]
purchase of lands by, **13**, [544]

**Commissioners under Commissioners
Clauses Act**
accounts—
  annual meeting, at, **10**, [394]
  annual statement of, **10**, [393]
  appeal, **10**, [396]
  auditor, appointing, **10**, [395]
  clerk, transmitted to, **10**, [397]
  receipts and disbursements, of, **10**, [392]
actions brought in name of, **10**, [364]
appointment, defect in, **10**, [355]
borrowing at low rate of interest, **10**, [383]
byelaws, making—
  breach, **10**, [399]
  conduct of officers, for, **10**, [398]
  penalties, **10**, [399]
constitution of body of, **10**, [308]
contracts—
  breach of, **10**, [361]
  power to enter into, **10**, [359]
  security, taking, **10**, [360]
  tenders for, **10**, [360]

**Commissioners under Commissioners
Clauses Act**—*contd*
conveyance of land by, **10**, [362]
Crown, saving of rights of, **10**, [405]
damages—
  recovery of, **10**, [404]
  reimbursement of, **10**, [366]
death, effect of on action, **10**, [364]
declaration—
  failure to make, **10**, [319]
  first meeting, made at, **10**, [317]
  form of, **10**, [316]
election—
  adjournment of, **10**, [336]
  annual meetings for, **10**, [324]
  conduct of, **10**, [331]
  declaration of poll, **10**, [333]
  early closing of poll, **10**, [332]
  inspection of books and papers, **10**, [334]
  mode of voting, **10**, [331]
  more than one ward, in, **10**, [335]
  poll books, examination of, **10**, [333]
  polling places, **10**, [326]
  presiding officer—
    expenses, **10**, [338]
    want of title, **10**, [337]
  questions to voters, **10**, [330]
  rate collectors, etc, ascertaining rights,
    10, [330]
  rateable value, vote based on, **10**, [327]
  re-election, **10**, [321]
  returning officer, **10**, [325], [338]
  rotation, **10**, [320]
  scale of votes, **10**, [327]
  voters, lists of, **10**, [329]
  voting papers, **10**, [326], [408]
  wards, voting in, **10**, [328]
execution levied on, **10**, [365]
indictment, preferring, **10**, [367]
liability of, **10**, [363]
meaning, **10**, [308]
meetings—
  absence from, **10**, [319]
  adjournment, **10**, [344]
  annual, **10**, [343]
  chairman, election of, **10**, [340]
  committees, **10**, [352]
  expenses, **10**, [351]
  first, **10**, [339]
  monthly, **10**, [343]
    extraordinary business at, **10**, [346]
    ordinary business for, **10**, [345]
  notices of, **10**, [350]
  quorum, **10**, [342]
  resolutions, revocation of, **10**, [347]
  special, **10**, [348]
  special notice, **10**, [349]
  special order, resolution, confirming,
    10, [349]
  vacancies, effect of, **10**, [354]
  voting, **10**, [341]
mortgages—
  arrears, payment of, **10**, [389]
  books of account, inspection of, **10**, [391]
  form of, **10**, [409]

Commissioners under Commissioners Clauses Act—*contd*
  mortgages—*contd*
    interest on, **10**, [382]
    notice of paying of, **10**, [386]
    paying off, determination by lot, **10**, [388]
    rates of, **10**, [378]
    receiver, appointment of, **10**, [390]
    register of, **10**, [379]
    register of transfers, **10**, [381]
    repayment, **10**, [384]
    sinking fund, **10**, [387]
    transfer, **10**, [379], [410]
  notices—
    advertisement, by, **10**, [401]
    authentication of, **10**, [402]
    service of, **10**, [400]
  office—
    daily attendance at, **10**, [357]
    holding, disqualification of, **10**, [314]
  officers—
    absconding, warrant against, **10**, [376]
    accounts, furnishing, **10**, [372]
    appointment, **10**, [368]
    balance of money, paying over, **10**, [373]
    clerk and treasurer to be different, **10**, [369]
    conduct, byelaws for, **10**, [398]
    fees, taking, **10**, [370]
    monies, paying over, **10**, [372]
    power to imprison, **10**, [375]
    refusal to account, **10**, [375]
    salaries, **10**, [368]
    security taken from, **10**, [371]
    summary proceedings against, **10**, [374]
    surety, remedy against, **10**, [377]
  proceedings, records of, **10**, [358]
  proof of debts in bankruptcy, **10**, [403]
  property, injury to, **10**, [367]
  public offices, providing, **10**, [356]
  qualifications—
    acting without, **10**, [318]
    bankrupt, disqualification of, **10**, [313]
    owner and occupier, as, **10**, [312]
    rating, dependent on, **10**, [311]
  refusal to act, deemed, **10**, [319]
  rotation list, **10**, [323]
  service of notices on, **10**, [400]
  shareholders as, **10**, [315]
  sinking fund, having, **10**, [387]
  Special Act—
    copies of, **10**, [406]–[407]
    meaning, **10**, [308]
  vacancies, filling, **10**, [322]

Commissions for Local Administration
  accommodation for, **25(2)**, [335]
  advice and guidance by, **25(2)**, [307]
  annual reports of, **25(2)**, [308], [875]
  chairman and vice-chairman, **25(2)**, [307]
  delegation by, **25(2)**, [335]
  establishment, **25(1)**, [1]; **25(2)**, [307]
  expenses, **25(2)**, [330], [874]
  financial provisions, **25(2)**, [335]

Commissions for Local Administration—*contd*
  Local Commissioner. *See* **Local Commissioner**
  Parliamentary Commissioner as member of, **25(2)**, [307]
  proceedings of, **25(2)**, [335]
  reports, **25(2)**, [307], [308]
  representative bodies—
    designation, **25(2)**, [307]
    reports for, **25(2)**, [308]
  staff, appointment, **25(2)**, [335]

committal
  either way offence, **12(1)**, [1085]
  proceedings—
    depositions at trial, use of, **11(3)**, [214], [218]
    evidence, **11(2)**, [408]
    general nature of, **11(2)**, [408]
    indictable-only offences, none for, **11(3)**, [236]
    notice following, **11(2)**, [416]
    open court, to be in, **11(2)**, [408]
    restrictions on reports, **11(2)**, [418]
    single justice, before, **11(2)**, [408]
    summary trial—
      change from, **11(2)**, [441]
      change to, **11(2)**, [449]
    written statements—
      evidence in, **11(2)**, [270]
      use of, at trial, **11(3)**, [214], [218]
  same arrears, more than once in respect of, **27**, [320]
  sentence, for, incorrigible rogue, **11(2)**, [214]
  trial, for—
    bail, on, **11(2)**, [416]
    custody, to, **11(2)**, [416]
    evidence, whether considering, **11(2)**, [416]
    meaning, **41**, [605]
    place of trial, specifying, **11(2)**, [417]

Committee of Public Accounts
  Comptroller and Auditor General considering proposals of, **19(2)**, [974]
  construction of references to, **19(2)**, [983]

Committee on Climate Change
  advice or assistance, provision on request, **35(S)**, 86
  advice, publication of, **35(S)**, 130
  ancillary powers, **35(S)**, 87
  carbon budgets, advice in connection with, **35(S)**, 82–3
  emissions from international aviation or shipping, advice on, **35(S)**, 84
  establishment of, **35(S)**, 81
  grants to, **35(S)**, 87
  impact report, advice on, **35(S)**, 97
  level of 2050 target, advice on, **35(S)**, 82
  members, **35(S)**, 126–7
  national authorities—
    directions, power to give, **35(S)**, 89
    guidance, power to give, **35(S)**, 88

Committee on Climate Change—*contd*
national authorities—*contd*
information, provision of, **35(S)**, 130
proceedings, **35(S)**, 128
proof of documents, **35(S)**, 129
reports and accounts, **35(S)**, 129
reports on progress—
contents of, **35(S)**, 84–5
laying before Parliament, **35(S)**, 84
responses to, **35(S)**, 85–6
staff, **35(S)**, 127
status, **35(S)**, 130
sub-committees, **35(S)**, 127–9
summary of provisions, **35(S)**, 47

commodity futures
charge to tax, **44(1)**, [103]
losses, **44(1)**, [203]
meaning, **44(1)**, [203]

common agricultural policy
assured markets, **18**, [7]
levies, provisions as to, **18**, [7]
refunds on exported goods, **18**, [7]

Common Council of City of London
committee, appointment of, **23**, [537]
court premises, duties on, **11(2)**, [249]
See also **London, City of, Common
Council**

common employment
defence of, abolition, **45**, [945], [946]
doctrine, **45**, [946]

common informer
abolition of actions, **12(1)**, [274]

common investment fund
distributions, **43(1)**, [432]
income arising to, **43(1)**, [432]
provisions for, **11(2)**, [881]
schemes—
defaults, **11(2)**, [882]
establishment of, **11(2)**, [881]
investment manager, **11(2)**, [881]
money, investment of, **11(2)**, [881]

common (land)
access to, public right, **20**, [793]
acquisition for allotments, **1(1)**, [244]
appropriation—
powers of, **25(2)**, [120]
restriction on, **1(1)**, [244]
appropriation of, **32**, [285]
land for planning purposes, **46**, [493]
approvement, abolition of power of, **24**, [490]
boundaries of authorities, on, **25(2)**, [166]
byelaws, **20**, [414]–[416], [469]; **24**, [492]
camping on, **20**, [793]
caravans on. *See* **caravan site**
commonable rights, extinction, **9**, [56], [298]
Commons Commissioners—
appeal from, **21**, [284]
appointing, **21**, [283]

common (land)—*contd*
Commons Commissioners—*contd*
assessors, **21**, [283]
procedure, **21**, [283]
commons councils—
ancillary powers, **24**, [475]
body corporate, as, **24**, [469]
consent to persons with interest in land,
action without, **24**, [476]
consequential provision, **24**, [479]
constitution—
standard, **24**, [472]
terms of, **24**, [473]
establishment of, **24**, [469]
establishment orders, variation and
revocation of, **24**, [480]
functions, **24**, [474]
money, raising, **24**, [475]
procedure for establishment, **24**, [470]
property of, **24**, [471]
rules—
enforcement of, **24**, [477]
power to make, **24**, [478]
revocation, **24**, [478]
status, **24**, [471]
compulsory acquisition of, **20**, [1]
commoners, meeting of—
committee—
appointment by, **9**, [59], [298]
payment of compensation to, **9**, [59],
[298]
convening, **9**, [59]
negotiations with, **9**, [61], [298]
compensation for, **9**, [56]–[58], [281], [298]
conveyance on payment of compensation,
9, [57], [298]
deed poll, vesting by, **9**, [57], [64], [298]
determination, **9**, [298]
disputes as to compensation, **9**, [62], [298]
exchange of lands, certificate as to,
9, [432], [453]
compulsory purchase, **32**, [285]
Crown, provisions binding, **24**, [501]
entire animals turned out on, **20**, [485], [486]
extinguishment of rights—
compensation money—
deposit of orders, **20**, [444]
land, schedule of, **20**, [446]
lawful use of, **20**, [443]
recreation grounds and field gardens, use
for, **20**, [442]
forest law, rights arising in, **10**, [84]
half-yearly or yearly, let, **20**, [55]
highway authority, acquisition by, **36**, [1285],
[1286]
inclosure. *See* **inclosure of commons**
inclosure of, restrictions, **20**, [794]
See also **inclosure of commons**
interpretation, **24**, [502]
land not held of a manor, **9**, [58], [298]
London boroughs, powers, **20**, [432]
Management, commons councils. *See*
commons councils *above*
meaning, **24**, [496]; **9**, [432]

common (land)—*contd*
metropolitan—
claim to inclose, notice of, **20**, [433]
compensation for estate or rights,
20, [372], [373]
Crown rights, **20**, [383]
draft scheme—
approval of, **20**, [370]
final settlement of, **20**, [370]
inquiry on, **20**, [368]
objections and suggestions, **20**, [367]
preparing, **20**, [365]
printing and publishing, **20**, [366]
report on, **20**, [369]
Duchy of Cornwall, rights of, **20**, [383]
Duchy of Lancaster, rights of, **20**, [383]
generally, **20**, [1]
illegal inclosures, **20**, [423]
inclosure—
land given in exchange, **25(1)**, [632]
road widening, for, **25(1)**, [632]
local authority, **20**, [359], [387]
local rate, **20**, [359], [387]
meaning, **20**, [360]
memorial—
expenses, **20**, [379]
extension of right, **20**, [391]
presentation of, **20**, [363]
subject matter of, **20**, [364]
Metropolitan Police District, situate in,
20, [361]
person interested in—
absence of, **20**, [382]
agent, appointing, **20**, [384], [388]
disability of, **20**, [382]
proceedings, **20**, [362]
rights of common, Crown granting,
20, [385]
stamp duty land tax exemption,
20, [386]
scheme—
amending scheme, **20**, [381]
appeal from Commissioners, **20**, [373]
approval of, **20**, [370]
certified, **20**, [375]
draft. *See* draft scheme *above*
expenses, **20**, [379]
local authority contribution to, **20**, [380]
operation of, **20**, [377]
petition against, **20**, [378]
publication, **20**, [376]
rights affected, stating, **20**, [371]
sale of copies, **20**, [374]
National Trust, powers of. *See* **National Trust**
Natural England, reference to, **24**, [499]
open cast coal compulsory rights order,
effect, **17(1)**, [192]
orders and regulations, **24**, [500]
pasture, of, allotment schemes, **1(1)**, [203]
power to amend enactments—
common land or greens, relating to,
24, [495]
national authorities, conferring functions
on, **24**, [496]

common (land)—*contd*
prescription period for claiming rights—
infant or other person under disability, in
case of, **20**, [67]
interruption to, **20**, [63]
pleadings, **20**, [65]
presumption, restricting, **20**, [66]
sixty years, absolute right after, **20**, [61]
thirty years' enjoyment, **20**, [61]
preservation, **9**, [432]
special parliamentary procedure for,
9, [432], [453]
vesting of land, **9**, [57], [64], [298]
procedure for taking, **32**, [285]
rams, dates for remaining on, **20**, [53]
recreational facilities on, **32**, [260]
registration—
application, **21**, [272]
authorities, **21**, [270]; **24**, [447]
cancellation of, **21**, [274]
common land, meaning of, **21**, [288]
Crown interest, **21**, [289]
deregistration and exchange—
applications, **24**, [459]
orders, **24**, [460]
disputed claims, **21**, [274]
Duchy interest, **21**, [289]
effect of, **21**, [276]
Epping Forest, **21**, [277]
exemption, **21**, [277]
expenses, **21**, [290]
Forest of Dean, **21**, [277]
generally, **21**, [269]
grazing rights, **21**, [281]
interruptions, disregard of, **21**, [282]
land registration, effect of, **21**, [278]
land to which applying, **24**, [448]
New Forest, **20**, [445]; **21**, [277]
notification of, **21**, [273]
objections to, **21**, [273]
ownership, **21**, [269], [288]
previous legislation—
mistake under, **24**, [506]
non-registration under, **24**, [506]
provisional, **21**, [272]
register—
amendment of, **21**, [279]
application for amendment, regulations,
24, [467]
common land, of, **21**, [271]
conclusiveness, **24**, [461]
contents of, **24**, [446]
copies of entries, inspecting, **21**, [273]
correction, **24**, [462]
electronic, **24**, [468]
inspection and copying, **24**, [463]
maintenance of, **21**, [271]; **24**, [444]
official copies, admissibility in evidence,
24, [464]
purpose of, **24**, [445]
rectification of, **21**, [280]
reference to, **24**, [498]
town or village greens, of, **21**, [271]
regulations, **21**, [285]
requisitioned land, **21**, [282]

common (land)—*contd*

registration—*contd*

rights of common, of. *See* rights of
common *below*

scheme, procedure for making, **20**, [462]

statutory dispositions, **24**, [457]

town greens, **21**, [269]; **24**, [458]

transitional provision, **24**, [507]

undisputed, finality of, **21**, [275]

village greens, **21**, [269]; **24**, [458]

regulated—

district council acquiring property in,
20, [466]

gravel digging, **20**, [467]

inclosed, not to be, **20**, [426]

management of, **20**, [463]

regulation of—

allotment for labouring poor, providing,
20, [430]

byelaws, **20**, [414]–[416], [469]

compensation, **20**, [465]

draft scheme, **20**, [462]

expenses raised by sale of part, **20**, [429]

generally, **20**, [1]

gravel digging, provisions on, **20**, [418]

schemes for **24**, [492]

amendment of, **20**, [468]

approval of, **20**, [462]

district council, powers of, **20**, [461],
[466]

expenses, **20**, [470]

parish contributing to expenses,
20, [464]

procedure, **20**, [462]

revocation, **20**, [468]

savings, **20**, [472]

urban district council contributing to
expenses, **20**, [471]

rights of common—

apportionment, **24**, [451]

attached rights, re-allocation of **24**, [454]

attachment, **24**, [453]

creation of, **24**, [449]

district council powers as to, **25(1)**, [81]

extinguishment, **24**, [456]

meaning, **21**, [288]

registration of, **21**, [269]

severance, **24**, [452], [505]

surrender, **24**, [456]

transfer in gross, **24**, [455]

variation, **24**, [450]

stinted—

depasturing with sheep, **20**, [52]

improving wastes, **20**, [48]

opening and closing, **20**, [49], [50]

persons not consenting to regulations,
20, [51]

postponed opening, **20**, [49]

rights of, extinguishment, **20**, [794]

unauthorised agricultural activities on,
24, [489]

unclaimed land, powers of local authority
over, **24**, [488]

waste land of a manor, meaning, **20**, [427]

common (land)—*contd*

works—

amendment of local or personal Acts,
24, [487]

consent to—

application, determining, **24**, [482]

conditions, **24**, [482]

exemption from requirement, **24**, [486]

need for, **24**, [481]

procedure, **24**, [483]

enforcement of provisions, **24**, [484]

National Trust property, in, **24**, [508]

new parishes, **24**, [508]

restricted, **24**, [481]

schemes, **24**, [485]

transitional provision, **24**, [508]

without consent, prohibition, **24**, [481]

common law

offences abolished, **12(1)**, [1000]

common lodging house

infectious disease at, duty to notify,
35(1), [480]

inmate—

medical examination of, **35(1)**, [481]

removal to hospital, **35(1)**, [482]

meaning, **35(1)**, [514]

notifiable disease—

closure on account of, **35(1)**, [483]

inmate suffering from—

medical examination of, **35(1)**, [481]

removal to hospital of, **35(1)**, [482]

common market. *See* **European
Communities**

common of pasture

land improvement affecting, **1(1)**, [1369]

opening and closing, days and times,
45, [926]

common ownership enterprise

nature of, **47**, [278]

common, rights of

grant of land subject to, **14**, 399–400

Common Serjeant

circuit judge, becoming, **11(2)**, [260]

oath, taking, **11(2)**, [210]

qualifications, **11(2)**, [209]

remuneration and benefits, **11(2)**, [262]

commonhold

advice regarding, financial assistance for,
24, [62]

approved ombudsman scheme, **24**, [42]

association—

constitution of, **24**, [34]

directors—

assessment by, **24**, [38]

duty to manage, **24**, [35]

documents, rectification of, **24**, [40]

expenses of, **24**, [38]

commonhold—*contd*
  association—*contd*
    liquidator, **24**, [48]
    meaning, **24**, [34]
    membership, **24**, [146]
    memorandum and articles of association,
      24, [145]
      amendment of, **8(1)**, [1359]
    name, **24**, [147]
    object of, **24**, [69]
    ombudsman scheme, membership of,
      24, [42]
    private company limited by guarantee, as,
      24, [34]
    reserve fund, **24**, [39]
      release of, **24**, [56]
    resolution, voting for, **24**, [36]
    RTM company, unable to be, **24**, [73]
    statutory declaration, **24**, [147]
    succession order—
      application for, **24**, [51]
      assets and liabilities, provision for,
        24, [52]
      transfer of responsibility by, **24**, [53]
    termination application—
      meaning, **24**, [46]
      Registrar, action of, **24**, [49]
    termination statement—
      contents of, **24**, [47]
      termination application, accompanying,
        24, [46]
    termination-statement resolution—
      agreement as to, **24**, [44], [45]
      meaning, **24**, [43]
      passing., **24**, [43]
    winding-up by court, **24**, [50]
    winding-up resolution—
      agreement as to, **24**, [44], [45]
      meaning, **24**, [43]
      passing., **24**, [43]
  breach of duty, limitation of action,
    19(3), [747]
  common parts—
    additions to, **24**, [30]
    charge over, not to be made, **24**, [28]
    commonhold community statement. *See*
      community statements *below*
    definition, **24**, [25]
    new legal mortgage of, **24**, [29]
    transactions, **24**, [27]
    use and maintenance of, **24**, [26]
  community statements—
    amendment, **24**, [33]
    common parts, provision for, **24**, [25]–[27]
    contents of, **24**, [11], [31]
      regulations, **24**, [32]
    development rights, conferring, **24**, [58]
    form, **24**, [31]
    meaning, **24**, [31]
    requirement, not complying with, **24**, [49]
    use and maintenance of units, provision
      regulating, **24**, [14]
  Crown, provisions binding, **24**, [63]
  defined expressions, index of, **24**, [70]
  enlargement, **24**, [41]

commonhold—*contd*
  jurisdiction, **24**, [66]
  land—
    adding, **24**, [41]
    advice as to, **24**, [62]
    compulsory purchase, **24**, [60]
    development rights, **24**, [58], [148]
      succession to, **24**, [59]
    excluded land, **24**, [4], [144]
    extinguished lease, liability for loss, **24**, [10]
    freehold estate, registration of—
      application for, **24**, [2]
        documents, **24**, [143]
      consent to, **24**, [3]
      error, in, **24**, [6]
      procedure, **24**, [65]
      register, **24**, [67]
      registered details, **24**, [5]
      unit-holders, with, **24**, [9]
      unit-holders, without, **24**, [7]
    home rights in, **24**, [61]
    meaning, **24**, [1]
    transitional period, **24**, [8]
  multiple site, **24**, [57]
  orders and regulations, **24**, [64]
  rights and duties, enforcement of, **24**, [37]
  summary of provisions, **20**, [1]
  termination, **24**, [54], [55]
  unit—
    definition, **24**, [11]
    extent of, **24**, [11]
    leasing—
      non-residential, **24**, [18]
      regulations, **24**, [19]
      residential, **24**, [17]
      tenant, obligations on, **24**, [19]
    part—
      charge over, **24**, [22]
      interest in, **24**, [21]
    size, changing, **24**, [23]
      charged unit, of, **24**, [24]
    transactions in, **24**, [20]
    transfer, **24**, [15], [16]
    use and maintenance of, **24**, [14]
  unit-holders—
    default by, **24**, [35]
    former, **24**, [16]
    joint, **24**, [13]
    meaning, **24**, [12]
    registration with, **24**, [9]
    registration without, **24**, [7]
    transactions by, **24**, [20]

Commonwealth. *See also names of*
Commonwealth countries
  Acts extending to, **32**, [848]
  certain countries of, jurisdiction, omission of
    references to, **41**, [524]
  citizen—
    meaning, **31**, [181]; **41**, [480]
    right of abode in UK, **31**, [73]
      deprivation of, **31**, [74]
  citizenship—
    countries to which applicable, **31**, [186]
    persons qualifying for, **31**, [164]

Commonwealth—*contd*
country, meaning, **3**, [1223]
diplomatic representatives, **10**, [1000], [1032]
extradition of offenders. *See* **extradition**
government security, issue unstamped,
  penalty, **41**, [42]
Ireland, cessation of membership, **31**, [622]
legislation affecting, by consent, **41**, [480]
letters of administration granted in, **18**, [595]
summary of provisions, **7(2)**, [350]
terrorism provisions applied, **18**, [754]

Commonwealth Development Corporation
accounts and audit, **7(2)**, [810]
borrowing—
  advances made by Secretary of State,
    7(2), [805]
  interest, **7(2)**, [685]
  new loans, **7(2)**, [806]
  old loans, **7(2)**, [805]
  powers, **7(2)**, [683]
  repayment, **7(2)**, [685]
  Treasury guarantees, **7(2)**, [684],
    [807]–[808]
Companies Act 1985, registration under—
  certificate, **7(2)**, [801]
  day for, appointing, **7(2)**, [800]
  documents, filing, **7(2)**, [799], [825]
  effect of, **7(2)**, [802]
  initial steps, **7(2)**, [798]
  modification of provisions,
    7(2), [826]–[827]
  registrar of companies, duty of, **7(2)**, [801]
  shares, initial allotment of, **7(2)**, [803]
company associated with, **7(2)**, [821]
constitution of, **7(2)**, [682]
Crown shareholding in, **7(2)**, [815]
dividends, payment of, **7(2)**, [818]
government assistance, limit on, **7(2)**, [812]
liabilities, extinguishment of, **7(2)**, [811]
repealed provisions, **7(2)**, [804]
securities—
  acquisition of, **7(2)**, [814]
  Crown, held by or for, **7(2)**, [816]
  issue of, **7(2)**, [813]
  meaning, **7(2)**, [822]
taxation, **7(2)**, [828]
Treasury consent, where required, **7(2)**, [819]

commonwealth force
absence from, **3**, [1193]
air force law, subject to, **3**, [981]
desertion from, **3**, [1193]
meaning, **3**, [723], [995]
military law, subject to, **3**, [708]
naval attachment to, **3**, [1198]
naval law, subject to, **3**, [1191]

Commonwealth Institute
management, enactments ceasing to apply,
  7(2), [849], [853]
staff superannuation, **33(1)**, [190]

commonwealth naval forces
navy, acting with, **3**, [1]

Commonwealth Scholarship Commission
annual reports, **15(2)**, [338]
committees, **15(2)**, [338]
functions, **15(2)**, [333]
members, **15(2)**, [332], [338]
proceedings, **15(2)**, [338]
committees, **15(2)**, [338]
functions, **15(2)**, [333]
members, **15(2)**, [332], [338]
proceedings, **15(2)**, [338]

Commonwealth Secretariat
arbitration, disputes referred to, **7(2)**, [577]
immunities and privileges, **7(2)**, [577], [579],
  [581]
income tax exemption, **10**, [1241]
legal capacity, **7(2)**, [577]
meaning, **7(2)**, [577]
privileges and immunities, **10**, [1239]
staff, **7(2)**, [580]

**Commonwealth Secretariat Arbitral
Tribunal**
privileges and immunities, **10**, [1240]

Commonwealth Telecommunications
Bureau, incorporation, **45**, [38]
  legal capacity, **45**, [38]
Cable and Wireless Ltd. *See under*
  telecommunications

Commonwealth War Graves Commission
protection of, **25(2)**, [271]

commorientes
survivorship, presumption of, **20**, [785]

communications. *See also* **electronic
communications**
data—
  disclosure of—
    authorisations, form and duration of,
      45, [351]
    grounds for, **45**, [350]
    lawful, **45**, [349]
    payments, arrangements for, **45**, [352]
  lawful acquisition of, **45**, [349]
  meaning, **45**, [349]
  obtaining—
    authorisations, form and duration of,
      45, [351]
    grounds for, **45**, [350]
    payments, arrangements for, **45**, [352]
interception—
  capability, maintenance of, **45**, [340]
  Commissioner—
    appointment, **45**, [385]
    co-operation with, **45**, [386]
    functions, **45**, [385]
    reports, **45**, [386]
    summary of provisions, **45**, [1]
  costs, grants for, **45**, [342]
  lawful—
    power to provide for, **45**, [332]

communications—*contd*
  interception—*contd*
    lawful—*contd*
      warrant—
        with, **45**, [333]
        without, **45**, [331]
      legal proceedings—
        exclusion of matters from, **45**, [345]
          exceptions, **45**, [346]
      location, **45**, [330]
      meaning, **45**, [330]
      safeguards—
        certificated warrants, extra in case of,
          45, [344]
        general, **45**, [343]
      summary of provisions, **45**, [1]
      Technical Advisory Board, **45**, [341]
      unauthorised disclosures, **45**, [347]
    unlawful, **45**, [329]
    warrant for—
      application for, **45**, [334]
      cancellation, **45**, [337]
      certificates, modification of, **45**, [338]
      contents of, **45**, [336]
      duration, **45**, [337]
      implementation of, **45**, [339]
      issue of, **45**, [335]
      modification of, **45**, [338]
      renewal, **45**, [337]
      Secretary of State, issued by, **45**, [333]
      without, **45**, [331]
  telecommunications. *See*
    telecommunications

communications data
  meaning, **12(3)**, [136]
  retention—
    agreements, **12(3)**, [131]
    codes of practice—
      issue and revision of, **12(3)**, [131]
      procedure for, **12(3)**, [132]
    costs, arrangement for payment of,
      12(3), [135]
    directions, **12(3)**, [133]
    lapsing of powers, **12(3)**, [134]

communion. *See* **Holy Communion**

community amateur sports clubs
  tax relief for—
    donors, reliefs for, **43(2)**, [159]
    entitlement to be registered, **43(2)**, [157]
    interpretation, **43(2)**, [162]
    introduction of, **43(2)**, [107]
    property ceasing to be held for qualifying
      purposes, chargeable gains on,
      43(2), [160]
    registered clubs, exemptions for,
      43(2), [158]
    registration, **43(2)**, [161]

community bus service. *See under* **bus
  services**

community care. *See also* **local authority**
  assessment of needs, **40(2)**, [448]
  carers—
    assessment—
      ability to provide care, of, **40(2)**, [42]
      carer and person cared for, of,
        40(2), [268]
      co-operation between authorities,
        40(2), [482]
      right to, **40(2)**, [265]
        local authority's duty to inform of,
          40(2), [270]
    direct payments to, **40(2)**, [320]
    disabled children, for,
      40(1), [1]. *See also* **disabled person**
    meaning, **40(2)**, [42]
    services for—
      carer and person cared for, for,
        40(2), [268]
      local authority, from, **40(2)**, [266]
      vouchers, issue of, **40(2)**, [267]
  delayed discharge payments—
    definitions, **40(2)**, [456]
    dispute resolution, **40(2)**, [453]
    liability to make, **40(2)**, [450]
    matters taken into account, **40(2)**, [451]
    NHS body—
      duties of, **40(2)**, [449]
      meaning, **40(2)**, [445]
      payment made to, **40(2)**, [451]
    NHS patients in care homes, application of
      provisions to, **40(2)**, [457]
    ordinary residence, dispute as to,
      40(2), [452]
    qualifying hospital patient, meaning,
      40(2), [445]
    regulations and orders, **40(2)**, [455]
    social services authorities, adjustments
      between, **40(2)**, [454]
  direct payments, **40(2)**, [320]
  general note, **40(1)**, [1]
  likely need for services, notice of,
    40(2), [446], [447]
  responsible authority, duties of,
    40(2), [448]
  responsible NHS body, duties of,
    40(2), [449]
  local authority services—
    England, free provision in, **40(2)**, [458]
    Wales, free provision in, **40(2)**, [459]
  nursing care, exclusion of, **40(2)**, [313]

community charges
  abolition, **26(1)**, [87]
  local authority members owing, restriction on
    voting by, **26(1)**, [90]
  summary of provisions, **25(1)**, [1]

community council. *See under* **Wales**
  community, meaning, **35(1)**, [118]
  expenses for traffic calming works,
    contributions to, **36**, [1322]
  parking places, provision of, **37**, [229]–[232]
  public health, exercise of powers as to,
    35(1), [118]

community council—*contd*
traffic signs, **37**, [245]

community development finance institutions
accreditation—
application for, **44(4)**, [348]
criteria for, **44(4)**, [348]
loss of, no claim after, **44(4)**, [364]
period of, **44(4)**, [350]
terms and conditions of, **44(4)**, [349]
investor—
beneficial ownership, must have, **44(4)**, [359]
no control by, **44(4)**, [358]
share in partnership, no acquisition of, **44(4)**, [360]
receipts of value from—
amount of, **44(4)**, [375]
connected persons, by or from, **44(4)**, [378]
future claims, effect on, **44(4)**, [377]
insignificant, added together, **44(4)**, [373]
loans, **44(4)**, [371]
meaning, **44(4)**, [374]
more than one investment, where, **44(4)**, [376]
securities, **44(4)**, [372]
shares, **44(4)**, [372]

Community Health Council
abolition of, **30**, [633]
documents, access to, **30**, [510]
England, abolition in, **28**, [745]
meetings, access to, **30**, [510]
members, access to information relating to, **30**, [511]

community home
accommodation in, provision of, **6**, [323]
approved institution becoming, **6**, [139]
assisted—
cessation, compensation payable, **6**, [374]
closure by local authority, **6**, [373]
discontinuance, **6**, [372]
disposal on cessation, **6**, [374]
disputes, determination of, **6**, [371]
financial provisions on cessation, **6**, [374]
home designated as, **6**, [370]
management—
generally, **6**, [447]
instrument of, **6**, [446]
regional plan, under, **6**, [188]
regulations, **6**, [448]
controlled—
cessation—
compensation payable, **6**, [374]
financial provisions, **6**, [374]
closure by local authority, **6**, [373]
designation, **6**, [370]
detention in, **6**, [127]
discontinuance, **6**, [372]
disposal on cessation, **6**, [374]
disputes relating to, determination, **6**, [371]
home designated as, **6**, [370]

community home—*contd*
controlled—*contd*
management—
generally, **6**, [447]
instrument of, **6**, [446]
regional plan, under, **6**, [188]
regulations, **6**, [448]
detention in, **6**, [127]
differing purposes, for, **6**, [370]
establishment of, **6**, [130]
financial provisions, **6**, [139]
generally, **6**, [1]
maintenance of children in, **6**, [375]
nature of, **6**, [370]
provision of, **6**, [370]
staff, **6**, [139]
voluntary organisation, provision by, **6**, [370]
young offender detained in, **6**, [127]

Community Infrastructure Levy
amended provisions, **46(S)**, 217
appeals, **46(S)**, 208
application of, **46(S)**, 209
charging authorities—
charge by, **46(S)**, 200
joint committees, **46(S)**, 201
charging schedule—
approval of, **46(S)**, 207
draft, examination of, **46(S)**, 206
effect of, **46(S)**, 207
issue of, **46(S)**, 204–5
regulations, **46(S)**, 205
collection of, **46(S)**, 210
damages caused by enforcement action, compensation for, **46(S)**, 212–13
enforcement, **46(S)**, 211–12
imposition, provision for, **46(S)**, 199
liability to—
amount of, **46(S)**, 202
assumption of, **46(S)**, 201
charities, exemption, **46(S)**, 203–4
interpretation, **46(S)**, 202–3
owner or developer, of, **46(S)**, 202
procedures, **46(S)**, 213–14
regulations and orders—
making of, **46(S)**, 215
other powers, relationship with, **46(S)**, 216
provisions of, **46(S)**, 215
repeals, **46(S)**, 217
Secretary of State, guidance from, **46(S)**, 215
summary of provisions, **46(S)**, 14–15

community interest company
Appeal Officer—
appeal to, **8(1)**, [29]
appointment, **8(1)**, [29]
functions, **8(1)**, [29]
payments to, **8(1)**, [74]
procedure, **8(1)**, [74]
remuneration and pensions, **8(1)**, [74]
terms of appointment, **8(1)**, [74]
audit, **8(1)**, [44]
ceasing to be, **8(1)**, [54]
charitable purposes, for, **8(1)**, [27]

community interest company—*contd*
  charity or Scottish charity, becoming—
    decision as to, **8(1)**, [56]
    requirements, **8(1)**, [55]
  civil proceedings on behalf of, **8(1)**, [45]
  company interest test, **8(1)**, [36]
  director—
    appointment of, **8(1)**, [46]
    removal, **8(1)**, [47]
  dissolution and striking off, **8(1)**, [52]
  distributions and interest, cap on, **8(1)**, [31]
  establishment of, **8(1)**, [27]
  excluded companies, **8(1)**, [36]
  existing companies—
    charitable, **8(1)**, [40]
    decision of Regulator, **8(1)**, [39]
    eligibility, **8(1)**, [39]
    prescribed conversion documents,
      8(1), [38]
    requirements for becoming, **8(1)**, [38]
    Scottish charitable, **8(1)**, [41]
  extension of provisions as to, **8(1)**, [59]
  formation, **8(1)**, [37]
  industrial and provident society, becoming,
    8(1), [57]
  investigations—
    documents and information, power to
      require, **8(1)**, [77]
    evidence, information in, **8(1)**, [77]
    false information, provision of, **8(1)**, [77]
    privileged information, **8(1)**, [77]
  limited company becoming, **8(1)**, [84]
  manager—
    appointment of, **8(1)**, [48]
    functions, **8(1)**, [48]
  memorandum and articles, **8(1)**, [33]
  name of, **8(1)**, [34], [76]
  new, **8(1)**, [37]
  offences, **8(1)**, [61]
  Official Property Holder—
    appointment, **8(1)**, [30]
    finance, **8(1)**, [74]
    functions, **8(1)**, [30]
    property, holding, **8(1)**, [75]
    relationship with Regulator, **8(1)**, [75]
    reports, **8(1)**, [75]
    status, **8(1)**, [75]
    vacancy in office, **8(1)**, [75]
    vesting of property in, **8(1)**, [49]
  prescribed formation documents, **8(1)**, [37]
  property, vesting of, **8(1)**, [49]
  re-registration, **8(1)**, [53]
  regulations, **8(1)**, [63]
  Regulator—
    appointment, **8(1)**, [28]
    audit, order for, **8(1)**, [44]
    civil proceedings on behalf of company,
      bringing, **8(1)**, [45]
    delegation of functions, **8(1)**, [73]
    director—
      appointment of, **8(1)**, [46]
      removal, **8(1)**, [47]
    dissolution and striking off, application
      for, **8(1)**, [52]

community interest company—*contd*
  Regulator—*contd*
    eligibility of exiting companies, deciding,
      8(1), [39]
    fees, charging, **8(1)**, [58]
    functions, **8(1)**, [28]
    guidance, issue of, **8(1)**, [28]
    information to, **8(1)**, [60]
    investigation by, **8(1)**, [43]
    manager, appointment of, **8(1)**, [48]
    Official Property Holder, relationship
      with, **8(1)**, [75]
    orders by, **8(1)**, [62]
    payments to, **8(1)**, [73]
    property, vesting of, **8(1)**, [49]
    remuneration and pensions, **8(1)**, [73]
    reports and information, **8(1)**, [73]
    shares, transfer of, **8(1)**, [50]
    staff, **8(1)**, [73]
    supervisory powers, conditions for exercise
      of, **8(1)**, [42]
    terms of appointment, **8(1)**, [73]
    winding up, presentation of petition for,
      8(1), [51]
  reports, **8(1)**, [35]
  shares, transfer of, **8(1)**, [50]
  status, change of, **8(1)**, [53]–[57]
  summary of provisions, **8(1)**, [1]
  winding up—
    distribution of assets on, **8(1)**, [32]
    petition for, **8(1)**, [51]

community investment tax relief
  "5 year period", meaning, **44(4)**, [346]
  amount of, **44(4)**, [343]
  associate, meaning, **43(2)**, [156]; **44(4)**, [389]
  attribution of—
    bonus shares, **44(4)**, [366]
    generally, **44(4)**, [365]
  bank, investor as, **43(S)**, 880
  community development finance institution—
    accreditation—
      application for, **44(4)**, [348]
      criteria for, **44(4)**, [348]
      loss of, no claim after, **44(4)**, [364]
      period of, **44(4)**, [350]
      terms and conditions of, **44(4)**, [349]
    accredited, **43(2)**, [150]
    control of, **43(2)**, [152]
    investor—
      beneficial ownership, must have,
        44(4), [359]
      no control by, **44(4)**, [358]
      share in partnership, no acquisition of,
        44(4), [360]
    receipts of value from—
      amount of, **44(4)**, [375]
      connected persons, by or from,
        44(4), [378]
      future claims, effect on, **44(4)**, [377]
      insignificant, added together,
        44(4), [373]
      loans, **44(4)**, [371]
      meaning, **44(4)**, [374]

community investment tax relief—*contd*
  community development finance
    institution—*contd*
      receipts of value from—*contd*
        more than one investment, where,
          44(4), [376]
        securities, **44(4)**, [372]
        shares, **44(4)**, [372]
      restructuring, **43(2)**, [155]
    definitions, **43(2)**, [156]
    disclosure, **43(2)**, [156]
    disposal—
      identification of securities or shares on,
        43(2), [156]; **44(4)**, [385]
      meaning, **43(2)**, [156]; **44(4)**, [387]
    eligibility for, **43(2)**, [149]; **44(4)**, [342]
    five year period, meaning, **43(2)**, [149]
    form of, **43(2)**, [153]; **44(4)**, [343]
    general conditions, **43(2)**, [152]
    information—
      disclosure of, **44(4)**, [382]
      investor, to be provided by, **44(4)**, [381]
    introduction of, **43(2)**, [103]
    "invested amount", meaning, **44(4)**, [345]
    "investment date", meaning, **44(4)**, [346]
    investment held continuously, meaning,
      43(2), [156]
    investment, meaning, **43(2)**, [149]
    investor, information provided by,
      43(2), [156]
    issue of securities or shares, meaning,
      43(2), [156]; **44(4)**, [386]
    loans—
      disposal of—
        during 5 year period, withdrawal or
          reduction on, **44(4)**, [368]
        no claim after, **44(4)**, [362]
      excessive repayment or receipts of value, no
        claim after, **44(4)**, [362]
      nominees, **44(4)**, [383]
      repaid during 5 year period, withdrawal or
        reduction on, **44(4)**, [370]
      value received by investor during 6 year
        period, withdrawal or reduction on,
        44(4), [371]
    "making an investment", meaning,
      44(4), [344]
    meaning, **44(4)**, [341]
    no claim for—
      disposal of loan, after, **44(4)**, [362]
      excessive repayment or receipts of value of
        loan, after, **44(4)**, [362]
      loss of accreditation by CDFI, after,
        44(4), [364]
      securities, disposal of, after, **44(4)**, [363]
      shares, disposal of, after, **44(4)**, [363]
    nominees, **43(2)**, [156]
    postponement of tax pending appeal,
      application for, **43(2)**, [156]; **44(4)**, [384]
    qualifying investments, **43(2)**, [151]
      loans, conditions to be met, **44(4)**, [353]
      meaning, **44(4)**, [352]
      risks, no pre-arranged protection against,
        44(4), [357]

community investment tax relief—*contd*
  qualifying investments—*contd*
    securities, conditions to be met,
      44(4), [354]
    shares, conditions to be met, **44(4)**, [355]
    tax relief certificates, **44(4)**, [356]
  securities—
    disposed of during 5 year period,
      withdrawal or reduction of, **44(4)**, [369]
    held continuously, meaning, **44(4)**, [388]
    nominees, **44(4)**, [383]
    receipt of value during 6 year period,
      withdrawal or reduction on, **44(4)**, [372]
  shares—
    disposed of during 5 year period,
      withdrawal or reduction on, **44(4)**, [369]
    held continuously, meaning, **44(4)**, [388]
    nominees, **44(4)**, [383]
    receipt of value during 6 year period,
      withdrawal or reduction on, **44(4)**, [372]
  tax avoidance, and, **44(4)**, [361]
  withdrawal of, **43(2)**, [154]
  withdrawal or reduction of—
    loans—
      disposed of during 5 year period,
        44(4), [368]
      repayment of during 5 year period,
        44(4), [370]
      value received by investor during 6 year
        period, **44(4)**, [371]
    manner of, **44(4)**, [380]
    not due, subsequently found not to have
      been, **44(4)**, [379]
    overview, **44(4)**, [367]
    receipts of value from CDFI—
      amount of, **44(4)**, [375]
      connected persons, by or from,
        44(4), [378]
      future claims, effect on, **44(4)**, [377]
      insignificant, added together,
        44(4), [373]
      loans, from, **44(4)**, [371]
      meaning, **44(4)**, [374]
      more than one investment, where,
        44(4), [376]
      securities, from, **44(4)**, [372]
      shares, from, **44(4)**, [372]
    securities—
      disposed of during 5 year period,
        44(4), [369]
      value received by investor during 6 year
        period, **44(4)**, [372]
    shares—
      disposed of during 5 year period,
        44(4), [369]
      value received by investor during 6 year
        period, **44(4)**, [372]

Community law. *See* **European
Communities**

Community Legal Service. *See under* **Legal
Services Commission**

community licence. *See under* **driving licence**

community orders. *See also* **attendance centre order; combination order; community service order; curfew order; probation**
activity requirement, **12(3)**, [932]
alcohol treatment requirement, **12(3)**, [943]
amendment, **12(2)**, [846]; **12(3)**, [1060]
appeal, on, **12(2)**, [843]
appeal, pending, **12(3)**, [1062]
attendance centre requirement, **12(3)**, [945]
breach, loss of social security benefit on, **40(2)**, [280]
breach of requirement of, **12(3)**, [1058]
    attendance centre order, imposition of, **12(2)**, [844]
    community punishment order, imposition of, **12(2)**, [844]
    Crown Court, powers, **12(2)**, [844]
    exclusions, **12(2)**, [844]
    magistrates' courts, powers, **12(2)**, [844]
    summons or warrant, issue, **12(2)**, [844]
    supplemental provisions, **12(2)**, [844]
court review, power to provide for, **12(3)**, [909]
curfew requirement, **12(3)**, [935]
date by which requirements must be complied with, **12(3)**, [908]
default orders, **11(3)**, [453]
definitions, **12(2)**, [843]
drug rehabilitation requirement, **12(3)**, [940]–[942]
electronic monitoring requirement, **12(3)**, [946]
    imposition of, **12(3)**, [908]
exclusion requirement, **12(3)**, [936]
interpretation, **12(3)**, [1057]
limits of requirements, amendment of, **12(3)**, [954]
local justice area, specification of, **12(3)**, [947]
mental health treatment requirement, **12(3)**, [938], [939]
Northern Ireland, transfer to, **12(3)**, [1064], [1065]
programme requirement, **12(3)**, [933]
prohibited activity requirement, **12(3)**, [934]
provision of copies of, **12(3)**, [950], [1079]
provisions ceasing to have effect, **12(4)**, [469]
religious beliefs, avoidance of conflict with, **12(3)**, [948]
requirements, **12(3)**, [908]
residence requirement, **12(3)**, [937]
responsible officer—
    duties of, **12(3)**, [929]
    duty of offender to keep in touch with, **12(3)**, [951]
    meaning, **12(3)**, [928]
restrictions on power to make, **12(4)**, [473]
revocation, **12(2)**, [845]; **12(3)**, [1059]
rules, **12(3)**, [953]
Scotland, transfer to, **12(3)**, [1063], [1065]
subsequent conviction, powers of court in relation to, **12(3)**, [1061]
supervision requirement, **12(3)**, [944]

community orders—*contd*
transitional provisions and savings, **12(2)**, [121], [127]
unpaid work requirement—
    extension of, **12(3)**, [1060]
    local area, availability in, **12(3)**, [949]
    meaning, **12(3)**, [930]
    obligations of person subject to, **12(3)**, [931]
work or education times, avoidance of conflict with, **12(3)**, [948]

Community Patent Convention. *See* **patent**

community punishment and rehabilitation order
breach, revocation and amendment. *See* **community orders**
combination order renamed as, **12(2)**, [993]

community punishment order
breach of community order, imposed for, **12(2)**, [844]
breach, revocation and amendment. *See* **community orders**
community service order renamed as, **12(2)**, [992]
fines on, **11(2)**, [508]

community rehabilitation order
breach, revocation and amendment. *See* **community orders**
probation order renamed as, **12(2)**, [991]

Community Relations Commission
transitional provisions, **7(1)**, [215]

community school
admissions—
    ability, restriction on selection by, **15(2)**, [774]
    code for, **15(2)**, [775]
    pupil banding, **15(2)**, [775]
alterations to, **15(2)**, [754]–[755]
    foundation proposals, governing body to determine, **15(2)**, [758]
    restrictions on, **15(2)**, [764]
collective worship—
    exceptions and special arrangements, **15(2)**, [59]
    requirements, **15(2)**, [58], [159]
concern, causing—
    closure of school, **15(2)**, [788]
    governing body—
        additional governors, appointment of, **15(2)**, [787]
        interim executive members, consisting of, **15(2)**, [790], [905]
    intervention—
        eligible for, **15(2)**, [780]–[782]
        LEA, by, **15(2)**, [783]–[786]
        Secretary of State, by, **15(2)**, [787]–[789]
development work and experiments, **15(2)**, [404]

community school—*contd*
discontinuance, proposals for, **15(2)**, [751], [897]–[898]
discontinuance of, restrictions on, **15(2)**, [764]
establishment or alteration, proposals for, **15(2)**, [29], [30], [35]
governing body—
  exemption order from education legislation requirements—
    application for, **15(2)**, [342]
    generally, **15(2)**, [340]
    revocation of, **15(2)**, [341]
    variation of, **15(2)**, [341]
  general duties of, **15(2)**, [773]
  individual pupils' performance, provision of information about, **15(1)**, [671]
  information, power of Secretary of State to require, **15(1)**, [670]
  provision of information to Secretary of State, **15(1)**, [673]
  teaching services for day nurseries, provision of, **15(1)**, [669]
new—
  establishment of, **15(2)**, [744]
    consultation on, **15(2)**, [745]
    notices as to, **15(2)**, [745]
    proposals for, **15(2)**, [897]
      adjudicator, consideration by, **15(2)**, [898]
      implementation of, **15(2)**, [899]
      local authority, consideration by, **15(2)**, [898]
    proposals, publication of, **15(2)**, [746]
    relevant LEA, outside area of, **15(2)**, [749]
    restrictions on, **15(2)**, [764]
religious education, duty to secure provision of, **15(2)**, [57]
religious worship, sixth form pupils excused from attendance at, **15(2)**, [777]
significant improvement, requiring, **15(2)**, [781]
special measures, requiring, **15(2)**, [782]
special. *See* **community special school**
staffing, **15(2)**, [376], [525]

community sentence
fine default, on, **12(2)**, [578]
meaning, **12(2)**, [750]; **12(3)**, [878]
offences punishable with imprisonment, **12(3)**, [882]
offender remanded in custody, passed on, **12(3)**, [880]
persistent offender previously fined, for, **12(3)**, [882], [883]
pre-sentence drug testing, **12(3)**, [891]
pre-sentence reports—
  disclosure, **12(3)**, [889]
  meaning, **12(3)**, [888]
  requirement, **12(3)**, [886]
restriction on imposing, **12(3)**, [879]
sentence fixed by law, not available, where, **12(3)**, [881]
youth offending team, report of, **12(3)**, [890]

community service order. *See now* **community punishment order**
community punishment order, renamed as, **12(2)**, [992]
enforcement, **12(1)**, [783]
Northern Ireland, made in, England and Wales or Scotland, person residing in, **12(1)**, [795]
powers, **12(1)**, [783]
Scotland, person residing in, **12(1)**, [795]

community special school
alterations to, **15(2)**, [754]–[755]
  foundation proposals, governing body to determine, **15(2)**, [758]
  restrictions on, **15(2)**, [764]
concern, causing—
  closure of school, **15(2)**, [788]
  governing body—
    additional governors, appointment of, **15(2)**, [787]
    interim executive members, consisting of, **15(2)**, [790], [905]
  intervention—
    eligible for, **15(2)**, [780]–[782]
    LEA, by, **15(2)**, [783]–[786]
    Secretary of State, by, **15(2)**, [787]–[789]
discontinuance—
  consultation on, **15(2)**, [752]
  direction requiring, **15(2)**, [753]
  proposals for, **15(2)**, [751], [897]–[898]
  restrictions on, **15(2)**, [764]
governing body, general duties of, **15(2)**, [773]
new—
  establishment of, **15(2)**, [744]
    consultation on, **15(2)**, [745]
    notices as to, **15(2)**, [745]
    proposals for, **15(2)**, [897]
      adjudicator, consideration by, **15(2)**, [898]
      implementation of, **15(2)**, [899]
      local authority, consideration by, **15(2)**, [898]
    proposals, publication of, **15(2)**, [746]
    relevant LEA, outside area of, **15(2)**, [749]
    restrictions on, **15(2)**, [764]
significant improvement, requiring, **15(2)**, [781]
special measures, requiring, **15(2)**, [782]

community treatment order
conditions, **29**, [41]
duration, **29**, [42]
effect of, **29**, [43]
expiry of, **29**, [52]
meaning, **29**, [40]
period, **29**, [51]
recall to hospital, powers of, **29**, [44]
recalled patients, powers in respect of, **29**, [45]
relevant criteria, **29**, [40]
revocation, **29**, [46]

companies
accounting periods, **44(1)**, [7]
accounting reference date—
  alteration of, **8(1)**, [470]
  meaning, **8(1)**, [469]
accounting reference period, **8(1)**, [469]
accounts. *See* **accounting records; accounts**
acquisition of own shares. *See* **purchase of own shares**
administration, in, tax on, **44(1)**, [175]
alternative finance arrangements. *See* **alternative finance arrangements**
annual return—
  company having share capital, of, **8**, 764–5
  contents, **8**, 419–21
  copy of, for registrar, **8**, 417
  default as to, **8**, 417, 925
  regulations, **8**, 421
  share capital, particulars of, **8**, 420–1
  shareholders, particulars of, **8**, 420–1
appointments, duty to notify—
  failure, offence of, **8(1)**, [1233]
  requirement, **8(1)**, [1232]
arrangement—
  allotment, providing for, **8**, 177
  application of provisions, **8**, 767–76
  company reconstruction, in connection with, **8**, 468–9
  date and consequences of, **8**, 772
  directors, by, value of, **8**, 400–1
  directors' report, **8**, 769
  documents and information made available, **8**, 768–9
  documents, inspection of, **8**, 771
  exceptions, **8**, 773
  expert's report, **8**, 770
  information to be circulated, **8**, 467–8
  meaning, **8**, 177, 466
  meeting to vote on, **8**, 465
  mergers, in relation to, **8**, 470–1
  own shares, transferee company holding, **8**, 772
  public company divisions, and mergers, **8**, 470–1
  special rights attached to securities, **8**, 772
  transfer company, transferee holding shares in, **8**, 774–5
articles of association. *See* **articles of association**
assessment, **43(1)**, [362]
assets—
  changes in, statement in directors' report, **8**, 665
  current, valuation, **8**, 624, 679–80, 705
  depreciation rules, **8**, 625–6, 681–2, 707, 737
  development costs shown as, **8**, 353
  distribution of, restriction on, **8**, 349—
    See also distribution *below*
  excess of money owed over value, **8**, 623, 680
  fixed, treatment of, **8**, 623–4, 679, 703–5
  non-cash—
    director's interest in, **8**, 382–3
    distribution of, **8**, 359

companies—*contd*
assets—*contd*
  non-cash—*contd*
    meaning, **8**, 600
    transfer to public company, **8**, 177–81
  payment of debts out of, **8**, 251
  treatment in relevant accounts, **8**, 358–9
associated—
  link to shares of, **44(1)**, [111]
  meaning, **44(1)**, [110], [230], [511]
  number, determining, **44(1)**, [8]
audit. *See* **audit; auditors**
banking group, meaning, **8(1)**, [1242]
banking, meaning, **8(1)**, [1242]
basic profits, **44(1)**, [8]
beginning or discontinuance of trade, **44(1)**, [169]
bill of exchange made, accepted or endorsed by, **8(1)**, [130]
books—
  entry and search for, **8**, 494–6
  falsification, **8**, 500–1
  information obtained from, security, **8**, 496–9
  inspection where offence suspected, **8**, 585
  meaning, **8**, 602
  mutilation etc, penalty, **8**, 500–1
  production of—
    direction by Minister for, **8**, 493–4
    inspectors, to, **8**, 484–5
    seizure of, warrant for, **8**, 494–6
borrowing powers—
  companies clauses. *See* **Companies Clauses Acts**
  maintenance of, **8**, 209
  serious loss of, directors' duties, **8**, 209
  share. *See* **share capital**
Business Names Act, application of, **48**, 95
capacity—
  constitutional limitations—
    charities, **8(1)**, [120]
    transactions involving directors, **8(1)**, [119]
  validity of acts, calling into question, **8(1)**, [117]
capital gains tax, not liable to, **44(1)**, [1]
certificate—
  business, to do, **8**, 189
  incorporation, of—
    issue of, **8**, 116; **8(1)**, [93]
    new, on change of name, **8(1)**, [158]
    public notice of, **8(1)**, [1142]
    re-registration, issue on—
      private company re-registered as public, **8(1)**, [174]
      private limited company as unlimited, **8(1)**, [182]
      private unlimited company as limited, **8(1)**, [185]
      public company as private, **8(1)**, [179], [743]
      public company becoming private and unlimited, **8(1)**, [189]
      public company becoming private, **8**, 154

companies—*contd*
certificate—*contd*
incorporation, of—*contd*
issue of—*contd*
right to, **8(1)**, [1143]
re-registration of private company,
8, 146–7
registration, of, **8**, 461
share capital, as to, **8**, 189
shares. *See* **Companies Clauses Acts**
transfer of shares, of, **8**, 244–5
chairman—
directors, of, **8**, 48
emoluments, disclosure in accounts,
8, 654–7
general meeting, at, **8**, 41
charges. *See also* **company charges**
company's own shares, on, **8**, 214–15
company's property, ceasing to affect,
8, 908
date of creation, **8**, 916
debentures, on, **8**, 457
definitions, **8**, 561–2
floating. *See* **floating charge**
instruments creating—
copy to be kept, **8**, 463, 560, 914–15
inspection, right of, **8**, 464, 914
oversea company—
created by, **8**, 465
situation of property of, **8**, 560–1
power of sale, effect of exercise of,
8, 910–11
property outside UK, on, **8**, 458
receiver, appointment, effect of, **8**, 461
register—
company to keep, **8**, 463, 914–15
inspection of, **8**, 461, 464, 914
notice of matters disclosed on, **8**, 917
rectification of, **8**, 462
registrar to keep, **8**, 460, 555, 903
registration of—
additional information, **8**, 559
book debts, on, **8**, 456
certificate, endorsement on debentures,
8, 461
certification of, **8**, 461
charges requiring, **8**, 456, 555, 900–2
debentures, for receiving, **8**, 457, 559
formalities, **8**, 457
duty of company as to, **8**, 458–9
enforcement of security, **8**, 462–3
floating charge, **8**, 456, 559
necessity for, **8**, 454–5
particulars—
duty to deliver, **8**, 556, 904
errors and omissions, **8**, 558, 907–8
failure to deliver, **8**, 558, 904–5
further, delivery of, **8**, 559, 906–7
issue of debentures, taking up,
8, 911–12
late delivery, **8**, 558, 905
prescribed, **8**, 917
registrar to whom delivered, **8**, 557–8
signature, power of court to dispense
with, **8**, 917

companies—*contd*
charges—*contd*
registration of—*contd*
property acquired, charge existing on,
8, 459
receiver or manager, appointment of,
8, 912
regulations—
further provision by, **8**, 560
power to make, **8**, 915–16
release, memorandum of, **8**, 461, 908
satisfaction, entry on register of, **8**, 482
ship, on, **8**, 456
time for, **8**, 457
extension by court, **8**, 462
uncalled share capital, on, **8**, 456
void unless registered, **8**, 454–5
voidness, **8**, 559
obligation secured, effect on, **8**, 911
restrictions on, **8**, 909–10
unregistered charges, exclusion of,
8, 909–10
charges on income—
charity, donations to, **44(1)**, [173]
loss, computing, **44(1)**, [197]
meaning, **44(1)**, [172]
total profits, deduction from, **44(1)**, [171]
charities, gift of shares, securities and real
property to, **44(1)**, [422]–[424]
civil proceedings on behalf of, repeal of power
of Secretary of State to bring, **8(1)**, [1254]
close. *See* **close company**
commission, payment of—
amount of, **8**, 173
authorised by articles, **8**, 173
barred, when, **8**, 174
power to make, **8**, 174
common seal, **8(1)**, [123]
communications by—
agreed forms of, **8(1)**, [1390]
application of schedule, **8(1)**, [1386]
death or bankruptcy of shareholder, effect
of, **8(1)**, [1391]
electronic form, in, **8(1)**, [1388]
hard copy form, in, **8(1)**, [1387]
joint holders, to, **8(1)**, [1391]
website, by means of, **8(1)**, [1389]
communications provisions—
effect of, **8(1)**, [1221]
interpretation, **8(1)**, [1226]
community interest. *See* **community interest
company**
Companies Acts, within, **8**, 2–8
companies annual general meeting—
business of, **8**, 430–1
default in calling, **8**, 422–3
duty to hold, **8**, 422
general provisions as to, **8**, 426
notice of, length of, **8**, 425–6
private company dispensing with, **8**, 422–3
Secretary of State, calling by, **8**, 423
time for, **8**, 422
companies legislation, not formed under—
joint stock company, definition,
8(1), [1119]

companies—*contd*
companies legislation, not formed
under—*contd*
registration—
authorisation, **8(1)**, [1118]
regulations, power to make provision
by, **8(1)**, [1120]
compensation for disturbance to business of
where shareholders over sixty, **9**, [345]
compromise—
applications of provisions, **8**, 767–76
company reconstruction, in connection
with, **8**, 468–9
date and consequences of, **8**, 772
directors' report, **8**, 770
documents and information made
available, **8**, 768–9
documents, inspection of, **8**, 771
exceptions, **8**, 773
expert's report, **8**, 770
information to be circulated, **8**, 467–8
meeting to vote on, **8**, 465
mergers, in relation to, **8**, 470–1
own shares, transferor company holding,
8, 772
power to, **8**, 465
public company divisions and mergers,
8, 470–1
special rights attached to securities, **8**, 772
transfer company, transferee holding shares
in, **8**, 774–5
compromise or arrangement with creditors or
members—
application of provisions, **8(1)**, [973]
articles, obligations of company with
respect to, **8(1)**, [979]
court sanction for, **8(1)**, [977]
debenture holders, statement to, **8(1)**, [975]
director and trustees, provision of
information by, **8(1)**, [976]
meetings—
court order for holding, **8(1)**, [974]
notice and statement, circulation of,
8(1), [975]
mergers. *See* **mergers**
connected persons, **44(1)**, [132]
connected, meaning, **44(1)**, [621]
consortium—
meaning, **44(1)**, [222]
owned by, **44(1)**, [227]
constitution—
alteration, notice to registrar—
enactment, by, **8(1)**, [112]
order, by, **8(1)**, [113]
articles. *See* **articles of association**
components of, **8(1)**, [95]
effect of, **8(1)**, [111]
meaning, **8(1)**, [335]
members, documents provided to,
8(1), [110]
objects, statement of, **8(1)**, [109]
order affecting, delivery to registrar,
8(1), [1076]–[1077]
references to, **8(1)**, [335]

companies—*contd*
constitution—*contd*
resolutions and agreements affecting—
application of provisions, **8(1)**, [107]
meaning, **8(1)**, [107]
order sanctioning compromise or
arrangement, obligations relating to,
8(1), [979]
order sanctioning reconstruction or
amalgamation, obligations relating to,
8(1), [979]
registrar, to be forwarded to, **8(1)**, [108]
continuity of law, **8(1)**, [1373]
contract—
capacity to enter into, **8**, 137
change of name, effect of, **8**, 80–1
debentures, for, enforcement, **8**, 251
directors' interest in, disclosure, **8**, 379
oversea company, **8**, 922–3
power to make, **8**, 49–50
pre-incorporation, **8**, 137
qualifications not affected by, **8**, 45–6
sole members who are directors, with,
8, 386–7
contract by, **8(1)**, [121]
control of—
Crown, by, **44(1)**, [228]
meaning, **44(1)**, [622]
controlled foreign. *See* **controlled foreign
company**
conversion of friendly society to, **19(1)**, [379]
corporation tax. *See* **corporation tax**
cost-book company, obsolete provisions
repealed, **8**, 830
court—
meaning, **8(1)**, [1234]
relief, power to grant, **8(1)**, [1235]
credit union, conversion to, **19(1)**, [588]
Crown, controlled by, **44(1)**, [228]
deeds, execution of—
attorney, by, **8(1)**, [125]
delivery, **8(1)**, [124]
valid, **8(1)**, [124]
defunct—
restoration to register, **8**, 520
striking off, **8**, 513
demergers—
capital gains tax relief, **42**, [1322]
exempt distribution, **42**, [1322]
See **demergers**
derivative claims—
meaning, **8(1)**, [338]
member, by. *See* **members of company**
directors and secretaries, confidentiality
orders, **12(3)**, [27]
dissolution—
bona vacantia, property to be, **8**, 521–2
disclaimer by Crown, **8**, 523
rentcharge, liability for, after, **8**, 524
revival, effect of, **8**, 522–3
void, power to declare, **8**, 511–12, 925–6
dissolved—
bona vacantia. *See* **bona vacantia**
liability for rentcharge on land after,
8(1), [1101]

companies—*contd*
  dissolved—*contd*
    records, preservation of, **8(1)**, [1162]
  distribution—
    articles providing for, **8**, 360
    assets, of, restriction on, **8**, 349
    banking company, by, **8**, 360
    bonus issue following repayment of share
      capital, **44(1)**, [113]
    chargeable payment—
      advance clearance, **44(1)**, [119]
      meaning, **44(1)**, [118]
    corporation tax treatment. *See*
    distributions
    development costs, treatment of, **8**, 353
    exempt—
      advance clearance, **44(1)**, [119]
      chargeable payments connected with,
        44(1), [118]
      conditions, **44(1)**, [116]
      information, inspector requiring,
        44(1), [121]
      meaning, **44(1)**, [116]
      returns, **44(1)**, [120]
    expenses of close company, **44(1)**, [232]
    extension of provisions, **8**, 352
    information relating to, **44(1)**, [139], [140]
    initial accounts for, **8**, 356–7
    insurance company, by, **8**, 352–3, 360
    interim accounts for, **8**, 356–7
    investment company, by, **8**, 350
    justification of, **8**, 353–4
    kind, in, **8**, 359
    last annual accounts, requirement for,
      8, 354–5
    matters not being—
      demergers,
        44(1), [116]–[122]. *See* **demerger**
      interest in respect of securities,
        44(1), [115]
    meaning, **8**, 349; **44(1)**, [110]
    mutual arrangements for, **44(1)**, [146]
    mutual business, **44(1)**, [330]
    non-cash assets, **8**, 349
    non-qualifying, returns as to, **44(1)**, [139],
      [145]
    profits, to be out of, **8**, 348
    purchase of own shares. *See* **shares**
    recipient, information furnished to,
      44(1), [139], [140]
    repayments of share capital, **44(1)**, [114]
    restraint on, saving for, **8**, 361
    securities held by other company, in respect
      of, **44(1)**, [110]
    stock dividends, **44(1)**, [134]
    successive, provisions applying, **8**, 357–8
    tax credit—
      borrower under stock lending agreement,
        no tax credit for, **44(1)**, [136]
      entitlement to, **44(1)**, [135]
      excessive, rectification of, **44(1)**, [144]
      interim holder under repurchase
        agreement, no tax credit for,
        44(1), [136]

companies—*contd*
  distribution—*contd*
    tax credit—*contd*
      original owner under repurchase
        agreement, no tax credit for certain
        manufactured dividends, **44(1)**, [137]
      passing on value of, **44(1)**, [138]
    taxation of, **44(1)**, [109]
    undistributable reserves, **8**, 349
    unlawful, consequences of, **8**, 359–60
  disturbance to business of, shareholders over
    sixty, compensation where, **9**, [345]
  division. *See* **division of company**
  documents, execution of—
    attorney, by, **8(1)**, [125]
    England and Wales, law of, **8(1)**, [122]
    Northern Ireland, law of, **8(1)**, [122]
  documents or information, sending or
    supplying—
    agreed forms of communication,
      8(1), [1385]
    application of schedule, **8(1)**, [1382]
    authentication, requirement of,
      8(1), [1224]
    communications provisions, **8(1)**, [1221]
    deemed delivery, **8(1)**, [1225]
    electronic form, in, **8(1)**, [1384]
    electronic form, meaning, **8(1)**, [1246]
    hard copy form, in, **8(1)**, [1383]
    hard copy, meaning, **8(1)**, [1246]
    hard copy version, right to, **8(1)**, [1223]
    interpretation, **8(1)**, [1226]
    requirements, **8(1)**, [1222]
  domicile, **11(2)**, [834]–[835], [848]
  dormant—
    audit, exemption from—
      conditions for, **8(1)**, [558]
      exclusions, **8(1)**, [559]
    auditors, resolution not to appoint,
      8, 329–30, 445
    meaning, **8(1)**, [1247]
  dual resident investing—
    appeals, **44(1)**, [648]
    charges on income, early payment of,
      44(1), [648]
    component accounting periods,
      44(1), [647]
    group relief, limitation of, **44(1)**, [220]
    interest, early payment of, **44(1)**, [648]
    straddling period—
      charges in income in, **44(1)**, [647]
      meaning, **44(1)**, [647]
  EEA, meaning, **8(1)**, [1248]
  employee-controlled, loans for shares in,
    42, [935]
  employees—
    disabled persons, disclosure as to, **8**, 667–8
    interest of, regard to be given to, **8**, 374
    involvement, disclosure as to, **8**, 668
    particulars to be given of, **8**, 632–3, 749
    provision for on cessation or transfer of
      business, **8**, 583; **8(1)**, [325]
    share scheme—
      allotment in pursuance of, **8**, 158
      invitation to subscribe, **8**, 157

companies—*contd*
  employees—*contd*
    share scheme—*contd*
      meaning, **8**, 602
      residual interests, **8**, 609, 611–12
      shares excluded from share capital,
        8, 189
      shares held on trust for, **8**, 610
  exchange of securities, **42**, [1234]
  existing company—
    meaning, **8**, 594
    registration. *See* **registration**
  expert, meaning, **8**, 158
  facilities for disabled persons, formation for
    provision of, **16**, [10]
  false information, furnishing, penalty, **8**, 501
  filing obligations, enforcement of,
    8(1), [1191]
  financial limits in provisions, power to
    increase, **8(1)**, [336]
  financial year, **8**, 284
    determining, **8(1)**, [468]
    first and subsequent, **8(1)**, [468]
  foreign law, transactions under, **8**, 406;
    8(1), [337]
  forged transfer, compensation for,
    19(1), [132]
  formation—
    method of, **8(1)**, [85]
    unlawful purpose, not to be for, **8(1)**, [85]
  formation of company—
    former Companies Acts, under, **8**, 525–6
    kinds of companies, **8**, 103–4
    mode of, **8**, 103–4
  formation of SE by merger, transfer of
    qualifying assets during, **43(1)**, [1199]
  franked investment income—
    distribution after 6th April 1999,
      attributable to, **43(1)**, [339]
    losses not to be set against, **43(1)**, [313]
  general meeting—
    annual. *See* annual general meeting *above*
    clauses Acts. *See* **Companies Clauses Acts**
    extraordinary—
      requisition by members for, **8**, 424
      serious loss of capital, in case of, **8**, 209
      time for calling, **8**, 424
    general provisions as to, **8**, 426
    notice of, length of, **8**, 425
    quorum at, **8**, 427
    variation of class rights, for, **8**, 195
    voting capacity, **8**, 427
  goods of, where immediate tenant a director,
    no privilege from distress for rent,
    13, [1201]
  goodwill, internally-generated, **43(S)**, 1399
  group—
    business assets, replacement of, **42**, [1309]
    business tenancy held by, **21**, [206]
    company ceasing to be member—
      degrouping charge, roll-over of,
        42, [1316], [1470]
      gain or loss accruing, reallocation of,
        42, [1315]
      post-appointed day cases, **42**, [1314]

companies—*contd*
  group—*contd*
    definitions, **42**, [1304]
    depreciatory transactions in, **42**, [1310]
    disposal or acquisition outside, **42**, [1308]
    dividend stripping, **42**, [1311]
    meaning, **19(2)**, [497]
    mergers, effect of, **42**, [1317]
    pre-entry gains, restrictions on set-off of,
      42, [1469]
    pre-entry losses, restriction on set-off of—
      application and construction of
        provisions, **42**, [1468]
      company changing group on transfers of
        shares, **42**, [1468]
      company's nature, change of, **42**, [1468]
      continuity provisions, **42**, [1468]
      deduction, restrictions on, **42**, [1468]
      gains from which deductible, **42**, [1468]
      market value, calculation by reference
        to, **42**, [1468]
      pooled assets, disposal of, **42**, [1468]
      pre-entry losses not to be treated as
        post-entry losses, **42**, [1468]
      proportion of losses on assets, **42**, [1468]
      relevant group, identification of,
        42, [1468]
      stock in trade, appropriation to,
        42, [1468]
    relief. *See* **group relief**
    tax, recovery from another member or
      controlling director, **42**, [1321]
    tax refund surrendered within, **42**, [983]
    transfers within, **42**, [1305]
      notional, **42**, [1306]
      trading stock, of, **42**, [1307]
  group accounts—
    acquisition and merger accounting,
      8, 638–40
    associated undertakings, **8**, 641–2
    companies not required to prepare,
      disclosure, **8**, 644–8
    companies required to prepare, disclosure,
      8, 648–53
    content of, **8**, 637–42
    disclosure of information—
      companies not required to prepare group
        accounts, **8**, 644–8
      companies required to prepare group
        accounts, **8**, 648–53
      directors, dealings in favour of, **8**, 660–3
    form of, **8**, 637–42
  group transactions, elimination of, **8**, 638
    individual profit and loss account, treatment
      of, **8**, 293
    joint ventures, **8**, 641
    minority interests, **8**, 640–1
    parent company in accounts of larger
      group, exemption for, **8**, 290–1
    preparation of, **8**, 289
    small and medium-sized groups—
      exemption for, **8**, 321
      qualification as, **8**, 318–19
      small company, prepared by, **8**, 322
    subsidiary companies included in, **8**, 292–3

companies—*contd*
  group transactions, elimination of—*contd*
    subsidiary undertakings excluded from
      consolidation, interests in, **8**, 641
    true and fair view, to give, **8**, 289
  group relief. *See* **group relief**
  hedging arrangements, **44(1)**, [112]
  holding, meaning, **44(1)**, [122], [133]
  income, exclusion of deductions, **44(1)**, [170]
  income tax, and, **44(4)**, [5]
  income tax provisions not applying to,
    44(1), [1]
  insolvency. *See* **company insolvency**
  inspectors—
    appointment, **8**, 481
    attendance before, **8**, 484
    disclosure of information to, **8**, 501–2
    documents to be produced to, **8**, 484–5
    examination on oath, powers, **8**, 484–5
    investigations by. *See* investigation *below*
    obstruction of, **8**, 485–6
    powers of, **8**, 484–6
    reasons for appointing, **8**, 484–5
    report of—
      copies, furnishing of, **8**, 486
      costs, recommendation as to, **8**, 488
      evidence, as, **8**, 489
      insider dealing, into, **8**, 862
      interim and final, **8**, 486
      not for publication, **8**, 483
      publication of, **8**, 486
  insurance. *See also* **insurance company**
    meaning, **8(1)**, [1243]
  intangible fixed assets—
    gains and losses from, **43(S)**, 69–72
      change of accounting policy, adjustment
        on, **43(2)**, [194]
      commencement and transitional
        provisions, **43(2)**, [195]
      credits and debits given effect,
        43(2), [186]
      credits in respect of, **43(2)**, [183], [750]
      debits in respect of, **43(2)**, [182], [750]
      excluded assets, **43(2)**, [190]
      groups of companies, **43(2)**, [188]–[189]
      interpretation, **43(2)**, [196]
      introduction, **43(2)**, [181]
      meaning, **43(2)**, [181]
      realisation of, **43(2)**, [184]
      related parties, transactions between,
        43(2), [192]
      roll-over relief, **43(2)**, [187]
      SE, formed by merger, **43(2)**, [191]
      supplementary provisions, **43(2)**, [193]
      tax written down value, calculation of,
        43(2), [185]
      transfer of business or trade, **43(2)**, [191]
    internally-generated, **43(S)**, 1399
    records—
      duty to keep and preserve, **43(1)**, [394]
      failure to keep and preserve, penalty
        for, **43(1)**, [394]
      information kept instead of, **43(1)**, [394]
    related parties, persons treated as,
      43(S), 890–1

companies—*contd*
  investigation—
    application for—
      company, by, **8**, 481
      members, by, **8**, 481
      security, requirement for, **8**, 481
    circumstances for, **8**, 481–3
    civil proceedings arising from, **8**, 487
    company ownership, into, **8**, 489–90
    costs of, liability for, **8**, 488
    destruction or mutilation of documents,
      8, 500–1
    disqualification of director after, **8**, 845–6
    documents and information, power to
      require, **8(1)**, [22]
    documents, production of, **8**, 484–5, 493–4
    evidence, information in, **8(1)**, [72]
    examination on oath, **8**, 484–5
    failure to comply with requirements,
      8(1), [25]
    false information, provision of, **8(1)**, [72]
    information—
      disclosure to Secretary of State or
        inspector, **8**, 501–2
      false, furnishing of, **8**, 501
      privileged, **8**, 502–3
      provided to Secretary of State, protected
        disclosure, **8(1)**, [23]
      security, provision for, **8**, 496–9
    insider dealing, into, **8**, 861–2
    inspectors. *See* inspectors *above*
    interest in shares, as to, **8**, 271–2
      inspection of report on, **8**, 277
      report to members on, **8**, 274
      requisition by members for, **8**, 273
    Minister, initiation by, **8**, 482–3
    order by court, on, **8**, 481
    other powers of, available to Minister,
      8, 489–91
    oversea company, **8**, 503–4
    ownership of shares or debentures, as to,
      8, 491
    premises—
      entry and search of, **8**, 494–6
      power to inspector or investigator to
        enter and remain on, **8(1)**, [24]
    report on. *See* inspectors *above*
    restrictions on shares etc, **8**, 491–2
    security of information, **8(1)**, [72]
    share dealings, **8**, 492–3
  investigations, application of Police and
    Criminal Evidence Act, **12(1)**, [922]
  investment. *See* **investment company**
  investment business—
    giving effect to allowances, **43(1)**, [832]
    managing investments of, **43(1)**, [569]
    with, corporation tax computation,
      42, [952]
  investment business, with—
    expenses of management, **44(1)**, [42]
      accounting period to which referable,
        44(1), [43]
      amounts reversing, charge to tax,
        44(1), [44]

companies—*contd*
  investment business, with—*contd*
    expenses of management—*contd*
      Financial Services and Markets Act 2000,
        levies and repayments under,
        44(1), [47]
      meaning, **44(1)**, [105]
  investment trust, meaning, **44(1)**, [626]
  joint stock, definition, **8(1)**, [1119]
  land charges, money secured by, **20**, [1]
  landlord, as, disclosure of details of, **22**, [505],
    [510]
  legal proceedings—
    costs, security for, **8**, 588
    court's power to control, **8**, 827
    officers, against, relief in, **8**, 589
  limited—
    acquisition of own shares. *See* **purchase of**
     own shares
    guarantee, by—
      community interest company,
        becoming, **8(1)**, [84]
      meaning, **8(1)**, [81]
      right to participate in profits, **8(1)**, [115]
      share capital, having, **8(1)**, [83]
      statement of guarantee, **8(1)**, [89]
    meaning, **8(1)**, [81]
    name. *See* **company name**
  link, meaning, **44(1)**, [222]
  link to shares of, **44(1)**, [111]
  liquidation, in, tax on, **44(1)**, [174]
  loans—
    director, to. *See* **directors**
    inter-company, **8**, 396
    money-lending company by, **8**, 398–9
  local authority interest in. *See* **local**
   authority
  major change in nature or conduct of trade,
    44(1), [503]
  meaning, **8(1)**, [79]; **44(1)**, [615];
    44(4), [1000]
  medium-sized—
    exclusion from being, **8(1)**, [545]
    parent companies, **8(1)**, [544]
    qualification as, **8(1)**, [543]
    shares, by—
      community interest company,
        becoming, **8(1)**, [84]
      meaning, **8(1)**, [81]
  meetings—
    annual general. *See* **annual general**
     meeting
    auditors' right to attend, **8**, 447
    chairman, election of, **8**, 426
    class, application of provisions to,
     8(1), [412]
      quoted company, meetings of,
       8(1), [430]
      records, **8(1)**, [437]
      share capital, company without,
       8(1), [413]
    Clauses Act, under. *See* **Companies**
     Clauses Acts
    corporations, representation of, at,
     8, 429–30

companies—*contd*
  meetings—*contd*
    court's power to order, **8**, 427
    general. *See* **general meetings**
    minute books—
      form of, **8**, 586
      inspection of, **8**, 440
    minutes of, **8**, 438–9
    notice of, **8**, 426
    poll. *See* poll *below*
    provisions regulating, **8**, 426
    proxies—
      audience, right of, **8**, 428
      poll, demand for, **8**, 429
      power to appoint, **8**, 428
    records of proceedings, **8**, 438–40
    requisition for—
      members, by, **8**, 424
      resigning auditor, by, **8**, 438–9
    resolutions. *See* resolutions *below*
    vote, right to, **8**, 427
  members. *See also* **members of company**
    accounts, rights to copy of, **8**, 302–3
    chartered company. *See* **chartered**
     company
    index of names, **8**, 411–12
    investigation respecting, **8**, 489–91
    meaning, **8**, 121; **44(1)**, [122]
    memorandum or articles—
      alteration, effect of, **8**, 118
      copies to be given to, **8**, 120
    minimum number for carrying on
     business, **8**, 124
    principal, **44(1)**, [229]
    register of—
      application for rectification, **8**, 414–15
      closing, **8**, 414
      contents, **8**, 409
      copies, charges for, **8**, 413
      default respecting, **8**, 409, 414
      entries in, **8**, 409
      evidence, as, **8**, 415
      index to, **8**, 411–12
      inspection, **8**, 413
      location of, **8**, 411
      non-compliance with provisions, **8**, 414
      obligation to keep, **8**, 409
      overseas branch, of—
        countries where kept, **8**, 761
        discontinuance of, **8**, 762
        duplication of, **8**, 762
        general provisions respecting, **8**, 416,
         762–3
        rectification, **8**, 762
      share warrants, entries as to, **8**, 412
      statement that company has only one
       member, **8**, 410
      trusts excluded from, **8**, 415
    requisition for meeting by, **8**, 424
    unfairly prejudiced, orders respecting—
      effect of, **8**, 510
      members' application, on, **8**, 508
      Minister's application, on, **8**, 509
  memorandum of association. *See*
   memorandum of association

companies—*contd*
mergers. *See also* **mergers**
  draft terms of, **8**, 767–8
  share premium account relief, **8**, 199–200
migration—
  capital gains tax on. *See* **capital gains tax**
  offences, **44(1)**, [497]
  outstanding tax, payment of—
    penalties, **42**, [926]
    persons liable for, **42**, [927]
    securing, **42**, [925]
    Treasury consent, **42**, [925]
  unlawful transactions, **44(1)**, [495]
minor definitions, **8(1)**, [1251]
minute books—
  form of, **8**, 586
  inspection of, **8**, 440
money-lending company—
  loans or quasi-loans by, **8**, 398–9
  meaning, **8**, 398
mortgage, borrowing by. *See* **Companies
Clauses Acts**
mutual business, carrying on, **44(1)**, [329]
name. *See also* **company name**
  "and reduced", adding to, **8**, 204–5
  approval of, **48**, 212
  certain names, prohibition of, **8**, 125–6
  "chamber of commerce", including, **48**, 21
  change of—
    actions not to abate on, **8**, 80–1
    alteration of register, **8**, 127–8, 133
    continuance of powers as to, **8**, 80
    contracts etc, preservation of, **8**, 81
    direction by minister for, **8**, 127–8,
    131–2
      application to set aside, **8**, 132
    misleading name, **8**, 132–3
    registration, for, **8**, 529
    saving of rights, **8**, 81
    similarity to another, where, **8**, 128
    special resolution, by, **8**, 127–8
  correspondence, to appear on, **8**, 407–8
  documents, on, **8**, 408
  general requirements, **8**, 533
  index of names, **8**, 577–8
  "limited"—
    exemption from requirement, **8**, 130–2
    improper use, penalty, **8**, 134
    inclusion in, **8**, 533
    Welsh equivalent, **8**, 131
  memorandum, as stated in, **8**, 125
  misleading—
    direction to change, **8**, 128
    old public company, of, **8**, 823
    requirement to abandon, **8**, 132–3
    trading under, prohibition, **8**, 133
  objection to, **8**, 129
  offences relating to, **8**, 407
  oversea companies, regulation of, **8**, 543–4
  place of business, to be shown on,
    8, 406–7
  "plc" to be included in, **8**, 408, 533
  public company, **8**, 125
  "public limited company", inclusion of,
    8, 408, 533

companies—*contd*
name—*contd*
  publication of, **8**, 408
  registrar's index, **8**, 577–8
  regulations governing, **8**, 129
  seal, to appear on, **8**, 408
  statutory designations, alternatives, **8**, 127
  Welsh company, **8**, 131, 134, 533
non-cash asset, meaning, **8(1)**, [1241]
non-resident companies, group relief for
  overseas losses of, **44(1)**, [218], [219]
non-resident—
  charge to corporation tax, **44(1)**, [5]
  permanent establishment—
    arms' length transactions, **44(1)**, [633]
    goods or services, provision of,
      44(1), [633]
    profits attributable to, **44(1)**, [5], [6]
    prohibited deductions, **44(1)**, [633]
    separate enterprise principle,
      44(1), [632]
objects—
  auditors. *See* **auditors**
  bodies corporate, by, **8**, 592–3, 849
  director failing to disclose age, **8**, 370
  disqualification order, in relation to,
    8, 848–9
  documents, mutilation etc, **8**, 500–1
  financial assistance in purchase of own
    shares, **8**, 215
  information, false, furnishing, **8**, 501
  interest in shares, failure to notify, **8**, 268
  loans to directors, **8**, 402
  misleading name, trading under, **8**, 133
  name, relating to, **8**, 407
  non-disclosure by director, **8**, 379
  oversea company, by, **8**, 548
  own shares, company acquiring, **8**, 209–10
  penalties, **8**, 64–5
  prosecution by public authorities, **8**, 592
  punishment—
    generally, **8**, 590–1
    schedule of, **8**, 796–814
  schedule of, **8**, 796–814
  share transactions by directors, **8**, 389
  statement of, **8(1)**, [109]
  summary proceedings, **8**, 591
  suspected, inspection of books where,
    8, 585
  transient offenders, **8**, 65
  unincorporated body, by, **8**, 593
offences—
  amended provisions, **8(1)**, [1381]
  daily default fine, meaning, **8(1)**, [1203]
  legal professional privilege, **8(1)**, [1207]
  liability of directors for, **22**, [546]
  officer in default—
    bodies other than companies, provisions
      applying, **8(1)**, [1201]
    liability of company as, **8(1)**, [1200]
    liability of, **8(1)**, [1199]
  production and inspection of documents,
    8(1), [1210]
  prosecution, consent required for,
    8(1), [1204]

companies—*contd*
offences—*contd*
summary conviction, imprisonment on,
8(1), [1209]
summary proceedings—
time limit for, **8(1)**, [1206]
venue for, **8(1)**, [1205]
transitional provisions, **8(1)**, [1211]
offences by, **12(1)**, [569]; **12(2)**, [162]
officer—
absconding, arrest of, **8**, 55
chartered company. *See* **chartered
company**
companies clauses. *See* **Companies
Clauses Acts**
examination on oath, **8**, 484
false statement by, **12(1)**, [570]
home provided for outside UK,
43(S), 873–4
meaning, **8**, 602
penalties, liability for, **43(S)**, 1337
proceedings against, relief in, **8**, 589
proper, person being, **42**, [248]
responsibility of, **42**, [248]
secretary. *See* secretary *below*
officers—
in default—
bodies other than companies, provisions
applying, **8(1)**, [1201]
liability of, **8(1)**, [1199]
liability of company as, **8(1)**, [1200]
proposed, statement of, **8(1)**, [90]
official seal—
share certificates, for, **8(1)**, [128]
use abroad, for, **8(1)**, [127]
old public company—
meaning, **8**, 818–19
memorandum, alteration of, **8**, 819
misleading name, trading under, **8**, 823
new classification, failure to obtain, **8**, 822
offences and penalties, **8**, 822
official seal, use of, **8**, 824
private company, becoming, **8**, 821
references to, in principal Act, **8**, 818–19
re-registration—
application to be made, **8**, 819–20
conditions for, **8**, 820–1
resolution by directors for, **8**, 819
resolution not to re-register, **8**, 821
share capital, payment for, **8**, 823–4
shares, own, charge on, **8**, 822–3
other Member State, in, transfer of UK
trade, **43(1)**, [1198]
overseas. *See* **overseas companies**
overseas branch—
register—
countries where kept, **8**, 761
discontinuance of, **8**, 762
general provisions for, **8**, 762–3
Great Britain, kept in, **8**, 763–4
keeping of, **8**, 416
meaning, **8**, 416
rectification, **8**, 762
ownership, change in—
assets transferred within group, **44(1)**, [506]

companies—*contd*
ownership, change in—*contd*
corporation tax, **44(1)**, [499]–[501]
information regarding, **44(1)**, [502]
investment company, **44(1)**, [505]
property business, company carrying on,
44(1), [507]
rules for ascertaining, **44(1)**, [509]
trading losses, disallowance of, **44(1)**, [503]
carry back, **44(1)**, [504]
unused non-trading loss on intangible fixed
assets, company with, **44(1)**, [508]
parent—
meaning, **8(1)**, [1251]
undertakings, **8(1)**, [1240], [1393]
parent and subsidiary undertakings,
19(2), [496]
partner, as. *See* **partnership**
payment made by, treatment of, **44(1)**, [2]
payments to, **44(4)**, [985]
periodical statement, repeal of requirement to
publish, **8(1)**, [1256]
persons dealing with, **8(1)**, [118]
political contributions, disclosure in directors'
report, **8**, 666
political donations and expenditure. *See*
political donations and expenditure
poll—
proxy may demand, **8**, 429
right to demand, **8**, 429
voting on, **8**, 429
power of directors to bind, **8(1)**, [118]
pre-entry losses, restriction on set-off of,
43(1), [6]
pre-incorporation contracts, deeds and
obligations, **8(1)**, [129]
prescribed, meaning, **8(1)**, [1245]
private—
auditor. *See* **auditor**
company secretary, not requiring,
8(1), [348]
meaning, **8(1)**, [82]
public offers, prohibition of—
allotment or agreement to allot
securities, **8(1)**, [833]
enforcement, **8(1)**, [835]–[837]
meaning, **8(1)**, [834]
orders available to court after
contravention, **8(1)**, [836]
person connected with company,
meaning, **8(1)**, [834]
proposed contravention, order
restraining, **8(1)**, [835]
remedial order, **8(1)**, [837]
validity of allotment, **8(1)**, [838]
purchase of own shares. *See* **purchase of
own shares**
resolutions. *See* **resolutions**
meaning, **8(1)**, [82]
profit and loss account—
formats—
detailed, **8**, 615–18, 671–4, 699–701,
730–2
notes on, **8**, 618–19, 674–5, 701–2,
732–4

companies—*contd*
  profit and loss account—*contd*
    information supplementing—
      miscellaneous matters, **8**, 633, 686
      separate statement of certain items,
        8, 631, 747
      staff, as to, **8**, 632–3, 749
      tax, particulars of, **8**, 631–2, 714, 747–8
      turnover, particulars of, **8**, 632, 686
  profits—
    basic, **44(1)**, [8]
    computation of, **44(1)**, [8], [9], [170]
    distribution. *See* distribution *above*
    meaning, **44(1)**, [1]
    small companies' relief, **44(1)**, [8]
    taxation of, **44(1)**, [3]
  promissory note made, accepted or endorsed
    by, **8(1)**, [130]
  public—
    accounts and reports, laying before general
      meeting, **8(1)**, [515]
      failure, offence of, **8(1)**, [516]
    acquisition of own shares. *See* **purchase of
      own shares**
    annual general meetings. *See* **annual
      general meeting**
    auditor. *See* **auditor**
    company secretary. *See* **company
      secretary**
    lien or charge on shares of, **8(1)**, [748]
    meaning, **8(1)**, [82]
    resolutions. *See* **resolutions**
    share capital. *See* **share capital**
  public company—
    cancellation of shares by, **8**, 211–14
    financial assistance for purchase of own
      shares, **8**, 218
    listed, summary financial statement,
      provision of, **8**, 331
    meaning, **8**, 104
    minimum authorised capital, **8**, 114
    old. *See* old public company *above*
    private company, becoming—
      court powers as to, **8**, 151–2
      objection to, **8**, 152–3
      procedure, **8**, 151–2
    re-registration. *See* re-registration *below*
    share capital requirements, **8**, 189
    shares held by or for, treatment of,
      8, 211–14
  public limited company—
    name, requirements as to, **8**, 408, 533
    Welsh equivalent, **8**, 533
  qualifying change of ownership, meaning,
    43(S), 54–5
  quoted—
    accounts and reports, right of member or
      debenture holder to demand copies of,
      8(1), [510]
    annual accounts and reports, meaning,
      8(1), [549]
    directors' remuneration report. *See*
      director (company)
    filing obligations, **8(1)**, [525]

companies—*contd*
  quoted—*contd*
    general meetings. *See* **general meetings**
    meaning, **8(1)**, [439], [463], [609];
      44(1), [133]
    summary financial statement, form and
      content of, **8(1)**, [506]
    website, accounts and reports to be on,
      8(1), [508]
  reconstruction—
    capital gains tax. *See* **capital gains tax**
    change of ownership, without, **44(1)**, [176]
    leasing plant or machinery, involving
      business of, **44(1)**, [178]
    loss relief, **44(1)**, [199]
    ownership, **44(1)**, [179]
    relevant assets, **44(1)**, [179]
    relevant liabilities, **44(1)**, [179]
    relevant loan stock, **44(1)**, [179]
    share exchanges on, **43(2)**, [134]
    transfer of trade to obtain balancing
      allowances, **44(1)**, [177]
  reconstruction or amalgamation—
    articles, obligations of company with
      respect to, **8(1)**, [979]
    mergers. *See* **mergers**
    power of court to facilitate, **8(1)**, [978]
  records—
    copies, provision of, **8(1)**, [1215]
    duty to keep and preserve, **43(1)**, [395]
    falsification, duty to take precautions
      against, **8(1)**, [1216]
    form of, **8(1)**, [1213]
    information kept instead of, **43(1)**, [395]
    inspection—
      keeping available for, **8(1)**, [1214]
      regulations, **8(1)**, [1215]
    meaning, **8(1)**, [1212]
  redeemable shares—
    capital redemption reserve, **8**, 231–2
    power to issue, **8**, 223
  redemption of shares—
    purchase of own shares by company, **8**, 225
    See also **shares in company
      (company's own)**
  redemption—
    cancellation, treated as, **8**, 224
    failure in, effect of, **8**, 239
    financing of, **8**, 224–5
    fully paid, must be, **8**, 223
    premium payable on, **8**, 224
    private companies, **8**, 232–4
    regulations, power to make, **8**, 240
    terms and manner of, **8**, 223–4
    transitional cases, **8**, 241
  register—
    administrative restoration to—
      application for, **8(1)**, [1102]
      decision of registrar, **8(1)**, [1105]
      effect of, **8(1)**, [1106]
      requirements for, **8(1)**, [1103]
      statement of compliance, **8(1)**, [1104]
    annotation, **8(1)**, [1159]
    copy of material on—
      certification as accurate, **8(1)**, [1169]

companies—*contd*
register—*contd*
copy of material on—*contd*
form and manner in which provided, **8(1)**, [1168]
form of application for, **8(1)**, [1167]
right to, **8(1)**, [1164]
dissolved companies, records relating to, **8(1)**, [1162]
effect of restoration where property has vested as bona vacantia, **8(1)**, [1112]
inconsistencies, resolution of, **8(1)**, [1171]
inspection of—
application to made address unavailable, **8(1)**, [1166]
form of application for, **8(1)**, [1167]
material not available for, **8(1)**, [1165]
right of, **8(1)**, [1163]
name of company on restoration, **8(1)**, [1111]
original documents, preservation of, **8(1)**, [1161]
records in, **8(1)**, [1158]
rectification—
application, on, **8(1)**, [1173]
court order, under, **8(1)**, [1174]
removal of material from—
administrative, **8(1)**, [1172]
powers of court on ordering, **8(1)**, [1175]
public notice of, **8(1)**, [1176]
restoration to by court—
application for, **8(1)**, [1107]
decision on, **8(1)**, [1109]
effect of order, **8(1)**, [1110]
time for application, **8(1)**, [1108]
striking off. *See* striking off register *below*
unique identifiers, allocation of, **8(1)**, [1160]
registered number, **8(1)**, [1144]
registered office—
change of address, **8(1)**, [165]
change of, notice of, **8**, 363
register located at, **8**, 335
requirement to have, **8**, 363–4; **8(1)**, [164]
statement in memorandum, **8**, 105
Welsh companies, **8(1)**, [166]
registers—
charges, of. *See* charges *above*
computers, use of, **8**, 586–7
debenture holders, of, **8**, 247–9
defunct company—
restoration of, **8**, 520
striking off, **8**, 513
directors' interests, of, **8**, 389–90
directors, of, **8**, 364–5
particulars to be registered, **8**, 365–6
directors' shareholdings. *See* **director**
disqualification orders, **8**, 851–2
form of, **8**, 586
inspection, obligations of company, **8**, 587
interest in shares, of, **8**, 270–1
inspection, open to, **8**, 277
removal of entries, **8**, 276

companies—*contd*
registers—*contd*
members. *See* members *above*
overseas branch register—
countries where kept, **8**, 761
discontinuance of, **8**, 762
duplication of, **8**, 762
general provisions respecting, **8**, 762–3
keeping, **8**, 416
meaning, **8**, 416
rectification of, **8**, 762
private company—
striking off on application—
directors' duties following, **8**, 517–18
duties, **8**, 515–16
enforcement, **8**, 519–20
general, **8**, 515
offences, **8**, 520
restoration to register, **8**, 520–1
supplementary provisions, **8**, 518–19
secretaries, of, **8**, 364–5
particulars to be registered, **8**, 367
striking company off—
notices as to, **8**, 513
objection to, **8**, 520–1
restoration after, **8**, 520
registrar of companies—
accounts, copy to be delivered to, **8**, 306
annual return, delivery to, **8**, 417
appointment, **8**, 565
assistant and staff, **8**, 565
certificate of incorporation, **8**, 572
certificate of registration by, **8**, 116
companies' registered numbers, **8**, 566
company records—
inspection of, **8**, 571–2
keeping, **8**, 570
documents—
copies of, **8**, 574
deemed notice, exclusion of, **8**, 576
inspection of, **8**, 571–2
issue or receipt, public notice of, **8**, 574–5
legible form, delivery in, **8**, 567–8
meaning, **8**, 578
otherwise than in legible form, **8**, 568–9, 573
Welsh companies, relating to, **8**, 573–4
duty of, **8**, 115
fees payable to, **8**, 570–1
index of company names, **8**, 577–8
matters to be communicated to, **8**, 184–5
meaning, **8**, 603
notice to—
alteration of share capital, of, **8**, 192–3
cancellation of shares, **8**, 192–3
increased share capital, of, **8**, 193
reduction of share capital, of, **8**, 192
numbers, allocation of, to companies, **8**, 571
official seal, **8**, 565
oversea company accounts and reports, delivery of, **8**, 552–3
remuneration, **8**, 565
returns to, enforcement, **8**, 577

companies—*contd*
  registrar of companies—*contd*
    share capital—
      certificate, **8**, 189
      notice of alteration, **8**, 192–3
      valuer's report for, **8**, 184–5
  registration—
    agreements, of, **8**, 435–6
    alteration of articles or memorandum,
      8, 119
    application for, **8(1)**, [87]
    articles of association, **8**, 111, 113–14
    cancellation of, **19(1)**, [380]
    capital, statement, **8(1)**, [88]
    certificate of incorporation, **8**, 116, 572
      issue of, **8(1)**, [93]
    change of company name, of, **8(1)**, [158]
    charges, of. *See* charges *above*
    chartered companies. *See* **chartered**
      company
    class rights, special, of, **8**, 197
    companies authorised to register—
      actions pending, **8**, 777
      application for, **8**, 527
      capacity to register, **8**, 527
      capital structure of company, **8**, 778
      constitution of, **8**, 777–8
      existing liabilities, effect on, **8**, 777
      procedural requirements, **8**, 528–9
      provisions applicable to, **8**, 777–8
      vesting of property, **8**, 777
    companies capable of, **8**, 527
    company not formed under companies
      legislation—
      authorisation, **8(1)**, [1118]
      regulations, power to make provision
        by, **8(1)**, [1120]
    compliance, statement of, **8(1)**, [91]
    computerised records of, **8**, 586–7
    documents, delivery to registrar, **8(1)**, [87]
    effect of, **8(1)**, [94]
    existing company—
      addition of limited to name, **8**, 533
      certificate of, **8**, 533–4
      change of name on, **8**, 529
      deed of settlement in place of articles
        etc, **8**, 534
      effect of, **8**, 534
      meaning, **8**, 527
      procedural requirements, **8**, 528–9
    fees for, prescribed, **8**, 570
    formation by, **8(1)**, [85]
    former Companies Acts, under, **8**, 525–6
    guarantee, company limited by, **8**, 528
    initial shareholdings, statement of **8(1)**, [88]
    Joint Stock Companies Acts, under, **8**, 526
    joint stock company—
      public company, **8**, 531
      requirements for, **8**, 530–2
    memorandum of association—
      effect of, **8**, 116
      procedure, **8**, 113–14
    names, prohibition of certain, **8**, 125–6
    offices for, **8**, 565

companies—*contd*
  registration—*contd*
    oversea company. *See* **oversea company**
    proposed officers, statement of, **8(1)**, [90]
    reduction of capital order, **8**, 206
    re-registration. *See* re-registration *below*
    registrar, by, **8(1)**, [92]
    resolutions, of, **8**, 435–6
    statement of guarantee, **8(1)**, [89]
    transfer of shares, **8**, 242–3
  regulations and orders—
    affirmative resolution procedure,
      8(1), [1366]
    approval after making, **8(1)**, [1367]
    negative resolution procedure, **8(1)**, [1365]
    provisions in, **8(1)**, [1368]
    statutory instrument, by, **8(1)**, [1364]
  related party transactions, **43(2)**, [241]
  relief, transfer of, **42**, [304]
  repayment supplement, **44(1)**, [608]
  reports—
    scheme of provisions, **8(1)**, [458]
    small companies regime, companies subject
      to, **8(1)**, [459]
  re-registration—
    alteration of status by, **8(1)**, [167]
    certificate of, **8**, 146–7
    former Companies Acts, under, **8**, 526
    limited company as unlimited, **8**, 147–9
    old public company, of, **8**, 819–20
    private company as public—
      acquisition of own shares, **8(1)**, [746]
      application and accompanying
        documents, **8(1)**, [172]
      certificate of incorporation, issue of,
        8(1), [174]
      conditions for, **8(1)**, [168]
      means of, **8(1)**, [168]
      net assets, requirements, **8(1)**, [170]
      non-cash consideration, effect of recent
        allotment of share for, **8(1)**, [171]
      proposed secretary, statement of,
        8(1), [173]
      share capital requirements, **8(1)**, [169]
      valuation requirements,
        8(1), [1227]–[1231]
    private limited company as unlimited—
      application and accompanying
        documents, **8(1)**, [181]
      certificate of incorporation, issue of,
        8(1), [182]
      conditions for, **8(1)**, [189]
    private unlimited company as limited—
      application and accompanying
        documents, **8(1)**, [184]
      certificate of incorporation, issue of,
        8(1), [185]
      conditions for, **8(1)**, [183]
      statement of capital, **8(1)**, [186]
    public company as private—
      application and accompanying
        documents, **8(1)**, [178]
      cancellation of shares, in consequence
        of, **8(1)**, [742]–[745]

companies—*contd*

re-registration—*contd*

public company as private—*contd*

certificate of incorporation, issue of, **8(1)**, [179], [743]

conditions for, **8(1)**, [175]

court application or order, notice to registrar, **8(1)**, [177]

elective resolution, effect on, **8**, 434–5

expedited procedure, **8(1)**, [729]

means of, **8(1)**, [175]

objection to, **8**, 152–3

procedure, **8**, 151–2

special resolution, application to court for cancellation of, **8(1)**, [176]

public company becoming private and unlimited—

application and accompanying documents, **8(1)**, [188]

certificate of incorporation, issue of, **8(1)**, [189]

conditions for, **8(1)**, [187]

unlimited company as limited, **8**, 150–1

residence—

Taxes Act, for purposes of, **42**, [921]

exceptions to rule, **42**, [938]

registered office, transfer of to UK, **42**, [922]

residuary income, **44(1)**, [438]

resolutions. *See also* **resolutions**

adjourned meeting, passed at, **8**, 436

copy, entitlement to, **8**, 434–5

director—

appointment of, for, **8**, 368

removal of, for, **8**, 371

elective. *See* **private company**

extraordinary—

meaning, **8**, 432

notice of, **8**, 432

members', circulation of, **8**, 430–1

notice of—

generally, **8**, 430

when unnecessary, **8**, 431

registration of, **8**, 434–5

special. *See* special resolution *below*

special notice, requiring, **8**, 433

written. *See* **private company**

returns—

allotments, as to, **8**, 165–6

annual. *See* annual return *above*

chartered company, by. *See* **chartered company**

right of first refusal provisions, exclusion for, **22**, [701]

SE, formed by merger—

continuity, for transitional purposes, **43(2)**, [755]

intangible fixed assets, gains and losses from, **43(2)**, [191]

seal—

documents, execution of, **8**, 137, 139

name to be engraved on, **8**, 408

no requirement to have, **8**, 137

official, meaning, **8**, 603

pre-1979 company, use by, **8**, 824

companies—*contd*

seal—*contd*

share certificates, for, **8**, 139

use abroad, for, **8**, 138

secretary. *See also* **company secretary**

company required to have, **8**, 361–2

dual capacity, acts done in, **8**, 362

meaning, **8**, 15

particulars as to, **8**, 608

qualifications of, **8**, 362–3

register of secretaries—

contents, **8**, 367

duty to keep, **8**, 364–5

vacancy of office, **8**, 361–2

securitisation. *See* **securitisation company**

self-assessment. *See under* **corporation tax**

senior accounting officer—

appropriate tax accounting arrangements, meaning, **43(S)**, 1683

certificate for Commissioners, **43(S)**, 1680

failure to provide, **43(S)**, 1680

interpretation, **43(S)**, 1683–5

main duty of, **43(S)**, 1679

failure to comply with, **43(S)**, 1680

meaning, **43(S)**, 1684

more than one, company with, **43(S)**, 1681

name, notification to Commissioners, **43(S)**, 1680

failure to provide, **43(S)**, 1681

penalties—

assessment, **43(S)**, 1681–2

amount, power to change, **43(S)**, 1682

appeals, **43(S)**, 1682

enforcement, **43(S)**, 1682

failure to comply, reasonable excuse for, **43(S)**, 1681

qualifying company, **43(S)**, 1683–4

service addresses, **8(1)**, [1219]–[1220]

service of documents on, **8(1)**, [1217]

share capital—

reorganisation of, capital gains tax on. *See* **capital gains tax**

repayment of, **44(1)**, [113]

share capital, with. *See* **share capital; shares**

share certificate, official seal for, **8**, 139

share premium account—

application of, **8**, 198

group reconstructions, relief, **8**, 817

premiums payable from, **8**, 198

regulations as to, **8**, 201

relief from requirements—

extension, powers of, **8**, 202

group reconstructions, for, **8**, 200–1

mergers, in respect of, **8**, 199–200

share capital, as part of, **8**, 198

transfers to, **8**, 198

shares, limited by—

articles, **8**, 111

meaning, **8**, 103

memorandum, form, **8**, 106–7

name of, **8**, 125

single member—

application of provisions to, **8(1)**, [116]

contract with sole member, **8(1)**, [309]

companies—*contd*
  single member—*contd*
    decisions, records of, **8(1)**, [435]
    register of members, **8(1)**, [201]
  small and medium-sized—
    research and development tax relief—
      definition for, **43(S)**, 545
      larger, modifications for, **43(S)**, 545–6
    vaccine research relief, **43(S)**, 543–4
  small company—
    accounts—
      abbreviated—
        form and content, **8**, 688–89
        notes to, **8**, 690–1
      accounting policies, disclosure of,
        8, 683, 690
      accounting principles—
        departure from, **8**, 678
        generally, **8**, 678
      accounting rules, **8**, 678–81
        alternative, **8**, 681–3
      fixed assets, treatment of, **8**, 679
      form of, **8**, 671–8, 688–9
      general rules, **8**, 670–1
      notes to, **8**, 683–6, 690–1
    assets—
      current, valuation, **8**, 679–80
      depreciation rules, **8**, 681–2
      excess of money owed over value,
        8, 680
      fixed, treatment of, **8**, 679
    audit, exemptions from, **8**, 324–9
      conditions for, **8(1)**, [555]
      exclusions, **8(1)**, [556]
      group company, availability to,
        8(1), [557]
    balance sheet—
      formats—
        detailed, **8**, 671–4, 688–9
        examples, **8**, 671–4, 688–9
        general rules, **8**, 670–1, 688–9
        notes on, **8**, 674–5, 689
      information supplementing—
        fixed assets, as to, **8**, 683–4, 690–1
        guarantees and commitments,
          8, 685–6
        indebtedness, details of, **8**, 685, 691
        investments, as to, **8**, 684
        miscellaneous matters, **8**, 686
        reserves and provisions, **8**, 684–5
        share capital and debentures, **8**, 683,
          690
    filing obligations, **8(1)**, [522]
    group accounts, option to prepare,
      8(1), [476]
    parent companies, **8(1)**, [461]
    profit and loss account—
      formats—
        detailed, **8**, 671–4
        notes on, **8**, 674–5
      information supplementing—
        miscellaneous matters, **8**, 686
        turnover, particulars of, **8**, 686
    qualification as, **8**, 318–19; **8(1)**, [460]

companies—*contd*
  small company—*contd*
    regime—
      accounts and reports provisions,
        8(1), [459]
      exclusions from, **8(1)**, [462]
  small, corporation tax rate, **44(1)**, [8]
  special Act—
    companies incorporated by, **8**, 85
    meaning, **8**, 86
  special resolution—
    adoption in articles, **8**, 112
    alteration of, **8**, 111
    articles—
      alteration, for, **8**, 112
      amendments, for, **8**, 108
    financial assistance for purchase of shares—
      cancellation by court, **8**, 222
      general provisions for, **8**, 222
      requirement for, **8**, 219
    meaning, **8**, 432
    notice of, **8**, 432
    public company becoming private, for,
      8, 151–2
    purchase of company's own shares, for,
      8, 226–7
    purchase of company's own shares, for
      private company, **8**, 236–7
    registration of, **8**, 434–5
    re-registration—
      private company, for, **8**, 141–2
      unlimited company, for, **8**, 146, 150
    share capital—
      not to call up, **8**, 191
      reduction of, for, **8**, 202–3
    unlimited liability of director, for, **8**, 374
  stamp duties. *See* **stamp duty**
  status—
    alteration of. *See* re-registration *above*
    events affecting, **8**, 140–1
  statutory company—
    general note, **8**, 8
    meaning, **8**, 86
  striking off—
    company being wound up, **8(1)**, [1079]
    defunct company, **8(1)**, [1078]
    letter or notice, service of, **8(1)**, [1080]
    power of, **8(1)**, [1078]
    restoration to register. *See* register *above*
    voluntary—
      activities requiring continuance,
        8(1), [1082]
      application by company, **8(1)**, [1081]
      creditor, meaning, **8(1)**, [1089]
      creditors, notice to, **8(1)**, [1084]
      members, employees etc, notice to,
        8(1), [1084]
      new creditors, notice to, **8(1)**, [1085]
      new members, employees etc, notice
        to, **8(1)**, [1085]
      other proceedings not concluded, effect
        of, **8(1)**, [1083]
      service of documents, **8(1)**, [1086]
      withdrawal of application,
        8(1), [1087]–[1088]

companies—*contd*

subsidiaries—

75 per cent, determining, **44(1)**, [123], [227]

definitions, **44(1)**, [620]

determining existence of, **44(1)**, [110]

meaning, **42**, [13]

other bodies corporate, capital held through, **42**, [15]

subsidiary. *See* **subsidiary**

substantial shareholdings, capital gains tax exemption for disposals—

application of, **42**, [1471]

consequential provisions, **42**, [1475]

interpretation, **42**, [1474]

investing company and company invested in, requirements, **42**, [1473]

main exemption, **42**, [1471]

not applying, **42**, [1471]

subsidiary exemption, **42**, [1471]

substantial shareholding requirement, **42**, [1472]

takeover offers—

convertible securities, treatment of, **8**, 480–1

joint, **8**, 479

meaning, **8**, 472–3

minority shareholder—

right to be bought out—

effect of requirement, **8**, 477

general provisions, **8**, 476–7

joint offers, **8**, 479

right to buy out—

court, applications to, **8**, 478

joint offers, **8**, 479

notice of, **8**, 473–5

offeror, of, **8**, 473

shares, meaning, **8**, 472

shares of associates, not extending to, **8**, 479–80

substituted provisions, **8**, 861

terms for, **8**, 472

tax avoidance arrangements, **43(2)**, [241]

trading, meaning, **44(1)**, [122], [133]

transitional provisions and savings, **8(1)**, [1372]

UK resident companies, group relief for overseas losses of, **44(1)**, [217]

UK-registered, meaning, **8(1)**, [1236]

undertaking—

meaning, **8(1)**, [1239]

parent and subsidiary, **8(1)**, [1240], [1393]; **19(2)**, [496]

"participating interest", meaning, **19(2)**, [498]

related expressions, **8(1)**, [1239]

unlimited—

exemption from obligation to file accounts, **8(1)**, [526]

meaning, **8(1)**, [81]

unquoted—

accounts and reports, right of member or debenture holder to demand copies of, **8(1)**, [509]

companies—*contd*

unquoted—*contd*

annual accounts and reports, meaning, **8(1)**, [549]

filing obligations, **8(1)**, [524]

meaning, **8(1)**, [463]; **44(1)**, [122], [133]

purchase of own shares, **44(1)**, [123]

shares in. *See* **shares**

summary financial statement, form and content of, **8(1)**, [505]

unregistered, **8(1)**, [1121]

valuation requirements—

application of, **8(1)**, [1227]

associate, meaning, **8(1)**, [1230]

full disclosure, valuer entitled to, **8(1)**, [1231]

independence requirement, **8(1)**, [1229]

qualified independent person, valuation by, **8(1)**, [1228]

voting—

poll. *See* poll *above*

proxy. *See* **proxies**

rights, **8**, 427

water. *See* **water companies**

Companies Acts

companies within, **8**, 2–8

Financial Services Act, relationship to, **8**, 595

former, meaning, **8(1)**, [1249]

index of defined expressions, **8(1)**, [1394]

Insolvency Act, relationship to, **8**, 595

meaning, **8**, 831–3; **8(1)**, [80]

Northern Ireland, provisions extended to, **8(1)**, [1360]

requirements, references to, **8(1)**, [1250]

Companies Clauses Acts

absconding officer, arrest of, **8**, 55

accounts—

arbitrators may call for, **8**, 61

books—

access to, by mortgagees, **8**, 35

balancing of, **8**, 56

inspection by shareholders, **8**, 56

debenture stock, of, **8**, 79

keeping of, **8**, 56

officers, of, **8**, 54

action—

calls on shares, for, **8**, 23–4

interest, to recover, **8**, 78

not to abate on change of name, **8**, 80–1

recovery of damages, for, **8**, 63–4

advertisement—

closing of transfer register, **8**, 20

notice of general meeting, **8**, 40

notices generally, **8**, 63

application to all companies, **8**, 70

arbitration—

costs of, **8**, 61

questions to be determined by, **8**, 60

submission to, as rule of court, **8**, 61

umpire, appointment, **8**, 60

arbitrator—

appointment, **8**, 60

books etc, power to call for, **8**, 61

Companies Clauses Acts—*contd*
  arbitrator—*contd*
    vacancy in office, filling, **8**, 60
  auditors—
    accountants, power to employ, **8**, 53
    balance sheet, delivery to, **8**, 53
    duty of, **8**, 53
    election, **8**, 52
    failure to elect, **8**, 53
    powers, **8**, 53
    qualifications, **8**, 52
    rotation of, **8**, 52
    vacancies in office, filling, **8**, 52
  balance sheet—
    delivery to auditors, **8**, 53
    production at meeting, **8**, 57
  bankruptcy, proof of debts in, **8**, 63
  borrowing powers—
    authorisation of—
      evidence of, **8**, 30
      generally, **8**, 29
    bond—
      form of, **8**, 68
      holders, access to account books by,
        8, 35
      obligees, rights of, **8**, 31
      on security of, **8**, 29
      register of, **8**, 31
      stamping of, **8**, 30
      transfer of—
        form of, **8**, 68
        registration, **8**, 32
        stamping, **8**, 32
    debenture stock, extinguished to extent
      of, **8**, 79
    interest—
      arrears, enforcement, **8**, 34
      cessation on expiration of notice to pay,
        8, 34
      monies borrowed, on, **8**, 32
      transfer of, stamping, **8**, 33
    loans, conversion into capital, **8**, 35
    mortgage—
      deed, form of, **8**, 67
      form of transfer, **8**, 68
      register of, **8**, 31
      rights of mortgagees, **8**, 30–1
      stamping of, **8**, 30
      transfer of—
        registration, **8**, 32
        stamping, **8**, 32
    mortgagees—
      access to account books by, **8**, 35
      application of shares notwithstanding,
        8, 31
      rights of, **8**, 30–1
    re-borrowing, **8**, 29
    receiver, appointment, **8**, 34–5
    repayment—
      arrears, enforcement of, **8**, 34
      fixed time, at, **8**, 33
      no time fixed, where, **8**, 33
    special Act, under, **8**, 29
  byelaws—
    breach of, penalty, **8**, 59

Companies Clauses Acts—*contd*
  byelaws—*contd*
    evidence of, **8**, 59
    mitigation of penalties, provision for, **8**, 59
    officers, for, **8**, 58–9
    power to make, **8**, 58–9
  calls on shares—
    action for—
      declaration in, **8**, 24
      enforcement by, **8**, 23
      matters to be proved, **8**, 24
    application of, notwithstanding mortgages,
      8, 31
    enforcement, **8**, 23
    non-payment, effect of, **8**, 25
    payment—
      arrears, in, notwithstanding
        cancellation, **8**, 71
      before call, interest on, **8**, 22
      dividends, to precede, **8**, 58
      reversion of forfeited shares on, **8**, 27
      sale of shares to meet, **8**, 26
      times and places for, **8**, 22
      transfer of shares, before, **8**, 20
    power to make, **8**, 22
    unpaid, interest on, **8**, 23
    value of cancelled shares, deduction of,
      8, 71
  cancellation of shares. *See* shares *below*
  capital—
    additional, creation of, **8**, 72
    application of, **8**, 38
    conversion of loans into, **8**, 35
    dividends, reduction by, **8**, 58
    new shares deemed part of, **8**, 35–6
    shares, division into, **8**, 16
  certificate—
    debenture stock, **8**, 78
    share. *See* shares *below*
  chairman—
    directors, of, **8**, 48
    general meeting, at, **8**, 41
  committees of directors, **8**, 49
  contingencies fund, **8**, 58
  contracts—
    change of name, effect of, **8**, 80–1
    power to make, **8**, 49–50
    qualifications not affected by, **8**, 45–6
  damages—
    ascertainment of, **8**, 63–4
    how to be levied, **8**, 63–4
    distress, enforcement by, **8**, 63–4
    recovery of, summary proceedings, **8**, 64
  debenture stock—
    account, separate, to be kept, **8**, 79
    advances to meet, **8**, 82
    borrowing powers, effect on, **8**, 79
    certificates to holders, **8**, 78
    creation, regulations as to, **8**, 76, 82
    holders, rights etc, of, **8**, 79
    interest—
      action or suit to recover, **8**, 78
      amendments as to, **8**, 81
      arrears, enforcement of payment, **8**, 77
      priority charge, as, **8**, 77

Companies Clauses Acts—*contd*
  debenture stock—*contd*
    interest—*contd*
      restriction on rate of, **8**, 82
    issue of—
      discount, at, **8**, 82–3
      regulations for, **8**, 76, 82–3
    judicial factor, appointment and duties, **8**, 77
    money raised by, application of, **8**, 79
    mortgage, effect on, **8**, 77
    priority of, **8**, 77
    receiver, appointment and duties, **8**, 77
    redeemable, issue of, **8**, 85–6
    registration, necessity for, **8**, 78
    transmissible and transferable, **8**, 76
  directors—
    chairman of—
      appointment, **8**, 48
      occasional, **8**, 49
    committees of, **8**, 49
    contracts—
      power to make, **8**, 49–50
      qualification not affected by, **8**, 45–6
    death, resignation etc, **8**, 46
    disposal of shares by, **8**, 36
    election of, **8**, 44
    failure of election, **8**, 44
    indemnity of, **8**, 51
    informalities in appointment, **8**, 51
    meetings—
      chairman, **8**, 48
      convening, **8**, 39
      generally, **8**, 48
      minutes, **8**, 50–1
    number of, **8**, 43–4
    office of profit etc, holding, **8**, 45
    personal liability, relief from, **8**, 51
    powers exercised by, **8**, 47
    powers not exercisable by, **8**, 47
    qualifications, **8**, 45
    record of proceedings, **8**, 50–1
    rotation of, **8**, 46
    vacancies, occasional, filling, **8**, 46
    vacation of office, **8**, 45
    validity of proceedings, **8**, 51
  discount, shares issued at, **8**, 82–3
  dividends—
    calls to be paid before, **8**, 58
    capital not to be reduced by, **8**, 58
    declaration of, **8**, 57
    preference shares entitlement to, **8**, 73
    scheme to precede declaration, **8**, 57
  execution against shareholders, **8**, 28
  forfeiture of shares. *See* shares *below*
  funded debt, provisions applied, **8**, 80
  general meetings—
    adjournment, **8**, 41
    business at, **8**, 41
    chairman at, **8**, 41
    extraordinary—
      business at, **8**, 40
      convening by directors, **8**, 39
      meaning, **8**, 39
      place of holding, **8**, 39

Companies Clauses Acts—*contd*
  general meetings—*contd*
    extraordinary—*contd*
      requisition by shareholders, **8**, 40
    first, time of, **8**, 39
    notice of, **8**, 40
    ordinary—
      business at, **8**, 39
      meaning, **8**, 39
      time for holding, **8**, 39
    poll, demand for, **8**, 43
    quorum for, **8**, 40–1
    voting—
      form of proxy, **8**, 68
      incapacitated persons, **8**, 43
      joint shareholders, **8**, 42–3
      manner of, **8**, 42
      proxy, as, **8**, 42
      rights, **8**, 41–2
  investment business. *See* **investment business**
  loans, conversion into capital, **8**, 35
  meetings—
    directors, of. *See* directors *above*
    general. *See* general meetings *above*
  mortgage—
    borrowing on. *See* borrowing *above*
    effect of Act on, **8**, 79
    preference stock, provisions applied, **8**, 80
  name, change of—
    actions etc, not to abate, **8**, 80–1
    contracts etc, preservation of, **8**, 81
    powers as to, continuance of, **8**, 80
    saving of rights, **8**, 81
  notices—
    advertisement, by, **8**, 63
    authentication of, **8**, 63
    joint proprietors, to, **8**, 62
    meetings, of, **8**, 40
    service of—
      company, on, **8**, 62
      shareholders, on, **8**, 62
  offences—
    penalties for. *See* penalties *below*
    transient offenders, **8**, 65
  officers—
    absconding, warrant for arrest, **8**, 55
    accountability, **8**, 53–4
    conduct, byelaws regulating, **8**, 58–9
    failure to account, **8**, 54
    imprisonment of, **8**, 55
    refusal to deliver up documents, **8**, 55
    security to be taken from, **8**, 53
    summary remedy against, **8**, 54
    sureties, remedies against, **8**, 55
  penalties—
    appeal to Crown Court, **8**, 65–6
    publication of, **8**, 64
      defacing boards used for, **8**, 64–5
    recovery of, summary proceedings, **8**, 65
  proceedings not to abate on change of name, **8**, 80–1
  proxies—
    appointment, **8**, 84
    form of, **8**, 68
    papers, form of, **8**, 83

Companies Clauses Acts—*contd*
  proxies—*contd*
    revocation, **8**, 84
    shareholders, deemed to be, **8**, 83
    special appointment, **8**, 84
    voting by, **8**, 42
  receiver—
    appointment, **8**, 34
    arrears of interest etc, to enforce, **8**, 34
    duties, **8**, 77
  register—
    bonds and mortgages, of, **8**, 31
    debenture stock, **8**, 78
    shareholders, of, **8**, 16–17
    stock, of, **8**, 38
    transfer—
      bonds and mortgages, of, **8**, 32
      shares, of, **8**, 18–19
  secretary, meaning, **8**, 15
  security, officers by, **8**, 53
  shareholders—
    accounts, right to inspect, **8**, 56
    addresses, register of, **8**, 17
    execution against—
      extent of, **8**, 28
      reimbursement of overpayment, **8**, 28
    meaning, **8**, 15
    new shares to be offered to, **8**, 36
    persons deemed to be, **8**, 16
    proof of proprietorship, **8**, 24
    proxies deemed to be, **8**, 83
    register of, **8**, 16–17
    remedies against, **8**, 28
    service of notices on, **8**, 62
    voting—
      joint shareholders, **8**, 42–3
      rights, **8**, 41–2
  shares—
    calls on. *See* calls *above*
    cancellation—
      creation of shares in lieu, **8**, 72
      forfeited shares, **8**, 70
      new unissued shares, **8**, 74
      payment not to be made for, **8**, 72
      payment of calls notwithstanding, **8**, 71
    capital to be divided into, **8**, 16
    certificate—
      evidence of title, as, **8**, 18
      form of, **8**, 67
      issue of, **8**, 17
      renewal when destroyed, **8**, 18
      terms to be stated on, **8**, 74
    consolidation into stock, **8**, 37
    creation of—
      in lieu of cancelled shares, **8**, 72
      regulations for, **8**, 72
    forfeited—
      cancellation of, **8**, 71
      consent of holders, with, **8**, 71
      deduction of value from amount due, **8**, 71
      evidence of, **8**, 26–7
      reversion on payment of calls, **8**, 27
      sale of, **8**, 26

Companies Clauses Acts—*contd*
  shares—*contd*
    forfeiture—
      confirmation by general meeting, **8**, 26
      evidence as to, **8**, 26–7
      non-payment of call, for, **8**, 25
      notice before, **8**, 25
    issue of, at discount, **8**, 82–3
    new—
      cancelled etc shares, in lieu of, **8**, 72
      creation of, regulations for, **8**, 72
      disposal by company, **8**, 75
      disposal by directors, **8**, 36
      issue of, **8**, 36
      offer of—
        letter, to be made by, **8**, 74–5
        old shares at premium, where, **8**, 36, 74
        shareholders, to, **8**, 36
        time for accepting, **8**, 75
      original shares, considered to be, **8**, 35–6
      vesting in parties accepting, **8**, 36
      vesting on acceptance, **8**, 75
    personal estate, as, **8**, 16
    preference—
      creation of, **8**, 73
      dividends, entitlement to, **8**, 73
      terms to be stated on certificate, **8**, 74
    proprietorship, proof of, **8**, 24
    sale of, to meet calls, **8**, 26
    surrender of, **8**, 72
    transfer of—
      books, closure of, **8**, 20
      calls to be paid before, **8**, 20
      deed, by, stamping, **8**, 18–19
      form of, **8**, 67
      registration of, **8**, 19
      transmission other than by, **8**, 20–1
    transmission—
      marriage, will etc, by, proof of, **8**, 21
      other than by transfer, **8**, 20–1
    trust, subject to, no duty to regard, **8**, 21–2
    unissued, cancellation, **8**, 74
  special Act—
    access to, **8**, 66
    borrowing powers under, **8**, 29
    depositing, **8**, 66
    expenses of obtaining, **8**, 38
    failure to keep etc, penalty, **8**, 67
    inspection of, **8**, 66
    penalties imposed by, **8**, 64–5
  statutory company, meaning, **8**, 86
  stock—
    consolidation of shares into, **8**, 37
    debenture stock. *See* debenture stock *above*
    holders—
      dividends, entitlement to, **8**, 38
      powers of, to transfer, **8**, 37
      privileges of, **8**, 38
    new—
      creation, regulations for, **8**, 72
      disposal by company, **8**, 75
      offer of—
        letter, to be made by, **8**, 74–5
        old stock at premium, **8**, 74

Companies Clauses Acts—*contd*
stock—*contd*
new—*contd*
offer of—*contd*
time for accepting, **8**, 75
unissued, cancellation, **8**, 74
vesting on acceptance, **8**, 75
preference—
creation of, **8**, 73
redeemable, issue of, **8**, 85–6
register of, **8**, 38
transfer of, **8**, 37
form of, **8**, 67
trusts, company not bound to regard, **8**, 21–2
voting. *See* general meeting *above*

company charges
amendment of provisions, power of Secretary
of State, **8(1)**, [972]
company's register of—
entries in, **8(1)**, [954]
inspection, keeping available for,
8(1), [954]–[955]
debentures—
certificate endorsed on, **8(1)**, [943]
commission, allowance or discount,
additional requirements, **8(1)**, [942]
series of, **8(1)**, [941]
information-sharing arrangements, **8(1)**, [971]
instruments creating—
duty of company to keep, **8(1)**, [953]
inspection, keeping available for,
8(1), [955]
property acquired, on, **8(1)**, [940]
property in another UK jurisdiction, in or
over, **8(1)**, [945]
property in jurisdictions outside UK, in or
over, **8(1)**, [944]
register—
particulars in, **8(1)**, [947]
rectification, **8(1)**, [951]
registrar, kept by, **8(1)**, [947]
satisfaction and release, entry of,
8(1), [950]
special, power to make provision for
registration in, **8(1)**, [971]
registration—
applicant for, **8(1)**, [938]
charges subject to, **8(1)**, [938]
creation, on, **8(1)**, [938]
enforcement of security of, **8(1)**, [949]
failure of, avoidance on, **8(1)**, [952]
land, charges on, **8(1)**, [938]–[939]
Northern Ireland, affecting land in,
8(1), [946]
overseas company, by, **8(1)**, [1130]
period allowed for, **8(1)**, [948]
property acquired, as to, **8(1)**, [940]
requirement of, **8(1)**, [938]
repealed provisions, **8(1)**, [1258]

company insolvency. *See also* **bankruptcy**
administration, **4(2)**, [544]
air traffic licence company, protection of.
See **air traffic services**

company insolvency—*contd*
administration—*contd*
non-company, application of law to,
4(2), [590]
special regimes, **4(2)**, [588]
administration order—
former provisions, **4(2)**, [80]
revocation, disabilities on, **4(2)**, [519]
administrative receiver—
acts of, validity, **4(2)**, [268]
agent, deemed to be, **4(2)**, [97]
appointment—
exceptions to prohibition, **4(2)**, [546]
notices of, **4(2)**, [99]
prohibited, **4(2)**, [104]
attendance before creditors' committee,
4(2), [102]
contracts, liability for, **4(2)**, [97]
dealing with, in good faith, **4(2)**, [95]
floating charge holder, prohibition of
appointment by, **4(2)**, [104]
capital markets exception, **4(2)**, [105]
financial market exception, **4(2)**, [110]
project finance exception, **4(2)**, [109]
protected railway companies exception,
4(2), [112]
public-private partnership exception,
4(2), [106]
registered social landlord exception,
4(2), [111]
supplementary provisions, **4(2)**, [113]
urban regeneration projects exception,
4(2), [108]
utilities exception, **4(2)**, [107]
general powers, **4(2)**, [95]
indemnity, right to, **4(2)**, [97]
information to be given by, **4(2)**, [99]
meaning, **4(2)**, [82]
more than one person as, **4(2)**, [267]
powers, schedule of, **4(2)**, [545]
property, disposal of—
charged property, **4(2)**, [96]
order authorising, **4(2)**, [96]
powers of, **4(2)**, [96]
proceeds, application of, **4(2)**, [96]
proposals for, report of, **4(2)**, [101]
getting in, **4(2)**, [270]
powers as to, **4(2)**, [545]
qualification of, **4(2)**, [266]
references to, construction of, **4(2)**, [95]
removal from office, **4(2)**, [98]
remuneration on vacation of office,
4(2), [98]
report by—
default as to, **4(2)**, [101]
distribution of, **4(2)**, [101]
liquidation of company, on, **4(2)**, [101]
summary of statement in, **4(2)**, [101]
time for making, **4(2)**, [101]
statement of affairs for—
default in, penalty, **4(2)**, [100]
matters to be shown in, **4(2)**, [100]
persons required to submit, **4(2)**, [100]
time for making, **4(2)**, [100]

company insolvency—*contd*
  administrative receiver—*contd*
    vacation of office—
      notice to registrar of, **4(2)**, [98]
      when required, **4(2)**, [98]
      See also receiver or manager *below*
  administrator—
    appointment, **4(2)**, [544]
    functions, **4(2)**, [544]
    gas etc services, requirement for,
      4(2), [269]
      powers, schedule of, **4(2)**, [545]
    property, powers as to, **4(2)**, [545]
    proposals by, **4(2)**, [544]
  agent in respect of, **4(2)**, [97]
  amended provisions, **4(2)**, [603]
  banks etc, provisions applied, **4(2)**, [509]
  books, lien on, unenforceable, **4(2)**, [280]
  composition. *See* voluntary arrangement *below*
  conduct of, **4(2)**, [559]
  connected with company, meaning,
    4(2), [283]
  contracts, liability for—
    administrative receiver, **4(2)**, [97]
    receiver or manager, **4(2)**, [90]
  courts—
    co-operation between, **4(2)**, [513]
    information and records, **4(2)**, [559]
    rules for, **4(2)**, [559]
  creditors—
    committee, powers of, **4(2)**, [102]
    meeting—
      approval of arrangement by, **4(2)**, [72]
      chairman's report on, **4(2)**, [72]
      corporate representatives at, **4(2)**, [526]
      decisions of, **4(2)**, [72]
        challenge of, **4(2)**, [75]
      moratorium, under, **4(2)**, [542]
      nominee's report as to, **4(2)**, [70]
      proposals, to consider, revised proposals,
        4(2), [75]
      summoning, **4(2)**, [71]
    secured, meaning, **4(2)**, [282]
  Crown, application of provisions, **4(2)**, [524]
  dealings, inquiry into, **4(2)**, [272], [273]
  debts, payment out of assets, **4(2)**, [93]
  director, offences by, **4(2)**, [248]
  effect of, **4(2)**, [136]
  expenses, **4(2)**, [559]
  extortionate credit transactions, **4(2)**, [278]
  fees orders, **4(2)**, [498]
  floating charge—
    avoidance of, **4(2)**, [279]
    meaning, **4(2)**, [285]
  foreign company, application of law to,
    4(2), [589]
  insolvency rules—
    committee—
      constitution, **4(2)**, [497]
      consultations with, **4(2)**, [497]
    contents, **4(2)**, [496], [559]
    power to make, **4(2)**, [495]
    procedure for making, **4(2)**, [495]
  insolvency services account. *See* **Insolvency
    Services Account**

company insolvency—*contd*
  letter heads, matters to be shown on,
    4(2), [92]
  liquidation, go into, meaning, **4(2)**, [281]
  liquidator. *See* **liquidator**
  manager. *See* receiver or manager *below*
  meaning, **4(2)**, [281]
  members of company—
    liability as contributories, **4(2)**, [115]
    meaning, **4(2)**, [284]
  N. Ireland, provisions applied, **4(2)**, [534]
  non-company, application of law to,
    4(2), [590]
  notices etc, rules as to, **4(2)**, [559]
  offences—
    bodies corporate, by, **4(2)**, [522]
    director, by, **4(2)**, [248]
    schedule of, **4(2)**, [561]
    summary proceedings, **4(2)**, [521]
  office-holder—
    acts of, validity, **4(2)**, [268]
    disposal of, **4(2)**, [96], [101]
    duty to co-operate with, **4(2)**, [271]
    getting in, **4(2)**, [270]
  practitioner. *See* insolvency practitioner
  preferences given, order as to, **4(2)**, [275]
  preferential debts. categories of, **4(2)**, [469],
    [557]
  property—
    administrator's powers, **4(2)**, [545]
    getting in, **4(2)**, [270]
    services, power to require, **4(2)**, [269]
  receiver—
    administrative. *See* administrative receiver
      above
    body corporate disqualified as, **4(2)**, [83]
    official. *See* **official receiver**
  receiver or manager—
    accounts—
      default as to, **4(2)**, [91]
      delivery to registrar, **4(2)**, [91]
      duty as to, enforcement, **4(2)**, [94]
      form of, **4(2)**, [91]
    administrative. *See* administrative receiver
      above
    appointment—
      company's website, statement on,
        4(2), [92]
      debenture holders, on behalf of,
        4(2), [82]
      invalid, liability for, **4(2)**, [87]
      joint, **4(2)**, [86]
      letterheads, statement on, **4(2)**, [92]
      notification of, **4(2)**, [92]
      time from which effective, **4(2)**, [86]
    body corporate disqualified as, **4(2)**, [83]
    contracts, liability for, **4(2)**, [90]
    cross-border operations by, **4(2)**, [103]
    dealing with, in good faith, **4(2)**, [95]
    directions by court, **4(2)**, [88]
    disqualification to act as, **4(2)**, [83], [84]
    indemnity, right to, **4(2)**, [90]
    meaning, **4(2)**, [82]

company insolvency—*contd*
  receiver or manager—*contd*
    official. *See* **official receiver**
    remuneration—
      charge on property for, **4(2)**, [90]
      court's power to fix, **4(2)**, [89]
      overpayment, **4(2)**, [89]
      vacation of office, on, **4(2)**, [90]
      variation of order for, **4(2)**, [89]
    returns by, enforcement of, **4(2)**, [94]
    undischarged bankrupt as, **4(2)**, [84]
  regulations, **4(2)**, [505]
  returns etc, enforcement of, **4(2)**, [94]
  rules. *See* insolvency rules *above*
  scheme of arrangement. *See* voluntary
    arrangement *below*
  special regimes, **4(2)**, [588]
  statement of affairs—
    admissibility in evidence, **4(2)**, [523]
    contents, **4(2)**, [100]
    default as to, **4(2)**, [100]
    liability to submit, **4(2)**, [100]
    time for making, **4(2)**, [100]
    verification of, **4(2)**, [100]
  summary of provisions, **4(2)**, [1]
  transactions at undervalue—
    order to negative, **4(2)**, [274]
    relevant time for, **4(2)**, [276]
    requirements under orders, **4(2)**, [277]
  transitional provisions, **4(2)**, [531], [562]
  unregistered. *See* **unregistered company**
  voluntary arrangement—
    approval of—
      challenge of, **4(2)**, [75]
      effect of, **4(2)**, [74]
      false representations to obtain, **4(2)**, [76]
      generally, **4(2)**, [72], [73]
      revocation or suspension, **4(2)**, [75]
    delinquent officers, prosecution of,
      4(2), [78]
    meaning, **4(2)**, [68]
    meetings. *See* creditors' meeting *above*
    moratorium—
      committee, **4(2)**, [542]
      directors' actions, challenging,
        4(2), [543]
      effects of, **4(2)**, [540]
      eligible companies, **4(2)**, [538]
      extension, **4(2)**, [542]
      Financial Services Authority, functions
        of, **4(2)**, [543]
      interpretation, **4(2)**, [538]
      meetings during, **4(2)**, [542]
      nominee, role of, **4(2)**, [541]
      obtaining, **4(2)**, [69], [539]
      offences, **4(2)**, [543]
      regulations, **4(2)**, [543]
    nominee—
      authorisation, **4(2)**, [473]
      official receiver as, **4(2)**, [474], [560]
      qualification, **4(2)**, [68]
      replacement of, **4(2)**, [70]
      report to be made by, **4(2)**, [70]
    non-company, application of law to,
      4(2), [590]

company insolvency—*contd*
  voluntary arrangement—*contd*
    premature end, coming to, **4(2)**, [79]
    procedure, **4(2)**, [70]
    proposal for—
      approval, effect of, **4(2)**, [74]
      consideration of, **4(2)**, [72]
      implementation, **4(2)**, [68], [77]
      modification of, **4(2)**, [72]
      notice of, **4(2)**, [70]
      who may make, **4(2)**, [68]
    registration, **4(2)**, [559]
    stay of winding up, **4(2)**, [74]
    supervisor of—
      authorisation, **4(2)**, [473]
      meaning, **4(2)**, [77]
      official receiver as, **4(2)**, [474], [560]
      powers and duties, **4(2)**, [77]

company investigations
  disqualification of directors, **8(1)**, [1117]
  inspectors—
    documents, power to require production
      of, **8(1)**, [1116]
    former, power to obtain information
      from, **8(1)**, [1115]
    resignation, removal and replacement of,
      8(1), [1114]
    Secretary of State, directions by,
      8(1), [1113]

company name
  adjudicators—
    appeal from decision of, **8(1)**, [152]
    appointment, **8(1)**, [148]
    Chief, **8(1)**, [148]
    decision, making public, **8(1)**, [150]
    duties of, **8(1)**, [148]
    office, holding, **8(1)**, [148]
    order requiring change of name, making,
      8(1), [151]
    procedural rules, **8(1)**, [149]
  change of—
    articles, under provision in, **8(1)**, [157]
    effect of, **8(1)**, [159]
    exemption from requirement to use
      "limited", ceasing to be entitled to,
      8(1), [142]
    means of, **8(1)**, [155]
    misleading indication of activities, provision
      of, **8(1)**, [154]
    misleading information, provision of,
      8(1), [153]
    new certificate of incorporation, issue of,
      8(1), [158]
    notice to registrar, **8(1)**, [156]
    order by adjudicator, **8(1)**, [151]
    registration, **8(1)**, [158]
    similarity to existing name, in case of,
      8(1), [145]
    special resolution, by, **8(1)**, [155]–[156]
    undertaking or assurance, failure to fulfil,
      8(1), [153]
  display of, **8(1)**, [160]

company name—*contd*
exemption from requirement to use
"limited"—
amendment of articles, restriction on,
8(1), [141]
ceasing to be entitled to, change on,
8(1), [142]
conditions for, **8(1)**, [138]
existing companies—
guarantee, limited by, **8(1)**, [140]
shares, limited by, **8(1)**, [139]
indication of company type or legal form,
inappropriate use of, **8(1)**, [143]
limited companies, required limitations for—
private, **8(1)**, [137]
public, **8(1)**, [136]
limited, ending in, **8(1)**, [137]
minor variations in form, **8(1)**, [163]
other names, similarity to—
change, power to direct, **8(1)**, [145]
direction for, **8(1)**, [146]
goodwill, in which person having,
8(1), [147]
prohibition, **8(1)**, [144]
registered, objection to, **8(1)**, [147]
overseas company, of, **8(1)**, [1125]
alternative, **8(1)**, [1126]
permitted characters, **8(1)**, [135]
prohibited, **8(1)**, [131]
public limited company or p.l.c., ending in,
8(1), [136]
registered, objection to, **8(1)**, [147]
registrar's index of—
amendment of enactments, power of,
8(1), [1179]
maintenance of, **8(1)**, [1177]
right to inspect, **8(1)**, [1178]
restoration to register, on, **8(1)**, [1111]
sensitive words and expressions—
approval of Secretary of State for,
8(1), [133]
comments of government department or
other specified body, duty to seek,
8(1), [134]
government or public authority, suggesting
connection with, **8(1)**, [132]
trading disclosure—
failure to make—
civil consequences of, **8(1)**, [161]
criminal consequences of, **8(1)**, [162]
minor variations in form, **8(1)**, [163]
requirement of, **8(1)**, [160]
Welsh companies—
private limited, **8(1)**, [137]
public limited, **8(1)**, [136]

company secretary
dual capacity, acts by person in, **8(1)**, [358]
inability to act, discharge of functions,
8(1), [352]
private company not required to have,
8(1), [348]
public company—
direction to appoint, **8(1)**, [350]
qualifications, **8(1)**, [351]

company secretary—*contd*
public company—*contd*
requirement of, **8(1)**, [349]
register of—
duty to keep, **8(1)**, [353]
duty to notify registrar of changes,
8(1), [354]
inspection, available for, **8(1)**, [353]
particulars in—
corporate secretaries and firms, of,
8(1), [356]
individuals, of, **8(1)**, [355]
regulations, power to make, **8(1)**, [357]
service address, **8(1)**, [1219]–[1220]
service of documents on, **8(1)**, [1218]
vacancy in office, discharge of functions,
8(1), [352]

compensation. *See also subject matter of
compensation*
acquiring authorities, recovery of sums from,
46, [580]
acquisition of land, for—
advance payment—
interest on, **9**, [354]
mortgage, land subject to, **9**, [351]–[353]
exceeding 90% threshold, **9**, [352]
mortgagee, payments to, **9**, [353]
requests for, **9**, [353]
right to, **9**, [350]
common lands, in case of. *See* **common
(land)**
compulsory acquisition, for—
absent or untraced owners, where,
9, [23], [27], [265], [296]
advance payment of, **9**, [350]
agricultural holdings, **9**, [347]
application of—
amounts—
between £20 and £200, **9**, [34],
[295]
exceeding £20, **9**, [36]
not exceeding £20, **9**, [35], [295]
£200 and over, **9**, [32]
investment, **9**, [33], [295]
lease, paid in respect of, **9**, [37]
limited owners, where payable to,
9, [295]
order for, **9**, [33], [37], [295]
part of house, for, **9**, [360]
payable to parties where not
exceeding £20, **9**, [35], [295]
payment into court, **9**, [33]–[36],
[38]–[41]
persons under disability, **9**, [32]–[38],
[295]
reversion, paid in respect of, **9**, [37]
trustees, paid to, **9**, [34]–[36], [295]
appropriate alternative development—
certificate of—
appeal against, **9**, [233], [236]
extension of provisions, **9**, [234]
interpretation of provisions,
9, [237]
issue of, **9**, [232], [381]

compensation—*contd*
  acquisition of land, for—*contd*
    compulsory acquisition, for—*contd*
      appropriate alternative
        development—*contd*
        certificate of—*contd*
          prescription of matters, **9**, [235]
          special cases, **9**, [234]
      assessment—
        agricultural holding, **9**, [347]
        alterations, **9**, [411]
        business tenancy, land subject to,
          9, [346]
        depreciation through prospect of
          compulsory acquisition, **9**, [225]
        development—
          adjacent land—
            same ownership, in, **9**, [223],
              [257]
            subsequent acquisition, **9**, [224],
              [257]
          disregard in, **9**, [222], [257]
        development plans—
          assumptions as to planning
            permission not directly derived
            from, **9**, [230]
          certification as to alternative
            development, **9**, [232]
          special assumptions, certain lands
            comprised in, **9**, [231]
        disabled person, dwelling adapted
          for, **9**, [344]
        disturbance, **9**, [220], [345]
        improvements, where, **9**, [411]
        injurious affection, **9**, [343]
        Lands Tribunal, by, **9**, [216]
        market value of land as basis, **9**, [220]
        new town sites, **9**, [349]
        person over sixty, business of, **9**, [345]
        planning permission—
          assumptions as to, **9**, [229]–[230],
            [308]
          refusal of, **9**, [228]
          special assumptions, **9**, [231]
        statutory undertakers, land acquired
          by, **9**, [227]
        valuation date, **9**, [221]
      authority possessing compulsory purchase
        powers, meaning, **9**, [253]
      certificate of value, **9**, [249]
      costs, **9**, [219], [283]
      Crown, application to, **9**, [247]
      depreciation. *See under* **public works**
      development. *See under* appropriate
        alternative development; assessment
        above
      disabled person, dwelling specially adapted
        for, **9**, [344]
      disputed. reference to Lands Tribunal. *See*
        Lands Tribunal
      disturbance. *See* disturbance *below*
      divided land, **9**, [268]
      ecclesiastical property, **9**, [248], [289]
      entry, payable before, **9**, [271]

compensation—*contd*
  acquisition of land, for—*contd*
    injurious affection, for. *See* **injurious
      affection**
    interest on. *See* interest *below*
    interpretation of provisions, **9**, [253]
    land subject to business tenancy, **9**, [346]
    lease, apportionment of rent under,
      9, [216]
    local inquiries, **9**, [251]
    occupier rehoused, **9**, [348]
    payment into court. *See* payment into court
      below
    possession, refusal to give up, **9**, [273]
    rent, apportionment, **9**, [279]
    rights over land, acquisition by local
      authority, **9**, [371], [377]
    saving for earlier transactions, **9**, [255]
    saving for purchases of, **9**, [250]
    service of notices, **9**, [252]
    severance—
      assessment, **9**, [26], [267]
      lessee, to, **9**, [279]
      provisions to be observed, **9**, [268]
    statutory undertaking, meaning, **9**, [250]
    summary of provisions, **9**, [1]
    tenants, to, **9**, [280]
  apprehension of offenders, for assistance in,
    12(1), [34]
  building preservation notice, loss due to,
    46, [669]
  claims, determination of, **46**, [380]
  compulsory acquisition, for. *See* **compulsory
    acquisition**
  compulsory acquisition, for, due to another
    local authority, **22**, [402]
  Crown, application of provisions to, **9**, [247],
    [364]
  damage by local authority, for, **35(1)**, [41],
    [44], [175], [629]
  damage due to rights of entry, for, **46**, [599]
  defective dwelling, compulsory purchase,
    22, [365]
  Defence Act 1842, under, payment into
    court, **13**, [3]
  Defence of the Realm Acts, under. *See under*
    Defence of the Realm
  demolition of obstructive building, on,
    22, [401]
  demolition order, on, **22**, [398], [399]
  depreciation in value of interest in land, for,
    46, [379]
  determination of amount, **35(1)**, [63]
  development—
    additional, granted after acquisition—
      assessment of, **9**, [238]
      bar on, **9**, [238]
      claims, **9**, [239]
      Crown development, extension to,
        9, [241]
      devolution of rights to, **9**, [238]
      disturbance, severance and injurious
        affection, **9**, [260]
      entitlement to, **9**, [238]
      interest not provided for, **9**, [461]

compensation—*contd*
  development—*contd*
    additional, granted after acquisition—*contd*
      interest on, **9**, [238], [458], [462]
      interpretation of provisions, **9**, [244], [260]
      mortgaged land, application to, **9**, [260]
      notices, **9**, [239]
      payments on account—
        interest not provided for, **9**, [461]
        interest on, **9**, [458], [462]
      planning permission, extension to, **9**, [240]
      regulations as to, **9**, [243]
      settled land, application to, **9**, [260]
      value increase, contiguous or adjacent land, **9**, [260]
    public, **9**, [349]
    See also appropriate alternative development *above*
  development plan for purposes of, **46**, [619]
  development, planning decision restricting, for—
    buildings, alteration or removal of, **46**, [377]
    discontinuance of use, for, **46**, [377]
    mineral working, orders affecting, **46**, [378]
    works, alteration or removal of, **46**, [377]
    works not ranking for, **46**, [620]–[621]
  disinfection of premises or articles, where, **35(1)**, [472], [498]
  displaced proprietor. *See* **house in multiple occupation**
  disputes. *See* **Lands Tribunal**
  disturbance—
    additional development granted after acquisition, **9**, [238]
    assessment, **9**, [220], [342]
    business of person over sixty, **9**, [345]
    enjoyment of land or chattels, in, **9**, [212]
    entitlement, **9**, [341]
    payment, person displaced from land—
      amount, **9**, [342]
      interest on, **9**, [341]
    right to, **9**, [341]
  dwelling adapted for disabled person, **9**, [245]
  easement or right, loss of, **46**, [501]
  easements. *See* **easements**
  ecclesiastical property, in respect of, **46**, [588]
  emergency powers, exercise of. *See* **emergency powers**
  entry on land in respect of, **22**, [403]
  expenses of, defrayal of, **9**, [157]
  food, seizure of, **1(2)**, [424]
  freshwater fishery, damage caused by works, for, **1(2)**, [18]
  general vesting declaration, vesting of land by. *See* **general vesting declaration**
  highway, for loss of access to, **22**, [226]
  highway, land required for, **9**, [229]
  home loss payment. *See* **home loss payment**
  housing action trust, acquisition of land by, **22**, [863]
  injurious affection, for. *See* **injurious affection**

compensation—*contd*
  instalments, paid by, **12(2)**, [818]
  interest on—
    generally, **9**, [129]
    injurious affection, for, **9**, [321], [363]
  interests omitted from compulsory purchase, purchase after entry, mesne profits, compensation for, **9**, [82], [282]
  intersected land, **9**, [268]
  land vested in urban development corporation, for, **46**, [65], [104]
  listed building consent—
    assessment, **46**, [671]
    local planning authorities, **46**, [670]
    modification of, **46**, [668]
    revocation of, **46**, [668]
  listed building purchase notice, as to, **46**, [678]
  local authority, paid by, contributions to, **46**, [577]
  local government. *See* **local government officers and staff**
  local planning authority, claims to, **46**, [614]
  loss of office, for, on transfer of jurisdiction to Lands Tribunal, **9**, [185]
  loss of rights in clearance area, **22**, [254]
  mine-owner, for non-working, **9**, [451]
  miscarriage of justice, for, **12(4)**, [494], [580]
  mortgagee of land subject to compulsory purchase. *See* **mortgage**
  notice to treat. *See* **notice to treat**
  officers of trustees executing local Acts—
    determination of appointment, where, **35(1)**, [204]
    diminution of emoluments, where, **35(1)**, [204]
  oil—
    installations, land taken for, **9**, [195], [212]
    pipe-lines. *See* **pipe-lines**
  omission to pay. *See* interests omitted *above*
  operational land, for new town, for, **46**, [147], [213]
  order. *See* **compensation order**
  parties under disability, ascertainment, **9**, [9]
  payment by local authority, **35(1)**, [629]
  payment into Bank, **9**, [9]
  payment into Court—
    compensation, application of receipts, **9**, [33]–[36], [38]–[41], [295]
    costs in respect of money paid in, **9**, [285]
    failure to make title by owner, after, **9**, [269]
    in good faith, effect, **9**, [272]
    interest, carrying, **9**, [271]
    mortgagee, on failure by, **9**, [274], [276]
    references to, construction of, **9**, [284]
    refusal by owner to convey, after, **9**, [269]
    rentcharge, failure by person entitled, on, **9**, [278]
    Supreme Court, procedure, **9**, [284]
  period excluded, **9**, [379]
  pipe-lines. *See* **pipe-lines**
  planning permission—
    conditional grant of, **46**, [372]

compensation—*contd*

planning permission—*contd*

depreciation, for—

apportionment, **46**, [373]

registration, **46**, [374]

mineral, in relation to, **46**, [866]

old, **46**, [865]

revocation or modification of, **46**, [371]

subsequent development, recovery on, **46**, [375]–[376]

prohibition order, on, **22**, [398], [399]

public development, meaning, **9**, [349]

public health powers, by reason of exercise of, **35(1)**, [498]

public works, depreciation in land value. *See* **public works**

purchase notice, reduction due to, **46**, [389]

reinstatement in civil employment. *See* **reinstatement in civil employment**

release of rentcharge, on. *See* **rentcharge**

rental. *See* **rental compensation**

repayment—

demolition order, on revocation of, **22**, [398], [399]

prohibition order, on revocation of, **22**, [398], [399]

replanting of trees, requirement for, **46**, [464]

requisition. *See under* **emergency powers**

severance. *See* **severance**

sheriff, paid by, **12(1)**, [35]

shop-keepers in clearance areas, **22**, [400]

site of new town for, land in area designated as, **9**, [349]

statutory undertakers, right of. *See* **statutory undertakers**

stop notice, loss due to, **46**, [441]

subsidence, damage by, **22**, [563]

survey by local authority, damage resulting from, **9**, [373]

temporary stop notice, issue of, **46**, [425]

time for paying, **12(2)**, [818]

transferred officers of authorities, rights as to, **35(1)**, [203]

tree preservation order, in respect of, **46**, [463], [465]

unclaimed money, repayment, **9**, [374]

Wales, claims in, **46**, [615]

wayleave order. *See* **pipe-lines**

Compensation Act 2006

amendments to Part 2, **11(4)**, [365]

compensation order

annulment, **12(2)**, [809]

appeals, **12(2)**, [809]

bereavement, in respect of, **12(2)**, [807]

convicted person, amount of award against, **12(2)**, [807]

conviction restored on appeal, effect, **12(2)**, [809]

damages in civil proceedings, effect on, **12(2)**, [811]

death, made on, **12(2)**, [807]

enforcement, **12(2)**, [809]

compensation order—*contd*

forfeited property, application of proceeds of sale, **12(2)**, [822]

funeral expenses, payments for, **12(2)**, [807]

magistrates' court, limit on power of, **12(2)**, [808]

motor vehicle, damage arising from, **12(2)**, [807]

parent or guardian—

financial circumstances, statement of, **12(2)**, [813]

fixing of amount, **12(2)**, [815]

responsibility of for payment, **12(2)**, [814]

power to make, **12(2)**, [807]

review of, **12(2)**, [810]

competition

agreements preventing, restricting or distorting—

directions in relation to, **47**, [505]

enforcement of directions, **47**, [507]

excluded agreements—

broadcasting, **47**, [562]

generally, **47**, [483], [563]

exemptions—

block—

generally, **47**, [484]

procedure, **47**, [485], [571]

criteria, **47**, [486]

other agreements, **47**, [488]

parallel, **47**, [487], [571]

rules, **47**, [571]

interim measures, **47**, [508]

land agreements, **47**, [523]

limited immunity for small agreements, **47**, [512]

penalty, **47**, [509]–[511]

prohibition of, **47**, [482]

small agreements, limited immunity for, **47**, [512]

vertical agreements, **47**, [523]

appeal tribunal. *See* **Competition Appeal Tribunal**

appealable decisions, **47**, [518]

Article 22(1) investigation—

business premises, entry on—

under warrant, **47**, [545], [547]

without warrant, **47**, [544]

documents or information, OFT requiring, **47**, [543]

domestic premises, entry on, **47**, [546]–[547]

meaning, **47**, [541]

offences—

destroying or falsifying documents, **47**, [551]

false or misleading information, **47**, [552]

generally **47**, [550]

power to conduct, **47**, [542]

powers when conducting, **47**, [543]

privileged communications, **47**, [548]

statements, use in prosecution, **47**, [549]

broadcasting, application of provisions, **45**, [177]

competition—*contd*
  cartel offences—
    appropriate circumstances, **47**, [885]
    arrangements giving rise to, **47**, [884]
    bid-rigging arrangements, **47**, [884]
    criminal investigations—
      authorised person, exercise of powers
        by, **47**, [890]
      documents, power to require, **47**, [888]
      interpretation, **47**, [895]
      offences, **47**, [894]
      OFT, powers of, **47**, [887]–[888]
      premises, entry under warrant, **47**, [889]
      privileged information, **47**, [891]
      property, action in respect of, **47**, [893]
      statements, restriction on use in court,
        47, [892]
    penalty, **47**, [886]
    prosecution, **47**, [886]
  commitments—
    acceptance by OFT, **47**, [500], [564]
    effect of, **47**, [501]
    enforcement, **47**, [504]
    guidance on, **47**, [503]
    release, **47**, [565]
    review, **47**, [502]
    variation, **47**, [500], [564]
  Community law, reform of, **47**, [899]
  Crown application, **47**, [555]
  Director General of Fair Trading, scrutiny by.
    See **Director General of Fair Trading**
  directors, disqualification of, **47**, [896]
  dominant position, abuse of—
    decision, directions in relation to,
      47, [505]–[506]
    enactments replaced, **47**, [481]
    enforcement of directions, **47**, [507]
    excluded cases—
      concentrations, **47**, [561]
      generally, **47**, [490], [563]
      mergers, **47**, [560]
    interim measures, **47**, [508]
    limited immunity, **47**, [513]
    penalty, **47**, [509]–[511]
    prohibition of, **47**, [489]
  enforcement orders, modification of
    provisions, **47**, [898]
  Financial Services Authority, scrutiny by. *See*
    Financial Services Authority
  information, disclosure of. *See* **trade and
    industry**
  infringements, findings of, **47**, [529]
  inspections ordered by Commission
    decision—
      entry to premises under warrant—
        business, **47**, [533], [536]
        non-business premises **47**, [534]
        offences, **47**, [538]
        supplementary provisions, **47**, [537]
      interpretation, **47**, [532]
      powers in conducting, **47**, [535]
      privileged communications, **47**, [539]
      statements, use in prosecutions, **47**, [540]

competition—*contd*
  investigation—
    Article 22(1). *See* Article 22(1) investigation
      above
    decisions following, **47**, [499]
    entry to premises—
      under warrant, **47**, [494], [496]
      without warrant, **47**, [493]
    entry to domestic premises, under
      warrant, **47**, [495]–[496]
    OFT, power of, **47**, [491]
    powers when conducting, **47**, [492]
    privileged communications, **47**, [497]
  market investigations. *See* **Competition
    Commission; Office of Fair Trading**
  offences—
    body corporate, by, **47**, [554]
    destroying or falsifying documents,
      47, [515]
    false or misleading information, **47**, [516]
    generally, **47**, [514]
  Office of Fair Trading, scrutiny by. *See* **Office
    of Fair Trading**
  prize. *See* **prize competition**
  principles to be applied in determining
    questions, **47**, [531]
  procedural rules, **47**, [558]
  recognised clearing house, scrutiny of. *See*
    recognised clearing house
  recognised investment exchange, scrutiny of.
    See **recognised investment exchange**
  regulations and orders, **47**, [553]
  regulator other than OFT, super-complaint
    to, **47**, [897]
  sectoral enactments, amendments of, **47**, [955]
  sectoral regulators, application of provisions
    to, **47**, [956]
  statements, use in prosecution, **47**, [498]
  third party appeals, **47**, [519]
  transitional provisions and savings, **47**, [556],
    [574]–[580], [962]
  value added tax, exemption from, **50**, [153]

Competition Appeal Tribunal
  appealable decisions, **47**, [518]
  appeal from, **47**, [522]
  chairman, **47**, [702], [948]
  consumers, claims on behalf of, **47**, [521]
  decisions, **47**, [570], [702], [951]
  establishment, **47**, [700]
  members, **47**, [700], [948]
  monetary claims before, **47**, [520]
  particular purposes, constitution for, **47**, [702]
  President, **47**, [948]
  procedure, **47**, [570]
  Registrar, **47**, [700]
  rules, **47**, [703], [952]
  staff, accommodation and property, **47**, [948]
  third party appeals, **47**, [519]
  transfer of proceedings to and from, **47**, [704]

Competition Commission. *See also*
monopoly references
  accounts, **47**, [566]

Competition Commission—*contd*
air traffic services—
  direction—
    position following, **4(1)**, [392]
    power to give, **4(1)**, [391]
    safety, priority of duty of, **4(1)**, [393]
  Enterprise Act, application of provisions
    of, **4(1)**, [394]
  privilege attaching, **4(1)**, [394]
  reference to, **4(1)**, [386]
    Enterprise Act, application of provisions
      of, **4(1)**, [388]
    modifications to licence following
      report, **4(1)**, [390]
    reports, **4(1)**, [389]
    time limits, **4(1)**, [387]
airport charges, reference concerning—
  associated companies, in respect of,
    4(1), [323]
  authority to make, **4(1)**, [278]
  conditions imposed following, **4(1)**, [285]
  expenses of, **4(1)**, [286]
  information disclosed by, **4(1)**, [310]
  information to be given, **4(1)**, [281]
  investigations, requirement for, **4(1)**, [280]
  powers of investigation, **4(1)**, [283]
  public interest, **4(1)**, [280]
  questions to be referred, **4(1)**, [280]
  reports on, **4(1)**, [284]
  specified matters, **4(1)**, [281]
  supplementary provisions, **4(1)**, [281]
  time limits, **4(1)**, [282]
annual reports, **47**, [566]
anti-competitive practice. *See* **fair trading**
appeals, **47**, [570]
appeals to, summary of provisions, **17(1)**, [1]
appointment of undertakers—
  determination of conditions, **49**, [723],
    [1367]
  modification references—
    investigation, powers of, **49**, [727]
    procedure, **49**, [725]
    reports, **49**, [728]
    time limits, **49**, [726]
    veto following report, Commission's
      power of, **49**, [730]–[731]
assistance by Gas and Electricity Markets
  Authority in carrying out investigations,
  17(1), [650]
chairman and deputy, **47**, [566]
Competition Services, transfer of property
  between, **47**, [950]
Council, **47**, [566]
dissolution of Monopolies and Mergers
  Commission, **47**, [517]
electricity licences—
  references as to, **17(1)**, [747]
    investigative powers, **17(1)**, [749]
    time limits, **17(1)**, [748]
  reports on, **17(1)**, [750]
    modification following, **17(1)**, [751]
    power to veto modifications following
      report, **17(1)**, [752]

Competition Commission—*contd*
electricity supply licences—
  licensable activities, reference as to,
    17(1), [814]
    Enterprise Act 2002, application of,
      17(1), [816]
    reports, **17(1)**, [817]
    time limits, **17(1)**, [815]
Enterprise Act 2002, application of,
  19(2), [539]
establishment of, **47**, [517]
financial services, powers. *See* **financial
  services**
functions, performance of, **47**, [567]
gas transporter, modifications to licence—
  investigation, powers of, **17(1)**, [620]
  power to veto, **17(1)**, [623]
  reference as to, **17(1)**, [618]
  reports, modification following,
    17(1), [622]
  time limits, **17(1)**, [619]
general references to—
  public interest, protection of, **47**, [174]
  transitional provisions, **47**, [202]
licence conditions, adverse report on,
  11(1), [969]
licensable gas activities, references as to,
  17(1), [659]–[662]
  Enterprise Act provisions, application of,
    17(1), [661]
  reports, **17(1)**, [662]
  time limits, **17(1)**, [660]
market investigation references—
  adverse effects, duty to remedy, **47**, [835]
  consultation requirements. **47**, [866]
  contents of, **47**, [830]
  decisions, review of, **47**, [876]
  defamation, absolute privilege for purposes
    of, **47**, [870]
  enforcement undertakings and orders—
    applicable provisions, **47**, [861]
    consultation, **47**, [860]
    duty of OFT to monitor, **47**, [859]
    enforcement of, **47**, [864]
    final orders, **47**, [858]
    final undertakings, **47**, [856]
    in lieu of reference. *See* undertakings in
      lieu *below*
    interim orders, **47**, [855]
    interim undertakings, **47**, [854]
    not fulfilled, order-making power,
      47, [857]
    procedural requirements, **47**, [862]
    register, **47**, [863]
    undertakings, content of, **47**, [861]
  excisions from reports, **47**, [874]
  interpretation of provisions, **47**, [880]–[881]
  investigations, powers, **47**, [873]
  investigations and reports, **47**, [833]
    time-limits for, **47**, [834]
  meaning, **47**, [828]
  Ministerial power to make, **47**, [829]
  minority reports, **47**, [875]
  offences, **47**, [877]

Competition Commission—*contd*
  market investigation references—*contd*
    Office of Fair Trading—
      advice and information, preparation and
        publication of, **47**, [868]
      information duties, **47**, [867]
      investigation powers, **47**, [871]–[872]
      monitoring by, **47**, [859]
      power to make, **47**, [828]
      publicity requirements, **47**, [869]
      undertakings and orders, role as to,
        47, [860]
    orders, **47**, [878]
    procedural rules, **47**, [569]
    public interest cases—
      Commission, duties of, **47**, [849]
      considerations not finalised, restrictions,
        47, [842]
      general procedure, interaction of notices
        with, **47**, [848]
      intervention notices, **47**, [836]–[837],
        [846]
      investigations and reports, **47**, [839]
      national security considerations,
        47, [850]
      OFT, duties of, **47**, [849]
      publication of reports, **47**, [840]
      questions to be determined, **47**, [838]
      remedial action, **47**, [844]
      reversion to Commission, **47**, [845]
      Secretary of State, decision of, **47**, [843]
      time-limits, **47**, [841]
      veto, Secretary of State's power of,
        47, [847]
    questions to be determined, **47**, [831]
    regulated markets, **47**, [865]
    relevant authorities, duty of consultation,
      47, [866]
    service of documents, **47**, [879]
    undertakings in lieu of, **47**, [851]
      effect of, **47**, [853]
      procedural requirements, **47**, [852]
    variation, **47**, [832]
  members, **47**, [566]
  merger references. *See* **merger reference**
  monopoly reference. *See* **monopoly
    references**
  monopoly situation, reference of *See*
    monopoly references
  offences—
    bodies corporate, by, **47**, [192]
    time-limit for prosecutions, **47**, [191]
  Office of Rail Regulation—
    access charges by—
      changes following report, **38(1)**, [488]
      making of changes by Commission,
        38(1), [488]
      reference to, **38(1)**, [488]
      report on reference, **38(1)**, [488]
      reports transmitted to, **38(1)**, [416]
      review—
        adverse effect on interests of certain
          providers of railway services,
          notification of, **38(1)**, [488]

Competition Commission—*contd*
  Office of Rail Regulation—*contd*
    access charges by—*contd*
      review—*contd*
        desired outputs and finances—
          duty to have regard to information
            about, **38(1)**, [488]
          duty to notify ORR about,
            38(1), [488]
        future, suggestions about, **38(1)**, [488]
        notice of, **38(1)**, [488]
        response to request to carry out,
          38(1), [488]
        scope of, **38(1)**, [488]
        veto changes, Commission's power to,
          38(1), [488]
  patents references to, **11(1)**, [694]
  postal services, reference as to—
    Enterprise Act 2002, provisions applied,
      34, [626], [632]
    information, provision of, **34**, [624]
    intervention, power of, **34**, [630]
    modification following report, **34**, [629]
      exclusions from disclosure, **34**, [632]
      procedural requirements, **34**, [631]
    power to make, **34**, [624]
    report on, **34**, [627]–[628]
    time limits, **34**, [625]
    variation of, **34**, [624]
  powers, **47**, [566]
  procedure, **47**, [173], [567]
  proof of instruments, **47**, [566]
  property, transfers of, **47**, [950]
  public interest cases, merger references in. *See*
    merger reference
  railway assets operators' licences, modification
    of—
    making, **38(1)**, [363]
    reference of, **38(1)**, [357]
      Enterprise Act, application of provisions
        of, **38(1)**, [359]
      time limits, **38(1)**, [358]
    report on, **38(1)**, [360]
    supplementary provisions, **38(1)**, [364]
    veto, power to, following report,
      38(1), [362]
  railway services, references in relation to,
    38(1), [415]
  reports, consideration of, **19(2)**, [212], [373],
    [539]
  reports by—
    action on, **47**, [176]
    Director to receive copy, **47**, [175]
    interim order after, **47**, [177]
    made before appointed day, **47**, [202]
    monopoly references, on. *See* **monopoly
      references**
    order arising on, **47**, [199]–[200]
  seal, application of, **47**, [566]
  special public interest cases, merger references
    in. *See* **merger reference**
  specialist members of, **17(2)**, [347], [521];
    49, [1366]
  staff, **47**, [566]
  status, **47**, [566]

Competition Commission—*contd*
summary of provisions, **47**, [1]
transitional provisions, **47**, [202], [568]
Treasury, provision of information by,
19(2), [539]
water or sewerage undertakings, duty to refer merger of—
generally, **49**, [786]
provisions applying to, **49**, [788], [1044]
small mergers, exclusion of, **49**, [787]
water supply licences—
modification references—
generally, **49**, [743]
investigation, powers of, **49**, [745]
reports, **49**, [746]
time limits, **49**, [744]
veto following report, Commission's power of, **49**, [748]

Competition Service
accounts, **47**, [949]
chairman, **47**, [949]
Commission, transfer of property between, **47**, [950]
establishment of, **47**, [701]
membership, **47**, [949]
powers of, **47**, [949]
procedure, **47**, [949]
purpose of, **47**, [701]
staff, **47**, [949]

composition
transfer duty, for, **41**, [124]

Comptroller and Auditor General
accounts rendered to, **19(2)**, [611]
appointment of, **19(2)**, [610], [974]
audit fee, charging, **19(2)**, [978]
authorised officer, performance of functions by, **19(2)**, [834]
body mainly supported by public funds, examining, **19(2)**, [980]
Care Quality Commission, provision of material by, **30(S)**, NHS 78
cash accounts, examining, **19(2)**, [738]
Chief Inspector of Education and Training in Wales, examination of, **10**, [1300]
Committee of Public Accounts, considering proposals of, **19(2)**, [974]
consolidated fund, report on audit, **19(2)**, [868]
corporation sole, being, **19(2)**, [987]
credits on Exchequer accounts, granting, **19(2)**, [614], [615]
Customs and Excise accounts, examining, **19(2)**, [737]
discretion in carrying out functions, having, **19(2)**, [974]
documents and information, right to obtain, **19(2)**, [981]
duties of, **19(2)**, [609]
Environment Agency, functions relating to, **10**, [1287]
Exchange Equalisation Account, examination and certification of, **19(2)**, [965]

Comptroller and Auditor General—*contd*
Forestry Commissioners, examination of, **10**, [1301]
government departmental accounts—
examination by, **19(2)**, [1035], [1051]
examination of, **19(2)**, [1035], [1039]
information regarding, access to, **19(2)**, [1036]
reports by, as to, **19(2)**, [1052]
House of Commons, report to, **19(2)**, [982]
Inland Revenue accounts, examining, **19(2)**, [737]
National Audit office, head of, **19(2)**, [976]
National Loans Fund—
granting credits on, **19(2)**, [849]
report on audit, **19(2)**, [868]
other offices, not to hold, **19(2)**, [608]
peer not to hold office of, **19(2)**, [608]
public departments, examining, **19(2)**, [979]
Registrar, as, **48**, 158
reports by, **43(1)**, [377]
reports, presenting to House of Commons, **19(2)**, [982]
resource accounts—
examination of, **19(2)**, [1034]
sent to, **19(2)**, [1033]
salary, **19(2)**, [833]
Scottish functions, examination of pre-commencement enactments, **10**, [1430]
status of, **19(2)**, [974]
summary of provisions, **19(1)**, [1]
superannuation, provision for, **33(1)**, [134]
supplementary powers, **43(1)**, [378]
tenure of, **19(2)**, [608]
trade marks, reports on, **48**, 163
transfer of functions, **10**, [1284]
Treasury accounts rendered to, responsibility for, **19(2)**, [619]
vacancy in office of, **19(2)**, [610]
Welsh Consolidated Fund, examination of, **10**, [1601]

compulsory acquisition
acquiring authorities, recovery of sums from, **46**, [580]
acquiring authority, meaning, **9**, [253], [261], [387], [416]
aerodromes, for, by local authorities, **4(1)**, [81]
agricultural land. See **agricultural land**
ancient monuments etc, **22**, [408]; **32**, [334]
apparatus, vesting of, **46**, [693]
authorisation procedure—
notices, **9**, [415], [448]
preliminary, **9**, [409], [419]
authorities to which Acts apply, **9**, [408]
authority possessing powers of, **9**, [253]
blight notice, following. See **blight notice**
British Coal Corporation, interests, protection of, **17(2)**, [136]
British Railways Board, by, **36**, [691]
British Waterways Board, by, **36**, [691]
camping site, for, **32**, [261]
capital gains tax. See **capital gains tax**
car parking, land for, **37**, [214]

compulsory acquisition—*contd*
caravan site, land for, **32**, [237]
civil aviation, for purposes of—
compensation to statutory undertakers,
4(1), [102]
generally, **4(1)**, [81], [91]–[93], [100]
clearance area, land in or adjoining, order,
modification of, **22**, [394]
coast protection works, **49**, [384], [392]
common form land clauses, **36**, [210]
common land, of, **32**, [285]
compensation. *See* **compensation**
compulsory purchase order. *See* **compulsory
purchase orders**
confirming authority, meaning, **9**, [416]
corresponding amendment of other
enactments, **46**, [1042]
country park, for, **32**, [258]
Countryside Council for Wales, by, **32**, [256]
covenants, taking account, of, **21**, [328], [345]
Crown application, **46**, [1058]
Crown land, **23**, [534]
Defence Acts, under. *See* **Defence Acts**
enforcement officer—
enforcement by, **11(S)**, Courts 105–6;
11(4), [65]
warrants issued to, **11(S)**, Courts 107–8;
11(4), [66]
entry on land, powers, **22**, [397], [403]
Environment Agency, by—
compensation provisions, **49**, [1287]
compulsory works orders, in relation to,
49, [1288]
disposal, restrictions on, **49**, [1202]
fisheries purposes, for, **49**, [1201]
power of, **49**, [1199]
facilities in National Park, for, **32**, [148]
forestry, land for, **18**, [1131], [1146]–[1148]
gas supply, for purpose of. *See* **gas
transporter**
general vesting direction. *See* **general vesting
declaration**
generally, **46**, [1]
grant, sums reckonable for purposes of,
46, [581]
highway, land in connection with, **46**, [519]
highways, land for, of. *See* **highway
(acquisition)**
Homes and Communities Agency, by,
24, [853]
housing action trust, by, **22**, [863], [931]
housing provisions, under, enactments applied
to, **22**, [393]
incorporated enactments, modification of,
46, [510]
Integrated Transport Executive, by, **36**, [779]
interests omitted, **9**, [81], [282]
knacker's yard, for, **1(1)**, [875]
land acquired—
entry on, powers, **22**, [397]
short tenancies, determination of, **22**, [397]
land excluded from, **9**, [429], [454]
landlord's interest in flats, of. *See* **flats**
leasehold enfranchisement or extension, effect
on, **21**, [300]

compulsory acquisition—*contd*
listed building in need of repair, of—
compensation, **46**, [691]
deliberately left derelict, **46**, [692]
direction for minimum compensation,
46, [692]
order, **46**, [689]
repairs notice, requirement of, **46**, [690]
local authority, by. *See* **local authority**
local authority, power of—
adjoining land, **46**, [490]
authorisation, **46**, [490]
development, etc, for, **46**, [490]
market or fair, for, **27**, [123]
meaning, **9**, [408]
multiple occupation, house in, **22**, [395]
National Park authority, powers of, **46**, [509]
National Trust land, and, **32**, [200]
nationally significant infrastructure projects,
land for. *See* **nationally significant
infrastructure projects**
natural beauty, area of, **32**, [183]
nature reserve, for, **32**, [154], [190]
maintenance, for, **32**, [155]
new town, in—
development corporation, by—
power of, **46**, [142]
procedure, **46**, [203]
extinguishment of rights, **46**, [148]
highway authority, by, **46**, [143], [204]
local land charge, order as, **46**, [144]
modification of enactments, **46**, [146],
[211]–[212]
National Trust land, **46**, [206]
orders and certificates, validity and
operation of, **46**, [207]
Secretary of State, by, **46**, [205]
statutory undertakers, operational land of,
46, [145], [208]–[210]
compensation, **46**, [213]
objections, disregarded, **46**, [510]
open country, for access to—
local authority, by, **32**, [174]
Minister, by, **32**, [175]
open space, of, **32**, [1]
opencast coal working, protection for,
17(1), [200]
orders. *See* **compulsory purchase orders**
owner—
interests when not in occupation, expenses
of, **9**, [226]
meaning, **9**, [4], [136], [207], [416]
Passenger Transport Executive, by, **36**, [779]
picnic site, for, **32**, [261]
pipe-lines, for. *See* **pipe-line**
postal services, for, **34**, [747]–[749]
powers, exercise of, **32**, [190]
prisons, for, **12(1)**, [275AC]
purchase by Ministers, **9**, [448]
railway, for—
additional land, **36**, [240]
compensation, **36**, [265]
regional development agencies, by, **46**, [916],
[950]–[951]

compulsory acquisition—*contd*
rights over land. *See* **rights over land**
rights over land, extinguishment of, **46**, [500]
Secretary of State, by, **46**, [492]
security of tenure of business premises, effect on, **21**, [200]
slaughterhouse, for, **1(1)**, [875]
statutory undertakers, rights of, **46**, [536]–[537]
tenancies, continuance of, **22**, [396]
Thames flood barrier, for purposes of, **49**, [495]
three years after death, inheritance tax provisions, **42**, [734]
time limit, **9**, [264]
town development, for, **46**, [7]
transitional provisions, **9**, [446], [454]
urban development corporation, by, **46**, [105]
Urban Regeneration Agency, by, **46**, [836], [858]
vesting direction. *See* **general vesting declaration**
Thames flood barrier, for purposes of, **49**, [495]
waterways, for recreation on, **32**, [149]

compulsory purchase orders
aggrieved person, application to High Court, **9**, [435]
confirmation—
  acquiring authority, by, **9**, [427]
  joint, by confirming authority and Minister, **9**, [422], [443]
  local and other authorities, purchase by, **9**, [422]
  notice after, **9**, [428]
  provisions against, **9**, [429], [443], [453]
  provisions as to, **9**, [422]
  remaining objections, **9**, [423]–[424]
  stages, in, **9**, [425]
confirmed, acquisition without certificate, **9**, [443]
confirmed by Act of Parliament, exclusion, **9**, [439]
date of operation, **9**, [438]
High Court—
  application to, **9**, [435]
  powers of, **9**, [436]
local authority or other authority—
  land excluded from purchase, **9**, [430], [453], [454]
  meaning of local authority, **9**, [430], [453]
  purchase by—
    authorisation procedure, **9**, [409]
    confirmation, **9**, [422]
    form, **9**, [419]
    land not originally in, **9**, [426]
    map, **9**, [419]
    notice of—
      after confirmation, **9**, [428]
      before confirmation, **9**, [420]
      ecclesiastical property, **9**, [421]
      local inquiry, **9**, [412], [422]
      newspapers, in, **9**, [420], [428]
      objections, **9**, [422]

compulsory purchase orders—*contd*
local authority or other authority—*contd*
  purchase by—*contd*
    notice of—*contd*
      owners, lessees and occupiers, to, **9**, [421]
      remaining objections, **9**, [423]–[424]
      service, **9**, [415]
  purchase by information—
    offences relating to, **9**, [414]
    power to require, **9**, [413]
meaning, **9**, [408], [445]
Ministers, purchase by—
  authorisation procedure, **9**, [409], [448]
  draft—
    form, **9**, [419]
    land not included, **9**, [448]
    map, **9**, [419]
    notice of—
      ecclesiastical property, **9**, [448]
      newspapers, in, **9**, [420], [448]
      objections to, **9**, [448]
      owners, lessees and occupiers, to, **9**, [421], [448]
      service, **9**, [415]
  local inquiry, **9**, [412], [448]
  making of order, **9**, [448]
  notice after, **9**, [448]
  quashing, **9**, [436]
  special parliamentary procedure, subject to, **9**, [430]
  statutory undertakers' land, exclusion of, **9**, [429], [454]
  suspension of order, **9**, [436]
  validity, **9**, [435]–[439]
notices after making, **9**, [391], [448]
operation, date of, **9**, [438]
See also local authority; Ministers *above*
special kinds of land—
  commons, open spaces, fuel or field allotments, **9**, [432]
  land in more than one category, **9**, [433]
  local authorities, **9**, [430]
  National Trust, **9**, [431]
  statutory undertakers, **9**, [429]–[430]
suspension, **9**, [436]

compulsory rights orders. *See also* **rights over land**
Open Cast Coal Act, **9**, [441]

computer
company records, use for, **8**, 586–7
domestic jurisdiction—
  offences linked with, **12(2)**, [38]
  significant links with, **12(2)**, [39]
external law—
  inchoate offences related to offences under, **12(2)**, [41]
  relevance of, **12(2)**, [42]
impairment of operation, unauthorised acts with intent, **12(4)**, [271]
inchoate offences—
  external law offences, related to, **12(2)**, [41]

computer—*contd*
  inchoate offences—*contd*
    territorial scope of, **12(2)**, [40]
  information on, seizure of, **12(1)**, [854]
  local authority's, use of spare capacity,
    25(2), [370]
  material—
    modification of, unauthorised, **12(2)**, [36]
      conviction of offence, **12(2)**, [46]
      what constitutes, **12(2)**, [50]
    unauthorised access to, **12(4)**, [270]
      conviction, **12(2)**, [46]
      intention to commit further offences,
        12(2), [35], [46]
      methods, **12(2)**, [34], [50]
      offence of, **12(2)**, [34]
      penalties, **12(2)**, [35]
      proceedings, **12(2)**, [45]
      repeal of offence, **12(4)**, [418]
      search warrant, issue of, **12(2)**, [47]
      trial on indictment, **12(2)**, [46]
      what constitutes, **12(2)**, [50]
  meaning, **25(2)**, [370]
  misuse—
    attempt to commit offence, **12(1)**, [751]
    generally, **12(1)**, [1]
    Northern Ireland, application of
      provisions, **12(2)**, [48], [49]
    offence of, **12(2)**, [34]
  offences—
    attempt to commit, **12(1)**, [751];
      12(2), [40]
    British citizenship immaterial, **12(2)**, [43]
    conditions, satisfaction with, **12(2)**, [42]
    conspiracy to commit, **12(2)**, [40]
    inchoate, territorial scope of, **12(2)**, [40],
      [41]
    intention behind, **12(2)**, [35]
    making, supplying or obtaining articles for
      use in, **12(2)**, [37]
    search or seizure, powers of, **12(2)**, [44]
    territorial scope of, **12(2)**, [38]–[41]
  operation of, intent to impair, **12(2)**, [36]
  program or data, alteration or erasure of,
    12(2), [34], [50]
  records, requirement to produce,
    43(S), 948–9
  transitional and saving provisions, **12(4)**, [272]

computer equipment
  employee, provision to, **43(S)**, 46

computer software
  capital allowances, transitional provisions,
    43(1), [1224]
  disposal values—
    bringing into account, **43(1)**, [633]
    circumstances of grant, **43(1)**, [633]
    limit on, **43(1)**, [634]
  plant, treated as, **43(1)**, [632]
  rights to, **43(1)**, [632]

concealment
  limitation of actions, **19(3)**, [762]

conciliation officers. *See also* **Advisory,
  Conciliation and Arbitration Service**

conditional caution
  authorised person, by, **12(3)**, [813]
  code of practice, **12(3)**, [820]
  conditions, failure to comply with,
    12(3), [817]
    arrest for, **12(3)**, [818]
  financial penalty provision, **12(3)**, [815]
  meaning, **12(3)**, [813]
  PACE provisions, application of, **12(3)**, [819]
  power to give, **12(3)**, [813]
  requirements for, **12(3)**, [814]
  variation of conditions, **12(3)**, [816]

conditional discharge
  appeal, on, **12(2)**, [730]
  conviction, not, **12(2)**, [729]
  effect of, **12(2)**, [729]
    further offence, effect of, **12(2)**, [728]
    order for, **12(2)**, [727]
  period of, **12(2)**, [727]
  rehabilitation of offenders, effect on,
    12(1), [630], [634]

conditional sale agreement
  adverse possession, **39(1)**, [297]
  breach—
    condition, of, **39(1)**, [131]
    goods, possession of, **39(1)**, [253], [254]
  buyer under, position of, **1(1)**, [10]
  emergency laws, **50**, [262]
  entry on premises, **39(1)**, [255]
  installation charge, **39(1)**, [253], [263]
  land, relating to—
    breach of, **39(1)**, [255]
    termination of, **39(1)**, [262]
  meaning, **1(1)**, [10]; **9**, [136]; **13**, [1203];
    39(1), [68], [132], [353]; **44(1)**, [528]
  motor vehicle under, dealings, presumptions
    on, **39(1)**, [67]
  paid-up sum, determining, **39(1)**, [296]
  requisition of goods subject to, **9**, [132]
  return order, **39(1)**, [296]
  sale under, restriction on privilege from
    distress for rent, **13**, [1203]
  termination of—
    debtor, liability on, **39(1)**, [263]
    right of, **39(1)**, [262]
  time orders, **39(1)**, [290]
  total price, meaning, **39(1)**, [353]
  transfer order, **39(1)**, [296]

confession
  evidence for co-accused, given in, **18**, [252]
  evidence of, **18**, [251]
    hearsay rules, **18**, [396], [406]
  meaning, **18**, [259]
  mentally handicapped person, by, **18**, [253]
  oppression of person making, **18**, [251]

confinement. *See also* **pregnancy**

confirmation (church)
register of, custody of, **14**, 934

confiscation orders. *See* **drug trafficking; proceeds of crime**
bankrupt's estate, property excluded from, **4(2)**, [380]

conflict of laws
questions of law, deciding, **19(3)**, [12]

congenital disabilities
artificial insemination resulting in disablement of child, **45**, [957], [960]
birth, meaning, **45**, [960]
child born disabled, **45**, [956], [957], [959]
Crown, liability of, **45**, [961]
damages—
  minimum period of life, **45**, [960]
  reduction where responsibility shared, **45**, [956]
embryo—
  construction of references to, **45**, [960]
  placing in woman, effect, **45**, [957], [960]
infertility treatment, extension of provisions to, **45**, [957], [960]
ionising radiation causing, **45**, [959]
liability for—
  dependent on parent's, **45**, [956]
  infertility treatment, after, **45**, [957], [960]
  liability in tort, exclusion, **45**, [960]
  mother driving when pregnant, **45**, [958]
  personal injuries, as, **45**, [960]
  restrictions on, **45**, [956]
  when excluded, **45**, [956]
mother—
  driving when pregnant, liability, **45**, [958]
  exclusion of liability, **45**, [956]
Northern Ireland, application of provisions, **45**, [962]
nuclear incidents, due to, **45**, [959]
occurrences causing—
  actionable at suit of child, **45**, [956]
  nuclear radiation, involving, **45**, [959]
  occurrences deemed to be, **45**, [956]
  persons answerable for, **45**, [956]
pre-birth injury—
  answerable for, being, **45**, [956]
  mother driving when pregnant, **45**, [958]
  occurrences before conception, **45**, [956]
pregnancy, occurrences during, **45**, [956]
radiation, due to, **45**, [959]
risk known to parents, **45**, [956], [959]
summary of provisions, **45**, [945]

connected persons
determination of questions, **44(1)**, [621]
meaning, **44(1)**, [132]
provisions applied, **44(2)**, [719]

consecrated land
acquisition for civil aviation, **4(1)**, [105]
housing action trust, acquired by, **22**, [930]

consecrated land—*contd*
new town, use in, **46**, [152]
regional development agencies, vesting of land in, **46**, [952]
urban development area, use in, **46**, [107]
Urban Regeneration Agency, use by, **46**, [859]
use and development of, **46**, [502], [504]

consecration
bishop in foreign country, of, **14**, 147–8
certificate of, **14**, 148
oath of due obedience, dispensing with, **14**, 244
removal of legal effects, **14**, 1231–2
Crown land, **14**, 1232–3

conservancy authority
coast protection board, representation on, **49**, [381]
drainage arrangements with, **19(3)**, [188]
financial contributions, **49**, [1181]
flood defence arrangements with, **49**, [1174]
functions or property, transfer to Environment Agency, **49**, [1272]
land drainage affecting, **19(3)**, [259]
limitation of liability of, **39(2)**, [868]
meaning, **19(3)**, [247]; **39(2)**, [988]; **49**, [1267]

conservation. *See also* **wild animals; wild plants**
Antarctica, in. *See* **Antarctica**
energy. *See under* **energy**

conservation area
advertisements in, control of, **46**, [485]
amendment of provisions, **46**, [232]
consent—
  Crown, application by, **46**, [732], [734]
  meaning, **46**, [716]
control of demolition in, **46**, [716]–[717]
designation of, **46**, [711]–[712]
financial provisions, **46**, [742]
functions relating to, **25(2)**, [581]
general note, **46**, [1]
highway construction in, **36**, [1121]
meaning, **46**, [711]
planning application affecting, **46**, [715]
planning functions, **46**, [714]
preservation or enhancement—
  grants and loans for—
    power to make, **46**, [719]
    recovery of, **46**, [720]
  proposals for, **46**, [713]
trees in, dealing with, **46**, [471]–[474], [1038]
unoccupied buildings in, preservation of, **46**, [718]

conservation bodies. *See* **nature conservation**

consistory court
assessors—
  functions of, **14**, 579

consistory court—*contd*
  assessors—*contd*
    panel of, **14**, 580
    provision of, **14**, 614–15
    verdict, unable to agree, **14**, 580
  chancellor of diocese, proceedings heard by,
    14, 590
  criminal proceedings in, **14**, 605
  dissolved diocese, in, **14**, 927
  examiners—
    inquiry by, **14**, 577
    panel of, **14**, 580
    provision of, **14**, 614–15
  judge of—
    oath of, **14**, 614
    persons being, **14**, 558–9
  jurisdiction of, **14**, 557–8, 564
  obsolete jurisdiction, **14**, 611
  trial—
    censure, **14**, 579
    conduct of, **14**, 579
    judge, **14**, 579
    new, ordering, **14**, 580
    procedure, **14**, 579
  vacation of see, effect of, **14**, 570

consolidated fund
  audit and accounts, **19(2)**, [868]
  charges payable out of, **19(2)**, [600]–[603]
  daily balancing, **19(2)**, [864]
  exchequer account, payments to, **19(2)**, [864]
  fees paid into, **19(2)**, [602]
  Great Britain and Ireland, unification of,
    19(2), [592]
  liabilities arising from activities of Public
    Trustee, repeals, **48(S)**, Trusts 1
  National Insurance Fund, adjustment
    between, **40(1)**, [694]
  National Loans Fund, substitution of,
    19(1), [1]; **19(2)**, [850], [866], [872]
  OECD Agreement, payments made under,
    19(2), [950]
  Parliament, sums authorised by, **19(2)**, [615]
  payments into, **40(1)**, [691], [693]
    error, by, **19(2)**, [1032]
    generally, **19(1)**, [1]
  payments out of, **19(2)**, [1031]; **40(2)**, [191]
  perpetual annuities charged on, **19(2)**, [626]
  public trustee, discharging liabilities of,
    48, 239
  public-private partnership business, payments
    for, **19(2)**, [1045]
  quarter days, payments on, **19(2)**, [601]
  repayment of sums from, **19(2)**, [1017]
  salaries, etc, charged on, accrual of,
    19(2), [715]
  salary of Comptroller and Auditor General to
    be paid from, **19(2)**, [833]
  social fund, payments to and from,
    40(1), [698]
  standing services, payment out of,
    19(2), [613]
  sums charged on produce of, **19(2)**, [827]
  sums issued from, application of,
    19(2), [1029]

conspiracy
  acts in furtherance of trade dispute, **16**, [456]
  agreement to commit an offence, **12(1)**, [671]
  common law, at, **12(1)**, [676]
  criminal conduct, to commit, by member of
    services, **3(S)**, 61
  defraud, to, **12(1)**, [676], [1070]
  exemptions from liability, **12(1)**, [673]
  incitement to commit, **12(1)**, [676]
  institution of proceedings, **12(1)**, [675]
  offence of, **12(1)**, [671]; **12(2)**, [162], [166]
    meaning, **12(1)**, [671]
  offences outside United Kingdom, to
    commit, **12(1)**, [672]
  penalties, **12(1)**, [674]
  trespass, to, **12(1)**, [676]

constable. *See also* **police**
  assistance in enforcement of customs and
    excise matters, **13**, [598]
  closure order—
    enforcement, **19(3)**, [482]
    exemption from liability relating to,
      19(3), [662]
    termination of, **19(3)**, [479]
  detention in custody of, **12(1)**, [710]
  offences, right of entry to investigate,
    19(3), [672]
  reasonable force, using, **12(1)**, [924]
  revenue trader, entry on premises in presence
    of, **13**, [709]
  statutory undertaker, employed by, powers
    of, **12(1)**, [840]
  unlicensed premises, service of closure
    notice, **19(3)**, [476]

constitutional law
  boundaries of, **10**, [1]
  rule of law, provisions not adversely affecting,
    11(3), [456]

construction contract
  Crown application, **11(1)**, [381]
  deduction of sums from payments under,
    43(2), [293]
  dispute—
    adjudication, right to refer to, **11(1)**, [372]
    meaning, **11(1)**, [372]
  meaning, **11(1)**, [368]
  Northern Ireland, corresponding provisions,
    11(1), [384]
  notices, service of, **11(1)**, [379]
  operations, meaning, **11(1)**, [369]
  payment—
    conditional provisions, prohibition of,
      11(1), [377]
    dates for, **11(1)**, [374]
    notice of intention to withhold,
      11(1), [375]
    stages, in—
      entitlement to, **11(1)**, [373]
      duration of work, depending upon,
        11(1), [373]
    suspension of performance, when not
      given, **11(1)**, [376]

construction contract—*contd*
residential occupier, with—
meaning, **11(1)**, [370]
provisions inapplicable, **11(1)**, [370]
Scheme, **11(1)**, [378]
time periods, reckoning of, **11(1)**, [380]
writing, in, **11(1)**, [371]

construction industry
construction trade, meaning, **43(1)**, [348]
grants and guarantees, **47**, [433]
sub-contractors. *See* **sub-contractors**

construction sites
control of noise on, **35(1)**, [319]
work on, prior consent for, **35(1)**, [320]

Consul
administration of estates, **10**, [919]–[922]
aircraft, civil jurisdiction on, **10**, [994]
archives and documents, inviolability of,
10, [1005]
Commonwealth, **10**, [1001]
communication, freedom of, **10**, [1005]
consular bag, **10**, [1005]
consular officer, **10**, [1005]
notarial acts by, **18**, [180]
customs duties and inspection, exemption
from, **10**, [1005]
deceased person's property, powers,
10, [919]–[922]
diplomatic privilege and immunities. *See*
diplomatic privilege
duration of privileges, **10**, [1005]
estate of members, export of, **10**, [1005]
evidence, members giving, **10**, [1005]
fees and charges, **10**, [1005], [1063]
functions of—
diplomatic mission, exercised by,
10, [1005]
fees, **10**, [1063]
meaning, **10**, [1005]
grant of representation to, **10**, [919]–[922]
head of post, functions of, **10**, [1005]
honorary consular officer, headed by,
10, [1005]
income tax exemption, **44(2)**, [303]–[305]
Ireland, serving in, **10**, [1000]
Irish, **10**, [1001]
jurisdiction, immunity from, **10**, [1005]
land, acquisition and loss of, **10**, [1068]
notarial acts, doing, **10**, [998]
oath, administering, **10**, [998]
personal service, exemption from, **10**, [1005]
premises—
former, vesting of, **10**, [1069],
[1076]–[1077]
inviolability of, **10**, [1005]
protection of, **10**, [1005]
Secretary of State, sale by, **10**, [1070]
taxation, exemption, **10**, [1005]
private gainful employment of, **10**, [1005]
privileges and immunities. *See* **diplomatic
privilege**

Consul—*contd*
ship—
civil jurisdiction, **10**, [994]
criminal jurisdiction on, **10**, [995]
disciplinary offences, detention for,
10, [996]
social security exemption, **10**, [1005]
taxation, exemption from, **10**, [1005]
third states, transit through, **10**, [1005]

consular officer
income tax exemption, **44(3)**, [786]–[787]

consular relations
Vienna Convention, application of, **10**, [991],
[1005]

Consultative Councils
officers, continuity of employment,
17(1), [811]

Consumer Appeals Tribunal
allowances, **39(1)**, [360]
appeals, disposal of, **39(1)**, [362]
constitution, **39(1)**, [361]
decisions, **39(1)**, [362]
Deputy President, **39(1)**, [360]
evidence, **39(1)**, [362]
panels, **39(1)**, [360]
President, **39(1)**, [360]
procedure, rules on, **39(1)**, [362]
remuneration, **39(1)**, [360]
sittings, **39(1)**, [362]
staff and costs, **39(1)**, [360]
terms of office, **39(1)**, [360]

Consumer Council for Postal Services. *See*
postal services

Consumer Council for Water
abolition, designation for, **39(1)**, [698]
directions, **39(1)**, [703]
loss of office, compensation for,
39(1), [701]
transfer of property, rights and liabilities,
39(1), [702], [739]
accounts, **49**, [1042]
annual reports, **49**, [1003], [1042]
co-operation with—
Secretary of State, **49**, [768]
Water Services Regulation Authority,
49, [768]
constitution, **49**, [1042]
establishment of, **49**, [767], [1355]
financial provisions, **49**, [1042]
first financial year, **49**, [1042]
forward work programmes, **49**, [1002]
functions—
consumer matters, power to publish
information and advice about, **49**, [773]
customers, provision of information to,
49, [772]
information, acquisition and review of,
49, [770]
interests of consumers, **49**, [769]

Consumer Council for Water—*contd*
  functions—*contd*
    performance of, **49**, [1042]
    public authorities, provision of advice and
      information to, **49**, [771]
  information—
    provision by, **49**, [776]–[777]
    provision of, to, **49**, [774]–[775], [777]
  investigation, powers of, **49**, [780]
  members—
    appointment, **49**, [1042]
    pensions, **49**, [1042]
    remuneration, **49**, [1042]
  membership, **49**, [1042]
  regional committees, **49**, [1042]
    establishment of, **49**, [767]
    purpose of, **49**, [767]
  reports, **49**, [1003]
  staff, **49**, [1042]
  statistical information about complaints,
    publication of, **49**, [799]–[800]
  supplementary powers, **49**, [1042]
  transfer and abolition order—
    payment conditions, **39(1)**, [700]
    power to make, **39(1)**, [699]
  transfer orders, **39(1)**, [699], [700]

consumer credit
  advertisement—
    cash, goods not sold for, **39(1)**, [202]
    content of, **39(1)**, [201]
    credit brokerage, for, **39(1)**, [313]
    credit information services, **39(1)**, [653]
    debt-adjusting, for, **39(1)**, [313]
    debt-counselling, for, **39(1)**, [313]
    form of, **39(1)**, [201]
    meaning, **39(1)**, [353]
    offences, **39(1)**, [202]
    regulated, **39(1)**, [200]
  agent—
    duty of, **39(1)**, [337]
    person deemed to be, **39(1)**, [212], [337]
  agreement—
    action to enforce, **39(1)**, [305]
    cancellable, **39(1)**, [223], [353]
    cancellation—
      cooling-off period, **39(1)**, [224]
      goods, return of, **39(1)**, [228]
      interest, payment of, **39(1)**, [227]
      money, recovery of, on, **39(1)**, [226]
      notice of, **39(1)**, [225]
      part-exchange, goods given in,
        39(1), [229]
      repayment of credit, **39(1)**, [227]
      rights, notice of, **39(1)**, [220]
    consideration period, **39(1)**, [217]
    content of, **39(1)**, [216]
    contracting-out, **39(1)**, [335]
    cooling-off period, **39(1)**, [224]
    creditor and supplies, between, **39(1)**, [350]
    debtor-creditor, **39(1)**, [146]
      canvassing, **39(1)**, [205]
      exclusion from regulations, **39(1)**, [230]
      land mortgage, secured by, **39(1)**, [149]

consumer credit—*contd*
  agreement—*contd*
    debtor-creditor-supplier, **39(1)**, [145]
      cancellation of, **39(1)**, [225]
      canvassing, **39(1)**, [158]
      land, financing, **39(1)**, [149]
      money, recovery of on cancellation,
        39(1), [226]
      restricted-use credit, for, **39(1)**, [230]
      supplier and creditor, claims against,
        39(1), [231]
    documents, powers to require provision
      of, **39(1)**, [336]
    enforcement of—
      jurisdiction, **39(1)**, [304], [665]
      notice of, **39(1)**, [232]
    entry into—
      antecedent negotiations, **39(1)**, [212]
      exclusion from regulations, **39(1)**, [230]
      information, disclosure of, **39(1)**, [211]
    executed—
      copy, supply of, **39(1)**, [219]
      meaning, **39(1)**, [353]
    execution of, **39(1)**, [217]
      improper, **39(1)**, [221]
    exempt, **39(1)**, [149]–[151]
    fixed-sum credit—
      arrears—
        information sheets on, prepared by
          OFT, **39(1)**, [244], [666]
        notice of sums in, **39(1)**, [245]
          failure to give, **39(1)**, [247]
      default, information sheets prepared by
        OFT on, **39(1)**, [244], [666]
      default sum—
        interest on, **39(1)**, [249]
        meaning, **39(1)**, [351]
        notice of, **39(1)**, [248]
      information, giving, **39(1)**, [233]
      meaning, **39(1)**, [143]
      statements to be provided, **39(1)**, [234],
        [666]
      surety, information to, **39(1)**, [269]
    form of, **39(1)**, [216]
    improper execution of, **39(1)**, [221]
    information—
      disclosure of, **39(1)**, [211]
      goods, about, **39(1)**, [237]
      powers to require provision of,
        39(1), [336]
    modifying, **39(1)**, [239]
    more than one debtor or hirer, with,
      39(1), [348], [649]
    multiple, **39(1)**, [153]
    non-commercial, meaning, **39(1)**, [353]
    prospective, **39(1)**, [215]
    prospective land mortgage, withdrawal
      from, **39(1)**, [214]
    rate of interest on default, **39(1)**, [256]
    regulated, **39(1)**, [141], [353]
    rescission, notice of, **39(1)**, [265]
    restricted use—
      advertisements, **39(1)**, [202]
      meaning, **39(1)**, [144]

consumer credit—*contd*
 agreement—*contd*
  running-account credit—
   arrears—
    information sheets on, prepared by
     OFT, **39(1)**, [244], [666]
    notice of sums in, **39(1)**, [246]
     failure to give, **39(1)**, [247]
   default sum—
    interest on, **39(1)**, [249]
    meaning, **39(1)**, [351]
    notice of, **39(1)**, [248]
   information, giving, **39(1)**, [235]
    surety, to, **39(1)**, [270]
   limit, **39(1)**, [143]
   meaning, **39(1)**, [143]
   two or more debtors, with, **39(1)**, [348],
    [649]
  signing, **39(1)**, [217]
  small, meaning, **39(1)**, [152]
  termination—
   notice of, **39(1)**, [261]
   statement, **39(1)**, [266], [334]
  transitional provisions, **39(1)**, [366]
  two or more creditors, with, **39(1)**, [349]
  unexecuted, supply of copy of, **39(1)**, [218]
  unfair relationships between creditors and
   debtors, **39(1)**, [300]
   powers of court regarding, **39(1)**, [301],
    [666]
  unlicensed credit-broker, introduction by,
   39(1), [312], [366]
  unlicensed trader, made by, **39(1)**, [196],
   [266], [366]
  unrestricted-use, **39(1)**, [144]
  variation—
   court, by, **39(1)**, [299]
   notice of, **39(1)**, [239]
  void, when, **39(1)**, [212]
  withdrawal from, **39(1)**, [213]
 ancillary credit business—
  canvassing, **39(1)**, [315], [316]
  lawyer not treated as doing, **39(1)**, [309]
  licensing, **39(1)**, [310], [366]
  meaning, **39(1)**, [308]
  repeals, **39(1)**, [367]
  unlicensed credit-broker, introduction by,
   39(1), [312], [366]
  unlicensed trader, **39(1)**, [311], [366]
 antecedent negotiations—
  beginning of, **39(1)**, [212]
  meaning, **39(1)**, [212]
 appeal to Secretary of State, **39(1)**, [198]
 appropriation of payments, **39(1)**, [238]
 associates, meaning of, **39(1)**, [347]
 binding statements, **39(1)**, [334]
 breach of Act, sanction for, **39(1)**, [332]
 business, carrying on of—
  power to prohibit, **19(2)**, [255]
  power to restrict, **19(2)**, [256]
 canvassing off trade premises—
  ancillary credit business, **39(1)**, [315], [316]
  conditional sale agreement. *See*
   conditional sale agreement
  debtor-creditor agreements, **39(1)**, [205]

consumer credit—*contd*
 canvassing off trade premises—*contd*
  definition, **39(1)**, [204]
  overdrawing, enabling, **39(1)**, [205]
 conditions on orders, **39(1)**, [298]
 conduct of business regulations—
  credit-brokerage, **39(1)**, [314]
  debt-adjusting, **39(1)**, [314]
  debt-counselling, **39(1)**, [314]
  power to make, **39(1)**, [210]
 consumer hire. *See* **consumer hire**
 convictions, notification to OFT, **39(1)**, [328]
 copies, form of, **39(1)**, [343]
 county court, jurisdiction of—
  England and Wales, **39(1)**, [304], [665]
  Northern Ireland, **39(1)**, [306], [665]
 credit brokerage—
  agreements, entry into, **39(1)**, [318]
  canvassing, **39(1)**, [315], [316]
  conduct of business regulations,
   39(1), [314]
  fees, recovering, **39(1)**, [317]
  information, duty to give, **39(1)**, [314]
  meaning, **39(1)**, [308]
  quotations, **39(1)**, [314]
 credit, meaning, **39(1)**, [142]
 credit reference agency—
  business consumer, procedure for,
   39(1), [322]
  filed information, disclosing, **39(1)**, [320]
  meaning, **39(1)**, [308]
  name and address, disclosing, **39(1)**, [319]
  wrong information, correcting,
   39(1), [321]
 creditor, meaning, **39(1)**, [353]
 credit-sale agreement, meaning, **39(1)**, [353]
 credit-token agreement. *See* **credit-token**
 debt-adjusting—
  advertising, **39(1)**, [313]
  agreements, entry into, **39(1)**, [318]
  canvassing, **39(1)**, [315], [316]
  conduct of business regulations,
   39(1), [314]
  information, duty to give, **39(1)**, [314]
  meaning, **39(1)**, [308]
  quotations, **39(1)**, [314]
 debt-collecting, meaning, **39(1)**, [308]
 debt-counselling—
  advertising, **39(1)**, [313]
  agreements, entry into, **39(1)**, [318]
  canvassing, **39(1)**, [315], [316]
  conduct of business regulations,
   39(1), [314]
  information, duty to give, **39(1)**, [314]
  meaning, **39(1)**, [308]
  quotations, **39(1)**, [314]
 debtor—
  death of, **39(1)**, [243]
   enforcement order on, **39(1)**, [289]
  judgment debts, interest payable on,
   39(1), [293]
  meaning, **39(1)**, [353]
 default notice—
  compliance with, **39(1)**, [252]
  contents of, **39(1)**, [251]

consumer credit—*contd*
  default notice—*contd*
    effect of, **39(1)**, [251]
    need for, **39(1)**, [250]
    OFT information sheets on, **39(1)**, [244]
    service of, **39(1)**, [250]
    surety, given to, **39(1)**, [273]
    time order on, **39(1)**, [290], [651]
  defences, **39(1)**, [330]
  deposit, meaning of, **39(1)**, [353]
  determinations by OFT, **39(1)**, [346]
  Director General of Fair Trading, and. *See*
  Director General of Fair Trading
  documents, service of, **39(1)**, [338]
    electronic transmission of, **39(1)**, [339]
  EEA firm—
    application for licence by, **39(1)**, [165]
    meaning, **39(1)**, [354]
  enforcement authority—
    entry and inspection, power of,
      39(1), [324]
    loss, compensation for, **39(1)**, [325]
    meaning, **39(1)**, [323]
    obstruction of officer, **39(1)**, [327]
    test purchases, **39(1)**, [326]
  enforcement order—
    cancellable agreement, in case of,
      39(1), [288]
    death of debtor or hirer, on, **39(1)**, [289]
    infringement, in case of, **39(1)**, [288]
    rights of parties, **39(1)**, [305]
    time order on, **39(1)**, [290], [292], [651]
  facilities, liability for misuse of, **39(1)**, [240]
  financial provisions, **39(1)**, [355], [659]
  floating charge, fixing, **39(1)**, [250]
  hirer—
    death of, **39(1)**, [243]
      enforcement order on, **39(1)**, [289]
    judgment debts, interest payable on,
      39(1), [293]
    meaning, **39(1)**, [353]
  information—
    displaying, **39(1)**, [209]
    duty to give—
      ancillary credit business, **39(1)**, [314]
      payments ahead of time, on, **39(1)**, [260]
  judgment, notification to OFT, **39(1)**, [328]
  licence—
    ancillary credit business, **39(1)**, [310]
    appeals, **39(1)**, [197]–[199]
    application, **39(1)**, [164]
      charge for, **39(1)**, [139]
      EEA firm, by, **39(1)**, [165]
    assignable, not, **39(1)**, [157]
    bankrupt, holder becoming, **39(1)**, [190]
    businesses needing, **39(1)**, [156]
    changes, notifying, **39(1)**, [183], [184]
    charges before end of payment periods,
      39(1), [167]–[169]
    conduct of business, regulations on,
      39(1), [163]
    death of holder, **39(1)**, [190]
    financial services ombudsman scheme—
      applicable to, **39(1)**, [656]
      consequential amendments, **39(1)**, [658]

consumer credit—*contd*
  licence—*contd*
    financial services ombudsman
    scheme—*contd*
      funding by licensees, **39(1)**, [657]
    fit person, licensee to be, **39(1)**, [161]
      OFT guidance on fitness test,
        39(1), [162]
    group, **39(1)**, [157]
      exclusion from, **39(1)**, [166]
      supervisory bodies, OFT's power to
      impose requirements on,
        39(1), [176]–[179]
    information requirement—
      failure to comply with, **39(1)**, [188]
      OFT, by, **39(1)**, [185]
    issue, **39(1)**, [166]
    lawful activities, covering, **39(1)**, [158]
    licensee's premises—
      entry to premises under warrant,
        39(1), [187], [189]
      OFT's power to require access to,
        39(1), [186]
    licensees, OFT's power to impose
      requirements on, **39(1)**, [175],
      [177]–[179]
    name of business in, **39(1)**, [159]
    Northern Ireland, termination in,
      39(1), [191]
    offences, **39(1)**, [192]
    OFT, determination of application by,
      39(1), [164]
    patient, holder becoming, **39(1)**, [190]
    renewal, **39(1)**, [170]
      charge for, **39(1)**, [139]
    revocation, **39(1)**, [173]
    specific activities, covering, **39(1)**, [158]
    standard, **39(1)**, [157]
      applications for, **39(1)**, [160]
    suspension, **39(1)**, [173], [174]
    termination, **39(1)**, [190]
    transitional provisions, **39(1)**, [366]
    variation, **39(1)**, [171], [172]
    winding-up of standard licensee's business,
      39(1), [181]
  linked transactions, **39(1)**, [154], [259]
  local Acts, effect of Act on, **39(1)**, [341]
  minor, circular to, **39(1)**, [206]
  monetary limits, alteration of, **39(1)**, [344]
  Northern Ireland, arrangements for,
    39(1), [356]
  offences—
    body corporate, by, **39(1)**, [331]
    prosecution and punishment of,
      39(1), [329], [363]
  Office of Fair Trading. *See* **Office of Fair
  Trading**
  pawn. *See* **pawn**
  payments ahead of time—
    information, duty to give, **39(1)**, [260]
    linked transactions, effect on, **39(1)**, [259]
    rebate, **39(1)**, [258]
    right to make, **39(1)**, [257]
  pledge, pawn. *See* **pawn**
  proceedings, onus of proof in, **39(1)**, [333]

consumer credit—*contd*
  protection orders, **39(1)**, [296]
  quotations—
    ancillary credit business, **39(1)**, [314]
    regulations, **39(1)**, [208]
  register—
    inspection of, **39(1)**, [182]
    particulars on, **39(1)**, [182]
  registered charges, saving for, **39(1)**, [340]
  regulations and orders, **39(1)**, [345]
  secondary documents, form of, **39(1)**, [342]
  Secretary of State, powers of, **39(1)**, [136]
  security—
    Act not to be evaded by use of,
      39(1), [275]
    content of, **39(1)**, [267]
    debtor or hirer, information given to,
      39(1), [272]
    execution of instrument, **39(1)**, [267]
    form of, **39(1)**, [267]
    ineffective, **39(1)**, [268]
    land mortgage, enforcement of,
      39(1), [287]
    linked transactions, **39(1)**, [275]
    meaning, **39(1)**, [353]
    negotiable instruments use of,
      39(1), [284]–[286]
    prospective agreement, for, **39(1)**, [275]
    realisation of, **39(1)**, [274]
    surety—
      default notice given to, **39(1)**, [273]
      information given to, **39(1)**, [269]–[271]
      meaning, **39(1)**, [353]
    variation by court, **39(1)**, [299]
  suspension of orders, **39(1)**, [298]
  terminology, examples of, **39(1)**, [352], [364],
    [365]
  time order, **39(1)**, [290], [292], [651]
  total charge for credit, regulations,
    39(1), [155]

Consumer Credit Appeals Tribunal
  appeals from, **39(1)**, [199]
  establishment of, **39(1)**, [197]
  summary of provisions, **39(1)**, [1]
  establishment of, **39(1)**, [197]
  summary of provisions, **39(1)**, [1]

consumer hire
  adverse possession, **39(1)**, [297]
  advertisements, **39(1)**, [200]
  agreement—
    exempt, **39(1)**, [150], [151]
    meaning, **39(1)**, [148]
    meaning, **13**, [1203]
    surety, information given to, **39(1)**, [271]
    termination of—
      notice, period of, **39(1)**, [264]
      right of, **39(1)**, [264]
    time orders, **39(1)**, [290], [292], [651]
  business, meaning, **39(1)**, [353]
  conduct of business regulations, **39(1)**, [210]
  entry on premises, **39(1)**, [255]
  hirer, financial relief on recovery of
    possession, **39(1)**, [295]

consumer hire—*contd*
  information—
    displaying, **39(1)**, [209]
    duty to give, **39(1)**, [236]
  suspension of orders, **39(1)**, [298]

Consumer Panel
  annual report, **45**, [434]
  committees and other procedures, **45**, [436]
  establishment, **45**, [434]
  information to, provision of, **45**, [434]
  matters on which to advise, **45**, [434]
  membership, **45**, [435]
  remit of, power to amend, **45**, [437]

consumer protection. *See also* **fair trading**
  body corporate, infringements by, **47**, [912]
  Community infringements, **47**, [902]
    proceedings, **47**, [911]
  consumer, meaning, **47**, [900]
  contract concluded away from business
    premises, regulations, **39(1)**, [722]
  Crown, provisions binding, **47**, [926]
  defective products—
    actions, time limit, **19(3)**, [736]
    date of knowledge of facts, **19(3)**, [739]
    death caused by, **19(3)**, [757]
  domestic infringements, **47**, [901]
  enforcement orders—
    application for, **47**, [905]
      directions by OFT, **47**, [906]
    body corporate, against, **47**, [913]
    consultation, **47**, [904]
    content of, **47**, [907]
    further proceedings, **47**, [910]
    grant of, **47**, [907]
    interim, **47**, [908]
    requirements, **47**, [907]
    undertakings, **47**, [909]
  enforcers, **47**, [915]
  evidence, **47**, [918]
  financial assistance, **47**, [939]
  general enforcers, **47**, [903]
  goods and services, reference to, **47**, [922]
  information, disclosure of. *See* **trade and
    industry**
  Injunctions Directive, **47**, [925]
  interests of consumers. *See* **fair trading**
  listed directives, **47**, [958]
    provisions of, **47**, [959]
  London, service in, **25(2)**, [300]
  meaning of consumer, **47**, [195]
  notices—
    enforcement, **47**, [917]
    procedure, **47**, [916]
  orders and regulations, **39(1)**, [723]
  person supplying goods, **47**, [923]
  safety provisions. *See* **safety of goods**
  services, reference to supply of, **47**, [924]
  test purchases, power to make, **47**, [142]

Consumer Protection Advisory Committee
  financial provision for, **47**, [194]
  orders—
    limitation of effect of, **47**, [140]

Consumer Protection Advisory Committee—*contd*

orders—*contd*

report, in pursuance of, **47**, [136]

procedure of, **47**, [173]

references to—

investigation procedure, **47**, [173]

orders on. *See* **fair trading**

reports on, order in pursuance of, **47**, [136]

contact lenses

fitting of, rules as to, **28**, [547]

contact order. *See* **child**

contaminated land

additional relief for, **43(S)**, 1447–8

adjoining land, **35(1)**, [808]

contaminated state, meaning, **43(2)**, [74]

contaminating substances escaping to other land, liability for, **35(1)**, [796]

controlled waters, pollution of—

meaning, **35(1)**, [787]

restrictions on liability relating to, **35(1)**, [795]

guidance by Secretary of State—

Environment Agency to have regard to, **35(1)**, [807]

supplementary provisions, **35(1)**, [810]

identification of, **35(1)**, [788]

interaction of provisions, **35(1)**, [811]

Isles of Scilly, application of provisions to, **35(1)**, [809]

land in contaminated state, meaning, **43(S)**, 1444

landfill tax, exemption from, **35(2)**, [186], [187]

major interest in land, meaning, **43(S)**, 1449

meaning, **35(1)**, [787]

nuclear sites, **43(S)**, 1444

radioactivity provisions applying to, **35(1)**, [812]

remediation—

amended provisions, **43(S)**, 1159, 1443–52

cause of harm, enforcement action relating to, **35(1)**, [811]

enforcing authority—

duty of, to require, **35(1)**, [791]

powers of, to carry out, **35(1)**, [799]

recovery of cost by, **35(1)**, [800]

registers—

confidential information, exclusion of certain, **35(1)**, [804]

national security, exclusion of information affecting, **35(1)**, [803]

requirement to maintain, **35(1)**, [802]

security for cost, **35(1)**, [800]

expenditure—

artificially inflated claims, **43(2)**, [78]

capital expenditure, deduction for, **43(2)**, [74]

capital gains, exclusion for purposes of, **43(2)**, [76]

corporation tax claims, **43(1)**, [403]

employee costs, **43(2)**, [74]

contaminated land—*contd*

remediation—*contd*

expenditure—*contd*

entitlement to relief, **43(2)**, [75]

expenditure incurred because of contamination, **43(2)**, [74]

interpretation, **43(2)**, [78]

life assurance business, special provision for, **43(2)**, [77]

losses carried forward, restriction on, **43(2)**, [76]

materials, expenditure on, **43(2)**, [74]

qualifying, **43(2)**, [74]

relevant remediation, **43(2)**, [74]

relief for, generally, **43(2)**, [45]

Schedule A business or trade, deduction in computing profits of, **43(2)**, [76]

sub-contracted remediation, on, **43(2)**, [74]

subsidised expenditure, **43(2)**, [74]

tax credit—

amount of, **43(2)**, [76]

entitlement to, **43(2)**, [76]

funding, **43(2)**, [78]

income, not, **43(2)**, [76]

payment in respect of, **43(2)**, [76]

transitional provisions, **43(2)**, [78]

meaning, **35(1)**, [787]

notice—

appeals against, **35(1)**, [797]; **35(2)**, [543]

non-compliance with, offence of, **35(1)**, [798]

prohibitions on serving, **35(1)**, [794]

restrictions on serving, **35(1)**, [794]

rights of entry—

compensation for, **35(1)**, [793]

grant of, **35(1)**, [793]

responsibility for, determination of appropriate person to bear, **35(1)**, [792]

special sites, **35(1)**, [801]

reports on state of, by Environment Agency, **35(1)**, [805]

site-specific guidance by Environment Agency, **35(1)**, [806]

special sites—

designation of, **35(1)**, [789]

identification of, **35(1)**, [789]

meaning, **35(1)**, [787]

referral of decisions to Secretary of State, **35(1)**, [790]

remediation, **35(1)**, [801]

statutory nuisance, not being, **35(1)**, [813]

summary of provisions, **35(1)**, [1]

supplementary provisions, **35(1)**, [808]

two or more sites, **35(1)**, [808]

contempt of court

appeal, **11(2)**, [201]; **12(1)**, [437]

armed forces, by. *See* **armed forces**

attendance centre order, making, **11(2)**, [658]

committal—

application for, appeal, **11(2)**, [201]

period of, **11(2)**, [658]

county court, of, **11(2)**, [1000]

contempt of court—*contd*
court sitting in private, publication of
information on, **11(2)**, [200]
Courts and Legal Services Act, offences
under, **11(3)**, [124]
fine—
amount of, **11(2)**, [658]
enforcement, **11(2)**, [659]
Northern Ireland, **11(2)**, [667]
hospital order, **11(2)**, [658]
Judicial Committee of Privy Council, of,
11(2), [44], [62]
jury's deliberations, and, **11(2)**, [653]
legal aid, Northern Ireland, in, **11(2)**, [667]
Legal Services Ombudsman Investigations,
of, **11(3)**, [85]
magistrates' court, of, **11(2)**, [657], [660],
[666]
mental condition, remand for report on,
11(2), [658]
Northern Ireland, in, **11(2)**, [661], [667]
obstruction of inspector as, **8**, 485–6
penalties, **11(2)**, [658]
proceedings—
England and Wales, in, **11(2)**, [658]
Northern Ireland, in, **11(2)**, [667]
reporting restrictions, and, **11(2)**, [656]
sources of information, disclosing,
11(2), [655]
strict liability rule—
active proceedings, in, **11(2)**, [646], [665]
administration of justice, conduct
impeding, **11(2)**, [651]
common law defences, saving for,
11(2), [651]
contemporary report, defence of,
11(2), [649]
generally, **11(2)**, [1]
innocent distribution, defence of,
11(2), [648]
innocent publication, defence of,
11(2), [648]
institution of proceedings, consent for,
11(2), [652]
limitation of scope, **11(2)**, [647]
meaning, **11(2)**, [646]
public interest discussion, publication of,
11(2), [650]
publications, relating to, **11(2)**, [647]
tape recorder, using in court, **11(2)**, [654]
tribunal, of, **11(2)**, [663]
witness summons, disobeying, **12(1)**, [354]
young person, detention of, **12(2)**, [800]

Content Board
establishment and maintenance, **45**, [430]
functions, **45**, [431]

continental shelf. *See also* **offshore
installation**
British Coal Corporation, exploitation
rights, **17(2)**, [134]
design provisions applying, **11(1)**, [566]
design right provisions applying, **11(1)**, [1126]

continental shelf—*contd*
designated area—
establishment, **17(1)**, [290]
meaning, **44(1)**, [613]
employment connected with, application of
provisions, **16**, [104]
exploration and exploitation generally,
17(1), [290]
grants, **17(1)**, [454]
food safety, in relation to, **1(2)**, [470]
installations, meaning, **17(1)**, [295]
Isle of Man, share of revenue, **17(1)**, [382]
meaning, **13**, [806]
navigation, safety of, **17(1)**, [291]
Northern Ireland, share of revenue,
17(1), [382]
offences, prosecution of, **17(1)**, [294]
operations—
meaning, **40(1)**, [364]
social security benefits, and, **40(1)**, [364]
patents provisions applied, **11(1)**, [775]
pipe lines, damage to, **17(1)**, [293]
produce of, relief from customs duty,
13, [806]
radioactive substances—
designated areas, **17(1)**, [292]
treating for purposes of, **17(1)**, [292]
Republic of Ireland, area between UK and,
17(1), [718]
submarine cables, **17(1)**, [293]
UK sector, profits from activities in,
44(3), [891]

Contingencies Fund
Civil Contingencies Fund to be known as,
19(2), [891]
maximum capital of, **19(2)**, [937]

contract
agricultural tenancy. *See* **agricultural
tenancy**
applicable law—
1996 Accession Convention—
meaning, **11(1)**, [330]
text of, **11(1)**, [343]
Brussels Protocol—
meaning, **11(1)**, [330]
text of, **11(1)**, [341]
Conventions—
conflicts, applying in case of,
11(1), [331]
European Court decisions on,
11(1), [332]
force of law, to have, **11(1)**, [331]
interpretation of, **11(1)**, [332]
meaning, **11(1)**, [330]
revision of, **11(1)**, [333]
extent of Act, **11(1)**, [337]
Funchal Convention—
meaning, **11(1)**, [330]
text of, **11(1)**, [342]
Luxembourg Convention—
meaning, **11(1)**, [330]
text of, **11(1)**, [340]

contract—*contd*
  applicable law—*contd*
    Rome Convention—
      applicable law, scope of, **11(1)**, [339]
      burden of proof, **11(1)**, [339]
      Community law, precedence of,
        11(1), [339]
      consumer contracts, **11(1)**, [339]
      employment contracts, **11(1)**, [339]
      final provisions, **11(1)**, [339]
      force of law, Articles not having,
        11(1), [331]
      formal validity, **11(1)**, [339]
      freedom of choice, **11(1)**, [339]
      incapacity, **11(1)**, [339]
      mandatory rules, effect of, **11(1)**, [339]
      material validity, **11(1)**, [339]
      meaning, **11(1)**, [330]
      more than one legal system, States
        with, **11(1)**, [339]
      non-contracting States, application of law
        of, **11(1)**, [339]
      "ordre public", **11(1)**, [339]
      other conventions, relationship with,
        11(1), [339]
      Protocol, **11(1)**, [339]
      renvoi, exclusion of, **11(1)**, [339]
      reservations, **11(1)**, [339]
      retrospective effect, not having,
        11(1), [339]
      scope of, **11(1)**, [339]
      subrogations, **11(1)**, [339]
      text of, **11(1)**, [339]
      uniform interpretation, **11(1)**, [339]
      voluntary assignment, **11(1)**, [339]
  body corporate, made by seal, under,
    11(1), [305]
  breach—
    business liability, of, **11(1)**, [308]
    effect of, **11(1)**, [315]
    exclusion of liability, **11(1)**, [309]
    indemnity clause, **11(1)**, [311]
    negligence, arising from, **11(1)**, [308]
    reasonableness, requirement of, **11(1)**, [315]
  capacity, **11(1)**, [293]
  change in value added tax, adjustment for,
    50, [119]
  commercial debt, late payment—
    applicable contracts, **11(1)**, [388]
    compensation for, **11(1)**, [392]
    conflict of laws, **11(1)**, [399]
    contract price—
      advance payments of, treatment of,
        11(1), [398]
      date for payment of, **11(1)**, [401]
    qualifying, **11(1)**, [389]
    statutory interest—
      compensation in addition to,
        11(1), [392]
      generally, **11(1)**, [387]
      ousting of, circumstances permitting,
        11(1), [395]
      period of, **11(1)**, [390]
      rate of, **11(1)**, [393]
      remission of, **11(1)**, [391]

contract—*contd*
  commercial debt, late payment—*contd*
    statutory interest—*contd*
      variation of, circumstances permitting,
        11(1), [395]
      substantial remedy, meaning, **11(1)**, [396]
    summary of provisions, **11(1)**, [293]
  company, by, **8(1)**, [121]
  construction contract. *See* **construction
    contract**
  consumer—
    civil jurisdiction, **11(2)**, [854], [855]
      allocation of court, **11(2)**, [809]
    dealing as—
      indemnity clauses, **11(1)**, [311]
      meaning, **11(1)**, [318]
  county court jurisdiction, **11(2)**, [908]
  debts, guarantee for, **11(1)**, [297]
  derivative. *See* **derivative contracts**
  exclusion of liability—
    charterparty, **11(1)**, [327]
    choice of law clause, and, **11(1)**, [322]
    company constitution, and, **11(1)**, [327]
    employment contract, in, **11(1)**, [327]
    goods, transfer of ownership of,
      11(1), [314]
    insurance contract, in, **11(1)**, [327]
    intellectual property, and, **11(1)**, [327]
    international supply contract, in,
      11(1), [321]
    land, interest in, and, **11(1)**, [327]
    marine salvage or towage contract, in,
      11(1), [327]
    prohibition, **11(1)**, [309]
    sea carriage of goods, and, **11(1)**, [327]
    sea carriage of passengers, and, **11(1)**, [323]
    secondary contract, in, **11(1)**, [316]
    standard terms of business, in, **11(1)**, [309]
    varieties of clause, **11(1)**, [319]
  frustrated—
    Act, application of, **11(1)**, [303]
    benefit, recovery of, **11(1)**, [302]
    charterparty, relating to, **11(1)**, [303]
    Crown as party to, **11(1)**, [303]
    expenses incurred, **11(1)**, [302]
    insurance—
      effect of, **11(1)**, [302]
      relating to, **11(1)**, [303]
    payments, recovery of, **11(1)**, [302]
    perishable goods, and, **11(1)**, [303]
    provision providing for, **11(1)**, [303]
    rights and liabilities, adjustment of,
      11(1), [302]
    severance, **11(1)**, [303]
    sums paid under, **11(1)**, [302]
  gambling. *See* **gambling**
  guarantee. *See* **guarantee**
  indemnity clause, unreasonable, **11(1)**, [311]
  infant, by. *See* **minor**
  insurance, of. *See* **insurance**
  land, relating to. *See under* **land**
  limitation of actions, **19(3)**, [729]
  negligence under—
    exclusion of liability, **11(1)**, [309]–[310]
    indemnity clause, **11(1)**, [311], [327]

contract—*contd*
  negligence under—*contd*
    meaning, **11(1)**, [308]
  overseas company, provisions applying,
    8(1), [1123]
  pre-incorporation, **8(1)**, [129]
  racial discrimination, **7(1)**, [194]
  reasonableness test, **11(1)**, [317], [328]
  ship, for repair to, **11(1)**, [299]
  sole member of company, with, **8(1)**, [309]
  standard terms of business, **11(1)**, [310]
  supply of goods or services, for—
    refusal to deal on grounds of union
      exclusion, prohibition, **16**, [385]
    trade union membership, void provisions
      on, **16**, [338]
    union recognition requirement, void,
      16, [384]
  surety, assignment of securities to,
    11(1), [298]
  term, reasonableness of, **11(1)**, [317], [324]
  third parties, rights of—
    arbitration provisions, **11(1)**, [412]
    exceptions, **11(1)**, [410]
    Northern Ireland, application of provisions
      to, **11(1)**, [413]
    promisee—
      enforcement of contract, by,
        11(1), [408]
      meaning, **11(1)**, [405]
    promisor—
      defences available, to, **11(1)**, [407]
      double liability, protection from,
        11(1), [409]
      meaning, **11(1)**, [405]
    rescission, **11(1)**, [406]
    summary of provisions, **11(1)**, [293]
    supplementary provisions, **11(1)**, [411]
    terms, enforcement of, **11(1)**, [405]
    variation, **11(1)**, [406]
  timeshare. *See* **timeshare**
  war, effect of, **50**, [180]
  writing, in, **11(1)**, [294]–[295]

contract of employment
  breach, injunction to restrain, **16**, [448]
  contracting-out of statutory provisions,
    16, [851]
  Crown employee, of, **16**, [458]
  equality clause, **16**, [28]
  meaning, **16**, [503], [877], [964]
  sex discrimination in, validity and revision,
    7(1), [112]
  specific performance, no order for, **16**, [448]
  statement of terms of employment, exclusion
    from requirement, **16**, [103]
  women, in case of, **16**, [28]

contribution
  liability for same damage, where. *See* **damage**

contributory benefits
  descriptions of, **40(1)**, [259]

**contributory employment and support
allowance**
  notice period, payment in, **16**, [729]

contributory negligence. *See* **negligence**
  application to Crown proceedings, **13**, [13]

controlled foreign company
  acceptable distribution policy, **43(S)**, 889;
    44(1), [475], [672]
    exemption, abolition of, **43(S)**, 1539
  accounting period, **43(1)**, [20]; **44(1)**, [467]
  advance pricing agreements—
    branch or agency, attribution of income
      to, **43(1)**, [440]
    chargeable periods, **43(1)**, [441]
    determinations, **43(1)**, [441]
    double taxation arrangements, inconsistency
      with, **43(1)**, [441]
    misleading information, **43(1)**, [441]
    modification or revocation, **43(1)**, [441]
    non-parties, effect on, **43(1)**, [442]
    reports and information, provision of,
      43(1), [441]
    ring fence trade, meaning, **43(1)**, [440]
    scope of, **43(1)**, [440]
  amended provisions, **43(S)**, 888–90, 1160
  assessment on, **44(1)**, [474]
  assumptions, **44(1)**, [671]
  bare trustee, **44(1)**, [473]
  business establishment, **44(1)**, [673]
  chargeable profits—
    apportionment of, **44(1)**, [470]
    EEA business establishment, reduction in,
      for certain activities of, **44(1)**, [468],
      [469]
    imputation of, **43(S)**, 678, 888;
      44(1), [459]
    life assurance company, apportionment to,
      44(1), [477]
  commencement of provisions, **43(S)**, 682
  company tax return, meaning, **44(1)**, [481]
  control, meaning, **43(S)**, 888; **44(1)**, [480]
  creditable tax—
    apportionment of, **44(1)**, [470]
    imputation, **44(1)**, [459]
    life assurance company, apportionment to,
      44(1), [477]
    meaning, **44(1)**, [470]
  designer rate tax, **44(1)**, [466]
  determinations requiring Board's sanction,
    44(1), [476]
  direction-making power, limitations on,
    44(1), [672]–[674]
  discovery assessments, **43(S)**, 681
  dividends from, **44(1)**, [675]
  double taxation relief, **44(1)**, [679]
  EEA business establishments, reduction in
    chargeable profits for, **44(1)**, [468]
    applications for, **44(1)**, [469]
  EEA territory, meaning, **43(S)**, 681
  elections and designations, **43(S)**, 678
  exempt activities—
    definition, **43(S)**, 889

controlled foreign company—*contd*
exempt activities—*contd*
engaged in, **43(2)**, [247]; **44(1)**, [460], [673]
exemption, abolition, **43(S)**, 1540–5
test, **43(S)**, 681
financing income, reduction in chargeable profits for, **43(S)**, 1545–6
general insurance business accounted for on non-annual basis, **44(1)**, [478], [479]
holding company, **44(1)**, [673]
insurance business, **44(1)**, [673]
interests in, **44(1)**, [462], [464]
investment business, **44(1)**, [673]
liability to tax, **43(1)**, [392]
group relief, **44(1)**, [675]
reliefs, **44(1)**, [474]
trading losses, **44(1)**, [675]
lower level of taxation, **44(1)**, [466]
countries with, **43(S)**, 678
meaning, **44(1)**, [459]
postponement of tax, **44(1)**, [474]
profits, diversion of, **44(1)**, [460], [674]
provisions applying to, **43(S)**, 73–4
public quotation exemption, abolition, **43(S)**, 681
recovery of tax, **44(1)**, [474]
reduction in UK tax, transaction achieving, **44(1)**, [460], [674]
relevant interest in, **44(1)**, [471]
percentage of shares represented by, **44(1)**, [472]
residence of, **44(1)**, [462], [463]
share linked to, meaning, **44(1)**, [473]
shares in, gains on disposal of, **44(1)**, [675]
superior holding company, **44(1)**, [673]
territorial exclusions, **44(1)**, [461]
territory with lower level of taxation, resident in, **44(1)**, [465]
trading company, meaning, **44(1)**, [481]
40 per cent test, meaning, **44(1)**, [480]

controlled tenancy
regulated tenancy, converted into, **21**, [539], [610]
transitional provisions, **21**, [660]

controlled waters
pollution of—
anti-pollution works and operations, notices requiring—
meaning, **35(1)**, [787]
restrictions on liability relating to, **35(1)**, [795]

Convention on International Carriage by Rail. *See* **International Carriage by Rail**

Convention on International Recognition of Rights in Aircraft
order giving effect to, **4(1)**, [140]

Convention on International Trade in Endangered Species of Wild Fauna and Flora
legislation giving effect to, **13**, [566]–[583]. *See also* **animals**; **plants**
See also **animals**; **plants**

conversion
goods, of. *See* **wrongful interference with goods**

conveyance
age of parties to, presumption, **20**, [638]
conditions not implied, **20**, [677]
costs of, **9**, [45], [283]
deed, by, requirement, **20**, [1], [670]
description of, **20**, [675]
electronic—
communication and storage of documents, **23**, [735]
dispositions, **23**, [731]
land registry network—
access, **23**, [782]
authority, presumption of, **23**, [782]
do-it-yourself conveyancing, **23**, [782]
education and training in relation to, **23**, [782]
generally, **23**, [732]
transactions, **23**, [782]
simultaneous registration, power to require, **23**, [733]
summary of provisions, **20**, [1]
executor etc, by. *See* **administration of estates; executor (assent)**
form of, **9**, [44], [95]–[96], [299]
grant, effect of term, **9**, [88]
implied covenants. *See* **covenant**
manor, of, words implied, **20**, [680]
consular officer, notarial acts by, **18**, [180]
meanings—
Conveyancing Act 1881, **20**, [436]
Land Charges Act 1972, **21**, [407]
Law of Property Act 1925, **20**, [694], [804]
overreaching, **20**, [626]
refusal of, **9**, [39], [269]
registered land. *See* **land registration**
self, to, **20**, [1], [690]
stamp duty. *See* **stamp duty**
taxation of costs of, **9**, [46], [283]
technicalities, abolition, **20**, [678]
two or more persons, to themselves etc, **20**, [690]
words implied, **20**, [680]

conveyance (vehicle)
aggravated vehicle-taking, **12(1)**, [565]
taking without authority, **12(1)**, [564], [1084]

conveyancing and law of property
accumulations. *See* **accumulations**; *See also* perpetuities *below*
acknowledgment of documents, effect, **20**, [682]
all estate clause implied, **20**, [681]

conveyancing and law of property—*contd*
bargain and sale, conveyance by, abolition, **20**, [669]
building society, services by. *See* **building society**
concurrence of persons equitably entitled, **20**, [660], [661]
corporation—
  by or on behalf of, **20**, [691]
  property or interest, devolution, **20**, [781]
  sole, to, **20**, [678]
court—
  orders, conclusive, **20**, [803]
  payment into, jurisdiction and procedure, **20**, [802]
Crown, application of Law of Property Act, **20**, [806]
deed—
  description of, **20**, [675]
  requirement, **20**, [1], [670]
disposition—
  meaning, **20**, [804]
  voidable. *See* voidable dispositions *below*
documents, production and safe custody, **20**, [663], [682]
electronic conveyancing. *See* **conveyance (electronic)**
equitable interests. *See* **equitable interest and chose in action**
equitable powers—
  conveyances over-reaching, **20**, [626]
  enforcement, **20**, [627]
  meaning, **20**, [804]
equitable waste, **20**, [745]
estates and interests capable of, **20**, [625]
feoffment, abolition, **20**, [1], [669]
grant, lands to lie in, **20**, [669]
historical notes, **20**, [1]
home information packs. *See* **home information packs**
husband and wife, rights of, **20**, [656]
implied conditions, exclusion, **20**, [677]
incorporeal hereditaments, provisions applicable, **20**, [800]
interest passing to grantee, **20**, [678]
judgments etc affecting land, **20**, [795]
leasehold, period of title, **20**, [662]
limitation of actions, exclusion, **20**, [635]
limitation, without words of, **20**, [678]
livery and seisin, conveyance by, abolition, **20**, [669]
mentally disordered person, conveyance on behalf of, **20**, [641]
merger, equitable rule, **20**, [786]
mortgage. *See* **mortgage**
Northern Ireland, meanings and interpretation of words etc in, **20**, [436]
notice—
  application to court, **20**, [802]
  assignment of chose in action, **20**, [746]
  constructive, restrictions, **20**, [798]
  easements, **20**, [799]
  Land Charges Act, registration under, as, **20**, [797], [798]

conveyancing and law of property—*contd*
notice—*contd*
  person barred from calling for title, **20**, [662]
  regulations respecting, **20**, [796]
  restrictive covenants, of, **20**, [798]
  service, **20**, [796]
  trust corporations, nomination to receive, **20**, [748]
  writing, requirement, **20**, [796]
overreaching conveyances, **20**, [626]
parol, interests in land created by, **20**, [672]
  savings, **20**, [673]
parties, presumption as to ages, **20**, [638]
past transactions, deed confirming, **20**, [684]
perpetuities, rule against—
  double possibilities, abolition of rule, **20**, [771]
  restriction on, **20**, [772]
  right of entry, application to, **20**, [772]
  when inapplicable, **20**, [772]
possession, meaning, **20**, [804]
pre-emption, right of, **20**, [787]
production of documents, **20**, [663], [682]
property, meaning, **20**, [804]
purchaser—
  execution of conveyance, right to, **20**, [693]
  meaning, **20**, [804]
  voluntary disposition to defraud, **20**, [776]
  without notice, protection of, **20**, [626]
registration, requirement to cancel, **20**, [661]
self, to, **20**, [690]
solicitor—
  protection under Law of Property Act 1925, **20**, [783]
  purchaser or lessee, right of to employ, **20**, [666]
statutory conditions of sale, **20**, [663]
supplemental instruments, effect given to, **20**, [676]
technicalities, abolition, **20**, [678]
title, commencement, **20**, [662]; **21**, [368]
transitional provisions, **20**, [658], [808], [809]
trustee, protection, **20**, [783]
valuable consideration, meaning, **20**, [804]
vesting orders and disposition operating as, **20**, [633]
voidable dispositions—
  acquisition of reversions at under value, **20**, [777]
  voluntary, to defraud purchaser, **20**, [776]
writing, instruments required in, **20**, [671]
  savings, **20**, [673]

Conveyancing Appeal Tribunal
appeals from, **11(3)**, [100]
appeals to, **11(3)**, [100]
chairman of, **11(3)**, [100]
constitution of, **11(3)**, [100]
decisions taking effect, **11(3)**, [100]
members, qualifications, **11(3)**, [100]
powers of, **11(3)**, [154]
procedure, **11(3)**, [154]
staff, **11(3)**, [154]

Conveyancing Ombudsman
annual report, **11(3)**, [102]
appointment of, **11(3)**, [102]
duty of, **11(3)**, [102]
expenses, **11(3)**, [102]
Scheme, rules for, **11(3)**, [102], [155]

conveyancing services
Authorised Conveyancing Practitioners Board.
See **Authorised Conveyancing Practitioners Board**
authorised practitioners—
authorisation of—
Board of, **11(3)**, [96]
refusal of, **11(3)**, [97]
revocation of, **11(3)**, [98]
suspension of, **11(3)**, [98]
competence and conduct, regulations,
11(3), [99]
conditions, imposition of, **11(3)**, [97]
provision by, **11(3)**, [95]
register of, **11(3)**, [96]
clients' money, interest on, **11(3)**, [157];
11(4), [571]
compensation scheme, **11(3)**, [103]
Conveyancing Appeal Tribunal. *See*
Conveyancing Appeal Tribunal
Conveyancing Ombudsman Scheme. *See*
Conveyancing Ombudsman
Council for Licensed Conveyancers. *See*
Council for Licensed Conveyancers
inadequate professional services—
compensation, **11(3)**, [157]
costs, **11(3)**, [157]
failure to comply with direction,
11(3), [157]
fees, **11(3)**, [157]
steps against, **11(3)**, [157]
licensed conveyancer. *See* **licensed conveyancer**
meaning, **11(3)**, [141]; **11(4)**, [563]
Office of Fair Trading—
advisory and supervisory functions,
11(3), [104]
investigatory powers, **11(3)**, [105]
documents, alteration or destruction of,
11(3), [107]
notices, enforcement of, **11(3)**, [106]

conviction. *See also* **previous conviction**
admissible as evidence—
civil proceedings, in, **18**, [204]
defamation action, in, **18**, [206]
conclusiveness for defamation action,
18, [206]
evidence of commission of offence, as,
18, [249], [250]
previous. *See* **previous conviction**
previous, evidence of, **18**, [104]
proof of, **18**, [129], [248]
quashing on appeal, **12(1)**, [417]
spent. *See* **rehabilitation of offenders**
witness, of, proof of, **18**, [129], [249]

convocation
commission of—
bishop, trying, **14**, 583
finding of, proceedings on, **14**, 584
findings, review of, **14**, 569
inquiry into complaint by, **14**, 586–7
jurisdiction of, **14**, 567
constitution, power to amend, **14**, 809
Diocese in Europe represented in, **14**, 959–60
duration of, **14**, 650
General Synod, vesting functions and
authority in, **14**, 685, 692–3
lower house, amending constitution of,
14, 302
membership—
new diocese, from, **14**, 912
reorganisation scheme, after, **14**, 911
promulgation of canons by, **14**, 21–22
transfer of functions from, **14**, 767–8
upper house—
bishops, jurisdiction on trial of, **14**, 557
declaration by, recording, **14**, 609
suffragan bishops to be members of,
14, 809

co-operative
loans to invest in, relief for interest payments
on, **44(4)**, [409]–[410]

co-operative association
interest paid by, **44(1)**, [325]
meaning, **44(1)**, [325]

co-operative housing association. *See also*
housing co-operative
housing management, financial assistance for,
22, [412]
meaning, **22**, [5], [455]
provisions not applicable to, **22**, [99]

**co-ordinated on-line register of electors
(CORE)**
amended provisions, **15(S)**, Elections 4
electoral registration officer—
area for which acting, **15(3)**, [593]
provisions relating to, **15(3)**, [597]
registration information, supply of,
15(3), [593]
information—
identifying—
Electoral Commission, report by,
15(S), Elections 53–4
meaning, **15(S)**, Elections 50
obligatory provision of,
15(S), Elections 55–9
removal of name from register,
15(S), Elections 59
voluntary provision of,
15(S), Elections 50–2
use of, **15(3)**, [594]; **15(S)**, Elections 48–9
keeper—
corporate sole, establishment of,
15(S), Elections 46–7
duties of, **15(3)**, [593]
Electoral Commission as, **15(3)**, [596]

co-ordinated on-line register of electors (CORE)—*contd*
  keeper—*contd*
    facilities and equipment, **15(3)**, [597]
    grants to, **15(3)**, [595]
    information, supply of, **15(3)**, [597]
    payments to, **15(3)**, [597]
  payments under, **15(3)**, [597]
  registration information, supply of,
    15(3), [593]
  scheme—
    establishment, **15(3)**, [593]
    grants, **15(3)**, [595]
    procedure, **15(3)**, [598]
    provisions of, **15(3)**, [597]
    termination, **15(3)**, [593]

copyhold
  abolition, **20**, [1]
  enfranchisement—
    deemed date of, **20**, [801]
    provisions applying, **20**, [501]
  land, former. *See under* **mines and mining**
  service of customs, for, vesting of, **13**, [543]

copyright
  Act, extension of, **11(1)**, [592]–[593]
  action—
    author, presumption of, **11(1)**, [590]
    proof of facts, **11(1)**, [590]
    subsistence, presumption of, **11(1)**, [590]
  Acts and Measures, in, **11(1)**, [991]
  anonymous work, in—
    assumptions as to, **11(1)**, [863]
    building, reconstruction of, **11(1)**, [579]
    duration of, **11(1)**, [613]
    painting, etc, of, **11(1)**, [579]
    provisions applying to, **11(1)**, [581]
    unpublished, **11(1)**, [1000]
  archives, special exceptions for, **11(1)**, [577]
  artistic work—
    advertisement of sale of, **11(1)**, [869]
    building, meaning, **11(1)**, [790]
    cable broadcast as, **11(1)**, [579]
    cinematograph film, inclusion in,
      11(1), [579]
    design derived from, exploitation,
      11(1), [858]
    exceptions from protection, **11(1)**, [579]
    fair dealing, **11(1)**, [579]
    graphic work, meaning, **11(1)**, [790]
    incidental inclusion in, **11(1)**, [823]
    industrial design—
      false registration of, **11(1)**, [612]
      made from, **11(1)**, [580]
    infringement. *See* infringement *below*
    instruction or examination, acts for
      purposes of, **11(1)**, [830]
    judicial proceeding, used in, **11(1)**, [579]
    lending copies of, **11(1)**, [872]
      royalty or other sum payable for,
        11(1), [967]
    meaning, **11(1)**, [573], [790]
    ownership, **11(1)**, [574]
    period of, **11(1)**, [573], [800]

copyright—*contd*
  artistic work—*contd*
    presumptions, **11(1)**, [917]
    public display, on, representations of,
      11(1), [868]
    published, **11(1)**, [573]
    reproductions, **11(1)**, [605]
    restricted acts, **11(1)**, [573]
    same artist, subsequent works made by,
      11(1), [870]
    same author, copy by, **11(1)**, [579]
    summary of provisions, **11(1)**, [415]
    television broadcast, inclusion in,
      11(1), [579]
    temporary copies, making, **11(1)**, [820]
    three-dimensional copy, **11(1)**, [579]
    unpublished, **11(1)**, [573]
  assignment of, **11(1)**, [597], [620], [898],
    [1175]
  author—
    computer-generated work, of, **11(1)**, [797]
    employment, made during, **11(1)**, [574]
    entitlement of, **11(1)**, [574]
    meaning, **11(1)**, [797]
    moral rights. *See* **moral rights**
    presumptions, **11(1)**, [917]
    qualification by references to, **11(1)**, [981]
    transitional provisions, **11(1)**, [1175]
    unknown, **11(1)**, [797]
  authorship, false attribution of, **11(1)**, [605],
    [620]
  bankrupt owner, **4(2)**, [563]
  Board of Trade, regulations on copying,
    11(1), [577]
  body corporate, seal of, **11(1)**, [1008]
  British Library Board, delivery of publications
    to, **13**, [49]
  British works, protection of, **11(1)**, [596]
  broadcast—
    archival purposes, recording for,
      11(1), [883]
    cable re-transmission in, collective exercise
      of certain rights in relation to,
      11(1), [970]
    duration of, **11(1)**, [803]
    educational establishment—
      licences for, **11(1)**, [948]
      performing etc in activities of,
        11(1), [832]
      recording by, **11(1)**, [833]
    encrypted transmission, **11(1)**, [793]
    free public showing, **11(1)**, [879]
    incidental inclusion in, **11(1)**, [823]
    incidental recording for, **11(1)**, [875]
    joint ownership, work of, **11(1)**, [798]
    meaning, **11(1)**, [793]
    photographs of, **11(1)**, [878]
    programmes, provision of advance
      information about—
      copyright licensing, **11(1)**, [1187]
      duty to, **11(1)**, [1183]
      programme service, meaning,
        11(1), [1184]
    public reading or recitation, of,
      11(1), [865]

copyright—*contd*
  broadcast—*contd*
    repeat, **11(1)**, [803]
    restricted act, as, **11(1)**, [811]
    satellite—
      safeguards, **11(1)**, [794]
      transmission, place of, **11(1)**, [793]
    sound recordings, use of in. *See* sound
      recordings *below*
    sub-titled copies, provision on, **11(1)**, [882]
    supervision and control, recording for,
      11(1), [876]
    telecommunications system, relayed by,
      11(1), [793]
    time-shifting, **11(1)**, [877]
    use of information, **11(1)**, [1188]
    wireless broadcast by cable, reception and
      re-transmission in, **11(1)**, [880]
      royalty or other sum payable for,
        11(1), [881]
  building—
    reconstruction of, **11(1)**, [871]
    representation of, making, **11(1)**, [868]
  cable programme—
    Act, application to, **11(1)**, [608]
    entitlement to, **11(1)**, [585]
    judicial proceedings, used in, **11(1)**, [585]
    meaning, **11(1)**, [585], [795]
    paying audience, seen by, **11(1)**, [585]
    period of, **11(1)**, [585]
    repetition of, **11(1)**, [585]
    restricted acts, **11(1)**, [585]
    subsistence of, **11(1)**, [585]
    works used in, **11(1)**, [576]
  cable programme service—
    copyright not subsisting, where,
      11(1), [795]
    exceptions from definition of, **11(1)**, [795]
    meaning, **11(1)**, [795]
  cinematograph film—
    cable programme, in, **11(1)**, [602]
    judicial proceeding, used in, **11(1)**, [583]
    meaning, **11(1)**, [583]
    period of, **11(1)**, [583]
    cable programme, in, **11(1)**, [602]
    judicial proceeding, used in, **11(1)**, [583]
    meaning, **11(1)**, [583]
    period of, **11(1)**, [583]
    transitional provisions,
      11(1), [617]. *See also* film *below*
  college, rights conferred on, **11(1)**, [606]
  colonies, extension to, **11(1)**, [592]
  commissioned work, in, **11(1)**, [574]
    public reading or recitation in, **11(1)**, [865]
    reception and re-transmission of broadcast
      in, **11(1)**, [880]
    sound recordings, use of in. *See* sound
      recordings *below*
    sub-titled copies, provision on, **11(1)**, [882]
    supervision and control, recording for,
      11(1), [876]
    time-shifting, **11(1)**, [877]
  computer program—
    adaptation of, **11(1)**, [783]
    avoidance of certain terms, **11(1)**, [1161]

copyright—*contd*
  computer program—*contd*
    back up copies, **11(1)**, [852]
    circumvention of technical devices applied
      to, **11(1)**, [1153]
    computer storage, references to,
      11(1), [784]
    county court jurisdiction, **11(1)**, [930]
    decompilation, **11(1)**, [853]
    literary work, treated as, **11(1)**, [783]
    observing, **11(1)**, [854]
    other permitted acts, **11(1)**, [855]
    studying, **11(1)**, [854]
    testing, **11(1)**, [854]
  Copyright Tribunal. *See* **Copyright Tribunal**
  country of origin, meaning, **11(1)**, [805]
  Crown—
    entitlement of, **11(1)**, [600], [620]
    material communicated to, **11(1)**, [849]
    presumptions, **11(1)**, [919]
    subsistence of, **11(1)**, [990]
    transitional provisions, **11(1)**, [1175]
  database—
    avoidance of certain terms, **11(1)**, [1162]
    meaning, **11(1)**, [789]
    permitted acts, **11(1)**, [856]
  definitions, **11(1)**, [608], [1009]
  dependent territories, **11(1)**, [1175]
  designs—
    artistic work, derived from, exploitation,
      11(1), [858]
    documents and models, article made to,
      11(1), [857]
    registration, things done in reliance on,
      11(1), [859]
    transitional provisions, **11(1)**, [1175]
  dramatic work—
    adaptation, **11(1)**, [572], [578]
    anthologies for educational use, in,
      11(1), [831]
    broadcast, reproduction used for,
      11(1), [576]
    collection, part used in, **11(1)**, [576]
    criticism or review, used for, **11(1)**, [576],
      [822]
    current events, used for reporting,
      11(1), [576]
    educational establishment—
      performing etc in activities of,
        11(1), [832]
      reprographic copying by, **11(1)**, [834]
    exceptions, **11(1)**, [576]
    infringement. *See* infringement *below*
    instructions or examination, acts for
      purposes of, **11(1)**, [830]
    judicial proceeding, used in, **11(1)**, [576]
    lending copies of, **11(1)**, [872]
    royalty or other sum payable for,
      11(1), [967]
    meaning, **11(1)**, [608], [788]
    ownership, **11(1)**, [574]
    period of, **11(1)**, [572], [800]
    presumptions, **11(1)**, [917]
    public reading, **11(1)**, [576], [865]
    published editions, in each, **11(1)**, [586]

copyright—*contd*
  dramatic work—*contd*
    research or private study, used for,
      11(1), [576], [821]
    restricted acts, **11(1)**, [572]
    subsistence of, **11(1)**, [572]
    summary of provisions, **11(1)**, [415]
    temporary copies, making, **11(1)**, [820]
    words as part of musical work, **11(1)**, [578]
  drawing, in, commissioned, **11(1)**, [574]
  duration of, transitional provisions,
    11(1), [1175]
  education, material used for, **11(1)**, [603],
    [831]
  educational establishments—
    licences, **11(1)**, [948]
    meaning, **11(1)**, [1006]
  EEA, meaning, **11(1)**, [1004]
  electro-magnetic energy, broadcast by,
    11(1), [595]
  electronic rights management information—
    alteration of, **11(1)**, [1160]
    removal of, **11(1)**, [1160]
  enemy of, licence—
    comptroller, grant by, **50**, [208]
    validity of, **50**, [207]
    variation of, **50**, [207], [208]
  engraving, in—
    commissioned, **11(1)**, [574]
    period of, **11(1)**, [573]
  exclusive licence, subject to—
    licensee, rights of, **11(1)**, [589]
    meaning, **11(1)**, [589]
    proceedings, **11(1)**, [589]
  film—
    duration of, **11(1)**, [802]
    educational establishment, performing etc
      in activities of, **11(1)**, [832]
    expiry of copyright, acts permitted on
      assumption as to, **11(1)**, [873]
    incidental inclusion in, **11(1)**, [823]
    infringement. *See* infringement *below*
    lending copies of, **11(1)**, [872]
    meaning, **11(1)**, [792]
    presumptions, **11(1)**, [918]
    transfer of rental right—
      equitable remuneration for—
        Copyright Tribunal, reference of
          amount to, **11(1)**, [904]
        right to, **11(1)**, [903]
      presumption of, in production
        agreement, **11(1)**, [902]
  folklore, in, **11(1)**, [1000]
  folksongs, recordings of, **11(1)**, [867]
  foreign law not protecting, **11(1)**, [596]
  fraudulent reception of programmes—
    apparatus for, rights and remedies in respect
      of, **11(1)**, [1167]
    offence of, **11(1)**, [1163]
    rights and remedies in respect of apparatus
      for, **11(1)**, [1167]
    supplementary provisions, **11(1)**, [1168]
    unauthorised decoders, **11(1)**, [1164]
      forfeiture of, **11(1)**, [1166]
      search warrants for, **11(1)**, [1165]

copyright—*contd*
  future, agreement on, **11(1)**, [598]
  government department, work from,
    11(1), [600], [620]
  Hospital for Sick Children, provision for
    benefit of, **11(1)**, [602], [1181]
  industrial designs, exceptions in respect of,
    11(1), [580]
  infringement—
    account of profits, **11(1)**, [588]
    adaptation, by making, **11(1)**, [812]
    appeals, **11(1)**, [591]
    broadcasting, by, **11(1)**, [811]
    concurrent rights, exercise of, **11(1)**, [915]
    construction of building, by, **11(1)**, [588]
    copying, by, **11(1)**, [807]
    copyright, owner, actionable by,
      11(1), [907]
    damages, **11(1)**, [588], [908]
    delivery up, order for—
      civil proceedings, in, **11(1)**, [911]
      criminal proceedings, in, **11(1)**, [922]
      no longer available, where, **11(1)**, [927]
    electronic transmission, by, **11(1)**, [811]
    exceptions, **11(1)**, [576]
    exclusive licensee, rights and remedies of,
      11(1), [913]
    exhibition, by, **11(1)**, [587]
    forfeiture of copies, **11(1)**, [929]
    importation, by, **11(1)**, [575], [587], [813]
    injunction, **11(1)**, [588]
    issue of copies to the public, by,
      11(1), [808]
    lending to public, by, **11(1)**, [809]
    licence of right, undertaking to take,
      11(1), [910]
    non-exclusive licensee, infringements
      actionable by, **11(1)**, [914]
    offences—
      body corporate, by, **11(1)**, [924]
      county court jurisdiction, **11(1)**, [930]
      delivery up, order for, **11(1)**, [922]
      making or dealing with infringing
        articles, **11(1)**, [920]
      local weights and measures authority,
        enforcment by, **11(1)**, [921]
      search warrants, **11(1)**, [923]
      sheriff court jurisdiction, **11(1)**, [930]
    owner, action by, **11(1)**, [588]
    penalties, **11(1)**, [591]
    presumptions—
      Crown copyright, works subject to,
        11(1), [919]
      literary, dramatic, musical and artistic
        works, relevant to, **11(1)**, [917]
      sound recordings and films, as to,
        11(1), [918]
    public performance, by permitting,
      11(1), [575], [810]
    remedies, **11(1)**, [588]–[591]
    rental to public, by, **11(1)**, [809]
    secondary—
      apparatus, provision of, **11(1)**, [817]
      importing, **11(1)**, [813]
      possession or dealing, **11(1)**, [814]

copyright—*contd*
  infringement—*contd*
    secondary—*contd*
      premises for infringing performance,
        permitting use of, **11(1)**, [816]
      providing means to make infringing
        copies, **11(1)**, [815]
    service providers, injunctions against,
      11(1), [909]
    setting or letting for hire, by, **11(1)**, [575],
      [587]
    showing or playing of work in public, by,
      11(1), [810]
    transitional provisions, **11(1)**, [616], [1175]
  infringement authorised by Crown, liability
    for, **13**, [12]
  infringing copy—
    forfeiture, **11(1)**, [929]
    importing, **11(1)**, [813]
    meaning, **11(1)**, [818]
    order for disposal of, **11(1)**, [928]
    possession or dealing, **11(1)**, [814]
      derogatory treatment, as, **11(1)**, [890]
    prohibited goods, treated as,
      11(1), [925]–[926]
    providing means to make, **11(1)**, [815]
    seizure of, **11(1)**, [912]
  international organisations, **11(1)**, [594],
    [999], [1175]
  joint authorship, in case of, **11(1)**, [581],
    [614], [798]
  judicial proceedings, acts for purposes of,
    11(1), [846]
  legal deposit libraries, copying by, **13**, [461]
  libraries and archives—
    copy required as condition of export,
      11(1), [844]
    legal deposit libraries, copying by,
      11(1), [845]
    librarians, copying by—
      articles in periodicals, **11(1)**, [837]
      generally, **11(1)**, [577]
      multiple copies, restriction on,
        11(1), [839]
      other libraries, supply of copies to,
        11(1), [841]
      parts of published works, **11(1)**, [838]
      replacement copies, **11(1)**, [842]
      signed declaration by, **11(1)**, [836]
      unpublished works, **11(1)**, [843]
    person requesting copy, false declaration
      by, **11(1)**, [836]
    prescribed, **11(1)**, [836]
  licence—
    adverse Competition Commission report,
      exercise of powers, **11(1)**, [969]
    Copyright Tribunal, factors taken into
      account by. *See* **Copyright Tribunal**
    exclusive licensee, rights and remedies of,
      11(1), [900], [913]
    grant of, **11(1)**, [597], [620]
    right, of, undertaking to take, **11(1)**, [910]
    successor in title, binding on, **11(1)**, [898]
    transitional provisions, **11(1)**, [1175]

copyright—*contd*
  licensing—
    body—
      application of provisions, **11(1)**, [939]
      meaning, **11(1)**, [931]
      summary of provisions, **11(1)**, [415]
    Copyright Tribunal, reference to. *See*
      Copyright Tribunal
    excepted sound recordings, notification of
      licence for, **11(1)**, [944]–[945]
  licensing scheme—
    application of provisions, **11(1)**, [932]
    certification of, **11(1)**, [968]
    meaning, **11(1)**, [931]
    reprographic copying, for—
      appeals against orders, **11(1)**, [964]
      coverage of, power to extend,
        11(1), [962]
      implied indemnity, **11(1)**, [961]
      inquiries, **11(1)**, [965]
      statutory licence, **11(1)**, [966]
      variation or discharge of order
        extending, **11(1)**, [963]
    summary of provisions, **11(1)**, [415]
  literary work—
    adaptation, **11(1)**, [572], [812]
    anthologies for educational use, in,
      11(1), [831]
    broadcast, reproduction used for,
      11(1), [576]
    collection, part used in, **11(1)**, [576]
    criticism or review, used for, **11(1)**, [576],
      [822]
    current events, used for reporting,
      11(1), [576]
    educational establishment—
      performing etc in activities of,
        11(1), [832]
      reprographic copying by, **11(1)**, [834]
    exceptions, **11(1)**, [576]
    infringement. *See* infringement *above*
    instruction or examination, acts for
      purposes of, **11(1)**, [830]
    judicial proceeding, used in, **11(1)**, [576]
    lending copies of, **11(1)**, [872]
      royalty or other sum payable for,
        11(1), [967]
    meaning, **11(1)**, [788]
    ownership of, **11(1)**, [574]
    period of, **11(1)**, [572], [800]
    presumptions, **11(1)**, [917]
    public reading, **11(1)**, [576], [865]
    published editions, in each, **11(1)**, [586]
    research or private study, used for,
      11(1), [576], [821]
    restricted acts, **11(1)**, [572]
    school, performed in, **11(1)**, [603]
    subsistence of, **11(1)**, [572]
    summary of provisions, **11(1)**, [415]
    temporary copies, making, **11(1)**, [820]
    words as part of musical work, **11(1)**, [578]
  meaning, **11(1)**, [571], [786]
  moral rights. *See* **moral rights**
  musical work—
    adaptation, **11(1)**, [572], [812]

copyright—*contd*
 musical work—*contd*
  broadcast, reproduction used in,
   11(1), [576]
  criticism or review, used for, **11(1)**, [576],
   [822]
  current events, used for reporting,
   11(1), [576]
  educational establishment—
   performing etc in activities of,
    11(1), [832]
   reprographic copying by, **11(1)**, [834]
  exceptions, **11(1)**, [576]
  infringement. *See* infringement *above*
  instruction or examination, acts for
   purposes of, **11(1)**, [830]
  judicial proceeding, used in, **11(1)**, [576]
  lending copies of, **11(1)**, [872]
   royalty or other sum payable for,
    11(1), [967]
  meaning, **11(1)**, [788]
  ownership, **11(1)**, [574]
  period of, **11(1)**, [572], [800]
  presumptions, **11(1)**, [574]
  published editions, in each, **11(1)**, [586]
  record, and, **11(1)**, [578]
  research or private study, used for,
   11(1), [576], [821]
  restricted acts, **11(1)**, [572]
  royalties, **11(1)**, [578]
  school, performed in, **11(1)**, [603]
  subsistence of, **11(1)**, [572]
  summary of provisions, **11(1)**, [415]
  temporary copies, making, **11(1)**, [820]
 nature of, **11(1)**, [571]
 new work incorporating old work,
  11(1), [577]
 newsreel, in, **11(1)**, [583]
 Northern Ireland Assembly, Bills, in,
  11(1), [995]
 official register, material on, **11(1)**, [848]
 original works, in, **11(1)**, [572]
 owner—
  construction of references to, **11(1)**, [1005]
  exclusive rights of, **11(1)**, [806]
  first—
   meaning, **11(1)**, [799]
   transitional provisions, **11(1)**, [1175]
  person being, **11(1)**, [609]
 painting, in, commissioned, **11(1)**, [572]
 parliamentary—
  Bills, in, **11(1)**, [993]
  Houses of Parliament, provisions on,
   11(1), [998]
  subsistence of, **11(1)**, [992]
  transitional provisions, **11(1)**, [1175]
 parliamentary proceedings, acts for purposes
  of, **11(1)**, [846]
 performers' rights. *See* **performers' rights**
 Performing Right Tribunal. *See* **Performing
  Right Tribunal**
 periodical, article in, **11(1)**, [577]
 permitted acts—
  adaptations, **11(1)**, [884]

copyright—*contd*
 permitted acts—*contd*
  advertisement of sale of artistic work,
   11(1), [869]
  anonymous works, assumptions as to,
   11(1), [863]
  anthologies for educational use,
   11(1), [831]
  broadcasts—
   archival purposes, recording for,
    11(1), [883]
   free public showing, **11(1)**, [879]
   photographs of, **11(1)**, [878]
   reception and re-transmission of wireless
    broadcast by cable, **11(1)**, [880]
   sub-titled copies, provision on,
    11(1), [882]
   supervision and control, recording for,
    11(1), [876]
   time-shifting, **11(1)**, [877]
  buildings, reconstruction of, **11(1)**, [871]
  club or society, playing recordings for,
   11(1), [874]
  computer programs—
   back up copies, **11(1)**, [852]
   decompilation, **11(1)**, [853]
   other acts, **11(1)**, [855]
  criticism, **11(1)**, [822]
  Crown, material communicated to,
   11(1), [849]
  databases, **11(1)**, [856]
  design—
   artistic work, derived from,
    exploitation, **11(1)**, [858]
   documents and models, article made to,
    11(1), [606]
   registration, things done in reliance on,
    11(1), [859]
  educational establishment—
   performing etc in activities of,
    11(1), [832]
   recording by, **11(1)**, [833]
   reprographic copying by, **11(1)**, [834]
  electronic form, transfer of copies of works
   in, **11(1)**, [862]
  folksongs, recordings of, **11(1)**, [867]
  generally, **11(1)**, [819]
  incidental inclusion, **11(1)**, [823]
  incidental recording, **11(1)**, [875]
  instruction of examination, for purposes
   of, **11(1)**, [830]
  libraries and archives, by. *See* libraries and
   archives *above*
  news reporting, **11(1)**, [822]
  official register, material on, **11(1)**, [848]
  parliamentary or judicial proceedings, for,
   11(1), [846]
  pseudonymous works, assumptions as to,
   11(1), [863]
  public display, representation of artistic
   works on, **11(1)**, [868]
  public inspection, material open to,
   11(1), [848]
  public reading or recitation, **11(1)**, [865]
  public records, copies of, **11(1)**, [850]

copyright—*contd*
  permitted acts—*contd*
    research and private study, **11(1)**, [821]
    review, **11(1)**, [822]
    Royal Commissions and statutory inquiries, for, **11(1)**, [847]
    same artist, subsequent works made by, **11(1)**, [870]
    scientific or technical articles, abstracts of, **11(1)**, [866]
    spoken words, use of notes or recordings of, **11(1)**, [864]
    statutory authority, acts done under, **11(1)**, [851]
    typefaces—
      articles for producing material in, **11(1)**, [861]
      ordinary course of printing, use in, **11(1)**, [860]
  perpetual, **11(1)**, [1175]
  photograph, in—
    commissioned, **11(1)**, [574]
    meaning, **11(1)**, [790]
    period of, **11(1)**, [573]
  prospective ownership of, **11(1)**, [899]
  protection—
    British ships, aircraft and hovercraft, extension to, **11(1)**, [989]
    circumvention of—
      computer programs, technical devices applied to, **11(1)**, [1153]
      technological measures, **11(1)**, [1154]–[1159]
        remedy where prevention of permitted acts, **11(1)**, [1158], [1178]–[1180]
    colonies, countries ceasing to be, **11(1)**, [985]
    countries to which extending, **11(1)**, [984]
    denial where adequate protection not given to British works, **11(1)**, [987]
    foreign countries, in, **11(1)**, [593]
    Order in Council, application by, **11(1)**, [986]
    qualification by reference to—
      author, **11(1)**, [981]
      country of first publication, **11(1)**, [982]
      place of transmission, **11(1)**, [983]
    qualification for, **11(1)**, [980]
    territorial water and continental shelf, **11(1)**, [988]
    transitional provisions, **11(1)**, [1175]
  pseudonymous work, in—
    assumptions as to, **11(1)**, [863]
    duration of, **11(1)**, [613]
    provisions applying to, **11(1)**, [581]
  public inspection, material open to, **11(1)**, [848]
  public place, work in, **11(1)**, [579]
  public records, in, **11(1)**, [604], [850]
  publication—
    commercial, meaning, **11(1)**, [1007]
    meaning, **11(1)**, [609], [1007]
  qualified person, meaning, **11(1)**, [571]
  regulations, provisions on, **11(1)**, [607]

copyright—*contd*
  reproduction, meaning of, **11(1)**, [608]
  restricted acts—
    generally, **11(1)**, [806]
    infringement. *See* infringement *above*
  rights and privileges, savings for, **11(1)**, [1002]
  Royal Commissions, acts for purposes of, **11(1)**, [848]
  savings, **11(1)**, [1175]
  scientific or technical articles, abstracts of, **11(1)**, [866]
  Scottish Parliament, Bills, in, **11(1)**, [994]
  sculpture—
    meaning, **11(1)**, [790]
    representation of making, **11(1)**, [868]
    substance in, **11(1)**, [579]
  sheriff court jurisdiction, **11(1)**, [930]
  sound broadcast, in—
    cable programme service, transmission in, **11(1)**, [585], [601]
    entitlement to, **11(1)**, [584]
    extension of provisions, **11(1)**, [595]
    judicial proceedings, used in, **11(1)**, [584]
    meaning, **11(1)**, [584], [793]
    period of, **11(1)**, [584]
    public, heard in, **11(1)**, [601]
    restricted acts, **11(1)**, [584]
    subsistence of, **11(1)**, [584]
    See also broadcast *above*
  sound recording, in—
    action, facts in, **11(1)**, [590]
    broadcasts and cable programme services, right to use in—
      circumstances in which available, **11(1)**, [953]
      conditions, etc, references about, **11(1)**, [957]
      conditions of exercise, **11(1)**, [955]
      factors taken into account, **11(1)**, [959]
      notice of intention to exercise, **11(1)**, [954]
      payments, application to settle, **11(1)**, [956]
      review of order, application for, **11(1)**, [958]
    cable programme, in, **11(1)**, [602]
    club or society, playing for, **11(1)**, [874]
    commissioned, **11(1)**, [582]
    duration of, **11(1)**, [801]
    educational establishment, performing etc in activities of, **11(1)**, [832]
    entitlement to, **11(1)**, [582]
    folksongs, of, **11(1)**, [867]
    incidental inclusion in, **11(1)**, [823]
    infringement. *See* infringement *above*
    lending copies of, **11(1)**, [872]
    meaning, **11(1)**, [582], [791]
    period of, **11(1)**, [582], [583]
    presumptions, **11(1)**, [918]
    public, heard in, **11(1)**, [865]
    restricted acts, **11(1)**, [582]
    transitional provisions, **11(1)**, [617]
  spoken words, use of notes or recording of, **11(1)**, [864]

copyright—*contd*
statutory authority, acts done under,
 11(1), [851]
statutory inquiries, acts for purposes of,
 11(1), [847]
statutory recording licence abolition,
 11(1), [1175]
subsistence of, transitional provisions,
 11(1), [1175]
sufficient acknowledgment, meaning of,
 11(1), [576]
summary of provisions, **11(1)**, [415]
television broadcast, in—
 cable programme service, transmission in,
  11(1), [585], [601]
 entitlement to, **11(1)**, [584]
 extension of provisions, **11(1)**, [595]
 judicial proceedings, used in, **11(1)**, [584]
 meaning, **11(1)**, [584]
 organisations, **11(1)**, [615]
 period of, **11(1)**, [584]
 public, seen in, **11(1)**, [584], [601]
 repetition, **11(1)**, [584]
 restricted acts, **11(1)**, [584]
 subsistence of, **11(1)**, [584]
 transitional provisions, **11(1)**, [617]
 See also broadcast *above*
television organisations, appointment of,
 11(1), [615]
transitional provisions, **11(1)**, [616], [1001],
 [1175]
typefaces—
 articles for producing material in,
  11(1), [861]
 meaning, **11(1)**, [1009]
 ordinary course of printing, use in,
  11(1), [860]
typographical arrangement, in published
 edition—
 duration of, **11(1)**, [804]
 meaning, **11(1)**, [796]
university, rights conferred on, **11(1)**, [606]
unpublished works—
 anonymous, **11(1)**, [1000]
 passing by will with, **11(1)**, [599], [901]
visually impaired persons, making accessible
 copy for—
 infringement, limitations following,
  11(1), [828]
 intermediate copy, approved body holding,
  11(1), [826]
 licensing scheme, **11(1)**, [827]
 meaning, **11(1)**, [829]
 multiple, **11(1)**, [825]
 single, **11(1)**, [824]
Welsh Assembly—
 Bills, in, **11(1)**, [997]
 Measures, in, **11(1)**, [996]
will, passing under, **11(1)**, [599], [620]
 transitional provisions, **11(1)**, [1175]
 unpublished work, **11(1)**, [901]
works made before 1st July 1912, **11(1)**, [621]
works, rights subsisting in, **11(1)**, [787]

Copyright Tribunal
appeal from, **11(1)**, [979]
award of interest, **11(1)**, [978]
chairman, qualification as, **11(1)**, [971]
constitution, **11(1)**, [971], [974]
jurisdiction, **11(1)**, [975], [1059]
licences—
 conditions imposed by promoters of events,
  reflecting, **11(1)**, [949]
 educational establishments, for, **11(1)**, [948]
 payments in respect of underlying rights,
  reflecting, **11(1)**, [950]
 relevant considerations, having regard to,
  11(1), [952]
 reprographic copying, for, **11(1)**, [947]
 works included in re-transmission, in
  respect of, **11(1)**, [951]
licensing body, licence granted by—
 expiring reference of, **11(1)**, [941]
 order as to, effect of, **11(1)**, [943]
 proposed, reference of, **11(1)**, [940]
 review of order, application for,
  11(1), [942]
 unreasonable discrimination, having regard
  to, **11(1)**, [946]
licensing scheme—
 licence—
  application for, **11(1)**, [936]
  entitlement to, application for review of
   order, **11(1)**, [937]
 order as to, effect of, **11(1)**, [938]
 reference of—
  further, **11(1)**, [935]
  operation in, **11(1)**, [933]–[934]
  proposed, **11(1)**, [933]
 reprographic copying, for, appeal against
  extension, **11(1)**, [964]
 sound recordings, excepted, notification of
  licence for, **11(1)**, [944]–[945]
 summary of provisions, **11(1)**, [415]
 unreasonable discrimination, having regard
  to, **11(1)**, [946]
members—
 office of, **11(1)**, [972]
 removal of, **11(1)**, [972]
 remuneration, **11(1)**, [973]
 resignation, **11(1)**, [972]
 temporary, **11(1)**, [972]
orders, proof of, **11(1)**, [977]
performer, consent on behalf of,
 11(1), [1026]
Performing Right Tribunal renamed as,
 11(1), [971]
proceedings—
 constitution for, **11(1)**, [974]
 costs, **11(1)**, [977]
 pending on commencement, **11(1)**, [1175]
rules, general power to make, **11(1)**, [976]
sound recordings used in broadcasts—
 conditions, etc, references about,
  11(1), [957]
 factors taken into account, **11(1)**, [959]
 payments, applications to settle,
  11(1), [956]

Copyright Tribunal—*contd*
  sound recordings used in broadcasts—*contd*
    review of order, application for,
      11(1), [958]
  staff, **11(1)**, [972]

Corfe Castle
  lord of the manor, rights of, **25(1)**, [55]

corn. *See also* **cereals**
  returns of purchases, hundredweight,
    substitution of, **1(1)**, [861]
  sale of, weights for, **1(1)**, [861]
  weights for basis of payment, **1(1)**, [248]

corn rent
  apportionment, schemes for, **14**, 551
  annuities, redemption of, **14**, 20
  extinguishment, schemes, **14**, 551

Cornwall
  sea-sand, right to take, **49**, [2]–[3]

Cornwall, Duchy of
  administration of estates provisions,
    application, **18**, [561]
  agricultural housing, application of
    provisions, **21**, [486]
  coal mining etc provisions, application,
    17(2), [191]
  driver information system apparatus on land
    of, **38(1)**, [147]
  escheat to, abolition, **18**, [548]
  food emergency orders, exclusion of
    provisions, **1(2)**, [250]
  gas, controlled operations on underground
    storage, **17(1)**, [318]
  generally, **10**, [1]
  land drainage—
    provisions, application of, **19(3)**, [249]
    rights, saving of, **19(3)**, [249]; **20**, [316]
  land of—
    access to, **36**, [641]
    cycle tracks, application of provisions,
      37, [348]
    long distance routes over, **36**, [641]
    right of way over, **37**, [97]
  land, use for literary or scientific institution,
    13, [52]
  limitation of actions—
    application of provisions, **19(3)**, [767]
    foreign law, **19(3)**, [780]
  net revenues, meaning of, **10**, [222]
  opencast coal mining on lands, **17(1)**, [206]
  pesticides, control of, **1(2)**, [250]
  revenues, effect on civil list, **10**, [212]
  road traffic enactments, application, **37**, [303]
  shellfish fisheries, consent to orders as to,
    1(1), [689]
  solicitor for, privileges etc, saving for
    11(2), [369]; **11(4)**, [463]
  widow of Duke, civil list provision for,
    10, [218]

coronation
  oath, **10**, [33]–[36]

coroner
  accounts, **11(1)**, [1234]
  annual returns, **11(1)**, [1236]
  appointment of—
    additional, **11(1)**, [1209]
    deputy, **11(1)**, [1212]
    qualification for, **11(1)**, [1207]
    relevant council, by, **11(1)**, [1206]
  assistant deputy—
    appointment of, **11(1)**, [1212]
    functions of, **11(1)**, [1213]
  burial, order for, **36**, [35]
  circuit judge, eligible to be, **11(2)**, [261]
  councillors, disqualification of, **11(1)**, [1207]
  court records, preservation, **18**, [189], [194]
  cremation, saving for jurisdiction, **5(2)**, [437]
  deputy—
    appointment of, **11(1)**, [1212]
    functions of, **11(1)**, [1213]
  districts, **11(1)**, [1209]
    Wales, **11(1)**, [1210]
  exhumation, order for, **11(1)**, [1230]
  ex-officio, **11(1)**, [1241]
  expenses, payment of, **11(1)**, [1233]
  fees and allowances paid by, **11(1)**, [1231]
  fine imposed by, **11(3)**, [63]
  human tissue required for functions of,
    28, [777]
  indemnity, **11(1)**, [1235]
  inquest—
    duty to hold, **11(1)**, [1214]
    order to hold, **11(1)**, [1219]
    verdict, **11(1)**, [1217]
    See also **inquest**
  jurisdiction, **11(1)**, [1211]
  jurisdiction over, **11(1)**, [1241]
  offences by, **11(1)**, [1208]
  office of, **11(1)**, [1205]
  pensions, **11(1)**, [1208], [1246]
  post-mortem examination—
    direction of, **11(1)**, [1228]
    order for, **11(1)**, [1226]
    removal of body, order for, **11(1)**, [1229]
    request to specially qualified persons to
      make, **11(1)**, [1227]
  powers, basis of, **11(1)**, [1205]
  prisons, jurisdiction as to, **12(1)**, [275AA]
  qualifications, **11(1)**, [1207]
  Queen's household, of, **11(1)**, [1237], [1247]
  recognizances forfeited by, **11(3)**, [63]
  removal from office, **11(1)**, [1208]
  remuneration, **11(1)**, [1208]
  resignation, **11(1)**, [1208]
  salary, **11(1)**, [1208], [1246]
  special examinations, order for, **11(1)**, [1227]
  summary of provisions, **11(1)**, [1205]
  treasure trove jurisdiction, **11(1)**, [1238]
  vacancy in office of, **11(1)**, [1206]
  visiting force, jurisdiction over, **3**, [446]

corporal punishment
  no right to give, **15(1)**, [682]

corporate bonds
qualifying—
relevant transactions, **43(1)**, [431]
reorganisations involving, **43(1)**, [431]

corporate governance
rules, **8(1)**, [1347], [1351]

corporate venturing scheme
advance clearance, **43(1)**, [516]
amended provisions, **43(S)**, 1122–3, 1453
amendment of provisions, **43(1)**, [517];
43(2), [70]
associate, meaning, **43(1)**, [517]
company restructuring, **43(1)**, [515]
deferral relief, **43(1)**, [514]
disposal of shares—
identification of shares, **43(1)**, [517]
meaning, **43(1)**, [517]
relief for losses on, **43(1)**, [513]
employees of company in which investment
made, limit on, **43(S)**, 684
excluded activities—
coal production, **43(S)**, 1123
receipt of royalties and licence fees,
43(S), 687
shipbuilding, **43(S)**, 1123
steel production, **43(S)**, 1123
gross assets of issuers of shares or securities,
limits on, **43(S)**, 343
interpretation, **43(1)**, [517]
investing company—
chargeable assets, shares being, **43(1)**, [508]
meaning, **43(1)**, [508]
no control requirement, **43(1)**, [508]
no material interest requirement,
43(1), [508]
no reciprocal arrangements requirement,
43(1), [508]
no tax avoidance requirement, **43(1)**, [508]
non-financial activities requirement,
43(1), [508]
relevant preference shares, **43(1)**, [508]
investment relief—
attributable to shares, determination of
loss, **43(1)**, [517]
attribution to shares, **43(1)**, [511]
compliance certificates, **43(1)**, [511]
appeals, **43(1)**, [511]
fraudulent, **43(1)**, [511]
compliance statements, **43(1)**, [511]
fraudulent, **43(1)**, [511]
eligibility for, **43(1)**, [507]
entitlement to claim, **43(1)**, [511]
form of, **43(1)**, [511]
maximum not obtained, **43(1)**, [512]
meaning, **43(1)**, [507]
qualification period, **43(1)**, [507]
withdrawal—
appeal, **43(1)**, [512]
connected persons, receipts of value by
and from, **43(1)**, [512]
disposal of shares, on, **43(1)**, [512]
information, Inland Revenue requiring,
43(1), [512]

corporate venturing scheme—*contd*
investment relief—*contd*
withdrawal—*contd*
insignificant repayments, disregard of,
43(1), [512]
interest, **43(1)**, [512]
investing company—
information to be provided by,
43(1), [512]
value received by, **43(1)**, [512]
issuing company, information to be
provided by, **43(1)**, [512]
means of, **43(1)**, [512]
other persons value received by,
43(1), [512]
period of restriction, **43(1)**, [512]
put and call options, attributable to,
43(1), [512]
replacement value, receipt of,
43(1), [512]
time limits, **43(1)**, [512]
issue of shares, meaning, **43(1)**, [517]
issuing company—
excluded activities—
facilities for another business, provision
of, **43(1)**, [509]
hotels and comparable establishments,
43(1), [509]
nursing home, **43(1)**, [509]
property development, **43(1)**, [509]
residential care homes, **43(1)**, [509]
royalties and licence fees, receipt of,
43(1), [509]
ships, leasing, **43(1)**, [509]
wholesale and retail distribution,
43(1), [509]
gross assets requirement, **43(1)**, [509]
independence requirement, **43(1)**, [509]
individual-owners requirement,
43(1), [509]
meaning, **43(1)**, [509]
partnerships and joint ventures
requirement, **43(1)**, [509]
property managing subsidiaries
requirement, **43(1)**, [509]
qualifying subsidiaries requirement,
43(1), [509]
trading activities requirement, **43(1)**, [509]
unquoted status requirement, **43(1)**, [509]
money raised, requirement as to, **43(1)**, [510]
no pre-arranged exits requirement,
43(1), [510]
no tax avoidance requirement, **43(1)**, [510]
nominees, shares held by, **43(1)**, [517]
qualifying 90% subsidiary, meaning,
43(S), 690
risk capital schemes, limit on amount raised
by, **43(S)**, 685–6
shares held continuously, meaning,
43(1), [517]
shares, requirement as to, **43(1)**, [510]

corporation
associated, relief from duty on transfer of
shares between, **41**, [68]

corporation—*contd*
    deed, execution by or on behalf of, **20**, [691]
    dissolution, vesting of legal estate on,
        20, [782]
    execution of instrument as deed, **20**, [692]
    fee simple vested in, deemed absolute,
        20, [631]
    indecent display offences by, **12(1)**, [716]
    indecent photographs of children, offences
        of, **12(1)**, [702]
    joint tenant, power to hold as, **20**, [459]
    coal mining etc provisions, application,
        17(2), [191]
        markets and fairs, relating to, **27**, [121]
        procedure on, **11(2)**, [170], [464], [581]
    representative, meaning, **11(2)**, [170]
    seal, affixation, **20**, [691]
    seat of—
        domicile provisions, **11(2)**, [834]–[835],
            [848]
        exclusive jurisdiction provisions,
            11(2), [835]
    service of documents on, **17(2)**, [187]
    sole—
        property or interest, devolution of,
            20, [781]
        vacancy in office, **20**, [781]

corporation tax
    accounting periods, assessed for, **44(1)**, [3]
    Acts—
        BLAGAB group reinsurers, modification of
            provisions for, **44(1)**, [654]–[656]
        interpretation of, **44(1)**, [616]
        meaning, **41**, [605]
    advance—
        abolition, **43(1)**, [339], [386]
        qualifying distribution, meaning,
            44(1), [19]
        surrender, **42**, [304]
        unrelieved surplus, regulations, **43(1)**, [340]
    appeals—
        notice of, **43(1)**, [406]
        Special Commissioners, to, **43(1)**, [406]
    assessable amounts, **43(1)**, [393]
    assessment—
        accounting periods, **44(1)**, [7]
        amount discovered to be incorrect,
            determination of, **43(1)**, [397]
        appeal against, **43(1)**, [398]
        basis of, **44(1)**, [7], [38]
        discovery, **43(1)**, [397]
        double, **43(1)**, [398]
        excessive, **43(1)**, [398]
        fraudulent or negligent conduct, finding
            of, **43(1)**, [397]
        loss of tax, discovery of, **43(1)**, [397]
        procedure, **43(1)**, [397]
        time limit for, **43(1)**, [397]
    avoidance. *See* **tax avoidance**
    BAA successor company, **4(1)**, [314]
    building society. *See* **building society**
    calculation of, **43(1)**, [394]
    capital allowances, claims for, **43(1)**, [401]

corporation tax—*contd*
    changes in trading stock, effect on trade
        profits, **43(S)**, 1140–1
    charge of, **43(2)**, [577]; **43(S)**, 15, 514, 839,
        1357, 1369
    charge to, **42**, [1]
    chargeable gain or loss—
        reallocation within group, **43(S)**, 1478–80
        stock lending, effect of insolvency of
            borrower, **43(S)**, 1481–3
    chargeable gains. *See* **capital gains tax**
    charging section, **44(1)**, [1]
    claims—
        capital allowances, for, **43(1)**, [401]
        consequential, **43(1)**, [399]
        group relief, for, **43(1)**, [400]
        more than one accounting period, for,
            43(1), [399]
        quantified, **43(1)**, [399]
        remediation of contaminated land, for,
            43(1), [403]
        research and development tax credit, for,
            43(1), [402]
        return—
            included in, **43(1)**, [394]
                not to be made without, **43(1)**, [394]
        single accounting period, for, **43(1)**, [399]
        time limits, **43(1)**, [399]
    close company participator, in connection
        with loans to, **42**, [249]
    close investment-holding company,
        44(1), [10]
    collection, **42**, [1]
    company distribution, not chargeable on,
        44(1), [109]
    company tax return. *See* **tax return**
    computation, companies with investment
        business and insurance companies, **42**, [952]
    controlled foreign company. *See* **controlled
        foreign company**
    currency to be used for—
        accounts, meaning, **43(1)**, [13]
        basic rule, **43(1)**, [8]
        functional currency—
            meaning, **43(1)**, [13]
            translating amounts into, **43(1)**, [12]
        sterling—
            equivalents, translating amounts into,
                43(1), [12]
            operating in but preparing accounts in
                other currency, **43(1)**, [9]
            other than, **43(1)**, [491]
                accounts in, **43(1)**, [10]–[11]
        translating amounts, **43(1)**, [12]
    deductions—
        expenses of management—
            accounting period to which referable,
                44(1), [43]
            company with investment business, of,
                44(1), [42]
            insurance company, of, **44(1)**, [45]
            local enterprise agency, contribution to,
                44(1), [48]
            local enterprise companies, contributions
                to, **44(1)**, [49]

corporation tax—*contd*

  deductions—*contd*

    not allowable, **44(1)**, [41]

    research and development, expenditure on, **44(1)**, [51]

    research associations, payments to, **44(1)**, [52]

    training and enterprise councils, contributions to, **44(1)**, [49]

    universities, payments to, **44(1)**, [52]

    urban regeneration companies, contributions to, **44(1)**, [50]

  derivative contracts. *See* **derivative contracts**

  distribution. *See* **distributions**

  dividend, not chargeable on, **44(1)**, [109]

  double taxation. *See* **double taxation relief**

  due and payable date, **43(1)**, [338]

  elections, **43(1)**, [399]

  employee share acquisition, relief on. *See* **shares**

  energy-saving items, deduction for expenditure on, **43(S)**, 519–20

  Financial Services and Markets Act 2000, levies and repayments under, **44(1)**, [46]

  financial year, assessments in, **44(1)**, [3]

  foreign currency accounting—

    amended provisions, **43(S)**, 1551–8

    sterling equivalents—

      basic rule, **43(S)**, 1552

      carried-back amounts, **43(S)**, 1552, 1554–5

      carried-forward amounts, **43(S)**, 1553, 1554–5

      commencement and transitional provisions, **43(S)**, 1555–7

    sterling losses—

      carried-back amounts, **43(S)**, 1553–5

      carried-forward amounts, **43(S)**, 1554–5

      commencement and transitional provisions, **43(S)**, 1555–7

  foreign enterprises, UK residents involved in, **43(S)**, 885–6

  franked investment income. *See* **franked investment income**

  furnished holiday accommodation, letting, **44(1)**, [359]

  Gas Boards and Council, **44(1)**, [371]

  general scheme of, **44(1)**, [3]

  group relief. *See* **group relief**

  harbour reorganisation scheme, **44(1)**, [374]

  income, charges on for purposes of, **43(2)**, [747]

  income, computation of, **44(1)**, [4]

  income tax law, application of, **44(1)**, [4]

  income tax, set off of, **44(1)**, [2]

  Inland Revenue determination—

    actual self-assessment, superseded by, **43(1)**, [397]

    extent of power to make, **43(1)**, [397]

    no return delivered, where, **43(1)**, [397]

    part compliance, on, **43(1)**, [397]

    self-assessment, having effect as, **43(1)**, [397]

corporation tax—*contd*

  intangible fixed assets. *See* **companies**

  land outside UK, Schedule D Case V income from, **44(1)**, [39]

  life assurance business—

    policy holders' fraction of profits, **42**, [978]

    policy holders' share of profits, **42**, [979]

  long funding leases *See* **long funding leases**

  loss relief—

    Case VI losses, **44(1)**, [200]

    charges on income, **44(1)**, [196]

    claim for, **44(1)**, [196]

    company reconstructions, **44(1)**, [199]

    government expenditure, write-off of, **44(1)**, [204]

    leasing contracts, **44(1)**, [199]

    other than terminal losses, **44(1)**, [196]

    overseas property business, **44(1)**, [195]

    pre-trading expenditure, **44(1)**, [205]

    profits of same or earlier accounting period, set off against, **44(1)**, [197]

    ring fence trade, losses of, set off against profits of an earlier accounting period, **44(1)**, [198]

    Schedule A, **44(1)**, [194]

    trading income, **44(1)**, [196]

  losses, temporary extension of carry back, **43(S)**, 1442

  main rate of, **43(2)**, [88], [577]; **43(S)**, 15

  mineral rights, expenses in relation to, **44(1)**, [100]

  nature of, **42**, [1]

  non-corporate distribution, rate, **43(2)**, [275], [580]

    abolition, **43(S)**, 16

  non-resident companies, assessment, collection and recovery from, **43(2)**, [216]

  non-resident company, charge on, **44(1)**, [5]

  notice of chargeability, duty to give, **43(1)**, [393]

  notice of coming within charge, duty to give, **43(2)**, [291]

  oil and gas exploration and appraisal, meaning, **44(1)**, [618]

  overdue, interest on, **42**, [218]

  overpaid—

    interest on, **44(1)**, [609]

    recovery of—

      application of provisions, **43(S)**, 1414

      claims, **43(S)**, 1723–8

  overseas life insurance companies, **43(2)**, [221]

  partnership involving company—

    computation, **44(1)**, [90]

    relief, transferring, **44(1)**, [92]

  payment of, **42**, [197], [199]

    arrangements for, **43(1)**, [342]

    interest on, **44(1)**, [610]

    time for, **44(1)**, [691]

  profits—

    charge on, **44(1)**, [3]

    computation of, **44(1)**, [8], [9]

    change of basis. *See* **income tax**

  rate of, **43(S)**, 514, 839, 1357, 1369

  record-keeping requirements, **43(S)**, 1305–8

corporation tax—*contd*
   receipts from land, transitional provisions,
      43(1), [387]
   reference to, **42**, [199]
   remittance basis, non-resident company. *See*
      non-resident
   repayment, claim in advance of establishment
      of liability, **42**, [198]
   repayment supplement, **44(1)**, [608]
   research and development, **44(1)**, [51], [617]
   scientific research organisations—
      deduction for payments to, **43(2)**, [732]
      exemption for, **43(2)**, [730]
   self-assessment. *See* **assessment**
      company returns. *See* **return**
   shares acquired under EMI option, relief for,
      43(S), 89
   small companies rate, **43(2)**, [89], [578];
      44(1), [8]
   small companies' rate and fraction, **43(S)**, 15,
      515, 840, 1370
   small companies' relief, associated companies,
      43(S), 863
   starting rate, **43(1)**, [417]; **43(2)**, [90], [579]
      abolition, **43(S)**, 16
      fraction, **43(2)**, [90], [579]
   tax advantage, meaning, **44(1)**, [623]
   tax credits—
      research and development. *See* **research
         and development**
      vaccine research. *See* **research and
         development**
   thin capitalisation—
      commencement of provisions, **43(2)**, [277]
      transitional provisions, **43(2)**, [277]
   trading losses, deduction of, **42**, [1059]
   transfer pricing—
      commencement of provisions, **43(2)**, [277]
      penalties, temporary relaxation of liability
         to, **43(2)**, [276]
      transitional provisions, **43(2)**, [277]
   transitional provisions, **44(2)**, [775]
   unremittable overseas income, on,
      44(1), [419]
   winding-up, on, **44(1)**, [174]

corroboration
   abolition of rules, **18**, [287]
   evidence, of, when necessary, **18**, [75]
   perjury, in case of, **12(1)**, [204]

corrosive fluid
   throwing, **12(1)**, [85]

corrupt practices
   bribery, **15(3)**, [115]
   treating, **15(3)**, [116]
   undue influence, **15(3)**, [117]

corruption
   agents, in transactions with, **12(1)**, [189],
      [190]
   committed outside UK, **12(3)**, [138]
   Director of Serious Fraud Office, powers,
      12(1), [1058]

corruption—*contd*
   offices, in. *See* **office**
   penalty, **12(1)**, [173]
   presumption of, **12(1)**, [227]; **12(3)**, [139]
   public morals, conspiracy as to, **12(1)**, [676]

cosmetic piercing
   amendment of enactments, **26(2)**, [163]
   application of provisions, **26(2)**, [164]
   business of—
      byelaws as to, **35(1)**, [434]
      entry on premises, powers of, **35(1)**, [436]
      medical practitioner, under supervision of,
         35(1), [434]
      person or premises for carrying on—
         offences by, **35(1)**, [436]
         registration of—
            certificate of, **35(1)**, [434], [435]
            charge for, **35(1)**, [434]
            requirement of, **35(1)**, [434]
            suspension or cancellation,
               35(1), [435]
   entry, powers of, **25(2)**, [969]
   existing, application of provisions to,
      25(2), [970]
   licence—
      appeals, **25(2)**, [967]; **26(2)**, [163]
      application for, **25(2)**, [961]
      cancellation, **25(2)**, [963]
      conditions, **25(2)**, [960]
      enforcement, **25(2)**, [968]
      provisional grant, **25(2)**, [965]
      refusal of, **25(2)**, [962]
      renewal and transfer, **26(2)**, [163]
      requirement of, **25(2)**, [960]
      standard terms, conditions and restrictions,
         25(2), [964]
      transmission, **25(2)**, [963]
      variation, **25(2)**, [966]
   meaning, **25(2)**, [466]
   registration of premises, **25(2)**, [466]
      termination, **26(1)**, [238]
   regulation of business, **26(2)**, [323]
   special treatment premises, as, **25(2)**, [958]
      meaning, **26**, 787

costs
   accused, against, **12(1)**, [948]
   appeal, awards on—
      Court of Appeal, in, **12(1)**, [946]
      dismissal, on, **12(1)**, [948]
   central funds, out of—
      amount of, **12(1)**, [946], [947]
      appeal, on, **12(1)**, [946]
      case not proceeded with, where,
         12(1), [946]
      Court of Appeal, **12(1)**, [947]
      Crown Court, **12(1)**, [946], [947]
      defence, **12(1)**, [946]
      Divisional Court, **12(1)**, [947]
      prosecution, **12(1)**, [947]
      regulations, **12(1)**, [949]
      retrial, on, **12(1)**, [946]
      scales or rates of payment, **12(1)**, [952]
   conveyances, of, **9**, [45], [283]

costs—*contd*
county court, in. *See* **county court**
Court of Appeal, in, **11(2)**, [238]–[239], [724]
Crown Court—
   defence, **12(1)**, [946]
   instalments, payment by, **12(2)**, [818]
   time for payment, **12(2)**, [818]
Crown Court, in, **11(2)**, [238]–[239], [725]
Crown proceedings, **13**, [7], [27]
defence in criminal cases, **12(1)**, [946]
defendant's costs order, making of,
   12(1), [946]
distress. *See* **distress**
High Court, in. *See* **High Court**
House of Lords, in, **11(2)**, [238]
interpreter, payment of, **12(1)**, [620], [944],
   [949], [953]
Lands Tribunal, proceedings before, **9**, [183]
legal aid. *See* **legal aid and advice**
legal representative, against, **12(1)**, [950]
litigant in person, of, **11(2)**, [377]
magistrates' court—
   civil debt, as, **11(2)**, [239]
   recovery of, **11(2)**, [235], [238]–[239]
medical witness, of, **12(1)**, [387], [949]
money paid into court, in respect of, **9**, [285]
order, meaning, **12(1)**, [952]
parties, between, **12(1)**, [952]
payment of, **12(1)**, [946]
Privy Council Judicial Committee, before,
   11(2), [24], [48]
provision for orders as to, **12(1)**, [949]
regulations on, **12(1)**, [949], [952]
security for, action for sale of mortgaged
   property, **20**, [709]
solicitor. *See under* **solicitors**
third parties, award against, **12(1)**, [951]
title, verification to, **9**, [283]
unnecessarily incurred, **12(1)**, [949]
wasted, **12(1)**, [950]
witness, to, **12(1)**, [949]

cottage
garden, maximum size, **22**, [10]
hill farming. *See* **hill farming**

cottage holding. *See also* **allotments**
conditions of occupation, **1(1)**, [317]
land for, restrictions on, **1(1)**, [824]
meaning, **1(1)**, [319]
powers as to, revocation of, **1(1)**, [824]
provision of, **1(1)**, [317]
provisions—
   applicable to, **1(1)**, [253]
   excluded in respect of, **1(1)**, [437]

**Council for Healthcare Regulatory
Excellence**
constitution, **28(S)**, 21–2
Council for the Regulation of Health Care
   Professionals, renamed, **28(S)**, 21
devolved administrations, powers of,
   28(S), 23
powers and duties of, **28(S)**, 22–3
public, duty to inform and consult, **28(S)**, 24

**Council for Healthcare Regulatory
Excellence**—*contd*
reference of cases to court, **28(S)**, 24–6
Secretary of State, powers of, **28(S)**, 23
summary of provisions, **28(S)**, 3

Council for Licensed Conveyancers
accounts, **11(3)**, [45]; **11(4)**, [519]
body corporate, provision of services by,
   11(3), [25]
code of conduct, **11(3)**, [156]
constitution, **11(3)**, [45]; **11(4)**, [519]
conveyancing services bodies—
   management and control of, **11(4)**, [497],
      [498]
   meaning, **11(4)**, [498]
   provision of services by, **11(4)**, [497]
decisions of, appeals from, **11(3)**, [22];
   11(4), [494]
delegation, **11(3)**, [157]; **11(4)**, [571]
Discipline and Appeals Committee—
   appeals to, **11(3)**, [22]; **11(4)**, [494]
   establishment of, **11(3)**, [18]; **11(4)**, [490]
   evidence, **11(3)**, [46]; **11(4)**, [520]
   licence—
      disqualification from holding, removal
         of, **11(3)**, [20]; **11(4)**, [492]
      revocation of—
         error, on grounds of, **11(3)**, [21];
            11(4), [493]
         fraud, on grounds of, **11(3)**, [21];
            11(4), [493]
   orders, filing of, **11(3)**, [46]; **11(4)**, [520]
   procedure, rules of, **11(3)**, [46];
      11(4), [520]
   proceedings, **11(3)**, [19]; **11(4)**, [491]
   rules as to constitution of, **11(3)**, [18];
      11(4), [490]
   supplementary provisions, **11(3)**, [46]
Discipline and Appeals Committee, duty of,
   11(3), [157]
duties, **11(3)**, [5], [114]; **11(4)**, [538]
establishment of, **11(3)**, [5]; **11(4)**, [474]
expenses, **11(3)**, [45]; **11(4)**, [519]
files, power to examine, **11(3)**, [157];
   11(4), [571]
inadequate professional services—
   compensation, **11(3)**, [157]
   costs, **11(3)**, [157]
   failure to comply with direction,
      11(3), [157]
   fees, **11(3)**, [157]
   steps against, **11(3)**, [157]
incidental powers, **11(3)**, [45]; **11(4)**, [519]
interest on clients' money, **11(3)**, [157];
   11(4), [571]
intervention powers, **11(3)**, [157]
Investigating Committee—
   determination of allegations by,
      11(4), [489]
   establishment of, **11(3)**, [17]; **11(4)**, [488]
   functions of, **11(3)**, [17]; **11(4)**, [488]
   intervention by, **11(3)**, [24]; **11(4)**, [496]
   rules as to constitution of, **11(3)**, [18];
      11(4), [490]

Council for Licensed Conveyancers—*contd*
licence—
  additional fee for certain, **11(4)**, [479]
  application for, to, **11(3)**, [7], [156];
   11(4), [476], [570]
  conditional, **11(4)**, [570]
  conditions, **11(3)**, [9], [156]; **11(4)**, [478]
   imposition of, during currency, of,
    11(3), [10]; **11(4)**, [480]
   variation of, **11(4)**, [481]
  disqualification from holding, **11(3)**, [156];
   11(4), [570]
  issue of, **11(3)**, [8], [156]; **11(4)**, [477],
   [570]
  revocation on grounds of error or fraud,
   11(3), [156]; **11(4)**, [570]
  suspension of, **11(3)**, [11], [156];
   11(4), [482], [570]
  termination of, **11(3)**, [11]; **11(4)**, [482]
members—
  number of, **11(3)**, [45]; **11(4)**, [519]
  remuneration of, **11(3)**, [45]; **11(4)**, [519]
officers and staff, **11(3)**, [45]; **11(4)**, [519]
powers, **11(3)**, [114]; **11(4)**, [538]
practice, intervention in—
  circumstances allowing, **11(3)**, [47];
   11(4), [521]
  generally, **11(3)**, [24]; **11(4)**, [496]
  powers, **11(3)**, [48]; **11(4)**, [522]
proceedings, **11(3)**, [45]
qualification regulations, **11(3)**, [156];
  11(4), [570]
register, **11(3)**, [12]; **11(4)**, [483], [570]
register of licensed conveyancers, **11(3)**, [156]
rules—
  accounts, keeping and establishment of, as
   to, **11(3)**, [15]; **11(4)**, [486]
  compensation, as to, **11(3)**, [14];
   11(4), [485]
  conduct, as to, **11(3)**, [13]; **11(4)**, [484]
  Discipline and Appeals Committee, rules as
   to constitution of, **11(3)**, [18];
   11(4), [490]
  discipline, as to, **11(3)**, [13]; **11(4)**, [484]
  generally, **11(3)**, [31]; **11(4)**, [505]
  interest on client money, as to, **11(3)**, [16];
   11(4), [487]
  Investigating Committee, constitution of, as
   to, **11(3)**, [18]; **11(4)**, [490]
  professional indemnity, as to, **11(3)**, [14];
   11(4), [485]
  professional practice, as to, **11(3)**, [13];
   11(4), [484]
  training, for, **11(3)**, [6]; **11(4)**, [475]
status, **11(3)**, [45]; **11(4)**, [519]
supplementary provisions, **11(3)**, [45]

**Council for the Regulation of Health Care
Professionals**
accounts, **28**, [759]
constitution, **28**, [759]
Council for Healthcare Regulatory
  Excellence, renamed as, **28(S)**, 21
disciplinary cases, reference to court,
  28, [750]

**Council for the Regulation of Health Care
Professionals**—*contd*
employees, **28**, [759]
establishment, **28**, [746]
functions, **28**, [746]
loans to, **28**, [759]
members, **28**, [759]
payments to, **28**, [759]
powers and duties of, **28**, [747]
regulatory bodies—
  complaints about, **28**, [749]
  co-operation by, **28**, [748]
  meaning, **28**, [749]
reports, **28**, [759]
seal, application of, **28**, [759]
status, **28**, [759]

Council of European Communities. *See*
European Communities

Council of Industrial Design
Treasury grants, **47**, [46]

Council on Tribunals
abolition, **11(S)**, Courts 58; **11(4)**, [46]
annual report, **10**, [720]
composition of, **10**, [718]
continuation of, **10**, [717]
functions of, **10**, [717]
general supervision by, **10**, [717], [736]
members—
  expenses, **10**, [719]
  number of, **10**, [718]
  Parliamentary Commissioner for
   Administration as, **10**, [718]
  remuneration, **10**, [719]
  tenure of office, **10**, [719]
members of tribunals, recommending,
  10, [721]
reference by, **10**, [720]
report by, **10**, [720]
Scottish committee, **10**, [718]
  abolition, **11(S)**, Courts 58; **11(4)**, [46]

council tax
amount of—
  basic, **26(1)**, [10]
   calculation of, **26(1)**, [37]
   part of area, special items relating to,
    26(1), [38], [49]
   precepting authority, calculation by,
    26(1), [48]
   special items, **26(1)**, [39], [50]
  different categories of dwelling, for,
   26(1), [34]
  different valuation bands, calculation for,
   26(1), [40], [51]
  discounts, **26(1)**, [11]
   administration, **26(1)**, [99]
   persons disregarded, **26(1)**, [98]
  reduced, **26(1)**, [14]
  substitute calculations, **26(1)**, [41]
  substituted, **26(1)**, [35]
  time for setting, **26(1)**, [34]
armed forces, relief for, **43(S)**, 879

council tax—*contd*

authority, functions to be discharged by,
26(1), [84]

benefit. *See* **council tax benefit**

billing authority—

amount of tax payable, power to reduce,
26(1), [15]

amount payable by, calculation of,
26(1), [52]

budget requirement—

calculation of, 26(1), [36]

informing Secretary of State of,
26(1), [80]

payments ignored, 26(1), [36]

designated, duty of, 26(1), [65], [75]

designation. *See* designation of authorities
below

estimated future expenditure, 26(1), [36]

information, provision to Secretary of
State, 26(1), [80]

information supplied by, 26(1), [56]

information supplied to, 26(1), [42]

meaning, 26(1), [1]

nomination. *See* nomination of authorities
below

part of dwelling within area of, 26(1), [1]

ratepayers, duty to consult, 26(1), [82]

Wales, in, 26(1), [160]

collection of, 26(1), [99]

definitions, 26(1), [86]

designation of authorities—

alternative notional amounts, 26(1), [59]

authorities subject to, 26(1), [58]

budget requirement—

meaning, 26(1), [78]

net of precepts, to be, 26(1), [79]

designated billing authority, duty of,
26(1), [65], [75]

designated precepting authority, duty of,
26(1), [66], [76]

failure to substitute, 26(1), [67], [77]

information, 26(1), [80]

maximum amount—

acceptance of, 26(1), [63], [73]

challenging, 26(1), [62], [72]

no challenge or acceptance of,
26(1), [64], [74]

notification of, 26(1), [69]

notification, after, 26(1), [69]

maximum amount, 26(1), [72]–[74]

notification of, 26(1), [69]

power of, 26(1), [58]–[61]

previous designation, after, 26(1), [71]

maximum amount, 26(1), [72]–[74]

Wales, 26(1), [81]

year under consideration, for, 26(1), [61]

discounts, 26(1), [11]

England, special provision for, 26(1), [12]

second and empty homes, effect of
regulations, 26(2), [292]

Wales, special provision for, 26(1), [13]

dwelling—

chargeable, 26(1), [4]

Crown exemption, 26(1), [22]

different categories of, 26(1), [34]

council tax—*contd*

dwelling—*contd*

exempt, 26(1), [99]

meaning, 26(1), [4]

meaning, 26(1), [3]

new, completion of, 26(1), [20]

owner, meaning, 26(1), [6]

England and Wales, administration in,
26(1), [81]

exemption, provision of information as to,
22, [836]

grants—

payment of, 25(2), [789]

special, 25(2), [790]

Greater London Authority. *See* **Greater
London Authority**

information—

authority, supply by, 26(1), [99]

authority, supply to, 26(1), [99]

failure to supply, 26(1), [100]

person liable, supply by, 26(1), [101]

properties, about, 26(1), [31]

Secretary of State, required by, 26(1), [85]

use of, 26(1), [99]

judicial review, matters subject to, 26(1), [83]

liability to pay—

boat, in respect of, 26(1), [7]

caravan, in respect of, 26(1), [7]

changes, smoothing, 26(1), [16]

daily basis, determined on, 26(1), [2]

death of liable person, 26(1), [21]

joint and several, 26(1), [9]

persons liable to, 26(1), [6]

prescribed cases, in, 26(1), [8]

spouses, of, 26(1), [9]

limitation, 26(1), [424]

listing officer—

appointment of, 26(1), [23]

information, giving, 26(1), [32]

lists, functions relating to. *See* valuation list
below

living accommodation, paid for, 44(2), [318]

local authority members owing, restriction on
voting by, 26(1), [90]

lump sum payment, reductions for,
26(1), [99]

nomination of authorities—

alternative notional amounts, 26(1), [59]

authorities, reference to, 26(1), [57]

budget requirement—

meaning, 26(1), [78]

net of precepts, to be, 26(1), [79]

designation after, 26(1), [69]

information, 26(1), [80]

no designation after, 26(1), [70]

power of, 26(1), [58]–[61], [68]

Wales, 26(1), [81]

orders and regulations, 26(1), [91]

penalties, 26(1), [100]

precept—

amount payable by each billing authority,
calculation of, 26(1), [52]

billing authority, issue to, 26(1), [43]

council tax—*contd*
precept—*contd*
issue—
local precepting authority, by,
26(1), [45]
major precepting authority, by,
26(1), [44]
substituted, **26(1)**, [46]
precepting authority—
combined fire authorities, **26(2)**, [293]
designated, duty of, **26(1)**, [66], [76]
designation. *See* designation of authorities
above
information—
provision to Secretary of State,
26(1), [80]
supply of, **26(1)**, [42]
local—
bodies being, **26(1)**, [43]
budget requirement, calculation of,
26(1), [54]
informing Secretary of State of,
26(1), [80]
estimated future expenditure, **26(1)**, [54]
issue of precept by, **26(1)**, [45]
substitute calculations, **26(1)**, [55]
major—
bodies being, **26(1)**, [43]
budget requirement, calculation of,
26(1), [47]
informing Secretary of State of,
26(1), [80]
calculation of amount of tax—
basic, **26(1)**, [48]
different valuation bands, for,
26(1), [51]
part of area, special items relating to,
26(1), [49]
special items, **26(1)**, [50]
substitute, **26(1)**, [53]
estimated future expenditure, **26(1)**, [47]
issue of precept by, **26(1)**, [44]
ratepayers, duty to consult, **26(1)**, [82]
recovery of sums payable, **26(1)**, [101]
Secretary of State—
information required by, **26(1)**, [85]
supplemental provision by, **26(1)**, [92]
summary of provisions, **25(1)**, [1]
valuation bands, **26(1)**, [5]
valuation list—
alteration, **26(1)**, [29]
appeals, information concerning,
26(1), [33]
compilation and maintenance of,
26(1), [25]
contents of, **26(1)**, [28]
information concerning, **26(1)**, [32]
new, compilation and maintenance of,
26(1), [27]
omission from, **26(1)**, [28]
proposals, information concerning,
26(1), [33]
valuation for purposes of, **26(1)**, [24]
Welsh billing authorities, for, **26(1)**, [26]

council tax—*contd*
valuation officer—
meaning, **26(1)**, [30]
notice, service of, **26(1)**, [31]
powers of entry, **26(1)**, [30]

council tax benefit
administering authority—
information, supply of—
between, **40(1)**, [627]
by, **40(1)**, [626]
to, **40(1)**, [625]
subsidy to—
annual orders, no requirement for,
40(1), [661]
calculation of, **40(1)**, [656]
definitions, **40(1)**, [662]
expenditure, financing, **40(1)**, [660]
joint arrangements, financing,
40(1), [659]
meaning, **40(1)**, [655]
payment of, **40(1)**, [657]
rent rebate, **40(1)**, [658]
Secretary of State, by, **40(1)**, [655]
administration, **40(1)**, [505]
Audit Commission, interaction with,
40(1), [647]
directions, **40(1)**, [649], [650]
investigation, powers of, **40(1)**, [646]
reports on, **40(1)**, [645], [648]
arrangements for, **40(1)**, [644]
attainment of standards—
enforcement determinations, **40(1)**, [653],
[654]
enforcement notices, **40(1)**, [652]
information about, **40(1)**, [651]
claims and reviews, determination of,
40(2), [183]
couples, regulations as to, **40(1)**, [380]
decisions, revisions and appeals, **40(2)**, [294]
discretionary housing payments—
grants towards cost of, **40(2)**, [285]
power to make, **40(2)**, [284]
entitlement to, **40(1)**, [379]
errors, revisions and appeals, **40(2)**, [294]
excess, **40(1)**, [580]
income-related benefit, as, **40(1)**, [367]
information—
failure to supply, **40(2)**, [294]
supply of, expedited claims, **40(1)**, [635]
local authority scheme, availability of,
40(1), [367]
nature of, **40(1)**, [643]
other benefits, relationship with, **40(1)**, [506]
overpayments—
colluding employees, **40(1)**, [606]
penalty as alternative to prosecution,
40(1), [605], [606]
persons taking up employment, for,
40(2), [526]–[528]
polygamous marriage, effect of, **40(1)**, [381]
representative organisations, consultation
with, **40(1)**, [705]
shortfall in, **40(1)**, [581]

council tax benefit—*contd*
state pension credit, attaining qualifying age
for, **40(1)**, [385]
suspension, provision for, **40(2)**, [184], [294]
termination, provision for, **40(2)**, [294]

counsel
meaning, **18**, [132]
summing up evidence by, **18**, [125]

counterclaim
Admiralty proceedings, county court,
11(2), [919]

counterfeiting
materials and implements for, **12(1)**, [734]
meaning, **12(1)**, [743]
notes and coins—
custody and control of, **12(1)**, [733]
exportation, prohibiting, **12(1)**, [738]
importation, prohibiting, **12(1)**, [737]
meaning, **12(1)**, [743]
offence, **12(1)**, [731]
passing or tendering, **12(1)**, [732]
offences, **12(2)**, [162]
penalties, **12(1)**, [739]
search and seizure, **12(1)**, [740]

counter-inflation
information, disclosure of, **47**, [135]
offences—
bodies corporate, by, **47**, [131]
Northern Ireland provisions, **47**, [133]
unincorporated bodies, by, **47**, [132]

country park. *See also* **National Park**
byelaws, **32**, [273]
compulsory acquisition for, **32**, [258]
enactments not relating to, **32**, [258]
local authority providing, **32**, [257]–[259]
provision of, **32**, [1]

countryside. *See also* **environment**
access to—
access authority—
boundaries of access land, notices
indicating, **32**, [670]
byelaws, power to make, **32**, [668]
meaning, **32**, [653]
wardens, appointment of, **32**, [669]
access land—
boundaries of, notices indicating,
32, [670]
code of conduct relating to, **32**, [671]
dedication of land as, **32**, [667]
dogs, restrictions on, **32**, [674]
excepted land, **32**, [720]–[721]
meaning, **32**, [653]
notices deterring public use, offence of
displaying, **32**, [665]
owners, rights and liabilities of, **32**, [664]
public rights in relation to, **32**, [654],
[722]
restrictions on—
appeals, **32**, [681]

countryside—*contd*
access to—*contd*
access land—*contd*
restrictions on—*contd*
defence, for, **32**, [679]
directions by relevant authority,
32, [678]
emergency, in case of, **32**, [682]
fire, for avoidance of, **32**, [676]
heritage preservation, for, **32**, [677],
[680]
land management, **32**, [675]
national security, for, **32**, [679]
nature conservation, for, **32**, [677],
[680]
owners, by, **32**, [673]
public danger, **32**, [676]
regulations, **32**, [683]
rights of access to, **32**, [722]
wardens, **32**, [669]
byelaws, **32**, [668]
dogs, restrictions on, **32**, [674]
entry on land—
compensation for damage resulting
from, **32**, [692]
powers of, **32**, [691]
grouse moors, restriction of dogs in,
32, [674]
lambing, land for, restrictions of dogs in,
32, [674]
local access forums, **32**, [712]–[713]
maps—
conclusive form, in—
generally, **32**, [661]
review of, **32**, [662]
confirmed—
appeals against—
generally, **32**, [658]
procedure, **32**, [659]
Secretary of State, delegation of
functions, **32**, [660]
draft form, publication in, **32**, [657]
duty to prepare, **32**, [656]
entry on land, **32**, [691]
regulations, **32**, [663]
means of—
agreements regarding—
appeals, **32**, [689]
failure to comply with, **32**, [687]
generally, **32**, [686]
notices under, appeals relating to,
32, [689]
provision by access authority in
absence of, **32**, [688]
meaning, **32**, [685]
obstruction, order to remove, **32**, [690]
open country—
coastal land, power to extend to,
32, [655]
meaning, **32**, [653]
orders and regulations, **32**, [695]
previous legislation, repeal of, **32**, [697]
restrictions on—
appeals, **32**, [681]

countryside—*contd*
  access to—*contd*
    restrictions on—*contd*
      Countryside Agency, guidance to
        National Park authorities, **32**, [684]
      defence, for, **32**, [679]
      directions by relevant authority,
        32, [678]
      emergency, in case of, **32**, [682]
      fire, for avoidance of, **32**, [676]
      heritage preservation, for, **32**, [677],
        [680]
      land management, **32**, [675]
      landowners, by, **32**, [673]
      national security, for, **32**, [679]
      nature conservation, for, **32**, [677], [680]
      public danger, **32**, [676]
      reference to, **32**, [672]
      regulations, **32**, [683]
    rights of, under other enactments,
      32, [666]
  Agency. *See* **Countryside Agency**
  agriculture Ministers, duties of, **32**, [469]
  biological diversity in, **32**, [1]
  Coal Authority's duty as to, **17(2)**, [126]
  Crown land, **32**, [828]
  farm capital grant, application for, **32**, [469]
  functions relating to, **25(2)**, [582]
  highway construction in, **36**, [1121]
  interests, protection for, **32**, [271]
  landowners, agreements with, **32**, [277]
  local Act, amendment of, **32**, [276]
  local authority powers, **32**, [275]
  management agreements, **32**, [468]
  natural beauty in, **32**, [826]
  protection of—
    grants for, **32**, [616]
    hedgerows, **32**, [615]
    subordinate legislation regarding,
      consultation before making, **32**, [617]
  public places, references to, **32**, [693]
  special scientific interest, sites of. *See* **nature conservation**
  traffic regulation in special areas, **37**, [189]

Countryside Agency
  Commission for Rural Communities,
    temporary provision of staff to, **32**, [794]
  dissolution, **32**, [766]
  environmental impact assessment, procedure
    for, **36**, [1122]
  Forestry Commission, acting as agent for,
    18, [1152]
  former, exercise of functions of, **32**, [1]
  generally, **32**, [1]
  long-distance routes, functions, **36**, [633],
    [637]
  Natural England, temporary provision of staff
    to, **32**, [794]
  property, rights and liabilities, transfer of,
    32, [791]–[794], [838]
  public path creation order, application for,
    38(2), [64]
  public path diversion, consultation as to,
    36, [1159]

Countryside Agency—*contd*
  right of way improvement plan, consultation
    on, **38(2)**, [67]
  traffic regulation in special areas, submissions
    by, **37**, [189]

Countryside Commission
  transitional provisions, **32**, [592], [594]

Countryside Council for Wales
  deer, persons licensed to take, **2**, [659]
  Forestry Commission, acting as agent for,
    18, [1152]
  grants and loans by, **25(2)**, [305]
  right of way improvement plan, consultation
    on, **38(2)**, [67]
  right of way, long distance routes, functions,
    36, [632]
  sites of special interest, notification to water
    undertakers, **49**, [715]
  traffic regulation in special areas, **37**, [189]

county
  commission of the peace, **25(2)**, [172]
  coroner. *See* **coroner**
  electoral divisions, **25(2)**, [6]
  lieutenants—
    appointment of, **26(1)**, [271]
    areas, **26(1)**, [280]
    clerks, **26(1)**, [275]
    functions, **26(1)**, [276]
    lord-lieutenant—
      absence of, **26(1)**, [274]
      appointment of, **26(1)**, [271]
      deputies, **26(1)**, [272]
      vice, **26(1)**, [273]
    transitional provisions, **26(1)**, [281]
  local government areas, **25(2)**, [1]
  meaning, **25(2)**, [229]
  metropolitan. *See* **metropolitan county**
  sheriffs appointed for, **25(2)**, [173]

county council. *See also* **local authority**
  acquisition of land by, **22**, [32]
  borrowing powers, **36**, [1327]
  chairman—
    declaration to be made by, **25(2)**, [72]
    election of, **25(2)**, [3], [4]
  constitution of, **25(2)**, [2]
    election, **25(2)**, [7], [240]
    terms of office etc, **25(2)**, [6]
  contributions—
    district councils, to, **25(1)**, [563]
    parish council, to, **25(1)**, [563]
  councillors—
    election, **25(2)**, [7], [240]
    terms of office etc, **25(2)**, [6]
  county fund, keeping, **25(2)**, [150]
  delegation of financial powers, **25(1)**, [60]
  district council, contributions to, **36**, [1320]
  documents, authentication of, **36**, [1373]
  duties and liabilities, **25(1)**, [62]
  expenses of, defrayment, **25(1)**, [156]
  functions as to highways, reference to,
    36, [1383]

county council—*contd*
  grants to. *See* **local authority** (grants)
  housing accommodation—
    consent to provision of, **22**, [31]
    employees, for, **22**, [32]
    expenditure on, **22**, [31]
    management, **22**, [31]
    reserve powers to provide, **22**, [31]
  information furnished to, **36**, [1347], [1348]
  land drainage. *See* **local authority**
  land for housing association, provision of,
    22, [462]
  legal proceedings by, **36**, [1181]
  local Act functions, **36**, [1014]
  local taxation licence—
    duties, application of proceeds, **25(1)**, [59],
      [153]
    fees, amendments of, **25(1)**, [798]
    list of, **25(1)**, [70]
    powers and duties, **25(1)**, [59]
  materials, disposing of, **36**, [1345]
  members. *See* **local authority**
  name, change of, **25(2)**, [64]
  powers transferred to—
    construction of references, **25(1)**, [61]
    delegation of financial powers, **25(1)**, [60]
    general provisions as to, **25(1)**, [60]
  public health purposes, local authority for,
    35(1), [118]
  trunk roads, delegation of functions,
    36, [1010]
  vice-chairman, **25(2)**, [5]
  Welsh. *See* **Wales**

county court
  action, transfer to High Court, wrongful
    interference with goods, **45**, [971]
  adjournment, **11(2)**, [898]
  administration order—
    composition provisions, with, **11(2)**, [994]
    distress, right of, **11(2)**, [998]
    effect of, **11(2)**, [996]
    meaning, **11(2)**, [992]
    money paid under, **11(2)**, [999]
    notice of, **11(2)**, [995]
    power to make, **11(2)**, [992]–[993];
      11(3), [75]; **11(4)**, [534]
    proof of debt, **11(2)**, [995]
    provisions on, **11(2)**, [992]–[999]
    registrar, execution by, **11(2)**, [997]
  Admiralty proceedings—
    aircraft, involving, **11(2)**, [918]
    appeals, **11(2)**, [918], [960]
    arrest in, **11(2)**, [918]
    assessors, hearing with, **11(2)**, [960]
    claims, hearing and determination,
      11(2), [917]
    definitions, **11(2)**, [920]
    evidence in, **11(2)**, [943]
    in personam, restrictions, **11(2)**, [919]
    in rem, excluded, **11(2)**, [920]
    jurisdiction—
      counterclaims, **11(2)**, [919]
      districts for purposes of, **11(2)**, [916]
      exercise, mode of, **11(2)**, [918]

county court—*contd*
  Admiralty proceedings—*contd*
    jurisdiction—*contd*
      generally, **11(2)**, [917]
      limitation, **11(2)**, [917]
    Rhine Convention, exclusion of cases
      within, **11(2)**, [917]
    seamen's wages, **11(2)**, [920]
    transfer, **11(2)**, [918]
    trial without jury, **11(2)**, [950]
    wages, seamen. *See* **wages**
  affidavits in, **11(2)**, [942]
  appeal—
    agreement not to, **11(2)**, [961]
    Court of Appeal, to, **11(2)**, [176], [959]
      powers, **11(2)**, [963]
      probate proceedings, **11(2)**, [964]
    judge's note on, **11(2)**, [962]
    question of fact, on, **11(2)**, [959]
  arbitration, reference to, **11(2)**, [948]
  assessors, summoning, **21**, [224]
  attachment of debts, **11(2)**, [988]
  attachment order by, **19(3)**, [36]
  audience, solicitor's right **11(2)**, [297]
  auditor, appointment of, **11(2)**, [1012]
  authority of, pretending to be under,
    11(2), [1015]
  bailiff—
    acting under warrant, action against,
      11(2), [1008]
    execution, failing to levy, **11(2)**, [1006]
  bankruptcy jurisdiction. *See* **bankruptcy**
    (court)
  bill of costs, order to deliver, **11(2)**, [349];
    11(4), [448]
  buildings, **11(2)**, [899]
  certiorari—
    leave to apply, **11(2)**, [965]
    stay of proceedings, **11(2)**, [965]
  civil proceedings by or against Crown in—
    county court rules, in accordance with,
      13, [19]
    transfer to High Court, **13**, [23]
  committal—
    contempt, for, **11(2)**, [1000]
    discharge of debtor, **11(2)**, [1003]
    jurisdiction, execution outside,
      11(2), [1004]
    order or warrant, execution of,
      11(2), [1001]
    prison made to, **11(2)**, [1002]
  commonhold, jurisdiction over, **24**, [66]
  consumer credit action in, **39(1)**, [304], [665]
  contempt of, committal, **11(2)**, [1000]
  conversion of house into flats, authorisation
    of, **22**, [410]
  costs—
    death or incapacity of judge, on,
      11(3), [39]; **11(4)**, [513]
    discretion of court in, **11(2)**, [724]
    transferred proceedings, in, **11(2)**, [930]
  damages—
    interest on, **11(2)**, [953]
    provisional, order for, **11(2)**, [935]
  deeds of arrangement filed in, **4(2)**, [22]

county court—*contd*
definitions, **11(2)**, [1020], [1026]
derelict land, determination of tenancy of,
  21, [217]
discovery, **11(2)**, [936]–[938]
districts—
  division of country into, **11(2)**, [896]
  Lord Chancellor specifying, **11(2)**, [897]
division of causes of action, **11(2)**, [923]
document issuing from, falsely representing,
  11(2), [1015]
execution, warrant of—
  bills of exchange, etc, seized, **11(2)**, [973]
  effect of, **11(2)**, [981]
  execution out of jurisdiction, **11(2)**, [985]
  goods, against, **11(2)**, [967]
  information as to, **11(2)**, [986]
  payment—
    instalment, when by, **11(2)**, [968]
    superseded on, **11(2)**, [969]
  power to stay, **11(2)**, [970]
  seizure of goods—
    bailiff acting as broker, **11(2)**, [978]
    brokers or appraisers, **11(2)**, [977]
    claim for rent, **11(2)**, [984]
    claim made to, **11(2)**, [982]
    custody, **11(2)**, [972]
    interpleader by registrar, **11(2)**, [983]
    permitted goods, **11(2)**, [971]
    public sale, **11(2)**, [979]
    rescue of, **11(2)**, [974]
    sale, period before, **11(2)**, [975]
    title passing, **11(2)**, [981]
expenses of, **11(2)**, [1013]
Family Division of High Court as principal
  registry for certain purposes, **6**, [423]
Fees, payment and application of,
  11(2), [1011]
fine—
  enforcement of, **11(2)**, [1010]
  payment and application of, **11(2)**, [1011]
funds, management of, **11(2)**, [877]
garnishees, expenses of, **11(2)**, [989]
generally, **11(2)**, [1]
High Court—
  allocation of business, **11(3)**, [70];
    11(4), [529]
  cross judgments, set-off, **11(2)**, [956]
  judgment, no action on, **11(2)**, [924]
  practice, application of, **11(2)**, [958]
  transfer of proceedings from, provisions,
    11(2), [927]
  transfer of proceedings to—
    county court order, by, **11(2)**, [929]
    High Court order, by, **11(2)**, [928]
HMRC, institution of proceedings by,
  43(S), 972–3
interest, awarding—
  debts and damages, on, **11(2)**, [953]
  judgment debt, on, **11(2)**, [957]
interim payments, orders for, **11(2)**, [934]
judge—
  appeal, note on, **11(2)**, [962]
  circuit, **11(2)**, [900]

county court—*contd*
judge—*contd*
  death or incapacity, additional costs arising
    from, **11(3)**, [39]; **11(4)**, [529]
  district—
    appointment, **11(2)**, [901]
    deputy, **11(2)**, [902]
    office, creation of, **11(3)**, [128];
      11(4), [550]
    proceedings, record of, **11(2)**, [905]
    qualifications, **11(2)**, [903]
    references to, **11(3)**, [128]; **11(4)**, [550]
    registrar becoming, **11(3)**, [128];
      11(4), [550]
    tenure of office, **11(2)**, [904]
  district, for, **11(2)**, [900]
  foreign law, determining, **11(2)**, [952]
  jurisdiction, exercising, **11(2)**, [925]
  law and fact, determining questions of,
    11(2), [946]
  persons sitting as, **11(2)**, [900]
  registrar or referee, reference to,
    11(2), [949]
judgment debt, interest on, **11(2)**, [957]
judgment or order—
  execution. *See* execution, warrant of *above*
  finality of, **11(2)**, [954]
  non-attendance on summons, **11(2)**, [990]
  satisfaction of, **11(2)**, [955]
  set-off, **11(2)**, [955]
judgment summons, meaning, **11(2)**, [1026]
jurisdiction—
  abandonment of excess of claim,
    11(2), [910]
  access to neighbouring land, **23**, [74]
  acquisition of new leases, as to, **23**, [166]
  administration of estates, **11(2)**, [913]
  judge's order, effect of, **11(2)**, [922]
  Admiralty. *See* Admiralty proceedings *above*
  agreement, by, **11(2)**, [911]
  agricultural housing, **21**, [477]
  allocation of family proceedings within,
    11(3), [72]; **11(4)**, [531]
  business premises, over, **21**, [224]
  collective enfranchisement, as to, **23**, [166]
  commonhold, over, **24**, [66]
  contract, action in, **11(2)**, [908]
  copyright, as to, **11(1)**, [930]
  defective housing proceedings, **22**, [387]
  demolition order, recovery of expenses
    for, **22**, [243]
  demoted tenancies, **23**, [463]
  equity, **11(2)**, [913]–[914]
    agreement, by, **11(2)**, [914]
  family provision proceedings, in,
    11(2), [915]
  financial relief, for, **27**, [558]
  fraud or mistake, proceedings relating to,
    11(2), [913]
  hereditament, determining title to,
    11(2), [912]
  Housing Act 1988, under, **22**, [833]
  introductory tenancies, **23**, [444]
  judge exercising, **11(2)**, [925]
  land, action for recovery of, **11(2)**, [912]

county court—*contd*
jurisdiction—*contd*
Landlord and Tenant Act 1987, under,
22, [765]
libel action, **11(2)**, [908]
matrimonial proceedings, in. *See*
matrimonial causes
minor, maintenance or advancement of,
11(2), [913]
money recoverable by statute, **11(2)**, [909]
mortgage of dwelling-house, action on,
11(2), [912]
mortgage, proceedings relating to,
11(2), [913]
partnership, proceedings relating to,
11(2), [913]
performers' rights, in respect of,
11(1), [1059]
principal registry of Family Division,
exercised in, **27**, [571]
probate, **11(2)**, [720]
judge's order, effect of, **11(2)**, [922]
property, proceedings relating to,
11(2), [913]
protection of children, for, **27**, [558]
public sector landlord, acquisition of
interest of, 22, [899]
refusal of licence by landlord, **21**, [216]
regulated mortgages, over, **21**, [623]
Rent Act, under, general, **21**, [628]
right to buy provisions, 22, [201]
secure tenancies, as to, 22, [101]
service charges, right to appoint surveyor to
advise on, as to, **23**, [418]
slander, action in, **11(2)**, [908]
tenant's improvements, questions arising,
21, [216], [746]
toll, etc, determining title to, **11(2)**, [908]
tort, action in, **11(2)**, [908]
trusts, proceedings relating to, **11(2)**, [913]
unlawful eviction, proceedings for
damages, 22, [833]
war damage, on, **21**, [107]
jury—
foreign law, not determining, **11(2)**, [952]
impanelling and swearing, **11(2)**, [951]
issues requiring, **11(2)**, [950]
number of, **11(2)**, [951]
trial without, **11(2)**, [950]
leasehold enfranchisement or extension,
powers on, **21**, [317]
limit—
meaning, **11(2)**, [1026]
power to raise, **11(2)**, [1024]
Lord Chancellor's advisory committees,
11(2), [250]
meaning, **41**, [605]
non-payment of rent—
forfeiture, provisions on, **11(2)**, [1018]
re-entry, **11(2)**, [1019]
service of summons, **11(2)**, [1019]
Northern Ireland, consumer credit, action
in, **39(1)**, [306], [307], [665]
officers—
assaulting, **11(2)**, [907]

county court—*contd*
officers—*contd*
injury during discharge of duties,
11(2), [633]
legal representative, acting as, **11(2)**, [906]
pension, **11(2)**, [632]–[633]
trespass by, **11(2)**, [1007]
orders before action—
Crown, binding, **11(2)**, [938]
personal injuries case, in, **11(2)**, [937]
powers, **11(2)**, [936]
public interest, injurious to, **11(2)**, [938]
rules, **11(2)**, [938]
parties to action—
Crown, **11(2)**, [931]
persons jointly liable, **11(2)**, [932]
plaintiff, bankruptcy of, **11(2)**, [933]
personal injuries action—
discovery, **11(2)**, [937]
orders before action, **11(2)**, [937]
provisional damages, **11(2)**, [935]
plaintiff, bankruptcy of, **11(2)**, [933]
possession, warrant of, **11(2)**, [991]
proceedings for repair of chancel in,
14, 351-2
prohibition—
application to High Court, **11(2)**, [966]
leave to apply, **11(2)**, [966]
stay of proceedings, **11(2)**, [966]
public building used for, **11(2)**, [899]
receiver, appointing, **11(2)**, [987]
records, **11(2)**, [905]
records, preservation of, **18**, [189], [194]
recovery of tax in, **42**, [204]
referee, reference for inquiry and report,
11(2), [949]
registrar—
administration order, executing,
11(2), [997]
district judge, becoming, **11(3)**, [128];
11(4), [550]
pensions, **11(2)**, [627]
reference for inquiry and report,
11(2), [949]
responsibilities of, **11(2)**, [1005]
remedies available in, **11(2)**, [926]
remuneration for appearing in, **11(2)**, [1022]
rent limit, determining, **21**, [596]
repairing obligations, declaration on
application of, 22, [519]
replevin, **11(2)**, [1023], [1031]
right of audience—
Lord Chancellor, by direction of,
11(2), [945]
meaning, **11(3)**, [141]; **11(4)**, [563]
orders as to, **11(3)**, [74]; **11(4)**, [533]
persons having, **11(2)**, [944]
rules—
discovery and production of documents by
Crown, **13**, [31]
interrogatories, to and by Crown, **13**, [31]
salaries and expenses, payment of,
11(2), [1013]
security of tenure declarations, power to
make, **21**, [208]

county court—*contd*
service charge, declaration as to reasonable
incurrence of costs, **22**, [523]
sittings, **11(2)**, [898]
solicitor—
payment to, **11(2)**, [1022]
undertaking given by, **11(2)**, [1021]
summons—
lessee notifying, **11(2)**, [1017]
service, proof of, **11(2)**, [1014]
transitional provisions, **11(2)**, [1032]
warrant—
evidence of authority, as, **11(2)**, [1009]
irregularity in executing, **11(2)**, [1007]
witness—
abroad, examined, **11(2)**, [940]
prisoner as, **11(2)**, [941]
refusal to give evidence, **11(2)**, [939]
writ, information as to, **11(2)**, [986]

county school
governing body, documents, use in evidence,
15(1), [700]
maintenance as, by local authority,
15(1), [514]

court. *See also* **Admiralty Court, etc**
accommodation, provision of, **11(3)**, [324]
administration, inspectors of, **12(4)**, [267]
appointment of, **11(3)**, [373]
Chief—
appointment of, **11(3)**, [373]
functions, **11(3)**, [375]
entry and inspection, rights of, **11(3)**, [376]
functions, **11(3)**, [374]
payments to, **11(3)**, [373]
ancient, jurisdiction of, **11(2)**, [381],
[384]–[386]
appeal after private hearing, **11(2)**, [220]
bankers' books, order for inspection,
18, [145]
boards—
areas, for, **11(3)**, [325]
chairman, **11(3)**, [416]
constitution, **11(3)**, [416]
functions of, **11(3)**, [326]
guidance to, **11(3)**, [326]
members—
expenses, **11(3)**, [416]
tenure, **11(3)**, [416]
procedure, **11(3)**, [416]
recommendations by, **11(3)**, [326]
child, dealing with, general considerations,
6, [32]
contempt of. *See* **contempt of court**
Court of Appeal. *See* **Court of Appeal**
equity, administering, **11(2)**, [722]
expenses, rate of, **11(2)**, [379]
family courts. *See* **family courts**
fees and costs—
orders, **11(3)**, [401]
prescription of, **11(3)**, [401]
High Court. *See* **High Court**
interest, awarding, **11(2)**, [180]
law and equity, administration of, **11(2)**, [722]

court—*contd*
Lord Chancellor, general duty of, **11(3)**, [322]
magistrates' court. *See* **magistrates' court**
matters exempt from disclosure in, publication
of, **11(2)**, [656]
meaning, **6**, [423]
officers—
administration of oaths by, **18**, [154]
pensions. *See* **judicial pensions**
officers and staff—
appointment, **11(3)**, [323]
civil service pension arrangements,
11(3), [323]
offices, abolition of, substituted references,
11(2), [263]
opinion of—
adoption of, **18**, [122]
certification of copies, **18**, [120]
duty of court making remit, **18**, [121]
rejection on appeal, **18**, [122]
remission of cases for, **18**, [119]
President, Lord Chief Justice as, **11(3)**, [462]
private, sitting in, **11(2)**, [220]
proceedings—
active, **11(2)**, [647], [665]
children, relating to, reporting of,
11(3), [312]
contemporary reports of, **11(2)**, [649]
postponed report of, **11(2)**, [649]
private, publishing information on,
11(2), [200]
repeals and revocations, **11(3)**, [316]
records—
meaning, **18**, [194]
preservation of, **18**, [189], [194]
remission of cases from abroad, **18**, [119]
reporting restrictions, **11(2)**, [656]
Rule Committee members, **11(2)**, [381]
rule-making power, **11(3)**, [466]
rules of court, powers generally, **6**, [424]
rules, regulations and orders, **11(3)**, [411]
security officers—
assaulting, **11(3)**, [372]
exclusion, removal or restraint of persons,
powers of, **11(3)**, [368]
generally, **11(2)**, [1]
identification, **11(3)**, [366]
meaning, **11(3)**, [366]
Northern Ireland. *See* **Northern Ireland**
obstructing, **11(3)**, [372]
retention of articles surrendered or seized,
11(3), [371]
search, powers of, **11(3)**, [367]
seizure of articles by, **11(3)**, [370]
Supreme Court. *See* **Supreme Court**
surrender of articles, requiring, **11(3)**, [370]
sources of information, requiring disclosure
of, **11(2)**, [655]
superior, meaning, **11(2)**, [109]
superseded, references to, **11(2)**, [795]
tape recorder used in, **11(2)**, [654]

court common investment funds
share in investments, entitlement to,
43(2), [240]

Court of Appeal

appeal to—

Admiralty proceedings—

county court, from, **11(2)**, [918]

Trinity Masters, assistance, **11(2)**, [960]

either way offence, conviction for, **12(1)**, [1085]

reporting of proceedings or public access, as to orders on, **12(1)**, [1103]

assignment of appeals to, **11(3)**, [291]

Child Support Commissioner, appeal from, **6**, [487]

civil division—

assessors, **11(2)**, [727]

bond given under order of, **11(2)**, [781]

business, distribution of, **11(2)**, [726]

constitution of, **11(2)**, [727]

costs, **11(2)**, [724]

even number of judges, **11(2)**, [727]

fines, enforcement of, **11(2)**, [785]

forfeited recognizance, **11(2)**, [785]

incidental jurisdiction, calling into question of, **11(2)**, [732]

jurisdiction, **11(2)**, [727]

number of judges, **11(2)**, [727]

own judgment, judge sitting on appeal from, **11(2)**, [729]

presidents, **11(2)**, [670]

scientific advisors, **11(2)**, [727]

single judge, decisions of, **11(2)**, [732]

constitution of, **11(2)**, [668]

costs. *See* **costs**

costs, recovery of, **11(2)**, [238]–[239]

county court, appeal from—

High Court, instead of, **11(2)**, [177]

powers on, **11(2)**, [963]

probate proceedings, **11(2)**, [964]

Court of Protection, appeal from, **29**, [284]

criminal cases, appeal in. *See* **criminal appeal**

criminal division—

business, distribution of, **11(2)**, [726]

cases, allocation of, **11(2)**, [730]

constitution of, **11(2)**, [728]

Criminal Procedure Rules, **11(2)**, [761]

even number of judges sitting, **11(2)**, [728]

judgment, form of, **11(2)**, [733]

jurisdiction, **11(2)**, [726]

number of judges, **11(2)**, [728]

own judgment, judge sitting on appeal from, **11(2)**, [729]

president, **11(2)**, [670]

presiding judge delivering judgment, **11(2)**, [733]

rules of court, **11(2)**, [757]

two judges sitting in, **11(2)**, [728]

damages—

injunction, and, **11(2)**, [723]

power to award, **11(3)**, [71]; **11(4)**, [530]

specific performance, and, **11(2)**, [723]

divisions, **11(2)**, [670], [726]

Employment Appeal Tribunal, appeal from, **16**, [586]

ex-officio judges, **11(2)**, [669]

Court of Appeal—*contd*

High Court, appeal from, jurisdiction, **11(2)**, [683]

judge. *See* Lord Justice of Appeal *below*

judges of, ordinary, **11(3)**, [378]

judgment—

final or interlocutory, **11(2)**, [734]

presiding judge delivering, **11(2)**, [733]

jurisdiction, **11(2)**, [682]

Lord Justice of Appeal—

clerks and secretaries, **11(2)**, [771]

death or incapacity, additional costs arising from, **11(3)**, [39]; **11(4)**, [513]

number of, **11(2)**, [669]

precedence, **11(2)**, [680]

Privy Council Judicial Committee, member of, **11(2)**, [110]

qualifications, **11(2)**, [677]

selection of—

Lord Chancellor, options of, **11(3)**, [536]

panel, **11(3)**, [534]

process, **11(3)**, [533]

provisions applying, **11(3)**, [530]

reconsideration, **11(3)**, [537]–[538]

report, **11(3)**, [535]

request for, **11(3)**, [532]

vacancies, filling, **11(3)**, [531]

meaning, **41**, [605]

new trial, applications for, **11(2)**, [684]

proceedings, staying, **11(2)**, [722]

proceeds of crime. *See* **proceeds of crime**

reference on point of law after acquittal, **12(1)**, [611]

registrar, powers exercisable by, **12(1)**, [448]

procedural directions, **12(1)**, [449]

appeal against, **12(1)**, [450]

restriction on appeals, **11(2)**, [685]

sentences, review of. *See under* **criminal procedure and practice** (sentencing)

sittings, **11(2)**, [731]

superior court of record, as, **11(2)**, [682]

superseded courts, reference to, **11(2)**, [795]

Upper Tribunal, appeal from—

proceedings, **11(4)**, [15]; **11(S)**, Courts 24–5

right of, **11(4)**, [14]; **11(S)**, Courts 22–4

vacations, **11(2)**, [731]

Court of Chancery

Accountant-General, reference to, **11(2)**, [795]

Court of Commissioners

illegality of, **14**, 10

Court of Criminal Appeal

reference to, **11(2)**, [795]

Court of Delegates and Appeals for Prizes

records, custody of, **11(2)**, [49]

Court of Ecclesiastical Causes Reserved

advisers, **14**, 589

criminal proceedings in, **14**, 605

**Court of Ecclesiastical Causes
Reserved**—*contd*
findings, review of, **14**, 569, 591
judges of, **14**, 563
jurisdiction of, **14**, 558, 567–8
precedent, not bound by, **14**, 589
trial, conduct of, **14**, 588–9

Court of Exchequer
Accountant-General, reference to,
11(2), [795]

Court of Inquiry
appointment of, **16**, [418]
constitution, **16**, [419]
inquiry by, **16**, [418]
members, **16**, [419]
proceedings, **16**, [419]
report of, **16**, [418]

Court of Protection. *See also* **mentally
disordered person**
appeal from, **29**, [284]
applications to, **29**, [281]
capacity, declarations about, **29**, [239]
costs in, **29**, [286], [287]
deputies—
appointment of, **29**, [240], [244]
powers, **29**, [244]
qualifications, **29**, [244]
reimbursement, **29**, [244]
restrictions on, **29**, [245]
directions, interim, **29**, [279]
existing receivers, transitional provisions,
29, [335]
fees, **29**, [285], [287]
judges of, **29**, [277]
lasting power of attorney, powers as to—
operation, as to, **29**, [249]
validity, as to, **29**, [248]
new, establishment of, **29**, [276]
summary of provisions, **29**, [1]
official seal, **29**, [276]
orders—
general power and effect of, **29**, [278]
interim, **29**, [279]
person lacking capacity, powers relating to—
decisions, making, **29**, [240]
deputies, appointment of, **29**, [240]
patron of benefice, as, **29**, [320]
personal welfare, as to, **29**, [242]
preservation of interests in property,
29, [320]
property and affairs, as to, **29**, [243], [320]
vesting of settlements and stocks, **29**, [320]
will, making, **29**, [320]
persons under 18, transfer of proceedings
relating to, **29**, [246]
practice directions, **29**, [283]
reports, power to call for, **29**, [280]
Rules, **29**, [282]
superior court of record, as, **29**, [276]
Supreme Court office, ceasing to exist,
29, [276]
transitional provisions, **29**, [335]

Court of Protection.—*contd*
Visitors—
General, **29**, [292]
meaning, **29**, [292]
powers of, **29**, [292]
Special, **29**, [292]

Court of Referees
evidence on oath before, **32**, [1004]

Court of Session
Act of Union, after, **10**, [62]
Copyright Tribunal, appeal from, **11(1)**, [979]
Lord President, delegation of functions by,
11(4), [47]; **11(S)**, Courts 59

court of summary jurisdiction
meaning, **41**, [605]

court (yard)
appurtenant to building, paving and
drainage, **35(1)**, [606]
common, used in, sweeping and cleansing,
35(1), [130]
entrance to, circulation of air through,
35(1), [607]

court-martial
air force—
accused, challenges by, **3**, [853]
adjournment of, **3**, [852]
affirmations, **3**, [865]
alternative offences, **3**, [859], [999]
appeal. *See* appeal *below*
civil trial, debarring, **3**, [902]
civilians, offences by, **3**, [863]
copy of proceedings, accused's right to,
3, [910]
court administration officers—
convening by, **3**, [848]
meaning, **3**, [846]
custody—
amendments relating to, **3**, [1743]
of proceedings, **3**, [910]
decisions of, **3**, [857]
disposal of offence, **3**, [904]
dissolution of, **3**, [856]
district—
constitution of, **3**, [849]
convening, **3**, [848]
powers, **3**, [850]
evidence. *See* **evidence**
field general—
constitution of, **3**, [868]
convening, **3**, [867]
rules, **3**, [869]
trial by, **3**, [867]
finding of, **3**, [858]
promulgation, **3**, [909]
review of, **3**, [870]
authority, powers of, **3**, [871]
fitness to stand trial—
accused committed act, findings where,
3, [877]
questions as to, **3**, [876]

court-martial—*contd*
air force—*contd*
general—
constitution of, **3**, [849]
convening, **3**, [848]
powers, **3**, [850]
imprisonment in default of fine, **3**, [806],
[1375]
judge-advocate general, functions of,
3, [883]
judge advocates, **3**, [847]
juveniles—
custodial sentence, reasons for awarding,
3, [805]
punishment of, **3**, [803]
meaning, **3**, [995]
oath, administration of, **3**, [854]
offences in relation to, **3**, [787]
open court, sitting in, **3**, [855]
powers—
different types, of, **3**, [850]
election for court-martial trial, in case
of, **3**, [851]
proceedings—
custody during, **3**, [816]
right of penalised parent to, **3**, [911]
punishments, **3**, [802]
restitution or compensation, ordering,
3, [908], [1376]
retrial, **3**, [1358]
authorisation of, **3**, [872]
rules of procedure, **3**, [866]
sentences of. *See also* **sentence**, **3**, [858]
life, reasons for not passing, **3**, [801]
minimum—
guilty pleas, reduction for, **3**, [800]
reasons for not passing, **3**, [801]
promulgation, **3**, [909]
review of, **3**, [870]
authority, powers of, **3**, [871]
sitting, place of, **3**, [852]
witness—
attendance of, power to compel, **3**, [864]
privilege of, **3**, [862]
written statement, proof by, **3**, [861],
[1374]
young service offender—
custodial sentence, reasons for awarding,
3, [805]
punishment of, **3**, [804]
alibi, notice of, **12(1)**, [383]
Appeal Court. *See* **Courts-Martial Appeal
Court**
appeal to House of Lords—
application for leave, **3**, [1336]
bail, grant of, **3**, [1338]
costs, **3**, [1343]
detention of accused, **3**, [1339]
disposal of, **3**, [1337]
hearing, **3**, [1337]
presence of accused, **3**, [1340]
restitution of property order, effect on,
3, [1342]
right of, **3**, [1335]
sentence, effect on, **3**, [1341]

court-martial—*contd*
appeal to House of Lords—*contd*
single judge of Appeal Court, powers of,
3, [1344]
appeals—
appellants—
expenses of, **3**, [1327]
presence of, **3**, [1320]
application for leave, **3**, [1297]
army, **3**, [1]
assessor, appointment of, **3**, [1323]
bail, release on, pending outcome of,
3, [1732]
CCRC, following reference by, **3(S)**, 500
conviction on different charge, **3**, [1302],
[1307]
guilty plea, after, **3**, [1303]
costs, **3**, [1324]
deceased persons, on behalf of, **3**, [1345]
detention pending, **3(S)**, 502
disposal by Appeal Court, **3**, [1300]
documents, furnishing, **3**, [1333]
evidence at, **3**, [1321]
exclusion of retrial, **3**, [1309]
finding of insanity—
against, **3**, [1312]–[1313]
substitution of, **3**, [1305]
finding of unfitness to stand trial, against,
3, [1315]
hospital orders, against, **3**, [1317]–[1318]
House of Lords, to. *See* appeal to House of
Lords *above*
less serious conviction, substitution of,
3, [1304], [1307]
member of trial court, report by, **3**, [1322]
point of law, reference on, **3**, [1328]
presentation of case, **3**, [1319]
procedural directions, **3**, [1331]–[1332]
proceedings of trial court, furnishing,
3, [1333]
registrar, powers of, **3**, [1330]–[1331]
removal of prisoner to court, **3**, [1348]
retrial, power to authorise, **3**, [1310]
right of, **3**, [1296], [1746]
sentence—
adjustment of, **3**, [1301], [1307]
against, **3**, [1306]
service authorities, reference by, **3**, [1328]
single judge, powers of, **3**, [1329], [1331]
special commissioner, referral to, **3**, [1323]
UK, court held outside, **3**, [1298]
unfitness to stand trial—
hospital order—
disposal of appeal, **3**, [1318]
right of appeal against, **3**, [1317]
substitution of finding, **3**, [1305], [1314]
witnesses' expenses, **3**, [1326]
army—
adjournment of, **3**, [579]
affirmation before, **3**, [592]
age of offender, **3**, [699]
alternative offences, **3**, [586], [727]
appeal. *See* appeal *above*
board of inquiry report on desertion as,
3, [633]

court-martial—*contd*
  army—*contd*
    challenge by accused, **3**, [580]
    civil court, jurisdiction of, **3**, [629]
    civil offence, convicting of, **3**, [586]
    civilians, trial of. *See* **civilians**
    court administration officers—
      convening, **3**, [575]
      meaning, **3**, [573]
    custody, amendments relating to, **3**, [1743]
    decisions of, **3**, [584]
    dissolution of, **3**, [583]
    district—
      constitution of, **3**, [576]
      convening, **3**, [575]
      powers, **3**, [577]
    evidence. *See* **evidence**
    field general—
      constitution of, **3**, [595]
      convening, **3**, [594]
      rules, **3**, [596]
    finding—
      announcing, **3**, [585]
      promulgation, **3**, [636]
      review of, **3**, [597]
        authority, powers of, **3**, [598]
    fine, awarding, **3**, [529]
      imprisonment in default, **3**, [533],
        [1375]
    fitness to stand trial—
      accused did act, findings where, **3**, [604]
      insanity—
        findings of, **3**, [605], [878]
        Mental Health Act, orders under,
          3, [607], [880]
        person suffering from, power to deal
          with, **3**, [606], [879]
        supervision orders, **3**, [608], [881]
      questions as to, **3**, [603]
      registered medical practitioner, evidence
        from, **3**, [609], [882]
    general—
      constitution of, **3**, [576]
      convening, **3**, [575]
      generally, **3**, [1]
      powers, **3**, [577]
    judge advocates, **3**, [574]
    meaning, **3**, [723]
    oath, administration of, **3**, [581]
    objection to members, **3**, [580]
    offence—
      attempt to commit, conviction for,
        3, [586]
      by civilians in relation to, **3**, [590]
      other than charged, convicting on,
        3, [586], [727]
      relating to, **3**, [514]
    offender ceasing to be subject to military
      law, **3**, [627]
    open court, sitting in, **3**, [582]
    penalty on conviction, **3**, [1]
    powers—
      different types, of, **3**, [577]
      election for court-martial trial, in case
        of, **3**, [578]

court-martial—*contd*
  army—*contd*
    proof by written statement, **3**, [588]
    property obtained unlawfully—
      compensation for loss, **3**, [635], [1376]
      generally, **3**, [635]
      owner, delivery to, **3**, [635]
      restitution, **3**, [635], [1376]
    punishment—
      civil offences—
        guilty plea, reduction in minimum
          sentence for, **3**, [527]
        life sentence, not passing, **3**, [528]
      generally, **3**, [529]
      juveniles, **3**, [530]
      young service offenders, **3**, [531]–[532]
    record of proceedings—
      accused's right to copy, **3**, [637]
      generally, **3**, [637]–[638]
      penalised parent or guardian's right to
        copy, **3**, [638]
    retrial, **3**, [1357]
      authorisation of, **3**, [599]
    Rules of Procedure, **3**, [593]
      provisions of, **3**, [593]
    sentence—
      announcing, **3**, [585]
      promulgation, **3**, [636]
      review of, **3**, [597]
        authority, powers of, **3**, [598]
      See also **sentence**
    sitting, place of, **3**, [579]
    supervision and control, **3**, [1]
    witness on oath, **3**, [581]
      attendance of, power to enforce,
        3, [591]
      privilege of, **3**, [589]
    written statement, proof by, **3**, [1374]
    young offenders, custodial orders,
      3, [531]–[532]
  causing or allowing death of child or
    vulnerable adult, evidence and procedure,
    12(4), [5]
  charge allocated for, powers of DSP,
    3(S), 128–9
  charges, amendment of, **3(S)**, 159
  civilians. *See* **civilians**
  constitution, **3(S)**, 153
  coroner, application of enactments relating
    to, **3**, [624], [897]
  costs—
    legal representatives, against, **3**, [1729]
    provision for orders as to, **3**, [1728], [1730]
  court administration officer, **3(S)**, 326
  Court Martial Appeal Court, reference of
    cases to, **12(2)**, [284]
  criminal evidence—
    accused's failure or refusal to account for,
      18, [293]
    accused's silence, **18**, [293]
    criminal evidence, application of provisions,
      18, [260]
  cross-examination by accused, **18**, [357]
  custody, conditional release from, **3**, [1732]
  custody during proceedings of, **3(S)**, 116

court-martial—*contd*
  establishment of, **3(S)**, 152
  evidence before, **3**, [1], [1512]
  findings and sentence by, **3(S)**, 156
  formal admission, proof by, **12(1)**, [382], [383]
  hospital order—
    making, **3(S)**, 166
    meaning, **3(S)**, 166
    remission of accused for trial, **3(S)**, 168–9
  Judge Advocate, deputies, abolition of office of, **3**, [1745]
  judicial review, restriction of, **3**, [1727]
  jurisdiction, **3(S)**, 65
  legal representatives, costs against, **3**, [1729]
  medical witness, costs of, **12(1)**, [387]
  membership—
    lay, **3(S)**, 153
    officers and warrant officers ineligible for in particular circumstances, **3(S)**, 155
    officers and warrant officers qualified for, **3(S)**, 154
  miscarriages of justice, compensation for, **3(S)**, 255
    assessment of, **3**, [1536]
    assessors, **3(S)**, 377–8
    right to, **3**, [1521]
  navy—
    accused—
      challenge by, **3**, [1120]
      electing trial by, powers where, **3**, [1124]
    affirmation, administration of, **3**, [1121]
    alternative offences, **3**, [1142]
    appeal. *See* appeals *above*
    attempt, power to convict of, **3**, [1143]
    civilians. *See* **civilians**
    composition, **3**, [1115]
    contempt by civilians, **3**, [1137]
    conviction of, **3**, [1064]
    court administration officers—
      assembling, **3**, [1114]
      meaning, **3**, [1112]
    custody, amendments relating to, **3**, [1743]
    dissolution of, **3**, [1117]
    evidence—
      admissibility of, **3**, [1133]
      age, of, **3**, [1216]
      proceedings, of, **3**, [1214]
      service facts and records, proof by, **3**, [1135]
      written statement, proof by, **3**, [1134]
    finding, **3**, [1123]
      review of, **3**, [1144]
      reviewing authority—
        powers, **3**, [1145]
        review by, **3**, [1144]
    fitness to stand trial—
      accused committed act, findings where, **3**, [1126]
      insanity—
        findings of, **3**, [1127]
        Mental Health Act, orders under, **3**, [1129]
        person suffering from, power to deal with, **3**, [1128]

court-martial—*contd*
  navy—*contd*
    fitness to stand trial—*contd*
      insanity—*contd*
        supervision orders, **3**, [1130]
        questions as to, **3**, [1125]
        registered medical practitioner, evidence from, **3**, [1131]
    imprisonment in default of fine, **3**, [1375]
    judge advocate, appointment of, **3**, [1113]
    jurisdiction, **3**, [1087]
    juveniles, reasons for awarding custodial sentence, **3**, [1070]
    limit on time for, **3**, [1089]
    members, **3**, [1115]
    mitigated offence, power to convict of, **3**, [1141]
    oath, administration of, **3**, [1121]
    offences relating to, **3**, [1060]
    open court, in, **3**, [1122]
    ordering, **3**, [1114]
    persons no longer subject to Act, **3**, [1088]
    place of, **3**, [1116]
    punishment of civil offences—
      guilty plea, reduction in minimum sentence for, **3**, [1065]
      life sentence, not passing, **3**, [1066]
    quorum, **3**, [1118]
    re-trial, **3**, [1146], [1356]
    record of proceedings, **3**, [1139]
      penalised parent or guardian's right to, **3**, [1140]
    rules of procedure, **3**, [1119]
    sentence. *See also* **sentence**, **3**, [1123]
      reviewing authority—
        powers, **3**, [1145]
        review by, **3**, [1144]
    time of sitting, **3**, [1116]
    witnesses—
      attendance, power to compel, **3**, [1138]
      summoning, **3**, [1132]
    young service offender—
      custodial sentence, reasons for awarding, **3**, [1070]
      punishments, **3**, [1069]
  offences other than charged, conviction of, **3(S)**, 156–7
  open court, sitting in, **3(S)**, 155
  prisoners of war, **3**, [1360]
  punishments available to, **3(S)**, 160–1
    civilian offenders, **3(S)**, 351
    ex servicemen, **3(S)**, 352–3
  retrial, **3**, [1356]–[1358]
  retrial after acquittal, application of provisions, **12(3)**, [868]
  rules, **3(S)**, 157–9
  rulings and directions by, **3(S)**, 156
  sentences—
    commencement of, **3(S)**, 264
    individual, for each offence, **3(S)**, 238
    pre-sentence reports, **3(S)**, 238–40
  Service Civilian Court, appeal from—
    findings and sentence on, **3(S)**, 262
    hearing, **3(S)**, 261
    right of, **3(S)**, 260–1

court-martial—*contd*
  service parent or guardian, recognizance and
    fines by—
      amount of, **3(S)**, 219
      appeals, **3(S)**, 220
      duration, **3(S)**, 219
      forfeiture of recognizance, **3(S)**, 221–2
      order for, **3(S)**, 219
      variation and revocation, **3(S)**, 220
  service restraining order—
      appeals, **3(S)**, 218
      power to make, **3(S)**, 216
      remission of case to, **3(S)**, 217
      variation and revocation, **3(S)**, 218
  service supervision order—
      making, **3(S)**, 166
      meaning, **3(S)**, 167
      regulations, **3(S)**, 167–8
      requirements for, **3(S)**, 167
  sexual offences, anonymity of victims,
    application of provisions, **12(2)**, [141]
  sitting, place of, **3(S)**, 152
  suspended sentence of service detention,
    activation of, **3(S)**, 186–7
      appeals, **3(S)**, 187–8
  trial—
      election for—
        consequences of, **3(S)**, 133
        right of, **3(S)**, 132
        sentencing powers, **3(S)**, 162–3
        Service Civilian Court, instead of,
          3(S), 258
      fitness to stand, question of, **3(S)**, 163
        duly approved medical practitioners,
          3(S), 169–70
        remission of accused for trial,
          3(S), 168–9
        reports tendered in evidence,
          3(S), 169–70
      insanity, finding of, **3(S)**, 165
        mental health provisions, modifications
          of, **3(S)**, 354–5
        powers on, **3(S)**, 166
      remission of accused for, **3(S)**, 168–9
      unfitness to stand—
        determining, **3(S)**, 163
        findings on, **3(S)**, 164
        mental health provisions, modifications
          of, **3(S)**, 354–5
        powers on, **3(S)**, 166
  witnesses and persons attending, privileges and
    immunities of, **3(S)**, 157
  witnesses, warrants of arrest in respect of,
    33(2), [592]
  written statement, proof by, **12(1)**, [381],
    [383]

Courts-Martial Appeal Court
  amended provisions, **3(S)**, 366–76
  appeal to, **3(S)**, 252
  appellant, right to be present at hearing,
    3(S), 372
  application for leave, considering, **3**, [1299]
  cases dealt with, **3**, [600], [873], [1147]
  constitution of, **3**, [1293]

Courts-Martial Appeal Court—*contd*
  costs—
      legal representatives, against, **3**, [1729]
      provision for orders as to, **3**, [1728], [1730]
  Criminal Cases Review Commission, powers
    of, **3(S)**, 379–84
  evidence before, **3**, [1512]
  generally, **3**, [1289]
  hospital order, appeal against, **3(S)**, 371
  judges, **3**, [1290]
  protected prisoner of war, court-martial of,
    3(S), 374
  record of Court Martial proceedings,
    provision of, **3(S)**, 373
  registrar, duties of, **3**, [1347]
  regulations, power of Secretary of State to
    make, **3(S)**, 254
  retrial in, **3(S)**, 375
  retrial, power to authorise, **3**, [1146]
  right of appeal to, **3**, [1746]
  rules of court, **3**, [1346]
  senior judges as judge of, **3**, [1291]
  sentence, appeal against, **3(S)**, 368
  sentences reviewed by, **3**, [601], [874], [1148]
  sittings, **3**, [1292]
  some but not all convictions successfully
    appealed, power to re-sentence on,
    3(S), 367
  staff of, **3**, [1295]
  Supreme Court, reference of point of law to,
    3(S), 253–4
  unduly lenient sentence, review of,
    3(S), 252–3

Courts and Legal Services Act 1990
  amendments to, **11(4)**, [359], [361]

covenant
  alteration of user, against, **21**, [65]
  application for consent, passing on, **22**, [785]
  assignments—
      against, **21**, [65]; **22**, [784]
      benefit of, effects of becoming entitled to,
        23, [299]
      excluded, **23**, [288]
      liability under, effects of becoming subject
        to, **23**, [299]
      loss of benefit of, effects of, **23**, [300]
      meaning, **23**, [304]
      release from liability, effects of, **23**, [300]
  breach of—
      duty, **22**, [787]
      local authority, entry by, **21**, [768]
      rentcharge, of, remedies, **20**, [791]
      under-lessees, relief of, **21**, [75]
      vendor, duty to disclose, **20**, [663]
  charging, against, **21**, [65]
  charity, to. *See* **charity**
  consent under, duty to approve, **22**, [786]
  consequential amendments and repeals,
    23, [306]
  enforcement of, **23**, [292]
  excluded assignments, **23**, [288]
  forfeiture or disclaimer limited to part only of
    demised premises, **23**, [298]

covenant—*contd*
heir, binding on, **20**, [439]
indemnity, abolition of, implied by statute,
  23, [291]
implied—
  benefit of, annexation to estate, **20**, [694]
  construction of, **20**, [701]
  conveyance, in—
    beneficial owner, as, **20**, [815]–[818]
    beneficial owner, by, **20**, [694]
    entirety of land comprised in lease,
      20, [823]
    generally, **20**, [694]
    interest created by lease, **20**, [823], [824]
    mortgage, by way of, **20**, [694]
    mortgagee, by, **20**, [694]
    personal representative, as, **20**, [694],
      [820]
    settlor, by, **20**, [694], [819]
    subject to rents, **20**, [695]
    trustee, by, **20**, [694]
  lease, in—
    interest created, **20**, [823]
    residue of term, **20**, [824]
  rentcharge, land affected by, **20**, [821],
    [822]; **21**, [511]
  statutory mortgages, **20**, [734], [736]
  title, for—
    annexation of benefit of, **23**, [226]
    charges, incumbrances and third party
      rights, as to, **23**, [222]
    discharge of obligations, **23**, [224]
    disposition of property, on, **23**, [220]
    full title guarantee, **23**, [220]
    further assurance, **23**, [221]
    husband and wife, **20**, [694]
    lease, validity of, **23**, [223]
    leasehold land, **23**, [224]
    limited title guarantee, **23**, [220]
    new form, in, **23**, [231]
    no liability, where, **23**, [225]
    old form, in, **23**, [229], [230]
    operation, limitation or extension,
      23, [227]
    options, transitional provisions, **23**, [232]
    rentcharge, property subject to, **23**, [224]
    right to dispose, **23**, [221]
    statutory forms, modification of,
      23, [228]
    subject matter conveyed by directions,
      20, [694]
    variation or extension, **20**, [694]
    Welsh terms, **23**, [227]
  when excluded, **20**, [677]
improvements, against making without
  consent, **21**, [65]
indemnity, implied by statute, abolition of,
  23, [291]
interpretation provisions, **23**, [304]
land, relating to—
  benefit of, **20**, [696]
  binding, **20**, [698]
  burden of, **20**, [697]
  enforceability by local authorities, **21**, [768]

covenant—*contd*
lease, in—
  assignment, underletting etc., fine,
    exclusion, **20**, [754]
  benefit to run with reversion, **20**, [751]
  breach, relief against forfeiture on,
    20, [756]
  internal decorative repairs, as to, **20**, [757]
  observance, assumption on sale, **20**, [663]
  protection of rights, **20**, [630]
  under-lessees, relief of, **21**, [75]
  waiver, **20**, [758]
lessor's, obligation to run with reversion,
  20, [752]
liability—
  apportionment of, binding both assignor
    and assignee of tenancy or reversion,
    23, [286], [287]
  joint, **23**, [290]
  release from, effects of, **23**, [300]
  restriction on, of former tenant or his
    guarantor—
    rent or service charge, for, **23**, [294]
    tenancy subsequently varied, where,
      23, [295]
  tenant guaranteeing performance of
    covenant by assignee, **23**, [293]
loss of benefit of, effects of, **23**, [300]
management companies etc, with, **23**, [289]
meaning, **23**, [304]
miscellaneous savings, **23**, [302]
notices, **23**, [303]
overriding leases—
  parting with possession, against, **21**, [65];
    22, [784]
  right of former tenant or his guarantor to,
    23, [296]
  supplementary provisions, **23**, [297]
provisions applicable to, **23**, [279]
release of—
  reversion, landlords may be released on
    assignment of, **23**, [283]–[285]
  tenancy, tenant released on assignment of,
    23, [282]
rent, indemnity against, **20**, [790]
rentcharge, in—
  enforcement, **21**, [502]
  remedies for breach, **20**, [791]
repair, to. *See* **repairing covenant**
restrictive, affecting land—
  benefit of, **20**, [626], [696]
  burden of, **20**, [697]
  compensation for, **20**, [702]
  court, declaration by as to effect of,
    20, [702]
  discharge or modification, **20**, [702]
  enforcement, stay of proceedings, **20**, [702]
  land charges, as, **20**, [799]; **21**, [392]
  Lands Tribunal, powers, **20**, [702];
    21, [371]
  memorandum, purchaser not holding
    documents, **20**, [799]
  notice of, **20**, [799]
  registered land. *See* **land registration**
  registration as land charge, **20**, [799]

covenant—*contd*

restrictive, affecting land—*contd*

Royal parks, savings, **20**, [702]

running with the land, **20**, [698]

self and others, with, enforcement, **20**, [700]

stamp duty—

abolitions, **41**, [152], [157]

sale of right secured by, **41**, [39]

separate deed, **41**, [152], [157]

successor in title—

meaning, **20**, [696], [697]

when binding on, **20**, [696], [697]

summary of provisions, **20**, [1]

tenancies to which provisions apply, **23**, [278]

third party, **23**, [289]

title, for, inclusion in conveyance, **20**, [694], [815]

transmission of—

benefit and burden of, **23**, [280]

re-entry, landlord's rights of, **23**, [281]

two or more persons jointly, made with, **20**, [699]

underletting, against, **21**, [65]; **22**, [784]

voidness of agreements restricting operation of 1995 Act, **23**, [301]

war damage, effect of notices following, **21**, [102]

Covent Garden Market Authority

pension provisions, **33(1)**, [137], [147]

cows. *See* **cattle**

coypus

poison, use of against, **2**, [363]

crab. *See* **shellfish**

crane

requisition, compensation for, **9**, [123]

creative artist

fluctuating profits, averaging—

adjustment, **44(3)**, [223]–[225]

claim for—

circumstances for, **44(3)**, [222]

making, **44(3)**, [221]

credit

fraudulently obtaining, **4(2)**, [11]

meaning, **39(1)**, [142]

total charge for, **39(1)**, [155]

transaction associated with, **44(1)**, [537]

wrongful, dishonestly retaining, **12(1)**, [576]

credit institution

meaning, **8(1)**, [1251]

overseas, accounts and reports, **8(1)**, [1128]

credit reference agency

meaning, **7(1)**, [542]

right of access to personal data held by, **7(1)**, [478]

credit-sale agreement

emergency laws, **50**, [262]

credit-token

acceptance of, **39(1)**, [222]

agreement—

cancellation rights, notice of, **39(1)**, [220]

meaning, **39(1)**, [147]

supply of copy of, **39(1)**, [218], [219]

issue of, duty on, **39(1)**, [242]

loss arising from use of, **39(1)**, [241]

meaning, **39(1)**, [147]

misuse of, **39(1)**, [241]

proceedings, onus of proof, **39(1)**, [333]

unsolicited, prohibited, **39(1)**, [207]

credit union

accounts—

audit, modification of requirements, **19(1)**, [589]

production of, **19(1)**, [583]

unaudited, display of, **19(1)**, [589]

amalgamation of unions, **19(1)**, [586]

bank administration provisions applying, **19(S)**, Financial 217

bank insolvency provisions applying, **19(S)**, Financial 184–5

books, production of, **19(1)**, [583]

borrow money, power to, **19(1)**, [577]

company—

conversion to credit union, **19(1)**, [588]

credit union not to convert to, **19(1)**, [587]

deposit—

ancillary services, power to charge for, **19(1)**, [576]

general prohibition on taking, **19(1)**, [574]

persons under membership age, by, **19(1)**, [575]

dissolution, rules for, **19(1)**, [596]

dividends, payment of, **19(1)**, [581]

financial statement by, **19(1)**, [583]

income, computing, **44(1)**, [326]

information, duty to give, **19(1)**, [583]

inspector, power to appoint, **19(1)**, [584]

insurance, guarantee funds, **19(1)**, [582]

investigation of—

expenses of, **19(1)**, [584]

inspector, appointment of, **19(1)**, [584]

land, power to hold, **19(1)**, [580]

loans to members—

interest on, **19(1)**, [578]

secured, **19(1)**, [579]

meaning, **19(1)**, [593]; **44(1)**, [326]

meeting, special, power to call, **19(1)**, [584]

members—

common bond, necessity for, **19(1)**, [567]

individuals only may be, **19(1)**, [571]

minimum and maximum number, **19(1)**, [572]

non-qualifying, **19(1)**, [571], [586], [593]

qualifications of, **19(1)**, [567]

share qualification, **19(1)**, [571]

voting rights, **19(1)**, [571]

membership—

restriction of, **19(1)**, [567]

credit union—*contd*
  membership—*contd*
    rules for, **19(1)**, [596]
    termination of, **19(1)**, [596]
  name, essential element of, **19(1)**, [569]
  Northern Ireland, in, **19(1)**, [594]
  objects of, **19(1)**, [567]
    wholly charitable, not regarded as,
      19(1), [568]
  offences, **19(1)**, [591]
  profits—
    application of, **19(1)**, [581]
    computation of, **19(1)**, [581]
  registrar—
    information, power to obtain, **19(1)**, [583]
    orders by, **19(1)**, [592]
    petition for winding up by, **19(1)**, [585]
  registration—
    cancellation of, **19(1)**, [585]
    change of, **19(1)**, [568]
    conditions for, **19(1)**, [567]
    industrial and provident society, as,
      19(1), [567]
      cancellation of, **19(1)**, [568]
    number of members for, **19(1)**, [572]
    provisions to be complied with,
      19(1), [568]
    statutory provisions for, **19(1)**, [567]
    suspension of, **19(1)**, [585]
    transitional provisions, **19(1)**, [568]
  rules—
    fee for copy of, **19(1)**, [571]
    form and content, **19(1)**, [570]
    matters provided for in, **19(1)**, [596]
    provisions applied to, **19(1)**, [570]
  seal, custody and use, **19(1)**, [596]
  shares—
    denomination of, **19(1)**, [573]
    members' maximum holding, **19(1)**, [572]
    non-transferable, **19(1)**, [573]
    rules as to, **19(1)**, [596]
    transfer on death, **19(1)**, [573]
    withdrawal, **19(1)**, [573]
  special resolution regime, application of,
    19(S), Financial 146
  subsidiaries, prohibition on, **19(1)**, [590]
  summary of provisions, **19(1)**, [1]
  transfer of engagements, **19(1)**, [586]
  transfer of functions, **19(2)**, [413], [414]
  use of term, restriction on, **19(1)**, [569]
  voting rights, **19(1)**, [571]
  winding up, petition for, **19(1)**, [585]

creditors
  arrangements with. *See* **deed of**
    arrangement
  bankruptcy, in. *See* **bankruptcy**
  defrauding, **4(2)**, [11]
  meaning, **39(1)**, [353]
  payment of, disclosure of policy and practice
    of, **8**, 668–9
  surety, assignment by, **11(1)**, [298]

creditors—*contd*
  winding up, in. *See* **winding up**

cremation
  burial regulations applicable, **36**, [40]
  burial service—
    fees, fixing, **5(2)**, [438]
    certificate for, falsifying, **5(2)**, [434]
  fees—
    burial authority, charges by, **5(2)**, [436],
      [438]
    medical certificate, for, **5(2)**, [444]
  local authority, duty of, **35(1)**, [487]
  notification to registrar, **36**, [36]
  nuisance, commission or permitting,
    5(2), [439]
  provision for, **5(2)**, [431]
  registers, maintenance of, **5(2)**, [434]
  regulations, **5(2)**, [434]
  summary of provisions, **5(2)**, [319]
  unlawful, **5(2)**, [434]
  value added tax, exemption from, **50**, [153]

crematorium
  certification, **5(2)**, [442]
  coroner, saving for jurisdiction of, **5(2)**, [437]
  deductible payments, **44(1)**, [68]
  donations of land for, **5(2)**, [433]
  inspection, **5(2)**, [434]
  London—
    burial authority powers, **25(1)**, [1008]
    dwelling-house, proximity to, **25(1)**, [235],
      [1008]
    savings, **25(1)**, [237]
  maintenance—
    after transfer to burial authority,
      5(2), [446]
    regulations for, **5(2)**, [434]
  meaning, **5(2)**, [430]
  new, certification for use, **5(2)**, [442]
  provision of, **5(2)**, [431]
  site, control, **5(2)**, [432]
  trade profits—
    application of provisions, **44(3)**, [169]
    capital expenditure—
      ancillary, allocation of, **44(3)**, [171]
      deduction for, **44(3)**, [170]
    definitions, **44(3)**, [169]
    subsidies, met by, **44(3)**, [172]
  transfer, maintenance after, **5(2)**, [446]

crew (ship). *See also* **mariners**
  accommodation—
    meaning, **39(2)**, [710]
    regulations, **39(2)**, [710]
  agreement—
    exemption from requirement, **39(2)**, [692]
    provisions and form of, **39(2)**, [692]
    regulations, **39(2)**, [693]
    requirement of, **39(2)**, [692]
    wages due under—
      account of, **39(2)**, [698]
      disputes, **39(2)**, [700]
      payment of, **39(2)**, [697]
      regulations, **39(2)**, [699]

crew (ship)—*contd*
death of member, inquiry into, **39(2)**, [950]
English, knowledge of, **39(2)**, [718]
injuries, reports and inquiries, **39(2)**, [951]
lists of, **39(2)**, [744]
manning regulations, **39(2)**, [714]
relief costs, financial assistance for,
  39(2), [742]
young persons as, **39(2)**, [722]

crime against humanity
ancillary offence—
  investigation, rights during, **10**, [1224]
  meaning, **10**, [1193]
application of provisions, **10**, [1188]
commanders and other superiors,
  responsibility of, **10**, [1203]
committed outside the jurisdiction, conduct
  ancillary to, **10**, [1190]
elements of, **10**, [1231]
England and Wales, offence in, **10**, [1189]
extradition request in respect of, **18**, [956]
general principles of liability, application of,
  10, [1194]
International Criminal Court, offences in
  relation to, **10**, [1192]
meaning, **10**, [1188], [1231]
mental element, **10**, [1204]
Northern Ireland. *See* **Northern Ireland**
omission, act including, **10**, [1207]
person subject to UK service jurisdiction,
  meaning, **10**, [1205]
persons becoming resident in the jurisdiction,
  proceedings against, **10**, [1206]
trial and punishment of, **10**, [1191]
UK national, meaning, **10**, [1205]
UK resident, meaning, **10**, [1205]
victims and witnesses, protection of,
  10, [1195]

crime and disorder
guidance on matters of, **12(4)**, [263]
local authority committee—
  City of London, in, **12(4)**, [282]
  functions of, **12(4)**, [282]
  joint, **12(4)**, [264]
  meetings, **12(4)**, [282]
  reports, **12(4)**, [262]
  requirement to have, **12(4)**, [262]
  sub-committees, **12(4)**, [282]

crime and disorder strategy
authorities, consideration of implications by,
  12(2), [665]
formulation and implementation of,
  12(2), [663]
information, sharing, **12(2)**, [666]
reports, **12(2)**, [664]
responsibility for, **12(2)**, [662]

crime prevention
payments or grants for, **12(2)**, [247]
serious crime prevention order. *See* **serious
  crime prevention order**
summary of provisions, **12(1)**, [1]

crime reduction
contribution to, **12(3)**, [171]

criminal appeal
acquittal verdict, direction as to, **12(1)**, [424]
allowing, grounds for, **12(1)**, [417]
  guilty plea, after, **12(1)**, [419]
alternative verdict, substitution of,
  12(1), [418]
arraign, grant of leave to, **12(1)**, [424]
bail, provisions on, **12(1)**, [438]
community treatment order, continuation of,
  12(1), [319]
continued detention under Mental Health
  Act, ordering, **12(1)**, [432], [471]
conviction, quashing, **12(1)**, [417]
Criminal Cases Review Commission—
  direction for investigation by, **12(1)**, [443]
  dismissal following references by,
    12(1), [435]
death of appellant, **12(1)**, [461]
disability, against finding of, **12(1)**, [431]
effect of order, **12(1)**, [417]
groundless, disposal of, **12(1)**, [439]
grounds for, **12(1)**, [426]
hearing—
  appellant, right to be present, **12(1)**, [441]
  evidence at, **12(1)**, [442]
  preparation for, **12(1)**, [440]
  witness attending, **12(1)**, [442]
hospital order, against—
  disposal of, **12(1)**, [434]
  right of, **12(1)**, [433]
hospital order, making, **12(1)**, [341], [342],
  [422], [430]
  interim, **12(1)**, [446]
House of Lords, to—
  application for leave, **12(1)**, [316], [453]
  bail pending, **12(1)**, [317], [318], [455]
  sentence, computation of, **12(1)**, [320]
  community treatment order, continuation
    of, **12(1)**, [457]
  Crown, by, **12(1)**, [456]
  defendant—
    detention of, **12(1)**, [456]
    presence at hearing, **12(1)**, [321], [458]
  hearing and disposal, **12(1)**, [454]
  prosecutor, by, **12(1)**, [456]
  right of, **12(1)**, [315], [452]
  sentence, effect on, **12(1)**, [459]
insanity, against verdict of—
  disposal of, **12(1)**, [429]
  hospital order on, **12(1)**, [341], [342],
    [422], [430]
  proof of medical condition, **12(1)**, [465]
  right of, **12(1)**, [428]
  See also **insanity**
insanity, substitution of finding of,
  12(1), [422], [430]
leave, grant of, **12(1)**, [447]
notice of, **12(1)**, [436]
pardon, grant of, **12(1)**, [365]
prerogative of mercy, and, **12(1)**, [365]
procedure, **12(1)**, [436]

criminal appeal—*contd*
registrar, powers exercisable by, **12(1)**, [448]
  procedural directions, **12(1)**, [449]
    appeal against, **12(1)**, [450]
related offence, appellant remaining convicted
  of, **12(1)**, [420]
restitution of property order, suspension of,
  12(1), [445]
retrial—
  depositions, **12(1)**, [470]
  fresh indictment, referral of, **12(1)**, [424]
  oral evidence at, **12(1)**, [470]
  order for, application to set aside,
    12(1), [424]
  orders on, **12(1)**, [424]
  power to order, **12(1)**, [423]
  procedural provisions, **12(1)**, [424], [470]
  sentence on conviction at, **12(1)**, [470]
right of, **12(1)**, [416]
sentence—
  meaning, **12(1)**, [464]
  related offence, appellant remaining
    convicted of, **12(1)**, [420]
  severity, not increasing, **12(1)**, [427]
sentence, against—
  Court of Appeal, with leave of,
    12(1), [427]
  effect on, **12(1)**, [444]
  indictment, where convicted on,
    12(1), [425]
  indictment, where not convicted on,
    12(1), [426]
  interim hospital order, **12(1)**, [427]
  judge granting certificate for, **12(1)**, [427]
  magistrates' court, convicted in,
    12(1), [426]
  quashing, **12(1)**, [427]
  substitution of sentence, **12(1)**, [427]
  suspended sentence, dealing with,
    12(1), [427]
  two or more, passing, **12(1)**, [426]
single judge, powers exercisable by,
  12(1), [447], [460], [462]
  procedural directions, **12(1)**, [449]
    appeal against, **12(1)**, [450]
special verdict, against, **12(1)**, [421]
supervision order, against—
  disposal of, **12(1)**, [434]
  right of, **12(1)**, [433]
transcripts, **12(1)**, [451]
unfitness to plead. *See* **unfitness to plead**
unsafe, conviction being, **12(1)**, [417]
value, mistake of, **12(1)**, [416]

criminal assize court
transitional provisions, **11(2)**, [264]

Criminal Cases Review Commission
annual reports and accounts, **12(2)**, [305]
constitution, **12(2)**, [279]
court-martial appeals, powers as to,
  3(S), 379–84, 500
court-martial, cases dealt with by,
  12(2), [284]

Criminal Cases Review Commission—*contd*
Court of Appeal—
  direction for investigation by, **12(1)**, [443]
    investigation under, **12(2)**, [288]
  reference of cases to, dismissal of appeal
    following, **12(1)**, [435]; **12(2)**, [280]
    application, with or without,
      12(2), [287]
    conditions for, **12(2)**, [286]
    guilty but insane, former verdict of,
      12(2), [704]–[706]
    Northern Ireland, from, **12(2)**, [281]
    verdict of insanity, **12(2)**, [280]
Crown Court, reference of cases to,
  12(2), [282]
  application, with or without, **12(2)**, [287]
  conditions for, **12(2)**, [286]
  Northern Ireland, from, **12(2)**, [283]
dismissal of appeals following reference by,
  Northern Ireland, **12(4)**, [487]
documents, power to obtain, **12(2)**, [290]
  government, **12(2)**, [291]
evidence before, **12(2)**, [305]
expenses, **12(2)**, [305]
information obtained, disclosure of,
  12(2), [296]
  consent to, **12(2)**, [298]
  exceptions from obligation, **12(2)**, [297]
investigating officers—
  inquiries by, **12(2)**, [293]
  power to require appointment of,
    12(2), [292]
investigations by, **12(2)**, [288]
members—
  appointment, **12(2)**, [305]
  number of, **12(2)**, [279]
  qualifications, **12(2)**, [279]
  removal from office, **12(2)**, [305]
  remuneration and expenses, **12(2)**, [305]
powers of, **12(2)**, [294]
prerogative of mercy, assistance in connection
  with, **12(2)**, [289]
procedure, **12(2)**, [305]
protected material in relation to sexual
  offences, restrictions on disclosure,
  12(2), [553]
Service Civilian Court, cases dealt with by,
  12(2), [285]
staff, **12(2)**, [305]

criminal conduct
meaning, **6**, [880]
parental compensation order. *See* **parental
  compensation order**
parenting contract in respect of, **6**, [876]
parenting order in respect of, **6**, [877]

criminal damage
evidence, **12(1)**, [603]
generally, **12(1)**, [1]
imprisonment, **12(1)**, [599]
joinder of charge, **12(1)**, [1084]
lawful excuse, without, **12(1)**, [600]
magistrates' court jurisdiction, **12(1)**, [602]
offences, **12(1)**, [596]

criminal damage—*contd*
possessing anything with intent, **12(1)**, [598]
property—
destroying or damaging, **12(1)**, [596]
meaning, **12(1)**, [604]
punishment of offences, **12(1)**, [599]
racially or religiously aggravated, **12(2)**, [670]
search for thing intended for use in, **12(1)**, [601]
threatening, **12(1)**, [597]

Criminal Defence Service. *See under* **Legal Services Commission**

criminal injuries compensation
adjudicators, oaths by, **12(2)**, [364]
award of—
appeals, **12(2)**, [363]
basis of calculation, **12(2)**, [360]
claims, **12(2)**, [361]
inalienability of, **12(2)**, [366]
review of, **12(2)**, [362]
generally, **12(1)**, [1]
offenders, recovery from, **12(4)**, [49]
determinations, review of, **12(2)**, [369]
notices, **12(2)**, [368]
amount, **12(2)**, [367]
proceedings for, **12(2)**, [370]
regulations, **12(2)**, [367]
Scheme—
administration of, **12(2)**, [359]
administrative functions, **10**, [555]
annual reports and records, **12(2)**, [365]
financial provisions, **12(2)**, [371]
Parliamentary Commissioner, jurisdiction of, **12(2)**, [372]
parliamentary control, **12(2)**, [373]
transitional provisions, **12(2)**, [374]

criminal investigation
accused's defence statement, contents of, **12(4)**, [493]
code of practice—
disclosure provisions, **12(2)**, [448]
effect of, **12(2)**, [450]
operation and revision of, **12(2)**, [449]
preparation of, **12(2)**, [447]
provisions in, **12(2)**, [447]
common law rules, **12(2)**, [451]
defence witness—
notification of intention to call, **12(2)**, [428]
police interviews, code of practice, **12(2)**, [445]
disclosure—
accused—
application by, **12(2)**, [432]
authority of, deemed, **12(2)**, [430]
disclosure by—
compulsory, **12(2)**, [424]
failure to comply, warning, **12(2)**, [430]
faults in, **12(2)**, [434]
time limits, **12(2)**, [435]
updated, **12(2)**, [427]

criminal investigation—*contd*
disclosure—*contd*
accused—*contd*
disclosure by—*contd*
voluntary, **12(2)**, [425]
experts instructed by, notification of names of, **12(2)**, [429]
references to, **12(2)**, [421]
application of provisions, **12(2)**, [420]
common law rules, **12(2)**, [444]
confidentiality, **12(2)**, [440]
contravention of provisions, **12(2)**, [441]
Criminal Procedure Rules, **12(2)**, [457]
defence, by—
compulsory, **12(3)**, [823]
faults in, **12(3)**, [824]
defence statement, **12(2)**, [426]
defence witness, notification of intention to call, **12(2)**, [428]
departure from, **12(2)**, [458]
examples of provisions, **12(2)**, [448]
material, references to, **12(2)**, [421]
officers of Secretary of State, by, **12(1)**, [922]
opportunity to be heard, **12(2)**, [439]
prosecutor, by—
continuing duty of, **12(2)**, [431]
initial, **12(2)**, [422], [423]
references to, **12(2)**, [421]
time limits, **12(2)**, [435]
failure to observe, **12(2)**, [433]
transitional, **12(2)**, [436]
public interest review of orders—
generally, **12(2)**, [438]
summary trials, **12(2)**, [437]
rules of court, **12(2)**, [442]
statutory rules, **12(2)**, [443]
disclosure notice—
appropriate person, meaning, **12(4)**, [82]
authorisation, **12(4)**, [82]
banking business, in relation to, **12(4)**, [84]
documents, production of, **12(4)**, [83]
false or misleading statements, making, **12(4)**, [87]
giving of, **12(4)**, [80]
legal privilege, **12(4)**, [84]
legible form, production of information in, **12(4)**, [89]
manner of giving, **12(4)**, [88]
meaning, **12(4)**, [82]
offences, **12(4)**, [87]
power to give, **12(4)**, [82]
privileged documents, **12(4)**, [84]
privileged information, **12(4)**, [84]
privileged questions, **12(4)**, [84]
restrictions, **12(4)**, [84]
search warrant following—
conditions for, **12(4)**, [86]
meaning, **12(4)**, [87]
offences, **12(4)**, [87]
service of, **12(4)**, [88]
signature, **12(4)**, [82]
specified requirements, **12(4)**, [82]
statements, restriction on use of, **12(4)**, [85]

criminal investigation—*contd*
enforcement, power to enter and seize
documents, **12(4)**, [86]
international co-operation—
banking transactions. *See* **banking**
evidence. *See* **evidence; witness**
Investigatory Authorities—
delegation by, **12(4)**, [80]
disclosure notice. *See* disclosure notice *above*
meaning, **12(4)**, [80]
relevant offences, investigation of,
12(4), [81]
meaning, **12(2)**, [420], [446]
mutual assistance, provision for, **12(4)**, [114]
offender, assistance by—
immunity from prosecution, **12(4)**, [90]
sentence—
exclusion of public from proceedings,
12(4), [94]
live link, use of, **12(4)**, [95]
reduction in, **12(4)**, [92]
review, **12(4)**, [93]
use of evidence, undertakings as to,
12(4), [91]
protection of persons involved in—
arrangements, disclosure of information
about—
defences to liability, **12(4)**, [106]
national security, on grounds of,
12(4), [106]
offence, **12(4)**, [105]
interpretation, **12(4)**, [113]
persons assuming new identity, disclosure of
information about—
defences to liability, **12(4)**, [108]
offence, **12(4)**, [107]
protected person, representation relating
to, **12(4)**, [109]
protection provider—
arrangements by, **12(4)**, [101]
duty to assist, **12(4)**, [104]
information, provision of, **12(4)**, [112]
joint arrangements by, **12(4)**, [102]
meaning, **12(4)**, [101]
transfer of responsibility, **12(4)**, [103]
specified persons, **12(4)**, [145]
transitional provisions, **12(4)**, [110], [111]

criminal justice
Head and Deputy Head of, **11(3)**, [463]
recognition of financial penalties, international
co-operation—
central authority for Scotland, transfer of
certificates to, **11(S)**, Courts 27
interpretation, **11(S)**, Courts 29
issue of certificate, procedure on—
England and Wales, **11(S)**, Courts 18–19
Northern Ireland, **11(S)**, Courts 21
magistrates' court, modification of
provisions, **11(S)**, Courts 24
other member states, requests from—
England and Wales, **11(S)**, Courts 21–2
Northern Ireland, **11(S)**, Courts 24–7
other member states, requests to—
England and Wales, **11(S)**, Courts 16–17

criminal justice—*contd*
recognition of financial penalties, international
co-operation—*contd*
other member states, requests to—*contd*
Northern Ireland, **11(S)**, Courts 19–20
penalties suitable for enforcement,
11(S), Courts 40–3
receipt of certificate by designated officer,
procedure on, **11(S)**, Courts 23
refusal to enforce, grounds for,
11(S), Courts 43–6

criminal procedure and practice
criminal court, meaning, **11(3)**, [382]
information, disclosure of, **12(2)**, [690]
practice directions, **11(3)**, [389]
preliminary hearing, use of live link at—
application of provisions, **12(2)**, [680]
custody, accused in, **12(2)**, [681]
police station, accused at, **12(2)**, [682]
sentencing hearing following, **12(2)**, [683]
Rules—
amendment of legislation, **11(3)**, [388]
Committee—
expenses, **11(3)**, [384]
making by, **11(3)**, [383]
members of, **11(3)**, [384]
requirements, power to change,
11(3), [385]
Lord Chancellor, rules to be made if
required by, **11(3)**, [387]
power to make, **11(3)**, [383]
process for making, **11(3)**, [386]
to be made if required by
Lord Chancellor, **11(3)**, [387]
sentence, meaning, **12(1)**, [464], [1081]
sentencing—
review of—
application for, **12(1)**, [1113]
Attorney General, reference of cases by,
12(1), [1082]
cases in which applicable, **12(1)**, [1081]
costs, **12(1)**, [1113]
Court of Appeal, jurisdiction,
12(1), [1081], [1113]
custody of person concerned,
12(1), [1113]
generally, **12(1)**, [1081]
House of Lords, functions and powers,
12(1), [1082], [1113]
leave, by, **12(1)**, [1082], [1113]
Northern Ireland, **12(1)**, [1082], [1113]
point of law involved in, **12(1)**, [1082]
powers of court, **12(1)**, [1082]
presence of accused during,
12(1), [1113]
procedure, **12(1)**, [1113]
supplementary provisions, **12(1)**, [1113]
term of sentence passed on,
12(1), [1113]
sentencing hearing, use of live link at—
application of provisions, **12(2)**, [680]
direction for, **12(2)**, [684]
preliminary hearing, following,
12(2), [683]

Criminal Procedure Rule Committee
powers, **12(1)**, [220]

criminal proceedings. *See also particular subjects of proceedings*
accused's silence. *See* **evidence** (criminal proceedings)
acquittals, proof of, **18**, [248]
armed forces, provisions applied, **18**, [260]
child, involving. *See* **child**
confession, evidence of, **18**, [251]
conviction—
  evidence of commission of offences, as, **18**, [249], [250]
  proof of, **18**, [248]
documentary evidence. *See* **evidence** (criminal proceedings)
evidence in. *See* **evidence**
financial implications, information on, **12(2)**, [117]
magistrates' court, in, discontinuance, **12(1)**, [957], [958]
meaning, **18**, [247], [259]
minors—
  reporting of involvement in—
    offences, **18**, [347], [349]
      defences to, **18**, [348]
      penalties for, **18**, [347]
    restrictions as to, **18**, [342], [343], [345]
      dispensation of, **18**, [343]
  restrictions on reporting, **18**, [344]–[346]
    offences, **18**, [347], [349]
      defences to, **18**, [348]
      dispensation of, **18**, [344]
      penalties for, **18**, [347]
    public interest, in, **18**, [350]
mutual assistance, provision for, **12(4)**, [114]
preliminary stage of, **12(2)**, [478]
prisoner, evidence by, mutual transfer to or from overseas, **12(2)**, [21], [22]
prosecution. *See* **prosecution**
protection of persons involved in—
  arrangements, disclosure of information about—
    defences to liability, **12(4)**, [106]
    national security, on grounds of, **12(4)**, [106]
    offence, **12(4)**, [105]
  interpretation, **12(4)**, [113]
  persons assuming new identity, disclosure of information about—
    defences to liability, **12(4)**, [108]
    offence, **12(4)**, [107]
  protected person, representation relating to, **12(4)**, [109]
  protection provider—
    arrangements by, **12(4)**, [101]
    duty to assist, **12(4)**, [104]
    information, provision of, **12(4)**, [112]
    joint arrangements by, **12(4)**, [102]
    meaning, **12(4)**, [101]
    transfer of responsibility, **12(4)**, [103]
  specified persons, **12(4)**, [145]
  transitional provisions, **12(4)**, [110], [111]
public access, Crown Court, **12(1)**, [1103]

criminal proceedings—*contd*
reporting restrictions, **12(1)**, [1068], [1069]
reports of, Crown Court proceedings, **12(1)**, [1103]
sexual offences, complainant—
  application for leave to question, **18**, [341]
  definitions, **18**, [340], [358]
  protection of, **18**, [339]–[341]
  sexual history, restriction on questions regarding, **18**, [339]
time limits, power to set, **12(1)**, [954]
  persons under 18, in respect of, **12(1)**, [955]
  stayed proceedings, re-institution of, **12(1)**, [956]
trial on indictment—
  corroboration, abolition of rules, **18**, [287]
  right of reply, **18**, [201]
unfair evidence, exclusion of, **18**, [254]
Vienna Convention, **12(2)**, [25]–[27]
written charge, institution by—
  public prosecutor, by, **11(3)**, [434]
  requisition, issue of, **11(3)**, [434]
  rules, **11(3)**, [435]

criminal records
criminal conviction certificates, **33(2)**, [302]
  amended provisions, **33(S)**, Police 3–4
criminal record certificates—
  accuracy of, disputes about, **33(2)**, [314]
  amended provisions, **33(2)**, [590]; **33(S)**, Police 3–4
  code of practice, **33(2)**, [323]
  Crown employment, **33(2)**, [312]
  delegation of functions by Secretary of State, **33(2)**, [324]
  enhanced—
    Crown employment, for, **33(2)**, [313]
    generally, **33(2)**, [305]
    judicial appointment, for, **33(2)**, [313]
  generally, **33(2)**, [303]
  identity, evidence of, **33(2)**, [315]
  independent monitor, **33(2)**, [317]
  offences—
    disclosure, **33(2)**, [326]
    falsification, **33(2)**, [325]
    information obtained in connection with delegated functions, disclosure, **33(2)**, [327]
  register—
    inclusion in, **33(2)**, [318]
    removal from, **33(2)**, [320]
  registration—
    cancellation of, **33(2)**, [320]–[322]
    refusal of, **33(2)**, [321]
    regulations, **33(2)**, [319]
    suspension, **33(2)**, [321]–[322]
  regulations, **33(2)**, [328]
  sources of information, **33(2)**, [316]
  specified children's and adults' lists, urgent cases, **33(2)**, [310]
  suitability—
    adults, information relating to, **33(2)**, [309]
    children, relating to, **33(2)**, [305], [308]

criminal records—*contd*
  criminal record certificates—*contd*
    suitability—*contd*
      considerations, **33(2)**, [311]
      power to amend information,
        33(2), [307]
      vulnerable adults, information relating
        to, **33(2)**, [306]
      summary of provisions, **33(2)**, [17]

crofting community
  right to buy, stamp duty land tax on,
    41, [351]

crops. *See also* **coal mining subsidence**
  growing, seizure under distress, **20**, [229]
  opencast coal working, on land for, harvesting
    etc, **17(1)**, [170]
  pests and diseases injurious to. *See* **pests**

crossbow
  age for possessing, **12(1)**, [1048], [1049]
  detention of person or vehicle, powers,
    12(1), [1051]
  exception from provisions, **12(1)**, [1052]
  hire of, restriction, **12(1)**, [1048], [1049]
  Northern Ireland provisions, **12(1)**, [1054]
  penalties for offences, **12(1)**, [1053]
  possession, as offence, **12(1)**, [1050]
  purchase and hiring, **12(1)**, [1049]
  sale etc, restriction on, **12(1)**, [1048]
  search and seizure, powers, **12(1)**, [1051]

Crossrail
  arbitration provisions, **38(2)**, [603]
  burial grounds, use of land comprised in,
    38(2), [590], [637]
  closures, **38(2)**, [576]
  controller of railway assets, co-operation by—
    arbitration, **38(2)**, [580]
      multiple proceedings, **38(2)**, [581]
    duty of, **38(2)**, [579]
  controls, disapplication and modification of,
    38(2), [636]
  Crown land, disposal of, **38(2)**, [592]
  deposited plans—
    correction of, **38(2)**, [601]
    deviation from, **38(2)**, [550]
    limits shown on, acquisition of land
      between, **38(2)**, [555], [613], [614]
    meaning, **38(2)**, [604]
  deposited sections, meaning, **38(2)**, [604]
  discontinued facilities, reinstatement of,
    38(2), [638]
  extensions, provisions applying to,
    38(2), [597]
  franchising—
    Heathrow Express Order, disapplication of
      exemptions, **38(2)**, [575]
    public-sector operators, award to,
      38(2), [574]
  Heathrow Express Order, disapplication of
    exemptions, **38(2)**, [575]

Crossrail—*contd*
  heritage—
    disapplication and modification of
      controls, **38(2)**, [565], [621]
    rights of entry, **38(2)**, [622]
  highways—
    authorities, agreements with, **38(2)**, [610]
    bridges carrying, **38(2)**, [610]
    construction, **38(2)**, [610]
    maintenance, **38(2)**, [610]
    permanent obstruction, **38(2)**, [610]
    protective provisions, **38(2)**, [639]
    stopping up, **38(2)**, [610]
    street works, **38(2)**, [610]
    subsoil, use of, **38(2)**, [610]
    temporary interference, **38(2)**, [610]
    working sites in, **38(2)**, [610]
  injurious affection, compensation for,
    38(2), [594]
  interpretation, **38(2)**, [605]
  key system assets, **38(2)**, [577]
  land—
    acquisition of—
      functions relating to works, transfer of,
        38(2), [582]
      limits shown on deposited plans,
        between, **38(2)**, [555], [613], [614]
      power of, **38(2)**, [556]
    use—
      prohibitions or restrictions on,
        38(2), [593]
      temporary, **38(2)**, [612]
  landlord and tenant law, application of,
    38(2), [591]
  noise—
    construction sites, on, **38(2)**, [569]
    statutory nuisance proceedings, defence to,
      38(2), [570]
  nominated undertaker, holder of functions
    of, **38(2)**, [588]
  Office of Rail Regulation—
    objective of, **38(2)**, [571]
    reports, publication of, **38(2)**, [572]
  operator of railway assets, licensing,
    38(2), [573]
  overhead lines, **38(2)**, [553], [611]
  planning—
    applications, fees for, **38(2)**, [561]
    conditions—
      qualifying authorities, **38(2)**, [616]
      unitary authority, development in area
        of, **38(2)**, [617]
      unitary authority, development not in
        area of, **38(2)**, [618]
    disapplication of provision, power of,
      38(2), [562]
    environmental impact assessment,
      38(2), [563]
    permission, deemed, **38(2)**, [559]
    permitted development—
      extension of rights, **38(2)**, [564], [620]
      time limit for, **38(2)**, [560]
  private rights of way, extinguishment of,
    38(2), [557]

Crossrail—*contd*
  protected railway company, designation,
    38(2), [578]
  protective provisions—
    British Waterways Board, **38(2)**, [643]
    electricity, gas, water and sewerage
      undertakers, **38(2)**, [640]
    electronic communications code networks,
      38(2), [642]
    fisheries, **38(2)**, [641]
    flood defence, **38(2)**, [641]
    highways and traffic, **38(2)**, [639]
    land drainage, **38(2)**, [641]
    Port of London Authority, **38(2)**, [644]
    water resources, **38(2)**, [641]
  railway legislation, application of, **38(2)**, [623]
  rights of statutory undertakers, extinguishment
    of, **38(2)**, [558]
  Secretary of State, power to devolve functions
    of, **38(2)**, [600]
  service of documents, **38(2)**, [602]
  statutory authority, availability of defence of,
    38(2), [583]
  temporary possession agreements, **38(2)**, [596]
  transfer schemes—
    exempt public bodies, taxable public
      bodies, to, **38(2)**, [632]
    power to make, **38(2)**, [624]–[627]
    private persons, involving, **38(2)**, [634]
    tax provisions, **38(2)**, [629]–[635]
    taxable public bodies—
      between, **38(2)**, [630]
      exempt public bodies, to, **38(2)**, [631]
  Transport for London, provisions applying
    to, **38(2)**, [587]
  trees—
    disapplication of controls, **38(2)**, [568]
    on neighbouring land, power to deal
      with, **38(2)**, [567]
  water abstraction, compensation for,
    38(2), [595]
  works—
    additional, **38(2)**, [609]
    buildings, support of, **38(2)**, [609]
    entry for preparatory purposes,
      38(2), [609]
    highway accesses, **38(2)**, [610]
    mitigation and protection works,
      38(2), [609]
    overhead line diversion, **38(2)**, [609]
    scheduled—
      construction and maintenance of,
        38(2), [550]
      description of, **38(2)**, [608]
    water, discharge of, **38(2)**, [609]
    waterways, temporary interference with,
      38(2), [609]

Crown
  abdication, declaration of, **10**, [189]–[192]
  accession declaration, **10**, [173], [175]
  acquisition and disposal of land by, **9**, [364]
  additional development of land after
   acquisition, compensation, **9**, [241]

Crown—*contd*
  administration of estates provisions, application
    of, **18**, [561]
  advowson, grant by, **10**, [9]
  agricultural housing, application of
    provisions, **21**, [457], [486]; **22**, [660]
  agricultural workers, safety and health
    provisions applying, **1(1)**, [477]
  aids and prises, **10**, [9]
  air traffic provisions, application of,
    4(1), [481], [482]
  aircraft, provisions applicable, **4(1)**, [150],
    [511]
  arbitration—
    costs in, **13**, [7]
    international investment disputes, **2**, [854]
  armed forces, liability for death or injury to
    members of, **13**, [14], [45], [46]
  arrest, freedom from, **13**, [2]
  assignment, etc, consent to, **22**, [789]
  attachment of moneys payable by, **13**, [30]
  bona vacantia—
    disclaimer, **8**, 521–2
    dissolution of company, on, **8**, 523
    revival of company, effect of, **8**, 522–3
  Building Acts, application of provisions of,
    35(1), [609]
  building regulations, application of,
    35(1), [565]
  carriage of goods by road Convention,
    binding on, **36**, [763]
  child of, born abroad, **10**, [13]
  civil enforcement, application of provisions,
    38(2), [368]
  civil list. *See* **civil list**
  civil proceedings by or against—
    abolition of certain, **13**, [17], [43]
    appeals, **13**, [25]
    civil proceedings, meaning, **13**, [7]
    costs, **13**, [7], [27]
    county court, in—
      county court rules, in accordance with,
        13, [19]
      institution of, **13**, [19]
      transfer to High Court, **13**, [23]
    declaratory order in, **13**, [24]
    defence to proceedings, **13**, [33]
    demise of Crown, unaffected by, **13**, [34]
    documents, discovery and production,
      13, [31]
    financial provisions, **13**, [37]
    High Court, in—
      institution of, **13**, [17]
      revenue matters, summary applications
        in, **13**, [18]
      rules of court, in accordance with,
        13, [17], [36]
      transfer to county court, **13**, [23]
      transferred from county court, **13**, [23]
    intellectual property rights, infringement
      of, **13**, [12]
    interest on—
      costs, **13**, [27]
      damages, **13**, [31]
      judgment debts, **13**, [27]

Crown—*contd*
  civil proceedings by or against—*contd*
    interrogatories, **13**, [31]
    judgments and execution, **13**, [27]–[30]
    jurisdiction and procedure, **13**, [17]–[26]
    limitation, **13**, [17]
    meaning, **13**, [7], [26], [38]
    nature of relief in, **13**, [24]
    parties to, **13**, [21]
    private capacity of sovereign, **13**, [8]
    recovery of land or other property, order where, **13**, [24]
    service of documents, **13**, [22]
    stay of execution, **13**, [25]
    time for bringing, limitation on, **13**, [16]
    transitional provisions, **13**, [16]
  Coal Authority, relationship, **17(2)**, [124]
  coal mining etc provisions, application, **17(2)**, [191]
  coast protection work, application of provisions, **49**, [389], [410]
  coinage rights, **10**, [1]
  commercial rent recovery provisions binding, **24**, [534]
  commons legislation binding, **21**, [289]; **24**, [501]
  company, controlling, **44(1)**, [228]
  company wholly owned by, **7(2)**, [821]
  consecrated land, legal effects of removal, **14**, 1232–3
  contribution, application of law to, **13**, [13]
  contributory negligence, application of law to, **13**, [13]
  copyright, liability for, infringement, **13**, [12]
  coronation oath, **10**, [33]–[36]
  Counsellors of State—
    persons to be, **10**, [198]
    Queen Mother to be, **10**, [231]
  court order, not binding on, **18**, [231]
  data protection, application of provisions, **7(1)**, [535]
  debtor, parliamentary privilege of, **13**, [2]
  debts—
    distress for, **20**, [29]
    proof of, **18**, [88]
  defective premises, application of provisions, **21**, [388]
  defence to proceedings against, **13**, [33]
  demise of—
    persons to be, **10**, [198]
    Queen Mother to be, **10**, [231]
    Great Seal, effect on, **10**, [81]
    holding of office, effect on, **10**, [162]
    Parliament, effect on, **10**, [78]
    proceedings unaffected by, **13**, [34]
    writs and proceedings, continuation of, **10**, [93]
  design, liability for, infringement, **13**, [12]
  design right, liability for infringement, **13**, [12]
  designs, use of. *See* **designs**
  different capacities, rights and liabilities in, **10**, [1409]
  disability discrimination, application of provisions, **7(1)**, [439]

Crown—*contd*
  domicile of, **11(2)**, [838]
  driver information system apparatus on land of, **38(1)**, [147]
  driving offences outside UK, application of provisions, **38(2)**, [288]
  duties, alienating, **10**, [90]
  ecclesiastical patronage, **14**, 1157–9
  emergency, ownership of goods requisitioned, **9**, [133]
  employee, invention by, **11(1)**, [683]
  employers' liability for defective equipment, application, **16**, [19]
  employment—
    meaning, **16**, [587], [841]
    national minimum wage, **16**, [942]
    national security, provisions excluded in interests of, **16**, [487], [843]
    provisions applying to, **16**, [485], [587], [841]
  employment provisions binding, **16**, [488]
  environmental provisions, application of, **35(2)**, [154], [176]
  equal pay, extent of applicable provisions, **16**, [28]
  escheat to, abolition, **18**, [548]
  execution by, **13**, [29]
  Factories Act, application to, **18**, [1197]
  food emergency orders, exclusion of provisions, **1(2)**, [250]
  food safety provisions, application of, **1(2)**, [467]
  food standards provisions, application of, **1(2)**, [681]
  forest rights of, **2**, [153]
  forests, abolition of franchises, **10**, [84]
  game licence exemption, **2**, [193]
  health and safety at work, application of provisions, **18**, [1301]
  hereditaments, protection, **36**, [591]
  High Court, summary applications in certain revenue matters, **13**, [18]
  hunting provisions, application of, **2**, [743]
  incapacity, declaration of, **10**, [194]
  indemnity, application of law to, **13**, [13]
  Insolvency Act, application of, **4(2)**, [524]
  international carriage by air, application of provisions, **4(1)**, [15], [27]
  interpleader proceedings, relief by way of, **13**, [20]
  land. *See also* **Crown land**
    application of compensation provisions, **9**, [247], [364]
    grant of, **10**, [12]
  land drainage provisions, **19(3)**, [249]
  landlord, as—
    assured tenancy, exclusion of, **22**, [913]
    restricted contract, exclusion of, **21**, [540]
    tenancy not protected, **21**, [533]
  lands. *See* **Crown Lands**
  laws, dispensing with, **10**, [40]
  Licensing Act 2003, application of, **19(3)**, [687]
  light, right to, **21**, [255]

Crown—*contd*
  limitation of actions—
    application of provisions, **19(3)**, [721],
      [767]
    foreign law, **19(3)**, [780]
    recovery of land, involvement in,
      19(3), [773]
  loan of money to, **10**, [27]
  marriages, royal, **10**, [98]–[99]
  martial law proceedings, **10**, [29]
  mines, royal, **10**, [39], [44]–[46]
  money, levying without grant of Parliament,
    10, [40]
  Nominee Account, payments into, **10**, [453]
  Northern Ireland, acquisition of land in,
    9, [383]
  occupier of premises, as, liability—
    persons other than visitors, to **21**, [783]
    visitors, to, **21**, [247]
  order—
    against, satisfaction, **13**, [28]
    in favour of, enforcement, **13**, [29]
  Parliament, proroguing, **10**, [79]–[80]
  patent, liability for, infringement, **13**, [12]
  patent licence of right, **11(1)**, [460]
  Patents Act, application of, **11(1)**, [772]
  patronage. *See* **patronage**
  penalty, remitting by, **12(1)**, [58]
  personal injuries, liability of, **45**, [949]
  persons in service of, provisions not
    applying, **15(1)**, [695]
  plant breeder's rights, provisions applying,
    1(2), [624]
  pollution by sea, deposits, etc in, application
    of provisions to, **49**, [637]
  ports and harbours, application of provisions,
    39(2), [196]
  premises, smoke control provisions, application
    to, **35(2)**, [46]
  prerogative powers, saving for acts done
    under, **13**, [15]
  private estates. *See* **Crown private estates**
  proceedings—
    against—
      defence to, **13**, [33]
      in rem, exclusion of, **13**, [32]
      meaning, **13**, [38]
    Northern Ireland, provisions as to, **13**, [41]
  product liability, application of provisions on,
    39(1), [605]
  property—
    public health provisions, application,
      35(1), [215], [513]
    stamp duty, **41**, [45], [200]
  public departments, application of provisions
    to, **43(1)**, [22]
  racial discrimination, application of
    provisions, **7(1)**, [199]
  re-entry on land by, **13**, [4]
  regency—
    absence of Sovereign, in, **10**, [198]
    guardianship of Sovereign, **10**, [197]
    heir attaining full age, **10**, [230]
    illness, during, **10**, [198]
    oath, **10**, [196]

Crown—*contd*
  regency—*contd*
    partial incapacity, on, **10**, [198]
  Regent—
    Duke of Edinburgh as, **10**, [229]
    oath, **10**, [196], [200]
    person to be, **10**, [195]
    power of, **10**, [196]
    sovereign under eighteen, **10**, [193]
    total incapacity, on, **10**, [194]
  registered trade mark, liability for,
    infringement, **13**, [12]
  religious discrimination provisions, application
    of, **7(1)**, [821]
  reservoirs, application of provisions to,
    49, [607]
  right to petition, **10**, [40]
  right to sue, **13**, [10]
  reservoirs, application of provisions to,
    49, [607]
  road traffic—
    application of provisions, **38(1)**, [113]
    drivers' hours, **36**, [835]
    provisions applicable, **37**, [302], [799]
    regulation provisions, application of,
      37, [302]
    speed limits, **37**, [302]
  roads—
    application of enactments, **37**, [303]
    appropriate authority, meaning, **37**, [303]
    charging schemes, **38(2)**, [185]
    meaning, **37**, [303]
    special provisions as to, **37**, [304]
  royal—
    proclamations, **10**, [458]
    style, **10**, [1], [227]
    titles, **10**, [1], [227]
  royal functions—
    delegation of, **10**, [198]
    meaning, **10**, [199]
  saving for rights, **35(1)**, [64], [92]
  service of notices on, **46**, [604]
  settlement—
    Act of Settlement, **10**, [47]–[51]
    William and Mary, after, **10**, [47]–[51]
  sex discrimination, application of provisions,
    7(1), [119]
  shellfish fishery, consent to orders as to,
    1(1), [689]
  Shops, Offices and Railway Premises
    Act 1963, application, **18**, [1243]
  spiritual jurisdiction united to, **14**, 46
  sports grounds, safety of, **13**, [229], [364]
  statute, whether bound by, **10**, [2]
  statutory powers, saving for acts done under,
    13, [15]
  statutory provisions, application of certain to,
    13, [33]
  stock or dividends belonging to, **44(1)**, [32]
  street works, application of provisions
    generally, **38(1)**, [252]
  sturgeons, right to, **10**, [11], [84]
  style of, **10**, [1], [227]
  subordinate legislation, application of,
    46, [1040]

Crown—*contd*
  succession—
    Bill of Rights, **10**, [40]
    children born abroad, **10**, [13]
    Church of England, membership of,
      10, [50]
    generally, **10**, [1]
    hindering, **10**, [52]
    Princess Sophia of Hanover, heirs of,
      10, [48], [83]
    Roman Catholics, incapacity of, **10**, [40],
      [49]
    Union, after, **10**, [55]
    United Kingdom, of, **10**, [54]
  swans, right to, **10**, [84]
  taxable person for VAT, as, **50**, [55]
  telecommunications code, application,
    45, [72]
  titles, **10**, [1], [227]
  tort, liability for—
    death or injury to members of armed
      forces, **13**, [14], [45], [46]
    extent, **13**, [11]
  traffic regulation provisions, application of,
    37, [302]
  tree felling, application of provisions,
    18, [1124]
  trees in conservation areas, acts as to,
    46, [1038]
  unclaimed wreck, right to, **39(2)**, [919]
  use of inventions. *See* **patent**
  war-time breaches of planning control by,
    46, [572], [635]
  water provisions, application of, **49**, [1034]
  water resources, application of provisions,
    49, [1268]
  weights and measures provisions, **39(1)**, [541]
  whales and sturgeons, right to, **1(1)**, [124]
  whales, right to, **10**, [11], [84]
  wild creatures, abolition of right to, **10**, [84]
  William and Mary, recognising, **10**, [43]
  wrongful interference with goods, extent of
    application, **45**, [978]

Crown Agents
  accounts, **10**, [641]
    final, **10**, [780]
  activities, pre-funding, **10**, [627]
  administrative expenses, **10**, [648]
  ancillary powers, **10**, [625]
  annual reports of, **10**, [630]
    final, **10**, [780]
  audit, **10**, [641]
  authorised activities—
    agency, **10**, [623], [657]
    non-agency, **10**, [624]
  authorities, acting for, **10**, [655]–[656]
  bodies, acting for, **10**, [655]–[656]
  body corporate, as, **10**, [620]
  borrowing powers, **10**, [637]
  chairman of, **10**, [653]
  commencing capital debt, **10**, [636]
    repayment, **10**, [772]
  consent of minister, activities requiring,
    10, [625]

Crown Agents—*contd*
  constitution of, **10**, [620], [653]
  Crown, relationship with, **10**, [620]
  dissolution, **10**, [778]
  documents, proof of, **10**, [653]
  excess of revenue, having, **10**, [635]
  financial duties of, **10**, [632]
  financial matters, Minister directing on,
    10, [642]
  former—
    alienation by, **10**, [647]
    meaning, **10**, [647]
    revenue of, **10**, [647]
  functions of, **10**, [622]
  generally, **10**, [1]
  government agents, acting as, **10**, [626]
  grants to, **10**, [639]
  holding and realisation board. *See* **Crown
    Agents Holding and Realisation Board**
    accounts, **10**, [658]
    annual reports, **10**, [658]
    audit, **10**, [658]
    borrowing by, **10**, [658]
    corporation tax, exemption from, **10**, [646]
    dissolution of, **10**, [658]
    documents, proof of, **10**, [658]
    duty of, **10**, [644]
    excess of revenue, having, **10**, [645], [658]
    grants to, **10**, [658]
    indebtedness, limit on, **10**, [658]
    information, obtaining from, **10**, [658]
    insurance against financial risks, **10**, [658]
    liquid assets, management of, **10**, [658]
    loans to, **10**, [658]
    members, **10**, [644], [658]
    Minister instructing, **10**, [658]
    performance of functions, **10**, [658]
    powers of, **10**, [658]
    proceedings, **10**, [658]
    property vesting in, **10**, [658]
    repeal of provisions, effect of, **10**, [781]
    reports, **10**, [658]
    review of affairs, **10**, [658]
    seal, authentication of, **10**, [658]
    stamp duty exemption, **10**, [646]
    subsidiaries, control of, **10**, [658]
    Treasury guarantees, **10**, [658]
  information, furnishing, **10**, [629]
  insurance against financial risks, **10**, [643]
  investment by, **10**, [627]
  limit on liabilities of, **10**, [638]
  liquid assets, management of, **10**, [634]
  loans to, **10**, [639]
  members—
    appointment of, **10**, [653]
    disqualification for Parliament, **10**, [653]
    numbers of, **10**, [620]
    remuneration of, **10**, [653]
    tenure of, **10**, [653]
  Minister giving directions to, **10**, [633]
  name, changing, **10**, [620]
  performance of functions, **10**, [653]
  proceedings, **10**, [653]
  property vesting in, **10**, [621], [654]
  report of, **10**, [628]

Crown Agents—*contd*
reserves, allocating, **10**, [633]
residual functions, **10**, [778]
review of affairs, **10**, [628]
seal, authenticating, **10**, [653]
staff of, **10**, [653]
subsidiaries, control of, **10**, [631]
successor company—
    corporation tax, **10**, [777]
    "Crown Agents", use in name, **10**, [776]
    initial Government holding, **10**, [773]
    property, rights and liabilities, vesting of,
      10, [771], [786]
      foreign, **10**, [779]
    securities, Government investment in,
      10, [774]
    statutory accounts, **10**, [775]
Treasury guarantees, **10**, [640]
unincorporated—
    final accounts, **10**, [659]
    meaning, **10**, [620]
    recoverable grants, **10**, [645]

Crown Court
appeal as to forfeiture etc, **8**, 65–6
appeal from, **11(2)**, [695]; **12(1)**, [426]
    See also **criminal appeal**
appeal to—
    abandonment of, **11(2)**, [530]
    bail pending, **11(2)**, [534]
    Children and Young Persons Act 1933,
      6, [50]
    conviction, against, **11(2)**, [529]
    decision, enforcement of, **11(2)**, [531]
    drainage rates, against, **19(3)**, [220]
    food safety offences, **1(2)**, [452]
    judges and justices sitting, **11(2)**, [748]
    practice and procedure, **11(2)**, [753]
    provisions on, **11(2)**, [721]
    recognizance to keep the peace, on,
      11(2), [195]
    right of, **11(2)**, [195], [529]
    sentence, against, **11(2)**, [529]
    unauthorised entry, forfeiture on, as to,
      9, [272]
appearance before, compelling, **11(2)**, [754]
bail, granting, **11(2)**, [755]
cases, allocation of, **11(2)**, [749]
City of London, in, **11(2)**, [675]
committal for sentence, judges and justices
    sitting, **11(2)**, [748]
committal for trial—
    date of trial, **11(2)**, [751]
    place of trial, altering, **11(2)**, [750]
community orders, enforcement of,
    11(3), [317]
composition of, **11(2)**, [747]
costs—
    civil debt, enforced as, **11(2)**, [239]
    recovery of, **11(2)**, [238]–[239]
    rules, **11(2)**, [725]
    See also **costs**
distribution of business, **11(2)**, [750]
drug trafficking cases generally. *See* **drug
   trafficking**

Crown Court—*contd*
either way offences, committal for trial for,
    to, **12(1)**, [1085]
expert evidence—
    prior notice of, **18**, [258]
    rules of court, **18**, [220]
indictable-only offence, sent for trial for—
    absence of accused, power to proceed in,
      11(3), [248]
    criminal damage offences as summary
      offences, procedure for determining,
      11(3), [248]
    depositions—
      evidence, use of as, **11(3)**, [248]
      power of justice to take, **11(3)**, [248]
    dismissal, applications for, **11(3)**, [248]
    procedure where none remains,
      11(3), [248]
    regulations, **11(3)**, [248]
    reporting restrictions, **11(3)**, [248]
    summary offence, power to deal with,
      11(3), [248]
indictment, proceedings on—
    Admiralty, offences within jurisdiction of,
      11(2), [719]
    jurisdiction, **11(2)**, [719]
    practice and procedure, **11(2)**, [753]
interim hospital order, making, **11(2)**, [721]
judges—
    jurisdiction, exercising, **11(2)**, [675]
    rates case, acting in, **11(2)**, [681]
    rules, **11(2)**, [747]
    tax case, acting in, **11(2)**, [681]
jurisdiction—
    general, **11(2)**, [718]
    indictment, proceedings on, **11(2)**, [719]
    persons exercising, **11(2)**, [675]
meaning, **41**, [605]
Northern Ireland. *See* **Northern Ireland**
offences—
    abroad, **11(2)**, [720]
    ships, on, **11(2)**, [720]
officers, duties of, **11(2)**, [756]
places conducted in, **11(2)**, [752]
proceedings on case stated for opinion of
    High Court, **11(2)**, [696]
proceedings, reports of, **12(1)**, [1103]
public access to, **12(1)**, [1103]
Recorder—
    appointment of, **11(2)**, [246]
    assistant, **11(2)**, [248]
    oath taken by, **11(2)**, [247]
records of, **11(2)**, [756]
Rule Committee, **11(2)**, [758]
rules—
    appeals, relating to, **11(2)**, [761]
    costs, on, **11(2)**, [725]
    Lord Chancellor, made at request of,
      11(2), [760]
    process for making, **11(2)**, [759]
    provisions in, **11(2)**, [761]
serious etc fraud. *See* **serious or complex
   fraud**
sittings, **11(2)**, [752]

Crown Court—*contd*
trial—
  alteration of place fixed for, **11(3)**, [400]
    Northern Ireland, **11(3)**, [409]
  right of reply, **18**, [201]

Crown employee
social security benefits, **40(1)**, [359]
statutory adoption pay, **40(1)**, [444]
statutory maternity pay, **40(1)**, [420]
statutory paternity pay, **40(1)**, [435]
statutory sick pay, **40(1)**, [412]

Crown Estate Commissioners
accounts, **10**, [1], [234]
charitable purposes, grants for, **10**, [236]
constitution of, **10**, [243]
contingent liability to, satisfaction by Forestry
  Commissioners, **18**, [1133]
continuance of, **10**, [233]
functions of, **10**, [1]
generally, **10**, [1]
land open to public, regulations on, **10**, [238]
management, provisions on, **10**, [235]
meaning, **41**, [605]
powers and duties, **10**, [233]
property, consent to sale of, **14**, 379–81
public purposes, grants for, **10**, [236]
reports, **10**, [1], [234]
transactions by, **10**, [1]
Windsor Estate, management of, **10**, [237]
woods and forests of, management by Forestry
  Commissioners, **18**, [1090]

Crown immunity
health service bodies, removal from, **30**, [530]

Crown in Chancery
Clerk of—
  appointment, **10**, [448]
  duties of, **10**, [448]
  fees, **10**, [449]
  salary, **10**, [448]
  Secretary of Presentations, transfer of duties
    of, **10**, [475]
office—
  language of documents, rules as to,
    10, [458]
  meaning, **10**, [462]

Crown lands
access to, **36**, [641]
administration of. *See* **Crown Estate**
  Commissioners
agreements relating to, **46**, [565]
agricultural tenancies, **22**, [660]
allotments, for, **1(1)**, [207], [257]
ancient monument on, **32**, [371]
application of enactments, **46**, [1], [557]
appropriate authority, **46**, [558]
arms control and disarmament powers,
  10, [1083]
caravan site licences, provisions on, **32**, [240]
collective enfranchisement, application of
  provisions to, **23**, [171]

Crown lands—*contd*
Commissioner of Works—
  Battersea Park Commissioners,
    10, [147]–[148]
  bridge, conveying, **10**, [169]
  Civil Service Commission, office of,
    10, [158]
  incorporation, **10**, [123], [147]
  Inland Revenue lands. *See* **Inland**
    Revenue
  land, dealing with, **10**, [123]–[125]
  Millbank Prison, site of, **10**, [159]
  persons being, **10**, [119]
  powers and expenses, **10**, [184]
  royal parks—
    duties in relation to, **10**, [121], [122]
    exchanging houses, **10**, [180]
  sales and purchase by, **10**, [157]
  Surveyor General of Works, duties of,
    10, [120]
  treasury consenting to sale, etc, **10**, [126]
commons, orders relating to, **32**, [246]
compensation, provisions, **21**, [421]
compulsory acquisition provisions applying,
  46, [1058]
compulsory purchase powers, **23**, [534]
conservation area consent, application for,
  46, [732], [734]
continuance of use, planning permission for,
  46, [571]
control of development, **46**, [560]
Countryside Act applying to, **32**, [279]
countryside provisions, **32**, [828]
Crossrail, disposal relating to, **38(2)**, [592]
Crown Estate, Stirling, management of,
  10, [150]
cycle tracks, application of provisions as to,
  37, [348]
designated site, trespass on—
  access provisions not applying, **12(4)**, [126]
  arrest, power of, **12(4)**, [125]
  meaning, **12(4)**, [123]
  notices, **12(4)**, [126]
  offence, **12(4)**, [123]
  Scotland, **12(4)**, [124]
disposal, anticipation of—
  conservation area consent, application for,
    46, [734]
  hazardous substance consent, **46**, [789]
  listed building consent, application for,
    46, [734]
  planning application, **46**, [568]
  tree preservation order, **46**, [570]
Dunfermline Palace, management of,
  10, [150]
electricity provisions, application of,
  17(1), [829]
enforcement relating to, **46**, [563]
escheat, **10**, [240], [464]
farm business tenancies, **23**, [273]
foreshore, disputes on, **10**, [168]
forestry, application of certain provisions,
  18, [1124]
forfeitures of tenants, **10**, [23]–[25]
gardens, **32**, [6]

Crown lands—*contd*
  gas, controlled operations on underground
    storage, **17(1)**, [318]
  grant of, **10**, [89]
  hazardous substances—
    application of provisions to, **46**, [783]
    consent, application for, **46**, [788]
      disposal, in anticipation of, **46**, [789]
    enforcement, **46**, [785]
    exercise of powers in relation to, **46**, [787]
    interest, reference to, **46**, [786]
    rights of entry, **46**, [795]
    transitional provisions, **46**, [784]
  highways provisions, application of, **36**, [1379]
  interests in—
    disposal of, **22**, [389]
    information as to, **46**, [606]
    meaning, **46**, [729], [786]
    provisions as to, **46**, [566]
    reference to, **46**, [564], [731]
  Kew Green, management of, **10**, [170]
  land registration provisions, **23**, [719]–[725]
  lease, acquisition of new, application of
    provisions to, **23**, [171]
  leasehold valuation tribunal's jurisdiction over
    enfranchisement or lease extension,
    23, [164]
  Linlithgow Palace, management of, **10**, [150]
  listed buildings—
    consent, application for, **46**, [732], [734]
    enforcement, **46**, [730]
    notices as to, **46**, [733]
    provisions applying, **46**, [727]
    purchase notice, **46**, [673]
    transitional provisions, **46**, [1060]
    urgent works, **46**, [728]
  litter authority, **32**, [554]
  local planning authority functions, **46**, [614]
  long distance routes over, **36**, [641]
  meaning, **18**, [1124]; **23**, [534]; **32**, [554];
    46, [558], [729]; **49**, [410]
  milk quota, provisions on compensation,
    1(2), [401]
  National Park, in, **32**, [189]
  new lease of, **10**, [161]
  New Scotland Yard, extension of, **10**, [181]
  northern lands, consideration for, **10**, [185]
  old mining permissions relating to, **46**, [1039]
  opencast coal mining on, **17(1)**, [206]
  Osborne estate, **10**, [164]–[166], [176]
  Outer Circle, Regents Park, management of,
    10, [186]
  permit schemes, provisions applying,
    38(2), [331]
  pesticides, control of, **1(2)**, [250]
  planning control, war-time breaches of,
    46, [572], [635]
  planning obligations, **46**, [569]
  planning permission, application for, **46**, [567]
  powers, exercise of, **46**, [562], [733]
  private estates. *See* **Crown private estates**
  provisions applying to, **46**, [1058]
    Commonhold and Leasehold Reform
      Act 2002, under, **24**, [131]
    commonhold, as to, **24**, [63]

Crown lands—*contd*
  provisions applying to—*contd*
    Housing Act 1988, under, **22**, [838]
    Landlord and Tenant Act 1927, under,
      21, [69], [73]
    Landlord and Tenant Act 1987, under,
      22, [769]
    leasehold enfranchisement or extension,
      21, [333]
    Rent Act, under, **21**, [639], [760]
    requisition, on, **21**, [137], [146]
    right to manage, on, **24**, [107]
    security of tenure, on, **21**, [218], [241]
    transitional, **46**, [1059]–[1060]
    unlawful eviction, **22**, [838]
    war damage, on, **21**, [106]
  public offices, for, **10**, [182]–[185]
  recovery of possession, provisions applicable
    to, **21**, [672]
  Regents Park Zoo, management of, **10**, [239]
  registration of holdings, **25(2)**, [433]
  representation, **23**, [723]
  research councils occupying, **10**, [533]
  revenues, **10**, [1]
  Richmond Green, management of, **10**, [170]
  Richmond Terrace and Richmond Mews, use
    of, **10**, [181], [183], [188]
  right of way over, **37**, [97]
  right of entry on, **46**, [600], [740]
  Royal parks and gardens, protection under
    Law of Property Act 1922, **20**, [493]
  smallholdings, for, **1(1)**, [825]
  special enforcement notice, **46**, [560]–[561]
  Surveyor-General of Works, **10**, [120]
  transitional provisions, **10**, [244]–[245]
  urgent development on, **46**, [559]
  vesting, declaration of, **10**, [240]
  Wildlife and Countryside Act, application of,
    32, [481]–[482]

Crown office. *See* **Crown in chancery**

Crown private estates
  conveyance of manors, **10**, [104]
  copyholds, vesting of, **10**, [102]
  descent of, **10**, [105], [134]
  generally, **10**, [1]
  grants of, **10**, [103]
  inheritance, **10**, [142]
  leaseholds, vesting of, **10**, [102], [132]
  manors, etc, purchased by Crown, **10**, [101],
    [115]
  meaning, **10**, [130]
  monies from privy purse as, **10**, [110]
  Osborne ceasing to be, **10**, [165]
  personal estate, bequest of, **10**, [108]
  Queen consort, rights of, **10**, [109]
  restricted, not, **10**, [100], [131], [141]
  rights and remedies of Sovereign, **10**, [139]
  Scotland, legal proceedings in, **10**, [138],
    [143]
  taxation of, **10**, [106]–[107], [135]–[136]
  testamentary disposition, **10**, [133]
  trustees of, **10**, [102], [132], [137]

Crown property
exemption from London Building Acts,
25(1), [353]
flammable materials provisions, **25(1)**, [900]
public health provisions applied, **25(1)**, [252]
servicemen's interest in, **3**, [413]
streets etc, paving etc, **25(1)**, [19]
cesser of powers, **25(1)**, [183]

Crown Prosecution Service
areas, division into, **12(1)**, [933]
Chief Inspector—
appointment of, **12(2)**, [859]
co-operation, **12(2)**, [862]
functions, **12(2)**, [860], [862]
inspection programmes and frameworks,
12(2), [862]
inspectors and staff of, **12(2)**, [859]
Crown Prosecutor—
chief, **12(1)**, [933]
code, **12(1)**, [942]
designation of, **12(1)**, [933]
guidelines, **12(1)**, [942]
powers, other person exercising,
12(1), [937]
Crown Prosecutors, Law Society's
compensation fund, exemption from
contributions to, **11(2)**, [375]
Director of Public Prosecutions as head of,
12(1), [933]
establishment of, **12(1)**, [933]
fees and expenses, payment of, **12(1)**, [944]
members of, **12(1)**, [933]
non-legal staff, powers of, **12(1)**, [939]
prosecution on behalf of, **12(1)**, [936]
staff of, **12(1)**, [933]

Crown servant
foreign service allowance, exemption,
44(2), [302]

Crown Suits Act 1865
writ of summons under Part V, abolition,
13, [43]

Crown Suppliers
scheme for transfer of—
agreements and transactions, construction
of, **10**, [703]
certificate of vesting, **10**, [703]
making, **10**, [697]
stamp duty exemption, **10**, [703]
staff, transfer of, **10**, [698]
trading fund, winding up, **10**, [700]
transferee companies, **10**, [699]

cruelty to animals
animals protected, **2**, [773]
disqualification orders, breach, in Scotland,
2, [292]
films involving, prohibition, **2**, [265]
livestock. *See* **livestock** (welfare)
offences—
arrest, entry for purpose of, **2**, [795]
docking of dogs' tails, **2**, [777]

cruelty to animals—*contd*
offences—*contd*
entry and search under warrant, **2**, [794]
fighting, **2**, [779]
destruction of animals involved in,
2, [809]
reimbursement of expenses relating to
animals involved in, **2**, [810]
seizure of animals involved in, **2**, [793]
mutilation, **2**, [776]
poisons, administration of, **2**, [778]
protected animals, **2**, [773]
unnecessary suffering, **2**, [775]
poisoned feed, selling etc, **2**, [239]
summary of provisions, **2**, [140]
traps, power to inspect, **2**, [240]

cultural objects
dealing in, meaning, **13**, [450]
on loan, protected—
conditions, **13**, [526]
Crown application, **13**, [530]
effect of, **13**, [527]
interpretation, **13**, [529]
relevant museums and galleries, **13**, [528]
tainted—
body corporate, offences by, **13**, [452]
dealing in, offence, **13**, [448]
meaning, **13**, [449]
Revenue and Customs prosecutions,
13, [451]

cultural services
value added tax, exemption from, **50**, [153]

Cultural Strategy Group for London
capacity, **26(1)**, [794]
culture strategy, review of, **26(1)**, [720]
delegation of functions to, **26(1)**, [725]
documents, proof of, **26(1)**, [794]
establishment of, **26(1)**, [719]
financial provisions, **26(1)**, [794]
functions of, **26(1)**, [719]
members, **26(1)**, [794]
proceedings, **26(1)**, [794]
seal, **26(1)**, [794]
service of documents, **26(1)**, [794]
staff, **26(1)**, [794]
status, **26(1)**, [794]

culverts
alteration by railway company, etc,
35(1), [207]
dock undertakers, powers as to, **35(1)**, [168]
land drainage authority, saving for,
35(1), [168]
maintenance and cleansing, **35(1)**, [166]
railway company, powers as to, **35(1)**, [168]
watercourse or ditch for, where building
operations in prospect, **35(1)**, [164]
watercourse or stream, for, in accordance with
approved plans, **35(1)**, [164]

Cumulative List of Recommended International Nonproprietory Names
references to, **28**, [494]
specified publication, as, **28**, [160]

curacy
perpetual, oath on licence to, **14**, 201

curate
assistant—
  lecturer or preacher performing duties as, **14**, 171
  licensing for fixed term, **14**, 832–3
  office of, **14(S)**, 181–2
bishop, appointed by, **14**, 115–16
dismissal of, **14**, 118
grants, diocesan board of finance administering, **14**, 416–17
guild church, of, **14**, 453–4, 458
incumbent, duty of to provide, **14**, 173
licence for—
  particulars on application, **14**, 117
  registry, entry in, **14**, 119
  requirement of, **14**, 173
non-resident incumbent, interference by, **14**, 246–7
notice—
  giving, **14**, 119
  new incumbent, from, **14**, 118
occupations, restrictions on, **14**, 645–6
perpetual, oath on institution, **14**, 201
proceedings against. *See* **ecclesiastical offences**
removal by bishop, **14**, 119
residence—
  benefice, on, **14**, 116
  delivery up of, **14**, 118–19
  non-resident incumbent, where, **14**, 116
  parsonage house, in, **14**, 117–18
stipend, payment towards, **14**, 843
stipendiary—
  declaration of, **14**, 831–2
  guild church, in, **14**, 458

curfew order. *See further* **community orders**
breach of action plan or reparation order, imposed for, **12(2)**, [850]
breach of supervision order, imposed for, **12(2)**, [849]
breach, revocation and amendment, **12(3)**, [1096]
  See also **community orders**
electronic monitoring, **12(2)**, [751], [754]
making of, **12(2)**, [752]
notice, contravention of, **6**, [600]
requirements in, **12(2)**, [752]
scheme, **6**, [599]
supervision order, in addition to, **12(2)**, [762]

currency
acquired under emergency powers, bar on compensation for, **9**, [131]
bank notes deemed to be, **12(1)**, [742]

currency—*contd*
counterfeiting. *See* **counterfeiting**
decimal. *See* **decimal currency**
note, meaning, **12(1)**, [742]
reproduction of notes, offence of, **12(1)**, [735]
  directors' liability, **12(1)**, [741]
variation of conditions, **43(2)**, [236]

curriculum
amended provisions, **6(S)**, 152–4
assessment arrangements, meaning, **15(2)**, [390]
attainment targets, meaning, **15(2)**, [390]
basic, **15(2)**, [394]
complaints, **15(1)**, [573]
general requirements, **15(2)**, [392]
  duty to implement, **15(2)**, [393]
information, provision of, **15(1)**, [572]
National—
  establishment by order, **15(2)**, [401]
  exceptions—
    development work and experiments, **15(2)**, [404]
    regulations, by, **15(2)**, [405]
    special educational needs, pupils with, **15(2)**, [406]
    temporary, for individual pupils, **15(2)**, [407]–[409]
  foundation stage, **15(2)**, [395], [397]
  general note, **15(1)**, [1]
  implementation of, **15(2)**, [402]–[403]
  individual pupils, directions for temporary exceptions—
    appeals, **15(2)**, [409]
    conditions, **15(2)**, [407]
    information concerning, **15(2)**, [408]
    regulations, **15(2)**, [407]
  key stages, **15(2)**, [396]
    first, **15(2)**, [398]
    fourth, **15(2)**, [399]–[400], [794]
    second, **15(2)**, [398]
    third, **15(2)**, [398]
  nursery schools, implementation in respect of, **15(2)**, [403]
  order, establishment by, **15(2)**, [401]
  orders and regulations, procedure for making, **15(2)**, [410]
nursery education, meaning, **15(2)**, [391]
political indoctrination, forbidding, **15(1)**, [570]
political issues, balanced treatment of, **15(1)**, [571]
public examinations, obligation to enter pupils for, **15(1)**, [566]
religious education—
  agreed syllabus—
    Christian traditions, taking account of, **15(1)**, [556]
    conference to reconsider, **15(1)**, [718]
    continuation of, **15(1)**, [556]
    meaning, **15(1)**, [556]
    new, preparation of, **15(1)**, [718]
    reconsideration, **15(1)**, [718]

curriculum—*contd*
religious education—*contd*
standing advisory councils—
constitution of, **15(1)**, [557]
discharge of duty of, **15(1)**, [562]
functions of, **15(1)**, [558]
meetings and documents, access to,
15(1), [563]
members, **15(1)**, [557], [559]
proceedings, **15(1)**, [559]
requirement for collective worship not
applying, determinations, **15(1)**, [560]
review, **15(1)**, [561]
revocation, direction for, **15(1)**, [562]
Sunday school, no requirement of
attendance at, **15(1)**, [564]
trust deed, whether in accordance with,
15(1), [565]
school year, meaning, **15(2)**, [390]
sex education—
exemption from, **15(1)**, [569]
policy, statements of, **15(1)**, [568]
provision, manner of, **15(1)**, [567]
Wales, in. *See* **Wales**

**Curriculum and Assessment Authority for
Wales.** *See* **National Assembly for Wales**

curtesy
tenant by, abolition of, **18**, [548]

custodial sentence
discretionary—
general restrictions on imposing,
12(3), [884]
length of, **12(3)**, [885]
mentally disordered offenders, in case of,
12(3), [887]
pre-sentence reports—
disclosure, **12(3)**, [889]
meaning, **12(3)**, [888]
requirement, **12(3)**, [886]
probation board, report of, **12(3)**, [890]
probation service providers, report of,
12(3), [890]
requirements, **12(3)**, [886]
youth offending team, report of,
12(3), [890]
imprisonment. *See* **sentence**
meaning, **12(2)**, [774]
persons not legally represented, on,
12(2), [778]
pre-sentence reports. *See* **community
sentence**
sexual or violent offences, for, committed
before 30 September 1998, **12(2)**, [779]
third class A drug trafficking offence,
minimum sentence for, **12(2)**, [801]
appeal, previous conviction set aside on,
12(2), [803]
certificate of conviction, **12(2)**, [804]
day of offence, determination of,
12(2), [806]
service law, conviction under, **12(2)**, [805]

custodial sentence—*contd*
third domestic burglary, minimum for,
12(2), [802]
appeal, previous conviction set aside on,
12(2), [803]
certificate of conviction, **12(2)**, [804]
day of offence, determination of,
12(2), [806]
service law, conviction under, **12(2)**, [805]

custody
child, of. *See* **child**
death of person in, inquest on, **11(1)**, [1214]
legal, **12(1)**, [266]
orders. *See now* **child; family proceedings**

Custody (Luxembourg Convention)
access to child, **6**, [227]
application to United Kingdom, **6**, [207]
British Islands and colonies, application of
provisions, **6**, [224]
central authorities, **6**, [209]
contracting States, **6**, [208]
costs and expenses, administrative, **6**, [222],
[226]
courts—
interim powers, **6**, [214]
restriction on powers, **6**, [215]
rules of, **6**, [219]
suspension of powers, **6**, [215]
UK decisions, **6**, [218]
"custody orders"—
effect on, **6**, [215]
termination, **6**, [221]
variation, **6**, [215]
various, to which provisions apply,
6, [228], [232]
decisions—
enforcement, **6**, [1], [213], [227]
recognition, **6**, [1], [210], [227]
refusal of recognition etc, **6**, [227]
registration of, **6**, [211]
revocation, **6**, [212]
United Kingdom courts, **6**, [218]
variation, **6**, [212]
delivery up of child, **6**, [227]
evidence, **6**, [217]
generally, **6**, [1]
meaning of child, **6**, [227]
Northern Ireland, provisions as to, **6**, [230],
[232]
proof of documents, **6**, [217]
removal of child across frontier, **6**, [227]
reports, **6**, [216]
rules of court, **6**, [219]
Scotland, provisions as to, **6**, [229], [232]
text, **6**, [227]
whereabouts of child, disclosure, **6**, [220]

Customs and Excise. *See now* **Her Majesty's
Revenue and Customs**
Act of Union, duties after, **10**, [58]–[60]
agents, use of, **13**, [772]
air passenger duty, setting of rates of interest,
13, [1062]

Customs and Excise—*contd*
  airport. *See* **airport**
  arrest of persons—
    escape from, **13**, [743]
    legal proceedings, **13**, [750]
    powers of, **13**, [743]
    ship's crew, member of, **13**, [743]
  bond, security, **13**, [762]
  consequential amendments, **13**, [781], [786]
  consul, exemption from duties and
    inspection, **10**, [1005]
  control—
    areas, **13**, [599]–[616]
    baggage, examination, **13**, [674], [919]
    chargeable goods, meaning, **13**, [674]
    concealed goods, forfeiture of, **13**, [674]
    declaration required, **13**, [674]
    failure to declare, **13**, [674]
    Isle of Man, coming from, **13**, [674]
  Crown, alienation of duties by, **10**, [90]
  customs information—
    duty to share, **13(S)**, Customs 40
    meaning, **13(S)**, Customs 32
    personal, disclosure of—
      exceptions to prohibition,
        13(S), Customs 35
      further, prohibition on,
        13(S), Customs 36
      interpretation, **13(S)**, Customs 33
      prohibition, **13(S)**, Customs 33–4
      statutory provisions, application of,
        13(S), Customs 38
      wrongful, offence of,
        13(S), Customs 36–7
    use and disclosure of, **13(S)**, Customs 31–2
  decisions, review of. *See* review of decisions
    below
  declaration, untrue, **13**, [773]
  directions, provisions as to, **13**, [780]
  Director of Border Revenue. *See* **Director of
    Border Revenue**
  documents—
    counterfeiting, **13**, [774]
    order for production, **13**, [946]
    power of Commissioners to request,
      13, [944]
    procedure when removed, **13**, [947]
    untrue, **13**, [773]
  drawback—
    adjustment of right to, **13**, [898]–[900]
    calculation, **13**, [741]
    claim for—
      general provisions as to, **13**, [737]
      offences connected with, **13**, [740]
    composite imported articles, **13**, [730],
      [784]
    conditions of payment, **13**, [736]
    damaged goods, **13**, [738]
    destroyed goods, **13**, [738]
    entitlement to, power to provide for,
      13, [918]
    extension, **13**, [736]
    hydrocarbon oils, etc, **13**, [840], [851],
      [857]
    manufactured articles, **13**, [730], [784]

Customs and Excise—*contd*
  drawback—*contd*
    repayment, **13**, [898]
    shipment, **13**, [1075]
    time limit for payment, **13**, [739]
    waiver of repayment—
      denatured goods, **13**, [733]
      goods lost or destroyed, **13**, [734]
  dutiable or restricted goods, entry outwards.
    See **exportation**
  duties. *See* **customs duties; excise duties**
  emergency powers. *See* **emergency powers**
  enforcement—
    member States, movements between,
      13(S), Customs 9
    powers, **13**, [941]–[948]
  entry of premises—
    body corporate, by, **13**, [705]
    discontinuance of trade after, **13**, [706]
    making, **13**, [705]
    new or further, of same premises, **13**, [706]
    offences in connection with, **13**, [708]
    powers of, **13**, [945]
    proof as to, **13**, [707]
    revenue traders, **13**, [709], [718]
  exchequer, revenues paid to, **30**, [25]
  excise—
    duty. *See* **excise duties**
    licence. *See* **excise licence**
  exportation. *See* **exportation**
  extradition, powers as to, **18**, [939]
  facilities, provision of, **13**, [763]
  forfeiture—
    aircraft used in connection with goods
      liable to forfeiture, **13**, [746]
    cargo—
      jettisoning, **13**, [683]
      missing, inability to account for,
        13, [684]
    condemnation, proceedings for, **13**, [744],
      [785]
    detention of goods liable to, **13**, [744]
    See also seizure of goods liable to *below*
    goods—
      improperly imported, **13**, [633]
      liable to, seizure and detention of,
        13, [744], [785]
    importation, improper, for, **13**, [633]
    imported goods, for breach of conditions,
      13, [728]
    restoration of, **13**, [758]
    seizure of goods liable to—
      condemnation, **13**, [744], [749], [758],
        [785]
      notice of, **13**, [785]
      power of, **13**, [744]
      proof of, **13**, [785]
      protection of officers, **13**, [749]
      restoration after, **13**, [758]
    ship—
      large—
        penalty in lieu of, **13**, [748]
        special provision for, **13**, [747]
      used in connection with goods liable
        to, **13**, [746]

Customs and Excise—*contd*
  forfeiture—*contd*
    spirits, **13**, [745]
    vehicles used in connection with goods
      liable to forfeiture, **13**, [746]
  free zone—
    designation by order, **13**, [695]
    goods, examination and taking account of,
      13, [764]
    meaning, **13**, [695]
    person entering or leaving, questioning,
      13, [696]
    responsible authority for, **13**, [695]
    vehicle entering or leaving, boarding and
      search of, **13**, [696]
  general customs officials—
    designation of, **13(S)**, Customs 22–4
    directions by Secretary of State, compliance
      with, **13(S)**, Customs 25
    Director of Border Revenue, designation
      by, **13(S)**, Customs 29–31
    PACE orders, application of,
      13(S), Customs 41–3
  goods, examination and taking account of,
    13, [764]
  HM Inspectors of Constabulary, inspections
    by, **13(S)**, Customs 48–9
  hovercraft, application of provisions to,
    13, [591]. *See also* **hovercraft**
  hydrocarbon oil, duty on, **10**, [997], [1031]
  importation. *See* **importation**
  information—
    order for furnishing of, **13**, [946]
    power of Commissioners to request,
      13, [944]
  insurance premium tax, setting of rates of
    interest, **13**, [1062]
  interpretation of provisions, **13**, [590]–[593]
  Isle of Man, part of United Kingdom for
    customs purposes, **13**, [537]
  landfill tax, setting of rates of interest,
    13, [1062]
  legal proceedings—
    appeal to Crown Court, **13**, [753]
    averment, evidence, as, **13**, [759]
    burden of proof, **13**, [759]
    compounding, **13**, [758]
    imprisonment, maximum terms of,
      13, [755]
    joint offenders, **13**, [756]
    jurisdiction of court, **13**, [754]
    Northern Ireland, in, **13**, [753]
    penalties—
      application of, **13**, [757]
      imprisonment—
        in addition to, **13**, [755]
        non-payment, for, **13**, [755]
      mitigation, **13**, [758]
    persons who may conduct, **13**, [760]
    process, service of, **13**, [751]
    security no defence, **13**, [756]
    summary trial, **13**, [753]
    time limit for, **13**, [752]
    trial, place of, **13**, [754]
  lock fittings, provision of, **13**, [763]

Customs and Excise—*contd*
  Northern Ireland inspectors, inspections by,
    13(S), Customs 48–9
  offences—
    detained persons, short-term holding
      facilities, **13(S)**, Customs 44
    detention, **13(S)**, Customs 43–4
    general provisions as to, **13**, [778]
    investigation of, **13(S)**, Customs 43–4
    prosecution of, **13(S)**, Customs 51
  officers, funds available for, **13**, [538]
  overdue customs duty, setting of rates of
    interest, **13**, [1062]
  penalties, general provisions as to, **13**, [778]
  postal packets—
    application of enactments to, **34**, [717]
    contraband, containing, **34**, [718]
  power to modify enactments,
    13(S), Customs 55
  prohibitions and restrictions, evasion of,
    13, [775]
  Queen's warehouse—
    combustible goods in, charges for,
      13, [693]
    goods deposited in—
      cessation of warehouse approval, where,
        13, [692]
      combustible or inflammable goods,
        13, [693]
      destruction on non-sale, **13**, [693]
      examination and taking account of,
        13, [764]
      lawful removal without payment of
        duty, **13**, [694]
      removal, payment of duty and charges
        before, **13**, [693]
      rent for, **13**, [693]
      sale of, **13**, [692], [693]
      uncleared, **13**, [624]
      unlawful removal, **13**, [694]
    inflammable goods in, charges for,
      13, [693]
    meaning, **13**, [590]
    removal to, **13**, [618]
    unauthorised entry, **13**, [694]
    uncleared goods—
      removal to, **13**, [624]
      sale of, **13**, [624]
  records—
    admissibility as evidence, **13**, [943]
    requirement to keep, **13**, [942]
  registered excise dealers and shippers—
    contravention of regulations, **13**, [699]
    meaning, **13**, [697]
    registration, **13**, [697]
    regulations, **13**, [697], [698]
  regulations, procedure for making, **13**, [779]
  relief, temporary importations, **13**, [632]
  repeals, **13**, [787]
  resolution—
    not having statutory effect, duties under,
      42, [65]
    with statutory effect, rate altered by,
      42, [66]

Customs and Excise—*contd*
  revenue trader—
    concealed pipes, etc, search for, **13**, [710]
    distress against, **13**, [714]
    documents, production of, **13**, [717]
    entry on premises of, **13**, [709], [718]
    examination of premises, facilities for, **13**, [763]
    excise duty—
      execution or distress to recover, **13**, [714]
      payment, **13**, [701], [713]
    failure to comply with requirements, **13**, [721]
    information, furnishing, **13**, [717]
    liquor, prohibition of use in exciseable goods, **13**, [711]
    lock fittings, provision for premises, etc, **13**, [763]
    meaning, **13**, [590]
    offences, **13**, [722]
    ostensible owner, liability of, **13**, [715]
    principal manager, liability of, **13**, [715]
    recorded information of, order for access to, **13**, [719]
    records, duty to keep, **13**, [716]
    removal of documents from, **13**, [720]
    samples of products, taking, **13**, [765]
    sign, display on premises, **13**, [704]
    specimen on premises of, **13**, [712]
    substance prohibited for use in exciseable goods, **13**, [711]
    tobacco dealer as, **13**, [590]
  review of decisions—
    Betting and Gaming Duties Act 1981, under, **13**, [950]
    Community Customs Code etc, under, **13**, [950]
    Customs and Excise Management Act 1979, under, **13**, [950]
    Finance Act 1993, under, **13**, [950]
    Hydrocarbon Oil Duties Act 1979, **13**, [950]
    procedure, **13**, [936]
    requirement for, **13**, [935]
    Tobacco Products Duty Act 1979, under, **13**, [950]
  samples—
    disposal and accounting for, **13**, [765]
    hydrocarbon oil. *See* **hydrocarbon oil**
    payment for, **13**, [765]
    taking, **13**, [765]
    trade, relief from customs and excise duties for, **13**, [796]
  saving and transitional provisions, **13**, [761], [781], [789]
  Scottish inspectors, inspections by, **13(S)**, Customs 48–9
  search of—
    articles, **13**, [770]
    persons, **13**, [771], [919]
    premises—
      warrant for, **13**, [767]
      writ of assistance, for, **13**, [766]
    vehicles, **13**, [709], [769]

Customs and Excise—*contd*
  search of—*contd*
    vessels, **13**, [709], [769]
  Secretary of State, general functions of—
    concurrent exercise with Commissioners, **13(S)**, Customs 19–21
    power to modify, **13(S)**, Customs 21–2
  security, bond, by, **13**, [762]
  setting of rates of interest, **13**, [1062]
  smuggling. *See* **smuggling**
  statements, untrue, **13**, [773]
  supplemental provisions, **13**, [938]–[940]
  surcharges or rebates. *See* **excise duties**
  tobacco products. *See* **tobacco products**
  transit sheds—
    approval, **13**, [607]
    meaning, **13**, [608]
    powers of entry, **13**, [608]
  untrue declarations, etc, **13**, [773]
  vehicles—
    access to, powers of, **13**, [611]
    boarding, powers of, **13**, [610], [696], [919]
    concealed goods, forfeiture, **13**, [611]
    constructed for concealing goods, forfeiture of, **13**, [682]
    detention, **13**, [612], [919]
    entry and search, **13**, [709]
    free zone, entering or leaving, boarding and search, **13**, [696]
    marking, **13**, [611]
    meaning, **13**, [590]
    search of, **13**, [610]
  war damage, effect on duties, **50**, [205]
  warehouse—
    approval—
      cessation of, **13**, [692]
      conditions of, **13**, [686]
      customs warehouse, **13**, [686]
      excise warehouse, **13**, [686]
      non-renewal, **13**, [692]
      revocation, **13**, [686], [692]
      variation of, **13**, [686]
    concealment of entered goods, **13**, [694]
    customs—
      approval, **13**, [686]
      goods kept in, without warehousing, **13**, [686]
      meaning, **13**, [590], [686]
    entry—
      goods for warehousing, **13**, [623]
      payment of duty, without, **13**, [630]
    excise—
      alteration after approval, **13**, [686]
      approval, **13**, [686]
      meaning, **13**, [590], [686]
    goods deposited in—
      examination and taking account of, **13**, [764]
      lawful removal without payment of duty, **13**, [694]
      unlawful removal, **13**, [694]
    hydrocarbon oils, **13**, [856]
    loss or damage to goods in, restriction on compensation for, **13**, [691]

Customs and Excise—*contd*
warehouse—*contd*
  Queen's. *See* Queen's warehouse *above*
  regulations—
    making, **13**, [687]
    non-compliance with, **13**, [687]
    scope of, **13**, [687]
  removal from—
    deficiency occurring, **13**, [689]
    fraudulent intent, with, **13**, [694]
    goods not duly warehoused, **13**, [694]
  sale of goods in, **13**, [692], [693]
  stealing from, with connivance of officer,
    13, [691]
  unauthorised—
    entry to, **13**, [694]
    taking of goods to, **13**, [694]
  unlawful removal of goods from—
    forfeiture of goods where, **13**, [694]
    restriction on compensation where,
      13, [691]
  warehoused goods—
    deficiency in, **13**, [688]
    regulation of, **13**, [687]
whisky defined, **13**, [560], [563]

customs duties
ad valorem duty—
  Community rules, based on, **13**, [729]
  valuation of goods for, **13**, [729]
allowance—
  calculation, **13**, [741]
  goods damaged or destroyed, **13**, [738]
  offences as to claims for, **13**, [740]
  time limit for payment, **13**, [739]
bond, enforcement where goods removed
  without payment, **13**, [735]
Community. *See* **European Communities**
contravention of relevant rule, penalty for,
  13, [1104], [1105], [1107]
delivery of goods after payment, restriction
  on, **13**, [732]
denatured goods, remission or repayment of
  duty, **13**, [733]
dumped goods, on. *See* **dumped goods**
EC provisions, under, **18**, [6]
evasion—
  liability of directors where body corporate
    liable to penalty for, **13**, [1106]
  penalty for, **13**, [1103], [1107]
exemption from. *See* relief from *below*
fractions of penny, ignoring, **43(S)**, 996
fraudulent evasion, **13**, [775]
free zone goods. *See* **customs and excise**
goods not in free circulation in member States
  of European Communities, **13**, [585]
hydrocarbon oil, on. *See* **hydrocarbon oil**
interest on unpaid customs debts, **13**, [1076]
new or altered, effect on contract price,
  13, [551]
origin of goods—
  determination of, **13**, [724]
  proof of, **13**, [759]
payment deferred, **13**, [629]

customs duties—*contd*
penalties—
  admissibility of certain statements and
    documents, **13**, [1116]
  appeals to tribunal, **13**, [1114], [1115]
  demands for, **13**, [1108]
    time limits, **13**, [1109]
  reductions of, **13**, [1107]
  right to review certain decisions,
    13, [1111]–[1113]
  service of notices, **13**, [1117]
prize, ships and goods taken as, **11(2)**, [88]
prohibited and restricted goods, **13**, [535],
  [540], [546]
rebate—
  calculation, **13**, [741]
  certain duties, **13**, [555]
  offences as to, **13**, [740]
recovery, **13**, [742]
relief from—
  administration, **13**, [793]
  annual report to Parliament, **13**, [808]
  antiques, **13**, [797]
  cinematograph film, exposed, **13**, [790]
  Community—
    obligations, in conformity with,
      13, [790], [793]
    practices, referable to, **13**, [791]
  consequential amendments, **13**, [811]
  continental shelf—
    meaning, **13**, [806]
    produce of, **13**, [806]
  false statements in application for, **13**, [807]
  fish, whales, etc, **13**, [806]
  goods qualifying for, **13**, [792]
  immunities and privileges, persons
    enjoying, **13**, [803]–[805]
  imported legacies, **13**, [795]
  international obligations, **13**, [790]
  interpretation of provisions, **13**, [810]
  labels, **13**, [796]
  naval vessels, goods supplied to, **13**, [590],
    [801]
  orders as to, **13**, [809]
  particular importations, **13**, [792]
  persons entering UK, **13**, [802]
  prizes awarded abroad, **13**, [797]
  reciprocal arrangements, **13**, [790]
  regulations as to, **13**, [809]
  repayment of duty, **13**, [793]
  sea, produce of, **13**, [806]
  shipbuilders, **13**, [555]
    ending of, **13**, [1120]
  sound recordings, **13**, [790]
  trade samples, **13**, [796]
  transit or transhipment, goods entered for,
    13, [631]
remission—
  denatured goods, **13**, [733]
  goods lost or destroyed, **13**, [734]
  offences connected with, **13**, [740]
repayment—
  goods—
    denatured, **13**, [733]

customs duties—*contd*
  repayment—*contd*
    goods—*contd*
      importer, returned or destroyed by,
        13, [727]
      lost or destroyed, **13**, [734]
    interest on, **13**, [1077]
      periods to be disregarded in
        determining, **13**, [1078]
      repayment of overpaid, **13**, [1079]
    offences connected with, **13**, [740]
  security for—
    delivery of goods on giving, **13**, [723]
    duty depending on matters other than use,
      13, [725]
  security in proceedings, **43(S)**, 961
  subsidised goods, on. *See* **subsidies**
  use of goods—
    dependent on—
      Community provision for, **13**, [726]
      matters other than, **13**, [726]
      regulations where, **13**, [726]

cycle. *See* **bicycle**

cycle track
  agricultural land, restriction on crossing,
    37, [345]
  barriers in, provision of, **37**, [346]
  construction of, **36**, [1068]
  Crown land, application of provisions to,
    37, [348]
  expenses, **37**, [349]
  footpath converted into, **37**, [345]

cycle track—*contd*
  meaning, **36**, [1381]; **37**, [344]
  motor vehicles, bar on use of, **37**, [344]
  orders for conversion of footpath, **37**, [345]
  safety measures, **37**, [346]
  trunk road, in connection with, **36**, [1013]
  works—
    carrying out, **37**, [345]
    damage, compensation for, **37**, [347]
    safety, for, **37**, [346]

cyclist
  careless or inconsiderate cycling, **37**, [600]
  dangerous cycling, **37**, [599]
  drink or drugs, under influence of, **37**, [601]
  identification of, **37**, [286]
  name and address, failure to give or giving
    false information, **37**, [786]
  police, power to stop on road, **37**, [780]
  reckless or careless riding, **37**, [786]

Cyprus, Republic of
  accession to European Union, **18**, [54]
  citizenship, **7(2)**, [472]
    declaration as to, **31**, [189]
  Commonwealth—
    citizenship, **31**, [186]
    relationship to, **7(2)**, [473]
  existing laws, operation of, **7(2)**, [471]
  independent sovereign country, as, **7(2)**, [469]
  sovereign base areas, **7(2)**, [470]
  visiting forces in, **7(2)**, [475]

Czech Republic
  accession to European Union, **18**, [54]

D

damage
aircraft, by, liability, **4(1)**, [125]
animals, by. *See* **animals**
burglary, in course of, **12(1)**, [561]
criminal. *See* **criminal damage**
person liable in respect of—
  contribution from another liable for same
    damage—
      assessment of amount, **13**, [1126]
      Crown, position of, **13**, [1129]
      entitlement to, **13**, [1125]
      interpretation, **13**, [1130]
      saving provisions, **13**, [1131]
      meaning, **13**, [1125], [1130]
      successive actions against, **13**, [1128]
  proceedings against persons jointly liable for
    same damage, **13**, [1127]

damages
action for, personal injuries, **45**, [947]
Companies Clauses Acts, under, **8**, 63–5
contributory negligence, **31**, [589]
Crown proceedings, in, interest on, **13**, [27]
defamation actions. *See* **libel; slander**
fatal accidents, in case of. *See* **fatal accidents**
future loss, periodical payments for—
  continuity of payment, **11(3)**, [405]
  enhanced protection for, **11(3)**, [406]
  matters taken into account, **11(3)**, [405]
  order for, **11(3)**, [405]
    variation of, **11(3)**, [405]
  security, **11(3)**, [406]
  settlements, variation of, **11(3)**, [405]
injunction, with, **11(2)**, [723]
interest on, **11(2)**, [180], [705]
interference with goods. *See* **wrongful
  interference with goods**
meaning, **13**, [1124]
misrepresentation, for, **39(1)**, [71]
mitigation, effect of apology, **19(3)**, [272]
personal injuries, for—
  assessment—
    maintenance in hospital, etc, effect on,
      13, [1137]
    reduced expectation of life, **13**, [1136]
  expectation of life—
    loss of, abolition of right to damages
      for, **13**, [1136]
    reduced, assessment of damages where,
      13, [1136]
  investment of, assumed rate of return for,
    13, [1142]
  meaning, **13**, [1149]
  periodical payments—
    compensation awards, **44(3)**, [746]
    considerations regarding, **13**, [1144]
    enhanced protection for, **13**, [1147]

damages—*contd*
  personal injuries, for—*contd*
    periodical payments—*contd*
      exempt, **44(3)**, [745], [765]
      order for, **13**, [1143]
      persons entitled to exemption,
        44(3), [747]
      trusts, payment from, **44(3)**, [748]
      variations, **13**, [1145]
    provisional—
      award of, **13**, [1146]
      fatal accident claims, **13**, [1146]
      meaning, **13**, [1146]
    settlements, **13**, [1145]
      public sector, guarantees for, **13**, [1148],
        [1151]
provisional, order for, **11(2)**, [701], [935]
specific performance, with, **11(2)**, [723]
summary of provisions, **13**, [1124]

dangerous animals. *See* **animals**

dangerous buildings. *See* **buildings; London
Building Acts**

dangerous driving. *See* **road traffic offences**

dangerous goods
carriage by road, international conventions,
  36, [765]; **37**, [130]
Port of London, entry at, **39(2)**, [354]

dangerous offenders
dangerousness, assessment of—
  certificates of conviction, **12(3)**, [963]
  day when offence committed,
    determination of, **12(3)**, [965]
  previous conviction set aside, appeals,
    12(3), [962]
  relevant offence, **12(3)**, [960]
  service law, offences under, **12(3)**, [964]
detention, place and conditions of sentence
  of, **12(3)**, [966]
life sentence, **12(3)**, [956]
  persons under 18, **12(3)**, [957]
public protection, imprisonment for,
  12(3), [956]
  persons under 18, **12(3)**, [957]
risk posed by, assessment of—
  arrangements for, **12(3)**, [1035]
  interpretation, **12(3)**, [1037]
  review of arrangements, **12(3)**, [1036]
serious offence, meaning, **12(3)**, [955]
specified offence—
  England and Wales, under law of,
    12(3), [1082]
  meaning, **12(3)**, [955]

dangerous offenders—*contd*
  specified offence—*contd*
    Northern Ireland, **12(3)**, [1084], [1088], [1089]
    Scottish, **12(3)**, [1083], [1087]
    Service law, under, **12(3)**, [1085]
    sexual, **12(3)**, [1081]–[1087], [1089]
    violent, **12(3)**, [1080]–[1088]
  violent or sexual offences, extended sentence for, **12(3)**, [958]
  persons under 18, **12(3)**, [959]

dangerous structure order
  listed building, in respect of, **46**, [698]

dangerous substances
  hoaxes involving, **12(3)**, [145]
  meaning, **12(3)**, [146]
  pathogens and toxins. *See* **pathogens and toxins**
  summary of provisions, **35(1)**, [1]
  use to harm and intimidate, **12(3)**, [142]
    conduct, conditions as to, **12(3)**, [143]
    consent to prosecution, **12(3)**, [144]

Dartmoor
  entire animals turned out on, **20**, [486]

data
  accessible record—
    educational record. *See* **educational records**
    meaning, **7(1)**, [540]
    public, **7(1)**, [565]
  body corporate, director, liability of, **7(1)**, [534]
  Commissioner. *See* **Information Commissioner**
  controller—
    blocking of data by, **7(1)**, [484]
    certain information, duty to make available, **7(1)**, [494]
    destruction of data by, **7(1)**, [484]
    erasure of data by, **7(1)**, [484]
    failure to comply with certain requirements, compensation for, **7(1)**, [483]
    meaning, **7(1)**, [470]
    notification by—
      generally, **7(1)**, [488]
      offences, **7(1)**, [491]
      preliminary assessment by Commissioner, **7(1)**, [492]
      prohibition on processing without, **7(1)**, [487]
    register of—
      contents, **7(1)**, [489]
      duty to notify changes, **7(1)**, [490]
      inspection, available for, **7(1)**, [489]
      maintenance of, **7(1)**, [489]
    registrable particulars, **7(1)**, [486]
    regulations concerning, functions of Commissioner in relation to, **7(1)**, [495]
    service of notices, **7(1)**, [538]

data—*contd*
  controller—*contd*
    rectification of data by, **7(1)**, [484]
  Crown application, **7(1)**, [535]
  defined expressions, index of, **7(1)**, [543]
  educational records, **7(1)**, [564]
  electronic. *See* **electronic data**
  exemption from protection principles—
    armed forces, **7(1)**, [556]
    artistic material, in cases of, **7(1)**, [502]
    confidential references given by data controller, **7(1)**, [556]
    corporate finance, **7(1)**, [556]
    crime, used to fight, **7(1)**, [499]
    Crown employment, **7(1)**, [556]
    domestic purposes, held for, **7(1)**, [508]
    education, in relation to, **7(1)**, [500]
    enactment, required under, **7(1)**, [505]
    examination marks, **7(1)**, [556]
    further, Secretary of State's power to make, by, **7(1)**, [510]
    health of subject, concerning, **7(1)**, [500]
    journalistic material in public interest, in cases of, **7(1)**, [502]
    judicial appointments, relating to, **7(1)**, [556]
    legal proceedings, disclosures made in connection with, **7(1)**, [506]
    legal professional privilege, claim of, **7(1)**, [556]
    literary material, in cases of, **7(1)**, [502]
    manual data held by public authorities, **7(1)**, [504]
    Ministerial appointments, **7(1)**, [556]
    miscellaneous, **7(1)**, [509], [556]
    national security, on grounds of, **7(1)**, [498]
    parliamentary privilege, **7(1)**, [507]
    preliminary, **7(1)**, [497]
    regulatory activity, **7(1)**, [501]
    research, for, **7(1)**, [503]
    self-incrimination, **7(1)**, [556]
    social work, in relation to, **7(1)**, [500]
    special purposes, for—
      determination by Commissioner as to special purposes, **7(1)**, [517]
      meaning, **7(1)**, [472]
      restriction on enforcement in case of processing for, **7(1)**, [518]
    statistics, for preparing, **7(1)**, [503]
    taxes and duty, used in collecting, **7(1)**, [499]
    transitional relief, **7(1)**, [557]–[561]
  health records, access to. *See* **health records**
  meaning, **7(1)**, [470]
  minor and consequential amendments, **7(1)**, [546], [567]
  offences—
    directors, liability of, **7(1)**, [534]
    inspection and seizure, matters exempt from, **7(1)**, [562]
    penalties, **7(1)**, [533]
    prosecutions, **7(1)**, [533]
    warrants, **7(1)**, [562]
  orders, regulations and rules, **7(1)**, [539]

data—*contd*
Parliament, application of provisions to,
7(1), [536]
personal—
access to—
credit reference agency, held by,
7(1), [478]
jurisdiction and procedure, 7(1), [485]
prohibition of requirement as to
production of certain records,
7(1), [529]
right to, 7(1), [476], [477]
blocking of, 7(1), [484]
destruction of, 7(1), [484]
erasure of, 7(1), [484]
freedom of information, exemptions,
7(1), [641]
meaning, 7(1), [470]
processing. *See* processing *below*
rectification of, 7(1), [484]
sensitive, 7(1), [471], [551]
unlawful obtaining of, 7(1), [528]
unstructured, held by public authorities,
7(1), [479]
personal files, access to. *See* **personal files**
processing—
meaning, 7(1), [470]
personal data, of—
assessment, request for, 7(1), [514]
automated decision-taking, rights in
relation to, 7(1), [482]
damage or distress, right to prevent
causing, 7(1), [480]
direct marketing for, right to prevent,
7(1), [481]
first principle, conditions relevant for,
7(1), [550]
information notices, 7(1), [515]
notices, failure to comply with,
7(1), [519]
special purposes, for—
assistance by Commissioner in cases
involving, 7(1), [525], [563]
determination by Commissioner as
to, 7(1), [517]
restriction on enforcement in cases
of, 7(1), [518]
special information notices,
7(1), [516]
processor, meaning, 7(1), [470]
protection principles—
application of 1998 Act, 7(1), [474]
eighth principle—
interpretation of, 7(1), [549]
where not applicable, 7(1), [552]
enforcement notices, 7(1), [512]
cancellation, 7(1), [513]
failure to comply with certain
requirements, compensation for,
7(1), [483]
first principle—
interpretation of, 7(1), [549]
personal data, processing of, 7(1), [550]
sensitive personal data, processing of,
7(1), [551]

data—*contd*
protection principles—*contd*
fourth principle, 7(1), [549]
generally, 7(1), [473], [548]
international co-operation, 7(1), [526]
interpretation of, 7(1), [549]
second principle, 7(1), [549]
seventh principle, 7(1), [549]
sixth principle, 7(1), [549]
supervisors, power to make provision for
appointment of, 7(1), [493]
registrar. *See* **Information Registrar**
relevant filing system, meaning, 7(1), [470]
repeals, 7(1), [546], [568]
revocations, 7(1), [546], [569]
subject—
meaning, 7(1), [470]
rights of, 7(1), [566]
summary of provisions, 7(1), [1]
transitional provisions and savings, 7(1), [545],
[566]
transitional relief, 7(1), [557]–[561]
transmission of notices, 7(1), [537]
tribunal. *See* **Information Tribunal**

data protection
data controllers, monetary penalty imposed
on, 12(4), [541]
personal data, unlawfully obtaining—
journalism and special purposes, for,
12(4), [508]
penalty for, 12(4), [507]

Data Protection Commissioner. *See now*
Information Commissioner

Data Protection Tribunal. *See now*
Information Tribunal

database right
legal deposit libraries, copying by, 13, [461]

day
period represented by, 45, [918]

day nursery
meaning, 15(1), [652]
provision of teachers to, 15(1), [652], [669]

DBS. *See under* **Independent Broadcasting
Authority (services)**

deacon
admission, minimum age for, 14, 63
deaconess becoming, 14, 1175
non-residentiary canon, appointment of,
14, 1262
offences. *See* **ecclesiastical offences**
ordination. *See* **ordination**
qualification for office, 14, 643
residentiary canon, appointment of, 14, 1262
women, ordination of. *See* **ordination**

deaconess
dependants, 14, 958

deaconess—*contd*
  doctrine of Church of England, assent to,
    14, 814
  duties performed by, **14**, 803
  licence, revocation of, **14**, 1179
  licensing for fixed term, **14**, 804
  order of, provisions as to, **14**, 1176
  ordination as deacon, **14**, 1175
  pension for, **14**, 957–8

dead body
  burial. *See* **burial**
  disposal. *See* **notifiable disease**
  finding of, information required,
    36, [90]–[92]

dean. *See also* **cathedral**
  cathedral, functions in relation to, **14**, 1344
  newly appointed, payment towards expenses
    incurred by, **14**, 1354
  qualifications of, **14**, 133
  resignation of, **14**, 1310
  rural, **14**, 1376
  stipend, **14**, 1354

Dean of the Arches and Auditor
  appointment of, **14**, 561–2
  deputy, **14**, 563
  Master of faculties, as, **14**, 570
  official principal, as, **14**, 570

deanery
  pastoral scheme—
    dealing with, **14**, 985
    dissolving, **14**, 997–8
  patronage of, **14**, 133

deanery synod
  casual vacancies, **14**, 748–9
  cathedral clergy and laity on, **14**, 725
  Channel Islands, of—
    duties, **14**, 347
    lay representatives on, **14**, 348
    rules and procedure, **14**, 349
  constitution of, **14**, 689–90
  diocesan synod—
    delegation of functions by, **14**, 689–90
    information from, **14**, 688
    members, electing, **14**, 729–31
  ex-officio member being elected, **14**, 747
  functions of, **14**, 689–90
  house of clergy, members, **14**, 722
  house of laity—
    members, **14**, 722
    parochial church meeting, elected at,
      14, 706–7
    parochial representatives, election of,
      14, 724
  meaning of, **14**, 335
  procedure, **14**, 726
  resignation from, **14**, 750
  ruri-decanal conference, taking place of,
    14, 689
  total number of members, **14**, 724
  vacation of seat on, **14**, 745–6

deanery synod—*contd*
  variation of membership by scheme, **14**, 725

death
  capital punishment. *See* **capital punishment**
  concealment by guardian etc, **20**, [20]
  date of, burden of proof, **20**, [18]
  employee, of. *See* **employee**
  employer, of. *See* **employer**
  false statement of particulars, **12(1)**, [198]
  information on, obtaining, **40(1)**, [630]
  inheritance tax. *See* **inheritance tax**
  members of armed forces, liability of Crown
    where, **13**, [14], [45], [46]
  notification of, **30**, [1075], [1316];
    40(1), [632]
  person subject to military law, of. *See*
    military law
  presumption of, **20**, [16]–[18]
  property involved on, exemption from stamp
    duty on instruments, **41**, [151]
  register, forging, **12(1)**, [724]
  Registrar General, provision of information
    by, **30**, [1076], [1317]
  registration. *See* **death, registration of**
  service, in—
    presumption of, **3**, [432]
    treating person as alive, **3**, [439]
  visiting force, member of, **3**, [446]

death duties
  generally, **42**, [1]
  obsolete, abolition of, **42**, [323]

death penalty. *See* **death sentence**

death, registration of
  aircraft, death in, **4(1)**, [134]; **36**, [143]
  armed forces overseas, **36**, [142]
  army abroad, evidence of records, **36**, [23],
    [24]
  cause of death—
    certificate of, **36**, [95]
    coroner's certificate, **36**, [96]
  certificate—
    body removed into England and Wales,
      36, [98]
    cause of death, **36**, [95]
    duplicate, **36**, [98]
    falsification, **36**, [6]
    forgery, **36**, [6], [112]
    issue of, **36**, [98]
  charge, freedom from, **36**, [93]
  coroner's certificate—
    inquest, after, **36**, [96]
    post-mortem, after, **36**, [96]
  dead body—
    disposal, meaning, **36**, [116]
    finding of, **36**, [90]–[92]
  district register offices, provision and
    maintenance, **36**, [128]
  districts, organisation into, **36**, [125]
  documents, transmission of, **36**, [64], [115]
  house, at—
    death occurring, **36**, [89]

death, registration of—*contd*
  house, at—*contd*
    death other than, **36**, [90]
    industrial diseases, death from, **36**, [152]
    information—
      coroner, furnishing by, **36**, [96]
      dead body, finding of, **36**, [90]–[92]
      duty to give, **36**, [90]
      failure to give, penalty, **36**, [111]
      industrial diseases, death from, **36**, [152]
      person other than registrar, giving to, **36**, [97]
      preliminary notice, **36**, [91]
      registrar's power to require, **36**, [92]
      time allowed for, **36**, [89]
  local schemes—
    matters to be included, **36**, [132]
    preparation, **36**, [1], [133]
    submission and approval, **36**, [133]
  non-parochial registers—
    extracts, **36**, [7]–[11]
    searches, **36**, [3]
  offences, **36**, [6], [110]–[113]
    prosecution of, **36**, [113]
  offices, **36**, [129], [130]
  officials, employment status of, **36**, [204]
  particulars required, **36**, [88]
  registers—
    army and air force, validation of entries, **36**, [146]
    certified copies, **36**, [109]
    compilation, **36**, [1]
    custody, **36**, [102]
    deposit of, **36**, [16]
    errors, correction of, **36**, [103], [104]
    evidence, as, **36**, [4], [11], [109]
    filled, **36**, [102]
    fire-resisting boxes, provision, **36**, [131]
    forgery, **36**, [6]
    form, **36**, [99]
    non-parochial. *See* non-parochial registers *above*
    offences relating to, **36**, [6], [110], [111]
    preservation, **36**, [1]
    provision of, **36**, [99]
    search and inspection, **36**, [3], [107]
    wilful damage to, **36**, [6]
  registrars—
    appointment, **36**, [126]
    delivery up of books etc on ceasing to hold office, **36**, [134]
    deputies, **36**, [127]
    employment status of, **36**, [204]
    fees, **36**, [135]
    interim, **36**, [128]
    meaning, **36**, [116]
    offences by, **36**, [110]
    qualifications, **36**, [126]
    returns by, **36**, [100]
  registration districts, **36**, [125], [129]
  registration offices, **36**, [129], [130]
  regulations, power to make, **36**, [114], [137]
  service civilians overseas, **36**, [142]
  service department records, **36**, [144], [145]
  ships, H.M., death on board, **36**, [143]

death, registration of—*contd*
  sub-district register offices, **36**, [130]
  sub-districts, organisation into, **36**, [125]
  summary of provisions, **36**, [1]
  superintendent registrars—
    appointment, **36**, [126]
    delivery up of books etc on ceasing to hold office, **36**, [134]
    deputies, **36**, [127]
    employment status of, **36**, [204]
    fees, **36**, [135]
    indexes kept by, search and copies, **36**, [106]
    interim, **36**, [128]
    meaning, **36**, [116]
    prosecutions by, **36**, [113]
    qualifications, **36**, [126]
    returns—
      by, **36**, [101]
      to, **36**, [100]
  time allowed, **36**, [89], [94]
  twelve months, after, **36**, [94]

death sentence. *See also* **capital punishment**
  murder, for, abolition, **12(1)**, [358]

debenture
  advances, deposit to secure, **8(1)**, [831]
  allotment. *See also* **allotment (shares and debentures)**
    certificate, issue of, **8(1)**, [847]
    registration, **8(1)**, [819]
  certificate endorsed on, **8(1)**, [943]
  charge in series of, **8(1)**, [941]
  charge on, **8**, 457, 559
  commission, allowance or discount, registration requirements, **8(1)**, [942]
  companies clauses. *See* **Companies Clauses Acts**
  contract for, enforcement of, **8**, 251
  contract to subscribe for, enforcement, **8(1)**, [818]
  deed, right of holder to copy of, **8(1)**, [827]
  deposit of, as security for debt, **8**, 457
  director's interest in, disclosure, **8**, 388–9
  floating charge—
    priorities where secured by, **8(1)**, [832]
    secured by, **8**, 251
  holders. *See* **debenture holder**
  interest in—
    connected persons, **8(1)**, [1377]
    interpretation of, **8**, 757
  irredeemable, **8**, 250
  meaning, **8**, 602; **8(1)**, [816]
  offer to the public—
    exceptions from rule, **8**, 156
    private limited company, by, **8**, 160
    prospectus, deemed to be, **8**, 156
    rule governing, **8**, 176
    See also **prospectus**
  ownership, information as to, **8**, 491
  perpetual, **8(1)**, [817]
    validity, **8**, 250
  redeemed, power to re-issue, **8(1)**, [830]

debenture—*contd*
  register of holders—
    claims arising from entry in, time limit
     for, **8(1)**, [826]
    closure, **8(1)**, [822]
    contents of, **8(1)**, [822]
    inspection and requiring copy of—
     offences, **8(1)**, [825]
     refusal or default in, **8(1)**, [824]
     response to request for, **8(1)**, [823]
     right of, **8(1)**, [822]
    inspection, keeping for, **8(1)**, [821]
    notice to registrar, **8(1)**, [821]
  re-issue of—
    mortgagees, saving of rights of, **8**, 826
    priorities after, **8**, 250–1
    redemption, after, **8**, 250–1
    stamp duty, **8**, 250–1
  short-dated, offers of, **8**, 866
  takeover offer. *See* **takeover offer**
  taking up issue, registration of particulars,
   8, 911–12
  title to. *See* **securities**
  transfer—
    certificate issued on—
     default, court making good, **8(1)**, [860]
     duty of company, **8(1)**, [854]
     financial institution, allotment or transfer
      to, **8(1)**, [856]
     Stock Transfer Act, cases within,
      8(1), [855]
    certification of instrument of, **8(1)**, [853]
    grant of probate, evidence of, **8(1)**, [852]
    procedure on lodging, **8(1)**, [849]
    registration of, **8(1)**, [848]
  transfer of. *See* **shares in company**
  trustees, liability of, **8**, 249–50
    older provisions, saving for, **8(1)**, [829]
    provisions exempting, void, **8(1)**, [828]
    release, **8(1)**, [828]

debenture holder
  accounts, right to copy of, **8**, 302–3
  register of—
    closing, **8**, 248
    copies, right to, **8**, 248
    entries and deletions, **8**, 248–9
    inspection, right of, **8**, 248–9
    keeping of, **8**, 247–8
    situation of, **8**, 247–8

Debt Management Account
  accounts, **19(2)**, [874]
  borrowing and lending, **19(2)**, [874]
  establishment of, **19(1)**, [1]; **19(2)**, [874]
  general powers, **19(2)**, [874]
  National Loans Fund, payment into,
   19(2), [874]
  objects of, **19(2)**, [874]

debtor
  administration order against—
    power to make, **19(3)**, [40]
    securing payments under, **19(3)**, [41]
  arrest of, about to quit England, **4(2)**, [8]

debtor—*contd*
  attachment of earnings. *See* **attachment of**
   earnings
  bankruptcy, in. *See* **bankruptcy**
  Crown—
    arrest, freedom from, **13**, [2]
    parliamentary privilege, **13**, [2]
  fraudulent, **4(2)**, [11]
  imprisonment of—
    abolition, exceptions from, **4(2)**, [6]
    jurisdiction as to, **4(2)**, [48]
    maximum period, **4(2)**, [6]
    restrictions on, **4(2)**, [6], [48]
    small debts, committal for, **4(2)**, [7]
  insolvency, in. *See* **company insolvency;**
   individual insolvency
  judgment, meaning, **19(3)**, [25]
  means, proof of, **4(2)**, [7]
  power of HMRC to obtain contact details
   for, **43(S)**, 1700–2
  sequestration of property of, **4(2)**, [9]
  unlawful harassment of, **12(1)**, [591]
  summary of provisions, **4(2)**, [1]
  writ of attachment, discretion of court,
   4(2), [12]

debts
  administration enforcement restriction order,
   effect on management arrangements,
   11(4), [64]; **11(S)**, Courts 96–7
  administration order. *See* **administration**
   order
  capital gains tax treatment, **42**, [1396]
  conveyance in satisfaction of, stamp duty,
   41, [37], [136]
  credit card, on, **44(1)**, [180]
  Crown, recovery, **13**, [2]
  debt management scheme—
    approval of—
     alternatives to termination, **4(2)**, [624]
     application for, **4(2)**, [609]
     conditions to be met, **4(2)**, [608]
     end of, effects, **4(2)**, [625]
     supervising authority, by, **4(2)**, [608]
     termination of, **4(2)**, [622]–[624]
     terms of, **4(2)**, [610]
    approved, charges by operator of,
     4(2), [621]
    meaning, **4(2)**, [606]
    period of protection—
     charging of interest during, **4(2)**, [614]
     gas or electricity supplies, no stopping
      of, **4(2)**, [615]
     meaning, **4(2)**, [630]
     non-bankruptcy remedies during,
      4(2), [613]
    qualifying debts, **4(2)**, [629]
    registration, **4(2)**, [617]
    regulations, **4(2)**, [627]
    scope of, **4(2)**, [606]
    summary of provisions, **4(2)**, [1]
    supervising authority—
     approval by, **4(2)**, [608]
     meaning, **4(2)**, [626]

debts—*contd*
debt relief order—
applicant, false representations and
omissions by, **4(2)**, [300]
application for, **4(2)**, [286], [287]
approved intermediaries, **4(2)**, [306]
conditions for—
debtor who meets, **4(2)**, [344]
mandatory, **4(2)**, [550]
preferences, **4(2)**, [551]
transactions, entry into, **4(2)**, [551]
consequential amendments, **4(2)**, [634]
debtor—
business, engaging in, **4(2)**, [304]
concealment or falsification of
documents, **4(2)**, [301]
credit, obtaining, **4(2)**, [304]
dealings and property, inquiry into,
4(2), [299]
fraudulent disposal of property,
4(2), [302]
official receiver, provision of assistance
to, **4(2)**, [295]
penalties, **4(2)**, [305]
proceedings for offences, **4(2)**, [305]
property obtained on credit, fraudulent
dealing with, **4(2)**, [303]
determination of application—
official receiver, by, **4(2)**, [288]
presumptions, **4(2)**, [289]
interpretation, **4(2)**, [309]
making, **4(2)**, [290]
objections and investigations, **4(2)**, [296]
official receiver—
consideration and determination of
applications by, **4(2)**, [288]
debtor, assistance from, **4(2)**, [295]
revocation or amendment by, **4(2)**, [297]
other debt management arrangements,
effect on, **4(2)**, [291]
powers of court, **4(2)**, [298]
qualifying debts—
discharge from, **4(2)**, [294]
meaning, **4(2)**, [286], [629]
moratorium, **4(2)**, [292]–[294]
register of, **4(2)**, [308]
revocation or amendment, **4(2)**, [297]
debt relief restriction order—
application, timing, **4(2)**, [552]
conditions for, **4(2)**, [552]
duration, **4(2)**, [552]
interim, **4(2)**, [552]
making, **4(2)**, [552]
revocation of debt relief order, effect of,
4(2), [552]
undertakings, **4(2)**, [552]
debt repayment plan—
affected creditor, appeal by, **4(2)**, [619],
[621]
existing county court proceedings, staying,
4(2), [616]
meaning, **4(2)**, [607]
other debt management arrangements in
force, cessation of, **4(2)**, [618]

debts—*contd*
debt repayment plan—*contd*
presentation of bankruptcy petition during
currency of, **4(2)**, [612]
registration, **4(2)**, [617]
scope of, **4(2)**, [607]
specified debts, discharge from, **4(2)**, [611]
deductions, restrictions on, **44(1)**, [65]
discontinuance, recovery after, **44(1)**, [84]
enemy, written off—
recovery, effect of, **42**, [27]
treatment of, **42**, [26]
funding bond, issue of, **44(1)**, [418]
irrecoverable, **44(1)**, [66]
overdraft, **44(1)**, [180]
PAYE regulations, recovery under,
43(S), 1756–7
proceedings against persons jointly liable for
same, **13**, [1127]
released, treatment of, **44(1)**, [75]
trade, release of, **43(S)**, 1381
transactions in, **44(1)**, [35], [202]

deception
going equipped for, **12(1)**, [577]
Northern Ireland, provisions in, **12(1)**, [696]
offences involving, **12(2)**, [162]
penalties, **12(1)**, [694]
valuable security executed by, **12(1)**, [571]

decimal currency
bank balances, conversion of, **10**, [259]
Bills of Exchange Act, modification of,
10, [268]
bills of exchange in, **10**, [257]
calculation of corresponding amounts,
10, [273]
denominations of money, **10**, [291]
enactments, references to old currency in,
10, [265]–[266]
forms, modification of, **10**, [267]
friendly society contracts, payments under,
10, [261]–[262]
industrial assurance company contracts,
payments under, **10**, [261]–[262]
non-business days, special, **10**, [268]
payments due after transitional period,
10, [264]
periodical payments in, **10**, [260]
promissory note in, **10**, [257]
references in old currency, conversion of,
10, [258]
registered stock in multiples of one penny,
10, [263]

declaration. *See* **statutory declaration**
stamp duty on, **41**, [214]

decorations (medals)
disposal of on death, **3**, [231]
meaning, **3**, [723], [995]
offences relating to—
air force, **3**, [776]
army, **3**, [503]
navy, **3**, [1046]

decorations (medals)—*contd*
  unauthorised use and dealing, **3**, [697], [970]

deed
  abolition of stamp duty on, **41**, [152], [157]
  attestation, **20**, [769]
  attorney, execution by, **8(1)**, [125]
  company, execution by, **8(1)**, [124]
  confirmation of past transactions, **20**, [684]
  construction of expressions used, **20**, [679]
  conveyance by, **20**, [1], [670]
  description of, **20**, [675]
  executed, when treated as, **41**, [46]
  execution—
    abolished provisions, **23**, [1]
    corporation, by or on behalf of, **20**, [691]
    delivery of, **23**, [1]
  execution of instrument as, **20**, [692]
  indenture, effect as, **20**, [675]
  land registration. *See* **land registration**
  persons not party to, interest taken by,
    20, [674]
  pre-incorporation, **8(1)**, [129]
  receipt in—
    evidence of payment, **20**, [686]
    payment to solicitor, authority for,
      20, [687]
    sufficiency, **20**, [685]
  supplemental instruments, **20**, [676]
  technicalities, abolition, **20**, [678]
  words implied, **20**, [680]

deed of arrangement
  accounts—
    audit, **4(2)**, [27]
    inspection, open to, **4(2)**, [25]
    transmission to—
      Board of Trade, **4(2)**, [25]
      creditors, **4(2)**, [26]
  affidavits, swearing, **4(2)**, [38]
  avoidance of, **4(2)**, [15], [16]
    notice to creditors of, **4(2)**, [31]
  classes of, **4(2)**, [14]
  creditors—
    accounts to be sent to, **4(2)**, [26]
    assent of majority required, **4(2)**, [16]
    majority, calculation of, **4(2)**, [16]
    notice of avoidance of deed, **4(2)**, [31]
  enforcement of trusts, **4(2)**, [34]
  land, affecting—
    register of, **21**, [391]
    registration, **21**, [397]
  local registration, **4(2)**, [22]
  office copies, right to have, **4(2)**, [36]
  register—
    extracts, right to, **4(2)**, [37]
    form, **4(2)**, [18]
    inspection, **4(2)**, [21]
    particulars to be shown in, **4(2)**, [18]
    rectification, **4(2)**, [19]
  registration—
    fees, **4(2)**, [37]
    local county court, in, **4(2)**, [22]
    mode of, **4(2)**, [17]
    office for, **4(2)**, [41]

deed of arrangement—*contd*
  registration—*contd*
    time for, **4(2)**, [20]
  summary of provisions, **4(2)**, [1]
  trustee—
    accounts. *See* accounts *above*
    acting when deed void, penalty, **4(2)**, [24]
    duties, **4(2)**, [24]
    expenses, payment, **4(2)**, [32]
    failure to give security, **4(2)**, [23]
    payment by—
      preferential, offence of, **4(2)**, [29]
      undistributed money, into court,
        4(2), [628]
    protection under void deeds, **4(2)**, [30]
    security by, **4(2)**, [23]
    undistributed money, payment into court,
      4(2), [28]
  unregistered, void, **4(2)**, [15]

deed poll
  easement, compulsory acquisition by, **9**, [150]
  general provisions as to, **9**, [286]
  mortgagee's interest, vesting by, **9**, [274]
  rentcharge, extinguishing, **9**, [74], [278]
  vesting by—
    absent or untraced owner, **9**, [296], [377]
    acquiring authority, by, **9**, [274], [295]
    common land, **9**, [64], [298], [377]
    default of payment, **9**, [38]
    deposit being made, on, **9**, [40]
    general vesting declarations, **9**, [393]
    Lord of the Manor etc, **9**, [57]
    on deposit being made, **9**, [38]
    owners under incapacity, **9**, [295], [377]
    promoters of undertaking, by, **9**, [64]
    refusal or failure to convey, **9**, [269], [298],
      [377]

deep sea mining
  civil liability, breach of statutory duty,
    17(1), [526]
  disclosure of information, **17(1)**, [524]
  Dumping at Sea Act, effect, **17(1)**, [527]
  exploration and exploitation licences—
    deep sea bed, meaning, **17(1)**, [512]
    grant, **17(1)**, [513]
    interference with operations, **17(1)**, [515]
    meanings—
      exploitation, **17(1)**, [513]
      exploration licence, **17(1)**, [513]
    need for, **17(1)**, [512]
    period of, **17(1)**, [513]
    reciprocating countries, granted by,
      17(1), [514]
    terms and conditions, **17(1)**, [513]
    variation and revocation, **17(1)**, [517]
  foreign discriminatory action, **17(1)**, [519]
  freedom of the high seas, duty as to,
    17(1), [518]
  fund, establishment etc, **17(1)**, [521]
  inspectors—
    appointment, **17(1)**, [522]
    regulations relating to, **17(1)**, [530]

deep sea mining—*contd*
interference with licensed operations, prevention, **17(1)**, [515]
levy on, **17(1)**, [520]
marine environment, protection, **17(1)**, [516]
offences, **17(1)**, [525]
reciprocating countries—
designation, **17(1)**, [514]
licences, grant by, **17(1)**, [514]
regulations and orders—
power to make, **17(1)**, [523]
subject matter of, **17(1)**, [530]
statutory duty, breach of, **17(1)**, [526]
unlicensed—
penalty, **17(1)**, [512]
prohibition, **17(1)**, [512]

deer. *See also* **pests**
authorised person—
meaning, **2**, [652]
powers of, **2**, [652]
close seasons, **2**, [653], [670]
Countryside Council for Wales, persons licensed by, **2**, [659]
destructive, requirement to destroy, **1(1)**, [390]
forfeiture for offences, **2**, [664]
meaning, **2**, [667]
nightly close times, **2**, [654]
offences, **2**, [652]–[655]
attempt to commit, **2**, [656]
exceptions as to, **2**, [658]
occupiers of land, exceptions for, **2**, [658]
penalties, **2**, [660]
police powers, **2**, [663]
search, arrest and seizure, **2**, [663]
poaching—
arrest of suspects, **2**, [663]
forfeiture of animals and articles, **2**, [664]
offences of, **2**, [652]
penalties, **2**, [660]
search, arrest and seizure, **2**, [663]
taking or killing—
authorised persons, by, **2**, [652]
close season, in, **2**, [653]
licence for, **2**, [659]
night, at, **2**, [654]
orders, power to make, **2**, [666]
unlawful weapons, **2**, [655], [671]
traps, snares etc, use of, **2**, [655]
venison—
forfeiture for offences, **2**, [664]
licensed game dealer—
disqualifications, **2**, [664]
offences and penalties, **2**, [661]
records—
duty to keep, **2**, [662]
form, **2**, [672]
inspection, **2**, [662]
meaning, **2**, [667]
offences, **2**, [661]. [662]
bodies corporate, by, **2**, [665]
game dealer, by, **2**, [662]
prohibited period—
meaning, **2**, [661]

deer—*contd*
venison—*contd*
prohibited period—*contd*
selling during, restriction, **2**, [661]

defamation. *See also* **libel; slander**
convictions, conclusiveness for purpose of action, **18**, [206]
National Assembly for Wales, privileged statements and publications, **10**, [1507]
Public Services Ombudsman for Wales, protection from claims, **10**, [831]
rehabilitation of offenders, effect on action, **12(1)**, [637]
Scottish Parliament, privileged statements in, **10**, [1352]

defective equipment
injury attributable to, liability, **16**, [19]

defective housing. *See also* **unfit house**
alternative accommodation—
duty to provide, **22**, [371]
suitable—
meaning, **22**, [295]
must be, **22**, [371]
assistance for—
application for, **22**, [349]
when not entertained, **22**, [350]
availability, publicising, **22**, [377]
compulsory purchase, **22**, [365]
conditions of eligibility, **22**, [346]
contributions by Secretary of State, **22**, [384]
death of person eligible for, **22**, [380]
eligibility for, **22**, [342]
determination of, **22**, [351]
exceptions to, **22**, [348]
form of, determination of, **22**, [352]
grant, by. *See* **reinstatement grant**
mortgagees, extension to, **22**, [383]
qualifying defect, **22**, [343]
relevant percentage, varying, **22**, [385]
repurchase, by way of. *See* repurchase *below*
shared ownership, in case of, **22**, [382]
compensation payment—
generally, **22**, [365]
refusal of, **22**, [366]
compulsory purchase compensation, **22**, [365]
county court jurisdiction, **22**, [387]
designation of—
Gazette notice of, **22**, [344]
local schemes, under—
grounds for, **22**, [374]
matters to be specified, **22**, [374]
Ministerial control, **22**, [376]
variation or revocation, **22**, [375]
more than one, falling within—
later designation disregarded, **22**, [454]
procedure as to, **22**, [454]
Secretary of State, by, **22**, [343]
variation or revocation, **22**, [344]
local schemes, under, **22**, [375]
disposal, references to, **22**, [347]
dwelling, meaning, **22**, [390]

defective housing—*contd*

notices as to, service of, **22**, [386]

pre-April 1989 expenses, contributions in respect of, **23**, [185]

pre-emption, interest subject to right of, **22**, [364]

public sector authority—

disposal of, by, **22**, [378]

Crown interest, affecting, **22**, [389]

meaning, **22**, [388]

reinstatement—

local housing authority, by, **22**, [379]

See also **reinstatement grant**

relevant interest—

condition for assistance, **22**, [346]

meaning, **22**, [345]

repurchase—

agreement to, **22**, [451]

assistance by way of, **22**, [451]–[453]

compulsory, compensation, **22**, [365]

conveyance, effect of, **22**, [454]

demolition, for, **22**, [371]

determination of, notice of, **22**, [355]

draft agreement—

amended, service of, **22**, [452]

service of, **22**, [451]

expenses incidental to, **22**, [367]

grant conditions ceasing to have effect, **22**, [453]

interest to be acquired, **22**, [451]

Ministerial contributions, **22**, [384], [385]

notice requiring, **22**, [451]

other than housing authority, by, **22**, [363]

price payable, **22**, [452]

proposed terms, notice of, **22**, [451]

purchase price—

application of, **22**, [453]

payment into court, **22**, [453]

questions as to, settlement of, **22**, [366]

reconstruction, for, **22**, [371]

registration of title, **22**, [453]

settlement of terms, **22**, [451]

tenancy—

existing, effect on, **22**, [368]

former owner-occupier, grant to, **22**, [369]

former tenant, grant to, **22**, [370]

request for grant of, **22**, [372]

secure tenancy becoming, **22**, [368]

two or more persons qualifying for, **22**, [370]

value, determination of, **22**, [452]

unsafe for occupation, **22**, [371]

valuation of, **22**, [452]

defective premises

builder's liability, **21**, [384]

Crown, application of provisions, **21**, [388]

disposal, effect of—

duty of care, on, **21**, [386]

liability, on, **21**, [386]

disposal, meaning, **21**, [389]

duty of care, **21**, [384], [386]

landlord's duty of care, **21**, [387]

defective premises—*contd*

personal injury—

duty as to, safety, **21**, [387]

meaning, **21**, [389]

remedy—

cases excluded, **21**, [385]

schemes as to, **21**, [385]

remedying defects, powers of local authorities for, **35(1)**, [598]

repair, maintenance, etc, duty of care, **21**, [387]

right of action, accrual, **21**, [384]

summary of provisions, **31**, [588]

tenancy—

meaning, **21**, [389]

obligations under, **21**, [387]

defence

central organisation, **3**, [1]

Defence Act 1842

compensation money under, payment into court, **13**, [3]

Defence Acts. *See also* **emergency powers**

acquisition of land, application to, **9**, [211]

compulsory acquisition under—

agreement, by, **9**, [156]

easements, **9**, [147], [149]–[150], [159]

exchange of lands, by, **9**, [156]

land in lieu of land acquired, **9**, [156]

meaning, **9**, [159]

minerals, **9**, [148]

modification in relation to acquisitions, **9**, [147]

requisitioned land, compensation, **9**, [213]

restrictive rights, **9**, [147], [149]

reversionary interests, **9**, [148]

surface of land, **9**, [148]

works, removal, **9**, [151]

Defence Council

alcohol testing, power to make regulations regarding, **3**, [1734]

certificate of service by, **3**, [1476]

drugs testing, power to make regulations regarding, **3**, [1734]

establishment of, **10**, [528]

functions, **3**, [1]

service complaint to—

individual grievances, **3(S)**, 302–3

role on, **3(S)**, 304

transfer of functions, **10**, [528]

Defence, Ministry of

land drainage, saving for, rights of, **20**, [321]

Defence of the Realm Acts

building laws, application of, **9**, [108]

certificate of government department, evidence, as, **9**, [107]

compensation, **9**, [103], [106], [114], [152]

disposal of land, **9**, [104], [114]

easements, **9**, [118]

highways, **9**, [105], [117]

Defence of the Realm Acts—*contd*
interpretation, **9**, [109], [116]
lease of land, **9**, [102]
Northern Ireland, application to, **9**, [112]
permanent acquisition, power of, **9**, [102]
pre-emption—
  right of, **9**, [104], [115]
  settled land, where, **9**, [115]
purchase money, payment, **9**, [106]
restrictive covenant—
  compensation for breach of, **9**, [103]
  disposal of land free from, **9**, [114]
sale of land—
  acquired under Act, **9**, [104], [114]
  compensation claimed, where, **9**, [103]
  user of acquired land, **9**, [103]
successive works as one, **9**, [154]

defence organisations
immunities and privileges, **10**, [979]

Defence Police Federation
constitution and proceedings, **33(2)**, [135]
continuation of, **33(2)**, [135]
functions, **33(2)**, [135]

Defence Regulations
permanent effect, **50**, [218], [233],
  [257]–[275]

Defence, Secretary of State for
Admiralty, succeeding, **10**, [528]
Air Secretary and Council, succeeding,
  10, [528]
Army Council, succeeding, **10**, [528]
corporation sole, as, **10**, [529]
Defence, Minister of, succeeding, **10**, [529]
documents, proof of, **10**, [529]
land, holding, **10**, [625]
seal of, **10**, [529]
transfer of functions to, **10**, [528]–[530]
War, Secretary of State for, succeeding,
  10, [529]

defraud
conspiracy to, **12(2)**, [162], [166]

delict
foreign element involved, choice of applicable
  law—
  abolition of certain common law rules,
    45, [989]
  Crown application, **45**, [994]
  defamation claims, exclusion from
    provisions, **45**, [992]
  displacement of general rule, **45**, [991]
  general rule, **45**, [990]
  purpose of provisions, **45**, [988]
  summary of provisions, **45**, [945]
  transitional provisions and savings, **45**, [993]

demand with menaces
person making, punishment, **12(1)**, [572]

demerger
exempt distributions—
  advance clearance, **44(1)**, [119]
  chargeable payments, **44(1)**, [118]
  conditions, **44(1)**, [116]
  division of business, **44(1)**, [117]
  group, **44(1)**, [116]
  information, power to require, **44(1)**, [121]
  references to, **44(1)**, [116]
  returns, **44(1)**, [120]

demesne land
cautions against first registrations, **23**, [721]
compulsory registration of grants out of,
  23, [720]
meaning, **23**, [772]
voluntary registration, **23**, [719]

demolition
building—
  dangerous, **35(1)**, [599]
  notice, of—
    appeal against, **35(1)**, [605], [608]
    intended, of, **35(1)**, [602]
    local authority, by, **35(1)**, [603], [604]

demolition order
appeal against, **22**, [239]
  other courses of action, suggesting,
    22, [240]
breach of covenant, rights arising from,
  22, [265]
building subject to—
  offences as to, **22**, [241]
  reconstruction instead of demolition,
    22, [245]
  vacation of, **22**, [241]
cleansing before demolition, **22**, [244]
compensation, payment of, **22**, [398], [399]
condemned houses, temporary use of,
  22, [258]
contents, **22**, [237]
demolition in default of another, **22**, [270]
entry under—
  penalty for obstructing, **22**, [274]
  powers of, **22**, [273]
execution of, **22**, [242]
expenses of executing, **22**, [243]
expenses of obtaining possession, **22**, [241]
lease, determination by court, **22**, [271]
listed building, not made for, **22**, [262]
management order, substituted by, **22**, [246]
meaning, **22**, [237]
obstructive building—
  compensation to owner, **22**, [401]
  default, court order on, **22**, [270]
  owner, protection for, **22**, [265]
operative time, **22**, [238]
other courses of action, appeals suggesting,
  22, [240]
possession of building, obtaining, **22**, [241]
power to make, **22**, [236]
prohibition order, substitution of, **22**, [247]
re-construction by owner, permission for,
  22, [245]

demolition order—*contd*
re-development by owner, **22**, [266], [267]
revocation, compensation repayable, **22**, [398], [399]
service of, **22**, [238]
subsidy. *See* **slum clearance**
tribunal's powers on appeal, **22**, [239]

demoted tenancy
assignment, restriction on, **23**, [460]
conditions, **23**, [450]
county court jurisdiction, **23**, [463]
duration, **23**, [451]
dwelling house, meaning, **23**, [464]
information, provision by landlord, **23**, [462]
landlord, change of, **23**, [452]
members of family, meaning, **23**, [465]
no successor tenant, **23**, [458]
possession—
proceedings—
effect of, **23**, [456]
landlord, by, **23**, [453]
notice of, **23**, [454[
review of decision to seek, **23**, [455]
repairs, right to carry out, **23**, [461]
succession to, **23**, [457]
successor tenants, **23**, [459]
termination where no successor tenant, **23**, [458]

Dental Estimates Board
renamed. *See* **Dental Practice Board**

Dental Practitioners' Formulary
specified publication, as, **28**, [160]

dental services
charging for, **30**, [982]
exemptions, **30**, [983]
dental public health functions, **30**, [917]
general—
contracts, **30**, [745]
indemnity cover, **30**, [455]
remuneration, regulations as to, **30**, [501]
Local Dental Committees—
expenses of, **30**, [919]
recognition of, **30**, [919]
primary—
accommodation, provision of, **30**, [920]
assistance and support for, **30**, [918]
contract for—
disputes, **30**, [911]
enforcement, **30**, [911]
payments, **30**, [909]
persons eligible to enter into, **30**, [908]
provisions of, **30**, [906]
requirements, **30**, [907]
terms of, **30**, [910]
persons performing, lists of, **30**, [912]
premises for, provision of, **30**, [827]
Primary Care Trust—
assistance and support for, **30**, [918]
provision by, **30**, [827], [905]
remuneration, **30**, [1040]
requirement to provide, **30**, [907]

dental services—*contd*
primary—*contd*
Strategic Health Authority, arrangement for provision by—
agreements, requirements, **30**, [913]
interpretation, **30**, [914]
persons with whom made, **30**, [914]
regulations, **30**, [915]
transfer of liabilities, **30**, [916]
Wales. *See* **Wales**

dentists
business of dentistry—
bodies corporate—
directors, qualifications of, **28**, [450]
fees, payment of, **28**, [451]
financial penalties, **28**, [452]–[455]
information, provision of, **28**, [451]
withdrawal of privileges, **28**, [456]
carrying on—
bodies corporate, by, **28**, [450]–[456]
individuals, by, restriction on, **28**, [449]
meaning, **28**, [448]
continuing professional development cases, **28**, [473]
controlled drug—
directions as regards, **28**, [211]–[215]
exemption as regards, **28**, [205]
degree in dentistry—
basic training, completion of, **28**, [380]
examinations for, **28**, [374], [377]
fees for, **28**, [371]
grant of—
authority for, **28**, [373]
effect of, **28**, [374]
minimum age for, **28**, [373]
saving for, **28**, [370]
information as to, **28**, [375]
dental authority—
byelaws and regulations of, **28**, [372]
meaning, **28**, [370]
dental schools—
supervision of instruction at, **28**, [376]
visitors to, **28**, [376]
descriptions, use of, **28**, [392]
diploma, meaning, **28**, [465]
drugs, misuse of. *See* **drugs**
education—
examinations, **28**, [371]–[373]
particular theories, restriction on requirement to adopt, **28**, [379]
supervision, **28**, [375]–[379]
European diploma—
appropriate—
meaning, **28**, [382], [470]
qualification for registration, **28**, [382]
examinations—
admission to, **28**, [373]
authority to hold, **28**, [370], [372]
board of examiners—
appointment, **28**, [371]
conduct of examinations by, **28**, [371]
conduct of, **28**, [371]
course of study for, remedying inadequate, **28**, [378]

dentists—*contd*
  examinations—*contd*
    inadequacy, remedying, **28**, [378]
    information as to, **28**, [375]
    particular theories of dentistry, rejection
      of, **28**, [379]
    recognised overseas diplomas, holders of,
      28, [383]
    Royal College of Surgeons, holding by,
      28, [372]
    supervision, **28**, [377]
  exemptions for, **28**, [76], [82], [111], [205]
  fitness to practice—
    allegations relating to, **28**, [395]
    appeals, **28**, [400]
    guidance, **28**, [394]
    impaired, **28**, [395]
    investigation, **28**, [396], [397]
    notification and disclosure by Council,
      28, [407]
    suspension of registration, **28**, [404]
  general note, **28**, [1]
  health cases. *See* **General Dental Council**
  instruction to students—
    inadequate, provision for remedying,
      28, [378]
    supervision, **28**, [376]
  insurance, **28**, [393]
  licence in dentistry—
    basic training, completion of, **28**, [380]
    examinations for, **28**, [371], [373], [378]
    fees for, **28**, [371]
    grant of—
      authority for, **28**, [370], [372]
      effect of, **28**, [374]
      minimum age for, **28**, [373]
      saving for, **28**, [370]
    information as to, **28**, [375]
    Royal College of Surgeons of England,
      grant by, **28**, [372]
  licentiates in dentistry—
    list of, entry in, **28**, [370], [372]
    registration of, **28**, [382]
  meaning, **28**, [187]
  medical authority—
    degree, grant by, **28**, [370]
    examinations by, **28**, [370]
    licence, grant by, **28**, [370]
    meaning, **28**, [370]
  medicinal products on prescription only,
    28, [114], [115]
  notifications, service of, **28**, [459]
  overseas diploma, recognised—
    examinations for holder, **28**, [383]
    meaning, **28**, [382]
    visitors, appointment, **28**, [383]
  post-graduate institutions, supervision of
    instruction at, **28**, [376]
  practice of dentistry—
    meaning, **28**, [445]
    unqualified person, by, prohibition on,
      28, [446]
  Privy Council, exercise of powers, **28**, [463]
  professional conduct. *See* **General Dental
  Council**

dentists—*contd*
  professions complementary to. *See*
    professions complementary to dentistry
  register—
    directions, taking effect, **28**, [401]
    erasure from, **28**, [386], [389], [390], [400],
      [401]
    fees, **28**, [386]
    publication, **28**, [388]
    registrar, kept by, **28**, [381]
    registration in. *See* registration *below*
    regulations as to, **28**, [386]
    restoration to, **28**, [386],[389], [390], [399],
      [410]
  registration—
    appeals as to, **28**, [400], [471]
    conditional—
      directions, taking effect, **28**, [401]
      immediate, order for, **28**, [402]
      recording, **28**, [405]
    disqualification in relevant European state,
      effect on, **28**, [411]
    European State, national of, **28**, [411],
      [412], [470]
      application for, by, notification of result
        of, **28**, [387]
      qualification for, **28**, [382]
    graduate or licentiate in dentistry, **28**, [382]
    notification of results of application,
      28, [387]
    overseas diploma, recognised—
      holder of, **28**, [382], [383]
      temporary registration, **28**, [384]
    procedure, **28**, [385]
    qualifications for, **28**, [382], [383], [470]
    reciprocal arrangements with Republic of
      Ireland, **28**, [457]
    suspension, **28**, [400], [401]
      effect of, **28**, [404]
      immediate, order for, **28**, [402]
      recording, **28**, [405]
    transitional provisions, **28**, [481]
    visiting dentists from relevant European
      States, **28**, [474]
  regulations and orders, **28**, [464]
  sale of poisons to, **28**, [253]
  titles, use of, **28**, [392]
  transitional provisions and savings, **28**, [347],
    [467], [481]
  unqualified person, prohibition on—
    practice of dentistry, **28**, [446]
    use of titles, **28**, [447]
  veterinary treatment by, **28**, [35]
  visiting dentists from relevant European
    States—
    professional training and development
      requirements, **28**, [409]
    provision of services by, **28**, [474]
    registration, **28**, [474]
  visitors to dental schools, **28**, [376]

**Department for Environment, Food and
Rural Affairs**
  designated bodies, agreements with—
    agreement, definition, **32**, [824]

Department for Environment, Food and Rural Affairs—*contd*
  designated bodies, agreements with—*contd*
    designated body, meaning, **32**, [818], [844]
    maximum duration of, **32**, [820]
    other designated bodies, with, **32**, [817]
    particular powers, **32**, [821]
    reserved functions, **32**, [819]
    Secretary of State, with. **32**, [816]
    supplementary provisions, **32**, [823]
  financial assistance, giving, **32**, [825]
  local authorities, agreements with, **32**, [822]

Department of Social Security. *Now* **Department for Work and Pensions**
  references to, **40(1)**, [730]

deportation
  aircrew, exception in case of, **31**, [84]
  appeals—
    generally. *See* **immigration** (appeals)
    pending, no removal during, **31**, [420]
  armed forces members, provisions inapplicable, **31**, [84]
  arrest pending, **31**, [575]
  Channel Islands, from, **31**, [131]
  control of person awaiting, **31**, [130]
  conviction, after, **31**, [82]
  co-operation, **31**, [511]
  criminals, of—
    appeals, **31(S)**, Nationality 36
    automatic, **31(S)**, Nationality 33
    detention after period of imprisonment, **31(S)**, Nationality 37
    exceptions, **31(S)**, Nationality 34
    family of, **31(S)**, Nationality 37
    foreign criminal, meaning, **31(S)**, Nationality 62–3
    interpretation, **31(S)**, Nationality 38
    special immigration status—
      designated person, conditions imposed on, **31(S)**, Nationality 64
      designation, **31(S)**, Nationality 62
      effect of designation, **31(S)**, Nationality 63
      end of designation, **31(S)**, Nationality 67
      interpretation, **31(S)**, Nationality 68
      support, **31(S)**, Nationality 65–7
      timing, **31(S)**, Nationality 35–6
  detention pending, **31**, [130]
  diplomatic immunity, **31**, [84]
    cessation of, **31**, [85]
  exceptions, **31**, [84]
    cessation of, **31**, [85]
  exemptions for certain existing residents, **31**, [83]
  foreign criminals liable to, fingerprinting, **31(S)**, Nationality 98
  Isle of Man, from, **31**, [131]
  liability to, **31**, [75]
  national security, in interests of, **31**, [440]
  order—
    assisting entry to UK in breach of, **31**, [95]
    leaving UK without, expenses, **31**, [81]
    power to make, **31**, [81]

deportation—*contd*
  pending—
    detention or control of persons, **31**, [130]
    powers of courts, **31**, [130]
    restrictions on persons, **31**, [130]
  persons liable to removal from United Kingdom, **12(3)**, [995]
  procedure for, **31**, [81]
  recommendation by court, **31**, [82], [130]
  removal of persons liable to, **31**, [130]
  seamen, exception in case of, **31**, [84]
  special cases, exceptions, **31**, [84]

deposit. *See also* **deposit-taker**
  certificate of—
    disposal of right, charge to tax, **44(1)**, [35], [36]
    meaning, **44(1)**, [35]; **44(4)**, [1026]
    qualifying, **44(4)**, [873], [993]
    transactions in, **44(1)**, [35], [202]
  general client account, **44(4)**, [871]
  meaning, **44(4)**, [863], [991]
  qualifying time, **44(4)**, [874]

deposit funds. *See* **Church of England**

deposit society
  statement to be published by—
    form of, **8**, 794–5
    generally, **8**, 584

deposited money
  application of, **9**, [41]
  costs in cases of, **9**, [44]

deposition
  aircraft, as to offences committed on board, **4(1)**, [144]
  evidence, use of as, **11(3)**, [248]
  maintenance order, in proceedings relating to, **27**, [188]
  power of justice to take, **11(3)**, [248]

deposition from Holy Orders
  archbishop or bishop, of, **14**, 594
  censure of deprivation, with, **14**, 593–4
  effect of, **14**, 594
  pardon, restoration on, **14**, 594

depository receipts
  chargeable securities—
    instalments, payment by, **41**, [186]
    meaning, **41**, [187], [196]
    meanings excluded, **41**, [196]
    stamp duty abolition, when applicable, **41**, [210]
    stamp duty reserve tax—
      charge to, **41**, [186]
      clearance system, transfer with, **41**, [194]
      exceptions, **41**, [188]
      replacement securities, **41**, [189]
    value of, **41**, [187]
  clearance systems, transfers with, **41**, [165]
  foreign securities, interests in, **41**, [254]

depository receipts—*contd*
  relevant securities—
    instalments, payment by, **41**, [159]
    issue of, business of, **41**, [159]
    meaning, **41**, [161]
    notification requirements, **41**, [160], [210]
    stamp duty, **41**, [159], [161]
    transfer of, stamp duty, **41**, [159], [161]
  stocks and shares, for, meaning, **41**, [196]

deposit-taker
  accounting period—
    meaning, **44(4)**, [956]
    payments in, **44(4)**, [957]
    payments otherwise than in, **44(4)**, [958]
  amended return, payer's duty to deliver,
    44(4), [966]
  assessments, **44(4)**, [964]–[965], [968]
    time limits, **44(4)**, [967]
  authorised UK—
    meaning, **19(2)**, [568]
    property, rights and liabilities, transfer of—
      authorisations and permissions,
        19(2), [586]
      compensation, **19(2)**, [574], [576]
      foreign property, **19(2)**, [586]
      new rights, creation of, **19(2)**, [586]
      orders, power to make, **19(2)**, [573]
      pension schemes, rights under,
        19(2), [586]
      public sector, to, further transfers
        following, **19(2)**, [575]
      tax consequences, **19(2)**, [577]
      Treasury's powers as to, **19(2)**, [569]
    securities, transfer of—
      compensation, **19(2)**, [572], [576]
      delisting of, **19(2)**, [585]
      directors of deposit-taker, provisions as
        to, **19(2)**, [585]
      form in which held, conversion of,
        19(2), [585]
      new rights, creation of, **19(2)**, [585]
      orders, power to make, **19(2)**, [570]
      pension schemes, rights under,
        19(2), [585]
      public sector, to, further transfers
        following, **19(2)**, [575]
      subscription rights, extinguishment of,
        19(2), [571]
      tax consequences, **19(2)**, [577]
      terms of, alteration of, **19(2)**, [585]
      Treasury's powers, where exercisable,
        19(2), [569]
  collection and payment of tax, **44(4)**, [959]
  credit agreements, exemption of, **39(1)**, [149]
  discretionary or accumulation settlements,
    44(4), [881]
  duty to deduct sums, **44(4)**, [859]
    power to disapply, **44(4)**, [860]
  investment—
    held outside UK, **44(4)**, [876]
    meaning, **44(4)**, [863]
  Lloyd's premium trust funds, **44(4)**, [875]
  meaning, **39(1)**, [149]; **44(4)**, [861]

deposit-taker—*contd*
  non-UK residence, declarations of—
    individuals, **44(4)**, [866]
    inspection of, **44(4)**, [870]
    personal representatives, **44(4)**, [868]
    Scottish partnerships, **44(4)**, [867]
    settlements, **44(4)**, [869]
  power to prescribe persons as, **44(4)**, [862]
  qualifying uncertificated eligible debt security
    units, **44(4)**, [872]
  relevant investments, **44(4)**, [864]–[865]
  return periods, **44(4)**, [955]
  sale and repurchase of securities, **44(4)**, [877]
  set-off claim—
    conditions for, **44(4)**, [960]
    how it works, **44(4)**, [961]
    proceedings begun after, **44(4)**, [962]
    proceedings begun before, **44(4)**, [963]
  supplementary provisions, **44(4)**, [879]–[881]
  transitional provisions and savings,
    44(4), [1060]
  yearly interest payments excepted from
    deductions, **44(4)**, [884]

deprivation (ecclesiastical office)
  adultery, after finding of, **14**, 595–6
  affiliation order, after making of, **14**, 595–6
  archbishop, of—
    offence, after conviction of, **14**, 597–8
    pronounced on, **14**, 594
  bishop, of—
    offence, after conviction of, **14**, 597–8
    pronounced on, **14**, 594
  compensation. *See under* **clergy**
  declaration of—
    consequences of, **14**, 598
    making, **14**, 596
  deposition, with, **14**, 593–4
  divorce, after, **14**, 595–6
  effect, having, **14**, 592
  extent of disqualification, **14**, 592
  illegal trading, for, **14**, 101–2
  judicial separation, after, **14**, 595–6
  meaning, **14**, 591
  offence, after conviction of, **14**, 595–6
  pardon, restoration on, **14**, 594

deregulation
  health and safety provisions, power to repeal
    certain, **18**, [1339]

derelict land
  additional relief for, **43(S)**, 1447–8
  area of outstanding natural beauty, in,
    32, [512]
  clearance area, **32**, [512]
  determination of tenancy of, **21**, [217]
  development area, in, **32**, [512]
  financial provisions, **32**, [513]
  grants for, **32**, [512]
  land in derelict state, meaning, **43(S)**, 1444
  local authority for purposes of, **32**, [512]
  major interest in land, meaning, **43(S)**, 1449
  National Park, in, **32**, [512]
  relevant remediation **43(S)**, 1445

derelict land—*contd*
remediation, amended provisions,
   43(S), 1443–52
Secretary of State, powers of, **32**, [512]
treatment of, **32**, [183]

derivative contracts
amended provisions, **43(S)**, 1202
authorised investment funds, **43(2)**, [734]
chargeable gains basis, charged on,
   43(2), [178]
collective investment schemes, **43(2)**, [176]
companies—
   international accounting standards,
      changing to, **43(2)**, [178]
   partnerships involving, **43(2)**, [178]
computation of amounts, **43(2)**, [173]
creditor relationships, **43(2)**, [178]
deduction of tax, prevention of, **43(2)**, [178]
foreign exchange, anti-avoidance provisions,
   43(S), 1570–6
insurance and mutual trading companies,
   43(2), [177]
interpretation, **43(2)**, [179]
land, relating to, **43(2)**, [178]
liability, special provision for release of,
   43(2), [174]
loan relationships—
   derivatives embedded in, **43(2)**, [178]
   host contract treated as, **43(2)**, [178]
offshore funds, computation of UK equivalent
   profits, **43(2)**, [553]
profits arising from, **43(2)**, [170]
requirements, **43(2)**, [171]
special computational provisions, **43(2)**, [175]
tangible movable property, relating to,
   43(2), [178]
taxation, method of, **43(2)**, [172]
trade, held for purposes of, **43(2)**, [178]
transitional provisions, **43(2)**, [180]
underlying subject matter, nature of,
   43(2), [178]

Derwent Valley
statutes repealed, **41**, [694]

descent
British citizen by, meaning, **31**, [146]
British overseas territories citizen, meaning,
   31, [154]
citizenship by. *See* **citizenship**
previous rules of, abolition, **18**, [548]

desertion
air force, from—
   arrest, **3**, [957]
   certificate of arrest or surrender, **3**, [960],
      [1253]
   civil court, proceedings before, **3**, [958]
   confession of, **3**, [827]
   failure to report or apprehend, **3**, [768]
   forfeiture of service, **3**, [744]
   generally, **3**, [766]
   governor of civil prison, duties of, **3**, [961]
   limitation of time for trial, **3**, [901]

desertion—*contd*
air force, from—*contd*
   police, surrendering to, **3**, [959]
   pretence of, **3**, [964]
   procuring and assisting, **3**, [965]
army, from—
   arrest, **3**, [684]
   board of inquiry report, **3**, [633]
   certificate of arrest or surrender, **3**, [687],
      [1253]
   civil court, proceedings before, **3**, [685]
   confession to, **3**, [554]
   failure to report or apprehend, **3**, [495]
   forfeiture of service for, **3**, [471]
   generally, **3**, [493]
   limitation of time for trial, **3**, [628]
   NCO, confession by, **3**, [554]
   police, surrendering to, **3**, [686]
   pretence, punishment for, **3**, [691]
   prison, reception into, **3**, [688]
   procuring and assisting, **3**, [692]
   soldier, confession by, **3**, [554]
   warrant officer, confession by, **3**, [554]
colonial naval force, from, **3**, [1193]
commonwealth force, from, **3**, [1193]
matrimonial. *See* **divorce**
meaning, **3**, [723], [995], [1029]
navy, from—
   arrest, **3**, [1182]
   assisting, **3**, [1174]
   certificate of arrest, **3**, [1281]
   confession, **3**, [1151]
   dispensing with trial, **3**, [1151]
   failure to report, **3**, [1032]
   false pretence of, **3**, [1173]
   forfeiture of service, **3**, [1215]
   meaning, **3**, [1029]
   offences, **3**, [1030]
   police, surrendering to, **3**, [1185]
   procuring, **3**, [1174]
   time for trial, **3**, [1089]
reserve forces, from—
   arrest, **3**, [1676]
   certificates of arrest or surrender, **3**, [1676]
   duty or training, failure to attend for,
      3, [1640]
   false pretence of illegal absence, **3**, [1642]
   inducing a person to desert, **3**, [1644]
   prison governors' duties to receive
      deserters, **3**, [1676]
   proceedings before civil court where
      persons suspected of, **3**, [1676]
   punishment for, **3**, [1641]
   record of illegal absence, **3**, [1645]
   service, failure to attend for, **3**, [1639]
   surrender to police, **3**, [1676]
   treatment of, **3**, [1643]
Royal Marines, from, forfeiture of service,
   3, [1451]
Ulster Defence Regiment, from, **3**, [1440]
visiting force, member of, **3**, [452]

design
infringement authorised by Crown, liability
   for, **13**, [12]

design—*contd*
  proceedings, state involved in, **10**, [1046]

design centres
  grants to, **47**, [46]

design right
  appeals, **11(4)**, [69]; **11(S)**, Courts 111
  assignment—
    partial, **11(1)**, [1091]
    registered design, of, **11(1)**, [1093]
    transmission by, **11(1)**, [1091]
  British design, meaning, **11(1)**, [1131]
  commercial purposes, act done for,
    11(1), [1131]
  comptroller—
    court, reference of proceedings to,
      11(1), [1120]
    jurisdiction of, **11(1)**, [1115]
    licence of right, settlement of terms of,
      11(1), [1116]
    proceedings before, rules, **11(1)**, [1120]
  continental shelf, **11(1)**, [1126]
  copyright, infringement of, **11(1)**, [1105]
  Crown use—
    act incidental to, **11(1)**, [1111]
    compensation for loss of profit,
      11(1), [1112]
    disputes, reference of, **11(1)**, [1121]
    emergency, during, **11(1)**, [1113]
    entitlement to, **11(1)**, [1109]
    government department concerned,
      11(1), [1109]
    meaning, **11(1)**, [1109]
    payment for, meaning, **11(1)**, [1111]
    services, meaning, **11(1)**, [1109]
    settlement of terms for, **11(1)**, [1110]
    third parties, rights of, **11(1)**, [1111]
  design—
    documents, meaning, **11(1)**, [1131]
    meaning, **11(1)**, [1082]
  designer—
    meaning, **11(1)**, [1083]
    ownership by, **11(1)**, [1084]
    qualification by reference to, **11(1)**, [1087]
  duration of, **11(1)**, [1085]
  extent of provisions, **11(1)**, [1124]
  infringement—
    authorised by Crown, liability for, **13**, [12]
    concurrent rights, exercise of,
      11(1), [1104]
    county court jurisdiction, **11(1)**, [1101]
    groundless threat of proceedings,
      11(1), [1122]
    importing or dealing with infringing
      article, **11(1)**, [1096]
        meaning, **11(1)**, [1097]
    infringing article, disposal, order for,
      11(1), [1100]
    innocent, **11(1)**, [1102]
    international obligations, exceptions in
      relation to, **11(1)**, [1114]
    licence of right, undertaking as to,
      11(1), [1108]
    primary, **11(1)**, [1095]

design right—*contd*
  infringement—*contd*
    remedies for—
      delivery up, order for, **11(1)**, [1099]
      disposal of infringing articles, order for,
        11(1), [1100]
      exclusive licensee, of, **11(1)**, [1103]
      owner, rights of, **11(1)**, [1098]
    secondary, **11(1)**, [1096]
    sheriff court jurisdiction, **11(1)**, [1101]
  joint design, **11(1)**, [1128]
  kit form, articles in, **11(1)**, [1129]
  licence, **11(1)**, [1091]
    exclusive, **11(1)**, [1094]
    exclusive licensee, rights and remedies of,
      11(1), [1103]
    of right—
      appeals as to terms of, **11(1)**, [1118]
      application to settle terms of,
        11(1), [1116]
      connection with owner, licensee not to
        claim, **11(1)**, [1123]
      infringement proceedings, undertaking
        in, **11(1)**, [1108]
      last five years, available in, **11(1)**, [1106]
      public interest, powers exercisable for,
        11(1), [1107]
  nature of, **11(1)**, [1082]
  owner—
    construction of references to, **11(1)**, [1127]
    licensee of right not to claim connection
      with, **11(1)**, [1123]
    rights and remedies of, **11(1)**, [1098]
    unknown, settlement of terms of licence,
      11(1), [1117]
  ownership of—
    commissioned design, **11(1)**, [1084]
    designer, by, **11(1)**, [1084]
    employee, design of, **11(1)**, [1084]
    prospective, **11(1)**, [1092]
  qualification for protection—
    commissioner, by reference to,
      11(1), [1088]
    designer, by reference to, **11(1)**, [1087]
    employer, by reference to, **11(1)**, [1088]
    first marketing, by reference to,
      11(1), [1089]
    further provision, power to make,
      11(1), [1090]
    qualifying country, **11(1)**, [1086]
    qualifying individual, **11(1)**, [1086]
    qualifying person, **11(1)**, [1086]
  reciprocal protection, **11(1)**, [1125]
  registered design, subsisting in, **11(1)**, [533]
  rules—
    comptroller, proceedings before,
      11(1), [1120]
    signature of instruments, **11(1)**, [1130]
  subsistence of, **11(1)**, [1082]
  territorial waters, **11(1)**, [1126]
  summary of provisions, **11(1)**, [415]

designs. *See also* **patent**
  Appeal Tribunal—
    jurisdiction, **11(1)**, [548]

designs—*contd*
  Appeal Tribunal—*contd*
    temporary additional judges—
      appointment, **11(1)**, [638]
      remuneration, **11(1)**, [638]
  assignee, meaning, **11(1)**, [563]
  assignment—
    effect on proprietorship, **11(1)**, [503]
    registration of, **11(1)**, [533]
  continental shelf, **11(1)**, [566]
  convention countries—
    designation of, **11(1)**, [525]
    Orders in Council as to, **11(1)**, [525]
    protection in—
      application for, **11(1)**, [526]
        extension of time for, **11(1)**, [527]
      registration for, **11(1)**, [526]
  courts having jurisdiction, **11(1)**, [547]
  Crown—
    rights, **11(1)**, [562]
    use—
      disputes as to, **11(1)**, [570]
      emergency, during, **11(1)**, [570]
      loss of profit, compensation for,
        11(1), [570]
      payments, **11(1)**, [570]
      registered proprietor, informing,
        11(1), [570]
      services of, for, **11(1)**, [570]
      third parties, rights of, **11(1)**, [570]
  defence purposes, for, **11(1)**, [509]
  expenses, tax deduction for, **44(3)**, [89]
  fees for registration etc, **11(1)**, [559]
  individual character, **11(1)**, [500]
  infringement—
    action for, **11(1)**, [538]
    exclusive licensee, rights and remedies of,
      11(1), [543]
    infringing article—
      delivery up, **11(1)**, [540]
      disposal of, **11(1)**, [541]
      meaning, **11(1)**, [544]
    innocent infringer, exemption from
      liability, **11(1)**, [539]
    liability, exemption of innocent infringer
      from, **11(1)**, [539]
    Northern Ireland, county court jurisdiction
      for proceedings in, **11(1)**, [542]
    proceedings—
      county court jurisdiction in Northern
        Ireland, **11(1)**, [542]
      groundless threats of, **11(1)**, [546]
      sheriff court jurisdiction in Scotland,
        11(1), [542]
    rights and remedies of exclusive licensee,
      11(1), [543]
  inspection—
    designs, of, **11(1)**, [536]
    register, of, **11(1)**, [531]
  Isle of Man, provisions applied, **11(1)**, [565]
  jurisdiction—
    Appeal Tribunal, of, **11(1)**, [548]
    courts, of, **11(1)**, [547]
  lapsed rights, restoration of, **11(1)**, [513]
    order, effect of, **11(1)**, [514]

designs—*contd*
  market investigations, powers exercisable
    following, **11(1)**, [523]
  meaning, **11(1)**, [499]
  merger investigations, powers exercisable
    following, **11(1)**, [523]
  Northern Ireland, provisions applied,
    11(1), [564]
  notices etc, service of, **11(1)**, [560]
  novelty, of, **11(1)**, [500]
  offences—
    body corporate, by, **11(1)**, [555]
    false representation of registration,
      11(1), [554]
    falsification of register, **11(1)**, [553]
    secrecy, as to, **11(1)**, [552]
  proceedings—
    Appeal Tribunal, **11(1)**, [548]
    costs and security for, **11(1)**, [550]
    courts for, **11(1)**, [547]
    disputes as to Crown use, **11(1)**, [570]
    evidence before registrar, **11(1)**, [551]
    rules relating to, **11(1)**, [547]–[548]
  proprietorship, **11(1)**, [503]
  public interest, powers for protection of,
    11(1), [522]
  public policy or morality, contrary to,
    11(1), [502]
  register—
    certification of entries, **11(1)**, [531]
    clerical errors, correction, **11(1)**, [535]
    contents, **11(1)**, [531]
    copies of entries, **11(1)**, [531]
    falsification of, **11(1)**, [553]
    form of, **11(1)**, [531]
    inspection, right of, **11(1)**, [531]
    prima facie evidence, as, **11(1)**, [531]
    rectification, **11(1)**, [534]
    variation or deletion of entries,
      11(1), [534]
  registered—
    applications for, **11(1)**, [529]
    assignment of, **11(1)**, [529]
      right carrying design right, **11(1)**, [1093]
    design right subsisting in, **11(1)**, [533]
    enemy character, evidence of, **50**, [213]
    enemy, of—
      licence—
        comptroller, grant by, **50**, [208]
        variation of, **50**, [208]
    exclusive licences, **11(1)**, [530]
    existence of rights, information as to,
      11(1), [537]
    falsely describing mark as, **11(1)**, [554]
    information as to, **11(1)**, [537]
    inspection of, **11(1)**, [536]
    licence, terms of, **11(1)**, [1133]
    nature of, **11(1)**, [528]
    post office, transitional provisions relating
      to, **34**, [590]
    rights, duration of, **11(1)**, [512]
    summary of provisions, **11(1)**, [415]
    time limits, extension in war
      circumstances, **50**, [212]
    use for Crown services, **11(1)**, [570]

designs—*contd*
  registrar—
    annual report of, **11(1)**, [561]
    appeal from, **11(1)**, [508], [548]
    costs, power to award, **11(1)**, [550]
    discretionary powers of, **11(1)**, [549]
    evidence in proceedings, **11(1)**, [551]
    secrecy, direction for, **11(1)**, [509]
  registration—
    application for—
      appeals, **11(1)**, [508]
      date of, **11(1)**, [507]
      determination of, **11(1)**, [505]
      generally, **11(1)**, [504]
      modification of, **11(1)**, [506]
      outside UK, **11(1)**, [509]
    assignments, of, **11(1)**, [533]
    cancellation, **11(1)**, [515]
    cancellation of—
      appeals, **11(1)**, [521]
      effect of, **11(1)**, [520]
    certificate of, **11(1)**, [532]
    effect of, **11(1)**, [510]
    emblems, refusal to register, **11(1)**, [569]
    false representation of, **11(1)**, [554]
    fees, **11(1)**, [559]
    generally, **11(1)**, [499]
    individual character, requirement of,
      11(1), [500]
    invalidation of—
      appeals, **11(1)**, [521]
      applications for, **11(1)**, [517]–[518]
      effect of, **11(1)**, [520]
      grounds for, **11(1)**, [516]
    merger and market investigations,
      11(1), [523]
    modification of, **11(1)**, [519]
    novelty, requirement of, **11(1)**, [500]
    public policy or morality, contrary to,
      11(1), [502]
    refusal, grounds for, **11(1)**, [569]
    rights—
      given by, **11(1)**, [510]
      infringement of, **11(1)**, [511]
      lapsed, restoration of, **11(1)**, [513]
    summary of provisions, **11(1)**, [415]
    technical function, **11(1)**, [501]
    title, of, **11(1)**, [533]
    Union Jack, refusal to register designs
      using, **11(1)**, [569]
    validity, certificate of, **11(1)**, [545]
  right. *See* **design right**
  rules—
    power to make, **11(1)**, [556]
    provisions of, **11(1)**, [556]–[557]
  secrecy of certain designs, **11(1)**, [509]
    offences as to, **11(1)**, [552]
  technical function, **11(1)**, [501]
  territorial waters, **11(1)**, [566]
  title, registration of, **11(1)**, [533]

destructive insects and pests. *See* **pests**

detention and training order. *See under*
  young offenders

detention centre. *See under* **young offenders**
  change of name, **12(1)**, [1114]

detinue
  abolition, **45**, [945], [954]

development. *See also* **compensation**
  additional, granted after acquisition,
    compensation. *See under* **compensation**
  adjacent land in same ownership, **9**, [223],
    [257]
  appropriate alternative. *See under*
    compensation
  compulsory acquisition for. *See* **compulsory
    acquisition**
  consent, nationally significant infrastructure
    projects, for. *See* **nationally significant
    infrastructure projects**
  consultation, duty to respond to, **46**, [1006]
  correction of errors in decisions—
    correctable error, meaning, **46**, [1011]
    correction notice, **46**, [1009]
    decision document, meaning, **46**, [1011]
    effect of, **46**, [1010]
    inspector, meaning, **46**, [1011]
    power of, **46**, [1008]
  Crown land—
    control of, **46**, [560]
    enforcement, **46**, [563]
    urgent, **46**, [559]
  discontinuance of use, order for—
    compensation in respect of, **46**, [377]
    confirmation of, **46**, [366]
    contravention of, **46**, [446]
    enforcement, **46**, [447]
    power to make, **46**, [365]
    Secretary of State, by, **46**, [367]
  disregard, **9**, [222]
  environmental effects, assessment of, **46**, [332]
  existing use of development, certificate of
    lawfulness—
    appeal against decisions, **46**, [452]–[453]
    application for, **46**, [450]
    development order, provision by, **46**, [450]
    effect, **46**, [448]
    offences, **46**, [451]
    purpose of, **46**, [448]
    revocation, **46**, [450]
    Secretary of State, appeals and references
      to, **46**, [452]–[453]
  general note, **46**, [1]
  initiation of, **46**, [316]
  internal operations, including, **46**, [1003]
  land held for planning purposes, of, **46**, [499]
  local—
    annual monitoring report, **46**, [991]
    documents—
      adoption of, **46**, [979]
      amended provisions, **46(S)**, 170–1
      contents of, **46**, [973]
      default powers, **46**, [983]
      independent examination of, **46**, [976],
        [1046]
      joint, **46**, [984]
      meaning, **46**, [993]

development—*contd*
  local—*contd*
    documents—*contd*
      preparation of, **46**, [975]
      regional strategy, conformity with,
        46, [980]
      revision, **46**, [982]
      revocation, **46**, [981]
      Secretary of State—
        default power, **46**, [983]
        intervention by, **46**, [977]
        specified in scheme, **46**, [973]
        withdrawal, **46**, [976]
    guidance, **46**, [990]
    interpretation, **46**, [993]
    joint committees—
      agreement to establish, **46**, [985]
      dissolution, **46**, [987]
      functions, **46**, [986]
      Secretary of State, order for constitution
        by, **46**, [985]
    local planning authorities, **46**, [993]
    orders. *See* **development order**
    regulations, **46**, [992]
    representations, excluded, **46**, [988]
    scheme—
      contents of, **46**, [971]
      documents specified in, **46**, [973]
      minerals and waste, **46**, [972]
      regulations, **46**, [971]
      requirement to prepare and maintain,
        46, [971]
    statement of community involvement,
      46, [974]
    survey—
      county council, by, **46**, [970]
      local planning authority, by, **46**, [969]
    urban development corporation, provisions
      not applying in area of, **46**, [989]
  meaning, **9**, [253]; **46**, [315]
  operations not involving, **46**, [315]
  planning permission. *See* **planning
    permission**
  proposed use or development, certificate of
    lawfulness—
      appeal against decisions, **46**, [452]–[453]
      application for, **46**, [450]
      development order, provision by, **46**, [450]
      offences, **46**, [451]
      purpose of, **46**, [449]
      revocation, **46**, [450]
      Secretary of State, appeals and references
        to, **46**, [452]–[453]
  public—
    meaning, **9**, [349]
    new town, as site for, **9**, [349]
  regeneration, financial assistance for—
    forms of, **46**, [870]
    power of Secretary of State to give,
      46, [869]
    terms of, **46**, [871]
  regional agencies. *See* **regional development
    agencies**
  sustainable, **46**, [995]
    good design, **46(S)**, 173

development—*contd*
  town. *See* **town development**
  uses not involving, **46**, [315]

development areas. *See also* **industrial
  development**
  assisted areas. *See* **industrial development**
  basic services, improvement of, **47**, [380]
  ceasing to be, effect of, **47**, [385]
  designations of, **47**, [373]
  industrial buildings—
    meaning of, **47**, [382]
    Minister's powers as to, **47**, [381]
    sites, provision of, **47**, [381]
  intermediate area, designation as, **47**, [373]
  premises in, provision of, **47**, [381]
  Secretary of State—
    accounts etc of, **47**, [384]
    annual reports by, **47**, [383]
  specification of, **47**, [373]
  urban. *See* **inner urban area; urban
    development area**

Development Board for Rural Wales
  ceasing to exist, **10**, [1271]
  functions ceasing to exist, **10**, [1268]
  new town code. *See* **new town**
  transitional provisions, **10**, [1270]
  Welsh Development Agency, transfer of
    property and staff to, **10**, [1269]

development charge
  generally, **42**, [1]

Development Commission
  functions, powers of Secretary of State,
    46, [933]
  regional development agencies, scheme for
    transfer of property etc to, **46**, [932], [955]
    corporation tax, **46**, [936]
    stamp duty, **46**, [937]
    stamp duty land tax, **46**, [938]

development corporation
  application of provisions to, **22**, [33]
  construction or maintenance work, direction
    to publish information, **25(2)**, [430]
  defective dwelling—
    repurchase of, **22**, [363]
    See further **defective housing**
  functions of, **47**, [394]
  grants and loans, power to make, **47**, [395]
  housing authority, as, **22**, [4]
  housing subsidy. *See* **housing subsidy**
  information, direction to publish, **25(2)**, [430]
  land held by, provisions applied, **25(2)**, [450]
  Landlord and Tenant Act 1987, exemption
    for, **22**, [771]
  landlord, as—
    assured tenancy, exclusion of, **22**, [913]
    protected tenancy, exclusion of, **21**, [534]
  landlord authority, as, **22**, [105]
  new town, for. *See* **new town**
  stamp duty—
    sale of house at discount, **41**, [138], [145]

development corporation—*contd*
stamp duty—*contd*
shared ownership lease, **41**, [134], [139]
urban. *See* **urban development area**
works contracts. *See* **local authority**

development council
accounts of, **47**, [43]
administrative expenses, **47**, [47]
chairman, **47**, [38]
constitution, **47**, [38]
dissolution, **47**, [44]
establishment—
consultations on, **47**, [37]
orders for, **47**, [37]
powers as to, **47**, [37]
functions assignable to, **47**, [37], [51]
general provisions, **47**, [52]
industries, activities treated as, **47**, [48]
information to—
enforcement, **47**, [42]
furnishing, **47**, [39]
improper disclosure, **47**, [41]
levies, **47**, [40]
members—
appointment, **47**, [38]
categories of, **47**, [38]
pensions, **47**, [38], [52]
remuneration, **47**, [38]
terms of office, **47**, [38]
officers etc, appointment, **47**, [52]
orders establishing—
amendment of, **47**, [44]
power to make, **47**, [37]
revocation, **47**, [44]
termination of, **47**, [44]
procedure, regulation of, **47**, [52]
registration of industrialists—
enforcement, **47**, [42]
requirement for, **47**, [39]
reports to Minister, **47**, [43]
returns, disclosure of, **47**, [41]
statement of accounts by, **47**, [43]
status of, **47**, [38]

development gains
abolition of tax on, **42**, [832]

development land tax
abolition of, **42**, [832]
generally, **42**, [1]
transitional provisions, **42**, [837]

development order
application for planning permission,
requirements, **46**, [327]
general, meaning, **46**, [316]
local—
National Assembly for Wales, intervention
by, **46**, [323]
planning permission, grant of, **46**, [322],
[324]
policies implemented by, **46**, [322]
procedure for making, **46**, [623]
provisions applying, **46**, [996]

development order—*contd*
local—*contd*
removal of requirement to implement
policies, **46(S)**, 176
revision or revocation, effect on incomplete
development, **46**, [325]
Secretary of State, intervention by,
46, [323]
withdrawal, compensation, **46(S)**, 176–8
new town, for, **46**, [139]
planning application, regulating dealing with,
46, [336]
planning permission granted by,
46, [319]–[321]
revision or revocation, effect on incomplete
development, **46**, [325]
withdrawal, compensation, **46(S)**, 176–8

development plan. *See also under*
compensation
assumptions as to planning permission—
not directly derived from, **9**, [230]
special, lands comprised in, **9**, [231]
climate change policies, **46(S)**, 172
compensation purposes, for, **46**, [619]
generally, **46**, [1]
Greater London, for, **46**, [283], [618]
land subject to, meaning, **9**, [231]
local planning authority, function of,
46, [614]
local plans. *See* **local plan**
meaning, **46**, [313], [994]
Greater London and metropolitan counties,
in, **46**, [283]
Wales, in, **46**, [284]
metropolitan county, for, **46**, [283]
old—
continuation in force, **46**, [616], [619]
discontinuance on adoption of local plan,
46, [619]
meaning, **46**, [619]
plans prevailing over, **46**, [619]
planning areas, survey of, **46**, [263]
rights of entry for, **46**, [598]
status of, **46**, [314]
structure plans. *See* **structure plan**
transitional provisions, **46**, [618]–[619], [827],
[1063]
unitary—
action area, designation of, **46**, [264]
adoption of, **46**, [268]
alteration or replacement, proposals for,
46, [274]
blighted land in, **46**, [632]
direction to reconsider proposals, **46**, [270]
general policies of, **46**, [264]
joint proposals, **46**, [276]
Wales, for, **46**, [277]
local inquiries, **46**, [269]
local plan, incorporation of, **46**, [616]
National Parks in Wales, for, **46**, [278]
joint, **46**, [279]
preparation of, **46**, [264]
public participation in, **46**, [266]
representations disregarded, **46**, [280]

development plan—*contd*
  unitary—*contd*
    Secretary of State—
      approval of, **46**, [272]
      calling in for approval, **46**, [271]
      default powers, **46**, [281]
      objections, considering, **46**, [273]
      regulations and directions, **46**, [282]
      transitional provisions, **46**, [285], [1063]
      Wales, **46**, [286]
    two parts, in, **46**, [264]
    urban development area, for, **46**, [265]
    validity, **46**, [549], [552]
    withdrawal of, **46**, [267]
  validity of, **46**, [549], [552], [1045]
  Wales. *See* **Wales**

devisee. *See* **will**

devolution
  general note, **41**, [480]
  real estate, personal representative, on,
    18, [513]

Devon
  sea-sand, right to take etc, **49**, [2]–[3]

die
  forged—
    detection of, **41**, [9]
    meaning, **41**, [14]
  fraudulent printing of, **41**, [8]
    meaning, **41**, [14]
  new, use of, **41**, [11]
  offences respecting, **41**, [8]
  stamp duty, for, discontinuance, **41**, [11], [54]

diem clausit extremum
  writ of, abolition, **13**, [35], [43]

diffuse mesothelioma
  disablement payments—
    conditions of entitlement, **40(1)**, [90]
    dependants, to, **40(1)**, [91]
    determination of claims, **40(1)**, [92]
    fraudulent statements, **40(1)**, [96]
    lump sum, **40(1)**, [1], [89]
    minors, for benefit of, **40(1)**, [94]
    reconsideration of determinations,
      40(1), [93]
    regulations, **40(1)**, [95]
    relevant employer, definition, **40(1)**, [99]

digging machine
  vehicle excise duty, **13**, [1044]

digital broadcasting
  additional services—
    ancillary service, meaning, **45**, [224]
    international obligations, compliance with,
      45, [701]
    licences—
      applications for, **45**, [225]
      conditions, **45**, [226]
      duration, **45**, [226]

digital broadcasting—*contd*
  additional services—*contd*
    licences—*contd*
      enforcement of, **45**, [227]
      meaning, **45**, [224]
    technical service, meaning, **45**, [224]
  available for reception by members of the
    public, meaning, **45**, [205], [723]
  Channel 3 licences, **45**, [594]
    existing, replacement of, **45**, [595]
  Channel 5 licences, **45**, [594]
    existing, replacement of, **45**, [595]
  competition between licensed providers,
    conditions relating to, **45**, [682], [689]
  financial penalties, power to vary, **45**, [232]
  foreign, proscription orders, **45**, [695]
  Gaelic programmes. *See* **Gaelic television**
  independent programmes, quotas for,
    45, [678]
  licences—
    award of, **45**, [207]
    BBC companies, held by, **45**, [231]
    conditions generally, **45**, [208]
    restrictions, **45**, [209]
  local digital television services, **45**, [623]
  local providers, OFCOM grants to, **45**, [722]
  multiplex services—
    available for reception by members of the
      public, meaning, **45**, [205], [723]
    frequencies, reserved for qualifying services,
      where, **45**, [622]
    licences—
      additional payments, **45**, [216]
      applications for, **45**, [210]
      award of, **45**, [211]
      conditional award, **45**, [213]
      conditions attached, **45**, [215]
      duration, **45**, [219]
      enforcement of, **45**, [220]
      failure to begin providing service,
        45, [214]
      Gaelic programmes, **45**, [229]
      renewal, **45**, [219]
      revocation of, financial penalties on,
        45, [214]
      two or more to be granted to one
        person, **45**, [212]
    meaning, **45**, [205]
    revenue—
      attribution to licence holder and others,
        45, [218]
      computation, **45**, [233], [306]
      definition of, **45**, [217]
      disputes, **45**, [306]
  programme and fairness standards, **45**, [693]
    advertisements and sponsorship—
      objectives for, **45**, [687]
      supplementary powers relating to,
        45, [688]
    fairness code, duty to observe, **45**, [692]
    OFCOM's standards code, **45**, [685]
      observance of, **45**, [691]
      setting and publication of, **45**, [690]
    special impartiality requirements, **45**, [686]

digital broadcasting—*contd*
  programme services—
    deaf and visually impaired, code relating
      to—
        duty to draw up, **45**, [672]
        issue and revision, procedure for,
          45, [673]
        observance of, **45**, [676]
        relevant date, meaning, **45**, [674]
        targets, power to modify, **45**, [675]
    international obligations, compliance with,
      45, [701]
    licences—
      applications for, **45**, [221]
      conditions, **45**, [222]
      duration, **45**, [222]
      enforcement of, **45**, [223]
      meaning, **45**, [205]
  proscription orders, effect of, **45**, [696]
  radio multiplex services—
    connected persons rules, **45**, [768]
    additional services provider, definition of,
      45, [250]
    digital sound programme service,
      meaning, **45**, [235]
    financial penalties, power to vary, **45**, [262]
    generally, **45**, [632]
    local—
      applications for, **45**, [244]
      award of, **45**, [245]
      conditions attached to, **45**, [248]
      duration of, **45**, [252]
      enforcement of, **45**, [253]
      meaning, **45**, [235]
      renewal of, **45**, [252]
      restriction on holding, **45**, [768]
      two or more to be granted to one
        person, power to require, **45**, [246]
    meaning, **45**, [235]
    national—
      additional payments to be made in
        respect of, **45**, [249]
      additional services provider, definition
        of, **45**, [250]
      applications for, **45**, [240]
      award of, **45**, [241]
      conditions attached to, **45**, [248]
      duration of, **45**, [252]
      enforcement of, **45**, [253]
      meaning, **45**, [235]
      programme provider, definition of,
        45, [250]
      renewal of, **45**, [252]
      restriction on holding, **45**, [768]
      revenue—
        attribution of, to licence holder and
          others, **45**, [251]
        computation of, **45**, [306]
        definition of, **45**, [250]
        disputes, **45**, [306]
    programme provider, definition of,
      45, [250]
    revenue—
      computation of, **45**, [307]
      disputes, **45**, [307]

digital broadcasting—*contd*
  review, **45**, [230]
  S4C digital service, **45**, [228]
  services—
    multiplex services. *See* multiplex services
      above
    programme services. *See* programme
      services *above*
  sound—
    complaints. *See* **Broadcasting Standards
      Commission**
    frequencies—
      reservation of capacity—
        BBC, for, **45**, [243]
        independent national broadcasters,
          for, **45**, [242]
    independent national broadcaster,
      meaning, **45**, [236]
    licences—
      additional services—
        applications for, **45**, [258]
        conditions, **45**, [259]
        definition, **45**, [257]
        duration, **45**, [259]
        enforcement, **45**, [260]
      conditions, **45**, [238]
      false information—
        disqualification for offence, **45**, [300],
          [301]
        offence of providing, **45**, [299]
      general provisions, **45**, [237]
      licensed service, failure to begin
        providing, **45**, [247]
      programme services—
        applications for, **45**, [254]
        conditions, **45**, [255]
        duration, **45**, [255]
        enforcement, **45**, [256]
      restrictions on holding, **45**, [239], [265]
      revocation, financial penalties on,
        45, [247]
      variation following change of control,
        45, [718]
    local services, restrictions on, **45**, [769]
    national radio multiplex, computation of
      revenue, **45**, [263]
    radio multiplex services. *See* radio multiplex
      services *above*
    review of, **45**, [261]
    simulcast radio service, meaning, **45**, [236]
    standards. *See* **Broadcasting Standards
      Commission**

dignity. *See also* **peer**
  payment etc to procure, **33(1)**, [15]

dilapidations (ecclesiastical)
  board. *See* **diocesan dilapidations board**
  liability for, **14**, 164
  notices, **14**, 327

diminished responsibility. *See also* **insanity**
  evidence of, **12(1)**, [343]

diocesan advisory committee
constitution, **14**, 1216, 1242–3
consultation with, **14**, 1225
continuation of, **14**, 1216
functions, **14**, 1216–17, 1243–4
members, **14**, 1242–3

Diocesan Board of Education
advice of, where required, **14**, 1247
alteration of educational endowments, advice
as to, **14**, 1248
consent of, where required, **14**, 1247
constitution, **14**, 1245–6
functions of, **14**, 1246–7
governing bodies, directions to, **14**, 1247
local education authority, consultation by,
14, 1248
members, **14**, 1253–4
proceedings, **14**, 1254
trustees of educational endowments, directions
to, **14**, 1250
voluntary aided church schools, directions to
governing bodies of, **14**, 1249

diocesan board of finance
accounts, Church Commissioners' powers
transferred to, **14**, 1374
acquisition of property, consenting to, **14**, 634
bishop as *ex officio* member, **14**, 333
Church Commissioners, substituted for in
enactments, **14(S)**, 97, 105–12
company, to be registered as, **14**, 333
constitution of, **14**, 332, 864
curate grants, transfer of administration,
14, 416–17
diocesan committee of enquiry, expenses of,
14, 897
diocesan widows and dependants committee,
14, 543
easements vesting in, **14**, 848
existing bodies, adoption of, **14**, 333–4
glebe land. *See* **glebe**
loans to, **14**, 862–3
meaning, **14**, 331
memorandum and articles, **14**, 332, 864
parsonage land, transfer of to, **14**, 860–1
powers and duties of, **14**, 334
property held in trust, dealing with,
14, 635–6
rent of parsonage house, payment of, to,
14, 858–9
transfer of property to, **14**, 334–5, 847–8,
1089
vesting of property in, **14**, 401, 490, 633–4

Diocesan Board of Patronage
constitution, **14**, 1171
continuance of, **14**, 1152
members—
election of, **14**, 1171
qualification, **14**, 1171
powers of, **14**, 1153
presentation to void benefice, **14**, 1153
vacancies, filling, **14**, 1171

diocesan committee of enquiry
disability of incumbent, enquiry into,
notification of action, after, **14**, 895
pastoral situation, enquiry into—
bishop, reporting to, **14**, 890
institution of, **14**, 885
notification of action, after, **14**, 895

diocesan conference
diocesan synod, transfer of functions to,
14, 688, 768

diocesan dilapidations board
exercise of powers, committee, by, **14**, 327
meaning, **14**, 326
parsonages fund, payment to, **14**, 787
transfer of functions, **14**, 793, 798–9

diocesan education committee
educational scheme, consenting to, **14**, 489

diocesan parsonages fund. *See* **parsonages
fund**

diocesan pastoral account
annual account, **14**, 1065
application of moneys, **14**, 1066
diocesan board of finance holding, **14**, 1065
loans, discharge from, **14**, 1089
payment of expenses from, **14**, 1065–6
transfer from general fund to, **14**, 1065–6

diocesan record office
care of items in, **14**, 943
designated places, **14**, 935
exhibition or research, making documents
available for, **14**, 944–5
manorial documents, deposit of, **14**, 936
more than one, providing, **14**, 935
notices and orders, service of, **14**, 950
parochial registers and records, deposit in—
faculty, without, **14**, 942
limited period, for, **14**, 944
old register books, closure of, **14**, 937–8
order for, **14**, 940–1
requirement of, **14**, 938–9
return to parochial custody, **14**, 942
provision of, **14**, 935
search of registers in, **14**, 946–8
transfer of records, **14**, 943

diocesan registrar
fees, **14**, 1238

diocesan stipends fund
annual accounts, **14**, 476
capital account—
allocation of money to, **14**, 472–3
application of money, **14**, 474
duties regarding, transferred to diocesan
board of finance, **14**, 1374
keeping, **14**, 472
property allocated to, **14**, 845
diocesan board of finance—
accounts, furnishing to, **14**, 476

diocesan stipends fund—*contd*
 diocesan board of finance—*contd*
  not regularly constituted, where, **14**, 477
 diocesan glebe land held for benefit of,
  14, 850
 income account—
  allocation of money to, **14**, 472–3
  application of money, **14**, 475
  income of endowment paid to, **14**, 867,
   871–2
  keeping, **14**, 472
 investments, moneys arising from, **14**, 862
 payments to, cessation of, **14(S)**, 44

diocesan synod
 accounts, considering, **14**, 1393
 annual budget, considering proposals for,
  14, 1393
 bishop consulting, **14**, 688
 bishops' council and standing committee
  discharging functions, **14**, 688
 buildings in diocese, providing for inspection
  of, **14**, 785
 casual vacancies, **14**, 748–9
 constitution of, **14**, 688
 deanery synod—
  delegation of functions to, **14**, 689–90
  election of members by, **14**, 729–31
  informing, **14**, 688
 diocesan conference, transfer of functions
  from, **14**, 688, 768
 electoral registration officer, **14**, 726–7
 ex-officio member being elected, **14**, 747
 functions of, **14**, 688
 house of bishops, members of, **14**, 727
 house of clergy—
  election—
   nomination, form of, **14**, 760–1
   notice of, **14**, 760
   voting paper, **14**, 761–2
  membership of, **14**, 727
 house of laity—
  elections—
   appeals, **14**, 742–4
   nomination, form of, **14**, 760–1
   notice of, **14**, 760
   voting paper, **14**, 761–2
  membership of, **14**, 727–8
 matters referred to, **14**, 695
 meaning, **14**, 331
 membership of—
  generally, **14**, 727–8
  new diocese, provisions on, **14**, 925–6
  nominated members, **14**, 728
  one only, belonging to, **14**, 729
 parsonages board, appointing, **14**, 774–5
 pastoral committee, indicating policy to,
  14, 967
 procedure, **14**, 733
 registrar, **14**, 733
 resignation from, **14**, 750
 scheme—
  approval of, **14**, 793
  bishop's duty to establish, **14**, 481
  inspection of church, for, **14**, 479–80

diocesan synod—*contd*
 scheme—*contd*
  provisions, **14**, 793
  regulation of building inspection and
   repairs, for, **14**, 781
 standing orders, **14**, 733
 vacation of seat on, **14**, 745–6

diocesan trust
 meaning, **14**, 335

diocese
 areas, scheme for division into—
  making, **14**, 915–16
  provision for, **14**, 914–15
  variation, **14**, 916–17
 boundaries—
  effect of change in, **14**, 1092–3
  scheme to alter, **14**, 1012–13
 chancellor of—
  chancellorships, limit on, **14**, 560
  deputy, **14**, 563
  generally, **14**, 558–9
  meaning, **14**, 330
  official principal, as, **14**, 570
  tenure of office, **14**, 1261
  trial judge, nominating, **14**, 578
 compensation, provisions on, **14**, 927
 dignitary—
  incapacity, alleged, **14**, 433–4
  meaning, **14**, 436
  retirement—
   incumbent, also being, **14**, 437–8
   notices, service of, **14**, 438
   pension rights, **14**, 435
   powers of bishop, **14**, 434
   report on, **14**, 433–4
   rules, **14**, 439
   vacancy, filling, **14**, 438
 diocesan body—
  discharge of functions, schemes,
   14(S), 143–5
  meaning, **14**, 920
  scheme for discharge of functions by,
   14, 920–2
 diocesan secretary, **14(S)**, 77
 diocesan widows and dependants committee,
  14, 543
 dissolved—
  compensation, rights of, **14**, 926
  consistory court proceedings in, **14**, 927
  provisions on, **14**, 925
 episcopal area—
  abolition or alteration, **14**, 925
  area synod for, **14**, 918–19
  meaning, **14**, 918
 Europe, in. *See* **Europe, Diocese in**
 glebe land. *See* **glebe**
 new—
  archdeaconries, **14**, 925
  cathedral church, provisions on, **14**, 924–5
  deaneries, **14**, 925
  diocesan synod, provisions on
   membership, **14**, 925–6

diocese—*contd*
new—*contd*
property, provisions for transfer of,
14, 926–7
stipend, Commissioners paying, **14**, 922
parish register books and records. *See*
parochial registers and records
pastoral committee. *See* **pastoral committee**
records, provisions for transfer of, **14**, 927
registrar. *See* **registrar (ecclesiastical)**
registry, copy of licence in, **14**, 125
reorganisation scheme—
application for, **14**, 908
coming into operation, **14**, 911
consideration of, **14**, 909
convocations, provisions on membership,
14, 912
draft, preparation of, **14**, 908–9
financial estimate, **14**, 909
General Synod, provisions on
membership, **14**, 912
interested parties, informing, **14**, 909
making, **14**, 910
Order in Council, confirmed by, **14**, 911
provisions of, **14**, 907, 924–7
revocation of, **14**, 911
variation of, **14**, 911
rural deanery, vacancy of, **14**, 1376

dioceses commission
advisory functions of, **14**, 906
annual report of, **14**, 906
appointment of, **14**, 906
committees, **14(S)**, 188
constitution, **14(S)**, 187
delegation of functions, **14**, 906
draft pastoral scheme or order, consideration
of, **14(S)**, 148–9
establishment of, **14(S)**, 127
membership, **14(S)**, 187–8
proceedings, **14(S)**, 188
provincial and diocesan structure, review of,
14(S), 127–8
reorganisation schemes—
application for, **14(S)**, 129
coming into operation, **14(S)**, 133
confirmation, **14(S)**, 133
contents of, **14(S)**, 189–94
draft, preparation of, **14(S)**, 130–1
duty as to, **14(S)**, 128
making of, **14(S)**, 132
preparation of, **14(S)**, 128
preparing, **14**, 907
variation or revocation, **14(S)**, 133
See also **diocese**
stipend of certain bishop, power to pay,
14(S), 145

diplomatic immunity
foreign service allowance, exemption,
44(2), [302]

diplomatic mission
deportation, exception in case of, **31**, [84]

diplomatic privilege
additional or reduced, agreements on,
10, [993]
archives and documents of mission, **10**, [990]
arms control and disarmament observers and
inspectors, of, **10**, [1078]
bilateral agreement, saving for, **10**, [988]
colonial laws, saving for, **10**, [1003]
Commonwealth countries, relating to,
10, [1000]–[1001], [1032]
communications, **10**, [990]
consular officers, extension to, **10**, [991]
criminal jurisdiction, immunity from,
10, [990]
customs duties, **10**, [990]
diplomatic agent, inviolability of, **10**, [990]
diplomatic bag, **10**, [990]
evidence of entitlement to, **10**, [986], [999]
families, extended to, **10**, [990]
Heads of State, extending to, **10**, [1059]
hydrocarbon oils, refund of duty on,
10, [997], [1031]
International Criminal Court, in relation to,
10, [1161]
international organisations. *See* **international
organisations**
Irish establishments, relating to,
10, [1000]–[1001], [1032]
land, acquisition and loss of, **10**, [1068]
notarial acts, **10**, [998]
oath, administration of, **10**, [998]
official acts, in respect of, **10**, [990]
Orders in Council, **10**, [987], [1002]
period of, **10**, [990]
premises—
former, vesting of, **10**, [1069],
[1076]–[1077]
protection of, **10**, [990]
Secretary of State, sale by, **10**, [1070]
private residence, **10**, [990]
restriction of, **10**, [985], [992]
servants, of, **10**, [990]
services, exemption from, **10**, [990]
social security provisions, **10**, [990]
state immunity, and, **10**, [1054]
taxation, exemption from, **10**, [990]
third State, travel through, **10**, [990]
Vienna Convention on Diplomatic Relations,
application of, **10**, [984], [990]
waiver, **10**, [984], [990], [1005]

diplomatic service
pension increase, **33(1)**, [112]

direct broadcasting by satellite (DBS)
IBA, transitional arrangements. *See under*
**Independent Broadcasting Authority
(services)**

direct marketing
processing of personal data for, right to
prevent, **7(1)**, [481]

direction post
pulling down or obliterating, **36**, [1186]

director
estate agent, orders as to. *See* **estate agency work**
financial services, powers. *See* **financial services**
merger situations. *See* **Competition Commission**
restrictive trade agreements. *See* **restrictive trade agreements**

director (company)
accounts, duty to prepare, **8**, 287–8
acts of, validity of, **8**, 362
age—
  duty to disclose, **8**, 370
  limit, **8**, 369
allotment of shares. *See* **shares**
appointment—
  defect in, **8(1)**, [239]
  direction requiring, **8(1)**, [234]
  life, for, removal of, **8**, 827
  minimum age for, **8(1)**, [235]
    exception, power to provide for, **8(1)**, [236]
    existing under-age, cessation of appointment, **8(1)**, [237]
  public company—
    individual vote on, **8(1)**, [238]
    number of, **8(1)**, [232]
  share qualification for, **8**, 367–8
  voting on individually, **8**, 368
approval and signing, **8(1)**, [497]
approval of members, transactions requiring—
  charitable companies, consent of Charity Commissioners, **8(1)**, [304]
  credit transactions. *See* credit transactions with *below*
  loans. *See* loans to *below*
  loss of office, payments for. *See* loss of office, payments for *below*
  memorandum not sent to all members, **8(1)**, [302]
  more than one provision, under, **8(1)**, [303]
  quasi-loans. *See* quasi-loans to *below*
  service contracts—
    contravention of provisions, civil consequences of, **8(1)**, [267]
    long-term, **8(1)**, [266]
    requirement, **8(1)**, [266]
  shadow director, provisions applying to, **8(1)**, [301]
  substantial property transactions—
    company in winding up or administration, exception for, **8(1)**, [271]
    contravention, civil consequences of, **8(1)**, [273]
    members, with, exception for, **8(1)**, [270]
    other group companies, with, exception for, **8(1)**, [270]
    requirement, **8(1)**, [268]
    subsequent affirmation, effect of, **8(1)**, [274]

director (company)—*contd*
approval of members, transactions requiring—*contd*
  substantial property transactions—*contd*
    substantial, meaning, **8(1)**, [269]
    transactions on recognised investment exchange, exception for, **8(1)**, [272]
  written resolution, made by, **8(1)**, [302]
arrangements by, value of, **8**, 400–1
assignment of office by, **8**, 374
benefits in kind. *See* **benefits in kind**
binding transactions, powers as to, **8**, 135
body corporate—
  associated, **8(1)**, [334]
  connected with, meaning, **8(1)**, [332]
  controlling, meaning, **8(1)**, [333]
chairman, **8**, 48
children of, provisions extended to, **8**, 391–2
Clauses Acts, under. *See* **Company Clauses Acts**
close company, meaning, **44(1)**, [231]
connected persons—
  body corporate as, **8**, 406
  loans etc to, **8**, 393–4
  meaning, **8**, 405
  transactions involving, **8**, 396
contracts with sole members who are, **8**, 386–7
conviction of—
  indictable offence, **8**, 839–40
  summary, effect of, **8**, 842
credit transactions by, **8**, 393–4
  meaning, **8**, 395
  minor, permissible, **8**, 396
  relevant amount, meaning, **8**, 399–400
credit transactions with—
  contravention of provisions, civil consequences of, **8(1)**, [291]
  meaning, **8(1)**, [280]
  members' approval not required for—
    company business, expenditure on, **8(1)**, [282]
    intra-group transactions, **8(1)**, [286]
    minor and business transactions, **8(1)**, [285]
    money-lending companies, **8(1)**, [287]
    proceedings, expenditure on defending, **8(1)**, [283]
    regulatory action or investigation, expenditure on, **8(1)**, [284]
  members' approval, requirement of, **8(1)**, [279]
  persons for whom entered into, **8(1)**, [290]
  related transactions, requirement of members, approval, **8(1)**, [281]
  relevant transactions or arrangements, **8(1)**, [288]
  subsequent affirmation, effect of, **8(1)**, [292]
  value of transactions, **8(1)**, [289]
delinquent, prosecution of, **4(2)**, [254]
disclosure—
  compensation payment, of, **8**, 376
  debentures, interest in, **8**, 388–9
  default, penalty, **8**, 379

director (company)—*contd*
  disclosure—*contd*
    interests, of. *See* interests *below*
    obligation not discharged, circumstances
      where, **8**, 759–60
    payments made to, of, **8**, 376
    register of, **8**, 389–90
    shareholdings in own company, **8**, 388–9
    period for disclosing, **8**, 759
    take-over, on, **8**, 376–7
    time for, **8**, 759
  disqualification. *See also* **disqualification of
    directors**
    amended provisions, **4(2)**, [585]
    Northern Irish orders, **4(2)**, [577]
    orders, **4(2)**, [575]
    undertakings, **4(2)**, [576]
  disqualification order—
    acting while under, **8**, 849–50
    administration order, failure to pay under,
      8, 848
    application for, **8**, 838–9, 850–1
    application for leave under, **8**, 851
    body corporate, offences by, **8**, 849
    building societies, application to, **8**, 854–5
    competition. *See* **directors'
      disqualification**
    concurrently, running, **8**, 838–9
    contravention of, **8**, 848–50
    conviction of offence, on, **8**, 839–40
    fraud in winding-up, for, **8**, 841
    friendly societies, application to
      incorporated, **8**, 855
    grounds for, **8**, 838–9
    Insolvency Act, interaction with, **8**, 853
    insolvent company, unfit directors of,
      8, 842–3
    investigation of company, after, **8**, 845–6
    period of, **8**, 838–9
    persistent breaches of legislation, for,
      8, 840–1
    persons subject to, **8**, 838–9
    power to make, **8**, 838–9
    register of, **8**, 851–2
    repealed enactments, special savings from,
      8, 852, 858
    reporting provisions, **8**, 844–5
    statements, admissibility in evidence, **8**, 853
    summary conviction, on, **8**, 842
    transitional provisions, **8**, 859
    unfitness, determining, **8**, 846–7, 856–7
    wrongful trading, participation in, **8**, 847
  documents, execution of, **8(1)**, [122]
  emoluments—
    disclosure in accounts, **8**, 295–6, 654–7,
      719–20
    tax-free, prohibited, **8**, 375, 827
  employees—
    interests of, **8**, 374
    provision for on cessation or transfer of
      business, **8(1)**, [325]
  excess retirement benefits, disclosure in
    accounts, **8**, 657

director (company)—*contd*
  existing transactions or arrangement,
    declaration of interest in—
    failure, offence of, **8(1)**, [261]
    general notice, sufficiency of, **8(1)**, [263]
    notice in writing, by, **8(1)**, [262]
    requirement, **8(1)**, [260]
    shadow director, by, **8(1)**, [265]
    sole director, company with, **8(1)**, [264]
  expenditure of—
    disclosures respecting, **8**, 397–8
    funding of, **8**, 397–8
    relevant amount, meaning, **8**, 399–400
  fair dealing by, **8**, 375 *et seq*
  financial limits in provisions, power to
    increase, **8(1)**, [336]
  foreign law, transactions under, **8(1)**, [337]
  full-time working, meaning, **44(2)**, [77]
  general duties of—
    benefits from third parties, not to accept,
      8(1), [254]
    breach, civil consequences of, **8(1)**, [256]
    cases within more than one of, **8(1)**, [257]
    charitable companies, modification of
      provisions for, **8(1)**, [259]
    common law rules and principles,
      8(1), [248]
    conflicts of interest, to avoid, **8(1)**, [253]
      consent, approval or authorisation by
        members, effect of, **8(1)**, [258]
    former director, of, **8(1)**, [248]
    independent judgment, to exercise,
      8(1), [251]
    interest in proposed transaction or
      arrangement, to declare, **8(1)**, [255]
      consent, approval or authorisation by
        members, effect of, **8(1)**, [258]
    powers, to act within, **8(1)**, [249]
    reasonable care, skill and diligence, to
      exercise, **8(1)**, [252]
    scope and nature of, **8(1)**, [248]
    success of company, to promote,
      8(1), [250]
  home provided for outside UK, **43(S)**, 873–4
  interest—
    contracts, in, disclosure, **8**, 379
    non-cash assets, **8**, 382–3
    register of, **8**, 389–90
    sanctions for non-compliance, **8**, 390
    shares in own company, in, **8**, 388–9
      references to, interpretation, **8**, 757–8
    statement in directors' report, **8**, 665
  liability—
    exemption from, avoidance of, **8**, 375
    expenditure on defending proceedings,
      funding, **8(1)**, [21]
    indemnity—
      copy of qualifying provision, availability
        for inspection, **8(1)**, [315]
      directors' report, qualifying provision to
        be disclosed in, **8(1)**, [314]
      provision of, void, **8(1)**, [310]
      qualifying pension scheme provision,
        8(1), [313]

director (company)—*contd*
liability—*contd*
indemnity—*contd*
qualifying third party provision,
8(1), [312]
right of member to inspect and request
copy, **8(1)**, [316]
insurance, provision of, **8(1)**, [311]
protection from, void, **8(1)**, [310]
provisions protecting from, relaxation of
prohibition, **8(1)**, [20]
ratification of acts giving rise to,
8(1), [317]
third party indemnity, **8(1)**, [20]
unlimited, when, **8**, 373
loans etc to—
accounts, to be shown in, **8**, 660–3
banking companies, **8**, 402
civil remedies as to, **8**, 401–2
connected persons, to—
company business, approval not required
for expenditure on, **8(1)**, [282]
contravention of provisions, civil
consequences of, **8(1)**, [291]
intra-group transactions, approval not
required for, **8(1)**, [286]
members' approval, requirement of,
8(1), [278]
minor and business transactions, approval
not requirement for expenditure on,
8(1), [285]
money-lending companies, exception
for, **8(1)**, [287]
persons for whom entered into,
8(1), [290]
proceedings, approval not required for
expenditure on defending, **8(1)**, [283]
regulatory action or investigation,
approval not required for expenditure
on, **8(1)**, [284]
related transactions, requirement of
members, approval, **8(1)**, [281]
relevant transactions or arrangements,
8(1), [288]
subsequent affirmation, effect of,
8(1), [292]
value of transactions, **8(1)**, [289]
contravention of provisions, civil
consequences of, **8(1)**, [291]
criminal penalties, **8**, 402
financial limits, power to increase, **8**, 404
general restriction on, **8**, 393–4
guarantee of, **8**, 393–4
holding company, transactions at behest
of, **8**, 397
inter-company, **8**, 396
members' approval not required for—
company business, expenditure on,
8(1), [282]
intra-group transactions, **8(1)**, [286]
minor and business transactions,
8(1), [285]
money-lending companies, **8(1)**, [287]
proceedings, expenditure on defending,
8(1), [283]

director (company)—*contd*
loans etc to—*contd*
members' approval not required for—*contd*
regulatory action or investigation,
expenditure on, **8(1)**, [284]
members' approval, requirement of,
8(1), [275]
money-lending company, by, **8**, 398–9
persons for whom entered into, **8(1)**, [290]
related transactions, requirement of
members, approval, **8(1)**, [281]
relevant amount, determination of,
8, 399–400
relevant transactions or arrangements,
8(1), [288]
restriction of money, **8**, 401
restriction on, **8**, 393–4
small loans, **8**, 396
subsequent affirmation, effect of,
8(1), [292]
value of transactions, **8(1)**, [289]
loss of office, compensation for—
amount, disclosure to members, **8**, 376
disclosure in company accounts, **8**, 657–8
take-over etc, on, **8**, 376–7
transfer of property as, **8**, 376
loss of office, payments for—
amounts taken to be, **8(1)**, [294]
approval of members, requiring, **8(1)**, [295]
payments in discharge of legal
obligations, exception for, **8(1)**, [298]
payments made without approval, civil
consequences of, **8(1)**, [300]
small payments, exception for,
8(1), [299]
discharge of legal obligations, in,
8(1), [298]
meaning, **8(1)**, [293]
share transfer, payments in connection
with, **8(1)**, [297]
small payments, **8(1)**, [299]
transfer of undertakings, in connection
with, **8(1)**, [296]
meaning, **8**, 600–1; **8(1)**, [328]; **44(2)**, [77]
meetings, minutes of—
evidence, as, **8(1)**, [327]
recording, **8(1)**, [326]
members of family, meaning, **8(1)**, [331]
minor transactions involving, **8**, 396–7
names of—
correspondence, on, **8**, 372–3
meaning, **8**, 608
natural person, requirement of, **8(1)**, [233]
notes to accounts, information in—
advances, credit and guarantees, **8(1)**, [491]
remuneration, **8(1)**, [490]
notice of general meetings, entitlement to
receive, **8(1)**, [388]
number of, **8**, 361; **8(1)**, [232]
offences in respect of insolvency, **4(2)**, [248]
particulars to be given as to, **8**, 607–8
past, liability of, **4(2)**, [116]
persons connected with, meaning, **8(1)**, [330]
power to bind company, **8(1)**, [118]

director (company)—*contd*
  property transactions involving—
    contravention of provisions, **8**, 384–5
    exceptions from provisions, **8**, 383–4
    substantial, prohibited, **8**, 382–3
  prospectus, particulars to be given in, **8**, 613
  quasi-loans to—
    connected persons, to—
      company business, approval not required
        for expenditure on, **8(1)**, [282]
      contravention of provisions, civil
        consequences of, **8(1)**, [291]
      intra-group transactions, approval not
        required for, **8(1)**, [286]
      members' approval, requirement of,
        8(1), [278]
      minor and business transactions, approval
        not required for expenditure on,
        8(1), [285]
      money-lending companies, exception
        for, **8(1)**, [287]
      persons for whom entered into,
        8(1), [290]
      proceedings, approval not required for
        expenditure on defending, **8(1)**, [283]
      regulatory action or investigation,
        approval not required for expenditure
        on, **8(1)**, [284]
      related transactions, requirement of
        members, approval, **8(1)**, [281]
      relevant transactions or arrangements,
        8(1), [288]
      subsequent affirmation, effect of,
        8(1), [292]
      value of transactions, **8(1)**, [289]
    contravention of provisions, civil
      consequences of, **8(1)**, [291]
    disclosure, **8**, 660–3
    interpretation, **8**, 394
    meaning, **8(1)**, [277]
    members' approval not required for—
      company business, expenditure on,
        8(1), [282]
      intra-group transactions, **8(1)**, [286]
      minor and business transactions,
        8(1), [285]
      money-lending companies, **8(1)**, [287]
      proceedings, expenditure on defending,
        8(1), [283]
      regulatory action or investigation,
        expenditure on, **8(1)**, [284]
    members' approval, requirement of,
      8(1), [276]
    money-lending company, by, **8**, 398–9
    persons for whom entered into, **8(1)**, [290]
    related transactions, requirement of
      members, approval, **8(1)**, [281]
    relevant transactions or arrangements,
      8(1), [288]
    short-term, **8**, 395–6
    subsequent affirmation, effect of,
      8(1), [292]
    value of transactions, **8(1)**, [289]

director (company)—*contd*
  register—
    changes, duty to notify registrar of,
      8(1), [245]
    particulars in—
      corporate directors and firms, of,
        8(1), [242]
      individuals, of, **8(1)**, [241]
      regulations, **8(1)**, [244]
    place of keeping, **8(1)**, [240]
    requirement to keep, **8(1)**, [240]
    residential addresses, of, **8(1)**, [243]
  register of—
    contents, **8**, 365–6
    duty to keep, **8**, 364–5
  removal of—
    resolution for, **8**, 371; **8(1)**, [246]
    right to protest against, **8**, 371–2;
      8(1), [247]
  remuneration—
    disclosure in accounts, **8**, 296, 656–7
    tax-free, prohibited, **8**, 375
  remuneration report—
    approval and signing, **8(1)**, [500]
    auditors' report on, **8(1)**, [575]
    contents of, **8(1)**, [499]
    defective—
      application to court, **8(1)**, [534]–[536]
      disclosure of information obtained under
        compulsory powers, **8(1)**, [538]–[540]
      documents, information and
        explanations, power of authorised
        person to require, **8(1)**, [537]
      revision, order for, **8(1)**, [534]
      Secretary of State's notice, **8(1)**, [533]
      tax authorities, disclosure of information
        by, **8(1)**, [536]
      voluntary revision of, **8(1)**, [532]
    duty to prepare, **8(1)**, [498]
    false or misleading statements in, liability
      for, **8(1)**, [541]
    filing, obligation of quoted company,
      8(1), [525]
    members' approval of, **8(1)**, [517]
    procedure for approval, offences,
      8(1), [518]
    regulations, procedure for, **8(1)**, [551]
  repealed provisions, **8(1)**, [1255]
  report of—
    approval and signing, **8**, 299
    arrangement or compromise, in, **8**, 769
    assets, changes in, statement of, **8**, 665
    charitable gifts, disclosure of, **8**, 666
    company acquiring own shares, disclosure,
      8, 667
    contents, **8**, 297–8
    copy, right to demand, **8**, 303
    disabled persons, employment etc of,
      8, 667–8
    duty to prepare, **8**, 297–8
    employee involvement, **8**, 668
    general meeting, laid before company in,
      8, 305
    interests to be stated in, **8**, 665

director (company)—*contd*
report of—*contd*
payment of creditors, policy and practice on, **8**, 668–9
persons entitled to obtain, **8**, 302
political gifts, disclosure of, **8**, 666
registrar, delivery to, **8**, 306–8
voluntary revision of, **8**, 311–12
reports—
auditors' report on, **8(1)**, [574]
circulation of—
default in, offence of, **8(1)**, [503]
duty of, **8(1)**, [501]
time allowed for, **8(1)**, [502]
company having securities admitted to trading on regulated market, disclosure requirements, **8(1)**, [1070]
content of—
business review, **8(1)**, [495]
disclosure to auditors, statement as to, **8(1)**, [496]
general, **8(1)**, [494]
defective—
application to court, **8(1)**, [534]–[536]
disclosure of information obtained under compulsory powers, **8(1)**, [538]–[540]
documents, information and explanations, power of authorised person to require, **8(1)**, [537]
revision, order for, **8(1)**, [534]
Secretary of State's notice, **8(1)**, [533]
tax authorities, disclosure of information by, **8(1)**, [536]
voluntary revision of, **8(1)**, [532]
Directive disclosure requirements, subject to, **8(1)**, [1156]
disclosure of information to auditors, statement as to, **8(1)**, [10]
duty to prepare, **8(1)**, [493]
false or misleading statements in, liability for, **8(1)**, [541]
filing—
default in, **8(1)**, [529]–[531]
medium-sized companies, obligations of, **8(1)**, [523]
period allowed for, **8(1)**, [520]–[521]
quoted companies, obligations of, **8(1)**, [525]
registrar, with, **8(1)**, [519]
small companies regime, companies subject to, **8(1)**, [522]
unlimited companies, exempt, **8(1)**, [526]
unquoted companies, obligations of, **8(1)**, [524]
further provision, power to make, **8(1)**, [546]
group, **8(1)**, [493]
name of signatory to be stated in, **8(1)**, [511]
overseas company, of, **8(1)**, [1127]
public company, laying before general meeting, **8(1)**, [515]
failure, offence of, **8(1)**, [516]
publication, meaning, **8(1)**, [514]

director (company)—*contd*
reports—*contd*
qualifying indemnity provision, disclosure of, **8(1)**, [314]
quoted company, publication on website of, **8(1)**, [508]
regulations, procedure for, **8(1)**, [551]
reporting standards, power to specify bodies to issue, **8(1)**, [14]
right of member or debenture holder to demand copies of—
quoted companies, **8(1)**, [510]
unquoted companies, **8(1)**, [509]
requirement to have, **8(1)**, [232]
residential address—
protected information—
court order, disclosure under, **8(1)**, [322]
meaning, **8(1)**, [318]
permitted use or disclosure by registrar, **8(1)**, [321]
registrar, restriction on use or disclosure by, **8(1)**, [320]
restriction on use or disclosure of, **8(1)**, [319]
public record, putting on—
circumstances for, **8(1)**, [323]
registrar, by, **8(1)**, [324]
register of, **8(1)**, [243]
secretary and, acts in dual capacity, **8**, 362
service address, **8(1)**, [1219]–[1220]
service contract—
approval of members, requiring—
contravention of provisions, civil consequences of, **8(1)**, [267]
long-term, **8(1)**, [266]
copy, place of keeping, **8**, 380
inspection—
copies to be available for, **8(1)**, [306]
to be open to, **8**, 380
meaning, **8(1)**, [305]
member, right of to inspect and request copy, **8(1)**, [307]
more than five years, for, **8**, 381–2
non-compliance with provisions, **8**, 380
oral, memorandum of, **8**, 380
shadow director, provisions applying to, **8(1)**, [308]
service of documents on, **8(1)**, [1218]
shadow director—
contract of service, **8**, 382
meaning, **8**, 600–1
property transactions involving, **8**, 380
shadow, meaning, **8(1)**, [329]
share qualifications, **8**, 367–8
share transactions—
interpretation, rules for, **8**, 757–8
notification to stock exchange, **8**, 393
offences respecting, **8**, 389
share options, dealing in, **8**, 387–8
share transfer, payments in connection with, **8(1)**, [297]
shareholdings of—
duty to disclose, **8**, 388–9
interpretation, rules for, **8**, 757–8
notification to stock exchange, **8**, 393

director (company)—*contd*
  shareholdings of—*contd*
    obligations not discharged, **8**, 759–60
    register of—
      company to keep, **8**, 760
      form of, **8**, 760
      index of names in, **8**, 760
      inspection of, **8**, 760
      location of, **8**, 760
    spouses or children, provisions extended
      to, **8**, 391–2
    time for disclosing, **8**, 759
  sole member, contract with, **8(1)**, [309]
  statutory company. *See* **Companies
  Clauses Acts**
  substantial property transactions—
    approval of members, requiring—
      company in winding up or
        administration, exception for,
        8(1), [271]
      contravention, civil consequences of,
        8(1), [273]
      members, with, exception for,
        8(1), [270]
      other group companies, with, exception
        for, **8(1)**, [270]
      requirement, **8(1)**, [268]
      transactions on recognised investment
        exchange, exception for, **8(1)**, [272]
    subsequent affirmation, effect of,
      8(1), [274]
    substantial, meaning, **8(1)**, [269]
  tax paid by employer, benefit in kind,
    44(2), [224]
  tax-free payments to, **8**, 375, 827
  transactions by—
    foreign law, under, **8**, 406
    record of, **8**, 402–4
    validity, **8**, 385–6
    value of, **8**, 400–1
  transactions involving, limitations, **8(1)**, [119]
  transfer of undertakings, payments in
    connection with, **8(1)**, [296]
  undischarged bankrupt acting as, **8**, 847–8
  unlimited liability—
    memorandum providing for, **8**, 373
    notice to be given of, **8**, 373
    special resolution as to, **8**, 374
  vacation of office, age for, **8**, 369
  validity of acts of, **8**, 362; **8(1)**, [239]
  winding up, liability in, **4(2)**, [116]
  wrongful trading, liability for, **4(2)**, [250]

Director General of Electricity Supply
  abolition of office, **17(2)**, [331]
  Gas and Electricity Markets Authority, transfer
    of functions to, **17(2)**, [332]

Director General of Fair Trading. *See now*
Office of Fair Trading
  abolition of office, **47**, [691]

Director General of Fair Trading—*contd*
  anti-competitive practices, report on,
    47, [338]
    See further **fair trading**
  consumer credit licence, order on unlicensed
    trader, **39(1)**, [196]
  copies of reports, receiving, **47**, [175]
  defamation, absolute privileges against,
    47, [527]
  financial provision for, **47**, [194]
  Office of Fair Trading, transfer of functions
    to, **47**, [691]
  restrictive trade agreements—
    registrar, transfer of functions of, **47**, [184],
      [202]
    See further **restrictive trade agreements**
  undertakings as alternative—
    enforcement, **47**, [182]
    merger reference, to—
      acceptance of, **47**, [168]
      failure to fulfil, **47**, [171]
      publication, **47**, [169]
      review, **47**, [170]

Director General of Gas Supply. *See* **Gas
and Electricity Markets Authority**
  abolition of office, **17(2)**, [331]
  Gas and Electricity Markets Authority, transfer
    of functions to, **17(2)**, [332]

Director General of Water Services
  annual report, **49**, [1358]
  appointment of, **49**, [710]
  competition, functions respecting, **49**, [785]
  complaints, duty respecting, **49**, [781]
  continuation of office, **49**, [710]
  customer service committees—
    complaints by, **49**, [781]
    consumer complaints, **49**, [1362]
    duties as to, **49**, [1362]
    maintenance of, **49**, [778]
  customers, protection of—
    directions, giving, **49**, [766]
    disputes, determination of, **49**, [784]
    general duty, **49**, [766]
  disputes, determining, **49**, [784]
  expenses, **49**, [1037]
  investigations by, **49**, [785]
  levels of performance, information as to,
    49, [798], [889]
  official seal, **49**, [1037]
  pension, **49**, [1037]
  register maintained by, **49**, [1006]
  remuneration and allowances, **49**, [1037]
  reports, **49**, [1004], [1358]
  resignation, **49**, [711]
  sewerage undertakers, appointment of. *See*
    sewerage undertaker
  resignation, **49**, [711]
  water industry—
    environmental and recreational duties,
      49, [714]
    general duties, **49**, [712]
  Water Services Regulation Authority,
    functions transferred to, **49**, [1356], [1401]

Director General of Water Services—*contd*
water undertakers, appointment of. *See* **water undertaker**

Director of Border Revenue
children's welfare, duty as to,
  31(S), Nationality 100
Consolidated Fund, payments into,
  13(S), Customs 53–4
customs revenue functions—
  concurrent exercise with Commissioners,
    13(S), Customs 25–7
  customs revenue matter, meaning,
    13(S), Customs 25–6
  delegation of, **13(S)**, Customs 28
  power to Treasury to modify,
    13(S), Customs 27
delegation of functions, **13(S)**, Customs 28
designation of, **13(S)**, Customs 25
directions by Secretary of State, compliance
  with, **13(S)**, Customs 31
directions by Treasury, compliance with,
  13(S), Customs 28
general customs officials—
  designation of, **13(S)**, Customs 29–31
  HM Revenue and Customs Commissions,
    payment of revenue to,
    13(S), Customs 52–3

Director of Fair Access to Higher Education
accounts, **15(2)**, [592]
appointment, **15(2)**, [564], [592]
functions, **15(2)**, [564]
Higher Education Funding Council for
  England, arrangements with, **15(2)**, [592]
payments to, **15(2)**, [592]
provision of information to, **15(2)**, [573]
relevant authority, duties of, **15(2)**, [565]
remuneration, **15(2)**, [592]
reports, **15(2)**, [592]
staff, **15(2)**, [592]
status, **15(2)**, [592]

Director of Passenger Rail Franchising
railway companies, not regarded as shadow
  directors of, **38(1)**, [458]
Strategic Rail Authority, transfer of functions
  to, **38(2)**, [189]
transfer schemes—
  accounting provisions, **38(1)**, [441]
  agreements, etc, construction of,
    38(1), [493]
  compensation, **38(1)**, [438]
  documents of title, production of,
    38(1), [493]
  employees, assignment of, **38(1)**, [440]
  foreign property, rights and liabilities,
    vesting, **38(1)**, [493]
  information, power to require, **38(1)**, [442]
  land, restrictions on dealing with,
    38(1), [493]
  power to make, **38(1)**, [433]
  proof of title by certificate, **38(1)**, [493]

Director of Passenger Rail Franchising—*contd*
transfer schemes—*contd*
  property, rights and liabilities, allocation
    of, **38(1)**, [493]
  provisions of, **38(1)**, [438]
  Secretary of State—
    functions of, **38(1)**, [443]
    transfer of function to, **38(1)**, [434]
  stamp duty and stamp duty reserve tax
    provisions, **38(1)**, [494]
  variation by agreement, **38(1)**, [493]
  vesting provisions, third parties affected
    by, **38(1)**, [493]

Director of Public Prosecutions
appeal, appearing on, **12(1)**, [935]
appointment, **12(1)**, [934]
appointments by, **12(1)**, [936]
Attorney General, reporting to, **12(1)**, [941]
chief officers of police making reports to,
  12(1), [940]
consent to prosecutions, **12(1)**, [960], [961]
corporate manslaughter proceedings, consent
  to, **12(4)**, [305]
crime reduction, contribution to, **12(3)**, [171]
Crown Prosecution Service, head of,
  12(1), [933]
delivery of documents to, **12(1)**, [938]
duties of, **12(1)**, [935]
functions of, **12(1)**, [935]
information—
  disclosure by, **12(3)**, [513]
  disclosure to, **12(3)**, [511], [512]
  Lord Advocate and Scottish Ministers,
    disclosure to and by, **12(3)**, [514]–[516]
  use of, **12(3)**, [510]
investigatory powers. *See* **criminal investigations**
private prosecutions, and, **12(1)**, [937]
proceedings—
  discontinuing, **12(1)**, [957], [958]
  instituting, **12(1)**, [935]
prosecutions on behalf of, **12(1)**, [936]
qualifications, **12(1)**, [934]
recognisance, delivery to, **12(1)**, [938]
remuneration, **12(1)**, [933]
reports by, **12(1)**, [941]
retrial after acquittal, functions in case of,
  12(3), [866]
serious crime prevention order, application
  for, **12(4)**, [365]
  See also **serious crime prevention order**
staff, activities authorised to be done by,
  12(3), [173]
staff, transfer of, **12(1)**, [943]
taking over actions by, **12(1)**, [935]

Director of Revenue and Customs Prosecutions
criminal investigation by Serious Organised
  Crime Agency, criminal proceedings
  following, **33(2)**, [555]
designated offence, functions as to persons
  arrested for, **33(2)**, [557]

Director of Revenue and Customs Prosecutions—*contd*
investigatory powers. *See* **criminal investigations**
prosecution of offences, **13(S)**, Customs 51
reference of cases and proceedings to appropriate prosecutor, **33(2)**, [556]
serious crime prevention order, application for, **12(4)**, [365]
See also **serious crime prevention order**

Director of Savings
appointment of, **19(2)**, [917]
bonds, lost or destroyed, replacement of, **19(2)**, [926]
disclosure of information, **19(2)**, [903]
expenses, **19(2)**, [917]
sums included in, **19(2)**, [910]
functions of, **19(2)**, [917]
National Savings Bank, carrying on business of, **19(2)**, [893]
national savings certificates, issuing, **19(2)**, [885]
National Savings Stock Register, keeping, **19(2)**, [884], [918]
Postmaster General, references to, **19(2)**, [883]
raising of money, regulations on, **19(2)**, [925]

Director of Service Prosecutions
appointment of, **3(S)**, 327
bringing of charge, power to direct, **3(S)**, 126
charge allocated for Court Martial trial, powers in respect of, **3(S)**, 128–9
charge allocated for Service Civilian Court, powers in respect of, **3(S)**, 130
charge brought at direction of, **3(S)**, 126
further proceedings, directions barring, **3(S)**, 131
prosecuting officers, appointment of, **3(S)**, 327–8
qualifications, **3(S)**, 327
referral to—
commanding officer, by, **3(S)**, 125
commanding officer, notification of, **3(S)**, 123
investigation by service or civilian police, following, **3(S)**, 121–2
multiple offences or offenders, of, **3(S)**, 122

directors' disqualification
competition order, **47**, [896]

directory
entries in—
agreement for, contents, **47**, [119]
invoices, form of, **47**, [119]
offences as to—
corporations, by, **47**, [120]
penalty, **47**, [118]
order for, **47**, [118]
particulars to be given as to, **47**, [118]
regulations as to, **47**, [119]

directory—*contd*
entries in—*contd*
unsolicited—
no liability to pay for, **47**, [118]
recovery of sums paid, **47**, [118]

disability appeal tribunal
appeal to, medical examinations, **40(1)**, [557]
appeals from, **40(1)**, [536]
chairmen—
nomination of, **40(1)**, [545]
remuneration, **40(1)**, [726]
tenure of office, **40(1)**, [726]
clerks to, **40(1)**, [726]
constitution, **40(1)**, [545]
decisions, certificate of, **40(1)**, [726]
members—
appointment of, **40(1)**, [544]
disabled, **40(1)**, [545]
period of office, **40(1)**, [544]
same sex as claimant, one to be, **40(1)**, [545]
officers and staff, **40(1)**, [726]
panels for appointment to, **40(1)**, [544]
President—
administrative duties, **40(1)**, [726]
appointment of, **40(1)**, [553]
remuneration, **40(1)**, [726]
tenure of office, **40(1)**, [726]
procedure, regulations as to, **40(1)**, [727]
questions first arising on appeal, **40(1)**, [538]
regional chairmen, appointment of, **40(1)**, [553]

disability discrimination. *See also* **disabled person**
advocates, by—
adjustments, duty to make, **7(1)**, [307]
harassment, **7(1)**, [306]
unlawful, **7(1)**, [306]
aggrieved persons, help for, **7(1)**, [432]
barrister or barrister's clerk, by—
adjustments, duty to make, **7(1)**, [305]
harassment, **7(1)**, [304]
unlawful, **7(1)**, [304]
collective agreements—
meaning, **7(1)**, [457]
terms of, **7(1)**, [456]
contract terms, validity and revision of, **7(1)**, [455]
Crown application, **7(1)**, [439]
discriminatory advertisements, **7(1)**, [318]
dwelling houses, improvements to, **7(1)**, [430]
education, in—
accessibility strategies and plans, preparation of, **7(1)**, [362]
procedure, **7(1)**, [363]
admission decisions, **7(1)**, [369]
definitions, **7(1)**, [374]
disabled pupils and prospective pupils, against, **7(1)**, [359]
substantially disadvantaged, not to be, **7(1)**, [361]
education authority, duty of, **7(1)**, [364]
residual, **7(1)**, [365]

disability discrimination—*contd*
education, in—*contd*
enforcement, **7(1)**, [383]
exclusion decisions, **7(1)**, [370]
further and higher—
adjustments to practices and provisions, responsible bodies to make, **7(1)**, [378]
definitions, **7(1)**, [386]
disabled students and prospective students, against, **7(1)**, [375]
discriminatory advertisements, **7(1)**, [382]
educational institutions, occupation of premises by, **7(1)**, [384]
harassment, meaning, **7(1)**, [377]
instructions to discriminate, **7(1)**, [381]
local education authorities and schools, provided by, **7(1)**, [379], [464]
meaning of discrimination, **7(1)**, [376]
modifications, **7(1)**, [465]
pressure to discriminate, **7(1)**, [381]
proceedings, **7(1)**, [453]
relationships which have come to an end, **7(1)**, [380]
responsible bodies, validity and revision of agreements, **7(1)**, [385]
Scotland, modifications for, **7(1)**, [466], [467]
general note, **7(1)**, [1]
general qualifications bodies, by—
adjustments to provisions or practices, duty to make, **7(1)**, [390]
claims, **7(1)**, [393]
enforcement, **7(1)**, [391]
generally, **7(1)**, [387]
harassment by, **7(1)**, [387]
meaning, **7(1)**, [389]
meaning of discrimination, **7(1)**, [388]
premises occupied under leases—
alterations to premises, **7(1)**, [392]
modifications to leases, **7(1)**, [393]
procedures, **7(1)**, [391]
regulations as to, Secretary of State to consult before making, **7(1)**, [394]
remedies, **7(1)**, [391]
Isles of Scilly, application to, **7(1)**, [395]
meaning of discrimination, **7(1)**, [360]
premises, alterations to, **7(1)**, [460]
proceedings, **7(1)**, [452]
remedies, **7(1)**, [383]
responsible bodies—
list of, **7(1)**, [462], [463]
validity and revision of agreements, **7(1)**, [373], [385]
Scotland, civil proceedings in, **7(1)**, [372]
Secretary of State, role of, **7(1)**, [371]
Special Educational Needs and Disability Tribunal. *See* **Special Educational Needs and Disability Tribunal**
Welsh Ministers, role of, **7(1)**, [371]
employers, by—
adjustments, duty of employer to make, **7(1)**, [290]
advertisements suggesting, **7(1)**, [318]

disability discrimination—*contd*
employers, by—*contd*
advisers, appointment by Secretary of State of, **7(1)**, [437]
applicants, against, **7(1)**, [289]
charities, exception for, **7(1)**, [324]
contract workers, **7(1)**, [291]
Disabled Persons (Employment) Act 1944, amendment of, **7(1)**, [438]
Disabled Persons (Employment) Act Northern Ireland 1945, amendment of, **7(1)**, [469]
discrimination, meaning, **7(1)**, [287]
employees, against, **7(1)**, [289]
enforcement of provisions against—
general, **7(1)**, [320]
proceedings, **7(1)**, [450]
generally, **7(1)**, [1]
harassment, meaning, **7(1)**, [288]
liability of employers and principals, **7(1)**, [434]
procedure against—
evidence, **7(1)**, [450], [451]
general, **7(1)**, [320]
period within which brought, **7(1)**, [451]
restriction on, **7(1)**, [450]
remedies against, **7(1)**, [320]
support for particular groups of persons, exception for, **7(1)**, [324]
enforcement of provisions—
general, **7(1)**, [356]
proceedings—
compensation for injury to feelings, **7(1)**, [451]
period within which, must be brought, **7(1)**, [450]
restriction on, **7(1)**, [451]
facilities, provision of—
agreements, validity and revision of certain, **7(1)**, [357]
general, **7(1)**, [327]
financial provisions, **7(1)**, [446]
generally, **7(1)**, [1]
goods, provision of—
agreements, validity and revision of certain, **7(1)**, [357]
general, **7(1)**, [327]
instructions to discriminate, **7(1)**, [319]
interpretation provisions, **7(1)**, [445]
locally-electable authorities, by—
adjustments, duty to make, **7(1)**, [316]
discrimination towards members, **7(1)**, [315]
harassment of members, **7(1)**, [315]
more favourable treatment, no requirement of, **7(1)**, [325]
national security, not unlawful in case of, **7(1)**, [435]
Northern Ireland, modification of provisions in relation to, **7(1)**, [469]
occupational pension schemes—
adjustments, duty to make, **7(1)**, [297]
complaint as to, **7(1)**, [298]
non-discrimination rule, **7(1)**, [296]

disability discrimination—*contd*
occupational pension schemes—*contd*
relevant disabled persons, **7(1)**, [300]
remedies, **7(1)**, [299]
office-holders, against—
adjustments, duty to make, **7(1)**, [294]
appointment of, **7(1)**, [292]
conditions, **7(1)**, [292]
discrimination, **7(1)**, [293]
election, **7(1)**, [295]
harassment, **7(1)**, [293]
relevant person, meaning, **7(1)**, [295]
Parliament, application to, **7(1)**, [441]
partnerships—
adjustments, duty to make, **7(1)**, [302]
harassment, **7(1)**, [301]
limited liability partnership, **7(1)**, [303]
limited partnership, **7(1)**, [303]
proposed partnership, **7(1)**, [303]
unlawful, **7(1)**, [301]
police, application to, **7(1)**, [440]
practical work experience, in relation to—
adjustments, duty to make, **7(1)**, [313]
harassment, **7(1)**, [312]
unlawful, **7(1)**, [312]
premises—
alterations to premises occupied under
leases, **7(1)**, [322], [323], [358],
[458]–[460]
commonholds, **7(1)**, [341]
exemptions, **7(1)**, [355]
general, **7(1)**, [340]
let—
controller of, by—
adjustment of, **7(1)**, [347]
auxiliary aids or services, duty to
provide, **7(1)**, [346]
duties, non-compliance with,
7(1), [344]
justification of, **7(1)**, [353]
exceptions, **7(1)**, [345]
meaning, **7(1)**, [344]
occupier, victimisation of, **7(1)**, [349]
policies and procedure, adjustments
to, **7(1)**, [347]
terms of letting, adjustments to,
7(1), [347]
small dwellings exemptions, power to
modify or end, **7(1)**, [741]
supplementary provisions, **7(1)**, [354]
meaning of discrimination in relation to,
7(1), [343]
provision of, other than in relation to
employment, **7(1)**, [326]
service provider's duty to make adjustments
to, **7(1)**, [329]
small dwellings, exemption for, **7(1)**, [342]
to let—
potential lessees, towards, **7(1)**, [350]
controller's duties as to, **7(1)**, [352]
non-compliance with, justification
of, **7(1)**, [353]
exceptions, **7(1)**, [351]
supplementary provisions, **7(1)**, [354]
pressure to discriminate, **7(1)**, [319]

disability discrimination—*contd*
private clubs, by, **7(1)**, [336]
associate, meaning, **7(1)**, [339]
guest, meaning, **7(1)**, [339]
meaning of discrimination in relation to,
7(1), [337]
member, meaning, **7(1)**, [339]
policies and procedure, duty to adjust,
7(1), [338]
premises, duty to adjust, **7(1)**, [459]
procedure—
general, **7(1)**, [356]
proceedings, **7(1)**, [450], [451]
proceedings and national security, **7(1)**, [436]
public authorities, **7(1)**, [332]
discrimination, meaning, **7(1)**, [334]
exceptions, **7(1)**, [333]
general duty as to, **7(1)**, [426]
exceptions from, **7(1)**, [428]
meaning, **7(1)**, [427]
policies and procedure, duty to adjust,
7(1), [335]
premises, duty to adjust, **7(1)**, [459]
proceedings, **7(1)**, [451]
specific duties, Secretary of State's power to
impose, **7(1)**, [429]
qualifications bodies, by—
adjustments, duty to make, **7(1)**, [311]
harassment, **7(1)**, [310]
premises, duty to adjust, **7(1)**, [311], [461]
proceedings, **7(1)**, [454]
unlawful, **7(1)**, [310]
rail vehicles—
accessibility compliance certificates,
7(1), [739]
accessibility regulations, application of,
7(1), [738]
enforcement and penalties, **7(1)**, [740]
regulations and orders, **7(1)**, [442]
relationships which have come to an end,
7(1), [317]
remedies against, **7(1)**, [356]
rules of undertakings, terms of, **7(1)**, [456]
services, provider of—
adjustments to premises, duty to make,
7(1), [329], [459]
employment services, **7(1)**, [331]
general, **7(1)**, [327]
meaning of discrimination in relation to,
7(1), [328]
transport services, **7(1)**, [330]
statutory authority, not unlawful in case of,
7(1), [435]
summary of provisions, **7(1)**, [1]
trade organisations, by—
adjustments, duty to make, **7(1)**, [309]
general, **7(1)**, [308]
harassment, **7(1)**, [308]
unlawful acts, aiding, **7(1)**, [433]
victimisation, **7(1)**, [431]

disability living allowance
adjudication. *See* **social security
adjudication**
care component, **40(1)**, [319]

disability living allowance—*contd*
components of, **40(1)**, [318]
entitlement to, **40(1)**, [318], [323]
medical examination and report, reference of
claim for, **40(1)**, [556]
mobility component—
conditions for, **40(1)**, [320]
invalid carriages, persons eligible for,
40(1), [321]
rates of, **40(1)**, [320]
terminally ill person, for, **40(1)**, [320]
period preceding claim, for, **40(1)**, [323]
persons aged over 65, for, **40(1)**, [322]
persons awarded, medical examination,
40(1), [560]
rate of, **40(1)**, [318]
transitional provisions, **40(2)**, [10]

Disability Living Allowance Advisory Board
continuation of, **40(1)**, [704]
expenses, **40(1)**, [704]
functions of, **40(1)**, [704]

Disability Rights Commission
consolidation of functions, **7(1)**, [79]
dissolution, power of, **7(1)**, [781]
transfer of property of, **7(1)**, [782], [783]
transitional provisions, **7(1)**, [787]

disability working allowance. *See also*
disabled person's tax credit
adjudication. *See* **social security**
adjudication
dependency increases, entitlement to after
termination of employment, **40(1)**, [338]
medical examination and report, reference of
claim for, **40(1)**, [556]

disabled facilities grant. *See also* **housing**
grants
application for, approval of, **23**, [582]
occupier's, certificates required, **23**, [580]
owner's, **23**, [576]
certificate required, **23**, [578]
tenants', **23**, [576]
certificates required, **23**, [579]
disabled occupier, **23**, [577]
change of circumstances, **23**, [594]
means testing of owner-occupier or tenant,
23, [584]
purposes of, **23**, [581]

disabled person. *See also* **disability**
discrimination
access to premises, provision for. *See* **access**
advisory committees, on, **16**, [45]
assistance for, meaning, **45**, [724]
authorised representatives of—
appointment of, **40(1)**, [161]
local authority, duties of, **40(1)**, [162]
meaning, **40(1)**, [161]
regulations, **40(1)**, [161]
rights of, **40(1)**, [162]
termination of appointment, **40(1)**, [161]
visits by, **40(1)**, [162]

disabled person—*contd*
badge—
display on vehicles, **36**, [892]
issued outside Great Britain, recognition
of, **36**, [893]
meaning, **37**, [315]
recognised, concessions, **36**, [894]
regulations and interpretation, **36**, [895]
wrongful misuse by others, **37**, [289]
carer, abilities of, **40(1)**, [168]; **40(2)**, [42]
carers, general note, **40(1)**, [1]
child—
application of provisions to, **40(1)**, [53]
assessment of needs, **40(2)**, [42]
carers, **40(1)**, [1]
education—
expected leaving dates, review of,
40(1), [166]
special requirements, **40(1)**, [165]
meaning, **40(1)**, [165]
persons with parental responsibility—
assessments, **40(2)**, [269]
right to, local authority's duty to
inform of, **40(2)**, [270]
direct payments to, **40(2)**, [271]
vouchers, **40(2)**, [271]
responsible authority, meaning, **40(1)**, [165]
committees, co-option of persons representing
interests of, **40(1)**, [169]
companies providing facilities for, formation,
16, [10]
co-option to local authority committees,
25(1), [990]
definition of expressions, **16**, [47]; **36**, [896];
40(1), [52]
development providing for, **46**, [338]
disability, meaning, **7(1)**, [284]
discrimination against. *See* **disability**
discrimination
driving instructor, as. *See* **driving**
instruction
driving licence, issue to. *See under* **driving**
licence
dwelling, acquisition for, compensation,
9, [244]
dwelling-house, right to buy, **22**, [436]
dwelling house, let, improvements to,
7(1), [430]
educational establishments, access to,
15(1), [265]
employee, automatic car for, **43(S)**, 1388–9
employees, provision of cars for, **44(2)**, [247]
employment and training, Secretary of State,
functions, **16**, [65], [74]
equality of opportunity, promotion of,
7(1), [753]
ex-service men and women, facilities for,
16, [11], [74]
facilities, grant for. *See* **disabled facilities**
grant
gas meters for, **17(1)**, [693]
goods sold as made by—
disablement, references to, **47**, [54]
exempted bodies, **47**, [53]

disabled person—*contd*
  goods sold as made by—*contd*
    house to house or post, by, control of,
     47, [53]
    offences, **47**, [53]
     body corporate, by, **47**, [53]
  guidance issued by Secretary of State,
   7(1), [286]
  highway works, regard to needs in case of,
   36, [1241]; **38(1)**, [199], [204]
  hire car services at designated transport
   facilities to follow taxi accessibility
   regulations, **7(1)**, [397]
  hire cars, provision of, **43(S)**, 1466
  housing accommodation needs, **21**, [381]
  housing authorities, duties of, **21**, [381]
  impairments, **7(1)**, [448]
  industrial training, **16**, [65], [74]
  interpretation of provisions, **16**, [47]
  invalid carriage. *See* **invalid carriage**
  local authorities, provision of sheltered
   employment by, **16**, [16], [18]
  local authority—
   duty, **25(1)**, [990]
   grants to organisations concerned with,
    40(2), [20]
   needs—
    assessment of, **40(1)**, [163]
    duty to consider, **40(1)**, [164]
    special education, requiring, **40(1)**, [165]
  meaning, **7(1)**, [284], [753]; **16**, [47];
   23, [611]; **38(2)**, [136]; **42**, [258];
   43(S), 1466
  meaning of disability, **37**, [729]
  motor vehicles used by—
   badge on, **36**, [892]
    issued outside Great Britain, recognition
     of, **36**, [893]
    recognised, concessions, **36**, [894]
    regulations and interpretation, **36**, [895]
    wrongful use of, **37**, [289]
   immobilisation, exemption from, **37**, [278]
   meaning of vehicle, **37**, [315]
  National Advisory Council—
   duties, **16**, [46]
   training, duties as to advice on, **16**, [46]
  National Disability Council, abolition of,
   7(1), [1]
  National Disability Council. *See* **National
  Disability Council**
  Northern Ireland, provisions as to, **16**, [14]
  officers and servants, appointment and
   remuneration, **16**, [12]
  own account, work on, **16**, [10]
  parking facilities for, **35(1)**, [285], [288]
  parking place for vehicles, misuse by others,
   37, [289]
  party to legal proceedings, assisting—
   conditions, **7(1)**, [773]
   costs, **7(1)**, [774]
  passenger transport services, regard to needs
   in, **37**, [401]
  past disabilities, **7(1)**, [285], [449]
  persons deemed to be, **7(1)**, [448]
  power to define, **21**, [382]; **25(1)**, [991]

disabled person—*contd*
  private hire vehicles, carrying assistance dogs
   in, **7(1)**, [402], [700]
  property used for, exemption from
   non-domestic rates, **25(2)**, [835]
  public transport—
   public service vehicle accessibility
    regulations—
    appeals, **7(1)**, [408]
    approval certificates, **7(1)**, [406]
    certificates, **7(1)**, [405]
    exemption certificate, appeal against
     refusal of, **7(1)**, [403]
    fees, **7(1)**, [409]
    forgery and false statements, **7(1)**, [425]
    general, **7(1)**, [404]
    offences by bodies corporate, **7(1)**, [424]
    reviews, **7(1)**, [408]
    special authorisations, **7(1)**, [407]
  rail vehicle accessibility regulations—
   application of, **7(1)**, [738]
   compliance certificates, **7(1)**, [739]
    fees, **7(1)**, [414]
   generally, **7(1)**, [412], [413]
   using rail vehicle in breach of
    requirements, **7(1)**, [417]
   using rail vehicle without, penalty
    for, **7(1)**, [415], [420], [421]
    appeals, **7(1)**, [422]
   Disabled Persons Transport Advisory
    Committee, Secretary of State to
    consult with, **7(1)**, [443]
   exemption from, **7(1)**, [411]
    orders, annual report on, **7(1)**, [444]
   general, **7(1)**, [410]
   offences by bodies corporate, **7(1)**, [424]
   vehicles not complying with—
    inspection of, **7(1)**, [418]
    notices as to, **7(1)**, [419]
    penalty for, **7(1)**, [416]
     amount of, **7(1)**, [420]
     appeals, **7(1)**, [422]
     procedure, **7(1)**, [421]
     recovery of amounts, **7(1)**, [420]
  taxis—
   accessibility regulations—
    exemptions from, **7(1)**, [399]
    forgery and false statements,
     7(1), [425]
    general, **7(1)**, [396]
    new licences conditional on
     compliance with, **7(1)**, [398]
   guide dogs, carrying of, **7(1)**, [401]
   hearing dogs, carrying of, **7(1)**, [401]
   wheelchairs, carrying of passengers in,
    7(1), [400]; **38(2)**, [675], [676]
  regulations and orders, **16**, [13]
  sanitary conveniences for, **35(1)**, [286], [287]
  seat belts, payments in respect of applicants for
   exemption from wearing, **37**, [142]
  seriously disabled, special provisions, **16**, [10]
  sheltered employment, arrangements by local
   authority, **16**, [16], [18]
  television services, code for—
   duty to draw up, **45**, [672]

disabled person—*contd*

television services, code for—*contd*

issue and revision, procedure for, **45**, [673]

observance of, **45**, [676]

relevant date, meaning, **45**, [674]

targets, power to modify, **45**, [675]

Transport Advisory Committee, consultation with, **7(1)**, [443]

Transport Advisory Committee. *See* **Disabled Persons Transport Advisory Committee**

transport facilities for, **36**, [778]; **37**, [440], [442]

travel concession, **37**, [430]; **38(2)**, [134]

trustee, etc, liability to tax, **42**, [210]

vehicle excise duty, exemption from, **13**, [1049], [1051]

vehicle maintenance grant, exemption from tax, **44(3)**, [795]

vehicles providing local services, wheelchairs, carrying of passengers in, **38(2)**, [675], [676]

welfare arrangements for—

local authority, **40(1)**, [13]

voluntary organisations, by, **40(1)**, [14]

welfare services—

information as to need for, **40(1)**, [48]

matters being, **40(1)**, [49]

provision of, **40(1)**, [49]

work and home, transport between, **44(2)**, [246]

youth employment, representation on advisory body, **16**, [44]

disabled persons

aids for, zero-rating, **50**, [151]

disabled person's tax credit. *See also* **tax credits**

abolition of, **40(2)**, [361]

Disabled Persons Transport Advisory Committee

administration, **37**, [474]

annual report, **37**, [453]

constitution, **37**, [474]

consultation with, **7(1)**, [443]

duties, **37**, [453]

establishment, **37**, [453]

guidance to, **37**, [453]

members, **37**, [453]

procedure, **37**, [474]

disablement benefit. *See* **industrial injuries benefit**

disadvantaged areas

land in—

exemptions from stamp duty, **41**, [290], [296], [297]

partly in, **41**, [422]

wholly in, **41**, [421]

meaning, **41**, [420]

renovation of business premises in, capital allowances for, **43(2)**, [640], [655]

residential property, in, **41**, [291], [292]

meaning, **41**, [292]

disadvantaged areas—*contd*

stamp duty land tax, relief for, **41**, [328]

disaffection. *See* **incitement to disaffection**

disaster

tax unpaid in case of, interest relief, **43(S)**, 970–1

discharge

absolute. *See* **absolute discharge**

conditional. *See* **conditional discharge**

order for, power to make, **12(2)**, [727]

disclosure

director, by. *See* **director**

interest in shares. *See* **shares**

discount

sale of house at, stamp duty, **41**, [138], [145]

Schedule D Case III, charge under, **44(1)**, [13]

discrimination

civil partner, against, **7(1)**, [34]

Commission for Equality and Human Rights. *See* **Commission for Equality and Human Rights**

disability. *See* **disabled person**

equality enactments—

meaning, **7(1)**, [778]

unlawful, meaning, **7(1)**, [779]

general note, **7(1)**, [1]

married person, against, **7(1)**, [34]

maternity leave, on ground of, **7(1)**, [35]

pregnancy, on ground of, **7(1)**, [35]

prohibition of, Convention right on, **7(1)**, [592]

racial. *See* **racial discrimination**

religion or belief, on grounds of—

acts of, **7(1)**, [789]

belief, meaning, **7(1)**, [788], [822]

contracts, validity and revision of, **7(1)**, [816]

Crown, application to, **7(1)**, [821]

discriminatory advertisements, **7(1)**, [798]

discriminatory practices, **7(1)**, [797]

education authorities, by, **7(1)**, [795]

educational establishments, by, **7(1)**, [793]

exceptions, **7(1)**, [794]

faith schools, exception for, **7(1)**, [803]

employers' liability, **7(1)**, [818]

enforcement—

contracts, validity and revision of, **7(1)**, [816]

evidence in proceedings, **7(1)**, [814]

immigration proceedings, question raised in, **7(1)**, [811]

national security, interests of, **7(1)**, [815]

remedies, **7(1)**, [812]

restriction of proceedings, **7(1)**, [809]

timing of proceedings, **7(1)**, [813]

unlawful action, claim of, **7(1)**, [810]

exceptions—

amendment, **7(1)**, [808]

discrimination—*contd*
  religion or belief, on grounds of—*contd*
    exceptions—*contd*
      charities relating to religion or belief,
        7(1), [802]
      education, training and welfare,
        7(1), [805]
      faith schools, **7(1)**, [803]
      family, care within, **7(1)**, [806]
      membership requirement, **7(1)**, [804]
      national security, **7(1)**, [807]
      organisations relating to religion or
        belief, **7(1)**, [801]
      statutory requirements, **7(1)**, [800]
    general note, **7(1)**, [80]
    goods, facilities and services, in provision
      of, **7(1)**, [790]
    indirect provision of benefit, application
      to, **7(1)**, [820]
    instructing or causing, **7(1)**, [799]
    interpretation, **7(1)**, [822]
    local education authorities, by, **7(1)**, [795]
    meaning, **7(1)**, [788]
    police, application of provisions to,
      7(1), [819]
    premises, in disposal of, **7(1)**, [791]
      exceptions, **7(1)**, [792]
    principals' liability, **7(1)**, [818]
    public authorities, by, **7(1)**, [796]
    religion, meaning, **7(1)**, [788], [822]
    remedies, **7(1)**, [812]
    summary of provisions, **7(1)**, [1]
    territorial application, **7(1)**, [823]
    unlawful acts, aiding, **7(1)**, [817]
  sex. *See* **sex discrimination**
  sexual orientation, on grounds of—
    meaning, **7(1)**, [780]
    Northern Ireland, regulations for,
      7(1), [825]
    regulations, **7(1)**, [81], [824]
    summary of provisions, **7(1)**, [1]
  victimisation, by, **7(1)**, [127]
  vocational training, against person
    undergoing, **7(1)**, [140]

disease
  control of—
    regulations for, **35(1)**, [454]
    infectious. *See* **infectious disease;
      notifiable disease**
  information and lectures on, **35(1)**, [495]
  notifiable. *See* **notifiable disease**

diseases of animals
  aircraft, detention, **2**, [522]
  animals affected by provisions, **2**, [437]
  antigens, antitoxins, manufacture of, **2**, [556]
  arrest of offenders, **2**, [510]
  attested areas, declaration of, **2**, [431]
  biosecurity—
    compliance, **2**, [433]
    guidance, **2**, [432]
  brucellosis—
    control of, **2**, [431]
    eradication, **2**, [346]

diseases of animals—*contd*
  brucellosis—*contd*
    offences, **2**, [347]
  carcase—
    meaning, **2**, [548]
    offences respecting, **2**, [472]
    seizure and disposal, **2**, [472]
    treatment of, **2**, [454]
    washed ashore, burial, **2**, [507]
  cattle plague—
    meaning, **2**, [548]
    slaughter in case of, **2**, [464], [559]
  civil debt, recovery of, **2**, [536]
  compensation—
    deduction from insurance, **2**, [471]
    scrapie, provisions relating to, **2**, [484]
    seizure, for, **2**, [473]
    slaughtered animals, **2**, [471]
  control protocol—
    exercise of powers, **2**, [468]
    publication of, **2**, [467]
    requirement to prepare, **2**, [467]
  deliberate infection, **2**, [460], [461]
  destruction of wild life to prevent—
    entry etc, for purposes of, **2**, [453]
    methods, specified, **2**, [452]
    orders requiring, **2**, [452]
  diseases defined, **2**, [547]
  dogs. *See* **rabies**
  enforcement of provisions—
    default of local authority, on, **2**, [509]
    police powers and duties, **2**, [510]
  eradication—
    areas, designation, **2**, [431]
    expenditure on, **2**, [428]
    import controls, **2**, [437]
  export—
    member States, to, control of, **2**, [439]
    quarantine stations, **2**, [440]
  exposure to infection, treatment after,
    2, [446]
  false statements, penalties, **2**, [429]
  foot-and-mouth disease—
    animals in transit, found in, **2**, [457]
    national contingency plan, **2**, [443]
    payment of tax, deferment of, **10**, [796]
    slaughter in case of, **2**, [464], [559]
    vaccinated animals, slaughter of, **2**, [447]
    vaccination, duty to consider, **2**, [444]
  hovercraft, provisions applied to, **2**, [549]
  human health, risk to, **2**, [462]
  importation—
    annual review of controls, **2**, [438]
    control orders, **2**, [437], [557]
    customs and excise offences, **2**, [535]
    wharves etc for purposes of, **2**, [504]
  infected animals—
    seizure and disposal, **2**, [459]
    separation of, **2**, [445]
  infected places and areas—
    cancellation of designation, **2**, [449]
    designation orders, **2**, [448]
    exclusion of strangers from, **2**, [458]
    movement in, control of, **2**, [454]
    orders affecting, **2**, [454]

diseases of animals—*contd*
  infected places and areas—*contd*
    powers, **2**, [448]
  inspection of animals, **2**, [428]
    before exporting, **2**, [440]
  inspectors—
    appointment, **2**, [502]
    Community obligations, powers relating
      to, **2**, [521]
    duties, **2**, [502]
    entry, powers of, **2**, [446]
    general powers, **2**, [519]
    obstruction etc, **2**, [524], [525]
    refusal to admit, **2**, [524], [525]
    vehicles, inspection of, **2**, [523]
    vessels and aircraft, power to detain,
      2, [522]
  lairs and sheds—
    cleansing and disinfecting, **2**, [434]
    provision of, **2**, [504]
  licences—
    false statements to obtain, **2**, [528]
    falsification, **2**, [526]
    issue of, in blank, **2**, [527]
  local authority—
    borrowing powers, **2**, [503]
    charges by, **2**, [504]
    default powers of Minister, **2**, [509]
    districts, **2**, [501]
    inspectors, appointment, **2**, [504]
    land acquisition, **2**, [505]
    meaning, **2**, [500]
    regulations by, **2**, [427], [508]
    wharves etc to be provided, **2**, [504]
  markets—
    cleansing and disinfection, **2**, [434]
    regulating or prohibiting holding, **2**, [435]
  marking of animals, **2**, [435]
  meaning—
    animals, **2**, [546]
    disease, **2**, [547]
    Minister, **2**, [545]
    poultry, **2**, [546]
  Minister—
    annual returns by, **2**, [539]
    fees prescribed by, **2**, [543]
    meaning, **2**, [545]
    orders, procedure as to, **2**, [550]
    reports by local authority to, **2**, [540]
  movement of animals—
    diseased or suspected animals, **2**, [456]
    prohibition in specific cases, **2**, [436]
    regulation of, **2**, [435]
  myxomatosis, spreading, **2**, [296]
  notices, form and service, **2**, [542]
  offences—
    appeals respecting, **2**, [537]
    control orders, under, **2**, [435]
    customs and excise, **2**, [533]
    diseased carcase, as to, **2**, [472]
    entry on premises, relating to, **2**, [483]
    evidence and procedure, **2**, [538]
    failure to notify disease, **2**, [445]
    false statements, making, **2**, [429]
    generally, **2**, [532]

diseases of animals—*contd*
  offences—*contd*
    licences, as to, **2**, [526]–[529]
    obstruction of inspection, **2**, [429]
    prosecution, time limit, **2**, [530]
    restriction notice, relating to, **2**, [479]
    summary, penalty, **2**, [534]
    therapeutic substances, as to, **2**, [556]
    triable either way, **2**, [535]
  orders—
    general power to make, **2**, [426]
    list of, **2**, [426]
    procedure as to, **2**, [550]
    specific matters of, **2**, [557]
  outbreak—
    national contingency plan, **2**, [443]
    notice of, **2**, [445]
    separation of animals, **2**, [445]
  pleuro-pneumonia—
    animals in transit, found in, **2**, [457]
    slaughter in case of, **2**, [464], [559]
  police, powers and duties, **2**, [480], [510],
    [511]
  poultry. *See* **poultry**
  rabies. *See* **rabies**
  scrapie—
    compensation provisions, **2**, [484]
    genetically susceptible sheep—
      breeding from, restriction on, **2**, [476]
      identification of, **2**, [475]
    offences, **2**, [483]
    orders and regulations, **2**, [485]
    powers of entry, **2**, [480], [481]
    restriction notice—
      appeals, **2**, [477]
      enforcement, **2**, [478]
      making of, **2**, [476]
      offences, **2**, [479]
    sheep genotypes, power to specify, **2**, [474]
    warrants, issue of, **2**, [481], [482]
  separation of affected animals, **2**, [445]
  serum treatment, **2**, [446]
  sheep dipping facilities, **2**, [506]
  sheep scab, prevention, **2**, [442]
  slaughter in case of—
    compensation, **2**, [471]
    disease control protocol, **2**, [467]
    diseases subject to, **2**, [559]
    powers of entry, **2**, [513]
    preventive, explanation of, **2**, [469]
    specified diseases, **2**, [464], [465]
    spread, to prevent, **2**, [466]
    warrants, issue of, **2**, [514]
  specified, **2**, [558]
  stamp duty exemption, **2**, [544]
  suffering, prevention, **2**, [487]
  summary of provisions, **2**, [140]
  suspected animals—
    seizure and disposal, **2**, [459]
    separation of, **2**, [445]
  swine-fever—
    meaning, **2**, [548]
    slaughter in case of, **2**, [464], [559]
  tests and samples—
    powers of entry, **2**, [516]

diseases of animals—*contd*
tests and samples—*contd*
warrants, issue of, **2**, [517]
therapeutic substances—
importation, **2**, [556]
licence to manufacture, **2**, [556]
meaning, **2**, [556]
offences relating to, **2**, [556]
orders as to, **2**, [556], [557]
provision of, **2**, [430]
vaccine treatment, **2**, [446]
slaughter of animals, **2**, [447]
vehicles, inspection of, **2**, [523]
vessels, power to detain, **2**, [522]
veterinary inspectors—
pet shops, inspection, **2**, [282]
tests and samples—
powers of entry, **2**, [516], [518]
warrants, issue of, **2**, [517]
veterinary services, provision of, **2**, [430]
wharves etc, provision of, **2**, [504]
zoonoses, control, **2**, [462]

dismissal (employment)
industrial action, in connection with,
16, [450]
redundancy. *See* **redundancy**
summary, **16**, [792]
teachers in aided schools, of, **16**, [786]
unfair. *See* **unfair dismissal**
unofficial industrial action, for taking,
16, [425], [449]
written statement of reasons for—
employment tribunal, complaint to,
16, [732]
evidence, admissibility in, **16**, [731]
right to, **16**, [731]

disorderly behaviour
on-the-spot penalties—
amount of, **12(3)**, [3]
enforcement, **12(3)**, [10]
maximum, increase in, **12(4)**, [9]
notice—
effect of, **12(3)**, [4]
form of, **12(3)**, [3]
meaning, **12(3)**, [2]
power of constable to give, **12(3)**, [2]
offences leading to, **12(3)**, [1]
payment of, **12(3)**, [7]
proceedings, restriction on, **12(3)**, [5]
registration certificate, **12(3)**, [8]
registration of sums payable in default,
12(3), [9]
Secretary of State, guidance of, **12(3)**, [6]

disorderly conduct
licensed premises, on, **19(3)**, [629]
refreshment house, permitting in, **19(3)**, [350]

dispensation (ecclesiastical)
Archbishop of Canterbury granting, **14**, 28
Archbishop of York granting, **14**, 33
assent of sovereign and council to, **14**, 28
bishop granting, **14**, 33

dispensation (ecclesiastical)—*contd*
charges for, **14**, 31–2
confirmation and enrolment of, **14**, 28
refusal to grant, appeal from, **14**, 34–5
registration of, **14**, 30
tax paid for, applying, **14**, 32–3
two prelates, grant by, **14**, 34–5
vacancy in see, during, **14**, 33

displaced persons
advances—
indemnity of lending authority, **21**, [419]
power to make, **21**, [418]
procedure for making, **21**, [418]
displacing authority, liability of, **21**, [419]
financial provisions, **21**, [422]
government departments, application of
provisions to, **21**, [421]
Housing Revenue Account dwelling,
rehousing in, **21**, [419]
moving expenses, power to pay, **21**, [415]
new dwellings, expenses of acquiring,
21, [420]
public works, during, **21**, [415]
rehousing—
caravan dwellers, **21**, [417]
financial provisions, **21**, [422]
indemnity by displacing authority,
21, [419]
relevant authority for purposes of,
21, [416]
residential occupiers, **21**, [416]
residential owner-occupiers—
advances to, **21**, [418]
duty to rehouse, **21**, [416]
meaning, **21**, [418]
treatment as displaced, **21**, [416]

display
indecent. *See* **indecent display**

disqualification. *See under* **offences**

disqualification of directors
bank administration, on, **19(S)**, Financial 214
bank insolvency, on, **19(S)**, Financial 178
foreign restrictions—
company's debts, liability for, **8(1)**, [1265]
court, meaning, **8(1)**, [1261]
disqualification—
breach, offence of, **8(1)**, [1264]
person subject to restrictions, of,
8(1), [1262]
statements to registrar, **8(1)**, [1267]
persons subject to, **8(1)**, [1260]
regulations, **8(1)**, [1263]
statements to registrar, **8(1)**, [1266]
disqualified person, from, **8(1)**, [1267]
making public, **8(1)**, [1268]
offences, **8(1)**, [1269]
UK company, meaning, **8(1)**, [1261]
investigation of company, after, **8(1)**, [1117]

distillers. *See* **spirits**

distillery
building near, London, **25(1)**, [175]

distraint
tax collector, by, **42**, [201]

distress
agricultural housing, restrictions in levy,
  21, [460]
assured tenancy, under, **22**, [814]
cattle—
  impounded, feeding by owner, **13**, [1156]
  sale, **13**, [1156]
chief rent, for, **20**, [31]
child support liability, **6**, [511]
compulsory acquisition, enforcement of
  possession on, **9**, [273]
Crown debts, for, **20**, [29]
damage feasant, **13**, [1156]
determination of lease, after, **20**, [27]
excess, **13**, [1154]
exchequer, debts to, **13**, [1156]
farming stock—
  execution, taken in—
    bankrupt, assignee of, restrictions on,
      13, [1185]
    bill of sale, assignee of, restrictions on,
      13, [1185]
    clover, etc, growing with corn,
      prohibition on sale of, **13**, [1181]
    protection for landlord or owner,
      13, [1175]
    sheriff—
      damages, restricted liability for,
        13, [1183]
      disposal of produce subject to
        agreement to use on land, **13**, [1177]
      executing process, sale contrary to
        covenant by, **13**, [1175]
      indemnity to, **13**, [1184]
      landlord or owner—
        action in name of, **13**, [1178]
        name and address, inquiries to
          sheriff as to, **13**, [1179]
        notice to, **13**, [1176]
      trespasser, not, **13**, [1184]
      written contract, removal from land in
        accordance with, **13**, [1177]
harbour rates, recovery by, **39(2)**, [43]
illegal—
  double damages for, **13**, [1160]
  punishment for, **13**, [1153]
irregularity in, **9**, [287]
limitation of action, **20**, [28]
market charges, levy by, **27**, [113]
personal representative, by, **18**, [529]
place of taking, restriction on, **13**, [1155]
rates, for, **11(2)**, [575]
reasonable, **13**, [1154]
recovery of toll by, **27**, [32]
removal from county, prohibition of,
  13, [1154]

distress—*contd*
rent, for—
  agricultural holdings. *See* **agricultural**
    holdings
  bailiff, by—
    certificate authorising—
      cancellation, **13**, [1194]
      duration, **13**, [1196]
      grant, **13**, [1192]
      penalty for acting without, **13**, [1195]
      rules as to, **13**, [1194]–[1196]
      voidance, **13**, [1194]
  cattle, **13**, [1168]
  corn, hay, etc—
    rent paid before cut, cessation of distress
      where, **13**, [1169]
    sale of, **13**, [1158]
  goods exempted from, **13**, [1189]
  goods fraudulently removed from
    premises—
    breaking in to seize, landlord's powers as
      to, **13**, [1167]
    fifty pounds in value, not exceeding,
      13, [1164]
    justices, recourse to, **13**, [1164]
    penalties where, **13**, [1161]–[1163]
    seizure and sale, **13**, [1161]
  illegal—
    double damages for, **13**, [1160]
    exempt goods seized, **13**, [1197]
    goods of under tenant or lodger,
      13, [1199]
  irregularity, subsequent, in effect of,
    13, [1174]
  lodger—
    protection of goods from distress,
      13, [1199], [1200]
    rent of, payment direct to superior
      landlord, **13**, [1201], [1205]
  notice of taking, **13**, [1157]
  pound-breach, treble damages for,
    13, [1159]
  premises—
    deserted by tenant, **13**, [1171], [1186]
    impounding and securing distress on,
      13, [1170]
    sale on, **13**, [1170]
    tenant holding, after giving notice to
      quit, double rent where, **13**, [1173]
    unoccupied or uncultivated, left by
      tenant, **13**, [1171], [1186]
  privilege from—
    exclusion of certain goods from—
      bill of sale, comprised in, **13**, [1203]
      company offices, in, where immediate
        tenant a director, **13**, [1202]
      conditional sale agreement, sale
        under, **13**, [1203]
      consumer hire agreement, bailed
        under, **13**, [1203]
      hire purchase agreement, bailed
        under, **13**, [1203]
      husband or wife of tenant, **13**, [1202]
      livestock, **13**, [1202]

distress—*contd*
rent, for—*contd*
privilege from—*contd*
exclusion of certain goods from—*contd*
office or warehouse premises, on,
13, [1202]
partner of immediate tenant,
13, [1202]
settlement, comprised in, **13**, [1202]
tenant reputed owner, **13**, [1202]
trade premises, on, **13**, [1202]
under tenants, certain, **13**, [1204]
lodger, of, on making declaration,
13, [1199]
under tenant, of, on making
declaration, **13**, [1199]
rescue, treble damages for, **13**, [1159]
sale of goods—
appraisement, after, **13**, [1157], [1168],
[1190]
corn, hay, etc, **13**, [1158], [1168]
removal to public auction for, **13**, [1190]
replevy, in default of, **13**, [1157]
right of, **13**, [1157], [1161], [1168]
stock, **13**, [1168]
under tenant—
protection of goods from distress,
13, [1199], [1200]
rent of, payment direct to superior
landlord, **13**, [1201], [1205]
rentcharge, recovery of, **20**, [668]
rents of assize, for, **20**, [31]
restriction on, **21**, [632]
revenue trader, against, **13**, [714]
sale of goods—
impounding—
cattle, **13**, [1156]
corn, hay, etc, **13**, [1158], [1168]
premises, on, **13**, [1170]
seck rent, for, **20**, [31]
sheep, not for, **13**, [1156]
special damage caused in levy of, **6**, [511]
summary of provisions, **13**, [1152]
warrant. *See* **warrant**

distress for rates. *See also* **distress**
magistrates' court, in, **11(2)**, [575]

distress or anxiety
causing, offence of, **12(1)**, [995], [996],
[1078]

distributions
accounting—
development costs, treatment of,
8(1), [922]
fixed assets, revaluation of, **8(1)**, [919]
long-term insurance business, realised
profits and losses of, **8(1)**, [921]
profit or loss in respect of asset,
determination where records incomplete,
8(1), [920]
realised profits and losses, **8(1)**, [919]
charge to tax, **43(S)**, 1483
amended provisions, **43(S)**, 1491–9

distributions—*contd*
charge to tax—*contd*
exemption, **43(S)**, 1485
anti-avoidance, **43(S)**, 1486—9
controlled companies, from, **43(S)**, 1485
election not to be exempt, **43(S)**, 1489
non-redeemable ordinary shares, in
respect of, **43(S)**, 1485
portfolio holdings, in respect of,
43(S), 1485
shares accounted for as liabilities,
dividends from, **43(S)**, 1486
transactions not designed to reduce tax,
43(S), 1485–6
commencement, **43(S)**, 1497
interpretation, **43(S)**, 1489–90
insurer receiving, **43(S)**, 1495
priority of provisions, **43(S)**, 1490
qualifying territory, meaning, **43(S)**, 1484
small companies, exemption, **43(S)**, 1484,
1489
definitions, **8(1)**, [931]
exclusions, **8(1)**, [907]
foreign income dividend, treatment as,
43(1), [319], [333]
foreign—
income tax credits, **43(S)**, 1558–62
tax credit, **43(S)**, 1125–30
franked investment income, losses not to be
set against, **43(1)**, [313]
friendly society, to, **43(1)**, [356]
investment company, by—
accumulated revenue profits, from,
8(1), [910]
holdings in other companies, condition as
to, **8(1)**, [912]
meaning, **8(1)**, [911]
power to extend provisions, **8(1)**, [913]
justification by reference to accounts—
initial accounts, use of, **8(1)**, [917]
interim accounts, use of, **8(1)**, [916]
last annual accounts, use of, **8(1)**, [915]
requirement of, **8(1)**, [914]
successive distributions, **8(1)**, [918]
kind, in—
determination of amount, **8(1)**, [923]
unrealised profits, treatment of, **8(1)**, [924]
meaning, **8(1)**, [907]
older profits or losses, treatment of,
8(1), [928]
older provisions in articles, saving for,
8(1), [926]
profits available for, **8(1)**, [908]
public company, by, net asset restrictions,
8(1), [909]
restrictions on, saving for, **8(1)**, [930]
rules of law restricting, application of,
8(1), [929]
tax arrangements, arising from, **43(S)**, 1196
tax credits—
amendment of provisions, **43(1)**, [316]
charities, transitional relief for, **43(1)**, [318]
treated as loan relationships, **43(S)**, 1198
UK, received by insurance company,
43(S), 1154–5

distributions—*contd*
unauthorised unit trust, by, **43(1)**, [315]
unlawful, consequences of, **8(1)**, [925]
unrealised profits—
distribution in kind, treatment for,
8(1), [924]
restriction on application of, **8(1)**, [927]

district church council
scheme for electing, **14**, 714–15

district council. *See also* **local authority**
area reviews by, chairman—
declaration to be made by, **25(2)**, [72]
election of, **25(2)**, [4]
borrowing powers, **36**, [1327]
bridleway, maintaining, **36**, [1046], [1064]
chairman, election of, **25(2)**, [4]
charter of incorporation—
effect of, **25(2)**, [209]
petition for, **25(2)**, [206]
civic restaurants, **25(1)**, [371], [372]
common, powers as to rights of, **25(1)**, [81]
constitution of, **25(2)**, [2]
councillors—
election, **25(2)**, [7], [240]
tenure of office, **25(2)**, [240]
terms of office etc, **25(2)**, [6]
depositories for documents, **25(2)**, [179]
expenses—
contributions by county council,
25(1), [563]
contributions to, **36**, [1320]
reimbursement of, **36**, [1410]
facilities, provision of, **22**, [16]
fairs, powers relating to, **25(1)**, [82]
footpath, maintaining, **36**, [1046], [1064]
grants to. *See* **local authority** (grants)
highways, maintenance of—
competent authority in relation to, as,
36, [1419]
counter-notice, service of, **36**, [1409]
indemnity, giving to county council,
36, [1409]
list, keeping, **36**, [1409]
notice of intention, **36**, [1409]
powers, **36**, [1046], [1409]
powers ceasing to be exercisable, **36**, [1409]
regulations, **36**, [1409]
reimbursement of expenses, **36**, [1410]
housing authority, as, **22**, [1]
See further **local housing authority**
information, furnishing, **36**, [1347], [1348]
land drainage. *See* **local authority**
legal proceedings by, **36**, [1181]
legal proceedings, powers as to, **25(1)**, [81]
meaning, **25(1)**, [80]
metropolitan. *See* **metropolitan district
council**
name, change of, **25(2)**, [64]
parish property, execution of works,
25(1), [154]
powers transferred to, **25(1)**, [82]
property etc transferred to, **25(1)**, [85]

district council—*contd*
public health purposes, local authority for,
35(1), [118]
restricted byway, maintaining, **36**, [1046]
rights of way, powers as to, **25(1)**, [81]
street collections, regulation of, **33(2)**, [60]
street trading powers. *See* **street trading**
urgent repairs to private street, carrying out,
36, [1276]
vice-chairman, **25(2)**, [5]
water supply, charge on land for,
20, [448]–[451]
Welsh. *See* **Wales**
works, restoration of powers as to,
25(2), [379], [381]

District Health Authority. *See also* **health
authority; Special Health Authority**
transfer of, **30**, [579]

District Judge. *See also* **stipendiary
magistrate**
legal aid, **11(3)**, [313]
retirement, **11(3)**, [313]

district planning authority
local planning authority, as, **46**, [251]

disturbance
compensation for. *See* **compensation**

ditch. *See also* **watercourse**
cleansing—
effect of order, **19(3)**, [198]
expenses, recovery of, **19(3)**, [198]
order requiring, **19(3)**, [197]
persons liable, **19(3)**, [197]
remedial work, meaning, **19(3)**, [197]
culverting, where building operations in
prospect, **35(1)**, [164]
drainage works affecting, **19(3)**, [199]
draining, cleansing, etc, power of parish
council or local authority as to, **35(1)**, [162]
foul—
offensive, and, near or forming boundary of
district, order for cleaning, **35(1)**, [163]
statutory nuisance, **35(1)**, [161]
land drainage authority, saving for,
35(1), [168]
meaning, **19(3)**, [197]

diver
trade profits, income taxed as, **44(3)**, [15]

divided land. *See also* **severance**
compulsory purchase, provisions, **9**, [268]
vesting declarations, provisions, **9**, [397], [403]

dividend
abnormal, **44(1)**, [445]
annual payments for, **44(1)**, [102]
building society, **44(3)**, [372]
controlled foreign company, from,
44(1), [675]

dividend—*contd*
corporation tax, not chargeable to,
44(1), [109]
date for payment, **44(1)**, [616]
distribution, as, **44(1)**, [109]
double taxation relief, **44(1)**, [541]
foreign coupons, sales of—
charge to tax, **44(3)**, [580]
foreign holdings, meaning, **44(3)**, [581]
income charged, **44(3)**, [582]
person liable, **44(3)**, [583]
foreign income—
election to be treated as, **43(1)**, [319],
[333]
unauthorised unit trust, by, **43(1)**, [315]
foreign, meaning, **44(1)**, [13]
income—
highest part of total income, treated as,
44(4), [16]
income tax charged on—
ordinary rate, **44(4)**, [8]
individuals, for, **44(4)**, [13]
other persons, for, **44(4)**, [14]
upper rate, **44(4)**, [8]
individuals, for, **44(4)**, [13]
meaning, **44(4)**, [19]
investment trusts, of, taxed as interest,
43(S), 1382–3
manufactured, **44(1)**, [455], [670]
amended provisions, **43(2)**, [552]
manufactured dividends on UK shares—
administrative provisions, powers about,
44(4), [594]
allowable deductions—
double-counting, restrictions on,
44(4), [583]
matching, **44(4)**, [582]
generally, **44(4)**, [581]
meaning, **44(4)**, [603]
Real Estate Investment Trusts, **44(4)**, [584]
relief, eligibility for, **44(4)**, [595]
statements about, **44(4)**, [585]
underlying payments, exceeded by,
44(4), [591]
manufactured overseas—
repos, **43(S)**, 1613–14
stock lending, **43(S)**, 1614
non-UK resident companies, from—
approved share incentive plans, shares in,
44(3), [405]–[408]
charge to tax, **44(3)**, [402]
income charged, **44(3)**, [403]
person liable, **44(3)**, [404]
overseas—
manufactured—
administrative provisions, powers about,
44(4), [594]
foreign payers, reverse charge,
44(4), [931]–[932]
generally, **44(4)**, [589]
gross amount, meaning, **44(4)**, [597]
powers about, **44(4)**, [590], [593]
relevant withholding tax, meaning,
44(4), [598]
relief, eligibility for, **44(4)**, [595]

dividend—*contd*
overseas—*contd*
manufactured—*contd*
set-off entitlement, power to provide,
44(4), [933]
supplementary provisions,
44(4), [934]–[935]
underlying payments—
exceeded by, **44(4)**, [591]
greater than, **44(4)**, [592]
meaning, **44(4)**, [575]
proportionate to amount paid up, **8**, 191
stock. *See also* **stock dividends**
distributions, **44(1)**, [134]
income, treated as, **44(1)**, [141]
returns, **44(1)**, [142]
tax underlying, double taxation, **43(S)**, 1391
Treasury, in name of, **44(1)**, [32]
UK resident companies, from—
amounts treated as, **44(3)**, [386]–[388]
approved share incentive plans, shares in,
44(3), [392]–[396]
authorised unit trust distributions,
44(3), [389]–[391]
charge to tax, **44(3)**, [383]
contents of provisions, **44(3)**, [382]
income charged, **44(3)**, [384]
non-qualifying distributions,
44(3), [400]–[401]
open-ended investment company,
distributions by, **44(3)**, [386]–[388]
person liable, **44(3)**, [385]
priority rule for, **44(2)**, [717]
tax credits—
increase in amount of value of
dividends, **44(3)**, [398]
persons not entitled to, distributions
received by, **44(3)**, [399]
qualifying distributions, for, **44(3)**, [397]
underlying tax. *See* **double taxation relief**
upper rate, income charged at, **43(S)**, 896
venture capital trusts dividends. *See* **venture
capital trust**

diving supervisor
trade profits, income taxed as, **44(3)**, [15]

division of company
application of provisions, **8(1)**, [980]
companies involved in—
meaning, **8(1)**, [997]
members—
approval of, **8(1)**, [1000]
documents, inspection of, **8(1)**, [1004]
compromise or arrangement with creditors or
members, relations of provisions to,
8(1), [981]
defaults, liability of transferee company for,
8(1), [1018]
Directive disclosure requirements, documents
subject to, **8(1)**, [1156]
directors' explanatory report on, **8(1)**, [1001]
documents, inspection of, **8(1)**, [1004]
expert's report on, **8(1)**, [1002]
associate, meaning, **8(1)**, [1015]

division of company—*contd*
  expert's report on—*contd*
    independence requirement, **8(1)**, [1014]
    valuation by another person, **8(1)**, [1013]
  material changes of assets of transferor
  company, report on, **8(1)**, [1005]
  meetings of members or creditors of transferee
  company, power of court to summon,
  8(1), [1016]
  new transferee company, approval of articles
  of, **8(1)**, [1006]
  nominee of transferee company, no allotment
  of shares to, **8(1)**, [1008]
  reconstruction or amalgamation, relationship
  of provisions to, **8(1)**, [981]
  scheme—
    draft terms of—
      particulars of, **8(1)**, [998]
      publication of, **8(1)**, [999]
    members of merging companies, approval
    of, **8(1)**, [1000]
  securities to which special rights attach,
  protection of holders of, **8(1)**, [1007]
  shares of transferor company held by
  transferee—
    agreement to dispense with reports,
    8(1), [1011]
    meeting of members of transferee not
    required, **8(1)**, [1010]
    meeting of members of transferor not
    required, **8(1)**, [1009]
    power of court to exclude requirements,
    8(1), [1012]
  supplementary accounting statement,
  8(1), [1003]
  transfer of undertaking of transferor company,
  power of court to fix date for, **8(1)**, [1017]
  transferee company, no allotment of shares
  to, **8(1)**, [1008]

division of land
  instrument effecting, stamp duty, **41**, [214],
  [262]

divorce
  adjournment of proceedings, **27**, [635]
  adultery—
    ground for divorce, as, **27**, [430]
    intolerability caused by, **27**, [430]
    parties—
      living together following, **27**, [431]
      proceedings, to, **27**, [486]
  agreements, consideration by court, **27**, [436],
  [559]
  arrangements between parties, rules as to,
  27, [436], [559]
  arrangements for future—
    court orders and agreements, **27**, [683]
    declarations, **27**, [683]
    exemptions, **27**, [683]
    financial arrangements, **27**, [683]
    negotiated agreements, **27**, [683]
    requirements as to, **27**, [630]
  connected proceedings, **27**, [644]
  custody of child, arising, **6**, [234]

divorce—*contd*
  decree—
    absolute—
      cause for not making, showing,
      27, [438]
      party against whom granted applying
      for, **27**, [438]
      separation cases, considerations in,
      27, [439]
      time for making, **27**, [430]
    court, powers of, **27**, [438]
    grant of, **27**, [430]
    nisi, proceedings following,
    27, [438]–[439], [440]
    protected states, of, validity, **27**, [582]
    religious marriages, **27**, [440]
  desertion—
    cohabitation prohibited, where, **27**, [433]
    ground for divorce, as, **27**, [430]
    period of, calculating, **27**, [431]
  financial provision. *See* **matrimonial causes**
  financial relief not granted, **18**, [613]
  five years separation, following—
    circumstances to be considered, **27**, [439]
    grave hardship caused by, **27**, [434]
    ground for divorce, as, **27**, [430]
  general principles underlying provisions,
  27, [622]
  information meetings, requirements about
  attendance at, **27**, [629]
  irretrievable breakdown of marriage, on,
  27, [430]
  judicial separation preceding, **27**, [433]
  jurisdiction of court, **27**, [638]
  living apart in same household, effect of,
  27, [431]
  marital breakdown—
    requirements to be met, **27**, [626]
    statement, **27**, [627]
  mediation, directions with respect to,
  27, [634]
  minor and consequential amendments,
  27, [691]
  one year of marriage, within, **27**, [432]
  orders—
    children, welfare of, **27**, [632]
    circumstances in which made, **27**, [624]
    conversion of separation order into,
    27, [625]
    hardship, orders preventing divorce in cases
    of, **27**, [631]
    power of court to make, **27**, [623]
    preventing divorce in cases of hardship,
    27, [631]
  parties to proceedings, **27**, [486]
  pension provisions, **33(1)**, [521]
  pensions, sharing, **43(1)**, [458]
  procedure, rules as to, **27**, [633]
  proceedings—
    jurisdiction, **27**, [496]
    pending outside England and Wales, effect
    of, **27**, [496], [499]
  property adjustment orders, meaning,
  27, [684]

divorce—*contd*
property involved, stamp duty on
instruments, **41**, [150]
Queen's Proctor, intervention by, **27**, [437]
recognition of decree—
British Isles, granted in, **27**, [581]
commencement of Act, grant before,
27, [589]
cross-proceedings, in, **27**, [584]
different systems of law, countries having,
27, [586]
generally, **27**, [127]
grounds for, **27**, [583]
legal separation, conversion from, **27**, [584]
proof of facts, **27**, [585]
refusal of, **27**, [588]
remarriage where not recognised, **27**, [587]
United Kingdom, in, **27**, [582]
reconciliation, attempts at, **27**, [435]
reflection and consideration, requirement for
period of, **27**, [628]
religious marriages, **27**, [695]
decree nisi, proceedings after, **27**, [440]
respondent, relief for, **27**, [450]
separate representation for children, provision
for, **27**, [679]
stay of proceedings—
ancillary matters, **27**, [685]
concurrent proceedings, duty to furnish
particulars of, **27**, [685]
discharge of orders, **27**, [685]
discretionary stays, **27**, [685]
interpretation provisions, **27**, [685]
summary of provisions, **27**, [127]
time when proceedings begin, **27**, [639]
transfer of certain tenancies on—
assured agricultural occupancy, **27**, [689]
assured tenancy, **27**, [689]
cases in which court may make order,
27, [688]
compensation, **27**, [690]
date when order made between spouses to
take effect, **27**, [690]
entitlement to occupy, references to,
27, [689]
interpretation provisions, **27**, [688]
liabilities and obligations in respect of
dwelling-house, **27**, [690]
matters to which court must have regard,
27, [688]
protected tenancy, **27**, [689]
remarriage of either spouse, **27**, [690]
rules of court, **27**, [690]
secure tenancy, **27**, [689]
statutory tenancy, **27**, [689]
transfer of tenancies on. *See* **matrimonial
home**
two years separation, following—
circumstances to be considered, **27**, [439]
consent, rules of court on, **27**, [431]
ground for divorce, as, **27**, [430]
respondent misled, where, **27**, [439]
unreasonable behaviour—
ground for divorce, as, **27**, [430]
parties living together following, **27**, [431]

dock
charge to tax, **44(1)**, [34]
owner, limitation of liability of, **39(2)**, [868]
pipe-line in, **17(1)**, [276]
rent payable in respect of, **44(1)**, [98]
street works near, display of lights,
38(1), [235]

Dock Labour Board. *See* **National Dock
Labour Board**

dock undertakers
culverting of stream or watercourse, saving as
to, **35(1)**, [168]
meaning, **36**, [1381]; **35(1)**, [216]
property of, reference to, **36**, [1381]
protection for works of, **35(1)**, [210], [650]
saving for works of, **36**, [1390]
sewers, etc, vested in local authority, power to
alter, **35(1)**, [207]

dock workers
contributions, Class 1, **40(1)**, [220]
registered, former, at dissolution of Board—
employment protection, **16**, [149]
temporarily unattached or suspended, at
dissolution of boards, **16**, [154]
temporary transfer, on, **16**, [154]

docks. *See* **dockyard ports; Port of London;
ports and harbours**

dockyard
paving, lighting etc, **25(1)**, [43]
police service at, **33(2)**, [27]
public stores in, offences as to, **12(1)**, [148]

dockyard ports. *See also* **ports and harbours**
Admiralty authority over, protection,
39(2), [119]
collisions in, prevention, **39(2)**, [137]
jurisdiction over vessels, **39(2)**, [148]
lights, **39(2)**, [137]
limits of, power to define, **39(2)**, [133]
meaning, **39(2)**, [132]
offences—
local jurisdiction, **39(2)**, [148]
service of summonses, **39(2)**, [147]
Orders in Council—
definition of limits by, **39(2)**, [133]
parliamentary procedure, **39(2)**, [151]
regulations by, **39(2)**, [135]
penalties—
application of, **39(2)**, [145]
generally, **39(2)**, [136]
recovery of expenses, **39(2)**, [143]
sale of vessel, raised by, **39(2)**, [146]
summary proceedings for, **39(2)**, [144]
Queen's harbour masters—
appointment, **39(2)**, [134]
powers—
fires and lights, as to, **39(2)**, [139]
search for gunpowder etc, **39(2)**, [139]
unmooring vessels, **39(2)**, [138]

dockyard ports—*contd*
Queen's harbour masters—*contd*
powers—*contd*
unserviceable vessels, removal,
39(2), [141]
wrecks and obstructions, removal,
39(2), [140]
regulations, power to make, **39(2)**, [135]
rights over property etc, savings,
39(2), [150]
wrecks and unserviceable vessels—
recovery of removal expenses,
39(2), [142]
removal, **39(2)**, [140]

dockyard services
company, provision by, **39(2)**, [531]
dockyard undertaking, meaning, **39(2)**, [531]
transfer—
application of provisions, **39(2)**, [531]
designated dockyard, **39(2)**, [531]
premises in use, **39(2)**, [533]
protection of employment, **39(2)**, [531]
Secretary of State, expenses, **39(2)**, [534]
trade union—
failure to inform, **39(2)**, [531]
information to and consultation with,
39(2), [531]
representations by, **39(2)**, [531]

document of title
documents included in, **1(1)**, [2]
exchange, rights acquired by, **1(1)**, [6]
general vesting declaration—
production and delivery, **9**, [399]
safe custody, **9**, [399]
possession—
owner's consent, deemed to be with,
1(1), [3]
when deemed to be in, **1(1)**, [2]
transferring, mode of, **1(1)**, [12]

documentary evidence. *See also* **documents;
evidence**
admissibility—
foreign and overseas documents, **18**, [172]
hearsay, **18**, [395]
public documents, certified, **18**, [105]
conviction, of, **18**, [248]–[250]
criminal proceedings. *See under* **evidence**
(criminal proceedings)
DEFRA, application of provisions to,
18, [163]
documents twenty years old, **18**, [175]
official documents—
admissibility, **18**, [151], [172]
London Gazette, by, **18**, [135]
summary of provisions, **18**, [75]

documents
administration of estates, in—
construction of, **18**, [554]
examination of persons as to, **18**, [649]
place for deposit of, **18**, [651]
subpoena to bring in, **18**, [650]

documents—*contd*
ancient, presumption as to, **18**, [175]
authentication of, **8**, 140
books. *See* **books**
building regulations, as to, register to be kept
by local authority, **35(1)**, [614]
concealment, fraudulent, **20**, [784]
conveyancing, production and safe custody,
20, [682]
delivery and service of, **42**, [255]
Director of Public Prosecutions, delivering
to, **12(1)**, [938]
discovery and production by Crown, **13**, [31]
duplicates and counterparts, stamp duty,
41, [262]
entry and search for, **8**, 494–6
execution by company, **8**, 137
false certification of, **18**, [106]
false entries, penalty, **8**, 501
false, issue of, **37**, [50], [139], [793]
falsification, relating to road traffic, **37**, [139]
foreign, proof and effect, **18**, [172], [198]
form of, **42**, [253]
inspection—
obligations of company, **8**, 587
offence suspected, where, **8**, 585
insurance company, relating to. *See* **insurance
company**
judge's signature, judicial notice of, **18**, [94]
legal estates, relating to, **20**, [636]
meaning, **8**, 602
microfilm copies, **18**, [246]
mutilation etc, penalty, **8**, 500–1
official—
communicating, **12(1)**, [210]
falsification, forgery, etc, of, **12(1)**, [229]
possessing, **12(1)**, [229]
retaining for prejudicial purpose,
12(1), [229]
tampering with, **12(1)**, [229]
otherwise than in legible form, **8**, 568–9, 573
powers of attorney, for, proof of, **18**, [178]
private, in court custody, transfer to Public
Record Office, **18**, [189]
production of—
acknowledgment, **20**, [663], [682]
direction by Minister for, **8**, 493–4
information obtained, security of, **8**, 496–9
inspector, to, **8**, 484–5
proof of—
colonies, in, **18**, [103], [172], [198]
England and Wales, in, **18**, [102]
Ireland, in, **18**, [101]
mode of proving, **18**, [135], [139]
statement contained in, **18**, [303], [409]
summary of provisions, **18**, [75]
public, copies admissible as evidence, **18**, [93]
public health—
authentication, **35(1)**, [178], [500], [616]
form of, **35(1)**, [499], [615]
register to be kept by local authority,
35(1), [614]
service, **35(1)**, [179], [501], [617]
Queen's Printer, printed by, **18**, [95], [151]
recitals, validity as evidence, **20**, [663]

documents—*contd*
  registration—
    inspection of, **8**, 571–2
    legible form, delivery in, **8**, 567–8
    receipt and issue, notice of, **8**, 574–5
  seal, proof of, **18**, [93]
  security of information from, **8**, 496–9
  serious fraud investigation, for, **12(1)**, [1057]
  service—
    application and interpretation of
      provisions, **41**, [531]
    by post, construction of reference to,
      41, [581]
    generally, **9**, [205], [391]
    recorded delivery, **41**, [530]–[534]
  service of, **8**, 588, 868–9
  stamping. *See* **stamp duty**
  suppression of, **12(1)**, [571]
  title, of—
    acknowledgment, **20**, [682]
    concealment or falsification, **20**, [784]
    custody—
      obligations, **20**, [682]
      right to, **20**, [682]
    delivery, **20**, [714]
    inspection by mortgagor, **20**, [714]
    loss or destruction—
      damages for, **20**, [682]
      responsibilities, **20**, [682]
    production—
      expenses of, **20**, [682]
      obligation, **20**, [682]
      order of court for, **20**, [682]
      regulations respecting, **20**, [714]
    vendor, retention by, **20**, [663]
  Welsh companies, relating to, **8**, 573–4

dogs
  breeding establishment—
    diseases, prevention of spread, **2**, [367]
    inspection, **2**, [367], [674]
      fees, **2**, [369]
    keeper, death of, **2**, [366]
    licence—
      breach of conditions, **2**, [366]
      cancellation, **2**, [368]
      conditions for granting, **2**, [366]
      disqualification for, **2**, [368]
      duration of, **2**, [366]
      grant of, **2**, [366]
      refusal of, appeal from, **2**, [366]
      requirement for, **2**, [366]
    meaning, **2**, [370], [717]
    offences and penalties, **2**, [368], [675]
    premises not covered by licence, inspection
      of, **2**, [674]
    sale of dogs from, offences, **2**, [717], [718]
  control orders—
    byelaws, **2**, [760]
    fixed penalty notices—
      amount of penalty, **2**, [757]
      contents of, **2**, [756]
      form of, **2**, [756]
      name and address, authorised officer
        requiring, **2**, [758]

dogs—*contd*
  control orders—*contd*
    fixed penalty notices—*contd*
      power to give, **2**, [756]
    land applicable to, **2**, [754]
    meaning, **2**, [752]
    offences, **2**, [752]
    overlapping powers, **2**, [759]
    penalties, **2**, [753]
    power to make, **2**, [752]
    primary and secondary authorities,
      meaning, **2**, [755]
    regulations, **2**, [753], [763]
  dangerous, order for destruction, **2**, [210],
    [643]
  delivery up, order for, **2**, [368]
  destruction orders—
    contingent, **2**, [681]
    conviction, otherwise than on, **2**, [682]
    generally, **2**, [680]
    transitional provisions, **2**, [714]
  disqualification for keeping, **2**, [680]
  docking of tails, offence of, **2**, [778]
  entry, powers of, **2**, [683]
  exceptions from liability, **2**, [354]
  ferocious and unmuzzled, **36**, [226], [385]
  fighting, bred for, **2**, [677]
  guard. *See* **guard dog**
  injury to cattle etc, liability, **2**, [234]
  killing to protect livestock, **2**, [358]
  lead, kept on, **2**, [685]
  livestock, worrying—
    entry and search, authorisation of, **2**, [289]
    injury by, liability, **2**, [234]
    killing or injuring, **2**, [352]
    meaning, **2**, [287]
    offence of, **2**, [287]
    penalty, **2**, [287]
    prevention of, **2**, [288], [358]
  mad, destruction of, **36**, [230]
  muzzling, **2**, [685]
  offences against badgers, used or present at,
    2, [702]
  pets. *See* **pet animal**
  poultry, liability for injuring, **2**, [254]
  proper control, keeping under, **2**, [679]
  rabies. *See* **rabies**
  registration scheme, regulations, provision
    for, **2**, [635]
  roads, on, control of, **37**, [598]
  sale of—
    offences, **2**, [717]
    penalties, **2**, [718]
  seizure of, **2**, [683]
  special dangerous, orders as to, **2**, [678]
  stray—
    control of, **2**, [636]
    Crown, application of provisions to,
      2, [647]
    delivery to police, **2**, [236], [646]
    disposal of, **2**, [645]
    finder, obligations of, **2**, [646]
    finder's right to keep, **2**, [236]
    local authority officer, delivery to, **2**, [646]
    notices, service of, **2**, [648]

dogs—*contd*
  stray—*contd*
    owner, notice on, **2**, [645]
    regulations, orders and directions, **2**, [649]
    seizure of, **2**, [235], [441], [645]
    termination of police responsibility for,
      2, [764]
    straying on highway, **2**, [357]
    street offences, **36**, [226], [385]
    summary of provisions, **2**, [140]
    young persons, owned by, **2**, [684]

domestic court and domestic proceedings.
See now **family proceedings**
  change of names, **6**, [423]

domestic fuel and power
  reduced rate VAT, **50**, [149]

domestic property
  meaning, **25(2)**, [756]

domestic servants
  health and safety at work, provisions
    excluded, **18**, [1304]
  redundancy provisions, application, **16**, [811]

domestic violence
  interpretation provisions, **27**, [678]
  minor and consequential amendments,
    27, [803]–[5]
  non-cohabiting couples, **12(4)**, [1]
  non-molestation orders—
    agreement to marry, evidence of, **27**, [659]
    appeals, **27**, [676]
    application for, **27**, [656]
    associated person, meaning of, **27**, [677]
    breach of—
      arrest for, **27**, [662]
      committal order, power of magistrates'
        court to suspend execution of,
        27, [665]
      guardianship, power of magistrates' court
        to order, **27**, [666]
      hospital admission, power of magistrates'
        court to order, **27**, [666]
      offence of, **27**, [657]
      remand—
        bail, on, **27**, [687]
        custody, in, **27**, [687]
        further, **27**, [687]
        medical examination and report, for,
          27, [663]
        postponement of taking of
          recognizance, **27**, [687]
    cohabitants, meaning of, **27**, [677]
    contempt proceedings for
      non-compliance, **27**, [673]
    criteria for, **27**, [656]
    discharge of, **27**, [664]
    ex parte orders, **27**, [660]
    generally, **27**, [127]
    jurisdiction of courts, **27**, [672]
    leave of court required for applications by
      children under sixteen, **27**, [658]

domestic violence—*contd*
  non-molestation orders—*contd*
    meaning, **27**, [656]
    relevant child, meaning of, **27**, [677]
    separate representation for children,
      provision of, **27**, [679]
    third parties acting on behalf of victims,
      application by, **27**, [675]
    undertakings, **27**, [661]
    variation of, **27**, [664]

domicile. *See also* **judgments (Conventions)**
  child, of—
    generally, **6**, [1]
    independent, **6**, [153]
    legitimation, effect of, **6**, [264]
    mother, living with, **6**, [154]
    See also **child**
  Contracting State, in, **11(2)**, [848]
  dispute as to, determination of, **44(2)**, [42]
    appeal, **44(2)**, [43]
  independent, age of acquiring, **6**, [153]
  tax purposes, for, **43(1)**, [248]
  United Kingdom, in—
    association, seat of, **11(2)**, [834]–[835]
    corporation, seat of, **11(2)**, [834]–[835]
    Crown, of, **11(2)**, [838]
    deemed, **11(2)**, [836]
    individual, **11(2)**, [833]
    trusts, of, **11(2)**, [837]

domiciliary care agency
  meaning, **35(2)**, [283]

Dominica
  Commonwealth citizenship, **31**, [186]

Dominion
  Acts extending to, **32**, [848]
  administration of estates, **18**, [489]
  courts of Admiralty, powers relating to,
    7(2), [428]
  documents, proof and effect, **18**, [172]
  extra-territorial law, making, **7(2)**, [426]
  government trading operations, taxation in
    respect of, **42**, [5]
  judgment obtained in—
    certified copy of, **19(3)**, [7]
    enforcement, **19(3)**, [6]
    reciprocal enforcement, **19(3)**, [29]
    registration provisions, **19(3)**, [20]
  laws, validity of, **7(2)**, [425]
  legislation by UK Parliament, **7(2)**, [427]
  meaning, **7(2)**, [355], [424]
  remission of cases for opinion of court,
    18, [119]

Doncaster Drainage District
  coal industry nationalisation, provisions
    applicable, **17(1)**, [14]
  mining subsidence, matters arising, **17(2)**, [34]

double taxation
  anti-fragmentation, **43(S)**, 1394
  dividends, tax underlying, **43(S)**, 1391

double taxation—*contd*
foreign tax, payments by reference to,
43(S), 1392–3

double taxation agreements
partners, resident, **44(3)**, [875]

double taxation relief
ADP dividend, separate streaming of,
44(1), [561]
agreement—
effect, **44(1)**, [539]
regulations, **44(1)**, [542]
transitional provisions, **44(1)**, [691]
Arbitration Convention, application of,
44(1), [601]
capital gains tax, agreement in respect of,
42, [1429]
claim for, **44(1)**, [539]
company loan relationships, disposals and
acquisitions of, **44(1)**, [588]
controlled foreign company, **44(1)**, [675]
credit, by—
code, interpretation of, **44(1)**, [543]
computation, **44(1)**, [547]
corporation tax, **44(1)**, [550]
trade income, **44(1)**, [554], [555]
disallowed, use as deduction, **44(1)**, [556]
election against, **44(1)**, [573]
foreign tax, minimisation of, **44(1)**, [548]
income tax, **44(1)**, [549]
trade income, **44(1)**, [553]
incorrectly paid, **44(1)**, [595]
no double relief, **44(1)**, [545]
overseas life insurance business, restriction
for, **44(1)**, [568]
reduction of UK tax, **44(1)**, [544]
residence requirements, **44(1)**, [546]
time limit for claims, **44(1)**, [574]
years of commencement, income arising
in, **44(1)**, [564]
disclosure of information, **42**, [992]
discretionary trusts, **44(1)**, [592]
dividend, separate streaming, **43(1)**, [544]
documents, inspection of, **44(1)**, [597]
eligible unrelieved foreign tax, **43(2)**, [79]
foreign dividends, **43(1)**, [544]
application of provisions to UK branch or
agency of non-UK resident person,
44(1), [584]
meaning, **44(1)**, [583]
qualifying, **44(1)**, [577]
foreign enterprises and UK residents,
44(1), [599]
foreign tax—
deduction where no credit allowable,
44(1), [593]
income subject to, computation of,
44(1), [547]
meaning, **44(1)**, [543]
minimisation of, **44(1)**, [548]
non-trading credit, items giving rise to—
intangible fixed assets, **44(1)**, [552]
loan relationships, **44(1)**, [551]
onshore pooling, **44(1)**, [577]

double taxation relief—*contd*
foreign tax—*contd*
relievable—
carry back of, **44(1)**, [579]
surrender by one group company to
another, **44(1)**, [582]
single entity, group as, **44(1)**, [563]
underlying tax, credit to be given for first,
44(1), [580]
unrelieved—
carry back of, **44(1)**, [585]–[586]
carry forward of, **44(1)**, [585]–[586]
eligible—
amounts being, **44(1)**, [576]
claims regarding, **44(1)**, [581]
dividends, falling on, **44(1)**, [575]
utilisation of, **44(1)**, [578]
income subject to foreign tax, computation
of, **43(2)**, [79]
information, disclosure of, **44(1)**, [602]
inheritance tax relief, **42**, [693], [694]
insurance companies—
credit, restriction of, **44(1)**, [569]
expenses, allocation of computations under
Case I Schedule D, **44(1)**, [570]–[572]
interest, special relationship provision,
44(1), [590]
limits on credit, **43(2)**, [638]
mutual agreement procedure, **44(1)**, [600]
non-UK trade, transfer of, **44(1)**, [598]
old law, arrangements under, **44(1)**, [540]
onshore pooling, **44(1)**, [577]
Order in Council, **44(1)**, [539]
petroleum revenue tax, relief for, **43(1)**, [45]
relief—
non-resident with branch or agency in UK,
for, **43(2)**, [79]
schemes and arrangements designed to
increase, **43(2)**, [639]
self-assessment, **43(1)**, [115]
royalties, special relationship provision,
44(1), [591]
schemes and arrangements designed to
increase, **44(1)**, [690]
notice as to, **44(1)**, [565]–[567]
schemes designed to increase, amendment,
43(S), 534
securities, transfer of, **44(1)**, [587]
special withholding tax, in respect of. *See*
special withholding tax
tax avoidance, **44(1)**, [596]
tax credits, **42**, [988]
trade income, foreign tax credit for,
43(S), 883
trading income, deduction of interest or
dividends from, **44(1)**, [589]
transferred profits, dividends paid out,
44(1), [560]
UK residents and foreign enterprises,
44(1), [599]
underlying tax—
computation of, **44(1)**, [557]
interest on loans, reflecting, **44(1)**, [562]
meaning, **44(1)**, [543]

double taxation relief—*contd*
  underlying tax—*contd*
    related companies, dividends between,
      44(1), [558]
    restriction of relief for, **43(1)**, [544];
      43(2), [79]; **44(1)**, [559]
    UK and third country taxes, **44(1)**, [558]
  unilateral, **44(1)**, [541], [546]
  unitary state, non-resident company associated
    with, **44(1)**, [594], [596]
  unrelieved foreign tax, **43(1)**, [544]
  years of commencement, income arising in,
    44(1), [564]

dower
  abolition of, **18**, [548]
  barring of—
    agreement against, **18**, [464]
    declaration in deed, by, **18**, [459]
    declaration in will, by, **18**, [460]
    devise of real estate, by, **18**, [462]
    personal estate, effect of bequest of,
      18, [463]
  estate disposed of by husband, from, **18**, [457]
  legacy in satisfaction of, **18**, [465]
  priority to partial estates etc, **18**, [458]
  restrictions, subject to, **18**, [461]
  savings, **18**, [466]
  title to, **18**, [456]
  widow's entitlement to, **18**, [455]

down
  public access to, **32**, [1]

drain. *See also* **sewer**
  adoption of, agreement for, **49**, [903]
  alteration by railway company, etc,
    35(1), [207]
  cleansing or repair, **35(1)**, [259]
  collegiate and corporate bodies, of,
    35(1), [212]
  defective, **35(1)**, [583]
  defective, investigation of, **49**, [917]
  disused, disconnection, **35(1)**, [586]
  examination and testing of suspected
    defective, **35(1)**, [125]
  execution of works, breaking open street for,
    35(1), [586], [624]
  general system, constructed as part of,
    49, [915]
  highway, use as sewers, **49**, [918]
  improper construction or repair, penalty for,
    35(1), [587]
  insufficiency, **35(1)**, [583]
  meaning, **35(1)**, [18], [216], [648]
  reconstruction, **35(1)**, [586]
    breaking open street for, **35(1)**, [586],
      [624]
  repair, power of local authority as to,
    35(1), [258]
  sewer, connection with, **35(1)**, [546], [586]
  stopped-up, requirement to owner or occupier
    to remedy, **35(1)**, [258]
  summary of provisions as to, **35(1)**, [1]
  system, alteration of, **49**, [916]

drain—*contd*
  tramway interfering with, **36**, [504]
  underground, repair, etc, notice as to,
    35(1), [585]
  works, power of local authority to execute,
    35(1), [173]

drainage
  buildings—
    combination, in, **35(1)**, [547]
    notice requiring provision for—
      appeal against—
        local authority to give effect to
          decision on, **35(1)**, [627]
        magistrates' court, to, **35(1)**, [626]
        procedure on, **35(1)**, [626]
      contents, **35(1)**, [583], [622]
      enforcement, **35(1)**, [583], [622]
      service by local authority, **35(1)**, [583]
  charges—
    agents for collection, etc, **49**, [1284]
    appeals, **49**, [1284]
    chargeable land, assessment of, **49**, [1284]
    commercial woodlands, partial exemption
      of, **49**, [1284]
    erroneous assessments, correction,
      49, [1284]
    general—
      amount of, **49**, [1190]
      assessment of, **49**, [1190]
      raising of, **49**, [1189]
    occupiers, liability of, **49**, [1284]
    owners, payment by, **49**, [1284]
    publication of, **49**, [1284]
    raising, **49**, [1284]
    recovery of, **49**, [1284]
    references to, **49**, [712], [896]
    returns with respect to land, **49**, [1284]
    special—
      agriculture, in interests of, **49**, [1191]
      amount of, **49**, [1192]
      levy of, **49**, [1192]
      schemes imposing, **49**, [1285]
  Coal Authority, acquisition of rights as to,
    17(1), [177]
  internal drainage boards—
    contributions from—
      appeals, **49**, [1194]
      precepts for recovery of, **49**, [1195]
      resolutions requiring, **49**, [1193]
    environmental and recreational duties,
      49, [714]
    transitory provisions, **49**, [1320]
  opencast coal working—
    acquisition of rights for, **17(1)**, [177]
    cessation of powers, **17(2)**, [176]
    entry on board's land for purposes of,
      17(1), [201]
    protection of board's apparatus and rights,
      17(1), [166], [172]
  passages and yards to building, **35(1)**, [606]
  soil pipes—
    use, **35(1)**, [584]
    ventilation, **35(1)**, [584]

drainage—*contd*
subsidence causing damage to. *See* **coal mining subsidence**
works, accretions of land resulting from, **49**, [1200]

drainage and improvement of land (private works)
adjoining land—
entry on, for repairs, **20**, [347]
interests in, **20**, [312]
sale of, **20**, [312]
applications—
costs of, **20**, [303]
Court, to, in case of dissent, **20**, [302]
dissenting from, **20**, [302]
expenses, included in charge, **20**, [329]
investigation of, **20**, [298]
persons under disability, representation of, **20**, [304]
sanction for improvements, **20**, [294]
forms of orders, **20**, [306]
assignment of charge—
form of, **20**, [354]
generally, **20**, [307], [339]
rentcharge, **20**, [339]
canal—
interference with, **20**, [300]
protection for, **20**, [326]
charge—
assignment, **20**, [307], [339], [354]
evidence of, **20**, [333]
execution of, **20**, [328]
expenses included in, **20**, [329]
form of, **20**, [331], [352], [353]
recoverable from lands, **20**, [344]
several charges in one order, **20**, [345]
improvement company, in favour of, **20**, [332]
inheritance, on, **20**, [328], [334]
interest on, **20**, [328]
landowner, in favour of, **20**, [307]
mansion house, on, **20**, [401]
merger in land charged, **20**, [337]
personal property, as, **20**, [337]
priority, **20**, [336]
rentcharge, by way of, **20**, [330]
repayment, period for, **20**, [481]
validity, evidence of, **20**, [333]
water supply, for, **20**, [448]–[451]. *See also* rentcharge *below*
church lands, consents necessary, **20**, [301]
Commissioners—
assistant, powers of, **20**, [288]
meaning, **20**, [286]
provisions applied, **20**, [287]
service of notices on, **20**, [289]
Crown rights, saving for, **20**, [314]
dissent as to—
application to court to override, **20**, [302]
representation of party under disability, **20**, [304]
Duchies, saving rights of, **20**, [316], [317]
easements over adjoining land, sale of, **20**, [312]

drainage and improvement of land (private works)—*contd*
entry—
authorisation of, **20**, [313]
neighbouring land, on, for repairs, **20**, [347]
powers of, **20**, [313]
execution of works—
adjoining land, on, **20**, [312]
authorisation of, **20**, [313]
Crown rights, saving for, **20**, [314]
entry for, **20**, [313]
foreshore etc, affecting, **20**, [319]
improvement company, by, **20**, [481]
inspection while in progress, **20**, [327]
materials for, **20**, [313]
notice requiring, **20**, [349]
rivers etc, protection for, **20**, [326]
specifications to be approved, **20**, [311]
Thames, affecting, **20**, [323]
waste, protection from impeachment, **20**, [313]
expenses—
charge, inclusion in, **20**, [329]
security for, **20**, [297]
survey, liability for, **20**, [320]
foreshore, works on, **20**, [319]
forms, issue of, **20**, [296]
harbour, works affecting, **20**, [319]
improvement company—
advances by, **20**, [481]
execution of works by, **20**, [481]
meaning, **20**, [483]
improvement of land—
detailed specifications, delivery of, **20**, [310]
maintenance of, **20**, [350]
meaning, **20**, [292]
infants—
protection for, **20**, [302]
representation of, **20**, [304]
inheritance, improvements charged on, **20**, [328], [334]
inspection of work, **20**, [327]
insurance—
farmhouse etc, liability for, **20**, [348]
mansion house, **20**, [404]
premium, liability for, **20**, [348]
landowner—
application for sanction by, **20**, [294], [295]
assessment for public works, **20**, [334]
death before completion, **20**, [308]
determination of interest of, effect, **20**, [308]
execution of works by, **19(3)**, [191]
meaning, **20**, [291]
security by, for expenses, **20**, [297]
survey expenses, liability for, **20**, [320]
maintenance of improvements, **20**, [350]
mansion house—
charge on, priority of, **20**, [405]
improvement—
increased value, calculation, **20**, [402]
maximum charge on, **20**, [401]
what deemed to be, **20**, [408]

drainage and improvement of land (private works)—*contd*

mansion house—*contd*

insurance against fire, **20**, [404]

suitability, certification of, **20**, [403]

materials, obtaining, **20**, [313]

Metropolitan Board of Works, protection for, **20**, [324]

Minister of Agriculture, saving for rights of, **20**, [315]

navigation, interference with, **19(3)**, [259]; **20**, [300]

notices—

proceedings, in, **20**, [482]

service of, **20**, [289], [290]

orders—

absolute—

charging assessment on inheritance, **20**, [334]

evidence of charge, as, **20**, [333]

form of, **20**, [335], [353]

modification of, **20**, [481]

priority of charges, **20**, [336]

term of, **20**, [335]

forms of, **20**, [306], [352], [353]

provisional—

assignment by endorsement on, **20**, [307]

charge, to create, **20**, [307]

form of, **20**, [352]

proceedings as to, notices in, **20**, [482]

proposals—

examination of, **20**, [298]

modification of, **20**, [299]

navigation etc, interfering with, **20**, [300]

rentcharge—

apportionment—

orders, form and registry, **20**, [343], [355]

several charges in one order, **20**, [345]

arrears, interest on, **20**, [338]

assignment, **20**, [339]

form of, **20**, [354]

charges made by way of, **20**, [330]

consent to be charged with, **20**, [341]

limited owner's duty to keep down, **20**, [340]

period for repayment, **20**, [481]

recovery of, **20**, [481]

release—

of part of land from, **20**, [342]

order, form of, **20**, [343], [356]

tenant for life to keep down, **20**, [340]

repair of works, entry for, **20**, [347]

river—

navigable—

abatement of works affecting, **20**, [351]

interference with, **20**, [300]

works affecting, **20**, [319]

protection for, **20**, [326]

sanction of improvements—

application for, **20**, [294], [295]

forms of orders, **20**, [306]

interest on cost, rate of, **20**, [305]

modification of scheme, **20**, [309]

drainage and improvement of land (private works)—*contd*

sanction of improvements—*contd*

provisional orders, **20**, [307]

form of, **20**, [352]

Secretary of State—

foreshore, consent to works on, **20**, [319]

saving for rights of, **20**, [318]

survey of works, expenses, **20**, [320]

settled land, provisions applied to, **20**, [447]

specifications, approval of, **20**, [311]

summary of provisions, **20**, [1]

survey, expenses of, **20**, [320]

Thames—

approval of works affecting, **20**, [323]

conservators, saving rights of, **20**, [323]

tidal waters—

abatement of works affecting, **20**, [351]

survey of works affecting, **20**, [320]

upholding improvements—

default as to, inspection, **20**, [349]

responsibility for, **20**, [346]

vesting order, form of, **20**, [357]

water undertakers, saving rights of, **20**, [325]

watercourses, duty to keep open, **20**, [346]

drainage and improvement of land (public works)

arrangements—

navigation and conservancy authorities, with, **19(3)**, [188]

other persons, with, **19(3)**, [189]

awards affecting, variation of, **19(3)**, [201]

byelaws. *See* **byelaws**

commutation of obligations—

financial consequences, **19(3)**, [203]

power of, **19(3)**, [202]

conservancy authority, arrangements for works by, **19(3)**, [188]

Crown, provisions applied, **19(3)**, [249]

definitions, **19(3)**, [165], [247]

districts. *See* **drainage districts**

ditches. *See* **ditch**

drainage—

board. *See* **drainage board**

rate. *See* **drainage rate**

entry, powers of—

internal drainage board by, **19(3)**, [183]

local authority, by, **19(3)**, [183]

expenses—

apportionment, **19(3)**, [162], [163]

excesses or deficiencies, carrying forward, **19(3)**, [164]

precepts in respect of, **19(3)**, [163]

flooding, to prevent, **19(3)**, [183]

grants, power to make, **19(3)**, [228]

information—

confidentiality of, **19(3)**, [245]

provisions as to, **19(3)**, [244]

injury arising from, compensation, **19(3)**, [183]

inquiries—

confidentiality of information, **19(3)**, [245]

costs, **19(3)**, [244]

power to hold, **19(3)**, [244]

drainage and improvement of land (public works)—*contd*
inquiries—*contd*
summons to attend, **19(3)**, [244]
internal drainage—
board. *See* **drainage board**
district. *See* **drainage district**
landowner, execution of works by, **19(3)**, [191]
local authority. *See* **local authority**
main river works—
disputes as to, **19(3)**, [248]
prohibition on, **19(3)**, [188]–[190]
Minister of Agriculture, power to make regulations, **19(3)**, [240]
navigation authority, arrangements with, **19(3)**, [188]
obligations—
commutation, **19(3)**, [202], [203]
variation. *See* variations of obligations *below*, **19(3)**, [201]
protective provisions, **19(3)**, [242], [259]
regulations and orders, power to make, **19(3)**, [240]
schemes—
drainage of small areas. *See* small areas *below*
reorganisation of districts, for, **19(3)**, [174]
variation of awards, for, **19(3)**, [201]
Scilly Isles, application to, **19(3)**, [250]
service of documents, **19(3)**, [246]
small areas, schemes for—
consultation, **19(3)**, [257]
contents, **19(3)**, [187]
Environment Agency, by, **19(3)**, [187]
expenses, **19(3)**, [187]
local authority, by, **19(3)**, [187]
local land charge, as, **19(3)**, [187]
making of, **19(3)**, [187], [257]
notice of, **19(3)**, [257]
objection to, **19(3)**, [257]
spoil, disposal of, **19(3)**, [184]
summary of provisions, **19(3)**, [161]; **20**, [1]
supervision of, **19(3)**, [178]
undertakings protected, **19(3)**, [242], [259]
variation of obligations, **19(3)**, [201]
order—
notice, **19(3)**, [256]
power to make, **19(3)**, [201], [256]
procedure for making, **19(3)**, [256]
unconfirmed, **19(3)**, [256]
schemes, **19(3)**, [201]

drainage authority. *See also* **drainage board; Environment Agency**
meaning, **36**, [1381]
rates, exemption from, **25(2)**, [835]
saving for works of, **36**, [1391]

drainage board
accounts of, **19(3)**, [255]
acquisition of land by, **19(3)**, [237]
annual reports, **19(3)**, [255]
arrangements between boards, **19(3)**, [182]
audit, **19(3)**, [255]
borrowing powers, **19(3)**, [224]

drainage board—*contd*
byelaws. *See* **byelaws**
coast protection work, consent to, **49**, [421]
committees, **19(3)**, [255]
commutation of obligations, financial consequences, **19(3)**, [203]
compulsory acquisition of land, **19(3)**, [237]
constitution, **19(3)**, [172]
construction or alteration of works—
consent to, **19(3)**, [178]
contravention of provisions as to, **19(3)**, [178]
continuation of, **19(3)**, [172]
default by—
Environment Agency powers, **19(3)**, [180]
exercise of powers by local authority, **19(3)**, [181]
disposal of land by, **19(3)**, [238]
employees—
compensation, loss of employment, **19(3)**, [177]
housing accommodation, **19(3)**, [255]
remuneration, **19(3)**, [255]
entry, powers of, **19(3)**, [239]
Environment Agency. *See* **Environment Agency**
environment and recreation—
codes of practice, **19(3)**, [235]
duties respecting, **19(3)**, [231]
Ministerial directions, **19(3)**, [234]
expenses—
apportionment of, **19(3)**, [206]
contributions by Environment Agency towards, **19(3)**, [226]
raising of, **19(3)**, [205]
sub-division of districts for raising, **19(3)**, [207], [208]
valuation of properties, **19(3)**, [206]
flood warning systems, default in connection with, **19(3)**, [180]
general drainage powers, **19(3)**, [183]
grants to, **19(3)**, [228]
incorporation, **19(3)**, [172]
land—
dealings in, **19(3)**, [238]
power to acquire, **19(3)**, [237]
powers of entry on, **19(3)**, [239]
land control, exemption from, **1(1)**, [652]
maintenance of works, **19(3)**, [183]
meetings, **19(3)**, [255]
members—
accidents to, insurance against, **19(3)**, [255]
appointed members, meaning, **19(3)**, [253]
appointment—
charging authorities, by, **19(3)**, [253]
generally, **19(3)**, [172], [252]
more than one charging authority, by, **19(3)**, [253]
elected member, meaning, **19(3)**, [254]
election of, **19(3)**, [172]
rules, **19(3)**, [252]
electors, **19(3)**, [252]
expenses incurred by, **19(3)**, [255]
interest to be disclosed, **19(3)**, [255]
qualification, **19(3)**, [252]

drainage board—*contd*

members—*contd*

resignation, **19(3)**, [254]

term of office, **19(3)**, [254]

vacancies, filling, **19(3)**, [254]

navigation authority—

arrangements with, **19(3)**, [188]

rights, variation of, **19(3)**, [204]

navigation tolls, power to levy, **19(3)**, [225]

new, constitution of, **19(3)**, [174]

new works, construction of, **19(3)**, [183]

officers and staff—

compensation for loss of office, **19(3)**, [177]

expenses incurred by, **19(3)**, [255]

housing accommodation for, **19(3)**, [255]

remuneration, **19(3)**, [255]

powers and duties, **19(3)**, [172], [183]

proceedings of, **19(3)**, [255]

rate levied by. *See* **drainage rate**

reorganisation schemes affecting, **19(3)**, [174]

sites of special scientific interest, duties respecting, **19(3)**, [233]

spoil, appropriation and disposal of, **19(3)**, [184]

spray irrigation, powers to facilitate, **19(3)**, [236]

supervision by Environment Agency, **19(3)**, [178]

watercourse, duty as to, **19(3)**, [190], [192]

works—

another area, in, **19(3)**, [183]

consent to, **19(3)**, [178]

outside area of, **19(3)**, [183]

drainage charge. *See* **drainage; drainage rate**

drainage districts

boundaries—

alteration by order, **19(3)**, [174]

review of, **19(3)**, [173]

constitution, **19(3)**, [172]

continuation of, **19(3)**, [172]

reorganisation—

compensation for loss of office, **19(3)**, [177]

objections to, **19(3)**, [256]

order for—

confirmation of, **19(3)**, [256]

making of, **19(3)**, [174]

Minister's powers, **19(3)**, [256]

procedure etc after making of, **19(3)**, [256]

proposed, notice of, **19(3)**, [256]

provisions of, **19(3)**, [174]

unconfirmed—

challenge of, **19(3)**, [256]

notice of, **19(3)**, [256]

public inquiry, **19(3)**, [256]

scheme for, **19(3)**, [174]

sub-division of, in raising expenses—

directions to board, **19(3)**, [208]

notice, **19(3)**, [208]

petition for order, **19(3)**, [208]

powers, **19(3)**, [207]

drainage etc of land

transfer of functions, **25(2)**, [586]

drainage rate

amendment of, **19(3)**, [219]

annual value—

adjustment to secure fair distribution, **19(3)**, [212]

assessment, **19(3)**, [209]

charge by reference to, **19(3)**, [210]

chargeable property, yearly rent of, **19(3)**, [210]

determination of—

appeal against, **19(3)**, [214]

cancellation of, **19(3)**, [214]

date of, **19(3)**, [211]

effect of, **19(3)**, [213]

effective date, **19(3)**, [213]

hearing of appeal, **19(3)**, [215]

notice of, **19(3)**, [213]

objection to, **19(3)**, [214]

yearly rent of holding, **19(3)**, [210]

fraction of pound, treatment of, **19(3)**, [218]

recalculation on appeal, **19(3)**, [215]

tenancy, nature of, **19(3)**, [210]

appeal against—

aggrieved person, by, **19(3)**, [220]

annual value determination, **19(3)**, [214]

contributions towards board's expenses, resolution as to, **19(3)**, [226]

Crown Court, to, **19(3)**, [220]

determination of board, **19(3)**, [214]

hearing of, **19(3)**, [215]

Lands Tribunal, to, **19(3)**, [215]

notice of, **19(3)**, [220]

persons entitled to appear, **19(3)**, [215]

procedure, **19(3)**, [215]

valuation tribunal, to, **19(3)**, [215]

arbitration, agreement to refer to, **19(3)**, [220]

arrears, recovery of, **19(3)**, [223]

assessment—

elements disregarded, **19(3)**, [210]

occupier, on, **19(3)**, [218]

persons to be assessed, **19(3)**, [218]

procedure, **19(3)**, [218]

uniform amount, **19(3)**, [210]

chargeable property, meaning, **19(3)**, [247]

differential rates, order, **19(3)**, [207]

enforcement of payment, proceedings, **19(3)**, [223]

errors in, amendment of, **19(3)**, [219]

exemption orders, **19(3)**, [216]

hereditament, registers of, **19(3)**, [221]

information, power to require, **19(3)**, [222]

levying of, **19(3)**, [209]

making of, procedure, **19(3)**, [217]

notice to be given of, **19(3)**, [217]

proceedings for recovery of, **19(3)**, [223]

special levies, **19(3)**, [207]

dredging

allowances. *See* **dredging allowances**

contributions, exclusion of, **43(1)**, [1170]

dredging—*contd*
meaning, **43(1)**, [1121]

dredging allowances
availability of, **43(1)**, [1121]
balancing allowances, entitlement to,
43(1), [1125]
contribution allowances, **43(1)**, [1180]
giving effect to, **43(1)**, [1126]
qualifying expenditure, meaning,
43(1), [1122]
qualifying trade, meaning, **43(1)**, [1121]
pre-trading expenditure, **43(1)**, [1123]
transitional provisions, **43(1)**, [1231]
writing-down, entitlement to, **43(1)**, [1124]

drink
driving under influence of. *See* **road traffic offences**

drinking banning orders
appeals, **12(4)**, [223]
approved courses—
approval of, **12(4)**, [225]
completion of, **12(4)**, [215], [226]
breach of, **12(4)**, [224]
county court proceedings, in—
application for, **12(4)**, [217]
consultation, **12(4)**, [217]
variation or discharge of, **12(4)**, [218]
criminal proceedings, on conviction in—
addition to other sentence or order, in,
12(4), [220]
conditions for, **12(4)**, [219]
evidence as to, **12(4)**, [220]
taking effect, **12(4)**, [220]
variation or discharge of, **12(4)**, [221]
duration, **12(4)**, [215]
interim, **12(4)**, [222]
interpretation, **12(4)**, [227]
magistrates' court, on application to—
conditions for, **12(4)**, [216]
variation or discharge of, **12(4)**, [218]
meaning, **12(4)**, [214]
prohibitions imposed by, **12(4)**, [215]

drinking fountains
streets or public places, provision in,
35(1), [93]

driver information systems
apparatus—
Crown or Duchy land, installation on,
38(1), [147]
installation, **38(1)**, [147]
other person's structure or apparatus, fixing
to, **38(1)**, [147]
undertakers' works affecting. *See*
undertakers' works *below*
authorisation, **38(1)**, [143]
meaning, **36**, [1381]; **38(1)**, [143]
offences, **38(1)**, [144], [146], [149], [154]
bodies corporate, by, **38(1)**, [149]
operating outside area, **38(1)**, [146]

driver information systems—*contd*
operators as statutory undertakers, **36**, [1231],
[1303]
operators' licence—
application of other Acts, **38(1)**, [148],
[153]
conditions, **38(1)**, [145]
duration, **38(1)**, [145]
grant, **38(1)**, [145]
payments, **38(1)**, [145]
requirement, **38(1)**, [144]
revocation or suspension, **38(1)**, [146]
regulations and orders, power to make,
38(1), [150]
scaffolding on highways, **36**, [1231]
undertakers' works affecting—
definitions, **38(1)**, [154]
execution, **38(1)**, [154]
notices and counter notices, **38(1)**, [154]
offences arising, **38(1)**, [154]
regulation of, **38(1)**, [150], [154]

drivers' hours
agricultural vehicles, provisions inapplicable,
36, [812]
authorised person, power to prohibit driving
of vehicle, **36**, [830]
Community Recording Equipment. *See*
recording equipment *below*
Community rules and regulations, **36**, [812],
[813]
control over, **36**, [811]
Crown, application of provisions, **36**, [835]
documents, inspection of, **36**, [823]
domestic drivers' hours code—
contravention of requirements, **36**, [812]
meaning, **36**, [812]
regulations as to, **36**, [811]
driver, meaning, **36**, [811]
drivers subject to control, **36**, [811]
driving of vehicle, prohibition—
duration of, **36**, [831]
failure to comply with, **36**, [832]
immobilisation, **38(2)**, [534]
power of, **36**, [830]
removal and disposal of vehicles,
38(2), [534]
removal of, **36**, [831]
emergency and special needs, **36**, [812]
examiners—
appointment, **37**, [649]
inspections by, **36**, [823]
exemptions—
agricultural vehicles, **36**, [812]
armed forces, **36**, [835]
defence vehicles, **36**, [835]
fire brigades, **36**, [835]
police, **36**, [835]
false statement, making, **36**, [823]
forestry vehicles, provisions inapplicable,
36, [812]
instructors and instruction businesses,
registration, **38(2)**, [535]
international agreements, **36**, [833]
interpretation, **36**, [839]

drivers' hours—*contd*
　modifications, orders, power to make,
　　36, [812]
　obstruction of examiner, **36**, [823]
　offences—
　　bodies corporate, by, **36**, [838]
　　partnerships, by, **36**, [837]
　　unincorporated associations, by, **36**, [837]
　orders, **36**, [812], [834]
　owner-drivers, **36**, [811]
　periods of duty, **36**, [812]
　permitted driving time, **36**, [812]
　recording equipment—
　　contravention of provisions, **36**, [812],
　　　[813]
　　data relating to—
　　　documents, seizure of, **36**, [829]
　　　false, recording, **36**, [828]
　　　inspection of, **36**, [824]
　　documents relating to, inspection of,
　　　36, [824]
　　driver cards, data downloaded from—
　　　access to, **36**, [821]
　　　hard copies of, driver to sign, **36**, [826]
　　　inspection of, **36**, [824]
　　　offences, **36**, [820]
　　　requirements as to, **36**, [819]
　　　retention of, **36**, [826]
　　　time limits, **36**, [818]
　　evidence, use of records in, **36**, [815]
　　forgery, alteration etc of seals, **36**, [814]
　　inspection of—
　　　obstruction of officer, **36**, [827]
　　　powers of entry for, **36**, [825]
　　　requirements for, non-compliance with,
　　　　36, [827]
　　installation, **36**, [813]
　　meaning, **36**, [813]
　　vehicle units, data downloaded from—
　　　access to, **36**, [821]
　　　offences, **36**, [820]
　　　requirements as to, **36**, [819]
　　　time limits, **36**, [817]
　records—
　　evidence, use in, **36**, [815]
　　inspection of, **36**, [823], [824]
　　sheets and printouts, delivery of, **36**, [816]
　　written, **36**, [822]
　regulations, **36**, [822], [834]
　rest intervals, **36**, [812]
　small goods vehicles—
　　exemptions, **36**, [822]
　　meaning, **36**, [839]
　summary of provisions, **36**, [210]
　supplementary provisions, **36**, [839]
　tramcars and trolley vehicles, exclusion,
　　36, [836]
　working day and working week, meanings,
　　36, [839]

driving instruction
　badge, use of, **37**, [745]
　definitions, **37**, [729]

driving instruction—*contd*
　disabled instructors—
　　emergency control assessment—
　　　application for, **37**, [730], [741]
　　　certificate, **37**, [729]
　　　　revocation, **37**, [741]
　　examination, **37**, [729]
　　further disability, disclosure, **37**, [742]
　　paid instruction, giving, **37**, [743]
　　practical experience, licence to obtain,
　　　37, [735]
　　registration—
　　　application for, **37**, [729], [730]
　　　conditions attaching, **37**, [727]
　　　grant, **37**, [729]
　disabled persons—
　　emergency vehicle control—
　　　assessment, **37**, [740]
　　　certificate—
　　　　grant, **37**, [740]
　　　　revocation, **37**, [741]
　　　further assessment, **37**, [741]
　　further disability, disclosure, **37**, [742]
　driver training courses—
　　compulsory, **37**, [688]
　　regulations, **37**, [690]
　　requirement to complete, **37**, [689]
　examination of instructor—
　　disabled instructor, **37**, [729]
　　licence, for, **37**, [735]
　　regulations, **37**, [738]
　　review of, **37**, [739]
　　test assistant present at, **37**, [779]
　fees etc, application of, **37**, [750]
　free of charge, **37**, [725]
　index of expressions used, **37**, [753]
　instructors and instruction businesses,
　　registration, **38(2)**, [535]
　licence to give—
　　application for, **37**, [727]
　　certificate, evidence in proceedings,
　　　38(1), [17]
　　duration, **37**, [731]
　　exhibition of, **37**, [725]
　　experience, to obtain, **37**, [735]
　　production to authorised person, **37**, [747]
　　refusal, **37**, [727]
　　requirement, **37**, [725]
　　revocation, **37**, [736], [744]
　　surrender of, **37**, [746]
　motor car, meaning, **37**, [752]
　notices, service of, **37**, [749]
　offences—
　　corporations, by, **37**, [748]
　　evidence in proceedings, **38(1)**, [17]
　　misuse of badge, certificate, etc, **37**, [745]
　　production of certificate or licence,
　　　failure, **37**, [747]
　　unregistered or unlicensed, by, **37**, [725]
　paid, **37**, [725]
　payment for, requirements, **37**, [725]
　police instructors, **37**, [726]
　practical experience, licence for gaining,
　　37, [735]
　qualification for giving, **37**, [725]

driving instruction—*contd*
  register—
    compilation and maintenance, **37**, [727]
      Northern Ireland, **37**, [727]
    entry in—
      alteration of conditions, **37**, [744]
      application for, **37**, [727]
      removal from, **37**, [731], [733], [744]
      re-entry after, **37**, [733]
    retention of name on, **37**, [731]
  registration of instructors—
    appeals against decisions, **37**, [737]
    application for, **37**, [727]
      evidence in proceedings, **38(1)**, [17]
    certificate—
      exhibition of, **37**, [725]
      form, **37**, [745]
      production to authorised person,
        37, [747]
      surrender, **37**, [746]
    conditions—
      alteration, powers, **37**, [744]
      generally, **37**, [727], [728]
    disabled instructor, **37**, [729]
    duration of—
      application for retention, **37**, [731]
      extension of, **37**, [732]
    necessity for, **37**, [725]
    qualification, **37**, [727]
    refusal, **37**, [732], [734]
    termination of, **37**, [734]
  regulations generally, power to make,
    37, [751]
  summary of provisions, **36**, [210]
  test of ability. *See* examination *above*
  title, use of, **37**, [745]

driving licence
  address on, incorrect, **37**, [687]
  age, requirement as to, **37**, [687], [697], [781]
    disqualification, persons under age,
      37, [697]
    table, **37**, [697]
  appeals relating to, **37**, [696]
  application for, **37**, [684]
    qualifying, **37**, [673]
  armed forces, exercise of functions as to,
    37, [799]
  British external licence—
    meaning, **37**, [673]
    possession, **37**, [673], [674]
    surrender, **37**, [684]
  British forces licence—
    meaning, **37**, [673]
    possession, **37**, [673], [674]
    surrender, **37**, [684]
  bus service vehicles, **37**, [373]
  classes of vehicles authorised, **37**, [674], [687]
  Community licence—
    counterpart, **37**, [692]
    meaning, **37**, [705]

driving licence—*contd*
  Community licence holder—
    authorisation to drive in Great Britain,
      37, [691]
      disability, revocation because of,
        37, [693], [694]
    disabilities, information relating to,
      37, [694]
    disqualification, **38(1)**, [111]
    endorsement of counterpart of licence,
      38(1), [112]
    foreign offence, production in relation to,
      38(2), [278]
    provisions applying to, **38(1)**, [111]
    resident, information about, **37**, [692]
    return of, **37**, [695]
  competence. *See* test *below*
  compulsory surrender of old-form, **37**, [686]
  counterpart, meaning, **37**, [705]
  Crown, application of provisions, **37**, [799]
  definitions, **37**, [705]
  disability—
    declaration of, **37**, [678]
    disclosure of, **37**, [678]
    information relating to, **37**, [694]
      revocation of licence, **37**, [693]
    information as to, provision of, **37**, [680]
    notice by Secretary of State arising from,
      37, [678]
    prospective, **37**, [679]
    provisional licence in case of, **37**, [684]
    revocation of licence because of, **37**, [679]
  disqualification—
    any offence, for, **12(2)**, [823]
    duplication of licences, prevention of,
      37, [698]
    generally, **37**, [673]
    large goods vehicles, **37**, [718]
    Northern Ireland, etc, in, **37**, [699]
    obtaining licence while disqualified,
      37, [700]
    offences outside UK. *See* **offences**
    passenger-carrying vehicles, **37**, [718]
    persons under age, **37**, [697]
    surrender of licence on, **37**, [687]
    vehicle used for crime, where, **12(2)**, [824]
    See also **offences**
  driving without, **37**, [672]
  duplication, prevention of, **37**, [698]
  duration, **37**, [687]
  endorsement—
    all drivers, **38(2)**, [501]
    Community licence holder, **38(1)**, [112]
    counterpart of licence, fixed penalty,
      payment of conditional offer, **38(1)**, [86]
    driving record—
      fixed penalty, payment of conditional
        offer, **38(1)**, [87]
      meaning, **38(1)**, [118]
    large goods vehicles, **37**, [720]
    Northern Ireland licence holder,
      38(1), [110]
    offences outside UK, **38(2)**, [281], [282]
    passenger carrying vehicles, **37**, [720]
    penalty points, **38(1)**, [65]

driving licence—*contd*
  endorsement—*contd*
    See also *under* **road traffic offences**
    error, issued in, **37**, [687]
    exchangeable licence—
      as driving licence, **37**, [674]
      meaning, **37**, [705]
      possession, **37**, [673], [674]
      surrender, **37**, [684]
    eyesight, defective, driving with, **37**, [683]
    fees, destination of, **37**, [703]
    foreign authorities, disclosure of information
      to, **38(2)**, [523]
    foreign offence, production in relation to—
      Community licence, **38(2)**, [278]
      Great Britain, **38(2)**, [276]
      Northern Ireland, **38(2)**, [277]
    forgery, **37**, [791]
    form of, **37**, [685]
    full, grant of, **38(2)**, [515]
    grant of, **37**, [684]
      classes and groups of vehicles, **37**, [674]
      test of competence, after, **37**, [674], [675]
    heavy goods and public service vehicles—
      existing licences, special provisions,
        38(1), [141]
      special licences, abolition, **38(1)**, [140]
    information, disclosure of, **12(3)**, [610]
    insurance refused, notification, **37**, [682]
    large goods vehicles and passenger-carrying
      vehicles—
      age of driver, **37**, [714]
      appeals, **37**, [721]
      applicants—
        attendance before commissioners,
          37, [713]
        conduct of. See conduct *below*
        information, supply of, **37**, [713]
      Community licence holders, **37**, [716]
      conditions, **37**, [714]
      conduct of applicants—
        fitness of, **37**, [712]
          referral of matters as to, **37**, [713]
        meaning of conduct, **37**, [723]
        traffic commissioners—
          functions, **37**, [711]
          referral of matters to, **37**, [713], [717]
      definitions, **37**, [710], [723]
      disqualification—
        appeal against, **37**, [721]
        Community licence holder, of, **37**, [719]
        removal of, **37**, [718]
        revocation of licence, on, **37**, [718]
      disqualified, meaning, **37**, [718]
      endorsement, **37**, [720]
      grant of, **37**, [710]
        failure or refusal, **37**, [713]
          appeals, **37**, [721]
        Northern Ireland, provisions as to,
          37, [724]
      provisional, **37**, [714]
      refusal, appeal against, **37**, [721]
      regulations, **37**, [722]
      revocation, **37**, [715]
        appeal against, **37**, [721]

driving licence—*contd*
  large goods vehicles and passenger-carrying
    vehicles—*contd*
    revocation—*contd*
      disqualification on, **37**, [718]
      referral to commissioners, **37**, [717]
      surrender of licence on, **37**, [720]
    suspension, **37**, [715]
      appeal against, **37**, [721]
      referral to commissioners, **37**, [717]
      surrender of licence on, **37**, [720]
    traffic commissioners—
      functions, **37**, [711]
      matters of conduct, referral to,
        37, [713], [717]
  limited, **37**, [678]
  meaning, **12(2)**, [823]
  motor cycles—
    provisional licence. See provisional *below*
    regulations as to, **37**, [684]
    training in driving, **37**, [674], [684]
  newly qualified drivers—
    fixed penalty offence, **38(1)**, [508]
    full and provisional licence, with—
      re-testing, **38(1)**, [520]
      revocation, **38(1)**, [520]
      surrender, **38(1)**, [520]
    offence, effect of committing, **38(1)**, [508]
    probationary period, **38(1)**, [507]
      early termination, **38(1)**, [513]
    provisional licence and test certificate,
      with—
      re-testing, **38(1)**, [519]
      revocation of certificate, **38(1)**, [519]
      surrender of certificate, **38(1)**, [519]
    provisions—
      application to Crown, **38(1)**, [514]
      interpretation, **38(1)**, [515]
    regulations, **38(1)**, [521]
    revocation, **38(1)**, [509]
      appeal, **38(1)**, [511]
      re-testing on, **38(1)**, [510]
      restoration, **38(1)**, [511]
    surrender, **38(1)**, [508]
    test certificate—
      holding, provisions applicable,
        38(1), [517]
      meaning, **38(1)**, [517]
      provision, duty as to, **38(1)**, [518]
      re-testing, **38(1)**, [510], [519]
      revocation, **38(1)**, [519]
      surrender of, **38(1)**, [519], [520]
    when becoming, **38(1)**, [507]
  Northern Ireland, granted in—
    endorsement, effect of, **38(1)**, [110]
    large goods and passenger carrying
      vehicles, **37**, [724]
    licence, possession of, **37**, [674]
    motor vehicles, **37**, [706]
    provisions applying, **38(1)**, [109]
    notices, service of, **37**, [704]
  old-form—
    compulsory surrender of, **37**, [686]
    surrender of, **38(2)**, [516]

driving licence—*contd*
  passenger-carrying vehicles. *See* large goods
    vehicles, etc *above*
  photocards, **37**, [685]
  physical fitness—
    declaration, **37**, [678]
    insurance, refusal of, **37**, [682]
    requirements, **37**, [678]
  production required by constable or
    examiner, **37**, [781], [786]
    failure in, **37**, [781]
  provisional—
    disability, in case of, **37**, [684]
    form, **37**, [685]
    grant of, **37**, [684]
    large goods vehicles, **37**, [714]
    motor cycles, training and tests, **37**, [674],
      [684]
    motor cyclists, **37**, [687]
    newly qualified driver. *See* newly qualified
      above
    passenger-carrying vehicles, **37**, [714]
    refusal, **37**, [684]
    supervising driver, particulars required after
      offence, **37**, [782]
  public service vehicles. *See* heavy goods and
    public service vehicles *above*
  records, access to, **12(2)**, [1000]
  refusal of—
    disability, on grounds of, **37**, [673], [678]
    driving after, **37**, [681]
    requirement, **37**, [672]
      alternative, **37**, [675]
      exceptions, **37**, [673]
  revocation, **37**, [687]
    disability, on grounds of, **37**, [679]
    driving after, **37**, [681]
    newly qualified driver, in case of,
      38(1), [509], [520]
  special licences, abolition, **38(1)**, [140]
  surrender, **37**, [687]
    newly qualified driver, in case of,
      38(1), [508], [520]
  test of competence—
    certificate—
      production of, power to obtain,
        37, [782]
      surrender by newly qualified driver,
        38(1), [519]
    classes and groups of vehicles, **37**, [674]
    court order for, **38(1)**, [42]
    disability—
      declaration of, **37**, [678]
      persons suffering from, **37**, [678], [680]
    disqualification, after, **38(1)**, [42]
    exchangeable licence, possession, **37**, [674]
    failing of, **37**, [674]
    fees—
      destination of, **37**, [703]
      regulations, **37**, [674]
      repayment, **37**, [677]
    heavy goods vehicle driver, **37**, [675]
    motor cyclists, required by, **37**, [674], [687]
    necessity for, **37**, [674]

driving licence—*contd*
  test of competence—*contd*
    newly qualified driver. *See* newly qualified
      above
    Northern Ireland, passing in, **37**, [674],
      [675]
    other licences, possession, **37**, [674]
    provision of vehicle, **37**, [674]
    provisional licence, provisions applicable,
      37, [674]
    public service vehicle, **37**, [675]
    regulations, **37**, [674]
    requirement, **37**, [674]
      alternative, **37**, [675]
      exemptions, **37**, [674]
    review of conduct of test, **37**, [676]
    test assistant present at, **37**, [779]
  vehicle driven without, power to seize,
    37, [783]
    retention, **37**, [784]

driving offences. *See* **road traffic offences**

droits of Admiralty
  colonial courts, **11(2)**, [130]

drought
  permits, **49**, [1138]
  plans, water undertakers' duty to prepare and
    review, **49**, [802]
  shortage, orders for meeting—
    abstractions and discharges, provisions as
      to, **49**, [1135]
    application for, **49**, [1132]
    charges, **49**, [1137]
    contents of, **49**, [1132]
    damage caused by, compensation,
      49, [1137], [1277]
    duration, **49**, [1132]
    emergency, in—
      duration, **49**, [1133]
      power to make, **49**, [1131]
      provisions of, **49**, [1133]
      works under, **49**, [1136]
    land, entry on, **49**, [1136]
    offences, **49**, [1139]
    power to make, **49**, [1131]
    proceedings on application for, **49**, [1276]
    provisions of, **49**, [1132]
    use of water, restricting, **49**, [1134]
    works under, **49**, [1136]
  Thames Water Authority, protection,
    49, [140], [243]

Drouly fund
  hospital bequest, vesting, **3**, [26]
  originating will, **3**, [29]
  powers of attorney, **3**, [28]
  transfer of, **3**, [25], [27]

drug abstinence order
  breach, revocation and amendment. *See*
    community orders

drug dependence
not considered as mental disorder, **29**, [23]

drug trafficking
arrest, delay in notifying, **12(1)**, [989]
See also **money laundering**
Commissioners for HM Revenue and
Customs—
enforcement powers, transfer of,
12(2), [168]
prosecutions by order of, **12(2)**, [264]
ships, enforcement of provisions against,
12(2), [25], [26]
confiscation of proceeds. *See under* proceeds
below
confiscation order, external—
enforcement, **12(2)**, [256]
registration, **12(2)**, [257]
Crown servants, extension of offences to,
12(2), [265]
investigation into—
information by government departments,
12(2), [262]
material, order to produce, **12(2)**, [258]
prejudicing, offence of, **12(2)**, [261]
search warrant, **12(2)**, [259]
supplementary provisions, **12(2)**, [260]
legislation, **12(1)**, [1]
meaning, **12(2)**, [263], [266]
offences—
British ships, on, **12(2)**, [25]
meaning of, **28**, [572]
sea, at, **12(2)**, [25]
scheduled substances—
manufacture of, **28**, [567]
regulations about, **28**, [568]
supply of, **28**, [567]
tables of, **28**, [574]
Vienna Convention, **28**, [567], [568]
sea, offence at—
British ship, on, **28**, [570]
enforcement powers, **28**, [570], [575]
illicit traffic, ship used for, **28**, [569]
jurisdiction, **28**, [571]
prosecutions, **28**, [571]
Vienna Convention, **28**, [569]–[571]
ship, offences on—
application of provisions, **12(2)**, [25]
divert and detain, powers, **12(2)**, [32]
enforcement powers, **12(2)**, [26]
force, use by enforcement officer,
12(2), [32]
information, power to obtain, **12(2)**, [32]
jurisdiction, **12(2)**, [27]
meaning of ship, **12(2)**, [28]
nature and punishment, **12(2)**, [32]
officers, protection of, **12(2)**, [32]
prosecutions, **12(2)**, [27]
search, power to, **12(2)**, [32]
stop and board, powers, **12(2)**, [32]
suspected, **12(2)**, [32]
territorial waters, powers within,
12(2), [27]
suspected offenders, remand of, **11(3)**, [64]

drug trafficking—*contd*
third class A offence, minimum sentence for,
12(2), [801]
appeal, previous conviction set aside on,
12(2), [803]
certificate of conviction, **12(2)**, [804]
day of offence, determination of,
12(2), [806]
service law, conviction under, **12(2)**, [805]
transitional provisions, **12(2)**, [268], [272]
travel restriction order—
contravention of, **12(3)**, [20]
meaning, **12(3)**, [17]
offences to which relating, **12(3)**, [18]
power to make, **12(3)**, [17]
power to remove person from UK, saving
for, **12(3)**, [21]
revocation, **12(3)**, [19]
suspension, **12(3)**, [19]

drug treatment and testing order
amendment, **12(2)**, [846]
breach and revocation of. *See* **community
orders**

druggists. *See also* **pharmaceutical chemist**
saving for, **28**, [347]
titles and emblems, restrictions on use,
28, [137], [138]

drugs. *See also* **drug trafficking; poisons**
abortion, to procure, **12(1)**, [99]
armed forces, testing for—
definitions, **3(S)**, 279
obtaining and analysis of samples,
3(S), 279–80
power of, **3(S)**, 276–7
serious incident, after, **3(S)**, 277–8
cannabis, meaning, **28**, [232]
cannabis resin, meaning, **28**, [232]
Class A—
assessment of misuse of—
bail provisions, relationship with,
12(4), [160]
disclosure of information about,
12(4), [158]
follow-up, **12(4)**, [153], [156], [157]
further analysis, samples submitted for,
12(4), [159]
initial, **12(4)**, [152], [155]
interpretation, **12(4)**, [162]
notice, **12(4)**, [154]
orders and guidance, **12(4)**, [161]
record of, **12(4)**, [154]
requirement to attend, **12(4)**, [154]
drugs being, **28**, [199], [237]
punishment of offences relating to,
28, [223], [245]
testing for presence of, **12(1)**, [913], [914];
12(4), [151]
trigger offences, **12(2)**, [1012]
Class B—
drugs being, **28**, [199], [238]
punishment of offences relating to,
28, [223], [245]

drugs—*contd*
  Class C—
    drugs being, **28**, [199], [239]
    punishment of offences relating to,
      28, [223], [245]
  controlled—
    administration of, illegal, **28**, [208]
    articles for administering or preparing,
      prohibition of supply, etc, **28**, [208]
    cannabis—
      cultivation of—
        authorisation of, **28**, [205]
        restriction on, **28**, [204]
      meaning, **28**, [232]
      use of premises for smoking, offence of
        permitting, **28**, [206]
    classification, **28**, [199], [237]–[239]
    convicted practitioner or pharmacist,
      prohibition on dealing with, **28**, [211]
    disposing of unwanted, **28**, [209]
    documentation of transactions involving,
      28, [209]
    entry to premises, powers of, **28**, [222],
      [844], [845]
    exemptions from control, **28**, [205]
    exportation, restriction on, **28**, [200]
    importation, restriction on, **28**, [200]
    inspection of books and documents relating
      to, **28**, [222]
    licence—
      dealing with, **28**, [200], [246]
      importation or exportation, for,
        28, [200]
      provisions as to, **28**, [227]
    management and use, supervision of—
      accountable officers, **28**, [841]
      Crown, provisions binding, **28**, [847]
      guidance on, **28**, [846]
      health bodies and other organisations,
        co-operation between, **28**, [842]
      interpretation, **28**, [849]
      powers of entry on premises, **28**, [844]
      relevant authorities, **28**, [848]
      relevant person, meaning, **28**, [843]
    meaning of, **28**, [199], [237]–[240]
    offences as to, **28**, [201]–[203],
      [206]–[208], [211]
      body corporate, by, **28**, [855]
      partnerships, by, **28**, [856]
      penalties, **28**, [857]
      unincorporated associations, by,
        28, [856]
    opium—
      smoking—
        offences connected with, **28**, [206],
          [207]
        use of premises in connection with,
          offence of permitting, **28**, [206]
    orders and regulations, **28**, [858]
    packaging and labelling, **28**, [209]
    pharmacist, convicted, prohibition on
      dealing with, **28**, [211]
    possession of—
      authorisation of, **28**, [205]
      restriction on, **28**, [203], [205]

drugs—*contd*
  controlled—*contd*
    practitioner prescribing, supplying, etc—
      directions prohibiting—
        advisory body—
          constitution, etc, **28**, [213], [215],
            [242]
          reference of case to, **28**, [213]
        cancelling, **28**, [211], [215]
        ceasing to have effect, **28**, [215]
        contravention of regulations, where,
          28, [212]
        conviction of practitioner, where,
          28, [211], [246]
        irresponsible supply, **28**, [212]
        professional panel—
          constitution, etc, **28**, [214], [215],
            [243]
          reference of case to, **28**, [214]
        suspension, **28**, [211], [215]
        temporary, **28**, [214]
        tribunal—
          constitution, etc, **28**, [213], [215],
            [241]
          reference of case to,
            28, [213]–[215]
      information, requirement to furnish,
        28, [216]
      practitioner, meaning, **28**, [232]
    prescriptions, **28**, [209]
    production—
      authorisation of, **28**, [205]
      restriction on, **28**, [201], [205]
      use of premises for, liability of occupier
        for permitting, **28**, [206]
    records and information on, **28**, [209]
    reference to, **12(3)**, [634]
    safe custody of, **28**, [210]
    scheduled substances—
      manufacture of, **28**, [567]
      regulations about, **28**, [568]
      supply of, **28**, [567]
      tables of, **28**, [574]
      Vienna Convention, **28**, [567], [568]
    search of persons and premises, **28**, [222]
    supply of—
      aggravation of offence, **28**, [202]
      authorisation of, **28**, [205]
      intention, proof of, **28**, [838]
      restriction on, **28**, [201], [205]
      use of premises for, liability of occupier
        for permitting, **28**, [206]
    transport of, **28**, [209]
  dispensing, units of measurement,
    39(1), [484]
  driving under influence of. *See* **road traffic
    offences**
  meaning, **37**, [578]
  misuse—
    addiction regulations—
      meaning, **28**, [246]
      saving for, **28**, [246]
    Advisory Council on—
      committees of, **28**, [236]
      constitution, **28**, [198], [236]

drugs—*contd*
  misuse—*contd*
    Advisory Council on—*contd*
      duties, **28**, [198]
      documents—
        production and seizure, **28**, [222]
        service, **28**, [226]
      extensive, information for practitioners or pharmacists where, **28**, [216]
      financial provisions, **28**, [230]
      misusing, construction of references to, **28**, [232]
      offences—
        body corporate, by, **28**, [220]
        connected with, **28**, [201], [206]–[208], [211]–[213], [217]–[220], [222]
        defence to proceedings, proof of lack of knowledge as, **28**, [225]
        enforcement provisions, **28**, [222]
        entry, powers of, **28**, [222]
        evidence of, **28**, [222]
        forfeiture on conviction, **28**, [224]
        incitement to commit, **28**, [218]
        outside UK, assisting or inducing commission of, **28**, [219]
        prosecution and punishment, **28**, [223], [245]
        search, powers of, **28**, [222]
      regulations as to, **28**, [209], [221], [228], [246]
      research into, **28**, [229]
      savings and transitional provisions, **28**, [234], [246]
      Single Convention on Narcotic Drugs, **28**, [231]
      social problems arising from, **28**, [198], [216]
    misuse of, grants to combat, **12(2)**, [172]
    premises where used unlawfully—
      clearing, securing or maintaining, reimbursement of costs, **12(3)**, [631]
      closed—
        access to other premises, **12(3)**, [630]
        meaning, **12(3)**, [634]
      closure notice—
        appeals, **12(3)**, [629]
        contents of, **12(3)**, [624]
        financial loss, compensation for, **12(3)**, [633]
        making, **12(3)**, [624]
        offences, **12(3)**, [627]
        service of, **12(3)**, [624]
      closure order—
        appeals, **12(3)**, [629]
        application for, **12(3)**, [625]
        discharge, **12(3)**, [628]
        enforcement, **12(3)**, [626]
        extension, **12(3)**, [628]
        financial loss, compensation for, **12(3)**, [633]
        making, **12(3)**, [625]
        meaning, **12(3)**, [634]
      damages, exemption of police from liability, **12(3)**, [632]

drugs—*contd*
    trafficking in. *See* **drug trafficking**
    ultrasound scan to detect, **12(1)**, [903]
    x-rays to detect, **12(1)**, [903]

drugs authority
    enforcement of Medicines Act 1968 by, **28**, [165]
    meaning, **28**, [165]
    microbiological examinations, provision of facilities for, **28**, [172]

drunkard
    habitual, prohibition on sale of liquor to, **19(3)**, [362]
    obtaining alcohol for, **19(3)**, [631]
    sale of alcohol to, **19(3)**, [630]

drunkenness. *See also* **road traffic offences** (drink or drugs)
    air force, **3**, [770]
    army, **3**, [497]
    child, in charge of, **19(3)**, [361]
    drunk person, supplying firearms to, **12(1)**, [501]
    hackney carriage driver, **36**, [217], [410]
    highway, in, **19(3)**, [355], [359]
    licensed premises, on, **19(3)**, [359]
    Licensing Acts, applied, **19(3)**, [359]
    navy, **3**, [1041]
    penalties, **19(3)**, [355], [359]
      increase, **19(3)**, [370]
    public place, in, **12(1)**, [396]
      apprehension, **19(3)**, [360]
      penalties, **19(3)**, [355], [359]
        increase, **19(3)**, [370]
    refreshment house, penalty for permitting in, **19(3)**, [350]
    sporting events, at, **12(1)**, [982]
    street offences, **36**, [228], [386]
    treatment centre, taking offender to, **12(1)**, [610]

Dublin Gazette
    royal proclamations in, **10**, [458]

Duchy land. *See* **Crown lands**
    coast protection work, application of provisions, **49**, [389], [410]
    pollution by sea, deposits etc, in, **49**, [637]

Duchy of Lancaster
    funds, investment of, **48**, 575

Duke of Cornwall
    manors, courts held for, **11(2)**, [381]

Duke of Edinburgh
    civil list provision, **10**, [215]
    Regent, to be, **10**, [229]

dumped goods
    customs duty on—
      additional to other duties, **13**, [588]
      ECSC products, in relation to, **13**, [588]

dumping at sea. *See* **pollution (sea)**

duplex querela
abolition of, **14**, 611

Durham, County of
bishopric interests, **10**, [128]
definition, **10**, [127]
foreshores, rents and proceeds, division of, **10**, [128]

dust
furnace, from. *See* **furnace**
nuisances from, byelaws for prevention of, **35(1)**, [133]

dustbins. *See also* **refuse**
charge for, **35(1)**, [248], [305]
infectious matter, prohibition on placing in, **35(1)**, [467]
meaning, **35(1)**, [216], [514]
requirements as to, **35(1)**, [305]

dwelling house. *See also* **house; housing**
agricultural. *See* **agricultural workers**
assignment, restriction on, **22**, [83]
assured tenancy of. *See* **assured tenancy**
City, in. *See* **London, City of**
coal mining subsidence, damage due to. *See* **coal mining subsidence**
common parts—
  grants for improvement or repair of, **46**, [228]
  meaning, **22**, [108]
defective. *See* **defective housing**
demoted tenancy. *See* **demoted tenancy**
depreciation in value through use of public works, **9**, [305], [311]
displacement from, home loss payment for. *See* **home loss payment**
disposal of—
  housing action trust, by, repayment of discount, **24**, [365]
  local authority, by, repayment of discount, **24**, [363]
energy efficiency, grants for, **40(1)**, [1], [214]
heating. *See* **heat, supply of**
improvement. *See* **improvement**
land and premises let with, including, **21**, [547]
land let with, treatment of, **22**, [204]
land treated as part of, **22**, [103]
meaning, **9**, [367]; **17(2)**, [46]; **21**, [379], [484]; **22**, [103], [203], [340], [494]; **23**, [410], [445], [464]
opencast coal working, protection, **17(1)**, [169]
overcrowded, possession of, **21**, [601]
owner, meaning, **22**, [340]; **23**, [610]
possession, action by mortgagee for possession, **21**, [377], [413]
professional, etc, services, provision of, **23**, [42]
protected tenancy of. *See* **protected tenancy**
registration of title, **22**, [162]

dwelling house—*contd*
rent or mortgage terms, acquisition on, duty, **41**, [223]
right to acquire on rent to mortgage terms—
  conveyance—
    duty of landlord, **22**, [154]
    terms and effect of, **22**, [155]
  deferred resale agreements, treatment of, **22**, [176]
  difficulty in exercising, **22**, [177]
  discount—
    amount landlord may demand, **22**, [165]
    cessation of liability to repay, **22**, [174]
    early disposal, repayment on, **22**, [163]
    initial—
      determination of, **22**, [152]
      notice of, **22**, [151]
    liability for as charge on premises, **22**, [167]
  disposals—
    compulsory, **22**, [173]
    exempted, **22**, [172]
    options, treatment of, **22**, [175]
    relevant, **22**, [171]
  exclusion of—
    entitlement to housing benefit, by, **22**, [145]
    minimum initial payment exceeding maximum initial payment, where, **22**, [146]
  exercise of—
    circumstances prohibiting, **22**, [145]
    claiming, **22**, [144]
  landlord's notices—
    admitting or denying claim, **22**, [148]
    complete, to—
      first, **22**, [158]
      second, **22**, [159]
    default, in, **22**, [150]
    initial discount, of, **22**, [151]
    landlord's share, of, **22**, [151]
  landlord's share—
    determination of, **22**, [152]
    notice of, **22**, [151]
    redemption of, **22**, [156]
    mortgage securing, **22**, [157]
  lease, grant of—
    duty of landlord, **22**, [154]
    terms and effect of, **22**, [155]
  registration of title, **22**, [162], [443]
    vesting order, on, **22**, [178]
  rent attributable to purchase price, payments of, **22**, [161]
  secure tenant, of, **22**, [144]
  tenant's notices—
    claiming right, **22**, [147]
      change of landlord after, **22**, [153]
    delay, of, **22**, [160]
    intention, of, **22**, [149]
  termination of, **22**, [143]
  treatment of options, **23**, [357]
right to buy—
  admission by landlord, **22**, [119]
  amended provisions, **46**, [224]

dwelling house—*contd*
  right to buy—*contd*
    anti-social behaviour, suspended in case
      of, **22**, [114]; **24**, [361]
    areas of natural beauty, in, **22**, [169];
      23, [356]
    change of tenant or landlord, **22**, [134],
      [135]
    charges for conveyance etc, **22**, [441]
    common use of facilities, **22**, [440]
    completion of purchase—
      deferment, abolition of right to,
        23, [181]
      demolition notice—
        final, effect where served before,
          22, [138]
        initial, effect where served before,
          22, [137]
      first notice to complete, **22**, [141]
      landlord's duty, **22**, [136]
      notice by landlord for, **22**, [141], [142]
      second notice requiring, **22**, [142]
    conveyance etc—
      common provisions, **22**, [438]
      covenants and conditions, **22**, [438]
      freehold, of, **22**, [439]
      leases, **22**, [440]
      rights of support etc, **22**, [438]
      rights of way, **22**, [438]
      terms and effect, **22**, [140]
      water rights, **22**, [438]
    costs in connection with, **22**, [198]
    county court jurisdiction, **22**, [201]
    covenants—
      discharge of, **22**, [181]
      landlord, by, **22**, [440]
      Minister's directions as to, **22**, [180]
      tenant, by, **22**, [440]
    deferred resale agreements, treatment of,
      22, [176]
    demolition notice—
      claim suspended or terminated by,
        24, [358]
      compensation where served, **22**, [139]
      final, effect where served before
        completion, **22**, [138]
      initial—
        effect where served before
          completion, **22**, [137]
        further, restriction on serving,
          22, [437]
        meaning, **22**, [437]
        revocation or termination of,
          22, [437]
        transfer, **22**, [437]
        validity, period of, **22**, [437]
    denying, notice by landlord, **22**, [119]
    difficulty in exercising, **22**, [177]
    discount—
      amount of—
        home improvements, affecting,
          22, [166]
        landlord may demand, **22**, [164]
        limits on, **22**, [133]
      cessation of liability to repay, **22**, [174]

dwelling house—*contd*
  right to buy—*contd*
    discount—*contd*
      cost floor, variation of, **22**, [904]
      covenant for repayment, **23**, [350]
        charge on house, liability as, **23**, [352]
        deferred resale agreements, treatment
          of, **23**, [359]
        increase in value attributable to home
          improvements disregarded, **23**, [351]
      entitlement to, **22**, [131]
      joint tenants, in case of, **22**, [131]
      liability for as charge on premises,
        22, [167]
      maximum, **22**, [131]
      previous, meaning and effect, **22**, [132]
      priority of charge for repayment,
        23, [353]
      reduction for previous discount,
        22, [132]
      repayment, early disposal, on, **22**, [163]
    disposal after—
      compulsory, meaning, **22**, [173]
      discount, repayment, **22**, [163]
      exempted disposals, **22**, [172]; **23**, [358]
      National Park, houses in, **22**, [169];
        23, [356]
      options, treatment of, **22**, [175];
        23, [357]
      relevant disposals, meaning, **22**, [171];
        23, [358]
      restriction on, **22**, [169]; **23**, [356]
    disposal to private sector landlord,
      preservation on, **46**, [227]
    duty to grant, **22**, [136]
    exception to—
      certain housing associations, **22**, [436]
      charities, **22**, [436]
      Crown tenancies, held on, **22**, [436]
      disabled persons, houses for, **22**, [436]
      employee accommodation, **22**, [436]
      house—
        demolished within 24 months, due to
          be, **22**, [436]
        elderly person, determination whether
          suitable for, **24**, [357]
      persons of pensionable age, **22**, [436]
    exercise of—
      circumstances prohibiting, **22**, [113]
      claim to, **22**, [117]
      information to help tenants decide,
        provision of, **22**, [115], [116]
    extension of, power to order, **22**, [184]
    extent of, **22**, [110]
    first refusal, landlord's right of, **24**, [360]
    freehold—
      determination of price, **22**, [195]
      duty to convey, **22**, [136]
      lease or, **22**, [110]
    joint tenants, in case of, **22**, [110]
    landlord—
      condition, **22**, [435]
      notice—
        improvement contributions, estimates
          and information about, **22**, [122]

dwelling house—*contd*
  right to buy—*contd*
    landlord—*contd*
      notice—*contd*
        purchase price, of, **22**, [120]
        reference period, **22**, [123]
        service charges, estimates and
          information about, **22**, [121]
        structural defects, stating, **22**, [120]
      right of first refusal for, **22**, [168]
        disposal, consideration for, **22**, [170]
      share, redemption of, **22**, [442]
    lease—
      avoidance of certain provisions, **22**, [440]
      charges respecting, **22**, [441]
    leasehold provisions excluded, **22**, [193]
    legal proceedings as to—
      assistance in, **22**, [183]
      costs, **22**, [183]
      jurisdiction in, **22**, [201]
    local Acts, power to repeal, **22**, [202]
    matters to be stated by landlord, **22**, [119]
    members of family, with, **22**, [118], [206]
    mortgage, abolition of right to, **23**, [181]
    National Park, houses in, **22**, [169];
      23, [356]
    notice claiming, **22**, [117]
      change of landlord after, **22**, [135]
      change of tenant after, **22**, [134]
    notices—
      errors and omissions, **22**, [197]
      form of, **22**, [196]
      service of, **22**, [196]
      tenant's, as to intention, landlord's notice
        in default, **22**, [125]
    private sector landlord, preservation on sale
      to—
      alternative accommodation, transfer of
        qualifying person to, **22**, [190]
      cases of, **22**, [185]
      consultations before, **22**, [434]
      disposal of landlord's interest, effect of,
        22, [188]
      generally, **22**, [443]
      modification of provisions, **22**, [187]
      notice claiming right to buy, disposal
        after, **22**, [192]
      qualifying disposal, **22**, [185]
      qualifying dwelling-houses, **22**, [186]
      qualifying persons, **22**, [186]
      termination of landlord's interest, effect
        of, **22**, [189]
    purchase price—
      calculation of, **22**, [126]
      notice of, **22**, [120]
    qualifying period, **22**, [111], [435]

dwelling house—*contd*
  right to buy—*contd*
    registered social landlord, tenant of,
      23, [360]–[362]
    registration of title, **22**, [162], [443]
      vesting order, on, **22**, [178]
    repayment of discount, periods and
      amounts applicable, **24**, [359]
    restriction in lease, avoidance of, **22**, [199]
    Secretary of State—
      assistance by, in legal proceedings,
        22, [183]
      covenants etc, powers as to, **22**, [180]
      further directions by, **22**, [179], [180]
      information, power to obtain, **22**, [182]
      intervention by, **22**, [177]
      vesting order by, **22**, [178]
    secure tenant, notice of intention, **22**, [124]
      landlord's notice in default, **22**, [125]
    service charge loans, **24**, [840]
    service charges etc payable after exercise
      of, **46**, [225]
    sharing of, **22**, [118]
    when right not exercisable, **22**, [113]
  separate dwelling, let as, **21**, [520]
  service charges—
    loans for, **22**, [327]
    statutory declarations, **22**, [200]
    tenant condition, **22**, [435]
    valuation, **22**, [120]
      assumptions in, **22**, [127]
      district valuer, by, **22**, [128]
      improvements disregarded, **22**, [127]
      review notices, **22**, [129]
      review of determination, **22**, [130]
      tenant requiring, **22**, [128]
  shared ownership lease—
    abolition of right to, **23**, [181]
    advances in respect of, **22**, [333], [481]
    costs in connection with, **22**, [198]
    jurisdiction respecting, **22**, [201]
    long lease at low rent, treated as, **22**, [194]
    meaning, **22**, [423], [494]
    notices—
      errors and omissions, **22**, [197]
      form of, **22**, [196]
    right to—
      abolition, **23**, [181]
      provisions restricting, **22**, [199]
    tenancy at low rent, as, **22**, [194]
  statutory tenancy of. *See* **statutory tenancy**
  subletting, restriction on, **22**, [82]
  time-sharing to constitute change of use,
    25(2), [530]
  vesting order, **22**, [178]

E

e-conveyancing
stamp duty land tax, **41**, [458]

ear-piercing
business of, local application of provisions as to, **35(1)**, [432]
registration of premises, **25(2)**, [466]

earnings
benefits code—
deductions from—
credit-token provided, where, **44(2)**, [374]
employment-related benefit, provision of, **44(2)**, [376]
living accommodation, provision of, **44(2)**, [375]
non-cash voucher provided, where, **44(2)**, [373]
scope of provisions, **44(2)**, [372]
definitions, **44(2)**, [76]
meaning, **44(2)**, [73]
relationship with, **44(2)**, [74]
chargeable overseas earnings, **44(2)**, [23]
deductions allowed—
benefits or reimbursed expenses, representing—
foreign accommodation and subsistence, for, **44(2)**, [387]
non-domiciled employees, duties performed in UK, **44(2)**, [384]–[386]
personal security assets and services, for, **44(2)**, [388]
scope of provisions, **44(2)**, [380]
travel costs and expenses where duties performed abroad, **44(2)**, [381]–[383]
deductibility provisions, meaning, **44(2)**, [342]
double, prevention of, **44(2)**, [340]
earnings, not to exceed, **44(2)**, [339]
expenses, for. *See* **expenses**
general, **44(2)**, [337]
income from which made, **44(2)**, [338]
order for making, **44(2)**, [341]
transitional provisions, **44(2)**, [769]
expenses treated as, **44(2)**, [82]
general—
delayed remittances, relief for, **44(2)**, [35]
claims, **44(2)**, [37]
election, **44(2)**, [36]
meaning, **44(2)**, [7]
money, receipt of, **44(2)**, [31]
non-money, receipt of, **44(2)**, [32]
overseas Crown employment subject to UK tax, from, **44(2)**, [28]
remitted to UK, **44(2)**, [33]
UK-linked debt, **44(2)**, [34]

earnings—*contd*
general—*contd*
tax year, for, **44(2)**, [29]
taxable. *See* taxable *below*
year in which employment not held, **44(2)**, [30]
meaning, **44(2)**, [72]
money's worth, meaning, **44(2)**, [72]
payments treated as—
director's tax, on account of, **44(2)**, [224]
restrictive undertakings, for, **44(2)**, [225]–[226]
sickness or disability, employee absent because of, **44(2)**, [222]
tax, on account of, where deduction not possible, **44(2)**, [223]
transitional provisions, **44(2)**, [767]
taxable—
employees not resident in UK, **44(2)**, [27]
employees resident and ordinarily resident but not domiciled in UK—
chargeable overseas earnings, calculation, **44(2)**, [23]
duties of associated employment performed in UK, **44(2)**, [24]
general provisions, **44(2)**, [21]–[22]
employees resident but not ordinarily resident in UK, **44(2)**, [25]–[26]
employees resident, ordinarily resident and domiciled in UK—
general earnings for year, **44(2)**, [15]
general provisions, **44(2)**, [14]
money, receipt of, **44(2)**, [18]
non-money, receipt of, **44(2)**, [19]
tax year, for, meaning, **44(2)**, [16]
year in which employment not held, treatment of, **44(2)**, [17]
employees resident, ordinarily resident or domiciled outside UK, **44(2)**, [20]–[41]
meaning, **44(2)**, [10], [20]
net, calculation of, **44(2)**, [11]
taxable specific—
meaning, **44(2)**, [10]
net, calculation of, **44(2)**, [12]
transitional provisions, **44(2)**, [767]

earnings factor
ascertainment of, **40(1)**, [262]
calculation of, **40(1)**, [264]
contributory benefits, for, **40(1)**, [261]
credits, **40(1)**, [288]
deemed, **40(1)**, [286], [287]
determining, **40(1)**, [198]
flat rate accrual amount, revaluation of, **40(1)**, [671]
low earnings threshold, revaluation of, **40(1)**, [670]

earnings factor—*contd*
modification, **40(2)**, [278]
regulations, **40(1)**, [198], [257]
revaluation of, **40(1)**, [669]; **40(2)**, [276]
state second pension derived from, **40(2)**, [275]
tables and rules for, **40(1)**, [262]

earn-out
securities, treated as, **43(2)**, [224]

earth-closet
care of, **35(1)**, [128]
meaning, **35(1)**, [140], [648]
provision in building, notice requiring, local authority, by, **35(1)**, [588]
water-closet replacing, **35(1)**, [590]

easement
acquisition—
oil installations, connected with, **9**, [195]
Thames flood barrier, of, **49**, [498]–[499]
under Defence Acts, **9**, [147], [149]–[150], [159], [195]
civil aviation, creation over land acquired for, **4(1)**, [95], [165]
clearance area, in, extinguishment, **22**, [253]
compensation for loss of, **46**, [501]
compulsory acquisition, advance payment of compensation where, **9**, [350]
created by uses, **20**, [12]
discharge or modification, **9**, [166]
enjoyment, **20**, [1]
equitable as land charge, **20**, [799]; **21**, [392]
Homes and Communities Agency land, power to override on, **24**, [855]
housing action trust, overridden by, **22**, [930]
legal, enuring for benefit of land, **20**, [788]
legal estate, as, **20**, [625]
nature of, **20**, [1]
opencast coal working—
compulsory rights order, effect, **17(1)**, [192], [220]
drainage and water supply, rights acquired, **17(1)**, [177]
possession of, **9**, [118]
power to override—
highway authority, **46**, [107]
new town, in, **46**, [151]
planning purposes, for, **46**, [501]
regional development agencies, transfers to, **46**, [952]
urban development corporation, **46**, [107]
Urban Regeneration Agency, **46**, [859]
prescription period for claiming—
forty years—
absolute right after, **20**, [62]
time excluded in computing, **20**, [68]
infant or other person under disability, in case of, **20**, [67]
interruption to, **20**, [61], [64]
nature of right, **20**, [61]
pleadings, **20**, [65]
presumption, restricting, **20**, [66]
twenty years' enjoyment, **20**, [62]

easement—*contd*
prisons, acquisition for, **12(1)**, [1106]
proceedings relating to, Limitation Acts exclusion, **20**, [635]
registration of grant, **9**, [150]
release, **9**, [151]
rent in respect of. *See* **rent**
Secretary of State, compulsory acquisition by, **46**, [492]

East Africa
loans, **41**, [567]

Easter
calculation, **45**, [918], [921]
Easter day—
application of Act, extent of, **45**, [931]–[933]
date of, **45**, [930]
table to find, **45**, [925]
provisions as to, **45**, [921]
rule for, **45**, [925]

eavesdropping
abolition of offence, **12(1)**, [369]

EC certificate of conformity. *See* **passenger transport services (light passenger vehicle)**

ecclesiastical charity
meaning, **25(1)**, [86]
parish council powers, **25(1)**, [77]

Ecclesiastical Commissioners. *See also* **Church Commissioners**
Church Commissioners, becoming, **14**, 418
common fund, transfer from, **14**, 424
dissolution of, **14**, 418
jurisdictions, abolishing, **14**, 91, 177
property, vesting of, **14**, 418–19

Ecclesiastical Committee of Parliament. *See* **Church Assembly**

ecclesiastical corporation
coast protection work, provision as to land belonging to, **49**, [411]
dilapidations, liability for, **14**, 164
disposal of land by—
contract, power to make, **14**, 188
money produced by, application of, **14**, 187–8, 198
powers of, **14**, 186
endowments, sale of, **14**, 138
lands of, agreeing boundaries of, **14**, 74
lease by. *See* **ecclesiastical lease**
licences and permissions, granting, **14**, 188
money in trust for, application of, **14**, 150
money, power to raise, **14**, 188
mortgage, entering into, **14**, 188
place of worship, grant of land for, **14**, 245
rentcharges, sale of, **14**, 376
site of church, grant of land for, **14**, 398
surplus income, application of, **14**, 195
surrenders, accepting, **14**, 188

ecclesiastical corporation—*contd*
Welsh Church, of, dissolution, **14**, 256

ecclesiastical courts. *See also* **ecclesiastical offences**
abolished, **14**, 611
appeal to Privy Council, **11(2)**, [62]
Arches Court of Canterbury. *See* **Arches Court of Canterbury**
Chancery Court of York. *See* **Chancery Court of York**
commissary. *See* **commissary court**
Commission of Review. *See* **Commission of Review**
conclusive, findings etc. deemed to be, **14**, 609
consistory. *See* **consistory court**
contempt of, **14**, 610
Court of Ecclesiastical Causes Reserved. *See* **Court of Ecclesiastical Causes Reserved**
criminal proceedings in, **14**, 605
deputy chancellors, **14(S)**, 95
duplex querela, jurisdiction as to, **14**, 611
enforcing repair of chancel, abolition, **14**, 350
evidence before, **14**, 610
expenses, **14**, 601
fees, **14**, 602
heresy, jurisdiction as to, **14**, 611
illegality of, **10**, [40]
judge—
oath of, **14**, 614
retiring age, **14**, 826
jurisdiction, amended provisions, **14(S)**, 94–5
meaning, **11(2)**, [51]
obsolete jurisdiction, **14**, 611
place of sitting, **14**, 610
powers of, **14**, 610
Privy Council, jurisdiction of, **14**, 558, 566
savings for, **14**, 612
Wales, in, **14**, 256–7

ecclesiastical fees
archbishop, reimbursement of, **14**, 1126
bishop, reimbursement of, **14**, 1126
Fees Advisory Commission—
constitution of, **14**, 1122
ecclesiastical judges fees orders, **14**, 1124–5
legal officers fees orders, **14**, 1123–5
members, **14**, 1122–3
orders—
ecclesiastical judges, **14**, 1124–5
legal officers, **14**, 1123–4
legal offices, **14**, 1123–4
parochial, **14**, 1119–20
parochial—
local acts inconsistent with, **14**, 1126, 1128–9
meaning, **14**, 1127
orders—
drafting of, **14**, 1119
General Synod, approval by, **14**, 1120
procedure for making, **14**, 1120
personal acts inconsistent with, **14**, 1126, 1128–9
persons to whom paid, **14**, 1121

ecclesiastical fees—*contd*
parochial—*contd*
private acts inconsistent with, **14**, 1126, 1128–9
powers under Tithe Acts, for, **14**, 549
recovery of, **14**, 1126

ecclesiastical land. *See also* **consecrated land**
landlord, exercise of powers of, **21**, [74]
leasehold enfranchisement or extension, provisions on, **21**, [330]

ecclesiastical lease
Act of Parliament, authorised by, **14**, 83
apportioned, power to grant, **14**, 158
building lease—
ecclesiastical corporation, grant by, **14**, 154–6
increased rent, power to reserve, **14**, 156
restrictions on, **14**, 154–6
streets and yards, land appropriated for, **14**, 156–7
certification of, **14**, 82
chapter property, increase in value, **14**, 161–2
consent to—
corporation, by, **14**, 167
crown patronage, in case of, **14**, 165
Duchy of Cornwall, where patronage attached to, **14**, 166
incapacity of patron, in case of, **14**, 166
more than one character, same party in, **14**, 167
party to deed, persons being, **14**, 165
patron, person considered to be, **14**, 167
validity, required for, **14**, 164–5
episcopal estates, increase in value, **14**, 161
exchange of lives, under, **14**, 83
existing powers, no restriction on, **14**, 160
expenses of, **14**, 189
fine or premium, avoidance for, **14**, 168
informality, void for, **14**, 158
mining leases, **14**, 159, 162
new, power to grant, **14**, 158
premiums, granted for, **14**, 186
rack rent, to be at, **14**, 160, 190
recitals—
absence of, effect of, **14**, 85
evidence of fact, as, **14**, 81, 85
false, **14**, 82
reference, agreement of—
disputed boundary, adjudication of, **14**, 74
ecclesiastical corporation, exercise of powers by, **14**, 75
entering into, **14**, 74
expenses, **14**, 77
persons under disability entering into, **14**, 75
quantity of manors, etc., adjudication on, **14**, 74
referees, investigation by, **14**, 75
registry, deposit of documents in, **14**, 76
validity, **14**, 74
rent—
application of, **14**, 187–8, 198
apportionment of, **14**, 190

ecclesiastical lease—*contd*
  rent—*contd*
    increased, reservation of, **14**, 156
    restrictions on grant of, **14**, 80–1
    running water, of, **14**, 157
    statutory terms, evidence of compliance
      with, **14**, 159–60
    surrender—
      acceptance of, **14**, 158, 188
      existing lease, of, **14**, 163
      under-lease, of, **14**, 163–4
    trust, held on, **14**, 167–8
    usual practice, conforming to, **14**, 82
    void, where, **14**, 84
    waterleaves, **14**, 157
    wayleaves, **14**, 157

ecclesiastical licence. *See* **dispensation**

ecclesiastical measure. *See also* **General
Synod**
  enactment of, **32**, [848]

ecclesiastical offences
  articles, content of, **14**, 578, 588
  bishop, duty of, **14**, 576, 585
  censure. *See* **censure**
  complaint—
    examiner, inquiry by, **14**, 577
    inquiry into, **14**, 586–7
    person promoting, **14**, 577, 588
    promotion of, **14**, 605
  conduct unbecoming, **14**, 571
  consistory court, trial in. *See* **consistory
    court**
  conviction, etc., deemed conclusive, **14**, 609
  costs—
    award of, **14**, 600
    central board, payment by, **14**, 601
    Church Commissioners, payment by,
      14, 599
    recovery of, **14**, 601
    security for, **14**, 600
  courts, etc., place of, **14**, 610
  fees, payment of, **14**, 602
  limitation, **14**, 572
  monition. *See* **monition**
  neglect of duty, **14**, 571
  place of, **14**, 572
  political opinions, not in respect of, **14**, 571
  powers of court, **14**, 610
  proceedings—
    archbishop, against. *See* **archbishop**
    bishop, against. *See* **bishop**
    instituting—
      complaint, by. *See* complaint *above*
      method of, **14**, 573
      persons, against, **14**, 572
    matter of doctrine, ritual or ceremonial,
      14, 576–80, 585–9
  sentence, pronouncing by consent, **14**, 580
  trial judge, **14**, 578

ecclesiastical offices
  age limits, **14**, 820–4, 954–5

ecclesiastical offices—*contd*
  common tenure, **14(S)**, 220–1
  deprivation. *See* **deprivation**
  misconduct, **14(S)**, 230
  office holders—
    common tenure, **14(S)**, 220–1
    corporation sole, as, **14(S)**, 230
    duration of appointments, **14(S)**, 223–4
    employer and employee, no relationship
      of, **14(S)**, 230
    houses of residence—
      acquisition and disposal of, **14(S)**, 227
      housing providers, transactions by,
        14(S), 227–9
      regulated transactions, **14(S)**, 234–5
      works, carrying out, **14(S)**, 227
    housing—
      providers, **14(S)**, 226
      provision of, **14(S)**, 225–6
    meaning, **14(S)**, 221
  terms and conditions—
    amended provisions, **14(S)**, 232, 236–8
    Codes of Practice, **14(S)**, 229–30
    duration of appointments, **14(S)**, 223–4
    regulations, **14(S)**, 221–3
    summary of provisions, **14(S)**, 219

ecclesiastical property
  abeyance, in, compensation for compulsory
    acquisition, **9**, [248]
  ancient monuments, provisions on, **32**, [372]
  archaeological area, in, **32**, [372]
  coal mining subsidence, damage due to,
    17(2), [20], [33]
  compulsory acquisition, **9**, [271], [289], [448]
    notices, service of, **9**, [421], [448]
  depreciation, compensation for, **9**, [317]
  entry on, **9**, [271]
  hazardous substances, provisions on, **46**, [790]
  meaning, **9**, [248], [317], [421], [448];
    17(1), [204]; **17(2)**, [20]; **46**, [588]
  new town, in, **46**, [193]
  notices, service of, **9**, [421], [448]; **46**, [735]
  opencast coal mining, **17(1)**, [204]
  pipe-lines, provisions as to, **17(1)**, [267]
  provisions relating to, **46**, [588]
  urban development area, in, **46**, [91]

ecclesiastical titles
  use of, **14**, 239

ecclesiastical trust
  diocesan authority, vesting of property in,
    14, 633–4
  ecclesiastical purposes, established for, **14**, 632
  guild church, for, **14**, 466–7
  personal property held on, **14**, 632
  place of worship, site of, **14**, 243

Edinburgh Gazette
  diplomatic agreements, publication of,
    10, [988]
  royal proclamations in, **10**, [458]

education. *See also* **college; school**
allowances in respect of, **15(2)**, [492]
alternative provisions, attendance orders
applicable to, **15(1)**, [587]
attendance notice—
  appeal arrangements, **15(S)**, Education 160
  attendance panel, **15(S)**, Education 159–60
  contents of, **15(S)**, Education 157
  education or training, description of,
    15(S), Education 158–9
  failure to comply with—
    offence, **15(S)**, Education 162
    penalty notice—
      appeal arrangements,
        15(S), Education 165–6
      issue of, **15(S)**, Education 164–5
      regulations, **15(S)**, Education 164–5
      proceedings restrictions on,
        15(S), Education 163
  initial operation of provisions, review of,
    15(S), Education 172
  issue of, **15(S)**, Education 157
  variation and revocation,
    15(S), Education 161
authorities. *See* **local education authority**
careers, information and advice as to,
  15(S), Education 192–4
charitable institutions, sex discrimination,
  7(1), [113]
children not receiving, local education
  authority's duties as to, **15(1)**, [578]
children's services authorities, co-operation
  by, **15(S)**, Education 196
companies to provide services for, general
  powers of Secretary of State in relation to,
  15(2), [351]
disabled person, of—
  expected leaving dates, review of,
    40(1), [166]
  special, requiring, **40(1)**, [165]
discrimination—
  disability. *See* **disability discrimination**
  racial, generally, **7(1)**, [145]
  sex. *See* sex discrimination *below*
duty to participate in—
  alternative ways of working,
    15(S), Education 173
  contract of employment, relevant,
    15(S), Education 134
  Crown employment,
    15(S), Education 173–4
  educational institution—
    good attendance, promotion of,
      15(S), Education 125
    information, duty to provide,
      15(S), Education 128–9
    meaning, **15(S)**, Education 127
  employers enabling. *See* employers *below*
  financial penalties, payment of,
    15(S), Education 176
  general note, **15(S)**, Education 101–4
  House of Commons staff,
    15(S), Education 175
  House of Lords staff, **15(S)**, Education 175
  interpretation, **15(S)**, Education 177

education—*contd*
duty to participate in—*contd*
  local education authority—
    fulfilment of duty, promotion of,
      15(S), Education 124
    guidance, issue of, **15(S)**, Education 133
    parenting contract, power to enter into,
      15(S), Education 151
    parenting order, power to apply for,
      15(S), Education 152
    public bodies, supply of information by,
      15(S), Education 131
    sharing and use of information
      supplied, **15(S)**, Education 132–3
    social security information supplied to,
      15(S), Education 129–30
    young persons not complying,
      notification of, **15(S)**, Education 126–8
    young persons not fulfilling duty,
      identification of, **15(S)**, Education 126
  non-participation fines. *See*
    non-participation fines *below*
  parenting contract—
    power to enter into,
      15(S), Education 151
    regulations, **15(S)**, Education 154
  parenting order—
    appeal against, **15(S)**, Education 153
    making of, **15(S)**, Education 152
    matters taken into account in making,
      15(S), Education 153
    meaning, **15(S)**, Education 152
    regulations, **15(S)**, Education 154
  Wales, provision for, **15(S)**, Education 178
  young persons—
    appropriate full-time education,
      15(S), Education 119
    attendance notice. *See* attendance notice
      above
    failure to fulfil duty—
      identification, **15(S)**, Education 126
      initial steps, **15(S)**, Education 155–6
    full-time occupation, person in,
      15(S), Education 120–1
    hours of guided learning to external
      qualification, assignment of,
      15(S), Education 124
    level 3 qualification,
      15(S), Education 118
    non-compliance, notification of,
      15(S), Education 126–8
    persons to whom provisions applying,
      15(S), Education 117
    relevant education, **15(S)**, Education 121
    relevant period, **15(S)**, Education 122
    scope of, **15(S)**, Education 117–18
    sufficient relevant education,
      15(S), Education 123
  employers—
    appropriate arrangements by,
      15(S), Education 135
    commencement of employment, before,
      15(S), Education 135–40
    penalty notices,
      15(S), Education 136–40

education—*contd*
  employers—*contd*
    duty to enable participation in—
      arrangements subsequently notified,
        15(S), Education 141–2
      enforcement notice—
        contravention of provisions, service
          on, **15(S)**, Education 143–4
        non-compliance with,
          15(S), Education 145–6
        withdrawal of, **15(S)**, Education 146
      initial arrangements,
        15(S), Education 140–1
      penalty notice—
        appeal against,
          15(S), Education 148–9
        non-compliance with enforcement
          notice, issue on,
          15(S), Education 145–6
        power to withdraw,
          15(S), Education 149
        withdrawal or variation of,
          15(S), Education 147–50
      persons reaching 18, extension for,
        15(S), Education 143
  exceptional provision of, **15(1)**, [517]
  external qualifications—
    approved, **15(2)**, [266]
      England, **15(S)**, Education 281
      Wales, **15(S)**, Education 281
    authorised bodies, **15(2)**, [268]
    enforcement of provisions,
      15(2), [269]–[270]
    persons over 19, **15(2)**, [265]
    persons under 19, **15(2)**, [264]
  financial assistance—
    Secretary of State, from—
      delegation of arrangements, **15(2)**, [355]
      forms of, **15(2)**, [353]
      power to give, **15(2)**, [352]
      terms, **15(2)**, [354]
  further. *See* **further education; higher and
    further education**
  grants, **15(2)**, [275]–[276]
    education standards, for, **15(1)**, [611]
    educational services or research, for,
      15(1), [612]
    payment of, **15(1)**, [616]
    promotion of learning or research, for,
      15(1), [613]
    Welsh, for education in, **15(1)**, [614]
  grants for, **46**, [575]
  higher. *See* **higher and further education**
  independent educational institutions—
    appeals—
      decision to deregister, against,
        15(S), Education 234
      decisions of Secretary of State, against,
        15(S), Education 235
      justice's order, against,
        15(S), Education 236
    colleges for 16 to 18 year olds—
      providers of education,
        15(S), Education 241–2
      regulations, **15(S)**, Education 243

education—*contd*
  independent educational institutions—*contd*
    England, application of provisions in,
      15(S), Education 207
    failure to meet standards—
      action plans, **15(S)**, Education 224–5
      enforcement action,
        15(S), Education 226–7
      relevant restrictions, imposition of,
        15(S), Education 227–8
    general note, **15(S)**, Education 106–8
    information, provision by proprietor,
      15(S), Education 230–2
    inspection—
      duty of—
        direction of Secretary of State, on,
          15(S), Education 220–1
        prescribed intervals, at,
          15(S), Education 219
      fees, **15(S)**, Education 222
      fees, failure to pay, **15(S)**, Education 223
      powers of entry, **15(S)**, Education 221
      reports, publication of,
        15(S), Education 224
    inspectorates—
      approval of, **15(S)**, Education 218
      quality assurance, **15(S)**, Education 219
    interpretation, **15(S)**, Education 245–6
    material change to registered details,
      approval of—
        definition, **15(S)**, Education 214
        determination of applications,
          15(S), Education 216
        inspection and report,
          15(S), Education 215
        requirement to apply for,
          15(S), Education 215
        unapproved change, power to deregister
          on, **15(S)**, Education 217
    meaning, **15(S)**, Education 206
    offences—
      bodies corporate, by,
        15(S), Education 244
      institution of proceedings for,
        15(S), Education 243
      unincorporated bodies, by,
        15(S), Education 244
    part-time, application of provisions to,
      15(S), Education 297
    participation in management—
      directions—
        appeal against, **15(S)**, Education 239
        information, provision of,
          15(S), Education 239–40
        notification, **15(S)**, Education 240
      prohibition, **15(S)**, Education 238, 248
    register of, **15(S)**, Education 209, 247
    registration—
      application for, **15(S)**, Education 211
      determination of applications,
        15(S), Education 212–13
      information required,
        15(S), Education 211–12
      power to deregister,
        15(S), Education 213–14

education—*contd*
  independent educational institutions—*contd*
    regulation and inspection, general note,
      15(S), Education 106–8
    relevant restrictions—
      appeals, **15(S)**, Education 234–6
      emergency, application for order in,
        15(S), Education 230
      imposition of, **15(S)**, Education 227–8
      justice of the peace, imposed by,
        15(S), Education 230–2
      meaning, **15(S)**, Education 227
      notification of order,
        15(S), Education 232–3
      Tribunal, imposed by,
        15(S), Education 237
    service of notices, **15(S)**, Education 245
    standards, **15(S)**, Education 208
    transitional provisions,
      15(S), Education 246–7
    unregistered—
      inspection of, **15(S)**, Education 210–11
      offence of conducting,
        15(S), Education 210
    unsuitable person working at or as
      proprietor, removal from register,
      15(S), Education 229
    Wales, in, **15(S)**, Education 298
  innovation, powers to facilitate—
    statutory requirements, order to suspend—
      annual report by Secretary of State,
        15(2), [343]
      applications for, **15(2)**, [342]
      effect of, **15(2)**, [340]
      generally, **15(2)**, [340]
      revocation of, **15(2)**, [341]
      variation of, **15(2)**, [341]
  learning agreements, **15(2)**, [493]
  London—
    higher education, functions, **25(1)**, [253]
    local education authorities, **25(1)**, [699]
    Westminster Technical Institute,
      25(1), [253]
    See also **Inner London Education
      Authority**
  London, in. *See* **London**
  member states, services for schools in,
    15(1), [361]
  non-participation fines—
    enforcement—
      normal powers, **15(S)**, Education 170
      normal provisions, **15(S)**, Education 170
      person aged 18 or over,
        15(S), Education 169
      person reaching 18,
        15(S), Education 167–8
    meaning, **15(S)**, Education 166
    sums recovered, application of,
      15(S), Education 171
  orders and regulations, **15(2)**, [307]
  outside school, funded, provision of
    information to Secretary of State,
    15(1), [672]
  parent—
    duty of to secure, **15(1)**, [502]

education—*contd*
  parent—*contd*
    representations of, local education authority
      to consider, **15(1)**, [511]
    wishes of, in accordance with, **15(1)**, [504]
  pensions—
    delegation, **15(2)**, [297]
    generally, **15(2)**, [295]
    interpretation, **15(2)**, [296]
  person not ordinarily resident in Great
    Britain, **7(1)**, [172]
  persons over 19, functions of local education
    authority, **15(1)**, [513]
  primary, meaning, **15(1)**, [497]
  qualifying accounts, **15(2)**, [271]
  qualifying arrangements, **15(2)**, [272]–[274]
  racial groups, special needs, **7(1)**, [173], [174]
  recognised awards, bodies designated as
    giving, **15(1)**, [355]
  records, regulations as to, **15(1)**, [697]
  religious trust for, orders arising from reverter
    of land, **22**, [689], [693]
  repeals, **15(1)**, [623]–[724]
  resident of accommodation centre, of,
    31, [391]–[392]
  revocations, **15(1)**, [725]
  secondary, meaning, **15(1)**, [497]; **15(2)**, [491]
  sex discrimination—
    boarding schools, **7(1)**, [69]
    charitable institutions, **7(1)**, [113]
    designated establishments, **7(1)**, [66]
    education authority, by, **7(1)**, [63]
    Further Education Councils, by, **7(1)**, [64],
      [146]
    further, in, **7(1)**, [61]
    general duty, **7(1)**, [67]
    Higher Education Funding Councils, by,
      7(1), [64], [146]
    higher, in, **7(1)**, [61]
    post-16 education and training, **7(1)**, [68]
    public authorities, by, **7(1)**, [60]
    pupil, meaning, **7(1)**, [62]
    Training and Development Agency for
      Schools, by, **7(1)**, [65], [147]
    transitional orders, **7(1)**, [123]
    types of, **7(1)**, [61]
    vocational training, **7(1)**, [52]
  single-sex establishments, **7(1)**, [69]
  sixteen to eighteen year olds, functions of
    local education authority, **15(1)**, [512]
  sixth-form, **15(2)**, [277]–[279], [316]–[318]
    admission—
      appeals, **15(S)**, Education 273–4
      preferences, **15(S)**, Education 257–9
    meaning, **15(S)**, Education 275
    restructuring, **15(2)**, [279], [319]
    significant improvement, requiring,
      15(2), [278], [316]–[318]
    proposals—
      implementation of, **15(2)**, [318]
      power to publish, **15(2)**, [316]
      publication of, **15(2)**, [317]
  Special Educational Needs and Disability
    Tribunal. *See* **Special Educational Needs
    and Disability Tribunal**

education—*contd*
special educational provision—
Academy, in, **15(1)**, [610]
general note, **15(1)**, [1]
local education authority, duty of,
15(1), [525]
meaning, **15(1)**, [519]
provision outside England and Wales,
15(1), [529]
review of arrangements for, **15(1)**, [522]
school—
mainstream, otherwise than in,
15(1), [524]
otherwise than in, **15(1)**, [528]
stages of, **15(1)**, [496]
statutes, generally, **15(1)**, [1]
supervision orders, **15(1)**, [592]
support for 13 to 19 year olds,
15(2), [280]–[287]
support for participation in—
conditional basis, provision on,
15(S), Education 182
educational institutions—
access and facilities,
15(S), Education 184–5
information, provision of,
15(S), Education 183–4
existing functions ceasing to have effect,
15(S), Education 190
general note, **15(S)**, Education 104–5
interpretation, **15(S)**, Education 189
learning and support agreements,
15(S), Education 182–3
learning difficulties, assessments relating
to, **15(S)**, Education 190–2
public bodies, supply of information by,
15(S), Education 188
services—
directions, **15(S)**, Education 180
inspection of, **15(S)**, Education 186
internet and telephone,
15(S), Education 185
local education authorities, provision
by, **15(S)**, Education 179
supplementary powers of authorities,
15(S), Education 181
social security information, provision to
young persons, **15(S)**, Education 187
training programmes, cessation of funding,
15(2), [300]
transitional provisions, **15(1)**, [726]–[728];
15(2), [306], [320]–[322]
travel—
local education authorities, exercise of
functions by, **15(S)**, Education 195
persons of sixth form age—
journey times for, **15(S)**, Education 195
religion or belief, duty to have regard
to, **15(S)**, Education 195
unrecognised degrees—
Channel Islands, **15(1)**, [356]
enforcement of provisions, **15(1)**, [354]
Northern Ireland, **15(1)**, [356]
offences, **15(1)**, [353]
value added tax, exemption from, **50**, [153]

education—*contd*
Wales—
learner travel arrangements. *See* **Wales**
local curriculum in. *See* **Wales**
Welsh Ministers—
directions, power to give,
15(S), Education 285, 299
functions of, **15(S)**, Education 283–5, 289
regulations by, **15(S)**, Education 308–10

education action zone
Education Action Forum for—
accounts, **15(2)**, [136]
chairman, **15(2)**, [136]
charitable status, **15(2)**, [136]
committees, **15(2)**, [136]
constitution, **15(2)**, [6]
establishment of, **15(2)**, [5]
exemption order from education legislation
requirements—
application for, **15(2)**, [342]
generally, **15(2)**, [340]
revocation of, **15(2)**, [341]
variation of, **15(2)**, [341]
expansion of zone, **15(2)**, [7]
functions of, **15(2)**, [10]
information relating to, **15(2)**, [9]
powers, **15(2)**, [136]
proceedings, **15(2)**, [136]
proof of documents, **15(2)**, [136]
removal from zone, **15(2)**, [8]
seal, **15(2)**, [136]
transitional provisions, **15(2)**, [528]
establishment of, **15(2)**, [4]
expansion of, **15(2)**, [7]
information relating to, **15(2)**, [9]
removal from, **15(2)**, [8]
schools in, pay and conditions orders, in
relation to, **15(2)**, [442]

Education and Library Board
sale of house at discount by, stamp duty,
41, [138], [145]

Education Assets Board
renamed. *See* **Education Transfer Council**

education authorities. *See* **local education
authorities**

education supervision order
application for, local education authority, by,
6, [349]
child in care, bar on order in case of, **6**, [349]
discharge of, **6**, [445]
duration, **6**, [445]
effect of, **6**, [445]
failure of child to comply, **6**, [445]
offences, **6**, [445]
parental duties, superseded, **6**, [445]
power to make, **6**, [349]
supervision order, where child subject to,
6, [445]
supervisor—
duties, **6**, [445]

education supervision order—*contd*
supervisor—*contd*
information, supply to, **6**, [445]

Education Transfer Council. *See also*
Funding Councils and Assets Board
alteration of functions, **15(2)**, [127]
constitution, **15(1)**, [341]
dissolution, provision for, **15(2)**, [127]
Education Assets Board, change of name
from, **15(2)**, [126]
property, transfer of, **15(1)**, [342], [376]
Secretary of State, assisting, **15(1)**, [343]

educational buildings
disabled, provisions for benefit of, **46**, [338]

educational establishment. *See also* **school**
body being, **44(3)**, [70]
building regulations, exemption from,
35(1), [530]
employee seconded to, **44(1)**, [60]
tax deduction for, **44(3)**, [69]
gifts to, deductions for, **44(1)**, [55]
meaning, **44(3)**, [69], [109]

educational records
data protection, **7(1)**, [564]

educational trust. *See also* **trusts, university**
and college
Endowed Schools Act, schemes under,
15(1), [687]
general provisions, **15(1)**, [268]
trustees, appointment of, **15(1)**, [180]

EEA market operator
meaning, **19(2)**, [383]
passport rights—
exercise of, **19(2)**, [380]
removal of, **19(2)**, [381]

EEA state
meaning, **8(1)**, [1248]
non-resident nationals, allowances for,
43(S), 897

eggs
British—
failure to mark, **1(1)**, [296]
meaning, **1(1)**, [299]
records of storage, **1(1)**, [296]
storage, restrictions on, **1(1)**, [296]
enforcement of provisions, **1(1)**, [297]
imported—
origin, indication of, **1(1)**, [296]
storage of, **1(1)**, [296]
preserved, marking, **1(1)**, [295]
storage—
British eggs, **1(1)**, [296]
chemical, meaning, **1(1)**, [299]
cold or chemical, **1(1)**, [296], [557]
imported eggs, **1(1)**, [296]
inspection of premises used for, **1(1)**, [296]
offences and penalties, **1(1)**, [296]

eggs—*contd*
storage—*contd*
registration of premises, **1(1)**, [296]
regulations and orders, **1(1)**, [298]

Eire. *See* **Ireland, Republic of**

EIS. *See* **enterprise investment scheme**

ejectment
cessation of proceedings, **20**, [235]
former remedies, saving for, **20**, [237]
jurisdiction, **20**, [238]
mesne profits, damages for, **20**, [236]
non-payment of rent, for, **20**, [232], [233]
notice of, by lessee to lessor, **20**, [755]
rent and costs, payment of, **20**, [234], [235]

elderly persons
meaning, **38(2)**, [136]
passenger transport services—
regard to needs in, **36**, [778]; **37**, [401]
travel concession, **37**, [430]; **38(2)**, [134],
[229]

election
absent voter—
changes relating to, **15(3)**, [283]
definite period, for, **15(3)**, [287]
entitlement to vote in person, **15(3)**, [624]
fresh signatures, provision of, **15(3)**, [605]
indefinite period, for, **15(3)**, [287]
list of, **15(3)**, [287]
local government elections, manner of
voting at, **15(3)**, [287]
manner of voting, **15(3)**, [287]
offences, **15(3)**, [287]
parliamentary elections, manner of voting
at, **15(3)**, [287]
particular election, at, **15(3)**, [287]
personal identifiers, **15(3)**, [605]
proxy, **15(3)**, [287]
access to documents—
conditions, **15(3)**, [628]
contravention of regulations, **15(3)**, [629]
interpretation, **15(3)**, [630]
relevant officers, **15(3)**, [630]
address, sending post free, **15(3)**, [100]
administration, **15(S)**, Elections 3
agent. *See* **election agent**
amendment of enactments,
pre-consolidation, **15(3)**, [645]
armed forces personnel voting, **3**, [1]
ballot paper—
postal, issue of, **15(3)**, [625]
tendered, **15(3)**, [626]
bribery—
acts amounting to, **15(3)**, [115]
licensed premises, on, **15(3)**, [159]
broadcasting—
during election, **15(3)**, [102]
local items during election period,
15(3), [102]
outside UK, from, **15(3)**, [101]

election—*contd*
  campaign expenditure. *See* **political parties**
  candidate. *See* **candidate**
  canvas period, falling within,
    15(S), Elections 39–41
  canvasser—
    payment of, **15(3)**, [113]
    police officer as, **15(3)**, [108]
  City of London, in. *See* **London, City of**
  combination of polls, **15(3)**, [237], [526]
  committee room, meaning, **15(3)**, [120]
  co-ordinated on-line register of electors. *See*
    co-ordinated on-line register of electors
    (CORE)
  corrupt practices—
    bribery, **15(3)**, [115]
    treating, **15(3)**, [116]
    undue influence, **15(3)**, [117]
  costs, rules on, **15(3)**, [179]
  custody, registration of person remanded in,
    15(3), [11]
  declarations, offences as to, **15(3)**, [60]
  defamatory statements, limitation on
    privilege, **19(3)**, [315]
  disregarded days, omission of reference to
    Maundy Thursday **15(3)**, [611], [656]
  documents—
    Scotland, disposal of in, **15(S)**, Elections 43
    supply of, **15(3)**, [67]
  donations to candidates, control of,
    15(3), [74]
  education as to, **15(S)**, Elections 15
  Electoral Commission. *See* **Electoral**
    Commission
  electoral fraud in Northern Ireland. *See*
    Northern Ireland
  electoral registration officer. *See* registration
    officer *below*
  European Parliament, to. *See* **European**
    Parliament
  exit polls, prohibitions on publication of,
    15(3), [66]
  expenses. *See* **election expenses**
  free postal services, remuneration for,
    15(3), [194]
  freedom of, **10**, [40]; **15(3)**, [2]
  imitation poll cards, sending out, **15(3)**, [103]
  legal incapacity to vote, abolition of common
    law rule, **15(3)**, [646]
  local government. *See* **local government**
    election
  London. *See* **London**
  meeting—
    disturbances at, **15(3)**, [106]
    schools and rooms for—
      local election, **15(3)**, [105]
      parliamentary election, **15(3)**, [104]
  members of the forces, provisions on,
    15(3), [57]
  mental patient—
    registration of, **15(3)**, [10]
    residence, **15(3)**, [10]
  nomination papers, false statements in,
    15(3), [64]

election—*contd*
  notices—
    payment for exhibition of, **15(3)**, [111]
    service of, **15(3)**, [180]
  offences—
    arrest, powers of, **15(3)**, [644]
    ballot paper, tampering with, **15(3)**, [63]
    bodies corporate, by, **15(3)**, [469]
    candidate, by, **15(3)**, [59]
    convictions, duty of court to report to
      Commission, **15(3)**, [471]
    declarations, as to, **15(3)**, [60], [236]
    Director of Public Prosecutions, duties of,
      15(3), [177]
    documents, failure to comply with
      conditions for supply of, **15(3)**, [67]
    false statements in nomination papers,
      15(3), [64]
    general, **15(3)**, [465]
    legal incapacity, voting while having,
      15(3), [59]
    more than once, voting, **15(3)**, [59]
    nomination papers, tampering with,
      15(3), [63]
    official duty, breach of, **15(3)**, [62]
    official guilty of, **15(3)**, [63]
    penalties, **15(3)**, [518]
    personation, **15(3)**, [58]
    postal and proxy votes, relating to
      application for, **15(3)**, [61]
    proxy voter, relating to, **15(3)**, [59]
    punishment, **15(3)**, [467]
    summary proceedings, **15(3)**, [468]
    unincorporated associations, by,
      15(3), [470]
  officials, not acting for candidate, **15(3)**, [107]
  parliamentary. *See* **parliamentary election**
  participation, encouraging, **15(3)**, [642]
  payments, illegal—
    illegal purposes, for, **15(3)**, [114]
    prosecution and penalties, **15(3)**, [170]
    withdrawal of candidate, for, **15(3)**, [110]
  persons disabled to vote, **10**, [82]
  petitions, trial of, judges, **11(2)**, [786]
  pilot regions, in, **15(3)**, [592]
  police officer, canvassing by, **15(3)**, [108]
  prosecutions—
    association, offence by, **15(3)**, [174]
    evidence of election, **15(3)**, [175]
    offences outside UK, **15(3)**, [173]
    registration, evidence of, **15(3)**, [176]
    summary, **15(3)**, [172]
    time limit, **15(3)**, [171], [643]
  publications—
    details to appear on, **15(3)**, [461]
    introduction of new law, **15(3)**, [524]
    printer's name and address to be on,
      15(3), [112], [174]
    restoration of previous law, **15(3)**, [523]
  register—
    alteration of—
      notice of, **15(3)**, [24]
      pending elections, **15(3)**, [25], [602],
        [654]
    combined, **15(3)**, [15]

election—*contd*
  register—*contd*
    conclusive effect of, **15(3)**, [50]
    electronic form, requirement to maintain
      in, **15(3)**, [52]
    generally, **15(3)**, [15]
    maintenance of—
      canvass, **15(3)**, [19]
      electors, registration of, **15(3)**, [22]
    misdescription in, **15(3)**, [51]
    Northern Ireland, in. *See* **Northern
    Ireland**
    publication of, **15(3)**, [23]
    reference to, construction of, **15(3)**, [220]
    regulations, **15(3)**, [53]
    steps necessary for compliance, **15(3)**, [16]
  registration appeals—
    England and Wales, **15(3)**, [55]
    Northern Ireland, **15(3)**, [56]
  registration of electors—
    anonymous, **15(3)**, [17], [653]
      removal of entry, **15(3)**, [18]
    false information, offences, **15(3)**, [606]
    objections, **15(3)**, [603]
    service qualification, with, **15(3)**, [604]
  registration officer—
    appointment of, **15(3)**, [14]
    claims for registration, determining,
      15(3), [22]
    data schemes—
      information, disclosure of,
        15(S), Elections 60
      orders, **15(S)**, Elections 60
      proposals, consultation and evaluation,
        15(S), Elections 61
      purpose of, **15(S)**, Elections 60
    deputy, **15(3)**, [52]
    determinations by, **15(3)**, [603]
    duties, **15(3)**, [15]
      discharge of, **15(3)**, [52]
      necessary steps for compliance, taking,
        15(3), [16]
    electronic form, requirement to keep
      register in, **15(3)**, [52]
    expenses, **15(3)**, [54]
    fees, accounting for, **15(3)**, [54]
    incapacity to act, **15(3)**, [52]
    Northern Ireland, for, **15(3)**, [14]
    reference to, construction of, **15(3)**, [220]
    register, preparing. *See* register *above*
    Scotland, for, **15(3)**, [14]
    summary of provisions, **15(S)**, Elections 4
    Wales, **15(3)**, [14]
  residence—
    determination of, **15(3)**, [8]
    generally, **15(3)**, [8]
    interruption of, **15(3)**, [8]
    local connection, declaration of—
      effect of, **15(3)**, [13]
      generally, **15(3)**, [12]
      offences as to, **15(3)**, [60]
    mental patients, of, **15(3)**, [10]
    merchant seamen, of, **15(3)**, [9]
    person remanded in custody, **15(3)**, [11]

election—*contd*
  returning officer, procedural errors, correction
    of, **15(3)**, [632]
  rules of procedure, **15(3)**, [178]
  secrecy, requirement of, **15(3)**, [65]
  service qualification—
    persons having, **15(3)**, [29]
    service declaration—
      attested, when, **15(3)**, [31]
      contents of, **15(3)**, [31]
      effect of, **15(3)**, [32]
      making, **15(3)**, [30]
      offences, **15(3)**, [60]
  Speaker's Committee. *See* **Speaker's
  Committee**
  Sunday, required to be held on, **45**, [929]
  time, computation of, **15(3)**, [46], [122],
    [182], [202]
  translation of documents, **15(3)**, [192]
  treating—
    licensed premises, on, **15(3)**, [159]
    offence of, **15(3)**, [116]
  undue influence, **15(3)**, [117]

election agent
  appointment of, **15(3)**, [68]
  candidate as, **15(3)**, [68], [71]
  claim by, **15(3)**, [84]
  corrupt, employing, **15(3)**, [161]
  death of, **15(3)**, [68], [71]
  default in appointment, **15(3)**, [71]
  disputed claim of, **15(3)**, [83]
  election expenses—
    authorising, **15(3)**, [78]
    incurring, **15(3)**, [82]
    payment of, otherwise than by, **15(3)**, [76]
    payment through, **15(3)**, [75]
  London Assembly election—
    default in appointment, **15(3)**, [72]
    sub-agent—
      nomination of, **15(3)**, [69]
      office, having, **15(3)**, [70]
  not required, where, **15(3)**, [73]
  office, having, **15(3)**, [70]
  sub-agent—
    nomination of, **15(3)**, [69]
    office, having, **15(3)**, [70]

election expenses
  agent, authorised by, **15(3)**, [78]
  agent not required, where, **15(3)**, [96]
  claim, time for sending in, **15(3)**, [82]
  creditors, rights of, **15(3)**, [118]
  disputed claims, **15(3)**, [83]
  Electoral Commission, guidance by,
    15(3), [216]
  exclusions, **15(3)**, [215]
  goods, free provision of, as, **15(3)**, [98]
  guidance as to, **15(S)**, Elections 39
  High Court jurisdiction, **15(3)**, [82]
  incurred otherwise than for, **15(3)**, [77]
  joint candidates, for, **15(3)**, [81]
  local election, at, **15(3)**, [213]
  matters, list of, **15(3)**, [214]
  maximum amount of, **15(3)**, [79]

election expenses—*contd*
  meaning, **15(3)**, [97]
  not authorised by election agent, prohibition
    of, **15(3)**, [78]
  offences, **15(3)**, [78]
  payment of—
    candidate, by, **15(3)**, [76]
    election agent, through, **15(3)**, [75]
    time for, **15(3)**, [82]
  pre-candidacy, **15(S)**, Elections 37–8
  property, free provision of, as, **15(3)**, [98]
  return and declaration—
    contents, **15(3)**, [617]
    declaration, making, **15(3)**, [86]
    Electoral Commission, forwarding to,
      15(3), [93]
    failure to make, **15(3)**, [88]
      agent, court requiring information
        from, **15(3)**, [92]
      Mayor of London, candidate for,
        15(3), [90]
      relief for, **15(3)**, [91]
    form of, **15(3)**, [212]
    inspection, **15(3)**, [95]
      time and place of, **15(3)**, [94]
    making, **15(3)**, [78], [85]
    meaning, **15(3)**, [120]
    not required, where, **15(3)**, [87]
    sitting and voting without making,
      15(3), [89]
  services, free provision of, as, **15(3)**, [98]
  third party, incurred by, **15(3)**, [616]
  variation of provisions, **15(3)**, [80], [456]

Electoral Commission
  accounting officer, **15(3)**, [482]
  accounts, **15(3)**, [482]
  accredited observers—
    attendance and conduct of, **15(3)**, [302]
    code of practice, **15(3)**, [303]
    individuals, **15(3)**, [300]
    organisations, **15(3)**, [301]
  advice from, **15(3)**, [310]
  advice of—
    direction for, **26(2)**, [220]
    exercise of functions, **26(2)**, [222]
    payments, **26(2)**, [223]
    preparation and submission of, **26(2)**, [221]
  annual examination by Comptroller and
    Auditor General, **15(3)**, [482]
  assistance for designated organisations—
    application for designation of, **15(3)**, [435]
    assistance available, **15(3)**, [436], [509]
    designation of, **15(3)**, [434]
  assistance from, **15(3)**, [310]
  audit, **15(3)**, [482]
  Boundary Commission—
    functions, transfer from, **15(3)**, [316],
      [484]–[485]
    property, transfer from, **15(3)**, [317]
  Boundary Committees—
    assessors to, **15(3)**, [314]
    establishment of, **15(3)**, [314]

Electoral Commission—*contd*
  Boundary Committees—*contd*
    Local Government Boundary Commission
      for Wales, transfer of functions to,
      15(3), [319]
    Local Government Commission for
      England, transfer of functions to,
      15(3), [318]
    number of, **15(3)**, [314]
  chairman, **15(3)**, [292], [294], [482]
  Commissioners—
    appointment, **15(3)**, [292], [294], [522]
    assistant, **15(3)**, [482]
    chairman, **15(S)**, Elections 10
    deputy, **15(3)**, [315], [482]
    nominated, **15(S)**, Elections 11
    number of, **15(3)**, [292];
      15(S), Elections 12
    parties, four to be put forward by,
      15(S), Elections 11
    political restrictions on, **15(S)**, Elections 13
    prospective, selection of,
      15(S), Elections 10
    salary, **15(3)**, [482]
    terms of office, **15(3)**, [482]
  committees, **15(3)**, [482]
  controls, monitoring compliance with,
    15(S), Elections 7
  convictions, duty of court to report to,
    15(3), [471]
  CORE keeper, as, **15(3)**, [320], [596]
  declarations and notifications to—
    generally, **15(3)**, [432]
    register, **15(3)**, [433], [466]
  delegation—
    committees, to, **15(3)**, [482]
    staff, to, **15(3)**, [482]
  democratic systems, education about,
    15(3), [313]
  documentary evidence, **15(3)**, [482]
  education regarding political systems,
    15(3), [313]
  electoral and political matters, reviews of,
    15(3), [297]
  electoral law, consultation with, regarding
    changes to, **15(3)**, [304]
  electoral procedures, involvement in changes
    in, **15(3)**, [306]
  electoral scheme—
    elections by halves—
      existing powers, Electoral Commission
        acting under, **26(2)**, [549]
      incidental provision, **26(2)**, [548]
      notice by council, **26(2)**, [540]
      order for, **26(2)**, [543, [544]
      publicity for order, **26(2)**, [550]
      requirement for electoral review,
        consideration of, **26(2)**, [541]
      transitional provisions, **26(2)**, [547]
      years in which held, **26(2)**, [543]
    elections by thirds—
      existing powers, Electoral Commission
        acting under, **26(2)**, [549]
      incidental provision, **26(2)**, [548]
      notice by council, **26(2)**, [540]

Electoral Commission—*contd*
electoral scheme—*contd*
elections by thirds—*contd*
order for, **26(2)**, [545], [546]
publicity for order, **26(2)**, [550]
requirement for electoral review,
consideration of, **26(2)**, [541]
transitional provisions, **26(2)**, [547]
years in which held, **26(2)**, [545]
new, order for, **26(2)**, [542]
whole council elections, for, notice by
council, **26(2)**, [534]
electoral systems, education about,
15(3), [313]
establishment of, **15(3)**, [292]
existing registered parties, assistance for,
15(3), [338]
expenditure information, requiring,
15(3), [309]
expenses, guidance on, **15(3)**, [216]
failure to deliver documents to, civil
sanctions, **15(S)**, Elections 9
combination of, **15(S)**, Elections 81
disclosure of information,
15(S), Elections 83
discretionary requirements,
15(S), Elections 75–7
enforcement provisions, **15(S)**, Elections 82
enforcement undertaking,
15(S), Elections 79
fixed monetary penalties,
15(S), Elections 73–5
interpretation, **15(S)**, Elections 83–4
penalties, payment into Consolidated
Fund, **15(S)**, Elections 82
reports on use of, **15(S)**, Elections 83
statements, use of, **15(S)**, Elections 81
stop notices, **15(S)**, Elections 77–9
supplementary provision, power to make,
15(S), Elections 79–81
unincorporated associations, amounts
payable by, **15(S)**, Elections 82
financing of, **15(3)**, [482]
five-year plan, **15(3)**, [482]
functions, controls, monitoring compliance
with, **15(S)**, Elections 7
identifying information for CORE, report
on, **15(S)**, Elections 53–4
investigatory powers—
annual report, **15(S)**, Elections 71–2
court orders, **15(S)**, Elections 68
disclosure, requiring, **15(S)**, Elections 66
documents, powers, **15(S)**, Elections 69–70
guidance, **15(S)**, Elections 71
inspection warrants, **15(S)**, Elections 66–7
offences, **15(S)**, Elections 71
provision for, **15(S)**, Elections 8
summary of provisions, **15(S)**, Elections 1
suspected offences or contravention,
powers, **15(S)**, Elections 67
Local Government Boundary Commission for
Wales, transfer of functions to, **15(3)**, [319]
Local Government Commission for England,
transfer of functions to, **15(3)**, [318]

Electoral Commission—*contd*
monitoring compliance with controls,
15(3), [462]
notifications to, **15(3)**, [432]–[433]
party political broadcasts, views on,
15(3), [311]
payments to, **26(2)**, [218], [223]
performance standards—
returns and reports, **15(3)**, [308]
setting, **15(3)**, [307]
policy development grants, **15(3)**, [312]
political parties, maintenance of register of,
15(3), [323]
powers, **15(3)**, [482]
procedure, **15(3)**, [482]
proceedings, **15(3)**, [482]
property, **15(3)**, [482]
recommendation of, for exercise of directions
regarding elections, **15(3)**, [305]
recommendations—
changes, as to, **26(1)**, [106]
duty to make, **26(1)**, [105]
implementation of, **26(1)**, [110]
orders, regulations for supplementing,
26(1), [111]
referendums—
advice as to, **26(2)**, [220]–[223]
encouragement of voting at, **26(2)**, [207]
expenditure, provision for, **26(2)**, [209]
voters, provision of information to,
26(2), [208]
registers—
declarations and notifications, of,
15(3), [433]
inspection, **15(3)**, [466]
third parties, notifications by, **15(3)**, [415]
regulations, **15(3)**, [482]
reports, **15(3)**, [482]
elections, on, **15(3)**, [296], [618]
referendums, on, **15(3)**, [296]
representatives—
attendance at election, **15(3)**, [298]
working practices, observation of,
15(3), [299]
reviews—
conduct of, **26(1)**, [105]
procedure, **26(1)**, [109]
single-member electoral areas—
direction for, **26(1)**, [108]
request for, **26(1)**, [107]
staff, **15(3)**, [482]
political restrictions on,
15(S), Elections 13–14
status, **15(3)**, [482]
superannuation, **15(3)**, [482]
supervisory powers, **15(3)**, [463]

electric line
wayleaves, rent in respect of, **44(1)**, [99]

electricity. *See also* **electricity distributors;**
electricity suppliers; electricity
transmitters; energy
abstracting, **12(1)**, [566]

electricity—*contd*
amenity and fisheries, preservation of,
  17(1), [873]
area boards, transfer of property of,
  17(1), [831], [874]
billing disputes—
  meaning, **17(1)**, [806]
  reference of, **17(1)**, [806]
Boards—
  references to property, rights and
    liabilities, **17(1)**, [848]
  rights of entry—
    restriction on, **17(1)**, [70]
    warrant to authorise, **17(1)**, [71]
body corporate, offences by, **17(1)**, [859]
British Energy plc. *See* **British Energy plc**
climate change levy. *See* **climate change
  levy**
concurrent proceedings, **17(1)**, [827]
Consultative Councils, officers, continuity of
  employment, **17(1)**, [811]
Consumers' Councils, members, continuity of
  employment, **17(1)**, [811]
Council—
  property, rights and liabilities, references
    to, **17(1)**, [848]
  transfer of property of, **17(1)**, [832], [874]
  transfer schemes, **17(1)**, [833]
    Secretary of State, functions of,
      17(1), [834]
Crown land, application of provisions to,
  17(1), [829]
directions, **17(1)**, [858]
Director-General. *See* **Director General of
  Electricity Supply**
disclosure of information, restriction on,
  17(2), [348]
disconnection, investigation of complaints by
  National Consumer Council, **39(1)**, [680]
distribution—
  distributor. *See* **electricity distributors**
  meaning, **17(1)**, [732]
  supply, separation of, **17(2)**, [357]
  unlicensed, prohibition of, **17(1)**, [732]
    exemptions, **17(1)**, [733]
distributors. *See* **electricity distributors**
documents, service of, **17(1)**, [861]
domestic microgeneration, renewables
  obligation certificate, **43(S)**, 522
electrical inspectors, appointment of,
  17(1), [775]
Electricity Supply Pension Scheme,
  17(1), [856], [877]
entry, power of, **17(1)**, [1]
existing bodies, taxation provisions,
  17(1), [875]
extraterritorial operation of Act, **17(1)**, [860]
false statements, making, **17(1)**, [825]
financial provisions, **17(1)**, [862]
fossil fuel—
  levy, **17(1)**, [782]; **17(2)**, [340]
  meaning, **17(1)**, [781I]
Gas and Electricity Consumer Council,
  replaced. *See now* **National Consumer
  Council**

electricity—*contd*
Gas and Electricity Markets Authority. *See*
  Gas and Electricity Markets Authority
Generating Board—
  transfer of property of, **17(1)**, [832], [874]
  transfer schemes, **17(1)**, [833]
    Secretary of State, functions of,
      17(1), [834]
generating stations—
  construction, extension of operation,
    consent for, **17(1)**, [785], [872]
  fuel stocks at, **17(1)**, [783], [784]
  fuelling, **17(1)**, [481]
  renewables obligation certificates,
    17(1), [779]
  sea, at—
    navigation—
      duties in relation to, **17(1)**, [787]
      extinguishing rights of, **17(1)**, [786]
generating stations, application of Factories
  Acts to, **18**, [1176]
generation—
  carbon emissions, target for reduction in,
    17(2), [346]
  licences, power to amend conditions,
    17(2), [675]–[677]
  small-scale low-carbon—
    feed-in tariffs for, **17(2)**, [634]–[636]
    promotion of, **17(2)**, [634]–[636]
generators—
  carbon emissions, reduction in,
    17(1), [796]
  overall targets, **17(2)**, [346]
  meaning, **17(1)**, [734]
green certificates—
  Great Britain, in, **17(2)**, [463]
  Northern Ireland, in, **17(2)**, [464]
high voltage line, meaning, **17(2)**, [524]
information, directions restricting use of
  certain, **17(1)**, [824]
interconnectors—
  licences—
    grant to existing operators, **17(2)**, [496]
    Secretary of State's powers,
      supplementary powers, **17(2)**, [530]
    standard conditions, **17(2)**, [495]
    summary of provisions, **17(1)**, [1]
local authority, generation by, **25(2)**, [363]
maximum prices for reselling, **17(1)**, [805];
  17(2), [341]
measurement, units of, **39(1)**, [559]
meter. *See* **electricity meter**
microgeneration—
  electricity generated by, sale of,
    17(2), [579], [580]
  installation of equipment, apparatus or
    appliances for, review of development
    orders to facilitate, **17(2)**, [581]
  meaning, **17(2)**, [590]
  national targets—
    designation, **17(2)**, [577], [578]
    meaning, **17(2)**, [577]
  sustainable energy reports, information
    in, **17(2)**, [578]

electricity—*contd*
microgeneration—*contd*
permitted development orders, review of, **17(2)**, [581]
system, meaning, **17(2)**, [577]
nationalisation, **17(1)**, [1]
nationally significant infrastructure projects, **46(S)**, 37. *See also* **nationally significant infrastructure projects**
new techniques, promotion in public interest, **17(1)**, [853]
Northern Ireland—
green certificates in, **17(2)**, [464]
regulator, Gas and Electricity Markets Authority power to act on behalf of, **17(2)**, [467]
guarantees of origin functions, **17(2)**, [468]
renewables obligation, **17(2)**, [633]
certificates, in, **17(1)**, [781B]
suppliers, distributions to, **17(2)**, [465]
nuclear installations, operators' liability, **17(1)**, [533]
nuclear liabilities, financial assistance, **17(1)**, [876]
offences committed outside Great Britain, **17(1)**, [860]
overhead lines, consent for, **17(1)**, [788], [872]
privatisation, **17(1)**, [1]
public electricity suppliers. *See* **electricity suppliers**
public inquiries, **17(1)**, [828]
regulations and orders, **17(1)**, [826], [857]
regulatory arrangements, **17(1)**, [1]
renewable sources—
renewables obligation, **17(2)**, [340], [630], [631]
certificates, electricity supplier's duty to produce, **17(2)**, [630]
Northern Ireland, **17(2)**, [633]
order, **17(2)**, [630]
renewables obligation—
banding provision **17(1)**, [781], [781A]
meaning, **17(1)**, [781I]
certificates **17(1)**, [779], [780]
Northern Ireland, in, **17(1)**, [781B]
costs, **17(1)**, [781E]
discharge by payment, **17(2)**, [462]
discharge payment **17(1)**, [781C]
amounts received, allocation of **17(1)**, [781D], [781E]
green certificates, issue of, **17(2)**, [588]
Great Britain, in, **17(2)**, [463]
Northern Ireland, in, **17(2)**, [464]
information, power to obtain **17(1)**, [781F]
meaning, **17(1)**, [781I]
Northern Ireland—
consultation in relation to orders, **17(2)**, [469]
guarantees of origin, Gas and Electricity Markets Authority power to act on behalf of regulator in connection with, **17(2)**, [468]

electricity—*contd*
renewables obligation—*contd*
orders **17(1)**, [777], [778], [781G]
procedure for making **17(1)**, [781H]
supplementary provision, **17(2)**, [466]
safety, **17(2)**, [690]
Health and Safety Executive, consultation with, **17(1)**, [730]
regulations on, **17(1)**, [774]
Scotland—
amenity and fisheries, preservation of, **17(1)**, [873]
roadworks in, **17(1)**, [869]
smart meters—
installation or operation of, licence required for, **17(1)**, [820], [821]
competitive tenders for, **17(1)**, [822]
licences for—
activities requiring, **17(2)**, [682]
conditions, power to amend, **17(2)**, [679]–[681]
stamp duty, **17(1)**, [855]
statistical information, provision of, **17(1)**, [852]
stock, rights and liabilities as to, **17(1)**, [847]
successor companies—
borrowings—
financial limits on, **17(1)**, [843]
temporary restrictions on, **17(1)**, [840]
flotation—
composite listing particulars, responsibility for, **17(1)**, [844]
Trustee Investments Act, application of, **17(1)**, [845]
Government lending to, **17(1)**, [841]
initial Government holding, **17(1)**, [836]
nominees of Treasury or Secretary of State, **17(1)**, [837]
statutory accounts, **17(1)**, [839]
statutory reserves, **17(1)**, [838]
Treasury guarantees, **17(1)**, [842]
suppliers. *See* **electricity suppliers**
supply—
distribution, separation of, **17(2)**, [357]
illegally taken, **17(1)**, [870]
licence—
activities requiring—
Competition Commission, references to, **17(1)**, [814]
Enterprise Act 2002, application of, **17(1)**, [816]
reports, **17(1)**, [817]
time limits, **17(1)**, [815]
exclusion—
application for, **17(1)**, [818]
consultation, **17(1)**, [819]
new, application for order including, **17(1)**, [813]
notices, service of, **17(1)**, [823]
power to alter, **17(1)**, [812]
smart meters, installation or operation of, **17(1)**, [820], [821]
competitive tenders for, **17(1)**, [822]
meaning, **17(1)**, [732]; **17(2)**, [523]

electricity—*contd*
  supply—*contd*
    restoration by councils, **25(2)**, [269], [369],
      [935], [938], [949], [952]
    security, **17(2)**, [690]
    security, directions for preserving,
      17(1), [850]
    unlicensed, prohibition of, **17(1)**, [732]
      exemptions, **17(1)**, [733]
    supply to baths, etc, favourable terms for,
      35(1), [156]
    trading, new arrangements, **17(2)**, [485]
    transitional provisions, **17(2)**, [357]
  transmission—
    charges, adjustment of, **17(2)**, [589]
    licence conditions, amendment of,
      17(2), [675]–[677], [688]
    meaning, **17(1)**, [732]
    offshore, **17(2)**, [637]
    security, directions for preserving,
      17(1), [850]
    transmitters. *See* **electricity transmitters**
    unlicensed, prohibition of, **17(1)**, [732]
      exemptions, **17(1)**, [733]
  transmitters—
    authorised—
      compulsory acquisition of land by,
        17(1), [867], [868]
      existing licences, **17(2)**, [358]
      interference, protection from,
        17(1), [869]
      land, entry on for exploration,
        17(1), [869]
      new arrangements, payments relating
        to, **17(2)**, [337]
      penalties, **17(1)**, [767]
        appeals against, **17(1)**, [771]
        interest and payment of instalments,
          17(1), [770]
        recovery of, **17(1)**, [772]
        statement of policy regarding,
          17(1), [768]
        time limits for imposition of
          financial, **17(1)**, [769]
      powers of, **17(1)**, [744]
      statement of remuneration and service
        standards, requirement for, **17(1)**, [801]
      street works by, **17(1)**, [869]
      trees, felling and lopping, **17(1)**, [869]
      wayleaves, acquisition of, **17(1)**, [869]
    charges for, adjustment of, **17(2)**, [526]
    licences authorising—
      applications, procedure for, **17(1)**, [736]
      compliance, orders for securing,
        17(1), [764]
      conditions, **17(1)**, [740]
      grant of, **17(1)**, [734]
      license holders, general duties,
        17(1), [743]
      modification—
        agreement, by, **17(1)**, [745]
        Competition Commission—
          investigative powers, **17(1)**, [749]
          power to veto modifications
            following report, **17(1)**, [752]

electricity—*contd*
  transmitters—*contd*
    licences authorising—*contd*
      modification—*contd*
        Competition Commission—*contd*
          references to, **17(1)**, [747], [748]
          new electricity trading arrangements,
            under, **17(1)**, [754]
          other enactments, under, **17(1)**, [753]
          report, following, **17(1)**, [751]
          reports on references, **17(1)**, [750]
          standard conditions, of, **17(1)**, [746]
        standard conditions, **17(1)**, [742];
          17(2), [339]
        transfer of, **17(1)**, [741]
      offshore, competitive tenders for licences
        authorising, **17(1)**, [737]

Electricity Consultative Council
  chairmen, remuneration of, **19(2)**, [943]

Electricity Consumers' Council
  members, continuity of employment,
    17(1), [811]

Electricity Council
  privatisation proposals, power to act in relation
    to, **49**, [655]

electricity distributors
  areas with high costs, assistance for,
    17(2), [525]
  authorised—
    compulsory acquisition of land by,
      17(1), [867], [868]
    interference, protection from, **17(1)**, [869]
    land, entry on for exploration, **17(1)**, [869]
    new arrangements, payments relating to,
      17(2), [337]
    penalties, **17(1)**, [767]
      appeals against, **17(1)**, [771]
      interest and payment of instalments,
        17(1), [770]
      recovery of, **17(1)**, [772]
      statement of policy regarding,
        17(1), [768]
      time limits for imposition of financial,
        17(1), [769]
    powers of, **17(1)**, [744]
    street works by, **17(1)**, [869]
    trees, felling and lopping, **17(1)**, [869]
    wayleaves, acquisition of, **17(1)**, [869]
  carbon emissions, reduction in, **17(1)**, [796]
  charges, adjustment to help disadvantaged
    groups of customers, **17(1)**, [803], [804]
  connection—
    additional terms, **17(1)**, [760]
    costs connected with offer of, **17(2)**, [689]
    entry during continuance of, **17(1)**, [870]
    entry during discontinuance of,
      17(1), [870]
    procedure for requiring, **17(1)**, [756]
    restoration of, without consent,
      17(1), [870]

electricity distributors—*contd*
connection—*contd*
special agreements with respect to,
17(1), [761]
disputes, determination of, **17(1)**, [762]
distress, plant etc not subject to, **17(1)**, [870]
duties, summary of provisions, **17(1)**, [1]
duty to connect on request, **17(1)**, [755]
exceptions, **17(1)**, [757]
expenditure, power to recover, **17(1)**, [758]
licences authorising—
applications, procedure for, **17(1)**, [735]
compliance, orders for securing,
17(1), [764]
conditions, **17(1)**, [740]
amendment of, **17(2)**, [675]–[677], [688]
grant of, **17(1)**, [734]
license holders, general duties, **17(1)**, [743]
modification—
agreement, by, **17(1)**, [745]
Competition Commission—
investigative powers, **17(1)**, [749]
power to veto modifications following
report, **17(1)**, [752]
references to, **17(1)**, [747], [748]
new electricity trading arrangements,
under, **17(1)**, [754]; **17(2)**, [486]
other enactments, under, **17(1)**, [753]
report, following, **17(1)**, [751]
reports on references, **17(1)**, [750]
small-scale low-carbon generation, for
promotion of, **17(2)**, [634]–[636]
standard conditions, of, **17(1)**, [746]
standard conditions, **17(1)**, [742];
17(2), [339]
transfer of, **17(1)**, [741]
meaning, **17(1)**, [734]
performance—
disputes concerning, **17(1)**, [792]
individual cases, in, **17(1)**, [791]
overall, **17(1)**, [794]
information to be given to customers
about, **17(1)**, [798]
standards—
complaints handling, information relating
to, **17(1)**, [800]
procedure for prescribing or
determining, **17(1)**, [795]
statistical information about, publication
of, **17(1)**, [799]
summary of provisions, **17(1)**, [1]
plant, damage to, **17(1)**, [870]
powers of entry, **17(1)**, [870]
replacement, repair or alteration of lines or
plant, entry for, **17(1)**, [870]
security, power to require, **17(1)**, [759]
statement of remuneration and service
standards, requirement for, **17(1)**, [801]
supplies illegally taken, recovery of value of,
17(1), [870]

electricity meter
certification of, **17(1)**, [871]
consumption to be ascertained by
appropriate, **17(1)**, [871]

electricity meter—*contd*
disabled persons, for, **17(1)**, [870]
distress, not to be subject to, **17(1)**, [870]
examiners, **17(1)**, [871]
Gas and Electricity Markets Authority,
functions transferred to Secretary of State,
17(2), [686]
interference with, **17(1)**, [871]
pre-payment, **17(1)**, [871]
presumptions and evidence, **17(1)**, [871]
proper order, keeping in, **17(1)**, [871]
restrictions on use of, **17(1)**, [871]
smart, licence required for installation or
operation of, **17(1)**, [820], [821]
testing, **17(1)**, [871]

electricity suppliers
authorised—
compulsory acquisition of land by,
17(1), [867], [868]
existing licences, **17(2)**, [358]
new arrangements, payments relating
to, **17(2)**, [337]
interference, protection from, **17(1)**, [869]
land, entry on for exploration, **17(1)**, [869]
penalties, statement of policy regarding,
17(1), [768]
powers of, **17(1)**, [744]
statement of remuneration and service
standards, requirement for, **17(1)**, [801]
street works by, **17(1)**, [869]
trees, felling and lopping, **17(1)**, [869]
wayleaves, acquisition of, **17(1)**, [869]
carbon emissions, reduction in, **17(1)**, [796]
overall targets, **17(2)**, [346]
charges—
adjustment to help disadvantaged groups of
customers, **17(1)**, [803], [804]
non-payment of, **17(1)**, [870]
connection, restoration without consent,
17(1), [870]
deemed contracts, **17(1)**, [870]
distress, plant etc not subject to, **17(1)**, [870]
enactments referring to, **17(2)**, [338]
entry during continuance of supply,
17(1), [870]
entry during discontinuance of supply,
17(1), [870]
former tariff customers, transitional
provisions, **17(2)**, [359]
licences authorising—
applications, procedure for, **17(1)**, [735]
compliance, orders for securing,
17(1), [764]
conditions, **17(1)**, [740]
amendment of, **17(2)**, [675]–[677]
standard, **17(2)**, [339]
grant of, **17(1)**, [734]
license holders—
penalties, **17(1)**, [767]
appeals against, **17(1)**, [771]
general duties, **17(1)**, [743]
interest and payment of instalments,
17(1), [770]
recovery of, **17(1)**, [772]

electricity suppliers—*contd*
  licences authorising—*contd*
    license holders—*contd*
      penalties—*contd*
        time limits for imposition of
          financial, **17(1)**, [769]
      modification—
        agreement, by, **17(1)**, [745]
        Competition Commission—
          investigative powers, **17(1)**, [749]
          power to veto modifications following
            report, **17(1)**, [752]
          references to, **17(1)**, [747], [748]
        new electricity trading arrangements,
          under, **17(1)**, [754]; **17(2)**, [486]
        other enactments, under, **17(1)**, [753]
        report, following, **17(1)**, [751]
        small-scale low-carbon generation, for
          promotion of, **17(2)**, [634]–[636]
      standard conditions, **17(1)**, [742], [746]
      transfer of, **17(1)**, [741]
  meaning, **17(1)**, [734]
  performance—
    disputes concerning, **17(1)**, [792]
    individual cases, in, **17(1)**, [790]
    levels, information as to, **17(1)**, [797]
    overall, **17(1)**, [793]
      information to be given to customers
        about, **17(1)**, [798]
    standards—
      complaints handling, information relating
        to, **17(1)**, [800]
      procedure for prescribing or
        determining, **17(1)**, [795]
    statistical information about, publication
      of, **17(1)**, [799]
    summary of provisions, **17(1)**, [1]
  powers of entry, **17(1)**, [870]

electricity transmitters
  licences authorising—
    applications, information to be provided to
      Secretary of State, **17(2)**, [490]
    existing, conversion of, **17(2)**, [488], [559]
    grant of, **17(2)**, [489]
    license holders, property arrangements
      schemes involving, **17(2)**, [491], [560]
    modification—
      new electricity trading arrangements,
        under, **17(2)**, [486]
      summary of provisions, **17(1)**, [1]
    new standard conditions for, **17(2)**, [487]
    special administration regime for, **17(1)**, [1]
  new trading and transmission arrangements,
    17(2), [485]
  offshore—
    licences authorising—
      competitive tenders for—
        payments in relation to, **17(1)**, [738]
      property schemes in respect of,
        17(1), [739], [866]
        applications for, **17(1)**, [866]
        effect of, **17(1)**, [866]
        notification of, **17(1)**, [866]
        terms of, **17(1)**, [866]

electricity undertakers
  land drainage affecting, **19(3)**, [259]
  London—
    infilling of cellars affecting, **25(2)**, [668]
    overground wires. *See* **overground wires**
    walkways—
      apparatus, removal of, **25(1)**, [951]
      liability of, **25(1)**, [953]
      notices to be given to, **25(1)**, [950]
      particular provisions as to, **25(1)**, [950]
      works in, **25(1)**, [876], [949]
  working minerals, application for restriction
    on, **17(1)**, [372]

electro-convulsive therapy
  treatment for mental disorder, used as,
    29, [96]

electrolysis
  business of—
    byelaws as to, **35(1)**, [434]
    entry on premises, powers of, **35(1)**, [436]
    local application of provisions as to,
      35(1), [432]
    medical practitioner, under supervision of,
      35(1), [434]
    person or premises for carrying on—
      offences by, **35(1)**, [436]
      registration of—
        certificate of, **35(1)**, [434], [435]
        charge for, **35(1)**, [434]
        requirement of, **35(1)**, [434]
        suspension or cancellation,
          35(1), [435]

electronic communications
  apparatus—
    OFCOM's duty to encourage availability of
      easily usable, **45**, [428]
    sharing use of, **45**, [491]
  available for reception by members of the
    public, meaning, **45**, [723]
  code. *See* **electronic communications code**
  company directors, criminal liability of,
    45, [747]
  documents—
    electronic form, in, **45**, [739]
    service of, **45**, [738]
  Duchy of Lancaster land, purchase of,
    45, [741]
  electronic form, licences in, **24**, [393]
  electronic signatures and related certificates,
    45, [314]
  incentives for, **43(1)**, [546]
    power to provide, **43(1)**, [494]
  information, restrictions on disclosure,
    45, [737]
  key escrow requirements, **45**, [319]
  legislation, modification of—
    National Assembly for Wales, by, **45**, [317]
    Scottish Ministers, by, **45**, [316]
    Secretary of State, by, **45**, [315], [316]
    Treasury, by, **45**, [315], [316]
  licences, destination of fees, **45**, [743]
  mandatory e-filing, **43(2)**, [125]

electronic communications—*contd*
minor and consequential amendments,
　45, [749], [772]
networks and services—
　administrative charges imposed on
　　providers—
　　fixing of, **45**, [456], [457]
　　non-payment—
　　　notification of, **45**, [458]
　　　penalties for, **45**, [459]
　　　suspending service for, **45**, [460],
　　　　[461]
　advance notification to OFCOM, **45**, [451]
　　contravention, **45**, [453]–[455]
　　designations and requirements, **45**, [452]
　conditional access systems, **45**, [493]
　conditions of entitlement to provide—
　　access-related conditions—
　　　modification of, **45**, [494]
　　　network access, **45**, [523]
　　　permitted subject matter, **45**, [491]
　　　revocation of, **45**, [494]
　　　specific types of, **45**, [492]
　　　test for setting or modifying,
　　　　45, [465]
　　copies of notifications, delivery of,
　　　45, [468]
　　customer interests, relating to,
　　　45, [470]–[473]
　　directions and approvals for purposes of,
　　　45, [467]
　　general, **45**, [469]
　　must-carry obligations, **45**, [482]
　　OFCOM's power to set, **45**, [463]
　　persons to whom applicable, **45**, [464]
　　privileged supplier conditions, **45**, [495]
　　procedure for setting, modifying and
　　　revoking, **45**, [466]
　　SMP conditions. *See* **SMP conditions**
　　universal services. *See* **universal
　　　services**
　consumer consultation, **45**, [434]
　consumer research into, **45**, [432], [433]
　dishonestly obtaining services, **45**, [543],
　　[544]
　end-to-end connectivity, **45**, [492]
　improper use of public network, **45**, [545]
　information requirement of OFCOM,
　　45, [553], [554]
　　contravention of—
　　　apparatus supply, suspension of,
　　　　45, [559]–[561]
　　　notification of, **45**, [556]
　　　penalties, **45**, [557]
　　　service provision, suspension of,
　　　　45, [558], [560], [561]
　　　enforcement of directions, **45**, [561]
　　　offences, **45**, [562]
　　　restrictions on imposing, **45**, [555]
　　　statement of policy on, **45**, [563]
　interpretation provisions, **45**, [568]
　leases, restrictions on, **45**, [552]
　licences, restrictions on, **45**, [552]
　local authorities' powers in connection
　　with, **45**, [565]

electronic communications—*contd*
networks and services—*contd*
　location of things done by means of,
　　45, [740]
　meaning, **45**, [450]
　misuse, persistent—
　　enforcement notification for stopping,
　　　45, [547]
　　notification of, **45**, [546]
　　penalties, **45**, [548]
　　statement of policy on, **45**, [549]
　Northern Ireland, grants for—
　　Department of Enterprise, Trade and
　　　Investment, by, **45**, [566]
　　district councils, by, **45**, [567]
　premium rate services, *See* **premium rate
　　services**
　protected programme service, **45**, [493]
　provider's entitlement, power to require
　　suspension or restriction of, **45**, [550],
　　[551]
　provision of information by OFCOM,
　　45, [564]
　publicly accessible register of providers,
　　OFCOM's duty to keep, **45**, [462]
　summary of provisions, **45**, [1]
　telephone numbers. *See* **telephone
　　numbers**
　timing of things done by means of,
　　45, [740]
notifications—
　electronic form, in, **45**, [739]
　service of, **45**, [738]
orders and regulations, power to make,
　45, [745]
other provisions, use under, **43(1)**, [452];
　43(2), [126]
penalties—
　Consolidated Fund, paid into, **45**, [743]
　destination of, **45**, [743]
　imposed by OFCOM, **45**, [736]
pre-consolidation amendments, **45**, [750]
programme guides, code of practice for,
　45, [679]
　compliance with, **45**, [680]
regulations implementing Directives,
　modifications consequential on, **45**, [752]
Secretary of State—
　annual report on functions of, **45**, [734]
　orders and regulations, power to make,
　　45, [745]
services. *See* networks and services *above*
specified information, delivery of,
　43(2), [125]
territorial sea, application of provisions to,
　45, [753]
things done electronically, timing and location
　of, **24**, [394]
transitional provision, **45**, [773]

electronic communications apparatus
meaning, **45**, [428]

electronic communications code
application of, **45**, [524]
  cessation—
    notification of, **45**, [534]
    transitional schemes on, **45**, [535]
  modification of, **45**, [533]
  revocation of, **45**, [533]
  suspension of, **45**, [531], [532]
assistance in certain proceedings, power to
  give, **45**, [537]
compulsory acquisition of land, **45**, [536],
  [757]
entry on land for exploratory purposes,
  45, [757]
procedure for directions applying, **45**, [525]
register of applicable persons, **45**, [526]
restrictions and conditions—
  contravention—
    enforcement notification, **45**, [529]
    penalties, **45**, [530]
  enforcement of, **45**, [528]
  subject to which code applies, **45**, [527]

electronic communications code network
drainage works affecting, protection,
  19(3), [259]

electronic data
protected by encryption—
  appropriate permission, persons having,
    45, [412]
  chief officers of police, duties, **45**, [383]
  Commissioners of Revenue and Customs,
    duties, **45**, [383]
  Director General of the Scottish Crime and
    Drug Enforcement Agency, duties,
    45, [383]
  Director General of the Serious Organised
    Crime Agency, duties, **45**, [383]
  disclosure—
    effect of, **45**, [378]
    notices—
      failure to comply with, **45**, [381]
      requiring, **45**, [377]
      tipping off, **45**, [382]
    payments for, **45**, [380]
    requirements, **45**, [377]
  key, requirement of, **45**, [379]
  Secretary of State, duties, **45**, [383]
  specified authorities, duties of, **45**, [383]
  summary of provisions, **45**, [1]

electronic media
OFCOM's duty to promote media literacy,
  45, [429]

electronic payments
large employers, by, **43(2)**, [248]
other provisions, under, **43(2)**, [249]
pension schemes, **43(2)**, [657]

electronic programme guide
meaning, **45**, [492], [612]

electronic rights management information
alteration of, **11(1)**, [1160]
removal of, **11(1)**, [1160]

emblements
extension of tenancy in lieu, **22**, [586]

emblems
trade mark registration, protection from—
  Convention countries, of, **48**, 154
  international organisations, of, **48**, 155
  national, **48**, 112–3, 154
  notification of, **48**, 156

embryos. *See also* **human fertilisation**
consent to use of, **28**, [633]
crime, keeping and examining in connection
  with, **28**, [625]
female germ cells—
  meaning, **28**, [581]
  prohibition on use of, **28**, [581]
human reproductive cloning, offence of,
  28, [742]
meaning, **28**, [576]
prohibitions in connection with, **28**, [580]

emergency
tax unpaid in case of, interest relief,
  43(S), 970–1

emergency laws
affidavits and declarations, taking, **3**, [459]

emergency powers
acquisition of property other than land. *See*
  requisition *below*
action taken, **9**, [120]
agricultural land—
  amount in case of, **9**, [121]
  meaning, **9**, [136]
annual value of land, work diminishing,
  9, [122], [154], [173]
authorisations, **50**, [264]
Channel Islands, extension to, **9**, [138]
compensation—
  claims, determination, **9**, [126]
  damage to requisitioned land—
    amount, **9**, [120], [191], [216]
    calculation, **9**, [170]
    making good, cost of, **9**, [120], [170]
    value, reference to, **9**, [213]
  land, taking possession of, **9**, [120], [171]
  lien, goods subject to, **9**, [133]
  requisition—
    fair wear and tear—
      disregarded, **9**, [123]
      meaning, **9**, [136]
    land of, **9**, [120], [170]
    machinery, **9**, [123]
      damage caused by removal, **9**, [153]
    ownership of goods deemed in Crown,
      9, [133]
    summary of provisions, **9**, [1]
  work done on land, repayment by
    instalments, **9**, [122]

emergency powers—*contd*
  conditional sale agreement, goods subject to,
    9, [132]
  corporations, offences by, **50**, [268]
  currency, exclusion of, **9**, [131]
  directions, **50**, [263]
  disputes as to, determination of, **9**, [126]
  documents—
    false, **50**, [266]
    production of, **50**, [275]
    proof of, **50**, [264]
  double payments, avoidance of, **9**, [134]
  emergency regulations—
    conditions for making, **50**, [313]
    devolved administrations, consultation
      with, **50**, [321]
    duration, **50**, [318]
    Emergency Coordinators, **50**, [316]
    limitations of, **50**, [315]
    National Assembly for Wales, consultation
      with, **50**, [321]
    Northern Ireland, consultation with First
      Minister, **50**, [321]
    parliamentary scrutiny, **50**, [319]–[320]
    power to make, **50**, [312]
    procedure for making, **50**, [322]
    Regional Nominated Coordinators,
      50, [316]
    scope of, **50**, [314]
    Scottish ministers, consultation with,
      50, [321]
    tribunal, establishing, **50**, [317]
  emergency, meaning, **50**, [295], [311]
  environment, threat of damage to, **50**, [311]
  exclusion in certain cases, **9**, [133]
  false documents and statement, **50**, [266]
  fixed plant and machinery, for removal of,
    9, [153]
  highways, stopping up or diversion, *See*
    highway
  hire-purchase agreement, goods subject to,
    9, [132]
  human welfare, threat of damage to, **50**, [311]
  importation and exportation of goods—
    charges, imposition of, **50**, [182]
    control of, **50**, [181]
    prohibited goods, **50**, [183]
  income tax, treatment of rental compensation
    for, **9**, [121]
  information, disclosure of, **50**, [267]
  interest on, **9**, [129]
  interpretation of provisions, **9**, [136]
  Isle of Man, extension to, **9**, [138]
  legal proceedings, **50**, [270]
  legislation, **50**, [180]
  meaning, **9**, [136]
  mortgage, pledge, etc, property subject to,
    9, [132]
  Northern Ireland, application to, **9**, [137];
    50, [273]
  notices, service of, **9**, [135]; **48**, 952–3;
    50, [264]
  orders, **50**, [263]
  payable apart from statute, **9**, [134]
  penalties, **50**, [269]

emergency powers—*contd*
  permanent effect, enactments having,
    50, [218], [237]–[238]
  rental compensation for requisitioned land,
    9, [121], [170]
  repeals, **50**, [332]–[333]
  requisition—
    agricultural equipment, **9**, [123]
    aircraft, **9**, [123]
    crane, **9**, [123]
    damage, compensation for, **9**, [121], [153],
      [170]
    excavator, **9**, [123]
    goods, **9**, [125]
    meaning, **9**, [136]
    mining or quarrying machinery, **9**, [123]
    ship, **9**, [120], [124]
    space and accommodation in, aircraft,
      9, [120], [124]
    vehicle, **9**, [123]
    vessel, **9**, [123]
  securities, exclusion of, **9**, [131]
  Shipping Claims Tribunal—
    constitution, **9**, [127]
    powers, **9**, [128]
  special constables, appointment of, **50**, [220]
  territorial extent, **50**, [265]
  time limit for claiming, **9**, [130]
  wartime, in, **50**, [180]
  work done on land—
    diminishing annual value, **9**, [122], [154],
      [173]
    lump sum payment, **9**, [122], [155], [173]
    successive works, **9**, [154]

emergency workers
  obstructing or hindering—
    means of effecting, **50(S)**, War 3
    offence, **50(S)**, War 1–2
    penalties, **50(S)**, War 4
    power to modify provisions, **50(S)**, War 4
  persons assisting, obstructing or hindering—
    means of effecting, **50(S)**, War 3
    offence, **50(S)**, War 3
    penalties, **50(S)**, War 4
    power to modify provisions, **50(S)**, War 4

emissions trading
  allocations, charge for, **35(2)**, [622]
  EU, criminal offences, **43(S)**, 997

employee
  annual leave, right to, **16**, [1022]
  benefits in kind. *See* **benefits in kind**
  cash shortages or stock deficiencies—
    cash shortage, meaning, **16**, [620]
    deductions—
      amount and time, limits on, **16**, [621]
      references to, **16**, [620]
    determination of wages, **16**, [622]
    final instalment of wages, **16**, [625]
    payments—
      amount of, limits on, **16**, [624]
      method and time of, limits on, **16**, [623]
    retail employment, meaning, **16**, [620]

employee—*contd*
  cash shortages or stock deficiencies—*contd*
    stock deficiency, meaning, **16**, [620]
  computer equipment provided to, **43(S)**, 46
  counselling services—
    cost, relief for, **44(1)**, [426]
    qualifying, **44(1)**, [427]
  death of, **16**, [500]
    institution or continuance of proceedings,
      16, [854]
    redundancy payments, effect on, **16**, [826]
    rights and liabilities accruing after,
      16, [855]
    termination of employment, effect on,
      16, [785]
  different categories, provisions requiring
    different treatment, repeal etc, **16**, [155],
    [163]
  disabled, automatic car for, **43(S)**, 1388–9
  earning £8,500 or more, benefits in kind. *See*
    benefits in kind
  earnings, return of, **42**, [119]
  exempt benefits, use of non-cash vouchers or
    credit-tokens with obtain, **43(S)**, 48
  eye tests and special glasses, **43(S)**, 47
  family or domestic reasons, leave for,
    detriment, right not to suffer, **16**, [668]
  former, deductions for liabilities—
    connected contracts, **44(2)**, [586]
    deductible payment, meaning, **44(2)**, [583]
    definitions, **44(2)**, [588]
    former employer, borne by, **44(2)**, [582]
    former employment, relating to,
      44(2), [584]
    meaning, **44(2)**, [587]
    net income, from, **44(2)**, [580]
      time limits, outside, **44(2)**, [581]
    office-holders, **44(2)**, [589]
    qualifying insurance contract, meaning,
      44(2), [585]
    relevant liabilities, **44(2)**, [584]
  individual, rights of, **16**, [979]
  information and consultation, regulations,
    16, [1011]
    Northern Ireland, **16**, [1012]
  inventions by. *See* **invention**
  liabilities, deductions for, **43(S)**, 1396–7
  living accommodation. *See* **living**
  accommodation
  meaning, **16**, [19], [22], [75], [113], [503],
    [877], [964]
  mobile telephone provided to, **43(S)**, 45–6
  notes to accounts, information in, **8(1)**, [489]
  persons treated as, returns of, **42**, [314]
  protected disclosure—
    conditions for protection, **16**, [653]
    contractual duties of confidentiality, and,
      16, [655]
    detriment, right not to suffer, **16**, [667]
    disclosures qualifying for protection,
      16, [648]
    employer or other responsible person, to,
      16, [649]
    exceptionally serious failure, of, **16**, [654]
    good faith, in, **16**, [653]

employee—*contd*
  protected disclosure—*contd*
    legal adviser, to, **16**, [650]
    meaning, **16**, [647]
    Minister of the Crown, to, **16**, [651]
    Northern Ireland, **16**, [904]
    personal gain, for, **16**, [658]
    police, application to, **16**, [657]
    prescribed person, to, **16**, [652]
    reasonableness, **16**, [654]
    unfair dismissal for reasons of, **16**, [753]
    worker, meaning, **16**, [656]
  rights—
    complaints and disputes, **16**, [1]
    protection, **16**, [1]
  securities, anti-avoidance, **43(2)**, [762]
  share schemes. *See* **employee share
  ownership trusts; employee share
  scheme**
  training courses for, relief for cost of,
    44(1), [425]
  trust—
    inheritance tax, **42**, [618]
    property becoming subject to, inheritance
      tax, **42**, [606]
    relevant property, **43(S)**, 397
    settled property held on, inheritance tax,
      42, [603]

employee benefit contributions
  restriction of deductions for, **43(2)**, [261];
    43(S), 533

Employee Benefit Trust
  application of provisions, **44(2)**, [574]
  attribution of interests in company,
    44(2), [577]
    appropriate percentage, meaning,
      44(2), [578]
    further, **44(2)**, [579]
  meaning, **44(2)**, [575]
  qualifying disposals, meaning, **44(2)**, [576]

employee incentive scheme
  conditional interests in shares, capital gains tax
    treatment of, **42**, [1267]

employee share ownership trusts
  beneficiaries, **42**, [996]
  capital gains tax—
    chargeable events—
      bonds, ownership of, **42**, [1373]
      replacement assets, ownership of,
        42, [1371]
      replacement property, ownership of,
        42, [1372]
    double charge, prevention of, **42**, [1375]
    dwelling-house, asset being, **42**, [1369]
    information, requirement of, **42**, [1374]
    relief, claim for, **42**, [1368]
    roll-over relief, conditions for, **42**, [1366],
      [1367]
    shares in, **42**, [1370]
  chargeable amounts—
    determining, **42**, [956]

employee share ownership trusts—*contd*
  chargeable amounts—*contd*
    limits on, **42**, [958]
  chargeable events—
    borrowing, **42**, [957]
    charge to tax, **42**, [954]
    events being, **42**, [955]
  continuation of, **42**, [996]
  costs of establishing, **44(1)**, [58]
  establishment of, **42**, [996]
  information, inspector requiring, **42**, [959]
  interpretation, **42**, [996]
  qualifying, **42**, [996]
  qualifying purposes, **42**, [953], [955]
  qualifying transfers, **42**, [955]
  tax relief, **42**, [953]
  trust deed—
    acquisition, rules on, **42**, [996]
    features of, **42**, [996]
    trustees, provision of, **42**, [996]
  trustees—
    functions, **42**, [996]
    securities acquired by, **42**, [996]
    sums received by, **42**, [996]
    trust deed, provision of, **42**, [996]

employee share scheme
  interest, exemption from income tax,
    44(3), [766]
  meaning, **8(1)**, [1244]

employer
  associated, **16**, [505], [878]
  attachment order. *See* **attachment of
    earnings**
  change of, effect on continuous
    employment, **16**, [865]
  death of, **16**, [500]
    institution or continuance of proceedings,
      16, [854]
    lay-off and short-time working, effect on,
      16, [825]
    redundancy payments, effect on, **16**, [824]
    rights and liabilities accruing after,
      16, [855]
    termination of employment, effect on,
      16, [785]
  duties towards employees. *See* **health and
    safety at work**
  health and safety of employees, liability for,
    16, [1]
  industrial training levy on, **16**, [118], [125]
  information, obligation to supply, **16**, [120],
    [121]
  insolvency of—
    employee's rights on, **16**, [832]
      maximum amount of week's pay, increase
        of, **16**, [1023]
    generally, **16**, [1]
    meaning, **16**, [833]
    National Insurance Fund, payments from—
      appropriate date, **16**, [835]
      debts to which provisions apply,
        16, [834]

employer—*contd*
  insolvency of—*contd*
    National Insurance Fund, payments
      from—*contd*
        employment tribunal, complaint to,
          16, [838]
        indexation, **16**, [982]
        information, power to obtain, **16**, [840]
        limits on amount payable, **16**, [836]
        relevant officer, role of, **16**, [837]
        right to, **16**, [832]
        rights and remedies, transfer to Secretary
          of State, **16**, [839]
    large, mandatory electronic payments by,
      43(2), [248]
    meaning, **16**, [503], [877], [964]
    successor, **16**, [882]

employers' associations
  administration provisions, **16**, [325]
  amalgamation, **16**, [327]
  Certification Officer—
    appeal against decisions of, **16**, [320]
    list, keeping, **16**, [317]
  combinations, **16**, [316]
  corporate or quasi-corporate status, **16**, [321]
  federated, **16**, [329]
  list of—
    appeal against decisions, **16**, [320]
    application to enter name on, **16**, [318]
    certificate of inclusion, **16**, [317]
    Certification Officer, kept by, **16**, [317]
    inclusion of name in, **16**, [317]
    removal from, **16**, [319]
  meaning, **16**, [316]
  name, change of, **16**, [328]
  officer, meaning, **16**, [330]
  political objects, application of funds for,
    16, [326]
  property of—
    enforcement of awards against, restrictions
      on, **16**, [324]
    provisions applying to, **16**, [323]
  restraint of trade, exclusion of common law
    rules, **16**, [322]
  tax exemption, **44(1)**, [315]
  transfer of engagements, **16**, [327]

employers' liability
  defective equipment, injuries attributable to,
    16, [19]
  health and safety, **16**, [1]
  personal injuries, for. *See* **personal injury**

employment
  careers, promotion of, **47**, [379]
  chargeable endowments. *See* **Schedule E**
  child, of—
    abroad, travelling for purposes of,
      6, [16]–[17]
    byelaws, **6**, [11], [18], [150]
      confirmation of, **6**, [18]
    education authority, supervision by,
      6, [148]
    evidence of wages, **6**, [49]

employment—*contd*
  child, of—*contd*
    generally, **6**, [1]
    meaning of child, **6**, [149]
    notice containing particulars, **6**, [148]
    offences and penalties, **6**, [13], [17], [148]
    particulars required, **6**, [148]
    powers of entry, **6**, [19]
    proceedings against employer, **6**, [13]
    prohibition and restriction, **15(1)**, [693]
    prohibitions, **6**, [148]
    regulation of, **6**, [147]
    regulations, **6**, [150]
    restrictions on, **6**, [11], [151]
    street trading, in, **6**, [12], [80]
    time limits, **6**, [11]
    unsuitable employment, **6**, [148]
    work experience, as, **15(1)**, [694]
  civil, reinstatement in. *See* **reinstatement in civil employment**
  continuous—
    break in, **16**, [857]
    change of employer, effect of, **16**, [865]
    computing, weeks counting in, **16**, [859]
    determination of questions, **16**, [857]
    dismissed employee, reinstatement or re-engagement of, **16**, [866]
    industrial disputes, effect of, **16**, [863]
    intervals in employment, **16**, [860]
    military service, reinstatement after, **16**, [864]
    month, meaning, **16**, [857]
    overseas employment, **16**, [862]
    period of, **16**, [858]
    presumption as to, **16**, [857]
    redundancy payments, provision for, **16**, [861]
    references to, **16**, [857]
    year, meaning, **16**, [857]
  contracting out of provisions, **16**, [498], [851]
  Crown—
    meaning, **16**, [587], [841]
    national security, provisions excluded in interests of, **16**, [487], [843]
    provisions applying to, **16**, [485], [587], [841]
  detriment, right to not suffer—
    employee representatives, **16**, [664]
    employment tribunals, complaints to—
      presentation of, **16**, [671]
      remedies, **16**, [672]
    family and domestic reasons, leave for, **16**, [668]
    flexible working, application for, **16**, [670]
    health and safety cases, **16**, [660]
    jury service, summoned for, **16**, [659]
    occupational pension schemes, trustees of, **16**, [663]
    protected disclosure, in case of, **16**, [667]
    study or training—
      employees in England aged 16 to 17, **16**, [666]
      exercising right to time off for, **16**, [665]
    Sunday working, **16**, [661]
    tax credits, right to, **16**, [669]

employment—*contd*
  detriment, right to not suffer—*contd*
    working time cases, **16**, [662]
  disability discrimination. *See* **disability discrimination**
  earnings, deductions for payment of maintenance, **6**, [507]–[508]
  excluded classes, provision as to, **16**, [496]
  fixed-term, regulations, **16**, [998]
    Northern Ireland, **16**, [999]
  flexible working. *See* **flexible working**
  foreign law, governed by, **16**, [499]
  health and safety. *See* **health and safety at work; office premises; railway** (premises); **shops**
  House of Commons staff, **16**, [490], [588], [845]
  House of Lords staff, **16**, [489], [588], [844]
  infringement of rights, remedy for, **16**, [853]
  investment scheme, relief withdrawn or reduced, date from which interest payable, **43(S)**, 1418–19
  law governing, **16**, [852]
  loss relief. *See* **loss relief**
  loss relief against general income—
    CGT loss, unused part treated as, **44(4)**, [133]
    claim for, **44(4)**, [131]
    deductions, how made, **44(4)**, [132]
  meaning, **7(1)**, [46], [116], [207]; **16**, [75], [113], [877]
  offshore—
    employment legislation, power to extend, **16**, [849]
    meaning, **16**, [497], [949]
    national minimum wage provisions, **16**, [949]
    provisions applying to, **16**, [497]
  orders and regulations, **16**, [883], [1000]
  outside Great Britain, provisions applying to, **16**, [495]
  part-time—
    code of practice, **16**, [977], [978]
    protection against discrimination, **16**, [976]
  partnerships, **16**, [980]
  periods of, **16**, [893]
  protection entitlement—
    earnings, to be, **40(1)**, [356]
    meaning, **40(1)**, [356]
  racial discrimination. *See* **racial discrimination**
  refusal on grounds of union membership, **16**, [331]
  regulations, **16**, [501]
  reinstatement in. *See* **reinstatement in civil employment**
  restrictive undertaking, consideration for, **42**, [923]
  securities and options granted in relation to, **43(2)**, [253]
  sex discrimination. *See* **sex discrimination**
  share fishermen, of, **16**, [494]
  short-term—
    provisions applying to, **16**, [846]
    redundancy provisions, **16**, [493]

employment—*contd*
    statement of changes, **16**, [605]
    statement of initial particulars—
        alternative documents, use of, **16**, [609]
            given before start of employment,
                16, [610]
        bodies and authorities excluded, **16**, [602]
        contents of, **16**, [602]
        disciplinary procedures and pension, note
            about, **16**, [604]
        employment tribunals, reference to—
            determination of, **16**, [615]
            requirement of, **16**, [614]
        exclusion from right to, **16**, [606]
        further matters, power to require particulars
            of, **16**, [608]
        no particulars to be entered in, **16**, [603]
        other document, reference to, **16**, [603]
        readily accessible document, meaning,
            16, [607]
        right to, **16**, [602]
    statutory adoption pay. *See* **statutory
        adoption pay**
    statutory paternity pay. *See* **statutory
        paternity pay**
    statutory provisions, power to amend,
        16, [856]
    termination. *See* **termination of
        employment**
    young persons. *See under* **young persons**

employment agencies and businesses
    body corporate, offences by, **16**, [57]
    charges and fees—
        regulation of, **16**, [53]
        restriction on, **16**, [54]
    conduct of, general regulations, **16**, [53]
    employment, meaning, **16**, [61]
    entry in documents, false, **16**, [56]
    ex-service personnel, provisions inapplicable,
        16, [61]
    information—
        obtaining and disclosure, **16**, [66]
        unlawful disclosure, **16**, [55], [66]
    inspection, **16**, [55], [992]
    licence, application to Secretary of State,
        16, [90]
    local authorities, exclusion of functions,
        16, [61]
    meaning, **7(1)**, [116], [207]; **16**, [61]
    obstruction of officers, **16**, [55]
    offences—
        bodies corporate, by, **16**, [57]
        cost of investigation, payment of, **16**, [59]
        extension of time limit, **16**, [58]
        organisations excluded, **16**, [61]
    premises, inspection, **16**, [55]
    prohibition order—
        appeals, **16**, [52]
        enforcement, **16**, [50]
        power to make, **16**, [49]
        revocation, **16**, [51]
        variation, **16**, [51]
    racial discrimination by, **7(1)**, [141]

employment agencies and businesses—*contd*
    records—
        fraudulent entries, **16**, [56]
        keeping, **16**, [53]
    refusal of service on grounds related to union
        membership, **16**, [332]
    regulations and orders, **16**, [53], [60]
    services excluded from provisions, **16**, [61]
    sex discrimination by, **7(1)**, [53]
    supply worker working with vulnerable adults,
        duty to refer, **35(2)**, [341]

employment and support allowance
    advance claims, **40(2)**, [551]
    benefit, treatment as, **40(2)**, [551]
    both forms, claimant entitled to, **40(2)**, [501]
    conditionality—
        functions of Secretary of State, contracting
            out, **40(2)**, [511]
        work-focused health-related assessments,
            40(2), [506]
        work-focused interviews—
            action plans, **40(2)**, [509]
            meaning, **40(2)**, [507]
            regulations, **40(2)**, [507]
        work-related activity—
            directions, **40(2)**, [510]
            limited capacity for, **40(2)**, [551]
            meaning, **40(2)**, [508]
            regulations, **40(2)**, [508]
    contributory allowance—
        absence from Great Britain, effect of,
            40(2), [551]
        amount of, **40(2)**, [497]
        conditions, **40(2)**, [549]
        deductions from, **40(2)**, [498]
        meaning, **40(2)**, [496]
        ship, vessel, hovercraft or aircraft,
            employment on, **40(2)**, [551]
        support component, entitlement
            conditions, **40(2)**, [497]
    disqualification from receiving, **40(2)**, [513]
    entitlement—
        assessments, report on, **40(2)**, [505]
        conditions, **40(2)**, [496]
        deemed, **40(2)**, [516]
        forces, members of, **40(2)**, [551]
        linking periods, **40(2)**, [551]
        periods of less than a week, in,
            40(2), [551]
        presence in Great Britain, **40(2)**, [551]
        work—
            effect of, **40(2)**, [551]
            limited capability for, **40(2)**, [503]
            work-related activity, limited capability
                for, **40(2)**, [504]
    financial provisions, **40(2)**, [522]
    income and capital of claimant, calculation
        of, **40(2)**, [512]
    income-related allowance—
        absence from Great Britain, effect of,
            40(2), [551]
        advance award of, **40(2)**, [500]
        amount of, **40(2)**, [499]
        conditions, **40(2)**, [550]

employment and support allowance—*contd*
  income-related allowance—*contd*
    meaning, **40(2)**, [496]
    interpretation, **40(2)**, [519]
    introduction of, **40(2)**, [496]
    limited capacity for work, person with,
      40(2), [551]
    maintenance, recovery of sums in respect of,
      40(2), [518]
    payments below prescribed minimum,
      exclusion of, **40(2)**, [502]
    pilot schemes, **40(2)**, [514]
    regulations—
      Parliamentary control, **40(2)**, [521]
      power to make, **40(2)**, [520]
    statutory payments, relationship with,
      40(2), [515]
    transitional provisions, **40(2)**, [553]
    waiting days, **40(2)**, [551]

Employment Appeal Tribunal
  appeals from, **16**, [586]
  composition of, **16**, [576]
  conduct of hearings, **16**, [577]
  continuation of, **16**, [567]
  costs and expenses, award of, **16**, [583]
  decisions, enforcement, **16**, [585]
  disability cases, restriction of publicity in,
    16, [581]
  employment agency or business, prohibition
    order, **16**, [52]
  interpretation of terms, **16**, [591]
  jurisdiction, **16**, [568]
  members—
    appointed—
      meaning, **16**, [569]
      number of, **16**, [569]
      qualifications of, **16**, [569]
      remuneration, pensions and allowances,
        16, [575]
      tenure, **16**, [574]
    guidance, **16**, [572]
    judges, **16**, [569], [571]
    oaths, **16**, [573]
    temporary, **16**, [570], [571]
    training, **16**, [572]
    welfare, **16**, [572]
  official seal, **16**, [567]
  orders, regulations and rules, **16**, [590]
  power to amend provisions, **16**, [589]
  powers of, **16**, [584]
  practice directions, **16**, [578]
  President, **16**, [569]
  procedure rules, **16**, [579]
  sexual misconduct, restriction of publicity in
    cases involving, **16**, [580]
  summary of provisions, **16**, [1]
  superior court of record, as, **16**, [567]
  time and place of sittings, **16**, [567]
  vexatious proceedings, restriction of, **16**, [582]

employment business
  supply worker working with vulnerable adults,
    duty to refer, **35(2)**, [341]

employment contract
  Rome Convention, application of,
    11(1), [339]

employment-related benefit scheme
  equal treatment, **40(1)**, [205]
  limited, meaning, **40(1)**, [205]
  meaning, **40(1)**, [205]
  personal, meaning, **40(1)**, [205]

employment-related securities
  acquisition, consideration for, **44(2)**, [435]
  application of provisions, **44(2)**, [429]
  artificially depressed market value, with—
    acquisition, tax charge on, **44(2)**, [465]
      amount of, **44(2)**, [466]
      convertible securities, **44(2)**, [467]
      restricted or restricted interest
        securities, **44(2)**, [467]–[468]
    application of provisions, **44(2)**, [464]
    consideration or benefit received,
      adjustment of, **44(2)**, [472]
    definitions, **44(2)**, [474]
    exceptions from charges, disapplication of,
      44(2), [473]
    market value, adjustment of—
      conditional interests, **44(2)**, [469]
      entitlement to convert, consideration
        for, **44(2)**, [470]
  artificially enhanced market value, with—
    application of provisions, **44(2)**, [475]
    definitions, **44(2)**, [481]
    exceptions from charges, disapplication of,
      44(2), [479]
    non-commercial increases, charge on,
      44(2), [476]
    relevant period, subject to restriction
      during, **44(2)**, [478], [480]
    valuation date, subject to restriction on,
      44(2), [477], [480]
  associated persons, **44(2)**, [430]
  changes in interest, **44(2)**, [431]
  consideration, meaning, **44(2)**, [428]
  convertible—
    acquisition, tax relief on, **44(2)**, [455]
    application of provisions, **44(2)**, [453]
    artificially depressed market value, with,
      44(2), [467]
    definitions, **44(2)**, [463]
    meaning, **44(2)**, [454]
    post-acquisition chargeable events—
      amount of charge on, **44(2)**, [458]
      cases outside charge, **44(2)**, [462]
      charge on occurrence of, **44(2)**, [456]
      entitlement to covert, consideration for,
        44(2), [460]
      events being, **44(2)**, [457]
      gain, amount of, **44(2)**, [459]
      secondary Class 1 contributions met by
        employee, relief for, **44(2)**, [461]
  employee-controlled, meaning, **44(2)**, [434]
  employee resident outside UK, exclusion,
    44(2), [432]
  excluded contract of insurance, **44(2)**, [426]
  exclusions from provisions, **44(2)**, [432]–[433]

employment-related securities—*contd*
  information, duty to provide, **44(2)**, [436]
  less than market value, acquired for—
    application of provisions, **44(2)**, [482]
    case outside provisions, **44(2)**, [483]
    definitions, **44(2)**, [489]
    notional loan—
      amount of, **44(2)**, [485]
      discharge, **44(2)**, [486]
      treatment of, **44(2)**, [484]
    other income tax charges, charge in
      addition to, **44(2)**, [488]
    pre-acquisition avoidance cases,
      44(2), [487]
  market value, meaning, **44(2)**, [427]
  meaning, **44(2)**, [426]
  more than market value, disposal of for—
    amount treated as income, **44(2)**, [491]
    application of provisions, **44(2)**, [490]
    definitions, **44(2)**, [492]
  negative amounts, treatment of, **44(2)**, [425]
  PAYE on, **44(2)**, [699]
  persons to whom applying, **44(2)**, [438]
  post-acquisition benefits—
    case outside provisions, **44(2)**, [495]
    definitions, **44(2)**, [496]
    other chargeable benefits, charge on,
      44(2), [493]
      amount of, **44(2)**, [494]
  public offers, exclusion, **44(2)**, [433]
  related provisions, **44(2)**, [424]
  replacement and additional, **44(2)**, [431]
  reportable events, **44(2)**, [437]
  restricted—
    acquisition, no tax charge on, **44(2)**, [442]
    application of provisions, **44(2)**, [439]
    approved plan or scheme, shares under,
      44(2), [450]
    artificially depressed market value, with,
      44(2), [467]–[468]
    definitions, **44(2)**, [440], [452]
    employment-related securities, exclusion
      of, **44(2)**, [441]
    full or partial disapplication of Chapter,
      election for, **44(2)**, [449]
    post-acquisition chargeable events—
      amount of charge on, **44(2)**, [445]
      cases outside charge, **44(2)**, [447]
      charge on occurrence of, **44(2)**, [443]
      events being, **44(2)**, [444]
      outstanding restrictions, election to
        ignore, **44(2)**, [448]
      secondary Class 1 contributions met by
        employee, relief for, **44(2)**, [446]
    relevant period, subject to restriction
      during, **44(2)**, [478], [480]
    tax avoidance, acquisition for purposes of,
      44(2), [451]
    valuation date, subject to restriction on,
      44(2), [477], [480]
  restricted securities, not, **44(2)**, [441]
  scope of provisions, **44(2)**, [423]
  transitional provisions, **44(2)**, [771]

Employment Service Agency
  abolition, **16**, [109]

employment tribunal
  access to wages records, complaint on refusal
    to allow access, **16**, [916]
  appeals from. *See* **Employment Appeal
    Tribunal**
  assessors, **16**, [548]
  awards—
    enforcement, **16**, [561]
    interest on, **16**, [560]
    social security benefits, recoupment of,
      16, [562], [563]
  chairman and one member, hearing by,
    16, [898]
  composition of, **16**, [541]
  conciliation—
    officer, duties of, **16**, [564]
    procedure, **16**, [565]
    proceedings, **16**, [564]
    sums payable under compromises, recovery
      of, **16**, [566]
  conduct of hearings, **16**, [547]
  confidential information, evidence being,
    16, [554]
  contract cases, procedure in, **16**, [551]
  costs and expenses, award of, **16**, [558]
    preparation time, payments in respect of,
      16, [559]
  death of employer or employee—
    institution or continuance of proceedings,
      16, [854]
    rights and liabilities accruing after,
      16, [855]
  deductions, complaint as to—
    determination of, **16**, [627], [628]
    presentation of, **16**, [626]
    remedies, **16**, [629]
  disability cases, restriction of publicity in,
    16, [557]
  disciplinary and grievance hearing, complaint
    of failure to allow union members to be
    accompanied to, **16**, [971]
  employment agency or business, prohibition
    order, **16**, [49]
    appeals, **16**, [52]
  Employment Judge, meaning, **16**, [540]
  equal pay, disputes as to, **16**, [30]–[34]
  establishment, **16**, [537]
  exclusion or expulsion from union, complaint
    as to—
    interpretation of terms, **16**, [375]
    presentation of, **16**, [372]
    remedies, **16**, [374]
    time limit for proceedings, **16**, [373]
  failure to provide statements, reference of—
    determination of, **16**, [615]
    requirement of, **16**, [614]
  flexible working, complaint as to, **16**, [723]
    remedies, **16**, [724]
  guarantee payments, complaint as to,
    16, [637]
  inducements, complaint relating to—
    collective bargaining, relating to, **16**, [341]

employment tribunal—*contd*
  inducements, complaint relating to—*contd*
    consideration of, **16**, [343]
    interpretation of terms, **16**, [345]
    remedies, **16**, [344]
    time limit for proceedings, **16**, [342]
    union membership or activities, as to,
      16, [340]
  industrial training levy, appeal against,
    16, [118], [126]
  industrial tribunals, change of name, **16**, [897]
  interpretation of terms, **16**, [591]
  judicial assistance, **16**, [546]
  jurisdiction—
    enactments conferring, **16**, [538]
    further, power to confer, **16**, [539]
    racial discrimination complaint, **7(1)**, [180]
      See also under **racial discrimination**
    sex discrimination complaint,
      7(1), [101]–[103]
      See also under **sex discrimination**
  mediation, **16**, [550]
  members—
    Employment Judge, **16**, [540]
    guidance, **16**, [543]
    hearing by, **16**, [541]
    oaths, **16**, [545]
    removal from office, **16**, [544]
    remuneration, fees and allowances,
      16, [542]
    training, **16**, [543]
    welfare, **16**, [543]
  national security—
    procedure, **16**, [553]
    publicity, restriction of, **16**, [555]
  orders, regulations and rules, **16**, [591]
  parental leave, complaint as to, **16**, [713]
  payments on insolvency of employer,
    complaint as to, **16**, [838]
  pensions—
    chairman, **11(2)**, [598]
    President, **11(2)**, [597]
  power to amend provisions, **16**, [589]
  practice directions, **16**, [549]
  pre-hearing reviews, **16**, [552], [994]
  preliminary matters, **16**, [552]
  procedure regulations, **16**, [548]
  redundancy—
    failure to comply with consultation
      requirements, complaint of, **16**, [388]
    protective award—
      entitlement under, **16**, [389]
      failure to pay under, complaint of,
        16, [391]
      power to make, **16**, [388]
  redundancy payments, reference of questions
    to, **16**, [813]
    equivalent payments, **16**, [827]
    Secretary of State's payments, **16**, [820]
  regulations, **16**, [537]
  right not to suffer detriment, complaint as
    to—
    national minimum wage, as to, **16**, [934],
      [935]
    presentation of, **16**, [671]

employment tribunal—*contd*
  right not to suffer detriment, complaint as
    to—*contd*
    remedies, **16**, [672]
  right to time off work, complaint as to—
    ante-natal care, for, **16**, [681]
    dependants, for, **16**, [683]
    employee representatives, **16**, [689]
    pension scheme trustees, **16**, [686]
    public duties, performance of, **16**, [675]
    study or training, for, **16**, [692]
    training, to arrange, **16**, [678]
    work, to look for, **16**, [678]
  sexual misconduct, restriction of publicity in
    cases involving, **16**, [556]
  statement of employment particulars, effect of
    failure to give, **16**, [995], [1005]
  summary of provisions, **16**, [1]
  sums payable under compromises, recovery
    of, **11(4)**, [68]; **11(S)**, Courts 109–90
  suspension from work, complaint as to,
    16, [699]
  time off for union duties or activities,
    complaint as to—
    interpretation of terms, **16**, [371]
    presentation of, **16**, [365]
    remedies, **16**, [370]
    time limit for proceedings, **16**, [369]
    union learning representatives, for,
      16, [366]
  trade union membership, complaints as to—
    contributory fault, assessment of, **16**, [355]
    detriment, on grounds of—
      consideration of complaint, **16**, [348]
      interpretation of terms, **16**, [351]
      prohibition of, **16**, [346]
      remedies, **16**, [349]
      third parties, awards against, **16**, [350]
      time limit for proceedings, **16**, [347]
    employer and employment agency, against,
      16, [335]
    employment agency, refusal of service of,
      16, [332]
    interpretation of terms, **16**, [337]
    refusal of employment on grounds of,
      16, [331]
    remedies, **16**, [334]
    third parties, awards against, **16**, [336]
    time limit for, **16**, [333]
    unfair dismissal—
      continuation of employment, order for,
        16, [361]
      contributory fault, assessment of,
        16, [355]
      failure to comply with order, **16**, [363]
      interim relief, application for, **16**, [358]
      interpretation of terms, **16**, [364]
      minimum basic award, **16**, [356]
      order, making, **16**, [360]
      procedure on hearing of application,
        16, [360]
      prompt determination of applications,
        16, [359]
      qualifying period, disapplication of
        requirement for, **16**, [354]

employment tribunal—*contd*
  trade union membership, complaints as
    to—*contd*
    unfair dismissal—*contd*
      third parties, awards against, **16**, [357]
      upper age limit, disapplication of,
        16, [354]
      variation or revocation of order,
        application for, **16**, [362]
  unfair dismissal, complaint of—
    choice and terms of order, **16**, [769]
    compensation, award of—
      adjustments, **16**, [778]
      basic, **16**, [772]–[775]
      compensatory, **16**, [776], [777]
      components of, **16**, [771]
      discriminatory, act also being, **16**, [779]
      enforcement, **16**, [770]
    interim relief—
      continuation of contract of employment,
        order for, **16**, [782]
      determination of complaint, pending,
        16, [780]
      failure to comply with order, **16**, [784]
      order, making, **16**, [781]
      procedure on hearing, **16**, [781]
      variation or revocation of order,
        application for, **16**, [783]
    orders and compensation, **16**, [765]
    presentation of, **16**, [764]
    re-engagement, order for, **16**, [766], [768]
    reinstatement, order for, **16**, [766], [767]
    written statement of reasons for dismissal,
      complaint as to, **16**, [732]

enactment
  consequential amendments, power to make,
    8(1), [1370]
  meaning, **8(1)**, [1369]

endangered species
  importation and exportation, restrictions on.
    See **animals**; **plants**

endemic disease
  prevention of spread of, **35(1)**, [454]
  treatment of persons affected with,
    35(1), [454]

endorsement of licence. *See under* **road
traffic offences**

endowments
  amended provisions, **14(S)**, 82
  annual personal grants from, **14**, 838
  benefices held in plurality, **14**, 839
  bishopric, re-endowment of, **14**, 375
  church educational funds, investment of,
    14, 495
  collegiate churches, for, **14**, 769
  determining what constitutes, **14**, 841–2
  diocesan board of finance, transfer to,
    14, 847–8
  diversion of, **14**, 871–2
  episcopal, vesting of, **14**, 409

endowments—*contd*
  sinecure rectory, of, vesting, **14**, 136, 144
  stipends, payment towards, **14**, 837–8

end-to-end connectivity
  meaning, **45**, [492]

enduring power of attorney
  attorney—
    actual or impending incapacity of donor,
      action on, **29**, [328]
    donor, ill-treatment or neglect of, **29**, [275]
    joint and joint and several, **29**, [333]
    protection of, **29**, [332]
    scope of authority, **29**, [327]
  characteristics of, **29**, [327]
  mental incapacity of surviving donor,
    29, [327]
  provisions ceasing to have effect, **29**, [297]
  register of, **29**, [330]
  registration—
    cancellation, **29**, [331]
    effect and proof of, **29**, [331]
    instrument, of, **29**, [330]
    legal position following, **29**, [331]
    notification prior to, **29**, [329]
  third party, protection of, **29**, [332]
  transitional provisions, **29**, [335]

enemy
  aiding, **12(1)**, [210]
  assisting, **3**, [478], [751], [1014]
  character, evidence in registers, **50**, [213]
  chose in action, assignment of, **50**, [190]
  copyright licence—
    comptroller, grant by, **50**, [208]
    validity, **50**, [207]
    variation, **50**, [207], [208]
  currency, purchasing, **50**, [192]
  debt—
    collection of, **50**, [193]
    German, **50**, [227], [230]
  design—
    licence—
      comptroller, grant by, **50**, [208]
      validity, **50**, [207]
      variation, **50**, [207], [208]
    registration, **50**, [210]
  information, giving to, **12(1)**, [210]
    See also **official secrets**
  meaning, **3**, [1282]; **48**, 940, 971; **50**, [184],
    [187]
  negotiable instrument, transfer of, **50**, [190]
  patent—
    grant to, **50**, [210]
    licence—
      comptroller, grant by, **50**, [208]
      validity of, **50**, [207]
      variation of, **50**, [207], [208]
  property—
    custodian of, **50**, [193], [239]
    generally, **50**, [180]
    German—
      administrator, **50**, [221]
      collection and realisation of, **50**, [221]

enemy—*contd*
  property—*contd*
    German—*contd*
      colony, etc, in, **50**, [224]
      conflicting claims, resolving, **50**, [223]
      distribution of, **50**, [221]
      meaning, **50**, [227]
      offences relating to, **50**, [222]
      Orders in Council, **50**, [225]
      Palestine Custodian of Enemy Property,
        held by, **50**, [224]
    meaning, **50**, [193]
  security, transfer and allotment of, **50**, [191]
  subject, meaning, **50**, [184], [199]
  territory, meaning, **50**, [184], [199]
  trade mark—
    registration of, **50**, [210]
    rights, suspension of, **50**, [209]
  trading with. *See* **enemy, trading with**

enemy, trading with
  Act, extension of, **50**, [198]
  authority, evidence of, **50**, [197]
  controller of business, powers of, **50**, [189]
  corporation, offence by, **50**, [195]
  Crown rights, saving for, **50**, [200]
  false statements, **50**, [194]
  generally, **50**, [180]
  income tax. *See* **income tax**
  inspection of books, **50**, [188]
  law relating to, **42**, [18]
  meaning, **50**, [186]
  obstruction, **50**, [194]
  penalties, **50**, [186]
  person acting for, including, **50**, [186]
  prosecution, instituting, **50**, [186]
  restriction order, **50**, [189]
  sanction, evidence of, **50**, [197]
  supervision of business, **50**, [188]
  winding up order, **50**, [189]

energy. *See also* **electricity; gas**
  climate change, summary of provisions,
    17(1), [1]
  Community obligations, **17(1)**, [492]
  community projects, promotion of,
    17(2), [585]
  conservation. *See* **energy conservation**
  conservation and control—
    administration of Act, **17(1)**, [484], [491]
      financial provisions, **17(1)**, [486]
    authority—
      area of, **17(2)**, [211]
      guidance of Secretary of State,
        17(2), [214]
      meaning, **17(2)**, [211]
    measures, meaning, **17(2)**, [211]
    Northern Ireland, application of provisions
      to, **17(2)**, [218]
    reports—
      contents of, **17(2)**, [212]
      duty to make, **17(2)**, [212]
      house-boats and houses in multiple
        occupation, on, **17(2)**, [235]
      modification of, **17(2)**, [215]

energy—*contd*
  conservation and control—*contd*
    reports—*contd*
      Secretary of State, functions of,
        17(2), [213]
    enforcement provisions, **17(1)**, [484], [491]
    general powers, **17(1)**, [476]
    government directions for, **17(1)**, [474]
    offences in respect of, **17(1)**, [484]
      penalties, **17(1)**, [485]
      proceedings for, **17(1)**, [491]
    orders—
      general control, **17(1)**, [473]
      general provisions, **17(1)**, [483]
      scope of, **17(1)**, [473]
    reserve powers—
      implementation of, **17(1)**, [475]
      Minister, of, **17(1)**, [474]
      territorial application, **17(1)**, [477]
    road traffic and transport law, relaxations,
      17(1), [490]
    substances etc subject to, **17(1)**, [473]
    summary of provisions, **17(1)**, [1]
  documents—
    power to call for, **17(1)**, [491]
    proof of, **17(1)**, [491]
  domestic microgeneration, renewables
    obligation certificate, **43(S)**, 522
  efficiency—
    grants for improvement, **40(1)**, [1], [214]
    increased in residential accommodation,
      17(2), [570]
  fuel. *See* **fuel**
  fuel reserves, maintenance of, **17(1)**, [478]
  functions, charges imposed to fund,
    17(2), [527]
  generating station, fuelling, **17(1)**, [481]
  heat from renewable sources, promotion of
    use of, **17(2)**, [587]
  information—
    disclosure, restriction on, **17(1)**, [491]
    power to obtain, **17(1)**, [491]
  information on measures, local authorities to
    have regard to, **17(2)**, [575]–[576]
  licensees, special administration regime for—
    administration orders—
      applications for, **17(2)**, [501]
      court powers, **17(2)**, [502]
      guarantees where made, **17(2)**, [512]
      meaning, **17(2)**, [499]
      ordinary, restrictions on making,
        17(2), [507]
    administrators, **17(2)**, [503]
      appointments by creditors, restrictions
        on, **17(2)**, [508]
    companies in administration—
      grants and loans, **17(2)**, [510]
      indemnities, **17(2)**, [511]
    conduct of, **17(2)**, [504]
    Enterprise Act 2002, **17(2)**, [515]
    licences—
      funding, conditions to secure,
        17(2), [514]
      modification of, **17(2)**, [513]

energy—*contd*
  licensees, special administration regime
    for—*contd*
    licences—*contd*
      supplementary provisions regarding
        powers, **17(2)**, [530]
      objective of, **17(2)**, [500]
      security, restrictions on enforcement,
        17(2), [509]
      transfer schemes, **17(2)**, [504], [566]
      winding up—
        orders—
          restrictions on, **17(2)**, [505]
          Schedule B1 to the Insolvency
            Act 1986—
              application of, **17(2)**, [562]
              modifications, **17(2)**, [563]–[565]
          voluntary, restrictions on, **17(2)**, [506]
  natural gas—
    disposal by flaring etc, **17(1)**, [480]
    ethane, **17(1)**, [479]
    fuelling of new and converted power
      stations, **17(1)**, [481]
    meaning, **17(1)**, [487]
    methane, **17(1)**, [479]
    offshore—
      administrative provisions, **17(1)**, [484]
      disposal by flaring etc, **17(1)**, [480]
      liquefaction, **17(1)**, [479]
      meaning, **17(1)**, [479]
      price regulation, **17(1)**, [473]
      releasing unignited, **17(1)**, [480]
  offshore installations—
    decommissioning—
      documents, duty to provide,
        17(2), [459]
      information requirements, **17(2)**, [459]
      programmes for—
        approval of, **17(2)**, [450]
        carrying out, **17(2)**, [453]
          default in, **17(2)**, [454]
        contents of, **17(2)**, [448]
        failure to submit, **17(2)**, [451]
        funds for, protection of, **17(2)**, [455],
          [456]
        modification of, **17(2)**, [452]
        notices as to, **17(2)**, [449]
        offences relating to, **17(2)**, [460]
        rejection of, **17(2)**, [451]
        requirement to prepare, **17(2)**, [448],
          [449]
        reviews and revisions of, **17(2)**, [452]
      regulations about, **17(2)**, [457]
      relevant object, responsibility for,
        17(2), [458]
    Petroleum Act 1998, modified for purpose
      of international agreements, **17(2)**, [528]
  offshore production—
    1989 Act licences, activities requiring,
      17(2), [437]
    distribution licences, modification of,
      17(2), [438]
    GB internal waters, **17(2)**, [637]
    generating stations, consents for,
      17(2), [440]

energy—*contd*
  offshore production—*contd*
    navigation, **17(2)**, [445], [446]
    relevant offshore line, **17(2)**, [637]
    renewable energy installations—
      civil law, applied to, **17(2)**, [435], [436]
      criminal law, applied to, **17(2)**, [433],
        [436]
      decommissioning—
        notices relating to, **17(2)**, [662]
        obligations, security for, **17(2)**, [663]
      meaning, **17(2)**, [447]
      offences committed on, **17(2)**, [434]
      safety zones—
        designation of, **17(2)**, [441]
        notices, **17(2)**, [558]
        offences relating to, **17(2)**, [443],
          [444]
        prohibited activities in, **17(2)**, [442]
    renewable energy zones, designation of,
      17(2), [432]
    territorial sea, exploitation of areas
      outside, **17(2)**, [432]
    transmission licences—
      extension offshore, **17(2)**, [439]
      modification of, **17(2)**, [438]
  petroleum—
    fuelling of new and converted power
      stations, **17(1)**, [481]
    passenger car consumption, **17(1)**, [482]
    reserves, maintenance of, **17(1)**, [478]
    summary of provisions, **17(1)**, [1]
    See also **petroleum**
  premises, access to, **17(1)**, [491]
  price control enforcement, **17(1)**, [491]
  prices, regulation of, **17(1)**, [473]
  regulation—
    documents in electronic form, **17(2)**, [533]
    notifications—
      electronic form, in, **17(2)**, [533]
      service of, **17(2)**, [532]
    Secretary of State's functions, **17(2)**, [529]
    statutory instrument, powers exercisable
      by, **17(2)**, [531]
    things done electronically, timing of,
      17(2), [534]
  renewable heat incentives, **17(2)**, [691]
  security of supply, annual report on,
    17(2), [517]
  sustainable—
    aims—
      annual reports on, **17(2)**, [370]
        amendment of provisions,
          17(2), [678]
      meaning, **17(2)**, [371]
      residential accommodation—
        energy conservation authorities'
          duties, **17(2)**, [373]
        National Assembly for Wales's duties as
          to, **17(2)**, [372]
        Secretary of State's duties as to,
          17(2), [371]
    CHP targets, **17(2)**, [374]
    Gas and Electricity Markets Authority, use
      of money held by, **17(2)**, [375]

energy—*contd*
  sustainable—*contd*
    microgeneration, **17(2)**, [431]
    summary of provisions, **17(1)**, [1]

energy products
  excise duty, **13**, [922]

energy-saving items
  corporation tax deduction for expenditure
    on, **43(S)**, 519–20
  expenditure on, treatment of, **44(1)**, [19]–[21]
  income tax deduction for expenditure on,
    43(S), 521

energy-saving materials
  installation of, reduced rate VAT, **50**, [149]

Enfield Chase, Middlesex
  statute affecting, deemed not repealed,
    41, [664]

enforcement notice
  appeal against—
    defect etc in, correcting, **46**, [431]
    determination, giving effect to, **46**, [431]
    dismissal, **46**, [431]
    grounds for, **46**, [429]
    planning permission, provisions on,
      46, [432]
    procedure, **46**, [430]
    writing, to be in, **46**, [429]
  copy, service of, **46**, [426]
  cost of compliance, **46**, [433]
  Crown land, and, **46**, [560]–[561]
  deemed planning permission following
    compliance with, **46**, [427]
  effect of, **46**, [427]
  failure to serve, **46**, [430]
  High Court, appeals to, **46**, [554]
  limitation period for, **46**, [419]
  listed building. *See* **listed building**
  local planning authority, execution of works
    by, **46**, [433]
  matters specified in, **46**, [427]
  meaning, **46**, [426]
  non-compliance with, **46**, [434]
  permanent effect of, **46**, [436]
  planning permission, effect of, **46**, [435]
  power to issue, **46**, [426]
  register of, **46**, [445]
  Secretary of State, issue by, **46**, [437]
  subsequent development, effect against,
    46, [436]
  time limits on action, **46**, [813]
  validity of, **46**, [550]
  variation, **46**, [428]
  withdrawal, **46**, [428]

enforcement of judgment
  county court—
    transfer of enforcement, **19(3)**, [94]
    warrants of control, **19(3)**, [96]
  goods, taking control of—
    amended provisions, **19(3)**, [121]

enforcement of judgment—*contd*
  goods, taking control of—*contd*
    application of proceeds, **19(3)**, [120]
    assignee or nominee, application to,
      19(3), [120]
    best price, obtaining, **19(3)**, [120]
    binding property in goods, **19(3)**, [120]
    care of goods, **19(3)**, [120]
    common law rules, replacement of,
      19(3), [92]
    costs, **19(3)**, [120]
    creditor, remedies available to, **19(3)**, [120]
    Crown preference, abolition, **19(3)**, [98]
    debtor, remedies available to, **19(3)**, [120]
    enactment, writ or warrant, procedure
      under, **19(3)**, [89]
    enforcement agents—
      acting as, **19(3)**, [90]
      certificate to act as, **19(3)**, [91]
      entry on premises, **19(3)**, [120]
      exempt individuals, **19(3)**, [90]
      inventory by, **19(3)**, [120]
      meaning, **19(3)**, [119]
      reasonable force, use of, **19(3)**, [120]
    goods other than securities, abandonment,
      19(3), [120]
    goods which may be taken, **19(3)**, [120]
    highway, goods on, **19(3)**, [120]
    insolvency provisions, relation to,
      19(3), [120]
    interpretation, **19(3)**, [119]
    limitation of liability, **19(3)**, [120]
    means of, **19(3)**, [120]
    notice of enforcement, **19(3)**, [120]
    offence, **19(3)**, [120]
    payment of amount outstanding,
      19(3), [120]
    power of High Court to stay execution,
      19(3), [97]
    pre-commencement enforcement,
      19(3), [93]
    procedure, **19(3)**, [119], [120]
    regulations, **19(3)**, [100]
    sale, **19(3)**, [120]
    securities—
      abandonment, **19(3)**, [120]
      holding and disposal of, **19(3)**, [120]
    summary of provisions, **19(3)**, [1]
    third party, goods claimed by, **19(3)**, [120]
    time limit, **19(3)**, [120]
    title, passing, **19(3)**, [120]
    valuation, **19(3)**, [120]
    value of goods, **19(3)**, [120]
  landlord's lien, restriction on, **19(3)**, [5]
  magistrates' courts, warrants of control,
    19(3), [95]
  meaning, **19(3)**, [1]
  money and bank notes, seizure of, **19(3)**, [2]
  summary of provisions, **19(3)**, [1]

engineering construction
  Factories Act, application of provisions,
    18, [1180]
  work of, meaning, **18**, [1200]

England
meaning, **41**, [605]
Scotland, union with. *See* **Scotland**

English Industrial Estates Corporation
dissolution, **46**, [851]
financial provisions, extension of, **47**, [410]

English information
abolition, **13**, [43]

English Nature
area of special scientific interest, and. *See*
  nature conservation
Commission for Rural Communities,
  temporary provision of staff to, **32**, [794]
dissolution, **32**, [766]
highway construction, opinion as to,
  36, [1122]
Joint Nature Conservation Committee. *See*
  Joint Nature Conservation Committee
Natural England, temporary provision of staff
  to, **32**, [794]
property, rights and liabilities, transfer of,
  32, [791]–[794], [838]
special scientific interest, site of, water
  undertakers, notification to, **49**, [715]

English Tourist Board. *See* **tourism**

Enlistment. *See also* **foreign enlistment**
air force, in—
  attestation paper—
    evidence, as, **3**, [971]
    false answers, **3**, [746]
    generally, **3**, [736], [997]
  consent to, **3**, [736]
  false statement, **3**, [789]
  general service, **3**, [737]
  generally, **3**, [1]
  procedure, **3**, [736]
  regulations, **3**, [748]
  terms, **3**, [1263]
  validity, **3**, [745]
aliens, of, **3**, [474]
army, in—
  appropriate minimum age, **3**, [463]
  attestation—
    evidence, as, **3**, [698]
    false answers, **3**, [473], [516]
    notice of, **3**, [463]
    procedure for, **3**, [725]
    validity, calling into question, **3**, [472]
  consent to, **3**, [463]
  false statement made on, **3**, [267], [516]
  general or corps service, **3**, [464]
  generally, **3**, [1], [463]
  regulations, **3**, [475]
  terms, **3**, [1263]
  validity, calling into question, **3**, [472]
foreign, **3**, [1]

entail
barring of—
  after possibility of issue extinct, **20**, [76]

entail—*contd*
barring of—*contd*
  issue heritable, by, restriction, **20**, [78]
  power, **20**, [75]
  remainderman, rights of, **20**, [75]
base fee—
  bankruptcy of tenant, disposition on,
    20, [103]
  disposition, consent to, **20**, [88]
  enlargement—
    consent to, **20**, [88]
    power, **20**, [77]
    sale or conveyance under Bankruptcy
      Acts, subsequent to, **20**, [106]
    saving of rights on, **20**, [77]
    subsequent to disposition, **20**, [105]
    union with immediate reversion,
      20, [93]
  fine, created by, **20**, [5]
  meaning, **20**, [74]
  union with immediate reversion, **20**, [93]
created by Statute of Westminster the
  Second, **20**, [5]
disentailing assurance—
  consent to, **20**, [95]
  deed, by, **20**, [94]
disposition—
  consent to, **20**, [95]–[98]
  court jurisdiction excluded, **20**, [99]
  Court of Protection as protector, by,
    20, [100]
  deed, by, **20**, [94]
  subsequent, confirmation of voidable
    disposition by, **20**, [92]
donor's will, observance of, **20**, [5]
entailed interest—
  barring of, **20**, [741]
  base fee, equivalent to, **20**, [741]
  contract relating to land, as subject of,
    20, [660]
  creation, **20**, [1], [741]
  devolution, **20**, [1], [741]
  equitable interest, devolution as, **20**, [741]
  meaning, **20**, [741]
  personal estates, in, dealings with, **20**, [741]
  statutory provisions applicable, **20**, [741]
estate—
  confirmed or restored by settlement,
    20, [82]
  meaning, **20**, [74]
estate tail—
  creation, **20**, [6]
  historical note, **20**, [1]
  limitation by deed, **20**, [678]
  meaning, **20**, [74]
  nature of, **20**, [1]
  tenements capable of being held in, **20**, [6]
heir in tail—
  fine no bar, **20**, [5]
  reverter of land, **20**, [5]
interest equivalent to, **20**, [741]
leases at rent created or confirmed by
  settlement, **20**, [83]
money to be invested, meaning, **20**, [74]
person, meaning, **20**, [74]

entail—*contd*
  protector of the settlement—
    appointment by settlor, **20**, [86]
    consent of—
      bankruptcy, in case of, **20**, [104]
      Court of Protection, by, **20**, [100], [101]
      discretion as to, **20**, [90]
      joint protector, by, **20**, [100]
      revocation, prohibition on, **20**, [97]
      unqualified, **20**, [96]
      when needed, **20**, [88], [89], [95]
    Court of Protection as, **20**, [87], [100], [101]
    Lord Chancellor as, **20**, [87]
    married woman, as, **20**, [98]
    mental disorder, **20**, [87], [100], [101]
    owner of prior estate as, **20**, [80]
      when excluded, **20**, [85]
    persons barred, **20**, [84]
    tenant in tail, transactions with, **20**, [91]
    two or more persons running prior estate, **20**, [81]
    who may be, **20**, [80]–[84]
  reverter. *See under* **land**
  Shelley's case, abilition of rule in, **20**, [742]
  tenant in tail—
    actual, meaning, **20**, [74]
    bankruptcy of—
      acts and deeds, when void, **20**, [108]
      assignees, recovery and powers, **20**, [111]
      base fee, disposition, **20**, [103]
      consent to disposition on, **20**, [102]
      death of bankrupt, **20**, [110]
      disposal in case of, **20**, [102]
      disposition—
        powers of, **20**, [109]
        voidable after, **20**, [107]
      land to which provisions applicable, **20**, [114], [115]
      Northern Ireland, application of provisions, **20**, [112]–[115]
      trustee in bankruptcy, powers, **20**, [102]
    disposition—
      deed, by, **20**, [94]
      fee simple, of, **20**, [75]
      restriction on, **20**, [76]
      voidable, confirmation of, **20**, [92], [107]
    meaning, **20**, [74], [779]
    mortgage by, estate created, **20**, [79]
    protector, transactions with, **20**, [91]
    testamentary powers, **20**, [779]

enterprise investment scheme
  amended provisions, **43(S)**, 1123, 1452–3
  amendments, **43(2)**, [68]
  arrangements, meaning, **43(1)**, [519]
  capital gains tax relief, **42**, [1270], [1271]
    reduction of, **42**, [1271]
    reinvestment—
      application of provisions, **42**, [1464]
      chargeable events, **42**, [1464]
        gains accruing on, **42**, [1464]
      claims, **42**, [1464]
      conditions of application, failure of, **42**, [1464]

enterprise investment scheme—*contd*
  capital gains tax relief—*contd*
    reinvestment—*contd*
      disregarded receipts, **42**, [1464]
      information, **42**, [1464]
      insignificant repayments, **42**, [1464]
      interpretation, **42**, [1464]
      investment-linked loans, **42**, [1464]
      investor, value received by, **42**, [1464]
      new company, acquisition of share capital by, **42**, [1464]
      options, **42**, [1464]
      original gain, postponement of, **42**, [1464]
      other persons, value received by, **42**, [1464]
      person to whom gain accrued, **42**, [1464]
      pre-arranged exits, **42**, [1464]
      reconstructions and amalgamations, **42**, [1464]
      reorganisation, **42**, [1464]
      replacement value, receipt of, **42**, [1464]
      same company, in, **42**, [1464]
      trustees, **42**, [1464]
      taper, **42**, [1465]
  carry back of relief, maximum amount, **43(S)**, 344
  corporate trades, relief for investment in, **43(1)**, [78]
  deferral relief, amended provisions, **43(2)**, [546]
  excluded activities—
    coal production, **43(S)**, 1123
    receipt of royalties and licence fees, **43(S)**, 688
    shipbuilding, **43(S)**, 1123
    steel production, **43(S)**, 1123
  gross assets of issuers of shares or securities, limits on, **43(S)**, 342
  increase in, **43(S)**, 859
  loss relief, **43(2)**, [68]
  maximum subscriptions, **43(S)**, 344
  qualifying 90% subsidiary, meaning, **43(S)**, 691
  qualifying companies, amendment of provisions, **43(1)**, [518]
  qualifying trades, **43(1)**, [351]
  reinvestment, **43(S)**, 686
  research and development, meaning, **43(1)**, [519]

enterprise investment scheme relief
  administration or receivership, company in—
    meaning, **44(4)**, [257]
    trading requirement, failure to meet because of, **44(4)**, [186]
  amount of, **44(4)**, [161]
  bare trustees, **44(4)**, [255]
  civil partners, transfers of shares between, **44(4)**, [250]
  claim for—
    compliance certificates, **44(4)**, [209]
    fraudulent, **44(4)**, [212]
    refusal to authorise, appeals, **44(4)**, [211]

enterprise investment scheme relief—*contd*
claim for—*contd*
  compliance statements, **44(4)**, [210]
  fraudulent, **44(4)**, [212]
  entitlement to, **44(4)**, [208]
  time for making, **44(4)**, [207]
eligibility for, **44(4)**, [160]
form of, **44(4)**, [161]
investor—
  issuing company, connection with—
    capital of, interest in, **44(4)**, [173]
    director, as, **44(4)**, [170]
    excluded from connection, **44(4)**, [171]
      relief, qualifying for, **44(4)**, [172]
    employee, as, **44(4)**, [170]
    meaning, **44(4)**, [169]
    partner, as, **44(4)**, [170]
    prohibited, **44(4)**, [166]
    subscription for shares, **44(4)**, [174]
  linked loans, none to be made to, **44(4)**, [167]
  requirements for, **44(4)**, [165]
  tax avoidance, subscription for shares not to be for, **44(4)**, [168]
issuing company, acquisition of—
  by new company, continuity of relief, **44(4)**, [252]
  new shares—
    carry over of obligations where relief attributed to, **44(4)**, [253]
    substituted for old, **44(4)**, [254]
meaning, **44(4)**, [154], [159]
nominees, **44(4)**, [255]
  approved investment fund as, **44(4)**, [256]
other tax reliefs, **44(4)**, [164]
qualifying business activity—
  issuing company to carry on, **44(4)**, [187]
  meaning, **44(4)**, [183]
  minimum period for carrying on, **44(4)**, [180]
risk capital schemes requirement, maximum amount raised through, **44(4)**, [177]
shares—
  attribution to, **44(4)**, [206]
  disposal of—
    civil partners, transfers between, **44(4)**, [250]
    identification of, **44(4)**, [251]
    meaning, **44(4)**, [259]
    spouses, transfers between, **44(4)**, [250]
    withdrawal or reduction of, on, **44(4)**, [214]
  issue—
    pre-arranged exits, not allowed, **44(4)**, [181]
    purpose of, **44(4)**, [178]
    tax avoidance, not allowed for, **44(4)**, [182]
    use of money raised, **44(4)**, [179]
  issuing company—
    control, requirements as to, **44(4)**, [189]
    employees, number of, **44(4)**, [191]

enterprise investment scheme relief—*contd*
shares—*contd*
  issuing company—*contd*
    excluded activities—
      facilities for another business, providing, **44(4)**, [204]
      guest houses, **44(4)**, [203]
      hotels, **44(4)**, [202]
      licence fees, receipt of, **44(4)**, [200]
      meaning, **44(4)**, [197]
      nursing homes, **44(4)**, [203]
      property development, **44(4)**, [201]
      residential care homes, **44(4)**, [203]
      royalties, receipt of, **44(4)**, [200]
      services for another business, providing, **44(4)**, [204]
      ships, leasing of, **44(4)**, [199]
      wholesale and retail distribution, **44(4)**, [198]
    gross assets, **44(4)**, [190]
    independence, requirements as to, **44(4)**, [189]
    property managing subsidiaries, **44(4)**, [193]
    qualifying subsidiaries, **44(4)**, [192], [195]–[196]
    qualifying trade—
      carrying on, **44(4)**, [187]
      meaning, **44(4)**, [194]
    trading requirement, **44(4)**, [185]
      administration or receivership, ceasing to meet because of, **44(4)**, [186]
    unquoted status, **44(4)**, [188]
  not attributable to—
    new, **44(4)**, [139]
    qualifying trading companies, **44(4)**, [137]
      exchange of shares for shares in another company, **44(4)**, [148]
      new shares substituted for old shares, **44(4)**, [149]
    subscriptions for, **44(4)**, [138]
  periods in which issued, **44(4)**, [162]
  requirements for, **44(4)**, [176]
  termination date, meaning, **44(4)**, [261]
spouses, transfers of shares between, **44(4)**, [250]
transitional provisions and savings, **44(4)**, [1052]
withdrawal or reduction of—
  acquisition of share capital, **44(4)**, [238]
  assessments—
    time limits for, **44(4)**, [242]
    when not to be made, **44(4)**, [243]
  assessments for, **44(4)**, [240]
  call options, **44(4)**, [216]
  disposal of shares, on, **44(4)**, [214]
    call options, **44(4)**, [216]
    put options, **44(4)**, [217]
  information—
    HM Revenue and Customs, power to require, **44(4)**, [247]–[248]
    investor, provided by, **44(4)**, [245]
    issuing company, provided by, **44(4)**, [246]

enterprise investment scheme relief—*contd*
withdrawal or reduction of—*contd*
information—*contd*
secrecy obligations, **44(4)**, [249]
interest, date from which chargeable,
44(4), [244]
investor, value received by, **44(4)**, [218]
amount, **44(4)**, [222]
connected persons, by and from,
44(4), [226]
maximum relief not obtained,
44(4), [225]
receipts of insignificant value,
44(4), [219]–[220]
replacement value, **44(4)**, [227]–[228]
share issue—
more than one, **44(4)**, [223]
previous tax year, treated as made in,
44(4), [224]
when, **44(4)**, [221]
maximum relief not obtained, **44(4)**, [215]
meaning, **44(4)**, [262]
put options, **44(4)**, [217]
relief found not to have been due, when,
44(4), [239]
appeals, **44(4)**, [241]
repayments of share capital, **44(4)**, [229]
amount where more than one issue of
shares, **44(4)**, [231]
authorised minimum to be repaid within
12 months, **44(4)**, [235]
insignificant, **44(4)**, [230]
maximum relief not obtained,
44(4), [234]
restriction on, **44(4)**, [236]
single issue—
more than one person, affecting,
44(4), [232]
previous tax year, treated as made
partly in, **44(4)**, [233]
restriction on, repayments of share capital,
44(4), [236]
trade or trading assets, upon acquisition
of, **44(4)**, [237]

enterprise management incentives
coal producing, exclusion of, **43(S)**, 861
excluded activities, **43(S)**, 558
number of employees requirement, **43(S)**, 861
qualifying companies, **43(S)**, 860–2
shipbuilding, exclusion of, **43(S)**, 861
steel, producing, exclusion of, **43(S)**, 861

enterprise zone
authority—
change of, **46**, [115]
modification of scheme by, **46**, [115]
planning authority, as, **46**, [256]
commercial buildings in, **43(1)**, [860]
designation of—
publicity, **46**, [114]
scheme for—
adoption of, **46**, [114]
draft, preparation of, **46**, [114]
invitation to prepare, **46**, [114]

enterprise zone—*contd*
designation of—*contd*
scheme for—*contd*
modification of, **46**, [115], [352]
planning permission, grant of, **46**, [351]
rights of entry, **46**, [114]
termination, **46**, [352]
validity, questioning, **46**, [114]
Secretary of State, by, **46**, [114]
generally, **46**, [1]
industrial training levy on employers,
exemption in, **16**, [130]
local plan, **46**, [311]
planning control, **46**, [116]
qualifying expenditure. *See* **industrial
buildings allowance**
qualifying expenditure, transitional provision,
43(S), 914
structure plan, **46**, [311]

entertainer
income, attribution of, **44(1)**, [389]
payment of tax, **44(1)**, [390]
trade, activity treated as, **44(1)**, [389]
valuation, **44(1)**, [390]

entertainment. *See also* **cinema; theatre**
amusement machines at, **5(1)**, [97]
child, employment of, in. *See* **child**
food given as prize at, **1(2)**, [418]
football. *See* **football matches**
gaming at. *See* **gaming**
hypnotism. *See* **hypnotism**
licensed by Crown, fee for assistance,
26(2), [182]
local authority, provision by, **25(2)**, [147]
London—
booking office licensing, **25(2)**, [394]
concert halls—
cinematograph shows in, **25(1)**, [378]
provision of, **25(1)**, [377]
fire, means of escape, **25(1)**, [809]
open spaces, in, **25(1)**, [379], [842]
power to provide, **25(1)**, [378]
walkways, on, **25(1)**, [875], [948]
lottery at. *See* **lottery**
meaning, **1(2)**, [418]
places of, provision of sanitary appliances at.
See **sanitary appliance**
prizes, with. *See* **amusements with prizes**
safety of child at, **6**, [8]
sport. *See* **sport**
Sunday, on. *See* **Sunday**

enticement
actions, abolition, **45**, [954]

entrances
removal of refuse, access for, **35(1)**, [548]

entrepreneur's relief
amended provisions, **43(S)**, 1028
amount of, **43(S)**, 1024–6
business assets, material disposal of,
43(S), 1021–4

entrepreneur's relief—*contd*
  commencement, **43(S)**, 1028
  interpretation, **43(S)**, 1027–8
  introduction of, **43(S)**, 1021
  reorganisations, **43(S)**, 1026–7
  transitional provisions, **43(S)**, 1028–30
  trust business assets, disposal of,
    43(S), 1022–3

entry and search
  powers. *See under* **police**
  without search warrant, **12(1)**, [851], [960]

entry on land or premises. *See also* **highway;
  search warrant**
  acquiring authority, power of, **9**, [271], [377],
    [393]
  acupuncture, etc, in relation to, **35(1)**, [436]
  advertising in vicinity of London Olympic
    Games, enforcement of regulations,
    13, [493]
  agricultural holding, landlord's right of,
    22, [588]
  agricultural holding, part of, notice of. *See*
    agricultural holding
  agricultural land, **1(1)**, [396]
  alcohol, licensed for, **5(1)**, [590]
  alternative procedure for, **9**, [271], [297]
  articles with blade or point, for, **12(1)**, [1097]
  authorisation of, **22**, [273], [290]
  authority, production of, **9**, [212]
  boarding school, **6**, [415]
  bond, on giving, **9**, [48], [297]
  broadcasting studio, **6**, [19]
  care establishments and agencies, inspection
    of, **35(2)**, [309]
  care homes, **6**, [414]
  Care Quality Commission, power of,
    30(S), NHS 69–71
  Chief Inspector of Schools, person authorised
    by—
      consent to entry, requirements for,
        6(S), 128
      power of constable to assist, **6(S)**, 129
      powers of, **6(S)**, 127
  child support inspectors, by, **6**, [479]
  civil aviation, powers for purposes of,
    4(1), [95], [101]
  climate change levy, in relation to,
    35(2), [380]
  club premises, **19(3)**, [586]
  coast protection authority, powers, **49**, [403]
  compensation for damage, **35(1)**, [340]
  compulsory purchase, in connection with,
    22, [403]
  consent—
      owner or occupier, to, **9**, [271]
      without, penalty for, **9**, [50], [272]
  contaminated land, **35(1)**, [793]
  control of disease, for purposes of,
    35(1), [502]
  control of pests, for purposes of, **35(1)**, [241]
  controlled drugs, securing safe, appropriate
    and effective management of—
      offences, **28**, [845]

entry on land or premises—*contd*
  controlled drugs, securing safe, appropriate
    and effective management of—*contd*
      powers, **28**, [844]
  criminal investigation, for, **12(4)**, [86]
  crossbows, in search for, **12(1)**, [1051]
  Crown, application of provisions, **6**, [536]
  damage arising from, **9**, [271]
  dangerous excavations, dealing with,
    35(1), [388]
  dangerous substances, relating to security of,
    12(3), [111]
  dangerous trees, dealing with, **35(1)**, [385],
    [386]
  deposit in court, on making, **9**, [48], [297]
  drainage boards and local authorities,
    19(3), [239]
  drought, during periods of, **49**, [1136]
  drugs offences, **28**, [222]
  ecclesiastical property, **9**, [271]
  egg storage, to inspect, **1(1)**, [296]
  employment of child, in relation to, **6**, [19]
  Environment Agency, by. *See* **Environment
    Agency**
  estate agency work, for purposes of, **21**, [687]
  evidence of authority, production before,
    35(1), [340]
  fee simple subject to right of, **20**, [631]
  fertilisers and feeding stuffs inspectors,
    1(1), [842]
  Financial Services Authority, warrant for,
    19(1), [849]
  fish and fish eggs, powers as to importation
    of, **1(2)**, [151]
  fish or foodstuff, suspected offences as to,
    1(1), [355]
  fishery officer, **1(2)**, [213]
  food, enforcement of provisions as to,
    1(2), [245]
  food safety, rights connected with, **1(2)**, [446]
  Food Standards Agency, powers of,
    1(2), [654], [657]
  force, by, **49**, [336]
  Forestry Commission, powers, **18**, [1137]
  gambling, in connection with. *See* **gambling**
  gangmasters enforcement or compliance
    officers, **1(2)**, [715]
  gas supplier, by. *See under* **gas**
  goods vehicles, on, **38(1)**, [562], [588]
  grading of produce, for purposes of,
    1(1), [590]
  hill farming land, **1(1)**, [374]
  housing authority, powers of, **22**, [60];
    24, [385]
  human fertilisation offences, relating to,
    28, [622]
  Human Tissue Act, for purposes of, **28**, [834]
  hypnotism, exhibition of, **13**, [120]
  improvement area, premises in, **22**, [232]
  independent hospitals, **6**, [414]
  International Carriage of Perishable Foodstuffs
    Agreement, powers under, **1(2)**, [65]
  investigator for Financial Services Authority,
    power of, **19(2)**, [226]
  knives, search for, **12(2)**, [540]

entry on land or premises—*contd*
land acquired or appropriated, **22**, [397], [403]
land drainage, for repairs etc, **19(3)**, [183]; **20**, [313], [347]
landfill tax, in connection with, **35(2)**, [221]
landmines. *See* **landmines**
Lands Tribunal, by members of, **9**, [217]
licensable activities, to investigate, **19(3)**, [671]
local authority officer, by, **35(1)**, [618]
local authority, right of, **49**, [871]
Medicines Act 1968, to enforce, **28**, [167], [170]
metering, for purposes of, **49**, [981]
milk cessation payment, in relation to, **1(2)**, [235]
mineral workings, former, entry on land of, **17(1)**, [550]
ministerial authority, under, **9**, [203]
noise, in relation to, **35(2)**, [240]
notice to treat, after, **9**, [271]
nuclear weapons inspections, for, **12(2)**, [606], [607]
obstruction of, **22**, [61], [233], [274], [404]; **23**, [35], [385]; **24**, [387]; **35(1)**, [340]; **49**, [336]
OFCOM, powers, **45**, [180], [833]
offences, to investigate, **19(3)**, [672]
offensive weapons, search for, **12(1)**, [1097], [1100]
opencast coal working—
notification, **17(1)**, [166], [213]
purposes of, **17(1)**, [201]
overcrowding provisions, under, **22**, [290], [293]
party wall, execution of work on, **35(2)**, [253]
payment before, **9**, [47]
persons and equipment, taking on, **35(1)**, [340]
pest inspectors, **1(1)**, [396], [631]
pesticides, in relation to, **1(2)**, [249]
poisons, in relation to, **28**, [258]
pollution control, in relation to, **35(2)**, [147], [174]
pollution, enforcement officers, by, **49**, [632], [646]
poultry, in connection with slaughter of, **1(1)**, [677]
proceeds of crime, investigation of, **12(3)**, [458]
rabbit clearance areas, **1(1)**, [464]
radioactive material transport inspection, **38(1)**, [272]
Relevant Authority, powers of, **23**, [384]
removal of refuse, in relation to, **35(1)**, [408]
renewal area, in, **23**, [35]
reservoir construction or alteration, **49**, [595], [607]
right of, **35(1)**, [39], [180], [339]
Rural Development Board, by, **1(1)**, [657]
seals, as to conservation of, **1(1)**, [790]
search warrant. *See* **search warrant**
security, on giving, **9**, [48], [297]

entry on land or premises—*contd*
seeds, inspection etc, **1(1)**, [570], [577]
sewerage, for purposes of, **49**, [980]
sex offender, home address of, **12(3)**, [761]
sheriff's warrant, on, **9**, [273], [377]
slaughterhouse or knacker's yards, **1(1)**, [883]
smoking regulations, for enforcement of, **35(2)**, [585]
social security purposes, for, **40(1)**, [27], [592]
sports ground, **13**, [224], [359]
statutory nuisance, in relation to, **35(1)**, [863]
street trading in vicinity of London Olympic Games, enforcement of regulations, **13**, [497]
survey and examination, for, **22**, [60]; **23**, [35]
survey, for—
before proposal to acquire, **9**, [306]
claim, after submission, **9**, [306]
nature of soil, to ascertain, **9**, [271]
powers of, **9**, [48]
temporary event notice, in case of, **19(3)**, [597]
Thames Water Authority, **49**, [550]
theatres, **13**, [191]
tips, disused, **17(1)**, [395], [400]
traffic signs, in connection with, **37**, [244]
unauthorised, **9**, [272], [377]
unoccupied premises, **35(1)**, [339], [437]
vessel, to, **35(1)**, [339]
video recordings, search for, **13**, [325]
voluntary organisation, of, **6**, [378]
warrant authorising, **35(1)**, [180], [339], [618]
warrant to authorise, **24**, [386]
water authority officer, **1(2)**, [31]
water bailiff, powers, **1(2)**, [31]
water undertakers, by, **49**, [32]
permitted hours, **49**, [52]
powers generally, **49**, [369a]
See also **undertakers**
wayleave orders, connected with, **9**, [196]–[197]
weeds, to control, **1(1)**, [545]
weights and measures authorities, powers **11(2)**, [301]
workplace parking levy, in relation to, **38(2)**, [179]
works notice, under, **49**, [1208]

environment
aerodromes, factors considered in licensing, **4(1)**, [58]
Agency. *See* **Environment Agency**
assessment—
construction and maintenance of highways, **36**, [1121]–[1123]
decisions, validity of, **36**, [1124]
other EEA States, impact on, **36**, [1123]
procedure, **36**, [1122]
special roads, **36**, [1122]
built—
Commission for Architecture and the Built Environment. *See* **Commission for Architecture and the Built Environment**

environment—*contd*
  built—*contd*
    financial assistance, **2**, [1019]
    meaning, **2**, [1013]
  damage to, meaning, **35(1)**, [822]
  drainage board—
    codes of practice, **19(3)**, [235]
    duties of, **19(3)**, [231]
    Ministerial directions, **19(3)**, [234]
  goods vehicles, matters involving licensing,
    38(1), [536], [541], [556]
  local authority's duties as to conservation,
    17(2), [126]
  meaning, **35(1)**, [709], [733], [822];
    35(2), [128]
  planning permission, coal-mining proposals in,
    duties as to, **17(2)**, [177]
  protection of—
    advisory committees. *See under*
      Environment Agency
    minor and consequential amendments,
      35(2), [159], [177]
    pollution control. *See* **pollution**
    statutory nuisance. *See* **statutory nuisance**
  restoration of land after mining operations—
    obligations, **17(2)**, [178]
    proposals in planning application,
      17(2), [177]
  substance released into, **35(1)**, [709]
  water industry, duties in relation to—
    general, **49**, [714]
    sites of special interest, with respect to,
      49, [715]

Environment Agency. *See under* **freshwater
fisheries**
  abstraction and impounding by, **49**, [1123]
  accounts, **35(2)**, [117]
  advisory committees—
    environment protection—
      approved membership schemes—
        approval of, **35(2)**, [169]
        duty to prepare and submit, for each
          region, **35(2)**, [169]
        meaning of, **35(2)**, [97]
        replacement of, **35(2)**, [169]
        variation of, **35(2)**, [169]
      constitution, **35(2)**, [97]
      consultation with, **35(2)**, [97]
      establishment of, **35(2)**, [97]
      maintenance of, **35(2)**, [97]
      members—
        allowances, **35(2)**, [169]
        appointment of, **35(2)**, [169]
        defective appointments, **35(2)**, [169]
        remuneration, **35(2)**, [169]
        vacancies, **35(2)**, [169]
    fisheries, local and regional, **35(2)**, [98]
    Wales, for, **35(2)**, [97]
  air quality. *See* **air quality**
  annual report, **35(2)**, [124]
  application of seal and proof of instruments,
    35(2), [165]
  audit, **35(2)**, [118]

Environment Agency—*contd*
  borrowing—
    government guarantees, **35(2)**, [122]
    government loans, **35(2)**, [121]
    powers, **35(2)**, [120]
  breach of duty owed to, **49**, [1225]
  bridge or tunnel construction, objection to,
    36, [1126]
  byelaws—
    commencement of, **49**, [1296]
    confirmation of, **49**, [1296]
    confirmed, availability of, **49**, [1296]
    enforcement of, **49**, [1261]
    fisheries—
      compensation in respect of, **49**, [1262]
      contributions, **49**, [1196]
      functions, for, **49**, [1295]
      marine or aquatic environmental
        purposes, for, **49**, [1295]
      restrictions on power to make,
        49, [1295]
    flood defence and drainage purposes, for,
      49, [1295]
    inland waters, regulation of use of,
      49, [1295]
    navigable waters, regulating use of,
      49, [1295]
    pollution, control of, **49**, [1295]
    power to make, **49**, [1260]
    proof of, **49**, [1296]
    relevant Minister, meaning, **49**, [1296]
    revocation, **49**, [1296]
    waterways, regulating use of, **49**, [1295]
  chairman, **35(2)**, [165]
  charges, incidental power to impose,
    35(2), [115]
  charging schemes—
    approval of, **35(2)**, [114]
    greenhouse gas emissions permits, in
      respect of, **35(2)**, [113]
    power to make, **35(2)**, [112]
    transitional provisions, **35(2)**, [178]
  coastal waters—
    conservation, **35(2)**, [92]
    enhancement, **35(2)**, [92]
  commutation of obligations, financial
    consequences, **19(3)**, [203]
  compensation—
    assessment, **49**, [1290]
    discharges for works purposes, for,
      49, [1290]
    exercise of works powers, for, **49**, [1226]
    flood defence and drainage works, for,
      49, [1290]
    pipe-laying works, for, **49**, [1290]
    street works powers, for, **49**, [1290]
  compulsory works orders—
    application for, **49**, [1217], [1288]
    compensation, **49**, [1288]
    compulsory acquisition provisions,
      49, [1288]
    discharges of water, authority for,
      49, [1217]
    draft, supply of copies, **49**, [1288]
    notice after making, **49**, [1288]

Environment Agency—*contd*
  compulsory works orders—*contd*
    objections, consideration of, **49**, [1288]
    power to grant, **49**, [1217]
    provisions of, **49**, [1217]
    public undertakings, protection of,
      49, [1288]
  constitution, **35(2)**, [87]
  consultations with, **32**, [259], [263], [284]
  contaminated land—
    guidance by Secretary of State, to have
      regard to, **35(1)**, [807]
    reports on state of, by, **35(1)**, [805]
    site-specific guidance by, **35(1)**, [806]
    special sites—
      designation of, **35(1)**, [789]
      identification of, **35(1)**, [789]
      remediation notice adopted by,
        35(1), [801]
  co-operation between water regulators,
    49, [1365]
  costs and benefits in exercising powers,
    general duty to have regard to, **35(2)**, [110]
  delegation of powers, **35(2)**, [165]
  deputy chairman, **35(2)**, [165]
  directions to, **35(2)**, [161]
  discharges of water—
    consents for, **49**, [1213]
    works purposes, for, **49**, [1212]
  drainage board, as—
    allocation of revenue for purposes of,
      19(3), [227]
    compensation for loss of office,
      19(3), [177]
    concurrent powers, **19(3)**, [179]
    default powers of, **19(3)**, [180]
    directions by, **19(3)**, [178]
    order—
      confirmation, **19(3)**, [256]
      making of, **19(3)**, [175]
      Minister's powers, **19(3)**, [175], [256]
      objection to, **19(3)**, [256]
      powers to make, **19(3)**, [175]
      procedure with respect to, **19(3)**, [256]
      proposed, notice of, **19(3)**, [256]
      provisions of, **19(3)**, [175]
      public inquiry before making,
        19(3), [256]
      transfers of powers, liabilities, etc—
        back from, **19(3)**, [176]
        to, **19(3)**, [175]
      unconfirmed, **19(3)**, [256]
    petition for, **19(3)**, [175]
    supervision by, **19(3)**, [178]
  drainage boards—
    agreements between, **19(3)**, [182]
    concurrent powers, **19(3)**, [179]
    default powers over, **19(3)**, [180]
    expenses of, contributions towards,
      19(3), [226]
    supervision of, **19(3)**, [178]
  drainage districts—
    boundaries, review of, **19(3)**, [173]
    reorganisation scheme, **19(3)**, [174]

Environment Agency—*contd*
  drainage of small areas, schemes for,
    19(3), [187]
  drought orders. *See* **drought**
  enforcement of provisions by, **49**, [1263]
  environmental duties—
    codes of practice, **35(2)**, [95]
    general, **35(2)**, [93]
    sites of special interest, with respect to,
      35(2), [94]
  escapes of water, civil liability for, **49**, [1258]
  establishment of, **35(2)**, [87]
  financial duties, **35(2)**, [116]
    flood defence revenue, with respect to,
      49, [1179]
    local enactments, funds raised under,
      49, [1180]
    other authorities, contributions between,
      49, [1181]
  fisheries—
    advisory committees—
      local, **35(2)**, [98]
      regional, **35(2)**, [98]
    functions in respect of, **35(2)**, [92]
    orders, **49**, [1177]
  flood defence—
    general supervision over, **35(2)**, [92]
    local committees—
      composition of, **35(2)**, [105]
      documents, authentication of,
        35(2), [172]
      general, **35(2)**, [104]
      membership—
        casual vacancies, appointments to fill,
          35(2), [171]
        chairmen, past and present, payments
          to, **35(2)**, [171]
        constituent council, membership of, as
          qualification for, **35(2)**, [171]
        deputies, appointment of, **35(2)**, [171]
        disqualification for, **35(2)**, [171]
        interest, declarations of, **35(2)**, [172]
        payments to members, **35(2)**, [171]
        re-appointment, eligibility of previous
          members for, **35(2)**, [171]
        resignation of, **35(2)**, [171]
        terms of, **35(2)**, [171]
        vacation of office by disqualifying
          event, **35(2)**, [171]
      proof and validity of proceedings,
        35(2), [172]
      rules of procedure, **35(2)**, [172]
      sub-committees—
        appointment of, **35(2)**, [172]
        delegation of functions to,
          35(2), [172]
    local schemes—
      composition of, **35(2)**, [105]
      general, **35(2)**, [104]
      revocation of, **35(2)**, [106]
      savings in relation to, **35(2)**, [179]

Environment Agency—*contd*
flood defence—*contd*
regional committees—
alteration or amalgamation of
boundaries—
consultation and notice of intention to
make order, **35(2)**, [170]
notice after making of order,
35(2), [170]
objections to draft order and making
of order, **35(2)**, [170]
power to make orders, **35(2)**, [170]
procedure for making of order,
35(2), [170]
questioning of orders in courts,
35(2), [170]
change in composition of, **35(2)**, [101]
composition of, **35(2)**, [100]
in Wales, power to alter, **35(2)**, [102],
[103]
documents, authentication of,
35(2), [172]
general, **35(2)**, [99]
membership—
chairmen, past and present, payments
to, **35(2)**, [171]
constituent council, membership of as
qualification for, **35(2)**, [171]
deputies, appointment of, **35(2)**, [171]
disqualification for, **35(2)**, [171], [179]
interest, declarations of, **35(2)**, [172]
payments to members, **35(2)**, [171]
resignation of, **35(2)**, [171]
terms of, **35(2)**, [171]
vacation of office by disqualifying
event, **35(2)**, [171]
proof and validity of proceedings,
35(2), [172]
rules of procedure, **35(2)**, [172]
sub-committees—
appointment of, **35(2)**, [172]
delegation of functions to,
35(2), [172]
Wales, in, power to alter composition
of, **35(2)**, [102], [103]
territorial sea adjacent to England and
Wales, extension of functions to,
35(2), [92]
See also **flood**
fresh-water limits, maps of, **49**, [1242]
functions—
continuity of exercise of, **35(2)**, [127]
delegation of, by Ministers, **35(2)**, [109]
discharge of, **35(1)**, [712]
exercise of, **35(1)**, [712]
incidental, **35(2)**, [96], [108]
scope of, **35(1)**, [712]
functions, carrying out, **49**, [1030]
functions or property transferred to,
49, [1272]
functions transferred to, **19(3)**, [161]; **20**, [1]
gauges, notice of, **49**, [1250]
government loans to, **35(2)**, [121]
grants to, **35(2)**, [119]
harm, power to remedy, **35(1)**, [731]

Environment Agency—*contd*
information—
abstraction, with respect to, **49**, [1251],
[1375]
annual report, **35(2)**, [124]
disclosure of, **35(2)**, [152]
duty to publish, **49**, [1236]
false statements, **49**, [1256]
obtaining, **35(1)**, [723]
permitted disclosure, **49**, [1293]
pollution control, as to, **49**, [1252]
pollution incidents, about, **49**, [1253]
provision of, **35(2)**, [123]
restrictions on disclosure of, **49**, [1254]
underground water—
about, **49**, [1247]
confidentiality of, **49**, [1255]
water flow, concerning, **49**, [1246]
information obtained by, confidentiality,
19(3), [245]
inland waters—
conservation, **35(2)**, [92]
enhancement, **35(2)**, [92]
inquiries and other hearings, **35(2)**, [125]
interpretation provisions, **35(2)**, [128]
land—
compulsory purchase of—
compensation provisions, **49**, [1287]
compulsory works orders, in relation
to, **49**, [1288]
disposal, restrictions on, **49**, [1202]
power of, **49**, [1199]
drainage works, accretions resulting from,
49, [1200]
fisheries purposes, acquisition for,
49, [1201]
powers of entry—
compensation, **49**, [1289]
designated persons, by, **49**, [1221]
enforcement purposes, for, **49**, [1218]
exercise of, **49**, [1289]
impersonation of persons exercising,
49, [1223]
notice of entry, **49**, [1289]
person exercising, obstruction of,
49, [1289]
premises, duty to secure, **49**, [1289]
surveys, to carry out, **49**, [1220]
warrant to exercise, **49**, [1289]
water, to search for, **49**, [1220]
works purposes, for, **49**, [1219]
provisions applied, **25(2)**, [450]
land drainage powers, London, exercise of,
19(3), [185]
legal proceedings, appearance in, **35(2)**, [126]
levies, power to authorise issue of, **49**, [1188]
local authorities powers, supervision of,
19(3), [186]
main river functions—
powers as to, **49**, [1170]
transfer to—
orders, **49**, [1283]
schemes for, **49**, [1171]
members—
appointment of, **35(2)**, [165]

Environment Agency—*contd*
members—*contd*
chairman, **35(2)**, [165]
defective appointments, **35(2)**, [165]
deputy chairman, **35(2)**, [165]
interests of, **35(2)**, [165]
meaning of, **35(2)**, [165]
pensions, **35(2)**, [165]
removal of, **35(2)**, [165]
remuneration, **35(2)**, [165]
resignation of, **35(2)**, [165]
vacancies, **35(2)**, [165]
mineral rights—
acquisition of, **49**, [1231], [1292]
injury, liability for, **49**, [1292]
mining communications, **49**, [1292]
powers of entry, **49**, [1292]
severance, compensation relating to,
49, [1292]
underlying mine, notice of working,
49, [1292]
mining operations affecting water
conservation, notice of, **49**, [1248]
Ministerial directions to, **35(2)**, [111]
minor and consequential amendments,
35(2), [159], [177]
minutes of proceedings, **35(2)**, [165]
national security, directions in interest of,
49, [1257]
navigation authority rights, variation of,
19(3), [204]
navigation tolls—
orders, **49**, [1286]
power to levy, **49**, [1197]
objectives, **35(2)**, [90]
obligations, variation of, schemes,
19(3), [201]
pipes vested in, **49**, [1224]
planning controls, saving for, **49**, [1232]
pollution. *See* **pollution**
pollution control, general functions with
respect to, **35(2)**, [91]
principal aim, **35(2)**, [90]
proceedings of, **35(2)**, [165]
records, **35(2)**, [117]
recreational duties—
codes of practice, **35(2)**, [95]
general, **35(2)**, [93]
registers—
abstraction licences, of, **49**, [1237]
confidential information, exclusion of,
49, [1241]
impounding licences, of, **49**, [1237]
information affecting national security,
exclusion of, **49**, [1240]
pollution control, **49**, [1238]
works discharges, for purposes of,
49, [1239]
repeals and revocations, **35(2)**, [159], [180]
reservoirs in Wales, recreational facilities made
available with, **49**, [1233]
resources—
management schemes, **49**, [1061]
other abstractors, arrangements with,
49, [1062]

Environment Agency—*contd*
resources—*contd*
management schemes—*contd*
Secretary of State, referral to, **49**, [1063]
minimum acceptable flows—
consideration of, **49**, [1066]
inland waters, of, **49**, [1067]
statement on, **49**, [1065], [1273]
protected rights, liability for derogation
from, **49**, [1118]
samples and abstractions, evidence of,
49, [1259]
service of documents, **35(2)**, [162], [165]
sites of special interest, environmental duties
with respect to, **35(2)**, [94]
staff, **35(2)**, [165]
summary of provisions, **35(1)**, [1]
tax provisions, summary of, **43(S)**, 505
tidal lands, works in, **49**, [1230]
trade effluent, powers and duties relating to.
See **trade effluent**
transfer schemes—
consequential provisions, **35(2)**, [167]
consideration, provision for, **35(2)**, [168]
continuity, **35(2)**, [168]
foreign property, rights and liabilities,
perfection of vesting of, **35(2)**, [168]
incidental provisions, **35(2)**, [167]
information and assistance in connection
with, provision of, **35(2)**, [167]
modification of, **35(2)**, [167]
property—
description of, **35(2)**, [167]
division of, **35(2)**, [167]
stamp duty not chargeable, **35(2)**, [158]
supplemental provisions, **35(2)**, [167]
transfer to—
continuity, **35(2)**, [168]
contracts of employment, **35(2)**, [166]
foreign property, rights and liabilities,
perfection of vesting of, **35(2)**, [168]
functions, **35(2)**, [88]
liabilities, **35(2)**, [89]
property, **35(2)**, [89], [165]
remedies, **35(2)**, [168]
rights, **35(2)**, [89]
transitional and transitory provisions,
35(2), [178]
undertakings, protection for, **19(3)**, [259];
49, [1291]
waste regulation, **35(1)**, [734]
water authorities, transfer of provisions
relating to, **19(3)**, [161]; **20**, [1]
water industry, general duties with respect to,
49, [1060]
water resources—
augmentation, **35(2)**, [92]
conservation, **35(2)**, [92]
redistribution, **35(2)**, [92]
works, interference with, **49**, [1225]
working minerals, restriction on, application
for, **17(1)**, [372]

**Environment Protection Advisory
Committees.** *See* **Environment Agency**

environmental protection
Agency. *See* **Environment Agency**
Community obligations, giving effect to,
  35(1), [850]
Crown, application of provisions to,
  35(1), [853]
documents, service of, **32**, [619]
enforcement provisions, **35(1)**, [703]
enforcing authority—
  information, obtaining, **35(1)**, [723]
  public registers of information—
    confidential information, exclusion of,
      35(1), [726]
    information affecting national security,
      exclusion of, **35(1)**, [725]
    maintenance of, **35(1)**, [724]
functions, exercise of, **35(1)**, [712]
grants for purposes of, **32**, [616]
hazardous substances, potentially—
  advisory committee, **35(1)**, [845], [864]
  information, power to obtain, **35(1)**, [845]
hedgerows, protection of, **32**, [615]
information, obtaining, **35(1)**, [723]
injurious substances—
  advisory committee, **35(1)**, [864]
  importation, use, supply or storage,
    prohibition or restriction of, **35(1)**, [843]
institutions, financial assistance to,
  35(1), [848]
international obligations, giving effect to,
  35(1), [850]
London borough, application of provisions,
  26(1), [262]
notices, service of, **32**, [584]; **35(1)**, [854]
offences—
  body corporate, by, **32**, [581]; **35(1)**, [851]
  fault of others, due to, **32**, [582];
    35(1), [852]
  generally, **35(1)**, [703], [727]
  High Court, enforcement measures by,
    35(1), [728]
  penalties, **35(1)**, [727]
  remedy, order for, **35(1)**, [730]
  techniques and evidence, onus of proof,
    35(1), [729]
orders, **35(1)**, [855]
prescribed processes—
  authorisation—
    appeals, **35(1)**, [722]
    application for, **35(1)**, [713], [859]
    conditions, **35(1)**, [714]
    fees and charges, **35(1)**, [715]
    grant of, **35(1)**, [713]
    other statutory controls, and,
      35(1), [732]
    review of conditions, **35(1)**, [713]
    revocation, **35(1)**, [719]
    transfer of, **35(1)**, [716]
    variation of, **35(1)**, [717], [860]
    variation of conditions, application for,
      35(1), [718]
  determination date, **35(2)**, [40]
  enforcement notices, **35(1)**, [720]
  prescription of, **35(1)**, [710]
  prohibition notices, **35(1)**, [721]

environmental protection—*contd*
prescribed processes—*contd*
  registers—
    confidential information, exclusion of,
      35(1), [726]
    information affecting national security,
      exclusion of, **35(1)**, [725]
    maintenance of, **35(1)**, [724]
prescribed substances—
  meaning, **35(1)**, [710]
  prescription of, **35(1)**, [710]
quality objectives, **35(1)**, [711]
registers—
  access to, **35(1)**, [688]
  entries in, **35(1)**, [690]
  maintenance of, **35(1)**, [688]
  prescribed processes, of—
    confidential information, exclusion of,
      35(1), [726]
    information affecting national security,
      exclusion of, **35(1)**, [725]
    maintenance of, **35(1)**, [724]
  responsible authorities, **35(1)**, [689]
  trade secrets, protection of, **35(1)**, [691]
regulations, **35(1)**, [704], [855]
regulations and orders, **32**, [585]
subordinate legislation regarding, consultation
  before making, **32**, [617]

environmentally sensitive area
consultation as to, **1(2)**, [396]
designation of, **1(2)**, [396]

epidemic
prevention of spread of, **35(1)**, [454]
treatment of persons affected with,
  35(1), [454]

Epping Forest
access to, provisions relating to, **32**, [199]
Countryside Act, application to, **32**, [278]

Equal Opportunities Commission
dissolution, power of, **7(1)**, [781]
replaced. *See now* **Commission for Equality
  and Human Rights**
transfer of property of, **7(1)**, [782], [783]
transitional provisions, **7(1)**, [787]

equal pay
agricultural wages orders, effect, **16**, [35]
collective agreements—
  reference to Central Arbitration
    Committee, **16**, [35]
  repeal of certain provisions, **7(1)**, [218]
complainant, **16**, [41]
Crown, extent of application to, **16**, [28]
discrimination, factors justifying, **7(1)**, [217]
disputes—
  complainant, **16**, [41]
  Crown, extent of application to, **16**, [28]
  employer, questioning, **16**, [41]
  employment tribunal—
    panel of experts, **16**, [34]
    procedure before, **16**, [34]

equal pay—*contd*
  employment tribunal—*contd*
    reference of disputes to, **16**, [30]
      arrears date, **16**, [32]
      qualifying date, **16**, [31]
      Scotland, determination of period in,
        16, [33]
  enforcement of requirements, **16**, [30]
  equality clauses in contracts—
    nature of, **16**, [28]
    pensions, in matters of, **16**, [36]
    provisions from which excluded, **16**, [36]
  equality treatment, **16**, [28]
  evaluation of work, **16**, [28], [34]
  government departments, etc, service in,
    16, [28]
  House of Commons staff, application of
    provisions to, **16**, [28]
  House of Lords staff, application of provisions
    to, **16**, [28]
  like work, employment on, **16**, [28]
  men, equality of treatment for, **16**, [28]
  men in the same employment, **16**, [28]
  pay structures, provisions amended,
    7(1), [218]
  pensions, exclusion as to, **16**, [36]
  political office, meaning, **16**, [29]
  service pay and conditions, **16**, [37]
    arrears date, **16**, [39]
    qualifying date, **16**, [38]
    Scotland, determination of period in,
      16, [40]
  summary of provisions, **16**, [1]
  women, equality of treatment, **16**, [28]
  work rated as equivalent, **16**, [28]

Equality Commission for Northern Ireland
  annual report, **31**, [1143]
  Commissioners—
    additional, **31**, [1143]
    appointment of, **31**, [1107]
    salary, **31**, [1143]
    tenure of office, **31**, [1143]
  discrimination, effect of certificates,
    31, [1123]
  enforcement of duties, **31**, [1144]
  establishment, **31**, [1107]
  financial provision, **31**, [1143]
  functions, **31**, [1108]
  members of, **31**, [1107]
  procedure, **31**, [1143]
  public authorities, statutory duty on,
    31, [1109]
  staff, **31**, [1143]
  status, **31**, [1143]

equitable interest and chose in action
  assignment, **20**, [746]
  capable of subsisting as a legal estate,
    meaning, **20**, [804]
  classification of, **20**, [625]
  contingent, creation and disposition, **20**, [628]
  contract relating to land, as subject of,
    20, [660]
  conversion of legal estates into, **20**, [808]

equitable interest and chose in action—*contd*
  conveyances overreaching, **20**, [626]
  creation of, **20**, [625], [628]
  dealings with—
    generally, **20**, [747]
    meaning, **20**, [747]
  disposition—
    generally, **20**, [628]
    writing, necessity for, **20**, [671]
      savings, **20**, [673]
  enforcement, **20**, [627]
  entailed interest, devolution as, **20**, [741]
  estate owner, notice of, **20**, [627]
  estate taking effect as, **20**, [625]
  executory limitations, restriction on, **20**, [744]
  future, creation and disposition, **20**, [628]
  heir, effect of limitation to, **20**, [743]
  legal estates, conversion of into, **20**, [658]
  life interests, dealings with, **20**, [747]
  meaning, **20**, [804]
  notice of dealings with, **20**, [746], [747]
  over-reachable—
    omission from abstract of title, **20**, [626]
    removed from title, **20**, [1], [634]
  owner, concurrence in conveyance, **20**, [661]
  possibility coupled with, disposition, **20**, [628]
  priority of competing interests, **20**, [747]
  protection of registration, **20**, [661]
  purchaser with notice, **20**, [626]
  Shelley's case, abolition of rule, **20**, [742]
  transitional provisions, **20**, [658]

escheat
  abolition of, **18**, [548]
  real estate, **18**, [493]

escuage
  abolition of, **10**, [7]

esplanades
  byelaws as to, **35(1)**, [73]

essential commodities
  commodities declared to be, **47**, [18]
  information—
    default in giving, **47**, [14]
    improper disclosure, **47**, [12]
    power to obtain, **47**, [12]
  meaning, **47**, [16]
  orders as to, **47**, [15]
  reserves—
    creation of, **47**, [13]
    loans to traders for, **47**, [13]
  returns—
    enforcement, **47**, [14]
    power to require, **47**, [12]
  stocks—
    acquisition etc, **47**, [13]
    returns of, **47**, [12]
  storage facilities—
    grants to improve, **47**, [13]
    returns as to, **47**, [12]

Essex County Council
Port of London Act, protection under,
39(2), [390]

Essex River Authority
Port of London Act, protection in,
39(2), [395]

estate
partition or division, stamp duty on
instrument, **41**, [262]

estate agency work. *See also* **estate agent**
advertisements, **21**, [678]
agent of another, by, **21**, [680]
authorised officer—
entry and inspection by, **21**, [687]
obstruction or personation of, **21**, [706]
bankrupt not to engage in, **21**, [700]
books, inspection and copying, **21**, [687]
clients' money. *See* **estate agent**
competence to conduct, **21**, [699]
controller, meaning, **21**, [710]
credit brokerage, in course of, **21**, [678]
discrimination in—
actions deemed to be, **21**, [715]
prohibition, **21**, [680]
employee, performed by, **21**, [678]
enforcement authority—
entry and inspection by, **21**, [687]
meaning, **21**, [705]
exceptions from provisions, **21**, [678]
financial provisions, **21**, [713]
home information packs. *See* **home
information packs**
insurance broker, by, **21**, [678]
interest in land, disposal of, **21**, [679]
meaning, **21**, [678]
offences—
general provisions, **21**, [707]
interest, failure to disclose, **21**, [680]
non-insurance of clients' money, **21**, [693]
obstruction and personation of authorised
officer, **21**, [706]
prohibition order, non-compliance with,
21, [680]
Office of Fair Trading—
applications to, **21**, [717]
enforcement authority, as, **21**, [705]
general duties, **21**, [704]
information to be furnished to, **21**, [686]
orders by—
appeals, **21**, [684]
decision to make, **21**, [716]
notification, **21**, [716]
partnership, against, **21**, [682]
procedure for making, **21**, [716]
proposal to make, notice of, **21**, [716]
register of, **21**, [685]
representations as to, **21**, [716]
revocation, **21**, [683]
unfit persons, prohibiting, **21**, [680]
variation, **21**, [683]
warning orders, **21**, [681]

estate agency work—*contd*
permanent records, requirement to keep,
21, [698]
premises—
entry and inspection, **21**, [687]
information to be displayed on, **21**, [693]
prohibition orders. *See* unfitness *below*
property misdescription. *See* **property
misdescription**
regulations, **21**, [709]
remuneration for, particulars to be given of,
21, [695]
service of notices, **21**, [708]
solicitor, by, **21**, [678]
unfitness for—
deemed, **21**, [680]
limited prohibitions, **21**, [680]
prohibition order, **21**, [680]
non-compliance with, **21**, [680]
revocation or variation, **21**, [683]
supplementary provisions, **21**, [715]
spent conviction, disregard of, **21**, [715]

estate agent. *See also* **estate agency work**
acting as, **24**, [331]
associate, meaning, **21**, [711]
bankrupt not to act as, **21**, [700]
business associate, **21**, [710]
business of. *See* **estate agency work**
client account, **21**, [691]
clients' money—
insurance cover—
appeals, **21**, [694]
exemption from requirements, **21**, [694]
generally, **21**, [693]
interest on, **21**, [692]
meaning, **21**, [689]
prohibition on holding, **21**, [690]
trust, deemed held on, **21**, [690]
trustee, appointment, **21**, [690]
competence, standards of, **21**, [699]
contract deposit, meaning, **21**, [689]
See further clients' money *above*
contract with, **21**, [695]
definitions, **21**, [712]
duly authorised officer, failure to produce
information to, **21**, [688]
general note, **1(1)**, [1]
home information packs. *See* **home
information packs**
information to be given to client—
personal interest, of, **21**, [697]
prospective liabilities, of, **21**, [695]
interest in land, disposal of—
interest of agent, disclosure of, **21**, [697]
meaning, **21**, [679]
Office of Fair Trading, notification of breach
of duty, **24**, [353]
person acting as, responsibility of, **24**, [333]
personal interest in transactions, **21**, [697]
place of business of, **21**, [693]
pre-contract deposit—
meaning, **21**, [689]
prescribed limit, **21**, [696]

estate agent—*contd*
  redress scheme—
    approval of, **21**, [718]
    approved, **21**, [701]
    complaints, **21**, [701]
    penalty charge notices, **21**, [702], [719]
    requirement to belong to, **21**, [701]
    residential property, meaning, **21**, [703]
    withdrawal of approval of, **21**, [718]
  remuneration, information as to, **21**, [695]
  residential property, responsibility for
    marketing, **24**, [332]
  seller, acting for, **24**, [340]
  service of notices on, **21**, [708]
  summary of provisions, **20**, [1]
  title, use of, **21**, [693]
  unfitness. *See* **estate agency work**

estate contract
  land charge, as, **20**, [799]; **21**, [392]
  Law of Property Act, provisions inapplicable,
    20, [626]
  meaning, **21**, [392]

estate duty
  abolition, **42**, [1], [322]
  inheritance tax, transition to, **42**, [829]
  property accepted in lieu, **42**, [907]

estate management schemes
  advice concerning, provision of **23**, [417]
  charges under, **24**, [124]
  general, **23**, [147]
  leasehold valuation tribunal, approval by—
    applications for—
      conservation areas, by public bodies in,
        23, [151]
      expiry of two-year period, after,
        23, [150]
      joint, by landlords in neighbouring
        areas, **23**, [149]
    precedence over initial notice for collective
      enfranchisement, **23**, [152]
    requirement for, **23**, [148]
  modifying provisions, **23**, [424]
  variation of existing schemes, **23**, [153]

estate pur autre vie
  cesqui que vie—
    presumed death, revesting of title if proved
      alive, **20**, [18]
    presumption of death, **20**, [17]
  grant of, **20**, [17]

estate tail. *See* **entail**

estates, university and college
  advowson—
    gratuitous transfer of, **21**, [37]
    power to sell, **21**, [33]
    purchase of, **21**, [34]
  application of Act, **21**, [1], [40]
  benefice—
    augmentation by, **21**, [33]
    endowment, substitution of lands, **21**, [35]

estates, university and college—*contd*
  benefice—*contd*
    headship, severance from, **21**, [36]
  capital money—
    application of, **21**, [26]
    income, application of, **21**, [26]
    land purchased with, **21**, [26]
    lease, paid for, **21**, [29]
    repayment of loan, used for, **21**, [26]
    replacement, provisions on, **21**, [46]
    reversion, paid for, **21**, [29]
    sinking fund, in, **21**, [32], [264]
    transfer of, **21**, [261]
  claims and disputes, compromising, **21**, [17]
  consideration in money or otherwise, **21**, [20]
  contract, power to enter into, **21**, [24]
  court, money payable into, **21**, [28]
  Ecclesiastical Leases Acts not applying to,
    21, [259]
  exchange of land—
    England and Wales, in, **21**, [4]
    Minister, consideration paid to, **21**, [5]
    powers of, **21**, [2]
    regulations, **21**, [4]
  existing powers, saving for, **21**, [41]
  grant of land—
    apportionment of rent, **21**, [19]
    public and charitable purposes, for, **21**, [15]
    variation of, **21**, [18]
  interpretation of terms, **21**, [42]
  lands vested in members, transfer of, **21**, [39]
  lease of land—
    building, for—
      duration, **21**, [6]
      regulations, **21**, [9]
      variation of, **21**, [11]
    duration of, **21**, [6]
    mining—
      duration, **21**, [6]
      option on, **21**, [23]
      regulations, **21**, [10]
      rents, etc, application of, **21**, [12]
      variation of, **21**, [11]
    regrant of, **21**, [13]
    regulations, **21**, [7]
    rent, apportionment of, **21**, [19]
    special objects, for, **21**, [8]
    surrender of, **21**, [13]
    variation of, **21**, [18]
  mineral workings on, **21**, [2]
  Minister, consent of, **21**, [38]
  money in court, use of, **21**, [27]
  money, raising—
    discharge of, provision for, **21**, [32]
    improvements, for, **21**, [30], [45]
    non-renewal of lease, compensation for,
      21, [31]
    power of, **21**, [30]
  option, grant of, **21**, [23]
  patronage, vesting of, **21**, [33]
  public or charitable purpose, grant for,
    21, [15]
  restrictions, lifting of, **21**, [260]
  restrictions on land, releasing, **21**, [17]
  rights over land, dealing with, **21**, [23]

estates, university and college—*contd*
sale of lands—
  auction, at, **21**, [3]
  Minister, consideration paid by, **21**, [5]
  money, for best consideration in, **21**, [3]
  powers of, **21**, [2]
  rent, for **21**, [3]
streets, etc, land appropriated for, **21**, [16]
surface and minerals, separate dealings,
  21, [22]
transactions—
  extent of, **21**, [21], [25]
  Minister effecting, **21**, [21]
trustees, money paid to, **21**, [28]
water rights, grant to statutory authority,
  21, [14]

Estonia
accession to European Union, **18**, [54]

Estray Court for Lordship of Denbigh
jurisdiction, **11(2)**, [381]

ethane
fractionation, **42**, [446]
meaning, **42**, [446]
new price formula, **42**, [450]
petrochemical purposes, alternative valuation
  of, **42**, [446], [450]

EU Treaty
approval of, **18**, [32]

Euratom
classified information, disclosure, **18**, [8]
Treaty establishing, **18**, [1], [10]
See also **European Community**

Euro
adoption of, regulations, **43(1)**, [382]
enterprise management initiatives, adoption,
  possible, **43(2)**, [529]

Eurocontrol
air navigation. *See* **air navigation**

Europe, Diocese in
bishop—
  residence for, **14**, 961
  stipend of, **14**, 961
convocations, represented in, **14**, 959–60
diocesan electors of, **14**, 734
extension of measures to, **14**, 961
Gibraltar, incorporating diocese of,
  14, 959–60
house of laity, representation in, **14**, 960

European Assembly. *See now* **European
Parliament**
change of name, **18**, [29]

European Central Bank
building society, financial assistance to,
  19(S), Financial 279–80
charges, registration of, **19(S)**, Financial 280

European Coal and Steel Community
products, anti-dumping measures, **13**, [588]
Treaty establishing, **18**, [1], [10]

European Commission
detached national experts, subsistence
  allowance, **44(2)**, [307]
provision of information by OFCOM to,
  45, [443]

European Community/Union. *See also*
**Euratom; European Coal and Steel
Community; European Economic
Community**
Andorra, mutual assistance provisions,
  43(2), [528]
Austria, accession of, **18**, [47]
banking and credit directives, amendments
  arising, **12(2)**, [170]
Bulgaria, accession of, **18**, [57]
Channel Islands, position of, **18**, [3], [5]
Commission—
  information from UK for, **18**, [35]
  Treaty establishing, **18**, [10]
common agricultural policy—
  assured markets, **18**, [7]
  levies, provisions as to, **18**, [7]
  refunds on exported goods, **18**, [7]
Community Customs Code etc, review of
  decisions under, **13**, [935], [950]
Community obligations, orders, rules and
  schemes relating to, **18**, [60]
Community relief—
  customs duties—
    administration, **13**, [793]
    imported legacies, **13**, [795]
    meaning, **13**, [795], [802]
    supplementing, **13**, [795], [802]
Community transit goods, meaning, **13**, [590]
Council of. *See* **Council of European
Communities**
Courts of Justice. *See* **European Court of
First Instance; European Court of
Justice**
customs documents, meaning, **13**, [647]
customs duties—
  ad valorem, based on rules of, **13**, [729]
  amendment of law, **18**, [5]
  charge of, **13**, [585]
  enforcement powers, **13**, [919]
  imports into UK, **18**, [6]
  obligations, implementing, **13**, [596]
  rates of, **13**, [627]
  relief from—
    administration of, **13**, [793]
    obligations, in conformity with,
      13, [790], [793]
    practices, referable to, **13**, [791]
Cyprus, accession of, **18**, [54]
Czech Republic, accession of, **18**, [54]
decisions, Parliamentary control of, **18**, [70]
definitions relating to, **18**, [10], [11]
documents, proof of, **18**, [4]
EC certificate of conformity. *See* **passenger
transport services** (light passenger vehicle)

European Community/Union—*contd*
  economic and monetary union, move to, **43(1)**, [450]
  establishment, **18**, [1], [10]
  Estonia, accession of, **18**, [54]
  exportation—
    authentication of customs document, **13**, [647]
    operative date for purposes of, **13**, [646]
  fertilisers and feeding stuffs, implementation of instruments as to, **1(1)**, [840]
  Finland, accession of, **18**, [47]
  food, sources and contact materials, enforcement of provisions as to, **1(2)**, [432]
  free zone, provisions as to, **13**, [695]
  Gibraltar, position of, **18**, [3]
  Greece, accession of, **18**, [27]
  horticultural produce, grading rules, **1(1)**, [588]
  Hungary, accession of, **18**, [54]
  implementation regulations, **12(2)**, [170]
  information to, furnishing, **18**, [9]
  instruments—
    decisions on, and proof of, **18**, [4]
    evidence of, **18**, [4]
    meaning, **18**, [11]
    proof of, **18**, [4]
  Isle of Man, position of, **18**, [3], [5]
  Latvia, accession of, **18**, [54]
  Lithuania, accession of, **18**, [54]
  Malta, accession of, **18**, [54]
  meaning, **18**, [2]
  medical and maternity treatment in, reimbursement of cost, **40(1)**, [1], [144]
  Member States—
    movements of capital between residents of, **44(1)**, [496]
    services for schools in, **15(1)**, [361]
    See **European Economic Community**
  monetary union. *See* **European Monetary Union**
  motor vehicles, drivers' hours rules, **36**, [812], [813]
  nationals of, British citizenship, **31**, [140]
  Northern Ireland, provisions as to, **18**, [3], [5], [12]
  Norway, accession of, **18**, [47]
  obligations, financial provisions, **18**, [3]
  offences, proceedings for, **18**, [8]
  Official Journal, judicial notice of, **18**, [4]
  origin of goods, evidenced under law or practice of, **13**, [676]
  other Member states, recovery of tax due in, **43(2)**, [124], [201]
  packaged goods, marking of, **50**, [396]
  Poland, accession of, **18**, [54]
  Portugal, accession of, **18**, [28]
  regulations, United Kingdom, of, **18**, [12]
  Romania, accession of, **18**, [57]
  Single European Act, meaning, **18**, [30]
  Slovak Republic, accession of, **18**, [54]
  Slovenia, accession of, **18**, [54]
  Spain, accession of, **18**, [28]
  stamp duty exemptions, **42**, [835]

European Community/Union—*contd*
  suckler cow premiums, additional grants for persons entitled to, **1(2)**, [481]
  Sweden, accession of, **18**, [47]
  tax authorities in other member States, information for, **42**, [1028]
  taxation, offences in connection with, **12(2)**, [171]
  terminology, changes of, **18**, [67], [73], [74]
  third pillar, implementation of, **12(3)**, [140], [141]
  Treaties—
    bodies established under, privileges and immunities, **10**, [1011]
    decisions on, **18**, [4]
    definitions relating to, **18**, [10], [11]
    founding, amendment, **18**, [69]
    implementation by UK, **18**, [3]
    judicial notice of, **18**, [4]
    meaning, **18**, [2], [10], [11]
    proof of, **18**, [4]
    questions of law arising, **18**, [4]
  Treaty of Lisbon, meaning, **18**, [66]
  Treaty of Nice, incorporation of provisions of, **18**, [51]
  United Kingdom—
    accession, treaty relating to, **18**, [2]
    amendment of law, **18**, [5]
    Bank of England, annual report by, **18**, [34]
    Committee of Regions, appointment of member to, **18**, [37]
    convergence criteria, assessment of deficits, **18**, [36]
    orders and regulations—
      classified lists of, **18**, [3]
      power to make, **18**, [3]
    Protocol on Social Policy, commencement of, **18**, [38]
    subordinate legislation, **18**, [12]
    workers, free movement of, **18**, [55], [58]
  value added tax provisions. *See* **value added tax**
  veterinary surgeons from—
    knowledge and skill, **28**, [19]
    refusal to register, appeals, **28**, [20]
    registration of, **28**, [18]
  weights and measures obligations, **39(1)**, [529]

European Company/SE
  petition for winding up, **4(2)**, [165]

European Cooperative Society
  petition for winding up, **4(2)**, [166]

European Council. *See* **Council of European Communities; European Economic Community**

European Court of Human Rights. *See* **human rights**

European Court of Justice
  Community law. *See* **European Community**

European Court of Justice—*contd*
　evidence of instruments, **18**, [4]
　false evidence before, **18**, [8]

European Economic Area
　Agreement on—
　　implementation of, **18**, [41]
　　law, consistent application to whole of
　　　EEA, **18**, [40], [46]
　　meaning, **18**, [44]
　export of medicinal products to, **28**, [105]
　free movement of workers, **18**, [55], [58]
　medical practitioner—
　　disqualification, effect of, **28**, [331]
　　fees, recovery of, **28**, [312], [336]
　　full registration without acquired rights
　　　certificate, **28**, [286]
　　medical services in UK by, **28**, [336]
　　primary European qualifications, **28**, [277],
　　　[290], [292], [293]
　　provisional registration, **28**, [288], [294]
　　registration in United Kingdom, **28**, [277],
　　　[292], [356]
　regulations, **18**, [43]

European Economic Community. *See*
European Community
　Community, law. *See* **European**
　Community
　Council. *See* **Council of European**
　Communities
　value added tax provisions. *See* **value added**
　tax

European Economic Interest Grouping
　assessment to tax, **42**, [115]
　charge to tax, **44(1)**, [370]
　income tax liability, **44(4)**, [850]
　meaning, **42**, [115]
　penalties, **43(1)**, [406]
　returns—
　　failure to make, **42**, [231]
　　making, **42**, [115]

European International Convention . . .
Co-operation for Safety of Air
Navigation. *See* **air navigation**
(Eurocontrol)

European Monetary Union
　notification for UK to move to third stage,
　　requirement for approval by Act of
　　Parliament, **18**, [33]

European Parliament
　approval of treaties increasing powers, **18**, [49]
　change of name from European Assembly,
　　18, [29]
　elections—
　　date of, **15(3)**, [539]
　　double voting at, **15(3)**, [544]
　　entitlement to vote, **15(3)**, [543]
　　generally, **15(3)**, [1]
　　Northern Ireland—
　　　filling vacant seats in, **15(S)**, Elections 44

European Parliament—*contd*
　elections—*contd*
　　Northern Ireland—*contd*
　　　voting in, **15(3)**, [228]
　　overseas electors voting at, **15(3)**, [233]
　　peer voting at, **15(3)**, [233], [543]
　　postal-only voting, pilot schemes—
　　　conduct of, **15(3)**, [580], [657]
　　　declaration of identity, **15(3)**, [580]
　　　Electoral Commission report,
　　　　15(3), [583]
　　　interpretation, **15(3)**, [588]
　　　personation, offence of, **15(3)**, [585]
　　　pilot order, **15(3)**, [581]
　　　pilot regions, **15(3)**, [580]
　　　prosecution of offences, time limit,
　　　　15(3), [586]
　　　revision of procedures, **15(3)**, [584]
　　regulations, **15(3)**, [542], [548]
　　returning officers, **15(3)**, [541];
　　　15(S), Elections 45
　　right to vote in, **15(3)**, 1330
　　vacant seats, filling, **15(3)**, [540]
　electoral regions, **15(3)**, [535]
　elector, meaning, **15(3)**, [561]
　England, in, **15(3)**, [554]
　Gibraltar, in, **15(3)**, [554], [564]
　expenses in connection with, **18**, [24]
　financial provisions, **15(3)**, [577]; **18**, [24]
　Gibraltar—
　　capacity of Gibraltar legislature, effect of
　　　statutory powers, **15(3)**, [576]
　　electoral regions, **15(3)**, [554]
　　entitlement to be registered, **15(3)**, [571]
　　existing electoral region, combination
　　　with, **15(3)**, [564]
　　　consequential provision, power to
　　　　make, **15(3)**, [567]
　　　Electoral Commission
　　　　recommendations, **15(3)**, [565]
	　　establishment of region, **15(3)**, [566]
　　　orders, **15(3)**, [567]–[568]
　　franchise for elections, **15(3)**, [570]
　　jurisdiction of courts, **15(3)**, [575]
　　provisions extended to, **15(3)**, [574]
　　register of electors, **15(3)**, [569]
　　regulations, **15(3)**, [572]–[573]
　　voting system, **15(3)**, [537]
　increase in powers—
　　approval of, **18**, [52], [68]
　　ratification of treaties, **15(3)**, [547]
　interpretation, **15(3)**, [552], [578]
　MEP's pay, allowances and pensions, tax
　　relief, **43(S)**, 1390–1
　pensions increase, **33(1)**, [112]
　Representatives—
　　allowances to, **18**, [18]
　　grants to, on losing seat, **18**, [19], [20]
　　meaning, **18**, [25]
　　payment of salaries and pensions, costs,
　　　18, [24]
　　pensions, **18**, [21]–[23]
　　resettlement grants, **18**, [19], [20]
　　salaries of, **18**, [17], [22]

European Parliament—*contd*
Single European Act, construction of
references to, **18**, [30]
transitional provisions, **15(3)**, [556]
UK MEPs—
changes in number of—
changes under Community law,
references to, **15(3)**, [559]
orders implementing, **15(3)**, [562]–[563]
disqualification from office, **15(3)**, [545]
judicial determination of, **15(3)**, [546]
distribution—
periodic review, **15(3)**, [555]
recommendations by Electoral
Commission, **15(3)**, [560]
Northern Ireland, voting system in,
15(3), [538]
number of, **15(3)**, [535]
voting system—
Gibraltar, in, **15(3)**, [537]
Great Britain, in, **15(3)**, [537]
Northern Ireland, in, **15(3)**, [538]

European Patent Convention
financial provisions, **11(1)**, [739]
judicial notice of, **11(1)**, [735]
meaning, **11(1)**, [773]
proceedings under—
costs in, **11(1)**, [737]
evidence for, obtaining, **11(1)**, [736]
provisions of, effect of, **11(1)**, [724]

European Patent Office
information to—
communication of, **11(1)**, [738]
duty to give, **11(1)**, [760]
proceedings in—
evidence for use in, **11(1)**, [736]
language in which conducted, **11(1)**, [727]
orders for costs, enforcement, **11(1)**, [737]

European Pharmacopoeia
specified publication, as, **28**, [160]
standards in monograph, compliance with,
28, [122]

eviction
agricultural employees, of, **21**, [666]
civil proceedings, saving for, **21**, [662]
court, jurisdiction of, **21**, [671]
due process of law, requiring, **21**, [664]
excluded tenancies and licences, **21**, [665]
notices, services of, **21**, [669]
prosecution of offences, **21**, [668]
rental purchase agreement, following,
21, [765]
residential occupier, of, **21**, [662]
unlawful—
Crown property, application of provision
to, **22**, [838]
damages for—
county court jurisdiction, **22**, [833]
landlord, liability of, **22**, [824]
measure of, **22**, [825]
offence of, **21**, [662], [668]

evidence. *See also* **witness**
abroad—
Hague Convention, **18**, [75]
obtaining, **18**, [75]
Admiralty proceedings in county court, in,
11(2), [943]
admissibility, **38(1)**, [12]
civil partner, by, **18**, [256], [257]
conviction. *See* conviction *below*
documents. *See* **documentary evidence**
expert and non-expert opinion, **18**, [221]
hearsay, **18**, [295]
public documents, copies of, **18**, [93]
spouse, by, **18**, [110], [256], [257]
witness beyond jurisdiction, **18**, [118]
adultery, finding of, as evidence, **18**, [205]
affirmation. *See* **affirmation**
age, of, **3**, [699], [972], [1216]
air force—
affidavits, officers taking, **3**, [978]
court-martial, at, **3**, [860]
proceedings, in, **3**, [971]
proceedings, of, **3**, [974]
rules, **3**, [860]
aircraft, proceedings in connection with,
4(1), [144], [145]
appeal hearing, at, **12(1)**, [442]
application to court to obtain, **18**, [225]
army—
affidavits, officers taking, **3**, [705]
board of inquiry, before, **3**, [632]
court-martial, before, **3**, [587]
declarations, officers taking, **3**, [705]
general provisions, **3**, [587], [698]
bad character, of—
armed forces, provisions applying, **18**, [428]
common law rules, abolition, **18**, [377]
defendant, of—
adverse effect of, **18**, [379]
another person's character, in event of
attack on, **18**, [384]
child, offences committed when,
18, [386]
circumstances for, **18**, [379]
contaminated, evidence being, **18**, [385]
false impression, to correct, **18**, [383]
important explanatory evidence,
meaning, **18**, [380]
matter in issue between defendant and
co-defendant, meaning, **18**, [382]
matter in issue between defendant and
prosecution, meaning, **18**, [381]
meaning, **18**, [390]
definitions, **18**, [390]
meaning, **18**, [376]
non-defendant, of, **18**, [378]
relevant or probative value, assumption of
truth, **18**, [387]
rules of court, **18**, [389]
rulings, duty to give reasons for, **18**, [388]
bankers' books. *See* **bank and banking**
banks and banking proceedings, **19(1)**, [600]

evidence—*contd*
blood tests. *See* **parentage**
bodily samples. *See* **parentage**
certificate, by, **12(1)**, [263]
  See also **road traffic offences**
child giving. *See* **child**
civil actions—
  conviction as evidence in, **18**, [204]
  expert reports etc, **18**, [220]
  foreign law, expert opinion on, **18**, [222]
  meaning, **18**, [305]
  paternity, finding of, admissible, **18**, [205]
  rules of court, **18**, [306]
  statements. *See* statement *below*
civil proceedings, meaning, **18**, [210], [305]
colonial judgments etc, **18**, [100]
compellability, spouses, **18**, [111], [256]
confession—
  evidence for co-accused, given in,
    18, [252]
  hearsay rules, **18**, [396], [406]
  meaning, **18**, [259]
  mentally handicapped person, by, **18**, [251]
  See also criminal proceedings *below.*
contradictory statements by witness, **18**, [127]
conviction—
  defamation action, in, **18**, [206]
  evidence in civil proceedings, **18**, [204]
  evidence of commission of offence, as,
    18, [249], [250]
  previous, as to, **18**, [104]
  proof of, **18**, [248]
  witness, of, **18**, [129]
corroboration, when necessary, **18**, [75]
county court, in, **11(2)**, [939], [941]
court-martial—
  appeal, at, **3**, [1321]
  before, **3**, [1512]
  proceedings, of, **3**, [701]
credit of witness, impeaching, **18**, [126]
criminal damage, **12(1)**, [603]
criminal intent, inferring, **12(1)**, [380]
criminal proceedings—
  accused's evidence, time for taking,
    18, [255]
  accused's failure or refusal to account for—
    interpretation provisions, **18**, [292]
    objects, substances or marks, **18**, [290]
    presence at a particular place, **18**, [291]
  accused's silence—
    armed forces, application of provisions
      to, **18**, [293]
    at trial, **18**, [289]
    inferences from, transitional provisions
      and savings, **18**, [369]
    interpretation provisions, **18**, [292]
    when questioned or charged, **18**, [288]
  acquittal, proof of, **18**, [248]
  answers given under compulsion, restriction
    on use of, **18**, [356], [366]
  armed forces, provisions applied, **18**, [260]
  bad character, of. *See* bad character, of *above*
  child as witness. *See under* **witness**
  civil partner of accused, by, **18**, [256],
    [257]

evidence—*contd*
criminal proceedings—*contd*
  competency to give, **18**, [165], [351]
    determination of, **18**, [352]
  confession—
    documentary evidence of, inadmissible,
      18, [406]
    evidence for co-accused, given in,
      18, [252]
    evidence of, **18**, [251]
    exclusion of, **18**, [251]
    meaning, **18**, [259]
    mentally handicapped person, by,
      18, [253]
    oppression, obtained by, **18**, [251]
    prosecution, use by, **18**, [251]
  conviction. *See* conviction *above*
  corroboration, abolition of rules, **18**, [287]
  defence, witnesses for, **18**, [166]
  defendants, unrepresented—
    cross-examination, restrictions on,
      18, [75]
    legal representatives, provision of,
      18, [75]
  documents—
    copy, meaning, **18**, [247]
    microfilm copies, **18**, [246]
  expert reports—
    admissibility, **18**, [270]
    meaning, **18**, [270]
  form of, **18**, [271]
  glossaries, **18**, [271]
  hearsay. *See* hearsay *below*
  incriminating questions, **18**, [98], [207]
  meaning, **18**, [259]
  mentally handicapped person. *See under*
    witness
  meaning, **18**, [259]
  person charged, by, **18**, [166]
  previous conviction, proof of, **18**, [104]
  regulations and orders, **18**, [360]
  sexual offences, protection of complainant
    in—
    sexual history, questions regarding,
      18, [339]
    transitional provisions and savings,
      18, [369]
  spouse of accused, by, **18**, [111], [256],
    [257]
  summing up in, **18**, [125]
  supplementary provisions, **18**, [361]
  television link—
    child witness, by, **18**, [320]
    offences to which applicable, **18**, [272]
    rules of court, **18**, [272]
    trials and proceedings applicable,
      18, [272]
    witness outside U.K., by, **18**, [272]
  transitional provisions and savings,
    18, [363], [369]
  trial, right of reply, **18**, [201]
  unfair evidence, exclusion of, **18**, [254]
  unsworn—
    false, penalty for giving, **18**, [355]
    reception of, **18**, [354]

evidence—*contd*
  criminal proceedings—*contd*
    video recorded evidence in chief, **18**, [323]
    video recording, meaning, **18**, [359]
  cross-examination—
    previous statements, on, **18**, [128]
    video recording, in, **18**, [324]
  Crown debts, of, **18**, [88]
  diminished responsibility, of, **12(1)**, [343]
  disqualification to give, **18**, [75]
  documentary. *See* **documentary evidence**
  enforcement of attendance to give, **18**, [75]
  European Court of Justice, instruments
    before, **18**, [4]
  expert—
    hearsay, **18**, [396]
    opinion, admissibility, **18**, [221]
      preparatory work, **18**, [405]
    prior notice of, **18**, [258]
    rules of court, **18**, [220]
  extradition proceedings. *See* **extradition**
  Factories Acts, offences under, **18**, [1191]
  foreign—
    acts of state etc, **18**, [100]
    court, for proceedings in, **18**, [244]
    documents, proof and effect of, **18**, [172],
      [198]
    judgments, of, **18**, [100]
    law, of, **18**, [75], [222]
    notarial acts, of, **18**, [180]
    proceedings—
      obtaining for, **18**, [244]
      required for, **18**, [195]
    registers etc, **18**, [172], [198]
  formal admission as, **12(1)**, [382]
  freezing order. *See* **freezing order**
  government war work or use, certificate of
    Minister as, **9**, [158]
  handling stolen goods, of, **12(1)**, [579]
  hearsay—
    admissibility of, **18**, [295], [392]
      common law categories, preservation
        of, **18**, [396]
    agent, admission by, **18**, [396]
    armed forces, provisions applying, **18**, [429]
    business and other documents, **18**, [395]
    capability to make statement, **18**, [401]
    character, reputation as to, **18**, [396]
    common enterprise, **18**, [396]
    common law exceptions, **18**, [301]
    competence, **18**, [299]
    confessions, **18**, [396], [406]
    credibility, **18**, [299], [402]
    cross-examination, power to call witness
      for, **18**, [297]
    definitions, **18**, [410]
    discretion to exclude, **18**, [404]
    exhibits, documents produced as, **18**, [400]
    expert, **18**, [396]
      preparatory work, **18**, [405]
    inconsistent statements, **18**, [397]
    meaning, **18**, [295]
    multiple, admission of, **18**, [399]
    notice of proposal to adduce, **18**, [296]
    original statement, meaning, **18**, [307]

evidence—*contd*
  hearsay—*contd*
    previous statements of witness, **18**, [300],
      [398]
    proof of statement in document, **18**, [409]
    public information, **18**, [396]
    representation other than by person,
      18, [407]
    reputation or family tradition, **18**, [396]
    res gestae, **18**, [396]
    rules of court, **18**, [408]
    statements and matters stated, **18**, [393]
    summary of provisions, **18**, [75]
    unconvincing, stopping case where,
      18, [403]
    weighing of, considerations relevant to,
      18, [298]
    witness unavailable, where, **18**, [394]
  incriminating questions, **18**, [75], [98], [207]
  indebtedness of witness, as to, **18**, [78]
  inquest, at, **11(1)**, [1216]–[1217],
    [1227]–[1228]
  insanity, of, **12(1)**, [343]
  instrument not duly stamped, production of,
    41, [28]
  instruments—
    attestation, requiring, proof of, **18**, [174]
    proof of, where attestation not required,
      18, [130]
  international proceedings, for—
    meaning, **18**, [229]
    power to obtain, **18**, [229]
  Ireland, proof of documents from, **18**, [101]
  Lands Tribunal, before, **9**, [183]
  legitimacy and illegitimacy, **18**, [218]
  libel action, effect of apology in, **19(3)**, [272]
  live link, given by—
    criminal proceedings, in, **18**, [330]
    definitions, **18**, [375]
    direction for, **18**, [330], [332], [370]
    effect of direction, **18**, [371]
    jury, warning to, **18**, [373]
    magistrates' court, removal to other
      location, **18**, [372]
    meaning, **18**, [331]
    rescission of direction, **18**, [371]
    rules of court, **18**, [374]
  meaning, **18**, [75]
  membership of visiting force, of, **3**, [450]
  motor vehicle driver's record of driving
    hours, **36**, [815]
  mutual assistance, provision for, **12(4)**, [114]
  mutual provision, United Kingdom and
    overseas, **12(2)**, [21], [22]
  nationality, of, **31**, [176]
  navy—
    court-martial, before, **3**, [1133]
    proceedings, of, **3**, [1214]
  notarial acts abroad, of, **18**, [180]
  oath, on. *See* **oaths**
  obtaining abroad, assistance in—
    domestic freezing order—
      power to make, **12(3)**, [573]
      revocation, **12(3)**, [575]
      sending, **12(3)**, [574]

evidence—*contd*
  obtaining abroad, assistance in—*contd*
    domestic freezing order—*contd*
      variation, **12(3)**, [575]
      nature of, **12(3)**, [570]
      request for—
        application, **12(3)**, [570]
        sending, **12(3)**, [571]
      use of evidence obtained, **12(3)**, [572]
  Ogden Tables—
    admissibility of, **18**, [304]
    proof of, **18**, [304]
  opinion, expert, **18**, [221]
  oral—
    civil proceedings, in, written statement
      after, **18**, [279]
    criminal proceedings. *See* criminal
      proceedings *above*
  orders and rules, **18**, [418]
  other jurisdictions, for proceedings in—
    applications for, **18**, [225]
      power to give effect to, **18**, [226]
    blood samples, requirement for, **18**, [226]
    documents, production, **18**, [226]
    examination of witnesses, **18**, [226]
    extension of High Court powers, **18**, [228]
    medical examination, order for, **18**, [226]
    order for obtaining, **18**, [226]
    overseas court, for, **18**, [229]
    privilege of witnesses, **18**, [227]
    restriction as to, **18**, [244]
    rules of court, **18**, [230]
    witness, warrant for attendance, **18**, [76],
      [228]
  overseas authorities, assisting—
    exercise of powers by others, **12(3)**, [590]
    nominated court, proceedings of,
      12(3), [618]
    nomination of court to receive,
      12(3), [578]
    obtaining, power to arrange, **12(3)**, [577]
    request for, **12(3)**, [576]
    seized evidence, sending, **12(3)**, [582]
    statutory search powers, extension of,
      12(3), [579]
    warrants, issue of—
      England and Wales, in, **12(3)**, [580]
      Northern Ireland, in, **12(3)**, [580]
      powers under, **12(3)**, [589]
      Scotland, in, **12(3)**, [581]
  overseas freezing order. *See* **freezing order**
  overseas, use in United Kingdom—
    prisoner, by, **12(2)**, [21]
    rules of court, **12(2)**, [24]
  paternity, of. *See* **parentage**
  physical or mental condition of child, of,
    6, [77]
  polygraph sessions, from, **12(4)**, [337]
  previous conviction, of, **12(1)**, [141]
  prisoner, by, transfer—
    from United Kingdom overseas, **12(2)**, [21]
    to United Kingdom, from overseas,
      12(2), [22]
  prisoner giving, **12(1)**, [54]

evidence—*contd*
  privy council judicial committee, before,
    11(2), [20]
  proof—
    business or public authority records,
      18, [303]
    European Communities instruments,
      18, [4]
    foreign etc documents, **18**, [172], [198]
    instruments creating powers of attorney,
      18, [178]
  public records. *See* **public records**
  Queen's Printer, documents admissible as,
    18, [95], [151]
  re-examination, video recording, in, **18**, [324]
  records of business or public authority, proof
    of, **18**, [303]
  regimental inquiry, at, **3**, [634]
  requisition, compensation for, **9**, [123]
  retrial, at, **12(1)**, [470]
  rules of court—
    evidence for use in other jurisdictions,
      18, [230]
    expert reports etc, as to, **18**, [220]
  seal of documents, of, **18**, [93]
  self-incrimination—
    criminal damage, **12(1)**, [603]
    protection, **6**, [429]
    theft offences, **12(1)**, [581]
  special measures—
    prejudice to, warning to jury against,
      18, [328]
    status of, under, **18**, [327]
    transitional provisions and savings, **18**, [369]
  spouse or civil partner of party, by, **18**, [110],
    [256]
    non compellable, where, **18**, [257]
  spouse or civil partner, of, theft offences,
    12(1), [580]
  Standing Civilian Court, in, **3**, [1381]
  statement—
    oral evidence by witness, as to, **18**, [279]
    rules of court, **18**, [279]
  statements contained in documents, proof of,
    18, [302]
  subpoena. *See* **witness**
  summary of provisions, **18**, [75]
  summing up in criminal proceedings,
    18, [125]
  telephone, hearing by, **12(3)**, [594], [620]
  television links, through—
    procedure, **12(3)**, [619]
    witnesses abroad, of, **12(3)**, [592]
    witnesses in UK, of, **12(3)**, [593]
  theatre play script as, **13**, [188]
  theft, of, **12(1)**, [579]
  unfair, exclusion of, **18**, [254]
  vulnerable accused, of, live link directions,
    12(4), [274]
  will, of execution of, **18**, [87]
  witnesses. *See* **witness**
  writing, disputed, comparison of, **18**, [131]
  written statement as—
    false, **12(1)**, [395]
    generally, **12(1)**, [381]

evidence—*contd*
written statement as—*contd*
Scotland or Northern Ireland, made in,
12(1), [612]
written statement, by, **3**, [861], [1374]

excavation
dangerous—
entry on land in connection with,
35(1), [388]
powers with respect to, **35(1)**, [387], [388]
London. *See* **London streets**

excavator
requisition, compensation for, **9**, [123]

excess profits levy
assessment, terminal date for, **42**, [39]
generally, **42**, [1]

excess profits tax
assessment, terminal date for, **42**, [39]
generally, **42**, [1]

exchange
rates, foreign currency, **41**, [20], [154]

exchange control
abolition of enactments, **19(2)**, [1004]
generally, **19(1)**, [1]

Exchange Equalisation Account
annual accounts, **19(2)**, [965]
Comptroller and Auditor General,
examination and certification by,
19(2), [965]
continuation of, **19(2)**, [962]
creation of, **19(1)**, [1]
investment of funds, **19(2)**, [964]
National Loans Fund, issue of sums from,
19(2), [963]
purposes of use of, **19(2)**, [962]

exchange gains and losses
loan relationships, from, **43(1)**, [199]
not on arm's length terms, **43(1)**, [257]

Exchequer
accountant, meaning, **19(2)**, [607]
bond, lost or destroyed, **19(2)**, [729]
casual receipts paid to, **19(2)**, [622]
Comptroller and Auditor General, returns sent
to, **19(2)**, [611]
one general fund, moneys paid into forming,
19(2), [612]
public moneys payable to, **19(2)**, [611]
revenues paid to, **19(2)**, [611]
royal order, sums issued on, **19(2)**, [614]

exchequer accounts
meaning, **43(S)**, 993
payments from—
financial claims, **43(S)**, 993
mechanism for, **43(S)**, 994
power of Treasury to make, **43(S)**, 993

exchequer bond
lost or destroyed, replacement of, **42**, [3]

excise duties. *See also* **beer; cider; spirits;
wine**
abolition of certain, **19(3)**, [461]
ad valorem, valuation for purposes of,
13, [729]
allowance—
calculation, **13**, [741]
goods destroyed or damaged, **13**, [738]
offences as to claims for, **13**, [740]
time limit for payment, **13**, [739]
assessments to, **13**, [931]–[933], [1073]
bioblends, on, **13**, [824]
biodiesel, on, **13**, [823]
bioethanol, on, **13**, [826]
bond, enforcement where goods removed
without payment, **13**, [735]
calculation, **13**, [741]
composite imported articles, **13**, [730], [784]
deferred payment, **13**, [731]
delivery of goods after payment, restriction
on, **13**, [732]
denatured goods, remission or repayment of
duty, **13**, [733]
distress for, **13**, [714]
dog licence. *See* **dogs**
drawback. *See* **customs and excise**
enforcement of payment, **13**, [1065]
error or delay by Commissioners—
appeals, **13**, [1094]
general, **13**, [1095]
interest, **13**, [1093]
payments, **13**, [1092]
evasion, **13**, [775], [777], [926]
excise licence, **13**, [700]–[704]
execution for, **13**, [714]
fractions of penny, ignoring, **43(S)**, 996
fraudulent evasion, **13**, [775]
game licence. *See* **game**
High Court, summary application by Crown
to, in matters of, **13**, [18]
hydrocarbon oil, on. *See* **hydrocarbon oil**
male servant duty, repeal, **2**, [267]
manufactured articles, **13**, [730], [784]
new or altered, effect on contract price,
13, [551]
origin of goods, determination of, **13**, [724]
overpaid, recovery of, **13**, [742]
overpayment of, unjust enrichment,
13, [1068]
payment—
cheque, by, **13**, [701]
deferred, **13**, [731]
revenue trader, by, **13**, [713]
time for, powers to fix, **13**, [917]
penalties—
assessments to, **13**, [934]
contravention of statutory requirements,
for—
exceptions to liability, **13**, [928]
general, **13**, [927]
controlled goods agreements, for breaches
of, **13**, [929]

excise duties—*contd*
  penalties—*contd*
    evasion, for, **13**, [926]
    walking possession agreements, for breaches
      of, **13**, [930]
  point, powers to fix, **13**, [917]
  preparatory steps for evasion, offence of,
    13, [777]
  rebates on, **13**, [740], [898]–[900]
  relief from—
    annual report to Parliament, **13**, [808]
    antiques, **13**, [797]
    consequential amendments, **13**, [811]
    immunities and privileges, persons
      enjoying, **13**, [803]–[805]
    imported legacies, **13**, [795]
    interpretation of provisions, **13**, [810]
    labels, **13**, [796]
    naval vessels, goods supplied to, **13**, [590],
      [801]
    orders as to, **13**, [809]
    persons entering UK, **13**, [802]
    prizes awarded abroad, **13**, [797]
    regulations as to, **13**, [809]
    re-imported goods—
      foreign goods, **13**, [799]
      testing etc, for, **13**, [800]
      United Kingdom goods, **13**, [798]
    shipbuilders, **13**, [555]
      ending of, **13**, [1120]
    trade samples, **13**, [796]
  remission—
    denatured goods, **13**, [733]
    goods lost or destroyed, **13**, [734]
    offences connected with, **13**, [740]
  repayment—
    denatured goods, **13**, [733]
    destroyed goods, **13**, [727]
    goods damaged, lost or destroyed,
      13, [734], [738]
    offences connected with, **13**, [740]
    returned goods, **13**, [727]
  revenue trader. *See* **customs and excise**
  security for, delivery of goods on giving,
    13, [723]
  security in proceedings, **43(S)**, 961
  surcharges or rebates—
    enactments applied, **13**, [900]
    groups of duties affected, **13**, [898]
    orders providing for, **13**, [898]–[900]
  tobacco products. *See* **tobacco products**
  unpaid—
    handling goods subject to, **43(S)**, 1331–2
    offence of handling goods subject to,
      13, [776]
  use of goods, dependent on matters other
    than, **13**, [726]
  vehicle. *See* **vehicle excise duty**
  warehoused goods, **13**, [687]
  wrongdoing, penalties,
    43(S), 1328–39. *See also* **tax penalty**

excise labels
  offences relating to, **41**, [12]

excise licence
  cheque—
    dishonoured, voidance and delivery up of
      licence where, **13**, [701]
    payment of duty by, **13**, [701]
  date of, **13**, [702]
  death of holder, transfer on, **13**, [703]
  delivery up, where cheque for duty
    dishonoured, **13**, [701]
  duty, **13**, [700]–[704]
  form and contents, **13**, [700]
  grant of, compliance with conditions,
    37, [648]
  paper for, fraud as to, **41**, [55]
  partnership, for, **13**, [700]
  production, **13**, [700]
  removal, **13**, [703]
  renewal, **13**, [702]
  revenue trader. *See* **customs and excise**
  tobacco dealer carrying on, **13**, [590]
  trade—
    meaning, **13**, [590]
    partnership, carrying on, **13**, [700]
    removal, **13**, [703]
    sign, display of, **13**, [704]
  transfer, **13**, [703]
  two or more premises, for, **13**, [700]
  voidance, where cheque for duty
    dishonoured, **13**, [701]

exclusion order
  monitoring of persons subject to, **12(2)**, [757]
  power to make, **12(2)**, [755]

exclusion zone
  constable, power of, **12(4)**, [117]

excommunication
  imprisonment, abolition of, **14**, 611

execution of judgment or order
  Crown, by, **13**, [29]
  judgment or order against literary or scientific
    institution, of, **13**, [68]
  revenue trader, against,
    13, [714]. *See also* **distress**
  rights of creditors, restriction, **4(2)**, [221]
  tenant's goods, payment of rent for, **21**, [25]

executor. *See also* **administrator; personal
representative**
  actions by or against, **18**, [529]
  appointment—
    minor, of, **18**, [645]
    special executor, **18**, [525]
  appropriation, powers as to, **18**, [544]
  assent or conveyance by—
    court powers, **18**, [541]
    effect of, **18**, [539]
    right to follow property after, **18**, [541]
    statement in writing as to, **18**, [539]
    validity on revocation of representation,
      18, [540]
  assets. *See* **administration of estates**
  cessation of executorship, **18**, [516]

executor—*contd*
chain in representation, break in, **18**, [518]
conveyance by. *See* assent *above*
creditor, of debtor as, **18**, [524]
death without proving will, **18**, [516]
debtor as, **18**, [524]
demise land, power to, **18**, [543]
distress by, **18**, [529]
distribution by. *See* **administration of estates**
duties generally, **18**, [528]
executor of original testator representing, **18**, [518]
expenses of, **18**, [537]
fatal accident, action in case of, **31**, [610]
fraud in respect of estate, **18**, [531]
liability of estate of, **18**, [532]
management, powers of, **18**, [542]
meaning, **18**, [559]
minor as, **18**, [645]
not to act while administration in force, **18**, [521]
notices affecting land, service of, to, **18**, [680]
number to whom probate granted, **18**, [641]
possession of land—
    court's powers as to, **18**, [546]
    meaning, **18**, [559]
    obligation to give, **18**, [546]
preference, right of, abolition, **18**, [594]
proving, right to exercise powers, **18**, [519]
Public Trustee, vesting of estate in, where lack of, **18**, [678]
raising money, powers of, **18**, [481]–[484], [543]
renunciation of probate—
    cesser of rights, **18**, [516]
    court summons as to, **18**, [639]
    withdrawal, **18**, [517]
representation—
    amounts disposable without, **18**, [573], [579]–[581]
        power to increase, **18**, [576], [577]
    chain of, **18**, [518]
    collaterals, amongst, **18**, [450]
    date of taking out, **18**, [625]
    evidence of, **18**, [590]
    meaning, **18**, [559]
    Northern Ireland, recognition in, **18**, [588], [589]
    revocation, validity of conveyance, effect on, **18**, [540]
    Scotland, recognition in, **18**, [589]
retainer, right of, abolished, **18**, [594]
rules of court, **18**, [534]
settled land—
    meaning, **18**, [525]
    power to dispose of, **18**, [527]
    renunciation of probate, **18**, [526]
special—
    appointment, **18**, [525]
    right of disposal, **18**, [527]
    rules of court, **18**, [526]
    settled land, as respects, **18**, [525]
spouse's life interest, redemption of, **18**, [551]
substitute personal representative as, **18**, [661]

executor—*contd*
summary of provisions, **18**, [447]
summons to, to prove or renounce, **18**, [639]
surviving spouse or civil partner—
    life interest, redemption of, **18**, [551]
    matrimonial home, rights as to, **18**, [569], [572]
    powers respecting, **18**, [552]
trust corporation as, **18**, [642]
waste, liability for, **18**, [532]

exhibition
film. *See under* **cinemas**
London—
    application of Shops Act, **25(2)**, [467], [473]
    licensing, **25(1)**, [808]
    premises requiring licence, **25(1)**, [820]
    walkways, on, **25(1)**, [875], [948]
removal of articles from, **12(1)**, [563]

exhumation
power to order, **11(1)**, [1230]

expedition
illegal, **12(1)**, [116]
licence, fitting out without, **12(1)**, [119]

expenses
business entertainment, **44(1)**, [411]
    allowed, **44(2)**, [368]
    disallowance of, **44(2)**, [366]
    employer's expenses disallowed, **44(2)**, [367]
contributions to, **46**, [578]
county councils, of, **46**, [584]
crime, expenditure involving, **44(1)**, [412]
employees—
    annual subscriptions, **44(2)**, [354]
        decision of officer of Revenue and Customs as to, **44(2)**, [355]
    application of provisions, **44(2)**, [80], [345]
    deduction provisions, application of, **44(2)**, [343]
    earnings, sums treated as, **44(2)**, [82]
    employee liabilities—
        allowable, **44(2)**, [356]
        connected contracts, **44(2)**, [360]
        liabilities relating to employment, **44(2)**, [358]
        payments after leaving employment, **44(2)**, [357]
        qualifying insurance contract, meaning, **44(2)**, [359]
    entertainers, agency fees, **44(2)**, [362]
    fixed sum—
        public revenue, payable from, **44(2)**, [379]
        scope of provisions, **44(2)**, [377]
        Treasury, sums fixed by, **44(2)**, [378]
        work equipment, repairing and maintaining, **44(2)**, [378]
    foreign element, earnings with, **44(2)**, [363]–[365]
    general rule, **44(2)**, [346]

expenses—*contd*
employees—*contd*
government departments, of, **46**, [582]
paid or put at disposal by reason of
employment, **44(2)**, [81]
professional membership fees, **44(2)**, [353]
qualifying insurance contracts, **44(2)**, [359]
reimbursement, effect of, **44(2)**, [344]
scope of provisions, **44(2)**, [343]

experimental traffic schemes. *See under*
traffic regulation

explosives. *See further* **gunpowder**
accessories, punishment of, **12(1)**, [164]
aggravated burglary, using in, **12(1)**, [562]
aiding and abetting offences, **12(1)**, [164]
attempt to cause explosion—
imprisonment, **12(1)**, [686]
offence, **12(1)**, [162]
bodily injury, causing, **12(1)**, [84]
boundaries, jurisdiction on, **18**, [709]
building, placing near, **12(1)**, [86]
carriage coastwise, **13**, [666]
carriage of. *See* conveyance *below*
children, sale to, **18**, [695]
conveyance, inspection during, **18**, [705]
Crown, held for, **3**, [1]
definition of, **18**, [717]
exportation, **13**, [666]
factory—
Government, exemption for, **18**, [713]
occupier, meaning, **18**, [718]
fireworks. *See* **fireworks**
forfeiture—
disposal after, **18**, [712]
proceedings for, **18**, [708]
seizure for, **18**, [704]
government contracts, conveyance for,
48, 943; **50**, [220]
Government premises, exemption for,
18, [713]
gunpowder, provisions applied to, **18**, [692],
[697], [698]. *See further* **gunpowder**
hawking, restriction on, **18**, [694]
highway, sale or exposing on, **18**, [694]
inquiry by Attorney-General into offences,
12(1), [165]
inspectors—
inspection of explosives in transit, **18**, [705]
samples, powers as to, **18**, [700]
search, powers of, **18**, [703]
seizure and detention by, **18**, [704]
keeping, **12(1)**, [162]
liability, saving clause, **18**, [715]
licence, other than for gunpowder, **18**, [698]
life or property, endangering—
imprisonment, **12(1)**, [686]
intention of, **12(1)**, [162]
offence, **12(1)**, [161]
local Acts, repeal of, **18**, [716]
local authority—
duties and powers, **18**, [702]
meaning, **18**, [701]

explosives—*contd*
London—
byelaws—
arrest of offenders, **25(1)**, [92], [97]
enforcement, **25(1)**, [90], [95]
conveyance—
byelaws, **25(1)**, [90]
ferries, by, **25(1)**, [90]
tunnels through, **25(1)**, [95]
inspection and search, **25(1)**, [91], [96]
magazine—
Government, exemption for, **18**, [713]
meaning, **18**, [718]
making—
commit offence, to, **12(1)**, [162]
suspicious circumstances, under,
12(1), [163]
meaning, **12(1)**, [168]; **18**, [692]
occupier of premises, meaning, **18**, [718]
offences—
penalties, application of, **18**, [712]
proceedings for, **18**, [710]
search etc, powers of, **18**, [703]
ship, involving, **18**, [711]
Orders in Council respecting, **18**, [707]
possessing—
aggravated burglary, during, **12(1)**, [562]
suspicious circumstances, under,
12(1), [163]
prosecution by leave of Attorney-General,
12(1), [166]
sale of—
children, to, **18**, [695]
containers, to be in, **18**, [696]
highways etc, on, **18**, [694]
search for, **12(1)**, [167]
search, powers of officers, **18**, [703]
search warrant, **12(1)**, [103]
seizure, **12(1)**, [167]
seizure and detention of, **18**, [704]
ship—
distress for unpaid penalties, **18**, [711]
emergency measures, **18**, [714]
master, meaning, **18**, [718]
specially dangerous, prohibitions as to,
18, [699]
store, meaning, **18**, [718]
substance, meaning, **12(1)**, [168]
substances deemed to be, **18**, [692]
summary of provisions, **18**, [690]
supply, prohibited, **18**, [744]
terrorism, use in, **18**, [757]
tidal waters, jurisdiction in, **18**, [709]
unauthorised access to premises, precautions
against, **18**, [693]
witnesses, absconding, **12(1)**, [165]

Export Credit Guarantee Department
commitment limits, **47**, [456]
delegation of functions, **47**, [462]
exports of goods and services, assistance in
connection with, **47**, [451]
financial management, **47**, [453]
overseas investment, insurance in connection
with, **47**, [452]

Export Credit Guarantee Department—*contd*
payments to, deduction of, **44(1)**, [64]; **44(3)**, [90]
reports and returns, **47**, [457]
Secretary of State, functions of, **47**, [463]
services and information, provision of, **47**, [455]
terms and conditions of transactions, **47**, [454]
transfer of functions—
certificate of vesting, **47**, [466]
construction of agreements, **47**, [466]
reinsurance, **47**, [461]
scheme, **47**, [458]
staff, transferred, **47**, [459]
vehicle companies, **47**, [460]

export guarantees. *See* **Export Credit Guarantee Department**

Export Guarantees Advisory Council
Secretary of State, functions of, **47**, [463]

exportation
aircraft, **13**, [645], [655]
animals—
certificate or licence for, **2**, [489]
control of, **2**, [439], [440]
member States, to, **2**, [439]
offences, **2**, [533]–[535]
assistance in connection with, **47(S)**, 14
certain items, restriction on, **13**, [566]
clearance outward of ships and aircraft—
boarding, officer's power of, **13**, [653]
departure without obtaining, **13**, [653]
loading before applying for, **13**, [653]
necessity for, **13**, [653]
procedure for obtaining, **13**, [653]
refusal or cancellation, **13**, [654]
ship in ballast, **13**, [653]
Community—
customs documents, authentication, **13**, [647]
purposes, operative date for, **13**, [646]
control of, **13**, [636]–[659]
annual reports, **50**, [288]
freedoms, protection of certain, **50**, [286]
generally, **50**, [279]
goods subject to, **50**, [294]
military equipment, **50**, [294]
orders, guidance regarding exercise of functions under, **50**, [287]
public information, protection regarding, **50**, [286]
restriction on—
exceptions from, **50**, [284]
powers as to, **50**, [283]
scientific research, protection regarding information about, **50**, [286]
supplementary provisions, **50**, [285]
technical assistance controls, **50**, [281], [294]
trade controls, **50**, [282]
transfer controls, **50**, [280]
weapons of mass destruction, **50**, [294]

exportation—*contd*
destination of goods, untrue declaration as to, **13**, [670]
documents, furnishing, **13**, [651]
drugs, controlled, penalties on, **13**, [657], [775], [783]
endangered species, restriction on. *See* **animals; plants**
entry outwards—
correction and cancellation, **13**, [639]
dutiable or restricted goods—
acceptance of, **13**, [637]
cancellation, **13**, [639]
correction of, **13**, [639]
delivery by owner of ship or aircraft, **13**, [641]
failure to export, **13**, [640]
hovercraft, approved, **13**, [649]
incomplete, acceptance of, **13**, [638]
meaning, **13**, [636]
requirement of, **13**, [637], [652]
security for, **13**, [637]
shipment before delivery, **13**, [637]
ships, minimum tonnage, **13**, [649]
substituted—
acceptance, **13**, [638]
correction by, **13**, [639]
requirements, **13**, [637]
examination and taking account of goods, **13**, [764]
failure to export, **13**, [640]
goods other than Community transit goods, provisions as to, **13**, [637]. *See also* dutiable or restricted goods *above*
incomplete, acceptance, **13**, [638]
non-dutiable or restricted goods, shipping without, **13**, [642], [644]
putting goods alongside for loading—
regulations as to, **13**, [648]
written authority for, **13**, [648]
requirement of, **13**, [637]
ship, **13**, [652]
shipping without, by registered exporter, **13**, [642]–[644]
ship's stores, goods as, **13**, [637]
stiffening order, **13**, [652]
explosives, entry of, **13**, [666]
export goods—
additional restrictions as to, **13**, [649]
Community transit goods, meaning, **13**, [590]
documents as to, furnishing, **13**, [651]
information as to, power to require, **13**, [651]
number identifying, **13**, [651]
exporter, meaning, **13**, [590]
failure to export, after entry, **13**, [640]
horses. *See* **horses**
information—
Community law or practice, **13**, [676]
evidence in support of, **13**, [675]
firearms, relating to, **13**, [672]
goods subject to certain transit arrangements, relating to, **13**, [673]
power to require, **13**, [651], [670]–[673]

exportation—*contd*
local control, **13**, [643]
Northern Ireland—
proof required as to, **13**, [659]
regulation of movement into and out of,
13, [609]
offences—
evasion of agricultural levy, **13**, [658]
prohibited goods, **13**, [657]
restricted goods, **13**, [657]
shipment as stores, **13**, [657]
unauthorised unloading in UK, **13**, [656]
origin of goods—
certificate of, **13**, [675]
evidenced under Community law or
practice, **13**, [676]
pipe-line—
application of customs and excise provisions
to, **13**, [592]
by, **13**, [645]
meaning, **13**, [590]
time of, **13**, [594]
ponies, **2**, [491]
records relating to—
firearms, **13**, [668]
general, **13**, [667]
goods subject to certain transit
arrangements, **13**, [669]
registered exporter—
conditions to be observed by, **13**, [642]
number assigned to, **13**, [642], [643]
records and accounts, **13**, [642], [643]
register, maintenance of, **13**, [642]
specification of goods, delivery by,
13, [644]
suspension or cancellation of registration,
13, [642], [644]
regulation of, **13**, [655]
salmon and trout, restrictions, **1(2)**, [23]
ship, **13**, [645], [652]–[654]
simplified clearance procedure, **13**, [642]
stores. *See* **aircraft; ship**
time of, **13**, [594]
trade, development of, **47**, [45]

ex-service men and women
disabled, facilities and training, **16**, [11], [74]
employment. *See* **employment** (civil)

extent
writ of, abolition, **13**, [35], [43]

extradition
article 95 alerts, transitional provision,
18, [969]
bail, magistrates' court decisions, powers of
High Court, **18**, [996]
British overseas territories, from, **18**, [941]
British overseas territories, to, **18**, [942]
Category 1 territories, to—
appeal—
decisions questioned by, **18**, [795]
detention pending conclusion of,
18, [790], [794]
discharge, against, **18**, [788]–[790]

extradition—*contd*
Category 1 territories, to—*contd*
appeal—*contd*
extradition following, **18**, [797]
High Court, to, **18**, [791]
House of Lords, to, **18**, [792], [793]
order, against, **18**, [786]
powers of court, **18**, [787], [[789]
start, time limit for, **18**, [791]
withdrawal of warrant pending,
18, [803], [804]
arrest—
bringing arrested person before judge,
18, [764]
copy of warrant, supply of, **18**, [762]
discharge of person arrested, **18**, [762],
[764]
identity of person arrested, **18**, [765]
provisional, **18**, [763]
remand under, **18**, [766]
warrant, under, **18**, [761]
asylum claim, person making, **18**, [800]
certificate relating to, **18**, [801]
bars to—
age, consideration of, **18**, [773]
double jeopardy, rule against, **18**, [770]
earlier extradition, **18**, [776], [777]
extraneous considerations, **18**, [771]
forum, by reason of, **18**, [779]
hostage-taking considerations, **18**, [774]
International Criminal Court, earlier
transfer to UK from, **18**, [778]
list of, **18**, [769]
passage of time, **18**, [772]
speciality, **18**, [775]
consent to, **18**, [806]
extradition following, **18**, [808]
order following, **18**, [807]
other warrant, issue of, **18**, [809]–[811]
costs—
discharge ordered, where, **18**, [822],
[823]
extradition ordered, where, **18**, [821]
deferral for competing claim, following,
18, [814]
designation, **18**, [759]
double jeopardy, rule against, **18**, [770]
earlier extradition, barred by—
category 1 territory, from, **18**, [776]
non-category 1 territory, from, **18**, [777]
extradition hearing—
conviction, effect of, **18**, [780]
human rights considerations, **18**, [781]
initial stage, **18**, [768]
judge, powers of, **18**, [767]
person charged with offence in UK,
adjournment in case of, **18**, [782]
person serving sentence in UK at time
of, **18**, [783]
physical or mental condition at time of,
18, [785]
further, consent to—
category 1 territory, to, **18**, [817], [818]
category 2 territory, to, **18**, [819]

extradition—*contd*
  Category 1 territories, to—*contd*
    further, consent to—*contd*
      hearing, questions for decision at,
        18, [818]
      request for, **18**, [817]
    hearing, meaning, **18**, [829]
    initial hearing, **18**, [765], [766]
    International Criminal Court, earlier
      transfer to UK from, **18**, [778]
    offence—
      appropriate authority, **18**, [827]
      appropriate judge, **18**, [828]
      person not sentenced for, **18**, [825]
      person sentenced for, **18**, [826]
      relevant law and proceedings, **18**, [827]
    other offence being dealt with, consent
      to—
      hearing, questions for decision at,
        18, [816]
      request for, **18**, [815]
    person serving sentence outside territory
      where convicted, **18**, [824]
    persons serving sentence, undertaking as
      to, **18**, [813]
    remainder of sentence, return of person to
      serve, **18**, [820]
    repatriation cases, **18**, [824]
    request for, **18**, [784]
      consent, following, **18**, [812]
    time for—
      deferral for competing claim, after,
        18, [799]
      following appeal, **18**, [797]
      no appeal, where, **18**, [796]
      person serving sentence, undertaking in
        relation to, **18**, [798]
    unlawfully at large, meaning, **18**, [830]
    warrant—
      arrest under, **18**, [761]–[764]
      certificate, issue of, **18**, [760]
      competing, **18**, [805]
      consent, following, **18**, [809]
      disposal of, **18**, [970]
      information in, **18**, [760]
      meaning, **18**, [760]
      receipt of, **18**, [760]
      statement in, **18**, [760]
      withdrawal of, **18**, [802]–[804]
  Category 2 territories, to—
    appeal—
      decisions questioned by, **18**, [881]
      detention pending conclusion of,
        18, [876], [880]
      discharge by Secretary of State, against,
        18, [874]–[876]
      discharge, against, **18**, [869]–[871]
      extradition following, **18**, [883]
      High Court, to, **18**, [877]
      House of Lords, to, **18**, [878], [880]
      order, against, **18**, [872], [873]
      Secretary of State, case sent to,
        18, [867], [868]
      start, time limit for, **18**, [877]

extradition—*contd*
  Category 2 territories, to—*contd*
    appeal—*contd*
      withdrawal of warrant pending,
        18, [889], [890]
    arrest warrant—
      copy, supply of, **18**, [834]
      discharge of person arrested, **18**, [834]
      provisional, **18**, [835], [836]
      request, following, **18**, [833]
    asylum claim, person making, **18**, [886]
    bars to—
      double jeopardy, rule against, **18**, [842]
      extraneous considerations, **18**, [843]
      forum, by reason of, **18**, [846]
      hostage-taking considerations, **18**, [845]
      International Criminal Court, earlier
        transfer to UK from, **18**, [860]
      list of, **18**, [841]
      passage of time, **18**, [844]
    competing claims, **18**, [853]
    consent to, **18**, [892]
      case sent to Secretary of State, before,
        18, [893]
    costs—
      discharge ordered, where, **18**, [899],
        [900]
      extradition ordered, where, **18**, [898]
    death sentence, to face, **18**, [857]
    designation, **18**, [831]
    discharge, order for, **18**, [865]
    double jeopardy, rule against, **18**, [842]
    earlier extradition to UK, effect of,
      18, [859]
    extradition hearing—
      conviction in person's absence, **18**, [849]
      conviction, effect of, **18**, [848]
      date of, **18**, [837], [838]
      human rights considerations, **18**, [850]
      initial stages, **18**, [840]
      judge, powers of, **18**, [839]
      no conviction, effect of, **18**, [847]
      person charged with offence in UK,
        adjournment in case of, **18**, [851]
      person serving sentence in UK at time
        of, **18**, [852]
      physical or mental condition at time of,
        18, [854]
    further, consent to—
      category 1 territory, to, **18**, [896]
      category 2 territory, to, **18**, [895]
    hearing, meaning, **18**, [905]
    International Criminal Court, earlier
      transfer to UK from, **18**, [860]
    offence—
      appropriate judge, **18**, [904]
      person not sentenced for, **18**, [902]
      person sentenced for, **18**, [903]
    order for, **18**, [865]
    other offence being dealt with, consent to,
      18, [894]
    person serving sentence outside territory
      where convicted, **18**, [901]
    remainder of sentence, return of person to
      serve, **18**, [897]

extradition—*contd*
  Category 2 territories, to—*contd*
    repatriation cases, **18**, [901]
    request—
      appeal, withdrawal pending, **18**, [889], [890]
      approved way, in, **18**, [832]
      arrest under, **18**, [833]
      British overseas territory, to, **18**, [832]
      certificate, issue of, **18**, [832]
      competing, **18**, [891]
      disposal of, **18**, [970]
      receipt of, **18**, [832]
      validity, **18**, [832]
      withdrawal of, **18**, [887]
    Scotland, references to Secretary of State, **18**, [907]
    Secretary of State, case sent to—
      appeal, **18**, [867], [868]
      appropriate day, **18**, [866]
      consent to extradition before, **18**, [893]
      consideration by, **18**, [856]
      deferral, **18**, [861], [862]
      information, provision of, **18**, [864]
      remand for decision, **18**, [855]
      time limit for order, **18**, [863]
      withdrawal of request following, **18**, [888]
    speciality arrangements, absence of, **18**, [858]
    time for—
      deferral for competing claim, after, **18**, [885]
      following appeal, **18**, [883]
      no appeal, where, **18**, [882]
      person serving sentence, undertaking in relation to, **18**, [884]
    United States, designation of, **18**, [990]
    unlawfully at large, meaning, **18**, [906]
  charge, disposal of, **18**, [971]
  competing claims, **18**, [943]
  crimes. *See* offences *below*
  crimes against humanity, in respect of, **18**, [956]
  custody, remand in, **18**, [957]
  customs officers, powers of, **18**, [939]
  deferred, proceedings on, **18**, [945]
  deferred warrant or request, proceedings on, **18**, [944]
  designation of territories, **18**, [953]
  documents, form of, **18**, [974]
  European framework list, **18**, [972], [987]
  evidence—
    burden and standard of proof, **18**, [963]
    electronic transmission of documents, **18**, [961]
    facsimile, documents sent by, **18**, [960]
    receivable documents, **18**, [959]
    written statements and admissions, **18**, [962]
  extradited prisoners, **12(3)**, [974]
  genocide, offence of, **18**, [956]
  hostage-taking, offence of, **12(1)**, [767]
  human rights proceedings, appropriate tribunal, **18**, [955]

extradition—*contd*
  international Convention, parties to, **18**, [953]
  interpretation, **18**, [973]
  Ireland, to. *See* **Ireland, Republic of**
  legal aid, **18**, [946], [947]
  legislation ceasing to have effect, **18**, [975]
  legal aid, **18**, [946], [947]
  legislation ceasing to have effect, **18**, [975]
  Northern Ireland, transfer of functions in, **31(S)**, N Ireland 7
  offences—
    aircraft, on, **18**, [752], [757]
    Channel Tunnel, relating to, **18**, [757]
  orders and regulations, **18**, [980], [991]
  Orders in Council, **18**, [981]
  police powers—
    arrest—
      entry and search of premises after, **18**, [931]
      entry and search of premises for purposes of, **18**, [928]
      entry and search of premises on, **18**, [929]
      fingerprints and samples, taking, **18**, [932]
      photographs, taking, **18**, [934]
      search of persons on, **18**, [930]
      searches and examination following, **18**, [933]
      treatment and rights of persons under, **18**, [935]
    codes of practice, **18**, [937]
    excluded material, warrant for, **18**, [927]
    interpretation, **18**, [938]
    production orders—
      application for, **18**, [924]
      computer information, for, **18**, [926]
      power to make, **18**, [924]
      requirements for, **18**, [925]
    search and seizure warrants, **18**, [923]
    seized property, delivery of, **18**, [936]
    special procedure material, warrant for, **18**, [927]
  proceedings, conduct of, Northern Ireland, in, **18**, [952]
  re-extradition—
    category 1 territories, to, **18**, [950], [985]
    category 2 territories, to, **18**, [951], [986]
    conditions, **18**, [948]
    hearing, **18**, [949]
    modification of provisions, **18**, [985], [986]
  reasonable force, use of, **18**, [966]
  rules of court, **18**, [967]
  Scottish jurisdiction, **18**, [751]
  service of notices, **18**, [968]
  service policemen, powers of, **18**, [940]
  serving prisoner, of, **18**, [958]
  special arrangements, **18**, [954]
  summary of provisions, **18**, [751]
  trial in United Kingdom more appropriate, **18**, [995]
  United Kingdom, to—
    appropriate judge, **18**, [915]
    bail, restriction on, **18**, [920]

extradition—*contd*
  United Kingdom, to—*contd*
    Category 1 territories not applying
      framework decision to old cases, **18**, [922]
    Category 2 territories, from—
      Commonwealth countries, **18**, [916]
      other offences, dealing with person for,
        18, [917]
    consent to, effect of, **18**, [913]
    extraditing territory, return to serve
      sentence, **18**, [910]
    extradition offences, **18**, [914]
    Part 3 warrant—
      certificate, **18**, [908]
      issue of, **18**, [908]
      meaning, **18**, [908]
      other offence, dealing with person for,
        18, [912]
      person serving sentence, undertaking as
        to, **18**, [909]
      statement in, **18**, [908]
      territory executing, service of sentence
        in, **18**, [911]

extradition—*contd*
  United Kingdom, to—*contd*
    person acquitted or not tried, return of,
      18, [919]
    person serving sentence, undertaking as
      to, **18**, [909]
    remission of punishment for other
      offences, **18**, [918]
    service personnel, **18**, [921]
  war crimes, in respect of, **18**, [956]

extra-parochial district
  army chaplain appointed in, **14**, 212
  chapel in, **14**, 212
  jurisdiction of archbishop or bishop, under,
    14, 213
  setting out, **14**, 211

eye tests
  provided by employer, exemption for,
    44(2), [329]

F

fabric advisory committee. *See* **cathedral**

face-value vouchers
VAT treatment of—
  nature of supply, **50**, [156]
  postage stamps, **50**, [156]
  retailer vouchers, **50**, [156]
  vouchers supplied free with goods or
    services, **50**, [156]

factor
  mercantile. *See* **mercantile agent**

factories and workshops
Act—
  application generally, **18**, [1196]
  Crown, application to, **18**, [1197]
  transitional provisions, **18**, [1207]
agreements, power of court to modify,
  18, [1193]
alterations—
  expenses, apportionment, **18**, [1194]
  modification of agreements, **18**, [1193]
Arbitration Act 1996, extent of application,
  18, [1195]
building operations—
  meaning, **18**, [1200]
  provisions applicable, **18**, [1180]
charitable institutions, application of Acts to,
  18, [1177]
children—
  construction of references to, **18**, [1192]
  employment of, offences arising, **18**, [1192]
  See also **young persons**
cotton cloth, meaning, **18**, [1200]
county court—
  apportionment of expenses between owner
    and occupier, **18**, [1194]
  modification of agreements, **18**, [1193]
Crown, application of provisions, **18**, [1197]
defective equipment, employers' liability,
  16, [19]
disabled person, provision for, at, **35(1)**, [289]
district council medical officer of health,
  annual report, **18**, [1184]
docks, provisions applicable to, **18**, [1178]
electrical stations, application of Acts to,
  18, [1176]
employment—
  meaning of period of, **18**, [1200]
  young persons. *See* **young persons**
employment of women in, soon after giving
  birth, **35(1)**, [147]
engineering construction—
  meaning, **18**, [1200]
  provisions applicable, **18**, [1180]
fencing, teagle openings and doors, **18**, [1168]

factories and workshops—*contd*
fumes, meaning, **18**, [1200]
gasholders, water sealed—
  meaning, **18**, [1169]
  precautions, **18**, [1169]
health, safety and welfare—
  fencing. *See* fencing *above*
  medical examination of persons, **18**, [1166]
  special regulations, power to make,
    18, [1171]
  welfare regulations, **18**, [1170]
  See also **health and safety at work**
hours of employment, exemptions from
  provisions regulating, **18**, [1172]
humid, meaning, **18**, [1200]
information, unauthorised disclosure,
  18, [1185], [1186]
inspectors—
  appointment, powers etc. *See under* **health
    and safety at work**
  fitness for work by young persons, powers
    as to, **18**, [1173]
institutions, charitable or reformatory,
  application of Acts, **18**, [1177]
lead, processes involving use of, employment
  of women and young persons, **18**, [1252]
machinery driving belt, meaning, **18**, [1200]
meaning, **18**, [1199]
mechanical power, use of, notification,
  18, [1181]
medical advisers, examination by, **18**, [1166]
medical examination of persons, **18**, [1166]
medical supervision, power to require,
  18, [1167]
occupation of, notice of, **18**, [1181]
occupier—
  agreement with owner, modification by
    court, **18**, [1193]
  liability for offences, **18**, [1187]
offences—
  children—
    construction of references to, **18**, [1192]
    employment of, in respect of, **18**, [1192]
  defence by owner or occupier, **18**, [1187]
  evidence, special provisions as to,
    18, [1191]
  information, disclosure of, **18**, [1185],
    [1186]
  liability for—
    owner of machine, **18**, [1190]
    owners or occupiers, **18**, [1187], [1190]
    parent of young person, **18**, [1188]
  parent of young person, by, **18**, [1188]
  meaning of parent, **18**, [1200]
  persons not primarily liable, proceedings
    against, **18**, [1189]

factories and workshops—*contd*
  offences—*contd*
    young person's employment, respecting,
      18, [1192]
  orders generally, **18**, [1202]
  part of building, let as separate factory,
    18, [1175]
  pipe-lines in, **17(1)**, [274]
  registers—
    general, **18**, [1182]
    preservation, **18**, [1183]
  regulations—
    generally, **18**, [1202]
    special, procedure for, **18**, [1206]
  safety. *See* health, safety and welfare *above*
  sanitary convenience, meaning, **18**, [1200]
  ships, provisions applicable, **18**, [1179]
  summary of provisions, **18**, [1165]
  tenement—
    application of Acts to, **18**, [1174]
    meaning, **18**, [1200]
  transmission machinery, meaning, **18**, [1200]
  welfare. *See* health, safety and welfare *above*
  wharves and quays, provisions applicable to,
    18, [1178]
  young persons, employment of. *See under*
    young persons

faculty
  building licensed for public worship, for,
    14, 639–40
  cases, jurisdiction in, **14**, 637–8
  costs, enforcement of orders, **14**, 641
  defaults, orders in relation to, **14**, 1222–3
  demolition, for, **14**, 1226–8
  grant of, **14**, 1222
    archdeacons, delegation of powers to,
      14, 1224
  guild church, in, **14**, 466
  jurisdiction, **14**, 1221
  monument, affecting, **14**, 638
  obtaining, proceedings for, **14**, 1225–6
  proceedings, bishop and chancellor disposing
    of, **14**, 590
  sale of parochial library books, for, **14**, 639
  sepulture, rights of, on, **14**, 641
  vesting of privately-owned church, for,
    14, 637–8

Fahrenheit
  replacement by Celsius in customs and excise
    Acts, **13**, [584]

fair trading. *See also* **food prices**
  advisory committee. *See* **Consumer**
    Protection Advisory Committee
  anti-competitive practices—
    orders and regulations, **47**, [340]
    report on—
      absolute privilege in, **47**, [338]
      general provisions, **47**, [338]
      laying before Parliament, **47**, [339]
      publication of, **47**, [339]
  consumer, meaning, **47**, [195]

fair trading—*contd*
  consumer trade practice, references of. *See*
    Consumer Protection Advisory
    Committee
  Director. *See* **Director General of Fair**
    Trading
  goods—
    seizure of—
      compensation, **47**, [146]
      powers, **47**, [143]
      test purchases, **47**, [142]
      testing, notice of, **47**, [145]
  monopoly references. *See* **monopoly**
    references
  offences—
    bodies corporate, by, **47**, [192]
    default of another, due to, **47**, [138]
    false information, **47**, [144]
    generally, **47**, [144]
    obstructing authorised officers, **47**, [144]
    penalties, **47**, [144]
    prosecutions, time-limit for, **47**, [191]
  orders—
    contravention, penalties for, **47**, [137]
    defences in proceedings, **47**, [139]
    documents, inspection etc of, **47**, [143]
    effect of, limitation of, **47**, [140]
    enforcement—
      authorities responsible for, **47**, [141]
      entry etc, powers of, **47**, [143]
      justices' warrant for, **47**, [143]
      legal privilege as to, **47**, [143]
      obstruction of, **47**, [144]
      offences in connection with, **47**, [144]
      seizure of goods, **47**, [143]
      test purchases, power to make, **47**, [142]
  provisions ceasing to have effect, **47**, [698]
  pyramid schemes. *See* **pyramid selling**
    scheme
  regulators—
    generally, **47**, [526]
    prohibitions—
      electricity, **47**, [572]
      gas, **47**, [572]
      Northern Ireland, **47**, [573]
      railways, **47**, [572]
      water, **47**, [572]
  seizure of goods—
    compensation for loss, **47**, [146]
    enforcement by, **47**, [143]
  test purchases, power to make, **47**, [142]
  testing of goods, **47**, [145]
  toll roads, application of enactments,
    38(1), [168]
  trading scheme, meaning, **47**, [185]

fair wear and tear
  compensation, excluded in payment of,
    9, [121], [123]
  meaning, **9**, [136]

fairground
  equipment—
    meaning, **18**, [1307]
    safety requirement, **18**, [1260]

fairs. *See also* **markets and fairs**
byelaws as to, **35(1)**, [384]
meaning, **5(1)**, [566]
rent payable in respect of, **44(1)**, [98]
rights, charge to tax, **44(1)**, [34]
travelling—
  gaming machines in, **5(1)**, [567]
  meaning, **5(1)**, [566]
  prize gaming in, **5(1)**, [572]

falconry
exempt from hunting provisions, **2**, [749]

Falkland Islands
British citizenship, acquisition of. *See under*
  citizenship

false accounting
offences, **12(1)**, [568]; **12(2)**, [162]

false instrument. *See* **forgery**

false statements or information
Act of Parliament, where made under,
  12(1), [194]
aiding and abetting, **12(1)**, [201]
benefit, to obtain, **40(1)**, [26]
birth, relating to particulars of, **12(1)**, [198]
company officer, by, **12(1)**, [570];
  12(2), [162]
corroboration, **12(1)**, [204]
corrupt practice, as, **12(1)**, [207]
dangerous or careless driving, name and
  address in case of, **37**, [786]
death, relating to particulars of, **12(1)**, [198]
evidence, in, **12(1)**, [395]
financial circumstances, as to, **12(2)**, [70]
goods vehicles operating licences, as to,
  38(1), [561]
indictment, form of, **12(1)**, [203]
interim possession order, as to, **12(2)**, [209]
liability for, **12(1)**, [207]
licence or permit, to obtain, **37**, [49], [458]
marriage, relating to, **12(1)**, [197]
oath, on—
  judicial proceeding, in, **12(1)**, [194]
  otherwise than in judicial proceeding,
    12(1), [196]
official secrets offences, **12(1)**, [229]
outside United Kingdom, made, **12(1)**, [202]
perjury. *See* **perjury**
private hire vehicles in London, as to,
  38(2), [37]
prohibited place, admission to by,
  12(1), [229]
registration, for obtaining, **12(1)**, [200]
statutory declaration, in, **12(1)**, [199]
unsworn, **12(1)**, [195]
without oath, **12(1)**, [199]

falsification
road traffic, relating to, **37**, [139], [793]

family
children, provision for separate representation
  for, **27**, [679]
disputes, mediation, legal aid for, general
  principles underlying provisions, **27**, [622]
domestic violence. *See* **domestic violence**

family assistance order
cessation of effect, **6**, [237]
power to make, **6**, [315]

family courts
CAFCASS—
  functions, **11(3)**, [373]
  meaning, **11(3)**, [373]
Family Justice, Head and Deputy Head of,
  11(3), [464]

Family Division, High Court
principal registry as a county court, **6**, [423]

Family Health Services Appeal Authority
conditions of use of services, **30**, [977]
constitution, **30**, [1104]
continuation of, **30**, [975]
expenses, **30**, [976]
functions, **30**, [975]
procedure, **30**, [1104]

Family Health Services Authority. *See now*
health authority; Special Health Authority
indicative amounts, specification of, **30**, [529]
transfer of, **30**, [579]

family procedure
practice directions, **11(3)**, [397]
Rules—
  amendment of legislation, **11(3)**, [396]
  Committee—
    making by, **11(3)**, [390]
    members of, **11(3)**, [392]
    requirements, power to change,
      11(3), [393]
  Lord Chancellor, rules to be made if
    required by, **11(3)**, [395]
  other rules, applying, **11(3)**, [392]
  power to make, **11(3)**, [390]
  process for making, **11(3)**, [394]
  scope of, **11(3)**, [391]
  to be made if required by
    Lord Chancellor, **11(3)**, [395]

family proceedings
change of name to, **6**, [423]
child involved in, privacy for, **6**, [428]
child, order relating to—
  contact activity conditions—
    conditions for making, **6(S)**, 7–8
    financial assistance, **6(S)**, 8–9
    monitoring, **6(S)**, 10
    parent, on, **6(S)**, 7
    power to make, **6(S)**, 6
  contact activity directions—
    conditions for making, **6(S)**, 7–8
    excepted contract order, **6(S)**, 5

family proceedings—*contd*
  child, order relating to—*contd*
    contact activity directions—*contd*
      financial assistance, **6(S)**, 8–9
      making of, **6(S)**, 3–4
      monitoring, **6(S)**, 10
      no power to make, where, **6(S)**, 4
      summary of provisions, **6(S)**, 1
    commencement, **6**, [453A]
    court powers in certain proceedings, **6**, [350]
    domestic proceedings change to, **6**, [423]
    generally, **6**, [453A]
    meaning, **6**, [301]
    officers, risk assessments, **6(S)**, 18
    orders arising from. *See* **child; care order;
      supervision order**
    rules of court, **6**, [424]
    single justice, hearings by, **6**, [453A]
    transfer of, **6**, [453A]
    Wales, in. *See* **Wales**

family proceedings orders. *See also* **child**
  application for, refusal, **6**, [236]
  British overseas territories, application of
    provisions, **6**, [262]
  civil partnership proceedings, **6**, [234], [238],
    [261]
  delivery up of child, **6**, [253]
  divorce proceedings, matter arising in,
    6, [234]
  duration of, **6**, [237], [243]
  education, provisions as to, **6**, [232]
  enforcement—
    dismissal of proceedings, **6**, [250]
    powers, **6**, [248]
    stay or sist of proceedings, **6**, [249]
  family law, application, **6**, [232]
  habitual residence—
    after removal from jurisdiction, **6**, [260]
    Northern Ireland, **6**, [241]
    on relevant date, **6**, [235]
  interpretation of provisions, **6**, [238], [261]
  judicial separation, matter arising in, **6**, [234]
  jurisdiction—
    exclusive, **6**, [234], [237]
    general, **6**, [1], [233]
    requirements, **6**, [234]
    Scotland, **6**, [232]
  marriage of parents, proceedings involving,
    6, [234]
  matrimonial proceedings, **6**, [234], [261]
  meaning of child, **6**, [238], [244]
  Northern Ireland—
    civil partnership proceedings, matter arising
      in, **6**, [240]
    divorce proceedings, matter arising in,
      6, [240]
    duration and variation, **6**, [243]
    education, provision as to, **6**, [232]
    habitual residence of child, **6**, [241]
    jurisdiction, **6**, [232], [239]
    made in, effect of, **6**, [237]
    matrimonial proceedings, **6**, [240]
    meaning of child, **6**, [244]
    presence of child, **6**, [241]

family proceedings orders—*contd*
  Northern Ireland—*contd*
    refusal of application and stay, **6**, [242]
  nullity proceedings, **6**, [234]
  orders to which provisions apply, **6**, [232],
    [301]
  other proceedings, furnishing of particulars,
    6, [258]
  power to make, **6**, [232]–[234]
  presence of child on relevant date, **6**, [235]
  recognition of, **6**, [245]
  recovery of child, **6**, [253], [454]
  registration—
    application for, **6**, [246]
    cancellation and variation of, **6**, [247]
  removal of child from jurisdiction—
    effect of order, **6**, [255]
    habitual residence after, **6**, [260]
    passports, surrender of, **6**, [256]
    power to restrict, **6**, [254]
  residence of child, relevance of, **6**, [235]
  Scotland, made in, effect of, **6**, [237]
  stay of proceedings, **6**, [236]
  variation of, **6**, [237], [243]
  whereabouts of child, disclosure, **6**, [252]

family provision
  applicant—
    immediate need, in, **18**, [604]
    interim payments to, **18**, [604]
  application for—
    attempts to defeat, **18**, [609]
    contracts intended to defeat, **18**, [610]
    disposition intended to defeat, **18**, [609],
      [611]
    grounds for, **18**, [600]
    matters to be regarded by court, **18**, [602]
    obligations of deceased, **18**, [602]
    persons who may make, **18**, [600]
    time-limit for, **18**, [603]
    variation etc of order, for, **18**, [605]
  beneficiary—
    application for variation etc of order,
      18, [605]
    meaning, **18**, [627]
  contracts to leave property by will, **18**, [610]
  directions by court, **18**, [611]
  disposition intended to defeat application,
    18, [609], [611]
  dissolution of civil partnership—
    absence of financial relief on, **18**, [614]
    court powers available in, **18**, [622]
    restrictions imposed in, **18**, [616], [618]
  divorce proceedings—
    absence of financial relief in, **18**, [613]
    restrictions imposed in, **18**, [615]
  financial resources of applicant, **18**, [602]
  illegitimacy, removal of, general principle,
    18, [665]
  illegitimate children—
    parents, succession by, **18**, [585]
    property rights, **18**, [585], [666], [667]
    statutory references to relationship,
      18, [665]
    succession on intestacy, **18**, [666]

family provision—*contd*
   inheritance tax, **18**, [607]
   joint tenancy, property held on, **18**, [608]
   lump sum payment—
      instalments, payment by, **18**, [606]
      order for, **18**, [601]
   maintenance agreement—
      meaning, **18**, [620]
      variation or revocation, **18**, [620]
   matrimonial proceedings—
      court powers available in, **18**, [621]
      orders in, **18**, [619]
      periodical payments orders in, **18**, [619]
      restrictions imposed in, **18**, [617]
   net estate—
      meaning, **18**, [627]
      property treated as, **18**, [607]
   non-marital birth, provisions as to,
      18, [665]–[667]
   nullity of marriage—
      absence of financial relief in, **18**, [613]
      restrictions imposed in, **18**, [615]
   orders—
      consequential provisions, **18**, [611]
      considerations in making, **18**, [602]
      contracts intended to avoid, **18**, [610]
      discharge of, **18**, [605]
      duration of, **18**, [623]
      effect of, **18**, [623]
      form of, **18**, [623]
      interim order, **18**, [604]
      kinds of, **18**, [601]
      lump sum payments, for, **18**, [601]
      payment by instalments, **18**, [606]
      periodical payments, for, **18**, [601]
      power of court to make, **18**, [601]
      trustees, on, **18**, [612]
      variation of, **18**, [605]
   periodical payments—
      discharge of order for, **18**, [605]
      variation or discharge, **18**, [605]
   personal representatives, provisions as to,
      18, [624]
   property available for—
      inheritance tax deduction, **18**, [607]
      joint tenancy, property held on, **18**, [608]
      meaning, **18**, [627]
      net estate, **18**, [607]
   reasonable financial provision—
      failure of deceased to make, **18**, [601],
         [602]
      meaning, **18**, [600]
   remarriage, provisions as to, **18**, [627]
   representation, date of taking out, **18**, [625]
   spouse—
      intestacy, sum payable on, **18**, [583]
      provision for, **18**, [583]
      surviving—
         life interest, redemption of, **18**, [551]
         personal representative's powers,
            18, [552]
   succession, order of, **18**, [549]
   trustees, orders against, **18**, [612]
   urgent cases, **18**, [604]

family provision—*contd*
   widow, provision from intestate's property,
      18, [497]–[499]
   wife, for. *See* spouse *above*

farm. *See also* **agricultural land; agriculture**
   clergy taking for occupation, **14**, 99–100
   stock, execution, taken in. *See* **distress**

farm animal
   herd basis, **44(1)**, [636]
   See also **herd basis**
   tax treatment of, **44(1)**, [78]
   trading stock, as, **44(1)**, [636]

farm business tenancy
   agreements, limited owner's power to give,
      23, [269]
   Agricultural Holdings Act 1986, exclusion
      of, **23**, [242]
   agriculture conditions, **23**, [239]
   arbitration—
      general provisions, **23**, [268]
      reference of dispute to, **23**, [266]
      right to refer claim not applying, **23**, [267]
   best rent, estimation of, **23**, [271]
   buildings, tenant's right to remove, **23**, [246]
   business conditions, **23**, [239]
   capital money, power to apply and raise,
      23, [270]
   consents, limited owner's power to give,
      23, [269]
   Crown land, application of provisions to,
      23, [273]
   defined expressions, index of, **23**, [275]
   disputes, resolution of, **23**, [266]–[268]
   fixtures, tenant's right to remove, **23**, [246]
   Landlord and Tenant Act 1954, exclusion from
      Part II, **21**, [207]
   meaning, **23**, [239]
   notice conditions—
      outline of, **23**, [239]
      surrender and re-grant, compliance in case
         of, **23**, [241]
   rent review—
      amount of rent, **23**, [251]
      application of provisions, **23**, [247]
      arbitrator, appointment of, **23**, [250]
      interpretation, **23**, [252]
      new tenancy of severed part of reversion,
         date where, **23**, [249]
      statutory, notice requiring, **23**, [248]
   service of notices, **23**, [272]
   tenancies not being, **23**, [240]
   termination of—
      meaning, **23**, [274]
      notice to quit, length of, **23**, [244]
      option to terminate tenancy or resume
         possession of part, notice for exercise of,
         23, [245]
      tenancy for more than two years to
         continue from year to year, **23**, [243]
   tenants' improvements, compensation for—
      amount of, **23**, [258]

farm business tenancy—*contd*
  termination of—*contd*
    tenants' improvements, compensation
     for—*contd*
      extent to which recoverable under
       agreements, **23**, [264]
      improvements, meaning, **23**, [253]
      landlord's consent as condition of,
       23, [255]
      part of holding, resumption of possession
       of, **23**, [262]
      planning permission—
       amount for, **23**, [259]
       conditions as to, **23**, [256]
      refusal or failure to give consent or of
       conditions, reference to arbitration,
       23, [257]
      reversionary estate in holding severed,
       on, **23**, [263]
      right to, **23**, [254]
      settlement of claims, **23**, [260]
      successive tenancies, **23**, [261]

farm land
  meaning, **44(1)**, [615]

farm premises
  inspection of, **2**, [799]

farm stock
  execution, taken in. *See* **distress**

farmers
  value added tax regime, **50**, [76]

farming
  fluctuating profits, averaging—
   adjustment, **44(3)**, [223]–[225]
   claim for—
    circumstances for, **44(3)**, [222]
    making, **44(3)**, [221]
  herd basis, **44(1)**, [636]
   See also **herd basis**
  loss relief, **44(1)**, [201]
  meaning, **44(1)**, [201]; **44(4)**, [1004]
  partnerships, **44(3)**, [876]
  short rotation coppice, cultivation of,
   43(1), [164]
  trade, as, **44(1)**, [33]
  trade losses—
   losses in previous tax years, determining,
    44(4), [70]
   reasonable expectation of profit test,
    44(4), [68]
   restrictions on, **44(4)**, [67]
   trade treated as same, whether, **44(4)**, [69]
  trade profits, income taxed as, **44(3)**, [9]

farriers. *See also* **Farriers Registration
Council**
  competence, securing, **2**, [373]
  examinations—
   approval of, **2**, [385]
   supervision of, **2**, [386]

farriers—*contd*
  farriery—
   meaning, **2**, [393]
   persons entitled to practice, **2**, [391]
   unregistered person, by, **2**, [391]
  qualifications for registration—
   approval of, **2**, [385]
   corresponding, **2**, [380]
   determination of questions, **2**, [383]
   experience as, **2**, [379], [380]
  register. *See* **Farriers Registration Council**
  registration—
   application for, determination, **2**, [381]
   certificate of, **2**, [384]
   entitlement, **2**, [379]
  shoeing smith, use of title, **2**, [390]
  style and title, unlawful use, **2**, [390]
  training courses—
   approval, **2**, [385]
   institutions, supervision of, **2**, [385]
  unregistered, offences by, **2**, [391]

Farriers Company
  functions, **2**, [373]
  meaning, **2**, [393]
  register of, availability to Council, **2**, [382]

Farriers Registration Council
  accounts, **2**, [396]
  approvals required of, **2**, [385]
  auditors, qualifications, **2**, [396]
  committees, power to set up, **2**, [396]
  constitution, **2**, [395]
  Disciplinary Committee—
   assessors to assist, **2**, [399]
   constitution, **2**, [398]
   direction for removal from register, **2**, [389]
   establishment, **2**, [388]
   functions, **2**, [388]
   Investigating Committee—
    constitution, **2**, [397]
    establishment, **2**, [387]
    functions, **2**, [387]
   proceedings of, **2**, [398]
   rules of procedure, **2**, [399]
  members, **2**, [395]
  register—
   entries in, **2**, [376]
   establishment and maintenance, **2**, [375]
   fees for entry in, **2**, [376]
   fraudulent entry, **2**, [377]
   parts of, qualifications for entry in, **2**, [379]
   printing and publishing, **2**, [375]
   public inspection, **2**, [375]
   qualifications for entry in. *See* **farriers**
   removal of names—
    appeals respecting, **2**, [389]
    death, on, **2**, [378]
    direction by Committee for, **2**, [389]
    misconduct, for, **2**, [389]
    non-payment of fee, for, **2**, [376]
    restoration after, **2**, [376]
   rules respecting, **2**, [376]
  registrar, appointment, **2**, [396]
  status of, **2**, [374]

Farriers Registration Council—*contd*
training courses approved by, **2**, [385]

fatal accident
action—
bereavement, claim for damages, **31**, [609]
executor or administrator, by, **31**, [610]
persons with right of, **31**, [608], [610]
actions, limitation of time, **19(3)**, [737],
[738], [764]
aircraft, involving, **4(1)**, [4], [17]
bereavement, claims for, **31**, [609]
contributory negligence in case of, **31**, [613]
damages—
apportionment, **31**, [611]
assessment, **31**, [611]–[612]
benefits, disregard of, **31**, [612]
bereavement, for, **31**, [609]
contributory negligence, reduction for,
31, [613]
funeral expenses, inclusion, **31**, [611]
payment into court, **31**, [611]
remarriage, prospects discounted, **31**, [611]
dependants—
benefit of action, **31**, [608]
meaning, **31**, [608]
executor or administrator, action by, **31**, [610]
funeral expenses, recovery, **31**, [611]
injury, construction of reference to, **31**, [608]
summary of provisions, **31**, [588]
wrongful act causing death, right of action,
31, [608]

father. *See also* **parent**
natural guardian, as, abolition of principle,
6, [294]
parental responsibility—
acquisition, **6**, [296], [837]
duration of order, **6**, [422]
unmarried, custody of child, **6**, [1]

fault
meaning, **16**, [19]

fee simple
coal and coal mines, vesting, note, **17(1)**, [1]
corporation, vested in, **20**, [678]
disposition by tenant in tail, **20**, [75]
divested, estates liable to be, **20**, [631]
legal estate, as, **20**, [625]
long term, enlargement of residue into fee
simple estate, **20**, [763]
mortgage of, **20**, [1]
use of words, **20**, [678]

fee tail
creation, **20**, [5]

feeding stuffs. *See* **fertilisers and feeding
stuffs**

Fellowship of Engineering
grants to, **15(1)**, [289]

felony
conviction of before abolition, **12(1)**, [368]
enactments referring to, adaptation,
12(1), [371]
misdemeanour, abolition of distinction,
12(1), [360]
transitional provisions, **12(1)**, [368]

fencing
burial grounds, **35(1)**, [48]
factory, in. *See* **factories and workshops**
lands adjoining streets, **35(1)**, [67]

feoffment
conveyancing by, abolition, **20**, [669]

female genital mutilation
assisting girl in self-mutilation, offence of,
12(3), [556]
definitions, **12(3)**, [560]
extra-territorial acts, extension of provisions
to, **12(3)**, [558]
non-UK person, assisting overseas,
12(3), [557]
offence of, **12(3)**, [555]
surgical operations, exclusion for,
12(3), [555]
penalties, **12(3)**, [559]

ferry
acquisition of—
integrated transport executive, by, **36**, [779]
passenger transport executive, by, **36**, [779]
charge to tax, **44(1)**, [34]
Crown rights, saving for, **36**, [591]
existing—
local authority, acquired by, **36**, [589]
meaning, **36**, [589]
passengers and public, regulations for
protection of, **36**, [590]
London—
byelaws, enforcement, **25(1)**, [74]
explosives—
byelaws, arrest of offenders, **25(1)**, [92]
conveyance of, **25(1)**, [90]
search for, **25(1)**, [91]
long-distance right of way, provision on,
36, [635]
provision of, Ministerial control, **25(2)**, [448]
rent payable in respect of, **44(1)**, [98]
road-ferry—
experiments for improving, **36**, [1332]
meaning, **36**, [1381]
new, provision of, **36**, [1028]
services—
assistance for, **36**, [792]
meaning, **36**, [871]
taxation. *See* **income tax**
toll—
exemptions, **36**, [592]
local authority, powers of, **36**, [589]

fertilisers and feeding stuffs
accident, offence due to, **1(1)**, [848]

fertilisers and feeding stuffs—*contd*
agricultural analysts—
appointment, **1(1)**, [831]
certificate of, **1(1)**, [843], [844]
deputy, **1(1)**, [831]
division of samples and analysis, **1(1)**, [843]
meaning, **1(1)**, [830]
qualification, **1(1)**, [831]
analysis—
certificate of—
agricultural analyst, by, **1(1)**, [843], [844]
Government chemist, by, **1(1)**, [844]
court order for, **1(1)**, [844]
division of, **1(1)**, [843]
fees, **1(1)**, [844]
Government chemist, by, **1(1)**, [844]
meaning, **1(1)**, [830]
purchaser's right to, **1(1)**, [841]
taking, regulations, **1(1)**, [845]
attributes claimed, particulars required, **1(1)**, [835]
chemicals. *See* **agriculture**
corporations, offences by, **1(1)**, [854]
dangerous feeding stuffs, **1(1)**, [838]
definitions, **1(1)**, [830]
deleterious ingredients, **1(1)**, [837]
delivery, what constitutes, **1(1)**, [830]
descriptions, **1(1)**, [834]
disclosure of trade secret, etc, **1(1)**, [849]
enforcement authorities, **1(1)**, [831]
exportation, restriction, **1(1)**, [840]
feeding stuff, meaning, **1(1)**, [830]
Government chemist—
certificate of, **1(1)**, [844]
submission of samples to, **1(1)**, [844]
importation, restriction, **1(1)**, [840]
inspectors—
appointment, **1(1)**, [831]
entry, power of, **1(1)**, [842]
exercise of powers, **1(1)**, [849]
information, powers to require, **1(1)**, [842]
obstruction of, **1(1)**, [849]
samples, power to take, **1(1)**, [842]
kitchen waste, collection, **1(1)**, [460]
marking, materials prepared for sale—
generally, **1(1)**, [833]
mis-statements, effect of, **1(1)**, [839]
register of marks, **1(1)**, [833]
when deemed marked, **1(1)**, [835]
marks, **1(1)**, [833]
mis-statement as to nature, quality, etc, **1(1)**, [839]
mistake, offence due to, **1(1)**, [848]
name, sale by, **1(1)**, [834]
Northern Ireland, application of provisions, **1(1)**, [852]
offences—
defence, **1(1)**, [848]
fault of another, due to, **1(1)**, [847]
prosecutions, **1(1)**, [846]
body corporate, by, **1(1)**, [854]
pet animals, feeding stuff dangerous to, **1(1)**, [830]
prosecutions, institution of, **1(1)**, [846]

fertilisers and feeding stuffs—*contd*
purchaser, right to samples and analysis, **1(1)**, [841]
register of marks, **1(1)**, [833]
regulations—
making of, **1(1)**, [850]
power to make, **1(1)**, [840]
supplementary provisions, **1(1)**, [845]
sale—
certain sales, exemption of, **1(1)**, [851]
material treated as sold, **1(1)**, [830]
sampled portion—
deleterious ingredient in, **1(1)**, [837]
failure to accord with description, **1(1)**, [835]
meaning, **1(1)**, [830]
samples—
analysis of, **1(1)**, [843]
division of, **1(1)**, [843]
Government chemist, submission to, **1(1)**, [844]
handling, etc, regulations, **1(1)**, [845]
inspector's power to take, **1(1)**, [842]
purchaser's right to, **1(1)**, [841]
tampering with, **1(1)**, [845]
statutory statement—
mis-statement in, **1(1)**, [839]
seller, by, **1(1)**, [832]
unwholesome, sale of, **1(1)**, [838]
warranty—
fitness of feeding stuffs, **1(1)**, [836]
implied, **1(1)**, [834]
mis-statements, limits of variation, **1(1)**, [839]

feudal tenures
abolition, **20**, [15]
historical note, **20**, [1]

field garden
generally, **1(1)**, [124]
meaning, **1(1)**, [124]

Fiji
British ship registered in, **7(2)**, [653]
Commonwealth citizenship, **31**, [186]
fully responsible status of, **7(2)**, [648]
legislative powers of, **7(2)**, [652]
visiting forces in, **7(2)**, [653]

film relief. *See* **cinematograph films**

films. *See also* **cinema; cinematograph film**
amended provisions, **43(S)**, 188–90
British, certification of, **43(S)**, 184–7
co-producer, meaning, **43(S)**, 23
commencement of provisions, **43(S)**, 35
definitions, **42**, [1501]
exhibition, mandatory conditions—
club premises certificate, in, **19(3)**, [563]
premises licence, in, **19(3)**, [506]
existing tax reliefs, withdrawal of—
corporation tax, **43(S)**, 29
income tax, **43(S)**, 30
expenditure, relief for, **43(1)**, [324]

films—*contd*
  exploitation of—
    capital gains relief, restrictions on,
      44(4), [119]
    sideways relief, restrictions on, **44(4)**, [82],
      [119]
  film-making activities, meaning, **43(S)**, 21
  film production company—
    meaning, **43(S)**, 20
    special film rules, election out of,
      43(S), 554
    taxation of activities of, **43(S)**, 178–80
  film tax relief—
    claims for, **43(S)**, 189
    conditions of—
      British film, **43(S)**, 25
      intended theatrical release, **43(S)**, 24
      UK expenditure, **43(S)**, 25
    entitlement to, **43(S)**, 180–3
    films qualifying for, **43(S)**, 23
    provisional entitlement, **43(S)**, 190–2
  in production, application of provisions to,
    43(S), 34–5
  intangible fixed assets, as, **43(S)**, 33–4
  leases, long funding, **43(S)**, 1631–2
  limited-budget, meaning, **43(S)**, 21–2
  losses—
    later periods, use in, **43(S)**, 27
    restriction on use while film in
      production, **43(S)**, 26
    terminal, **43(S)**, 28
  master versions, expenditure on, **42**, [1495]
  meaning, **43(S)**, 19
  non-trade business—
    calculation of income, **44(3)**, [622]
    charge to tax, **44(3)**, [619]
    income charged, **44(3)**, [620]
    person liable for tax, **44(3)**, [621]
    trading income rules, application of,
      44(3), [623]
  partnership, interest relief, **43(S)**, 67–9
  partnerships, loans for investing in, relief for
    interest payments on, **44(4)**, [408]
  periods, allocation of expenditure to,
    42, [1496]
    election against, **42**, [1498]
    not applying, where, **42**, [1497]
  preliminary expenditure, relief for, **42**, [1499]
  production and acquisition, relief for,
    43(1), [324]
  production expenditure, meaning, **43(S)**, 21
  production or acquisition expenditure, relief
    for, **42**, [1500]
  qualifying co-production, meaning, **43(S)**, 23
  "qualifying film expenditure", meaning,
    44(4), [107]
  sound track, defamatory words in,
    19(3), [261]
  trading losses, individuals claiming sideways or
    capital gains relief for, **44(4)**, [805]
    capital contribution by a partner, exclusion
      of amounts in calculating, **44(4)**, [810]
    "capital contribution", meaning,
      44(4), [809]

films—*contd*
  trading losses, individuals claiming sideways or
    capital gains relief for—*contd*
    charge to tax on income receivable under,
      44(4), [804]
    "disposal of right of individual to profits",
      meaning, **44(4)**, [807]
    double counting, prohibition against,
      44(4), [811]
    "film-related losses", meaning, **44(4)**, [808]
    "non-taxable consideration", meaning,
      44(4), [806]
  UK expenditure, meaning, **43(S)**, 22

finance
  alternative arrangements. *See* **alternative
    finance arrangements**
  value added tax, exemption from, **50**, [153]

finance lease
  accountancy rental earnings, **43(1)**, [298]
  assessments and adjustments, **43(1)**, [298]
  capital form, return in, **43(1)**, [295]
  connected persons, arrangements between,
    43(1), [298]
  existing schemes, **43(1)**, [298]
  insurance companies, assets of, **43(1)**, [297]
  interpretation, **43(1)**, [298]
  leased assets, assets representing, **43(1)**, [298]
  lessor's interest, charge to tax, **43(1)**, [296]
  machinery and plant. *See* **machinery and
    plant allowances**
  new schemes, **43(1)**, [298]
  normal rent, **43(1)**, [298]
  parent undertaking, accounting purposes,
    43(1), [298]
  periods of account—
    straddling 26th November 1996,
      43(1), [298]
    time apportionment, **43(1)**, [298]
  rental earnings, **43(1)**, [298]

financial assistance
  building society, to, **19(S)**, Financial 279–80
  meaning, **19(S)**, Financial 284

financial collateral arrangements
  meaning, **19(S)**, Financial 282
  regulations, **19(S)**, Financial 282–3

financial futures
  charge to tax, **44(1)**, [103]
  investment, as, **44(1)**, [433]
  losses, **44(1)**, [203]
  meaning, **44(1)**, [203]

financial institution
  institution not to be treated as,
    19(S), Financial 266
  meaning, **8(1)**, [1251]
  overseas, accounts and reports, **8(1)**, [1128]

financial instruments
  debt contracts and options. *See* **debt**
  exchange gains and losses. *See* **exchange gains and losses**
  loan relationships, application of provisions, **43(1)**, [222]
  meaning, **19(2)**, [388]
  suspension or removal from trading—
    Authority's power of, **19(2)**, [385]
    notification, **19(2)**, [387]
    procedure, **19(2)**, [386]

financial markets
  operations, safeguarding, **19(1)**, [776]

financial penalty
  enforcement order, **3**, [630], [903]
  meaning, **3**, [630]

financial promotion
  restrictions on, **19(2)**, [21]
  rules, **19(2)**, [194]
    contravention, **19(2)**, [25]

financial reporting order
  coming into force, **12(4)**, [96]
  disclosure of report, **12(4)**, [100]
  duration of, **12(4)**, [96]
  effect of, **12(4)**, [98]
  failure to comply with, **12(4)**, [98]
  Northern Ireland, in, **12(4)**, [97]
  person subject to, report by, **12(4)**, [98]
  power to make, **12(4)**, [96]
  relevant offences, **12(4)**, [96]
  revocation, **12(4)**, [99]
  variation, **12(4)**, [99]
  verification, **12(4)**, [100]

financial services
  civil proceedings, jurisdiction, **19(2)**, [491]
  compensation scheme. *See* **Financial Services Compensation Scheme**
  consequential and supplementary provisions, **19(2)**, [504]
  definitions, **19(2)**, [493]
  gaming contracts, **19(2)**, [486]
  Gibraltar, provisions applying to, **19(2)**, [484]
  independent inquiries, arrangements for—
    appointment of persons to hold, **19(2)**, [15]
    cases of, **19(2)**, [14]
    conclusion of, **19(2)**, [17]
    contempt of, **19(2)**, [18]
    obstruction of, **19(2)**, [18]
    power of appointed person, **19(2)**, [16]
    procedure, **19(2)**, [16]
  international obligations, compatibility with, **19(2)**, [485]
  investment business, carrying on by insurance companies. *See under* **insurance company** (regulated)
  investment firm, meaning, **19(2)**, [502]
  members of the professions, provision by—
    Authority, general duty of, **19(2)**, [400]

financial services—*contd*
  members of the professions, provision by—*contd*
    general prohibition—
      consultations, **19(2)**, [405]
      directions, **19(2)**, [403]
      exemption from, **19(2)**, [402]
      false claims as to, **19(2)**, [408]
      orders, **19(2)**, [404], [406]
      rules as to, **19(2)**, [407]
    professional bodies, designation of, **19(2)**, [401]
  offences—
    Authority, misleading, **19(2)**, [473]
    body corporate, by, **19(2)**, [475]
    false and misleading statements, **19(2)**, [472]
    jurisdiction and procedure, **19(2)**, [478]
    Office of Fair Trading, misleading, **19(2)**, [474]
    proceedings, **19(2)**, [476], [477]
  Ombudsman scheme—
    administration, **19(2)**, [277]
    annual reports, **19(2)**, [544]
    budget, **19(2)**, [544]
    Chief Ombudsman, **19(2)**, [544]
    compulsory jurisdiction, **19(2)**, [278], [545]
      awards, **19(2)**, [282]
      determination under, **19(2)**, [281]
    constitution, **19(2)**, [544]
    consumer credit jurisdiction, **19(2)**, [279], [546]
      awards, **19(2)**, [282]
      funding, **19(2)**, [287]
    consumer credit licences—
      applicable to, **39(1)**, [656]
      consequential amendments, **39(1)**, [658]
      funding by licensees, **39(1)**, [657]
    establishment of, **19(2)**, [277], [544]
    funding, **19(2)**, [286], [287]
    information, power to require, **19(2)**, [284]
      court, power of, **19(2)**, [285]
    liability in damages, exemption from, **19(2)**, [544]
    operator—
      administration by, **19(2)**, [277]
      constitution, **19(2)**, [544]
      costs rules, **19(2)**, [283]
      guidance, **19(2)**, [544]
      status, **19(2)**, [544]
    panel, **19(2)**, [544]
    privilege, **19(2)**, [544]
    voluntary jurisdiction, **19(2)**, [280], [547]
  power to require documents, limitation on, **19(2)**, [489]
  regulations, power to make, **19(2)**, [506]
  repeals, **19(2)**, [550]
  service of notices, **19(2)**, [490]
  single regulator, **19(1)**, [1]
  third country decisions, implementing—
    directions, **19(2)**, [480]
    consequences of, **19(2)**, [482]
    interpretation, **19(2)**, [481]
    EFTA firms, **19(2)**, [483]
  transitional provisions, **19(2)**, [505], [549]

financial services—*contd*
undertaking—
   controller of, **19(2)**, [499]
   "participating interest", meaning,
      19(2), [498]

Financial Services and Markets Tribunal
appeal on point of law from, **19(2)**, [187]
applications referred to, **19(2)**, [56]
approval of arrangements, applications relating
   to, **19(2)**, [63]
constitution, **19(2)**, [537]
costs, **19(2)**, [538]
decisions of, **19(2)**, [538]
disciplinary measures, references concerning,
   19(2), [68]
establishment of, **19(2)**, [182]
evidence, **19(2)**, [538]
functions, **19(2)**, [182]
legal assistance scheme—
   establishment of, **19(2)**, [184]
   funding, **19(2)**, [186]
   provisions of, **19(2)**, [185]
market abuse penalties, reference as to,
   19(2), [175]
members—
   expenses, **19(2)**, [536]
   remuneration, **19(2)**, [536]
   terms of office, **19(2)**, [536]
panels, **19(2)**, [536]
practice directions, **19(2)**, [538]
president, **19(2)**, [536]
procedure before, **19(2)**, [538]
proceedings before, **19(2)**, [183]
prohibition order, application relating to,
   19(2), [59]
recognised investment exchanges and clearing
   houses, extension of functions, **19(2)**, [355]
references, **19(2)**, [183]
staff, **19(2)**, [536]

Financial Services Authority
administration order—
   administrator—
      appointed by company or directors,
         19(2), [437]
      report by, **19(2)**, [435]
   application for, **19(2)**, [433]
   insurers, **19(2)**, [434]
   participation in proceedings, **19(2)**, [436]
annual public meeting, **19(2)**, [512]
annual report, **19(2)**, [512]
authorised persons. *See* **regulated activities**
Bank of England functions, transfer of,
   19(1), [1019], [1038]
bankruptcy—
   insolvency practitioner, report of,
      19(2), [448]
   participation in proceedings, **19(2)**, [449]
   petition, presentation of, **19(2)**, [447]
building societies—
   accounts, furnishing, **19(1)**, [679]
   amalgamations, confirmation of,
      19(1), [693], [695], [758]

Financial Services Authority—*contd*
building societies—*contd*
   disclosure of information—
      inspections and investigations, from,
         19(1), [635]
      restrictions on, **19(1)**, [634]
   documents, directions for form of,
      19(1), [721]
   functions relating to, **19(1)**, [615]
   investigations, **4(2)**, [584]
   investigations on behalf of, **19(1)**, [636]
   name, approval, **19(1)**, [712]
   notices to—
      amalgamation proposals, **19(1)**, [757]
      dissolution, of, **19(1)**, [684]
      proposed merger, of, **19(1)**, [757]
      transfer of business, of, **19(1)**, [697]
   public files, preparation and maintenance,
      19(1), [711]
   registration, cancellation of, **19(1)**, [708]
   settlement of disputes, right to be heard,
      19(1), [747]
   transfer of business to company—
      confirmation, **19(1)**, [697], [698], [761]
      direction for, **19(1)**, [735], [736]
   transfer of engagements, confirmation and
      registration of certificate, **19(1)**, [694]
Building Societies Commission, transfer of
   functions, **19(2)**, [411], [414]
Building Societies Investor Protection Board,
   transfer of functions, **19(2)**, [412], [414]
competent authority, as—
   general duty, **19(2)**, [74]
   official listing. *See* **securities**
competition scrutiny—
   Competition Act 1998, application of
      prohibitions in, **19(2)**, [214]
   Competition Commission, consideration of
      reports by, **19(2)**, [212], [539]
   Office of Fair Trading—
      information, power to request,
         19(2), [211]
      reports by, **19(2)**, [210]
   regulating provisions, **19(2)**, [210]
   Treasury, role of, **19(2)**, [213]
compliance of EEA firm with requirements
   under markets in financial instruments
   directive, home state regulator's primary
   responsibility for securing, **19(2)**, [247]
compliance of EEA firm with UK branch
   with requirements under markets in financial
   instruments directive, responsibility for
   securing, **19(2)**, [245]
constitution, **19(2)**, [512]
consultation, duty of, **19(2)**, [8]
Consumer Panel—
   appointment, **19(2)**, [10]
   chairman, **19(2)**, [10]
   consumers, meaning, **19(2)**, [10]
   membership, **19(2)**, [10]
   National Consumer Council member,
      appointment of, **39(1)**, [706]
   representations by, consideration of,
      19(2), [10]
co-operation, duty of, **19(2)**, [429]

Financial Services Authority—*contd*
credit unions, transfer of functions,
   19(2), [413], [414]
debt avoidance, provisions against,
   19(2), [450]
decision notices—
   access to material, **19(2)**, [469]
   application of provisions, **19(2)**, [467]
   contents of, **19(2)**, [461]
   power to issue, **19(2)**, [463]
   procedures, determination of, **19(2)**, [470]
      statements, consultation on, **19(2)**, [471]
   publication, **19(2)**, [466]
   third party rights, **19(2)**, [468]
disciplinary measures—
   decision notices, **19(2)**, [261]
   financial penalties, **19(2)**, [258]
   proposal to take, **19(2)**, [259]
   public censure, **19(2)**, [257]
   statements of policy, **19(2)**, [70], [262],
      [263]
   Tribunal, right to refer to, **19(2)**, [68]
disciplinary powers—
   action, taking, **19(2)**, [67]
   procedure, **19(2)**, [68]
   statements, publication of, **19(2)**, [69]
discontinuance of proceedings, notice of,
   19(2), [464]
economy, efficiency and effectiveness, review
   of—
   conduct of, **19(2)**, [12]
   documents and information, right to
      obtain, **19(2)**, [13]
   report, **19(2)**, [12]
entry of premises under warrant, power of,
   19(1), [633]
establishment of, **19(2)**, [1]
final notices, **19(2)**, [465]
financial penalties, imposition of, **19(2)**, [258]
friendly societies—
   Commission, transfer of functions of,
      19(2), [409], [414]
   functions relating to. *See* **friendly society**
functions of, **19(S)**, Financial 278
general duties, **19(2)**, [2]
governing body—
   functions of, **19(2)**, [512]
   non-executive members of, **19(2)**, [512]
guidance—
   outsourcing by investment firms and credit
      institutions, on, **19(2)**, [208]
   power to give, **19(2)**, [206]
   publication, **19(2)**, [206]
   summary of provisions, **19(1)**, [1]
   Treasury, notification to, **19(2)**, [207]
incoming firms, intervention—
   EEA firms, in respect of, **19(2)**, [251]
   grounds for exercise of, **19(2)**, [244]
   meaning, **19(2)**, [243]
   notice, **19(2)**, [249]
   overseas insurance company, application for
      injunction in respect of, **19(2)**, [250]
   overseas regulator, in support of,
      19(2), [253]
   procedure on exercise of, **19(2)**, [249]

Financial Services Authority—*contd*
incoming firms, intervention—*contd*
   requirements, **19(2)**, [253]
      contravention of, **19(2)**, [254]
      other persons, effect on, **19(2)**, [253]
      rescission and variation of requirements,
         19(2), [252]
   requirements, imposition of, **19(2)**, [248]
industrial and provident societies, transfer of
   functions, **19(2)**, [413], [414]
information—
   auditors or actuaries, from, **19(2)**, [417],
      [418]
   authorised person, from, **19(2)**, [215]
   collection of, **19(S)**, Financial 279
   competition, **19(2)**, [426]
   confidential, restrictions on disclosure of,
      19(2), [423]
      exceptions, **19(2)**, [424]
   HM Revenue and Customs, disclosure by,
      19(2), [425]
   offences, **19(2)**, [427]
   power to require, **19(2)**, [215];
      19(S), Financial 230
   protected items, **19(2)**, [489]
   restrictions on disclosure, removal of,
      19(2), [428]
   rules for, **19(2)**, [540], [541]
   skilled persons, reports by, **19(2)**, [216]
information and documents, power to
   obtain, **19(1)**, [632]
injunction, obtaining, **19(2)**, [455]
   application for, **19(1)**, [1]
   market abuse, in case of, **19(2)**, [456]
inter-bank payment systems, role as to,
   19(S), Financial 240
investigations—
   arrangements for, **19(2)**, [512]
   complaints, of, **19(2)**, [512]
   conduct of, **19(2)**, [220]
   information and documents, power to
      require, **19(2)**, [223], [225]
   investigators—
      appointment, **19(2)**, [217], [218]
      attendance before, power to require,
         19(2), [221], [222]
      investigating authority, meaning,
         19(2), [220]
      meaning, **19(2)**, [221]
      notice of appointment, **19(2)**, [220]
      powers, **19(2)**, [221]–[223]
      reports, **19(2)**, [220]
      statements made to, admissibility,
         19(2), [224]
   offences, **19(2)**, [227]
   overseas regulator, in support of,
      19(2), [219]
   persons to carry out, appointment of,
      19(2), [217], [218]
   premises, entry of under warrant,
      19(2), [226]
   rules for, **19(2)**, [540], [541]
liability, **19(1)**, [1023]
liability in damages, exemption from,
   19(2), [515]

Financial Services Authority—*contd*
Lloyd's, general duty as to,
 19(2), [323]. *See also* **Lloyd's**
market abuse, control of. *See* **market abuse**
market abuse, summary of provisions,
 19(1), [1]
misleading, **19(2)**, [473]
monitoring and enforcement by, **19(2)**, [512]
Ombudsman Scheme, summary of
 provisions, **19(1)**, [1]
open-ended investment companies, powers.
 See **open-ended investment company**
overseas regulator—
 exercise of power in support of, **19(2)**, [48]
  intervention, of, **19(2)**, [246]
 investigations in support of, **19(2)**, [219]
past business, schemes for reviewing,
 19(2), [479]
penalties and fees, **19(2)**, [514]
Practitioner Panel—
 appointment, **19(2)**, [9]
 establishment of, **19(2)**, [9]
 representations by, consideration of,
  19(2), [11]
principles of good governance, duty to
 follow, **19(2)**, [7]
proceedings, institution of, **19(2)**, [477]
prohibition orders—
 activities to which relating, **19(2)**, [57]
 applications, **19(2)**, [59]
 breach of, **19(2)**, [57]
 by, **19(1)**, [627]
 meaning, **19(2)**, [114]
 power to make, **19(2)**, [57]
 procedure, **19(2)**, [58]
 Tribunal, reference to, **19(2)**, [58]
 variation or revocation of, **19(2)**, [57]
public censure, power of, **19(2)**, [257]
publication of notices, **19(2)**, [466]
receivership—
 participation in proceedings, **19(2)**, [438]
 receiver, report by, **19(2)**, [439]
records, **19(2)**, [512]
Registry of Friendly Societies, transfer of
 functions, **19(2)**, [410], [414]
regulated activities, authorisation and
 permission. *See* **regulated activities**
regulatory objectives, **19(2)**, [2]
 market confidence, **19(2)**, [3]
 protection of consumers, **19(2)**, [5]
 public awareness, **19(2)**, [4]
 reduction of financial crime, **19(2)**, [6]
restitution—
 decision notices, **19(2)**, [461]
 order, obtaining, **19(2)**, [457]
  market abuse, in case of, **19(2)**, [458]
 power to require, **19(2)**, [459]
 warning notices, **19(2)**, [460]
rules—
 clients' money, as to, **19(2)**, [189]
 collective investment scheme managers,
  restricting, **19(2)**, [190]
 consultation on, **19(2)**, [204]
 contravention—
  damages, action for, **19(2)**, [199]

Financial Services Authority—*contd*
rules—*contd*
 contravention—*contd*
  evidential provision, **19(2)**, [198]
  limits on effects, **19(2)**, [200]
 control of information, **19(2)**, [196]
 draft, **19(2)**, [204]
 financial promotion, **19(2)**, [194]
 general, **19(2)**, [188]
 instruments making, **19(2)**, [202]
 insurance business, as to, **19(2)**, [191]
  regulations supplementing, **19(2)**, [192]
 modification or waiver, **19(2)**, [197]
 money laundering, **19(2)**, [195]
 power to make, **19(2)**, [188]
 price stabilising, **19(2)**, [193]
 supplementary powers, **19(2)**, [205]
 Treasury, notification to, **19(2)**, [201]
 unit trust scheme managers, restricting,
  19(2), [190]
 verification of, **19(2)**, [203]
statements of policy, **19(2)**, [70]
 procedure, **19(2)**, [71]
status, **19(1)**, [1022]; **19(2)**, [513]
summary of provisions, **19(1)**, [1]
supervisory notices—
 meaning, **19(2)**, [470]
 procedures, determination of, **19(2)**, [470]
  statements, consultation on, **19(2)**, [471]
 publication, **19(2)**, [466]
trade-matching and reporting systems,
 approval and monitoring of, **19(2)**, [487],
 [488]
voluntary arrangements, participation in—
 company, **19(2)**, [431]
 individual, **19(2)**, [432]
voluntary winding up—
 insurers, of, **19(2)**, [441]
 participation in proceedings, **19(2)**, [440]
warning notices—
 access to material, **19(2)**, [469]
 application of provisions, **19(2)**, [467]
 contents of, **19(2)**, [462]
 power to issue, **19(2)**, [462]
 procedures, determination of, **19(2)**, [470]
  statements, consultation on, **19(2)**, [471]
 publication, **19(2)**, [466]
 third party rights, **19(2)**, [468]
winding up by court—
 insurers, of, **19(2)**, [444]
 liquidator, report by, **19(2)**, [445]
 participation in proceedings, **19(2)**, [446]
 petition, presentation of, **19(2)**, [442]–[444]
winding up petition by, **19(1)**, [628]

Financial Services Compensation Scheme
amendment of provisions, overview,
 19(S), Financial 223
bank insolvency, role in, **19(S)**, Financial 180
claims, procedure for, **19(S)**, Financial 228
contingency funding, **19(S)**, Financial 223–4
continuation of long-term insurance policies,
 provision for, **19(2)**, [268]
costs of special resolution regime, contribution
 to, **19(S)**, Financial 224–6

Financial Services Compensation
Scheme—*contd*
determination of matters relating to,
19(2), [266]
establishment of, 19(2), [265]
information requirements, powers of court,
19(2), [273]
insolvency, rights in, 19(2), [267];
19(S), Financial 229
insurance in connection with pensions,
intervention in relation to, 43(S), 1405
insurers in financial difficulties, provision on,
19(2), [269]
interest, payments representing, 43(S), 1376–7
levies, 19(S), Financial 51–2
management expenses, 19(2), [275]
manager—
annual report, 19(2), [270]
constitution, 19(2), [264]
documents held by Official Receiver,
power to inspect, 19(2), [276]
establishment, 19(2), [264]
information held by liquidator, etc, power
to inspect, 19(2), [272]
information, power to require, 19(2), [271]
powers of, 19(2), [265]
statutory immunity, 19(2), [274]
National Loans Fund—
borrowing from, 19(S), Financial 227–8,
231
payments from, 19(S), Financial 226–7
provisions of, 19(2), [266]
rules, 19(2), [265]
scheme manager, delegation of functions,
19(S), Financial 232
summary of provisions, 19(1), [1]

financial year
determination of, 8, 284
oversea company, of, 8, 552

fine
attachment of earnings orders, 11(3), [422]
benefit deductions—
application for, 11(3), [422]
disclosure of information with application
for, 11(S), Courts 7–8
collection, 11(3), [402], [421]
orders—
contents of, 11(3), [423]
defaulters, further steps in relation to,
11(3), [427]
first default, effect of, 11(3), [425]
making of, 11(3), [423]
reserve terms, containing, 11(3), [426]
variation, 11(3), [424]
regulations, 11(3), [428]
Crown Court—
enforcement of, 12(2), [817]
power of, 12(2), [816]
search for money, ordering, 12(2), [819]
Crown proceedings for recovery, 13, [29]
default—
attendance centre requirement, power to
impose, 11(S), Courts 6

fine—*contd*
default—*contd*
community sentence for, 12(2), [578]
driving disqualification for, 12(2), [579]
periods of imprisonment or detention,
12(2), [816]
financial circumstances of offender—
false statements, 12(2), [70]
inquiry into, 12(3), [896]
statement as to, power to order,
12(3), [894]
fixing of, 12(3), [896]
imposition of, 12(1), [656]
increase of, 12(1), [397]; 12(2), [241]
maximum, 12(1), [685]
offences, 11(3), [428]
offender convicted on indictment, imposed
on, 12(3), [895]
remission, 12(3), [897]
unpaid work, discharge by, 11(3), [402],
[429]
vagrancy offences, 12(1), [784]; 12(2), [71]
young offenders—
magistrates' courts, limit on power of,
12(2), [812]
parent or guardian—
financial circumstances, power to order
statement as to, 12(2), [813]
fixing of amount, 12(2), [815]
responsibility of for payment,
12(2), [814]

fingerprints
amended provisions, 12(4), [119]
consent for taking, 12(1), [908]
destruction of, 12(1), [915]
certificate of, 12(1), [915]
palm print, including, 12(1), [917]
requirement to give, 12(1), [861]
taking electronically, 12(3), [51]
use and destruction, restrictions on,
12(3), [53]

Finland
accession to European Union, 18, [47]
peace treaty, 10, [916]

fire
danger or annoyance caused by, 36, [1223]
escape. *See* **fire escape**
false alarm, giving, 18, [1070]
highway, lighting on, 36, [1186]
means of escape. *See* **fire precautions**
salvage force, establishment for London,
18, [1004]

fire and rescue authority
advisory bodies, payments in respect of,
18, [1071]
bodies acting as, 18, [1023]
charging, powers as to, 18, [1041]
combined—
body corporate, as, 18, [1025]
Fire Services Act 1947, schemes approved
under, 18, [1026]

fire and rescue authority—*contd*
  combined—*contd*
    powers, **18**, [1027]
    scheme for creation of, **18**, [1024]
  death or injury, power to respond to situation causing, **18**, [1033]
  discharge of functions—
    by others, arrangements for, **18**, [1038], [1039]
    other employers of fire-fighters, arrangements with, **18**, [1037]
    reinforcement schemes—
      directions as to, **18**, [1036]
      meaning, **18**, [1035]
      provisions of, **18**, [1035]
  emergency—
    meaning, **18**, [1079]
    other, responding to, **18**, [1031]
      directions relating to, **18**, [1032]
    powers in event of, **18**, [1065]
  employment—
    conditions of service—
      negotiating bodies—
        establishment of, **18**, [1053]
        guidance to, **18**, [1054]
        local negotiation arrangements, **18**, [1053]
        meaning, **18**, [1054]
        variation by Secretary of State, **18**, [1020]
    police, prohibition on, **18**, [1058]
  environmental harm, power to respond to situation causing, **18**, [1033]
  equipment, provision and maintenance of, **18**, [1050]
  facilities—
    provision and maintenance of, **18**, [1050]
    use or disposal of, **18**, [1051]
  false alarm of fire, giving, **18**, [1070]
  Fire and Rescue National Framework. *See* **Fire and Rescue National Framework**
  fire hydrants—
    location of, water undertaker's duty to mark, **18**, [1063]
    works affecting, notice of, **18**, [1064]
  fire safety, promotion of, **18**, [1028]
  fire-fighting, **18**, [1029]
    directions relating to, **18**, [1032]
  Firemen's Pension Scheme. *See* **Firemen's Pension Scheme**
  information—
    duty to provide, **18**, [1048]
    inspectors appointed to obtain, **18**, [1049]
    powers of entry for obtaining, **18**, [1066], [1067]
  local authority, meaning, **18**, [1078]
  London Fire and Emergency Planning Authority, **18**, [1023]
  organisations promoting economy, efficiency, effectiveness, establishment and maintenance of, **18**, [1050]
  other services, provision of, **18**, [1034]
  pensions—
    employment, other employment reckoned as, **18**, [1055]

fire and rescue authority—*contd*
  pensions—*contd*
    information in connection with, **18**, [1056]
    offences in connection with, **18**, [1055]
    opting or transferring out, **18**, [1056]
    schemes for, **18**, [1055]
  police, prohibition on employment of, **18**, [1058]
  powers of entry—
    information, for obtaining, **18**, [1066], [1067]
    investigating fires, for, **18**, [1066], [1067]
    notices—
      delivery of, **18**, [1068]
      generally, **18**, [1068]
      given electronically, **18**, [1069]
  public safety, directions from Secretary of State as to, **18**, [1051]
  road traffic accidents, rescuing people from, **18**, [1030]
  sea, exercise of powers at, **18**, [1042]
  services, provision and maintenance of, **18**, [1050]
  summary of provisions, **18**, [997]
  supervision of, information—
    duty to provide to Secretary of State, **18**, [1048]
    inspectors to obtain, **18**, [1049]
  training centres, establishment of, **18**, [1040]
  training institutions and centres, **18**, [1052]
  vehicles, speed limit exemption, **37**, [261]
  Wales, application of provisions to, **18**, [1083]
  water supply—
    duty to secure, **18**, [1059]
    emergency, in, **18**, [1061]
    other persons, by, **18**, [1062]
    water undertaker, by—
      agreement for, **18**, [1060]
      emergency, obligations in case of, **18**, [1061]
    fire hydrants—
      duty to mark location of, **18**, [1063]
      notice of works affecting, **18**, [1064]
    works affecting, notice of, **18**, [1064]

Fire and Rescue National Framework
  adherence to—
    best value, **18**, [1046]
    failure, intervention by Secretary of State in case of, **18**, [1044]
      protocol for, **18**, [1045]
    report by Secretary of State on, **18**, [1047]
  purpose of, **18**, [1043]
  Secretary of State—
    compliance with, powers to ensure, **18**, [1044], [1045]
    prepared by, **18**, [1043]
    reports as to, **18**, [1047]
  summary of provisions, **18**, [997]

fire authority
  auditors. *See* **Audit Commission**
  capital expenditure. *See* **local authority**
  combined, as precepting authority, **26(2)**, [293]

fire authority—*contd*
flammable material, powers. *See* **flammable material**
Greater London, in, **25(1)**, [708]
information—
access to. *See* **local authority**
duty to publish, **25(2)**, [428]
Wales, in, **26(1)**, [151]

fire brigade
central advisory council, abolition of, **18**, [1072]
employment, transfers to or from service, **18**, [1015]
firemen. *See* **firemen**
London—
information, giving to insurance officers, **18**, [1005]
salvage force, assisting, **18**, [1004]
transfers to or from service, **18**, [1015]
water supply. *See* **fire authority, water supply**

Fire Brigades Union
local authority fire service employers, June 2003 agreement with, **18**, [1021]

fire engine
vehicle excise duty, exemption from, **13**, [1049]

fire escape. *See* **fire precautions**

fire fighting
charges for use of water, **49**, [954]
supply of water for, **49**, [828]
water for, abstraction of, **49**, [1081]

fire grate
child in room with, **6**, [7]

fire hydrant
specially requested, fixing, **49**, [829]
water supply for. *See under* **water supply**

fire insurance
accidental fire, protection as to, **19(1)**, [10]
application of money received, **19(1)**, [9]

fire precautions
building regulations as to, relaxation, **35(1)**, [541]
capital allowances, repealed provisions, **43(S)**, 895
London buildings. *See* **London Building Acts**
means of escape in case of fire, high buildings, **35(1)**, [594]

fire safety
expenditure, allowances for, **43(1)**, [580]

fire services
regulations, **18**, [1008]

fire services—*contd*
summary of provisions, **18**, [997]
transfer to or from, pensions on, **18**, [1015]

firearm certificate
appeals, **12(1)**, [528], [549]
application for, **12(1)**, [502], [546]
cancellation of, **12(1)**, [536]
coterminous, grant of, **12(1)**, [1124]
document, failure to produce on demand, **12(1)**, [532]
European firearm pass—
cancellation, **12(1)**, [516]
documents, issue of, **12(1)**, [514]
endorsement, **12(1)**, [526]
expired, **12(1)**, [515]
form of, **12(1)**, [514]
issue, **12(1)**, [514]
loss or theft of, **12(1)**, [516]
meaning, **12(1)**, [541]
particulars required, **12(1)**, [514]
period for, **12(1)**, [514]
renewal, **12(1)**, [515]
shot guns, **12(1)**, [514]
surrender of, **12(1)**, [515]
variation of, **12(1)**, [516]
European states, purchase in, **12(1)**, [1132]
exemptions, **12(1)**, [481]–[488]
false, use of, **12(1)**, [476]
false statement concerning, **12(1)**, [476], [506]
fees, **12(1)**, [513]
form of, **12(1)**, [504]
grant of, **12(1)**, [504]
meaning, **12(1)**, [541]
Northern Ireland, issued in, **12(1)**, [488]
period in force, **12(1)**, [506]
person under eighteen, conditions for grant to, **12(1)**, [504]
personation of holder, **12(1)**, [476]
photograph of applicant, **12(1)**, [1123]
pistol club, muzzle-loading, exemption, **12(1)**, [1127]
production, demanding, **12(1)**, [532]
prohibited weapon, for, **12(1)**, [512]
prosecution and punishment of offences, table, **12(1)**, [550]
reasons for grant, **12(1)**, [504]
refusal of, appeal, **12(1)**, [506]
register of holders, **12(2)**, [521]
renewal, **12(1)**, [506]
requirement of, **12(1)**, [474]
revocation of, **12(1)**, [508], [509], [511], [1125]
rifle club, exemption, **12(1)**, [498], [1127]
rules prescribing, **12(1)**, [537]
shot gun, for, **12(1)**, [475]
statements in support, **12(1)**, [502]
target shooting, firearms used for, **12(2)**, [522]
variation of, **12(1)**, [507]
visitors' permits, **12(1)**, [1131]

firearms
adaptation, **12(1)**, [478]

firearms—*contd*

administrative expenses, **12(1)**, [1137]
  museums, in, **12(1)**, [1141]
aggravated burglary, using in, **12(1)**, [562]
air weapon—
  prohibited, **12(3)**, [654]
  public place, possession in, **12(3)**, [654]
aircraft's equipment, as, **12(1)**, [487]
ammunition—
  certificate, requiring, **12(1)**, [474]
  constable, handing over to, **12(1)**, [531]
  Crown Servants, application of Act to,
    12(1), [538]
  dealing in, **12(1)**, [474], [476]
  drunk or insane person, supplying to,
    12(1), [501]
  European member state, purchase in,
    12(1), [514]
  expanding, military use, **12(1)**, [478], [479]
  forfeiture and disposal, **12(1)**, [536]
  meaning, **12(1)**, [541]
  military use, for, unlawful possession,
    12(1), [478]
  minor—
    acquisition or possession by,
      12(1), [497], [498]
    supplying to, **12(1)**, [499]
  missiles, various, for, unlawful possession,
    12(1), [478]
  movement of, prohibiting, **12(1)**, [480]
  noxious thing, containing, **12(1)**, [478]
  pawning, **12(1)**, [476]
  person previously convicted of crime
    having, **12(1)**, [495]
  possession with intent to injure,
    12(1), [489]
  primers, restriction on sale and purchase
    of, **12(4)**, [231]
  prohibited, **12(1)**, [478], [1118]
  prohibition, general, **12(1)**, [478], [479]
  removal to Northern Ireland, **12(1)**, [480]
  rifle clubs, **12(1)**, [1127]
  search for, **12(1)**, [530]
  smooth bore guns, restriction of sale,
    12(1), [1119]
  stop and search powers, **12(1)**, [531]
  traffic in, **12(1)**, [533]
  treating animals, for, **12(2)**, [511]
  visitors' permit, **12(1)**, [1131]
antique, **12(1)**, [542]
appeals, **12(1)**, [528], [549]
armed forces personnel, held by, **3**, [1]
armour piercing weapons, unlawful
  possession, **12(1)**, [478]
arrest—
  powers of, **12(1)**, [542]
  using to resist, **12(1)**, [491]
auctioneer, in possession of, **12(1)**, [483],
  [1126]
authorised dealing, **12(1)**, [482]
barrel, length of, **12(1)**, [541], [1120]
burglary, having during, **12(1)**, [562]
carrier, in possession of, **12(1)**, [483], [1126]

firearms—*contd*

certificate. *See* **firearm certificate**
cinematograph film, used in producing,
  12(1), [486]
compressed carbon dioxide, powered by,
  12(2), [524]
constable, handing over to, **12(1)**, [531]
consultative committee, establishment and
  functions, **12(1)**, [1136]
conversion of, **12(1)**, [477], [1121]
conviction of crime, previous, ban in case of,
  12(1), [495], [546]
criminal intent, carrying with, **12(1)**, [492]
Crown servants, application of Act to,
  12(1), [538]
de-activated, **12(1)**, [1122]
  notification of, **12(2)**, [518]
dealer—
  authorised, **12(1)**, [482]
  compulsory register of transactions,
    12(1), [524], [547]
  expanding ammunition, transactions in,
    12(1), [479]
  export, acquired for, **12(1)**, [1132]
  in possession of, **12(1)**, [482]
  meaning, **12(1)**, [541]
  offence, convicted of, **12(1)**, [529]
  police register—
    conditions, **12(1)**, [520]
    details on, **12(1)**, [517]
    false statements, **12(1)**, [523]
    fees, **12(1)**, [519], [527]
    new place of business, entering,
      12(1), [521]
    offences, **12(1)**, [523]
    refusal to register, **12(1)**, [518]
    removal from, **12(1)**, [522]
    registration, **12(1)**, [517]
  sale of firearms for export, notice of,
    12(1), [1132]
  transactions without registration,
    12(1), [476]
dealings with, **12(1)**, [476]
destruction, notification of, **12(2)**, [518]
disguised as another object, **12(1)**, [478]
drunk person, supplying to, **12(1)**, [501]
dwelling, discharge near, **36**, [227]
European member state, purchase in,
  12(1), [514], [1132]
European weapons directive—
  firearms pass. *See under* **firearms**
    certificates
  use under, **12(1)**, [541]
events taking place outside Great Britain,
  notification of, **12(2)**, [519]
exhibition, collection as part of, **12(1)**, [479]
export, acquired for, European directive,
  12(1), [1132]
exportation—
  information powers relating to, **13**, [672]
  records relating to, **13**, [668]
fishing, prohibition of use in, **1(2)**, [1]
forfeiture and disposal, **12(1)**, [536], [551]
game licence, effect on, **12(1)**, [542]
general prohibition, subject to, **12(1)**, [478]

firearms—*contd*
  generally, **12(1)**, [1]
  highway, discharge on or near, **36**, [1186], [1222]
  historic interest, of, **12(2)**, [510]
  humane killing of animals, for, **12(2)**, [506]
  imitation—
    arrest, using to resist, **12(1)**, [491]
    burglary, having during, **12(1)**, [562]
    convertible to firearm, **12(1)**, [770]–[772]
    criminal intent, carrying with, **12(1)**, [492]
    intent to cause fear of violence, possession with, **12(1)**, [490]
    meaning, **12(1)**, [541]
    minors, supply to, **12(1)**, [500]; **12(4)**, [236]
    possessing, maximum sentence for, **12(4)**, [237]
    realistic, manufacture, import and sale of—
      defences, **12(4)**, [233]
      offences, **12(4)**, [232]
      regulations, **12(4)**, [232]
    realistic, meaning, **12(4)**, [234]
    specification for, **12(4)**, [235]
  importation—
    information powers relating to, **13**, [672]
    records relating to, **13**, [668]
  insane person, supply to, **12(1)**, [501]
  loss, notification of, **12(2)**, [518]
  meaning, **12(1)**, [541], [562]
  military, unlawful possession, **12(1)**, [478]
  miniature rifle range, in, **12(1)**, [485]
  minor—
    acquisition or possession by, **12(1)**, [497], [498]
    imitation firearm, supply of, **12(1)**, [500]
    supplying to, **12(1)**, [499]
  missiles, unlawful possession, **12(1)**, [478]
  movement of—
    police powers, **12(1)**, [533]
    prohibiting, **12(1)**, [480]
  museums etc, in, **12(1)**, [1141]
  muzzle-loading pistol club, **12(1)**, [1127]; **12(2)**, [523]
  name and address, constable requiring, **12(1)**, [532]
  Northern Ireland—
    provisions applicable, **12(1)**, [1139]; **12(2)**, [133], [178]
    removal to, **12(1)**, [480]
  notices, service of, **12(1)**, [540]
  noxious liquid or gas, designed for, prohibition, **12(1)**, [478]
  offences—
    importation or exportation, **12(3)**, [1023]
    minimum sentence, **12(1)**, [535]
      persons under 18, **12(3)**, [1022]
    penalties, **12(2)**, [520]
    police suspecting, **12(1)**, [531]
    prosecution and punishment, **12(1)**, [534], [550], [551]
    trial, **12(1)**, [551]
  pawning, **12(1)**, [476]
  person previously convicted of crime, sale to, **12(1)**, [495], [546]

firearms—*contd*
  police functions, exercise of, **12(1)**, [539]
  police permit, **12(1)**, [481]
  possession of—
    intent to cause fear of violence, with, **12(1)**, [490]
    intent to injure, with, **12(1)**, [489]
    minor, by, **12(1)**, [497], [498]
    offence, while committing, **12(1)**, [545]
    person previously convicted, by, **12(1)**, [495], [546]
  prohibited, **12(1)**, [474], [1118], [1135]
  proof houses, saving for, **12(1)**, [542]
  public place, carrying in, **12(1)**, [493]
  pump action, **12(1)**, [478]
  register of. *See* dealer (police register) *above*
  removal from place to place, **12(1)**, [480]
  "repeaters", **12(1)**, [478]
  rifle club, in, **12(1)**, [485], [1127]
    approved, **12(2)**, [523]
  rifle, meaning, **12(1)**, [541]
  rifles on private premises, borrowing of, **12(1)**, [1128]
  rocket, explosive, possession etc of, **12(1)**, [478]
  rocket launcher or mortar, **12(1)**, [478]
  rules, power to make, **12(1)**, [537]
  search warrant, issue of, **12(1)**, [530]
  Secretary of State, expenses and receipts, **12(1)**, [1137]
  self loading, **12(1)**, [478]
  service premises, in, **12(1)**, [1129], [1130]
  ship's equipment, as, **12(1)**, [487]
  shot gun. *See* **shot gun**
  shot pistol for shooting vermin, **12(2)**, [507]
  signalling apparatus, as, **12(1)**, [487]
  slaughter of animals, for, **12(1)**, [479], [484], [541]; **12(2)**, [505]
  small, prohibition of, **12(2)**, [504]
    ancillary equipment, **12(2)**, [514]
    compensation schemes, **12(2)**, [515]
    payments for, **12(2)**, [513]
    surrender, **12(2)**, [512]
  smooth bore gun—
    ammunition for, restriction on sale, **12(1)**, [1119]
    prohibition on, **12(1)**, [478]
    shortening of barrels, **12(1)**, [1120]
  sporting purposes, for, **12(1)**, [485]
  starting pistol, **12(1)**, [485]; **12(2)**, [508]
  stop and search for, **12(1)**, [531]
  street, discharging in, **36**, [226], [385]
  summary of provisions, **12(1)**, [1]
  theatrical performance, used in, **12(1)**, [486]
  traffic in, **12(1)**, [533]
  transactions—
    compulsory register of, **12(1)**, [524], [547]
    offences, **12(1)**, [476]
  transfers—
    notification of, **12(2)**, [517]
    person, in, **12(2)**, [516]
  treating animals, for, **12(2)**, [511]
  trespassing with, **12(1)**, [494]
  unsound mind, supplying to person of, **12(1)**, [501]

firearms—*contd*
  visitors' permits—
    certificate, exemption, **12(1)**, [1131]
    competition, for entry in, **12(1)**, [1131]
    fees, **12(1)**, [1131]
    grant of, **12(1)**, [1131]
    group application, **12(1)**, [1131]
    transactions under, information as to,
      12(1), [526]
  war trophies, **12(2)**, [509]
  warehouseman, in possession of, **12(1)**, [483],
    [1126]
  weapons, general prohibition—
    exemptions from requirements,
      12(1), [479]
    subject to, **12(1)**, [478]

firemen
  war service—
    civil pay, making up, **33(2)**, [66]
    death on—
      officially reported, **33(2)**, [78]
      presumption of, **33(2)**, [78]
    death or incapacity—
      grants in case of, **33(2)**, [68], [76]
      pensions, provisions for, **33(2)**, [67]
    exception from provisions, **33(2)**, [70]
    injuries, presumption as to, **33(2)**, [72]
    medical appeals, **33(2)**, [77]
    pay during, reckoning, **33(2)**, [69]
    questions as to, determination of,
      33(2), [77]
    reckoning of, **33(2)**, [67]
    retirement on pension, suspension of
      right, **33(2)**, [71]
    superannuation, reckoning for, **33(2)**, [67]
    time limits, alteration of, **33(2)**, [79]
    training, person under, **33(2)**, [73]

Firemen's Pension Scheme
  contributions, return or application of,
    18, [1006], [1014]
  dismissal, payments on, **18**, [1006]
  employment—
    meaning, **18**, [1006]
    other employment reckoned as, **18**, [1006]
    purposes of scheme, for, **18**, [1006]
    temporary instructor, person becoming,
      18, [1016]
  establishment of, **18**, [1006]
  information in connection with, provisions as
    to, **18**, [1007]
  maiming or injuring oneself, provisions on,
    18, [1006]
  opting out—
    information in connection with, provisions
      as to, **18**, [1007]
    meaning, **18**, [1007]
  pension—
    conditions of payment, varying, **18**, [1014]
    provisions on payment, **18**, [1011]
    summary of provisions, **18**, [997]
  preservation of, **18**, [1057]
  provisions in, **18**, [1006], [1014]
  retirement, provisions on, **18**, [1014]

Firemen's Pension Scheme—*contd*
  Secretary of State, powers of, **18**, [1006],
    [1012]
  transferring out—
    information in connection with, provisions
      as to, **18**, [1007]
    meaning, **18**, [1007]
  transfers to or from service, **18**, [1015]
  variation of, **18**, [1014]

fireworks. *See also* **explosives**
  dangerous—
    destruction of, **18**, [719]
    factory licence, power to determine,
      18, [720]
    standard for judging, **18**, [721]
  enforcement of provisions, **18**, [742]
  importation, prohibition, **18**, [739]
  information, provision of, **18**, [738]
  marking—
    defacing marks, penalty, **18**, [723]
    exempted types, **18**, [722], [727]
    exports, exemption for, **18**, [728]
    offences, **18**, [722]
    requirements as to, **18**, [722]
  meaning, **18**, [731]
  notices, service of, **18**, [724]
  offences, **18**, [722], [741]
  privileges, savings for, **18**, [743]
  prohibited, **18**, [735]
  public displays, conditions for, **18**, [736]
  regulations, parliamentary procedure,
    18, [732], [746]
  samples, power to take, **18**, [719]
  sporting events, possessing at, **12(1)**, [983]
  street offences, **36**, [226], [385]
  summary of provisions, **18**, [690]
  suppliers, licensing, **18**, [737]
  supply—
    certain fireworks, prohibited, **18**, [735]
    circumstances in which prohibited,
      18, [734]
    reference to, **18**, [731]
    young persons, to, prohibition, **18**, [733]
  throwing in public place, **18**, [706]
  training courses, **18**, [740]
  young persons, prohibition of supply to,
    18, [733]

First-tier Tribunal
  application to—
    cases when made, **29**, [116]
    conditionally discharged restricted patient,
      as to, **29**, [126]
    general provisions, **29**, [128]
    guardianship order, concerning patient
      subject to, **29**, [120]
    hospital order, concerning patient subject
      to, **29**, [120]
    relevant period for making, **29**, [116]
    restricted patient, by, **29**, [121], [124],
      [125]
    transfer direction, by person subject to,
      29, [118]
    who may make, **29**, [116]

First-tier Tribunal—*contd*
  application to—*contd*
    withdrawal, **29**, [118]
  discharge of patient—
    conditional, **29**, [125]
    power to direct, **29**, [123], [124]
    restricted patients, **29**, [124], [125]
  examining patients, **29**, [127]
  leave of absence, recommendation for,
    29, [123]
  reference to—
    hospital managers, by, **29**, [118]
    information for purposes of, **29**, [118]
    restricted patients, concerning, **29**, [122]
    Secretary of State, by, **29**, [117], [122]
    time limit for, **29**, [118]
      power to reduce, **29**, [119]
  restricted patients, discharge of, **29**, [124],
    [125]
  summary of provisions, **29**, [1]
  visiting patients, **29**, [127]

first-time buyers. *See under* **house**

fiscal stability
  annual budget documents, **43(1)**, [377]
  code for, **43(1)**, [376]
  Comptroller and Auditor General,
    supplementary powers, **43(1)**, [378]

fish
  customs duty, relief from, **13**, [806]
  diseases of. *See* **freshwater fisheries**
  farming, *See* **fish farming**
  importation and exportation, restriction on.
    See **animals**
  meaning, **1(2)**, [466]
  non-native, importing—
    entry and inspection of premises,
      1(2), [151]
    live fish and eggs, **1(2)**, [150]
    offences, **1(2)**, [152]
    orders relating to, **1(2)**, [150]
  sale, etc, restriction on. *See* **animals**
  taking or destroying, **12(1)**, [582], [587]

fish farm
  non-domestic rates, exemption from,
    25(2), [835]

fish farming
  advice and instruction on, **1(2)**, [177]
  belief that fish produced by, **1(2)**, [178]
  business of, meaning, **1(1)**, [359]
  conservation offences, exclusion of,
    1(2), [178]
  diseases of fish, prevention. *See* **freshwater
    fisheries**
  farm, meaning, **1(1)**, [359]
  financial assistance scheme, **1(2)**, [176]
  financial provisions, **1(2)**, [184]
  information—
    disclosure of, **1(2)**, [225]
    enforcement of provisions, **1(2)**, [224]
    power to require, **1(2)**, [223]

fish farming—*contd*
  marketing, grants for—
    false statements to obtain, **1(2)**, [520]
    generally, **1(2)**, [519]
    Northern Ireland, extension of provisions
      to, **1(2)**, [184]
  meaning, **1(2)**, [176], [178], [223], [519]
  notices, service of, **1(1)**, [356]
  offences, exemption, **1(2)**, [178], [190], [191]
  research and development, **1(2)**, [177]

fisheries
  acquisition of land for purposes of, **49**, [1201]
  Board of Agriculture, transfer to, **10**, [477]
  byelaws—
    compensation in respect of, **49**, [1262]
    contravention of, **49**, [1261]
    marine or aquatic environmental purposes,
      for, **49**, [1295]
    purposes of, **49**, [1295]
    restrictions on, **49**, [1295]
  contributions, **49**, [1196]
  Environment Agency—
    advisory committees—
      local, **35(2)**, [98]
      regional, **35(2)**, [98]
    functions in respect of, **35(2)**, [92]
  facilities, financial assistance for construction
    etc, **39(2)**, [161]
  freshwater. *See* **freshwater fisheries**
  herring. *See* **herring fisheries**
  industry, powers relating to, **10**, [468]
  international obligations, giving effect to,
    49, [1178]
  National Rivers Authority, functions
    transferred to, **49**, [681], [700]
  salmon. *See* **freshwater fisheries**
  sea. *See* **sea fisheries**
  seal. *See* **seal fisheries**
  summary of provisions, **1(1)**, [124]
  Thames, jurisdiction relating to, **39(2)**, [308]
  transitional provisions, **49**, [705]

fishery board
  coast protection board, representation on,
    49, [381]
  examination of waters on demand of,
    1(1), [354]
  meaning, **1(1)**, [359]
  powers and duties of, **1(1)**, [351]

fishery harbours
  application of Acts, **39(2)**, [152]
  charges, **39(2)**, [179]
  construction, repair, etc, financial assistance
    for, **39(2)**, [161]
  England and Wales, in, list, **39(2)**, [154]
  harbour, meaning, **39(2)**, [152]
  meaning, **39(2)**, [152]
  order, charges uncompleted at time of,
    39(2), [183]
  summary of provisions, **39(2)**, [1]
  works—
    application of enactments, **39(2)**, [152]
    financial assistance, **39(2)**, [161]

fishery produce
  grade designation, **1(1)**, [293]
  meaning, **1(1)**, [299]
  metrication, adaptation to, **1(2)**, [52]
  provisions applied to, **1(1)**, [313]

fishing boat
  fuel for, repayment of duty on, **13**, [843],
    [869], [898]
  sea fisheries. *See* **sea fisheries**

fishing vessel
  catch, account of, **39(2)**, [781]
  certificate—
    alterations, notice of, **39(2)**, [794]
    copy, display of, **39(2)**, [792]
    delivery up, **39(2)**, [792]
    evidence, admissible in, **39(2)**, [792]
    going to sea without, **39(2)**, [793]
    issue of, **39(2)**, [791]
    offences, **39(2)**, [792]
    production of, **39(2)**, [785]
  construction rules, **39(2)**, [789]
  crew agreements, **39(2)**, [778]
  disciplinary offences, **39(2)**, [787]
  documents of qualification, production of,
    39(2), [785]
  exemptions from provisions, power to grant,
    39(2), [788]
  forfeiture, **39(2)**, [683]
  hours of work, **39(2)**, [784]
  liquor, unauthorised, on, **39(2)**, [786]
  masters and seamen, provisions on,
    39(2), [691]
  meaning, **39(2)**, [988]
  registration—
    enforcement, **39(2)**, [683]
    entitlement, **39(2)**, [677]
    failure to register, **39(2)**, [683]
    termination, marks displayed after,
      39(2), [683]
  safety matters, training in, **39(2)**, [795]
  Scottish officers, **39(2)**, [935]
  summary of provisions, **39(2)**, [1]
  survey rules, **39(2)**, [790]
  United Kingdom, meaning, **39(2)**, [669]
  wages—
    account of, **39(2)**, [781]
    assignment and charge on, restriction of,
      39(2), [782]
    deductions, **39(2)**, [780]
    loss of right to, **39(2)**, [783]
    payment of, **39(2)**, [779]
    right to, **39(2)**, [783]

fishings
  charge to tax, **44(1)**, [34]
  rent payable in respect of, **44(1)**, [98]

fixed penalties. *See under* **road traffic
  offences**

fixed platform
  destroying, **39(2)**, [577]
  meaning, **39(2)**, [583]

fixed platform—*contd*
  safety, endangering, **39(2)**, [577]
  seizing or exercising control of, **39(2)**, [576]
  threats, offences involving, **39(2)**, [579]

fixtures
  acquisition of ownership—
    assignee of energy services provider, by,
      43(1), [764]
    assignee of equipment lessor, by,
      43(1), [762]
    client under energy services agreement,
      by, **43(1)**, [765]
    equipment lessee, by, **43(1)**, [763]
    lease or licence, on termination of,
      43(1), [761]
  appeals, **43(1)**, [774]
  apportionment, election to fix—
    capital sum on grant of lease, of,
      43(1), [769]
    effect of, **43(1)**, [770]
    irrevocable, being, **43(1)**, [770]
    procedure, **43(1)**, [771]
    reduction of amount, **43(1)**, [770]
    sale of qualifying interest, on, **43(1)**, [768]
  capital allowances, transitional provisions,
    43(1), [1224]
  cessation of ownership—
    equipment lessor, of, **43(1)**, [759]
    incoming lessee entitled to allowances,
      where, **43(1)**, [757]
    person ceasing to have qualifying interest,
      43(1), [755]
    qualifying interest, identification of,
      43(1), [756]
    severance, on, **43(1)**, [758]
  claim, **43(1)**, [772]
    other claims, interaction between,
      43(1), [560]
  disposal values—
    avoidance cases, in, **43(1)**, [767]
    table of, **43(1)**, [766]
  energy services agreement—
    client, acquisition of ownership by,
      43(1), [765]
    energy services provider—
      assignee, acquisition of ownership by,
        43(1), [764]
      ownership by, cessation of, **43(1)**, [760]
      treatment of, **43(1)**, [746]
    meaning, **43(1)**, [740]
    purchaser of land discharging obligations of
      client under, **43(1)**, [749]
  entitlement to allowance, **43(1)**, [772]
  equipment lease—
    affordable warmth programme, as part of,
      43(1), [745]
    meaning, **43(1)**, [738]
  equipment lessee—
    acquisition of ownership by, **43(1)**, [763]
    meaning, **43(1)**, [738]
    purchaser of land discharging obligations
      of, **43(1)**, [748]
    qualifying activity, for, **43(1)**, [743]
    severance, right of, **43(1)**, [744]

fixtures—*contd*
equipment lessor—
assignee, acquisition of ownership by, **43(1)**, [761]
cessation of ownership of, **43(1)**, [759]
meaning, **43(1)**, [738]
treatment of, **43(1)**, [742]
interest in land—
meaning, **43(1)**, [739]
person having interest in—
meaning, **43(1)**, [741]
qualifying activity, having fixture for purposes of, **43(1)**, [741]
lease, meaning, **43(1)**, [738]
long-life assets, exclusion, **43(1)**, [653]
meaning, **43(1)**, [737]
purchaser of land—
consideration given by, **43(1)**, [747]
obligations of equipment lessee, discharging obligations of, **43(1)**, [748]
qualifying expenditure, restrictions on amount of—
industrial buildings allowance made, where, **43(1)**, [753]
plant and machinery allowance claimed, where, **43(1)**, [752]
research and development allowance claimed, where, **43(1)**, [754]
relevant land—
incoming lessee, rights of—
lessor entitled to allowances, where, **43(1)**, [750]
lessor not entitled to allowances, where, **43(1)**, [751]
meaning, **43(1)**, [737]
returns, amendment of, **43(1)**, [773]
scope of provisions, **43(1)**, [736]

flags
trade mark registration, protection from—
Convention countries, of, **48**, 154
international organisations, of, **48**, 155
national, **48**, 112–13, 154
notification of, **48**, 156

flammable material
London—
Crown premises, **25(1)**, [900]
entry for inspection, **25(1)**, [895]
meaning, **25(1)**, [891]
offences and penalties, **25(1)**, [896]
plastics, special provisions, **25(2)**, [407]
stacks—
exemption for certain, **25(1)**, [898]
general provisions, **25(1)**, [897]
not to contain room etc, **25(1)**, [894]
storage, consent to—
appeals respecting, **25(1)**, [893]
application for, **25(1)**, [892]
conditions attached, **25(1)**, [892]
deemed to be given, **25(1)**, [897]
requirement for, **25(1)**, [892]
when not required, **25(1)**, [897]

flat conversion allowances
availability of, **43(1)**, [1003]
balancing adjustments—
avoidance affecting, **43(1)**, [1209]
balancing events, **43(1)**, [1172]–[1173]
calculation of, **43(1)**, [1018]
where made, **43(1)**, [1015]
demolition costs, **43(1)**, [1021]
dwelling, meaning, **43(1)**, [1003]
high value flats, **43(1)**, [1007]
initial, **43(1)**, [1010]
writing off, **43(1)**, [1020]
lease, meaning, **43(1)**, [1025]
non-qualifying assets, apportionment of sums partly referable to, **43(1)**, [1023]
qualifying building—
business use, ground floor authorised for, **43(1)**, [1005]
meaning, **43(1)**, [1005]
qualifying expenditure—
exclusions, **43(1)**, [1004]
meaning, **43(1)**, [1004]
residue of, **43(1)**, [1014]
writing off, **43(1)**, [1020]
qualifying flat—
flat not being, **43(1)**, [1011]
meaning, **43(1)**, [1006]
relevant interest in—
completion of conversion, acquired on, **43(1)**, [1009]
general rule, **43(1)**, [1008]
sale before letting, **43(1)**, [1011]
termination of lease, **43(1)**, [1024]
writing off, **43(1)**, [1019]–[1021]
writing-down, **43(1)**, [1012]–[1014]

flats
collective enfranchisement. *See* **collective enfranchisement (leasehold reform)**
conversion of house, authorisation of, **22**, [410]
landlord of—
exempt, **22**, [771]
resident, **22**, [771]
landlord's interest, compulsory acquisition of—
acquisition order—
application for, **22**, [743]
conditions for making, **22**, [744]
content of, **22**, [745]
discharge of, **22**, [749]
landlord not found, where, **22**, [748]
leasehold valuation tribunals, determination of terms by, **22**, [746]
meaning, **22**, [740]
nominated person, references to, **22**, [745]
premises in, **22**, [744]
consent required for, **22**, [745]
mortgages, discharge of, **22**, [747], [777]
premises liable to, **22**, [740]
tenant—
preliminary notice by, **22**, [742]
qualifying, **22**, [741]
qualifying tenant, of, **22**, [741]

flats—*contd*
landlord's interest, compulsory acquisition
 of—*contd*
  tenant—*contd*
   requisite majority of qualifying,
    22, [742]
   withdrawal by, **22**, [749]
 lease—
  acquisition of new. *See* **lease (acquisition
   of new)**
  long, meaning, **22**, [750]
  service charge, provision for computation
   of, **22**, [750]
  variation of—
   application for, **22**, [750]
   effect of order, **22**, [754]
   majority of parties, application by,
    22, [752]
   order for, **22**, [753]
   other leases, application for, **22**, [751]
 manager, appointment of—
  application to court, **22**, [738]
  court, by, **22**, [739]
  functions of, **22**, [739]
  landlord, service of notice on, **22**, [737]
  order, contents of, **22**, [739]
  preliminary notice, **22**, [737]
  premises managed, **22**, [739]
  tenant's right to apply, **22**, [736]
 meaning, **22**, [203], [772], [916]; **23**, [178]
 nominated person, notice of withdrawal by,
  22, [718]
 purpose-built block, **22**, [771], [916]
 reasonable standard of accommodation, factors
  for, **22**, [750]
 right of first refusal—
  acceptance notice, **22**, [710]
  appurtenant premises, **22**, [702]
  contracts, application of provisions to,
   22, [703]
  covenant affecting landlord's power to
   dispose, **22**, [717]
  enforcement of obligations, **22**, [734]
  excluded disposals, **22**, [702]
  landlord—
   covenant affecting land power to
    dispose, **22**, [717]
   lapse of offer by, **22**, [720]
   meaning, **22**, [700]
   notice of withdrawal by, **22**, [719]
   obligations—
    acceptance and nomination, in case
     of, **22**, [712]
    election in case of sale at auction,
     22, [714]
    general provisions, **22**, [713]
   superior, **22**, [700]
  leasehold valuation tribunal, determination
   of questions by, **22**, [728]
  nominated person—
   disposal to, **22**, [710]
   failure to make nomination, **22**, [711]
   replacement of, **22**, [710]
   supplementary provisions, **22**, [727]
   withdrawal of, **22**, [729]

flats—*contd*
 right of first refusal—*contd*
  notice accepting, **22**, [710]
  notice conferring. *See* offer notice *below*
  notices served by prospective purchasers to
   ensure rights do not arise, **22**, [732]
  offences, **22**, [721]
  offer notice—
   compliance with requirements, **22**, [704]
   conveyance—
    requirements where contract to be
     completed by, **22**, [705]
    requirements where not preceded by
     contract, **22**, [708]
   disposal for non-monetary
    consideration—
     election where, **22**, [715]
     requirements where, **22**, [709]
   failure to accept or make nomination,
    22, [711]
   lapse of, **22**, [720]
   period for accepting offer in, **22**, [704]
   pre-emption, option or right of—
    disposal in pursuance of, **22**, [716]
    requirements where, **22**, [707]
   sale by auction—
    landlord's obligations where, **22**, [714]
    requirements where, **22**, [706]
   service of, **22**, [704]
  premises qualifying, **22**, [699]
  procedure for exercise of, **23**, [416]
  prospective purchases, notice by, **22**, [732]
  protected interest, **22**, [735]
  purchase notice—
   mortgage, discharge of, **22**, [776]
   service of, **22**, [725]
  purchaser—
   circumstances in which tenant' rights
    enforceable against, **22**, [722]
   contract, right of qualifying tenants to
    take benefit of, **22**, [724]
   information regarding terms of disposal
    from, right to, **22**, [723]
   new tenancy, grant of, **22**, [726]
   sale by, right of qualifying tenants to
    compel, **22**, [725]
   termination of rights against, **22**, [731]
  regulations, **22**, [735]
  relevant disposals—
   meaning, **22**, [702]
   mortgage, by, **22**, [702]
  subsequent purchaser—
   rights of qualifying tenants against,
    22, [730]
   termination of rights against, **22**, [731]
  tenant—
   body corporate as, **22**, [701]
   nominated person, disposal to, **22**, [710]
   qualifying, **22**, [701]
   qualifying tenant, of, **22**, [699]
   references to, **22**, [735]
   requisite majority of qualifying,
    22, [733]
   sale by purchaser, compelling, **22**, [725]

flats—*contd*
service charge. *See* **service charge**

flexible working
contract variation, statutory right to request, **16**, [721]
detriment, right to not suffer, **16**, [670]
employer, duties of, **16**, [722]
employment tribunal, complaint to, **16**, [723]
remedies, **16**, [724]
regulations, **16**, [722]
unfair dismissal for reasons related to, **16**, [757]

flick gun
importing, **12(1)**, [304]
manufacturing, selling etc, **12(1)**, [304]
Northern Ireland, importing into, **12(1)**, [327]

flick knife
importing, **12(1)**, [304]
manufacturing, selling, etc, **12(1)**, [304]
Northern Ireland, importing into, **12(1)**, [327]

floating charge
crystallisation, notice of, **8**, 912–13
registration of, **8**, 456, 559
winding up, effect in, **8**, 828

flood and flooding
conservancy authorities, arrangements with, **49**, [1174]
damage, mitigation of, **19(3)**, [183]
defence—
committees—
functions carried out through, **49**, [1169]
membership in Wales, **49**, [1373]
regional, **49**, [1374]
Environment Agency, functions of, **49**, [1168]
functions, meaning, **49**, [1267]
National Rivers Authority, functions of, **49**, [680]
power to revoke local schemes, **49**, [1372]
protective provisions, **49**, [995], [1228]
provisions, meaning, **49**, [1267]
railways, protection for, **49**, [1291]
regulations, **49**, [1175]
transitory provisions, **49**, [1320]
defence and drainage works—
byelaws, **49**, [1295]
compensation for, **49**, [1290]
Environment Agency, power of to carry out, **49**, [1214]
drainage board, default by, **19(3)**, [180]
drainage obligations, savings for, **49**, [1234]
large raised reservoirs, flood plans for, **49**, [589]–[590]
local authorities, defrayment of expenses, **19(3)**, [230]
large raised reservoirs, flood plans for, **49**, [589]–[590]

flood and flooding—*contd*
main river—
functions—
Environment Agency—
powers of, **49**, [1170]
transfer to—
orders, **49**, [1283]
schemes for, **49**, [1171]
Land Drainage Act 1991, under, **49**, [1170]
meaning, **49**, [1176]
structures in, over and under—
applications for consents and approval, **49**, [1172]–[1173]
works, consent for, **49**, [1172]
National Rivers Authority, defence functions, **49**, [680]
navigation authorities, arrangements with, **49**, [1174]
powers, exercise of, **19(3)**, [183]
regional defence committee—
directions, compliance with, **49**, [1169]
transitory provisions, **49**, [1320]
revenues, duty of Environment Agency, **49**, [1179]
spoil, disposal of, **49**, [1216]
Thames river. *See* **Thames river**
warning system—
Environment Agency, works by, **49**, [1215]
meaning, **49**, [465]
provision of, **49**, [465]
Scotland, areas adjoining England, **49**, [465]

flood prevention
London. *See* **Greater London; Thames flood barrier**
transfer of functions, **25(2)**, [586]

flowers. *See* **horticultural produce**
theft of, **12(1)**, [556]

fluoridation. *See under* **water supply**

fly-posting
defacement removal notices—
appeals against, **35(2)**, [435]
exemption from liability, **35(2)**, [436]
expenditure, recovery of, **35(2)**, [433]
guidance issued by Secretary of State, **35(2)**, [434]
issue of, **35(2)**, [432]
meaning, **35(2)**, [432]
relevant surface, **35(2)**, [432]
penalty notices for—
effect of, **35(2)**, [426]
issue of, **35(2)**, [426]
payment of penalty, **35(2)**, [430]
penalty under, **35(2)**, [426]
relevant offence, meaning, **35(2)**, [429]

flying accident. *See under* **aircraft**

foliage
theft of, **12(1)**, [556]

food

contamination of, offence of, **12(1)**, [1042]

hawkers, unregistered, penalties, **25(2)**, [512], [515]

infestation—

  containers, in, **35(1)**, [234], [235]

  directions for preventing or mitigating—

    appeal against, **35(1)**, [236]

    failure to comply with—

      offence of, **35(1)**, [237], [243]

      powers of Minister on, **35(1)**, [237]

    power of Minister to give, **35(1)**, [235]

    scope of, **35(1)**, [235]

  entry, powers of, **35(1)**, [241]

  financial provisions, **35(1)**, [244]

  legal proceedings, **35(1)**, [243]

  meaning, **35(1)**, [245]

  notice of occurrence of, **35(1)**, [234]

  offences, **35(1)**, [238]

  regulations as to, **35(1)**, [234]

  ships and aircraft—

    application of provisions to, **35(1)**, [242]

    inspection of ships, charges for, **35(1)**, [251]

  structural works, direction to carry out, **35(1)**, [236]

meaning, **35(1)**, [245]

premises—

  London, insanitary—

    closing order, **25(2)**, [298]

    improved premises, certificate of, **25(2)**, [298]

    interim closing order, **25(2)**, [298]

    offences, fines for, **25(2)**, [298], [527]

price regulation. *See* **food prices**

safety. *See* **food and food safety**

shortages, orders for alleviating—

  consultations on making, **39(1)**, [369]

  penalties under, **39(1)**, [368]

  temporary requirements, **39(1)**, [372]

storage accommodation—

  notice requiring—

    appeal against, **35(1)**, [593], [625]

    local authority, given by, **35(1)**, [593]

street trading. *See* **street trading**

weights, etc. *See* **weights and measures**

zero-rating, **50**, [151]

food and food safety

abstraction of constituent, **1(2)**, [422]

additives, offences, **1(2)**, [422]

advertisement—

  false or misleading, **1(2)**, [430]

  meaning, **1(2)**, [466]

  offence arising, defence to, **1(2)**, [437]

  regulations on, **1(2)**, [431]

aircraft, on, entry to inspect, **1(2)**, [245], [261], [475]

  transitional provisions affecting, **1(2)**, [475]

analysis—

  certificate of, **1(2)**, [444]

  food analyst, meaning, **1(2)**, [444]

  Government Chemist, by, **1(2)**, [445]

  meaning, **1(2)**, [466]

  regulation of, **1(2)**, [445]

food and food safety—*contd*

analysis—*contd*

  samples, of, **1(2)**, [444]

  analysts, appointment etc. *See* **public analyst**

appeal—

  Crown Court, to, **1(2)**, [452]

  enforcement authority, from decision of, **1(2)**, [440], [451]

  improvement notice, against, **1(2)**, [453]

  magistrates' court, to, **1(2)**, [440], [451]

  regulations as to procedure, **1(2)**, [440]

  tribunal constituted under regulations, to, **1(2)**, [440], [451]

artificial technique, modification of food sources by, **1(2)**, [433]

authorised officer—

  decision of, appeal from, **1(2)**, [440]

  emergency prohibition notice, issue of, **1(2)**, [427]

  expenses of, **1(2)**, [460]

  food authority, of, **1(2)**, [420]

  good faith, acting in, **1(2)**, [458]

  improvement notice, issue of, **1(2)**, [425]

  inspection and seizure by, **1(2)**, [424]

  meaning, **1(2)**, [420]

  premises, right to enter, **1(2)**, [446]

  samples, taking of, **1(2)**, [443]

authority—

  charges by, regulations, **1(2)**, [459]

  enforcement of provisions by, **1(2)**, [421]

  England and Wales, in, **1(2)**, [420]

  in default, **1(2)**, [456]

  liability for acts of officers, **1(2)**, [458]

  local authority as, **1(2)**, [420]

  public analysts, appointment, **1(2)**, [441]

business—

  entry on premises of, **1(2)**, [446]

  improvement notice, service on proprietor, **1(2)**, [425]

  meaning, **1(2)**, [417]

  prohibition on, **1(2)**, [426]

  undertakings included in term, **1(2)**, [417]

Channel Islands, application of provisions to, **1(2)**, [469]

codes of practice, issue of, **1(2)**, [454]

cold storage, amendment provisions as to, **1(2)**, [465]

commercial operation—

  hygienic conditions, observance of, in, **1(2)**, [425]

  injurious to health, emergency control order, **1(2)**, [428]

  meaning, **1(2)**, [417]

  records and returns, **1(2)**, [440]

  regulations as to, **1(2)**, [431], [440]

Community provisions, application of, **1(2)**, [432]

compensation—

  destruction of suspected food, **1(2)**, [424]

  prohibition notice, on compliance with, **1(2)**, [427]

  seizure, for, **1(2)**, 424]

composition of food, regulations as to, **1(2)**, [431], [473]

food and food safety—*contd*
consumer protection—
false description or presentation,
1(2), [430]
food not of nature or quality demanded,
1(2), [429]
food premises, licensing of, **1(2)**, [434]
regulations for, **1(2)**, [431]
contact materials—
commercial operations with respect to,
1(2), [431], [432]
meaning, **1(2)**, [417]
container—
contamination, powers relating to,
1(2), [261]
meaning, **1(2)**, [466]
contamination of—
defences, **1(2)**, [252]
designating authority, **1(2)**, [242]
emergency order—
contravening, **1(2)**, [242], [243]
Crown and Duchy land, application to,
1(2), [250]
directions, giving, **1(2)**, [243]
meaning, **1(2)**, [242]
Ministers, powers of, **1(2)**, [243]
power to make, **1(2)**, [242]
emergency prohibitions—
activities affected, **1(2)**, [258]–[260]
contravention of, **1(2)**, [242]
meaning, **1(2)**, [242]
movement of food, on, **1(2)**, [259]
financial provisions, **1(2)**, [253]
investigating and enforcement officers—
aircraft, powers relating to, **1(2)**, [261]
assistants, **1(2)**, [261]
authorisation of, **1(2)**, [244]
authority, evidence of, **1(2)**, [261]
British sea-fishery officer as, **1(2)**, [244]
containers, powers relating to,
1(2), [261]
dwellings, entry into, **1(2)**, [261]
false statements to, **1(2)**, [261]
force, using, **1(2)**, [261]
obstructing, **1(2)**, [261]
powers of, **1(2)**, [245]
protection from proceedings, **1(2)**, [261]
questioning, powers of, **1(2)**, [261]
requirement of, failure to comply with,
1(2), [261]
time of performance of functions,
1(2), [261]
vessels, etc, powers relating to,
1(2), [261]
offences, **1(2)**, [251]
continental shelf, provisions relating to,
1(2), [470]
county councils, expenses of, **1(2)**, [460]
Crown, application of provisions to,
1(2), [250], [467]
death, continuation of registration or licence
on, **1(2)**, [457]
default powers of Minister, **1(2)**, [456]
documents—
form and authentication, **1(2)**, [463]

food and food safety—*contd*
documents—*contd*
service of, **1(2)**, [464]
emergency control order—
issue of, **1(2)**, [428]
Secretary of State—
directions by, **1(2)**, [428]
issue by, **1(2)**, [428]
emergency prohibition notices and order—
matters covered by, **1(2)**, [258]–[260]
power to make, **1(2)**, [242]
procedure, **1(2)**, [427]
enforcement action—
entry powers for persons monitoring,
1(2), [657]
information relating to, power to request,
1(2), [656]
monitoring of, **1(2)**, [655]
offences, **1(2)**, [659]
enforcement authority—
appeal from decision of. *See* appeal *above*
duties, **1(2)**, 421]
emergency prohibition notices and orders,
service of, **1(2)**, [427]
improvement notice—
appeal against, **1(2)**, [453]
issue by officer, **1(2)**, [425]
meaning, **1(2)**, [421], [658]
proceedings, institution of, **1(2)**, [421]
enforcement of provisions, **1(2)**, [421]
entertainment, given away at, **1(2)**, [418]
entry, powers of—
authorised officer, **1(1)**, [355]; **1(2)**, [245],
[446]
diseased animals or birds, premises in which
kept, **1(2)**, [446]
dwelling house, in case of, **1(2)**, [446]
information obtained during,
non-disclosure of, **1(2)**, [446]
obstruction of officers, **1(2)**, [447]
records—
inspection of **1(2)**, [446]
seizure of, **1(2)**, [446]
warrant, issue of, **1(2)**, [446]
examinations—
facilities for, provision of, **1(2)**, [442]
meaning, **1(2)**, [442]
examiner, food, **1(2)**, [444]
false description or presentation of food,
1(2), [430]
false or misleading information, furnishing
of, **1(2)**, [447]
food authority. *See* authority *above*
food business. *See* business *above*
hazard, likely creation of, emergency powers,
1(2), [242]
health risk, what constitutes, **1(2)**, [426]
human consumption, for—
fitness for, regulations, **1(2)**, [431]
meaning, **1(2)**, [466]
presumption of, **1(2)**, [419]
sale for, when falsely described, **1(2)**, [430]
unfit for—
disposal, **1(2)**, [473]

food and food safety—*contd*
human consumption, for—*contd*
unfit for—*contd*
safety requirements, failure to comply
with, **1(2)**, [423]
hygiene—
observance in commercial operations,
1(2), [425]
regulations, **1(2)**, [431], [473]
requirements for, **1(2)**, [473]
training in—
provision of, **1(2)**, [438]
regulations, **1(2)**, [473]
hygienic conditions in dealing with food,
regulations, **1(2)**, [425], [431]
importation of food—
meaning, **1(2)**, [466]
prohibition by regulation, **1(2)**, [433]
improvement notice, service on proprietor of
food business, **1(2)**, [425]
information—
disclosure of, **1(2)**, [446]
false or misleading, furnishing, **1(2)**, [447]
obtained under power of entry, **1(2)**, [446]
injurious to health—
conditions giving rise to injury, **1(2)**, [426]
operations being, **1(2)**, [422]
rendering food, **1(2)**, [422]
risk, emergency control order in case of,
1(2), [428]
inspection, authorised officer's powers,
1(2), [424], [473]
Isles of Scilly, application of provisions to,
1(2), [469]
knacker's yard, slaughter in, **1(2)**, [423]
label, false description or presentation on,
1(2), [430]
labelling, marking and advertising, regulations
as to, **1(2)**, [431]
licences—
appeals. *See* appeal *above*
conditions, subject to, **1(2)**, [440]
continuance on death, **1(2)**, [457]
milk producers and sellers, **1(2)**, [433]
premises, **1(2)**, [434]
local authority as food authority, **1(2)**, [420]
local inquiry, default of food authority, into,
1(2), [456]
meaning, **1(2)**, [417]
meat, prohibited sale from knacker's yard,
1(2), [423]
microbiological standards regulations as to,
1(2), [431]
milk—
producers and sellers, licences, **1(2)**, [433]
special designations, **1(2)**, [433]
Minister, powers of—
codes of practice, issue of, **1(2)**, [454]
default powers, **1(2)**, [456]
regulations by. *See* regulations *below*
returns, power to require, **1(2)**, [455]
statutory functions ceasing to be exercisable
by, **1(2)**, [669]
misleading presentation, **1(2)**, [430]

food and food safety—*contd*
novel foods—
meaning, **1(2)**, [433]
regulations as to operations as to,
1(2), [433]
offences—
body corporate, by, **1(2)**, [450]
defences—
advertisement, offence in relation to,
1(2), [437]
due diligence, of, **1(2)**, [436]
fault of another person, due to,
1(2), [435]
publication in course of business,
1(2), [437]
directions by Minister, failure to comply
with, **1(2)**, [428]
emergency control order, contravention
of, **1(2)**, [428]
emergency prohibition, relating to,
1(2), [242], [258]–[260], [427]
false description or presentation,
1(2), [430]
false or misleading information, furnishing
of, **1(2)**, [447]
improvement notice, failure to comply
with, **1(2)**, [425]
label, false description etc, by, **1(2)**, [430]
misleading presentation, **1(2)**, [430]
obstruction of officers, **1(2)**, [447]
penalties, regulations as to liability for,
1(2), [440]
proceedings—
limitation period, **1(2)**, [231]
trial, regulations governing, **1(2)**, [440]
prohibition order, contravention of,
1(2), [426]
prosecutions, time limit for, **1(2)**, [448]
punishment of, **1(2)**, [449]
rendering food injurious to health,
1(2), [422]
requirements, food not complying with,
1(2), [423]
safety requirements, non-compliance with,
1(2), [423]
Slaughterhouses Act, licensee under, by,
1(2), [449]
officers—
acting in good faith, protection of,
1(2), [458]
obstruction of, **1(2)**, [447]
orders—
consultation before making, **1(2)**, [462]
enforcement, **1(2)**, [421]
supplementary provisions, **1(2)**, [440],
[462]
perishable, international carriage of. *See*
**international carriage of perishable
foodstuffs**
premises—
entry on, powers, **1(2)**, [446]
hygiene requirements, **1(2)**, [473]
licensing of, **1(2)**, [434]
meaning, **1(2)**, [417]

food and food safety—*contd*
  premises—*contd*
    registration—
      continuance on death, **1(2)**, [457]
      requirement, **1(2)**, [434]
  preparation—
    improvement notice as to, **1(2)**, [425]
    meaning, **1(2)**, [466]
    regulation of, **1(2)**, [431]
  presentation—
    false, **1(2)**, [430]
    meaning, **1(2)**, [466]
  prize or reward, given as, **1(2)**, [418]
  processing, regulations as to, **1(2)**, [473]
  prohibition notice, emergency, **1(2)**, [427]
    cessation of, **1(2)**, [427]
    compensation, when payable, **1(2)**, [427]
  prohibition order—
    affixing copy on premises, **1(2)**, [426],
      [427]
    certificate after satisfaction, **1(2)**, [426]
    cessation, **1(2)**, [426], [427]
    court, powers of, **1(2)**, [426]
    directions by court, **1(2)**, [426]
    emergency, **1(2)**, [427]
    manager of business, making against,
      1(2), [426]
    proprietor of food business—
      conviction of, effect, **1(2)**, [426]
      emergency notice, service on,
        1(2), [427]
      imposition against, **1(2)**, [426]
    when called for, **1(2)**, [426]
  proprietor, meaning, **1(2)**, [466]
  public analyst, appointment etc. *See* **public
  analyst**
  registers, regulations as to keeping of,
    1(2), [440]
  regulations—
    charges, as to, **1(2)**, [459]
    Community obligations, as to, **1(2)**, [432]
    consultation before making, when
      required, **1(2)**, [462]
    documents, prescribing, **1(2)**, [463]
    enforcement, **1(2)**, [421]
    matters covered by, **1(2)**, [431], [473]
    modification etc of enactments by,
      1(2), [462]
    particular foods, special provisions,
      1(2), [433]
    power to make, **1(2)**, [431]
    sampling and analysis, **1(2)**, [445]
    supplementary provisions, **1(2)**, [440]
  requirements, food not complying with,
    1(2), [423]
  returns, required by Minister, **1(2)**, [455]
  sale and related expressions, meaning,
    1(2), [418]
  sale of food—
    falsely described or presented food,
      1(2), [430]
    human consumption, presumed for,
      1(2), [419]
    nature, substance or quality demanded,
      food not of, **1(2)**, [429]

food and food safety—*contd*
  sale of food—*contd*
    unfit, **1(2)**, [423]
  samples—
    analysis of, **1(2)**, [444]
    facilities for examination of, **1(2)**, [442]
    Government Chemist, examination by,
      1(2), [445]
    meaning, **1(2)**, [444]
    procurement of, **1(2)**, [443]
    public analyst, submitted to, **1(2)**, [444]
    purchase of food to procure, **1(2)**, [443]
    regulation of sampling, **1(2)**, [445]
    taking of, **1(2)**, [443]
  seizure of suspected food, **1(2)**, [424]
  service of documents, **1(2)**, [464]
  shellfish. *See* **shellfish**
  ships, on—
    authorised officer entering, **1(2)**, [245],
      [261]
    entry on, power, **1(2)**, [475]
    home-going, **1(2)**, [475]
    meaning, **1(2)**, [466]
  sources of food—
    Community provisions as to, **1(2)**, [432]
    genetically modified, **1(2)**, [433]
    inspection of, **1(2)**, [473]
    meaning, **1(2)**, [417]
    production, **1(2)**, [473]
    regulations as to, **1(2)**, [431], [473]
  standards—
    Food Standards Agency—
      accounts, **1(2)**, [692]
      advice, information and assistance,
        provision of, **1(2)**, [650]
      advisory committees, **1(2)**, [648], [688]
      animal feedingstuffs—
        general functions in relation to,
          1(2), [652]
        Great Britain, **1(2)**, [673]
        meaning, **1(2)**, [679]
        Northern Ireland, **1(2)**, [674]
      annual report, **1(2)**, [647]
      audit, **1(2)**, [692]
      benefits, consideration of, **1(2)**, [666]
      breach of duty, directions relating to,
        1(2), [667]
      chief executive, appointment of,
        1(2), [646]
      constitution, **1(2)**, [687]
      costs, consideration of, **1(2)**, [666]
      Crown application, **1(2)**, [681]
      delegation of powers, **1(2)**, [687]
      devolution in Scotland and Northern
        Ireland, **1(2)**, [678]
      directors, **1(2)**, [646]
      disclosure of information, power to
        modify enactments about, **1(2)**, [668]
      emergency orders, delegation of powers
        to make, **1(2)**, [660]
      enforcement action—
        entry powers for persons monitoring,
          1(2), [657]
        information relating to, power to
          request, **1(2)**, [656]

food and food safety—*contd*
  standards—*contd*
    Food Standards Agency—*contd*
      enforcement action—*contd*
        monitoring of, **1(2)**, [655]
        offences, **1(2)**, [659]
      establishment of, **1(2)**, [644]
      financial provisions, **1(2)**, [682]
      food policy, development of, **1(2)**, [649]
      Food Safety Promotion Board, duty to
        take account of functions of,
        1(2), [677]
      food-borne diseases—
        notification of tests for, **1(2)**, [670]
        power to issue guidance on control
          of, **1(2)**, [663]
      food-borne zoonoses, arrangements for
        sharing information about, **1(2)**, [671]
      functions, **1(2)**, [644]
        under other enactments, **1(2)**, [661],
          [689]–[691]
      information, acquisition and review of,
        1(2), [651]
      international obligations, directions
        relating to, **1(2)**, [667]
      loss of certain functions, consequences
        of, **1(2)**, [676]
      members—
        appointment of, **1(2)**, [645]
        number of, **1(2)**, [645]
        pensions, **1(2)**, [687]
        remuneration, **1(2)**, [687]
        tenure of office, **1(2)**, [687]
      modification of provisions, **1(2)**, [675]
      objectives—
        consideration of, **1(2)**, [666]
        main, **1(2)**, [644]
        statement of, **1(2)**, [665]
      observations—
        entry powers for persons carrying
          out, **1(2)**, [654]
        power to carry out, **1(2)**, [653]
      practices, statement of, **1(2)**, [665]
      proceedings, **1(2)**, [687]
      publication of advice and information,
        1(2), [662]
      reports, **1(2)**, [647]
      risks, consideration of, **1(2)**, [666]
      staff, **1(2)**, [687]
      status, **1(2)**, [687]
      supplementary powers, **1(2)**, [664]
      transfer of property, rights and liabilities
        to, **1(2)**, [684]
      veterinary products, consultation on,
        1(2), [672]
  subordinate legislation, **1(2)**, [680]
  substance or quality demanded, food not
    being of, **1(2)**, [429]
  substance, meaning, **1(2)**, [466]
  sugar beet. *See* **sugar beet**
  summary of provisions, **1(1)**, [124]
  suspected food—
    compensation of owner, **1(2)**, [424]
    justices' powers, **1(2)**, [424]
    notices, **1(2)**, [424]

food and food safety—*contd*
  suspected food—*contd*
    seizure of, **1(2)**, [424]
  territorial waters, in relation to, **1(2)**, [470]
  transitional provisions, **1(2)**, [471], [475]
  treatment of food—
    meaning, **1(2)**, [466]
    regulations, **1(2)**, [473]
  tribunals constituted under regulations—
    appeal from, **1(2)**, [440], [451]
    remuneration of chairmen, **1(2)**, [461]
  unfit for human consumption—
    sale of, **1(2)**, [423]
    seizure and inspection of, **1(2)**, [424]
    See also human consumption *above*
  water supply, provisions applicable, **1(2)**, [468]

Food from Britain
  accounts, **1(2)**, [198]
  annual reports, **1(2)**, [198]
  borrowing powers, **1(2)**, [199]
  charges for services, **1(2)**, [203]
  committees to assist, **1(2)**, [203]
  contributions—
    bodies authorised to make, **1(2)**, [197]
    power to accept, **1(2)**, [203]
  council—
    establishment, **1(2)**, [194]
    procedure, **1(2)**, [203]
  food, meaning, **1(2)**, [201]
  functions, **1(2)**, [195]
    transferred, general provisions, **1(2)**, [204]
  funding, **1(2)**, [392]
  grants or loans—
    by, power to make, **1(2)**, [199]
    to, by ministers, **1(2)**, [200]
  members—
    appointment, **1(2)**, [194]
    interest, duty to disclose, **1(2)**, [203]
    remuneration, **1(2)**, [203]
    terms of office, **1(2)**, [203]
  officers and servants, **1(2)**, [203]
  reports by, **1(2)**, [198]
  status of, **1(2)**, [203]

food, Minister of. *See* **Agriculture, Fisheries
and Food, Minister of**

food poisoning
  medical practitioner—
    certificate by, **35(1)**, [453]
    duty to report, **35(1)**, [452]
  tracing source of, occupier to furnish
    information for, **35(1)**, [459]

food prices
  enforcement of provisions, **47**, [208]
  marking of prices, **47**, [204]
  offences, **47**, [208]
  regulation of, enforcement, **47**, [208]
  subsidies, enforcement, **47**, [208]

Food Standards Agency. *See* **food and food
safety**

foot-and-mouth disease. *See* **diseases of animals**

football club
transfer fees, tax treatment, **43(1)**, [429]

football grounds
improvements, pools payments for, **42**, [1029]

Football Licensing Authority
accounts and audit, **13**, [406]
documents and seal, **13**, [406]
establishment, **13**, [374]
expenses, **13**, [374]
functions, **13**, [374]
inspectors, appointment, **13**, [379], [406]
local authority, co-operation in safety
  measures, **13**, [379]
members—
  appointment, **13**, [374], [406]
  number, **13**, [374]
  remuneration and pensions, **13**, [406]
  tenure of, **13**, [406]
officers and employees, **13**, [406]
proceedings, **13**, [406]
safety at football grounds, powers as to,
  13, [379]
status and capacity, **13**, [406]

football match. *See also* **sporting events**
admission to premises—
  hours of, **13**, [373]
  licences. *See* licences *below*
  restriction on, **13**, [373]
  unlicensed premises, **13**, [375]
alcohol at. *See* **sporting events**
banning order, **12(4)**, [255]
  additional requirements, **13**, [387]
  appeals, **13**, [384]
  complaint, made on, **13**, [382]
  enforcing authority, functions of, **13**, [391]
  exempting authority—
    functions, **13**, [393]
    powers, **13**, [392]
  generally, **13**, [385]
  information as to, requirements, **13**, [390]
  local police, functions of, **13**, [391]
  meaning, **13**, [380]
  offences, **13**, [389]
    failure to comply with orders, **13**, [391]
    made on conviction of, **13**, [381]
  outside England and Wales—
    Orders in Council, **13**, [398]
    proceedings, **13**, [398]
  period of, **13**, [386]
  police, exemption from requirements,
    13, [392]
  regulated matches, **13**, [392]
  supplementary, **13**, [383]
  termination of, **13**, [388]
cancellation, **13**, [373]
chanting, indecent or racialist, **13**, [409]
control period—
  meaning, **13**, [380]

football match—*contd*
control period—*contd*
  summary measures—
    compensation, **13**, [397]
    detention, **13**, [394]
    references to a court, **13**, [395]
    supplementary, **13**, [396]
  designated, meaning, **13**, [373], [407]
  designation of—
    orders, **13**, [373], [376]
    annulment by Parliament, **13**, [407]
  exclusion order—
    extension to other events, **12(1)**, [1041]
    photograph of offender, **12(1)**, [1040]
    prescribed matches, **12(1)**, [1041]
  financial provision, **13**, [403]
  Football Licensing Authority. *See* **Football Licensing Authority**
  indecent chanting, **13**, [409]
  inspectors—
    appointment, **13**, [379], [406]
    authority, production, **13**, [379]
  licences—
    entitlement under, **13**, [376]
    seating, conditions, **13**, [377]
  licences to admit spectators—
    application for, **13**, [376]
    fees, **13**, [376]
    generally, **13**, [376]
    grant, **13**, [376]
    matters to be regarded, **13**, [376]
    refusal, **13**, [376]
    revocation, **13**, [376], [378]
    specific matches, **13**, [376]
    suspension, **13**, [376], [378]
    terms and conditions, **13**, [376]
    variation of, **13**, [376]
    See also **Football Licensing Authority**
  Licensing Authority. *See* **Football Licensing Authority**
  missiles, throwing of, **13**, [408]
  offences—
    bodies corporate, by, **13**, [401]
    chanting, indecent or racialist, **13**, [409]
    licences, contravention of terms, **13**, [376]
    list of, **13**, [405]
    missiles, throwing of, **13**, [408]
    playing area, going onto, **13**, [410]
    relevance, declarations of—
      appeal against, **13**, [400]
      further provisions, **13**, [400]
  offences in connection with, **12(1)**, [426]
  "pitch, invasion of", **13**, [410]
  playing area, going onto, **13**, [410]
  postponed, **13**, [373]
  racialist chanting, **13**, [409]
  regulated, meaning, **13**, [380]
  safety at grounds, **13**, [379]
  seating, conditions relating to, **13**, [377]
  Secretary of State—
    designation of matches, powers, **13**, [373]
    designation orders by, **13**, [373], [407]
    seating, power to require conditions,
      13, [377]
  service of documents, **13**, [402]

football match—*contd*

spectators—

    admission to premises. *See* admission *above*

    offences. *See* offences *above*

unlicensed premises, admission to, penalties, **13**, [375]

violence or disorder, prevention of, **13**, [440]

football pools

child—

    employment to provide facilities, **5(1)**, [333]

    invitation to participate, **5(1)**, [338]

footpath

agricultural land, passing over—

    ploughing, **36**, [1190]

    works on, authorisation, **36**, [1191]

amenities, provision. *See* **highway (services etc)**

creation of. *See* **public path**

cycle track, converted into, **37**, [345]

dedication of, **36**, [1029]

dedication of, **36**, [1029]

diversion of. *See* **public path**

evidence of, **37**, [89]

excepted highways, **38(2)**, [60]

dedication of, **36**, [1029]

extinguishment. *See* **public path**

field-edge path, **36**, [1381]

horse, riding or leading, **37**, [301]

local authority using vehicles on, **36**, [1350]

maintenance and repair—

    highway authority, default powers of, **36**, [1061]

    liability, enforcement of, **36**, [1060]

    proceedings for order, **36**, [1060]

    public expense, at, **36**, [1041]

    surface, making good—

        entry on land, **36**, [1419]

        expenses, **36**, [1419]

        requirement, **36**, [1419]

making up, **36**, [1031]

meaning, **36**, [1381]; **37**, [96], [178], [301], [808]

motor vehicles, driving on, **37**, [301], [605]

notice deterring public use, penalty for, **36**, [638]

open to all traffic, **37**, [301]

orders—

    confirmation of, **46**, [633]

    notice of, **36**, [1407]

    procedure for making, **36**, [1407]

    publicity, **46**, [634]

    validity and operation, **36**, [1408]

parish or community council maintaining, **36**, [1047]

ploughing—

    enforcement provisions, **36**, [1190]

    expenses, **38(1)**, [156]

    making good, **36**, [1190], [1419]

    period allowed for, **36**, [1190]

    right to, **36**, [1190]

    temporary diversion, **36**, [1191]

power of entry on, **36**, [1343]

footpath—*contd*

privately maintainable, **36**, [1054]

public right of way, extinguishment of, **46**, [523]

public right of way over, **37**, [808]

rail crossing diversion orders, **36**, [1154]

railway, crossing, stopping up, **36**, [1149]

    See further **rail crossing; railway**

railway or tramway, over, **38(1)**, [327]

recreation or refreshment facilities on, **36**, [1137]

repairs. *See* maintenance and repair *above*

right of way orders affecting, **37**, [95], [108]

services and amenities on. *See* **highway**

signposting, **36**, [773]

stile or gate on—

    erection, authorisation of, **36**, [1210]

    maintenance of, **36**, [1209]

stopping up, **36**, [1147]

stopping up or diversion, **46**, [522]

surface, disturbance of, **36**, [1190], [1419]

    unlawful, **36**, [1187]

survey of, **36**, [1031]

temporary prohibition or restriction of traffic, **37**, [178]

tramway, crossing, **38(1)**, [327]

walkway. *See* **walkway**

wardens, appointment of, **37**, [94]

widening, power of, **36**, [1075]

works, carrying out, **36**, [1031]

young riders using, **6**, [458]

footway. *See also under* **highway**

London—

    parking on, penalty, **25(2)**, [345]

    vehicles on, for street cleansing, **25(1)**, [655]

parking of heavy goods vehicles on, **37**, [589]

footwear

zero-rating, **50**, [151]

forecourt

London, maintenance—

    local authority, by, **25(1)**, [418]

    expenses, recovery, **25(1)**, [420]

    notice requiring, **25(1)**, [418]

foreign company. *See* **oversea company**

foreign compensation

governments of other countries, payable by, **10**, [926]

international organisations, payable by, **10**, [926]

Foreign Compensation Commission

accounts of, **10**, [929]

administrative provisions, **10**, [930]

annual report, **10**, [929]

body corporate, as, **10**, [925]

constitution of, **10**, [925]

contempt of, **10**, [928]

determinations of, **10**, [1028]

documents, production to, **10**, [928]

Foreign Compensation Commission—*contd*
financial provisions, **10**, [930]
information, furnishing to, **10**, [928]
members—
  office, holding, **10**, [925]
  pensions, **10**, [977]
Orders in Council, **10**, [931]
procedure, **10**, [927]
staff—
  pensions, **10**, [977]
  remuneration of, **10**, [930]
witnesses, attendance of, **10**, [928]

foreign corporations
corporate status, recognition of, **8**, 959–60
general note, **8**, 9

foreign country
British court in, **7(2)**, [408]
meaning, **7(2)**, [413]
Republic of Ireland not, **7(2)**, [452]
will executed in. *See* **will**

foreign currency
stamp duty expressed in, **41**, [20], [154]

foreign enlistment
accessory to, **12(1)**, [120]
application of provisions, **12(1)**, [111]
appeals, **12(1)**, [135]
definitions, **12(1)**, [138]
detention of ships, **12(1)**, [131], [132]
equipment of foreign ships, **12(1)**, [118]
false representations as to service, **12(1)**, [114]
forfeiture of ships, **12(1)**, [127]
illegal prize, **12(1)**, [122]
illegally enlisted persons on ship, taking,
  12(1), [115]
imprisonment, **12(1)**, [121]
intention as to, **12(1)**, [113]
jurisdiction for offences, **12(1)**, [124]
leaving Her Majesty's dominions for,
  12(1), [113]
licence, grant of, **12(1)**, [123]
offender, removing for trial, **12(1)**, [126]
penalty, **12(1)**, [112]
place of offence, **12(1)**, [125]
seizure of ships, **12(1)**, [129]
  powers of officers, **12(1)**, [130]
shipbuilding—
  evidence, **12(1)**, [117]
  illegal, **12(1)**, [116]

foreign exchange
anti-avoidance provisions—
  derivative contracts, **43(S)**, 1570–6
  loan relationships, **43(S)**, 1566–5
loan relationships, gains and losses from,
  43(2), [168]

foreign income
arising basis, charged on—
  annual payments, **44(3)**, [856]
  backdated pensions, **44(3)**, [857]
  expenses, **44(3)**, [855]

foreign income—*contd*
overview of provisions, **44(3)**, [846]
relevant, meaning, **44(3)**, [847]
remittance basis—
  charge on, **44(3)**, [849]
  claims to be charged on, **44(3)**, [848]
  delayed remittance, **44(3)**, [852]–[854]
  partners, **44(3)**, [874]
  UK-linked debts, repayment of,
    44(3), [850]–[851]
transitional provisions, **44(3)**, [913]
unremittable—
  application of provisions, **44(3)**, [858]
  claim for relief, **44(3)**, [859]
  source ceasing, income charged on,
    44(3), [859]
  valuing, **44(3)**, [862]
  withdrawal of relief, **44(3)**, [860]

foreign judgment. *See also* **judgments
(Conventions)**
arbitration awards, **19(3)**, [24]
awards expressed in foreign currency,
  19(3), [78]
enforcement—
  arbitration awards, **19(3)**, [24]
  exceptions from, **19(3)**, [22]
  reciprocal. *See* **judgment**
  registration necessary to, **19(3)**, [19]
enforcement, route licences, **4(1)**, [123]
general effect of, **19(3)**, [21]
in personam, jurisdiction of courts,
  19(3), [17]
reciprocal enforcement. *See* **judgment**
registration—
  application for, **19(3)**, [15]
  dominions, extension to, **19(3)**, [20]
  effect of, **19(3)**, [15]
  extension of provisions, **19(3)**, [14]
  judgments eligible for, **19(3)**, [14]
  judgments of courts outside England and
    Wales, **19(3)**, [28]
  mandated territory, extension to,
    19(3), [20]
  protectorates, extension to, **19(3)**, [20]
  required for enforcement, **19(3)**, [19]
  rules of court, **19(3)**, [16]
  security for costs, **19(3)**, [16]
  setting aside—
    appeal pending, where, **19(3)**, [18]
    application for, court's powers on,
      19(3), [18]
    cases for, **19(3)**, [17]
    grounds for, **19(3)**, [17]
    provision with regard to, **19(3)**, [16]
rules of court, **19(3)**, [8], [16]
summary of provisions, **19(3)**, [1]
unenforceable in UK, **19(3)**, [22]

foreign jurisdiction
British court, assignment to, **7(2)**, [408]
British subjects, over, **7(2)**, [401]
consolidation of Acts, **7(2)**, [399]
courts, Admiralty jurisdiction, **11(2)**, [134]
definitions, **7(2)**, [413]

foreign jurisdiction—*contd*
  evidence of, **7(2)**, [403]
  exercise of, **7(2)**, [400]
  extension of enactments, **7(2)**, [404], [415],
    [418], [420]
  Order in Council—
    act done under, **7(2)**, [407]
    amendment, **7(2)**, [409]
    laying before Parliament, **7(2)**, [410]
    void for repugnancy, **7(2)**, [411]
  place of punishment of offenders, **7(2)**, [406]
  protection of person acting in, **7(2)**, [412]
  trial in British possession, **7(2)**, [405]
  validity of acts, **7(2)**, [402]

foreign lawyers. *See under* **Law Society**

foreign marriage
  caveat against, **27**, [141]
  chaplains of HM forces, solemnized by,
    27, [155], [203]
  consent to, **27**, [140]
  dominions, provisions as to, **27**, [203]
  evidence of, **27**, [149]
  fees, **27**, [145], [153]
  forbidding, means of, **27**, [140]
  foreigner, with. *See* **marriage**
  hours for solemnisation, **27**, [144]
  intended, notice of, **27**, [138]
  international law, effect of inconsistency
    with, **27**, [152]
  marriage officer—
    caveat lodged with, **27**, [141]
    districts, **27**, [147]
    fee, entitlement to, **27**, [145], [153]
    filing and posting of notice by, **27**, [139]
    marriage warrant, authorised by, **27**, [147]
    notice to, **27**, [138]
    official house of, **27**, [157]
    persons being, **27**, [147]
    registration in duplicate by, **27**, [145]–[146]
    seal of, **27**, [147]
    Secretary of State, forwarding copy of
      register to, **27**, [146]
    solemnisation by, **27**, [144]
  notice of—
    filing and posting, **27**, [139]
    marriage officer, to, **27**, [138]
    new, requirement of after three months,
      27, [142]
  oath before, **27**, [143]
  objections to, avoidance, **27**, [148]
  proof of, **18**, [172]
  registration of—
    duplicate, in, **27**, [145]–[146]
    HM forces serving abroad, solemnisation by
      chaplain of, **27**, [155], [203]
    local law, where solemnised under,
      27, [151]
    provisions applying to, **27**, [150]
  regulations, power to make, **27**, [154]
  solemnisation, **27**, [144]
  validity of, **27**, [137]
  void, being, **27**, [444]
  witnesses to, **27**, [144]

foreign prison
  goods made in, importation prohibited,
    13, [546]

foreign security
  unstamped, issue of, **41**, [42]

foreign state
  administration of estates, **18**, [489]
  documents, proof and effect, **18**, [172], [198]
  enlisting in service of. *See* **foreign
    enlistment**
  evidence involving. *See under* **evidence**
  evidence, mutual provision of, **12(2)**, [21],
    [22]
  extradition from and to. *See* **extradition**
  meaning, **12(1)**, [138]
  probate, sealing in UK, **18**, [508]
  ships, offences as to. *See* **ship**

foreign tax
  information and inspection powers,
    43(S), 1412–13, 1692–8

foreign vehicles. *See* **international traffic;
  motor vehicles**

foreshore
  drainage works, consent to, **20**, [319]
  harbours, docks etc, consents to construction
    on, **39(2)**, [13]

forest
  abrogation of law, **10**, [84]
  Crown rights, abolition of, **10**, [84]
  rights of common, **10**, [84]
  verderers, appointment and functions of,
    10, [84]

Forest of Dean
  acquisition and disposal of land in, **18**, [1130]
  byelaws, provisions on, **18**, [1136]
  verderers, **10**, [84]

forestry
  acquisition of land for—
    agreement, by, **18**, [1130], [1145]
    amenity, for, **18**, [1153]
    compulsory purchase, by—
      procedure, **18**, [1148]
      provisions on, **18**, [1131], [1146]
      validity and operation of orders,
        18, [1147]
    Minister, powers of, **18**, [1130]
  camping etc sites, aid for, **1(1)**, [649]
  Commission. *See* **Forestry Commission**
  Commission, co-operation with Rural
    Development Boards, **1(1)**, [648]
  control by Rural Development Board,
    1(1), [654]
  Crown Estate, satisfaction of contingent
    liability to, **18**, [1133]
  dedication agreement. *See* **forestry
    dedication agreement**

forestry—*contd*

dedication covenant. *See* **forestry dedication covenant**

disposal of land, **18**, [1130]

fund. *See* **forestry fund**

land—

agricultural land excluded, **21**, [481]

management of, **18**, [1090]

meaning, **21**, [453]

metrication of measurements, **18**, [1159]

Minister—

acquisition and disposal of land by, **18**, [1130]

directions, giving, **18**, [1088]

felling directions, failure to comply with, **18**, [1115]

general duty of, **18**, [1096]

information, failure to provide, **18**, [1121]

public open space, **18**, [1097], [1153]

rabbits etc, failure to prevent damage by, **18**, [1093]

savings, **18**, [1151]

transitional provisions, **18**, [1139], [1149]

unauthorised tree felling, **18**, [1105]

public paths orders, protection under, **36**, [1033], [1160]

rabbits and hares, failure to destroy, **18**, [1093]

summary of provisions, **18**, [1087]

trees, planting, **1(1)**, [654]

vehicles used, driver's hours, when provisions inapplicable, **36**, [812]

vermin—

failure to destroy, **18**, [1093]

squirrels included in, **18**, [1093]

Forestry Commission

administration of, **18**, [1141]

advisory committees—

allowances, payment of, **18**, [1129]

composition of, **18**, [1129]

conservancy, for, **18**, [1128]

maintenance of, **18**, [1128]

annual report, **18**, [1134]

body corporate, formation and participation in, **18**, [1094], [1154]

byelaws, power to make, **18**, [1135], [1152]

charitable trust, establishment of, **18**, [1094], [1154]

Commissioners—

constitution, **18**, [1089]

directions of Ministers, complying with, **18**, [1088]

duties of, **18**, [1088]

special knowledge of, **18**, [1089]

committees—

allowances, **18**, [1141]

appointing, **18**, [1089]

quorum and procedure, **18**, [1141]

reference, of, **18**, [1118]

continuing in existence, **18**, [1088]

Countryside Agency acting as agent for, **18**, [1152]

Forestry Commission—*contd*

Crown Estate Commissioners—

contingent liability to, satisfaction of, **18**, [1133]

woods and forests belonging to, management of, **18**, [1090]

damage by rabbits, hares and vermin, preventing, **18**, [1093]

enforcement, powers of, **18**, [1137]

entry, powers of, **18**, [1137]

facilities, providing, **18**, [1152]

finance, **18**, [1132]–[1134]

forestry fund. *See* **forestry fund**

forestry land, management of, **18**, [1090]

gifts to, **18**, [1132]

grants and loans, making, **18**, [1158]

haulage facilities, provision for, **18**, [1092]

Home Grown Timber Advisory Committee—

allowances, payment of, **18**, [1129]

composition of, **18**, [1129]

consultation with, **18**, [1128]

maintenance of, **18**, [1128]

incidental powers, **18**, [1094], [1154]

instruction and training, promoting, **18**, [1095]

ironstone workings restoration, payments by British Steel, **17(1)**, [548]

land, tree preservation order in respect of, **46**, [460], [1037]

loans by, **18**, [1094], [1154]

obstruction of officers, **18**, [1137]

pollution of water, avoidance of, **32**, [272]

procedure of, **18**, [1141]

replanting, grant or loan for, **46**, [464]

seal of, **18**, [1141]

service of documents, **18**, [1121]

staff, **18**, [1141]

statistics, powers relating to, **18**, [1095]

superannuation provisions, **18**, [1142]

timber—

adequate supply of, ensuring, **18**, [1095]

dealing with, **18**, [1090]

tree felling, control of. *See* **tree felling**

woodland industries, establishing and carrying on, **18**, [1090]

forestry dedication agreement

compulsory purchase, land not subject to, **18**, [1131]

entry into, **18**, [1091]

meaning, **18**, [1091]

plan for tree felling under, **18**, [1102]

purpose of, **18**, [1091]

Scotland, in respect of land in, **18**, [1091]

forestry dedication covenant

Commissioners, rights of, **18**, [1091]

compulsory purchase, land not subject to, **18**, [1131]

conveyancing provisions, **18**, [1143]

enforcement of, **18**, [1091]

entry into, **18**, [1091]

Lands Tribunal, exclusion of powers of, **18**, [1091]

meaning, **18**, [1091]

forestry dedication covenant—*contd*
plan for tree felling under, **18**, [1102]
purpose of, **18**, [1091]

forestry fund
capital sums paid into, **18**, [1132]
grants and loans for, **18**, [1158]
payments into and out of, **18**, [1132]

forestry society
rules, registration of, **19(1)**, [336]

forestry workers
housing—
generally. *See* **agricultural workers**
information as to availability, **21**, [481]
permit workers, **21**, [494]
provisions, date of operation, **21**, [453],
[494]
temporary provisions, **21**, [494]
transitional provisions, **21**, [499]
whole time workers, **21**, [494]

forfeiture
appeal against, **9**, [91]
breach of repairing covenant, on, **21**, [64]
chemical weapons offences, **12(2)**, [406]
counterfeit notes and coin, **12(1)**, [740]
Crown, to, savings under Colonial Courts of
Admiralty Act, **11(2)**, [130]
drugs, **28**, [224]
due process of law, requirement of, **21**, [664]
false instrument, **12(1)**, [726]
forgery, object used for, **12(1)**, [726]
goods and land, of, abolition, **12(1)**, [1]
indecent photographs of children, of,
12(1), [704], [709]; **12(4)**, [273]
industrial assurance benefits, **19(1)**, [249]
inheritance, of, after unlawful killing,
12(1), [1]
knives and publications, of, **12(2)**, [541],
[542]
landmines, material relating to, **12(2)**, [638]
non-payment of rent, for—
county court, in, **11(2)**, [1018]
High Court, in, **11(2)**, [708]
obscene publications, **12(1)**, [312], [335]
overseas orders, enforcement of, **12(2)**, [23]
pension or allowance, of, **12(1)**, [267]
recovery, **9**, [90]
relief against, **20**, [1]
restrictions on, **20**, [1]
rule—
application for financial provision, and,
12(1), [776]
meaning, **12(1)**, [774]
murder, person convicted of, **12(1)**, [778]
Northern Ireland, **12(1)**, [779]
pensions and social benefits, **12(1)**, [777]
power to modify, **12(1)**, [775]
social security benefits, application to,
12(1), [777]
serious crime prevention order, failure to
comply with, **12(4)**, [383]
sound equipment, of, **12(2)**, [205]

forfeiture—*contd*
terrorist cash, of, **12(3)**, [73], [155]
terrorist property, of,
12(2), [896]. *See also* **terrorism**
unlawful killing, after, **12(1)**, [774], [775]
vehicle, ship or aircraft used for trafficking for
sexual exploitation, **12(3)**, [722], [724]

forgery. *See also* **counterfeiting**
birth certificate, **36**, [6]
common law, abolition of, **12(1)**, [730]
counterfeiting. *See* **counterfeiting**
death certificate, **36**, [6]
driving licences and certificates, **37**, [791]
false instruments—
cheque card, **12(1)**, [724]
cheques, **12(1)**, [724]
copying, **12(1)**, [721]
credit cards, **12(1)**, [724]
false, meaning, **12(1)**, [728]
Inland Revenue stamps, **12(1)**, [724]
instrument, meaning, **12(1)**, [727]
making, **12(1)**, [720], [728]
means of making, having, **12(1)**, [724]
money orders, **12(1)**, [724]
passport, **12(1)**, [724]
postage stamps, **12(1)**, [724]
postal order, **12(1)**, [724]
prejudice, inducing, **12(1)**, [729]
register entries, relating to, **12(1)**, [724]
share certificate, **12(1)**, [724]
sound recording, including, **12(1)**, [727]
tape, information on, **12(1)**, [727]
travellers' cheques, **12(1)**, [724]
using, **12(1)**, [722]
using copy of, **12(1)**, [723]
forfeiture, **12(1)**, [726]
goods vehicles, documents connected with,
38(1), [560]
grade designation marks, **1(1)**, [294]
marriage certificate, **36**, [6]
motor vehicle documents etc, **37**, [791]
offences of, **12(1)**, [720]–[724]; **12(2)**, [162]
penalties, **12(1)**, [725]
permits and licences, **37**, [48], [458]
register of births, etc, of, **12(1)**, [66]
seals on recording equipment, of, **36**, [814]
search and seizure, **12(1)**, [726]
test certificates, **37**, [791]
vehicle testing documents, **37**, [48], [138],
[791]

foster parents and fostering
agency—
meaning, **35(2)**, [283]
persons carrying on or managing,
notification of matters relating to,
6(S), 466–7
amended provisions, **6(S)**, 430
application for section 8 order, **6**, [302]
boarded out child with, **6**, [454]
complaints and representations, **6**, [451]
exemptions by local authority, **6**, [451]
foster-care relief—
adjustment of assessment, **44(3)**, [836]

foster parents and fostering—*contd*
　foster-care relief—*contd*
　　alternative calculation of profits—
　　　application of provisions, **44(3)**, [832]
　　　election for, **44(3)**, [835]
　　　income not otherwise charged,
　　　　44(3), [834]
　　　periods of account not ending on 5th
　　　　April, **44(3)**, [840]
　　　trading income, **44(3)**, [833]
　　amount per child, **44(3)**, [828]
　　capital allowances—
　　　carried forward unrelieved qualifying
　　　　expenditure, **44(3)**, [842]
　　　definitions, **44(3)**, [841]
　　　excluded capital expenditure,
　　　　44(3), [843]–[844]
　　full—
　　　application of provisions, **44(3)**, [829]
　　　income not otherwise charged,
　　　　44(3), [831]
　　　trading income, **44(3)**, [830]
　　individual's limit, **44(3)**, [825]–[828]
　　means of providing care, **44(3)**, [823]
　　overlap profit, **44(3)**, [845]
　　overview of provisions, **44(3)**, [820]
　　periods of account not ending on 5th
　　　April, **44(3)**, [837]–[840]
　　person qualifying for, **44(3)**, [821]
　　providing care, meaning, **44(3)**, [823]
　　receipts—
　　　meaning, **44(3)**, [822]
　　　total, calculation of, **44(3)**, [824]
　　　trading income, from, **44(3)**, [23]
　　transitional provisions, **44(3)**, [912]
　fostering, meaning, **6**, [451]
　inspection of premises, **6**, [384], [638]
　limit in number of children—
　　appeals, **6**, [452]
　　exceeding, effect of, **6**, [451]
　　usual, **6**, [451]
　local authority—
　　placing children with, **6**, [441]
　　regulation of exercise of functions by,
　　　6, [639]
　meaning, **6**, [368]
　number of children permitted, **6**, [451]
　offences and penalties, **6**, [387]
　payments to, **6**, [1], [961]
　placing child with, powers, **6**, [323], [441]
　private fostering—
　　advertisements, prohibition, **6**, [452]
　　appeals arising, **6**, [452]
　　consent to, **6**, [385]
　　disqualified, **6**, [385]
　　fostering child privately, meaning, **6**, [383]
　　generally, **6**, [1]
　　local authority's powers and duties,
　　　6, [386], [452]
　　prohibition, powers as to, **6**, [386]
　　unsatisfactory, **6**, [384]
　privately fostered child—
　　appeals arising, **6**, [452]
　　exemptions, **6**, [452]
　　imposition of requirements, **6**, [452]

foster parents and fostering—*contd*
　privately fostered child—*contd*
　　inspection of premises, Secretary of State's
　　　powers, **6**, [409]
　　life insurance, avoidance, **6**, [452]
　　meaning, **6**, [383]
　　notification, **6**, [452]
　　regulations, **6**, [383]
　　school children during holidays, **6**, [452]
　　visitation, **6**, [384]
　　welfare, **6**, [384]
　　when not regarded as, **6**, [383], [452]
　refuge for child at risk, as, **6**, [368]
　registration scheme—
　　power to establish, **6**, [957]–[959]
　　regulations, period allowed for, **6(S)**, 472
　regulated activity, **6(S)**, 223–4
　siblings, **6**, [451]
　transitional provisions, **6**, [454]; **35(2)**, [364]
　usual fostering limit, **6**, [451]
　voluntary organisation, placing children by,
　　6, [375]

foundation bodies
　further education corporation, transfer of
　　property to, **15(1)**, [399]

foundation school
　admissions—
　　ability, restriction on selection by,
　　　15(2), [774]
　　code for, **15(2)**, [775]
　　pupil banding, **15(2)**, [775]
　alterations to, **15(2)**, [754]–[755]
　　proposals—
　　　implementation of, **15(2)**, [760]
　　　interested bodies, rights of, **15(2)**, [759]
　　　restriction on publication of,
　　　　15(2), [756]–[757]
　　　restrictions on, **15(2)**, [764]
　charity trustees, Secretary of State's powers in
　　relation to, **15(2)**, [25]
　collective worship—
　　exceptions and special arrangements,
　　　15(2), [59]
　　requirements, **15(2)**, [58], [159]
　concern, causing—
　　closure of school, **15(2)**, [788]
　　governing body—
　　　additional governors, appointment of,
　　　　15(2), [787]
　　　interim executive members, consisting
　　　　of, **15(2)**, [790], [905]
　　intervention—
　　　eligible for, **15(2)**, [780]–[782]
　　　LEA, by, **15(2)**, [783]–[786]
　　　Secretary of State, by,
　　　　15(2), [787]–[789]
　conditions for, **15(2)**, [24]
　discontinuance—
　　disposal of land on, **15(2)**, [64],
　　　[163]–[167], [771], [902]–[903]
　　further provisions, **15(2)**, [35]
　　notice by governing body, **15(2)**, [32]

foundation school—*contd*
discontinuance—*contd*
proposals for, **15(2)**, [31], [144]–[148], [751], [897]–[898]
restrictions on, **15(2)**, [764]
establishment or alteration, proposals for, **15(2)**, [29], [30], [35], [144]–[148]
foundation—
governors, reduction in—
implementation, **15(2)**, [763]
procedure, **15(2)**, [762]
proposals for, **15(2)**, [761]
removal of—
implementation, **15(2)**, [763]
procedure, **15(2)**, [762]
proposals for, **15(2)**, [761]
requirements as to, **15(2)**, [769]
funding, **15(2)**, [139], [141]
governing body—
exemption order from education legislation requirements—
application for, **15(2)**, [342]
generally, **15(2)**, [340]
revocation of, **15(2)**, [341]
variation of, **15(2)**, [341]
general duties of, **15(2)**, [773]
individual pupils' performance, provision of information about, **15(1)**, [671]
information, power of Secretary of State to require, **15(1)**, [670]
provision of information to Secretary of State, **15(1)**, [673]
teaching services for day nurseries, provision of, **15(1)**, [669]
governors as ex officio trustees, **15(2)**, [72]
new—
establishment of—
consultation on, **15(2)**, [745]
notices as to, **15(2)**, [745]
premises, provision of, **15(2)**, [900]
proposals for, **15(2)**, [897]
adjudicator, consideration by, **15(2)**, [898]
implementation of, **15(2)**, [899]
invitations for, **15(2)**, [743], [897]
local authority, consideration by, **15(2)**, [898]
publication of, **15(2)**, [746], [747]
relevant LEA, outside area of, **15(2)**, [749]
restrictions on, **15(2)**, [764]
parent councils, **15(2)**, [362]
religious character, teachers at schools with, **15(2)**, [53], [772]
religious education, duty to secure provision of, **15(2)**, [57]
religious opinions of staff, **15(2)**, [52]
religious worship, sixth form pupils excused from attendance at, **15(2)**, [777]
significant improvement, requiring, **15(2)**, [781]
special measures, requiring, **15(2)**, [782]
staffing, **15(2)**, [377], [526]
types of, **15(2)**, [21]

foundation special school
alterations to, **15(2)**, [754]–[755]
restrictions on, **15(2)**, [764]
charity trustees, Secretary of State's powers in relation to, **15(2)**, [25]
concern, causing—
closure of school, **15(2)**, [788]
governing body—
additional governors, appointment of, **15(2)**, [787]
interim executive members, consisting of, **15(2)**, [790], [905]
intervention—
eligible for, **15(2)**, [780]–[782]
LEA, by, **15(2)**, [783]–[786]
Secretary of State, by, **15(2)**, [787]–[789]
conditions for, **15(2)**, [24]
discontinuance—
consultation on, **15(2)**, [752]
direction requiring, **15(2)**, [753]
disposal of land on, **15(2)**, [771], [902]–[903]
proposals for, **15(2)**, [751], [897]–[898]
restrictions on, **15(2)**, [764]
foundation—
governors, reduction in—
implementation, **15(2)**, [763]
procedure, **15(2)**, [762]
proposals for, **15(2)**, [761]
removal of—
implementation, **15(2)**, [763]
procedure, **15(2)**, [762]
proposals for, **15(2)**, [761]
requirements as to, **15(2)**, [769]
governing body, general duties of, **15(2)**, [773]
new—
establishment of—
consultation on, **15(2)**, [745]
premises, provision of, **15(2)**, [900]
proposals, publication of, **15(2)**, [747]
proposals for, **15(2)**, [897]
adjudicator, consideration by, **15(2)**, [898]
implementation of, **15(2)**, [899]
local authority, consideration by, **15(2)**, [898]
relevant LEA, outside area of, **15(2)**, [749]
restrictions on, **15(2)**, [764]
parent councils, **15(2)**, [362]
significant improvement, requiring, **15(2)**, [781]
special measures, requiring, **15(2)**, [782]

foxes
destruction in rabies infected area, **2**, [450]

franked investment income
insurance company, of, **44(1)**, [260]
meaning, **44(1)**, [615]

fraud
abuse of position, by, **12(4)**, [198]

fraud—*contd*
administration of estates, in, **18**, [531]
agricultural charge, in creation of, **1(1)**, [308]
anti-fraud organisation—
   disclosure of information by public
     authority to, **12(4)**, [425]
      code of practice, **12(4)**, [428]
      data matching, **12(4)**, [454], [455]
      data protection rules, **12(4)**, [429]
      further disclosure, offence, **12(4)**, [426],
       [427]
     meaning, **12(4)**, [425]
articles for use in—
   making or supplying, **12(4)**, [201]
   meaning, **12(4)**, [202]
   possession or control of, **12(4)**, [200]
benefit, local authority power to prosecute,
   40(1), [608]
cabman, defrauding of, **36**, [570]
conspiracy to defraud, **12(1)**, [1070]
credit obtained by, **4(2)**, [11]
creditors, against, **4(2)**, [243], [249]
evidence relating to, **12(4)**, [207]
failing to disclose information, by,
   12(4), [197]
false representation, by, **12(4)**, [196]
fraudulent business, participation in—
   company, carried on by, **12(4)**, [204]
   sole trader, carried on by, **12(4)**, [203]
friendly society matters, in, **19(1)**, [536]
gain and loss, reference to, **12(4)**, [199]
health in pregnancy grant, as to, **40(1)**, [728]
insolvency, in, **4(2)**, [510]–[512]
limitation of actions, postponement in case
   of, **19(3)**, [762]
offence of, **12(4)**, [195]
offences by company, liability of officer for,
   12(4), [206]
prevention and verification, supply of
   information for—
     government, **40(1)**, [624]
     tax authorities, held by, **40(1)**, [621]
punishment for, **12(4)**, [195]
serious or complex. *See* **serious or complex
   fraud**
services, obtaining dishonestly, **12(4)**, [205]
solicitor, conviction for **11(2)**, [291];
   11(4), [386]
stamp duty, in relation to, **41**, [10], [21]
stamps, adhesive, in relation to, **41**, [21]
transitional provisions and savings,
   12(4), [212]
winding up, in, **4(2)**, [242]

fraudulent trading
offence of, **8(1)**, [1071]

freebench
abolition, **18**, [548]

freedom of information
code of practice—
   consultation, **7(1)**, [646]
   contents of, **7(1)**, [646]
   Lord Chancellor, issue by, **7(1)**, [647]

freedom of information—*contd*
code of practice—*contd*
   Secretary of state, issue by, **7(1)**, [646]
defamatory matter, **7(1)**, [675]
definitions, **7(1)**, [680]
enactments prohibiting disclosure, power to
   amend or repeal, **7(1)**, [670]
environmental information, **7(1)**, [640], [669]
exemptions—
   administrations within UK, prejudicing,
     7(1), [629]
   audit functions, concerning, **7(1)**, [634]
   bodies dealing with security matters,
     concerning, **7(1)**, [624], [626]
   commercial interests, **7(1)**, [644]
   conduct of public affairs, prejudicing,
     7(1), [637]
   confidence, information provided in,
     7(1), [642]
   cost of compliance exceeding appropriate
     limit, **7(1)**, [613]
   court records, **7(1)**, [633]
   Crown, communications with, **7(1)**, [638]
   defence, prejudicing, **7(1)**, [627]
   economy, prejudicing, **7(1)**, [630]
   effect of, **7(1)**, [603]
   environmental information, **7(1)**, [640]
   formulation of government policy, relating
     to, **7(1)**, [636]
   future publication, intended for, **7(1)**, [623]
   health and safety, endangering, **7(1)**, [639]
   honours, as to, **7(1)**, [638]
   information accessible by other means,
     7(1), [622]
   international relations, prejudicing,
     7(1), [628]
   investigations and proceedings, for,
     7(1), [631]
   law enforcement, prejudicing, **7(1)**, [632]
   legal professional privilege, **7(1)**, [643]
   national security, safeguarding, **7(1)**, [625],
     [626]
     certificate, appeal against, **7(1)**, [661]
   parliamentary privilege, **7(1)**, [635]
   personal information, **7(1)**, [641]
   prohibition on disclosure, **7(1)**, [645]
   trade secrets, **7(1)**, [644]
general note, **7(1)**, [1]
government departments, treatment of,
   7(1), [677]
historical records—
   discretionary disclosure, refusal of,
     7(1), [666]
   exempt information, not, **7(1)**, [664], [665]
   meaning, **7(1)**, [663]
orders and regulations, **7(1)**, [678]
public authorities—
   additions to schedule, **7(1)**, [605]
   advice and assistance, duty to provide,
     7(1), [617]
   alteration of records to prevent disclosure,
     7(1), [673]
   audit functions, **7(1)**, [634]
   companies, publicly-owned, **7(1)**, [607]

freedom of information—*contd*
  public authorities—*contd*
    decision notice—
      appeal against, **7(1)**, [658]
      duty to comply with, exceptions from,
        7(1), [654]
      failure to comply with, **7(1)**, [655]
      service of, **7(1)**, [651]
    designation, power of, **7(1)**, [606]
    enforcement notice—
      appeal against, **7(1)**, [658]
      duty to comply with, exceptions from,
        7(1), [654]
      failure to comply with, **7(1)**, [655]
      service of, **7(1)**, [653]
    existing powers, saving for, **7(1)**, [674]
    general right of access to information held
      by, **7(1)**, [602]
    good practice, recommendations as to,
      7(1), [649]
    information notice—
      appeal against, **7(1)**, [658]
      failure to comply with, **7(1)**, [655]
      service of, **7(1)**, [652]
    investigations and proceedings, information
      relating to, **7(1)**, [631]
    limited application of provisions,
      7(1), [608]
    meaning, **7(1)**, [604]
    publication schemes—
      adoption and maintenance of,
        7(1), [620]
      approval of, **7(1)**, [620]
      contents of, **7(1)**, [620]
      model, **7(1)**, [621]
    request for information. *See* request for
      information *below*
    right of action against, **7(1)**, [657]
    schedule of, **7(1)**, [685]–[691]
    Welsh, meaning, **7(1)**, [679]
  repeals, **7(1)**, [695]–[697]
  request for information—
    communication, means of, **7(1)**, [612]
    cost of compliance exceeding appropriate
      limit—
        exemption, **7(1)**, [613]
        fees for disclosure, **7(1)**, [614]
    fees, **7(1)**, [610]
    meaning, **7(1)**, [609]
    Public Record Office, public records
      transferred to, **7(1)**, [616], [667]
    refusal of, **7(1)**, [618]
    repeated, **7(1)**, [615]
    time for compliance with, **7(1)**, [611]
    vexatious, **7(1)**, [615]
  Scotland, provisions applying, **7(1)**, [676]

freehold land
  registration of. *See* **land registration**
  satisfied term of years, **20**, [629]

freemen
  honorary, **25(2)**, [212]
  rights etc of, **25(2)**, [211]

freezing order
  amending orders, power to make, **12(3)**, [82]
  compensation for, **12(3)**, [159]
  conditions for, **12(3)**, [75]
  contents of, **12(3)**, [76]
  Crown, binding, **12(3)**, [86]
  de-hybridisation of, **12(3)**, [84]
  duration, **12(3)**, [79]
  evidence for use abroad, in respect of—
    power to make, **12(3)**, [573]
    revocation, **12(3)**, [575]
    sending, **12(3)**, [574]
    variation, **12(3)**, [575]
  funds, **12(3)**, [159]
  information and documents, **12(3)**, [159]
  licences, **12(3)**, [159]
  meaning, **12(3)**, [76]
  nationals and residence, meaning, **12(3)**, [80]
  offences, **12(3)**, [159]
  overseas—
    certificate accompanying, **12(3)**, [583]
    consideration by court, **12(3)**, [584]
    evidence seized under—
      release of, **12(3)**, [588]
      retention of, **12(3)**, [587]
    giving effect to, **12(3)**, [585]
    making **12(3)**, [583]
    meaning, **12(3)**, [583]
    postponed effect, **12(3)**, [586]
    warrants, powers under, **12(3)**, [589]
  power to make, **12(3)**, [75]
  procedure for making, **12(3)**, [81]
  property—
    application for, **12(3)**, [336]
    conditions for making, **12(3)**, [336]
    exclusions from, **12(3)**, [338]
    legal expenses, exclusion of, **12(3)**, [390]
      regulations, **12(3)**, [391]
    meaning, **12(3)**, [336]
    proceedings and remedies, restriction on,
      12(3), [339]
    receives, **12(3)**, [340]–[342]
    setting aside, **12(3)**, [337]
    variation, **12(3)**, [337]
  reasons, giving, **12(3)**, [159]
  review of, **12(3)**, [78]
  revocation of, **12(3)**, [83]
  terrorist property, **12(3)**, [621]

Freightliners Limited
  controlling interest, transfer of, **36**, [967]

frequencies. *See* **independent television;**
radio services

freshwater fisheries
  close season and close time—
    byelaws, **1(2)**, [44]
    eels, for, **1(2)**, [19]
    fixed engine, removal during, **1(2)**, [20]
    freshwater fish, for, **1(2)**, [19], [44]
    offences, **1(2)**, [19]
    putts and pitchers, for, **1(2)**, [19]
    rainbow trout, for, **1(2)**, [19], [44]
    salmon, for, **1(2)**, [19], [44]

freshwater fisheries—*contd*
  close season and close time—*contd*
    trout, for, **1(2)**, [19], [44]
  compensation arising, **1(2)**, [18]
  dam—
    boxes and cribs in, use of, **1(2)**, [16]
    damage to, **1(2)**, [18]
    destruction of, **1(2)**, [5]
    fish pass, duty to make and maintain,
      1(2), [9]
    meaning, **1(2)**, [41]
    salmon or trout, obstructing, **1(2)**, [8]
    Severn navigation, provisions on, **1(2)**, [40]
  designated area—
    authority to remove fish, **1(1)**, [350]
    power to designate, **1(1)**, [348]
    removal of fish, direction for, **1(1)**, [349]
  diseases of fish—
    notices, **1(1)**, [356]
    prevention of spreading, **1(1)**, [348]
    See also infected waters *below*
  eels—
    annual close season, **1(2)**, [19]
    baskets, prohibition on use, **1(2)**, [21]
    licence, **1(2)**, [25]
  eggs of fish, importation restriction,
    1(1), [347]
  electrical device, using, **1(2)**, [5]
  Environment Agency—
    additional constables, requiring, **1(2)**, [46]
    byelaws, close seasons and times, as to,
      1(2), [44]
    compensation, paying, **1(2)**, [18]
    fish pass, constructing or altering,
      1(2), [10], [18]
    land, entry on, **1(2)**, [31]
    legal proceedings, taking, **1(2)**, [46]
    screens, use of to limit movements of
      salmon and trout, **1(2)**, [15]
    suspected premises, entry on, **1(2)**, [32]
  Esk river, application of provisions to,
    1(2), [39]
  examination of waters, **1(1)**, [354]
  explosives, using, **1(2)**, [5]
  firearm, prohibition of use, **1(2)**, [1]
  fish farming. *See under* **fish**
  fish pass or free gap—
    constructing and altering, **1(2)**, [10]
    duty to make and maintain, **1(2)**, [9]
    injury to—
      penalty, **1(2)**, [12]
      repair of, **1(2)**, [10]
    Minister, approval or consent of, **1(2)**, [11]
    notice of application for, **1(2)**, [18]
    obstructing, **1(2)**, [12]
  fish roe, using for bait, **1(2)**, [2]
  fishery board—
    infected waters, powers on suspecting,
      1(1), [351]
    meaning, **1(1)**, [359]
  fishing licence. *See* licence *below*
  fishing mill dam—
    box or crib in, **1(2)**, [16]
    meaning, **1(2)**, [41]
    passing of fish, obstructing, **1(2)**, [8]

freshwater fisheries—*contd*
  fishing mill dam—*contd*
    salmon or trout, taking in, **1(2)**, [8]
  fishing weir—
    box or crib in, **1(2)**, [16]
    meaning, **1(2)**, [41]
    passage of fish, obstructing, **1(2)**, [8]
    salmon or trout, taking in, **1(2)**, [7]
  fixed engine—
    close season, removal during, **1(2)**, [20]
    meaning, **1(2)**, [41]
    salmon or trout, using to take, **1(2)**, [6],
      [405]
    unauthorised, use of, **1(2)**, [6]
  flood-gate, destroying, **1(2)**, [5]
  freshwater fish—
    annual close season, **1(2)**, [19], [44]
    meaning, **1(1)**, [359]
  gaff, use of, **1(2)**, [1]
  illegal night fishing, arrest for, **1(2)**, [33]
  immature fish, taking, **1(2)**, [2]
  implements prohibited in taking etc fish,
    1(2), [1]
  importation, restrictions on, **1(1)**, [347]
  infected fish, meaning, **1(1)**, [359], [361]
  infected waters—
    agents, authority of, **1(1)**, [356]
    designated area, as, **1(1)**, [348]
    entry and inspection, powers of,
      1(1), [355]
    examination of on suspicion, **1(1)**, [355]
    fish, eggs or foodstuff taken into or out of,
      1(1), [352]
    fishery board suspecting, powers on,
      1(1), [351]
    inland, **1(1)**, [352]
    inspector, powers of, **1(1)**, [355]
    meaning, **1(1)**, [359]
    notice served on occupier, **1(1)**, [352]
    notices, service of, **1(1)**, [356]
    preliminary precautions—
      inland waters, **1(1)**, [352]
      marine waters **1(1)**, [353]
    samples of fish, taking, **1(1)**, [355]
    suspicion of, reporting, **1(1)**, [352]
  inland waters, introduction of fish into,
    1(2), [29]
  killing of fish—
    immature fish, **1(2)**, [2]
    prohibited implements, **1(2)**, [1]
    unclean fish, **1(2)**, [2]
  legal proceedings, power of taking,
    1(1), [162], [357]
  licence—
    duty on, **1(2)**, [45]
    exclusive right, for, **1(2)**, [25]
    fishing without, **1(2)**, [27]
    forfeiture or surrender, **1(2)**, [48]
    general, **1(2)**, [25]
    grant of, **1(2)**, [25], [45]
    importation of fish and eggs, for,
      1(1), [347]
    instruments for fishing, for use of,
      1(2), [25]
    limitation of, **1(2)**, [26]

freshwater fisheries—*contd*
licence—*contd*
matters provided for in, **1(2)**, [25]
name and address entered on, **1(2)**, [45]
production of, power to require, **1(2)**, [34]
rearing, for, **1(2)**, [28]
regulations on, powers to make, **1(1)**, [358]
salmon and trout, regulation of fishing for,
1(2), [25]
servant or agent of holder, person being,
1(2), [45]
temporary, **1(2)**, [45]
light, use of in taking fish, **1(2)**, [1]
live fish, importation restriction, **1(1)**, [347]
meaning, **1(1)**, [359]
mill race, salmon or trout, taking in,
1(2), [17]
nets—
limitation, **1(2)**, [3]
mesh, size of, **1(2)**, [3]
salmon, review of use of, **1(2)**, [406]
night, illegal fishing by, **1(2)**, [33]
noxious substance, using, **1(2)**, [5]
offences—
exclusions, **1(2)**, [178], [190]
fish farming, exemptions for, **1(2)**, [190]
fixed penalty notice for, **1(2)**, [37]
forfeiture of fish, **1(2)**, [48]
importation of fish and eggs, **1(1)**, [347]
legal proceedings, **1(1)**, [357]
obstruction, **1(2)**, [18]
penalties, **1(1)**, [357]
procedure, **1(2)**, [48]
prosecution of, **1(2)**, [36], [47]
punishment of, **1(2)**, [47]
otter lath or jack, prohibition of use, **1(2)**, [1]
passage of fish, obstructing—
fish pass. *See* fish pass *above*
fishing mill dam, by, **1(2)**, [8]
fishing weir, by, **1(2)**, [7]
fixed engine, by, **1(2)**, [6]
poison, using, **1(2)**, [5]
poisonous matter, putting in waters, **1(2)**, [4]
polluting effluent, putting in waters, **1(2)**, [4]
prohibited implements, **1(2)**, [1]
rainbow trout, annual close season, **1(2)**, [19],
[44]
regulations, power to make, **1(1)**, [358]
roe, using for bait, **1(2)**, [2]
salmon—
annual close season, **1(2)**, [19], [44]
boxes and cribs, use in taking of, **1(2)**, [16]
byelaws as to, **1(2)**, [405]
consignment of, marking, **1(2)**, [24]
deal, meaning, **1(2)**, [403]
dealers, licensing of, **1(2)**, [403]
export, prohibitions on, **1(2)**, [23]
fishing, restriction on, **1(1)**, [738]
handling in suspicious circumstances,
1(2), [404]
importation, restriction on, **1(1)**, [347]
licence to fish, **1(2)**, [25]
meaning, **1(2)**, [405], [407]
nets—
review of use of, **1(2)**, [406]

freshwater fisheries—*contd*
salmon—*contd*
nets—*contd*
use of, **1(2)**, [3]
packaging, marking, **1(2)**, [24]
sale, when prohibited, **1(2)**, [22]
suspicious circumstances, handling in,
1(2), [404]
unlicensed dealer, purchasing from,
1(2), [403]
water bailiff, powers, **1(2)**, [404]
weekly close time, **1(2)**, [19], [44]
screens—
meaning, **1(2)**, [41]
movement of salmon and trout, limiting,
1(2), [15]
offences, **1(2)**, [14]
setline, prohibition of use, **1(2)**, [1]
Severn river, application of provisions to,
1(2), [40]
sluice, when to be kept shut, **1(2)**, [13]
Solway Firth, application of provisions to,
1(2), [39]
spawn, disturbing, **1(2)**, [2]
spawning fish, disturbing, **1(2)**, [2]
spear, prohibition of use, **1(2)**, 1]
stroke-haul or snatch, prohibition of use,
1(2), [1]
summary of provisions, **1(1)**, [124]
trout—
annual close season, **1(2)**, [19], [44]
boxes and cribs in taking of, **1(2)**, [16]
consignment of, marking, **1(2)**, [24]
export of, **1(2)**, [23]
fishing, restriction on, **1(1)**, [738]
licence, **1(2)**, [25]
meaning, **1(2)**, [41]
packaging, marking, **1(2)**, [24]
rainbow, close season for, **1(2)**, [19], [44]
sale, when prohibited, **1(2)**, [22]
weekly close time, **1(2)**, [19], [44]
Tweed River, application of provisions to,
1(2), [39]
unclean fish—
meaning, **1(2)**, [41]
taking, prohibition of, **1(2)**, [2]
unlicensed, **1(2)**, [27]
water bailiff—
constable, deemed to be, **1(2)**, [35]
examination, powers of, **1(2)**, [30]
fishing licence, requiring production of,
1(2), [34]
land, entry on, **1(2)**, [31]
obstruction of, **1(2)**, [30]
offences, fixed penalty notice for, **1(2)**, [37]
persons illegally fishing at night,
apprehending, **1(2)**, [33]
powers of, **1(2)**, [30], [404]
salmon, power as to, **1(2)**, [404]
seizure, powers of, **1(2)**, [30]
stop and search powers, **1(2)**, [30]
suspected premises, entry on, **1(2)**, [32]
works below high water mark, authorisation
of, **1(2)**, [38]

Friendly Societies Commission
inspections by—
  definitions, **19(1)**, [853]
  duties as to, **19(1)**, [853]
  powers, **19(1)**, [852]
  reports, **19(1)**, [853]
modification of provisions, order for, **19(1)**, [898]
orders and regulations, **19(1)**, [918]
transfer of functions of, **19(2)**, [409], [414]

friendly society
accounting records, **19(1)**, [854]
accounts—
  accountant's report, obtaining, **19(1)**, [480]
  appointed actuary, information on, **19(1)**, [878]
  approval and signing, **19(1)**, [877]
  audit—
    exempt societies, **19(1)**, [471]
    past years, of, **19(1)**, [482]
    requirements, **19(1)**, [467]
  auditor remuneration, disclosure of, **19(1)**, [867], [941]
  balance sheet, **19(1)**, [856]
  consistency, requirement for, **19(1)**, [863]
  employees, disclosures relating to, **19(1)**, [864], [938]
  group—
    balance sheet, **19(1)**, [860]
    contents and form of, **19(1)**, [861]
    duty to prepare, **19(1)**, [859]
    IAS, **19(1)**, [862]
    income and expenditure account, **19(1)**, [860]
  individual—
    contents and form of, **19(1)**, [857]
    duty to prepare, **19(1)**, [855]
    IAS, **19(1)**, [858]
    income and expenditure account, **19(1)**, [856]
  keeping of, **19(1)**, [467]
  laying and furnishing, **19(1)**, [879]
  members of committee of management, disclosures relating to, **19(1)**, [864], [937]
  off-balance-sheet arrangements, disclosures relating to, **19(1)**, [866]
  publication of, **19(1)**, [469]
  related undertakings, disclosures about, **19(1)**, [865], [939], [940]
  revenue, **19(1)**, [468]
  year of account, meaning, **19(1)**, [548]
activities of, **19(1)**, [923]
amalgamation, **19(1)**, [884]
  confirmation—
    application for, **19(1)**, [944]
    Authority, by, **19(1)**, [944]
    relevant requirements, failure to comply with, **19(1)**, [944]
  special resolution for, **19(1)**, [520]
    registration of, **19(1)**, [524]
  stamp duty land tax, exemption from, **19(1)**, [543], [901]
  statements relating to, **19(1)**, [943]
amended provisions, **43(S)**, 1167–8

friendly society—*contd*
annual returns—
  contents, **19(1)**, [486]
  copies, supply of, **19(1)**, [487]
  period covered, **19(1)**, [486]
  requirement, **19(1)**, [486]
  statement on, **19(1)**, [486]
annuity, societies assuring, **19(1)**, [449]
armed forces, protection of members joining, **19(1)**, [545]
associate, meaning of, **19(1)**, [916]
auditors—
  access to books, right of, **19(1)**, [479]
  appointment, **19(1)**, [870], [942]
    obligation, **19(1)**, [470], [472], [480]
    procedure, **19(1)**, [475]
    resolutions for, **19(1)**, [474]
    restrictions, **19(1)**, [477]
  cessation of office, duty to notify appropriate audit authority, **19(1)**, [942]
  eligibility, **19(1)**, [942]
  exempt societies, **19(1)**, [471]
  ineligibility, effect of, **19(1)**, [942]
  information, right to, **19(1)**, [876]
  meetings, attendance at, **19(1)**, [479], [876]
  no exemptions from liability, **19(1)**, [902]
  not re-appointed, rights of, **19(1)**, [942]
  partnership as, **19(1)**, [942]
  person ceasing to hold office, statement by, **19(1)**, [942]
  persons disqualified, **19(1)**, [477]
  qualifications, **19(1)**, [476], [870]
  re-appointment, **19(1)**, [473]
  recognised supervisory body, not required to be member of, **19(1)**, [942]
  regulations as to, **19(1)**, [470]
  removal, **19(1)**, [473], [942]
  removed, rights of, **19(1)**, [942]
  remuneration, **19(1)**, [483], [942]
  remuneration, disclosure of, **19(1)**, [867]
  report by, **19(1)**, [478]
    contents of, **19(1)**, [871]
    laying and furnishing, **19(1)**, [879]
    names to be stated in published or filed copies of, **19(1)**, [874], [875]
    signature, **19(1)**, [872]
      senior statutory auditor, of, **19(1)**, [873]
  resignation, **19(1)**, [942]
  second audit, power to require, **19(1)**, [942]
  tenure, **19(1)**, [870]
balance sheets—
  copies, supply of, **19(1)**, [488]
  display of, **19(1)**, [488]
  falsification, **19(1)**, [537]
  general provisions, **19(1)**, [468]
  offences as to, **19(1)**, [468]
  publication of, **19(1)**, [469]
  true and fair view, **19(1)**, [468]
benefits—
  group insurance business, **19(1)**, [509]
  provision of, **19(1)**, [510]
benevolent societies. *See* **benevolent societies**

friendly society—*contd*

books—
  inspection by members, **19(1)**, [506]
  keeping, duties as to, **19(1)**, [467]
  production, inspector's powers, **19(1)**, [526]
branches—
  conversion of society into, **19(1)**, [523]
  dissolution. *See* dissolution *below*
  expelled, use of name by, **19(1)**, [453]
  meaning, **19(1)**, [548]
  new, establishment, **19(1)**, [451]
  registration—
    acknowledgement, **19(1)**, [454]
    appeals, **19(1)**, [455]
    applications, **19(1)**, [450]
    generally, **19(1)**, [448]
    restrictions, **19(1)**, [448]
    separate societies, as, **19(1)**, [452]
  rules. *See* rules *below*
  seceding, use of name by, **19(1)**, [453]
business review, requirement for, **19(1)**, [869]
Channel Islands—
  application of provisions, **19(1)**, [550], [921]
  contracts of insurance, **19(1)**, [614]
  legal representative in, payments to, **19(1)**, [551]
charities, contributions to, **19(1)**, [495]
chief executive—
  appointment, **19(1)**, [839]
  requirement of, **19(1)**, [839]
Chief Registrar, regulated societies, powers as to. *See* regulated *below*
children under 10, insurance of lives of, **19(1)**, [896]
combinations of business, restriction of, **19(1)**, [842]
commencement of proceedings, time limit for, **19(1)**, [903]
committee of management—
  Authority, notification of officers to, **19(1)**, [840]
  chairman, **19(1)**, [838]
  disclosures relating to, **19(1)**, [864]
  members, **19(1)**, [838]
    age, notice of, **19(1)**, [934]
    date of election, **19(1)**, [934]
    dealings with, **19(1)**, [935]
    eligibility, **19(1)**, [934]
    retirement, **19(1)**, [934]
    no exemptions from liability, **19(1)**, [902]
    offences, **19(1)**, [904]
    report on affairs by, **19(1)**, [868]
    laying and furnishing, **19(1)**, [879]
company, conversion of society into, **19(1)**, [521], [890]
  confirmation—
    application for, **19(1)**, [944]
    Authority, by, **19(1)**, [944]
    relevant requirements, failure to comply with, **19(1)**, [944]
    statements relating to, **19(1)**, [943]
company law, assimilation of, **19(1)**, [897]
compensation for loss of office, **19(1)**, [891]

friendly society—*contd*

contributions to charities and other societies, **19(1)**, [495]
controllers, supervision of, **19(1)**, [846]
conversion—
  branch, into, **19(1)**, [523]
  company, into, **19(1)**, [521], [944]
  industrial and provident society, to, **19(1)**, [522], [558]
death—
  payments on—
    devolution, **19(1)**, [513]
    illegitimacy of member, **19(1)**, [513]
    nominee. *See* nomination *below*
definitions, **19(1)**, [915]
disputes—
  appeals to High Court. *See* **High Court**
  arbitration, determination by, **19(1)**, [881]
  court, reference to, **19(1)**, [515]
  decision of, generally, **19(1)**, [515]
  discovery of documents, **19(1)**, [516]
  loans of surplus funds, arising from, **19(1)**, [883]
  loans, arising out of, **19(1)**, [518]
  meaning, **19(1)**, [515], [881]
  rules, settlement under, **19(1)**, [515]
  statement of case in respect of, **19(1)**, [516]
disqualification orders, **8**, 855
dissolution—
  annuities, protection, **19(1)**, [529]
  award, by, **19(1)**, [529], [531]–[533]
  consent to, **19(1)**, [529]
  distribution of funds on, **19(1)**, [529], [533]
  effective date, **19(1)**, [531]
  finality of award, **19(1)**, [533]
  instrument of, **19(1)**, [530]
  notice of, **19(1)**, [531]
  setting aside, proceedings for, **19(1)**, [534]
  ways of, **19(1)**, [529]
distributions to, **43(1)**, [356]
division of funds, special provisions, **19(1)**, [449]
documents—
  deposit of, **19(1)**, [547]
  discovery of, **19(1)**, [516]
  evidence of, **19(1)**, [547]
  form of, **19(1)**, [910]
  stamp duty exemption, **19(1)**, [542], [900]
establishment generally, **19(1)**, [448]
exempt 'other' business, transfers of, **43(S)**, 1167–8
fees for inspection or copying of documents, **19(1)**, [541]
Financial Services Authority—
  cancellation or suspension of registration by, **19(1)**, [527]
  decision notices, **19(1)**, [847]
  dissolution of society, award, **19(1)**, [531]
  entry on premises, warrant for, **19(1)**, [849]
  functions of, **19(1)**, [1], [815]
  information, powers to obtain, **19(1)**, [848]
  inspectors, appointment by, **19(1)**, [526]
  investigations on behalf of, **19(1)**, [851]

friendly society—*contd*
  Financial Services Authority—*contd*
    notices from, **19(1)**, [847]
    notification of officers to, **19(1)**, [840]
    second audit, power to require,
      19(1), [942]
    transfer of engagements—
      alteration of requirements, **19(1)**, [888]
      power to effect, **19(1)**, [889]
    warning notices, **19(1)**, [847]
    winding-up petition by, **19(1)**, [525], [843]
  financial year, **19(1)**, [914]
  first-time house buyers, assistance to,
    22, [325]
  fraud, punishment of, **19(1)**, [536]
  funds—
    distribution on dissolution, **19(1)**, [529],
      [533]
    investment of, **19(1)**, [489]
    surplus, disputes arising out of loans of,
      19(1), [518]
  government securities, purchase of,
    19(1), [490]
  group insurance business—
    carrying on, **19(1)**, [509]
    meaning, **19(1)**, [509]
    supervision of, **19(1)**, [845]
  housing associations, investment in,
    19(1), [494]
  incorporated—
    additional activities, **19(1)**, [926]
    assets of, **44(1)**, [313]
    assured members, loans to, **19(1)**, [828]
    benefits, terms of, **19(1)**, [829]
    bodies corporate—
      assistance to, **19(1)**, [827]
      control of, **19(1)**, [824], [928]
      offences, **19(1)**, [904]
    capacity, **19(1)**, [816]
    contracts, making, **19(1)**, [927]
    dissolution—
      consent, by, **19(1)**, [831]
      modes of, **19(1)**, [830]
      void, declared, **19(1)**, [836]
      winding up, after, **19(1)**, [933]
    documents, execution of, **19(1)**, [927]
    establishment, **19(1)**, [816], [924]
    exemption, qualifying for, **44(1)**, [305]
    funds, investment of, **19(1)**, [825]
    general note, **19(1)**, [1]
    Government Securities, funds for purchase
      of, **19(1)**, [926]
    group insurance business, **19(1)**, [822]
    housing associations, investment of funds
      in, **19(1)**, [926]
    interest in property, transfer or grant of,
      19(1), [820]
    land, holding, **19(1)**, [826]
    meaning, **19(1)**, [912]; **44(1)**, [305]
    members—
      nominations by, **19(1)**, [929]
      records, inspection of, **19(1)**, [924]
      register of, **19(1)**, [924]
      winding up, as contributories in,
        19(1), [931]

friendly society—*contd*
  incorporated—*contd*
    memorandum—
      alteration of, **19(1)**, [924]
      effect of, **19(1)**, [819]
      requirements of, **19(1)**, [924]
    purposes and powers of, **19(1)**, [818]
    qualifying status, withdrawal of,
      44(1), [307]
    registration, cancellation of, **19(1)**, [837]
    reinsurance business, **19(1)**, [823]
    requirements for, **19(1)**, [924]
    rules—
      alteration of, **19(1)**, [924]
      copies, supply of, **19(1)**, [924]
      effect of, **19(1)**, [820]
      requirements of, **19(1)**, [924]
    separate loan fund, loans from, **19(1)**, [926]
    social and benevolent activities,
      19(1), [821]
    subscriptions, **19(1)**, [926]
    subsidiaries—
      assistance to, **19(1)**, [827]
      control of, **19(1)**, [824], [928]
      supervision of activities, **19(1)**, [844]
    surplus contributions, accumulation of,
      19(1), [926]
    taxation, **44(1)**, [306]
    winding up—
      Authority, petition by, **19(1)**, [843]
      contributories, members as, **19(1)**, [931]
      court, by, **19(1)**, [833], [931]
      dissolution after, **19(1)**, [933]
      High court, by, **19(1)**, [932]
      insolvency rules and fees, application of,
        19(1), [933]
      legislation, application of, **19(1)**, [834],
        [930]
      long term business, continuation of,
        19(1), [835]
      modes of, **19(1)**, [830]
      penal provisions, **19(1)**, [931]
      preferential debts, **19(1)**, [931]
      voluntary, **19(1)**, [832], [931]
  incorporation—
    members, rights of, **42**, [1352]
    subsequent disposal of assets, **42**, [1353]
    transfer of assets on, **42**, [1351]
  industrial and provident society, conversion
    to, **19(1)**, [522], [558]
  industrial assurance. *See* **industrial assurance**
  information—
    auditor's right to, **19(1)**, [876]
    disclosure, **19(1)**, [850]
    entry on premises to obtain, **19(1)**, [849]
    powers to obtain, **19(1)**, [848]
    social security, for purposes of, **19(1)**, [911]
  inspection—
    costs, security for, **19(1)**, [526]
    definitions, **19(1)**, [853]
    duties as to, **19(1)**, [853]
    powers, **19(1)**, [852]
    reports, **19(1)**, [853]
  inspectors, appointment, **19(1)**, [526]

friendly society—*contd*

insurance—
  contracts, validation of, **19(1)**, [612]
  definitions, **19(1)**, [913]
  law, assimilation of, **19(1)**, [897]
  margins of solvency, actuary's report,
    19(1), [886]
insurance business of, **42**, [499]
insurance company, transfer to—
  commencement, **43(S)**, 663
  exempt life or endowment business,
    43(S), 660–1
  non-life or endowment exempt business,
    43(S), 661–3
investigations—
  Authority, on behalf of, **19(1)**, [851]
  body under, meaning, **19(1)**, [853]
  powers, **19(1)**, [852]
investments—
  consent to, **19(1)**, [489]
  government securities, in, **19(1)**, [490]
  housing associations, in, **19(1)**, [494]
Isle of Man—
  application of provisions, **19(1)**, [549],
    [921]
  contracts of insurance, **19(1)**, [614]
  legal representative in, payments to,
    19(1), [551]
land—
  meaning, **19(1)**, [548]
  power to hold, **19(1)**, [496]
  vesting of, **19(1)**, [497]
legal proceedings, conduct of, **19(1)**, [540]
legislation, **19(1)**, [1]
library or reading room maintained by,
  offences in, **13**, [80]–[83]
life assurance premium payable to,
  44(1), [642]
life or endowment business, **19(1)**, [612]
loans—
  disputes arising out of, **19(1)**, [518]
  members, to, **19(1)**, [491]
  other societies or branches, **19(1)**, [493]
  separate loan fund, from, **19(1)**, [492]
long-term business carried on by, **43(S)**, 1168
long term business, transfer, actuary's report
  on, **19(1)**, [887]
magistrates' courts in Northern Ireland,
  jurisdiction of, **19(1)**, [539]
manager, meaning, **19(2)**, [500]
maximum benefits, **19(1)**, [613]
meaning, **19(1)**, [1], [912]
meetings—
  annual general, **19(1)**, [936]
  auditors—
    attendance of, **19(1)**, [479]
    rights of, **19(1)**, [481]
  notice, **19(1)**, [936]
  poll, right to demand, **19(1)**, [936]
  special, calling of, **19(1)**, [526]
  special notice, resolutions requiring,
    19(1), [936]
  special resolutions, **19(1)**, [936]
  voting, **19(1)**, [936]

friendly society—*contd*

members—
  books, inspection of, by, **19(1)**, [506]
  complaints by, **19(1)**, [882]
  legal proceedings by, **19(1)**, [540]
  liability of, **19(1)**, [924]
  loans to, **19(1)**, [491]
  membership, **19(1)**, [924]
  minors as, **19(1)**, [504]
  register of, **19(1)**, [508]
  subscriptions—
    irrecoverable at law, **19(1)**, [505]
    surplus, accumulation of, **19(1)**, [507]
minor—
  as member, **19(1)**, [504]
  disqualification for office, **19(1)**, [465]
misrepresentation, punishment, **19(1)**, [536]
mortgages—
  discharge of, **19(1)**, [500], [501]
  receipt of, endorsement on, **19(1)**, [500],
    [556]
name—
  change of, **19(1)**, [519], [924]
  offences, **19(1)**, [924]
  requirements, **19(1)**, [924]
  seceding or expelled branch, use by,
    19(1), [453]
national insurance, provisions as to
  information, **19(1)**, [301], [544]
new, meaning, **44(1)**, [314]
nomination—
  amount, **19(1)**, [511]
  devolution when not made, **19(1)**, [513]
  illegitimacy of nominator, **19(1)**, [513]
  marriage, effect of, **19(1)**, [511]
  payment on death of nominator,
    19(1), [512]
  power to make, **19(1)**, [511]
  validity of payments, **19(1)**, [514]
  variation or revocation, **19(1)**, [511]
non-annual actuarial investigations,
  43(1), [405]
Northern Ireland—
  application of provisions, **19(1)**, [920]
  winding up—
    contributories, members as, **19(1)**, [932]
    penal provisions, **19(1)**, [932]
    preferential debts, **19(1)**, [932]
    voluntary, **19(1)**, [932]
  magistrates' courts' jurisdiction over,
    19(1), [906]
obsolete provisions, repeal of, **43(S)**, 1168
offences—
  balance sheet, falsification, **19(1)**, [537]
  bodies corporate, etc, by, **19(1)**, [904]
  costs, recovery, **19(1)**, [538]
  due diligence, defence of, **19(1)**, [905]
  evidence, **19(1)**, [907]
  fraud, punishment of, **19(1)**, [536]
  generally, **19(1)**, [535]
  magistrates' court jurisdiction in Northern
    Ireland, **19(1)**, [906]
  misapplication of property, **19(1)**, [536]
  misrepresentation, **19(1)**, [536]
  prosecution of, **19(1)**, [538]

friendly society—*contd*
  officers—
    appointment, proof of, **19(1)**, [466]
    bankruptcy, priority on, **19(1)**, [503]
    death of, priority on, **19(1)**, [503]
    execution against, priority on, **19(1)**, [503]
    legal proceedings, conduct of, **19(1)**, [540]
  old, business of, **44(1)**, [312]
  person assured resident outside UK and Isle of
    Man, **19(1)**, [557]
  PHI business, **43(S)**, 1167
  postal ballots, **19(1)**, [936]
  property—
    dealing in, **19(1)**, [496]
    devolution on death etc of trustee,
      19(1), [502]
    legal proceedings concerning, **19(1)**, [499]
    meaning, **19(1)**, [548]
    misapplied, recovery, **19(1)**, [536]
    vesting of, **19(1)**, [500]
  public file, **19(1)**, [899]
  Public Trustee, holding of securities by,
    19(1), [498]
  qualifying club, as, **19(3)**, [554]
  qualifying policies, **42**, [1071]; **43(1)**, [170]
  qualifying policy, **44(1)**, [644]
  records, **19(1)**, [908]
  registered—
    amalgamation, formed by, **44(1)**, [304],
      [314]
    company, conversion into, **44(1)**, [303],
      [304]
    incorporation, **19(1)**, [817]
      branches, effect on, **19(1)**, [925]
      consequences of transfer, **19(1)**, [925]
      definitions, **19(1)**, [925]
      effect of, **19(1)**, [925]
      schemes, **19(1)**, [925]
      treatment of assets after, **44(1)**, [313]
    life or endowment business—
      meaning, **44(1)**, [314]
      tax exempt, **44(1)**, [303]
        conditions for, **44(1)**, [309]
        meaning, **44(1)**, [314]
    long-term business, application of
      Corporation Tax Acts to, **44(1)**, [310]
    meaning, **19(1)**, [912]
    members—
      maximum benefit payable to,
        44(1), [311]
      statutory declaration, **44(1)**, [311]
    profits, taxation of, **44(1)**, [304]–[310]
    transfers of other business, **44(1)**, [308]
  registered office, change of, **19(1)**, [924]
  Registrars. *See* assistant registrars; Chief
    Registrar *above*
  registration—
    acknowledgement, **19(1)**, [454]
    branches. *See* branches *above*
    cancellation—
    cancellation—
      appeal against, **19(1)**, [528]
      Financial Services Authority's powers,
        19(1), [527]
      reasons for, **19(1)**, [527]

friendly society—*contd*
  registration—*contd*
    existing societies, **19(1)**, [892]
    generally, **19(1)**, [448]
    Northern Ireland, extension of provisions
      to, **19(1)**, [895]
    refusal, appeal against, **19(1)**, [455]
    restrictions on, **19(1)**, [448]
    suspension—
      appeal against, **19(1)**, [528]
      Financial Services Authority's powers,
        19(1), [527]
      reasons for, **19(1)**, [527]
    validation and ratification of actions,
      19(1), [893]
  Registry, transfer of functions, **19(2)**, [410],
    [414]
  regulations, power to make, **19(1)**, [546]
  reinsurance, **19(1)**, [463]
  resolutions—
    auditors, appointment etc of, **19(1)**, [474]
    special. *See* special resolution *below*
  revenue accounts, **19(1)**, [468]
  rules—
    amendments—
      registration of, **19(1)**, [457], [458]
        appeal from refusal of, **19(1)**, [459]
    binding nature of, **19(1)**, [461]
    conversion of society into branch, effect,
      19(1), [523]
    copies, supply, **19(1)**, [460]
    matters to be provided for, **19(1)**, [448],
      [554], [555]
    registration, **19(1)**, [456]
    reinsurance, provision for, **19(1)**, [463]
    special provisions in, **19(1)**, [462]
  secretary—
    appointment, **19(1)**, [839]
    requirement of, **19(1)**, [839]
  securities—
    government, purchase of, **19(1)**, [490]
    holding by Public Trustee, **19(1)**, [498]
  service of notices, **19(1)**, [909]
  social security, provisions as to information,
    19(1), [544]
  special meetings, **19(1)**, [852]
    calling, by Authority, **19(1)**, [526]
  special resolution—
    amalgamation, for, **19(1)**, [520]
      registration of, **19(1)**, [524]
    meaning, **19(1)**, [524]
    transfer of engagements, for, **19(1)**, [520]
  stamp duty exemption, **19(1)**, [542], [900]
  summary of provisions, **19(1)**, [1]
  tax exempt business, **43(S)**, 541
  termination. *See* dissolution *above*
  trade union, application of provisions to,
    16, [192]
  trade union, provision of information on
    claim for benefit from, **19(1)**, [301]
  transfer of engagement—
    Authority—
      alteration of requirements by,
        19(1), [888]
      power to effect, **19(1)**, [889]

friendly society—*contd*
transfer of engagement—*contd*
confirmation—
application for, **19(1)**, [944]
Authority, by, **19(1)**, [944]
policy holders, rights of, **19(1)**, [944]
margin of solvency, report as to,
19(1), [886]
procedure, **19(1)**, [885]
relevant requirements, failure to comply
with, **19(1)**, [944]
special resolution for, **19(1)**, [520]
stamp duty land tax, exemption from,
19(1), [543], [901]
statements relating to, **19(1)**, [943]
trustees—
appointment, **19(1)**, [464]
death, resignation, etc, devolution of
property on, **19(1)**, [502]
legal proceedings by, **19(1)**, [499], [540]
proof of appointment, **19(1)**, [466]
receipt by, in discharge of mortgage,
19(1), [500]
vesting of property in, **19(1)**, [497]
unregistered, exemption from tax,
44(1), [302]
valuations—
dispensation with provisions, **19(1)**, [484]
exemptions, **19(1)**, [484]
five yearly, **19(1)**, [484]
regulations and directions, **19(1)**, [485]
report on, **19(1)**, [484]
three yearly, **19(1)**, [485]
valuers, appointment, **19(1)**, [484]
winding up petition, **19(1)**, [525]

fruit. *See also* **horticultural produce**
theft of, **12(1)**, [556]

fuel
building regulations, use of, compliance report
relating to, **17(2)**, [582]
liquid, weights and measures for, **39(1)**, [578]
poverty—
meaning, **17(2)**, [362]
strategy, **17(2)**, [363]
private use, for, **50**, [78]
renewable transport fuel—
certificates, **17(2)**, [476]
determination of amounts, **17(2)**, [475]
information held by HM Revenue and
Customs—
disclosure of, **17(2)**, [481], [482]
offences, **17(2)**, [483]
obligations—
discharge by payment, **17(2)**, [477]
imposition of, **17(2)**, [470]
RTF orders, **17(2)**, [470]
Administrator—
appointment of, **17(2)**, [471]
functions, **17(2)**, [472], [473]
transfer to new Administrator,
17(2), [474]
civil penalties—
appeals against, **17(2)**, [480]

fuel—*contd*
renewable transport fuel—*contd*
RTF orders—*contd*
civil penalties—*contd*
imposition of, **17(2)**, [478]
notices, **17(2)**, [478]
objections to, **17(2)**, [479]
powers, **17(2)**, [471]
solid. *See* **solid fuel**
wood fuel, sale by weight, **39(1)**, [581]

fuel allotment
summary of provisions, **1(1)**, [124]

fuel and power
liquid, weights and measures for, **39(1)**, [578]
private use, for, **50**, [78]
solid. *See* **solid fuel**
wood fuel, sale by weight, **39(1)**, [581]

Fuel and Power, Minister of
appointment, **10**, [502]
duties of, **10**, [502]
functions of, **10**, [502]

fuel or field garden allotment
compulsory acquisition—
exchange of lands, certificate as to,
9, [432], [453]
special parliamentary procedure for,
9, [432], [453]
meaning, **9**, [159], [432]

fuel substitutes
charge of excise duty on, **13**, [829]

fumes
furnaces, from, provisions as to, **35(2)**, [47]
meaning, **35(2)**, [64]
public works, from, compensation for,
9, [304]. *See also* **public works**

Funding Agency for Schools
dissolution, **15(2)**, [125]

funding bond
appropriate, lack of, **43(S)**, 969–70
interest on debt, issued in respect of,
44(1), [418]
retained, tender by Commissioners,
43(S), 969–70
retention where issue treated as payment of
interest, duty of, **44(4)**, [947]–[948]

Funding Councils and Assets Board
accounts, **15(1)**, [374]
chief officer, **15(1)**, [374]
committees, **15(1)**, [374]
delegation of functions, **15(1)**, [374]
instruments, proof of, **15(1)**, [374]
members—
qualification of, **15(1)**, [374]
salaries, allowances and pensions,
15(1), [374]
tenure of office, **15(1)**, [374]

Funding Councils and Assets Board—*contd*
powers of, **15(1)**, [374]
proceedings, **15(1)**, [374]
references to, **15(1)**, [374]
seal, application of, **15(1)**, [374]
staff, **15(1)**, [374]

funeral benefits
payments for, relief for—
police organisations, to, **44(4)**, [466]
residence of claimants, to, **44(4)**, [468]
trade unions, to, **44(4)**, [465]

funeral service
conduct of, **14**, 1257

fur farming
entry, powers of, **2**, [725]
existing businesses, compensation for, **2**, [726]
forfeiture orders, **2**, [723], [724]
offence, **2**, [722]

furnace
chimney—
dark smoke, emission from,
35(2), [1]. *See also* **smoke**
height of, **35(2)**, [14]–[16]
served by single, one furnace, as,
35(2), [64]
domestic, meaning, **35(2)**, [64]
fuel consumed in, information as to,
35(2), [12]
fumes. *See* **fumes**
grit and dust—
arrestment plant—
exemptions from provisions, **35(2)**, [7]
new non-domestic furnaces, for,
35(2), [6]
refusal of approval for, appeal, **35(2)**, [9]
solid fuel, for burning, **35(2)**, [8]
emission from, limits on rates of, **35(2)**, [5]
measurement of—
local authorities, by, **35(2)**, [11]
occupiers, by, **35(2)**, [10]
information as to, requirement to give,
35(2), [12]
new—
fumes, to be free of, **35(2)**, [47]
grit and dust—
measurement, **35(2)**, [10], [11]
plant for arresting, approval by local
authority, **35(2)**, [6]
oil fuel for, limit on sulphur content of,
35(2), [30]
outdoor—
grit and dust from—
emission of, limits on, **35(2)**, [13]
measurement, **35(2)**, [13]
plant for arresting, fitting, **35(2)**, [13]
information as to, **35(2)**, [13]

furnished holiday letting
averaging treatment, claim for, **44(1)**, [360]
business—
giving effect to allowances, **43(1)**, [828]

furnished holiday letting—*contd*
business—*contd*
meaning, **43(1)**, [568]
commercial, **44(1)**, [360]
commercial letting—
capital allowances, **44(3)**, [327]
introduction to provisions, **44(3)**, [322]
loss relief, **44(3)**, [327]
meaning, **44(3)**, [323]
pension purposes, relevant UK earnings
for, **44(3)**, [328]
qualifying accommodation, **44(3)**, [325]
relevant period, meaning, **44(3)**, [324]
under-used accommodation, averaging
election, **44(3)**, [326]
holiday accommodation, treatment as,
44(1), [360]
letting, meaning, **44(1)**, [360]
qualifying accommodation, **44(1)**, [360]
trade, treatment as, income tax purposes, for,
44(1), [359]

furnished lettings
profits of, **44(3)**, [308]

furniture and fittings
provision by local authority, **22**, [11], [469]
sale by hire-purchase, **22**, [11]

further education. *See also* **higher and
further education**
Adult Learning Inspectorate, general note,
15(1), [1]
corporations. *See* **further education
corporation**
fees, regulations on, **15(1)**, [279]
general note, **15(1)**, [1]
governors—
appointment, **15(2)**, [191], [219]
minimum age of, **15(1)**, [293]
inspections, **15(2)**, [838]
general note, **15(1)**, [1]
institutions—
accounts, inspection of, **15(1)**, [422]
agreements before date of transfer, effect
of, **15(1)**, [447]
breach of duty, intervention in case of,
15(1), [425]
collective worship, **15(1)**, [413]
designated—
companies, conducted by, **15(1)**, [404]
conduct of, **15(1)**, [402]
disposals of land, generally, **15(2)**, [302]
generally, **15(2)**, [301]
government of, **15(1)**, [402]
loan liabilities, **15(1)**, [411]
meaning, **15(1)**, [401]
surpluses and deficits, attribution of,
15(1), [410]
transfer of property to,
15(1), [405]–[406], [409]
designation, **15(1)**, [401]
distribution of information about,
15(1), [675]
disturbance in, **15(1)**, [449]

further education—*contd*
  institutions—*contd*
    employees, remuneration of, **15(1)**, [412]
    employment in, contractual terms,
      avoidance of, **15(1)**, [417]
    enrolment numbers—
      calculation of, **15(1)**, [462]
      meaning, **15(1)**, [462]
      non-EEC students, exclusion of,
        15(1), [462]
    failure to reach acceptable standards,
      intervention in case of, **15(1)**, [425]
    foundation degrees, power to award,
      15(S), Education 24–5
    governing body—
      consultation by, **15(S)**, Education 27
      liability, **15(2)**, [303]
      meaning, **15(1)**, [456]
      travelling and subsistence allowance,
        15(1), [655]
    hazardous material, **15(2)**, [510]
    health and fitness, **15(2)**, [454]
    higher education sector, transfer to,
      15(1), [439]
    information, publication of, **15(1)**, [418]
    inspection of, **15(2)**, [839]
    intervention in—
      England, in, **15(S)**, Education 20–2
      Wales, in, **15(S)**, Education 23
    loan liabilities, **15(1)**, [411]
    mismanagement, intervention in case of,
      15(1), [425]
    named individuals, duty to provide for,
      15(1), [420]
    new sector—
      additional property made available for,
        15(1), [407]
      meaning, **15(1)**, [407]
    nuisance in, **15(1)**, [449]
    principals—
      qualifications of, **15(S)**, Education 28
      specified qualification, to have,
        15(2), [450]
    property, rights and liabilities, transfer of—
      construction of agreements, **15(1)**, [465]
      division and apportionment, **15(1)**, [464]
      documents of title, **15(1)**, [464]
      generally, **15(1)**, [405]–[406]
      identification, **15(1)**, [464]
      title, proof of, **15(1)**, [465]
      transferee, delivery of documents to,
        15(1), [464]
      vesting provisions, third parties affected
        by, **15(1)**, [464]
    records, **15(2)**, [508]–[509]
    reference to, **15(1)**, [457]
    religious education, **15(1)**, [414]
    secondary education, duty to safeguard
      pupils receiving, **15(1)**, [421]
    special provision for certain, **15(1)**, [403]
    staff—
      force, power to use, **15(1)**, [451]
      voluntary transfers of, **15(1)**, [408]
    summary of provisions, **15(S)**, Education 2

further education—*contd*
  institutions—*contd*
    surpluses and deficits, attribution of,
      15(1), [410]
    training in provision of, **15(2)**, [451]
    trust deeds, variation of, **15(1)**, [415]
    voluntary origin, of, **15(1)**, [413]
    weakness, intervention in case of,
      15(1), [425]
  maintained schools, collaboration
    arrangements with, **15(2)**, [875]
  meaning, **15(1)**, [497]
  schools, reorganisation of, **15(1)**, [426]
  Secretary of State, duty of, **15(1)**, [505]
  supply of goods and services—
    accounts, **15(1)**, [284]
    loan of money for, **15(1)**, [284]
    local education authority, powers of,
      15(1), [283]
    meaning, **15(1)**, [282]
    open market value, **15(1)**, [283]
    weapons, searching students for,
      15(1), [450]
  Wales, in. *See* **Wales**

further education corporation
  accounts, inspection of, **15(1)**, [422]
  bodies corporate, formation or involvement
    in, **15(S)**, Education 26–7
  charitable status of, **15(1)**, [395]
  constitution, **15(1)**, [392]
  dissolution, **15(1)**, [400]; **15(S)**, Education 18
  higher education corporation, transfer of,
    15(1), [416]
  incorporation, **15(S)**, Education 17
    initial, **15(1)**, [387]
    operative date, **15(1)**, [389]
    orders for, **15(1)**, [388]
  institutions—
    conduct of, **15(1)**, [392]
    goods and services, supply of, **15(1)**, [397]
    land held for purposes of, **15(1)**, [397]
    local authority, rights and liabilities of,
      15(1), [397]
    property, transfer of, **15(1)**, [396], [409]
  instruments and articles of government,
    15(1), [463]
    initial, **15(1)**, [393]
    subsequent, **15(1)**, [394]
  meaning, **15(1)**, [389]
  powers of—
    principal, **15(1)**, [390]
    supplementary, **15(1)**, [391]
  property, transfer to—
    foundation bodies, from, **15(1)**, [398]
    generally, **15(1)**, [409]
    institutions maintained by local education
      authorities, from, **15(1)**, [396]
  proposals, publication of, **15(1)**, [419];
    15(S), Education 19
  reference to, **15(1)**, [457]
  schools, reorganisation of, **15(1)**, [426]
  secondary education, duty to safeguard pupils
    receiving, **15(1)**, [421]
  staff, transfer of, **15(1)**, [399]

further education corporation—*contd*
transfers to, stamp duty exemption,
15(1), [453]

Further Education Funding Councils
accounts, **15(1)**, [461]
chief officer, **15(1)**, [461]
committees, **15(1)**, [461]
delegation of functions, **15(1)**, [461]
dissolution, **15(2)**, [258]
efficiency studies, **15(1)**, [446]
information, duty to give, **15(1)**, [423]
instruments, proof of, **15(1)**, [461]
joint exercise of functions, **15(1)**, [445]
members—
 salaries, allowances and pensions,
  15(1), [461]
 tenure, **15(1)**, [461]
proceedings, **15(1)**, [461]
seal, **15(1)**, [461]

Further Education Funding Councils—*contd*
staff, **15(1)**, [461]
status, **15(1)**, [461]
supplementary powers, **15(1)**, [461]
transfers—
 contracts of employment, **15(2)**, [263]
 stamp duty not chargeable on, **15(2)**, [261]
transitional provisions, **15(2)**, [320]–[321]

Further Education Unit
grants to, **15(1)**, [289]
staff superannuation, **15(1)**, [360]

futures. *See also* **commodity futures;
financial futures**
disposals involving guaranteed returns, charge
 to tax. *See* **savings and investment
 income**
gains from, exempt, **44(3)**, [794]
investments, as, **44(1)**, [433]

G

Gaelic Media Service (Seirbheis nam Meadhanan Gàidhlig)
functions, **45**, [590]
membership of, **45**, [173]

Gaelic television
Comataidh Telebhisien Gaidhlig—
Channel 3, Scotland, broadcasting on, **45**, [174]
Committee—
accounts and audit, **45**, [201]
annual reports, **45**, [201]
documents and seal, **45**, [201]
employees, **45**, [201]
establishment, **45**, [172]
expenses, **45**, [201]
financial provision, **45**, [172], [201]
functions, **45**, [172]
members, **45**, [201]
proceedings, **45**, [201]
status and capacity, **45**, [201]
Fund—
establishment, **45**, [172]
grants from, purposes, **45**, [172]
management, **45**, [172]
payments—
into, **45**, [172]
out of, **45**, [172], [201]
funded Gaelic productions, **45**, [172]
meaning, **45**, [172]
OFCOM—
financing by, **45**, [172]
powers as to, **45**, [172]
programmes in Gaelic—
broadcasting of, **45**, [174]
making, **45**, [172]
research, **45**, [172]
digital broadcasting, **45**, [229]
Gaelic Media Service. *See* **Gaelic Media Service**

gallery
assistance for, **26(1)**, [721]
value added tax, relief from, **50**, [46]

Gambia, The
British ship registered in, **7(2)**, [573]
Commonwealth citizenship, **31**, [186]
fully responsible status of, **7(2)**, [568]
legislative powers of, **7(2)**, [572]
republic, becoming—
existing law, operation of, **7(2)**, [645]
Privy Council, jurisdiction of, **7(2)**, [646]
visiting forces in, **7(2)**, [573]

gambling
advertising—
broadcasting, **5(1)**, [609]
foreign gambling, of, **5(1)**, [611]
meaning, **5(1)**, [607]
regulations, **5(1)**, [608]
territorial application—
non-remote advertising, **5(1)**, [612]
remote advertising, **5(1)**, [613]
unlawful gambling, of, **5(1)**, [610]
aircraft, on, **5(1)**, [639]
authorised persons—
compliance, activities for, **5(1)**, [585]
meaning, **5(1)**, [584]
obstruction of, **5(1)**, [606]
powers of, **5(1)**, [597]
premises, entry on—
authorisation, evidence of, **5(1)**, [601]
dwellings, exclusion of, **5(1)**, [598]
family entertainment centre, **5(1)**, [589]
force, use of, **5(1)**, [603]
information, provision of, **5(1)**, [602]
inspection, for, **5(1)**, [587]
licensed premises, **5(1)**, [593]
lotteries, inquiries in connection with, **5(1)**, [594]
persons accompanying, **5(1)**, [604]
prize gaming permit, application for, **5(1)**, [591]
records of, **5(1)**, [599]
securing premises after, **5(1)**, [605]
temporary use notice, having, **5(1)**, [595]
timing, **5(1)**, [600]
chain-gift schemes, **5(1)**, [324]
cheating, **5(1)**, [323]
children and young persons—
age, reasonable belief about, **5(1)**, [344]
bingo and club premises, employment on, **5(1)**, [334]
casino, etc, employment in, **5(1)**, [336]
definitions, **5(1)**, [326]
employment, reference to, **5(1)**, [342]
employment to provide facilities, **5(1)**, [332]
enforcement operations, use in, **5(1)**, [345]
facilities for gambling, provision of, **5(1)**, [331]
football pools—
employment for, **5(1)**, [333]
invitation to participate in, **5(1)**, [338]
gambling by, **5(1)**, [329]
gaming machines, age limit for, **5(1)**, [340]
invitation to enter premises, **5(1)**, [328]
invitation to gamble, **5(1)**, [327]
lottery—
employment for, **5(1)**, [333]

gambling—*contd*
  children and young persons—*contd*
    lottery—*contd*
      invitation to participate in, **5(1)**, [337]
      offences relating to, penalty, **5(1)**, [343]
      premises, entering, **5(1)**, [330]
      premises with gaming machines,
        employment on, **5(1)**, [335]
      stake, return of, **5(1)**, [339], [364]
  codes of practice, **5(1)**, [305]
    compliance with, condition of operating
      licence, **5(1)**, [363]
  constable—
    authorisations, power to require,
      5(1), [596]
    compliance, activities for, **5(1)**, [585]
    obstruction of, **5(1)**, [606]
    powers of, **5(1)**, [597]
    premises, entry on—
      club or miners' welfare institute,
        5(1), [592]
      dwellings, exclusion of, **5(1)**, [598]
      family entertainment centre, **5(1)**, [589]
      force, use of, **5(1)**, [603]
      information, provision of, **5(1)**, [602]
      inspection, for, **5(1)**, [587]
      licensed premises, **5(1)**, [593]
      operating licence holder, of, **5(1)**, [588]
      persons accompanying, **5(1)**, [604]
      prize gaming permit, application for,
        5(1), [591]
      records of, **5(1)**, [599]
      securing premises after, **5(1)**, [605]
      suspicion of offence, on, **5(1)**, [586]
      temporary use notice, having,
        5(1), [595]
      timing, **5(1)**, [600]
  contracts—
    bet, avoidance of, **5(1)**, [616]
      appeal, **5(1)**, [617]
      interim moratorium, **5(1)**, [618]
    enforceability, **5(1)**, [615]
    general note, **5(1)**, [1]
    provisions preventing enforcement, repeal,
      5(1), [614]
  Crown, provisions binding, **5(1)**, [634]
  data protection, **5(1)**, [631]
  employment, reference to, **5(1)**, [342]
  enforcement officers—
    authorisations, power to require,
      5(1), [596]
    compliance, activities for, **5(1)**, [585]
    designation of, **5(1)**, [583]
    obstruction of, **5(1)**, [606]
    payment, **5(1)**, [583]
    powers of, **5(1)**, [597]
    premises, entry on—
      authorisation, evidence of, **5(1)**, [601]
      club or miners' welfare institute,
        5(1), [592]
      dwellings, exclusion of, **5(1)**, [598]
      family entertainment centre, **5(1)**, [589]
      force, use of, **5(1)**, [603]
      information, provision of, **5(1)**, [602]
      inspection, for, **5(1)**, [587]

gambling—*contd*
  enforcement officers—*contd*
    premises, entry on—*contd*
      licensed premises, **5(1)**, [593]
      lotteries, inquiries in connection with,
        5(1), [594]
      operating licence holder, of, **5(1)**, [588]
      persons accompanying, **5(1)**, [604]
      prize gaming permit, application for,
        5(1), [591]
      records of, **5(1)**, [599]
      securing premises after, **5(1)**, [605]
      suspicion of offence, on, **5(1)**, [586]
      temporary use notice, having,
        5(1), [595]
      timing, **5(1)**, [600]
  excluded premises, **5(1)**, [627]
  facilities for, **5(1)**, [286]
    abroad, unlawful, **5(1)**, [325]
    child or young person, employment of,
      5(1), [332]
    offences, **5(1)**, [314]
    provision of, **5(1)**, [314]
    remote equipment, **5(1)**, [317], [325]
    territorial application of provisions,
      5(1), [317]
    young person, provision by, **5(1)**, [331]
  general note, **5(1)**, [1]
  information, exchange of, **5(1)**, [629],
    [646]–[649]
  inspection, **5(1)**, [587]
  interpretation, **5(1)**, [633]
  licensing authorities—
    information, Commission requiring from,
      5(1), [310]
    meaning, **5(1)**, [283]
    premises licence. *See* premises licence *below*
    prosecution by, **5(1)**, [625]
    three-year licensing policy, **5(1)**, [628]
  licensing objectives—
    Commission, promotion by, **5(1)**, [303]
    meaning, **5(1)**, [282]
  meaning, **5(1)**, [284]
  occasional use notice—
    betting premises licence, treatment as,
      5(1), [341]
    day of effect, **5(1)**, [320]
    maximum number of, **5(1)**, [320]
    meaning, **5(1)**, [320]
    requirements, **5(1)**, [320]
  offences—
    body corporate or unincorporate, by,
      5(1), [620]
    false information, giving, **5(1)**, [621]
    forfeiture, power of, **5(1)**, [624]
    general note, **5(1)**, [1]
    prosecution, limitation, **5(1)**, [626]
  operating licence—
    amendment, submission for, **5(1)**, [386]
    annual fee, **5(1)**, [381]
    annual levy, **5(1)**, [404]
    application for, **5(1)**, [350]
      consideration of, **5(1)**, [351]–[353]
      criminal record, applicant having,
        5(1), [352]

gambling—*contd*
  operating licence—*contd*
    application for—*contd*
      demand, having regard to, **5(1)**, [353]
      determination of, **5(1)**, [355]
      procedure for considering, **5(1)**, [354]
    bingo, **5(1)**, [372]
    casino, **5(1)**, [371]
    children, return of stake to, **5(1)**, [339], [364]
    combined, **5(1)**, [349]
    conditions—
      breach, financial penalty for, **5(1)**, [402]
      children, return of stakes to, **5(1)**, [364]
      code of practice, compliance with, **5(1)**, [363]
      credit, as to, **5(1)**, [362]
      equipment, as to, **5(1)**, [366]
      gaming machines, relating to, **5(1)**, [367]
      general, **5(1)**, [356]–[357]
      individual, **5(1)**, [358]
      inducements, as to, **5(1)**, [362]
      information, requiring provision of, **5(1)**, [369]
      management office, relating to, **5(1)**, [361]
      membership, as to, **5(1)**, [368]
      operational function, relating to, **5(1)**, [361]
      premises, as to, **5(1)**, [365]
      procedure, **5(1)**, [357]
      scope of power to attach, **5(1)**, [360]
      Secretary of State, imposed by, **5(1)**, [359]
    copy, issue of, **5(1)**, [388]
    duration—
      indefinite, **5(1)**, [391]
      power to limit, **5(1)**, [392]
    forfeiture, **5(1)**, [396]
    form of, **5(1)**, [347]
    general betting, **5(1)**, [373]
    holder—
      amendment, submission for, **5(1)**, [386]
      annual levy, payment of, **5(1)**, [404]
      application to vary by, **5(1)**, [385]
      authorisations, production of, **5(1)**, [596]
      breach, financial penalty for, **5(1)**, [402]
      change of circumstance, notification, **5(1)**, [382]
      corporate control, change of, **5(1)**, [383]–[384]
      information, provision of, **5(1)**, [403]
      inspection of premises, **5(1)**, [588]
      meaning, **5(1)**, [407]
      offence, conviction of, **5(1)**, [390], [396]
      production, requirement of, **5(1)**, [389]
      warning to, **5(1)**, [398]
    horse-race pool betting, **5(1)**, [375]
    lapse, **5(1)**, [395]
    lottery, **5(1)**, [379]–[380]
    meaning, **5(1)**, [346]
    nature of, **5(1)**, [346]
    personal, requirement for, **5(1)**, [361]
    pool betting, **5(1)**, [374]
    production, requirement of, **5(1)**, [389]

gambling—*contd*
  operating licence—*contd*
    register of, **5(1)**, [387]
    regulatory powers, **5(1)**, [398]
    relevant offences, disapplication of rehabilitation, **5(1)**, [406], [650]–[651]
    remote, **5(1)**, [370]
    remote gambling, for, **5(1)**, [348]
    renewal, **5(1)**, [393]
    requirement, **5(1)**, [346]
    review by Commission, **5(1)**, [397]
    revocation, **5(1)**, [400]
      conditions for, **5(1)**, [401]
    small-scale operators, exemption for, **5(1)**, [410]
    software, for, **5(1)**, [378]
    summary of provisions, **5(1)**, [1]
    surrender, **5(1)**, [394]
    suspension, **5(1)**, [399]
      conditions for, **5(1)**, [401]
    types of, **5(1)**, [346]
    variation, application for, **5(1)**, [385]
  participation fee, **5(1)**, [623]
  participation in prize competition, exclusion, **5(1)**, [619]
  personal licence—
    application of provisions, **5(1)**, [409]
    applications, **5(1)**, [411]
    condition, breach of, **5(1)**, [420]
    disqualification from holding, **5(1)**, [417]
    duration, **5(1)**, [412]
    fees, **5(1)**, [413]
    forfeiture, **5(1)**, [417]
    holder, conviction of offence, **5(1)**, [419]
    multiple, **5(1)**, [414]
    nature of, **5(1)**, [408]
    production, requirement of, **5(1)**, [415]
    regulations, **5(1)**, [409]
    review, provision not applying, **5(1)**, [416]
    summary of provisions, **5(1)**, [1]
    suspension or revocation of, **5(1)**, [418]
  premises—
    activity on, amendment of provisions, **5(1)**, [319]
    child, employment of, **5(1)**, [333]
    football pools, relating to, **5(1)**, [321]
    responsible authorities for, **5(1)**, [438]
    temporary use of, **5(1)**, [1]
    use of, offences, **5(1)**, [318]–[319]
  premises licence—
    annual fee, **5(1)**, [465]
    appeal—
      further, **5(1)**, [490]
      process, **5(1)**, [488]
      right of, **5(1)**, [487]
      stay pending, **5(1)**, [489]
    application for—
      determination of, **5(1)**, [444]
      entry on premises, **5(1)**, [593]
      form of, **5(1)**, [440]
      grant of, **5(1)**, [445]
      hearing, requirement for, **5(1)**, [443]
      making, **5(1)**, [440]
      notice of, **5(1)**, [441]
      rejection of, **5(1)**, [446]

gambling—*contd*
  premises licence—*contd*
    application for—*contd*
      representations, **5(1)**, [442]
      area of track, for, **5(1)**, [433]
      betting machines, number of, **5(1)**, [462]
      bingo, **5(1)**, [453]
        credit, licensee not to give, **5(1)**, [458]
      casino—
        children, access by, **5(1)**, [457]
        credit, licensee not to give, **5(1)**, [458]
        issue of, **5(1)**, [455]
        machines in, **5(1)**, [455]
        overall limits, **5(1)**, [456]
        resolution not to issue, **5(1)**, [447]
      Christmas Day, exclusion of betting on,
        5(1), [464]
      combined, **5(1)**, [433]
      conditions—
        default, **5(1)**, [449]
        licensing authority, imposed or excluded
          by, **5(1)**, [450]
        mandatory, **5(1)**, [448]
        membership, as to, **5(1)**, [451]
        stakes, fees, winnings or prizes, no limits
          on, **5(1)**, [452]
      copy, issue of, **5(1)**, [471]
      door supervision requirement, **5(1)**, [459]
      duration, initial, **5(1)**, [472]
      failure to pay fee, revocation for,
        5(1), [474]
      fees, **5(1)**, [493]
      form of, **5(1)**, [432]
      gaming machines, for, **5(1)**, [453]
      holder—
        application to vary by, **5(1)**, [468]
        change of circumstance, notification of,
          5(1), [467]
      interested parties, **5(1)**, [439]
      lapse, **5(1)**, [475]
        reinstatement, **5(1)**, [476]–[477]
      licensing authority—
        delegation of functions,
          5(1), [435]–[436]
        principles to be applied, **5(1)**, [434]
        register, maintenance of, **5(1)**, [437]
      nature of, **5(1)**, [431]
      planning permission, decisions as to,
        5(1), [491]
      pool betting—
        dog racing, **5(1)**, [461]
        track, on, **5(1)**, [460]
      premises, to be kept on, **5(1)**, [466]
      provisional statement—
        application for, **5(1)**, [485]
        effect of, **5(1)**, [486]
      register of, **5(1)**, [437]
      review—
        action following, **5(1)**, [483]
        application for, **5(1)**, [478]
        conduct of, **5(1)**, [482]
        determination of, **5(1)**, [484]
        grant of application, **5(1)**, [480]
        licensing authorities, initiation by,
          5(1), [481]

gambling—*contd*
  premises licence—*contd*
    review—*contd*
      purpose of, **5(1)**, [482]
      rejection of application, **5(1)**, [479]
    subsidiary and main, **5(1)**, [433]
    summary of provisions, **5(1)**, [1]
    surrender, **5(1)**, [473]
    transfer, **5(1)**, [469]–[470]
    variation of, **5(1)**, [468]
    vehicle, exclusion of, **5(1)**, [492]
    vessel, for, **5(1)**, [492]
    virtual gaming, for, **5(1)**, [454]
  prize, value of, **5(1)**, [622]
  regulations, orders and rules, **5(1)**, [635]
  remote—
    meaning, **5(1)**, [285]
    operating licence, **5(1)**, [348], [370]
  small-scale operators, **5(1)**, [410]
  software—
    offences, **5(1)**, [322]
    operating licence, **5(1)**, [378]
  summary of provisions, **5(1)**, [1]
  tax, meaning, **5(1)**, [79]
  temporary use notice—
    acknowledgement of, **5(1)**, [501]
    appeals, **5(1)**, [507]
    consideration by licensing authority,
      5(1), [509]
    counter-notice, **5(1)**, [505]
    display of, **5(1)**, [510]
    effect of, **5(1)**, [498]
    endorsement, **5(1)**, [508]
    form of, **5(1)**, [497]
    giving, **5(1)**, [500]
    licensing authority functions, delegation
      of, **5(1)**, [513]–[514]
    maximum permitted period, **5(1)**, [499]
    modification by agreement, **5(1)**, [504]
    nature of, **5(1)**, [496]
    objections to—
      dismissal of, **5(1)**, [506]
      hearing, **5(1)**, [503]
      notice of, **5(1)**, [502]
    permitted activities, **5(1)**, [495]
    premises, entry on to assess effects,
      5(1), [595]
    premises licence, treatment as, **5(1)**, [341]
    procedure, **5(1)**, [500]
    production of, **5(1)**, [510]
    register of, **5(1)**, [515]
    vehicle, exclusion of, **5(1)**, [512]
    vessel, for, **5(1)**, [512]
    withdrawal, **5(1)**, [511]
  transitional provisions, **5(1)**, [670]–[671]
  vessels, on, **5(1)**, [638]

Gambling Appeals Tribunal
  appeal from, **5(1)**, [424]
  appeal to—
    avoidance of bet, as to, **5(1)**, [617]
    costs, enforcement, **5(1)**, [430]
    decision of Commission, from, **5(1)**, [422]
    fees, **5(1)**, [428]
    legal assistance, scheme for, **5(1)**, [429]

Gambling Appeals Tribunal—*contd*
  appeal to—*contd*
    powers on, **5(1)**, [425]
    rules, **5(1)**, [427]
    stay pending, **5(1)**, [426]
    timing, **5(1)**, [423]
  establishment of, **5(1)**, [421]
  financial provisions, **5(1)**, [652]
  members, **5(1)**, [652]
  President, **5(1)**, [652]
  procedure, **5(1)**, [652]
  sittings, **5(1)**, [652]
  staff, **5(1)**, [652]

Gambling Commission
  annual report, **5(1)**, [644]
  appeal from decision of, **5(1)**, [422]
  bet, avoidance of, **5(1)**, [616]
    appeal, **5(1)**, [617]
    interim moratorium, **5(1)**, [618]
  chairman, **5(1)**, [302]
  codes of practice, **5(1)**, [305]
    compliance with, condition of operating
      licence, **5(1)**, [363]
  Commissioners for HM Revenue and
    Customs, consultation with, **5(1)**, [313]
  compliance, activities for, **5(1)**, [308]
  constitution, **5(1)**, [644]
  directions and requirements by, **5(1)**, [405]
  establishment of, **5(1)**, [301]
  false information given to, **5(1)**, [621]
  financial provisions, **5(1)**, [644]
  Gaming Board, transfer of functions, rights
    and liabilities, **5(1)**, [302], [645]
  information—
    exchange of, **5(1)**, [311]
    holder of operating licence, from,
      5(1), [403]
    licensing authorities, required from,
      5(1), [310]
  licensing objectives, duty to promote,
    5(1), [303]
  local authorities, guidance to, **5(1)**, [306]
  members—
    payments to, **5(1)**, [644]
    tenure, **5(1)**, [644]
  National Lottery Commission, consultation
    with, **5(1)**, [129], [313]
  offences, investigation and promotion of,
    5(1), [309]
  operating licence—
    issue of, **5(1)**, [346]. *See also* **gambling**
    regulatory powers, **5(1)**, [398]
    review of, **5(1)**, [397]
    revocation, **5(1)**, [400]
      conditions for, **5(1)**, [401]
    suspension, **5(1)**, [399]
      conditions for, **5(1)**, [401]
  personal licence, suspension or revocation of,
    5(1), [418]
  proceedings, **5(1)**, [644]
  Secretary of State, duty to advise, **5(1)**, [307]
  staff, **5(1)**, [644]
  statement of principles for regulation and
    licensing, **5(1)**, [304]

Gambling Commission—*contd*
  status, **5(1)**, [644]
  summary of provisions, **5(1)**, [1]

game
  agreement—
    not to kill, **2**, [186]
    reserving game rights, **2**, [152]
  cattlegate owners, rights of, **2**, [154]
  certificate. *See* game certificate *below*
  Christmas Day, taking or killing on, **2**, [147]
  close season—
    buying or selling during, **2**, [148]
    period of, **2**, [147]
    taking or killing game in, **2**, [147]
  common rights, owners of, **2**, [154]
  Crown—
    forest rights, **2**, [153]
    licence exemption, **2**, [193]
  dealers—
    board to be displayed by, **2**, [162]
    buying or selling, **2**, [148]
    conviction of, effect of, **2**, [165]
    licence—
      conditions of, **2**, [203]
      dealing without, **2**, [202]
      duration and expiration, **2**, [204]
      duty on, **2**, [190]
      falsification, **2**, [526]
      feigning to be holder, **2**, [170]
      grant of, **2**, [163]
      holders, list of, **2**, [203]
      partnership, for, **2**, [163]
      Post Office, issue by, **2**, [339]
      selling without, **2**, [163]
      voidance for conviction, **2**, [164]
    licensed—
      buying from unauthorised person,
        2, [170]
      sale to, **2**, [161]
      sales on account of another, **2**, [171]
      servants of, buying and selling by,
        2, [171]
    unlicensed, buying game from, **2**, [170]
    See further under **deer**
  deer. *See* **deer**
  eggs, taking, destroying etc, **2**, [166]
  game certificate—
    authority conferred by, **2**, [150]
    duty on, **2**, [190]
    form etc, **2**, [204]
    killing or taking without, **2**, [165]
    meaning, **2**, [194]
    Northern Ireland, of, availability in GB,
      2, [244]
    requirement for, **2**, [149]
    sale under, to unlicensed dealer, **2**, [167]
  gamekeeper—
    appointment—
      lord of manor, by, **2**, [157]
      registration, **2**, [160]
      termination of, **2**, [160]
      Wales, in, **2**, [159]
      who may appoint, **2**, [158]
    arrest of poachers by, **2**, [141]

game—*contd*
  gamekeeper—*contd*
    certificate, scope of, **2**, [150]
    change of, effect on licence, **2**, [196]
    licence, duty on, **2**, [190]
    male servant duty, repeal of, **2**, [267]
    powers and duties, **2**, [158]
    sale of game by, **2**, [161]
  ground game—
    agreements with moorland owners,
      2, [233]
    meaning, **2**, [220]
    night shooting, prohibition, **2**, [218]
    non-occupier, rights, **2**, [219]
    occupier's rights—
      agreements contravening, **2**, [215]
      extension of, **2**, [232]
      kill, to, **2**, [213]
      licence, exemption from, **2**, [216]
      poison, prohibition of use, **2**, [218]
      tenant's rights, saving for, **2**, [217]
  hares. *See* **hares**
  hunting, saving for, **2**, [177]
  innkeeper, sale of game by, **2**, [168]
  landlord—
    authorisation of others to kill game,
      2, [155]
    right to game, **2**, [151]
  lessor, right to game, **2**, [151]
  licence to kill or take—
    date of expiration, **2**, [225]
    duration and expiration, **2**, [204]
    duty on, **2**, [190]
    exceptions and exemptions, **2**, [193]
    failure to have, **2**, [191]
    falsification, **2**, [526]
    form of, **2**, [204]
    gamekeepers, for, **2**, [195]
    lists of holders, publication of, **2**, [200]
    local authority responsibility for, **2**, [338]
    Post Office, issue by, **2**, [339]
    production, **2**, [198]
    requirement for, **2**, [191]
    servants, for, **2**, [197]
    short periods, for, **2**, [226]
    voidance on conviction, **2**, [199]
  licences generally—
    false statements to obtain, **2**, [528]
    form etc, **2**, [204]
    issue of, in blank, **2**, [527]
    See also specific licences above
  lord of manor—
    meaning, **2**, [146]
    wastes, right to game on, **2**, [154]
  meaning, **2**, [145], [146], [206], [302]
    variations of, **2**, [140]
  occupier—
    exclusion of rights of, **2**, [156]
    killing game by, **2**, [156]
  offences—
    enforcement of penalties, **2**, [208]
    prosecutions, time for, **2**, [179]
    summary, penalty, **2**, [534]
  poaching. *See* taking etc *below*
  poison, use to kill, **2**, [147]

game—*contd*
  rabbits. *See* **rabbits**
  sale of—
    close season, during, **2**, [148]
    gamekeeper, by, **2**, [161]
  search, constable's powers, **2**, [207]
  summary of provisions, **2**, [140]
  Sunday, taking or killing on, **2**, [147]
  taking etc, unlawfully—
    close season, during, **2**, [147]
    daytime, offences and penalties, **2**, [172]
    equipment etc, seizure of, **2**, [157]
    meaning of game, **2**, [145]
    night, at—
      arrest of offenders, **2**, [142], [300]
      highways, on, **2**, [182]
      meaning of night, **2**, [144]
      penalty, **2**, [141]
      three or more persons armed, **2**, [143]
    poison, use of, **2**, [147]
    Sunday or Christmas Day, on, **2**, [147]
  trespassing in search of—
    arrest for, **2**, [172]
    civil action for, **2**, [180]
    daytime—
      five or more armed persons, by, **2**, [175]
      meaning of daytime, **2**, [176]
      offence of, **2**, [172]
      requirement to quit land, **2**, [173]
    entry on land by police, **2**, [300]
    guns etc, seizure and forfeiture, **2**, [302]
    hunting excluded from, **2**, [177]
    night-time. *See* taking etc *above*
    police, powers of, **2**, [174], [300], [301]
    search of persons, powers, **2**, [207]
    seizure of arms etc, **2**, [302]
    seizure of game taken, **2**, [178]
    vehicles, forfeiture, **2**, [303]

gametes. *See also* **human fertilisation**
  consent to use of, **28**, [633]
  crime, keeping and examining in connection
    with, **28**, [625]
  donor, parental orders in favour of, **28**, [612]
  meaning, **28**, [576]
  prohibitions in connection with, **28**, [582]

gaming. *See also* **betting; lottery**
  bingo. *See* **bingo**
  casino—
    child, employment of, **5(1)**, [336]
    large—
      classification as, **5(1)**, [288]
      overall limits, **5(1)**, [456]
      premises licence, **5(1)**, [431], [453]
    meaning, **5(1)**, [288]
    operating licence, **5(1)**, [371]
    premises licence—
      applications for, **5(1)**, [653]
      children, access by, **5(1)**, [457]
      credit, licensee not to give, **5(1)**, [458]
      large, **5(1)**, [431], [453]
      machines in, **5(1)**, [455]
      nature of, **5(1)**, [431]
      overall limits, **5(1)**, [456]

gaming—*contd*
  casino—*contd*
    premises licence—*contd*
      regional, **5(1)**, [431], [453]
      resolution not to issue, **5(1)**, [447]
      small, **5(1)**, [431], [453]
      See also **gambling**
    regional—
      classification as, **5(1)**, [288]
      overall limits, **5(1)**, [456]
      premises licence, **5(1)**, [431], [453]
    small—
      classification as, **5(1)**, [288]
      overall limits, **5(1)**, [456]
      premises licence, **5(1)**, [431], [453]
    use of premises for, offences,
      5(1), [318]–[319]
  casino game—
    meaning, **5(1)**, [288]
    regulations, **5(1)**, [288]
  club. *See also* **club**
  cross-category activities—
    betting, **5(1)**, [297]
    lotteries, **5(1)**, [298]
  duty—
    accounting periods, **5(1)**, [208]
    amended provisions, **5(S)**, Betting 5–6
    evidence, **5(1)**, [208]
    groups, **5(1)**, [207]
    information, disclosure of, **5(1)**, [208]
    interpretation of provisions, **5(1)**, [204]
    liability to pay, **5(1)**, [201]
    licence duty, replacing, **5(1)**, [199]
    offences, **5(1)**, [208]
    officers, protection of, **5(1)**, [208]
    premises, notification of, **5(1)**, [207]
    rate of, **5(1)**, [200]; **5(S)**, Betting 1;
      43(S), 852
    register, **5(1)**, [207]
    registration, **5(1)**, [207]
    remote. *See* remote gaming duty *below*
    returns, **5(1)**, [208]
    subordinate legislation, **5(1)**, [203]
    summary of provisions, **5(1)**, [1]
  equal chance—
    meaning, **5(1)**, [289]; **5(S)**, Betting 6
    premises with alcohol licence, in,
      5(1), [559]–[560]
      exemption, removal of, **5(1)**, [564]
  gambling. *See* **gambling**
  game of chance, meaning, **5(1)**, [287]
  licence duty, replacement of, **5(1)**, [199]
  machine. *See* **gaming machine**
  meaning, **5(1)**, [287]; **5(S)**, Betting 7
  non-commercial—
    equal chance—
      conditions for, **5(1)**, [580]
      facilities for, provision of, **5(1)**, [578]
    facilities for, provision of, **5(1)**, [578]
    meaning, **5(1)**, [577]
    prize—
      conditions for, **5(1)**, [579]
      facilities for, provision of, **5(1)**, [578]
      profits, misusing, **5(1)**, [581]

gaming—*contd*
  offences and penalties, bodies corporate, by,
    5(1), [86]
  participation fees, VAT exemption,
    50(S), VAT 30
  private—
    conditions for, **5(1)**, [665]
    facilities for, provision of, **5(1)**, [576]
  prizes, for—
    application for permit, entry on premises,
      5(1), [591]
    bingo halls, in, **5(1)**, [571]
    conditions for, **5(1)**, [573]
    exemptions, power to restrict, **5(1)**, [574]
    gaming and entertainment centres, in,
      5(1), [570]
    meaning, **5(1)**, [287], [568]
    non-commercial. *See* non-commercial *above*
    permits, **5(1)**, [569], [664]
    travelling fair, in, **5(1)**, [572]
  remote—
    duty. *See* remote gaming duty *below*
    registration of persons providing facilities,
      5(1), [81]
    returns, **5(1)**, [82]
  remote gaming duty—
    accounting periods, **5(1)**, [75]
    amended provisions, **5(1)**, [684], [689]
    amounts in currencies other than sterling,
      5(1), [85]
    appeals. **5(1)**, [84]
    charge of, **5(1)**, [73]
    enforcement, **5(1)**, [83]
    evasion of, **5(1)**, [83]
    exemptions, **5(1)**, [79]
    liability to pay, **5(1)**, [80]
    losses, **5(1)**, [78]
    meaning, **5(1)**, [72]
    rate of, **5(1)**, [74]
    receipts, **5(1)**, [76]
    returns, **5(1)**, [82]
    review of appeal as to liability, **5(1)**, [84]
    winning, **5(1)**, [77]
  transitional provisions, **5(1)**, [670]–[671]
  use of premises, offences, **5(1)**, [318]–[319]
  value added tax, exemption from, **50**, [153]

Gaming Board
  Gambling Commission, transfer of functions,
    rights and liabilities to, **5(1)**, [302], [645]

gaming machine
  adult gaming centre—
    meaning, **5(1)**, [518]
    premises licence, **5(1)**, [453]
  categories of, **5(1)**, [517]
  Category D, age limit for, **5(1)**, [340]
  centre, premises licence—
    adult centre, for, **5(1)**, [453]
    number of machines, **5(1)**, [453]
    See also **gambling**
  club permit. *See* **club**
  computers, **5(1)**, [516]

gaming machine—*contd*
family entertainment centre—
enforcement, entry on premises for,
5(1), [589]
meaning, **5(1)**, [519]
permit, **5(1)**, [527]
appeals, **5(1)**, [654]
application for, **5(1)**, [654]
duration, **5(1)**, [654]
form of, **5(1)**, [654]
interpretation, **5(1)**, [654]
maintenance, **5(1)**, [654]
register, **5(1)**, [654]
renewal, **5(1)**, [654]
vehicles and vessels, not applying to,
5(1), [654]
premises licence, **5(1)**, [453]
licensed premises gaming machine permit,
5(1), [563]
machines not being, **5(1)**, [516]
meaning, **5(1)**, [516]; **5(S)**, Betting 7–8;
50, [153]
offences and penalties—
family entertainment centre gaming
machine permit, having, **5(1)**, [527]
limited prize, exclusion for, **5(1)**, [529]
linked machine, making available,
5(1), [525]
making available for use, **5(1)**, [523]
manufacture, supply, installation, adaptation,
maintenance or repair without licence,
5(1), [524]
no prize offered, exclusion for, **5(1)**, [528]
penalty, **5(1)**, [526]
single-machine supply and maintenance
permit, having, **5(1)**, [530]
opening, power to require, **50**, [157]
operating licence—
requirement, **5(1)**, [346]
technical, standards, **5(1)**, [377]
See also **gambling**
premises, employment of child, **5(1)**, [335]
premises licence—
adult centre, for, **5(1)**, [453]
family entertainment centre, for,
5(1), [453]
prize, meaning, **5(1)**, [520]
provision of, **5(1)**, [316]
pubs, in, **5(1)**, [562]
exemption, removal of, **5(1)**, [564]
permits—
appeals, **5(1)**, [663]
application for, **5(1)**, [663]
cancellation and forfeiture, **5(1)**, [663]
form of, **5(1)**, [663]
maintenance, **5(1)**, [663]
register of, **5(1)**, [663]
transfer, **5(1)**, [663]
variation, **5(1)**, [663]
regulations, for use of, **5(1)**, [521]
supply, installation, adaptation, maintenance or
repair, regulations, **5(1)**, [522]
territorial application of provisions,
5(1), [531]
travelling fair, in, **5(1)**, [567]

gaming machine—*contd*
value added tax, **50**, [33]
VAT provisions, **50(S)**, VAT 1–3

garden
chemicals used in—
analysis, evidence of, **1(1)**, [686]
classes of, **1(1)**, [684]
labelling and marking, **1(1)**, [683]
penalties for offences, **1(1)**, [685]
unlabelled, sale of, **1(1)**, [685]
generally, **32**, [1]
Historic Buildings and Ancient Monuments
Commission, acquisition by, **32**, [210]
historic interest, of—
acquisition, grants for, **32**, [211]
endowment of, **32**, [215]
preservation, grants and loans for, **32**, [207]
register of, **32**, [216]
square, in—
byelaws for management of, **32**, [4]
corporate authority, taken charge of by,
32, [2]
Crown property, exclusion of, **32**, [6]
encroachment, protection from, **32**, [3]
injuring, penalty for, **32**, [5]
vesting of, **32**, [2]

garnishee proceedings
child support liability, enforcement by,
6, [512]

gas. *See also* **energy**
Act 1986—
extraterritorial operation of, **17(1)**, [687]
transfer date, provisions coming into effect
on, **17(1)**, [698]
transitional provisions, **17(1)**, [690]
activities relating to gas, licensing of,
17(1), [586], [587], [692]
administrative expenses, Secretary of State,
17(1), [688]
antifluctuators, use of, **17(1)**, [693]
bridges, breaking up, **17(1)**, [696]
calorific value—
apparatus, tests of, **17(1)**, [601]
change in, alteration of burners,
17(1), [693]
charges, basis for, **17(1)**, [600]
meaning, **17(1)**, [600]
carbon dioxide. *See* **carbon dioxide**
charges—
billing disputes, **17(1)**, [602]
disadvantaged groups of consumers,
adjustment to help—
information, supply of, **17(1)**, [656]
notices, **17(1)**, [656]
schemes, **17(1)**, [655]
recovery, **17(1)**, [693]
security for payment, **17(1)**, [599]
climate change levy. *See* **climate change
levy**
code. *See* **gas code**
combustible, importation and storage of—
abandoned well, **17(2)**, [296]

gas—*contd*
  combustible, importation and storage
    of—*contd*
      criminal proceedings, **17(2)**, [607]
      inspectors, **17(2)**, [606]
      licences—
        activities carried on partly on land,
          exception for, **17(2)**, [596]
        applications, **17(2)**, [598]
        breach of regulations, injunctions
          restraining, **17(2)**, [605]
        conditions, **17(2)**, [599]
        directions from Secretary of State—
          following non-compliance with,
            17(2), [603], [604]
          petroleum licensing requirements,
            interaction with, **17(2)**, [608]
        grant of, **17(2)**, [597]
        model clauses for, **17(2)**, [600]
        offences, **17(2)**, [601], [602]
        terms, **17(2)**, [599]
        unlicensed activities—
          offence to carry on, **17(2)**, [601]
          prohibition on, **17(2)**, [595]
  compulsory acquisition of land. *See under* **gas**
    transporter
  connection—
    obligation as to, **17(1)**, [597]
    request for, duty as to, **17(1)**, [597]
    required by owner or occupier,
      17(1), [597]
    security for payment, **17(1)**, [599]
  consumers, council. *See* **National Consumer**
    Council
    undue preference, avoidance, **17(1)**, [596]
  controlled operations. *See* underground
    storage *below*
  Corporation. *See* **British Gas Corporation**
  disconnection, investigation of complaints by
    National Consumer Council, **39(1)**, [680]
  distribution main, meaning, **17(1)**, [674]
  documents, production of, **17(1)**, [653]
  downstream pipes—
    construction of railway, works due to,
      36, [277]–[282]
    tramway, attention for purpose of,
      36, [503]
  entry—
    authorised officers, powers, regulations as
      to, **17(1)**, [605]
    continuance of supply, during, **17(1)**, [693]
    discontinuance of supply, on, **17(1)**, [693]
    obstruction, penalty, **17(1)**, [605]
    power of—
      provisions as to, **17(1)**, [693]
      regulations as to, **17(1)**, [605]
      summary of provisions, **17(1)**, [1]
      warrant to authorise, **17(1)**, [71], [330]
    See also under underground storage *below*
  escape regulations, **17(1)**, [606]
  fittings—
    distress, not subject to, **17(1)**, [693]
    injury to, **17(1)**, [693]
    meaning, **17(1)**, [674]
    removal, entry for, **17(1)**, [693]

gas—*contd*
  importation—
    areas outside territorial sea, exploitation
      of, **17(2)**, [594]
    combustible gas. *See* combustible *above*
  improper use of, **17(1)**, [693]
  information—
    collection and publication, **17(1)**, [647]
    disclosure, restrictions on, **17(2)**, [348]
    Gas and Electricity Markets Authority—
      functions as to, **17(1)**, [647]
      power to require, **17(1)**, [653]
  infrastructure, third party access to,
    17(2), [669]
  inquiries, power to hold, **17(1)**, [456]
  interconnectors—
    licences—
      grant to existing operators, **17(2)**, [498]
      licences for operation of, **17(1)**, [589]
      Secretary of State's powers,
        supplementary provisions, **17(2)**, [530]
      standard conditions, **17(2)**, [497]
  leakage, underground storage, from,
    17(1), [310]
  levy, reduction and abolition, **17(2)**, [316]
  licensing of activities relating to, **17(1)**, [586],
    [692]
    application for order excluding,
      17(1), [663]
    Competition Commission, reference to,
      17(1), [659]–[662]
    consultation for Secretary of State,
      17(1), [664]
    interconnectors, **17(1)**, [589]
    new, application for order including,
      17(1), [658]
    new arrangements, payments relating to,
      17(2), [337]
    payment conditions, meaning, **17(2)**, [337]
    power to alter, **17(1)**, [657]
    smart meters, installation or operation of,
      17(1), [665], [666]
      competitive tenders for, **17(1)**, [667]
  lighting of streets, etc, by, **35(1)**, [23]
  LNG facilities—
    acquisition of rights to use, **17(1)**, [611]
    application of provisions, **17(1)**, [610]
    information, provision of, **17(1)**, [612]
  manufacture of, pollution of water in. *See*
    pollution
  meaning, **17(1)**, [674]
  measuring equipment, functions of Gas and
    Electricity Markets Authority and Secretary
    of State with respect to, **17(1)**, [651]
  meters—
    consumption to be ascertained by,
      17(1), [693]
    disabled persons, for, **17(1)**, [693]
    disconnection of, failure to notify,
      17(1), [693]
    distress, not subject to, **17(1)**, [693]
    evidence of quantity supplied, as,
      17(1), [693]
    examiners, appointment and duties,
      17(1), [604]

gas—*contd*
  meters—*contd*
    Gas and Electricity Markets Authority,
      functions transferred to Secretary of
      State, **17(2)**, [683]
    installation in new premises, **17(1)**, [693]
    interference with, **17(1)**, [693]
    pre-payment, **17(1)**, [693]
    proper order, to be kept in, **17(1)**, [693]
    removal, entry for, **17(1)**, [693]
    testing and stamping, **17(1)**, [604];
      17(2), [233]
  mining operations, control, **17(1)**, [298]
  nationally significant infrastructure projects,
    46(S), 38–41. *See also* **nationally significant
    infrastructure projects**
  natural—
    British Coal Corporation, exploitation
      rights, **17(2)**, [135]
    disposal by flaring etc, **17(1)**, [480]
    ethane, **17(1)**, [479]
    fuelling of new and converted power
      stations, **17(1)**, [481]
    meaning, **17(1)**, [321], [487]
    methane, **17(1)**, [479]
    offshore—
      disposal by flaring etc, **17(1)**, [480]
      liquefaction, **17(1)**, [479]
      meaning, **17(1)**, [479]
    offshore installations. *See* **offshore
      installations**
    price regulation, **17(1)**, [473]
    releasing unignited, **17(1)**, [480]
    underground storage, **17(1)**, [297]
  notices, service of, **17(1)**, [672]
  offences—
    corporations, by, **17(1)**, [671]
    false or reckless statements, **17(1)**, [669]
  operations, planning applications, **25(2)**, [262]
  orders, provisions as to, **17(1)**, [686]
  pipe-lines—
    capacity etc, increase of—
      directions as to, **17(1)**, [614]
        effect of, **17(1)**, [615]
      generally, **17(1)**, [614]
    construction—
      directions as to, effect of, **17(1)**, [615]
      notice to be given, **17(1)**, [616]
    cost of supplying and laying, **17(1)**, [597]
    infrastructure, third party access to,
      17(2), [669]
    modification of, **17(2)**, [670]
    replacement, repair or alteration, entry for,
      17(1), [693]
    restriction on use of, **17(1)**, [598]
    safety regulations, **17(1)**, [605]
    service—
      connection or disconnection, failure to
        notify, **17(1)**, [693]; **17(2)**, [233]
      maintenance of, **17(1)**, [693]
    use of, acquisition of rights to—
      directions, **17(1)**, [607]
        effect of, **17(1)**, [615]
      generally, **17(1)**, [607]
  pipes, removal, **35(1)**, [21], [176]

gas—*contd*
  processing facilities, acquisition of rights to
    use, **17(2)**, [224]
  quality, standards of, **17(1)**, [603]
  regulations, provisions as to, **17(1)**, [673]
  safety—
    duties of Secretary of State and Authority,
      17(1), [582]
    regulations, **17(1)**, [605]
  Secretary of State—
    expenses and financial provisions,
      17(1), [688]
    health and safety duties, **17(1)**, [584]
    order excluding licensable activities,
      consultation, **17(1)**, [664]
    principal objective and general duties,
      17(1), [582]
    social and environmental matters, guidance
      on, **17(1)**, [583]
  service standards and remuneration,
    17(1), [646]
  sewers and drains, opening and breaking up,
    17(1), [696]
  smart meters—
    installation or operation of, licence required
      for, **17(1)**, [665], [666]
      competitive tenders for, **17(1)**, [667]
    licences—
      activities requiring, **17(2)**, [682]
      conditions, power to amend,
        17(2), [679]–[681]
    summary of provisions, **17(1)**, [1]
  storage underground, acquisition of rights
    for, **9**, [442]
  storage facilities—
    acquisition of rights to use, **17(1)**, [609]
      exemption, application for, **17(1)**, [608]
    areas outside territorial sea, exploitation
      of, **17(2)**, [594]
    definitions, **17(1)**, [613]
    summary of provisions, **17(1)**, [1]
    underground. *See* underground storage
      below
  streets, breaking up, **17(1)**, [696]
  supplier. *See* **gas supplier**
  supply—
    authorisation—
      charges for. *See* charges *above*
      gas suppliers. *See under* **gas supplier**
    charges for. *See* charges *above*
    consumer in default, no obligation to
      restore where, **17(1)**, [693]
    deemed contracts, **17(1)**, [693]
      excess of 25,000 therms per annum, in,
        17(1), [594]
    false statements in connection with,
      17(1), [669]
    illegally taken, **17(1)**, [693]
    inquiries, provisions applicable,
      17(1), [456]
    licences, register of, **17(1)**, [649]
    restoration without consent, **17(1)**, [693]
    restriction on use of pipe-lines,
      17(1), [598]
    therms, method of calculating, **17(1)**, [600]

gas—*contd*
  supply—*contd*
    undue preference or discrimination,
      avoidance, **17(1)**, [596]
  supply, restoration or continuance—
    borough councils' powers, **25(2)**, [269],
      [935], [938], [949], [952]
    instigation of local authority, by,
      25(2), [369]
    recovery of charges, **25(2)**, [369]
  tariffs. *See* charges *above*
  therm, meaning, **17(1)**, [674]
  underground storage—
    accidents—
      inquiry into, **17(1)**, [310], [329]
      notification of, **17(1)**, [310]
      offences and penalties, **17(1)**, [309]
    authorisation order—
      application for—
        form, **17(1)**, [323]
        formal, **17(1)**, [324]
      compensation for effect of, **17(1)**, [300]
      making of, **17(1)**, [324]
      power to make, **17(1)**, [297]
      procedure for making, **17(1)**, [324]
      protective area, enlargement by,
        17(1), [324]
      provisions as to, **17(1)**, [298]
      variation, **17(1)**, [297], [325]
    Church Commissioners, matters involving,
      17(1), [319]
    coal mine, disused, acquisition of land
      forming part of, **17(1)**, [306]
    compensation—
      assessment—
        generally, **17(1)**, [316]
        Lands Tribunal, by, **17(1)**, [303]
      compulsory acquisition of rights,
        17(1), [303], [316]
      double, exclusion of, **17(1)**, [303]
      effect of order on land, **17(1)**, [300]
      grounds for, **17(1)**, [300]
      mortgage, where land subject to,
        17(1), [317]
      payment, special provisions, **17(1)**, [317]
      refusal of consent, **17(1)**, [301]
      repayment, **17(1)**, [304]
      variation of conditions, **17(1)**, [302]
      water pollution, **17(1)**, [308]
      water supply, interference with,
        17(1), [308]
      withdrawal of consent, **17(1)**, [302]
    controlled operations—
      abstraction of water—
        assumption, **17(1)**, [301]
        statutory licence for, **17(1)**, [326]
      consent to—
        application for, **17(1)**, [298]
        compensation for refusal, **17(1)**, [301]
        conditions attaching, **17(1)**, [298],
          [302]
        Minister, by, **17(1)**, [298]
        refusal or revocation, **17(1)**, [298],
          [301]
        variation of conditions, **17(1)**, [392]

gas—*contd*
  underground storage—*contd*
    controlled operations—*contd*
      consent to—*contd*
        withdrawal, **17(1)**, [302]
      Crown or Duchy land, on, **17(1)**, [318]
      default, works to remedy, **17(1)**, [299]
      detection and supervision, **17(1)**, [330]
      gas supplier's responsibilities, **17(1)**, [298]
      meaning, **17(1)**, [298]
      planning permission—
        application for certificate, **17(1)**, [326]
        assumption, **17(1)**, [301]
        certificates, generally, **17(1)**, [326]
      provisions applicable, **17(1)**, [298]
      unauthorised, **17(1)**, [299]
    Crown or Duchy land, application of
      provisions, **17(1)**, [318]
    damage caused by, **17(1)**, [307]
    danger, meaning, **17(1)**, [321]
    discontinuance—
      failure to comply, **17(1)**, [311]
      order for, **17(1)**, [311]
    ecclesiastical property, on, **17(1)**, [319]
    entry, power of—
      compensation, payment of, **17(1)**, [330]
      information obtained, unlawful
        disclosure, **17(1)**, [330]
      obstruction, **17(1)**, [330]
      provisions applicable, **17(1)**, [313]
      reinstatement of land, duty as to,
        17(1), [330]
      sites, search for, **17(1)**, [330]
      supplementary provisions, **17(1)**, [330]
      survey, for purposes of, **17(1)**, [330]
      warrant to authorise, **17(1)**, [330]
    gas transporter's liabilities and
      responsibilities, **17(1)**, [297], [308]
    inquiries, power to hold, **17(1)**, [315],
      [456]
    inspectors—
      appointment, remuneration, etc,
        17(1), [312]
      powers and duties, **17(1)**, [312]
    land charges arising, **17(1)**, [298], [305]
    leakages, **17(1)**, [310]
    liability for damage caused by, **17(1)**, [307]
    meaning, **17(1)**, [298]
    natural gas, **17(1)**, [297]
    nature of gas stored, **17(1)**, [297], [325]
    nuisance, liability for, **17(1)**, [297]
    offences and penalties, generally,
      17(1), [314]
    orders. *See* authorisation order *above*
    planning permission for, deemed,
      17(1), [297], [301], [324]
    proposals for—
      contents, **17(1)**, [324]
      formulation, matters to be considered
        during, **17(1)**, [297]
      preliminary submission, **17(1)**, [324]
    protective area—
      detection and supervision of operations
        in, **17(1)**, [330]
      enlargement of, **17(1)**, [324]

gas—*contd*
  underground storage—*contd*
    protective area—*contd*
      meaning, **17(1)**, [298]
      mining and other operations in,
        17(1), [299]
      reinstatement of land after works,
        17(1), [330]
      rights—
        compulsory acquisition, **17(1)**, [303],
          [306]
        disposal of, restrictions, **17(1)**, [305]
        local land charges, registration as,
          17(1), [320]
        registration as land charge, **17(1)**, [305]
        related, **17(1)**, [305]
      rights of way in connection with,
        17(1), [306]
      safety conditions, power to impose,
        17(1), [309]
      sites, search for, **17(1)**, [330]
      statutory undertakers, meaning,
        17(1), [321]
      storage area—
        compulsory acquisition of rights in,
          17(1), [327]
        detection and supervision of operations
          in, **17(1)**, [330]
        mining and other operations in,
          17(1), [299]
      transfer of functions between suppliers,
        17(1), [325]
      water—
        abstraction, **17(1)**, [306]
        pollution, responsibilities for,
          17(1), [308]
        supplies—
          compulsory purchase affecting,
            17(1), [306], [328]
          interference with, **17(1)**, [308]
      wells, boreholes and shafts, compulsory
        acquisition of rights, **17(1)**, [306], [328]
      works associated with planning approval,
        17(1), [297], [324]
  unlicensed activities relating to gas,
    prohibition on, **17(1)**, [586], [587], [692]
  valves, use of, **17(1)**, [693]
  washings, pollution of water by, penalty for,
    35(1), [20]

Gas and Electricity Consumer Council
  abolished. *See now* **National Consumer
  Council**
  Gas and Electricity Markets Authority, service
    of notices by, **17(1)**, [668]
  information—
    disclosure, restriction on, **17(2)**, [348]
    power to require, **17(1)**, [653]
  service of notices on, **17(1)**, [668]

Gas and Electricity Markets Authority
  annual reports, **17(2)**, [334]
  billing disputes, reference of, **17(1)**, [806]
  carbon emissions, reduction in targets for,
    17(2), [346]

**Gas and Electricity Markets
Authority**—*contd*
  chairman, **17(2)**, [354]
  committees, **17(2)**, [354]
  Competition Commission—
    appeals to, **17(1)**, [1]
    assisting in carrying out investigations,
      17(1), [650]
  competition, functions as to, **17(1)**, [802]
  complaints handling—
    enforcement of requirements, **39(1)**, [719]
    standards for—
      compliance, information as to,
        39(1), [712], [740]
      consumers, supply of information to,
        39(1), [713]
      prescription of, **39(1)**, [710]
      regulations, making, **39(1)**, [711]
  compliance, orders for securing—
    power to make, **17(1)**, [764]
    procedural requirements, **17(1)**, [765]
    validity and effect of, **17(1)**, [766]
  co-operation with National Consumer
    Council, **17(2)**, [336]
  decisions—
    appeals from—
      Competition Commission, to,
        17(2), [518]
        determination of, **17(2)**, [520]
      funding, modification of standard
        conditions for, **17(2)**, [522]
      procedure on, **17(2)**, [519], [567]
  Director General of Gas Supply and Director
    General of Electricity Supply, transfer of
    functions, **17(2)**, [332], [355]
  disputes, determination of, **17(2)**, [60]
  documents, power to require production of,
    17(1), [653]
  duties of, **17(2)**, [674]
  electricity meter legislation, functions under,
    transferred to Secretary of State, **17(2)**, [686]
  energy, regulation, functions, **17(2)**, [529]
  establishment of, **17(2)**, [331]
  forward work programmes, **17(2)**, [33]
  functions—
    advice and assistance by, **17(1)**, [647]
    competition, with respect to, **17(1)**, [650]
    gas measuring equipment, with respect to,
      17(1), [651]
    generally, **17(2)**, [331]
    information—
      collection, **17(1)**, [647]
      power to require, **17(1)**, [653]
      publication of, **17(1)**, [648]
    performance, **17(2)**, [354]
    prices, fixing of maximum, **17(1)**, [652]
    priorities in performance of, **17(1)**, [647]
    registers, maintenance of, **17(1)**, [649]
    transferred to, **17(2)**, [355]
  Gas and Electricity Consumer Council,
    service of notices on, **17(1)**, [668]
  gas meter legislation, functions under,
    transferred to Secretary of State, **17(2)**, [683]
  gas quality, standards of, **17(1)**, [603]

**Gas and Electricity Markets
Authority**—*contd*
general duties and objective of, **17(1)**, [728]
exceptions, **17(1)**, [731]
general functions, **17(1)**, [807]
health and safety duties, **17(1)**, [584]
impact assessment, duty to carry out,
17(2), [335]
information—
disclosure, restriction on, **17(2)**, [348]
power to require, **17(1)**, [773]
publication of, **17(1)**, [808]
licence, activities requiring—
Competition Commission, references to,
17(1), [814]
Enterprise Act 2002, application of,
17(1), [816]
reports, **17(1)**, [817]
time limits, **17(1)**, [815]
exclusion—
application for, **17(1)**, [818]
consultation, **17(1)**, [808]
new, application for order including,
17(1), [813]
notices, service of, **17(1)**, [823]
power to alter, **17(1)**, [812]
maximum prices for reselling electricity,
direction of, **17(1)**, [805]; **17(2)**, [341]
members—
number of, **17(2)**, [354]
pensions, **17(2)**, [354]
remuneration, **17(2)**, [354]
terms of appointment, **17(2)**, [354]
money held by, use of certain, **17(2)**, [375]
National Consumer Council, co-operation
with, **17(2)**, [336]
new licensable activities—
application for order excluding,
17(1), [663]
application for order including,
17(1), [658]
Competition Commission, reference to,
17(1), [659]–[662]
Northern Ireland regulator, power to act on
behalf of, **17(2)**, [467]
objectives, **17(1)**, [1]
penalties imposed by, **17(1)**, [767]
appeals against, **17(1)**, [771]
interest and payment of instalments,
17(1), [770]
recovery of, **17(1)**, [772]
statement of policy regarding, **17(1)**, [768]
time limits for imposition of financial,
17(1), [769]
performance of functions, **17(2)**, [354]
powers, **17(2)**, [354]
prices, fixing of, **17(1)**, [652]
principal objective and general duties,
17(1), [582]
proceedings, **17(2)**, [354]
reasons for decisions—
duty to give, **17(1)**, [654]
publication of, **17(1)**, [810]

**Gas and Electricity Markets
Authority**—*contd*
redress schemes—
approval of—
application for, **39(1)**, [717]
considerations, **39(1)**, [716]
refusal or withdrawal, procedure for,
39(1), [718]
interpretation, **39(1)**, [715]
membership of, **39(1)**, [714], [715]
qualifying, **39(1)**, [715]
register, keeping, **17(1)**, [809]
relevant regulator, as, **39(1)**, [709]
reports, **17(2)**, [334]
Secretary of State, duty to advise, **17(2)**, [225]
social and environmental matters, guidance
on, **17(1)**, [583], [729]
staff, **17(2)**, [354]
standards of performance—
compliance with, collection of information
on, **17(1)**, [645]
disputes, **17(1)**, [637]
gas transporters, of, **17(1)**, [636], [639]
information, **17(1)**, [642]
overall, **17(1)**, [638]
prescribing or determining, procedures
for, **17(1)**, [640]
regulations, **17(1)**, [635]
statistical information, publication of,
17(1), [644]
statement of remuneration and service
standards from licence holders, requirement
for, **17(1)**, [801]
summary of provisions, **17(1)**, [1]
supplementary powers, **17(2)**, [354]
transitional provisions, **17(2)**, [360]

Gas and Markets Authority
references to, **35(2)**, [382]

gas banking scheme
taxation, **42**, [403], [431]

gas board
corporation tax, **44(1)**, [371]

gas code
antifluctuators and valves, use of, **17(1)**, [693];
17(2), [233]
application, **17(1)**, [595]; **17(2)**, [222]
calorific value, change in, alteration of
burners, **17(1)**, [693]
charges, recovery of, **17(1)**, [693];
17(2), [233]
fittings—
distress, not subject to, **17(1)**, [693]
injury to, **17(1)**, [693]
removal, entry for, **17(1)**, [693]
meters—
consumption to be ascertained by,
17(1), [693]
disabled persons, for, **17(1)**, [693]
disconnection of, failure to notify,
17(1), [693]
distress, not subject to, **17(1)**, [693]

gas code—*contd*
  meters—*contd*
    evidence of quantity supplied, as,
      17(1), [693]
    installation in new premises, **17(1)**, [693]
    interference with, **17(1)**, [693]
    pre-payment, **17(1)**, [693]
    proper order, to be kept in, **17(1)**, [693]
    removal, entry for, **17(1)**, [693]
  pipes, entry for replacement, repair or
    alteration, **17(1)**, [693]
  service pipes—
    connection or disconnection, failure to
      notify, **17(1)**, [693]; **17(2)**, [233]
    maintenance of, **17(1)**, [693]
  shipping arrangements, failure to maintain,
    17(1), [693]
  supply—
    continuance of, entry during, **17(1)**, [693]
    deemed contracts, **17(1)**, [693]
    discontinuance of, entry on, **17(1)**, [693]
    illegally taken, **17(1)**, [693]
    no obligation to restore where consumer in
      default, **17(1)**, [693]
    restoration without consent, **17(1)**, [693];
      17(2), [233]

Gas Consultative Council
  chairmen, remuneration of, **19(2)**, [943]

Gas Consumers' Council. *See* **Gas and
Electricity Markets Authority**
  National Council, compensation for loss of
    office etc, **17(1)**, [670]
  Regional Councils, compensation for loss of
    office etc, **17(1)**, [670]

Gas Council
  corporation tax, **44(1)**, [371]

gas shipper. *See also* **gas**
  licences—
    generally, **17(1)**, [590], [591]; **17(2)**, [221]
    register of, **17(1)**, [649]
    standard conditions, **17(2)**, [358]
    transfer of, **17(1)**, [593]

gas supplier. *See also* **gas; public gas supplier**
  carbon emissions—
    promotion of reduction in, **17(1)**, [641]
    targets for reduction in, **17(2)**, [346]
  licences, **17(2)**, [221]
  licences assignment of—
    conditions attaching to—
      enforcement—
        appeals, **17(1)**, [633]
        effect of orders for, **17(1)**, [628]
        final order for, **17(1)**, [626]
        penalties, **17(1)**, [629]–[634]
          interest, **17(1)**, [632]
          payment of instalments,
            17(1), [632]
          recovery of, **17(1)**, [634]
          statement of policy as to,
            17(1), [630]

gas supplier—*contd*
  licences assignment of—*contd*
    conditions attaching to—*contd*
      enforcement—*contd*
        penalties—*contd*
          time limits on imposition of,
            17(1), [631]
          procedural requirements, **17(1)**, [627]
          validity of orders, **17(1)**, [628]
    generally, **17(1)**, [590], [591]
    register of, **17(1)**, [649]
    standard conditions, **17(1)**, [592]
    transfer of, **17(1)**, [593]
  remuneration, **17(1)**, [646]
  standards of performance—
    disputes, **17(1)**, [637]
    efficient use of gas, for promoting,
      17(2), [233]
    gas transporters, of, **17(1)**, [636], [639]
    information, **17(1)**, [642]
    overall, **17(1)**, [638]
      information to be given to customers
        about, **17(1)**, [643]
    prescribing or determining, procedures
      for, **17(1)**, [640]
    regulations, **17(1)**, [635]
    statistical information, publication of,
      17(1), [644]
  working minerals, application for restriction
    on, **17(1)**, [372]

gas supply
  connection to, reduced rate VAT, **50**, [149]

gas transporter. *See also* **gas**
  authorised areas, **17(2)**, [343]
  bridges, breaking up, provisions applicable,
    17(1), [696]
  carbon emissions—
    promotion of reduction in, **17(1)**, [641]
    targets for reduction in, **17(2)**, [346]
  compulsory acquisition of land by—
    Acts applicable, adaptation of, **17(1)**, [695]
    authorisation, **17(1)**, [694]
    compensation—
      assessment, **17(1)**, [695]
      new rights, **17(1)**, [695]
    disposal after, **17(1)**, [694]
    entry, power of, **17(1)**, [695]
    injurious affection arising, **17(1)**, [695]
    interests of others, protection, **17(1)**, [695]
    new rights, **17(1)**, [694]
    rights over land, **17(1)**, [694]
    severance arising, protection, **17(1)**, [695]
  disputes, determination of, **17(1)**, [625]
  duties and functions—
    connection, as to, **17(1)**, [597]
    generally, **17(1)**, [596]
  enforcement orders. *See* licences *below*
  entry, right of. *See under* **gas**
  licences—
    conditions attaching to—
      compliance. *See* enforcement *below*
      enforcement—
        appeals, **17(1)**, [633]

gas transporter—*contd*
  licences—*contd*
    conditions attaching to—*contd*
      enforcement—*contd*
        effect of orders for, **17(1)**, [628]
        final order for, **17(1)**, [626]
        penalties, **17(1)**, [629]–[634]
          interest, **17(1)**, [632]
          payment of instalments,
            17(1), [632]
          recovery of, **17(1)**, [634]
          statement of policy as to,
            17(1), [630]
          time limits on imposition of,
            17(1), [631]
        procedural requirements, **17(1)**, [627]
        validity of orders, **17(1)**, [628]
      generally, **17(1)**, [588]
      modification—
        agreement, by, **17(1)**, [617]
        Competition Commission—
          action following report by,
            17(1), [622]
          power to veto, **17(1)**, [623]
          references to, **17(1)**, [618]–[620]
          report on references, **17(1)**, [621]
        enactments, under other, **17(1)**, [624]
        order, by, **17(1)**, [624]
      register of, **17(1)**, [649]
      special administration regime for, summary
        of provisions, **17(1)**, [1]
      standard, **17(2)**, [344], [358]
      transitional provisions, **17(2)**, [232]
  meaning, **17(1)**, [588]
  powers generally, **17(1)**, [596]
  standards of performance, **17(1)**, [636], [639]
    overall, information to be given to
      customers about, **17(1)**, [643]
    statistical information, publication of,
      17(1), [644]
  storage authorisation. *See under* **gas**
    (underground)
  streets, breaking up, provisions applicable,
    17(1), [696]
  supply by. *See* **gas**
  underground storage. *See under* **gas**

gas undertakers
  land drainage works affecting, **19(3)**, [259]
  London Passenger Transport Act, protection
    under, **36**, [612]

gasworks
  London, buildings near, **25(1)**, [175]
  charge to tax, **44(1)**, [34]

gauges
  water flow, etc, measuring, **49**, [1250]

gavelkind
  abolition, **18**, [548]

Geffrye Museum
  vesting on abolition of GLC, **25(2)**, [604]

gender recognition certificate
  application for—
    acquired gender, meaning, **7(1)**, [702]
    appeals, **7(1)**, [710]
    determination of, **7(1)**, [703]
    evidence in, **7(1)**, [704]
    fees, **7(1)**, [709]
    form of, **7(1)**, [709]
    grant of, **7(1)**, [705]
    making, **7(1)**, [702]
    reports in, **7(1)**, [704]
    successful, **7(1)**, [705]
    two years of commencement, within,
      7(1), [729]
  benefits and pensions, effect on—
    application of provisions, **7(1)**, [735]
    occupational pension schemes, under,
      7(1), [737]
    State benefits, **7(1)**, [736]
  disclosure of information, prohibition,
    7(1), [724]
  effect of, **7(1)**, [711]
  errors in, **7(1)**, [708]
  foreign post-recognition marriage, **7(1)**, [723]
  full, issue of, **7(1)**, [705]
    civil partner, when applicant has been,
      7(1), [707]
    married, when applicant has been,
      7(1), [706]
  gender-specific offences, effect on, **7(1)**, [722]
  interim, **7(1)**, [705]
  interpretation, **7(1)**, [727]
  orders and regulations, **7(1)**, [726]
  parenthood, not affecting, **7(1)**, [714]
  peerage, etc, descent of, **7(1)**, [718]
  personal representatives, duty of, **7(1)**, [719]
  registration, **7(1)**, [712], [733]
    Northern Ireland, **7(1)**, [734]
  sport, effect on, **7(1)**, [721]
  statutory provisions, power to modify,
    7(1), [725]
  succession before appointed day, not
    affecting, **7(1)**, [717]
  trustees, duty of, **7(1)**, [719]
  will, devolution of property under,
    7(1), [720]

Gender Recognition Panel
  constitution, **7(1)**, [732]
  gender recognition certificate, application for.
    See **gender recognition certificate**
  membership, **7(1)**, [732]

General Chiropractic Council. *See also*
chiropractors
  accounts, **28**, [723]
  appeals against decisions of, **28**, [713]
  appeals against decisions of Registrar to,
    28, [712]
  audit, **28**, [723]
  Chairman, **28**, [727], [729]
  Code of Practice, **28**, [702]
  constitution, **28**, [727]

General Chiropractic Council—*contd*
Council for the Regulation of Health Care
Professionals. *See* **Council for the
Regulation of Health Care Professionals**
duties, **28**, [683]
Education Committee—
duties, **28**, [694]
establishment of, **28**, [683]
general, **28**, [728]
information to be given to, by institutions,
28, [701]
members, **28**, [728]
members of Council appointed by,
28, [727]
revocation of interim suspension orders,
28, [708]
visitors, **28**, [695]
establishment of, **28**, [683]
Health Committee—
appeals against decisions of, **28**, [714]
consideration of allegations by, **28**, [706]
establishment of, **28**, [683]
general, **28**, [728]
interim suspension powers of, **28**, [707]
investigation of allegations, procedural rules
for, **28**, [709]
legal assessors, advice from, **28**, [710]
medical assessors, advice from, **28**, [711]
members, **28**, [728]
revocation of interim suspension orders,
28, [708]
interpretation provisions, **28**, [725]
Investigating Committee—
allegations against professional conduct and
fitness to practise, **28**, [703]
establishment of, **28**, [683]
general, **28**, [728]
interim suspension powers of, **28**, [704]
legal assessors, advice from, **28**, [710]
medical assessors, advice from, **28**, [711]
members, **28**, [728]
revocation of interim suspension orders,
28, [708]
legal assessors, appointment of, **28**, [710]
medical assessors, appointment of, **28**, [711]
members—
chiropractic, **28**, [729]
education, **28**, [729]
fully registered chiropractors, elected by,
28, [727]
lay, **28**, [729]
Privy Council, appointed by, **28**, [727],
[729]
Secretary of State, appointed by, **28**, [727],
[729]
membership—
general, **28**, [727]
initial, **28**, [729]
transitional periods, **28**, [729]
post registration training, **28**, [700]
powers of, **28**, [727]
Privy Council—
default powers of, **28**, [718]
exercise of powers of, **28**, [720]

General Chiropractic Council—*contd*
Privy Council—*contd*
members of General Council appointed
by, **28**, [727], [729]
rules by General Council, requirement for
approval by, **28**, [719]
Professional Conduct Committee—
appeals against decisions of, **28**, [715]
consideration of allegations by, **28**, [705]
establishment of, **28**, [683]
general, **28**, [728]
interim suspension powers of, **28**, [707]
investigation of allegations, procedural rules
for, **28**, [709]
legal assessors, advice from, **28**, [710]
members, **28**, [728]
restoration to register, applications referred
to, **28**, [691]
revocation of suspension orders, **28**, [708]
professional indemnity insurance, rules
requiring, **28**, [721]
proficiency, standards of, **28**, [696]
qualifications—
recognition of, **28**, [697], [698]
withdrawal of recognition, **28**, [699]
register, provision of access to, **28**, [692]
Registrar, legal assessors, advice from,
28, [710]
registration rules. *See* **chiropractors**
transitional provisions, **28**, [726]

General Claims Tribunal
abolition and transfer of jurisdiction, **9**, [204]

general commercial company
objects, statement of, **8**, 107

General Commissioners
allowances, **42**, [90]
appeal to, **42**, [157]
appointment of, **42**, [90]
assignment of proceedings to, **42**, [265]
change of name, **42**, [1511]
clerk—
compensation for loss of office, **42**, [293]
employment of, **42**, [92]
indemnity, **42**, [93]
declaration on taking office, **42**, [97], [261],
[272]
determinations, conclusive nature of,
42, [173]
divisions, for—
areas of, **42**, [90]
boundaries, **42**, [306]
generally, **42**, [1]
indemnity, **42**, [93]
interest in proceedings, having, **42**, [96]
jurisdiction, **42**, [173]; **43(1)**, [406]
legal proceedings, costs and expenses in,
42, [91]
Northern Ireland, for, **42**, [928]
penalty proceedings before, **42**, [238]
proceedings before, **42**, [173]
retirement age, **42**, [90]

General Council of the Bar
rights of audience, grant of, **11(3)**, [89]

General Dental Council
accounts, **28**, [368]
annual reports, **28**, [367]
board of examiners, appointment by,
  28, [371]
competent authority, as, **28**, [413]
complaints, investigation and resolution of,
  28, [369]
constitution, **28**, [469]
continuation, **28**, [364]
Continuing Professional Development
  Committee, **28**, [473]
co-operation, duty of, **28**, [366]
Council for the Regulation of Health Care
  Professionals. *See* **Council for the**
  Regulation of Health Care Professionals
courses of study inadequate, powers as to,
  28, [378]
Directive, functions under, **28**, [475]
disclosure of information, power to require,
  28, [406], [439]
duties, general, **28**, [364]
examinations inadequate, powers as to,
  28, [378]
fees, **28**, [414]
fitness to practice—
  allegations relating to, **28**, [395], [428]
  appeals, **28**, [400], [433]
  guidance, **28**, [394], [427]
  impaired, **28**, [395]
  investigation, **28**, [396], [397]
  notification and disclosure by Council,
    28, [407], [440]
  supplementary provisions, **28**, [437]
  suspension of registration, **28**, [404]
Health Committee—
  appeal from, **28**, [400]
  establishment, **28**, [365]
  interim orders, **28**, [403], [436]
  legal advisers, **28**, [479]
  medical advisers, **28**, [479]
  professional advisers, **28**, [479]
  unfitness to practice, reference, **28**, [396]
information to, **28**, [375]
Interim Orders Committee—
  constitution, **28**, [365]
  interim orders, **28**, [403], [436]
  legal advisers, **28**, [479]
  medical advisers, **28**, [479]
  proceedings before, **28**, [472], [477]
  professional advisers, **28**, [479]
Investigating Committee—
  allegations relating to fitness to practice,
    reference, **28**, [395], [429]
  constitution, **28**, [365]
  investigation by, **28**, [396]
  legal advisers, **28**, [479]
  medical advisers, **28**, [479]
  powers of, **28**, [396]
  proceedings before, **28**, [472], [477]
  professional advisers, **28**, [479]
  warning, issue of, **28**, [396]

General Dental Council—*contd*
legal advisers, **28**, [479]
medical advisers, **28**, [479]
members, **28**, [469]
particular theories, powers as to adoption or
  rejection, **28**, [379]
powers, general, **28**, [469]
Practice Committees—
  allegations relating to fitness to practice,
    reference, **28**, [430]
  appeal from, **28**, [400], [433]
  constitution, **28**, [365]
  directions, taking effect, **28**, [434]
  interim orders, **28**, [403]
  investigation by, **28**, [397]
  meaning, **28**, [365]
  proceedings before, **28**, [472], [477]
  publication of information, **28**, [460]
  resumed hearings, **28**, [398], [431]
procedure, rules of, **28**, [469]
professional advisers, **28**, [479]
professional conduct, guidance, **28**, [394],
  [427]
Professional Conduct Committee—
  appeal from, **28**, [400], [433]
  body corporate carrying on dental business,
    withdrawal of privilege from, **28**, [456]
  constitution, **28**, [365]
  directions, taking effect, **28**, [434]
  erasure from register, functions of,
    28, [390]
  interim orders, **28**, [403], [436]
  legal advisers, **28**, [479]
  medical advisers, **28**, [479]
  professional advisers, **28**, [479]
  suspension of registration, supplementary
    provisions, **28**, [404]
Professional Performance Committee—
  constitution, **28**, [365]
  interim orders, **28**, [403], [436]
  legal advisers, **28**, [479]
  medical advisers, **28**, [479]
  professional advisers, **28**, [479]
  reference to, **28**, [396]
professional training and development
  requirements, **28**, [408]
  restoration of name to register, **28**, [410]
  visiting dentists from relevant European
    countries, **28**, [409]
professions complementary to dentistry. *See*
  professions complementary to dentistry
publication of information, **28**, [460]
Registration Appeals Committee—
  appeals from, **28**, [471], [476]
  appeals to, **28**, [471], [476]
  constitution, **28**, [365]
  legal advisers, **28**, [479]
  medical advisers, **28**, [479]
  professional advisers, **28**, [479]
reports, **28**, [367]
rules—
  consultation requirements, **28**, [462]
  power to make, **28**, [461]
visitors to dental schools, appointment by,
  28, [376]

general improvement area. *See also* **housing action area**
area ceasing to be, **23**, [36]
cessation of power to declare, **23**, [36]
contributions by Secretary of State, **22**, [229]
declaration of—
cancellation of, **22**, [228]
conditions for, **22**, [223]
steps taken after, **22**, [224]
definition of, **22**, [223]
entry of premises—
obstruction of, **22**, [233]
powers of, **22**, [232]
expenditure on, **22**, [229]
grants. *See* **improvement grant**
highways, stopping use of, **22**, [226]
information, duty to publish, **22**, [227]
land—
comprised in, **22**, [223]
exclusion from, **22**, [228]
incorporation in housing action area, **22**, [212]
powers in respect of, **22**, [225]
notice to Secretary of State of, **22**, [224]
owner of premises, meaning, **22**, [234]
powers of housing authority in, **22**, [225]
resolution declaring—
conditions for, **22**, [223]
effect of, **22**, [230], [231]
notice of, publication of, **22**, [224]
publication of, **22**, [224]
steps to be taken in, **22**, [224]
termination of, **22**, [228]

General Lighthouse Fund
accounts and audit, **39(2)**, [888]
expenses paid from, **39(2)**, [888]
charges relating to, **39(2)**, [1008]
further powers in relation to, **39(2)**, [1008]
light dues paid to, **39(2)**, [888]
lighthouse authorities, sums paid to, **39(2)**, [889]
pension rights, **39(2)**, [891]

General Medical Council
annual report, **28**, [345]
appealable decisions of, **28**, [326]
borrowing powers, **28**, [351]
branch councils, **28**, [354]
chairman, **28**, [351]
competent authority, as, **28**, [341]
conduct, performance or ethics, power to advise on, **28**, [317]
constitution, **28**, [275], [351]
continuation, **28**, [275]
Council for the Regulation of Health Care Professionals. *See* **Council for the Regulation of Health Care Professionals**
Directive, functions under, **28**, [360]
Education Committee—
constitution, **28**, [275], [353]
general functions of, **28**, [279]
information to, **28**, [280]
inspectors—
appointment by, **28**, [280]

General Medical Council—*contd*
Education Committee—*contd*
inspectors—*contd*
attendance at examinations, **28**, [280]
reports by, **28**, [280]
medical schools, visitors of, **28**, [281]
orders, proof of, **28**, [346]
Privy Council, powers where standards not maintained, **28**, [283]
provisionally registered doctors, programmes for, **28**, [284]
qualifying examinations, recommendations for further, **28**, [282]
standards of proficiency, determination by, **28**, [279], [282], [283]
visitors, medical schools of, **28**, [281]
financial provisions, **28**, [351]
fitness to practice—
disclosure of information, power to require, **28**, [318]
notification of decisions regarding, by, **28**, [319]
power to advise on, **28**, [317]
Fitness to Practice Panels—
appeals, **28**, [326]
constitution, **28**, [275], [353]
directions, **28**, [322], [323]
evidence, **28**, [359]
functions of, **28**, [322]
interim orders, **28**, [328]
proceedings before, **28**, [359]
professional performance assessments, **28**, [359]
restoration to register, direction for, **28**, [327]
incidental powers, **28**, [351]
Interim Orders Panels—
constitution, **28**, [275], [353]
evidence, **28**, [359]
orders by, **28**, [328]
proceedings before, **28**, [359]
Investigation Committee—
constitution, **28**, [275], [353]
evidence, **28**, [359]
fitness to practice, determining, **28**, [320]
functions of, **28**, [320]
licence to practice, reference of matters, **28**, [302]
proceedings before, **28**, [359]
professional performance assessments, **28**, [359]
references to, **28**, [358]
rules, **28**, [321]
licence to practice. *See* **medical practitioner**
medical register, regulations as to, **28**, [309]–[312]
members, **28**, [351]
Office of Health Professional Adjudicator, fees payable to, **28(S)**, 17–18
officers, **28**, [352]
president, **28**, [351]
proceedings of, **28**, [351]
registrar, appointment, **28**, [351]
Registration Appeals Panels—
appeals from, **28**, [357]

General Medical Council—*contd*
　Registration Appeals Panels—*contd*
　　appeals to, **28**, [358]
　　constitution, **28**, [275], [353]
　Registration Panels, constitution, **28**, [275], [353]
　regulations—
　　medical registers, as to, **28**, [310]
　　proof of, **28**, [346]

general meetings
　adjourned, resolution passed at, **8(1)**, [410]
　adjournment, vote on, **8(1)**, [399]
　annual. *See* **annual general meeting**
　calling—
　　directors' duty to call when required by members, **8(1)**, [382]
　　directors, power of, **8(1)**, [380]
　　members' power to call at company's expense, **8(1)**, [383]
　　members' power to require, **8(1)**, [381]
　chairman—
　　declaration on show of hands, **8(1)**, [398]
　　election of, **8(1)**, [397]
　　proxy as, **8(1)**, [406]
　computation of periods of notice, **8(1)**, [438]
　corporation, representation of, **8(1)**, [401]
　electronic form, documents in, **8(1)**, [411]
　members' statements—
　　circulation of—
　　　application not to circulate, **8(1)**, [395]
　　　duty of company, **8(1)**, [393]
　　　expenses of, **8(1)**, [394]
　　　power to require, **8(1)**, [392]
　more extensive rights conferred by articles, saving for, **8(1)**, [409]
　notice of—
　　accidental failure to give, **8(1)**, [391]
　　computation of periods of, **8(1)**, [438]
　　contents of, **8(1)**, [389]
　　electronic form, in, **8(1)**, [411]
　　manner of giving, **8(1)**, [386]
　　persons entitled to receive, **8(1)**, [388]
　　requirement, **8(1)**, [385]
　　right to appoint proxy, statement of, **8(1)**, [403]
　　special, resolution requiring, **8(1)**, [390]
　　website, publication on, **8(1)**, [387]
　poll—
　　right of proxy to demand, **8(1)**, [407]
　　right to demand, **8(1)**, [399]
　　voting on, **8(1)**, [400]
　power of court to order, **8(1)**, [384]
　proxy—
　　appointment of—
　　　company-sponsored invitation, **8(1)**, [404]
　　　notice of meeting, rights to appear in, **8(1)**, [403]
　　　notice of, **8(1)**, [405]
　　　right of, **8(1)**, [402]
　　meeting, chairing, **8(1)**, [406]
　　more extensive rights conferred by articles, saving for, **8(1)**, [409]
　　poll, right to demand, **8(1)**, [407]

general meetings—*contd*
　proxy—*contd*
　　termination of authority, notice of, **8(1)**, [408]
　public company, of—
　　accounts and reports, laying, **8(1)**, [515]
　　failure, offence of, **8(1)**, [516]
　quorum, **8(1)**, [396]
　quoted company, of—
　　extension of provisions to other types of company, **8(1)**, [432]
　　independent report on poll—
　　　assessor—
　　　　appointment of, **8(1)**, [421]
　　　　associate of, **8(1)**, [423]
　　　　independence requirement, **8(1)**, [422]
　　　　information, right to, **8(1)**, [427]
　　　　meeting, right to attend, **8(1)**, [426]
　　　　partnership as, **8(1)**, [424]
　　　　provision of information to, offences, **8(1)**, [428]
　　　　report, **8(1)**, [425]
　　　class meetings, provisions applying to, **8(1)**, [430]
　　　members' power to require, **8(1)**, [420]
　　　website availability, **8(1)**, [431]
　　　website, information on, **8(1)**, [429]
　　poll—
　　　class meetings, provisions applying to, **8(1)**, [430]
　　　independent report on. *See* independent report on poll *above*
　　　website availability, **8(1)**, [431]
　　　website, publication of results on, **8(1)**, [419]
　records of—
　　class of members, of, **8(1)**, [437]
　　inspection of, **8(1)**, [436]
　　preservation, time for, **8(1)**, [433]
　　requirement to keep, **8(1)**, [433]
　　sole member, of decisions by, **8(1)**, [435]
　resolutions passed at, **8(1)**, [379]
　right of auditor to attend or be heard, **8(1)**, [580]

General Optical Council. *See also* **opticians**
　accounts, **28**, [556]
　committees, general power to appoint, **28**, [509]
　Companies Committee, **28**, [502]
　constitution, **28**, [500], [564]
　Council for the Regulation of Health Care Professionals, functions of. *See* **Council for the Regulation of Health Care Professionals**
　delegation, powers of, **28**, [510]
　education and training—
　　competencies, **28**, [523]
　　content and standards of, **28**, [523]
　　continuing, scheme for—
　　　failure to satisfy requirements, **28**, [522]
　　　rules, **28**, [521]
　　supervision, **28**, [524]

General Optical Council—*contd*
  Education Committee—
    constitution, **28**, [501]
    consultation, **28**, [523]
  expenses, **28**, [556]
  fitness to practice—
    allegation as to—
      disclosure of information, power to
        require, **28**, [526]
      nature of, **28**, [528]
      notification and disclosure, **28**, [527]
    financial penalty order, imposition of,
      28, [532]
    guidance, provision of, **28**, [525]
    impaired, **28**, [528]
  Fitness to Practice Committee—
    appeals from, **28**, [544]
      date of decision, **28**, [545]
    clinical and specialist advisers, **28**, [542]
    constitution, **28**, [507]
    directions by, **28**, [531]
    immediate suspension, order for, **28**, [533]
    interim orders, **28**, [536]
    legal advisers, **28**, [541]
    powers of, **28**, [530]
    procedure, **28**, [539]
    reference to, **28**, [528]
    rules of procedure and evidence, **28**, [540]
  functions of, **28**, [500]
  Hearings Panel, constitution, **28**, [508]
  Investigation Committee—
    directions by, **28**, [528]
    exercise of functions of, **28**, [529]
    constitution, **28**, [503]
    investigations by, **28**, [528]
  legal proceedings, **28**, [553]
  members, **28**, [564]
  Office of Health Professional Adjudicator, fees
    payable to, **28(S)**, 17–18
  powers of, **28**, [564]
  Privy Council's power to alter membership
    of, **28**, [564]
  registrar, **28**, [500], [564]
    functions of Investigation Committee,
      exercise of, **28**, [529]
  Registration Appeals Committee—
    appeals from, **28**, [544]
      date of decision, **28**, [545]
    appeals to, **28**, [565]
    clinical and specialist advisers, **28**, [542]
    constitution, **28**, [505]
    legal advisers, **28**, [541]
    procedure, **28**, [539]
    restoration to register, order for, **28**, [535]
    rules of procedure and evidence, **28**, [540]
  Registration Committee, constitution,
    28, [504]
  rules, **28**, [554], [555]
  Standards Committee—
    constitution, **28**, [506]
    consultation, **28**, [523]

General Osteopathic Council. *See also*
osteopaths
  accounts, financial provisions as to, **28**, [677]

General Osteopathic Council—*contd*
  appeals against decisions of, **28**, [667]
  chairman, **28**, [680]
  Code of Practice, requirement to produce,
    28, [656]
  constitution, **28**, [680]
  Council for the Regulation of Health Care
    Professionals, functions of. *See* **Council for
    the Regulation of Health Care
    Professionals**
  Education Committee—
    constitution, **28**, [681]
    duties, **28**, [648]
    establishment of, **28**, [637]
    members, **28**, [681]
    visitors to educational institutions,
      appointment of, **28**, [649]
  educational institutions, requirement for
    information from, **28**, [655]
  establishment of, **28**, [637]
  Health Committee—
    constitution, **28**, [681]
    establishment of, **28**, [637]
    members, **28**, [681]
  initial membership of, **28**, [682]
  Investigating Committee—
    constitution, **28**, [681]
    establishment of, **28**, [637]
    members, **28**, [681]
  members, **28**, [680]
  post registration training, rules regarding,
    28, [654]
  powers of, **28**, [680]
    default powers of, **28**, [672]
    exercise of powers of, **28**, [674]
    rules, requirement for approval by,
      28, [673]
  professional conduct and fitness to practise—
    Health Committee—
      appeals against decisions of, **28**, [668]
      consideration of allegations, **28**, [660]
      interim suspension—
        powers of, **28**, [661]
        revocation of orders, **28**, [662]
      investigations of allegations, procedural
        rules of, **28**, [663]
      legal assessors, advice from, **28**, [664]
      medical assessors, advice from, **28**, [665]
    Investigating Committee—
      first referral to, **28**, [657]
      Health Committee, referral to, **28**, [657]
      interim suspension powers of, **28**, [658]
      legal assessors, advice from, **28**, [664]
      medical assessors, advice from, **28**, [665]
      Professional Conduct Committee,
        referral to, **28**, [657]
    Professional Conduct Committee—
      appeals against decisions of, **28**, [669]
      consideration of allegations, **28**, [659]
      interim suspension—
        powers of, **28**, [661]
        revocation of orders, **28**, [662]
      investigations of allegations, procedural
        rules of, **28**, [663]
      legal assessors, advice from, **28**, [664]

General Osteopathic Council—*contd*
professional conduct and fitness to
practise—*contd*
Professional Conduct Committee—*contd*
medical assessors, advice from, **28**, [665]
Professional Conduct Committee—
establishment of, **28**, [637]
membership, **28**, [681]
qualifications, recognition of—
general, **28**, [651]
supplemental, **28**, [652]
withdrawal of, **28**, [653]
register of osteopaths—
requirement to make available to public,
28, [646]
restoration to, **28**, [645]
suspension of, **28**, [644]
Registrar of Osteopaths, appointment of,
28, [638]
standard of proficiency, determination of,
28, [650]
transitional periods, **28**, [682]
transitional provisions, **28**, [682]

General Practice Finance Corporation
property, etc, vesting of, **30**, [527]
successor company—
corporation tax, **30**, [516]
statutory accounts, **30**, [515]
transfer to, **30**, [527]
Treasury guarantees, **30**, [514]

General Social Care Council
accounts, **35(2)**, [363]
chief officer, **35(2)**, [363]
codes of practice, **35(2)**, [327]
delegation of functions, **35(2)**, [363]
directions to, **35(2)**, [319]
duties of, **35(2)**, [319]
establishment of, **35(2)**, [319]
execution of documents, **35(2)**, [363]
general duty of, **35(2)**, [363]
general powers of, **35(2)**, [363]
members—
appointment, **35(2)**, [363]
remuneration and allowances, **35(2)**, [363]
membership, **35(2)**, [363]
payments to, **35(2)**, [363]
procedure, **35(2)**, [363]
reports and information, **35(2)**, [363]
rules, power to make, **35(2)**, [337]
seal, application of, **35(2)**, [363]
social care workers, registers of,
35(2), [321]. *See also* **social care workers**
staff, **35(2)**, [363]
status, **35(2)**, [363]
training—
courses, approval of, **35(2)**, [328]
examinations, conduct of, **35(2)**, [328]
Minister, functions of, **35(2)**, [332]
post-registration, **35(2)**, [330]
qualifications gained outside area,
35(2), [329]
Tribunal, appeals to, **35(2)**, [334]
visitors, appointment of, **35(2)**, [331]

General Social Care Council—*contd*
use of staff, arrangements for, **35(2)**, [363]

General Synod
Appointments Committee of the Church of
England, **14**, 1330
Business Committee, **14**, 1330
canons, making etc., **14**, 685
chair, **14(S)**, 96
choirmasters, appointment, **14**, 1179
Church Assembly reconstituted as, **14**, 686,
768
Church Commissioners' report and accounts
before, **14**, 426
clergy pensions, making regulations on,
14, 806–7
committees etc, of—
generally, **14**, 696
restriction on membership, **14**, 1330
constitution of, **14**, 6, 693–7
convocations—
amending constitution of, **14**, 809
functions and authority, vesting, **14**, 685,
692–3
diocesan synods—
constitution and function of, **14**, 688–9
referring matters to, **14**, 695, 1393
See also **diocesan synods**
dioceses commission, appointing, **14**, 906
dissolution of, **14**, 693
ecclesiastical jurisdiction measures, powers
exercised under, **14**, 687
ecumenical relations—
Act of Uniformity, exclusion of, **14**, 1186
buildings, use by other churches,
14, 1183–4
canon relating to, **14**, 1183–4
churches to which provisions apply,
14, 1186
joint worship, provision for, **14**, 1183–4
local projects—
meaning, **14**, 1186
participation in, **14**, 1184–5
overseas clergymen etc, **14**, 1185
restrictions relating to, **14**, 1185–6
functions of, **14**, 694–5
house of bishops—
matters referred to, **14**, 695
meaning, **14**, 331
upper house, as, **14**, 693
house of clergy—
lower house, as, **14**, 693
meaning, **14**, 331
house of laity—
casual vacancies, **14**, 748–9
co-opted members, **14**, 740–1
Diocese in Europe, representation of,
14, 960
elected members—
number of, **14**, 735–6
province, from dioceses in, **14**, 734
qualifications of, **14**, 736
term of office, **14**, 740
elections, **14**, 693
appeal, **14**, 742–4

General Synod—*contd*
house of laity—*contd*
elections—*contd*
chairman and vice-chairman, of, **14**, 696
conduct of, **14**, 737–9
constraints in, **14**, 750
electoral areas, **14**, 737
presiding officers' rules, **14**, 739
ex-officio members, **14**, 740, 747
meaning, **14**, 331
members of, **14**, 734
new diocese, from, **14**, 912
reorganisation of diocese, during,
14, 912
representative members, **14**, 734–5
term of office, **14**, 740
resignation from, **14**, 750
vacation of seat, **14**, 745–6
legislative committee, **14**, 7, 696
licences—
ministers etc, revocation of, **14**, 1179
power to revoke, **14**, 13
meaning, **14**, 331
Measures—
force and effect, **41**, [480]
interpretation, **41**, [480], [597]
passing, date of, **14**, 332
proof of, **14**, 332
meetings of, **14**, 693
membership of convocations, temporary
provision as to, **14(S)**, 134
motions, passing, **14**, 694
organists, appointment, **14**, 1179
prayer book measures, powers exercised
under, **14**, 687
presidents of, **14**, 694
procedure, making provision by canon for,
14, 831–2
registrars of, **14**, 694
regulation, meaning, **14**, 331
Royal Writ dissolving and bringing into
being, **14**, 685
standing orders, **14**, 695, 1329
Vacation of Benefices Rule Committee,
14, 898
voting, **14(S)**, 96
widows' pensions, making regulations on,
14, 806–7

General Teaching Council
accounts, **15(1)**, [812]
additional functions, **15(1)**, [790]
advisory functions, **15(1)**, [783]
ancillary functions, **15(1)**, [790]
annual reports, **15(1)**, [812]
chairman, **15(1)**, [812]
committees, **15(1)**, [812]
delegation of functions, **15(1)**, [812]
disciplinary powers—
appeals against disciplinary orders,
15(1), [813]
conditional registration orders, **15(1)**, [813]
disciplinary orders, **15(1)**, [813]
investigation, hearing and determination of
disciplinary cases, **15(1)**, [813]

General Teaching Council—*contd*
disciplinary powers—*contd*
prohibition orders, **15(1)**, [813]
supplementary provisions, **15(1)**, [813]
suspension orders, **15(1)**, [813]
establishment of, **15(1)**, [782]
finance, **15(1)**, [812]
functions, **15(1)**, [782]
members—
appointment, **15(1)**, [812]
interests reflected by, **15(1)**, [782]
salaries and allowances, **15(1)**, [812]
powers, **15(1)**, [812]
proceedings, **15(1)**, [812]
proof of instruments, **15(1)**, [812]
register of teachers—
establishment and maintenance of,
15(1), [784]
registration—
appeals against refusal of, **15(1)**, [786]
eligibility for, **15(1)**, [784]
fees, **15(1)**, [794]
regulations, **15(1)**, [785]
registered teachers—
code of practice, **15(1)**, [787]
disciplinary powers in relation to,
15(1), [788]
seal, **15(1)**, [812]
staff, **15(1)**, [812]
status, **15(1)**, [812]
supply of information relating to teachers—
agency, by, **15(1)**, [797]
contractor, by, **15(1)**, [797]
dismissal or resignation, as to, **15(1)**, [796]
generally, **15(1)**, [795]
teaching profession, power to promote,
15(1), [789]

General Teaching Council for Wales
establishment of, **15(1)**, [791]
functions, **15(1)**, [792]–[793]
supply of information relating to teachers—
agency, by, **15(1)**, [797]
contractor, by, **15(1)**, [797]
dismissal or resignation, as to, **15(1)**, [796]
generally, **15(1)**, [795]

general vesting declaration
acquiring authority—
liability arising on vesting, **9**, [395]
meaning, **9**, [387]
vesting of land in, **9**, [393]
application of provisions, **9**, [386]
compensation—
liability for, **9**, [395]
overpaid, recovery, **9**, [396]
questions as to, determination by Lands
Tribunal, **9**, [395]
confirmation, statutory notice of, **9**, [388]
construction of provisions, **9**, [387]
constructive notice to treat, **9**, [392]
deed poll, **9**, [393]

general vesting declaration—*contd*
divided land, provisions applicable, **9**, [397], [403]
See also severance *below*
documents of title—
production and delivery, **9**, [399]
safe custody, **9**, [399]
effect of, **9**, [1], [392]–[394]
entry, right of, **9**, [393]–[394]
execution of—
earliest date for, **9**, [390]
notices after, **9**, [391]
notices prior to, **9**, [388]
vesting date, **9**, [389]
interpretation, **9**, [387]
land, meaning, **9**, [387]
Local Government, etc, Act 1980, s 141
orders, application to, **9**, [400], [405]
long tenancy about to expire—
meaning, **9**, [387]
right of entry where, **9**, [394]
meaning, **9**, [387]
minor tenancy—
meaning, **9**, [387]
right of entry where, **9**, [394]
notice to treat, constructive, **9**, [392]
notices—
execution, after, **9**, [391]
objection to severance. *See* severance *below*
preliminary, **9**, [388]
statutory notice of confirmation, meaning, **9**, [388]
particulars in, **9**, [388]
possession, right to take, **9**, [393]–[394]
preliminary notice, local land charge, as, **9**, [388]
rent, recovery of mistaken payment, **9**, [398]
rentcharge, recovery of mistaken payment, **9**, [398]
severance—
objection to—
notice of—
effect of, **9**, [403]
late service of, **9**, [403]
meaning, **9**, [403]
reference to Lands Tribunal, **9**, [403]
service of, **9**, [403]
rentcharges, **9**, [404]
response by acquiring authority to, **9**, [403]
tenancies, **9**, [404]
transitional provisions, **9**, [406]
vesting date—
meaning, **9**, [389]
possession, taking on, **9**, [393]–[394]
right to enter on, **9**, [393]–[391]
vesting in acquiring authority on, **9**, [393]–[394]

generating station
construction, extension or operation of, consent for, **17(1)**, [785], [872]
fuel stocks, **17(1)**, [783], [784]
fuelling, **17(1)**, [481]
green certificates, **17(1)**, [779]

generating station—*contd*
Nuclear Decommissioning Authority's power to operate, **17(2)**, [387]
sea, at—
navigation—
duties in relation to, **17(1)**, [787]
extinguishing rights of, **17(1)**, [786]

genetically modified organism
acquisition of, **35(1)**, [824]
advisory committee, **35(1)**, [839]
biological matter, meaning, **35(1)**, [821]
consents—
application for, **35(1)**, [826]
conditions, **35(1)**, [826]
exemptions, **35(1)**, [826]
fees and charges, **35(1)**, [828]
implied conditions, **35(1)**, [827]
importation, acquisition, release or marketing, for, **35(1)**, [826]
limitations, **35(1)**, [827]
requirement of, **35(1)**, [826]
control of person, under, **35(1)**, [822]
enforcement powers, delegation of, **35(1)**, [840]
escape or release, prevention of damage from, **35(1)**, [821]
genetically modified, meaning, **35(1)**, [821]
harm, capable of causing, **35(1)**, [822]
importation of, **35(1)**, [824]
information, obtaining, **35(1)**, [831]
inspectors—
appointment of, **35(1)**, [829]
entry and inspection, rights of, **35(1)**, [830]
imminent danger of damage, dealing with, **35(1)**, [832]
powers of, **35(1)**, [830]
keeping of, **35(1)**, [824]
notification requirements, **35(1)**, [823]
offences—
body corporate, by, **35(1)**, [851]
cause, remedying, **35(1)**, [835]
fault of others, due to, **35(1)**, [852]
generally, **35(1)**, [833]
onus of proof, **35(1)**, [834]
organism, meaning, **35(1)**, [821]
penalties, **35(1)**, [833]
prohibition notices, **35(1)**, [825]
register of information—
exclusion of information from, **35(1)**, [838]
maintenance of, **35(1)**, [837]
release of, **35(1)**, [824]
reproduction, reference to, **35(1)**, [821]
risk assessment, **35(1)**, [823]
Secretary of State—
enforcement powers, delegation of, **35(1)**, [840]
harm, power to remedy, **35(1)**, [836]
information, obtaining, **35(1)**, [831]
mode of exercise of functions, **35(1)**, [841]

Geneva Conventions
additional distinctive emblem, adoption of, **10(S)**, 126–30
amended provisions, **10(S)**, 123–4

Geneva Conventions—*contd*
generally, **10**, [1]
grave breaches of, **10**, [944]
trial and punishment of, **10**, [945]
prisoner of war, trial of. *See* **prisoner of war**
text of, **10**, [954]–[976]

Geneva Cross
use of emblem, **10**, [950]–[951], [954], [971]

genocide
ancillary offence—
investigation, rights during, **10**, [1224]
meaning, **10**, [1193]
application of provisions, **10**, [1188]
commanders and other superiors,
responsibility of, **10**, [1203]
committed outside the jurisdiction, conduct
ancillary to, **10**, [1190]
elements of, **10**, [1231]
England and Wales, offence in, **10**, [1189]
extradition request in respect of, **18**, [956]
general principles of liability, application of,
10, [1194]
International Criminal Court, offences in
relation to, **10**, [1192]
meaning, **10**, [1188], [1231]
mental element, **10**, [1204]
Northern Ireland. *See* **Northern Ireland**
omission, act including, **10**, [1207]
person subject to UK service jurisdiction,
meaning, **10**, [1205]
persons becoming resident in the jurisdiction,
proceedings against, **10**, [1206]
trial and punishment of, **10**, [1191]
UK national, meaning, **10**, [1205]
UK resident, meaning, **10**, [1205]
victims and witnesses, protection of,
10, [1195]

Germany, Federal Republic of
Arbitral Commission, immunities and
privileges, **10**, [940]
Arbitration Tribunal, immunities and
privileges, **10**, [940]
Bonn Conventions, **10**, [939]
customs law, enforcement of, **10**, [941]
Supreme Restitution Court, immunities and
privileges, **10**, [940]

Ghana
British ship registered in, **7(2)**, [462]
citizenship, cesser of former provisions as to,
31, [53]
Commonwealth citizenship, **31**, [186]
fully responsible status of, **7(2)**, [458]
legislative powers of, **7(2)**, [461]
republic, becoming, existing law, operation
of, **7(2)**, [467]
visiting forces in, **7(2)**, [462]

Gibraltar
diocese in. *See* **Europe, Diocese in**
disqualification while disqualified in, **37**, [699]

Gibraltar—*contd*
European Parliament, representation in. *See*
European Parliament
financial services provisions applying to,
19(2), [484]

gift
business, charge to tax, **44(1)**, [411]
inter vivos, abolition of stamp duty, **41**, [149]
inter vivos, relationship between persons,
6, [280]
reduction of National Debt, for, exemption
from stamp duty, **41**, [66]

gift aid
benefits associated with a gift—
admission rights—
disregard of certain, **44(4)**, [428]–[429]
meaning, **44(4)**, [428]
meaning, **44(4)**, [425]
periods of less than 12 months, linked to,
44(4), [427]
restrictions on, **44(4)**, [426]
carry back relief, election to, **44(4)**, [434]
charged amount, meaning, **44(4)**, [435]
charity, meaning, **44(4)**, [438]
donor's liability not less than tax treated as
deducted—
measures to ensure—
charge to tax, **44(4)**, [432]
income tax, total amount to which
charged, **44(4)**, [433]
restriction of reliefs, **44(4)**, [431]
entitlement to, **44(4)**, [422]
"gift aid declaration", meaning, **44(4)**, [436]
grossed up amount, meaning, **44(4)**, [423]
income tax basic rate, transitional relief on
reduction of, **43(S)**, 1170–2
overseas gifts, disqualified, **44(4)**, [430]
overview, **44(4)**, [421]
qualifying donation, meaning, **44(4)**, [424]
self-assessment return, giving through,
44(4), [437]

Gilbert Islands
Kiribati, becoming, **7(2)**, [708]

gipsy encampment
local authority, provision by, **32**, [1]
repeal of provisions, **32**, [596]

girls
Royal Hospital School, admission regardless of
seafaring family connection, **3**, [1519]

glebe
amended provisions, **14(S)**, 82, 103
buildings, parsonage. *See* **parsonage**
corn sown on, profits of, **14**, 43
diocesan board of finance—
information, requiring, **14**, 849
transfer to, **14**, 848–9
diocesan glebe land—
acquisition, **14(S)**, 92
acquisition of land for, **14**, 849–90

glebe—*contd*
diocesan glebe land—*contd*
appropriation of, **14**, 855
Church Commissioners—
grant to, **14**, 855
information given to, **14**, 858
diocesan board of finance, powers of,
14, 851–3
diocesan stipends fund, held for, **14**, 850
disposition of land—
Commissioners' consent to, **14**, 851–2
surveyor's report on, **14**, 852
income, account of, **14**, 857
meaning, **14**, 865
mines and minerals, account of, **14**, 857
money arising from dealings, payment of,
14, 856
rent of parsonage house, provisions on,
14, 858–9
restrictive covenant, enforcement of,
14, 855
scheme for management of, **14**, 850
team vicar, rent free house for, on, **14**, 856
housing grants, **23**, [608]
injurious affection, compensation, **9**, [289]
land, meaning, **14**, 865
not sown, right to have, **14**, 43
smallholdings, for, **1(1)**, [825]

Godalming Navigation
management of, **32**, [309]
meaning, **32**, [308]

gold
acquired under emergency powers, no
compensation for, **9**, [131]
carat, use of term, **48**, 74
supplies, customers accounting for value added
tax on, **50**, [77]
zero-rating, **50**, [151]

Gold Coast
Ghana, becoming, **7(2)**, [458]

goods
carriage by sea. *See* **carriage of goods by
sea**
consumer use, in, **11(1)**, [312]
contamination, offences as to, **12(1)**, [1042]
contracts as to—
refusal to deal on grounds of union
exclusion, **16**, [385]
union membership requirement in, void,
16, [338], [339]
union recognition requirement in, void,
16, [384]
country of origin, **39(1)**, [110]
dangerous, carriage by sea. *See* **carriage of
goods by sea**
fair trading. *See* **fair trading**
hire, contract for—
bailee, meaning, **39(1)**, [472]
bailor, meaning, **39(1)**, [472]
excepted, **39(1)**, [454]

goods—*contd*
hire, contract for—*contd*
implied terms—
description, hire by, **39(1)**, [456]
exclusion of, **39(1)**, [460]
fitness for purpose, **39(1)**, [457]
possession, right to transfer, **39(1)**, [455]
quiet possession, **39(1)**, [455]
sample, by, **39(1)**, [458]
satisfactory quality, **39(1)**, [457]
meaning, **39(1)**, [454]
non-consumer, breach of condition in,
39(1), [459]
interference with. *See* **wrongful interference
with goods**
meaning, **1(1)**, [2]; **12(1)**, [1042]; **36**, [871];
37, [808]
possession or ownership passing, implied
undertakings, **11(1)**, [314]
prices. *See* **prices**
requisitioning under emergency powers—
compensation for, **9**, [125]
ownership, vesting in Crown, **9**, [133]
restrictive agreements. *See* **restrictive trade
agreement**
safety of. *See* **safety**
sale of. *See* **sale of goods**
slander of, **19(3)**, [310], [318]
stolen. *See* **stolen goods**
supply of—
civil rights, saving for, **39(1)**, [109]
guarantee, exclusion in, **11(1)**, [312]
meaning, **39(1)**, [633]; **47**, [195]
title to. *See* **document of title**
transfer, contract for—
consumer cases, rights in—
application of provisions, **39(1)**, [461]
conformity with contract, **39(1)**, [466]
court, powers of, **39(1)**, [465]
other remedies, relation to, **39(1)**, [464]
purchase price, reduction of,
39(1), [463]
repair or replacement of goods,
39(1), [462]
rescission of contract, **39(1)**, [463]
excepted, meaning, **39(1)**, [448]
implied terms—
charge or encumbrance, freedom from,
39(1), [449]
description, goods corresponding to,
39(1), [450]
exclusion of, **39(1)**, [460]
fitness for purpose, **39(1)**, [451]
quiet enjoyment, **39(1)**, [449]
sample, by, **39(1)**, [451], [452]
satisfactory quality, **39(1)**, [451]
title, as to, **39(1)**, [449]
meaning, **39(1)**, [448]
non-consumer, breach of condition in,
39(1), [453]
transferee and transferor, meaning,
39(1), [472]
unsolicited—
corporation, offence by, **39(1)**, [122]
offences, prosecution of, **47**, [209]

goods—*contd*
  unsolicited—*contd*
    payment, demands and threats for,
      39(1), [121]

goods vehicles. *See also* **motor vehicle**
  ADR Convention, inspections, **37**, [130]
  articulated, meaning, **37**, [705]
  authorised vehicles, **38(1)**, [527]
  brakes, breach of requirement as to, **37**, [613]
  check-weighing—
    meaning, **39(1)**, [547]
    power to require, **39(1)**, [517]
  companies and subsidiaries as licensed
    operators, **38(1)**, [568]
  condition, satisfactory, tests of, **37**, [627]
  consignment notes, **38(1)**, [588]
  constable's powers, **38(1)**, [564]
    exercise by authorised persons, **37**, [781],
      [782]
  construction and use, regulation of—
    contravention, **37**, [618]
    matters to be included, **37**, [613]
    powers, **37**, [613]
    temporary exemption, **37**, [619]
  driver—
    meaning, **38(1)**, [578]
    names and addresses of, power to obtain
      from, **37**, [782]
  drivers' hours. *See* **drivers hours**
  driving licence. *See* **driving licence**
  entry on premises, right of, **37**, [651];
    38(1), [562], [588]
  examinations, records of, **38(2)**, [522]
  examiner—
    appointment, **37**, [649]
    entry on premises, powers, **37**, [651]
    goods vehicle, entry and inspection,
      37, [651]
    powers, **37**, [651], [782]
    production of documents etc, to, **37**, [781],
      [785]
    See also **vehicle testing**
  exceptional dimension of loads, **37**, [620]
  excise duty—
    conveying machines, vehicles for,
      13, [1048]
    exceptions, **13**, [1048]
    island goods vehicle, meaning of,
      13, [1048]
    reduced plated weight, vehicles with,
      13, [1048]
    rigid, exceeding 7,500 kilos plated gross
      weight or relevant maximum weight,
      13, [1048], [1082]
    tractive units exceeding 7,500 kilos train
      weight, **13**, [1048]
    trailer, meaning of, **13**, [1048]
  exempt—
    benefits or money obtained in connection
      with, **44(2)**, [270]
    payment of expenses, **44(2)**, [240]
  foreign, certain prohibitions. *See* **motor**
  vehicles (foreign)

goods vehicles—*contd*
  forgery etc of documents, penalties,
    38(1), [560]
  goods, meaning, **38(1)**, [578]
  heavy commercial vehicles—
    meaning, **37**, [311], [590]
    weight, **37**, [311]
  heavy goods vehicles—
    driving licences. *See* **driving licence**
    meaning, **36**, [1135]
    parking on verges etc, **37**, [589]
    parking places, provision of, **36**, [1134]
  inquiries, power to hold, **38(1)**, [557]
  inspection—
    examiner, by, **37**, [651]
    operator's duty, **37**, [659]
    powers, **37**, [651]
    records of, operator's duty, **37**, [659]
  insurance, production of evidence of,
    37, [782]
  international road haulage permits. *See*
    international road haulage
  large—
    consignment notes, **38(1)**, [588]
    documents required, **38(1)**, [572], [588]
    entry and inspection, **38(1)**, [588]
    falsification, **38(1)**, [588]
    meaning, **38(1)**, [588]
  locomotives. *See under* **motor vehicles**
  maintenance facilities, inspection, **38(1)**, [562]
  meaning, **13**, [1032]; **36**, [905], [919];
    37, [311], [808]; **38(1)**, [578]
  modest private use of, **44(2)**, [238]
  nuisance, saving for law of, **38(1)**, [575]
  operating centres—
    area of, **38(1)**, [527], [529]
    entry, officer's right of, **38(1)**, [562]
    environmental matters—
      determination, **38(1)**, [556]
      objections, **38(1)**, [536], [541]
    location, **38(1)**, [529]
    meaning, **38(1)**, [529]
    objections to, **38(1)**, [534]
      environmental grounds, on, **38(1)**, [536],
        [541]
    removal on review, **38(1)**, [553]
    review—
      condition, attachment of, on,
        38(1), [554]
      periods, **38(1)**, [552]
      removal on, **38(1)**, [553]
    specification in licence, **38(1)**, [529]
    transfer of, **38(1)**, [555]
      new licences, in connection with,
        38(1), [587]
      variation of licences, on, **38(1)**, [587]
    use of, **38(1)**, [535]
      conditions, **38(1)**, [545]
    variation of licence with respect to,
      38(1), [539]
  operator, duties, **37**, [659]
  operators' licence—
    addition of vehicles, **38(2)**, [200]
    appeals in connection with, **38(1)**, [559]

goods vehicles—*contd*
  operators' licence—*contd*
    applicant—
      financial standing, **38(1)**, [586]
      good repute as requirement,
        38(1), [535], [586]
      professional competence, **38(1)**, [586]
    application for—
      determination, **38(1)**, [535]
        environmental grounds, objection
          on, **38(1)**, [536]
      fees, **38(1)**, [567]
      generally, **38(1)**, [530]
      information required, **38(1)**, [530], [585]
      notice of, **38(1)**, [532], [533]
      objections to, **38(1)**, [534]
        environmental grounds, on,
          38(1), [536]
        persons and bodies raising,
          38(1), [534]
      particulars required, **38(1)**, [530]
      qualifications required, **38(1)**, [586]
      representation against, **38(1)**, [534]
    area of operation, **38(1)**, [527]
      meaning, **38(1)**, [578]
      separate areas, licences for, **38(1)**, [530]
    assignment, prohibition, **38(1)**, [570]
    companies and subsidiaries, as, **38(1)**, [568]
    conditions attached—
      commissioner, matters requiring
        notification to, **38(1)**, [544]
      operating centres, use of, **38(1)**, [545]
      road safety, as to, **38(1)**, [543]
      suspension or curtailment, on,
        38(1), [548]
    conviction, notification of, **38(1)**, [531],
      [585]
    curtailment, **38(1)**, [548], [585]
      order, **38(1)**, [548]
    definitions, **38(1)**, [578]
    disqualification, **38(1)**, [550]
    documents—
      forgery, **38(1)**, [560]
      seizure, **38(1)**, [563]
    duration, **38(1)**, [538]
    emergency use, temporary exemption,
      38(1), [526]
    environmental matters—
      determinations as to, **38(1)**, [556]
      objections on grounds of, **38(1)**, [536],
        [541]
    European Community member State,
      certificate of qualification, **38(1)**, [571]
    evidence by certificate, **38(1)**, [565]
    exemptions, temporary, **38(1)**, [526]
    false statements as to, **38(1)**, [561]
    fees, **38(1)**, [567]
    financial questions, assessor to assist
      commissioners, **38(1)**, [566]
    forgery etc of documents, penalties,
      38(1), [560]
    grant, **38(1)**, [537]
      review by Commissioners, **38(1)**, [558]

goods vehicles—*contd*
  operators' licence—*contd*
    holding companies and subsidiaries,
      38(1), [568]
      meaning, **38(1)**, [589]
      restricted licence, **38(1)**, [525]
    information required, **38(1)**, [530], [585]
    inquiries, Commissioners, by, **38(1)**, [557]
    interim—
      application for, **38(1)**, [1185]
      termination, **38(1)**, [546]
      variation, **38(1)**, [547]
    international carriage, provisions
      inapplicable, **38(1)**, [523]
    issue, **38(1)**, [537]
      objection to, **38(1)**, [534]
      terms of, **38(1)**, [537]
    local authority, provisions applicable,
      38(1), [523]
    non-transferability, **38(1)**, [570]
    obligation to hold, **38(1)**, [523]
    officer, meaning, **38(1)**, [564]
    operating centres. *See* operating centres
      above
    partnerships, **38(1)**, [569]
    public authority, provisions applicable,
      38(1), [523]
    public interests, protection, **38(1)**, [576]
    qualifications for, **38(1)**, [535], [571]
    refusal, **38(1)**, [535]
      review by Commissioners, **38(1)**, [558]
    regulations and orders, **38(1)**, [577]
    restricted, **38(1)**, [525]
      application for, **38(1)**, [535]
      variation, application for, **38(1)**, [542]
    review, periods of, **38(1)**, [552]
    revocation—
      conviction, on, **38(1)**, [548]
      disqualification on, **38(1)**, [550]
      grounds for, **38(1)**, [548], [585]
      small goods vehicles, provisions
        inapplicable to, **38(1)**, [523]
      standard licence, **38(1)**, [549]
      supplementary provisions, **38(1)**, [551]
    small goods vehicles. *See* small *below*
    standard—
      authorised use under, **38(1)**, [525]
      conditions attached, **38(1)**, [544]
      nature, **38(1)**, [525]
      qualifications for, **38(1)**, [586]
      revocation, **38(1)**, [549]
        supplementary provisions, **38(1)**, [551]
      variation, application for, **38(1)**, [539],
        [542]
        environmental grounds, objection
          on, **38(1)**, [541]
        publication of notice, **38(1)**, [540]
    subsidiary companies. *See* holding
      companies *above*
    suspension—
      grounds for, **38(1)**, [548], [585]
      order, **38(1)**, [548]
    temporary exemptions, **38(1)**, [526]
    termination—
      by request, **38(1)**, [538]

goods vehicles—*contd*
  operators' licence—*contd*
    termination—*contd*
      on earlier date, **38(1)**, [538]
    testing stations, provision of, **37**, [657]
    traffic commissioners—
      assessors, assistance by, **38(1)**, [566]
      functions, **38(1)**, [522]
      inquiries by, **38(1)**, [557]
      matters notified to, **38(1)**, [544]
      reviews by, **38(1)**, [558]
    transfer, prohibition, **38(1)**, [570]
    transitional provisions, **38(1)**, [579], [589]
    transport manager—
      meaning, **38(1)**, [578]
      notification of proceedings, **38(1)**, [586]
      reputation and competence of,
        38(1), [586]
    variation—
      application for—
        generally, **38(1)**, [539]
        notice of, **38(1)**, [539]
        objection to, **38(1)**, [541]
      conditions attached, **38(1)**, [543]–[545]
      environmental grounds, objection on,
        38(1), [541]
      information, duty to give, **38(1)**, [539]
      interim licences, **38(1)**, [547]
      objection to, grounds, **38(1)**, [541]
      refusal, **38(1)**, [541]
    vehicle testing business, holder barred,
      37, [126]
    vehicles—
      authorised for use under, **38(1)**, [527]
        maximum number, **38(1)**, [528]
      used without, detention, **38(1)**, [524],
        [584]
  overloaded—
    driving of, prohibition, **37**, [654]
    offences in connection with, **37**, [655]
  owner, meaning, **38(1)**, [578]
  partnerships as licensed operators, **38(1)**, [569]
  police constable, powers, **38(1)**, [564]
  proceedings, evidence by certificate in,
    38(1), [565]
  recording equipment, instillation and use. *See*
    under **drivers' hours**
  regulations and orders, power to make,
    38(1), [577]
  seizure of documents, **38(1)**, [563]
  small—
    meaning, **36**, [905], [919]; **37**, [705];
      38(1), [583]
    plated weight, **38(1)**, [583]
    provisions inapplicable, **38(1)**, [523]
    trailer, meaning, **38(1)**, [583]
  special, authorisation of use, **37**, [620]
  steering-gear, breach of requirement as to,
    37, [613]
  summary proceedings, time for bringing,
    38(1), [573]
  summary of provisions, **36**, [210]
  testing. *See* **vehicle testing**
  TIR Convention, inspections, **37**, [130]

goods vehicles—*contd*
  trailer. *See* **trailer**
  tyres, breach of requirement as to, **37**, [613]
  unfit—
    contravention of provisions, **37**, [655]
    driving, prohibition, **37**, [652]
    inspection, **37**, [652]
    notice of, **37**, [652]
    powers as to, **37**, [652]
    removal—
      appeal against refusal, **37**, [656]
      notice, **37**, [656], [658]
      when fit, **37**, [656]
    supplementary provisions, **37**, [658]
  weighing, when required, **37**, [664]
  weight—
    calculation, methods, **38(1)**, [574]
    plated—
      alteration, **37**, [643]
      determination, **37**, [134], [627]
      meaning, **38(1)**, [578]
    regulation of—
      breach of requirement as to, **37**, [615]
      powers, **37**, [613]
      temporary exemption, **37**, [619]
    unauthorised, using, **37**, [644]

gorse
  burning, regulation of, **1(1)**, [372]

government
  fees and charges, **19(2)**, [1006]

government accounts
  Comptroller and Auditor General, **19(1)**, [1]
    See also **Comptroller and Auditor**
      General
  consolidated accounts, preparation of,
    19(1), [1]
  information regarding, preparation of,
    19(2), [1038]
  national health service, summarised accounts,
    19(2), [1040]
  preparation of, **19(1)**, [1]; **19(2)**, [1033],
    [1035], [1037]
  public-private partnership business—
    expenditure as to, **19(2)**, [1042], [1045]
    investment, limit for, **19(2)**, [1044]
    meaning, **19(2)**, [1043]
  resource accounts—
    Advisory Board for, **19(2)**, [1050]
    scrutiny of, **19(2)**, [1034]
  scrutiny of, **19(2)**, [1039]
  timetable for, alteration of, **19(2)**, [1048]
  VAT, supplies by government departments, for
    purposes of, **19(2)**, [1047]
  Wales—
    provisions regarding, **19(2)**, [1041]
    timetables for, alteration of, **19(2)**, [1058]

Government Annuities Investment Fund
  annuities charged on, **19(2)**, [740], [761]
  insurances charged on, **19(2)**, [761]
  provisions as to, **19(2)**, [783]

government annuity
Bank of England, allowances to, **19(2)**, [755]
certificates—
    false statements, **19(2)**, [757]
    forgery of, **19(2)**, [758]
    form of, **19(2)**, [752]
certification of amounts payable, **19(2)**, [746]
death of nominee, sum paid on, **19(2)**, [741], [743]
declarations as to—
    evidence of, **19(2)**, [750]
    false statements, **19(2)**, [757]
    forgery of, **19(2)**, [758]
    form of, **19(2)**, [752]
errors, correction of, **19(2)**, [753]
executors and administrators, validity of payments to, **19(2)**, [747]
false statement, making, **19(2)**, [757]
forgery of documents, **19(2)**, [758]
improper receipt, penalty for, **19(2)**, [756]
National Loans Fund, charged on, **19(2)**, [740], [855]
payment—
    mode of, **19(2)**, [742], [743]
    small sums, of, **19(2)**, [748]
    time for, **19(2)**, [741]
penalties, recovery of, **19(2)**, [759]
regulations, power to make, **19(2)**, [754]
stamp duty, exemption from, **19(2)**, [749]
termination of powers, **19(2)**, [838]
transfer of, **19(2)**, [744]
unclaimed, account of, **19(2)**, [745]
warrants, provisions as to, **19(2)**, [751]

government borrowing
alternative finance arrangements, **43(S)**, 992
    ancillary arrangements, **43(S)**, 1353
    decision to raise money, **43(S)**, 1353
    interpretation, **43(S)**, 1355
    liabilities, **43(S)**, 1354
    money raised, treatment of, **43(S)**, 1354
    other legislation, modification, **43(S)**, 1355
    persons other than Treasury, involvement of, **43(S)**, 1353
    powers and duties, **43(S)**, 1354
    property, **43(S)**, 1354
    regulations, **43(S)**, 1353, 1355
    terms, conditions and procedures, **43(S)**, 1353
    things to be done other than in regulations, **43(S)**, 1355
non-FOTRA securities, **43**, [381]
Treasury, securities, position regarding own, **43**, [379]

government chemist
analysis of samples by, **1(2)**, [445]

Government Communications Headquarters
Director, **10**, [747]
functions of, **10**, [746]
warrants—
    authorisation of actions by, **10**, [748]
    duration of, **10**, [749]

Government Communications Headquarters—*contd*
warrants—*contd*
    procedure for issue, **10**, [749]

government department. *See also under names of Ministers*
sale of houses at discount, stamp duty, **41**, [138], [145]

government departments. *See also under names of Ministers*
authorised, for Crown proceedings, **13**, [21]
changes in, **10**, [595]
charge for services, **10**, [563]
records. *See* **public records**

government investment
write-off of, **44(1)**, [204]

government stock
administration, **43(2)**, [130]
bank accounts for, **19(2)**, [616]
Bank of England, discharge of functions in place of Bank of Ireland, **43(2)**, [128]
bearer bonds in respect of, **19(2)**, [840]
certificates of investment, exchange of, **19(2)**, [930]
creation of, **19(2)**, [859]
dealings in, provisions on, **19(2)**, [733]
death of person entitled to, procedure on, **19(2)**, [727]
descriptions of, **19(2)**, [809]
dividends—
    payment, **19(2)**, [631]
    unclaimed, **19(2)**, [829]
documents of title, issue of, **19(2)**, [807]
exchange of, **19(2)**, [859]
exchequer bonds, lost or destroyed, **19(2)**, [729]
inscribed, transfer of, **19(2)**, [801], [803]
Issue Department of Bank of England, held in, **19(2)**, [860]
issue of, **19(2)**, [859]
meaning, **19(2)**, [928], [1025]
minors, held by, **19(2)**, [940]
national debt, annuities as part of. *See* **national debt**
National Savings Stock Register, closing, **19(1)**, [1024]
purchase of, **19(2)**, [807]
redemption, closure of register for, **19(2)**, [920]
register. *See* **National Savings Stock Register**
registers kept in Ireland, closure of, **43(2)**, [129]
registrar. *See* **Registrar of Government Stock**
registration of, **19(2)**, [807], [862]
sale of, **19(2)**, [807]
surrender of, **19(2)**, [859]
transfer of—
    Channel Islands, probate issued in, **19(2)**, [825], [921]

government stock—*contd*
transfer of—*contd*
court order, on authority of, **19(2)**, [730]
indemnity, **19(2)**, [731]
Isle of Man, probate issued in,
19(2), [825], [921]
regulations, **19(2)**, [807]
stock and registered bonds, **19(2)**, [862]
unclaimed, where, **19(2)**, [829]
unclaimed sum—
investigation of, **19(2)**, [829]
transfer of, **19(2)**, [829]
variation of terms, **19(2)**, [859]
warrant for exchange of, **19(2)**, [799]

Governor
citizenship, exercise of functions as to,
31, [127], [173]
meaning, **31**, [180]

Governor General
meaning, **41**, [605]

graffiti
defacement removal notices—
appeals against, **35(2)**, [435]
exemption from liability, **35(2)**, [436]
expenditure, recovery of, **35(2)**, [433]
guidance issued by Secretary of State,
35(2), [434]
issue of, **35(2)**, [432]
meaning, **35(2)**, [432]
relevant surface, **35(2)**, [432]
penalty notices for—
amount of penalty, **35(2)**, [427]
effect of, **35(2)**, [426]
issue of, **35(2)**, [426]
name and address, power to require,
35(2), [428]
payment of penalty, **35(2)**, [430]
penalty under, **35(2)**, [426]
relevant offence, meaning, **35(2)**, [429]

grant-maintained school
curriculum. *See* **curriculum**
premises, prescribed standards, relaxation,
15(1), [677]
religious education. *See* **curriculum**
special. *See* **special school**

grants. *See also* **housing grants**
Secretary of State, by, **16**, [65]

grass
burning—
covenants against, relaxation of, **1(1)**, [373]
regulation of, **1(1)**, [372]
regulations and orders, **1(1)**, [377]

grass cutting machine
motor vehicle, not treated as, **37**, [805]

gravel pit
charge to tax, **44(1)**, [34]
rent payable in respect of, **44(1)**, [98]

gravity knife
importing, **12(1)**, [304]
manufacturing, selling etc, **12(1)**, [304]
Northern Ireland, importing into,
12(1), [327]

Gray's Inn
administrative position, **25(1)**, [1]
exemption from Building Acts, **25(1)**, [354]
overground wires, placing, **25(1)**, [213]

Great Britain
union with Ireland. *See under* **Ireland**

Great Seal
Act of Union, after, **10**, [66]
authority for passing instruments under,
10, [466]
clerk of the patents, transfer of duties of,
10, [447]
clerk of the petty bag, transfer of duties of,
10, [446]
commissioners for, **10**, [37]–[38]
cursitor, transfer of duties of, **10**, [446]
death of Sovereign, on, **10**, [81]
messenger, transfer of duties of, **10**, [445]
use of, **10**, [37]–[38]
wafer, **10**, [459]

Greater London. *See also* **Greater London
Authority; London; London borough;
London government**
acupuncturists, registration, **25(2)**, [466]
adaptations of enactments, **25(1)**, [721], [735],
[766]
administration of justice—
adaptation of enactments to, **25(1)**, [766]
financial provisions, **25(1)**, [761]
youth courts, **25(1)**, [758]
administrative area—
boundaries of, **25(1)**, [732]
constitution, **25(1)**, [695]
generally, **25(1)**, [1]
schedule of, **25(1)**, [731]
agricultural wages provisions, **1(1)**, [422]
amenities, publicity for, **25(1)**, [718]
animal diseases, authority for, **2**, [500]
application of planning provisions, **46**, [261]
authorities, exercise of functions, **25(1)**, [697]
Authority. *See* **Greater London Authority**
borough boundaries, **25(1)**, [732]
brown tail moth, control of, **25(2)**, [421]
building control, **25(2)**, [639]
building operations—
public safety, affecting, **25(1)**, [814]
directors, liability of, **25(1)**, [817]
offences, liability for, **25(1)**, [816]
proceedings, **25(1)**, [818]
See also **London Building Acts**
burial ground, closed—
chapel in, **5(2)**, [383]
See also **burial ground**
byelaws. *See* **London government**
caravan sites, **25(1)**, [735]

Greater London—*contd*
 cellars—
  access to, **25(2)**, [664]
  appeals in respect of, **25(2)**, [667]
  infilling—
   control of, **25(2)**, [665]
   electricity undertakers, protection,
    25(2), [668]
 cemetery—
  generally, **25(1)**, [705]
  meaning, **25(2)**, [377]
  performance of services in, **25(1)**, [996]
  rights of interment—
   extinguishment, **25(2)**, [377]
   grant of, **25(1)**, [967]
  tombstones, removal of, **25(2)**, [377]
 child care expenses, **25(2)**, [301]
 civic restaurant authorities, **25(1)**, [371], [372]
 commercial buildings, provision of, **22**, [17]
 conference premises, Shops Act applied,
  25(2), [467], [473]
 consumer protection service, **25(2)**, [300]
 continuation of plans, **46**, [618]
 cosmetic piercing, registration for,
  25(2), [466]
 council. *See* **Greater London Council**
 crematoria, **25(1)**, [237], [1008]
 dangerous buildings—
  application of provisions, **26(2)**, [178]
  occupants removed, priority housing,
   25(2), [558]
  removal of occupants, **25(2)**, [556]
  See also **London Building Acts**
 development plan, **46**, [283], [618]
 education. *See* **education**
 elections. *See* **elections**
 entertainments. *See* **entertainment**
 explosives in. *See* **explosives**
 Festival Hall etc, vesting of, **25(2)**, [606]
 fines for summary offences, increase,
  25(2), [525], [527]
 Fire and Civil Defence Authority—
  establishment, **25(2)**, [590]
  functions transferred to, **25(2)**, [598]
   See also new authorities *below*
 fire authorities, **25(1)**, [708]
 fire brigade. *See* **fire brigade**
 flammable material. *See* **flammable material**
 flood prevention—
  defences, **25(2)**, [662]
  functions, **25(1)**, [681]
  general provisions, **25(2)**, [662]
  officers, obstruction of, **25(2)**, [527]
  payments, **25(1)**, [682]
  service of notices, **25(1)**, [681]
 footways—
  parking on, **25(2)**, [345]
  vehicles on, for street cleaning, **25(1)**, [655]
 functions—
  delegation of, **25(1)**, [697]
  exercise of, **25(1)**, [696]
 grass verges—
  parking on, **25(2)**, [345]
   offences, increased penalties, **25(2)**, [527]
  powers as to, **25(2)**, [344]

Greater London—*contd*
 Grosvenor Square. *See* **Grosvenor Square**
 hairdressers, registration, **25(1)**, [834];
  25(2), [527]
 heat, supply of. *See* **heat, supply of**
 heaths, military drill on, **25(1)**, [72]
 highway authorities. *See* **highway authority**
 Historic Buildings etc Commission,
  functions, **25(2)**, [635]
 hostels—
  appeal against notice, **25(2)**, [457]
  entry by authorised officers, **25(2)**, [461]
  exemption for certain purposes,
   25(2), [463]
  meaning, **25(2)**, [455]
  notice to be exhibited, **25(2)**, [458]
  offences and penalties, **25(2)**, [459]
  overcrowding—
   control of, **25(2)**, [456]
   evidence in proceedings, **25(2)**, [462]
  withdrawal of notice, **25(2)**, [460]
 housing—
  nomination of tenants, **25(2)**, [624]
  transfer orders, **25(2)**, [624]
  See **housing**
 housing authorities in, additional powers,
  22, [17]
 housing estates, parking on, **25(2)**, [355]
 insanitary food premises—
  closing order, **25(2)**, [298]
  improved premises, certificate of,
   25(2), [298]
  interim order, **25(2)**, [298]
  offences as to, **25(2)**, [298], [527]
 insolvency district, **4(2)**, [457]
 joint authorities—
  chairman and vice-chairman—
   allowances to, **25(2)**, [596]
   appointment, **25(2)**, [595]
   casual vacancy, filling, **25(2)**, [596]
  clerk, appointment, **25(2)**, [595]
  constituent councils, **25(2)**, [640]–[645]
  discharge of functions, **25(2)**, [601]
  members—
   disqualification, **25(2)**, [596]
   notice of appointment, **25(2)**, [597]
   number of, **25(2)**, [592], [640]–[645]
   replacement of, **25(2)**, [593]
   vacancies, filling, **25(2)**, [594]
  See also new authorities *below*
 joint planning committee for, **46**, [253]
 landing places. *See* **Thames**
 laundries, self-operated—
  closing orders, **25(2)**, [299]
  dangerous substances used in, **25(2)**, [299]
  machinery, inspection of, **25(2)**, [299]
  meaning, **25(2)**, [299]
 libraries. *See* **public library**
 listed buildings, amended provisions,
  25(2), [635]
 listed buildings in, **46**, [710]
 local Acts and instruments, **25(1)**, [724]
 local education authorities, **25(1)**, [699]
 local inquiries, **25(1)**, [725]
 local plans, **46**, [618]

Greater London—*contd*
lost property. *See* **London Regional Transport**
meaning, **25(1)**, [1]
museums, vesting of, **25(2)**, [603]–[605]
National Film Theatre, vesting of, **25(2)**, [606]
national parks functions, **25(2)**, [582]
new authorities—
  accounts and audit, **25(2)**, [618]
  Bills, restriction on promoting, **25(2)**, [60]
  financial administration, **25(2)**, [619], [859]
  financial provisions, **25(2)**, [618]–[620]
  provisions applied to, **25(2)**, [621]
  transfers to, orders for, **25(2)**, [628]
  See also **Greater London Council (successor authorities)**
night cafés. *See* **night cafés**
overground wires. *See* **overground wires**
parks and open spaces—
  byelaws, enforcement, **25(1)**, [854]
  commons, restrictions as to, **25(1)**, [847]
  competitions etc, use for, **25(1)**, [848]
  entertainments in, **25(1)**, [842]
  exchange of adjoining land, **25(1)**, [850]
  licences to use land in, **25(1)**, [843]
  powers generally, **25(1)**, [846]
  private owners of land, powers for, **25(1)**, [851]
  public recreation, facilities for, **25(1)**, [842]
  public rights, restriction of, **25(1)**, [844]
  street improvements, use for, **25(1)**, [852]
  Sunday closing, **25(2)**, [397]
  transfers between authorities, **25(1)**, [849]
  uniformity of law, **25(1)**, [839]–[855]
  use of, charges for, **25(1)**, [845]
petroleum depots. *See* **petroleum**
petroleum functions, **25(2)**, [646]
police authority. *See* **police authority**
Public Health Acts—
  application, **25(1)**, [702]
  modification and re-enactment, **25(1)**, [733], [734]
  See also **public health**
public recreation, facilities for, **25(1)**, [842]
rates and rating—
  enactments amended and applied, **25(1)**, [716]
  recovery of, **25(2)**, [296]
  unpaid, charge on premises, **25(2)**, [297]
refuse. *See* **refuse**
research schemes, **25(2)**, [623]
residuary body—
  access to documents, **25(2)**, [647]
  acquisition of land by, **25(2)**, [647]
  annual reports by, **25(2)**, [647]
  authentication of documents, **25(2)**, [647]
  borrowing powers, **25(2)**, [612]
  capital etc, treatment of, **25(2)**, [620]
  information, duty to furnish, **25(2)**, [647]
  land, powers as to, **25(2)**, [647]
  local authority, treated as, **25(2)**, [647]
  local government provisions applied, **25(2)**, [647]

Greater London—*contd*
residuary body—*contd*
  members—
    disqualifications, **25(2)**, [647]
    remuneration, **25(2)**, [647]
    tenure of office, **25(2)**, [647]
  pensions, liability as to, **25(2)**, [613], [614]
  proceedings, regulation of, **25(2)**, [647]
  repayment of loans to, **25(2)**, [612]
  residuary property etc, custody of, **25(2)**, [615]
  rights and liabilities, **25(2)**, [612]
  services, powers to provide, **25(2)**, [647]
  status, **25(2)**, [647]
  transfer of property etc, **25(2)**, [617]
  orders for, **25(2)**, [628]
  winding up, **25(2)**, [617]
  See also new authorities *above*
retaining walls—
  appeals in respect of, **25(2)**, [667]
  powers as to, **25(2)**, [666]
road traffic. *See* **road traffic**
  transfer of property etc, **25(2)**, [617]
  orders for, **25(2)**, [628]
  winding up, **25(2)**, [617]
scaffolding—
  licence to erect—
    bodies not requiring, **25(1)**, [1004]
    requirement for, **25(1)**, [1004]
  lighting at night, **25(1)**, [1004]
  unlicensed, fines for, **25(2)**, [527]
school, superannuation of non-teaching staff, **25(1)**, [258], [543]
sewers. *See* **sewers and drains**
sex establishments, amendments relating to, **25(2)**, [670], [673]
sheriff of, appointment, **25(1)**, [759]; **25(2)**, [173]
sleeping accommodation. *See* **sleeping accommodation**
smallholdings, allotments etc, **25(1)**, [710]
South Bank properties, vesting of, **25(2)**, [606]
spatial development strategy, conformity with, **46**, [275]
squares—
  railings for, contributions for, **25(2)**, [268]
  See also **Grosvenor Square**
stagnant water, drainage etc, **25(1)**, [734]
statues. *See* **statues**
street trading. *See* **street trading**
streets, power to lay out, **22**, [17]
swimming baths, provision of, **25(1)**, [842]
tattooists, registration, **25(2)**, [466]
temporary sleeping accommodation—
  change of use, as, **25(2)**, [295]
  meaning, **25(2)**, [295]
tenement house—
  common staircase, lighting, **25(1)**, [515]
  meaning, **25(1)**, [515]
time-sharing constituting change of use, **25(2)**, [530]
town development functions, **25(1)**, [714]
traffic control and regulation. *See* **traffic regulation**

Greater London—*contd*
transport. *See* **London transport**
travel concessions. *See* **London passenger transport services**
underground room—
appeals relating to, **25(2)**, [667]
infilling, **25(2)**, [665]
unitary development plan, incorporation of local plan in, **46**, [618]
vaults—
appeals in respect of, **25(2)**, [667]
infilling—
control of, **25(2)**, [665]
electricity undertaking, protection, **25(2)**, [668]
walkways. *See* **walkways**
waste disposal—
authorities, duties of, **26(2)**, [490]
joint arrangements for, **25(2)**, [585]
London Waste and Recycling Board. *See* **London Waste and Recycling Board**
transfer of functions, **25(2)**, [584]
water authority for, **25(1)**, [1]
weights and measures authorities, joint, **39(1)**, [594]
works under streets, demolition, **25(2)**, [663]
appeals as to, **25(2)**, [667]
electricity undertakers, protection, **25(2)**, [668]
youth courts, **25(1)**, [758]

Greater London Authority
accommodation, **26(1)**, [739]
administrative, professional and technical services, **26(1)**, [740]
auditors' reports and recommendations—
consideration of, **26(1)**, [329]
meetings, publicity for, **26(1)**, [330]
Bills—
consent to inclusion of provisions in, **26(1)**, [510]
promoted by London local authorities, power to request provisions in, **26(1)**, [509]
promotion or opposition to, **26(1)**, [508], [773]
body corporate, as, **26(1)**, [431]
budget—
deemed component requirements for last old financial year, **26(2)**, [481]
monitoring, **26(2)**, [260]
budget requirements—
amounts brought into account, **26(1)**, [512]
component and consolidated, calculation of, **26(1)**, [511]
consolidated, determining, **26(1)**, [774]
emergencies and disasters, recalculation for, **26(1)**, [519]
estimated future expenditure, meaning, **26(1)**, [512]
levy, taking into account, **26(1)**, [512]
procedure for determining, **26(1)**, [774]
chief finance officer, **26(1)**, [536]; **26(2)**, [480]
constitution, **26(1)**, [432]

Greater London Authority—*contd*
consultation by, **26(1)**, [464]
continuity of functions, **26(1)**, [754]
council tax—
basic amount, calculation of, **26(1)**, [514]
Metropolitan Police Authority—
minimum budget, **26(1)**, [517], [518]
special expense of, **26(1)**, [516]
special items for part of Greater London—
calculation of, **26(1)**, [515]
meaning, **26(1)**, [516]
substitute calculation—
emergencies and disasters, recalculation for, **26(1)**, [519]
Mayor's final draft, **26(1)**, [775]
Mayor's first draft, **26(1)**, [775]
Metropolitan Police Authority, minimum budget for, **26(1)**, [517], [518]
procedure for making, **26(1)**, [775]
publication, **26(1)**, [775]
cultural functions, delegation of, **26(1)**, [725]
disposal of land, restriction on, **26(1)**, [562]
ethical standards, guidance on, **26(1)**, [500]
expenditure grants, **26(2)**, [262]
expenditure not to be incurred by, **26(1)**, [463]
financial reports—
investigation—
report on, **25(2)**, [319], [321]
subject to, **25(2)**, [310]
Mayor of London and London Assembly, duties of, **25(2)**, [808]
functional bodies—
accommodation, **26(1)**, [739]
accounting for grants, **26(1)**, [525]
annual spending plan—
information, supply of, **26(1)**, [533]
statement in, **26(1)**, [530]
capital grants, **26(1)**, [528]
capital receipts, power to redistribute, **26(1)**, [527]
distribution of grants, **26(1)**, [524]
information, advice and assistance, provision of, **26(1)**, [734]
meaning, **26(1)**, [762]
property, rights and liabilities, transfer of—
contracts of employment, **26(1)**, [749]
foreign, **26(1)**, [753]
modification of instruments, **26(1)**, [752]
pensions, **26(1)**, [750]
provision for, **26(1)**, [747]
schemes, **26(1)**, [748], [796]
stamp duty and stamp duty reserve tax exemptions, **26(1)**, [756]
transfer or pension instruments, common provisions, **26(1)**, [751]
provision of information by, **26(1)**, [526]
relevant authority—
chief finance officer, **26(1)**, [535]
meaning, **26(1)**, [535]
revenue grants, **26(1)**, [529]
summary statement of accounts—
information for purposes of, **26(1)**, [538]
preparation of, **26(1)**, [537]

Greater London Authority—*contd*
functions, exercise of—
joint committees, by, **26(1)**, [471]
Mayor, Assembly or both, by, **26(1)**, [467]
Mayor, by, **26(1)**, [539]
Mayor, delegation by, **26(1)**, [470]
vacancy in office of Mayor, during,
26(1), [469]
general note, **25(1)**, [1]
general power of, **26(1)**, [462]
limits of, **26(1)**, [463]
grants—
Authority and financial bodies, distribution
between, **26(1)**, [524]
capital, **26(1)**, [528]
functional bodies, accounting to,
26(1), [525]
general GLA, **26(1)**, [522]
revenue, **26(1)**, [529]
transport, **26(1)**, [523]
Health Adviser—
appointment, **26(1)**, [660]
deputy—
appointment, **26(1)**, [662]
establishment of office, **26(1)**, [661]
person being, **26(1)**, [662]
establishment of office, **26(1)**, [659]
functions, **26(1)**, [659]
person being, **26(1)**, [660]
improvements in health, promotion of,
26(1), [462]
information, collection of, **26(1)**, [735]
local development schemes, **26(2)**, [484]
London Olympic Games, powers as to,
13, [505], [506]
members, **26(1)**, [432]
salaries, **26(1)**, [456]
monitoring officer, **26(1)**, [506]; **26(2)**, [479]
non-discrimination by, **26(1)**, [743]
paid service, head of, **26(2)**, [478]
Parliament Square—
byelaws, **26(1)**, [730]
transfer of land and functions, **26(1)**, [729]
principal council, treatment as, **26(1)**, [507]
principal purposes of, **26(1)**, [462]
property, rights and liabilities, transfer of—
contracts of employment, **26(1)**, [749]
foreign, **26(1)**, [753]
modification of instruments, **26(1)**, [752]
pensions, **26(1)**, [750]
provision for, **26(1)**, [747]
schemes, **26(1)**, [748], [796]
stamp duty and stamp duty reserve tax
exemptions, **26(1)**, [756]
transfer or pension instruments, common
provisions, **26(1)**, [751]
rail franchise documents, amendment of,
26(1), [592]
referendum—
ballot paper, form of, **26(1)**, [317]
conduct of, **26(1)**, [307]
counting officers, **26(1)**, [306]
entitlement to vote, **26(1)**, [305]
expenditure, grants towards, **26(1)**, [308],
[314]

Greater London Authority—*contd*
referendum—*contd*
holding of, **26(1)**, [304]
legal proceedings, exclusion of,
26(1), [309]
ordinary election, at time of, **26(1)**, [307]
relevant authority—
chief finance officer, **26(1)**, [535]
meaning, **26(1)**, [535]
research, **26(1)**, [735]
roads. *See* **London streets**
Secretary of State—
exercise of functions by, **26(1)**, [746]
guidance from, **26(1)**, [462]
severance payments, **43(S)**, 880
staff—
appointment of, **26(1)**, [501]; **26(2)**, [477]
disqualification and political restriction,
26(1), [502]
interests in contracts, disclosure of,
26(1), [504]
monitoring officer, **26(1)**, [506]
paid service, head of, **26(1)**, [505]
terms and conditions of employment,
26(1), [503]
standing orders, **26(1)**, [468]
subsidiaries, control of, **26(1)**, [563]
subsidiary powers, **26(1)**, [466]
summary statement of accounts—
information for purposes of, **26(1)**, [538]
preparation of, **26(1)**, [537]
provisions applying to, **26(1)**, [537]
superannuation provisions, **26(1)**, [732], [733]
tourism—
advice, provision of, **26(1)**, [724]
delegation of functions, **26(1)**, [725]
functions, meaning, **26(1)**, [727]
grants for, **26(1)**, [726]
promotion of, **26(1)**, [723]
Trafalgar Square—
byelaws, **26(1)**, [730]
transfer of functions, **26(1)**, [728]
transport—
facilities and services, **26(1)**, [540]
general duty, **26(1)**, [540]

Greater London Council
For functions etc following abolition, see **Greater
London**
abolition—
acts preceding, validity, **25(2)**, [627]
charity property, vesting of, **25(2)**, [625]
continuity of exercise of functions,
25(2), [627]
date of, **25(2)**, [579]
loans outstanding on, **25(2)**, [612]
loss of employment on, **25(2)**, [609]
pensions provisions, **25(2)**, [613], [614]
provisions having effect from date of,
25(2), [580]
residuary property etc on, **25(2)**, [615]
transitional provisions, **25(2)**, [629]
byelaws, continuity of, **25(2)**, [627]
development of, **25(1)**, [1]

Greater London Council—*contd*
documents—
  destruction of, time for, **25(1)**, [963]
  electronic, mechanical or other
    equipment, **25(1)**, [965]
  meaning, **25(1)**, [966]
  microfilming of, **25(1)**, [964]
members, allowances, **25(2)**, [293]
office, compensation on abolition of,
  25(1), [142], [907]
staff—
  compensation for loss of office etc,
    25(2), [609]
  transfer of, **25(2)**, [608]
  voluntary transfer, continuity of
    employment, **25(2)**, [610]

**Greater London Magistrates' Courts
Authority**
establishment of, **11(3)**, [313]
payments by local authorities to, **26(2)**, [449]
transfer of property to, schemes for,
  11(3), [313]

Greece
accession to European Communities, **18**, [27]

Green Belt
alternative land, provision of, **32**, [96]
area, meaning, **32**, [91]
building—
  meaning, **32**, [91]
  restriction on erection of, **32**, [99]
  savings, **32**, [102]
  statutory purposes, erection for, **32**, [101]
byelaws, **32**, [106]
capital money, application of, **32**, [114]
consents, giving of, **32**, [113]
county council—
  meaning, **32**, [91]
  saving for, **32**, [121]
covenants—
  enforcement of, **32**, [111]
  land, relating to, **32**, [92]
declaration of, **32**, [92]
deed made before commencement of Act,
  32, [110]
differences, settlement of, **32**, [115]
land—
  acquisition of, **32**, [92]
  charitable trusts, held on, **32**, [109]
  compensation for, **32**, [98]
  exchange of, **32**, [104]–[105]
  highway authorities, saving for, **32**, [97]
  meaning, **32**, [91]
  plans, deposit of, **32**, [93]
  private owners of, **32**, [107]
  statutory powers of acquisition, saving for,
    32, [95]
  user, **32**, [116]
Land Charges Act, saving for, **32**, [120]
leasehold land, **32**, [92], [103]
lines, saving for, **32**, [100]

Green Belt—*contd*
local authority—
  alienation of land by, restrictions on,
    32, [94]
  contributing, **32**, [91]
  cumulative powers of, **32**, [123]
  exchange of land by, **32**, [104]
  meaning, **32**, [91]
local inquiries, holding, **32**, [122]
London, round, **32**, [91]
nationally significant infrastructure project,
  grant of development consent for,
    46(S), 146
parish council, meaning, **32**, [91]
pipes, saving for, **32**, [100]
Postmaster-General, saving for, **32**, [119]
private owners of land, powers for, **32**, [107]
questions, settlement of, **32**, [115]
restrictions on—
  enforcement of, **32**, [112]
  purposes of, **32**, [117]
rights, saving for, **32**, [118]
sewers, saving for, **32**, [100]
statutory undertakers, meaning, **32**, [91]
tenants for, life, powers of, **32**, [108]

greenhouse gas
emissions—
  annual statement of, **35(S)**, 67–8
  international aviation or shipping, from,
    35(S), 79–81
    Committee on Climate Change, advice
      of, **35(S)**, 84
  measurement of, **35(S)**, 119
  offsetting, power of Ministers and
    departments, **35(S)**, 116
  permits, charging schemes for, **35(2)**, [113]
  reporting, guidance on, **35(S)**, 114
  territorial scope of provisions, **35(S)**, 117
  trading—
    EU Scheme, charges for allocations,
      35(2), [622]
    UK Scheme 2002, penalty provisions
      of, **35(2)**, [419]
  trading schemes—
    activities to which applying, **35(S)**, 90–1
    administration and enforcement,
      35(S), 139–43
    encouraging activities, **35(S)**, 136–9
    information, power to require,
      35(S), 147–8
    interpretation, **35(S)**, 96
    limiting activities, **35(S)**, 133–6
    matters provided for in regulations,
      35(S), 91
    meaning, **35(S)**, 90
    national authorities—
      administrators and participants, grants
        to, **35(S)**, 95
      consequential provision, making,
        35(S), 95
      directions, powers to give, **35(S)**, 95
      guidance, powers to give, **35(S)**, 94
      regulations, procedure for making,
        35(S), 93

greenhouse gas—*contd*
emissions—*contd*
  trading schemes—*contd*
    national authorities—*contd*
      relevant, **35(S)**, 92
      Order in Council, provision by,
        35(S), 145–6
      regulations, **35(S)**, 90
      single national authority, regulations
        by, **35(S)**, 144
      summary of provisions, **35(S)**, 48
      two or more national authorities,
        regulations by, **35(S)**, 145
  UK, meaning, **35(S)**, 79
  meaning, **35(S)**, 119
  targeted—
    base years for, **35(S)**, 75
    meaning, **35(S)**, 74

Greenwich Hospital
accounts—
  audit of, **3**, [146]
  laying before Parliament, **3**, [147]
Admiralty, protection of, **3**, [148]
admission to, **3**, [168], [1422]
capital account—
  generally, **3**, [139]
  investment of, **3**, [1287]
daughters of seamen, provision for, **3**, [175]
distribution of money without probate,
  3, [357]
dividends, payment of, **3**, [141]
expenditure defrayed from revenue of,
  3, [196]
financial provisions, **3**, [1379]
government of, **3**, [134]
income—
  account, **3**, [172]
  payment in of, **3**, [143]
invalids, transfer to, **3**, [169]
land—
  benefit of, held for, **3**, [135]
  public purposes, used for, **3**, [138]
  quitrents, etc, subject to, **3**, [136]
  sale of, **3**, [139]
leases, powers of Secretary of State to grant,
  3, [1698]
leases, protection of, **3**, [137]
naval pensions of inmates, **3**, [173]
officers of, **3**, [134]
pensions—
  decisions of Admiralty, **3**, [187]
  extension of powers, **3**, [356], [359]
  granting, **3**, [184]
  maintenance, substitution for, **3**, [170]
  name of, **3**, [132]
  power to appoint, **3**, [131]
  regulations, **3**, [186]
property vested in Her Majesty, **3**, [142]
schools, **3**, [134]
seafaring family connection, power of Royal
  Hospital School to disregard, **3**, [1519]
sons and daughters of deceased officers,
  provision for, **3**, [176], [197]
sons of seamen, provision for, **3**, [185]

Greenwich Hospital—*contd*
stock—
  conversion of, **3**, [144]
  transfer to Admiralty, **3**, [140]
transfer between accounts, **3**, [145]
visitor and governor, **3**, [133]
widow's gratuities, **3**, [131]

Grenada
Commonwealth citizenship, **31**, [186]

grievous bodily harm
burglary, in course of, **12(1)**, [561]
inflicting, **12(1)**, [76]
murder, alternative verdict to, **12(1)**, [364]
poison, inflicting by, **12(1)**, [79], [81]
wounding with intent to cause, **12(1)**, [76]

grit
furnace, from. *See* **furnace**

Grosvenor Square
enforcement of provisions, **25(1)**, [367]
expenses, **25(1)**, [369]
extinguishment of certain rights,
  compensation, **25(1)**, [364]
laying out and use of, **25(1)**, [362]
liability of persons interested in, **25(1)**, [368]
management and maintenance, **25(1)**, [362]
public, use by, **25(1)**, [362]
Roosevelt Memorial—
  erection, **25(1)**, [362]
  maintenance, **25(1)**, [362]
subsoil, rights as to, **25(1)**, [365]
underground works in, **25(1)**, [365]
Water Authority, saving powers of,
  25(1), [366]

Groundwork Foundation
superannuation, **35(1)**, [849]

group ministry
grant council, scheme for, **14**, 720
more than one diocese, benefices from,
  14, 1011
parochial church council, members of,
  14, 711
parochial church meeting, attending,
  14, 703–4
pastoral scheme—
  altering, **14**, 994–5
  establishing, **14**, 992–3, 1086
  terminating, **14**, 994–5

group of companies
approved share option scheme, **44(1)**, [637]
chargeable gain or loss, reallocation of,
  43(S), 1478–80
degrouping charge, roll-over of, **43(2)**, [92]
differing accounting practices, use of,
  43(2), [288]
financing costs and income—
  anti-avoidance, **43(S)**, 1518–20
  application of provisions, **43(S)**, 1499–1505
  available amount, meaning, **43(S)**, 1530–1

group of companies—*contd*
  financing costs and income—*contd*
    charities, **43(S)**, 1527
    commencement, **43(S)**, 1538
    consequential amendments, **43(S)**, 1537
    disallowance of deductions, **43(S)**, 1506–9
    educational and public bodies, **43(S)**, 1527
    exemption of financing income,
      43(S), 1510–14
    financing expense amounts, **43(S)**, 1521
    financing income amounts, **43(S)**, 1521–2
    group treasury companies, **43(S)**, 1522–3
    interpretation, **43(S)**, 1532–7
    intra-group financing income where payer
      denied deduction, **43(S)**, 1515–17
    intra-group short-term finance,
      43(S), 1524
    oil extraction activities, companies engaged
      in, **43(S)**, 1524
    overview of provisions, **43(S)**, 1498
    real estate investment trusts, **43(S)**, 1523–4
    short-term loan relationships, **43(S)**, 1525
    small net financing deduction or income,
      companies with, **43(S)**, 1529
    stranded deficits in non-trading loan
      relationships, **43(S)**, 1525–6
    stranded management expenses,
      43(S), 1526–7
    tested expense amount, **43(S)**, 1529
    tested income amount, **43(S)**, 1529
    transitional provisions, **43(S)**, 1538
  intangible fixed assets, **43(2)**, [188]–[189]
  member, meaning, **44(1)**, [222]
  profit sharing scheme, **44(1)**, [637]
  purchase of own shares, **44(1)**, [126]
  relief. *See* **group relief**
  research and development expenditure, tax
    relief for, **43(2)**, [142]
  90 per cent, **44(1)**, [146]

group relief
  amendment of provisions, **42**, [1517]
  amounts eligible for, **44(1)**, [207]
    consortium cases, **44(1)**, [215]
    excess capital allowances, **44(1)**, [209]
    gross profits, computation of, **44(1)**, [212]
    non-trading deficit on loan relationships,
      44(1), [210]
    other, **44(1)**, [211]
    trading losses, **44(1)**, [208]
  availability of, **44(1)**, [206]
  claims for, **43(1)**, [400]
  consortium claim—
    group claim, priority of, **44(1)**, [221]
    group member, by, **44(1)**, [222]
    link company, by, **44(1)**, [222]
    meaning, **44(1)**, [206]
  double allowance, exclusion of, **44(1)**, [225]
  dual resident companies, in respect of,
    44(1), [220], [647]–[649]
  equity holders, **44(1)**, [650]
  excessive, **44(1)**, [226]
    assessment to recover, **43(1)**, [400]

group relief—*contd*
  group claim—
    consortium claim, priority over,
      44(1), [221]
    meaning, **44(1)**, [206]
    potential relief attributable to, **44(1)**, [221]
  limits on, **44(1)**, [213]
    apportionments, **44(1)**, [214]
  meaning, **44(1)**, [206]
  non-resident companies, for, **44(1)**, [216]
    overseas losses of, **44(1)**, [218], [219],
      [651]–[653]
  other relief, and, **44(1)**, [223]
  overseas losses—
    non-resident companies, for, **44(1)**, [218],
      [219], [651]–[653]
    UK resident companies, for, **44(1)**, [217]
  payment, treatment of, **44(1)**, [206]
  preference shares, amended provisions,
    43(S), 1455–7
  restrictions on, **43(1)**, [334]
  surrender—
    consent to, **43(1)**, [400]
    reduction in amount available for,
      43(1), [400]
  surrendering company not resident in UK,
    where—
    availability of, **43(S)**, 161–2
    claims, **43(S)**, 171–2
    commencement of provisions, **43(S)**, 172
    conditions—
      EEA tax loss, **43(S)**, 165–6
      equivalence, **43(S)**, 165
      meaning, **43(S)**, 165–71
      precedence, **43(S)**, 168
      qualifying loss, **43(S)**, 166
    current and previous periods, qualifying
      for, **43(S)**, 166–7
    equity holders and profits or assets available
      for distribution, **43(S)**, 164
    future periods, qualifying for, **43(S)**, 167
    intepretation, **43(S)**, 170–1
    limits on, **43(S)**, 162
    non-resident companies within charge to
      corporation tax, **43(S)**, 163
    overseas losses of non-resident companies,
      43(S), 163–4
    territory outside UK, amount not given
      other relief under, **43(S)**, 167
    UK rules applied, **43(S)**, 168–70
  transfer of company, **44(1)**, [224]

guarantee
  exclusion clause in, **11(1)**, [312]
  meaning, **11(1)**, [312]
  writing, in, **11(1)**, [297]

guarantee, company limited by
  articles—
    form of, **8**, 111
    general provisions, **8**, 118
    See also **articles of association**
  meaning, **8**, 103–4
  memorandum—
    form of, **8**, 106–7

guarantee, company limited by—*contd*
memorandum—*contd*
general provisions, **8**, 118
See also **memorandum of association**
name of, **8**, 125, 130–1
pre-1901 companies, **8**, 824
registration, **8**, 528

guarantee payment. *See under* **wages**

guard dog
civil liability respecting, **2**, [404]
control of, generally, **2**, [400]
handler to be in attendance, **2**, [400]
kennel—
licence, requirement for, **2**, [402]
meaning, **2**, [406]
licence to keep, **2**, [401]
appeals, **2**, [403]
meaning, **2**, [406]
offences, **2**, [404]
regulations, **2**, [405]
warning notice of, **2**, [400]

guardian. *See also* **guardian's allowance**
appointment of—
court, by, **6**, [298]
disclaimer of, **6**, [299]
order for, duration, **6**, [422]
person other than court, by, **6**, [298]
residence order requirement, **6**, [298]
revocation, **6**, [299]
termination, **6**, [299]
transitional provisions, **6**, [454]
will, by, **6**, [298]
attendance at court by, **6**, [24]
contact with child under care, **6**, [347]
death of, **6**, [298]
financial relief order against, **6**, [439]
mentally disordered person. *See* **mentally
disordered person or patient**
parental responsibility of, **6**, [298]
rights, powers etc, passing to person having
parental responsibility, **6**, [295]
special—
death of, **6**, [298]
generally, **6**, [1]
requirements for being, **6**, [308]
special guardianship orders—
amended provisions, **6(S)**, 430
application for, **6**, [308]
care orders, discharging, **6**, [422]
discharge, **6**, [311]
effect, **6**, [310]
entitlement of relative to apply for,
6(S), 473
financial relief under, **6**, [439]
jurisdiction, **6**, [233]
making, **6**, [309]
meaning, **6**, [308]
power to make, **6**, [232]
supplementary provisions, **6**, [312]
support services, **6**, [313]
timetables for determining questions,
6, [312]

guardian—*contd*
special—*contd*
special guardianship orders—*contd*
variation of, **6**, [311]
support services, **6**, [313]

guardian's allowance
conditions for, **40(1)**, [324]
entitlement to, **40(1)**, [324]
functions of Secretary of State transferred to
Treasury, **40(2)**, [409]
HM Revenue and Customs—
functions of Secretary of State transferred
to, **40(2)**, [410]
information, provision of, **40(2)**, [429]
payment and management by, **40(2)**, [413]
transfer of property, rights and liabilities
to, **40(2)**, [412]
transitional provisions, **40(2)**, [414]
information—
administrative arrangements, **40(2)**, [415]
exchange of, **40(2)**, [429]
powers to use, **40(2)**, [429]
provision by HM Revenue and Customs,
40(2), [429]
parent, exclusion of, **40(1)**, [324]
rate of, **40(1)**, [467]
regulations, **40(1)**, [324]
termination of entitlement, **40(1)**, [324]

Guernsey
consolidated fund, payments out of,
7(2), [442]
Jethou, including, **7(2)**, [442]

guided transport system
drink or drugs, offences involving—
application of provisions, **38(1)**, [310]
employee, by, **38(1)**, [311]
evidence—
documentary, **38(1)**, [320]
specimens, use of, **38(1)**, [319]
maintenance worker, by, **38(1)**, [311]
operator, by, **38(1)**, [312]
penalties, **38(1)**, [321]
police, powers of—
breath tests, **38(1)**, [313]
entry and arrest, of, **38(1)**, [314]
hospital patients, protection for,
38(1), [318]
persons incapable of consenting,
specimens of blood from, **38(1)**, [316]
specimens for analysis, requirement of,
38(1), [315]
two specimens of breath, choice of,
38(1), [317]
prescribed limit, **38(1)**, [322]
principal, **38(1)**, [311]
meaning, **38(1)**, [323]
modes of, prescription of, **38(1)**, [291]
orders—
applications for, **38(1)**, [295]
compulsory purchase, authorisation of,
38(1), [302]
consents under enactments, **38(1)**, [305]

guided transport system—*contd*
orders—*contd*
Crown land, **38(1)**, [309]
inquiries and hearings, **38(1)**, [301]
made other than on application,
38(1), [297]
making, **38(1)**, [303]
model clauses, **38(1)**, [298]
national significance, schemes of,
38(1), [299]
objections to, **38(1)**, [300]
other Member States affected, where,
38(1), [296]
power to apply for or object to,
38(1), [306]
power to make, **38(1)**, [290]
publicity, **38(1)**, [304]
refusal of, **38(1)**, [303]
special parliamentary procedure,
38(1), [302]
subject-matter of, **38(1)**, [294], [345]
validity of, **38(1)**, [307]
safety—
bodies corporate, offences by, **38(1)**, [335]
Health and Safety at Work etc Act,
application of provisions of, **38(1)**, [460]
insurance, directions requiring, **38(1)**, [325]
prosecutions, consent to, **38(1)**, [334]
speeds and loads, directions limiting,
38(1), [324]
works, plant and equipment, approval of,
38(1), [323]
service of notices, **38(1)**, [338]

guild church
additional designation of, **14**, 511
baptism in, **14**, 465
certificate given to, **14**, 451
churchwardens, **14**, 462, 1389
clerk, **14**, 463
constitution of, **14**, 452–3
council—
body corporate, as, **14**, 459
constitution of, **14**, 452–3
lay representatives, **14**, 452–3, 460–1
members of, **14**, 459
curate, **14**, 458
designation as, **14**, 451, 470
electoral roll, person entitled to be on,
14, 458
establishment as, **14**, 451, 470
faculties, **14**, 466
freehold of, **14**, 452
goods and ornaments, vesting of, **14**, 462
marriage in, **14**, 464
meaning, **14**, 450
meetings, **14**, 459
patronage, rights of—
exercise of, **14**, 454–5
generally, **14**, 453–4
lapse, **14**, 455
new benefice, creation of, **14**, 468–9, 471
transfer of, **14**, 513
patrons of, **14**, 453–4
presentation to, suspension of, **14**, 512

guild church—*contd*
purpose of, **14**, 452
redundancy, declaration of, **14**, 1077–8
registers and records, custody of, **14**, 465
scheme for representation of laity, **14**, 460–1
sidesmen, **14**, 463
status of, **14**, 452
trusts and trustees, **14**, 466–7
vacancy in, **14**, 454
vicar of—
licensing, **14**, 453–4
rights and duties, **14**, 456–7
vacancy in office, **14**, 457
ward church—
alteration of, **14**, 514–15
designation as, **14**, 467–8

Guildhall Museum. *See* **Museum of London**

gullies
cleansing and repair, **35(1)**, [259]

gun barrel
convention proof mark—
exemption for, **48**, 32
meaning, **48**, 31
offences, proceedings for, **48**, 33
register, **48**, 31
transitional provisions, **48**, 91–3
converted—
provisional mark on, **48**, 22
unproved, deemed, **48**, 23
double barrel—
meaning, **48**, 18
reduction in strength, **48**, 21
explosive substances, sent for proof
containing, **48**, 29
guardians—
generally, **48**, 48–9
regulations by, **48**, 90
interpretation of terms, **48**, 17–18
mark—
defaced, **48**, 22
meaning, **48**, 18
provisional—
converted barrel, on, **48**, 22–3
meaning, **48**, 18
Military barrel, on, **48**, 22
removal of, **48**, 22
Military, removal of provisional proof from,
48, 22
offences, **48**, 26–9, 89
officers, fraud by, **48**, 36
penalties, **48**, 27–8, 30, 89
proof—
Act, expenses of, **48**, 50
application of Act, **48**, 25
charges, **48**, 24
companies—
marking, etc, by, **48**, 20
meaning, **48**, 17
generally, **48**, 11–12
meaning, **48**, 18
measurements, **48**, 90
reduction following, **48**, 21

gun barrel—*contd*
  proof—*contd*
    regulations, **48**, 20
    rules, regulations and scale, **48**, 23–4
  proof house—
    branch, establishment of, **48**, 90
    establishment of, **48**, 17
  proof master—
    convention mark, keeping register of,
      48, 31
    declaration by, **48**, 19
    responsibility of, **48**, 19
  small arm—
    detained, disposal of, **48**, 35
    meaning, **48**, 17
    pawn of, **48**, 21
    sale or export of, **48**, 21
  stamp—
    forged—
      detention of barrels, **48**, 35
      disposal, **48**, 35
      property in, **48**, 31
      warrant for seizure of, **48**, 33–4
    meaning, **48**, 18
    removal of, **48**, 36

gunpowder. *See also* **explosives**
  building, placing near, **12(1)**, [86]
  byelaws. *See* **explosives**
  causing injury by, **12(1)**, [84]
  causing to explode, **12(1)**, [85]
  conveyance. *See* **explosives**
  factory. *See* **explosives**
  hawking, prohibition of, **18**, [694]

gunpowder—*contd*
  licence. *See* **explosives**
  magazine. *See* **explosives**
  making to commit offence, **12(1)**, [102]
  modification of provisions, **18**, [698]
  provisions applied to other explosives,
    18, [692], [697], [698]
  safety precautions, **18**, [698]
  sale of—
    children, to, **18**, [695]
    containers, to be in, **18**, [696]
    highways etc, on, **18**, [694]
  samples, power to take, **18**, [700]
  search for, powers of, **18**, [703]
  search warrant, **12(1)**, [103]
  store. *See* **explosives**

gutter
  draining, cleansing, etc, power of parish
    council or local authority as to, **35(1)**, [162]
  foul, statutory nuisance, **35(1)**, [161]

Guyana
  British ship registered in, **7(2)**, [588]
  certificate of naturalisation, effect of,
    7(2), [583]
  Commonwealth citizenship, **31**, [186]
  fully responsible status of, **7(2)**, [582]
  legislative powers of, **7(2)**, [587]
  republic, becoming, existing law, operation
    of, **7(2)**, [638]
  visiting forces in, **7(2)**, [588]

gypsies and travellers
  accommodation needs of, duties of local
    housing authorities as to, **24**, [373], [374]

H

habeas corpus
  application—
    appeal, **7(1)**, [25]
    meaning, **7(1)**, [26]
    procedure, **7(1)**, [24]
    vacation, in, **7(1)**, [9]
  bail, grant of, **7(1)**, [3]
  bankruptcy, in case of, **7(1)**, [14]
  capital crime committed outside England,
    7(1), [12]
  Cinque ports, in, **7(1)**, [10], [20]
  civil cause, person charged in, **7(1)**, [7]
  civil procedure, application to, **7(1)**, [16]–[21]
  counties palatine, in, **7(1)**, [10], [20]
  criminal matter, person committed for,
    7(1), [8]
  debt, person charged in, **7(1)**, [7]
  discharge on recognizance, **7(1)**, [3]
  general note, **7(1)**, [1]
  Northern Ireland. *See* **Northern Ireland**
  Northern Ireland, in, **7(1)**, [27], [29], [30]
  offences, limitation for prosecution, **7(1)**, [13]
  prisoner sent into Scotland, etc, **7(1)**, [11]
  recommitment, **7(1)**, [6]
  scope of, **7(1)**, [21]
  three days, prisoner brought up in, **7(1)**, [2]
  true cause of imprisonment, certifying,
    7(1), [3]
  witness, prisoner as, **7(1)**, [15]
  writ of—
    colony with competent court, issue into,
      7(1), [22]
    Commissioners, bringing person before,
      7(1), [14]
    court martial, bringing person before,
      7(1), [14]
    dominions, not issuing in, **7(1)**, [22]
    marking, **7(1)**, [3]
    non-obedience to, **7(1)**, [5], [17]
    prisoners only removed by, **7(1)**, [8]
    truth of facts in return, **7(1)**, [18], [19]
    vacation time, in, **7(1)**, [4], [16]
      non-obedience, **7(1)**, [17]
      return of, **7(1)**, [17]
      undue denial, **7(1)**, [9]

hackney carriage. *See also* **taxis and taxicabs**
  accident to, notification of, **36**, [933]
  Acts—
    application of, **36**, [244], [928], [961]
    construction, **36**, [433]
    continuation in force, **36**, [491]
    execution of, **36**, [488]
    incorporation with special Acts, **36**, [375]
    interpretation, **36**, [377]
    limits, **36**, [432]
    summary of provisions, **36**, [210]

hackney carriage—*contd*
  advertisements on, **36**, [428]
  amendment of enactments, **26(1)**, [787]
  appeals—
    drivers, by, **36**, [942], [944]
    general provisions, **36**, [960]
  area of application, **37**, [365]
  authorised officer—
    inspection and testing by, **36**, [951]
    meaning, **36**, [963]
    obstruction of, **36**, [956]
  byelaws regulating, **36**, [416]
  cabs, licensing of. *See* licence *below*
  compensation for damage—
    driver, by, **36**, [412]
    hirer, by, **36**, [213]
    recovery from driver, **36**, [256], [412]
  complaint—
    driver's licence, production on, **36**, [397]
    hearing of, **36**, [259]
    time limits for, **36**, [258]
    withdrawal of, compensation on, **36**, [218],
      [414]
  construction of statutory terms, **36**, [219],
    [243], [963]
  defrauding cabmen, **36**, [570]
  distance required to drive, **36**, [425]
  distinguishing marks—
    identification by, **36**, [931]
    return of plate etc, on expiry of licence,
      36, [941]
  district councils, provisions adopted by,
    36, [928]
  driver—
    abstract of laws, issue to, **36**, [245]
    acting without consent of proprietor,
      36, [255]
    appeals by, **36**, [942], [944]
    badges—
      byelaws as to, **36**, [416]
      delivery up of, **36**, [250]
      issue, **36**, [245], [938]
      lost or defaced, **36**, [251]
      return of, **36**, [944]
      wearing of, **36**, [245], [249]
    compensation—
      complaints, on withdrawal of, **36**, [218],
        [414]
      hirer, refusal to pay or causing damage,
        36, [213]
      recovery of, from, **36**, [256], [412]
      when improperly summoned, **36**, [3];
        37, [3]; **38(1)**, [3]
    damage by, **36**, [256], [412]
    deposit for waiting time, **36**, [214], [406]
    distance required to drive, **36**, [425]
    drunkenness, **36**, [217], [410]

hackney carriage—*contd*
 driver—*contd*
 furious driving by, **36**, [217], [256], [410]
 licence—
  acting without, penalty, **36**, [396]
  application for, **36**, [940]
   information, submission, **36**, [940]
  duration, **36**, [484], [936]
  fee, **36**, [936]
  generally, **36**, [930]
  grant of, **36**, [245]
  requirement, **36**, [389], [395], [484]
  retention or return by proprietor,
   36, [397], [398]
  revocation, return of plate or disc,
   36, [941]
  suspension or revocation, **36**, [944]
  See also **driving licence**
 loitering, **36**, [257]
 misbehaviour by, **36**, [217], [256], [398]
 obstructing other drivers, **36**, [413]
 obstruction by, penalty, **36**, [257]
 permitting persons to ride without hirer's
  consent, **36**, [215], [408]
 qualifications, **36**, [942]
 quitting service, proceedings, **36**, [253]
 refusal of hire by, **36**, [211]
 refusal to drive, **36**, [402], [429]
 ticket—
  numbered plate, **36**, [388]
  return of plate or disc, **36**, [941]
 unauthorised person acting as, **36**, [409]
 uncivil language by, **36**, [212]
 unlicensed, penalty, **36**, [246], [394]–[396]
 wait, refusal to, **36**, [214]
 waiting period, **36**, [214], [406]
 driver of, shelter for, **35(1)**, [54]
 false information in respect of, **36**, [247],
  [940]
 fares—
  demanding more than agreed, **36**, [403]
  depriving other drivers of, **36**, [216]
  extra, demanding, penalty for, **36**, [429]
  fixed sum, agreement, **36**, [405]
  fixing of, **36**, [948]
  illegal, demanding, **36**, [257]
  legal, agreement to more than, **36**, [404]
  long journeys, **36**, [949]
  overcharging, **36**, [407], [429]
  refusal to pay, **36**, [213]
  table of, **36**, [948]
  taxi fares byelaws, **36**, [416]
  taximeter cabs, **36**, [585]
  unpaid, recovery, **36**, [415]
 fitness, inspection and testing for, **36**, [951]
 furious driving, **36**, [217], [256], [410]
 hire—
  driver refusing, **36**, [211]
  plying for—
   when deemed, **36**, [211]
   without licence, **36**, [394]
 hirer—
  damage by, **36**, [213]
  injury by, **36**, [213]
   to, **36**, [256]

hackney carriage—*contd*
 hirer—*contd*
 persons riding without consent of,
  36, [215]
 refusing to pay fare, **36**, [213]
 identification plate or disc, **36**, [388], [941]
 injury or endangering life, **36**, [217]
  hirer, by, **36**, [213]
  to, **36**, [256]
 inspection and testing—
  fitness, for, **36**, [951]
  presentation for, **36**, [933]
 licence—
  appeals arising, **36**, [254]; **37**, [367]
  application for, **36**, [247]
   requisition required, **36**, [247], [389]
  authentication of, **36**, [962]
  badge—
   issue of, **36**, [245]
   lost or defaced, **36**, [251]
   wearing of, **36**, [249]
  conditions attaching to, **36**, [930]
  delivery up on discontinuation of,
   36, [250]
  duration, **35(1)**, [26]; **36**, [392], [482]
  endorsement, **36**, [252]
  expiry, return of distinguishing plate etc,
   36, [941]
  false representation relating to, **36**, [247]
  fees for, **36**, [279], [953]; **37**, [80]
  grant of, **36**, [245], [387], [482], [487]
  information required of applicant, **36**, [940]
  matters to be specified in, **36**, [390]
  particulars, record of, **36**, [248]
  plying for hire without, **36**, [394]
  production on complaint, **36**, [397]
  quitting service by driver, proceedings,
   36, [253]
  registration of, **36**, [391]
  requirement, **36**, [389]
  requisition required, **36**, [389]
  retention by proprietor, **36**, [252], [397]
  return by proprietor, **36**, [398]
  revocation of—
   appeal against, **36**, [254]
   conviction, on, **36**, [254], [399]
   grounds for, **36**, [944]
   misbehaviour, **36**, [217]
  suspension of—
   appeal against, **36**, [254]
   conviction, on, **36**, [254]
   grounds for, **36**, [424], [944]
  transfer, **36**, [482], [930]
 licensing generally, **36**, [387], [930]
 loitering, **36**, [257]
 London—
  complaints, time limits for, **26(2)**, [805]
  directional taxi ranks, power to designate,
   26(2), [800]
  drivers' badges, **26(2)**, [802]
  fixed penalty offences—
   financial provisions, **26(2)**, [842]
   levels of penalty, **26(2)**, [811]
   notice, **26(2)**, [808], [810]
   regulations, power to make, **26(2)**, [813]

hackney carriage—*contd*
London—*contd*
fixed penalty offences—*contd*
schedule of offences, **26(2)**, [809], [841]
Secretary of State, reserve powers,
26(2), [812]
journeys ending outside London, fares for,
26(2), [806]
licence, public register not to include
holders' addresses, **26(2)**, [803]
replacement badges, cost of, **26(2)**, [804]
rest ranks, power to designate, **26(2)**, [801]
unfit cabs, **26(2)**, [807]
London cabs—
defrauding cabmen, **36**, [570]
meaning, **36**, [571]
non-obligatory journeys, **36**, [768]
obligatory journeys, **36**, [769]
order, meaning, **36**, [771]
parking, **36**, [770]
privileged cab system, abolition, **36**, [586]
taximeters, fixing of, **36**, [585]
London, limits of application of Act of 1869,
36, [480]
luggage, quantity, **36**, [427]
magistrates—
jurisdiction, **36**, [430]
power as to disputes, **36**, [259]
meaning, **36**, [388], [481]
Metropolis, limits of application of Act of
1869, **36**, [480]
metropolitan police district, provisions on
alteration of, **26(1)**, [644]
number of persons permitted, **36**, [400], [426]
painting on vehicle, **36**, [400], [401], [426]
refusal to carry, **36**, [429]
numbered plate on, **36**, [388]
return of, **36**, [941]
obstruction by, **36**, [257]
authorised officer of, **36**, [956]
offences. *See* **offences**
operators' licence. *See* licence *above*
overcharging, **36**, [407]
passengers or property endangered, **36**, [217],
[410]
penalties—
generally, **36**, [431], [486], [959]
magistrates' powers, **36**, [259]
recovery, generally, **36**, [489]
pictures, placards etc, on, **36**, [428]
placards as to, on lamp posts, **36**, [490]
place of keeping of, notification, **36**, [933]
private hire, use for, **36**, [929], [950]
prolongation of journey, unnecessary,
36, [952]
proprietor—
abode, change of, **36**, [393]
general provisions, **36**, [933]
meaning, **36**, [243], [963]
misbehaviour by, **36**, [217]
more than one, proceedings where,
36, [260]
particulars specified in licence, **36**, [390]
permitting persons to ride without hirer's
consent, **36**, [215], [408]

hackney carriage—*contd*
proprietor—*contd*
unlicensed driver, penalty for employment
of, **36**, [394]
railway stations, at, **35(1)**, [101]
regulations, **36**, [485]
roof-signs, **36**, [995]
savings—
certain businesses, **36**, [957]
certain vehicles, **36**, [958]
special Act—
incorporation of Acts with, **36**, [375]
meaning, **36**, [376]
speed, **36**, [429]
standing, deemed to be plying for hire,
36, [211]
stands—
appointment and regulation of, **36**, [422],
[946]
other vehicles on, prohibition, **36**, [947]
summary of provisions, **36**, [210]
taxis and taximeters. *See* **taxis and taxicabs**
transfer of functions, **26(1)**, [787]
transfer of, notification, **36**, [932]
transitional provisions, **26(1)**, [788]
Transport for London, functions transferred
to, **26(1)**, [643]
unattended, **36**, [411]
unfitness for use, **36**, [424], [429], [943]
unlicensed, penalty for use of, **36**, [483]
vehicles deemed to be, **36**, [388]
waiting—
deposit, demand for, **36**, [214], [406]
driver, refusal by, **36**, [214]

hairdressing
byelaws as to, **35(1)**, [272]
Council—
accounts, **47**, [91]
approval of courses etc, **47**, [82]
constitution of, **47**, [95]
disciplinary committee—
assessor to assist, **47**, [98]
constitution of, **47**, [97]
duty of, **47**, [86]
procedure of, **47**, [98]
establishment, **47**, [79]
investigating committee—
constitution of, **47**, [97]
duty of, **47**, [86]
limitation on powers, **47**, [92]
members—
qualifications of, **47**, [95]
terms of office, **47**, [96]
powers of, **47**, [92], [96]
status, **47**, [96]
supplementary provisions, **47**, [96]
London—
offences, increased fines, **25(2)**, [527]
registration of, **25(1)**, [834]
meaning, **47**, [93]
notices, service of, **47**, [90]
register of hairdressers—
contents, **47**, [80]
establishment and maintenance, **47**, [80]

hairdressing—*contd*
  register of hairdressers—*contd*
    publication of, **47**, [85]
    registration in—
      certificate of, **47**, [81]
      qualifications for, **47**, [81]
      removal from—
        effect of, **47**, [87]
        grounds for, **47**, [87]
        return of certificate on, **47**, [88]
      rules as to, **47**, [84]
  registrar, appointment, **47**, [90]
  summary of provisions, **47**, [1]
  training institutions—
    courses etc, approval of, **47**, [82]
    supervision of, **47**, [83]

hallmark
  Act, enforcement of, **48**, 61
  ancient mark, **48**, 60
  approved—
    alteration to article bearing, **48**, 58
    conditions for, **48**, 55–7
    meaning, **48**, 53
    one metal, article comprised of, **48**, 75–6
    precious metal and other materials, article
      comprised of, **48**, 78
    schedule of, **48**, 75–8
    shield, etc, enclosed in, **48**, 78
    striking, **48**, 56
    two or more metals, article comprised of,
      48, 77
  assay towns—
    Birmingham as, **48**, 13–15
    generally, **48**, 11
    Sheffield as, **48**, 13–15
  charge for, **48**, 63
  convention, **48**, 53
  die or mark, counterfeiting, **48**, 59
  improper alteration, **48**, 53
  law relating to, **48**, 10–11
  local Act, repeal of, **48**, 66–7
  local inquiries, **48**, 67–8
  notices, display of, **48**, 62
  offences, **48**, 79
  regulations, power to make, **48**, 57, 68
  sponsors' mark, **48**, 54–5, 70
  unauthorised, treatment of, **48**, 60
  unhallmarked articles—
    amendment of provisions, **48**, 75
    exempted, **48**, 72–3
    meaning, **48**, 53
    permissible descriptions, **48**, 71
    prohibited descriptions of, **48**, 52

handicapped persons. *See* **disabled person**

harassment
  civil remedy for, **12(2)**, [561]
  conduct regarded as, **7(1)**, [37]
  course of conduct amounting to, **12(2)**, [559]
  court, jurisdiction of, **21**, [671]
  employer, by, **7(1)**, [39]
  injunctions to protect against, **12(2)**, [562]
  interpretation of provisions, **12(2)**, [566]

harassment—*contd*
  national security, matters relating to,
    12(2), [567]
  Northern Ireland, provisions applying,
    12(2), [568]
  offence of, **21**, [662], [668]
  person in home, of—
    offence of, **12(3)**, [26]
    police directions stopping, **12(3)**, [25]
  prohibition, **12(2)**, [559]
  public order offence, as, **12(1)**, [995], [996]
  racially or religiously aggravated, **12(2)**, [672]
  rental purchase agreement, following,
    21, [765]
  residential occupier, of, **21**, [662]
  restraining orders, **12(2)**, [564]; **12(4)**, [7]
    acquittal, on, **12(2)**, [565]
  sexual—
    Highlands and Islands Enterprise, by,
      7(1), [54]
    Scottish Enterprise, by, **7(1)**, [54]
  violence, putting people in fear of,
    12(2), [563]

harbour authorities. *See also* **ports and
harbours**
  accounts and audit, **39(2)**, [526]
  accounts, preparation, **39(2)**, [186]
  activities—
    meaning, **39(2)**, [186]
    reports on, **39(2)**, [186]
  Associated British Ports. *See* **Associated
    British Ports**
  borrowing powers—
    approval required, **39(2)**, [104]
    generally, **39(2)**, [214], [525]
    priority debts, payment of, **39(2)**, [129]
    supplemental provisions, **39(2)**, [527]
    when unrestrained, **39(2)**, [124]
  business, power to acquire, **39(2)**, [212]
  charges. *See under* **ports and harbours**
  coast protection—
    board, representation on, **49**, [381]
    works, **49**, [395]
  competent, **39(2)**, [536]
  constitution, power to vary, **39(2)**, [168]
  dangerous vessels, liability as to, **39(2)**, [518]
  debts of Boards, transfer of, to, **39(2)**, [216]
  depots, provision of, **39(2)**, [211]
  discharge of oil in exercise of powers of,
    39(2), [807]
  drainage authority not regarded as,
    39(2), [201]
  drainage works affecting, protection,
    19(3), [259]
  dues, transfer of, to—
    borrowing powers to effect, **39(2)**, [108]
    evidence of transfer, **39(2)**, [107]
    intended, notice, **39(2)**, [106]
    powers, **39(2)**, [105]
  efficiency, orders to secure, **39(2)**, [166],
    [167]
  environmental duties, **39(2)**, [193]
  financial contributions, **49**, [1181]

harbour authorities—*contd*
functions or property, transfer to Environment Agency, **49**, [1272]
herring fisheries, use for, **1(1)**, [125]
inland clearance depots, provision, **39(2)**, [211]
limitation of liability, **39(2)**, [868]
loans to—
  capital debts, to pay off, **39(2)**, [447]
  execution of works, for, **39(2)**, [164]
  expenses incurred, **39(2)**, [215]
  limitation, **39(2)**, [165], [450]
  National Loans Fund, issues from, **39(2)**, [164], [187]
  overdrafts, to pay off, **39(2)**, [447]
  past loans, **39(2)**, [449]
  power to make, **39(2)**, [104]
  priority of security, **39(2)**, [126]–[129]
  purposes for which made, **39(2)**, [104]
  repayment, **39(2)**, [187]
  temporary, **39(2)**, [447]
local fisheries committee—
  acting as, **1(1)**, [623]
  contributions by, **1(1)**, [618]
mail-bags—
  control, not to be subject to, **34**, [710]
  harbour charges, **34**, [709]
maximum fines, provision for, **11(3)**, [61]
meaning, **35(1)**, [112]; **39(2)**, [103], [200], [988]; **44(1)**, [374]; **49**, [1267]
national defence, powers in interest of, **39(2)**, [513]
National Ports Council dissolution—
  charging schemes, **39(2)**, [481], [492]
  contributions towards expenses of, **39(2)**, [480]
nationally significant infrastructure project, creation on grant of development consent for, **46(S)**, 144–5
oil discharge, protection, **49**, [469], [475]
operations—
  meaning, **39(2)**, [200]
  miscellaneous powers as to, **39(2)**, [213]
powers, miscellaneous, **39(2)**, [213]
removal of wreck by, **39(2)**, [930]
reports, preparation, **39(2)**, [186]
river authority not regarded as, **39(2)**, [201]
searches in harbour areas, promotion of, **39(2)**, [588]
services and facilities provided, use of, **39(2)**, [184]
shares in harbour business, acquisition, **39(2)**, [212]
shipping purposes, meaning, **39(2)**, [103]
statutory—
  accounts and reports, **39(2)**, [186]
  local lighthouse authorities, as, **39(2)**, [879]
  local lighthouses, individual transfers of, **39(2)**, [880]
  meaning, **39(2)**, [186], [988]
tidal works, licensing, **39(2)**, [570]
transfer of business, capital gains tax on, **42**, [1357]
transfer of trade to, **44(1)**, [374]

harbour master. *See under* **ports and harbours**

harbour reorganisation scheme
corporation tax, **44(1)**, [374]
meaning, **44(1)**, [374]
transfers under, stamp duty, **41**, [112]

harbour undertakers. *See also* **ports and harbours**
meaning, **36**, [1381]
property of, reference to, **36**, [1381]
saving for works of, **36**, [1390]

harbouring
spouse or child, action for, abolition, **45**, [954]

harbours. *See* **ports and harbours**
meaning, **35(1)**, [112]

hard labour
abolition, **12(1)**, [259]

hares. *See also* **game**
agreements not to kill, **2**, [186]
authority to kill—
  limitations of, **2**, [184]
  persons having, **2**, [183]
close season for, **2**, [228]
coursing—
  offences—
    body corporate, by, **2**, [741]
    Crown application, **2**, [743]
    forfeiture, **2**, [740]
    generally, **2**, [737]
    penalties, **2**, [739]
    search and seizure, power of, **2**, [739]
destruction, rights as to, **2**, [213], [233]
firearms, killing by night with, **2**, [185]
open trapping, **2**, [295]
poisoning, prohibition of, **2**, [185]
shot, retrieval of, **2**, [749]

haulage vehicle
excise duty, **13**, [1047]

hawker. *See also* **pedlar**
food, of, unregistered, penalties, **25(2)**, [512], [515]
highway, pitching booth on, **36**, [1213]

hawking
explosives, restriction on, **18**, [694]

hazardous substances
appeals, determination of, **46**, [801]
authority—
  application of provisions to, **46**, [782]
  council as, **46**, [751]–[752]
  register, keeping, **46**, [780]
consent—
  application for—
    appeals, **46**, [770]

hazardous substances—*contd*
  consent—*contd*
    application for—*contd*
      applicant's status, certificate as to, **46**, [757]
      appropriate consultations, **46**, [756]
      determination of, **46**, [758]
      disposal of Crown land, in anticipation of, **46**, [789]
      fees, **46**, [778]
      grant on, **46**, [755]
      regulations, **46**, [756]
      Secretary of State, reference to, **46**, [769]
      validity of decisions, **46**, [771]
      without condition attached to previous consent, **46**, [762]
    change of control of land, **46**, [766]
    compensation for modification or revocation, **46**, [765]
    conditions, **46**, [759]
    content of, **46**, [758]
    continuation, application for, **46**, [767]–[768]
    deemed—
      established presence, where, **46**, [760]
      government authorisation, on, **46**, [761]
    government department, authorisation of, **46**, [761]
    health and safety requirements, **46**, [781]
    land, enuring for benefit of, **46**, [755]
    meaning, **46**, [753]
    modification of, **46**, [763]–[765]
    person in control of land, change in, **46**, [766]
    previous conditions, without compliance with, **46**, [762]
    requirement of, **46**, [753]
    revocation of, **46**, [763]–[766]
  contravention notice—
    appeals, **46**, [775]
    copy, service of, **46**, [773]
    health and safety requirements, **46**, [781]
    injunctions, **46**, [777]
    matters specified in, **46**, [773]
    meaning, **46**, [773]
    power to issue, **46**, [773]
    regulations, **46**, [775]
    requirement as to removal of substance, **46**, [773]
    transitional exemptions, **46**, [776]
    variation, **46**, [774]
    withdrawal of, **46**, [773]
  control, contravention of, **46**, [772]
  Crown land—
    application of provisions to, **46**, [783]
    consent, application for, **46**, [788]
      disposal, in anticipation of, **46**, [789]
    enforcement, **46**, [785]
    exercise of powers in relation to, **46**, [787]
    interest, reference to, **46**, [786]
    rights of entry, **46**, [795]
    transitional provisions, **46**, [784]
  ecclesiastical property, on, **46**, [790]
  financial provisions, **46**, [797]
  generally, **46**, [1]

hazardous substances—*contd*
  Isles of Scilly, provisions applying to, **46**, [791]
  local inquiries, **46**, [801]
  offences, **46**, [772]
  power to prescribe, **46**, [754]
  provisions applying to, **46**, [796]
  regulations, **46**, [799]
  rights of entry, **46**, [792]–[795]
  specification of, **46**, [754]
  temporary presence of, **46**, [779]
  warrants to enter land, **46**, [793]

health and safety at work
  agriculture, in. *See* **agricultural workers**
  articles for use at work, meaning, **18**, [1307]
  breach of duty in respect of, **18**, [1300]
  charges and levies against employees, prohibition, **18**, [1263]
  civil liabilities in respect of, **18**, [1300]
  codes of practice—
    approval and issue, **18**, [1270]
    use in criminal proceedings, **18**, [1271]
  Commission. *See* **Health and Safety Commission**
  Commissioners for Revenue and Customs, disclosure of information, **18**, [1283]
  conditional sale agreement, articles supplied under, **18**, [1307]
  contract of employment, meaning, **18**, [1307]
  credit-sale agreement, articles supplied under, **18**, [1307]
  Crown, application of provisions to, **18**, [1301]
  customs officer, powers to facilitate enforcement, **18**, [1280]
  damage caused by breach of duty, **18**, [1300]
  defective equipment, injuries attributable to, **16**, [19]
  deregulation, power to repeal certain provisions under, **18**, [1339]
  detriment, right to not suffer, **16**, [660]
  domestic—
    employment, exclusion, **18**, [1304]
    premises, meaning, **18**, [1307]
  employees—
    charges or levies on, prohibition, **18**, [1263]
    general duties of, **18**, [1261]
  employers—
    general duties—
      employees, to, **18**, [1257]
      persons other than employees, **18**, [1258]
    liability, **16**, [19]
    statement of policy by, **18**, [1257]
  enforcement of provisions, authorities responsible, **18**, [1272]
  enforcing authorities—
    default in duties, **18**, [1298]
    directions to, **18**, [1298]
    expenses, **18**, [1295]
    information—
      power to obtain, **18**, [1282]
      restriction on disclosure, **18**, [1284]
    meaning, **18**, [1272]
    powers, **18**, [1272]

health and safety at work—*contd*

entertainment, duties as to articles in connection with, duties as to, **18**, [1260]

examination of manufactured articles, duties, **18**, [1260]

Executive. *See* **Health and Safety Executive**

existing enactments, **18**, [1314]

factories, in. *See* **factories**

fairground equipment—

  meaning, **18**, [1307]

  safety requirement, **18**, [1260]

fees, regulations as to, **18**, [1295]

financial provisions, **18**, [1295]

general duties—

  employees—

    by, **18**, [1261]

    to, **18**, [1257]

  employers, **18**, [1257], [1258]

  manufacturers, of, **18**, [1260]

  persons other than employees, to, **18**, [1259]

  self-employed, of, **18**, [1258]

  users of premises, **18**, [1259]

hire-purchase agreement, articles supplied under, **18**, [1307]

imminent danger, power to deal with, **18**, [1279]

improvement notice—

  appeal against, **18**, [1278]

  directions in, **18**, [1277]

  measures to be taken under, **18**, [1275]

  service of, **18**, [1275]

information—

  power to obtain, **18**, [1282]

  restriction on disclosure, **18**, [1284]

inspectors—

  appointment, **18**, [1273]

  books etc, inspection, **18**, [1274]

  harmful articles or substances, removal, **18**, [1274]

  impersonation, **18**, [1285]

  improvement notice, service of, **18**, [1275]

  indemnification of, **18**, [1281]

  information required by, **18**, [1274]

  obstruction of, **18**, [1274], [1285]

  powers, **18**, [1274]

  prohibition notice, service of, **18**, [1276]

  prosecutions by, **18**, [1291]

interference or misuse of things provided, **18**, [1262]

licences under relevant statutes—

  appeals in respect of, **18**, [1297]

  nuclear site licences, exclusion, **18**, [1297]

local authorities, enforcement by, **18**, [1272]

Medical Advisory Service. *See* **Medical Advisory Service**

metric units, adaptation of enactments to, **18**, [1302]

mining. *See* **mines and mining (safety etc)**

notices, service of, **18**, [1299]

offences—

  bodies corporate, by, **18**, [1289]

  court's powers, **18**, [1294]

  corporate manslaughter or homicide charge in same proceedings for, **12(4)**, [307]

health and safety at work—*contd*

offences—*contd*

  Crown, by, **18**, [1288]

  evidence, **18**, [1293]

    onus of proof, **18**, [1292]

  false statement, making, **18**, [1285]

  fault of another, due to, **18**, [1288]

  forfeiture by court order, **18**, [1294]

  forgery of documents, **18**, [1285]

  generally, **18**, [1285]

  jurisdiction as to, **18**, [1290]

  mode of trial **18**, [1317]

  penalties, **18**, [1285], [1317]

  proceedings for, **18**, [1290]

  prosecutions by inspectors, **18**, [1291]

  remedy, court order for, **18**, [1294]

  summary proceedings—

    penalty in case of, **18**, [1285]

    time for bringing, **18**, [1286]

  venue, **18**, [1287]

office premises. *See* **office premises**

offshore installation, meaning, **18**, [1307]

personal injury, meaning, **18**, [1307]

police, application of provisions to, **16**, [673]; **18**, [1305]

premises, meaning, **18**, [1307]

prohibition notice—

  appeal against, **18**, [1278]

  directions in, **18**, [1277]

  service of, **18**, [1276]

purpose of provisions, **18**, [1256]

railway premises. *See under* **railway**

regulations—

  application of, **18**, [1269]

  contravention of, **18**, [1269]

  exemptions, power to provide, **18**, [1269]

  matters to be provided for, **18**, [1269]

  metric units, conversion to, **18**, [1302]

  offences and defences, **18**, [1269]

  power to make, **18**, [1269], [1311]

  relevant statutory provisions, under, **18**, [1303]

  repeals or modification of provisions by, **18**, [1269], [1309]

  subject matters, schedule of, **18**, [1316]

safety representatives, **16**, [92]

Scilly Isles, application of provisions, **18**, [1308]

self-employed—

  as domestic servant, exclusion of provisions, **18**, [1304]

  general duties, **18**, [1258]

  meaning, **18**, [1307]

shops, in. *See* **shops**

summary of provisions, **16**, [1]

unfair dismissal for reasons of, **16**, [747]

work, meaning, **18**, [1306]

Health and Safety Commission. *See now* **Health and Safety Executive**

Health and Safety Executive

accounts, **18**, [1315]

civil proceedings, **18**, [1264]

Health and Safety Executive—*contd*
Coal Authority, co-operation with,
17(2), [127]
codes of practice—
approval and issue, **18**, [1270]
notification of, **18**, [1270]
committees, appointment, **18**, [1267]
constitution, **18**, [1315]
control by Secretary of State, **18**, [1266]
duties, **18**, [1265]
electricity safety issues, consultation on,
17(1), [730]
enforcement powers, **18**, [1272]
establishment, **18**, [1264]
functions, **16**, [79]
general, **18**, [1265]
performance, **18**, [1264], [1315]
information, provision by, **18**, [1265]
inquiries by, **18**, [1268]
investigations by, **18**, [1268]
members—
appointment, **18**, [1315]
remuneration, **18**, [1315]
tenure of office, **18**, [1315]
mines, faulty plans, action on, **17(1)**, [87]
nuclear installations. *See* **nuclear installations**
offshore installations, safety zones, proposals
as, **17(1)**, [710]
petroleum and petroleum products, security
preservation, consultations, **17(2)**, [57]
powers generally, **18**, [1267]
proceedings, **18**, [1315]
receipts by, disposal, **16**, [110]
reports, **18**, [1315]
research, duties as to, **18**, [1265], [1267]
responsibility towards, **16**, [79]
services and facilities, provision of, **18**, [1267]
staff, **18**, [1315]

health authority. *See also* **national health
service; Special Health Authority**
AIDS and HIV reports, **30**, [505], [509]
family health services, duty in relation to,
30, [446]
general ophthalmic services. *See* **ophthalmic
optician; ophthalmic services**
information, supply by, **16**, [84]
inspection of premises etc, Secretary of State's
powers, **6**, [409]
instruction, provision of, **30**, [430]
mental patient—
discharge from hospital, notification of,
40(1), [167]
needs, assessment of, **40(1)**, [167]
repeals and revocations, **30**, [572]
Strategic. *See* **Strategic Health Authority**
transitional provisions and savings, **30**, [571],
[579]

Health Board
instruction, provision of, **30**, [430]

health care
associated professions, regulation—
Orders in Council, **28**, [741]

health care—*contd*
associated professions, regulation—*contd*
power of, **28**, [735]
regulations and orders, **28**, [736]
regulation—
Orders in Council, **28**, [741]
power of, **28**, [735]
regulations and orders, **28**, [736]

health care workers
designated bodies, co-operation between,
28(S), 34–5
extension of statutory powers, **28(S)**, 70–3
responsible officers—
Crown, provisions binding, **28(S)**, 30
regulations, **28(S)**, 29–32
requirement to nominate or appoint,
28(S), 26–7
responsibilities of, **28(S)**, 28–9, 32–3

health in pregnancy grant
administration, **40(2)**, [593]
amount of, **40(1)**, [391]
application, necessity for, **40(1)**, [513]
entitlement to, **40(1)**, [390]
fraud, civil penalty for, **40(1)**, [728]
payment and management, responsibility for,
40(2), [595]

health professional
meaning, **7(1)**, [541]

Health Professions Wales
establishment of, **30**, [647]
functions, **30**, [647]
further provisions about, **30**, [648]

health records
access to—
application for, **7(1)**, [239]
fees, **7(1)**, [239]
right of—
court, application to, **7(1)**, [244]
generally, **7(1)**, [239]
partially excluded, **7(1)**, [241]
wholly excluded, **7(1)**, [240]
contractual term etc, purporting to require,
7(1), [245], [530]
health professionals—
holder of records, as, **7(1)**, [237]
meaning, **7(1)**, [238], [541]
health service bodies—
duty to seek advice, **7(1)**, [243]
meaning, **7(1)**, [247]
holder—
health professional as, **7(1)**, [237]
meaning, **7(1)**, [237]
inaccurate, correction of, **7(1)**, [242]
information including expression of opinion,
7(1), [247]
interpretation of terms, **7(1)**, [247]
meaning, **7(1)**, [237]
patient, meaning, **7(1)**, [237]
regulations and orders, power to make,
7(1), [246]

Health Protection Agency
accounts, **35(2)**, [508]
annual report, **35(2)**, [508]
appropriate authority for, **35(2)**, [500]
biological substances, functions in relation to,
　35(S), Public Health 2, 26–8
chairman, **35(2)**, [508]
charges, **35(2)**, [498]
chief executive, **35(2)**, [508]
co-operation with other bodies, **35(2)**, [499]
devolved authorities, **35(2)**, [508]
directions to, **35(2)**, [498], [503]
disclosure of information, **35(2)**, [498]
establishment of, **35(2)**, [495]
exercise of functions, powers, **35(2)**, [498]
finance, **35(2)**, [508]
health care provision, standards for,
　35(2), [504]
health functions, **35(2)**, [496]
members—
　appointment, **35(2)**, [508]
　disqualification for appointment,
　　35(2), [508]
　number of, **35(2)**, [508]
　terms of appointment, **35(2)**, [508]
proceedings, **35(2)**, [508]
property, rights and liabilities, transfer to—
　employment, continuity of, **35(2)**, [509]
　schemes, **35(2)**, [502], [509]
　time of, **35(2)**, [509]
　transitional, **35(2)**, [509]
publication of information, **35(2)**, [501]
radiation protection functions, **35(2)**, [497]
regulations, **35(2)**, [508]
seal, **35(2)**, [508]
staff, **35(2)**, [508]
status, **35(2)**, [508]

health service
change of employer, **16**, [865]
employers, **16**, [865]
practitioners, employment provisions,
　16, [491]

health service bodies
accounts and audit, **30**, [1108]
co-operation between, **30**, [878]
complaints about health care, **30**, [699], [701]
Crown immunities, removal of, **30**, [530]
employment in, validity of clearance for,
　30, [750]
directed partnership arrangements—
　directions, **30**, [885]
　Secretary of State, power of, **30**, [884]
directions and regulations, **30**, [879]
goods and services, supply of, Secretary of
　State, power of, **30**, [886]–[887]
intervention orders—
　effect of, **30**, [873]
　power to make, **30**, [872]
　suspension of members under, **30**, [873]
local authorities, arrangements with,
　30, [881], [1111]
losses and liabilities, scheme for meeting,
　30, [877]

health service bodies—*contd*
meaning, **30**, [814]–[815]; **44(1)**, [376]
members—
　allowances, **30**, [1039]
　protection from personal liability, **30**, [875]
NHS foundation trusts. *See* **NHS foundation
　trust**
NHS Trust. *See* **NHS Trust**
Northern Ireland, in, **30**, [816]
patient information—
　Advisory Group, **30**, [1058]
　control of, **30**, [1057]
　meaning, **30**, [1057]
Primary Care Trust. *See* **Primary Care Trust**
quality in health care—
　duty to attain, **30**, [661]
　standards set by—
　　Assembly, **30**, [663]
　　Secretary of State, **30**, [662]
residual liabilities, transfer of, **30**, [876]
Secretary of State—
　default powers, **30**, [874]
　directions by, **30**, [814]
Special Health Authority. *See* **Special Health
　Authority**
Strategic Health Authority. *See* **Strategic
　Health Authority**
subject to investigation by Health Service
　Commissioner, **30**, [544]
tax exemption, **44(1)**, [376]
taxation, **30**, [531]
Wales. *See* **Wales**

Health Service Commissioners
Local Commissioners, collaborative working
　with, **25(2)**, [325]
other commissioners, consultation with,
　25(2), [324]

health services
indemnity schemes, **30(S)**, NHS 105
local involvement networks—
　annual reports, **26(2)**, [638]
　contractual arrangements for, **26(2)**, [632],
　　[633]
　further provision, power to make,
　　26(2), [634]
　local authority, meaning, **26(2)**, [640]
　meaning, **26(2)**, [633]
　service-providers, duties of—
　　entry, to allow, **26(2)**, [636]
　　respond, to, **26(2)**, [635]
　social care matters, referrals of, **26(2)**, [637]
　transitional arrangements, **26(2)**, [639]
qualifying bodies—
　financial assistance to—
　　company, power to form,
　　　30(S), NHS 114
　　forms of, **30(S)**, NHS 112
　　interpretation, **30(S)**, NHS 115
　　power to give, **30(S)**, NHS 110–11
　　terms of, **30(S)**, NHS 113
　　third parties, arrangements with,
　　　30(S), NHS 114
　　meaning, **30(S)**, NHS 111–12

health services—*contd*
  users, duty to, **26(2)**, [644]
  value added tax, exemption from, **50**, [153]

Health Services Board
  abolition of, **30**, [483]

Health Services Commissioner
  advisers, **30**, [568]
  appointment of, **30**, [568]
  complaints to—
    individuals and bodies entitled to make,
      30, [551]
    referral by health service body, **30**, [553]
    requirements to be complied with,
      30, [552]
    transitional provisions, **30**, [615]
  expenses, **30**, [568]
  generally, **30**, [543]
  investigations by—
    confidentiality of information obtained,
      30, [558]
    consultation during, **30**, [561]
    evidence, **30**, [555]
    exclusions from—
      general health services and service
        committees, **30**, [549]
      other remedy, availability of, **30**, [548]
      personnel, **30**, [550]
    health service bodies subject to, **30**, [544]
    health service providers subject to,
      30, [545]
    independent providers subject to, **30**, [546]
    information obtained in—
      confidentiality of, **30**, [558]
      disclosure to Information
        Commissioner, **30**, [563]
      safety of State, prejudicial to, **30**, [559]
      use in other capacity, **30**, [560]
    obstruction and contempt, **30**, [556]
    procedure, **30**, [554]
    remit, general, **30**, [547]
  other Commissioners, collaborative working
    with, **30**, [562]
  Parliamentary Commissioner, consultations
    with, **10**, [553]
  pensions and other benefits, **30**, [568]
  redress scheme, remit as to, **30**, [1377]
  reports by, **30**, [557]
  salaries, **30**, [568]
  staff, **30**, [568]
  Welsh, abolition of office, **10**, [835]

hearing aids
  Council—
    accounts and audit, **28**, [63]
    constitution, **28**, [52], [67]
    Disciplinary Committee of—
      appeal to against refusal of registration,
        28, [53], [61]
      assessors to—
        appointment, **28**, [62]
        rules as to functions, **28**, [62]
      erasure from registers by direction of,
        28, [58]

hearing aids—*contd*
  Council—*contd*
    Disciplinary Committee of—*contd*
      evidence in proceedings before, **28**, [61]
      functions, **28**, [53], [57]
      procedure of, **28**, [61]
      restoration to registers by direction of,
        28, [59]
      rules as to constitution, **28**, [57]
    dissolution, **28(S)**, 4, 36–7
    establishment, **28**, [52]
    functions, **28**, [52]
    Investigating Committee of—
      functions, **28**, [56]
      rules as to constitution, **28**, [56]
      setting up, **28**, [56]
    powers, **28**, [53], [67]
    registers, rules as to form and keeping,
      28, [55]
    standards of competence and codes of
      practice—
        approval of, **28**, [52]
        drawing up by, **28**, [52]
        publication by, **28**, [52]
  dispenser—
    employer of, meaning, **28**, [65]
    hearing aids, of, meaning, **28**, [65]
  meaning, **28**, [65]
  Northern Ireland, modifications of Act in
    application to, **28**, [273]
  registers of dispensers and employers—
    appeal against erasure from, **28**, [60]
    contents, **28**, [53]
    entries in, **28**, [55]
    erasure from, **28**, [58]
    establishment and maintenance, **28**, [53]
    form and keeping of, rules as to, **28**, [55]
    public inspection of, **28**, [53]
    registration in—
      appeal against refusal of, **28**, [53]
      application for, **28**, [53], [55]
      certificates of, **28**, [55]
      fees for, **28**, [55]
      qualifications for, **28**, [53]
    removal from, **28**, [55]
    restoration to, **28**, [55], [59], [61]
    unregistered persons, offences by, **28**, [54]

heat
  waste, production from, **35(1)**, [311]

heat, supply of (London)
  accounts—
    combination of undertakings for,
      25(1), [453]
    separate, **25(1)**, [445]
  Act of 1936, under, **25(1)**, [459]
  alteration of temperatures etc, **25(1)**, [455]
  apparatus, interference with, **25(1)**, [457]
  arbitration, provision for, **25(1)**, [466]
  breaking open streets for, **25(1)**, [430]
    notice to police commissioner, **25(1)**, [431]
  bridge, works affecting, **25(1)**, [452]
  byelaws as to wasting water, **25(1)**, [439]

heat, supply of (London)—*contd*
charges—
prescription of, **25(1)**, [443]
recovery of, **25(1)**, [444]
tenant, payable by, **25(1)**, [443]
conditions of supply, **25(1)**, [441]
cutting off for non-payment, **25(1)**, [444]
disputes between authorities, **25(1)**, [446]
efficiency of, **25(1)**, [454]
embankment, works affecting, **25(1)**, [452]
entry, powers of, **25(1)**, [456]
existing schemes, **25(1)**, [447]
extension of provisions, **25(1)**, [968]
generally, **25(1)**, [428]
government departments, consent of,
25(1), [463]
heating authority—
consultations by, **25(1)**, [434]
discharge of steam etc by, **25(1)**, [438]
discrimination by, **25(1)**, [441]
electricity—
excess, sale of, **25(1)**, [429]
power to generate, **25(1)**, [428]
general powers, **25(1)**, [428]
investments by, **25(1)**, [450]
meaning, **25(1)**, [425]
repairs equalisation fund, **25(1)**, [449]
reports by, **25(1)**, [446]
reserve funds—
investment of, **25(1)**, [450]
provision and purpose of, **25(1)**, [448]
separate accounts to be kept, **25(1)**, [445]
heating undertakings—
establishment, **25(1)**, [426]
approval of Minister, **25(1)**, [432]
scope of, **25(1)**, [427]
hot water, provision of, **25(1)**, [428]
houses etc eligible for, **25(1)**, [427]
inquiries, power to hold, **25(1)**, [465]
interference with, **25(1)**, [457]
interpretation of expressions, **25(1)**, [425]
mains, laying of, **25(1)**, [430]
methods of, **25(1)**, [427]
nuisance, proceedings for, **25(1)**, [462]
offences, increased fines, **25(2)**, [527]
outer London boroughs, in, **25(1)**, [968]
pipes—
borough council powers, **25(1)**, [451]
laying in streets, **25(1)**, [430]
laying in subways, **25(1)**, [451]
Port of London, protection, **25(1)**, [442]
pressure, alteration of, **25(1)**, [455]
proposals subject to Minister's approval,
25(1), [432]
reports and returns, **25(1)**, [446]
sewers—
discharge of steam etc into, **25(1)**, [438]
protection of, **25(1)**, [437]
special roads, saving for, **25(1)**, [460]
station for providing, construction—
counter-notice as to, **25(1)**, [433]
proposal for, **25(1)**, [433]
subways, protection of, **25(1)**, [437]
surplus, supply to other authorities,
25(1), [429]

heat, supply of (London)—*contd*
temperatures, maximum and minimum,
25(1), [455]
Transport Commission, protection of,
25(1), [435]
undertakers—
consultation with, **25(1)**, [434]
discrimination by, **25(1)**, [441]
information required by, **25(1)**, [434]
meaning, **25(1)**, [425], [436]
protection of, **25(1)**, [436]
undertaking—
combining for accounts purposes,
25(1), [453]
establishment of, **25(1)**, [426], [432]
maintenance, **25(1)**, [454]
scope of, **25(1)**, [427]
undue preference in, **25(1)**, [441]
water supply for, preventing waste,
25(1), [439]
water undertakers, protection of, **25(1)**, [440]
watercourse, discharge into, **25(1)**, [438]
works, execution of—
bridges etc, affecting, **25(1)**, [452]
consultations as to, **25(1)**, [434]
sewers etc, affecting, **25(1)**, [437]

heath
public access to, **32**, [1]

heather burning
covenants against, relaxation of, **1(1)**, [373]
regulation of, **1(1)**, [372]
regulations and orders, **1(1)**, [377]

Heathrow Airport
Animal Quarantine Station, **25(2)**, [698]

heating authorities
charges by, **22**, [98]
meaning, **22**, [98]

heating equipment
grant-funded installation of, reduced rate
VAT, **50**, [149]

heavy goods vehicles. *See also* **goods vehicles**
exempt—
benefits or money obtained in connection
with, **44(2)**, [270]
payment of expenses, **44(2)**, [240]
modest private use of, **44(2)**, [238]

hedgerows
protection of, **32**, [1], [615]

hedges
high—
appeals—
determination of, **24**, [171]
powers of entry, **24**, [172]
procedure, **24**, [170]
right of, **24**, [169]
withdrawal, **24**, [171]

hedges—*contd*
  high—*contd*
    complaints, **24**, [163]
      amendment of provisions, **24**, [181]
      powers of entry, **24**, [172]
      procedure, **24**, [166]
    domestic property, meaning, **24**, [165]
    electronic form, documents in, **24**, [178],
      [179]
    meaning, **24**, [164]
    occupier, power to require permitting of
      action by owner, **24**, [174]
    offences, **24**, [173]
      body corporate, by, **24**, [176]
    orders and regulations, **24**, [184]
    powers of entry, **24**, [172]
    relevant authority, action by, **24**, [175]
    remedial notices—
      appeals, **24**, [169]–[171]
      matters in, **24**, [167]
      meaning, **24**, [167]
      withdrawal or relaxation of
        requirements, **24**, [168]
    service of documents, **24**, [177]

heir
  in tale. *See* **entail**
  limitation in favour of, effect, **20**, [743]

heirlooms
  sale, proceeds as entailed interest, **20**, [741]

helmets and head gear. *See under* **motor
cycles**

**Her Majesty's Chief Inspector of
Education, Children's Services and Skills**
  child care functions, **15(2)**, [461]–[463]
  complaints about schools—
    investigation of—
      information from local authority,
        15(2), [607]
      parents' meetings, calling, **15(2)**, [607]
      powers as to, **15(2)**, [606]
      reports of, **15(2)**, [608]
  discretion, inspection at, **15(2)**, [602]
  duty to inspect schools, **15(2)**, [595]–[599]
  duty to notify parents of inspection,
    15(2), [600]
  inspection reports, publication of,
    15(2), [605]
  inspections, support for 13 to 19 year olds,
    15(2), [284]
    See also **school**
  maintained schools, destination of report on,
    15(2), [611]
  non-maintained schools, destination of report
    on, **15(2)**, [613]
  powers of entry, **15(2)**, [604]
  school causing concern, duties on,
    15(2), [610]
  special measures, report requiring,
    15(2), [612]
  view of certain persons, duty to have regard
    to, **15(2)**, [601]

**Her Majesty's Chief Inspector of Education
and Training in Wales**
  additional functions, **15(2)**, [246]
  advisory panel, establishment of, **15(2)**, [619]
  annual plan, **15(2)**, [256]
  annual and other reports by, **15(2)**, [618]
  annual reports, **15(2)**, [255]
  appointment, **15(2)**, [616]
  delegation of functions, **15(2)**, [714]–[715]
  directions from National Assembly,
    15(2), [254]
  duty to arrange for inspections, **15(2)**, [621]
  extended remit, **15(2)**, [245]
  fees, payment of, **15(2)**, [627]
  functions of, **15(2)**, [617]
  general powers, **15(2)**, [248]
  inspections—
    action plans, **15(2)**, [250], [253]
    area inspections, **15(2)**, [252]
    publication of reports, **15(2)**, [626]
    reporting on, **15(2)**, [247], [251]
    right of entry and offences, **15(2)**, [249]
    support for 11 to 25 year olds,
      15(2), [292]–[293]
  official seal, **15(2)**, [714]–[715]
  powers of entry, **15(2)**, [620]
  regular inspection of schools, duty to
    arrange, **15(2)**, [625]
  remuneration and pensions,
    15(2), [714]–[715]
  renamed as, **15(2)**, [222]–[243]
  staff, **15(2)**, [714]–[715]
    inspectors—
      additional, **15(2)**, [714]–[715]
      obstructing, **15(2)**, [717]
      parents, meeting, **15(2)**, [717]
      registration, **15(2)**, [622]
      registration appeals, **15(2)**, [624], [716]
      removal from register, **15(2)**, [623]
      replacement, **15(2)**, [717]
      rights of entry, **15(2)**, [717]
      selection of, **15(2)**, [717]
      teams, **15(2)**, [717]
      training, **15(2)**, [717]

HM Inspectorate of Court Administration
  generally, **11(2)**, [1]

Her Majesty's Inspectorate of Schools. *See
now* **Her Majesty's Chief Inspector of
Education, Children's Services and Skills;
Her Majesty's Chief Inspector of
Education and Training in Wales; Office
for Standards in Education, Children's
Services and Skills**
  Chief Inspector in England, abolition of
    office, **15(2)**, [827]
  Inspectors, HM Inspectors of Education,
    Children's Services and Skills, becoming,
    15(2), [828]
  local education authorities, inspection of—
    Audit Commission, collaboration of,
      15(1), [752]
    powers as to, **15(1)**, [749]
    reports, **15(1)**, [750]

**Her Majesty's Inspectorate of
Schools**—*contd*
local education authorities, inspection
of—*contd*
rights of entry, **15(1)**, [751]

HM Revenue and Customs
accounts, examination of, **19(2)**, [737]
administration by, **42**, [1]
assets, power to mark, **43(S)**, 1282
businesses, power to inspect, **43(S)**, 1279–81
cash recovery proceedings, power for
prosecutors to appear in,. **12(4)**, [432]
certificate of debt, **43(S)**, 973, 1347–8
Charter of standards and values, preparation
of, **43(S)**, 1408–9
chemical weapons prosecutions, **12(2)**, [407]
child benefit—
functions of Secretary of State transferred
to, **40(2)**, [410]
transfer of property, rights and liabilities,
40(2), [412]
transitional provisions, **40(2)**, [414]
civil proceedings, conduct of, **43(2)**, [686]
collectors—
City of London, for, **42**, [22]
compensation allowances to, **42**, [9]
demand note, issue of, **42**, [200]
distraint by, **42**, [201]
proceedings, continuation of, **42**, [90]
receipt, giving, **42**, [200]
Commissioners—
accounts, **43(2)**, [707]
ancillary powers, **43(2)**, [670]
appointment of, **43(2)**, [662]
civil servants, as, **43(2)**, [662]
conduct of proceedings, **43(2)**, [673]
Consolidated Fund—
payments into, **43(2)**, [705]
payments out of, **43(2)**, [708]
declaration of confidentiality, **43(2)**, [664]
disclosure of information, **42**, [991]
EU Mutual Assistance Directive, duties
under, **43(2)**, [757]
expenditure, **43(2)**, [704]
functions—
delegation of, **43(2)**, [675]
initial, **43(2)**, [666]
officers, exercise by, **43(2)**, [674]
power to transfer, **43(2)**, [669]
restrictions, **43(2)**, [720]
impersonation, **43(2)**, [691]
instruments, notifications of, **43(2)**, [757]
Northern Ireland, treatment in,
43(2), [676]
remuneration, **43(2)**, [706]
resignation, **43(2)**, [662]
rewards, payment of, **43(2)**, [687]
Scotland, treatment in, **43(2)**, [676]
statistical purposes, disclosure of
information for, **42**, [77]
taxes, responsibility for, **42**, [89]
transfer of property, rights and liabilities
to, **43(2)**, [709]

HM Revenue and Customs—*contd*
Commissioners—*contd*
Treasury directions, compliance with,
43(2), [672]
complaints, inspection by Independent Police
Complaints Commission, **43(2)**, [688]
computer records, requiring production of,
43(S), 948–9
consolidated fund, payments out of,
19(2), [603]
containers, power to open or unpack,
43(S), 951
contract settlement, meaning, **43(S)**, 974
contributions etc information—
disclosure of, **40(1)**, [623]
held by Secretary of State, supply to,
40(1), [620]
held by, supply of, **40(1)**, [619]
powers to call for documents, **40(1)**, [593]
contributions, transfer of functions,
40(2), [214]
exercise of, **40(2)**, [215]
modification of enactments, **40(2)**, [224]
Northern Ireland, **40(2)**, [232]
Order in Council, by, **40(2)**, [231]
orders and regulations, **40(2)**, [233]
property, rights and liabilities, transfer of,
40(2), [229]
contributions, transfer of functions,
40(2), [214]
exercise of, **40(2)**, [215]
modification of enactments, **40(2)**, [224]
Northern Ireland, **40(2)**, [232]
Order in Council, by, **40(2)**, [231]
orders and regulations, **40(2)**, [233]
property, rights and liabilities, transfer of,
40(2), [229]
county court proceedings, **43(S)**, 972–3
criminal investigation powers, **43(S)**, 562–4
restriction on exercise of functions,
43(S), 565
Scotland, in. *See* **Scotland**
cross-border exercise of powers, **43(S)**, 566–7
debtors, power to obtain contact details for,
43(S), 1700–2
decisions, review and appeals, **43(S)**, 959–60
deliberate tax defaulters, publication of details
of, **43(S)**, 1410–11
designated office, meaning, **43(S)**, 567
detention, persons in, bail, **12(1)**, [1101]
Director, investigatory powers. *See* **criminal
investigations**
Director of Border Revenue. *See* **Director of
Border Revenue**
Director of Prosecutions—
crime reduction, contribution to,
12(3), [171]
staff, activities authorised to be done by,
12(3), [173]
disclosure of information, **12(4)**, [433];
19(2), [425]; **42**, [991]
documents—
business, inspection of, **43(S)**, 1285
evidence of, **43(2)**, [685]
old, restrictions on powers, **43(S)**, 1283

HM Revenue and Customs—*contd*
documents—*contd*
power to copy, **43(S)**, 1282
power to remove, **43(S)**, 1282
reference to Commissioners of Customs
and Excise in, **43(2)**, [711]
employment schemes, supply of tax
information to assess, **40(1)**, [622]
enforcement—
goods, taking control of, **43(S)**, 962,
1344–6
summary warrant, **43(S)**, 962–3, 1346–7
Exchequer, revenues paid to, **19(2)**, [611]
existing concession—
meaning, **43(S)**, 995
power to give statutory effect to,
43(S), 994–5
extension of powers—
amendment and repeal of provisions,
43(S), 718–19
Scotland, **43(S)**, 719–20
facilities and services, making available,
13(S), Customs 46
fee for payment to, **43(S)**, 972
fraud prevention and verification, supply of
information held for, **40(1)**, [621]
general customs functions—
concurrent exercise with Secretary of
State, **13(S)**, Customs 19–21
power to modify, **13(S)**, Customs 21–2
general customs officials—
designation of, **13(S)**, Customs 22–4
directions by Secretary of State, compliance
with, **13(S)**, Customs 25
PACE orders, application of,
13(S), Customs 41–3
guardian's allowance—
functions of Secretary of State transferred
to, **40(2)**, [410]
transitional provisions, **40(2)**, [414]
health in pregnancy grant, responsibility for
payment and maintenance of, **40(2)**, [595]
importation of wireless telegraphy apparatus,
powers, **45**, [839]
information—
confidentiality, **43(2)**, [679]
data protection, **43(2)**, [683]
disclosure by, **12(3)**, [513]
disclosure to, **12(3)**, [511], [512]
freedom of, **43(2)**, [684]
prosecuting authority, disclosure to,
43(2), [682]
public interest disclosure, **43(2)**, [681]
restrictions, **43(2)**, [721]
use of, **43(2)**, [678]
wrongful disclosure, **43(2)**, [680]
information and documents, power to
obtain—
approval of notices, **43(S)**, 1276
auditors, position of, **43(S)**, 1284–5
authorised officers, **43(S)**, 1298
business, reference to, **43(S)**, 1298
chargeable period, meaning, **43(S)**, 1298
concealment etc of documents, offences,
43(S), 1296

HM Revenue and Customs—*contd*
information and documents, power to
obtain—*contd*
consequential provisions, **43(S)**, 1300–4
copies of documents, producing,
43(S), 1278
information notice—
appeal against, **43(S)**, 1287
auditors, not requiring information
from, **43(S)**, 1284
compliance with, **43(S)**, 1277
concealment etc of documents,
offences, **43(S)**, 1296
deceased person, checking tax position
of, **43(S)**, 1284
meaning, **43(S)**, 1277
penalties, **43(S)**, 1291–4
special cases, **43(S)**, 1288–90
tax advisers, not requiring information
from, **43(S)**, 1285
interpretation, **43(S)**, 1297
penalties, **43(S)**, 1291–5
persons whose identity is not known,
about, **43(S)**, 1277
privileged communications, **43(S)**, 1283
regulations, **43(S)**, 1297
statutory records, meaning, **43(S)**, 1298
tax advisors, position of, **43(S)**, 1285
tax, meaning, **43(S)**, 1299
tax position, meaning, **43(S)**, 1299
taxpayer, from, **43(S)**, 1275
third party, from, **43(S)**, 1276
third party notice, copying to taxpayer,
43(S), 1276
information and inspection powers—
amended provisions, **43(S)**, 1685–91
extension of, **43(S)**, 1412–13, 1692–8
involved third parties, provisions applying,
43(S), 1694–8
land transaction return, taxpayer notices
following, **43(S)**, 1694
registered pension schemes, **43(S)**, 1695–6
valuation, inspection of property for,
43(S), 1692–3
information, power to record, **43(S)**, 1282
inspection—
confidentiality, **43(2)**, [690]
Independent Police Complaints
Commission, functions of, **43(2)**, [688]
Inspectors of Constabulary, functions of,
43(2), [688]
Northern Ireland inspectors, functions of,
43(2), [688]
Scottish inspectors, functions of,
43(2), [688]
inspector, accounts, etc, calling for, **42**, [127]
investigatory powers, regulation of,
12(4), [461]
land transactions—
individual and financial institution,
alternative property arrangements
between, **41**, [345]–[348]
registered social landlords, acquisitions by,
41, [344]

HM Revenue and Customs—*contd*
landmines, prosecutions in relation to,
  12(2), [637]
managed payment plans, **43(S)**, 1423–5
nuclear weapons offences, prosecution of,
  12(3), [99]
office, meaning, **43(S)**, 567
officer, meaning, **12(3)**, [531]
officers—
  appointment of, **43(2)**, [663]
  arrest, power of, **12(1)**, [1102]; **43(2)**, [694]
  assaulting, **43(2)**, [693]
  assessments by, **42**, [151]
  Commissioners' functions, exercise of,
    43(2), [674]
  decisions by, **40(2)**, [217]
    appeals against, **40(2)**, [220]
      regulations, **40(2)**, [222]
      right of, exercise of, **40(2)**, [221]
    discharge of functions, arrangements
      for, **40(2)**, [226]
    matters arising, **40(2)**, [223]
    Pension Schemes Act, under,
      40(2), [225]
    regulations, **40(2)**, [218]
    varying or superseding earlier decisions,
      40(2), [219]
  disclosure of information, **42**, [991]
  documents—
    failure to produce to, **42**, [227]
    power to call for, **42**, [126]
  functions—
    former Inland Revenue matters,
      43(2), [668], [719]
    initial, **43(2)**, [667]
    restrictions, **43(2)**, [720]
  impersonation, **43(2)**, [691]
  obstruction of, **43(2)**, [692]
  penalties, determination of, **42**, [235], [236]
  provision of accommodation for,
    39(2), [15], [353]
orders and regulations by, **44(3)**, [890]
Police and Criminal Evidence Act applying
  to, **12(1)**, [921]
Port of London—
  arrangements with Authority, **39(2)**, [246]
  entry of goods, **39(2)**, [350]
powers, saving for, **25(1)**, [65]
proceedings—
  conduct of, **43(2)**, [673], [686]
  evidence in, **43(2)**, [685]
  Northern Ireland, in, **42**, [11]
proceeds of crime, prosecutions relating to,
  12(3), [527]
production of documents, application for,
  43(S), 562–3
Prosecutions Office—
  confidentiality of information, **43(2)**, [701]
  Director of Revenue and Customs
    Prosecution—
      annual report, **43(2)**, [722]
      appointment of, **43(2)**, [695], [722]
      Code for Crown Prosecutors, having
        regard to, **43(2)**, [697]

HM Revenue and Customs—*contd*
Prosecutions Office—*contd*
  Director of Revenue and Customs
    Prosecution—*contd*
      disclosure of information to,
        43(2), [702]
      functions, **43(2)**, [696]–[697]
      remuneration, **43(2)**, [722]
      status, **43(2)**, [722]
      transfer of property, rights and liabilities
        to, **43(2)**, [710]
    financial year, **43(2)**, [722]
    information—
      confidentiality of, **43(2)**, [701]
      Director of Revenue and Customs
        Prosecutions, disclosure to, **43(2)**, [702]
    inspection, **43(2)**, [703]
    non-legal staff, designation, **43(2)**, [700]
    prosecutions, conduct of, **43(2)**, [699]
    Prosecutor, designation of, **43(2)**, [698]
  reference to, **43(2)**, [665]
repayment interest on sums to be paid by—
  application of provisions, **43(S)**, 1415–16
  date on which due and payable,
    43(S), 1417
  provision for, **43(S)**, 1417–18
  rates of, **43(S)**, 1416–17
repayments, attribution of, **43(S)**, 1736
start date—
  general rule, **43(S)**, 1734–5
  special provision, **43(S)**, 1735–6
resolution—
  not having statutory effect, duties under,
    42, [65]
  with statutory effect, rate altered by,
    42, [66]
restrictions on powers, **43(S)**, 1283–5
retained funding bonds, tender of,
  43(S), 969–70
retrospective non-charging provision, power
  to make, **43(S)**, 1406
returns, enquiry into, **43(S)**, 578
safety legislation—
  detention of goods, **39(1)**, [619]
  information, disclosure of, **39(1)**, [625]
search warrants, execution in Scotland,
  43(S), 566
Secretary of State, issues referred by,
  40(2), [156], [173]
seizure, powers of, **12(3)**, [47]
set-off—
  England and Wales, in, **43(S)**, 964
  insolvency procedure, exclusion in case of,
    43(S), 965–6
  Northern Ireland, in, **43(S)**, 964
  oil profits, against, **43(S)**, 1274–5
  transfer of right to be paid sum, in case
    of, **43(S)**, 967–8
  VAT, requirement in case of, **43(S)**, 966
social security adjudication, issues referred to,
  40(2), [156], [173]
staff, **43(2)**, [663]
statutory adoption pay—
  fraud, penalties for, **40(2)**, [435]
  appeals, **40(2)**, [444]

HM Revenue and Customs—*contd*
statutory adoption pay—*contd*
fraud, penalties for—*contd*
procedure, **40(2)**, [444]
funding of employers' liability for,
40(2), [431]
information—
requirements, **40(2)**, [433]
non-compliance with, penalties for,
40(2), [434]
appeals, **40(2)**, [444]
procedure, **40(2)**, [444]
supplied by, **40(2)**, [436]
used by, **40(2)**, [438]
payment of, regulations about, **40(2)**, [432]
statutory paternity pay—
fraud, penalties for, **40(2)**, [435]
appeals, **40(2)**, [444]
procedure, **40(2)**, [444]
funding of employers' liability for,
40(2), [431]
information—
requirements, **40(2)**, [433]
non-compliance with, penalties for,
40(2), [434]
appeals, **40(2)**, [444]
procedure, **40(2)**, [444]
supplied by, **40(2)**, [436]
used by, **40(2)**, [438]
payment of, regulations about, **40(2)**, [432]
sums due to, late payment interest on—
amount carrying, **43(S)**, 1728–9
application of provisions, **43(S)**, 1414–15
date from which running, **43(S)**, 1732–3
date on which due and payable,
43(S), 1417
inheritance tax, **43(S)**, 1730–1, 1733
provision for, **43(S)**, 1417–18
rates of, **43(S)**, 1416–17
reliefs, effect on, **43(S)**, 1733–4
start date, **43(S)**, 1730–2
taxpayer, death of, **43(S)**, 1732
VAT, **43(S)**, 1731
tax credits—
annual reports to Treasury, **40(2)**, [400]
decisions on—
after final notice, **40(2)**, [378]
appeals against, **40(2)**, [398], [399]
temporary modifications, **40(2)**, [420]
initial, **40(2)**, [374]
notice of, **40(2)**, [383]
official error, subject to, **40(2)**, [381]
revisions—
after notifications, **40(2)**, [375]
on discovery, **40(2)**, [380]
other, **40(2)**, [376]
enquire, power to, **40(2)**, [379]
final notice by, **40(2)**, [377]
information requirements, **40(2)**, [382]
notices, giving of, **40(2)**, [406]
overpayment of, **40(2)**, [388], [389]
interest on, **40(2)**, [397]
payment and management of, **40(2)**, [362]
payment of, **40(2)**, [384]
underpayment of, **40(2)**, [390]

HM Revenue and Customs—*contd*
training schemes, supply of tax information to
assess, **40(1)**, [622]
transfer of functions, expenditure for
facilitating, **40(2)**, [196]
transitional provisions, **43(2)**, [715]–[716]
travelling expenses, payment of, **40(1)**, [709]
UK Border Agency, transfers to—
property, rights and liabilities.
13(S), Customs 45–6
summary of provisions,
13(S), Customs 15–17
Valuation Office, **43(2)**, [671]
watch-houses, provision and maintenance,
39(2), [15], [16]
Welsh title, **43(2)**, [665]

Her Majesty's Stationery Office
documents printed by, as evidence, **18**, [151]

herbal remedies
exemptions for, **28**, [79], [112]

herbalist
medicinal products, licensing, exemption
from, **28**, [79]

herd basis
abuse of rules, preventing, **44(3)**, [126]
addition of animals, **44(3)**, [114]
application of rules, election for, **44(3)**, [110]
definitions, **44(3)**, [111]–[112]
disease control order—
old animals slaughtered under, **44(3)**, [116]
slaughter under, **44(3)**, [125]
election, information relating to,
43(S), 1688–9
elections, **44(3)**, [123]–[125]
five year gap when no production herd kept,
44(3), [124]
further assessment, **44(3)**, [128]
information, provision of, **44(3)**, [127]
initial cost, **44(3)**, [113]
replacement of animals, **44(3)**, [115]
sale of animals—
acquisition of new herd within 5 years of,
44(3), [119]–[120]
profits, calculation of, **44(3)**, [117]
reasons outside farmer's control, for,
44(3), [120], [122]
replacement of part within 5 years of,
44(3), [121]
whole or substantial part of herd,
44(3), [118]
tax treatment of animals, **44(1)**, [636]
value of herd, **44(3)**, [113]

hereditament
change in state of, **25(2)**, [813]
non-domestic rates. *See* **non-domestic rates**

Hereford
statutes repealed, **41**, [709]

heritage maintenance settlement
income from—
  double taxation, prevention of, **44(4)**, [519]
  elections by trustees, **44(4)**, [516]
    change of circumstances affecting,
      44(4), [517]
  non-heritage purposes, used for—
    rate of tax, **44(4)**, [523]
  tax charged on, **44(4)**, [520]–[521]
  property maintenance, sums applied for,
    44(4), [518]
meaning, **44(4)**, [515]
non-heritage purposes, application of property
for—
  rate of tax, **44(4)**, [523]
    transfer of property between
      settlements, **44(4)**, [524]
  tax charged on, **44(4)**, [520]–[521]
    exemptions, **44(4)**, [525]
  transfer of property between settlements,
    44(4), [524]

herring fisheries
artificial ports and harbours, dues for,
  1(1), [126]
ports and harbours, free use of, **1(1)**, [125]

Herring Industry Board
abolition of, **1(2)**, [167]
Sea Fish Industry Authority, transfer to,
  1(2), [189]
validation of charges by, **1(2)**, [695]

Hertfordshire
water undertakings, provisions for, **49**, [208],
  [258], [277]

Heydon's Case
rule in, **41**, [480]

High Commission Court
generally, **14**, 10

High Court. *See further* **probate**
Admiralty Court, business of, **11(2)**, [736]
Admiralty jurisdiction. *See* **Admiralty
  jurisdiction**
Agricultural Land Tribunal, reference to by,
  1(1), [459]
appeal—
  Conveyancing Appeal tribunal, from,
    11(3), [101]
  Copyright Tribunal, from, **11(1)**, [979]
  Court of Appeal, jurisdiction of,
    11(2), [683]
  Crown Court, from, **11(2)**, [695]
  House of Lords, to—
    certificate, granting, **11(2)**, [226], [229]
    leave, granting, **11(2)**, [227]
    provisions on, **11(2)**, [228]
    Northern Ireland, **11(2)**, [230]
  prize court, when acting as, **11(2)**, [683]
  restrictions on, **11(2)**, [685]
appeals to, **42**, [187], [188]
application for charging order, **19(3)**, [81]

High Court—*contd*
applications to, grounds for, **9**, [435]
arbitrator, powers of exercised by,
  11(2), [716]
assessors in, **11(2)**, [744]
attachment of earnings orders, **19(3)**, [36]
bail, granting or varying, **12(1)**, [385]
bill of costs, order to deliver **11(2)**, [349];
  11(4), [448]
bond given under order of, **11(2)**, [781]
case stated for opinion of, by magistrates'
  court of Crown Court, **11(2)**, [696]
certiorari orders. *See* quashing orders *below*
chambers, proceedings in, **11(2)**, [741]
Chancellor—
  appointment of, **11(2)**, [677]
  precedence, **11(2)**, [680]
Chancery Division—
  distribution of business, **11(2)**, [791]
  judges, **11(2)**, [672]
  Patents Court, **11(2)**, [673]
civil proceedings by or against Crown in—
  institution of, **13**, [17]
  rules, in accordance with, **13**, [17], [36]
  transferred from county court, **13**, [23]
Commercial Court, business of, **11(2)**, [736]
committal, power to vary, **11(2)**, [715]
commonhold, jurisdiction, over, **24**, [66]
constitution of, **11(2)**, [671]
costs—
  discretion of court, in, **11(2)**, [724]
  recovery of, **11(2)**, [235], [238]–[239]
  transferred proceedings, **11(2)**, [930]
county court—
  allocation of business, **11(3)**, [70];
    11(4), [529]
  transfer of proceedings from—
    county court order, by, **11(2)**, [929]
    High Court order by, **11(2)**, [928]
  transfer of proceedings to, provisions,
    11(2), [927]
court, business in, **11(2)**, [741]
criminal information, abolition of proceedings
  by, **12(1)**, [364]
damages—
  injunction, and, **11(2)**, [723]
  interest on, **11(2)**, [705]
  specific performance, and, **11(2)**, [723]
district judges—
  another, acting for, **11(2)**, [773]
  appointment, **11(2)**, [773]
  deputy, **11(2)**, [774]
district probate registries, **11(2)**, [775]
district registries, **11(2)**, [772]
divisional courts, **11(2)**, [740]
divisions—
  alteration of, **11(2)**, [674]
  courts, transfer of, **11(2)**, [674]
  distribution of business, **11(2)**, [234], [735],
    [791]
  generally, **11(2)**, [672]
  plaintiff, choice of by, **11(2)**, [738]
  transfer between, **11(2)**, [739]

High Court—*contd*
  estates of deceased persons and trusts,
    proceedings relating to—
      counsel's opinion, action taken in reliance
        on, **11(3)**, [38]; **11(4)**, [512]
      persons not parties to action, binding on,
        11(3), [37]; **11(4)**, [511]
  execution of instrument, ordering,
    11(2), [709]
  Family Division—
    distribution of business, **11(2)**, [791]
    judges, **11(2)**, [672]
    registrar of principal registry, **11(3)**, [128];
      11(4), [550]
  fines, enforcement of, **11(2)**, [785]
  forfeited recognizance, **11(2)**, [785]
  forfeiture, relief against, **11(2)**, [708]
  funds in, management of, **11(2)**, [877]
  garnishees, expenses, **11(2)**, [711]
  heads of Divisions, selection of, **11(3)**, [521]
  inheritance tax appeals, **42**, [766]
  injunction, granting—
    office-holder, against, **11(2)**, [698]
    powers, **11(2)**, [707]
  inquest, order to hold, **11(1)**, [1219]
  interest, power to order, **11(2)**, [705], [875]
  judges—
    clerks and secretaries, **11(2)**, [771]
    death or incapacity, additional costs arising
      from, **11(3)**, [39]; **11(4)**, [513]
    deputy, **11(2)**, [676]
    extraordinary functions, **11(2)**, [717]
    generally, **11(2)**, [671]
    precedence, **11(2)**, [680]
    specially nominated, **11(2)**, [737]
  judgment, no action in county court on,
    11(2), [924]
  judicial review—
    application for, **11(2)**, [699]
    jurisdiction, **11(2)**, [697]
  jurisdiction—
    admiralty, **11(2)**, [687]
      mode of exercise of, **11(2)**, [688]
      Rhine Convention—
        exclusion of cases within, **11(2)**, [690]
        meaning, **11(2)**, [691]
    attachment of debts, **11(2)**, [710]
    business premises, over, **21**, [224]
    general, **11(2)**, [686]
    judges exercising, **11(2)**, [742]
    judicial review, **11(2)**, [697]
    mandatory orders, **11(2)**, [697]
    matrimonial, **11(2)**, [693]
    prize, **11(2)**, [694]
    probate, **11(2)**, [692]
    prohibiting orders, **11(2)**, [697]
    quashing orders, **11(2)**, [697]
    single judge, exercise by, **11(2)**, [686]
  mandatory orders, **11(2)**, [697]
  matrimonial jurisdiction, **27**, [127]
  meaning, **41**, [605]
  new trial, application for, hearing,
    11(2), [684]

High Court—*contd*
  orders—
    commencement of action, before,
      11(2), [702], [704]
    Crown, binding, **11(2)**, [704]
    documents, for disclosure of, **11(2)**, [703]
    interim payment, for, **11(2)**, [700]
    provisional damages for personal injuries,
      11(2), [701]
    public interest, injurious to, **11(2)**, [704]
    rules of court, **11(2)**, [704]
  orders, enforcement of, **8**, 590
  Patent Court—
    business of, **11(2)**, [736]
    constitution, **11(2)**, [673]
    scientific advisers, **11(2)**, [744]
  personal injuries action—
    disclosure of documents, **11(2)**, [703]
    inspection of property, **11(2)**, [703]
    provisional damages, ordering, **11(2)**, [701]
  powers, **9**, [436]
    commencement of action, exercisable
      before, **11(2)**, [702], [704]
    committal, variation of, **11(2)**, [715]
  proceedings, staying, **11(2)**, [722]
  prohibiting orders, **11(2)**, [697]
  prohibition, jurisdiction, **11(2)**, [697]
  quashing orders, **11(2)**, [697]
    variation of sentence on application for,
      11(2), [714]
  Queen's Bench Division—
    Admiralty Court, **11(2)**, [673]
    Commercial Court, **11(2)**, [673]
    distribution of business, **11(2)**, [791]
    judges, **11(2)**, [672]
    jury, trial by, **11(2)**, [743]
  receiver, appointing, **11(2)**, [707]
  recovery of tax in, **42**, [205]
  rules, Crown proceedings in accordance
    with, **13**, [17], [36]
  self-incrimination in, **11(2)**, [746]
  sittings, **11(2)**, [745]
  solicitors, appeal, suspension of certificate,
    on, **11(4)**, [386]
  subpoena issued by, **11(2)**, [706]
  summary application by Crown to, in certain
    revenue matters, **13**, [18]
  superior court of record, as, **11(2)**, [686]
  superseded courts, reference to, **11(2)**, [795]
  vacations, **11(2)**, [745]
  vexatious legal proceedings, restricting,
    11(2), [713]
  ward of court, order on, **11(2)**, [712]
  winding up jurisdiction, **4(2)**, [158]
    case stated for, **4(2)**, [160]
  writ of execution—
    enforcement officers, **11(3)**, [430]
    goods, against, **11(3)**, [430]
    regulations, **11(3)**, [430]
    requirement to be directed to sheriff,
      abolition of, **11(3)**, [404]

High Court of Admiralty. *See* **Prize Court**

high judicial office
holders, pensions for. *See* **judicial pensions**
meaning, **11(2)**, [121], [588]

high net worth debtors and hirers
credit or hire agreements, exemption of,
39(1), [150]

higher and further education
accounts, inspection of, **15(1)**, [320]
advanced further education, meaning,
15(1), [301]
Arts and Humanities Research Council. *See*
Arts and Humanities Research Council
arts and humanities, research in, **15(2)**, [543]
company, institutions run by, **15(1)**, [322]
designated assisted institution—
government and conduct of, **15(1)**, [322]
trust deeds, variation of, **15(1)**, [323]
Director of Fair Access to Higher Education.
See **Director of Fair Access to**
Education
educational provision, information with
respect to, **15(1)**, [325]
financial support to students—
arrangements for, **15(1)**, [800]
transfer or delegation of functions,
15(1), [801]
transitional arrangements, **15(1)**, [803]
full-time equivalent enrolment number,
15(1), [326], [375]
further education corporation, transfer to
higher education sector, **15(1)**, [303]
general note, **15(1)**, [1]
higher education corporation—
accounts, **15(1)**, [307], [320], [372]
allowances, **15(1)**, [372], [373]
bodies corporate, formation or involvement
in, **15(S)**, Education 32
chairman, election of, **15(1)**, [372]
charitable status of, **15(1)**, [311]
committees, **15(1)**, [372], [373]
conduct of, **15(1)**, [306]
constitution, **15(1)**, [306]
dissolution of, **15(1)**, [314]
establishment, **15(1)**, [372]
financial year, **15(1)**, [442]
further education sector, transfer to,
15(1), [416]
initial constitution, **15(1)**, [372]
instruments of government, **15(1)**, [373]
instruments, proof of, **15(1)**, [372]
meaning, **15(1)**, [456]
members—
allowances, **15(1)**, [372], [373]
initial, **15(1)**, [308], [372]
qualifications, **15(1)**, [372]
subsequent appointments, **15(1)**, [372]
tenure of office, **15(1)**, [372]
membership, **15(1)**, [373]
numbers, determination of, **15(1)**, [372]
name, **15(1)**, [373]
officers, **15(1)**, [373]

higher and further education—*contd*
higher education corporation—*contd*
orders incorporating, **15(1)**, [302]
powers of, **15(1)**, [305]
Privy Council, exercise of powers of,
15(1), [309]
proceedings, **15(1)**, [372]
property, transfer of, **15(1)**, [312], [342],
[376]
references to, **15(1)**, [304], [457]
seal, application of, **15(1)**, [372], [373]
staff, transfer of, **15(1)**, [313]
successor company, **15(1)**, [315]
transfers to—
stamp duty exemption, **15(1)**, [453]
stamp duty land tax exemption,
15(1), [454]
Higher Education Funding Councils. *See*
Higher Education Funding Councils
higher education institution—
accounts, inspection of, **15(1)**, [320]
agreements before date of transfer, effect
of, **15(1)**, [447]
articles of government, **15(1)**, [310]
degrees, power to award, **15(1)**, [440]
denominational, **15(1)**, [432]
designated, **15(1)**, [437]
disturbance in, **15(1)**, [449]
enrolment numbers—
calculation of, **15(1)**, [462]
meaning, **15(1)**, [462]
non-EEC students, exclusion of,
15(1), [462]
governing body, meaning, **15(1)**, [456]
land held for purposes of, **15(1)**, [321]
nuisance in, **15(1)**, [449]
property, rights and liabilities, transfer of,
15(1), [465]
quality of education, assessment of,
15(1), [436]
reference to, **15(1)**, [427]
teachers, power to use force, **15(1)**, [451]
university, use of title, **15(1)**, [441]
weapons, searching students for,
15(1), [450]
inspections, **15(2)**, [838]
action plans following, **15(2)**, [841]
area, **15(2)**, [842]
action plans following, **15(2)**, [844]
reports of, **15(2)**, [843]
documents, of, **15(2)**, [846]
framework for, **15(2)**, [847]
general note, **15(1)**, [1]
powers of entry, **15(2)**, [845]
institutions, conditions as to fees, **15(1)**, [804]
institutions for funding—
companies, conducted by, **15(1)**, [317]
designation of, **15(1)**, [315]
government and conduct of, **15(1)**, [316]
transfer of property to, **15(1)**, [318]
local education authorities—
courses referred to, **15(1)**, [371]
functions of, **15(1)**, [300]
locally funded, finance and government of,
15(1), [448]

higher and further education—*contd*
orders and regulations, **15(1)**, [455], [807];
15(2), [579]
Polytechnics and Colleges Funding Council.
See **Polytechnics and Colleges Funding
Council**
reports and returns, **15(1)**, [324]
staff disputes, exclusion of visitor's
jurisdiction, **15(2)**, [578]
student complaints scheme—
changes to, **15(2)**, [589]
compliance with, **15(2)**, [589]
conditions to be met by,
15(2), [587]–[588]
defamation, privilege as to, **15(2)**, [550]
discrimination proceedings, extension of
time for bringing, **15(2)**, [552]
fees, **15(2)**, [588]
interpretation, **15(2)**, [554]
operator—
annual report, **15(2)**, [589]
conditions to be met by, **15(2)**, [587]
designation of, **15(2)**, [546]
duties of, **15(2)**, [547], [589]
information, supply of, **15(2)**, [589]
period for compliance with duties,
15(2), [589]
termination of designation, **15(2)**, [549],
[551], [590]–[591]
provision of, **15(2)**, [589]
publication of, **15(2)**, [589]
qualifying complaint, meaning,
15(2), [545]
qualifying institution—
duties of, **15(2)**, [548]
meaning, **15(2)**, [544]
review, **15(2)**, [588]–[589]
visitor's jurisdiction, extension of,
15(2), [553]
student fees—
basic or higher amount, regulations relating
to, **15(2)**, [559]
conditions—
basic amount, fees not to exceed,
15(2), [558]
duty of Secretary of State to impose,
15(2), [556]
English funding bodies, imposed by,
15(2), [557]
Higher Education Funding Council for
Wales, imposed by, **15(2)**, [561]
inapplicable, **15(2)**, [562]
interpretation, **15(2)**, [557]
National Assembly for Wales, imposed
by, **15(2)**, [560]
Training and Development Agency for
Schools, **15(2)**, [561]
interpretation, **15(2)**, [574]
plan—
approval of, **15(2)**, [567]
contents of, **15(2)**, [566]
duration, **15(2)**, [568]
enforcement—
England, in, **15(2)**, [570]
Wales, in, **15(2)**, [571]

higher and further education—*contd*
student fees—*contd*
plan—*contd*
interpretation, **15(2)**, [566]
meaning, **15(2)**, [555]
variation, **15(2)**, [569]
qualifying course, descriptions of,
15(2), [562]
relevant authority—
decisions, review of, **15(2)**, [572]
meaning, **15(2)**, [563]
student support—
authority, supply of information held by,
15(2), [577]
bankruptcy, effect of, **15(2)**, [575]
National Assembly for Wales, transfer of
functions to, **15(2)**, [576]
Teachers, employment of, regulations as to,
15(1), [357]
trust deeds, variation of, **15(1)**, [323]
Universities Funding Council. *See*
Universities Funding Council

**Higher Education Funding Council for
Wales**
Assembly, directions by, **15(2)**, [682]
efficiency studies, **15(2)**, [684]
funding—
discretion, exercise of, **15(2)**, [677]
grants, loans and other payments,
15(2), [677]
qualifying activities and eligible
institutions, **15(2)**, [676]
grants to, **15(2)**, [679]
information, provision of, **15(2)**, [685]
joint exercise of functions, **15(2)**, [683]
research, power to carry out or commission,
15(2), [680]
supplementary and ancillary functions,
15(2), [681]

Higher Education Funding Councils
accounts, **15(1)**, [461]
advisory services, provision of, **15(1)**, [435]
chief officer, **15(1)**, [461]
committees, **15(1)**, [461]
delegation of functions, **15(1)**, [461]
directions, compliance with, **15(1)**, [444]
efficiency studies, **15(2)**, [684]
establishment of, **15(1)**, [429]
existing councils, transfer of property, rights
and liabilities of, **15(1)**, [430]
funds—
activities eligible for, **15(1)**, [431]
administration of, **15(1)**, [431]–[432]
review of activities, **15(1)**, [435]
grants and loans by—
balance, maintenance of, **15(1)**, [432]
consultation on, **15(1)**, [432]
power to make, **15(1)**, [431]
terms and conditions, **15(1)**, [431]
grants to, **15(1)**, [434]
information and advice, provision to Secretary
of State, **15(1)**, [435]
information provided to, **15(1)**, [443]

Higher Education Funding Councils—*contd*
  instruments, proof of, **15(1)**, [461]
  joint exercise of functions, **15(1)**, [445];
    15(2), [683]
  members—
    number of, **15(1)**, [429]
    qualifications, **15(1)**, [429]
    salaries, allowances and pensions,
      15(1), [461]
    tenure, **15(1)**, [461]
  new employer, as, **15(1)**, [430]
  proceedings, **15(1)**, [461]
  property, exercise of functions in relation to,
    15(1), [435]
  Quality Assessment Committee—
    establishment of, **15(1)**, [436]
    members, **15(1)**, [436]
  quality of education, assessment of,
    15(1), [436]
  reference to, **15(1)**, [427], [429], [457]
  seal, **15(1)**, [461]
  staff, **15(1)**, [461]
  status, **15(1)**, [461]
  supplementary powers, **15(1)**, [461]
  teacher training. *See* **teacher training**

highway. *See also* **road**
  access to or from—
    acquisition of land for, **36**, [1287]
    advances by Minister to provide, **36**, [1319]
    crossing over footways and verges,
      36, [1247]
    facilities and amenities, restrictions,
      36, [1138]
    fencing obstructing, **36**, [1083]
    premises, **36**, [1126], [1168], [1169]
    stopping up—
      agreement, by, **36**, [1171]
      compensation for damage, **36**, [1170]
      new means of access, provision of,
        36, [1173]
      obstruction, avoiding, **36**, [1170]
      order for, **36**, [1168]
        date of operation, **36**, [1400]
        other orders, powers under,
          36, [1169]
        validity, **36**, [1400]
      regulations on, **36**, [1168]
      use after, penalty for, **36**, [1172]
    watercourse, diversion to provide,
      36, [1126]
    works obstructing, **36**, [1069]
  acquisition of land for—
    access to premises, for, **36**, [1304]
    advances by Minister for, **36**, [1319]
    adverse effects, mitigation, **36**, [1293],
      [1331]
    authorities' buildings and facilities, for,
      36, [1291]
    bridge, for, **36**, [1288], [1294], [1301]
    buildings needed for functions, for,
      36, [1291]
    cattle-grid or by-pass, for, **36**, [1289]
    clearance of title, **36**, [1306]
    common land, **36**, [1285], [1286]

highway—*contd*
  acquisition of land for—*contd*
    compensation—
      assumptions made in assessing,
        36, [1308]
      matters taken into consideration,
        36, [1307]
    compulsorily, **36**, [1293]
    compulsory purchase order—
      concurrent proceedings, **36**, [1304]
      creation of rights, extending to,
        36, [1297]
      objections to, **36**, [1305]
      title, clearance of, **36**, [1306]
    construction, for, **36**, [1285]
    distance limits applicable to, **36**, [1296],
      [1425], [1426]
    enjoyment, where affected, **36**, [1293]
    exchange, for purposes of, **36**, [1285],
      [1286]
    frontages, for, **36**, [1285], [1286]
    fuel or field garden allotment, **36**, [1285],
      [1286]
    generally, **36**, [1285], [1286]
    improvement, for, **36**, [1285]
    improvement line and street boundary,
      between, **36**, [1287]
    local authority, property of, **36**, [1301]
    lorry area, for, **36**, [1286]
    Minister, by, **36**, [1285]
    mitigation of adverse effects, for,
      36, [1293], [1331]
    navigable watercourse, for diversion of,
      36, [1286]
    objections to, **36**, [1305]
    open space, **36**, [1285], [1286]
    picnic area, for, **36**, [1286]
    procedure, **36**, [1294]
    public conveniences, for, **36**, [1286]
    purposes of, **36**, [1285], [1286]
    related schemes and orders, with,
      36, [1304], [1428]
      concurrent proceedings, **36**, [1304]
    requirements, in advance of, **36**, [1295]
      purposes of, **36**, [1424]
    road-ferry, for, **36**, [1290]
    special road authority, by, **36**, [1285]
    traffic management purposes, buildings
      needed for, **36**, [1292]
    transitional provisions, **36**, [1433]
    works, in connection with, **36**, [1285]
  acquisition of rights over land for—
    bridge, for, **36**, [1288], [1294]
    compensation, **36**, [1307]
    compulsory purchase order, **36**, [1297],
      [1309], [1427]
    enactments, adaptation of, **36**, [1427]
    exchange, in, **36**, [1285]
    expenses, liability for, **36**, [1302]
    level crossing replaced by bridge, for,
      36, [1302]
    local authority, property of, **36**, [1301]
    powers extended to, **36**, [1297]
    road drainage, for, **36**, [1301]

highway—*contd*
  acquisition of rights over land for—*contd*
    statutory undertakers, property of,
      36, [1301]
    successive owners, binding on, **36**, [1298]
    whole interest, right to require acquisition
      of, **36**, [1299]
  adjoining land—
    agreements for use of, **36**, [1300]
    barbed wire on, **36**, [1226]
    exchange for adjustment of boundary,
      36, [1303]
    fencing off, **36**, [1055]
    meaning, **36**, [1381]
    source of danger on, **36**, [1227]
  adoption—
    agreement, by, **36**, [1043]
    private street, **36**, [1044], [1274]
  advances for purposes of, **36**, [1319]
  amenities, provision. *See* services and
    amenities *below*
  animals straying on, **2**, [357]; **36**, [1220]
  annoyance, penalty for causing, **36**, [1222]
  apparatus in or under—
    exchange of land, effect of, **36**, [1303],
      [1416]
    meaning, **36**, [1381]
    statutory undertakers—
      exchange of land, affected by,
        36, [1303], [1416]
      extinguishment of rights, **36**, [1026],
        [1405], [1406]
  appeals—
    Crown Court, to, **36**, [1369]
    decision in, effect of, **36**, [1370]
    magistrates' court, to, **36**, [1368]
    notice of right of, **36**, [1367]
  arch under, control of, **36**, [1246]
  authority. *See* **highway authority**
  authority, records, keeping of, **9**, [318]
  barbed wire on land adjoining, **36**, [1226]
  barrier—
    emergency, erection in, **36**, [1337]
    erection, **36**, [1065]
    footway, in, **36**, [1069]
    hazards of nature, protecting against,
      36, [1117]
  barbed wire on land adjoining, **36**, [1226]
  barrier—
    emergency, erection in, **36**, [1337]
    erection, **36**, [1065]
    footway, in, **36**, [1069]
    hazards of nature, protecting against,
      36, [1117]
  boundary—
    exchange of land for adjusting, **36**, [1303],
      [1416]
    posts, provision of, **36**, [1084]
  bridge, on. *See* **bridge**
  bridges in two districts, **25(2)**, [637]
  bridleway. *See* **bridleway**
  bridleway, stopping up or diversion of,
    46, [522]
  building line—
    compensation for injury, **36**, [1077]

highway—*contd*
  building line—*contd*
    power to prescribe, **36**, [1077]
    prescription of, **36**, [1412]
    revocation of, **36**, [1077], [1412]
    undertakers, effect on, **36**, [1077]
  building on. *See* **building**
  building operations on—
    hoarding, erection of, **36**, [1237]
    materials—
      charge for occupation by,
        36, [1234]–[1236]; **38(2)**, [348]
      deposit of, **36**, [1233]
    meaning, **36**, [1230]
    public safety, affecting, **36**, [1230]
    scaffolding, control of, **36**, [1231]
      charges for occupation by,
        36, [1234]–[1236]; **38(2)**, [348]
  byway. *See* **byway**
  carriage of, alteration, **9**, [312], [318]
  carriageway—
    dual, construction of, **36**, [1067]
    made-up, meaning, **36**, [1381]
    meaning, **36**, [1381]
    surface, making good, **36**, [1419]
    widening, **36**, [1078], [1384]
  cart, driving on, **36**, [222]
  cattle-grid. *See* **cattle-grid**
  cellar—
    construction, control of, **36**, [1245]
    obstruction, removal of, **36**, [1217]
    openings, control of, **36**, [1246]
  cement, mixing on, **36**, [1232]
  centre line, provisions on, **36**, [1376]
  classes of vehicles on, testing, **36**, [1332]
  cleaning—
    highway or local authority—
      duty as to, **35(1)**, [312]
      prohibition of parking to facilitate,
        35(1), [313]
  closing in improvement area, **22**, [226]
  Coast Protection Act, saving for, **36**, [1388]
  common land, acquisition of, **36**, [1285],
    [1286]
  compensation—
    acquisition of land, for, **36**, [1307], [1308]
    disputes, settlement of—
      arbitration, by, **36**, [1360]
      county courts, by, **36**, [1360]
      Upper Tribunal, by, **36**, [1359]
    interest subject to mortgage, depreciation
      of, **36**, [1361]
  compulsory acquisition of land, and, **46**, [519]
  concession agreements, roads subject to. *See*
    special roads (new roads)
  concurrent proceedings, **46**, [520]
  connection notice, service of, **46**, [839], [920]
  connection of private streets to, notice by
    regional development agency, **46**, [920]
  conservation area, construction in, **36**, [1121]
  construction—
    advances by Minister for, **36**, [1319]
    adverse effects, mitigating, **36**, [1293]
    blighted land, on, **36**, [1293]

highway—*contd*
construction—*contd*
environmental assessment,
36, [1121]–[1123]
experiments for improving, **36**, [1332]
highway authority, by, **36**, [1028]
Minister, by, **36**, [1028]
conversion into footpath or bridleway,
36, [210]
corners—
cutting off, **36**, [1081]
notices restraining building, etc, **36**, [1082]
obstruction to view, prevention of,
36, [1082]
countryside, construction in,
36, [1121]–[1123]
creation of, **36**, [210]
crops, encroachment by, **36**, [1197]
Crown Court, appeal to, **36**, [1369]
Crown land, application of provisions to,
36, [1379]
damage to—
deposit, by, **36**, [1186]
excavation, by, **36**, [1189]
exclusion of sun and wind, consequent
on, **36**, [1194]
extraordinary traffic, by, **36**, [1063]
fire, lighting, **36**, [1186]
firearm or firework, discharging, **36**, [1186]
footway, to, **36**, [1189]
forms of, **36**, [1186]
penalty, **36**, [1186]
soil or turf, removing, **36**, [1186]
surface, disturbance of, **36**, [1187]
unauthorised marks on, **36**, [1188]
danger—
penalty for causing, **36**, [1222]
things constituting, removal, **36**, [1214]
dangerous land adjoining, **36**, [1227]
dedication of—
evidence of, **36**, [1037]
maintainable at public expense, becoming,
36, [1042]
map and statement of, deposit by
landowner, **36**, [1035]
maps, statements and declarations, register
of, **36**, [1036]
notice negativing intention, **36**, [1035]
parish or community council, agreement
with, **36**, [1034], [1075]
presumption and proof of, **36**, [210],
[1035]
public use for 20 years, after, **36**, [1035]
Defence of the Realm Acts, powers under,
9, [105], [117]
deposit on—
damage, causing, **36**, [1186]
danger, causing, **36**, [1222]
nuisance, constituting, **36**, [1214]
penalty for, **36**, [1213]
depreciation in land value through use of,
compensation for. *See* **public works**
disabled or blind, regards to needs of,
36, [1241]

highway—*contd*
ditch—
making of, unlawful, **36**, [1186]
meaning, **36**, [1116]
power to fill in, **36**, [1116]
diversion. *See* stopping up or diversion *below*
door opening outwards on, **36**, [1218]
drainage—
charges for, **49**, [953]
compensation for damage, **36**, [1115]
construction and maintenance, **36**, [1115]
discharge of water, **36**, [1115], [1349]
drain—
meaning, **36**, [1115]
mortar, etc, entering, **36**, [1232]
obstruction etc of, **36**, [1115]
vesting of, **36**, [1310]
highway authority, powers of, **36**, [1115]
drunkenness in, penalty, **19(3)**, [355], [359]
dual carriageways, powers, **36**, [1067]
dust, mitigating nuisance of, **36**, [1119]
dustbins on, **35(1)**, [305]
emergency powers, stopped up or diverted
under. *See* stopping up or diversion *below*
encamping on, **36**, [1213]
entry on land—
apparatus, placing, **36**, [1340]
authorisation of, **36**, [1339]
compensation for damage, **36**, [1342]
notice of, **36**, [1340]
offences, **36**, [1342]
re-surfacing, purposes of, **36**, [1419]
structures and works, to maintain,
36, [1341]
survey, for, **36**, [1339], [1340]
works, for, **36**, [1340]
excavations in—
charges for making, **36**, [1234]–[1236];
38(2), [348]
control of, **36**, [1233]
damage by, **36**, [1189]
undertaken by, **36**, [1076], [1077]
exchange of land for adjustment of
boundaries, **36**, [1303]
expenses, recovery of—
council, by, **36**, [1357]
extraordinary traffic, due to, **36**, [1063]
highway authority, by, **36**, [1357]
proceedings for, **36**, [1358]
rents, deduction from, by occupiers,
36, [1420]
experiments, conduct of, **36**, [1332]
extraordinary traffic on, **36**, [1063]
fence—
access, preventing, **36**, [1083]
alteration or removal, **36**, [1083]
obstruction, causing, **36**, [1083], [1217]
power to erect, **36**, [1083], [1111]
unlawful, penalty for, **36**, [1198]
fencing off, effect of, **36**, [1055]
fire, lighting on or near, **36**, [1186], [1223]
firearm or firework, discharging, **36**, [1186],
[1222]
flagpole, etc, erected on, **36**, [1207]

highway—*contd*
  flooding—
    depth, provision of posts indicating, **36**, [1118]
    protection against, **36**, [1117]
  football, playing on, **36**, [1222]
  footbridge over, **36**, [1073]
  footpath. *See* **footpath**
  footway—
    barriers, etc, in, **36**, [1069]
    cellar openings, control of, **36**, [1246]
    damage to, **36**, [1189]
    lighting systems, **36**, [1069], [1317]
    local authority using vehicles on, **36**, [1350]
    meaning, **36**, [1381]
    provision of, **36**, [1069]
    vehicle crossing on—
      conditions for use, **36**, [1247]
      construction of, **36**, [1247]
      notices, **36**, [1247], [1421]
      request for, **36**, [1247]
      transitional provisions, **36**, [1433]
      unauthorised, penalty for, **36**, [1247]
    ventilators and lights, control of, **36**, [1246]
    widening, **36**, [1078]
  forecourt abutting on, **36**, [1229]
  fuel or field garden allotment, acquisition of, **36**, [1285], [1286]
  functions transferred, **25(2)**, [583]
  games, playing on, **36**, [1222]
  gates across, **36**, [1208]
  gating orders—
    availability of, **36**, [1178]
    circumstances for, **36**, [1174]
    effect of, **36**, [1175]
    interpretation, **36**, [1180]
    procedure, **36**, [1176]
    publication of, **36**, [1178]
    revocation, **36**, [1179]
    summary of provisions, **36**, [210]
    validity, **36**, [1177]
    variation, **36**, [1179]
  grass margin—
    horses and livestock, for, **36**, [1074]
    laying out, **36**, [1111]
  Greater London, in, improving, **36**, [1335]
  guard-rails—
    private street, in, **36**, [1070]
    provision of, **36**, [1069]
    trees etc protection, for, **36**, [1111]
  hazards of nature, protection against, **36**, [1117]
  hedge, planting in, **36**, [1198]
  hoardings—
    building operations, erected in, **36**, [1237]
    secure, to be, **36**, [1238]
  horses and livestock, margin for, **36**, [1074]
  housing action trust, powers of, **22**, [856]
  improvement, **9**, [140]
  improvement line—
    building on, **36**, [1076]
    compensation for injury, **36**, [1076]
    prescription of, **36**, [1076], [1412]
    revocation of, **36**, [1076], [1412]

highway—*contd*
  improvement line—*contd*
    undertakers, effect on, **36**, [1076]
  improvement of—
    advances by Minister for, **36**, [1319]
    adverse effects, **36**, [1293], [1331]
    environmental assessment, **36**, [210]
    general powers, **36**, [1065]
    Greater London, in, **36**, [1335]
    meaning, **36**, [1381]
    parish or community council, by, **36**, [1034]
    power of, **36**, [1065]
    trees and shrubs, planting, **36**, [1065], [1067], [1111]
    widening as, **36**, [1384]
    works deemed to be, **36**, [1065]
  inquiry, **36**, [1354], [1397]
  interference with rights and liabilities, **36**, [1385]
  Isles of Scilly, application of provisions to, **36**, [1395]
  land—
    acquisition of. *See* acquisition of land *above*
    entry on. *See* entry *above*
    exchange to adjust boundaries, **36**, [1303]
    meaning, **36**, [1381]
    nearby, agreements for use of, **36**, [1300]
    ownership, information as to, **36**, [1347]
    rights over, acquisition of. *See* acquisition of rights over land *above*
  land required for, blight notice in respect of, **46**, [632]
  landslide, protection against, **36**, [1117]
  levelling, works for, **36**, [1079]
  levels, alteration of, **36**, [1080]
  lighting—
    authority, meaning, **36**, [1381]
    buildings, lamps attached to, **36**, [1112]
    footway lighting system, **36**, [1317]
    footways, of, **36**, [1069]
    lighting authority—
      delegation of functions to, **36**, [1113]
      meaning, **36**, [1381]
      powers of, **36**, [1351]
      works by, **36**, [1113]
    obstructions, warning of, **36**, [1215]
    provision of, **36**, [1067], [1112]
    road lighting system, **36**, [1317]
    scaffolding, of, **36**, [1231]
    subways, of, **36**, [1072]
    transfer of systems, **36**, [1317]
  livestock, margins for, **36**, [1074]
  London. *See* **London streets**
  lorry area. *See* **lorry area**
  loss of access to, compensation, **22**, [226]
  magistrates' court, appeal from, **36**, [1369]
    orders as to maintenance, **36**, [1052], [1060]
  maintainable—
    designation, declaration of, **38(1)**, [230]
    meaning, **38(1)**, [230]
  maintenance and repair—
    advances by Minister for, **36**, [1319]

highway—*contd*
　maintenance and repair—*contd*
　　agreement between authorities for,
　　　36, [1011]
　　compound, meaning, **36**, [1381]
　　default in—
　　　damages, action for, **36**, [1062]
　　　highway authority, powers of, **36**, [1061]
　　district council, by. *See* **district council**
　　environmental assessment,
　　　36, [1121]–[1123]
　　extraordinary traffic, due to, **36**, [1063]
　　generally, **36**, [210]
　　highway authority undertaking, **36**, [1009]
　　magistrates' courts, power to order,
　　　36, [1052], [1060]
　　materials, power to get, **36**, [1049], [1050]
　　meaning, **36**, [1381]
　　parish or community council, by,
　　　36, [1034]
　　person liable, agreement by, **36**, [1048]
　　private—
　　　bridges, approaches to, **36**, [1053]
　　　diversion, extinguishment of liability
　　　　on, **36**, [1058]
　　　highway authority, default powers of,
　　　　36, [1061]
　　　liability, magistrates' court
　　　　extinguishing, **36**, [1057]
　　　repair, materials for, **36**, [1056]
　　proceedings to repair, **36**, [1060]
　　public expense, at—
　　　authority, duty of, **36**, [1041]
　　　becoming, **36**, [1041]
　　　bridge carrying, construction of,
　　　　36, [1105]
　　　carriageway, works in, **36**, [1067]
　　　county council, reimbursement by,
　　　　36, [1046]
　　　cycle track in, **36**, [1068]
　　　dedication, on, **36**, [1042]
　　　district council, by, **36**, [1046]
　　　　empowering regulations, **36**, [1064]
　　　duty of, **36**, [1045]
　　　enclosure, effect of, **36**, [1055]
　　　excavation of materials for, **36**, [1050]
　　　extraordinary traffic, expenses due to,
　　　　36, [1063]
　　　highway authority adopting, **36**, [1043]
　　　list of, council keeping, **36**, [1041]
　　　magistrates' court ordering, **36**, [1052]
　　　meaning, **36**, [1381]
　　　non-repair, defence in action for,
　　　　36, [1062]
　　　person liable, agreement of, **36**, [1048]
　　　private street, adoption of, **36**, [1044],
　　　　[1274]
　　　repair, power to get materials for,
　　　　36, [1049], [1050]
　　　road lamps in, **36**, [1112]
　　　safety provisions, **36**, [1069]
　　　unnecessary, declared, **36**, [1051]
　　　vesting of, **36**, [1309]
　　surface, making good—
　　　entry on land for, **36**, [1419]

highway—*contd*
　maintenance and repair—*contd*
　　surface, making good—*contd*
　　　expenses, **36**, [1419]
　　　requirement, **36**, [1419]
　　　transitional provisions, **36**, [1433]
　　margins for horses and livestock, **36**, [1074]
　　marks, placing, unauthorised, **36**, [1188]
　　materials for—
　　　excavation, got by, **36**, [1050]
　　　left on road, liability for, **36**, [1240]
　　　maintenance and repair, for, **36**, [1049],
　　　　[1050]
　　　privately maintainable highway, for,
　　　　36, [1056]
　　meaning, **36**, [210], [1380]
　　metalling, **36**, [1114]
　　metropolitan roads, cessation as, **25(2)**, [637]
　　minerals under, saving for, **36**, [1387]
　　mobility problems, improvements for benefit
　　　of persons with, **36**, [1211]
　　mortar, mixing on, **36**, [1232]
　　National Park or nature reserve, in, **36**, [1121]
　　nationally significant infrastructure projects,
　　　46(S), 42–3. *See also* **nationally significant
　　infrastructure projects**
　　new, construction of, **36**, [1028]
　　notices—
　　　form of, **36**, [1372]
　　　service of, **36**, [1374], [1397]
　　nuisance, removal of things being, **36**, [1214]
　　object or structure placed in—
　　　charges for, **36**, [1140]
　　　consents, unreasonably withholding,
　　　　36, [1143]
　　　consultation of authorities, **36**, [1142]
　　　council, power of, **36**, [1135]
　　　notice of, **36**, [1141]
　　　persons other than councils, by, **36**, [1139]
　　　records of, **38(2)**, [346]
　　　terms of permission, failure to comply
　　　　with, **36**, [1144]
　　obstructing execution of Act, **36**, [1355]
　　obstruction of—
　　　animals, straying, **36**, [1220]
　　　builders' skip, by. *See* **builders' skip**
　　　building, erecting in, **36**, [1198]
　　　doors, etc, opening outwards on,
　　　　36, [1218]
　　　fence, erecting, **36**, [1198]
　　　forecourt, abutting, **36**, [1229]
　　　hedge, planting, **36**, [1198]
　　　lighting, **36**, [1215]
　　　offender, power to order removal by,
　　　　36, [1196]
　　　overhanging trees, etc, **36**, [1219]
　　　prevention of, **36**, [1181]
　　　projections from buildings, **36**, [1217]
　　　removal of structure, **36**, [1206]
　　　rights and liabilities, saving for, **36**, [1385]
　　　snow, by, **36**, [1215]
　　　soil, by, **36**, [1215], [1216]
　　　tree or shrub, restriction on planting,
　　　　36, [1204]
　　　warning of, **36**, [1215]

highway—*contd*

  obstruction of—*contd*

    wilful, penalty for, **36**, [1195]

  offences—

    body corporate, by, **36**, [1365]; **38(2)**, [389]

    builders' skip, relating to, **36**, [1199], [1200]

    building operation affecting public safety, **36**, [1230]

    building over, unlawful, **36**, [1243]

    continuing, **36**, [1363], [1433]

    danger or annoyance, causing, **36**, [1222], [1223]

    deposit or excavation in, **36**, [1233]

    fixed penalties, **36**, [1366], [1431], [1432]; **38(2)**, [345]

    institution of proceedings, restriction on, **36**, [1364], [1430]

    judges and justices, qualification to hear, **36**, [1371]

    obstructing execution of Act, **36**, [1355]

    openings under, **36**, [1246]

    penalties, **36**, [221], [222]

    retaining walls, relating to, **36**, [1229]

    road-side sales, relating to, **36**, [926], [1212]

    rope or wire, placing across, **36**, [1224]

    scaffolding, relating to, **36**, [1231]

    summary proceedings, **36**, [1362]

    works, tampering with warning of, **36**, [1239]

  offensive matter on, **36**, [1222]

  oil pipe-line passing under, **9**, [175]

  open space, acquisition of, **36**, [1285], [1286]

  orders—

    confirmation of, **36**, [1397]

    date of operation, **36**, [1400]

    documents, service of copies of, **36**, [1397]

    draft, publication of, **36**, [1397]

    local inquiry, **36**, [1397]

    modifications, **36**, [1397]

    objections to, **36**, [1397]

    procedure for making, **36**, [1376], [1377]

    publicity for, **36**, [1399]

    revocation and variation, **36**, [1378]

    service on specified persons, **36**, [1397]

    stopping up and diversion, for, **36**, [1397]

    validity, **36**, [1400]

  overhead beam, etc, restriction on, **36**, [1244]

  owner in relation to premises, meaning, **36**, [1381]

  pavement lights, control of, **36**, [1246]

  pedestrians, measure for safety etc of, **36**, [1069]

  periods, reckoning, **36**, [1375]

  permit schemes. *See* **highway authority**

  planning permission, land for, **9**, [229]

  private street converted into, **36**, [1039]

  prohibition of traffic on, **36**, [1135]

  proposed, meaning, **36**, [1381]

  public access, restriction of, **36**, [1138]

  Public Health Act, amendment of, **36**, [1393], [1430]

  public rights, protection of, **36**, [1181]

highway—*contd*

  public safety, operations affecting, **36**, [1069], [1230]

  public user, extent of, **36**, [210]

  rail over, restriction on, **36**, [1244]

  recreation facilities—

    consents, unreasonably withholding, **36**, [1143]

    consultation of authorities, **36**, [1142]

    notice of, **36**, [1141]

    permission to operate, charge for, **36**, [1140]

    provision of, **36**, [1137]

    terms of permission, failure to comply with, **36**, [1144]

    works and use, persons other than councils, **36**, [1139]

  refreshment facilities—

    consents, unreasonably withholding, **36**, [1143]

    consultation of authorities, **36**, [1142]

    notice of, **36**, [1141]

    permission to operate, charge for, **36**, [1140]

    provision of, **36**, [1137]

    terms of permission, failure to comply with, **36**, [1144]

    works and use, persons other than councils, **36**, [1139]

  refuges, provision of, **36**, [1071]

  refuse bins, provision of, **36**, [1248]

  renewal area, in, extinguishment of rights, **23**, [32]

  rents, deduction from, recovery of expenses by occupiers, **36**, [1420]

  repairable by inhabitants at large, **9**, [140]

  retaining walls, powers on, **36**, [1229]

  reversioners, protection of rights of, **36**, [1038]

  ribbon development, repayment of compensation for restriction of, **9**, [140]

  right of way proceedings, **36**, [1181]

  rights of public, protection, **36**, [1181]

  rights over land, acquisition. *See* acquisition of rights *above*

  road humps. *See* **road humps**

  roadside sales. *See* **road-side sales**

  roadside waste, encroachment on, **36**, [1181]

  rope or wire, placing across, **36**, [1224]

  roundabouts, **36**, [1067]

  rubbish, charge for deposit on, **36**, [1234]–[1236]; **38(2)**, [348]

  safety provisions, **36**, [1069]

  scaffolding on, control of, **36**, [1231]

  schemes—

    procedure for making, **36**, [1376], [1377]

    revocation and variation, **36**, [1378]

  service area—

    acquisition of land for, **36**, [1285]

    compulsory purchase of land for, **36**, [1308]

    development, meaning, **36**, [1308]

    meaning, **36**, [1381]

    title to land, clearance of, **36**, [1306]

highway—*contd*
services and amenities—
charge for grant of permissions, **36**, [1140]
consents, unreasonably withholding,
36, [1143]
consultation of authorities, **36**, [1142]
frontagers, interests of, **36**, [1135]
notices to be given, **36**, [1141]
persons other than councils, provision by,
36, [1041]
provision of, **36**, [1136]
public access, restricting, **36**, [1138]
scope of provision, **36**, [1135]
terms of permission, failure to comply
with, **36**, [1144]
works and use, persons other than
councils, **36**, [1139]
sewer, vesting of, **36**, [1310]
snow—
protection against, **36**, [1117]
removal of, **36**, [1215]
soil—
removal of, **36**, [1215]
washing onto street, prevention of,
36, [1216]
special roads. *See* **special roads**
statutory undertakers, meaning, **36**, [1381]
stopping up and diversion, in interests of civil
aviation, **4(1)**, [99]
stopping up or diversion—
authorisation of, **9**, [140], [165]
cables, etc, provision as to, **9**, [140]
compensation for orders, **46**, [515]
development, for, **46**, [512]
emergency powers, under, **9**, [140]
expenditure, defrayal of, **9**, [140]
footpaths and bridleways, **46**, [522]
local authority, notice proposed order to,
9, [142]
main highway, crossing or entering,
46, [513]
mineral workings, in relation to, **46**, [526]
orders, **46**, [512]
copies of, **9**, [143]
date of operation, **9**, [143]
duration of, **9**, [144]
making, notice of, **9**, [143]
notice of proposal to make, **9**, [142]
person aggrieved by, **9**, [143]
proposed, **9**, [142]
provision made by, **9**, [140]
quashing, **9**, [143]
suspension of operation, **9**, [143]
validity of, **9**, [143]
permanent, **9**, [140], [165]
planning permission, in anticipation of,
46, [518]
proposal for—
objection to, **9**, [143]
publication, **9**, [140], [142]
retention of railway, etc where no, **9**, [141]
savings, **9**, [145]
telecommunications apparatus, powers as
to, **46**, [521], [525]

highway—*contd*
stopping up or diverting—
access land, on, **38(2)**, [65]
aircraft, use for manufacture of, **36**, [666]
classified road, where crossing or joining,
36, [1017]
crime prevention, for purposes of—
diversion, **36**, [1155]
stopping up, **36**, [1150]
defence purposes, for, **36**, [666]
emergency powers, in exercise of, **36**, [667]
existing highway, **38(2)**, [65]
magistrates' court ordering, **36**, [1145]
Northern Ireland, in, **36**, [668], [671]
notice of proposal, **36**, [1145]
orders—
application on behalf of another,
36, [1146]
display of copy of, **36**, [1397]
making, **36**, [1415]
person requesting application for,
36, [1146]
power conferred by enactments, saving
for, **36**, [1167]
prevention of, **36**, [1181]
provision for, **36**, [210]
relevant authority, **38(2)**, [65]
special diversion order—
appeals, **36**, [1164], [1165]
application for, **36**, [1161]
compensation for, **36**, [1160]
confirmation, **36**, [1155]
consultation on, **36**, [1159]
contribution to, **36**, [1160]
council declining to determine
applications, **36**, [1163]
determinations, delegation of functions,
36, [1418]
form of, **36**, [1155]
meaning, **36**, [1155]
notices to be given, **36**, [1407]
power to make, **36**, [1155], [1159]
procedure for making, **36**, [1407]
register of applications, **36**, [1162]
school proprietor, application by,
36, [1156]
statutory undertakers, apparatus of,
36, [1160]
validity and operation of, **36**, [1408]
special extinguishment order—
appeals, **36**, [1164], [1165]
application for, **36**, [1161]
compensation for, **36**, [1160]
confirmation, **36**, [1150]
consultation on, **36**, [1150], [1159]
contribution to, **36**, [1160]
council declining to determine
applications, **36**, [1163]
determinations, delegation of functions,
36, [1418]
form of, **36**, [1150]
meaning, **36**, [1150]
notices to be given, **36**, [1407]
power to make, **36**, [1150], [1159]
procedure for making, **36**, [1407]

highway—*contd*
stopping up or diverting—*contd*
special extinguishment order—*contd*
register of applications, **36**, [1162]
school proprietor, application by, **36**, [1151]
statutory undertakers, apparatus of, **36**, [1160]
validity and operation of, **36**, [1408]
special road, where crossing or joining, **36**, [1024]
SSSI diversion order—
appeals, **36**, [1164], [1165]
application for, **36**, [1158], [1161]
compensation for, **36**, [1160]
confirmation, **36**, [1157]
contribution to, **36**, [1157], [1160]
council declining to determine applications, **36**, [1163]
determinations, delegation of functions, **36**, [1418]
form, **36**, [1158]
notice of intention to make, **36**, [1158]
notices to be given, **36**, [1407]
power to make, **36**, [1157], [1159]
procedure for making, **36**, [1407]
provisions applying to, **36**, [1158]
register of applications, **36**, [1162]
statutory undertakers, apparatus of, **36**, [1160]
validity and operation of, **36**, [1408]
statutory undertakers—
apparatus, effect on, **36**, [1145], [1416]
meaning, **36**, [1145]
substitution of, **36**, [667]
telecommunication apparatus, provisions on, **36**, [1398]
temporary, **36**, [666], [1166]
trunk road, where crossing or joining, **36**, [1017]
stopping up, Thames flood barrier, **49**, [549]
storage bins, provision of, **36**, [1248]
structures—
occupation by, charge for, **36**, [1234]–[1236]; **38(2)**, [348]
removal of, **36**, [1206]
substituted highway where, **9**, [140]
subway, provision of, **36**, [1072]
surface water, drainage of, **36**, [1115]
telecommunications code system, rights relating to, **36**, [1398]
temporary, construction of, **36**, [210]
temporary diversion of, **36**, [666], [1166]
transitional provisions, **36**, [1433]
transport undertakers, meaning, **36**, [1381]
trees and shrubs—
adverse effects of construction, mitigating, **36**, [1331]
dead or diseased, removal of, **36**, [1219]
guard-rails, **36**, [1111]
land adjoining, on, **36**, [1300]
licence to plant, **36**, [1205]
overhanging, cutting or felling, **36**, [1219]
planting without licence, **36**, [1205]
plants, including, **36**, [1111]

highway—*contd*
trees and shrubs—*contd*
power to plant, **36**, [1065], [1111]
restriction on planting, **36**, [1204]
trunk road, **9**, [140]
metropolitan road becoming, **25(2)**, [637]
See also **trunk road**
types of, **36**, [210]
unauthorised marks on, **36**, [1188]
undertakers, meaning, **36**, [1145], [1381]
users, danger or annoyance to—
barbed wire on land adjoining, **36**, [1226]
dangerous land adjoining, **36**, [1227]
deposit of thing, by, **36**, [1222]
fire, lighting, **36**, [1186], [1223]
firearm or firework, discharging, **36**, [1186], [1222]
forecourt, abutting, **36**, [1229]
games, playing, **36**, [1222]
offensive matter flowing on, **36**, [1222]
retaining walls, powers relating to, **36**, [1229]
rope or wire, placing across, **36**, [1224]
water flowing on to road, **36**, [1225]
vaults, control of, **36**, [1246]
vehicles, extinguishment of right to use, **46**, [514]
ventilators in, control of, **36**, [1246]
verge—
vehicle crossing on—
conditions for use, **36**, [1247]
construction of, **36**, [1247]
notices, **36**, [1421]
request for, **36**, [1247]
transitional provisions, **36**, [1433]
unauthorised, penalty for, **36**, [1247]
vesting of, **36**, [1309]
waggon, driving on, **36**, [222]
water—
discharge of, **36**, [1115], [1349]
flowing on, **36**, [1225]
widening—
bridge, part on, **36**, [1078]
carriageway, of, **36**, [1078], [1384]
footway, of, **36**, [1078]
improvement line. *See* improvement line *above*
parish or community council, power of, **36**, [1075]
power of, **36**, [1075]
width—
minimum and maximum, **36**, [1419]
re-surfacing within limits, **36**, [1419]
works—
adverse effects, mitigating, **36**, [1293], [1331]
agreements as to execution, **36**, [1326]
blighted land, on, **36**, [1293]
consents for, **36**, [1411]
disabled or blind, regard to needs of, **36**, [1241]
drainage authorities consent for, **36**, [1391], [1430]
execution on behalf of another, **36**, [1346]

highway—*contd*
  works—*contd*
    gas and water pipes, power to move, **36**, [1338], [1430]
    guard-rails during, **36**, [1069]
    occupier required to permit, **36**, [1356]
    persons displaced by, **21**, [415]
    rent, deductions from, **36**, [1420]
    statutory undertakers, by, **36**, [1382]
    undertakers' consent for, **36**, [1390], [1430]
      See also **street works**
  works for road purposes, meaning, **38(1)**, [229]

highway authority. *See also* **traffic authority**
  acquisition of land by. *See* **highway**
  advances to—
    district council, to, **36**, [1320]
    grant or loan, by, **36**, [1319]
    Minister, making to himself, **36**, [1319]
    purposes of, **36**, [1319]
  agreements between authorities—
    contributions, provision for payment of, **36**, [1008]
    maintenance and improvement, for, **36**, [1009], [1011]
    secondment of staff and facilities for, **36**, [1021]
    trunk road construction or improvement, for, **36**, [1008]
    works, for, **36**, [1011], [1326]
  air-space above land, dealing with, **36**, [1244]
  appeal from decision of—
    magistrates' court, to, **36**, [1368]
    notice of, **36**, [1367]
  approach to bridge, for, **36**, [1007]
  bridges, for, **36**, [1007]
  buildings and facilities, acquisition of land for, **36**, [1291]
  coast protection board, representation on, **49**, [381]
  Common Council as, **36**, [1005]
  competent authority in relation to highways, as, **36**, [1419]
  concession agreements. *See* **special roads (new roads)**
  county council as, **36**, [1005]
  default powers, **36**, [1061]
  documents, authentication of, **36**, [1373]
  drainage authorities' consent for works, **36**, [1391], [1430]
  entry, power of—
    authorising, **36**, [1340]
    compensation for damage, **36**, [1342]
    offences, **36**, [1342]
    premises, in, **36**, [1344], [1430]
    structures and works, to maintain, **36**, [1341]
    survey, for, **36**, [1339]
  expenses—
    contributions to, **46**, [578]
      bridge, maintenance of, **36**, [1321]
      community council, by, **36**, [1322]
      council, by, **36**, [1321]

highway authority—*contd*
  expenses—*contd*
    contributions to—*contd*
      county council, to district council, **36**, [1320]
      parish council, by, **36**, [1322]
    footways and bridleways, in connection with, **36**, [1322]
    recovery of—
      annual instalments, paid in, **36**, [1357]
      appeals, **36**, [1358]
      local land charge, as, **36**, [1357]
      owner of premises, from, **36**, [1357]
      summary proceedings, **36**, [1362]
  expenses, contributions to, **46**, [578]
  footpaths, bridleways and restricted byways, for, **36**, [1031]
  improving highways, power of, **36**, [210]
  lighting functions, delegation of, **36**, [1113]
  local sums paid to, **36**, [1328]
  London—
    additional powers, **25(2)**, [344]
    agreements for highway construction, **25(1)**, [910]
    fencing of lands, **25(1)**, [510]
    footway—
      meaning, **25(1)**, [576]
      use of vehicles etc on, **25(1)**, [576]
    meaning, **25(1)**, [576], [633]; **25(2)**, [344]
  London borough council as, **36**, [1005]
  lorry area, providing, **36**, [210], [1134]
  material for repair of publicly maintainable highway, getting, **36**, [1049], [1050]
  meaning, **37**, [808]
  metropolitan district council as, **36**, [1005]
  Minister being, **36**, [1005]
  navigable watercourse, diverting. *See* **watercourse**
  new town, in. *See* **new town**
  non-repair by, **36**, [1062]
  notice to enforce duty—
    application procedure, **36**, [1184]
    costs, **36**, [1185]
    hearing, **36**, [1184]
    orders following, **36**, [1183]
    service of, **36**, [1182]
  notices, etc, form of, **36**, [1372]
  objects in highways, records of, **38(2)**, [346]
  obstruction, removing, **36**, [1215]
  oil and tar, use of, **49**, [859]
  ownership of land, requiring information on, **36**, [1347]
  permit schemes—
    approval, **38(2)**, [327]
    Crown, provisions applying, **38(2)**, [331]
    generally, **36**, [210]
    implementation, **38(2)**, [327], [328]
    interpretation, **38(2)**, [332]
    meaning, **38(2)**, [325]
    preparation of, **38(2)**, [326]
    provisions, **38(2)**, [325]
    regulations, **38(2)**, [330]
    revocation, **38(2)**, [329]
    variation, **38(2)**, [329]
  predecessor authority, acts by, **36**, [1433]

highway authority—*contd*
  removal of things on highway by, **36**, [1214]
  road-side sales, controlling, **36**, [926]
  scaffolding, licensing of, **25(1)**, [1004]
  sewerage undertaker, exercise of powers of,
    by, **36**, [1115]
  special road, providing. *See* **special road**
  survey, powers on entry for, **36**, [1339]
  toll rights, transfer to, **36**, [1318]
  Transport for London as, **36**, [1005]
  trunk road, for—
    cessation as, **36**, [1006]
    delegation of functions, **36**, [1010]
    Minister as, **36**, [1005]
    road ceasing to be, for, **36**, [1006]
  undertakers' consent required for works,
    36, [1390], [1430]
  urban development area, in. *See* **urban
    development area**
  Wales, in, county council or borough as,
    36, [1005]
  Water Acts, exercise of powers under,
    36, [1115]
  water, right to discharge, **36**, [1349]
  works executed by—
    another, on behalf of, **36**, [1346]
    compensation for damage, **36**, [1026],
      [1027]

Highway Code
  continuation and revision, **37**, [609]
  failure to observe, **37**, [609]

highway undertakings
  carrying on, meaning, **43(1)**, [920]
  concession—
    balancing adjustment on ending of,
      43(1), [922]
    extended, treated as, **43(1)**, [923]
    meaning, **43(1)**, [920]
  relevant interest, **43(1)**, [921]

Highways Acts
  agreements under, stamp duty exemption,
    41, [152], [157]

hijacking
  aircraft, of, **4(1)**, [178], [183]

hill farming
  development boards. *See* **Rural
    Development Boards**
  entry and inspection of land, **1(1)**, [374]
  ministerial expenses respecting,
    1(1), [375] [376], [447]
  obstruction of authorised persons, **1(1)**, [374]
  regulations and orders, **1(1)**, [377]
  sums due to minister, recovery of, **1(1)**, [375]

hire agreement
  emergency laws, **50**, [262]

hire purchase
  adverse possession, **39(1)**, [297]

hire purchase—*contd*
  agreement—
    breach, goods, possession of, **39(1)**, [253],
      [254]
    exemption from stamp duty, **41**, [62]
    goods bailed under, restriction on privilege
      from distress for rent, **13**, [1203]
    installation charge, **39(1)**, [253], [263]
    leased assets subject to, **44(1)**, [528]
    meaning, **9**, [136]; **13**, [1203]; **39(1)**, [68],
      [132]; **44(1)**, [528]
    requisition of goods subject to, **9**, [133]
    terms, implied, **39(1)**, [125]
    title, implied terms as to, **39(1)**, [125]
    total price, meaning, **39(1)**, [353]
  breach of statutory conditions, modification of
    remedies for, **39(1)**, [129]
  capital gains tax, **42**, [1109]
  description of goods, **39(1)**, [126]
  emergency laws, **50**, [262]
  entry on premises, **39(1)**, [255]
  fitness, implied undertakings on, **39(1)**, [127]
  implied terms and conditions, express,
    exclusion by, **39(1)**, [130]
  machinery and plant. *See* **machinery and
    plant allowances**
  motor vehicle—
    debtor, disposal by, **39(1)**, [66]
    presumptions, **39(1)**, [67]
  paid-up sum, determining, **39(1)**, [296]
  quality, implied undertakings on, **39(1)**, [127]
  return order, **39(1)**, [296]
  sample, goods bailed by reference to,
    39(1), [128]
  termination of agreement—
    debtor, liability of, **39(1)**, [263]
    right of, **39(1)**, [262]
  time orders, **39(1)**, [290], [292], [651]
  transfer order, **39(1)**, [296]

hire vehicles. *See* **private hire vehicles; taxis
  and taxicabs**

historic building. *See also* **listed building**
  acquisition of—
    Commission, by, **32**, [210]
    grants for, **32**, [211]
    London, **25(1)**, [402], [674]
    Minister, by, **32**, [209]
  administrative expenses, **32**, [218]
  Commission. *See* **Historic Buildings and
    Ancient Monuments Commission for
    England**
  Council, establishment, **32**, [1]
  demolition under London Building Acts,
    25(1), [336]
  endowment of, Minister accepting, **32**, [213]
  generally, **32**, [1]
  land adjoining—
    Minister, acquisition by, **32**, [209]
    preservation, grants and loans for, **32**, [206]
  loans for preservation of, **46**, [20]
  maintenance funds, stamp duty exemption,
    41, [135]
  Minister, acquisition by, **32**, [209]

historic building—*contd*
preservation, grants and loans for—
Commission, by, **32**, [206]
Minister, by, **32**, [207]
recovery of, **32**, [208]

Historic Buildings and Monuments Commission
ancient monuments, functions, **25(2)**, [635]
functions transferred to, **25(2)**, [581]
Greater London archaeological service, grants towards, **13**, [344]
properties vested in, **25(2)**, [603]

Historic Buildings and Ancient Monuments Commission for England
accounts, **32**, [551]
acquisition of buildings and land by, **32**, [210]
advice, giving, **32**, [539]
ancient monument—
acquiring, **32**, [335]
agreements concerning, **32**, [341]
expenditure on, **32**, [346], [353]
guardianship, under, maintaining, **32**, [337]
investigations, expenditure on, **32**, [367]
land in vicinity of, control of, **32**, [339]
preservation, securing, **32**, [539]
transfer, consultation on, **32**, [345]
annual reports, **32**, [551]
archaeological areas—
designating, **32**, [355]
expenditure on investigations, **32**, [367]
investigating authority, as, **32**, [356]
Architectural Heritage Fund, grants to, **32**, [370]
auditor, **32**, [551]
borrowing powers, **32**, [539]
building preservation notice, powers as to, **46**, [643]–[644]
buildings of special architectural or historical interest, listing, **46**, [641]
See also **listed building**
capacity, **32**, [539]
capital gains tax exemption, **42**, [1420]
charges, making, **32**, [539]
charitable purposes, body for, **42**, [465]
committees, **32**, [551]
companies, power to form, **32**, [544]
conservation area—
designating, **46**, [712]
grants and loans for, **46**, [719]
designation order by, **32**, [387]
documents of, **32**, [551]
duties of, **32**, [539]
endowments, power to accept, **32**, [214]
entry, powers of—
damage caused by, **32**, [545]
recording purposes, for, **32**, [545]
establishment of, **32**, [538]
financial provisions, **32**, [547]
foreign monuments and buildings, functions, **32**, [540]
gardens of historic interest. *See* **gardens**
generally, **32**, [1]

Historic Buildings and Ancient Monuments Commission for England—*contd*
grants by—
acquisition, for, **32**, [211]
preservation, for, **32**, [206]
information, giving, **32**, [551]
intangible assets, exploitation of, **32**, [541]
loans for preservation of buildings, etc, by, **32**, [206]
London, listed building enforcement notice in, **46**, [710]
members—
appointment, **32**, [551]
remuneration, **32**, [551]
tenure of office, **32**, [551]
ministerial functions, exercising, **32**, [543], [734]
monuments partly situated in England, functions relating to, **32**, [546]
proceedings, **32**, [551]
protected wrecks, assistance in relation to, **32**, [542]
scheduled monuments—
consultation, **32**, [323]
powers of entry, **32**, [330]
staff of, **32**, [551]
stamp duty reserve tax exemption, **41**, [183]
status of, **32**, [551]
tax exemption, **44(1)**, [366]
town scheme, grants for repair of buildings in, **46**, [721]–[722]
urgent works to preserve building, and, **46**, [696]
vesting of redundant building in, **14**, 1054–6

Historic House Museums
meaning, **25(2)**, [603]
vesting of, on abolition of GLC, **25(2)**, [603]

HIV
meaning, **28**, [495]
periodical reports, **30**, [505], [509]
testing kits and services—
meaning, **28**, [495]
offences as to supplying, **28**, [495]
penalties for supplying, **28**, [495]

holding company
accounts—
company's own, **8**, 633
group. *See* **group accounts**
amendment of definitions, **8**, 599
meaning, **8**, 596–7
membership of, **8**, 122–3
references to, **8**, 926–7
subsidiary as member of—
authorised dealer in securities, acting as—
prohibition not applying, **8(1)**, [219]
third parties, protection of, **8(1)**, [220]
companies not limited by shares, provisions applying to, **8(1)**, [221]
employer's right of recovery under pension scheme or employees' share scheme, disregarding, **8(1)**, [218]

holding company—*contd*

subsidiary as member of—*contd*

nominees, provisions applying to,
8(1), [222]

personal representative or trustee, acting
as, **8(1)**, [216]–[218]

prohibition, **8(1)**, [214]

residual interest under pension scheme or
employees' share scheme, disregarding,
8(1), [217]

shares acquired before prohibition
applicable, **8(1)**, [215]

holidays

statement as to, in terms etc of employment,
16, [99]

young persons, removal of restrictions,
16, [156]

Holy Communion

mode of administering, **14**, 44–5

persons admitted to, **14**, 773

Home Guard

pensions and grants, **3**, [1443]

home information packs

authenticity of documents, duty to endure,
24, [339]

contents of, **24**, [344]

copy, provision on request, **24**, [337]

conditions, compliance with, **24**, [338]

definitions, **24**, [355], [356]

duty to have, **24**, [336]

enforcement of provisions—

authorities, **24**, [347]

body corporate, offences by, **24**, [397]

offences, **24**, [350]

penalty charge notices, **24**, [349], [437]

private action, right of, **24**, [351]

estate agent acting for seller, duties of,
24, [340]

exceptions, power to provide for, **24**, [342]

grants, **24**, [354]

home condition report—

meaning, **24**, [345]

register of, **24**, [346]

regulations for, **24**, [345]

Isles of Scilly, provisions applying, **24**, [414]

market, references to, **24**, [330]

meaning, **24**, [329]

offences, **24**, [350]

penalty charge notices, **24**, [349], [437]

private action, right of, **24**, [351]

production, power to require, **24**, [348]

residential property—

marketing, responsibility for, **24**, [332]

meaning, **24**, [329]

not available with vacant possession,
exemption from provisions, **24**, [341]

seller, responsibility of, **24**, [334]

responsible person, duties of, **24**, [335]

sub-divided buildings, for, **24**, [352]

suspension of duties relating to, **24**, [343]

home loss payment

person displaced from dwelling, for—

advance payment, **9**, [328]

amount, **9**, [327]–[328]

appurtenances, **9**, [327]

authority liable to make, **9**, [325]

caravan dweller, **9**, [329]

claim for, **9**, [328]

compulsory acquisition of interest, **9**, [325]

conditions, **9**, [325], [328]

death of person without claiming, **9**, [328]

improvement, for, **9**, [325]

interests and rights applicable, **9**, [325]

landlord obtaining possession, by, **9**, [328]

limitation of action, **9**, [328]

market value, determination, **9**, [327]

Northern Ireland, **9**, [459]

possession order, on making of, **9**, [325]

right to, **9**, [325]

several persons, **9**, [328]

spouses with occupation rights, **9**, [326]

time for making, **9**, [328]

homeless persons. *See also* **displaced persons**

accommodation—

available for occupation, meaning,
23, [489]

priority for. *See* priority need *below*

reasonableness of continuing to occupy,
23, [490]

suitability of, **23**, [521]

tenancy of, **22**, [427]

advisory services, duty of local housing
authority to provide, **23**, [492]

associated persons, meaning, **23**, [491]

asylum-seekers, **23**, [499]

change of circumstances, notification of,
23, [526]

co-operation between authorities, **23**, [524]

children, cases involving, **23**, [525]

discharge of functions—

applicable provisions, **23**, [517]

local housing authority, by, **23**, [518]

out-of-area placements, **23**, [519]

private landlord, arrangements with,
23, [520]

domestic or other violence, fear of, **23**, [490]

duties of housing authority—

housing register, abolition of duty to
maintain, **23**, [634]

minimum period subject to, abolition of,
23, [632]

strategy for—

formulation of, **23**, [628]

meaning, **23**, [630]

provisions of, **23**, [630]

false statements, **23**, [526]

guidance by Secretary of State as to, **23**, [495]

homelessness—

assistance—

application for, **23**, [496]

persons not eligible for, **23**, [498]

inquiries into, **23**, [497]

intentionally becoming, **23**, [503], [504]

threat of, **23**, [508]

homeless persons—*contd*

homelessness—*contd*

meaning, **23**, [488]

review of, by local housing authority, **23**, [629]

strategy for—

formulation of, **23**, [628]

meaning, **23**, [628]

provisions of, **23**, [630]

threatened—

duties as to, **23**, [507]

inquiries as to, **23**, [497]

intentional homelessness, **23**, [508]

meaning, **23**, [488]

information—

provision by Secretary of State, **23**, [500]

withholding, **23**, [526]

interim duty to accommodate, **23**, [501]

private landlord, arrangements with, **23**, [520]

local connection, meaning, **23**, [510]

priority need for accommodation—

order by Minister as to, **23**, [502]

persons having, **23**, [502]

persons not intentionally homeless—

advice and assistance, **23**, [505]

duty to, **23**, [506]

property of, protection of, **23**, [522], [523]

referral to another authority—

conditions for, **23**, [509]

duty of notified authority, **23**, [511]

Scotland, cases arising in, **23**, [512]

regulations and orders, **23**, [527]

review of decisions—

appeal on point of law, **23**, [515], [516]

procedure, **23**, [514]

right to request, **23**, [513]

transitional provisions, **23**, [528]

voluntary organisations concerned with, assistance for, **23**, [493], [494]

Wales, in, **23**, [635]

Homes and Communities Agency

advice, education and training, provision of, **24**, [578]

agent, acting as, **24**, [582]

derelict land, in respect of, **24**, [566]

regeneration and development, in respect of, **24**, [565]

borrowing powers—

currency of, **24**, [559]

European Investment Bank, from, **24**, [559]

financial limits, **24**, [562]

Secretary of State—

guarantees by, **24**, [561]

loans from, **24**, [559], [560]

short-term management, for, **24**, [559]

business, carrying on, **24**, [567]

committees, **24**, [852]

community services, provision of, **24**, [569]

companies, forming or acquiring interests in, **24**, [568]

delegation of functions, **24**, [852]

determinations by, **23**, [400]

approval, requiring, **23**, [401]

Homes and Communities Agency—*contd*

establishment of, **24**, [540]

financial assistance, power to give, **24**, [558]

financial provision, **24**, [852]

former Commission for the New Towns functions, role as to, **24**, [591]

general determinations, **22**, [843]

guidance from, **24**, [579]

information services, **24**, [577]

interpretation of provisions, **24**, [596], [597]

land—

acquired—

main powers as to, **24**, [550]

statutory undertakers, powers, **24**, [551]

acquisition by agreement, **24**, [854]

acquisition of, **24**, [548]

burial grounds, powers as to, **24**, [857]

compulsory acquisition, **24**, [853]

consecrated, powers as to, **24**, [857]

derelict, as agent in respect of, **24**, [566]

development powers, **24**, [545]

disposal, **24**, [549]

easements etc, power to override, **24**, [855]

effective use of, powers, **24**, [545]

entry and survey, power of, **24**, [556], [557]

housing, provision of, **24**, [544]

power to deal with, **24**, [547]

provision of, **24**, [544]

public rights of way, power to extinguish, **24**, [856]

regeneration powers, **24**, [545]

statutory undertakers—

extension or modification or functions, **24**, [860]

extinguishment or removal powers, **24**, [858]

notice to carry out works, **24**, [859]

obligations, relieving of, **24**, [861]

orders and directions, **24**, [862]

Landlord and Tenant Act 1987, exclusion of, **22**, [771]

landlord's interest, acquiring, **22**, [828]

local government involvement, **24**, [583]

local planning authority, as, **24**, [554]

members, **24**, [852]

notices, **24**, [594]

objects of, **24**, [541]

other persons acting with, **24**, [582]

planning—

designation order—

consultation on, **24**, [552]

contents of, **24**, [553]

draft, **24**, [552]

permitted purposes, **24**, [552]

power of Secretary of State to make, **24**, [552]

local involvement, statement of, **24**, [554]

regional, **24**, [555]

powers of—

borrowing—

currency of, **24**, [559]

European Investment Bank, from, **24**, [559]

financial limits, **24**, [562]

Homes and Communities Agency—*contd*
powers of—*contd*
borrowing—*contd*
guarantees by Secretary of State,
24, [561]
Secretary of State, from, **24**, [559], [560]
short-term management, for, **24**, [559]
charge, to, **24**, [563]
companies, to form or acquire interests in,
24, [568]
dealing with land. *See* land *above*
exercise of, **24**, [543]
financial assistance, to give, **24**, [558]
infrastructure, as to, **24**, [546]
land, regeneration, development or effective
use of, **24**, [545]
principal, **24**, [542]
specific, **24**, [543]
procedure, **24**, [852]
property, rights and liabilities, transfer to—
Commission for the New Towns, of—
interim arrangements, **24**, [592]
scheme for, **24**, [590], [864]
taxation, **24**, [865]
Housing Corporation, of—
interim arrangements, **24**, [605]
scheme for, **24**, [604], [864]
taxation, **24**, [865]
transitional arrangements, **24**, [606]
new towns development corporation, of,
24, [591]
regional development agency, of, scheme
for, **24**, [590], [864]
taxation, **24**, [865]
Urban Regeneration Agency, of—
interim arrangements, **24**, [592]
scheme for, **24**, [590], [864]
taxation, **24**, [865]
registered providers—
enforcement notice, notification of,
24, [761]
penalty notice, notification of, **24**, [771]
Regulator of Social Housing—
co-operation with, **24**, [644]
directions from, **24**, [645]
reports and accounts, **24**, [852]
Secretary of State—
consents, **24**, [587]
directions by, **24**, [586]
guarantees by, **24**, [561]
guidance from, **24**, [585]
loans from, **24**, [559], [560]
social housing—
assistance, recovery of—
determinations, **24**, [573]
interest on, **24**, [572]
power of, **24**, [571]
successors in title, from, **24**, [572]
disposals, financial assistance in respect of,
24, [574]
duties as to, **24**, [570]
information, supply of, **24**, [575]
low cost rental accommodation, provision
of, **24**, [570]

Homes and Communities Agency—*contd*
social housing—*contd*
Regulator of Social Housing, co-operation
with, **24**, [576]
staff, **24**, [852]
subsidiaries, control of, **24**, [580]
support services, provision of, **24**, [584]
surplus funds, directions as to, **24**, [564]
urban development corporation, agency
arrangements with, **24**, [581]
validity of transactions by, **24**, [593]

homeworker
additional household expenses, exemption
from tax liability, **44(2)**, [321]

homicide
corporate—
armed forces, application of provisions to,
12(4), [300]
conviction, publicising, **12(4)**, [298]
convictions for offences and under health
and safety legislation, **12(4)**, [307]
criminal procedure and evidence,
12(4), [303]
Crown bodies, no immunity from
prosecution, **12(4)**, [299]
exclusions from relevant duty of care—
child-protection functions, **12(4)**, [295]
emergency, in response to, **12(4)**, [294]
exclusively public function, in exercise
of, **12(4)**, [291]
military activities, **12(4)**, [292]
policing and law enforcement, in respect
of, **12(4)**, [293]
probation functions, **12(4)**, [295]
public policy decisions, **12(4)**, [291]
statutory inspections, **12(4)**, [291]
extension of offence to other
organisations, **12(4)**, [309]
Government departments, list of,
12(4), [318]
power to amend, **12(4)**, [310]
interpretation, **12(4)**, [313]
no individual liability for, **12(4)**, [306]
offence, **12(4)**, [289]
partnerships, application of provisions to,
12(4), [302]
police forces, application of provisions to,
12(4), [301]
relevant duty of care—
exclusions. *See* exclusions from relevant
duty of care *above*
gross breach, factors for jury,
12(4), [296]
meaning, **12(4)**, [290]
power to extend provisions, **12(4)**, [311]
remedy of breach, order for,
12(4), [297]
Scotland, offence in, **12(4)**, [289]
sentencing, **12(4)**, [303]
transfer of functions, proceedings in case
of, **12(4)**, [304]
domestic homicide review, **12(4)**, [6]

homosexual act
armed forces, members of, **12(2)**, [239], [240]
merchant ships, on, **12(2)**, [239], [240]
premises resorted to, **12(1)**, [378]

Hong Kong
British citizenship. *See* **citizenship**
British overseas territories citizenship,
exclusion of, **31**, [369]
British sovereignty, ending of—
adaptation of law on, **7(2)**, [766]
date of, **7(2)**, [764]
diplomatic privilege following, **7(2)**, [766]
general note, **7(2)**, [350]
nationality, effect on, **7(2)**, [766]
nationals of, status, **31**, [180]
probate, provisions applied, **18**, [506]

Hong Kong Economic and Trade Office
application of provisions to, **10**, [1127]
exemptions and reliefs, **10**, [1129]
general note, **10**, [1]
legal proceedings, **10**, [1129]
premises and archives, **10**, [1129]
privileges and immunities, **10**, [1129]

Hong Kong overseas public servants
meaning, **33(1)**, [539]
payments under Orders in Council,
33(1), [541]
pension supplements, **33(1)**, [540]

honours. *See also* **peerage**
abuse in connection with grant of, **33(1)**, [15]

hop-pickers
byelaws as to, **35(1)**, [172]

hops
male plants, requirement to destroy, **1(2)**, [51]
marketing scheme, power to amend,
1(1), [490]
metrication, adaptation to, **1(2)**, [52]
seedless, production of, **1(2)**, [51]

Horley
general provisions, **25(2)**, [339]
parish council, **25(2)**, [338]
part transferred to Surrey, **25(2)**, [338]

Horniman Museum
vesting on abolition of GLC, **25(2)**, [604]

horse
damage to, by dogs, **2**, [352]
diseases. *See* **diseases of animals**
docked, restriction on landing, **2**, [277]
docking, meaning, **2**, [278]
drinking fountains for, **35(1)**, [93]
export—
certification for, **2**, [498]
enforcement of provisions, **2**, [499]
injury on board ship, **2**, [496]
marking animals for, **2**, [495]
restrictions on, **2**, [490]

horse—*contd*
export—*contd*
thoroughbreds, **2**, [497]
farrier. *See* **farrier**
furious riding of, **36**, [222]
long-distance routes, riding on, **36**, [633]
meaning, **2**, [278], [548]; **36**, [1381]; **37**, [96]
pony. *See* **pony**
riding establishments. *See* **riding**
establishment
riding or leading, right of way when, **37**, [89]
road side margins for, **36**, [1074]
slaughter—
examination, on, **2**, [494]
injured on ship, where, **2**, [496]
street offences, **36**, [385]
summary of provisions, **2**, [140]

horse racecourse. *See also* **betting (track)**
approval by Levy Board, **5(1)**, [23]
bets. *See* **betting**
pool betting. *See* **pool betting**
totalisator on, financing, **5(1)**, [23]

horse riding
horse, meaning, **6**, [458]
protective headgear, young riders—
Northern Ireland provisions, **6**, [459]
regulations, **6**, [457]
requirement, **6**, [456]
road, meaning, **6**, [458]

horse-drawn vehicles
brakes on, regulation of, **37**, [667]

Horserace Betting Levy Board
appeals—
costs, **5(1)**, [16]
determinations, against, **5(1)**, [29]
approval of racecourse by, **5(1)**, [23]
Bookmakers' Committee—
constitution of, **5(1)**, [7]
schemes for, **5(1)**, [8]
composition of, **5(1)**, [5]
determination of schemes by, **5(1)**, [14]
establishment, **5(1)**, [5]
functions, **5(1)**, [5]
information to, disclosure by Commissioners
for HM Revenue and Customs, **13**, [561]
levy. *See under* **bookmaker**
members—
appointment, **5(1)**, [5], [19]
government-appointed, exercise of
functions, **5(1)**, [25]
remuneration, **5(1)**, [5]
terms of office, **5(1)**, [5]
powers and duties, **5(1)**, [6]
powers transferred to, **5(1)**, [24]
procedure, regulation of, **5(1)**, [5]
property, rights and liabilities, transfer scheme
for—
accounts, **5(1)**, [276]
ancillary powers, **5(1)**, [276]
certificate of title, **5(1)**, [276]
coming into force, **5(1)**, [349]

Horserace Betting Levy Board—*contd*
property, rights and liabilities, transfer scheme
for—*contd*
consultations and consent, **5(1)**, [276]
content of, **5(1)**, [276]
direction for, **5(1)**, [248]
information and assistance as to, **5(1)**, [276]
modification, **5(1)**, [276]
tax provisions, **5(1)**, [250]
transfer of undertakings, **5(1)**, [276]
status of, **5(1)**, [5]

Horserace Betting Levy System
abolition—
consequential amendments, **5(1)**, [277]
order for, **5(1)**, [247]

Horserace Totalisator Board. *See* **Totalisator Board**

Horticultural Development Council
power to dissolve, **1(2)**, [734]

horticultural produce. *See also* **horticulture**
co-operative activities—
grants in respect of, **1(1)**, [555]
promotion of, **1(1)**, [555], [659]
containers, meaning, **1(1)**, [600]
Council. *See* **Central Council for Agricultural and Horticultural Co-operation**
Food from Britain. *See* **Food from Britain**
fresh—
authorised officer—
obstruction of, **1(1)**, [592]
regrading by, **1(1)**, [590]
entry on premises, powers, **1(1)**, [590]
grades—
duties as to, **1(1)**, [589]
EEC rules, **1(1)**, [588]
label—
indication by, **1(1)**, [588]
meaning, **1(1)**, [600]
offences in connection with—
act of another, due to, **1(1)**, [595]
commission of offence by another,
leading to, **1(1)**, [593]
corporations, by, **1(1)**, [596]
defences in proceedings, **1(1)**, [594]
generally, **1(1)**, [591]
mistake, pleading, **1(1)**, [595]
movement, prohibiting, **1(2)**, [385]
meaning, **1(1)**, [600]
provisions applying, **1(1)**, [598]
regulations and orders, **1(1)**, [599]
sale, restrictions on, **1(1)**, [589]
samples, power to take, **1(1)**, [590]
stalls, etc, sale from, **1(1)**, [590]
London—
empty containers—
licence for keeping, **25(1)**, [619]
meaning, **25(1)**, [614]
local authority, trading by, **25(1)**, [621]
market area—
entry of premises, **25(1)**, [620]

horticultural produce—*contd*
London—*contd*
market area—*contd*
leasing of accommodation in,
25(1), [617]
meaning, **25(1)**, [614]
market storage facilities—
acquisition of land for, **25(1)**, [607],
[615]
buildings, erection etc, for, **25(1)**, [616]
byelaws, **25(1)**, [608], [616]
charges for use of, **25(1)**, [616]
provision of, **25(1)**, [606]
sufficiency, certification of, **25(1)**, [618]
marketing—
grants. *See also* **agricultural marketing**
Northern Ireland, extension of provisions
to, **1(2)**, [184]
provision for, **1(2)**, [519]
meaning, **1(1)**, [276], [662]
(London), **25(1)**, [605]
metrication, adaptation to, **1(2)**, [52]
movement, control of—
consents to—
authorised officer, by, **1(2)**, [385]
circumstances, change of, **1(2)**, [386]
interpretation, **1(2)**, [3]
offences, **1(2)**, [387], [388]
power of, **1(2)**, [384]
price support, annual report, **1(2)**, [527]
sales on commission—
advice note by consignor, **1(1)**, [274]
agent appointed for purposes of,
1(1), [276]
buying by salesmen, **1(1)**, [274]
offences and penalties, **1(1)**, [274]
particulars to be given to owner,
1(1), [274]
theft of, **12(1)**, [556]

horticultural society
rules, registration of, **19(1)**, [336]

horticulture
bank loans, grants respecting, **1(1)**, [662]
chemicals used in. *See* **agriculture**
heavy oil used in, repayment of duty on,
13, [841], [857], [869], [898]
horticultural—
produce, meaning, **13**, [866]
producer, meaning, **13**, [841]
horticultural business—
bank guarantees, grants as to, **1(1)**, [662]
meaning, **1(1)**, [662]
improvement scheme, grants under, false
statement to obtain, **1(1)**, [665]
produce. *See* **horticultural produce**

hosepipes
restriction or prohibition of use, **49**, [863]

hospital
accommodation—
part payment for, **30**, [995], [1253]
private practice, use for, **30**, [475], [1073]

hospital—*contd*
  charges, recovery of, **30**, [995]
  complaints procedure, **30**, [498]
  corrupt election to, **14**, 47–8
  definition, **40(1)**, [33]
  extra-parochial service at, **14**, 654
  independent—
    clinic, **35(2)**, [281]
    listed services, **35(2)**, [281]
    meaning, **35(2)**, [281]
    medical agency, **35(2)**, [281]
    registration and regulation. *See* **care**
      establishments and agencies
  infected person—
    detention in, **35(1)**, [479]
    removal to, **35(1)**, [478]
  marriage in, **14**, 654–5
  meaning, **35(1)**, [452], [514]; **35(2)**, [281]
  medical examinations, payments for,
    30, [1042]
  notifiable disease—
    in, **35(1)**, [452]
    inmate of common lodging house with,
      removal to, **35(1)**, [482]
    person dying in, with, provisions as to,
      35(1), [484]
  officers, superannuation, **30**, [1041]
  pay beds, provisions on, **30**, [483]
  person admitted to, protection of property,
    40(1), [23]
  premises, causing nuisance or disturbance
    on—
    HSS premises, **12(4)**, [574]
    offence, **12(4)**, [533]
    removal of persons, power of, **12(4)**, [534]
      guidance, **12(4)**, [535]
  teaching, special trustees, **30**, [1018], [1276]
  university, special trustees, **30**, [1018], [1276]
  use, sale of poisons for, **28**, [253]
  voluntary—
    Charity Commissioners—
      part paying patients, provision for,
        30, [416]
      rules, power to make, **30**, [418]
      trusts, protection of, **30**, [417]
    committee of management, **30**, [414]
    funds, application of, **30**, [416]–[418]
    meaning, **30**, [414]
    paying patients in—
      accommodation for, **30**, [415]
      charges, **30**, [415]
      part payment by, **30**, [416]
    trusts, protection of, **30**, [417]

Hospital for Sick Children
  Peter Pan, continuing right to royalties,
    11(1), [1169], [1181]

hostage-taking
  extradition, **12(1)**, [767]
  extradition proceedings, **18**, [774], [845]
  imprisonment, **12(1)**, [765]
  institution of proceedings, **12(1)**, [766]
  offence of, **12(1)**, [765]

hostel
  London—
    entry by authorised officer, **25(2)**, [461]
    exemption for certain purposes,
      25(2), [463]
    inspection, **25(2)**, [461]
    meaning, **25(2)**, [455]
    notice to be exhibited, **25(2)**, [458]
    offences and penalties, **25(2)**, [458]
    overcrowding—
      appeal against notice of, **25(2)**, [457]
      evidence in proceedings, **25(2)**, [462]
      notice to occupier etc, **25(2)**, [456],
        [460]
  meaning, **22**, [494]; **23**, [410]
  protection from eviction, exclusion from,
    21, [665]
  provision by Corporation, **22**, [488]

hotel. *See also* **inn; innkeeper; tourism**
  development grant—
    enforcement of conditions, **47**, [114]
    information, Boards calling for, **47**, [114]
    offences by bodies corporate, **47**, [114]
    premises, entry and inspection, **47**, [114]
  industrial buildings allowance—
    balancing event, **43(1)**, [896]
    exclusions, **43(1)**, [856]
    qualifying for, **43(1)**, [858]
  loss of damage to guest's property, making
    good, **26(2)**, [450]
  meaning, **19(3)**, [366]
  proprietor, duties of, **19(3)**, [366]
  summary of provisions, **19(3)**, [349]

hours. *See* **working hours**

house. *See also* **accommodation; dwelling**
house; housing
  acquisition of land for, **22**, [18]
  bathroom, requirement to provide, **22**, [58]
  charge on. *See* **charging order**
  cleansing before demolition, **22**, [244]
  condemned, use for temporary
    accommodation, **22**, [258]
  control order. *See* **house in multiple**
    occupation
  Crown property, Building Act applied,
    35(1), [609]
  defective. *See* **defective housing**
  disposal of—
    avoidance of, **22**, [52]
    compulsory disposals, **22**, [78]
      meaning, **22**, [48]
    consent of Minister, **22**, [51]
    covenants terminated on, **22**, [49]
    deferred resale agreements, treatment of,
      22, [47]
    matrimonial order for, **22**, [46]
    options, treatment of, **22**, [50]
    without consent, avoidance of, **22**, [52]

house—*contd*
 disposal of—*contd*
  See also **dwelling-house** (right to buy)
 disposal of, by local authority—
  charge on the premises—
   approved lending institutions for,
    22, [41]
   approved purposes, **22**, [41]
   liability to repay discount, **22**, [41]
   priority of, **22**, [41]
  consents required, **22**, [37]
  covenants and conditions, **22**, [36]
  discount, repayment, **22**, [39]
  exempted disposals, **22**, [46]
  general powers, **22**, [35]
  letting on secure tenancy, where, **22**, [51]
  levy on, **23**, [183]
  National Parks etc, in, restriction on,
   22, [44]
  relevant disposals, **22**, [45]
  requirement to co-operate, **22**, [38]
  restrictions on, **22**, [44]
  sale etc of, right of first refusal, **22**, [42]
   consideration payable, **22**, [43]
  transitional provisions, **23**, [184]
 erection, minimum standards in, **22**, [58]
 first-time buyers—
  assistance to—
   advances by Minister for, **22**, [322]
   forms of, **22**, [323]
   minimum loan for purposes of, **22**, [323]
   qualifying conditions, **22**, [323]
   winding up of scheme, **23**, [43]
  recognised lending institutions—
   advances to, by Minister, **22**, [322]
   indemnity to, **22**, [326]
   meaning, **22**, [324], [391]
   terms of advances, **22**, [326]
  recognised savings institutions—
   meaning, **22**, [325]
   savings with, as condition for assistance,
    22, [323]
 flats, conversion into, **22**, [410]
 food storage accommodation in—
  notice requiring—
   appeal against, **35(1)**, [593], [626]
   local authority, given by, **35(1)**, [593]
 land for, sale or lease of, **22**, [34]
 licensing of—
  licences—
   application for, **24**, [268]
   conditions, **24**, [271], [426]
   decisions regarding, appeals against,
    24, [275], [429]
   duration, **24**, [272]
   electronic form, in, **24**, [393]
   general requirements, **24**, [272]
   grant of, **24**, [269]
    requirements before, **24**, [427]
   holders of, tests for fitness as, **24**, [270]
   procedural requirements regarding,
    24, [275], [427]
   refusal of, **24**, [269]
   register of, **24**, [378]
   revocation, **24**, [274], [428]

house—*contd*
 licensing of—*contd*
  licences—*contd*
   satisfactory manager, tests verifying,
    24, [270]
   variation, **24**, [273], [428]
  local housing authority, by, **24**, [260]
  offences—
   generally, **24**, [276]
   unlicensed house, operating, **24**, [276]
   rent repayment orders, **24**, [277],
    [278]
    terminating tenancies, restriction on,
     24, [279]
  requirement for, **24**, [266]
  temporary exemption from, **24**, [267]
 local authority, sale etc of—
  early disposal—
   home improvements increasing value,
    disregarding, **22**, [40]
   repayment of discount, **22**, [39]
  power of, **22**, [35]
 management. *See* **management (housing)**
 meaning, **22**, [62], [203], [335], [494];
  24, [280]; **35(1)**, [18]
 minimum standards, **22**, [58]
 more than one authorities' district, in, **22**, [3]
 multiple occupation. *See* **house in multiple**
  occupation
 name of street, painting on, **35(1)**, [6], [22],
  [66], [97]
 numbering, **35(1)**, [6], [7]
 overcrowding. *See* **overcrowding**
 owner, meaning, **22**, [234]
 part of—
  acquiring authority, required to purchase
   whole, **9**, [403]
  no requirement to sell, **9**, [53]
  proposal for compulsory acquisition,
   determination of material detriment,
   9, [360]
 prefabs, provisions applied to, **22**, [59]
 provision of—
  county council, by. *See* **county council**
  environmental considerations, **22**, [407]
  methods of, **22**, [10]
 purchase, assistance in, **22**, [26]
 reinstatement. *See* **reinstatement grant**
 repairs—
  grants. *See* **repairs**
  secure tenant, by. *See* **secure tenancy**
 right to buy. *See* **dwelling-house**
 rights of possession, overriding, **46**, [506]
 service charge. *See* **service charge**
 services, powers as to, **23**, [42]
 shared ownership. *See* **dwelling house**
 situated in more than one district, **22**, [3]
 small dwellings. *See* **small dwellings**
 subsidence, compensation, **22**, [563]
 subsidy. *See* **housing subsidy**
 survey and examination, **22**, [60]
 unfit. *See* **unfit house**
 unfit for human habitation. *See* **unfit house**
 water supply to, **35(1)**, [550]
 welfare provisions, **23**, [182]

house—*contd*
  yards and passages to, paving and drainage,
    35(1), [606]

house agent. *See* **accommodation agency;**
  estate agent

house doves
  built-up areas, in, reduction of numbers,
    35(1), [269]

house in multiple occupation
  amenities, provision of, **22**, [214]
  buildings not being, **24**, [441]
  compulsory purchase order, effect of,
    22, [395]
  declarations—
    revocation of, **24**, [402]
    tests for making, **24**, [401]
  fire hazard—
    fire and rescue authorities, local housing
      authority's consultation with regarding,
      24, [196]
    repeal of certain provisions, **24**, [234]
  flats, converted blocks of, **24**, [403]
  housing conditions, consideration of,
    22, [395]
  licensing of—
    additional—
      designation of areas subject to, **24**, [237]
        confirmation or approval of, **24**, [239]
        duration of, **24**, [241]
        further considerations, **24**, [238]
        notification requirements, **24**, [240]
        proof of, **24**, [395]
        review of, **24**, [241]
        revocation of, **24**, [241]
    fitness as licence holder, tests for, **24**, [247]
    generally, **24**, [236]
    licence—
      appeals, **24**, [252], [429]
      application for, **24**, [244]
      conditions of, **24**, [248], [426]
      duration, **24**, [249]
      electronic form, in, **24**, [393]
      general requirements, **24**, [249]
      grant of, **24**, [245]
        requirements before, **24**, [427]
      refusal of, **24**, [245]
      register of, **24**, [378]
      revocation of, **24**, [251], [428]
      variation of, **24**, [250], [428]
    management arrangements, tests for fitness
      of, **24**, [247]
    offences—
      generally, **24**, [253]
      rent repayment orders, **24**, [254], [255]
      unlicensed HMO, operating,
      24, [253]–[256]
    requirement for, **24**, [242]
      temporary exemption from, **24**, [243]
    suitability, tests as to, **24**, [246]
    transitional arrangements regarding,
      24, [257]

house in multiple occupation—*contd*
  licensing of—*contd*
    unlicensed—
      meaning, **24**, [254]
      operating, **24**, [253]
        terminating tenancies, restriction on,
        24, [256]
      rent repayment orders, **24**, [254], [255]
  main residence, persons treated as occupying
    main premises as, **24**, [405]
  management—
    codes of practice as to, approval of,
      24, [379]
    regulations, **24**, [380]
  meaning, **22**, [340]; **24**, [258], [400]
  number of occupants, calculation of, **24**, [410]
  overcrowding. *See* **overcrowding**
  repealed provisions, **23**, [412]
  significant use condition, **24**, [406]
  single household, persons not forming,
    24, [404]
  sole use condition, **24**, [406]
  suitability as, tests for, **24**, [246]

House of Commons
  bankruptcy, disqualification for, **4(2)**, [514]
    Northern Ireland or Scotland, order in,
      4(2), [517], [595]
  certificate of vacancy, **32**, [944], [948]
  clergy, removal of disqualification from,
    32, [986]
  clerk assistant, **32**, [877]
  commission—
    chairman of, **32**, [954]
    delegation of functions, **32**, [954]
    dissolution of Parliament, on, **32**, [954]
    establishment of, **32**, [848]
    financial provisions, **32**, [951]
    functions of, **32**, [950]
    House Departments, dealing with,
      32, [952]
    incorporation, **32**, [954]
    members of, **32**, [949], [954]
    proceedings, **32**, [954]
  constitution, provision for, **32**, [848]
  copyright provisions, **11(1)**, [998]
  Corporate Officer—
    establishment, **32**, [971]
    gifts to, **32**, [975]
    joint departments—
      establishment of, **32**, [1009A]
      functions, in connection with,
      32, [1009B]
      staff employment, **32**, [1009C]
        application of enactments,
        32, [1009E]
      staff transfers, **32**, [1009G]
    powers of, **32**, [971]
    schemes for transfer of property to,
      32, [972], [974]
    seal, **32**, [971]
    staff transferred to, **32**, [973]
    status of, **32**, [971]
    transitional provisions, **32**, [978]

House of Commons—*contd*
  costs—
    Bills other than private, for, **32**, [1003]
    consequential and transitional provisions,
      32, [1005], [1009]
    disputed, assessment of—
      application for, **32**, [991]
      certificate of responsible officer,
        32, [996]
      complaints about report, **32**, [995]
      duty of, **32**, [992]–[993]
      responsible officer, report to, **32**, [994]
    meaning, **32**, [1006]
    private Bill—
      Court of Referees, evidence to,
        32, [1004]
      petitioner opposing, award to, **32**, [998]
      promoter, award to, **32**, [997]
    representatives' charges, authorisation of,
      32, [990]
    taxing officer—
      appointment, **32**, [969]
      complaints about report, **32**, [995]
      duty to assess, **32**, [992]–[993]
      fees, **32**, [1001]
      functions of, **32**, [1001]
      responsible officer, report to, **32**, [994]
      vexatious proceedings, assessment and
        certification for, **32**, [1000]
    vexatious proceedings—
      assessment, application for, **32**, [999]
      duty to assess and certify costs,
        32, [1000]
      petitioner opposing private Bill,
        32, [998]
      private Bill, promoter of, **32**, [997]
  court of appeal, as, **32**, [848]
  disqualification from—
    armed forces, members of, **32**, [928], [930]
    bodies, members of, **32**, [939]–[941]
    Chiltern Hundreds, steward of, **32**, [931]
    Civil Service, members of, **32**, [928]
    clergy, removal of disqualification, **32**, [986]
    constituencies, for, **32**, [941]
    effect of, **32**, [933], [962]
    generally, **32**, [848]
    hereditary peers, removal of
      disqualification, **32**, [980]
    Irish House of Commons, **32**, [869]
    judicial office, holder of, **32**, [928], [938]
    Manor of Northstead, steward of, **32**, [931]
    obligation to accept office, relaxation of,
      32, [935]
    other legislature, member of, **32**, [928]
    peers, **32**, [848]
    police force, members of, **32**, [928]
    power to amend provisions, **32**, [932]
    prisoners, of, **32**, [961]
    Privy Council, jurisdiction of, **32**, [934]
    relief, provision for, **32**, [933]
    Speaker, notice given to, **32**, [944]
    United Parliament, from, **32**, [868]–[870]
  election petition, trying, **32**, [848]
  House Departments, **32**, [952]

House of Commons—*contd*
  joint departments—
    establishment of, **32**, [1009A]
    functions of, **32**, [1009A]
    staff employment, **32**, [1009C]
      application of enactments, **32**, [1009E]
    staff transfers, **32**, [1009G]
  member of, freedom from arrest for debt,
    13, [2]
  Members' fund—
    accounts, **32**, [909]
    establishment of, **32**, [848], [907]
    hardship, alleviation of, **33(1)**, [187]
    payments from, **32**, [907], [911], [957]
    property, trustees accepting, **32**, [909],
      [918]
    rate of payment, **32**, [958]
    report on, **32**, [909]
    special hardship, cases of, **32**, [917]
    sums paid into, **32**, [907], [916]
    Treasury, contributions of, **32**, [922], [959]
    trustees—
      accounts, **32**, [909]
      custodian, **32**, [909]
      documents, custody of, **32**, [912]
      investment powers, **32**, [924]
      management powers, **32**, [912]
      managing, **32**, [908]
      number of, **32**, [908]
      procedure of, **32**, [908]
      property, accepting, **32**, [909], [918]
    widowers of past members, payment to,
      32, [915]
  members' pensions. *See* **parliamentary
    pensions**
  membership, **32**, [848]
  ministerial offices, **32**, [929], [942]
  Northern Ireland, provisions as to. *See*
    Northern Ireland
  oath of allegiance, **32**, [848]
  parliamentary constituencies, **32**, [848]
  pensions. *See* **parliamentary pensions**
  privilege, application of insolvency provisions
    irrespective of, **4(2)**, [516]
  privileges, **32**, [848]
  recess, writs issued during, **32**, [943]
  resolution, temporary statutory effect of,
    42, [1], [63], [67]
  road traffic near, regulation of, **36**, [224]
  Speaker—
    Commission, chairman of, **32**, [949], [954]
    dependants' pensions, **33(1)**, [152]
    Deputy—
      acts, validity of, **32**, [874]
      Commission, acting on, **32**, [955]
      office, not to appoint to, **32**, [875]
    disqualifying office, notification of,
      32, [945]
    election, approbation of, **32**, [848]
    members, powers exercised by, **32**, [946]
    pension of, **33(1)**, [151]
    writ, issue during recess, **32**, [943]
  staff—
    data processing, **7(1)**, [536]
    disability discrimination, **7(1)**, [441]

House of Commons—*contd*
staff—*contd*
employment of, **16**, [490], [588], [845]
equal pay, **16**, [28]
political office, meaning, **16**, [29]
national minimum wage, **16**, [946]
racial discrimination, **7(1)**, [200]
sex discrimination, **7(1)**, [120]
witnesses, examination on oath, **32**, [892]

House of Lords
appeal to—
cases in which lying, **11(2)**, [101]
dissolution or prorogation of Parliament, during, **11(2)**, [105]–[106]
exclusion of cases, **11(2)**, [108]
form of, **11(2)**, [102]
generally, **11(2)**, [1]
hearing, **11(2)**, [105]–[106]
High Court, from—
certificate, grant of, **11(2)**, [226], [229]
leave, grant of, **11(2)**, [227]
provisions, **11(2)**, [228]
leave for, **11(2)**, [176]
Lords of Appeal, number of, **11(2)**, [103]
Northern Ireland, from. *See* **Northern Ireland**
procedure, **11(2)**, [107]
assessors, **11(2)**, [137]
bankruptcy, disqualification for, **4(2)**, [514]
Northern Ireland or Scotland, order in, **4(2)**, [517], [595]
Bill—
consent not required for, **32**, [848]
Money. *See* Money Bill *below*
Clerk of the Parliaments—
appointment of, **32**, [871]
clerks appointed by, **32**, [872]–[873]
committees, oaths administered to witnesses before, **32**, [878]
consent, Bills not requiring, **32**, [848]
Corporate Officer—
establishment, **32**, [970]
gifts to, **32**, [975]
joint departments—
establishment of, **32**, [1009A]
functions, in connection with, **32**, [1009B]
staff employment, **32**, [1009C]
application of enactments, **32**, [1009E]
staff transfers, **32**, [1009G]
powers of, **32**, [970]
schemes for transfer of property to, **32**, [972], [974]
seal, **32**, [970]
staff transferred to, **32**, [973]
status of, **32**, [970]
transitional provisions, **32**, [978]
costs—
Bills other than private, for, **32**, [1003]
consequential and transitional provisions, **32**, [1005], [1009]
disputed, assessment of—
application for, **32**, [991]

House of Lords—*contd*
costs—*contd*
disputed, assessment of—*contd*
certificate of responsible officer, **32**, [996]
complaints about report, **32**, [995]
duty of, **32**, [992]–[993]
responsible officer, report to, **32**, [994]
meaning, **32**, [1006]
private Bill—
Court of Referees, evidence to, **32**, [1004]
petitioner opposing, award to, **32**, [998]
promoter, award to, **32**, [997]
representatives' charges, authorisation of, **32**, [990]
taxing officer—
appointment, **32**, [969]
complaints about report, **32**, [995]
duty to assess, **32**, [992]–[993]
fees, **32**, [1001]
functions of, **32**, [1001]
responsible officer, report to, **32**, [994]
vexatious proceedings, assessment and certification for, **32**, [1000]
vexatious proceedings—
assessment, application for, **32**, [999]
duty to assess and certify costs, **32**, [1000]
petitioner opposing private Bill, **32**, [998]
private Bill, promoter of, **32**, [997]
costs, recovery of, **11(2)**, [238]
court of record, as, **32**, [848]
court-martial, appeal on. *See* **court-martial**
criminal appeal to. *See* **criminal appeal**
disqualifications, **32**, [848]
exclusion from, **32**, [848]
extradition appeal to—
Category 1 territories, as to—
composition for, **18**, [792]
leave for, **18**, [792]
powers of, **18**, [793]
where lying, **18**, [792]
withdrawal of warrant pending, **18**, [804]
Category 2 territories, as to—
composition for, **18**, [878]
leave for, **18**, [878]
powers of, **18**, [879]
where lying, **18**, [878]
withdrawal of request pending, **18**, [890]
hereditary peers—
exclusion from—
exemptions, **32**, [979]
generally, **32**, [848], [978]
number exempted from, **32**, [979]
Weatherill amendment, **32**, [848]
joint departments—
establishment of, **32**, [1009A]
functions of, **32**, [1009A]
staff employment, **32**, [1009C]
application of enactments, **32**, [1009E]
staff transfers, **32**, [1009G]
judicial capacity, **32**, [848]

House of Lords—*contd*
Lords of Appeal in Ordinary—
appointment of, **11(2)**, [104]
attendance of, **11(2)**, [103]
Baron, becoming, **11(2)**, [104]
Judicial Committee of Privy Council, on,
11(2), [104]
number of, **11(2)**, [217]
precedence, **11(2)**, [680]
prorogation, taking seat during,
11(2), [119]
qualifications of, **11(2)**, [104]
relevant service, **11(2)**, [588], [603]
retirement—
age, **11(2)**, [197]
incapacity, **11(2)**, [275]
salary, **11(2)**, [274]
vacancies, **11(2)**, [191]
Lords Spiritual, **32**, [848]
Lords Temporal, **32**, [848]
membership of, **32**, [848]
ministerial salaries, **10**, [707]
Money Bill—
certificate of Speaker as to, **32**, [898], [900]
meaning, **32**, [898]
powers on, **32**, [848], [898]
restriction of powers, **32**, [899], [920]
oath of allegiance, **32**, [848]
office-holders, allowances, **10**, [707]
parliamentary standards provisions not
affecting, **32(S)**, Parliament 3
peerage claims, jurisdiction as to, **32**, [848]
precedence in. *See* **peerage**
privilege, application of insolvency provisions
irrespective of, **4(2)**, [516]
reference on point of law after acquittal,
12(1), [611]
review of sentencing, functions and powers,
12(1), [1082], [1113]
Speakership, amendment of provisions,
11(3), [472], [601]
staff—
data processing, **7(1)**, [536]
disability discrimination, **7(1)**, [441]
employment of, **16**, [489], [588], [844]
equal pay, **16**, [28]
political office, meaning, **16**, [29]
national minimum wage, **16**, [945]
racial discrimination, **7(1)**, [201]
sex discrimination, **7(1)**, [121]

house of residence
acquisition of land for, **14**, 397
adverse possession, penalty for, **14**, 114
building—
incumbent, powers of, **14**, 382–3
notices, **14**, 384–5
certification by bishop, **14**, 389
colleges lending for, **14**, 62, 97
contracts for letting, **14**, 114
conveyance of land for—
grant, form of, **14**, 243
life tenant, by, **14**, 245–6
person under disability, by, **14**, 242
powers, **14**, 240–1

house of residence—*contd*
conveyance of land for—*contd*
public body, by, **14**, 245
purchase money, payment of, **14**, 241–2
curate—
circumstances of residence, **14**, 116
delivery up by, **14**, 118–19
direction to reside in, **14**, 117–18
division of, **14**, 383–4
episcopal—
alteration, stating reason for, **14**, 149
church commissioners dealing with,
14, 409
contents of, dealing with, **14**, 150
freehold fixtures, **14**, 150
insurance of, **14**, 151
sale of, **14**, 149
taking down or rebuilding, **14**, 149
trust money, use of, **14**, 150
exchange, powers of, **14**, 379–81, 516
exercise of powers, notice of, **14**, 384–5
extension of, land for, **14**, 397
fixtures, articles deemed to be, **14**, 150
garden etc. not to be leased, **14**, 160–1
guild church vicar, for, **14**, 456
historical etc. interest, of, **14**, 410–11
improvement of, **14**, 382–3
interest-free loan for, **14**, 97
leased, not to be, **14**, 160–1
leasehold enfranchisement, **14**, 298–301
new, erecting or purchasing, **14**, 382–3
non-residence in—
exemption from penalties, **14**, 104
licence for—
grant of, **14**, 107
grantor, death or removal of, **14**, 108
petition for, **14**, 106
registry, filed in, **14**, 109
revocation of, **14**, 109
sovereign, transmitted to, **14**, 109–10
validity of, **14**, 109–10
penalty for, **14**, 102–3, 113
sequestration of living, **14**, 110–11
temporary, privileges for, **14**, 104–5
tenant occupying, **14**, 115
parochial church council, exercise of powers
of, **14**, 390
parsonage. *See* **parsonage**
patron lending money for, **14**, 97
pensions board, provision by, **14**, 535–6,
652–3
possession on dissolution of benefice, **14**, 998
power to purchase, **14**, 431
purchase money, application of, **14**, 151–2
Queen Anne's Bounty, purchased from,
14, 103
rectory. *See* **rectory**
return of land granted for, **14**, 520
reversionary interests, acquisition of,
14, 299–300
sale of—
conveyance, **14**, 388–9
corporation, by, **14**, 151–2
Crown patronage, in, **14**, 392
exchange regarded as, **14**, 379–81, 516

house of residence—*contd*
  sale of—*contd*
    interim income from, **14**, 387
    moneys, application of, **14**, 381, 385–6
    person under disability, by, **14**, 151–2
    power of, **14**, 379–81
    rules for, **14**, 390–1
  sharing agreements, **14**, 676
  stamp duty exemptions, **14**, 62
  surveyor's report on, **14**, 382
  unfit, **14**, 103
  widow continuing in, **14**, 104

house to house collection
  charitable purposes, meaning, **5(2)**, [492]
  chief office of police—
    certificate granted by, **5(2)**, [483]
    delegation of functions by, **5(2)**, [489]
    metropolitan police district, in, **5(2)**, [491]
  collector—
    acting without licence, **5(2)**, [483]
    badges—
      requirement for, **5(2)**, [486]
      unauthorised use, **5(2)**, [487]
    conduct etc, regulation of, **5(2)**, [486]
    name etc to be given on demand,
      5(2), [488]
  licence—
    appeals, **5(2)**, [484]
    application for, **5(2)**, [484]
    exemption, **5(2)**, [485]
    licensing authority, meaning, **5(2)**, [484]
    period of, **5(2)**, [484]
    refusal or revocation, **5(2)**, [484]
    requirement for, **5(2)**, [483]
  local character, of, **5(2)**, [483]
  meaning, **5(2)**, [492]
  offences and penalties, **5(2)**, [490], [494]
  promoter—
    conduct, regulation of, **5(2)**, [486]
    meaning, **5(2)**, [492]
  regulations, **5(2)**, [486]
  wide area, over, **5(2)**, [485]

houseboat
  certificates—
    conditions as to, **38(1)**, [607]
    general terms of, **38(1)**, [606], [621]–[623]
  City of London, in—
    byelaws, **25(1)**, [187]
    meaning, **25(1)**, [187]
    registration, **25(1)**, [187]
  right to use, **44(1)**, [12]

household article
  meaning, **35(1)**, [262]
  verminous—
    disinfection or destruction, **35(1)**, [262]
    sale, etc, prohibition of, **35(1)**, [262]

housing
  agricultural workers. *See* **agricultural
    workers**

housing—*contd*
  allocation—
    applications for housing accommodation,
      23, [479]
    eligible persons, to, **23**, [478]
    provisions not applying, where, **23**, [477]
    regulations, **23**, [485]
    rules as to, **22**, [96]; **23**, [476]
    scheme—
      in accordance with, **23**, [480]
      information about, **23**, [481]
      priorities, **23**, [480]
      proposal for, **23**, [480]
  appropriate national authority, meaning,
    24, [407]
  armed forces—
    loans to, **3**, [1261]
    married persons, for, **3**, [374]
    security of tenure. *See* **civil interests of
      servicemen**
  body corporate, offences by, **24**, [397]
  definitions, **24**, [355], [356], [408], [409]
  disabled facilities grant. *See* **disabled facilities
    grant**
  forestry workers. *See* **agricultural workers;
    forestry workers**
  forms, power to prescribe, **24**, [390]
  heating. *See* **heat, supply of** (London)
  hill farming. *See* **hill farming**
  home information packs. *See* **home
    information packs**
  London—
    advances reserve fund—
      application of, **25(1)**, [959]
      setting up, **25(1)**, [959]
    City, in. *See* **London, City of**
    heating. *See* **heat, supply of**
    land held for, transfer of, **25(1)**, [698]
    low-lying land, building on, **25(1)**, [176],
      [177]
    safety in the home, promotion of,
      25(1), [643]
  management. *See* **management (housing)**
  notices, power to dispense with, **24**, [391]
  orders and regulations, **24**, [396]
  rent to mortgage terms, acquisition on, stamp
    duty, **41**, [223]
  safety in the home, promotion of,
    25(1), [643]
  service of documents, **24**, [392]
  social. *See* **social housing**
  summary of provisions, **20**, [1]
  sustainability certificate—
    authorised assessors, **24**, [820]
    breach of duty, penalty charge notice,
      24, [824], [868]
    disclosure, **24**, [828]
    enforcement authorities, **24**, [822]
    enforcement officers, offences relating to,
      24, [825]
    extension of provisions, power of, **24**, [830]
    grants, **24**, [826]
    interim, **24**, [818]
    interpretation, **24**, [831], [832]
    meaning, **24**, [818]

housing—*contd*
  sustainability certificate—*contd*
    none, statement to effect of—
      production, power to require, **24**, [823]
      residential property, supply for, **24**, [818]
    production, power to require, **24**, [823]
    register of, **24**, [821]
    regulations, general power to make, **24**, [829]
    residential property, supply for, **24**, [818]
    suspension of duties, **24**, [827]
    sustainability, meaning, **24**, [819]
  time-sharing, change of use, as, **25(2)**, [530]
  underground rooms. *See* **underground room**

housing action area
  acquisition of land in, **22**, [213]
  amenities in, improving, **22**, [214]
  area ceasing to be, effect of, **23**, [36]
  assistance to persons in, **22**, [214]
  cessation of power to declare, **23**, [36]
  compulsory improvement. *See* **improvement**
  contributions by Secretary of State, **22**, [215]
  declaration of, **22**, [209]
    cancellation of, **22**, [211]
    duration of, **22**, [209]
    resolution for, **22**, [209]
  duration of, **22**, [209], [221]
  environmental works, **22**, [214]
  exclusion of land from, **22**, [220]
  general powers of housing authority, **22**, [213]
  guidance as to, by Minister, **22**, [209]
  housing accommodation—
    inclusion of, in, **22**, [217]
    meaning, **22**, [222]
    ownership etc, changes in, **22**, [217]
  incorporation of other land in, **22**, [212]
  information as to, publication of, **22**, [216]
  land in—
    acquisition of, **22**, [213]
    activities on, **22**, [213]
    exclusion from, **22**, [220]
  local planning authority for, **46**, [258]
  notification of changes as to—
    acknowledgment of, **22**, [217]
    contents of, **22**, [218]
    default in giving, penalty, **22**, [219]
    exceptions from, **22**, [217]
    form of, **22**, [218]
    matters to be notified, **22**, [217]
  requirements for, **22**, [209]
  resolution—
    declaring area to be, **22**, [209]
    effect of, **22**, [230], [231]
    termination of area as, **22**, [220]
  Secretary of State—
    contribution by, **22**, [215]
    functions of, **22**, [211]
    statement etc to be sent to, **22**, [211]
  steps to be taken in, **22**, [210]
  termination of, **22**, [220]

housing action trust
  accounts, **22**, [926]

housing action trust—*contd*
  achievement of objects, dissolution on, **22**, [874]
  agency agreements, **22**, [873]
  annual report, **22**, [926]
  area. *See* **housing action trust area**
  assured tenancy, exclusion of, **22**, [913]
  audit, **22**, [926]
  body corporate, as, **22**, [849]
  borrowing by, **22**, [925]
  Chairman and Deputy Chairman, **22**, [923]
  debt, assumed, **22**, [925]
  disposals by—
    land, of, **22**, [853]
    repayment of discount other than right to buy, **24**, [365]
  dissolution, **22**, [874]
  establishment of, **22**, [849]
  financial assistance, power to give, **22**, [857]
  financial duties, **22**, [925]
  financial limits, **22**, [925]
  financial year, **22**, [924]
  functions—
    agency agreement as to, **22**, [873]
    directions as to, **22**, [858]
    highways, as to, **22**, [856]
    local housing authority, of, **22**, [852]
    public health, as to, **22**, [855]
    transfer of, **22**, [859]
  general powers of, **22**, [850]
  government grants, **22**, [925]
  grants and loans, accounts of, **22**, [925]
  housing authority, as, **22**, [852]
  instruments, **22**, [923]
  introductory tenancy. *See* **introductory tenancy**
  land—
    acquisition of, **22**, [863], [929]
    burial grounds, acquisition of, **22**, [930]
    compulsory purchase of, **22**, [863]
    consecrated, acquisition of, **22**, [930]
    displacement of persons, **22**, [930]
    disposal of—
      charges, obligation to repay, **22**, [932]
      compulsory, **22**, [932]
      consent for, **22**, [865]
      consent, without, **22**, [866]
      deferred resale agreements, treatment of, **22**, [932]
      discount, repayment or early disposal, **22**, [932]
      exempted, **22**, [932]
      first refusal, right of, **22**, [932]
      meaning, **22**, [865]
      options, treatment of, **22**, [932]
      relevant, **22**, [932]
      secure tenancy, subject to, **22**, [869]
        order, transfer by, **22**, [870]
      subsequent, consent for, **22**, [867]
      tenants, legal assistance for, **22**, [868]
    easements, overriding, **22**, [930]
    open spaces, **22**, [930]
    provisions applied, **25(2)**, [540]
    public rights of way, extinguishment of, **22**, [930]

housing action trust—*contd*
land—*contd*
rights, acquisition of, **22**, [931]
rights over, extinguishment, **22**, [930]
statutory undertakers, rights vested in, **22**, [930]
telegraphic lines across, **22**, [930]
transfers to, **22**, [860], [861]
vesting orders, **22**, [862], [927], [928]
Landlord and Tenant Act 1987, exemption from, **22**, [771]
landlord authority, as, **22**, [105]
meaning, **22**, [4]
meetings, **22**, [923]
members—
appointment of, **22**, [923]
removal from office, **22**, [923]
remuneration, **22**, [923]
notices, service of, **22**, [877]
objects of, **22**, [850]
planning authority, as, **22**, [854]
planning control, **22**, [853]
proceedings, **22**, [923]
proposals, publication of, **22**, [851]
rents—
charge of, **22**, [871]
increase where tenancy not secure, **22**, [872]
reasonable, charge of, **22**, [871]
sale of houses at discount, stamp duty, **41**, [138], [145]
staff, **22**, [923]
status of, **22**, [849]
surplus funds, **22**, [925]
tenancy—
rents, **22**, [871]
status of, **22**, [828]
Treasury guarantees, **22**, [925]
urban development corporation, supply of goods and services, **22**, [875]

housing action trust area
designation—
consultation, **22**, [848]
land in, **22**, [847]
matters taken into account, **22**, [847]
order, **22**, [847]
local authority, supply of information by, **22**, [876]
proposals, publicity for, **22**, [848]

housing association
agreements with, variation or termination, **22**, [470]
allocation of housing, rules, **22**, [96]
arrangements under repealed Acts, **22**, [472], [497], [565]
assistance to—
local authorities, by, **22**, [468]
restricted to registered associations, **22**, [469]
assured tenancy, exclusion of, **22**, [913]
charitable, disposal of houses by, **22**, [459]
contributions from Minister, **22**, [500]

housing association—*contd*
co-operative—
approval of, **44(1)**, [327]
claim, provisions on, **44(1)**, [327]
meaning, **22**, [5], [455]
provisions not applicable to, **22**, [99]
secure tenancy provisions not applying to, **22**, [99]
defective dwelling, repurchase of, **22**, [363]
See further **defective housing**
disposals by, **42**, [1355]
expressions defined, **22**, [467], [474]
formation—
financial assistance, **22**, [486]
local authority, by, **22**, [468]
fully mutual, meaning, **22**, [5], [455]
furniture for tenants of, **22**, [469]
gifts to—
capital gains tax relief, **42**, [1402]
inheritance tax relief, **42**, [546]
grant-aided land—
dispositions, control of, **22**, [458]
meaning, **22**, [496]
payments creating, **22**, [496]
grants—
discontinued, **23**, [375]
formation etc, for, **22**, [486]
general determinations, **22**, [843]
local authorities, by, **22**, [468]
recovery of, **22**, [842]
Relevant Authority, by, **22**, [840]
revenue deficit, for, **22**, [841]
tax relief, for affording, **22**, [844]
unification of conditions, **22**, [501]
hostels. *See* **hostel**
houses—
disposal of—
avoidance of, **22**, [460]
charity, by, **22**, [459]
consent required, **22**, [459]
control by Housing Corporation, **22**, [458]
discount given, where, **22**, [459]
exceptions from control, **22**, [459]
without consent, **22**, [460]
housing activities, meaning, **22**, [494]
Housing Corporation, disposals between, **42**, [1354]
improvement or re-development by—
disturbance payment to displaced person, **9**, [341]
home loss payment, to person displaced by, **9**, [325]
investment by friendly societies in, **19(1)**, [494], [926]
land—
acquisition of, **22**, [462]
county councils, provision by, **22**, [462]
housing management agreement, subject to, **22**, [471]
Landlord and Tenant Act 1987, exemption from, **22**, [771]
landlord, as—
protection, tenancy excluded from, **21**, [535]

housing association—*contd*
  landlord, as—*contd*
    restricted contract, exclusion of, **21**, [540]
  landlord's interest, acquiring, **22**, [828]
  lease granted by, exclusion from
    enfranchisement or extension, **21**, [347]
  loans to—
    Housing Corporation, by, **22**, [479]
    land securing, disposal of, **22**, [503]
    purposes of, **22**, [480]
  management, financial assistance, **22**, [486]
  meaning, **9**, [367]; **21**, [589]; **22**, [5], [455]
  Northern Ireland, disposals by, **42**, [1356]
  registered, meaning, **22**, [457]
  registration, references to, **22**, [5]
  Relevant Authority for, **22**, [7]
  rent—
    book, false entry in, **21**, [594]
    excess, recovery of, **21**, [594]
    increase without notice to quit, **21**, [593]
    limit—
      determination of, **21**, [591], [596]
      meaning, **21**, [591]
      previous tenancy, statement of rent
        under, **21**, [595]
      rates, addition of, **21**, [591]
    registrable, to be, **21**, [591]
    registration, provisions applying to,
      21, [591]
      See also **rent registration**
    rental periods, adjustment between,
      21, [596]
  repealed enactments, arrangements under,
    22, [472], [498], [565]
  residual subsidies, commutation of payments,
    23, [376]
  revenue deficit incurred by, **22**, [841]
  sale of house at discount, stamp duty,
    41, [138], [145]
  Scilly Isles, provisions applied, **22**, [492]
  self-build society, meaning, **22**, [5], [455]
  service of notices on, **22**, [196]
  shared ownership lease, stamp duty, **41**, [134],
    [139]
  subsidies—
    administrative provisions, **22**, [499]
    agreements with local authority, **22**, [498]
    amount, determination of, **22**, [499]
    building schemes, for, **22**, [502]
    disposal of dwelling, effect of, **22**, [499]
    factors governing, **22**, [499]
    improvement schemes, for, **22**, [502]
    residual, entitlement to, **22**, [499]
  summary of provisions, **20**, [1]
  tax provisions, **22**, [844]
  tenancy—
    ceasing to be, **22**, [831]
    conditions, **22**, [828]
    meaning, **21**, [589]; **22**, [828]
    regulated tenancy, conversion to, **21**, [592],
      [650]
    special regimes, removal of, **22**, [828]
    status of, **22**, [828]
  tenants, security of tenure. *See* **secure
    tenancy**

housing association—*contd*
  unregistered—
    lease, grant of, **22**, [459]
    meaning, **22**, [457]

housing authority
  local. *See* **local housing authority**
  meaning, **22**, [4], [551]
  offences, prosecuting, **22**, [547]
  sale of house at discount, stamp duty,
    41, [138], [145]

housing benefit
  administering authority—
    information, supply of—
      between, **40(1)**, [627]
      by, **40(1)**, [626]
      to, **40(1)**, [625]
    subsidy to—
      annual orders, no requirement for,
        40(1), [661]
      calculation of, **40(1)**, [656]
      definitions, **40(1)**, [662]
      expenditure, financing, **40(1)**, [660]
      joint arrangements, financing,
        40(1), [659]
      meaning, **40(1)**, [655]
      payment of, **40(1)**, [657]
      rent rebate, **40(1)**, [658]
      Secretary of State, by, **40(1)**, [655]
  administration, **23**, [554]; **40(1)**, [505]
  Audit Commission, interaction with,
    40(1), [647]
    directions, **40(1)**, [649], [650]
    investigation, powers of, **40(1)**, [646]
    reports on, **40(1)**, [645], [648]
  appropriate maximum, **40(1)**, [372]
  arrangements for, **40(1)**, [642]
  attainment of standards—
    enforcement determinations, **40(1)**, [653],
      [654]
    enforcement notices, **40(1)**, [652]
    information about, **40(1)**, [651]
  Auditor General for Wales, inspection reports
    by, **40(2)**, [530]
  claims and reviews, determination of,
    40(2), [183]
  decisions, revisions and appeals, **40(2)**, [294]
  determinations, validation of, **40(2)**, [192]
  discretionary housing payments—
    grants towards cost of, **40(2)**, [285]
    power to make, **40(2)**, [284]
  entitlement to, **40(1)**, [371]
  errors, revisions and appeals, **40(2)**, [294]
  eviction for anti-social behaviour, etc, loss
    on, **40(2)**, [525]
  eviction, loss following—
    conditions, **40(1)**, [373]
    couples, conditions for entitlement of,
      40(1), [376]
    information provision, **40(1)**, [377]
    pilot schemes, **40(1)**, [378]
    regulations, **40(1)**, [375]
    relevant orders for possession, **40(1)**, [374]
  income-related benefit, as, **40(1)**, [367]

housing benefit—*contd*
  information—
    failure to provide, **40(2)**, [294]
    supply of, expedited claims, **40(1)**, [635]
  landlords and agents, power to require
    information from, **40(1)**, [634]
  local authority scheme, availability of,
    40(1), [367]
  overpayment of, **40(1)**, [579]
    colluding employees, **40(1)**, [606]
    penalty as alternative to prosecution,
      40(1), [605], [606]
  payment, arrangements for, **40(2)**, [529]
  persons taking up employment, for,
    40(2), [526]–[528]
  rebates and allowances, **40(1)**, [642]
  rent officers, functions of, **23**, [426]
  rent officers, supply of information by,
    40(1), [628]
  representative organisations, consultation
    with, **40(1)**, [705]
  scheme, **40(1)**, [642]
  state pension credit, attaining qualifying age
    for, **40(1)**, [385]
  suspension, provision for, **40(2)**, [184], [294]
  termination for failure to furnish
    information, **40(2)**, [294]
  transitional provisions and savings, **40(2)**, [10]
  under-occupation, measures to reduce,
    40(2), [252]

housing conditions
  assessing, new system for, **24**, [187]
  category 1 hazard—
    demolition orders. *See* **demolition order**
    emergency remedial action—
      appeals relating to, **24**, [231]
      charging for, local authority's powers as
        to, **24**, [232], [233]
      expenses, recovery of, **24**, [228]
      local housing authority taking, **24**, [226]
      meaning, **24**, [226]
      notice of, **24**, [227]
    enforcement action—
      duties, operation of, **24**, [192]
      local authority to take, **24**, [191]
      meaning, **24**, [191]
    existence of, local housing authority to
      inspect, **24**, [190]
    hazard awareness notices—
      local authority's duty to serve, **24**, [214]
        charging for, **24**, [232], [233]
      meaning, **24**, [214]
    improvement notices—
      appeals, **24**, [204], [419]
      breach of covenant, saving for rights
        arising from, **24**, [224]
      change in person liable to comply with,
        24, [205]
      contents of, **24**, [199]
      duty of local housing authority to
        serve, **24**, [197]
      enforcement action—
        court's powers to order, **24**, [221],
          [222]

housing conditions—*contd*
  category 1 hazard—*contd*
    improvement notices—*contd*
      enforcement action—*contd*
        expenses, recovery of, **24**, [425]
        local authority's power to charge for,
          24, [232], [233]
        management orders, effect of,
          24, [225]
        power to take, **24**, [217]
        taken by agreement, **24**, [423]
        taken without agreement, **24**, [424]
      failure to comply with, **24**, [216]
      local land charges, as, **24**, [223]
      meaning, **24**, [197]
      operation of, **24**, [201]
      revocation and variation of, **24**, [202]
        notices relating to, service of,
          24, [418]
      service of, **24**, [204], [417]
      suspension of, **24**, [200]
        review of, **24**, [203]
    meaning, **24**, [188]
    prohibition orders—
      appeals, **24**, [213], [422]
      breach of covenant, saving for rights
        arising from, **24**, [224]
      compliance with—
        failure, **24**, [218]
        possession of premises, recovery of,
          24, [219]
      contents of, **24**, [208]
      emergency—
        contents of, **24**, [230]
        local authority's power to make,
          24, [229]
        meaning, **24**, [229]
      enforcement action—
        court's powers to order, **24**, [221],
          [222]
        local authority's power to charge for,
          24, [232], [233]
        management orders, effect of,
          24, [225]
      lease, determination or variation of,
        24, [220]
      local housing authority, duty to make,
        24, [206]
      local land charges, as, **24**, [223]
      meaning, **24**, [206]
      operation of, **24**, [210]
      revocation and variation of, **24**, [211]
        notices relating to, service of,
          24, [421]
      service of, **24**, [213], [420]
      suspension of, **24**, [209]
        review of, **24**, [212]
    category 2 hazard—
      demolition orders. *See* **demolition order**
      enforcement action—
        power to take, **24**, [193]
        reason for taking, **24**, [194]
      existence of, local housing authority to
        inspect, **24**, [190]

housing conditions—*contd*
  category 2 hazard—*contd*
    hazard awareness notices—
      local authority's power to serve,
      24, [215], [232], [233]
      meaning, **24**, [215]
    improvement notices—
      appeals, **24**, [204], [419]
      breach of covenant, saving for rights
      arising from, **24**, [224]
      change in person liable to comply with,
      24, [205]
      contents of, **24**, [199]
      enforcement action—
        court's powers to order, **24**, [221],
        [222]
        expenses, recovery of, **24**, [425]
        local authority's power to charge for,
        24, [232], [233]
        management orders, effect of,
        24, [225]
        power to take, **24**, [217]
        taken by agreement, **24**, [423]
        taken without agreement, **24**, [424]
      failure to comply with, **24**, [216]
      local land charges, as, **24**, [223]
      meaning, **24**, [198]
      operation of, **24**, [201]
      power of local housing authority to
      serve, **24**, [198]
      revocation and variation of, **24**, [202]
        notices relating to, service of,
        24, [418]
      service of, **24**, [204]
      suspension of, **24**, [200]
        review of, **24**, [203]
    meaning, **24**, [188]
    prohibition orders—
      appeals, **24**, [213], [422]
      breach of covenant, saving for rights
      arising from, **24**, [224]
      compliance with—
        failure, **24**, [218]
        possession of premises, recovery of,
        24, [219]
      contents of, **24**, [208]
      enforcement action—
        court's powers to order, **24**, [221],
        [222]
        local authority's power to charge for,
        24, [232], [233]
        management orders, effect of,
        24, [225]
      lease, determination or variation of,
      24, [220]
      local authority's power to make,
      24, [207]
      local land charges, as, **24**, [223]
      meaning, **24**, [207]
      operation of, **24**, [210]
      revocation and variation of, **24**, [211]
        notices relating to, service of,
        24, [421]
      service of, **24**, [213], [420]

housing conditions—*contd*
  category 2 hazard—*contd*
    prohibition orders—*contd*
      suspension of, **24**, [209]
        review of, **24**, [212]
    fire and rescue authorities, local housing
    authority's consultation with, **24**, [196]
    local housing authority—
      duty to review, **24**, [189]
      enforcement action—
        category 1 hazard—
          duties, **24**, [192]
          taking, **24**, [191]
        category 2 hazard—
          power to take, **24**, [193]
          reason for taking, **24**, [194]
        guidance as to, **24**, [195]
      fire and rescue authorities, consultation
      with, **24**, [196]
      inspections by, **24**, [190]
        guidance as to, **24**, [195]
    prohibition orders—
      compensation, payment of, **22**, [398], [399]
      demolition order, substitution for, **22**, [247]
      house subject to, use for temporary housing
      accommodation, **22**, [258]
      revocation and variation of, compensation
      repayable, **22**, [398], [399]
    reviewed by local housing authority, **24**, [189]
    standards, enforcing, **24**, [187]

housing co-operative
  agreements with housing authority, **22**, [29]
  landlord, as, tenancy not protected, **21**, [536]
  meaning, **22**, [29]
  tenancies, status of, **22**, [828]

Housing Corporation. *See further* **housing
association**
  acquisition of land by, **22**, [487]
  advisory service, provision of, **22**, [478]
  agreements to indemnify lenders, **22**, [484]
  approved persons, register of, **22**, [880]
  control powers over associations, **22**, [458]
  delegation of functions, **24**, [515]
  delegation of functions to, **22**, [845]
  directions to, by Secretary of State, **22**, [477]
  dissolution, **24**, [603]
  dwellings, power to provide or improve,
  22, [488]
  functions—
    general, **22**, [476]
    particular, **22**, [487]–[489]
  grants to housing associations—
    formation and management, for, **22**, [486]
    See further **housing association**
  guarantee of loans by, **22**, [483]
  hostels, provision of, **22**, [488]
  insolvency of registered social landlord. *See*
  registered social landlord
  land—
    acquisition of, **22**, [487]
    clearance and development, **22**, [488]
    disposal of, **22**, [489]

Housing Corporation—*contd*
landlord, as—
protection, tenancy excluded from,
21, [535]
restricted contract, exclusion of, **21**, [540]
lenders, agreement to indemnify, **22**, [484]
loans by—
eligible bodies, **22**, [479]
further, power to make, **22**, [482]
guaranteeing, **22**, [483]
land securing, disposal of, **22**, [503]
made under 1964 Act, **22**, [482], [503]
security for, **22**, [480]
self-build societies, to, **22**, [480]
shared ownership lease, disposal on,
22, [481]
management, powers as to, **22**, [488]
meaning, **22**, [475]
property, rights and liabilities, transfer of—
Homes and Communities Agency, to—
interim arrangements, **24**, [605]
scheme for, **24**, [604], [864]
taxation, **24**, [865]
transitional arrangements, **24**, [606]
regulator, to—
interim arrangements, **24**, [605]
scheme for, **24**, [604], [864]
taxation, **24**, [865]
transitional arrangements, **24**, [606]
public sector authority, as, **22**, [388]
public sector landlord, purchase of interest
of—
approval, **22**, [880]
information etc, as to, **22**, [892]
legal assistance for tenants, **22**, [893]
relevant authority, as, **22**, [475]
rent. *See* **housing association**
sale of house at discount, stamp duty,
41, [138], [145]
Scilly Isles, provisions applied, **22**, [492]
social housing grants by. *See* **registered
social landlord**
tenancies, status of, **22**, [828]
tenant's right to buy from. *See*
dwelling-house
tenant, security of tenure. *See* **secure
tenancy**
transferred tenant, legal assistance for,
22, [868]

Housing for Wales
ceasing to exist, **10**, [1279]
rent. *See* **housing association**
Secretary of State, transfer of functions etc
to, **10**, [1276]
transitional provisions, **10**, [1277]
winding down, **10**, [1278]

housing grants. *See also kinds of grants*
amount of—
landlord's application, determination in case
of, **23**, [585]
maximum, specification of, **23**, [586]
applicant, death of, **23**, [601]
applications for, **23**, [574]

housing grants—*contd*
charities, **23**, [608]
conditions—
cessation of, **23**, [600]
compensation, repayment in case of,
23, [598]
meaning, **23**, [597]
period, meaning, **23**, [597]
power to impose, **23**, [599]
consent of Secretary of State, **23**, [607]
decision on—
approval, **23**, [587]
notification of, **23**, [587]
refusal, **23**, [587]
exemption from tax, **44(3)**, [784]
glebe land, **23**, [608]
improvements, for. *See* **improvement grant**
ineligible applicants, **23**, [575]
means testing of owner-occupier or tenant,
23, [584]
parsonages, **23**, [608]
payment—
applicant ceasing to be entitled before,
23, [593]
carrying out of works, conditions,
23, [590]
contractors employed, condition as to,
23, [591]
contractor, to, **23**, [592]
delayed, **23**, [589]
generally, **23**, [588]
re-calculation, **23**, [595]
reinstatement, for. *See* **reinstatement grant**
repairs for. *See* **repairs**
repayment—
applicant not entitled, where, **23**, [596]
cases of, **23**, [595]
compensation, in case of payment of,
23, [599]
conditions, cessation of, **23**, [600]
social—
bodies other than registered social
landlords, to, **23**, [373], [374]
conditions, **23**, [363]
housing management agreement, land
subject to, **23**, [364]
recovery of, **23**, [372]
reduction, suspension or cancellation of,
23, [372]
superseded, **22**, [444]
tax exemption, **44(1)**, [413]
transitional provisions, **23**, [613]
water supply service pipe, for, **22**, [338]
withholding, **23**, [595]
works—
already begun, restrictions for, **23**, [583]
carrying out, condition of, **23**, [590]
local housing authority carrying out,
23, [602]

housing management bodies
rights of audience of employees of,
11(4), [306]

housing ombudsman
appointment and status, **23**, [551]
communications, privileged, **23**, [551]
determinations by, **23**, [551]
Wales, for. *See* **Social Housing Ombudsman for Wales**

housing order
meaning, **9**, [325]
persons displaced by—
disturbance payment, **9**, [341]
home loss payment, **9**, [325]

Housing Repairs Account
accounting, directions for, **23**, [12]
competitive tendering, accounting for work subject to, **23**, [14]
debits to, **23**, [11]
items referable to property, **23**, [13]
keeping of, **23**, [11]
service charges, treatment of, **23**, [13]
sums to be credited to, **23**, [11]

Housing Revenue Account
appropriation of land, adjustment on, **23**, [52]
balance for 1989–90, **23**, [52]
business plans, **24**, [158]
competitive tendering, accounting for work subject to, **23**, [14]
contributions in respect of land, **23**, [52]
credits to, **23**, [50]
debit balance, duty to prevent, **23**, [10]
debits to, **23**, [51]
dwelling, housing displaced person in, **21**, [419]
information as to state of, **23**, [53]
items referable to property, **23**, [13]
keeping of, **23**, [8]
less than market value, disposal of land at, **23**, [52]
London authorities, transfers between, **23**, [52]
orders amending provisions, **23**, [26]
residual debt subsidy, 1989–90, **23**, [20]
calculation of, **23**, [21]
recoupment of, **23**, [24]
service charges, treatment of, **23**, [13]
statutory provisions, modifying etc, **23**, [53]
subsidy—
agreements to exclude certain authorities or property, **23**, [19]
calculation of, **23**, [16]
credit balance where none payable, **23**, [52]
final decision on, **23**, [18]
negative amounts payable to appropriate person, **23**, [17]
payment of, **23**, [15]
recoupment of, **23**, [24]
welfare services, provision of, **23**, [52]
whole community, amenities shared by, **23**, [52]

housing subsidy
adjustment for, 1989–90, **23**, [22]

housing subsidy—*contd*
development corporation, to—
base amount, **22**, [300]
calculation of, **22**, [301]
claim to be made for, **22**, [298]
costs differential, **22**, [301]
housing account, credited to, **22**, [298]
local contribution differential, **22**, [302]
management agreement, land subject to, **22**, [304]
payment, **22**, [298]
reckonable expenditure for, **22**, [301]
housing association. *See* **housing association**
Housing Revenue Account. *See* **Housing Revenue Account**
local housing authorities, calculation for, **22**, [299]
recoupment in certain cases, **22**, [303]; **23**, [24]
residual debt, 1989–90, **23**, [20]

housing trust
housing management, financial assistance for, **22**, [307]
Landlord and Tenant Act 1987, exemption from, **22**, [771]
landlord, as, tenancy not protected where, **21**, [535], [763]
landlord authority, as, **22**, [105]
landlord's interest, acquiring, **22**, [828]
lease of houses to housing authority, **22**, [463]
legal proceedings, institution of, **22**, [464]
meaning, **22**, [6], [456]
rent. *See* **housing association**
tenancies, status of, **22**, [828]
tenancy ceasing to be, provisions on, **21**, [763]

Housing for Wales
approved persons, register of, **22**, [880]

hover vehicle
use of term, **37**, [804]

hovercraft
Admiralty jurisdiction, **39(2)**, [426]
animals diseases provisions applied, **2**, [549]
application of provisions to, **37**, [312], [804]
approval, for export goods, **13**, [649]
British, meaning, **10**, [1211]
captain, meaning, **49**, [641]
Civil Aviation Act—
application, **4(1)**, [149]
savings under, **4(1)**, [176]
customs and excise provisions, application to, **13**, [591]
dumping at sea by. *See* **pollution** (sea)
entry and search, **13**, [709]
export of goods by, **13**, [649]
forfeiture, **13**, [746]–[748]
maritime liens, law on, **39(2)**, [426]
meaning, **39(2)**, [428]
movement, customs and excise control of, **13**, [605]

hovercraft—*contd*
  oil pollution, application of provisions,
    49, [486]
  Orders in Council, power to make,
    39(2), [425]
  provisions applying to, **39(2)**, [427], [432],
    [987]
  public health provisions, application to,
    35(1), [283]
  smuggling by. *See* **smuggling**
  stores, **13**, [650]
  summary of provisions, **39(2)**, [1]

human cloning
  offence of, **28**, [782]

human fertilisation
  amended provisions, **28(S)**, 85–9
  assisted reproduction—
    agreed fatherhood conditions, **28(S)**, 151
      application of, **28(S)**, 150
      no other person treated as father,
        28(S), 152
    amended provisions, **28(S)**, 206–17
    application of provisions, **28(S)**, 148
    death of husband not providing sperm,
      embryo transferred after, **28(S)**, 154–5
    death of man providing sperm, use of
      sperm or transfer of embryos after,
      28(S), 153
    election as to other parent, late, **28(S)**, 167
    father, meaning—
      agreed fatherhood conditions,
        28(S), 150–2
      interpretation of references, **28(S)**, 168
      woman married at time of treatment,
        where, **28(S)**, 149
    mother, meaning, **28(S)**, 147
    Northern Ireland, provisions in,
      28(S), 223–31
    parent of child, effect of provisions,
      28(S), 164–5
    parental order—
      applicants, **28(S)**, 169
      application for, **28(S)**, 169–70
      regulations, **28(S)**, 171
    parenthood, general note, **28(S)**, 89–90
    persons not treated as father, **28(S)**, 156
    prohibited degrees of relationship,
      28(S), 173
    references to parties to civil partnership,
      meaning of, **28(S)**, 166
    references to parties to marriage, meaning
      of, **28(S)**, 165
    registration of parent, **28(S)**, 208
    relevant register of births, meaning,
      28(S), 167
    Scotland, provisions in, **28(S)**, 219–23
    subsequent civil partnership, legitimation of
      child by, **28(S)**, 212
    woman as other parent—
      agreed female parenthood conditions,
        28(S), 160
      agreement as to, **28(S)**, 158

human fertilisation—*contd*
  assisted reproduction—*contd*
    woman as other parent—*contd*
      egg donation, not to be treated as solely
        due to, **28(S)**, 163
      legitimacy of child, **28(S)**, 161
      no man treated as father, **28(S)**, 161
      parental responsibility, acquisition of,
        28(S), 214
      transfer of embryo after death of civil
        partner or intended female parent,
        28(S), 161–2
      woman in civil partnership at time of
        treatment, **28(S)**, 157
  Authority. *See* **Human Fertilisation and
    Embryology Authority**
  code of practice, **28(S)**, 123
    generally, **28**, [607]
    procedure for approval of, **28**, [608]
  conscientious objection, **28**, [620]
  consent to prosecution, **28**, [624]
  consequential provision, power to make,
    28(S), 145
  directions—
    general, **28**, [605]
    meaning, **28**, [578]
    particular matters, as to, **28**, [606];
      28(S), 121–2
  Directives, reference to, **28**, [57]
  eggs, permitted, **28(S)**, 97
  embryos—
    consent to use of, **28**, [633]
    consent to use or storage of, **28(S)**, 186–98
    crime, keeping and examining in
      connection with, **28**, [625]
    female germ cells—
      meaning, **28**, [581]
      prohibition on use of, **28**, [581]
    human admixed, consent to use or storage
      of, **28(S)**, 186–98
    meaning, **28**, [576]; **28(S)**, 94–5
    organism, exclusion from definition of,
      28(S), 175
    permitted, **28(S)**, 97
    prohibited activities, **28(S)**, 96
    prohibitions in connection with, **28**, [580]
  entry of premises, powers relating to,
    28, [622]
  father—
    deceased, **28**, [764]
    meaning, **28**, [610]
  fertility services, meaning, **28**, [581]
  foetus, prohibition on use of female germ cells
    from, **28**, [581]
  gametes—
    consent to use of, **28**, [633]
    consent to use or storage of, **28(S)**, 186–98
    crime, keeping and examining in
      connection with, **28**, [625]
    donor, parental order in favour of,
      28, [612]
    meaning, **28**, [576]; **28(S)**, 94–5
    prohibitions in connection with, **28**, [582]
  general note, **28**, [1]

human fertilisation—*contd*
  genetic material not of human origin,
    prohibitions, **28(S)**, 98–100
  index of expressions, **28**, [628]
  information—
    authority's register of, **28**, [613]; **28(S)**, 124
    disclosure of—
      consent required for authorisation of,
        28(S), 136
      exceptions, **28(S)**, 137
      justice, in interests of—
        congenital disabilities, **28**, [619]
        generally, **28**, [618]
      medical or other research, for purposes
        of, **28(S)**, 137–9
      restriction on, **28**, [617]; **28(S)**, 133–5
    Registrar General, provided to, **28**, [616]
  licences—
    activities for which granted, **28**, [632]
    applications, **28(S)**, 117
    committees, **28**, [588]
    decisions—
      notification of, **28(S)**, 116–17
      point of law, appeal on, **28(S)**, 121
      procedure for, **28(S)**, 116
      reconsideration—
        procedure, **28(S)**, 120
        right to, **28(S)**, 119
    embryo testing, for, **28(S)**, 182
    general conditions, **28**, [591]; **28(S)**, 106
    grant of, **28**, [598]; **28(S)**, 112
    human application, conditions, **28**, [595],
      [634]
    meaning, **28**, [578]
    non-medical fertility services, for,
      28(S), 183
      activities covered, **28**, [632]
      conditions of, **28**, [593]
      duration, **28**, [632]
      power of Authority to grant, **28**, [590]
    person responsible, **28**, [599]; **28(S)**, 113
    purposes for which activities licensed,
      28(S), 184
    refusal, procedure for, **28**, [601]
    register of, **28**, [614]
    research, for—
      activities covered, **28**, [632]
      amended provisions, **28(S)**, 184
      conditions of, **28**, [596]
      duration, **28**, [632]
      power of Authority to grant, **28**, [590]
      revocation, **28(S)**, 114
    revocation—
      generally, **28**, [600]
      procedure for, **28**, [601]
    scope of, **28(S)**, 106
    sex selection, for, **28(S)**, 183
    storage, for—
      activities covered, **28**, [632]
      amended provisions, **28(S)**, 183
      conditions of, **28**, [594]; **28(S)**, 111
      duration, **28**, [632]
      power of Authority to grant, **28**, [590]
    suspension, power of, **28(S)**, 118
    temporary suspension of, **28**, [604]

human fertilisation—*contd*
  licences—*contd*
    treatment, for—
      activities covered, **28**, [632]
      amended provisions, **28(S)**, 181–2;
        28(S), 107–9
      conditions of, **28**, [592]
      counselling, offer of required as
        condition of, **28(S)**, 200–1
      duration, **28**, [632]
      power of Authority to grant, **28**, [590]
    variation, **28(S)**, 114
      generally, **28**, [600]
      procedure for, **28**, [601]
  mitochondrial donation, **28(S)**, 139
  mother, meaning, **28**, [609]
  Northern Ireland, application of provisions
    to, **28**, [629]
  notices, **28**, [627]
  nuclear DNA, meaning, **28(S)**, 96
  offences, **28**, [623]; **28(S)**, 142–3
  orders, **28(S)**, 146–7
  prosecution, consent to, **28**, [624]
  regulations, **28**, [626]; **28(S)**, 144
  sperm, permitted, **28(S)**, 97
  status—
    dignity or title of honour, succession to
      any, **28**, [611]
    father, meaning, **28**, [610]
    gamete donor, parental order in favour of,
      28, [612]
    mother, meaning, **28**, [609]
    property, devolution of any, **28**, [611]
  third party agreements, **28**, [579]
  treatment services, meaning, **28**, [578]

**Human Fertilisation and Embryology
Authority**. *See also* **human fertilisation**
  accounts, **28**, [584]
  agency arrangements, **28(S)**, 102
  appeals—
    committee, **28(S)**, 119
    Court of Session, to, **28**, [603]
    High Court, to, **28**, [603]
    licence committee, against determination
      of, **28**, [602]
  audit, **28**, [584]
  authority, meaning, **28**, [578]
  committees, **28**, [588]
    delegation to, **28(S)**, 105
    establishment of, **28(S)**, 105
  competent authorities of other EEA states,
    communication with, **28**, [587]
  constitution, **28**, [583]
  Court of Session, appeal to, **28**, [603]
  donor, information to—
    request for information, as to, **28(S)**, 128
    resulting children, as to, **28(S)**, 128–30
  donor-conceived genetic siblings, provision of
    information as to, **28(S)**, 130–1
  employees, powers of, **28**, [621]
  entry, inspection and search, powers of,
    28(S), 141–2, 202–5
  expenses, **28**, [631]
  fees, charging, **28(S)**, 140–1

Human Fertilisation and Embryology Authority—*contd*

functions of—
  additional general, **28(S)**, 101
  contracting out, **28(S)**, 103
  duties in carrying out, **28(S)**, 102
  exercise by others, disclosure of information, **28(S)**, 104
general functions of, **28**, [586]
general note, **28**, [1]
High Court, appeal to, **28**, [603]
information, register of, **28**, [613]; **28(S)**, 124
instruments, **28**, [631]
licence committee—
  appeal against determination of, **28**, [602]
  functions, **28**, [588]
licence. *See* **human fertilisation**
  membership, **28**, [588]
licensing procedure, **28**, [589]
members—
  appointment, **28(S)**, 180
  appointment of, **28**, [631]
  other public authorities, power to assist, **28(S)**, 105
  pensions, **28**, [631]
  powers of, **28**, [621]
  remuneration, **28**, [631]
  tenure of office, **28**, [631]
Parliamentary Commissioner, investigation by, **28**, [631]
powers, **28**, [631]
proceedings, **28**, [631]
request for information to—
  genetic parentage, as to, **28(S)**, 125
  intended spouse, as to, **28(S)**, 126–7
  power to inform donor of, **28(S)**, 128
Secretary of State, reports to, **28**, [585]
serious adverse event—
  duties relating to, **28**, [598]
  meaning, **28**, [578]
  register of, **28**, [615]
serious adverse reaction—
  duties relating to, **28**, [598]
  meaning, **28**, [578]
  register of, **28**, [615]
services, provision of, **28(S)**, 102
staff, **28**, [631]
status, **28**, [631]
supplementary provisions, **28**, [631]
voluntary contact register—
  persons setting up, financial assistance for, **28(S)**, 132
  power to keep, **28(S)**, 131–2

human organs

removal, storage and use of—
  adults lacking capacity to consent, from, **28**, [772]
  appropriate consent for—
    adults, for, **28**, [769]
    children, for, **28**, [768]
  coroners, functions of, **28**, [777]
  donated material, restriction of activities, **28**, [774]
  excepted material, meaning, **28**, [778]

human organs—*contd*

removal, storage and use of—*contd*
  existing anatomical specimens, **28**, [776]
  existing holdings, **28**, [775]
  need for consent, power to dispense with, **28**, [773]
  nominated representatives—
    appointment of, **28**, [770]
    powers of, general or limited, **28**, [770]
  prohibition of activities without consent, **28**, [771]
  scheduled purposes—
    authorisation of activities for, **28**, [767]
    consent, requiring, **28**, [828], [829]
trafficking people for exploitation, **31**, [493]–[494]
transplantation—
  information about operations, requirement of, **28**, [800]
  involving live donor, restriction on, **28**, [799]
  material for, prohibition of commercial dealings in, **28**, [798]
  meaning, **28**, [820]
  preservation for, **28**, [809]

human remains

disposal of, **14**, 1052–3, 1102–3
power to de-accession, **28**, [813]

human reproduction

cloning, offence of, **28**, [742]

human rights

Commission for Equality and Human Rights. *See* **Commission for Equality and Human Rights**
Convention rights—
  abuse of rights, prohibition of, **7(1)**, [592]
  assembly and association, freedom of, **7(1)**, [592]
  death penalty, abolition of, **7(1)**, [594]
  discrimination, prohibition of, **7(1)**, [592]
  education, right to, **7(1)**, [593]
  expression, freedom of, **7(1)**, [581], [592]
  fair trial, right to, **7(1)**, [592]
  forced labour, prohibition of, **7(1)**, [592]
  free elections, right to, **7(1)**, [593]
  generally, **7(1)**, [570]
  interpretation of, **7(1)**, [571]
  liberty and security, right to, **7(1)**, [592]
  life, right to, **7(1)**, [592]
  marry, right to, **7(1)**, [592]
  no punishment without law, **7(1)**, [592]
  political activity of aliens, restrictions on, **7(1)**, [592]
  private and family life, right to respect, **7(1)**, [592]
  property, protection of, **7(1)**, [593]
  slavery, prohibition of, **7(1)**, [592]
  thought, conscience and religion, freedom of, **7(1)**, [582], [592]
  torture, prohibition of, **7(1)**, [592]
  use of restrictions on rights, limitations on, **7(1)**, [592]

human rights—*contd*
derogations from Convention, **7(1)**, [583], [585]
European Court of—
appointment to, **7(1)**, [587]
judges of, **7(1)**, [587]
judicial pensions, **7(1)**, [597]
extradition proceedings, consideration in, **18**, [781], [850]
interpretation provisions, **7(1)**, [590]
legislation—
incompatibility with Convention right—
Crown right to intervene, **7(1)**, [574]
declaration of, **7(1)**, [573]
remedial action, power to take, **7(1)**, [579], [595]
interpretation of, **7(1)**, [572]
statements of compatibility with Convention, **7(1)**, [588]
orders under 1998 Act, **7(1)**, [589]
proceedings, appropriate tribunal, **18**, [955]
public authorities—
acts incompatible with Convention right—
judicial acts, **7(1)**, [578]
judicial remedies, **7(1)**, [577]
proceedings against, **7(1)**, [576]
unlawful, **7(1)**, [575]
reservations to Convention, **7(1)**, [584], [596]
periodic review of, **7(1)**, [586]
safeguard for existing, **7(1)**, [580]
Scotland, action in, **7(1)**, [752]
social care, provision of, **40(2)**, [596]
summary of provisions, **7(1)**, [1]

human tissue
activities involving, regulation of—
conduct, requirements for, **28**, [789]
licence—
applications, **28**, [831]
breach of requirement, **28**, [791]
change of circumstances, **28**, [790]
characteristics of, **28**, [831]
conditions of, **28**, [831]
criminal justice purposes, things done for, **28**, [805]
decisions, procedure, **28**, [831]
designated individual, duty of, **28**, [784]
notification of decisions, **28**, [831]
permission for purpose of conditions, **28**, [831]
person to whom applying, **28**, [783]
point of law, appeal on, **28**, [788]
power to grant, **28**, [831]
pre-conditions to grant, **28**, [831]
reconsideration of decision, right to, **28**, [785]
requirement, **28**, [782]
revocation, power of, **28**, [831]
suspension, power of, **28**, [831]
variation, power of, **28**, [831]
religious relics, provisions applying to, **28**, [806]
storage of relevant material, **28**, [782]
anatomical examination, carrying out of, **28**, [807]

human tissue—*contd*
anatomical specimen—
former, possession away from licensed premises, **28**, [797]
meaning, **28**, [807]
possession away from licensed premises, **28**, [796]
Authority. *See* **Human Tissue Authority**
Community obligations, power to give effect to, **28**, [812]
definitions, **28**, [820]
DNA, non-consensual analysis of, **28**, [811], [832]–[833]
inspection, entry, search and seizure, powers of, **28**, [834]
offences—
body corporate, by, **28**, [815]
Northern Ireland, in, **28**, [817]
prosecutions, **28**, [816]
orders and regulations, **28**, [818]
relevant material, meaning, **28**, [819]
religious relics, provisions applying to, **28**, [806]
removal, storage and use of—
adults lacking capacity to consent, from, **28**, [772]
appropriate consent for—
adults, for, **28**, [769]
children, for, **28**, [768]
obtaining, standards for, **28**, [793]
coroners, functions of, **28**, [777]
donated material, restriction of activities, **28**, [774]
excepted material, meaning, **28**, [778]
existing anatomical specimens, **28**, [776]
existing holdings, **28**, [775]
need for consent, power to dispense with, **28**, [773]
nominated representatives—
appointment of, **28**, [770]
powers of, general or limited, **28**, [770]
prohibition of activities without consent, **28**, [771]
scheduled purposes—
authorisation of activities for, **28**, [767]
consent, requiring, **28**, [828], [829]
surplus, treatment as waste, **28**, [810]
transitional provisions, **28**, [824]
transplantation—
information about operations, requirement of, **28**, [800]
involving live donor, restriction on, **28**, [799]
material for, prohibition of commercial dealings in, **28**, [798]
meaning, **28**, [820]
preservation for, **28**, [809]

Human Tissue Authority
accounts and audit, **28**, [830]
agency arrangements, **28**, [801]
annual report, **28**, [802]
appeals committees—
maintenance of, **28**, [786]
members, **28**, [786]

Human Tissue Authority—*contd*
  appeals committees—*contd*
    reconsideration by, **28**, [787]
  codes of practice—
    approval of, **28**, [795]
    consent, as to, **28**, [793]
    effect of, **28**, [794]
    preparation of, **28**, [792]
    publication, **28**, [792]
    review, **28**, [792]
    Secretary of State, functions of, **28**, [795]
  criminal justice purposes, things done for, **28**, [805]
  directions by, **28**, [803]
  establishment of, **28**, [779]
  finance, **28**, [830]
  functions, duties as to carrying out, **28**, [804]
  general functions, **28**, [781]
  licences for activities involving human tissue—
    applications, **28**, [831]
    characteristics of, **28**, [831]
    conditions of, **28**, [831]
    decisions, procedure, **28**, [831]
    notification of decisions, **28**, [831]
    permission for purpose of conditions, **28**, [831]
    power to grant, **28**, [831]
    pre-conditions to grant, **28**, [831]
    reconsideration of decision, **28**, [785]
    revocation, power of, **28**, [831]
    suspension, power of, **28**, [831]
    variation, power of, **28**, [831]
  members, **28**, [830]
  obtaining of consent, standards for, **28**, [793]
  other public authorities, power to assist, **28**, [808]
  proceedings, **28**, [830]
  provision of services by another authority, **28**, [801]
  remit, activities within, **28**, [780]
  staff, **28**, [830]
  status, **28**, [830]
  supplementary powers, **28**, [830]
  use of human tissue or organs, direction for, **28**, [773]

Hungary
  accession to European Union, **18**, [54]
  peace treaty, **10**, [916]

hunting. *See* **falconry; hares; rabbits; rats; wild mammals**

husband and wife
  actions in tort between, **27**, [334]
  connected persons, as, **44(1)**, [621]
  dependent domicile, abolition of, **27**, [495]
  enticement action, abolition, **45**, [954]
  evidence. *See* **evidence**
  evidence—
    criminal proceedings, in, **18**, [256], [257]
    proceedings between, in, **27**, [485]
  "former" of either, meaning, **18**, [627]
  home loss payments, right to, **9**, [326]

husband and wife—*contd*
  housekeeping allowance, ownership of, **27**, [336]
  incrimination of self or spouse, privilege against, **18**, [207]
  life assurance premiums, **44(1)**, [642]
  life interest, redemption, **18**, [551]
  maintenance, liability for, **40(1)**, [19]
  married woman. *See* **married woman**
  matrimonial home, rights as to, **18**, [569], [572]
    See also **matrimonial home**
  property—
    common law rule, **27**, [127]
    determination of questions as to, **27**, [133], [310], [373]
    generally, **27**, [127]
    improvement of, contribution to, **27**, [372]
    interests in, rights as to, **20**, [656]
  surviving spouse—
    life interest, redemption of, **18**, [551]
    personal representative's powers, **18**, [552]
  tenant, of, goods of, not privileged from distress for rent, **13**, [1202]
  theft offences, **12(1)**, [580]
  wife's services, abolition of action for loss of, **45**, [983]
  witnesses—
    admissibility as, **18**, [110], [256]
    compellable, not, **18**, [257]
    evidence, failure to give, **18**, [257]

hydrocarbon oil
  accidentally mixed, **13**, [845]
  aviation gasoline—
    meaning, **13**, [822]
    rate of excise duty on, **13**, [822], [857]
  biodiesel—
    excise duty on, **13**, [823], [1096]
    meaning, **13**, [817]
  bioethanol—
    blends, excise duty on, **13**, [826]
    excise duty on, **13**, [826]
  classes of—
    regulations for different, **13**, [851]
    testing for ascertaining, **13**, [816]
  contaminated, **13**, [845]
  control of duty-free and rebated oil, **13**, [857], [869]
  definitions, **13**, [815]
    power to amend, **13**, [819]
    provisions supplementing, **13**, [816]
  energy products, extension of 1979 Act to, **13**, [922]
  excise duty—
    charge of, **13**, [822]
    drawback on exportation, etc—
      certain goods, **13**, [840]
      regulations as to, **13**, [851], [857]
    production without delivery, charge on, **13**, [1070]
    rate of, **13**, [822]
    rebates—
      control of use of rebated oil, **13**, [857]

hydrocarbon oil—*contd*
  excise duty—*contd*
    rebates—*contd*
      heavy oil. *See under* heavy oil *below*
      kerosene. *See under* kerosene *below*
      light oil. *See under* light oil *below*
      mixing of rebated oils, **13**, [847]
      regulations as to, **13**, [857]
      road vehicles, fuel for, not allowed on,
        13, [834]
      unleaded petrol, **13**, [838]
      volume, measurement of, **13**, [923]
    relief from—
      forfeiture for misuse, **13**, [832]
      home use, delivery of oil for, **13**, [831]
      industrial purposes, for use in, **13**, [831]
      offences and penalties, **13**, [832]
      regulations controlling, **13**, [849], [850]
      restrictions on use of duty-free oil,
        13, [832]
      shipbuilders, **13**, [555], [557]
        ending of, **13**, [1120]
      use not qualifying for, **13**, [831]
    repayment, **13**, [904]
      accidentally mixed, different
        descriptions, **13**, [845]
      biodiesel used otherwise than as road
        fuel, **13**, [842]
      contaminated oil, **13**, [845]
      energy for refinery, fuel for producing,
        13, [844], [857], [869]
      fishing boats, fuel for, **13**, [843], [857],
        [869], [898]
      horticultural producers, **13**, [841], [857],
        [869], [898]
      lifeboat, fuel for, **13**, [857], [869], [898]
      regulations controlling, **13**, [857], [869]
      use not qualifying for relief, **13**, [831],
        [857]
    surcharges or rebates, **13**, [898]–[900]
    volume, measurement of, **13**, [923]
  fuel substitutes, charge of excise duty on,
    13, [829]
  fuel testing, power to allow reliefs for,
    13, [850]
  gas oil, meaning, **13**, [815]
  heavy oil—
    bioblends, excise duty on, **13**, [824]
    duty on—
      charge of, **13**, [822]
      rebate—
        home use, for, **13**, [833]
        misuse of rebated, **13**, [835]
        offences and penalties, **13**, [835]
        regulating trade in, **13**, [1097]
        road vehicle fuel, not allowed for,
          13, [834]
    repayment to horticultural producer,
      13, [841], [857], [869], [898]
    horticulture, used in, repayment of duty
      on, **13**, [841], [857], [869], [898]
    meaning, **13**, [815]
  home use, delivery for, relief from duty
    where, **13**, [831], [832], [857], [869]

hydrocarbon oil—*contd*
  horticulture, used in, repayment of duty on,
    13, [841], [857], [869], [898]
  imported, excise duty on, **13**, [822]
  imported goods, as ingredient of, **13**, [820]
  industrial purposes, for, relief from duty
    where, **13**, [831], [832], [857], [869]
  kerosene—
    rebate of duty—
      misuse of rebated, **13**, [837]
      restrictions on use of rebated, **13**, [836]
  licences required, **13**, [857], [867]
  lifeboat, fuel for, repayment of duty on,
    13, [843], [857], [869], [898]
  light oil—
    bioethanol, used for same purposes as,
      13, [818]
    duty on—
      charge of, **13**, [822]
      rebate on use as furnace fuel, **13**, [839],
        [857]
    meaning, **13**, [815]
  marked oil, penalties for misuse of, **13**, [859]
  markers in—
    evidence as to, **13**, [857]
    regulations as to, **13**, [869]
  mixing of oils—
    accidental, **13**, [845]
    adjustment of duty, **13**, [846]
    rebated oil, **13**, [847], [848]
  petrol substitutes—
    excise duty on, surcharges or rebates,
      13, [898]–[900]
    regulations as to, **13**, [851], [857]
    use without payment of duty, prohibition
      of, **13**, [822]
  power methylated spirits, excise duty,
    surcharges or rebates, **13**, [898]–[900]
  production of, what included in, **13**, [820]
  rebate of duty. *See under* excise duty *above*
  refineries, fuel for producing energy for,
    13, [844]
  regulations—
    duty-free and rebated oil, as to control of,
      13, [857], [869]
    hydrocarbon oil, **13**, [851]
    petrol substitutes, **13**, [851]
    procedure for making, **13**, [860]
    reliefs, allowing, **13**, [849], [850]
    road fuel gas, **13**, [851]
    subjects for, **13**, [867]–[869]
    traders in controlled oils, **13**, [854–855],
      [858]
  road fuel gas—
    excise duty on—
      charge of, **13**, [830]
      surcharges or rebates, **13**, [898]–[900]
    licence to produce and deal in, **13**, [868]
    meaning, **13**, [821]
    regulations as to, **13**, [851], [857], [868]
    use without payment of duty, prohibition
      of, **13**, [853],[857]
  road vehicle—
    excepted vehicles, **13**, [865]

hydrocarbon oil—*contd*
  road vehicle—*contd*
    fuel for, rebate not allowed on, **13**, [834], [839]
    meaning, **13**, [862]
    road fuel gas used in, **13**, [821], [830]
  sample taking, provisions as to, **13**, [857], [870]
  storage, etc, control of, **13**, [857], [869]
  ultra low sulphur diesel, meaning, **13**, [815]
  unleaded petrol, rebate on, **13**, [838]
  warehousing, **13**, [856]

hydrocarbon oil duties
  aircraft, fuel used in, **43(S)**, 1045–7
  amended provisions, **13(S)**, Customs 10
  bioblend, on, **43(S)**, 1039–44
  biodiesel, on, **43(S)**, 1039–44
  engine fuel, heavy oil used for, **43(S)**, 1050–1
  heating, heavy oil used for, **43(S)**, 1050–1
  private pleasure craft, fuel used in, **43(S)**, 1047–9
  rates of—
    aircraft and boats, for, **43(S)**, 847
    engines, fuel for, **43(S)**, 847
    heating oil, **43(S)**, 847
    September 2009, from, **13(S)**, Customs 8
    Spring 2009, from, **13(S)**, Customs 7
    simplification, **43(S)**, 844
    1 October 2008, increase from, **43(S)**, 846

hydrocarbon oil duties—*contd*
  rebates—
    September 2009, from, **13(S)**, Customs 8
    Spring 2009, from, **13(S)**, Customs 7
    simplification, **43(S)**, 844
    1 October 2008, increase from, **43(S)**, 846
  ultra low sulphur diesel, definitions, **43(S)**, 995
  wrongdoing, penalties, **43(S)**, 1328–39. *See also* **tax penalty**

hygiene
  summary of provisions, **35(1)**, [1]

hypnotism
  authorisation, fee for, **26(1)**, [209]
  controlling authority, **13**, [117]
    fee for application to, **13**, [118]
  demonstrations, control—
    places other than public entertainment, **13**, [117]
    public entertainment, places licensed for, **13**, [116]
  entry of premises, **13**, [120]
  meaning, **13**, [122]
  persons under eighteen, on, prohibition, **13**, [119]
  plays, demonstrations in, **13**, [117]
  scientific purposes, saving for, **13**, [121]

I

identity cards
civil penalties, imposition of, **36**, [188]
  appeals, **36**, [190]
  code of practice, **36**, [191]
  objection to, **36**, [189]
compulsorily registered persons, for, **36**, [165]
cost of scheme, report to Parliament,
  36, [193]
designated documents—
  application for, **36**, [163]
  designation, **36**, [162]
  false, etc, possession of, **36**, [183]
  issue as part of, **36**, [164]
  persons issuing, functions of, **36**, [166]
functions, fees for, **36**, [192]
Intelligence Services Commissioner and
  Tribunal, jurisdiction of, **36**, [182]
interpretation, **36**, [198]
invalidity, **36**, [169]
issue of, **36**, [164]
meaning, **36**, [164]
orders and regulations, **36**, [196]
requirement to produce, prohibition,
  36, [174]
Scotland, use in, **36**, [199]
summary of provisions, **36**, [1]
surrender, **36**, [169]
unauthorised disclosure of information,
  36, [185]

identity checks
public services conditional on, power to
  make, **36**, [171]
  regulations, **36**, [172]
Register, on, **36**, [173]

identity documents
false, etc, possession of, **36**, [183]
meaning, **36**, [184]
unauthorised disclosure of information,
  36, [185]

idle and disorderly person
appeal to Crown Court, **12(1)**, [30]
house of correction, committal to, **12(1)**, [26]
meaning, **12(1)**, [27]
offender deemed to be, **12(1)**, [27]
rogue and vagabond, deemed to be,
  12(1), [27]

illegitimacy. *See also* **legitimacy**
presumption as to, rebuttal, **18**, [218]
removal of, **6**, [1]

illegitimate child. *See* **child; parentage**
birth, registration. *See* **birth, registration of**

illuminated signs
overground wires for, London, **25(1)**, [216]

immigration. *See also* **citizenship**
abode in the UK—
  deprivation of right, **31**, [74]
  right of, statement of, **31**, [73]
  those having right of, freedom of
    movement, **31**, [72]
accommodation centre. *See* **accommodation
centre**
administration—
  expenses, **31**, [119]
  offences in connection with, **31**, [98]
  rules as to, **31**, [72]
Advisory Panel on Country Information,
  31, [477]
aircraft—
  captain etc, supplementary duties, **31**, [128]
  freight, information on, **31**, [558]
  liability of owners etc, **31**, [128]
  offences involving, **31**, [101]
    detention, **31**, [97]
    forfeiture, **31**, [96]
  passenger information—
    non-EEA arrivals, notice of, **31**, [128]
    power to require, **31**, [128], [557]
  search of, **31**, [128]
aircrew, exceptions, **31**, [128]
appeals—
  abandonment, **31**, [536]
  Asylum and Immigration Tribunal. *See*
    Asylum and Immigration Tribunal
  bail—
    applications for, **31**, [269]
    arrest of appellants released on, **31**, [129]
    hearings, summary of provisions, **31**, [1]
    pending, grant of, **31**, [129]
    recognizances, forfeiture, **31**, [129]
    restrictions on grant, **31**, [129]
  certification of claims as unfounded,
    monitor of, **31**, [454]
  Community treaties, person having right
    under, **31**, [453]
  decision—
    meaning, **31**, [423]
    notice of, **31**, [449]
  determination of, **31**, [428]
  earlier right of, **31**, [438]
  effect of, **31**, [129]
  entry clearance, refusal of, **31**, [431], [533]
  exceptions—
    national security decisions, **31**, [439]
    non-family visitor, **31**, [433]

immigration—*contd*
  appeals—*contd*
    exceptions—*contd*
      pending appeal, **31**, [442]
      public good, grounds of, **31**, [441]
      students, **31**, [434]
      visitor or student without entry
        clearance, **31**, [432]
    forged documents, use of, **31**, [452]
    grounds of, **31**, [426], [530]
    ineligibility, **31**, [430]–[431], [532]
    matters to be considered, **31**, [427]
    outside UK, from, **31**, [437]
    patriality, refusal of certificate of, **31**, [189]
    pending—
      meaning, **31**, [448]
      no removal during, **31**, [421]
    recognizances, forfeiture, **31**, [129]
    regulations, **31**, [455], [534]
    right of, **31**, [423]
    rules, **31**, [90], [450]
    Special Commission. *See* **Special**
      Immigration Appeals Commission
    successful, direction on, **31**, [429]
    summary of provisions, **31**, [1]
    transitional provisions, **31**, [488]
    Tribunal. *See* **Asylum and Immigration**
      Tribunal
    unification of system, **31**, [509]
    within United Kingdom, from—
      general, **31**, [435]
      unfounded human rights or asylum
        claim, **31**, [436], [458], [539]
  Appeals Tribunal. *See* **Immigration Appeals**
  Tribunal
  application—
    additional grounds for, **31**, [460]
    fees, **31**, [573]–[574], [586]
    meaning, **31**, [464]
    physical data, provision of, **31**, [464]–[465]
    procedural requirements as to, **31**, [120],
      [572]
  applications for leave to remain in UK,
    charges for, **31**, [239]
  armed forces members, provisions
    inapplicable, **31**, [84]
  arrest, powers of, **31**, [128], [130], [501]
  authorised person, search by, **31**, [565]–[566]
  authority-to-carry scheme, **31**, [462]
  biometric registration—
    information, use and retention of,
      31(S), Nationality 15
    interpretation, **31(S)**, Nationality 20
    non-compliance, **31(S)**, Nationality 14
    penalty for failure to comply with
      requirements—
      appeals, **31(S)**, Nationality 17
      code of practice, **31(S)**, Nationality 19
      enforcement, **31(S)**, Nationality 18
      notice, **31(S)**, Nationality 15–16
      objection to, **31(S)**, Nationality 16–17
      prescribed matters, **31(S)**, Nationality 19
    persons subject to control, meaning,
      31(S), Nationality 20
    regulations, **31(S)**, Nationality 10–13

immigration—*contd*
  biometric registration—*contd*
    summary of provisions,
      31(S), Nationality 1–2
  Border and Immigration Agency. *See* **Border**
    and Immigration Agency
  breach of laws, references to,
    31(S), Nationality 93–5
  British citizenship, proof of, **31**, [75]
  carriers' liability, **31**, [490]
  Channel Islands, freedom of travel, **31**, [72]
  children—
    code of practice for ensuring safety of,
      31(S), Nationality 25
    code of practice relating to,
      13(S), Customs 54
    welfare, duty as to, **31(S)**, Nationality 100
  civil partnership, duty to report suspicious,
    31, [250]
  claims etc, fees for, **31(S)**, Nationality 25
  clandestine entry, carriers' liability—
    code of practice, **31**, [257]
    defences, **31**, [258]
    penalty, **31**, [255]
      appeal, **31**, [260]
      code of practice, **31**, [256]
      detention in default of payment,
        31, [262]
      detention of vehicles in connection
        with, **31**, [261]
      procedure for, **31**, [259]
    summary of provisions, **31**, [1]
    transporters—
      release of, **31**, [263]
      sale of, **31**, [343]
  common travel area—
    meaning, **31**, [72]
    provisions applicable, **31**, [87]
  Commonwealth citizens, right of abode in
    UK, **31**, [73]
    deprivation of, **31**, [74]
  Community rights, person exercising,
    31, [196]
  complaints and misconduct, IPCC functions,
    13(S), Customs 50
  conditional leave to enter or remain,
    31(S), Nationality 21
  consequential amendments, **31**, [354]
  control—
    administration of, **31**, [75], [80]
    charges, **31**, [252]
    EEA ports, at, **31**, [476]
    general provisions, **31**, [75]
    ports, at, facilities for, **31**, [251]
  decision, meaning, **31**, [495]
  deportation. *See* **deportation**
  detained property, forfeiture of,
    31(S), Nationality 29
  detention centre, change of name, **31**, [411]
  detention of persons—
    bail—
      accommodation on release, **31**, [238]
      application for, **31**, [269]
      power to release on, **31**, [413]
      release on, **31**, [128]

immigration—*contd*
    detention of persons—*contd*
        detainee custody officers, **31**, [329], [351], [352]
        escorts and custody, arrangement for, **31**, [331], [353]
        persons liable to, construction of references to, **31**, [412]
        powers, **31**, [128]
        Secretary of State, authority of, **31**, [410]
        short-term holding facilities, **31**, [332]
        summary of provisions, **31**, [1]
        wrongful disclosure of information, **31**, [332]
    documents—
        deliberate destruction or disposal of, **31**, [492]
        entering UK without, **31**, [492]
        meaning, **31**, [492]
        production and examination of, **31**, [128]
    employment—
        body corporate, offences by, **31**, [218], [548]
        discrimination, code of practice, **31**, [549]
        employer—
            defences, by, **31**, [218]
            offences, by, **31**, [218]
            unlawful discrimination, **31**, [219]
        penalty—
            appeals, **31**, [543]
            code of practice, **31**, [545]
            employer, notice given to, **31**, [541]
            enforcement, **31**, [544]
            objection to, **31**, [542]
            orders, **31**, [546]
        person subject to control, of, **31**, [541]
            offences, **31**, [547]–[548]
        restrictions on, **31**, [218]
    employment document—
        fee for, **31**, [461]
        meaning, **31**, [461]
    entrant, meaning, **31**, [122]
    entry into UK—
        clearance for—
            meaning, **31**, [122]
            refusals, monitoring of, **31**, [248]
            restricted right of appeal, **31**, [531]
            security on grant of, **31**, [244]
        construction of references to, **31**, [89]
        control—
            administration of, **31**, [75], [80]
            examination of documents, **31**, [553]
            general provisions, **31**, [75]
            rules as to, **31**, [75]
        deception as to means of, penalty, **31**, [92]
        disembarkation, effected by, **31**, [89]
        electronic monitoring, **31**, [512]
        entitlement, certificate of, **31**, [75]
        excluded person—
            meaning, **31**, [86]
            provisions applicable, **31**, [86]
        general principles, **31**, [72]
        illegal—
            assisting, penalty, **31**, [93]–[95]

immigration—*contd*
    entry into UK—*contd*
        illegal—*contd*
            deportation or exclusion order, assisting in breach of, **31**, [95]
            Islands, from, **31**, [131]
            penalty for, **31**, [91]
            removal of entrants, **31**, [128]
        lapse of leave, **31**, [75]
        leave, by—
            common travel area, **31**, [87]
            excluded person, **31**, [86]
            extension of, provision of further security on, **31**, [245]
            grant of, **31**, [75]–[76]
            notice of, **31**, [128]
            refusal, **31**, [128]
            removal of persons refused, **31**, [128]
            revocation, **31**, [418]
                continuation following, **31**, [79]
            statutorily extended, removal of persons with, **31**, [571]
            summary of provisions, **31**, [1]
            variation of, **31**, [75]–[76]
                charges for, **31**, [239]
                continuation of, pending decision as to, **31**, [78], [537]
        limited period, for, **31**, [75]
        local journeys, **31**, [87]
        medical examination after, **31**, [128]
        otherwise than by sea and air, **31**, [88]
        prohibition, **31**, [75]
        proper documents, without, charges for, **31**, [264]
            appeal, **31**, [266]
            notification and objection, **31**, [265]
            transporters, sale of, **31**, [343]
        refusal, appeal against. *See* appeals *above*
        summary of provisions, **31**, [1]
        temporary admission, **31**, [128], [550]
            accommodation for, **31**, [238]
        what constitutes, **31**, [89]
    examination of passengers prior to arrival, **31**, [197]
    examination of persons—
        detention for, **31**, [128]
        powers, **31**, [128]
    failed asylum-seekers, support for, **31(S)**, Nationality 21–3
    fees, **31**, [513]
    functions, discrimination in carrying out, **7(1)**, [151], [152]
    HM Revenue and Customs, supply of information by—
        confidentiality, **31(S)**, Nationality 41–2
        purpose of, **31(S)**, Nationality 39
        wrongful disclosure, **31(S)**, Nationality 42–3
    human trafficking, **31(S)**, Nationality 32
    Convention against, **31(S)**, Nationality 69
    illegal entry—
        arrest without warrant, powers of, **31**, [103]
        assisting—
            entry and search of premises, **31**, [110]

immigration—*contd*
  illegal entry—*contd*
    assisting—*contd*
      penalty, **31**, [93]–[95]
    clandestine. *See* clandestine entry *above*
    deception as to means of, penalty, **31**, [92]
    Islands, from, **31**, [131]
    penalty, **31**, [91]
    removal of entrant, **31**, [128]
  information—
    disclosure—
      Commissioners for HM Revenue and
        Customs, by, **31**, [467]
      employer, by, **31**, [470]
      financial institution, by, **31**, [471]
      law enforcement agencies, to, **31**, [564]
      local authority, by, **31**, [466]
      medical inspectors, by, **31**, [469]
      notice requiring, **31**, [472]
      offences, **31**, [473]–[474]
      police, by, **31**, [468]
      security purposes, for, **31**, [563]
      self-incrimination, privilege against,
        31, [475]
    duty to share, **31**, [561]
      code of practice, **31**, [562]
    embarking passengers, **31**, [567]
    power to require, **31**, [128], [560]
    supply of—
      by Secretary of State, **31**, [247]
      to Secretary of State, **31**, [246]
  international projects, **31**, [409]
  Ireland, freedom of travel to and from,
    31, [72]
  Islands—
    deportation from, **31**, [131]
    law, integration of, **31**, [131]
    leave to enter, **31**, [87], [131]
    meaning, **31**, [72], [122]
  Isle of Man, freedom of travel, **31**, [72]
  judicial review applications, transfer of,
    13(S), Customs 60
  laws—
    integration of, **31**, [131]
    meaning, **31**, [122], [180]
    transitional and temporary provisions,
      31, [123]
  leave to remain in UK—
    charges for application for, **31**, [239]
    grant of, **31**, [75], [77]
    lapse of, **31**, [75], [77]
    revocation, continuation following, **31**, [79]
    variation of, **31**, [75]
      continuation of, pending decision as to,
        31, [78]
  local journeys, **31**, [72]
  marriage—
    abolition of certificate by licence, **31**, [335]
    consequential amendments, **31**, [354]
    duty to report suspicious, **31**, [249]
    Northern Ireland, **31**, [506]–[507]
    notice of, **31**, [336]
    permission, application for, **31**, [508]
    procedure, **31**, [504]
    refusal to issue certificate, **31**, [337]

immigration—*contd*
  marriage—*contd*
    regulations, **31**, [507]
    residence, declaration of, **31**, [505]
  medical examination—
    after entry, **31**, [128]
    on entry, **31**, [128]
  medical inspectors—
    appointment, **31**, [128]
    examination of persons by, **31**, [128]
  member state, to, unlawful, **31**, [93]
  nationals of member states, **31**, [196]
  offences and penalties—
    administration of Act, in connection with,
      31, [98]
    arrest—
      business premises, entry to, **31**, [107]
      warrant for—
        by, **31**, [104]
        grant of, **31**, [105]
        without, **31**, [103], [106]
    arrested person, search of, **31**, [113]–[114],
      [128]
    assisting illegal entry, **31**, [93]–[95]
    clandestine entrants, for carrying,
      31, [255]–[256]
    deception, **31**, [92]
    defences based on Article 31(1) of the
      Refugee Convention, **31**, [254]
    detention of ship, aircraft or vehicle,
      31, [97]
    entry and search of premises—
      arrest, following, **31**, [109]–[110]
      business, **31**, [107]
      conditions permitting, **31**, [108]
      execution of, **31**, [117]
      personnel records, search for,
        31, [111]–[112]
      powers, **31**, [128]
      seized material, access to and copies of,
        31, [115], [128]
      warrant for—
        grant of, **31**, [105], [108]
        personnel records, relating to,
          31, [112]
        safeguards, **31**, [116]
        with, **31**, [104]
        without, **31**, [106]
    illegal entry, **31**, [91]
    proceedings, **31**, [102]
    ships or aircraft, involving, **31**, [96]–[97],
      [101]
    stamp, possession of, **31**, [100]
    unlawful, assisting, **31**, [93]
  offences, **31**, [559]
    enforcement, **31(S)**, Nationality 9
  officers—
    appointment, **31**, [128]
    arrest, power of, **31**, [501]
    assaulting—
      offence of, **31(S)**, Nationality 27
      powers of arrest, **31(S)**, Nationality 27
    cash, seizure of, **31(S)**, Nationality 28
    codes of practice, **31**, [319]

immigration—*contd*
  officers—*contd*
    designated—
      detention of individuals by,
        31(S), Nationality 8
      power of designation,
        31(S), Nationality 7
    disposal of property,
      31(S), Nationality 29–30
    documents, retention of, **31**, [503]
    examination of persons, **31**, [128]
    exercise of functions, **31**, [128]
    information to be given to, **31**, [128],
      [556]
    meaning, **31**, [514]
    passengers, power to obtain information
      about, **31**, [502]
    use of force, **31**, [320]
  Orders in Council, general provisions,
    31, [121]
  overstayers, treatment of, **31**, [240]
  patriality, certificate of, **31**, [189]
  personal records, search for,
    31(S), Nationality 29–31
  points-based applications, no new evidence on
    appeal, **31(S)**, Nationality 23–4
  police information, supply of,
    31(S), Nationality 44
  port, meaning, **31(S)**, Nationality 10
  ports—
    control at, facilities for, **31**, [251]
    EEA, **31**, [476]
    officials, duties of, **31**, [128]
  racial discrimination claims, **7(1)**, [185]
  reform, summary of provisions,
    31(S), Nationality 77–8
  registration card, **31**, [99]
  regulation of, general provisions, **31**, [75]
  regulations and orders, **31**, [338]
  removal centres—
    alcohol, **31**, [352]
    assisting detained persons to escape,
      31, [352]
    constables acting outside jurisdiction,
      31, [334]
    contracted out functions at directly
      managed centres, **31**, [324]
    contracting out, **31**, [323]
    custodial functions, **31**, [330]
    detention centre, change of name from,
      31, [411]
    discipline, **31**, [330], [352]
    inspection of, **31**, [326], [570]
    management of, **31**, [322]
    measuring and photographing detained
      persons, **31**, [352]
    medical examinations, **31**, [352]
    penalties, notice of, **31**, [352]
    rules, **31**, [327]
    Secretary of State, intervention by,
      31, [325]
    summary of provisions, **31**, 9–10
    testing for drugs or alcohol, **31**, [352]
    visiting committees, **31**, [326]

immigration—*contd*
  removal centres—*contd*
    work done, exclusion from national
      minimum wage, **31**, [328], [579]
    wrongful disclosure of information,
      31, [333]
  removal from UK—
    asylum claimants, proof of identity of
      persons, **31**, [242]
    bail, grant of, pending, **31**, [129]
    detention for, **31**, [128]
    escorts for persons to be removed under
      directions, **31**, [243]
    illegal entrants, **31**, [128]
    overstayers, treatment of, **31**, [240]
    persons refused leave, **31**, [128]
    persons unlawfully in UK, **31**, [241]
    proof of identity of persons, **31**, [242]
    summary of provisions, **31**, [1]
    See also **deportation**
  reporting restriction—
    imposition of, **31**, [415]
    meaning, **31**, [415]
    travelling expenses, payment of, **31**, [414]
  Revenue and Customs Prosecution Office,
    supply of information by—
    confidentiality, **31(S)**, Nationality 41–2
    purpose of, **31(S)**, Nationality 39–40
    wrongful disclosure,
      31(S), Nationality 42–3
  right of abode, **31**, [73]
    certificate of entitlement, **31**, [367]
    deprivation of, **31**, [74]
    polygamy, restriction in case of, **31**, [195]
  Scotland, provisions extended to,
    31(S), Nationality 98–9
  seamen, exceptions, **31**, [128]
  serious criminal, removal of, **31**, [417]
  services—
    advertising, offences, **31**, [282]
    Commissioner—
      accounts and records, **31**, [345]
      annual report, **31**, [345]
      appointment, **31**, [271]
      Code of Standards, **31**, [344]
      compensation, **31**, [345]
      complaints, **31**, [344]
      Deputy, **31**, [345]
      duties, **31**, [271]
      enforcement of provisions, **31**, [280]
      expenditure, **31**, [345]
      expenses, **31**, [345]
      functions, **31**, [271]
      information, disclosure of, **31**, [283]
      pensions, **31**, [345]
      period of office, **31**, [345]
      premises, power to enter, **31**, [281],
        [344]
      proof of instruments, **31**, [345]
      receipts, **31**, [345]
      remuneration, **31**, [345]
      rules of, **31**, [344]
      staff, **31**, [345]
      status, **31**, [345]

immigration—*contd*
  services—*contd*
    Commissioner—*contd*
      terms and conditions of appointment,
        31, [345]
      designated professional bodies, **31**, [274]
      disciplinary bodies, orders by, **31**, [278]
      meaning, **31**, [270]
      offences, **31**, [279]
      provision of, **31**, [272]
      registration—
        applications for, **31**, [346]
        disqualification of certain persons,
          31, [346]
        exemption by Commissioner, **31**, [273]
        fees, **31**, [346]
        open registers, **31**, [346]
        review of qualifications, **31**, [346]
        variation, **31**, [346]
      summary of provisions, **31**, [1]
  ships—
    captain, supplementary duties, **31**, [128]
    freight, information on, **31**, [558]
    liability of owners etc, **31**, [128]
    offences involving, **31**, [101]
      detention, **31**, [97]
      forfeiture, **31**, [96]
    passenger information—
      non-EEA arrivals, notice of, **31**, [128]
      power to require, **31**, [128], [557]
    search of, **31**, [128]
  Special Immigration Appeals Commission. *See*
    **Special Immigration Appeals
    Commission**
  special status—
    designated person—
      conditions imposed on,
        31(S), Nationality 64
      support, **31(S)**, Nationality 65–7
    designation, **31(S)**, Nationality 62
      effect of, **31(S)**, Nationality 63
      end of, **31(S)**, Nationality 67
    foreign criminal, meaning,
      31(S), Nationality 62–3
    interpretation, **31(S)**, Nationality 68
  stamp, possession of, **31**, [100]
  studies, restriction on, **31(S)**, Nationality 97
  summary of provisions, **31**, [1]
  trafficking people for exploitation,
    31, [493]–[494]; **31(S)**, Nationality 99
  transit passengers, visa for, **31**, [267]
  transitional provisions and savings, **31**, [355]
  travel documents, charges for, **31**, [253]
  Tribunal. *See* **Immigration Services
    Tribunal**
  unlawful—
    assisting, **31**, [93]
    facilitating, **31(S)**, Nationality 32
  unlawful presence in United Kingdom,
    31, [368]
  vehicles—
    detention, **31**, [97]
    forfeiture, **31**, [96]
    freight, information on, **31**, [558]
  visas for transit passengers, **31**, [267]

immigration—*contd*
  work permit, meaning, **31**, [122]

Immigration and Asylum Act 1999
  amendments to, **11(4)**, [363]

Immigration Services Tribunal. *See also*
  immigration (services)
  appeals to—
    relevant decisions, **31**, [275], [347]
    upheld, **31**, [276]
  disciplinary charge upheld by, **31**, [277]
  establishment, **31**, [275]
  expenditure, **31**, [347]
  members—
    appointment, **31**, [347]
    expenses, **31**, [347]
    legally qualified, meaning of, **31**, [347]
    President, **31**, [347]
    remuneration, **31**, [347]
    terms and conditions of appointment,
      31, [347]
  proceedings, **31**, [347]
  relevant decision, suspending effect of,
    31, [347]
  rules of procedure, **31**, [347]
  staff, **31**, [347]

Imperial Institute. *See* **Commonwealth
  Institute**

Imperial War Museum
  Board of Trustees—
    companies, power to form, **13**, [86]
    constitution, **13**, [84], [90], [124]
    establishment, **13**, [84]
    membership, **13**, [90]
    powers and duties, **13**, [85]
    proceedings, **13**, [90]
  British Museum, transfers from, **13**, [87]
  committees, **13**, [90]
  curator, **13**, [88]
  Director-General, **13**, [88]
  expenses, **13**, [88]
  grants, **13**, [431], [432]
  history of, **13**, [49]
  land—
    dealings in, **13**, [85]
    transfer of, **13**, [430]
  loans by, **13**, [125]
  objects—
    disposal, **13**, [85]
    transfer to, **13**, [87]
    vesting of, **13**, [87]
  officers and staff, **13**, [88]
  President, **13**, [90]
  rules, power to make, **13**, [85], [90]
  Vice-President, **13**, [90]

impersonation
  examiners, of, **37**, [794]
  Port of London police constable, of,
    39(2), [365]
  traffic officer, of, **38(2)**, [304]
  vehicle testing inspector, of, **37**, [140]

importation

agricultural produce. *See* **agricultural produce**

animals—

control orders, **2**, [437], [557]

customs and excise offences, **2**, [533]

wharves etc for purposes of, **2**, [504]

bees, hives etc, control of, **2**, [420]

certain items, restriction on, **13**, [566], [569]

control of, **13**, [617]–[635]

drugs, controlled, penalties on, **13**, [657], [775], [783]

duty—

Community customs duties, **13**, [627]

deferred payment, **13**, [629], [731]

destroyed goods, waste or debris from, **13**, [627]

goods subject to, **13**, [627]

rates of, **13**, [627]

re-imported goods, **13**, [627]

relief from. *See* **customs duties**

removal of goods, payment before, **13**, [627]

samples, **13**, [627]

standing deposits to cover, **13**, [628]

temporarily imported goods, relief from, **13**, [632]

transit or transhipment, goods entered for, relief from, **13**, [631]

warehousing without payment, **13**, [630]

eggs, **1(1)**, [296]

endangered species, restriction on. *See* **animals; plants**

entry of goods on—

cancellation of, **13**, [622]

correction of, **13**, [622]

free circulation, for, **13**, [622]

home use, for, **13**, [622]

initial, **13**, [619]

non-compliance with provisions as to, **13**, [625]

payment of duty on, **13**, [627]

postponed, **13**, [620]

report inward—

aircraft, **13**, [617]

ship, **13**, [617]

requirement, **13**, [620]

samples, taking for purpose of, **13**, [627]

substituted, **13**, [627]

supplementary, **13**, [619], [621]

surplus stores, **13**, [623]

transit or transhipment—

for, **13**, [631]

meaning, **13**, [590]

warehousing, for, **13**; [624], [630]

fish and fish eggs, limitation, **1(2)**, [150]

horses, docked, restriction on, **2**, [277]

horticultural produce. *See* **horticultural produce**

imported goods—

Community transit goods, meaning, **13**, [590]

control of movement, **13**, [613], [614]

delivery on giving security for duty, **13**, [723]

importation—*contd*

imported goods—*contd*

destroyed or returned, repayment of excise duty where, **13**, [727]

dumped. *See* **dumped goods**

duty on. *See* duty *above*

examination, **13**, [764]

forfeiture, breach of conditions, for, **13**, [728]

information, disclosure of, **13**, [915]

inland clearance depot, control of movements to, **13**, [614]

origin of, determination, **13**, [724]

restrictions where duty dependent on other than use, **13**, [726]

subsidised. *See* **subsidies**

taking account of, **13**, [764]

unloading, removal, etc, regulation of, **13**, [616]

valuation for ad valorem duties, **13**, [729]

importer, meaning, **13**, [590]

improper—

forfeiture of goods, **13**, [633]

penalty for, **13**, [634]

information—

evidence in support of, **13**, [675]

firearms, relating to, **13**, [672]

goods subject to certain transit arrangements, relating to, **13**, [673]

power to require, **13**, [670]–[673]

landing of goods, regulation of, **13**, [626]

livestock—

control of, **1(1)**, [481]

offences and penalties, **1(1)**, [482]

musk rats, **2**, [256]

Northern Ireland—

proof required as to, **13**, [635]

regulation of movement into and out of, **13**, [609], [919]

origin of goods, determination of, **13**, [724]

pipe-lines—

application of customs and excise provisions to, **13**, [592]

meaning, **13**, [590]

time of, **13**, [594]

procedure on, regulation of, **13**, [626]

records relating to—

general, **13**, [667]

goods subject to certain transit arrangements, **13**, [669]

re-exportation, **13**, [632]

re-imported goods—

duty on, **13**, [627]

relief from excise duty, **13**, [798]

salmon, restrictions, **1(1)**, [347]

seal skins, penalties on, **13**, [775]

time of, **13**, [594]

uncleared goods—

clearance, time allowed for, **13**, [624]

removal to Queen's warehouse, **13**, [624]

sale of, **13**, [624]

unloading of goods, regulation of, **13**, [626]

imprisonment. *See also* **prison; prisoner;**
sentence
  bail offences, for, **12(4)**, [269]
  consecutive terms, **12(4)**, [476]
  conviction on indictment, liability on,
    12(2), [775]
  debt, for. *See* **bankruptcy**
  illegal, declarations against, **10**, [6], [16]
  impose, meaning, **12(2)**, [776]
  less than 12 months, sentence for—
    conditions for, **12(3)**, [912]
    custodial period, specification of,
      12(3), [912]
    custody plus order—
      activity requirement, **12(3)**, [932]
      alcohol treatment requirement,
        12(3), [943]
      amendment, **12(3)**, [1066]
      attendance centre requirement,
        12(3), [945]
      curfew requirement, **12(3)**, [935]
      drug rehabilitation requirement,
        12(3), [940]–[942]
      electronic monitoring requirement,
        12(3), [946]
      exclusion requirement, **12(3)**, [936]
      licence conditions, **12(3)**, [913]
      limits of requirements, amendment of,
        12(3), [954]
      local justice area, specification of,
        12(3), [947]
      meaning, **12(3)**, [912]
      mental health treatment requirement,
        12(3), [938], [939]
      Northern Ireland, transfer to,
        12(3), [1069], [1070]
      programme requirement, **12(3)**, [933]
      prohibited activity requirement,
        12(3), [934]
      provision of copies of, **12(3)**, [950],
        [1079]
      religious beliefs, avoidance of conflict
        with, **12(3)**, [948]
      residence requirement, **12(3)**, [937]
      responsible officer, **12(3)**, [928], [929]
      revocation, **12(3)**, [1066]
      Scotland, transfer to, **12(3)**, [1067],
        [1068], [1070], [1071]
      supervision requirement, **12(3)**, [944]
      unpaid work requirement, **12(3)**, [930],
        [931], [949]
      work or education times, avoidance of
        conflict with, **12(3)**, [948]
    exercise of power to impose, **12(3)**, [912]
    intermittent custody order—
      activity requirement, **12(3)**, [932]
      alcohol treatment requirement,
        12(3), [943]
      attendance centre requirement,
        12(3), [945]
      curfew requirement, **12(3)**, [935]
      drug rehabilitation requirement,
        12(3), [940]–[942]
      electronic monitoring requirement,
        12(3), [946]

imprisonment—*contd*
  less than 12 months, sentence for—*contd*
    intermittent custody order—*contd*
      exclusion requirement, **12(3)**, [936]
      imposition of, **12(3)**, [914]
      licence conditions, **12(3)**, [916]
      limits of requirements, amendment of,
        12(3), [954]
      local justice area, specification of,
        12(3), [947]
      meaning, **12(3)**, [914]
      mental health treatment requirement,
        12(3), [938], [939]
      Northern Ireland, transfer to,
        12(3), [1069]–[1071]
      programme requirement, **12(3)**, [933]
      prohibited activity requirement,
        12(3), [934]
      provision of copies of, **12(3)**, [950],
        [1079]
      provisions applying to, **12(3)**, [917]
      religious beliefs, avoidance of conflict
        with, **12(3)**, [948]
      residence requirement, **12(3)**, [937]
      responsible officer, **12(3)**, [928], [929]
      restriction on power to make,
        12(3), [915]
      revocation, **12(3)**, [1066]
      revocation or amendment, **12(3)**, [918]
      Scotland, transfer to, **12(3)**, [1067],
        [1068], [1070], [1071]
      supervision requirement, **12(3)**, [944]
      unpaid work requirement, **12(3)**, [930],
        [931], [949]
      work or education times, avoidance of
        conflict with, **12(3)**, [948]
    rules, **12(3)**, [953]
    suspended, order for—
      activity requirement, **12(3)**, [932]
      alcohol treatment requirement,
        12(3), [943]
      amendment of, **12(3)**, [1074]
      attendance centre requirement,
        12(3), [945]
      breach of, **12(3)**, [1072], [1073]
      curfew requirement, **12(3)**, [935]
      drug rehabilitation requirement,
        12(3), [940]–[942]
      electronic monitoring requirement,
        12(3), [946]
      exclusion requirement, **12(3)**, [936]
      imposition of requirements by,
        12(3), [921]
      limits of requirements, amendment of,
        12(3), [954]
      local justice area, specification of,
        12(3), [947]
      mental health treatment requirement,
        12(3), [938], [939]
      Northern Ireland, transfer to,
        12(3), [1076]–[1078]
      periodic review, **12(3)**, [923]
      programme requirement, **12(3)**, [933]
      prohibited activity requirement,
        12(3), [934]

imprisonment—*contd*

less than 12 months, sentence for—*contd*
  suspended, order for—*contd*
    provision of copies of, **12(3)**, [950], [1079]
    religious beliefs, avoidance of conflict with, **12(3)**, [948]
    residence requirement, **12(3)**, [937]
    responsible officer, duty of offender to keep in touch with, **12(3)**, [951]
    review of, **12(3)**, [922]
    Scotland, transfer to, **12(3)**, [1075], [1077], [1078]
    supervision period, **12(3)**, [920]
    supervision requirement, **12(3)**, [944]
    unpaid work requirement, **12(3)**, [930], [931], [949]
    work or education times, avoidance of conflict with, **12(3)**, [948]
magistrates' court, general limit on power of, **12(2)**, [776]
meaning, **12(1)**, [328G]
offence punishable with, **12(3)**, [1029]
offences for which abolished, **12(3)**, [1093]
penal servitude, abolition, **12(1)**, [178]
period of remand on bail, credit for—
  release, amended provisions **12(4)**, [478]
  terms of imprisonment and detention, **12(4)**, [477]
  transitional provisions, **12(4)**, [479], [564]
person not legally represented, on, **12(2)**, [778]
release. *See under* **prisoner**
road traffic offences, for, **38(1)**, [32]
sentence—
  calculation of term of, **12(1)**, [275W]
  concurrent terms, **12(3)**, [1000]
  consecutive terms, **12(3)**, [1001]
    intermittent custody, **12(3)**, [1002]
    released prisoners, for, **12(3)**, [1003]
  life—
    mandatory, transitional cases, **12(3)**, [1092]
    meaning, **12(3)**, [1012]
  meaning, **12(1)**, [328G]; **12(3)**, [973], [1029]
  penal servitude, abolition and substitution, **12(1)**, [178]
  serious offences, for, **12(3)**, [956]
  persons under 18, **12(3)**, [957]
summary offences not subject to, **12(3)**, [1015], [1093]
young offenders. *See* **young offenders**

improvement

area. *See* **general improvement area**
business premises, to. *See* **business premises**
consent for—
  county court jurisdiction, **21**, [216]
  unreasonably withholding, **21**, [65], [742]
covenant against, **21**, [65]
disturbance payment, to person displaced from land, **9**, [341]
expenditure on, control of, **22**, [308]

improvement—*contd*

grants. *See* **improvement grant**
home loss payment, to person displaced from dwelling, **9**, [325]
housing action area. *See* **housing action area**
improvements for sale scheme, **22**, [306]
loans for purposes of, **22**, [331]
meaning, **9**, [325]; **22**, [207]
rent increase for, restriction on, **22**, [91]
secure tenant, by—
  compensation for—
    persons qualifying for, **22**, [89]
    regulations, **22**, [88]
    right to, **22**, [88]
  conditional consent to, **22**, [87]
  consent to—
    refusal of, **22**, [86]
    requirement for, **22**, [85]
  reimbursement of cost, **22**, [90]
  rent not to be increased, **22**, [91]
  withholding consent to, **22**, [85], [86]
works authorised by tribunal, **22**, [272]

improvement grant

exchequer contributions, **22**, [445]
letting conditions, **22**, [907]

improvement line. *See under* **highway**

improvement of land. *See* **drainage and improvement of land**

in forma pauperis. *See* **legal aid and advice**

in personam proceedings

restrictions on, county court, **11(2)**, [919]

in rem proceedings

county court jurisdiction excluded, **11(2)**, [920]

inalienable land

compulsory acquisition, **9**, [418], [431]

incapacitated persons. *See* **disabled person**

incapacity benefit

contribution conditions, **40(1)**, [260]
contributory, being, **40(1)**, [259]
councillor's allowance, reduction for, **40(1)**, [270]
days and periods of incapacity for work, **40(1)**, [267]
days of entitlement, references to, **40(1)**, [268]
entitlement to, **40(1)**, [265]
increase—
  adult dependents, for, **40(1)**, [331]
  entitlement to, **40(1)**, [331]
  reduced contributions, associated pension attributable to, **40(1)**, [332]
pension payments, reduction for, **40(1)**, [269]
PPF periodic payments, reduction for, **40(1)**, [269]
rate of, **40(1)**, [266], [465]; **40(2)**, [30]

incapacity benefit—*contd*
short-term—
contribution conditions, **40(1)**, [463]
entitlement to, **40(1)**, [265]
higher rate, at, **40(1)**, [266]
notice period, payment in, **16**, [729]
rate of, **40(1)**, [266]
statutory maternity pay, relationship with,
40(1), [495]
statutory sick pay, relationship with,
40(1), [494]
transition to, power to provide for,
40(2), [31]
widowers, long-term benefit for—
entitlement to, **40(1)**, [282]
period of employment or training for work,
after, **40(1)**, [283]
widows, long-term benefit for—
entitlement to, **40(1)**, [281]
period of employment or training for work,
after, **40(1)**, [283]

incest
anonymity rule, when inapplicable,
12(2), [138]
armed forces, members of, **12(2)**, [239], [240]
merchant ships, on, **12(2)**, [239], [240]

incineration. *See* **pollution (sea)**

incitement
common law offence, abolition, **12(4)**, [416],
[452]
criminal conduct by member of services,
3(S), 62
offence, trial of, **11(2)**, [463]
service offence, to commit, **3(S)**, 57

incitement to disaffection
detection of, **12(1)**, [246]
dissemination of documents, **12(1)**, [246]
offence, **12(1)**, [245]
prevention of, **12(1)**, [246]
prosecution of offence, **12(1)**, [247]
punishment, **12(1)**, [247]
search warrant, **12(1)**, [246]
seizure of documents, **12(1)**, [246]

Inclosure Commission. *See under* **inclosure of commons**

inclosure of commons
actions, relevant court for, **20**, [58]
agreement of owners under disability, **20**, [54]
allotment—
award, confirmation of, **20**, [164]
Charity Commissioners, power of,
20, [417]
compensation for previous rights, **20**, [165]
exchange, **20**, [245]
exercise and recreation, for—
fencing, **20**, [243]
nuisance, prevention of, **20**, [277]
places for, **20**, [156]
use for, **20**, [141]

inclosure of commons—*contd*
allotment—*contd*
fencing—
cost of, **20**, [159]
dispensing with, **20**, [270]
field gardens—
compensation money applied to,
20, [442]
letting, **20**, [419]
managers, reports by, **20**, [421]
modification of provisions, **20**, [475]
surplus rents, application of, **20**, [420],
[474]
herbage, right to, **20**, [157]
labouring poor, for, **20**, [156]
letting—
determination of tenancy, **20**, [169]
field garden. *See* field gardens *above*
letting, **20**, [168]
management of, **20**, [167]
recovery of possession, **20**, [170]
recreation grounds. *See* recreation
grounds *below*
rent, recovery and application of,
20, [171]
maintenance of, **20**, [157]
neighbour, fencing etc done by, **20**, [216]
public purposes, for, **20**, [156]
modification of provisions, **20**, [475]
recreation grounds, for—
compensation money applied to,
20, [442]
managers, reports by, **20**, [421]
modification of provisions, **20**, [475]
surplus rents, application of, **20**, [420],
[435], [474]
rent-charge, payment of, **20**, [158]
repair of roads, for, **20**, [155]
shares paid in respect of, **20**, [283]
supplemental orders, **20**, [166]
tenure of, **20**, [161]
unfenced, provisions on, **20**, [271]
wills and settlements, etc, effect on,
20, [160]
attorney, appointment by person interested
in, **20**, [147]
award—
application of parties, on, **20**, [202]
confirmation of, **20**, [164]
copies of, **20**, [184]
dispensing with, **20**, [270]
leasehold and copyhold land,
distinguishing, **20**, [201]
boundaries, marking, **20**, [141]
claims—
determination of, appeal to High Court,
20, [151]
service of, **20**, [272]
commissioners. *See* inclosure commissioners
below
common law, at, **20**, [1]
common rights, compensation for, **20**, [246]
compensation, apportionment of—
Bank of England, paid into, **20**, [262]
committee, money paid to, **20**, [261]

inclosure of commons—*contd*
  compensation, apportionment of—*contd*
    provision for, **20**, [465]
    share under £20, **20**, [266]
    trustees, shares paid to, **20**, [265]
    value of shares, **20**, [263]
  compulsory acquisition, by, **20**, [1]
  consent to—
    dispute over title, **20**, [207]
    lord of the manor, **20**, [149]
    more than one interested person, **20**, [208]
    occupiers, **20**, [57]
  cottagers—
    parts of common fields allotted to, **20**, [41]
    rights, not excluded from, **20**, [40]
  Crown, interest of, **20**, [143]
  dispute over title, **20**, [207]
  distress—
    informality, not unlawful for, **20**, [193]
    levying, **20**, [192]
  division—
    intermixed lands, **20**, [186]
    orders of, **20**, [244]
    party in possession under exchange, etc,
      by, **20**, [253]
  Duke of Cornwall, interest of, **20**, [144]
  embankment, making, **20**, [138]
  encroachment, jurisdiction of county court,
    20, [423]
  exchange of lands—
    allowable, **20**, [185], [187], [204], [245]
    Crown interested in reversion, where,
      20, [274]
    easements, reservation of, **20**, [209]
    expenses, **20**, [189]
    inconvenient allotments, of, **20**, [187]
    land under separate titles, **20**, [225]
    minerals, reservation of, **20**, [209]
    notice of, **20**, [188]
    order for, **20**, [244]
    party in possession under exchange, etc,
      by, **20**, [253]
    railway etc companies, by, **20**, [273]
    rights, of, **20**, [224]
    validity of, **20**, [424]
  false evidence, giving, **20**, [197]
  fencing—
    dispensing with, **20**, [270]
    expenses, **20**, 36], [159]
    open arable land, **20**, [33]
    rules, **20**, [34]
    village green, **20**, [141], [243]
  field master, **20**, [35]
  field reeves, **20**, [37], [38], [175], [176]
  fifteen miles from London, land within,
    20, [140]
  Forest of Dean, exemption of, **20**, [139]
  franchises, effect on, **20**, [162]
  illegal, **20**, [423]
  inclosure commissioners—
    application for provisional order—
      duty of Commissioners, **20**, [412]
      evidence furnished with, **20**, [412]
      local inquiry, **20**, [413]

inclosure of commons—*contd*
  inclosure commissioners—*contd*
    application for provisional order—*contd*
      neighbourhood, provisions for benefit
        of, **20**, [411]
      publication of notices, **20**, [412]
      rules, **20**, [412]
      writing, in, **20**, [412]
    assistant, **20**, [136]
      draft award, framing, **20**, [201]
      salaries, **20**, [180]
    award, correction of, **20**, [247]
    costs and expenses, **20**, [264]
    decision, appeals against, **20**, [151]
    documents of tithe commissioners, using,
      20, [135]
    inquiry, costs of, **20**, [182], [389]
    interpretation, **20**, [198]
    maps, production, signing and sealing,
      20, [205]
    notice of proceedings, giving, **20**, [183]
    witnesses, calling, **20**, [135]
  inclosure, meaning of, **20**, [198]
  infant interested in, **20**, [146]
  inquiry, expenses of, **20**, [182], [389]
  intermixed lands, **20**, [201]
  land—
    leasehold and copyhold, distinguishing,
      20, [202]
    meaning, **20**, [251]
    minerals under, right to, **20**, [163]
    rights, including, **20**, [254]
    subject to inclosure, **20**, [137]
    towns, near, **20**, [140]
  local Acts reducing trustees, **20**, [190]
  local inquiry—
    report after, **20**, [413]
    rules as to, **20**, [413]
  lord of the manor—
    consent, giving, **20**, [203]
    interests of, **20**, [149]
    mines, power to work, **20**, [279]
    rights, saving, **20**, [60]
  manorial jurisdictions, effect on, **20**, [162]
  meetings. *See also* local inquiry *above*
    adjournment, **20**, [210], [476]
    expenses—
      attendees, of, **20**, [181]
      witnesses, of, **20**, [182]
  minerals, right to, **20**, [163]
  mines—
    damage, assessment of, **20**, [280]
    damages, payment of, **20**, [281]
    distress, levy of, **20**, [282]
    power to work, **20**, [279]
  New Forest, exemption of, **20**, [139]
  notices—
    giving, **20**, [194]
    Secretary of Commissioners giving,
      20, [211]
    service of, **20**, [272]
  occupation roads—
    rating officer—
      appointment of, **20**, [214]
      duties of, **20**, [215]

inclosure of commons—*contd*
occupation roads—*contd*
rating officer—*contd*
occupiers' liability to, **20**, [215]
setting out, **20**, [213]
order, form of, **20**, [200]
Parliament, authority of, **20**, [242]
partition—
orders of, **20**, [244]
party in possession under exchange, etc,
by, **20**, [253]
rights, of, **20**, [224]
validity of, **20**, [424]
patronage of benefice, **20**, [284]
penalties and forfeitures, recovering, **20**, [191]
person interested in—
Crown, **20**, [143]
dispute over, **20**, [207]
Duke of Cornwall, **20**, [144]
generally, **20**, [142]
joint interests, **20**, [145]
lessee, **20**, [252]
unsound mind, of, **20**, [146]
ploughing of balks, slades and meers,
20, [43]–[46]
private roads—
expenses, **20**, [154]
maintenance of, **20**, [215]
rating officer—
appointment of, **20**, [214]
duties of, **20**, [215]
occupiers' liability to, **20**, [215]
setting out, **20**, [213]
proportional value of interests, **20**, [148]
provisions ceasing to have effect, **24**, [491]
public roads—
fencing, no need for, **20**, [255]
hard materials, no need for, **20**, [255]
repairing, **20**, [153], [255]
rams, dates of remaining on, **20**, [53]
rates and assessments, recovery of, **20**, [70]
appeal, **20**, [72]
regulated pasture—
byelaws, **20**, [414]
field reeves, **20**, [175], [176]
management expenses, **20**, [178]
procedure, **20**, [172]
proportionate value of stints, **20**, [173]
rights of pasture, change in, **20**, [177]
soil, property of, **20**, [174]
stock found on, **20**, [248]
rent—
apportionment of—
application for, **20**, [256]
expenses, **20**, [260]
order of, **20**, [257], [258]
recovery of, **20**, [259]
chargeable lands, **20**, [258]
rentcharge—
deficiency in value of land, and, **20**, [276]
priority of, **20**, [275]
recovery of, **20**, [275]
restrictions, **20**, [794]
rights of common, cottagers not excluded,
20, [40]

inclosure of commons—*contd*
roads—
repair of, **20**, [155]
See also private roads, public roads *above*
royalties, effect on, **20**, [162]
seigniories, effect on, **20**, [162]
separate sheep walk in, **20**, [42]
stamp duty land tax on agreements,
exemption **20**, [196]
stamp duty on agreements, exemption,
20, [195]
summary of provisions, **20**, [1]
summons, form of, **20**, [200]
surveyor, costs and expenses, **20**, [264]
surveys, etc, power to enter for, **20**, [179]
times of opening lands, **20**, [39]
titles, determining, **20**, [150]
use of owner, for, **20**, [59]
validity of agreements, **20**, [56]
validity of grant, **20**, [477]
valuer—
costs and expenses, **20**, [264]
private roads, powers on, **20**, [154]
watercourses, etc, making, **20**, [152]
village green—
encroachment on, **20**, [422]
exemption of, **20**, [141]
fencing, **20**, [141], [243]
nuisance, prevention of, **20**, [277]
public nuisance on, **20**, [423]
warrant of distress, form of, **20**, [71], [73]
wastes—
leasing, **20**, [47]
protection of, **20**, [138]
Westminster, bringing actions at, **20**, [58]

income
agreement to waive or forgo, **44(1)**, [537]
corporation tax, charges on, **43(2)**, [747]
corporation tax purposes, disapplication of
provisions for, **44(3)**, [896]
dividend. *See* **dividend**
modified net, meaning, **44(4)**, [1032], [1033]
overseas—
meaning, **44(1)**, [419]
unremittable, relief for, **44(1)**, [419]
possessions out of the UK, arising from,
44(1), [13]
property. *See* **property income**
return of. *See* **return**
savings. *See* **savings income**
savings, from, lower rate of tax, application
of, **43(1)**, [192]
securities, from, **42**, [138]; **44(1)**, [13]
source, charge to tax, **44(1)**, [615]
sources of, within charge to income or
corporation tax, **44(4)**, [1017]
total, relationship between rules on highest
part of, **44(4)**, [1019]
trading. *See* **trading income**

income stream, transfers of
amendments and repeals, **43(S)**, 1605–6
company transferees. *See* **loan relationships**
company transferors, **43(S)**, 1599–1

income stream, transfers of—*contd*
non-corporate transferors, **43(S)**, 1601–4

income support
back to work bonus—
expedited claims, **40(2)**, [76]
long-term unemployed, employment of,
40(2), [75]
meaning, **40(2)**, [74]
pilot schemes, **40(2)**, [77]
qualifying employees, **40(2)**, [75]
regulations, **40(2)**, [74]
breach of community order, loss on,
40(2), [280]
conditions for, **40(1)**, [368]
duty to maintain, failure of, **40(1)**, [585]
entitlement to, **40(1)**, [368]
income-related benefit, as, **40(1)**, [367]
increases in—
attainment of certain age, due to,
40(1), [687]
component rates, alteration in, **40(1)**, [683]
loss of—
benefits offence, on commission of,
40(2), [302]
breach of community order, on,
40(2), [280]
maintenance payments collected by Secretary
of State, payment where, **40(1)**, [578]
mortgage interest, payments in respect of,
40(1), [517]; **40(2)**, [13]
notification of taxable amount, **44(1)**, [106]
person liable for maintenance, recovery
from—
additional amounts, **40(1)**, [587]
enforcement, **40(1)**, [588]
order for, **40(1)**, [586]
transfer of orders, **40(1)**, [587]
personal representatives, information from,
40(1), [633]
recovery of, payment made after prescribed
date, **40(1)**, [577]
termination of awards, **40(2)**, [79]
trade disputes, during—
calculation of, **40(1)**, [369]
return to work, effect of, **40(1)**, [370]

income tax
additional rate, **43(S)**, 1369
annual payments. *See also* **annual payment**
maintenance payments—
assessments, **42**, [1504]
existing obligations, **43(1)**, [421]
existing obligations, under—
meaning, **42**, [917]
1989–90 onwards, **42**, [918]
1989–90 onwards, **42**, [918]
annual tax, **44(4)**, [4]
assessment. *See* **assessment**
assessors, abolition of office, **42**, [24]
basic rate, **43(2)**, [84], [575]; **43(S)**, 514,
1367; **44(4)**, [6]
individuals, for, **44(4)**, [10]
persons other than, **44(4)**, [11]

income tax—*contd*
basic rate—*contd*
limit, **43(S)**, 1367; **44(4)**, [20]
indexation of, **44(4)**, [21]
meaning, **44(1)**, [1]
benefits in kind, medical insurance premiums,
withdrawal of relief on, **43(1)**, [312]
bodies of persons, charge on, **42**, [209]
capital allowances, agreements, **43(1)**, [1203]
changes in trading stock, effect on trade
profits, **43(S)**, 1138–40
charge of, **42**, [1]; **43(2)**, [575]; **43(S)**, 15
charge to, **43(S)**, 1357, 1367; **44(2)**, [1]
charges, overview of, **44(3)**, [1]; **44(4)**, [3]
charitable trust. *See* **charitable trust**
community investment tax relief. *See*
community investment tax relief
companies, and, **44(4)**, [5]
corporation tax, set off against, **44(1)**, [2]
deduction at source—
annual payments—
"applicable rate", meaning, **44(4)**, [910]
commercial payments made by
individuals, **44(4)**, [908]
dividends or non-taxable consideration,
for, **44(4)**, [912]
overview, **44(4)**, [906]
payments made by other persons,
44(4), [909]
qualifying, meaning, **44(4)**, [907]
building societies—
accounting period—
meaning, **44(4)**, [956]
payments in, **44(4)**, [957]
payments otherwise than in,
44(4), [958]
amended return, payer's duty to deliver,
44(4), [966]
assessments, **44(4)**, [964]–[965], [968]
time limits, **44(4)**, [967]
collection and payment of tax,
44(4), [959]
declarations of non-UK residence—
individuals, **44(4)**, [866]
inspection of, **44(4)**, [870]
personal representatives, **44(4)**, [868]
Scottish partnerships, **44(4)**, [867]
settlements, **44(4)**, [869]
discretionary or accumulation
settlements, **44(4)**, [881]
duty to deduct sums, **44(4)**, [859]
power to disapply, **44(4)**, [860]
general client account deposits,
44(4), [871]
"investment", meaning, **44(4)**, [863]
Lloyd's premium trust funds,
44(4), [875]
other investments, **44(4)**, [878]
outside UK, investments held,
44(4), [876]
overview, **44(4)**, [858]
qualifying uncertificated eligible debt
security units, **44(4)**, [872]
relevant investments, **44(4)**, [864]–[865]
return periods, **44(4)**, [955]

income tax—*contd*
  deduction at source—*contd*
    building societies—*contd*
      sale and repurchase of securities,
        44(4), [877]
      securities, payments in respect of,
        44(4), [897]
      set-off claim—
        conditions for, **44(4)**, [960]
        how it works, **44(4)**, [961]
        proceedings begun after, **44(4)**, [962]
        proceedings begun before,
          44(4), [963]
        supplementary provisions,
          44(4), [879]–[881]
    certain payments by other persons,
      collection of tax on, **44(4)**, [971]
    companies, payments to, **44(4)**, [985]
    deposit—
      meaning, **44(4)**, [863], [991]
      qualifying certificate, **44(4)**, [873], [993]
      qualifying time deposits, **44(4)**, [874]
    deposit-takers—
      accounting period—
        meaning, **44(4)**, [956]
        payments in, **44(4)**, [957]
        payments otherwise than in,
          44(4), [958]
      amended return, payer's duty to deliver,
        44(4), [966]
      assessments, **44(4)**, [964]–[965], [968]
        time limits, **44(4)**, [967]
      collection and payment of tax,
        44(4), [959]
      declarations of non-UK residence—
        individuals, **44(4)**, [866]
        inspection of, **44(4)**, [870]
        personal representatives, **44(4)**, [868]
        Scottish partnerships, **44(4)**, [867]
        settlements, **44(4)**, [869]
      discretionary or accumulation
        settlements, **44(4)**, [881]
      duty to deduct sums, **44(4)**, [859]
        power to disapply, **44(4)**, [860]
      general client account deposits,
        44(4), [871]
      "investment", meaning, **44(4)**, [863]
      Lloyd's premium trust funds,
        44(4), [875]
      meaning, **44(4)**, [861]
      other investments, **44(4)**, [878]
      outside UK, investments held,
        44(4), [876]
      overview, **44(4)**, [858]
      power to prescribe persons as,
        44(4), [862]
      qualifying uncertificated eligible debt
        security units, **44(4)**, [872]
      relevant investments, **44(4)**, [864]–[865]
      return periods, **44(4)**, [955]
      sale and repurchase of securities,
        44(4), [877]
      set-off claim—
        conditions for, **44(4)**, [960]
        how it works, **44(4)**, [961]

income tax—*contd*
  deduction at source—*contd*
    deposit-takers—*contd*
      set-off claim—*contd*
        proceedings begun after, **44(4)**, [962]
        proceedings begun before,
          44(4), [963]
        supplementary provisions,
          44(4), [879]–[881]
    derivative contracts, **44(4)**, [988]
    designated international organisations,
      44(4), [987]
    "financial instrument", meaning,
      44(4), [992]
    foreign currency securities, **44(4)**, [989]
    funding bonds, retention where issue
      treated as payment of interest, duty of,
      44(4), [947]–[948]
    gross amounts, calculation by reference to,
      44(4), [990]
    income tax paid by recipient, treated as,
      44(4), [856]
    interaction with other Income Tax Acts,
      44(4), [857]
    manufactured dividends—
      overseas—
        foreign payers, reverse charge,
          44(4), [931]–[932]
        set-off entitlement, power to provide,
          44(4), [933]
        UK residents, payments by,
          44(4), [930]
        supplementary provisions,
          44(4), [934]–[939]
      UK shares, on: Real Estate Investments
        Trusts, **44(4)**, [926]
    manufactured interest—
      foreign payers, reverse charge,
        44(4), [928]
      supplementary provisions,
        44(4), [934]–[935]
      UK securities, on, payments by UK
        residents, **44(4)**, [927]
      underlying securities paid gross, cases
        where, **44(4)**, [929]
    non-commercial payments by companies,
      44(4), [936]
    non-resident landlords, **44(4)**, [979]–[980]
    overview, **44(4)**, [855]
    patent right, proceeds of sale to non-UK
      residents, **44(4)**, [918]
    patent royalties, **44(4)**, [906], [911]
      double taxation arrangements, deduction
        at treaty rate, **44(4)**, [919]–[921]
      qualifying, meaning, **44(4)**, [907]
    payments between companies—
      excepted payments—
        incorrect belief that payment is
          excepted, **44(4)**, [946]
        non-UK resident companies,
          44(4), [942]
        partnerships, **44(4)**, [945]
        PEP and ISA managers, **44(4)**, [943]
        recipients who are to be paid gross,
          44(4), [944]

income tax—*contd*
  deduction at source—*contd*
    payments between companies—*contd*
      excepted payments—*contd*
        UK resident companies, **44(4)**, [941]
        exception from duty to deduct,
          44(4), [937]–[940]
        "qualifying partnership", meaning,
          44(4), [940]
      payments of interest less tax or at specified
        rate, arrangements for, **44(4)**, [984]
      payments to non-UK residents, directions
        for deduction from, **44(4)**, [952]
      public departments, **44(4)**, [986]
      "qualifying uncertificated eligible debt
        security unit", meaning, **44(4)**, [994]
      "quoted Eurobond", meaning, **44(4)**, [995]
      Real Estate Investment Trusts,
        44(4), [981]–[982]
      royalty payments—
        discretion to make payments gross—
          EU companies, **44(4)**, [922]–[923]
          payee's duty to notify if payment not
            exempt., **44(4)**, [924]
          supplementary provisions, **44(4)**, [925]
        double taxation arrangements, deduction
          at treaty rate, **44(4)**, [919]–[921]
        further provision, **44(4)**, [917]
        UK resident agents, made through,
          44(4), [916]
        where usual place of owner's abode is
          abroad, **44(4)**, [914]
      self-assessment return, collection through,
        44(4), [972]
      statements about, **44(4)**, [983]
      transitional provisions and savings,
        44(4), [1060]
      UK public revenue dividends, **44(4)**, [898],
        [900]
        meaning, **44(4)**, [899]
        payments which are payable at gross,
          44(4), [901]
        Treasury directions, **44(4)**, [902]
        regulations, power to make, **44(4)**, [905]
        source application—
          deduction at, **44(4)**, [903]
          withdrawal of, **44(4)**, [904]
      unauthorised unit trusts—
        calculation of trustees' income pool,
          44(4), [951]
        collection of tax from trustees,
          44(4), [950]
        deemed deductions, **44(4)**, [949]
        deemed payments to unit holders,
          44(4), [949]
        treatment of income, **44(4)**, [512]
        trustees of—
          affected by s 733 ICTA, special rules
            for, **44(4)**, [514]
          relief for, **44(4)**, [513]
      visiting performer, **44(4)**, [973]–[978]
      yearly interest payments, **44(4)**, [882]
        excepted—
          advances from banks, interest paid
            on, **44(4)**, [887]

income tax—*contd*
  deduction at source—*contd*
    yearly interest payments—*contd*
      excepted—*contd*
        advances from building societies,
          interest paid on, **44(4)**, [888]
        authorised persons dealing financial
          instruments, **44(4)**, [893]
        banks, paid by, **44(4)**, [886]
        building societies, paid by,
          44(4), [883]
        deposit-takers, paid by, **44(4)**, [884]
        industrial and provident societies,
          44(4), [895]
        life annuity, interest on loan to buy,
          44(4), [891]
        National Savings Bank interest,
          44(4), [889]
        quoted Eurobond interest,
          44(4), [890]
        recognised clearing houses, paid by,
          44(4), [894]
        relevant foreign income, **44(4)**, [892]
        statutory interest, **44(4)**, [896]
        UK public revenue dividends,
          44(4), [885]
  deduction of, refusal to allow, **42**, [246]
  deductions—
    computing profits or gains, not allowed in,
      44(1), [603]
    non-property business—
      business entertaining and gifts, for,
        44(3), [777]
      crime-related payments, **44(3)**, [887]
      employee benefit contributions, for,
        44(3), [883]
    non-trades—
      business entertaining and gifts, for,
        44(3), [884]
      crime-related payments, **44(3)**, [887]
      employee benefit contributions, for,
        44(3), [883]
      penalties, interest and VAT surcharges,
        44(3), [886]
      social security contributions,
        44(3), [885]
    under-deductions before annual Act,
      44(1), [605]
    unpaid remuneration, for, **44(3)**, [882]
  dividend additional rate, **43(S)**, 1435
  dividend ordinary rate, **44(4)**, [8]
    individuals, for, **44(4)**, [13]
    other persons, for, **44(4)**, [14]
  dividend trust rate, **43(S)**, 1369; **44(4)**, [9]
    income charged at, **44(4)**, [15]
  dividend upper rate, **43(S)**, 1369, 1432–4;
    44(4), [8]
    income charged at, **43(S)**, 896
    individuals, for, **44(4)**, [13]
  double taxation. *See* **double taxation relief**
  employment income, of, remittance basis,
    43(S), 1069–78
  employment income, on—
    agency workers. *See* **agency**
    amount charged to tax, **44(2)**, [9]

income tax—*contd*
　employment income, on—*contd*
　　charge, nature of, **44(2)**, [6]
　　earnings. *See* **earnings**
　　employment, meaning, **44(2)**, [4]
　　exempt, meaning, **44(2)**, [8]
　　exemptions—
　　　annual parties and functions,
　　　　44(2), [265]
　　　armed forces, **44(2)**, [298]–[301]
　　　childcare,
　　　　44(2), [323]–[327]. *See also* **childcare**
　　　consuls and foreign agents,
　　　　44(2), [303]–[305]
　　　counselling, **44(2)**, [314]
　　　Crown employees, **44(2)**, [302]
　　　cycles and cyclist's safety equipment,
　　　　44(2), [244]
　　　detached national experts, **44(2)**, [307]
　　　disabled employees, transport for,
　　　　44(2), [246]–[247]
　　　earnings-only, meaning, **44(2)**, [227]
　　　education and training. *See* **training**
　　　effect of, **44(2)**, [228]
　　　employment income, meaning,
　　　　44(2), [227]
　　　failure of car-sharing arrangements,
　　　　transport on, **44(2)**, [248]
　　　health and employment insurance
　　　　payments, **44(2)**, [335]
　　　homeworker, additional household
　　　　expenses of, **44(2)**, [321]
　　　incidental overnight expenses and
　　　　benefits, **44(2)**, [240]–[241]
　　　late-night work, transport home after,
　　　　44(2), [248]
　　　long service awards, **44(2)**, [332]
　　　Members of Parliament etc, payments
　　　　to, **44(2)**, [293]–[297]
　　　mileage allowances. *See* **car**
　　　miners, **44(2)**, [309]
　　　ministers of religion, **44(2)**, [292]
　　　mobile telephones, **44(2)**, [328]
　　　offshore workers, **44(2)**, [308]
　　　outplacement services, **44(2)**, [314]
　　　overseas medical treatment, **44(2)**, [334]
　　　passenger payments. *See* **car**
　　　pension provision, **44(2)**, [310]–[312]
　　　public bus services, support for,
　　　　44(2), [243]
　　　public transport strikes, travelling and
　　　　subsistence during, **44(2)**, [245]
　　　recreational facilities, **44(2)**, [262]–[264]
　　　removal expenses. *See* **benefits in kind**
　　　retraining courses, **44(2)**, [315]–[316]
　　　sale of asset, expenses incidental to,
　　　　44(2), [336]
　　　scope of provisions, **44(2)**, [227]
　　　statutory redundancy payments,
　　　　44(2), [313]
　　　subsidised meals, **44(2)**, [322]
　　　suggestion awards, **44(2)**, [330]–[331]
　　　third party entertainment, **44(2)**, [266]
　　　third party, small gifts from, **44(2)**, [333]
　　　transitional provisions, **44(2)**, [768]

income tax—*contd*
　employment income, on—*contd*
　　exemptions—*contd*
　　　visiting forces, **44(2)**, [306]
　　　vouches. *See* **vouchers**
　　　works transport services, **44(2)**, [242]
　　intermediary, services provided though. *See*
　　　intermediaries
　　meaning, **44(2)**, [7]
　　offices and office-holders, **44(2)**, [5]
　　person liable for, **44(2)**, [13]
　　place of performance of duties—
　　　duties in UK incidental to duties outside
　　　　UK, **44(2)**, [39]
　　　period of absence from, **44(2)**, [38]
　　　UK sector of continental shelf, in,
　　　　44(2), [41]
　　　vessel or aircraft, on, **44(2)**, [40]
　　specific, meaning, **44(2)**, [7]
　　structure of provisions, **44(2)**, [3]
　　transitional provisions, **44(2)**, [766]–[771]
　enemy, trading with—
　　custodian—
　　　Commissioners, furnishing information
　　　　to, **42**, [21]
　　　income payable to, **42**, [20]
　　　meaning, **42**, [21]
　　　payment of tax by, **42**, [20]
　　　release of property or income by,
　　　　42, [20]
　　effect of, **42**, [18]
　　income, provisions on, **42**, [20]
　　time limits, relaxation of, **42**, [20]
　energy-saving items, deduction for
　　expenditure on, **43(S)**, 521
　enforcement of payment, **4(2)**, [48], [51]
　enterprise investment scheme. *See* **enterprise
　　investment scheme; enterprise
　　investment scheme relief**
　exempt income—
　　annual payments. *See* **annual payments**
　　approved share incentive plan distribution,
　　　44(3), [785]
　　commodity and financial futures, gains on,
　　　44(3), [794]
　　consular officers and employees, relevant
　　　foreign income of, **44(3)**, [786]–[787]
　　disabled person's vehicle maintenance
　　　grant, **44(3)**, [795]
　　domestic microgeneration, **44(3)**, [798]
　　　renewables obligation certificate for,
　　　　44(3), [799]
　　electronic communications, incentives to
　　　use, **44(3)**, [793]
　　employee share schemes, from, **44(3)**, [766]
　　employment zone programme, payments
　　　under, **44(3)**, [797]
　　foreign interest securities owned by
　　　non-UK residents, interest on,
　　　44(3), [769]–[770]
　　FOTRA securities, from. *See* **securities**
　　funding bonds, redemption of, **44(3)**, [768]
　　general disregard, **44(3)**, [800]
　　housing grants, **44(3)**, [784]

income tax—*contd*
  exempt income—*contd*
    individual investment plans, from—
      duties of foreign institution, discharge
        of, **44(3)**, [712]
      foreign managers, **44(3)**, [711]
      information, provision of, **44(3)**, [714]
      non-entitlement to exemption,
        44(3), [713]
      plan managers, **44(3)**, [710]
      provision for, **44(3)**, [707]
      regulations, **44(3)**, [715]
      specification of, **44(3)**, [709]
    interest and royalty payments between
      associated companies of different Member
      states—
      anti-avoidance, **44(3)**, [780]
      companies being 25% associated,
        44(3), [776]
      conditions for, **44(3)**, [773]
      exemption notices, **44(3)**, [777]
      interpretation, **44(3)**, [781]
      person beneficially entitled, **44(3)**, [775]
      person making, **44(3)**, [774]
      power to amend Directive, **44(3)**, [782]
      provision for, **44(3)**, [772]
      special relationships, **44(3)**, [778]–[779]
    interest on certain deposits of victims of
      National-Socialist persecution,
      44(3), [771]
    national debt, towards reducing,
      44(3), [790]
    National Savings. *See* **National Savings
      Bank**
    New Deal 50plus, payments under,
      44(3), [796]
    non-UK residents, of—
      designated international organisations,
        securities issued by, **44(3)**, [789]
      Inter-American Development Bank
        securities, **44(3)**, [788]
    overview of provisions, **44(3)**, [704]
    personal injury damages, from, **44(3)**, [765]
    purchased life annuity payments. *See*
      purchased life annuity
    repayment supplements, paid under,
      44(3), [763]
    SAYE. *See* **Save As You Earn**
    scholarship, **44(3)**, [791]
    sight testing provided by employer, exempt
      from, **44(2)**, [329]
    student loan, interest on repayment of,
      44(3), [767]
    tax reserve certificates, from, **44(3)**, [764]
    transitional provisions, **44(3)**, [911]
    VAT repayment supplements, **44(3)**, [792]
    venture capital trusts dividends. *See* **venture
      capital trust**
    victims of National-Socialist persecution,
      interest on certain deposits of,
      44(3), [771]
    woodlands, commercial occupation of,
      44(3), [783]
  foreign distributions, credits for,
    43(S), 1558–62

income tax—*contd*
  foreign enterprises, UK residents involved in,
    43(S), 885–6
  foreign income. *See* **foreign income**
  fraudulent evasion, **43(1)**, [495]
  generally, **42**, [1]
  higher rate, **43(2)**, [84], [575]; **43(S)**, 514,
    1367; **44(4)**, [6]
    individuals, for, **44(4)**, [10]
  husband and wife maintenance payments. *See*
    annual payments *above*
  indexed rate bands, **43(2)**, [85]
  inheritance tax allowing for, **42**, [533]
  liability to. *See* **income tax liability**
  liability to, notice of, **42**, [98]
  loan interest relief—
    commercially let property, for, abolition,
      43(1), [127]
    home loans—
      higher rate relief, abolition of,
        42, [1045]
      payment under deduction of tax,
        qualifying lenders, **43(1)**, [80]
      qualifying maximum, **43(1)**, [68]
      withdrawal of, **43(1)**, [422]
  long funding leases. *See* **long funding leases**
  loss relief. *See* **loss relief**
  losses, temporary extension of carry back,
    43(S), 1440–2
  lower rate. *See under* savings rate *below*
  managed payment plans, **43(S)**, 1423–5
  married couple's allowance, **43(1)**, [67]
    effect of provisions, **43(1)**, [418]
    persons over 65, restricted to, **43(1)**, [418]
  miscellaneous income—
    annual payments. *See* **annual payments**
    estates in administration, beneficiaries'
      income from. *See* **administration of
      estates**
    films. *See* **films**
    intellectual property, from. *See* **intellectual
      property; know-how; patents**
    losses, calculation of, **44(3)**, [889]
    not otherwise charged to tax,
      44(3), [701]–[703]
    overview of provisions, **44(3)**, [584]
    priority of provisions, **44(3)**, [585]–[586]
    profits, apportionment, **44(3)**, [888]
    settlements. *See* **settlement**
    sound recordings. *See* **sound recordings**
    telecommunications. *See*
      telecommunications
    territorial scope of charges, **44(3)**, [587]
    transitional provisions, **44(3)**, [910]
  non-domiciled persons, exemption from
    liability—
    conditions, **43(S)**, 1386
    interpretation, **43(S)**, 1387
    means of giving, **43(S)**, 1386
  non-liability, certificate of, **42**, [234]
  non-resident, charge on. *See* **non-resident**
  non-resident companies, extent of charge,
    43(2), [217]
  non-residents, charged on, **43(1)**, [156]
  notice of liability, **42**, [98]

income tax—*contd*
  overdue, interest on, **42**, [216]; **43(1)**, [149]
  overpaid, recovery of—
    application of provisions, **43(S)**, 1414
    claims, **43(S)**, 1717–23
  partnership. *See* **partnership**
  PAYE deductions, **43(2)**, [207]
  payment of, **42**, [195]
  payments on account, **42**, [194]; **43(2)**, [544];
    43(S), 896
  personal allowance. *See also under* **personal
    reliefs**
    non-residents', abolition of, **43(S)**, 1432–4
    persons over 65, for, **43(2)**, [87], [576];
      43(S), 838
    persons under 65, for, **43(2)**, [86];
      43(S), 837, 1367
    persons with income exceeding £100, 000,
      reduction for, **43(S)**, 1368
  personal reliefs. *See* **personal reliefs**
  priority rules, establishment of, **44(3)**, [2]
  profits, computation of—
    change of basis, adjustment on,
      43(2), [108]
    calculation of, **43(2)**, [164]
    commencement, **43(2)**, [167]
    partnerships, **43(2)**, [166]
    special rules, **43(2)**, [165]
    mark to market, postponement of change
      to, **43(2)**, [109]
      election to continue, **43(2)**, [110]
  property income. *See* **property income**
  provisional repayment regime, end of,
    43(2), [51]
  rates of, **43(1)**, [191]; **43(S)**, 15, 1435–9
    amended provisions, **43(S)**, 1435–9
    basic, **43(2)**, [575]; **44(4)**, [6]
    basic rate, **43(S)**, 837
      individuals, for, **44(4)**, [10]
      limit, **43(S)**, 838; **44(4)**, [20]
        indexation of, **44(4)**, [21]
      reduction, transitional relief for gift aid
        charities, **43(S)**, 1170–2
      repayment when paid at, instead of
        starting or savings rate, **44(4)**, [17]
    dividend income, for, determining,
      44(4), [16]
    dividend ordinary rate, **44(4)**, [8]
      individuals, for, **44(4)**, [13]
      other persons, for, **44(4)**, [14]
    dividend trust rate, income charged at,
      44(4), [15]
    dividend upper rate, **44(4)**, [8]
      individuals, for, **44(4)**, [13]
    higher, **43(2)**, [575]; **43(S)**, 837; **44(4)**, [6]
    higher rate, individuals, for, **44(4)**, [10]
    lower, **43(2)**, [575]
    saving, abolition, **43(S)**, 839, Sch 1
    savings income, for, determining,
      44(4), [16]
    savings, on, **44(4)**, [7], [12]
    starting, **44(4)**, [6]
    starting rate—
      abolition, **43(S)**, 839
      individuals, for, **44(4)**, [10]

income tax—*contd*
  rates of—*contd*
    starting rate—*contd*
      limit, **44(4)**, [20]
        indexation of, **44(4)**, [21]
      savings, for—
        amendment of provisions,
          43(S), 998–1005
        creation of, **43(S)**, 839, 998–1005
        income charged at, **43(S)**, 999
        indexation, **43(S)**, 999
      transitional provisions and savings,
        44(4), [1048]
      trust, **44(4)**, [9]
        income charged at, **44(4)**, [15]
    record-keeping requirements, **43(S)**, 1305–8
    reduced and composite rate orders, **42**, [1506]
    reliefs, allowances and exemptions, **42**, [1]
    remittance basis, amended provisions,
      43(S), 1608–12
    rental compensation, on, **9**, [121]
    repayment, basic rate instead of starting or
      savings rate, where paid at, **44(4)**, [17]
    return. *See* **return**
    savings and investment income. *See* **savings
      and investment income**
    savings rate, **44(4)**, [7]
      income charged at, **44(4)**, [12]
    Schedule A—
      income chargeable under, substitution of
        provisions, **43(1)**, [168]
      information for purposes of, **42**, [125]
    Schedule C—
      abolition of charge, **43(1)**, [193]
      transfer of charge to Schedule D,
        43(1), [255]
    Schedule D computation, **42**, [951]
    Schedules, generally, **42**, [1]
      See **Schedule A, etc**
    scientific research organisations, deduction for
      payments to, **43(2)**, [731]
    social security pension lump sums, on,
      43(2), [725]
    starting rate, **43(2)**, [84], [575]; **43(S)**, 514;
      44(4), [6]
      individuals, for, **44(4)**, [10]
      limit, **44(4)**, [20]
        2001–2, **43(2)**, [35]
        indexation of, **44(4)**, [21]
    summary of provisions, **43(S)**, 1
    territorial extension of charge, **42**, [305],
      [308]
    trading income. *See* **trading income**
    trading losses, deduction of, **42**, [1058]
    transitional provisions, **44(3)**, [903]
    trust rate, **43(S)**, 1369
    trusts—
      income tax rate, **44(4)**, [9]
        income charged on, **44(4)**, [15]
    unpaid, surcharges on, **43(1)**, [148]
    widow's bereavement allowance, abolition,
      43(1), [420]

Income Tax Acts
  abbreviations, **44(2)**, [726]

Income Tax Acts—*contd*
application from year to year, **44(1)**, [604]
defined expressions, index of, **44(2)**, [727]
definitions—
"bank", **44(4)**, [999]
"company", **44(4)**, [1000]
"connected" persons, **44(4)**, [1001]–[1002], [1028]
"control", **44(4)**, [1003], [1028]
"debenture", **44(4)**, [1029]
"double taxation arrangements", **44(4)**, [1030]
"farming" and related expressions, **44(4)**, [1004]
"generally accepted accounting practice", **44(4)**, [1005]
"gilt-edged securities", **44(4)**, [1031]
"grossing up", **44(4)**, [1006]
index of, **44(4)**, [1064]
"local authority", **44(4)**, [1007]
"local authority association", **44(4)**, [1008]
"modified net income", **44(4)**, [1032], [1033]
"offshore installation", **44(4)**, [1009]–[1010]
"oil and gas exploration and appraisal", **44(4)**, [1011]
"property investment LLP", **44(4)**, [1012]
"recognised stock exchange", **44(4)**, [1013]
"research and development", **44(4)**, [1014]
"unit trust scheme", **44(4)**, [1015]
final provisions, **44(4)**, [1034]–[1042]
meaning, **44(1)**, [614]
minor and consequential amendments, **44(4)**, [1043]–[1045]
old and new law, continuity etc of, **44(1)**, [691]
orders and regulations, **44(4)**, [1021]
over-deductions before passing of, **44(1)**, [606]
overview, **44(4)**, [1]–[2]
repeals and revocations, **44(4)**, [1062]–[1063]
territorial sea of UK, **44(4)**, [1020]
transitional provisions and savings, **44(4)**, [1046]–[1061]
under-deductions before passing of, **44(1)**, [605]

Income Tax (Earnings and Pensions) Act 2003
overview of, **44(4)**, [1]

income tax liability
additional tax, **44(4)**, [30]
allowances deductible, **44(4)**, [24]–[25]
annual payments, restriction of deductions for, **44(4)**, [851]
calculation of, **44(4)**, [23]
liabilities not included in, **44(4)**, [32]
civil partners, reductions for, **44(4)**, [26]
European Economic Interest Groupings, **44(4)**, [850]
extra return to be treated as interest, **44(4)**, [853]–[854]

income tax liability—*contd*
government securities held by non-UK resident central banks, **44(4)**, [848]
industrial building allowances, **44(4)**, [24]
jointly held property, **44(4)**, [844]
unequal beneficial interest, declaration of, **44(4)**, [845]
letters patent, **44(4)**, [852]
limits on, for non-UK residents—
"beneficial entitlement", meaning, **44(4)**, [830]
broker conditions, independent, **44(4)**, [825]
companies, **44(4)**, [823]
"disregarded company income", meaning, **44(4)**, [824]
"disregarded annual payments", meaning, **44(4)**, [834]
"disregarded savings and investment income", meaning, **44(4)**, [833]
independent investment manager—
brokers, transactions through, **44(4)**, [836]
conditions, **44(4)**, [826]
20% rule—
collective investment schemes, application to, **44(4)**, [832]
requirements of, **44(4)**, [827]
where not met, **44(4)**, [831]
meaning, **44(4)**, [835]
transactions through, **44(4)**, [836]
individuals, trustees etc, **44(4)**, [819]
cases where not applicable, **44(4)**, [820]
"disregarded income", meaning, **44(4)**, [821]
"disregarded transaction income", meaning, **44(4)**, [822]
independent investment manager—
brokers, transactions through, **44(4)**, [836]
conditions, **44(4)**, [826]
20% rule—
collective investment schemes, application to, **44(4)**, [832]
requirements of, **44(4)**, [827]
where not met, **44(4)**, [831]
meaning, **44(4)**, [835]
transactions through, **44(4)**, [836]
"investment transaction", **44(4)**, [835]
"qualifying period", meaning, **44(4)**, [828]
"relevant disregarded income", meaning, **44(4)**, [829]
local authorities, **44(4)**, [846]
local authority associations, **44(4)**, [846]
married couples, reductions for, **44(4)**, [26]
official agents of Commonwealth countries, **44(4)**, [849]
patents—
allowances, **44(4)**, [24]
expenses, **44(4)**, [24]
royalties—
gross amount of payment, meaning, **44(4)**, [460]
receipts, spreading, **44(4)**, [469]

income tax liability—*contd*
  patents—*contd*
    royalties—*contd*
      relief for—
        individuals, for, **44(4)**, [456]
        other persons, for, **44(4)**, [457]
        overview, **44(4)**, [455]
        payments ineligible for, **44(4)**, [458]
        s 733 ICTA, special rule for persons
          affected by, **44(4)**, [459]
  plant and machinery allowances, **44(4)**, [24]
  reliefs deductible, **44(4)**, [24]–[25]
  Reserve Bank of India, issue department of,
    44(4), [847]
  residence—
    employment income of individuals in UK
      for temporary purpose, **44(4)**, [840]
    foreign income of individuals in UK for
      temporary purpose, **44(4)**, [839]
    personal representatives, **44(4)**, [842]
    staff of designated allied headquarters,
      44(4), [841]
    temporarily abroad, **44(4)**, [837]
    trustees and companies, **44(4)**, [843]
    visiting forces, **44(4)**, [841]
    working abroad, **44(4)**, [838]
  State Bank of Pakistan, issue department of,
    44(4), [847]
  tax reductions, **44(4)**, [26], [29]
    order of deducting, **44(4)**, [27]–[28]
  total income, calculating, **44(4)**, [31]

Income Tax (Trading and Other Income) Act 2005
  overview of, **44(4)**, [1]

inconsiderate driving
  death, caused by, **37**, [560]
  meaning, **37**, [562]
  offence of, **37**, [561]

incorrigible rogue
  committal for sentence, **11(2)**, [214]
  committal for trial, **12(1)**, [28]
  persons being, **12(1)**, [28]
  sentence, **12(1)**, [29]

incumbent. *See also* **clergy**
  acquisition of property, consent of diocesan
    authority to, **14**, 634
  annual personal grant to, **14**, 838, 841
  benefices held in plurality—
    designation of, **14**, 996
    resigning, **14**, 984–5
  chancel, abolition of obligation to repair,
    14, 328
  corn sown by, profits of, **14**, 43
  covenant over land, entering into, **14**, 518–19
  curate—
    dismissing, **14**, 118
    failing to appoint, **14**, 115–16
  diocesan surveyor's report, sent to, **14**, 777–8
  disability—
    bishop, powers of, **14**, 893–4
    enquiry into, **14**, 887

incumbent—*contd*
  disability—*contd*
    inhibition in cases of, **14**, 891
    medical examination, **14**, 889
    notification of action, **14**, 895
    pension, **14**, 896
    plurality of benefices, holding, **14**, 894
    report on, **14**, 890
    resignation on, **14**, 893–4
  easement, entering into agreement for,
    14, 519
  group ministry, in, **14**, 992–3
  highway, dedicating land for, **14**, 520
  interest in trust, holding, **14**, 633
  medical examination, **14**, 889
  new benefice, of, **14**, 996
  non-resident—
    curates, requiring, **14**, 246–7
    penalties, **14**, 102–3
    return, not to, **14**, 246–7
    See also **house of residence**
  parsonage house, obligations and duties to,
    14, 783
  pastoral scheme or order, designated by,
    14, 1087–8
  pastoral situation, breakdown in—
    compensation on vacation of benefice,
      14, 895–6, 902–4
    discharge on, **14**, 892–3
    meaning, **14**, 899
    notification of action, **14**, 895
    pension after, **14**, 896
    rebuke on, **14**, 892
    resignation before, **14**, 886
    See also **parish**
    Vacation of Benefices Rule Committee,
      14, 898
  payments to, **14**, 521
  property given to, transfer of, **14**, 847
  provincial tribunals, enquiries referred to,
    14, 1266
  residence—
    benefice, in, *See* **benefice; house of
      residence**
    more than one, liable for, **14**, 69
    power of sale. *See* **house of residence**
  sequestrated benefice, of, **14**, 237
  service of documents on, **14**, 406
  stipend. *See* **stipend**
  vesting of land in, **14**, 400–1, 517

incumbrance
  meaning, **17(1)**, [211]; **20**, [436], [804]
  registered land, on. *See* **land registration**
  sale etc of land, on, discharge by court,
    20, [668]

indecency. *See* **child; sexual offences**
  street offences, **36**, [228], [385], [386]

indecent assault. *See under* **assault**

indecent display
  corporation, offence by, **12(1)**, [716]
  entry and seizure, **12(1)**, [715]

indecent display—*contd*
offences, **12(1)**, [714]
penalties, **12(1)**, [717]
public, deemed to be, **12(1)**, [714]
public place, in, meaning, **12(1)**, [714]
warning notice, **12(1)**, [714]

indemnity
application to Crown proceedings, **13**, [13]

indenture
deed taking effect as, **20**, [674]
description of, **20**, [675]

Independent Barring Board
accounts, **6(S)**, 236
adults' barred list—
appeals as to, **6(S)**, 177
barred persons, meaning, **6(S)**, 177
establishment and maintenance of,
6(S), 176
inclusion in, **6(S)**, 241–3
information, Board requiring,
6(S), 245–6
prescribed criteria, **6(S)**, 246–7
procedure, **6(S)**, 243
representations as to, **6(S)**, 244
review of, **6(S)**, 244–5
children's barred list—
appeals as to, **6(S)**, 177
barred persons, meaning, **6(S)**, 176
establishment and maintenance of,
6(S), 176
inclusion in, **6(S)**, 239–41
information, Board requiring,
6(S), 245–6
prescribed criteria, **6(S)**, 246–7
procedure, **6(S)**, 243
representations as to, **6(S)**, 244
review of, **6(S)**, 244–5
delegation of functions, **6(S)**, 236
documents received in evidence, **6(S)**, 237
establishment of, **6(S)**, 176
funding, **6(S)**, 236
incidental powers, **6(S)**, 237
local authority—
duty to provide information on request,
6(S), 211
prescribed information, duty to refer,
6(S), 210–11
maladministration, **6(S)**, 237
membership, **6(S)**, 234
prescribed information, duty to refer—
findings of fact, immaterial, **6(S)**, 223
local authority, of, **6(S)**, 210–11
offences, **6(S)**, 210
personnel suppliers, by, **6(S)**, 208
regulated activity providers, of, **6(S)**, 207
relevant register, keeper of, **6(S)**, 212–13
supervisory authorities, of, **6(S)**, 216–18
regulated activity providers—
duty to provide information on request,
6(S), 209
prescribed information, duty to refer,
6(S), 207

Independent Barring Board—*contd*
relevant register, keeper of—
duty to provide information on request,
6(S), 214
prescribed information, duty to refer,
6(S), 212–13
remuneration and allowances, **6(S)**, 235
reports, **6(S)**, 236
staff, **6(S)**, 235
status, **6(S)**, 237
supervisory authorities—
duty to provide information on request,
6(S), 218
prescribed information, duty to refer,
6(S), 216–18
provision of information to, **6(S)**, 222
tenure of office, **6(S)**, 234
transfers to, schemes for, **6(S)**, 238

Independent Broadcasting Authority
assets, transfer of—
generally, **45**, [155]
scheme, **45**, [194]
vesting of property on, **45**, [194]
chairman and members, cessation of office,
45, [155]
continuance until transfer date, **45**, [155]
final accounts and annual report, **45**, [194]
liabilities, contingent, discharge of, **45**, [194]
pension fund, division of, control, **45**, [194]
property, vesting after transfer scheme,
45, [194]
radio service, transitional arrangements. *See*
sound broadcasting *below*
services, transitional arrangements—
Broadcasting Complaints Commission,
provisions, **45**, [197]
Broadcasting Standards Council,
provisions, **45**, [197]
DBS—
additional payments by licence holders,
45, [198]
additional services licences, **45**, [198]
contracts, **45**, [158], [198]
equipment, disposal, **45**, [160]
provisions as to, **45**, [158], [197]
replacement, **45**, [198]
teletext contracts, **45**, [198]
generally, **45**, [157], [197]
ITC—
Channel 4, **45**, [197]
DBS services, **45**, [197]
generally, **45**, [155], [196]
local delivery services, **45**, [197]
programme contracts, **45**, [197]
provision of services by, **45**, [197]
teletext services, **45**, [197]
Welsh programmes, **45**, [197]
advertisements on, **45**, [197]
local sound broadcasting, exercise of
functions, **45**, [161]
programme contracts, variation, **45**, [158],
[159]

Independent Broadcasting Authority—*contd*
services, transitional arrangements—*contd*
  radio service. *See* sound broadcasting *below*
sound broadcasting service, transitional
  arrangements—
    Broadcasting Complaints Commission,
      provisions, **45**, [197], [199]
    generally, **45**, [155], [199]
    local delivery service, **45**, [197], [199]
    local licences, **45**, [200]
    local services—
      contracts—
        preservation, **45**, [199]
        provision of, **45**, [199]
        replacement, **45**, [200]
        terminated, liabilities under, **45**, [200]
transfer of undertakings—
  bodies to which transferred, **45**, [155],
    [194]
  generally, **45**, [155]
  nominated company, to—
    borrowing by, temporary restrictions,
      45, [167]
    functions, exercise of, **45**, [163]
    generally, **45**, [155], [162]
    Government holding in—
      initial, **45**, [162]
      target investment limit, **45**, [164]
    loans to, **45**, [166]
    reserves, **45**, [165]
  scheme, **45**, [194]
transitional arrangements. *See* services *above*

independent hospitals
children's accommodation in, notification,
  6, [414]
entry by authorised person, **6**, [414]

**Independent Police Complaints
Commission**
accounts, **33(2)**, [397]
appeals, **33(2)**, [401]
  review and re-investigation following,
    33(2), [401]
authentication of seal, **33(2)**, [397]
borrowing, **33(2)**, [397]
chairman, **33(2)**, [397]
  appointment, **33(2)**, [348]
chief executive, **33(2)**, [397]
conduct matters, reference to, **33(2)**, [399]
  duties of Commission, **33(2)**, [399]
constitution, **33(2)**, [348]
deputy chairman, **33(2)**, [397]
establishment of, **33(2)**, [348], [369]
evidence of documents, **33(2)**, [397]
financial year, **33(2)**, [397]
general functions, **33(2)**, [349]
guidance, power to issue, **33(2)**, [362]
immigration and asylum enforcement
  functions, **33(2)**, [619]
immigration, investigation of complaints
  relating to, **13(S)**, Customs 50
information, provision of, to, **33(2)**, [357]
inspection of police premises on behalf of,
  33(2), [358]

**Independent Police Complaints
Commission**—*contd*
investigation—
  accelerated procedure, **33(2)**, [401]
  action in response to report, **33(2)**, [401]
  appeals, **33(2)**, [401]
  assistance from police authorities and chief
    officers, **33(2)**, [354]–[355]
  complainant, duty to keep informed,
    33(2), [360]
  covert human intelligence sources, use of,
    33(2), [359]
  directed or intrusive surveillance, use of,
    33(2), [359]
  discontinue, power to, **33(2)**, [401]
  generally, **33(2)**, [401]
  National Policing Improvement Agency
    involvement, **33(2)**, [356]
  payment for assistance with, **33(2)**, [355]
  power to determine form of, **33(2)**, [401]
  regulations, **33(2)**, [363]
    consultation on, **33(2)**, [364]
  relatives, duty to provide information for,
    33(2), [361]
members—
  appointment, **33(2)**, [348]
  ordinary, **33(2)**, [397]
  pensions, **33(2)**, [397]
  remuneration, **33(2)**, [397]
payments by Secretary of State, **33(2)**, [397]
proceedings, **33(2)**, [397]
reference of complaints to, **33(2)**, [398]
  duties of Commission, **33(2)**, [398]
regional offices, power to set up, **33(2)**, [397]
reports, to Secretary of State, **33(2)**, [350]
staff—
  appointment of, **33(2)**, [397]
  conduct of, **33(2)**, [368]
  insurance, **33(2)**, [397]
  National Policing Improvement Agency,
    agreement for corresponding procedures,
    33(2), [367]
  seconded, liability for acts of, **33(2)**, [397]
  Serious Organised Crime Agency,
    agreement for corresponding procedures,
    33(2), [366]
  superannuation, **33(2)**, [397]
summary of provisions, **33(2)**, [17]
transitional arrangements, **33(2)**, [369]

independent radio services. *See* **radio
services**

independent schools
assisted places at—
  abolition, **15(1)**, [768]
  meaning, **15(1)**, [769]
  participation agreement, meaning,
    15(1), [771]
  transitional arrangements—
    generally, **15(1)**, [769]
    regulations for purposes of, **15(1)**, [770]
child with special educational needs,
  admission of, **15(1)**, [553]
early years provision, **6(S)**, 93

independent schools—*contd*
general note, **15(1)**, [1]
governing body, individual pupils'
  performance, provision of information
  about, **15(1)**, [671]
information—
  registration authority requiring,
    15(2), [482]
  Secretary of State requiring, **15(1)**, [670]
inspection, **15(2)**, [471]–[472]
management, prohibition on participation in,
  15(2), [877]–[878]
meaning, **15(1)**, [607]
offences—
  bodies corporate, by, **15(2)**, [484]
  proceedings for, **15(2)**, [483]
  unincorporated bodies, by, **15(2)**, [485]
register—
  appeals against removal from,
    15(2), [476]–[477]
  deletion of school from, **15(2)**, [475], [486]
  meaning, **15(2)**, [488]
  requirement for, **15(2)**, [466]
registered—
  changes to details, **15(2)**, [470]
  information, provision of, **15(2)**, [482]
  inspect, power to, **15(2)**, [471]–[472]
  participation in management, prohibition
    on, **15(2)**, [478]–[481]
  removal from register, **15(2)**, [475]
    appeals against, **15(2)**, [476]–[477]
    service of notice, **15(2)**, [487]
    unsuitable persons, **15(2)**, [486]
  standards, failure to meet, **15(2)**, [475]
registration of—
  applications for, **15(2)**, [468]–[469]
  changes to registered details, **15(2)**, [470]
  registers, **15(2)**, [466]
  unregistered schools, **15(2)**, [467]
religious character, having—
  designation of, **15(2)**, [122]
  employment of teachers at, **15(2)**, [121]
special educational needs, pupil with,
  15(1), [553]
standards—
  failure to meet, **15(2)**, [475]
  generally, **15(2)**, [465]
unregistered schools, **15(2)**, [467]
Wales, in. *See* **Wales**

independent sound broadcasting. *See* **radio
services**

independent television
additional services—
  broadcasting frequencies, provided on,
    45, [102]
  frequencies, spare, use in transmission,
    45, [103]
  interference with other transmissions,
    prohibition, **45**, [108]
  licences—
    additional payments in respect of,
      45, [106]
    application for, **45**, [104]

independent television—*contd*
additional services—*contd*
  licences—*contd*
    award of, **45**, [105]
    cash bids, **45**, [105]
    conditions in use of frequencies, as to,
      45, [103]
    consideration procedure, **45**, [105]
    duration, **45**, [107]
    enforcement of, **45**, [109]
    fees, **45**, [104], [106], [107]
    notices as to, **45**, [104]
    payments, **45**, [104], [106], [107]
    renewal, **45**, [107]
    revocation, **45**, [105]
    spare frequencies, use of, inclusion of
      provisions in, **45**, [103]
  licensing generally, **45**, [103]
  meaning, **45**, [102]
  telecommunication signals, sending of, by,
    45, [102]
  teletext. *See* **teletext services**
broadcasting frequencies, additional services
  on. *See* additional services *above*
Channel 3—
  additional services. *See* additional services
    above
  apology, direction to broadcast, **45**, [97]
  application for licence—
    consideration procedure, **45**, [85]
    generally, **45**, [84]
    guidance on, **45**, [84]
    news, particulars as to, **45**, [85]
    programme proposals, **45**, [85]
    proposals in, **45**, [84], [85]
    requirements as to contents, **45**, [85]
    Secretary of State, referred to, **45**, [86]
  area served, **45**, [83], [767]
    additional, temporary provision of,
      45, [91]
    provisions relating to, application,
      45, [95]
  cash bid for licence—
    accompanying application, **45**, [84]
    further, submission of, **45**, [86]
    highest, award on, **45**, [86]
    less than highest, award, **45**, [86]
  control, change of—
    control, meaning, **45**, [720]
    notification to OFCOM, **45**, [714]
    restrictions, **45**, [90]
    review by OFCOM, **45**, [714]
    variation of licence following, **45**, [715]
  correction, direction to broadcast, **45**, [97]
  employees, proposals as to, **45**, [84]
  establishment, **45**, [83]
  failure by, financial penalty, **45**, [88], [98]
  international obligations, compliance with,
    45, [701]
  licence—
    additional payments, **45**, [89]
    application for. *See* application for
      licence *above*
    appointment of news providers by
      holders of, **45**, [265]

independent television—*contd*
  Channel 3—*contd*
    licence—*contd*
      award—
        conditions attached, **45**, [87]
        generally, **45**, [86]
      cash bid. *See* cash bid for licence *above*
      conditions attached, **45**, [80], [89]
      digital, **45**, [594]
      enforcement, **45**, [97]
      fees, **45**, [80], [84]
        additional, payment of, **45**, [89]
        qualifying revenue, **45**, [84], [89]
      grant, notice of proposal, **45**, [84]
      initial expiry date, meaning, **45**, [604]
      new licensing round, report in
        anticipation of, **45**, [609]
      newspaper proprietors banned from
        holding, **45**, [767]
      payments received under, additional
        payments arising, **45**, [89]
      refusal, **45**, [90]
      renewal, **45**, [596]
        financial terms, **45**, [597]
        orders suspending rights of, **45**, [610]
      replacement of existing, **45**, [595]
      restrictions, relaxation of, **45**, [713]
      reviews relating to, **45**, [605]–[608]
      revocation, **45**, [88], [99]
      shortening of period as penalty, **45**, [98]
      source of funds, **45**, [86]
    licensed services, failure to provide,
      penalty, **45**, [88]
    networking arrangements—
      appeals against decisions relating to the
        competition test, **45**, [763]
      approved—
        obligation as to making and
          continuance of, **45**, [662]
        review of, **45**, [664]
      duty to refuse approval, **45**, [763]
      imposition of, notification of decisions
        on, **45**, [763]
      information for OFCOM, **45**, [763]
      modifications, approval required for,
        45, [763]
      OFCOM's decisions regarding approval,
        45, [763]
      OFCOM's power to impose, **45**, [663]
      proposals for, **45**, [661]
      supplemental provisions, **45**, [665]
    news programmes. *See* news programmes
      below
    participation in, restrictions for newspaper
      proprietors, **45**, [767]
    programme schedules, announcement,
      45, [96]
    regional basis, **45**, [83]
    regional licences—
      networking agreements—
        competition legislation, **45**, [177]
        modification, **45**, [177]
    regional programmes, **45**, [657], [658]
    Scotland, programmes in Gaelic, **45**, [174]

independent television—*contd*
  Channel 3—*contd*
    teletext service. *See* **teletext services**
  Channel 4—
    additional services. *See* additional services
      above
    apology, direction to broadcast, **45**, [97]
    Channel Four Television Corporation. *See*
      Channel Four Television Corporation
      below
    correction, direction to broadcast, **45**, [97]
    failure by, financial penalty, **45**, [98]
    IBA programmes, transitional
      arrangements, **45**, [157], [197]
    international obligations, compliance with,
      45, [701]
    licence—
      enforcement, **45**, [97]
      replacement of, **45**, [611]
      shortening of period as penalty, **45**, [98]
    licensed service, provision of, **45**, [93]
    programmes, schedules, announcement,
      45, [96]
    regional programme-making for, **45**, [659]
    school programmes, **45**, [667]
    teletext service. *See* **teletext services**
    Welsh Authority, provision of programmes
      for, **45**, [111]
  Channel Four Television Corporation—
    accounts and audit, **45**, [190]
    annual reports, **45**, [190]
    borrowing limit, **45**, [584]
    documents, authentication and seal,
      45, [190]
    employees, **45**, [190]
    formation, **45**, [92]
    functions, **45**, [92], [583], [759]
    licensed service, provision of, **45**, [93]
    members—
      appointment, **45**, [190]
      remuneration and pensions, **45**, [190]
      tenure of office, **45**, [190]
    OFCOM, functions transferred to,
      45, [755]
    proceedings, **45**, [190]
    programme-making, involvement in,
      45, [666]
    shares in, **45**, [93]
    status and capacity, **45**, [190]
  Channel 5—
    area service, determination, **45**, [94]
    change of control—
      control, meaning, **45**, [720]
      notification to OFCOM, **45**, [716]
      review by OFCOM, **45**, [716]
      variation of licence following, **45**, [717]
    correction or apology, direction to
      broadcast, **45**, [97]
    days and times of service, determination,
      45, [94]
    failure by, financial penalty, **45**, [98]
    international obligations, compliance with,
      45, [701]
    licences—
      additional payments, **45**, [89]

independent television—*contd*
Channel 5—*contd*
licences—*contd*
applications, **45**, [84]
award of licence, **45**, [86]
conditions attached, **45**, [87]
control, changes in, restriction, **45**, [90]
digital, **45**, [594]
enforcement, **45**, [97]
failure to provide service, **45**, [88]
grant of, **45**, [86], [94]
initial expiry date, meaning, **45**, [604]
new licensing round, report in
anticipation of, **45**, [609]
provisions applicable, generally, **45**, [94]
renewal of, **45**, [596], [597]
replacement of existing, **45**, [595]
reviews relating to, **45**, [605]–[608]
revocation, **45**, [99]
penalties on, **45**, [88]
shortening of period as penalty, **45**, [98]
regional programme-making for, **45**, [657]
setting up of service, **45**, [94]
Commission. *See* **Independent Television
Commission**
competition between licensed providers,
conditions relating to, **45**, [682], [689]
digital broadcasting. *See* **digital broadcasting**
distribution of services, requirements,
45, [117]
equal opportunities in employment,
promotion of, **45**, [703]
frequencies—
assignment of, additional services, **45**, [102]
spare, use, **45**, [103]
licences—
abolition of separate licences for certain
television services, **45**, [620]
conditional, **45**, [80]
conditions generally, **45**, [80]
disqualification from holding, **45**, [189]
modification of, **45**, [712]
false information—
disqualification for offence, **45**, [300],
[301]
offence of providing, **45**, [299]
fees, **45**, [80]
general provisions, **45**, [79]
holding of—
disqualification, **45**, [189], [712]
religious bodies—
approval required, **45**, [770]
disqualification, **45**, [189]
restrictions, **45**, [81], [188]
relaxation of, **45**, [713]
requirements, **45**, [79], [80]
variation, **45**, [79]
following change of control, **45**, [715]
licensed service—
failure to provide, penalty, **45**, [88]
Government requirement for, **45**, [702]
local delivery services, licence, abolition of,
45, [593]
local digital television services, **45**, [623]
monitoring of programmes, **45**, [700]

independent television—*contd*
must-offer obligations—
networks, in relation to, **45**, [643]
satellite services, in relation to, **45**, [644]
securing of must-provide services in certain
areas, **45**, [645], [646]
news programmes—
Channel 3—
appointed of news providers, **45**, [651]
disqualified, **45**, [652]
power to repeal or modify news provider
provisions, **45**, [653]
restrictive trade practices, **45**, [178]
Channel 5 news providers, **45**, [654]
particulars required in licence application,
45, [85]
party political broadcasts, **45**, [699]
programme and fairness standards, **45**, [693]
advertisements and sponsorship
objectives for, **45**, [687]
supplementary powers relating to,
45, [688]
fairness code, duty to observe, **45**, [692]
OFCOM's standards code, **45**, [685]
observance of, **45**, [691]
setting and publication of, **45**, [690]
special impartiality requirements, **45**, [686]
public service remit—
enforcement of, **45**, [641]
licensed providers, of, **45**, [636]
OFCOM to report on fulfilment of,
45, [635]
power to amend, **45**, [642]
programme policy—
changes of, **45**, [638]
statements of, **45**, [637]
restricted services—
licensing, **45**, [101]
meaning, **45**, [100]
revenue, qualifying—
computation, **45**, [119]
statement of, **45**, [192]
services—
annual report by OFCOM on, **45**, [721]
assigning television frequencies, abolition of
function of, **45**, [592]
licensed. *See* licensed service *above*
regulation of, **45**, [591]
transmission and distribution,
requirements, **45**, [117]
unlicensed, prohibition, **45**, [82]
telecommunication signals, transmission of
additional services by. *See* additional services
above
teletext service, provision. *See* **teletext
services**
television licensable content service—
international obligations, compliance with,
45, [701]
licences—
abolition of separate licences for certain
television services, **45**, [620]
application for, **45**, [615]

independent television—*contd*
  television licensable content service—*contd*
    licences—*contd*
      contravention of condition or
        direction—
          penalties for, **45**, [617]
          revocation of licence, **45**, [618]
      crime or disorder, action against licence
        holders who incite, **45**, [619]
      remedial action, direction to licensee to
        take, **45**, [616]
      meaning, **45**, [612], [614]
      services not being, **45**, [613], [614]
    transmission of services, requirements,
      45, [117]
  Welsh. *See* **Welsh Authority**

Independent Television Commission
  Cable Authority, transfer of property, rights
    and liabilities of to, **45**, [156], [195]
  functions generally. *See* **independent**
    television
  Gaelic, programmes in—
    payments to Fund, **45**, [172]
    powers as to, **45**, [172]
  IBA services, transitional arrangements—
    generally, **45**, [155], [197]
    provision, **45**, [197]
    See further under **Independent**
      Broadcasting Authority
  OFCOM, functions transferred to, **45**, [755]

India
  Commonwealth citizenship, **31**, [186]
  existing laws, **7(2)**, [440]
  new dominions—
    legislation for, **7(2)**, [437]
    meaning, **7(2)**, [436]
    setting up, effect of, **7(2)**, [438]
  pensions, judges, increase of, **33(1)**, [102],
    [112], [116]
  republic, becoming, existing law, operation
    of, **7(2)**, [456]
  Secretary of State for, legal proceedings,
    7(2), [439]

indictable offence
  meaning, **41**, [605]

indictment
  amendment of, **12(1)**, [223]
  arraigning person in custody, **12(1)**, [106]
  assault or battery proceedings on, **12(1)**, [97]
  bill, preferring, **12(1)**, [242]
  content of, **12(1)**, [221]
  due process of law, with, **12(1)**, [3]
  false statement, for, **12(1)**, [203]
  form of, **12(1)**, [203]
  joinder of charges in, **12(1)**, [222], [1084]
  procedure for, **12(1)**, [242]
  retrial, on, **12(1)**, [424]
  separate trial on, **12(1)**, [223]
  statement of offence in, **12(1)**, [221]
  treason, for, limitation on, **12(1)**, [10]

individual
  personal reliefs. *See* **personal reliefs**

individual insolvency
  administration—
    expenses, **4(2)**, [345]
    rules, **4(2)**, [560]
  annual report for Parliament, **4(2)**, [462]
  appeals, jurisdiction to hear, **4(2)**, [458]
  associate of person, meaning, **4(2)**, [528]
  bankruptcy order. *See* **bankruptcy**
  county court jurisdiction, **4(2)**, [456]
  court rules, **4(2)**, [560]
  courts—
    co-operation between, **4(2)**, [513]
    information and records, **4(2)**, [560]
  creditors—
    meaning, **4(2)**, [466]
    meeting—
      approval of arrangement by, **4(2)**, [317]
      decisions of—
        challenging, **4(2)**, [321]
        report of, to court, **4(2)**, [318]
      irregularity as to, **4(2)**, [321]
      summoning, **4(2)**, [316]
    orders protecting, **4(2)**, [512]
    persons deemed to be, **4(2)**, [316]
    transactions defrauding, **4(2)**, [510]–[512]
  Crown, provisions applied, **4(2)**, [524]
  debtor—
    absconding, arrest, **4(2)**, [8], [447]
    delinquent, prosecution of, **4(2)**, [323]
    false representations by, **4(2)**, [322]
    information to be given by, **4(2)**, [314]
    meaning, **4(2)**, [468]
    proposal by, **4(2)**, [315]
    stay of action against, **4(2)**, [312]
    undischarged bankrupt, where, **4(2)**, [320]
  deceased persons' estates, **4(2)**, [507]
    joint tenancies, **4(2)**, [508]
  districts—
    bankruptcy districts becoming, **4(2)**, [457]
    designation, **4(2)**, [457]
    London district, **4(2)**, [457]
  documents, stamp duty exemption,
    4(2), [461]
  fees order, **4(2)**, [499]
  High Court jurisdiction, **4(2)**, [456]
  interim order—
    application for, **4(2)**, [311]
    circumstances for making, **4(2)**, [313]
    discharge of, **4(2)**, [314]
    effect of, **4(2)**, [310]
    extension of period of, **4(2)**, [314]
    not making, procedure, **4(2)**, [315]
    power to make, **4(2)**, [310]
    provisions of, **4(2)**, [313]
    undischarged bankrupt, in case of,
      4(2), [313]
  jurisdiction—
    appeals from courts having, **4(2)**, [458]
    co-operation between courts, **4(2)**, [513]
    county court, **4(2)**, [456]
    High Court, **4(2)**, [456]
  N. Ireland, provisions applied, **4(2)**, [534]

individual insolvency—*contd*
nominee's report, **4(2)**, [315]
notices etc, rules, **4(2)**, [560]
offences and penalties, **4(2)**, [561]
office-holders—
  gas etc services, right to, **4(2)**, [455]
  meaning, **4(2)**, [455]
  powers of, **4(2)**, [455]
partnerships, **4(2)**, [506]
practitioner. *See* **insolvency practitioner**
preferential debts—
  categories of, **4(2)**, [469], [557]
  priorities, **4(2)**, [317]
  relevant date as to, **4(2)**, [470]
receiver or manager, **4(2)**, [560]
regulations, **4(2)**, [505]
rules—
  committee, constitution, **4(2)**, [497]
  contents, **4(2)**, [496], [560]
  power to make, **4(2)**, [496]
  procedure for making, **4(2)**, [496]
scheme or arrangement. *See* voluntary
  arrangement *below*
services account. *See* **Insolvency Services
  Account**
statement of affairs as evidence, **4(2)**, [523]
summary of provisions, **4(2)**, [1]
time limits, extension, **4(2)**, [459]
transactions defrauding creditors,
  4(2), [510]–[512]
transitional provisions, **4(2)**, [531], [563]
voluntary arrangement—
  administration expenses, **4(2)**, [345]
  approval of—
    effect of, **4(2)**, [319]
    generally, **4(2)**, [317]
    revocation or suspension of, **4(2)**, [321]
  default in respect of, **4(2)**, [345]
  false representations, **4(2)**, [322]
  fast-track—
    approval of, **4(2)**, [329]
    availability of, **4(2)**, [326]
    decision, **4(2)**, [327]
    implementation, **4(2)**, [330]
    offences, **4(2)**, [332]
    result, report on, **4(2)**, [328]
    revocation, **4(2)**, [331]
  implementation, **4(2)**, [325]
  insolvency practitioner—
    appointment of, **4(2)**, [325]
    See further **insolvency practitioner**
  intention to make, effect, **4(2)**, [312]
  interim order. *See* interim order *above*
  meaning, **4(2)**, [311]
  modification of, **4(2)**, [317]
  nominee—
    authorisation, **4(2)**, [473]
    official receiver as, **4(2)**, [474], [560]
    person to act as, **4(2)**, [311]
    report by, **4(2)**, [314], [315]
    statement by debtor to, **4(2)**, [314]
  premature end, coming to, **4(2)**, [324]
  registration rules, **4(2)**, [560]
  revision of, **4(2)**, [321]
  supervision of, **4(2)**, [325], [368]

individual insolvency—*contd*
voluntary arrangement—*contd*
  supervisor—
    authorisation, **4(2)**, [473]
    official receiver as, **4(2)**, [474], [560]
    undischarged bankrupt, in case of,
    4(2), [320]

individual savings accounts
business, meaning, **43(S)**, 611
tax credits, **43(1)**, [354]

induction
more than one parish church, where,
  14, 1063–4
plurality, of benefices held in, **14**, 1063–4

industrial action. *See* **strike; trade unions**
(ballots, secret)
ballot before—
  action having support of, **16**, [428], [443]
  ceasing to be effective, period of, **16**, [444]
  conduct of, **16**, [436]
  contract of employment, references to,
    16, [446]
  entitlement to vote, **16**, [432]
    member denied, inducement of,
    16, [441]
  failure to comply, small accidental,
    16, [442]
  notice of, **16**, [429]
  overseas members, of, **16**, [440]
  requirement of, **16**, [428]
  result, information as to, **16**, [437], [438]
  sample voting paper, **16**, [429]
  scrutineer, appointment of, **16**, [430]
  scrutineer's report, **16**, [439]
  separate workplaces, in, **16**, [433], [434]
  small, **16**, [431]
  support of, **16**, [443]
  voting paper, **16**, [435]
conciliation and mediation matters, **16**, [452]
continuous employment, effect on, **16**, [863]
criminal offences—
  conspiracy, **16**, [456]
  injury to persons or property, breach of
    contract involving, **16**, [454]
  intimidation or annoyance, **16**, [455]
dismissal for taking unofficial action, taken
  because of, **16**, [425]
dismissals in connection with, **16**, [450]
employers, notice to, **16**, [445]
official, participation in, **16**, [451]
peaceful picketing, **16**, [422]
provisions in collective agreement restricting
  right to take, effect of, **16**, [378]
secondary, **16**, [426]
supply of goods or services to individual,
  affecting—
  court, power of, **16**, [447]
  order, application for, **16**, [447]
  support of ballot, with, **16**, [443]
trade union membership, to enforce,
  16, [424]
unfair dismissal rights, loss of, **16**, [449]–[453]

industrial action—*contd*
 union recognition requirement, pressure to
 impose, **16**, [427]
 unofficial—
  dismissal for taking part in, **16**, [449]
  action taken because of, **16**, [425]

industrial and provident society
 accountant—
  appointment to inspect books, **19(1)**, [374]
  report, **19(1)**, [423]
  rights of, **19(1)**, [424]
 accounts—
  access to, by auditors, **19(1)**, [422]
  accountants' report on, **19(1)**, [423]
  auditors' report on, **19(1)**, [422]
   See also auditors *below*
  books, form of, **19(1)**, [413]
  falsification, guarding against, **19(1)**, [413]
  group. *See* group accounts *below*
  investigation of, **19(1)**, [422]
  keeping, obligation, **19(1)**, [412], [413]
  offences relating to, **19(1)**, [414], [432]
  production of, **19(1)**, [375]
  publication, **19(1)**, [415]
  regulations, **19(1)**, [433]
  revenue, general requirements, **19(1)**, [414]
  transitional provisions, **19(1)**, [438]
 actuary, appointment to inspect books,
  19(1), [374]
 advances to members, **19(1)**, [345]
 agricultural society rules, registration,
  19(1), [336]
 amalgamation—
  company, with, **19(1)**, [379]
  creditors' rights, saving for, **19(1)**, [381]
  powers of, **19(1)**, [377]
  special resolution for, **19(1)**, [377]
 annual returns—
  contents, **19(1)**, [427]
  copy, right to obtain, **19(1)**, [366]
  form of, **19(1)**, [427]
  making, **19(1)**, [366]
 appeal as to registration, **19(1)**, [342]
 audit of accounts—
  exception from requirements, **19(1)**, [416]
  group accounts, **19(1)**, [429]
  past years, for, **19(1)**, [425]
  rules for, **19(1)**, [404]
 auditors—
  access to books, right of, **19(1)**, [422]
  appointment, **19(1)**, [416]
   disapplication of provisions, **19(1)**, [417]
   exempt society, by, **19(1)**, [416]
   representations as to, **19(1)**, [419]
   resolution for, **19(1)**, [419]
   restrictions on, **19(1)**, [421]
  ineligibility for appointment, **19(1)**, [418]
  investigations by, **19(1)**, [422]
  meetings, attendance at, **19(1)**, [422]
  prohibited persons, **19(1)**, [421]
  qualification, **19(1)**, [420]
  re-appointment, **19(1)**, [418]
  removal of, **19(1)**, [418]
   resolution for, **19(1)**, [419]

industrial and provident society—*contd*
 auditors—*contd*
  remuneration, **19(1)**, [426]
  report by, **19(1)**, [422]
 authority of committee, no duty to enquire
  into, **19(1)**, [329]
 balance sheet—
  display of, **19(1)**, [367]
  falsification, **19(1)**, [392]
  publication, **19(1)**, [415]
 banking business—
  engaging in, statement as to, **19(1)**, [326]
  offences as to, **19(1)**, [326]
  restriction on, **19(1)**, [326]
  statement for carrying on, **19(1)**, [405]
 bills of exchange, making etc, **19(1)**, [352]
 bond for security by officers, **19(1)**, [407]
 books—
  accounts, of. *See* accounts *above*
  falsification, **19(1)**, [392]
  inspection—
   accountant or actuary, by, **19(1)**, [374]
   inspectors, by, **19(1)**, [376]
   members, by, **19(1)**, [373]
   order of Financial Services Authority,
    by, **19(1)**, [374]
   restriction on, **19(1)**, [372]
  production of, **19(1)**, [375]
 business, letters, name to appear on,
  19(1), [323]
 capacity—
  no duty to enquire as to, **19(1)**, [329]
  rules, not limited by, **19(1)**, [327]
 Channel Islands, application of provisions to,
  19(1), [400], [436]; **19(2)**, [552]
 charge on property—
  agricultural, **19(1)**, [409]
  creation of, **19(1)**, [408]
  evidence of, **19(1)**, [408]
  recording of, procedure, **19(1)**, [408]
 charitable—
  capacity, **19(1)**, [330]
  power of committee to bind, **19(1)**, [328],
   [330]
  status to appear on correspondence,
   19(1), [324]
 charitable incorporated organisation,
  conversion to—
  application for, **5(2)**, [635]
  consideration of application, **5(2)**, [636]
  refusal of, **5(2)**, [636]
  registration, **5(2)**, [637]
 co-operative nature of, **19(1)**, [319]
 committee members, transaction with in
  excess of powers, **19(1)**, [331], [332]
 common seal, no need for, **19(1)**, [355]
 community benefit societies—
  Channel Islands, application of provisions
   to, **19(2)**, [558]
  use of assets, power to restrict, **19(2)**, [554]
 community interest company becoming,
  8(1), [57]
 company—
  amalgamation with, **19(1)**, [379]
  conversion of society into, **19(1)**, [379]

industrial and provident society—*contd*
company—*contd*
law, assimilation of provisions relating to industrial and provident societies with, **19(2)**, [551]
society, conversion into, **19(1)**, [380]
contract, making etc, **19(1)**, [353]
county court registrar, remuneration, **19(1)**, [396]
credit unions. *See* **credit union**
debts, recovery from member, **19(1)**, [346]
deeds and documents, execution of, **19(1)**, [356], [357]
deposits with—
alteration of limits, **19(1)**, [564], [565]
bank business, when not deemed to be, **19(1)**, [326]
rules as to, **19(1)**, [326]
disputes—
hearing, procedure, **19(1)**, [387]
magistrates' court, reference to, **19(1)**, [387]
settlement of, **19(1)**, [387]
dissolution—
See also winding up *below*
advertisement of, **19(1)**, [385]
instrument of, **19(1)**, [385]
offences in connection with, **19(1)**, [385]
operative date, **19(1)**, [385]
proceedings to set aside, **19(1)**, [385]
resolution for, **19(1)**, [382]
restriction on, **19(1)**, [386]
documents—
deposit, **19(1)**, [398]
evidence of, **19(1)**, [398]
falsification, **19(1)**, [392]
forms, **19(1)**, [398]
inspection and copying of, fees for, **19(1)**, [397]
production of, **19(1)**, [375]
falsification—
accounts, **19(1)**, [413]
documents, **19(1)**, [392]
Financial Services Authority—
directions by, contravention of, **19(1)**, [340]
expenses of, **19(1)**, [376]
winding up on petition by, **19(1)**, [383]
forestry societies, registration of rules, **19(1)**, [336]
friendly society, conversion of, **19(1)**, [522], [558]
fund for purchase of government securities, **19(1)**, [335]
group accounts—
audit of, **19(1)**, [429]
contents, **19(1)**, [429]
exemption from requirements, **19(1)**, [430]
meaning, **19(1)**, [429]
registrar, to be sent to, **19(1)**, [429]
right to copy of, **19(1)**, [429]
horticultural societies, rules, registration of, **19(1)**, [336]
incorporation of, **19(1)**, [321]
inspectors—
appointment, **19(1)**, [376]

industrial and provident society—*contd*
inspectors—*contd*
production of books etc to, **19(1)**, [376]
investments, authorised, **19(1)**, [362]
Isle of Man, provisions applying to, **19(1)**, [436]
land—
holding of, **19(1)**, [361]
meaning, **19(1)**, [399]
liability, limitation of, **19(1)**, [321]
library or reading room maintained by, offences in, **13**, [80]–[83]
limited, use of word in name, **19(1)**, [323]
manager, duties, **19(1)**, [369]
meetings—
auditors' right to attend, **19(1)**, [422]
rules for, **19(1)**, [404]
special, calling of, **19(1)**, [376]
members—
advances to, **19(1)**, [345]
debts, recovery of, **19(1)**, [346]
fines on, **19(1)**, [337]
inspection of books by, **19(1)**, [373]
intestacy, disposal of property on, **19(1)**, [349]
mentally incapable, **19(1)**, [350]
nomination by. *See* nomination *below*
number, minimum, **19(1)**, [320]
offences in general by, **19(1)**, [388]
register of, **19(1)**, [371]
rules binding on, **19(1)**, [338]
shareholdings by, maximum, **19(1)**, [325]
alteration of, **19(1)**, [561], [562]
membership—
evidence of, **19(1)**, [371]
withdrawal, **19(1)**, [404]
mentally incapable member, payments to, **19(1)**, [350]
mortgage—
discharge of, **19(1)**, [364]
receipt, form of, **19(1)**, [365], [406]
name—
change of—
procedure, **19(1)**, [323]
registration of, **19(1)**, [334]
displaying on documents etc, **19(1)**, [323]
"limited" as part of, **19(1)**, [323]
nomination to property in—
nominator, death of, **19(1)**, [348]
procedure, **19(1)**, [347]
variation or revocation, **19(1)**, [347]
Northern Ireland, application of provisions, **19(1)**, [401]
offences—
accounts etc, as to, **19(1)**, [432]
continuing, **19(1)**, [390]
false representation, **19(1)**, [391]
falsification of documents, **19(1)**, [392]
misappropriation, **19(1)**, [391]
officers, by, **19(1)**, [389]
proceedings, institution of, **19(1)**, [393]
societies, generally, **19(1)**, [388]
officers—
accounting by, **19(1)**, [368], [369]
auditors, may not act as, **19(1)**, [421]

industrial and provident society—*contd*
officers—*contd*
bond for security, forms of, **19(1)**, [407]
meaning, **19(1)**, [399]
name, failure to display, **19(1)**, [323]
neglect or refusal by, **19(1)**, [369]
offences in general by, **19(1)**, [388]
register of, **19(1)**, [371]
security by, **19(1)**, [368], [407]
official seal for use abroad, **19(1)**, [358]–[360]
operations of, **19(1)**, [326]
payments—
mentally incapable person, to, **19(1)**, [350]
money secured, of, receipt for,
19(1), [365], [406]
person apparently entitled, to, **19(1)**, [351]
treatment as interest, **44(3)**, [379]
proceedings—
costs, recovery of, **19(1)**, [394]
fines, for recovery of, **19(1)**, [394]
institution of, **19(1)**, [393]
process, service of, **19(1)**, [395]
promissory note, making etc, **19(1)**, [352]
property—
meaning, **19(1)**, [399]
misappropriation etc, **19(1)**, [391]
nomination to, **19(1)**, [347]
proxy voting, **19(1)**, [363]
purported contracts, deeds and obligations,
19(1), [354]
qualifying club, as, **19(3)**, [554]
receiver or manager, duties, **19(1)**, [370]
register—
duplicate to be kept, **19(1)**, [371]
evidence, as, **19(1)**, [371]
form of, **19(1)**, [371]
inspection of, **19(1)**, [371]
members and officers, of, **19(1)**, [371]
registered—
corporation as members of, **19(1)**, [343]
deeds and documents, execution of,
19(2), [555]
meaning, **44(1)**, [325]
members—
age limits, **19(1)**, [344]
bodies corporate as, **19(1)**, [343]
office—
change of situation, **19(1)**, [334]
name, exhibition of, **19(1)**, [323]
share or loan interest, **44(1)**, [325]
registered provider of social housing, as—
accounts—
disclosure of information, **24**, [682]
failure to comply with direction,
provision or requirement, **24**, [681]
non-audited society, of, **24**, [673]
offences, **24**, [680]
amalgamation, instrument of, **24**, [794]
change of rules, **24**, [751]
company, conversion of, **24**, [700]
dissolution, **24**, [704]
manager to implement proposals in
insolvency, powers of, **24**, [696]
restructuring, **24**, [702]
winding up, **24**, [703]

industrial and provident society—*contd*
registered social landlord, as. *See* **registered
social landlord**
registrar—
disputes, settlement of, **19(1)**, [387]
group accounts sent to, **19(1)**, [429]
registration—
acknowledgment of, **19(1)**, [320]
amendment of rules, of, **19(1)**, [334]
application for, procedure, **19(1)**, [320]
cancellation—
appeal against, **19(1)**, [342]
conversion into company, on,
19(1), [379]
dissolution, on, **19(1)**, [386]
effect of, **19(1)**, [340]
Gazette notice of, **19(1)**, [340]
grounds for, **19(1)**, [340]
proposed, notice as to, **19(1)**, [340]
suspension in lieu of, **19(1)**, [341]
change of name, **19(1)**, [334]
conditions to be fulfilled, **19(1)**, [319]
credit unions. *See* **credit union**
earlier statutes, under, **19(1)**, [322]
existing societies, **19(1)**, [322]
instrument of dissolution, **19(1)**, [385]
number of members required for,
19(1), [320]
qualifications for, **19(1)**, [319]
refusal of, appeal against, **19(1)**, [342]
rules, of, acknowledgment of, **19(1)**, [333]
special resolution, of, **19(1)**, [378]
suspension of, **19(1)**, [341]
regulations, power to make, **19(1)**, [433]
returns—
annual, **19(1)**, [366]
contents, **19(1)**, [427]
form of, **19(1)**, [427]
revenue accounts, **19(1)**, [414]
rules—
accounts, as to, **19(1)**, [428]
advances, as to, **19(1)**, [345]
amendment—
meaning, **19(1)**, [399]
registration of, **19(1)**, [334]
binding on members, **19(1)**, [338]
cancellation, representations as to,
19(1), [340]
copies, right to obtain, **19(1)**, [339]
deposits, permitting, **19(1)**, [326]
disputes, for settlement of, **19(1)**, [387]
false pretences as to, **19(1)**, [339]
government securities, for purchase of,
19(1), [335]
matters specified in, **19(1)**, [404]
non-compliance with, fines for,
19(1), [337]
registration of, acknowledgment of,
19(1), [333]
shareholdings, for, **19(1)**, [325]
seal, custody and use, **19(1)**, [404]
shares—
corporations as holders, **19(1)**, [343]
lien on, for debts, **19(1)**, [346]

industrial and provident society—*contd*
shares—*contd*
maximum holding by members,
19(1), [325]
alteration of, **19(1)**, [561], [562]
special resolution—
amalgamation, for, **19(1)**, [377]
transfer of engagements, for, **19(1)**, [378]
subsidiary companies, **19(1)**, [430], [431]
transaction in excess of powers, **19(1)**, [331],
[332]
transfer of engagements—
company, to, **19(1)**, [379]
special resolution for, **19(1)**, [378]
transfer of functions, **19(2)**, [413], [414]
voting by proxy, **19(1)**, [363]
winding up—
debts and liabilities, payment, **19(1)**, [384]
Financial Services Authority's petition, on,
19(1), [383]
liability of members in, **19(1)**, [384]
yearly interest excepted from deductions,
44(4), [895]

industrial assurance
business—
application of provisions, **19(1)**, [242]
company ceasing to effect, **19(1)**, [242]
conduct, **19(1)**, [1]
excepted matters, **19(1)**, [242]
claims, payment of, **19(1)**, [252]
collecting book, meaning, **19(1)**, [257]
collecting society—
disputes, determination of, **19(1)**, [254]
meaning, **19(1)**, [1], [242]
offences and penalties, **19(1)**, [255], [283]
policies. *See* policies *below*
transfer of members, **19(1)**, [251]
collectors—
meaning, **19(1)**, [257]
offences and penalties, **19(1)**, [255]
company—
disputes, determination of, **19(1)**, [254]
life assurance premium payable to,
44(1), [642]
meaning, **19(1)**, [242]
memorandum and articles, provisions
over-riding, **19(1)**, [245]
offences and penalties, **19(1)**, [255], [283]
policies. *See* policies *below*
transfer of—
assured person, **19(1)**, [251]
one to another, **19(1)**, [251]
valuation procedure, **19(1)**, [258]
contract of, meaning, **19(1)**, [242]
documents, inspection and return,
19(1), [247]
false representation, on part of proposer,
19(1), [244]
forfeiture—
default in premium, for, **19(1)**, [249]
notice of, **19(1)**, [248]
rights of policy holder on, **19(1)**, [249]
juvenile society—
exemption from provisions, **19(1)**, [1]

industrial assurance—*contd*
juvenile society—*contd*
meaning, **19(1)**, [1]
legislation, **19(1)**, [1]
meaning, **19(1)**, [1]
national insurance, information for purposes
of, **19(1)**, [301]
notices, service of, **19(1)**, [256]
offences and penalties, generally, **19(1)**, [283]
policies—
emergency protection, **19(1)**, [284]
forfeiture. *See* forfeiture *above*
health, prohibition on restriction of liability
on grounds of, **19(1)**, [281]
illegal, **19(1)**, [244]
penalties arising, **19(1)**, [255]
inspection, return after, **19(1)**, [247]
liability under, limitation on restriction,
19(1), [281]
meaning, **19(1)**, [242], [285]
misstatements in proposal, **19(1)**, [246]
owner, meaning, **19(1)**, [257]
paid up—
amount, **19(1)**, [249]
issue on forfeiture, **19(1)**, [248]
substitution, entitlement arising,
19(1), [250]
proposal as to—
form, completion by employee,
19(1), [246]
meaning, **19(1)**, [285]
requirements, **19(1)**, [246]
substitution, **19(1)**, [250]
surrender value, **19(1)**, [251]
taking possession of, receipt for, and
return, **19(1)**, [247]
valuation, ascertainment, **19(1)**, [253]
variations, **19(1)**, [243]
premium—
default, forfeiture for, **19(1)**, [248], [249]
meaning, **19(1)**, [257]
receipt book—
form, regulations as to, **19(1)**, [278]
inspection, return after, **19(1)**, [247]
matters to be set out in, **19(1)**, [282],
[287]
meaning, **19(1)**, [257]
provision of, requirement, **19(1)**, [278]
receipt, contents of, **19(1)**, [279]
taking possession of, receipt and return,
19(1), [247]
statement recording, **19(1)**, [280], [288]
repealed provisions, **19(2)**, [492]
trade union, application of provisions to,
16, [192]

industrial building
allowance. *See* **industrial building
allowance**
carrying on trade as developer, meaning,
43(1), [872]
cessation of use, **43(1)**, [864]
commercial buildings in enterprise zones,
43(1), [860]
demolition costs, **43(1)**, [919]

industrial building—*contd*
dwelling-houses, exclusion of, **43(1)**, [856]
meaning, **43(1)**, [850]
miners, for, **43(1)**, [934]
more than one licensee, used by, **43(1)**, [857]
non-industrial part, disregard of, **43(1)**, [862]
offices, exclusion of, **43(1)**, [856]
outside UK, **43(1)**, [861]
qualifying trades, **43(1)**, [853]
relevant interest in—
completion of construction, acquired on,
43(1), [866]
elections, **43(1)**, [870]
general rule, **43(1)**, [865]
grant of lease exceeding 50 years, treatment
as sale, **43(1)**, [869]
lease exceeding 50 years, election to treat as
sale, **43(1)**, [869]
leasehold, merger of, **43(1)**, [868]
sale, calculation of allowance after,
43(1), [890]
subordinate interest, effect of creating,
43(1), [867]
retail shops, exclusion of, **43(1)**, [856]
roads on industrial estates as, **43(1)**, [863]
showrooms, exclusion of, **43(1)**, [856]
sports pavilions, qualifying, **43(1)**, [859]
temporarily out of use, **43(1)**, [933]
temporary disuse, **43(1)**, [864]
thermal insulation of, **43(1)**, [579]
welfare of workers, used for, **43(1)**, [854]

industrial building allowance
abolition from 2011, **43(S)**, 911
consequential amendments, **43(S)**, 1237–40
savings, **43(S)**, 1241
additional VAT liabilities—
initial allowance, and, **43(1)**, [925]
meaning, **43(1)**, [924]
writing-down allowance, and, **43(1)**, [926]
writing off initial allowances, **43(1)**, [927]
additional VAT rebates—
balancing adjustments, **43(1)**, [929]
meaning, **43(1)**, [924]
writing-down allowance, and, **43(1)**, [928]
writing off qualifying expenditure,
43(1), [930]
artificial effect on pricing, arrangements
having, **43(1)**, [936]
availability of, **43(1)**, [850]
balancing adjustments—
additional VAT rebates, **43(1)**, [929]
adjusted net cost, **43(1)**, [902]
avoidance, affecting, **43(1)**, [1209]
calculation of—
building being industrial throughout,
43(1), [897]
building not being industrial
throughout, **43(1)**, [898]
overall limit, **43(1)**, [899]
main balancing events—
hotel not qualifying for 2 years,
43(1), [896]
list of, **43(1)**, [894]
proceeds from, **43(1)**, [895]

industrial building allowance—*contd*
balancing adjustments—*contd*
qualifying enterprise zone expenditure,
effect of realising capital value—
application of provisions, **43(1)**, [906]
definitions, **43(1)**, [910]
payments more than 7 years after
agreement, **43(1)**, [909]
realisation, **43(1)**, [907]
subordinate interest, attributable to,
43(1), [908]
qualifying expenditure, **43(S)**, 535–6
relevant period of ownership, meaning,
43(1), [900]
starting expenditure, **43(1)**, [901]
subordinate interest, sale subject to,
43(1), [904]
when made, **43(1)**, [893]
writing off or increase of expenditure,
43(1), [916]
buildings and structures—
construction, expenditure on, **43(1)**, [851]
meaning, **43(1)**, [850]
temporarily out of use, for, **43(1)**, [933]
contribution allowances, **43(1)**, [1176]
expenditure—
construction of building, on, **43(1)**, [851]
preparation of site for plant or machinery,
for, **43(1)**, [852]
fixture on which claimed, **43(1)**, [753]
highway undertakings. *See* **highway
undertakings**
hotels—
balancing event, **43(1)**, [896]
exclusion of, **43(1)**, [856]
qualifying, **43(1)**, [858]
initial—
additional VAT liabilities, **43(1)**, [925]
amount of, **43(1)**, [885]
building not industrial when first used,
where, **43(1)**, [886]
grants affecting entitlement to, **43(1)**, [887]
period for which made, **43(1)**, [885]
qualifying enterprise zone expenditure,
for, **43(1)**, [884]
writing off, **43(1)**, [912]
additional VAT liabilities, **43(1)**, [927]
lease—
meaning, **43(1)**, [939]
termination, provisions applying on,
43(1), [938]
lessors and licensees, for, **43(1)**, [932]
miners, buildings for, **43(1)**, [934]
net, amount of, **43(1)**, [903]
non-qualifying assets, apportionment of sums
partly referable to, **43(1)**, [935]
phasing out—
abolition, before, **43(S)**, 911–13
anti-avoidance, **43(S)**, 914–15
qualifying expenditure—
balancing adjustments, increase or writing
off on, **43(1)**, [916]
construction, capital expenditure on,
43(1), [873]

industrial building allowance—*contd*
qualifying expenditure—*contd*
enterprise zone—
balancing adjustments. *See* balancing
adjustments *above*
construction of building, capital
expenditure on, **43(1)**, [877]
initial allowances, **43(1)**, [884]
part within time limit for,
43(1), [881]–[883]
purchase of building within 2 years of
first use, **43(1)**, [880], [882]–[883]
time limit, **43(1)**, [877]
unused buildings, purchase of,
43(1), [880], [882]
meaning, **43(1)**, [871]
residue allowance limited to, **43(1)**, [891]
meaning, **43(1)**, [892]
unused building, purchase of—
developer not involved, where,
43(1), [874]
developer, sale by, **43(1)**, [875]
used building, purchase from developer,
43(1), [876]
writing off—
additional VAT rebates, **43(1)**, [930]
balancing adjustment made, where,
43(1), [916]
building not industrial, where,
43(1), [915]
demolition costs, **43(1)**, [919]
extent and time of, **43(1)**, [912]
initial allowances, **43(1)**, [912]
realised capital value, of, **43(1)**, [917]
relevant interest, Crown or person not
within charge to tax entitled to,
43(1), [918]
research and development allowances,
43(1), [914]
writing-down allowances, **43(1)**, [913]
qualifying trades—
meaning, **43(1)**, [853]
parts of, **43(1)**, [855]
table of, **43(1)**, [853]
requisitioned land, for, **43(1)**, [937]
trades, giving effect to for, **43(1)**, [931]
transitional charging period, **43(S)**, 911–13
transitional provisions, **43(1)**, [1226]
writing-down—
additional VAT liabilities, **43(1)**, [926]
additional VAT rebates, **43(1)**, [928]
calculation of—
basic rule, **43(1)**, [889]
sale of relevant interest, after,
43(1), [890]
entitlement to, **43(1)**, [888]
residue of qualifying expenditure, limited
to, **43(1)**, [891]
meaning, **43(1)**, [892]
writing off, **43(1)**, [915]

industrial design
copyright, and, **11(1)**, [580]
false registration of, **11(1)**, [612]

industrial development. *See also* **development
areas**
advice, provision for giving, **47**, [378]
assisted areas—
designation of, **47**, [373], [403]
financial assistance for—
aggregate amount, **47**, [375]
foreign currency liabilities, **47**, [376]
purposes of, **47**, [374]
selective, **47**, [374]–[375]
terms and conditions of, **47**, [374]
careers in industry, promotion of, **47**, [379]
councils. *See* **development council**
design centres, grants to, **47**, [46]
development organisations, grants to,
47, [395]
export trade, promotion of, **47**, [45]
functions relating to, **47**, [51]
industries, activities treated as, **47**, [48]
levies—
power to impose, **47**, [40]
purposes of, **47**, [45]
Northern Ireland provisions, **47**, [49]
regional development grants, conditions, new
scheme of, **47**, [404]
registration of industrialists, **47**, [42]
reports on, **47**, [43]
returns—
improper disclosure of, **47**, [41]
requirement to make, **47**, [39]
selective financial assistance, increase in limit,
47(S), 13
summary of provisions, **47**, [1]
Wales. *See* **Welsh Development Agency**

Industrial Development Act
grants under, **44(1)**, [74]

Industrial Development Advisory Board
constitution of, **47**, [377]
functions of, **47**, [377]
recommendations by, **47**, [377]

industrial disease. *See also* **industrial
accident; personal injury**
adjudication, **40(1)**, [565]
death from, certification of, **36**, [152]
regulations, **40(1)**, [220], [488]; **40(2)**, [181]
schemes, **40(1)**, [488]

industrial estates companies
pensions provisions, **47**, [128]

industrial estates corporation. *See also*
English Industrial Estates Corporation
re-naming of, **47**, [129]

industrial injuries. *See also* **personal injury**
regulations, **40(1)**, [220]
research on, **40(1)**, [715]
transitional provisions and savings,
40(1), [113]; **40(2)**, [10]

Industrial Injuries Advisory Council
advice, giving, **40(1)**, [700]

Industrial Injuries Advisory Council—*contd*
chronically sick and disabled, member with
  experience of, **40(1)**, [50]
constitution, **40(1)**, [732]
continuation of, **40(1)**, [700]
members, **40(1)**, [732]
regulations—
  consultation not required, where,
    40(1), [702], [734]
  consultation on, **40(1)**, [701]

industrial injuries benefit
accidents—
  another's misconduct, caused by,
    40(1), [346]
  breach of regulations, earner in,
    40(1), [343]
  declaration of, **40(1)**, [546]
  emergency, while meeting, **40(1)**, [345]
  employer's transport, earner travelling in,
    40(1), [344]
  employment, during, **40(1)**, [339]
  illegal employments, in course of,
    40(1), [342]
  notification of, **40(1)**, [509]
  outside Great Britain, **40(1)**, [339]
  successive, adjustments for, **40(1)**, [351]
adjudicating medical practitioners,
  40(1), [551]
benefits being, **40(1)**, [339]
death benefit, **40(1)**, [487]
definitions, **40(1)**, [490]
disablement benefit—
  claimants—
    medical examinations, **40(1)**, [510]
    obligations of, **40(1)**, [511]
    treatment of, **40(1)**, [510]
  lump sum payments, **40(1)**, [1]
disablement gratuity—
  entitlement to, **40(1)**, [483]
  hospital treatment, increase during,
    40(1), [484]
  reduced earnings allowance, **40(1)**, [485]
disablement pension—
  constant attendance, requirement of,
    40(1), [348]
  disablement, assessment of extent of,
    40(1), [481]
  entitlement to, **40(1)**, [347]
  exceptionally severe disablement, increase
    for, **40(1)**, [349]
disablement questions—
  determination of, **40(1)**, [547]
  meaning, **40(1)**, [547]
  medical appeals and references, **40(1)**, [548]
  medical decisions, review of, **40(1)**, [549]
  question of law, appeal on, **40(1)**, [550]
employed earners' employment—
  breach of regulations, earner in,
    40(1), [343]
  meaning, **40(1)**, [341]
employers, persons treated as, **40(1)**, [341]
general note, **40(1)**, [1]

industrial injuries benefit—*contd*
industrial accidents, decisions as to,
  40(2), [178]
  effect of, **40(2)**, [179]
notice period, payment in, **16**, [729]
prescribed industrial diseases, for—
  conditions for, **40(1)**, [353]
  payment of, **40(1)**, [352]
  respiratory diseases, **40(1)**, [354]
rate of, **40(1)**, [469]
relevant employments, **40(1)**, [340]
retirement allowance, **40(1)**, [486]
right to, **40(1)**, [339]
time qualification, subject to, **40(1)**, [350]
unemployability supplement, **40(1)**, [482]

industrial premises
smoke, dark, prohibition of emission,
  35(2), [2]

industrial relations
ACAS. *See* **Advisory, Conciliation and
  Arbitration Service**

industrial scholarship
award of, **15(1)**, [276]
meaning, **15(1)**, [276]

industrial training
abroad—
  activities overseas, advice as to, **16**, [119]
  employment, for, **16**, [124]
accidents happening during, **16**, [132]
activities, transfer from one industry to
  another, **16**, [115]
advice, Secretary of State's power to obtain,
  16, [67]
age for, **16**, [113]
amended provisions, **15(S)**, Education 37–8
ancillary provisions, **16**, [74]
boards—
  accounts, keeping of, **16**, [122]
  advice by, **16**, [119]
  annual reports by, **16**, [122]
  chairman and deputy, **16**, [136]
  combined pension fund, **16**, [133]
  committees—
    appointment, **16**, [114]
    attendance at, **16**, [136]
    chairmen, **16**, [114]
    pensions and allowances, **16**, [114]
    procedure and quorum, **16**, [114]
  constitution, **16**, [158]
  contracts of service or apprenticeship, entry
    into, **16**, [119]
  establishment, **16**, [113]
  functions, **16**, [119]
  grants and loans to, **16**, [131]
  incorporation, **16**, [136]
  information—
    disclosure of, to, **16**, [66]
    power to require, **16**, [120], [121]
  injury or disease, payments in respect of,
    16, [73]
  joint committees, **16**, [114]

industrial training—*contd*
  boards—*contd*
    meetings, attendance at, **16**, [136]
    members—
      appointment, **16**, [136], [158]
      consultations before appointment,
        16, [136]
      reconstitution of membership, **16**, [158]
      remuneration, pensions, etc, **16**, [114],
        [136]
      voting by, restrictions on, **16**, [136]
    officers and servants, **16**, [136]
    orders relating to, **16**, [136]
    procedure and quorum, **16**, [136]
    proposals by—
      default powers of Secretary of State,
        16, [129]
      submission to Secretary of State,
        16, [119], [125]
      unsatisfactory, **16**, [129]
    returns by employers to, **16**, [120]
    staff, transfer of, **16**, [117]
    transfer of establishments' activities
      between, **16**, [115]
    travelling and subsistence allowances,
      payment by, **16**, [74]
    winding up, **16**, [118]
  consultations, **16**, [113], [143]
  courses, attendance at, payment of
    allowances, **16**, [119]
  disabled persons, **16**, [65], [74]
    young, representation on advisory bodies,
      16, [44]
  education authorities, provision of services,
    16, [70]
  Employment Service Agency, abolition,
    16, [109]
  facilities and payments, Secretary of State's
    functions, **16**, [65], [142]
  grants and loans, **16**, [65]
  information—
    boards' power to require, **16**, [120], [121]
    disclosure, **16**, [66], [120]
    employers, obligation to supply, **16**, [120],
      [121]
    publication of, **16**, [123]
  injuries sustained in course of, **16**, [132]
  levies—
    amount, **16**, [125]
    appeal against, **16**, [118], [126]
    board members, voting restriction,
      16, [136]
    conditions, **16**, [125]
    enterprise zones, exemption within,
      16, [130]
    exemption—
      criteria, **16**, [127]
      enterprise zones, **16**, [130]
      proposals as to, **16**, [125]
    exemption certificates—
      cessation of effect, **16**, [128]
      decision as to, dissatisfaction with,
        16, [128]
      effect, **16**, [125], [127]
      issue, **16**, [128]

industrial training—*contd*
  levies—*contd*
    exemption certificates—*contd*
      post-school education, in respect of,
        16, [127]
      proposals for, **16**, [127]
      provisions in, **16**, [128]
    imposition, **16**, [118]
    liability of employers, **16**, [118], [125]
    orders—
      amendment proposals, **16**, [126]
      duration of, **15(S)**, Education 30–1
      new, **16**, [126]
      provisions in, **16**, [126]
    proposals, conditions, **15(S)**, Education 29
    proposals by boards, **16**, [125], [127]
      approval of, **16**, [125]
      information to be included, **16**, [126]
      one or more periods for, **16**, [125]
    summary of provisions, **15(S)**, Education 3
  local education authorities, careers services.
    See **local education authority**
  maintenance and travelling allowances,
    payment of, **16**, [74], [119]
  medical advisory service, availability of,
    16, [79]
  Northern Ireland, activities in, **16**, [119]
  orders—
    amendment or revocation—
      powers, **16**, [113]
      transfer of assets on, **16**, [116]
      winding up of boards on revocation,
        16, [118]
    consultations before making of, **16**, [113]
    levy, as to, **16**, [125], [126]
    power to make, **16**, [113]
  outside Great Britain, functions as to,
    16, [119], [124]
  overseas employment, for, **16**, [124]
  payments, Secretary of State's powers, **16**, [65]
  post-school education—
    meaning, **16**, [119]
    provision of—
      arrangements for, **16**, [127]
      fees for, **16**, [119]
      levy exemption, grant of, **16**, [128]
  powers, **16**, [119]
  publication of, **16**, [123]
  purposes, **16**, [113]
  research connected with, **16**, [67], [119]
  Secretary of State's functions generally. *See*
    **Secretary of State for Education and
    Employment**
  social security benefits, **16**, [74]
  statistics, compilation of, **16**, [66]
  tests and certificates, **16**, [119]
  trainees, status of, **16**, [142]
  training, meaning, **16**, [75]
  Training Services Agency, abolition, **16**, [109]
  transitional provisions, **16**, [134], [137]
  travelling and subsistence allowances, **16**, [74],
    [119]
  women and girls, **16**, [65]

Industrial Training Board
pension provisions, **33(1)**, [137], [147]

industrial tribunal. *Now* **employment tribunal**
employment tribunal, change of name to, **16**, [897]

industry
documents, service of, **47**, [223]
important manufacturing undertaking—
change of control—
meaning, **47**, [212]
prohibition order—
conditions for making, **47**, [213]
contravention of, **47**, [217]
Parliamentary control, **47**, [215]
power to make, **47**, [213]
territorial scope of, **47**, [218]
relevant events for, **47**, [211]
compensation orders—
arbitration of disputes, **47**, [220], [227]–[228]
contents of, **47**, [219]
vesting order to be preceded by, **47**, [219]
meaning, **47**, [212]
vesting order—
arbitration of disputes, **47**, [220]
compensation rights, **47**, [219]
contents of, **47**, [216]
disputes arising from, **47**, [220], [227]–[228]
draft, laying of, **47**, [215]
effect of, **47**, [213]
extension to other holdings, **47**, [214]
Gazette notice of, **47**, [216]
grounds for making, **47**, [213]
power to make, **47**, [213]
information, disclosure of, **47**, [221], [229]
manufacturing industry, engagement in, **47**, [224]

industry, rationalisation of
certification of scheme—
cancellation of, **44(1)**, [394]
conditions for, **44(1)**, [391]
contributions—
deduction of, **44(1)**, [391]
meaning, **44(1)**, [391]
repayment of, **44(1)**, [392]
damage payments, **44(1)**, [393]
interpretation, **44(1)**, [667]
post-cessation payments, **44(1)**, [393]
payments, relief for, **44(1)**, [668]
scheme, exclusion of relief, **44(1)**, [669]
statutory redundancy schemes, **44(1)**, [395]
trading receipt, payments as, **44(1)**, [393]

infant. *See also* **child, minor, young person**
tax liability, **42**, [211]

infanticide
alternative verdict, **12(1)**, [240]

infanticide—*contd*
inquest into death of person by, **11(1)**, [1217], [1222]–[1223]
offence, **12(1)**, [240], [256]

infectious disease
aerodrome, at, **35(1)**, [455]
aircraft, in, **35(1)**, [454]
canal boat, in—
duties of local and port health authorities, **35(1)**, [492]
entry and inspection, **35(1)**, [491], [503]
offences, prosecution of, **35(1)**, [493]
prevention of spread, **35(1)**, [490]
regulations as to, **35(1)**, [490]
common lodging house, in, notification of, **35(1)**, [480]
complaint, magistrates' court, application to and appeals from, **35(1)**, [507]
control of, regulations for—
Channel Islands, extension to, **35(1)**, [516]
contravention, **35(1)**, [456]
enforcement and execution, **35(1)**, [454]
entry, powers of, for executing, etc, **35(1)**, [454]
Isle of Man, extension to, **35(1)**, [516]
making by Secretary of State, **35(1)**, [454]
scope of, **35(1)**, [454]
Crown property, application of provisions to, **35(1)**, [513]
cumulative effect of statutory provisions, **35(1)**, [512]
default powers of Secretary of State, **35(1)**, [511]
disinfecting stations, provision of, **35(1)**, [468]
documents—
authentication of, **35(1)**, [500]
form of, **35(1)**, [499]
service of, **35(1)**, [501]
entry of premises, powers of, **35(1)**, [502]
infested articles, books, **13**, [49]
infected premises—
disinfection of, **35(1)**, [472]
removal of persons from, **35(1)**, [473]
Inner and Middle Temples, provisions as to, **35(1)**, [515]
local inquiry, holding by Secretary of State, **35(1)**, [510]
notices—
authentication of, **35(1)**, [500]
form of, **35(1)**, [499]
service of, **35(1)**, [501]
notifiable. *See* **notifiable disease**
offences—
continuing, daily penalties for, **35(1)**, [506]
obstruction, **35(1)**, [504]
prosecution of, restriction on right of, **35(1)**, [505]
personal liability of members and staff of local authority, etc, protection from, **35(1)**, [509]
prevention of spread of, **35(1)**, [454]
spread by occupants of tents, etc, byelaws for preventing, **35(1)**, [497]
transitional provisions and savings, **35(1)**, [520]

infectious disease—*contd*
treatment of persons affected with,
35(1), [454]
vessel, in, **35(1)**, [454]

infertility treatment
resulting in child born disabled, **45**, [957]

infestation
food. *See* **food**

information
access to. *See* **local authority; public
authority**
failure to answer, **11(2)**, [114]
limitation of time, **11(2)**, [555]
mines, mining etc. *See under* **Coal Authority;
mines and mining**
summary trial of. *See* **summary trial**
summons, issue of, **11(2)**, [405]

Information Commissioner
accounts, **7(1)**, [553]
annual report, **7(1)**, [650]
application for decision by, **7(1)**, [651]
appointment of, **7(1)**, [475]
authentication of seal, **7(1)**, [553]
capacity, **7(1)**, [553]
codes of practice, **7(1)**, [524]
confidentiality of information provided to,
7(1), [532]
Data Protection Commissioner becoming,
7(1), [619], [692]
decision notice—
appeal against, **7(1)**, [658]
duty to comply with, exceptions from,
7(1), [654]
failure to comply with, **7(1)**, [655]
service of, **7(1)**, [651]
disclosure of information to, **7(1)**, [531]
Local Commissioner, by, **25(2)**, [326]
Parliamentary Commissioner, by, **10**, [554]
duties of, **7(1)**, [523]
enforcement notice—
appeal against, **7(1)**, [658]
duty to comply with, exceptions from,
7(1), [654]
failure to comply with, **7(1)**, [655]
service of, **7(1)**, [653]
entry and inspection, powers of, **7(1)**, [693]
fees payable to, **7(1)**, [496]
functions of, **7(1)**, [648]
good practice, recommendations as to,
7(1), [649]
information notice—
appeal against, **7(1)**, [658]
failure to comply with, **7(1)**, [655]
service of, **7(1)**, [652]
information obtained from, **25(2)**, [323]
international co-operation, **7(1)**, [526]
money, **7(1)**, [553]
notification regulations, functions in relation
to making of, **7(1)**, [495]
officers, **7(1)**, [553]

Information Commissioner—*contd*
ombudsmen, disclosure of information
between, **7(1)**, [671]
overseas information systems, inspection of,
7(1), [527]
presumption of authenticity of documents
issued by, **7(1)**, [553]
publication scheme, approval of, **7(1)**, [620]
reports by, **7(1)**, [524]
salary, **7(1)**, [553]
Scottish Information Commissioner, disclosure
of information between, **7(1)**, [672]
service of notices by, **7(1)**, [538]
special purposes, processing of personal data
for—
assistance by, in cases involving, **7(1)**, [525],
[563]
determination as to, **7(1)**, [517]
staff, **7(1)**, [553]
status, **7(1)**, [553]
tenure of office, **7(1)**, [553]
vacation of office, **7(1)**, [619]
Welsh Administration Ombudsman,
consultation with, **10**, 1178

Information Tribunal
appeal from, **7(1)**, [660]
appeal to, **7(1)**, [520], [555], [658]
chairman, **7(1)**, [475]
constitution, **7(1)**, [475]
Data Protection Tribunal becoming,
7(1), [619], [692]
decision notice, appeal against, **7(1)**, [658]
determination of appeals, **7(1)**, [521], [659]
disclosure of information to, **7(1)**, [531]
enforcement notice, appeal against,
7(1), [658]
expenses, **7(1)**, [554]
information notice, appeal against, **7(1)**, [658]
members—
appointment of, **7(1)**, [475]
salary, **7(1)**, [554]
tenure of office, **7(1)**, [554]
national security certificate, appeal against,
7(1), [661]
officers and staff, **7(1)**, [554]

Infrastructure Planning Commission
accounts, **46(S)**, 237–8
assistance, arrangements for, **46(S)**, 236
chief executive, **46(S)**, 236
code of conduct, issue of, **46(S)**, 25
Commissioners' interests, register of,
46(S), 25
Council, **46(S)**, 234–6
delegation of functions, **46(S)**, 236–7
establishment of, **46(S)**, 24
funding, **46(S)**, 237
fees, charging, **46(S)**, 26
members, **46(S)**, 233–4
nationally significant infrastructure projects,
development consent for—
application for order granting—
acceptance of, **46(S)**, 71–5
accepted, notification of, **46(S)**, 73

Infrastructure Planning Commission—*contd*
  nationally significant infrastructure projects,
    development consent for—*contd*
      application for order granting—*contd*
        categories of persons to be notified of
          acceptance, **46(S)**, 74
        consultation report, **46(S)**, 57
        Crown, by, **46(S)**, 59
        local impact reports, **46(S)**, 77
        model provisions, **46(S)**, 58
        request relates, notice, **46(S)**, 76
        register of, **46(S)**, 59
        requirement for, **46(S)**, 57
        standards, **46(S)**, 57
        summary of provisions, **46(S)**, 7–9
      deciding application for order granting—
        Council, decision by, **46(S)**, 95
        Panel. *See* Panel *below*
        persons appointed to chair, delegation of
          functions by, **46(S)**, 80
        single Commissioner procedure. *See*
          single Commissioner *below*
      decisions on—
        decision-maker, meaning, **46(S)**, 108
        errors, correction of, **46(S)**, 251–3
        matters disregarded, **46(S)**, 110
        Panel and Council, of, **46(S)**, 108–9
        Secretary of State, by, **46(S)**, 108, 110
        timetable for, **46(S)**, 111
      examination of application for order
        granting—
        assessors, **46(S)**, 105
        completion of, **46(S)**, 105
        compulsory acquisition hearings,
          46(S), 99
        Examining Authority—
          control by, **46(S)**, 96
          decision by, **46(S)**, 97
        hearings—
          costs, **46(S)**, 102
          disruption, **46(S)**, 102
          general provisions, **46(S)**, 100–1
          supervision, **46(S)**, 102
        initial assessment of issues, **46(S)**, 96–7
        interested parties, **46(S)**, 106
        legal advice and assistance, **46(S)**, 106
        open-floor hearings, **46(S)**, 100
        Panel or Single Commissioner, by,
          46(S), 95
        preliminary meeting, **46(S)**, 96–7
        procedure rules, **46(S)**, 103
        relevant local authority, **46(S)**, 107
        relevant representations, **46(S)**, 107
        specific issues, hearing about, **46(S)**, 98
        timetable for, **46(S)**, 104
        written representations, **46(S)**, 98, 103
      order granting—
        development for which granted,
          46(S), 118
        formalities, **46(S)**, 119
        legal challenges to, **46(S)**, 120–1
        legislation powers, proposed exercise of,
          46(S), 123–4
        making, **46(S)**, 117
        reasons for decision, **46(S)**, 119

Infrastructure Planning Commission—*contd*
  nationally significant infrastructure projects,
    development consent for—*contd*
      Panel—
        additional appointments, **46(S)**, 84
        allocation of functions within, **46(S)**, 89
        changes in, consequences of, **46(S)**, 87
        decision or recommendations by,
          46(S), 88
        decision-making by, **46(S)**, 88
        each application, for, **46(S)**, 81
        examination by, **46(S)**, 95
        exercise of powers for examining
          application, **46(S)**, 89–90
        land in Wales, membership for,
          46(S), 85
        lead member—
          appointment of, **46(S)**, 81–2
          ceasing to be, **46(S)**, 82
          replacement, **46(S)**, 85
        member continuing though ceasing to be
          Commissioner, **46(S)**, 83
        members—
          appointment of, **46(S)**, 81–2
          ceasing to be, **46(S)**, 82
          Panel ceasing to have, **46(S)**, 86
        or single Commissioner, choice of,
          46(S), 78
        switch from single Commissioner,
          46(S), 79, 86
      potential applicants and others, advice for,
        46(S), 66
      pre-application procedure—
        guidance, **46(S)**, 66
        proposed application, duty to notify,
          46(S), 63
      refusal of—
        order for, **46(S)**, 117
        reasons for decision, **46(S)**, 119
      review of national policy statement,
        suspension of decision-making during,
        46(S), 112
      rights of entry, **46(S)**, 69–70
        Crown land, **46(S)**, 71
      Secretary of State, intervention by—
        defence and national security, in interests
          of, **46(S)**, 114
        effect of, **46(S)**, 116, 248–50
        other circumstances, specifying,
          46(S), 115
        power of, **46(S)**, 115
        significant change in circumstances, on,
          46(S), 113
      single Commissioner—
        application, handling, **46(S)**, 90
        appointment, **46(S)**, 91
        ceasing to be, **46(S)**, 91
        continuing though ceasing to be
          Commissioner, **46(S)**, 92
        Council—
          decision by, **46(S)**, 95
          report referred to, **46(S)**, 94
        examination and report by, **46(S)**, 93
        examination by, **46(S)**, 95
        or Panel choice of, **46(S)**, 78

Infrastructure Planning Commission—*contd*
nationally significant infrastructure projects,
  development consent for—*contd*
  single Commissioner—*contd*
    replacement, appointment of, **46(S)**, 93
    switch to Panel from, **46(S)**, 79, 86
proof of documents, **46(S)**, 238
reports, **46(S)**, 237
staff, **46(S)**, 236
status, **46(S)**, 238
summary of provisions, **46(S)**, 5
validity of proceedings, **46(S)**, 238

inheritance
death of person attainted, after, **18**, [476]
definitions, **18**, [467]
descent—
  before 1 January 1834, **18**, [477], [478]
  brother or sister, to, **18**, [471]
  failure of heirs of purchaser, on, **18**, [486]
  half blood, traced by, **18**, [475]
  male ancestors, remoteness, **18**, [474]
  male line preferred, **18**, [473]
  rules and canons abolished, **18**, [548]
  tracing from purchaser, **18**, [468]
heir—
  right to take beneficially, **18**, [555]
  taking as devisee, **18**, [469]
  taking by purchase under limitations to
    heirs of ancestor, **18**, [470]
interest acquired through, compensation for
  depreciation where, **9**, [314], [379]
lineal ancestor as heir, **18**, [472]
order of succession, **18**, [549]
tax—
  deduction of, **18**, [607], [609]
  unpaid, refusal of grant where, **18**, [636]

inheritance tax
acceptance of property in lieu, property of
  historic interest, undertakings, **43(1)**, [409]
accounts—
  defective, **42**, [754]
  delivery of, **42**, [753]
  documents supporting, **42**, [799]
  errors, failure to remedy, **42**, [790]
  failure to deliver, **42**, [787]
  form of, **42**, [799]
  inventories, **42**, [803]
  personal representatives, delivery by,
    42, [753]
  probate registry, delivered to, **42**, [799]
  regulations, **42**, [798]
active service, death on, **42**, [689]
agricultural property—
  allocation of exemptions, **42**, [565]
  grant of tenancy of, **42**, [537]
alternatively secured pensions, amended
  provisions, **43(S)**, 704–6
amendments, **42**, [1520]
annual budget documents, **43(1)**, [377]
annual exemption, **42**, [540]
appeal—
  determination, against, **42**, [763]
  High Court, to, **42**, [766]

inheritance tax—*contd*
appeal—*contd*
  out of time, **42**, [764]
  procedure before Special Commissioners,
    42, [765]
  regulation-making powers, **42**, [767]
  Special Commissioners, from, **42**, [766]
  summary penalties, against, **42**, [793]
Apsley House, relief for, **42**, [691]
associated operations, **42**, [811]
burden of on death, **42**, [748]
capital transfer tax to be known as, **42**, [850]
certificate of tax paid, **42**, [751]
chargeable transfer—
  charge on, **42**, [521]
  death within three years of, **42**, [823]
  meaning, **42**, [522]
  more than one property, affecting,
    42, [807]
  one day, more than one on, **42**, [808]
  Stock Exchange reforms, effect of,
    42, [858]
  voidable, **42**, [685]
Chevening Estate, relief for, **42**, [691]
close company—
  capital, alteration of, **42**, [630], [632]
  employees, disposition for benefit of,
    42, [534]
  liability for tax, **42**, [740]
  meaning, **42**, [634]
  settled property of—
    capital, alterations of, **42**, [630]
    interest in possession in, **42**, [633]
    trustees, participators being, **42**, [632]
  transfer by—
    group, within, **42**, [629]
    participator, charge on, **42**, [626]
    preference shares, disregard of, **42**, [628]
    two companies, in, **42**, [627]
commencement provisions, **42**, [817], [830]
company, control of, **42**, [812]
conditional exemption, relief, **43(S)**, 405–6
conditionally exempt transfer—
  associated properties, **42**, [556]
  chargeable events, **42**, [555]
  cumulative total, reinstatement of, **42**, [558]
  death before 7 April 1976, on, **42**, [559],
    [828]
  designation, **42**, [554]
  liability for tax, **42**, [744]
  meaning, **42**, [553]
  property, amount of charge on, **42**, [557]
  reduction of tax, **42**, [823]
  ten-yearly charge, exemption from,
    42, [610]
  undertakings, **42**, [554]
    variation, **42**, [560]
  works of art, etc, **42**, [608], [609]
connected persons, **42**, [813]
corporation sole, property of, **42**, [814]
determination—
  appeal against, **42**, [763]
  notice of, **42**, [762]
discharge, certificate of, **42**, [781]

inheritance tax—*contd*

dispositions on death, instruments varying, **42**, [756]

dividend, waiver of, **42**, [536]

documents—

appeal against requirement to produce, **42**, [759]

power to call for, **42**, [758]

service of, **42**, [800]

double charges, avoiding, **42**, [857]

double taxation relief—

convention, by, **42**, [693]

unilateral, **42**, [694]

EEA land, reliefs for, **43(S)**, 1425–6

employee trust, **42**, [618]

estate—

changes in distribution, **42**, [538]

death, changes occurring on, **42**, [706]

debts and incumbrances, treatment of, **42**, [856]

dispositions, alteration of, **42**, [679]

expenses incurred abroad, **42**, [708]

funeral expenses, deduction for, **42**, [707]

future payments, liability to make, **42**, [710]

income tax, allowance for, **42**, [709]

Inheritance (Provision for Family and Dependants) Act, order under, **42**, [683]

inheritance tax, existing liability for, **42**, [709]

legatee, transfer in accordance with testator's wishes by, **42**, [680]

legitim, claim of, **42**, [684]

meaning, **42**, [526]

property settled by will, distribution from, **42**, [681]

related property, sale of, **42**, [711]

sale of land from—

beneficiaries, sale to, **42**, [733]

compulsory acquisition more than three years after death, **42**, [734]

date of sale or purchase, **42**, [736]

death and sale, changes between, **42**, [730]

definitions, **42**, [727]

exchanges, **42**, [733]

fourth year after death, in, **42**, [735]

leases, **42**, [731]

other interests, valuation by reference to, **42**, [732]

purchases, effect of, **42**, [729]

relief, **42**, [728]

sale of shares etc from—

calls, payment of, **42**, [717]

cancelled investment, **42**, [722]

capital receipts, **42**, [716]

date of sale or purchase, **42**, [726]

definitions, **42**, [713]

exchanges, **42**, [719]

holdings, changes in, **42**, [718]

like investments, acquisition of, **42**, [720]

loss, limitation of, **42**, [725]

part of fund, value of, **42**, [721]

purchase by claimant, effect of, **42**, [715]

relief, **42**, [714]

inheritance tax—*contd*

estate—*contd*

sale of shares etc from—*contd*

specific investment, attribution of value to, **42**, [724]

suspended investment, **42**, [723]

Scottish agricultural lease, accounting for, **42**, [712]

surviving spouse's life interest, redemption of, **42**, [682]

estate duty, transition from, **42**, [829]

evidence, provisions on, **42**, [796]

excluded property, **42**, [527]

exempt transfer—

annual amount, **42**, [540]

beneficiary's resources, claim settled from, **42**, [552]

charities, gifts to, **42**, [544]

conditional. *See* conditionally exempt transfer *above*

employee trust, to, **42**, [550]

housing association, gifts to, **42**, [546]

loans, **42**, [551]

maintenance fund for historic buildings, to, **42**, [549]

marriage, gifts in consideration of, **42**, [543]

meaning, **42**, [522]

national purposes, gift for, **42**, [547], [824]

normal expenditure out of income, **42**, [542]

political party, gifts to, **42**, [545]

potential. *See* potentially exempt transfer *below*

small gifts, **42**, [541]

spouses, between, **42**, [539]

exemptions, allocation of—

determination of questions, **42**, [561]

gifts—

abatement of, **42**, [562]

agricultural relief, and, **42**, [565]

business relief, and, **42**, [565]

chargeable, gain on disposal of, **42**, [1403]

different funds, made from, **42**, [566]

housing association, to, **42**, [1402]

meaning, **42**, [568]

own tax, bearing, **42**, [568]

residuary, attribution of value to, **42**, [564]

specific, attribution of value to, **42**, [563]

value of, **42**, [568]

tax, burden of, **42**, [567]

family, disposition for maintenance of, **42**, [532]

five years, two or more transfers within, **42**, [678]

fiscal stability, code for, **43(1)**, [376]

foreign trusts, purchase of interests in, **43(S)**, 152–3

future payments, charge in respect of, **42**, [804]

general note, **42**, [1]

gratuitous benefit, dispositions not conferring, **42**, [531]

inheritance tax—*contd*

High Court, summary application by Crown to, in matters of, **13**, [18]

historic building, maintenance fund for—
property comprised in, **42**, [827]
property leaving—
charge to tax, **42**, [826]
exceptions from charge, **42**, [826]
interest in possession, following, **42**, [826]
rates of tax, **42**, [826]
reduction of tax, **42**, [823]
transfer of value to, **42**, [549]
Treasury directions—
conditions, **42**, [825]
giving, **42**, [825]
information, **42**, [825]
trusts, enforcement of, **42**, [825]
withdrawal of, **42**, [825]

income tax, disposition allowable for, **42**, [533]

information—
failure to provide, **42**, [788]
errors, failure to remedy, **42**, [790]
incorrect, provision of, **42**, [789]
other countries, exchange with, **42**, [761]
power to require, **42**, [757]

information and inspection powers, **43(S)**, 1412–13, 1692–8

Inland Revenue Regulation Act, provisions not applying, **42**, [802]

instalments—
interest on, **42**, [776]
payment by—
generally, **42**, [768]
shares, relating to, **42**, [770]
refund by, **42**, [750]
woodlands, **42**, [771]

interest—
instalments, on, **42**, [776]
overpaid tax, on, **42**, [777]
repayable tax, on, **42**, [777]
special cases, **42**, [778]
unpaid tax, on, **42**, [775]

interest in possession—
settlement, extension of transitional period, **43(S)**, 978
termination of, charge on where new interest acquired, **43(S)**, 974

introduction of, **42**, [1]

liability for—
close company transactions, on, **42**, [740]
conditional exemption, on, **42**, [744]
death, transfer on, **42**, [738]
disposition by transferor, on, **42**, [737]
limitation of, **42**, [742]
more than one person, of, **42**, [743]
pension rights, in relation to, **42**, [747]
personal representative, of, **42**, [738], [742]
Scotland, effect of succession in, **42**, [746]
settled property, transfer of, **42**, [739], [742]
spouse, of, **42**, [741]
trustee, of, **42**, [742]
woodlands, in respect of, **42**, [745]

inheritance tax—*contd*

life policy, annuity purchased in conjunction with, **42**, [805]

limited liability partnership, charge on, **42**, [810]

loan to pay, relief for interest payments on, **44(4)**, [411]–[413]

lump sum death benefits, property applied to pay, **43(S)**, 715

management of, **42**, [752]

newspaper trust, **42**, [619]

nil-rate band, transfer between spouses—
amended provisions, **43(S)**, 1033–7
commencement, **43(S)**, 1037
deceased person died before 25 July 1986, modification in case of, **43(S)**, 1037–9

non-resident trustee, return of, **42**, [755]

non-resident's bank account, treatment of, **42**, [692]

non-UK pension schemes, treatment of, **43(S)**, 1254

old and new law, continuity and references to, **42**, [818]

overpaid, interest on, **42**, [777]

overpayment of, **42**, [783]

payment of—
acceptance of property in lieu, **42**, [772]
administration actions, and, **42**, [774]
general rules, **42**, [768]
instalments, by—
generally, **42**, [769]
shares, relating to, **42**, [770]
woodlands, relating to, **42**, [771]
personal representatives, by, **42**, [768]
transfer of property to satisfy, **42**, [773]

penalties—
accounts, failure to deliver, **42**, [787]
errors, failure to remedy, **42**, [790]
HM Revenue and Customs, recovery by, **42**, [794]
incorrect information, provision of, **42**, [789]
information, failure to provide, **42**, [788]
mitigation of, **42**, [795]
recovery of, **42**, [791]
time limit, for, **42**, [792]
summary, appeal against, **42**, [793]

penalty regime, amendments, **43(2)**, [511]

pension schemes—
amended provisions, **43(S)**, 441–6
cash option, **42**, [687]
overseas, **42**, [688]
rights under, treatment of, **42**, [686]

persons domiciled in UK, **42**, [809]

potentially exempt transfer—
death within seven years of, **42**, [823]
designation, claim for, **42**, [554]
generally, **42**, [1]
lifetime transfers, **42**, [851]
meaning, **42**, [524]
national purposes, property subsequently held for, **42**, [548]
settled property, affecting, **42**, [582], [583]
seven years before death of transferor, made, **42**, [524]

inheritance tax—*contd*
  power to raise, **42**, [749]
  previous view of law, determination of
    question on, **42**, [797]
  proceedings for recovery, **42**, [784]–[786]
  property accepted in lieu, **42**, [907]
  property, inspection of, **42**, [760]
  property subject to reservation, termination of
    interests in possession, **43(S)**, 403–4
  rate bands, indexation of, **42**, [529]
  rates and rate bands, **43(2)**, [642];
    43(S), 151–2, 516
  rates of, **42**, [528], [822], [878]
  records, inspection of, **42**, [801]
  recovery of, **42**, [784], [785]
  reduction of—
    chargeable transfer, death within three years
      of, **42**, [823]
    conditionally exempt transfer, after,
      42, [823]
    historic buildings, maintenance fund for,
      42, [823]
    meaning, **42**, [823]
    potentially exempt transfer, death within
      seven years of, **42**, [823]
    settlement without interest in possession,
      42, [823]
    trees and underwood, disposal of, **42**, [823]
  regulations, **42**, [798]
  remuneration, waiver of, **42**, [535]
  reservation, gift with—
    agricultural property, of, **42**, [865], [879]
    benefit, exclusion of, **42**, [865]
    business property, of, **42**, [865], [879]
    interpretation, **42**, [865]
    land, interest in, **42**, [853]
      relevant period, **42**, [855]
      share of, **42**, [854]
      supplemental provisions, **42**, [855]
    material date, donee predeceasing,
      42, [865]
    meaning, **42**, [865]
    provisions relating to, **42**, [852]
    securities, of, **42**, [879]
    settlement, in, **42**, [865]
    substitutions and accretions, **42**, [865]
  retirement benefits, disposition conferring,
    42, [533]
  Scotland—
    agricultural leases, **42**, [712]
    inventories, delivery of, **42**, [803]
    legitim, claim of, **42**, [684]
    recovery in, **42**, [785]
  settlement—
    annual charges, credit for, **42**, [617]
    commencement, references to, **42**, [591]
    death, vesting on, **42**, [615]
    disabled persons, trust for, **42**, [621]
    excluded property, **42**, [614]
    liability for tax, **42**, [739], [742]
    meaning, **42**, [569]
    power—
      meaning, **42**, [574]
      purchased, **42**, [585]
    property moving between, **42**, [613]

inheritance tax—*contd*
  settlement—*contd*
    related, **42**, [593]
    return relating to, **42**, [755]
    reversionary interest—
      beneficiary, acquired by, **42**, [584]
      excluded property, as, **42**, [575]
      meaning, **42**, [573]
      transfer, property given in consideration
        of, **42**, [575]
    settled property—
      accumulation and maintenance trusts,
        held on, **42**, [602]
      charitable purposes—
        interest applied for, **42**, [616]
        property held for, **42**, [607]
      close company, of. *See* close company
        above
      disabled persons, pre-1981 trusts for,
        42, [605]
      employee trust, on, **42**, [603], [618]
        property becoming subject to,
        42, [606]
      exemptions—
        application of, **42**, [587]
        exclusion of, **42**, [586]
      interest in possession, **42**, [572]
        administration period, in, **42**, [623]
        consideration for, treatment of,
          42, [576]
        death, exceptions from charge on,
          42, [581]
        disclaimer of, **42**, [625]
        disposal of, **42**, [578]
        exceptions from charge, **42**, [580]
        maintenance fund, **42**, [588]
        part only, of, **42**, [577]
        potentially exempt transfer, affected
          by, **42**, [582]
        qualifying, **42**, [590]
        termination, charge on, **42**, [579]
        treatment of, **42**, [576]
      newspaper trusts, on, **42**, [603], [619]
      pre-1978 protective trust, held on,
        42, [604]
      protective trust, on, **42**, [620]
      temporary charitable purposes, held for,
        42, [601]
      undertakings, variation of, **42**, [611]
      without interest in possession—
        added property, **42**, [598]
        charge to tax, **42**, [595], [596]
        relevant property, **42**, [589]
    settlor—
      initial interest of, **42**, [612]
      meaning, **42**, [570]
    ten-year anniversary—
      charge at, **42**, [595]
      exemption from charge, **42**, [610]
      first, rate before, **42**, [599]
      meaning, **42**, [592]
      rate between, **42**, [600]
      rate of charge, **42**, [597]
    trustee—
      annuities, **42**, [622]

inheritance tax—*contd*
  settlement—*contd*
    trustee—*contd*
      meaning, **42**, [571]
  settlements and trusts, amendments,
    43(S), 390–401
  successive charges, **42**, [678]
  sums due, late payment interest on—
    instalments, **43(S)**, 1730–1
    property accepted in lieu, **43(S)**, 1733
    underpaid amounts, **43(S)**, 1731
  survivorship clause, effect of, **42**, [624]
  three years of death, transfer within—
    close company transactions, **42**, [673]
    land, interests in, **42**, [674]
    leases, value of, **42**, [675]
    market value, **42**, [668]
    property, market value of, **42**, [676]
    qualifying sale, **42**, [668]
    relief, **42**, [668]
    shares—
      capital receipts for, **42**, [670]
      payment of calls on, **42**, [670]
      reorganisation of share capital, **42**, [672]
    wasting assets, **42**, [669]
  time limits for assessments, claims, etc,
    amendment, **43(S)**, 1707–9
  transfer of value—
    agricultural property—
      agricultural value, **42**, [649]
      company—
        assets, part of, **42**, [656]
        occupation by, **42**, [653], [657]
        use by, **42**, [657]
      contracts for sale, **42**, [658]
      death of transferor, transfer within seven
        years of, **42**, [659]
      double relief, avoidance of, **42**, [648]
      habitat schemes, land in, **42**, [661]
      horses, breeding etc, **42**, [649]
      meaning, **42**, [648]
      occupation or ownership, minimum
        period of, **42**, [651]
      partnership, occupation by, **42**, [653]
      relief, **42**, [650]
      replacements, **42**, [652], [660]
      succession to, **42**, [654]
      successive transfers, **42**, [655]
    business property, of—
      contracts for sale, effect of, **42**, [645]
      double relief, avoidance of, **42**, [648]
      excepted assets, exclusion of value,
        42, [644]
      market maker, of, **42**, [637]
      meaning, **42**, [635]
      ownership, minimum period of,
        42, [638]
      relevant, **42**, [637]
      relief, **42**, [636]
      replacements, **42**, [639], [647]
      seven years of death of transferor,
        within, **42**, [646]
      shares and securities, value of, **42**, [643]
      succession to, **42**, [640]
      successive transfers, **42**, [641]

inheritance tax—*contd*
  transfer of value—*contd*
    business property, of—*contd*
      value of business, **42**, [642]
    chargeable, **42**, [522]
    death, on, **42**, [525]
    dispositions not being, **42**, [531]–[538]
    expenses, treatment of, **42**, [699]
    late, reported, **42**, [806]
    meaning, **42**, [523]
    potentially exempt. *See* potentially exempt
      transfer *above*
    Stock Exchange reforms, effect of,
      42, [858]
  transitional provisions, **42**, [864]
  underpayment of, **42**, [782]
  unpaid—
    Inland Revenue charge for—
      imposition of, **42**, [779]
      purchases, effect of, **42**, [780]
    interest on, **42**, [775]
    refusal of grant of probate, **43(2)**, [510]
  valuation—
    capital gains tax, reduction by, **42**, [700]
    creditors' rights, **42**, [701]
    expenses, treatment of, **42**, [699]
    farm cottages, of, **42**, [704]
    freedom to dispose, restriction on,
      42, [698]
    leases for life, of, **42**, [705]
    liabilities, taking account of, **42**, [697]
    life policies, of, **42**, [702]
    market value, **42**, [695]
    related property, and, **42**, [696]
    unquoted shares and securities, of,
      42, [703]
  visiting forces, and, **42**, [689]
  woodlands—
    amount on which charged, **42**, [664]
    credit for tax charged, **42**, [666]
    death, value transferred on, **42**, [667]
    expenses allowable, **42**, [667]
    instalments, payment by, **42**, [771]
    liability for tax, **42**, [745]
    net proceeds of sale, **42**, [667]
    rate of charge, **42**, [665]
    relief, **42**, [662]
    trees or underwood, disposal of, **42**, [663]

inhibition
  exercise of function after, **14**, 591–2
  meaning, **14**, 591
  pendente lite, **14**, 608
  performance of duties during, **14**, 605–6
  readmission to benefice after, **14**, 591–2
  restrictions during, **14**, 607
  rights of patronage during, **14**, 608
  sequestration, during, **14**, 237

injunction
  acts in contemplation or furtherance of trade
    dispute, protection in relation to, **16**, [423]
  anti-social behaviour, against—
    arrest, power of, **23**, [468], [471], [472],
      [474], [555]

injunction—*contd*
anti-social behaviour, against—*contd*
breach of tenancy agreement, **23**, [469]
conditions, **23**, [466]
discharge, **23**, [470]
ex parte applications, **23**, [471]
exclusion order, **23**, [468]
medical examination and report, remand for, **23**, [473]
remand, **23**, [472], [473], [555]
unlawful use of premises, **23**, [467]
variation, **23**, [470]
breach of contract of employment, to restrain, **16**, [448]
Crown, against, declaratory order instead of, **13**, [24]
High Court jurisdiction, **11(2)**, [707]

injuries in war
administration of pensions, **3**, [296]
civilians, compensation, to, **3**, [269]
mariners, **3**, [339]
payment of pensions in advance, **3**, [297]
Pensions Appeal Tribunal—
appeal to, **3**, [299], [316]
constitution of, **3**, [302]
jurisdiction of, **3**, [302]
procedure of, **3**, [302]
persons disabled abroad, **3**, [273]
statutory right to pension, **3**, [298]

injurious affection
additional development after acquisition, compensation, **9**, [260]
compensation—
assessment of, **9**, [343]
ecclesiastical property, **9**, [289]
estimating, **9**, [26]
glebe land, **9**, [289]
interest, payment of, **9**, [321], [363]
local authority land, **9**, [372]
measure of, **9**, [267]
restrictions, **9**, [311]
Lands Tribunal jurisdiction, **9**, [181], [270]
limitation on time, **9**, [379]
right to, **9**, [270]

inland navigation
charge to tax, **44(1)**, [34]
street works near, display of lights, **38(1)**, [235]
towing path or way, street works involving, **38(1)**, [234]
undertakers, property of, meaning in relation to highways, **36**, [1381]

Inland Revenue. *See now* **HM Revenue and Customs**
advance pricing agreements—
branch or agency, attribution of income to, **43(1)**, [440]
chargeable periods, **43(1)**, [441]
determinations, **43(1)**, [441]
double taxation arrangements, inconsistency with, **43(1)**, [441]

Inland Revenue—*contd*
advance pricing agreements—*contd*
misleading information, **43(1)**, [442]
modification or revocation, **43(1)**, [442]
non-parties, effect on, **43(1)**, [442]
reports and information, provision of, **43(1)**, [441]
ring fence trade, meaning, **43(1)**, [440]
scope of, **43(1)**, [440]
Board—
determinations requiring sanction of, **43(1)**, [359]
income tax, directions for purposes of, **43(1)**, [360]
potential claimants, notice to, **43(1)**, [360]
Commissioners, account of. *See*
Commissioners
contracts, completion of, **10**, [154]
lands—
Commissioners of Works—
purchase by, **10**, [155]–[156]
vesting in, **10**, [152]
copyholds, vesting of, **10**, [153]
social security authorities, obtaining information from, **43(1)**, [289]
windfall tax, administration of, **43(1)**, [309], [329]

inland waters
byelaws regulating use of, **49**, [1295]
diseases of fish. *See* **freshwater fisheries**
Environment Agency's promotion of conservation and enhancement, **35(2)**, [92]
meaning, **1(1)**, [359]; **11(2)**, [919]; **35(1)**, [216]; **49**, [1267]
minimum acceptable flow—
meaning, **49**, [1267]
statements on, procedure relating to, **49**, [1273]
vessels lying in, public health provisions applicable to, **35(1)**, [169]

inland waterway. *See also* **canal**
Amenity Advisory Council, Inland Waterways Advisory Council, renamed as, **38(2)**, [496]
amenity purposes, maintenance for, **36**, [853]
arbitration, **38(1)**, [615]
Board. *See* **British Waterways Board**
bodies taking over, **36**, [845]
bridge over—
load-bearing capacity, **36**, [856]
maintenance, responsibility for, **36**, [855]
owner, duties of, **36**, [856]
trunk or special road, carrying, **36**, [858]
undertakers, provisions applied to, **36**, [859]
Waterways Board—
duties of, **36**, [856]
works by, **36**, [857]
byelaws, **36**, [852]
certificates, conditions as to, **38(1)**, [607]
classification of, **36**, [840]
commercial, meaning, **36**, [840], [882]
commercial transport, national policy for, **36**, [966]

inland waterway—*contd*

Crown rights, **38(1)**, [617]

cruising, meaning, **36**, [840], [883]

cutting, running in, **36**, [860]

economical manner, to be dealt with in, **36**, [843]

enforcement of duties, **36**, [842]

financial assistance, **38(2)**, [202]

freight haulage, grants for provision of facilities, **38(1)**, [472]

legal proceedings, **38(1)**, [616]

licences, conditions as to, **38(1)**, [607]

maintenance of, **36**, [841]

meaning, **38(1)**, [593]

moorings—

    control of, **38(1)**, [611]

    private, provisions as to, **38(1)**, [610]

navigation authority, meaning, **36**, [1381]

navigation, right of, **36**, [854]

nuisance, prevention of, **36**, [844]

obstruction by vessels, **38(1)**, [608]

orders—

    applications for, **38(1)**, [295]

    compulsory purchase, authorisation of, **38(1)**, [302]

    consents under enactments, **38(1)**, [305]

    consultation on, **36**, [884]

    Crown land, **38(1)**, [309]

    inquiries and hearings, **38(1)**, [301]

    made other than on application, **38(1)**, [297]

    making, **38(1)**, [303]

    model clauses, **38(1)**, [298]

    national significance, schemes of, **38(1)**, [299]

    objections to, **36**, [884]; **38(1)**, [300]

    other Member States affected, where, **38(1)**, [296]

    power to apply for or object to, **38(1)**, [306]

    power to make, **36**, [840]; **38(1)**, [292]

    publication of, **36**, [884]

    publicity, **38(1)**, [304]

    refusal of, **38(1)**, [303]

    special parliamentary procedure, **38(1)**, [302]

    subject-matter of, **38(1)**, [294], [345]

    validity of, **38(1)**, [307]

    works, description of, **38(1)**, [293]

private rights, extinguishment of, **36**, [841]

qualified body, owned or managed by, **36**, [852]

Scotland, application of provisions to, **38(1)**, [620]

statutory right of navigation, extinguishment of, **36**, [841]

tunnel, carried by, **36**, [860]

undertakings, charges schemes of, **36**, [716]

vessels using, provisions on, **36**, [841]

watercourse, being, **36**, [844]

inland waterway undertaking

meaning, **39(2)**, [158]

revision of charges, **39(2)**, [155]

Inland Waterways Advisory Council

constitution, **36**, [846]

functions, **36**, [848]

    Scotland, **36**, [849]

members—

    expenses, **36**, [847]

    remuneration, **36**, [847]

    term of office, **36**, [847]

Inland Waterways Amenity Advisory Council. *See now* **Inland Waterways Advisory Council**

INMARSAT

capital gains tax exemption, **42**, [1420]

inn. *See also* **innkeeper**

hotel deemed to be, **19(3)**, [366]

Inner London. *See also* **Greater London**

building regulations—

    application of provisions, **35(1)**, [610], [660]

    repeal or modification of Acts relating to, **35(1)**, [610]

buildings in, demolition, byelaws as to, **35(1)**, [662]

byelaws as to, demolition of buildings, **35(1)**, [662]

Inner London Education Authority. *See also* **Greater London (new authorities)**

chargeability of certain expenses, **25(1)**, [908]

charitable property held by, **15(1)**, [338]

compensation payments, responsibility for, **15(1)**, [335]

exercise of functions, continuity, **15(1)**, [339]

higher education functions, **25(1)**, [253]

information, duty to publish, **25(2)**, [428]

new constitution etc, **25(1)**, [1]

pensions and pensions increase, payment of, **15(1)**, [333]

property, rights and liabilities, transfer of, **15(1)**, [328]

residuary property, custody of, **15(1)**, [334]

staff—

    continuity of employment, **15(1)**, [332]

    employment or emoluments, compensation for loss, **15(1)**, [331]

    power to transfer, **15(1)**, [330]

Westminster Technical Institute, powers as to, **25(1)**, [253]

Inner Temple

administration of justice, **25(1)**, [760]

building provisions, application to, **35(1)**, [610]

City, inclusion in, **25(1)**, [1]

City of London general rate, contribution to, **25(1)**, [113]

exemption from Building Acts, **25(1)**, [354]

functions exercisable by, **25(2)**, [626]

overground wires, placing, **25(1)**, [213]

Port of London Act, savings under, **39(2)**, [389]

Inner Temple—*contd*
  public health purposes, local authority for,
    35(1), [118]
  references concerning, construction of,
    35(1), [515], [649]
  ward elections, **25(1)**, [641]
  welfare services functions, **25(1)**, [706]

inner urban area
  designated district—
    acquisition of land, loan for, **46**, [37]
    authority—
      expenditure, power to incur, **46**, [47]
      improvement area. *See* improvement area
        below
      loans by, **46**, [37]–[38]
      meaning, **46**, [36]
    common ownership, loans and grants for,
      46, [38]
    co-operative enterprises, loans and grants
      for, **46**, [38]
    Secretary of State, by, **46**, [36]
    special area—
      building in, grant towards rent, **46**, [45]
      loan interest, grants towards, **46**, [46]
      order specifying, **46**, [43]
      site preparation, loans for, **46**, [44]
      small firm, loan interest of, **46**, [46]
    works, loan for, **46**, [37]
  generally, **46**, [1]
  improvement area—
    amenities, loans etc for improving, **46**, [40]
    buildings, converting or improving,
      46, [41]
    declaration of, **46**, [39], [52]
    meaning, **46**, [39]
  orders and directions, **46**, [48]
  procedure for declaring, **46**, [39], [52]
  relevant land—
    meaning, **46**, [82]
    urban development corporation, powers
      of, **46**, [82]
  special social need, arrangements for, **46**, [42]

innkeeper
  deposit of property with, disposal,
    19(3), [356]
  game, sale of, by, **2**, [168]
  hotel proprietor, as, **19(3)**, [366]
  liability of—
    loss or damage to guest's property, for,
      19(3), [341], [366]
    modifications, **19(3)**, [366]
  lien, **19(3)**, [367]
  rights and liabilities, **19(3)**, [367]
  war damage, liability for, **50**, [204]

inquest
  accommodation for, **11(1)**, [1239]
  adjournment of—
    criminal proceedings, in event of,
      11(1), [1222]
    judicial enquiry, in event of, **11(1)**, [1224]
  body destroyed or irrecoverable, where,
    11(1), [1221]

inquest—*contd*
  coroner. *See* **coroner**
  death of person by murder, manslaughter or
    infanticide, into, **11(1)**, [1217],
    [1222]–[1223]
  death of person in custody, on, **11(1)**, [1214]
  district of coroner, within, **11(1)**, [1211]
  fees and allowances, payment of,
    11(1), [1231]
  findings, certificate of, **11(1)**, [1217]
  inquisition, **11(1)**, [1217]
  jurisdiction, out of, **11(1)**, [1220]
  jurors—
    attendance of, **11(1)**, [1216]
    payments to, **11(1)**, [1232]
    qualification of, **11(1)**, [1215]
    Queen's household, inquest held by
      coroner of, **11(1)**, [1237]
  jury—
    failure to agree, **11(1)**, [1218]
    medical witnesses, requiring summoning
      of, **11(1)**, [1228]
    summoning, **11(1)**, [1214]
    verdict, **11(1)**, [1217]
  offence, person killed in commission of,
    11(1), [1217], [1222]–[1223]
  order to hold, **11(1)**, [1219]
  prisoner, on death of, **11(1)**, [1214]
  proceedings at, **11(1)**, [1217]
  railway, into person killed on, **11(1)**, [1217]
  road deaths in London, into, **11(1)**, [1225]
  rules, power to make, **11(1)**, [1240]
  summary of provisions, **11(1)**, [1205]
  treasure trove, **11(1)**, [1238]
  verdict, **11(1)**, [1217]
  where required, **11(1)**, [1214]
  witnesses—
    attendance of, **11(1)**, [1216]
    examination on oath, **11(1)**, [1217]
    medical, **11(1)**, [1227]–[1228]

inquiry. *See also* **Courts of Inquiry**
  accidents, into, **37**, [797]
  board of. *See* **board of inquiry**
  breach of notice, enforcement, **10**, [887]
  change of responsibility for, **10**, [885]
  conversion—
    consultation, **10**, [867]
    obligations arising, **10**, [867]
    original members, **10**, [867]
    other inquiry, of, **10**, [866]
    terms of reference, **10**, [866]
  Crown, provisions binding, **10**, [900]
  damage to economy, information risking to be
    withheld, **10**, [874]
  end of, **10**, [865]
  expenses of, **36**, [549]
    payment of, **10**, [890]
  Financial Services and Markets Act, under,
    10, [897]
  general provisions, **37**, [796]
  immunity from suit, **10**, [888]
  information, access to, **10**, [869]
  inland waterways, objections to orders as to,
    36, [884]

inquiry—*contd*
  interpretation, **10**, [894]
  joint, **10**, [883]
  judicial review of decisions, time limit for
    applying for, **10**, [889]
  liability, no determination of, **10**, [853]
  local—
    Acts providing for, **25(2)**, [656]
    appeal, as to, **46**, [626]
    appointed representative, exclusion in case
      of, **46**, [592]
    Boundary Commission, by, **25(2)**, [55]
    cancelled, costs in connection with,
      25(2), [656]
    coast protection work, **49**, [386], [420]
    costs of, **25(2)**, [213]; **46**, [574],
      [594]–[596]
    hallmarking, relating to, **48**, 67–8
    hazardous substances, as to, **46**, [801]
    local plan, objections to, **46**, [302]
    Minister of Health, by, **35(1)**, [199]
    Ministers' costs—
      costs treated as, **25(2)**, [656]
      recovery of, **25(2)**, [656]
      standard daily amount, **25(2)**, [656]
    national security considerations, **46**, [1032]
    new town, relating to, **46**, [191]
    payments in connection with appointments,
      validation, **46**, [867]
    planning inquiry, as, **46**, [591]
    Planning Inquiry Commission holding,
      46, [628]
    power of Secretary of State to hold,
      35(1), [510], [641]; **35(2)**, [59]
    power to direct, **25(2)**, [213]
    power to hold, **22**, [416]; **46**, [590], [626]
    public, to be in, **46**, [591]
    Secretary of State, by, **35(1)**, [60]
    simplified planning zone scheme, as to,
      46, [627]
    summons to attend, **25(2)**, [213]
    Thames flood barrier, **49**, [562]
    unitary development plan, as to, **46**, [269]
    Wales, in, **46**, [593], [1033]
  Minister establishing, duty to inform
    Parliament or Assembly, **10**, [857]
  more than one administration, as to, **10**, [884]
  Northern Ireland, **10**, [881]
    suspension of devolved government,
      functions during, **10**, [896]
  Northern Ireland matters, as to, **10**, [878]
  Notices, **10**, [893]
  offences, **10**, [886]
  panel—
    appointment, **10**, [855]
    assessors assisting, **10**, [862]
    duration of appointment, **10**, [863]
    further appointments to, **10**, [858]
    impartiality, requirement of, **10**, [860]
    judge as member of, **10**, [861]
    meaning, **10**, [854]
    suitability of, **10**, [859]
  pipe-line, as to, **17(1)**, [263]
  power to establish, **10**, [852]
  power to hold, **37**, [796]

inquiry—*contd*
  proceedings—
    evidence, **10**, [868]
      privileged information, **10**, [873]
      production, chairman requiring,
        10, [872]
    procedure, **10**, [868]
    public access to, **10**, [869]
      restriction orders and notices,
        10, [870]–[871]
  public—
    meaning, **12(1)**, [182]
    witness—
      obstructing or intimidating, **12(1)**, [183]
      prosecution, costs and compensation,
        12(1), [185]
  public local—
    commons, open spaces etc, as to, **9**, [432]
    National Trust land, rights over, acquisition
      of, **9**, [453]
    objections, hearing of, **9**, [422], [448]
    power to hold, **9**, [412]
  regimental, generally, **3**, [634]
  relevant administration, consultation with,
    10, [878]
  relevant part of United Kingdom, applicable
    rules, **10**, [882]
  reports—
    interim, **10**, [875]
    Parliament or Assembly, laying before,
      10, [877]
    publication, **10**, [876]
    submission of, **10**, [875]
  road user charging scheme, as to, **38(2)**, [157]
  rules, **10**, [892]
  Scottish, **10**, [879]
  Scottish or Welsh matters, as to, **10**, [878]
  Secretary of State, by, **37**, [796]
  Secretary of State for Transport, power of,
    36, [548]
  setting-up date, **10**, [856]
  special Act, under, **36**, [548]
  statutory—
    procedure, **10**, [725]
    reason for decision, Minister giving,
      10, [726]
  summary of provisions, **10**, [1]
  suspension, power of, **10**, [864]
  terms of reference, **10**, [856]
  traffic commissioners, by, **37**, [38];
    38(1), [557]
  tramway, as to, **36**, [532]
  transport systems, orders for, **38(1)**, [301]
  United Kingdom, **10**, [878]
  Welsh, **10**, [880]
  witness, expenses of, **10**, [891]
  workplace parking levy licensing schemes, as
    to, **38(2)**, [174]

inquisition
  re-entry by Crown on land without, **13**, [4]

insanity
  acquittal on grounds of, **12(1)**, [170], [338];
    12(2), [62]

insanity—*contd*
arms or ammunition, supply to insane person, **12(1)**, [501]
diminished responsibility, evidence of, **12(1)**, [343]
evidence by prosecution in murder charge, **12(1)**, [343]
finding of—
appeal against—
disposal of, **12(1)**, [429]
hospital order on, **12(1)**, [341], [342], [430]
right of, **12(1)**, [427]
persons not guilty by reason of, **12(1)**, [341], [422]
substitution for, **12(1)**, [422]
substitution of on appeal, **12(1)**, [422]
summary of provisions, **12(1)**, [1]
supervision order—
amendment, **12(1)**, [347]
appeal, on, **12(1)**, [430]
making and effect of, **12(1)**, [346]
medical treatment requirement, **12(1)**, [346]
meaning, **12(1)**, [345]
power to make, **12(1)**, [341], [422]
requirements, **12(1)**, [345]
residence requirement, **12(1)**, [346]
revocation, **12(1)**, [347]
unfitness to plead, **12(1)**, [339]
See further **unfitness to plead**
guilty but insane, former verdict of, **12(2)**, [704]–[706]
hospital order—
disposal of appeal, **12(1)**, [434]
interim, **12(1)**, [342], [446]
power to make, **12(1)**, [341], [342]
restriction order, with, **12(1)**, [341]
right of appeal against, **12(1)**, [433]
murder, in trial for, evidence, **12(1)**, [343]
not guilty by reason of, finding of, **12(1)**, [341]
proof of medical condition, **12(1)**, [465]
special verdict, **12(1)**, [170], [338]; **12(2)**, [62]
supervision and treatment order—
amendment, **12(1)**, [347]
appeal, on, **12(1)**, [430]
making and effect of, **12(1)**, [341], [346]
medical treatment requirement, **12(1)**, [346]
meaning, **12(1)**, [345]
power to make, **12(1)**, [341]
requirements, **12(1)**, [345]
residence requirement, **12(1)**, [346]
revocation, **12(1)**, [347]

insects
importation and exportation, restriction on. *See* **animals**

insemination
artificial, status of child resulting from, **6**, [281]
time of—
belief that marriage was valid, **6**, [156]

insemination—*contd*
time of—*contd*
reckoning of time from, **6**, [277]

insider dealings. *See* **securities**

insolvency
bank. *See* **bank insolvency**
building society. *See* **building society**
charges, power to make provisions about, **19(1)**, [795]
charitable incorporated organisation, **5(2)**, [642]
company. *See* **company insolvency**
cross-border, model law on, **4(2)**, [579]
definitions, **19(2)**, [430]
employer, of. *See* **employer**
exchange or clearing house proceedings, precedence of, **19(1)**, [780]
Financial Services Authority, participation by. *See* **Financial Services Authority**
financial services compensation scheme, rights of, **19(2)**, [267]
individual. *See* **individual insolvency**
investment bank regulations—
procedure, **19(S)**, Financial 270
provisions of, **19(S)**, Financial 267–70
review, **19(S)**, Financial 271
market charge—
administration provisions not applying to, **19(1)**, [794]
insolvency law, modification of, **19(1)**, [793]
See also **insolvency**
market contracts, modification of law for, **19(1)**, [779]
proceedings—
beginning of, **19(1)**, [779]
other jurisdictions, in, **19(1)**, [802]
protected railway company, restrictions as to, **38(1)**, [410]
registered provider, of—
assistance by regulator, **24**, [697]
court, applications to **24**, [698]
creditor, application to court by, **24**, [698]
manager—
appointment, **24**, [694]
industrial and provident society, of, **24**, [696]
interim, **24**, [690]
powers, **24**, [695]
remuneration and expenses, **24**, [694]
moratorium—
consent to disposal of land, **24**, [687]
disposal of land, on, **24**, [684]
disposals without consent, void, **24**, [689]
duration, **24**, [685]
effect of, **24**, [687]
exempted disposals, **24**, [688]
further, **24**, [686]
interim manager, appointment of, **24**, [690]
proposals. *See* proposals *below*
steps, **24**, [684]

insolvency—*contd*
  registered provider, of—*contd*
    preliminary steps, notice, **24**, [683]
    proposals—
      effect of, **24**, [693]
      implementation, **24**, [693]
      procedure for, **24**, [692]
      regulator, by, **24**, [691]
  registered social landlord, of. *See* **registered social landlord**
  rules, meaning, **19(2)**, [267]
  set-off of debit and credit, exclusion of, **43(S)**, 965–6
  stock lending and repurchase arrangements, stamp taxes—
    application of provisions, **41(S)**, Stamp Duties 6–7
    replacement stock, **41(S)**, Stamp Duties 9
    stamp duty, **41(S)**, Stamp Duties 9
    stamp duty reserve tax, **41(S)**, Stamp Duties 10–12
  summary of provisions, **4(2)**, [1]

insolvency practitioner
  acting, as—
    meaning, **4(2)**, [471]
    qualification, without, **4(2)**, [472]
  administrative receiver etc, as, **4(2)**, [266]
  appointment on debtor's petition, **4(2)**, [342]
  authorisation—
    application for, **4(2)**, [477]
    competent authority for, **4(2)**, [477]
    grant of, **4(2)**, [478]
    notices as to, **4(2)**, [479]
    refusal of, **4(2)**, [478]
      without reference to Tribunal, **4(2)**, [483]
    representations by applicant, **4(2)**, [480]
    withdrawal of, **4(2)**, [478], [483]
  bankrupt disqualified as, **4(2)**, [475]
  company, in relation to, **4(2)**, [471]
  competent authority—
    meaning, **4(2)**, [477]
    reports to be made to, **4(2)**, [482]
  disqualifications to act as, **4(2)**, [475]
  individual, in relation to, **4(2)**, [471]
  insolvent partnership, in relation to, **4(2)**, [471]
  interim receiver, as, **4(2)**, [357]
  liquidator as, **4(2)**, [266]
  nominee under company arrangement, **4(2)**, [68]
  office holders to be, **4(2)**, [266]
  professional body, recognised—
    meaning, **4(2)**, [476]
    membership requirement, **4(2)**, [475]
  regulations or orders, **4(2)**, [505]
  report of, action on, **4(2)**, [343]
  restrictive practices affecting, **4(2)**, [518]
  transitional provisions, **4(2)**, [531], [565]
  Tribunal—
    action on reference, **4(2)**, [482]
    continuance of, **4(2)**, [481]
    panels of members, **4(2)**, [558]
    procedure of, **4(2)**, [558]

insolvency practitioner—*contd*
  Tribunal—*contd*
    references to, **4(2)**, [481]
    remuneration, **4(2)**, [558]
    sittings of, **4(2)**, [558]

Insolvency Services Account
  adjustment of balances, **4(2)**, [492]
  excess money in, **4(2)**, [488]
  Investment Account—
    adjustment of balances, **4(2)**, [492]
    annual financial statement, **4(2)**, [493]
    audit of, **4(2)**, [493]
    income in, application of, **4(2)**, [489]
    moneys in, investment of, **4(2)**, [489]
    payments into, **4(2)**, [489]
  money received by liquidators, **4(2)**, [490]
  payments into, **4**, [1087]
  unclaimed dividends in, **4(2)**, [491]
  undistributed balances in, **4(2)**, [491]

inspector
  company. *See* **companies**
  factory. *See* **factories and workshops**
  friendly society. *See* **friendly society**
  weights and measures. *See* **weights and measures**

institution
  bishop refusing—
    appeal, **14**, 250–1
    grounds, **14**, 250, 801
  deeds of, issuing, **14**, 831–2

instrument. *See also* **deed; documents**
  attestation, requiring, proof of, **18**, [174]
  European Communities, of, proof of, **18**, [4]
  executed or execution, meaning, **41**, [46]
  inter vivos, construction, **18**, [554]
  meaning, **20**, [436], [804]
  powers of attorney, creating, proof of, **18**, [178]
  proof of, where attestation not required, **18**, [130]

insubordinate behaviour
  air force, **3**, [760]
  army, **3**, [487]
  navy, **3**, [1022]

insulation
  building affected by public works—
    grants towards cost of, **35(1)**, [298]
    regulations providing for, **35(1)**, [298]

insurance. *See also* **friendly society; industrial assurance**
  agreements as to liability, avoidance, **37**, [764]
  ambulances, exception, **37**, [755]
  aviation. *See* **war risks insurance**
  bankruptcy etc of insured, effect, **37**, [768]
  bankruptcy, rights in, **4(2)**, [43]–[46]

insurance—*contd*
  broker. *See* **insurance broker**
  business. *See* **insurance company**
  capitals gains tax—
    allowable losses, **42**, [1336]
    deferred annuity, **42**, [1335]
    life assurance policy, **42**, [1335]
    losses, ringing fencing of, **42**, [1336]
    policy, rights under, **42**, [1333]
    premiums, disallowance as expenses,
      42, [1334]
    securities, disposal and acquisition,
      42, [1337]
    transfers of business, **42**, [1338]
      unused losses, transfer of, **42**, [1339]
    transitional provisions, **42**, [1343], [1344]
    venture capital investment partnership,
      from, **42**, [1476]
  car-sharing agreements, **37**, [765]
  Care Quality Commission inspection
    vehicles, **37**, [755]
  casualties, treatment of—
    emergency, payment for, **37**, [773]
    hospital, payment for, **37**, [772]
    meaning of hospital, **37**, [777]
    supplementary provisions, **37**, [774]
  certificates of—
    issue, **37**, [762]
    surrender, **37**, [762]
  claim, notification by tenant, **22**, [554]
  definitions, **19(2)**, [501]; **37**, [777]
  director's liabilities, against, **8(1)**, [311]
  double, marine insurance, **19(1)**, [177]
  employers' liability. *See under* **personal injury**
  European Communities, provision in. *See*
  European Communities
  evidence of—
    on application for licence, **37**, [771]
    production to police, **37**, [782]
  excluded liability, **37**, [766]
  expenditure met by, **43(1)**, [1172]
  group policies, validation of, **19(1)**, [446]
  health service bodies, **37**, [755]
  industrial. *See* **industrial assurance**
  information, disclosure of, **37**, [775]
  information, provision to claimant, **37**, [769],
    [790]
  insurable interest—
    life policy. *See* **life assurance**
    marine policy. *See* **marine insurance**
    meaning, **19(1)**, [150]
  judgments, satisfaction of, **37**, [766]
  landlord's choice of insurers, challenge to,
    22, [554]
  liability towards passengers, avoidance of
    agreements as to, **37**, [764]
  life. *See* **life assurance**
  local authority vehicles, **37**, [755]
  marine. *See* **marine insurance**
  mark to market, postponement of change to,
    43(2), [109]
    election to continue, **43(2)**, [110]
  medical, benefit in kind. *See* **income tax**
  medical, withdrawal of relief on premiums,
    43(1), [312]

insurance—*contd*
  motor, access to certain information,
    47, [614]
  Motor Insurers' Information Centre,
    information, duty to disclose, **37**, [775]
  pensions, relating to, Financial Services
    Compensation Scheme intervention,
    43(S), 1405
  personal, summary of provisions, **19(1)**, [1]
  police vehicles, **37**, [755]
  policies—
    authorised insurers, by, **37**, [760]
    exceptions, avoidance of, **37**, [763]
    inspection of, **22**, [554]
    meaning, **37**, [777]
    requirements, **37**, [760]
  property, generally, **19(1)**, [1]
  refusal on grounds of health, notification,
    37, [682]
  registered friendly societies, business of,
    42, [499]
  regulations, power to make, **37**, [776]
  re-insurance, marine policy, **19(1)**, [154]
  salvage operations vehicles, **37**, [755]
    meaning, **37**, [777]
  secured person, effect of bankruptcy of,
    37, [768]
  security against third party risks—
    certificates of, **37**, [762]
    compulsory, **37**, [754]
    deposits—
      application of, **37**, [770]
      provisions as to, **37**, [755]
    duty of persons giving—
      application of provisions, **37**, [766]
      exceptions, **37**, [767]
    evidence of, on application for licence,
      37, [771]
    exceptions from requirement, **37**, [755]
      avoidance, **37**, [763]
    information, provision to claimant,
      37, [769]
    requirements, **37**, [761]
  sex discrimination in, **7(1)**, [90]
  status of vehicle, disclosure of information
    about, **33(2)**, [582]
  summary of provisions, **19(1)**, [1]
  superior landlord, effected by, **22**, [554]
  tenants, rights of, **22**, [542], [554]
  terrorism, reinsurance in respect of—
    arrangements for, **19(1)**, [948]
    obligations, financing, **19(1)**, [947]
  third party risks—
    certificates, use and surrender of, **37**, [762]
    compulsory, **37**, [754]
    duty of insurers—
      application of provisions, **37**, [766]
      exceptions, **37**, [767]
    evidence of, **37**, [771]
    hospital treatment of casualties,
      37, [772]–[774]
    information, duty to give, **37**, [769], [775],
      [789]
    interpretation of provisions, **37**, [738],
      [777]

insurance—_contd_
  third party risks—_contd_
    private use of vehicles, **37**, [765]
    regulations, **37**, [776]
    requirement, **37**, [761]
      exceptions from, **37**, [755]
    requirements, **37**, [754]
      vehicle not meeting—
        exceptions, **37**, [757]
        fixed penalty notices, **37**, [758]
        immobilisation, **37**, [759], [817]
        offence of, **37**, [756]
        removal and disposal of, **37**, [759],
          [817]
      satisfaction of judgments, in, **37**, [766]
        exceptions, **37**, [767]
      use of vehicle by another person, **37**, [754]
    trustee, powers of, **48**, 470, 648, 655
    value added tax, exemption from, **50**, [153]
    variation of lease regarding, **22**, [750], [755]
    vehicle driven without, power to seize,
      37, [783]
      retention, **37**, [784]
    verification of compliance with
      requirements, **37**, [789]
    war risks. _See_ **war risks insurance**

insurance broker
  estate agency work by, **21**, [678]
  marine policy premium, responsible for,
    19(1), [198]

insurance business
  long-term, realised profits and losses of,
    8(1), [921]
  rules, **19(2)**, [191]
    regulations supplementing, **19(2)**, [192]
  transfer scheme. _See_ **business transfer
    scheme**

insurance company
  accounts—
    accounting principles—
      departure from, **8**, 735
      generally, **8**, 734
    accounting rules—
      current value—
        additional information to be
          provided, **8**, 737
        assets, valuation of, **8**, 735
        depreciation rules, application of,
          8, 737
        meaning, **8**, 736–7
        revaluation reserve, **8**, 737–8
      historical cost—
        assets, valuation of, **8**, 738–9
        miscellaneous and supplemental,
          8, 739–41
      outstanding claims, rules for, **8**, 741–3
    disclosure requirements, modification of,
      8, 337
    form of, **8**, 723–34
    general rules, **8**, 721–3
    generally, **8**, 335
    group accounts, **8**, 337

insurance company—_contd_
  accounts—_contd_
    modification of provisions, **8**, 755–6
    notes to, generally, **8**, 743–9
  acquisitions, disregarded, **43(1)**, [437]
  amended provisions, **43(1)**, [169];
    43(S), 1145–62
  amendment of provisions, **43(S)**, 648–56
  annuity. _See_ **annuity**
  annuity business—
    general—
      charges on income, **44(1)**, [264]
      meaning, **44(1)**, [247]
    meaning, **44(1)**, [237]
    steep-reduction annuity, meaning,
      44(1), [265]
  apportionment, participating funds,
    43(S), 295
  apportionments, **43(S)**, 1153–4
    income and gains, of, **43(S)**, 1155
    inherited estates rules, abolition,
      43(S), 1158
  assets—
    linked, meaning, **44(1)**, [251]
    securities as, **44(1)**, [268]
    transfer of, **44(1)**, [267]
  balance sheet—
    formats—
      detailed, **8**, 723–5
      examples, **8**, 723–5
      general rules, **8**, 721–2
      notes on, **8**, 725–9
      special rules, **8**, 729–30
    information supplementing—
      assets, **8**, 744–5
      guarantees and commitments, **8**, 746–7
      indebtedness, details of, **8**, 746
      investments, **8**, 745
      miscellaneous matters, **8**, 747
      reserves and provisions, **8**, 745–6
      share capital and debentures, **8**, 744
      tax, provision for, **8**, 746
  basis of taxation—
    amended provisions, **43(S)**, 629–34
    life assurance business and other business,
      company carrying on, **43(S)**, 629
    life assurance business, company carrying
      on, **43(S)**, 629
    modifications of, **43(S)**, 630–1
  BLAGAB profits, **43(S)**, 1157
  business, specification of place of, **19(1)**, [24]
  business transfer schemes, commencement of
    Order, **43(S)**, 1162
  capital redemption business, meaning,
    44(1), [237]
  Case I profits, **43(2)**, [266]
  charges on income, **43(S)**, 1159
  child trust fund business, meaning, **43(S)**, 611
  Community State, in. _See_ **European
    Communities**
  consolidated accounts, **8**, 751–2
  contaminated land, remediation of,
    43(S), 1159
  contingent loan to, **42**, [969]
  contingent loans, **43(S)**, 648

insurance company—*contd*

contingent losses, **43(S)**, 307–8

contract, law applicable in certain. *See under*
insurance

contributions to London Fire and Civil
Defence Authority by—
amount of, ascertaining, **18**, [1000]
books, examination of, **18**, [1002]
enforcing, **18**, [999]
information of fires, having, **18**, [1005]
penalties, recovery of, **18**, [1003]
returns, failure to make, **18**, [1001]
salvage force, establishment of, **18**, [1004]

controlled foreign companies, **43(S)**, 1160

corporation tax computation, **42**, [952]

definitions, generalisation, **43(S)**, 653

demutualisation, stamp duty relief **41**, [242],
[336]

deposit back arrangements, **43(S)**, 1152

derivative contracts, **43(S)**, 1153

disposal of authorised investment funds to
connected manager, losses on, **43(S)**, 650–1

distributions by, **8**, 352–3, 360

effect of orders, continuing, **43(S)**, 295

equalisation reserves—
application of rules, **44(1)**, [301]
general business, for, **44(1)**, [298]
mutual business, for, **44(1)**, [299]
non-annual accounting, **44(1)**, [300]
non-resident companies, **44(1)**, [299]
overseas business, for, **44(1)**, [299]

excess adjusted Case I profits, **43(S)**, 632

expenses, **43(S)**, 1150–1

expenses of management, **44(1)**, [45]

fair value provisions, **43(S)**, 653

financial difficulties, insurers in, **19(2)**, [269]

financial reinsurance arrangement—
apportionment and redefining, **43(S)**, 1148
reduction or increase in liabilities,
43(S), 1148

financial resources—
assets. *See* assets *above*
solvency. *See* solvency *below*

financing-arrangement-funded transfers—
amended provisions, **43(S)**, 1148–50
contingent losses, **43(S)**, 1587
relevant period of account, charge in,
43(S), 1146–7
subsequent periods of account, deduction
in, **43(S)**, 1147–8
transfers of business, **43(S)**, 1148–9

foreign business assets, **43(S)**, 1152–3
apportionment, **43(S)**, 1587–8
election that assets not be, **44(1)**, [238]
meaning, **44(1)**, [237]

foreign currency assets, **43(S)**, 1153

franked investment income, **43(1)**, [330]

free assets amount, meaning, **44(1)**, [237]

friendly society, transfer from—
commencement, **43(S)**, 663
exempt life or endowment business,
43(S), 660–1
non-life or endowment exempt business,
43(S), 661–3

insurance company—*contd*

general business. *See generally*, business *above*

general insurance business, non-annual
accounting, **43(1)**, [405]

general insurers, technical provisions made
by—
commencement, **43(S)**, 659
definitions, **43(S)**, 658–9
enforcement, **43(S)**, 657
restriction on amount of, **43(S)**, 657

general reserves, **43(1)**, [492]

gross roll-up business, **43(S)**, 1162
amended provisions, **43(S)**, 537, 609–24
gains referable to not to be chargeable
gains, **43(S)**, 617–18
meaning, **43(S)**, 611
non-participating funds, apportionment,
43(S), 614–15
profits, separate charge on, **43(S)**, 617–18
transfers-in, apportionment, **43(S)**, 616–17
transitional provisions, **43(S)**, 626–8
unused non-pension business losses, carry
forward, **43(S)**, 627–8
unused pension business losses, carry
forward, **43(S)**, 626–7

group policies, validation of, **19(1)**, [446]

group relief, gross profits excluding relevant
profits, **43(S)**, 1158

individual savings account business, meaning,
43(S), 611

internal linked fund, meaning, **44(1)**, [237]

internal linked funds and net value,
43(S), 652

liabilities, meaning, **44(1)**, [237]

life—
amendment of provisions, **44(1)**, [239]
linked assets, **44(1)**, [237]
overseas, meaning, **44(1)**, [237]
tax basis—
change of, **44(1)**, [270]
I minus E of, **44(1)**, [248]

life assurance—
income, apportionment of, **42**, [1034]
overseas business, **42**, [1035]

life assurance business. *See also* **life assurance
business; life policy**
acquisition expenses, spreading of relief,
42, [976]
allowances and charges—
application of provisions, **43(1)**, [833]
apportionment, **43(1)**, [834]
different categories, rules for,
43(1), [835]
giving effect to, **43(1)**, [835]
brought into account, meaning, **42**, [972]
contaminated land remediation
expenditure, **43(2)**, [77]
corporation tax—
policy holders' fraction of profits,
42, [978]
policy holders' share of profits, **42**, [979]
expenses payable, restriction on carrying
forward, **43(2)**, [77]
I minus E basis, **42**, [1507]
investment assets, **43(1)**, [1182]

insurance company—*contd*
  life assurance business—*contd*
    leased assets, taxation of, **43(1)**, [297]
    long term insurance fund—
      amounts added to in excess of loss,
        42, [970]
      receipts taken into account, **42**, [968]
      transfer of business, treatment of surplus
        on, **42**, [971]
    management assets, **43(1)**, [1181]
    meaning, **42**, [974]
    overseas companies, of, **42**, [1001]
    profits—
      basic business, charge of receipts of,
        42, [975]
      calculation of—
        bonuses, etc, **42**, [964]
        policy holders' tax, **42**, [965]
      receipts taken into account, **42**, [968]
    reverse premiums, receipt of, **43(1)**, [457]
    special leasing, **43(1)**, [840]
    See also **life assurance business; life
      policy**
  life insurance. *See* **life assurance**
  liquidation, in—
    assets, treatment of, **19(2)**, [453]
    long-term contracts, continuation of,
      19(2), [451]
    reducing value of contracts, **19(2)**, [452]
    winding-up rules, **19(2)**, [454]
  Lloyd's underwriters. *See* **Lloyd's**
  loan relationships, **43(1)**, [259]
  loans, meaning, **8**, 750
  long-term business other than life—
    computing profits of, **44(1)**, [250]
    Insurance Prudential Sourcebook, effect of
      change in, **44(1)**, [250]
  long-term policies, continuation of,
    19(2), [268]
  loss relief, limitations on, **44(1)**, [261]
  losses, computation of, **44(1)**, [261]
  management expenses—
    amounts reversing, charge to tax,
      43(2), [282]
    consequential amendments, power to
      make, **43(2)**, [283]
    transitional provisions, **43(2)**, [281]
  materiality, meaning, **8**, 750
  meaning, **8(1)**, [1243]; **44(1)**, [237]
  mutual and former mutual business, surpluses
    of, **43(S)**, 297–303
  non-annual actuarial investigations,
    43(1), [405]
  non-profit companies, non-profit and
    with-profit funds, **43(S)**, 652
  non-profit funds, limits on loss relief for
    addition to, **43(S)**, 1584–7
  non technical account, transfers from,
    43(S), 1584
  obsolete provisions, **43(S)**, 655
  offshore income gains, **43(S)**, 1160
  overseas—
    application of provisions to, **42**, [1477]
    deemed disposal and reacquisition,
      43(1), [50]

insurance company—*contd*
  overseas—*contd*
    power of intervention in respect of,
      19(2), [250]
  overseas business, **44(1)**, [272]
    equalisation reserves, **44(1)**, [299]
    property business—
      losses from, **44(1)**, [254]
      treated as carrying on separate,
        44(1), [253]
  overseas life insurance business, amended
    provisions, **43(S)**, 1160
  pension business—
    exemption from tax, **44(1)**, [266]
    meaning, **43(2)**, [772]; **44(1)**, [240]
    transitional provisions, **44(1)**, [691]
  pension schemes. *See* **pension schemes**
  periodic return, meaning, **44(1)**, [237]
  periodical return, **43(S)**, 1161
  periodical statement by, **8**, 584
    form of, **8**, 794–5
  policy, long term. *See* long term policy *above*
  priority of provisions, **43(S)**, 651
  profit and loss account—
    formats—
      detailed, **8**, 730–2
      notes on, **8**, 732–4
    information supplementing—
      separate statement of certain items,
        8, 747
      staff, as to, **8**, 749
      tax, particulars of, **8**, 747–8
  profits, computing, **44(1)**, [260]
  provisions, meaning, **8**, 750
  R & D relief, **43(S)**, 1161
  recognised accounts, changes in, **42**, [973]
  reinsurance contracts, **42**, [967]
  related expressions, **8(1)**, [1243]
  reorganisation of mutual business, gains
    ineligible for taper relief, **42**, [1347]
  research and development expenditure, tax
    relief for, **43(2)**, [141]
  restriction on expenses of management,
    43(S), 526
  risk reinsured, taxation of investment return,
    44(1), [273]
  Schedule A business—
    losses from, **44(1)**, [254]
    treated as carrying on separate, **44(1)**, [253]
  Scots land tenure, meaning, **8**, 750
  securities, dealing in. *See* **securities**
  special purpose vehicles, **43(S)**, 1158
  staff costs, meaning, **8**, 750–1
  structural assets, **43(S)**, 648–50, 1151
  trades in I minus E, **43(S)**, 1160
  transfer of business, **43(2)**, [266], [772];
    43(S), 1161
    anti-avoidance rule, **43(S)**, 642–5
    assets brought into account, changes in
      value, **43(S)**, 304–7
    capital allowances, **43(1)**, [1197]
    anti-avoidance rule, **43(S)**, 642–5
    excess of assets or liabilities, **43(S)**, 296
    expenses and losses etc, **43(S)**, 637

insurance company—*contd*
> transfer of business—*contd*
>> long-term insurance fund, assets added to, **43(S)**, 645
>> modification of provisions, **43(S)**, 296
>> no gain/no loss on, **43(S)**, 646
>> old annuity contracts, **43(S)**, 646
>> old reinsurance business, **43(S)**, 646
>> part, scheme for, **43(S)**, 640
>> power to amend provisions, **43(S)**, 646
>> receipts, taking into account, **43(S)**, 303–4, 645
>> relevant non-transferred assets, **43(S)**, 639
>> retained assets, **43(S)**, 640
>> scheme, definition, **43(S)**, 636
>> transferee, taxation of, **43(S)**, 641
>> transferor's period of account, **43(S)**, 641
>> transferor, taxation of, **43(S)**, 638–9
>> value shifting attributable to, **43(S)**, 1588
> transitional relief—
>> chargeable gains, for, **42**, [1070]
>> old general annuity contracts, for, **42**, [1070]
>> unrelieved general annuity losses, for, **42**, [1070]
> UK distributions received by, **43(S)**, 1154
> taxation of, **44(1)**, [77]
> underwriter, Lloyd's. *See* **Lloyd's**
> unit trusts, deemed disposals of, **43(1)**, [7]
> vaccine research expenditure, relief for, **43(2)**, [147]
> valuation, unappropriated surplus, **42**, [966]
> with-profits policy holders, capital allocations to, **43(S)**, 1584

insurance policy
> disposal of rights, gains accruing on, **43(S)**, 65–6
> marine, reference to, **41**, [93]
> qualifying, method for calculating benefits, **43(S)**, 85
> sum recovered under as trade receipt, **44(3)**, [105]

insurance premium tax
> appeals, **19(1)**, [964]
> assessment of, **19(1)**, [962], [991]
> charge of, **19(1)**, [951]
> chargeable amount, **19(1)**, [952]
> commencement, **43(1)**, [257]
> Commissioners for HM Revenue and Customs—
>> administration by, **19(1)**, [950]
>> decision, review of, **19(1)**, [963], [965]
>> evidence by certificate, **19(1)**, [991]
>> information—
>>> disclosure of, **19(1)**, [991]
>>> requiring, **19(1)**, [986]
>> interest payable by, **19(1)**, [990]
>> records, **19(1)**, [986]
> contracts—
>> adjustment of, **19(1)**, [991]
>> not taxable, **19(1)**, [992]
> criminal offences, **19(1)**, [989]
> criminal proceedings, **19(1)**, [989]

insurance premium tax—*contd*
> documents, removal by authorised person, **19(1)**, [987]
> entry on premises for purposes of, **19(1)**, [987]
> fraud offence, arrest for, **19(1)**, [987]
> increase in, **43(1)**, [375]
> information and inspection powers, **43(S)**, 1412–13, 1692–8
> information, furnishing of, **19(1)**, [986]
> insured, liability of, **19(1)**, [969]
> insurers—
>> bankruptcy, **19(1)**, [966]
>> cancellation of registration, **19(1)**, [957]
>> credit, **19(1)**, [961]
>> groups of companies, **19(1)**, [967]
>> Lloyd's underwriters, **19(1)**, [966]
>> partnerships, **19(1)**, [966]
>> registration of, **19(1)**, [957]
>> transfer of business, **19(1)**, [966]
>> unincorporated body as, **19(1)**, [966]
> interest on, **19(1)**, [990]
> liability to pay, **19(1)**, [955]
> notices, service of, **19(1)**, [991]
> orders and regulations, **19(1)**, [981]
> overpaid, recovery of, **19(1)**, [988]
> overseas insurers, liability of insured, **43(S)**, 979
> payment, time for, **19(1)**, [960]
> penalties—
>> assessment, **19(1)**, [991]
>> civil, **19(1)**, [989]
>> criminal, **19(1)**, [989]
> pre-emption, prevention of, **43(1)**, [276]
> premium—
>> amount, directions as to, **19(1)**, [969]
>> deemed date of receipt, **19(1)**, [971]
>> meaning, **19(1)**, [979]
>> open market conditions, received in, **19(1)**, [970]
>> other than money, in, **19(1)**, [970], [979]
>> repayment, credit for, **19(1)**, [961]
> provisional collection, **19(1)**, [991]
> rates of—
>> announced increase—
>>> contracts treated as made on date of, **19(1)**, [973]
>>> exceptions and apportionments, **19(1)**, [974]
>>> premiums treated as made on date of, **19(1)**, [972]
>> charge to tax where different, **19(1)**, [976]
>> higher—
>>> amount, **19(1)**, [953]
>>> cars and motor cycles, insurance relating to, **19(1)**, [985]
>>> charge to, **19(1)**, [953]
>>> contract, meaning, **19(1)**, [956]
>>> divided company, insurance provided by, **19(1)**, [985]
>>> domestic appliances, insurance relating to, **19(1)**, [985]
>>> fees to be treated as premiums under, **19(1)**, [956]

insurance premium tax—*contd*
rates of—*contd*
higher—*contd*
premiums liable to, **19(1)**, [954], [984], [985]
travel insurance, **19(1)**, [985]
standard, **19(1)**, [953]
receipt of premium, charged on, **19(1)**, [951]
recorded information, access to, **19(1)**, [987]
record-keeping, **43(S)**, 1702–3
records, **19(1)**, [986]
recovery of, **19(1)**, [988]
registrable person—
accounting for tax, **19(1)**, [960]
cancellation of registration, **19(1)**, [957]
register, keeping up to date, **19(1)**, [959]
registration of, **19(1)**, [957]
return—
failure to make, **19(1)**, [962]
requirement to make, **19(1)**, [960]
security for, **19(1)**, [991]
setting of rates of interest, **13**, [1062]
special accounting schemes, **19(1)**, [975]
summary of provisions, **19(1)**, [1]
tax representatives, repealed provisions, **43(S)**, 979
taxable insurance contract—
definition, power to change, **19(1)**, [978]
meaning, **19(1)**, [977]
taxable intermediaries—
cancellation of registration, **19(1)**, [958]
credit, **19(1)**, [961]
registration of, **19(1)**, [958]
time limits for assessments, claims, etc, amendment, **43(S)**, 1707

insurer
credit agreements, exemption of, **39(1)**, [149]
meaning, **39(1)**, [149]

intangible fixed assets. *See* **companies**

integrated transport areas
agreements with other areas, **36**, [777]
workplace parking levy licensing schemes, as to, **38(2)**, [174]
designation of, **36**, [777]
Director General, appointment, **36**, [777]
dissolution of, **38(2)**, [696]
consents required, **38(2)**, [697]
guidance from Secretary of State as to, **38(2)**, [702]
interconnected bodies corporate, disqualification of persons connected with, **36**, [778]
metropolitan counties as, **36**, [777]
orders as to—
incidental provisions, **38(2)**, [698]
procedure for making, **38(2)**, [698]
passenger transport areas, renamed as, **38(2)**, [682]
well-being of, promotion of, **38(2)**, [703], [704]

Integrated Transport Authority
airports transferred to, **25(2)**, [600]
annual reports, **36**, [786]
approval by, of acts by Executive, **36**, [779], [784]
arrangements relating to—
constitutional, **38(2)**, [689]
review of, **38(2)**, [687]
Secretary of State's power to direct, **38(2)**, [688]
competition, bar on inhibition of, **37**, [417]
designation of, **38(2)**, [683]
disqualification for membership, **25(2)**, [596]
duties, **36**, [778]
duty, role of metropolitan district councils, **38(2)**, [82]
England and Wales, **36**, [777]
establishment, **25(2)**, [591]; **36**, [777]
expenditure, when defrayed by Executive, **37**, [464]
functions, **36**, [778], [784]; **37**, [464]
functions transferred to, **25(2)**, [599]
members, number of, **25(2)**, [640]–[645]
grants to, **38(2)**, [144]
grants to Executive by, **36**, [782]
guidance from Secretary of State, **38(2)**, [702]
loans to Executive by, **36**, [781]
local authority functions, delegation to, **38(2)**, [692]
local transport plans, review and alteration of, **38(2)**, [77]
membership of, **38(2)**, [689]
orders as to, **38(2)**, [690]
name, change of, **38(2)**, [702]
new—
orders for, provisions contained in, **38(2)**, [684]
power to establish, **38(2)**, [683]
review by county and district councils, **38(2)**, [685]
Secretary of State's power to direct, **38(2)**, [686]
orders as to—
consultation before making, **38(2)**, [697]
incidental provisions, **38(2)**, [698]
membership, regarding, **38(2)**, [690]
powers of direction, conferring, **38(2)**, [693], [694]
procedure for making, **38(2)**, [698]
Passenger Transport Authority, renamed as, **38(2)**, [682]
policies, formulation of, **36**, [778]
powers of direction, conferred on, **38(2)**, [693], [694]
quality contracts scheme, power to make, **38(2)**, [95]
road charging schemes, information as to, duty to provide, **38(2)**, [166]
Secretary of State's functions, delegation to, **38(2)**, [691]
travel concession scheme, **37**, [430]
well-being of area, power to promote, **38(2)**, [703]
enactments obstructing, amendment or repeal of, **38(2)**, [705], [706]

Integrated Transport Authority—*contd*
well-being of area, power to promote—*contd*
limits on, **38(2)**, [704]

Integrated Transport Executive
accounts, **36**, [783]
agency agreements, **36**, [779]
agreements, power to enter into, **36**, [778]
annual reports, **36**, [786]
approval by Authority of acts by, **36**, [779],
[784]
borrowing powers, **36**, [781]
compulsory purchase of land by, **36**, [779]
consents and directions by Minister, **36**, [789]
control over, **36**, [785]
duties, **36**, [778]
establishment, **36**, [777]
estimates of income and expenditure,
36, [784]
ferries, acquisition of, **36**, [779]
financial duty of, **36**, [780]
functions, **36**, [778]
general powers, **36**, [779]
grants by Authority to, **36**, [782]
land, powers as to, **36**, [779]
loans to, **36**, [781]
members, **36**, [777]
disqualification, **36**, [778]
orders relating to, power to make, **36**, [777]
organisation of undertaking, review of,
36, [785]
powers, **36**, [779]
railway passenger services, special duties with
respect to, **36**, [787]
review of activities of, **36**, [785]
subsidiaries, control over, **36**, [779]
subsidiary activities—
generally, **36**, [779]
improper conduct, prevention, **36**, [786]

intellectual property
non-trading income, charge to tax—
charge to tax, **44(3)**, [589]
contents of provisions, **44(3)**, [588]
deductions, **44(3)**, [592]
person liable, **44(3)**, [591]

Intelligence and Security Committee
annual report, **10**, [751]
functions of, **10**, [751]
information, access to, **10**, [754]
members—
appointment of, **10**, [751]
tenure of office, **10**, [754]
procedure, **10**, [754]
sensitive information, **10**, [754]

Intelligence Service
acts outside British Islands, authorisation of,
10, [750]
Chief of, **10**, [745]
Commissioner—
appointment of, **45**, [387]
co-operation with, **45**, [388]
reports, **45**, [388]

Intelligence Service—*contd*
Commissioner—*contd*
summary of provisions, **45**, [1]
functions of, **10**, [744]
warrants—
authorisation of actions by, **10**, [748]
duration of, **10**, [749]
procedure for issue, **10**, [749]

Intelligence Services Commissioner
jurisdiction, **36**, [182]

Intelligence Services Tribunal
jurisdiction, **36**, [182]

Inter-American Development Bank
capital gains tax exemption, **42**, [1415]
income from securities, **44(3)**, [788]
security issued by, place of, **42**, [359]
stamp duty exemption, **41**, [132]

inter-bank payment systems
closure, **19(S)**, Financial 245
de-recognition, **19(S)**, Financial 237
Financial Services Authority, role of,
19(S), Financial 240
general note, **19(S)**, Financial 52–3
informal oversight, **19(S)**, Financial 250
information, requirement of,
19(S), Financial 248–9
interpretation, **19(S)**, Financial 234
meaning, **19(S)**, Financial 223
meaning, **19(S)**, Financial 234
operation of—
codes of practice, **19(S)**, Financial 238
compliance failure—
closure on, **19(S)**, Financial 245
meaning, **19(S)**, Financial 243
penalty for, **19(S)**, Financial 244
publication of details,
19(S), Financial 243–4
directions, **19(S)**, Financial 239
expert, report by, **19(S)**, Financial 242–3
fees, **19(S)**, Financial 248
inspection of—
appointment of persons for,
19(S), Financial 241
warrant, **19(S)**, Financial 241–2
management disqualification,
19(S), Financial 246
principles, **19(S)**, Financial 238
sanctions—
appeals, **19(S)**, Financial 247
warning, **19(S)**, Financial 247
overview, **19(S)**, Financial 233
pretending to be recognised, offence,
19(S), Financial 250
recognition order—
power to make, **19(S)**, Financial 235
procedure for making, **19(S)**, Financial 236
recognition criteria, **19(S)**, Financial 235–6
revocation, **19(S)**, Financial 237
specification of, **19(S)**, Financial 235
system rules, **19(S)**, Financial 239

interdicts
acts in contemplation or furtherance of trade dispute, protection in relation to, **16**, [423]

interesse termini
abolition of doctrine, **20**, [759]

interest
arrangements appearing very likely to produce post-tax advantage, **43(S)**, 1615–17
borrower, arrangements minimising risk to, **43(S)**, 1615–17
building society, payment by. *See* **building society**
capital charged to, **42**, [1124]
compensation, payable on—
    entry on land, after, **9**, [246]
    generally, **9**, [129], [321], [363]
debts, damages and costs, on, in Crown proceedings, **13**, [27]
deduction, not allowed as, **42**, [829]
deposits, on, deduction of tax from, **43(1)**, [143]
deposit-taker, payment by. *See* **deposit-taker**
disallowance of relief for, **42**, [219]
disposal of right to receive, charge to tax, **44(1)**, [35]
distributions of offshore funds taxed as, **43(S)**, 1379
distributions, payments deemed to be, **43(1)**, [144]
dividends of investment trusts taxed as, **43(S)**, 1382–3
double relief for, restriction of, **44(3)**, [51]
double taxation relief, special relationship provision, **44(1)**, [590]
exchange restrictions, arrears due to, **42**, [221]
exempt income—
    employee share schemes, from, **44(3)**, [766]
    foreign interest securities owned by non-UK residents, on, **44(3)**, [769]–[770]
    funding bonds, redemption of, **44(3)**, [768]
    personal injury damages, from, **44(3)**, [765]
    pool betting duty, payments by persons liable to, **44(3)**, [762]
    repayment supplements, paid under, **44(3)**, [763]
    student loan, repayment of, **44(3)**, [767]
    tax reserve certificates, from, **44(3)**, [764]
exempt payments between associated companies of different Member states—
    anti-avoidance, **44(3)**, [780]
    companies being 25% associated, **44(3)**, [776]
    conditions for, **44(3)**, [773]
    exemption notices, **44(3)**, [777]
    interpretation, **44(3)**, [781]
    person beneficially entitled, **44(3)**, [775]
    person making, **44(3)**, [774]
    power to amend Directive, **44(3)**, [782]
    provision for, **44(3)**, [772]
    special relationships, **44(3)**, [778]–[779]
exemption of payments from tax, claim for tax deducted at source from, **43(2)**, [326]
gilt-edged securities, paid on, **43(1)**, [320]

interest—*contd*
income tax, without deduction of—
    banks, etc, paid or credited by, **42**, [122]
    notice of, **42**, [123]
indirect taxation, on, **4(1)**, [372]
industrial and provident society, paid by, **44(1)**, [325]
inheritance tax, on, **42**, [775]–[778]
late payment of tax, on sums due to HMRC—
    amount carrying, **43(S)**, 1728–9
    application of provisions, **43(S)**, 1414–15
    date from which running, **43(S)**, 1732–3
    date on which due and payable, **43(S)**, 1417
    inheritance tax, **43(S)**, 1730–1, 1733
    provision for, **43(S)**, 1417–18
    rates of, **43(S)**, 1416–17
    reliefs, effect on, **43(S)**, 1733–4
    start date, **43(S)**, 1730–2
    taxpayer, death of, **43(S)**, 1732
    VAT, **43(S)**, 1731
loan relationships. *See* **loan relationships**
manufactured, **44(1)**, [670]
    credits and debits, **43(S)**, 1620
    payments, **43(1)**, [218], [294]
meaning, **44(1)**, [615]
over-deductions, **44(1)**, [606]
overdue tax, on, **43(1)**, [149]
    company payments, on, **42**, [217]
    corporation tax, **42**, [218]
    income tax and capital gains tax, **42**, [216]
    provisions on, **42**, [905]
overpaid tax, on, **44(1)**, [609]
payments, restrictions on relief for, **43(S)**, 1202
penalties, on, **42**, [243]
petroleum revenue tax, on, **42**, [346]
rates of, **42**, [990]
recovery of, **42**, [206]
relief. *See* **interest relief**
reliefs, effect of, **42**, [220]
repayment, on sums to be paid by HMRC—
    application of provisions, **43(S)**, 1415–16
    date on which due and payable, **43(S)**, 1417
    provision for, **43(S)**, 1417–18
    rates of, **43(S)**, 1416–17
    repayments, attribution of, **43(S)**, 1736
    start date—
        general rule, **43(S)**, 1734–5
        special provision, **43(S)**, 1735–6
revenue nature, item of, **44(3)**, [29]
savings and investment income, as—
    authorised unit trust distributions, **44(3)**, [376]–[378]
    building society dividends, **44(3)**, [372]
    charge to tax, **44(3)**, [369]
    discounts as, **44(3)**, [381]
    funding bonds, issue of, **44(3)**, [380]
    income charged, **44(3)**, [370]
    industrial and provident society payments, **44(3)**, [379]
    open-ended investment company, distributions by, **44(3)**, [373]–[375]

interest—*contd*
  savings and investment income, as—*contd*
    person liable, **44(3)**, [371]
    Schedule D Case III, charge under,
      44(1), [13]
    Stock Exchange reforms, effect of, **42**, [859]
    transfer of securities with. *See* **securities**
    under-deductions, **44(1)**, [605]
    underlying tax reflecting, **44(1)**, [562]
    windfall tax, on, **43(1)**, [329]

interest payments
  relief for—
    business successions—
      other, **44(4)**, [418]
      partnerships, between, **44(4)**, [417]
    commercial woodlands, occupation of—
      ineligible for, **44(4)**, [419]
    double relief, exclusion of, **44(4)**, [395]
    entitlement to, **44(4)**, [391]
    general restrictions, **44(4)**, [392]
    information requirements, **44(4)**, [420]
    loans—
      business reorganisations, for, **44(4)**, [418]
      business successions, for, **44(4)**, [417]
      close companies, to buy interest in,
        44(4), [400]
        associate, meaning, **44(4)**, [403]
        eligibility requirements, **44(4)**, [401]
        material interest, meaning,
          44(4), [402]
      co-operatives, to invest in,
        44(4), [409]–[410]
      employee-controlled company, to buy
        interest in, **44(4)**, [404]
        eligibility requirements, **44(4)**, [405]
      film partnerships, **44(4)**, [408]
      general provisions, **44(4)**, [393]
      inheritance tax, to pay,
        44(4), [411]–[413]
      partly meeting requirements,
        44(4), [394]
      partnership, to invest in, **44(4)**, [406]
        business successions between
          partnerships, **44(4)**, [417]
      plant or machinery, to buy—
        eligibility requirements, **44(4)**, [397],
          [399]
        employment use, for,
          44(4), [398]–[399]
        partnership use, for,
          44(4), [396]–[397]
      qualifying for, **44(4)**, [391]
      recovery of capital—
        effect of, **44(4)**, [414]
        events counting as, **44(4)**, [415]
        replacement, **44(4)**, [416]
    partnerships—
      loans to invest in, **44(4)**, [406]
        business successions between,
          44(4), [417]
  yearly, **44(4)**, [882]
    exception from deductions—
      advances from banks, interest paid on,
        44(4), [887]

interest payments—*contd*
  yearly—*contd*
    exception from deductions—*contd*
      advances from building societies, interest
        paid on, **44(4)**, [888]
      authorised persons dealing financial
        instruments, **44(4)**, [893]
      banks, paid by, **44(4)**, [886]
      building societies, paid by, **44(4)**, [883]
      deposit-takers, paid by, **44(4)**, [884]
      industrial and provident societies,
        44(4), [895]
      life annuity, interest on loan to buy,
        44(4), [891]
      National Savings Bank interest,
        44(4), [889]
      quoted Eurobond interest, **44(4)**, [890]
      recognised clearing houses, paid by,
        44(4), [894]
      relevant foreign income, **44(4)**, [892]
      statutory interest, **44(4)**, [896]
      UK public revenue dividends,
        44(4), [885]

interest relief
  deduction of, **44(1)**, [180]
  general provision, **44(1)**, [180]
  information, **44(1)**, [182]
  loan, life annuity, for, **44(1)**, [181]
  mortgage. *See* **mortgage interest relief**
  restriction of, **44(1)**, [538]
  tax avoidance, **44(1)**, [538]

**Intergovernmental Commission and Safety
Authority**
  channel tunnel—
    supervision of construction and operation
      of, **37**, [499]
    supplementary provisions, **37**, [500]

interlocutory order
  detention of goods, relief where, **45**, [966]

intermediary
  associate, meaning, **44(2)**, [60]
  distributions by, **44(2)**, [58]
  multiple, **44(2)**, [59]
  payments by, PAYE income, **44(2)**, [687]
  profits, calculation of, **43(1)**, [504]
  provision of services through, **43(2)**, [208]
    company, being, **44(2)**, [51]
    deemed employment payment—
      calculation of, **44(2)**, [54]
      earlier date of, **44(2)**, [57]
      Income Tax Acts, application of,
        44(2), [56]
    earnings from employment—
      application of rules, **44(2)**, [55]
      worker treated as receiving, **44(2)**, [50]
    engagements to which provisions apply,
      44(2), [49]
    individual, being, **44(2)**, [53]
    partnership, being, **44(2)**, [52], [61]
    scope of provisions, **44(2)**, [48]

internal drainage board. *See* **drainage board**

international agreements
pollution, as to, power to give effect to, **35(2)**, [48]

International Bank for Reconstruction and Development
establishment of, **19(1)**, [1]
immunities and privileges of, **19(2)**, [1064]
transfer of stock, exemption from stamp duty, **41**, [86]

International Carriage by Rail
convention concerning—
giving effect to, **38(2)**, [249], [264]
international transport conventions, revision of, **37**, [159]
modification of, **38(2)**, [264]
rights under, exercise of, **38(2)**, [264]
sanctions, **38(2)**, [264]
special drawing rights, conversion of, **38(2)**, [264]

international carriage of perishable foodstuffs
Agreement—
amendment of, **1(2)**, [75]
documents admissible as evidence, **1(2)**, [74]
financial provisions, **1(2)**, [77]
foreign goods vehicle—
driving, prohibiting, **1(2)**, [70]
meaning, **1(2)**, [78]
offences, **1(2)**, [70]
interpretation of terms, **1(2)**, [78]
Jersey, provisions extending to, **1(2)**, [76]
meaning, **1(2)**, [78]
regulations—
examination and testing, on, **1(2)**, [61]
making, **1(2)**, [79]
offences against, **1(2)**, [66]
power to make, **1(2)**, [62]
standards for transport equipment, on, **1(2)**, [60]
standards, regulation of, **1(2)**, [60]
goods vehicle, meaning, **1(2)**, [78]
meanings, **1(2)**, [78]
motor vehicle, meaning, **1(2)**, [78]
offences—
body corporate, by, **1(2)**, [72]
certificate of compliance—
forgery of, **1(2)**, [68]
unauthorised use, **1(2)**, [66]
certification plate—
forgery of, **1(2)**, [68]
unauthorised use, **1(2)**, [66]
certification, use of vehicle without, **1(2)**, [66]
defences, **1(2)**, [66]
designated mark—
failing to exhibit, **1(2)**, [66]
unauthorised use, **1(2)**, [67]
false statements, **1(2)**, [69]
fines, **1(2)**, [66]

international carriage of perishable foodstuffs—*contd*
offences—*contd*
jurisdiction of courts, **1(2)**, [73]
material information, withholding, **1(2)**, [69]
regulations, against, **1(2)**, [66]
standards, regulation of, **1(2)**, [60]
summary proceedings, time limit for, **1(2)**, [71]
transport equipment—
certificate of compliance—
false statement to obtain, making, **1(2)**, [69]
forgery of, **1(2)**, [68]
issue of, **1(2)**, [61], [62]
meaning, **1(2)**, [78]
production, examiner requiring, **1(2)**, [65]
unauthorised use, **1(2)**, [66]
use of vehicle without, **1(2)**, [66]
certification of, **1(2)**, [61]
certification plate—
false statement to obtain, making, **1(2)**, [69]
forgery of, **1(2)**, [68]
inspection of, **1(2)**, [65]
issue of, **1(2)**, [61]
meaning, **1(2)**, [78]
unauthorised use, **1(2)**, [66]
use of vehicle without, **1(2)**, [66]
container, meaning, **1(2)**, [78]
designated mark—
affixing of, **1(2)**, [61]
failing to exhibit, **1(2)**, [66]
prescription of, **1(2)**, [61]
unauthorised use, **1(2)**, [66]
designated station—
loans for, **1(2)**, [64]
provision of, **1(2)**, [61]
entry on premises, power, **1(2)**, [65]
examination and testing—
apparatus for, **1(2)**, [61]
designated stations for, **1(2)**, [61]
qualified persons for, **1(2)**, [61]
records, keeping, **1(2)**, [61]
regulations on, **1(2)**, [62]
examiner—
appointment, **1(2)**, [65]
authorisation, **1(2)**, [62]
authority, production, **1(2)**, [65]
foreign goods vehicle, prohibiting use of, **1(2)**, [70]
obstruction of, **1(2)**, [65]
powers of, **1(2)**, [65]
exemption from regulations, **1(2)**, [62]
foreign documents and plates, recognition of, **1(2)**, [62]
foreign vehicles. *See* Agreement (foreign goods vehicle) *above*
type vehicle, **1(2)**, [63]
vehicle not registered in UK, **1(2)**, [78]

International Cocoa Agreement
implementation, legislation to enable,
  13, [564]
meaning, **13**, [564]

International Court of Justice
priority of telecommunications, **10**, [1015]

International Criminal Court
appropriate judicial officer, meaning,
  10, [1164]
arrest—
  bail, grant of, **10**, [1154]
    competent court in England and Wales,
      grant by, **10**, [1155]
    consultation on, **10**, [1156]
    custody, remand in, **10**, [1155]–[1158]
    provisional, request for, **10**, [1141]
    provisional warrant, under, **10**, [1142]
    request for, **10**, [1140]
    warrant. *See* warrant *below*
assistance to—
  entry, search and seizure, **10**, [1171]
  evidence, taking or production of,
    10, [1167]–[1168]
  exhumation, order for, **10**, [1173]
  fingerprints, taking, **10**, [1172], [1225]
  freezing orders, **10**, [1176], [1229]
  non-intimate sample, taking, **10**, [1172],
    [1225]
  proceeds of crime, investigation of,
    10, [1175], [1226]–[1228]
  process, service of, **10**, [1169]
  provision of, **10**, [1165]
  questioning, **10**, [1166]
  records and documents, provision of,
    10, [1174]
  transfer of prisoner, **10**, [1170]
  transmission of material to Court,
    10, [1179]
  verification of material, **10**, [1178]
competent court, meaning, **10**, [1164]
crime—
  meaning, **10**, [1139]
  proceeds, investigation of, **10**, [1175]
Crown, provisions binding, **10**, [1213]
delivery order—
  competent court, proceedings before,
    10, [1144]
  decisions as to making, **10**, [1143]
  effect of, **10**, [1153]
  making, procedure on, **10**, [1148]
  meaning, **10**, [1143]
  person not delivered up, discharge of,
    10, [1157]
  proceedings for, **10**, [1143]
  refusal of, **10**, [1146]
    appeal against, **10**, [1147]–[1148]
    review, right to, **10**, [1150]
    waiver, **10**, [1151]
diplomatic immunity, provisions on,
  10, [1161]
enforcement of orders, provision for,
  10, [1187]
extradition proceedings, **10**, [1222]

International Criminal Court—*contd*
general note, **10**, [1]
judges, UK, **10**, [1220]
legal capacity, **10**, [1220]
national security of UK, production or
  disclosure of material prejudicial to,
  10, [1177]
offences against, **10**, [1232]
orders, proof of, **10**, [1220]
person subject to criminal proceedings,
  delivery up of, **10**, [1162], [1221]–[1223]
privileges and immunities, **10**, [1220]
proceedings and orders, evidence of,
  10, [1220]
rules of procedure and evidence, **10**, [1220]
scope of provisions, **10**, [1214]
Scotland, provision in relation to, **10**, [1215]
sentences of imprisonment—
  detention in UK in pursuance of,
    10, [1180]
    domestic provisions not applicable on,
      10, [1230]
  domestic sentence current at end of,
    10, [1184]
  other part of the UK, transfer to,
    10, [1182]–[1183]
  person being detained in UK, reference
    to, **10**, [1186]
  prisoner in transit, custody of, **10**, [1185]
  temporary return or transfer to another
    state, **10**, [1181]
sittings in UK, **10**, [1220]
state immunity, provisions on, **10**, [1161]
Statute, meaning, **10**, [1139]
surrender—
  consent to, **10**, [1145]
  person no longer required, discharge of,
    10, [1158]
  request for, **10**, [1140]
transit of surrendered person—
  request for, **10**, [1159]
  unscheduled landing, **10**, [1160]
warrant—
  arrest, **10**, [1140]
  documents, **10**, [1163]
  effect of, **10**, [1152]
  provisional, **10**, [1141]
    dealing with persons under, **10**, [1142]
  section 2, **10**, [1140], [1142]
  transfer, **10**, [1170]

international development. *See* **overseas
development**

International Development Association
establishment of, **19(1)**, [1]
immunities and privileges of, **19(2)**, [1064]

International Finance Corporation
establishment of, **19(1)**, [1]
immunities and privileges of, **19(2)**, [1064]

international headquarters
Abortion Act applying to, **12(1)**, [411]
immunities and privileges, **10**, [979]

international headquarters—*contd*
visiting forces in. *See* **visiting forces**

International Monetary Fund
Bretton Woods Agreement Act, continuation
of orders under, **19(2)**, [958]
establishment of, **19(1)**, [1]
immunities and privileges, provisions on,
19(2), [957]
international support operations, indemnities
for, **19(2)**, [992]
loans to, **19(2)**, [954]
notes and obligations issued to, **19(2)**, [956]
payments to, **19(2)**, [953]
receipts from, **19(2)**, [955]

international obligations
giving effect to—
fisheries, in respect of, **49**, [1178]
pollution, in respect of, **49**, [1165]
power of, **49**, [881]

**International Oil Pollution Compensation
Fund**
Admiralty jurisdiction, **39(2)**, [851]
application of International Organisations
Act 1968 to, **39(2)**, [1029]
claim, extinguishment of, **39(2)**, [852]
contributions to, **39(2)**, [845]
evidence of documents, etc, **39(2)**, [854]
Fund Convention—
country, **39(2)**, [844]
meaning, **39(2)**, [844]
information, power to obtain, **39(2)**, [846]
judgment against, **39(2)**, [851]
liability of—
conditions, **39(2)**, [847]
limit on, **39(2)**, [848]
overall limit on, **39(2)**, [996], [997]
transitional provisions, **39(2)**, [856]
transitory text, **39(2)**, [856]
rights of recourse, **39(2)**, [841]
subrogation, acquisition of rights by,
39(2), [853]
Supplementary Fund—
Admiralty jurisdiction, **39(2)**, [851]
claim, extinguishment of, **39(2)**, [852]
evidence of documents, etc, **39(2)**, [854]
liability of—
conditions, **39(2)**, [849], [998]
limit on, **39(2)**, [850]
meaning, **39(2)**, [844]
subrogation, acquisition of rights by,
39(2), [853]

international organisations
assemblies, UK representatives to, **10**, [1065]
commodity organisations, **10**, [1010]
compensation payable by, **10**, [926]
conferences in United Kingdom, **10**, [1013]
designated, securities, issue of, **42**, [1027]
evidence of entitlement to privileges,
10, [1016]
financial provisions, **10**, [1017]
income from securities, **44(3)**, [789]

international organisations—*contd*
intellectual property grants, **48**, 103
International Sugar Organisation, **10**, [1034]
Orders in Council, **10**, [1018]
parliamentary, register of, **32**, [967]
privileges and immunities—
death, taxes on, **10**, [1026]
families of staffs, **10**, [1025]
generally, **10**, [1012]
officers and servants, of, **10**, [1024]
official staffs, of, **10**, [1025]
organisation, of, **10**, [1022]
representatives and officers, of, **10**, [1023]
Treaty on European Union, established
under, **10**, [1011]
United Kingdom as member of, **10**, [1007]
United Kingdom not member of, **10**, [1009]
United Nations, specialised agencies of,
10, [1008]

International Pharmacopoeia
specified publication, as, **28**, [160]

international proceedings
evidence for use in, **18**, [229]
meaning, **18**, [229]

international road haulage
documents, production of, **36**, [919]
examiner—
meaning, **36**, [919]
obstruction of, **36**, [919]
powers, **36**, [919], [920]
goods vehicle, meaning, **36**, [919]
operator's licence provisions inapplicable,
38(1), [523]
permit—
journeys necessitating, **36**, [919]
meaning, **37**, [808]; **37**, [808]
production of, **36**, [919]
using vehicle without, **36**, [919]
prohibition on vehicle leaving UK, **36**, [920]
regulations, power to make, **36**, [919]
removal of vehicle out of the UK, **36**, [920]
trade plates, presumption as to use of,
36, [919]
trailers—
document required for, **36**, [919]
meaning, **36**, [919]
vehicles registered in UK, presumption,
36, [919]

international traffic. *See also* **international
road haulage**
Conventions. *See* **carriage of goods by
road (Convention)**
extent of powers as to, **36**, [766]
foreign vehicles. *See under* **motor vehicles**
Northern Ireland, **36**, [649]
Orders in Council, **36**, [648], [766]
residents in the UK, travel abroad by,
36, [648]
residents outside UK, vehicles brought into
UK, **36**, [648]
summary of provisions, **36**, [210]

international tribunal
  meaning, **10**, [1012]
  proceedings before, **10**, [1012]

International Tribunal for Rwanda
  provisions applied in, **10**, [1212]

International Tribunal for the Former Yugoslavia
  provisions applied in, **10**, [1212]

International Tribunal for the Law of the Sea
  establishment of, **39(2)**, [1030]
  international organisation, as, **10**, [1244]
  members, **39(2)**, [1030]

internee
  protected, meaning, **10**, [952]
  reduction of sentence, **10**, [949]
  sentence of death, appeal against, **10**, [948]
  trial—
    legal representation, **10**, [947]
    notice of, **10**, [946]

internet
  tickets, sale and disposal of, **12(2)**, [244]

interpleader proceedings
  relief to Crown by way of, **13**, [20]

interpreter
  court costs, payment, **12(1)**, [620], [944], [949], [953]
  Northern Ireland, in, **12(1)**, [620]
  perjury by, **12(1)**, [194]

interrogatories
  Crown to answer, **13**, [31]

intersected land. *See also* **severance**
  owners, insistence on sale, **9**, [54]
  promoters of undertaking, insistence on purchase, **9**, [55]

Intervention Board for Agricultural Produce
  agricultural levies to, **13**, [907]

intestacy. *See* **administration of estates**

intimidation
  offence of, **12(2)**, [191]

intoxicating liquor
  alcohol disorder zone. *See* **alcohol disorder zone**
  alcohol education etc. *See* **Alcohol Education and Research Council**
  alcohol licence—
    application for, entry on premises, **5(1)**, [590]
    meaning, **5(1)**, [557]

intoxicating liquor—*contd*
  alcohol licence—*contd*
    premises with. *See* **public house**
    Scottish, **5(1)**, [557]
  alcohol, meaning, **19(3)**, [683]
  alcohol related disorder, individuals representing risk of, directions to, **19(3)**, [715]
  armed forces canteen, sale in, **3**, [1]
  beer. *See* **beer**
  child under five, given to, **6**, [5]
  children and young persons—
    consumption by, **19(3)**, [641]
    delivery to, **19(3)**, [642]
    liqueur confectionery, sale to, **19(3)**, [639]
    purchase by or on behalf of, **19(3)**, [640]
    sale to—
      allowing, **19(3)**, [636]
      persistent, **19(3)**, [637]
        closure notices, **19(3)**, [660], [661]
        premises licence, suspension of, **19(3)**, [638]
      prohibition, **19(3)**, [635]
    sending to obtain, **19(3)**, [643]
    unaccompanied, prohibition from premises, **19(3)**, [634]
    unsupervised sales by, **19(3)**, [644]
    weights and measures authorities, enforcement role of, **19(3)**, [645]
  cider. *See* **cider**
  clubs, sale and supply by. *See* **club**
  compensation authorities. *See* justices' licence (old on-licence) *below*
  confiscation from minor, **6**, [586]
  Crown, provisions binding, **19(3)**, [687]
  drunkard. *See* **drunkard**
  duties. *See* **alcoholic liquor duties; beer; cider; spirits; wine**
  garages, prohibition of sale at, **19(3)**, [668]
  justices' licence—
    new towns, in. *See* **new towns**
    old on-licence. *See* old on-licence *below*
  licence. *See* justices' licence *above*
  licensable activities—
    alcohol, unauthorised sale of—
      due diligence, defence of, **19(3)**, [628]
      exposing for, **19(3)**, [626]
      keeping on premises for, **19(3)**, [627]
    authorisation, **19(3)**, [488]
    certain locations, activities not licensable in, **19(3)**, [665]
    incidental non-commercial lottery, exemption for, **19(3)**, [667]
    late night refreshment, provision of, **19(3)**, [487], [697]
    meaning, **19(3)**, [487]
    permitted temporary. *See* permitted temporary activities *below*
    regulated entertainment, provision of, **19(3)**, [487]
      definitions, **19(3)**, [694]
      exemptions, **19(3)**, [695]
      interpretation, **19(3)**, [696]
    right of entry to investigate, **19(3)**, [671]

intoxicating liquor—*contd*
  licensable activities—*contd*
    unauthorised—
      due diligence, defence of, **19(3)**, [628]
      meaning, **19(3)**, [625]
      offences, **19(3)**, [625]
  licensed premises—
    closure order—
      appeals, **19(3)**, [656], [702]
      area experiencing disorder, order in,
        19(3), [650]
      cancellation of, **19(3)**, [653]
      consideration by magistrates' court,
        19(3), [655]
      enforcement, **19(3)**, [659]
      extension of, **19(3)**, [652]
      identified premises, for, **19(3)**, [651]
      interpretation, **19(3)**, [663]
      liability for damages, exemption of
        constable, **19(3)**, [662]
      magistrates' court, application to by
        police, **19(3)**, [654]
      review of premises licence following,
        19(3), [657], [658]
      summary of provisions, **19(3)**, [349]
    convicted persons, exclusion, **19(3)**, [440]
    disorderly conduct, allowing, **19(3)**, [629]
    drunk and disorderly person failing to leave,
      offence, **19(3)**, [632]
    drunkenness on, **19(3)**, [360]
    exclusion order—
      copy to licensee, **19(3)**, [443]
      non-compliance with, penalty,
        19(3), [441]
      power to make, **19(3)**, [440]
    expulsion of persons from, **19(3)**, [442]
    meaning, **19(3)**, [364]
    new towns, in. *See* **new town**
    open, being, **19(3)**, [663]
    premises licence. *See* premises licence *below*
    small, dancing and live music at,
      19(3), [669]
    tenancy—
      assured, not, **22**, [913]
      Landlord and Tenant Act 1954 Pt II,
        application of, **23**, [58]
      protected, not, **21**, [531]
      secure, not, **22**, [427]
  Licensed Trade Charities Trust, transfer of
    compensation fund to, **19(3)**, [452]
  licensing committee—
    consulting, **19(3)**, [493]
    delegation to, **19(3)**, [493]
    establishment of, **19(3)**, [492]
    proceedings, **19(3)**, [495]
    sub-delegation of functions by, **19(3)**, [496]
  licensing, false statements for purposes of,
    19(3), [648]
  licensing guidance, **19(3)**, [674]
  licensing justices—
    appeals from decisions of, **19(3)**, [673]
    area of, **19(3)**, [489]
    bodies being, **19(3)**, [489]
    delegation of functions, **19(3)**, [493]
    duties of, **19(3)**, [490]

intoxicating liquor—*contd*
  licensing justices—*contd*
    exercise of functions, **19(3)**, [493]
    hearings, **19(3)**, [675]
    information, provision of, **19(3)**, [677]
    licence document, updating, **19(3)**, [545]
    licensing committee. *See* licensing
      committee *above*
    information, provision of, **19(3)**, [677]
    licence document, updating, **19(3)**, [545]
    statement of licensing policy, **19(3)**, [491]
  licensing matters, right of freeholder to be
    notified of, **19(3)**, [670]
  moving vehicles, prohibition of sale on,
    19(3), [646]
  national security, certifying premises on
    grounds of, **19(3)**, [666]
  new towns, provisions as to. *See* **new towns**
  notices, service of, **19(3)**, [676]
  occasional permissions. *See under* justices'
    licence *above*
  offences—
    bodies corporate, by, **19(3)**, [679]
    drunkenness. *See* **drunkenness**
    jurisdiction and procedure, **19(3)**, [680]
    proceedings for, **19(3)**, [678]
    right of entry to investigate, **19(3)**, [672]
    summary of provisions, **19(3)**, [349]
    unincorporated associations, by,
      19(3), [680]
  old on-licence—
    compensation authorities—
      abolition, **19(3)**, [445]
      dissolution, **19(3)**, [448]
      final accounts, **19(3)**, [447]
      loss of office, compensation, **19(3)**, [448]
    compensation fund liquidator—
      accounts and audit, **19(3)**, [454]
      appointment, **19(3)**, [446]
      funds in hands of, **19(3)**, [449]
      powers, **19(3)**, [447]
      repayment scheme, **19(3)**, [453]
    compensation funds, application,
      19(3), [449]
  permitted hours, relaxation for special
    occasions, **19(3)**, [664]
  permitted temporary activities—
    conditions, **19(3)**, [587]
    meaning, **19(3)**, [587]
    period of time between, **19(3)**, [590]
    relevant licensing authority, **19(3)**, [588]
    temporary event notice. *See* temporary
      event notice *below*
  personal licence—
    appeals, **19(3)**, [702]
    applications and notices, form of,
      19(3), [622]
    change of name or address, notification of,
      19(3), [616]
    false statements for purposes of,
      19(3), [648]
    foreign offence—
      meaning, **19(3)**, [602]
      spent convictions, **19(3)**, [603]
    form of, **19(3)**, [614]

intoxicating liquor—*contd*
personal licence—*contd*
grant, application for, **19(3)**, [606]
convictions coming to light after,
19(3), [613]
convictions during period of, duty to
notify, **19(3)**, [612]
determination of, **19(3)**, [609]
notification of determinations,
19(3), [611]
licensing qualification, meaning,
19(3), [609]
meaning, **19(3)**, [600]
one only, individual, holding, **19(3)**, [607]
period of validity, **19(3)**, [604]
production, duty of, **19(3)**, [624]
relevant licensing authority, **19(3)**, [601]
relevant offence—
list of, **19(3)**, [699]
meaning, **19(3)**, [602]
spent convictions, **19(3)**, [603]
relevant offence, conviction for—
appellate court, powers of suspension,
19(3), [619]
duty to notify court of licence,
19(3), [617]
forfeiture or suspension on, **19(3)**, [618]
licensing authority, duty of court to
notify, **19(3)**, [620]
licensing authority, duty of holder to
notify, **19(3)**, [621]
renewal, application for, **19(3)**, [606]
continuation pending, **19(3)**, [608]
convictions coming to light after,
19(3), [613]
convictions during period of, duty to
notify, **19(3)**, [612]
determination of, **19(3)**, [610]
notification of determinations,
19(3), [611]
summary of provisions, **19(3)**, [349]
supply of alcohol, meaning, **19(3)**, [600]
surrender, **19(3)**, [605]
theft or loss of, **19(3)**, [615]
transitional provisions, **19(3)**, [707]
updating, **19(3)**, [623]
premises licence—
appeals, **19(3)**, [700]
applicant for, **19(3)**, [502]
application for—
advertising, **19(3)**, [503]
determination of, **19(3)**, [504]
documents accompanying, **19(3)**, [503]
grant or rejection of, **19(3)**, [509]
making, **19(3)**, [503]
operating schedule, **19(3)**, [503]
authorised persons, meaning, **19(3)**, [499]
certified copy of, **19(3)**, [547]
dancing and live music, permitting,
19(3), [669]
designated premises supervisor—
change of name or address, notification
of, **19(3)**, [519]
meaning, **19(3)**, [501]
request to be removed as, **19(3)**, [527]

intoxicating liquor—*contd*
premises licence—*contd*
designated premises supervisor—*contd*
transfer of licence, duty to notify,
19(3), [532]
variation of licence to specify,
19(3), [523]–[526]
document, updating, **19(3)**, [545]
duty to keep and produce, **19(3)**, [546]
false statements for purposes of,
19(3), [648]
fees, **19(3)**, [544]
form of, **19(3)**, [510]
form of applications, **19(3)**, [543]
holder—
change of name or address, notification
of, **19(3)**, [519]
death, incapacity or insolvency of,
19(3), [513]
interim authority notice. *See* interim
authority notice *below*
reinstatement of licence on transfer,
19(3), [536]
variation, duty following, **19(3)**, [526]
inspection of premises before grant of,
19(3), [548]
interested party, meaning, **19(3)**, [499]
interim authority notice—
death etc of holder, following,
19(3), [533]
definitions, **19(3)**, [533]
meaning, **19(3)**, [533]
notification, **19(3)**, [535]
person giving, issue of licence and
summary to, **19(3)**, [535]
police objection, cancellation following,
19(3), [534]
supplementary provisions, **19(3)**, [535]
lapse, **19(3)**, [533]
mandatory conditions—
door supervision, for, **19(3)**, [507]
exhibition of films, for, **19(3)**, [506]
supply of alcohol, where authorising,
19(3), [505]
meaning, **19(3)**, [497]
period of validity, **19(3)**, [512]
plays, for performance of, **19(3)**, [508]
provisional statement—
advertisement of application,
19(3), [516]
application for, where premises being
built, **19(3)**, [515]
determination of application,
19(3), [517]
representations following, restriction on,
19(3), [518]
relevant licensing authority, **19(3)**, [498]
responsible authority, meaning, **19(3)**, [499]
review—
application for, **19(3)**, [537]
closure order, following, **19(3)**, [657],
[658]
determination of application,
19(3), [538]
relevant representations, **19(3)**, [538]

intoxicating liquor—*contd*
  premises licence—*contd*
    review—*contd*
      supplementary provisions, **19(3)**, [539]
    summary, **19(3)**, [510]
    summary of provisions, **19(3)**, [349]
    summary reviews—
      application for, by senior police officer, **19(3)**, [540]
      determination of—
        interim steps pending, **19(3)**, [541]
        notifications, **19(3)**, [542]
    supply of alcohol—
      mandatory conditions for, **19(3)**, [505]
      meaning, **19(3)**, [500]
    surrender, **19(3)**, [514]
    theft or loss of, **19(3)**, [511]
    transfer—
      application for, **19(3)**, [528]
      designated premises supervisor, duty to notify, **19(3)**, [532]
      determination of application, **19(3)**, [530]
      interim effect, **19(3)**, [529]
      notification of determination, **19(3)**, [531]
      reinstatement on, **19(3)**, [536]
    transitional provisions, **19(3)**, [705]
    variation—
      application for, **19(3)**, [520]
      determination of application, **19(3)**, [521], [522]
      interim effect, **19(3)**, [524]
      premises supervisor, to specify individual as, **19(3)**, [523]–[526]
      relevant representations, **19(3)**, [521]
  regulations and orders, **19(3)**, [689]
  relevant premises, meaning, **19(3)**, [649]
  retail containers, duty stamps on, **19(3)**, [436]
  sale of—
    by retail, meaning, **19(3)**, [684]
    habitual drunkard, to, **19(3)**, [362]
    permitted hours, relaxation of, **19(3)**, [664]
  sales of alcohol, location of, **19(3)**, [682]
  service areas, prohibition of sale at, **19(3)**, [668]
  smuggled goods, keeping, **19(3)**, [633]
  special occasions, relaxation of opening hours for, **19(3)**, [664]
  spirits. *See* **spirits**
  sports events, at. *See* **sporting events**
  supply of alcohol, meaning, **19(3)**, [500]
  table meal, meaning, **19(3)**, [649]
  temporary event notice—
    acknowledgement of, **19(3)**, [591]
    appeals, **19(3)**, [702]
    contents of, **19(3)**, [589]
    duty to keep and produce, **19(3)**, [598]
    false statements for purposes of, **19(3)**, [648]
    form of, **19(3)**, [589]
    meaning, **19(3)**, [589]
    period of time between, **19(3)**, [590]
    permitted limits, exceeding, **19(3)**, [596]

intoxicating liquor—*contd*
  temporary event notice—*contd*
    police objections to, **19(3)**, [593]
      counternotice, **19(3)**, [594]
      modification of notice following, **19(3)**, [595]
    requirement to give, **19(3)**, [589]
    right of entry in case of, **19(3)**, [597]
    theft or loss of, **19(3)**, [599]
    withdrawal, **19(3)**, [592]
  tenancy of licensed premises, exclusion from protection, **21**, [531]
  tenancy of licensed premises not assured, **22**, [913]
  trains, power to prohibit of sale on, **19(3)**, [647]
  unlicensed premises—
    closure notice, **19(3)**, [476]
    closure order—
      appeals, **19(3)**, [481]
      application for, **19(3)**, [477]
      body corporate, offences by, **19(3)**, [483]
      complaint, **19(3)**, [477]
      conditions, **19(3)**, [478]
      discharge of, **19(3)**, [480]
      enforcement, **19(3)**, [482]
      interpretation, **19(3)**, [485]
      making of, **19(3)**, [478]
      service of notices, **19(3)**, [484]
      termination of, **19(3)**, [479]
  wine. *See* **wine**

intoxicating substances
  supplying to persons under 18—
    offence of, **12(1)**, [967]
    penalties, **12(1)**, [967]

introductory tenancy
  allocation of accommodation, **23**, [476]
    provisions not applying, where, **23**, [477]
  application of provisions to, **22**, [102]
  assignment, **23**, [440]
  consequential amendments, **23**, [447]
  county court jurisdiction, **23**, [444]
  duration, **23**, [429]
  dwelling-house, meaning, **23**, [445]
  housing management, consultation on matters of, **23**, [443]
  information, provision of, **23**, [442]
  joint tenants, **23**, [429]
  licences, **23**, [432]
  meaning, **22**, [107]
  members of a person's family, meaning, **23**, [446]
  periodic tenancy as, **23**, [428]
  members of a person's family, meaning, **23**, [446]
  periodic tenancy as, **23**, [428]
  repairs, **23**, [441]
  secure tenancy, not, **22**, [427]
  succession on death of tenant—
    persons qualified to succeed, **23**, [437]
    rules for, **23**, [439]
    tenant successor, where, **23**, [438]

introductory tenancy—*contd*
trial period, **23**, [429]
extension by 6 months, **23**, [430]
review of decision to extend, **23**, [431]

invalid carriage
badges—
display of, **36**, [892]
issued outside Great Britain, recognition,
36, [893]
recognised, concessions, **36**, [894]
regulations and interpretation, **36**, [895]
highway, use on, **36**, [891]
interpretation of expressions, **36**, [896]
meaning, **30**, [661]; **36**, [677], [891];
37, [309], [801]
persons eligible for, mobility component of
disability living allowance for, **40(1)**, [321]
provision of, **30**, [498], [661]
Secretary of State, powers of, **30**, [661]

invention. *See also* **National Research
Development Corporation**
abstract, purpose of, **11(1)**, [654]
addition to, **11(1)**, [448]
alteration of, **11(1)**, [448]
biotechnological, patents for, **11(1)**, [415],
[704], [723], [776]–[777]
communication, previous, **11(1)**, [470]
Crown use of, **11(1)**, [465]–[468]
disclosure in specification, **11(1)**, [654]
employee, by—
benefit from, calculation of, **11(1)**, [683]
collective agreement affecting, **11(1)**, [682]
compensation for—
amount, determination, **11(1)**, [683]
lump sum or periodical, **11(1)**, [683]
provisions for, **11(1)**, [682]
contracts relating to, **11(1)**, [684]
course of employment, made in,
11(1), [681]
Crown employee, **11(1)**, [683], [684]
disputes as to, **11(1)**, [474]
employer's right to, **11(1)**, [681]
made before appointed day, **11(1)**, [685]
supplementary provisions, **11(1)**, [685]
extent of, **11(1)**, [768]
immoral or anti-social, **11(1)**, [640]
improvement or modification, **11(1)**, [448]
inventor—
mention of, in patent, **11(1)**, [438], [653]
statement for Patent Office, **11(1)**, [653]
matter constituting, disclosure of, **11(1)**, [641]
meaning, **11(1)**, [491]
patentable. *See* **patent**
secrecy under 1949 Act, **11(1)**, [440]
two or more linked as one, **11(1)**, [654]

investment
business. *See* **investment business**
collective scheme. *See* **collective investment
scheme**

investment—*contd*
unlisted securities. *See* **unlisted securities**

investment bank
conditions, **19(S)**, Financial 267
insolvency regulations—
procedure, **19(S)**, Financial 270
provisions of, **19(S)**, Financial 267–70
review, **19(S)**, Financial 271
meaning, **19(S)**, Financial 267

investment bonds
alternative finance, stamp duty and stamp duty
reserve tax on, **43(S)**, 988–9

investment business
clearing house—
insolvency. *See* **insolvency**
market contracts. *See* **insolvency**
collective investment scheme. *See* **collective
investment scheme**
companies with—
giving effect to allowances, **43(1)**, [832]
managing investments of, **43(1)**, [569]
exempted persons—
friendly societies, by. *See* **friendly society**
insurance companies, by. *See* **insurance
company (regulated)**.
intervention, powers of, Tribunal, reference of
case to. *See* **Financial Services Tribunal**
investment exchange, insolvency. *See*
insolvency
overseas regulatory authority. *See* **overseas
regulatory authority**
securities. *See* **securities**

investment company. *See also* **investment
business**
accounts of, **8**, 633–4
change in ownership, deductions—
amounts in issue, **44(1)**, [684], [687]
apportionments, **44(1)**, [685], [688]
company capital, significant increase in,
44(1), [683]
disallowed debits, **44(1)**, [686]
generally, **44(1)**, [505]
non-trading deficits, **44(1)**, [686]
distributions by, **8**, 350
See also **distributions**
Export Credit Guarantee Department,
payments to, **44(1)**, [64]
local enterprise company, contribution to,
44(1), [49]
management expenses—
amounts reversing, charge to tax,
43(2), [282]
consequential amendments, power to
make, **43(2)**, [283]
restriction on, **43(S)**, 526
transitional provisions, **43(2)**, [280]
meaning, **8**, 351; **8(1)**, [911]; **44(1)**, [105]
open-ended, **43(1)**, [162]
corporation tax rate, **44(1)**, [317]
dividend distributions, **44(3)**, [386]–[388]
interest distributions, **44(3)**, [373]–[375]

investment company—*contd*
open-ended—*contd*
loan relationships, **43(1)**, [258]
meaning, **44(1)**, [317]
umbrella, **44(1)**, [317]
regional development grant made to,
44(1), [73]

investment exchange
composition by, transfer duty, **41**, [124]
stamp duty exemption, **41**, [219]
stamp duty reserve tax exemption, **41**, [220]
transfers to, stamp duty, **41**, [179]

investment firm
meaning, **19(2)**, [502]

investment fund. *See* **authorised investment
fund**

investment gold
value added tax, exemption from, **50**, [153]

investment income
losses etc not to be set against surplus
franked, **43(1)**, [313]

investment life insurance contract
company gains from—
commencement of provisions,
43(S), 1133–4
consequential amendments, **43(S)**, 1135–7
loan relationship, as, **43(S)**, 1132
non-trading credits, increased,
43(S), 1132–3
meaning, **43(S)**, 1131

investment manager
non-resident—
agent of independent status, eligibility to
be, **43(S)**, 1142–3
commencement of provisions, **43(S)**, 1145
liability to tax, disregarded investment
income or profits, **43(S)**, 1143–4
UK representative, eligibility to be,
43(S), 1142

investment plan
individual, regulations, **43(S)**, 868
regulations, **44(1)**, [168]

investment trust
dividends taxed as interest, **43(S)**, 1382–3
housing, repealed provisions, **43(S)**, 133
meaning, **43(S)**, 1383; **44(1)**, [626]
real estate. *See* **real estate investment trusts**

Ireland. *See also* **Ireland, Republic of;
Northern Ireland**
Agreement of 1922, **31**, [622]
English law, introduction into, **31**, [622]
historical notes, **31**, [622]
Home Rule bills, **31**, [622]
Irish Free State, emergence, **31**, [622]
loan guarantees, **41**, [567]

Ireland—*contd*
Parliament of Great Britain, former right and
authority of, **31**, [622]
Parliament of, independence of, **31**, [622]
Poynings' law, operation of, **31**, [622]
repeals, **41**, [649]
separate legislatures, **31**, [622]
Southern, proposals, **31**, [622]
statutes, references in, to, **41**, [482], [524]
union with Great Britain, **31**, [635]

Ireland, Church of
disestablishment of, **14**, 19

Ireland, Republic of
Armed Forces Act, extension to, **3**, [1277]
citizens of—
continuance as British subjects, **31**, [12],
[159]
limitation of criminal liability, **31**, [13]
status of, **31**, [12]
Commonwealth membership, cessation of,
31, [622]
constitutional provisions, **7(2)**, [451]
diplomatic representations, **10**, [1000]–[1001],
[1032]
double taxation, **31**, [637]
extra-territorial offences—
criminal liability for, in NI, **31**, [700]
escape or rescue from detention, **31**, [702]
evidence taken in NI, **31**, [704], [716]
examination of witnesses in NI, **31**, [716]
hijacking, penalty, **31**, [701]
inchoate offences, **31**, [705]
list, **31**, [712]
meaning, **31**, [702]
prosecution of, **31**, [708]
trial of, **31**, [703], [715]
venue of trial, right to opt for, **31**, [715]
written statements, admissibility of,
31, [706]
foreign country, not, **7(2)**, [452]
freedom of travel to and from, **31**, [72]
Irish Free State—
adaptation of enactments, **31**, [638]
Articles of Agreement, **31**, [622]
change of name, **31**, [622]
emergence of, **31**, [622]
formation, **31**, [622]
livestock imported from, **1(1)**, [481]
nationality, transitional provisions on,
7(2), [454]
offences in, triable in NI, **31**, [712]–[713]
proof of documents, **18**, [101]
United Kingdom and colonial laws,
7(2), [453]

Irish Free State. *See* **Ireland, Republic of**

iron and steel
Corporation. *See* **British Steel Corporation**
information, restriction on disclosure,
47, [366]
offences—
bodies corporate, by, **47**, [367]

iron and steel—*contd*
  offences—*contd*
    disclosure of information, **47**, [366]

ironstone workings
  agricultural land, arrangements affecting,
    17(1), [547]
  derelict land, treatment, **17(1)**, [550]
  districts, schedule of, **17(1)**, [555]
  extraction in, **17(1)**, [546]
  former mining land—
    entry on, **17(1)**, [550]
    work on, **17(1)**, [551]
  historical note, **17(1)**, [1]
  mining leases, comprised in, **17(1)**, [48]
  restoration of land—
    entry on former mining land, **17(1)**, [550]
    local authorities, by, **17(1)**, [550]
    payments, **17(1)**, [548]
      in lieu, **17(1)**, [48]

ironworks
  charge to tax, **44(1)**, [34]
  rent payable in respect of, **44(1)**, [98]

Isle of Man
  Acts not extending to, **14**, 248
  Acts of Tynwald, proof of, **7(2)**, [725]
  adoption in—
    registration, **6**, [864]
    regulations, **6**, [834]
  Air Force Act, application of, **3**, [989]
  air traffic provisions applied, **4(1)**, [483]
  application to—
    Carriage of Goods by Road Act 1965,
      36, [760]
    disqualification while disqualified in,
      37, [699]
  arbitration, international investment disputes,
    application, **2**, [859]
  Army Act, application of, **3**, [717]
  British Colony, interpreted as, **18**, [109]
  children, orders affecting, effect, **6**, [431]
  citizenship, application of provisions, **31**, [43]
  civil jurisdiction, **11(2)**, [832], [844]
  Commission for Social Care Inspection,
    arrangements with, **35(2)**, [480]
  common duties—
    arrest in relation to, **7(2)**, [719]
    bankers' books, evidence of, **7(2)**, [725]
    disclosure of information, **7(2)**, [723]
    enforcement of judgments, **7(2)**, [718]
    meaning of, **7(2)**, [715]
    offences, **7(2)**, [719]
    proceedings, **7(2)**, [719]
    recovery of, **7(2)**, [717]
    share of, **7(2)**, [716]
    summons, **7(2)**, [719]
  companies incorporated in, **8**, 549
  continental shelf, share of revenue,
    17(1), [382]
  Copyright Act, extension of, **11(1)**, [592]
  customs and excise—
    amended provisions, **7(2)**, [726]
    disclosure of information, **7(2)**, [723]

Isle of Man—*contd*
  customs and excise—*contd*
    goods removed from United Kingdom,
      7(2), [722]
    goods removed to United Kingdom,
      7(2), [721]
    meaning of, **7(2)**, [727]
  customs control, entry from, **13**, [674]
  deportation from, **31**, [131]
  designs provisions applied, **11(1)**, [565],
    [1124]
  employment, reciprocal arrangements,
    16, [886]
  EEC, position as to, **18**, [3], [5]
  evidence in criminal proceedings, provisions as
    to, **18**, [422]
  execution of warrant in, **11(2)**, [554]
  fishery limits, provisions extending to,
    1(2), [136]
  freedom of travel, **31**, [72]
  friendly societies, provisions applying,
    19(1), [549], [921]
  industrial and provident societies, **19(1)**, [436]
  infectious diseases, regulations as to,
    35(1), [516]
  livestock imported from, **1(1)**, [481]
  measures of general synod applied to, **14**, 5
  mentally disordered patients—
    absence from hospital in, **29**, [153]
    community patients—
      removed or transferred to, **29**, [144]
      responsibility for, transfer to England and
        Wales from, **29**, [148]
    conditionally discharged—
      responsibilities for—
        transfer from, **29**, [149]
        transfer to, **29**, [145]
  Naval Discipline Act, application of, **3**, [1201]
  nuclear installations, **17(1)**, [361]
  offenders found to be insane in, England and
    Wales, transferred to, **29**, [146]
  offshore installations, adjacent to, **17(2)**, [206]
  oil pollution, provisions as to, **49**, [480]
  Panel on Takeovers and Mergers, power to
    extend provisions as to, **8(1)**, [1043]
  part of United Kingdom for customs
    purposes, **13**, [537]
  patents provisions applied, **11(1)**, [358], [494],
    [775]
  Police Act 1997, extension to, **33(2)**, [47]
  pollution, application of provisions, **49**, [643],
    [644]
  Post Office Acts, application of provisions,
    generally, **34**, [588], [598]
  post office privileges, surrender of, **34**, [587]
  prisoners, transfer of, **12(2)**, [589]
  prize, extension of Acts to, **11(2)**, [185], [189]
  provisions on opting-in and opting-out
    resolutions, power to extend to, **8(1)**, [1051]
  reinstatement in civil employment, **3**, [1484]
  sea fisheries—
    extension of provisions, **1(1)**, [563], [772];
      1(2), [220]
    regulations on, **1(1)**, [743]
  sentencing, provisions applying, **12(3)**, [1050]

Isle of Man—*contd*

serious fraud, request for investigation,
12(1), [1057]

Services Acts, application of, **3**, [1532]

shellfish, provisions applying to, **1(1)**, [711]

statutes—

repealing Acts, lists, **41**, [659], [661], [662]

revision generally, **41**, [659]

when applicable to, **41**, [560], [628], [645], [692], [703], [731], [780]

teachers, superannuation of, **15(1)**, [178]

telecommunications, extension of provisions, **45**, [4], [46], [49], [50], [68]

terrorism provisions extended to, **18**, [754]

time, **45**, [943]

torture, application of provisions, **12(1)**, [1094]

tourism, promotion of, **47**, [106]

action arising from—

person taking, **47**, [158]

recommendations, **47**, [158]

transfer of functions to, **7(2)**, [724]

Uniform Laws on sale of goods, application of, **39(1)**, [78]

value added tax, provisions on, **7(2)**, [720]

visiting forces in, **3**, [454]

weighing equipment, stamping, **39(1)**, [485]

whales and whaling, extension of provisions to, **1(1)**, [337]

Isles of Scilly

Acts applying to—

Ancient Monuments and Archaeological Areas, **32**, [373]

Countryside and Rights of Way, **32**, [715]

Environment Act 1995, **32**, [612]

National Parks and Access to the Countryside, **32**, [197]

Wildlife and Countryside, **32**, [438], [483]

agricultural wages provisions, **1(1)**, [423]

air quality, application of provisions, **35(2)**, [139]

application of provisions to, **49**, [1035]

Homelessness Act 2002, **23**, [639]

Housing Act 1985, **22**, [420]

Housing Act 1988, **22**, [910]

Housing Act 1996, **23**, [538]

Housing Act 2004, **24**, [414]

Housing Associations Act 1985, **22**, [492]

Landlord and Tenant Act 1985, **22**, [548]

Landlord and Tenant Act 1987, **22**, [768]

leasehold reform, **23**, [180]

Local Government and Housing Act 1989, **23**, [48]

possession, recovery of, **21**, [673]

Rent Act, under, **21**, [638]

unlawful eviction, as to, **22**, [910]

bus services, assistance for, **36**, [792]

carers, assessment of ability of, **40(2)**, [43]

child support, application of provisions, **6**, [537]

children, application of provisions, **6**, [136]

Civic Amenities Act 1967, application of, **46**, [21]

Clean Air Act, application of, **35(2)**, [65]

Isles of Scilly—*contd*

contaminated land, provisions applying, **35(1)**, [809]

Control of Pollution Act, application of, **35(1)**, [352]

Cornwall, as part of, **25(2)**, [172]

Coroners Act, application of, **11(1)**, [1242]

Council—

audit of accounts. *See* **Audit Commission for Local Authorities**

capital expenditure. *See* **local authority**

constitution, **25(2)**, [224]

continuance of, **25(2)**, [224]

financial provisions applied, **25(1)**, [738]

grants, right to, **25(2)**, [306]

information, duty to publish, **25(2)**, [428]

land, powers as to, **25(1)**, [690]

meetings, provisions applied, **25(1)**, [626]

social services provisions, **25(1)**, [984]

county council, sale of houses at discount, stamp duty, **41**, [138], [145]

disability discrimination, application of provisions, **7(1)**, [395]

education provisions, application of, **15(1)**, [712]

environmental protection provisions, **35(1)**, [707]; **35(2)**, [156]

food safety, application of provisions to, **1(2)**, [469]

hazardous substances, provisions on, **46**, [791]

health and safety provisions, application of, **18**, [1308]

Highways Act applying to, **36**, [1395]

housing, agricultural workers, **21**, [485]

housing authority for, **22**, [4]

See further **local housing authority**

land drainage, application of provisions, **19(3)**, [250]

land, local authority powers, **25(1)**, [591], [599]

licence fees, amendments of, **25(1)**, [798]

litter, provisions on, **32**, [533]

Local Commissioner for, **25(2)**, [307]

Local Government Act 1972 applied, **25(2)**, [224]

Local Government Act 1992 applied, **26(1)**, [112]

Local Government Act 2003 applied, **26(2)**, [315]

Local Government and Housing Act applied, **25(2)**, [895]

local government elections, **15(3)**, [197]

local government officers, compensation, **25(1)**, [409]

local government reviews, **26(2)**, [219]

National Assistance Act, application of, **40(1)**, [34], [46]

nationally significant infrastructure projects in, **46(S)**, 163

Offices, Shops and Railway Premises Act 1963, application, **18**, [1247]

provisions applying to, **46**, [589], [744], [1047]

public libraries, **13**, [161]

publicity, provisions as to, **25(2)**, [652]

Isles of Scilly—*contd*
refuse, disposal of, **35(1)**, [409]
rights of way, application of provisions on, **36**, [644]; **37**, [98]; **38(2)**, [72]
road traffic, application of provisions, **37**, [308]
theatres, application of provisions, **13**, [195]
war memorials, expenditure on, **25(1)**, [408]
waste, provisions on, **35(1)**, [784]
water provisions, application of, **49**, [695]
water resources provisions, application of, **49**, [1270]
weights and measures authority, **39(1)**, [522]
youth community order, application of provisions, **12(2)**, [766]

Isles of Scilly—*contd*
youth rehabilitation orders, provisions applying, **12(4)**, [471]

isolation hospital
committees, transferred officers of, compensation and superannuation rights of, **35(1)**, [203]

issuing house
chargeable gains, **42**, [139]

Italy
peace treaty, **10**, [916]

J

jactitation of marriage
jurisdiction, **27**, [595]

Jamaica
British ship registered in, **7(2)**, [510]
Commonwealth citizenship, **31**, [186]
fully responsible status of, **7(2)**, [505]
islands included in, **7(2)**, [507]
legislative powers of, **7(2)**, [509]
meaning, **7(2)**, [507]
visiting forces in, **7(2)**, [510]

Japan
peace treaty, **10**, [934]

Jersey
consolidated fund, payments out of,
   7(2), [442]
International Carriage of Perishable Foodstuffs
   Agreement, application, **1(2)**, [76]
teachers, superannuation of,
   15(1), [172]–[176]

Jethou. *See* **Guernsey**

Jewish marriage
registration, **36**, [53]

Jews
burial grounds, discontinuance of use,
   5(2), [386]
marriage between, **27**, [166]
right of presentation, holding, **14**, 185
Sunday trading, **18**, [1336]
superintendent registrar's certificate, marriage
   under, **27**, [232]

jobseeker's allowance
additional conditions, **40(2)**, [87]
alteration of rates, effect of, **40(1)**, [684]
   state pension credit, on, **40(1)**, [685]
amount payable, **40(2)**, [51]
another person, responsibility for, **40(2)**, [87]
attendance, requirement of, **40(2)**, [56]
back to work bonus—
   expedited claims, **40(2)**, [76]
   long-term unemployed, employment of,
      40(2), [75]
   meaning, **40(2)**, [74]
   pilot schemes, **40(2)**, [77]
   qualifying employees, **40(2)**, [75]
   regulations, **40(2)**, [74]
benefit, as, **40(2)**, [87]
breach of community order, loss on,
   40(2), [280]
   joint-claim allowance, **40(2)**, [281]
calculation of periods, **40(2)**, [87]

jobseeker's allowance—*contd*
claimants, special schemes for, **40(2)**, [249]
contribution-based—
   conditions, **40(2)**, [47]
   duration of, **40(2)**, [53]
   meaning, **40(2)**, [46]
definition of terms, **40(2)**, [80]
denial of—
   circumstances of, **40(2)**, [67]
   exemptions, **40(2)**, [68]
   joint-claim couples, **40(2)**, [69], [70]
   voluntary redundancy, in case of,
      40(2), [67]
education, relevant, **40(2)**, [87]
employment—
   actively seeking, meaning, **40(2)**, [55]
   availability for, **40(2)**, [54]
   employed earner's, meaning, **40(2)**, [54]
   protection sums, **40(2)**, [87]
   ships, on, **40(2)**, [87]
entitlement to, **40(2)**, [46]
financial arrangements, **40(2)**, [83]
Great Britain, presence in or absence from,
   40(2), [87]
households, members of, **40(2)**, [87]
income and capital for purposes of,
   40(2), [60]
income-based—
   attainment of particular ages, increases due
      to, **40(1)**, [688]
   claims yet to be determined, **40(2)**, [87]
   conditions, **40(2)**, [48]
   entitlement, calculating, **40(2)**, [63]
   exemptions from requirements, **40(2)**, [87]
   income and capital for purposes of,
      40(2), [61]
   meaning, **40(2)**, [46]
   personal representatives, information from,
      40(1), [633]
   suspended payments, **40(2)**, [87]
   young person, reduced payments,
      40(2), [66]
information, provision of, **40(2)**, [56]
jobseeker's agreement—
   appeals, **40(2)**, [59]
   meaning, **40(2)**, [57]
   requirements, **40(2)**, [57]
   reviews, **40(2)**, [59]
   variation, **40(2)**, [58]
joint-claim couples—
   amount payable, **40(2)**, [51], [52]
   attendance, information and evidence,
      40(2), [56]
   community order, effect of breach of,
      40(2), [281]
   conditions for claims by, **40(2)**, [49]
   continuity of claims, **40(2)**, [87]

jobseeker's allowance—*contd*
  joint-claim couples—*contd*
    denial or reduction of allowance,
      40(2), [69], [70]
    loss of allowance, **40(2)**, [281]
    nominated member, **40(2)**, [50]
    offence, effect of, **40(2)**, [303]
    trade disputes, effect of, **40(2)**, [64]
  limited capacity for work, **40(2)**, [87]
  linking periods, **40(2)**, [87]
  loss of—
    benefits offence, on commission of,
      40(2), [302]
    breach of community order, on,
      40(2), [280]
  maintenance payments collected by Secretary
    of State, payment where, **40(1)**, [578];
    40(2), [73]
  members of the forces, application to,
    40(2), [72]
  Northern Ireland, provision for, **40(2)**, [84]
  notification of taxable amount, **44(1)**, [106]
  pension payments, **40(2)**, [87]
  periods of less than a week, for, **40(2)**, [87]
  recovery of amount of, **40(1)**, [575]
  regulations and orders, **40(2)**, [81]
  remunerative work, **40(2)**, [87]
  resettlement places, grants for, **40(1)**, [1];
    40(2), [78]
  severe hardship direction—
    meaning, **40(1)**, [575]
    revocation, **40(1)**, [575]; **40(2)**, [65]
    Secretary of State making, **40(2)**, [65]
    young person, reduced payments,
      40(2), [66]
  termination of income support award,
    40(2), [79]
  trade disputes, effect of, **40(2)**, [62]
    joint-claim couples, **40(2)**, [64]
    other claimants, **40(2)**, [63]
  transitional provisions, **40(2)**, [85]
  waiting days, **40(2)**, [87]

John F Kennedy Memorial
  Runnymede, site at, **32**, [247]–[251]
  scholarship, **32**, [247]
  trustees, functions of, **32**, [249]

joint authorities. *See also* **Greater London;**
  metropolitan counties
  information, access to. *See* **local authority**

joint board
  acquisition of land by, **25(1)**, [591], [599]
  borrowing powers of, **35(1)**, [122]
  default, in, provisions where, **35(1)**, [201],
    [638]
  expenses of, **35(1)**, [196]
  meaning, **35(1)**, [216]
  members and officers, protection from
    personal liability, **35(1)**, [195], [637]
  order constituting, **35(1)**, [121]
  reports and returns, **25(2)**, [182]
  sewerage functions, conferment by order on,
    35(1), [294]

joint board—*contd*
  transferred officers of, compensation and
    superannuation rights of, **35(1)**, [203]
  united district, for, **35(1)**, [119]

joint committee. *See* **local authority**

Joint Nature Conservation Committee
  advice from, **32**, [800]
  annual reports, **32**, [839]
  company, formation of, **32**, [839]
  continuation of, **32**, [796]
  directions to, **32**, [803]
  discharge of functions, **32**, [839]
  funding, **32**, [839]
  members—
    appointment, **32**, [839]
    remuneration and allowances, **32**, [839]
    term of office, **32**, [839]
  procedure, **32**, [839]
  staff, **32**, [839]
  summary of provisions, **32**, [1]

joint stock companies
  Acts—
    meaning, **8**, 594
    registration under, **8**, 525–6
  meaning, **8**, 529–30
  registration—
    public company, as, **8**, 531
    requirements for, **8**, 530–2

joint tenants
  corporations, power to hold as, **20**, [459]
  husband and wife, **20**, [656]
  legal estate, beneficially limited to, **20**, [1]
  release of interest by, **20**, [655]
  severance of tenancy, **20**, [655]
  survivor—
    right to deal with legal estate, **20**, [655]
    sale by, assumptions on, **21**, [265]
  transitional provisions, **20**, [658]
  trust of legal estate limited to, **20**, [655]

judge. *See also* **High Court, etc**
  appointment. *See* **judicial office**
  chief justice, representations to Parliament,
    11(3), [460]
  circuit—
    allowances, **11(2)**, [243]
    appointment of, **11(2)**, [241]
    Common Serjeant becoming, **11(2)**, [260]
    deputy, **11(2)**, [248]
      appointment of, **11(4)**, [56];
      11(S), Courts 73–4
    disqualifications, **11(2)**, [242]
    health of, **11(2)**, [241]
    number of, **11(2)**, [241]
    oath taken by, **11(2)**, [247]
    office holders becoming, **11(2)**, [260]
    pensions, **11(2)**, [244], [592]
      transitory provisions, **11(2)**, [638]
    presiding judges for, **11(4)**, [548]
    Recorder of London, becoming,
      11(2), [260]

judge—*contd*
  circuit—*contd*
    relevant service, **11(2)**, [603]
    removal of, **11(2)**, [242]
    retiring age, **11(2)**, [242]
    salary, **11(2)**, [243]
  circuits, presiding judges for, **11(3)**, [126]
  confidential information, disclosure of,
    11(3), [582]
  Criminal Justice, Head and Deputy Head of,
    11(3), [463]
  death or incapacity, costs arising from,
    11(3), [39]; **11(4)**, [513]
  disqualification, liability to rates not being,
    35(1), [194], [335], [508], [628]
  District (Magistrates' Court)—
    acting alone, **11(3)**, [347]
    appointment, **11(3)**, [343]
    Deputy, **11(3)**, [345]
    functions of, **11(3)**, [420]
    judges having power of, **11(3)**, [381]
    justice of the peace, as, **11(3)**, [346]
    reference to, **11(3)**, [380]
    Senior, **11(3)**, [344]
  European or international courts, holding
    office in, **11(3)**, [292]
  Family Justice, Head and Deputy Head of,
    11(3), [464]
  Head of Civil Justice—
    appointment of, **11(3)**, [377]
    Deputy, **11(3)**, [377]
    eligibility, **11(3)**, [377]
  High Court jurisdiction, exercising,
    11(2), [742]
  judicial—
    designated directions, power to give,
      11(3), [595]–[596]
    designated rules, power to make,
      11(3), [593]–[594]
    disciplinary powers—
      exercise of, **11(3)**, [561]
      interpretation, **11(3)**, [562]
      Ombudsman, complaint to. *See* **Judicial
        Appointments and Conduct
        Ombudsman**
    misconduct by judicial office holders,
      investigation of allegations of—
      delegation of functions, **11(3)**, [572]
      extension of provisions, **11(3)**, [571]
      Northern Ireland, **11(3)**, [573]
      procedural rules, **11(3)**, [570]
      procedure, **11(3)**, [568]
      regulations, **11(3)**, [569]
    oaths, **11(3)**, [130]; **11(4)**, [552]
    pensions. *See* **judicial pension**
    representations to Parliament, **11(3)**, [460]
    selection of, **11(3)**, [521]
    salary, **11(2)**, [99], [274]
    titles, power to alter, **11(3)**, [379]
    vacancy or incapacity in office,
      11(3), [470]
      vacancy in office, filling, **11(3)**, [522]
  legal practice, barred from, **11(3)**, [129],
    [158]; **11(4)**, [551], [572]

judge—*contd*
  liability for damages, exemption from,
    11(3), [123]
  Lord Chancellor. *See* **Lord Chancellor**
  Lord Chief Justice, disciplinary powers,
    Ombudsman, complaint to. *See* **Judicial
    Appointments and Conduct
    Ombudsman**
  Lord Justice of Appeal. *See* **Court of Appeal**
  Lord of Appeal in Ordinary. *See* **House of
    Lords**
  Parliamentary disqualification, **11(3)**, [580]
  parliamentary election petitions, for trial of,
    11(2), [786]
  pensions. *See* **judicial pension**
  presiding, **11(3)**, [126]; **11(4)**, [548]
  repeals and revocations, **11(3)**, [316]
  retirement—
    age, **11(2)**, [197]
    completion of proceedings after,
      11(3), [199]
    date for holders of certain judicial offices,
      11(3), [198]
    dates, transitional provisions, **11(3)**, [212]
    incapacity, in case of, **11(2)**, [275]
    relevant offices, **11(3)**, [211]
  selection—
    Commission. *See* **Judicial Appointments
      Commission**
    diversity, encouragement of, **11(3)**, [518]
    good character, **11(3)**, [517]
    guidance, **11(3)**, [519]–[520]
    Lord Chancellor, options of, **11(3)**, [527]
    merit, on, **11(3)**, [517]
    reconsideration, **11(3)**, [528]–[529]
    request by Lord Chancellor, **11(3)**, [523]
  signature, judicial notice of, **18**, [94]
  Supreme Court, of. *See* **Supreme Court**
  Vice-president of Queen's Bench Division,
    11(3), [293]

Judge Advocate General
  appointment of, **3**, [380]
  Assistants—
    generally, **3**, [381]
    pensions, **3**, [385]
  functions of, **3**, [610], [883]
  pension, **11(2)**, [594]–[595]
  qualification as, **3**, [382]
  relevant service, **11(2)**, [603]
  removing, **3**, [383]
  salary, **3**, [384]
  temporary assistants, appointment of,
    11(4), [59]; **11(S)**, Courts 75
  vacation of office, **3**, [383]
  vice—
    generally, **3**, [381]
    pension, **3**, [385]

Judge Advocate of the Fleet
  appointment, **3**, [379]
  saving for functions of, **3**, [1150]

judgment. *See also* **judgments (Conventions)**
  action on, enforcement by, **19(3)**, [1]

judgment—*contd*

arbitration awards, **19(3)**, [24]

attachment to enforce. *See* **attachment of earnings**

certified copy of UK judgment, **19(3)**, [7], [23]

Convention on. *See* **judgments (Conventions)**

copies of, issue of, **19(3)**, [7], [23]

debt. *See* **judgment debt**

decrees to have effect as, **19(3)**, [4]

enforcement—

  action, by, **19(3)**, [1]

  attachment, by. *See* **attachment of earnings**

  charging order, by, **19(3)**, [1]

  execution, by. *See* **execution of judgment**

  literary or scientific institution, against, **13**, [68]

  reciprocal. *See* reciprocal enforcement *below*

  servicemen, against, **3**, [388]

  summary of provisions, **19(3)**, [1]

  time limit for action, **19(3)**, [752]

foreign. *See* **foreign judgment**

foreign currency, expressed in, **19(3)**, [78]

foreign law, questions of, **19(3)**, [12]

in personam, jurisdiction of foreign courts, **19(3)**, [17]

interest on. *See* **judgment debt**

land, affecting, **20**, [795]; **21**, [396]

mandated territories, obtained in, **19(3)**, [20]

meaning, **19(3)**, [9]

orders having effect as, **19(3)**, [4]

reciprocal enforcement—

  application to protectorates, **19(3)**, [10]

  British Dominions judgments, **19(3)**, [6], [29]

  certificates obtained in UK, **19(3)**, [23]

  copies of judgment, issue of, **19(3)**, [7]

  dominions, modifications respecting, **19(3)**, [6], [29]

  extent of provisions, **19(3)**, [11]

  lack of, effect, **19(3)**, [22]

  Northern Ireland, application to, **19(3)**, [26]

  Orders in Council, making of, **19(3)**, [14]

  power to extend provisions, **19(3)**, [14]

registration—

  dominions judgments, **19(3)**, [6], [20]

  foreign judgment. *See* **foreign judgment**

summary of provisions, **19(3)**, [1]

judgment debt

action to recover, application for information—

  power to make, **19(3)**, [104]

  unauthorised use or disclosure of information, **19(3)**, [111]

  use of information, **19(3)**, [110]

committal order, effect of, **19(3)**, [39]

court, action by, **19(3)**, [105]

Crown proceedings, in, interest on, **13**, [27]

deduction for, **3**, [651], [924], [1208]

judgment debt—*contd*

departmental information request—

  information requested, **19(3)**, [106]

  meaning, **19(3)**, [106]

  power to make, **19(3)**, [106]

  responding to, **19(3)**, [108]

information order—

  meaning, **19(3)**, [107]

  power to make, **19(3)**, [107]

  required information not held, failure to disclose in case of, **19(3)**, [109]

information regulations, **19(3)**, [112]

interest on—

  provisions for, **19(3)**, [1]

  rate of, **19(3)**, [3], [33]

    expressed in currencies other than sterling, **19(3)**, [34]

meaning, **19(3)**, [38]

recovery, limitation of action for, **19(3)**, [752]

witness at enquiry, costs etc awarded, as, **12(1)**, [186]

judgments (Conventions)

Note. The following entries relate to the provisions implementing the Brussels Convention on jurisdiction and the enforcement of judgments. For references to the Convention itself *see* **civil jurisdiction conventions**

Accession, scope, **11(2)**, [850]

admissibility of, **11(2)**, [810]

Brussels Conventions—

  1968 Convention—

    application, **11(2)**, [848]

    arrangement of provisions, **11(2)**, [848]

    domicile of party—

      association, **11(2)**, [848]

      corporation, **11(2)**, [848]

      individual, **11(2)**, [848]

      internal law applying, **11(2)**, [848]

      trust, of, **11(2)**, [848]

    duration, **11(2)**, [848]

    EEC members required to accept, **11(2)**, [848]

    entry into force, **11(2)**, [848]

    exclusion from provisions, **11(2)**, [848]

    general provisions, **11(2)**, [848]

    interpretation, rulings on, **11(2)**, [849]

    maritime matters, in, **11(2)**, [848]

    other conventions, relation to, **11(2)**, [848]

    preamble, **11(2)**, [848]

    protocol—

      amended, **11(2)**, [849]

      duration, **11(2)**, [849]

      EEC member required to accept, **11(2)**, [849]

      entry into force, **11(2)**, [849]

      interpretation, preliminary ruling on, **11(2)**, [849]

      ratification, **11(2)**, [849]

      revision, requesting, **11(2)**, [849]

      text, **11(2)**, [848]

    ratification, **11(2)**, [848]

    revision of, requesting, **11(2)**, [848]

judgments (Conventions)—*contd*
Brussels Conventions—*contd*
1968 Convention—*contd*
scope, **11(2)**, [848]
transitional provisions, **11(2)**, [848]
Accession—
1982—
ratification, **11(2)**, [851]
text, **11(2)**, [851]
1989—
ratification, **11(2)**, [852]
text of, **11(2)**, [852]
1996—
ratification of, **11(2)**, [853]
text of, **11(2)**, [853]
entry into force, **11(2)**, [850]
ratification, **11(2)**, [850]
text, **11(2)**, [850]
Channel Islands, application of provisions,
11(2), [832]
domicile of party—
association, **11(2)**, [834]–[835]
corporation, **11(2)**, [834]–[835]
Crown, **11(2)**, [838]
deemed, **11(2)**, [836]
individual, **11(2)**, [833]
trust, of, **11(2)**, [837]
European court decision modifying,
11(2), [839]
force of law, having, **11(2)**, [799]
interpretation of, **11(2)**, [800]
Isle of Man, application of provisions,
11(2), [832]
maintenance orders, enforcement of,
11(2), [840]
meaning, **11(2)**, [798]
reports on, **11(2)**, [800]
rules of court, **11(2)**, [840]
certificate relating to, issue of, **11(2)**, [811]
Channel Islands, application of provisions,
11(2), [844]
Contracting State, meaning, **11(2)**, [798]
copies of, issue of, provision for, **11(2)**, [811]
Crown, binding, **11(2)**, [843]
enforcement—
authentic instruments, modifications to
cover, **11(2)**, [812]
court settlements, modifications to cover,
11(2), [812]
other parts of UK, in, **11(2)**, [857]
reciprocal. *See* **judgment**
UK judgments—
money provisions, **11(2)**, [857]
non-money provisions, **11(2)**, [858]
other parts of UK, in, **11(2)**, [817]
Isle of Man, application of provisions,
11(2), [844]
Lugano Convention—
domicile of party—
association, **11(2)**, [834]–[835]
corporation, **11(2)**, [834]–[835]
Crown, **11(2)**, [838]
deemed, **11(2)**, [836]
individual, **11(2)**, [833]
trust, of, **11(2)**, [837]

judgments (Conventions)—*contd*
Lugano Convention—*contd*
enforcement of, **11(2)**, [803]
force of law, having, **11(2)**, [801]
interpretation of, **11(2)**, [802]
maintenance orders—
appeals, **11(2)**, [805]
recognition and enforcement of,
11(2), [804], [840]
meaning, **11(2)**, [798]
rules of court, **11(2)**, [840]
maintenance order—
minor amendments relating to, **11(2)**, [831]
Northern Ireland, registration in,
11(2), [830]
sums payable under, currency of,
11(2), [807]
Northern Ireland, Act extending to,
11(2), [844]
overseas—
bar to further proceedings, when,
11(2), [828]
breach of agreement proceedings, in,
11(2), [826]
given against states etc, **11(2)**, [825]
minor amendments relating to, **11(2)**, [829]
submission to jurisdiction, **11(2)**, [827]
provisions, coming into effect, **11(2)**, [810]
reciprocal enforcement. *See* **foreign
judgment**
recognition, other parts of UK, in,
11(2), [818]
registered, interest on, **11(2)**, [806]
revision of, modifications on, **11(2)**, [813]

judgments and orders
register of—
body corporate, kept by, **11(3)**, [403]
maintenance of, **11(3)**, [403]
regulations, **11(3)**, [403]

**Judicial Appointments and Conduct
Ombudsman**
acting, **11(3)**, [615]
appointment, **11(3)**, [615]
assistance, arrangements for, **11(3)**, [615]
code of conduct, **11(3)**, [615]
complaint to—
investigation of, **11(3)**, [555]
Lord Chancellor, reference by, **11(3)**, [558]
report and recommendations, **11(3)**, [556]
report procedure, **11(3)**, [557]
transferred, **11(3)**, [555]
delegation of functions, **11(3)**, [615]
documentary evidence, **11(3)**, [615]
establishment of, **11(3)**, [516]
financial provisions and directions,
11(3), [615]
information provided to, **11(3)**, [560]
Lord Chancellor, arrangements by,
11(3), [615]
powers of, **11(3)**, [615]
reports, **11(3)**, [615]
review of regulated disciplinary function—
application for, **11(3)**, [563]

Judicial Appointments and Conduct Ombudsman—*contd*
review of regulated disciplinary
function—*contd*
carrying out, **11(3)**, [564]
conduct, reference on, **11(3)**, [566]
procedure, **11(3)**, [564]
reports, **11(3)**, [565]
salaries, allowances and expenses, **11(3)**, [615]
status, **11(3)**, [615]
term of office, **11(3)**, [615]

Judicial Appointments Commission
accounts and audit, **11(3)**, [614]
assistance—
arrangements for, **11(3)**, [614]
provision of, **11(3)**, [552]
code of conduct, **11(3)**, [613]
committees, **11(3)**, [614]
complaint—
Lord Chancellor, to, **11(3)**, [554]
meaning, **11(3)**, [553]
Ombudsman, to, **11(3)**, [555]
See also **Judicial Appointments and Conduct Ombudsman**
constitution, **11(3)**, [613]
delegation of functions, **11(3)**, [614]
disclosure of information to, **11(3)**, [560]
Northern Ireland, **11(3)**, [575]
diversity, encouragement of, **11(3)**, [518]
establishment of, **11(3)**, [515]
financial provisions and directions, **11(3)**, [614]
guidance to, **11(3)**, [519]–[520]
inspection of documents, **11(3)**, [614]
Lord Chancellor, appointments and arrangements by, **11(3)**, [614]
Lord Justices of Appeal, selection of—
Lord Chancellor, options of, **11(3)**, [536]
panel, **11(3)**, [534]
process, **11(3)**, [533]
report, **11(3)**, [535]
request for, **11(3)**, [533]
members of, **11(3)**, [613]
orders permitting disclosure, to, **11(4)**, [62]; **11(S)**, Courts 77
panels, **11(3)**, [613]
powers of, **11(3)**, [614]
procedure and proceedings, **11(3)**, [614]
procedure rules, **11(3)**, [519]
property, **11(3)**, [614]
puisne judges, selection of—
consultations, **11(3)**, [541], [552]
process, **11(3)**, [542]
report, **11(3)**, [543]
request for, **11(3)**, [541], [548]
relevant offices and enactments, schedule of—
appointments by Lord Chancellor, **11(3)**, [617]–[618]
appointments by Queen, **11(3)**, [616]
reports, **11(3)**, [614]
requests for selection to, **11(3)**, [523], [533]
identification of persons, **11(3)**, [548]
withdrawal and modification of, **11(3)**, [549]

Judicial Appointments Commission—*contd*
salaries, allowances and expenses, **11(3)**, [613]
seal, **11(3)**, [614]
selection of commissioners, **11(3)**, [613]
process, **11(3)**, [524]
selection panel—
appointment, **11(3)**, [524]
members of, **11(3)**, [525]
nominees, **11(3)**, [525]
report by, **11(3)**, [526]
selection by, **11(3)**, [613]
Senior President of tribunals, selection of, **11(4)**, [77]; **11(S)**, Courts 117–20
staff, **11(3)**, [614]
status, **11(3)**, [614]
superannuation functions, delegation and contracting out, **11(3)**, [614]
term of office, **11(3)**, [613]
transfer of staff to, **11(3)**, [614]
vice-chairmen, **11(3)**, [613]

Judicial Committee of the Privy Council
amended provisions, **11(3)**, [619]
appeals from Colonial Courts of Admiralty, **11(2)**, [128]
members, **11(3)**, [619]
Northern Ireland legislation, reference of to, **31**, [671]
prize courts, appeals from, **11(2)**, [74]
registrar, **11(3)**, [619]

judicial office
appointment—
amended provisions, **11(4)**, [104], [105]; **11(S)**, Courts 192–204
Appeals Commissions, members of, **11(4)**, [60]; **11(S)**, Courts 76
deputy circuit judge, **11(4)**, [56]; **11(S)**, Courts 73–4
deputy district judges, **11(4)**, [57], [106]; **11(S)**, Courts 205–8
deputy masters, **11(4)**, [58]; **11(S)**, Courts 74–5
district judges, **11(4)**, [106]; **11(S)**, Courts 205–8
eligibility condition—
gain experience in law, meaning, **11(4)**, [53]; **11(S)**, Courts 66–6
qualifying period, **11(4)**, [53]; **11(S)**, Courts 63
relevant qualification,' **11(4)**, [51], [52]; **11(S)**, Courts 63–6
Judge Advocate General, temporary assistants to, **11(4)**, [59]; **11(S)**, Courts 75
Law Commission, Chairman of, **11(4)**, [61]; **11(S)**, Courts 77
summary of provisions, **11(4)**, [1]; **11(S)**, Courts 2–3
temporary additional masters, **11(4)**, [58]; **11(S)**, Courts 74–5
fee-paid, transfer from salaried to—
courts, **11(4)**, [54]; **11(S)**, Courts 67
tribunals, **11(4)**, [54]; **11(S)**, Courts 67–71
normal retirement sate, continuation after, **11(4)**, [55]; **11(S)**, Courts 72–3

judicial pension
abatement, disregarding, **11(2)**, [616];
  11(3), [188]
accrued benefits, transfer of,
  11(2), [635]–[637]
  general, **11(3)**, [194]
  generally, **11(3)**, [207]
  regulations, **11(3)**, [207]
  transfers in—
    application for, **11(3)**, [209]
    regulations, **11(3)**, [209]
  transfers out—
    cash benefit, method of taking,
      11(3), [208]
    cash equivalents, calculation of,
      11(3), [208]
    exercise of option—
      cancellation of, **11(3)**, [209]
      time limit, **11(3)**, [208]
      writing, in, **11(3)**, [208]
    qualifying members, **11(3)**, [208]
    qualifying member's right to transfer
      payment, **11(3)**, [208]
  values, **11(3)**, [207]
annual rate, appropriate, **11(3)**, [175]
appeals, **11(3)**, [191]
application of provisions, **11(3)**, [173]
armed forces, service in, **11(2)**, [634]
benefit—
  marriage after retirement, on, **11(2)**, [632]
  spouse or dependant, allocation to,
    11(2), [632]
children's—
  appeals, **11(2)**, [624]
  beneficiaries, **11(2)**, [609]
  childhood and full-time education, period
    of, **11(2)**, [610]; **11(3)**, [179]
  contributions, **11(2)**, [612]; **11(3)**, [181]
  grant of, **11(2)**, [606]; **11(3)**, [178]
  payment of, **11(3)**, [178]
    mode of, **11(2)**, [611]
  rate of, **11(2)**, [611]; **11(3)**, [180]
circuit judge—
  City of London, in, **11(2)**, [628]
  exclusion of—
    Common Serjeant, **11(3)**, [187]
    Recorder of London, **11(3)**, [187]
  grant to, **11(2)**, [244], [592]
civil partner's, surviving—
  contributions, **11(3)**, [181]
  entitlement, **11(3)**, [177]
  transitional provisions, **11(3)**, [206]
civil service scheme, option of, **11(2)**, [631]
Comptroller and Auditor General's
  entitlement, **11(3)**, [197]
Consolidated Fund—
  paid from, **11(2)**, [622]
  payments charged on, **11(3)**, [200]
county court registrars, **11(2)**, [627]
death, distribution on, **11(2)**, [634]
derivative benefits, **11(2)**, [639]–[640]
earnings in excess of pension-capped salary,
  benefits in respect of, **11(3)**, [190]
employment tribunal, president or chairman
  of, **11(2)**, [598]

judicial pension—*contd*
entitlement to, **11(3)**, [174]
financial provisions, **11(2)**, [623]
former office-holder, of, **11(2)**, [590]
Health Service Commissioners, **11(3)**, [197]
high judicial office, meaning of, **11(2)**, [588]
higher judiciary—
  double, provision against, **11(2)**, [591]
  election by, **11(2)**, [590]
  rates of, **11(2)**, [589]
  transitory provisions, **11(2)**, [638]
increase of, **33(1)**, [112]–[113]
inefficiency, discharge for, **11(2)**, [632]
injury, allowances on, **11(2)**, [633]
Judge Advocate General—
  civil service scheme, option of,
    11(2), [594]
  special provision, **11(2)**, [595]
judicial office—
  meaning, **11(2)**, [603]; **33(1)**, [82]
  woman, held by, **11(2)**, [613]
Lands Tribunal members, **11(2)**, [596]
local authorities, payable by, **11(3)**, [192]
Lord Chancellor's entitlement, **11(3)**, [186]
lump sum, payment of, **11(2)**, [605];
  11(3), [176]
Minister—
  determination of questions by, **11(2)**, [634]
  power to grant, delegating, **11(2)**, [634]
  recommendation of, requiring, **11(2)**, [618]
nullity decrees, effect of certain, **11(3)**, [189]
officers, status of, **11(2)**, [767]
Parliamentary Commissioner for
  Administration, generally, **11(3)**, [197]
pension credits, **11(3)**, [195], [210]
pension credits, restriction on payments of,
  11(2), [620]
pensions appeal tribunal, president of,
  11(2), [597]
Pensions (Increase) Act 1971, application of,
  11(3), [193]
personal, **11(2)**, [632]
personal pension scheme, election of, instead
  of, **11(3)**, [185]
President of Transport Tribunal, **11(2)**, [631],
  [634]
provisions applied, **33(1)**, [82]
qualifying judicial offices—
  court officers, **11(3)**, [205]
  judges, **11(3)**, [204]
  members of tribunals, **11(3)**, [205]
  other offices, **11(3)**, [205]
Registrar of Criminal Appeals, **11(2)**, [600]
relevant service, meaning of, **11(2)**, [588],
  [603], [631]
repeals and revocations, **11(3)**, [213]
retirement—
  abolition of office, on, **11(2)**, [632]
  ill-health, for, **11(2)**, [632]
  qualifying, before, **11(2)**, [632]
  re-employment after, **11(2)**, [632]
  service after, **11(2)**, [614]
Social Security Commissioners, **11(2)**, [599]
spouse's, surviving—
  contributions, **11(3)**, [181]

judicial pension—*contd*
  spouse's, surviving—*contd*
    entitlement, **11(3)**, [177]
    stipendiary magistrate, **11(2)**, [593], [625]
    Supreme Court officers, **11(2)**, [631]
  surviving civil partner's, **11(2)**, [642]
    appeals, **11(2)**, [624]
    formation of civil partnership after relevant
      service, **11(2)**, [608]
    grant of, **11(2)**, [606]–[608]
    marriage or formation of subsequent civil
      partnership on, cessation upon,
      11(2), [608]
  temporary abatement of salary, **11(2)**, [634]
  transfer of rights into, **11(3)**, [184]
  transfers in, **11(2)**, [637]
  transfers out, **11(2)**, [636]
  transitory provisions, **11(2)**, [638]–[642]
  two or more schemes, provisions against
    pensions under, **11(3)**, [183]
  voidable marriage, effect of, **11(2)**, [617]
  voluntary contributions, **11(2)**, [626]
    additional benefits from, **11(3)**, [182]
  widowers', **11(2)**, [641]; **11(3)**, [132];
    11(4), [554]
    appeals, **11(2)**, [624]
    grant of, **11(2)**, [606]–[608]
    marriage after relevant service, **11(2)**, [608]
    re-marriage, cessation upon, **11(2)**, [608]
  widow's—
    appeals, **11(2)**, [624]
    contributions, **11(2)**, [612]
    grant of, **11(2)**, [606], [608]
    marriage after relevant service, **11(2)**, [608]
    re-marriage, cessation upon, **11(2)**, [608]
  woman, office held by, **11(2)**, [613]

judicial proceedings
  reports, restriction on publication,
    12(1), [237]

judicial review
  application to High Court, **11(2)**, [699]
  county court jurisdiction, **11(2)**, [697]
  decision, power to substitute, **11(4)**, [67];
    11(S), Courts 108
  High Court jurisdiction, **11(2)**, [697]
  tribunal, in. *See* **tribunal**

judicial separation
  custody of child, arising, **6**, [234]
  See also **separation**

judiciary
  judicial independence, guarantee of,
    11(3), [458]
    Northern Ireland, **11(3)**, [459]
  office. *See* **judicial office**
  training, guidance or welfare, co-operation,
    11(4), [48]; **11(S)**, Courts 60

jurisdiction
  foreign. *See* **foreign jurisdiction**
  See also, generally, matters subject to jurisdiction

jury
  age limit for service, **19(3)**, [125], [127]
  alien, disqualification of, **31**, [8]
  armed forces members, excusal of,
    19(3), [135]
  attendance—
    certificate of, **19(3)**, [134]
    default in, penalty, **19(3)**, [149]
    deferral of, **19(3)**, [136]
    period of, **19(3)**, [133]
  autrefois acquit and autrefois convict, plea,
    decision without jury, **19(3)**, [157]
  ballot, selection by, **19(3)**, [140]
  causes for which required, **19(3)**, [125]
  challenge—
    array, to the, **19(3)**, [141]
    cause, for, **19(3)**, [141]
    county court, in, **19(3)**, [141]
    Crown, by, **19(3)**, [126], [141]
    hearing of, **19(3)**, [156]
    peremptory, abolition of, **19(3)**, [156]
  coroner's jury, payments to, **19(3)**, [148]
  county court, in, **11(2)**, [950]
  death of juror, effect, **19(3)**, [145]
  deferral of attendance, discretionary,
    19(3), [136]
    guidance, issue of, **19(3)**, [137]
  deliberations, confidentiality of, **11(2)**, [653]
  discharge of juror—
    continuation of trial after, **19(3)**, [145]
    incapacity, for, **19(3)**, [138], [139]
  drunkenness etc, penalty, **19(3)**, [149]
  English language, knowledge of, **19(3)**, [139]
  evasion of service, penalty, **19(3)**, [149]
  excusal from service—
    armed forces, **19(3)**, [135]
    discretionary, **19(3)**, [135]
    guidance, issue of, **19(3)**, [137]
    prescribed period for, **19(3)**, [134]
    previous service, for, **19(3)**, [134]
    refusal of, appeal from, **19(3)**, [135]
  false representation to avoid service,
    19(3), [149]
  grand, **12(1)**, [1]
  historical development, **19(3)**, [125]
  illness of juror, **19(3)**, [145]
  incapacity for service, **19(3)**, [138], [139]
  inquest, for. *See* **inquest**
  intimidation of juror, **12(2)**, [191]
  judgment after verdict, unaffected by
    irregularities, **19(3)**, [147]
  libel prosecutions, in—
    functions, **19(3)**, [262]
    general verdict, **19(3)**, [262]
    special verdict, **19(3)**, [264]
    trial by, **19(3)**, [261]
  majority verdicts—
    allowance for, **19(3)**, [125], [146]
    civil proceedings, in, **19(3)**, [146]
    number required, **19(3)**, [146]

jury—*contd*

mentally disordered, exemption of, **19(3)**, [153]

offences by jurors, **19(3)**, [149]

orders and writs, **19(3)**, [150]

panels—

    inspection, right of, **19(3)**, [131]

    preparation of, **19(3)**, [131]

payment to jurors—

    amount, determination of, **19(3)**, [148]

    coroners jury, to, **19(3)**, [148]

    entitlement, **19(3)**, [148]

    travelling etc allowances, **19(3)**, [148]

personation, objection to verdict for, **19(3)**, [148]

persons disqualified—

    bail, on, **19(3)**, [154]

    mentally disordered, **19(3)**, [153]

    sentence, having served, **19(3)**, [154]

physical disability, discharge of summons in case of, **19(3)**, [138]

Pyx, trial of, no payment for attendance of juror, **19(3)**, [148]

Queen's Bench Division, in, **11(2)**, [743]

question of fitness to plead, trying, **12(1)**, [339]

refreshment, court may allow, **19(3)**, [144]

selection of—

    ballot, by, **19(3)**, [140]

    electoral register as basis for, **19(3)**, [129]

separation of, before verdict, **19(3)**, [142]

service—

    age limits, **19(3)**, [125], [127]

    attendance for, **19(3)**, [133]

    bail, persons on, **19(3)**, [154]

    certification of, **19(3)**, [134]

    disqualified persons, **19(3)**, [153], [154]

    employee summoned for—

        right not to suffer detriment, **16**, [659]

        unfair dismissal, **16**, [745]

    evading, penalty for, **19(3)**, [149]

    excusal from. *See* excusal *above*

    incapacity etc for, **19(3)**, [138], [139]

    liability for, **19(3)**, [125], [127]

    member of VAT tribunal, exemption of, **50**, [159]

    payment for. *See* payment *above*

    places of, no restriction on, **19(3)**, [128]

    qualification for, **19(3)**, [125], [127]

    records of, **19(3)**, [134]

special plea, trial of, **19(3)**, [140]

special verdict of, appeal against, **12(1)**, [422]

summary of provisions, **19(3)**, [125]

summoning—

    alteration of summons, **19(3)**, [130]

    discharge for incapacity, **19(3)**, [138], [139]

    exceptional circumstances, in, **19(3)**, [132]

    failure to attend, penalty, **19(3)**, [149]

    irregularity etc in, **19(3)**, [147]

    notice, service of, **19(3)**, [128]

    responsibility for, **19(3)**, [128]

    service of summons, **19(3)**, [128]

    withdrawal of summons, **19(3)**, [130]

    without notice, **19(3)**, [132]

swearing of, **19(3)**, [140]

jury—*contd*

tampering—

    appeals, **12(3)**, [829]

    danger of, **12(3)**, [826]

    discharge because of, **12(3)**, [828]

trial without. *See* **trial**

two or more cases, trial of, **19(3)**, [140]

view by, **19(3)**, [143]

jus patronatus

proceedings on, **14**, 563

jus tertii

rule, abolition, **45**, [970]

justice of the peace. *See also* **magistrate**

Act of Settlement, effect of, **11(3)**, [363]

adjournment, bench following, **11(2)**, [542]

administration of oaths by, **18**, [84], [673]

bail—

    dealing with, restriction on sitting after, **11(2)**, [458]

    power to grant, where police bail has been granted, **11(2)**, [461]

City of London, in. *See* **London, City of**

commission of the peace, England and Wales, for, **11(3)**, [328]

committal proceedings. *See* **committal**

completion of market, certifying, **27**, [26]

Crown Court, sitting in, **11(2)**, [748]

decision, affidavit of ground for, **11(2)**, [96]

deserted premises, giving possession of, **11(2)**, [37]

disqualification, liability to rates not being, **35(1)**, [31], [194], [335], [508], [628]

District Judge (Magistrates' Court) as, **11(3)**, [346]

examining justices—

    adjournment of inquiry, **11(2)**, [409]

    discharge by, **11(2)**, [416]

    evidence—

        before, **11(2)**, [408]

        whether considering, **11(2)**, [416]

    jurisdiction, **11(2)**, [406]

    open court, sitting in, **11(2)**, [408]

    single justice, functions discharged by, **11(2)**, [408]

    trial, committal for, **11(2)**, [416]

fair, declaring illegal, **27**, [3]

family proceedings court, authorised to sit as member of, **11(2)**, [487]

immunity for acts—

    beyond jurisdiction, **11(3)**, [353]

    costs in legal proceedings, **11(3)**, [355]

    proceedings, striking out, **11(3)**, [354]

    within jurisdiction, **11(3)**, [352]

indemnifiable amount, **11(3)**, [356]

jurisdiction, **6**, [423], [453A]

    barrators, over, **11(2)**, [1A]

    rioters, over, **11(2)**, [1A]

    vagabond, over, **11(2)**, [1A]

justices' clerk—

    assignment to area, **11(3)**, [348]

    assistant, **11(3)**, [348]

    functions of, **11(3)**, [349]

justice of the peace—*contd*
justices' clerk—*contd*
immunity—
acts beyond jurisdiction in good faith,
for, **11(3)**, [353]
acts within jurisdiction, for, **11(3)**, [352]
costs in legal proceedings, **11(3)**, [355]
proceedings, striking out, **11(3)**, [354]
indemnifiable amount, **11(3)**, [356]
independence, **11(3)**, [32]
meaning, **11(3)**, [348]
qualification as, **11(3)**, [348]
lay justice—
allowances, **11(3)**, [336]
appointment, **11(3)**, [331]
chairman—
right to preside, **11(3)**, [339]
selection, **11(3)**, [338]
deputy chairman—
right to preside, **11(3)**, [339]
selection, **11(3)**, [338]
duty to consult, **11(3)**, [342]
meaning, **11(3)**, [330]
members of local authorities,
disqualification, **11(3)**, [362]
records, **11(3)**, [337]
removal, **11(3)**, [332]
resignation, **11(3)**, [332]
size of bench, **11(3)**, [339]
supplemental list—
entry of names in, **11(3)**, [334]
generally, **11(3)**, [333]
removal of names from, **11(3)**, [335]
training, development and appraisal,
11(3), [340]

justice of the peace—*contd*
local justice areas, **11(3)**, [329]
oath, administering, **11(2)**, [2]
peace, keeping, **11(2)**, [10]
petty sessions. *See* **petty sessions**
local justice areas, **11(3)**, [329]
Scotland, for, **10**, [76]
search warrant, issue of, **12(1)**, [103]
single, limit on powers, **11(2)**, [542]
solicitor, practising as **11(2)**, [319];
11(4), [412]
summons, issuing. *See* **summons**
warrant, issue of. *See* **warrant**
witness summons, issuing, **11(2)**, [519]–[520]

justices' chief executive
transfer of clerks' functions to, **11(3)**, [296],
[308], [313]

justices' clerk
justices' chief executive, transfer of functions
to, **11(3)**, [296], [308], [313]
qualifications, **11(2)**, [193]
solicitor, as, **11(2)**, [193]

justices' licence. *See* **intoxicating liquor**

juvenile court. *See now* **youth court**
change of name, **6**, [1], [550]

juveniles
court-martial—
custodial sentence, reason for awarding,
3, [805], [1070]
punishment at, **3**, [530], [803], [1068]

K

Kent
references to, in enactments, **25(1)**, [64]

Kent River Authority
Port of London Act, protection under, **39(2)**, [395]

Kenwood House
vesting of, on abolition of GLC, **25(2)**, [603]

Kenya
British ship registered in, **7(2)**, [539]
Commonwealth citizenship, **31**, [186]
fully responsible status of, **7(2)**, [534]
legislative powers of, **7(2)**, [538]
republic, becoming, existing law, operation of, **7(2)**, [574]
visiting forces in, **7(2)**, [539]

kerb-crawling
soliciting of women by, **12(1)**, [969]

kerosene
rebate of duty—
misuse of rebated, **13**, [837]
restrictions on use of rebated, **13**, [836]

Kew Gardens. *See* **Royal Botanic Gardens, Kew**

Kew Green
management of, **10**, [170]

kidnapping
institution of proceedings, **12(1)**, [814]

Kiribati
British ship registered in, **7(2)**, [710]
Commonwealth citizenship, **31**, [186]
constitution as republic, **7(2)**, [705]
existing law, operation of, **7(2)**, [706]
independence for, **7(2)**, [704]
Privy Council, appeals to, **7(2)**, [707]
territories of, **7(2)**, [708]
visiting forces in, **7(2)**, [710]

kite
flying, street offence of, **36**, [226]

knacker's yard
animals awaiting slaughter, conditions for, **1(1)**, [880]
codes of practice, **1(1)**, [882]
compulsory purchase of land, **1(1)**, [875]
construction of, regulations as to, **1(1)**, [880]

knacker's yard—*contd*
enforcement of provisions, **1(1)**, [881];
1(2), [539], [542]
entry, powers of, **1(1)**, [883]
horse, premises for slaughter of. *See* **horse**
licence, cancellation for offence, **1(1)**, [880]
local authority—
compulsory purchase of land by, **1(1)**, [875]
meaning, **1(1)**, [873]
local inquiry, **1(1)**, [876]
meaning, **1(1)**, [886]; **1(2)**, [466]
offences—
prosecution and punishment, **1(1)**, [1038], [884]
regulations, against, **1(1)**, [880]
port, **1(1)**, [879]
premises, regulations on, **1(1)**, [880]
public health provisions, incorporation of, **1(1)**, [877]
regulations—
compliance with, **1(2)**, [431]
making, **1(1)**, [885]
slaughter—
food deemed unfit, **1(2)**, [423]
humane conditions of, regulations for, **1(1)**, [880]
transitional provisions, **1(1)**, [888], [890]

knives. *See also* **flick knife**
combat, suitable for, **12(2)**, [544]
forfeiture, **12(2)**, [541], [542]
marketing—
bodies corporate, offences by, **12(2)**, [543]
defences, **12(2)**, [538], [539]
entry, seizure and retention, powers of, **12(2)**, [540]
exempt trades, **12(2)**, [538]
publications relating to, **12(2)**, [537]
unlawful, **12(2)**, [536]
meaning, **12(2)**, [544]
offensive weapons, as, **12(1)**, [1095], [1099]
sale, amended provisions, **12(4)**, [238]
sale to persons under sixteen, **12(1)**, [1099]
violent behaviour, likely to stimulate, **12(2)**, [544]

know-how
allowances. *See* **know-how allowance**
Capital Allowances Act 2001, application of, **44(1)**, [383]
disposal—
charge to tax on income from, **44(3)**, [593]
exceptions, **44(3)**, [594]
income charged, **44(3)**, [595]
persons liable for tax, **44(3)**, [596]
part of disposal of trade, as, **44(3)**, [194]

know-how—*contd*
  disposal—*contd*
    seller controlled by buyer, where,
      44(3), [195]
    trade continuing to be carried on,
      44(3), [193]
  disposal of, **44(1)**, [382]
  meaning, **43(1)**, [1089]; **44(1)**, [384];
    44(3), [192]
  property, as, **43(1)**, [1090]
  restrictive undertakings, **44(1)**, [382]
  trading receipts, **44(1)**, [382]

know-how allowance
  availability of, **43(1)**, [1089]
  balancing adjustments—
    amount of, **43(1)**, [1095]

know-how allowance—*contd*
  balancing adjustments—*contd*
    entitlement or liability, determination of,
      43(1), [1094]
  disposal values, **43(1)**, [1099]
  entitlement or liability, determination of,
    43(1), [1094]
  giving effect to, **43(1)**, [1100]
  qualifying expenditure—
    available, **43(1)**, [1096]
    exclusions, **43(1)**, [1092]
    meaning, **43(1)**, [1091]
    pooling, **43(1)**, [1093]
    pools, allocation to, **43(1)**, [1097]
    unrelieved, **43(1)**, [1098]
  writing-down—
    amount of, **43(1)**, [1095]
    entitlement to, **43(1)**, [1094]

L

labels

exported goods, with, relief from customs and excise duties on, **13**, [796]

laity

house of. *See* **General Synod**

rules for representation of, meaning, **14**, 331

lake

National Park, in, control of, **32**, [264]

park or pleasure ground, in, pleasure boats in, **35(1)**, [56], [380]

Lambeth Palace

Cardinal Morton's Tower, preserving, **14**, 204

library, maintenance of, **14**, 203

Lollards Tower, preserving, **14**, 204

maintenance of, **14**, 336

Lancaster, Duchy of

acquisition of land of, by local authority, **25(2)**, [128]

administration of estates provisions, **18**, [561]

agricultural housing, application of provisions, **21**, [486]

Chancellor, salary of, **10**, [609]

crown rights within liberties of, **10**, [464]

driver information system apparatus on land of, **38(1)**, [147]

Duchy solicitor, **10**, [494]

escheat to, abolition, **18**, [548]

foreshore, disputes on, **10**, [168]

forestal, purchases of, **10**, [84]

gas, controlled operations on underground storage, **17(1)**, [318]

generally, **10**, [1]

intestate's estates provisions applied, **18**, [495]

land drainage—

provisions, application of, **19(3)**, [249]

rights, saving of, **19(3)**, [249]; **20**, [317]

land of—

access to, **36**, [641]

cycle tracks, application of provisions, **37**, [348]

leasing powers, **10**, [690]

long distance routes over, **36**, [641]

right of way over, **37**, [97]

sale of, Port of London Authority, to, **39(2)**, [385]

land, use for literary or scientific institution, **13**, [51]

limitation of actions—

application of provisions, **19(3)**, [767]

foreign law, **19(3)**, [780]

opencast coal mining on lands, **17(1)**, [206]

personal estate, entitlement to, **10**, [494]

pesticides, control of, **1(2)**, [250]

Lancaster, Duchy of—*contd*

powers of investment, extension of, **10**, [493]

road traffic enactments, application, **37**, [303]

shellfish fishery, consent to orders, **1(1)**, [689]

land. *See also* **property**

accretions from sea, annexation, **25(2)**, [62]

acquisition. *See* **acquisition of land**

agricultural. *See* **agricultural land**

amenity of neighbourhood, adversely affecting—

proper maintenance—

appeal against notice, **46**, [481]–[482]

execution and cost of works, **46**, [483]

non-compliance with notice, **46**, [480]

power to require, **46**, [479]

annual sum charged on, distress for, service of customs, for, vesting, **13**, [542]

annual value, business expense, allowance as, **44(1)**, [691]

appropriation by local authorities—

adjustment of accounts on, **25(1)**, [593]

common land, **25(2)**, [120]

parish or community council, by, **25(2)**, [124]

part of open space, **25(1)**, [592]

principal councils, by, **25(2)**, [120]

appropriation of, **22**, [20]

common, etc, part of, **46**, [493]

disposal, **46**, [497]–[498]

house, possession of, **46**, [506]

planning purposes, held for, **46**, [496], [511]

body corporate, sale etc by, **22**, [34]

byelaws for use of, **22**, [23]

capital gains tax. *See* **capital gains tax**

civil aviation, for purposes of. *See* **civil aviation**

commercial basis, occupation on, **44(1)**, [33]

commercial occupation of, **44(3)**, [110]

commercial rent of, **44(1)**, [523]

compulsory acquisition, orders. *See* **compensation; orders**

consecrated. *See* **consecrated land**

contracts relating to—

Bain v Fothergill, abolition of rule in **23**, [3]

land charges, affected by, **21**, [369]. *See also* **land charge**

statutory period of title, **21**, [368]

compulsory powers, purchaser having, **20**, [660]

entailed interest in possession, **20**, [660]

equitable interests, **20**, [660], [661]

generally, **20**, [1]

mortgage terms, **20**, [660]

provisions generally, **20**, [660]

registration, rights protected by, **20**, [661]

land—*contd*

contracts relating to—*contd*

rescission—

purchaser, by, restrictions, **20**, [660]

rights of, **20**, [661]

sale, for—

conditions of—

forms, **20**, [664]

generally, **20**, [663]

title, as to, **20**, [662]

court, applications by vendor and

purchaser, **20**, [667]

expenses, borne by purchaser, **20**, [663]

forms, **20**, [664]

insurance, application after completion,

20, [665]

signed writing, to be made by, **23**, [2]

stipulations—

costs, **20**, [660]

outstanding estate, **20**, [660]

solicitor, void restrictions on

employment, **20**, [666]

title, **20**, [660]

whether of the essence, **20**, [659]

undivided share, to convey, **20**, [660]

title, commencement, **20**, [662]; **21**, [368]

dealing in, computation of profits or gains,

44(1), [80]

depreciation caused by public works. *See*

public works

development. *See* **development**

disposal of, by local authority. *See* **local**

authority

disposal of, held for housing purposes—

consent of Secretary of State, **22**, [37]

covenants and conditions, **22**, [36]

early disposal—

home improvements increasing value,

disregarding, **22**, [40]

repayment of discount, **22**, [39]

manner of, **22**, [35]

option, under, **22**, [35]

pre-emption, reserving right of, **22**, [36]

requirement to co-operate, **22**, [38]

surplus land, **22**, [35]

divided—

compulsory purchase, provisions, **9**, [268]

vesting declaration, provisions as to,

9, [397], [403]

See also **severance**

dwelling-house, let with, **22**, [204]

estate or interest in, transfer of, **44(1)**, [523]

exchange of, contracts for. *See* contracts *above*

extinction of title after expiration of time,

19(3), [744]

fee simple—

corporation, vested in, **20**, [631]

legal estate as, **20**, [625]

right of entry, subject to, **20**, [631]

Homes and Communities Agency, powers of.

See **Homes and Communities Agency**

Housing Corporation and housing

association—

disposals between, **42**, [1354]

disposals by, **42**, [1355]

land—*contd*

interest in, partition or division, stamp duty

on instrument, **41**, [262]

interests in—

acquisition or sale of, **46**, [612]

creation by parol, **20**, [672]

savings, **20**, [673]

information as to, **46**, [605]

instruments required in writing, **20**, [671]

savings, **20**, [673]

persons not named in conveyance etc,

20, [674]

lease. *See* **lease**

legal estate. *See* **legal estate**

material change of use, meaning, **46**, [315]

meanings, **9**, [416]; **12(2)**, [195]; **19(3)**, [768];

36, [377]; **41**, [605]

Conveyancing Act 1881, **20**, [436]

Fines and Recoveries Act 1833, **20**, [74]

Land Charges Act 1972, **21**, [407]

Law of Property Act 1922, **20**, [497]

Law of Property Act 1925, **20**, [804]

Local Land Charges Act 1975, **21**, [447]

neighbouring, access to—

access orders—

application for, **23**, [68]

breach, damages for, **23**, [73]

contracting out, bar on, **23**, [71]

effect of, **23**, [70]

inspection of land, **23**, [68]

making of, **23**, [68]

payment under, **23**, [69]

persons bound by, **23**, [71]

registration, **23**, [72]

terms and conditions, **23**, [69]

unidentified persons, against, **23**, [71]

variation, **23**, [73]

waste, provision for, **23**, [70]

allocation of proceedings, **23**, [74]

entry on land, meaning, **23**, [75]

jurisdiction, **23**, [74]

occupier's liability, **21**, [782]

Northern Ireland housing association,

disposals by, **42**, [1356]

notices, service of, **46**, [603]

Crown, on, **46**, [604]

open spaces, use and development for,

46, [505]

owner, meaning, **46**, [612]

parol, interests created by, **20**, [672]

savings, **20**, [673]

person in possession, interests of, **20**, [637]

planning purposes, held for—

appropriation of, **46**, [496]

development of, **46**, [499]

disposal, **46**, [497]–[498]

easements and rights, overriding, **46**, [501]

joint body, by, **46**, [507]–[508]

National Park authority, powers of,

46, [509]

public rights of way, extinguishment of,

46, [523]

proceedings relating to, exclusion of

Limitation Acts, **20**, [635]

land—*contd*

property business. *See* **property business**

public bodies, held by. *See* **public bodies**

public right of way, extinguishment of, **46**, [516], [523]

receipts from, taxation of, **43(1)**, [343], [387]

recovery of, limitation of time—

   accrual of rights—

      adverse possession, in case of, **19(3)**, [772]

      forfeiture or breach of condition, **19(3)**, [772]

      future interests, **19(3)**, [742], [772]

      present interests, **19(3)**, [742], [772]

   administration, dating back to death, **19(3)**, [753]

   corporation sole, involvement of, **19(3)**, [773]

   Crown involvement, **19(3)**, [773]

   possession of beneficiary not being adverse, **19(3)**, [772]

   right of action, construction of references to, **19(3)**, [768]

   settled land, **19(3)**, [745], [772]

   time limit, **19(3)**, [742]

   trust land, **19(3)**, [745], [772]

recovery of, time limit, **23**, [736]

registration of title. *See* **land registration**

repeals, **41**, [653]

requisitioned. *See* **requisitioned land**

reverter, right of—

   beneficiaries—

      claims outstanding, **22**, [695]

      limitation on rights, **22**, [689]

   Charity Commissioners schemes—

      appeal against order, **22**, [692]

      application for, **22**, [691]

      conditions attaching, **22**, [690]

      establishment, **22**, [690]

      notice, **22**, [690], [692]

      order by Commission, **22**, [690], [692]

      refusal, **22**, [690]

   general note, **20**, [1]

   historical origin, **20**, [5]

   minister and churchwardens as trustees, **22**, [689]

   religious education, trust for, **22**, [689]

   replacement, **20**, [627]; **22**, [689]

   status etc of land before, **22**, [694]

   trust as replacement for, **22**, [689]

   trustees, who are, **22**, [689]

   trusts arising, **22**, [689]

rights of entry—

   Crown land, **46**, [600]

   enterprise zone scheme, to prepare, **46**, [114]

   new town, in, **46**, [190]

   provisions as to, **46**, [599]

   purposes of, **46**, [598]

   survey, power of, **46**, [598]

   urban development area, in, **46**, [89]

rights over. *See* **rights over land**

rights over, as to highway. *See* **highway** (acquisition of rights)

land—*contd*

sale and leaseback. *See* **lease**

sale of. *See* contracts *above*; *see also* **sale of land**

sale of—

   receipts and outgoings, apportionment of, **44(1)**, [29]

   recovery of proceeds, **19(3)**, [748]

   right of reconveyance, with, **44(1)**, [24], [30]

settled. *See* **settlement**

special enactments as to, **46**, [611]

statutory trusts, **20**, [654]

superfluous. *See* **superfluous land**

taxable premiums, etc, treatment of, **44(1)**, [62], [63]

tenure—

   copyhold, abolition, **20**, [1]

   feudal—

      abolition, **20**, [15]

      historical note, **20**, [1]

   free and common socage, grant in, **20**, [15]

theft of, **12(1)**, [556]

title, commencement of, **20**, [662]; **21**, [368]

transactions in—

   capital gains on, **44(1)**, [520], [521]

   disposing of land—

      income treated as arising when gains obtained from some, **44(4)**, [764]–[765]

      meaning, **44(4)**, [761]

   gains from, charge to tax on, **44(4)**, [763]

   "another person", meaning, **44(4)**, [771]

   apportionments, **44(4)**, [772]

   clearance procedure, **44(4)**, [778]

   exemptions—

      disposals of shares in companies holding land as trading stock, **44(4)**, [774]

      gain attributable to period before intention to develop formed, **44(4)**, [773]

      private residences, **44(4)**, [775]

   income charged, **44(4)**, [766]

   information, power to obtain, **44(4)**, [779]

   method of calculating gain, **44(4)**, [768]

   person liable, **44(4)**, [767]

   relevant transactions, sales and realisations, **44(4)**, [769]

   tracing value, **44(4)**, [770]

   valuations, **44(4)**, [772]

   overview, **44(4)**, [760]

   priority of other income tax provisions, **44(4)**, [762]

   recovery of tax—

      certificates of tax paid, **44(4)**, [777]

      person not assessed, where consideration receivable by, **44(4)**, [776]

transfer, stamp on. *See* **lease**; **stamp duty**

trespassers, power to remove, **12(2)**, [195]

   alternative site available, **12(2)**, [197]

   common land, provisions applying, **12(2)**, [200]

land—*contd*

trespassers, power to remove—*contd*
failure to comply with direction—
offences, **12(2)**, [198]
seizure of articles, **12(2)**, [196], [199]
interpretation, **12(2)**, [201]
undivided shares—
creation, restriction on, **20**, [652]
party structures, **20**, [657]
settlement of, **20**, [652]
statutory trusts, **20**, [654]
use—
conditions for, **46**, [365]
discontinuance of, **46**, [365], [377]
validity of order, **46**, [549]
established. *See* **established use**
generally, **46**, [1]
uses, requirement as to conveyance by,
20, [625]
valuation, power of entry for, **42**, [250]
value added tax, exemption from, **50**, [153]
VAT provisions, **50(S)**, VAT 1, 3–4
winning and working of minerals as,
46, [365]

Land Authority for Wales. *See under* **Wales**

land charge. *See also* **land registration**
annuities. *See* **annuities**
bankruptcy order, registration of, **21**, [396]
bankruptcy petition, registration of, **21**, [395]
class A charges, schedule of, **21**, [411]
classes of, **21**, [392]
company, created by, **20**, [1]
contracts for purchase of land, **21**, [369]
creation of, **20**, [625]
Crown, application of provisions, **21**, [405]
deeds of arrangement—
register of, **21**, [391]
registration, **21**, [397]
drainage of land. *See* **drainage and
improvement of land** (private works)
equitable—
charge as, **21**, [392]
easement, **21**, [392]
estate contract, **20**, [799]; **21**, [392]
Inland Revenue charge, **21**, [392]
judgment affecting land, registration,
21, [396]
land improvement charge, meaning, **21**, [407]
limited owner's charges, **21**, [392]
local—
administrative expenses, **21**, [446]
advance payment of compensation,
particulars as, **9**, [350]
compulsory rights order as to opencast
coal, **17(1)**, [171]
Crown, application of provisions to,
21, [451]
drainage of small areas, **19(3)**, [187]
failure to register—
effect generally, **21**, [440]
enforceability unaffected by, **21**, [440]
loss resulting, compensation, **21**, [440]

land charge—*contd*
local—*contd*
failure to register—*contd*
mortgagee, claims in respect of,
21, [441]
protection of solicitors etc, **21**, [443]
settled land, interest in, **21**, [441]
trust of land, **21**, [441]
general note, **20**, [1]
highway works agreements, arising,
36, [1326]
land acquired for civil aviation, **4(1)**, [106]
local Acts, power to amend, **21**, [449]
matters not deemed to be, **21**, [432]
meaning, **21**, [431]
notices prior to general vesting
declaration, **9**, [388]
originating authorities, **21**, [435]
particulars of retained land as, **9**, [311]
pipe-lines, **9**, [174], [194]
private street works, **36**, [1270]
prospectively maintainable highway
declaration, **38(1)**, [230]
register—
appropriate, for entries, **21**, [434]
exclusions from, **21**, [432]
indexes of, **21**, [433]
office copies as evidence, **21**, [442]
requirement to keep, **21**, [433]
searches. *See* searches *below*
registering authorities, **21**, [433]
fees, specification of, **21**, [444]
registration—
cancellation, **21**, [435]
duty as to, **21**, [435]
effect of, **21**, [437]
failure as to. *See* failure *above*
financial charges, **21**, [437]
general charges against land, **21**, [436]
Land Charges Act 1972, under,
21, [435]
rules as to, power to make, **21**, [445]
saving as regards, **35(1)**, [651]
searches—
defective certificates—
compensation, **21**, [440]
mortgagee, claims by, **21**, [441]
protection of solicitors etc, **21**, [443]
official—
certificates, issue, **21**, [439]
defective certificates. *See* defective
certificates *above*
fees, **21**, [440]
generally, **21**, [440]
personal, **21**, [438]
services, fees for, **21**, [444]
transitional provisions, **21**, [450]
wayleave order as, **9**, [199]
matrimonial homes, charges affecting,
21, [392]
overreaching powers, savings, **21**, [403]
pending actions—
land actions, **21**, [395]
meaning, **21**, [407]
register of, **21**, [391]

land charge—*contd*
  pending actions—*contd*
    registration, **21**, [395]
  personal representatives, protection, **21**, [402]
  priority notices, **21**, [401]
  puisne mortgages, **21**, [392]
  purchaser—
    loss due to undisclosed charges, **21**, [370]
    meaning, **21**, [369], [407]
    protection, **21**, [394]
  receiving orders, **21**, [396]
  register—
    classes of charges, **20**, [1]
    entries, copies as evidence, **21**, [391]
    index of entries, **21**, [391]
    search. *See* searches *below*
    types to be kept, **21**, [391]
  registered land—
    matters affecting, exclusion, **21**, [404]
    See also **land registration**
  registered, meaning, **21**, [369]
  registration—
    access orders, **21**, [396]
    actual notice, as, **20**, [797]
    cancellation, purchaser's right to require, **20**, [661]
    Companies Acts, under, **21**, [393]
    constructive notice, restrictions, **20**, [798]
    Crown debt, **20**, [795]
    date of creation, effect, **21**, [392]
    deeds of arrangement, **21**, [397]
    effect of, **21**, [394]
    effective, date of, **21**, [401]
    equitable easements, **20**, [799]; **21**, [392]
    estate contract, **20**, [799]
    estate owner, in name of, **21**, [393]
    expenses, **21**, [393]
    expiry, time for, **21**, [398]
    gas underground storage rights. *See* **gas**
    generally, **21**, [393]
    matters excluded, **21**, [404]
    name to be entered, **21**, [393]
    overreaching powers, savings, **21**, [403]
    pre-emption, right of, **20**, [630]
    priority notices, **21**, [401]
    receiving orders, **21**, [396]
    recognisance, **20**, [795]
    renewal, **21**, [398]
    restrictive covenants, **20**, [799]; **21**, [392]
    writs and orders affecting land, **21**, [396]
  restrictive covenants, **20**, [799]; **21**, [392]
  rules, power to make, **21**, [406]
  searches—
    official—
      certificate, issue of, **21**, [400]
      fees, **21**, [400]
      generally, **21**, [400]
      regulation of, **21**, [406]
      requisition for, **21**, [400]
    right to make, **21**, [399]
  solicitors, protection, **21**, [402]
  summary of provisions, **20**, [1]
  trustees, protection, **21**, [402]
  undisclosed, compensation for loss due to, **21**, [370]

land charge—*contd*
  writs and orders—
    register of, **21**, [391]
    registration, **21**, [396]

Land Commission
  compulsory acquisition by. *See* **compulsory acquisition**

land drainage. *See also* **drainage; local authority**
  byelaws, **32**, [827]
  Coal Authority, powers, **17(1)**, [177]
  subsidence causing damage to. *See* **coal mining subsidence**
  town development, works during, **46**, [14]

land drainage authority
  meaning, **35(1)**, [216]
  protection for works of, **35(1)**, [211]
  sewers, etc, vested in local authority, power to alter, **35(1)**, [207]

land registration
  access order, **23**, [72]
  adverse possession—
    defences, **23**, [738]
    meaning, **23**, [783]
    periods of limitation, disapplication of, **23**, [736]
    registration of adverse possessor, **23**, [783]
    transition provisions, **23**, [789]
  bona vacantia, registered estate or charge, passing as, **23**, [725]
  cancellation, requirement on conveyance, **20**, [661]
  caution—
    first registration, against—
      alteration of register by court, **23**, [660]
      alteration of register by registrar, **23**, [661]
      cancellation of, **23**, [658]
      cautioner, meaning, **23**, [662]
      demesne land, **23**, [721]
      effect, **23**, [656]
      register, **23**, [659]
      right to lodge, **23**, [655]
      transition, **23**, [789]
      withdrawal of, **23**, [657]
    register, **23**, [659]
      alteration by court, **23**, [660]
      alteration by registrar, **23**, [661]
    summary of provisions, **20**, [1]
  charge on registered land—
    bona vacantia, **23**, [725]
    chargee, powers as, **23**, [691], [692]
    disponees, protection of, **23**, [692]
    joint proprietors, receipt in case of, **23**, [696]
    local land charges, **23**, [695]
    overriding statutory charges, duty of notification, **23**, [690]
    proceeds of sale, chargee's duty as to, **23**, [694]
    priority, order of entry, **23**, [688]

land registration—*contd*

charge on registered land—*contd*

registration, effect of completion by, **23**, [698]

right of consolidation, entry in register of, **23**, [697]

sub-chargee, powers as, **23**, [693]

tacking and further advances, **23**, [689]

compulsory registration—

demesne land, of grants out of, **23**, [720]

first registration, **23**, [643]–[648]

covenant, implied, rules, power to make, **23**, [788]

Crown, provisions applicable, **23**, [719]–[725]

deeds of arrangement, **23**, [727]

demesne land—

cautions against first registrations, **23**, [721]

compulsory registration of grants out of, **23**, [720]

meaning, **23**, [772]

voluntary registration, **23**, [719]

dependent estates, **23**, [699]

disposition—

conclusiveness of filed copies, **23**, [760]

disponees, protection of, **23**, [666]

electronic, **23**, [731]

modes of, **23**, [665]

owner's powers, **23**, [663]

right to exercise, **23**, [664]

registered. *See* registered disposition *below*

registrable, **23**, [667], [678], [778], [779]

vesting order. *See* vesting order *below*

district registries. *See* **Land Registry**

Duchy land, disapplication of requirements relating to, **23**, [724]

duty to act reasonably, **23**, [717]

electronic conveyancing—

communication and storage of documents, **23**, [735]

dispositions, **23**, [731]

land registry network—

access, **23**, [782]

authority, presumption of, **23**, [782]

do-it-yourself conveyancing, **23**, [782]

education and training in relation to, **23**, [782]

generally, **23**, [732]

transactions, **23**, [782]

settlement, **23**, [734]

simultaneous registration, power to require, **23**, [733]

escheat, **23**, [722]

freehold land—

charge on. *See* charge on registered land *above*

registered. *See* registered disposition *below*

registration, first—

effect of, **23**, [651]

unregistered interests which override, **23**, [777]

implied covenants, power to make rules, **23**, [788]

incorporeal hereditaments, **23**, [728]

incumbrances, meaning, **20**, [436]

land registration—*contd*

indemnity, **23**, [785]

transitional provisions, **23**, [789]

internal waters, application of provisions to, **23**, [770]

interpretation provisions, **23**, [772]

land actions, pending, **23**, [726], [727]

land certificate, power to make rules, **23**, [788]

leasehold land—

charge on. *See* charge on registered land *above*

registration, first—

effect of, **23**, [652]

unregistered interests which override, **23**, [777]

manors, power to deregister, **23**, [759]

Minor Interests Index, abolition, **22**, [687]

notices—

entry on application, **23**, [674]

excluded interests, **23**, [673]

form and content, **23**, [679]

nature and effect, **23**, [672]

registrable dispositions, **23**, [678]

rules, **23**, [788]

unilateral, **23**, [675]

cancellation, **23**, [676]

unregistered interests, **23**, [677]

offences—

information, suppression of, **23**, [763]

registers, improper alteration of, **23**, [764]

self-incrimination, privilege against, **23**, [765]

orders—

laying before Parliament, **23**, [768]

pending, **23**, [727]

PPP leases relating to transport in London, **23**, [730]

proceedings—

costs, **23**, [716]

documents, production of, **23**, [715]

proprietor, **23**, [698], [699]

in possession, **23**, [771]

record of title. *See* title *below*

register—

alteration of—

application for, **23**, [781]

court order, pursuant to, **23**, [781]

improper, offence of, **23**, [764]

mistake, correction of, **23**, [781]

non-rectification cases, costs in, **23**, [781]

rectification and derivative interests, **23**, [781]

continuation of, **23**, [641]

defects in title, use of to record, **23**, [704]

information included in, **23**, [641]

inspection of, **23**, [706]

official copies as evidence, **23**, [707]

official searches of, **23**, [710]

registered disposition—

charges, effect on, **23**, [670]

Inland Revenue charges, effect on, **23**, [671]

leasehold land, effect of, **23**, [669]

land registration—*contd*
  registered disposition—*contd*
    priority of interest, effect on,
      23, [668]–[671]
    summary of provisions, **20**, [1]
    unregistered interests which override,
      23, [780]
  registered land—
    bona vacantia, **23**, [725]
    boundaries—
      accretion and diluvion, **23**, [701]
      general, **23**, [700]
    charge on. *See* charge on registered land
      above
    mere equities, **23**, [756]
    pre-emption, rights of, **23**, [755]
    proprietary estoppel, **23**, [756]
  registrar—
    Chief. *See* **Land Registry**
    company, formation of, **23**, [746]
    consultancy and advisory services, provision
      of, **23**, [745]
    costs, orders for, **23**, [716]
    documents, production of, **23**, [715]
    electronic settlement, provision of system
      of, **23**, [734]
    general information about land, publication
      of, **23**, [744]
    historical information, provision by,
      23, [709]
    index, requirement to keep, **23**, [708]
    notice of trust not to affect, **23**, [718]
    registrar of companies, forwarding of
      applications to, **23**, [761]
  registration—
    adverse possessor, of, **23**, [783]
    compulsory. *See* compulsory registration
      above
    disposition. *See* disposition *above*
    electronic settlement, **23**, [734]
    leaseholds. *See* leasehold land *above*
  registry. *See* **Land Registry**
  restriction—
    applications to enter, **23**, [683]
    effect, **23**, [681]
    entry on register, **23**, [682]
    nature, **23**, [680]
    notifiable applications, **23**, [685]
    obligatory, **23**, [684]
    power of court to order entry, **23**, [686]
    withdrawal, **23**, [687]
  rights protected on, **20**, [661]
  rules—
    general, power to make, **23**, [767], [768],
      [788]
    implied covenant, **23**, [787]
    land certificates, **23**, [787]
  settled land, rules as to registration, **23**, [729]
  summary of provisions, **20**, [1]
  title—
    commencement of, **20**, [1]
    defects in, use of register to record,
      23, [704]

land registration—*contd*
  title—*contd*
    examination. *See* examination *above*
    first registration—
      applications for—
        objections, **23**, [713]
        priority protection, **23**, [712]
        unregistered interests, duty to
          disclose, **23**, [711]
      appurtenant rights and charges, **23**, [653]
      cautions. *See* caution *above*
      compulsory, **23**, [644]–[648]
        dealings with estates subject to,
          23, [787]
        duty to apply for, **23**, [646]
        void transfers, liability for making
          good, **23**, [648]
      effective date of, **23**, [714]
      freehold estates—
        effect of, **23**, [651]
        titles to, **23**, [649]
      leasehold estates—
        effect of, **23**, [652]
        titles to, **23**, [650]
      rules, **23**, [654]
      voluntary, **23**, [643]
    registrable titles, **20**, [1]
    scope of registration, **23**, [642]
    upgrade—
      effect of, **23**, [703]
      power to, **23**, [702]
  unregistered interests with automatic
    protection, reduction in, **23**, [757]
  writs, pending, **23**, [727]

Land Registry
  adjudicator—
    appeals against decision of, **23**, [751]
    appointment, **23**, [747]
    conduct of business, **23**, [786]
    disputes, functions in relation to, **23**, [750]
    enforcement of orders, **23**, [752]
    fees, **23**, [753]
    finances, **23**, [786]
    holding of office, **23**, [786]
    jurisdiction, **23**, [748]
    parliamentary disqualification, **23**, [786]
    procedure, **23**, [749]
    remuneration, **23**, [786]
    staff, **23**, [786]
  annual report, **23**, [741]
  Chief Land Registrar—
    holding of office by, **23**, [784]
    remuneration, **23**, [784]
  conduct of business, **23**, [740]
  constitution, **23**, [739]
  continuance of, **23**, [739]
  documentary evidence, **23**, [784]
  electronic communications network—
    access, **23**, [782]
    authority, presumption of, **23**, [782]
    do-it-yourself conveyancing, **23**, [782]
    education and training in relation to,
      23, [782]
    generally, **23**, [732]

Land Registry—*contd*
 electronic communications network—*contd*
  transactions, **23**, [782]
 fee orders, **23**, [742]
 members, indemnity for, **23**, [784]
 Middlesex Register. *See* **Middlesex Deeds Register**
 parliamentary disqualification, **23**, [784]
 register. *See* **land registration**
 registrar. *See* **land registration**
 Registrar of, proceedings by or against, **13**, [26]
 repeal of 1862 Act, **23**, [762]
 seal, **23**, [784]
 staff, **23**, [784]
 summary of provisions, **20**, [1]
 Yorkshire. *See* **Yorkshire Deeds Registries**

land tax
 assessors, abolition of office, **42**, [24]
 generally, **42**, [1]

landfill tax
 access to recorded information, order for, **35(2)**, [221]
 accounting for, **35(2)**, [195]
 activities subject to, **35(2)**, [215]
 adjustments—
  contracts, of, **35(2)**, [226]
  rent, of, **35(2)**, [226]
 amount of, **35(2)**, [184]
 appeals against, **35(2)**, [201], [202]
 arrest, powers of, **35(2)**, [221]
 assessment—
  powers, **35(2)**, [196]
  supplementary, **35(2)**, [226]
  time limits, **35(2)**, [226]
 bankruptcy, **35(2)**, [204]
 charge to tax, **35(2)**, [182]
 civil penalties—
  assessments to, **35(2)**, [226]
  breach of regulations, **35(2)**, [224]
  evasion, **35(2)**, [224]
  mitigation of, **35(2)**, [224]
  registration, failure to comply with regulations, **35(2)**, [224]
  walking possession agreements, **35(2)**, [224]
 Commisioners' decisions—
  appeals against, **35(2)**, [202]
  review of, **35(2)**, [200]
 companies, groups of, **35(2)**, [205]
 contracts, adjustment of, **35(2)**, [226]
 controllers of sites—
  credit, entitlement to, **35(2)**, [227]
  interest payable by, **35(2)**, [227]
  meaning, **35(2)**, [227]
  notice that person is or is no longer, **35(2)**, [227]
  secondary liability, **35(2)**, [227]
 credit—
  bad debts, **35(2)**, [198]
  environmental bodies, **35(2)**, [199]
  general, **35(2)**, [197]
  withdrawal of approval of environmental bodies, **43(S)**, 986

landfill tax—*contd*
 criminal—
  offences, **35(2)**, [223]
  penalties, **35(2)**, [223]
  proceedings, **35(2)**, [223]
 customs and excise, setting of rates of interest, **13**, [1062]
 disposal by way of, definition of, **35(2)**, [211]
 entry and search, powers of, **35(2)**, [221]
 evasion, penalty for, **35(2)**, [224]
 evidence of registration by certificate, **35(2)**, [226]
 exemptions—
  contaminated land, **35(2)**, [186], [187]
  material removed from water, **35(2)**, [185]
  mining, **35(2)**, [189]
  pet cemeteries, **35(2)**, [191]
  power to vary, **35(2)**, [192]
  quarrying, **35(2)**, [189], [190]
  site restoration, **35(2)**, [188]
 generally, **35(2)**, [181]
 groups of companies, **35(2)**, [205]
 information and inspection powers, **43(S)**, 1412–13, 1692–8
 information, requirement to furnish—
  disclosure of, **35(2)**, [226]
  documents, **35(2)**, [220]
  failure to meet, civil penalty for, **35(2)**, [224]
  general, **35(2)**, [220]
  records, **35(2)**, [220]
 register—
  publication, **35(2)**, [226]
  to keep up to date, **35(2)**, [194]
 interest—
  Commissioners, payable by, **35(2)**, [225]
  under-declared, on, **35(2)**, [225]
  unpaid, on, **35(2)**, [225]
 invoices, amounts shown as tax on, **35(2)**, [226]
 landfill sites—
  definition of, **35(2)**, [212]
  operators of, **35(2)**, [213]
 liability to pay, **35(2)**, [183]
 material removed from water exempted, **35(2)**, [185]
 mining exempted, **35(2)**, [189]
 misdeclaration or neglect, penalty for, **35(2)**, [224]
 operators of landfill sites, **35(2)**, [213]
 orders and regulations, **35(2)**, [217]
 overpaid, recovery of, **35(2)**, [222]
 partnerships, **35(2)**, [204]
 payment, time for, **35(2)**, [195]
 penalties—
  civil—
   assessments to, **35(2)**, [226]
   breach of regulations, **35(2)**, [224]
   evasion, **35(2)**, [224]
   mitigation of, **35(2)**, [224]
   registration, failure to comply with regulations, **35(2)**, [224]
   walking possession agreements, **35(2)**, [224]
  criminal, **35(2)**, [223]

landfill tax—*contd*

pet cemeteries exempted, **35(2)**, [191]

prescribed site activities, **35(S)**, 180–3

quarrying exempted, **35(2)**, [189], [190]

rates of, **35(2)**, [621]; **35(S)**, 174; **43(S)**, 849

record-keeping, **43(S)**, 1706

recovery of, **35(2)**, [222]

reduced rate—

    amount, **35(2)**, [184]

    qualifying materials, **35(2)**, [209]

register—

    information required to keep up to date,
    35(2), [194]

    publication, **35(2)**, [226]

registration, **35(2)**, [193], [224]

regulations, penalty for breach of,
35(2), [224]

removal of documents, **35(2)**, [221]

rent, adjustment of, **35(2)**, [226]

review of Commissioners' decisions. *See*
Commissioners' decisions *above*

samples, power to take, **35(2)**, [221]

secondary liability for, **35(2)**, [227]

security for, **35(2)**, [226]

service of notices, **35(2)**, [226]

set-off of amounts, **35(2)**, [226]

summary of provisions, **35(1)**, [1]

taxable disposals—

    regulations, **35(2)**, [208]

    special provisions, **35(2)**, [207]

    weight of material disposed of, **35(2)**, [214]

time for payment, **35(2)**, [195]

time limits for assessments, claims, etc,
amendment, **43(S)**, 1715

transfer of business, **35(2)**, [204]

under-declared, interest on, **35(2)**, [225]

unpaid, interest on, **35(2)**, [225]

walking possession agreements, penalty for
breach of, **35(2)**, [224]

waste, disposal of material as, definition of,
35(2), [210]

wrongdoing, penalties,
43(S), 1328–39. *See also* **tax penalty**

landlord

access, implied term as to, **21**, [633]

agents, service of notices on, **21**, [636]

agricultural tenancy. *See* **agricultural
tenancy**

assignment of interest, informing tenant of,
22, [506]

business premises of, meaning, **21**, [209]

choice of insurers, challenge to, **22**, [554]

collective enfranchisement, provisions on. *See*
**collective enfranchisement (leasehold
reform)**

corporate, disclosure of details of—

    tenant requesting, **22**, [505]

    weekly rent, premises occupied at,
    22, [510]

defective premises, duty of care, **21**, [387]

demand for rent, name and address to be in,
22, [762]

landlord—*contd*

distress for rent by. *See* **distress**

entry, power of—

    condition of premises, to view, **22**, [512]

    implied term as to, **21**, [633]

flats. *See* **flats**

identity, disclosure of, **22**, [504]

Landlord and Tenant Act 1987, exemption,
22, [771]

lease, acquisition of new. *See* **lease
(acquisition of new)**

leasehold enfranchisement or extension,
provisions on. *See* **leasehold
enfranchisement; leasehold extension**

managing agents, consultation on, **22**, [543]

meaning, **21**, [70], [637]; **22**, [773], [839]

name and address to be in demand for rent,
22, [762]

notices, service of—

    agent, on, **21**, [636]

    last known place of abode or business,
    reference to, **22**, [764]

    notification of address for, **22**, [763]

    Protection from Eviction Act, under,
    21, [669]

offences, **22**, [511]

overcrowding—

    duty to notify authority of, **22**, [286]

    liability for, **22**, [284]

possible right to acquire landlord's interest,
informing tenant of, **22**, [507]

power to determine tenancy, **22**, [839]

protected long tenancy, of. *See* **protected
long tenancy**

public sector. *See* **public sector landlord**

registered social. *See* **registered social
landlord**

rent book, duty to provide, **22**, [508]

repairing obligations, specific performance
of, **22**, [521], [545]

repairs, access for, **22**, [811]

resident—

    assured tenancy, exclusion of, **22**, [913],
    [915]

    meaning, **22**, [771]

    protected tenancy, exclusion of, **21**, [532],
    [644]

statutory tenant, in relation to, **22**, [550]

trustees as, **22**, [506]

landlord and tenant

agricultural holdings or housing. *See*
**agricultural tenancies; agricultural
workers**

landlord authority. *See also particular authorities*

exemption certificate as to, **22**, [105]

meaning, **22**, [105]

landmines

amendment of provisions, **12(2)**, [640]

anti-handling device, meaning, **12(2)**, [617]

anti-personnel mine—

    components of, **12(2)**, [617]

landmines—*contd*
anti-personnel mine—*contd*
destruction, securing—
compensation, **12(2)**, [627]
entry on premises, **12(2)**, [626]
offences, **12(2)**, [628]
removal or immobilisation of objects,
12(2), [624]
removed objects, of, **12(2)**, [625]
suspicious objects, **12(2)**, [623]
international military operations, conduct
in course of, **12(2)**, [621]
meaning, **12(2)**, [617]
offences, **12(2)**, [618]–[622]
defences, **12(2)**, [622]
permitted conduct, **12(2)**, [620]
places outside UK, application of
prohibitions to, **12(2)**, [619]
prohibited conduct, **12(2)**, [618]
bodies corporate, offences by, **12(2)**, [639]
Crown, provisions binding, **12(2)**, [644]
disclosure of information, **12(2)**, [635]
evidence, power to search for and obtain,
12(2), [634]
fact-finding missions—
expenditure, reimbursement of,
12(2), [632]
offence relating to, **12(2)**, [630]
privileges and immunities, **12(2)**, [631]
right of entry for, **12(2)**, [629]
forfeiture of material, **12(2)**, [638]
HM Revenue and Customs prosecutions,
12(2), [637]
interpretation, **12(2)**, [643]
meaning, **12(2)**, [617]
notices, service of, **12(2)**, [642]
Ottawa Convention—
fact-finding missions. *See* fact-finding
missions *above*
information and records for, **12(2)**, [633]
prosecutions, consent to, **12(2)**, [636]

landowner
land drainage by. *See under* **drainage and
improvement of land** (private works)

Lands Clauses Acts
adaptation of references to, **9**, [292]
application, **9**, [2]
compensation under. *See* **compensation**
incorporation with other Acts, **9**, [2]
interpretation of terms, **9**, [3]–[4]
note on effect etc, **9**, [1]
penalties under, **9**, [90]
special Act—
access to, **9**, [92]–[93]
incorporation with, **9**, [3]
meaning, **9**, [3]

Lands Tribunal
agricultural. *See* **Agricultural Land
Tribunal**
agricultural land, acquisition of part, reference
of questions to, counter notices, **9**, [356],
[358]

Lands Tribunal—*contd*
arbitrator, acting as, **9**, [181], [183]
assessment of compensation—
date for valuation, **9**, [221]
rules, **9**, [220]
assessors to assist, **9**, [183], [184]
basic loss payment, determination of disputes
as to, **9**, [338]
certificate, as to access of light. *See* **light**
certificate of value, issue by, **9**, [249]
coal mining subsidence, reference of disputes
to, **17(2)**, [6], [37], [171]
coast protection work, questions relating to,
reference of, **49**, [402]
compensation, determination of disputes as
to—
amount, **9**, [265], [373], [451]
assessment, **9**, [216], [220], [266]
consolidation of proceedings, **9**, [218]
costs, **9**, [219]
divided land, **9**, [268]
entry, as to power of, **9**, [271]
injurious affection, **9**, [270]
jurisdiction, **9**, [181]
mortgaged lands, value of, **9**, [275]
procedure, **9**, [217]
public works, depreciation caused by,
9, [319]
reference of, **9**, [126], [216], [265], [319]
rent charges, **9**, [278]
submission of claims, **9**, [266]
tenants at will, **9**, [280]
compensation disputes, settlement by,
37, [347]
consolidation of proceedings before, **9**, [218]
constitution, **9**, [182]
costs, **9**, [183], [219]
counter-notice as to part of agricultural
holding, reference to, **9**, [358]
decisions of—
appeal by case stated from, **9**, [126], [183]
finality of, **9**, [126], [183]
form of, **9**, [183]
oral hearing, without, **9**, [183], [217]
depreciation caused by public works,
disputes, **9**, [319]
disputes as to compensation. *See* compensation
above
disturbance payment, determination of dispute
as to, **9**, [342]
divided land, disputes arising as to, **9**, [268],
[358]
drainage rate appeals, **19(3)**, [215]
entry by member, power of, **9**, [217]
entry on land, disputes as to, **9**, [271], [373]
establishment, **9**, [1], [181]
evidence before, **9**, [183], [217]
expenses, **9**, [182], [183]
expert witnesses before, **9**, [217]
fees, **9**, [183]
general vesting declaration, disputes as to
compensation, **9**, [395]
injurious affection, disputes arising, **9**, [270]
jurisdiction—
compensation disputes generally, **9**, [216]

Lands Tribunal—*contd*
  jurisdiction—*contd*
    exercise of, **9**, [181], [184]
    extension by Order in Council, **9**, [184]
    extent of, **9**, [181]
    generally, **9**, [126], [181]
    referees, panel of, **9**, [181]
    statutory tribunal, of, determination by,
      9, [184]
    transfer to—
      compensation for loss of office, **9**, [185]
      General Claims Tribunal, from, **9**, [204]
      Order in Council, by, **9**, [184]
      savings on, **9**, [186]
  member—
    pension, **11(2)**, [596]
    relevant service, **11(2)**, [603]
  members, **9**, [182]
  mines and minerals, disputed compensation,
    9, [451]
  mortgaged land, disputes involving, **9**, [275],
    [278]
  Northern Ireland, application, **9**, [188]
  notice to treat, matters arising, **9**, [266]
  occupier's loss payment, determination of
    disputes as to, **9**, [338]
  officers and servants, **9**, [182]
  oral hearing, determination without, **9**, [183],
    [217]
  pensions, **11(2)**, [596]
  president, **9**, [182]
  procedure, **9**, [183], [184], [217]
  public, to sit in, **9**, [217]
  remuneration and allowances to members,
    9, [182]
  rent under lease, apportionment by, **9**, [279]
  rentcharges, disputes as to, **9**, [278]
  reservoirs, reference of disputes as to damage
    etc to, **49**, [597]
  restrictive covenants—
    discharge or modification by, **20**, [702]
    powers in relation to, **20**, [702]; **21**, [371]
  rules—
    Reference Committee, of, **9**, [183]
    regulating proceedings, **9**, [183]
  savings in, **9**, [183]
  sittings, **9**, [217]
  statutory tribunal—
    jurisdiction of, transfer to, **9**, [184]
    meaning, **9**, [184]
  summary of provisions, **9**, [1]
  surveyor, selection from members of, **9**, [23],
    [181], [183]
  surveys, entry for purposes of, **9**, [271], [373]
  tenants at will, disputes involving, **9**, [280]
  time for instituting proceedings before,
    9, [183]
  tree felling, determination of matters on,
    18, [1122]
  value of land, determining questions of,
    42, [179]
  wayleave orders, determination of
    compensation for, **9**, [200]

lasting power of attorney
  alteration in registered powers, records of,
    29, [317]
  Court of Protection, powers of—
    operation, as to, **29**, [249]
    validity, as to, **29**, [248]
  creation of, requirements, **29**, [233]
  donee—
    appointment, **29**, [234]
    donor, ill-treatment or neglect of, **29**, [275]
    gifts, making, **29**, [236]
    joint or several, **29**, [234]
    personal welfare of donor, making decisions
      about, **29**, [236]
    purported exercise of power, acting in,
      29, [238]
    registration, protection on, **29**, [238]
    replacement of, **29**, [317]
    restraint of donor by, **29**, [235]
  ineffective instruments, **29**, [315]
  instruments, making, **29**, [314]
  meaning, **29**, [233]
  registration of—
    applications and procedure, **29**, [315]
    cancellation of, **29**, [316]
    deputy already appointed, where, **29**, [315]
    donee, objections by, **29**, [315]
    donor, objections by, **29**, [315]
    evidence of, **29**, [315]
    notification of, **29**, [315]
  restrictions on, **29**, [235]
  revocation, **29**, [237]
  scope of, **29**, [233], [236]

Latin information
  abolition, **13**, [43]

Latvia
  accession to European Union, **18**, [54]

laudanum
  using in offence, **12(1)**, [78]

laundering of proceeds of crime. *See*
money laundering

laundry
  infected articles, restriction on sending to,
    35(1), [465]
  self-operated, **25(2)**, [299]

lavatories. *See* **sanitary conveniences**

law
  confirmation of, **10**, [51]

Law Commission
  Chairman, appointment, **11(4)**, [61];
    11(S), Courts 77
  Commissioners—
    pensions etc, **41**, [539]
    qualifications, **41**, [537]
    remuneration, **41**, [539]
    terms of office, **41**, [537]
  constitution, **41**, [537]

Law Commission—*contd*
  expenses of, **41**, [540]
  functions of, **41**, [480], [538]
  Northern Ireland. *See* **Northern Ireland**
  officers and staff, **41**, [540]
  proposals for reform of law, **41**, [538]
  reports to be made by, **41**, [538]

law ecclesiastical
  offences against,
  14, 571. *See also* **ecclesiastical offences**

law officers. *See also* **Attorney General;**
Solicitor General
  fees, application of, **10**, [440]
  meaning of, **10**, [441]
  prosecutions, consent to, **12(1)**, [960], [961]
  Scottish—
    appointment or removal, **10**, [1358]
    Lord Advocate—
      property and liabilities of, **10**, [1371]
      retained functions of, **10**, [1363]
      transfer of property to, **10**, [1373]
    Scottish Parliament, participation in,
    10, [1338]

law report
  person other than barrister, by, **11(3)**, [139];
  11(4), [561]

Law Society
  bankruptcy of solicitor, powers, **11(2)**, [364],
  [372]; **11(4)**, [458], [466]
  Charter—
    grant of, **11(2)**, [367]
    meaning, **11(2)**, [367]; **11(4)**, [462]
  committees—
    functions, **11(2)**, [360]
    power to appoint, **11(2)**, [360]
  compensation fund—
    administration, **11(2)**, [375]
    application of money in, **11(2)**, [375]
    borrowing for purposes of, **11(2)**, [375]
    contributions to, **11(2)**, [375]
    contributions to, by incorporated practice,
    11(3), [44]; **11(4)**, [518]
    costs of administering, **11(2)**, [375]
    establishment of, **11(4)**, [410]
    foreign lawyers, by, **11(3)**, [160]
    grants from—
      criteria for, **11(4)**, [409]
      purposes of, **11(2)**, [316]
      refusal of, **11(2)**, [316]
      rules concerning, **11(4)**, [409]
      subrogation of Society, **11(2)**, [316]
      terms and conditions, **11(2)**, [316]
    insurance in respect of, **11(2)**, [375]
    investment of moneys in, **11(2)**, [375]
    investments, **11(4)**, [410]
    loans from, **11(2)**, [316]
    maintenance of, **11(2)**, [316], [374];
    11(4), [410]
    purposes of, **11(4)**, [410]
    reduced subscriptions, **11(2)**, [375]
    rules as to, power to make, **11(2)**, [316]

Law Society—*contd*
  compensation fund—*contd*
    special levy for, **11(2)**, [375]
  complaint to—
    intervention following, **11(2)**, [372];
    11(4), [466]
    investigation, **11(2)**, [325]–[326]
  conduct of solicitors, power in relation to,
  11(3), [284], [306]
  Council—
    acting on behalf of Society, **11(2)**, [361];
    11(4), [457]
    committees and sub-committees,
    11(2), [360]; **11(4)**, [456]
    delegation of functions, **11(2)**, [361];
    11(4), [457]
    disciplinary powers, **11(4)**, [422], [518]
    documents, signature to, **11(2)**, [362]
  fees to—
    accounting for, **11(2)**, [286]
    application of, **11(2)**, [286]
  files, inspection, **11(2)**, [329]
  foreign lawyers—
    accountants' reports, **11(3)**, [160];
    11(4), [574]
    bankruptcy, effect of, **11(3)**, [160];
    11(4), [574]
    compensation fund, contributions to
    11(3), [160]; **11(4)**, [574]
    disciplinary action, effect of, **11(3)**, [160];
    11(4), [574]
    Disciplinary Tribunal—
      appeals from, **11(3)**, [160]; **11(4)**, [574]
      assistance to, **11(3)**, [160]; **11(4)**, [574]
      jurisdiction and powers of, **11(3)**, [160];
      11(4), [574]
    incorporated practices, rules, **11(3)**, [2]
    intervention in practice, **11(3)**, [160];
    11(4), [574]
    meaning, **11(3)**, [134]; **11(4)**, [556]
    powers in relation to, **11(3)**, [306]
    registered, meaning, **11(3)**, [2]
    registration—
      application for, **11(3)**, [134], [159];
      11(4), [556], [573]
      duration of, **11(3)**, [159]; **11(4)**, [573]
      evidence as to, **11(3)**, [159]; **11(4)**, [573]
    solicitors, partnerships with, **11(3)**, [134];
    11(4), [556]
  inadequate professional services, provision as
  to. *See under* **solicitors**
  incorporated practice, recognition of,
  11(3), [2]
  individual, exercise of Committee's powers
  by, **11(2)**, [360]; **11(4)**, [456]
  intervention in solicitor's practice—
    circumstances for, **11(2)**, [372];
    11(4), [466]
    complaint, on, **11(2)**, [372]; **11(4)**, [466]
    documents, delivery up of, **11(2)**, [373];
    11(4), [467]
    electronic communications, re-direction to
    Society, **11(4)**, [467]
    generally, **11(2)**, [373]; **11(4)**, [467]

Law Society—*contd*
  intervention in solicitor's practice—*contd*
    High Court—
      applications to, **11(2)**, [373];
        11(4), [467]
      disposition in chambers, **11(2)**, [373];
        11(4), [467]
      incorporated practice, **11(3)**, [44];
        11(4), [518]
      mail, re-direction to Society, **11(2)**, [373];
        11(4), [467]
      money, control of, **11(2)**, [373];
        11(4), [467]
      notice preceding, **11(2)**, [372]; **11(4)**, [466]
      powers exercisable on, **11(2)**, [315], [372];
        11(4), [466]
      practising certificate, suspension arising,
        11(2), [293]
      trustee, substitution of, **11(2)**, [373];
        11(4), [466]
    members—
      non-practising solicitors, **11(2)**, [357]
      suspension, **11(2)**, [359]
    membership—
      cessation and suspension, **11(2)**, [359]
      eligibility for, **11(2)**, [357]
    orders of court, **11(2)**, [332]
    practising certificate, register of holders of,
      11(4), [380]
    practising certificates—
      applications, register of, **11(2)**, [284]
      intervention, suspension arising,
        11(2), [293]
    professional indemnity rules, **11(4)**, [411]
    regulations, making of, **11(4)**, [398]
    resolutions, evidence of, **11(2)**, [362]
    rights of audience, grant of, **11(3)**, [89]–[90]
    roll, keeping of, **11(2)**, [281]; **11(4)**, [375]
    rules—
      accountant's report, **11(2)**, [314];
        11(4), [405]
      accounts, for, **11(2)**, [311]; **11(4)**, [402]
      client's money, for, **11(2)**, [311];
        11(4), [402]
      foreign lawyers, power to make, **11(3)**, [2]
      incorporated practices, for, **11(3)**, [2];
        11(4), [470]
      legal service bodies, **11(4)**, [470]
      multi-disciplinary and multi-national
        practices, **11(3)**, [2]
      professional conduct etc, **11(2)**, [310]
      sole solicitors, employees of, **11(4)**, [406],
        [407]
    staff, exercise of committee's functions by
      member of, **11(2)**, [361]
    sub-committees, appointment, **11(2)**, [360]
    subscriptions to, **11(2)**, [358]
    Tribunal orders—
      filing, **11(2)**, [329]; **11(4)**, [427]
      Gazette notice of, **11(2)**, [329]

lay officers
  doctrine of Church of England, assent to,
    14, 814
  meaning, **14**, 814

lay workers
  duties performed by, **14**, 803
  licences—
    fixed term, for, **14**, 804
    revocation of, **14**, 1179
  meaning, **14**, 958
  pension for, **14**, 957–8
  stipend, payment towards, **14**, 843

layman
  recovery of penalties, **14**, 124

Learning and Skills Council for England
  academic years, plans for, **15(S)**, Education 13
  accounts, **15(2)**, [312]
  adult learning committee, provisions ceasing
    to have effect, **15(S)**, Education 11
  annual report, **15(2)**, [209]
  apprenticeship, functions as to,
    15(S), Education 194
  assessments and means tests, **15(2)**, [189]
  bodies corporate, formation or involvement
    in, **15(S)**, Education 13–14
  chief executive, **15(2)**, [312]
  committees—
    adult learning committee,
      15(2), [314]–[315]
    generally, **15(2)**, [314]–[315]
    members—
      allowances, **15(2)**, [314]–[315]
      tenure, **15(2)**, [314]–[315]
    other, **15(2)**, [314]–[315]
    proceedings, **15(2)**, [314]–[315]
    young people's learning committee,
      15(2), [314]–[315]
  constitution, **15(2)**, [177]
  consultation by, **15(S)**, Education 12
  delegation of functions, **15(2)**, [312]
  directions, **15(S)**, Education 14
  directions from Secretary of State,
    15(2), [206]
  diversity and choice, duty as to,
    15(S), Education 12
  education and training for persons—
    aged 16 to 19, **15(2)**, [178]
      additional entitlement,
        15(2), [182]–[183]
      core entitlement, **15(2)**, [181], [183]
      entitlement to, **15(2)**, [180]
      support schemes relating to, **15(2)**, [192]
    encouragement of, **15(2)**, [184]
    over 19, **15(2)**, [179]
  efficiency studies, **15(1)**, [446]; **15(2)**, [684]
  employment and training, assistance with,
    15(S), Education 16
    Northern Ireland, **15(S)**, Education 16
  equality of opportunity, **15(2)**, [195]
  establishment, **15(2)**, [177]
  financial resources—
    conditions, **15(2)**, [186]
    provision of, **15(2)**, [185]
  financial year, **15(2)**, [210]
  functions, strategies for—
    duty to carry out, **15(S)**, Education 10
    England, in, **15(S)**, Education 8

Learning and Skills Council for England—*contd*
  functions, strategies for—*contd*
    London, in, **15(S)**, Education 9
  governors, appointment of, **15(2)**, [191]
  grants to, **15(2)**, [208]
  joint exercise of functions, **15(2)**, [683]
  learning difficulties, having regard for persons with, **15(2)**, [194]
  links between education and training and employment, **15(2)**, [188]
  local councils—
    abolition, **15(S)**, Education 8
    constitution, **15(2)**, [200]
    delegation of functions, **15(2)**, [313]
    director, **15(2)**, [313]
    establishment of, **15(2)**, [200]
    functions, **15(2)**, [201]
    guidance to, **15(2)**, [202], [205]
    members—
      allowances, **15(2)**, [313]
      tenure, **15(2)**, [313]
    plans, **15(2)**, [203]
    proceedings, **15(2)**, [313]
    staff, **15(2)**, [313]
  members—
    interests of, **15(2)**, [312]
    number of, **15(S)**, Education 5
    pensions, **15(2)**, [312]
    salaries, **15(2)**, [312]
    tenure, **15(2)**, [312]
  plans, **15(2)**, [196]
  proceedings, **15(2)**, [312]
  qualifying accounts and arrangements, **15(2)**, [190]
  reference to, **15(1)**, [428]
  regional councils—
    establishment of, **15(S)**, Education 6
    functions, **15(S)**, Education 6–7
    guidance to, **15(S)**, Education 7
    regulations, **15(S)**, Education 6
  research and information, **15(2)**, [193]
  school sixth-forms, funding of, **15(2)**, [187]
  seal and proof of instruments, **15(2)**, [312]
  services, provision of, **15(S)**, Education 14–15
  staff, **15(2)**, [312]
  status, **15(2)**, [312]
  strategy, **15(2)**, [197]
  summary of provisions, **15(S)**, Education 1
  supplementary functions, **15(2)**, [199]
  transfer of property, rights and liabilities to—
    contracts of employment, **15(2)**, [263]
    Further Education Funding Councils, from, **15(2)**, [258]
    Secretary of State, from, **15(2)**, [259]–[260]
    stamp duty land tax not chargeable on, **15(2)**, [262]
    stamp duty not chargeable on, **15(2)**, [261]
  transitional provisions, **15(2)**, [320]–[321]
  use of information by, **15(2)**, [198]
  young people's learning committee, provisions ceasing to have effect, **15(S)**, Education 11

learning disability
  meaning, **29**, [23]

learning disability—*contd*
  not considered as mental disorder, **29**, [23]

lease
  acquisition of new. *See* **lease (acquisition of new)**
  administration charges, **24**, [154]
  agreements for, time for presenting for stamping, **41**, [226]
  agricultural buildings. *See* **agricultural buildings**
  agricultural land, surrender, **9**, [356]
  agricultural, war damage provisions. *See* **war damage**
  assignment—
    implied covenant, **20**, [695]
    licence for, **20**, [754]
    See also **assignment**
  assured tenancy. *See* **assured tenancy; assured tenancy allowances**
  attornment of lessees, **20**, [761]
  capital gains tax. *See* **capital gains tax**
  compensation arising from, application of, **9**, [37]
  compulsory purchase of land subject to—
    compensation to tenant where, **9**, [77]–[78], [279]
    lease or grant, production by tenant at will, **9**, [79], [280]
    limit of time for, **9**, [80]
    part only of land taken, apportionment of rent where, **9**, [76], [279]
    qualifying tenancies, **9**, [315]–[316]
    tenant from year to year, compensation to, **9**, [78], [280]
  cost of, **21**, [250]
  covenants in. *See* **covenants**
  decorative repairs, notice to effect, relief, **20**, [757]
  duration of, **44(1)**, [27], [691]
  ecclesiastical. *See* **ecclesiastical lease**
  enfranchisement. *See* **leasehold enfranchisement**
  enfranchisement or extension, compensation for depreciation where tenant entitled to, **9**, [315]–[316], [379]
  extension of. *See* **leasehold extension**
  flat, of. *See* **flats**
  forfeiture—
    bankruptcy of lessee, on, **20**, [756]
    lessor's costs and expenses, **20**, [756]
    relief against—
      application for, **20**, [756]
      court's discretion, **20**, [756]
    under-lease, **20**, [756]
    See also **forfeiture**
  grant or transfer, production of instrument of, **41**, [70], [74]
  ground—
    meaning, **17(2)**, [46]
    war damage. *See* **war damage**
  holding over after determination, penalty for, **20**, [30]

lease—*contd*

industrial buildings. *See* **industrial buildings**

inheritance tax. *See* **inheritance tax**

insurance provisions, application for variation of, **22**, [750], [755]

interesse termini, abolition of doctrine, **20**, [759]

invalidation, non-compliance with terms of powers, **20**, [762]

lessee—

  grant of licence to, **20**, [753]

  meaning, **20**, [756]

lessor, meaning, **20**, [756]

licence—

  assignment, for, **20**, [754]

  grant to lessee, effect, **20**, [753]

life, for, conversion, **20**, [759]

long—

  collective enfranchisement. *See* **collective enfranchisement**

  determination of breach, no forfeiture notice before, **24**, [128], [129]

  insurance other than with landlord's insurer, **24**, [125]

  meaning, **22**, [755], [773]

  rent due, duty to notify, **24**, [126]

  right of re-entry or forfeiture, power to prescribe additional or different requirements, **24**, [130]

  small amount for short period, failure to pay, **24**, [127]

long term, enlargement of residue into fee simple, **20**, [763]

meaning, **20**, [756]; **21**, [70]; **23**, [542]; **42**, [1482]

mental disorders, persons with, avoidance of provisions preventing occupation by, **23**, [165]

mining—

  meaning, **21**, [70]

  security of tenure, exclusion from, **21**, [207]

  war damage. *See* **war damage**

  See **mining lease**

mortgagor or mortgagee in possession, by, **20**, [632], [717]

multiple, war damage provisions. *See* **war damage**

Northern Ireland, production of documents, **41**, [231], [232]

parol, created by, **20**, [672]

  savings, **20**, [673]

peppercorn rent, at, **20**, [717]

perpetually renewable—

  contract to grant or renew, effect of, **20**, [500]

  conversion to long term, **20**, [496], [500]

  disposition purporting to create, effect of, **20**, [500]

  existing contract, effect of, **20**, [500]

  meaning, **20**, [498]

  power to grant, effect of, **20**, [500]

  small holdings and allotments, savings for, **20**, [500]

lease—*contd*

persons with mental disorders, avoidance of provisions preventing occupation by, **23**, [165]

plant or machinery, of. *See* **machinery and plant**

powers, non-compliance with terms of, **20**, [762]

pre-1963, provisions applying to, **44(1)**, [28]

premiums. *See* **lease premium; property income**

re-entry—

  conditions running with reversion, **20**, [751]

  due process of law for, **21**, [663]

  right of, **20**, [750], [756]

references to, **44(1)**, [17]

registration. *See* **land registration**

rent to shared ownership—

  scheme, meaning, **41(S)**, Stamp Duties 5

  stamp duty land tax provisions, **41(S)**, Stamp Duties 5–6

  trust, meaning, **41(S)**, Stamp Duties 5–6

rent under, apportionment on acquisition of part of land, **9**, [279]

rentcharge, to enforce, **20**, [632]

reversion—

  extinguishment, effect, **20**, [749]

  rent and benefit of covenants running with, **20**, [751]

  severance, appointment of conditions on, **20**, [750]

  surrender or merger, effect, **20**, [749]

reversionary, **20**, [759]

right to buy. *See* **dwelling-house**

sale—

  assumption of due grant, **20**, [663]

  covenants, assumption as to observance, **20**, [663]

  own solicitor, right to employ, **20**, [666]

  underlease, **20**, [663]

sale and leaseback—

  commercial rent, **44(1)**, [523]

  consideration, taxation of, **44(1)**, [524]

  tax reliefs, limitation on, **44(1)**, [523]

satisfied terms, **20**, [629]

Schedule A, charge under, **44(1)**, [12]

service charge. *See* **service charge**

shared ownership, **46**, [229], [239]

  exclusion of leasehold enfranchisement or extension, **21**, [334], [347]

  protected tenancy, not being, **21**, [525]

  protection for hard to replace houses, protection for, **24**, [837]

  restricted contract, exclusion of, **21**, [540]

stamp duty—

  agreement, on, **41**, [41], [146], [226], [235], [261]

    exemption from duty, **41**, [235]

    term exceeding 35 years, **41**, [146]

    time for stamping, **41**, [226]

  associated bodies, **41**, [235]

  charge, **41**, [261]

  charities, exemption for, **41**, [141]

lease—*contd*
  stamp duty—*contd*
    consideration, where not ascertainable,
      41, [229]
    exempt instruments, **41**, [155]
    exemption, **41**, [235]
    further consideration, **41**, [64]
    market rent expected, **41**, [229]
    rates, **41**, [261]
    rent to mortgage terms, acquired on,
      41, [223]
    rent, where not ascertainable, **41**, [229]
    right to buy under Housing Act,
      application of provisions, **41**, [138]
    seven years, on, **41**, [287]
    shared ownership lease, **41**, [134], [139],
      [199]
    stamping—
      after execution, penalty, **41**, [29]
      requirements before treatment as,
        41, [227]
      surrender, agreement to, **41**, [230]
      time for presenting for, **41**, [226]
    surrender, on, **41**, [281]
    treatment as duly stamped, **41**, [227]
  stamp duty land tax, **41**, [404], [454]
  See also **stamp duty land tax**
  summary of provisions, **20**, [1]
  surrender—
    mortgagee and mortgagor in possession,
      acceptance by, **20**, [718]
    mortgagor or mortgagee, to, validity,
      20, [718]
    new grant, with view to, **20**, [760]
    requirements, **20**, [670]
  taxed, tenants under—
    application of provisions, **44(3)**, [59]
    corporation tax receipts, treatment of,
      44(3), [65]–[66]
    employment for purposes of trade,
      44(3), [62]
    expenses, deduction of, **44(3)**, [59]
    lease premium receipts, **44(3)**, [63]
    mineral extraction allowance, entitled to,
      44(3), [61]
    part of premises, lease of, **44(3)**, [64]
    trade, occupation of land for purpose of,
      44(3), [60]
  tenant for life, powers of. *See* **tenant for life**
  term of, commencement and effect, **20**, [756]
  term of years absolute, meaning, **20**, [804]
  title, period of, **20**, [662]
  under-lease—
    forfeiture, relief against, **20**, [756]
    meaning, **20**, [756]
    sale, assumption on, **20**, [663]
    surrender of head lease, effect, **20**, [760]
  underletting, covenant against, **21**, [65]
  undervalue, granted at, assignment of,
    44(1), [23], [30]
  war damage, effect of. *See* **war damage**
  work, requiring, **44(1)**, [22]
  writing, when necessary, **20**, [671]
    savings, **20**, [673]

lease (acquisition of new). *See also* **collective**
enfranchisement (leasehold reform)
  amendment of rights, **24**, [117]
  cathedral precinct, saving for property
    within, **23**, [173]
  contracting out of right to, prohibition of,
    23, [169]
  costs to be paid by tenant, **23**, [141]
  county court—
    enforcement of obligations, **23**, [168]
    jurisdiction of, **23**, [166]
  Crown land, application of provisions to,
    23, [171]
  grant of—
    amounts payable to owners of intermediate
      leasehold interests, **23**, [217]
    further renewal after, **23**, [140]
    mortgage, where interest of landlord or
      tenant is subject to, **23**, [138]
    obligation of, **23**, [136]
    premium payable for, **23**, [216]
    priority of interests on, **23**, [139]
    terms, **23**, [137]
  ineffective claims, landlord's right to
    compensation for, **23**, [143], [144], [423]
  Isles of Scilly, application of provisions to,
    23, [180]
  landlord—
    absent, qualifying tenant's application to
      court for vesting order when, **23**, [130],
      [131]
    compensation, right to, in relation to
      ineffective claims, **23**, [143], [144], [423]
    counter-notice—
      details of, **23**, [125]
      failure to give, **23**, [129]
    court, application to over failure to enter
      into new lease, **23**, [128]
    custodian trustee, vested in, **23**, [192]
    definition, **23**, [120]
    disability, under, **23**, [192]
    ecclesiastical, **23**, [192]
    interest of—
      mortgagee in possession of, **23**, [192]
      settlement, subject to, **23**, [192]
      trust, held in, **23**, [192]
    leasehold valuation tribunal, application to
      over disputes relating to terms of
      acquisition, **23**, [128]
    redevelopment by—
      application to defeat tenant's claim
        where, **23**, [127]
      right to terminate new lease on grounds
        of, **23**, [142], [218]
    university or college, **23**, [192]
  leasehold valuation tribunal—
    disputes relating to terms of acquisition—
      landlord's application to, over, **23**, [128]
      tenant's application to, over, **23**, [128]
    jurisdiction of, **23**, [167]
  low rent test, alternative to, **23**, [421]
  National Trust, saving for, **23**, [172]
  orders and regulations, power of Secretary of
    State to make, **23**, [177]

lease (acquisition of new)—*contd*
premises—
  access by landlords to for valuation
    purposes, **23**, [124]
  redevelopment by landlord—
    failure of tenant's claim where, **23**, [127]
    right to terminate new lease on grounds
      of, **23**, [142], [218]
  procedure for, power of Secretary of State to
    prescribe, **23**, [175]
  right of qualifying tenant of flat to acquire,
    23, [119]
tenant, qualifying—
  absent landlord, applications to court for
    vesting order when, **23**, [130], [131]
  compensation for landlord's termination of
    new lease, **23**, [218]
  costs incurred, **23**, [141]
  counter-notice, applications to county
    court where landlord fails to give,
    23, [129]
  court, application to over failure to enter
    into new lease, **23**, [128]
  failure of claim where landlord intends to
    redevelop, **23**, [127]
  general, **23**, [119]
  grant of new lease—
    amounts payable to owners of
      intermediate leasehold interests,
      23, [217]
    premium payable for, **23**, [216]
  ineffective claims by, landlord's right to
    compensation for, **23**, [143], [144], [423]
  leasehold valuation tribunal, application to
    over disputes relating to terms of
    acquisition, **23**, [128]
  notice by—
    competent landlord not tenant's
      immediate landlord, where, **23**, [211],
      [212]
    compulsory acquisition procedures, effect
      on, **23**, [135]
    details of, **23**, [122]
    forfeitures, effect on, **23**, [213]
    general provisions as to effect of,
      23, [123]
    giving of, provision for, **23**, [176]
    inaccuracies or misrepresentations in,
      23, [214]
    notices, effect on other, **23**, [213]
    orders for possession, effect on, **23**, [213]
    registration of, **23**, [174]
    suspension of during currency of notice
      for collective enfranchisement,
      23, [134]
    validity of, proceedings relating to,
      23, [126]
    withdrawal of, deemed, **23**, [133]
  superior interests, right to obtain
    information about, **23**, [121]
  trustees, powers of, **23**, [170]
  withdrawal from acquisition, **23**, [132]
term dates for periodical tenancies, **23**, [179]

lease (acquisition of new)—*contd*
  termination of new lease, landlord's right to
    on grounds of redevelopment, **23**, [142],
    [218]

leasehold enfranchisement
  agricultural holding, exclusion of, **21**, [292]
  amendment of provisions, **24**, [118]
  betterment levy, liability to, **21**, [321]
  boundary, adjustment of, **21**, [296]
  claim for—
    contracts, releasing landlord from, **21**, [300]
    court, powers of, **21**, [317]
    good faith, not made in, **21**, [317], [342]
    ineffective, termination after, **21**, [325],
      [326], [343]
    invalid, becoming, **21**, [300], [343]
    notice of. *See* notice requiring *below*
    notice terminating tenancy, after, **21**, [343]
    re-entry or forfeiture during, **21**, [343]
    restrictions on, **21**, [343]
    sub-tenancy, in respect of, **21**, [341]
  collective. *See* **collective enfranchisement**
  compensation for loss of—
    amount of, **21**, [342]
    date payable on, **21**, [342]
    tenant's rights, for, **21**, [320]
  compensation to landlord, **21**, [317], [321],
    [322], [325], [326]
  compulsory acquisition—
    covenants, taking account of, **21**, [328],
      [345]
    effect of, **21**, [300]
  conveyance—
    covenants restricting development in,
      21, [328], [345]
    effect of, **21**, [304]
    landlord not found, where, **21**, [324]
    local authority, reservation of right to
      develop by, **21**, [328], [345]
    mortgage, discharging, **21**, [309]
    rights in, **21**, [307], [318]
    sale of interest transferred, deemed to be
      on, **21**, [322]
  costs, tenant bearing, **21**, [305]
  county court jurisdiction, **21**, [317]
  court, payment of money into, **21**, [310]
  Crown land, provisions on, **21**, [333], [341]
  default, powers on, **21**, [317]
  delay, powers on, **21**, [317]
  documents, acknowledgment for production
    of, **21**, [307]
  easements, grant of, **21**, [307]
  ecclesiastical property, provisions on, **21**, [330]
  entitlement to, **21**, [292]–[295]
  estate management schemes. *See* **estate
    management schemes**
  exclusions, **21**, [292]
  house—
    meaning, **21**, [296]
    premises, and, **21**, [296]
  incumbrances, grant to be free of, **21**, [304]
  Isles of Scilly, application of provisions to,
    23, [180]

leasehold enfranchisement—*contd*
  landlord—
    breach of covenant, limitation of liability
      for, **21**, [307]
    compensation to, **21**, [317], [321], [322]
    custodian trustee, interest vested in,
      21, [323]
    disability, under, **21**, [323]
    lien for purchase price, **21**, [305]
    management scheme by, **21**, [316]
    missing, **21**, [324]
    mortgage—
      discharge of, **21**, [309]
      payment into court in respect of,
        21, [310]
      relief in respect of, **21**, [335]
  Landlord and Tenant Act 1954, proceedings
    under, **21**, [337]
  leasehold valuation tribunal, jurisdiction of,
    21, [318]
  low rent test—
    abolition, **24**, [835]
    extension of rights, **23**, [421]
  management powers, retention of, **21**, [316],
    [425]
  members of tenant's family—
    meaning, **21**, [303]
    rights of, **21**, [303]
  minerals, exclusion of right to, **21**, [296]
  mortgagee in possession, effect of, **21**, [322]
  National Trust property, saving for, **21**, [331]
  new town, in, pre-emption of rights,
    21, [329]
  new towns residuary body, re-acquisition for
    development by, **21**, [328], [345]
  notice requiring—
    charge, given to person having, **21**, [344]
    forfeiture, tenancy subject to, **21**, [319]
    form and contents, **21**, [344]
    good faith, not made in, **21**, [317]
    landlord's notice in reply, **21**, [344]
    late, given, **21**, [319]
    misrepresentation etc in, **21**, [317]
    procedure giving effect to, **21**, [319]
    service of, **21**, [344]
    sub-tenant, given by, **21**, [341]
  notice terminating tenancy, effect of,
    21, [344]
    obligation to enfranchise, **21**, [304]
    payment received by, application of,
      21, [321]
    residential rights, **21**, [315]
    successors, rights extending to, **21**, [300]
    unidentified landlord, where, **21**, [324]
  obligation to enfranchise, **21**, [304]
  order for possession, effect of, **21**, [342]
  orders and regulations concerning, powers of
    Secretary of State to make, **23**, [177]
  overspill area, in, pre-emption of rights,
    21, [329]
  period of occupation, **21**, [292]
  personal representatives, rights of, **21**, [302]
  places of public worship, **21**, [339]
  previous contract, effect on, **21**, [300]

leasehold enfranchisement—*contd*
  property transferred for public benefit,
    exclusion of, **21**, [332]
  public purposes, land required for, **21**, [327]
  purchase price—
    amount of, **21**, [305]
    application of, **21**, [321]
    consideration for disposition of interest, as,
      21, [322]
    defect in title, deduction for, **21**, [305]
    leasehold valuation tribunal determining,
      21, [318]
    superior interest, effect of creation of,
      21, [720]
  rateable value—
    ascertainment of, **21**, [336]
    limit on, **21**, [292]–[294]
    tenant's improvements, taking account of,
      21, [305], [427]
  receiver in possession, effect of, **21**, [322]
  registration of notice, **21**, [300]
  rent—
    apportionment of, **21**, [298], [317]
    determination of questions as to, **21**, [298]
    limits—
      alternative, **21**, [299]
      applicable, exceeding, **21**, [293], [294],
        [306]
    low, meaning, **21**, [298]
  rentcharge—
    discharge from, **21**, [308]
    estate to be free of, **21**, [304]
    redemption of, **21**, [308]
    release from, **21**, [308]
  restrictive covenants, provisions on, **21**, [307]
  rights of way, provisions on, **21**, [307]
  settled land, **21**, [301]
  sub-tenant, by, **21**, [341]
  tenancy—
    death or marriage, rights in cases
      terminable after, **21**, [295]
    expectation of possession carried by,
      21, [341]
    long, meaning, **21**, [297]
    meaning, **21**, [336]
    new, grant of, **21**, [320]
    shared ownership, exclusion of, **21**, [346]
    sub-demise, granted by, **21**, [300], [313]
    surrender, agreement for, **21**, [320]
    two or more parts of house, of, **21**, [297]
  tenant—
    artificial person as, **21**, [336]
    charge on premises, duty to redeem,
      21, [309]
    costs, bearing, **21**, [305]
    entitlement to, **21**, [292]–[295]
    mortgage, payment into court in respect
      of, **21**, [309]
    purchaser for valuable consideration,
      being, **21**, [305]
    residence, occupying house as, **21**, [292]
    rights conveyed to, **21**, [307], [318]
    rights of, agreement excluding or
      modifying, **21**, [320]
    successors, rights extending to, **21**, [300]

leasehold enfranchisement—*contd*
  trustees, rights of, **21**, [301]
  university body, re-acquisition for
    development by, **21**, [327], [345]

leasehold extension
  agricultural holding, exclusion of, **21**, [292]
  amendment of provisions, **24**, [118]
  amount payable for, **21**, [311], [318]
  boundary, adjustment of, **21**, [296]
  charge on landlord's estate, effect of, **21**, [311]
  claim for—
    contracts, releasing landlord from, **21**, [300]
    court, powers of, **21**, [317]
    good faith, not made in, **21**, [317], [342]
    ineffective, termination after, **21**, [325],
      [343]
    invalid, becoming, **21**, [300], [343]
    notice of. *See* notice requiring *below*
    notice terminating tenancy, after, **21**, [343]
    previous contract, obligations under,
      21, [300]
    re-entry or forfeiture during, **21**, [343]
    restrictions on, **21**, [343]
    sub-tenancy, in respect of, **21**, [341]
  compensation on termination—
    amount payable, **21**, [314], [315], [342]
    date payable on, **21**, [342]
    leasehold valuation tribunal determining,
      21, [318]
    mortgagee, paid to, **21**, [322]
    tenant's rights, for, **21**, [320]
  compensation to landlord, **21**, [317], [321],
    [322], [325], [326]
  compulsory acquisition, taking account of
    covenants, **21**, [328], [345]
  costs of, **21**, [311]
  county court jurisdiction, **21**, [317]
  Crown land, provisions on, **21**, [333]
  default, powers on, **21**, [317]
  delay, powers on, **21**, [317]
  duration of, **21**, [311]
  ecclesiastical property, provisions on, **21**, [330]
  entitlement to, **21**, [292]
  exclusions, **21**, [292]
  freehold, tenant wishing to have, **21**, [300],
    [313]
  further rights, exclusion of, **21**, [313]
  house—
    meaning, **21**, [296]
    premises, and, **21**, [296]
  instrument—
    charge, evidencing, delivery of, **21**, [311]
    covenants restricting development in,
      21, [328], [345]
    statement of extension in, **21**, [313]
  landlord—
    compensation to, **21**, [317], [321], [322]
    covenant for title, obligations as to,
      21, [312]
    custodian trustee, interest vested in,
      21, [323]
    disability, under, **21**, [323]
    insurance, liability for, **21**, [312]
    management scheme by, **21**, [316]

leasehold extension—*contd*
  landlord—*contd*
    mortgage—
      payment into court in respect of,
        21, [310]
      relief for, **21**, [335]
    notice terminating tenancy, effect of,
      21, [344]
    obligation to grant, **21**, [311]
    redevelopment rights, **21**, [314]
    repairs and maintenance, liability for,
      21, [312]
    residential rights, **21**, [315]
    services, provision by, **21**, [312]
    successors, rights extending to, **21**, [300]
  Landlord and Tenant Act 1954, proceedings
    under, **21**, [337]
  leasehold valuation tribunal, jurisdiction of,
    21, [318]
  letting value, **21**, [312]
  local authority, reservation of right to develop
    by, **21**, [328], [345]
  management powers, retention of, **21**, [316],
    [425]
  members of tenant's family—
    meaning, **21**, [303]
    rights of, **21**, [303]
  minerals, exclusion of right to, **21**, [296]
  mortgagee in possession, effect of, **21**, [322]
  new town, in, pre-emption of rights,
    21, [329]
  new towns residuary body, re-acquisition for
    development by, **21**, [328], [345]
  notice requiring—
    charge, given to person having, **21**, [344]
    forfeiture, tenancy subject to, **21**, [319]
    form and contents, **21**, [344]
    good faith, not made in, **21**, [317]
    landlord's notice in reply, **21**, [344]
    late, given, **21**, [319]
    misrepresentation, etc in, **21**, [317]
    procedure giving effect to, **21**, [319]
    service of, **21**, [344]
    sub-tenant, given by, **21**, [341]
  obligation to grant, **21**, [311]
  order for possession, effect of, **21**, [342]
  overspill area, in, pre-emption of rights,
    21, [329]
  period of occupation, **21**, [292]
  personal representatives, rights of, **21**, [302]
  postponement of termination, compensation
    for, in connection with ineffective claims,
    21, [325], [326], [887]
  previous contract, effect on, **21**, [300]
  public benefit, exclusion of property
    transferred for, **21**, [332]
  public purposes, land required for, **21**, [327]
  rateable value—
    ascertainment of, **21**, [336]
    limit on, **21**, [292]
    tenant's improvements, taking account of,
      21, [427]
  receiver in possession, effect of, **21**, [322]
  registration of notice, **21**, [300]

leasehold extension—*contd*
rent—
apportionment of, **21**, [298], [317]
ascertainment of, **21**, [312]
determination of questions as to, **21**, [298]
low, meaning, **21**, [298]
Rent Act, application of, **21**, [313]
settled land, **21**, [301]
statement as to, truth of, **21**, [320]
sub-demise, rights under, **21**, [300], [313]
sub-tenancy, provisions applying to, **21**, [313]
sub-tenant, by, **21**, [341]
tenancy—
expectation of possession carried by,
21, [341]
long, meaning, **21**, [297]
meaning, **21**, [336]
new, grant of, **21**, [320]
shared ownership, exclusion of, **21**, [334],
[346]
sub-demise, rights under, **21**, [300], [313]
surrender, agreement for, **21**, [320]
terms of, **21**, [312]
two or more parts of house, of, **21**, [297]
tenant—
artificial person as, **21**, [336]
brothel, using premises as, **21**, [312]
costs, bearing, **21**, [311]
depreciation, compensation for, **9**, [379]
entitlement to, **21**, [292]–[295]
freehold, wishing to purchase, **21**, [300],
[313]
residence, occupying house as, **21**, [292]
rights, agreements excluding or
modifying, **21**, [320]
successors, rights extending to, **21**, [300]
trustees, rights of, **21**, [301]
university body, re-acquisition for
development by, **21**, [327], [346]

leasehold house
insurance obligations, **24**, [125]

leasehold land
registered. *See* **land registration**
satisfied term of years, **20**, [629]

leasehold valuation tribunal
acquisition order, determination of terms of,
22, [746]
appeals, **24**, [134]
applications and fees, **23**, [553]
approval of estate management schemes,
23, [148]
jurisdiction, **21**, [318]; **22**, [538], [728];
23, [164], [167], [553]; **24**, [132]
liability to pay service charge, determining,
22, [538]
managers, appointment of, by, **23**, [553]
procedure, **24**, [155]
rent assessment committee as, **21**, [750]

leasing
allowable deductions, **44(1)**, [526]

leasing—*contd*
allowances. *See* **machinery and plant**
apportionment of payments, **44(1)**, [527]
asset, meaning, **44(1)**, [529]
associated persons, **44(1)**, [527]
capital sum, meaning, **44(1)**, [529]
commercial rent, **44(1)**, [526]
expenses—
amount of, **43(S)**, 881
relief for, **43(S)**, 882
hire-purchase agreement, assets subject to,
44(1), [528]
interest, sum obtained in respect of,
44(1), [527]
lease, meaning, **44(1)**, [529]
lessor companies, sale of, **43(S)**, 881–2
loss relief, **44(1)**, [199]
meaning, **43(1)**, [665]
overseas. *See* **overseas leasing**
partnership, business carried on in, **43(S)**, 881
partnerships, restriction on use of losses,
44(1), [530]
plant or machinery—
business of, meaning, **44(1)**, [531]
capital payments, **44(1)**, [533], [534]
capital receipts treated as income,
44(1), [533]
meaning, **44(1)**, [534]
relevant income, meaning, **44(1)**, [531]
rent factoring, **44(1)**, [532]
tax relief, deductions by way of, **44(1)**, [525]

leasing arrangement. *See* **finance lease**

lecturers in Holy Orders
clerical or ministerial duties, undertaking,
14, 171
licensed, to be, **14**, 53

Lee Conservancy Board
pension provisions, **33(1)**, [136]

legacy
imported, relief from customs and excise
duties, **13**, [795]

legacy duty
generally, **42**, [1]

legal advice
commonhold land law, as to, **24**, [62]
general, concerning residential tenancies,
23, [417]

legal aid
criminal—
financial eligibility, assessment of, disclosure
of information to enable,
11(S), Courts 12–14
pilot schemes, **11(S)**, Courts 14–16
right to representation, provisional grant
of, **11(S)**, Courts 10–12

legal aid and advice
  complaints, **11(3)**, [44]; **11(4)**, [518]
    barristers—
      conduct of, **11(3)**, [34]; **11(4)**, [508]
      work, exclusion from, **11(3)**, [35]
    meaning, **11(3)**, [33]; **11(4)**, [507]
    solicitors, against, **11(3)**, [36]; **11(4)**, [510]
    Solicitors Disciplinary Tribunal, jurisdiction
      and powers, **11(3)**, [36]
    See also **Solicitors Disciplinary
      Tribunal**
  contempt proceedings, in, Northern Ireland,
    11(2), [667]
  costs order, regulations, **12(1)**, [949]
  exclusion of solicitor from, **11(2)**, [328]
  extradition proceedings, **18**, [946], [947]
  family matters, for mediation in, general
    principles underlying provisions, **27**, [622]
  International Child Abduction Convention,
    6, [206]
  Legal Aid Commission, establishment of,
    14, 1298
  Legal Aid Fund, maintenance of, **14**, 1298
  proceedings for which given, **14**, 1304–5
  rules, **14**, 1301–2
  supplementary provisions, **14**, 1300–1
  work, exclusion of barristers from,
    11(3), [35]; **11(4)**, [509]

legal capacity
  child, of, **6**, [1]

legal deposit libraries
  activities in relation to publications,
    exemption from liability, **13**, [463]
  deposit of publications—
    British Library, **13**, [457]
    enforcement, **13**, [456]
    exemption from liability, **13**, [462]
    new and alternative editions, **13**, [455]
    non-print—
      copyright, **13**, [461]
      database right, **13**, [461]
      regulations, **13**, [459]
      restriction on activities, **13**, [460]
    request for, **13**, [458]
    requirement, **13**, [454]
  meaning, **13**, [467]
  regulations, **13**, [464]–[466]

legal estate
  actions as to, limitation of time, **20**, [635]
  administration of, **20**, [455]
  appropriation, satisfaction of legacy or share,
    20, [457]
  concurrent subsistence, **20**, [625]
  conversion into equitable interests, **20**, [808]
  conveyance overreaching, **20**, [626]
  conveyance subject to—
    estate not in existence, effect, **20**, [683]
    prior interests, **21**, [47]
  creation—
    deed, requirement of, **20**, [670]
    generally, **20**, [625], [633]
  devolution on death, **20**, [454]

legal estate—*contd*
  dispositions operating as conveyances,
    20, [633]
  documents, effect of possession, **20**, [636]
  easement, **20**, [625], [788]
  equitable interests and powers—
    conversion into, **20**, [658]
    enforcement against owner, **20**, [627]
  estate owner, meaning, **20**, [625], [804]
  fee simple. See **fee simple**
  joint tenancy, severance prohibited, **20**, [655]
  joint tenants—
    beneficially limited to, **20**, [1]
    held in trust for, **20**, [655]
  meaning, **20**, [625], [804]
  minor—
    incapacity to hold, **20**, [1], [625]
    vested in, transitional provisions, **20**, [810]
  outstanding, void stipulations in, **20**, [660]
  past transactions, confirmation, **20**, [684]
  person in possession, interests of, **20**, [637]
  purchaser, protection, **20**, [456]
  rentcharge in possession, **20**, [625]
  reservation, **20**, [683]
  reverter, rights of, replacement, **20**, [627]
    See also **land**
  term of years absolute, **20**, [625]
  title to be shown, **20**, [634]
  transfer to heir or devisee, **20**, [456]
  undivided shares, in, prohibitions, **20**, [625]
  vesting—
    corporation, on dissolution of, **20**, [782]
    infant, transitional provisions, **20**, [810]
    orders operating as conveyances, **20**, [633]
    transitional provisions, **20**, [809]
  vesting of, **25(1)**, [27]

legal proceedings
  bankers' books, inspection, **18**, [145]
  evidence in. See **evidence**

legal professional privilege
  bankruptcy proceedings, in, **4(2)**, [527]

legal representative
  costs against, **12(1)**, [950]
  meaning, **12(1)**, [950]

legal separation. See **separation**

legal services
  advocates—
    duties of, **11(4)**, [303]
    employed, **11(4)**, [304]
      by Legal Services Commission, rights of
        audience and to conduct litigation,
        11(4), [536]
  alternative business structures, licensing of—
    appeals, **11(4)**, [195], [196]
    procedural requirements, **11(4)**, [196]
  appellate bodies—
    Discipline and Appeals Committee, as,
      11(4), [195]
    functions of, **11(4)**, [195]

legal services—*contd*
  alternative business structures, licensing
    of—*contd*
    appellate bodies—*contd*
      Solicitors Disciplinary Tribunal, as,
        11(4), [195]
    licence—
      application for, **11(4)**, [199]
        determination of, **11(4)**, [345]
        form and manner of, **11(4)**, [345]
        Legal Services Board, to, **11(4)**, [349]
      bodies holding, registers of, **11(4)**, [202]
      continuity of, **11(4)**, [345]
      evidence of having, **11(4)**, [203]
      modification of, **11(4)**, [201], [345]
      period of, **11(4)**, [345]
      renewal, **11(4)**, [345]
      revocation of, **11(4)**, [216]
      rules, **11(4)**, [348]
      suspension of, **11(4)**, [216]
      terms of, **11(4)**, [200]
    licensed bodies—
      controlled interest in, **11(4)**, [350]
      divestiture, **11(4)**, [354]
      employees of—
        disqualification from being,
          11(4), [214], [215]
        duties, **11(4)**, [205]
        referral of, to appropriate regulator,
          11(4), [213]
      enforcement of conditions, **11(4)**, [354]
      financial penalties, **11(4)**, [210]
        appeals, **11(4)**, [211]
        recovery of, **11(4)**, [212]
      Head of Finance and Administration—
        disqualification as, **11(4)**, [214], [215]
        duties of, **11(4)**, [207]
      Head of Legal Practice—
        disqualification as, **11(4)**, [214], [215]
        duties of, **11(4)**, [206]
      information, duty to provide,
        11(4), [208], [209]
      legal professional privilege, applied to
        communications from, **11(4)**, [305]
      manager of, disqualification from being,
        11(4), [214], [215]
      material interest in, **11(4)**, [350]
      meaning, **11(4)**, [187]
      non-authorised persons, duties of,
        11(4), [205]
      ownership of, **11(4)**, [204], [350]
      registers of, **11(4)**, [202]
      restricted interests in, **11(4)**, [350]
        approval of—
          after licence is issued, **11(4)**, [352]
          on application for licence,
            11(4), [351]
      share limit, power to impose,
        11(4), [353]
      voting limit, power to impose,
        11(4), [353]

legal services—*contd*
  alternative business structures, licensing
    of—*contd*
    licensing authority—
      approved regulator, designation as,
        11(4), [189]
        cancellation of, **11(4)**, [192]
        automatic, **11(4)**, [190]
        Board's power to recommend,
          11(4), [193]
        order, by, **11(4)**, [191], [344]
        powers of entry, **11(4)**, [194]
      Board as, regulatory conflict and,
        11(4), [218]
      financial penalties, imposition of,
        11(4), [210]
        appeals against, **11(4)**, [211]
        recovery of, **11(4)**, [212]
      information, power to require,
        11(4), [208], [209]
      intervention powers, **11(4)**, [217], [355]
        communications, **11(4)**, [355]
        costs, **11(4)**, [355]
        documents—
          notice to produce or deliver,
            11(4), [355]
          order to produce or deliver,
            11(4), [355]
        mail, as to, **11(4)**, [355]
        money, as to, **11(4)**, [355]
        trusts, as to, **11(4)**, [355]
      meaning, **11(4)**, [188]
      policy statements, duty to issue,
        11(4), [197]
      regulatory conflict—
        Board, and, **11(4)**, [218]
        prevention of, **11(4)**, [219]
        relevant, meaning, **11(4)**, [188]
    low risk bodies—
      meaning, **11(4)**, [223]
      modification of rules for, **11(4)**, [221],
        [222]
    reporting requirements of Board,
      11(4), [225]
    rules, **11(4)**, [198], [345]
      disqualifications, **11(4)**, [348]
      fees, **11(4)**, [348]
      financial penalties, **11(4)**, [348]
      Head of Finance and Administration,
        requirement as to, **11(4)**, [346]
      Head of Legal Practice, requirement as
        to, **11(4)**, [346]
      licences, suspension or revocation of,
        11(4), [348]
      management, requirements as to,
        11(4), [346]
      modification of—
        community interest companies, for,
          11(4), [221], [222]
        foreign bodies, for, **11(4)**, [224]
        low risk bodies, for, **11(4)**, [221],
          [222]
        meaning, **11(4)**, [223]
        not for profit bodies, for,
          11(4), [221], [222]

legal services—*contd*

alternative business structures, licensing
of—*contd*

rules—*contd*

modification of—*contd*

trade unions, for, **11(4)**, [221], [222]

practice requirements, **11(4)**, [347]

structural requirements, **11(4)**, [346]

status, evidence of, **11(4)**, [203]

summary of provisions, **11(4)**, [1]

trade unions, exemptions for, **11(4)**, [220]

approved regulators—

bodies as—

applications to Legal Services Board,
11(4), [333]

advice, publication of, **11(4)**, [333]

applicant, representations by,
11(4), [333]

consultees, information obtained by,
11(4), [333]

Consumer Panel, advice from,
regarding, **11(4)**, [333]

determination of, **11(4)**, [333]

grant of, **11(4)**, [333]

Lord Chief Justice, advice from,
regarding, **11(4)**, [333]

OFT, advice from, regarding,
11(4), [333]

orders designating, **11(4)**, [333]

cancellation of designation as,
11(4), [160]–[162], [342]

advice regarding—

Consumer Panel, from, **11(4)**, [342]

Legal Services Board's duty to seek,
11(4), [342]

Lord Chief Justice, from, **11(4)**, [342]

OFT, from, **11(4)**, [342]

publication of, **11(4)**, [342]

consultees—

advice from, **11(4)**, [342]

information obtained by, **11(4)**, [342]

decisions as to, **11(4)**, [342]

powers of entry, **11(4)**, [163]

representations by, **11(4)**, [342]

transfer arrangements, **11(4)**, [161]

warning notices, **11(4)**, [342]

censure of—

procedure for, **11(4)**, [151]

public, **11(4)**, [150], [151]

statement from Board, **11(4)**, [150]

Competition Commission—

duties of, **11(4)**, [175]

reports referred to, **11(4)**, [174]

directions to remedy failures—

advice—

Consumer Panel, from, **11(4)**, [339]

Legal Services Board's duty to seek,
11(4), [339]

Lord Chancellor, from, **11(4)**, [339]

Lord Chief Justice, from, **11(4)**, [339]

OFT, from, **11(4)**, [339]

publication of, **11(4)**, [339]

consultees—

advice from, **11(4)**, [339]

legal services—*contd*

approved regulators—*contd*

directions to remedy failures—*contd*

consultees—*contd*

information, power to request,
11(4), [339]

enforcement of, **11(4)**, [149]

Legal Services Board, from, **11(4)**, [147]

procedure, **11(4)**, [148], [339]

representations by, **11(4)**, [339]

warning notices to, **11(4)**, [339]

duties generally, **11(4)**, [143]

existing, **11(4)**, [332]

financial penalties for—

appeals against, **11(4)**, [154]

procedure, **11(4)**, [153]

recovery of, **11(4)**, [155]

rules as to, **11(4)**, [152]

functions—

modification of, **11(4)**, [184]

procedural requirements relating to,
11(4), [185]

immigration advice—

Immigration and Asylum Act 1999,
amendments to, **11(4)**, [363]

qualifying regulators, as, **11(4)**, [301],
[362]

applications to be, **11(4)**, [362]

consultation as to, **11(4)**, [362]

loss of status as, **11(4)**, [362]

representations as to, **11(4)**, [362]

transitional provisions, **11(4)**, [364]

information, duty to provide to Board,
11(4), [170], [171]

internal governance rules for, **11(4)**, [145]

intervention directions—

advice—

Consumer Panel, from, **11(4)**, [340]

Legal Services Board's duty to seek,
11(4), [340]

Lord Chancellor, from, **11(4)**, [340]

Lord Chief Justice, from, **11(4)**, [340]

OFT, from, **11(4)**, [340]

publication of, **11(4)**, [340]

circumstances in which Board may
give, **11(4)**, [156], [340]

consultees—

advice from, **11(4)**, [340]

information, power to request,
11(4), [340]

decisions of Legal Services Board,
11(4), [340]

enforcement, **11(4)**, [158]

meaning, **11(4)**, [156]

powers of entry under, **11(4)**, [157]

procedure for, **11(4)**, [156], [340]

representations by, **11(4)**, [340]

revocation of, **11(4)**, [159]

advice as to—

Consumer Panel, from,
11(4), [341]

Legal Services Board's duty to
seek, **11(4)**, [341]

Lord Chancellor, from,
11(4), [341]

legal services—*contd*
  approved regulators—*contd*
    intervention directions—*contd*
      revocation of—*contd*
        advice as to—*contd*
          Lord Chief Justice, from,
            11(4), [341]
          OFT, from, **11(4)**, [341]
          publication of, **11(4)**, [341]
        consultees—
          advice from, **11(4)**, [341]
          information obtained by,
            11(4), [341]
        decisions as to, **11(4)**, [341]
        representations by approved
          regulators, **11(4)**, [341]
        warning notices, **11(4)**, [340]
    Legal Services Board. *See* **Legal Services Board**
    licensing authority, designation as,
      11(4), [189], [343]
      cancellation of, **11(4)**, [190]–[192]
      Board's power to recommend,
        11(4), [193]
      powers of entry, **11(4)**, [194]
    meaning, **11(4)**, [135]
    OFT, reports by, **11(4)**, [172]
      Board's response to, **11(4)**, [173]
      Competition Commission, referral to,
        11(4), [174]
      Lord Chancellor's directions to Board
        following, **11(4)**, [176]
    performance targets, **11(4)**, [146]
    policy statements from Board—
      preparation of, **11(4)**, [164]
      procedure for issuing, **11(4)**, [165]
    practising fees—
      control of, **11(4)**, [166]
      meaning, **11(4)**, [166]
    professional principles, **11(4)**, [116]
    provisional designation as, **11(4)**, [140]
    regulated persons, duties in relation to,
      11(4), [291]
    regulation of, summary of provisions,
      11(4), [1]
    regulatory arrangements, alteration of—
      advice regarding, **11(4)**, [334]
      application to Legal Services Board,
        11(4), [334]
        decisions as to, **11(4)**, [334]
        grant of, **11(4)**, [334]
      approval of, **11(4)**, [334]
      initial determinations, **11(4)**, [334]
    regulatory conflict with—
      external, meaning, **11(4)**, [169]
      meaning, **11(4)**, [167]
      modification of provision made about,
        11(4), [168]
      other regulatory regimes, with,
        11(4), [169]
      prevention of, **11(4)**, [167], [218]
    regulatory functions—
      meaning, **11(4)**, [142]
      representative functions, separate from,
        11(4), [145]

legal services—*contd*
  approved regulators—*contd*
    regulatory functions—*contd*
      rules governing, **11(4)**, [145]
    regulatory objectives—
      guiding, **11(4)**, [116]
      promotion of, **11(4)**, [143]
    relevant, meaning, **11(4)**, [135]
    representative functions—
      interference from Board in, prohibition
        of, **11(4)**, [144]
      meaning, **11(4)**, [142]
      regulatory functions, separate from,
        11(4), [145]
    reserved legal activity, authorisation from to
      carry on, **11(4)**, [133]
  audience, right of—
    advocates and litigators employed by Legal
      Services Commission, **11(4)**, [536]
    barrister, of, **11(3)**, [86], [89]
    court's powers, **11(4)**, [307]
    employed advocates, **11(3)**, [90]
    general principle, **11(3)**, [77]
    housing management bodies, for employees
      of, **11(4)**, [306]
    Law Society, granted by, **11(3)**, [89]
    meaning, **11(4)**, [330]
    person having, determination of,
      11(3), [86]
    references to, **11(3)**, [125]; **11(4)**, [547]
    statutory duty, **11(3)**, [78]
    unauthorised practitioners, **11(3)**, [124]
    where existing, **11(3)**, [86]
  authorised bodies—
    application to be, **11(3)**, [149]
    change of, **11(3)**, [92]; **11(4)**, [537]
    designation of, **11(3)**, [87], [152], [278]
      revocation of, **11(3)**, [152]
    qualification regulations or rules of
      conduct, alteration of—
        approval of, **11(3)**, [150]
        order of Secretary of State, by,
          11(3), [151]
    regulations and rules, **11(3)**, [88]
      advocates and litigators employed by
        Legal Services Commission, for,
        11(3), [91]
      approval of, **11(3)**, [278]
      transitional provisions, **11(3)**, [311]
  Authorised Conveyancing Practitioners Board.
    See **Authorised Conveyancing
    Practitioners Board**
  Board. *See* **Legal Services Board**
  bodies corporate, offences by, **11(4)**, [311]
  claims management services—
    Compensation Act 2006, amendments to
      Part 2, **11(4)**, [365]
    reserved legal activity, treated as,
      11(4), [276]
  Commission. *See* **Legal Services
    Commission**
  Commissioners for Oaths, right to use title
    of, **11(4)**, [298]
  compensation arrangements, meaning,
    11(4), [136]

legal services—contd
  complaints—
    continuity of, **11(4)**, [247]
    Office for Legal Complaints. See **Office
      for Legal Complaints**
    ombudsman scheme. See under **Office for
      Legal Complaints**
    procedures, authorised persons, for,
      11(4), [227]
    scheme for dealing with, **11(4)**, [1], [228]
      claims management services, extension
        to, **11(4)**, [276]
      voluntary, **11(4)**, [279]
        operation of, **11(4)**, [281]
        orders as to, **11(4)**, [280]
  conditional fee agreements,
    11(3), [116]–[117], [311]; **11(4)**, [540], [541]
    conditions, **11(3)**, [116]; **11(4)**, [540]
    exempted proceedings, **11(3)**, [117];
      11(4), [541]
  consequential amendments, **11(3)**, [162];
    11(4), [576]
  Consolidated Fund, payments into,
    11(4), [290]
  Consultative Panel—
    appointment of persons to, **11(3)**, [79]
    duties, **11(3)**, [79]
    publication of recommendations and
      advice, **11(3)**, [79]
  conveyancing. See **conveyancing services**
  costs—
    insurance premiums by way of, recovery
      of, **11(3)**, [276]
    liabilities, recovery where body undertakes
      to meet, **11(3)**, [277]
  documents—
    electronic form, in, **11(4)**, [317]
    giving, **11(4)**, [316]
    meaning, **11(4)**, [315]
  General Council of the Bar. See **General
    Council of the Bar**
  judicial appointments, qualifications for,
    11(3), [125]; **11(4)**, [547]
  Law Society. See **Law Society**
  legal activity, meaning, **11(4)**, [127]
  legal professional privilege, **11(3)**, [121];
    11(4), [305]
  Legal Services Commission. See **Legal
    Services Commission**
  Legal Services Complaints Commissioner. See
    **Legal Services Complaints
    Commissioner**
  litigation—
    conduct of, meaning, **11(4)**, [330]
    funding agreements, **11(3)**, [118];
      11(4), [542]
    right to conduct, **11(3)**, [87]
      court's powers in relation to,
        11(4), [307]
      statutory duty, **11(3)**, [78]
  litigators—
    duties of, **11(4)**, [303]
    employed by Legal Services Commission,
      right of audience and to conduct
      litigation, **11(4)**, [536]

legal services—contd
  minor amendments, **11(3)**, [161];
    11(4), [366], [575]
  notary—
    ecclesiastical, Public Notaries Act,
      exemption from, **11(2)**, [4]
    public—
      Act, **11(2)**, [3]–[4], [52]–[56]
        exemptions from, **11(2)**, [4]
      admittance of, **11(2)**, [3]
      enrolment of, **11(2)**, [3]
      Master of Faculties—
        oath, power to issue commission to
          take, **11(2)**, [55]
        refusal to grant, **11(2)**, [53]
        testimonial of ability, requirement by,
          for, **11(2)**, [52]
      oath, **11(2)**, [54]
      unauthorised person practising as,
        offences and penalties, **11(2)**, [56]
  notices—
    electronic form, in, **11(4)**, [317]
    giving, **11(4)**, [316]
    writing, to be in, **11(4)**, [314]
  oaths, fees charged in administration of,
    11(4), [298]
  offences, **11(3)**, [124]
    bodies corporate, by, **11(4)**, [311]
    local weights and measures authorities,
      proceedings instituted by, **11(4)**, [312]
  Ombudsman. See **Legal Services
    Ombudsman**
  orders and regulations, parliamentary control
    of, **11(4)**, [320]
  pro bono representation, payments in respect
    of, **11(4)**, [309]
  regulated persons, duties of, **11(4)**, [291]
  regulations and orders, **11(3)**, [142];
    11(4), [564]
  regulatory arrangements, meaning,
    11(4), [136]
  regulatory objectives, **11(4)**, [116]
  repeals, **11(4)**, [368], [578]
  repeals and revocations, **11(3)**, [164], [315]
  reserved legal activity—
    additions to, **11(4)**, [139], [338]
    alteration of—
      advice as to, **11(4)**, [338]
      investigation by Legal Services Board—
        decision to hold, **11(4)**, [338]
        reports following, **11(4)**, [338]
        requests for, **11(4)**, [338]
        preliminary inquiries held by Legal
          Services Board, **11(4)**, [338]
    audience, rights of, **11(4)**, [330]
    authorisation to carry on, **11(4)**, [133]
      exempt persons, **11(4)**, [134], [331]
      employers acting through,
        11(4), [331]
      European lawyers, **11(4)**, [331]
      litigation, right to conduct,
        11(4), [331]
      notarial activities, **11(4)**, [331]
      oaths, administration of, **11(4)**, [331]
      probate activities, **11(4)**, [331]

legal services—*contd*
  reserved legal activity—*contd*
    authorisation to carry on—*contd*
      exempt persons—*contd*
        reserved instrument activities,
          11(4), [331]
        rights of audience, exercising,
          11(4), [331]
     authorised person—
      legal professional privilege, applied to
        communications from, **11(4)**, [305]
      licensable body as, **11(4)**, [133]
      meaning, **11(4)**, [133]
     carrying on—
      employees, by, **11(4)**, [130]
      employers, by, **11(4)**, [130]
      entitlement to, **11(4)**, [128]
        pretence of having, **11(4)**, [132]
      existing rights, continuity of,
        11(4), [137]
        audience, rights of, **11(4)**, [335]
        conveyancing services, **11(4)**, [335]
        transitional period, during,
          11(4), [336]
      non-commercial bodies, transitional
        protection for, **11(4)**, [138]
      offences, **11(4)**, [129], [131], [132]
      person not entitled, through,
        11(4), [131]
     ceasing to be, recommendations as to,
      11(4), [141], [338]
     claims management services, to be treated
      as, **11(4)**, [276]
     employees, references to, **11(4)**, [130]
     employers, references to, **11(4)**, [130]
     exempt persons, **11(4)**, [134]
     extension of, **11(4)**, [139], [338]
     litigation, conduct of, **11(4)**, [330]
     meaning, **11(4)**, [127]
     notarial activities, **11(4)**, [330]
     oaths, administration of, **11(4)**, [330]
     probate activities, **11(4)**, [330]
     provisional reserved activities, application to
      carry on, **11(4)**, [140]
     qualification regulations, **11(4)**, [136]
     regulatory arrangements, meaning,
      11(4), [136]
     reserved instrument activities, **11(4)**, [330]
     summary of provisions, **11(4)**, [1]
  rules—
    consultation requirements for, **11(4)**, [319]
    making, **11(4)**, [318]
  Scottish and Northern Ireland lawyers,
    practice in England and Wales, **11(3)**, [119];
    11(4), [543], [544]
  statutory duty, **11(3)**, [78]
  statutory objective, meaning, **11(3)**, [77]
  transitional provisions, **11(3)**, [163];
    11(4), [367], [577]

Legal Services Board
  accounts, **11(4)**, [329]
  annual report by, **11(4)**, [121], [225]
  application of seal, **11(4)**, [329]

Legal Services Board—*contd*
  approved regulators—
    designation as, **11(4)**, [177]
      cancellation of, **11(4)**, [180]
      circumstances for, **11(4)**, [178]
      effect of, **11(4)**, [182]
      modification of functions, **11(4)**, [179]
      regulatory conflict, and, **11(4)**, [183],
        [218]
    documents, duties as to, **11(4)**, [170]
    enforcement, **11(4)**, [171]
    information, duty to provide to,
      11(4), [170]
    enforcement, **11(4)**, [171]
  assistance to, arrangements for, **11(4)**, [329]
  borrowing money, **11(4)**, [329]
  chairman, **11(4)**, [329]
  Chief Executive, **11(4)**, [329]
  committees, **11(4)**, [329]
  Consolidated Fund, payments into,
    11(4), [290]
  Consumer Panel—
    advisory functions, **11(4)**, [126]
    chairman, **11(4)**, [123]
    committees, **11(4)**, [124]
    establishment of, **11(4)**, [123]
    members, **11(4)**, [123]
    procedure of, **11(4)**, [124]
    representations by, **11(4)**, [125]
    research functions, **11(4)**, [126]
  corporate governance, and, **11(4)**, [120]
  data protection, and, **11(4)**, [285]
  education and training—
    development of standards, **11(4)**, [119]
    maintenance of standards, **11(4)**, [119]
  expenditure, levy on approved regulators to
    fund, **11(4)**, [288], [289]
  functions—
    delegation of, **11(4)**, [329]
    generally, **11(4)**, [118]
  funding, **11(4)**, [287]
  guidance from, **11(4)**, [277]
  information—
    disclosure to, **11(4)**, [284]
    freedom of, **11(4)**, [329]
    restricted, **11(4)**, [282], [283]
    use of, **11(4)**, [286]
  liability in damages, exemption from,
    11(4), [329]
  members—
    number of, **11(4)**, [329]
    ordinary, **11(4)**, [329]
    remuneration of, **11(4)**, [329]
    tenure of, **11(4)**, [329]
    terms of appointment, **11(4)**, [329]
  notices—
    electronic form, in, **11(4)**, [317]
    giving, **11(4)**, [316]
    writing, to be in, **11(4)**, [314]
  Office for Legal Complaints, reporting from,
    11(4), [235]
  proceedings, **11(4)**, [329]
  proof of instruments, **11(4)**, [329]
  regulatory objectives—
    guided by, **11(4)**, [116]

Legal Services Board—*contd*
  regulatory objectives—*contd*
    promotion of, **11(4)**, [118]
  Solicitors Disciplinary Tribunal, directions to,
    power to give, **11(4)**, [294]
  staff, **11(4)**, [329]
  status, **11(4)**, [329]
  supplementary powers, **11(4)**, [122]
  voluntary arrangements, power to enter into,
    11(4), [278]

Legal Services Commission
  accounts, **11(3)**, [303]
  administration, funding of, **11(3)**, [303]
  advocates and litigators employed by,
    11(3), [91]
    rights of audience and to conduct
      litigation, **11(4)**, [536]
  annual plan, **11(3)**, [303]
  annual report, **11(3)**, [303]
  audit, **11(3)**, [303]
  Community Legal Service—
    disclosure of information, restriction of,
      11(3), [269]
    establishment of, **11(3)**, [252]
    excluded services, **11(3)**, [304]
    foreign law, **11(3)**, [268]
    funded services—
      code about provision of, **11(3)**, [256]
      costs in funded cases, **11(3)**, [259]
      generally, **11(3)**, [253]
      individuals for whom services may be
        funded, **11(3)**, [255]
      priority of, **11(3)**, [254]
      terms of provision of, **11(3)**, [258]
      ways of funding, **11(3)**, [254]
    funding of, **11(3)**, [252]–[253]
      code, procedure relating to, **11(3)**, [257]
    misrepresentation, **11(3)**, [270]
    replacement of Commission by,
      11(3), [250]
    service providers and other parties, position
      of, **11(3)**, [271]
  consequential amendments, **11(3)**, [273]
  constitution, **11(3)**, [249]
  Criminal Defence Service—
    advice and assistance, **11(3)**, [261]
    code of conduct, **11(3)**, [264]
    criminal proceedings, meaning,
      11(3), [260]
    disclosure of information, restriction of,
      11(3), [269]
    establishment of, **11(3)**, [260]
    foreign law, **11(3)**, [268]
    funded services—
      contribution towards, orders for,
        11(3), [266]
      terms of provision of, **11(3)**, [265]
    funding of, **11(3)**, [260], [267]
    misrepresentation, **11(3)**, [270]
    replacement of Commission by,
      11(3), [250]
    representation—
      contribution orders, **11(3)**, [266]
      generally, **11(3)**, [262]

Legal Services Commission—*contd*
  Criminal Defence Service—*contd*
    representation—*contd*
      right to—
        appeals, **11(3)**, [305]
        consequential amendments,
          11(3), [632]
        contribution orders, **11(3)**, [631]
        financial eligibility, **11(3)**, [630]
        grant of, **11(3)**, [305], [629]
        individual to whom may be granted,
          11(3), [305]
      representative, selection of, **11(3)**, [263]
      service providers and other parties,
        position of, **11(3)**, [271]
  defamation, not funding, **19(3)**, [261]
  functions, **11(3)**, [249]
  generally, **11(2)**, [1]
  guidance from Lord Chancellor, **11(3)**, [272]
  incorporation, **11(3)**, [303]
  information, provision of, **11(3)**, [303]
  instruments, **11(3)**, [303]
  interpretation provisions, **11(3)**, [275]
  members—
    remuneration, **11(3)**, [303]
    tenure of, **11(3)**, [303]
  membership, **11(3)**, [249]
  orders, regulations and directions, **11(3)**, [274]
  powers, **11(3)**, [251]
  proceedings, **11(3)**, [303]
  repeals and revocations, **11(3)**, [314]
  staff, **11(3)**, [303]
  status, **11(3)**, [303]
  transitional provisions, **11(3)**, [310]

Legal Services Complaints Commissioner
  abolition of, **11(4)**, [274]
  accounts, **11(3)**, [307]
  acting, **11(3)**, [307]
  annual and other reports, **11(3)**, [307]
  appointment of, **11(3)**, [285]
  audit, **11(3)**, [307]
  delegation of functions, **11(3)**, [307]
  discharge of functions, **11(3)**, [307]
  financial provisions, **11(3)**, [307]
  functions, **11(3)**, [285]
  generally, **11(2)**, [1]
  remuneration, **11(3)**, [307]
  staff, **11(3)**, [307]

Legal Services Consultative Panel
  generally, **11(2)**, [1]

Legal Services Ombudsman
  abolition of, **11(4)**, [274]
  accounts and audit, **11(3)**, [148]
  acting, appointment of, **11(3)**, [148]
  advisory functions, **11(3)**, [83]
  allegations—
    excluded investigations, **11(3)**, [81]
    investigation of, **11(3)**, [81]
    properly made, **11(3)**, [81]
  annual reports, **11(3)**, [148]
  appointment of, **11(3)**, [80]
  delegation of functions, **11(3)**, [148]

Legal Services Ombudsman—*contd*
directions for discharge of duties, **11(3)**, [148]
expenses, recovery of, **11(3)**, [82]
financial provisions, **11(3)**, [148]
functions of, **11(3)**, [81]
generally, **11(2)**, [1]
investigations—
allegations, of, **11(3)**, [81]
contempt of, **11(3)**, [84]
information, requiring, **11(3)**, [84]
witnesses, powers as to, **11(3)**, [84]
recommendations—
failure to comply with, **11(3)**, [82]
professional body, to, **11(3)**, [82]
reasons for, **11(3)**, [82]
report, in, **11(3)**, [82]
remit, extension of, **11(3)**, [85]
remuneration, **11(3)**, [148]
report—
conclusions, of, **11(3)**, [82]
generally, **11(3)**, [148]
privileged, **11(3)**, [82]
Scottish, **11(3)**, [81]; **11(4)**, [310]
staff, **11(3)**, [148]

legal tender. *See also* **coinage**
bank notes as, **19(1)**, [298]
unpresented note ceasing to be, writing
off, **19(1)**, [609]

legislation. *See also* **Parliament**
amendments, consequential, **22**, [563]
consolidating Acts—
meaning, **22**, [555]
references to corresponding provisions,
22, [556]
savings as to, **22**, [565]
transitional provisions, **22**, [564]
repealed—
continuity of law, **22**, [556]
schedule of, **22**, [561], [562]

legislative reform
order-making powers—
affirmative resolution procedure, **41**, [767]
burdens, power to reduce or remove,
41, [716], [751]
consultation, **41**, [763]
draft order and explanatory document,
laying before Parliament, **41**, [762], [764]
European Communities Act, combination
with powers under, **41**, [770]
negative resolution procedure, **41**, [766]
Parliamentary procedure, determination
of, **41**, [765]
regulatory principles, promotion of,
41, [751]
repeals, **41**, [772], [776]
restrictions—
criminal penalties—
as to, **41**, [756]
excepted enactments, **41**, [758]
forcible entry, compelling, **41**, [757]
giving of evidence, enforcing, **41**, [757]
Northern Ireland legislation, **41**, [760]

legislative reform—*contd*
order-making powers—*contd*
restrictions—*contd*
preconditions, **41**, [753]
Scottish Parliament, matters within
competence of, **41**, [759]
taxation provisions, **41**, [755]
Wales, relating to, **41**, [761]
statutory instruments, orders made by,
41, [762]
subordinate legislation, **41**, [754]
super-affirmative resolution procedure,
41, [768]
time periods, calculation of, **41**, [769]

legitimacy. *See also* **parentage**
declaration of—
application for, **6**, [264]
Attorney General, powers, **6**, [267]
effect of, **6**, [266]
making of, **6**, [266]
supplementary provisions, **6**, [268]
non-marital birth, provisions as to,
18, [665]–[667]
presumption of rebuttal, **18**, [218]
proceedings, restriction of publicity for,
27, [340]

legitimation
adopted child, of, **6**, [1], [159]
adoption order, revocation of, **6**, [159]
child of void marriage, **6**, [1], [156]
death before, **6**, [160]
disposition of property—
date of birth, dependent on, **6**, [161]
effect on, **6**, [160]
meaning, **6**, [165]
personal representatives, protection of,
6, [162]
trustees, protection of, **6**, [162]
extraneous law, by, **6**, [158]
generally, **6**, [1]
personal rights and obligations, effect on,
6, [1], [163]
property interests, effect on, **6**, [160]
re-registration of birth, **6**, [164]; **36**, [86]
service departments, persons in, registration of
births, **36**, [147]
status after, **6**, [277]
subsequent marriage of parents by, **6**, [1],
[157], [164]
void marriage—
belief that marriage valid, **6**, [156]
child of, **6**, [156]

Lesotho
Commonwealth citizenship, **31**, [186]
existing law, operation of, **7(2)**, [597]
kingdom, establishment of, **7(2)**, [596]
visiting forces in, **7(2)**, [599]

lessee
meaning, **20**, [498]

lessor
  meaning, **20**, [498]

letters
  carriage etc. *See* **post office**
  interception. *See* **communications**

Letters Mandatory
  procedure for issuing, **14**, 831–2

letters of administration
  application for, **18**, [632]
    false or misleading statement in, **18**, [671]
  British possession, granted in, **18**, [508], [510]
  colonial, sealing in UK, **18**, [507], [595]
  Commonwealth, sealing of, **18**, [595]
  failure to take out, **18**, [453]
  meaning, **18**, [671], [673]
  Northern Ireland, granted in, recognition of, **18**, [589]
  oaths and affidavits, administration or taking of, **18**, [673]
  preparation of, unqualified persons, by, bar on **11(2)**, [302]
  recognition in England, **18**, [587]

Letters Patent
  claim of, **10**, [22]
  companies, as to. *See* **chartered company**
  income tax liability, **44(4)**, [852]

Letters Testimonial
  procedure for exhibiting, **14**, 831–2

level crossing. *See also* **rail crossing**
  appeal against consent to, **36**, [313]
  approaches, duties as to, **36**, [314], [315]
  barriers, contributions to expenses of, **36**, [861]
  bridge, Secretary of State requiring, **36**, [441]
  fences, provision of, **36**, [314], [315]
  gates—
    closed, kept, **36**, [300]
    generally, **36**, [210]
    maintenance of, **36**, [223]
    provision of, **36**, [223], [300], [314], [315]
    railway, kept closed across, **36**, [625]
    roads, closed across, **36**, [238]
  justices' consent to, **36**, [312], [313]
  lodge, duty to erect, **36**, [440]
  modernisation of, **36**, [210]
  orders, delegation of power to make, **38(2)**, [526]
  power to make, **36**, [299]
  private, barriers at, **36**, [210]
  safety orders, **37**, [163]
  station, adjoining, **36**, [301]
  stile, provision of, **36**, [314], [315]
  train—
    approaching speed of, **36**, [625]
    shunted over, not to be, **36**, [439]

libel. *See also* **defamation**
  actions—
    consolidation, **19(3)**, [303], [318]

libel—*contd*
  actions—*contd*
    defence of justification, **19(3)**, [312]
    law Officers, commencement by, **19(3)**, [283]
    parties, interpretation of terms, **19(3)**, [278]
  agent, publication by, **19(3)**, [277]
  amends, offer of, **19(3)**, [311], [329]
    acceptance of, **19(3)**, [330]
    failure to accept, **19(3)**, [331]
    payment into court as, **19(3)**, [280]
  apology for, **19(3)**, [311]
    mitigation of damages, **19(3)**, [272]
  author, meaning, **19(3)**, [328]
  blasphemous—
    abolition of common law offence, **12(4)**, [509]
    copies—
      disposal of, **19(3)**, [267]
      order for seizure, **19(3)**, [266]
      restoration, where arrest of judgment, **19(3)**, [267]
  broadcasting, **19(3)**, [324]
    extension of defences, **19(3)**, [314]
  civil proceedings, **19(3)**, [261]
  claim, summary disposal of—
    Northern Ireland, **19(3)**, [336]
    power of, **19(3)**, [333]
    rules of court, **19(3)**, [335]
    summary relief, meaning, **19(3)**, [334]
  company or association meetings, report of proceedings, **19(3)**, [346]
  criminal proceedings—
    arrest of judgment, defendant's right, **19(3)**, [265]
    judge, directions to jury, **19(3)**, [263]
    jury—
      functions, **19(3)**, [262]
      general verdict, **19(3)**, [262]
      special verdict, **19(3)**, [264]
      trial by, **19(3)**, [261]
    remedy in, **19(3)**, [261]
  damages—
    actions for same libel, in case of, **19(3)**, [317]
    consolidation of actions, assessment in, **19(3)**, [303]
    evidence in mitigation, **19(3)**, [317]
    mitigation of, apology, **19(3)**, [272]
  editor, meaning, **19(3)**, [328]
  elections, limitation on privilege, **19(3)**, [315]
  evidence, **19(3)**, [261]
  fair comment, defence of, **19(3)**, [313]
  film sound track, defamatory words in, **19(3)**, [261]
  indemnity, agreements firm, **19(3)**, [316]
  justification, defence of, **19(3)**, [312]
  known to be false, publication, **19(3)**, [274]
  limitation of actions—
    discretionary exclusion of, **19(3)**, [763]
    generally, **19(3)**, [261]
    period, **19(3)**, [728]
  local authority proceedings, reports, **19(3)**, [346]

libel—*contd*
local government election candidate, of,
19(3), [315]
malice, publication without, **19(3)**, [273]
malicious, penalties, **19(3)**, [275]
negligence, publication in newspaper
without, **19(3)**, [273]
newspaper—
action against—
apology, effect of, **19(3)**, [273]
defence, **19(3)**, [273]
institution of, judge's order for,
19(3), [304]
bodies and persons, privileged, **19(3)**, [302]
copies, retention of, **19(3)**, [283]
discovery of proprietor, printer, etc,
19(3), [283]
proprietor, prosecution of, **19(3)**, [304]
public benefit, for, inquiry, **19(3)**, [285]
public meetings, privileged reports of
proceedings, **19(3)**, [302]
truth, evidence of, **19(3)**, [285]
parliamentary election candidate, of,
19(3), [315]
parliamentary papers—
absolute privilege, **19(3)**, [268]
abstract, printing of, **19(3)**, [270]
authenticated reports, **19(3)**, [269]
broadcasting, **19(3)**, [314]
exemption, **19(3)**, [283]
extracts, printing of, **19(3)**, [270]
payment into court, **19(3)**, [280]
penalties, recovery and application,
19(3), [283]
printer's imprint—
exemptions and relaxations, **19(3)**, [283],
[322]
failure to print, penalties, **19(3)**, [283]
university presses, in case of, **19(3)**, [283]
privilege—
absolute, parliamentary papers, **19(3)**, [271]
court proceedings, reports of, **19(3)**, [338]
elections, limitation in case of, **19(3)**, [315]
National Assembly for Wales, statements
in, **19(3)**, [261]
Northern Ireland Assembly, statements in,
19(3), [261]
parliamentary papers, **19(3)**, [268]–[271],
[314]
public meetings and proceedings,
19(3), [302]
qualified, reports protected by,
19(3), [339], [345]–[347]
Scottish Parliament, statements in,
19(3), [261]
statutory, **19(3)**, [261], [338]
subject to explanation or contradiction,
19(3), [346]
proceedings in Parliament, evidence
concerning, **19(3)**, [337]
publication—
meaning, **19(3)**, [341]
responsibility for, **19(3)**, [328]
without authority or consent, **19(3)**, [277]
publisher, meaning, **19(3)**, [328]

libel—*contd*
rehabilitation of offenders, effect on action,
12(1), [637]
seditious copies—
disposal, **19(3)**, [267]
restoration, where arrest of judgment,
19(3), [267]
slander distinguished, **19(3)**, [261]
statutes, summary of, **19(3)**, [261]
truth of—
defence, as, **19(3)**, [276]
evidence of, **19(3)**, [285]
inquiry into, **19(3)**, [276]
unintentional defamation, **19(3)**, [311]

libraries. See also **British Library; legal
deposit libraries; public library**
assistance for, **26(1)**, [721]
books, notifiable diseases, provisions as to,
35(1), [466]
summary of provisions, **13**, [49]

licence. See also *particular subject matters of
licensing*
Archbishop of Canterbury, granted by,
14, 28–9
Archbishop of York, granted by, **14**, 33
bishop, granted by, **14**, 33
charges for, **14**, 31–2
children, legitimacy of, **14**, 28–9
cocoa beans and products, to import,
13, [564]
confirmation and enrolment of, **14**, 28–9
excise. See **excise licence**
importation or exportation of certain animals
and plants, for, **13**, [566] See also **animals;
plants**
near beer. See **London**
night cafe. See **London**
refusal to grant, appeal from, **14**, 34–5
registration of, **14**, 30
sale, etc, of certain animals and plants, for,
13, [569] See also **animals; plants**
street trading in. See **London**
tax paid for, applying, **14**, 32–3
two prelates, grant by, **14**, 34–5
uncleared goods, to move, **13**, [613]
vacancy in see, during, **14**, 33

licences. See **driving licence; motor vehicles
and under specific type of vehicle**

licensed conveyancer
Administration of Justice Act 1985,
amendments to, **11(4)**, [360]
body corporate—
offences, **11(3)**, [29]; **11(4)**, [503]
penalties, **11(3)**, [29]; **11(4)**, [503]
pretending to be, for, **11(3)**, [28]
provision of services by, **11(3)**, [25]
supplementary provisions, **11(3)**, [49]
conveyancing services bodies—
management and control of,
11(4), [497]–[498]
meaning, **11(4)**, [498]

licensed conveyancer—*contd*
  conveyancing services bodies—*contd*
    provision of services by, **11(4)**, [497]
    supplementary provisions, **11(4)**, [523]
  Courts and Legal Services Act 1990,
    amendments to, **11(4)**, [361]
  disciplinary cases, proceedings in, **11(3)**, [19];
    11(4), [491]
  documents, service of, **11(3)**, [30];
    11(4), [504]
  existing enactments, modification of,
    11(3), [27]; **11(4)**, [501]
  legal professional privilege, **11(3)**, [26];
    11(4), [499]
  licence—
    additional fee for certain, **11(4)**, [479]
    application for, **11(3)**, [7]; **11(4)**, [476]
    conditions, **11(3)**, [9]; **11(4)**, [478]
      imposition of, during currency, of,
        11(3), [10]; **11(4)**, [480]
      variation of, **11(4)**, [481]
    disqualification from holding, removal of,
      11(3), [20]; **11(4)**, [492]
    issue of, **11(3)**, [8]; **11(4)**, [477]
    revocation of, **11(3)**, [21]; **11(4)**, [493]
    suspension of, **11(3)**, [11]; **11(4)**, [482]
    termination of, **11(3)**, [11]; **11(4)**, [482]
  meaning, **11(3)**, [4]; **11(4)**, [473]
  oaths, administration of, by, **11(4)**, [500]
  offences, **11(3)**, [28]–[29]; **11(4)**, [503]
  penalties, **11(3)**, [29]; **11(4)**, [503]
    pretending to be, for, **11(3)**, [28];
      11(4), [502]
  practice of, intervention by Council,
    11(3), [24]; **11(4)**, [496]
  register of, **11(3)**, [12]; **11(4)**, [483]
  rules—
    accounts, keeping and establishment of, as
      to, **11(3)**, [15]; **11(4)**, [486]
    compensation, as to, **11(3)**, [14];
      11(4), [485]
    interest on client money, as to, **11(3)**, [16];
      11(4), [487]
    professional indemnity, as to, **11(3)**, [14];
      11(4), [485]
    training, of, as to, **11(3)**, [6]; **11(4)**, [475]
  services, provision of, by, **11(3)**, [4];
    11(4), [473]

licensed premises. *See* **intoxicating liquor**

Licensed Trade Charities Trust
  transfer of compensation fund to, **19(3)**, [452]

licensed water suppliers
  domestic supply by, **49**, [835]
  non-domestic supply by, **49**, [836]
  prohibition on unauthorised introduction of
    water, **49**, [851]
  unauthorised use of supply system, **49**, [850]
  licensing of, **49**, [1402]
    conditions, **49**, [739]–[740]
      financial penalties for contravention of—
        appeals, **49**, [760]
        generally, **49**, [756]

licensed water suppliers—*contd*
  licensing of—*contd*
    conditions—*contd*
      financial penalties for contravention
        of—*contd*
        interest and payment of instalments,
          49, [759]
        recovery of, **49**, [761]
        statement of policy with respect to,
          49, [757]
        time limits on imposition, **49**, [758]
    determinations by Authority, **49**, [737]
    granting of, **49**, [733]
    household premises, meaning of, **49**, [735]
    minor and consequential amendments,
      49, [1408]
    modification of—
      agreement, by, **49**, [741]
      by order under other enactments,
        49, [750]
      following report, **49**, [747]
      references to Competition Commission,
        49, [743]–[746]
      standard conditions, **49**, [742]
      veto following report, Commission's
        power of, **49**, [748]
    procedure for granting, **49**, [738]
    requirements, **49**, [733]
    supplementary, **49**, [734]
    threshold requirement, **49**, [736]

licensing justices. *See under* **intoxicating liquor**

lien
  acquisition of property subject to, **9**, [133]
  London port rates, for, **39(2)**, [264]
  property subject to, requisition during
    emergency, **9**, [133]

Lieutenant Governors
  citizenship, exercise of functions as to,
    31, [173]

life annuity
  purchased, self-assessment, **43(S)**, 542

life assurance. *See also, generally,* **insurance**
  amount recoverable by insured, **19(1)**, [7]
  business. *See* **life assurance business**
  company—
    meaning, **19(1)**, [142]
    payment into court, **19(1)**, [143]
      proper officer, receipt of, **19(1)**, [144]
    See also **insurance company**
  gains, rate of tax on, **43(2)**, [234]
  goods or merchandise, exclusion as to,
    19(1), [8]
  group policies, validation of, **19(1)**, [446]
  insurable interest, requirement for, **19(1)**, [5]
  personal portfolio bonds—
    annual calculation—
      gains, showing, **44(3)**, [533]
      method for making, **44(3)**, [530]
      requirement for, **44(3)**, [523]

life assurance—*contd*
  personal portfolio bonds—*contd*
    excess, total amount of, **44(3)**, [531]
    index categories, **44(3)**, [526]
    index selection conditions, **44(3)**, [527]
    meaning, **44(3)**, [524]
    part surrender gains, total amount of,
      44(3), [532]
    policies and contracts not being,
      44(3), [525]
    property categories, **44(3)**, [528]
    property selection conditions, **44(3)**, [529]
    regulations, power to make, **44(3)**, [534]
  policies and contracts, gains arising from—
    application of provisions to, **44(3)**, [481]
    assignment—
      chargeable events, calculations showing
        gains, **44(3)**, [517]
      co-ownership, involving, **44(3)**, [513]
      co-ownership transactions, on,
        44(3), [514]
      final insurance year, in, **44(3)**, [521]
      periodic calculations, **44(3)**, [506], [515]
      transaction-related calculations,
        44(3), [518]–[522]
      value of rights, **44(3)**, [516]
    calculation of gain—
      company debts, policies held as security
        for, **44(3)**, [504]
      disregarded amounts, **44(3)**, [503]
      general rules, **44(3)**, [499]
      total allowable deductions, **44(3)**, [502]
      total benefit value, **44(3)**, [500]
      trivial inducement benefits, disregard of,
        44(3), [505]
      value of policy or contract, **44(3)**, [501]
    charge to tax, **44(3)**, [468]
    chargeable events—
      alteration of terms, events after,
        44(3), [496]
      assignments disregarded, **44(3)**, [495]
      disregarded, **44(3)**, [493]
      maturity of capital redemption policies,
        exclusion, **44(3)**, [494]
      occurrence of, **44(3)**, [492]
    companies interested, where, **44(3)**, [554]
    credit union group policies, exclusion of,
      44(3), [491]
    deficiencies—
      calculation of, **44(3)**, [549]
      events following calculation events,
        44(3), [548]
      relief for, **44(3)**, [547]
    definitions, **44(3)**, [555]
    European Economic Area insurers, with—
      comparable EEA charge, meaning,
        44(3), [541]
      relief for, **44(3)**, [540]
    excepted group life policies—
      benefits, conditions about, **44(3)**, [489]
      exclusion of, **44(3)**, [488]
      persons entitled to benefit, conditions
        about, **44(3)**, [490]
    foreign tax chargeable, relief for,
      44(3), [542]

life assurance—*contd*
  policies and contracts, gains arising
  from—*contd*
    income charged, **44(3)**, [470]
    income tax treated as paid,
      44(3), [538]–[539]
    insurance year, definitions, **44(3)**, [507]
    last payment under guaranteed income
      bonds, **44(3)**, [498]
    mortgage repayment policies, exclusion of,
      44(3), [486]
    part surrender—
      chargeable events, calculations showing
        gains, **44(3)**, [517]
      events treated as, **44(3)**, [508]
      final insurance year, in, **44(3)**, [521]
      guaranteed income bonds, payments
        under, **44(3)**, [512]
      life annuity, loan to buy, **44(3)**, [510]
      loans, **44(3)**, [509]
      periodic calculations, **44(3)**, [506], [515]
      qualifying policies, loans under,
        44(3), [511]
      transaction-related calculations,
        44(3), [518]–[522]
      value of rights, **44(3)**, [516]
    pension policies, exclusion of, **44(3)**, [487]
    person liable—
      amounts liable treated as highest part of
        total income, **44(3)**, [473]
      foreign institutions, **44(3)**, [476]
      individuals, **44(3)**, [472]
      introduction to provisions, **44(3)**, [471]
      non-UK resident trustees, **44(3)**, [476]
      personal representatives, **44(3)**, [474]
      UK resident trustees, **44(3)**, [475]
    personal portfolio bonds. *See* personal
      portfolio bonds *above*
    policy terms, alteration of—
      conditions applicable to, **44(3)**, [497]
      disregard of events after, **44(3)**, [496]
    qualifying policies—
      replacement of, **44(3)**, [552]
      replacing foreign policy, issue time of,
        44(3), [553]
    rebated commission, effect of,
      44(3), [550]–[551]
    reduction from, **44(3)**, [535]–[537]
    reinvested commission, effect of,
      44(3), [550]–[551]
    shares and rights, determination of,
      44(3), [479]
    special rules—
      foreign policies, **44(3)**, [484]
      older policies and contracts,
        44(3), [485], [556]
      personal portfolio bonds, **44(3)**, [483]
      qualifying policies, **44(3)**, [482]
    top slicing relief, **44(3)**, [543]
    top slicing relieved liability—
      one chargeable event, **44(3)**, [544]
      two or more chargeable events,
        44(3), [545]
    trustees, recovery of tax from, **44(3)**, [546]

life assurance—*contd*

policies and contracts, gains arising
from—*contd*
two or more persons interested in,
44(3), [477]–[478]
two or more persons, trusts created by,
44(3), [480]
when arising, **44(3)**, [469]
policy—
action on, equitable defence, **19(1)**, [22]
assignees, suing by, **19(1)**, [21]
assignment—
acknowledgment of notices, **19(1)**, [26]
mode of, **19(1)**, [25], [30]
notice of, **19(1)**, [23]
company's office to be stated, **19(1)**, [24]
gains arising from. *See* **life assurance**
meaning, **19(1)**, [27]
names to be inserted, **19(1)**, [6]
place of business specified in, **19(1)**, [24]
savings as to certain contracts, **19(1)**, [28]
servicemen, protection. *See* **civil interests
of servicemen**
premium contributions—
amended provisions, commencement,
43(S), 697–9
meaning, **43(S)**, 696–7
relievable pensions contributions, not to
be, **43(S)**, 696
ship etc, exclusion as to, **19(1)**, [8]
unnamed person, for benefit of, **19(1)**, [446]

life assurance business

apportionment—
business transfer-in, **44(1)**, [259]
income and gains, of, **44(1)**, [252]
non-participating funds, net amount,
44(1), [256]
participating funds, **44(1)**, [257]
receipts brought into account, **44(1)**, [255]
reduction of amount, **44(1)**, [258]
basic, meaning, **44(1)**, [247]
basis of taxation, **43(S)**, 629
BLAGAB group reinsurers—
Corporation Tax Acts, modification of
provisions for, **44(1)**, [654]–[656]
meaning, **44(1)**, [654]
child trust fund business, meaning,
44(1), [241]
companies carrying on, **43(1)**, [129]
demutualisation surplus, **44(1)**, [291]
relevant receipts reduction, **44(1)**, [295]
unappropriated surplus—
meaning, **44(1)**, [297]
reduction in, **44(1)**, [294]
expenses, allocation of computations under
Case I Schedule D, **44(1)**, [571]
gross roll-up business—
gains non-chargeable, **44(1)**, [263]
meaning, **44(1)**, [246]
mutual surplus, **44(1)**, [296]
relevant receipts reduction, **44(1)**, [295]
profits, separate charge on, **44(1)**, [262]
individual savings account business, meaning,
44(1), [242]

life assurance business—*contd*

losses, **43(1)**, [265]
meaning, **44(1)**, [237]
overseas—
double taxation relief, restriction of,
44(1), [568]
meaning, **44(1)**, [244]
regulations, **44(1)**, [245]
UK companies, of, **44(1)**, [272]
reinsurance business—
meaning, **44(1)**, [243]
risk reinsured, taxation of risk where,
44(1), [273]
Schedule D Case I, tax charged under,
44(1), [248], [249], [269], [270]
transfer of, **43(1)**, [130]
transfers of business, **44(1)**, [274]
anti-avoidance rule, **44(1)**, [284], [287]
assets—
relevant non-transferred, **44(1)**, [278]
retained, **44(1)**, [279]
clearance by HMRC Commissioners,
44(1), [290]
deemed periodical return, **44(1)**, [276]
demutualisation transfer surplus,
44(1), [292], [293]
FAFTS, **44(1)**, [283]
no avoidance or group advantage,
44(1), [290]
transferee—
Case I advantage, **44(1)**, [286], [289]
reduction of income of, **44(1)**, [282]
transferor—
Case I advantage, **44(1)**, [285], [288]
Case I losses, **44(1)**, [276]
Case VI losses, **44(1)**, [275]
conditions on, **44(1)**, [277]
election for transferee to pay tax of,
44(1), [280]
period if account including transfer,
44(1), [281]

life assurance relief

endowment, **44(1)**, [644]
family income policy, **44(1)**, [644]
friendly society policy, **44(1)**, [642], [644]
industrial assurance policy, **44(1)**, [642], [644]
mortgage protection policy, **44(1)**, [644]
premium—
civil partners, **44(1)**, [642]
employer, paid by, **44(1)**, [158]
husband and wife, **44(1)**, [642]
limit on, **44(1)**, [166]
non-resident, relief for, **44(1)**, [157]
not qualifying for relief, **44(1)**, [157]
qualifying policies, **44(1)**, [159]
regulations, **44(1)**, [643]
relief for, **44(1)**, [157], [643]
short-term, **44(1)**, [644]
term, **44(1)**, [644]
whole life, **44(1)**, [644]

life insurance
payments for, relief for—
family members, for benefit of,
44(4), [467]
police organisations, to, **44(4)**, [466]
residence of claimants, **44(4)**, [468]
trade unions, to, **44(4)**, [465]

life insurance contract
losses from, no loss relief for, **43(S)**, 1398

life insurance policy
civil partner, for benefit of, **27**, [766]
Northern Ireland, **27**, [833]
exceptional risk of disability, charges for,
43(2), [233]
gain on maturity, rollover into new policy,
43(2), [268]
group, amended provisions, **43(2)**, [267]

life policy
early conversion or surrender, effect of,
44(1), [160], [162]
foreign, **43(1)**, [169]
four years, surrender or falling due after,
44(1), [161]
insurers, information given by, **44(1)**, [385],
[386]
mortgage, securing, **44(1)**, [157]
non-resident, **44(1)**, [646]
overseas, insurers, tax representatives for,
44(1), [387], [388]
premium—
employer, paid by, **44(1)**, [158]
relief for, **44(1)**, [157], [159]
protection of. *See* **civil interests of
servicemen**
qualifying, **43(1)**, [132]
additional, **44(1)**, [644]
certification of, **44(1)**, [645]
conditions, **44(1)**, [644]
connected policies, **44(1)**, [644]
exceptional mortality risk, **44(1)**, [644]
personal accident, **44(1)**, [644]
substituted, **44(1)**, [644]
sums due under previous policies,
premiums from, **44(1)**, [644]
variation of, **44(1)**, [644]
rebated or reinvested commission, effect of,
43(S), 527–9
relevant excepted benefit, **43(1)**, [282]
relevant meaning, **43(1)**, [282]
substitution of, **44(1)**, [643]
surrender—
collection of sums due, **44(1)**, [164]
deemed, **44(1)**, [163]
early, **44(1)**, [160], [162]
four years, after, **44(1)**, [161]
variation of, **44(1)**, [643]

lifeboat
fuel for, repayment of duty on, **13**, [843],
[857], [869], [898]

light
access and use—
obstruction of—
registration of notice in lieu of—
application for, **21**, [253]
Crown land, **21**, [255]
effect of, **21**, [254]
interpretation of terms, **21**, [257]
proceedings, **21**, [254]
rules, power to make, **21**, [256]
right to—
prescriptive period for claiming—
infant or other person under disability,
in case of, **20**, [67]
interruption to, **20**, [63]
pleadings, **20**, [65]
presumption, restricting, **20**, [66]
twenty years' enjoyment, **20**, [63]

light goods vehicle
vehicle excise duty, **13**, [1041]

light passenger vehicle. *See also* **passenger
transports service**
vehicle excise duty, **13**, [1040]

lighter
unsafe, use of, **39(2)**, [763]

lighthouse
additions to, **39(2)**, [875]
areas, **39(2)**, [871]
authority—
bodies being, **39(2)**, [871]
general—
accounts, **39(2)**, [895]
bodies being, **39(2)**, [871]
borrowing powers, **39(2)**, [892], [893]
disclosure of information to,
39(2), [900]
establishments, **39(2)**, [889]
expenses, **39(2)**, [890]
General Lighthouse Fund, sums paid
from, **39(2)**, [888]
light dues, **39(2)**, [882]
ships, exemption from harbour dues,
39(2), [899]
harbour dues, exemption from,
39(2), [899]
joint discharge of functions, **39(2)**, [874]
land, powers as to, **39(2)**, [875]
local—
bodies being, **39(2)**, [871]
harbour authorities, powers of,
39(2), [879]
light dues, **39(2)**, [177], [220]
meaning, **39(2)**, [200]
local authority, controlling, **39(2)**, [877]
management, general function of,
39(2), [873]
powers of, **39(2)**, [875]
property, holding, **39(2)**, [873]
removal of wreck by, **39(2)**, [931]
returns by, **39(2)**, [872]

lighthouse—*contd*
Commissioners of Northern Lighthouses, body of, **39(2)**, [1004]
damage to, **39(2)**, [896]
erection, sanction required for, **39(2)**, [75]
expenses, payment of, **39(2)**, [888]
false lights, prevention of, **39(2)**, [897]
General Lighthouse Fund. *See* **General Lighthouse Fund**
inspection of, **39(2)**, [876]
light dues—
   application of, **39(2)**, [887]
   collection of, **39(2)**, [882]
   distress for, **39(2)**, [885]
   general, levy of, **39(2)**, [882]
   general lighthouse authorities, leviable by, **39(2)**, [882]
   information to determine, **39(2)**, [883]
   local, **39(2)**, [887]
      objections, **39(2)**, [1005]
   payment of, **39(2)**, [887]
   receipt for, **39(2)**, [886]
   recovery of, **39(2)**, [884]
   regulations, inspection of, **39(2)**, [882]
local, harbour authorities, individual transfers to, **39(2)**, [880]
meaning, **39(2)**, [901]
Secretary of State—
   guarantees by, **39(2)**, [894]
   power of inspection by, **39(2)**, [878]
summary of provisions, **39(2)**, [1]
surrender of, **39(2)**, [881]
taxes, duties and rates, exemption from, **39(2)**, [896]

lighthouse authority
civil aviation, protection of rights etc arising from, **4(1)**, [176]
local light dues, **39(2)**, [177], [220]
local, meaning, **39(2)**, [200]

limestone pavement
orders, procedure in connection with, **32**, [508]
power of entry, **32**, [478]
preservation of, **32**, [1], [462]
protection of, **32**, [508]

limitation of action
account, action for, **19(3)**, [751]
acknowledgment—
   effect on third parties, **19(3)**, [761]
   formal provisions on, **19(3)**, [760]
   fresh accrual of action on, **19(3)**, [759]
action, meaning, **19(3)**, [720], [768]
assurance, disentailing, **19(3)**, [754]
award, enforcement of, **19(3)**, [731]
breach of duty, in case of, **19(3)**, [735]
building society proceedings, **19(1)**, [716]
charge, recovery of money secured by, **19(3)**, [748]
commonhold duty, breach of, **19(3)**, [747]
concealment, postponement in case of, **19(3)**, [762]
contract, **19(3)**, [729]

limitation of action—*contd*
contribution, claiming, **19(3)**, [734]
Crown—
   application of provisions, **19(3)**, [721], [767]
   recovery of land, involvement in, **19(3)**, [773]
damage, recovery of contribution in respect of, **19(3)**, [734]
deceased person, claiming personal estate of, **19(3)**, [750]
defamation action—
   discretionary exclusion of, **19(3)**, [763]
   period, **19(3)**, [728]
defective products. *See* **consumer protection**
disability, extension in case of, **19(3)**, [757]
Duchy of Cornwall, application of provisions, **19(3)**, [767]
Duchy of Lancaster, application of provisions, **19(3)**, [767]
enactments as to, saving, **19(3)**, [769]
enemy—
   Crown, application of provisions to, **19(3)**, [721]
   meaning, **19(3)**, [720]
   Northern Ireland, application of provisions to, **19(3)**, [722]
   suspension of period in case of, **19(3)**, [719]
enemy territory—
   meaning, **19(3)**, [720]
   prisoners of war, suspension of period in case of, **19(3)**, [719]
enforcement of judgment, for, **19(3)**, [752]
equitable relief, claims for, **19(3)**, [766]
external order, recovery of property for purposes of, **19(3)**, [756]
fatal accidents, **19(3)**, [737]–[739], [764]
foreign limitation law—
   application—
      Crown and Duchies, to, **19(3)**, [780]
      exceptions, **19(3)**, [777]
      generally, **19(3)**, [776]
      public policy, conflicting with, **19(3)**, [777]
   foreign judgments on, **19(3)**, [778]
   meaning, **19(3)**, [779]
   summary of provisions, **19(3)**, [718]
fraud, postponement in case of, **19(3)**, [762]
government departments, application of provisions, **19(3)**, [767]
infant, persons regarded as being under disability, **19(3)**, [768]
judgment debt, recovery of, **19(3)**, [752]
land. *See* **land**
latent damage. *See* negligence *below*
law relating to, meaning, **19(3)**, [779]
libel action—
   discretionary exclusion of, **19(3)**, [763]
   generally, **19(3)**, [261]
   period, **19(3)**, [728]
loans, special limit for, **19(3)**, [730]
malicious falsehood, action for—
   discretionary exclusion of, **19(3)**, [763]
   period, **19(3)**, [728]

limitation of action—*contd*
mistake, postponement in case of,
  19(3), [762]
mortgage, recovery of money secured by,
  19(3), [748]
mortgagee, against, **19(3)**, [743]
negligence, in case of—
  cause not known at date of accrual,
    19(3), [740], [758]
  extension of time, **19(3)**, [758]
  personal injury, involving, **19(3)**, [735]
  personal injury, not involving—
    overriding time limit, **19(3)**, [741]
    relevant facts not known at time,
      19(3), [740]
    special time limit, **19(3)**, [741]
  property, to, **19(3)**, [783]
  special time limit, **19(3)**, [740]
  summary of provisions, **19(3)**, [718]
  transitional provisions, **19(3)**, [784]
nuisance, in case of, **19(3)**, [735]
part payment—
  effect on third parties, **19(3)**, [761]
  formal provisions, **19(3)**, [760]
  fresh accrual of action, **19(3)**, [759]
pending actions, new claims in, **19(3)**, [765]
period of limitation—
  actions for mistake relating to direct tax,
    for, **43(S)**, 583
  extension—
    disability, in case of, **19(3)**, [757]
    foreign law, where disregarded,
      19(3), [777]
    generally, **19(3)**, [718], [724]
    libel or slander action, **19(3)**, [763]
    malicious falsehood action, **19(3)**, [763]
  foreign law, under. *See* foreign limitation
    law *above*
  generally, **19(3)**, [724]
  ordinary time limits, **19(3)**, [718]
  special time limit—
    contribution, claiming, **19(3)**, [734]
    fatal accidents, **19(3)**, [737]–[739]
    loans, **19(3)**, [730]
    personal injury actions, **19(3)**, [735]
    speciality, action on, **19(3)**, [732]
    theft, **19(3)**, [727]
  sums recoverable by statute, where,
    19(3), [733]
  suspension—
    enemy or person detained in enemy
      territory, **19(3)**, [719]
    prisoners of war, in case of, **19(3)**, [719]
  tort, action founded on, **19(3)**, [725]
personal estate of deceased person, claim for,
  19(3), [750]
personal injuries—
  actions in respect of, **19(3)**, [735]
  discretionary exclusion of time,
    19(3), [764]
  meaning, **19(3)**, [768]
postponement, **19(3)**, [762]
printer, action against, **19(3)**, [283]
prisoners of war, suspension of period in case
  of, **19(3)**, [719]

limitation of action—*contd*
private international law, **19(3)**, [718], [776]
proceedings generally, **20**, [635]
property obtained through unlawful conduct,
  recovery of, **19(3)**, [755]
redemption action, **19(3)**, [743]
rent—
  part payment, effect, **19(3)**, [759]
  recovery, action for, **19(3)**, [746]
right of action, construction of references to,
  19(3), [768]
simple contract, action based on, **19(3)**, [729]
slander action—
  discretionary exclusion of, **19(3)**, [763]
  generally, **19(3)**, [261]
  period, **19(3)**, [728]
specialty, action on, **19(3)**, [732]
specific performance, claim for, **19(3)**, [766]
statute of limitation, meaning, **19(3)**, [720]
summary of provisions, **19(3)**, [718]
sums recoverable by statute, where,
  19(3), [733]
theft, in case of, **19(3)**, [727]
title, extinction after expiration of time,
  19(3), [744]
tort, in case of, **19(3)**, [725]
transitional provisions, **19(3)**, [770], [774]
trust property, in respect of, **19(3)**, [749]

limited liability partnership
contribution to—
  amounts excluded when calculating,
    44(4), [117]–[118]
  meaning, **44(4)**, [111]
  non-active partners, by, **44(4)**, [114]
income from, treatment of, **44(1)**, [434]
incorporation, stamp duty land tax
  exemption, **41**, [338]
members of—
  restrictions on loss reliefs for, **44(4)**, [110]
  unrelieved losses brought forward,
    44(4), [112]
non-active members of—
  contribution to the firm, meaning,
    44(4), [114]
  restrictions on loss reliefs for, **44(4)**, [113]
property investment—
  meaning, **44(1)**, [628]
  treatment of income from, **44(1)**, [434]
"property investment LLP", meaning,
  44(4), [1012]
restriction on relief, **44(1)**, [95]
taxation of, **44(3)**, [880]
trade, member's contribution to, **44(1)**, [96]
treatment of, **44(1)**, [94]
unrelieved losses, carry forward of, **44(1)**, [97]

limited owner
charge—
  as land charge, **21**, [392]
  meaning, **21**, [392]
  overreaching, **20**, [626]

limited partnership
members, number of, **8**, 581

Lincoln's Inn
administrative position, **25(1)**, [1]
exemption from Building Acts, **25(1)**, [354]

liner conferences
Code—
appropriate authority, **39(2)**, [509]
conciliation procedure, rules for,
39(2), [512]
conciliators, recognition and enforcement
of recommendations of, **39(2)**, [508]
conference agreements, contents of,
39(2), [512]
Contracting Parties, **39(2)**, [503]
disputes, settlement of, **39(2)**, [512]
fighting ships, **39(2)**, [512]
freight rates, **39(2)**, [512]
head office of conference, **39(2)**, [512]
loyalty arrangements, contents of,
39(2), [512]
meaning, **39(2)**, [503]
member lines, relations among,
39(2), [512]
proceedings—
liability of members in, **39(2)**, [504]
restrictions on, **39(2)**, [506]
time for bringing, **39(2)**, [507]
unincorporated conference, by or
against, **39(2)**, [505]
representation, **39(2)**, [512]
service, adequacy of, **39(2)**, [512]
shippers, relations with, **39(2)**, [512]
text of, **39(2)**, [512]
trade participation agreements, contents
of, **39(2)**, [512]
conciliation proceedings, **39(2)**, [510]
meaning, **39(2)**, [512]
summary of provisions, **39(2)**, [1]
unincorporated, proceedings by or against,
39(2), [505]

liquidator
accounts for, enforcement, **4(2)**, [94]
acts of, validity, **4(2)**, [268]
appointment, corruption in, **4(2)**, [201]
default by, **4(2)**, [206]
delinquent, remedy against, **4(2)**, [248]
duties, enforcement of, **4(2)**, [206]
more than one person as, **4(2)**, [267]
offences by, **4(2)**, [248]
pending liquidation, information as to,
4(2), [230]
property, getting in, **4(2)**, [270]
provisional, **4(2)**, [177]
qualification of, **4(2)**, [266]
style and title, **4(2)**, [200]
winding-up, in. *See* **winding up by court;
winding up, voluntary**

liquor licensing
near beer—
application of provisions, **26(1)**, [223]
definitions, **26(1)**, [222]
enforcement, **26(1)**, [234]

liquor licensing—*contd*
near beer—*contd*
licence—
appeals, **26(1)**, [232], [233]
application for, **26(1)**, [225]
cancellation, **26(1)**, [228]
fee for, **26(1)**, [225]
provisional grant, **26(1)**, [230]
refusal of, **26(1)**, [227]
renewal, **26(1)**, [226]
requirement of, **26(1)**, [224]
standard terms, conditions and
restrictions, **26(1)**, [229]
transmission, **26(1)**, [228]
variation, **26(1)**, [231]
premises—
existing, **26(1)**, [237]
meaning, **26(1)**, [222]
powers of entry, **26(1)**, [235]
seizure of apparatus and equipment on,
26(1), [236]

listed building
amendment of provisions, **46**, [232]
ancient monuments, exception for, **46**, [703]
building preservation order, previously subject
to, **46**, [747]
cathedral church, application for consent
relating to, **14**, 1205–6
clearance area, in, **22**, [263], [264]
Commission, functions of, **46**, [687]
consent—
appeal against enforcement notice, granted
on, **46**, [682]
appeals—
determination of, **46**, [663], [749]
form of, **46**, [662]
grounds for, **46**, [662]
local planning authorities, functions of,
46, [661]
right of, **46**, [660]
application—
certificate accompanying, **46**, [651]
Commission, notification of, **46**, [654]
Crown land, for, **46**, [732], [734]
decision on, **46**, [656]
directions concerning notification,
46, [655]
form of, **46**, [651]
making of, **46**, [650]
notification of Secretary of State,
46, [653]
overlapping, power to decline, **46**, [725]
Secretary of State, reference to, **46**, [652]
subsequent, power to decline, **46**, [724]
building, enuring for benefit of, **46**, [656]
conditional grant, purchase notice on,
46, [672]
conditions, **46**, [657]
variation or discharge, application for,
46, [659]
default of decision, **46**, [660]
demolition, for, **46**, [648]
duration, limit of, **46**, [658], [1004]

listed building—*contd*
  consent—*contd*
    enforcement notice—
      deemed grant in, **46**, [679]
      effect on, **46**, [685]
    failure to comply with, **46**, [649]
    meaning, **46**, [648]
    modification of, **46**, [664]
      compensation, **46**, [668], [670]
      opposition to, **46**, [665]
      Secretary of State, by, **46**, [667]
      unopposed cases, **46**, [666]
      validity, **46**, [704]
    refusal—
      appeal against, **46**, [654], [662]
      purchase notice, **46**, [672]
    revocation of, **46**, [664]
      compensation, **46**, [668], [670]
      opposition to, **46**, [665]
      Secretary of State, by, **46**, [667]
      unopposed cases, **46**, [666]
      validity, **46**, [704]
    works, authorisation of, **46**, [648]
  certificate that building is not intended to
    be, **46**, [646]
  control of works, **46**, [647]–[649]
  Crown land—
    consent, application for, **46**, [732], [734]
    enforcement, **46**, [730]
    exercise of powers, **46**, [733]
    expressions relating to, **46**, [729]
    interest, reference to, **46**, [731]
    provisions applying, **46**, [727]
    transitional provisions, **46**, [1060]
    urgent works, **46**, [728]
  damage, acts likely to cause, **46**, [701]
  dangerous structure order in respect of,
    46, [698]
  demolition of—
    consent for, **46**, [648]
    offence of, **46**, [649]
  demolition order not to be made for,
    22, [262]
  ecclesiastical, exclusion of, **46**, [702]
  enforcement notice—
    appeal—
      determination, **46**, [682], [749]
      dismissal of, **46**, [682]
      grounds for, **46**, [680]
      procedure, **46**, [681]
      writing, to be in, **46**, [680]
    consent, deemed grant of, **46**, [679]
    consent, effect of, **46**, [685]
    copy, service of, **46**, [679]
    cost of works, **46**, [683]
    Crown land, and, **46**, [733]
    effective date of, **46**, [679]
    High Court, appeals to, **46**, [707]
    local planning authority, execution of works
      by, **46**, [683]
    London, in, **46**, [687]
    meaning, **46**, [679]
    non-compliance with, **46**, [684]
    power to issue, **46**, [679]
    Secretary of State, issue by, **46**, [688]

listed building—*contd*
  enforcement notice—*contd*
    validity of, **46**, [706]
    withdrawal of, **46**, [679]
  financial provisions, **46**, [742]
  functions relating to, **25(2)**, [581]
  general note, **46**, [1]
  Greater London, in, **46**, [710]
  lists of—
    approval of, **46**, [641]
    compilation of, **46**, [641]
    copy, deposit of, **46**, [642]
    publication of, **46**, [642]
    rights of entry, **46**, [737]–[740]
  local planning authorities—
    application of provisions to, **46**, [726]
    overlapping application, power to decline,
      46, [725]
    reference to, **46**, [723]
    subsequent application, power to decline,
      46, [724]
  meaning, **22**, [261]; **46**, [641]
  notice, service of, **46**, [642]
  offences—
    consent, failure to comply with, **46**, [649]
    damage, act causing or likely to result in,
      46, [701]
    defences, **46**, [649]
    demolition, **46**, [649]
    injunctions, **46**, [686]
    penalties, **46**, [649]
  planning application affecting, **46**, [709]
  planning functions, general duty in exercise
    of, **46**, [708]
  preservation—
    acquisition by agreement, **46**, [694]
    compulsory acquisition for—
      compensation, **46**, [691]
      deliberately left derelict, where,
        46, [692]
      minimum compensation, direction for,
        46, [692]
      order, **46**, [689]
      repairs notice, requirement of, **46**, [690]
      rights over land, ending of, **46**, [693]
    contributions to, **46**, [699]
    features, of, **46**, [641]
    management etc for, **46**, [695]
    recovery of grants, **46**, [700]
  purchase notice—
    compensation, **46**, [678]
    council, action by, **46**, [674]
    Crown land, **46**, [673]
    refusal or conditional grant of consent, on,
      46, [672]
    Secretary of State—
      action by, **46**, [676]
      confirmation, **46**, [677]
      effect of action, **46**, [677]
      reference to, **46**, [675]
  redundant churches, exclusion of, **46**, [702]
  repairs notice, **46**, [690]
  rights of entry, **46**, [737]–[740]
  Secretary of State, consultation by, **46**, [641]
  settled land, as, **46**, [736]

listed building—*contd*
  temporary listing. *See* **building**
  urgent works to preserve—
    carrying out, **46**, [696]
    expenses, recovery of, **46**, [697]
  validity of orders, **46**, [704]–[705]
  warrant to enter land, **46**, [738]
  works—
    authorisation of. *See* consent *above*
    restriction on, **46**, [647]

literary and scientific institutions
  amalgamation, **13**, [72]
  buildings, disposal, **13**, [104]
  byelaws, power to make, **13**, [69]
  dissolution, **13**, [74]
  governing body, constitution, **13**, [77]
  institutions to which Act applicable, **13**, [78]
  joint stock companies, proviso for on
    dissolution, **13**, [75]
  judgments against, enforcement, **13**, [68]
  land—
    cessation of use for, reverter, **13**, [53]
    conveyance as sites for—
      commissioners, by, **13**, [55]
      corporation, by, **13**, [55]
      Duchy of Cornwall, **13**, [52]
      Duchy of Lancaster, **13**, [51]
      form of, **13**, [61]
      generally, **13**, [50]
      justices, by, **13**, [55]
      landlords of unsold parts, remedies,
        13, [58]
      mode of, **13**, [56]
      number of sites granted, unlimited,
        13, [59]
      part only, lands subject to rent or lease,
        13, [57]
      persons under incapacity, **13**, [54]
      tenants of unsold parts, liabilities,
        13, [58]
      trustee, by, **13**, [55]
    ecclesiastical corporation sole, sale by,
      13, [55], [62]
    purchase money, application of, **13**, [62],
      [63]
  members—
    meaning, **13**, [76]
    offences by, **13**, [71]
    subscriptions in arrears, **13**, [70], [76]
    suits against, as strangers, **13**, [70]
  property of—
    dealings in, **13**, [64]
    vesting, **13**, [66]
    See also land *above*
  purposes, alteration, extension, etc, powers,
    13, [72]
    Secretary of State, of, **13**, [73]
  sites—
    conveyance of land for. *See* land *above*
    corporations or trustees, grants to, **13**, [60]
    form of grants, etc, **13**, [61]
    separate institutions, grants for, **13**, [59]
  specially authorised societies, **13**, [72]
  suits by and against, **13**, [67]

literary and scientific institutions—*contd*
  summary of provisions, **13**, [49]
  trustees—
    conveyance by, **13**, [55]
    dealing in property, powers, **13**, [64]
    grant of sites to, **13**, [60]
    indemnification, **13**, [65]
  unincorporated, grant of site for, **13**, [60]

Lithuania
  accession to European Union, **18**, [54]

litigant in person
  costs, **11(2)**, [377]
  county court, right of audience, **11(2)**, [944]
  expenses, **11(2)**, [377]

litigators
  duties of, **11(4)**, [303]
  employed by Legal Services Commission,
    right of audience and to conduct litigation,
    11(4), [536]

litter
  abatement, **35(1)**, [314]
    consultation and proposals for, **32**, [528]
    notice, **32**, [559]
    order, **32**, [558]
  application of provisions, **32**, [568]
  authority—
    bins, duties relating to, **32**, [529]
    consent to works by, **32**, [536]
    consultations by, **32**, [528]
    meaning, **32**, [528], [532]
  bins, **32**, [529]
  clearing notices—
    appeal against, **32**, [561]
    failure to comply with, **32**, [562]
    fixed penalty notices, **32**, [565]
    service of, **32**, [560]
  Crown land—
    authority for, **32**, [554]
    meaning, **32**, [554]
  designated land, free distribution of printed
    matter on, **32**, [589]
  discouraging, grants for, **32**, [527]
  duty to keep land and highways clear of,
    32, [557], [569]
  exclusion of liability, **32**, [571]
  expenditure, contributions to, **32**, [530]
  fixed penalty notices, **32**, [556], [565], [570]
  generally, **32**, [1]
  offence of leaving, **26(2)**, [162]; **32**, [555]
  orders relating to, making, **32**, [531]
  persons aggrieved by, summary proceedings
    by, **32**, [558]
  principal litter authorities—
    meaning, **32**, [554]
    relevant land of, **32**, [554]
    summary proceedings by, **32**, [559]
  regulations, **32**, [568]
  relevant highways, **32**, [554]
  relevant land—
    cleaning, **26(2)**, [160]

litter—*contd*
relevant land—*contd*
designated educational institution, of, **32**, [554]
keeping clear, **32**, [557]
litter control area of local authority, within, **32**, [554]
principal litter authority, of, **32**, [554]
statutory undertaker, of, **32**, [554]
remedial action, power of authority to take, **35(2)**, [440]
street litter control notice—
appeal against, **32**, [564]
failure to comply with, **32**, [564]
fixed penalty notices, **32**, [565]
land, description of, **32**, [564]
premises, description of, **32**, [564]
register of, **32**, [567]
requirements imposed by, **32**, [564]
service of, **32**, [563]

livery and seisin
conveyance by, abolition, **20**, [669]

livestock
accommodation, suitability, **2**, [329]
artificial breeding—
control of, **2**, [596], [597]
offences and penalties, **2**, [596]
regulations, **2**, [596]
artificial insemination research, **2**, [274]
bleeding, prohibition, **2**, [329]
brucellosis, eradication, **2**, [346]
carcase—
burying of, **2**, [507]
meaning, **2**, [548]
seizure and disposal, **2**, [472]
cattle. *See* **cattle**
development scheme. *See* **Meat and Livestock Commission**
diseases. *See* **diseases of animals**
distress for rent, no privilege from, **13**, [1202]
dogs worrying. *See* **dogs**
importation—
control of, **1(1)**, [481]
offences and penalties, **1(1)**, [481]
injury to, by dogs, **2**, [352]
meaning, **1(1)**, [399]; **21**, [453]
owner, meaning, **2**, [353]
protection against dogs, **2**, [358]
rearing—
improvement—
list of improvements, **1(1)**, [381]
meaning, **1(1)**, [367]
operations deemed to be, **1(1)**, [367]
rights of common, affecting, **1(1)**, [369]
schemes, **1(1)**, [381]
settled land, **1(1)**, [368]
meaning, **1(1)**, [367]
rearing purposes, meaning, **1(1)**, [367]
regulations and orders, **1(1)**, [377]
statistical information, requirement for, **1(2)**, [142]
trespassing—
detention of, **2**, [356]

livestock—*contd*
trespassing—*contd*
exceptions from liability, **2**, [354]
highway on, **2**, [357]
liability for, **2**, [357]
sale of, **2**, [356]
welfare—
codes of recommendations, **2**, [330]
entry and inspection for purposes of, **2**, [331]
offences and penalties, **2**, [332]
regulations, **2**, [329]

livestock market
Meat and Livestock Commission, controlled by, **27**, [1]

living accommodation
lease premiums, **43(S)**, 1400–3
local authority, provided by, **44(2)**, [109]
more than one employee, provided for, **44(2)**, [119]
person involved in providing, meaning, **44(2)**, [123]
priority of rules applying to, **44(2)**, [120]

Lloyd's
assessment and collection of tax, **43(2)**, [753]
core provisions, **19(2)**, [392]
corporate and partnership members—
equalisation reserves, **43(S)**, 1384
meaning, **43(S)**, 1384
corporate members—
cessation of business, **43(S)**, 539–40
group relief, restriction of, **43(S)**, 531–2
transfer of underwriting business without change of ownership, **43(S)**, 539–40
Council—
consultation, **19(2)**, [394]
exercise of powers through, **19(2)**, [393]
Financial Services Authority—
direction by, **19(2)**, [391]
general duty of, **19(2)**, [389]
former underwriting members—
meaning, **19(2)**, [399]
requirements, **19(2)**, [395], [396]
rules applicable to, **19(2)**, [397]
members' agent pooling arrangements—
meaning, **43(1)**, [439]
payment of amount, reference to, **43(1)**, [439]
tax treatment, **43(1)**, [438]
Society, authorisation and permissions, **19(2)**, [390]
summary of provisions, **19(1)**, [1]
transfer schemes, **19(2)**, [398]

loan
employment-related—
aggregation, loans by close company to director, **44(2)**, [197]
cash equivalent, apportionment, **44(2)**, [195]
classes of, **44(2)**, [184]
death of employee, **44(2)**, [200]

loan—*contd*

employment-related—*contd*

earnings, benefit treated as, **44(2)**, [185], [190]

exclusions, **44(2)**, [186]

fixed rate of interest, at, **44(2)**, [187]

interest treated as paid, **44(2)**, [194]

meaning, **44(2)**, [184]

necessary expenses, advances for, **44(2)**, [189]

official rate of interest—

alternative method of calculation, **44(2)**, [193]

meaning, **44(2)**, [191]

normal method of calculation, **44(2)**, [192]

ordinary commercial terms, on, **44(2)**, [186]

person making, **44(2)**, [184]

provisions applied to, **44(2)**, [183]

release or writing off, **44(2)**, [198]

double charge, exception, **44(2)**, [199]

relief, claim for taking account of event after assessment, **44(2)**, [201]

replacement, **44(2)**, [196]

tax relief, qualification for, **44(2)**, [188]

interest relief. *See* **interest relief**

local—

automatic charge for, **19(2)**, [844], [847]

limit for, **19(2)**, [852]

new form of, **19(2)**, [844], [847]

public works loan. *See* **public works loan**

Public Works Loan Commissioners. *See*
Public Works Loan Commissioners

rates of interest, **19(2)**, [851], [853], [854]

re-borrowing, **19(2)**, [842]

meaning, **44(2)**, [183]

national debt. *See* **national debt**

National Loans Fund. *See* **National Loans
Fund**

public works, for. *See* **public works loan**

residential property. *See* **residential property
loan**

Secretary of State, by, **16**, [65]

society. *See* **loan society**

tax avoidance, **44(1)**, [537]

loan capital

meaning, **41**, [169]

transfer, stamp duty, **41**, [169], [170]

stamp duty, **43(S)**, 932

loan creditor

close company, meaning, **44(1)**, [231]

loan relationships

accounting methods—

adjustment on change of, **43(1)**, [257]

assets or liabilities, change of accounting basis for, **43(1)**, [206]

connection, parties having, **43(1)**, [202]

control, meaning, **43(1)**, [203]

exemption, **43(1)**, [204]

generally accepted practice, computation in accordance with, **43(1)**, [200]

loan relationships—*contd*

accounting methods—*contd*

rate of interest reset, where, **43(1)**, [205]

amended provisions, **43(2)**, [269], [534]

amendment of provisions, **43(1)**, [261]

authorised investment funds, **43(2)**, [734]

capital redemption policies, removal of exclusion from computations, **43(2)**, [770]

close companies, deeply discounted securities of, **43(1)**, [257]

collective investment schemes—

authorised unit trusts, **43(1)**, [258]

company holdings, **43(1)**, [258]

computational provisions, amended provisions, **43(2)**, [535]

investment trusts, **43(1)**, [258]

non-qualifying investments test, **43(1)**, [258]

offshore funds—

distributing, **43(1)**, [328]–[9]

meaning, **43(1)**, [258]

orders, powers to make, **43(1)**, [258]

venture capital trusts, **43(1)**, [258]

connected debtor and creditor, treated differently by, **43(S)**, 1201–2

connected parties, amended provisions, **43(S)**, 1562–5

continuity of treatment, **43(1)**, [257]

convertible securities, treatment of, **43(1)**, [262]

corporate members of Lloyds, of, **43(1)**, [260]

credits—

bringing into account, **43(1)**, [198], [257]

generally accepted accounting practice, in accordance with, **43(1)**, [200]

capital expenditure, relating to, **43(1)**, [257]

companies, partnerships involving, **43(1)**, [257]

consortium relief, **43(1)**, [257]

debtor relationship, release of liability, **43(1)**, [257]

deeply discounted securities, **43(1)**, [257]

distributions, treated as, **43(1)**, [257]

equity, recognised in, **43(1)**, [257]

exchange gains and losses, **43(1)**, [257]

government investments, writing off, **43(1)**, [257]

impaired debt, **43(1)**, [257]

impairment losses, **43(1)**, [257]

imported losses, **43(1)**, [257]

life assurance policies, **43(1)**, [257]

major interests, references to, **43(1)**, [257]

options, **43(1)**, [257]

overseas sovereign debt, **43(1)**, [262]

repo transactions, **43(1)**, [257]

shareholders' funds, recognised in, **43(1)**, [257]

stock lending, **43(1)**, [257]

transactions not at arm's length, **43(1)**, [257]

credits and debits brought into account—

amounts not fully recognised for accounting purposes, **43(S)**, 1617–18

loan relationships—*contd*
credits and debits brought into account—*contd*
counterfactual currency movement
assumptions, **43(S)**, 1567–8
exchange gains and losses, **43(S)**, 1571–5
one-way exchange effect, arrangements
having, **43(S)**, 1566–70
options, treatment, of, **43(S)**, 1568
debits—
bringing into account, **43(1)**, [198], [257]
generally accepted accounting practice,
in accordance with, **43(1)**, [200]
revaluation, restriction following,
43(1), [257]
capital expenditure, relating to,
43(1), [257]
companies, partnerships involving,
43(1), [257]
consortium relief, **43(1)**, [257]
debtor relationship, release of liability,
43(1), [257]
deeply discounted securities, **43(1)**, [257]
distributions, treated as, **43(1)**, [257]
equity, recognised in, **43(1)**, [257]
exchange gains and losses, **43(1)**, [257]
impaired debt, **43(1)**, [257]
impairment losses, **43(1)**, [257]
imported losses, **43(1)**, [257]
late interest, **43(1)**, [257]
life assurance policies, **43(1)**, [257]
major interests, references to, **43(1)**, [257]
non-trading, **43(1)**, [196]
options, **43(1)**, [257]
overseas sovereign debt, **43(1)**, [262]
repo transactions, **43(1)**, [257]
shareholders' funds, recognised in,
43(1), [257]
stock lending, **43(1)**, [257]
transactions not at arm's length,
43(1), [257]
unallowable purposes, **43(1)**, [257]
deep discount securities, **43(1)**, [262]
deep gain securities, **43(1)**, [262]
deficits—
bringing into account, **43(1)**, [196]
carry-back of, **43(1)**, [322]
claims, **43(1)**, [256]
non-trading, **43(1)**, [197]
definitions, **43(1)**, [223]
derivatives,—
connected debtor and creditor, different
treatment by, **43(S)**, 1619
embedded in, **43(2)**, [178], [769]
disguised interest—
excluded shares, **43(S)**, 1591–2
no tax avoidance purpose, arrangement
having, **43(S)**, 1590
overview of provisions, **43(S)**, 1589
profit, regarded as, **43(S)**, 1589–90
return otherwise taxable, exclusion,
43(S), 1590
distributions treated as, **43(S)**, 1198
embedded derivatives, with, **43(1)**, [215]
exchange gains and losses from, **43(1)**, [199];
43(2), [769]

loan relationships—*contd*
financial instruments, application of
provisions, **43(1)**, [222]
foreign exchange gains and losses from,
transitional provisions, **43(2)**, [168]
gains, bringing into account, **43(1)**, [196]
gilt strips, represented by, **43(1)**, [216]
gilts, rules for, **43(1)**, [214]
impairment losses, **43(1)**, [257]
indexed gilt-edged securities, represented by,
43(1), [214]
insurance companies—
accruals basis, election for, **43(1)**, [259]
apportionments, **43(1)**, [259]
deficit, treatment of, **43(1)**, [259]
different categories of business, **43(1)**, [259]
I minus E basis, **43(1)**, [259]
investment life insurance contract as,
43(S), 1132
losses, determining, amounts recognised in,
43(1), [201]
manufactured interest, treatment of,
43(1), [218]
meaning, **43(1)**, [194]
money debt—
lending of money, not arising from,
43(1), [221]
meaning, **43(1)**, [195]
payments or interest under, references to,
43(1), [195]
profits—
bringing into account, **43(1)**, [196]
determining, amounts recognised in,
43(1), [201]
rate of interest reset, accounting method,
43(2), [111]
related transaction, meaning, **43(1)**, [198]
replacement of transferor, transferee leaving
group after, **43(1)**, [257]
Schedule 28AA to Taxes Act 1988, amounts
imputed under, **43(1)**, [257]
SE, formation by merger, **43(1)**, [257]
shares accounted for as liabilities—
amendments and repeals, **43(S)**, 1595–7
application of provisions, **43(S)**, 1592–4
commencement, **43(S)**, 1597
excepted shares, **43(S)**, 1594
rights under creditor relationship,
43(S), 1593
shares ceasing to be, **43(S)**, 1595
unallowable purpose, **43(S)**, 1594
shares treated as—
non-qualifying, **43(1)**, [208]
ceasing to be, **43(1)**, [213]
conditions for, **43(1)**, [209]–[212]
outstanding third party obligations, subject
to, **43(1)**, [207], [213]
taxation of, **43(1)**, [194]
termination before 1st April, 1996,
43(1), [262]
transferred income streams, **43(S)**, 1604–5
transitional provisions, **43(1)**, [299];
43(2), [114], [169]
transitional provisions and savings—
corporation tax, **43(1)**, [262]

loan relationships—*contd*
  transitional provisions and savings—*contd*
    income tax and capital gains tax,
    43(1), [263]
  UK resident, assignment of assets and liabilities
    on company ceasing to be, **43(1)**, [257]
  unallowable purposes, **43(1)**, [257]

lobster. *See* **shellfish**

local Act
  amendment, adaptation or repeal, **35(1)**, [38],
    [89], [197], [198], [274]
  buildings, as to, facilities for inspection of,
    35(1), [612]
  double and treble costs, allowing, **11(2)**, [38]
  meaning, **35(1)**, [90]
  planning enactments, subject to, **46**, [31]
  plea of general issue, allowing, **11(2)**, [39]
  trade effluents, adaptation as to, **35(1)**, [219]

Local Authorities' Mutual Investment Trust
  investment powers, **48**, 592–3
  scheme, **48**, 594

local authority. *See further* **Local
Commissioner; local government**
  Note. *This heading includes matters common to
  most authorities, but readers are advised to look
  under the names of authorities, eg* **London
  borough council; parish council** *etc.*
  abduction of child, report on, **6**, [201]
  access to information. *See* information *below*
  accommodation—
    authority liable for, **40(1)**, [11]
    charges for, **40(1)**, [9]
    community care services, transfer of staff
      from health services, **40(1)**, [210]
    contributions—
      charge of arrears of, **40(1)**, [126]
      charges on land instead of, **40(2)**, [318]
    conveyance to and from, **40(1)**, [8]
    cross-border placements, **40(2)**, [319]
    duty to provide, **40(1)**, [8]
    failure to maintain, provision due to,
      40(1), [25]
    financial adjustments between authorities,
      40(1), [16]
    management of, **40(1)**, [8]
    more expensive, funding by resident,
      40(2), [317]
    needs, assessment of, **40(1)**, [208]
    person in, disposal of assets by, **40(1)**, [125]
    person in need of care and attention,
      removal to suitable premises, **40(1)**, [22],
      [38]
    plans for, **40(1)**, [207]
    premises—
      inspection of, **40(1)**, [209]
      management of, **40(1)**, [10]
    residence, based on, **40(1)**, [11]
    Scotland, in, of persons under 65,
      40(1), [51]
    transfer of responsibilities for, **40(2)**, [314]

local authority—*contd*
  accommodation—*contd*
    voluntary organisations, premises
      maintained by, **40(1)**, [12]
  accounting practice, **26(2)**, [252]
  accounts—
    funds, of, **25(2)**, [150]
    inspection, open to, **25(2)**, [180]
    separate, of certain expenditure,
      25(2), [135]
  acquisition of land—
    agreement, by—
      community council, by, **25(2)**, [122]
      jointly by two councils, **25(2)**, [118]
      parish council, by, **25(2)**, [122]
      principal councils, by, **25(2)**, [118]
      purposes of, **25(2)**, [118]
    compensation provisions, **25(2)**, [127]
    compulsory—
      authorisation, **25(2)**, [119]
      community council, for, **25(2)**, [123]
      more than one purpose for, **25(2)**, [119]
      parish council, for, **25(2)**, [123]
      principal councils, by, **25(2)**, [119]
      restrictions on, **25(2)**, [119]
    Duchy of Lancaster lands, **25(2)**, [128]
    exercise of powers, **25(1)**, [591]
    powers, summary of, **25(1)**, [1]
    protection of purchasers, **25(2)**, [126]
    summary of provisions, **25(1)**, [1]
  adaptation of enactments, **25(2)**, [261]
  advances by. *See* mortgage *below*
  aerodromes, powers as to, **4(1)**, [81]
  agriculture pests control, **1(1)**, [633], [862]
  airports. *See* **airport**
  aldermen, **25(2)**, [212]
  allotments. *See* **allotments**
  allowances to members—
    approved duty for purposes of, **25(2)**, [160]
    attendance, **25(2)**, [156], [870]
    authorities authorised to pay, **25(2)**, [161]
    conferences etc, attending, **25(2)**, [159]
    courtesy visits etc expenses, **25(2)**, [160]
    financial loss, **25(2)**, [156]
      right to opt for, **25(2)**, [157]
    overseas meetings, attending, **25(2)**, [159]
    regulations as to, **25(2)**, [162]; **26(2)**, [136]
    schemes for, **25(2)**, [870]
    special responsibility payment, **25(2)**, [870]
    subsistence, **25(2)**, [158]
    travelling, **25(2)**, [158]
    official and courtesy visits, **25(2)**, [160]
  applications to, **46**, [608]
  appropriation of land—
    adjustment of accounts on, **25(1)**, [593]
    common land, **25(2)**, [120]
    exercise of powers, **25(1)**, [592]
    open space, part of, **25(1)**, [592];
      25(2), [120]
    parish or community council, by,
      25(2), [124]
    powers, exercise of, **25(1)**, [592]
    principal councils, by, **25(2)**, [120]
  areas. *See* **local government areas**
  armorial bearings, transfer of, **25(2)**, [210]

local authority—*contd*
 association—
  capital gains tax exemption, **42**, [1420]
  meaning, **44(1)**, [375]; **44(4)**, [1008]
  no income tax liability for, **44(4)**, [846]
  tax exemption, **44(1)**, [375]
 association of—
  officers, transfer of, **25(2)**, [218]
  subscriptions to, **25(2)**, [145]
  See **local authority association**
 Audit Commission. *See* **Audit Commission for Local Authorities**
 benefit fraud, power to prosecute,
  40(1), [608]
 best value—
  accounts, **26(1)**, [418]
  Audit Commission, references to,
   26(1), [417]
  authorities being, **26(1)**, [391]
  charging or trading, power to modify
   enactments, **26(2)**, [299]
    orders, procedure for, **26(2)**, [300]
  commencement of provisions, **26(1)**, [421]
  contracting out of provisions, **26(1)**, [415]
  contracts, exclusion of non-commercial
   considerations, **26(1)**, [416]
  discretionary services, power to charge for,
   26(2), [295]
    disapplication of provision, **26(2)**, [296]
   extension or disapplication of provisions,
    26(1), [392]
     Wales, authorities in, **26(1)**, [393]
  function-related activities, trade though
   company, **26(2)**, [297]
  general duty of, **26(1)**, [394]
  grants to, **26(2)**, [265], [266]
  guidance, **26(1)**, [420]
  inspections, **26(1)**, [403]
    Auditor-General for Wales, by,
     26(1), [404]
    co-ordination, **26(1)**, [419]
    fees, **26(1)**, [406], [407]
    powers and duties of inspectors,
     26(1), [405]
    reports, **26(1)**, [408], [409]
    Secretary of State, powers of,
     26(1), [410]
  local representatives, involvement of,
   26(1), [395]
  meaning, **26(1)**, [391]
  modification of enactments,
   26(1), [411]–[414]
  new powers, conferring, **26(1)**, [411]–[414]
  orders and regulations, **26(1)**, [422]
  performance plans. *See* **Wales**
  performance reviews, abolition,
   26(2), [607]
  staff transfer matters—
   general, **26(2)**, [303]
   pensions, **26(2)**, [304]
  trading powers, regulation of, **26(2)**, [298]
  Wales, in, **26(1)**, [423]

local authority—*contd*
 billing authority—
  levies. *See* levy *below*
  Secretary of State, information for,
   25(2), [821]
  special authority, as, **25(2)**, [826]
  See also **council tax**
 Bills in Parliament—
  power to promote or oppose, **25(2)**, [199]
  restriction on promoting, **25(2)**, [60]
 block grants. *See under* **rates**
 bodies being, **26(2)**, [254], [263]
 borrowing—
  affordable limits, duty to determine,
   26(2), [234]
  control of, **26(2)**, [233]
  external funds, for purpose of, **26(2)**, [248]
  lenders, protection of, **26(2)**, [237]
  limits, imposition of, **26(2)**, [235]
  powers, **26(2)**, [232]
  receiver, appointment of, **26(2)**, [244]
  security for, **26(2)**, [244]
  temporary, **26(2)**, [236]
 borrowing by. *See* **loan**
 borrowing, for housing purposes, **22**, [305]
 budget calculations—
  inadequacy of controlled reserve, report
   on, **26(2)**, [258]
  robustness of estimates, report on,
   26(2), [256]
 budget monitoring—
  generally, **26(2)**, [259]
  Greater London Authority, **26(2)**, [260]
 building regulations, registers regarding, to be
  kept by, **35(1)**, [614]
 buildings, power to provide, **25(2)**, [131]
 burial authorities, deemed to be, **5(2)**, [455]
  See further **burial authority**
 bus services, abolition of special control over
  provision of, **36**, [791]
 byelaws of. *See also* **byelaws**
  abolished councils, of, **25(2)**, [627]
  alternative procedure for, **25(2)**, [189];
   26(2), [604]
  authorities qualified to make, **25(2)**, [187]
  breach, powers of community support
   officers, **26(2)**, [605]
  confirming authority, **25(2)**, [187]
  copy of, right to, **25(2)**, [188]
  evidence of, **25(2)**, [198]
  existing, saving for, **25(1)**, [69]
  fixed penalties—
   amount of, **25(2)**, [193]
   guidance, **25(2)**, [196]
   name and address, requirement to give,
    25(2), [194]
   notices, **25(2)**, [192]
   receipts, use of, **25(2)**, [195]
   regulations and orders, **25(2)**, [197]
  nuisances, suppression of, **25(2)**, [187]
  offences and penalties, **25(2)**, [191]
   fixed penalty. *See* fixed penalties *above*
  pleasure boats, **25(2)**, [442]
  power to make, **25(2)**, [187]
  procedure for making, **25(2)**, [188], [189]

local authority—*contd*
byelaws of—*contd*
proceedings for offences, **25(2)**, [474]
revocation, **25(2)**, [190]
capital expenditure, meaning, **26(2)**, [247]
capital gains tax exemption, **42**, [1420]
capital receipts—
meaning, **26(2)**, [240]
non-money, **26(2)**, [241]
use of, regulations, **26(2)**, [242]
care order. *See* **care order**
central government control, **25(1)**, [1]
chairman, casual vacancy in office, **25(2)**, [77]
change of name, transfer of securities on,
25(2), [148]
charges by—
excepted functions in respect of,
25(2), [888]
library services, **25(2)**, [889]
power to allow, **25(2)**, [886]
provisions for, power to amend,
25(2), [887]
regulation of, **25(2)**, [886]
relevant authorities for making,
25(2), [888]
charging authorities, meaning, **25(2)**, [826]
charitable contributions by, **25(2)**, [135]
charitable trustees, as, **25(2)**, [170]
charities, local—
areas, enlargement of, **5(2)**, [692]
co-operation between, **5(2)**, [664]
index of, **5(2)**, [662]
meaning, **5(2)**, [683]
reviews of, **5(2)**, [663]
charter trustees—
accounts, audit. *See* **Audit Commission**
continuation of, **25(2)**, [577]
powers and duties, **25(2)**, [209]
chief finance officer, meaning, **25(2)**, [857]
child in care—
See further children *below*
abroad, arrangements to live, **6**, [441]
apprenticeship deeds or articles, guarantee
of, **6**, [441]
authorities for purposes of, **6**, [45]
ceasing to be looked after, preparation for,
6, [441]
contact with family, **6**, [441]
death of, **6**, [441]
education supervision order, bar on,
6, [349]
educational achievement, promotion of,
6, [322]
matters to be considered, **6**, [322]
public, protection from injury, **6**, [322]
remand—
on bail, report where, **6**, [123]
conditions, breaking, **6**, [122]
to, **6**, [120]
visitor for, appointment of, **6**, [441]
visits to or by, **6**, [441]
child leaving care—
advice and assistance, **6**, [685]
exclusion from benefits, **6**, [686]

local authority—*contd*
child looked after by—
accommodation and maintenance, provision
of, **6(S)**, 441–2
accommodation, manner of provisions,
6, [574]
change of address, persons with parental
responsibility notifying, **6**, [573]
contact with, duty to ensure, **6(S)**, 450–1
duty to, **6**, [572]
former relevant child, further assistance to
pursue education or training,
6(S), 458–60
higher education, entitlement to payment
for, **6(S)**, 457
independent reviewing officer—
appointment of, **6(S)**, 445
functions of, **6(S)**, 446
further provision, power to make,
6(S), 447–50
referred cases, **6(S)**, 446
independent visitors for, **6(S)**, 452
personal adviser, extension of entitlements
to, **6(S)**, 460
regulations, **6(S)**, 443
review of case, **6(S)**, 442
school for, designated member of staff at,
6(S), 456
sufficient accommodation, general duty to
secure, **6(S)**, 444–5
support for, **6(S)**, 455
visits to, duty to ensure, **6(S)**, 450–1
child minders. *See under* **child**
children, powers and duties as to—
abandoned child, **6**, [320]
abscond, child likely to, **6**, [334]
accommodation for—
age of child, **6**, [320]
assessment of need, **6**, [440]
charges for, **6**, [97]–[98]
contact with family, **6**, [441]
costs, recoupment, **6**, [341]
detention, child in, **6**, [321], [546]
disabled children, **6**, [323], [440]
inquiries into, **6**, [335]
local education authority, consultation
with, **6**, [340]
meaning, **6**, [135], [322]
nature of, **6**, [323]
police protection, child under, **6**, [321],
[363]
protection of child, for, **6**, [440]
provision, **6**, [320], [322], [440]
regulations, **6**, [323], [441]
remands to, **6**, [120], [545]
security requirements, **6**, [120]
removal from, **6**, [320]
secure—
detention in, **6**, [546]–[547]
grants towards costs, **6**, [410], [547]
meaning, **6**, [120]
placing in, **6**, [120]
provision of, **6**, [334], [546]
advice for, duty as to, **6**, [329], [330]
advocacy services, **6**, [338]

local authority—*contd*

  children, powers and duties as to—*contd*

    amendment of provisions, powers as to, **6(S)**, 54

    assistance for, duty as to, **6**, [329], [330]

    befriending, **6**, [330]

    breaks from caring for, **6(S)**, 461

    care proceedings, reduction of need for, **6**, [440]

    child's wishes, duty to ascertain, **6**, [316]

    childcare, provision of. *See* **child care**

    co-operation between authorities, **6**, [339]

    complaints, procedure for, **6**, [333]

    cost of services, recoupment, **6**, [341]

    day care. *See under* **child**

    disabled—

      accommodation for, **6**, [323], [440]

      register of, **6**, [440]

      services for, provision, **6**, [440]

    early childhood services, meaning, **6(S)**, 51

    education—

      achievement, duty to promote, **6**, [322]

      assistance as to, **6**, [331]

    employment, assistance as to, **6**, [331]

    expenses, **6**, [97], [341]

      See also maintenance costs *below*

    family centres, provision of, **6**, [440]

    family home, maintenance of, **6**, [440]

    family of—

      assistance to, **6**, [316]

      cost of services to, **6**, [341]

      identification of children in need, **6**, [440]

      meaning, **6**, [316]

      provision of information, **6**, [440]

      provision of services for—

        child living with family, **6**, [440]

        powers, **6**, [316], [322], [440]

      social security benefits, **6**, [316]

    family, placing child with, **6**, [323]

    formerly in care—

      duty to keep in touch with, **6**, [325]

      functions in respect of, **6**, [325], [326]

      pathway plans for, **6**, [325], [328]

      personal adviser, duty to appoint, **6**, [325]

      responsibility towards, **6**, [324]

    foster parent, placing with, **6**, [441]

    general duty towards, **6**, [1], [322]

    in need, extension of powers to make payments in cash, **6(S)**, 461

    information, advice and assistance, duty to provide—

      England, in, **6(S)**, 61

      Wales, in, **6(S)**, 73

    information, duty to give to other authorities, **6**, [332]

    injury to self or others, child likely to cause, **6**, [334]

    inquiries into representations—

      Commission for Social Care Inspection, by, **6**, [336]

      disclosure of information for, authorisation of, **6**, [336]

      payments, **6**, [336]

local authority—*contd*

  children, powers and duties as to—*contd*

    inquiries into representations—*contd*

      procedure, **6**, [335]

      regulations as to, **6**, [335]

      Wales, in, **6**, [337]

    investigation into circumstances, **6**, [350]

    leaving care. *See* child leaving care *above*

    liberty, restriction of, **6**, [334]

    local education authorities, consultation with, **6**, [340]

    maintenance costs—

      agreed contributions towards, **6**, [442]

      contribution orders, **6**, [442]

      contribution towards, **6**, [439]

      contributors, liability, **6**, [442]

      recovery, **6**, [442]

    maintenance, provision of, **6**, [323]

    need, assessment of, **6**, [440]

    neglect and abuse, prevention of, **6**, [440]

    other local authority, recoupment of costs from, **6**, [341]

    particular facilities, homes providing—

      financial support, **6**, [410]

      maintenance in, **6**, [323], [410]

      provision of, **6**, [323], [410]

    pathway plans, **6**, [328]

    personal advisers, appointment of, **6**, [327]

    placing with friend, relative etc, **6**, [323], [441]

    proper performance—

      powers of National Assembly of Wales to secure, **6(S)**, 75

      powers of Secretary of State to secure, **6(S)**, 64

    racial groups, duty as to, **6**, [440]

    relevant partners, duty to work with, **6(S)**, 53–4

    representations, procedure for, **6**, [333]

    residence in relation to, **6**, [320], [342], [350]

    review of cases, **6**, [335]

    secure accommodation for. *See* accommodation *above*

    services, provision of, powers, **6**, [316]

    sibling, accommodation with, **6**, [323]

    specific duties, **6(S)**, 52

    statutory duty as to, failure in, **6**, [412]

    training, assistance as to, **6**, [331]

    welfare, duties as to, **6**, [316]

    well-being of young children, duties, **6(S)**, 50

  children's home. *See* **children's home**

  civic restaurants, **25(1)**, [371], [372]

  collection fund—

    establishment, **25(2)**, [792]

    payments to be met from, **25(2)**, [794]

    regulations for, **25(2)**, [801]

    sums payable into, **25(2)**, [794]

    transfer of sums to general fund, **25(2)**, [799], [800]

    use of sums in, **25(2)**, [792]

    Welsh authorities, of, **25(2)**, [793]

  combined applications to, **46**, [608]

local authority—*contd*
  committal to care of—
    accommodation. See *under* children etc
      above
    Channel Islands, transfer to, **6**, [125]
    expenses, **6**, [97]
    Isle of Man, transfer to, **6**, [125]
    residence of child, **6**, [97]
    training school, from, **6**, [124]
  committees—
    advisory committees, **25(2)**, [102]
    appointment, **25(2)**, [102]
    discharge of functions by, **25(2)**, [101]
    joint committees—
      appointment, **25(2)**, [102]
      area changes, effect of, **25(2)**, [223]
      expenses of, **25(2)**, [103]
      reports and returns by, **25(2)**, [182]
      voting rights, **25(2)**, [866]
    meaning, **25(2)**, [93]
    meetings—
      admission of public, **25(1)**, [625]
      failure to attend, **25(2)**, [74]
      general provisions, **25(2)**, [253]
    members—
      ceasing to be, **25(2)**, [102]
      disqualification of, **25(2)**, [104]
      interest in contracts etc, **25(2)**, [105]
      non-voting, **25(2)**, [866]
      voting rights, **25(2)**, [866]
    parish meeting, of, **25(2)**, [108]
    political balance on—
      bodies to which provisions apply,
        25(2), [898]
      duty to ensure, **25(2)**, [867]
      exceptions and extensions, **25(2)**, [869]
      regulations for, **25(2)**, [898]
    provisions applied to, **25(2)**, [93]
    references to, **6**, [45]
    social services. See social services *below*
    standing orders, **25(2)**, [106]
    voting, disability for, **25(2)**, [105]
  community home. See **community home**
  companies—
    arm's length companies, **25(2)**, [878]
    authorised companies—
      directors of, **25(2)**, [881]
      information, power to acquire,
        25(2), [881]
      meaning, **25(2)**, [881]
    authorities subject to provisions,
      25(2), [877]
    companies affected by provisions,
      25(2), [877]
    controlled by local authority—
      authorities acting jointly, **25(2)**, [883]
      deemed to be, **25(2)**, [878]
      generally, **25(2)**, [878]
      requirements as to, **25(2)**, [880]
    group control of, **25(2)**, [883]
    kinds of companies, **25(2)**, [877]
    minority interests, control of, **25(2)**, [881]
    orders, power to make, **25(2)**, [877]
    provision for, **26(2)**, [249]
    restriction of powers, **25(2)**, [881]

local authority—*contd*
  companies—*contd*
    subject to local authority influence—
      business relationship of, **25(2)**, [879]
      nature of, **25(2)**, [879]
      requirements as to, **25(2)**, [880]
      trusts, provisions applied, **25(2)**, [882]
  complaints about social services, **30**, [700],
    [701]
  compulsory acquisition by. See
    compensation; orders
  computers, use of spare capacity of,
    25(2), [370]
  conduct of members—
    Adjudication Panels, **26(2)**, [115]
    case tribunals—
      adjudications by, **26(2)**, [117]
      decisions of—
        England, **26(2)**, [119], [120]
        Wales, **26(2)**, [121]
      interim, **26(2)**, [116]
        decisions of, **26(2)**, [118]
      recommendations, **26(2)**, [122]
      references to, **26(2)**, [116]
    code of—
      conduct covered by, **26(2)**, [612]
      duty to adopt, **26(2)**, [81]
      duty to comply with, **26(2)**, [82]
      model, **26(2)**, [80]
    monitoring officers—
      delegation of functions, **26(2)**, [125]
      ombudsmen, consultation with,
        26(2), [107]
      matters referred to, **26(2)**, [103], [113]
    principles governing, **26(2)**, [79]
    Standards Board for England, investigations
      by. See **Standards Board for England**
    standards committee, **26(2)**, [83]–[87]
    See also standards committee *below*
  conferences, facilities for, **25(2)**, [146]
  contracting out of functions—
    amendment of provisions, **10**, [770]
    certified contracts, **26(1)**, [301]
    disclosure of information, **10**, [762], [769];
      26(1), [198], [205]
    effect of, **10**, [759]; **26(1)**, [196]
    exclusions, **26(1)**, [195]
    financial provisions, **10**, [767]
    interpretation, **10**, [766]
    Northern Ireland, **10**, [765]
    order for, **26(1)**, [194], [199]
    termination, **10**, [760]
    termination of, **26(1)**, [197]
  contracts—
    certified—
      audit reviews, **26(1)**, [297], [300]
      certificate, **26(1)**, [296]
      certification period, **26(1)**, [294]
      certification requirements, **26(1)**, [295]
      contracting out of functions,
        26(1), [301]
      discharge terms, **26(1)**, [298]
        absence of, **26(1)**, [299]
      intra vires, **26(1)**, [294]
      judicial review, **26(1)**, [297]

local authority—*contd*
  contracts—*contd*
    certified—*contd*
      regulations, **26(1)**, [302]
    interest in. *See* members *below*
    power to enter into, **26(1)**, [293]
    standing orders, **25(2)**, [133]
  contracts, competitive tendering, public supply
    etc, for. *See* public supply or works contracts
    below
  contributions by, concurrent functions
    expenditure, **25(2)**, [134]
  contributions to expenses—
    Minister, by, **46**, [577]
    other authorities, of, **46**, [578]
  control of, relaxation etc, **25(2)**, [328], [427],
    [447]
  councillors, paid time off, **26(2)**, [310]
  county council. *See* **county council**
  covenant relating to land, enforcement of,
    by, **21**, [768]
  credit agreements, exemption of, **39(1)**, [149]
  credit arrangements—
    control of, **26(2)**, [239]
    meaning, **26(2)**, [238]
  crime and disorder committee—
    City of London, in, **12(4)**, [282]
    functions of, **12(4)**, [282]
    joint, **12(4)**, [264]
    meetings, **12(4)**, [282]
    reference of local matters to, **26(2)**, [601]
    requirement to have, **12(4)**, [262]
    sub-committees, **12(4)**, [282]
  crime and disorder matters, guidance on,
    12(4), [263]
  crime and disorder strategy. *See* **crime and
    disorder strategy**
  custody of child, report on, **6**, [216]
  damage by, compensation for, **35(1)**, [41],
    [44], [175], [629]
  dance halls etc, provision of, **25(2)**, [147]
  day care, functions regarding, **6**, [406]
  debts, extinguishment, **25(2)**, [891]
  default powers of Secretary of State, **6**, [412]
  definition of, **42**, [1030]
  development, deemed planning permission
    for, **46**, [318], [353]
  directed partnership arrangements—
    directions, **30**, [885]
    Secretary of State, power of, **30**, [884]
  directions to, **26(2)**, [251]
  disabled person—
    authorised representatives, duties to,
      40(1), [162]
    carer, taking abilities into account,
      40(1), [168]
    needs—
      assessment of, **40(1)**, [163]
      duty to consider, **40(1)**, [164]
  disabled persons, provision of sheltered
    employment for, **16**, [16], [18]
  diseases, control of, **35(1)**, [442]
  diseases of animals, for. *See* **diseases of
  animals**

local authority—*contd*
  displaced officers, compensation of,
    40(1), [29]
  disposal of houses. *See* **house**
  disposal of land—
    direction for, **25(2)**, [437], [438]
    exercise of powers, **25(1)**, [594]
    meaning of disposal, **25(1)**, [597]
    parish or community council, by,
      25(2), [125]
    principal councils, by, **25(2)**, [121]
    protection of purchasers, **25(2)**, [126]
    transactions requiring consent, **25(1)**, [595],
      [596]
  disqualification for membership. *See* members
    below
  dissolved by order—
    definitions, **26(2)**, [528]
    directions—
      consideration taken into account,
        26(2), [525]
      contravention of, **26(2)**, [526]
      disposals, contracts and reserves, control
        of, **26(2)**, [522]
      meaning, **26(2)**, [524]
      reserves, as to, **26(2)**, [523]
      substitution of sums, **26(2)**, [527]
  district council. *See* **district council**
  documents—
    authentication, **25(2)**, [186]
    copy, meaning, **25(2)**, [100]
    custody of, **25(2)**, [176]
    defamatory matter in, **25(2)**, [97]
    deposit with proper officer, **25(2)**, [177]
    depositories for, **25(2)**, [179]
    inspection—
      after meetings, **25(2)**, [91]
      background papers, **25(2)**, [92]
      council members, by, **25(2)**, [95]
      fee chargeable for, **25(2)**, [97]
      functions exercisable by members,
        records relating to, **25(2)**, [94]
      obstruction of, **25(2)**, [97]
      reports, **25(2)**, [90]
      time for, **25(2)**, [90], [97]
      to be open for, **25(2)**, [180]
    parish or community, **25(2)**, [178]
    photographic copies, **25(2)**, [181]
    service of, **25(2)**, [183]
    supply to press, **25(2)**, [90]
  documents etc—
    form of, **35(1)**, [615]
    register of, duty to keep, **35(1)**, [614]
  drainage. *See* land drainage *below*
  drainage board, exercise of powers in case of
    default by, **19(3)**, [181]
  economic, social or environmental well-being,
    promotion of—
    amendment or repeal of enactments—
      orders, procedure for, **26(2)**, [9]
      Wales, **26(2)**, [10]
    plans, concerning, **26(2)**, [7]
      Wales, **26(2)**, [8]
    power of, **26(2)**, [6]
    limits on power, **26(2)**, [3]

local authority—*contd*
  economic, social or environmental well-being,
    promotion of—*contd*
      power of, **26(2)**, [2]
      strategies for, **26(2)**, [4]
        parish council, **26(2)**, [5]
  electricity, power to generate, **25(2)**, [363]
  emergencies or disasters, financial assistance
    for, **25(2)**, [890]
  emergency payment of benefits, **40(1)**, [518]
  employees—
      code of conduct, **26(2)**, [124]
      paid leave for local authority duties,
        25(2), [863]
      staff records, **25(2)**, [864]
      terms and conditions, negotiation of,
        25(2), [865]
  employment and training arrangements,
    25(2), [476]
  England, in—
      adoption and fostering functions, premises
        with, inspection of, **15(2)**, [861]
      annual review of, **15(2)**, [852]
      inspection of, **15(2)**, [850]–[851]
        documents, **15(2)**, [854]
        information, provision of, **15(2)**, [855]
        powers of entry, Chief Inspector, of,
          15(2), [853]
      payment of annual fee to Chief Inspector,
        15(2), [869]
  entertainments, provision of, **25(2)**, [147]
  entities controlled by—
      amended provisions, **26(2)**, [668]
      definition of terms, **26(2)**, [628], [629]
      orders, **26(2)**, [623], [625]
        exemptions, **26(2)**, [626]
      trusts, **26(2)**, [624]
  entry, powers of. *See* **entry on land and
    premises**
  executives. *See* **local authority executives**
  expenditure—
      appropriate sum, **25(2)**, [260]
      capital. *See* capital expenditure *above*
      discretionary, **25(2)**, [135]
      emergency or disaster, **25(2)**, [137]
      inter-authority contributions, **25(2)**, [135]
      limit on, **25(2)**, [135]
      power to incur, **25(2)**, [135]
      publicity, on, **25(2)**, [135], [649]–[652]
      purposes not authorised, **25(2)**, [135]
      voluntary organisations, assistance to,
        25(2), [135]
  expenses—
      grants, of providing, **25(2)**, [330]
      parish and community councils,
        25(2), [151]
      records, in connection with, **25(1)**, [664]
      recovery of establishment charges,
        25(2), [329]
  explosives provisions. *See* **explosives**
  external funds, **26(2)**, [248]
  facilities, power to provide, **25(2)**, [146]
  family assistance. *See under* **child**
  ferries, Ministerial control, **25(2)**, [448]

local authority—*contd*
  ferry, acquiring—
      Crown rights, saving for, **36**, [591]
      existing, **36**, [589]
      passengers and public, regulations for
        protection of, **36**, [590]
  fertilisers and feeding stuffs, enforcement
    authority for, **1(1)**, [831]
  financial administration—
      authorities to which provisions apply,
        25(2), [802]
      certain combined authorities, **25(2)**, [803]
      chief finance officer, report by,
        25(2), [804]
      meetings, information about, **25(2)**, [810]
      regulations, **25(2)**, [825]
      reports—
          duties of executive, **25(2)**, [809]
          duty of authorities, **25(2)**, [807]
      responsible officer—
          duties, **25(2)**, [805]
          functions of, **25(2)**, [805], [806]
          local authorities operating executive
            arrangements, **25(2)**, [806]
          qualifications of, **25(2)**, [804]
          reports by, **25(2)**, [805], [806]
      supplementary provisions, power to make,
        25(2), [829]
  financial provisions—
      administration of finances, **25(2)**, [152]
      borrowing powers. *See* borrowing *above*
      credit arrangements. *See* credit
        arrangements *above*
      financial assistance—
          conditions for giving, **25(2)**, [136]
          meaning, **25(2)**, [136]
      funds. *See* funds *below*
      local Acts, power to amend, **25(1)**, [737]
      returns to be made, **25(2)**, [154]
      revenue from undertakings, **25(2)**, [153]
      separate, England and Wales, **25(2)**, [822]
      summary of, **25(1)**, [1]
      See also expenditure *above*
  financial years, **25(2)**, [827]
  fixed penalty receipts, use of—
      higher tier authorities, **35(2)**, [539], [541]
      lower tier authorities, **35(2)**, [540], [541]
  flood prevention works, **19(3)**, [183]
  forged transfer, compensation for,
    19(1), [132]
  functions—
      commons, **25(2)**, [166]
      control, relaxation etc, **25(2)**, [328]
      discharge of—
          arrangements for, **25(2)**, [101]
          jointly by two authorities, **25(2)**, [101]
      environmental, **25(2)**, [164]–[167]
      ordnance survey, **25(2)**, [167]
      research into, **40(1)**, [15]
      social services. *See* social services *below*
      subsidiary powers, **25(2)**, [110]
      summary of, **25(1)**, [1]
      traffic and transportation, **25(2)**, [164]
      transfer of, general provisions, **25(2)**, [163]
      village greens, **25(2)**, [166]

local authority—*contd*
  funds—
    general fund, **25(2)**, [795]
    regulations for, **25(2)**, [801]
    transfers between, **25(2)**, [799], [800]
    types of, **25(2)**, [150]
    See also collection fund *above*; general fund
     below
  garages, provision of, **25(1)**, [686]
  general fund—
    authorities liable to establish, **25(2)**, [795]
    establishment, **25(2)**, [795]
    payments to or from, **25(2)**, [795]
    regulations for, **25(2)**, [796], [801]
    transfer of moneys to, **25(2)**, [799]
  general rate fund, discontinuance of,
    25(2), [795]
  generally accepted accounting practice,
    amendment or repeal of enactments by
    reference to, **26(2)**, [312]
  gifts, power to accept, **25(2)**, [138]
  goods and services—
    accounts in respect of, **25(1)**, [972]
    forms of, **25(1)**, [971]
    power to provide, **25(1)**, [971]
  goods and services, supply by water
    authorities, **49**, [566]
  goods and services, supply of, **30**, [448], [880]
  grants—
    authorities for purposes of, **25(2)**, [306]
    commutation, power as to, **25(2)**, [891]
    commuted payment, calculation of,
     25(2), [891]
    designation for service excellence, in
     connection with, **26(2)**, [264]
    ethnic minorities, in respect of,
     25(1), [797]
    expenditure—
     bodies being local authorities,
      26(2), [263]
     Greater London Authority, **26(2)**, [262]
     power to pay, **26(2)**, [261]
    National Parks, for, **25(2)**, [305]
    rate support. *See* **rates**
    social services, for, **25(1)**, [982]
    special. *See* special grants *below*
    special social need, for, **25(1)**, [913]
    specific purposes, for, **25(2)**, [334]
    transport purposes, **25(2)**, [303], [333]
  grants to housing association, power to
    make, **22**, [468]
    See further **housing association**
  guidance from Secretary of State, **26(2)**, [246]
  health and social care, joint strategic needs
    assessments, **26(2)**, [596]
  heat, production and supply of, **25(2)**, [363],
    [364]
  highway authority, as, **25(2)**, [165]
  houses, right to buy. *See* **dwelling-house**
  houses sold at discount, stamp duty,
    41, [138], [145]
  housing. *See* **housing**
  indebtedness, payments towards, **26(2)**, [268]

local authority—*contd*
  information—
    access to—
     agendas, right to inspect, **25(2)**, [90]
     council members, by, **25(2)**, [95]
     employees, relating to, **25(2)**, [254]
     exception from—
      confidential information, **25(2)**, [89]
      descriptions of exempt information,
       25(2), [254]–[259]
      provision for, **25(2)**, [98]
     rights, summary of, **25(2)**, [96]
    collection of, **25(2)**, [143]
    electronic access to, **40(1)**, [595]
    on energy measures, to have regard to,
     17(2), [575]–[576]
    power to publish, **21**, [634]
    provision of, **25(2)**, [144]
    provision to Secretary of State, **26(2)**, [245]
    publication—
     codes of practice, **25(2)**, [428], [429]
     direction by Minister, **25(2)**, [430]
     duty as to, **25(2)**, [428]
     regulations requiring, **25(2)**, [429]
    returns of, generally, **6**, [411]
    supply of, **22**, [876]
  inquiries, power to direct, **25(2)**, [213]
  insurance—
    generally, **25(2)**, [142]
    members' accident, **25(2)**, [139]
    probation assistants, for, **25(2)**, [141]
    voluntary assistants, for, **25(2)**, [140]
  investigation, subject to, **25(2)**, [310]
    See further **Local Commissioner**
  investment by, **48**, 217
  investment powers, **26(2)**, [243]
  investment schemes, **48**, 576, 592–4
  ironstone workings restoration, **17(1)**, [550]
  joint authorities—
    information, duty to publish, **25(2)**, [428]
    meetings, **25(2)**, [248]
    status of, **25(2)**, [149]
  joint boards—
    continuance of, **25(2)**, [223]
    provisions applied, **25(2)**, [201]
  joint bodies, transfers between, exemption
    from stamp duty, **41**, [88]
  joint committees, voting rights, **25(2)**, [866]
  justices members of, not disqualified,
    35(1), [31], [194]
  land—
    acquisition. *See* acquisition *above*
    advances for development, **25(1)**, [684]
     mortgage to secure, **25(1)**, [684]
    appropriation. *See* appropriation *above*
    areas in which provisions operate,
     25(2), [432]
    building agreements, advances under,
     25(1), [685]
    compulsory acquisition, special
     parliamentary procedure, **9**, [430], [433],
     [453]
    consent to dealings in, **25(2)**, [126]
    development—
     assessment for, **25(2)**, [441]

local authority—*contd*
land—*contd*
development—*contd*
powers of, **25(1)**, [683]
disposal of. *See* disposal *above*
entry on, powers of, **25(2)**, [439]
erection of buildings, advances for,
25(1), [684]
exclusion from compulsory purchase,
9, [454]
garages, provision of, **25(1)**, [686]
information—
entries, about, **25(2)**, [435]
Minister requiring, **25(2)**, [436]
power to obtain, **25(2)**, [365]
local Acts, amendment of, **25(1)**, [688]
meaning, **25(1)**, [692]
persons interested in, particulars of,
25(2), [365]
powers relating to, **25(1)**, [1]
public access to information, **25(1)**, [1];
25(2), [434]
public bodies, provisions applied to,
25(2), [431]
See further **public bodies**
registration of holdings, **25(2)**, [433]–[435]
rights over, special parliamentary procedure
where, **9**, [453]
transactions—
compensation provisions, **25(2)**, [127]
protection of purchasers, **25(2)**, [126]
savings in respect of, **25(2)**, [129]
under-used, register of, **25(2)**, [433]
land drainage—
agreements to execute work, **19(3)**, [188]
borrowing for purposes of, **19(3)**, [224]
byelaws. *See* **byelaws**
county council, exercise by, **19(3)**, [185]
entry, powers of, **19(3)**, [239]
environment and recreation, duties
respecting, **19(3)**, [232]
expenses—
contribution to, **19(3)**, [229]
defrayment, **19(3)**, [167], [230]
general powers, **19(3)**, [183]
grants for, **19(3)**, [228]
land, power to acquire, **19(3)**, [237]
maintenance of works, **19(3)**, [183]
new works, construction of, **19(3)**, [183]
outside area of, **19(3)**, [183]
supervision of, **19(3)**, [186]
powers—
exercise by Environment Agency,
19(3), [185]
exercise of, **19(3)**, [185]
general discharge of, **19(3)**, [183]
precepts, issue of, **19(3)**, [163]
small areas, **19(3)**, [187]
spoil, disposal of, **19(3)**, [184]
supervision, **19(3)**, [186]
spray irrigation, powers to facilitate,
19(3), [236]
summary of provisions, **19(3)**, [161]
supervision of, **19(3)**, [186]

local authority—*contd*
Landlord and Tenant Act 1987, exemption
from, **22**, [771]
landlord, as—
assured tenancy, exclusion of, **22**, [913]
restricted contract, exclusion of, **21**, [540]
tenancy not protected, **21**, [534]
legal proceedings—
appearance in, **25(2)**, [175]
photographic copies, use of, **25(2)**, [181]
powers in respect of, **25(2)**, [174]
legislation—
Acts repealed, **25(2)**, [263]
adaptations to 1972 Act, **25(2)**, [261]
amendments, **25(2)**, [261]
library. *See* **public library**
licences, responsibility for, **2**, [338]
loans, extinguishment, **25(2)**, [891]
local Acts—
application of, **25(2)**, [222]
repeal or amendment, **25(2)**, [478]
local area agreements—
draft—
approval by Secretary of state,
26(2), [589]
duty to prepare and submit, **26(2)**, [588]
information, duty to publish, **26(2)**, [595]
local improvement targets—
designated, **26(2)**, [591]
designated, revision proposals,
26(2), [593]
duty to have regard to, **26(2)**, [590]
meaning, **26(2)**, [587]
revision and addition of, **26(2)**, [592]
partner authorities, **26(2)**, [586]
responsible authorities, **26(2)**, [585]
revision proposals—
approval of, **26(2)**, [594]
designated targets, as to, **26(2)**, [593]
transitional provisions, **26(2)**, [598]
Local Better Regulation Office. *See* **Local
Better Regulation Office**
local education authority—
consultation with, **6**, [340]
functions concurrent with, **6**, [342]
local implementation plan—
meaning, **38(2)**, [1]
reports, **38(2)**, [2]
local licence duties—
application of proceeds, **25(1)**, [59]
payment over to county council,
25(1), [59]
local partners, co-operation with—
community strategy. *See* community
strategy *above*
community strategy, health and social care,
26(2), [596]
local area agreements. *See* local area
agreements *above*
local polls by, **26(2)**, [311]
local road traffic—
meaning, **38(2)**, [1]
reports, duty to make, **38(2)**, [2]

local authority—*contd*
London. *See* **London**
lost or uncollected property, dealing with,
  25(2), [475]
lotteries promoted by. *See* **lottery** (local)
maladministration—
  complaints of, **25(1)**, [1]
  investigation, **25(2)**, [311]
  payments, **26(2)**, [132]
market authority, as. *See* **markets and fairs**
meaning, **6**, [135], [223], [435]; **8(1)**, [132],
  [1271]; **9**, [375], [416]; **10**, [766]; **22**, [4];
  40(1), [17], [45]; **41**, [499]; **44(1)**, [627];
  44(4), [1007]
  co-ordination of regulatory enforcement,
    for, **26(2)**, [771]
  Deregulation and Contracting Out
    Act 1994, **26(1)**, [201]–[203]
  Emergency Provisions Act, **25(1)**, [131]
  Local Authorities (Goods and Services)
    Act 1970, **25(1)**, [971]
  Local Better Regulation Office, for
    purposes of, **26(2)**, [751]
  Local Government Act 1999, **26(1)**, [391]
  Local Government Act 2000, **26(2)**, [1]
  Local Government Act 2003, **26(2)**, [254],
    [263]
  Local Government and Housing Act 1989,
    25(2), [873], [877], [890]
  Local Government (Contracts) Act 1997,
    26(1), [293]
  Local Government (Miscellaneous
    Provisions) Act 1976, **25(2)**, [373]
  Local Government (Overseas Assistance)
    Act 1993, **26(1)**, [137]
  local involvement networks, for purposes
    of, **26(2)**, [640]
  social services provisions, **25(1)**, [974]
  War Memorials etc Act, **25(1)**, [145]
meetings—
  admission of press, **25(2)**, [88]
  admission of press and news agencies,
    25(1), [625]
  admission of public, **25(1)**, [1], [625];
    25(2), [88], [89]
    committee meetings, **25(2)**, [93]
    principal council meetings, **25(2)**, [89]
  agenda—
    copy, right to, **25(2)**, [90]
    inspection of, **25(2)**, [90]
    provision of, **25(1)**, [625]
    time for inspection, **25(2)**, [90]
  annual, **25(2)**, [247]
  attendance, record of, **25(2)**, [253]
  chairman, **25(2)**, [247]
  exclusion of public, **25(1)**, [625]
    circumstances for, **25(2)**, [89]
    disorderly conduct etc, to prevent,
      25(2), [89]
    part of proceedings, from, **25(2)**, [89]
    resolution for, **25(2)**, [89]
  extraordinary meetings, **25(2)**, [247]
  failure to attend, **25(2)**, [74]
  general provisions, **25(2)**, [253]

local authority—*contd*
meetings—*contd*
  minutes of proceedings—
    evidence of, **25(2)**, [372]
    inspection of, **25(2)**, [91]
    procedure for keeping, **25(2)**, [253]
  notice of, **25(2)**, [247]
  parish council, **25(2)**, [249]
  photography, ban on, **25(2)**, [89]
  press, admission of, **25(1)**, [625];
    25(2), [88]
  principal councils, of, **25(2)**, [247]
  public notice of, **25(1)**, [625]; **25(2)**, [89]
  quorum, **25(2)**, [247]
  standing orders, **25(2)**, [253], [872]
  voting—
    disability for, **25(2)**, [82]
    removal of disability, **25(2)**, [85]
members—
  acceptance of office, **25(2)**, [72]
  access to information, **25(2)**, [95]
  age qualification, **25(2)**, [68]
  allowances to. *See* allowances *above*
  approved duty, meaning, **25(2)**, [161]
  bankrupt disqualified as, **25(2)**, [69]
  casual vacancy—
    chairman, in case of, **25(2)**, [77]
    date of occurrence of, **25(2)**, [76]
    filling, **25(2)**, [77]
    person filling, term of office, **25(2)**, [79]
  conduct of. *See* conduct of members *above*
  courtesy visits, expenses, **25(2)**, [160]
  declaration to be made by, **25(2)**, [72]
  disqualification—
    generally, **25(2)**, [69]
    joint authority, for, **25(2)**, [69], [596]
    office holders liable to, **25(2)**, [851]
    proceedings for, **25(2)**, [81]
  functions exercisable by, inspection of
    records, **25(2)**, [94]
  general provisions, **25(1)**, [1]
  indemnification, **26(2)**, [137]
  insurance against accidents, **25(2)**, [139]
  interest in contract etc—
    disability to vote by, **25(2)**, [82]
    disclosure of, **25(2)**, [82]; **26(2)**, [123]
    general notice in respect of, **25(2)**, [84],
      [871]
    matters deemed to be, **25(2)**, [83]
    offences as to, penalty, **25(2)**, [82], [871]
    record of disclosures, **25(2)**, [84]
    registration, **26(2)**, [123]
    regulations as to, **25(2)**, [871]
    removal or exclusion of disability to
      vote, **25(2)**, [85]
  meetings, failure to attend, **25(2)**, [74]
  misconduct, references to Adjudication
    Panel, **26(2)**, [104]
  pensions, **26(2)**, [135]
  politically restricted post—
    disqualification for holding, **25(2)**, [851]
    lists of posts, **25(2)**, [852]
    meaning, **25(2)**, [852]
    protection from personal liability,
      35(1), [32], [195], [391], [509], [637]

local authority—*contd*
　members—*contd*
　　qualifications for election, **25(2)**, [68]
　　references to, **26(2)**, [126]
　　register of, **25(2)**, [96]
　　resignation of, **25(2)**, [73]
　　teachers, qualification of, **25(2)**, [70]
　　temporary appointment, **25(2)**, [80]
　　unqualified, validity of acts by, **25(2)**, [71]
　　vacation of office—
　　　declaration of, **25(2)**, [75]
　　　non-attendance, for, **25(2)**, [74]
　　voting—
　　　disability for, **25(2)**, [82]
　　　removal or exclusion of disability,
　　　　25(2), [85]
　　　rights, **25(2)**, [866]
　　written allegations against—
　　　decision not to act, right to request
　　　　review of, **26(2)**, [91]
　　　initial assessment, **26(2)**, [90]
　　　right to make, **26(2)**, [90]
　　　Standard Board, referred to, **26(2)**, [94]
　　　standards committee's functions, power
　　　　to suspend, **26(2)**, [93]
　　　subject of, information to, **26(2)**, [92]
　mental patient—
　　discharge from hospital, notification of,
　　　40(1), [167]
　　needs, assessment of, **40(1)**, [167]
　mines and quarries disused tips, functions. *See*
　　tips
　minimum reserves, **26(2)**, [257]
　Ministerial controls, relaxation—
　　Ferries, **25(2)**, [448]
　　road traffic, **25(2)**, [449]
　minutes of proceedings—
　　evidence of, **25(2)**, [372]
　　inspection of, **25(2)**, [91]
　　procedure for keeping, **25(2)**, [253]
　misrepresentation, recovery of expenditure in
　　case of, **40(1)**, [21]
　mortgage—
　　abolition of right to, **23**, [181]
　　advances—
　　　fitness of premises for, **22**, [316]
　　　power to make, **22**, [312]
　　　property requiring repair etc, **22**, [318]
　　　purposes of, **22**, [312]
　　　requirements as to, **22**, [316]
　　　terms of, **22**, [313]
　　agreement to indemnify mortgagee,
　　　22, [319]
　　costs, contributions to, **22**, [320], [321]
　　deed, provisions in, **22**, [313]
　　　interest rates, **22**, [315], [447]
　　　leaving amount outstanding on,
　　　　22, [314]
　　　waiver or reduction of payments,
　　　　22, [318]
　　transfer of, **25(2)**, [653]
　mortgaged property, maintenance etc of,
　　22, [317]
　museums and art galleries, provision of,
　　13, [49]

local authority—*contd*
　name, change of, **25(2)**, [64]
　new councils—
　　chairman, **25(2)**, [240]
　　establishment of, **25(2)**, [23]
　　London. *See* **Greater London**
　　metropolitan. *See* **metropolitan counties**
　NHS bodies—
　　arrangements with, **30**, [881], [1111]
　　co-operation with, **30**, [888]
　　delegation arrangements, **30**, [883]
　　payments to, **30**, [882]
　new town development corporation, transfer
　　of undertaking by, **46**, [170]
　no income tax liability for, **44(4)**, [846]
　noise, summary procedure for dealing with.
　　See **noise**
　non-disclosure, recovery of expenditure in
　　case of, **40(1)**, [21]
　notice of proposed stopping up or diversion of
　　highway to, **9**, [142]
　notices—
　　authentication of, **25(2)**, [186]
　　public, giving, **25(2)**, [184]
　　service by, **25(2)**, [185]
　　service on, **25(2)**, [183]
　nursing homes. *See* **nursing home**
　obstruction of, **35(1)**, [40]
　offences, prosecuting, **21**, [635]
　officers. *See* **local government officers and
　　staff**
　officers, appointment of, **35(1)**, [69]
　offices, provision of, **25(2)**, [130]
　old people, promotion of welfare of,
　　40(1), [45]
　omnibus shelter, providing, **36**, [652]–[654]
　orders by—
　　appeals, **35(1)**, [61], [190]–[192]
　　effect of, **35(1)**, [36]
　　provisional, **35(1)**, [35]–[37]
　　publication, **35(1)**, [36]
　orders by Secretary of State, **25(2)**, [200]
　ordnance survey provisions, **25(2)**, [167]
　overseas assistance by, **26(1)**, [137]
　overview and scrutiny committees—
　　Common Council of City of London,
　　　establishment by, **30**, [1053]
　　exempt information, **30**, [1052]
　　functions of, **30**, [1050]
　　joint, **30**, [1051]
　　Wales. *See* **Wales**
　parenting contract, entry into, **6(S)**, 276
　parenting order, application for, **6(S)**, 279–80
　　county court proceedings, in, **6(S)**, 281
　parish. *See* **parish council**
　payment into court of purchase price etc,
　　9, [39], [269], [296]
　　repayment when unclaimed, **9**, [374]
　performance, categorisation by reference to—
　　Audit Commission, by, **26(2)**, [301]
　　exercise of powers by reference to,
　　　26(2), [302]
　pleasure boats byelaws, **25(2)**, [442]

local authority—*contd*
poisons, functions as regards. *See* **poisons**
police authority, provisions applied,
25(2), [107]
political groups—
  allocation of seats to—
    bodies affected by provisions,
      25(2), [898]
    exceptions as to, 25(2), [869]
    extension of requirements, 25(2), [869]
    general duty as to, 25(2), [867]
    giving effect to, 25(2), [868]
  assistants for, appointment, 25(2), [862]
  regulations as to, 25(2), [898]
political publicity, prohibition, 25(2), [649]
powers—
  gifts, to accept, 25(2), [138]
  subsidiary, 25(2), [110]
  summary of, 25(1), [1]
  transfer from public bodies, 25(2), [216]
  See also functions *above*
precepting authorities—
  meaning, 25(2), [826]
  powers, limitation of, 25(2), [496]
precepts. *See* **precept**
primary—
  advice and guidance by, 26(2), [775]
  enforcement action—
    exclusions, 26(2), [777]
    notification to, 26(2), [776]
    referred to LBRO, 26(2), [791]
  fees, charging, 26(2), [779]
  inspection plans, 26(2), [778]
  LBRO support, 26(2), [780]
  nomination of, 26(2), [774]
principal authority, meaning, 26(2), [499]
principal councils—
  bodies deemed to be, 25(2), [99]
  chairmen of, 25(2), [3], [4]
  constitution of, 25(2), [2]
  councillors, 25(2), [6], [7]
  funds of, 25(2), [150]
  meaning, 25(2), [229]
  meetings of, 25(2), [247]
  vice-chairmen, 25(2), [5]
private supply notice—
  confirmation of, 49, [868]
  enforcement of, 49, [869]
  power to serve, 49, [867]
  steps required by, 49, [867]
  variation of, 49, [869]
proceedings, institution by, 38(1), [4]
proceedings, institution of, 6, [47]
promotion etc of housing associations,
  22, [468]
promotion or protection of interests of
  inhabitants, proceedings for, 12(3), [657]
proper officer—
  documents, deposit with, 25(2), [177]
  meaning, 25(2), [229]
property—
  gifts of, power to accept, 25(2), [138]
  transfer of, orders for, 25(2), [628]
property of persons admitted to hospital,
  temporary protection for, 40(1), [23]

local authority—*contd*
provisional orders relating to, 25(2), [200]
public health purposes, for, 35(1), [118]
public inquiries, representations in,
  25(2), [174]
public notices, mode of giving, 25(2), [184]
public service vehicles undertaking,
  acquisition or disposal, 36, [793]
public supply or works contracts—
  contractors, meaning, 25(2), [702]
  decisions as to, reasons for, 25(2), [705]
  interpretation of terms, 25(2), [702]
  lists of contractors, 25(2), [702]
    compilation, 25(2), [706]
    existing lists, 25(2), [706]
    inclusion in or exclusion from,
      25(2), [702]
    no charge for inclusion in, 25(2), [707]
  meaning, 25(2), [702]
  miscellaneous provisions, 25(2), [704]
  non-commercial considerations—
    exclusion of, 25(2), [702]
    meaning, 25(2), [702]
  public authorities for purposes of,
    25(2), [715]
  race relations matters, 25(2), [703]
publicity—
  codes of recommended practice,
    25(2), [650]
  expenditure on, 25(2), [135]
    account of, 25(2), [651]
    appropriate sum, 25(2), [260]
  local services, of, 25(2), [144]
  meaning, 25(2), [652]
  political, prohibition, 25(2), [649]
racial discrimination by—
  general statutory duty, 7(1), [191]–[193]
  planning authority, as, 7(1), [148]
rate support grant. *See* **rates**
receiving authority—
  meaning, 25(2), [761], [823]
  payments to and from authorities,
    25(2), [823]
  revenue support grant. *See* revenue support
    grant *below*
records—
  acquisition of, 25(1), [663]
  adequate use of, powers as to, 25(1), [662]
  custody of, 25(1), [663]
  deposit of, 25(1), [663]
    public library etc, with, 25(1), [667]
  expenses respecting, 25(1), [664]
  local Acts relating to, 25(1), [665]
  meaning, 25(1), [668]
  orders as to, 25(1), [666]
  transfer to Public Record Office etc,
    25(1), [667]
  use of, promotion of, 25(1), [662]
registered social landlords, assistance to,
  23, [367]
regulatory burdens—
  regulatory enforcement by, 25(1), [1]
  co-ordination of—
    orders, 26(2), [782]

local authority—*contd*

regulatory enforcement by—*contd*

co-ordination of—*contd*

relevant function, meaning, **26(2)**, [752], [772]

scope of provisions, **26(2)**, [770]

reports—

duty to make, **25(2)**, [182]

"not for publication", **25(2)**, [90]

power to inspect, **25(2)**, [90]

reports of proceedings, libel, **19(3)**, [346]

research, conduct of, **6**, [411]

research powers, **25(2)**, [143]

resolutions, evidence of, **25(2)**, [372]

returns, duty to make, **25(2)**, [182]

revenue account, meaning, **26(2)**, [253]

revenue support grant—

additional grant—

application of provisions, **25(2)**, [782]

distribution of, **25(2)**, [784]

provision for, **25(2)**, [783]

amount, calculation of, **25(2)**, [766]

amending report, under, **25(2)**, [769]

approval by Parliament, **25(2)**, [765]

determinations as to, **25(2)**, [763]

England, provisions applying, **25(2)**, [762]

instalments, payment in, **25(2)**, [767]

payment of, **25(2)**, [767]

amending report, under, **25(2)**, [770]

power to pay, **25(2)**, [763]

report, **25(2)**, [764]

amending, **25(2)**, [768]–[770]

effect of approval, **25(2)**, [765]

Wales, provisions applying. *See* **Wales**

rights over land, compulsory acquisition of, **9**, [371]

road liabilities etc, transfer of, **25(1)**, [155]

road safety grants to, from national transport authority, **37**, [611]

road traffic functions, exercise of, **37**, [290]

safety in the home, promotion of, **25(1)**, [643]

sale of materials by, **35(1)**, [174]

sanctions etc, mode of giving, **25(1)**, [130]

schoolrooms etc, power to use, **25(2)**, [132]

Scotland, accommodation of persons under 65 in, **40(1)**, [51]

securities—

register, **25(2)**, [371]

transfer on alteration of area etc, **25(2)**, [148]

trusts attaching to, **25(2)**, [371]

service of notices on, **25(2)**, [183]

services, charge for—

charge on land for, **40(1)**, [126]

England and Wales, in, **40(1)**, [124]

interest, securing, **40(1)**, [127]

recovery of sums, **40(1)**, [125]

sewer maps provided to, **49**, [1012]

sewerage functions, performance of, **49**, [893]

smallholdings authority, as. *See* **smallholding**

social services—

authorities for purposes of, **25(1)**, [974]; **25(2)**, [168]

local authority—*contd*

social services—*contd*

chronically sick and disabled persons, **25(1)**, [990]

committees, functions of, **25(1)**, [975], [988]

default powers, **25(1)**, [981]

exercise, direction as to, **25(1)**, [978]

complaints about, **30**, [700], [701]

complaints procedure, **25(1)**, [979]

director of, **25(1)**, [976]

grants for, **25(1)**, [982]

inquiries, **25(1)**, [980]

Ministerial control, **25(1)**, [977]

nature of, **25(1)**, [988]

orders and regulations, **25(1)**, [985]

performance rating, of, **6**, [937]

Scilly Isles, in, **25(1)**, [984]

staff, protection of interests of, **25(1)**, [983]

welfare services, grants for, **26(2)**, [133]

social welfare in Scotland, **6**, [96]

staff. *See* **local government officers and staff**

standards committee—

community councils, for, **26(2)**, [87]

establishment of, **26(2)**, [83]

functions of, **26(2)**, [84]

power to suspend, **26(2)**, [93]

guidance to, **26(2)**, [83]

members of, **26(2)**, [83]

parish councils, for, **26(2)**, [86]

regulations, **26(2)**, [83]

sub-committees—

community councils, for, **26(2)**, [87]

establishment, **26(2)**, [85]

members of, **26(2)**, [85]

parish councils, for, **26(2)**, [86]

written allegations to, **26(2)**, [90]

standing orders for regulation of proceedings, **25(2)**, [253]

duty to adopt, **25(2)**, [872]

statutory order, support or opposition to, **41**, [496]

stock transfers, stamp duty exemption, **41**, [88]

summary of provisions, **25(1)**, [1]

sums due to, recovery of, **40(1)**, [28]

superannuation. *See* **local government officers**

supervision order. *See* **supervision order**

survey of land to be compulsorily acquired, **9**, [373]

sustainable communities—

action plans, **26(2)**, [469]

local spending reports, **26(2)**, [471]

promotion of sustainability, **26(2)**, [466]

proposals for—

interpretation, **26(2)**, [473]

making of, **26(2)**, [467]

regulations, **26(2)**, [470]

relevant matters, **26(2)**, [476]

short-list, decision on, **26(2)**, [468]

sustainable community strategy, **26(2)**, [472]

tax exemption, **44(1)**, [375]

local authority—*contd*

tobacco, sale to child, enforcement action, **6**, [463]

trade fairs, facilities for, **25(2)**, [146]

traffic and transportation functions, **25(2)**, [164]

tramways. *See* **tramway**

transferred officers, compensation and superannuation rights of, **35(1)**, [203]

transfers of property etc, orders for, **25(2)**, [628]

transport grants—

calculation, basis of, **25(2)**, [787]

councils eligible for, **25(2)**, [788]

relevant expenditure for, **25(2)**, [788]

urban development corporation, transfer of undertaking of, **46**, [85]

valuation list, apportionment of expenditure with reference to, **25(1)**, [152]

value added tax—

registration for, **50**, [56]

relief from, **50**, [45]

vehicle licences functions, compensation on transfer from, **36**, [888]

vesting of mortgaged house in—

compensation and accounting, **22**, [448]

effect of, **22**, [448]

leave of court, with, **22**, [448]

where power of sale, **22**, [332]

visitors to area, encouragement of, **25(2)**, [146]

voluntary assistants—

insurance of, **25(2)**, [140]

meaning, **25(2)**, [140]

voluntary home. *See* **voluntary home**

voluntary organisation, assistance to, **25(2)**, [135]

voluntary organisations, assisting, **30**, [432]

voluntary organisations, duties as to, **6**, [378]

war memorial—

alteration, expenditure on, **25(1)**, [408]

maintenance etc, **25(1)**, [143]

water, functions as to—

information, power to obtain, **49**, [872]

private supplies—

application of powers in relation to, **49**, [870]

remedial powers, **49**, [867]

quality, as to, **49**, [864]

supplies insufficient or unwholesome, where, **49**, [866]

undertakers' supplies, in relation to, **49**, [865]

watercourse, powers as to, **19(3)**, [194]

weeds, powers respecting, **1(1)**, [546]

welfare arrangements for blind, deaf, dumb and crippled persons, **40(1)**, [13]

welfare of child—

generally, **6**, [1]

promotion of, **6**, [322]

report on, **6**, [300]

welfare services—

information as to, need for, **40(1)**, [48]

matters being, **40(1)**, [49]

provision of, **40(1)**, [49]

local authority—*contd*

welfare services—*contd*

Scotland, accommodation of persons under 65 in, **40(1)**, [51]

Welsh Ministers, advice to, **26(2)**, [758]

works—

contract. *See* contracts, competitive tendering; direct labour organisation *above*

execution outside area, **25(2)**, [368]

powers as to, restoration of, **25(2)**, [379], [381]

young persons. *See* **young offenders; young person**

youth justice. *See* **youth justice**

zoos. *See* **zoo**

local authority executives

arrangements—

alternative—

application of provisions, **26(2)**, [38]

authorities to which applying, **26(2)**, [38]

ceasing to operate, **26(2)**, [556], [558]

executive, move to, **26(2)**, [43]

failure to cease operating, **26(2)**, [557], 558]

nature of, **26(2)**, [39]

operation of, **26(2)**, [40]

proposals for, **26(2)**, [38]

specification of, **26(2)**, [39]

variation of, **26(2)**, [44]

different, operation of, **26(2)**, [37]

functions, provision for, **26(2)**, [14]

mayoral, variation of, **26(2)**, [54]

meaning, **26(2)**, [11]

move to—

alternative arrangements, from, **26(2)**, [43]

general requirements, **26(2)**, [49]

new form of, **26(2)**, [50]

operation of, **26(2)**, [36]

overview and scrutiny committees, provision for, **26(2)**, [22]

proposals for operation of—

directions, **26(2)**, [32]

drawing up, **26(2)**, [32]

elected mayor, involving, **26(2)**, [34]

outline fall-back, approval of, **26(2)**, [35]

referendum, not requiring, **26(2)**, [33]

publicity, **26(2)**, [36]

regulations, **26(2)**, [74]

transitional provisions, **26(2)**, [603]

constitution, **26(2)**, [59]

decisions, record of, **26(2)**, [28]

elections—

entitlement to vote, **26(2)**, [65]

procedure, **26(2)**, [144]

regulations, **26(2)**, [66]

time of, **26(2)**, [63]

voting at, **26(2)**, [64]

forms of, **26(2)**, [12]

additional, **26(2)**, [13]

functions—

arrangements for, **26(2)**, [14]

local authority executives—*contd*
functions—*contd*
  discharge of—
    another local authority, of and by,
      26(2), [20]
    area committee, by, **26(2)**, [19]
    leader and cabinet executive, by,
      26(2), [15], [143]
      Wales, **26(2)**, [16]
    mayor and cabinet executive, by,
      26(2), [15], [143]
    mayor and council manager executive,
      by, **26(2)**, [17], [143]
    prescribed form of executive, by,
      26(2), [18]
  joint exercise of, **26(2)**, [21]
  meaning, **26(2)**, [14]
  responsibility for, **26(2)**, [14]
governance arrangements—
  changing—
    alternative, variation of, **26(2)**, [44]
    different forms of, **26(2)**, [41]
    directions, **26(2)**, [49]
    executive, move to, **26(2)**, [43]
    implementation, **26(2)**, [47], [48]
    interpretation, **26(2)**, [55]
    petition, referendum following,
      26(2), [56]
    proposals for, **26(2)**, [45]
    referendum, not subject to approval in,
      26(2), [52]
    referendum, subject to approval in,
      26(2), [51], [53]
    resolution for, **26(2)**, [46]
    variation of, **26(2)**, [42]
guidance, **26(2)**, [60]
information, access to, **26(2)**, [28]
interpretation, **26(2)**, [78]
leader—
  councillor, continuing to hold office as,
    26(2), [72]
  election of—
    means of, **26(2)**, [73]
    partial-council election, **26(2)**, [68]
    whole-council election, **26(2)**, [67]
  removal of, **26(2)**, [69], [73]
  term of office—
    partial-council election, **26(2)**, [71]
    whole-council election, **26(2)**, [70]
  transitional provisions, **26(2)**, [659]
mayors—
  elected—
    assistant, **26(2)**, [143]
    election of, **26(2)**, [62]–[66], [144]
    meaning, **26(2)**, [61]
    member or councillor, treated as,
      26(2), [61]
    proposals involving, referendum,
      26(2), [34]
    style, **26(2)**, [61]
    term, **26(2)**, [61]
  mayoral arrangements, variation of,
    26(2), [54]
  transitional provisions, **26(2)**, [660]

local authority executives—*contd*
meetings—
  access to, **26(2)**, [28]
  entitlement to attend and speak,
    26(2), [143]
members—
  elected executive—
    election, **26(2)**, [62]–[66]
    meaning, **26(2)**, [61]
    term, **26(2)**, [61]
  exclusions, **26(2)**, [12]
  number of, **26(2)**, [12]
overview and scrutiny committees—
  consequential amendments, **26(2)**, [602]
  co-opted members, voting rights,
    26(2), [143]
  education functions, **26(2)**, [143]
  functions of, **26(2)**, [22]
  joint, local improvement targets,
    26(2), [600]
  partner authorities—
    functions with respect to, **26(2)**, [27]
    information, provision of, **26(2)**, [29]
    power to require information from,
      26(2), [599]
    relevant, meaning, **26(2)**, [25], [27]
    reports and recommendations, duties as
      to, **26(2)**, [25]
  powers of, **26(2)**, [22]
  provision for, **26(2)**, [22]
  reference of matters to, **26(2)**, [23]
  reports and recommendations—
    confidential and exempt information,
      26(2), [26]
    partner authorities, duties of, **26(2)**, [25]
  response to—
    authority or executive, duty of,
      26(2), [24]
    confidential and exempt information,
      26(2), [26]
  sub-committees, **26(2)**, [22]
political balance, absence of requirement for,
  26(2), [31]
procedure, **26(2)**, [143]
referendum—
  direction, following, **26(2)**, [57]
  elected mayor, proposals involving,
    26(2), [34]
  entitlement to vote, **26(2)**, [75]
  number of, **26(2)**, [75]
  order, following, **26(2)**, [58]
  petition, following, **26(2)**, [56]
  proposals not requiring, **26(2)**, [33]
  regulations, **26(2)**, [75]

Local Better Regulation Office
accounts, **26(2)**, [788]
ancillary powers, **26(2)**, [762]
annual report, **26(2)**, [788]
burdens, duty not to impose, **26(2)**, [761]
committees, **26(2)**, [788]
company—
  dissolution, **26(2)**, [750]
  replacement of, **26(2)**, [789]

Local Better Regulation Office—*contd*
  delegation of functions, **26(2)**, [788]
    review of, **26(2)**, [765]
  dissolution—
    power of, **26(2)**, [766]
    tax provisions, **26(2)**, [767]
  employees, **26(2)**, [788]
  enforcement action referred to, **26(2)**, [791]
  enforcement priorities, **26(2)**, [759]
  establishment of, **26(2)**, [749]
  financial year, **26(2)**, [788]
  freedom of information, **26(2)**, [788]
  funding, **26(2)**, [788]
  general functions, objective, **26(2)**, [753]
  guidance or directions to—
    Secretary of State, by, **26(2)**, [763]
    Welsh Ministers, by, **26(2)**, [764]
  instruments and authorisations, **26(2)**, [788]
  investigation of, **26(2)**, [788]
  local authorities—
    financial support and assistance to,
      26(2), [756]
    guidance to, **26(2)**, [781]
      enforcement, **26(2)**, [755]
      function of, **26(2)**, [754]
    primary—
      nomination of, **26(2)**, [773]
      support for, **26(2)**, [780]
  members, **26(2)**, [788]
  Ministers of the Crown, advice to,
    26(2), [757]
  orders relating to, making, **26(2)**, [768]
  other regulators, relationship with,
    26(2), [760]
  parliamentary disqualification, **26(2)**, [788]
  proceedings, **26(2)**, [788]
  records, **26(2)**, [788]
  specified enactments, **26(2)**, [790]
  status, **26(2)**, [788]
  transitional provisions, **26(2)**, [788]
  Welsh Ministers, advice to, **26(2)**, [758]

Local Commissioner. *See also* **Commission
for Local Administration**
  appointment, **25(2)**, [307]
  areas for operation of, **25(2)**, [307]
  complaints—
    complainants, **25(2)**, [312]
    general provisions, **25(2)**, [318]
    procedure for making, **25(2)**, [313]
    referral by authorities, **25(2)**, [314]
  consultation with other commissioners,
    25(2), [324]
  defamation, privilege, **25(2)**, [323]
  disclosure of information to Information
    Commissioner, **25(2)**, [326]
  disqualification for appointment, **25(2)**, [335]
  documents, production of, **25(2)**, [318]
  information—
    power to obtain, **25(2)**, [318]
    privileges, **25(2)**, [323]
  injustice, report of, **25(2)**, [320]
  investigation by—
    adverse report—
      action on, notification of, **25(2)**, [320]

Local Commissioner—*contd*
  investigation by—*contd*
    adverse report—*contd*
      consideration by authority, **25(2)**, [321]
      further report, **25(2)**, [321]
      statement to be made on, **25(2)**, [320]
    anonymity in reports on, **25(2)**, [319]
    authorities subject to, **25(2)**, [310]
    decision not to hold, **25(2)**, [319]
    discretion as to, **25(2)**, [311]
    information, power to obtain, **25(2)**, [318]
    matters coming to attention of
      Commissioner, **25(2)**, [315]
    matters not subject to, **25(2)**, [336]
    matters subject to, **25(2)**, [311]
    member of the public, meaning,
      25(2), [316]
    payments to persons attending, **25(2)**, [317]
    power of, **25(2)**, [309]
    procedure, **25(2)**, [317]
    publication of report, **25(2)**, [322]
    recommendations, **25(2)**, [320]
    reports on, **25(2)**, [319]–[323]
    restrictions on, **25(2)**, [311]
  maladministration, complaints of, **25(2)**, [1]
  meaning, **25(2)**, [307]
  obstruction of, **25(2)**, [318]
  other Commissioners—
    collaborative working with, **25(2)**, [325]
    consultation with, **25(2)**, [324]
  removal from office, **25(2)**, [307]
  remuneration, **25(2)**, [335]
  staff to assist, **25(2)**, [335]

local communities
  sustainability—
    action plans, **26(2)**, [469]
    local spending reports, **26(2)**, [471]
    promotion of, **26(2)**, [466]
    proposals by local authorities—
      interpretation, **26(2)**, [473]
      making of, **26(2)**, [467]
      regulations, **26(2)**, [470]
      relevant matters, **26(2)**, [476]
      short-list, decision on, **26(2)**, [468]
    sustainable community strategy, **26(2)**, [472]

local constituency association
  reorganisation, tax reliefs on, **42**, [1413]
  stamp duty relief for, **41**, [143]

local education authority
  advisory services, power to require LEA to
    obtain, **15(2)**, [384]–[386]
  areas, **15(1)**, [507]
  awards—
    allowances, supplemental, **15(1)**, [269]
    designated courses, for, **15(1)**, [248]
    ordinary residence, requirement of,
      15(1), [248], [255]
    other courses, for, **15(1)**, [249]
    regulations on, **15(1)**, [250]
    rules of eligibility, **15(1)**, [280]
  births and deaths, supply of information in
    register of, **15(1)**, [698]

local education authority—*contd*

breakdown of discipline, reserve power to prevent, **15(2)**, [55]

careers service—

ancillary goods and services, **16**, [71]

arrangements for, **16**, [70]

inspection, **16**, [72]

provision, **16**, [68]

relevant education, **16**, [68]

relevant services—

meaning, **16**, [68]

securing provision of, **16**, [69]

certain contractual terms, avoidance of, **15(1)**, [359]

chief education officer, appointment of, **15(1)**, [667]

child care—

duties in respect of, **15(2)**, [117]

partnerships, establishment of, **15(2)**, [118]

children not receiving education, duty to identify, **15(1)**, [578]

children's accommodation, notification, **6**, [413]

community purposes, expenditure incurred for, **15(2)**, [47]

compulsory purchase of land by, **15(1)**, [665]

council as, **15(1)**, [507]

day nursery, provision of teachers to, **15(1)**, [652]

default, powers on, **15(1)**, [622]

disabled child, special education for, **40(1)**, [165]

discrimination by, **7(1)**, [141], [145]

diversity in provision of schools, promoting, **15(2)**, [741]

documents, use in evidence, **15(1)**, [700]

duties—

diversity in provision of schools, securing, **15(2)**, [741]

fulfilment of potential, promoting, **15(2)**, [740]

high standards, promoting, **15(2)**, [740]

parental choice, promoting, **15(2)**, [741]

school improvement partner, appointment of, **15(2)**, [742]

duties of, **15(1)**, [508]

education, responsibility for, **15(1)**, [508]

education support grant. *See* **education support grant**

educational conferences, organising, **15(1)**, [663]

educational research, provision for, **15(1)**, [662]

exemption order from education legislation requirements—

application for, **15(2)**, [342]

generally, **15(2)**, [340]

revocation of, **15(2)**, [341]

variation of, **15(2)**, [341]

expenses of, **6**, [45]

financial schemes, **15(2)**, [43]

financial schemes, revision of, **15(2)**, [156]

fulfilment of potential, promoting, **15(2)**, [740]

local education authority—*contd*

further education, providing facilities for. *See* **further education; higher and further education**

gifts, accepting, **15(1)**, [664]

grant-maintained schools. *See* **grant-maintained school**

high standards in primary and secondary education, duty to promote, **15(1)**, [509]

high standards, promoting, **15(2)**, [740]

higher and further education. *See* **higher and further education**

information, provision of, **15(1)**, [518]

inspection of, **6**, [963], [982]; **6(S)**, 64, 74

Audit Commission, collaboration of, **15(1)**, [752]

Auditor General for Wales, collaboration of, **15(1)**, [753]

powers as to, **15(1)**, [749]

reports, **15(1)**, [750]

rights of entry, **15(1)**, [751]

institutions—

inspection of, **15(1)**, [424]

meaning, **15(1)**, [424]

quality of education, review of, **15(1)**, [424]

intervention in school causing concern—

additional governors, power to appoint, **15(2)**, [13]

cases for, **15(2)**, [12]

delegated budget, suspension of right to, **15(2)**, [15]

interim executive members for governing body, power to provide for, **15(2)**, [14], [19], [137]

power of, **15(2)**, [11]

land, power to acquire, **15(1)**, [666]

loan liabilities excepted from transfer, **15(1)**, [343]

local authority—

consultation with, **6**, [340]

functions concurrent with, **6**, [342]

London. *See* **London**

maintained school. *See* **maintained school**

meals—

free—

children entitled to, **15(1)**, [720]

providing, **15(1)**, [648]

power to charge for, **15(1)**, [647]

providing, **15(1)**, [646]

governing bodies, functions transferred to, **15(1)**, [649]

medical officer, **15(1)**, [710]

members, power of Secretary of State to direct appointment, **15(1)**, [627]

milk—

free, providing, **15(1)**, [648]

providing, **15(1)**, [646]

non-maintained school, arrangements with, **15(1)**, [516]

nursery education—

early years development partnerships, **15(2)**, [118]

general duty as respects availability of, **15(2)**, [116]

local education authority—*contd*
 opposite side of Welsh border, restrictions on
  establishment of schools, **15(2)**, [662]
 parental choice, increasing opportunities for,
  15(2), [741]
 participation in education and training, role as
  to. *See* **education; training**
 passenger transport services, co-operation in
  provision of, **37**, [425]
 person belonging to area of, **15(1)**, [710]
 persons over 19, functions as to, **15(1)**, [513]
 primary schools, providing. *See* **primary and
  secondary schools**
 proceedings, institution of, **6**, [47]
 proper performance of functions—
  duties as to, **15(1)**, [624]
  Secretary of State's power to secure,
   15(1), [623]–[625]
 property, holding and administering trust for,
  15(1), [664]
 pupils over school age, scholarships etc, to,
  15(1), [654]
 qualifications, award or authentication of,
  15(2), [500]
 recoupment—
  adjustment between authorities,
   15(2), [513]–[514]
  cross-border, **15(1)**, [618]
  excluded pupils, **15(1)**, [619]
  special cases, **15(2)**, [515]
 recreational facilities, providing—
  persons aged 13 to 19, for, **15(1)**, [630]
  persons aged 20 to 24, for, **15(1)**, [630]
  persons under 13, for, **15(1)**, [629]
 religion or belief, discrimination on grounds
  of, **7(1)**, [795]
 scheme for financing schools, financial
  delegation, general note, **15(1)**, [1]
 school—
  assistance to, **15(1)**, [710]
  reorganisation of, **15(1)**, [426]
 school fees and expenses, payment of,
  15(1), [654]
 school forums, establishment of, **15(2)**, [42]
 school improvement partner, appointment of,
  15(2), [742]
 school organisation committees, establishment
  of, **15(2)**, [26]
 schools forums—
  constitution of, **15(S)**, Education 287
  travel functions, exercise of,
   15(S), Education 195
 secondary schools, providing. *See* **primary
  and secondary schools**
 sex discrimination, duties as to, **7(1)**, [67]
 sixteen to eighteen year old, functions in
  respect of full-time education for,
  15(1), [512]
 special education, providing. *See* **education**
 special educational needs, identifying child
  with. *See* **child**
 specified budgets, determination of,
  15(2), [40]
 standards, duty to promote high, **15(2)**, [740]
 sufficient schools, providing, **15(1)**, [510]

local education authority—*contd*
 support for 13 to 19 year olds, **15(2)**, [282]
 targets, **15(2)**, [692]–[693]
 transport—
  adult learners, provided for certain,
   15(1), [637]
  arrangements, making, **15(1)**, [633]–[635]
  belief, duty to consider in exercise of
   functions as to, **15(1)**, [642]
  disabled persons, providing for,
   15(1), [640]
  eligible child, for, meaning, **15(1)**, [720]
  learning difficulties, persons with, providing
   for, **15(1)**, [640]
  nursery education otherwise than at school,
   arrangements for children receiving,
   15(1), [643]
  persons of sixth form age—
   meaning, **15(1)**, [641]
   providing for, **15(1)**, [639]–[640]
  religion, duty to consider in exercise of
   functions as to, **15(1)**, [642]
  school schemes—
   amendment of, **15(1)**, [721]
   charges, **15(1)**, [721]
   commencement of, **15(1)**, [721]
   duties as to, **15(1)**, [636]
   power to make, **15(1)**, [721]
  sustainable modes of, promotion of,
   15(1), [632]
 Wales, in. *See under* **Wales**
 welfare of children, duties regarding,
  15(2), [489]

local election. *See also* **local government
 election**
 application of provisions to, **15(3)**, [183]
 date of general election, on, postponement,
  15(3), [238]
 ordinary day of, **15(3)**, [239]
 timing of, **15(3)**, [240]
 voting offences, **15(3)**, [184]

local enterprise agency
 contribution to, **44(1)**, [48]

local enterprise companies
 contributions to, **44(1)**, [49]

local enterprise organisations
 agency, approval of, **44(3)**, [83]–[84]
 meaning, **44(3)**, [82]
 payments to, tax deduction for, **44(3)**, [81]

local government. *See also* **local authority**
 adaptation of enactments, **25(1)**, [163]
 administration—
  advice and guidance, **25(2)**, [307]
  commissions. *See* **Commissions for Local
   Administration**
  summary of provisions, **25(1)**, [1]
 appropriate Minister for, **25(2)**, [229]
 areas. *See* **local government areas**
 associations, subscriptions to, **25(2)**, [145]

local government—*contd*
  boundary changes—
    authorities dissolved by order—
      directions, **26(2)**, [524]–[526]
      disposals, contracts and reserves, control
        of, **26(2)**, [522]
      reserves, directions, **26(2)**, [523]
    correction of orders, **26(2)**, [518]
    definitions, **26(2)**, [521]
    implementation of—
      agreements as to incidental matters,
        26(2), [514]
      billing authorities, county councils as,
        26(2), [517]
      incidental provision, **26(2)**, [513]
      membership of authorities on,
        26(2), [510]
      orders, **26(2)**, [509], [511], [512]
      regulations, **26(2)**, [512]
      residuary bodies, establishment of,
        26(2), [515]
      staff commissions, establishment of,
        26(2), [516]
    meaning, **26(2)**, [506]
    pre-commencement invitations,
      26(2), [519]
  historical summary, **25(1)**, [1]
  inquiries—
    Secretary of State, by, **25(1)**, [157]
    social services, as to, **25(1)**, [980]
  National Code of Conduct, **25(2)**, [876]
  orders etc, provisions as to, **25(1)**, [158]
  regional assemblies. *See* **regional assemblies**
    Electoral Commission. *See* **Electoral
      Commission**
  regulations, provisions as to, **25(1)**, [158]
  review. *See* **Boundary Commission for
    England**
  sanctions, simplified mode of giving,
    25(1), [130]
  single tier—
    meaning, **26(2)**, [499]
    proposals for—
      Boundary Commission, powers of. *See*
        **Boundary Commission for
        England**
      directions for, **26(2)**, [500], [501]
      implementation by order, **26(2)**, [505]
      invitations for, **26(2)**, [500], [501]
      types of, **26(2)**, [500]
  summary of provisions, **25(1)**, [1]
  Wales, improvement in. *See* **Wales**

local government areas
  accretions from sea, annexation, **25(2)**, [62]
  alteration of—
    Bills for, restriction on, **25(2)**, [60]
    effect of, **25(2)**, [58]
    recommendation of, **26(1)**, [106]
    transfer of functions on, **25(2)**, [163]
    transfer of securities on, **25(2)**, [148]
    water-course, alteration of on, **25(2)**, [63]
    See also **Local Government Commission
      for England**
  boundaries, rules as to, **25(2)**, [236]

local government areas—*contd*
  Charlwood, alteration of, **25(2)**, [338], [339]
  county divisions, **25(2)**, [1]
  electoral arrangements for, **26(1)**, [114]
  electoral divisions, **25(2)**, [6]
  Horley, alteration of, **25(2)**, [338], [339]
  meaning, **25(2)**, [229]
  metropolitan counties and districts—
    divisions of, **25(2)**, [1]
    schedule of, **25(2)**, [234]
    See also **metropolitan county**
  name, change of, **26(2)**, [553]
  non-metropolitan counties—
    Boundary Commission proposals,
      25(2), [240]
    division into districts, **25(2)**, [240]
    establishment, **25(2)**, [1]
    list of, **25(2)**, [235]
  orders, variation or revocation, **25(2)**, [59]
  review of—
    conduct of, **26(2)**, [506]
    consultation, **26(2)**, [507]
    recommendations, **26(2)**, [507], [508]
    See also **Local Government Commission
      for England**
  schedule of, **25(2)**, [235]
  seaward boundaries, **25(2)**, [61]
  Wales, in—
    changes in. *See* **Local Government
      Boundary Commission**
    generally. *See* **Wales**

Local Government Boundary Commission
  England, for—
    electoral arrangements, rules in respect of,
      25(2), [246]
    non-metropolitan counties, proposals for,
      25(2), [240]
  Wales, for—
    assistant commissioner, appointment etc,
      25(2), [56]
    constitution of, **25(2)**, [245]
    delegation of functions, **25(2)**, [56]
    documents, proof of, **25(2)**, [245]
    electoral arrangements—
      meaning, **25(2)**, [67]
      review of, **25(2)**, [51]
      rules to be observed, **25(2)**, [246]
      substantive changes in, **25(2)**, [51]
    establishment, **25(2)**, [47]
    expenses, defrayment, **25(2)**, [245]
    local inquiry, power to hold, **25(2)**, [55]
    members, appointment etc, **25(2)**, [245]
    new town orders, effect of, **25(2)**, [49]
    officers, appointment etc, **25(2)**, [245]
    proposals by—
      changes, for, **25(2)**, [48]
      general provisions, **25(2)**, [54]
      implementation, **25(2)**, [52]
    recommendations by, **25(2)**, [49]
    reports by, **25(2)**, [52]
    reviews by—
      conduct of, **25(2)**, [54]
      directions as to, **25(2)**, [50], [53]

Local Government Boundary Commission—*contd*

Wales, for—*contd*

reviews by—*contd*

electoral arrangements, affecting, **25(2)**, [51]

extent of, **25(2)**, [52]

intervals for, **25(2)**, [51]

procedure for, **25(2)**, [54]

proposals consequent on, **25(2)**, [38]

request by local authority for, **25(2)**, [49]

seaward boundaries, **25(2)**, [61]

transitional arrangements, **25(2)**, [57]

Local Government Commission for England

constitution, **26(1)**, [118]

directions to, **26(1)**, [313]

establishment of, **26(1)**, [104]

functions of, **26(1)**, [310]

Greater London Authority, report on electoral arrangements—

submission of, **26(1)**, [311]

supplementary, **26(1)**, [312]

payments to, **26(1)**, [314]

local government election

agent. *See* **election**

candidate—

corrupt or illegal practice, guilty of, **15(3)**, [154]

void, election declared, **15(3)**, [155]

donations. *See* **election**

casual vacancies, filling, **25(2)**, [77]–[79]

change of years in which held, **26(2)**, [130]

City of London. *See* **London, City of**

combined, **15(3)**, [43]

computation of time for, **25(2)**, [203]

corrupt practice—

avoidance for, **15(3)**, [160]

candidate guilty of. *See* candidate *above*

illegal practice, found guilty of on charge of, **15(3)**, [166]

incapacity—

conviction, on, **15(3)**, [167]

mitigation, **15(3)**, [169]

remission, **15(3)**, [169]

Scotland, in, **15(3)**, [168]

justice of the peace guilty of, **15(3)**, [157]

legal profession, member guilty of, **15(3)**, [158]

licensed premises, on, **15(3)**, [159]

persons guilty of, provisions on, **15(3)**, [155]–[156]

professional person guilty of, **15(3)**, [158]

prosecution and penalties, **15(3)**, [164]

relief, claim for, **15(3)**, [163]

date, change of to date of European Parliamentary election, **26(2)**, [554]

definitions, **26(2)**, [127]

disenfranchisement—

mental hospitals, offenders in, **15(3)**, [6]

prison, offenders in, **15(3)**, [5]

local government election—*contd*

elector—

convicted person, incapacity of, **15(3)**, [5]

entitlement to be registered as, **15(3)**, [7]

one vote only, having, **15(3)**, [4]

electoral arrangements, meaning, **25(2)**, [67]

See further **Local Government Boundary Commission**

electoral scheme—

elections by halves—

Electoral Commission, notice to, **26(2)**, [540]

existing powers, Electoral Commission acting under, **26(2)**, [549]

incidental provision, **26(2)**, [548]

meaning, **26(2)**, [529]

order for, **26(2)**, [543], [544]

ordinary elections, councillors elected at, **26(2)**, [544]

publicity for order, **26(2)**, [550]

publicity for resolution, **26(2)**, [539]

requirement for electoral review, consideration of, **26(2)**, [541]

resolution for, **26(2)**, [535], [536]

transitional provisions, **26(2)**, [547]

years in which held, **26(2)**, [543]

elections by thirds—

Electoral Commission, notice to, **26(2)**, [540]

existing powers, Electoral Commission acting under, **26(2)**, [549]

incidental provision, **26(2)**, [548]

meaning, **26(2)**, [529]

order for, **26(2)**, [545], [546]

ordinary elections, councillors elected at, **26(2)**, [546]

publicity for order, **26(2)**, [550]

publicity for resolution, **26(2)**, [539]

requirement for electoral review, consideration of, **26(2)**, [541]

resolution for, **26(2)**, [537], [538]

transitional provisions, **26(2)**, [547]

years in which held, **26(2)**, [545]

new, order for, **26(2)**, [542]

ordinary elections, for, amendment, **26(2)**, [552]

whole council elections—

Electoral Commission, notice to, **26(2)**, [534]

meaning, **26(2)**, [529]

operation of scheme, **26(2)**, [532]

publicity for resolution, **26(2)**, [533]

resolution for, **26(2)**, [530], [531]

England and Wales, in—

conduct of, **15(3)**, [43]

postponement of, **15(3)**, [46]

timing of, provisions on, **15(3)**, [46]

void, where, **15(3)**, [45]

entitlement to vote in, **15(3)**, [4]

executive, for. *See* **local authority executives**

exit polls, prohibitions on publication of, **15(3)**, [66]

expenses. *See* **election**

general note, **15(3)**, [1]

local government election—*contd*
illegal practices—
  avoidance for, **15(3)**, [160]
  candidate guilty of. *See* candidate *above*
  corrupt practice, charge of, **15(3)**, [166]
  incapacity—
    conviction, on, **15(3)**, [167]
    election court, imposed after report of, **15(3)**, [156]
    mitigation, **15(3)**, [169]
    remission, **15(3)**, [169]
  persons guilty of, provisions on, **15(3)**, [155]–[156]
  prosecution and penalties, **15(3)**, [165]
  relief, claim for, **15(3)**, [163]
incidental provisions, **26(2)**, [131]
interpretation of terms, **15(3)**, [181], [197]
loan of equipment for, **15(3)**, [48]
London borough divisions, **25(2)**, [240]
new areas—
  county councillors, **25(2)**, [7], [240]
  district councillors, **25(2)**, [7], [240]
  suspension of, **25(2)**, [240]
offences punishable summarily, **15(3)**, [172]
options for, **26(2)**, [128]
ordinary day of, **15(3)**, [44]
parish councillors, **25(2)**, [20]
parliamentary election rules, adaptation of, **15(3)**, [43]
periods for, **25(2)**, [7]
petition—
  amendment of, **15(3)**, [131]
  appeal, leave for, **15(3)**, [153]
  case, stating, **15(3)**, [148]
  corrupt practice—
    alleging, **15(3)**, [131]
    costs, **15(3)**, [152]
    report on, **15(3)**, [146], [154]
  costs—
    corrupt practices, provisions on, **15(3)**, [152]
    illegal practices, provisions on, **15(3)**, [152]
    neglect or refusal to pay, **15(3)**, [151]
    orders on, **15(3)**, [150]
    security for, **15(3)**, [138]
  election court, **15(3)**, [132]
    accommodation of, **15(3)**, [133]
    attendance on, **15(3)**, [133]
    corrupt or illegal practice, finding, **15(3)**, [154]
    expenses, orders on, **15(3)**, [135]
    remuneration and allowances, **15(3)**, [134]
    shorthand writer, attendance of, **15(3)**, [133]
  High Court jurisdiction, **15(3)**, [130], [153]
  illegal practice—
    alleging, **15(3)**, [131]
    costs, **15(3)**, [152]
    report on, **15(3)**, [146], [154]
  issue, when at, **15(3)**, [139]
  list of, **15(3)**, [140]
  presentation of, **15(3)**, [130]

local government election—*contd*
petition—*contd*
  publication of, **15(3)**, [131]
  questioning of by, **15(3)**, [129]
  respondent to, **15(3)**, [130]
  rules on, **15(3)**, [153]
  same election, relating to, **15(3)**, [141]
  security for costs, **15(3)**, [138]
  special case, hearing of, **15(3)**, [148]
  time for presenting, **15(3)**, [131]
  trial—
    corrupt practice, evidence of, **15(3)**, [141]
    determination, certificate on, **15(3)**, [146]
    High Court, certificate sent to, **15(3)**, [146]
    open court, in, **15(3)**, [141]
    respondent ceasing to hold office, effect of, **15(3)**, [141]
    undue election, evidence of, **15(3)**, [141]
    witnesses—
      attendance of, **15(3)**, [142]
      examination of, **15(3)**, [142]
      expenses, **15(3)**, [144]
      questions, duty to answer, **15(3)**, [143]
  two or more candidates as respondents, **15(3)**, [140]
  void, declaring election, **15(3)**, [136]
  withdrawal of, **15(3)**, [149]
polling districts, division into, **15(3)**, [41]
postal-only voting, pilot schemes—
  conduct of, **15(3)**, [580]
  declaration of identity, **15(3)**, [580]
  Electoral Commission report, **15(3)**, [583]
  generally, **15(3)**, [281]
  interpretation, **15(3)**, [588]
  personation, offence of, **15(3)**, [585]
  pilot order, **15(3)**, [581]
  pilot regions, **15(3)**, [580]
  previous provisions, under, **15(3)**, [582]
  prosecution of offences, time limit, **15(3)**, [586]
  revision of procedures, **15(3)**, [282], [584]
power to change date of—
  England, **26(2)**, [305]
  Wales, **26(2)**, [306]
qualifications of candidates, **25(2)**, [68]
questioning, method of, **15(3)**, [129]
regional assemblies. *See* **regional assemblies**
related electoral areas, in, **15(3)**, [43]
returning officer—
  England and Wales, in, person being, **15(3)**, [42]
  expenditure incurred by, **15(3)**, [43]
  expenses of, **15(3)**, [49]
  reference to, construction of, **15(3)**, [220]
  vote, entitled to, **15(3)**, [47]
rules for, **15(3)**, [43]
scheme, power to specify, **26(2)**, [129]
timing of, **25(2)**, [203]
validity of, **15(3)**, [49]

Enquiry Bureau   hsieb@lexisnexis.co.uk

local government election—*contd*
  voting at, **15(3)**, [47]
    absent. *See* **election**
  voting paper, inaccuracy in, **25(2)**, [202]
  Wales, in, **25(2)**, [30], [32]

local government officers and staff
  abolished councils, of. *See* **Greater London
    Council; metropolitan county council**
  accountability, **25(2)**, [114]
  administrators, as, indemnity for, **25(2)**, [367]
  appointment—
    members disqualified for, **25(2)**, [115]
    merit, to be by, **25(2)**, [860]
    political activities, regard to, **25(2)**, [861]
    statutory provisions, **25(2)**, [860]
    terms and conditions, **25(2)**, [111]
  compensation for loss of office, **25(1)**, [409];
    25(2), [220]
    abolition of councils, on, **25(2)**, [609]
    early retirement in lieu of, **25(2)**, [221]
  confidential records, **25(2)**, [864]
  Data Protection Act exemptions, **26(2)**, [613]
  deceased officer—
    advances of remuneration paid to,
      25(2), [366]
    funeral expenses, **25(2)**, [117]
    payments due to, **25(2)**, [117]
  dependants, gratuities etc to, **25(2)**, [117]
  deputies, as, indemnity for, **25(2)**, [367]
  deputy chief officer, meaning, **25(2)**, [852]
  disqualification for appointment, **25(2)**, [115]
  ethical standards officers. *See* **Standards
    Board for England**
  gratuities—
    family for purposes of, **25(1)**, [181]
    non-pensionable staff, to, **25(1)**, [181]
  head of paid service, **25(2)**, [856]
  housing staff, (London), transfer of,
    25(2), [420]
  indemnification, **26(2)**, [137]
  interest in contracts, disclosure, **25(2)**, [116]
  leave for local authority duties, **25(2)**, [863]
  legislation, summary of, **25(1)**, [1]
  local councillors, exercise of functions by,
    arrangements for, **26(2)**, [647]
  loss of office—
    abolition of councils, on, **25(2)**, [609]
    compensation, **25(1)**, [409]; **25(2)**, [220];
      33(1), [139]
    early retirement, provision for, **25(2)**, [221]
  members disqualified, **25(2)**, [115]
  monitoring officer—
    delegation of functions, **26(2)**, [125]
    designation of, **25(2)**, [857]
    duties to and of, **25(2)**, [857]
    matters referred to, **26(2)**, [103], [113]
    ombudsmen, consultation with,
      26(2), [107]
    reports by, **25(2)**, [857]
      local authorities operating executive
        arrangements, **25(2)**, [858]
  non-statutory chief officer, meaning,
    25(2), [852]

local government officers and staff—*contd*
  officers—
    payment of expenses of, **25(1)**, [736]
    resignation of, **25(2)**, [73]
  personal information, confidentiality,
    25(2), [864]
  politically restricted posts—
    disqualification of holders of, **25(2)**, [851]
    exemption, application for, **25(2)**, [854]
      Scotland and Wales, **25(2)**, [853]
    general advise as to, **25(2)**, [855]
    lists of posts—
      deposit of, **25(2)**, [852]
      direction to include posts in,
        25(2), [853], [854]
      preparation and maintenance,
        25(2), [852]
      removal from, **25(2)**, [853], [854]
    person to supervise, **25(2)**, [853], [854]
    persons deemed to hold, **25(2)**, [852]
  retirement—
    early, provision for, **25(2)**, [221]
    normal age of, meaning, **25(2)**, [221]
  seconded to other authorities, **25(2)**, [112]
  security to be taken, **25(2)**, [113]
  service with other authorities, **25(2)**, [112]
  Staff Commission—
    establishment, **25(2)**, [420]
    general provisions, **25(2)**, [420]
  staff negotiations, conflict of interests,
    25(2), [865]
  staff records, confidentiality, **25(2)**, [864]
  standing orders, adoption of, **25(2)**, [861]
  statutory chief officer—
    meaning, **25(2)**, [852]
    politically restricted post, holding,
      25(2), [852]
  superannuation—
    death from war service, **25(1)**, [129]
    increase of pensions, **33(1)**, [113], [115],
      [128]
    London—
      application of certain provisions,
        25(1), [960]
      borough councils, application to,
        25(1), [905]
      Common Council, application to,
        25(1), [906]
      dependants, qualifying, **25(1)**, [912]
      employment, transfer of, **25(1)**, [904]
      funds—
        division of, **25(1)**, [909]
        investment of, **25(1)**, [829]–[831],
          [961]
      general provisions, **25(1)**, [901]
      pensionable age, meaning, **25(1)**, [902]
      retirement, premature, **25(1)**, [902]
      rights of certain contributors,
        preservation, **25(1)**, [1000]
      transfer value, payment, **25(1)**, [904]
      trustees, sums to be paid to,
        25(1), [903], [912]
    provision for, **33(1)**, [128]
    questions as to, determination of,
      33(1), [132]

local government officers and staff—*contd*
  superannuation—*contd*
    reckonable service, meaning, **25(2)**, [221]
    regulations as to, **33(1)**, [128]
      retrospective effect, **33(1)**, [133]
      transitional provisions, **33(1)**, [543]
  terms of office, **25(2)**, [111]
  transfer of officers—
    abolished councils, from, **25(2)**, [608]
    compensation, **25(1)**, [564]
    orders as to, **25(2)**, [218]
    voluntary, continuity of employment,
      25(2), [219], [610]

Local Health Board
  amended provisions, **30**, [791]
  employment in, validity of clearance for,
    30, [750]
  local authorities, payments from, **30**, [882]
  quality in health care—
    duty to attain, **30**, [661]
    standards set by—
      Assembly, **30**, [663]
      Secretary of State, **30**, [662]
  taxation, **30**, [531]
  Wales. *See* **Wales**

local housing authority
  accommodation. *See* **accommodation**
  acquisition of land by, **22**, [18]
  agreements with co-operatives, **22**, [29]
  allocation of housing—
    applications for housing accommodation,
      23, [479]
    eligible persons, to, **23**, [478]
    provisions not applying, where, **23**, [477]
    regulations, **23**, [485]
    rules as to, **22**, [96]; **23**, [476]
    scheme—
      in accordance with, **23**, [480]
      information about, **23**, [481]
      priorities, **23**, [480]
      proposal for, **23**, [480]
  anti-social behaviour. *See* **anti-social
    behaviour; injunctions**
  appropriation of land by, **22**, [20]
  area improvement. *See* **general
    improvement area**
  authorisations for enforcement, **24**, [389]
  authorities other than, meaning, **22**, [4]
  borrowing powers, **22**, [305]
  buildings acquired for housing purposes,
    duties, **22**, [19]
  byelaws, power to make, **22**, [23]
  clearance area. *See* **clearance area**
  conversions etc, control of expenditure on,
    22, [308]
  covenants with, enforcement, **22**, [409]
  disabled persons, needs of, **21**, [381]
  district—
    buildings in more than one, **22**, [3]
    exercise of powers outside, **22**, [16]
    meaning, **22**, [2]
  documents—
    power to require production of, **24**, [381]

local housing authority—*contd*
  documents—*contd*
    service of, **24**, [392]
    electronic form, issue of licences and
      documents in, **24**, [393]
    timing and location, regulations, **24**, [394]
  empty dwelling management orders—
    final—
      appeals, **24**, [436]
      duties once in force, **24**, [318]
      general effect of, **24**, [434], [435]
      making, **24**, [317]
      management scheme, having, **24**, [434]
      meaning, **24**, [313]
      operation of, **24**, [434]
    interim—
      appeals, **24**, [436]
      compensation payable to third parties,
        24, [319]
      duties once in force, **24**, [316]
      general effect of, **24**, [433], [435]
      making, **24**, [314]
        authorisation for, **24**, [315]
      meaning, **24**, [313]
      operation of, **24**, [433]
  entry, powers of. *See* **entry**
  environmental considerations, **22**, [407]
  facilities, provision of. *See* **accommodation**
  false statements, **23**, [484]
  final management orders—
    accounts, **24**, [300]
    appeals, **24**, [304], [432]
    compensation payable to third parties,
      24, [309]
    duties whilst in force, **24**, [296]
    effect of—
      agreements and legal proceedings, on,
        24, [306]
      furniture, on, **24**, [307]
      occupiers, on, **24**, [305]
    furniture—
      effect on, **24**, [307]
      power to supply, **24**, [308]
    general effect of, **24**, [297]
      immediate landlords and mortgagees,
        24, [299]
      leases and licences granted by authority,
        24, [298]
    making, **24**, [294]
    management scheme—
      containing, **24**, [300]
      enforcement by landlord, **24**, [301]
    meaning, **24**, [282]
    operation of, **24**, [295]
    powers of entry, **24**, [312]
    procedural requirements, **24**, [304], [430]
    register of, **24**, [378]
    review of, **24**, [296]
    revocation of, **24**, [303], [431]
    termination of—
      agreements, effect on, **24**, [311]
      financial arrangements on, **24**, [310]
      leases, effect on, **24**, [311]
      proceedings, effect on, **24**, [311]
    variation of, **24**, [302], [431]

local housing authority—*contd*
functions—
  generally, **22**, [9]–[17]
  overcrowding, as to. *See* **overcrowding**
group repair scheme. *See* **group repair
  scheme**
gypsies and travellers, duties regarding. *See*
  gypsies and travellers
heating, charges for, **22**, [98]
homelessness. *See* **homeless persons**
housing—
  account. *See* **housing revenue account**
  conditions. *See* **housing conditions**
  management. *See* **management**
  needs, reviews of, **22**, [9]
  rents, **24**, [159]
  repairs account. *See* **Housing Repairs
    Account**
  statements as to, **24**, [157]
  strategy for, **24**, [157]
housing action trust as, **22**, [852]
housing action trust, transfer of land and
  property to, **22**, [860], [861]
housing subsidy, calculation of, **22**, [298]
improvements, control of expenditure,
  22, [308]
information—
  enforcement of powers to obtain, **24**, [382]
  false or misleading, **24**, [384]
  other statutory purposes, used for,
    24, [383]
  power to require, **24**, [381]
  supply to Secretary of State, **23**, [23]
  withholding, **23**, [484]
interim management orders—
  appeals, **24**, [304], [432]
  compensation payable to third parties,
    24, [309]
  duties whilst in force, **24**, [287]
  effect of—
    agreements and legal proceedings, on,
      24, [306]
    furniture, on, **24**, [307]
    occupiers, on, **24**, [305]
  financial arrangements whilst in force,
    24, [291]
  furniture—
    effect on, **24**, [307]
    power to supply, **24**, [308]
  general effect of, **24**, [288]
  immediate landlords and mortgagees,
    24, [290]
  leases and licences granted by authority,
    24, [289]
  health and safety condition, **24**, [285]
  making, **24**, [283]
  meaning, **24**, [282]
  operation of, **24**, [286]
  powers of entry, **24**, [312]
  procedural requirements, **24**, [304], [430]
  register of, **24**, [378]
  revocation of, **24**, [293], [431]
  special, **24**, [284]
  supplementary provisions, **24**, [326]

local housing authority—*contd*
interim management orders—*contd*
  termination of—
    agreements, effect on, **24**, [311]
    financial arrangements on, **24**, [310]
    leases, effect on, **24**, [311]
    proceedings, effect on, **24**, [311]
  time limits, **24**, [286]
  variation of, **24**, [292], [431]
introductory tenancy. *See* **introductory
  tenancy**
landlord authority, as, **22**, [105]
leases to, by housing trust, **22**, [463]
management—
  consultation, **22**, [30]
  powers, **22**, [22]
  meaning, **22**, [1], [493]; **24**, [407]
notices, additional requirements for protection
  of owners, **24**, [388]
obstructive building. *See* **demolition order**
payments to tenants, **23**, [556]
powers and duties—
  housing action area, in, **22**, [213]
  improvement area, in, **22**, [225]
  miscellaneous, **22**, [411]
  principal, **22**, [9]–[17]
  shops, provision of, **22**, [14]
powers of entry, **24**, [385]
privately let accommodation, financial
  assistance for—
    consent for, **22**, [780], [781]
    power to provide, **22**, [779]
registered social landlords, co-operation with,
  23, [483]
reinstatement of defective dwelling by,
  22, [379]
renewal areas. *See* **renewal area**
rent—
  increase of, **22**, [25]
  power to charge, **22**, [24]
  reviews of, **22**, [24]
Secretary of State, guidance from, **23**, [482]
service charges, loan for, **22**, [328], [329]
services for owners and occupiers, powers as
  to, **23**, [42]
slum clearance. *See* **slum clearance**
subsequent disposals, consent for, **22**, [908]
tenancies, status of, **22**, [828]
tenants—
  payments for obtaining other
    accommodation, **22**, [906]
  removal expenses, contributions to,
    22, [26]
works attracting grant, carrying out, **23**, [602]

local inquiry. *See* **inquiry**

local land charge. *See* **land charge**
notice in lieu of obstruction of access to light,
  registration as, **21**, [253]

local plan
action area, for, **46**, [297]
adoption of, **46**, [303]
alteration, **46**, [300]

local plan—*contd*
approval of, **46**, [305]
conformity, **46**, [306]
content of, **46**, [297]
enterprise zone, in, **46**, [311]
inquiries, power to hold, **46**, [302]
joint, **46**, [308]
local inquiries, power to hold, **46**, [302]
minerals, **46**, [298]
objections to, **46**, [302]
old development plan, discontinuance on
adoption, **46**, [619]
other enactments, development authorised
by, **46**, [307]
preparation of, **46**, [297]
proposals—
adoption of, **46**, [303]
approval of, **46**, [305]
calling in for approval, **46**, [304]
structure plan, conforming with, **46**, [306]
public participation, **46**, [301]
regulations as to, **46**, [312]
replacement, **46**, [300]
Secretary of State—
approval by, **46**, [305]
calling in for approval, **46**, [304]
default powers, **46**, [309]
street authorisation map as, **46**, [619]
structure plan, conformity with, **46**, [306]
transitional provisions, **46**, [616]–[619], [1063]
unitary development plan, incorporation in,
46, [616]
urban development area, in, **46**, [310]
validity, **46**, [549], [552]
Wales. *See* **Wales**
waste policies, **46**, [299]

local planning area
structure plan. *See* **structure plan**

local planning authority
annual monitoring report, **46**, [991]
appeal relating to planning permission,
functions in, **46**, [343]
application of provisions to—
listed buildings, as to, **46**, [726]
planning control, as to, **46**, [586]
body being, **46**, [251], [993]
Broads, for, **46**, [255]
buildings, requiring alteration or removal of.
See **building**
consequential and supplementary provisions,
46, [260]
conservation area, designating, **46**, [711]
consultation, duty of person to respond to,
46, [1006]
Crown land, exercise of powers as to,
46, [733]
discontinuance of use, requiring. *See*
development
displaced persons, providing accommodation
for, **46**, [365]
energy policies, **46(S)**, 1–2
enterprise zone authority as, **46**, [256]
expenses, contributions to, **46**, [578]

local planning authority—*contd*
functions—
authorities exercising, **46**, [251], [750]
compensation, **46**, [614]
Crown, as to, **46**, [614]
development plans, **46**, [614]
distribution of, **46**, [614]
planning and special control, **46**, [614]
Wales, in, **46**, [615]
housing action area, for, **46**, [258]
inquiries, costs of, **46**, [574]
joint boards—
area of, **46**, [252]
constitution, **46**, [252]
National Park, for, **46**, [254]
order constituting, **46**, [252]
joint plans, **46**, [276]
Wales, for, **46**, [277]
National Parks in, **46**, [279]
local development scheme, preparation and
maintenance of, **46**, [971]
local plans. *See* **local plan**
London. *See* **Greater London**
metropolitan areas. *See* **metropolitan
counties**
metropolitan district, for, **46**, [251]
National Park, for, **46**, [254]
new town, for, **46**, [139]
non-metropolitan county, for, **46**, [251]
planning applications to. *See* **planning
permission**
planning area, survey of, **46**, [263], [288]
planning functions, distribution of, **46**, [54]
Scotland, for, **46**, [877]
simplified planning zone, in, **46**, [346]
statutory undertakers, as, **46**, [587]
survey by, **46**, [263], [969]
tree preservation order, making. *See* **tree**
urban development corporation as, **46**, [257]
Urban Regeneration Agency as, **46**, [259],
[845]
Wales, in, **46**, [262]

local probation boards. *See* **probation**

local social services authority
care and after-care by, **30**, [1113]
functions of, **30**, [1060]
home help, providing, **30**, [1113]
laundry facilities, providing, **30**, [1113]
mothers and young children, care of,
30, [1113]
prevention of illness, arrangements for,
30, [1113]
Primary Care Trust, payments by, **30**, [1062]
research by, **30**, [1113]
residential accommodation, provision of,
30, [1060]
Wales, **30**, [1308], [1347]

local taxation licence
duties—
application of proceeds, **25(1)**, [153]
payment over to county council,
25(1), [59]

local taxation licence—*contd*
  fees, amendments of, **25(1)**, [798]
  list of, **25(1)**, [70]

local transport authority
  local transport plans. *See* **local transport plans**

local transport plans
  guidance, having regard to, **38(2)**, [81]
  Integrated Transport Authority, review and alteration by, **38(2)**, [77]
  new, **38(2)**, [77]
  policies, requirement to develop, **38(2)**, [76]
  preparation of, **38(2)**, [76], [651]
  review and alteration of, **38(2)**, [77]
  Wales, in—
    approval by National Assembly, **38(2)**, [78]
    directions issued to local transport authorities as to functions, **38(2)**, [84]
    provisions regarding, modification of, **38(2)**, [83]
    replacement plans, **38(2)**, [79]
    review and alteration of, **38(2)**, [79]
    transitional provisions, **38(2)**, [80]

local weights and measures authority. *See* **weights and measures authority**

locally-electable authorities
  disability discrimination. *See under* **disability discrimination**

locomotive. *See under* **motor vehicle**

lodger
  goods of, protection from distress, **13**, [1199], [1200]
  rent, payment direct to superior landlord, **13**, [1201], [1205]
  secure tenancy, in case of, **22**, [81]

loitering
  intent, with, abolition, **12(1)**, [758]
  prostitute, by, **12(1)**, [306], [307]

London. *See also* **Greater London; London borough council; London, City of**
  administrative county, area of, **25(1)**, [1]
  advertisements—
    designation of areas, **26(2)**, [695]
    fly posting—
      certificate of conviction, **26(2)**, [697]
      day on which offence committed, determination of, **26(2)**, [698]
      third conviction, minimum fine for, **26(2)**, [696]
    portable—
      meaning, **26(2)**, [694]
      restrictions on, **26(2)**, [694]
    seizure of relevant objects—
      disposal orders, **26(2)**, [703]
      forfeiture, **26(2)**, [704]
      power of, **26(2)**, [701]
      return and disposal of, **26(2)**, [702]

London—*contd*
  advertisements—*contd*
    seizure of relevant objects—*contd*
      unlawful, compensation for, **26(2)**, [705]
    shroud, meaning, **26(2)**, [693]
    shroud offence—
      certificate of conviction, **26(2)**, [697]
      day on which committed, determination of, **26(2)**, [698]
      meaning, **26(2)**, [693]
      third conviction, minimum fine for, **26(2)**, [696]
    surfaces, measures taken on, **26(2)**, [699], [745]
      railway undertakings, provision for, **26(2)**, [700]
  ambulances, false calls, **25(1)**, [247]
  animals, imported, **25(1)**, [709]
  borough council, exercise of powers affecting other authority's roads, **36**, [1352]
  boroughs. *See* **London borough**
  bridges, management of, **49**, [186]
  building regulations. *See* **London Building Acts**
  burial grounds. *See* **burial ground**
  busking. *See* **busking**
  byelaws. *See* **London government**
  canals in. *See* **canal**
  caravan sites, **25(1)**, [735]
  cemeteries. *See* **Greater London**
  Chelsea, provision of studios, **25(1)**, [464]
  City of. *See* **London, City of**
  Common Council—
    port health authority, as, **35(1)**, [448]
    public health duties, **35(1)**, [118]
  costermongers, storage accommodation, **25(1)**, [477]
  crematoria, **25(1)**, [237], [1008]
  Crown rights, saving for, **25(1)**, [254]
  cultural bodies, contributions to, **25(1)**, [400]
  dangerous lands, fencing, **25(1)**, [419]
  dangerous structures. *See* **London Building Acts**
  development, planning provisions, **25(1)**, [403]
  dilapidated structures. *See* **London Building Acts**
  elections—
    Assembly, for. *See* **London Assembly**
    Mayor of London, determination in respect of, **15(3)**, [147]
  enclosure of land adjoining streets, **25(1)**, [150]
  entertainments. *See* **entertainment**
  explosives in. *See* **explosives**
  fencing of land—
    dangerous lands, **25(1)**, [419]
    expenses of, **25(1)**, [510]
    interference with, penalty, **25(1)**, [419]
    lighting of, **25(1)**, [419]
  fire authorities, **25(1)**, [708]
  fire brigade. *See* **fire brigade**
  flammable material. *See* **flammable material**
  flood prevention. *See* **Thames flood barrier; Thames river**

London—*contd*
  forecourts, maintenance—
    execution by borough council, **25(1)**, [418]
      expenses of, **25(1)**, [420]
    notice to owner requiring, **25(1)**, [418]
  gardens, enclosed, property in, **25(1)**, [18]
  government. *See* **London government**
  Greater London Magistrates' Courts
    Authority. *See* **Greater London**
    Magistrates' Courts Authority
  green belt. *See* **Green Belt**
  guild church. *See* **guild church**
  heat, supply of. *See* **heat, supply of**
  highway authorities. *See* **highway authority**
  highway authorities in, **36**, [1005]
  historic buildings—
    acquisition by borough council,
      25(1), [402]
    restoration, **25(1)**, [336]
  hostels. *See* **hostel**
  hostess bars, licensing—
    amended provisions, **26(2)**, [720]
    existing premises, **26(2)**, [721]
    meaning, **26(2)**, [720]
  houses. *See* **housing**
  ILEA. *See* **Inner London Education**
    Authority
  inner. *See* **Inner London**
  land drainage, provisions relating to,
    19(3), [171]
  libraries. *See* **public library**
  local education authority—
    councils being, **15(1)**, [327]
    property, rights and liabilities, transfer of,
      15(1), [328]
    staff—
      commission, establishment and
        functions, **15(1)**, [329]
      continuity of employment, **15(1)**, [332]
      loss of employment or emoluments,
        compensation for, **15(1)**, [331]
      power to transfer, **15(1)**, [330]
  Lord Mayor. *See* **London, City of**
  meaning, **25(1)**, [1]
  near beer premises, provisions ceasing to have
    effect, **26(2)**, [722]
  night café. *See* **night café**
  occasional sales. *See* **street trading**
  overhead wires. *See* **overground wires**
  owner of vehicle, disclosure of information as
    to, **26(2)**, [346]
  parking. *See* **parking**
  parking places. *See* **London, City of;**
    parking
  parks. *See* **Greater London**
  petrol filling station. *See* **petroleum**
  police districts, **25(1)**, [1]
  polytechnics, superannuation provisions,
    25(1), [166]
  Port of. *See* **Port of London**
  public health. *See* **public health**
  public health and environment,
    interpretation, **26(2)**, [693]
  rendering certain rents by corporation of,
    13, [5]

London—*contd*
  repeals affecting, **41**, [786]
  Residuary Body. *See* **London Residuary**
    Body
  right of way improvement plan, **38(2)**, [68]
  road death, inquest into, **11(1)**, [1225]
  road humps, **36**, [1097]
  road improvements in, **36**, [1335]
  roadside amenities, **25(1)**, [476]
  sanitation, aged etc persons, cleansing of,
    25(1), [487]
  sewers. *See* **sewer**
  sleeping accommodation. *See* **sleeping**
    accommodation
  statues. *See* **statues**
  strategic roads—
    initial designation, **38(2)**, [343]
    orders changing, **38(2)**, [344]
  street trading. *See* **street trading**
  temporary sleeping accommodation, powers
    of entry, search and seizure, **26(2)**, [736]
  traffic calming works, **36**, [1102]
  transport. *See* **London transport**
  tunnels, explosives in, **25(1)**, [95]
  vegetation, planning provisions applied to,
    26(2), [719]
  vehicle crossings over footways and verges,
    26(2), [342]
  water supply. *See* **Thames Water Authority**
  wine, etc, gauging of, **39(1)**, [543]
  youth courts, **25(1)**, [758]

London Assembly
  annual report, **26(1)**, [499]
  Chair—
    appointment, **26(1)**, [483]
    Deputy—
      appointment, **26(1)**, [483]
      functions, **26(1)**, [482]
      office of, **26(1)**, [482]
    functions, **26(1)**, [482]
    office of, **26(1)**, [482]
    vacancy in office, **26(1)**, [483]
  climate change, duties with respect to,
    26(1), [705]
  committees—
    advisory, **26(1)**, [487]
    appointment, **26(1)**, [487]
    exercise of functions by, **26(1)**, [486]
    openness, **26(1)**, [490]
    political composition, **26(1)**, [489]
    sub-committees—
      appointment, **26(1)**, [487]
      openness, **26(1)**, [490]
  constituencies, **26(1)**, [432]
    changes to, **26(1)**, [764]
    comprehensive review of, **26(1)**, [764]
    directions, **26(1)**, [764]
    orders, **26(1)**, [765]
    report, preparation and submission of,
      26(1), [764]
    rules, **26(1)**, [764]
  elections—
    agent—
      default in appointment, **15(3)**, [72]

London Assembly—*contd*
　elections—*contd*
　　agent—*contd*
　　　sub-agent—
　　　　nomination of, **15(3)**, [69]
　　　　office, having, **15(3)**, [70]
　　constituency member, determination in
　　　respect of election of, **15(3)**, [147]
　　election of members being declared void,
　　　consequences of, **15(3)**, [137]
　　expenses of members, **15(3)**, [99]
　　return of members being declared void,
　　　consequences of, **15(3)**, [137]
　financial reports, **25(2)**, [808]
　Greater London Authority functions, exercise
　　of, **26(1)**, [467]
　London Transport Users' Committee,
　　directions to, **26(1)**, [635]
　Mayor—
　　periodic report by, **26(1)**, [477]
　　proposals to, **26(1)**, [492]
　　review of functions of, **26(1)**, [491]
　meetings—
　　attendance at—
　　　information given, restriction of,
　　　　26(1), [496]
　　　openness, **26(1)**, [498]
　　　power to require, **26(1)**, [494]
　　　procedure for requiring, **26(1)**, [495]
　　failure to attend, **26(1)**, [497]
　　minutes of, **26(1)**, [488]
　　openness, **26(1)**, [490]
　　procedure, **26(1)**, [485]
　　whole Assembly, of, **26(1)**, [484]
　members—
　　constituency, **26(1)**, [432]
　　　vacancy, filling, **26(1)**, [440]
　　declaration of acceptance of office,
　　　26(1), [460]
　　disqualification—
　　　bankrupt, of, **26(1)**, [452]
　　　grounds for, **26(1)**, [452]
　　　paid officer of London borough council,
　　　　of, **26(1)**, [452]
　　　proceedings for, **26(1)**, [454]
　　exercise of functions by, **26(1)**, [486]
　　failure to attend meetings, **26(1)**, [436]
　　London, **26(1)**, [432], [441]
　　　calculation of figure, **26(1)**, [767]
　　　individual candidates, **26(1)**, [767]
　　　party lists, **26(1)**, [767]
　　　prescribed percentage of total vote,
　　　　failure to poll, **26(1)**, [767]
　　　return of, **26(1)**, [767]
　　Mayor, election as, **26(1)**, [438]
　　number of, **26(1)**, [432]
　　payments on ceasing to hold office,
　　　26(1), [458]
　　pensions, **26(1)**, [457]
　　qualification to be, **26(1)**, [451]
　　remuneration, publication of information as
　　　to, **26(1)**, [459]
　　resignation, **26(1)**, [435]
　　salaries and expenses, **26(1)**, [455]
　　term of office, **26(1)**, [432]

London Assembly—*contd*
　members—*contd*
　　unqualified person, acts by, **26(1)**, [453]
　ordinary election for, **26(1)**, [432]
　　constituency member, return of,
　　　26(1), [434]
　　cost, recovery of, **26(1)**, [449]
　　definitions, **26(1)**, [461]
　　London vote, **26(1)**, [434]
　　Secretary of State, expenditure of,
　　　26(1), [450]
　　time of, **26(1)**, [433]
　　voting at, **26(1)**, [434]
　People's Question Time, holding, **26(1)**, [480]
　procedure, **26(1)**, [485]
　staff—
　　appointment of, **26(1)**, [501]
　　disqualification and political restriction,
　　　26(1), [502]
　　terms and conditions of employment,
　　　26(1), [503]
　vacancy in—
　　casual, date of, **26(1)**, [439]
　　declaration of, **26(1)**, [437]

London borough
　adaptations of enactments, **25(1)**, [721], [735]
　application of provisions, **26(2)**, [164]
　areas of, **25(1)**, [731]
　authorised officer, obstruction of, **26(1)**, [265]
　boundaries, **25(1)**, [732]
　bus lanes—
　　penalty charges—
　　　emergency vehicles, exemption of,
　　　　26(1), [249]
　　　enforcement notices, **26(1)**, [250], [269]
　　　financial provisions, **26(1)**, [270]
　　　fixing, **26(1)**, [251A]
　　　not payable, where, **26(1)**, [252]
　　　notices, service of, **26(1)**, [248]
　charter, power to grant, **25(1)**, [694]
　councils. *See* **London borough council**
　electoral arrangements, **25(2)**, [246]
　electoral divisions and wards, **25(2)**, [239]
　environmental protection, **26(1)**, [262]
　establishment, **25(1)**, [694]
　exercise of powers affecting other authority's
　　roads, **36**, [1352]
　floodlighting etc buildings, **25(1)**, [751]
　green belt land, **25(1)**, [711]
　illuminations, powers as to, **25(1)**, [751]
　incorporation orders, **25(1)**, [694]
　mail forwarding business, restrictions on,
　　26(2), [739]
　mayor, **25(2)**, [239]
　meaning, **41**, [605]
　name, change of, **25(2)**, [64]
　names of, **25(1)**, [731]
　night cafés. *See* **night cafés**
　offences, due diligence defence, **26(1)**, [266];
　　26(2), [184]
　parking places, off-street, **25(1)**, [880]
　parks and open spaces, **25(1)**, [711]
　　See also **Greater London**
　smallholding, allotments etc, **25(1)**, [710]

London borough—*contd*
special treatment premises—
  amendment of enactments, **26(2)**, [163]
  entry, powers of, **25(2)**, [969]
  existing, application of provisions to,
    25(2), [970]
  licence—
    appeals, **25(2)**, [967]; **26(2)**, [163]
    application for, **25(2)**, [961]
    cancellation, **25(2)**, [963]
    conditions, **25(2)**, [960]
    enforcement, **25(2)**, [968]
    provisional grant, **25(2)**, [965]
    renewal and transfer, **26(2)**, [163]
    refusal of, **25(2)**, [962]
    requirement of, **25(2)**, [960]
    standard terms, conditions and
      restrictions, **25(2)**, [964]
    transmission, **25(2)**, [963]
    variation, **25(2)**, [966]
  meaning, **25(2)**, [958]
  termination of registration, **26(1)**, [238]
street trading. *See* **street trading**
streets. *See* **London streets**

London borough council. *See also* **Greater
London (new authorities); local authority;
London government**
abandoned vehicles—
  disposal of, **26(2)**, [715]
  expenses of removal, recovery of,
    26(2), [435]
  information, disclosure of, **26(2)**, [438]
  owner, meaning, **26(2)**, [436]
  powers of entry, **26(2)**, [437]
  removal, no notice required, **26(2)**, [714]
  transitional provision, **26(2)**, [439]
abroad, power to raise money, **25(1)**, [827]
acquisition of land—
  agreement, by, **25(1)**, [832]
  allowances for removal, **25(1)**, [575]
  walkway, for, **25(1)**, [947]
advances by—
  erection etc of buildings, for, **25(1)**, [559]
  securing repayment, **25(1)**, [559]
aged and feeble persons, power to cleanse,
  25(1), [487]
agreements with, binding on successive
  owners, **25(2)**, [346]
amenities, publicity for, **25(1)**, [718]
annual reports, **25(1)**, [488]
appointed council—
  meaning, **25(1)**, [962]
  purposes and powers, **25(1)**, [962]
authorised officer—
  meaning, **26(2)**, [347], [452]
  obstruction, **26(2)**, [183], [348], [453]
  provision of information to, **26(2)**, [349],
    [451]
bearer bonds, raising money on, **25(1)**, [826]
bills, raising money by issue of, **25(1)**, [825]
birds, nuisance from, **26(2)**, [440], [457]
body corporate, offences by, **26(2)**, [455]
booking offices, licensing, **25(2)**, [394]

London borough council—*contd*
borrowing—
  abroad, from, **25(1)**, [827]
  methods of, **25(1)**, [827]
  procedure, **25(1)**, [962]
  rate of interest, **25(1)**, [962]
brown tail moth, control of, **25(2)**, [421]
buildings—
  defacement of—
    railway and waterway undertakers,
      protection of, **26(2)**, [443]
    universal postal service providers,
      protection of, **26(2)**, [442]
  erection of—
    advances for, **25(1)**, [559]
    extended power, **25(1)**, [507]
burial grounds—
  human remains, disturbing, **26(2)**, [738]
  maintenance, powers, **25(1)**, [231], [508]
  outer boroughs, in, **25(2)**, [270]
byelaws—
  fees under Building Acts, **25(1)**, [503]
  fixed penalties—
    financial provisions, **26(2)**, [459]
    level of, **26(2)**, [446]
    notices, **26(2)**, [445], [458]
    power to discharge liability, **26(2)**, [444]
    Secretary of State reserve powers of,
      26(2), [447]
  massage etc establishments, **25(1)**, [471]
  military drill, for, **25(1)**, [72]
  overground wires, **25(1)**, [200]
  parking etc on housing estates, **25(2)**, [355]
  public health, **25(1)**, [734]
  street trading, **25(1)**, [553]
  tenement houses, **25(1)**, [515]
ceremonies, expenses of, **25(1)**, [475]
chairman—
  declaration to be made by, **25(2)**, [72]
  references to, **25(2)**, [229]
charges by, under Building Acts, **25(2)**, [509]
child care expenses, **25(2)**, [301]
civil amenity sites, deposit of waste in,
  26(2), [713]
commissioners of lieutenancies, **26(1)**, [277]
concert halls, provision of, **25(1)**, [377]
constitution, **25(2)**, [8], [239]
consumer advisory and protection service,
  25(2), [300]
costermongers, storage accommodation for,
  25(1), [477]
councillors—
  election, **25(2)**, [8]
  number of, **25(2)**, [239]
  retirement of, **25(2)**, [239]
  term of office, **25(2)**, [239]
countryside functions transferred to,
  25(2), [582]
courtesy visits, expenses, **25(1)**, [475]
crematoria, powers as to, **25(1)**, [1008]
crime prevention, **25(2)**, [950]
cultural bodies, contributions to, **25(1)**, [400]
dangerous structures, demolition, **26(2)**, [441]

London borough council—*contd*
  defacement of buildings, notice as to,
    26(1), [219]
    indemnity, **26(1)**, [220]
    operational land, entry on, **26(1)**, [221]
  development funds—
    application of, **25(2)**, [302]
    establishment, **25(2)**, [302]
    investment of, **25(2)**, [302]
  disused burial ground authority, **25(1)**, [58]
  documents—
    destruction of, time for, **25(1)**, [963]
    electronic, mechanical or other
      equipment, **25(1)**, [965]
    evidence as to, **25(2)**, [395]
    meaning, **25(1)**, [966]
    microfilming of, **25(1)**, [964]
  door supervisors, registration of. *See* **licensed
    premises**
  electricity supply, power to restore,
    25(2), [269], [935], [938], [949], [952]
  enclosure of land by, **25(1)**, [150]
  enforcement action zones—
    designation, **26(2)**, [716]
    designation procedure, **26(2)**, [717]
    modification of enactments, **26(2)**, [718],
      [746], [747]
  entertainments, provision of, **25(1)**, [378]
  fencing lands, expenses, **25(1)**, [510]
  financial provisions, **25(1)**, [810]
  fixed penalties—
    financial provisions, **26(2)**, [459]
    level of, **26(2)**, [446]
    notices, **26(2)**, [445], [458]
    power to discharge liability, **26(2)**, [444]
    Secretary of State, reserve powers of,
      26(2), [447]
  floodlighting etc, powers as to, **25(1)**, [751]
  foreign loans reserve fund, **25(2)**, [356]
  functions—
    Common Council, discharge of,
      25(1), [697]
    exercise of, **25(1)**, [696]
    flood prevention, **25(1)**, [681], [682]
    green belt land, **25(1)**, [712]
    miscellaneous, **25(1)**, [715]
    National Parks, **25(1)**, [713]
    parks and open spaces, **25(1)**, [711]
    town development, **25(1)**, [714]
  functions transferred to—
    building control, **25(2)**, [639]
    countryside, **25(2)**, [582]
    highways, **25(2)**, [583]
    land drainage, **25(2)**, [586]
    local statutory provisions, under,
      25(2), [588]
    miscellaneous, **25(2)**, [639]
    National Parks, **25(2)**, [582]
    reorganisation of, **25(2)**, [602]
    road traffic, **25(2)**, [583]
    waste regulation and disposal, **25(2)**, [584]
  funds, investment of, **25(2)**, [266]
  gas services, power to restore, **25(2)**, [269],
    [935], [938], [949], [952]

London borough council—*contd*
  grants—
    right to, **25(2)**, [306]
    voluntary organisations, to, **25(2)**, [607]
  gratuities—
    family for purposes of, **25(1)**, [181]
    non-pensionable employees, to,
      25(1), [181]
  hairdressers, registration, **25(1)**, [834];
    25(2), [527]
  heat, supply of. *See* **heat, supply of**
  highway, bridges in two districts, **25(2)**, [637]
  historic buildings, acquisition, **25(1)**, [402]
  hostels. *See* **hostel**
  housing authority—
    secure tenancy, in case of, **22**, [81]
    See further **local housing authority**
  housing powers, **22**, [17]
  housing provisions, **25(2)**, [639]
  housing staff, transfer of, **25(2)**, [420]
  insurance fund, establishment, **25(1)**, [1007]
  insurance of property, **25(1)**, [506]
  investment, powers of, **25(2)**, [266]
  joint committee, meaning, **26(2)**, [727]
  land—
    agreements binding on successive owners,
      25(2), [346]
    vesting in, **25(1)**, [698]
  land drainage—
    powers, **19(3)**, [185]
    supervision of, **19(3)**, [186]
  land drainage function, **25(2)**, [586]
  lending by, **25(1)**, [962]
  littering from vehicles, penalty for,
    26(2), [711]
  local Bills, promotion of, **25(2)**, [622]
  national parks functions, **25(2)**, [582]
  nuisance vehicles, removal of—
    disposal of, **26(2)**, [715]
    notice, no requirement of, **26(2)**, [714]
  offences, due diligence defence, **26(2)**, [454]
  office—
    accommodation, power to erect,
      25(1), [507]
    compensation on abolition, **25(1)**, [142]
  officers—
    decisions of, evidence as to, **25(2)**, [395]
    injury etc compensation, **25(1)**, [719]
    transfer of, **25(1)**, [723]
    See also **local government officers and
      staff**
  payments on behalf of, **25(1)**, [1003]
  penalty charges—
    adjudicators, **26(2)**, [730]
    enforcement—
      certificated bailiffs, **26(2)**, [732]
      regulations, **26(2)**, [731]
    financial provisions, **26(2)**, [748]
    interpretation, **26(2)**, [854]
    levels of, **26(2)**, [733]
    notice—
      appeals, **26(2)**, [729]
      contents of, **26(2)**, [728]
      representations, **26(2)**, [729]
      service of, **26(2)**, [728]

London borough council—*contd*
  penalty charges—*contd*
    Secretary of State, reserve powers of,
      26(2), [734]
  pipe subways, charges for, **26(2)**, [737]
  placards and posters, removal of, **26(1)**, [221]
    operational land, entry on, **26(1)**, [221]
  private sewers, charges, **26(2)**, [740]
  public exhibitions, licensing, **25(1)**, [808]
  public health purposes, local authority for,
    35(1), [118]
  public receptions, expenses of, **25(1)**, [475]
  railings at squares etc, contributions for,
    25(2), [268]
  rates—
    recovery from tenants and lodgers,
      25(2), [296]
    unpaid, charge on premises, **25(2)**, [297]
  research, schemes for, **25(2)**, [623]
  residuary functions of, **25(2)**, [616]
  resolution, proof of, **26(2)**, [742]
  retaining walls, powers as to, **25(2)**, [666]
  return, financial, **25(1)**, [488]
  road traffic—
    functions as to, **25(2)**, [583]
    powers, guidance in exercise of,
      25(2), [638]
  roadside amenities, improvement, **25(1)**, [476]
  small dwellings expenses, **25(1)**, [401]
  soliciting for custom, prohibited, **26(2)**, [448]
  staff—
    transfer of, to, **25(2)**, [608]
    See also **local government officers and
      staff**
  street names. *See* **London streets**
  street trading. *See* **street trading**
  subways, provision of shops in, **25(1)**, [750]
  superannuation fund—
    charges on, **25(1)**, [246]
    investment, **25(1)**, [829]–[831]
    provisions applied, **25(1)**, [905]
    See further **local government officers
      and staff**
  Trophy Tax, levy of, **26(1)**, [277]
  unauthorised advertisement hoardings,
    removal of, **26(1)**, [218]
    operational land, entry on, **26(1)**, [221]
  voluntary organisations, contributions to,
    25(1), [1003]
  waste, receptables for—
    commercial—
      placing of, **26(2)**, [708]
      regulations, **26(2)**, [709]
    enforcement of regulations, **26(2)**, [710]
    household—
      placing of, **26(2)**, [706]
      regulations, **26(2)**, [707]
    industrial—
      placing of, **26(2)**, [708]
      regulations, **26(2)**, [709]
  waste unlawfully deposited, power to require
    removal of, **26(2)**, [712]
  water supply, restoration after cutting off,
    25(1), [835]
  works under street, demolition, **25(2)**, [663]

London Bridge
  trunk road, not being, **36**, [1013]

London Building Acts
  additions to buildings, **25(1)**, [339]
  adjoining owner. *See* owner *below*
  alterations in building—
    appeal respecting, **25(1)**, [286]
    conformation to Act, **25(1)**, [338]
    fire precautions, **25(1)**, [283]
  appeals. *See* tribunal of appeal *below*
  application of, **25(1)**, [351]
  architect. *See* superintending architect *below*
  architectural etc interest, buildings, of,
    25(1), [336]
  basement storey, meaning, **25(1)**, [172]
  building notice. *See* notices *below*
  building operations—
    public safety, affecting, **25(1)**, [814]
      directors, liability of, **25(1)**, [817]
      offences, liability for, **25(1)**, [816]
      proceedings, **25(1)**, [818]
  buildings—
    numbering or naming, **25(1)**, [269]
    special. *See* special buildings *below*
  byelaws—
    additional matters of, **25(1)**, [310]
    notices of making, **25(1)**, [241]
    objections to, **25(1)**, [241]
    procedure as to making, **25(1)**, [241]
    public inspection, **25(1)**, [241]
    references to, construction of, **25(1)**, [263]
    safety of persons, **25(1)**, [310]
    sealing, **25(1)**, [241]
  consents under—
    charges for, **25(2)**, [509]
    conditions, power to annex, **25(1)**, [347]
    meaning, **25(2)**, [509]
    owners not to be found, where,
      25(1), [346]
  construction of buildings—
    erected before commencement of Act,
      25(1), [356]
    subject to rules, **25(1)**, [357]
  conversions, rules for, **25(1)**, [343]
  county court—
    appeal from, **25(1)**, [312]
    apportionment of expenses by, **25(1)**, [316]
    jurisdiction, **25(1)**, [312]
  cubical extent—
    limitation of, **25(1)**, [274]
    meaning, **25(1)**, [263]
  damage, arbitration as to incidence of,
    25(1), [285]
  dangerous business—
    building near—
      permitted distance, **25(1)**, [173]
      regulations for, **25(1)**, [173]
    fees, **26(1)**, [209]
    meaning, **25(1)**, [172]
    places deemed not to be, **25(1)**, [173]
    relaxation of provisions, **25(1)**, [173]
    restriction on establishing, **25(1)**, [173]
  dangerous structures—
    application of provisions, **25(1)**, [500]

London Building Acts—*contd*
  dangerous structures—*contd*
    arbitration as to, **25(1)**, [291]
      order made notwithstanding,
        25(1), [293]
    certification of, **25(1)**, [290]
    court order as to, **25(1)**, [293]
    disputes as to, **25(1)**, [291]
    entry, powers of, **25(1)**, [501]
    expenses—
      apportionment, **25(1)**, [499]
      interest payable on, **25(1)**, [498]
      occupant, liability of, **25(1)**, [498]
      owner's liability, **25(1)**, [294]
      recovery, **25(1)**, [498]
      repayment to local authority,
        25(1), [298]
    fees payable to local authority,
      25(1), [306], [502]
      byelaws as to, **25(1)**, [503]
      schedule of, **25(1)**, [360]
    functions, transfer of, **25(1)**, [571]–[573]
    information as to, **25(1)**, [289]
    inmates—
      priority housing, **25(1)**, [904];
        25(2), [558]
      removal of, **25(1)**, [295], [903];
        25(2), [557]
      temporary accommodation for,
        25(1), [573]
    inspection or examination, **25(1)**, [501]
    interpretation of provisions, **25(1)**, [497]
    notice to owner to remedy—
      enforcement, **25(1)**, [292]
      service of, **25(1)**, [290]
    proceedings against owner, **25(1)**, [292]
    removal of occupants, **25(1)**, [295];
      25(2), [557]
    service of notices, **25(1)**, [334]
    shoring up etc, **25(1)**, [290]
      public streets, on, **25(1)**, [296]
    survey, requirement for, **25(1)**, [289]
  demolition of buildings, **25(1)**, [313]
  dilapidated structures. *See* neglected structures
    below
  distilleries, buildings near, **25(1)**, [175]
  district surveyor—
    duties, **25(1)**, [301], [574]
    entry, powers of, **25(1)**, [345]
    fees, recovery of, **25(1)**, [309]
    meaning, **25(1)**, [263]
    notice of irregularity—
      after completion, **25(1)**, [304]
      amendment, requiring, **25(1)**, [303]
      non-compliance with, **25(1)**, [305]
    survey fees, **25(1)**, [359]
  division wall—
    buildings requiring, **25(1)**, [274]
    walls deemed to be, **25(1)**, [274]
  documents—
    authentication, **25(1)**, [331]
    service of, **25(1)**, [332]–[334]
  dwelling-house—
    low-lying land, on, **25(1)**, [176], [177]
    meaning, **25(1)**, [172]

London Building Acts—*contd*
  effect of, in Greater London, **25(1)**, [704]
  entry—
    authorised officers, by, **25(1)**, [345]
    execution of works, for, **25(1)**, [344]
    refusal of, penalties, **25(1)**, [350]
  exemptions from—
    Crown buildings, **25(1)**, [353]
    duration of, **25(1)**, [355]
    generally, **25(1)**, [351]
    Inns of Court, **25(1)**, [354]
  expenses—
    apportionment, **25(1)**, [316]
    proceedings for recovery, **25(1)**, [311]
  expressions defined, **25(1)**, [172], [263]
  extent of, **25(1)**, [171]
  factories, exemptions from fire precautions,
    25(1), [287]
  fees—
    abatement, **25(1)**, [308]
    accrual of, **25(1)**, [307]
    apportionment, **25(1)**, [316]
    dangerous structures, in respect of,
      25(1), [306]
    recovery of, **25(1)**, [309]
    remission, **25(1)**, [308]
    schedule of, **25(1)**, [359]
  fire, partial destruction by, **25(1)**, [340]
  fire precautions—
    additional conditions as to, **25(1)**, [274]
    alterations, in case of, **25(1)**, [283]
    apparatus etc, provision of, **25(1)**, [274]
    appeals respecting, **25(1)**, [286]
    conditions, imposition of, **25(1)**, [274]
    excepted buildings, **25(1)**, [274]
    factory, building used as, **25(1)**, [287]
    means of escape—
      access to roof, **25(1)**, [282]
      buildings exempt from provisions,
        25(1), [352]
      maintenance of, **25(1)**, [337]
      new buildings, meaning, **25(1)**, [279]
      old buildings—
        alternative proposals by owner,
          25(1), [280]
        exceptions, **25(1)**, [280]
        meaning, **25(1)**, [279]
        notice requiring provision of,
          25(1), [280]
        offences, **25(1)**, [280]
        provisions applied, **25(1)**, [809]
      offences and penalties, **25(1)**, [350]
      projecting shops, **25(1)**, [281]
      special fire risk area—
        conditions imposed for, **25(1)**, [274]
        meaning, **25(1)**, [274]
      works, damage by, **25(1)**, [285]
  functions under, transfer of,
    25(1), [571]–[573]
  gasworks, buildings near, **25(1)**, [175]
  height—
    meaning, **25(1)**, [263]
    measurement of, **25(1)**, [274]
    restrictions as to, **25(1)**, [274]
  historic interest, buildings of, **25(1)**, [336]

London Building Acts—*contd*

Inns of Court, exemption for, **25(1)**, [354]

irregularity of work—
  after completion, **25(1)**, [304]
  amendment, requiring, **25(1)**, [303]
  non-compliance with notice, **25(1)**, [305]
  service of notice, **25(1)**, [302]

local authority—
  functions transferred to, **25(1)**, [571]–[573]
  meaning, **25(1)**, [571]

London, references to, in, **25(1)**, [704]

low-lying land, building on, **25(1)**, [176], [177]

materials—
  removal and disposal, **25(1)**, [315]
  sale of, surplus proceeds, **25(1)**, [314]

modifications of, **25(1)**, [704]

neglected structures—
  entry, powers of, **25(1)**, [501]
  expenses of local authority, **25(1)**, [298]
    apportionment, **25(1)**, [499]
    interest payable on, **25(1)**, [498]
    occupier's liability, **25(1)**, [498]
    recovery, **25(1)**, [498]
  fees payable to local authority,
    25(1), [306], [502]; **26(1)**, [209]
    accrual of, **25(1)**, [307]
    byelaws as to, **25(1)**, [503]
    proceedings for, **25(1)**, [309]
    recovery of, **25(1)**, [309]
    schedule of, **25(1)**, [359]
  functions, transfer of, **25(1)**, [571]–[573]
  inspection or examination, **25(1)**, [501]
  interpretation of provisions, **25(1)**, [497]
  removal of, **25(1)**, [297]
  repayment of expenses incurred,
    25(1), [298]
  service of notices, **25(1)**, [334]

notices under—
  authentication, **25(1)**, [331]
  dangerous structures, as to, **25(1)**, [334]
  fees relating to, **25(1)**, [359]
  neglected structures, as to, **25(1)**, [334]
  objection to building notice, of,
    25(1), [302]
  ownership, information of, **25(1)**, [335]
  service of—
    by local authority, **25(1)**, [333]
    on local authority, **25(1)**, [332]
    writing, to be in, **25(1)**, [330]

noxious business—
  buildings near, **25(1)**, [174]
  meaning, **25(1)**, [262]

offences—
  actual offender, effect of conviction of,
    25(1), [284]
  fines and penalties, **25(2)**, [408], [414], [415]
  fines etc, recovery of, **25(1)**, [311]
  schedule of, **25(1)**, [350]

owner—
  entry by, powers of, **25(1)**, [344]
  service of notices on, **25(1)**, [333]

ownership, information concerning,
  25(1), [335]

London Building Acts—*contd*

party wall—
  meaning, **25(1)**, [262]
  taken down for rebuilding, **25(1)**, [342]

penalties, schedule of, **25(1)**, [350]

plans—
  property in, **25(1)**, [349]
  submission, regulations for, **25(1)**, [348]

proceedings—
  fines etc, recovery of, **25(1)**, [311]
  roof, removal of, not to affect, **25(1)**, [317]

projecting shops, fire precautions, **25(1)**, [281]

public building, meaning, **25(1)**, [262]

rebuilding—
  fire etc, after, **25(1)**, [340], [341]
  party walls taken down for, **25(1)**, [342]

roof—
  access to, fire precautions, **25(1)**, [282]
  removal not to affect proceedings,
    25(1), [317]

sale of buildings etc, surplus proceeds,
  25(1), [314]

special buildings—
  application of provisions, **25(1)**, [276]
  consent required, **25(1)**, [277]
  court orders as to, **25(1)**, [278]
  exceptions from provisions, **25(1)**, [277]
  meaning, **25(1)**, [276]

streets, naming. *See* **London streets**

structure—
  dangerous. *See* dangerous structures *above*
  meaning, **25(1)**, [288]
  neglected. *See* neglected structures *above*

superintending architect—
  appointment, **25(1)**, [299]
  assistants, appointment, **25(1)**, [299]
  deputy, **25(1)**, [300]
  duties, **25(1)**, [301]
  meaning, **25(1)**, [262]

surveyor—
  district. *See* district surveyor *above*
  survey of dangerous structure, **25(1)**, [290]

temporary buildings—
  consent required, **25(1)**, [277]
  court orders as to, **25(1)**, [278]
  exceptions from provisions, **25(1)**, [277]

transfer of functions under—
  dangerous or neglected structures,
    25(1), [572], [573]
  interpretation of provisions for,
    25(1), [571]

tribunal of appeal—
  case stated for High Court, **25(1)**, [325]
  constitution, **25(1)**, [318]
  decisions—
    enforcement, **25(1)**, [327]
    majority, **25(1)**, [318]
    publication of, **25(1)**, [322]
    questioning, **25(1)**, [325]
    register of, **25(1)**, [322]
  existing, abolition of, **25(1)**, [329]
  expenses, **25(1)**, [328]
  fees, **25(1)**, [326], [328]
  hearings, **25(1)**, [324]
  jurisdiction, **25(1)**, [324]

London Building Acts—*contd*
  tribunal of appeal—*contd*
    local authority powers as to, **25(1)**, [323]
    members—
      appointment, **25(1)**, [318]
      deputies for, **25(1)**, [318]
      remuneration, **25(1)**, [318]
    office accommodation, **25(1)**, [320]
    officers etc, appointment, **25(1)**, [319]
    procedure, regulation of, **25(1)**, [326]
    professional advice for, **25(1)**, [321]
    sittings of, **25(1)**, [320]
  uniting of buildings, **25(1)**, [275]
  warehouse class buildings, **25(1)**, [274]
  works, execution of—
    county court jurisdiction, **25(1)**, [312]
    default by owner, on, fees, **25(1)**, [360]
    entry for purposes of, **25(1)**, [344]
    irregularity of, **25(1)**, [303]
    notice of objection, **25(1)**, [302]

London cab
  meaning, **36**, [571]
  order, meaning, **36**, [771]
  See generally **hackney carriages, taxis**

London, City of. *See also* **Greater London**
  acquisition of land—
    agreement, by, **25(1)**, [585], [832]
    market storage facilities, for, **25(1)**, [607]
    requirements, in advance of, **25(1)**, [586]
    walkways, for, **25(1)**, [874]
  ambulances, false calls, **25(1)**, [247]
  amenities—
    improvement of, **25(1)**, [480]
    powers as to, **25(1)**, [480]
    publicity for, **25(1)**, [718]
    undertakers' apparatus, protection,
      25(1), [483]
  architectural interest, buildings of—
    acquisition of, **25(1)**, [402], [674]
    demolition under Building Acts,
      25(1), [336]
  building operations—
    public safety, affecting, **25(1)**, [775]
      directors, liability of, **25(1)**, [777]
      offences as to, **25(1)**, [775]
      owner, exemption from liability,
        25(1), [776]
      penalties for offences, **25(1)**, [775]
    See also **London Building Acts**
  byelaws. *See* **London government**
  car parks, provision of, **25(1)**, [537]
  catering facilities in certain buildings,
    25(1), [887]
  cemetery, funeral services in, **25(1)**, [996]
  children, powers and duties of Common
    Council as to, **6**, [46]
  churchyards, closed, maintenance,
    25(1), [481]
  Common Council, land drainage powers,
    19(3), [185]
    See also **London, City of, Common
    Council**

London, City of—*contd*
  consumer advisory and protection service,
    25(2), [300]
  corporate office, avoidance of election to,
    15(3), [191]
  corporation. *See* **London, City of,
    Corporation**
  crime and disorder committee, **12(4)**, [282]
  dangerous containers, disposal of, **25(1)**, [658]
  disused burial ground, **25(1)**, [58]
  drainage—
    byelaws, **25(2)**, [695]
    fines, **25(2)**, [697]
    works, charges for, **25(2)**, [696]
  dustbins, provision of, **25(1)**, [789]
  elections—
    aldermen, **25(1)**, [1]
    candidate, qualification of, **25(1)**, [530]
    electors, qualification of, **25(1)**, [531]
    interpretation of provisions, **25(1)**, [529]
    provisions applied to, **25(1)**, [533]
    registers of electors, preparation of,
      25(1), [886]
    repeal and amendment of provisions,
      25(1), [536]
    town clerk—
      duties, **25(1)**, [532]
      expenses of, **25(1)**, [535]
      meaning, **25(1)**, [529]
    transfer of functions, **25(1)**, [886]
    voting, manner of, **25(1)**, [533]
    ward election—
      Inner and Middle Temples, **25(1)**, [641]
      voting qualification, **25(1)**, [531]
    ward lists—
      appeals as to, **25(1)**, [534]
      application for inclusion in, **25(1)**, [532]
      inspection of, **25(1)**, [532]
      preparation and publication, **25(1)**, [532]
      provisional list, **25(1)**, [532]
  electoral area, **15(3)**, [185]
  excavations near streets—
    distance for purposes of provisions,
      25(1), [774]
    offences and penalties, **25(1)**, [774]
    withdrawal of support by, **25(1)**, [774]
  expenses, **49**, [341]
  furnaces, emissions from, **25(1)**, [1011]
  garage accommodation, provision of,
    25(1), [537]
  general rate, contribution by Inner and
    Middle Temples, **25(1)**, [113]
  good rule and government byelaws,
    25(1), [657]
  historic buildings—
    acquisition by Corporation, **25(1)**, [674]
    demolition under Building Acts,
      25(1), [336]
  horticultural produce. *See* **horticultural
    produce**
  houseboats—
    byelaws, **25(1)**, [187]
    meaning, **25(1)**, [187]
    registration, **25(1)**, [187]

London, City of—*contd*
houses—
  dangerous business, near, **25(1)**, [173]
  low-lying land, on, **25(1)**, [176]
  noxious business, near, **25(1)**, [174]
  Inns of Court within, **25(1)**, [1]
itinerant traders, **25(1)**, [785]; **25(2)**, [689]
land—
  acquisition. *See* acquisition *above*
  improvement, **25(1)**, [480]
liberties and customs, confirmation of, **10**, [5]
litter bins in streets, **25(1)**, [1015]
liverymen, election, **25(1)**, [1]
liverymen, election by, candidate's expenses, **15(3)**, [190]
Local Government Board, inquiries by, **25(1)**, [111]
Lord Mayor—
  appointment, **25(1)**, [1]
  justice, ex officio, as, **25(1)**, [1]
  presentation and swearing of, **25(1)**, [604]
Lord Mayor, annual admission and swearing, **45**, [928]
market storage facilities—
  acquisition of land for, **25(1)**, [607]
  borrowing for provision of, **25(1)**, [606]
  market area, meaning, **25(1)**, [614]
  powers of entry, **25(1)**, [620]
  meaning, **25(1)**, [605]
markets or fairs, trading in, **25(1)**, [787]; **25(2)**, [691]
massage establishments. *See* **massage etc establishments**
medical officers of health, **25(1)**, [703]
militia—
  courts of lieutenancy, **25(1)**, [10]
  expenses, tax to defray, **25(1)**, [4]
  headquarters, building, **25(1)**, [8]
  leases of ground etc, acceptance, **25(1)**, [9]
  lieutenants, powers of, **25(1)**, [2]
  rights and privileges, **25(1)**, [3]
  trained bands, listing and levying, **25(1)**, [2]
  trophy tax—
    charges on, **25(1)**, [9]
    collectors, neglect of duty, **25(1)**, [7]
    security, **25(1)**, [6]
    treasurer etc for, **25(1)**, [5]
municipal elections—
  application of provisions to, **15(3)**, [185]
  broadcasting, provisions on, **15(3)**, [187]
  costs and expenses, **15(3)**, [189], [213]
  meetings, disturbances at, **15(3)**, [188]
  personation, **15(3)**, [186]
  voting offences, **15(3)**, [186]
municipality, as, **25(1)**, [1]
newsvenders, saving for, **25(1)**, [785]; **25(2)**, [689]
night café. *See* **night café**
noise abatement, **25(1)**, [657]
nuisances, suppression of, **25(1)**, [657]
parishes—
  overseers, **25(1)**, [104]
  union of, **25(1)**, [103], [117]

London, City of—*contd*
parishes—*contd*
  vestry, transfer of powers, etc, of, **25(1)**, [106]
parking places—
  charges for use, **25(1)**, [638]
  classes of vehicles to use, **25(1)**, [638]
  off-street, **25(1)**, [880]
  provision of, **25(1)**, [537]
  regulation of, **25(1)**, [638]
police—
  districts, **25(1)**, [1]
  metropolitan district, acting in, **25(1)**, [482]
Port of London Act, savings as to privileges under, **39(2)**, [388]
ports and harbours, savings as to rights, **39(2)**, [92]
precept, issue of, **25(1)**, [105]
public health—
  enactments applied, **25(1)**, [1012]
  inspectors, **25(1)**, [703]
  sulphur gas, emission of, **25(1)**, [1011]
public safety, building operations affecting, **25(1)**, [775]
rates—
  existing exemptions, saving for, **25(1)**, [116]
  expenses, payment from, **25(1)**, [112]
  making, **25(1)**, [108]
  publication of, **25(1)**, [108]
  railway companies, saving for, **25(1)**, [115]
  scheme for, **25(1)**, [109]
  vestry of Saint Giles Cripplegate, saving for, **25(1)**, [114]
  ward expenses, payment of, **25(1)**, [110]
refuse bins in streets, **25(1)**, [1015]
secondary of, **25(1)**, [886]
sanitary accommodation, charges for, **25(2)**, [696]
sanitation byelaws, fines, **25(2)**, [697]
sheriff, appointment of, **39(1)**, [764]
street trading. *See* **street trading**
streets—
  closure to vehicles, **25(1)**, [757]
  improvement—
    boundary walls, weatherproofing etc, **25(1)**, [771]
    damage to property, compensation, **25(1)**, [772]
    meaning, **25(1)**, [770]
    part building demolished by, **25(1)**, [771]
    underpinning houses near—
      Corporation's powers, **25(1)**, [772]
      disputes, arbitration of, **25(1)**, [772]
      inadequacy of, **25(1)**, [772]
      obstruction, penalty, **25(1)**, [773]
    undertakers' apparatus affected by, **25(1)**, [772]
  vehicular access, restriction of, **25(1)**, [757]
  See also **London streets**
subways, provision of shops etc in, **25(1)**, [750]
sulphur gas, emission of, **25(1)**, [1011]

London, City of—*contd*
tax collectors, appointment of, **42**, [22]
Temples included in for certain purposes, **25(1)**, [760]
Tower Bridge, byelaws, **25(1)**, [189]
town clerk—
election duties, **25(1)**, [532]
functions transferred to, **25(1)**, [886]
Trophy Tax, issue of precepts, **25(1)**, [108]
trunk road, highway in not being, **36**, [1013]
ward elections—
broadcasting, provisions on, **15(3)**, [187]
candidate's expenses, **15(3)**, [190]
costs and expenses, **15(3)**, [189]
definitions, **26(2)**, [190]
existing system, interim saving, **26(2)**, [198]
provisions for, **15(3)**, [218]
qualifying body—
exclusion of Crown bodies, **26(2)**, [194]
ward lists, **26(2)**, [196]
reports, **26(2)**, [195]
voters—
allocation of appointments, **26(2)**, [192]
connections with city, **26(2)**, [193]
qualification of, **26(2)**, [191]
ward lists, **26(2)**, [196]
weights and measures authority, **39(1)**, [522]
youth courts, **25(1)**, [758]

London, City of, Common Council
abroad, power to raise money, **25(1)**, [827]
acquisition of land. *See* **London, City of**
adaptations of enactments, **25(1)**, [721], [735]
auditors. *See* **Audit Commission**
bearer bonds, raising money on, **25(1)**, [826]
bills, raising money by issue of, **25(1)**, [825]
buildings, power to erect, **25(1)**, [507]
byelaws. *See* **London government**
capital expenditure. *See* **local authority**
ceremonies, expenses of, **25(1)**, [475]
child care expenses, **25(2)**, [301]
City fund—
establishment, **25(2)**, [797]
other funds, relationship with, **25(2)**, [798]
payments to and from, **25(2)**, [797]
regulations as to, **25(2)**, [798]
transfers between funds, **25(2)**, [799]
contributions in respect of railings, **25(2)**, [268]
Court of, constitution, **25(1)**, [1]
courtesy visits, expenses, **25(1)**, [475]
crematoria, powers as to, **25(1)**, [1008]
cultural bodies, contributions to, **25(1)**, [400]
documents—
acquisition, **25(1)**, [672]
destruction of, time for, **25(1)**, [963]
electronic, mechanical or other equipment, **25(1)**, [965]
meaning, **25(1)**, [966]
microfilming of, **25(1)**, [964]
preservation, **25(1)**, [672]
publication, **25(1)**, [672]
elections. *See* **London, City of**
financial administration officer, **25(2)**, [859]

London, City of, Common Council—*contd*
financial provisions applicable, **25(1)**, [717]
flood prevention functions, **25(1)**, [681]
foreign loans reserve fund, **25(2)**, [356]
functions—
delegation of, **25(1)**, [697]
exercise of, **25(1)**, [696]
functions transferred to—
local Acts, under, **25(2)**, [588]
miscellaneous, **25(2)**, [639]
road traffic, **25(2)**, [583]
waste regulation and disposal, **25(2)**, [584], [585]
funds, investment of, **25(2)**, [266]
grants, right to, **25(2)**, [306]
gratuities—
family for purposes of, **25(1)**, [181]
non-pensionable employees, to, **25(1)**, [181]
housing authority, as, **22**, [1]
housing committee, **22**, [418]; **23**, [537]
See further **local housing authority**
information, duty to publish, **25(2)**, [428]
insurance fund, establishment, **25(1)**, [1007]
insurance of property, **25(1)**, [506]
investment, powers of, **25(2)**, [266]
land, power to acquire, **25(1)**, [591], [599]
legal proceedings, powers as to, **25(2)**, [174], [175]
levy—
bodies for issuing, **25(2)**, [759]
decisions, judicial review of, **25(2)**, [819]
meaning, **25(2)**, [828]
power to issue, **25(2)**, [759]
regulations, **25(2)**, [759]
special—
meaning, **25(2)**, [828]
power to issue, **25(2)**, [760]
levying body, meaning, **25(2)**, [759], [828]
local Bills, promotion of, **25(2)**, [622]
meetings, expenses of, **25(1)**, [538]
officers, transfer of, **25(1)**, [723]
offices, compensation on abolition, **25(1)**, [142]
overseers, as, **25(1)**, [104]
port health authority, as—
functions, exercise of, **25(1)**, [1014]
provisions applied, **25(1)**, [1012]
precepts, **25(1)**, [105]
public exhibitions, licensing, **25(1)**, [808]
public receptions, expenses of, **25(1)**, [475]
rate books, references to, **25(1)**, [640]
rate, power to levy, **25(1)**, [716]
records, powers as to, **25(1)**, [663]
references to, interpretation of, **25(1)**, [584]
reports and returns by, **25(1)**, [589]
research, schemes for, **25(2)**, [623]
superannuation—
fund, charges on, **25(1)**, [246]
provisions applied, **25(1)**, [906]
See further **local government officers and staff**
Temples, functions respecting, **25(2)**, [626]
transfer of staff to, **25(2)**, [608]

London, City of, Common Council—*contd*
travelling and subsistence allowances,
25(1), [538]

London, City of, Corporation
acquisition of land. *See* **London, City of**
agreements binding successive owners,
25(1), [639]
aldermen—
  Court of, **25(1)**, [1]
  number and election, **25(1)**, [1]
appeal against decisions etc, **25(1)**, [660]
assemblies of, **25(1)**, [1]
borrowing—
  abroad, from, **25(1)**, [995]
  bearer bonds, by, **25(1)**, [995]
  bonds, by issue of, **25(2)**, [277]
  interest, raising money for payment of,
    25(1), [792]
  market storage, to provide, **25(1)**, [606]
  promissory notes, on, **25(1)**, [793]
  repayment, suspension of provision for,
    25(1), [792]
  securities, transfer of, **25(1)**, [794]
  Treasury powers as to, **25(1)**, [590], [609]
byelaws. *See* **London government**
catering facilities, provision of, **25(1)**, [887]
charities pool, **25(1)**, [924]
Common Hall, Court of, **25(1)**, [1]
conferences, powers as to, **25(1)**, [538]
constitution, **25(1)**, [1]
decisions of, appeal from, **25(1)**, [660]
dustbins, power to provide, **25(1)**, [650],
  [789]
garages, power to provide, **25(1)**, [537]
land, disposal of, **25(1)**, [587]
loans fund, **25(2)**, [385]
meetings etc, expenses of attending,
  25(1), [538]
notices by—
  appeal against, **25(1)**, [659]
  enforcement, **25(1)**, [659]
officers. *See* **local government officers and
  staff**
orders, appeal against, **25(1)**, [660]
parking places, provision of, **25(1)**, [537]
raising money—
  abroad, **25(1)**, [995]
  bearer bonds, by issue of, **25(1)**, [995]
  See also borrowing *above*
securities, transfer of, **25(1)**, [794]
sinking fund, provision as to, **25(2)**, [385]
staff appointment, provisions applied,
  25(2), [387]
stock regulations, application, **25(2)**, [384]
street trading functions. *See* **street trading**
subscriptions to learned societies etc,
  25(1), [673]
tithe stock, **25(2)**, [386]
trustees of, investment powers, **25(1)**, [924]
undertakings, binding nature, **25(1)**, [639]
vehicular access, power to restrict,
  25(1), [757]

London, City of, Corporation—*contd*
walkways, construction etc, responsible for,
  25(1), [866]
  See further **walkways**

London County Council
former jurisdiction, **25(1)**, [1]

London Development Agency
annual reports, **46**, [913]
audit, **46**, [911]
Bills, power to promote or oppose, **46**, [923],
  [953]
chief finance officer, **26(1)**, [502]
constitution, **46**, [895], [946]
delegation of functions to, **26(1)**, [470],
  [725]; **46**, [900], [948]
functional body, as, **26(1)**, [762]
guidance and directions to, **46**, [902]
interests in land, power to requirement
  information as to, **26(2)**, [328]
meaning, **46**, [940]
members, **46**, [895], [946]
  allowances, **26(2)**, [482]
  transitional provisions, **46**, [947]
property, rights and liabilities, transfer of—
  contracts of employment, **26(1)**, [749]
  foreign, **26(1)**, [753]
  modification of instruments, **26(1)**, [752]
  pensions, **26(1)**, [750]
  provision for, **26(1)**, [747]
  schemes, **26(1)**, [748], [796]
  stamp duty and stamp duty reserve tax
    exemptions, **26(1)**, [756]
  transfer or pension instruments, common
    provisions, **26(1)**, [751]
staff, **46**, [946]
strategy—
  formulation and submission of, **46**, [902]
  Mayor of London, guidance and directions
    from, **46**, [902]
  revisions, **46**, [902]
  Secretary of State, functions of, **46**, [903]
superannuation provisions, **26(1)**, [732], [733]

London Ecology Committee
abolition, **26(1)**, [718]

London Electricity Board
deep tube shelters, provisions relating to,
  50, [252]

London Fire and Civil Defence Authority
compensation to servants of, **26(2)**, [180]
contributions by insurance company to—
  amount of, ascertaining, **18**, [1000]
  books, examination of, **18**, [1002]
  enforcing, **18**, [999]
  payment of, **18**, [998]
  penalties, recovery of, **18**, [1003]
  returns, failure to make, **18**, [1001]
reconstitution, **26(1)**, [671]

London Fire and Emergency Planning Authority

Bill, promotion of, **25(2)**, [60]
functional body, as, **26(1)**, [762]
local authority, treatment for tax purposes, **26(1)**, [757]
Mayor of London—
  directions from, **26(1)**, [672]
  Secretary of State, directions from, **26(1)**, [673]
members, **26(1)**, [792]
proceedings, **26(1)**, [792]
provisions applied to, **25(2)**, [205], [646]
reconstitution, **26(1)**, [671]
unqualified persons, acts by, **26(1)**, [792]
vacancies, filling, **26(1)**, [792]

London Gazette

diplomatic agreements, publication of, **10**, [988]
proof of documents by, **18**, [135]
royal proclamations in, **10**, [458]

London government

acquisition of land—
  agreement, by, **25(1)**, [832]
  walkway, for, **25(1)**, [947]
adaptation of enactments, **25(1)**, [721]
administrative areas, **25(1)**, [694]
aged etc persons, cleansing, **25(1)**, [487]
amenities, publicity for, **25(1)**, [718]
building Acts. *See* **London Building Acts**
burial grounds. *See* **burial ground**
byelaws—
  bridges, **25(1)**, [75]
  Building Acts. *See* **London Building Acts**
  drainage, **25(2)**, [695]
  explosives, **25(1)**, [90]–[97]
  fees under Building Acts, **25(1)**, [503]
  ferries, **25(1)**, [74]
  good rule and government, **25(1)**, [657]
  horticultural market storage, **25(1)**, [608], [616]
  houseboats, **25(1)**, [187]
  market storage facilities, **25(1)**, [608], [616]
  massage establishments, **25(1)**, [137], [257], [471]
  military drilling, **25(1)**, [72]
  noise abatement, **25(1)**, [657]
  nuisances, suppression of, **25(1)**, [657]
  offences, proceedings for, **25(1)**, [190]
  overground wires, **25(1)**, [200]
  parking, **25(2)**, [355]
  Parliament Square, **26(1)**, [730]
  public health, **25(1)**, [734]
  street trading, **25(1)**, [99], [553], [782]; **25(2)**, [684]
  tenement houses, **25(1)**, [515]
  Thames landing places, **25(2)**, [283]
  Tower Bridge, **25(1)**, [189]
  Trafalgar Square, **26(1)**, [730]
  walkways, **25(1)**, [870]
  wasting water, **25(1)**, [439]
development of, **25(1)**, [1]
early position as to, **25(1)**, [1]

London government—*contd*

education. *See* **education**
fire authorities. *See* **fire authority**
functions—
  delegation of, **25(1)**, [697]
  exercise of, **25(1)**, [696]
  green belt country, **25(1)**, [712]
  health and welfare services, **25(1)**, [706]
housing. *See* **housing**
interpretation of expressions, **25(1)**, [726]
land, derelict or neglected, **25(1)**, [734]
local Acts and instruments, **25(1)**, [724]
local inquiries, **25(1)**, [725]
medical officers of health, **25(1)**, [703]
ministerial expenses, **25(1)**, [728]
National Parks provisions, **25(1)**, [711]
officers—
  injury etc compensation, **25(1)**, [719]
  transfer—
    compensation, provision for, **25(1)**, [723]
    orders as to, **25(1)**, [723]
parks and open spaces. *See* **Greater London**
public health—
  Acts, application of, **25(1)**, [702]
  inspectors, **25(1)**, [703]
raising money—
  abroad, **25(1)**, [827]
  bearer bonds, by, **25(1)**, [826]
  bills, by issue of, **25(1)**, [825]
rates. *See* **Greater London**
reforms, **25(1)**, [1]
re-organisation, **25(1)**, [1]
road traffic. *See* **road traffic**
Royal Commission on, recommendations, **25(1)**, [1]
sewerage and sewage—
  application of enactments, **25(1)**, [701]
  modifications of Public Health Acts, **25(1)**, [733], [734]
  vesting of land, **25(1)**, [700]
sewers. *See* **sewer**
streets. *See* **London streets**
structure of, **25(1)**, [1]
superannuation—
  funds, investment, **25(1)**, [829]–[831]
  provisions, **25(1)**, [505]
supplementary provision, **25(1)**, [722]
town development functions, **25(1)**, [714]
transitional provisions, **25(1)**, [722]

London Museum. *See* **Museum of London**

London Olympic Games

advertising in vicinity of—
  arrest of offenders, **13**, [510]
  control of, **13**, [490]
  enforcement of regulations, powers of entry, **13**, [493]
  local planning authority, notification of consent by, **13**, [495]
  offences, **13**, [492]
  Olympic Delivery Authority, role of, **13**, [494]
  regulations, **13**, [490], [491]

London Olympic Games—*contd*
  British Olympic Association, meaning,
    13, [472]
  competitors and staff, tax exemptions,
    13, [523]
  event, meaning, **13**, [472]
  functions affecting, **13**, [484]
  Greater London Authority, powers of,
    13, [505], [506]
  Host City Contract, meaning, **13**, [472]
  International Olympic Committee, permanent
    establishment of, **13**, [522]
  London Olympic association right, **13**, [519]
  London Organising Committee (LOCOG)—
    exemptions from tax, **13**, [520], [521]
    meaning, **13**, [472], [520]
    regulations, **13**, [521]
  meaning, **13**, [472]
  Northern Ireland, provisions applying to,
    13, [509]
  Office of Rail Regulation, objectives of,
    13, [488]
  Olympic Charter, meaning, **13**, [472]
  Olympic Delivery Authority—
    advertising regulation, functions as to,
      13, [494]
    annual report, **13**, [515]
    co-operation with, **13**, [483]
    committees, **13**, [514]
    compensation for land, payment of,
      13, [475]
    conflict of interests, **13**, [515]
    delegation, **13**, [515]
    dissolution, provision for, **13**, [480]
    effect of regulations, authorities giving
      information as to, **13**, [501]
    establishment of, **13**, [474]
    financial provisions, **13**, [516]
    general functions, **13**, [475]
    members—
      accounts, **13**, [516]
      appointment, **13**, [514]
      remuneration, **13**, [516]
      tenure, **13**, [514]
    non-discrimination, **13**, [515]
    Olympic Transport Plan, preparation of. *See*
      Olympic Transport Plan *below*
    planning provisions, **13**, [476]
    proceedings, **13**, [515]
    records, **13**, [515]
    Secretary of State, guidance and directions
      from, **13**, [515]
    security, having regard to, **13**, [477]
    self-regulation, **13**, [515]
    specified property, rights and liabilities,
      transfer scheme for, **13**, [479], [517]
    staff, **13**, [514]
    status, **13**, [514]
    street lighting and cleaning, provision for,
      13, [478]
    street trading regulation, functions as to,
      13, [500]
    summary of provisions, **13**, [49]
    supervision, **13**, [514]

London Olympic Games—*contd*
  Olympic Delivery Authority—*contd*
    traffic regulation orders, making, **13**, [485]
    enforcement, **13**, [486]
  Olympic documents, alteration of, **13**, [473]
  Olympic Route Network—
    designation of, **13**, [482]
    functions affecting, **13**, [484]
  Olympic Symbol, protection of, **13**, [518]
  Olympic Transport Plan—
    co-operation in implementation of,
      13, [483]
    consultations, **13**, [481]
    contents of, **13**, [481]
    functions affecting, **13**, [484]
    preparation and review, **13**, [481]
  Paralympic Games, meaning, **13**, [472]
  period, meaning, **13**, [472]
  regional development agencies, purposes of,
    13, [507]
  road closures for, **13**, [487]
  Scotland, provisions applying to, **13**, [508]
  street trading in vicinity of—
    arrest of offenders, **13**, [510]
    enforcement of regulations, powers of
      entry, **13**, [499]
    offences, **13**, [498]
    Olympic Delivery Authority, role of,
      13, [500]
    regulations, **13**, [496]
  summary of provisions, **13**, [49]
  tickets, sale of, **13**, [502]

London Passenger Transport Board
  London Passenger Transport Area, map
    showing extent, **36**, [614], [624]
  statutory gas and water undertakers,
    protection, **36**, [612]
  Tramways Act 1870, former application to,
    36, [613]
  undertakings transferred to, **36**, [611],
    [618]–[623]
    bye-laws etc, savings, **36**, [615]

London passenger transport services. *See
also* **London Regional Transport**
  bus service—
    London local services—
      agreements and permits, validity of,
        26(1), [587]
      definitions, **26(1)**, [573]
      provision of, **26(1)**, [574]
    London network—
      additions or variation, **26(1)**, [577]
      determination of services, **26(1)**, [575]
      discontinuance, **26(1)**, [578]
      local service agreements, **26(1)**, [576]
    London service permits—
      appeals, **26(1)**, [583]
      conditions, **26(1)**, [581]
      duration, **26(1)**, [584]
      grant of, **26(1)**, [580]
      guidance document, **26(1)**, [579], [585],
        [586]
      meaning, **26(1)**, [579]

London passenger transport services—*contd*
bus service—*contd*
  London service permits—*contd*
    operators' licences, provisions applying
    to, **26(1)**, [588]
    provision of service, for, **26(1)**, [579]
    revocation, **26(1)**, [582]
    validity, **26(1)**, [587]
    penalty fares, **26(1)**, [785]
  companies for. *See* **London Regional
  Transport**
  concessionary fares. *See* travel concessions
  below
  London Transport Users' Committee—
    appointment, **26(1)**, [631]
    Assembly, directions by, **26(1)**, [635]
    establishment of, **26(1)**, [631]
    Rail Passengers' Committee, role as,
    26(1), [636]
    railway matters, keeping under review,
    26(1), [637]
    recommendations, **26(1)**, [634]
    references to, investigations, **26(1)**, [638]
      action on, **26(1)**, [639]
      exclusions from duties, power to make,
      26(1), [641]
      reports, **26(1)**, [640]
    reports of, **26(1)**, [634]
    representations to, **26(1)**, [632]
    transport providers, voluntary arrangements
    with, **26(1)**, [633]
  lost property. *See* **London Regional
  Transport**
  passenger consultation. *See* **London
  Regional Passengers' Committee**
  penalty fares, **26(1)**, [785]
    levels of, **26(2)**, [818]
  public-private partnership (PPP) agreements.
  See **public-private partnership (PPP)
  agreements**
  rail services—
    Croydon Tramlink, transfer orders,
    26(1), [595]
    Docklands Light Railway, transfer orders,
    26(1), [594]
    facility exemptions, **26(1)**, [590]
    licences, exemptions, **26(1)**, [590]
    railway access contracts, **26(1)**, [591]
    reserved, contracting out, **26(1)**, [593]
    Strategic Rail Authority—
      extra services and facilities, provision of,
      26(1), [571]
      Transport for London, co-operation with,
      26(1), [569]
  streets. *See* **London streets**
  Transport for London—
    co-operation with other persons,
    26(1), [570]
    extra services and facilities, provision of,
    26(1), [571]
    fares and services, structure of, **26(1)**, [568]
    information and publicity, provision of,
    26(1), [572]
    provision by, **26(1)**, [567]

London passenger transport services—*contd*
Transport for London—*contd*
  Strategic Rail Authority, co-operation
  with, **26(1)**, [569]
travel concessions—
  benefit of, **26(1)**, [628]
  guidance on, **26(1)**, [625]
  joint committee, exercise of functions by,
  26(1), [629]
  journeys in and around Greater London,
  26(1), [625]
  reserve free travel scheme—
    annual report, **26(1)**, [784]
    blind persons, **26(1)**, [784]
    eligible England residents, for,
    26(1), [626], [784]
    eligible London residents, for, **26(1)**, [784]
    London authorities, payments by,
    26(1), [784]
    London Local Transport Network, on,
    26(1), [627]
    London residents, for, **26(1)**, [626]
    notification, **26(1)**, [784]
    permits, **26(1)**, [784]
    scope of, **26(1)**, [628]
    uniformity of arrangements, **26(1)**, [628]

London Pensions Fund Authority
  appointments to, **26(1)**, [742]
  budget, setting, **26(1)**, [741]
  Mayor of London, functions of, **26(1)**, [742]
  statements prepared by, **26(1)**, [741]

London, Port of. *See* **Port of London**

London Regional Passengers' Committee
  amendment of enactments, **26(1)**, [787]

London Regional Transport
  byelaws, making, **36**, [721]
  dissolution, **26(1)**, [657]
  historical records, transfer and disposal of,
  36, [867]
  levy, discontinuance of, **25(2)**, [816]
  London Passenger Transport—
    area map, **36**, [614], [624]
    byelaws and regulations, savings, **36**, [615]
    definitions, **36**, [616]
    undertakings transferred, **36**, [611],
    [618]–[623]
  operational land, entry on, **26(1)**, [221]
  parking places, provision for cabs, **36**, [770]
  pension schemes—
    amendment, **26(1)**, [796]
    consent of trustees, power to dispense
    with, **26(1)**, [796]
    interpretation, **26(1)**, [796]
    transferred employees, protection of,
    26(1), [796]
  Port of London Acts, saving in, **39(2)**, [386],
  [436]
  predecessors, former employees of,
  26(1), [796]
  private street works, exemption from
  provisions, **36**, [1265]

London Regional Transport—*contd*
property, rights and liabilities, transfer of—
contracts of employment, **26(1)**, [749]
foreign, **26(1)**, [753]
modification of instruments, **26(1)**, [752]
pensions, **26(1)**, [750]
provision for, **26(1)**, [747]
schemes, **26(1)**, [748], [796]
stamp duty and stamp duty reserve tax
exemptions, **26(1)**, [756]
transfer or pension instruments, common
provisions, **26(1)**, [751]
refreshment shelters etc, **25(1)**, [557]
repeal and re-enactment of provisions,
26(1), [755]
subsidiaries, joint, **36**, [804]
Transport for London, transition to. *See*
Transport for London
welfare schemes, **26(1)**, [796]

London Residuary Body
financial provisions, **15(1)**, [336]
ILEA—
compensation payments, **15(1)**, [335]
pensions and pensions increase, payment
of, **15(1)**, [333]
residuary property, custody of, **15(1)**, [334]
winding-up, **15(1)**, [337]

London streets
abandoned apparatus, removal of,
26(2), [851], [867]
access, vehicular, restriction etc, **25(1)**, [633],
[757]
Acts—
cumulative powers, **36**, [466]
placards as to execution of Acts, **36**, [465],
[490]
advertisements, restriction on carriage of,
36, [464]
buildings—
defacing with slogans etc, **25(1)**, [493]
numbering or naming—
exempted buildings, **25(1)**, [269]
marking of, **25(1)**, [270]
offences respecting, **25(1)**, [272]
owner's liability, **25(1)**, [269]
proceedings by local authority,
25(1), [273]
record of, **25(1)**, [272]
regulations, **25(1)**, [270]
unsuitable, changing, **25(1)**, [269]
cattle—
driving through, restriction, **36**, [463]
meaning, **36**, [461]
cleansing—
driving on footpaths for, **25(1)**, [655]
removal of vehicles for—
charges for, **25(2)**, [348]
notices of, **25(2)**, [348]
obstructing, fines for, **25(2)**, [527]
powers as to, **25(2)**, [348]
closure to vehicles, **25(1)**, [633], [757]
Crown rights, saving for, **25(1)**, [634]

London streets—*contd*
defacement with slogans etc, **25(1)**, [493]
expenses of removing, **25(1)**, [493]
increased fines, **25(2)**, [527]
deposit of goods on, **36**, [462], [468]
distribution containers on, **25(2)**, [972]
easements or rights, acquisition, **25(1)**, [746]
excavations near—
City, in. *See* **London, City of**
distance for purposes of provisions,
25(1), [812]
liability as to, **25(1)**, [812]
owner, exemption of, **25(1)**, [816]
meaning, **25(1)**, [811]
offences and penalties, **25(1)**, [815]
proceedings in respect of, **25(1)**, [815]
river authorities, by, **25(1)**, [813]
withdrawal of support by, **25(1)**, [811]
filming, prohibition or restriction in
connection with, **26(2)**, [852]
floodlighting buildings, **25(1)**, [751]
footways—
driving on, for street cleansing,
25(1), [655]
parking on, **25(2)**, [345]
power to use vehicles and appliances on,
26(2), [830]
further powers of authorities, **25(2)**, [344]
GLA roads—
amenities and services on—
consents for, **26(2)**, [836], [837]
limit of powers, **26(2)**, [834]
notice before exercise of, **26(2)**, [835]
planning provisions, saving for,
26(2), [838]
recreation and refreshment facilities,
26(2), [833]
scope of provisions, **26(2)**, [831]
Transport for London, provision by,
26(2), [831]–[838]
barriers, power to erect in case of
emergency, **26(2)**, [829]
dangerous land adjoining, **26(2)**, [826]
flag poles, etc, power to erect on,
26(2), [824]
forecourts abutting on, **26(2)**, [827]
former, local and private Act functions,
26(2), [822]
order affecting, special parliamentary
procedure, **26(2)**, [821]
prevention of soil etc being washed on,
26(2), [825]
privately maintainable bridges carrying,
26(2), [823]
retaining walls near, **26(2)**, [828]
grass verges—
offences, increased fines, **25(2)**, [527]
parking on, **25(2)**, [345]
powers as to, **25(2)**, [344]
gritting or salting, vehicles for, **25(1)**, [655]
highway construction etc, agreements for,
25(1), [910]
highway, removal of things deposited on—
notice—
appeals, **26(2)**, [343]

London streets—*contd*
highway, removal of things deposited
on—*contd*
notice—*contd*
power to serve, **26(2)**, [343]
service of, **26(2)**, [345]
improvement—
agreements between authorities,
25(1), [910]
application of Street Works Act,
25(1), [752]
boundary walls, weatherproofing etc,
25(1), [745]
City, in. *See* **London, City of**
common, for partial inclosure of,
25(1), [632]
Crown rights, saving for, **25(1)**, [753]
damage of property, compensation,
25(1), [747]
easements etc, acquisition, **25(1)**, [746]
financial provisions, **25(1)**, [824]–[831]
meaning, **25(1)**, [744]
obstructing, penalty, **25(2)**, [527]
open space, use of for, **25(1)**, [852]
part building demolished by, **25(1)**, [745]
underpinning houses near, **25(1)**, [747]
disputes, arbitration of, **25(1)**, [747]
inadequacy of, **25(1)**, [747]
obstructing, penalty, **25(1)**, [748]
vehicular access, restriction of, **25(1)**, [633]
land adjoining, enclosure of, **25(1)**, [150]
litter bins, power to place, **25(1)**, [1015]
meaning of street, **36**, [461]
milk bottles, recovery of, **25(1)**, [560]
names—
assignment of, **25(1)**, [265]
notice in respect of, **25(1)**, [264]
offences respecting, **25(1)**, [268]
proceedings by local authority, **25(1)**, [273]
record of, **25(1)**, [272]
setting up of—
destruction etc, after, **25(1)**, [266]
regulations, **25(1)**, [267]
requirements for, **25(1)**, [266]
wrongful, **25(1)**, [268]
notice, service of, **26(2)**, [179]
orders and notices, restrictions on,
26(2), [853]
parking. *See* **parking**
refuse bins, fixing to buildings, **25(1)**, [1015]
road user charges—
changes in eligibility for exemption, failure
to notify, **26(2)**, [799]
imposition of, **26(1)**, [650]
schemes—
enforcement provisions, extension of
power to include, **26(2)**, [797]
power to suspend, **26(2)**, [798]
requirement, contravention of,
26(2), [796]
schemes for, **26(1)**, [789]
roadside amenities, improvement of,
25(1), [476]
sludge main, stopping up for laying,
25(1), [931]

London streets—*contd*
stopping up—
court order for, **25(2)**, [465]
notice of application as to, **25(2)**, [465]
rescinding or modifying order, **25(2)**, [465]
vehicular access by certain bodies,
25(2), [465]
subways—
advertisement displays in, **25(1)**, [750]
shops etc in, provision of, **25(1)**, [750]
traders, **36**, [468]
trees and shrubs on, **25(1)**, [476]; **25(2)**, [344]
vehicular access, restriction of, **25(1)**, [633],
[757]
walkways. *See* **walkway**
wires over. *See* **overground wires**
works under, demolition of—
appeals as to, **25(2)**, [667]
consent required, **25(2)**, [663]
electricity undertakers, protection,
25(2), [668]

London traffic control system
London borough council, transfer to,
37, [248]
meaning, **37**, [248]
Secretary of State and Transport for London,
transfer between, **37**, [249]

London Transport. *See* **bus services; London
Regional Transport; passenger transport
service**

London Transport Board
British Transport Commission, vesting of
property etc of assets, **36**, [707]

London Transport Executive. *Became*
London Regional Transport; *see now*
Transport for London
members, termination payments, **36**, [727]

London Transport Users' Committee
accommodation, **26(1)**, [786]
accounts, **26(1)**, [786]
chairman, **26(1)**, [786]
constitution, **26(1)**, [786]
meetings, admission of public to, **26(1)**, [786]
members, **26(1)**, [786]
officers, **26(1)**, [786]
pensions, **26(1)**, [786]
procedure, **26(1)**, [786]
property, rights and liabilities, transfer of—
contracts of employment, **26(1)**, [749]
foreign, **26(1)**, [753]
modification of instruments, **26(1)**, [752]
pensions, **26(1)**, [750]
provision for, **26(1)**, [747]
schemes, **26(1)**, [748], [796]
stamp duty and stamp duty reserve tax
exemptions, **26(1)**, [756]
transfer or pension instruments, common
provisions, **26(1)**, [751]
remuneration, **26(1)**, [786]
superannuation provisions, **26(1)**, [732], [733]

London, University of. *See also* **universities and colleges**
medical school, scheme for, **30**, [421]

London Waste and Recycling Board
constitution, **26(1)**, [700]
establishment of, **26(1)**, [699]
grants to, **26(1)**, [700]

London Waste Regulation Authority
transfer of functions to Environment Agency. *See* **Environment Agency**

long-distance routes. *See* **right of way**

long funding leases
asset under construction, **43(S)**, 264
capital allowances. *See* **machinery and plant**
combined assets and constituent assets, **43(S)**, 264
commencement of provisions, **43(S)**, 259–65
corporation tax, special rules for, **43(S)**, 244–51
election for lease to be treated as, **43(S)**, 261
events beyond control of parties, **43(S)**, 262
excepted leases, **43(S)**, 261
expenditure incurred before passing of Act, **43(S)**, 263
extended time limit, **43(S)**, 261–2
finalisation of lease, **43(S)**, 264
income tax, special rules for, **43(S)**, 252–8
mixed leases, **43(S)**, 265
pre-existing heads of agreement, **43(S)**, 262
property business, profits of, **43(S)**, 258
transitional provisions, **43(S)**, 259–65

long-life assets
anti-avoidance—
disposal values, **43(1)**, [664]
later claims, **43(1)**, [663]
capital allowances, transitional provisions, **43(1)**, [1224]
disposal values, **43(1)**, [664]
expenditure—
application of provision to, **43(1)**, [650]
exclusions—
cars, **43(1)**, [656]
fixtures, **43(1)**, [653]
railway assets, **43(1)**, [655]
ships, **43(1)**, [654]
meaning, **43(1)**, [651]
monetary limit—
application to, **43(1)**, [658]
exceeding, **43(1)**, [660]
meaning, **43(1)**, [659]
relevant, within, **43(1)**, [657]
later claims, **43(1)**, [663]
meaning, **43(1)**, [651]
pool, **43(1)**, [661]
writing-down allowances, **43(1)**, [662]

looting
air force, in, **3**, [757]
army, in, **3**, [484]
navy, in, **3**, [1016]

Lord Chamberlain
censorship of plays, abolition, **13**, [181]

Lord Chancellor
advisory committee, **11(2)**, [250]
Advisory Committee on Legal Education and Conduct. *See* **Advisory Committee on Legal Education and Conduct**
agricultural land tribunals, functions, **1(1)**, [534], [539], [540]
annuity, **10**, [295]
Chancery Division, president of, **11(2)**, [672]
coroner, removal from office, **11(1)**, [1208]
court boards, guidance to, **11(3)**, [326]
court system, duty to maintain, **11(3)**, [322]
disciplinary powers—
exercise of, **11(3)**, [561]
interpretation, **11(3)**, [562]
Ombudsman, complaint to. *See* **Judicial Appointments and Conduct Ombudsman**
ecclesiastical committee members, nominating, **14**, 296
expenditure, levy on approved regulators to fund, **11(4)**, [288], [289]
funding—
Legal Services Board, to, **11(4)**, [287]
Office for Legal Complaints, to, **11(4)**, [287]
Great Seal, using, **10**, [38]
incidental etc provisions, power to make, **11(4)**, [71]; **11(S)**, Courts 113–14
judges, selection of—
acceptance, effect of, **11(3)**, [550]
options for, **11(3)**, [527]
Lord Justices of Appeal, **11(3)**, [536]
puisne, **11(3)**, [544]
Supreme Court, **11(3)**, [483]
reconsideration, **11(3)**, [545]–[546]
Judicial Appointments and Conduct Ombudsman, reference to, **11(3)**, [558]
Judicial Appointments Commission, complaint about, **11(3)**, [554]
judicial independence, guarantee of, **11(3)**, [458]
Legal Services Commission, guidance to, **11(3)**, [272]
Lords Commissioners representing, **11(2)**, [776], [1025]
meaning, **41**, [605], [606]
modification of office, rule of law, provisions not adversely affecting, **11(3)**, [456]
modification or abolition of functions by order, **11(3)**, [473]
oath, **10**, [426]; **11(3)**, [471]
pension of, **33(1)**, [153], [206]
precedence of, **33(1)**, [5]
protected functions, **11(4)**, [70], [313]; **11(S)**, Courts 112–13
qualifications for office, **11(3)**, [457]
relevant service, **11(2)**, [603]
request for selection of judge, **11(3)**, [523]
retirement, **11(2)**, [615]
Roman Catholic as, **10**, [578]–[579]; **14**, 71

Lord Chancellor—*contd*
   salary, **10**, [605]
      alteration of, **10**, [606]–[607]
   Speakership of House of Lords, amendment of
      provisions, **11(3)**, [472], [601]
   Supreme Court rules submitted to,
      11(3), [500]
   transfer of functions—
      appointment, of, **11(3)**, [468], [597]
      Northern Ireland, relating to, **11(3)**, [600]
      order, by, **11(3)**, [473]
      protected functions, **11(3)**, [474]–[475],
         [602]
      provision for, **11(3)**, [469]–[470],
         [598]–[599]
      supplementary provisions, **11(3)**, [476]

Lord Chief Justice
   appointment of, **11(2)**, [677]
   clerk and secretary to, **11(2)**, [771]
   Court of Appeal criminal division, president
      of, **11(2)**, [670]
   delegation of functions by, **11(4)**, [47];
      11(S), Courts 59
   precedence, **11(2)**, [680]
   Queen's Bench Division, president of,
      11(2), [672]

lord of the manor. *See also under* **inclosure of
   common**
   compensation for loss, **9**, [57], [298]
   conveyance by, **9**, [298]
   game rights, **2**, [154]
   meaning, **2**, [146]

Lord President of the Council
   salary, **10**, [612]

Lord Privy Seal
   salary, **10**, [612]

lorries
   road-user charge, **43(2)**, [127]

lorry area
   acquisition of land for, **36**, [1286]
   compensation for land, **36**, [1308]
   compulsory purchase of land for, **36**, [1308]
   delegation of powers, **36**, [1134]
   development, meaning, **36**, [1308]
   facilities, provision of, **36**, [1134]
   lease of, **36**, [1134]
   meaning, **36**, [1134]
   provision of, **36**, [1134]
   provisions applicable to, **36**, [1134]
   title to land, clearance of, **36**, [1306]

loss relief
   capital redemption policy, no loss relief for,
      43(S), 1398
   carry back, temporary extension of—
      corporation tax, **43(S)**, 1442
      income tax, **43(S)**, 1440–2
   commodity futures, **44(1)**, [203]

loss relief—*contd*
   corporation tax. *See* **corporation tax**
   debts, transactions in, **44(1)**, [202]
   deposits, transactions in, **44(1)**, [202]
   employment, **43(S)**, 1397
      See also **employment**
   farming, in, **44(1)**, [201]
   financial futures, **44(1)**, [203]
   government investment, write-off of,
      44(1), [204]
   insurance company, limitation for,
      44(1), [261]
   life annuity contracts, losses from, **43(S)**, 1398
   life insurance contracts, losses from,
      43(S), 1398
   market gardening, in, **44(1)**, [201]
   miscellaneous income, against—
      claims for, **44(4)**, [155]
         time limits, **44(4)**, [158]
      deductions, how made, **44(4)**, [156]
      deposit rights, transactions in, **44(4)**, [157]
   oil extraction activities, **44(1)**, [331]
   partnerships—
      chargeable amount, computing,
         43(2), [631]
      excess, recovery of, **43(2)**, [630]
      transitional provision, **43(2)**, [633]
   pre-trading expenditure, for, **44(1)**, [205]
   qualifying options, **44(1)**, [203]
   shares, on. *See under* **shares**
   terminal, transfer of trade to obtain,
      43(S), 1395
   trade loss relief. *See* **trade loss relief**
   trading loss, carry-back of, **43(1)**, [321]
   transitional provisions, **44(1)**, [691]
   unquoted shares, on—
      companies, for, **44(1)**, [396]
      exclusion of, **44(1)**, [397]

losses
   trade profits, calculation on same basis of,
      44(3), [26]

lost property
   local authority's powers and duties,
      25(2), [475]
   Transport for London. *See* **Transport for
      London**

lottery
   child—
      employment to provide facilities,
         5(1), [333]
      invitation to participate to, **5(1)**, [337]
   complex, meaning, **5(1)**, [295]
   cross-category activities—
      betting, **5(1)**, [299]
      gaming, **5(1)**, [298]
   customer, **5(1)**, [657]
   draw, meaning, **5(1)**, [535]
   duty—
      administration, **5(1)**, [114]
      amount of, **5(1)**, [111]
      body corporate, offences by, **5(1)**, [117]
      charge of, **5(1)**, [110]

lottery—*contd*
  duty—*contd*
    enforcement, **5(1)**, [114]
    information, disclosure of, **5(1)**, [121]
    offences, **5(1)**, [116]
    persons liable for, **5(1)**, [113]
    regulations and orders, **5(1)**, [122]
    summary of provisions, **5(1)**, [1]
    time for payment, **5(1)**, [112]
  exempt—
    additional restrictions, power to impose,
      5(1), [660]
    customer, **5(1)**, [657]
    incidental non-commercial, **5(1)**, [655]
    interpretation, **5(1)**, [661]
    local authority, registration with,
      5(1), [659]
    private, **5(1)**, [656]
    profits, misusing, **5(1)**, [541]
    small society, **5(1)**, [658]
  external manager, acting as, **5(1)**, [537]
  facilitating, **5(1)**, [539]
  facilities for, provision of, **5(1)**, [315]
  meaning, **5(1)**, [295]
  National. *See* **National Lottery**
  non-commercial, incidental, **5(1)**, [655]
    licensable activities, exclusion, **19(3)**, [667]
  notices, etc, as to, importation prohibited,
    13, [549]
  offences—
    bodies corporate, by, **5(1)**, [117]
    evidence, **5(1)**, [120]
    facilitating, **5(1)**, [539]
    forfeitures, **5(1)**, [118]
    general, **5(1)**, [116]
    penalties, **5(1)**, [118], [543]
    proceedings for, **5(1)**, [119]
    profits, misusing, **5(1)**, [540]
      exempt lottery, **5(1)**, [541]
    promotion, **5(1)**, [538]
    small society lottery, breach of condition,
      5(1), [542]
  operating licence—
    conditions, **5(1)**, [379]
    issue of, **5(1)**, [379]
    mandatory conditions, **5(1)**, [380]
    requirement, **5(1)**, [346]
    society or authority, issue to, **5(1)**, [379]

lottery—*contd*
  payment to enter, definition, **5(1)**, [643]
  private, meaning, **5(1)**, [295]
  proceeds of, **5(1)**, [534]
  profits of—
    meaning, **5(1)**, [534]
    misusing, **5(1)**, [540]
      exempt lottery, **5(1)**, [541]
  promoters, registration, **5(1)**, [115]
  promotion of—
    meaning, **5(1)**, [532]
    offences, **5(1)**, [538]
  rollover, meaning, **5(1)**, [536]
  securities issued under National Loans Act,
    exemption of, **19(2)**, [831]
  simple, meaning, **5(1)**, [295]
  society—
    premises, entry on, **5(1)**, [594]
    small, **5(1)**, [658]
      breach of condition, **5(1)**, [542]
  territorial application of provisions,
    5(1), [545]
  tickets, meaning, **5(1)**, [533]
  value added tax, exemption from, **50**, [153]

loudspeakers
  street, in, restriction on operation of,
    35(1), [321]

Low Pay Commission
  appointment, **16**, [913]
  facilities, **16**, [967]
  financial provisions, **16**, [967]
  membership, **16**, [967]
  proceedings, **16**, [967]
  referral of matters to—
    consultations, **16**, [912]
    regulations, as to, **16**, [910]
    report, **16**, [911], [912]
  staff, **16**, [967]

Lugano Convention. *See* **civil jurisdiction Conventions**

luggage trolleys
  abandoned, **32**, [573], [590]
    transitional provision, **35(2)**, [542]

M

M2 improvement works
acquisition of land for, **38(1)**, [675], [708]
blight, compensation for pre-enactment
acquisition, **38(1)**, [676]
authorised, **38(1)**, [674]
description of, **38(1)**, [705]
new roads, regulation of traffic on,
38(1), [707]
operation and works, status of, **38(1)**, [707]
status of new highways, **38(1)**, [707]
stopping up of highways and private
access, **38(1)**, [706]
temporary interference with highways,
38(1), [706]

machinery and plant. *See also* **capital
allowances**
annual investment allowance, **43(S)**, 902
anti-avoidance, **43(S)**, 1185–7
assessments, adjustment of, **43(1)**, [810]
connected person—
meaning, **43(1)**, [811]
transactions between, **43(1)**, [784]
finance lease—
chargeable period, allocation of
expenditure to, **43(1)**, [790]
meaning, **43(1)**, [789]
first-year allowances, restricted,
43(1), [786]–[788]
hire purchase, **43(1)**, [808]
lease and finance leasebacks, further
operating lease, subject to, **43(1)**, [807]
manufacturers and suppliers, **43(1)**, [809]
qualifying expenditure, restriction on,
43(1), [788]
relevant transactions, **43(1)**, [783]
sale and finance leasebacks—
accounts of lessee, not accounted for as
finance lease in, **43(1)**, [805]
application of provisions, **43(1)**, [799]
definitions, **43(1)**, [806]
disposal value, restriction on,
43(1), [792]
first-year allowance not made,
43(1), [793]
further operating lease, subject to,
43(1), [807]
lease, subject to, **43(1)**, [804]
lessee's income or profits—
deductions, **43(1)**, [800]
termination of leaseback, **43(1)**, [801]
lessor's income or profits, **43(1)**, [802]
termination of leaseback, **43(1)**, [803]
meaning, **43(1)**, [791]
non-compliance risk, lessor not
bearing, **43(1)**, [795]

machinery and plant—*contd*
anti-avoidance—*contd*
sale and finance leasebacks—*contd*
qualifying expenditure, restriction on,
43(1), [794]
special treatment, election for,
43(1), [797]–[798], [824]
subsequent transaction, qualifying
expenditure limited in, **43(1)**, [796]
VAT liabilities, additional, **43(1)**, [822]
sale and leaseback, **43(1)**, [786]
transactions to obtain allowances,
43(1), [785]
VAT liabilities and rebates, **43(1)**, [812]
availability of allowances, general conditions,
43(1), [562]
balancing allowances and charges—
amount of, **43(1)**, [617]
entitlement or liability, determination of,
43(1), [616]
business entertainment, use for, **43(1)**, [848]
cars. *See* **motor cars**
chargeable period, allocation of expenditure
to, **43(S)**, 274–5
companies with investment businesses, for,
43(1), [832]
computer software. *See* **computer software**
connected persons, transactions between,
43(1), [784]
contribution allowances, **43(1)**, [1175]
demolition, costs of, **43(1)**, [577]
depreciation, sums payable in respect of,
43(1), [588]
disposal event—
disposal values, and, **43(1)**, [622]
meaning, **43(1)**, [621]
disposal receipt, meaning, **43(1)**, [621]
disposal values—
additional VAT rebates—
generated by, **43(1)**, [817]
limit, **43(1)**, [818]
amount of, **43(1)**, [622]
bringing into account, **43(1)**, [622]
general limit on, **43(1)**, [623]
nil, being, **43(1)**, [624]
not brought into account, where,
43(1), [625]
notional ownership, on cessation of,
43(1), [629]
provisions concerning, **43(1)**, [627]
double relief, exclusion of, **43(1)**, [558]
employee's, withdrawal of capital allowances.
See **motor cars**
employments and offices, for, **43(1)**, [841]
expenditure, notification of, **43(1)**, [75]
fencing of. *See* **factories and workshops**
final chargeable period, **43(1)**, [626]

machinery and plant—*contd*

finance lease—

  chargeable period, allocation of expenditure
    to, **43(1)**, [790]

  meaning, **43(1)**, [789]; **43(S)**, 274

first-year allowances—

  amount of, **43(1)**, [613]

  entitlement to, **43(1)**, [613]

  gas refuelling stations, **43(S)**, 905

  low carbon dioxide emissions, cars with,
    43(S), 902–5

  small and medium-sized enterprises,
    discontinued for, **43(S)**, 902–3

  spent, repeal, **43(S)**, 903–4

first-year qualifying expenditure—

  cars with low carbon dioxide emissions,
    on, **43(1)**, [600]

  energy-saving plant or machinery, on,
    43(1), [597]

    certification, **43(1)**, [598]

    components, **43(1)**, [599]

  environmentally beneficial plant or
    machinery, on, **43(1)**, [604]

    certification, **43(1)**, [605]

    components, **43(1)**, [606]

  gas refuelling station, for, **43(1)**, [601]

  general exclusions, **43(1)**, [607]

  generally, **43(1)**, [590]

  information and communications
    technology, incurred by small enterprises
    on, **43(1)**, [596]

  Northern Ireland purposes, incurred by
    small or medium-sized enterprises for,
    43(1), [591]–[593].

    See also **Northern Ireland**

  ring fence trade, plant and machinery for
    use in, **43(1)**, [602]–[603]

  small and medium-sized enterprises, of—

    businesses, **43(1)**, [609]

    companies, **43(1)**, [608]

    incurred by, **43(1)**, [595]

    large or medium-sized group, company
      as member of, **43(1)**, [610]

    Northern Ireland purposes, incurred
      for, **43(1)**, [591]–[593].

      See also **Northern Ireland**

  time of incurring, **43(1)**, [611]

  UK tax authorities, disclosure of
    information between, **43(1)**, [612]

fixed, removal under emergency powers,
  compensation for, **9**, [153]

fixtures. *See* **fixtures**

gifts, **43(1)**, [565]

hire purchase, **43(1)**, [630]

installation, building alterations connected
  with, **43(1)**, [576]

lease and finance leasebacks—

  further operating lease, subject to,
    43(1), [807]

  subject to, **43(S)**, 604

leases—

  amended provisions, **43(S)**, 266–75

  capital receipts treated as income,
    43(S), 1627

machinery and plant—*contd*

leases—*contd*

  disposal values—

    long funding finance lease,
      commencement of, **43(S)**, 1625

    termination of long funding lease,
      43(S), 1625–7

    finance leaseback, **43(S)**, 1630

    transfer and long funding leaseback,
      restrictions on lessee's allowances,
      43(S), 1628

    transfer followed by hire purchase, etc,
      restrictions on hirer's allowances,
      43(S), 1629

  first year allowance, withdrawal of,
    43(S), 273

  rent factoring, **43(S)**, 203

leasing—

  anti-avoidance, **43(S)**, 1185–7

  arrangements, **43(S)**, 269

  capital receipts treated as income,
    43(S), 1173–7

  company carrying on business of—

    reconstructions without change of
      ownership, **43(S)**, 606–7

    sale of, anti-avoidance, **43(S)**, 607–9

  expectation that capital payment will not be
    paid, **43(S)**, 1174, 1177

  lease and finance leaseback, **43(S)**, 1178–80

  long funding lease—

    deemed disposals, **43(S)**, 1178

    election for application of rules,
      restriction on, **43(S)**, 1180

    grant of, **43(S)**, 1177

    lessors under, avoidance, **43(S)**, 1180–3

  loss relief, **44(1)**, [199]

  other property, and, **43(S)**, 1174, 1176

  rent factoring, **43(S)**, 1177, 1195

  sale and finance leaseback, **43(S)**, 1177–80

  trading stock, held as, **43(S)**, 1180, 1182

lessee, provided by, **43(1)**, [631]

lessees—

  long funding finance leases, under—

    deductions, limit on, **44(1)**, [355]

    termination, **44(1)**, [356]

  long funding operating lease, under,
    44(1), [357]

lessor companies, sale of—

  amended provisions, **43(S)**, 1457–60

  anti-avoidance provisions, **43(S)**, 1621–4

  principal company's interest in consortium
    company unchanged, where, **43(S)**, 1458

lessor company—

  anti-avoidance, **43(S)**, 291–2

  carried forward loss, relief for expenses
    otherwise giving rise to, **43(S)**, 292

  corporation tax purposes, provision for,
    43(S), 276

  definitions, **43(S)**, 293–4

  leasing business carried out by company
    alone, **43(S)**, 277–85

  leasing business carried out by company in
    partnership, **43(S)**, 286–91

  relationship with other provisions,
    43(S), 292–3

machinery and plant—*contd*

lessors—

long funding finance lease, under—

avoidance—

lessee under non-long funding lease, lessor also, **44(1)**, [353]

machinery or plant held as trading stock, **44(1)**, [352]

other, **44(1)**, [354]

exceptional items, **44(1)**, [347]

rental earnings, **44(1)**, [346]

termination payment, making, **44(1)**, [348]

long funding operating lease, under—

additional expenditure, **44(3)**, [142]; **44(1)**, [350]

avoidance—

lessee under non-long funding lease, lessor also, **44(1)**, [353]

machinery or plant held as trading stock, **44(1)**, [352]

other, **44(1)**, [354]

periodic deduction, **44(1)**, [349]

termination of lease, **44(1)**, [351]

life insurance business, for—

allowances and charges, apportionment, **43(1)**, [834]

application of provisions, **43(1)**, [833]

different categories, rules for, **43(1)**, [835]

giving effect to allowances, **43(1)**, [835]

long funding lease, capital allowances—

accountancy classification, change to, **43(S)**, 235

additional expenditure, allowances for lessee, **43(S)**, 222

application of provisions, **43(S)**, 242

background plant or machinery for building, **43(S)**, 230

commencement, disposal events and disposal values, **43(S)**, 220

deemed disposals and re-acquisition, **43(S)**, 267

derived leases, terms and rentals, **43(S)**, 228

disposal events and disposal values, **43(S)**, 223

expenditure not qualifying expenditure, **43(S)**, 220

finance lease, amount of capital expenditure, **43(S)**, 221–2

finance lease test, **43(S)**, 228

funding lease, **43(S)**, 226

general definitions, **43(S)**, 240–3

general exclusions, **43(S)**, 220

international leasing, involving, **43(S)**, 232

land, plant or machinery leased with, **43(S)**, 231–2

lease payments test, **43(S)**, 229

lessees, entitlement to allowances, **43(S)**, 220–4

losses, restriction of, **43(S)**, 268

machinery or plant lease, meaning, **43(S)**, 226–7

meaning, **43(S)**, 224

machinery and plant—*contd*

long funding lease, capital allowances—*contd*

minimum lease payments, meaning, **43(S)**, 238

operating lease—

amount of capital expenditure, **43(S)**, 221

extension of term, **43(S)**, 236

plant or machinery leased with other assets, separate derived leases, **43(S)**, 227

previous use for, use for other purposes **43(S)**, 219

right of lessor to claim allowances, exclusion by, **43(S)**, 229–30

sale and leaseback or lease and leaseback by lessor, **43(S)**, 234–5

short lease, construction of, **43(S)**, 225

short life asset treatment, ruling out, **43(S)**, 242

tax return, requirement for, **43(S)**, 224–5

term, **43(S)**, 238

term and rentals, **43(S)**, 228

termination amount, **43(S)**, 239

termination value, **43(S)**, 240

transfers etc by lessee, effect of, **43(S)**, 233–4

transfers etc by lessor, effect of, **43(S)**, 233

useful economic life test, **43(S)**, 229

long-life assets. *See* **long-life assets**

market value, definition, **43(S)**, 269

mines and transport undertakings, etc, for, **43(1)**, [831]

mining and oil industries. *See* **mining and oil industries**

motor cars. *See* **motor car**

net present value of rentals, determining, **43(S)**, 82–3

noise from, regulation of, **35(1)**, [327]

notional ownership, disposal value on cessation of, **43(1)**, [629]

overseas leasing. *See* **overseas leasing**

overseas rules, phasing out, **43(S)**, 274

partial depreciation subsidy—

first-year allowances, reduction of, **43(1)**, [780]

meaning, **43(1)**, [779]

single asset pool—

qualifying expenditure allocated to, **43(1)**, [781]

reduction of allowances and charges, **43(1)**, [782]

person entitled to benefit of contract, treated as owned by, **43(1)**, [628]; **43(S)**, 273–4

preparation of site for, allowances, **43(1)**, [852]

professions and vocations, for, **43(1)**, [830]

property business, giving effect for—

furnished holiday lettings business, **43(1)**, [828]

ordinary property businesses, **43(1)**, [827]

overseas, **43(1)**, [829]

qualifying activity—

assets provided or used partly for—

allowances and charges on expenditure, reduction of, **43(1)**, [777]

machinery and plant—*contd*
  qualifying activity—*contd*
    assets provided or used partly for—*contd*
      first-year allowance, reduction of, **43(1)**, [775]
      significant reduction, effect of, **43(1)**, [778]
      single asset pool, allocation of expenditure to, **43(1)**, [776]
    calculation for, **43(1)**, [562]
    companies with investment business, managing investments of, **43(1)**, [569]
    expenditure incurred before carrying on of, **43(1)**, [563]
    furnished holiday lettings business, **43(1)**, [570]
    gift, use of, **43(1)**, [565]
    list of, **43(1)**, [566]
    meaning, **43(1)**, [566]
    offices and employments, meaning, **43(1)**, [571]
    ordinary property businesses, **43(1)**, [567]
    partnership, carried on in, **43(1)**, [842]
    plant or machinery supplied for other purpose, use of, **43(1)**, [564]
    special leasing, **43(1)**, [570]
    successions—
      beneficiaries, by, **43(1)**, [847]
      connected persons, predecessor and successor being, **43(1)**, [845]
      effect of election, **43(1)**, [846]
      relevant property, **43(1)**, [844]
  qualifying expenditure—
    available, **43(1)**, [618]
    demolition, costs of, **43(1)**, [577]
    exclusions—
      acquisition of interest in land, **43(1)**, [575]
      buildings, **43(1)**, [572]
      depreciations, sums payable for, **43(1)**, [588]
      dwelling-house, expenditure on plant or machinery for use in, **43(1)**, [586]
      employment or office, in case of, **43(1)**, [587]
      expenditure unaffected by, **43(1)**, [574]
      MPs and members of regional assemblies, accommodation for, **43(1)**, [585]
      production animals, on, **43(1)**, [589]
      structures, assets and works, **43(1)**, [573]
    fire precautions, repealed provisions, **43(S)**, 899
    first-year. *See* first-year qualifying expenditure *above*
    integral features, on, **43(S)**, 899–901
    pooling, **43(1)**, [614]–[615]
    pools, initial allocation to, **43(1)**, [619]
    restrictions on, **43(1)**, [788]
    safety measures, on—
      application of provisions, **43(1)**, [578]
      designated sports grounds. *See* **sports grounds**
      fire safety, **43(1)**, [580]
      personal security, **43(1)**, [584]

machinery and plant—*contd*
  qualifying expenditure—*contd*
    safety measures, on—*contd*
      sports grounds. *See* **sports ground**
    thermal insulation of buildings, **43(S)**, 897–8
    thermal insulation, on—
      application of provisions, **43(1)**, [578]
      industrial buildings, of, **43(1)**, [579]
    unrelieved, **43(1)**, [620]
  requisition, compensation for, **9**, [123]
  ring fence trade, for use in, **43(S)**, 941
  safety precautions. *See under* **factories and workshops**
  sale and finance leasebacks—
    accounts of lessee, not accounted for as finance lease in, **43(1)**, [805]
    application of provisions, **43(1)**, [799]
    definitions, **43(1)**, [806]
    disposal value, restriction on, **43(1)**, [792]
    first-year allowance not made, **43(1)**, [793]
    further operating lease, subject to, **43(1)**, [807]
    lease, subject to, **43(1)**, [804]
    lessee's income or profits—
      deductions, **43(1)**, [800]
      termination of leaseback, **43(1)**, [801]
    lessor's income or profits, **43(1)**, [802]
      termination of leaseback, **43(1)**, [803]
    meaning, **43(1)**, [791]
    non-compliance risk, lessor not bearing, **43(1)**, [795]
    qualifying expenditure, restriction on, **43(1)**, [794]
    special treatment, election for, **43(1)**, [797]–[798], [824]
      additional VAT liability, effect on, **43(1)**, [824]
      circumstances for, **43(1)**, [797]
      effect of, **43(1)**, [798]
    subsequent transaction, qualifying expenditure limited in, **43(1)**, [796]
    VAT liabilities, additional, **43(1)**, [822]
  sale and leaseback, **43(1)**, [786]
  shares in, application of provisions, **43(1)**, [849]
  ships. *See* **ship**
  short-life assets. *See* **short-life assets**
  small pools, for, **43(S)**, 908
  special leasing—
    corporation tax—
      excess allowances, **43(1)**, [839]
      generally, **43(1)**, [838]
    income tax, **43(1)**, [837]
    life assurance business, **43(1)**, [840]
  special rate expenditure, existing long-life asset expenditure treated as, **43(S)**, 909–10
  subject to lease where income retained, disposal of, **43(S)**, 81–3
  successions where predecessor and successor are connected persons, **43(S)**, 84
  trade, treatment for, **43(1)**, [826]
  transactions to obtain, **43(1)**, [785]
  transitional provisions, **43(1)**, [1224]

machinery and plant—*contd*
VAT liability, additional—
anti-avoidance, **43(1)**, [812], [820]
assessments and adjustments, **43(1)**, [825]
election for special treatment, effect of,
43(1), [824]
first-year allowance, generating,
43(1), [815]
exceptions, **43(1)**, [816]
no first year allowance in respect of,
43(1), [820]
qualifying expenditure, restriction on—
generally, **43(1)**, [821]
non-compliance risk, lessor not
bearing, **43(1)**, [823]
sale and finance leaseback, **43(1)**, [822]
qualifying expenditure, treated as,
43(1), [814]
short-life assets, **43(1)**, [819]
VAT rebate, additional—
anti-avoidance, and, **43(1)**, [813], [820]
disposal value—
generating, **43(1)**, [817]
limit on, **43(1)**, [818]
meaning, **43(1)**, [813]
writing-down allowances—
amount of, **43(1)**, [617]
entitlement or liability, determination of,
43(1), [616]
main rate of, **43(S)**, 906–8
small pools, for, **43(S)**, 908

machinery and plant allowances
cars. *See* **motor cars**
environmentally beneficial, first-year
allowances for, **43(2)**, [264]
finance leasebacks, **43(2)**, [351]
transitional provision, **43(2)**, [551]
mining and oil industries. *See* **mining and
oil industries**
ships. *See* **ship**

madeira
use of term, **48**, 13, 37

magistrate. *See also* **justice of the peace;
stipendiary magistrate**
assault on, **12(1)**, [93]
Crown Court, sitting in, **11(2)**, [748]
sheriff not to act as, **39(1)**, [755]
stipendiary—
pension, **11(2)**, [593], [625]
relevant service, **11(2)**, [603]
salary, **11(2)**, [274]
transitory provisions, **11(2)**, [638]

magistrates' court
accommodation, provision of, **11(3)**, [324]
adjournment—
composition following, **11(2)**, [542]
inquiry, of, **11(2)**, [409]
administration, inspectors of—
appointment of, **11(3)**, [373]
Chief—
appointment of, **11(3)**, [373]

magistrates' court—*contd*
administration, inspectors of—*contd*
Chief—*contd*
functions, **11(3)**, [375]
entry and inspection, rights of, **11(3)**, [376]
functions, **11(3)**, [374]
payments to, **11(3)**, [373]
age of offender, determining, **11(2)**, [574]
appeals from, **6**, [425]
control of infectious diseases, as to,
35(1), [507]
See also **Crown Court**
attachment order. *See* **attachment of
earnings**
bail, grant of. *See* **bail**
binding over. *See* **recognizance to keep the
peace**
boards—
areas, for, **11(3)**, [325]
chairman, **11(3)**, [416]
constitution, **11(3)**, [325], [416]
functions of, **11(3)**, [326]
guidance to, **11(3)**, [326]
members—
expenses, **11(3)**, [416]
tenure, **11(3)**, [416]
procedure, **11(3)**, [416]
recommendations by, **11(3)**, [326]
case stated by. *See* **case stated**
child or young person—
Crown Court, sending cases to,
11(3), [237]
notices given in cases involving,
11(3), [239]
child, proceedings against, **11(2)**, [444]
children involved in proceedings, privacy for,
6, [428]
civil debt—
costs, enforcement of order, as,
11(2), [484]
money recoverable as, **11(2)**, [476]
non-payment, complaint for, **11(2)**, [517]
order for recovery of, **11(2)**, [470], [476]
civil proceedings, transfer to another court,
powers as to, **11(2)**, [475]
closure order—
application to by police, **19(3)**, [654]
consideration of, **19(3)**, [655]
collecting officer of—
functions of, **27**, [293]
meaning, **27**, [302]
commission areas, **11(3)**, [313]
consequential provisions, **11(3)**, [294]
transitional provisions and savings,
11(3), [313]
committal. *See* **committal**
committals for sentence, **11(3)**, [313]
committee—
joint authorities, number of members,
25(2), [592], [640]–[645]
joint committee, appointments to be made
by, **25(2)**, [593]
committee areas, **11(3)**, [313]

magistrates' court—*contd*
committees—
abolition, **11(3)**, [327], [417]–[419]
property transfer schemes, **11(3)**, [417]
staff transfers, **11(3)**, [418]
areas for, **11(3)**, [313]
Greater London Magistrates' Courts
Authority. *See* **Greater London
Magistrates' Courts Authority**
inner London, for. *See* **committee of
magistrates**
staff, pensions etc of, in inner London
area, **11(3)**, [313]
compensation order, limit on amount of,
12(2), [808]
compensation, recovery of, **11(2)**, [235],
[238]
complaint—
civil debt, non-payment of, **11(2)**, [517]
construction of references to, **11(2)**, [467]
enforcement of maintenance order by,
27, [323]
hearing—
adjournment of, **11(2)**, [471]
both parties, non-appearance of,
11(2), [474]
complainant, non-appearance of,
11(2), [473]
defendant—
non-appearance of, **11(2)**, [472]
remanding, **11(2)**, [472]
order, making, **11(2)**, [470]
procedure, **11(2)**, [470]
issue of summons on, **11(2)**, [468]
jurisdiction to deal with, **11(2)**, [469]
limitation, **11(2)**, [555]
confiscation order by, **12(4)**, [115]
constitution of, **11(2)**, [542]
contempt of, **11(2)**, [657]
conviction, sum adjudged to be paid by—
application of, **11(2)**, [565]
detention in police station overnight,
11(2), [564]
distress warrant, defect in, **11(2)**, [496]
enforcement, **11(2)**, [494]
High Court or county courts enforcement
by, **11(2)**, [506]
imprisonment in default, **11(2)**, [494],
[512], [582]
hearing, securing attendance of offender
at, **11(2)**, [501]
reduction of period, **11(2)**, [497]
release from, **11(2)**, [497]
restriction on, **11(2)**, [500]
inquiry into means, **11(2)**, [500]
day for, court fixing, **11(2)**, [505]
instalments, by, **11(2)**, [493]
meaning, **11(2)**, [574]
money found on defaulter, application of,
11(2), [498]
payment—
effect of, **11(2)**, [497]
methods of, **11(2)**, [493]
persons aged 17 to 20, provisions applying
to, **11(2)**, [518]

magistrates' court—*contd*
conviction, sum adjudged to be paid
by—*contd*
supervision pending payment, **11(2)**, [508]
transfer of fine order, **11(2)**, [509]
variation of instalments, **11(2)**, [504]
warrant, postponement of issue of,
11(2), [495]
young offender, enforcement of fines on,
11(2), [499]
corporation charged with offence before,
11(2), [464], [581]
costs—
award of, **11(2)**, [484]
civil debt, recovered as, **11(2)**, [239]
complaint not proceeded with, where,
11(2), [254]
enforcement of, **11(2)**, [484]
legal representative, order against,
11(2), [571]
maintenance order, awarded in complaint
for, **11(2)**, [484]
recovery of, **11(2)**, [235], [238]–[239]
criminal proceedings, power to transfer to
another court, **11(2)**, [452]
Crown Court, sending cases to—
children or young persons, involving,
11(3), [237]
serious or complex fraud cases,
11(3), [238]
custodial sentence, general limit on power to
impose, **12(2)**, [776]
designated officers, arrears of payments,
proceedings by, **11(2)**, [478]
Crown Court, sending cases to—
children or young persons, involving,
11(3), [237]
serious or complex fraud cases,
11(3), [238]
periodical payments made to, **11(2)**, [478]
receipts, application of, **11(3)**, [359]
detention, imposing for one day, **11(2)**, [563]
disclosure order, power to make, **11(2)**, [551]
discontinuance of proceedings, **12(1)**, [957],
[958]
distress for rates in, **11(2)**, [575]
district judges. *See also* **judge**
appointment, **11(3)**, [313]
legal aid, **11(3)**, [313]
pensions, **11(3)**, [313]
retirement, **11(3)**, [313]
early administrative hearings, **11(3)**, [234]
evidence in—
admissible, **11(2)**, [410]–[415]
copy, production of as proof,
11(2), [415]
depositions, **11(2)**, [412]
documents, **11(2)**, [414]
prima facie evidence, **11(2)**, [414]
statements, **11(2)**, [413]
written statements, **11(2)**, [270], [411]
child, of, in sexual offences, **11(2)**, [525]
exceptions, etc, proof of, **11(2)**, [524]
false written statement, **11(2)**, [527]
non-payment of sum, of, **11(2)**, [522]

magistrates' court—*contd*
  evidence in—*contd*
    oath, on, **11(2)**, [521]
    statement of wages as, **11(2)**, [523]
    summons or warrant, at variance with,
      11(2), [544]
    witness refusing to give, **11(2)**, [519]–[520]
  false statements, **11(2)**, [527]–[528]
  family proceedings court, as, **11(2)**, [486]
  family proceedings in—
    composition for, **11(2)**, [486]
    in camera, held, **11(2)**, [488]
    indecent evidence, hearing, **11(2)**, [488]
    inner London, in, **11(2)**, [489]
    meaning, **11(2)**, [485]; **11(3)**, [73];
      11(4), [532]
    newspaper reports, restriction on,
      11(2), [490]
    non-represented party, examination of
      witness by, **11(2)**, [491]
    persons entitled to be present, **11(2)**, [488]
    proceedings treated as, **11(2)**, [485]
    reasons for decisions, **11(2)**, [492]
    rules, **11(3)**, [73]; **11(4)**, [532]
    sittings, **11(2)**, [488]
  fees, **11(3)**, [401]
  fines—
    attachment of earnings, **11(3)**, [422]
    benefit deductions, application for,
      11(3), [422]
    collection, **11(3)**, [402], [421]
      orders—
        contents of, **11(3)**, [423]
        defaulters, further steps in relation to,
          11(3), [427]
        first default, effect of, **11(3)**, [425]
        making of, **11(3)**, [423]
        reserve terms, containing, **11(3)**, [426]
        variation, **11(3)**, [424]
      regulations, **11(3)**, [428]
    companies, on, **11(2)**, [507]
    defaulters—
      community orders, **11(3)**, [453]
      curfew requirement, imposition of,
        11(3), [439], [453]
      driving disqualification, **11(3)**, [440]
      unpaid work requirement, imposition
        of, **11(3)**, [439], [453]
    enforcement—
      county court, by, **11(2)**, [506]
      expenses of, **11(2)**, [506]
      High Court, by, **11(2)**, [506]
      Northern Ireland, **11(2)**, [510]–[511]
      Scotland, **11(2)**, [510]–[511]
      young offenders, provisions applying to,
        11(2), [518]
    general increase in, **11(2)**, [866]–[868]
    imprisonment in default—
      offender, presence of at hearing,
        11(2), [501]
      police station, detention in, **11(2)**, [564]
      restriction on, **11(2)**, [500]
    income support, recovery by deduction
      from, **11(3)**, [169]
    maximum, **11(2)**, [582]

magistrates' court—*contd*
  fines—*contd*
    meaning, **11(2)**, [574]
    offences, **11(3)**, [428]
    officers, **11(3)**, [357]
    pecuniary penalty, including, **11(2)**, [402]
    power to alter, **11(2)**, [568], [585]
    receipts, application of, **11(3)**, [359]–[360]
    remission of, **11(2)**, [503]
    secondary subordinate instruments, under,
      11(3), [60]
    standard scale, **11(2)**, [865]
      existing enactments, application to,
        11(2), [869]
    statutory maximum—
      exceptionally high, power to alter,
        11(3), [62]
      offences triable either way, for,
        11(3), [57]
      summary offences, for, **11(3)**, [58]
    subordinate instruments, under,
      11(2), [864], [868]; **11(3)**, [58]
    summary offences, for, **11(2)**, [396]
    supervision pending payment, **11(2)**, [508]
    transfer order, **11(2)**, [400], [509]
    transitional provisions, **11(2)**, [404]
    unpaid work, discharge by, **11(3)**, [402],
      [429]
    young offender, imposed on, **11(2)**, [499]
  fines in respect of young offenders, limit on
    amount of, **12(2)**, [812]
  forfeited items, disposal of, **11(2)**, [566]
  generally, **11(2)**, [1]
  Greater London Magistrates' Court
    Authority, **11(3)**, [313]
  highway—
    maintenance, power to order, **36**, [1052],
      [1060]
    stopping up or diversion, authorisation,
      36, [1145]
  imprisonment, imposing—
    consecutive terms, **11(2)**, [562]
    limit on power, **11(3)**, [437]
    meaning, **11(2)**, [574]
    minimum term, **11(2)**, [561]
    one day, detention for, **11(2)**, [563]
  incorrigible rogue, committal on bail,
    11(2), [214]
  jurisdiction, **6**, [423]
    complaint, dealing with, **11(2)**, [469]
    generally, **11(2)**, [1]
    indictable offence, over, **11(2)**, [406]
    matrimonial causes, in, **27**, [520]
    offence triable either way, over,
      11(2), [406]
    summary offences, to try, **11(2)**, [406]
  maintenance orders. *See* **maintenance order**
  matrimonial proceedings in. *See* **matrimonial
    causes**
  meaning, **11(2)**, [573]; **11(3)**, [358]; **41**, [605]
  medical examination, remand by for,
    12(2), [726]
  mistake, re-opening case to rectify,
    11(2), [567]

magistrates' court—*contd*
notices given—
children, cases involving, **11(3)**, [239]
offences, of, **11(3)**, [240]
place of trial, of, **11(3)**, [240]
serious or complex fraud cases, in,
11(3), [238]
offences—
triable either way—
meaning, **11(3)**, [241]
order of consideration, **11(3)**, [235]
officers and staff, appointment, **11(3)**, [323]
open court, sitting in, **11(2)**, [542]
orders—
affiliation. *See* affiliation order *above*
disobeying, penalty for, **11(2)**, [483]
financial provision, for. *See* **matrimonial
causes**
hearing of complaint, made on,
11(2), [470]
periodical payments, for. *See* **periodical
payments, order for below**
power to make, **11(2)**, [483]
sum adjudged to be paid by—
arrears, complaint for, **11(2)**, [513]
distress warrant, defect in, **11(2)**, [496]
enforcement, **11(2)**, [494]
imprisonment in default, **11(2)**, [494]
restriction on, **11(2)**, [512]
payment, effect of, **11(2)**, [496]
orders and regulations, **11(3)**, [215]
orders of, disobedience to, **11(2)**, [660], [666]
payment by instalments, ordering,
11(2), [493]
pedlar—
appeal against refusal of certificate by,
27, [68]
certificate, depriving of, **27**, [69]
offences, summary proceedings for,
27, [71]
periodical payments, order for—
arrears, recovery of, **11(2)**, [478]
breach, penalty for, **11(2)**, [479]
child, made to, **11(2)**, [482]
designated officer—
payment to, **11(2)**, [478]
proceedings by, **11(2)**, [478]
matrimonial proceedings, in. *See*
matrimonial causes
meaning, **11(2)**, [481]
means of payment, **11(2)**, [477]
more than one order, payment under,
11(2), [481]
qualifying maintenance order, under,
11(2), [477]
revival, **11(2)**, [480]
revocation, **11(2)**, [480]
variation, **11(2)**, [480]
person aged 17 to 21, committal of,
11(2), [518]
person in custody brought before,
11(2), [460]
petty session areas, **11(3)**, [313]
powers exercisable by single justice,
11(3), [233]

magistrates' court—*contd*
pre-trial hearings, rulings at, **11(3)**, [364]
previous convictions, proof of, **11(2)**, [526]
private, sitting in, where children involved,
6, [428]
proceedings on case stated for opinion of
High Court, **11(2)**, [696]
proceedings relating to children, transmission
of particulars to Secretary of State, **6**, [411]
process—
death, etc, of justice issuing, **11(2)**, [545]
defect in, **11(2)**, [544]
indorsement, **11(2)**, [114], [118]
issue of, **11(2)**, [114]
meaning, **11(2)**, [117]
Scotland, service and execution in,
11(2), [114]–[115], [271]
service and execution, **11(2)**, [114]–[115]
witness, to procure attendance of,
11(2), [114]
property, ordering return to accused,
11(2), [466]
prosecutor, rules as to furnishing of
information by, **11(2)**, [401]
recognizance, entering into—
enforcement of, **11(2)**, [541]
forfeiture, **11(2)**, [541]
good behaviour, to be of. *See*
recognizance to keep the peace
keep the peace, to. *See* **recognizance to
keep the peace**
mode of entering into, **11(2)**, [158]
postponement, **11(2)**, [540]
release on bail, **11(2)**, [538]
records, preservation of, **18**, [189], [194]
recovery of tax in, **42**, [203]
remand by—
absence of accused, in, **11(2)**, [558], [871]
adjournment, on, **11(2)**, [556]
drug trafficking offences, on suspicion of,
11(3), [64]
further, **11(2)**, [556], [558]
hearings, transfer of, **11(2)**, [559], [584]
more than eight days, for, **11(2)**, [557]
period of, **11(2)**, [556]
person already in custody, of, **11(2)**, [560]
police station, detention at, **11(2)**, [556]
powers, **11(2)**, [556]
remission for sentence—
another magistrates' court, by, **12(2)**, [725]
young offender reaching 18, **12(2)**, [724]
repeals and revocations, **11(3)**, [318]
reporting restrictions—
dealing with, **11(3)**, [243]
offences, **11(3)**, [244]
representation before, **11(2)**, [543]
rule committee, **11(2)**, [569]
rules, **11(3)**, [341]
power to make, **11(2)**, [569]–[569A]
provisions in, **11(2)**, [570]
Summary Jurisdiction (Process) Act 1881,
extending, **11(2)**, [159]
youth courts, relating to, **11(2)**, [572]
security officers—
assaulting, **11(3)**, [372]

magistrates' court—*contd*
security officers—*contd*
exclusion, removal or restraint of persons, powers of, **11(3)**, [368]
identification, **11(3)**, [366]
meaning, **11(3)**, [366]
obstructing, **11(3)**, [372]
retention of articles surrendered or seized, **11(3)**, [370]
search, powers of, **11(3)**, [367]
seizure of articles by, **11(3)**, [369]
surrender of articles, requiring, **11(3)**, [369]
serious fraud, transfer of cases to Crown Court. *See* **serious or complex fraud**
single justice, limit on powers, **11(2)**, [542]
sittings—
open court, in, **11(2)**, [542]
places, dates and times of, **11(3)**, [351]
specified sums, power to alter, **11(2)**, [568]
statement of means, requiring, **11(2)**, [502]
summary trial. *See* **summary trial**
system, maintenance of, **11(3)**, [322]
transitional provisions, **11(2)**, [586]
warrant, issue of. *See* **warrant**
young offender, trial of, **11(2)**, [444]
youth courts, **11(3)**, [313], [365]
See also **youth courts**

Magna Carta
confirmation of, **10**, [1], [8], [14], [19]
text of, **10**, [3]–[7]

mail
carriage etc. *See* **post office**
interception. *See* **communications**

mail bag
stealing, **12(1)**, [567]

maintained school
accounts, **15(2)**, [381]–[382]
adjudicators, **15(2)**, [27], [143]
allocation of existing schools to categories, **15(2)**, [138]
alternative education provision, **15(S)**, Education 277
assessment arrangements, duty to implement, **15(S)**, Education 278
boarding hostels, approval of, **15(1)**, [678]
categories of, **15(2)**, [20]
change of category, **15(2)**, [37], [154]
charges—
boarding schools, board and lodging at, **15(1)**, [602]
civil debt, recovery as, **15(1)**, [605]
information, provision of, **15(1)**, [603]
permitted—
generally, **15(1)**, [599]
regulations of, **15(1)**, [600]
policy, **15(1)**, [601]
prohibition of—
admission, for, **15(1)**, [594]
education, for, **15(1)**, [595]
examinations, for, **15(1)**, [597]
incidental, **15(1)**, [598]

maintained school—*contd*
charges—*contd*
remissions policy, **15(1)**, [601]
voluntary contributions, **15(1)**, [604]
charitable status, **15(2)**, [23]
closure of, Secretary of State's power to direct, **15(2)**, [18]
communication with, **15(2)**, [379]
consultation with pupils, existing functions, **15(S)**, Education 280
curriculum—
basic, **15(2)**, [394]
general requirements, **15(2)**, [392]–[393]
National. *See* **curriculum**
early years provision, charges for, **6(S)**, 66
financing—
accounts, **15(2)**, [381]–[382]
budget shares—
allocation of, **15(2)**, [39]
determination of, **15(2)**, [41]
community purposes, expenditure incurred for, **15(2)**, [47]
delegation—
delegated budgets, **15(2)**, [44]
effect of, **15(2)**, [45]
employment law, application of, **15(2)**, [70]
suspension for mismanagement, **15(2)**, [46], [157]
financial schemes, **15(2)**, [43]
financial schemes, revision of, **15(2)**, [155]
financial statements—
certification by Audit Commission, **15(2)**, [49]
making of, **15(2)**, [48]
LEA, determination of specified budgets of, **15(2)**, [40]
minimum schools budget for LEA, Secretary of State's power to set, **15(2)**, [62]–[63]
schools budget, power to require LEAs to determine, **15(2)**, [40A]–[40C]
funding, **15(2)**, [733]–[734]
further education bodies, collaboration arrangements with, **15(2)**, [875]
governing bodies—
accounts, **15(2)**, [381]–[382]
additional functions, **15(2)**, [369]
clerk, **15(2)**, [361]
collaboration between schools, **15(2)**, [365]
community facilities, power to provide, **15(2)**, [366]
companies to provide services, formation of or investment in—
limits on powers, **15(2)**, [350]
powers, **15(2)**, [349]
conduct of school, responsibility for, **15(2)**, [359]
constitution, **15(2)**, [357]
consultation with pupils, **15(2)**, [490]
discipline, responsibility for, **15(2)**, [54]
dissolution, **15(2)**, [524]
documents, use in evidence, **15(1)**, [700]

maintained school—*contd*
  governing bodies—*contd*
    education provision for improving
      behaviour, powers,
      15(S), Education 275–6
    federations of schools, **15(2)**, [363]–[364]
    functions of, **15(2)**, [357], [359], [369]
    further education, provision of, **15(2)**, [69]
    higher education, power to provide,
      15(2), [368]
    individual pupils' performance, provision of
      information about, **15(1)**, [671]
    information, Secretary of State requiring,
      15(1), [670]
    meals, provision of, **15(1)**, [668]
    name and seal, **15(2)**, [524]
    new school, for, **15(2)**, [375]
    powers, **15(2)**, [524]
    premises, control of, **15(2)**, [372]
    provision of information to Secretary of
      State, **15(1)**, [673]
    pupils' views, inviting and considering,
      15(S), Education 279
    regulations, **15(2)**, [357]
    school premises, control of, **15(2)**, [38],
      [155]
    school profiles, preparation and publication
      of, **15(2)**, [371]
    training and support, **15(2)**, [360]
    welfare of children, duties regarding,
      15(2), [489]
  home-school agreements, **15(2)**, [111]–[112]
  instruments of government—
    making of, **15(2)**, [358]
    regulations, **15(2)**, [358]
    review, **15(2)**, [358]
    variation, **15(2)**, [358]
  intervention—
    LEA, by—
      additional governors, power to appoint,
        15(2), [13]
      cases for, **15(2)**, [12]
      delegated budget, suspension of right
        to, **15(2)**, [15]
      interim executive members for governing
        body, power to provide for, **15(2)**, [14],
        [19], [137]
    Secretary of State, by—
      additional governors, power to appoint,
        15(2), [16]
      interim executive members for governing
        body, power to provide for, **15(2)**, [17],
        [19], [137]
  local education authority, consultation with
    pupils, **15(2)**, [490]
  maintenance and funding, **15(2)**, [22]
  meaning, **15(1)**, [593]; **15(2)**, [380]
  minor authorities, **15(2)**, [131]
  nursery education in, **15(1)**, [485]
  parent councils, **15(2)**, [362]
  potentially harmful materials and apparatus,
    control of, **15(1)**, [680]
  premises—
    approval of, **15(1)**, [678]

maintained school—*contd*
  premises—*contd*
    building byelaws, exemption from,
      15(1), [679]
    control by governing body, **15(2)**, [372]
    nuisance or disturbance on, **15(1)**, [681]
    prescribed standards, **15(1)**, [676]
  pupils—
    admission of, charges, prohibition of,
      15(1), [594]
    exclusion of, generally, **15(2)**, [383]
    public examinations—
      charge for, **15(1)**, [599]
      wasted fees, recovery of, **15(1)**, [597]
  rating, **15(2)**, [66]
  school organisation committees, **15(2)**, [26],
    [142]
  school performance, exemptions relating to—
    application for orders for, **15(2)**, [346]
    curriculum, **15(2)**, [345]
    pay and conditions, **15(2)**, [345]
    determination of, during and after
      exemption, **15(2)**, [348]
    qualifying schools, **15(2)**, [344]
    removal of, **15(2)**, [347]
  school workforce, provision of training for,
    15(2), [686]
  staffing—
    delegated budget, suspension of,
      15(2), [525]
    dismissal, payments in respect of,
      15(2), [378]
    generally, **15(2)**, [376]–[377]
    religious opinions, **15(2)**, [52]
  terms and holidays, fixing dates of,
    15(2), [373]
  times of sessions, fixing, **15(2)**, [373]
  Wales, in. *See* **Wales**
  wasted examination fees, recovery of,
    15(1), [597]

maintenance
  abolition of offence, **12(1)**, [369]
  agreement, **18**, [620]
    alteration by court—
      death of one party, after, **27**, [477]
      lives of parties, during, **27**, [476]
      meaning, **27**, [475]
      transitional provisions, **27**, [491]
      validity of, **27**, [475]
  armed forces—
    assessment, deductions from pay, **3**, [649],
      [922]
    deductions from pay, **3**, [648], [921]
    limits on deductions, **3**, [652], [925]
    wife or child, deductions from pay for,
      3, [650], [923]
  child, of, **40(1)**, [19]
  civil rights in respect of, abolition, **45**, [945],
    [952]
  convention country—
    declaration of, **27**, [396]
    evidence for use in—
      exclusion of enactments, **27**, [424]
      request for, **27**, [419]

maintenance—*contd*
  convention country—*contd*
    evidence given in—
      admissibility, **27**, [417]
      United Kingdom court requesting,
        27, [418]
    recovery by person in—
      England and Wales, in, against person
        in, **27**, [398]–[402]
      Northern Ireland, in, against person in,
        27, [404]–[409]
    recovery in, application for, **27**, [397]
    transfer of order, **27**, [410]
  cost of assistance, recovery of, **40(1)**, [20]
  failure to maintain, **40(1)**, [585]
    offence of, **40(1)**, [25]
  family. *See* **family provision**
  husband and wife, liability of, **40(1)**, [19]
  jurisdiction, references to, **27**, [427]
  non-payment, committal for, **4(2)**, [48]
  Northern Ireland, provisions applying to,
    27, [428]
  order. *See* **maintenance order**
  Orders in Council, **27**, [425]
  payments collected by Secretary of State,
    payment of benefits, **40(1)**, [578]
  pending suit—
    anti-avoidance provisions, **27**, [478]
    arrears, enforcement of payment, **27**, [472]
    order for, **27**, [453]
    repayment, order for, **27**, [473]
    variation, discharge etc, **27**, [471]
  person liable for, recovery of income support
    from—
      additional amounts, **40(1)**, [587]
      enforcement, **40(1)**, [588]
      order for, **40(1)**, [586]
      transfer of orders, **40(1)**, [587]
  proceedings—
    furnishing of addresses for, **40(1)**, [641]
    restriction of publicity for, **27**, [340]

maintenance order
  1965 Act, made under, **27**, [493]
  appeals, **27**, [385]
  application for, **19(3)**, [39]
  armed forces—
    deductions from pay, **3**, [366], [647], [650]
    service of process, **3**, [653], [926], [1178]
  breach, penalty for, **11(2)**, [479]
  change of address, payer giving notice of,
    27, [292]
  collecting officer—
    functions of, **27**, [293]
    payment through, **27**, [293]
  committal to enforce—
    review of, magistrates' court, by, **27**, [321]
    same arrears, more than once in respect
      of, **27**, [320]
  costs—
    award of, **11(2)**, [484]
    payment deemed part of, **27**, [313]
  court of summary jurisdiction, procedure in,
    27, [299]

maintenance order—*contd*
  depositions as evidence in proceedings,
    27, [188]
  documents, proof of, **27**, [187], [300]
  enforcement, **11(2)**, [840]
  enforcement of—
    application of enactments, **27**, [290], [861]
    complaint, by, **27**, [323]
    dominions, where made in, **27**, [179]
    magistrates' court, by, **27**, [185]
    mode of, **27**, [185]
    other countries, application of 1972 Act
      to, **27**, [422]
    reciprocal provisions, **27**, [191], [609]
    reciprocating countries—
      confirmation of order in, **27**, [377]
      designation of, **27**, [375]
      evidence given in, admission of,
        27, [386], [424]
      High Court, order registered in,
        27, [394]
      orders and proceedings under 1920 Act,
        and, **27**, [394]–[395]
      proof not necessary, **27**, [388]
      transmission of order to, **27**, [376]
      variation or revocation in United
        Kingdom, **27**, [378]
    registered order, of, **27**, [292], [316]
    United Kingdom, in another part of,
      27, [290]
  evidence relating to—
    exclusion of enactments, **27**, [424]
    reciprocating country—
      given in, **27**, [386]
      required in, **27**, [387]
  generally, **27**, [127]
  interim—
    appeals, **27**, [519]
    parties living together, effect of, **27**, [515]
    power to make, **27**, [509], [544]
    variation or revocation, **27**, [510]
  jurisdiction, provisions as to, **27**, [301]
  magistrates' court—
    arrears—
      committal, effect of, **11(2)**, [514]
      complaint for, **11(2)**, [513]
      English, meaning, **11(2)**, [516]
      interest on, **11(2)**, [515]
      payment, manner of, **11(2)**, [516]
      remission of, **11(2)**, [516]
    imprisonment in default, **11(2)**, [512]
    proceedings, **27**, [390]
    rules, **27**, [391], [420]
  meaning, **4(2)**, [49], [52]; **19(3)**, [38];
    27, [189], [392], [604]
  Northern Ireland, in—
    application of provisions, **27**, [190]
    collecting officer, payment to, **27**, [293]
    enforcement of, **27**, [290], [292]
    registration—
      revocation of, by magistrates' courts,
        27, [416]
      variation of, by magistrates' courts,
        27, [414], [416]
    service of process, **27**, [289], [303]

maintenance order—*contd*
  orders applicable, **19(3)**, [71]
  Orders in Council, review of, **27**, [322]
  payments, attachment of earnings for,
    19(3), [39]
    See further **attachment of earnings**
  periodical—
    attachment of earnings, **27**, [604]
    generally, **27**, [127]
    meaning, **27**, [604]
    means of payment order, **27**, [604]
    order for, **11(2)**, [477]
    payment, means of, **27**, [604]
    qualifying, meaning, **27**, [604]
  person entitled to receive payments,
    meaning, **27**, [324]
  process, service of, **27**, [305]
  provisional—
    appeal not lying from, **27**, [385]
    confirmation of, **27**, [181]
    meaning, **27**, [392]
    person resident in dominions, against,
      27, [181]
    person residing in reciprocating country,
      against, **27**, [377]
    regulations for facilitating communications,
      power to make, **27**, [184]
    remarriage, effect of, **27**, [423]
    revocation of, **27**, [183]
    United Kingdom court—
      confirmed in, **27**, [380]
      variation or revocation of order by,
        27, [382]
    variation of, **27**, [183]
  registration—
    application for, **27**, [291], [314]
    arrears, enforcement of, **27**, [294]
    cancellation of, **27**, [298], [319]
    clerk entitled to receive payments,
      application by, **27**, [323]
    collecting officer, functions of, **27**, [293]
    county court, made in, **27**, [313]–[314]
    court other than court making, in—
      enforcement, **27**, [411]
      variation and revocation, **27**, [412]
    court to which order sent, **27**, [291]
    discharge—
      court of summary jurisdiction, power
        of, **27**, [296]
      notice of, **27**, [297]
      sheriff court, power of, **27**, [296]
      superior court, power of, **27**, [295]
    High Court, made in, **27**, [313]–[314]
    interest, recovery of, **27**, [315]
    magistrates' court, made in,
      27, [313]–[314], [314]
    Northern Ireland, in, **27**, [533]
    original court, in, **27**, [314]
    place of residence of payer, in, **27**, [291]
    reciprocating country, order made in,
      27, [379]
    Scotland or Northern Ireland, made in,
      27, [313]
    variation of—
      appeal, after, **27**, [317]

maintenance order—*contd*
  registration—*contd*
    variation of—*contd*
      High Court, in, **27**, [318]
      magistrates' court, in, **27**, [296], [317],
        [323], [413], [415]
      notice of, **27**, [297]
      original court, by, **27**, [317]
      rate of payments, in, **27**, [296]
      sheriff court, power of, **27**, [296]
      superior court, power of, **27**, [295]
    remarriage, ceasing on, **27**, [371]
    transmission outside England or Ireland,
      27, [180]
    United Kingdom court, registered in—
      cancellation of, **27**, [383]
      confirmation of, **27**, [380]
      enforcement, **27**, [381]
      foreign currency, payable in, **27**, [389]
      payer—
        non-resident, found to be, **27**, [384]
        removal out of jurisdiction, **27**, [383]
      payment of, provisions on, **27**, [389]
      procedure, **27**, [379]
      revocation of, **27**, [382]
      transfer of, **27**, [383]
      variation of, **27**, [382]

maintenance payment
  air force pay, deduction for, **3**, [1522]
  army pay, deduction for, **3**, [1522]
  child support, **44(4)**, [463]
  navy pay, deduction for, **3**, [1522]
  qualifying—
    meaning, **44(4)**, [462]
    tax reduction for, **44(4)**, [461]
  recovery of benefit, payments under orders
    for, **44(4)**, [464]

maize. *See* **cereals**

Malacca
  Federation of Malaya, forming part of,
    7(2), [463]

Malawi
  British ship registered in, **7(2)**, [555]
  Commonwealth citizenship, **31**, [186]
  constitutional provisions, **7(2)**, [554]
  fully responsible status of, **7(2)**, [550]
  legislative powers, **7(2)**, [554]
  republic, becoming, existing law, operation
    of, **7(2)**, [589]
  visiting forces in, **7(2)**, [555]

Malay States
  formation of, **7(2)**, [463]

Malaya, Federation of
  British ship registered in, **7(2)**, [466]
  existing law, operation of, **7(2)**, [464]
  formation of, **7(2)**, [529]
  independent sovereign country, as, **7(2)**, [463]
  visiting forces in, **7(2)**, [466]

Malaysia
Commonwealth citizenship, **31**, [186]

Malaysia, Federation of
existing law, operation of, **7(2)**, [530]–[531], [533]

Maldives
Commonwealth citizenship, **31**, [186]

malice
libel, in. *See* **libel**

malicious communication
Northern Ireland, provisions applicable, **12(1)**, [1079]
sending or delivering, **12(1)**, [1078]

malicious damage
Admiralty jurisdiction, offences committed within, **12(1)**, [64]
owner of property, malice against, **12(1)**, [63]
railway, to, **12(1)**, [61], [62]

malicious falsehood
action, no need to prove special damage, **19(3)**, [310]
limitation of action—
discretionary exclusion of, **19(3)**, [763]
period, **19(3)**, [728]

malingering
armed forces—
aiding, **3**, [694], [967]
generally, **3**, [496], [1040]

Malta
accession to European Union, **18**, [54]
British ship registered in, **7(2)**, [567]
Commonwealth citizenship, **31**, [186]
existing law, operation of, **7(2)**, [670]
fully responsible status of, **7(2)**, [562]
legislative powers of, **7(2)**, [566]
meaning of, **7(2)**, [564]
republic, becoming, **7(2)**, [670]
visiting forces in, **7(2)**, [567]

mammals. *See also* **wild mammals**
importation and exportation, restriction on. *See* **animals**
protected, list of, **32**, [503]
sale, etc, restriction on. *See* **animals**

man
meaning, **7(1)**, [38]
sex discrimination against, **7(1)**, [32]

man trap
offences, **12(1)**, [87]

managed service companies
associate, meaning, **44(2)**, [70]
distributions by, **44(2)**, [69]
meaning, **44(2)**, [63]

managed service companies—*contd*
provider, meaning, **44(2)**, [63]
provision of services through—
deemed employment payment—
calculation of, **44(2)**, [66]
Income Tax Acts, application of, **44(2)**, [68]
earnings from employment—
application of rules, **44(2)**, [67]
worker treated as receiving, **44(2)**, [65]

managed service companies
deemed employment payments, deduction for, **44(3)**, [164]; **43(S)**, 595

management (housing)
agreement—
housing association grant, and, **22**, [471]
meaning, **22**, [27]
performance of functions under, **22**, [27]
power to make, **22**, [27]
Secretary of State, approval of, **22**, [27]
tenant management organisations, with, **22**, [28]
terms of, **22**, [27]
allocation of houses, **22**, [96]
application of provisions, **22**, [21]
arrangements for, publication of, **22**, [95]
byelaws as to, **22**, [23]
consultations respecting, **22**, [30], [95]
county council housing, **22**, [31]
financial assistance, **22**, [307]
general powers, **22**, [22]
houses in multiple occupation. *See* **house in multiple occupation**
matters concerning—
consultation on, **22**, [95]
meaning, **22**, [95]

manager. *See* **receiver or manager**

managing agent
meaning, **22**, [543]
recognised tenant's association, right to be consulted, **22**, [543]

Manchester Ship Canal
bridges, exclusion of provisions, **36**, [1109]
land, acquisition for bridge, **36**, [1301]

mandamus
child care, directions of Secretary of State enforcement by, **6**, [412]
Crown proceedings, saving in, **13**, [39]

mandated territory
enactments, application to, **7(2)**, [449]
judgments obtained in, **19(3)**, [20]

manoeuvres (armed forces)
commission—
constitution, **3**, [1243]
directions, powers to give, **3**, [1244]–[1245]
compensation following, **3**, [1246]
highway, power to close, **3**, [1242]

manoeuvres (armed forces)—*contd*
offences, **3**, [1247]
power to authorise, **3**, [1240]
purposes of, **3**, [1241]

manor
conveyance, general words implied, **20**, [680]
deregister, power to, **23**, [759]
Law of Property Act, application, **20**, [800]
lordship included in, **20**, [436]

Manor of Laxton, court leet
jurisdiction, **11(2)**, [381]

manorial documents
Court Rolls, inspection, **20**, [494]
custody, **20**, [495]
diocesan record office, placed in, **14**, 936
extinguishment, **20**, [495]
meaning, **20**, [495]

mansion house
improvement. *See* **drainage and improvement of land (private works)**

manslaughter
abroad, committed, **12(1)**, [71]
aiding suicide, verdict of, **12(1)**, [330]
corporate—
armed forces, application of provisions to, **12(4)**, [300]
consent of DPP to proceedings, **12(4)**, [305]
conviction, publicising, **12(4)**, [298]
convictions for offences and under health and safety legislation, **12(4)**, [307]
criminal procedure and evidence, **12(4)**, [303]
Crown bodies, no immunity from prosecution, **12(4)**, [299]
exclusions from relevant duty of care—
child-protection functions, **12(4)**, [295]
emergency, in response to, **12(4)**, [294]
exclusively public function, in exercise of, **12(4)**, [291]
military activities, **12(4)**, [292]
policing and law enforcement, in respect of, **12(4)**, [293]
probation functions, **12(4)**, [295]
public policy decisions, **12(4)**, [291]
statutory inspections, **12(4)**, [291]
extension of offence to other organisations, **12(4)**, [309]
Government departments, list of, **12(4)**, [318]
power to amend, **12(4)**, [310]
interpretation, **12(4)**, [313]
no individual liability for, **12(4)**, [306], [419]
offence of, **12(4)**, [289]
partnerships, application of provisions to, **12(4)**, [302]
police forces, application of provisions to, **12(4)**, [301]

manslaughter—*contd*
corporate—*contd*
relevant duty of care—
exclusions. *See* exclusions from relevant duty of care *above*
gross breach, factors for jury, **12(4)**, [296]
meaning, **12(4)**, [290]
power to extend provisions, **12(4)**, [311]
remedy of breach, order for, **12(4)**, [297]
sentencing, **12(4)**, [303]
transfer of functions, proceedings in case of, **12(4)**, [304]
diminished responsibility, on grounds of, **12(1)**, [299]
England or Ireland, death in, **12(1)**, [72]
liability of corporations at common law, abolition, **12(4)**, [308]
life sentence for, **12(1)**, [70]
murder, alternative verdict to, **12(1)**, [364]
suicide pact, in course of, **12(1)**, [301]

manufacture
medicinal products, **28**, [75]

manufactured payments
administrative provisions, powers about, **44(4)**, [594]
anti-avoidance, **43(S)**, 1207–10
avoidance arrangements, meaning, **43(S)**, 1208
deduction of tax, deemed, **44(4)**, [611]
dividends on UK shares—
allowable deductions—
double-counting, restrictions on, **44(4)**, [583]
matching, **44(4)**, [582]
generally, **44(4)**, [581]
Real Estate Investment Trusts, **44(4)**, [584], [926]
statements about, **44(4)**, [585]
interest on UK securities—
allowable deductions—
double counting, restriction on, **44(4)**, [588]
matching, **44(4)**, [587]
foreign payers, reverse charge, **44(4)**, [928]
generally, **44(4)**, [586]
payments by UK residents, **44(4)**, [927]
underlying securities paid gross, cases where, **44(4)**, [929]
overseas dividend—
administrative provisions, powers about, **44(4)**, [594]
foreign payers, reverse charge, **44(4)**, [931]–[932]
generally, **44(4)**, [589]
gross amount, meaning, **44(4)**, [597]
power to deal with, **44(4)**, [593]
powers about, **44(4)**, [590]
relevant withholding tax, meaning, **44(4)**, [598]
relief, eligibility for, **44(4)**, [595]

manufactured payments—*contd*
  overseas dividend—*contd*
    set-off entitlement, power to provide,
      44(4), [933]
    supplementary provisions,
      44(4), [934]–[935]
    underlying payments—
      exceeded by, **44(4)**, [591]
      greater than, **44(4)**, [592]
  overview of, **44(4)**, [580]
  power to deal with, **44(4)**, [593]
  relief, eligibility for, **44(4)**, [595]
  repos deemed, **44(4)**, [610]
  transitional provisions and savings,
    44(4), [1057]
  unallowable purpose, arrangements having,
    43(2), [353]
  underlying payments—
    exceeded by, **44(4)**, [591]
    greater than, **44(4)**, [592]

manure
  removal from mews, stables, etc, **35(1)**, [132]

maps
  fresh-water limits, of, **49**, [1242]
  main river—
    amendment of, **49**, [1244]
    evidence, as, **49**, [1243]
    keeping, **49**, [1243]
    meaning, **49**, [1243]
  pipes, showing location of, **35(1)**, [315]
  waterworks, of, **49**, [1245]

Marble Hill House
  vesting on abolition of GLC, **25(2)**, [603]

marine accidents
  Chief Inspector of, **39(2)**, [946]
  inspector of—
    appointment of, **39(2)**, [946]
    powers of, **39(2)**, [946]
  investigation of—
    appeals, rules for, **39(2)**, [949]
    formal, **39(2)**, [947]
    re-hearing and appeal, **39(2)**, [948]
    regulations, **39(2)**, [946]
    rules for conduct of, **39(2)**, [949]
    summary of provisions, **39(2)**, [1]
  regulations, **39(2)**, [946]

marine insurance
  abandonment—
    effect of, **19(1)**, [208]
    notice of, **19(1)**, [207]
  advance freight, **19(1)**, [157]
  adventure, implied warranty as to legality of,
    19(1), [186]
  agent, disclosure by, **19(1)**, [164]
  arrest of kings, princes etc, meaning,
    19(1), [238]
  at and from, meaning, **19(1)**, [238]
  barratry, meaning, **19(1)**, [238]
  bottomry, insurable interest of lender,
    19(1), [155]

marine insurance—*contd*
  charges, inclusion of, **19(1)**, [158]
  common law rules, application, **19(1)**, [236]
  compulsory insurance or security,
    39(2), [870]
  contingent interest, **19(1)**, [152]
  contract—
    good faith essential to, **19(1)**, [162]
    implied obligations, variation of,
      19(1), [232]
    policy, to be embodied in, **19(1)**, [167]
    ratification, **19(1)**, [231]
    representations pending negotiation,
      19(1), [165]
    when deemed concluded, **19(1)**, [166]
  contribution—
    general average, **19(1)**, [218]
    insurer's right to, **19(1)**, [225]
  defeasible interest, **19(1)**, [152]
  delay in voyage, **19(1)**, [193]
  deviation—
    excuses for, **19(1)**, [194]
    meaning and effect, **19(1)**, [191]
  disclosure—
    agent of assured, by, **19(1)**, [164]
    assured, by, **19(1)**, [163]
  double insurance, **19(1)**, [177]
  evidence of, **19(1)**, [234]
  excepted losses, meaning, **19(1)**, [238]
  floating policy by ship or ships, **19(1)**, [174]
  freight—
    advance, insurable interest, **19(1)**, [157]
    insurable value, **19(1)**, [161]
    insured "at and from", **19(1)**, [238]
    meaning, **19(1)**, [235], [238]
    partial loss, **19(1)**, [215]
  fundamental principles, **19(1)**, [1]
  gambling policies, prohibition, **19(1)**, [239]
  gaming or wagering contracts, **19(1)**, [149]
  general average—
    contributions, **19(1)**, [218]
    loss, **19(1)**, [211]
  goods and merchandise—
    meaning, **19(1)**, [238]
    partial loss of, **19(1)**, [216]
    sea-worthiness, absence of implied
      warranty, **19(1)**, [185]
  implied obligations, variation, **19(1)**, [232]
  indemnity, measure of, **19(1)**, [177], [212]
    general provisions as to, **19(1)**, [220]
  insurable interest—
    advance freight, in, **19(1)**, [157]
    assignment, **19(1)**, [160]
    bottomry, in case of, **19(1)**, [155]
    charges of insurance, **19(1)**, [158]
    defensible or contingent interest,
      19(1), [152]
    extent of, **19(1)**, [159]
    loss, acquired after, **19(1)**, [151]
    meaning, **19(1)**, [150]
    mortgagor, of, **19(1)**, [159]
    partial interest, **19(1)**, [153]
    quantum of interest, **19(1)**, [159]
    re-insurance, in case of, **19(1)**, [154]
    wagering etc contract void, **19(1)**, [149]

marine insurance—*contd*
insurable interest—*contd*
wages of master and seamen, **19(1)**, [156]
when attachable, **19(1)**, [151]
insurable value, measure of, **19(1)**, [161]
insurer—
liability, extent of, **19(1)**, [200], [212]
rights of, on payment, **19(1)**, [224]–[226]
land and sea risks mixed, **19(1)**, [147]
law merchant, application of rules,
19(1), [236]
loss—
general average, **19(1)**, [211]
goods and merchandise, **19(1)**, [216]
included and excluded, **19(1)**, [200]
liability of insurer, extent of, **19(1)**, [200],
[212]
partial. *See* partial loss *below*
particular average, **19(1)**, [209]
salvage charges as, **19(1)**, [210]
successive losses, **19(1)**, [222]
total. *See* total loss *below*
lost or not lost, meaning, **19(1)**, [151], [238]
marine adventure, meaning, **19(1)**, [148]
maritime perils, meaning, **19(1)**, [148]
material circumstances, disclosure of,
19(1), [163]
meaning, **19(1)**, [146]
misconduct of assured, **19(1)**, [200]
mutual insurance, **19(1)**, [230]
negligence of assured, **19(1)**, [200]
neutrality, warranty of, **19(1)**, [181]
over-insurance, **19(1)**, [177]
partial loss—
abandonment, on, **19(1)**, [207]
freight, **19(1)**, [215]
goods and merchandise, **19(1)**, [216]
meaning, **19(1)**, [201]
measure of indemnity, **19(1)**, [214]–[216]
particular average loss as, **19(1)**, [209]
ship, of, **19(1)**, [214]
particular average—
loss, **19(1)**, [209]
warranties, **19(1)**, [221]
perils of the sea, meaning, **19(1)**, [238]
pirates, meaning, **19(1)**, [238]
policy—
all other perils, meaning, **19(1)**, [238]
assignment—
generally, **19(1)**, [195]
inoperative, when, **19(1)**, [196]
broker, effected through, **19(1)**, [198]
construction, rules for, **19(1)**, [238]
contract embodied in, **19(1)**, [167]
covering note, as evidence, **19(1)**, [234]
designation of subject-matter, **19(1)**, [171]
floating, **19(1)**, [174]
form of, **19(1)**, [238]
gambling polices, prohibition, **19(1)**, [239]
land risks included in, **19(1)**, [147]
losses included or excluded, **19(1)**, [200]
name to be specified in, **19(1)**, [168]
payment required for issue, **19(1)**, [197]
ship not declared in, **19(1)**, [174]
signature of insurer, **19(1)**, [169]

marine insurance—*contd*
policy—*contd*
slip as evidence of, **19(1)**, [234]
suing and labouring clause, **19(1)**, [223]
terms, construction of, **19(1)**, [175], [235]
time, meaning, **19(1)**, [170]
unvalued, meaning, **19(1)**, [173]
valued, meaning, **19(1)**, [172]
voyage and time policies, **19(1)**, [170]
premium—
arrangement, **19(1)**, [176]
broker responsible for, **19(1)**, [198]
failure of consideration, return for,
19(1), [229]
no arrangement for, **19(1)**, [176]
reasonable, must be, **19(1)**, [176]
receipt on, effect of, **19(1)**, [199]
return of, **19(1)**, [227]–[229]
time for paying, **19(1)**, [197]
ratification of contract, **19(1)**, [231]
reasonable time etc, question of fact,
19(1), [233]
re-insurance, **19(1)**, [289]
representations pending contract, **19(1)**, [165]
risk—
commencement, implied condition,
19(1), [187]
sea and land, mixed, **19(1)**, [147]
when attaching, **19(1)**, [238]
salvage charges—
liability, measure of, **19(1)**, [218]
recovery of, **19(1)**, [210]
sea and land risks mixed, **19(1)**, [147]
ship—
abandonment of, **19(1)**, [207], [208]
changed destination, sailing for,
19(1), [189]
deviation on voyage, **19(1)**, [191]
meaning, **19(1)**, [238]
missing, total loss presumed, **19(1)**, [203]
nationality, no implied warranty of,
19(1), [182]
neutral, warranty of, **19(1)**, [181]
ports of discharge, several, **19(1)**, [192]
repairs, cost of, **19(1)**, [214]
seaworthiness, **19(1)**, [184]
stranding of, **19(1)**, [238]
stamp duty exemptions, **19(1)**, [294]
subject-matter—
abandonment of, **19(1)**, [207], [208]
designation of, **19(1)**, [171]
subrogation, insurer's right of, **19(1)**, [224]
suing and labouring clause, **19(1)**, [223]
summary of provisions, **19(1)**, [1]
thieves, meaning, **19(1)**, [238]
third parties, liabilities to, **19(1)**, [219]
total loss—
actual, **19(1)**, [202]
constructive—
covered by policy, **19(1)**, [201]
definition of, **19(1)**, [205]
effect of, **19(1)**, [206]
when arising, **19(1)**, [203]
measure of indemnity, **19(1)**, [213]

marine insurance—*contd*
  total loss—*contd*
    presumption when ship missing,
      19(1), [203]
    transhipment, effect of, **19(1)**, [204]
    uberrima fides as essential of, **19(1)**, [162]
    under insurance, effect of, **19(1)**, [226]
    unvalued policies, **19(1)**, [173]
    valuation, apportionment, **19(1)**, [217]
    valued policies, **19(1)**, [172]
    voyage—
      change of, voluntary, **19(1)**, [190]
      commencement, implied condition,
        19(1), [187]
      delay in—
        effect of, **19(1)**, [193]
        excuses for, **19(1)**, [194]
      destination, different, sailing for,
        19(1), [189]
      deviation—
        excuses for, **19(1)**, [194]
        meaning and effect, **19(1)**, [191]
      interruption of, transhipment on,
        19(1), [204]
      place of departure, alteration, **19(1)**, [188]
      time, and, policies, **19(1)**, [170]
    wagering or gaming contracts, **19(1)**, [149]
    wages of master and seamen, **19(1)**, [156]
    warranty—
      breach of, when excused, **19(1)**, [179]
      express, **19(1)**, [180]
      free from particular average, of,
        19(1), [221]
      good safety, of, **19(1)**, [183]
      implied, **19(1)**, [178]
      legality of adventure, of, **19(1)**, [186]
      nationality, of, not implied, **19(1)**, [182]
      nature of, **19(1)**, [178]
      neutrality, of, **19(1)**, [181]
      seaworthiness, of, **19(1)**, [184], [185]
      waiver of, **19(1)**, [179]

marine structure
  dumping at sea from. *See* **pollution** (sea)
  meaning, **49**, [641]

Marines. *See* **Royal Marines**

maritime claims
  Convention on Limitation of Liability for—
    Limitation Fund, **39(2)**, [1002]
    provisions having effect with, **39(2)**, [1003]
    text of, **39(2)**, [1002]
  force of law, having, **39(2)**, [862]
  Her Majesty's ships, in case of, **39(2)**, [869]
  liability for—
    apportionment, **39(2)**, [864]
    exclusion of, **39(2)**, [863]
    joint and several, **39(2)**, [865]
    limitation of, **39(2)**, [862]
    loss of life or personal injuries, for—
      contribution, right of, **39(2)**, [866]
      joint and several, **39(2)**, [865]
    time limit for proceedings, **39(2)**, [867]
  summary of provisions, **39(2)**, [1]

maritime services
  funding of, **39(2)**, [980], [1008]

market abuse
  applicable behaviours, **19(2)**, [163], [164]
  code—
    City Code, provisions included by reference
      to, **19(2)**, [168]
    contents of, **19(2)**, [167]
    draft, **19(2)**, [169]
    effect of, **19(2)**, [170]
    preparation and issue of, **19(2)**, [167]
  disregarded behaviour, **19(2)**, [164]
  guidance, issue of, **19(2)**, [178]
  injunctions, **19(2)**, [456]
  inside information, meaning, **19(2)**, [166]
  insiders, meaning, **19(2)**, [165]
  investigation by exchange or clearing house,
    suspension of, **19(2)**, [176]
  meaning, **19(2)**, [163]
  penalties—
    court, imposition by, **19(2)**, [177]
    decision notices, **19(2)**, [175]
    effect on transactions, **19(2)**, [180]
    power to impose, **19(2)**, [171]
    statement of policy, **19(2)**, [172]
      procedure for issuing, **19(2)**, [173]
    Tribunal, right to refer to, **19(2)**, [175]
    warning notices, **19(2)**, [174]
  protected disclosures, **19(2)**, [181]
  restitution orders, **19(2)**, [458]

market charge
  insolvency provisions. *See* **insolvency;**
  recognised clearing house

market contract. *See* **recognised clearing**
house

market garden. *See also* **agricultural holding;**
agricultural tenancy
  agreement to let holding as, effect, **22**, [644]
  Agricultural Land Tribunal, powers, **22**, [645]
  compensation—
    agreement as to, **22**, [646]
    Evesham custom, **22**, [646]
    improvements, for, **22**, [644], [682]
  fruit trees and bushes, removal, **22**, [644]
  old tenancy, provision applicable, **22**, [683]

market gardening
  land, meaning, **44(1)**, [615]
  loss relief, **44(1)**, [201]
  meaning, **44(1)**, [201]
  trade, as, **44(1)**, [33]
  trade losses—
    losses in previous tax years, determining,
      44(4), [70]
    reasonable expectation of profit test,
      44(4), [68]
    restrictions on, **44(4)**, [67]
    trade treated as same, whether, **44(4)**, [69]
  trade profits, income taxed as, **44(3)**, [9]

market maker
meaning, **44(1)**, [453]

market property. *See* **recognised clearing house**

marketable security
ad valorem duty in respect of, **41**, [35]
exempt property, transferred for, **41**, [280]
instruments relating to, stamp duty on, **41**, [409], [456]
meaning, **41**, [46]
stamp duty, **41**, [35]
stock including, **41**, [175]

marketing board
reserve fund, treatment of, **44(1)**, [368]

markets and fairs
abolition, order for, **27**, [55]–[56]
amendments to enactments as to, **1(2)**, [465]
annual accounts, undertakers making up, **27**, [43]
annual returns, **27**, [1]
byelaws—
application for allowance, notice of, **27**, [39]
approval of, **27**, [38]
confirmation of, **27**, [38]
enforcement, **27**, [37]
local authority making, **27**, [118]
powers to make, **27**, [36]
proof of publication, **27**, [42]
proposed, inspection of, **27**, [40]
provisions in, **27**, [36]
publication of, **27**, [41]
carts, weighing, **27**, [24]
cattle. *See* **cattle**
cleansing and disinfection, **2**, [434]
completion, certificate of justices, **27**, [26]
corporation, offences by, **27**, [121]
days for holding, **45**, [922]
alteration of, **27**, [80]
appointment of, **27**, [17]
published in certain newspapers, **27**, [81]
district council functions, **25(1)**, [82]
holding, regulating, or prohibiting, **2**, [435]
lighting, provision for, **35(1)**, [23]
local authority—
acquisition by, **27**, [108]
byelaws, making, **27**, [118]
charges—
determining, **27**, [103], [111]
display of, **27**, [111]
excessive, demanding, **27**, [111]
payment, time for, **27**, [112]
recovery of, **27**, [113]
cold store, provision of, **27**, [116]
compulsory purchase of land, **27**, [123]
days and hours for, appointing, **27**, [103], [110]
establishment by, **27**, [108]
meaning, **27**, [119]
sale to, power of, **27**, [109]
temporary market, powers on, **27**, [106]

markets and fairs—*contd*
local authority—*contd*
weighing—
charges for, **27**, [112]
machines and scales, providing, **27**, [115]
London—
horticultural. *See* **horticultural produce**
street. *See* **street trading**
Market and Fairs Clauses Act 1847—
application of, **27**, [5]
Railways Clauses Acts 1845, incorporation of, **27**, [44]
market authority, meaning, **27**, [119]
See also local authority *above*
market officer—
authorised, meaning, **27**, [119]
distress, recovering charges by, **27**, [113]
information given to, **27**, [117]
metropolitan police district—
fairs in—
declaration of illegality—
magistrate making, **27**, [3]
suspension until trial by Queen's Bench, **27**, [4]
inquiry into, **27**, [3]
seven years, not held for, **27**, [49]
time for holding, **27**, [1], [2]
notice of opening, **27**, [15]
offences—
corporations, by, **27**, [121]
proceedings, institution of, **27**, [122]
summarily, triable, **27**, [120]
owner, meaning, **27**, [54], [79]
prohibited sales, **27**, [114]
rent—
collector, obstruction of, **27**, [34]
demand on completion of market, **27**, [25]
disputes, determination of, **27**, [33]
distress, recovery by, **27**, [32]
list of, publishing, **27**, [35]
payment of, **27**, [27]
variation, **27**, [30]
rent payable in respect of, **44(1)**, [98]
rights, charge to tax, **44(1)**, [34]
slaughter-houses in. *See* **slaughter-houses**
special Act—
acquisition of land subject to, **27**, [9]
alterations, certified copies of, **27**, [11]
copies, inspection of, **27**, [46]
Crown rights, saving for, **27**, [45]
errors and omissions, correction of, **27**, [10]
meaning, **27**, [6]
stallage—
collector, obstruction of, **27**, [34]
demand on completion of market, **27**, [25]
disputes, determination of, **27**, [33]
distress, recovery by, **27**, [32]
list of, publishing, **27**, [35]
payment of, **27**, [25], [27]
variation, **27**, [30]
summary offences, **27**, [120]
Sunday Fairs Act 1448, effect of repeal, **41**, [546]

markets and fairs—*contd*
superintendent, assaulting or obstructing, **27**, [18]
temporary, **27**, [106]
tolls—
 cattle, in respect of, **27**, [29], [89], [100]
 collector, obstruction of, **27**, [34]
 demand on completion of market, **27**, [25]
 disputes, determination of, **27**, [33]
 distress, recovery by, **27**, [32]
 greater than authorised, penalty for taking, **27**, [31]
 list of, publishing, **27**, [35]
 payment of, **27**, [25], [27]
 variation, **27**, [30]
 weighing, for, **27**, [28], [89]
undertakers—
 acquisition of land by, **27**, [9]
 additional land, appropriating, **27**, [12]
 annual accounts, **27**, [43]
 byelaws, publishing. *See* byelaws *above*
 damage by, satisfaction for, **27**, [14]
 execution of works by, **27**, [13]
 local authority, power to sell to, **27**, [109]
 notice of opening, giving, **27**, [15]
 slaughter-houses, powers on. *See*
  slaughter-houses
 special Act, failure to keep copies of, **27**, [47]
 weighing places, providing, **27**, [22]
unlicensed person, sales by, **27**, [16], [114]
weighing—
 carts, machines for, **27**, [24]
 charges for, **27**, [112]
 market authority, provision of machines and scales by, **27**, [115]
 provision of places for, **27**, [22]
 request of buyer, at, **27**, [23]
 tolls for, **27**, [28]
weights and measures, provision of, **27**, [1]

marriage
acquired gender, involving persons of, **27**, [211]
approved premises—
 offences, **27**, [273]
 regulations for, **27**, [258]
 solemnisation in, **27**, [259]
army overseas, evidence of records, **36**, [23], [24]
banns in other church, where, **14**, 1092
banns. *See* **banns of marriage**
birth outside, **6**, [277]
breach of promise, abolition of action, **27**, [346]
British subjects, between, facilities for, **27**, [174], [177]
certificate—
 falsification, **36**, [6]
 forgery, **36**, [6]
certificate by licence, abolition of, **31**, [335]
change of gender, following, **7(1)**, [723]
chapel—
 authorised, meaning, **27**, [275]
 extra-parochial place, in, **27**, [227]

marriage—*contd*
chapel—*contd*
 licensed, lists of, **27**, [271]
 licensing, **27**, [226]
 naval, military or air force. *See* naval, military and air force chapels *below*
 public, meaning, **27**, [226]
Church of England, according to rites of—
 benefices held in plurality, in, **27**, [229], [577]
 generally, **27**, [127]
 methods of authorising, **27**, [209]
 naval, military and air force chapels, licensing, **27**, [267]
 witnesses to, **27**, [228]
citizenship by virtue of. *See* **citizenship**
common licence, by—
 caveat entered against grant, **27**, [222]
 grant of, **27**, [222]
 meaning, **27**, [209]
 no impediment of affinity, declaration of, **27**, [222]
 places for solemnisation, **27**, [221]
 residence, proof of not necessary, **27**, [230]
 surrogate, grant by, **27**, [222]
 within three months, to be, **27**, [222]
consequential amendments, **31**, [354]
counselling, provision of, **27**, [642]
customary church or chapel, solemnised in, **27**, [128]
death, presumption of, **27**, [449]
detained person—
 meaning, **27**, [275], [539]
 place of residence, at, **27**, [232], [234], [539]
  meaning, **27**, [275]
 provisions applying to, **27**, [539]
 solemnisation, **27**, [256]
 statement accompanying notice of, **27**, [234]
 superintendent registrar's certificate, under, **27**, [232]
dissolution, presumption of death, on, **27**, [449]
distinct or district parish church, solemnised in, **27**, [130]
divorce. *See* **divorce**
divorced person, remarriage of, **27**, [338]
documents, sending by post, **36**, [64]
doubtful validity, of, **27**, [127], [163], [619]
engagement—
 property, ownership of, **27**, [347]
 ring, gift of, **27**, [348]
 termination, effect of, **27**, [347]
evidence of, savings in certain repeals, **41**, [571]
evidence, required by superintendent registrar, **27**, [238]
extra-parochial place, in, **27**, [227]
false statement relating to, **12(1)**, [197]
forced marriage protection order—
 appeals, **27(S)**, Matrimonial 14
 application for, **27(S)**, Matrimonial 4–5
 contempt proceedings, **27(S)**, Matrimonial 14

marriage—*contd*
forced marriage protection order—*contd*
contents of, **27(S)**, Matrimonial 3
duration of, **27(S)**, Matrimonial 7
ex parte, **27(S)**, Matrimonial 6
guidance, issue of, **27(S)**, Matrimonial 15
interpretation, **27(S)**, Matrimonial 16
jurisdiction—
High Court, of **27(S)**, Matrimonial 12
magistrates' courts, extension to,
27(S), Matrimonial 13
Northern Ireland—
appeals, **27(S)**, Matrimonial 22–3
application for,
27(S), Matrimonial 19–20
contempt proceedings,
27(S), Matrimonial 22
contents of, **27(S)**, Matrimonial 19
duration of, **27(S)**, Matrimonial 20
enforcement, **27(S)**, Matrimonial 21
ex parte, **27(S)**, Matrimonial 20
guidance, issue of,
27(S), Matrimonial 24
interpretation, **27(S)**, Matrimonial 25
jurisdiction, **27(S)**, Matrimonial 22
occasions for making,
27(S), Matrimonial 19–20
orders, **27(S)**, Matrimonial 24
other protection or assistance, not
affecting, **27(S)**, Matrimonial 25
power to make,
27(S), Matrimonial 18–19
variation and discharge,
27(S), Matrimonial 21
occasions for making,
27(S), Matrimonial 4–5
other protection or assistance, not
affecting, **27(S)**, Matrimonial 15
power of arrest, attachment of—
arrest under, **27(S)**, Matrimonial 9
power of, **27(S)**, Matrimonial 8–9
power to make, **27(S)**, Matrimonial 2
remand of arrested person—
medical examination and report, for,
27(S), Matrimonial 12
powers of court, **27(S)**, Matrimonial 11
supplementary provisions,
27(S), Matrimonial 17
undertakings in place of,
27(S), Matrimonial 7
variation and discharge,
27(S), Matrimonial 8
warrant, arrest under,
27(S), Matrimonial 10
foreign. *See* **foreign marriage**
foreigner, with—
abroad, **27**, [165]
caveat, entering, **27**, [165], [171]
certificate showing no impediment,
obtaining, **27**, [165]
conditions for obtaining certificate,
27, [165], [171]
forbidding, **27**, [171]
generally, **27**, [127]
Jewish, both parties being, **27**, [166]

marriage—*contd*
foreigner, with—*contd*
notice of, **27**, [165]
regulations, power to make, **27**, [167]
United Kingdom, in, **27**, [166]
generally, **27**, [127]
Greek, **27**, [596]
guild church, in, **14**, 464
hours for solemnisation, **27**, [208]
house-bound person—
meaning, **27**, [275], [539]
medical certificate accompanying notice
of, **27**, [234]
place of residence, at, **27**, [232], [234],
[539]
meaning, **27**, [275]
provisions applying to, **27**, [539]
solemnisation of, **27**, [256]
superintendent registrar's certificate, under,
27, [232]
immigration control, party subject to—
Northern Ireland, **31**, [506]–[507]
permission, application for, **31**, [508]
procedure, **31**, [504]
regulations, **31**, [505]
residence, declaration of, **31**, [505]
information on, obtaining, **40(1)**, [630]
inter-denominational building, in, **14**, 674–5
jactitation of, **27**, [595]
Jewish, registration of, **36**, [53]
Jews—
between, **27**, [166]
superintendent registrar's certificate, under,
27, [232]
judicial separation. *See* **separation**
licence, common, **14(S)**, 213–14
marital status, declaration as to—
application for, **27**, [591]
Attorney-General, papers sent to, **27**, [593]
effect of, **27**, [592]
form of, **27**, [594]
generally, **27**, [127]
hearing in camera, **27**, [594]
jurisdiction, **27**, [591]
making, **27**, [592]
rules of court, **27**, [594]
types of, **27**, [591]
matters not necessary to validity, proof of,
27, [261]
minor, of, consent to—
evidence of, **27**, [343]
persons giving, **27**, [207]
Registrar General's licence, marriage on,
27, [356]
naval, military and air force chapels, in—
authorisation of, **27**, [266]
certified chapels, **27**, [266]
Church of England rites, according to,
27, [267]
evidence of, **27**, [269]
provisions applying to, **27**, [281]–[284]
qualified persons, **27**, [266]
registration, **27**, [268]
notice book, **27**, [233]
notice of, **31**, [336]

marriage—*contd*
nullity of—
decrees nisi—
decrees to be, **27**, [691]
proceedings after, general powers of
court, **27**, [691]
financial provision orders, **27**, [684]
generally, **27**, [127]
property adjustment orders, **27**, [684]
Queen's Proctor, intervention of, **27**, [691]
stay of proceedings, **27**, [685]
offences—
authorised persons, by, **27**, [274]
Registrar General's licence, solemnisation
on, **27**, [366]
solemnisation, relating to, **27**, [273]
order, removal of doubt by, **27**, [127], [163],
[193]
outside England & Wales, proof, **18**, [172]
parish—
adjoining, church etc, in registration in
books of, **36**, [53]
meaning, **36**, [68]
parish church, in, **14**, 1000
persons of acquired gender, involving,
27, [211]
persons under age, between, **27**, [206]
polygamous—
matrimonial relief in case of, **27**, [484]
potentially, validity in English law,
27, [615]–[616]
validity, declaration of, **27**, [484]
void, being, **27**, [441]
prohibited degrees, within—
child of the family, person not being,
27, [279]
common licence, grant of, **27**, [222]
superintendent registrar's certificate,
under, **27**, [235]
void, not to be, **27**, [579]
parent or child of dead spouse, to,
27, [205], [280]
common licence, grant of, **27**, [222]
superintendent registrar's certificate,
under, **27**, [236]
void, not to be, **27**, [579]
statutory exemptions, **27**, [329]
void, being, **27**, [205], [210], [278], [441]
property transfers in connection with, stamp
duty exemption, **41**, [150]
Quaker, registration of, **36**, [53]
refusal to issue certificate, **31**, [337]
register as evidence of, **27**, [129]
register books—
any church etc in same parish, **36**, [53]
custody of, **36**, [57]
disposal of, **36**, [60]
entries, certified copies—
fees, **36**, [55]
Registrar General, returns to, **36**, [56]
superintendent registrar, returns to,
36, [55]
entries, persons authorised to make,
36, [53]
errors, correction of, **36**, [59]

marriage—*contd*
register books—*contd*
filled, custody of, **36**, [58]
form of, **36**, [53]
indexes, searches of, **36**, [62], [63]
particular search, meaning, **36**, [65]
provision of, **36**, [52]
searches and fees, **36**, [61]
See also registers *below*
register, making false instrument, **12(1)**, [724]
register of—
custody of, **14**, 934
provision of, **14**, 949
search in, **14**, 946–8
register office, in—
religious ceremony following, **27**, [257]
solemnisation, **27**, [255]
registered building, in—
authorised persons, appointment of,
27, [253]; **36**, [50]
cancellation of registration, **27**, [252]
certificate and licence, custody of,
27, [263]
lists of, **27**, [271]
not certified, effect of, **27**, [262]
registration, **27**, [251]
solemnisation in, **27**, [254]
registers—
army, air force and marine registers,
validation of entries, **36**, [146]
compilation, **36**, [1]
deposit of, **36**, [16]
evidence, as, **36**, [4], [11]
falsification, **36**, [6]
fire-resisting boxes, provision, **36**, [131]
non-parochial—
extracts, **36**, [7]–[11]
searches, **36**, [3]
preservation, **36**, [1]
See also register books *above*
Registrar General's licence, by—
application for, reporting, **27**, [354]
caveat, entering, **27**, [355]
evidence of capacity, etc, **27**, [353]
fees, **27**, [367]
issue of, **27**, [357]
licence, period of validity, **27**, [358]
manner of solemnisation, **27**, [360]
marriages applying to, **27**, [351]
notice of, **27**, [352]
offences relating to, **27**, [366]
person to whom authority delivered,
27, [364]
person under eighteen, consent to,
27, [356]
place of, **27**, [359]
registration, **27**, [365]
regulations, power to make, **27**, [368]
religious ceremony following, **27**, [361]
seriously ill person, of, **27**, [353]
validity of licence, period of, **27**, [358]
validity, proof of matters not necessary to,
27, [362]
void, provisions on, **27**, [363]
registrar, fee of, **27**, [264]

marriage—*contd*
  registrars—
    delivery up of books etc on ceasing to hold office, **36**, [134]
    deputies, **36**, [127]
    fees, **36**, [135]
  registration—
    adjoining parish, church etc in, books of, **36**, [53]
    any church etc in same parish, in books of, **36**, [53]
    armed forces overseas, **36**, [1], [23], [24]
    clergyman not incumbent of church etc, by, **36**, [53]
    district register offices, **36**, [129]
    districts, organisation into, **36**, [1]
    duplicate, **36**, [53]
    local schemes—
      matters to be included, **36**, [132]
      preparation, **36**, [1], [133]
      submission and approval, **36**, [133]
    manner of, **36**, [53]
    offences and penalties, **36**, [67]
    officials, employment status of, **36**, [204]
    particulars, power to ask for, **36**, [54]
    persons by whom to be registered, **36**, [51], [53]
    quarterly returns, **36**, [55], [56]
    regulations, power to make, **36**, [66], [137]
    service civilians overseas, **36**, [142]
    sub-district register offices, **36**, [130]
    sub-districts, organisation into, **36**, [1]
    summary of provisions, **36**, [1]
  registration of, **27**, [127]
  regulations, power to make, **27**, [272]
  repair and rebuilding of church, solemnisation during, **27**, [224]
  royal, **10**, [98]–[99]
  Scotland—
    one party residing in, **27**, [201], [307]
    parent of one party residing in, **27**, [307]
  separation. *See* **separation**
  service chapel, in, **3**, [1]
  sex change of one party, following, **27**, [249]
  shared church buildings, in, **14**, 674–5
  Society of Friends, according to usage of, **36**, [53]
  solemnisation—
    approval of premises for, **27**, [258]
    church in parish with which party has qualifying connection, in, **14(S)**, 211–13
    divorced person, remarriage of, **27**, [338]
    hours for, **27**, [208]
    offences relating to, **27**, [273]
  solemnisation of, persons qualified for, **14**, 1187
  special licence, grant of, **27**, [209], [276], [369]
  superintendent registrars—
    delivery up of books etc on ceasing to hold office, **36**, [134]
    fees, **36**, [135]
    indexes kept by, searches, **36**, [62]
    meaning, **36**, [65]

marriage—*contd*
  superintendent registrars—*contd*
    quarterly returns—
      by, **36**, [56]
      to, **36**, [55]
  superintendent registrar's certificate, under—
    applicable period, to be within, **27**, [243]
    authorisation by, **27**, [209]
    caveat, entry of, **27**, [239]
    church or chapel, in, **27**, [223]
    declaration of affinal relationship, after, **27**, [235]
    detained person, of, **27**, [232], [234], [539]
    evidence required for, **27**, [238]
    fee for, **27**, [233], [264]
    forbidding issue of, **27**, [240]
    forms of, **27**, [250]
    HM ship, issue on board, **27**, [248]
    house-bound person, of, **27**, [232], [234], [539]
    Jewish marriage, under, **27**, [232]
    licence, without, **27**, [241]
      appeals, **27**, [242]
    Northern Ireland, one party residing in, **27**, [247]
    notice of, **27**, [233]
    offences, **27**, [273]
    parent or child of dead spouse, to, **27**, [236]
    person to whom delivered, **27**, [263]
    registration district, in—
      neither party residing in, **27**, [245]
      one party residing in, **27**, [244]
    Scotland, one party residing in, **27**, [246]
    solemn declaration with notice, **27**, [237]
    solemnisation, where permitted, **27**, [223], [232]
    usual place of worship, in, **27**, [245]
  support services, funding for, **27**, [641]
  suspicious, duty to report, **31**, [249]
  usual place of worship, in, **27**, [245], [270]
  validity of, colonial laws, **7(2)**, [364]
  void—
    belief that marriage was valid, **6**, [156]
    legitimacy of child of, **6**, [1], [156]
    meaning, **6**, [165]
    See also **void marriage**
  voidable. *See* **voidable marriage**
  Wales and Monmouthshire, in, **14**, 293
  war damage, where church injured by, **27**, [225]
  ward of court, consent to, **27**, [207]
  Welsh language, in, **27**, [265]
  will—
    dissolution, effect of, **50**, [497]
    made in contemplation of, **50**, [496]
    revoked by, **50**, [496]
  witnesses to, **27**, [228]; **36**, [53]

married couple
  connected persons, meaning, **44(4)**, [1001]–[1002], [1028]
  income tax liability, reductions for, **44(4)**, [26]
  references to married persons, **44(4)**, [1018]

married couple—*contd*
tax reductions for. *See under* **personal reliefs**

married woman. *See also* **husband and wife**
bankruptcy, subject to law of, **27**, [195]
capacity, **27**, [195]
children, policy of assurance benefiting,
    27, [132]
contract—
    ante-nuptial, liability for, **27**, [197]
    capacity to sue and be sued, **27**, [195]
dependent domicile, abolition of, **27**, [495]
housekeeping allowance, money and property
    derived from, **27**, [336]
husband's money, fraudulent investment with,
    27, [131]
independent domicile, having, **27**, [495]
judgments and orders against, enforcement,
    27, [195]
life insurance policy and part of estate of,
    27, [132]
property—
    capacity to deal with, **27**, [195]
    husband, holding jointly with, **27**, [198]
    questions as to, orders on, **27**, [133], [310]
    restraint upon anticipation, abolition of,
        27, [287]
    separate, dealing with, **27**, [196]
protector of the settlement, as, **20**, [98]
tort—
    capacity to sue and be sued, **27**, [195]
    husband's liability for, abolition of,
        27, [197]
will, provisions on, **27**, [160]

Marshall Aid
Commemoration Commission, **15(1)**, [244]
scholarships, **15(1)**, [243]
    increase in, **15(1)**, [246]

massage etc establishments (London)
advertising—
    offences, **25(1)**, [138]
    restrictions, **25(1)**, [257]
amendment of enactments, **26(2)**, [163]
application of provisions, **26(2)**, [164]
byelaws—
    advertising, **25(1)**, [257]
    exhibition of, **25(1)**, [137]
    power to make, **25(1)**, [137], [471]
charges, scales of, **25(1)**, [471]
entry by officer, **25(1)**, [136]
entry, powers of, **25(2)**, [969]
existing, application of provisions to,
    25(2), [970]
inspection—
    obstruction of, **25(1)**, [138]
    powers of, **25(1)**, [136]
licence—
    appeals, **25(2)**, [967]; **26(2)**, [163]
    applicant—
        fees to be paid by, **25(1)**, [135];
        25(2), [409]
        matters to be stated by, **25(1)**, [135]

massage etc establishments (London)—*contd*
licence—*contd*
    applicant—*contd*
        misrepresentation by, **25(1)**, [138]
        application for, **25(2)**, [961]
    cancellation, **25(2)**, [963]
    conditions, **25(2)**, [960]
    enforcement, **25(2)**, [968]
    necessity for, **25(1)**, [135]
    operating without, **25(1)**, [138]
    particulars required for, **25(1)**, [135]
    period of, **25(1)**, [135]
    provisional grant, **25(2)**, [965]
    refusal of, **25(2)**, [962]
    refusal or revocation—
        appeal against, **25(1)**, [135]
        grounds for, **25(1)**, [135]
    renewal and transfer, **26(2)**, [163]
    requirement of, **25(2)**, [960]
    standard terms, conditions and restrictions,
        25(2), [964]
    temporary, fees for, **25(2)**, [410]
    transmission, **25(2)**, [963]
    variation, **25(2)**, [966]
licensing—
    authority, meaning, **25(1)**, [134]
    exemptions, **25(1)**, [140]; **25(2)**, [559],
        [669]
    local enactments, modification of,
        25(2), [416]
local enactments—
    modified, **25(2)**, [567], [670], [673]
    repealed, **25(2)**, [568]
meaning, **25(1)**, [134]
offences and penalties, **25(1)**, [138]
    directors' liability, **25(1)**, [139]
    increased fines, **25(2)**, [525], [527]
premises exempt from provisions,
    25(1), [140]; **25(2)**, [559], [669]
special treatment premises, as, **25(2)**, [958]
termination of registration, **26(1)**, [238]

master (of ship)
application of provisions, **39(2)**, [691]
arrest, power of, **39(2)**, [773]
change of, handing over of documents,
    39(2), [747]
dangerously unsafe ship, liability for,
    39(2), [762]
delivery of offender by, **39(2)**, [581]
disbursements, lien for, **39(2)**, [708]
drink or drugs, capacity affected by,
    39(2), [1044]
    arrest without warrant, **39(2)**, [1051]
    Crown service, application of provisions
        to, **39(2)**, [1055]
    detention pending arrival of police,
        39(2), [1050]
    drug, meaning, **39(2)**, [1054]
    enforcement, **39(2)**, [1048]
    orders and regulations, **39(2)**, [1053]
    prescribed limit, **39(2)**, [1047]
    right of entry on ship, **39(2)**, [1052]
    specimens, provision of, **39(2)**, [1049]
    territorial application, **39(2)**, [1056]

master (of ship)—*contd*
offenders, return of, **39(2)**, [960]
passengers, returns as to, **39(2)**, [775]
remuneration, lien for, **39(2)**, [708]

Master of the Rolls
administrative functions, delegation of,
　11(3), [127]; **11(4)**, [549]
appointment of, **11(2)**, [677]
clerk and secretary to, **11(2)**, [771]
Court of Appeal civil division, president of,
　11(2), [670]
manorial documents, custody of, **20**, [495]
precedence, **11(2)**, [680]
public records for which responsible,
　18, [188]
solicitors—
　admission, application for, to, **11(2)**, [280];
　　11(4), [374]
　appeal—
　　disciplinary proceedings, in, **11(2)**, [330]
　　practising certificate, in connection
　　　with, **11(2)**, [288]
　　removal or restoration of name, as to,
　　　11(2), [283]
　　right of, **11(2)**, [307]
　　suspension of certificate, on, **11(2)**, [291]
　jurisdiction over, protection, **11(2)**, [328],
　　[331]; **11(4)**, [426]
　practice rules, approval of, **11(2)**, [310]
　regulations, **11(2)**, [307]

matches
manufacture—
　licence to—
　　duty, no charge of, **13**, [911]
　　surrender or revocation, **13**, [911]

maternity. *See also* **confinement; pregnancy**
leave—
　additional, **16**, [702]
　compulsory, **16**, [701]
　ordinary, **16**, [700]
　redundancy and dismissal during, **16**, [703]
　regulations, **16**, [704]
　sex discrimination during, **7(1)**, [40]
　unfair dismissal relating to, **16**, [746]
information on, obtaining, **40(1)**, [630]
pay. *See* **statutory maternity pay**
suspension from work on grounds of—
　alternative work, right to offer of,
　　16, [696]
　meaning, **16**, [695]
　remuneration—
　　calculation of, **16**, [697]
　　right to, **16**, [698]
unfair dismissal for reasons of, **16**, [746]
unfair employment-related benefit scheme
　provisions, **40(1)**, [205]

maternity allowance
appropriate weekly rate, **40(1)**, [272]
confinement, meaning, **40(1)**, [271]
contribution conditions, **40(1)**, [260]
contributory, being, **40(1)**, [259]

maternity allowance—*contd*
entitlement to, **40(1)**, [271]

maternity home. *See* **nursing home**

maternity treatment
European Community, in, **40(1)**, [1], [144]

matrimonial causes
adultery, finding of, **18**, [205]
child—
　county court jurisdiction, **27**, [558]
　orders under 1965 Act, **27**, [493]
　satisfaction with arrangements for,
　　27, [483]
　welfare, consideration of, **27**, [508]
circuit judge, jurisdiction of, **27**, [560]
county court—
　jurisdiction, **27**, [496], [557]
　magistrates' court orders, powers relating
　　to, **27**, [518]
family business—
　meaning, **27**, [556]
　transfer of—
　　county court, to, **27**, [565]
　　directions as to, **27**, [566]
　　High Court, to, **27**, [567], [599]
family proceedings—
　meaning, **27**, [556]
　principal registry of Family Division,
　　commencement in, **27**, [571]
　rules—
　　Lord Chancellor, made upon request
　　　of, **27**, [570]
　　power to make, **27**, [568]
　　process for making, **27**, [569]
financial provision not made, relief, **18**, [613]
financial provision order—
　age limit of child for purposes of,
　　27, [469], [505]
　agreement between parties on, **27**, [506]
　anti-avoidance provisions, **27**, [478]
　arrangements regarding, **27**, [636]
　arrears—
　　enforcement of payment, **27**, [472]
　　remission of, **27**, [471]
　child, for benefit of, **27**, [454], [469], [502]
　child of the family, consideration of
　　welfare, **27**, [460]
　civil partnership, effect of formation of,
　　27, [504]
　commencement of proceedings, **27**, [466]
　consent order, **27**, [474]
　county court, in, **27**, [451], [558]
　decree, on grant of, **27**, [454]
　discharge of, **27**, [471]
　duration of, **27**, [468], [504]
　enforcement, **27**, [522]
　formation of civil partnership, effect of,
　　27, [468]
　grounds of application for, **27**, [501]
　magistrates' court, in, **27**, [637]
　High Court, case more suitable for,
　　27, [517]
　interim, **27**, [509]

matrimonial causes—*contd*
  financial provision order—*contd*
    lump sum order—
      instalments, paid in, **27**, [454]
        variation of, **27**, [513]
      maximum amount, **27**, [502]
        exceeding, **27**, [510]
      power to make, **27**, [451], [454], [502]
    made under 1965 Act, **27**, [493]
    maintenance agreements. *See* **maintenance**
    matters to be considered, **27**, [460], [503]
    meaning, **27**, [451], [684]
    mentally disordered person, in favour of,
      27, [481]
    neglect to maintain, in case of, **27**, [467]
    overseas proceedings, after—
      anti-avoidance provisions, **27**, [553]
      application for, **27**, [542]
      child, for benefit of, **27**, [548]
      consent order, **27**, [549]
      England and Wales, whether proper
        venue, **27**, [546]
      interim, **27**, [544]
      jurisdiction, **27**, [545]
      leave to apply for, **27**, [543]
      matrimonial home in England or Wales,
        jurisdiction founded on, **27**, [550]
      matters to be considered, **27**, [548]
      power to make, **27**, [547]
      prospective applications, transactions to
        defeat, **27**, [553]
    parties living apart by agreement, where,
      27, [507]
    parties living together, effect on, **27**, [515]
    pensions—
      generally, **27**, [462]
      lump sums, **27**, [463]
      Pension Protection Fund, **27**, [465]
      supplementary, **27**, [464]
    periodical payments, for—
      death of payer, **27**, [471]
      power to make, **27**, [451], [454], [502]
      variation, revival and revocation,
        27, [510]–[512]
    power of court to make, **27**, [454], [502]
    reconciliation, possibility of, **27**, [516]
    remarriage, effect of, **27**, [468], [504]
    repayment, order for, **27**, [473], [479],
      [523]
    sale of property, order for, **27**, [456]
    secured and unsecured payments orders,
      27, [684]
    suspension of, **27**, [471]
    termination of financial obligations,
      27, [461]
    variation of, **27**, [471]
  generally, **27**, [127]
  High Court—
    appeals to, **27**, [519]
    jurisdiction, **27**, [496]
    magistrates' court orders, powers relating
      to, **27**, [518]
  magistrates' court, in—
    appeals, **27**, [519]
    constitution of, **27**, [521]

matrimonial causes—*contd*
  magistrates' court, in—*contd*
    enforcement of orders, **27**, [522]
    financial provision order, making. *See*
      financial provision order *above*
    jurisdiction of, **27**, [520]
    orders, powers of High Court and county
      court in relation to, **27**, [518]
    transitional provisions, **27**, [528]
  orders made under 1965 Act, **27**, [493]
  pension sharing order—
    charges, apportionment of, **27**, [459]
    generally, **27**, [452], [457]
    stay, duty to, **27**, [458]
  proceedings—
    meaning, **18**, [205]
    staying, **27**, [499]
  property adjustment order—
    anti-avoidance provisions, **27**, [451]
    bankruptcy of settlor, effect of, **27**, [480]
    child in favour of, **27**, [455], [469]
    child of the family, consideration of
      welfare, **27**, [460]
    commencement of proceedings, **27**, [466]
    consent order, powers over, **27**, [474]
    county court jurisdiction, **27**, [558]
    decree, on grant of, **27**, [455]
    discharge of, **27**, [471]
    formation of civil partnership, effect of,
      27, [468]
    instrument for effecting, settling, **27**, [470]
    matters to be considered, **27**, [460]
    meaning, **27**, [451]
    mentally disordered person, in favour of,
      27, [481]
    overseas proceedings, after—
      anti-avoidance provisions, **27**, [553]
      application for, **27**, [542]
      child, for benefit of, **27**, [548]
      consent order, **27**, [549]
      England and Wales, whether proper
        venue, **27**, [546]
      jurisdiction, **27**, [545]
      leave to apply for, **27**, [543]
      matrimonial home in England and Wales,
        jurisdiction founded on, **27**, [550]
      matters to be considered, **27**, [548]
      power to make, **27**, [547]
      prospective applications, transactions to
        prevent, **27**, [554]
    pensions—
      generally, **27**, [462]
      lump sums, **27**, [463]
      Pension Protection Fund, **27**, [465]
      supplementary, **27**, [464]
    remarriage, effect of, **27**, [468]
    sale of property, order for, **27**, [456]
    suspension of, **27**, [471]
    termination of financial obligations,
      27, [461]
    variation of, **27**, [471]
  transitional provisions, **27**, [491]–[493]

matrimonial home
charge on—
  priority, postponement of, **27**, [686]
  registration of—
    cancellation of—
      contract for sale, on, **27**, [686]
      termination of marriage, on, **27**, [686]
    restriction where spouse entitled to more
      than one charge, **27**, [686]
    rights of occupation as, **27**, [646], [649]
dwelling house—
  mortgage, where subject to, **27**, [669]
  rights of occupation as charge on,
    27, [646]
generally, **27**, [127]
interpretation provisions, **27**, [678]
land charge arising, **21**, [392]
minor and consequential amendments,
  27, [803]–[5]
non-molestation orders, contempt proceedings
  for non-compliance, **27**, [673]
occupation orders—
  agreement to marry, evidence of, **27**, [659]
  appeals, **27**, [676]
  applicant has estate or interest, where,
    27, [648]
  associated person, meaning of, **27**, [677]
  breach of—
    arrest for, **27**, [662]
    committal order, power of magistrates'
      court to suspend execution of,
      27, [665]
    contempt proceedings, **27**, [673]
    guardianship, power of magistrates' court
      to order, **27**, [666]
    hospital admission, power of magistrates'
      court to order, **27**, [666]
    remand—
      bail, on, **27**, [687]
      custody, in, **27**, [687]
      further, **27**, [687]
      medical examination and report, for,
        27, [663]
      postponement of taking of
        recognizance, **27**, [687]
  cohabitants, meaning of, **27**, [677]
  discharge of, **27**, [664]
  discharge of rent, mortgage payments etc,
    obligations as to, **27**, [655]
  ex parte orders, **27**, [660]
  furniture or other contents, obligations as
    to, **27**, [655]
  generally, **27**, [127]
  jurisdiction of courts, **27**, [672]
  meaning, **27**, [654]
  neither cohabitant or former cohabitant
    entitled to occupy, **27**, [653]
  neither spouse entitled to occupy, **27**, [652]
  one cohabitant or former cohabitant with
    no existing right to occupy, where,
    27, [651]
  one former civil partner with no existing
    right to occupy, where, **27**, [650]
  one former spouse with no existing right
    to occupy, where, **27**, [650]

matrimonial home—*contd*
occupation orders—*contd*
  relevant child, meaning of, **27**, [677]
  repair and maintenance, obligations as to,
    27, [655]
  separate representation for children,
    provision of, **27**, [679]
  supplementary provisions, **27**, [654]
  third parties acting on behalf of victims of
    domestic violence, application by,
    27, [675]
  undertakings, **27**, [661]
  variation of, **27**, [664]
rights—
  charge, occupation as, **27**, [646]
  court orders. *See* occupation orders *above*
  generally, **27**, [127]
  jurisdiction of courts, **27**, [672]
  one spouse having no estate, where,
    27, [645]
  release of, **27**, [686]
rights of occupation, **21**, [600], [608];
  22, [801]
surviving spouse or civil partner's rights as
  to, **18**, [569], [572]
transfer of tenancies on divorce. *See* **divorce**
  orders, **27**, [552]

matrimonial proceedings
custody of child, arising in course of. *See*
  child
meaning, **6**, [238]

Mauritius
British ship registered in, **7(2)**, [625]
Commonwealth citizenship, **31**, [186]
existing law, operation of, **7(2)**, [792]
fully responsible status of, **7(2)**, [620]
Judicial Committee of Privy Council,
  jurisdiction, **7(2)**, [793]
legislative powers of, **7(2)**, [624]
meaning, **7(2)**, [622]
visiting forces in, **7(2)**, [625]

mayor. *See* **London borough**

Mayor of London
acting, **26(1)**, [770]
air quality strategy—
  consultations, **26(1)**, [710]
  contents of, **26(1)**, [710]
  directions to local authorities, **26(1)**, [713]
  information, advice and assistance, provision
    of, **26(1)**, [713]
  local authorities taking account of,
    26(1), [713]
  preparation and publication of, **26(1)**, [710]
  Secretary of State, directions by,
    26(1), [711]
annual report, **26(1)**, [478]
annual spending plan—
  admissible factors in preparing, **26(1)**, [532]
  form and contents of, **26(1)**, [530]
  functional bodies, statement for,
    26(1), [530]

Mayor of London—*contd*
  annual spending plan—*contd*
    information, supply of, **26(1)**, [533]
    preparation of, **26(1)**, [531]
  appointments by, confirmation hearings,
    26(1), [493], [772]
  Assembly, periodic report to, **26(1)**, [477]
  aviation noise, consultation on, **26(1)**, [716]
  Biodiversity Action Plan, **26(1)**, [694]
  chairman of principal council, treatment as,
    26(1), [507]
  climate change—
    adaptation strategy—
      directions to revise, **26(1)**, [709]
      preparation and publication of,
        26(1), [708]
    duties with respect to, **26(1)**, [705]
    London climate change mitigation and
      energy strategy—
      directions to revise, **26(1)**, [707]
      preparation and publication of,
        26(1), [706]
  consultation by, **26(1)**, [473], [474]
  cultural bodies, exercise of powers of
    appointment, **26(1)**, [722]
  declaration of acceptance of office,
    26(1), [460]
  delegation of functions, **26(1)**, [470]
  Deputy, **26(1)**, [481], [770]
  disqualification—
    bankrupt, of, **26(1)**, [452]
    grounds for, **26(1)**, [452]
    paid officer of London borough council,
      of, **26(1)**, [452]
    proceedings for, **26(1)**, [454]
  draft housing strategy, submission to Secretary
    of State, **26(2)**, [483]
  election of—
    first preference vote, **26(1)**, [766]
    second preference vote, **26(1)**, [766]
    three or more candidates, where,
      26(1), [766]
  failure to attend meetings, **26(1)**, [443]
  functions, exercise of—
    Authority, on behalf of, **26(1)**, [539]
    review by Assembly, **26(1)**, [491]
  grants, distribution of, **26(1)**, [524]
  Greater London Authority—
    as member of, **26(1)**, [432]
    functions, exercise of, **26(1)**, [467]
  guidance to, **46**, [928]
  health inequalities strategy—
    persons living in Greater London,
      inequalities between, **26(1)**, [664]
    preparation and publication of, **26(1)**, [663]
    procedure, **26(1)**, [665]
    relevant bodies or persons, **26(1)**, [663]
    revision, **26(1)**, [665]
    Secretary of State, directions by,
      26(1), [666]
  information schemes—
    authorities, binding on, **26(1)**, [737]
    power to make, **26(1)**, [736]
    provisions in, **26(1)**, [736]
    revocation, **26(1)**, [738]

Mayor of London—*contd*
  information schemes—*contd*
    variation, **26(1)**, [738]
  London ambient noise strategy, **26(1)**, [715]
  London Assembly member, election of,
    26(1), [438]
  London bus service permit, guidance
    document for, **26(1)**, [579], [585], [586]
  London Fire and Emergency Planning
    Authority—
    directions to, **26(1)**, [672]
    Secretary of State, directions from,
      26(1), [673]
  London housing strategy—
    draft, submission to Secretary of State,
      26(1), [675]
    Homes and Communities Agency, duties
      of, **26(1)**, [677]
    preparation and publication of, **26(1)**, [674]
    reviews, **26(1)**, [676]
  London Pensions Fund Authority, functions
    relating to, **26(1)**, [742]
  London Regional Development Agency. *See*
    London Development Agency
  municipal waste strategy plan—
    consultations, **26(1)**, [695]
    implementation, directions for, **26(1)**, [698]
    preparation and publication of, **26(1)**, [695]
    Secretary of State, directions by,
      26(1), [696]
    waste collection and disposal authorities
      having regard to, **26(1)**, [697]
  museums and galleries, assistance for,
    26(1), [721]
  ordinary election for, **26(1)**, [432]
    addresses, free delivery of, **26(1)**, [448],
      [768]
    cost, recovery of, **26(1)**, [449]
    definitions, **26(1)**, [461]
    Secretary of State, expenditure of,
      26(1), [450]
    time of, **26(1)**, [433]
    voting at, **26(1)**, [434]
  payments on ceasing to hold office,
    26(1), [458]
  pensions, **26(1)**, [457]
  People's Question Time, holding, **26(1)**, [480]
  planning applications—
    determining, **26(2)**, [485]
    obligations, agreeing, **26(2)**, [486], [488]
    representation hearings, **26(2)**, [489]
  planning, functions as to, **26(1)**, [690]
  political advisers, **26(1)**, [501]
  proposals to, **26(1)**, [492]
  qualification to be, **26(1)**, [451]
  remuneration, publication of information as
    to, **26(1)**, [459]
  resignation, **26(1)**, [442]
  salaries and expenses, **26(1)**, [455]
  severance payments, **43(S)**, 880
  staff—
    appointment of, **26(1)**, [501]
    disqualification and political restriction,
      26(1), [502]

Mayor of London—*contd*
  staff—*contd*
    terms and conditions of employment,
      26(1), [503]
  State of London debate, holding, **26(1)**, [479]
  state of the environment report, **26(1)**, [693]
  strategies—
    air quality. *See* air quality strategy *above*
    availability of, **26(1)**, [475]
    climate charge. *See* climate change *above*
    consultation on, **26(1)**, [473], [474]
    culture, **26(1)**, [720]
    current version, meaning, **26(1)**, [475]
    functional bodies to have regard to,
      26(1), [717]
    general duties, **26(1)**, [472]
    health. *See* health inequalities strategy *above*
    housing. *See* London housing strategy *above*
    improvements in health, promotion of,
      26(1), [472]
    matters to be considered, **26(1)**, [472]
    noise. *See* London ambient noise strategy
      above
    publicity for, **26(1)**, [475]
    Secretary of State, directions by,
      26(1), [476]
    spatial development—
      alteration, **26(1)**, [685]
      contents of, **26(1)**, [678]
      data collection, **26(1)**, [688]
      examination in public, **26(1)**, [682]
      functional bodies having regard to,
        26(1), [689]
      implementation, monitoring,
        26(1), [688]
      matters affecting, **26(1)**, [686]
      preparation of, **26(1)**, [678]
      public participation, **26(1)**, [679]
      publication, **26(1)**, [681]
      regulations, **26(1)**, [687]
      replacement, **26(1)**, [685]
      review of, **26(1)**, [684]
      review of matters affecting, **26(1)**, [683]
      statements in, **26(1)**, [678]
      withdrawal, **26(1)**, [680]
    transport. *See* transport strategy *below*
    waste. *See* municipal waste strategy plan
      above
  temporary incapacity—
    exercise of functions during, **26(1)**, [771]
    meaning, **26(1)**, [769]
  term of office, **26(1)**, [432]
  transport—
    general duty, **26(1)**, [540]
    policies for, **26(1)**, [540]
    strategy. *See* transport strategy *below*
  Transport for London—
    directions to, **26(1)**, [554]
    transfer of functions, **26(1)**, [557]
  transport strategy—
    local implementation plan—
      approval of, **26(1)**, [545]
      consultation, **26(1)**, [544]
      directions, issue of, **26(1)**, [552]

Mayor of London—*contd*
  transport strategy—*contd*
    local implementation plan—*contd*
      implementation by borough council,
        26(1), [550]
      implementation by Mayor, **26(1)**, [551]
      mayor, preparation by, **26(1)**, [546]
      preparation of, **26(1)**, [544]
      revised, power of Mayor to prepare,
        26(1), [548]
      revision of, **26(1)**, [547], [548]
    London borough councils, duties of,
      26(1), [543]
    preparation and publication of, **26(1)**, [541]
    Secretary of State, directions by,
      26(1), [542]
  unqualified person, acts by, **26(1)**, [453]
  vacancy in office—
    casual, date of, **26(1)**, [445]
    declaration of, **26(1)**, [444]
    exercise of functions during, **26(1)**, [770]
    filling, **26(1)**, [446]
  waste contracts, information about—
    confidentiality, **26(1)**, [703]
    existing, **26(1)**, [701]
    interpretation, **26(1)**, [704]
    new, **26(1)**, [702]

Mayor's and City of London Court
  accommodation of, **11(2)**, [249]
  county court, becoming, **11(2)**, [251]
  recorder, **11(2)**, [209]

meals
  provision by housing authority, **22**, [12]

measures. *See* **Church Assembly; General
Synod**

meat
  meaning, **1(1)**, [639]

Meat and Livestock Commission
  Food from Britain, contributions to,
    1(2), [197]
  pig industry levy scheme—
    expenses relating to, **1(2)**, [206]
    power to make, **1(2)**, [206]
    See further **pig industry**
  power to dissolve, **1(2)**, [734]

mechanically propelled vehicle
  accident whilst driving, **37**, [788]
    inquiry into, **37**, [797]
  careless driving of, **37**, [561], [786]
    causing death by, **37**, [560]
    meaning, **37**, [562]
  causing death whilst driving—
    alcohol, under influence of, **37**, [564]
    disqualified drivers, **37**, [563]
    drugs, under influence of, **37**, [564]
    uninsured drivers, **37**, [563]
    unlicensed drivers, **37**, [563]
  dangerous driving of, **37**, [558]
  driver, user or owner, evidence of, **38(1)**, [10]

mechanically propelled vehicle—*contd*
excise duty in respect of—
shipbuilders', relief for, **13**, [555], [557]
ending of, **13**, [1120]
motor car as, **37**, [665], [801]
police power to stop, **37**, [780]
regulation of, **36**, [210]

medals. *See* **decorations**

mediation
tribunals, in, **11(4)**, [25]; **11(S)**, Courts 37

medical advisers
appointment and qualification, **16**, [80]
fees, **16**, [81]

Medical Advisory Service
accounts, keeping of, **16**, [83]
application of provisions, **16**, [87]
appointments, **16**, [80]
authority responsible for, **16**, [80]
expenses and receipts, **16**, [85]
fees, **16**, [81]
financial provisions, **16**, [82]
functions of authority as to, **16**, [79]
maintenance, responsibility for, **16**, [79]
regulations as to, power to make, **16**, [86]
reports by authority, **16**, [83]
school medical records, furnishing of
particulars, **16**, [84]
supplementary provisions, **16**, [84]

medical appeal tribunal
appeal from, **40(1)**, [550]
chairmen—
nomination of, **40(1)**, [552]
remuneration, **40(1)**, [726]
tenure of office, **40(1)**, [726]
constitution, **40(1)**, [552]
decisions, review of, **40(1)**, [549]
members, appointment of, **40(1)**, [552]
officers and staff, **40(1)**, [726]
President—
administrative duties, **40(1)**, [726]
appointment of, **40(1)**, [553]
remuneration, **40(1)**, [726]
tenure of office, **40(1)**, [726]
procedure, regulations as to, **40(1)**, [727]
reference of questions to, **40(1)**, [548]
regional chairmen, appointment of,
40(1), [553]

medical examination
infected person, **35(1)**, [476]
group of persons suspected of comprising
carrier, **35(1)**, [477]

medical insurance premiums
withdrawal of relief on, **43(1)**, [312]

medical practice
goodwill, sale of, **30**, [1065], [1114]
loss of right to sell, compensation for,
30, [422]

Medical Practices Committee
abolition of, **30**, [617]

medical practitioner
approved practice settlings, **28**, [335]
charges, recovery of, **28**, [336]
conduct and performance, **28(S)**, 4
controlled drugs—
information on, requirement to furnish,
28, [216]
prohibition on dealing with. *See* **drugs**
convicted, prohibition on dealing with
controlled drugs, **28**, [211]
death caused by negligence of, post-mortem
examination, **11(1)**, [1227]
death certificate, issue of, **36**, [98]
designated bodies, co-operation between,
28(S), 34–5
disqualification of—
conditions, **30**, [460]
efficiency cases, **30**, [460]–[461]
fraud cases, **30**, [460]–[462]
duty to report—
food poisoning, **35(1)**, [452]
notifiable disease, **35(1)**, [452]
EC practitioner. *See* **European Economic
Community**
exemptions, **28**, [76], [82], [111], [205]
experience—
alternative requirements, **28**, [285]
registration, required for, **28**, [277]
resident medical capacity, employment in,
28, [287]
United Kingdom, acquired outside,
28, [285]
fitness to practice—
appeals, **28**, [326]
exempt persons, sufficient evidence as to,
28, [333]
impaired, **28**, [320]
information, provision of, **28**, [332]
restoration of name to register, **28**, [327]
rules, **28**, [321]
suspension of registration, **28**, [322]–[324]
fraud and unsuitability, **30**, [462]
fully registered—
appointments restricted to, **28**, [337]
certificates signed by, **28**, [338]
EEA nationals with overseas primary
qualifications, **28**, [292]
EEA nationals with overseas qualifications
accepted by relevant European State,
28, [293]
EEA nationals without acquired rights
certificates, **28**, [286]
meaning, **28**, [348]
privileges of, **28**, [336]–[340]
registration as, **28**, [276], [277], [292]
See also **medical register**
general medical services. *See* **medical
services**
general note, **28**, [1]
indicative amounts, **30**, [529]
licence to practice—
appeals, **28**, [305], [358]

medical practitioner—*contd*
  licence to practice—*contd*
    directions or orders, effect of, **28**, [329]
    evidence as to, **28**, [304]
    fees, **28**, [308]
    grant of, **28**, [301]
    guidance, publication of, **28**, [308]
    indemnity arrangements, **28**, [334]
    Investigation Committee, reference to, **28**, [302]
    licensing authority, **28**, [300]
    meaning, **28**, [300]
    notices, **28**, [307]
    pretending to hold, penalty for, **28**, [340]
    refusal of, **28**, [301]
    regulations, **28**, [300], [308]
    restoration, **28**, [303]
    revalidation appeals, **28**, [357]
    withdrawal of, **28**, [301]
  local medical committee, representation by, **30**, [459]
  meaning, **30**, [478]
  medical education, **28**, [279]–[283].
    See also **General Medical Council**
  medical examinations, payments for, **30**, [1042]
  medical reports. *See* **medical reports**
  medicinal products on prescription only, **28**, [114], [115]
  mental patients, duties of. *See* **mentally disordered person**
  ophthalmic services, qualification for, **30**, [451]
  prescribing rights, other health professional, extension to, **30**, [619]
  primary—
    accommodation, provision of, **30**, [904]
    assistance and support for, **30**, [902]
    persons performing, lists of, **30**, [897]
    premises for, provision of, **30**, [827]
    Primary Care Trust—
      assistance and support by, **30**, [902]
      contract by, **30**, [890]
      duty of, **30**, [889]
      provision by, **30**, [827]
    remuneration, **30**, [1040]
    requirement to provide, **30**, [891]
    Strategic Health Authority, arrangement for provision by—
      agreements, requirements, **30**, [898]
      interpretation, **30**, [899]
      persons with whom made, **30**, [899]
      regulations, **30**, [900]
      transfer of liabilities, **30**, [901]
  professional conduct—
    General Council to advise on, **28**, [317]
    information regarding, General Council to require disclosure of, **28**, [318]
    notifications and disclosure by General Council, **28**, [319]
  provisional registration, **28**, [276], [287]
    acceptable programmes for, **28**, [284]
    EEA nationals, **28**, [288]
  qualifications—
    acceptable overseas, meaning, **28**, [348]

medical practitioner—*contd*
  qualifications—*contd*
    meaning, **28**, [348]
    overseas—
      primary, **28**, [292]
      registration of, **28**, [289]
    primary European—
      certificates and declarations required, **28**, [290]
      entitling to registration, **28**, [277]
      meaning, **28**, [290]
      registration of, **28**, [289]
    primary United Kingdom—
      entitling to registration, **28**, [277]
      meaning, **28**, [278]
      registration of, **28**, [289]
      standards for grant of, **28**, [279], [282]
    proof of, **28**, [356]
    registration of, **28**, [289]
    required for, **28**, [276], [277]
  qualifying examination—
    bodies entitled to hold, **28**, [278]
    examination deemed not to be, **28**, [283]
    further, addition of, **28**, [282]
    inspectors, attendance at, **28**, [280]
    meaning, **28**, [278]
    passing, necessity for, **28**, [277]
    standard of proficiency at, **28**, [279], [282]
  qualifying overseas. *See* **medical register**
  re-employment after attaining 65, reduction of pension, **30**, [518]
  registered, falsely pretending to be, **28**, [339]
  registration. *See* **medical register**
  remuneration, **30**, [501]
  responsible officers—
    Crown, provisions binding, **28(S)**, 30
    regulations, **28(S)**, 29–32
    requirement to nominate or appoint, **28(S)**, 26–7
    responsibilities of, **28(S)**, 28–9, 32–3
  sale of poisons to, **28**, [253]
  sight testing, arrangements for, **30**, [450]
  transitional and saving provisions, **28**, [349], [361]
  veterinary operation by, **28**, [35]
  visiting EC practitioner. *See* **European Economic Community**
  visiting, from relevant European State, **28**, [355]
  Wales. *See* **Wales**
  witness, as, costs, **12(1)**, [387]

medical register
  alterations to, **28**, [309], [310], [356]
  appeals, **28**, [326]
  contents, **28**, [276], [309]
  entries in, **28**, [310], [356]
  erasure from—
    appeal against, **28**, [310], [326], [357]
    application of practitioner, on, **28**, [312]
    death, on, **28**, [309]
    entries fraudulently or incorrectly procured, **28**, [325]
    error, for, **28**, [325]
    fraud, for, **28**, [325]

medical register—*contd*
  erasure from—*contd*
    incorrect entries, **28**, [325]
    licence to practice, effect on, **28**, [329]
    non-payment of fees, for, **28**, [312]
    regulations as to, **28**, [310]
    voluntary removal, **28**, [311]
  form, **28**, [310]
  fraud or error in, **28**, [325]
  keeping, **28**, [276], [309], [310]
  lists, **28**, [276], [309]
  overseas practitioner—
    full registration—
      EEA nationals with overseas primary
        qualifications, **28**, [292]
      EEA nationals with overseas
        qualifications accepted by relevant
        European State, **28**, [293]
      persons with overseas qualification,
        28, [295]
      temporary, **28**, [298]
    provisional registration—
      EEA nationals with overseas
        qualifications, **28**, [294]
      overseas qualification, persons with,
        28, [296]
    qualifications, registration of, **28**, [297]
    specialists, temporary registration of,
      28, [298]
  publication, **28**, [314]
  registration—
    appeals, **28**, [316], [357]
    application for, **28**, [356]
    certificate of, issue of, **28**, [356]
    conditional, interim, **28**, [328]
    disqualification in member State, effect
      on, **28**, [331]
    EC practitioners. *See* **European
      Economic Community**
    entitlement to, **28**, [277]
    experience required for. *See* **medical
      practitioner**
    falsely pretending, **28**, [339]
    fees, regulations as to charging of, **28**, [312]
    full, entitlement to, **28**, [277]
    interim orders, **28**, [328]
    proof of, **28**, [315]
    provisional, **28**, [287]
    qualifications required for, **28**, [277].
      See also **medical practitioner**
    qualifying examinations for. *See* **medical
      practitioner**
    special purpose, **28**, [299]
    suspension—
      appeal against, **28**, [326]
      appointment not terminated by,
        28, [337]
      disqualification in member State,
        28, [331]
      fitness to practice, impairment of,
        28, [322]–[324]
      licence to practice, effect on, **28**, [329]
  regulations as respects, **28**, [309], [310]
  restoration to, **28**, [310], [312], [327]

medical register—*contd*
  transitional and saving provisions, **28**, [349],
    [361]
  voluntary removal from, **28**, [311]

medical reports
  access to—
    application to court as to, **28**, [490]
    exemptions, **28**, [489]
    interpretation of terms, **28**, [484]
    references to, interpretation of, **28**, [486]
    right of, **28**, [483]
    supply of report subject to, **28**, [486]
  employment or insurance purposes, for—
    amendment, request for, **28**, [487]
    consent to—
      conditional on access to, **28**, [486]
      requirement for, **28**, [485]
    meaning, **28**, [484]
    notification of application for, **28**, [485]
    retention of reports by practitioner,
      28, [488]
  errors etc, correction of, **28**, [487]
  meaning, **28**, [484]

Medical Research Council
  establishment of, **10**, [532]
  expenses of, **10**, [533]
  hearing research, institute for, **30**, [440]
  report and accounts, **10**, [539]

medical school
  visitors of—
    appointment, **28**, [281]
    instruction at, report on sufficiency of,
      28, [281]

medical services
  general—
    arrangements for, **30**, [519]
    contract for—
      disputes, **30**, [896]
      drugs, prescription of, **30**, [894]
      enforcement, **30**, [896]
      payments, **30**, [893]
      persons eligible to enter into, **30**, [892]
      Primary Care Trust, by, **30**, [890]
      required terms, **30**, [895]
      requirements, **30**, [891]
    indemnity cover, **30**, [455]
    remuneration, regulations as to, **30**, [501]
    transitional provisions, **30**, [746]
    Local Medical Committees, **30**, [903]

medical supplies
  price control—
    enforcement, **30**, [1071]
    maximum prices, **30**, [1066], [1115]
    powers of, **30**, [1068], [1072]
    statutory schemes, **30**, [1069]–[1070]
    territorial extent of provisions, **30**, [1077]
    voluntary schemes, powers relating to,
      30, [1067]

medicinal products
  administration, **28**, [68], [117]
  adulteration, **28**, [120]
  advertisement—
    copies of, power of licensing authority to
      require, **28**, [155]
    issue of, **28**, [150]
    meaning, **28**, [150]
    offences, **28**, [151]
    practitioner, to—
      data sheet, requirements as to, **28**, [154]
      restrictions on delivery, **28**, [154]
    product licence, consent of holder to,
      28, [152]
    regulations as to, **28**, [153]
    representation—
      false or misleading, **28**, [151]
      meaning, **28**, [151]
      regulations as to, **28**, [153]
      unauthorised recommendations,
        including, **28**, [151]
  animal feeding stuffs. *See* **feeding stuffs**
  articles and substances not, application of
    legislation to certain, **28**, [161]
  books and documents, production, **28**, [168]
  British Pharmacopoeia. *See* **British
    Pharmacopoeia**
  business, extension of references to carrying
    on, **28**, [163]
  colour, **28**, [147]
  committee—
    annual reports, **28**, [72]
    establishment, **28**, [71]
    licensing authority—
      consultation with, **28**, [87]
      hearing before person appointed,
        28, [90]
      procedure on reference to, **28**, [88], [89]
    regulations as to, **28**, [192]
  container—
    breaking open, **28**, [168]
    distinctive marks on, **28**, [144]
    false or misleading descriptions on,
      28, [144]
    inspection, right of, **28**, [168]
    labelling, **28**, [144], [187]
    meaning, **28**, [187]
    offences and penalties, **28**, [149]
    requirements as to, **28**, [146]
  dealing with—
    regulation of, further powers for, **28**, [123]
    restrictions on, **28**, [74]
      exemptions, **28**, [76]
  dentist, exemptions for, **28**, [76], [111]
  disqualification for certain offences, **28**, [125]
  distinctive marks on, **28**, [147]
  documents—
    seizure, **28**, [168]
    service, **28**, [182]
  enforcement—
    authority, protection for officers of,
      28, [175]
    legislative provisions, **28**, [165], [166]
  exemption for—
    dentists, **28**, [76], [111]

medicinal products—*contd*
  exemption for—*contd*
    extension or modification, **28**, [82]
    herbal remedies, **28**, [79], [112]
    imports, certain, **28**, [76]–[84]
    medical practitioners, **28**, [76], 544
    midwives, **28**, [78], [111]
    nurses, **28**, [78], [111]
    pharmacists, **28**, [77], [107]–[109]
    re-exports, **28**, [81]
    transitional exemptions, **28**, [83]
      termination of, **28**, [84]
  exportation—
    certain products, special provisions as to,
      28, [74], [82], [104]
    certificate for, **28**, [106]
    EEA States, to, **28**, [105]
    restrictions on, **28**, [74]
      exemptions, **28**, [76]–[84]
      postponement, **28**, [103]
    unlawful, forfeiture for, **28**, [173]
  financial provisions, **28**, [183]
  forfeiture for improper importation or
    exportation, **28**, [173]
  general sale list, on—
    automatic machine section, **28**, [107],
      [109], [110]
    meaning, **28**, [107]
    sale or supply of—
      not on, **28**, [108]
        exemptions, **28**, [111]–[113]
      on, **28**, [109]
        exemptions, **28**, [111]–[113]
    specification of, **28**, [107]
  general note, **28**, [1]
  herbal remedy—
    exemption for, **28**, [79], [112]
    meaning, **28**, [187]
  homeopathic—
    exportation, **28**, [74]
    manufacture, **28**, [74]
    meaning, **28**, [74]
    sale or supply, **28**, [74]
  importation, **28**, [74], [80], 544, 546
    improper, forfeiture for, **28**, [173]
    prohibition for safety reasons, **28**, [119]
    restrictions on, **28**, [74]
      exemptions, **28**, [76]–[84]
  information—
    licensing authority, to, **28**, [99]
    wrongful disclosure, **28**, [174]
  inspection, right of, **28**, [168]
  label—
    inspection, power of, **28**, [168]
    meaning, **28**, [187]
  leaflets—
    false or misleading, **28**, [145]
    inspection, power of, **28**, [168]
    offences and penalties, **28**, [149]
    regulations as to, **28**, [145]
  licence of right—
    application for, proceedings on, **28**, [94]
    entitlement to, **28**, [93]
    fee for, **28**, [248], [493]
    grant, **28**, [94], [104]

medicinal products—*contd*
  licence of right—*contd*
    meaning, **28**, [93]
    refusal, **28**, [94]
  licensing authority—
    advertisements, power to require copies of, **28**, [155]
    advice to, **28**, [71]
    certificate for exporter of, issue by, **28**, [106]
    constitution, **28**, [73]
    consultation with, appropriate committee, **28**, [87]
    entry, authorised by, **28**, [167]
    licences granted by. *See* manufacturer's licence; product licence; wholesale dealer's licence *below*
    meaning, **28**, [73]
    standard provisions, incorporation in licences, **28**, [102]
    suspension, variation or revocation of, licences, **28**, [95]–[97], [193]
    validity of decisions, **28**, [164]
  manufacture—
    meaning, **28**, [187]
    restrictions on, **28**, [74], [98]
      exemptions from, **28**, [76]–[84]
  manufacturer's licence—
    application for—
      factors relevant to determination of, **28**, [86]
      hearing before person appointed, **28**, [90]
      licensing authority, to, **28**, [85]
      procedure, **28**, [88], [89]
    duration, **28**, [92]
    effect of, **28**, [91]
    fee for, **28**, [248], [493]
    grant of, **28**, [87]
    meaning, **28**, [75]
    new, grant of, **28**, [92]
    product licence, in addition to, **28**, [91]
    refusal, **28**, [87]–[89]
    renewal, **28**, [92]
    requirement of, **28**, [75]
      exemptions, **28**, [76]–[84]
    revocation, **28**, [95], [96], [193]
    suspension, **28**, [95], [96], [193]
    validity of, **28**, [164]
    variation, **28**, [95]–[97], [193]
  meaning, **28**, [185]
  medical practitioner, exemption for, **28**, [76], 544
  medicinal purposes, meaning, **28**, [185]
  midwife, exemption for, **28**, [78], [111]
  monographs, standards in, compliance with, **28**, [122]
  new, special provisions as to, **28**, [116]
  Northern Ireland, enforcement of provisions in, **28**, [166]
  Nurses, exemption for, **28**, [78], [111]
  offences—
    analysis under directions of court, **28**, [194]
    body corporate, by, **28**, [179]

medicinal products—*contd*
  offences—*contd*
    certificate of analysis, in relation to, **28**, [178]
    dealings with, **28**, [124]
    licences and certificates, as to, **28**, [100], [101]
    presumptions as to, **28**, [181]
    prosecutions for, **28**, [180]
    third party, due to default by, **28**, [176]
    warranties—
      defence, as, **28**, [177]
      in relation to, **28**, [178]
  offences and penalties, **28**, [100], [124]
    defences, **28**, [101]
  on the market in UK at particular time, **28**, [187]
  orders and regulations, **28**, [184]
  other substances, application of provisions to, **28**, [162]
  packages—
    breaking open, **28**, [168]
    distinctive marks on, **28**, [144]
    false or misleading descriptions on, **28**, [144]
    inspection, right of, **28**, [168]
    labelling—
      meaning, **28**, [187]
      requirement as to, **28**, [144]
    meaning, **28**, [187]
    offences and penalties, **28**, [149]
  persons to be supplied with, special restrictions on, **28**, [118]
  pharmacists, exemptions for, **28**, [77], [107]–[109]
  premises—
    annual return of, **28**, [136], [143]
    requirements for, prescribing, **28**, [123]
  prescription by nurses, **30**, [540], [541]
    specification, **28**, [114], [115]
  product licence—
    advertisement, consent of holder to, **28**, [152]
    application for—
      factors relevant to determination of, **28**, [86]
      hearing before person appointed, **28**, [90]
      licensing authority, to, **28**, [85]
      procedure, **28**, [88], [89]
    duration, **28**, [92]
    effect, **28**, [103]
    fee for, **28**, [248], [493]
    grant, **28**, [87], [98], [103], [104]
    manufacturer's licence, in addition to, **28**, [91]
    new, grant of, **28**, [92]
    offences by holder, **28**, [100]
      special defences, **28**, [101]
    refusal, **28**, [87]
    renewal, **28**, [92]
    requirement of, **28**, [74]
      exemptions, **28**, [76]–[84]
    revocation, **28**, [95], [96], [193]

medicinal products—*contd*
  product licence—*contd*
    standard provisions—
      incorporation in, **28**, [102]
      operative, meaning, **28**, [102]
    suspension, **28**, [95], [96], [193]
    validity of, **28**, [164]
    variation, **28**, [95]–[97], [193]
  proprietary, meaning, **28**, [74]
  publications—
    monographs, compliance with standards
      in, **28**, [122]
    relating to, **28**, [156]–[160]
  purchasers, protection of, **28**, [121]
  re-exports, exemption for, **28**, [81]
  retail, sale by, **28**, [107]–[109], [113], [117],
    [186]
  safekeeping, **28**, [123]
  sale or supply—
    automatic machine, by, **28**, [109], [110],
      [123], [148]
    general list—
      not on, **28**, [108], [111]–[113]
      on, **28**, [109]
    precautions before, **28**, [123]
    prohibition for safety reasons, **28**, [119]
    records as to, **28**, [123]
    restricted, **28**, [118]
    restrictions on, **28**, [74], [98]
      exemptions, **28**, [76]–[84]
    samples, distributed as, **28**, [123]
    wholesale dealer's licence for, **28**, [75]
      exemptions, **28**, [76]–[84]
  samples—
    analysis—
      certificate of, **28**, [171], [178], [194]
      fee for, **28**, [171]
      Government Chemist, by, **28**, [194]
      meaning, **28**, [187]
      submission for, **28**, [171], [194]
    automatic machine, from, **28**, [194]
    distribution as, **28**, [123]
    division into parts, **28**, [169], [194]
    evidence, provisions as to, **28**, [194]
    examination, **28**, [194]
    microbiological examinations of drugs,
      provision of facilities for, **28**, [172]
    modification of provisions, **28**, [194]
    notice to person named on container,
      28, [194]
    payment for, **28**, [194]
    protection of purchaser of, **28**, [194]
    public analyst—
      analysis by, **28**, [171], [194]
      certificate of, **28**, [171], [194]
      fee of, **28**, [171]
      meaning, **28**, [171], [194]
    right to take, **28**, [168]
    sampling officer, meaning, **28**, [194]
    setting aside, **28**, [169], [194]
    treating substance or article as, **28**, [169],
      [194]
  shape, **28**, [147]
  standards in monographs, compliance with,
    28, [122]

medicinal products—*contd*
  storage, **28**, [123]
  substances excluded from, **28**, [74]
  unusable, disposal of, **28**, [123]
  vending machine—
    breaking open, **28**, [168]
    seizure from, **28**, [168]
  veterinary surgeon or practitioner, exemption
    for, **28**, [205]
  wholesale dealer's licence—
    application for—
      hearing before person appointed,
        28, [90]
      licensing authority, to, **28**, [86], [87]
      procedure, **28**, [88], [89]
    duration, **28**, [92]
    fee for, **28**, [248], [493]
    grant of, **28**, [87]
    meaning, **28**, [75]
    new, grant of, **28**, [92]
    refusal, **28**, [87]–[89]
    renewal, **28**, [92]
    requirement of, **28**, [75]
      exemptions, **28**, [76]–[84]
    revocation, **28**, [95], [193]
    standard provisions—
      incorporation in, **28**, [102]
      operative, meaning, **28**, [102]
    suspension, **28**, [95], [193]
    validity of, **28**, [164]
    variation, **28**, [95], [193]
  wholesale dealing, meaning, **28**, [186]
  zero-rating, **50**, [151]

medical supplies and equipment
  gifts from trading stock, tax relief for,
    43(2), [101]

medical treatment
  advance decision as to. *See* **advance decision**
  mental disorder, for, **29**, [254]

Medicines Commission
  British Pharmacopoeia and compendia etc,
    functions as to, **28**, [156]
  committees—
    appointment, **28**, [192]
    British Pharmacopoeia and compendia, etc,
      functions as to, **28**, [156]
    members, **28**, [192]
    procedure, **28**, [192]
    staff and accommodation, **28**, [192]
    sub-committees, **28**, [192]
    validity of proceedings, **28**, [192]
  procedure, **28**, [192]
  reports by, **28**, [72]
  staff and accommodation, **28**, [192]
  validity of proceedings, **28**, [192]

Medway
  Port of London powers not exercisable within
    area, **39(2)**, [384], [419]

meeting
company. *See* **companies**
endeavouring to break up, **12(1)**, [192]
local authority. *See* **local authority**
parish. *See* **parish meeting**
public bodies. *See* **public bodies**

Member of Parliament. *See also* **House of Commons**
accommodation, expenditure on,
   43(1), [585]; **44(2)**, [370]
European travel expenses, **44(2)**, [296]
overnight expenses allowances, **44(2)**, [294]
pension fund. *See* **pensions**
termination payments to, **44(2)**, [293]

members of company
amendment of articles, effect of, **8(1)**, [103]
audit, right to require, **8(1)**, [554]
class meetings, provisions applying to,
   8(1), [412]
   share capital, company without, **8(1)**, [413]
constitutional documents provided to,
   8(1), [110]
damages against company, shareholding no bar
   to, **8(1)**, [733]
derivative claims—
   England and Wales, proceedings in—
      application of provisions, **8(1)**, [338]
      brought by another member, application
         for permission to continue, **8(1)**, [342]
      cause of action, **8(1)**, [338]
      grant of permission, factors taken into
         account, **8(1)**, [341]
      permission to continue claim as,
         application for, **8(1)**, [340]
      permission to continue, application for,
         8(1), [339]
      meaning, **8(1)**, [338]
   Northern Ireland, proceedings in—
      application of provisions, **8(1)**, [338]
      brought by another member, application
         for permission to continue, **8(1)**, [342]
      cause of action, **8(1)**, [338]
      grant of permission, factors taken into
         account, **8(1)**, [341]
      permission to continue claim as,
         application for, **8(1)**, [340]
      permission to continue, application for,
         8(1), [339]
director's service contract, right to inspect and
   request copy, **8(1)**, [307]
index of—
   inspection and requirement of copies—
      information as to state of, **8(1)**, [198]
      request, **8(1)**, [194]
      rights, **8(1)**, [194]
   inspection, to be kept available for,
      8(1), [193]
   requirement to keep, **8(1)**, [193]
information rights—
   form in which copies provided, **8(1)**, [225]
   nomination of person to enjoy—
      status of rights conferred, **8(1)**, [228]
      termination or suspension, **8(1)**, [226]

members of company—*contd*
information rights—*contd*
   nomination of person to enjoy—*contd*
      traded companies, in, **8(1)**, [224]
   power to amend provisions, **8(1)**, [229]
   voting rights, as to, **8(1)**, [227]
memorandum, subscribers to, **8(1)**, [86]
notice of general meetings, entitlement to
   receive, **8(1)**, [388]
overseas branch register—
   countries and territories to which
      provisions applying, **8(1)**, [207]
   discontinuance, **8(1)**, [213]
   inspection, to be kept for in UK,
      8(1), [210]
   keeping of, **8(1)**, [207]
   local courts, jurisdiction of, **8(1)**, [212]
   main register, as part of, **8(1)**, [209]
   modification of provisions, **8(1)**, [209]
   notice of opening, **8(1)**, [208]
   transactions in shares registered in,
      8(1), [211]
persons being, **8(1)**, [190]
register—
   claims arising from entry in, time limit,
      8(1), [206]
   evidence of matters in, as, **8(1)**, [205]
   former members, removal of entries,
      8(1), [199]
   inspection and requirement of copies—
      default in, **8(1)**, [196]
      information as to state of, **8(1)**, [198]
      offences, **8(1)**, [197]
      refusal of, **8(1)**, [196]
      request, **8(1)**, [194]
      response to request, **8(1)**, [195]
      rights, **8(1)**, [194]
   inspection, to be kept available for,
      8(1), [192]
   overseas branch. *See* overseas branch register
      above
   particulars in, **8(1)**, [191]
   place of keeping, **8(1)**, [192]
   power of court to rectify, **8(1)**, [203]
   requirement to keep, **8(1)**, [191]
   share warrants, entry of details of,
      8(1), [200]
   shares held, statement of, **8(1)**, [191]
   single member companies, **8(1)**, [201]
   treasury shares, company holding own
      shares as, **8(1)**, [202]
   trusts not to entered on, **8(1)**, [204]
rights, exercise of—
   articles, provisions in, **8(1)**, [223]
   audit, to require, **8(1)**, [554]
   information rights. *See* information rights
      above
   shares held on behalf of others, where—
      different ways, in, **8(1)**, [230]
      members' requests, **8(1)**, [231]
statement of capital provided to, **8(1)**, [110]
subsidiary as member of holding company—
   authorised dealer in securities, acting as—
      prohibition not applying, **8(1)**, [219]
   third parties, protection of, **8(1)**, [220]

members of company—*contd*
subsidiary as member of holding
company—*contd*
companies not limited by shares, provisions
applying to, **8(1)**, [221]
employer's right of recovery under pension
scheme or employees' share scheme,
disregarding, **8(1)**, [218]
nominees, provisions applying to,
8(1), [222]
personal representative or trustee, acting
as, **8(1)**, [216]–[218]
prohibition, **8(1)**, [214]
residual interest under pension scheme or
employees' share scheme, disregarding,
8(1), [217]
shares acquired before prohibition
applicable, **8(1)**, [215]
transactions with directors requiring approval
of. *See* **director (company)**
unfair prejudice, protection against—
general rule-making powers, application
of, **8(1)**, [1075]
order affecting company's constitution,
delivery to registrar, **8(1)**, [1076]–[1077]
petition—
member, by, **8(1)**, [1072]
Secretary of State, by, **8(1)**, [1073]
powers of court, **8(1)**, [1074]

memorandum of association
alteration—
cancellation of, **8**, 108
confirmation by court, **8**, 108
copies, to be embodied in, **8**, 120–1
matters which could have been in articles,
8, 119
members of company, effect on, **8**, 118
objecting to, procedure, **8**, 108–9
registrar, to be sent to, **8**, 109–10
registration of, **8**, 119
restriction on, **8**, 106
special resolution, by, **8**, 108
validity of, **8**, 110
capacity not limited by, **8**, 134
commonhold association, of, amendment,
8(1), [1359]
company limited by guarantee, **8**, 118
copies—
alterations to be embodied in, **8**, 120–1
members to be provided with, **8**, 120
documents to be sent to registrar, **8**, 113–14
effect of, **8**, 117
existing companies, provisions treated as
provisions of articles, **8(1)**, [106]
form of, **8(1)**, [86]
forms of, **8**, 106–7
liability of members, statement of, **8**, 105
meaning, **8(1)**, [86]
name as stated in, **8**, 125
name clause, **8**, 105
objects, statement of—
general commercial company, **8**, 107
generally, **8**, 105
resolution to alter, **8**, 108

memorandum of association—*contd*
registered office, statement of, **8**, 105
registration—
effect of, **8**, 116
procedure, **8**, 113–14
requirements respecting, **8**, 105
share capital, statement of, **8**, 105, 114
signatures to, **8**, 105
statement to accompany—
contents, **8**, 114
particulars of directors, **8**, 607–8
secretaries, particulars to be given, **8**, 608
subscribers—
identification of, **8(1)**, [88]
members of company, as, **8(1)**, [190]
number required, **8**, 105
payment for shares, **8(1)**, [662]
shares issued to, **8**, 181
shares to be taken by, **8**, 105
subscribing to, **8(1)**, [85]

mental capacity
codes of practice—
duty to have regard to, **29**, [273]
failure to comply with, **29**, [273]
procedure for, **29**, [274]
revision, **29**, [273]
subjects of, **29**, [273]
Court of Protection. *See* **Court of
Protection**
declarations about, **29**, [239]
family relationships, decisions relating to,
29, [253]
independent advocates—
adjustment of role of, **29**, [272]
appointment of, **29**, [261]
functions of, **29**, [262]
proposal for serious medical treatment by
NHS body, acting for patient, **29**, [263]
provision of accommodation for patient,
representation—
local authority, by, **29**, [265]
NHS body, by, **29**, [264]
person nominated for consultation, no
requirement on, **29**, [271]
lasting power of attorney. *See* **lasting power
of attorney**
murder or manslaughter, provisions not
affecting law of, **29**, [293]
persons lacking—
accommodation, provision for—
local authority by, **29**, [265]
NHS body, by, **29**, [264]
person consulted on, nomination of,
29, [271]
balance of probabilities, decided on,
29, [224]
best interests, determining, **29**, [226]
care or treatment, acts in connection
with—
expenditure, **29**, [232]
liability for, **29**, [229]
limitations, **29**, [230]
restraint of patient, **29**, [230]

mental capacity—*contd*
  persons lacking—*contd*
    family relationships, decisions relating to, **29**, [253]
    ill-treatment or neglect of, **29**, [275]
    impairment or disturbance of mind or brain, due to, **29**, [224]
    inability to make decisions, **29**, [225]
    intrusive research on—
      approval, requirements for, **29**, [257]
      carer, consulting, **29**, [258]
      clinical trial not being, **29**, [256]
      loss of capacity during, **29**, [60]
      safeguards, **29**, [259]
      unlawful, **29**, [256]
    liberty, deprivation of—
      authorisations—
        conditions, **29**, [301]
        detained resident, meaning, **29**, [302]
        independent mental capacity advocates, **29**, [311]
        information, disclosure of, **29**, [312]
        interested persons, meaning, **29**, [313]
        meaning, **29**, [302]
        notices, **29**, [312]
        persons becoming subject to, **29**, [266], [267]
        powers of court, **29**, [247]
        qualifying requirements, **29**, [303]
        regulations, **29**, [312]
        relevant person—
          meaning, **29**, [302]
          representative of, **29**, [310]
        standard, **29**, [304]
          assessments, **29**, [309]
          change in supervisory responsibility, **29**, [307]
          review, **29**, [308]
          suspension of, **29**, [306]
        unrepresented persons subject to, **29**, [268]
        urgent, **29**, [305]
        without paid representative, persons subject to, **29**, [269], [270]
      ineligible persons, **29**, [318]
      life-sustaining treatment, where necessary for, **29**, [228]
      restriction on, **29**, [227]
      welfare orders, and, **29**, [241]
    material time, at, **29**, [224]
    necessary goods and services, payment for, **29**, [231]
    serious medical treatment proposed by NHS body, **29**, [263]
    summary of provisions, **29**, [1]
    voting rights, **29**, [255]
    will, **29**, [320]
  principles, **29**, [223]
  summary of provisions, **29**, [1]

mental disorder. *See also* **insanity**
  alcohol dependence not considered as, **29**, [23]
  armed forces personnel subject to, **3**, [1], [1452]

mental disorder—*contd*
  drug dependence not considered as, **29**, [23]
  learning disability not considered as, **29**, [23]
  meaning, **29**, [23]
  medical treatment for, **29**, [254]

Mental Health Act Commission
  biennial reports by, **29**, [169]
  consultation with Secretary of State, **29**, [169]
  establishment and continuation, **29**, [169]
  functions of, **29**, [169]
  postal packet, withholding, review of decision as to, **29**, [169]

mental health professionals
  education and training, **28(S)**, 39

Mental Health Review Tribunal. *See* **First-tier Tribunal**

Mental Health Review Tribunal for Wales
  accommodation for, **29**, [115]
  appeals from, Upper Tribunal, to, **29**, [130]
  application to—
    advising patients as to, **29**, [127]
    cases when made, **29**, [116]
    conditionally discharged restricted patient, as to, **29**, [126]
    formal hearing, disposal without, **29**, [129]
    general provisions, **29**, [128]
    guardianship order, concerning patient subject to, **29**, [120]
    hospital order, concerning patient subject to, **29**, [120]
    information relevant to, **29**, [129]
    postponement of consideration, **29**, [129]
    procedure for making, **29**, [129]
    relevant period for making, **29**, [116]
    restricted patient, by, **29**, [121], [124], [125]
    restriction direction, by restricted patient subject to, **29**, [125]
    transfer direction, by person subject to, **29**, [118]
    who may make, **29**, [116], [120]
    withdrawal, **29**, [118]
  chairman, **29**, [129], [207]
  constitution, **29**, [115], [207]
  decisions, reasons to be given for, **29**, [129]
  discharge of patient—
    conditional, **29**, [124], [125]
    power to direct, **29**, [123], [124]
    restricted patients, **29**, [124], [125]
  documents, right of applicant to copies of, **29**, [129]
  examining patients, **29**, [127]
  jurisdiction, exercise of, **29**, [115]
  leave of absence, recommendation for, **29**, [123]
  members—
    legal and medical, **29**, [207]
    remuneration and allowances, **29**, [115]
    restriction, particular application, for, **29**, [129]
    tenure of office, **29**, [207]

Mental Health Review Tribunal for Wales—*contd*

officers and servants, **29**, [115]

president, **29**, [129], [207]

proceedings of, rules as to, **29**, [129]

public, exclusion from proceedings, **29**, [129]

reference to—

    conditionally discharged restricted patient, as to, **29**, [125]

    hospital managers, by, **29**, [118]

    information for purposes of, **29**, [118]

    procedure on, **29**, [129]

    restricted patients, concerning, **29**, [122]

    Secretary of State, by, **29**, [117], [122]

    time limit for, **29**, [118]

        power to reduce, **29**, [119]

reports of proceedings, prohibition on publication, **29**, [129]

representation before, **29**, [129]

restricted patients—

    discharge of, **29**, [124], [125]

    meaning, **29**, [131]

    procedure in case of, **29**, [129]

    reference to, by Secretary of State, concerning, **29**, [122]

special case, stating, **29**, [129]

summary of provisions, **29**, [1]

Upper Tribunal, appeals to, **29**, [130]

visiting patients, **29**, [127], [129]

mental nursing home

patient in. *See* **mentally disordered person or patient**

mental patient

legal incapacity to vote, abolition of common law rule, **15(3)**, [646]

residence for electoral purposes, **15(3)**, [10]

mentally disordered person or patient. *See also* **insanity**

action statements, **29**, [166]

acts done in pursuance of Act, protection for, **29**, [192]

after-care under supervision, duty to provide, **29**, [161]

amended provisions, **30(S)**, NHS 134–8

approvals, regulations as to, **29**, [196]

approved clinician—

    approvals, regulations as to, **29**, [196]

    meaning, **29**, [200]

approved mental health professionals—

    access to patient by, **29**, [30]

    application by, guardianship, for, **29**, [33], [36]

    approval of, **29**, [157]

    code of practice for guidance of, **29**, [162]

    courses for, approval of, **29**, [158]

    entry and inspection of premises by, **29**, [159]

    guardianship application by, **29**, [36]

    meaning, **29**, [157]

approved social worker—

    application by, for admission or guardianship, **29**, [26], [33]

mentally disordered person or patient—*contd*

approved social worker—*contd*

    emergency application by, **29**, [26]

categories of, removal, **29**, [339]

Channel Islands—

    absence from hospital in, **29**, [153]

    community patients—

        removed or transferred to, **29**, [144]

        responsibility for, transfer to England and Wales from, **29**, [148]

    conditionally discharged patients—

        transfer of responsibilities—

            from, **29**, [149]

            to, **29**, [145]

    removal of patients to or from, **29**, [147]

child or young person, visiting, **29**, [160]

clinician, responsible—

    meaning, **29**, [68]

    report of, opposing discharge of patient, **29**, [59]

code of practice—

    guidance of medical practitioners, etc, for, **29**, [162]

    preparation and revision, **29**, [162]

    withdrawal, **29**, [162]

convicted, escape of, **12(1)**, [394]

correspondence, review of decision to withdraw, **30(S)**, NHS 138

criminal proceedings, concerned in—

    accused person, who is, **29**, [69], [70]

    Channel Islands, offenders found to be insane in, England and Wales, transferred to, **29**, [146]

    detainees—

        hospital order, in respect of, **29**, [87]

        provisions as to, **29**, [87]

    guardianship order—

        appeal against, **29**, [80]

        application to tribunal as to, **29**, [76]

        application to tribunals as to, **29**, [118]

        authority conferred by, **29**, [75]

        conditions for making, **29**, [71]

        effect of, **29**, [75]

        information to facilitate, **29**, [74]

        power to make, **29**, [71]

        quashing of conviction, effect of, **29**, [75]

    hospital—

        admission, power of courts to direct, **29**, [81]

        conditional discharge from, **29**, [220]

        direction—

            effect of, **29**, [82]

            medical evidence required for, **29**, [81]

            power of higher courts as to, **29**, [81]

        order—

            after-care, **29**, [161]

            appeal against, **29**, [80]

            application to tribunal as to, **29**, [76], [118]

            conditions for making, **29**, [71]

            custody, instead of committal to, **29**, [79]

mentally disordered person or
patient—*contd*
criminal proceedings, concerned in—*contd*
hospital—*contd*
order—*contd*
discharge from hospital, restriction on.
See restriction order *below*
effect of, **29**, [75]
information as to hospitals, **29**, [73]
interim—
absconding, **29**, [72]
duration and renewal, **29**, [72]
effect of, **29**, [75]
power to make, **29**, [72]
power to make, **29**, [71], [87]
quashing of conviction, effect of,
29, [75]
reduction of period for making,
29, [91]
restriction order, with or without,
29, [78]
power to specify, **29**, [219]
units, power to specify, **29**, [219]
Isle of Man, offenders found to be insane
in, England and Wales, transferred to,
29, [146]
limitation direction—
effect of, **29**, [82]
medical evidence required for, **29**, [81]
power of higher courts as to, **29**, [81]
medical evidence, requirements as to,
29, [90]
medical report on, **29**, [69], [70]
remand to hospital—
absconding on, **29**, [69]
further remand, **29**, [69], [70]
period of, **29**, [69]
powers of court to, **29**, [69], [71]
report on medical condition, for,
29, [69]
treatment, for, **29**, [70]
restricted patient—
absconding on, **29**, [69]
further remand, **29**, [69], [70]
period of, **29**, [69]
powers of court to, **29**, [69], [71]
report on medical condition, for,
29, [69]
treatment, for, **29**, [70]
discharge of patient, **29**, [77]
higher courts, powers of, regarding,
29, [76]
hospital order, without, **29**, [78]
power to make, **29**, [76]
review of treatment of person subject
to, **29**, [99]
Secretary of State, powers of, **29**, [77]
special restrictions—
imposed by, **29**, [76], [205]–[206]
patients not subject to, **29**, [205]
patients subject to, **29**, [206]
restriction direction imposing,
29, [85]
Scotland, removal from, **29**, [135]
summary of provisions, **29**, [1]

mentally disordered person or
patient—*contd*
criminal proceedings, concerned in—*contd*
transfer direction—
absence without leave, effect of, **29**, [86]
accused remanded by magistrates' court,
29, [88]
after-care, **29**, [161]
aliens, **29**, [84], [89]
application to tribunals where, **29**, [118]
civil prisoners, **29**, [84], [89]
discharge of prisoners, restriction on,
29, [85]
duration, **29**, [83]
expiry, **29**, [87], [88]
hospital order, effect as, **29**, [83]
medical reports for, **29**, [84]
persons subject to, **29**, [83], [84]
power to make, **29**, [83]
remand, persons on, **29**, [84]
remission to prison where, **29**, [125]
removal of patients where, **29**, [138],
[147]
restriction direction and—
expiry, **29**, [87], [88]
prisoners under sentence, **29**, [86]
warrant giving, **29**, [85]
restriction on discharge of prisoner
removed to hospital, **29**, [85]
custody—
constable, power to take into, **29**, [190]
legal—
escaping from, retaking of patient,
29, [191]
person deemed to be in, **29**, [190]
patient escaping from, retaking, **29**, [191]
deprivation of liberty. *See* liberty, deprivation
of *below*
detention—
complaints, investigation of, **29**, [164]
legal custody, in, **29**, [191]
review of powers of, **29**, [164]
visits to patients in, **29**, [164]
discharge from hospital, notification to health
authority, **40(1)**, [167]
discretionary custodial sentence, requirements
for, **12(3)**, [887]
general protection of patients,
30(S), NHS 135
guardian, local social services authority as,
29, [32]
guardianship—
absence without leave—
custody, taking into, **29**, [47], [54], [55]
return to place of guardianship, **29**, [47],
[54], [55]
special provisions as to, **29**, [53]
application—
amendment, **29**, [30]
effect of, **29**, [30]
general provisions, **29**, [33]
grounds for, **29**, [29]
patient in custody, where, **29**, [56]
who may make, **29**, [33]

mentally disordered person or patient—*contd*
  guardianship—*contd*
    discharge from—
      examination of patient for, **29**, [58]
      order for, **29**, [57]
      Tribunals, by, **29**, [123]
      visiting of patient, **29**, [58]
    duration of authority for, **29**, [50]
    escape while in, **29**, [191]
    local social services authority, by, **29**, [29], [57]
    medical recommendation for, **29**, [29], [30]
      regulations as to, **29**, [66]
    reference to tribunals, person subject to, **29**, [117]
    regulations as to, **29**, [31], [66]
    removal of patient subject to, **29**, [138], [147]
    renewal of authority for, **29**, [50]
    summary of provisions, **29**, [1]
    transfer—
      death, incapacity etc of guardian, on, **29**, [32]
      hospital, to or from, **29**, [48]
      into, recommendation of Tribunals for, **29**, [123]
    visiting persons subject to, **29**, [31], [58], [160], [211]
  hospital—
    absence without leave—
      assisting, **29**, [174]
      Channel Islands hospital, from, **29**, [153]
      custody, taken into—
        after more than 28 days, **29**, [55]
        within 28 days, **29**, [54]
      custody, taking into, **29**, [47]
      Isle of Man hospital, from, **29**, [153]
      Northern Ireland hospital, from, **29**, [151]
      return—
        after more than 28 days, **29**, [55]
        re-admission, and, **29**, [47]
        within 28 days, **29**, [54]
      special provisions as to, **29**, [53]
    admission to—
      application for—
        assessment, for, **29**, [24]
        authority conferred by, **29**, [28]
        conflicts of interest, **29**, [33], [35]
        effect of, **29**, [28]
        emergency, **29**, [26]
        general provisions, **29**, [33]
        in-patient, in respect of, **29**, [27]
        medical recommendations, **29**, [24], [34], [66]
        patient in custody, where, **29**, [56]
        rectification, **29**, [38]
        regulations as to, **29**, [66]
        treatment, for, **29**, [25]
        ward of court, **29**, [67]
        who may make, **29**, [33]
      assessment, for—
        application for, **29**, [24]
        detention, period of, **29**, [24]

mentally disordered person or patient—*contd*
  hospital—*contd*
    admission to—*contd*
      assessment, for—*contd*
        emergency, in case of, **29**, [26]
        grounds for, **29**, [24]
        medical recommendations for, **29**, [24], [33], [38]
      report by approved mental health professional on, **29**, [37]
      summary of provisions, **29**, [1]
      treatment, for—
        application for, **29**, [25]
        grounds for, **29**, [25]
        in-patient, in respect of, **29**, [27]
        medical recommendation for, **29**, [25], [33], [38], [66]
    detention in—
      assessment, for, period of, **29**, [24]
      authority for, **29**, [28]
      duration of authority for, **29**, [50]
      in-patient, **29**, [27]
      renewal of authority for, **29**, [50]
      treatment, for, **29**, [25]
    discharge from—
      nearest relative, by, **29**, [57]
        restrictions on, **29**, [59]
      order for, **29**, [57]
      responsible clinician, by, **29**, [57]
      visiting and examination of patients for, **29**, [58]
    escaping from, **29**, [191]
    in-patients—
      applications for admission in respect of, **29**, [27]
      pocket money for, **29**, [170]
    leave of absence—
      grant of, **29**, [39]
      recall, **29**, [76]
      recommendation of Tribunals for, **29**, [123]
      restriction on granting, **29**, [76]
    managers—
      action statements, produced by, **29**, [166]
      code of practice for guidance of, **29**, [162]
      discharge of patient, to inform nearest relative of, **29**, [185]
      evidence by, **29**, [90]
      information, duty to provide, **29**, [167]
      meaning, **29**, [200], [212]
      reference of cases to tribunals by, **29**, [118]
    meaning, **29**, [200], [212]
    patients. *See* patients *below*
    recall of community patients to, **29**, [44]
      treatment upon, **29**, [101]
    reception of special cases, having arrangements for, notification of, **29**, [193]
    registered establishment included in references to, **29**, [68]
    social reports on patients in, **29**, [37]

mentally disordered person or
patient—*contd*
hospital—*contd*
special—
postal packet addressed to patient in,
29, [186]
transfers to and from, **29**, [171]
staff, code of practice for guidance of,
29, [162]
transfer of patients. *See* patients *below*
visiting patients in, **29**, [58], [160], [211]
imprisonment, sentenced to, effect of,
29, [56]
independent mental health advocates—
appointment of, **29**, [177]
assistance from—
arrangements for provision of, **29**, [178]
patients qualifying for, **29**, [179]
information about, duty to give, **29**, [180]
visits from, **29**, [178]
investigation reports—
information required for, provision of,
29, [167]
regulatory authority, published by,
29, [165]
Isle of Man—
community patients—
removed or transferred to, **29**, [144]
responsibility for, transfer to England and
Wales from, **29**, [148]
conditionally discharged patients—
transfer of responsibilities—
from, **29**, [149]
to, **29**, [145]
removal of patients to or from, **29**, [147]
jury service, excusal from, **19(3)**, [153]
liberty, deprivation of—
authorisations—
conditions, **29**, [301]
detained resident, meaning, **29**, [302]
independent mental capacity advocates,
29, [311]
information, disclosure of, **29**, [312]
interested persons, meaning, **29**, [313]
meaning, **29**, [302]
notices, **29**, [312]
persons becoming subject to, **29**, [266],
[267]
powers of court, **29**, [247]
qualifying requirements, **29**, [303]
regulations, **29**, [312]
relevant person—
meaning, **29**, [302]
representative of, **29**, [310]
standard, **29**, [304]
assessments, **29**, [309]
change in supervisory responsibility,
29, [307]
review, **29**, [308]
suspension of, **29**, [306]
unrepresented persons subject to,
29, [268]
urgent, **29**, [305]
without paid representative—
persons subject to, **29**, [269], [270]

mentally disordered person or
patient—*contd*
liberty, deprivation of—*contd*
ineligible persons, **29**, [318]
life-sustaining treatment, where necessary
for, **29**, [228]
restriction on, **29**, [227]
welfare orders, and, **29**, [241]
local Acts, power to amend, **29**, [199]
local authority—
children in care of, **29**, [61], [160]
nearest relative, as, **29**, [61]
prosecutions by, **29**, [176]
visiting patients, **29**, [160], [211]
local social services authority—
action statements, produced by, **29**, [166]
default by, **29**, [4]
guardianship by, **29**, [29], [57]
hospital admission and guardianship,
functions regarding, **29**, [33]
information, duty to provide, **29**, [167]
nearest relative, acting as, **29**, [61], [64]
power and duties, **29**, [2]
prosecutions for offences by, **29**, [3]
managers of NHS foundation trusts,
delegation of powers, **29**, [197]
medical practitioners—
code of practice for guidance of, **29**, [162]
remuneration, etc of, **29**, [163]
visiting patients, **29**, [163]
member of Parliament—
complaint by, investigation of, **29**, [164]
detention, notice to Speaker of, **29**, [194]
vacation of seat, **29**, [194]
mental disorder, meaning, **29**, [210]
minor—
guardianship, under, nearest relative of,
29, [62]
informal admission to hospital, **29**, [181]
murder, mental condition of person accused
of, expenses, etc, of medical practitioner in
making a report on, **29**, [14]
nearest relative—
acting, appointment by county court—
application for—
order on, **29**, [63]
discharge or variation of, **29**, [64]
expiry of, **29**, [64]
procedure on, **29**, [65]
application by—
admission to hospital, for, **29**, [26], [33]
guardianship, for, **29**, [33]
tribunals, to, **29**, [116], [120]
child in care of, **29**, [61]
discharge of patient, to be informed of,
29, [185]
emergency application for hospital
admission by, **29**, [26]
meaning, **29**, [60], [212]
minor under guardianship, of, **29**, [62]
objection to application by, **29**, [33]
relative, meaning, **29**, [60]
necessaries, contract for, **39(1)**, [375]
needs, assessment of, **40(1)**, [167]

mentally disordered person or patient—*contd*

Northern Ireland—
  absence without leave from hospital in, **29**, [151]
  application of Act to, **29**, [202]
  removal of patients to or from, **29**, [138]
offences—
  assisting absentees from hospital, **29**, [174]
  documents, regarding, **29**, [172]
  false statements, **29**, [172]
  ill-treatment of patients, **29**, [173]
  obstruction, **29**, [175]
  penalties for, **29**, [172], [175]
  prosecution by local authorities, **29**, [176]
offender—
  dealing with, **12(3)**, [898]
  directions, duration of, **12(3)**, [1024]
  Parole Board, access to, **12(3)**, [1025]
Parliament, reports to, **40(1)**, [170]
patients—
  absence—
    leave of, **29**, [39]
    without leave, **29**, [47], [54], [55]
  children, suitable accommodation for, provision of, **29**, [182]
  community—
    assignment of responsibility for, regulations as to, **29**, [49]
    discharge of, **29**, [57]
    information to be given to, **29**, [184]
    meaning, **29**, [40]
    Northern Ireland, removed to, **29**, [139]
    not recalled to hospital—
      adults—
        lacking capacity, **29**, [107]
        negligence, liability for, **29**, [112]
        treatment of, **29**, [105], [106]
        relating to, **29**, [111]
        to, consideration of, **29**, [113]
      capacity or competence, lacking, **29**, [107], [109]
        emergency treatment, **29**, [110]
        meaning, **29**, [114]
      child—
        lacking competence, **29**, [109]
        negligence, liability for, **29**, [112]
        treatment of, **29**, [108]
        relating to, **29**, [111]
      objection to treatment, consideration of, **29**, [113]
      summary of provisions, **29**, [1]
    recall to hospital, powers of, **29**, [44]
    recalled patients, powers in respect of, **29**, [45]
    relevant treatment, meaning, **29**, [104]
    Scotland—
      responsibilities for, transferred to, **29**, [133]
  community treatment order—
    conditions, **29**, [41]
    duration, **29**, [42]
    effect of, **29**, [43]
    expiry of, **29**, [52]
    meaning, **29**, [40]

mentally disordered person or patient—*contd*

patients—*contd*
  community treatment order—*contd*
    period, **29**, [51]
    recall to hospital, powers of, **29**, [44]
    recalled patients, powers in respect of, **29**, [45]
    relevant criteria, **29**, [40]
    revocation, **29**, [46]
    treatment upon, **29**, [101]
  complaints by, investigation, **29**, [164]
  conditionally discharged—
    Northern Ireland, responsibilities for, transferred to England and Wales, **29**, [142]
    Scotland, responsibilities for, transferred to, **29**, [134]
  conveyance, **29**, [190]
  correspondence of, **29**, [186]
    withholding, review of decisions as to, **29**, [187]
  detained, information to be given to, **29**, [183]
  discharge—
    examination for, **29**, [50], [58]
    hospital or guardianship, from, **29**, [57]
    restriction on, **29**, [76]
  examination, discharge, for, **29**, [58]
  ill-treated or neglected, removal to place of safety, **29**, [188]
  ill-treatment, **29**, [173]
  informal admission to hospital, **29**, [181]
  meaning, **29**, [200], [212]
  Northern Ireland—
    community patients, removed to, **29**, [139]
    England and Wales, removal of, to, **29**, [141]
    responsibility transferred to, **29**, [140]
  property of. *See* property and affairs, management of *below*
  removal. *See* removal of patients *below*
  social report on, **29**, [37]
  transfer of—
    another hospital, to, **29**, [48]
    guardianship to hospital, **29**, [48]
    hospital to guardianship, **29**, [48]
    regulations as to, **29**, [48]
    restriction on granting, **29**, [76]
  visiting, **29**, [31], [58], [160], [211]
  warrant to search for and remove, **29**, [188]
  welfare, **29**, [160], [211]
pay, pensions, etc, application of, **29**, [195]
property and affairs, management of—
  Court for. *See* **Court of Protection**
  pay, pensions etc, application of, **29**, [195]
  Public Trustee, by, **29**, [215]
public place, found in, **29**, [189]
receiver for, council officers acting as, expenses of, **40(1)**, [24]
regulations—
  powers as to making, **29**, [66], [154]
  rules and orders, general provisions as to, **29**, [198]

mentally disordered person or patient—*contd*
regulatory authority—
annual reports by, **29**, [168]
investigation reports by, **29**, [165]
removal of patients—
aliens, **29**, [150]
another hospital, to, **29**, [48]
Channel Islands, from, **29**, [147]
England and Wales—
from—
authorisation, **29**, [132], [138]
general provisions, **29**, [155]
to—
Channel Islands, from, **29**, [147]
Isle of Man, from, **29**, [147]
Isle of Man, from, **29**, [147]
Northern Ireland, to, authorisation for, **29**, [138]
place of safety, to, **29**, [188], [189]
Scotland—
authorisation of removal to, **29**, [132]
compulsion in the community, patients subject to, **29**, [136]
conditionally discharged patients transferred from, **29**, [137]
from, **29**, [135]
summary of provisions, **29**, [1]
restriction order—
conditional discharge, recall after, **29**, [77], [124]
public inquiry, attendance of patient for purposes of, **29**, [77]
Scotland, application of Act to, **29**, [201]
Secretary of State—
Care Quality Commission, consultation with, **29**, [165]
code of practice, preparation by, **29**, [162]
detained persons, protection of, **29**, [164]
medical practitioners, remuneration, etc to, provision for, **29**, [163]
reference of cases to tribunals by, **29**, [118]
sexual offence against. *See* **sexual offences**
special hospitals, visits to patients in, travelling expenses payable for, **29**, [12]
transfer of patients, another hospital to, recommendation of tribunals for, **29**, [123]
transferred patients, transitional provisions, **29**, [11]
transitional provisions, **29**, [203], [208], [362]
treatment—
admission for. *See* hospital *above*
consent to—
capacity to give, **29**, [94], [95]
incapacity to give, **29**, [95]
patients to whom provisions applicable, **29**, [93]
plan of, **29**, [97]
requiring, **29**, [95]
second opinion and, requiring, **29**, [94]
second opinion or, requiring, **29**, [95]
summary of provisions, **29**, [1]
when not required, **29**, [102]

mentally disordered person or patient—*contd*
treatment—*contd*
consent to—*contd*
withdrawal, **29**, [98]
continuation of treatment after, **29**, [98]
electro-convulsive therapy, **29**, [96]
medical report on, **29**, [99]
review of, **29**, [99]
understanding by patient of, **29**, [94], [95]
urgent, **29**, [100]
ward of court, admission to hospital, **29**, [67]
welfare authorities, functions of, **29**, [2]

mentally handicapped person
confession of crime by, **18**, [253]
meaning, **18**, [253]
witness, as, assistance, **18**, [312]

mercantile agent
authorised acts, **1(1)**, [2]
clerk, agreement with through, **1(1)**, [7]
common law powers, **1(1)**, [14]
consignors and consignees, provisions as to, **1(1)**, [8]
disposition of goods—
buyer obtaining possession by, **1(1)**, [10]
consideration for, **1(1)**, [6]
general powers, **1(1)**, [3]
seller remaining in possession, by, **1(1)**, [9]
stoppage in transit, **1(1)**, [11]
documents of title—
documents included in, **1(1)**, [2]
exchange, rights acquired by, **1(1)**, [6]
possession—
owner's consent, deemed to be with, **1(1)**, [3]
when deemed to be in, **1(1)**, [2]
transferring, mode of, **1(1)**, [12]
general note, **1(1)**, [1]
goods—
disposition. *See* disposition of goods *above*
exchange, rights acquired by, **1(1)**, [6]
possession, when deemed to be in, **1(1)**, [2]
liability, not exempted from, **1(1)**, [13]
meaning, **1(1)**, [2]
owner of goods—
consent to disposition presumed, **1(1)**, [3]
possession given by, **1(1)**, [9]
rights, saving for, **1(1)**, [13]
pledge by—
antecedent debts, for, **1(1)**, [5]
effect of, **1(1)**, [4]
meaning, **1(1)**, [2]
validity, **1(1)**, [3]

mercantile marine superintendent
appointment and functions, **39(2)**, [973]

merchant navy
homosexual acts in, **12(2)**, [239], [240]

Merchant Navy Reserve
maintenance of, **39(2)**, [748]
members of, **39(2)**, [748]
payment to, **39(2)**, [749]
service in, **39(2)**, [749]
training and certification, **39(2)**, [749]

merchant navy uniform
regulations as to, **39(2)**, [724]

merchant seaman
residence for electoral purposes, **15(3)**, [9]

merchant ship. *See* **ship**

merchant shipping
Admiralty jurisdiction. *See* **Admiralty jurisdiction**
certificate of competency—
failure to deliver up, **39(2)**, [733]
false statements, **39(2)**, [721]
holder, disqualification of, **39(2)**, [729]
restoration of, **39(2)**, [734]
special, **39(2)**, [721]
Consolidated Fund, payments to be made into, **39(2)**, [982]
documents, admissibility in evidence, **39(2)**, [964], [965]
fees, **39(2)**, [979]
foreign ship, application of Act to, **39(2)**, [984]
inspector—
appointment of, **39(2)**, [934]
offences relating to, **39(2)**, [939]
powers of, **39(2)**, [938]
jurisdiction. *See* **Admiralty jurisdiction**
legal proceedings—
British seamen, offences by, **39(2)**, [959]
copies of documents admissible in evidence, **39(2)**, [966]
depositions of persons abroad, **39(2)**, [963]
documents admissible in evidence, **39(2)**, [964]
exemptions, etc, proof of, **39(2)**, [967]
jurisdiction—
offences, in relation to, **39(2)**, [956]
ship, offences on board, **39(2)**, [958]
ships lying off coast, over, **39(2)**, [957]
offenders, return of, **39(2)**, [960]
officers of body corporate, offences by, **39(2)**, [955]
summary offences, time limit for, **39(2)**, [953]
summary orders, time limit for, **39(2)**, [954]
maritime claims. *See* **maritime claims**
offences—
body corporate, by officers of, **39(2)**, [955]
jurisdiction, **39(2)**, [956]
on board, committed, **39(2)**, [958]
coast, lying off, **39(2)**, [957]
summary proceedings, limitation of time for, **39(2)**, [953]
time limits, **39(2)**, [953]
Orders in Council, **39(2)**, [983]

merchant shipping—*contd*
regulations, making, **39(2)**, [983]
Secretary of State—
advisory committees, **39(2)**, [978]
forms, preparation of, **39(2)**, [977]
general functions of, **39(2)**, [969]
regulations, rules and orders, making, **39(2)**, [983]
returns to, **39(2)**, [976]
service of documents, **39(2)**, [968]
summary of provisions, **39(2)**, [1]
training, financial assistance for, **39(2)**, [723]
transitional provisions, **39(2)**, [1011]

merger. *See also* **Competition Commission**
absorption, by, **8(1)**, [993]
application of provisions, **8(1)**, [980]
compromise or arrangement with creditors or members, relations of provisions to, **8(1)**, [981]
Directive disclosure requirements, documents subject to, **8(1)**, [1156]
directors' explanatory report on, **8(1)**, [986]
documents, inspection of, **8(1)**, [989]
equitable rule, **20**, [786]
expert's report on, **8(1)**, [987]
associate, meaning, **8(1)**, [1015]
independence requirement, **8(1)**, [1014]
valuation by another person, **8(1)**, [1013]
meeting of members of transferee not required—
conditions for, **8(1)**, [996]
shares of transferor company held by transferee, where, **8(1)**, [994]
meetings of members or creditors of transferee company, power of court to summon, **8(1)**, [1016]
Merger Directive regulations, power to make, **43(S)**, 590
merging companies—
meaning, **8(1)**, [982]
members—
approval of, **8(1)**, [985]
documents, inspection of, **8(1)**, [989]
new transferee company, approval of articles of, **8(1)**, [990]
notice—
meaning, **47**, [788]
modification of provisions, **47**, [794]
Office of Fair Trading, functions of, **47**, [791]
period for considering, **47**, [789]
extension of, **47**, [789]–[790]
protection given by, exceptions to, **47**, [792]
regulations, **47**, [793]
requirement to give, **47**, [788]
Secretary of State, functions of, **47**, [791]
nominee of transferee company, no allotment of shares to, **8(1)**, [992]
Panel. *See* **Panel on Takeovers and Mergers**
reconstruction or amalgamation, relationship of provisions to, **8(1)**, [981]

merger—*contd*
scheme—
draft terms of—
particulars of, **8(1)**, [983]
publication of, **8(1)**, [984]
meaning, **8(1)**, [982]
members of merging companies, approval
of, **8(1)**, [985]
securities to which special rights attach,
protection of holders of, **8(1)**, [991]
shares of transferor company held by
transferee—
meeting of members of transferee not
required, **8(1)**, [994]
no meetings required, **8(1)**, [995]
particulars and reports not required,
8(1), [993]
supplementary accounting statement,
8(1), [988]
transfer of undertaking of transferor company,
power of court to fix date for, **8(1)**, [1017]
transferee company, no allotment of shares
to, **8(1)**, [992]
venture capital trust, of, **43(2)**, [198]

merger reference
anticipated mergers—
cancellation and variation of, **47**, [723]
duty to make, **47**, [717]
effects, duty to remedy, **47**, [727]
European Commission, duty of OFT
where case referred by, **47**, [719]
final determination, meaning, **47**, [771]
information powers, **47**, [720]
interest in shares, time of acquisition of,
47, [771]
interim orders, **47**, [773]
investigations and reports, **47**, [724]
time-limits for, **47**, [725]–[726]
orders relating to, **47**, [718]
power of Secretary of State, **47**, [161]
questions to be determined, **47**, [722]
share dealings, restrictions on, **47**, [770],
[787]
undertakings in lieu of reference, **47**, [765]
effect of, **47**, [766]
interim, **47**, [772]
not fulfilled, order-making power on,
47, [767]–[768]
See also undertakings *below*
assets—
limit of, for investigation, **47**, [149]
taken over, valuation of, **47**, [153]
associated persons, treatment of, **47**, [824]
body corporate, offences by, **47**, [822]
Competition Commission—
final orders by, **47**, [776]
general information duties, **47**, [798]
investigation powers—
documents, production of, **47**, [804]
enforcement, **47**, [805]
witnesses, attendance of, **47**, [804]
minority reports, **47**, [814]
penalties, **47**, [806]–[807]
appeals, **47**, [809]

merger reference—*contd*
Competition Commission—*contd*
penalties—*contd*
payment, **47**, [808]
recovery of, **47**, [810]
publicity requirements, **47**, [802]
statement of policy, **47**, [811]
completed mergers—
cancellation and variation of, **47**, [723]
dealings, restrictions on, **47**, [769], [787]
distinct, enterprises ceasing to be, **47**, [710]
time of, **47**, [711]
duty to make, **47**, [706]
effects, duty to remedy, **47**, [727]
enforcement orders, initial, **47**, [764]
final determination, meaning, **47**, [771]
information powers, **47**, [715]
interest in shares, time of acquisition of,
47, [771]
interim orders, **47**, [773]
investigations and reports, **47**, [724]
time-limits for, **47**, [725]–[726]
prior notice, **47**, [708]
questions to be determined, **47**, [721]
regulations, power to make, **47**, [716]
relevant customer benefits, **47**, [714]
relevant merger situations, **47**, [707]
stages, obtaining control by, **47**, [713]
time-limits, **47**, [708]
extension, **47**, [709]
turnover test, **47**, [712]
undertakings—
initial, **47**, [763]
interim, **47**, [772]
See also undertakings *below*
undertakings in lieu of reference, **47**, [765]
effect of, **47**, [766]
not fulfilled, order-making power on,
47, [767]–[768]
conditions for, **47**, [149]
consultation, duty of, **47**, [796]
defamation, privilege in relation to, **47**, [803]
enforcement orders—
completed mergers, initial, **47**, [764]
contents of, **47**, [780], [954]
directions, delegated power of, **47**, [779]
effect of, **47**, [778]
enforcement, right of, **47**, [786]
meaning, **47**, [778]
Office of Fair Trading—
consultation by, **47**, [785]
monitoring by, **47**, [784]
procedural requirements, **47**, [954]
register of, **47**, [783]
scope of, **47**, [778]
enterprises—
distinct, ceasing to be, **47**, [150]
time of, **47**, [151]
meaning, **47**, [148]
European mergers—
legitimate interests, intervention to
protect, **47**, [760]
scheme for, **47**, [761]
expedition, duty of, **47**, [795]

merger reference—*contd*
  false or misleading information, supply of, **47**, [812]
  fees, **47**, [818]
  functions of Director as to, **47**, [172]
  interim orders, making, **47**, [773]
  interpretation, **47**, [826]–[827]
  investigation—
    action resulting from, **47**, [158]
    limitation of, **47**, [155]
    situations subject to, **47**, [149]
  market for services, reference to, **47**, [825]
  media mergers—
    advice and information as to, **47**, [800]
    consultation in case of, **47**, [797]
    media enterprise, meaning, **47**, [749]
    OFCOM, additional investigation and report by, **47**, [731], [754]
    OFT, monitoring role of, **47**, [816]
  OFCOM—
    additional investigation and report by, **47**, [731], [754]
    advice and information from, **47**, [800]
    functions of, **47**, [815]
    general advisory function, **47**, [801]
    general information duties, **47**, [798]
  Office of Fair Trading—
    advice and information from, **47**, [799]
      Community law, primacy of, **47**, [819]
    case referred by European Commission, duty in case of, **47**, [719]
    general information duties, **47**, [798]
    information, power to request, **47**, [720]
    publicity requirements, **47**, [802]
    undertakings—
      consultation, **47**, [785]
      monitoring, **47**, [784]
  orders and regulations, **47**, [821]
  orders resulting from—
    cessation of effect, **47**, [160]
    conditions warranting, **47**, [159]
    draft, laying of, **47**, [201]
    enforcement of, **47**, [181]
    general provisions, **47**, [178]
    interim orders, **47**, [160]
    investigation of company, **47**, [180]
    powers exercisable by, **47**, [159]
    procedure relating to, **47**, [179]
    time-limit for making, **47**, [160]
  other than newspapers, **47**, [148]
  prior notice of—
    amendment of provisions, power of, **47**, [167]
    Director, role of, **47**, [163]
    interpretation of provisions, **47**, [166]
    power to refer unaffected, where, **47**, [164]
    regulations, **47**, [165]
    restriction of power to make, **47**, [162]
  procedural rules, **47**, [569]
  public interest cases, in—
    cessation of intervention, **47**, [746]
    Competition Commission, reference to, **47**, [732]–[733]
      cancellation, **47**, [738]
      European Commission, by, **47**, [734]

merger reference—*contd*
  public interest cases, in—*contd*
    Competition Commission, reference to—*contd*
      information, Office of Fair Trading requesting, **47**, [736]
      investigations and reports, **47**, [740]
      preliminary assessment period, extension of, **47**, [735]
      questions to be determined, **47**, [737]
      regulations, **47**, [742]
      restrictions on action, **47**, [743]
      time-limits, **47**, [741]–[742]
      variation of, **47**, [739]
    enforcement regime, **47**, [777], [953]
    excisions from reports, **47**, [813]
    investigation and report, **47**, [730]
    media mergers, **47**, [731]
    media considerations, **47**, [730]
    media enterprises, **47**, [749]
    Secretary of State—
      decisions of, **47**, [744]
      enforcement action by, **47**, [745]
      intervention by, **47**, [728]–[729]
      matters to be brought to attention of, **47**, [747]
    special. *See* special public interest cases *below*
    specified considerations, **47**, [748]–[749]
  publication of, **47**, [149]
  publicity requirements, **47**, [802]
  questions for investigation, **47**, [154]
  report on—
    action by Director on, **47**, [176]
    action recommended by, **47**, [158]
    contents, **47**, [158]
    Director to receive copy, **47**, [175]
    interim order following, **47**, [177]
    matters to be included in, **47**, [158]
    recommendations in, **47**, [158]
    Secretary of State, by, **47**, [149]
    situations qualifying for, **47**, [149], [154]
    time-limit for, **47**, [156]
    variation of, **47**, [157]
  review of decisions, **47**, [817]
  service of documents, **47**, [823]
  share of supply test, power to alter, **47**, [820]
  special public interest cases, in—
    enforcement regime, **47**, [777], [953]
    excisions from reports, **47**, [813]
    initial investigation and report, **47**, [753]
    media mergers, **47**, [754]
    OFCOM, additional investigation and report by, **47**, [754]
    Secretary of State, by—
      cancellation and variation of, **47**, [757]
      decision by, **47**, [759]
      enforcement action, **47**, [759]
      intervention by, **47**, [750]–[752]
      investigations and reports, **47**, [758]
      questions to be decided on, **47**, [756]
  stages, obtaining control by, **47**, [152]
  supply of services, reference to, **47**, [825]
  transitional and transitory provisions, **47**, [962]
  types of, **47**, [155]

merger reference—*contd*
  undertakings—
    enforcement, right of, **47**, [786]
    final, **47**, [774]
      not fulfilled, order-making power on,
        47, [775]
    in lieu of reference, **47**, [765]
      effect of, **47**, [766]
      not fulfilled, order-making power on,
        47, [767]–[768]
    initial, completed merger, **47**, [764]
    interim, **47**, [772]
    Office of Fair Trading—
      consultation by, **47**, [785]
      monitoring by, **47**, [784]
    procedural requirements, **47**, [957]
    register of, **47**, [783]
    subject-matter of, **47**, [781]
  undertakings as alternative to—
    acceptance of, **47**, [168]
    failure to fulfil, **47**, [171]
    publication, **47**, [169]
    review, **47**, [170]
  water mergers, **47**, [762]

Mersey Docks and Harbour Company. *See
also, generally,* **ports and harbours**
  debts, reduction of indebtedness, **39(2)**, [515]
  financial assistance to, provision, **39(2)**, [467]

Mersey River
  saving for, **39(2)**, [120]

mesmerism. *See* **hypnotism**

mesne profits
  compensation for, **9**, [82], [282]
  meaning, **9**, [282]

mesothelioma
  damages for, **31(S)**, Negligence 2–4
  lump sum payments—
    appeals to First-tier Tribunal, **40(2)**, [587]
    claim for—
      dependant, by, **40(2)**, [583]
      determination of, **40(2)**, [585]
      making, **40(2)**, [583]
      reconsideration of, **40(2)**, [586]
    conditions of entitlement, **40(2)**, [584]
    minors, to trustees of, **40(2)**, [588]
    people lacking capacity, to trustees of,
      40(2), [588]
    regulations, **40(2)**, [589]

messages
  interception. *See* **communications**

metal
  application of Hallmarking Act to, **48**, 66
  carat, use of term, **48**, 74
  fineness—
    describing, **48**, 52, 74
    meaning, **48**, 69
  precious—
    fineness, describing, **48**, 52, 74

metal—*contd*
  precious—*contd*
    meaning, **48**, 70

metal detector
  restrictions on use, **32**, [364]

methane gas
  British Coal Corporation, exploitation
    rights, **17(2)**, [135]
  Coal Authority, exploration rights,
    17(2), [126]

methyl alcohol
  spirit, deemed not, **19(3)**, [372]

methylated spirits
  power, surcharges or rebates on excise duty,
    13, [898]–[900]

metric units. *See also* **weights and measures**
  adaptation of enactments, **1(1)**, [248];
    1(2), [52]

metropolis
  definition, **25(1)**, [1]

Metropolitan Board of Works. *See* **London
Fire and Civil Defence Authority**

metropolitan commons. *See* **common (land)**

metropolitan county. *See also* **metropolitan
district council**
  administrative area, as, **25(2)**, [1], [234]
  application of planning provisions, **46**, [261]
  development plan for, **46**, [283]
  fire and civil defence authorities—
    constituent councils in relation to,
      25(2), [590]
    constitution of, **25(2)**, [590]
    establishment, **25(2)**, [589]
    functions transferred to, **25(2)**, [598], [646]
    members, number of, **25(2)**, [640]–[645]
    See also new authorities *below*
  highways, transfer of functions, **25(2)**, [583]
  Integrated Transport Authorities—
    airports, transfer of, to, **25(2)**, [600]
    disqualification for membership,
      25(2), [596]
    establishment, **25(2)**, [591]
    functions transferred to, **25(2)**, [599]
    members, number of, **25(2)**, [640]–[645]
    provisions applied to, **25(2)**, [647]
    See also new authorities *below*
  joint authorities—
    chairman and vice-chairman—
      allowances to, **25(2)**, [595]
      appointment, **25(2)**, [595]
      casual vacancy, filling, **25(2)**, [595]
    clerk, appointment, **25(2)**, [595]
    constituent councils, **25(2)**, [640]–[645]
    discharge of functions, questions on,
      25(2), [601]

metropolitan county—*contd*
  joint authorities—*contd*
    members—
      disqualification, **25(2)**, [596]
      notice of appointment, **25(2)**, [597]
      number of, **25(2)**, [592], [640]–[645]
      replacement of, **25(2)**, [593]
      vacancies, filling, **25(2)**, [594]
      See also new authorities *below*
  local planning authority for, **46**, [251]
  museums etc, vesting of, **25(2)**, [605]
  National Parks. *See* **National Park**
  new authorities—
    accounts, **25(2)**, [618]
    financial administration, **25(2)**, [619]
    financial provisions, **25(2)**, [618]–[620]
    provisions applied to, **25(2)**, [621]
    transfers to, orders for, **25(2)**, [628]
  orders etc, procedure for making, **25(2)**, [631]
  passenger transport authorities. *See*
    Integrated Transport Authority
    See also new authorities *above*
  police authorities. *See* **police authority**
  research schemes, **25(2)**, [623]
  residuary bodies—
    access to documents, **25(2)**, [647]
    acquisition of land by, **25(2)**, [647]
    annual reports by, **25(2)**, [647]
    authentication of documents, **25(2)**, [647]
    capital etc, treatment of, **25(2)**, [620]
    information to be furnished by,
      25(2), [647]
    land, powers as to, **25(2)**, [647]
    local government provisions applied,
      25(2), [647]
    members—
      disqualifications, **25(2)**, [647]
      remuneration of, **25(2)**, [647]
      tenure of office, **25(2)**, [647]
    pensions, liability for, **25(2)**, [613], [614]
    proceedings, regulation of, **25(2)**, [647]
    repayment of loans to, **25(2)**, [612]
    residuary property, custody of, **25(2)**, [615]
    rights and liabilities, **25(2)**, [612]
    services, power to provide, **25(2)**, [647]
    status, **25(2)**, [647]
    transfer of property etc, **25(2)**, [617]
      orders for, **25(2)**, [628]
    winding up, **25(2)**, [617]
  road traffic control systems, Ministers'
    powers, **25(2)**, [638]
  waste disposal, joint arrangements for,
    25(2), [585]

metropolitan county council
  For functions etc following abolition see
    metropolitan county. *See also* **local**
    government officers and staff
  abolition—
    acts prior to, validity, **25(2)**, [627]
    charity property, vesting of, **25(2)**, [625]
    date of, **25(2)**, [579]
    loans outstanding on, **25(2)**, [612]
    loss of employment on, **25(2)**, [609]
    pensions provisions, **25(2)**, [613], [614]

metropolitan county council—*contd*
  abolition—*contd*
    provisions having effect from date of,
      25(2), [580]
    residuary property etc, custody of,
      25(2), [615]
    transitional provisions, **25(2)**, [629]
  byelaws, continuity of, **25(2)**, [627]
  new authorities. *See* **metropolitan county**
  staff—
    compensation for loss of office etc,
      25(2), [609]
    transfer of, **25(2)**, [608]
    voluntary transfer, continuity of
      employment, **25(2)**, [610]
    See also **local government officers and**
      staff

metropolitan district. *See also* **metropolitan**
county
  highway authority, as, **36**, [1005]

metropolitan district council. *See also*
metropolitan county
  administrative areas, **25(2)**, [1], [234]
  functions transferred to—
    airports, **25(2)**, [600]
    countryside, **25(2)**, [582]
    flood prevention, **25(2)**, [586]
    highways, **25(2)**, [583]
    land drainage, **25(2)**, [586]
    local statutory provisions, under,
      25(2), [588]
    miscellaneous, **25(2)**, [639]
    reorganisation of, **25(2)**, [602]
    road traffic, **25(2)**, [583]
    trading standards etc, **25(2)**, [639]
    waste regulation and disposal, **25(2)**, [584],
      [585]
  grants to voluntary organisations, **25(2)**, [607]
  highway—
    bridge in two districts, **25(2)**, [637]
    functions, **25(2)**, [583]
  land drainage—
    functions, **25(2)**, [586]
    works, **19(3)**, [185]
  local Bills, promotion of, **25(2)**, [622]
  National Parks, functions, **25(2)**, [582]
  research and collection of information,
    25(2), [623]
  residuary functions of, **25(2)**, [616]
  road traffic—
    functions, **25(2)**, [583]
    powers, guidance in exercising,
      25(2), [638]
  transfer of staff to, **25(2)**, [608]
  waste disposal functions, **25(2)**, [584], [585]

metropolitan police. *See also* **police authority**
  amendment of enactments, **26(1)**, [791]
  Authority—
    chairman, **33(2)**, [270]
    establishment of, **33(2)**, [162]
    functions, questions as to at London
      Assembly meetings, **33(2)**, [195]

metropolitan police—*contd*
Authority—*contd*
local policing—
objectives, **33(2)**, [169]
plans, **33(2)**, [170]
magistrates, appointment of, **33(2)**, [270]
members—
appointment of—
independent members, **33(2)**, [270]
Mayor, by, **33(2)**, [270]
magistrates, appointment of, **33(2)**, [270]
number, **33(2)**, [163], [270]
Royal Parks Constabulary, transfers from,
33(2), [606]
capital expenditure, grants for, **33(2)**, [226]
civil staffs—
meaning, **33(2)**, [96]
pension provisions, **33(2)**, [96]
commanders, appointment of, **33(2)**, [180]
Commissioner—
appointment, **33(2)**, [174]
assistants—
appointment, **33(2)**, [178]
duties, **33(2)**, [29]
removal, **33(2)**, [179]
remuneration, **33(2)**, [58]
Deputy—
appointment, **33(2)**, [176]
functions, **33(2)**, [175]
removal, **33(2)**, [177]
functions, **33(2)**, [173]
removal, **33(2)**, [177]
remuneration, **33(2)**, [58]
Commissioners and Commanders,
continuation in post, **26(1)**, [667]
complaints against. *See* **police**
constables—
employment at HM yards—
authorisation of, **33(2)**, [27]
expenses incurred in, **33(2)**, [30]
swearing in for, **33(2)**, [28]
district. *See* **Metropolitan Police District**
dockyards, employment at, **33(2)**, [27]
expenses—
examination and approval, **33(2)**, [21]
payable by Receiver, **33(2)**, [21]
grants for, **33(2)**, [225]
housing, **33(2)**, [391]
international functions—
generally, **33(2)**, [256]
reports, application of requirements relating
to, **33(2)**, [257]
London Assembly, questions regarding at
meetings of, **33(2)**, [195]
maintenance of, **33(2)**, [161]
members, **33(2)**, [270]
national functions—
generally, **33(2)**, [256]
reports, application of requirements relating
to, **33(2)**, [257]
national security, grants for safeguarding,
33(2), [227]
pensions. *See* **police pensions**
property, in possession of, **33(2)**, [54]
ranks, **33(2)**, [181]

metropolitan police—*contd*
Receiver. *See* **metropolitan police district**
special constables—
defence establishments, service at,
33(2), [63]
swearing in, **33(2)**, [63]
special services, provision of, **33(2)**, [200]
vehicles—
arrest of person in charge of, **33(2)**, [22]
detention of, **33(2)**, [22]
yards, Her Majesty's—
employment of constables at, **33(2)**, [27]
meaning, **33(2)**, [31]

Metropolitan Police Authority
functional body, as, **26(1)**, [762]
local authority, treatment for tax purposes,
26(1), [757]
minimum budget, **26(1)**, [517], [518]
special expense of, **26(1)**, [516]
superannuation provisions, **26(1)**, [732], [733]

metropolitan police court
fees and fines, application of, **11(2)**, [150]

Metropolitan Police District
areas of, **25(1)**, [1], [720]
city police acting in, **25(1)**, [482]
fairs in. *See* **markets and fairs**
jurisdiction of officers, **33(2)**, [260]
meaning, **33(2)**, [262]
offences in, summary conviction, **33(2)**, [24]
provisions on alteration of, **26(1)**, [644]
public statues. *See* **statues**
Receivers of—
abolition of office, **26(1)**, [670]
accounts—
audit of, **33(2)**, [20]
financial year for, **33(2)**, [35]
appointment, **33(2)**, [19]
Bank of England account, **33(2)**, [19]
borrowing powers, **33(2)**, [87]
buildings, power to construct, **33(2)**, [37]
corporation sole, as, **33(2)**, [32]
duties, **33(2)**, [19]
gifts, acceptance of, **33(2)**, [252]
grants to, **33(2)**, [225]–[227], [251]
leases, power to grant, **33(2)**, [51]
loans, acceptance of, **33(2)**, [252]
moneys received by, **33(2)**, [19]
payments to be made by, **33(2)**, [19]
powers, **33(2)**, [33]
property etc—
acquisition, powers, **33(2)**, [33]
disposal of, **33(2)**, [33]
land, purchase of, **33(2)**, [38]
Minister's approval as to, **33(2)**, [39]
remuneration, **33(2)**, [58]
riot compensation. *See* **riot**
salaries payable by, **33(2)**, [21]
temporary absence of, **33(2)**, [52]
secondments to, **26(1)**, [668]
street collections, regulation of, **33(2)**, [60]

metropolitan traffic area
formation, **37**, [2]

Metropolitan Water Board
abolition, **49**, [1]
See now **Thames Water Authority**
establishment, original, **49**, [196]

mews
removal of manure, etc, from, **35(1)**, [132]

mice. *See* **rats and mice**

microfilm
evidence, use in, **18**, [246]

microgeneration
electricity generated by, sale of, **17(2)**, [579], [580]
installation of equipment, apparatus or appliances for, review of development orders to facilitate, **17(2)**, [581]
meaning, **17(2)**, [590]
national targets—
designation, **17(2)**, [577], [578]
meaning, **17(2)**, [577]
sustainable energy reports, information in, **17(2)**, [578]
permitted development orders, review of, **17(2)**, [581]
system, meaning, **17(2)**, [577]

midden
room over, prohibition on use as living, sleeping or work room, **35(1)**, [126]

Middle Temple
administration of justice, **25(1)**, [760]
building provisions, application to, **35(1)**, [610]
City, inclusion in, **25(1)**, [1]
City of London general rate, contribution to, **25(1)**, [113]
exemption from Building Acts, **25(1)**, [354]
functions exercisable by, **25(2)**, [626]
overground wires, placing, **25(1)**, [213]
Port of London Act, saving in, **39(2)**, [389]
public health purposes, local authority for, **35(1)**, [118]
references concerning, construction of, **35(1)**, [515], [649]
ward elections, **25(1)**, [641]
welfare services functions, **25(1)**, [706]

Middlesex
references to, in enactments, **25(1)**, [64]

Middlesex Deeds Register
closing of, **21**, [110]
indemnification for loss, **21**, [112]
meaning, **21**, [114]
memorials registered in, proof of, **21**, [113]
puisne mortgages registered in, **21**, [111]
searches, discontinuance, **21**, [110]

midwives
medicinal products, exemption for, **28**, [78], [111]
sex discrimination, **7(1)**, [58], [124]

milestone
pulling down or obliterating, **36**, [1186]

military drill
London heaths, on, **25(1)**, [72]

military establishment
meaning, **3**, [640]
watching, lighting etc, **25(1)**, [43]

military law
air forces, application to, **3**, [731]
naval forces, application to, **3**, [731]
persons subject to—
air forces, attached members of, **3**, [710]
colonial forces, **3**, [709]
commonwealth forces, **3**, [708]
death of—
absentees, **3**, [243]
army paymaster, of, **3**, [242]
assets and money remitted, **3**, [235]
creditor's rights, **3**, [240]
deserter, of, **3**, [243]
discharge of paymaster, **3**, [237]
disposal of non-monetary effects, **3**, [232]
duty or residue, **3**, [236]
effects, securing, **3**, [221]
felon, of, **3**, [243]
insane person, of, **3**, [244]
intestacy, **3**, [241]
medals and decorations, disposal of, **3**, [231]
official administrator, interposition of, **3**, [234]
original will, probate of, **3**, [241]
payments of charges, **3**, [221]
personal estate, **3**, [223]
preferential charges, **3**, [222]–[226]
representative's rights, **3**, [239]
residue, disposal of, **3**, [227]–[230]
surplus, disposal of, **3**, [227]
undisposed residue, **3**, [230]
generally, **3**, [707]
naval forces, attached members of, **3**, [710]

military prison
meaning, **3**, [640]

military remains
application of provisions, **3**, [1497]
authorised person—
meaning, **3**, [1502]
powers, **3**, [1502]
controlled site—
designation of, **3**, [1497]
prohibited actions at, **3**, [1498]
designation of vessels as, **3**, [1497]
expenses of Minister, **3**, [1504]
jurisdiction, extraterritorial, **3**, [1499]

military remains—*contd*
  meaning, **3**, [1505]
  offences—
    actions deemed to be, **3**, [1498]
    international waters, in, **3**, [1499]
    penalties for, **3**, [1498]
    proceedings for, **3**, [1498]
    supplemental provisions, **3**, [1503]
    unlicensed operations, **3**, [1501]
  prohibited operations—
    generally, **3**, [1498]
    licence to carry out—
      application for, **3**, [1501]
      falsely obtaining, **3**, [1501]
      grant of, **3**, [1500]
  summary of provisions, **3**, [1]
  tampering etc with, **3**, [1498]

military services
  financial provisions, **10**, [676]

military stores
  unlawful purchase of, **3**, [695]

militia
  London. *See* **London, City of**

militia storehouses
  generally, **3**, [1450]

milk
  consumer's committee. *See further*
    agricultural marketing schemes
  marketing boards. *See* **milk marketing boards**
  marketing scheme—
    power to amend, **1(1)**, [490]
    revocation of—
      Agricultural Marketing Act 1958, restriction of, **1(2)**, [511]
      consequential amendments, **1(2)**, [513]
      generally, **1(2)**, [492]
      Northern Ireland, extension of provisions to, **1(2)**, [531]
      position of Board following, **1(2)**, [504]
  meaning, **1(2)**, [466]
  prices—
    producers and sellers, licensing of, **1(2)**, [433]
  production, ceasing or reducing—
    entry on land to determine, **1(2)**, [235]
    Northern Ireland, **1(2)**, [239]
    offences, **1(2)**, [236]
    payments on, **1(2)**, [234]
  quotas—
    arbitrations, provisions applying, **1(2)**, [394]
    meaning, **1(2)**, [234], [401]
    ministerial expenses, **1(2)**, [397]
    outgoing tenant, compensation to—
      amount of, **1(2)**, [400]
      assignment of tenancy, **1(2)**, [399]
      Crown land, application to, **1(2)**, [401]
      enforcement, **1(2)**, [401]
      limited owners, powers of, **1(2)**, [401]
      notices, **1(2)**, [401]

milk—*contd*
  quotas—*contd*
    outgoing tenant, compensation to—*contd*
      part of land, termination of tenancy of, **1(2)**, [401]
      payment of, **1(2)**, [393]
      reversionary estate, severing of, **1(2)**, [401]
      right to, **1(2)**, [399]
      settlement of claim, **1(2)**, [401]
      sub-tenancy, termination of, **1(2)**, [399]
      succession to tenancy, and, **1(2)**, [399]
    registered, **1(2)**, [401]
    standard—
      determination before end of tenancy, **1(2)**, [401]
      meaning, **1(2)**, [400]
    tenant's fraction—
      determination before end of tenancy, **1(2)**, [401]
      meaning, **1(2)**, [400]
    valuation, **1(2)**, [400]
  special designation of, **1(2)**, [433]

Milk Development Council
  power to dissolve, **1(2)**, [734]

milk marketing boards
  assets, acquisition by registered producers, **1(2)**, [535]
  capital allowances, apportionment of, **1(2)**, [535]
  capital losses, unallowed, **1(2)**, [535]
  change of location, restraints on, **1(2)**, [536]
  chargeable gains, **1(2)**, [535]
  depreciatory transactions, **1(2)**, [535]
  disclosure of information, **1(2)**, [536]
  distribution of profits from commercial activities, **1(2)**, [525]
  distributions, **1(2)**, [535]
  functions, overriding nature of, **1(2)**, [510]
  functions of appropriate authority before vesting day, **1(2)**, [501]
  land registration, **1(2)**, [536]
  levies, **1(2)**, [508], [535]
  losses, apportionment of, **1(2)**, [535]
  meaning, **1(2)**, [514]
  membership, **1(2)**, [507]
  Northern Ireland, extension of provisions to, **1(2)**, [531], [535]
  pension scheme, **1(2)**, [536]
  position—
    in absence of reorganisation, **1(2)**, [506]
    reorganisation, following, **1(2)**, [505]
    revocation of milk marketing scheme, following, **1(2)**, [504]
  preparatory work, power to carry out, **1(2)**, [509]
  procedure where scheme not one which should be approved, **1(2)**, [495]
  provisions of, effective on statutory vesting, **1(2)**, [536]
  reorganisation, **43(1)**, [251]
  reorganisation schemes—
    alienation, restraints on, **1(2)**, [536]

milk marketing boards—*contd*

reorganisation schemes—*contd*

allocated shares, application of Trustee
Investments Act 1961, **1(2)**, [536]

applications for approval—

determinations, **1(2)**, [494]

generally, **1(2)**, [493]

information, requirements for,
1(2), [498]

publicity for determinations, **1(2)**, [499]

scheme not one which ought to be
approved, procedure, **1(2)**, [495]

disposition of property, rights and
liabilities, **1(2)**, [534]

existing participants, rights of, **1(2)**, [534]

form, **1(2)**, [534]

information, disclosure of, **1(2)**, [534]

introductory, **1(2)**, [534]

new successor bodies, nature of, **1(2)**, [534]

other disposals, **1(2)**, [534]

qualifying, **1(2)**, [534]

relevant board, functions of, **1(2)**, [500]

residual functions, **1(2)**, [534]

transfer of board's undertakings, rights and
liabilities, **1(2)**, [534]

vesting day, **1(2)**, [534]

reserve funds, **1(2)**, [535]

roll-over relief, **1(2)**, [535]

service of documents, **1(2)**, [512]

stamp duty, **1(2)**, [535]

stamp duty reserve tax, **1(2)**, [535]

statutory accounts, **1(2)**, [536]

statutory transfer on vesting day, **1(2)**, [502],
[536]

taxation provisions, **1(2)**, [535]

transfer of undertakings regulations,
application of, **1(2)**, [536]

transfer to successor bodies, **1(2)**, [535]

transfers relevant to flotation, **1(2)**, [536]

trusts for registered producers, **1(2)**, [535]

variation of approved scheme before vesting
day, **1(2)**, [496]

vesting, certificate of, **1(2)**, [536]

withdrawal of approval before vesting day,
1(2), [497]

mill and milling

meanings, **1(2)**, [41]

water rights as to, protection, **1(2)**, [17]

mill dams

removal or alteration, **19(3)**, [183]

watercourse, causing obstruction of,
19(3), [192]

millibars

atmospheric pressure expressed in, in customs
and excise Acts, **13**, [584]

Millwall docks

London Building Acts, exemption from,
39(2), [376]

meaning, **39(2)**, [423]

minders

child. *See under* **child**

mineral extraction allowance

availability of, **43(1)**, [1026]

balancing allowance—

amount of, **43(1)**, [1055]

avoidance affecting entitlement to,
43(1), [1209]

ceasing to work mineral deposits, on,
43(1), [1065]

discontinuance of trade, on, **43(1)**, [1068]

disposal of asset, on, **43(1)**, [1067]

employees abroad, ceasing to use buildings
or works for benefit of, **43(1)**, [1066]

entitlement to, **43(1)**, [1054]

giving up exploration, search or inquiry,
on, **43(1)**, [1064]

pre-trading expenditure, for, **43(1)**, [1063]

balancing charge—

amount of, **43(1)**, [1055]

entitlement to, **43(1)**, [1054]

contribution allowances, **43(1)**, [1178]

demolition costs, treatment of, **43(1)**, [1070]

development, meaning, **43(1)**, [1073]

disposal receipt, meaning, **43(1)**, [1057]

disposal values—

amount of, **43(1)**, [1060]

capital sum, receipt of, **43(1)**, [1062]

disposal of or ceasing to use asset,
43(1), [1058]

disposal receipt, meaning, **43(1)**, [1057]

interest in land, of, **43(1)**, [1061]

permitted development, use of asset other
than for, **43(1)**, [1059]

first-year allowances—

artificially inflated claims, **43(1)**, [1053]

entitlement to, **43(1)**, [1052]

qualifying expenditure available for,
43(1), [1049]

ring fence trade, expenditure incurred for,
43(1), [1050]

giving effect to, **43(1)**, [1069]

mineral asset—

acquiring, qualifying expenditure—

buildings or structures ceasing to be
used, **43(1)**, [1037]

generally, **43(1)**, [1035]

premium relief previously allowed,
reduction on, **43(1)**, [1038]

previous trader, owned by, **43(1)**, [1039]

undeveloped market value of land,
exclusion of, **43(1)**, [1036]

group, transfer within,
43(1), [1044]–[1045]

meaning, **43(1)**, [1029]

mineral exploration and access—

meaning, **43(1)**, [1028]

qualifying expenditure—

nature of, **43(1)**, [1032]

plant or machinery, pre-trading
expenditure on, **43(1)**, [1033]–[1034]

pre-trading, **43(1)**, [1033]–[1034]

mineral extraction allowance—*contd*
  oil licence. *See* **oil licence**
  qualifying expenditure—
    employees abroad, contribution to buildings
      or works for benefit of, **43(1)**, [1047]
    excluded expenditure, **43(1)**, [1031]
    first-year allowances, **43(1)**, [1049]
    historic costs, limited by reference to—
      assets generally, **43(1)**, [1043]
      group, transfers of mineral assets within,
        43(1), [1044]
      UK oil licence, **43(1)**, [1042]
    main types of, relationship between,
      43(1), [1030]
    meaning, **43(1)**, [1027]
    mineral asset, on acquiring—
      buildings or structures ceasing to be
        used, **43(1)**, [1037]
      generally, **43(1)**, [1035]
      premium relief previously allowed,
        reduction on, **43(1)**, [1038]
      previous trader, owned by, **43(1)**, [1039]
      undeveloped market value of land,
        exclusion of, **43(1)**, [1036]
    mineral exploration and access, on—
      nature of, **43(1)**, [1032]
      plant or machinery, pre-trading
        expenditure on, **43(1)**, [1033]–[1034]
      pre-trading, **43(1)**, [1033]–[1034]
    restoration, on, **43(1)**, [1048]
    second-hand assets, on—
      non-traders, acquired from,
        43(1), [1041]
      oil licence, acquisition from non-trader,
        43(1), [1040]
      previous trader, mineral asset owned by,
        43(1), [1039]
    time when incurred, **43(1)**, [1051]
    unrelieved, **43(1)**, [1056]
    works likely to become valueless, on,
      43(1), [1046]
  relevant planning enactments, **43(1)**, [1073]
  shares in assets, application to, **43(1)**, [1072]
  time of incurring expenditure, **43(1)**, [1071]
  transitional provisions, **43(1)**, [1228]
  writing-down—
    amount of, **43(1)**, [1055]
    entitlement to, **43(1)**, [1054]

mineral extraction trade
  allowance. *See* **mineral extraction**
    allowances
  meaning, **43(1)**, [1026]

mineral planning authority
  aftercare scheme, approval of, **46**, [624]
  meaning, **46**, [251]
  resumption of development, prohibiting,
    46, [630]
  supplementary suspension order, making,
    46, [630]
  suspension order—
    confirmation of, **46**, [630]
    enforcement of, **46**, [447]
    local land charge, registration as, **46**, [630]

mineral planning authority—*contd*
  suspension order—*contd*
    making, **46**, [630]
    penalties, **46**, [446]
    resumption of development following,
      46, [630]
    reviews, **46**, [630]
    revocation of, **46**, [630]
    supplementary, **46**, [630]

mineral rights
  Environment Agency, acquisition by,
    49, [1231], [1292]
  management expenses, claim for, **44(1)**, [100]
  undertakers, acquisition by, **49**, [997], [1057]

mineral royalties
  Commissioners determining, **44(3)**, [343]
  loss relief, **42**, [1331]
  management expenses available for set-off
    against, **44(1)**, [100]
  meaning, **44(1)**, [101]
  Northern Ireland—
    application to, **44(1)**, [101]
    meaning in, **44(3)**, [342]
  property income, relief, **44(3)**, [319]
  relief in respect of, **44(1)**, [101]
  rent receivable, relief for, **44(3)**, [340]
  taxation of, **42**, [1330]
  trade profits, **44(3)**, [156]

minerals. *See also* **mines and mining**
  acquisition under Defence Acts, **9**, [148]
  ancillary rights, **17(1)**, [366]
  Antarctic. *See* **Antarctic Minerals**
  boreholes, depth, when notice of required,
    17(1), [10]
  compensation, modifications, **46**, [378]
  continental shelf. *See* **continental shelf**
  county matters, **46**, [614]
  deep sea mining for. *See* **deep sea mining**
  development scheme, **46**, [972]
  entry on land, **9**, [451]
  exclusion from compulsory purchase, **9**, [450]
  exploration—
    grants, **17(1)**, [454]
    Natural Environment Research Council,
      notice to, **17(1)**, [10]
  exploration and access—
    expenditure incurred on, **44(1)**, [72]
    trade profits, **44(3)**, [160]
  extraction allowance. *See* **mineral extraction**
    allowance
  former mining land—
    damage or loss resulting from entry,
      17(1), [550]
    entry on, **17(2)**, [202]
    warrant, entry under, **17(1)**, [550]
    works on, **17(1)**, [551]
  hard mineral resources, meaning, **17(1)**, [512]
  ironstone. *See* **ironstone workings**
  local plans, **46**, [298]
  meaning, **17(1)**, [211]; **44(1)**, [101]; **46**, [612]
  mining lease, meaning, **20**, [436], [804]
  mortgagee, powers of, **20**, [719]

minerals—*contd*
opencast coal working, compensation arising, **17(1)**, [195]
owner, meaning, **9**, [449]
protected—
communication works through, **9**, [451]
meaning, **9**, [451]
remedial works, **9**, [451]
restrictions on working, **9**, [175]
right to work, **17(1)**, [365]
search for, **9**, [373]
severed—
communication works through, **9**, [451]
expenses and losses where, payment of, **9**, [451]
shafts or boreholes, nature of sinking of, **17(1)**, [10]
underlying, meaning, **9**, [449]
value, expert witness as to, **9**, [217]
winning and working—
county matter, reference to, **46**, [614]
default powers, **46**, [630]
development, permanent cessation of, **46**, [630]
discontinuance, order requiring, **46**, [630]
modification of provisions, **46**, [585]
notification of applications, revocation or modification of, **46**, [625]
planning permission for—
aftercare conditions, **46**, [624]
conditions, **46**, [333]
duration of, **46**, [624]
regulations, **46**, [585]
resumption, prohibition of, **46**, [630]
steps for protection of the environment, **46**, [630]
suspension—
orders after, **46**, [630]
resumption following, **46**, [630]
supplementary order, **46**, [630]
temporary stopping up of highways for, **46**, [526]
use of land, as, **46**, [365]
working—
compensation for not, **9**, [451]
improper, damage or obstruction to undertaking by, **9**, [451]
notice of intention to work, **9**, [451]
working facilities, grant of—
ancillary rights, **17(1)**, [365], [366]
meaning, **17(1)**, [366]
application for rights, **17(1)**, [368]
several, for same rights, **17(1)**, [370]
compensation or consideration, **17(1)**, [369], [373]
court, by, **17(1)**, [365], [366]
effect of grant, **17(1)**, [375]
Environment Agency etc, savings for rights, **17(1)**, [372]
generally, **17(1)**, [365]
limitation on, **17(1)**, [367], [371]
other than coal, **17(1)**, [365]
Railways Clauses Acts, savings for rights under, **17(1)**, [377]

minerals—*contd*
working facilities, grant of—*contd*
Secretary of State and departments, duty, **17(1)**, [374]
support, required for, applications for, **17(1)**, [371], [372]
surface, meaning, **17(1)**, [378]
tables of rights, **17(1)**, [365]
tenants for life, provisions as to, **17(1)**, [376]

miners
free coal, allowance of and cash for, **44(2)**, [309]
former worker, for, **44(2)**, [644]
welfare trusts, **5(2)**, [502]

miners' welfare. *See also* **Coal Industry Social Welfare Organisation; mines and mining**
colliery welfare property. *See under* **Coal Industry Social Welfare Organisation**
Commission—
dissolution, **17(1)**, [51]
transfer of property, liabilities, etc, **17(1)**, [51]
generally. *See* **mines and mining** (safety etc)
institutes. *See* **gaming**
restructuring of industry, provisions applicable, **17(2)**, [148]
trusts, **5(2)**, [502]
trusts and other welfare bodies, provisions and savings, **17(2)**, [206]

Miners Welfare Fund
certain trusts, savings, **17(2)**, [206]
Charity Commission, application concerning to, **17(1)**, [702]
representative organisations, participation by, **17(1)**, [702]
trust property provided out of, power to vary, **17(1)**, [13]
winding up, **17(1)**, [52]

miners' welfare institute
bingo—
activities, as part of, **5(1)**, [555]
high turnover period, **5(1)**, [555]
enforcement, entry on premises for, **5(1)**, [592]
exempt gaming in, **5(1)**, [549]–[550]
gaming permit—
appeals, **5(1)**, [662]
application for, **5(1)**, [662]
area for gaming, **5(1)**, [552]
cancellation and forfeiture, **5(1)**, [662]
conditions, **5(1)**, [551]
duration, **5(1)**, [662]
form of, **5(1)**, [662]
licensing authority, functions of, **5(1)**, [662]
maintenance, **5(1)**, [662]
meaning, **5(1)**, [551]
procedure, **5(1)**, [554]
register of, **5(1)**, [662]
renewal, **5(1)**, [662]

miners' welfare institute—*contd*

gaming permit—*contd*

vehicles and vessels, not applying to, **5(1)**, [662]

machine permit—

appeals, **5(1)**, [662]

application for, **5(1)**, [662]

cancellation and forfeiture, **5(1)**, [662]

conditions, **5(1)**, [553]

duration, **5(1)**, [662]

form of, **5(1)**, [662]

licensing authority, functions of, **5(1)**, [662]

maintenance, **5(1)**, [662]

meaning, **5(1)**, [553]

register of, **5(1)**, [662]

renewal, **5(1)**, [662]

vehicles and vessels, not applying to, **5(1)**, [662]

meaning, **5(1)**, [548]

provision of facilities by, **5(1)**, [550]

mines and mining. *See also* **coal mine; minerals**

abandoned—

fencing, **17(1)**, [131]

plans and sections relating to tips, **17(1)**, [390]

abandonment—

meaning, **49**, [1153]

requirement to give notice of, **49**, [1154]

access, means, provision and maintenance, **17(1)**, [120]

accidents, workmen's inspection after, **17(1)**, [126]

Acts and regulations—

exemptions etc, provisions as to, **17(1)**, [148]

general savings, **17(1)**, [157]

information with respect to, furnishing of, **17(1)**, [127]

minor and consequential amendments, **17(1)**, [164]

administration of mining industry—

generally, **17(1)**, [2], [3], [6]

inquiries, **17(1)**, [5]

inter-departmental arrangements, **17(1)**, [6]

advisory committees, appointment, **17(1)**, [3]

Authority. *See* **Coal Authority**

below ground premises, Offices, Shops etc Act 1963, exclusion of application, **18**, [1245]

blasting materials and devices, **17(1)**, [111]

buildings and structures, safety of, **17(1)**, [119]

central rescue station, **17(1)**, [112]

certificate of competency—

cancellation or suspension, **17(1)**, [130]

inquiry into fitness of holder—

delivery up of certificate after, **17(1)**, [130], [163]

generally, **17(1)**, [130]

tribunal, **17(1)**, [130], [162]

offences and conviction, effect of, **17(1)**, [130]

charge to tax, **44(1)**, [34]

mines and mining—*contd*

colliery welfare. *See under* **Coal Industry Social Welfare Organisation**

common law rights of workmen, **17(1)**, [159]

concessional coal, payments in lieu, **17(2)**, [145]

conservation notices—

appeals, **49**, [1248]

form of, **49**, [1248]

continental shelf, search for coal in, **17(1)**, [290]

conveyors—

at working faces, charge of, **17(1)**, [97]

charge of, **17(1)**, [95]

safe operation, securing of, **17(1)**, [95]

copyhold land, former—

retained interests—

claims—

acceptance, **17(2)**, [204]

application of provisions, **17(2)**, [204]

costs of, **17(2)**, [204]

form, **17(2)**, [204]

rejection, **17(2)**, [204]

compensation—

agreements as to, **17(2)**, [204]

notice of, **17(2)**, [204]

payment of, **17(2)**, [204]

persons entitled, **17(2)**, [204]

provisions applicable, **17(2)**, [204]

disposition, saving for rights of, **17(2)**, [205]

miscellaneous provisions, **17(2)**, [205]

notices, **17(2)**, [173]

particulars required in, **17(2)**, [174]

rejection, challenge of, **17(2)**, [204]

rights generally, **17(2)**, [173]

transitional provisions, **17(2)**, [205]

working of coal in—

compensation, **17(2)**, [204]

notices, **17(2)**, [173]

rights generally, **17(2)**, [173]

danger—

area, entry to save life, **17(1)**, [115]

inflammable gas, amount of, **17(1)**, [115]

withdrawal of workmen in case of, **17(1)**, [115]

deep sea. *See* **deep sea mining**

Devon and Cornwall, in, **10**, [46]

disused, fencing, **17(1)**, [131]

drainage schemes, **17(1)**, [4]

drinking water, supply of, **17(1)**, [125]

expenses of Minister, **17(1)**, [149]

explosives, use of, **17(1)**, [111]

fencing—

disused and abandoned, **17(1)**, [131]

working places, where fall of two metres, **17(1)**, [120]

fire precautions—

fire fighting and rescue, **17(1)**, [112]

rooms at special risks, escape from, **17(1)**, [113]

health. *See* safety, health and welfare *below*

Health and Safety Executive. *See* **Health and Safety Executive**

mines and mining—*contd*
information—
  disclosure of, prevention, **17(1)**, [15]
  furnished to Authority, inaccurate,
    liability, **17(2)**, [182]
  held by Authority—
    confidentiality, **17(2)**, [183]
    public access to, **17(2)**, [181]
  use of, **17(1)**, [15]
inquiries, power to hold, **17(1)**, [5]
inspection on behalf of workmen,
  17(1), [126]
inspectors—
  meaning, **17(1)**, [153]
  notices served by, references upon,
    17(1), [144]
  powers, **17(1)**, [386]
interests in, Authority or Corporation, of,
  protection, **17(2)**, [136]
leases. *See* **mining lease**
licences—
  Authority's duties as to, **17(2)**, [125]
  See also **coal mining operations**
lighting—
  manager's duty, **17(1)**, [104]
  permitted lights, **17(1)**, [105]
    meaning, **17(1)**, [153]
  safety lamps, **17(1)**, [106]
machinery and apparatus—
  air, gas and steam containers, **17(1)**, [118]
  construction and maintenance, **17(1)**, [116]
  meanings, **17(1)**, [153]
  restrictions on use of certain engines,
    17(1), [117]
  winding and haulage, provision,
    17(1), [88], [95]
machinery, compensation for requisition of,
  9, [123]. *See also* **minerals**
manager—
  duties, **17(1)**, [386]
  transport rules, powers and duties as to,
    17(1), [91]
meaning of mine, **9**, [449]; **17(1)**, [151]
mining code, generally, **36**, [210], [594],
  [595]
museums, financial assistance for, **17(2)**, [185]
nationalisation. *See* **coal industry**
  nationalisation
notices—
  served by inspector, references upon,
    17(1), [144]
  service of, **17(2)**, [187]
nuisance, unfenced as, **17(1)**, [131]
offences—
  accessories to, **17(1)**, [133]
  certificate of competency, effect of
    conviction on, **17(1)**, [130]
  contravention, meaning, **17(1)**, [132],
    [134], [153]
  defence, offence not committed
    personally, **17(1)**, [136]
  employment of young persons, unlawful,
    liability for, **17(1)**, [143]
  generally, **17(1)**, [132]
  owner or manager, by, **17(1)**, [132]

mines and mining—*contd*
offences—*contd*
  penalty, no express penalty provided,
    17(1), [135]
  persons guilty of, **17(1)**, [132]
  proceedings, results of, duty to report,
    17(1), [142]
  separate contraventions, different persons,
    17(1), [134]
  servants, breaches of duty by, liability for,
    17(1), [138]
  unavoidable contravention, **17(1)**, [137]
opencast. *See* **opencast coal**
opencast planning permission, application
  for, **9**, [441]
operations. *See* **coal mining operations**
operations affecting water conservation, notice
  of, **49**, [1248]–[1249]
orders and rules—
  parliamentary control, **17(1)**, [147]
  revocation and variation, **17(1)**, [146]
outlets, signalling in, **17(1)**, [98]
output, meaning, **17(1)**, [7]
owner—
  breach of duty by servants, liability,
    17(1), [138]
  compensation for non-working, **9**, [451]
  general duties, **17(1)**, [386]
  meaning, **17(1)**, [152]
  offences by, **17(1)**, [132]
pipe-lines in, **17(1)**, [275]
pit closures, redundancy payments,
  17(1), [500], [557]
plans, faulty, **17(1)**, [87]
powers, transfer of, **17(1)**, [2]
profit sharing schemes, **17(1)**, [9]
property—
  Authority's duty as to, generally,
    17(2), [126]
  character and use, Authority's duty as to,
    17(2), [126]
railway as part of, **17(1)**, [151]
railway, under or near. *See* **railway**
redundant workers, payments to, **17(1)**, [557]
refuse from, combustion of, **35(2)**, [42]
regulations—
  information respecting, furnishing of,
    17(1), [127]
  parliamentary control, **17(1)**, [147]
  variation and revocation, **17(1)**, [129]
rent, charge to tax, **44(1)**, [98]
restructuring. *See under* **British Coal**
  Corporation; *see also* **coal mining**
  operations (licensing)
rights—
  registration of, **17(2)**, [180]
  working facilities. *See* working facilities
    below
roads—
  conveyors, use of, **17(1)**, [90]
  foot passengers in, safety of, **17(1)**, [92]
  refuge holes, provision, **17(1)**, [93]
  signalling in, **17(1)**, [99]
  transport rules, **17(1)**, [91]

mines and mining—*contd*
roads—*contd*
vehicles—
prohibition where no free movement,
17(1), [90]
safety measures in use of, **17(1)**, [94]
ropeway as part of, **17(1)**, [151]
royal, **10**, [39], [44]–[46]
safety, health and welfare—
access, means of, **17(1)**, [120]
blasting materials and devices, use of,
17(1), [111]
buildings and structures, **17(1)**, [119]
Coal Authority—
coal mine water discharge—
compulsory purchase of land,
17(2), [130], [197]
entry, powers of, **17(2)**, [129], [196]
powers with respect to, **17(2)**, [128]
duty with respect to safety, **17(2)**, [127]
drinking water, supply of, **17(1)**, [125]
dust precautions, **17(1)**, [114]
employment, safe means of, **17(1)**, [120]
fire precautions. *See* fire precautions *above*
lighting. *See* lighting *above*
matches and lighters, possession,
17(1), [109], [110]
rescue service, **17(2)**, [179]
roads. *See* roads *above*
sanitary conveniences, **17(1)**, [122]
shafts and outlets—
securing of, **17(1)**, [89]
signalling in, **17(1)**, [98]
smoking materials, possession, **17(1)**, [109]
staple-pits, **17(1)**, [89]
support. *See* support *below*
vehicles, in use of, **17(1)**, [94]
ventilation—
means of, **17(1)**, [102]
provision, **17(1)**, [100]
vermin and insects, measures against,
17(1), [123]
winding and haulage apparatus—
operation of, **17(1)**, [95], [96]
provision of, **17(1)**, [88]
safety lamps—
mine, meaning, **17(1)**, [153]
offences relating to, **17(1)**, [108]
prohibited lamps, **17(1)**, [107]
sanitary conveniences, provision, **17(1)**, [122]
service of documents, **17(2)**, [187]
severed, works involving, **9**, [451]
shafts—
depth, when notice required, **17(1)**, [10]
securing of, **17(1)**, [89]
signalling in, **17(1)**, [98]
unfenced, as statutory nuisance,
17(1), [131]
winding and haulage apparatus, **17(1)**, [88]
small mines, persons managing, savings,
17(1), [158]
smoking materials, possession of, prohibition,
17(1), [109]
stannaries. *See* **stannaries**
staple-pits, securing, **17(1)**, [89]

mines and mining—*contd*
statutory rights, savings, **17(2)**, [206]
subsidence. *See* **coal mining subsidence**
summary of provisions, **17(1)**, [1]
support—
minerals required for, restrictions on
working facilities, **17(1)**, [371], [372]
sufficiency, **17(1)**, [1]
withdrawal—
notice of, **17(2)**, [163]
provisions applicable, **17(2)**, [164]
right of, **17(2)**, [163]
revocation, **17(2)**, [166]
savings for special cases, **17(2)**, [165]
See also **coal mining subsidence**
third parties, protection, **17(1)**, [1]
tips. *See* **tips**
trade profits, income taxed as, **44(3)**, [12]
training mines, application of provisions to,
17(1), [154]
transport plans, **17(1)**, [91]
underground land, additional rights in relation
to, **17(2)**, [175]
unworked, rights in or relation to,
17(2), [124]
vehicles—
below ground, accompanying on foot,
17(1), [92]
prohibition on use where no free
movement in road, **17(1)**, [90]
safety measures in use of, **17(1)**, [94]
transport rules, **17(1)**, [91]
use in mines, **17(1)**, [91]
ventilation—
airways, use of, **17(1)**, [103]
apparatus, provision and maintenance,
17(1), [102]
exemptions permitted, **17(1)**, [102]
gas in waste, avoidance of danger,
17(1), [101]
interruption or cessation, **17(1)**, [100]
leakage of air between airways, prevention,
17(1), [103]
means of, **17(1)**, [102]
provision, duty as to, **17(1)**, [100]
vermin and insects, measures against,
17(1), [123]
waste, gas in, avoidance of danger,
17(1), [101]
waterworks, near. *See* **waterworks**
welfare. *See* safety, health and welfare *above*;
See also **Coal Industry Social Welfare**;
miners' welfare
Welsh language, knowledge of, provisions as
to, **17(1)**, [145]
winding and haulage apparatus—
charge of, when persons—
are carried, **17(1)**, [95]
not carried, **17(1)**, [96]
provision, **17(1)**, [88]
winding apparatus, meaning, **17(1)**, [153]
working, meaning, **17(1)**, [153]
working facilities, grant of—
adjoining mines, **17(1)**, [365]

mines and mining—*contd*
  working facilities, grant of—*contd*
    ancillary rights—
      generally, **17(1)**, [365]
      meaning, **17(1)**, [366]
    application for rights—
      generally, **17(1)**, [368]
      references to court, **17(1)**, [369]
      several, in respect of same rights,
        17(1), [370]
    compensation or consideration,
      17(1), [373]
      determination by court, **17(1)**, [369],
        [372]
      special provisions, **17(1)**, [372]
    court, by, **17(1)**, [365], [366]
    effect of grant of rights, **17(1)**, [375]
    Environment Agency etc, savings for
      rights, **17(1)**, [372]
    limitation on grant of rights, **17(1)**, [367],
      [371]
    minerals other than coal, **17(1)**, [365]
    Railways Clauses Acts, rights under,
      savings, **17(1)**, [377]
    Secretary of State and departments, duty
      of, **17(1)**, [374]
    support, minerals required for, restrictions,
      17(1), [371], [372]
    surface, meaning, **17(1)**, [378]
    tables of rights, **17(1)**, [365]
    tenants for life, provisions as to,
      17(1), [376]
  young persons, employment of. *See under*
  young persons

mining and oil industries
  capital allowances, transitional provisions,
    43(1), [1224]
  interests in oil fields, transfer of,
    anti-avoidance, **43(1)**, [730]
  mineral extraction trade—
    expenditure incurred for, **43(1)**, [720]
    expenditure wholly for, capital allowances,
      43(2), [107]
    meaning, **43(1)**, [719]
    pre-trading expenditure, **43(1)**, [721]
  offshore infrastructure—
    chargeable periods ending before 1st or 6th
      April, 2001, **43(2)**, [72]
    chargeable periods ending on or after 1st or
      6th April, 2001, **43(2)**, [73]
    decommissioning expenditure—
      allocation to pool, **43(1)**, [724]
      application of provisions,
        43(1), [724]–[725]
      meaning, **43(1)**, [723]
    meaning, **43(1)**, [722]
  oil production sharing contracts—
    application of provisions,
      43(1), [731]–[735]
    cessation of ownership, disposal values on,
      43(1), [735]
    oil-related use of plant or machinery,
      43(1), [731]

mining and oil industries—*contd*
  oil production sharing contracts—*contd*
    plant or machinery, expenditure incurred
      on—
      contractor, by, **43(1)**, [732]
      participator, by, **43(1)**, [733]–[734]
  ring fence trade—
    abandonment expenditure—
      cessation of trade, incurred before,
        43(1), [728]
      meaning, **43(1)**, [727]
      within three years of ceasing trade,
        43(1), [729]
    meaning, **43(1)**, [726]
    separate qualifying activity, as, **43(1)**, [726]

mining lease
  ironstone working comprised in, **17(1)**, [48]
  Landlord and Tenant Act 1954, exclusion from
    Part II, **21**, [207]
  war damage provisions. *See* **war damage**

mining operations
  meaning, **46**, [315]

minister of religion. *See also* **clergy**
  accommodation benefits, **44(2)**, [292]
  expenses, deduction for, **44(2)**, [361]
  institutions, ministry at, **14**, 654–5
  legal capacity of, **14**, 59–60
  meaning, **14**, 655, 753
  non-resident electors, ministry to, **14**, 654
  sex discrimination, **7(1)**, [57]
  trade profits, **44(3)**, [158]
  trades or occupations of, **14**, 645–6

Minister of Transport
  acquisition of land by, **36**, [1285]
  advances by, **36**, [1319]
  appeals to, **36**, [1279]
  bridge—
    construction of, **36**, [1105]
    maintenance, contributing to, **36**, [1325]
    transfer to, **36**, [1059], [1312]
  delegation of functions, **36**, [1010], [1092]
  experiments by, **36**, [1332]
  functions of highway authority, exercising,
    36, [1066]
  Greater London, executing improvements in,
    36, [1335]
  highway authority, as, **36**, [210], [1005]
  inquiries, **36**, [1354]
  new highway, construction of, **36**, [1028]
  secondment of staff to, **36**, [1021]
  trunk road system, reviewing, **36**, [1013]

Ministers. *See also under names of departments*
  contracting-out of functions—
    amendment of provisions, **10**, [770]
    disclosure of information, **10**, [762], [769]
    effect of, **10**, [759]
    excluded functions, **10**, [758]
    financial provisions, **10**, [767]
    interpretation, **10**, [766]
    Northern Ireland, **10**, [765]

Ministers—*contd*
  contracting-out of functions—*contd*
    order for, **10**, [757]
    termination, **10**, [760]
  corporation sole, as, **10**, [603]
  evidence of documents, **10**, [603]
  House of Lords, in, **10**, [707]
  oaths, taking, **10**, [603]
  Orders in Council, **10**, [598]
  salary, **10**, [605], [612]–[616]
    alteration of, **10**, [606]–[607]
  Scottish Executive, in. *See* **Scottish Executive**
  seal of, **10**, [603]
  staff of, **10**, [603]
  title, change of, **10**, [597]
  transfer of functions, **10**, [594]
  transport and subsistence expenses, **44(2)**, [297]

Ministry of Defence Police
  amended provisions, **33(S)**, Police 18–21
  arrest, search upon, **3**, [1718]
  British Transport Police—
    having powers of, **33(2)**, [131]
    providing assistance to, **33(2)**, [132]
  codes of practice, **3**, [1721]
  disaffection among members, causing, **33(2)**, [142]
  disciplinary matters—
    proceedings, representation at, **33(2)**, [137]; **33(S)**, Police 19
    regulations, **33(2)**, [136]
  dismissal, appeals against, **33(2)**, [138]; **33(S)**, Police 20–1
  establishment, **33(2)**, [130]
  impersonation, **33(2)**, [141]
  inspectors of constabulary—
    functions of, **33(2)**, [139]
    reports from, publication of, **33(2)**, [140]
  jurisdiction, **10**, [713]; **33(2)**, [131]
  membership, **33(2)**, [130]
  Northern Ireland police, powers and duties of, **33(2)**, [131]
  orders, **3**, [1721]
  other forces—
    assistance to, **33(2)**, [132]
    constables serving with, **33(2)**, [133]
  persons, powers to stop and search, **3**, [1710]–[1711]
  premises, entry and search of—
    arrest, for purposes of, **3**, [1717]
    commanding officer's power to authorise, **3**, [1715]
    judicial officer—
      power to authorise, **3**, [1713]
      review by, **3**, [1716]
    special provisions as to access, **3**, [1714]
  reasonable force, power to use, **3**, [1722]
  seizure—
    generally, **3**, [1719]
    property in possession of service police or commanding officer, **3**, [1720]
  Serious Organised Crime Agency, constables serving with, **33(2)**, [134]

Ministry of Defence Police—*contd*
  summary of provisions, **33(2)**, [17]
  supplementary provisions, **3**, [1724]
  vehicles, powers to stop and search, **3**, [1710]–[1711]
    commanding officer's powers, **3**, [1712]

Ministry of Defence Police Committee
  appointment of, **33(2)**, [130]

minor. *See also* **child, young person**
  application of income from property of, **20**, [438]
  beneficial interest, vesting order as to, **48**, 525
  building society membership, **19(1)**, [730]
  citizenship. *See* **citizenship**
  contracts—
    disapplication of relief Acts, **6**, [272]
    former provisions, **6**, [1]
    generally, **6**, [1]
    guarantees, **6**, [273]
    restitution of property after majority, **6**, [274]
  credit, offering to, **39(1)**, [206]
  executor, as, **18**, [645]
  firearms or ammunition—
    acquisition or possession by, **12(1)**, [497], [498]
    imitation, supply of, **12(1)**, [500]
    supply to, **12(1)**, [499]
  friendly society—
    as member of, **19(1)**, [504]
    disqualification for office in, **19(1)**, [465]
  independent domicile, acquiring, **6**, [153]
  legal estate—
    conveyance to, effect, **20**, [530]; **23**, [335]
    incapacity to hold, **20**, [1], [625]
    vested in, transitional provisions, **20**, [810]
  management of estate of, **18**, [542], [641]
  married, receipt by, **20**, [640]
  meaning, **6**, [1], [113]
  medical treatment, consent to, **6**, [111]
  necessaries, sale to, **39(1)**, [375]
  pawn taken from, **39(1)**, [276]
  property of, appointment of trustees, **18**, [545]
  settled land—
    management of, **20**, [603]
    powers relating to, **20**, [529]
  settlement for, **20**, [505]
  supervision order. *See* **supervision order**
  surgical, medical and dental treatment, consent to, **6**, [111]
  tattooing of, **6**, [106]
  trust income, application of, **48**, 487–9
  trustee, void appointment as, **20**, [639]
  trustees, appointment, **18**, [545]

Mint, the
  assay office, inspection of, **48**, 83
  authority of, coins made with, **10**, [284]
  Chancellor of the Exchequer as master of, **10**, [278], [576]
  consolidated fund, payments into, **10**, [278]
  expenses of, **10**, [278]

Mint, the—*contd*
trading funds for, **10**, [576]

miscarriage of justice
compensation for, **12(4)**, [494], [580]
amount, assessment of, **12(1)**, [1089], [1090]
application for, **12(1)**, [1089]
assessors—
appointment of, **12(1)**, [1089], [1115]
assessment by, **12(1)**, [1089]
qualification, **12(1)**, [1115]
removal from office, **12(1)**, [1115]
remuneration and allowances, **12(1)**, [1115]
determination of rights to, **12(1)**, [1089]
payment, **12(1)**, [1089]
person detained for at least 10 years, **12(1)**, [1091]

misdemeanour
felony, abolition of distinction, **12(1)**, [360]

misrepresentation
damages for, **39(1)**, [71]
friendly society matters, in, **19(1)**, [536]
liability for, excluding provisions, avoidance, **39(1)**, [72]
newspaper's annual return, in, **19(3)**, [291]
rescission of contracts, bars to, removal, **39(1)**, [70]
summary of provisions, **39(1)**, [1]

mission and pastoral committee
appointment, **14(S)**, 171
constitution, **14(S)**, 195
functions of, **14(S)**, 172

mistake
limitation of action, postponement in case of, **19(3)**, [762]

mobile crane
vehicle excise duty, **13**, [1044]

mobile home. *See also* **caravan**
meaning, **32**, [321]
owner, rights of, **32**, [1]
re-siting, **21**, [777]
site. *See* **caravan site**
summary of provisions, **20**, [1]

mobile telephones
benefit in kind, as, **44(2)**, [328]
employee, provision to, **43(S)**, 45–6
meaning, **44(2)**, [328]
re-programming—
offence of, **12(3)**, [552]
possession or supply of anything for purposes of, **12(3)**, [553]
unique device identifier, changing, **12(3)**, [552]

mobilisation
documents, illegal dealings, **3**, [696], [969]

mobilisation—*contd*
reserve forces. *See* **reserve forces (call out)**

molluscs
importation and exportation, restriction on. *See* **animals**
sale, etc, restriction on. *See* **animals**

monastery. *See* **religious houses**

money laundering
counter-terrorism provisions, general note, **12(S)**, 4–5
criminal conduct, meaning, **12(3)**, [451]
criminal property—
acquisition, use and possession of, **12(3)**, [434]
arrangement, retention, use or control of, **12(3)**, [433]
concealing, etc, offences, **12(3)**, [432]
meaning, **12(3)**, [451]
disclosures—
authorised, **12(3)**, [447]
form and manner of, **12(3)**, [448]
group, within, **12(3)**, [439]
institutions, permitted between, **12(3)**, [440]
permitted, **12(3)**, [439]–[442]
protected, **12(3)**, [446]
Serious Organised Crime Agency, to, **12(3)**, [449]
undertaking, within, **12(3)**, [439]
investigations, meaning, **12(3)**, [452]. *See also* **proceeds of crime**
offences, **12(3)**, [493]
penalties, **12(3)**, [443]
prohibited act, consent to—
appropriate, **12(3)**, [444]
nominated officer, by, **12(3)**, [445]
rules, **19(2)**, [195]
suspected, failure to disclose—
nominated officers, **12(3)**, [436], [437]
regulated sector, **12(3)**, [435], [436], [545]
supervisory authorities, **12(3)**, [546]
terrorist financing, directions—
conditions for giving, **12(S)**, 117–18
Crown, application to, **12(S)**, 138
definitions, **12(S)**, 118
enforcement—
civil penalties, **12(S)**, 130–2
information powers, **12(S)**, 126–9
offences, **12(S)**, 133–6
Financial Services Authority, functions of, **12(S)**, 138
guidance, preparation of, **12(S)**, 138
interpretation, **12(S)**, 139–40
licensing, **12(S)**, 124–5
notices, **12(S)**, 138
persons to whom given, **12(S)**, 119–21
procedural provisions, **12(S)**, 124–5
report to Parliament, **12(S)**, 137
requirements imposed by, **12(S)**, 121–4
supervisory authority, supervision by, **12(S)**, 137

money laundering—*contd*
  terrorist financing, directions—*contd*
    United Kingdom person, meaning,
     12(S), 138–9
  terrorist property and funds, **12(2)**, [880]
  threshold amounts, **12(3)**, [450]
  tipping-off, offences of, **12(3)**, [438]

money orders. *See under* **postal services**

moneylenders
  registration and licensing, **11(1)**, [1]

monition (ecclesiastical)
  meaning, **14**, 592
  notice of, **14**, 247
  regulations, **14**, 122
  residence enforced by, **14**, 110–11, 112
  sequestration not issuing after, **14**, 123

monopolies. *See also* **monopoly references**
  toll roads, application of enactments,
    38(1), [168]

Monopolies and Mergers Commission. *See
now* **Competition Commission**
  airport charges references. *See* **airport**
  dissolution of, **47**, [517]

**Monopolies and Restrictive Practices
Commission.** *Became* **Monopolies and
Mergers Commission.** *Now* **Competition
Commission**

monopoly
  offences, **47**, [538]

monopoly references
  false or misleading information furnished to,
    47, [183]
  orders—
    enforcement of, **47**, [181]
    general provisions, **47**, [178]
    powers exercisable as to, **47**, [199]–[200]
    procedure relating to, **47**, [179]
    unlawful agreements, making, **47**, [199]
  public bodies, involving—
    agricultural schemes, **47**, [337]
    bodies etc subject to, **47**, [331]
    body corporate, offences by, **47**, [334]
    false or misleading information, **47**, [334]
    general provisions, **47**, [331]
    interim orders, **47**, [335]
    investigation, powers of, **47**, [333]
    monopoly situations, **47**, [331]
    penalties, **47**, [333]
    provisions applied to, **47**, [331]
    public interest, protection of, **47**, [174]
    questions referable, **47**, [331]
    report on, orders following, **47**, [336]
    time limits, **47**, [332]
  reports—
    action on, **47**, [176]
    Director to receive copies, **47**, [175]
    interim order after, **47**, [177]

monopoly references—*contd*
  reports—*contd*
    made before appointed day, **47**, [202]
    transitional provisions, **47**, [202]

monstrans de droit
  proceedings against Crown by, abolition,
    13, [43]

month
  meaning, **41**, [605]; **45**, [918]
  See also **calendar; time**

Montreal Protocols
  carriage by air. *See* **carriage by air** (Warsaw
    Convention)

Montserrat
  court, powers of, **7(2)**, [613]

monument. *See also* **ancient monument**
  burial ground, in. *See* **burial ground**
  erection and maintenance in streets,
    35(1), [55]
  faculty for work on, **14**, 638
  meaning, **32**, [382]

monuments. *See* **burial ground**

moorings
  non-domestic rates, exemption from,
    25(2), [835]
  owner, **25(2)**, [753]

moorland
  public access to, **32**, [1]

moped
  application of motor cycle provisions to,
    37, [481]

moral rights
  assignable, not, **11(1)**, [905], [1071]
  author or director—
    consent to acts infringing, **11(1)**, [895]
    derogatory treatment of work, objection
     to—
      exceptions to, **11(1)**, [889]
      infringing article, possessing or dealing
       with, **11(1)**, [891]
      qualification of right, **11(1)**, [890]
      right of, **11(1)**, [888]
    duration of, **11(1)**, [894]
    false attribution of work, **11(1)**, [892]
    identification of—
      assertion of right, **11(1)**, [886]
      exceptions, **11(1)**, [887]
      rights of, **11(1)**, [885]
    joint works, application of provisions to,
     11(1), [896]
    part of works, **11(1)**, [897]
    waiver of, **11(1)**, [895]
  infringement, remedies for, **11(1)**, [916],
    [1073]

moral rights—*contd*
  performer—
    derogatory treatment of performance,
      objection to—
        exceptions to, **11(1)**, [1066]
        infringing article, possessing or dealing
          with, **11(1)**, [1067]
        right of, **11(1)**, [1065]
    identification of—
      assertion of right, **11(1)**, [1063]
      exceptions, **11(1)**, [1064]
      rights of, **11(1)**, [1062]
  photographs and films, right to privacy of,
    11(1), [893]
  subsistence of, **11(1)**, [787]
  summary of provisions, **11(1)**, [415]
  transitional provisions, **11(1)**, [1175]
  transmission on death, **11(1)**, [906], [1072]

Moravians
  affirmation by, right to, **18**, [75]

mortgage
  acquisition of property subject to, **9**, [133]
  advance payment of compensation where
    acquired land subject to, **9**, [350]
  aircraft, of, **4(1)**, [136]
  building society. *See* **building society**
  charge by way of legal mortgage—
    creation, **20**, [705]
    forms, **20**, [734]
    freehold, **20**, [703]
    leasehold, **20**, [704]
    legal estate, as, **20**, [625], [705]
    legal mortgage—
      generally, **20**, [705]
      interest, as, **20**, [625]
    mortgagee, powers and remedies, **20**, [705]
  coast protection charges, levy subject to,
    49, [389]
  commonhold, over common parts, **24**, [29]
  consolidation, **20**, [711]
  conversion into mortgage by demise,
    20, [658]
  conveyance by way of—
    implied covenants, **20**, [694]
    operation as demise, **20**, [704]
  costs, contributions to, **22**, [320], [321]
  discharge—
    forms, **20**, [826], [831]
    friendly society, **19(1)**, [500], [501]
    reconveyances, **20**, [732]
    statutory mortgage or charge, **20**, [733],
      [827], [831]
  discharge of—
    acquisition order, in pursuance of,
      22, [747], [777]
    purchase notice, in pursuance of, **22**, [702],
      [776]
  documents—
    first mortgagee's right to possession,
      20, [704], [705]
    inspection, production and delivery,
      20, [714]

mortgage—*contd*
  endorsed receipt, friendly society,
    19(1), [500], [556]
  equitable charges, realisation by court,
    20, [708]
  foreclosure—
    action for, order for sale, **20**, [709]
    order for, **20**, [706]
      power of sale, whether affecting,
        20, [724]
    trust following, **20**, [650]
  freehold—
    conversion into mortgage by demise,
      20, [658], [813]
    mode of effecting, **20**, [703]
    realisation of, **20**, [706]
    sale of mortgage, **20**, [706]
    term of, **20**, [703]
  improper investment in, **48**, 460
  incumbrancer—
    more than one, priorities, **20**, [712]
    mortgagor in possession, leasing powers as
      against, **20**, [717]
  indemnity by local authority, **22**, [319]
  insurance—
    amount, limitation on, **20**, [726]
    application of money received, **20**, [726],
      [727]
    mortgagee, by power to effect, **20**, [719]
    receiver, powers as to, **20**, [727]
  interest—
    benefit, payment of sums from,
      40(1), [517]; **40(2)**, [13]
    meaning, **40(1)**, [517]
  interest relief. *See* **mortgage interest relief**
  interest subject to, compensation for
    depreciation where, **9**, [307], [313]
  joint account, advance on, **20**, [729]
  land subject to compulsory purchase, of—
    additional development after acquisition,
      compensation, **9**, [260]
      mortgagee, to, **9**, [67], [274]–[277]
    deed poll, vesting of mortgagee's interest
      by, **9**, [67]–[70], [274]
    equity of redemption, **9**, [65], [274]
    mortgage—
      exceeding value of land, **9**, [67], [275]
      part of land subject to acquisition, of,
        9, [69], [276]
      repaid before due date, compensation
        where, **9**, [71], [277]
    mortgage money—
      court, payment into, **9**, [68], [274]–[275]
      notice of intention to pay, **9**, [65], [274]
      payment or tender to mortgagee,
        9, [65], [274]
    mortgagee—
      compensation to—
        early repayment of mortgage, **9**, [71],
          [277]
        mortgage exceeding value of land,
          9, [67], [275]
        part only of mortgaged land taken,
          9, [69], [276]

mortgage—*contd*
  land subject to compulsory purchase,
    of—*contd*
      mortgagee—*contd*
        mortgage money, recovery of residue,
          9, [70], [276]
        purchase or redemption of interest,
          9, [65], [274]
        refusal to accept mortgage or other
          money, **9**, [68], [70], [274]
        release of interest by, **9**, [65], [274]
        saving for rights of, **9**, [71], [275]
        vesting of interest under deed poll,
          9, [67]–[70], [274]
      payments into court, **9**, [68], [274]–[275]
      possession, taking, **9**, [274]
  leasehold—
    assignment of, operating as sub-demise,
      20, [704]
    conversion into mortgage by sub-demise,
      20, [658], [814]
    licence to sub-demise by way of, **20**, [704]
    mode of effecting, **20**, [704]
    purported assignment, operation, **20**, [704]
    realisation of, **20**, [707]
    rents and covenants, apportionment,
      20, [707]
    reversion, incumbrances affecting, **20**, [707]
    sale by mortgagee, **20**, [707]
    term of, **20**, [704]
  legal—
    charge by way of. *See* charge *above*
    meaning, **20**, [804]; **21**, [622], [624]
    priority, **20**, [715]
  loan in inner urban area, securing, **46**, [37]
  local authority. *See* **local authority**
  meaning, **17(1)**, [211]; **20**, [436], [804];
    21, [230], [678]
  mines and minerals—
    powers of mortgagee, **20**, [719]
    separate dealings with, **20**, [710]
  money secured by, limitation of action for,
    19(3), [748]
  mortgaged property, meaning, **20**, [709],
    [732]
  mortgagee—
    action for possession, **21**, [377], [413]
    charge by way of legal mortgage, powers
      and remedies, **20**, [705]
    conveyance by, **20**, [706], [707]
    dwelling house, action for possession,
      21, [377], [413]
    equitable, remedies available, **20**, [709]
    estate or interest of, powers incidental to,
      20, [719]
    fee simple, enlargement into term,
      20, [706]
    first, right to possession of documents,
      20, [704], [705]
    fixtures and chattels personal, rights as to,
      20, [706], [707]
    further advances, right to make, **20**, [712]
    in possession—
      lease by—
        powers, **20**, [632], [717]

mortgage—*contd*
  mortgagee—*contd*
    in possession—*contd*
      lease by—*contd*
        surrender, acceptance, **20**, [718]
        meaning, **20**, [804]
      insurance by, **20**, [719]
      mines and minerals, powers as to, **20**, [719]
      prior, tacking, **20**, [712]
      receipt by. *See* receipt *below*
      vesting declaration by, **20**, [633], [707]
  mortgagee, service of blight notice by,
    46, [408]
  mortgagor—
    action by, for possession, **20**, [716]
    bankruptcy of, **20**, [728]
    documents—
      delivery by, **20**, [714]
      right to inspect and copy, **20**, [714]
    in possession, lease by—
      powers, **20**, [632], [717]
      surrender, acceptance, **20**, [718]
      meaning, **20**, [718], [804]
    transfer, right to require, **20**, [713]
  notice of trusts affecting mortgage debts,
    20, [730]
  opencast coal mining, mortgaged land,
    17(1), [205]
  option scheme, termination of, **42**, [445]
  possession, action by mortgagor for, **20**, [716]
  prior—
    mortgagee, priority of ranking of further
      advances by, **20**, [712]
    right to create, **20**, [712]
  puisne—
    land charge, as, **21**, [392]
    meaning, **21**, [392]
    priorities between, **20**, [715]
    purchaser with notice taking subject to,
      20, [626]
  realisation—
    equitable charges, by court, **20**, [708]
    leasehold mortgage, **20**, [707]
  receipt—
    endorsed—
      reconveyance by, **20**, [732]
      transfer of mortgage, by, **20**, [732]
    forms, **20**, [826], [831]
    mortgagee, by, sufficiency, **20**, [725]
    survivor under joint account, by, **20**, [729]
  receiver—
    agent of mortgagor, as, **20**, [727]
    appointment, **20**, [719], [727]
    bankruptcy of mortgagor, effect of,
      20, [728]
    powers and duties, **20**, [727]
    remuneration, **20**, [727]
  reconveyance, alternative to, **20**, [713]
  redemption, **9**, [65], [274]
    action for, order for sale, **20**, [709]
    barred, trust of land, **20**, [650]
    cesser on, provision for, **20**, [703], [704]
    transfer, right to require, **20**, [713]

mortgage—*contd*
registered land, application of provisions,
  20, [703], [704]
  See also **land registration**
regulated—
  county court, jurisdiction of, 21, [623]
  hardship to mortgagor, mitigation of,
    21, [623]
  interest rate, limitation of, 21, [623]
  meaning, 21, [622]
  order, variation or revocation of terms of,
    21, [623]
  relevant date, created before, 21, [621]
  repayment, extension of time for, 21, [623]
  security, apportionment of, 21, [623]
  variation of terms of, 21, [623]
regulated agreement, as, 21, [378]
sale—
  action for redemption or foreclosure, in,
    20, [709]
  conveyance on, 20, [722]
  deposit to meet expenses, 20, [709]
  equitable mortgage, order of trust,
    20, [708]
  judgment or order for, 20, [709]
  mines and minerals, separate disposition,
    20, [710]
  power of—
    exercise of—
      generally, 20, [724]
      improper or irregular, 20, [722]
      persons entitled to, 20, [724]
      regulation of, 20, [721]
    foreclosure notwithstanding, 20, [724]
  proceeds, application, 20, [650], [723]
  security for costs, 20, [709]
  undivided shares, mortgages of, 20, [720]
second or subsequent, term, 20, [703], [704]
servicemen defaulting on, 3, [382], [388]
settled land, of, 20, [519]
ship, of. *See* **ship**
statutory—
  covenants implied, 20, [734], [736]
  discharge—
    form, 20, [737], [831]
    receipt on, form, 20, [831]
  forms, 20, [734], [827]–[831]
  joint mortgagors, 20, [736]
  transfer, 20, [735]
sub-mortgage—
  mode of effecting, 20, [703], [704]
  realisation, 20, [706], [707]
surrender, alternative to, 20, [713]
tacking, 20, [712]
tenant for life raising money by, 20, [573]
tenant in tail, by, estate created, 20, [79]
term—
  cesser, 20, [703], [704]
    on payment off, 20, [733]
  enlargement into fee simple, 20, [706]
  surrender, endorsed receipt operating as,
    20, [732]
timber, cutting and sale by mortgagee,
  20, [719]

mortgage—*contd*
transfer—
  alternative to reconveyance etc, 20, [713]
  deed, by, 20, [731]
  endorsed receipt, by, 20, [732]
  form, 20, [825]
  mortgagor, right to require, 20, [713]
  provisions operating, 20, [731]
  transferee, meaning, 20, [731]
trust for sale, by way of, 20, [703]
trust of land where redemption barred,
  20, [650]
trust property, on sale of, 48, 461
trustee—
  capital money, raising, 48, 469
  persons dealing with, protection of,
    48, 470
trusts affecting mortgage debts, notice,
  20, [730]
vesting declaration, mistaken payment after,
  9, [398]
vesting order consequential on, 48, 519

mortgage interest relief
deduction of tax, paid under, 44(1), [184]
joint borrowers, 44(1), [186]
limited loan, 44(1), [186]
payment under deduction of tax, qualifying
  lenders, 43(1), [80]
qualifying borrowers, 44(1), [190]
qualifying lenders, 44(1), [190]
  register of, 44(1), [191]
qualifying maximum, 43(1), [68]
  loan in excess of, 44(1), [186]
regulations, 44(1), [192]
relevant loan interest—
  conditions for deduction, 44(1), [187]
  interest—
    ceasing to be, 44(1), [189]
    never being, 44(1), [188]
  meaning, 44(1), [185]

mortmain
prohibition, 20, [8]

mortuary
byelaws as to, 35(1), [146]
provision of, 35(1), [146]
removal of infected body to, 35(1), [489]

mothers
nutrition, benefits under schemes for
  improving, 30, [748]

motor boat
petroleum-spirit, keeping and use for,
  regulations as to, 35(1), [107], [110]

motor car. *See also* **car (company); motor
vehicle**
anti-avoidance provisions, 43(1), [640]
appropriate percentage, car with CO_2
  emissions figure, 43(S), 43–5

motor car—*contd*

business expenditure, tax relief for—
avoidance cases, disposal value in,
43(S), 1463
capital allowances, **43(S)**, 1460–8
connected persons, **43(S)**, 1470, 1472–3
corporation tax, **43(S)**, 1471–6
hire expenses, restrictions on deductions
for, **43(S)**, 1469–77
short-term hiring out and long-term hiring
in, **43(S)**, 1470, 1472–3
special rate cars, **43(S)**, 1462
capital allowances, transitional provisions,
43(1), [1224]
disabled persons, hire cars for, **43(S)**, 1466
disposal values, bringing into account,
43(1), [640]
electrically-propelled vehicles—
meaning, **43(S)**, 1463–4
taxable benefits, **43(S)**, 1613
emissions, terms relating to, **43(S)**, 1464
employee's, withdrawal of capital allowances,
43(2), [37]
hire, qualifying, **43(1)**, [642]
inexpensive, pooling, **43(1)**, [482]
low carbon dioxide emissions, with,
43(1), [600]
main rate car, meaning, **43(S)**, 1461
meaning, **36**, [677]; **37**, [309], [752], [801];
43(1), [641]; **43(S)**, 1463
mileage allowance, **43(2)**, [36]
partial depreciation subsidy, effect of,
43(1), [639]
qualifying activity, partly used other than for,
43(1), [638]
qualifying expenditure—
other person, partly met by, **43(1)**, [637]
single asset pool, allocated to, **43(1)**, [635]
taxable benefits—
cars with CO_2 emissions figures,
appropriate percentage, **43(S)**, 1612
disabled employee, automatic car for,
43(S), 1388–9
electrically propelled cars, **43(S)**, 1613
price cap, abolition, **43(S)**, 1612
writing-down allowance, general limit on
amount of, **43(1)**, [636]

motor cycle. *See also* **car (company); motor
vehicle**

business expenditure, tax relief for—
capital allowances, **43(S)**, 1460–8
corporation tax, **43(S)**, 1471–6
hire expenses, restrictions on deductions
for, **43(S)**, 1469–77
carriage of persons on, restrictions, **37**, [594]
driving licence. *See* **driving licence**
EC certificate of conformity—
requirements as to, **37**, [645]
sale without, **37**, [647]
emissions, terms relating to, **43(S)**, 1464
exhaust systems—
offences and enforcement of provisions,
37, [482]
requirements, **37**, [480]

motor cycle—*contd*

head gear, wearing of—
authorisation of appliances, **37**, [588]
contravention of provisions, proceedings,
37, [588], [815]; **38(1)**, [4]
requirement, **37**, [586]
Sikh religion, persons of, exemption,
37, [586]
helmets, protective—
contravention of provisions, proceedings,
37, [588], [815]; **38(1)**, [4]
meaning of, **37**, [587]
meaning, **36**, [677]; **37**, [309], [481], [801];
43(S), 1463
noise control, **37**, [480]
parking places, **37**, [229]
safety equipment, offences, **38(1)**, [4]
sidecar as part of, **37**, [310], [802]
silencers, requirements, **37**, [480]
vehicle excise duty, **13**, [1042]

motor fuel

pollution by. *See* **air pollution**

motor racing

disapplication of provisions, **37**, [581]
public ways, on, **37**, [579]
regulation of events, **37**, [580]

motor salvage operator

amendment or repeal of provisions, **47**, [597]
entry and inspection of premises, right of,
47, [591]
false particulars on sale for salvage, offence of
giving, **47**, [594]
false statements, offence of, **47**, [592]
"fit and proper" test, application of, **47**, [595]
interpretation provisions, **47**, [598]
notification of destruction of motor vehicles,
47, [590]
offences, proceedings for, **47**, [596]
records, keeping of, **47**, [589]
registration of—
appeals, **47**, [588]
applications for, **47**, [585]
cancellation of, **47**, [586]
notification requirements, **47**, [593]
registers, **47**, [584]
renewal of, **47**, [585]
representations, right to make, **47**, [587]
requirement for, **47**, [583]

motor scooter

application of motor cycle provisions to,
37, [481]

motor tractor

meaning, **13**, [1032]; **36**, [677]; **37**, [801]

motor vehicle. *See also* **mechanically
propelled vehicle**

abandoned—
offence, **35(1)**, [398]
fixed penalty notice for—
amounts paid under, use of,
35(1), [401]

motor vehicle—*contd*
  abandoned—*contd*
    offence—*contd*
      fixed penalty notice for—*contd*
        contents, **35(1)**, [399]
        name and address power to require,
          35(1), [400]
        payment of, **35(1)**, [399]
      penalty where, **35(1)**, [398]
      removal of—
        charges for, **37**, [275]
        claimed by owner, **37**, [272]
        disposal after, **35(1)**, [403]
        duty of local authority as to,
          35(1), [402]
        entry powers in connection with,
          35(1), [408]
        expenses, **35(1)**, [405]
        guidance on, **35(1)**, [404]
        interim disposal, **37**, [271]
        loading area, from, **37**, [276]
        owner, right of to recover vehicle or
          proceeds of sale, **37**, [273]
        parking place, from, **37**, [275]
        powers, **37**, [270]
        representations and appeals, **37**, [274]
        safe custody after, **35(1)**, [402]
        ultimate disposal, **37**, [272]
  aggravated vehicle-taking, **38(1)**, [33]
    accident or damage arising, **12(1)**, [565]
    fine, power to impose, **12(2)**, [129]
    offence and punishment, **12(1)**, [565];
      12(2), [129]
  alarm, distress or annoyance, used in manner
    causing—
      retention, **33(2)**, [387]
      seizure, **33(2)**, [386]
  appliances and apparatus as part of, **37**, [310],
    [802]
  articulated, **37**, [311], [803]
  brakes, breach of requirement as to, **37**, [614]
  bridleway, driving on, **37**, [301], [605]
  broken down—
    removal of—
      charges for, **37**, [275]
      interim disposal, **37**, [271]
      owner, right of to recover vehicle or
        proceeds of sale, **37**, [273]
      parking area, from, **37**, [275]
      powers, **37**, [270]
      representations and appeals, **37**, [274]
  byway, driving on, **37**, [301]
  carriage, when deemed, **37**, [807]
  conditional sale agreement, under—
    dealings, presumptions on, **39(1)**, [67]
    debtor, disposal by, **39(1)**, [66]
  construction, regulation of—
    contravention, **37**, [618]
    definitions, **37**, [670]
      index of, **37**, [671]
    powers, **37**, [613]
    temporary exemption, **37**, [619]
  control of, breach of requirement as to,
    37, [617]

motor vehicle—*contd*
  Crown, in service of, provisions applied,
    37, [302]
  dangerous condition, in, using, **37**, [612]
  dangerous position, leaving in, **37**, [592]
  definitions, **36**, [677]
  design, construction, equipment etc, approval,
    See type *below*
  disabled person, use by. *See under* **disabled
    person**
  disqualified, driving while, **12(1)**, [1084]
  documents, forging and misuse. *See* **forgery;
    road traffic offences**
  driver—
    disqualification. *See under* **driving licence**
    identification of, **36**, [672], [674]
      corporation, offence by, **37**, [790]
      failure to give information, **37**, [786],
        [790]
      generally, **37**, [286]
      ignorance in, **37**, [790]
      information, duty to give, **37**, [789],
        [790]
      offences applicable, **37**, [790];
        38(1), [121]
      summary proceedings, in, **37**, [56];
        38(1), [11]
    instruction. *See* **driving instruction**
    licence. *See* **driving licence**
    meaning, **36**, [679], [811]; **37**, [315]
    name and address, failure to give or giving
      false information, **37**, [786], [790]
  drivers hours. *See* **driver's hours**
  driving—
    elsewhere than on roads, **37**, [301], [605]
    furious, **36**, [226], [256]
    licence. *See* **driving licence**
    offences. *See* **road traffic offences**
    test. *See* **driving licence**
  equipment, regulation of—
    contravention, **37**, [614], [615]
    powers, **37**, [613]
  examination and testing. *See* **vehicle testing**
  exceptional dimensions of loads, **37**, [620]
  footpaths, driving on, **37**, [301], [605]
  foreign vehicles—
    authorised inspector, powers, **36**, [901],
      [902]; **37**, [128]
    authorised person for purposes of,
      36, [905]
    damage or loss, responsibility for, **36**, [903]
    detention of, **36**, [903]
    documents, production of, **36**, [904]
    driver—
      fees, **36**, [902]
      meaning, **36**, [905]
      requirements as to, **36**, [908]
    driving prohibition, powers, **36**, [901]
    examiners—
      functions conferred on, **36**, [901], [907]
      meaning, **36**, [905]
      obstruction of, **36**, [910]
      powers, **36**, [901]
    goods vehicles—
      application of provisions, **36**, [901]

motor vehicle—*contd*
  foreign vehicles—*contd*
    goods vehicles—*contd*
      meaning, **36**, [905]
  goods. *See* **goods vehicles**
  heavy locomotive, meaning, **36**, [677];
    37, [309], [801]
  heavy motor car, meaning, **36**, [677];
    37, [801]
  hire-purchase agreement, under—
    dealings, presumption on, **39(1)**, [67]
    debtor, disposal by, **39(1)**, [66]
  immobilisation—
    device, meaning, **37**, [277]
    financial penalty deposits, **38(2)**, [502]
    when illegally parked. *See under* **parking**
      (illegal)
  incorrectly registered, offence, **33(2)**, [580]
  information, withholding, **37**, [786], [790]
  inspection—
    extension of provision as to, **37**, [11]
    fees, **36**, [902]
      power of, **36**, [901], [907]
      testing, **37**, [128]
      testing station, at, **36**, [902]
  inspector—
    construction of references to, **37**, [149]
    powers, **37**, [128]
  offences, **36**, [903]
  presumption as to, **36**, [905]
  prohibition on driving of—
    conditional exemption, **36**, [902]
    contravention, **36**, [902]
    enforcement, **36**, [903]
    notice of, **36**, [901], [902]
    power to impose, **36**, [901]
    removal, **36**, [902]; **37**, [128]
  removal to place of detention, **36**, [901],
    [903]
  suspicion as to an offence, **36**, [903]
  testing station—
    inspection at, **36**, [902]
    meaning, **36**, [905]
  trailers, **36**, [903], [905]
  vehicles carrying more than eight
    passengers, **37**, [652]
  weighing, powers as to, **36**, [901]
  insurance. *See* **insurance**
  insurance status, disclosure of information as
    to, **33(2)**, [582]
  interference with, **12(1)**, [759]
  international circulation—
    extent of powers, **36**, [766]
    facilitation, **36**, [648]
    Northern Ireland, **36**, [649]
  invalid carriages. *See* **invalid carriages**
  licence—
    excise, conditions for grant of, **37**, [648]
    insurance, evidence of in application for,
      37, [771]
    local authorities, transfer of functions
      from, **36**, [888]
    regulations, power to make, **36**, [888]

motor vehicle—*contd*
  licence—*contd*
    See also **driving licence; goods vehicles;**
      hackney carriages; public service
      vehicles; stage carriages
  locomotives—
    light, meaning, **36**, [677]; **37**, [309]
    meaning, **36**, [677]; **37**, [801]
    trailer drawn by, permitted weight,
      37, [188]
  marine salvage vehicles, speed limit variation,
    37, [306]
  meaning, **35(1)**, [112], [411]; **37**, [64], [309],
    [801]
  mobile telephones, breach of requirement as
    to, **37**, [617]
  Northern Ireland, application of provisions,
    36, [875], [886], [887]
  nuisance, savings for law of, **36**, [680];
    37, [316]; **38(1)**, [132]
  offences. *See* **road traffic offences**
  parking. *See* **parking**
  parts—
    approval mark, **37**, [665]
    defective or unsuitable, fitting and supply,
      37, [661]
    examination, **37**, [661]
    export of, **37**, [661]
    meaning, **37**, [670]
    vehicles sold without, **37**, [646]
  passenger carrying, other than public service
    vehicles, application of provisions, **37**, [11],
    [652]
  passenger vehicles weight, breach of
    requirement, **37**, [615]
  plated weights, determination, **37**, [134],
    [627]
  police constable—
    birth date of driver, power to require,
      37, [781], [782]
    documents, production of, to, **37**, [781]
    insurance, requirement to produce evidence
      of, **37**, [782]
    licence, production of, to, **37**, [781]
    names and addresses, power to obtain,
      37, [782]
    power to stop, **37**, [780]
    seizure of forged or false documents,
      37, [794]
    test certificate, production of, **37**, [782]
  private hire-cars. *See* **private hire vehicles**
  public service vehicles. *See* **public service**
    vehicles
  recording equipment, installation and use. *See*
    under **drivers' hours**
  reflectors, construction and use, **37**, [668]
  registration documents, power of constable to
    require, **33(2)**, [581]
  registration marks, obscured, **26(2)**, [849]
  regulations, general provisions, **36**, [889];
    37, [307]
  removal for street cleansing, London,
    25(2), [348]
  road fund, winding up, **36**, [664]

motor vehicle—*contd*
routes, Police Commissioners' powers, **36**, [224]
safety equipment for children. *See* **seat belts**
sale—
  dealer's responsibilities, **37**, [660]
  meaning, **37**, [670]
  unroadworthy vehicles, **37**, [660]
  used vehicles, testing condition, **37**, [662]
special, not complying with regulations, authorisation of use, **37**, [620]
speed—
  assessment detection devices, breach of requirement as to, **37**, [616]
  limit. *See* **speed limit**
steering-gear, breach of requirement as to, **37**, [614]
street offences under Acts of 1839 and 1847, **36**, [226], [385]
summary of provisions, **36**, [210]
tail lamps—
  construction and use, **37**, [668]
  meaning, **37**, [670]
  offences arising, **37**, [668]
taking without authority—
  aggravated. *See* aggravated vehicle-taking *above*
  offence and punishment, **12(1)**, [564], [1084]
tampering with, **37**, [596]
tax. *See* **car tax**
tests. *See* **vehicle testing**
third party insurance. *See* **insurance**
tractor, meaning, **36**, [677]
trailer. *See* **trailer**
type vehicles—
  alterations, notification of, **37**, [137], [630], [638]
  approval certificates—
    appeals, **37**, [639]
    cancellation, **37**, [635]
    conditions, **37**, [635]
    issue of, **37**, [634]
    Minister's, **37**, [637], [642]
    obligatory, **37**, [642]
    parts, sale without, **37**, [646]
    refusal, **37**, [635]
    sale without, **37**, [646]
    suspension of, **37**, [635]
  approval marks, **37**, [633]
  approval requirements—
    generally, **37**, [633]
    regulations, **37**, [640]
    supplementary provisions, **37**, [641]
  conformity, certificate of, **37**, [636], [638]
  EC certificate of conformity—
    compliance with, **37**, [642], [644]
    motor cycle, requirement, **37**, [645]
    tractor, requirement, **37**, [645]
  examinations, **37**, [640]
  goods vehicle, meaning, **37**, [641]
    conform, meaning, **37**, [634]
    obligatory certificates, **37**, [642]
    record of issues, **37**, [640]
    sale without, **37**, [646]

motor vehicle—*contd*
type vehicles—*contd*
  goods vehicle, meaning—*contd*
    supplementary provisions, **37**, [638]
  plated weights, determination, **37**, [134], [627]
  regulations generally, **37**, [640]
  tyres, breach of requirement as to, **37**, [614]
  unroadworthy—
    alteration, condition after, **37**, [660]
    sale, prohibition on, **37**, [660]
  use of, regulation of—
    contravention, **37**, [618]
    definitions, index of, **37**, [671]
    powers, **37**, [613]
  used, testing at sale rooms, **37**, [662]
  vehicles not treated as, **37**, [313], [805]
  weighing, when required—
    certificate, issue of, **37**, [664]
    provisions as to, **37**, [663], [664]
  weight—
    calculation of, **36**, [678]; **38(1)**, [574]
    plated, determination, **37**, [134], [627]
    regulation of—
      calculation, method of, **37**, [806]
      contravention, **37**, [615]
      powers, **37**, [613]
      temporary exemption, **37**, [619]
    regulations as to, **36**, [677]

motorway
nature of, **36**, [210]

mountains
public access to, **32**, [1]

moveable dwellings
erection and use of, licence for, **35(1)**, [171]
regulation of use, **35(1)**, [171]
sites for, licence to use land as, **35(1)**, [171]
summary of provisions, **35(1)**, [1]

moveable structures
Licensing Act 2003, application of, **19(3)**, [681]

Mozambique
Commonwealth—
  admission to, **7(2)**, [854]
  citizenship, **31**, [186]

multilateral development bank
meaning, **19(2)**, [1063]
relevant payment to, **19(2)**, [1063]

Multilateral Investment Guarantee Agency
Arbitration Act, application of, **19(2)**, [1013]
Convention—
  arbitration awards under, **19(2)**, [1011]
  meaning, **19(2)**, [1008]
  text of, **19(2)**, [1016]
Northern Ireland, provisions applying to, **19(2)**, [1014]
payments to and from, **19(2)**, [1009]
privileges and immunities, **19(2)**, [1010]

Multilateral Investment Guarantee Agency—*contd*
rules of court, **19(2)**, [1012]
status of, **19(2)**, [1010]

multilateral trading facility
EEA market operator—
meaning, **19(2)**, [384]
passport rights—
exercise of, **19(2)**, [380]
removal of, **19(2)**, [381]
meaning, **19(2)**, [384]

multi-national practices. *See under* **Solicitor**

municipal corporation
Alnwick, status of, **25(1)**, [53]
charitable trustee, as, **25(1)**, [28]
existing, saving for, **25(1)**, [41]
legal proceedings, **25(1)**, [37]
local Acts, powers under, **25(1)**, [32]
meaning, **25(1)**, [25]
members, appointment as trustees, **25(1)**, [29]
powers transferred to, **25(1)**, [30]
Romney Marsh, position of, **25(1)**, [52]

murder
abroad, committed, **12(1)**, [71]
aiding suicide, verdict of, **12(1)**, [330]
alternative verdicts, **12(1)**, [364]
arrest, in course of, **12(1)**, [298]
bail, conditions of, **12(1)**, [647]
conspiring to commit, **12(1)**, [69]
constructive malice, abolition of, **12(1)**, [298]
death penalty, abolition, **12(1)**, [358]
diminished responsibility—
defence, as, **12(1)**, [299]
evidence of, **12(1)**, [343]
England or Ireland, death in, **12(1)**, [72]
forfeiture rule, application of, **12(1)**, [778]
inquest into death of person by,
11(1), [1217], [1222]–[1223]
insanity, evidence of, **12(1)**, [343]
letter threatening, **12(1)**, [73]
life imprisonment for, **12(1)**, [358]
malice aforethought, **12(1)**, [298]
offence, in course of, **12(1)**, [298]
provocation, **12(1)**, [300]
soliciting, **12(1)**, [69]
threat to kill, **12(1)**, [73]

Museum of London
admission charges, power to make, **13**, [169]
archaeological services, provision, **13**, [168], [344]
Board of Governors—
archaeological services, **13**, [168], [344]
chairman, **13**, [180]
city appointees, **13**, [343]
composition, revised, **13**, [343]
constitution, **13**, [166]
functions, **13**, [168]
ministerial appointments, **13**, [343]
number of, **13**, [166], [343]
period and vacation of office, **13**, [180]

Museum of London—*contd*
Board of Governors—*contd*
procedure and quorum, **13**, [180]
secretary and treasurer, **13**, [174]
collections, maintenance, **13**, [169]
devises and bequests, **13**, [175]
director, **13**, [174]
expenditure, **13**, [177]
expenses, **13**, [345]
financial provisions, **13**, [177]
Guildhall Museum collections, transfer of,
13, [167]
land, acquisition or disposal, **13**, [168]
loans by, **13**, [171]
London, meaning, **13**, [168]
London Museum collections, transfer of,
13, [167]
moneys received, application, **13**, [176]
objects—
acquisition, **13**, [170]
disposal, **13**, [170]
exhibition of, places for, **13**, [168]
loan of, **13**, [171]
transfer to other organisations, **13**, [172]
other organisations, transfer of objects
between, **13**, [172]
premises—
acquisition, **13**, [168]
use of, **13**, [173]
staff, **13**, [174]
summary of provisions, **13**, [49]

museums. *See also* **Armed Forces Museums;
Armouries; British Museum; Imperial War
Museum; Museum of London; National
Maritime Museum; Natural History
Museum; Science Museum; Victoria and
Albert Museum; Wellington Museum**
assistance for, **26(1)**, [721]
coal-mining, financial assistance for,
17(2), [185]
human remains, power to de-accession,
28, [813]
loans by, indemnity for loss or damage,
13, [253], [254]
local authority—
admission charges, **13**, [153]
agreement with another authority,
13, [152]
authorities for purposes of, **13**, [204]
byelaws, **13**, [158]
exhibits—
amalgamation of funds for, **13**, [155],
[205]
expenses incurred by another body,
contributions towards, **13**, [154], [205]
funds for purchase of, **13**, [155]
management of funds for, **13**, [165]
premises, use for educational or cultural
events, **13**, [159]
provision and maintenance, **13**, [49],
[152]
Secretary of State, annual reports by,
13, [157]

museums—*contd*
  local authority—*contd*
    exhibits—*contd*
      transfer to another authority, **13**, [152], [205]
  specific institutions, **13**, [49]
  staff superannuation, **33(1)**, [89]
  summary of provisions, **13**, [49]
  Transport for London, powers of, **26(1)**, [777]
  value added tax, relief from, **50**, [46]

mushrooms
  meaning, **12(1)**, [604]
  theft of, **12(1)**, [556]

music and dancing
  licences. *See* **entertainments**

music tuition
  charges for, **15(2)**, [778]

musk rats
  at large, destruction of, **2**, [259]
  importation—
    control of, **2**, [256]
    licences, **2**, [257], [258]
    prohibit, power to, **2**, [256]
  keeping—
    exhibition, for, **2**, [262]
    power to prohibit, **2**, [256]

musk rats—*contd*
  keeping—*contd*
    prohibition, compensation on, **2**, [262]
    research etc, for, **2**, [262]
  offences, **2**, [260]
  provisions, extension to other animals, **2**, [264]

mutiny
  death penalty, **3**, [1365]
  failure to suppress, **3**, [486], [759], [1021]
  generally, **3**, [485], [758]
  navy—
    meaning, **3**, [1019]
    time for trial, **3**, [1089]

mutual business
  company carrying on, **44(1)**, [329]
  distributions, **44(1)**, [330]
  meaning, **44(1)**, [330]

mutual fund
  meaning, **43(S)**, 1578–9

mutual society
  meaning, **43(S)**, 1427
  transfers of business, tax consequences of, **43(S)**, 1427–8
  transfers to subsidiaries—
    distribution of funds, **19(2)**, [565]
    provisions facilitating, **19(2)**, [564]

N

Namibia
British ship registered in, **7(2)**, [791]
Commonwealth—
admission to, **7(2)**, [789]
citizenship, **31**, [186]
visiting forces in, **7(2)**, [791]

naphtha
spirit, deemed not, **19(3)**, [372]

National Assembly for Wales
accommodation, expenditure by members
on, **43(1)**, [585]
accounts—
Government of Wales, of, **10**, [1265]
preparation and audit, **10**, [1264]
publication of, **10**, [1609]
Acts—
commencement of provisions, **10**, [1570]
confirmation, **10**, [1651]
English and Welsh texts of, **10**, [1621]
general restrictions, **10**, [1643]
exceptions, **10**, [1644]
interpretation, **10**, [1619]
judicial notice of, **10**, [1572]
legislative competence, as to,
10, [1571]–[1574]
power to pass, **10**, [1572]
proposed, Bills, **10**, [1572]
See also Bills *below*
referendum as to provisions—
combination of polls, **10**, [1641]
conduct of, **10**, [1641]
date of, **10**, [1641]
entitlement to vote, **10**, [1641]
funding and accounts, **10**, [1641]
holding of, **10**, [1568]
material, **10**, [1641]
period for, **10**, [1641]
proposal for, **10**, [1569]
questions and statement, **10**, [1641]
result, no legal challenge to, **10**, [1641]
voters, provision of information to,
10, [1641]
voting, encouragement of, **10**, [1641]
retrospective decisions, power to remedy,
10, [1618]
subject matter of, **10**, [1642]
allowances for eligible persons, paying—
delegation of functions relating to,
15(2), [495]–[496]
education and training, in respect of,
15(2), [492]
learning agreements, **15(2)**, [493]
transfer of functions relating to,
15(2), [494]
annual reports, **30**, [716]

National Assembly for Wales—*contd*
Audit Committee, **10**, [1495]
reports, **10**, [1608]
audit reports, publication of, **10**, [1609]
Auditor General for Wales. *See* **Auditor
General for Wales**
Bills—
copyright in, **10**, [1651]
ECJ references, **10**, [1578]
interpretation, **10**, [1619]
introduction of, **10**, [1575]
proceedings on, **10**, [1576]
proposed Acts as, **10**, [1572]
Royal Assent, **10**, [1580]
Secretary of State, intervention by,
10, [1579]
Supreme Court, scrutiny by, **10**, [1577]
bodies awarding qualifications, levy on,
15(1), [748]
Budget motions—
annual, **10**, [1590], [1652]
supplementary, **10**, [1591], [1652]
Budget resolution, appropriations without,
10, [1592]
care. *See* **care**
Chief Inspector of Education and Training,
funding, **10**, [1266]
child care, functions, **15(2)**, [461]–[463]
children—
financial assistance to—
delegation of arrangements, **15(2)**, [355]
forms of, **15(2)**, [354]
power to give, **15(2)**, [352]
terms, **15(2)**, [354]
Clerk, **10**, [1491]
transitional provisions, **10**, [1652]
Commission—
accounting officers, **10**, [1603]
accounts, **10**, [1602]
annual report, **10**, [1633]
Crown status, **10**, [1633]
delegation of functions, **10**, [1633]
establishment of, **10**, [1492]
exercise of functions, **10**, [1633]
members, **10**, [1492]
membership, **10**, [1633]
powers of, **10**, [1633]
proceedings, **10**, [1633]
property of, **10**, [1633]
property, staff and services, provision of,
10, [1492]
public awareness, promotion of, **10**, [1633]
staff, **10**, [1633]
standing orders, **10**, [1492]
subsidiaries, accounts of, **10**, [1604]
transitional provisions, **10**, [1652]

National Assembly for Wales—*contd*
  Commission—*contd*
    use of resources, examinations into,
      10, [1605]
    validity of acts of, **10**, [1633]
  committees—
    composition, **10**, [1494]
    members, **10**, [1494]
    standing orders, **10**, [1493]
  communication with schools, **15(2)**, [379]
  Community law, implementation of,
    10, [1524]
  consequential provision, power to make,
    10, [1615]
  constituencies, **10**, [1467]
  co-operation with Commission for Healthcare
    Audit and Inspection, **30**, [719]
  Counsel General—
    acts, validity of, **10**, [1556]
    appointment, **10**, [1514]
    ceasing to hold office, **10**, [1514]
    construction of references to, **10**, [1550]
    contracts by, **10**, [1533]
    documents supplied by, charge for,
      10, [1534]
    financial assistance by, **10**, [1535]
    functions of—
      application of provisions, **10**, [1521]
      exercise of, **10**, [1522]
      facilitating, **10**, [1536]
      transfer of, **10**, [1523], [1634]–[1636]
      Wales, exercisable in relation to,
        10, [1620]
    legal proceedings, instituting, defending or
      appearing in, **10**, [1532]
    matters affecting Wales, representations as
      to, **10**, [1527]
    Measures, introduction of. *See* Measures
      below
    oath or affirmation, **10**, [1520]
    official secrets, Crown servants for purposes
      of, **10**, [1557]
    participation by, **10**, [1499]
    property, rights and liabilities of, **10**, [1552]
      transfer of, **10**, [1637]
    remuneration and allowances,
      10, [1518]–[1519]
    use of resources, examinations into,
      10, [1600]
  Crown right and liabilities in different
    capacities, **10**, [1554]
  curriculum, powers as to, **15(2)**, [882]
  defamation, privilege, **10**, [1507]
  Deputy Presiding Officer, **10**, [1490]
  devolution issues—
    costs, **10**, [1650]
    courts and tribunals, proceedings of,
      10, [1650]
    decision, references to, **10**, [1650]
    England and Wales, proceedings in,
      10, [1647]
    House of Lords proceedings, **10**, [1650]
    meaning, **10**, [1646]
    Northern Ireland, proceedings in,
      10, [1649]

National Assembly for Wales—*contd*
  devolution issues—*contd*
    Scotland, proceedings in, **10**, [1648]
    Supreme Court, direct references to,
      10, [1650]
  directions, power to give, **15(1)**, [746]
  documents—
    notice requirements, **10**, [1503]
    offences relating to, **10**, [1504]
    power to call for, **10**, [1502]
    transitional provisions, **10**, [1652]
  documents and information, power to
    require, **30**, [696], [697]
  education and children—
    exercise of functions, **15(2)**, [704]
    financial assistance to—
      delegation of arrangements, **15(2)**, [355]
      forms of, **15(2)**, [353]
      power to give, **15(2)**, [352]
      terms, **15(2)**, [354]
    framework power, **15(2)**, [882]–[883]
  education and training—
    amended provisions, **15(S)**, Education 32–4
    powers, **15(S)**, Education 109, 256–7
  elections—
    constituency vacancies, for, **10**, [1475]
    entitlement to vote, **10**, [1477]
    extraordinary general, **10**, [1470]
    general—
      candidates, **10**, [1472]
      constituency vote, **10**, [1471]
      electoral region figures, calculation of,
        10, [1473]
      electoral region vote, **10**, [1471]
      regional returning officer, **10**, [1472]
      voting at, **10**, [1471]
    ordinary general—
      poll, **10**, [1468]
      power to vary date of, **10**, [1469]
    power to make provision about, **10**, [1478]
    returns, questioning, **10**, [1478]
    transitional provisions, **10**, [1652]
  Electoral Commission, alteration of electoral
    regions by, **10**, [1632]
  electoral regions, **10**, [1467]
    alteration of, **10**, [1632], [1652]
    figures, calculation of, **10**, [1473]
    members, allocation of seats, **10**, [1474]
    vacancies, filling, **10**, [1476]
    voting for, **10**, [1471]
  English and Welsh languages, equality of
    treatment, **10**, [1500]
  entry, right of, **30**, [694]–[695]
  establishment, **10**, [1466]
  European Convention on Human Rights,
    compatibility of legislation with, **10**, [1546]
  existing instruments, savings for, **10**, [1652]
  First Minister—
    acts, validity of, **10**, [1556]
    appointment, **10**, [1511]
    ceasing to hold office, **10**, [1511]
    choice of, **10**, [1512]
    construction of references to, **10**, [1550]
    contracts by, **10**, [1533]

National Assembly for Wales—*contd*
First Minister—*contd*
documents supplied by, charge for,
10, [1534]
financial assistance by, 10, [1535]
functions of—
application of provisions, 10, [1521]
exercise of, 10, [1511], [1522]
facilitating, 10, [1536]
transfer of, 10, [1523], [1634]–[1636]
Wales, exercisable in relation to,
10, [1620]
matters affecting Wales, representations as
to, 10, [1527]
Measures, introduction of. *See* Measures
below
oath or affirmation, 10, [1520]
official secrets, Crown servants for purposes
of, 10, [1557]
property, rights and liabilities of, 10, [1552]
transfer of, 10, [1637]
remuneration and allowances,
10, [1518]–[1519]
transitional provisions, 10, [1652]
Forestry Commissioners, funding, 10, [1267]
functions—
curriculum and assessment, in relation to,
15(1), [743]
discharge of, 15(1), [745]
education and training, advancement of,
15(1), [742]
external vocational and academic
qualifications, in relation to, 15(1), [744]
general duties of, 35(2), [287]
Government—
establishment of, 10, [1510]
members of, 10, [1510]
staff of, 10, [1517]
Health Professions Wales. *See* **Health
Professions Wales**
housing legislation, reference in, 24, [602]
improvement in quality of services,
encouragement of, 35(2), [287]
information, use of, 30, [717]
inquiries by, 30, [718]; 35(2), [288]
interpretation of provisions, 10, [1623]
LEA, advisory services, power to require LEA
to obtain, 15(2), [385]–[386]
legal proceedings by or against, 10, [1506]
lending powers, 10, [1652]
Letters Patent, 10, [1581]
loans to, accounts, 10, [1260]
Measures—
Assembly Act provisions, effect of
commencement of, 10, [1571]
confirmation, 10, [1651]
copyright in, 10, [1651]
criminal offences, not creating, 10, [1639]
English and Welsh texts of, 10, [1621]
general restrictions, 10, [1639]
exceptions, 10, [1640]
interpretation, 10, [1619]
judicial notice of, 10, [1558]
laws, as, 10, [1558]
legislative competence, 10, [1559]–[1560]

National Assembly for Wales—*contd*
Measures—*contd*
power to pass, 10, [1558]
proposed—
approval of, 10, [1567]
ECJ references, 10, [1565]
introduction of, 10, [1562]
proceedings on, 10, [1563]
Secretary of State, intervention by,
10, [1566]
Supreme Court, scrutiny by, 10, [1564]
retrospective decisions, power to remedy,
10, [1618]
subject matter of, 10, [1638]
members—
accommodation expenses, 44(2), [370]
constituency, 10, [1466]
disqualification—
effect of, 10, [1483]
exceptions and relief, 10, [1482]
judicial proceedings as to, 10, [1484]
office holders, 10, [1481]
European travel expenses, 44(2), [296]
groups, assistance to, 10, [1489]
integrity, 10, [1501]
oath or affirmation of allegiance,
10, [1488]
overnight expenses, 44(2), [295]
regional, 10, [1466]
register of interests, 10, [1501]
remuneration—
information as to, 10, [1487]
limit on salaries, 10, [1486]
pensions, gratuities and allowances,
10, [1485]
provision for, 10, [1485]
resignation, 10, [1480]
return of, 10, [1466]
tax treatment, 43(1), [425]
term of office, 10, [1479]
transitional provisions, 10, [1652]
minor and consequential amendments,
10, [1651]
National Loans Fund lending, accounts,
10, [1261]
orders and directions, 10, [1622]
Orders in Council—
legislative competence, as to, 10, [1560]
scrutiny of, 10, [1561]
petitions, exemption from postage, 34, [712]
planning, powers relating to, 46(S), 195–6
post-16 education and training—
assessments and means tests, 15(2), [217]
encouragement of, 15(2), [213]
financial resources—
conditions, 15(2), [215]
provision of, 15(2), [214]
learning difficulties, having regard for
persons with, 15(2), [221]
persons aged over 19, for, 15(2), [212]
persons aged 16 to 19, for, 15(2), [211]
qualifying accounts and arrangements,
15(2), [218]
research and information, 15(2), [220]

National Assembly for Wales—*contd*
  Presiding Officer, **10**, [1490]
    transitional provisions, **10**, [1652]
  proceedings—
    meaning, **10**, [1466]
    standing orders, **10**, [1496]
  public body, as, **10**, [1509]
  Public Transport Users' Committee for
    Wales—
    establishment of, **38(2)**, [484]
    functions of, **38(2)**, [485]
    guidance and directions to, **38(2)**, [10]
  publications—
    contempt of court, **10**, [1508]
    defamation, privilege, **10**, [1507]
  registration authority, as, **35(2)**, [284]
  reporting to Secretary of State and
    Independent Regulator, **30**, [693]
  reports and statements, laying of, **10**, [1551]
  reviews and investigations into health care
    provision, **30**, [692]
  schools—
    admission of pupils, **15(2)**, [882]
    change of category, **15(2)**, [882]
    discipline, **15(2)**, [882]
    discontinuance, **15(2)**, [882]
    establishment, **15(2)**, [882]
    maintained by local education authorities,
      regulations as to, **15(2)**, [882]
    sixth-forms, funding of, **15(2)**, [216]
  Secretary of State for Wales, participation by,
    10, [1497]
  social services functions—
    additional, **35(2)**, [468]
    authorised persons—
      obstruction, **35(2)**, [471]
      right of entry, **35(2)**, [470], [471]
    economy, efficiency, etc, studies as to,
      35(2), [467]
    explanation, power to require, **35(2)**, [473]
    general considerations, **35(2)**, [469]
    improvement in social services,
      encouragement of, **35(2)**, [464]
    information, power to require, **35(2)**, [472]
    reviews and investigations by, **35(2)**, [466]
    studies and research, review of,
      35(2), [465]
  special educational needs, power to make
    proposals to secure regional provision for,
    15(2), [503]
  staff, **10**, [1652]
  standing orders—
    Bills, proceedings on, **10**, [1576]
    Commission, **10**, [1492]
    committees and sub-committees,
      10, [1493]
    Measures, proceedings on, **10**, [1563]
    proceedings, regulating, **10**, [1496]
    register of interests, provision for,
      10, [1501]
    transitional provisions, **10**, [1652]
  sub-committees—
    composition, **10**, [1494]
    members, **10**, [1494]
    standing orders, **10**, [1493]

National Assembly for Wales—*contd*
  subordinate legislation, **41**, [480]
  transitional provisions, **10**, [1652]
  transport—
    discharge of functions, arrangements for,
      38(2), [480]
    general duty, **38(2)**, [477]
    joint transport authority, establishment of,
      38(2), [481]
    local functions, financial assistance for,
      38(2), [482]
    public passenger services, provision of,
      38(2), [483]
    summary of provisions, **36**, [210]
    Wales Transport Strategy, preparation and
      publication of, **38(2)**, [478]
  UK Government's legislative programme,
    consultation about, **10**, [1498]
  UK ministers, participation by, **10**, [1497]
  ultra vires acts, remedying, **10**, [1616]
  Wales Centre for Health. *See* **Wales**
  water, intervention in functions by Secretary
    of State, **10**, [1617]
  Welsh Consolidated Fund—
    accounts, **10**, [1597]
    approvals to draw from, **10**, [1594]
    Comptroller and Auditor General,
      examinations by, **10**, [1601]
    contingencies, **10**, [1593], [1652]
    establishment of, **10**, [1582]
    lending to—
      accounts, **10**, [1588]
      National Loans Fund, from, **10**, [1587]
    Paymaster General, held by, **10**, [1582]
    payments into—
      destination of receipts, **10**, [1585]
      estimated, statements of, **10**, [1584]
      grants, **10**, [1583]
      mistake, by, **10**, [1595]
    payments out of, **10**, [1589]
    temporary excess of funds paid out,
      borrowing for, **10**, [1586]
    transitional provisions, **10**, [1652]
  Welsh Ministers—
    accounting officers, **10**, [1598]
    accounts, **10**, [1596]
    agency arrangements by, **10**, [1548]
    appointment, **10**, [1513]
    Auditor General, co-operation with,
      10, [1610]
    borrowing by, **10**, [1586]
    business scheme by, **10**, [1540]
    ceasing to hold office, **10**, [1513]
    Community law, implementation of,
      10, [1524]
    Community obligations, **10**, [1545]
    construction of references to, **10**, [1550]
    contracts by, **10**, [1533]
    cross-border bodies, consultations bout,
      10, [1528]
    culture, support of, **10**, [1526]
    Deputy, **10**, [1515]
    documents supplied by, charge for,
      10, [1534]
    documents, valid execution of, **10**, [1555]

National Assembly for Wales—*contd*
  Welsh Ministers—*contd*
    financial assistance by, **10**, [1535]
    functions of—
      agency arrangements for, **10**, [1548]
      application of provisions, **10**, [1521]
      different exercise of, **10**, [1549]
      equality of opportunity, exercise with
        regard to, **10**, [1542], [1652]
      exercise of, **10**, [1522]
      facilitating, **10**, [1536]
      transfer of, **10**, [1286], [1523],
        [1634]–[1636]
      transfer to, **10**, [1652]
      Wales, exercisable in relation to,
        10, [1620]
    international obligations, **10**, [1547]
    limit on numbers of, **10**, [1516]
    local government scheme by, **10**, [1538],
      [1652]
    matters affecting Wales, representations as
      to, **10**, [1527]
    Measures, introduction of. *See* Measures
      above
    oath or affirmation, **10**, [1520]
    official secrets, Crown servants for purposes
      of, **10**, [1557]
    Partnership Council for Wales,
      establishment of, **10**, [1537]
    private Bills, promotion of, **10**, [1530]
    property, rights and liabilities of, **10**, [1552]
      transfer of, **10**, [1637]
    public records, transfer of responsibility
      for, **10**, [1612]
    regulatory impact assessment code,
      10, [1541]
    remuneration and allowances,
      10, [1518]–[1519]
    subsidiaries, accounts of, **10**, [1599]
    sustainable development scheme by,
      10, [1544], [1652]
    Treasury, provision of information to,
      10, [1531]
    use of resources, examinations into,
      10, [1600]
    views of the public, polls for ascertaining,
      10, [1529]
    voluntary sector scheme by, **10**, [1539],
      [1652]
    well-being, promotion of, **10**, [1525]
    Welsh language strategy and scheme,
      10, [1543], [1652]
  Welsh public bodies, reform of, **10**, [1259],
    [1296]–[1299]
  Welsh Seal, **10**, [1581]
  whole of Government accounts, **10**, [1606]
  witness—
    allowances and expenses, **10**, [1505]
    notice requirements, **10**, [1503]
    oath or affirmation, **10**, [1505]
    offences, **10**, [1504]
    power to call, **10**, [1502]
    transitional provisions, **10**, [1652]

national assistance
  transitional provisions, **40(1)**, [37]

National Audit Office
  accounts, **19(2)**, [977]
  auditor—
    appointment of, **19(2)**, [977]
    powers of, **19(2)**, [988]
    qualifications of, **19(2)**, [988]
    resource account, examination of,
      19(2), [988]
  breach of duty, payment of sums for,
    19(2), [977]
  constitution of, **19(2)**, [976]
  Exchequer and Audit Department, transfer of
    staff of, **19(2)**, [987]
  expenses, **19(2)**, [977]
  staff, appointment of, **19(2)**, [976]

National Biological Standards Board
  biological substances—
    meaning, **28**, [270]
    standards for, **28**, [266]
  establishment, **28**, [266]
  financial provisions, **28**, [268]
  functions, **28**, [266]
  members, **28**, [267], [272]
  staff, **28**, [272]
  tax exemption, **28**, [267]

National Bus Company. *See also* **bus services**
  disposal of undertaking—
    dissolution of company on completion,
      37, [393]
    transfer schemes, **37**, [460]
  dissolution of—
    generally, **37**, [393]
    Secretary of State, expenses incurred,
      37, [469]
  transfer of undertaking. *See* disposal *above*

National Care Standards Commission. *See*
care

National Coal Board
  change of name etc. *See now* **British Coal
  Corporation**

National Consumer Council
  accounts, **39(1)**, [735]
  advice, information and guidance, issue of,
    39(1), [686]
  annual report, **39(1)**, [674]
  assistance, arrangements for, **39(1)**, [732]
  Chief Executive, **39(1)**, [732]
  co-operation arrangements, duty to enter
    into, **39(1)**, [687]
  committees, **39(1)**, [733]
  consumer matters, meaning, **39(1)**, [670]
  consumer, meaning, **39(1)**, [670]
  delegation by, **39(1)**, [734]
  designated consumer—
    meaning, **39(1)**, [671]
    vulnerable, investigation of complaints by,
      39(1), [679]

National Consumer Council—*contd*
  establishment of, **39(1)**, [668]
  Financial Services Consumer Panel,
    appointment of member to, **39(1)**, [706]
  forward work programmes—
    content of, **39(1)**, [672]
    functions, having regard to in exercise of,
      39(1), [673]
    notice of, **39(1)**, [672]
    publication of, **39(1)**, [672]
  functions—
    extension of, **39(1)**, [704]
    information, **39(1)**, [677]
    matters to be considered, **39(1)**, [673]
    Northern Ireland, in relation to,
      39(1), [705]
    representative, **39(1)**, [675]
    research, **39(1)**, [676]
  functions transferred to, **17(2)**, [355]
  funding, **39(1)**, [735]
  Gas and Electricity Markets Authority,
    co-operation with, **17(2)**, [336]
  information—
    disclosure of, **39(1)**, [696]
    notice to provide—
      enforcement, **39(1)**, [692], [693], [737]
      power to issue, **39(1)**, [691]
    provision by—
      authorised person requiring, **39(1)**, [694]
      exemption from requirement,
        39(1), [695]
    provision to, **39(1)**, [691]
  investigation of complaints—
    disconnection of gas or electricity, as to,
      39(1), [680]
    Gas and Electricity Markets Authority,
      reference of matters to, **39(1)**, [681]
    general powers of, **39(1)**, [678]
    Postal Services Commission, reference of
      matters to, **39(1)**, [682]
    public post offices, as to, **39(1)**, [683]
    vulnerable designated consumers, by,
      39(1), [679]
  liability in damages, exemption from,
    39(1), [736]
  membership, **39(1)**, [731]
  OFCOM Consumer Panel, appointment of
    member to, **39(1)**, [706]
  offices, **39(1)**, [734]
  power to co-operate and give assistance,
    39(1), [688]
  procedure, **39(1)**, [734]
  regional committees—
    constitution, **39(1)**, [733]
    establishment of, **39(1)**, [733]
  reports—
    requirement to prepare, **39(1)**, [684]
    Secretary of State's power to require,
      39(1), [685]
  seal, application of, **39(1)**, [734]
  staff, **39(1)**, [732]
  status of, **39(1)**, [736]
  summary of provisions, **39(1)**, [1]
  superannuation schemes, **39(1)**, [732]
  supplementary powers, **39(1)**, [690]

National Consumer Council—*contd*
  territorial committees—
    constitution, **39(1)**, [733]
    establishment of, **39(1)**, [668]
    functions of, **39(1)**, [669]
  transfer and abolition order—
    payment conditions, **39(1)**, [700]
    power to make, **39(1)**, [699]
  voluntary activities, **39(1)**, [689]

**National Council for Education and
Training for Wales**
  efficiency studies, **15(2)**, [684]
  joint exercise of functions, **15(2)**, [683]

**National Council for Vocational
Qualifications**
  transfer of staff from, **15(1)**, [747]

national court
  meaning, **10**, [1210]

National Crime Squad
  ceasing to exist, **33(2)**, [518]

National Criminal Intelligence Service
  ceasing to exist, **33(2)**, [518]

National Curriculum Council. *See also*
Curriculum and Assessment Councils

national debt
  account for sum bequeathed to reduce,
    19(2), [598]
  annuities—
    continuance of, **19(2)**, [625]
    donations or bequests, purchased by,
      19(2), [605]
    joint stock, as, **19(2)**, [627]
  bearer bonds, **19(2)**, [787], [840]
  Commissioners, persons being, **19(1)**, [1]
  consolidation of, **19(2)**, [592]
  conversion loan—
    guarantee of, **19(2)**, [795]
    sinking fund with respect to, **19(2)**, [735]
  dividends—
    balance, striking—
      effect of, **19(2)**, [717]
      payment after, **19(2)**, [718]
      time for, **19(2)**, [717]
    fractions of a penny, accumulating,
      19(2), [702]
    infant entitled to, **19(2)**, [719]
    issue of money, for, **19(2)**, [628]
    payment, regulations as to, **19(2)**, [711]
    quarterly, paid, **19(2)**, [699]
    unclaimed—
      application, advertisement of,
        19(2), [797]
      transfers of, **19(2)**, [633]
  National Loans fund. *See* **National Loans
    Fund**
  origin of, **19(1)**, [1]
  permanent funded debt, continuance of,
    19(2), [625]

national debt—*contd*
reduction, gifts for, exemption from stamp duty, **41**, [66]
reduction of, sums bequeathed for, **19(2)**, [598]
service of, payments for, **19(2)**, [861]
stock—
 bearer bonds in respect of, **19(2)**, [787], [840]
 claimant—
  petition by, **19(2)**, [634]
  second, **19(2)**, [636], [637]
 creation of, **19(2)**, [700]
 dividends. *See* dividends *above*
 entitlement to, proof of, **19(2)**, [634]
 joint, **19(2)**, [627]
 meaning, **19(2)**, [624]
 new, denomination and incidents of, **19(2)**, [709]
 re-transfer of, **19(2)**, [634]
 transfer—
  Bank of England and Ireland, indemnity to, **19(2)**, [638]
  second claimant to, **19(2)**, [636]
 unclaimed—
  application, advertisement of, **19(2)**, [797]
  transfer of, **19(2)**, [633]
summary of provisions, **19(1)**, [1]
trust funds for reduction of, **48**, 552

National Debt Commissioners
accounts, **11(2)**, [884]; **19(2)**, [970]
clerks, employment of, by, **19(2)**, [588]
discharge given to, regulations on, **19(2)**, [724]
expenses—
 deduction of, **19(2)**, [970]
 sums included in, **19(2)**, [910]
government stock, payment of unclaimed sums on, **19(2)**, [829]
liability, discharging, **19(2)**, [970]
Lord Chief Justice, as, **19(2)**, [590]
meaning, **41**, [605]
money transferred to, **11(2)**, [878]
National Insurance Fund, investment of, **40(1)**, [690]
payment orders, by, **19(2)**, [589]
payments made to, regulations on, **19(2)**, [724]
persons being, **19(2)**, [587], [590]
re-investment by, **19(2)**, [970]
sums issued to, repayment to National Loans Fund, **43(S)**, 996
tax exemption, **44(1)**, [32]
three empowered to act, **19(2)**, [597]
transfer of stock to, **19(2)**, [633]
United Kingdom, for, **19(2)**, [595]

National Debt Office
consolidated fund, payments out of, **19(2)**, [603]

national development bond
power to issue, **19(2)**, [857]

National Disability Council
abolition, **7(1)**, [1]
codes of practice, Northern Ireland, further provisions in relation to, **7(1)**, [469]

National Dock Labour Board. *See also* **dock workers**
documents relating to, transitional provisions, **16**, [154]
indebtedness, reduction, **16**, [139]
local boards, effect of documents, **16**, [154]

National Endowment for Science, Technology and the Arts
accounts, **5(1)**, [220]
annual report, **5(1)**, [219]
capital gains tax exemption, **42**, [1420]
delegation of functions, **5(1)**, [225]
establishment of, **5(1)**, [213]
evidence of documents, **5(1)**, [225]
financial directions to, **5(1)**, [218]
forward plans, **5(1)**, [219]
general duties and powers, **5(1)**, [215]
initial and subsequent endowment, **5(1)**, [216]
investment of money, **5(1)**, [217]
membership, **5(1)**, [225]
objects of, **5(1)**, [214]
prior consultation, **5(1)**, [225]
proceedings, **5(1)**, [225]
reimbursement of payments, **5(1)**, [225]
remuneration and allowances, **5(1)**, [225]
seal, **5(1)**, [225]
solicitation of gifts, **5(1)**, [217]
staff, **5(1)**, [225]
stamp duty exemption, **41**, [141]
stamp duty reserve tax exemption, **41**, [183]
status, **5(1)**, [225]
tenure of office, **5(1)**, [225]

National Enterprise Board
dissolution, **47**, [439]
public dividend capital—
 meaning, **47**, [361]
 reduction of, **47**, [361]
successor company—
 borrowing, temporary restriction on, **47**, [438]
 corporation tax, **47**, [440]
 financial structure, **47**, [437]
 vesting of property in, **47**, [436], [446]
transitional provisions, **47**, [450]

National Film Finance Corporation
dissolution, **13**, [336]
property, rights and payments, vesting of, on, **13**, [336]

National Film Theatre
vesting on abolition of GLC, **25(2)**, [606]

National Freight Company Limited
British Transport Commission, vesting of property etc of, **36**, [707]
transfer of undertakings to, **36**, [210]

National Freight Corporation
capital grants, **36**, [968]
employees, travel concessions for, **36**, [969]
employment, compensation for loss of,
  36, [863]
generally, **36**, [210]
members, loss of office, **36**, [999]
pension scheme—
  amendment of, **36**, [993]
  debt, cancellation of, **36**, [992]
  relevant obligations—
    meaning, **36**, [980], [987]
    payments as to, **36**, [982]–[986]
    proportion corresponding to, **36**, [989]
    supplementation scheme, in respect of,
      36, [990]
    unfunded, **36**, [988]
  transfer of, **36**, [999]
  transfer values, exclusion of payments in
    respect of, **36**, [991]
rights and liabilities, transfer of, **36**, [967]
successor company—
  initial government holding in, **36**, [978]
  pension obligations, funding, **36**, [979]
  rights and liabilities, transfer to, **36**, [999]
  transfer of undertaking to, **36**, [977]
transfer of assets, **44(1)**, [372]
undertaking, transfer of, **36**, [977]

National Galleries of Scotland
admission charges, power to make, **13**, [207]
land, transfer of, **13**, [430]

National Gallery
Angerstein collection, **13**, [49]
Board of Trustees, new—
  accounts and audit, **13**, [422]
  agreements, party to, **13**, [413]
  allowances, **13**, [424]
  companies, power to form, **13**, [415]
  establishment, **13**, [413]
  general functions, **13**, [414]
  land, transfer of, **13**, [420], [430]
    stamp duty exemption, **13**, [421]
    stamp duty land tax exemption,
      13, [421]
  membership, **13**, [424]
  pictures and relevant objects—
    acquisition and disposal of, **13**, [416]
    lending and borrowing, **13**, [417]
    transfer between institutions, **13**, [296],
      [297], [418]
  predecessor, meaning, **13**, [413]
  proceedings, **13**, [424]
  reports, **13**, [424]
  sealing of instruments, **13**, [424]
  status, **13**, [424]
  vesting of property, rights and liabilities in,
    13, [413]
companies, objects of, **13**, [415]
control of, **13**, [49]
custodian trustee, **13**, [413]
director, **13**, [424]
establishment, **13**, [49]
finances, **13**, [422]

National Gallery—*contd*
grants, **13**, [422], [431], [432]
history, **13**, [49]
land acquired, **13**, [49]
loans by, **13**, [49]
staff, **13**, [424]
Tate Gallery—
  separation, **13**, [49]
  transfer of responsibility for, **13**, [49]
will, gifts by, **13**, [419]

National Health Service
accommodation—
  private practice, use for, **30**, [475], [1073],
    [1314]
  See also **hospital**
Appointments Commission—
  accounts, **30**, [801]
  advice, giving, **30**, [784]
  annual report, **30**, [786]
  appointment functions, exercise of—
    jointly exercisable, direction as to,
      30, [778]
    manner of, **30**, [781]
    National Assembly for Wales, of,
      30, [780]
    Privy Council, of, **30**, [779]
    Secretary of State, of, **30**, [777]
  assisting other bodies with appointments,
    30, [783]
  Board, **30**, [801]
  chairman, **30**, [801]
  chief executive, **30**, [801]
  committees, **30**, [801]
  directions to, **30**, [789]
  establishment of, **30**, [776]
  exercise of functions, powers, **30**, [785]
  financing, **30**, [801]
  Health and Social Care Committee,
    30, [801]
  interpretation, **30**, [790]
  members, **30**, [801]
  mentoring and assistance, providing,
    30, [783]
  prescribed functions, **30**, [784]
  proceedings, **30**, [801]
  property, rights and liabilities, transfer of,
    30, [804]
  regulatory bodies, list of, **30**, [803]
  reports and information, providing,
    30, [787]
  seal, authentication of, **30**, [801]
  staff, **30**, [801]
  status, **30**, [801]
  statutory bodies, list of, **30**, [802]
  training, provision of, **30**, [783]
  transfer of staff to, **30**, [804]
  vice-chairman, **30**, [801]
authorities. *See* **Health Authority; Special
  Health Authority; Strategic Health
  Authority**
births, notification of, **30**, [1075]
bodies, directions to, **30(S)**, NHS 113
Care Trust, designation of body as, **30**, [883]

National Health Service—*contd*
certificates—
appeal against certificate or waiver
decision, **30**, [732]–[734]
applications for, **30**, [726]–[727]
information contained in, **30**, [728]
review of, **30**, [731]
charges—
dental services, for, **30**, [982]
exemptions, **30**, [983]
designated services or facilities, for,
30, [993]
drugs, medicines and appliances, for,
30, [978]
employed patients, **30**, [996]
general, exemption from, **30**, [979]
hospitals or ambulance trusts, payment to,
30, [737]
liability to pay, **30**, [725]
more expensive supplies for, **30**, [991]
non-residents, in respect of, **30**, [981]
offences, **30**, [1000]
optical appliances, for, **30**, [985]–[987]
part payment, hospital accommodation on,
30, [995]
payment of, **30**, [729]
penalties for non-payment, **30**, [999]
pharmaceutical services, for, **30**, [984]
pre-payment certificates, **30**, [980]
recovery of, **30**, [730], [767]
goods and services, for, **30**, [998]
information—
provision of, **30**, [735]
use of, by Secretary of State or
Scottish Ministers, **30**, [736]
insurers' liability, **30**, [739]
lump sums, regulations governing,
30, [738]
non-health service hospitals, **30**, [740]
periodical payments, regulations
governing, **30**, [738]
remission and repayment of, **30**, [988],
[990]
repairs and replacements, for, **30**, [992]
sums otherwise payable to persons
providing services, **30**, [994]
travelling expenses, **30**, [989]–[990]
chronically sick—
elderly person, separation from younger,
30, [438]
references to, **30**, [441]
community care services, transfer of staff for,
40(1), [210]
community services, payments towards
expenditure on, **30**, [1062]
voluntary organisations, services provided
by, **30**, [1063]
complaints, independent advocacy services
for, **30**, [1054], [1303]
consolidating Acts—
consequential amendments, **30**, [1357]
continuity of law, **30**, [1358]
meaning, **30**, [1349]
transitional modifications,
30, [1360]–[1361]

National Health Service—*contd*
consolidating Acts—*contd*
transitional provisions and savings,
30, [1358]–[1358]
contraceptive services, provision of,
30, [1085], [1326]
contracts—
arrangements treated as, **30**, [817]
commissioners, **30**, [815]
meaning, **30**, [815]
providers, **30**, [815]
contributions, allocation from, **40(1)**, [691]
Crown immunities, removal of, **30**, [530]
deaths, notification of, **30**, [1075]
development, persons displaced by, **30**, [1074]
directions, making, **30**, [477]
disabled—
elderly person, separation from younger,
30, [438]
interpretation of, **30**, [441]
research and development, annual report
on, **30**, [439]
disabled persons, provision of vehicles for,
30, [1085], [1326]
emergency powers, **30**, [1059]
employees, compensation for loss of office,
33(1), [139]
English and Scottish border provisions,
30, [605]
exempt information—
descriptions of, **30**, [1108]
interpretation, **30**, [1110]
qualifications, **30**, [1109]
family health services, Health Authority's duty
as to, **30**, [446]
foundation trusts, establishment of, **30**, [413]
fraud and unlawful activities, protection
from—
compulsory disclosure of documents,
30, [1001]
disclosure notice—
contents of, **30**, [1003]
delegation of functions,
30, [1005]–[1006]
disclosure of information obtained,
30, [1007]
manner of service, **30**, [1009]
personal information, protection of,
30, [1008]
power to serve, **30**, [1003]
production of documents, **30**, [1004]
interpretation, **30**, [1016]
offences—
bodies corporate, by, **30**, [1012]
disclosure or use of information,
30, [1011]
partnership, by, **30**, [1013]
penalties, **30**, [1014]
production of documents, relating to,
30, [1010]
unincorporated association, by,
30, [1013]
orders and regulations, **30**, [1015]
persons and bodies, provisions applying to,
30, [1002]

National Health Service—*contd*
  functions—
    distribution of, **30**, [813]
    performance outside England, **30**, [812]
  general dental services. *See* **dental services**
  general medical services. *See* **medical**
    services
  general ophthalmic services. *See* **ophthalmic**
    services
  health care and associated professions, Council
    for the Regulation of Health Care
    Professionals. *See* **Council for the**
    Regulation of Health Care Professionals
  health care associated infections, prevention
    and control of—
      code of practice, **30**, [664]
      consultation on, **30**, [665]
      effect of, **30**, [666]
  Health Service Commissioners. *See* **Health**
    Service Commissioners
  hearing research, institute for, **30**, [440]
  high security psychiatric services, provision
    of, **30**, [810]
  hospital. *See* **hospital**
  interpretation, **30**, [1081]–[1082]
  local administration, power to make changes
    to, **30**, [482]
  medical inspection of pupils, **30**, [1085]
  medical practitioners. *See* **medical**
    practitioner
  medical supplies, maximum price of—
    authorisations, **30**, [1115]
    control of, **30**, [1066]
      powers of, **30**, [1068], [1072]
    corporation, offence by, **30**, [1115]
    documents, production and proof of,
      30, [1115]
    enforcement, **30**, [1071]
    false documents and statements, **30**, [1115]
    information, disclosure of, **30**, [1115]
    orders and directions, **30**, [1115]
    penalties, **30**, [1115]
    statutory schemes, **30**, [1069]–[1070]
    territorial extent of provisions, **30**, [1077],
      [1115]
    voluntary schemes, powers relating to,
      30, [1067]
  money, raising, **30**, [1028]
  NHS trust. *See* **NHS trust**
  Northern Ireland, agreement with, **30**, [443],
    [445]
  nutrition, benefits under schemes for
    improving, **30**, [748]
  offences—
    body corporate, by, **30**, [792]
    partnerships, by, **30**, [793]
    penalties, **30**, [794]
    unincorporated associations, by, **30**, [793]
  orders and regulations, **30**, [477], [795],
    [1078]–[1079]
  patented inventions, user of, **11(1)**, [636]
  patient information—
    Advisory Group, **30**, [1058]
    control of, **30**, [1057]
    meaning, **30**, [1057]

National Health Service—*contd*
  pharmaceutical services. *See* **pharmaceutical**
    services
  prescribing rights of doctors, extension to
    other health professionals, **30**, [619]
  Primary Care Trust. *See* **Primary Care Trust**
  prison service, joint working with,
    30, [1055], [1304]
  property, acquisition, use and maintenance
    of, **30**, [1017]
  property transferred under 1946 Act—
    free of trusts, **30**, [1025]
    general hospital purposes, previously held
      for, **30**, [1026]
    voluntary hospitals, **30**, [1027]
  public-private partnerships, **30**, [1029]
  redress scheme—
    application of, **30**, [1364]
    commencement of proceedings, **30**, [1366]
    complaints, handling, **30**, [1376]
    co-operation, duties of, **30**, [1375]
    Health Commissioner, remit of, **30**, [1377]
    individuals, assistance for, **30**, [1371]
    interpretation, **30**, [1379]
    legal advice, provision of, **30**, [1370]
    limitation period, suspension of, **30**, [1369]
    medical experts, provision of, **30**, [1370]
    members, **30**, [1372]
    potential application, duty to consider,
      30, [1367]
    power to establish, **30**, [1363]
    proceedings under, **30**, [1368]
    redress under, **30**, [1365]
    regulations, **30**, [1378]
    resolution, general duty to promote,
      30, [1374]
    Special Health Authority, functions of,
      30, [1373]
  redress, Wales—
    accessing, **30(S)**, NHS 212
    arrangements—
      functions with regard to,
        30(S), NHS 215–16
      potential application, duty to consider,
        30(S), NHS 212
    complaints, **30(S)**, NHS 215–17
    delivery, method of, **30(S)**, NHS 213
    general note, **30(S)**, NHS 207–8
    individuals, assistance for, **30(S)**, NHS 215
    interpretation, **30(S)**, NHS 215–18
    legal advice, provision of, **30(S)**, NHS 214
    limitation period, suspension of,
      30(S), NHS 214
    medical experts, services of,
      30(S), NHS 214
    orders, power to make,
      30(S), NHS 215–17
    regulations—
      power to make, **30(S)**, NHS 209, 217
      redress under, **30(S)**, NHS 211
    settlement agreement, **30(S)**, NHS 213
    supplementary and consequential
      provisions, **30(S)**, NHS 215–18
  regulations, making, **30**, [477]
  reorganisation, **30**, [413]

National Health Service—*contd*
scrutiny of health service provision. *See* **local authority**
Secretary of State—
  duty of to promote, **30**, [807]
  emergency powers, **30**, [1059]
  financial powers, **30**, [517]
  general power of, **30**, [808]
  goods and services, supply of, **30**, [886]–[887]
  health service bodies, directions to, **30**, [814]
  high security psychiatric services, provision of, **30**, [810]
  other bodies, arrangements with, **30**, [818]
  particular services, provision of, **30**, [809]
  performance of functions outside England, **30**, [812]
  research, powers as to, **30**, [1085]
  services provided by, **30**, [1085]
  standing advisory committees, constituting, **30**, [1056], [1112]
  supplies not readily obtainable, making available, **30**, [1061]
  supply of goods and services by, **30**, [448]
services, supply of. *See* supply of goods and services *below*
Special Health Authority. *See* **Special Health Authority**
staff, transfer of, **30**, [520]
Strategic Health Authority. *See* **Strategic Health Authority**
summarised accounts, **19(2)**, [1040]
summary of provisions, **30**, [413]
superannuation provisions, **30**, [428]
supplementary regulatory powers, **30**, [1080]
territorial extent of provisions, **30**, [1077]
traffic casualties, treatment of—
trust. *See* **NHS trust**
trust property, transfers of—
  application of, **30**, [1022]
  apportionment of, **30**, [1019]
  discretion, exercise of, **30**, [1022]
  general hospital purposes, previously held for, **30**, [1026]
  hospital, private trusts for, **30**, [1024]
  rights and liabilities, of, **30**, [1023]
  Secretary of State, powers of, **30**, [1019]
  special trustees, **30**, [1020]–[1021]
  voluntary hospitals, religious denomination and character of, **30**, [1027]
Wales. *See* **Wales**
university clinical teaching and research facilities, **30**, [1064]
video recordings, supply for purposes of, **13**, [305]
voluntary organisations—
  financial assistance—
    local authorities, by, **30**, [432]
    Minister of Health, by, **30**, [431]
  meaning, **30**, [431], [432]
  premises and services of local authority, using, **30**, [432]
  provision of services, arrangements for, **30**, [818]

National Health Service—*contd*
Wales. *See also* **Wales**
  Health Professions Wales. *See* **Health Professions Wales**
  Wales Centre for Health. *See* **Wales**
welfare food schemes, replacement of, **30**, [748]
Welsh NHS bodies—
  audit—
    Auditor General for Wales, by, **26(2)**, [407]
    officers, of, **26(2)**, [409]
  auditors, **26(2)**, [424]
  Care Quality Commission, provision of information by, **26(2)**, [410]
  meaning, **26(2)**, [406]

National Heritage Memorial Fund
annual report and accounts, **13**, [252]
application of—
  archives, towards, **13**, [248]
  exhibitions, towards, **13**, [248]
  generally, **13**, [249]
  property, towards, **13**, [247], [249]
capital gains tax exemption, **42**, [1420]
charitable purposes, trustees for, **42**, [405]
establishment of, **13**, [245]
generally, **32**, [1]
gifts, acceptance of, **13**, [250]
ministerial functions, transfer of, **42**, [397]
National Land Fund, succeeding, **13**, [245]
payments into, **13**, [246]
stamp duty exemption, **41**, [141]
stamp duty reserve tax exemption, **41**, [183]
summary of provisions, **13**, [49]
tax exemption, **44(1)**, [366]
Trustees—
  annual report and accounts, making, **13**, [252]
  appointment of, **13**, [245]
  chairman, terms of office, **13**, [257]
  expenses and allowances, **13**, [257]
  financial assistance, power to give, **13**, [247]
  investment, powers of, **13**, [251]
  proceedings, **13**, [257]
  remuneration, **13**, [257]
  staff, **13**, [257]
  status of, **13**, [257]
  tenure of office, **13**, [257]

National Identity Register
changes affecting accuracy, notification of, **36**, [168]
checks on, provision for, **36**, [173]
civil penalties, imposition of, **36**, [188]
  appeals, **36**, [190]
  code of practice, **36**, [191]
  objection to, **36**, [189]
designation of documents for purposes of registration, **36**, [162]
entries in—
  applications relating to, **36**, [163]
  information, provision of—
    false, **36**, [186]

National Identity Register—*contd*
  entries in—*contd*
    information, provision of—*contd*
      inaccurate or incomplete, correcting, **36**, [177]
      individual's consent without, **36**, [179]
      power to authorise, **36**, [178]
      prevention and detection of crime, for, **36**, [176]
      public authorities, to, **36**, [175]
    personal information, **36**, [201]
    personal reference numbers, **36**, [201]
    record history, **36**, [201]
    registration and ID card history, **36**, [201]
    residential status, **36**, [201]
    security information, **36**, [201]
    validation information, **36**, [201]
    verification, provision of information for, **36**, [170]
  establishment of, **36**, [159]
  functions, fees for, **36**, [192]
  identity, meaning, **36**, [159]
  individuals entered in, **36**, [160]
  information recorded in, **36**, [161]
  purposes of, **36**, [159]
  registrable fact, meaning, **36**, [159]
  residential status, meaning, **36**, [159]
  summary of provisions, **36**, [1]
  tampering with, **36**, [187]
  validating, power to require information for, **36**, [167]

National Identity Scheme Commissioner
  appointment of, **36**, [180]
  functions, **36**, [180]
  reports, **36**, [181]

National Information Governance Board for Health and Social Care
  annual reports, **30(S)**, NHS 118
  consultation with, **30(S)**, NHS 119
  establishment of, **30(S)**, NHS 116
  functions of, **30(S)**, NHS 116–17
  regulations as to, **30(S)**, NHS 117–18
  summary of provisions, **30(S)**, NHS 6
  Wales, functions in, **30(S)**, NHS 117

National Institute for Research in Nuclear Science
  staff pensions, **17(1)**, [228]

National Institute of Agricultural Botany
  employees, pension scheme, **1(1)**, [553]

National Insurance. *See also* **social security**
  agreements, **40(2)**, [463], [492]
    joint elections, **40(2)**, [463], [492]
  contributions—
    administration, transfer of functions, **40(2)**, [264]
    annual review, **40(1)**, [663]
    avoidance arrangements, disclosure of, **40(1)**, [640]
    benefits, conditions for—
      bereavement payment, **40(1)**, [463]

National Insurance—*contd*
  contributions—*contd*
    benefits, conditions for—*contd*
      child's special allowance, **40(1)**, [463]
      early years of contribution, satisfaction in, **40(1)**, [464]
      retirement pension, **40(1)**, [463]
      short-term incapacity benefit, **40(1)**, [463]
      widowed mother's allowance, **40(1)**, [463]
      widowed parent's allowance, **40(1)**, [463]
      widow's pension, **40(1)**, [463]
    benefits in kind, in respect of—
      Northern Ireland, **40(2)**, [288], [289]
      regulations, **40(2)**, [286]
      third party providers, **40(2)**, [287], [289]
    Class 1—
      calculations of amounts, **40(1)**, [461]
      earnings limits, **40(1)**, [238]
      earnings not paid at normal intervals, **40(1)**, [461]
      generally, **40(1)**, [231]
      more than one employment, earner in, **40(1)**, [461]
      payment—
        error, in, **40(1)**, [258]
        method of, **40(1)**, [461]
      powers to call for documents, **40(1)**, [593]
      primary—
        calculation of, **40(1)**, [242]
        liability for, **40(1)**, [239]
        notional payment, **40(1)**, [240]
        power to alter, **40(1)**, [667]
      regulations, **40(1)**, [461]
      secondary—
        calculation of, **40(1)**, [243]
        liability for, **40(1)**, [239]
        power to alter, **40(1)**, [667]
      secondary contributor, meaning, **40(1)**, [241]
      share options, liability to pay on, **40(2)**, [332]
        roll-overs, **40(2)**, [333]
      thresholds, **40(1)**, [238]
      transfer of liability, earner bearing, **40(1)**, [461]
      Treasury, alterations by, **40(1)**, [668]
      upper earnings limit, **40(2)**, [610]
    Class 1A—
      benefits in kind, on, **40(1)**, [244]
      generally, **40(1)**, [231]
      liability for, **40(1)**, [244]
      modification of enactments, **40(1)**, [244]
      more than one employment, earner in, **40(1)**, [461]
      non-cash vouchers provided by third parties, in respect of, **40(1)**, [246]
      payment of, **40(1)**, [244]
        error, in, **40(1)**, [258]
      percentage, **40(1)**, [244]
      powers to call for documents, **40(1)**, [593]
      regulations, **40(1)**, [461]

National Insurance—*contd*
contributions—*contd*
  Class 1A—*contd*
    relevant payment of earnings, meaning,
      40(1), [244]
    retrospective tax legislation, provisions
      made in consequence of, **40(1)**, [247]
    third party provider of benefits, liability
      of, **40(1)**, [245]
  Class 1B—
    amount of, **40(1)**, [248]
    chargeable emoluments, **40(1)**, [248]
    generally, **40(1)**, [231]
    payment of, **40(1)**, [248]
      error, in, **40(1)**, [258]
    percentage, **40(1)**, [248]
    powers to call for documents,
      40(1), [593]
    regulations, **40(1)**, [461]
  Class 2—
    annual review, **40(1)**, [663]
    generally, **40(1)**, [231]
    late paid, **40(1)**, [250]
    liability for, **40(1)**, [249]
    powers to call for documents,
      40(1), [593]
  Class 3—
    additional, right to pay,
      33(S), Pensions 201–3
    amount of, **40(1)**, [251]
    annual review, **40(1)**, [663]
    generally, **40(1)**, [231]
    payment of, **40(1)**, [251]
    restriction on right to pay, **40(1)**, [252]
  Class 4—
    annual review, **40(1)**, [663]
    deferment of, **40(1)**, [255]
    destination of, **40(1)**, [254]
    exceptions from charge, **40(1)**, [255]
    generally, **40(1)**, [231]
    husband and wife, provisions on,
      40(1), [462]
    incidental matters, regulations on,
      40(1), [255]
    Income Tax Acts—
      application of, **40(1)**, [254]
      recoverable under, **40(1)**, [253], [462]
    partnerships, from, **40(1)**, [462]
    profits or gains, computing, **40(1)**, [462]
    regulations, recoverable under,
      40(1), [256]
    reliefs, **40(1)**, [462]
    trustees, from, **40(1)**, [462]
  classes of, **40(1)**, [231]
  collection other than through PAYE
    system, **40(1)**, [461]
  Commissioners of Her Majesty's Revenue
    and Customs, transfer of functions to. *See*
    HM Revenue and Customs
    See also **National Insurance Fund**
  destination of, **40(1)**, [691]
    See also **National Insurance Fund**
  dock workers, of, **40(1)**, [220]
  earner, meaning, **40(1)**, [233]

National Insurance—*contd*
contributions—*contd*
  earnings—
    meaning, **40(1)**, [233]
    payments treated as, **40(1)**, [234];
      40(2), [190]
    records of, **40(1)**, [264]
    regulations, **40(1)**, [233]
    retrospective tax legislation, provisions
      made in consequence of, **40(1)**, [236],
      [237]
    workers provided by service companies,
      of, **40(1)**, [235]
  earnings factor—
    ascertainment of, **40(1)**, [262]
    calculation of, **40(1)**, [264]
    contributory benefits, for, **40(1)**, [261]
    credits, **40(1)**, [288]
    deemed, **40(1)**, [286], [287]
    determining, **40(1)**, [198]
    flat rate accrual amount, revaluation of,
      40(1), [671]
    low earnings threshold, revaluation of,
      40(1), [670]
    modification, **40(2)**, [278]
    regulations, **40(1)**, [198], [257]
    revaluation of, **40(1)**, [669]; **40(2)**, [276]
    State second pension derived from,
      40(2), [275]
    tables and rules for, **40(1)**, [262]
  employed earner—
    meaning, **40(1)**, [232]
    treatment as, **40(1)**, [232]
  employer's, prohibition on recovery of,
    40(1), [461]
  employment, disregarded, **40(1)**, [232]
  general note, **40(1)**, [1]
  national health service allocation,
    40(1), [691]
  National Insurance Fund, adjusting level
    of, **40(1)**, [665], [666]
  offences, **40(1)**, [603]
  orders for, **40(1)**, [664]
  payment in error, **40(1)**, [310]
  pension, deduction from, **40(1)**, [461]
  questions relating to, **40(2)**, [9]
  rates of—
    alteration of, **40(1)**, [231]
    regulations, **40(1)**, [231]
    residence condition, **40(1)**, [231]
  regulations—
    amounts and rates, as to, **40(1)**, [231]
    Class 4 contributions, relating to,
      40(1), [255]
    earnings, as to, **40(1)**, [233]
    liability, as to, **40(1)**, [257]
    power to make, **40(1)**, [461]
    workers provided by service companies,
      as to, **40(1)**, [235]
  remuneration—
    payments treated as, **40(1)**, [234];
      40(2), [190]
    sickness payment treated as, **40(1)**, [461]
  returns, penalties, **40(1)**, [461]

National Insurance—*contd*
  contributions—*contd*
    self-employed earner—
      meaning, **40(1)**, [232]
      treatment as, **40(1)**, [232]
    share options, notice of right to acquire—
      effect of, **40(2)**, [332]
      person giving, **40(2)**, [331]
      requirement to give, **40(2)**, [331]
      roll-overs, **40(2)**, [333]
    system, outline of, **40(1)**, [231]
    tax, collection with, **40(1)**, [461]
    unpaid—
      convictions, **40(1)**, [614]
      directors, liability of, **40(1)**, [616]
      evidence of non-payment, **40(1)**, [611]
      notices, service of, **40(1)**, [614]
      personal liability notice—
        appeals, **40(1)**, [617]
        meaning, **40(1)**, [616]
        service of, **40(1)**, [616]
      previous offences, proof of, **40(1)**, [613]
      prosecution, recovery on, **40(1)**, [612]
      recovery of, **40(1)**, [615]
  employee, contributions met by—
    capital gains tax relief, **43(2)**, [543]
    consequential amendments, **43(2)**, [543]
    corporation tax relief, **43(2)**, [543]
  number, requirement to apply for,
    40(1), [714]
  surcharge, abolition of, **40(1)**, [141]

National Insurance Commissioners
  Social Security Commissioners, becoming,
    40(1), [103]

National Insurance Fund
  accounts, **40(1)**, [690]
  adjustment to level of, **40(1)**, [665], [666]
  Consolidated Fund, adjustments between,
    40(1), [694]
  contributions paid into, **40(1)**, [691]
  control and management of, **40(1)**, [690]
  jobseeker's allowance, amount paid out for,
    40(2), [83]
  maintenance of, **40(1)**, [690]
  money purchase contracted-out pension
    schemes, payments in respect of,
    40(2), [228]
  National Debt Commissioners, investment
    by, **40(1)**, [690]
  payments from, **40(1)**, [692]
  payments into, **40(1)**, [693]; **40(2)**, [15]
  Redundancy Fund, replacing, **16**, [170]
  repayments, destination of, **40(1)**, [693]
  social fund, payments to and from,
    40(1), [698]

National Land Fund
  National Heritage Memorial Fund
    succeeding, **13**, [245]

National Library of Scotland
  land, transfer of, **13**, [430]
  legal deposit library, as, **13**, [467]

National Library of Wales
  legal deposit library, as, **13**, [467]

national loans. *See* **government borrowing**

National Loans Fund
  amendment of provisions, **43(1)**, [410]
  assets, **19(2)**, [865]
  audit and accounts, **19(2)**, [868]
  consolidated fund, substitution for,
    19(2), [850], [866], [872]
  conversion loan, sinking fund with respect
    to, **19(2)**, [735]
  creation of, **19(2)**, [849]
  credits on, **19(2)**, [849]
  daily payments into, **19(2)**, [864]
  Debt Management Account, payment from,
    19(2), [874]
  dividends, payment of, **19(2)**, [631]
  Exchange Equalisation Account, issue of sums
    to, **19(2)**, [963]
  government annuities charged on,
    19(2), [855]
  HM Revenue and Customs, loans from,
    19(2), [1024]
  International Monetary Fund, payments to
    and from, **19(2)**, [953], [955]
  Irish land purchase annuities, payment of sum
    in respect of, **19(2)**, [851]
  liabilities, **19(2)**, [865]
  local loan, issue of sums for, **19(2)**, [852]
  national debt—
    charge on, as, **19(2)**, [858]
    payments into for service of, **19(2)**, [861]
  new town development loan, suspension of,
    19(2), [972]
  OECD Agreement, payments made under,
    19(2), [949]
  payments into—
    error, by, **19(2)**, [1032]
    generally, **19(1)**, [1]
    out of, **19(2)**, [1031]
  perpetual annuities charged on, **19(2)**, [626],
    [704]
  ports and harbours, loans for purposes of,
    39(2), [164], [187], [216]
  profits of Issue Department of Bank of
    England paid into, **19(2)**, [856]
  repayment of sums issued to National Debt
    Commissioners, **43(S)**, 996
  Revenue accounts, loans from, **19(2)**, [1024]
  summary of provisions, **19(1)**, [1]
  terms on which held, **19(2)**, [857]
  Treasury bill paid out of, **19(2)**, [687]
  War Loan charged on, **19(2)**, [927]

National Lottery
  bet on outcome of lottery forming part of,
    5(1), [376]
  Big Lottery Fund—
    advice, power to give, **5(1)**, [177]
    committees, **5(1)**, [191]
    directions to, **5(1)**, [178]

National Lottery—*contd*
  Big Lottery Fund—*contd*
    distribution of dormant account money
      to, **19(S)**, Financial 16
    advice, giving, **19(S)**, Financial 38
    arrangements, power to enter into,
      19(S), Financial 24
    consultation, **19(S)**, Financial 37
    delegation of functions,
      19(S), Financial 34–5
    directions to, **19(S)**, Financial 21
    expenses, **19(S)**, Financial 24–5
    information, publication of,
      19(S), Financial 37
    power to solicit applications,
      19(S), Financial 37
    reports and accounts, **19(S)**, Financial 36
    strategic plans, **19(S)**, Financial 31–3
  establishment of, **5(1)**, [174]
  finance, **5(1)**, [193]
  membership, **5(1)**, [191]
  non-lottery funds, distribution of,
    5(1), [176]
  power to distribute funds, **5(1)**, [175]
  proceedings, **5(1)**, [192]
  records, **5(1)**, [192]
  remuneration and allowances, **5(1)**, [193]
  staff, **5(1)**, [191]
  status, **5(1)**, [191]
  tenure of office, **5(1)**, [191]
  Charities Board, dissolution, power of,
    5(1), [675]
  Commission—
    annual report, **5(1)**, [146]
    capacity, **5(1)**, [187]
    chairman, **5(1)**, [187]
    decisions, reasons for, **5(1)**, [187]
    delegation by, **5(1)**, [187]
    directions to, **5(1)**, [143]
    Director General, replacement of,
      5(1), [210], [224]
    establishment of, **5(1)**, [127]
    evidence of documents, **5(1)**, [187]
    finance and accounts, **5(1)**, [187]
    Gambling Commission, consultation with,
      5(1), [129], [313]
    information, disclosure of, **5(1)**, [130]
      wrongful, **5(1)**, [131]
    licences, grant of. *See* licences *below*
    membership, **5(1)**, [187]
    overriding duties of, **5(1)**, [128]
    proceedings, **5(1)**, [187]
    promotion, licensing of body for,
      5(1), [133], [135]
    remuneration and allowances, **5(1)**, [187]
    seal, **5(1)**, [187]
    staff, **5(1)**, [187]
    status, **5(1)**, [187]
    tenure of office, **5(1)**, [187]
  distributing bodies—
    accounts, **5(1)**, [172]
    annual reports, **5(1)**, [171]
    application of money by, **5(1)**, [156]
    directions to, **5(1)**, [162]
      Scotland, **5(1)**, [163]

National Lottery—*contd*
  distributing bodies—*contd*
    joint schemes for distribution by,
      5(1), [158], [109]
    old—
      dissolution of, **5(1)**, [675]
      outstanding balances, allocation of,
        5(1), [677]
      transfer of property, rights and
        liabilities, **5(1)**, [676]
    payment to, **5(1)**, [155]
    percentage of funds for, **5(1)**, [154], [165]
    power of distribution, delegation of,
      5(1), [157]
    prohibition of distribution, power of,
      5(1), [164]
    publicity, **5(1)**, [161]
    reallocation of funds, **5(1)**, [167]
    strategic plans, **5(1)**, [159]
      Scotland, **5(1)**, [160]
    substitution and addition of, **5(1)**, [166]
  Distribution Fund—
    accounts, **5(1)**, [170]
    apportionment of money in, **5(1)**, [153],
      [674]
    distributing bodies, payment to, **5(1)**, [155]
    establishment of, **5(1)**, [152]
    expenses, payments for, **5(1)**, [168]
    investment, **5(1)**, [169]
    re-allocation of money in,
      5(1), [211]–[212]
  false representations, **5(1)**, [148]
  licences—
    amended provisions, **5(1)**, [682]
    annual fee, **5(1)**, [136], [672]
    annual levy, **5(1)**, [142]
    competition for, **5(1)**, [134]
    conditions—
      appeals against penalties, **5(1)**, [141]
      breach, financial penalties for,
        5(1), [140]
      enforcement, **5(1)**, [138]
      subject matter of, **5(1)**, [135]
      variation, **5(1)**, [137]
    Horserace Totaliser Board, powers of,
      5(1), [149]
    persons to run lottery, of, **5(1)**, [132],
      [135]
    promotion, person for, **5(1)**, [133], [135]
    revocation, **5(1)**, [139], [188]–[189]
  licensing structure, **5(1)**, [673]
  lotteries forming part of, **5(1)**, [126]
  lottery offences, exclusion from, **5(1)**, [544]
  meaning, **5(1)**, [126]
  National Endowment for Science, Technology
    and the Arts. *See* **National Endowment
    for Science, Technology and the Arts**
  national heritage, expenditure for, **5(1)**, [179]
  Northern Ireland, provisions applied,
    5(1), [183]
  Olympic Lottery—
    changes in Olympic procedure, provision
      for, **5(1)**, [267]
    Distribution Fund—
      establishment of, **5(1)**, [255]

National Lottery—*contd*
  Olympic Lottery—*contd*
    Distribution Fund—*contd*
      investment, **5(1)**, [259]
      lottery proceeds, payments from,
        5(1), [256]
      National Lottery Distribution Fund,
        payments from, **5(1)**, [257]
      payments out of, **5(1)**, [258]
      winding up, provision for, **5(1)**, [260]
    Distributor—
      accounts, **5(1)**, [280]
      annual report, **5(1)**, [279]
      committees, **5(1)**, [278]
      constitution, **5(1)**, [278]
      dissolution, provision for, **5(1)**, [264]
      distribution by, **5(1)**, [262]
      distribution policy, **5(1)**, [263]
      establishment of, **5(1)**, [261]
      grants or loans by, **5(1)**, [263]
      investment by, **5(1)**, [280]
      membership, **5(1)**, [278]
      payments by, **5(1)**, [280]
      proceedings, **5(1)**, [279]
      receipts, **5(1)**, [280]
      remuneration, **5(1)**, [280]
      staff, **5(1)**, [278]
      status, **5(1)**, [278]
      tenure, **5(1)**, [278]
    licensing—
      designation, **5(1)**, [253]
      power of, **5(1)**, [253]
      timing, **5(1)**, [254]
    Olympic Games, reference to, **5(1)**, [265]
    regulations and orders, **5(1)**, [268]
    summary of provisions, **5(1)**, [1]
  orders and regulations, **5(1)**, [180]
  participation in, nature of, **5(1)**, [296]
  promotion, regulations as to, **5(1)**, [144]
  regulations—
    contravention, offence of, **5(1)**, [145]
    power to make, **5(1)**, [180]
    promotion, as to, **5(1)**, [144]
  rehabilitation of offenders, restriction of
    enactments, **5(1)**, [150]
  Secretary of State—
    directions by—
      Big Lottery Fund, to, **5(1)**, [178]
      Commission, to, **5(1)**, [143]
      distributing bodies, to, **5(1)**, [162]–[163]
      National Endowment for Science,
        Technology and the Arts, to,
        5(1), [218]
    information, power to require, **5(1)**, [147]
    overriding duties of, **5(1)**, [128]
    prohibition of distribution, power of,
      5(1), [164]
  summary of provisions, **5(1)**, [1]

National Maritime Museum
  control and management, **13**, [92]
  director, **13**, [95]
  establishment, **13**, [91]
  financial provisions, **13**, [96]
  grants, **13**, [431], [432]

National Maritime Museum—*contd*
  history, **13**, [49]
  land—
    for use of, **13**, [98]
    transfer of, **13**, [430]
  loans by, **13**, [92]
  objects—
    disposal, **13**, [92]
    loan or transfer—
      by, **13**, [92]
      to, **13**, [94]
    vesting of, **13**, [93]
  officers and servants, **13**, [95]
  staff, **13**, [95]
  trustees—
    constitution of Board, **13**, [92], [99]
    establishment, **13**, [92]
    functions, **13**, [371]
    powers, **13**, [92]
    proceedings, **13**, [99]
    transfer of land to, **13**, [370]
    vesting of collection in, **13**, [93]

national minimum wage
  information, use of, **43(1)**, [498]

National Museums of Scotland
  admission charges, power to make, **13**, [207]
  land, transfer of, **13**, [430]

national ownership
  undertaking under, transfer of stock, stamp
    duty exemption, **41**, [81]

National Park
  access agreement, **32**, [162]
  access order, **32**, [163]
  accommodation, meals and refreshment in,
    32, [148]
  acquisition of land, powers of, **46**, [509]
  administration, **32**, [1]
  agricultural housing, application of
    provisions, **21**, [457]
  areas of, **32**, [143]
  authorities—
    chairman and deputy chairman, **32**, [622]
    committees, **32**, [622]
    constitution, **32**, [622]
    documents and records, **32**, [622]
    duties of, **32**, [147]
    emergency financial assistance, **32**, [815]
    establishment of, **32**, [600]
    existing, **32**, [614]
    general powers of, **32**, [623]
    general purposes and powers, **32**, [602]
    grants to, **32**, [608]
    land, powers in relation to, **32**, [623]
    levying bodies, as, **32**, [607]
    meetings and proceedings, **32**, [622]
    members, **32**, [622]
    officers, **32**, [622]
    parish and community councils, liaison
      with, **32**, [622]

National Park—*contd*
  authorities—*contd*
    planning authority functions—
      National Parks legislation, under,
        32, [604]
      Wildlife and Countryside Act, under,
        32, [605]
    relevant orders, **32**, [622]
    status of, **32**, [622]
    statutory functions, **32**, [606], [624]
    sub-committees, **32**, [622]
    Wales, in, **32**, [601]
  byelaws, **32**, [184]
    continuity of, **25(2)**, [636]
  campsites in, **32**, [148]
  committees, political balance on, **25(2)**, [898]
  Crown land in, **32**, [189]
  Crown, provisions applying to, **32**, [618]
  derelict land in, grant for, **32**, [512]
  designation of, **32**, [144]–[145]
  development plans relating to, **32**, [146]
  expenditure relating to, grants to local
    authorities for, **32**, [609]
  farm capital grant, duties on application for,
    32, [469]
  functions relating to, **25(2)**, [582]
  generally, **32**, [1]
  grants—
    Countryside Council for Wales, by,
      25(2), [305]
    supplementary, **25(2)**, [303]
  highway construction in, **36**, [1121]
  houses in, restriction on disposal, **22**, [44],
    [169]; **23**, [356]
  incidental matters, agreements on, **32**, [611]
  information on, provision of, **32**, [181]
  inquiries, **32**, [195]
  lakes in, powers relating to, **32**, [264]
  land control, exemption from, **1(1)**, [652]
  land in, acquisition by Minister, **32**, [150]
  litter in, abatement, **35(1)**, [314]
  local authority, financial contributions by,
    32, [187]
  local communities within, **32**, [147]
  local planning authority—
    facilities provided by, **32**, [148], [263]
    for, **46**, [254]
    grants by, **32**, [473]
    loans by, **32**, [473]
    maps, preparing, **32**, [472]
    other bodies, functions carried out by,
      32, [311]
    water, works facilitating use of, **32**, [263]
  long distance routes in, **36**, [633]
  Management Plans, **32**, [603]
  moor and heath—
    agricultural operations, notification of,
      32, [471]
    maps showing, **32**, [472]
    power of entry, **32**, [478]
  Natural England, duties of, **32**, [144]
  notices, service of, **32**, [195]
  Officer, **32**, [622]
  order designating—
    consultation before, **32**, [145], [203]

National Park—*contd*
  order designating—*contd*
    notice of, **32**, [203]
    validity, **32**, [204]
    variation of, **32**, [145], [474]
  orders, power to make, **32**, [610]
  parking places in—
    byelaws, **32**, [184]
    provision of, **32**, [148]
  planning functions, **46**, [254]
  purchase notice provisions, **46**, [393]
  purposes of, **32**, [598]
    bodies and persons having regard to,
      32, [147], [599]
  service of notices, **32**, [486]–[487]
  sites of special interest, notification to water
    undertakers, **49**, [715]
  summary prosecutions, **32**, [479]
  traffic regulation in, **37**, [189]
  variation of area, **32**, [600]
  Wales, in, unitary development plans,
    46, [278]
    joint, **46**, [279]
  Wales, provisions applying to, **32**, [142], [470]
  wardens, **32**, [274], [476]
  waterways, access to, **32**, [172]

National Parks Commission
  establishment of, **32**, [1]

National Policing Improvement Agency
  accounts, **33(2)**, [628]
  annual plans, **33(2)**, [625]
  annual reports, **33(2)**, [627]
  Assets Recovery Agency, transfers from,
    12(4), [458]
  chief executive, **33(2)**, [626]
  consultation, **33(2)**, [625]
  establishment of, **33(2)**, [610]
  financial investigators, accreditation of,
    12(3), [174]
  financial provisions, **33(2)**, [628]
  Independent Police Complaints
    Commission—
      investigations, involvement with,
        33(2), [356]
      staff, agreement for corresponding
        procedures, **33(2)**, [367]
  inspections, **33(2)**, [627]
  interpretation, **33(2)**, [630]
  members of, **33(2)**, [626]
  objects and powers of, **33(2)**, [625]
  procedure, **33(2)**, [626]
  reports, **33(2)**, [627]
  staff, **33(2)**, [626]
  status, **33(2)**, [626]
  strategic priorities, **33(2)**, [625]
  summary of provisions, **33(2)**, [17]
  transfer schemes, **33(2)**, [629]

National Portrait Gallery
  Board of Trustees, new—
    accounts and audit, **13**, [422]
    agreements, party to, **13**, [413]
    allowances, **13**, [426]

National Portrait Gallery—*contd*
  Board of Trustees, new—*contd*
    British works, maintenance of collection
      of, **13**, [414]
    companies, power to form, **13**, [415]
    establishment, **13**, [413]
    general functions, **13**, [414]
    land, transfer of, **13**, [421], [430]
      stamp duty exemption, **13**, [421]
      stamp duty land tax exemption,
        13, [421]
    membership, **13**, [426]
    pictures and relevant objects—
      acquisition and disposal of, **13**, [416]
      lending and borrowing, **13**, [417]
      transfer between institutions, **13**, [418],
        [428], [429]
    predecessor, meaning, **13**, [413]
    proceedings, **13**, [426]
    reports, **13**, [426]
    sealing of instruments, **13**, [426]
    status, **13**, [426]
    vesting of property, rights and liabilities in,
      13, [413]
  companies, objects of, **13**, [415]
  director, **13**, [426]
  establishment and government, **13**, [49]
  finances, **13**, [422]
  grants, **13**, [422], [431], [432]
  portraits, collection of, **13**, [414]
  staff, **13**, [426]
  will, gifts by, **13**, [419]

National Ports Council
  dissolution—
    agreements and documents, modification,
      39(2), [491]
    charging schemes arising, **39(2)**, [481],
      [492]
    compensation, loss of office etc,
      39(2), [491]
    council's duty as to, **39(2)**, [491]
    debts, repayment, **39(2)**, [479]
    disposal of documents, **39(2)**, [491]
    final accounts, **39(2)**, [491]
    generally, **39(2)**, [479]
    harbour reorganisation scheme, pending,
      39(2), [491]
    local enactments, adjustment, **39(2)**, [491]
    pending proceedings, **39(2)**, [491]
    pension scheme, provisions as to,
      39(2), [491]
    repayments under charging schemes,
      39(2), [492]
    residual functions, **39(2)**, [491]

National Probation Service. *See also*
probation
  aim of, **12(2)**, [976]
  purpose of provisions, **12(2)**, [975]
  Secretary of State, functions of, **12(2)**, [977]

National Radiological Protection Board
  cessation of certain enactments, **43(2)**, [754]

National Research Development
Corporation
  chairman, appointment, **47**, [99]
  common seal, **47**, [101]
  constitution, **47**, [99]
  dissolution, **47**, [439]
  establishment, **47**, [99]
  managing director, appointment, **47**, [99]
  members—
    appointment, **47**, [99]
    qualifications, **47**, [99]
  procedure, regulation of, **47**, [101]
  regulations concerning, **47**, [101]
  successor company—
    corporation tax, **47**, [440]
    financial structure, **47**, [437]
    temporary restriction on, **47**, [438]
    vesting of property in, **47**, [436], [446]
  tax liability, **47**, [101]
  transitional provisions, **47**, [450]

National Rivers Authority. *See* **freshwater**
fisheries (Environment Agency);
Environment Agency
  land control, exemption from, **1(1)**, [652]
  local authorities, arrangements with, **49**, [707]
  local statutory provisions, effect of, **49**, [680]
  pipes—
    land apart from streets, power to lay in,
      49, [1205]
    streets, power to lay in, **49**, [1204]
  recreational activities, **49**, [707]
  reservoir undertakers, as, **49**, [577]
  sites of special interest, notification to water
    undertakers, **49**, [715]
  transfer of functions to Environment Agency,
    35(2), [88]
  water authorities functions, transfer of,
    49, [660]

National Savings
  ordinary accounts, surplus funds, **43(S)**, 1429
  repayment to National Loans Fund,
    43(S), 996

National Savings and Investments
  statutory adjudicator, abolition of,
    43(2), [758]

National Savings Bank
  business of, Director of Savings carrying on,
    19(2), [893]
  continuation of, **19(2)**, [893]
  death, payment without representation on,
    19(2), [901]
  deposit—
    charities, by, **19(2)**, [905]
    investment—
      interest on, **19(2)**, [898]
        meaning, **19(2)**, [913]
      minimum balance, **19(2)**, [896]
      National Loans Fund, payment into,
        19(2), [968], [970]
      regulations, **19(2)**, [894]
      terms and conditions, **19(2)**, [902]

National Savings Bank—*contd*
deposit—*contd*
limit on amount of, **19(2)**, [896]
ordinary—
annual statement, **19(2)**, [908]
application of, **19(2)**, [906]
balances, adjustment of, **19(2)**, [909]
Consolidated Fund, repayment from,
19(2), [911]
interest on, **19(2)**, [897]
investment in securities, **19(2)**, [907]
regulations, **19(2)**, [895]
overseas savings banks, transfer to and
from, **19(2)**, [904]
penny savings bank, by, **19(2)**, [905]
withdrawal of, **19(2)**, [899]
depositor—
certificate of birth, death or marriage of,
19(2), [705]
certificate of civil partnership, **19(2)**, [706],
[707]
deposits, attachment of, **11(2)**, [784]
exempt income, ordinary account interest,
44(3), [705]
re-investment of sums, **19(2)**, [970]
regulations—
power to make, **19(2)**, [894], [900]
procedure for, **19(2)**, [912]
secrecy, **19(2)**, [903]
summary of provisions, **19(1)**, [1]
yearly interest excepted from deductions,
44(4), [889]

national savings certificates
exempt income from, **44(3)**, [706]
extension terms, Treasury powers regarding,
19(2), [1027]
interest, rate of, **19(2)**, [922]
national savings gift tokens, **19(2)**, [924]
national savings stamps, **19(2)**, [924]
power to issue, **19(2)**, [857], [885]
references to, **19(2)**, [922]
repayment, conditions as to, **19(2)**, [922]

National Savings Stock Register
Director of Savings, kept by, **19(2)**, [884],
[918]
gilts, closure to, **19(1)**, [1024]
maintenance of, **19(2)**, [918]
probate issued in Isle of Man or Channel
Islands, acceptances of, **19(2)**, [921]
redemption of stock, closure preceding,
19(2), [920]
regulations, powers to make, **19(2)**, [919]
statute repeal affecting, **41**, [666]
transfer of stock, **19(2)**, [1001]

national security
Crown employment, exclusion of provisions
in interests of, **16**, [487], [843]
directions in interest of, **49**, [1020], [1257]
disclosure of information, restrictions on,
16, [850]
employment tribunal—
procedure, **16**, [553]

national security—*contd*
employment tribunal—*contd*
restriction of publicity, **16**, [555]
flood plans and, **49**, [590]
information excluded from registers,
49, [1240]
Postal Services Commission, directions to,
34, [713]
telecommunications, directions in interests
of, **45**, [61], [67]
undertaker, grants to, **49**, [961]

national service
employment, reinstatement in. *See*
employment
firemen's pensions, **3**, [415]

**National Society for the Prevention of
Cruelty to Children**
authorised person for purposes of care or
supervision, **6**, [343]
care order, application for, **6**, [343]

National Television Archive
maintenance and funding, **45**, [175]

National Theatre
cost, Treasury contribution, **13**, [111]

national transport authority
road safety grants, **37**, [611]

National Trust
accounts, **32**, [86], [302]
amenity lands—
grant of, **32**, [127]
inalienable, to be, **32**, [132]
Association—
books, etc, use of, **32**, [54]
contracts of, **32**, [52]
deeds of, saving for, **32**, [55]
dissolution of, **32**, [46]
liabilities of, **32**, [53]
meaning, **32**, [45]
memorandum and articles, voidance of,
32, [50]
property, vesting of, **32**, [49]
rights and liabilities of, **32**, [51]
assurances of land, **32**, [83]
audit, **32**, [303]
benefactors, **32**, [300]
books of account, **32**, [301]
borrowing powers, **32**, [58]
business tenancy, modification of provisions,
21, [219]
byelaws—
buildings, as to, **32**, [66], [88]
exhibition of, **32**, [67]
local authority provisions applying to,
32, [89]
purposes of, **32**, [305]
river and drainage authorities, saving for,
32, [305]
capital money, use of, **32**, [62]
charity scheme, **32**, [72], [74]

National Trust—*contd*
collective enfranchisement, exclusion of,
23, [172]
commons—
digging, restriction on, **32**, [68]
powers over, **32**, [304]
rights, saving of, **32**, [69]
compulsory purchase, land not subject to,
18, [1131]
constitution, **32**, [300]
council, meaning, **32**, [45]
Countryside Act applying to, **32**, [278]
generally, **32**, [1]
Godalming Navigation, management of,
32, [309]
historic buildings, grants for—
acquisition, for—
Historic Buildings and Ancient
Monuments Commission, by, **32**, [211]
Minister, by, **32**, [212]
preservation, for—
Historic Buildings and Ancient
Monuments Commission, by, **32**, [206]
Minister, by, **32**, [207]
recovery of, **32**, [208]
incorporation, **32**, [46]
investment powers, **32**, [82], [223]
land—
agreements restricting use of, **32**, [85]
assurances of, **32**, [83]
compulsory purchase, special parliamentary
procedure for, **9**, [431], [433], [453]
exemption from control, **1(1)**, [652]
holding, **32**, [47]
inalienable, compulsory purchase of,
32, [200]
nationally significant infrastructure projects,
compulsory acquisition, for **46(S)**, 131
traffic regulation, **37**, [189], [192]
leasehold enfranchisement, exclusion of,
21, [331]
local authority—
arrangements with, **32**, [65]
grants and contributions by, **32**, [84]
meaning, **9**, [416]; **18**, [1138]; **32**, [45]
members—
classes of, **32**, [300]
corporate, **32**, [300]
family, **32**, [300]
junior, **32**, [300]
liability, **32**, [56]
life, **32**, [300]
ordinary subscribing, **32**, [300]
original, **32**, [46]
profits not accruing to, **32**, [48]
property, occupying, **32**, [306]
subscriptions, **32**, [222]
mortgages, provisions relating to, **32**, [59]
notices, services of, **32**, [134]
principal mansion house—
grant of—
conditions of, **32**, [128]
court, consent of, **32**, [131]
lease of, **32**, [129]
power of, **32**, [127]

National Trust—*contd*
principal mansion house—*contd*
grant of—*contd*
Trustees, consent of, **32**, [128], [130]
inalienable, to be, **32**, [132]
meaning, **32**, [126]
statutory owner, powers of, **32**, [133]
trustees for sale, powers of, **32**, [133]
profits not to be divided, **32**, [48]
property—
admission, power to charge for, **32**, [64]
alienable, **32**, [71]
application of, **32**, [87]
easements, grant of, **32**, [136]
inalienable, to be, **32**, [57], [70], [132]
meaning, **32**, [45]
occupation by member, **32**, [306]
power to hold, **32**, [47], [82]
powers exercisable over, **32**, [63]
restrictions for protection of, **32**, [307]
vesting of, **32**, [49]
purposes of, **32**, [47], [81]
receiver, power to appoint, **32**, [60]
residents, arrangements with, **32**, [65]
revenue, application of, **32**, [61]
service of documents on, **9**, [415]
trustee, acting as, **32**, [137]
Wey Navigation, management of, **32**, [309]

National Water Council
dissolution provisions—
agreements, effect on, **49**, [620]
documents, construction of, **49**, [620]
employees—
compensation, **49**, [620]
superannuation commitments, **49**, [620]
expenses of Secretary of State, **49**, [615]
final accounts and reports, **49**, [620]
functions, transfer of, **49**, [614]
general duties of Council, **49**, [620]
legal remedies and pending proceedings,
49, [620]
orders, power to make, **49**, [614], [617]
property, rights and liabilities, transfer of,
49, [614]

nationalisation
schemes, stamp duty exemptions, **41**, [79]

nationalist-socialist persecution
victims of—
deposits of, interest on, **43(S)**, 49–50
disposal, gains accruing on, **43(S)**, 50–1
treatment of payments to, **43(S)**, 49–51

nationality
births, registration, application of provisions,
31, [169]
British—
citizenship, by virtue of, **31**, [11]
declaration of retention, failure to make,
former provisions, **31**, [26]
good character, requirement of, **31**, [578]
loss of—
marriage, by, **31**, [25]

nationality—*contd*
British—*contd*
loss of—*contd*
parent, by, **31**, [27]
British protected persons—
designation by Order, **31**, [165]
former provisions, **31**, [40], [64]
meaning, **31**, [42], [180]
citizenship. *See* **citizenship**
Commonwealth citizenship, persons
qualifying, **31**, [164]
deaths, registration, application of provisions,
31, [169]
documents, seizure of,
31(S), Nationality 46–7
dual, renunciation by reason of, former
provisions, **31**, [30]
evidence of, **31**, [176]
false statements, **31**, [177]
fees, regulations as to, **31**, [169]
full capacity, waiver of requirement for,
31, [175]
functions, discrimination in carrying out,
7(1), [151], [152]
generally, **31**, [179]
Governors etc—
discretion in matters of, **31**, [174]
exercise of functions by, **31**, [173]
meaning of expressions, **31**, [181]
Northern Ireland, application of provisions,
31, [189]
offences and proceedings, **31**, [177]
Orders in Council, power to make, **31**, [169]
protectorates and protected states—
designation by Order, **31**, [165]
former provisions, **31**, [40]
regulations, power to make, **31**, [169]
search for evidence of—
documents, seizure of,
31(S), Nationality 46–7
police civilians, by, **31(S)**, Nationality 47
premises, entry on, **31(S)**, Nationality 45–6
suspicion of commission of offence, on,
31(S), Nationality 44–5
summary of provisions, **31**, [1]
transitional provisions, **31**, [189]

nationally significant infrastructure projects
advice and assistance, grants for, **46(S)**, 168
airports, **46(S)**, 43–4
appropriate Crown authority, meaning,
46(S), 218–19
areas of, **46(S)**, 36
Crown land, meaning, **46(S)**, 218
Crown, provisions binding, **46(S)**, 218–29
dams and reservoirs, **46(S)**, 48
development—
meaning, **46(S)**, 52
unauthorised, notice of—
execution of works required,
46(S), 161–2
service of, **46(S)**, 160
without consent, offence, **46(S)**, 154
development consent—
amended provisions, **46(S)**, 240–7

**nationally significant infrastructure
projects**—*contd*
development consent—*contd*
application for order granting—
consultation report, **46(S)**, 57
Crown, by, **46(S)**, 59
deciding. *See* **Infrastructure Planning
Commission**
local impact reports, **46(S)**, 77
model provisions, **46(S)**, 58
power to decline to determine,
46(S), 261–3
register of, **46(S)**, 59
requirement for, **46(S)**, 57
standards, **46(S)**, 57
summary of provisions, **46(S)**, 7–9
beginning of development, **46(S)**, 152
blighted land, **46(S)**, 166–7
buildings for which granted, as of,
46(S), 153
compulsory acquisition—
application of provisions, **46(S)**, 126
authorisation, notice of, **46(S)**, 136–7
commons, **46(S)**, 132–5
compensation, **46(S)**, 127
Crown land, interest in, **46(S)**, 138
guidance as to authorisation, **46(S)**, 126
land to which relating, **46(S)**, 125
local authority and statutory undertakers'
land, **46(S)**, 129–31
National Trust land, **46(S)**, 131
open spaces, **46(S)**, 132–5
purpose for which authorised,
46(S), 124
statutory undertakers' land, **46(S)**, 127–8
underground gas storage facilities, rights
in connection with, **46(S)**, 136
consultation—
categories of persons to consult,
46(S), 62
duty of, **46(S)**, 61
local authorities, with, **46(S)**, 61
local community, with, **46(S)**, 64
responses, duty to take account of,
46(S), 65
timetable for, **46(S)**, 63
directions, **46(S)**, 55–6
enforcement, summary of provisions,
46(S), 11
errors in decisions, correction of,
46(S), 251–3
grant of—
information about interests in land,
obtaining, **46(S)**, 67–8
nuisance, statutory authority for,
46(S), 153
order granting—
benefit of, **46(S)**, 152
breach of terms of, **46(S)**, 155
changes to, **46(S)**, 256–61
Coast Protection Act, deemed consent
for, **46(S)**, 147
common land, effect on, **46(S)**, 142
compulsory acquisition. *See* compulsory
acquisition *above*

nationally significant infrastructure projects—*contd*
development consent—*contd*
order granting—*contd*
consent requirements, removal of, **46(S)**, 148
development for which granted, **46(S)**, 118
discharge of water, authorising, **46(S)**, 146
duration of, **46(S)**, 151
electric lines installed above grounds, authorising, **46(S)**, 143
existing regime, liability under, **46(S)**, 149
Food and Environment Protection Act, deemed licence under, **46(S)**, 148
formalities, **46(S)**, 119
Green Belt land, development of, **46(S)**, 146
harbour authority, creation of, **46(S)**, 144–5
highway tolls, authorisation of, **46(S)**, 144
legal challenges to, **46(S)**, 120–1
legislation powers, proposed exercise of, **46(S)**, 123–4
making of, **46(S)**, 117
matters ancillary to development, **46(S)**, 253–6
nuisance, compensation for no right to claim in, **46(S)**, 149–50
operation of generating stations, authorisation of, **46(S)**, 142
public right of way, extinguishment of, **46(S)**, 139
public right of way, statutory undertakers' apparatus etc on, **46(S)**, 139–40
reasons for decision, **46(S)**, 119
requirements included in, **46(S)**, 122–3
revocation, **46(S)**, 256–61
rights of common, effect on, **46(S)**, 142
statutory undertakers, extinguishment of rights and removal of apparatus, **46(S)**, 141
summary of provisions, **46(S)**, 9–11
underground gas storage facilities, use of, **46(S)**, 143
watercourses, diversion of, **46(S)**, 143
other consent regimes, impact on, **46(S)**, 53–4
planning obligations, **46(S)**, 164–5
potential applicants and others, advice for, **46(S)**, 66
pre-application procedure—
application of provisions, **46(S)**, 60
consultation. *See* consultation *above*
guidance, **46(S)**, 66
proposed application, duty to notify Commission, **46(S)**, 63
publicity. *See* publicity *below*
publicity—
duty to publicise, **46(S)**, 65

nationally significant infrastructure projects—*contd*
development consent—*contd*
publicity—*contd*
responses, duty to take account of, **46(S)**, 65
refusal of—
order for, **46(S)**, 117
reasons for decision, **46(S)**, 119
requirement for, **46(S)**, 6
rights of entry, **46(S)**, 69–70
Crown land, **46(S)**, 71
when required, **46(S)**, 51
electric lines, installation of, **46(S)**, 37
existing planning regimes, changes to—
blighted land, **46(S)**, 166–7
local development documents, **46(S)**, 170–1
planning obligations, **46(S)**, 164–5
regional planning bodies, delegation of functions of, **46(S)**, 168–9
summary of provisions, **46(S)**, 12–14
fields of, **46(S)**, 36
gas reception facilities, **46(S)**, 40
gas transporter pipe-lines, **46(S)**, 41
generating stations, **46(S)**, 37
harbour facilities, **46(S)**, 45
hazardous waste facilities, **46(S)**, 50–1
highways, **46(S)**, 42–3
information—
notice, offences as to, **46(S)**, 160
power to require, **46(S)**, 159
Infrastructure Planning Commission. *See* **Infrastructure Planning Commission**
injunction, activity prohibited by, **46(S)**, 162
Isles of Scilly, land in, **46(S)**, 163
list of, **46(S)**, 35
LNG facilities, **46(S)**, 39
meaning, **46(S)**, 35–6
national policy statements—
consultation—
publicity requirements, on, **46(S)**, 30
requirements, **46(S)**, 29
designation of statement as, **46(S)**, 27
legal challenges to, **46(S)**, 34
meaning, **46(S)**, 27
parliamentary requirements, **46(S)**, 31
policy in, **46(S)**, 27
pre-commencement statements, **46(S)**, 33
publicity—
consultation on requirements, **46(S)**, 30
requirements, **46(S)**, 29
review, **46(S)**, 28–9
suspension of decision-making process during, **46(S)**, 112
summary of provisions, **46(S)**, 5
suspension pending review, **46(S)**, 32–3
sustainable development, achievement of, **46(S)**, 32
offences—
breach of terms of order, **46(S)**, 155
development without consent, offence, **46(S)**, 154
information notice, relating to, **46(S)**, 160

nationally significant infrastructure projects—*contd*
offences—*contd*
right to enter—
Crown land, not applying to, **46(S)**, 158
damage, causing, **46(S)**, 158
evidence of authority, **46(S)**, 158
obstruction, **46(S)**, 158
warrant, under, **46(S)**, 157
warrant, without, **46(S)**, 156
time limits, **46(S)**, 155–6
pipe-lines, **46(S)**, 41–2
rail freight interchanges, **46(S)**, 47–8
railways, **46(S)**, 46
relevant local planning authority, **46(S)**, 163–4
Scotland, application of provisions in, **46(S)**, 278–83
service of notices—
Crown and Parliament, on, **46(S)**, 223
means of, **46(S)**, 220–1
persons interested in or occupying premises, on, **46(S)**, 222
summary of provisions, **46(S)**, 6
underground gas storage facilities, **46(S)**, 38–9. *See also* **nationally significant infrastructure projects**
waste water treatment plants, **46(S)**, 49–50
water resources, transfer of, **46(S)**, 49
Welsh offshore generating station, for, **46(S)**, 55

natural beauty, areas of. *See also* **area of outstanding natural beauty**
areas of. *See* **area of outstanding natural beauty**
conservation of, **32**, [262]
houses in, restriction on disposal, **22**, [44], [169]; **23**, [356]
preservation, references to, **32**, [201]

Natural England
access land, code of conduct relating to, **32**, [671]
advice from, **32**, [800]
advisory functions, **32**, [769]
areas of natural beauty—
advice on, **32**, [180]
designation of—
generally, **32**, [700]
orders, procedure for, **32**, [701]
functions relating to, **32**, [702]
information services, **32**, [181]
byelaws, making, **32**, [273]
compulsory acquisition by, **32**, [256], [266]
consultations with, **32**, [263]
consultancy services and training, **32**, [775]
committees and sub-committees, **32**, [836]
countryside interests, protection for, **32**, [271]
criminal proceedings, power to institute, **32**, [777]
deer, persons licensed to take, **2**, [659]
directions to, **32**, [803]
discharge of functions, **32**, [836]

Natural England—*contd*
diseases of animals, consultations as to, **2**, [452], [453]
disposal of land by, **32**, [256]
establishment of, functions of, **32**, [766]
experimental projects by, **32**, [256]
experimental schemes by, **32**, [773]
financial and other assistance by, **32**, [771]
functions of, **32**, [766]
national or international importance of, **32**, [799]
purpose of, **32**, [798]
wildlife, as to, **32**, [801]
general note, **32**, [1]
general purpose of, **32**, [767]
incidental powers, **32**, [778], [802]
information services, providing, **32**, [181], [255], [774]
interests in countryside, protection for, **32**, [271]
landowners, agreements with, **32**, [277]
management agreements by, **32**, [772]
maps—
conclusive form, in—
generally, **32**, [661]
review of, **32**, [662]
confirmed—
appeals against—
generally, **32**, [658]
procedure, **32**, [659]
Secretary of State, delegation of functions, **32**, [660], [723]
draft form, publication in, **32**, [657]
duty to prepare, **32**, [656]
regulations, **32**, [663]
marine nature reserve—
byelaws, making, **32**, [466]
managing, **32**, [465]
members—
appointment, **32**, [836]
remuneration and pensions, **32**, [836]
term of office, **32**, [836]
national nature reserve, declaring, **32**, [464]
National Park—
designation of, **32**, [145]
duties relating to, **32**, [144]
orders, securing copies for inspection, **32**, [145]
nature reserves, **32**, [836]
pollution of water, prevention of, **32**, [272]
payment for agreements, **32**, [477]
procedure, **32**, [836]
proof of documents, **32**, [836]
proposals, carrying out, **32**, [770]
reference to, **24**, [499]
reports and accounts, **32**, [836]
research by, **32**, [768]
review of matters by, **32**, [768]
seal, application of, **32**, [836]
Secretary of State—
directions by, **32**, [781]
grants by, **32**, [779]
guidance from, **32**, [780]
services and licences, power to charge for, **32**, [776]

Natural England—*contd*
  special scientific interest, site of—
    addition of extra land, notification of,
      32, [442]
    byelaws, making, **32**, [457]
    compulsory purchase of land in, **32**, [454]
    denotification of, **32**, [444]
    enlargement of, notification of, **32**, [443]
    generally, **32**, [1]
    landowners and occupiers, notification of
      change of, **32**, [456]
    management notices, **32**, [451]
      appeals, **32**, [452], [507]
    management schemes for, **32**, [450]
    notification of, **32**, [440]
      variation of, **32**, [441]
    offences relating to, **32**, [455]
    payment for operations, **32**, [453]
    signs and notices, **32**, [458]
  staff, **32**, [836]
  status, **32**, [836]

Natural Environment Research Council
  establishment of, **10**, [532]
  geological information, supply of, to,
    17(1), [454]
  land control, exemption from, **1(1)**, [652]
  mineral exploration, notice of, to, **17(1)**, [10]
  National Oceanographic Council, taking
    over, **10**, [534], [540]
  Natural Conservancy Council replacing,
    32, [316]
  report and accounts, **10**, [539]

natural gas. *See under* **gas**

Natural History Museum
  admission charges, power to make, **13**, [207]
  British Museum—
    application of statutory provisions as to,
      13, [134]
    separation from, **13**, [134]
      transitional provisions, **13**, [139]
    transfer of objects to and from, **13**, [135]
  byelaws, ordinances, statutes or rules,
    validity, **13**, [137]
  capital gains tax exemption, **42**, [1420]
  collections—
    included, **13**, [49]
    keeping and inspection, **13**, [129]
  director, **13**, [132]
  exemption from tax, **44(1)**, [366]
  grants, **13**, [431], [432]
  land—
    transfer of, **13**, [430]
    trustees' powers, **13**, [128]
  loans by, **13**, [130]
  objects—
    disposal of, **13**, [131]
    loan of, **13**, [130]
    storage of, **13**, [129]
    temporary removal, **13**, [129]
  officers and servants, **13**, [132]
  repositories—
    access by public to, **13**, [129]

Natural History Museum—*contd*
  repositories—*contd*
    authorised, **13**, [136]
    sites, **13**, [136], [141]
    storage of objects in, **13**, [129]
  staff, **13**, [132]
  transfer of objects to and from British
    Museum, **13**, [135]
  trustees—
    appointment, **13**, [134]
    composition, **13**, [134]
    powers, generally, **13**, [128]
    proceedings, **13**, [138]
    reports, **13**, [134]
    tenure of office, **13**, [138]

naturalisation. *See also* **citizenship;
nationality**
  application for—
    former provisions, **31**, [29]
    pending at commencement of Act,
      31, [29], [189]
  certificate, grant of, **31**, [21], [170], [179]
  citizenship by. *See* **citizenship**
  evidence of, **31**, [176]
  false statements, penalty, **31**, [177]
  fee, **31**, [171]
  generally, **31**, [179]
  oath of allegiance, requirement and form of,
    31, [170], [187]
  offences and proceedings, **31**, [177]
  persons regarded as naturalised, **31**, [180]
  qualifications for—
    former provisions, **31**, [21], [46], [66]
    general provisions, **31**, [170], [189]
  registration, **31**, [170]
  timing, **31**, [172]

Nature Conservancy Council. *See now*
English Nature
  transitional provisions, **32**, [316], [593]–[594]

nature conservation
  conservation body—
    advice from, **32**, [800]
    appropriate, meaning, **32**, [152]
    compulsory acquisition of land by,
      32, [154], [190]
      maintenance, for, **32**, [155]
    endangered species, advising on, **32**, [418]
    functions of—
      national or international importance of,
        32, [799]
      purpose of, **32**, [797]
      wildlife, as to, **32**, [801]
    incidental powers, **32**, [802]
    licensing, consultation on, **32**, [419]
    meaning, **32**, [797]
  countryside, restrictions on access to for
    purposes of, **32**, [677], [680]
  generally, **32**, [1]
  grants for purposes of, **32**, [616]
  hedgerows, protection of, **32**, [615]
  limestone pavement—
    orders, **32**, [508]

nature conservation—*contd*
  limestone pavement—*contd*
    power of entry, **32**, [478]
    preservation of, **32**, [1], [462]
    protection of, **32**, [508]
    meaning, **32**, [577]
  natural beauty, area of. *See* **area of**
  outstanding natural beauty
  public paths order, protection under,
    36, [1033], [1160]
  service of notices, **32**, [486]–[487]
  special scientific interest, site of—
    addition of extra land, notification of,
      32, [442]
    agreements on, **32**, [265]
    agriculture Ministers, duties of, **32**, [460]
    byelaws, **32**, [457]
    codes of guidance, **32**, [461]
    compulsory acquisition of land in,
      32, [266]
    compulsory purchase of land by Natural
      England **32**, [454]
    denotification, **32**, [444]
    enlargement of, notification of, **32**, [443]
    farm capital grant, application for,
      32, [460]
    generally, **32**, [698]
    landowners and occupiers—
      appeals, **32**, [446], [507]
      change of, **32**, [456]
      duties of, **32**, [445]
    management notices, **32**, [451]
      appeals, **32**, [452], [507]
    management schemes for, **32**, [450]
    notification of, **32**, [440]
      variation of, **32**, [441]
    offences relating to, **32**, [455]
    payment for operations, **32**, [477]
    powers of entry, **32**, [478]
    restoration following damage to, **32**, [459]
    signs and notices, **32**, [458]
    statutory undertakers—
      duties, **32**, [447]–[449]
      operations—
        authorising, **32**, [449]
        carrying out, **32**, [448]
    transitional provisions and savings, **32**, [724]
  subordinate legislation regarding, consultation
    before making, **32**, [617]
  summary prosecutions, **32**, [479]

nature reserve
  appropriate conservation body, meaning,
    32, [463]
  areas declared to be, **32**, [156]
  byelaws, **32**, [157], [192]
  compensation in respect of, **32**, [157], [193]
  compulsory acquisition of land for, **32**, [154]
    maintenance, for, **32**, [155]
  district council, establishment by, **32**, [313]
  drainage authority, work by, **32**, [159]
  establishment of, local authority, by, **32**, [158]
  management, agreements for, **32**, [153]
  marine—
    byelaws, **32**, [466]

nature reserve—*contd*
  marine—*contd*
    management of, **32**, [465]
    orders, **32**, [509]
    meaning, **32**, [151]
    national, **32**, [464]
    Natural England, management by, **32**, [836]
    owners, etc, of land, exercise of rights by,
      32, [157]

Nauru
  British ship registered in, **7(2)**, [740]
  Commonwealth—
    citizenship, **31**, [186]
    Commonwealth, entry into, **7(2)**, [737]
  visiting forces in, **7(2)**, [740]

Nautical Almanack
  publication of, **39(2)**, [2]

nautical mile
  meaning, **49**, [650]

naval prize. *See* **prize**

navigable waters. *See also* **inland waterway,**
  watercourse
  bridge or tunnel—
    construction, order or scheme for,
      36, [1125]
    navigation, reasonable requirements of,
      36, [1126]
    objections to, **36**, [1126]
    plans or specifications of, **36**, [1126]
    scheme—
      confirmation of, **36**, [1398]
      date of operation, **36**, [1400]
      inquiry, **36**, [1398]
      modifications, **36**, [1398]
      objections to, **36**, [1398]
      proposed, publication of, **36**, [1398]
      publicity for, **36**, [1399]
      validity, **36**, [1400]
  meaning, **36**, [1130]

navigation
  Act of Union, rights after, **10**, [57]
  coast protection work detrimental to. *See*
    coast protection work
  continental shelf, safety provisions applicable,
    17(1), [291]
  land drainage interfering with, **19(3)**, [259];
    20, [300]
  rights, saving for, **35(1)**, [43]
  Thames. *See* **Thames flood barrier**
  tolls—
    orders, **49**, [1286]
    levy of, **19(3)**, [225]
    power to levy, **49**, [1197]

navigation authority
  bridge construction, objection to, **36**, [1126]
  coast protection board, representation on,
    49, [381]
  drainage arrangements with, **19(3)**, [188]

navigation authority—*contd*
  financial contributions, **49**, [1181]
  flood defence arrangements with, **49**, [1174]
  functions or property, transfer to Environment
    Agency, **49**, [1272]
  land drainage affecting, **19(3)**, [259]
  meaning, **19(3)**, [247]; **49**, [347], [352],
    [1267]
  overground wires, placing of, **25(1)**, [215]
  rights, variation of—
    order as to—
      confirmation of, **19(3)**, [256]
      notice of, **19(3)**, [256]
      objections to, **19(3)**, [256]
      power to make, **19(3)**, [204]
      procedure, **19(3)**, [256]
      unconfirmed, **19(3)**, [256]
    power of, **19(3)**, [204]
  sewers, power to divert, **19(3)**, [243]
  streets or bridges controlled by, breaking up
    by water authorities, **49**, [366]
  water courses, diversion of, **49**, [1229]

navy
  absence without leave. *See* **absence without
    leave**
  active service, on—
    generally, **3**, [1278]
    meaning, **3**, [1222]
  Admiralty Board administrating, **3**, [1]
  air force, attachment to, **3**, [1197]
  aircraft—
    damage to, **3**, [1043]
    hazarding, **3**, [1033]
    inaccurate certification, **3**, [1039]
    loss of, **3**, [1043]
  alcohol offences, **3**, [1]
  annoyance by flying, **3**, [1036]
  arrest—
    absentees, of, **3**, [1182]
    certificate of, **3**, [1187]
    civil court, offence punishable by, **3**, [1183]
    deserter, of, **3**, [1182]
    entry to premises for, **3**, [1717]
    evidence of, **3**, [1073]
    generally, **3**, [1]
    person unlawfully at large, **3**, [1181]
    powers of, **3**, [1072]
    resisting, **3**, [1050]
    search upon, **3**, [1718]
    warrant of naval authority, under, **3**, [1180]
  attachment to forces, **3**, [1229]
  award, review of, **3**, [1149]
  billeting. *See* **billeting**
  Channel Islands, application of Act to,
    3, [1201]
  charges—
    amendment or substitution of, **3**, [1090]
    commanding officer—
      cases referred back to, **3**, [1109]
      investigation by, **3**, [1090], [1093]
    court-martial trial, opting for, **3**, [1092]
    higher authority, reference to, **3**, [1091]
    summary appeal court. *See* summary appeal
      court *below*

navy—*contd*
  charges—*contd*
    summary dealings, generally, **3**, [552]
    summary finding, review of, **3**, [1149]
    summary trial for—
      generally, **3**, [1092]
      regulations, **3**, [1095]
      sentence of detention awarded on,
        3, [1161]
  children of personnel, caring for, **3**, [294]
  civil offences—
    conviction of, **3**, [1064]
    guilty plea, reduction in minimum sentence
      for, **3**, [1065]
    life sentence, not passing, **3**, [1066]
  civil trial, proof of outcome, **3**, [1213]
  colonial forces acting with, **3**, [1]
  colonies, application of Act to, **3**, [1202]
  Commonwealth forces—
    acting with, **3**, [1]
    attachment to, **3**, [1198]
  complaints, redress of, **3**, [1217]
  confinement, escape from, **3**, [1051]
  continuation of service, in time of danger,
    3, [1266]
  court-martial. *See* **court-martial**
  cowardice, showing, **3**, [1013]
  Crown's prerogative, **3**, [1]
  dangerous flying, **3**, [1034]
  desertion. *See* **desertion**
  disabled—
    gifts for assisting, **3**, [284]
    provision for, **3**, [278]
  discharge, postponement of, **3**, [1265]
  disciplinary proceedings, evidence in,
    3, [1512]
  discipline—
    conduct to prejudice, **3**, [1061]
      generally, **3**, [1]
  disgraceful conduct, **3**, [1059]
  disobedience to lawful commands, **3**, [1023]
  documents, falsifying, **3**, [1054]
  drugs—
    offences, **3**, [1]
    testing for, failure to provide sample,
      3, [1024]–[1025]
  drunkenness, **3**, [1041]
  enemy, assisting, **3**, [1014]
  entry into—
    consent to young person's, **3**, [1270]
    false statements, **3**, [1053], [1269]
    generally, **3**, [1]
    terms, **3**, [1263]
    validity of, **3**, [1271]
  equipment, interference with, **3**, [1044]
  failure to attend for duty, **3**, [1018]
  false air signal, giving, **3**, [1015]
  fighting and quarrelling, **3**, [1026]
  financial penalty enforcement orders,
    3, [1209]
  fines, imprisonment in default, **3**, [1071]
  forfeited service, **3**, [1215]
  ill-treatment, **3**, [1058]
  information, unauthorised disclosure,
    3, [1052]

navy—*contd*
  insubordinate behaviour, **3**, [1022]
  Isle of Man, application of Act to, **3**, [1201]
  law—
    person subject to—
      attached forces, **3**, [1190]
      civilians, **3**, [1195], [1231]
      colonial naval forces, **3**, [1192]
      Commonwealth forces, **3**, [1191]
      marines, **3**, [1189]
      naval forces, **3**, [1188]
      sentenced offenders, **3**, [1196]
      ships, passengers in, **3**, [1194]
      trainees, **3**, [1188]
      UK, outside, **3**, [1230]
      volunteers, **3**, [1188]
  looting, **3**, [1016]
  low flying, **3**, [1035]
  maintenance order, service of proceedings,
    3, [1178]
  malingering, **3**, [1040]
  marine forces, application of Act to, **3**, [1228]
  medical compassionate fund, **3**, [276]
  mental disorder, treatment for, **3**, [1452]
  messages and signals, interference with,
    3, [1044]
  military forces, attachment to, **3**, [1197]
  misconduct in action, **3**, [1013]
  mutiny—
    failure to suppress, **3**, [1021]
    offences, **3**, [1020]
    time for trial, **3**, [1089]
  Naval Detention Quarters Rules, **3**, [1156]
  neglect of duty, **3**, [1018]
  Northern Ireland, application of Act to,
    3, [1200]
  offences—
    aiding and abetting, **3**, [1063]
    attempt to commit, **3**, [1062]
    billeting, relating to, **3**, [1047]
    civilians, against, **3**, [1055]
    commanding officers, **3**, [1090], [1093]
    decorations, relating to, **3**, [1046]
    equipment, interference with, **3**, [1044]
    generally, **3**, [1]
    inciting, **3**, [1063]
    issues, relating to, **3**, [1046]
    jurisdiction of civil courts, **3**, [1211]
    messages and signals, interference with,
      3, [1044]
    morale, against, **3**, [1056]
    required custodial sentences, **3**, [1726],
      [1742]
    sentences, review of, **3**, [1]
    summary appeal court, eligibility of warrant
      officers for membership, **3**, [1725]
    superior authorities, officers acting as,
      3, [1094]
  offenders, bringing to justice, **3**, [1072]
  officer—
    arrest of, **3**, [1072]
    cruelty by, **3**, [1057]
    meaning, **3**, [1221]
    scandalous conduct by, **3**, [1057]

navy—*contd*
  official documents, illegal dealings in,
    3, [1176]
  operations, obstructing, **3**, [1015]
  overseas authority, person arrested by,
    3, [1274]
  pensioners—
    recall of, **3**, [1405]
      notices, **3**, [1401]
  powers of command, **3**, [1199]
  prisoner, assisting escape or harbouring after,
    12(1), [328A]
  prisoners—
    escape, permitting, **3**, [1049]
    unlawful release, **3**, [1049]
  prize. *See* **prize**
  property—
    damage to, **3**, [1042]
    equipment, interference with, **3**, [1044]
    execution, exemption from, **3**, [1179]
    loss of, **3**, [1042]
    misapplication and waste, **3**, [1045]
    unlawful purchase of, **3**, [1175]
  property of deceased—
    Admiralty, discharge from liability, **3**, [164]
    medals and decorations, **3**, [162]
    Orders in Council, **3**, [165]
    probate duty, exemption from, **3**, [163]
    residue, disposal of, **3**, [152]
      civil service member, of, **3**, [153]
      creditor, representation by, **3**, [156]
      debts, payment of, **3**, [160]
      nominee of representative, **3**, [158]
      payment to representatives, **3**, [154]
      representation not taken out, **3**, [157]
      three months, after, **3**, [159]
    undisposed residue, **3**, [198]
    unsold effects, **3**, [161]
  prosecuting authority—
    appointment of, **3**, [1107]
    commanding officer, power to refer cases
      back to, **3**, [1109]
    functions of, **3**, [1108]
    police, power to advise, **3**, [1110]
    prosecuting officers, **3**, [1111]
    qualification as, **3**, [1107]
  protectorates, etc, application of Act to,
    3, [1203]
  provost officer, obstructing, **3**, [1027]
  public worship, **3**, [1012]
  punishments—
    generally, **3**, [1], [1067]
    juveniles, **3**, [1068]
    young service offenders, **3**, [1069]
  rating—
    discharge, **3**, [1267]
    meaning, **3**, [1221]
    transfer to Reserve, **3**, [1268]
  reserve, postponement of transfer to, **3**, [1265]
  salvors, crews acting as, **3**, [111]
  sentries, offences relating to, **3**, [1017]
  Service Acts, continuation of, **3**, [1709]
  ship—
    hazarding, **3**, [1033]
    inaccurate certification, **3**, [1039]

navy—*contd*
ships under convoy, **3**, [1219]
sleeping on duty, **3**, [1013]
spying—
  abolition of death penalty, **3**, [1453]
  generally, **3**, [1170]
standing orders, disobeying, **3**, [1028]
summary appeal court—
  appeals—
    constitution for, **3**, [1099]
    hearings, **3**, [1101]
    right of, **3**, [1100]
  decisions from, **3**, [1103]
  generally, **3**, [1]
  judge advocates, appointment of, **3**, [1097]
  members—
    generally, **3**, [1096]
    oaths administered to, **3**, [1105]
    officers qualifying as, **3**, [1098]
  powers, **3**, [1102]
  rules of, **3**, [1104]
  witnesses, privileges of, **3**, [1106]
summary court, proceedings before, **3**, [1186]
summary fines, **3**, [1177]
surrender of offender, **3**, [1073]
theft—
  compensation, **3**, [1153], [1376]
    appeal, **3**, [1154]
  restitution, **3**, [1153], [1376]
    appeal, **3**, [1154]
trial and punishment, **3**, [1]
vehicles, requisitioning. *See* **vehicles**
young offenders, amendment of law as to,
  6, [551]

neglect
child, of, **6**, [2], [440]

negligence
apology, effect of, **31(S)**, Negligence 2
contract, under—
  exclusion of liability, **11(1)**, [309]–[310]
  indemnity clause, **11(1)**, [311], [327]
  meaning, **11(1)**, [308]
contributory—
  apportionment of liability, **31**, [589]
  carriage by air, in case of, **4(1)**, [8], [17],
    [19], [21], [37]
  damage, meaning, **31**, [591]
  damages, apportionment, **31**, [589]
  defence in proceedings as to banking,
    19(1), [597]
  fatal accident, effect on claim for damages,
    31, [613]
  fault, meaning, **31**, [591]
  Maritime Convention Act, claims,
    non-application, **31**, [590]
  wrongful interference with goods, in regard
    to, **45**, [967], [973]
fault, meaning, **16**, [19]
injury attributable to, **16**, [19]
limitation of action for. *See* **limitation of
  action**
meaning, **11(1)**, [308]
occupiers' liability, **11(1)**, [308]

negligence—*contd*
offer of treatment or other redress, effect of,
  31(S), Negligence 2
potential liability, deterrent effect,
  31(S), Negligence 1
summary of provisions, **31**, [588]

negotiable instrument
bill of exchange. *See* **bill of exchange**
consumer credit transaction, in,
  39(1), [284]–[286]

Nevis. *See* **Anguilla**

New Deal 50plus
payments under, exemption from tax,
  44(3), [796]

new drivers. *See under* **driving licence**

New Forest
allotment gardens, in, **1(1)**, [263]
byelaws—
  offences against, **18**, [1135]
  verderers, powers of, **18**, [1136]

New Hebrides
British ship registered in, **7(2)**, [743]
independence of, **7(2)**, [741]
visiting forces in, **7(2)**, [743]

New River Company
provisions inapplicable to, **49**, [152]
special provisions, **49**, [203]
transfer of undertaking of—
  compensation, **49**, [203]
  exceptions, **49**, [203]
  interest and estate included in, **49**, [203]
  water stock—
    distribution of, **49**, [203]
    issue of, **49**, [203], [211]

new roads. *See under* **special roads**

new street
provision in housing development, **22**, [15]

new town
appropriate Minister, **46**, [195]
area—
  designation of, **9**, [349]; **46**, [133], [200]
  reduction of, **46**, [134], [201]
Commission. *See* **New Towns Commission**
compulsory acquisition, compensation,
  9, [258]
  See also **compensation**
development corporation—
  accounts, **46**, [184]
  acquisition of land by, **46**, [142]
  advances to, **46**, [172]
  annual report, **46**, [187]
  audit, **46**, [185]
  borrowing powers, **46**, [137], [174]
    limit on, **46**, [174]
  burial grounds, use of, **46**, [152]

new town—*contd*

development corporation—*contd*

chairmen, pension benefits for, **46**, [202]

Commission, transfer of property to, **46**, [171], [216]

consecrated land, use of, **46**, [152]

constitution, **46**, [135]

development proposals by, **46**, [139]

disposal of land by, **46**, [181]

conditions, **46**, [149]

dissolution of, **46**, [171]

pre-acquisition occupiers, to, **46**, [150]

easements and rights, power to override, **46**, [151]

establishment of, **46**, [135]

functions, allocation or transfer of, **46**, [138]

general powers of, **46**, [136]

grants to, **46**, [173]

housing stock—

meaning, **46**, [245]

property etc associated with, **46**, [245]

subsequent disposals, consent for, **46**, [246]

transfer of, **46**, [245]

information, provision of, **46**, [188]

instruments of, **46**, [202]

loan obligations—

power to extinguish, **46**, [178]

suspension of, **46**, [179]

meetings, **46**, [202]

members, **46**, [202]

objects, **46**, [136]

open spaces, use of, **46**, [153]

possession of houses by, **46**, [154]

proceedings, **46**, [202]

Secretary of State—

directions by, **46**, [137]

payments to, **46**, [180]–[183]

stamp duty, exemption from, **46**, [189]

surplus funds, disposal of, **46**, [182]–[183]

taxes, liability for, **46**, [135]

transfer of housing. *See* transfer scheme *below*

transfer of undertakings by, **46**, [170]

Treasury guarantees, **46**, [177]

trolley vehicle service, operation of, **46**, [164]

district council—

stamp duty, exemption from, **46**, [189]

transfer of housing to. *See* transfer scheme *below*

ecclesiastical property in, **46**, [193]

features of special architectural or historical interest, directions on, **46**, [140]

frontages and abutments, agreement as to, **46**, [141]

highway authority—

burial grounds, use of, **46**, [152]

compulsory acquisition procedure, **46**, [143]

consecrated land, use of, **46**, [152]

easements and rights, power to override, **46**, [151]

open spaces, use of, **46**, [153]

new town—*contd*

highway authority—*contd*

possession of houses by, **46**, [154]

legislation, **46**, [1]

local inquiries, **46**, [191]

National Loans Fund, sums advanced from, **46**, [176]

notices, service of, **46**, [192]

planning authority, **46**, [139]

planning control, **46**, [139]

public health, district for purposes of, **46**, [165]

public rights of way, extinguishment of, **46**, [155]

regulations and orders, **46**, [194]

rights of entry, **46**, [190]

Secretary of State, accounts of, **46**, [186]

statutory undertakers—

extinguishment of rights, **46**, [158]–[159]

functions, extension or modification of, **46**, [160]–[161]

meaning, **46**, [196]

objections to orders, **46**, [163], [214]

obligations rendered impracticable, relief from, **46**, [162]

operational land, acquisition of, **46**, [145], [208]–[210]

apparatus, rights as to, **46**, [158]–[159]

compensation, **46**, [147], [213]

extinguishment of rights, **46**, [148], [158]–[159]

functions, extension or modification of, **46**, [160]–[161]

impracticable obligations, relief from, **46**, [162]

meaning, **46**, [196]

objections, dealing with, **46**, [163]

telegraphic lines, provisions relating to, **46**, [156]

transfer scheme, employees, protection of, **46**, [219]

transitional provisions, **46**, [217]

trunk roads, power to create, **46**, [157]

new town corporation. *See also* **housing authority**

application of provisions to, **22**, [33]

conversions, control of expenditure, **22**, [308]

defective housing, disposal of, **22**, [378]

first-time buyers, assistance to, **22**, [322]–[326]

housing authority, as, **22**, [4]

See further **local housing authority**

housing subsidy to, **22**, [298]

See further **housing subsidy**

tenant, security of tenure. *See* **secure tenancy**

New Towns Commission

abolition, **24**, [589]

amended provisions, **24**, [863]

accounts, **46**, [184]

advances to, **46**, [172]

annual report, **46**, [187]

audit, **46**, [185]

New Towns Commission—*contd*
borrowing powers, **46**, [168], [174]
limit on, **46**, [174]
committees, **46**, [215]
continuation of, **46**, [166]
delegation of powers, **46**, [215]
disposal of property by, **46**, [168]
dissolution, power of, **46**, [215]
documents of, **46**, [215]
former functions, role of Homes and
Communities Agency, **24**, [591]
functions of, **46**, [167]
restrictions on, **46**, [168]
grants to, **46**, [173]
information—
direction to publish, **25(2)**, [430]
provision of, **46**, [188]
investigation, subject to, **25(2)**, [310]
See also **Local Commission**
loan obligations, suspension of, **46**, [179]
local authorities, work by, **46**, [169]
members, **46**, [215]
proceedings, **46**, [215]
property of development corporation, transfer
of, **46**, [171], [216]
property, rights and liabilities, transfer to
Homes and Communities Agency—
interim arrangements, **24**, [592]
scheme for, **24**, [590], [864]
taxation, **24**, [865]
Secretary of State—
accounts, **46**, [186]
directions of, **46**, [168]
payments to, **46**, [180]–[183]
stamp duty—
exemption from, **46**, [189]
sale of houses at discount, **41**, [138], [145]
shared ownership lease, **41**, [134], [139]
status of, **46**, [166]
surplus funds, disposal of, **46**, [182]–[183]
taxes, liability for, **46**, [166]
Treasury guarantees, **46**, [177]
works contracts. *See* **local authority**

new towns development corporation
meaning, **24**, [591]
property, rights and liabilities, transfer to
Homes and Communities Agency, **24**, [591]

new towns residuary body
landlord, as, exclusion of protected tenancy,
21, [534]; **22**, [913]
leasehold enfranchisement or extension—
future right to develop, reservation of,
21, [328], [345]
pre-exemption rights, **21**, [329]
meaning, **21**, [336]

New Zealand
Commonwealth citizenship, **31**, [186]
constitution, amendment, **7(2)**, [430]
Statute of Westminster, adopting, **7(2)**, [432]

Newfoundland
Statute of Westminster, adopting, **7(2)**, [432]

Newport, Pembroke
corporation, saving for, **25(1)**, [54]

newspaper
annual return—
failure to make, **19(3)**, [289]
fees, **19(3)**, [293]
form, **19(3)**, [299], [300]
misrepresentation, wilful, **19(3)**, [291]
omission from, wilful, **19(3)**, [291]
register, entry in, **19(3)**, [292]
requirement, **19(3)**, [288]
competitions. *See* **prize competition**
joint stock company, belonging to,
19(3), [296]
libel action against. *See* **libel**
local market shares, **45**, [767]
meaning, **19(3)**, [284], [301]
merger. *See* **Competition Commission**
national shares, **45**, [767]
orders, enforcement, **19(3)**, [295]
penalties, recovery, **19(3)**, [295]
printer—
name and address of employer, **19(3)**, [283]
preservation of copies, **19(3)**, [283]
privileged reports of public meetings,
19(3), [302]
proprietor—
ceasing to be, return of, **19(3)**, [290], [296]
Channel 3—
licences, banned from holding, **45**, [767]
participation in, restrictions on,
45, [767]
libel action against, judge's order,
19(3), [304]
meaning, **19(3)**, [284]
new, return as to, **19(3)**, [290], [296]
registration of names, **19(3)**, [287]
exceptions, **19(3)**, [286], [296]
representative, **19(3)**, [286]
publisher, discovery of, **19(3)**, [283]
register—
copies of entries—
evidence, as, **19(3)**, [294]
right to, **19(3)**, [292]
entries in, **19(3)**, [292]
establishment, **19(3)**, [287]
searches, **19(3)**, [292]
registrar—
duties, **19(3)**, [292]
meaning, **19(3)**, [284]
registration—
exceptions, **19(3)**, [287], [296]
proprietors, **19(3)**, [287]
registry office, meaning, **19(3)**, [284]
report—
committal proceedings, restriction on,
11(2), [418]
domestic proceedings, of, **11(2)**, [490]
running, meaning, **45**, [767]
sexual offences, anonymity of victims,
application of provisions, **12(2)**, [139]
share or interest in, return as to changes,
19(3), [290]
zero-rating, **50**, [151]

newsvendors
  rights of, London, **25(1)**, [395], [785];
    25(2), [689]

NHS foundation trust
  amendments relating to, **30**, [753]
  application to become, **30**, [840]
  audit of accounts, **30**, [1101]
  authorisation of—
    conditions for, **30**, [841]
    effect of, **30**, [842]
    variation of, **30**, [844]
  authorised services, **30**, [849]
  board of governors, elections for
    membership—
    conduct of, **30**, [865]
    representative membership, **30**, [867]
    standing for, **30**, [866]
    voting in, **30**, [866]
  borrowing by—
    powers, **30**, [852]
    prudential code, **30**, [847]
  complaints about health care, **30**, [699], [701]
  constitution, amendments of, **30**, [843]
  dissolution of, **30**, [860]–[861]
  employment in, validity of clearance for,
    30, [750]
  failing, **30**, [858]
  general duty of, **30**, [869]
  general powers, **30**, [853]
  goods and services, provision of—
    authorisation of, **30**, [849]
    restriction of, **30**, [850]
  Health Service Commissioner, subject to
    investigation by, **30**, [544]
  Independent Regulator—
    annual fee paid to, **30**, [856]
    authorisation by, **30**, [841], 862]–[863]
    certificate of incorporation, issue of,
      30, [840]
    continuation of, **30**, [837]
    disclosure of information to, **30**, [854]
    dissolution by, **30**, [860]–[861]
    entry and inspection of premises by,
      30, [855]
    failing trust, powers as to, **30**, [858]
    finance, **30**, [1099]
    functions, delegation of, **30**, [1099]
    general duty, **30**, [838]
    general powers, **30**, [1099]
    membership, **30**, [1099]
    mergers, authorisation of, **30**, [862]–[863]
    pensions, **30**, [1099]
    remuneration, **30**, [1099]
    reports, **30**, [1099]
    seal and evidence, **30**, [1099]
    specific powers, **30**, [1099]
    staff, **30**, [1099]
    tenure of office, **30**, [1099]
    voluntary arrangements, requiring,
      30, [859], [861]
  information, disclosure of, **30**, [854]
  interpretation, **30**, [871]
  meaning, **30**, [836]
  mergers, **30**, [862]–[863]

NHS foundation trust—*contd*
  NHS trust applying to be, **30**, [839]
  orders and regulations, **30**, [870]
  Patients' Forum. *See* **Patients' Forum**
  private health care, income from, **30**, [850]
  property, protection of, **30**, [851]
  public benefit corporation. *See* **public
    benefit corporation**
  public dividend capital, **30**, [848]
  public involvement and consultation,
    30, [1048]
  register of, **30**, [845]
  Secretary of State, financial assistance by,
    30, [846]
  staff, transfer of, **30**, [1100]
  taxation of, **30**, [531], [864]
  trustees—
    appointment of, **30**, [857]
    transfer of property to, **30**, [857]
  voluntary arrangements, entering into,
    30, [859], [861]

NHS trust
  AIDS and HIV reports, **30**, [505], [509]
  board of directors, **30**, [1092]
  borrowing, **30**, [1096]
  Care Trust, designation as, **30**, [883]
  complaints about health care, **30**, [699], [701]
  compulsory acquisition, **30**, [1093]
  consecrated land and burial grounds, use and
    development of, **30**, [1095]
  contracts, **30**, [815]
  conversion of initial loan, **30**, [603]
  dissolution, **30**, [1094]
  employment in, validity of clearance for,
    30, [750]
  establishment of, **30**, [831]
    orders, **30**, [602]
    prior to operational date, **30**, [1092]
  financial obligations, **30**, [1096]
  financial provisions, **30**, [833]
  first trust order, **30**, [1092]
  foundation. *See* **NHS foundation trust**
  general duty of, **30**, [832]
  Health Service Commissioner, subject to
    investigation by, **30**, [544]
  investments, **30**, [1096]
  local authorities, co-operation with, **30**, [888]
  members, **30**, [1092]
  originating capital, **30**, [1096]
  Patients' Forum. *See* **Patients' Forum**
  powers and duties, **30**, [1093]
  property and liabilities, transfer of, **30**, [1092]
  public dividend capital, **30**, [1096]
  public involvement and consultation,
    30, [1048]
  quality in health care—
    duty to attain, **30**, [661]
    standards set by—
      Assembly, **30**, [663]
      Secretary of State, **30**, [662]
  regulations, **30**, [1092]
  reports and information, **30**, [1092]
  residual liabilities, transfer of, **30**, [876]
  staff, **30**, [1092]–[1093]

NHS trust—*contd*
status, **30**, [1092]
statutory undertaker, as, **9**, [430]
taxation, **30**, [531]
trust funds and trustees, **30**, [1092]
Wales. *See* **Wales**

Nigeria
British ship registered in, **7(2)**, [481]
Commonwealth citizenship, **31**, [186]
existing law, operation of, **7(2)**, [544]
fully responsible status of, **7(2)**, [476]
legislative powers in, **7(2)**, [480]
naval forces, service in, **7(2)**, [478]
overseas service in, **7(2)**, [478]
republic, becoming, **7(2)**, [544]
visiting forces in, **7(2)**, [481]

night
period of time, **45**, [918]

night cafés (London)
offences, increased fines, **25(2)**, [527]

night walker
common, abolition of offence, **12(1)**, [369]

nitrate sensitive areas
agreements in, **49**, [1158]
consents, regulations in relation to, **49**, [1159]
designation of, **49**, [1157]
orders—
application for, **49**, [1280]
mandatory provisions in, **49**, [1281]

noise
abatement—
London, byelaws, **25(1)**, [657]
order, meaning, **35(1)**, [322]
summary of provisions, **35(1)**, [1]
zones—
designation by local authority, **35(1)**, [322], [355]
noise level—
exceeding registered level—
restriction on, **35(1)**, [324]
works, execution where, **35(1)**, [324], [328]
measurement of, **35(1)**, [323]
new buildings, in case of, **35(1)**, [326]
reduction of—
execution of works by local authority for, **35(1)**, [328]
order for, **35(1)**, [325]
register—
copies of entries in, **35(1)**, [323]
meaning, **35(1)**, [323]
public inspection, open to, **35(1)**, [323]
recording of levels in, **35(1)**, [323]
regulations as to, **35(1)**, [323]
aircraft—
caused by, exclusion of, **35(1)**, [332]

noise—*contd*
aircraft—*contd*
from. *See* **aircraft**
appeals to—
magistrates' court, **35(1)**, [329]
Secretary of State, **35(1)**, [329]
audible intruder alarms. *See* **audible intruder alarms**
aviation, consultation on, **26(1)**, [716]
best practicable means—
construction of expression, **35(1)**, [331]
for controlling, **35(1)**, [319]
test of, **35(1)**, [331]
construction sites, on, **35(1)**, [319]
control of, regulations governing appeals as to, **35(1)**, [329]
insulation against, in building affected by public works, **35(1)**, [298]
local authorities responsible, **35(1)**, [332]
local inquiries, power to hold, **35(1)**, [344]
London ambient noise strategy, **26(1)**, [715]
machinery, from, regulation of, **35(1)**, [327]
minimising—
codes of practice for—
best practicable means, relevance of, **35(1)**, [331]
preparation and approval, **35(1)**, [330]
construction sites, on, **35(1)**, [319]
noisy premises, closure of—
cancellation of order, **35(2)**, [424]
power of, **35(2)**, [423]
penalties for offences, **35(1)**, [333]
periodical inspections by local authority, **35(1)**, [318]
plant, from, regulation of, **35(1)**, [327]
public works, from, compensation for, **9**, [304]
See also **public works**
seizure of equipment used to make noise unlawfully—
entry and seizure, powers of, **35(2)**, [240]
forfeiture, **35(2)**, [245]
personal liability of officer, protection from, **35(2)**, [242]
retention, **35(2)**, [245]
return of seized equipment, **35(2)**, [245]
sound-proofing grants, **9**, [307]
streets, in—
abatement notice for, **35(1)**, [815]
audible intruder alarms, **35(2)**, [77], [83]
expenses recoverable from owner to be charge on premises, **35(1)**, [817]
loudspeakers—
local authority's consent, **35(2)**, [76], [82]
operation of, **35(2)**, [76]
summary procedure for dealing with noise at night—
investigation of complaints of noise, **35(2)**, [229]
offence—
evidence, **35(2)**, [235]
fixed penalty notices—
amounts in, **35(2)**, [237]
delivering, **35(2)**, [236]

noise—*contd*
summary procedure for dealing with noise at night—*contd*
offence—*contd*
fixed penalty notices—*contd*
form of, **35(2)**, [239]
name and address, power to require, **35(2)**, [238]
payment of, **35(2)**, [236]
supplementary provisions, **35(2)**, [239]
noise exceeds permitted level after notice—
dwelling, from, **35(2)**, [231]
other premises, from, **35(2)**, [232]
permitted level—
determination of, **35(2)**, [233]
dwelling, from, offence where noise exceeds after notice, **35(2)**, [231]
measuring devices, approval of, **35(2)**, [234]
other premises, from, offence where noise exceeds after notice, **35(2)**, [232]
warning notices, **35(2)**, [230]
two or more persons responsible for, **35(1)**, [332]

non obstantes
dispensation by, **10**, [42]

nonconformist churches
legislation relating to, **14**, 19–20

non-domestic rates
accounts, **25(2)**, [840]; **26(1)**, [125]
authority, functions discharged by, **25(2)**, [820]
billing authorities, **25(2)**, [826]
business improvement districts—
billing authority, arrangements by—
additional contributions and action, **26(2)**, [272]
commencement, **26(2)**, [282]
duration of, **26(2)**, [283]
duty to comply with, **26(2)**, [273]
joint, **26(2)**, [271]
power to make, **26(2)**, [270]
purpose of, **26(2)**, [270]
Crown, provisions binding, **26(2)**, [286]
further provision, power to make, **26(2)**, [285]
interpretation, **26(2)**, [288]
levy—
administration, **26(2)**, [277]
Business Rate Supplement, interaction with, **25(S)**, 19–20, 36–40
imposition of, **26(2)**, [274]
liability for, **26(2)**, [275]
proposals—
appeal against veto, **26(2)**, [281]
approval in ballot, **26(2)**, [279]
ballot regulations, **26(2)**, [284]
regulations, **26(2)**, [278]
requirement for, **26(2)**, [278]
veto, power of, **26(2)**, [280]

non-domestic rates—*contd*
business improvement districts—*contd*
Revenue Account—
meaning, **26(2)**, [276]
requirement to keep, **26(2)**, [276]
Wales, application of provisions to, **26(2)**, [287]
Business Rate Supplement—
administrative expenses, **25(S)**, 25
ballot—
approval by, **25(S)**, 10
holding, **25(S)**, 9–10
regulations, **25(S)**, 11
BID levy, interaction with, **25(S)**, 19–20, 36–40
billing authorities, notice to—
before start of financial year, **25(S)**, 21
during of financial year, **25(S)**, 22
calculation for financial year, **25(S)**, 23
chargeable amount—
formula, **25(S)**, 16–17
interpretation, **25(S)**, 17–18
collection, **25(S)**, 24
conditions for imposing, **25(S)**, 7
consequential provision, power to make, **25(S)**, 30
consultation as to, **25(S)**, 8–9
enforcement, **25(S)**, 24
interpretation, **25(S)**, 32
levying authority—
accounting, **25(S)**, 41–2
bodies being, **25(S)**, 4–5
guidance to, **25(S)**, 28
information, requiring, **25(S)**, 27
liability to—
non-domestic ratepayers, of, **25(S)**, 14
rateable value conditions, **25(S)**, 15–16
power to cancel, **25(S)**, 26
power to impose, **25(S)**, 4
prospectus, **25(S)**, 8, 34–6
regulations, **25(S)**, 31
relief from, **25(S)**, 19
special introduction provision, **25(S)**, 29
summary of provisions, **25(S)**, 1–2
use of money raised, **25(S)**, 5–6
variations, **25(S)**, 12–13
charging authorities, **25(2)**, [826]
collection and recovery, **25(2)**, [843]
contributions, **25(2)**, [841]; **26(1)**, [125]
in aid, **25(2)**, [747]
death of ratepayer, **25(2)**, [752]
decreasing, **26(1)**, [123]
discretionary relief, **25(2)**, [734], [735]
distributable amount, **26(1)**, [124]
distribution, **25(2)**, [842]
England and Wales, separate administration in, **25(2)**, [822], [893]
exemption from, **25(2)**, [835]
financial years, **25(2)**, [827]
hereditaments—
Crown property, **25(2)**, [755]
defined, **26(1)**, [121]
domestic property, **25(2)**, [756]
interpretation, **25(2)**, [758]
meaning, **25(2)**, [753]

non-domestic rates—*contd*
  hereditaments—*contd*
    non-domestic, meaning, **25(2)**, [753]
    occupied—
      joint, **25(2)**, [737]
      liability, **25(2)**, [727]
      meaning, **25(2)**, [754]
      multiplier, **25(2)**, [728]
      rateable value, **25(2)**, [728]
    owner—
      joint, **25(2)**, [737]
      meaning, **25(2)**, [754]
    partly occupied, **25(2)**, [729]
    rateable value, **25(2)**, [836]
    relevant, **25(2)**, [753]
    unoccupied—
      change in state of property, disregard of, **25(2)**, [757]
      elections, used for, **25(2)**, [754]
      liability, **25(2)**, [730]
      multiplier, **25(2)**, [732]
      new buildings, **25(2)**, [733]
      plant, machinery or equipment kept in, **25(2)**, [754]
      rateable value, **25(2)**, [732]
      zero-rating, **25(2)**, [731]
  increase in 1993, limit on, **26(1)**, [131]
  increase in 1994, limit on, **26(1)**, [141]
  increasing, **26(1)**, [122]
  information, **25(2)**, [843]
    disclosure of, **26(1)**, [243]
    Secretary of State requiring, **25(2)**, [821]
  introduction of, **25(1)**, [1]
  judicial review, **25(2)**, [819]
  multipliers, **25(1)**, [1]
    general, **25(2)**, [837]
    special authority, of, **25(2)**, [838]
    special provision for 1990–95, **25(2)**, [837]
  new buildings, completion dates, **25(2)**, [834]
  orders and regulations, **25(2)**, [825]
  payments to and from authorities, **25(2)**, [823]
  place of religious worship, exemption of, **26(2)**, [289]
  pooling, **25(2)**, [842]; **26(1)**, [124], [132], [142]
  powers of entry, **25(2)**, [843]
  rateable values, removal of power of Secretary of State to prescribe, **26(2)**, [290]
  reduction or remission of liability, **25(2)**, [736]
  special provision for 1995 onwards, **25(2)**, [746]
  supplementary provisions, power to make, **25(2)**, [829]
  transitional period, **25(2)**, [839]
  transitional provision for 2005 onwards, **25(2)**, [745]
  unoccupied hereditaments, amended provisions, **26(2)**, [464]

non-metropolitan county
  application of planning provisions, **46**, [287]
  Boundary Commission proposals, **25(2)**, [240]
  division into districts, **25(2)**, [240]

non-metropolitan county—*contd*
  establishment, **25(2)**, [1]
  list of, **25(2)**, [235]
  local planning authority for, **46**, [251]
  meaning, **25(2)**, [229]

non-resident
  bank account, inheritance tax provisions, **42**, [692]
  branch or agency in UK, double taxation relief, **43(2)**, [79]
  company. *See also* **company**
    broker, investment manager or Lloyd's agent, transactions through, **43(2)**, [218], [262]
    chargeable gains of, **43(1)**, [541]–[543]
    consequential amendments, **43(2)**, [220]
    corporation tax—
      assessment, collection and recovery of, **43(2)**, [216]
      income tax, extent of charge to, **43(2)**, [217]
      permanent establishment—
        agent, carrying on business through, **43(2)**, [215]
        branch or agency, replacement of references to, **43(2)**, [219]
        fixed place of business, **43(2)**, [215]
        meaning, **43(2)**, [215]
    gifts of assets, **42**, [1293]
    group relief, **43(1)**, [539]
    local tax, reduction of, **43(2)**, [752]
    notice of particulars, **42**, [142]
    recovery of tax payable by, **43(1)**, [540]
    remittance basis—
      accrued income profits, **43(S)**, 1110
      market value of assets, **43(S)**, 1113
      members, attribution of gains to, **43(S)**, 1094–5
      offshore income gains, **43(S)**, 1091–4
      transfer of assets abroad, **43(S)**, 1111–13
    replacement of business assets, **42**, [1288]
    tax, recovery of, **42**, [1321]
    treated as, **43(1)**, [107]–[109]
  company treated as—
    capital allowances provisions applying, **43(1)**, [1204]
    generally, **43(1)**, [107]–[108]
    repeals, **43(1)**, [109]
  EEA state nationals, allowances for, **43(S)**, 897
  entertainer. *See* **entertainer**
  gift to, **42**, [1404]
  interest and dividends, restriction on deduction of, **44(1)**, [589]
  life assurance premium, relief for, **44(1)**, [157]
  limits on income chargeable on, income tax, **43(1)**, [156]
  limits on income tax liability—
    "beneficial entitlement", meaning, **44(4)**, [830]
    broker conditions, independent, **44(4)**, [825]

non-resident—*contd*
limits on income tax liability—*contd*
companies, **44(4)**, [823]
"disregarded company income",
meaning, **44(4)**, [824]
"disregarded annual payments", meaning,
44(4), [834]
"disregarded savings and investment
income", meaning, **44(4)**, [833]
independent investment manager—
brokers, transactions through,
44(4), [836]
conditions, **44(4)**, [826]
20% rule—
collective investment schemes,
application to, **44(4)**, [832]
requirements of, **44(4)**, [827]
where not met, **44(4)**, [831]
meaning, **44(4)**, [835]
transactions through, **44(4)**, [836]
individuals, trustees etc, **44(4)**, [819]
cases where not applicable, **44(4)**, [820]
"disregarded income", meaning,
44(4), [821]
"disregarded transaction income",
meaning, **44(4)**, [822]
"investment transaction", meaning,
44(4), [835]
"qualifying period", meaning, **44(4)**, [828]
"relevant disregarded income", meaning,
44(4), [829]
offshore income gain, **44(1)**, [490]
partner, **44(1)**, [91]
patent rights, sale of, **44(1)**, [377]
personal reliefs, abolition, **43(S)**, 1432–4
reliefs, claim for, **44(1)**, [167]
sportsman. *See* **sportsman**
temporary, **42**, [1091]
trust. *See* **trust**
UK representatives—
branch or agency, **43(1)**, [154]
obligations of, **43(1)**, [177]
persons not treated as, **43(1)**, [155]

Norfolk and Suffolk Broads
long distance routes, powers, **36**, [645]

North Borneo
Malaysia, forming part of, **7(2)**, [529]

North Sea fisheries
Belgian Declaration—
commission appointed under, powers of,
1(1), [158]
confirmation of, **1(1)**, [157]
report or certificate under, **1(1)**, [159]
text of, **1(1)**, [164]
convention on policing of fisheries—
confirmation of, **1(1)**, [145]
text of, **1(1)**, [156]
fishing gear, fouling or interfering with,
1(1), [160], [164]
liquor trade in—
British vessel—
purchase by person on, **1(1)**, [167]

North Sea fisheries—*contd*
liquor trade in—*contd*
British vessel—*contd*
supply by person on, **1(1)**, [166]
convention—
confirmation of, **1(1)**, [165]
text of, **1(1)**, [176]
enforcement of provisions, **1(1)**, [170]
evidence of statement, **1(1)**, [172]
legal proceedings, **1(1)**, [171]
licence—
breach of, **1(1)**, [168]
regulations on, **1(1)**, [169]
regulations on, **1(1)**, [169]
spirituous liquors, meaning, **1(1)**, [173]
North Sea limits, meaning, **1(1)**, [173]

Northern Ireland
accommodation centre in, **31**, [396]
Accountant General. *See under* Supreme Court
below
accounts, **31**, [1097]
appropriation. *See* appropriation accounts
below
loans, of, **31**, [733]
accounts and audit of charitable companies,
repeal of special provisions, **8(1)**, [1396]
accredited community-based restorative justice
schemes, register of,
31(S), Northern Ireland 96
acquisition by Crown of land in, **9**, [383]
acquittal on indictment, reference of point of
law after, **31**, [891], [912]
action of ejectment, **42**, [257]
Admiralty jurisdiction—
bail, **31**, [652]
exclusive, **31**, [764]
exercise, mode of, **31**, [652]
generally, **31**, [652]
in personam, **31**, [652]
Advocate General—
Attorney General for England and Wales
as, **31**, [1280]
functions, **31**, [1281], [1339]
affidavits, taking of, **31**, [850]
aggregates levy, transitional tax credit,
43(2), [16], [509]
agricultural and horticultural produce,
provisions applying, **1(1)**, [668]
agricultural levies, goods in, **13**, [659]
Agricultural Marketing Reorganisation
Commission, **1(1)**, [513]
agricultural marketing scheme, **1(1)**, [524]
AIDS and HIV reports, **30**, [506]
Air Force Act, application to, **3**, [988]
animal feedingstuffs, orders, **1(2)**, [674]
appeals and decisions, provision for,
40(2), [203]
appellant, criminal appeal. *See* criminal appeal
below
appropriation accounts—
annual accounts, preparation of, **31**, [1397]
Comptroller and Auditor-General,
objections by, **31**, [1402]
disposition of balances, **31**, [1398]

Northern Ireland—*contd*

appropriation accounts—*contd*

examination of, **31**, [1400]

explanatory statement, **31**, [1399]

unauthorised expenditure, treatment of, **31**, [1401]

arbitration—

foreign awards, enforcement in, **2**, [850]

international investment disputes, **2**, [860]

arms decommissioning, amnesty period, **31(S)**, Northern Ireland 9

Army Act, application to, **3**, [716]

army in, terms and conditions of service, **3**, [1539]

Assembly. *See* **Northern Ireland Assembly**

assisted reproduction, provisions applying, **28(S)**, 223–31

assize courts, abolition, **31**, [779]

Associated British Ports, provisions applicable, **39(2)**, [484]

asylum-seekers, exclusion from homelessness provisions, **31**, [308]

atomic energy provisions, **17(1)**, [40], [82]

Attorney General—

annual report, **31**, [1279]

appointment, **31**, [1275]

Assembly proceedings, participation in, **31**, [1278]

Director of Public Prosecutions, appointment and removal of, **31**, [1296]

exercise of functions of, **10**, [791]

functions, **31**, [1275]

reference of point of law by, **31**, [891]

removal from office, **31**, [1277]

staff, **31**, [1275]

terms of appointment, **31**, [1276]

Audit Office, **31**, [1101]

aviation security, application to, **4(1)**, [153], [155], [232]

bail—

appeal, pending, **31**, [894]

Crown Court, power to admit to, **31**, [784]

House of Lords, appeal pending, **31**, [863], [913]

prosecution right of appeal against grant of, **31**, [1362]

retrial, pending, **31**, [883]

scheduled offences, in relation to—

legal aid, **31**, [1178]

limitation, **31**, [1177]

Terrorism Act, under—

absconding, **31**, [1373]

duty to surrender to custody, **31**, [1363]

persons arrested without warrant, **31**, [1373]

summary trial, offences suitable for, **31**, [1373]

bank administration provisions applying, **19(S)**, Financial 221–2

bank insolvency provisions applying, **19(S)**, Financial 186–7

bank notes, issue of. *See* **bank note**

bank notes issued in, **19(1)**, [262]

Bank of England Act applied, **19(1)**, [1032]

Northern Ireland—*contd*

bankruptcy provisions, **4(2)**, [534]

banns of marriage published in, **27**, [219]

bar, Attorney General and Solicitor General of England having right of audience, **31**, [669]

barrister—

conveyancing counsel, **31**, [851]

qualification for office, **31**, [845]

right to enter into contract for services, **31**, [1366]

solicitor becoming, **31**, [845]

binding over proceedings, **31**, [1297]

bingo duty, **5(1)**, [106]

biodegradable municipal waste sent to landfill, strategy for reducing, **35(2)**, [402]

bona vacantia, Crown disclaimer of property vesting as, **8(1)**, [1093]–[1097]

British-Irish Intergovernmental Conference, **31**, [1089]

building societies, application of provisions, **19(1)**, [727]

burial grounds, provisions on, **32**, [40]

calendar, **31**, [634]

cancellation of corporation tax advantage, proceedings, **44(1)**, [448]

carriage by air, application of Warsaw Convention, **4(1)**, [14]

carriage of goods by road Convention, application, **36**, [761]

causing or allowing death of child or vulnerable adult, evidence and procedure, **12(4)**, [4]

census provisions, **36**, [154]

certiorari, order of—

application for, **31**, [754]

sentence, power to vary on, **31**, [757]

charges affecting land in, registration, **8(1)**, [946]

charity regulator, disclosure of information to and by, **5(2)**, [745]

Chief Inspector of Criminal Justice, **31(S)**, Northern Ireland 101

annual report, **31**, [1340]

appointment, **31**, [1298]

delegation of functions, **31**, [1340]

financial provisions, **31**, [1340]

functions of, **31**, [1299]–[1300]

inspections by—

inspectors, powers of, **31**, [1301]

programme for, **31**, [1300]

scope of, **31**, [1299]

office of, **31**, [1298]

police service, inspections of, **31**, [1340]

reports, **31**, [1302]

salary, **31**, [1340]

seal, **31**, [1340]

staff, **31**, [1340]

status and property, **31**, [1340]

tenure, **31**, [1340]

child—

abduction proceedings, **12(1)**, [816]

harbouring of, abolition of action for, **31**, [943]

support—

arrangements, **31**, [1121]

Northern Ireland—*contd*
  child—*contd*
    support—*contd*
      Commissioners, **6**, [484], [541]
      provisions and co-ordination with,
        6, [535], [537], [568]
  children, orders affecting, taken to live in,
    6, [431]
  Children's Commissioner, functions of,
    6, [920]
  chose in action, assignment of, **31**, [830]
  citizenship, application of provisions, **31**, [169]
  Civic Forum, **31**, [1091]
  civil interests of servicemen in, **3**, [435]
  civil law—
    chose in action, assignment, **31**, [830]
    contracts, stipulations in, **31**, [831]
    Crown proceedings, application to,
      31, [857]
    debts, assignment of, **31**, [830]
    district judges, jurisdiction, **31**, [839]
    ejectment, relief from, **31**, [837]
    equitable waste by tenant for life, **31**, [833]
    incrimination of self or spouse, withdrawal
      of privilege against, **31**, [838]
    injunction. *See* injunction *below*
    merger of estates, **31**, [832]
    mortgagors, suits for possession by,
      31, [836]
    property, order for sale of, **31**, [834]
    receiver, Court's power to appoint,
      31, [834]
    specific performance, damages in addition,
      31, [835]
  civil partnership—
    agreements—
      meaning, **27**, [836]
      termination, effect on property,
        27, [837]
      unenforceable, **27**, [836]
    appeals, **27**, [828]
    assurance policy for benefit of partner,
      27, [833]
    children, orders affecting, restriction on
      making, **27**, [825]
    court, meaning, **27**, [827]
    declarations—
      Attorney General, papers sent to,
        27, [822]
      form of, **27**, [823]
      hearings, **27**, [823]
      making and effect of, **27**, [821]
      proceedings for, **27**, [822]
      rules of court, **27**, [823]
      types of, **27**, [820]
    dissolution order—
      agreements or arrangements,
        consideration by court, **27**, [806]
      application for, time bar on, **27**, [804]
      conditional, period before making final,
        27, [801]
      Crown Solicitor, intervention by,
        27, [802]
      desertion, period of, **27**, [809]
      effect of, **27**, [800]

Northern Ireland—*contd*
  civil partnership—*contd*
    dissolution order—*contd*
      financial provision, **27**, [932]
      grounds for, **27**, [807]
      irretrievable breakdown, on, **27**, [807]
      orders affecting children, restriction on
        making, **27**, [825]
      pension sharing order, **27**, [934]
      power to make, **27**, [800]
      presumption of breakdown, facts
        raising, **27**, [808]
      previous separation order, effect of,
        27, [809]
      proceedings—
        before making final, **27**, [803]
        relief for respondent in, **27**, [824]
      property adjustment, **27**, [933]
      reconciliation, attempt at, **27**, [805]
      refusal in 5 year separation cases on
        grounds of grave hardship, **27**, [810]
      rules of court, **27**, [826]
    eligibility, **27**, [778]
    evidence, rules applying, **27**, [838]
    fees, **27**, [796]
    financial relief—
      arrears and repayments, **27**, [942]
      avoidance of transactions intended to
        prevent or reduce, **27**, [944]
      commencement and duration of orders,
        27, [940]
      consent orders, **27**, [943]
      courts of summary jurisdiction, in,
        27, [945]–[952]
      dissolution or nullity, following,
        27, [932]
      failure to maintain, **27**, [939]
      maintenance agreements, **27**, [943]
      maintenance pending outcome of
        proceedings, **27**, [938]
      matters to which court has regard,
        27, [935]
      miscellaneous and supplementary
        provisions, **27**, [944]
      overseas dissolution, after,
        27, [953]–[955]
      pension benefits, **27**, [936]
      Pension Protection Fund compensation,
        27, [937]
      variation of orders, **27**, [941]
    immigration control provisions, **27**, [962]
    interpretation, **27**, [799]
    list of, **27**, [780]
    notice book, **27**, [780]
    nullity order—
      conditional, period before making final,
        27, [801]
      Crown Solicitor, intervention by,
        27, [802]
      effect of, **27**, [800]
      financial provision, **27**, [932]
      orders affecting children, restriction on
        making, **27**, [825]
      pension sharing order, **27**, [934]
      power to make, **27**, [800]

Northern Ireland—*contd*
civil partnership—*contd*
nullity order—*contd*
proceedings before making final,
27, [803]
property adjustment, **27**, [933]
rules of court, **27**, [826]
void, grounds of, **27**, [812]
voidable, grounds of, **27**, [813]
offences, **27**, [797]
overseas relationships, jurisdiction—
court, meaning, **27**, [855]
dissolution, proceedings for, **27**, [856]
nullity, proceedings for, **27**, [856]
presumption of death order, proceedings
for, **27**, [857]
rules of court, **27**, [858]
separation order, proceedings for,
27, [856]
validity, application for directions as to,
27, [859]
person under 18, parental consent,
27, [785]
presumption of death order—
conditional, period before making final,
27, [801]
Crown Solicitor, intervention by,
27, [802]
effect of, **27**, [800]
power to make, **27**, [800], [817]
proceedings before making final,
27, [803]
proof of, **27**, [795]
property—
disputes, **27**, [830]
termination of agreement, effect of,
27, [837]
proposed, notice of, **27**, [779]
Registrar General—
annual report, **27**, [793]
records and documents, sending to,
27, [792]
registrars, **27**, [791]
registration—
authorities, **27**, [790]
detained persons, of, **27**, [789]
districts, **27**, [990]
formation by, **27**, [777]
persons under 18, consent for,
27, [929]–[931]
place of, **27**, [784]
prohibited degrees of relationship,
27, [928]
records, searches, **27**, [794]
validity, **27**, [786]
regulations, **27**, [798]
reports of proceedings, restrictions on
publicity, **27**, [839]
schedule, **27**, [783]
separation cases, protection for respondent
in, **27**, [811]
separation order—
agreements or arrangements,
consideration by court, **27**, [806]
application for, **27**, [818]

Northern Ireland—*contd*
civil partnership—*contd*
separation order—*contd*
effect of, **27**, [800], [819]
orders affecting children, restriction on
making, **27**, [825]
power to make, **27**, [800]
property adjustment, **27**, [933]
reconciliation, attempt at, **27**, [805]
rules of court, **27**, [826]
subsequent dissolution order, not
precluding, **27**, [809]
stepchildren, references to, **27**, [873], [875],
[959]
transfer of proceedings, **27**, [829]
validity—
declarations, **27**, [820]–[823]
partnership registered outside Northern
Ireland, **27**, [816]
proof of matters not necessary for,
27, [815]
void, grounds of, **27**, [812]
voidable—
bars to relief, **27**, [814]
grounds of, **27**, [813]
civil recovery order, proceedings for,
12(3), [333], [420]
See also **proceeds of crime**
civil rights, **31**, [622]
Civil Service, legislation, **10**, [742]
Clerk of the Crown, **15(3)**, [206]
climate change—
adaptation to, programme for, **35(S)**, 98
relevant department, meaning, **35(S)**, 120
commerce, English statutes extended to,
31, [632]
Commissioners for Her Majesty's Revenue
and Customs, treatment in, **43(2)**, [676]
Commissioners of Oaths—
appointment, **31**, [850]
fees, fixing, **31**, [854]
common law offences triable in NI, **31**, [712]
community orders, transfer of, **12(3)**, [1064],
[1065]
community safety—
local partnerships, **31**, [1315]
strategy, **31**, [1314]
companies—
common seal, **8(1)**, [123]
contract by, **8(1)**, [121]
deeds, execution of—
attorney, by, **8(1)**, [125]
valid, **8(1)**, [124]
documents, execution of, **8(1)**, [122]
provisions applicable to, **8**, 607
provisions excluded, **8**, 527
Companies Act 1989, provisions applying,
19(1), [811]
Comptroller and Auditor General—
adjustment of balances, **31**, [1411]
age limit, **31**, [1414]
appointment, **31**, [1100]
appropriation accounts, objections to,
31, [1402]
audit by, **31**, [1100], [1413]

Northern Ireland—*contd*

Comptroller and Auditor General—*contd*
books of account, access to, **31**, [1409]
dates for submission of accounts, **31**, [1417]
disallowance of matters in accounts, appeals, **31**, [1412]
examination of accounts, **31**, [1404]–[1405]
preparation and rendering of accounts to, **31**, [1407]
stock and store accounts, examination of, **31**, [1406]
compulsory acquisition of land by post office, **34**, [747], [749]
computer misuse offences, **12(2)**, [48]
search warrant, **12(2)**, [49]
congenital disabilities, application of provisions, **45**, [962]
consolidated fund—
appropriation of sums from, **31**, [1092]
audit of accounts, **31**, [1095]
borrowings on security of, **31**, [1430]
capital expenditure—
public services, accommodation of, **31**, [1440]
voluntary schools, charging on, **31**, [1439]
construction of references to, **31**, [1434]
credits charged on, **31**, [1393]
financial control, **31**, [1095]
government funds, advances to, **31**, [1438]
Irish Sailors and Soldiers Land Trust, issues to, **31**, [1441]
land purchase annuities, payment of, **31**, [1127]
loans to, **31**, [731]
increase of limits, **31(S)**, Northern Ireland 9
payments into, **31**, [677], [1093]
payments out of, **31**, [1094]
Thiepval War Memorial Fund, appropriation to, **31**, [1442]
constituencies, **15(3)**, [265]
constitutional status, **31**, [622]
construction contracts, **23**, [618]
Consumer Safety Act 1987], application of, **39(1)**, [636]
contempt of court, appeal, **31**, [777], [893]
continental shelf, share of revenue, **17(1)**, [382]
contracting-out of functions, **10**, [765]
contributions—
benefits in kind, in respect of, **40(2)**, [288], [289]
transfer of functions, **40(2)**, [232]
conveyancing, meanings and interpretation, in, **20**, [436]
coroner's court—
Court Service, **31**, [813]
Lord Chancellor, duty of, **31**, [812]
corresponding provisions, **8**, 929
County Court—
contempt of court, appeal, **31**, [777]
Court Service, **31**, [813]
district judges, civil jurisdiction, **31**, [839]
fees, fixing, **31**, [854]

Northern Ireland—*contd*

County Court—*contd*
judges—
Crown Court, as judges of, **31**, [739]
High Court, sitting as judges of, **31**, [741]
Lord Chancellor, duty of, **31**, [812]
payment into court, interim, **31**, [658]
proceedings in, **42**, [204]
remittal and removal of proceedings to, **31**, [765]
Court of Appeal—
appeals to—
costs, orders as to, **31**, [773]
jurisdiction to hear, **31**, [770]
leave required, when, **31**, [770]
power of court in, **31**, [773]
single judge, powers of, **31**, [772]
assessors, trial with, **31**, [804]
bonds, rules of court as to, **31**, [848]
composition of, **31**, [738], [771]
costs—
award of, **31**, [802]
discretion as to, **31**, [773]
taxation, **31**, [803]
Court Service, **31**, [813]
Criminal Cases Review Commission, power to order investigation, by, **31**, [903]
divisions, creation of, **31**, [740]
enforcement of judgments and orders, **31**, [773]
establishment, **31**, [736]
judges—
additional, **31**, [742]–[743]
allowances, **31**, [856]
criminal causes, **31**, [738]
equality of jurisdiction, **31**, [738]
number, **31**, [738]
qualifications, **31**, [744]
single, powers of, **31**, [772], [923]
See also Lords Justices of Appeal *below*
jurisdiction, generally, **31**, [738], [769]
officers and staff. *See* Supreme Court (statutory officers) *below*
reference of point of law to, **31**, [891]
rules of court for, **31**, [800]
sittings, regulation of, **31**, [801]
solicitor, right of audience, **31**, [844]
See also Supreme Court *below*
court security—
duty to secure, **31**, [1374]
exclusion, removal or restraint of persons, **31**, [1374]
officers—
assaulting or obstructing, **31**, [1374]
powers and duties of, **31**, [1319]
protection of, **31**, [1320]
retention of articles surrendered or seized, **31**, [1374]
search, powers of, **31**, [1374]
surrender and seizure of articles, **31**, [1374]
Court Service, **31**, [813]
court security, duty to ensure, **31**, [1318]
power to abolish, **31**, [1317]

Northern Ireland—*contd*
  courts—
    binding over, power of, **31**, [842]
    official seals, **31**, [853]
    Rhine Navigation Convention, ouster of
      jurisdiction, **31**, [652]
    substituted statutory references, **31**, [868],
      [870]
    transfer of certain functions to
      Lord Chancellor, **31**, [855]
    See also County Court; Court of Appeal
      above; Crown Court; Supreme Court
      below
  credit unions, **19(1)**, [594]
  Crime and Disorder Act, application of
    provisions, **12(2)**, [692]
  criminal appeal—
    amended provisions, **12(4)**, [565], [566]
    appellant—
      costs from public funds, **31**, [891]
      meaning, **31**, [908]
      presence of, **31**, [901]
    assessor to court, appointment, **31**, [904]
    bail—
      admission to, **31**, [894], [913]
      retrial, pending, **31**, [883]
    certificate by trial judge for, **31**, [876]
    community order, against, **31**, [885]
    composition of Court for, **31**, [922]
    contempt of court, against punishment
      for, **31**, [777], [893]
    conviction, against—
      allowed, order for retrial, **31**, [882]
      alteration of sentence, **31**, [880]
      alternative offence, substitution,
        31, [878]–[879]
      grounds for allowing, **31**, [877]
      guilty plea, substitution of conviction
        after, **31**, [879]
      indictment, on, **31**, [876]
      insanity, finding of, **31**, [887]
      order quashing, **31**, [877]
      right of, **31**, [876]
      special verdict, on, **31**, [881]
    costs—
      allowable, **31**, [906]
      preparation for hearing, **31**, [897]
      restriction on allowing, **31**, [906]
    Court of Appeal, jurisdiction generally,
      31, [921]
    Court of Criminal Appeal, abolition,
      31, [769]
    Criminal Cases Review Commission—
      death of appellant, **31**, [926]
      investigation by, **31**, [903]
      report by, **31**, [903]
    death of appellant, bringing or continuation
      of appeal by approved person, **31**, [926]
    documents—
      custody of, **31**, [899]
      examination and report on, **31**, [904]
      preparation of, **31**, [897]
      production, order for, **31**, [902]
      special commissioner, inquiry and report
        by, **31**, [904]

Northern Ireland—*contd*
  criminal appeal—*contd*
    documents—*contd*
      transcripts, **31**, [898]
      trial judge's notes, **31**, [900]
    evidence at, **31**, [902]
    groundless, disposal of, **31**, [895]
    grounds for, **31**, [877]
    habeas corpus proceedings, **31**, [778]
    hearing—
      preparation of case for, **31**, [897]
      presence of appellant, **31**, [901]
    hospital, detention in, pending, **31**, [863]
    House of Lords, to—
      application for leave, **31**, [910]
      bail pending, **31**, [863], [913]
      composition of House for, **31**, [774],
        [911]
      contempt of court, against punishment
        for, **31**, [777]
      costs—
        powers as to, **31**, [919]
        taxation of, **31**, [920]
      Crown, by, **31**, [914]
      decisions appealable, **31**, [774], [863]
      defendant—
        detention pending, **31**, [914]
        expenses incurred by, **31**, [919]
        meaning, **31**, [909]
        presence at hearing, **31**, [916]
      disposal of, **31**, [911]
      hearing—
        composition of House for, **31**, [911]
        matters preliminary to,
          31, [913]–[916]
        presence of defendant, **31**, [916]
      leave—
        application for, **31**, [863], [910]
        requirement, **31**, [774], [909]
      legal aid, **31**, [915]
      Mental Health Order, order under,
        31, [914]
      reference of points of law, **31**, [912]
      remission of case to court, **31**, [911]
      restitution of property, **31**, [918]
      right of, **31**, [909]
      rules of court, **31**, [863]
      sentence, computation of, **31**, [917]
    insanity, against finding of—
      admission to hospital, order for,
        31, [889], [932]
      disposal of appeal allowed, **31**, [889]
      order for detention in hospital,
        31, [889], [932]
      right of, **31**, [888]
      unfitness to be tried, **31**, [890]
    interpreter, employment of, **31**, [906]
    judgment, pronouncement of, **31**, [924]
    leave, application for, **31**, [863], [886]
    legal aid, **31**, [896]
    Master's duties, **31**, [897]
    Mental Health Order, court orders under,
      31, [887]–[889]
    mental hospital, detention in, pending,
      31, [863]

Northern Ireland—*contd*
  criminal appeal—*contd*
    new trial. *See* retrial *below*
    notice of, **31**, [892]
    orders of court, enforcement, **31**, [904]
    preparation of case for hearing, **31**, [897]
    prerogative of mercy, saving for, **31**, [927]
    reference on point of law, **31**, [891], [912]
    restitution of property, **31**, [905]
    retrial—
      bail pending, **31**, [883]
      conviction and sentence, **31**, [931]
      depositions, **31**, [931]
      legal aid, **31**, [931]
      mentally disordered person, **31**, [883]
      power to order, **31**, [882]
      procedure, **31**, [883]
      retention of property pending, **31**, [883]
      supplementary provisions, **31**, [883]
    right of appeal, **31**, [876]
    rules of court, compliance with, **31**, [925]
    sentence, against—
      alteration of, **31**, [880]
      computation, **31**, [907]
      different sentence, passing of, **31**, [886]
      leave required, **31**, [886]
      meaning, **31**, [908]
      mentally disordered person, **31**, [886]
      particular cases, in, **31**, [885]
      right of, **31**, [884]
      supplementary provisions, **31**, [886]
      two or more sentences, **31**, [886]
      when beginning to run, **31**, [907]
    single judge, jurisdiction, **31**, [923]
    unfitness to be tried—
      admission to hospital, order for,
        31, [890]
      appeal against finding, **31**, [890]
      effect of detention order, **31**, [932]
    warrants, issue of, **31**, [904]
    witnesses, examination of, **31**, [904]
  criminal care orders, transitional provisions,
    6, [124]
  Criminal Cases Review Commission—
    dismissal of appeals following reference by,
      12(4), [487]
    reference of cases to, **12(2)**, [281], [283]
  criminal justice organisations, guidance on
    human rights standards, **31**, [1361]
  criminal justice purposes, legislation for,
    12(1), [1107]
  Criminal Procedure and Investigations Act,
    application of, **12(2)**, [489]
  cross-border bodies, generally, **31**, [622]
  crossbow, provisions applied, **12(1)**, [1054]
  Crown Court—
    See also Supreme Court *below*
    appeal from. *See* criminal appeal *above*
    appearance before, process to compel,
      31, [784]
    audience, right of, **31**, [783]
    bail, power to admit to, **31**, [784]
    breach of recognizance to appear, **31**, [784]
    business, allocation of, **31**, [780]
    establishment, **31**, [739]

Northern Ireland—*contd*
  Crown Court—*contd*
    judges—
      persons deemed to be, **31**, [739], [780]
      single, exercise of jurisdiction by,
        31, [780]
    jurisdiction—
      exclusive in trial on indictment,
        31, [779]
      exercise of, **31**, [780]
      transferred, **31**, [781]
    proceedings in, transitional provisions,
      31, [871]
    Rules Committee—
      constitution, **31**, [794]
      secretary, **31**, [794]
    rules of court—
      making of, **31**, [795]
      power to make, **31**, [793]
    sentences and orders of, **31**, [782]
    solicitors, right of audience, **31**, [783]
    substituted references, **31**, [867]–[868]
    summons to appear, **31**, [784]
    trial on indictment—
      committal for, **31**, [781]
      exclusive jurisdiction, **31**, [779]
    venue, **31**, [781]
    warrant of arrest—
      appearance, to enforce, **31**, [784]
      bail, endorsement on, **31**, [784]
    witness summons—
      disobedience to, punishment for,
        31, [791]
      document, requiring advance production
        of, **31**, [786]
      ineffective, application to make,
        31, [788], [790]
      costs, **31**, [788]
      issue of, **31**, [785]
        Crown Court's own motion, of,
          31, [789]
      warrant of arrest, power to issue to
        secure appearance under, **31**, [792]
      when no longer needed, **31**, [787]
  Crown Proceedings Act, application,
    31, [857], [944]
  Crown Solicitor for, **31**, [675]
  Custody (Luxembourg Convention),
    provisions as to, **6**, [230]
  custody of children. *See* **child**
  custody plus order, transfer of, **12(3)**, [1069],
    [1070]
  customs and excise—
    exportation, proof as to, **13**, [659]
    importation or exportation—
      customs and excise stations—
        hovercraft proceeding to or from,
          control of movement of, **13**, [605]
        regulation of, **13**, [609]
      importation, proof as to, **13**, [635]
      movement of goods, regulation of,
        13, [626]
      proceedings in, **13**, [753]
  damages—
    award of, **31**, [756]

Northern Ireland—*contd*

damages—*contd*

personal injuries, for, **31**, [943]

damages for personal injuries, public sector settlements, guarantees by departments of, **13**, [1148], [1151]

dangerous dogs, provision for, **2**, [686]

death of person in, application of laws, **43(S)**, 320

death sentence. *See* criminal appeal (capital cases) *above*

deception offences, **12(1)**, [696]

debit and credit, set-off of, **43(S)**, 964

debts, assignment of, **31**, [830]

decommissioned articles—

inadmissibility of, as evidence, **31**, [960]

meaning, **31**, [965]

testing of, **31**, [961]

decommissioning—

Commission, **31**, [962]

methods of, **31**, [958]

scheme—

amnesty—

extension of period, **31**, [1247]

generally, **31**, [959]

offences covered by, **31**, [967]

duration of, **31**, [957]

England and Wales, in, **31**, [963]

expenses, **31**, [964]

meaning, **31**, [956]

provisions of, **31**, [958]

Scotland, in, **31**, [963]

delivery up or disposal of goods infringing trade mark, jurisdiction to order, **48**, 128

Department of Agriculture, communications to and from, **2**, [551]

departments, references to departments of government, **31**, [647]

deputy lieutenants, **31**, [676]

derivative claims, proceedings for—

brought by another member, application for permission to continue, **8(1)**, [342]

cause of action, **8(1)**, [338]

grant of permission, factors taken into account, **8(1)**, [341]

meaning, **8(1)**, [338]

permission to continue claim as, application for, **8(1)**, [340]

permission to continue, application for, **8(1)**, [339]

designs provisions applied, **11(1)**, [564], [1124]

devolution—

bail and legal aid in criminal proceedings, **31**, [1149]

courts and tribunals, procedure of, **31**, [1149]

delegation by First Minister, **31**, [1149]

England and Wales, proceedings in, **31**, [1147]

expenses, **31**, [1149]

House of Lords proceedings, **31**, [1149]

Judicial Committee proceedings, **31**, [1149]

meaning, **31**, [1145]

Northern Ireland—*contd*

devolution—*contd*

Northern Ireland, proceedings in, **31**, [1146]

orders, **31**, [1028]

restoration of government—

consequential provisions, power to make, **31**, [1384]

Ministers, selection of, **31**, [1383], [1389]

no order for selection of Ministers, **31**, [1390]

Parliamentary procedure for orders, **31**, [1385]

preparation for, **31**, [1382]

Scotland, proceedings in, **31**, [1148]

suspension, **31**, [1163]

accounts, **31**, [1172]

Assembly Commission, **31**, [1172]

audit, **31**, [1172]

ending, **31**, [1164]

executive functions, **31**, [1172]

further suspension by order, **31**, [1166]

implementation bodies, **31**, [1167], [1172]

legislation by Order in Council, **31**, [1172]

orders, **31**, [1169]

Parliamentary control of Order in Council, **31**, [1172]

political parties, financial assistance for, **31**, [1172]

provisions applicable during, **31**, [1172]

reports, **31**, [1172]

resource accounts, **31**, [1172]

resources, use of, **31**, [1172]

restoration, effect of, **31**, [1165]

subordinate instruments, **31**, [1172]

vacant offices, **31**, [1172]

devolved government, restoration of, **31(S)**, Northern Ireland 58–60

diplomatic and consular premises, vesting of, **10**, [1077]

direct rule, **31**, [622]

Director of Public Prosecutions—

annual reports, **31**, [1292]

appointment, **31**, [1283]

Attorney General—

appointment and removal by, **31**, [1296]

transfer of functions of, **31**, [1294]

code of practice, **31**, [1291]

conduct of prosecutions, **31**, [1284]

consent to prosecutions, **31**, [1288]

corporation sole, as, **31(S)**, 125

delegation of powers, **31**, [1290]

discontinuance of proceedings by, **31**, [1286]

extradition proceedings, conduct of, **31**, [1285]

independence, **31**, [1295]

information—

disclosure by, **12(3)**, [513]

disclosure to, **12(3)**, [511], [512]

Lord Advocate and Scottish Ministers, disclosure to and by, **12(3)**, [514]–[516]

Northern Ireland—*contd*
  Director of Public Prosecutions—*contd*
    information—*contd*
      use of, **12(3)**, [510]
      information for, **31**, [1289]
      investigatory powers. *See* **criminal investigations**
    office, holding, **31**, [1283]
    Public Prosecution Service, head of, **31**, [1282]
    qualifications, **31**, [1283]
    removal from office, **31**, [1293]
    serious crime prevention order, application for, **12(4)**, [365].
      See also **serious crime prevention order**
    superintendence of, **31**, [1293]
  directors disqualification orders, **4(2)**, [577]
  disability discrimination—
    codes of practice, further provisions about, **7(1)**, [469]
    consequential amendments, **7(1)**, [469]
    Disabled Persons (Employment) Act Northern Ireland 1945, amendment of, **7(1)**, [469]
    modification of provisions for, **7(1)**, [469]
    regulations and orders, **7(1)**, [469]
    repeals, **7(1)**, [469]
    taxi accessibility regulations, new licences conditional on compliance with, **7(1)**, [469]
  discrimination—
    avoidance of legislation containing, **31**, [670]–[671]
    effect of certificates, **31**, [1123]
    injunction to restrain, **31**, [672]
    interpretation, **31**, [673]
    meaning, **31**, [673]
    public authorities, by, **31**, [672]
  disqualification while disqualified in, **37**, [699]
  double taxation relief, **31**, [637]
  driver's licences granted in—
    counterparts, **37**, [707]
    disability or prospective disability, revocation of authorisation because of, **37**, [708]
    endorsement, effect of, **38(1)**, [110]
    information relating to disabilities, **37**, [709]
    motor vehicles, **37**, [706]
    provisions applying, **38(1)**, [109]
  drugs, provisions as to misuse of, **28**, [233], [244]
  ejectment, relief from, **31**, [837]
  election—
    Chief Electoral Officer—
      annual reports, **15(3)**, [664]
      tenure, **15(3)**, [663]
    combination of polls, **15(3)**, [237], [526]
    European Parliament, to, **15(3)**, [228], [538]
    interpretation of terms, **15(3)**, [198]
    registration—
      amended provisions, **15(3)**, [676]
      anonymous, **15(3)**, [661]

Northern Ireland—*contd*
  election—*contd*
    registration—*contd*
      appeals, **15(3)**, [676]
    election courts, **31**, [846]
    elections to Assembly. *See* **Northern Ireland Assembly**
  electoral identity cards, **15(3)**, [27]
  electoral register—
    alteration, pending elections, **15(3)**, [26], [662]
    false information, provision of, **15(3)**, [28]
    registration objectives, **15(3)**, [21]
    timing of canvass, **15(3)**, [20]
  electricity—
    apportionments, **42**, [1521]
    capital allowances, restriction of losses by reference to, **42**, [1521]
    capital losses, unallowed, **42**, [1521]
    green certificates, **17(2)**, [464]
    regulator, Gas and Electricity Markets Authority power to act on behalf of, **17(2)**, [467]
    guarantees of origin functions, **17(2)**, [468]
    renewables orders, consultation in relation to, **17(2)**, [469]
    roll-over relief, **42**, [1521]
    stamp duty reserve tax relief, **42**, [1521]
    successor company—
      arrangements in favour of, **42**, [1521]
      securities of, **42**, [1521]
      transfer to, **42**, [1521]
      transfers between, **42**, [1521]
    suppliers, distributions to, **17(2)**, [465]
  electronic communications networks and services—
    grants—
      Department of Enterprise, Trade and Investment, by, **45**, [566]
      district councils, by, **45**, [567]
  emergency laws—
    application of, **50**, [273]
    generally, **31**, [622]
  emergency powers—
    offences. *See* scheduled offences *below*
    proscribed organisations, application of criminal injuries provisions, **31**, [686]
    scheduled offences, court for trial of, **31**, [724]
    terrorism. *See* terrorism *below*
  employees, information and consultation regulations, **16**, [1012]
  employment—
    provisions applied, **16**, [159], [533]
    reciprocal arrangements, **16**, [502], [885]
  energy conservation provisions, **23**, [618]
  enticement, abolition of actions for, **31**, [943]
  Equality Commission. *See* **Equality Commission for Northern Ireland**
  European Communities, provisions as to, **18**, [3], [5], [12]
  evidence—
    criminal proceedings, in, **31**, [707]
    provisions as to, **18**, [273], [362], [422]

Northern Ireland—*contd*
evidence—*contd*
  expert, disclosure of, **31**, [945]
  foreign law, as to, **31**, [852]
Exchequer—
  additional—
    capital repayments from surplus, power to make, **31**, [1427]
  appropriations in aid, **31**, [1426]
  borrowings, unclaimed balances, **31**, [1433]
  capital deficits, meeting, **31**, [1425]
  capital purposes, meaning, **31**, [1423]
  capital receipts—
    application of, **31**, [1424]
    meaning, **31**, [1422]
  church temporalities, payment of moneys from, **31**, [1435]
  investment of moneys, **31**, [1432]
  issues from, **31**, [1426]
  public income and expenditure—
    annual accounts, **31**, [1420]
    declared surplus or deficit, **31**, [1421]
    meaning, **31**, [1419]
  receipts of revenue, examination of accounts, **31**, [1404]
  trading accounts, **31**, [1407]
  ways and means, credits for, **31**, [1394]
Exchequer Bank—
  daily returns, **31**, [1391]
  general fund, formation of, **31**, [1392]
  gross revenues, payment in, **31**, [1391]
  overdrafts, **31**, [1431]
execution of warrant in, **11(2)**, [554]
executive powers, exercise, former provisions, **31**, [668]
exempt gas supplies, **35(2)**, [370]
existing laws, saving for, **31**, [1128], [1151]
extra-territorial offences, generally. *See under*
Ireland, Republic of
extradition proceedings—
  conduct of, **18**, [952]
  legal aid, **18**, [946], [947]
fair trading provisions, **47**, [147]
family proceedings. *See* **family proceedings**
fertilisers and feeding stuffs, application of provisions, **1(1)**, [852]
financial reporting orders, **12(4)**, [97]
financial services provisions, application of, **19(2)**, [508]
firearms certificate issued in, **12(1)**, [488]
firearms provisions applicable, **12(1)**, [1139]; **12(2)**, [133], [178]
first-year allowances, qualifying expenditure—
  general exclusions, **43(1)**, [607]
  plant or machinery partly for use outside, exclusion of, **43(1)**, [593]
  small or medium-sized enterprises, incurred by, **43(1)**, [591]
    exclusions, **43(1)**, [591]
  subsequent use primarily outside NI, effect of, **43(1)**, [594]
fishery limits, provisions extending to, **1(2)**, [135]
fixed-term employment, regulations, **16**, [999]
Food Acts applying to, **1(2)**, [255]

Northern Ireland—*contd*
forced marriage protection order. *See* **marriage**
foreign disqualification—
  endorsement, **38(2)**, [282]
  power to suspend, **38(2)**, [275]
  production of licence, **38(2)**, [277]
  regulations, **38(2)**, [286]
foreign law, evidence as to, **31**, [852]
forfeited estates, statutes extended to, **31**, [632]
forfeiture rule, **12(1)**, [779]
formation, **31**, [622]
friendly society—
  magistrates' courts' jurisdiction over, **19(1)**, [906]
  provisions applying, **19(1)**, [920]
  registration of, **19(1)**, [895]
  winding up—
    contributories, members as, **19(1)**, [932]
    High court, by, **19(1)**, [932]
    penal provisions, **19(1)**, [932]
    preferential debts, **19(1)**, [932]
    voluntary, **19(1)**, [932]
funds in court. *See* Supreme Court *below*
game certificate, availability in GB, **2**, [244]
gangmasters provisions, application of, **1(2)**, [726], [729]
general betting duty, **5(1)**, [106]
General Commissioners for, **42**, [928]
genocide, crimes against humanity and war crimes—
  ancillary offence, meaning, **10**, [1200]
  committed outside the jurisdiction, conduct ancillary to, **10**, [1197]
  general principles of liability, application of, **10**, [1201]
  International Criminal Court, offences in relation to, **10**, [1199]
  offences, **10**, [1196]
  trial and punishment of, **10**, [1198]
  victims and witnesses, protection of, **10**, [1202]
Great Seal, facsimile impressions, **31**, [643]
guaranteed prices, powers on entry in relation to, **1(1)**, [666]
guilty but insane, reference of former verdict of, **12(2)**, [706]
Gun Barrel Proof Acts, extension of, **48**, 90
habeas corpus—
  appeals, **31**, [778]
  committal for same offence, prohibition on, **31**, [627]
  criminal offence, only removable by, **31**, [629]
  debt, non-application to, **31**, [628]
  limitation, **31**, [630]
  marking and signing, **31**, [624]
  neglect or refusal to return, **31**, [626]
  persons in custody, sheriff's duty, **31**, [623]
  procedure on complaint, **31**, [624]
  sheriff, duty of, **31**, [623]
  treason or arrestable offence, **31**, [631]
  vacation, imprisonment during, **31**, [625]

Northern Ireland—*contd*
  habeas corpus—*contd*
    writ—
      limitation on time, **31**, [630]
      marking of, **31**, [624]
      service of, **31**, [623]
  habitual residence in, **6**, [241]
  Health and Medicines Act 1988, application
    of certain provisions to, **28**, [497]
  health in pregnancy grant. *See* **health in
    pregnancy grant**
  health service agreement, **30**, [443], [445]
  health service bodies, **30**, [816]
  hearing aid provisions, application to,
    28, [273]
  heather or grass burning, **1(1)**, [379]
  High Court—
    See also Supreme Court *below*
    Admiralty jurisdiction. *See* jurisdiction *below*
    affidavits taken abroad, **31**, [809]
    appeals from. *See* Court of Appeal *above*
    assessors, trial with, **31**, [804]
    bonds, rules of court as to, **31**, [848]
    business, assignment to, **31**, [753]
    certiorari, order of—
      application for, **31**, [754]
      sentence, power to vary on, **31**, [761]
    Chancery Judge, **31**, [753]
    commencement of action, powers
      exercisable before, **31**, [659], [662]
    composition, **31**, [737]
    contempt of court, appeal, **31**, [777], [893]
    conveyancing counsel, appointment,
      31, [851]
    costs—
      award of, **31**, [802]
      taxation, **31**, [803]
    Court Service, **31**, [813]
    damages, award of, **31**, [756]
      interest on, power to award, **31**, [768]
    debts, award of interest on, **31**, [768]
    declaratory judgments, **31**, [759]
    disability, persons under, jurisdiction,
      31, [762]–[763]
    divisions of, **31**, [740]
    documents—
      disclosure of, **31**, [662]–[664]
      discovery of, **31**, [662]–[664]
    establishment, **31**, [736]
    execution of instruments by order of,
      31, [767]
    funds in court. *See under* Supreme Court
      below
    injunction—
      application for, **31**, [754]
      public office, concerning, **31**, [760]
    interim relief, grant of, **31**, [755]
    judges—
      additional, **31**, [742]–[743]
      allowances, **31**, [856]
      appointment, **31**, [747], [1252];
        31(S), 133
      Court of Appeal, as judge of, **31**, [738],
        [741]
      equal jurisdiction, **31**, [737]

Northern Ireland—*contd*
  High Court—*contd*
    judges—*contd*
      number, **31**, [737]
      precedence, **31**, [745]
      qualifications, **31**, [744]
      rates and taxes cases, acting in, **31**, [751]
      removal from office, tribunals to
        consider, **31**, [1256]
      temporary, **31**, [742]
      tenure of office, **31**, [748]–[749];
        31(S), 134–6
      vacation of office, **31**, [750]
    judgments of courts outside NI,
      registration, **31**, [653]
    judicial review—
      application for, **31**, [754]
      damages, award of, **31**, [756]
      forms of relief granted in, **31**, [754]
      remission or reversal of decisions,
        31, [757]
      stay and interim relief, **31**, [755]
    jurisdiction—
      Admiralty—
        bail, **31**, [652]
        exclusive, **31**, [764]
        exercise of, mode, **31**, [652]
        generally, **31**, [652]
        in personam, **31**, [652]
        wages, action for, **31**, [652]
      general, **31**, [752]
      shipping, **31**, [652]
    jury—
      civil action, in—
        challenge, trial of, **31**, [806]
        generally, **31**, [807]
        rules of court for, **31**, [808]
        trial with, **31**, [805]
        trial without, **31**, [805]
    modern constitutional position, **31**, [622]
    officers and staff. *See* Supreme Court
      (statutory officers) *below*
    payment into Court—
      Crown, application of provisions,
        31, [660]
      interim, order for, **31**, [658]
    personal injuries or death, discovery of
      documents, **31**, [663]
    property, order for inspection of, **31**, [663]
    remittal and removal of proceedings,
      31, [765]
    rules of court, **31**, [800]
    sittings, regulation of, **31**, [801]
    solicitor, right of audience, **31**, [844]
    stay of proceedings, **31**, [755]
    subpoenas in other parts of UK, **31**, [810]
    supervisory powers—
      extension, **31**, [758]
      generally, **31**, [754]
    vexatious actions, restriction on, **31**, [766]
    wards of court proceedings, **31**, [762]
  hijacking, penalty, **31**, [701]
  hill farming provisions applied, **1(1)**, [379]
  home loss payments, **9**, [459]

Northern Ireland—*contd*
horse riding, young riders protective
headgear, **6**, [459]
hospital premises, nuisance or disturbance
on, **12(4)**, [574]
House of Lords—
appeal to—
civil cases, in, **31**, [775]
contempt of court, **31**, [777], [893]
criminal matters. *See* criminal appeal
above
habeas corpus proceedings, **31**, [778]
High Court, from, **31**, [776]
housing association, disposal of land by,
42, [1356]
housing provisions, **23**, [539]
housing, stamp duty—
sales at discount, **41**, [138], [145]
shared ownership transactions, **41**, [134],
[139]
hovercraft, provisions on, **39(2)**, [429]
human fertilisation, application of Act to,
28, [629]
Human Rights Commission. *See* **Northern
Ireland Human Rights Commission**
Human Tissue Act, offences under, **28**, [817]
imitation firearms, specification, **12(4)**, [254]
incapacity for work, provision for, **40(2)**, [38]
inchoate offences, **31**, [705], [1231]
incrimination of self or spouse, withdrawal of
privilege against, **31**, [838]
Independent Assessor of Military Complaints
Procedure—
appointment, **31**, [1203]
functions, **31**, [1203]
information provided to, **31**, [1203]
remuneration, **31**, [1234]
reports, **31**, [1234]
staff, **31**, [1234]
tenure of office, **31**, [1234]
Independent Commission for the Location of
Victims' Remains—
disclosure of information, restrictions on,
31, [1160]
functions, **31**, [1157]
information given to, admissibility as
evidence, **31**, [1158]
meaning, **31**, [1156]
payments to, **31**, [1157]
privileges and immunities, **31**, [1157]
servants of, **31**, [1157]
indictment, acquittal on, reference of point of
law following, **31**, [891], [912]
industrial and provident societies, **19(1)**, [401]
industrial development provisions, **47**, [49]
injunction—
application for, **31**, [754]
damages in lieu or in addition, **31**, [835]
power to grant, **31**, [834]
public office, concerning, **31**, [760]
inquiries, **10**, [881]
suspension of devolved government,
functions during, **10**, [896]
insolvency provisions, **4(2)**, [534]
institution of proceedings, **31**, [1297]

Northern Ireland—*contd*
instruments, enrolment etc, **31**, [847]
intermittent custody order, **12(3)**, [1069],
[1070]
international traffic, **36**, [649]
Investigatory Powers Commissioner, **45**, [389]
jobseeker's allowance, provisions on,
40(2), [84]
Joint Authority, **31**, [1122]
judges. *See under name of court*
judgments—
reciprocal enforcement, **19(3)**, [26], [30]
registration of, **19(3)**, [32]
judicial appointments and removals,
31(S), 125
listed judicial offices, **31(S)**, 137–40
review of arrangements, **31(S)**, 149–50
transfer of appointments, **31(S)**, 140–4
judicial appointments, confidentiality,
31, [1266]
Judicial Appointments Commission—
annual report, **31**, [1334]
chairman, **31**, [1251]
committees, **31**, [1334]
complaints to, **31**, [1259]–[1260]
delegation of functions, **31**, [1334]
disclosure of information to, **11(3)**, [575];
31, [1254]
establishment of, **31**, [1251]
financial provisions, **31**, [1334]
Lord Chancellor, transfer of functions to
31, [1358]
members, **31**, [1251]
non-judicial members, salary of, **31**, [1334]
Ombudsman, provision of information to,
31, [1265]
proceedings, **31**, [1334]
seal, **31**, [1334]
staff, **31**, [1334]
status and property, **31**, [1334]
tenure, **31**, [1334]
Judicial Appointments Ombudsman—
acting, **31**, [1336]
appointment, **31**, [1258], [1336]
code of conduct, **31**, [1336]
complaint to, **31**, [1261]
information provided to, **31**, [1265]
Lord Chancellor, references by, **31**, [1264]
powers of, **31**, [1336]
recommendations, **31**, [1262]
reports, **31**, [1262]–[1263], [1336]
salaries, allowances and expenses,
31, [1336]
status, **31**, [1336]
term of office, **31**, [1336]
Judicial Committee of the Privy Council—
decisions of, **31**, [1116]
reference of legislation to, **31**, [671]
judicial independence, guarantee,
11(3), [459]; **31**, [1249]
judicial office holders, investigation of
allegations of misconduct, **11(3)**, [573]
judicial offices—
appointment, **31**, [1250], [1253], [1335]

Northern Ireland—*contd*

judicial offices—*contd*

  holders—

    complaints about, **31**, [1272]

    excepted matters, **31**, [1321]

    judicial oath or affirmation, **31**, [1274], [1338]

    removal from, **31**, [1250], [1255], [1360]

      tribunal to consider, **31**, [1256]

    schedule of, **31**, [1333]

    suspension from, **31**, [1360]

    vacancies, duty to fill,

      31(S), Northern Ireland 10–11

  judicial titles, power to alter, **11(3)**, [407]

  jury, trial without—

    applications, procedure, **12(3)**, [832]

    reporting restrictions, **12(3)**, [832]

  justices of the peace—

    appointment, **31**, [841]

    functions of, **31**, [1337]

    transfer of functions, **31**, [1267]

  land—

    Acts, payments under, **31**, [934]

    boundary adjustment, **1(1)**, [645]

    English statutes extended to, **31**, [632]

    power to require, **1(1)**, [645]

    purchase, transfer of functions, **31**, [654]

    title to—

      registration of, **31**, [645]

      when including seashore etc, **31**, [641]

    transfer, production of documents,

      41, [231], [232]

  Lands Clauses Act 1845, application, **31**, [869]

  large goods and passenger carrying vehicles,

    driver's licence, **37**, [724]

  law and equity—

    chose in action, assignment of, **31**, [830]

    concurrent administration, **31**, [829]

    debts, assignment of, **31**, [830]

    equitable waste, **31**, [833]

    execution, stay of, **31**, [829]

    merger of estates, **31**, [832]

    rules, conflict between, **31**, [829]

    stay of proceedings, **31**, [829]

    stipulations not being essence of contracts,

      31, [831]

    See also civil law *above*

  Law Commission. *See* **Northern Ireland**

  Law Commission

  lay magistrates—

    allowances, **31**, [1257]

    appointment, **31**, [1257]

    exercise of functions of, **31**, [1257]

    justice of the peace, transfer of functions

      of, **31**, [1267]

    presiding, **31**, [1271]

    removal from office, **31**, [1257]

  legal aid—

    criminal appeal—

      House of Lords, to, **31**, [863]

      order for retrial, **31**, [931]

      pending, **31**, [915]

  legal system, generally, **31**, [622]

Northern Ireland—*contd*

legislation—

  application to, **9**, [112], [137], [160], [178], [188], [368]

  discrimination in, avoidance of, **31**, [670]

  interpretation provisions applied, **41**, [601]

  meaning, **31**, [1132]

  Order in Council, by, **31**, [678]–[679]

  Parliament, laid before, **31**, [1449]

  subordinate, interpretation, **41**, [601]

  validity, procedure for determining,

    31, [671]

legislative functions, discharge during interim

  period, **31**, [691]

legislative powers, exercise, former

  provisions, **31**, [668]

licensed apothecaries in, saving for business

  of, **28**, [347]

lieutenants, **31**, [676]

Limitation Act, application of, **19(3)**, [722], [771]

loans—

  accounts, preparation, **31**, [733]

  capital purposes, for, **31**, [731]

  existing, **31**, [732]

local government elections, provisions on,

  15(3), [228]

local government provisions applied,

  25(2), [445]

London Olympic Games, provisions

  applying, **13**, [509]

Lord Chancellor—

  complaints to, **31**, [1260]

  court fees, fixing of, **31**, [854]

  functions transferred to, **31**, [855]

  Judicial Appointments Commission, transfer

    of functions relating to, **31**, [1358]

  Judicial Appointments Ombudsman—

    provision of information to, **31**, [1265]

    reference to, **31**, [1264]

  transfer of functions, **11(3)**, [600]

Lord Chief Justice—

  appointment, **31**, [747], [1250], [1252], [1359]; **31(S)**, 133

  Assembly, representations to, **11(3)**, [461]

  complaints about holders of judicial office,

    code of practice, **31**, [1272]

  delegation of functions by, **11(4)**, [47]; **11(S)**, Courts 59

  exercise of functions, **31**, [746]

  Judicial Appointments Commission,

    chairman of, **31**, [1251]

  office of, **11(3)**, [465]

  presiding county court judge, delegation of

    functions to, **31**, [1269]

  qualification for office, **31**, [744]

  removal from office, **31**, [1250]

    tribunal to consider, **31**, [1256]

  role of, **31**, [1268]

  tenure of office, **31**, [748]–[749]; **31(S)**, 133–4

  vacation of office, **31**, [750]

lord-lieutenants, **31**, [676]

Lord of Appeal in Ordinary—

  qualification for appointment, **31**, [1273]

Northern Ireland—*contd*
Lord of Appeal in Ordinary—*contd*
sitting in High Court or Court of Appeal,
31, [741]
Lords Justices of Appeal—
appointment, **31**, [747], [1250], [1252],
[1359]; **31(S)**, 133
precedence, **31**, [745]
qualifications, **31**, [744]
rates and taxes cases, acting in, **31**, [751]
removal from office, **31**, [1250]
tribunal to consider, **31**, [1256]
sitting as judge of the High Court,
31, [741]
style and title, **31**, [737]
tenure of office, **31**, [748]–[749];
31(S), 134–6
vacation of office, **31**, [750]
magistrates' courts—
committal by, to Crown Court, **31**, [781]
contempt of court, appeal, **31**, [777]
Court Service, **31**, [813]
jurisdiction, **11(3)**, [431]
Lord Chancellor, duty of, **31**, [812]
maintenance, courts' jurisdiction, **6**, [63]
maintenance orders. *See* **maintenance order**
maintenance, provisions applying to, **27**, [428]
maladministration, investigation into,
31, [1112]
malicious communications, provisions
applicable, **12(1)**, [1079]
malicious damage—
offence triable in NI, **31**, [712]
scheduled offence, as, **31**, 875
mandamus, order of, **31**, [754]
marriage, party subject to immigration
control, **31**, [506]–[507]
Measures—
discrimination in, avoidance,
31, [670]–[671]
reserved matters, legislation by Orders in
Council, **31**, [678]
Medicines Act 1968—
enforcement in, **28**, [166]
special provisions as to, **28**, [189], [195]
mentally disordered patients—
absent without leave, **29**, [151]
application of Act to, **29**, [202]
community patients, removed to, **29**, [139]
conditionally discharged, England and
Wales, transfer of responsibilities to,
29, [142]
England and Wales, removed to, **29**, [141]
removal to or from, **29**, [138]
responsibility for, transferred to, **29**, [140]
merger of estates, **31**, [832]
Military Lands Act, application to, **3**, [218]
milk cessation payments, **1(2)**, [239]
mineral royalties, **44(1)**, [101]
mineral workings, offshore, application of
provisions, **17(1)**, [450]
ministries, transfer of functions, **31**, [1418]
Ministry of Finance—
borrowing powers, **31**, [1429]
consolidation of accounts, **31**, [1396]

Northern Ireland—*contd*
Ministry of Finance—*contd*
finance accounts, **31**, [1428]
form of accounts, **31**, [1410]
government funds—
investment of, **31**, [1437]
temporary advances to, **31**, [1438]
loss of capital, provision against, **31**, [1436]
public accounts, determination of,
31, [1395]
public income and expenditure, accounts
of, **31**, [1420]
reports of, **31**, [1403]
Monitoring Commission—
capacity, **31**, [1353]
functions, **31**, [1353]
meaning, **31**, [1353]
prejudicial effects, duty to avoid, **31**, [1354]
privileges and immunities, **31**, [1353]
reports, laying before Parliament,
31, [1355]
servants of, **31**, [1353]
mortgages, devolution on death, **20**, [437]
mortgagor, suit for possession by, **31**, [836]
Multilateral Investment Guarantee Agency
Act, application to, **19(2)**, [1014]
murder, punishment for, **31**, [685]
National Insurance Fund, payments into,
40(2), [16]
National Loan Fund, advances from,
31, [1096]
National Lottery, application of provisions,
5(1), [183]
Naval Discipline Act, application to, **3**, [1200]
negotiable instruments, lost, indemnity for,
31, [849]
Northern Ireland Assembly, **32**, [848]
notaries public—
appointment, **31**, [850]
fees, fixing of, **31**, [854]
nuclear installations in, **17(1)**, [360]
oaths, administration of, **31**, [850]
occupier's liability, powers as to, **21**, [248]
offences—
aiding, abetting etc in Republic, **31**, [705]
consent to prosecution, **31**, [709]
evidence, **31**, [707]
examination of witnesses, **31**, [716]–[717]
inchoate, **31**, [705], [1231]
incrimination of self or spouse, withdrawal
of privilege against, **31**, [838]
list, **31**, [705], [712]–[713]
prosecution of, **31**, [708]
Republic of Ireland, committed in, triable
in NI, **31**, [712]–[713]
right to opt for trial in Republic, **31**, [715]
scheduled. *See under* emergency powers
above
written statements, admissibility—
outside NI, made, **31**, [723]
Republic, made in, **31**, [706], [723]
See also under specific offences
offences in relation to auditor's report,
guidance to regulatory and prosecuting
authorities, **8(1)**, [586]

Northern Ireland—*contd*
  offensive weapons, importing into,
    12(1), [327]
  official secrets, provisions as to, **12(1)**, [236],
    [258]; **12(2)**, [11]
  Official Solicitor, **11(3)**, [408]
    appointment, **31**, [819]
    powers and duties, **31**, [819]
  oil pollution, provisions as to, **49**, [485]
  open spaces, provisions on, **32**, [40]
  orders and regulations, **31**, [1130]
  Orders in Council—
    legislation by, **31**, [678]–[679]
    provision by, **31**, [1118]
    purposes of, **40(1)**, [148]
    temporary provision for government,
      31, [691]
  overseas regulatory authority, request for
    assistance by, **19(1)**, [772]
  Parades Commission—
    accounts, **31**, [990]
    annual report, **31**, [990]
    audit, **31**, [990]
    code of conduct, **31**, [970], [991]
    conditions on public processions, powers to
      impose, **31**, [975]
    contracts etc, **31**, [990]
    establishment, **31**, [968]
    evidence, **31**, [990]
    finance, **31**, [990]
    functions, **31**, [969]
    guidelines, **31**, [972], [991]
    membership, **31**, [990]
    procedural rules, **31**, [971], [991]
    procedure, **31**, [990]
    public protests, power to impose conditions
      on, **31**, [977]
      review of determination, **31**, [978]
    remuneration, **31**, [990]
    seal, **31**, [990]
    staff, **31**, [990]
    status, **31**, [990]
    term of office, **31**, [990]
    validity of proceedings, **31**, [990]
  paramilitary groups, decommissioning by,
    31, [622]
  Parliament of, former members, pension
    rights, **31**, [674]
  parliamentary election—
    ballot paper, refusal to deliver, **15(3)**, [225]
    declaration of identity, **15(3)**, [532]
    disabled voters, **15(3)**, [533]
    entitlement to vote, **15(3)**, [227]
    loans, regulation of, **15(3)**, [639]
    questions put to voters, **15(3)**, [531]
    returning officer, **15(3)**, [36]
    specified documents—
      meaning, **15(3)**, [224]
      offences relating to, **15(3)**, [226]
      production of, **15(3)**, [224]
  Parliamentary representation, **31**, [622]
  patents provisions applied, **11(1)**, [493], [774]
  pension arrangements, **31**, [1121]
  pension provisions, **40(2)**, [94], [259]
  personal injuries, damages for, **31**, [943]

Northern Ireland—*contd*
  pesticides, control of, **1(2)**, [255]
  pharmaceutical practitioners, corresponding
    provisions, **30**, [969], [1235]
  police—
    meaning, **31**, [1241]
    name of, **31**, [1239]
    Ombudsman—
      allowances, **31**, [1000]
      appointment, **31**, [1000]
      evidence, **31**, [1000]
      exercise of functions, **31**, [1000]
      finance, **31**, [1000]
      meaning, **31**, [993]
      members of police force, assistance by,
        31, [1000]
      office of, **31**, [994]
      officer of, meaning, **31**, [993]
      pensions, **31**, [1000]
      powers, **31**, [994]
      property, **31**, [1000]
      remuneration, **31**, [1000]
      retrial following investigations by,
        12(3), [860]
      staff, **31**, [1000]
    orders and regulations, **31**, [995], [1240]
    Reserve, **31**, [1239]
    Service, **31**, [1239]
    statutory reference to, transitional
      provisions, **31**, [1242], [1246]
  policing and justice, devolution—
    amended provisions,
      31(S), Northern Ireland 23
    conditions for, **31(S)**, Northern Ireland 3–4
    department with functions of—
      establishment of,
        31(S), Northern Ireland 5, 14–15
      minister and junior minister, rotation
        between,
        31(S), Northern Ireland 17–20
      modifications, power to make,
        31(S), Northern Ireland 20
      two ministers, in charge of,
        31(S), Northern Ireland 16–17
    entrenching enactments, provision for,
      31(S), Northern Ireland 8
    functions relating to extradition, transfer
      of, **31(S)**, Northern Ireland 7
    summary of provisions,
      31(S), Northern Ireland 1
    witnesses and documents, power of
      Assembly to call for,
      31(S), Northern Ireland 6
  policing and justice functions, departments
    with, **31(S)**, Northern Ireland 97–100
    amended provisions, **31(S)**, 127–32
    department in charge of Minister and
      Deputy Minister,
      31(S), Northern Ireland 108–12
    first, special provision applying to,
      31(S), 131–2

Northern Ireland—*contd*
  political discrimination in legislation,
    avoidance of, **31**, [670]
    See also discrimination *above*
  political purposes, donations for—
    commencement of provisions, **15(3)**, [665]
    donation reports—
      contents, duty not to disclose,
        15(3), [377]
      verification of, **15(3)**, [376]
    final disapplication period, **15(3)**, [666]
    interpretation, **15(3)**, [373]
    modifications during prescribed period,
      15(3), [668], [675]
    permissible donors—
      extension of categories of, **15(3)**, [374]
      Great Britain, in relation to, **15(3)**, [375]
      power to make provision, **15(3)**, [669]
  polls as to status, **31**, [1136]
  pollution, provisions as to, **49**, [642]
  pool betting duty, **5(1)**, [106]
  Post Office Act, application of provisions,
    34, [591], [604]
  Post Office, application of regulations to,
    19(2), [888]
  Poynings' Law—
    statutes adopted by, **31**, [622]
    text, **31**, [622]
  presiding resident magistrate, **31**, [1270]
  prices, application of provisions, **47**, [208]
  prisons, provisions applicable, **12(1)**, [328K]
  prisoners, transfer of—
    British Islands, within, **31**, [1364]
    conditions of, **31**, [1364]
    See also **prisoner**
  private security industry in—
    amended provisions,
      31(S), Northern Ireland 104
    appeals, **31(S)**, Northern Ireland 116
    change of personnel,
      31(S), Northern Ireland 116–17
    interim arrangements for regulating,
      31(S), Northern Ireland 103, 112–18
    licences, **31(S)**, Northern Ireland 113–16
    offences, **31(S)**, Northern Ireland 117
    records, **31(S)**, Northern Ireland 117
  private security services, **31**, [1236]
  probates, recognition of, **18**, [587]–[589]
  proceeds of crime, confiscation—
    absconding defendant—
      convicted or committed, **12(3)**, [274]
      discharge of order, **12(3)**, [277]
      not convicted or acquitted, **12(3)**, [275]
      variation of order, **12(3)**, [276]
    appeal—
      Court of Appeal, to, **12(3)**, [278], [279],
        [327]
      House of Lords, to, **12(3)**, [280], [328]
      powers of court, **12(3)**, [279]
      prosecutor, by, **12(3)**, [278]
    applications, **12(3)**, [324]
    code of practice, **12(3)**, [488]
    compensation, order for, **12(3)**, [310],
      [311]
    court, powers of, **12(3)**, [307]

Northern Ireland—*contd*
  proceeds of crime, confiscation—*contd*
    criminal conduct, meaning, **12(3)**, [314]
    criminal investigation, meaning,
      12(3), [326]
    criminal lifestyle—
      assumptions, **12(3)**, [257]
      conditions, **12(3)**, [313]
      defendant, provision of information by,
        12(3), [265]
      offences, **12(3)**, [541]
    Crown Court rules, **12(3)**, [329]
    Crown Court, sentencing by, **12(3)**, [309]
    defendant, meaning, **12(3)**, [326]
    enforcement—
      abroad, **12(3)**, [312]
      fine, as, **12(3)**, [281]
      imprisonment or detention, **12(3)**, [282]
      reconsideration, variation of term on,
        12(3), [283]
    financial investigators—
      appeals, **12(3)**, [306]
      applications, **12(3)**, [306]
    free property, **12(3)**, [320]
    gifts, value of, **12(3)**, [316]
    magistrates' court, committal by,
      12(3), [308]
    no order made—
      benefit, reconsideration of, **12(3)**, [267]
      case, reconsideration of, **12(3)**, [266]
    offence, reference to, **12(3)**, [326]
    order—
      available amount, **12(3)**, [256]
        inadequacy of, **12(3)**, [270], [271]
        reconsideration of, **12(3)**, [269]
        satisfaction of, **12(3)**, [325]
      benefit, reconsideration of, **12(3)**, [268]
      defendant, benefit of, **12(3)**, [255]
      making of, **12(3)**, [253]
      other powers of court, effect on,
        12(3), [260]
      payment, time for, **12(3)**, [258]
      recoverable amount, **12(3)**, [254]
      small amount outstanding, discharge on,
        12(3), [272]
      unpaid sums, interest on, **12(3)**, [259]
    postponement of proceedings, **12(3)**, [261]
      effect of, **12(3)**, [262]
    proceedings for offence, **12(3)**, [323]
    property—
      free, **12(3)**, [320]
      meaning, **12(3)**, [322]
      realisable, **12(3)**, [321]
    receiver—
      appeals, **12(3)**, [303], [304]
      applications by, **12(3)**, [300]
      discharge and variation of orders,
        12(3), [301]
      enforcement, **12(3)**, [293], [294], [298]
      management, **12(3)**, [291], [292], [302]
      powers, exercise of, **12(3)**, [307]
      protection of, **12(3)**, [299]
      sums received, application of,
        12(3), [295], [296]

Northern Ireland—*contd*
proceeds of crime, confiscation—*contd*
restraint order—
application for, **12(3)**, [286], [290]
application of, **12(3)**, [285]
Court of Appeal, appeal to, **12(3)**, [287]
discharge and variation, **12(3)**, [286]
exercise of powers, conditions for,
12(3), [284]
House of Lords, appeal to, **12(3)**, [288]
making of, **12(3)**, [285]
realisable property, seizure of,
12(3), [289]
registration, **12(3)**, [290]
restrictions, **12(3)**, [297]
restrictions—
enforcement receiver, **12(3)**, [298]
restraint order, **12(3)**, [297]
seized money, payment of, **12(3)**, [305]
statement of information—
court, given to, **12(3)**, [263], [273]
defendant's response to, **12(3)**, [264]
sums received, application of—
chief clerk, received by, **12(3)**, [296]
enforcement receiver, in hands of,
12(3), [295]
tainted gifts, **12(3)**, [315]
value of, **12(3)**, [319]
transfer of property, **12(3)**, [316]
value of property—
basic rule, **12(3)**, [317]
conduct, obtained from, **12(3)**, [318]
prohibition, order of, **31**, [754]
proscribed organisations. *See under* emergency
powers *above*
protection from harassment, provisions
applying, **12(2)**, [568]
provision extending to, **8**, 928–9
business names, as to, **8(1)**, [1363]
business organisations, relating to forms of,
8(1), [1362]
Companies Acts, **8(1)**, [1360]
European Public Limited-Liability
companies, as to, **8(1)**, [1361]
public authorities—
discrimination by, **31**, [1110]
equality of opportunity, statutory duty,
31, [1109]
unlawful oaths, **31**, [1111]
public banking accounts—
consolidation, **31**, [1396]
determination of, **31**, [1395]
public interest disclosure, **16**, [904]
public processions—
advance notice to be given, **31**, [973]
alcohol at, control of, **31**, [983]
breaking up, **31**, [984]
conditions on—
Commission's powers to impose,
31, [975]
determination of, by Commission—
constable, saving for powers of,
31, [979]
review by Secretary of State, **31**, [976]
constable's powers of arrest, **31**, [985]

Northern Ireland—*contd*
public processions—*contd*
interpretation provisions, **31**, [987]
orders, power to make, **31**, [986]
protest meetings related to—
advance notice to be given, **31**, [974]
power to impose conditions on,
31, [977]
review of determination, **31**, [978]
Secretary of State's power to prohibit,
31, [981]
registration of bands taking part in,
31, [982]
regulations, power to make, **31**, [986]
Secretary of State's powers to prohibit,
31, [980]
Public Prosecution Service—
establishment of, **31**, [1282]
head of, **31**, [1282]
members of, **31**, [1282]
prosecutor, influencing, **31**, [1287]
public records, **18**, [192]
public service pensions, **33(1)**, [203]
Qualifications and Curriculum Authority—
functions of, **15(S)**, Education 281–3
vocational qualifications, functions as to,
15(S), Education 286
Welsh language, access to education and
training through medium of,
15(S), Education 64, 78
radioactive material transport, corresponding
provisions, **38(1)**, [275]
radioactive substances, **17(2)**, [108], [117]
Railways Act 1993, application of,
38(1), [486]
receiver, power to appoint, **31**, [834]
recognition of financial penalties, international
co-operation—
issue of certificate, procedure on,
11(S), Courts 21
magistrates' court, modification of
provisions, **11(S)**, Courts 26
other member states—
requests from, **11(S)**, Courts 24–5
requests to, **11(S)**, Courts 19–20
penalties suitable for enforcement,
11(S), Courts 40–3
receipt of certificate by clerk of petty
sessions, procedure on,
11(S), Courts 25–6
refusal to enforce, grounds for,
11(S), Courts 43–6
recovery of benefits, **40(2)**, [130]–[132]
regional development grants, **43(1)**, [1171]
registered design infringements, jurisdiction of
county court, **11(1)**, [542]
registration appeals, **15(3)**, [56]
registration of title. *See* land *above*
registration officer for, **15(3)**, [14]
registration plate suppliers, regulation of,
38(2), [520]
release from imprisonment—
accelerated, **31**, [1010]
eligibility for—
application for declaration of, **31**, [1003]

Northern Ireland—*contd*
  release from imprisonment—*contd*
    eligibility for—*contd*
      fixed term prisoners, **31**, [1004]
      life prisoners, **31**, [1006]
      revocation of declaration, **31**, [1008]
    evidence or information, admissibility,
      31, [1014]
    fixed term prisoners—
      eligibility, **31**, [1004]
      meaning, **31**, [1012]
      special cases, **31**, [1005]
    licence for, conditions of, **31**, [1009]
    life prisoners—
      eligibility, **31**, [1006]
      meaning, **31**, [1012]
      specified dates, **31**, [1007]
    notice of decisions, **31**, [1011]
    orders and rules, **31**, [1018]
    sentence passed outside Northern Ireland,
      31, [1025]
    suspension or revival of orders, **31**, [1016]
    terrorism, meaning, **31**, [1013]
    victims, information for, **31**, [1015]
  religious discrimination in legislation—
    avoidance of, **31**, [670]
    See also discrimination *above*
  renewables obligation, certificates in,
    17(1), [781B]
  repatriation of prisoners, application of
    provisions, **12(1)**, [833]
  representation in Parliament of UK, **31**, [622]
  Requisitioned Land and War Works Act,
    application, **31**, [646], [649]
  requisitioned land, provisions on, **21**, [139]
  reserved matters. *See under* Measures *above*
  resident magistrate, title of,
    31(S), Northern Ireland 102
  retrial after acquittal, application of
    provisions, **12(3)**, [870]
  road traffic, application of provisions,
    36, [875], [886], [887]
  road traffic reduction, **38(2)**, [8]
  Royal Arms not to be displayed in
    courtrooms, **31**, [1308]
  salmon or migratory trout, landing in,
    1(1), [742]
  Saving Gateway accounts, **40(S)**, 23
  scientific procedures on animals, provisions
    applying to, **2**, [629]
  Scotch whisky provisions, **19(3)**, [465]
  sea and tidal waters, provisions as to, **31**, [641]
  seat belts, wearing by children, **37**, [555]
  Secretary of State, reports of, **31**, [1356]
  seduction, abolition of action for, **31**, [943]
  senior judicial officers—
    removal from listed office, **11(3)**, [577]
    tribunals for considering, **11(3)**, [578]
  sentence of imprisonment, reference to,
    31, [1313]
  Sentence Review Commissioners—
    allocation of cases, **31**, [1024]
    allowances, **31**, [1023]
    annual report, **31**, [1023]
    applications to, **31**, [1024]

Northern Ireland—*contd*
  Sentence Review Commissioners—*contd*
    appointment, **31**, [1001]
    chairman, **31**, [1023]
    conduct of proceedings, **31**, [1024]
    disqualification of Commissioners,
      31, [1023]
    evidence and information, provisions as
      to, **31**, [1024]
    exclusion of persons from proceedings,
      31, [1024]
    lawyer as, **31**, [1001]
    legal aid, **31**, [1024]
    procedure, **31**, [1002], [1024]
    psychiatrist as, **31**, [1001]
    psychologist as, **31**, [1001]
    remuneration, **31**, [1023]
    staff and premises, **31**, [1023]
    successive applications to, **31**, [1024]
    tenure, **31**, [1023]
  sentencing—
    provisions applicable, **12(3)**, [1049]
    review of, **12(1)**, [1082], [1113]
  serious crime, involvement in, **12(4)**, [360],
    [443]
    See also **serious crime prevention order**
  serious fraud investigations, **12(1)**, [1057],
    [1071]
  Serious Organised Crime and Police Act,
    extension of provisions of,
    31(S), Northern Ireland 10, 21–2
  sex discrimination in educational
    establishments, **7(1)**, [231]
  Sexual Offences Act, application of,
    12(3), [794]
  sexual orientation discrimination, regulations,
    7(1), [825]
  shares, acquisition by Crown, **17(1)**, [498]
  shipping—
    High Court jurisdiction, **31**, [652]
    wages, action for, **31**, [652]
  Social Security Act 1973, application of,
    40(1), [56]
  social security arrangements, **31**, [1121]
  Social Security Commissioners, transfer of
    functions, **40(1)**, [187]
  social security enactments, **40(1)**, [178]
  Solicitor General, **31**, [669]
  solicitors—
    audience, right of, **31**, [844]
    barrister becoming, **31**, [845]
    officers of the court, as, **31**, [843]
  special advocates, appointment of,
    12(S), 93–4
  special polling station—
    ballot papers, rules on, **15(3)**, [250]
    modification of enactments,
      15(3), [251]–[252]
    parliamentary election rules applying to,
      15(3), [250]
    provision of, **15(3)**, [234]
    right to vote at, **15(3)**, [249]
    rules relating to, **15(3)**, [250]
  specific performance, damages in addition,
    31, [835]

Northern Ireland—*contd*
St Andrews Agreement—
dates, alteration of,
31(S), Northern Ireland 75
summary of provisions,
31(S), Northern Ireland 27
timetable, compliance with,
31(S), Northern Ireland 30, 61
stamp duty provisions generally, **41**, [129]
Statistics Board—
authorisation of disclosure of information
by, **10(S)**, 47
authorisation of disclosure of information
to, **10(S)**, 43–4
status as part of UK—
declaration, **31**, [1026]
poll on change in, **31**, [1026]
statute law in—
generally, **31**, [622]
Measures of the Assembly, **31**, [622]
Orders in Council, **31**, [622]
Parliament of Northern Ireland, **31**, [622]
Parliament of the UK, of, **31**, [622]
Parliaments of England and of Great
Britain, of, **31**, [622], [632]–[634]
statutes—
interpretation, application generally,
41, [601]
repeals affecting, **41**, [554], [560], [613],
[628], [645], [703], [731], [780]
statutory sick pay provisions, **40(2)**, [28]
stay of proceedings, **31**, [755], [829]
still-birth, provisions on, **36**, [156]
stock transfer provisions, **19(1)**, [315]
stopping up and diversion of highways in,
36, [668], [671]
student loan provisions, **15(1)**, [777]
student loans, **15(1)**, [382], [482]
subordinate legislation—
extension of, **5(1)**, [104], [108]
making and control, **31**, [858]
summary proceedings in revenue cases,
42, [11]
summer time, **45**, [942]
Supreme Court—
Accountant General—
accounts, keeping of, **31**, [822]
appointment, **31**, [821]
bank account, **31**, [823]
investment of funds by, **31**, [825]
payments and transfers, **31**, [824]
property held by, **31**, [820]
bank account of, **31**, [823]
Court Service—
default of members, **31**, [828]
establishment, **31**, [813]
functions, **31**, [813]
departments—
business assigned to, **31**, [811]
establishment, **31**, [811]
schedule of, **31**, [864]
establishment, **31**, [736]
excepted and reserved matters, **11(3)**, [512]
expert evidence, disclosure of, **31**, [945]

Northern Ireland—*contd*
Supreme Court—*contd*
funds in court—
accounts of, **31**, [822]
application, **31**, [869]
investment of, **31**, [825]
National Debt Commissioners, transfer
to, **31**, [826]
rules as to, **31**, [826]
statutory deposits, **31**, [827]
transfers, **31**, [824]
generally, **31**, [622]
instruments, enrolment etc, **31**, [847]
Lord Chancellor, duty of, **31**, [812]
officers and staff. *See* statutory officers *below*
Official Solicitor—
appointment, **31**, [819]
powers and duties, **31**, [819]
renaming, miscellaneous amendments,
11(3), [611]
Rules Committee—
composition and functions, **31**, [796]
constitution, **31**, [1316]
rules of court—
disclosure of expert evidence, **31**, [945]
increased expenditure, involving,
31, [799]
making of, **31**, [798]
Parliamentary control over, **31**, [799]
publication of, **31**, [799]
subject matter of, **31**, [797]
seal, official, **31**, [853]
solicitors as officers of, **31**, [843]
statutory officers—
appointment, **31**, [814], [872]
barrister, bar on practice, **31**, [817]
civil servant, deemed to be, **31**, [816]
deputies, **31**, [818]
exceptional appointments, **31**, [814]
functions, **31**, [814]
transferred, **31**, [814], [865]
list of offices, **31**, [865]
meaning, **31**, [814]
property held by, **31**, [820]
qualification, **31**, [814]
solicitor, bar on practice, **31**, [817]
superannuation, **31**, [816], [866]
temporary appointments, **31**, [818]
tenure of office, **31**, [815]
See also Court of Appeal; Crown Court;
High Court *above*
surveillance, authorisations regarding,
45, [359]
suspended sentence order, transfer of,
12(3), [1076]–[1078]
suspension of devolved government. *See*
devolution *above*
tax cases, proceedings in, **42**, [11], [193]
taxation, double, relief from, **31**, [637]
telecommunications, application of
provisions, **45**, [47], [70]
terrorism. *See also* **terrorism**
additional powers, **31**, [1209]
arrest and seizure, power of—
armed forces, of, **31**, [1189]

Northern Ireland—*contd*
terrorism—*contd*
arrest and seizure, power of—*contd*
constable, of, **31**, [1188]
codes of practice, procedure for, **31**, [1205]
compensation, **31**, [1235]
consent to prosecution, **31**, [1218]
continuation of provisions, **31**, [1376]
defences, **31**, [1219]
detention of terrorist, transitional
provisions, **31**, [730]
documents, examination of—
procedure, **31**, [1194]
record of, **31**, [1194]
retention, **31**, [1193]
search, found on, **31**, [1193]
entry on premises—
explosives inspectors, by, **31**, [1191]
force, use of, **31**, [1201]
munitions and transmitters, search and
seizure, **31**, [1233]
offences, **31**, [1199]
preservation of peace or order, for,
31, [1196]
suspected terrorist, to arrest, **31**, [1187]
unlawfully detained persons, to find,
31, [1192]
expiry and revival of provisions, **31**, [1216]
inciting, **31**, [1174]
information, offences, **31**, [1207]
land, Secretary of State taking possession
of, **31**, [1197]
munitions and transmitters, search and
seizure, **31**, [1233]
order, maintenance of—
entry on premises, power of, **31**, [1196]
land, Secretary of State taking possession
of, **31**, [1197]
offences, **31**, [1199]
regulations, **31**, [1202]
road closure for, **31**, [1198]–[1201]
orders and regulations, **31**, [1222]
peace, preservation of—
entry on premises, power of, **31**, [1196]
land, Secretary of State taking possession
of, **31**, [1197]
offences, **31**, [1199]
regulations, **31**, [1202]
road closure for, **31**, [1198]–[1201]
police and army powers, code of practice,
31, [1204]–[1205]
police powers, record of exercise of,
31, [1208]
preventing. *See* **terrorism**
repealed provisions, **31**, [1377]
scheduled offences—
bail—
legal aid, **31**, [1178]
limited power to grant, **31**, [1177]
extra-territorial, **31**, [1232]
inchoate and related, **31**, [1231]
meaning, **31**, [1175], [1378]
possession of article, onus of proof,
31, [1184]
preliminary enquiry, **31**, [1176]

Northern Ireland—*contd*
terrorism—*contd*
scheduled offences—*contd*
preliminary proceedings, time limit for,
31, [1180]–[1181]
remand in custody, maximum period
of, **31**, [1179]
remission of sentence—
conviction during, **31**, [1186]
restricted, **31**, [1185]
substantive, **31**, [1230]
trial, court for, **31**, [1182]
trial on indictment, **31**, [1183]
specified organisations—
evidence of membership,
31, [1212]–[1214]
forfeiture orders, **31**, [1215], [1220]
inferences, **31**, [1213]
interpretation, **31**, [1211]
stopping and questioning persons, power
of, **31**, [1195]
suspects, post-charge questioning,
12(S), 31–2
temporary legislation ceasing to have
effect, **31**, [1173]
preserved provisions, **31**, [1229]
transitional provisions, **31**, [1217], [1226],
[1379]
vehicles, power to stop, **31**, [1201]
theft, aggravated, offence triable in NI,
31, [712]
tidal waters, provisions as to, **31**, [641]
title to land. *See* land *above*
torture, consent to prosecution for,
12(1), [1093]
tourism, promotion of, **47**, [106]
trade descriptions, **39(1)**, [113]
trade mark jurisdiction, **48**, 183
trade statistics, **47**, [35]
trade unions—
amalgamation or transfer, **16**, [304]
meaning, **16**, [314]
transfer of fines to or from,
11(2), [510]–[511]
Transport Act 1962, application of, **36**, [734],
[749], [750]
Transport Act 1968, application of, **36**, [875],
[886], [887]
treasure, provisions on, **32**, [638]
Treasury Bills, **31**, [1448]
trial by jury of certain counts only, provisions
applying, **12(4)**, [15], [56]
trial on indictment without jury—
amended provisions,
31(S), Northern Ireland 107
certificate, issue of—
challenge, limitation on,
31(S), Northern Ireland 86
conditions for,
31(S), Northern Ireland 80–1
court, lodging before,
31(S), Northern Ireland 82
court for, **31(S)**, Northern Ireland 83
Crown Court sitting in Belfast, at,
31(S), Northern Ireland 83

Northern Ireland—*contd*

trial on indictment without jury—*contd*

duration of provisions,
31(S), Northern Ireland 87
fitness, trial of question of,
31(S), Northern Ireland 86
mode of, **31(S)**, Northern Ireland 84–5
preliminary inquiry,
31(S), Northern Ireland 82
rules of court, **31(S)**, Northern Ireland 85
summary of provisions,
31(S), Northern Ireland 77

Tribunal—

appeals from, **31**, [1125]
chairman, **31**, [1150]
establishment, **31**, [1124]
expenses, **31**, [1150]
members, **31**, [1150]
proceedings, **31**, [1150]
rules, **31**, [1124]
staff, **31**, [1150]
tribunals, **16**, [900]
trusts, dissolution on death, **20**, [437]
Union of Great Britain and Ireland. *See under*
Ireland
United Kingdom, part of, **32**, [848]
unlawful oaths, **31**, [1111]
unrecognised degrees, **15(1)**, [356]
unregistered company, winding up,
4(2), [257], [260]
Upper Tribunal, provision for appeals to,
11(4), [35]; **11(S)**, Courts 47–8
vacant European Parliament seats, filling,
15(S), Elections 44
vaccine damage payments appeals,
40(2), [537]
value added tax, refund of, **50**, [130]
victim of mentally disordered persons,
information about discharge and leave of,
12(4), [39]
victims of crime—
discharge and leave of absence of mentally
disordered persons, information about,
31, [1311]
information schemes, **31**, [1309]
leave of absence, views on, **31**, [1312]
temporary release of prisoners, views on,
31, [1310]
victims' remains, location of—
Commission. *See* Independent Commission
for the location of Victims' Remains *above*
forensic testing, restrictions on, **31**, [1159]
powers of entry, **31**, [1161]
voter, production of specified documents,
15(3), [224]
vulnerable children and adults, provisions
applying, **6(S)**, 225
wards of court proceedings, **31**, [762]
warrant to obtain evidence for use abroad,
issue of, **12(3)**, [580]
warrants, backing, reciprocal arrangements,
31, [655]
waste, equitable, by tenant for life, **31**, [833]
water adjoining, fishery protection in,
1(2), [181]

Northern Ireland—*contd*

water and sewerage services, reorganisation
of, **43(2)**, [756]
weapons, provisions as to, **12(4)**, [254]
weights and measures provisions, **39(1)**, [548]
welfare food schemes, replacement of,
30, [748]
wireless telegraphy, application of provisions,
45, [34]
witnesses, examination of—
extra-territorial offence in Republic,
31, [716]
protection, **31**, [718]
Republic of Ireland, in, **31**, [717]
Yelverton's Act—
application of, **31**, [622]
provisions, **31**, [632]–[634]
young offenders. *See under* emergency powers
(scheduled offences) *above*
youth justice, provisions as to, **18**, [362]
youth justice system—
aims of, **31**, [1306]
extension to 17 year olds, **31**, [1307]
meaning, **31**, [1306]
youth rehabilitation order, transfer of,
12(4), [560], [561]

Northern Ireland Airports Limited

interpretation, **43(1)**, [118]
leasehold interests, **43(1)**, [118]
roll-over relief, **43(1)**, [118]
successor company—
Holding Company, transfer from,
43(1), [118]
meaning, **43(1)**, [118]
securities, **43(1)**, [118]
transfer to, **43(1)**, [118]
transfer of undertaking, **43(1)**, [111]

Northern Ireland Assembly

accommodation, expenditure by members
on, **43(1)**, [585]
Acts of—
generally, **31**, [1030]
interpretation, **31**, [1117]
Attorney General, participation by, **31**, [1278]
audit, **31**, [1100]
Bills—
consent by Secretary of State to, **31**, [1033]
ECJ, reference to, reconsideration where
made, **31**, [1037]
Royal Assent—
Parliamentary control, **31**, [1040]
passing into law on receipt of,
31, [1030]
submission for, **31**, [1039]
scrutiny—
Judicial Committee, by, **31**, [1036]
ministers, by, **31**, [1034]
Presiding Officer, by, **31**, [1035]
stages of, **31**, [1038]
British-Irish Council—
agreements by participants, **31**, [1088]
meetings, **31(S)**, Northern Ireland 43–6
members of, **31**, [1087]

Northern Ireland Assembly—*contd*
  censure resolutions, **31**, [1086]
  Commission—
    Crown status, **31**, [1140]
    delegation by, **31**, [1140]
    functions of, **31**, [1068]
    membership, **31**, [1140]
    powers, **31**, [1140]
    proceedings and business, **31**, [1140]
    staff, **31**, [1140]
    suspension of devolved government,
      during, **31**, [1172]
  constituencies, **31**, [1061]
  constitution, **31**, [622]
  copyright in Bills of, **11(1)**, [995]
  declarations against terrorism—
    breach of terms, **31**, [950]
    form of, **31**, [955]
    High Court, application to, **31**, [951]
    requirement of, **31**, [949]
  defamation, statements privileged for,
    31, [1081]
  departments, **31**, [1047]
  devolution of powers. *See* **Northern Ireland**
    (devolution)
  disqualification for membership—
    amendments, provision for, **31**, [694]
    armed forces, members of, **31**, [692]
    civil servants, **31**, [692]
    copy of Act, deposit, **31**, [694]
    exceptions, **31**, [692]
    foreign legislatures, members, **31**, [692]
    generally, **31**, [692]
    judicial office, **31**, [692], [697]
    listed offices—
      obligation to accept, relaxation,
        31, [695]
      schedule of, **31**, [697]–[699]
    police, **31**, [692]
    reserve and auxiliary forces, **31**, [693]
  dissolution, date for, **31**, [1059]
  draft budgets, **31**, [1099]
  Dublin Parliament, meetings with members
    of, **31**, [622]
  election to—
    dates of, **31**, [1059];
      31(S), Northern Ireland 31
    expenditure, **31**, [1346]
    extraordinary, **31**, [1060]
    postponement, **31**, [622]
    suspension, **31**, [1346]–[1352]
    timetable, **31**, [1346]
    voting, **31**, [1062]
  entrenched enactments, **31**, [1032]
  excepted matters—
    judicial office-holders, **31**, [1321]
    legislation dealing with, **31**, [1051]
    meaning, **31**, [1029]
    schedule of, **31**, [1137]
  Executive Committee, **31**, [1046]
    amended provisions,
      31(S), Northern Ireland 32–3
    functioning, committee to review,
      31(S), Northern Ireland 42

Northern Ireland Assembly—*contd*
  Executive Committee—*contd*
    Irish language strategy,
      31(S), Northern Ireland 48
    ministerial decisions referred to,
      31(S), Northern Ireland 34–5
    poverty and social exclusion strategy,
      31(S), Northern Ireland 48
    Ulster Scots language strategy,
      31(S), Northern Ireland 48
    witnesses and documents, power to call
      for, **31(S)**, Northern Ireland 47
  financial acts, **31**, [1098]
  First Minister—
    amended provisions,
      31(S), Northern Ireland 63–5
    appointment,
      31(S), Northern Ireland 36–40
    Deputy, **31**, [1041]
      amended provisions,
        31(S), Northern Ireland 63–5
      appointment,
        31(S), Northern Ireland 36–40
      nominations, **31(S)**, Northern Ireland 55
      statutory committee,
        31(S), Northern Ireland 41
      vacancies in office,
        31(S), Northern Ireland 37–8
    election, **31**, [1041]
    ministerial offices, determining, **31**, [1042]
    nominations, **31(S)**, Northern Ireland 55
    pledge of office, **31**, [1041], [1139]
    statutory committee,
      31(S), Northern Ireland 41
    vacancy in office, **31**, [1041];
      31(S), Northern Ireland 37–8
  functioning, committee to review,
    31(S), Northern Ireland 42
  generally, **31**, [622]
  implementation bodies, **31**, [1090]
  international obligations—
    compatibility of action with, **31**, [1052]
    quotas for purposes of, **31**, [1053]
  legislation—
    Community law, compatibility with,
      31, [1050]
    Convention rights, compatibility with,
      31, [1050]
    subordinate—
      Community law, compatibility with,
        31, [1050]
      Convention rights, compatibility with,
        31, [1050]
      excepted and reserved matters, dealing
        with, **31**, [1051]
  legislative competence, **31**, [1031]
  Letters Patent, **31**, [1080]
  Lord Chief Justice, representations by,
    11(3), [461]
  members—
    accommodation expenses, **44(2)**, [370]
    designation, change of,
      31(S), Northern Ireland 47
    disqualification—
      effect of, **31**, [1065]

Northern Ireland Assembly—*contd*
members—*contd*
disqualification—*contd*
judicial proceedings, **31**, [1066]
office, from, **31**, [1064]
relief, provisions for, **31**, [1065]
European travel expenses, **44(2)**, [296]
interests, register of, **31**, [1071]
number of, **31**, [1061]
overnight expenses, **44(2)**, [295]
pensions, **31**, [1079]
petition of concern, **31**, [1070]
remuneration, **31**, [1075], [1349];
31(S), Northern Ireland 32
directions, **31**, [1129], [1152]
reduction, **31**, [1076]–[1078]
resignation, **31**, [1082]
tax treatment, **43(1)**, [425]
vacancies, filling, **31**, [1063]
Ministerial Code—
amendments, **31(S)**, Northern Ireland 33
draft, **31(S)**, Northern Ireland 55
meaning, **31(S)**, Northern Ireland 33
provisions of, **31(S)**, Northern Ireland 33–4
Ministers—
amended provisions,
31(S), Northern Ireland 63–5
appointment,
31(S), Northern Ireland 36–40
censure resolutions, **31**, [1086]
code of conduct, **31**, [1139]
disqualifications from office, **31**, [1045]
exclusion from office, **31**, [1056]
directions, **31**, [1129], [1152]
exceptional circumstances, **31**, [1058]
Secretary of State, powers of,
31, [1057]–[1058]
junior, **31**, [1044]
nomination, **31**, [1043]
offices, **31**, [1042]
pledge of office, **31**, [1043], [1139]
modification of enactments, **31**, [1350]
North-South Ministerial Council—
agreements by participants, **31**, [1088]
meetings, **31(S)**, Northern Ireland 43–6
members of, **31**, [1087]
Ombudsman, appointment, **31**, [676]
Parliament buildings, **31**, 1086
policing and justice matters, devolution—
department, nomination of ministers,
31(S), Northern Ireland 66–9
report on progress,
31(S), Northern Ireland 49–50
political party, reduction of financial assistance
for—
directions, **31**, [1129], [1152]
resolutions, **31**, [1083]
Secretary of State, powers of, **31**, [1084]
specified periods and extensions, **31**, [1085]
prerogative and executive powers, exercise of,
31, [1049]
presiding officer, **31**, [1067]
prorogation, interim period, legislative
functions, **31**, [691]

Northern Ireland Assembly—*contd*
purposes consequential on Act, provision for,
31, [1120]
renewal of powers, **31**, [1351]
repealed provisions,
31(S), Northern Ireland 62–3
reserved matters—
legislation dealing with, **31**, [1051]
meaning, **31**, [1029]
new institutions, **31**, [1322]
provision dealing with, **31**, [1119]
schedule of, **31**, [1138]
transferred matters, becoming, **31**, [1029]
restoration of devolved government, on,
31, [1388]
retrospective decisions, power to vary,
31, [1115]
standing orders, **31**, [1069], [1141]
statutory committees, **31**, [1055]
statutory functions, **31**, [1048]
suspension of, **31**, [622]
transferred matters—
meaning, **31**, [1029]
reserved matters, becoming, **31**, [1029]
Transitional—
cross-community support, meaning,
31(S), Northern Ireland 58
draft standing orders,
31(S), Northern Ireland 55–6
meetings, **31(S)**, Northern Ireland 54
members of, **31(S)**, Northern Ireland 29
presiding officer,
31(S), Northern Ireland 56
privilege, **31(S)**, Northern Ireland 57
proceedings, **31(S)**, Northern Ireland 55
provision for, **31(S)**, Northern Ireland 29
roll of membership,
31(S), Northern Ireland 57–8
staff, **31(S)**, Northern Ireland 57
standing orders, **31(S)**, Northern Ireland 57
Treasury, provision of information to,
31, [1102]
UK and NI departments, agency
arrangements between, **31**, [1054]
ultra vires acts, power to remedy, **31**, [1114]
vacancy in, **31(S)**, Northern Ireland 49
witnesses and documents—
notice requirements, **31**, [1072]
oath, **31**, [1074]
offences, **31**, [1073]
power of Assembly to call for,
31(S), Northern Ireland 6
power to call for, **31**, [1072]

**Northern Ireland Human Rights
Commission**
amended provisions,
31(S), Northern Ireland 78
annual report, **31**, [1142]
application of rights, restrictions on,
31, [1106]
assistance in proceedings, **31**, [1105]
Commissioners—
appointment, **31**, [1103]
salary, **31**, [1142]

Northern Ireland Human Rights Commission—*contd*
Commissioners—*contd*
tenure of office, **31**, [1142]
establishment, **31**, [1103]
financial provision, **31**, [1142]
functions, **31**, [1104]
generally, **31**, [622]
investigations—
detention, places of,
31(S), Northern Ireland 92–3
duty to report, **31(S)**, Northern Ireland 95
evidence, **31(S)**, Northern Ireland 89
national security,
31(S), Northern Ireland 90–1
terms of reference,
31(S), Northern Ireland 94
timing, **31(S)**, Northern Ireland 95
legal proceedings, instituting or intervening
in, **31(S)**, Northern Ireland 88
members of, **31**, [1103]
procedure, **31**, [1142]
recommendations about functions,
31(S), Northern Ireland 95
staff, **31**, [1142]
status, **31**, [1142]

Northern Ireland Law Commission
chairman, **31**, [1303]
Commissioners—
appointment, **31**, [1303]
judicial office, holding, **31**, [1341]
salary, **31**, [1341]
tenure, **31**, [1341]
documents, **31**, [1341]
duties of, **31**, [1304]
establishment of, **31**, [1303]
exercise of functions, **31**, [1341]
financial provisions, **31**, [1341]
members, **31**, [1303]
reports, **31**, [1305]
review of law by, **31**, [1304]
seal, **31**, [1341]
staff, **31**, [1341]

Northern Rhodesia
Zambia, becoming, **7(2)**, [556]

Norway
accession to European Union, **18**, [47]

notarial acts
abroad, powers as to, **18**, [158], [197]
consular officers etc, by, **18**, [180]
faculties, applications for, oaths and
affirmations, **18**, [153]

notarial instrument
abolition of stamp duty, **41**, [152], [157]

notaries
district, **11(3)**, [115]
ecclesiastical, **11(2)**, [1]
general, **11(2)**, [1]; **11(4)**, [539]
administration of oaths by, **18**, [280]

notaries—*contd*
general—*contd*
meaning, **18**, [280]
generally, **11(3)**, [115]
Master of Faculties, **11(3)**, [115]; **11(4)**, [539]
oaths and affidavits, taking by, **18**, [75], [280]
public, **11(2)**, [1]
scriveners' monopoly, abolition of,
11(3), [287]

notary public
duly certified, meaning, **1(1)**, [20]
power of attorney, certificate as to, **1(1)**, [20]

notice to quit
agricultural holding. *See* **agricultural holding**
assured tenancy, **22**, [795]
business tenancy, **21**, [181]
contract for sale after, possession for, **21**, [651]
meaning, **21**, [230]
validity of, **21**, [667]
See also **agricultural holding**

notice to treat
absent or untraced owners, in case of,
9, [265], [296]
cessation of effect, **9**, [265]
compensation—
cessation of effect, on, **9**, [265]
withdrawal of notice, on, **9**, [245]
compensation, dispute as to, **9**, [23]
contents, **9**, [265]
disputes, reference to Lands Tribunal, **9**, [266]
easement, to acquire, **9**, [149], [159]
entry after, **9**, [271]
failure to treat after service of, **9**, [20]
general vesting declaration—
application of provisions, **9**, [355]
constructive, **9**, [392]
effect of 1981 Act, **9**, [1]
meaning, **9**, [265]
oil installations, land for, **9**, [195], [211]
period of, **9**, [265]
persons to be given, **9**, [265]
planning permission, assumptions as to,
9, [229]
refusal, **9**, [228]
requirement of, **9**, [17], [265]
service—
corporation aggregate, on, **9**, [19]
owners and occupiers, on, **9**, [18]
withdrawal, **9**, [245]

notices
additional requirements for protection of
owners, **24**, [388]
dispensing with, **22**, [415]; **24**, [391]
forms etc of, **22**, [414]
power to prescribe, **24**, [390]
service of, **22**, [417]

notifiable disease. *See also* **infectious disease**
categories of, **35(1)**, [451]

notifiable disease—*contd*
clothing, infected, exposure before
disinfection, **35(1)**, [458]
common lodging house—
closure on account of, **35(1)**, [483]
entry to, **35(1)**, [481], [503]
inmate—
medical examination of, **35(1)**, [481]
removal to hospital, **35(1)**, [482]
control of, regulations for—
contravention of, **35(1)**, [456]
enforcement and execution, **35(1)**, [454]
entry, power of, for executing, etc,
35(1), [454]
making by Secretary of State, **35(1)**, [454]
scope of, **35(1)**, [454]
dead body—
burial, **35(1)**, [487]–[489]
cremation, **35(1)**, [487]–[489]
death in hospital, **35(1)**, [484]
disposal, **35(1)**, [487]–[489]
embalming, **35(1)**, [488]
isolation of, **35(1)**, [485]
regulations as to, **35(1)**, [488]
removal to mortuary, **35(1)**, [489]
wake over, prohibition on holding,
35(1), [486]
death in hospital with, provisions as to,
35(1), [484]
infected articles—
cleaners, restriction on sending to,
35(1), [465]
disinfecting stations, provision of,
35(1), [468]
disinfection, **35(1)**, [468], [472]
dustbin, prohibition on placing in,
35(1), [467]
exposure before disinfection, **35(1)**, [458]
laundry, restriction on sending to,
35(1), [465]
library books, **35(1)**, [466]
public washhouse, restriction on sending
to, **35(1)**, [465]
infected person—
detention in hospital, **35(1)**, [479]
exposure of, **35(1)**, [458]
information as to, **35(1)**, [459]
medical examination, **35(1)**, [476]
group of persons suspected of
comprising carrier, **35(1)**, [477]
removal to hospital, **35(1)**, [478]
trading, etc, by, **35(1)**, [460]
infected premises—
disinfection, **35(1)**, [472]
letting of house or room, **35(1)**, [470]
person ceasing to occupy, duty of,
35(1), [471]
property disinfected, **35(1)**, [472]
meaning, **35(1)**, [470]
wearing apparel, prohibition as to,
35(1), [469]
work on, prohibition of, **35(1)**, [469]
infectious disease, order directing to be,
35(1), [457]

notifiable disease—*contd*
information in case of, occupier to furnish,
35(1), [459]
library books, provisions as to, **35(1)**, [466]
meaning, **35(1)**, [451]
medical practitioner, duty to report,
35(1), [452]
person dying with—
hospital, in, **35(1)**, [484]
isolation of body, **35(1)**, [485]
wakes, restriction of, **35(1)**, [486]
prevention of spread—
exclusion of children from places of
entertainment, **35(1)**, [464]
information, occupier to furnish for,
35(1), [459]
regulations for, **35(1)**, [454]
stopping of work for, **35(1)**, [461]
compensation for, **35(1)**, [461]
public conveyance—
disinfection, **35(1)**, [475]
owner, etc, duty of, **35(1)**, [474]
use by person with, **35(1)**, [474]
reporting—
certificate
duty of medical practitioner as to,
35(1), [452]
fee for, **35(1)**, [453]
medical practitioner, by, **35(1)**, [452]
school—
exclusion from, of child liable to convey,
35(1), [462]
having case of, list of day pupils at,
35(1), [463]
transitional provisions, **35(1)**, [520]

Nottingham
statutes repealed, **41**, [694]

noxious matter
removal from—
premises, **35(1)**, [131]
streets, byelaws as to, **35(1)**, [134]

Nuclear Corporation
shares, acquisition by Crown, **17(1)**, [498]

nuclear decommissioning
associated body corporates, meaning,
17(2), [660]
disregard for tax purposes of provisions—
BNFL company, **43(S)**, 97–9
Nuclear Decommissioning Authority,
recognised by, **43(S)**, 99–100
funding account—
establishment of, **17(2)**, [408]
examination of, **17(2)**, [409]
maintenance of, **17(2)**, [408]
funded decommissioning programme—
approval of, **17(2)**, [639]
information and documents, provision
of, **17(2)**, [645]

nuclear decommissioning—*contd*
  funded decommissioning programme—*contd*
    approved programme—
      modification of, **17(2)**, [641]
        information and documents, provision
          of, **17(2)**, [645]
        procedure for, **17(2)**, [642], [643]
        time when takes effect, **17(2)**, [644]
      non-compliance with—
        offence of, **17(2)**, [650]
        Secretary of State's power of
          direction, **17(2)**, [651]
      security under, protection of,
        17(2), [649]
      site use prohibited in absence of,
        17(2), [640]
    Department of the Environment for
      Northern Ireland, assistance from,
      17(2), [656]
    duty to submit, **17(2)**, [638]
    Environment Agency, assistance from,
      17(2), [656]
    financial matters, verification of,
      17(2), [648]
    guidance, publication of, **17(2)**, [647]
    hazardous material, disposal of, **17(2)**, [659]
    Health and Safety Executive, assistance
      from, **17(2)**, [656]
    information—
      Department of the Environment for
        Northern Ireland, assistance from,
        17(2), [656]
      disclosure of, **17(2)**, [652]
      Environment Agency, from, **17(2)**, [656]
      false, supplying, **17(2)**, [653]
      Health and Safety Executive, from,
        17(2), [656]
      provision of, **17(2)**, [645]
    obligations, continuity of, **17(2)**, [657]
    operation of, review of, **17(2)**, [646]
    other nuclear installations, applicable to,
      17(2), [655]
    prosecutions, restriction on, **17(2)**, [654]
    regulations, **17(2)**, [647]
    Secretary of State, co-operation with other
      public bodies, **17(2)**, [656]
  meaning, **17(2)**, [413]
  Nuclear Decommissioning Authority. *See*
  Nuclear Decommissioning Authority

Nuclear Decommissioning Authority
  accounts, **17(2)**, [403]
  annual plans, **17(2)**, [390]
    approval of, **17(2)**, [542]
    procedural requirements, **17(2)**, [542]
    publication of, **17(2)**, [542]
  annual reports, **17(2)**, [391]
  borrowing by—
    government guarantees for, **17(2)**, [402]
    limit on, **17(2)**, [401]
  committees, **17(2)**, [539]
  constitution, **17(2)**, [379]
  corporation tax—
    cancellation of provisions, disregarded,
      17(2), [406]

Nuclear Decommissioning Authority—*contd*
  corporation tax—*contd*
    Case VI, Schedule D, activities chargeable
      under, **17(2)**, [405]
    exempt activities, **17(2)**, [404], [543]
    provisions recognised by NDA,
      disregarded, **17(2)**, [407]
  designations—
    responsibilities under, **17(2)**, [380]–[382]
    Scotland, relating to, **17(2)**, [383]
  establishment, **17(2)**, [378]
  expenditure and receipts, **17(2)**, [399]
  financial responsibilities, **17(2)**, [398]
  functions—
    duties when carrying out, **17(2)**, [385]
    pensions, in relation to, **17(2)**, [385]
    powers for carrying out, **17(2)**, [387]
    research—
      decommissioning, into, **17(2)**, [384]
      powers, **17(2)**, [388]
    strategy for carrying out, **17(2)**, [388]
      approval of, **17(2)**, [541]
      consultation by, **17(2)**, [541]
      contents, **17(2)**, [389]
      procedural requirements, **17(2)**, [541]
      publication of, **17(2)**, [541]
    supplemental, **17(2)**, [384]
  funding account. *See* **Nuclear**
  Decommissioning Funding Account
  hazardous material, treatment of, **17(2)**, [393]
  installations—
    cleaning up, duties as to, **17(2)**, [392]
    decommissioning—
      duties as to, **17(2)**, [392]
      research into, **17(2)**, [384]
    duty to operate, **17(2)**, [393]
    person in control, directions to,
      17(2), [395]
    used for purposes of, **17(2)**, [394]
  members, **17(2)**, [379], [538]
    remuneration and pensions, **17(2)**, [538]
  pension scheme, modification of, **17(2)**, [550]
  proceedings, **17(2)**, [539]
  responsibilities—
    additional, **17(2)**, [381]
    designated, **17(2)**, [380]
  sites—
    cleaning up, duties as to, **17(2)**, [392]
    contaminated—
      directions as to, duty to comply with,
        17(2), [397]
      meaning, **17(2)**, [396]
      related site, treatment as, **17(2)**, [396]
    meaning, **17(2)**, [412]
    person in control—
      directions to, **17(2)**, [395]
      meaning, **17(2)**, [412]
  staff, **17(2)**, [538]
  summary of provisions, **17(1)**, [1]
  validity of transactions with, **17(2)**, [410]

**Nuclear Decommissioning Funding
Account**
  establishment of, **17(2)**, [408]
  examination of, **17(2)**, [409]

Nuclear Decommissioning Funding Account—*contd*
maintenance of, **17(2)**, [408]

nuclear explosions
amendment of provisions, **12(2)**, [613], [614]
bodies corporate, offences by, **12(2)**, [612]
causing—
offence, **12(2)**, [602]; **12(3)**, [93]
defences, **12(3)**, [95]
exceptions, **12(3)**, [94]
Crown, provisions binding, **12(2)**, [615]
evidence, power to search for and obtain,
12(2), [611]
inspections. *See also* **nuclear material**
on-site, meaning, **12(2)**, [605]
team, meaning, **12(2)**, [605]
institution of proceedings, **12(2)**, [604]
jurisdiction, **12(2)**, [603]
place of, **12(2)**, [603]
Scottish partnerships, offences by,
12(2), [612]

nuclear facilities
physical protection, amended provisions,
12(4), [505], [572], [573], [581]

Nuclear Fuels Company. *See also* **nuclear installations**
accounts of, **17(1)**, [437]
borrowing, Treasury guarantee, **17(1)**, [496]
employees—
conditions of employment, **17(1)**, [432]
contracts of employment, **17(1)**, [433]
transfer of, to, **17(1)**, [431]
financial limits, **17(1)**, [497]
lands etc, use by Atomic Energy Authority,
17(1), [428]
loans by Secretary of State to, **17(1)**, [435]
losses, extinguished for tax purposes,
17(2), [420]
Nuclear Liabilities Investment Portfolio,
transfer of, **17(2)**, [418]
pension scheme, **17(1)**, [440]
property, transfer from, **17(2)**, [414], [416]
services for, provision of, **17(1)**, [437]
shares, provisions relating to, **17(1)**, [434]
transfer of undertaking to—
certification of, **17(1)**, [429]
directions by Minister, **17(1)**, [429]
excepted parts, **17(1)**, [425]
exclusions from, **17(1)**, [427], [430]
parts transferred, **17(1)**, [425]
stamp duty exemption, **17(1)**, [442]
supplementary provisions, **17(1)**, [444]

nuclear industry
international obligations, amendments for
giving effect to, **17(2)**, [427]
security—
disclosures, prohibition of, **12(3)**, [124]
installations, repeal of provisions,
12(3), [123]
proceedings, institution of, **12(3)**, [126]
regulation of, **12(3)**, [122]

nuclear industry—*contd*
uranium enrichment technology, prohibition
of disclosures, **12(3)**, [125]

nuclear information
sensitive, security of, **17(2)**, [692]

nuclear installations. *See also* **atomic energy; Nuclear Fuels Company**
Act 1965, amendment of, **17(2)**, [658]
bodies corporate, offences by, **17(1)**, [356]
Channel Islands, in, **17(1)**, [361]
compensation for breach of duty—
agreement, under, **17(1)**, [342]
claims—
amount of, **17(1)**, [343]
authorities to which made, **17(1)**, [346]
High Court, reference to, **17(1)**, [347]
jurisdiction to determine, **17(1)**, [347]
satisfaction of, **17(1)**, [346]
thirty-year limit for, **17(1)**, [345]
time for bringing, **17(1)**, [345]
cover for—
carriage, in respect of, **17(1)**, [351]
cover period, **17(1)**, [349]
general, **17(1)**, [348]
licensee's, information on, **17(1)**, [350]
public funds, from, **17(1)**, [348]
special, for licensee's liability,
17(1), [349]
excluded cases, **17(1)**, [342]
extension in certain cases, **17(1)**, [342]
foreign contribution to, **17(1)**, [348]
foreign judgments, enforcement,
17(1), [347]
foreign operator, liability of, **17(1)**, [347]
injury etc partly due to other cause,
17(1), [342]
joint and several liability, **17(1)**, [347]
liability for, **17(1)**, [342]
maximum amount, **17(1)**, [347]
reduction, circumstances for, **17(1)**, [342]
right to, **17(1)**, [342]
shared liability, **17(1)**, [347]
ships and aircraft, protection for,
17(1), [344]
dangerous occurrences—
carriage, in course of, **17(1)**, [352]
meaning, **17(1)**, [359]
persons in area of, registration of,
17(1), [353]
reporting of, **17(1)**, [352]
decommissioning, **17(1)**, [1]
foreign operations, duty of, **17(1)**, [340]
funded decommissioning programmes. *See*
nuclear decommissioning (funded
decommissioning programme)
hazardous material, disposal of, **17(2)**, [659]
Health and Safety Executive, recovery of
expenses by, **17(1)**, [355], [722]
inspectors—
appointment, **17(1)**, [354]
payments by licensee, **17(1)**, [354]
powers of, **17(1)**, [354]
remuneration etc, **17(1)**, [354]

nuclear installations—*contd*
  Isle of Man, in, **17(1)**, [361]
  licensed site—
    installations restricted to, **17(1)**, [331]
    licensee. *See* site licensee *below*
    list of, maintenance of, **17(1)**, [336]
    processes restricted to, **17(1)**, [331]
  Minister's expenses, **17(1)**, [423]
  national security provisions, **17(1)**, [364]
  Northern Ireland, provisions applied,
    17(1), [360]
  Nuclear Decommissioning Authority. *See*
    Nuclear Decommissioning Authority
  nuclear matter—
    carriage of—
      compensation, cover for, **17(1)**, [351]
      foreign operator, by, **17(1)**, [340]
      occurrences during, reporting,
        17(1), [352]
      responsibility for, **17(1)**, [341]
    excepted matter, meaning, **17(1)**, [359]
    meaning, **17(1)**, [359]
    occurrences involving, **17(1)**, [337]
  offences, general, **17(1)**, [356]
  operators' liability, limitation of, **17(1)**, [533]
  orders, making of, **17(1)**, [357]
  permit—
    requirement for, **17(1)**, [332]
    variation or revocation, **17(1)**, [333]
  Safeguards Agreement—
    Agency inspectors—
      obstruction etc of, **17(1)**, [505]
      rights of, **17(1)**, [505]
    design information—
      examination of, **17(1)**, [505]
      general provisions, **17(1)**, [505]
    giving effect to in UK, **17(1)**, [504]
    regulations for, **17(1)**, [506]
    inspections under, **17(1)**, [505]
    offences by bodies corporate, **17(1)**, [507]
    parties to, **17(1)**, [504]
    protocol to, **17(1)**, [505]
  security provisions, **17(1)**, [364]
  site—
    Crown, duty of, in respect of, **17(1)**, [339]
    licence. *See* site licence *below*
    licensed. *See* licensed site *above*
    permit for. *See* permit *above*
  site licence—
    application, notice of, **17(1)**, [333]
    conditions—
      contravention of, **17(1)**, [334]
      display of, **17(1)**, [334]
      power to attach, **17(1)**, [334]
    exemption as to, **17(1)**, [331], [333]
    grant of, **17(1)**, [333]
    permit in addition to. *See* permit *above*
    requirement for, **17(1)**, [331]
    revocation or surrender, **17(1)**, [335]
    two or more installations, for, **17(1)**, [333]
    variation, **17(1)**, [333]
  site licensee—
    compensation cover, **17(1)**, [349]
    duty of, **17(1)**, [337]
    inspection costs, payment of, **17(1)**, [354]

nuclear installations—*contd*
  site licensee—*contd*
    liability insurance—
      amount of, **17(1)**, [349]
      information to be furnished,
        17(1), [350]
      offences and penalties, **17(1)**, [349]
    occurrences to be reported by, **17(1)**, [352]
    offences and penalties, **17(1)**, [349]
  special drawing rights, **17(1)**, [358]
  specified body corporate—
    meaning, **17(1)**, [364]
    national security, provisions for,
      17(1), [364]
  territories, provisions applied to, **17(1)**, [361]
  United Kingdom Atomic Energy Authority,
    duty as to, **17(1)**, [338]

nuclear material. *See also* **nuclear
  installations** (nuclear matter)
  armed forces, activities of, **12(1)**, [805]
  contemplated acts, **12(1)**, [803]
  damage to environment, offences relating to,
    12(1), [800]
  evidence, power to search for and obtain,
    12(2), [611]
  hazardous, disposal of, **17(2)**, [659]
  holding preparatory to acts, **12(1)**, [803]
  importing or exporting, extended
    jurisdiction, **12(1)**, [801]
  imprisonment for offences, **12(1)**, [803]
  inspections—
    expenditure, reimbursement of,
      12(2), [610]
    interpretation of provisions, **12(2)**, [605]
    offences, **12(2)**, [608]
    privileges and immunities, **12(2)**, [609]
    rights of entry, **12(2)**, [606], [607]
  institution of proceedings, **12(1)**, [804]
  investigations and proceedings, **12(1)**, [802]
  meaning, **12(1)**, [806], [809]
  offences outside United Kingdom,
    12(1), [798]
  peaceful purposes, used for, **12(1)**, [806]
  penalties, **12(1)**, [799]
  physical protection, amended provisions,
    12(4), [505], [572], [573], [581]
  threatening to use, **12(1)**, [803]

nuclear radiation
  congenital disability due to, **45**, [959]

nuclear safeguards
  Additional Protocol—
    information and records, **17(2)**, [321]
      false or misleading, **17(2)**, [326]
      persons having, identification,
        17(2), [322]
      restrictions on disclosure, **17(2)**, [325]
    meaning, **17(2)**, [320]
    powers of entry, **17(2)**, [323]
  Agency inspections, rights of access for,
    17(2), [324]
  evidence, power to search and obtain,
    17(2), [327]

nuclear safeguards—*contd*
offences, **17(2)**, [328]
service of notices, **17(2)**, [329]

nuclear transfer schemes
consultation before making, **17(2)**, [414]
effect of, **17(2)**, [544]
Nuclear Decommissioning Authority,
supplementary powers, **17(2)**, [424]
Nuclear Liabilities Investment Portfolio,
transfer of, **17(2)**, [418]
pensions, **17(2)**, [422], [547]
extension of certain, **17(2)**, [548]
other transfers, **17(2)**, [550]
public sector transfers of UKAEA pension
scheme members, **17(2)**, [549]
property in private ownership, recovery of,
17(2), [417]
property which may be transferred,
17(2), [544]
publicly owned assets, transfer of, **17(2)**, [415]
Secretary of State—
supplementary powers, **17(2)**, [424]
transferor's duty to assist, **17(2)**, [425]
stamp duty, **17(2)**, [516]
supplementary provisions, **17(2)**, [544]
supplementary powers, **17(2)**, [424]
transferor's duty to assist, **17(2)**, [425]
stamp duty, **17(2)**, [516]
supplementary provisions, **17(2)**, [544]
transferee companies—
finances and accounts, **17(2)**, [546]
provisions applying to, **17(2)**, [421]
structure of, **17(2)**, [545]
transferor—
only with consent of, **17(2)**, [416]
Secretary of State, duty to assist,
17(2), [425]
United Kingdom Atomic Energy Authority,
supplementary powers, **17(2)**, [424]

nuclear undertakings
extinguishment of, **17(2)**, [419]

nuclear weapons
dependencies, extension of provisions to,
12(3), [103]
extraterritorial application of provisions,
12(3), [97]
meaning, **12(3)**, [93]
UK person, meaning, **12(3)**, [102]
use of, offences, **12(3)**, [93]
body corporate, by, **12(3)**, [100]
consent to prosecutions, **12(3)**, [101]
defences, **12(3)**, [95]
exceptions, **12(3)**, [94]
false or misleading statements, **12(3)**, [100]
HM Revenue and Customs prosecutions,
12(3), [99]
powers of entry, **12(3)**, [98]
weapons-related acts abroad, assisting or
inducing, **12(3)**, [96]

nuisance
aircraft, by—
aerodrome, when on, **4(1)**, [126]
liability, **4(1)**, [125]
byelaws for prevention of certain, **35(1)**, [133]
higher and further education institutions, in,
15(1), [449]
immunity for actions for, **9**, [304], [320]
law of, saving in Road Traffic Acts, **36**, [680];
37, [316]; **38(1)**, [132], [575]
limitation of action, **19(3)**, [735]
London, suppression of, **25(1)**, [657]
mine or quarry, unfenced, as, **17(1)**, [131]
noise amounting to. *See* **noise**
parking. *See* **parking**
primary schools, in, **15(1)**, [681]
public service vehicles causing, saving as to,
37, [67]
secondary schools, in, **15(1)**, [681]
statutory. *See* **statutory nuisance**
Thames, abatement on, **39(2)**, [314]

nullity of marriage. *See also* **void marriage,
voidable marriage**
custody of child, arising, **6**, [234]
decrees nisi—
decrees to be, **27**, [691]
proceedings after, general powers of court,
27, [691]
financial provision orders, **27**, [684]
financial relief—
not granted, **18**, [613]
restrictions imposed on, **18**, [615]
generally, **27**, [127]
property adjustment orders, **27**, [684]
Queen's Proctor, intervention of, **27**, [691]
stay of proceedings, **27**, [685]

nursery education
admission for, **15(2)**, [99]
curriculum requirements not applying,
15(1), [574]
definition, **15(2)**, [115]
early years development partnerships,
15(2), [118]
funded—
code of practice, having regard to,
15(1), [488]
meaning, **15(1)**, [488]; **15(2)**, [391]
general note, **15(1)**, [1]
grants—
amount of, **15(1)**, [485]
arrangements for, **15(1)**, [485]
delegation of functions, **15(1)**, [486]
disclosure of education, **15(1)**, [494]
requirements, compliance with,
15(1), [487]
inspection, **15(2)**, [119], [172]
local education authority—
duty of, **15(2)**, [116]
powers, **15(1)**, [515]; **15(2)**, [464]
maintained school, at, **15(1)**, [485]
meaning, **15(1)**, [485]
orders and regulations, **15(1)**, [490]

nursery education—*contd*
  special education needs, children with,
    15(1), [488]
  special educational needs, child with,
    15(2), [120]
  travel arrangements for children receiving,
    otherwise than at school, **15(1)**, [643]

nursery school
  local education authority, powers of,
    15(1), [514]–[515]; **15(2)**, [464]
  maintained—
    alterations to, **15(2)**, [754]–[755]
      restrictions on, **15(2)**, [764]
    concern, causing—
      closure of school, **15(2)**, [788]
      governing body—
        additional governors, appointment
          of, **15(2)**, [787]
        interim executive members, consisting
          of, **15(2)**, [790], [905]
      intervention, eligible for,
        15(2), [780]–[782]
      LEA, by, **15(2)**, [783]–[786]
      Secretary of State, by,
        15(2), [787]–[789]
    curriculum—
      basic, **15(2)**, [394]
      general requirements, **15(2)**, [392]–[393]
      National, *See* **curriculum**
    discontinuance, proposals for, **15(2)**, [31],
      [751], [897]
    governing body—
      exemption order from education
        legislation requirements—
        application for, **15(2)**, [342]
        generally, **15(2)**, [340]
        revocation of, **15(2)**, [341]

nursery school—*contd*
  maintained—*contd*
    governing body—*contd*
      exemption order from education
        legislation requirements—*contd*
        variation of, **15(2)**, [341]
    new—
      proposals to establish, **15(2)**, [747]
      restrictions on alterations to,
        15(2), [764]
    proposals for discontinuance, **15(2)**, [31],
      [751], [897]
    significant improvement, requiring,
      15(2), [781]
    special measures, requiring, **15(2)**, [782]
    staffing, **15(2)**, [376], [525]
  meaning, **15(1)**, [501]
  National Curriculum, implementation in,
    15(2), [403], [424]

nurses
  medicinal products—
    exemption for, **28**, [111]
    licensing, exemption from, **28**, [78]

nurses agency
  Act, provisions ceasing to have effect,
    35(2), [351]
  meaning, **35(2)**, [283]

nursing home
  child accommodation by, **6**, [329]
  mental. *See* **mental nursing home**

nutrition
  schemes for improving, **40(1)**, [190]

Nyasaland
  Malawi, becoming, **7(2)**, [550]
  Rhodesia, dissolution of federation with,
    7(2), [526]

O

oath

administration—

abroad, **18**, [158], [196]

ambassador, by, **18**, [158], [196]

authorised person—

meaning, **18**, [280]

powers, **18**, [280]

commissioners, by, **18**, [153], [280]

fees, **11(4)**, [298]; **18**, [280]

foreign country, for, **18**, [195]

form and manner, **18**, [235]

interest in proceedings, person having, bar on, **18**, [280]

justices without jurisdiction, by, **18**, [84]

meaning, **11(4)**, [330]

necessity for, **18**, [82]

outside England, **18**, [155]

persons eligible to administer, **18**, [107], [154], [280]

prize proceedings, for, **18**, [156]

probate or letters of administration, required for, **18**, [673]

procedure, **18**, [235]

representative of protecting power, by, **18**, [196]

alien, taken on naturalisation, **10**, [433]

allegiance—

form of, **31**, [45], [187]

naturalisation, required on, **31**, [67], [170], [187]

allegiance, of—

form of, **10**, [420]

ministers taking, **10**, [603]

National Assembly of Wales, members of, **10**, [1488]

person taken before, **10**, [438]

persons to take, **10**, [423], [425], [435]

Scottish Parliament, members of, **10**, [1395]

substitution of, **10**, [428]

canonical obedience, of, **10**, [433]

Cinque Ports Salvage Commissioners, taken by, **11(2)**, [7]

circuit judge, taken by, **11(2)**, [247]

clerical, **10**, [433]

Commissioners for, right to use title, **11(4)**, [298]

Commissioners of Oaths—

appointment, revocation, **18**, [286]

powers, **18**, [153], [280]

use of title, **18**, [280]

Common Serjeant, taken by, **11(2)**, [210]

consular officer, administered by, **10**, [998]

coronation, **10**, [33]–[36]

court of justice, in, **18**, [82]

declaration substituted for—

acceptance by courts, **18**, [86]

oath—*contd*

declaration substituted for—*contd*

administration of, **18**, [84]

Bank of England, by, **18**, [85]

Crown debts, as to, **18**, [88]

false, **18**, [89]

fees payable, **18**, [90]

foreign territories, in, **18**, [86]

form of, **18**, [91], [92]

generally, **18**, [75], [79]

instrument, publication, **18**, [80]

oath not to be administered, **18**, [81]

Treasury, by, **18**, [79]

universities, by, **18**, [83]

will or codicil, proof of, **18**, [87]

declaration, substitution of—

alteration, power of, **10**, [434]

penalty on not making, **10**, [432]

regulations, **10**, [431]

declining to take, **10**, [427]

diplomatic agent, administered by, **10**, [998]

document, attesting, **10**, [433]

due obedience, of, **10**, [433]

ecclesiastical—

canonical obedience, of, **14**, 202

chancellor of diocese taking, **14**, 559, 614

consecration service, not administered during, **14**, 202

due obedience, of, dispensing with, **14**, 244

institution to benefice, on, **14**, 201

judge of ecclesiastical court, by, **14**, 614

licence to perpetual curacy, on, **14**, 201

ordination, on, **14**, 200

ordination service, not administered during, **14**, 202

overseas clergyman not taking, **14**, 658

vicar of guild church taking, **14**, 456

false statement on—

judicial proceeding, in, **12(1)**, [194]

otherwise than in judicial proceeding, **12(1)**, [196]

foreign marriage, before, **27**, [143]

homage, of, **10**, [433]

illegal—

Cambridge University, at, **15(1)**, [80]

Oxford University, at, **15(1)**, [54]

judicial, **11(3)**, [130]; **11(4)**, [552]

form of, **10**, [422]

person taken before, **10**, [438]

persons to take, **10**, [423], [436]

jurat to state where taken, **18**, [157], [280]

justice of the peace, administered by, **11(2)**, [2]

Lord Chancellor, of, **10**, [426]

master of faculties, power to issue commission to take, **11(2)**, [55]

oath—*contd*
meanings, **18**, [159]; **41**, [605]
objection to taking, **18**, [238]
official—
   form of, **10**, [421]
   ministers taking, **10**, [603]
   neglecting to take, **10**, [427]
   persons to take, **10**, [423], [425], [435]
only persons required or authorised taking,
   10, [429]
parliamentary, **10**, [433]
peers, taken by, **10**, [433]
privy councillor, taken by, **10**, [433]
public notary, taken by, **11(2)**, [54]
Recorder, taken by, **11(2)**, [247]
repealed Act, required under, **10**, [437]
Scottish Executive, by member of, **10**, [424]
servicemen, taken by, **10**, [433]
Sovereign, name of, in, **10**, [430]
swearing with uplifted hand, **18**, [236]
taking, method, **41**, [13], [53]
trial, in course of, **10**, [433]
unwillingness to take, **18**, [75]
validity of, **18**, [237]
Welsh language, in, **18**, [75]
Welsh Ministers, of, **10**, [1520]
witnesses before National Assembly of Wales,
   of, **10**, [1505]

oats. *See also* **cereals**
weights for basis of payment, **1(1)**, [248]

objects. *See also* **cultural objects**
Armouries, lending and borrowing, **13**, [281]
British Museum—
   disposal of, **13**, [131]
   loan of, **13**, [130]
   powers generally, **13**, [49]
   storage of, **13**, [129]
   temporary removal, **13**, [129]
Imperial War Museum—
   disposal, **13**, [85]
   transfer to, **13**, [87]
   vesting of, **13**, [87]
library authorities, loan of objects by,
   indemnity against loss or damage, **13**, [253],
   [254]
Museum of London—
   acquisition, **13**, [170]
   disposal, **13**, [170]
   exhibition of, places for, **13**, [168]
   loan of, **13**, [171]
   transfer to other organisations, **13**, [172]
National Maritime Museum—
   disposal, **13**, [92]
   loan or transfer—
      by, **13**, [92]
      to, **13**, [94]
   vesting of, **13**, [93]
Natural History Museum—
   disposal of, **13**, [131]
   loan of, **13**, [130]
   storage of, **13**, [129]
   temporary removal, **13**, [129]

objects. —*contd*
Royal Botanic Gardens, Kew—
   acquisition and disposal of, **13**, [287]
   lending and borrowing, **13**, [288]
Science Museum—
   acquisition and disposal of, **13**, [274]
   lending and borrowing, **13**, [275]
universities and colleges, loan of objects by,
   indemnity against loss or damage, **13**, [253],
   [254]
Victoria and Albert Museum—
   acquisition, **13**, [267]
   disposal, **13**, [267]
   lending and borrowing, **13**, [268]

obscene article
appeal against forfeiture, **12(1)**, [312], [335]
examination of, **12(1)**, [312], [335]
gain, intended for, **12(1)**, [312], [335]
meaning, **12(1)**, [310]
obscenity, test of, **12(1)**, [310]
production of, objects for, **12(1)**, [336]
publication of. *See* **obscene publication**
search and seizure, **12(1)**, [312], [335]
stall or vehicle, search of, **12(1)**, [312]

obscene publication
appeal, forfeiture after, **12(1)**, [335]
broadcasting, by, **12(1)**, [310]
   See further **broadcasting**
common law, offence at, **12(1)**, [311]
defences—
   article not examined, of, **12(1)**, [311],
      [335]
   public good, of, **12(1)**, [313]
Director of Public Prosecutions, consent of to
   proceedings, **12(1)**, [312]; **12(2)**, [58]
forfeiture, **12(1)**, [312], [335]
general note, **12(1)**, [1]
items used for production of, **12(1)**, [336]
maximum penalty for, **12(4)**, [502]
obscenity, test of, **12(1)**, [310]
prohibition of, **12(1)**, [311]
prosecution and punishment, **12(1)**, [311]
publication, meaning, **12(1)**, [310]
search, powers of, **12(1)**, [312]
search warrant, **12(1)**, [312], [386]
seizure, powers of, **12(1)**, [312], [335]

obscenity
plays—
   defence of public good, **13**, [183]
   prohibition of presentation, **13**, [182]
test for, **12(1)**, [310]

obstructions
bollards, placing on roads. *See* **bollards**
penalty for, **35(1)**, [181]
placing to prevent passage of vehicles,
   37, [264]
wilful, penalty for, **35(1)**, [634]

obstructive buildings. *See* **demolition order**

occasional sales. *See* **street trading**

occupational pension scheme
  activities of, **33(1)**, [849]
  actuary—
    appointment of, **33(1)**, [453]
    ineligibility of trustee to act as,
      33(1), [438]–[439]
  advertisements, form and content of,
    33(1), [349]
  advisory bodies, grants to, **33(1)**, [392]
  agreement excluding provisions, void,
    33(1), [380]
  anti-franking rules, alternative to, **33(1)**, [601]
  assets—
    deficiencies in, on winding up,
      33(1), [492]–[493]
    excess, winding up, on, **33(1)**, [494]
  auditor—
    appointment of, **33(1)**, [453]
    ineligibility of trustee to act as,
      33(1), [438]–[439]
  average salary method, **33(1)**, [414]
  bankruptcy, priority in, **33(1)**, [355], [415]
  basis of, **33(1)**, [298]
  bodies corporate, offences by, **33(1)**, [388]
  breach of regulations, **33(1)**, [387], [503]
  choice, schemes restricting to be void,
    33(1), [379]
  commutation payments, **42**, [285]
  compensation, Pensions Compensation Board.
    See **Pensions Compensation Board**
  contracted-out—
    alteration of rules of, **33(1)**, [251]
    benefit, entitlement to, **33(1)**, [223]
    ceasing to be—
      calculation of guaranteed minimum
        pensions preserved under approved
        arrangements, **33(1)**, [269]
      power of Inland Revenue to approve
        arrangements for scheme, **33(1)**, [268]
      state scheme premium—
        amount payable, **33(1)**, [276]
        calculations relating to, **33(1)**, [280]
        contributions equivalent—
          deduction of, from refund of
            scheme contributions,
            33(1), [278]
          election to pay, **33(1)**, [275]
        determination of questions as to,
          33(1), [389]–[391]
        effect of payment of, on rights,
          33(1), [277]
        no recovery of, from earners etc,
          33(1), [279]
        non-payment of, **33(1)**, [281]–[282]
        payment of, **33(1)**, [273]
        regulations, **33(1)**, [412]
    summary of provisions, **33(1)**, [25]
    supervision of schemes, **33(1)**, [270]
  certification requirements for—
    general, **33(1)**, [216]
    principal appointed day, **33(1)**, [514]

occupational pension scheme—*contd*
  contracted-out—*contd*
    certification requirements for—*contd*
      statutory standard, **33(1)**, [220]
      tax requirements prevailing over,
        33(1), [246]
    Class 1 contributions—
      additional pension and other benefits,
        33(1), [266]
      alteration of rates of, **33(1)**, [256]
      reduced rates of, **33(1)**, [255]
        scope of provisions, **33(1)**, [254]
        social security benefits, effect on,
          33(1), [266]
      review of rates of, **33(1)**, [256]
    commutation, **33(1)**, [222]
    determination of basis on which,
      33(1), [219]
    investments and resources, power for Board
      to impose conditions as to, **33(1)**, [235]
    meaning, **33(1)**, [215]
    money purchase benefits, **33(1)**, [217]
    persons who may establish, **33(1)**, [236]
    reference scheme, **33(1)**, [221]
    rules of, alteration of, **33(1)**, [251]
    transfer of, **33(1)**, [222]
  contracting-out certificate—
    cancellation of, **33(1)**, [248]
    elections as to employments covered by,
      33(1), [218]
    further—
      cancellation of, **33(1)**, [250]
      issue of, **33(1)**, [249]
    issue of, **33(1)**, [214]
    refusal of, **33(1)**, [248]
    summary of provisions, **33(1)**, [25]
    surrender of, **33(1)**, [248]
    variation of, **33(1)**, [248]
  contracting-out, defined contribution,
    abolition for, **33(S)**, Pensions 13, 31–44
  contribution notice—
    amended provisions,
      33(S), Pensions 261–71
    clearance statements, **33(1)**, [639]
    content and effect of, **33(1)**, [637]
    employer debt—
      avoidance of, **33(1)**, [635]
      relationship with, **33(1)**, [638]
    financial support directions,
      non-compliance with—
        content and effect of, **33(1)**, [646]
        employer debt, relationship with,
          33(1), [647]
        power to issue, **33(1)**, [644]
        sum specified in, **33(1)**, [645]
    material detriment test,
      33(S), Pensions 262–4
    partnerships and limited liability
      partnerships, provisions applying to,
      33(1), [654]
    restoration notice, failure to comply with,
      33(1), [652]–[653]
    review of operation of provisions,
      33(S), Pensions 197
    sum specified in, **33(1)**, [636]

occupational pension scheme—*contd*
contribution notice—*contd*
transfer of members of scheme,
33(S), Pensions 266–8
Crown application, **33(1)**, [508]
different employers, covering, **33(1)**, [412]
dispute resolution, arrangements, requirement
for, **33(1)**, [857]
early leavers—
cash transfer sum and contribution
refunds—
calculation, **33(1)**, [322]
exercise of right, **33(1)**, [320]
loss of right, **33(1)**, [325]
notification of right to, **33(1)**, [319]
permitted ways of using, **33(1)**, [321]
powers where right not exercised,
33(1), [324]
right to, **33(1)**, [318]
scope of provisions, **33(1)**, [317]
supplementary provisions, **33(1)**, [325]
trustees or managers, duties of,
33(1), [323]
earnings factors, revaluation of,
33(1), [228]
transfers out, exclusion of,
33(S), Pensions 200
employer, payment of surplus to, **33(1)**, [845]
employers, regulations for consultations by,
33(1), [853], [855]
equal treatment rule—
consequential alteration of schemes,
33(1), [466]
exceptions, **33(1)**, [465]
general, **33(1)**, [463]
overseas residents, **33(1)**, [468]
supplementary provisions, **33(1)**, [464]
terms of employment, effect on,
33(1), [467]
European Union, cross-border activities—
disposal of assets in other member States,
stopping, **33(1)**, [868]
European employer, contributions from—
approval of particular employer,
33(1), [863]
conditions for, **33(1)**, [861]
general authorisation to accept,
33(1), [862]
legal requirements of host member State,
notification of, **33(1)**, [864]
ring-fencing of assets, power to require,
33(1), [866]
trustees or managers, duty of to act
consistently with law of host,
33(1), [865]
other European regulators, assistance for,
33(1), [868]
summary of provisions, **33(1)**, [25]
UK employer, European scheme receiving
contributions from, **33(1)**, [867]
extra-statutory benefits, **33(1)**, [357]
fees for official services, **33(1)**, [394]
final salary method, **33(1)**, [414]
financial assistance scheme—
provision for, **33(1)**, [860]

occupational pension scheme—*contd*
financial assistance scheme—*contd*
qualifying pension scheme, **33(1)**, [860]
summary of provisions, **33(1)**, [25]
financial support directions—
amended provisions,
33(S), Pensions 261–71
clearance statements, **33(1)**, [643]
financial support, meaning, **33(1)**, [642]
insufficiently resourced, meaning,
33(1), [641]
interpretation, **33(1)**, [648]
issue of, **33(1)**, [640]
non-compliance, contribution notice on—
content and effect of, **33(1)**, [646]
employer debt, relationship with,
33(1), [647]
power to issue, **33(1)**, [644]
sum specified in, **33(1)**, [645]
partnerships and limited liability
partnerships, provisions applying to,
33(1), [654]
review of operation of provisions,
33(S), Pensions 197
service company, meaning, **33(1)**, [641]
transfer of members of scheme,
33(S), Pensions 268–9
fines or penalties, no indemnification for,
33(1), [850]
flat rate method, **33(1)**, [414]
foreign element, application of provisions to
cases with, **33(1)**, [384]
forfeiture, **33(1)**, [499]–[501]
freezing order—
action in contravention of, validation,
33(1), [628]
assessment period, effect of, **33(1)**, [631]
ceasing to have effect, power to give
direction on, **33(1)**, [632]
consequences of, **33(1)**, [626]
determination to wind up scheme, effect
of, **33(1)**, [629]
duration of, **33(1)**, [627]
effect of winding up order on, **33(1)**, [630]
power to make, **33(1)**, [625], [634]
trustees, managers, employers and members,
notification of, **33(1)**, [633]
fund manager—
appointment of, **33(1)**, [453]
meaning of, **33(1)**, [511]
funding—
actuarial valuations—
obtaining, **33(1)**, [821]
recovery plan, **33(1)**, [823]
reports, **33(1)**, [821]
technical provisions, certification of,
33(1), [822]
application of provisions, **33(1)**, [818]
modification of provisions, **33(1)**, [830]
recovery plan, **33(1)**, [823]
Regulator, powers of, **33(1)**, [828]
schedule of contributions—
advice of actuary, where required,
33(1), [827]

occupational pension scheme—*contd*
　funding—*contd*
　　schedule of contributions—*contd*
　　　agreement of employer, matters
　　　　requiring, **33(1)**, [826]
　　　failure to make payments, **33(1)**, [825]
　　　meaning, **33(1)**, [824]
　　　preparation and revision of, **33(1)**, [824]
　　　Regulator, powers of, **33(1)**, [828]
　　　statement of principles, **33(1)**, [820]
　　　statutory objective, **33(1)**, [819]
　　　summary of provisions, **33(1)**, [25]
　　　winding up procedure, requirements for,
　　　　33(1), [829]
　guaranteed minimum pension—
　　accrued rights, transfer of, **33(1)**, [232]
　　annual increases in, **33(1)**, [344]
　　benefits, securing of, **33(1)**, [234]
　　commutation, **33(1)**, [233]
　　conversion of—
　　　actuarial equivalence, **33(S)**, Pensions 8
　　　conditions, **33(S)**, Pensions 7–8
　　　enforcement of conditions,
　　　　33(S), Pensions 9–11
　　　interpretation, **33(S)**, Pensions 7
　　　power to amend schemes,
　　　　33(S), Pensions 9
　　　procedural requirements,
　　　　33(S), Pensions 8
　　　survivors' benefits, **33(S)**, Pensions 8
　　　transfer out, **33(S)**, Pensions 9
　　determination of questions as to,
　　　33(1), [389]–[391]
　　discharge of liability where secured by
　　　insurance policies or annuity contracts,
　　　33(1), [231]
　　earners, minimum pension for,
　　　33(1), [224]–[225]
　　earnings factors for early leavers, revaluation
　　　of, **33(1)**, [228]
　　effect of entitlement to,
　　　33(S), Pensions 176–7
　　forfeiture, **33(1)**, [233]
　　inalienability of, **33(1)**, [377]
　　increase of where commencement
　　　postponed, **33(1)**, [226]
　　increases in, protection of—
　　　appropriate addition, **33(1)**, [303]
　　　continued employment after ceasing to
　　　　be contracted-out, special provision
　　　　where, **33(1)**, [305]
　　　later earning addition, **33(1)**, [304]
　　　principle, **33(1)**, [301]
　　　relevant sum, **33(1)**, [302]
　　　summary of provisions, **33(1)**, [25]
　　　supplementary provisions, **33(1)**, [306]
　　　transitional provisions, **33(1)**, [420]
　　insignificant amounts, treatment of,
　　　33(1), [230]
　　meaning of, **33(1)**, [215]
　　pension debit, reduction in consequence
　　　of, **33(1)**, [227]
　　social security benefits, effect of entitlement
　　　to, on, **33(1)**, [264]–[265]
　　surrender, **33(1)**, [233]

occupational pension scheme—*contd*
　guaranteed minimum pension—*contd*
　　widows and widowers, minimum pensions
　　　for, **33(1)**, [229]
　hybrid, **33(1)**, [517]
　inalienability of, **33(1)**, [498]
　increases in rate of pension—
　　annual, **33(1)**, [457]
　　appropriate percentage, meaning,
　　　33(1), [458]
　　restrictions—
　　　annuity tied to investments, where,
　　　　33(1), [459]
　　　member is under 55, where,
　　　　33(1), [460]
　　statutory requirement, effect of increases
　　　above, **33(1)**, [461]
　　supplementary provisions, **33(1)**, [462]
　information about, **33(1)**, [372]–[376]
　Inland Revenue, reports by, **33(1)**, [391]
　insurer, meaning, **33(1)**, [399]
　internal controls, requirement for,
　　33(1), [844]
　interpretation provisions, **33(1)**, [400],
　　[510]–[512]
　levies—
　　general, **33(1)**, [393]
　　late payment, interest on,
　　　33(S), Pensions 272
　liabilities—
　　discharge of, by insurance, on winding up,
　　　33(1), [491]
　　preferential on winding up, **33(1)**, [488]
　linked qualifying service, **33(1)**, [397]
　long-term insurance business, meaning,
　　33(1), [399]
　managers—
　　actuary, appointment of, **33(1)**, [453]
　　auditor, appointment of, **33(1)**, [453]
　　breaches of law, duty to report,
　　　33(1), [667]
　　documents for members, provision of,
　　　33(1), [452]
　　employer-related investments, restriction
　　　on, **33(1)**, [451]
　　fund manager, appointment of,
　　　33(1), [453]
　　internal controls, **33(1)**, [844]
　　meaning of, **33(1)**, [511]
　　person treated as, **33(1)**, [396]
　　resolution of disputes, **33(1)**, [456]
　　winding up, records to be kept of decisions
　　　regarding, **33(1)**, [455]
　meaning, **33(1)**, [213]
　members, disclosure of information to—
　　default powers, **33(1)**, [348]
　　regulations, **33(1)**, [346], [594]
　　transfers, about, **33(1)**, [347]
　minimum payment, meaning of, **33(1)**, [215]
　misuse or misappropriation of assets—
　　injunction against, **33(1)**, [618]
　　restitution, order for, **33(1)**, [619]
　modification of enactments, **33(1)**, [370]

occupational pension scheme—*contd*
  modifications—
    Authority, powers of—
      intervention, **33(1)**, [477]
      order, to make, **33(1)**, [481]
      voidable modifications, **33(1)**, [476]
    grounds for applying, **33(1)**, [480]
    resolution, powers of trustees to modify
      by, **33(1)**, [479]
    subsisting rights provisions, **33(1)**, [469]
      actuarial equivalence requirements,
        33(1), [472]–[473]
      civil penalties, **33(1)**, [478]
      consent requirements, **33(1)**, [471]
      interpretation, **33(1)**, [470]
      reporting requirement, **33(1)**, [475]
      trustee approval requirement,
        33(1), [474]
    voidable, **33(1)**, [476]
    winding-up, to secure, **33(1)**, [483]
  money purchase method, **33(1)**, [414]
  money purchase schemes—
    application of further provisions to,
      33(1), [497]
    schedules of payments to,
      33(1), [495]–[496]
  non-European—
    representative to be treated as trustee,
      33(1), [848]
    trust with UK-resident trustee, as,
      33(1), [847]
  normal pension age, **33(1)**, [398]
  Occupational Pensions Regulatory Authority.
    See **Occupational Pensions Regulatory
    Authority**
  offences by bodies corporate and
    partnerships, **33(1)**, [502]
  overriding requirements, **33(1)**, [504], [878]
  overseas residents, prohibition on different
    rules for, **33(1)**, [468]
  payment under—
    earnings including, **40(1)**, [334]
    meaning, **40(1)**, [366]
  payments to employers, **33(S)**, Pensions 198
  pension credit benefit—
    alternatives to, **33(1)**, [329]
    annuity contracts, discharge of liability
      where secured by, **33(1)**, [330]
    basic principle as to, **33(1)**, [328]
    calculations, matters to be disregarded in,
      33(1), [339]
    cash equivalent—
      amount to be used, variation of,
        33(1), [337]
      calculation of, **33(1)**, [334]
      written statement of, **33(1)**, [333]
    form of, **33(1)**, [329]
    hybrid schemes, **33(1)**, [342]
    insurance policies, discharge of liability
      where secured by, **33(1)**, [330]
    meaning, **33(1)**, [327], [341]
    scope of provisions, **33(1)**, [326]
    service of notices, **33(1)**, [340]

occupational pension scheme—*contd*
  pension credit benefit—*contd*
    transfer notice—
      compliance with—
        time for, **33(1)**, [335]
        trustees' duties, effect on, **33(1)**, [338]
      power to give, **33(1)**, [331]
        restrictions on, **33(1)**, [332]
      withdrawal of, **33(1)**, [336]
  pension liberation—
    interpretation, **33(1)**, [621]
    repatriation orders, **33(1)**, [624]
    restitution, power to order, **33(1)**, [622]
    restraining orders, **33(1)**, [623]
  pensionable service, meaning of, **33(1)**, [511]
  perpetuities, exemption from rule against,
    33(1), [382]
  premises, inspection of—
    employers' obligations, in respect of,
      33(1), [671]
    exercise of powers, **33(1)**, [673]
    offences and penalties, **33(1)**, [674]
    powers of inspector, **33(1)**, [672]
    private dwelling-house, exclusion,
      33(1), [673]
    provisions under which made, **33(1)**, [670]
    warrant, issue of, **33(1)**, [675]
  preservation of benefits—
    bonus credits, meaning, **33(1)**, [293]
    long service benefit—
      discrimination, prohibition of,
        33(1), [290]
      increases in, **33(1)**, [294]
      meaning, **33(1)**, [288]
    purchased credits, meaning, **33(1)**, [293]
    regulations, **33(1)**, [296]
    requirements, **33(1)**, [287], [358]
    short service benefit—
      alternatives to, **33(1)**, [291]
      basic principle, **33(1)**, [289]
      computation, **33(1)**, [292]
      discharge of liability where secured by
        insurance policies or annuity contracts,
        33(1), [295]
      discrimination, prohibition of,
        33(1), [290]
      form of, **33(1)**, [291]
    summary of provisions, **33(1)**, [25]
    supplementary credits, meaning,
      33(1), [293]
  prospective and consequential amendments,
    33(1), [408]
  protected rights—
    discharge of, on winding up, **33(1)**, [245]
    effect to, ways of giving, **33(1)**, [238]
    extension of interim arrangements to,
      33(1), [516]
    forfeiture of, **33(1)**, [244]
    general, **33(1)**, [217]
    identification of, **33(1)**, [237]
    inalienability of, **33(1)**, [377]
    investment and resources, requirements as
      to, **33(1)**, [243]
    liability for, securing of, **33(1)**, [242]

occupational pension scheme—*contd*
  protected rights—*contd*
    occupational pension scheme, identification
      and valuation of, **33(1)**, [237]
    pension and annuity requirements,
      33(1), [241]
    suspension of, **33(1)**, [244]
    valuation of, **33(1)**, [237]
  provisions, powers to modify, **33(1)**, [505]
  public service schemes—
    modification of, **33(1)**, [484]
    winding up of, **33(1)**, [430]
  reciprocity with other countries, **33(1)**, [385]
  refund of contributions, taxation of, **42**, [285]
  register of—
    compilation and maintenance of,
      33(1), [656]
    information, provision of, **33(1)**, [658]
    inspection of, **33(1)**, [658]
    registrable information, **33(1)**, [657]
    reports, **33(1)**, [658]
    trustees or managers, duties of, **33(1)**, [659]
  regulations—
    breach of, **33(1)**, [387], [503]
    calculations etc under, **33(1)**, [506]
    commencement and termination of
      employment, **33(1)**, [412]
    consultation about, **33(1)**, [507]
    general power to make, **33(1)**, [253], [526]
    Parliamentary control, **33(1)**, [527]
  repeals, **33(1)**, [406], [416]–[418]
  requirements—
    conformity with, indirectly-applying,
      33(1), [359]
    extra-statutory benefits, **33(1)**, [357]
    overriding, **33(1)**, [356], [420]
  revaluation, **33(1)**, [298]
    percentage, **33(1)**, [414]
  safeguarded rights—
    generally, **33(1)**, [283]
    liability, power to control transfer or
      discharge of, **33(1)**, [286]
    non-complying schemes, reserve powers
      regarding, **33(1)**, [285]
    requirements relating to, **33(1)**, [284]
  salary related, meaning, **33(1)**, [512]
  scope of provisions, **33(1)**, [297]
  subordinate legislation regarding,
    33(1), [401]–[405]
  subsisting rights provisions—
    actuarial equivalence requirements,
      33(1), [472]–[473]
    application of, **33(1)**, [469]
    civil penalties, **33(1)**, [478]
    consent for modifications, **33(1)**, [471]
    interpretation, **33(1)**, [470]
    intervention powers, **33(1)**, [477]
    reporting requirement, **33(1)**, [475]
    trustee approval requirement, **33(1)**, [474]
    voidable modifications, powers of
      Authority, **33(1)**, [476]
  substituted benefit, not applicable to,
    33(1), [299]
  summary of provisions, **33(1)**, [25]
  supplementary provisions, **33(1)**, [300]

occupational pension scheme—*contd*
  transactions at undervalue—
    meaning, **33(1)**, [649]
    restoration notice—
      content and effect of, **33(1)**, [651]
      definitions, **33(1)**, [650]
      failure to comply with, contribution
        notice on., **33(1)**, [652]–[653]
      partnerships and limited liability
        partnerships, provisions applying to,
        33(1), [654]
      power to make, **33(1)**, [649]
      requirements in, **33(1)**, [650]
  transactions defrauding creditors, application
    for order, **33(1)**, [655]
  transfer of employment, protection on—
    conditions for, **33(1)**, [851]
    form of, **33(1)**, [852]
  transfer values—
    cash equivalent—
      application, withdrawal of, **33(1)**, [315]
      calculation of, **33(1)**, [312]
      exercise of option, trustees' duties after,
        33(1), [314]
      loss of rights to, **33(1)**, [313]
      right to, **33(1)**, [309]
      variation of rights to, **33(1)**, [313]
      ways of taking right to,
        33(1), [310]–[311]
    scope of provisions, **33(1)**, [307]
    statement of entitlement, right to,
      33(1), [308]
    supplementary provisions, **33(1)**, [316]
  transitional provisions and savings,
    33(1), [407], [419]–[420]
  transitory modifications, **33(1)**, [409], [422]
  trust—
    non-European scheme as with UK-resident
      trustee, **33(1)**, [847]
    UK-based scheme to be, **33(1)**, [846]
  trustees—
    actuary—
      appointment of, **33(1)**, [453]
      ineligibility to act as, **33(1)**, [438]–[439]
    appointment of, **33(1)**, [426];
      33(S), Pensions 198
    auditor—
      appointment of, **33(1)**, [453]
      ineligibility to act as, **33(1)**, [438]–[439]
    borrowing, restrictions on, **33(1)**, [447]
    breaches of law, duty to report,
      33(1), [667]
    civil penalties, against, **33(1)**, [429]
    company as—
      knowledge and understanding,
        requirement for, **33(1)**, [842]
      member-nominated directors,
        requirement for, **33(1)**, [839]
    corporate—
      decisions by majority, **33(1)**, [442]
      detriment, right to not suffer, **16**, [663]
      directions to, where employer fails to
        comply with requirements, **33(1)**, [433]
      disqualification, **33(1)**, [440]–[441]

occupational pension scheme—*contd*
  trustees—*contd*
    documents for members, provision of,
      33(1), [452]
    exercise of power by, **33(1)**, [450]
    fees and expenses, **33(1)**, [427]
    fund manager, appointment of,
      33(1), [453]
    independent—
      appointment of, **33(1)**, [436]
      general, **33(1)**, [434]
      insolvency practitioner to give
        information to, **33(1)**, [437]
      official receiver to give information to,
        33(1), [437]
      power to appoint, **33(1)**, [435]
      powers of, **33(1)**, [436]
    internal controls, **33(1)**, [844]
    investment powers—
      choosing investments, **33(1)**, [446]
      delegation of, **33(1)**, [444]
      duty of care, **33(1)**, [443]
      employer-related investments, restriction
        on, **33(1)**, [451]
      principles of investments, requirement
        for written statement of, **33(1)**, [445]
    knowledge and understanding, requirement
      for, **33(1)**, [841]–[843]
    meaning of, **33(1)**, [511]
    meetings, records to be kept of,
      33(1), [454]
    member-nominated, requirement for,
      33(1), [838], [840]
    modification of scheme by resolution,
      powers of, **33(1)**, [479]
    money received to be kept in separate
      account, **33(1)**, [454]
    offence of purporting to be, while
      prohibited or suspended, **33(1)**, [425]
    person treated as, **33(1)**, [396]
    prescribed transactions by, books and
      records to be kept of, **33(1)**, [454]
    prohibited, register of, **33(1)**, [663]–[664]
    prohibition order against person being,
      33(1), [423]
    removal of, property, powers to vest or
      transfer, **33(1)**, [428]
    resolution of disputes, **33(1)**, [456]
    restitution by, **33(1)**, [432]
    surplus, payment of to employer,
      33(1), [448]
    suspension of, **33(1)**, [424]
    time off work—
      employment tribunal, complaints to,
        16, [686]
      remuneration, **16**, [685]
      right to, **16**, [684]
    transitory provisions, **16**, [894]
    unfair dismissal, **16**, [751]
    winding up—
      power to defer, **33(1)**, [449]
      records to be kept of decisions
        regarding, **33(1)**, [455]

occupational pension scheme—*contd*
  unpaid contributions—
    payment by Secretary of State of,
      33(1), [350]–[354]
    recovery of, **33(1)**, [620]
  winding up of—
    assets—
      deficiencies in, **33(1)**, [492]–[493]
      excess on, **33(1)**, [494]
    Authority—
      directions by, for facilitating,
        33(1), [486]
        compliance with, **33(1)**, [487]
      reports to, regarding, **33(1)**, [485]
    deferment powers of trustees, **33(1)**, [449]
    directions by Authority for facilitating,
      33(1), [486]
    discharge of liabilities by insurance,
      33(1), [491]
    freezing order, effect on, **33(1)**, [629]
    operation of scheme during,
      33(1), [489]–[490]
    powers of Authority, **33(1)**, [430]
    preferential liabilities on, **33(1)**, [488],
      [490]
    recovery plan, requirements on preparation
      of, **33(1)**, [829]
    reports, **33(1)**, [485]

**Occupational Pensions Regulatory
Authority**
  dissolution, **33(1)**, [872]
  employees, transfer to Regulator, **33(1)**, [873]
  Pensions Regulator, transfer of functions to,
    33(1), [610]

occupier's liability
  access land, in respect of, **21**, [782]
  common duty of care, **21**, [244]
  fixed or moveable structures, when included,
    21, [781]
  highway, exclusion for persons using,
    21, [781]
  persons other than visitors, to—
    Crown, application of provisions to,
      21, [783]
    duty towards, **21**, [781]
  visitors, to—
    children, **21**, [244]
    common duty of care—
      extent of, **21**, [244]
      generally, **21**, [588]
    common law rules, **21**, [243]
    contract—
      entry under, effect, **21**, [245]
      implied terms, **21**, [246]
      liability under, **21**, [245]
    Crown, application to, **21**, [247], [248]
    danger due to state of premises, **21**, [588]
    fault due to contractor, **21**, [244]
    right of entry, persons having, **21**, [244]
    risks willingly taken, **21**, [244]
    tenancy,. terms governing, **21**, [245]
    tort, in, **21**, [243]
    warning given, **21**, [244]

occupier's loss payment
  agricultural land, **9**, [331]
    dual entitlement, **9**, [337]
  amounts, **9**, [331]–[332]
  claims, **9**, [334]
  death before claim made, **9**, [336]
  disputes as to, determined by Lands Tribunal,
    9, [338]
  exclusions, **9**, [333]
  insolvency proceedings instituted before claim
    made, **9**, [335]
  interest acquired by agreement, **9**, [339]
  notices, **9**, [333]
  other land, **9**, [332]
  payment of, **9**, [338]
  pre-commencement acquisition of interest in
    land, **9**, [464]
  regulations, **9**, [340]

OFCOM. *See* **Office of Communications**

offences. *See also headings relating to particular*
offences
  abolished, **12(1)**, [369]
  abroad, committed, **11(2)**, [407]
  arrestable, amended provisions, **12(4)**, [148]
  associated, meaning, **12(2)**, [832]
  attempting to commit. *See* **attempt**
  body corporate, by, **22**, [413]; **23**, [536];
    24, [397]
  child, against. *See* **child**
  child, by. *See* **child; young offenders**
  compounding, **12(1)**, [363]
  concealing, **12(1)**, [363]
  corporation charged with, **11(2)**, [170], [464],
    [581]
  criminal intent, proof of, **12(1)**, [380]
  Crown servants, extension to, **12(2)**, [173]
  demolition order, disregard of, **22**, [241]
  early administrative hearings, **12(1)**, [896]
  encouraging or assisting crime—
    acting reasonably, defence of, **12(4)**, [407]
    alternative verdicts, **12(4)**, [414]
    believing in commission of, **12(4)**, [402]
      one or more offences, of, **12(4)**, [403],
      [405]
    capability of offence being committed,
      12(4), [406]
    course of conduct, **12(4)**, [424]
    extra-territoriality, **12(4)**, [450]
    guilty plea, **12(4)**, [414]
    indirect, **12(4)**, [423]
    institution of proceedings, **12(4)**, [411]
    intentionally, **12(4)**, [401]
    interpretation, **12(4)**, [421]
    jurisdiction, **12(4)**, [409]
    listed offence, **12(4)**, [445]–[449]
    penalties, **12(4)**, [415]
    proof of offence, **12(4)**, [404], [405]
    prosecution, **12(4)**, [410]
    protective offences, **12(4)**, [408]
    request for assistance, failure to respond
      to, **12(4)**, [422]
    service law amendments, **12(4)**, [451]
    threat, by, **12(4)**, [422]

offences—*contd*
  encouraging or assisting crime—*contd*
    transitional and transitory provisions and
      savings, **12(4)**, [462]
  entry, obstructing, **22**, [61], [233], [274],
    [404]; **23**, [35]
  expressions relating to, construction, **41**, [605]
  false information, giving, **12(1)**, [363]
  fatal, institution of proceedings, **12(2)**, [418]
  fines for, up-rating, **24**, [398]
  foreign country, committed in, **12(1)**, [261]
  formal admission, proof by, **12(1)**, [382]
  friendly society, by. *See* **industrial and**
    provident society
  group A—
    external law, relevance of, **12(2)**, [167]
    jurisdiction, **12(2)**, 163]–[165]
    location of events, **12(2)**, [165]
    offences to which applicable, **12(2)**, [162]
    relevant events, **12(2)**, [163]
  group B—
    jurisdiction, questions immaterial to,
      12(2), [164]
    location of events, **12(2)**, [165]
    offences to which applicable, **12(2)**, [162]
  impeding apprehension or prosecution,
    12(1), [362]
  incitement, abolition of common law
    offence, **12(4)**, [416], [452]
  indictable—
    limitation, **11(2)**, [555]
    meaning, **11(2)**, [402]; **12(1)**, [689]
    summarily, tried, **11(2)**, [406]
  investigation. *See* **criminal investigation**
  jurisdiction of Admiralty, committed in,
    12(1), [154]
  lesser—
    finding of guilty, **12(1)**, [364]
    plea of guilty, **12(1)**, [364]
  local housing authority, by, **22**, [926];
    23, [484]
  markets and fairs, related to. *See* **markets and**
    fairs
  marriage, related to. *See* **marriage**
  money laundering. *See* **money laundering**
  overcrowding premises, **22**, [280], [284]
  pardon, **12(1)**, [365]
  penalties, remitted by Crown, **12(1)**, [58]
  persons employed abroad, by, **12(1)**, [13]
  proceeds of. *See* **proceeds of crime**
  property, against, **12(1)**, [1]
  public, against, **12(1)**, [1]
  racially or religiously aggravated—
    assaults, **12(2)**, [669]
    criminal damage, **12(2)**, [670]
    harassment, **12(2)**, [672]
    meaning, **12(2)**, [668]
    public order, **12(2)**, [671]
  road traffic. *See* **road traffic offences**
  sea, committed at, **12(1)**, [12]
  self-defence, reasonable force for purposes of,
    12(4), [506], [581]
  serious—
    court reasons for bail in case of,
      12(1), [663]

offences—*contd*
  serious—*contd*
    dangerous offenders. *See* **dangerous offenders**
  ship, committed on, **11(2)**, [407]
  state, against, **12(1)**, [1]
  summary—
    aiding and abetting, **11(2)**, [462]
    alteration of penalties, **12(3)**, [1016]
      enabling powers, **12(3)**, [1018], [1095]
      maximum term, increase in, **12(3)**, [1094]
    conversion of offences to, **12(3)**, [1097]
    enhanced penalties, abolition of, **11(2)**, [863]
    fines. *See* **magistrates' court**
    imprisonment, not punishable with, **12(3)**, [1015], [1093]
    incitement, **11(2)**, [463]
    jurisdiction to try, **11(2)**, [406]
    meaning, **11(2)**, [402]; **12(1)**, [689]
    mode of trial, **11(2)**, [395]
    offences being, **11(2)**, [393]
    penalties, **11(2)**, [394]–[395]
    statutory maximum fines, **11(3)**, [59]
  time of committing, **12(2)**, [481]
  tipping off. *See under* **money laundering**
  triable either way—
    aiding and abetting, **11(2)**, [462]
    allocation—
      amendment of provisions, **11(3)**, [436], [451]
      decision as to, **11(3)**, [451]
    jurisdiction over, **11(2)**, [406]
    maximum term on summary conviction, **12(3)**, [1017]
    meaning, **11(2)**, [402]; **12(1)**, [689]
    offences being, **11(2)**, [432], [579]
    order of consideration, **11(3)**, [235]
    penalties, **11(2)**, [394]
    sentence, committal for, **11(3)**, [451]
    statutory maximum fines, **11(3)**, [57]
    summary trial, suitability of, **11(3)**, [451]
    trial on indictment, suitability of, **11(3)**, [451]
    trial. *See* **summary trial**
  violent, meaning, **12(2)**, [832]
  written statement, proof by, **12(1)**, [381]
  year and a day rule, abolition, **12(2)**, [417]

offences against the person
  Admiralty jurisdiction, committed in, **12(1)**, [104]
  apprentices, providing for, **12(1)**, [82]
  assault. *See* **assault**
  battery. *See* **battery**
  child, abandoning or exposing, **12(1)**, [83]
  chloroform, using in offence, **12(1)**, [78]
  choking, suffocating or strangling, **12(1)**, [77]
  corrosive fluid, throwing, **12(1)**, [85]
  explosive substance, sending, **12(1)**, [85]
  furious driving of carriage, by, **12(1)**, [91]
  grievous bodily harm. *See* **grievous bodily harm**

offences against the person—*contd*
  gunpowder. *See* **gunpowder**
  laudanum, using in offence, **12(1)**, [78]
  man trap, setting, **12(1)**, [87]
  manslaughter. *See* **manslaughter**
  murder. *See* **murder**
  poison, administering, **12(1)**, [79], [81]
  railway, offences on, **12(1)**, [88]–[90]
  servant, providing for, **12(1)**, [82]
  sexual. *See* **sexual offences**
  spring gun, setting, **12(1)**, [87]
  summary of provisions, **12(1)**, [1]

offender
  assisting, penalty, **12(1)**, [362]
  fine, imposition of, **12(1)**, [656]
  rehabilitation. *See* **rehabilitation of offenders**

offensive matter
  removal from streets, byelaws as to, **35(1)**, [134]

offensive trade
  Public Health Act controls, termination of, **35(1)**, [820]

offensive weapon
  aggravated burglary, using in, **12(1)**, [562]
  armed forces and visiting forces, carrying by members of, **12(1)**, [1098]
  blade or pointed article—
    entry and search of premises for, **12(1)**, [1097]
    possession in public place, offence of, **12(1)**, [1095]
    sale to persons under sixteen, **12(1)**, [1099]
    school premises, having on, **12(1)**, [1096]
  carrying without lawful authority or excuse, **12(1)**, [276]
  defence to charge related to, **12(1)**, [1098]
  entry and search of premises, powers, **12(1)**, [1097], [1100]
  film, having for purposes of, **12(1)**, [1098]
  firearms. *See* **firearms**
  flick gun, **12(1)**, [304], [327]
  flick knife, **12(1)**, [304], [327]
  gravity knife, **12(1)**, [304], [327]
  importation, prohibition, **12(1)**, [1098]
  knives, **12(1)**, [1095], [1099]
    sale to persons under sixteen, **12(1)**, [1099]
    See also **knives**
  manufacture, sale or hire, **12(1)**, [1098]
  museums and galleries, provisions as to, **12(1)**, [1098]
  Northern Ireland, provisions, **12(1)**, [327], [1098]
  penalties, **12(1)**, [304]
  pocketknife, limitation in cutting edge, **12(1)**, [1095]
  school premises, having on, **12(1)**, [1096]
  seizure and retention, powers, **12(1)**, [1100]
  stop and search for, constable's power, **12(1)**, [835]

offensive weapon—*contd*
television programme production, having for purposes of, **12(1)**, [1098]
theatrical performance, having for purposes of, **12(1)**, [1098]
trespass with, **12(1)**, [679]

office
corruption in—
avoiding, **12(1)**, [7]
offence of, **12(1)**, [172]
penalty, **12(1)**, [173]
prosecution, **12(1)**, [175]
sale of—
abroad, offences committed, **12(1)**, [24]
agreement for, avoiding, **12(1)**, [8]
brokers or agents, advertising, **12(1)**, [20]
Crown offices, **12(1)**, [15]
deputation, excepting, **12(1)**, [22]
extension of provisions, **12(1)**, [15], [21]
forfeited right, **12(1)**, [16]
former holder, payment to, **12(1)**, [23]
generally, **12(1)**, [14]
house for negotiating, **12(1)**, [18]–[19]
misdemeanours, **12(1)**, [17]–[19]
penalties, **12(1)**, [7]
profiting from, **12(1)**, [17]
soliciting, **12(1)**, [18]
validity of acts, **12(1)**, [9]

Office for Legal Complaints
accounts, **11(4)**, [356]
annual report by, **11(4)**, [233]
application of seal, **11(4)**, [356]
assistance, arrangements to receive, **11(4)**, [356]
borrowing, **11(4)**, [356]
budget, **11(4)**, [356]
Chairman, **11(4)**, [356]
committees, **11(4)**, [356]
Consolidated Fund, payments into, **11(4)**, [290]
corporate governance, and, **11(4)**, [232]
data protection, **11(4)**, [268]
establishment of, **11(4)**, [229]
expenditure, levy on approved regulators to fund, **11(4)**, [288], [289]
freedom of information, **11(4)**, [356]
functions, delegation of, **11(4)**, [356]
funding, **11(4)**, [287]
general obligations, **11(4)**, [231]
information, duty to share, **11(4)**, [259]
interests in land, **11(4)**, [356]
Legal Services Board, reporting to, **11(4)**, [235]
liability in damages, exemption from, **11(4)**, [356]
members—
appointment of, **11(4)**, [356]
lay persons, majority to be, **11(4)**, [356]
number of, **11(4)**, [356]
remuneration of, **11(4)**, [356]
tenure of, **11(4)**, [356]
terms of appointment, **11(4)**, [356]
monitoring of, **11(4)**, [236]

Office for Legal Complaints—*contd*
ombudsman scheme—
administered by, **11(4)**, [230]
Chief Ombudsman—
appointment of, **11(4)**, [237]
report from—
additional, **11(4)**, [239]
annual, **11(4)**, [238]
claims management services, extension to, **11(4)**, [276]
complaints—
continuity of, **11(4)**, [247]
defamation claims, protection from, **11(4)**, [269]
determination of, **11(4)**, [252]
acceptance of, **11(4)**, [255]
rejection of, **11(4)**, [255]
excluded from—
notification requirements where, **11(4)**, [250]
respondent's complaints procedures not used, where, **11(4)**, [241]
scheme rules, by, **11(4)**, [242]
data protection, **11(4)**, [268]
directions under—
enforcement of, **11(4)**, [256]
court orders, reporting, **11(4)**, [257]
limit on value of, **11(4)**, [253]
alteration of, **11(4)**, [254]
employees, acts and omissions by, **11(4)**, [246]
information, sharing, **11(4)**, [259]
investigations under, reports of, **11(4)**, [265]
jurisdiction of, **11(4)**, [240]
misconduct, reporting, **11(4)**, [258]
ombudsmen—
assistant, appointment of, **11(4)**, [237]
documents—
power to require, **11(4)**, [262]
enforcement, **11(4)**, [264]
failures in compliance with, reporting, **11(4)**, [263]
functions, delegation of, **11(4)**, [249]
information—
duty to disclose, **11(4)**, [259]
power to require, **11(4)**, [262]
enforcement, **11(4)**, [264]
failures in compliance with, reporting, **11(4)**, [263]
restricted, **11(4)**, [266], [267]
investigations, co-operation with—
duties as to, **11(4)**, [260]
failures, reporting, **11(4)**, [261]
operation of, **11(4)**, [248]
orders relating to, **11(4)**, [245]
parties to complaint, conditions on, **11(4)**, [243]
pre-commencement acts, **11(4)**, [244]
redress, provisions not to be made for, **11(4)**, [272], [273]
respondents, charges payable by, **11(4)**, [251]
rules—
consent requirements for, **11(4)**, [270]

Office for Legal Complaints—*contd*
ombudsman scheme—*contd*
rules—*contd*
Legal Services Board, powers as to,
11(4), [271]
transitional provisions, **11(4)**, [244]
performance targets for, **11(4)**, [236]
proceedings, **11(4)**, [356]
proof of documents, **11(4)**, [356]
public records, **11(4)**, [356]
regulatory objectives guiding, **11(4)**, [116]
restricted information, **11(4)**, [266], [267],
[282], [283]
staff, **11(4)**, [356]
status, **11(4)**, [356]
supplementary powers, **11(4)**, [234]
voluntary schemes—
operation of, **11(4)**, [281]
power to establish, **11(4)**, [279]
orders, **11(4)**, [280]

Office for National Statistics
cessation of, **10(S)**, 48
Statistics Board, transfers to, **10(S)**, 49–50

**Office for Standards in Education,
Children's Services and Skills**
chairman—
appointment of, **15(2)**, [909]
remuneration of, **15(2)**, [909]
Children Rights Director, appointment of,
15(2), [834]
committees, **15(2)**, [909]
constitution of, **15(2)**, [909]
documents, execution of, **15(2)**, [909]
functions, **15(2)**, [826], [830], [909]
performance of, **15(2)**, [831]
higher and further education, inspection of,
15(2), [838]
inspectors—
additional, **15(2)**, [911]
appointment of, **15(2)**, [828]
Chief Inspector—
annual report, **15(2)**, [835]
appointment of, **15(2)**, [827]
CAFCASS, inspection of, **15(2)**, [857]
documents, power to inspect,
15(2), [859]
powers of entry, **15(2)**, [858]
CSCI functions, certain transferred to,
15(2), [862]
documents, power to inspect,
15(2), [846]
framework for inspections, duty to
devise, **15(2)**, [847]
functions, **15(2)**, [832]
performance of, **15(2)**, [833]
transferred to, **15(2)**, [836]
higher and further education—
action plans for, **15(2)**, [841]
area inspections, **15(2)**, [842]–[844]
duties as to, **15(2)**, [838]–[840]
local authorities in England—
annual review of, **15(2)**, [852]

**Office for Standards in Education,
Children's Services and Skills**—*contd*
inspectors—*contd*
Chief Inspector—*contd*
local authorities in England—*contd*
information, power to require,
15(2), [855]
inspection of, **15(2)**, [850]–[851]
documents, **15(2)**, [854]
powers of entry, **15(2)**, [853]
other authorities, interaction with,
15(2), [863], [912]
payment from local authorities,
15(2), [869]
pension, **15(2)**, [910]
powers of entry, **15(2)**, [845]
premises with adoption and fostering
functions, inspection of, **15(2)**, [861]
relationship with Office, **15(2)**, [910]
remuneration, **15(2)**, [910]
reports—
combined, **15(2)**, [866]
publication of, **15(2)**, [865]
schools' contribution to community
cohesion, on, **15(2)**, [868]
secure training centres, inspection of,
15(2), [860]
temporary appointment, **15(2)**, [910]
functions, delegation of, **15(2)**, [911]
members—
remuneration of, **15(2)**, [909]
terms of appointment, **15(2)**, [909]
procedure, **15(2)**, [909]
staff, **15(2)**, [909]

Office of Communications (OFCOM)
accounts, **45**, [418]
advances to, **45**, [418]
advisory committees, **45**, [418]
different parts of UK, for, **45**, [438]
elderly and disabled persons, on, **45**, [439]
annual report, **45**, [418]
audit, **45**, [418]
authentication of seal, **45**, [418]
BBC, functions in relation to, **45**, [582]
borrowing, Secretary of State guarantees for,
45, [447]
broadcasting functions, **45**, [441]
charging for services, general power, **45**, [446]
chief executive, **45**, [418]
code, meaning, **45**, [724]
committees, **45**, [418]
Community obligations, duties for purpose of
fulfilling, **45**, [422]
Community requirement to provide
information, **45**, [443]
Competition Act 1998, functions under,
45, [732]
competition functions, **45**, [730]
competition matters—
Broadcasting Act powers, exercise of,
45, [683]
fair and effective competition, conditions
ensuring, **45**, [682], [689]
review of powers, **45**, [684]

Office of Communications (OFCOM)—*contd*

complaints as to fairness to—
consideration of, **45**, [283]
duty to publicise functions, **45**, [694]
general functions in relation to, **45**, [280]
general provisions, **45**, [281]
persons attending hearings, power to pay
allowances to, **45**, [285]
publication of findings, **45**, [286]
qualified privilege, statements protected by
for purposes of defamation, **45**, [288]
recordings, duty to retain, **45**, [284]
reports on action taken voluntarily in
response to findings on complaints,
45, [287]
supplementary provisions, **45**, [282]
Consolidated Fund, payments into, **45**, [743]
constitution, **45**, [415]
consumer consultation, **45**, [434]
consumer information and advice, publication
of, **45**, [444]
Consumer Panel. *See also* **Consumer Panel**
National Consumer Council member,
appointment of, **39(1)**, [707]
consumer research, **45**, [432]
publishing and taking account of, duty of,
45, [433]
Content Board. *See* **Content Board**
deaf persons, code regarding services—
duty to draw up, **45**, [672]
issue and revision, procedure for, **45**, [673]
observance of, **45**, [676]
relevant date, meaning, **45**, [674]
targets, power to modify, **45**, [675]
delegation of functions, **45**, [418]
detention and disposal of property seized,
45, [875], [876]
dispute references, **45**, [569]
action on, **45**, [570]
appeals to Tribunal, **45**, [576], [758]
appeals from, **45**, [580]
decisions by, **45**, [579]
price control matters, reference of, to
Competition Commission, **45**, [577],
[578]
information on connection with, power to
require, **45**, [575]
legal proceedings about, **45**, [571]
other member States, involving, **45**, [573]
resolution of, **45**, [574]
resolving, procedure for, **45**, [572]
summary of provisions, **45**, [1]
disqualification, **45**, [418]
disqualification on grounds relating to political
objects, duties of, in cases involving,
45, [298]
electronic communications code. *See*
electronic communications code
employees, **45**, [418]
Enterprise Act 2002, functions under,
45, [731]
entry and search, powers, **45**, [180]
establishment of, **45**, [415]
fees and penalties, recovery of, **45**, [710]

Office of Communications (OFCOM)—*contd*

finances, **45**, [418]
functions, **45**, [419], [755]
general duties, **45**, [421]
general powers, **45**, [419]
grants from—
community radio providers, to, **45**, [722]
local digital television providers, to,
45, [722]
grants to, **45**, [418]
impact assessments, duty to carry out,
45, [425]
information provision by—
consumer information and advice,
publication of, **45**, [444]
European Commission, to, **45**, [443]
Secretary of State, to, **45**, [442]
international and other bodies, representation
on, **45**, [440]
licences—
conditions generally, **45**, [80]
disqualifications, **45**, [125], [189]
enforcement—
BBC companies, **45**, [118]
correction or apology, **45**, [141]
financial penalty, **45**, [142]
revocation, **45**, [143]
suspension or shorten, **45**, [142]
general provisions, **45**, [79]
held by BBC companies, enforcement,
45, [144]
provision of services without, **45**, [82]
restrictions, **45**, [81], [188]
satellite service, power to suspend,
45, [145]
licensing functions generally, **45**, [121]
listed events—
coverage of, **45**, [276]
EEA States, information regarding
relationship with, **45**, [277]
restriction on televising—
code of guidance, **45**, [275]
EEA States, in, **45**, [272]
penalties, **45**, [273]
report to Secretary of State, **45**, [274]
management of, **45**, [416]
media literacy, promotion of, **45**, [429]
media ownership, duty to review, **45**, [735]
members—
deputy chairman, **45**, [418]
number, **45**, [415]
pensions of non-executive members,
45, [418]
qualification for non-executive members,
45, [418]
remuneration of non-executive members,
45, [418]
tenure of office, **45**, [418]
terms and conditions of executive
members, **45**, [418]
National Telephone Numbering Plan, duty to
publish, **45**, [474]
networks, directions in respect of, **45**, [423]
notices, service of, **45**, [182]

**Office of Communications
(OFCOM)**—*contd*

Office of Fair Trading, concurrent powers
with, **45**, [731]

orders and regulations by, **45**, [896]

orders made by, **45**, [746]

penalties—
Consolidated Fund, payment into,
45, [743]
imposed by, **45**, [736]

pre-commencement regulators—
abolition of, **45**, [449]
transfer of function from, **45**, [420]
transfers of property from, **45**, [448]
transitional functions, **45**, [449]

privacy, code relating to infringement of,
45, [279]

proceedings, **45**, [418], [867]

promptness standards—
duty to publish and meet, **45**, [426]
Secretary of State's powers regarding,
45, [427]

qualifying revenue, computation, **45**, [193]

radio services, annual report on, **45**, [721]

radio spectrum functions—
advisory service, provision of, **45**, [778]
authorised use, limitations on, **45**, [803]
directions from Secretary of State—
general or specific, **45**, [779]
order, by, **45**, [779]
procedure for, **45**, [780]
directions in respect of, **45**, [423]
duties in carrying out, **45**, [777]
general, **45**, [775]
payments for, **45**, [802]
power to retain costs of carrying out,
45, [744]
recognised spectrum access, grant of—
application for, **45**, [792], [902]
bidding for, **45**, [797]
charges for, **45**, [795]
duration, **45**, [902]
effect of, **45**, [794]
grant, procedure for, **45**, [902]
making of, **45**, [792]
matters taken into account, **45**, [796]
recovery of sums, **45**, [798]
refusal, proposed, **45**, [902]
regulations, **45**, [799]
renewal, **45**, [800]
restrictions and conditions, **45**, [792]
revocation or variation, **45**, [902]
transfer of, **45**, [804]
wireless telegraphy licence, conversion to
and from, **45**, [801]
register of relevant information, **45**, [805]
regulations, **45**, [819]
spectrum trading, authorisation, **45**, [804]
statement of policy, **45**, [808]
statistical information—
failure to provide, offence, **45**, [807]
requirement to provide, **45**, [806]
television multiplexes, reservation of
frequencies for, **45**, [781]

**Office of Communications
(OFCOM)**—*contd*

radio spectrum functions—*contd*
UK Plan for Frequency Authorisation,
publication of, **45**, [776]
wireless telegraphy licences. *See* **wireless
telegraphy**

register, duty to keep publicly accessible,
45, [462]

regulations made by, **45**, [746]

regulatory bodies, duty to review, **45**, [424]

regulatory regimes, application of, **45**, [634]

Secretary of State, provision of information
to, **45**, [442]

standards code, **45**, [685]
observance of, **45**, [691]
setting and publication of, **45**, [690]

summary of provisions, **45**, [1]

telephone numbering functions, **45**, [481]
See also **telephone numbers**

television services, annual report on, **45**, [721]

transfer scheme, **45**, [756]

universal services. *See* **universal services**

validity of proceedings, **45**, [418]

visually impaired persons, code regarding
services—
duty to draw up, **45**, [672]
issue and revision, procedure for, **45**, [673]
observance of, **45**, [676]
relevant date, meaning, **45**, [674]
targets, power to modify, **45**, [675]

Welsh Authority, functions in relation to,
45, [585]

wireless telegraphy apparatus. *See* **wireless
telegraphy**

Office of Fair Trading

advice and information, **47**, [525], [919]

advice, disseminating, **39(1)**, [137]

air traffic services, functions—
concurrent with CAA, **4(1)**, [462], [465]
exercise of, **4(1)**, [465]
interpretation, **4(1)**, [461]

annual plan, **47**, [692]

annual reports, **47**, [693]

appeals to, **39(1)**, [199]

breach of Consumer Credit Act requirement,
and, **39(1)**, [332]

breach of duty of estate agent, notification
of, **24**, [353]

CAA functions, co-ordination of, **4(1)**, [295]

cartel offence, investigation of,
47, [887]–[888]

committees and sub-committees, **47**, [947]

competition disqualification order, **47**, [896]

competition investigations. *See* **competition**

competition scrutiny by, **19(2)**, [210],
[370]–[372]

consumer body, complaint by, **47**, [699]

Consumer Credit Act business—
power to prohibit, **19(2)**, [255], [484]
power to restrict, **19(2)**, [256], [542]

consumer credit applications to—
determination of, **39(1)**, [165]
form of, **39(1)**, [138]

Office of Fair Trading—*contd*
consumer credit convictions and judgments,
notification of, **39(1)**, [328]
consumer credit licence—
access to licensee's premises, power to
require, **39(1)**, [186], [189]
charges before end of payment periods,
39(1), [167]–[169]
civil penalties—
further provisions, **39(1)**, [194]
power to impose, **39(1)**, [193]
statement of policy regarding,
39(1), [195]
determinations by, **39(1)**, [346]
information requirement, **39(1)**, [185]
failure to comply with, **39(1)**, [188]
issue of, **39(1)**, [166]
licensees, power to impose requirements
on, **39(1)**, [175], [177]–[179]
renewal, **39(1)**, [170]
revocation, **39(1)**, [173]
supervisory bodies, power to impose
requirements on, **39(1)**, [176]–[179]
suspension, **39(1)**, [173], [174]
variation, **39(1)**, [171], [172]
winding-up of standard licensee's business,
39(1), [181]
consumer credit register—
amending, **39(1)**, [183]
establishment of, **39(1)**, [182]
consumer law enforcement order, directions as
to, **47**, [906]
conveyancing services—
advisory and supervisory functions,
11(3), [104]
investigatory powers, **11(3)**, [105]
documents, alteration or destruction of,
11(3), [107]
notices, enforcement of, **11(3)**, [106]
convictions and judgments, notice of to,
47, [921]
decisions, **47**, [571]
Director General of Fair Trading, transfer of
functions of, **47**, [691]
establishment, **47**, [690]
estate agency, orders as to. *See* **estate agency
work**
false information, giving to, **39(1)**, [140]
findings of fact, **47**, [528]
functions, **39(1)**, [135]; **47**, [690]
good consumer practice, promotion of,
47, [697]
information—
acquisition of, **47**, [694]
disseminating, **39(1)**, [137]
Ministers, provision to, **47**, [696]
power to request, **19(2)**, [211]
public, provision to, **47**, [695]
requiring, **47**, [914]
infringements, findings of, **47**, [529]
intended prosecution, notice to of, **47**, [920]
market investigation references. *See*
Competition Commission
members, **47**, [947]
merger notice, functions as to, **47**, [791]

Office of Fair Trading—*contd*
merger references. *See* **merger reference**
misleading, **19(2)**, [474]
Office of Rail Regulation, exercise of
functions by, **38(1)**, [416]
proceedings, **47**, [947]
reports, **19(2)**, [210]
Competition Commission, considered by,
19(2), [212]
representations to, **39(1)**, [180]
rules, **47**, [524], [571]
staff, **47**, [947]
super-complaint to, **47**, [699]
transitional and transitory provisions, **47**, [962]

Office of Health Professional Adjudicator
accounts, **28(S)**, 51
constitution, **28(S)**, 48–52
consultation requirements, **28(S)**, 16
employees, **28(S)**, 50
establishment of, **28(S)**, 7
fitness to practice panels—
administration of oaths, **28(S)**, 14
clinical advisers, **28(S)**, 12
functions discharged by, **28(S)**, 9
legal assessors, **28(S)**, 11
persons eligible for membership—
lists of, **28(S)**, 9–10
payments to, **28(S)**, 10–11
procedural rules, **28(S)**, 13
specialist advisers, **28(S)**, 12
witness summons, issue of, **28(S)**, 14
fitness to practice proceedings, standard of
proof, **28(S)**, 20
functions of, **28(S)**, 8
General Medical Council, fees payable by,
28(S), 17–18
General Optical Council, fees payable by,
28(S), 17–18
general powers, **28(S)**, 49
Medical Act 1983, adjudication functions
under, **28(S)**, 53–62
members, **28(S)**, 49–50
Northern Ireland, meetings in, **28(S)**, 52
Opticians Act 1989, adjudication functions
under, **28(S)**, 63–70
payments and loans to, **28(S)**, 51
procedure, **28(S)**, 50
public—
consultation with, **28(S)**, 16
publication of information to, **28(S)**, 15
reports, **28(S)**, 51
rules, power to make, **28(S)**, 16–17
status, **28(S)**, 48
summary of provisions, **28(S)**, 1–2

Office of Rail Regulation
access charges, review of, **38(1)**, [488];
38(2), [448]
transitional provisions, **38(2)**, [222]
access contract—
approval of, **38(1)**, [376]
directions on, **38(1)**, [375], [651]
annual report, **38(1)**, [424]

Office of Rail Regulation—*contd*
Authority, provision of information to,
  38(1), [418]
channel tunnel. *See* **channel tunnel**
committees, **38(2)**, [260]
compliance with condition or requirement,
  orders for, **38(2)**, [222]
  final, **38(1)**, [397]
  information, power to require, **38(1)**, [406]
  penalties—
    imposition of, **38(1)**, [400]
    interest and payment by instalments,
      38(1), [404]
    procedural requirements, **38(1)**, [402]
    statement of policy, **38(1)**, [401]
    time limits, **38(1)**, [403]
    validity and effect of, **38(1)**, [405]
  procedural requirements, **38(1)**, [398]
  provisional, **38(1)**, [397]
  revocation, **38(1)**, [398]
  validity and effect of, **38(1)**, [399]
constitution, **38(2)**, [260]
Crossrail. *See* **Crossrail**
disabled rail users, code of practice for
  interests of, **38(1)**, [420]
duty to furnish information to, **38(1)**, [427]
establishment of, **38(2)**, [246]
general duties, **38(1)**, [349]
general functions of, **38(1)**, [418]
information and advice, publication of,
  38(1), [419]
investigatory functions of, **38(1)**, [417]
licence conditions, review of, **38(2)**, [448]
London Olympic Games, objectives relating
  to, **13**, [488]
members—
  appointment, **38(2)**, [260]
  conflict of interest, **38(2)**, [260]
  ineligibility for appointment, **38(2)**, [253]
  payments to, **38(2)**, [260]
national authorities, duty to assist and advise,
  38(2), [435]
Office of Fair Trading, exercise of functions
  of, **38(1)**, [416]
operators' licences, grant of, **38(1)**, [352]
penalties, transitional provisions and savings,
  38(2), [222]
proceedings, **38(2)**, [260]
provision, improvement and development of
  railway facilities—
  directions on, **38(1)**, [366]
    applications for, **38(1)**, [368]
    code of practice, **38(1)**, [373]
    compliance with, **38(1)**, [372]
    consideration of, **38(1)**, [369]
    decisions on applications, **38(1)**, [370],
      [371]
    exemptions, **38(1)**, [367]
    revocation of, **38(1)**, [372]
    supplementary provisions, **38(1)**, [374]
    variation of, **38(1)**, [372]
references to—
  closure—
    non-ratification notice, issue of,
      38(2), [419]

Office of Rail Regulation—*contd*
references to—*contd*
  closure—*contd*
    ratification notice, issue of, **38(2)**, [419]
    requirements, **38(2)**, [420]
  making of, **38(2)**, [419]
register, keeping, **38(1)**, [421]
reports, **38(1)**, [424]
safety functions, transfer to, **38(2)**, [392],
  [447]
staff, **38(2)**, [260]
transfer of functions to, **38(2)**, [247]

office premises
disabled persons, provision for, at,
  35(1), [289]
health, safety and welfare provisions—
  agreements, modification, **18**, [1237]
  buildings—
    plurally owned, provisions as to,
      18, [1227]
    single ownership, in, provisions as to,
      18, [1226]
  cleanliness, **18**, [1211]
  clothing, accommodation and drying,
    18, [1219]
  complaint, appeal from order made on,
    18, [1236]
  Crown, application to, **18**, [1243]
  disclosure of information, restriction of,
    18, [1231]
    public authorities, exception for,
      18, [1232]
  drinking water, supply, **18**, [1218]
  eating facilities, **18**, [1222]
  employment of persons, notification,
    18, [1230]
  exemptions, power to grant, **18**, [1229]
  expenses—
    apportionment, **18**, [1237]
    Minister's, **18**, [1242]
  fish salerooms, limited application to,
    18, [1245]
  floors and passages, construction and
    maintenance, **18**, [1223]
  fuel storage, **18**, [1228]
  heavy work, prohibitions, **18**, [1225]
  hours worked, limited, exceptions where,
    18, [1210]
  lighting, **18**, [1215]
  local Act, exercise of powers under,
    18, [1240]
  machinery, fencing, **18**, [1224]
  offences—
    appeal against orders, **18**, [1236]
    defence available, **18**, [1234]
    generally, **18**, [1233]
    removal or defacement of documents,
      18, [1235]
  outworkers, exceptions for, **18**, [1209]
  overcrowding, **18**, [1212]
  premises to which provisions apply,
    18, [1208]
  regulations and orders, making of,
    18, [1241]

office premises—*contd*
  health, safety and welfare provisions—*contd*
    sanitary conveniences, **18**, [1216]
    seating facilities, **18**, [1220], [1221]
    stairs and steps, construction and
      maintenance, **18**, [1223]
    temperature, **18**, [1213]
    transitory purposes, exclusion where used
      for, **18**, [1246]
    ventilation, **18**, [1214]
    visiting forces, exclusion of application,
      18, [1244]
    washing facilities, **18**, [1217]

office-holder
  contracting-out of functions—
    amendment of provisions, **10**, [770]
    disclosure of information, **10**, [762], [769]
    effect of, **10**, [759]
    excluded functions, **10**, [758]
    financial provisions, **10**, [767]
    interpretation, **10**, [766]
    Northern Ireland, **10**, [765]
    order for, **10**, [757]
    powers of, **10**, [761]
    termination, **10**, [760]
  meaning, **10**, [761], [766]

officer
  Crown—
    liability for torts of, **13**, [11]
    meaning, **13**, [38]
  customs and excise. *See* **Commissioners for
    HM Revenue and Customs**

Official Custodian for Charities
  Supreme Court funds transferred to,
    11(2), [880]

official receiver
  appointment—
    court, by, **4(2)**, [85]
    Minister, by, **4(2)**, [484]
  attachment to court, **4(2)**, [484]
  authorisation to act, **4(2)**, [484]
  bankrupt's duties in relation to, **4(2)**, [362]
  business of, directions as to, **4(2)**, [484]
  co-operation with, duty as to, **4(2)**, [271]
  death etc, property vesting on, **4(2)**, [485]
  delivery of bankrupt's estate to, **4(2)**, [362]
  deputy, **4(2)**, [486]
  duties, **4(2)**, [178]
  examination of company officers, **4(2)**, [175]
  fees for services of, **4(2)**, [498]–[500]
  functions, **4(2)**, [485]
  investigatory duties, **4(2)**, [174], [360]
  liquidator, functions as to, **4(2)**, [178]
  manager of bankrupt's estate, as, **4(2)**, [358]
  meetings, power to summon, **4(2)**, [178]
  nominee or supervisor of voluntary
    arrangement, as, **4(2)**, [474], [560]
  public examination of bankrupt, **4(2)**, [361]
  remuneration, **4(2)**, [484]
  staff for, **4(2)**, [486]
  statement of affairs for, **4(2)**, [173]

official receiver—*contd*
  status, **4(2)**, [485]
  terms of office, **4(2)**, [484]

official referee
  meaning, **11(2)**, [742]

official secrets
  acts done abroad, **12(2)**, [15]
  Attorney-General, prosecution instituted by,
    12(1), [213]
  authorised disclosures, **12(2)**, [7]
  British possessions, in, **12(1)**, [216]
  Civil Aviation Authority, application of Act
    to, **4(1)**, [71]
  code word, use of, **12(1)**, [229]
  confidential information, disclosure—
    information resulting from, **12(2)**, [5]
    other States etc, entrusted in, **12(2)**, [6]
  crime investigation powers, **12(2)**, [4]
  Crown servant—
    damaging disclosure by, **12(2)**, [1]–[3]
    meaning, **12(2)**, [12]
  defence matters—
    damaging disclosures, **12(2)**, [2]
    meaning, **12(2)**, [2]
    offences, **12(2)**, [2]
  definitions, **12(1)**, [217]
  die, seal or stamp, using, **12(1)**, [229]
  disclosures, authorised, **12(2)**, [7]
  documents—
    communicating, **12(1)**, [229]
    retaining for prejudicial purpose,
      12(1), [229]
    safeguarding information, **12(2)**, [8]
    tampering with, **12(1)**, [229]
  false statement, making, **12(1)**, [229]
  foreign agents, communication with as
    evidence, **12(1)**, [230]
  government contractor—
    damaging disclosure by, **12(2)**, [1]–[3]
    meaning, **12(2)**, [12]
  information as to offences, giving,
    12(1), [232]
  international relations—
    damaging disclosures, **12(2)**, [3]
    meaning, **12(2)**, [3]
  investigation powers, **12(2)**, [4]
  Northern Ireland, provisions extending to,
    12(1), [236], [258]; **12(2)**, [11]
  obtaining, etc, **12(1)**, [210]
  offences—
    aiding and abetting, **12(1)**, [233]
    arrest, **12(2)**, [11]
    attempts, **12(1)**, [233]
    company, committed by, **12(1)**, [234]
    documents, relating to, **12(2)**, [8]
    generally, **12(1)**, [1]
    incitement, **12(1)**, [233]
    place of, **12(1)**, [215]
    prosecutions, **12(2)**, [9]
    punishment, **12(1)**, [234]; **12(2)**, [10]
    search, **12(1)**, [214]; **12(2)**, [11]
    trial, **12(1)**, [215]; **12(2)**, [11]
  password, use of, **12(1)**, [229]

official secrets—*contd*
personation of officers, **12(1)**, [229]
search warrant, **12(1)**, [214]; **12(2)**, [11]
security or intelligence offences, **12(2)**, [1]
spying—
　harbouring spies, **12(1)**, [212]
　penalties, **12(1)**, [210]
trial—
　place of, **12(1)**, [215]
　provisions as to, **12(1)**, [234]; **12(2)**, [11]
uniform, unauthorised use of, **12(1)**, [229]

official solicitor
powers and duties, **11(2)**, [764]

official statistics
Code of Practice—
　assessment, **10(S)**, 16
　　programme for, **10(S)**, 19
　　requests for, **10(S)**, 19
　duty to comply with, **10(S)**, 17
　interim period, **10(S)**, 21
　preparation and publication of, **10(S)**, 14
　re-assessment, **10(S)**, 18
　　programme for, **10(S)**, 19
　revision, **10(S)**, 21
definitions, **10(S)**, 13
devolved, meaning, **10(S)**, 57
meaning, **10(S)**, 11
monitoring and reporting, **10(S)**, 13
order, specified by, **10(S)**, 11
pre-release access, **10(S)**, 15
Statistics Board. *See* **Statistics Board**
summary of provisions, **10(S)**, 1

offshore fund
amended provisions, **43(2)**, [357]; **43(S)**, 554
Case VI losses, offsetting, **43(S)**, 553
certification—
　breaches of conditions, disregard of,
　　44(1), [677]
　conditions for, **44(1)**, [677]
　decisions, information on, **44(1)**, [679]
　distributing, exclusion of investments in,
　　44(1), [677]
　postponement of tax pending
　　determination, **44(1)**, [679]
　procedure for, **44(1)**, [678]
commodity income, **44(1)**, [676]
definition, **43(S)**, 553; **44(1)**, [482]
distributing, **44(1)**, [488]
distributions taxed as interest, **43(S)**, 1379
exchange of interests of different classes,
　44(1), [493]
full distribution policy, meaning, **44(1)**, [676]
loan relationships, **43(1)**, [258]
meaning, **43(1)**, [258]; **43(S)**, 1577
more than one class of interests—
　arrangements comprising, **43(S)**, 1578
　comprising, **44(1)**, [484], [682]
non-certification, effect of, **44(1)**, [679]
non-qualifying—
　equalisation arrangements, operating,
　　44(1), [486], [676]

offshore fund—*contd*
non-qualifying—*contd*
　material interests—
　　disposal of, **44(1)**, [485], [680]–[682]
　　realisation of, **44(1)**, [487]
　　references to, **44(1)**, [487]
　meaning, **44(1)**, [488]
offshore income gain. *See* **offshore income
gain**
participants, tax treatment of, **43(S)**, 1382
　amended provisions, **43(S)**, 869
　regulations, **43(S)**, 868–71
qualifying, meaning, **44(1)**, [677]
regulations, **43(S)**, 1580
relevant income-producing assets, meaning,
　43(S), 1579
taxable income, **44(1)**, [676]
TCGA 1992, application of, **43(S)**, 1581–4
transitional provision, **43(2)**, [553]
UK equivalent profits, **44(1)**, [676]
　Computation—
　　creditor relationships, **43(2)**, [553]
　　derivative contracts, **43(2)**, [553]
umbrella—
　arrangements, **43(S)**, 1578
　funds, **44(1)**, [483], [679], [682]
wholly-owned subsidiaries, with, **44(1)**, [677]

offshore income gain
capital gain, deduction in determining,
　44(1), [494]
charge to tax, **44(1)**, [489]
charity, of, **44(1)**, [489]
computation of, **44(1)**, [680]–[682]
equalisation element, disposal involving,
　44(1), [681]
material disposal giving rise to, **44(1)**, [680]
non-resident, accruing to, **44(1)**, [490]
post-1st January 1984, **44(1)**, [680]
remittance basis, **44(1)**, [492]
transfer of assets abroad provisions, application
　of, **44(1)**, [491]
unindexed, calculation of, **44(1)**, [680]

**offshore installations and submarine
pipelines**. *See also* **minerals; submarine
pipelines**
abandonment programmes—
　approval of, **17(2)**, [280]
　default in carrying out, **17(2)**, [285]
　duty to carry out, **17(2)**, [284]
　failure to submit, **17(2)**, [281]
　financial resources, **17(2)**, [286]
　funds, protection of, **17(2)**, [666]
　meaning, **17(2)**, [294], [295]
　notices, **17(2)**, [293]
　　service of, **17(2)**, [293]
　offences—
　　general, **17(2)**, [291]
　　penalties, **17(2)**, [290]
　persons required to submit, **17(2)**, [278],
　　[664]
　preparation of, **17(2)**, [277]
　protected assets, directions to provide
　　information about, **17(2)**, [288]

offshore installations and submarine pipelines—*contd*
abandonment programmes—*contd*
protection of funds set aside for, **17(2)**, [287]
regulations, power to make, **17(2)**, [289]
revisions, **17(2)**, [282]
Secretary of State—
expenses incurred by, **17(1)**, [711]
validity of acts of, **17(2)**, [292]
withdrawal of approval, **17(2)**, [283]
accidents involving, prevention of pollution after, **35(2)**, [272]
breach of duty, civil liability, **17(1)**, [449]
damage to pipelines, **17(1)**, [293]
expenses of Secretary of State, **17(1)**, [711]
fatal accidents, inquiries into, **17(1)**, [446]
health and safety. *See* safety, health and welfare regulations *below*
health and safety provisions, application of, **18**, [1319]–[1324]
inquiries, power to hold, **17(1)**, [453]
inspectors—
appointment, **17(1)**, [446]
powers and duties, **17(1)**, [453]
Isle of Man, adjacent to, **17(2)**, [206]
meanings, **35(2)**, [272]; **44(1)**, [619]; **44(4)**, [1009]–[1010]
Northern Ireland, application of provisions, **17(1)**, [450]
offences—
general provisions, **17(1)**, [448]
safety zones, arising, **17(1)**, [709]
owner, meaning, **17(1)**, [450]
pipe-lines, damage to, **17(1)**, [293]
regulations—
exclusion of provisions, powers, **17(1)**, [447]
general provisions, **17(1)**, [447]
safety, **17(1)**, [446]
safety, health and welfare regulations—
fatal accidents, inquiries into, **17(1)**, [446]
power to make, **17(1)**, [446]
subject matter of, **17(1)**, [453]
safety zones—
establishment—
automatic, **17(1)**, [707]
order, by, **17(1)**, [708]
exclusion from, order for, **17(1)**, [707]
Health and Safety Executive, proposals by, **17(1)**, [710]
offences arising, **17(1)**, [709]
supplementary provisions, **17(1)**, [710]
vessels—
entry by, **17(1)**, [709]
meaning, **17(1)**, [709]
security of, preservation, **17(2)**, [57]
Northern Ireland, provisions, **17(2)**, [58]
summary of provisions, **17(1)**, [1]

offshore natural gas. *See under* **gas**

oil
amended provisions, **43(S)**, 1678–9

oil—*contd*
assets put to other uses—
capital allowances, **43(S)**, 1664–5
petroleum revenue tax—
allowable expenditure, no reduction of, **43(S)**, 1663–4
chargeable tariff receipts, amounts not being, **43(S)**, 1663
decommissioning and restoration expenditure, **43(S)**, 1662–3
blended, taxation of, **43(S)**, 1651–3
capital allowances—
abandonment expenditure after ceasing ring fence trade, **43(S)**, 942–4
general decommissioning expenditure, **43(S)**, 941–2
ring fence trade, plant and machinery for use in, **43(S)**, 941
crude, power to make regulations, **43(S)**, 140
decommissioning expenditure—
assets put to other uses, **43(S)**, 1662–3
capital allowances, amended provisions, **43(S)**, 1648–51
consequential amendments, **43(S)**, 1273
definitions, **43(S)**, 1648–9
general, **43(S)**, 1664–5
field allowances—
change in equity share, **43(S)**, 1672–5
holding, **43(S)**, 1671
initial licensee holding, **43(S)**, 1671
no change in equity share, **43(S)**, 1672
pool of, **43(S)**, 1670
transfer, **43(S)**, 1674
unactivated amount, **43(S)**, 1671
gas fractionation, **43(S)**, 364
infrastructure, third party access to, **17(2)**, [669]
installations—
abandonment programmes, persons required to submit, **17(2)**, [664]
acquisition of land for, **9**, [195], [210], [211]
meaning, **9**, [207]
pipe-lines. *See* **pipe-lines**
investment management, no deduction for expenses of, **43(S)**, 946–7
market value, determining, **43(S)**, 134–40
aggregate, **43(S)**, 364–5
allowance of exploration and appraisal expenditure, **43(S)**, 362–3
assessable profits and allowable losses, **43(S)**, 362
designated fraction, **43(S)**, 366
oil disposed of or appropriated in certain circumstances, **43(S)**, 366–7
nomination excesses, corporation tax, **43(S)**, 145
nomination scheme, **43(S)**, 141
notional delivery day, **43(S)**, 134–40
petroleum revenue tax. *See* **petroleum revenue tax**
pipelines, modification of, **17(2)**, [670]
processing facilities—
associate, meaning, **17(2)**, [673]
third party access to, **17(2)**, [671], [672]

oil—*contd*

profits of earlier accounting [periods, losses set off against, **43(S)**, 945

regulations, power to make, **43(S)**, 365

returns by participators, **43(S)**, 364

ring fence trades—
assets, reinvestment of, **43(S)**, 1658–61
capital allowances, election to defer, **43(S)**, 147–9
cessation, after, **43(S)**, 1649–51
disposal event, meaning, **43(S)**, 148
expenditure supplement, **43(S)**, 149–51, 368–77
increase in rate of supplementary charge, **43(S)**, 146–7
meaning, **43(S)**, 148
roll-over relief, alternative to, **43(S)**, 1659–61
straddling periods, **43(S)**, 150

set-off against profit, consequential amendments, **43(S)**, 1274–5

shipped oil not sold at arm's length, date of delivery or appropriation, **43(S)**, 363

taxation, nominations, **43(S)**, 142–4

wells, decommissioning of, **17(2)**, [667]

oil and gas exploration and appraisal
meaning, **44(1)**, [618]

Oil and Pipe Lines Agency
accounts and audit, **17(1)**, [570]
annual reports, **17(1)**, [570]
authentication of documents, **17(1)**, [568]
borrowing powers, **17(1)**, [570]
British National Oil Corporation, property, rights etc, transfer, **17(1)**, [562], [569]
duties, **17(1)**, [560], [563], [564]
establishment, **17(1)**, [560]
functions generally, **17(1)**, [561]
grants to, **17(1)**, [570]
information, provision of, **17(1)**, [570]
investment powers, **17(1)**, [570]
loans to, **17(1)**, [570]
members—
appointment, **17(1)**, [568]
remuneration and payments, **17(1)**, [568]
tenure of office, **17(1)**, [568]
payments to Secretary of State, **17(1)**, [570]
proceedings, **17(1)**, [568]
property—
surplus, disposal of, **17(1)**, [563]
transfer from British National Oil Corporation, **17(1)**, [562], [569]
seal of, **17(1)**, [568]
staff, appointment etc, **17(1)**, [568]
taxation, liability to, **17(1)**, [560]
Treasury guarantees, **17(1)**, [570]

oil corporation. *See* **British National Oil Corporation**

oil extraction
trade profits, income taxed as, **44(3)**, [16]

oil extraction activities
assets, sale and leaseback of, **44(1)**, [334]
capital allowances, **44(1)**, [331]
exploration expenditure supplement, **44(1)**, [657]
application and interpretation, **44(1)**, [658]
post-commencement, **44(1)**, [660]
pre-commencement, **44(1)**, [659]
group relief, computation of amount available for surrender by way of, **44(1)**, [335]
loan relationships, **44(1)**, [333]
loss relief, **44(1)**, [331]
meaning, **44(1)**, [344]
petroleum revenue tax. *See* **petroleum revenue tax**
regional development grants, **44(1)**, [336]
ring fence expenditure supplement, **44(1)**, [661]
application and interpretation, **44(1)**, [662]
post-commencement, **44(1)**, [664]
pre-commencement, **44(1)**, [663]
ring fence income, meaning, **44(1)**, [344]
ring fence profits—
deductions against, **44(1)**, [333]
loss relief, **44(1)**, [331]
meaning, **44(1)**, [344]
ring fence trades—
meaning, **44(1)**, [344]
supplementary charge for—
assessment, **44(1)**, [343]
generally, **44(1)**, [342]
postponement of, **44(1)**, [343]
recovery of, **44(1)**, [343]
separate trade, as, **44(1)**, [331]
tariff receipts, **44(1)**, [337]
tax-exempting tariffing receipts, **44(1)**, [337]
tax purposes, treatment for, **44(1)**, [331]
valuation of oil, **44(1)**, [332]

oil field
abandoned, unrelieved loss from, **42**, [336]
allowable expenditure—
abortive exploration, on, **42**, [333], [351]
appeals, **42**, [349]
apportionment, **42**, [331]
assets, on—
associated, **42**, [492]
brought-in, **42**, [493]
dedicated mobile, **42**, [475]
exclusion of expenditure, **42**, [477]
long-term, **42**, [332], [476]
mobile, becoming dedicated, **42**, [493]
non-dedicated mobile, **42**, [474]
principal field, no longer in use for, **42**, [492]
remote associated, **42**, [492]
subsequent use not in connection with taxable field, **42**, [493]
two or more fields, acquired for, **42**, [493]
claims, **42**, [349], [350]
deballasting, on, **42**, [478], [494]
exempt gas, related to, **42**, [478]
expenditure not being, **42**, [331]
exploration and appraisal, on, **42**, [334]

oil field—*contd*
  allowable expenditure—*contd*
    meaning, **42**, [331], [493]
    participator, claim by, **42**, [350]
    reduction of, **42**, [348]
    reduction of uplift for, **42**, [381]
    research, on, **42**, [335], [884], [890]
    restriction on reliefs, **42**, [500]
    restrictions on, **42**, [348]
  asset—
    allowable expenditure. *See* allowable
      expenditure *above*
    business, replacement of, **42**, [1328]
    disposal of—
      acquisition otherwise than at arm's
        length, where, **42**, [494]
      avoidance schemes, **42**, [494]
      brought-in, in respect of, **42**, [494]
      connected persons, consideration
        received by, **42**, [494]
      consideration, apportionment of,
        42, [494]
      deballasting, use for, **42**, [494]
      gains on, **42**, [1327]
      insurance and compensation payments,
        42, [494]
      long-term, **42**, [348]
      oil disregarded, where, **42**, [494]
      oil field, ceasing to be used in
        connection with, **42**, [494]
      ring fence provisions, **42**, [1327]
    long-term, money received on loss or
      destruction, **42**, [348]
    participators, acquired jointly by, **42**, [348]
  capacity payments, **42**, [501]
  determination of, **42**, [329], [345], [447]
  final periods, adjustment for, **42**, [886]
  gas sales, treatment of payments, **42**, [501]
  light gases, market value of, **42**, [347]
  meaning, **42**, [343], [345]
  new, reduction of supplementary charge,
    43(S), 1408
    adjusted ring fence profits, **43(S)**, 1669
    adjustments, **43(S)**, 1675
    interpretation, **43(S)**, 1676–8
    orders, **43(S)**, 1675
  oil—
    blended, **42**, [883], [889]
    excluded, **42**, [341]
    market value—
      aggregate, **42**, [347]
      definition of, **42**, [347]
      determining, **42**, [347], [502], [882]
    meaning, **42**, [329]
    offshore in transit, treatment of, **42**, [347]
    person other than participator, owned by,
      42, [347]
    royalties, delivered in place of, **42**, [347]
    sale at arm's length, **42**, [330], [347]
  oil allowance—
    amount utilised, **42**, [338]
    determining, **42**, [338], [347]
    new fields, increased for, **42**, [463]
    onshore field, for, **42**, [929]
    receipts set against, **42**, [467]

oil field—*contd*
  oil allowance—*contd*
    Southern Basin, for, **42**, [929]
  participator—
    abandonment guarantees—
      expenditure on, **42**, [1053]
      meaning, **42**, [1062]
      reimbursement expenditure, relief for,
        42, [1054], [1064]
      restriction of expenditure relief,
        42, [1063]
    accumulated capital expenditure, **42**, [339]
    adjusted profit of, **42**, [339]
    allowable expenditure. *See* allowable
      expenditure *above*
    allowable losses, **42**, [330]
      abandoned field, unrelieved loss,
        42, [336]
      relief for, **42**, [337]
    amount debited or credited to, **42**, [330]
    appropriations, proceeds of, **42**, [881]
    assessable profits, **42**, [330]
    assets, disposal of. *See* asset *above*
    assets producing tariff receipts, disposals of,
      43(1), [105]
    associated company, transfer of rights to,
      42, [347]
    capital expenditure, spreading of, **42**, [429]
    chargeable tariff receipts, **42**, [480]
    claim for allowable expenditure, **42**, [350]
    cross-field allowance, **42**, [885],
      [891]–[894]
    decisions, re-opening, **42**, [490]
    defaulter's abandonment expenditure—
      expenditure in meeting, **42**, [1055]
      reimbursement of, **42**, [1056], [1065]
      ring fence provisions, **42**, [1327]
    disposal receipts, reduction of, **42**, [484]
    disposals—
      chargeable receipts from, **42**, [483]
      gains on, **42**, [1327]
      proceeds of, **42**, [881]
    electing, tax relief for receipts of,
      43(1), [101]
    elections by, **42**, [347]
    expenditure—
      chargeable periods, **43(1)**, [43]
      elected assets, on, **43(1)**, [100], [102]
      tariff receipts, **43(1)**, [44]
      taxable field use, allowance on assets
        limited by reference to, **43(1)**, [41]
      time of incurring, **43(1)**, [42]
    exploration and appraisal expenditure,
      transitional relief, **43(1)**, [40]
    failure to give information, **42**, [503]
    field interest, transfer of—
      allowable expenditure, **43(1)**, [446]
      disposal receipts, marginal tax on,
        43(1), [447]
      qualifying assets, **43(1)**, [448]
    foreign field assets, use of, **42**, [488], [496]
    former, default as to abandonment
      expenditure met by, **43(S)**, 934–6
      reimbursement, **43(S)**, 938
    incorrect return by, **42**, [346]

oil field—*contd*
  participator—*contd*
    loss, determinations of, **42**, [346]
    meaning, **42**, [343]; **43(S)**, 933
    nominated proceeds for the period, excess
      of, **42**, [881]
    nomination scheme—
      aggregate effective volume, **42**, [888]
      aggregate nominated proceeds, **42**, [888]
      amendments, **42**, [908], [910]
      blended oil, **42**, [888]
      content, **42**, [888]
      definitions, **42**, [888]
      effective period, **42**, [888]
      effective volume, **42**, [888]
      establishment of, **42**, [881]
      nominal volume, **42**, [888]
      price, **42**, [888]
      revision, **42**, [888]
      timing, **42**, [888]
      transactions, **42**, [888]
    operating expenditure, **42**, [340]
    payments on account by, **42**, [387]
      computation of, **42**, [389]
    profit or loss accruing to, **42**, [425]
      licence payments, treatment of,
        42, [330], [430]
    purchase at place of extraction, **42**, [494]
    qualifying assets, **42**, [485]
    qualifying date, **42**, [500]
    relief, spreading, **42**, [347]
    returns by, **42**, [346], [487], [882]
    sales at arm's length, information on,
      42, [502]
    tariff receipts allowance, **42**, [486], [495]
    tax-exempt tariffing receipts, **42**, [481]
    transactions between, **42**, [347]
    transfer of interests, expenditure
      supplement, **42**, [426]
    transitional provisions, **42**, [489]
  qualifying existing field, condition for being,
    42, [482]
  relevant assets, sale and lease-back of—
    allowable expenditure, **43(1)**, [445]
    disposal receipts, marginal tax on,
      43(1), [447]
    qualifying assets, **43(1)**, [448]
  relevant new field, increased allowance for,
    42, [463]
  reliefs, **42**, [464]
  responsible person—
    appointment of, **42**, [346]
    returns by, **42**, [346]
  transfer of interests in—
    abortive exploration expenditure, **42**, [409]
    accumulated capital expenditure, **42**, [408]
    advance payments, **42**, [409]
    excluded oil, **42**, [408]
    exclusion of rules, **42**, [407]
    exploration and appraisal expenditure,
      42, [409]
    long-term assets, disposal of, **42**, [409]
    meaning, **42**, [407]
    new participator, losses of, **42**, [409]
    notice of, **42**, [407]

oil field—*contd*
  transfer of interests in—*contd*
    oil allowance, **42**, [409]
    oil, transfer of, **42**, [409]
    partial, **42**, [407]
    payments on account, **42**, [409]
    period of, limit on tax payable, **42**, [409]
    provisional relief for expenditure, **42**, [409]
    research expenditure, **42**, [409]
    royalty payments, **42**, [409]
    share of oil, retention of, **42**, [409]
    successive, **42**, [408]
    terminal losses, **42**, [409]
    unused expenditure relief, **42**, [408]
    unused losses, **42**, [408]
  transmedian, **42**, [402]
  two or more, blend of oil from, **42**, [883]
  undeveloped area, licence relating to,
    42, [1324]

oil industry. *See* **mining and oil industries**

oil licence
  definitions, **43(1)**, [1193]
  exploitation value, disposal with,
    43(1), [1192]
  foreign oil concession, meaning, **43(1)**, [1189]
  interest in, meaning, **43(1)**, [1189]
  licence-consideration swaps, **43(S)**, 1655
  meaning, **43(1)**, [1189]
  mineral extraction allowance. *See* **mineral**
    extraction allowances
  mixed consideration—
    company giving, **43(S)**, 1656–7
    company receiving, **43(S)**, 1655–6
  swaps, **43(S)**, 1654
  UK, meaning, **43(1)**, [1189]
  undeveloped areas, relating to—
    circumstances of, **43(1)**, [1191]
    consideration treated as nil, **43(1)**, [1190]

oil pollution
  annual report by Secretary of State,
    39(2), [819]; **49**, [481]
  Channel Islands, provisions as to, **49**, [480]
  colonies and dependencies, provisions as to,
    49, [480]
  Conventions, enforcement of, **39(2)**, [816]
  detention of ships, **39(2)**, [813]
  discharge—
    defences to charge, **49**, [472]
    exploration, resulting from, **49**, [471]
    harbour, into, duty to report, **49**, [475]
    nature of, **49**, [470]
    pipe-lines, from, **49**, [471]
    place on land, from, **49**, [470]
    territorial waters, outside, **49**, [469]
    United Kingdom waters, into, **49**, [470]
  discharge into waters of harbours—
    discharges authorised by other enactments,
      39(2), [810]
    duty to report, **39(2)**, [809]
  discharge of oil, definitions, **39(2)**, [820]
  exemptions from provisions, power to grant,
    39(2), [817]

oil pollution—*contd*
　financial provisions, **49**, [483]
　fines—
　　application of, **39(2)**, [815]
　　enforcement of, **39(2)**, [812], [815]
　Government ships, provisions not applying
　　to, **39(2)**, [818]
　harbour—
　　authorities, protection, **49**, [474]
　　discharge into, duty to report, **49**, [475]
　harbour authorities, acts done in exercise of
　　powers of, **39(2)**, [807]
　hovercraft, application of provisions, **49**, [486]
　increased penalty for causing, **39(2)**, [1022]
　inspection, powers of, **49**, [477]
　institution of proceedings, **39(2)**, [814]
　international arrangements, revisions of,
　　39(2), [1063]
　International Fund. *See* **International Oil
　　Pollution Compensation Fund**
　Isle of Man, provisions as to, **49**, [480]
　Liability Convention, meaning, **39(2)**, [821]
　liability for—
　　bunker oil, by, **39(2)**, [823], [827]
　　　compulsory insurance against,
　　　　39(2), [835]
　　compulsory insurance—
　　　certificate, issue of, **39(2)**, [836]
　　　requirement, **39(2)**, [834], [835]
　　　third parties, rights against insurer,
　　　　39(2), [837]
　　concurrent, **39(2)**, [831]
　　exceptions, **39(2)**, [825]
　　foreign judgments, registration of,
　　　39(2), [838]
　　Government ships, provisions not applying
　　　to, **39(2)**, [839]
　　jurisdiction, **39(2)**, [838]
　　limitation of, **39(2)**, [828], [840]
　　　action, **39(2)**, [829]
　　　enforcement of claim after establishment
　　　　of fund, **39(2)**, [830]
　　　UK, fund established outside,
　　　　39(2), [832]
　　owner, of, **39(2)**, [824], [827]
　　restriction of, **39(2)**, [826]
　　tankers, in case of, **39(2)**, [822], [827]
　　time for claim, **39(2)**, [833]
　　transitional provisions, **39(2)**, [843]
　　transitory text, **39(2)**, [843]
　meanings of oil, **49**, [484]
　Northern Ireland, provisions as to, **49**, [485]
　offences—
　　body corporate, by, **49**, [478]
　　defence to charges, **49**, [472]
　　prosecutions, **49**, [478]
　offences, prosecution of, **39(2)**, [812]
　oil reception facilities, inspection, **49**, [477]
　oil record books, **39(2)**, [811]
　orders and Orders in Council, general
　　provisions, **49**, [482]
　prevention of—
　　exemption of certain ships, **49**, [479]
　　inspection, powers of, **49**, [477]
　　prosecution of offences, **49**, [478]

oil pollution—*contd*
　records, inspection of, **49**, [477]
　recourse action, saving for, **39(2)**, [841]
　regulations—
　　general provisions, **49**, [482]
　　power to make, **49**, [482]
　rights of action, savings, **49**, [487]
　summary of provisions, **39(2)**, [1]
　Supplementary Fund. *See under* **International
　　Oil Pollution Compensation Fund**
　surveyor of ships, appointment, **49**, [477]
　transfer of oil at night, restrictions on,
　　39(2), [808]
　United Kingdom waters, discharges into—
　　defences—
　　　occupier, of, **39(2)**, [806]
　　　owner or master, of, **39(2)**, [805]
　　offences, **39(2)**, [804]
　wrecks, consequent on removal of, **49**, [474]

oil refinery. *See* **generally petroleum and
petroleum spirit**
　meaning, **17(2)**, [57]
　security of, preservations, **17(2)**, [57]
　　Northern Ireland, provisions, **17(2)**, [58]

oil taxation
　excluded oil, **43(1)**, [444]
　qualifying assets, **43(1)**, [448]
　sale and lease-back, **43(1)**, [445]
　tax-exempt tariffing receipts, transitional
　　period, expenditure in, **43(2)**, [569]

Olympic Symbol
　definitions, **48**, 211
　offences—
　　counterfeit goods, forfeiture of, **48**, 209
　　goods, in relation to, **48**, 208
　　partnerships and bodies corporate, by,
　　　48, 209
　Olympic association right—
　　controlled representation, **48**, 202–5
　　creation of, **48**, 200
　　directions to proprietor, **48**, 210
　　infringement, **48**, 202
　　　action for, **48**, 206
　　　groundless threat of proceedings, **48**, 210
　　　infringing goods, materials or articles,
　　　　orders relating to, **48**, 207
　　limits on effect, **48**, 203–6
　　use of symbol, conferring exclusive rights
　　　to, **48**, 201
　protection of, **13**, [518]
　representation—
　　controlled, **48**, 202–5
　　offences, **48**, 208
　　use of, burden of proof, **48**, 211
　protection of, **48**, 13, 113

Ombudsman. *See* **Parliamentary
Commissioner for Administration**

omnibus. *See also* **bus services; local
authority**
　byelaws, **36**, [566]

omnibus—*contd*
drivers, provisions applicable in general,
  36, [564]
fares, **36**, [564], [604]
licence, short period, **36**, [565]
licensing generally, provisions extended to,
  36, [564]
local authorities, powers, **36**, [602]
meaning, **36**, [563]
National Bus Company. *See* **National Bus
  Company**
provisions applicable, **36**, [564]
queue barriers, maintenance of, **36**, [655]
shelter—
  consent to exercise of powers, **36**, [653]
  existing, maintenance of, **36**, [655]
  provision of, **36**, [210], [652]
  telecommunication apparatus, obstructing
    access to, **36**, [654]
  undertakers' apparatus, obstructing access
    to, **36**, [654]
stands, position of, **36**, [566]
Town Police Clauses Act, extension of
  provisions in, **36**, [564]

one-way traffic
trunk roads, **37**, [185]

onshore terminal. *See generally* **petroleum and
petroleum spirit**
meaning, **17(2)**, [57]
security of, preservation, **17(2)**, [57]
  Northern Ireland, provisions, **17(2)**, [58]

open country
access to—
  acquisition of land for—
    local authority, by, **32**, [174]
    Minister, by, **32**, [175]
  agreements—
    excepted land, not to convert into,
      32, [268]
    interested persons, effect on, **32**, [162],
      [164]
    making of, **32**, [162]
    provisions applied by, **32**, [161]
    restrictions in, **32**, [161]
    rights of way, effect on, **32**, [164]
  appropriation of land, **32**, [191]
  boundary notices, **32**, [178]
  byelaws—
    making of, **32**, [184], [192], [273]
    Secretary of State, default powers of,
      32, [185]
  danger areas, exclusion of, **32**, [177]
  disposal of land, **32**, [191]
  excepted land, **32**, [161], [174]–[175]
  fire risk, suspension to avoid, **32**, [167]
  generally, **32**, [1]
  inquiries, **32**, [195]
  local authority—
    contributions, **32**, [187]
    functions, **32**, [313]
  local planning authority—
    acquisition of land by, **32**, [174]

open country—*contd*
access to—*contd*
  local planning authority—*contd*
    contributions to work by, **32**, [179]
    enforcement by, **32**, [166]
    management, duties of, **32**, [174]
    maps—
      contributions to persons displaying,
        32, [269]
      preparing and up-dating, **32**, [176]
    notices, contributions to persons
      displaying, **32**, [269]
    work carried out by, **32**, [174]
  means, provision of, **32**, [165]
  order—
    compensation—
      calculation of, **32**, [193]
      claims, **32**, [170]
      disputes, **32**, [193]
      first five years, effect of, **32**, [169]
      interest, **32**, [170]
      right to, **32**, [168]
      special hardship, payment in case of,
        32, [171]
    Environment Agency, representations
      by, **32**, [203]
    interested persons, effect on, **32**, [164]
    internal drainage board, representations
      by, **32**, [203]
    land adjacent to, water in, **32**, [263]
    making of, **32**, [163]
    notice of, **32**, [203]
    provisions applied by, **32**, [161]
    restrictions in, **32**, [161]
    rights of way, effect on, **32**, [164]
    validity, **32**, [204]
    variation of, **32**, [196]
    work specified in, **32**, [173]
  powers of entry, **32**, [194]
  provision for, **32**, [160]
  restrictions, general, **32**, [205]
  service of notices, **32**, [195]
  wardens, **32**, [186], [274]
meaning, **32**, [160]
water, including, **32**, [267]
woodlands, including, **32**, [267]

open-ended investment company
collective investment business, regulations for
  carrying on of, **19(2)**, [315]
investment condition, **19(2)**, [289]
meaning, **19(2)**, [289]
property condition, **19(2)**, [289]
stamp duty land tax provisions applied to,
  41, [386]

open space
appropriation of part of, **25(1)**, [592]
appropriation, restriction on, **1(1)**, [244]
byelaws, **32**, [34]
compensation, provision for, **32**, [32]
compulsory acquisition—
  exchange of lands, certificate as to,
    9, [432], [453]

open space—*contd*
  compulsory acquisition—*contd*
    special parliamentary procedure for,
      9, [432]–[433], [453]
  contributions by county council for,
    25(1), [563]
  corporation, conveyance of land by, **32**, [26]
  definitions, **32**, [39]
  disposal of, **22**, [895]
  housing action trust, vested in, **22**, [930]
  Law of Property Act, transitional provisions,
    20, [812]
  local authority—
    acquisition by, **32**, [28]
    bodies being, **32**, [20]
    borrowing by, **32**, [37]
    expenses of, **32**, [36]
    jointly, acting, **32**, [35]
    maintenance by, **32**, [29]
    powers already vested in, **32**, [31]
    transfer to—
      charity trustees, by, **32**, [23]
      public recreation, land held for, **32**, [22]
      rights of user, subject to, **32**, [24]
      trustees under local Act, by, **32**, [21]
  London—
    byelaws, enforcement, **25(1)**, [854]
    commons, restrictions as to, **25(1)**, [847]
    competitions etc, use for, **25(1)**, [848]
    enforcement of provisions, **25(1)**, [853]
    entertainments in, **25(1)**, [842]
    exchange of adjoining land for,
      25(1), [850]
    licences to use land, **25(1)**, [843]
    powers as to—
      exercise of, **25(1)**, [846]
      restriction of, **25(1)**, [847]
    private owners of land, powers for,
      25(1), [851]
    public rights, restriction of, **25(1)**, [844]
    recreation, facilities for, **25(1)**, [842]
    street improvements, use for, **25(1)**, [852]
    Sunday closing, **25(2)**, [397]
    transfer between local authorities,
      25(1), [849]
    uniformity of law, **25(1)**, [839]–[855]
    use of, charges for, **25(1)**, [845]
  management, **32**, [1]
  meaning, **9**, [159], [432], [453]; **18**, [1097],
    [1153]; **32**, [39]
  new town, use in, **46**, [153]
  Northern Ireland, application of provisions
    to, **32**, [40]
  parish council powers, **25(1)**, [522]
  preservation, **9**, [432]–[433]
  provision of, in housing development,
    22, [15]
  regional development agencies, vesting of land
    in, **46**, [952]
  savings, **32**, [38]
  special resolution on, **32**, [27]
  tree felling, **18**, [1097]
  trust for, **32**, [1]
  urban development area, use in, **46**, [107]

open space—*contd*
  Urban Regeneration Agency, use by,
    46, [859]
  use and development of land, **46**, [505]

opencast coal
  Acquisition of Land Act 1981, application of
    provisions, **17(1)**, [177]
  agricultural—
    holdings, compulsory rights over, effect,
      17(1), [173]
    land, compensation. *See* compensation *below*
    tenancies, effect on, **17(1)**, [173]
      arbitration, **17(1)**, [173]
      rental value, **17(1)**, [173]
  allotments and allotment gardens,
    17(1), [203], [226]
  buildings protected, **17(1)**, [169]
  chattels, removal from land and disposal,
    17(1), [172]
  Coal Authority, compulsory rights orders. *See*
    compulsory rights order *below*
  compensation—
    accrues due, time when, **17(1)**, [197]
    agricultural land—
      annual borrowing cost, market value, by
        reference to, **17(1)**, [179]
      calculation, **17(1)**, [179]
      changes in right of occupation,
        17(1), [220]
      claim, notice of, **17(1)**, [184]
      cost of works—
        payment of, **17(1)**, [181]
        provisions as to, **17(1)**, [214]
      deductions from tenant's compensation,
        17(1), [185]
      diminution in value of holding,
        17(1), [182]
      forced sales, **17(1)**, [188]
      general provisions, **17(1)**, [178]
      improvements—
        long term, **17(1)**, [184]
        market gardens, **17(1)**, [189], [215]
        schedules of, **17(1)**, [217]
        short term, **17(1)**, [187]
        tenant's rights, **17(1)**, [184]
      market gardens, **17(1)**, [189], [218]
      market price, annual borrowing cost,
        17(1), [179]
      market value of rights, calculation by,
        17(1), [178]
      ownership of holding, division of,
        17(1), [220]
      person entitled, **17(1)**, [178]
      persons liable for payment, **17(1)**, [178],
        [187]
      re-occupation, additional compensation
        on, **17(1)**, [183]
      special system of farming, **17(1)**, [184]
      tenant's rights—
        deductions from compensation,
          17(1), [185]
        improvements, for, **17(1)**, [184]
        terminal compensation, **17(1)**, [180],
          [220]

opencast coal—*contd*
  compensation—*contd*
    agricultural land—*contd*
      time of year for payment, **17(1)**, [178]
    apportionment, parts of a year,
      17(1), [192], [197], [220]
    assessment, record of condition of land,
      17(1), [198]
    claims for, **17(1)**, [202]
    common or waste land, **17(1)**, [192]
    condition of land, record of, **17(1)**, [198]
    cost of works—
      payment of, **17(1)**, [181]
      procedure, **17(1)**, [214]
    depreciation of other land in same
      ownership, **17(1)**, [194], [220]
      annual value in calculation, **17(1)**, [194]
    disposable materials, in respect of,
      17(1), [193]
    disputes, **17(1)**, [202]
    easements etc, in respect of, **17(1)**, [192],
      [220]
    farm business tenancies, **17(1)**, [186]
    letting of land, **17(1)**, [220]
    licence to occupy land, right conferred
      by, **17(1)**, [220]
    market gardens, **17(1)**, [189], [218]
    minerals, in respect of, **17(1)**, [193], [219]
      amount payable, **17(1)**, [193], [195]
      notices, **17(1)**, [193]
    mortgage, land subject to, **17(1)**, [205]
    non-agricultural land—
      annual and terminal, **17(1)**, [190]
      application of 1927 Act, **17(1)**, [191]
      forced sales, **17(1)**, [190]
      tenant's improvements, **17(1)**, [191]
    payment, methods, **17(1)**, [197]
    record of condition of land, **17(1)**, [198]
    rights over land, in respect of, **17(1)**, [192]
    special cases, in, **17(1)**, [196], [220]
    terminal, **17(1)**, [180]
    time when accruing due, **17(1)**, [197]
    woodlands, **17(1)**, [220]
  compulsory purchase of land, authorised
    working protected from, **17(1)**, [200]
  compulsory rights order—
    Acquisition of Land Act 1981, provisions
      applicable, **17(1)**, [165]
    agricultural tenancies, provisions as to,
      17(1), [173]
    application for, **17(1)**, [165], [209]
      successor to original applicant,
        17(1), [166]
      transfer of, **17(1)**, [166]
    cessation of powers, **17(2)**, [176]
    compensation under. *See* compensation
      above
    concurrent, **17(1)**, [220]
    contravention of provisions, **17(1)**, [209]
    easements, effect on, **17(1)**, [192], [220]
    effect of—
      generally, **17(1)**, [166]
      limitations, **17(1)**, [166]
    entry date, notification, **17(1)**, [166], [213]
    exercise of rights conferred, **17(1)**, [166]

opencast coal—*contd*
  compulsory rights order—*contd*
    land charge, as, **17(1)**, [171]
    land exempt from inclusion, **17(1)**, [169]
    limitation on, **17(1)**, [165]
      general, **17(1)**, [166]
    limited, **17(1)**, [168], [220]
    notices—
      application for order, **17(1)**, [165]
      forms, **17(1)**, [165]
      person issuing etc, record required by,
        17(1), [198]
      provisions as to, **17(1)**, [166], [213]
      removal of chattels, for, **17(1)**, [172]
    operations permitted, **17(1)**, [165]
    period of effect, **17(1)**, [165]
    "persons entitled", "persons directly
      concerned", references to, meanings,
      17(1), [166], [168]
    planning permission requirement,
      17(1), [165]
    power to make, **17(1)**, [165]
    previous order, effect of, **17(1)**, [169]
    property exempt from inclusion,
      17(1), [169]
    publication, **17(1)**, [166], [213]
    registration, **17(1)**, [227]
    "relevant offer" in connection with,
      17(1), [209]
    restoration condition, subject to,
      17(1), [173]
    restructuring, before, savings, **17(2)**, [206]
    revocation, **17(1)**, [209]
    rights affected by, **17(1)**, [166]
    rights conferred by, exercise of,
      17(1), [166]
    rights of way. *See* right of way *below*
    statutory undertakers' rights protected,
      17(1), [166], [172]
    telecommunications, interference with
      excluded, **17(1)**, [207]
    time for making, **17(1)**, [165]
    variation and revocation, **17(1)**, [209]
  crops, harvesting and disposal of, **17(1)**, [170]
  Crown land, **17(1)**, [206]
  drainage, acquisition of rights of, **17(1)**, [177]
    cessation of powers, **17(2)**, [176]
    exercise of, **17(1)**, [177]
  drainage board, entry on land of, **17(1)**, [201]
  Duchy lands, **17(1)**, [206]
  dwelling house, exemption from order,
    17(1), [169]
  easements—
    compulsory rights order, effect,
      17(1), [192], [220]
    drainage and water supply, rights acquired,
      17(1), [177]
  ecclesiastical property—
    meaning, **17(1)**, [204]
    special provisions, **17(1)**, [204]
  entry on land—
    cessation of powers as to directions,
      17(2), [176]
    damage caused during, **17(1)**, [201]
    direction by Minister for, **17(1)**, [201]

opencast coal—*contd*
  entry on land—*contd*
    generally, **17(1)**, [201]
    limitation, **17(1)**, [201]
    notice, giving and fixing, **17(1)**, [201]
    notification, **17(1)**, [166], [213]
    revocation or variation of authority for,
      17(1), [201]
  farm business tenancies—
    compensation, right to, **17(1)**, [186]
    generally, **17(1)**, [174]
  fixtures, buildings etc, removal, **17(1)**, [170]
  landlords and tenants, adjustments between,
    17(1), [199], [221]–[225]
  licensed operator—
    application for compulsory rights order,
      17(1), [165]
    meaning, **17(1)**, [165]; **17(2)**, [189]
  minerals—
    compensation in respect of, **17(1)**, [193],
      [219]
    other than coal, **17(1)**, [170]
  mortgaged land, **17(1)**, [205]
  notices—
    provisions as to, **17(1)**, [208], [227]
    rights of way suspension, **17(1)**, [176]
    service of, **17(1)**, [165], [208]
  permitted activities, meaning, **17(1)**, [211]
  planning permission—
    application for, **9**, [441]
    compulsory rights order, **17(1)**, [165]
    entry on land in connection with,
      17(1), [201]
    meaning, **17(1)**, [211]
    person, reference to, meaning, **17(1)**, [211]
    rights of way suspension, provisions
      involving, **17(1)**, [175], [176]
    telecommunication apparatus, provision as
      to, **17(1)**, [207]
  power of Secretary of State to authorise
    working, abolition, **46**, [231]
  public inquiries, **17(1)**, [176], [208]
  regulations and orders, **17(1)**, [209]
  religious purposes, property held for,
    17(1), [204]
  restoration of land after operations—
    agricultural tenancies, provision as to,
      17(1), [173]
    environmental duties, **17(2)**, [177], [178]
    meaning, **17(1)**, [211]
    right of way, **17(1)**, [175]
  right of way, suspended—
    alternative way—
      land for, **17(1)**, [175]
      provision of, **17(1)**, [175]
    application for, **17(1)**, [175]
      copies, inspection, **17(1)**, [176]
      information to local authorities,
        17(1), [176]
      notices, publication before, **17(1)**, [176]
      successor to original applicant by,
        17(1), [175]
    cessation of power, **17(2)**, [176]
      successor to original applicant by,
        17(1), [175]

opencast coal—*contd*
  right of way, suspended—*contd*
    cessation of power—*contd*
      notices before, **17(1)**, [176]
      objection to, **17(1)**, [176]
      revocation, **17(1)**, [175]
    permitted activities, **17(1)**, [175]
    public local inquiry before, **17(1)**, [176]
    reconstruction of the way, **17(1)**, [175]
  rights protected, **17(1)**, [166]
  statutory undertakers—
    apparatus of, protection, **17(1)**, [172]
    land of, entry on, **17(1)**, [201]
  successor, meaning, **17(1)**, [211]
  summary of provisions, **17(1)**, [1]
  telegraph lines, **17(1)**, [207]
  temporary rights of occupation, orders,
    17(1), [165]
  timber, right to fell and dispose, **17(1)**, [170]
  water supply, acquisition of rights as to,
    17(1), [177]
    cessation of powers, **17(2)**, [176]
    exercise of, **17(1)**, [177]
  woodlands, **17(1)**, [220]

ophthalmic optician
  contingent removal from list, **30**, [461]
    appeals, **30**, [467]
    notification of decisions, **30**, [469]
    review of decisions regarding, **30**, [466]
  disqualification of—
    conditions, **30**, [460]
    efficiency cases, **30**, [460]–[461]
    fraud cases, **30**, [460]–[462]
    Northern Ireland, corresponding provisions
      in, **30**, [472]
    notification of decisions, **30**, [469]
    regulations, **30**, [471]
    Scotland, corresponding provisions in,
      30, [472]
    withdrawal from list, **30**, [470]
  fraud and unsuitability, **30**, [462]
  indemnity cover, **30**, [455]
  meaning, **30**, [478]
  national disqualification, **30**, [468]
  remuneration, regulations as to,
    30, [453]–[454], [476], [501]
  sight testing, arrangements for, **30**, [449]
  suspension, **30**, [463]
    appeals, **30**, [467]
    effect of, **30**, [465]
    notification of decisions, **30**, [469]
    pending appeal, **30**, [464]
    regulations, **30**, [471]
    review of, **30**, [466]
    withdrawal from list, **30**, [470]
  Wales. *See* **Wales**

ophthalmic services
  appliances, charging for, **30**, [985]–[987]
  general—
    accommodation, **30**, [473]
    arrangements for, **30**, [449]–[450], [519]
    assistance and support for, **30**, [930]
    conditional inclusion in list, **30**, [452]

ophthalmic services—*contd*
  general—*contd*
    contract for—
      disputes, **30**, [928]
      enforcement, **30**, [928]
      exclusion of contractors, **30**, [925]
      payments, **30**, [926]
      persons eligible to enter into, **30**, [924]
      required terms, **30**, [927]
      requirements, **30**, [923]
      services under, **30**, [923]
    disqualification of practitioners, **30**, [460]
    inadequate, provisions on, **30**, [474]
    indemnity cover, **30**, [455]
    Local Optical Committees, **30**, [931]
    premises, provision of, **30**, [447]
    Primary Care Trust—
      assistance and support for, **30**, [930]
      contract, entry into, **30**, [923]
    regulations, **30**, [450]
    remuneration, regulations as to,
      30, [453]–[454], [501]
    supplementary list, **30**, [456]
    suspension of practitioners, **30**, [463], [463]
    transitional provisions, **30**, [775]
  premises for, provision of, **30**, [827]
  primary—
    persons performing, lists of, **30**, [929]
    Primary Care Trust, duties of, **30**, [921]
    regulations, **30**, [921]–[922]
    remuneration, **30**, [1040]
    sight-testing, **30**, [921]
    transitional modifications, **30**, [1360]
  Wales. *See* **Wales**

opium
  smoking—
    offences connected with, **28**, [207]
    use of premises in connection with, liability
      of occupier for permitting, **28**, [206]

Opposition (Parliament)
  doubt as to, **10**, [608]
  leader of—
    meaning, **10**, [608]
    salary, **10**, [605], [617]–[618]
      alteration of, **10**, [606]–[607]
  whips—
    meaning, **10**, [608]
    salary, **10**, [605], [617]–[618]
      alteration of, **10**, [606]–[607]

optical appliance
  value added tax, exemption from, **50**, [153]

opticians. *See also* **General Optical Council**
  bodies corporate—
    carrying on business, list of, **28**, [517]
    meaning, **28**, [560]
    offences by, **28**, [552]
  contact lenses, fitting of, **28**, [547]
  education and training—
    competencies, **28**, [523]
    content and standards of, **28**, [523]

opticians—*contd*
  education and training—*contd*
    continuing, scheme for—
      failure to satisfy requirements, **28**, [522]
      rules, **28**, [521]
    supervision, **28**, [524]
  fitness to practice—
    Council, role of. *See* **General Optical
      Council**
    financial penalty order, imposition of,
      28, [532]
    findings as to, **28**, [530]
    immediate suspension, order for, **28**, [533]
  legal proceedings, **28**, [553]
  lists—
    bodies corporate carrying on business,
      28, [517]
    general provisions as to, **28**, [518]
    meaning, **28**, [560]
    publication of, **28**, [520]
  miscellaneous matters, **28**, [554]
  optical appliances, sale and supply of,
    28, [549]
  Privy Council—
    default powers of, **28**, [557]
    documents, **28**, [559]
    quorum, **28**, [559]
  proceedings and appeals, service of
    notification, **28**, [538]
  qualifications—
    approval of, **28**, [523]
    registration, for, **28**, [512]
    supervision of qualifying assessments,
      28, [524]
  registered—
    bankruptcy of, **28**, [551]
    death of, **28**, [551]
    insurance requirements, **28**, [519]
  registers—
    entitlement to be registered—
      visiting dispensing opticians, of,
        28, [516]
      visiting optometrists, of, **28**, [515]
    erasure from, **28**, [530], [531]
    fraud or error, removal on ground of,
      28, [534]
    general provisions as to, **28**, [518]
    immediate suspension, order for, **28**, [533]
    maintenance of, **28**, [511]
    meaning, **28**, [560]
    penalty for pretending to be registered,
      28, [550]
    proof of registration, **28**, [520]
    publication of, **28**, [520]
    qualifications for being registered, **28**, [512]
    registration appeals, **28**, [565]
    removal from, **28**, [530], [531]
    restoration to, **28**, [535]
    students, of, **28**, [513]
    suspension from, **28**, [530], [531]
      interim, **28**, [536], [537]
    visiting opticians from relevant European
      States, of, **28**, [514]
  sight testing—
    duties to be performed on, **28**, [548]

opticians—*contd*
  sight testing—*contd*
    meaning, **28**, [560]
    rules as to, **28**, [546]
  subordinate legislation procedure, **28**, [558]
  training institutions—
    approval of, **28**, [523]
    supervision of, **28**, [524]

options
  avoidance using, **43(S)**, 88
  capital gains tax—
    gains, **42**, [1249]
    pooling rules, **42**, [1213]
    taper relief, **42**, [1450]
  cash-settled, **42**, [1255]
  currency, variation of conditions, **43(2)**, [236]
  definitions, **42**, [1250]
  disposals involving guaranteed returns, charge
    to tax. *See* **savings and investment
    income**
  employee, **43(2)**, [253]
  employment, relating to. *See* **employment**
  enterprise management incentives. *See*
    enterprise management incentives
  exercise of—
    market value rule, application of,
      42, [1251]
    market value rule, exception to, **42**, [1252]
      alteration of to obtain tax advantage,
        42, [1254]
    non-commercial, **42**, [1253]
  financial, **42**, [1250]
  grant, capital gains tax on, **42**, [1250]
  guaranteed return involving,
    42, [1260]–[1262]
  investment, as, **44(1)**, [433]
  qualifying—
    charge to tax, **44(1)**, [103]
    losses, **44(1)**, [203]
    meaning, **44(1)**, [203]
  quoted. *See* **quoted option**
  share. *See* **share option**
  traded—
    closing purchases, **42**, [1259]
    gains arising on, **42**, [1249]
    meaning, **42**, [1250]
  wasting assets, rules on, **42**, [1257]

Orders in Council
  statutory, power to make, **41**, [480]

orders of court
  attachment. *See* **attachment of earnings**
  charging order. *See* **charging order**
  foreign currency, awards in, **19(3)**, [78]
  judgment, having effect as, **19(3)**, [4]

ordinary (ecclesiastical)
  powers over church fabric, etc. **14**, 193
  profits of benefice, receiving during vacancy,
    14, 42

ordination
  admission, before, **14**, 52

ordination—*contd*
  age for, **14**, 63, 644
  corrupt, **14**, 51
  deacons, women as, **14**, 1175–6
  divorced woman, effect of marriage to,
    14, 645
  illegitimacy, effect of, **14**, 644
  impediments, **14**, 645
  ministry overseas, for, **14**, 659
  oaths, taking before, **14**, 200
  procedure, providing by canon, **14**, 831–2
  re-marriage, effect of, **14**, 645
  women—
    deacon, as. *See* **deacon**
    priests, as—
      Canon—
        amendment of, **14**, 1277
        provision by, **14**, 1269–70
      declarations against—
        bishops, by, **14**, 1270–1
        contravention of, by bishop, priest or
          deacon, an ecclesiastical offence,
          14, 1275
        Crown benefices, **14**, 1275–6
      General Synod powers, **14**, 1175–6
      Isle of Man, application of Measure to,
        14, 1279
      Measure, amendment of, **14**, 1277
      provision for, **14**, 1269–70
      resignation because of opposition to—
        benefits—
          applications for, **14**, 1284
          Church Commissioners to finance,
            14, 1284–5
          declarations, **14**, 1284, 1289
          financial benefit, entitlement to,
            14, 1280
          housing, **14**, 1281
          payments—
            discretionary, **14**, 1283
            periodical, **14**, 1282, 1284
          pensions, **14**, 1176, 1285
          resettlement grants, **14**, 1281
          residential benefit, entitlement to,
            14, 1280
      resolutions against—
        contravention of, by bishop, priest or
          deacon, an ecclesiastical offence,
          14, 1275
        Crown benefices, **14**, 1275–6
        forms of, **14**, 1278
        parochial church councils, by,
          14, 1272
      sex discrimination against not unlawful,
        14, 1275

ordnance department
  Secretary of State for War, transfer to,
    10, [414]–[417]

ordnance factories
  building restrictions, **10**, [672]
  financial provisions, **10**, [677]
  nominee of Secretary of State, **10**, [667]
  planning restrictions, **10**, [672]

ordnance factories—*contd*
  successor company—
    government investment in, **10**, [666], [668]
    trustee investments in, **10**, [670]
  transfer scheme—
    certificate of vesting, **10**, [679]
    consideration, **10**, [662]
    consultation, **10**, [662]
    employment provisions, **10**, [680]
    expenses, **10**, [666]
    liabilities, extinguishing, **10**, [671]
    operation of, **10**, [664], [679]
    power to make, **10**, [662]
    property, rights and liabilities, **10**, [663]
    securities, **10**, [662], [666]
    stamp duty, **10**, [673]
    third party, affecting, **10**, [679]
    transaction, construction of, **10**, [679]
    winding-up, liabilities on, **10**, [669]

ordnance map
  meaning, **41**, [605]

ordnance survey
  boundaries—
    not changing, **10**, [303]
    stone, removing, **10**, [301]
  local authority functions, **25(2)**, [167]
  obstructing, **10**, [302]
  persons assisting—
    appointment by justices, **10**, [298]
    entry on land, **10**, [299]
    marks, fixing, **10**, [299]
  rights of property, not affecting, **10**, [303]
  surveyor, clerk of peace attending on,
    10, [300]

**Organisation for Economic Co-operation
and Development**
  Support Fund—
    agreement establishing, **19(2)**, [948]
    consolidated fund, payments into and out
      of, **19(2)**, [950]
    establishment and purpose of, **19(1)**, [1]
    National Loans Fund, payments into and
      out of, **19(2)**, [949]
    tax exemptions on securities, **19(2)**, [951]

**Organization for Security and
Co-operation in Europe**
  agreements with, **10**, [1242]

Osborne Estate
  class of persons used for, **10**, [176]
  hereditary revenues, part of, **10**, [165]

osteopaths. *See also* **General Osteopathic
Council**
  Code of Practice, **28**, [656]
  competition, **28**, [671]
  criminal convictions, requirement to declare,
    28, [676]
  education. *See* training *below*
  fitness to practice. *See* professional conduct
    and fitness to practise *below*

osteopaths—*contd*
  general note, **28**, [1]
  monopolies, **28**, [671]
  offences, **28**, [670]
  professional conduct and fitness to practise—
    general, **28**, [657]
    Health Committee—
      appeals against decisions of, **28**, [668]
      consideration of allegations, **28**, [660]
      interim suspension—
        powers of, **28**, [661]
        revocation of orders, **28**, [662]
      investigations of allegations, procedural
        rules of, **28**, [663]
      legal assessors, advice from, **28**, [664]
      medical assessors, advice from, **28**, [665]
    interim suspension powers of, **28**, [658]
    Investigating Committee—
      Health Committee, referral to, **28**, [657]
      legal assessors, advice from, **28**, [664]
      medical assessors, advice from, **28**, [665]
      Professional Conduct Committee,
        referral to, **28**, [657]
    Professional Conduct Committee—
      appeals against decisions of, **28**, [669]
      consideration of allegations, **28**, [659]
      investigations of allegations, procedural
        rules of, **28**, [663]
      legal assessors, advice from, **28**, [664]
      medical assessors, advice from, **28**, [665]
      revocation of orders, **28**, [662]
  professional indemnity insurance, requirement
    for, **28**, [675]
  register, public access to, **28**, [646]
  registration—
    conditional, **28**, [640]
    fraud or error in relation to, **28**, [647]
    full, **28**, [639]
    provisional, **28**, [641]
    Registrar of Osteopaths—
      appeal against decisions of, **28**, [666]
      appointment of, **28**, [638]
    restoration to register, **28**, [645]
    supplemental provision, **28**, [643]
    suspension of, **28**, [644]
    temporary, for visiting osteopaths from
      relevant European State, **28**, [642]
  training—
    Education Committee—
      role of, **28**, [648]
      visitors to educational institutions,
        appointment of, **28**, [649]
    educational institutions, information to be
      given by, **28**, [655]
    post registration, **28**, [654]
    qualifications, recognition of by General
      Osteopathic Council—
      general, **28**, [651]
      supplemental, **28**, [652]
      withdrawal of, **28**, [653]
    standard of proficiency, determination by
      General Osteopathic Council, **28**, [650]

outer space
 activities—
  cessation, power to order, **4(1)**, [336]
  damage by, indemnity as to, **4(1)**, [338]
  directions by Minister, **4(1)**, [336]
  insurance, requirement for, **4(1)**, [333]
  meaning, **4(1)**, [329]
  Treaty on, **4(1)**, [1]
  unlicensed—
   exceptions, **4(1)**, [331]
   offences and penalties, **4(1)**, [340]
   prohibition, **4(1)**, [331]
 application of provisions, **4(1)**, [329]
 conventions relating to, **4(1)**, [1]
 international obligations, direction to comply
  with, **4(1)**, [336]
 licensing of activities—
  conditions of, **4(1)**, [333]
  information to be given, **4(1)**, [333]
  licence—
   application and procedure, **4(1)**, [332]
   conditions contained in, **4(1)**, [333]
   grant of, **4(1)**, [332]
   requirement for, **4(1)**, [331]
   suspension of, **4(1)**, [334]
   termination of, **4(1)**, [334]
   terms of, **4(1)**, [333]
   transfer of, **4(1)**, [334]
   variation of, **4(1)**, [334]
   when not required, **4(1)**, [331]
  licensee's duties, **4(1)**, [333]
  meaning of activities, **4(1)**, [329]
  Minister's powers as to, **4(1)**, [332]
  regulations, **4(1)**, [332]
 meaning, **4(1)**, [341]
 offences relating to—
  generally, **4(1)**, [340]
  justice's warrant, **4(1)**, [337]
  proceedings for, **4(1)**, [340]
 persons affected by provisions, **4(1)**, [330]
 regulations, **4(1)**, [339]
 space objects—
  damage by, **4(1)**, [338]
  register of, **4(1)**, [335]
 summary of provisions, **4(1)**, [1]
 treaties and conventions, **4(1)**, [1]
 UN instruments on, **4(1)**, [1]

overcrowding
 abatement notice, **22**, [291]
 causing or permitting, penalty, **22**, [284]
 default in notifying, **22**, [288]
 determinations as to, **24**, [370]
 enforcement of provisions, **22**, [292]
 entry, obstruction of, **22**, [294]
 exceptions as to, **22**, [281]
 floor area, ascertainment of, **22**, [279]
 houses in multiple occupation—
  general requirements, **24**, [322]
  notice—
   appeal against, **24**, [324]
   contents of, **24**, [321]
   contravention, penalty, **24**, [320]
   general requirements, **24**, [322]

overcrowding—*contd*
 houses in multiple occupation—*contd*
  notice—*contd*
   new residents, requirement as to,
    24, [323]
   revocation or variation, **24**, [325]
   service of, **24**, [320]
 landlord—
  duty to report, **22**, [286]
  meaning, **22**, [296]
  liability for, **22**, [284]
 local housing authority—
  entry, powers of, **22**, [290], [293]
  information, power to require, **22**, [288]
  inspection and report by, **22**, [287]
  obstruction of, **22**, [294]
  rent book, power to inspect, **22**, [289]
 meaning, **22**, [277]
 notice to abate, **22**, [291]
 number permitted—
  children excepted from, **22**, [281]
  entry to determine, **22**, [290], [293]
  exceeding, licence to permit, **22**, [283]
  information required of, **22**, [288]
  rent book to show, **22**, [285]
  tables of, **22**, [279]
  visitors excepted from, **22**, [282]
 occupier, liability of, **22**, [280]
 offences, prosecution of, **22**, [292]
 orders regarding, **24**, [370]
 owner, meaning, **22**, [296]
 room standard, **22**, [278]
 sexes, separation of, **22**, [278]
 space standard, **22**, [279]
 suitable alternative accommodation—
  meaning, **22**, [295]
  offer of, **22**, [281]
 visiting members of family, **22**, [282]

overground wires (London)
 accidents, liability for, **25(1)**, [207]
 byelaws, **25(1)**, [200]
  enforcement, **25(1)**, [201]
 consent to—
  appeal respecting, **25(1)**, [198]
  terms and conditions, **25(1)**, [198]
 demands, recovery of, **25(1)**, [220]
 electricity undertakers, saving for,
  25(1), [210]
 electronic communications system, for,
  25(1), [209]
 enforcement of provisions, **25(1)**, [201]
 exemption of certain, **25(1)**, [212]
 illuminated signs, for, **25(1)**, [216]
 Inns of Court property, over, **25(1)**, [213]
 local authorities—
  byelaws by, **25(1)**, [200]
  expenses of, **25(1)**, [224]
  limit of powers, **25(1)**, [211]
  London County Council, powers of,
   25(1), [202]
  meaning, **25(1)**, [197]
  officers' powers, **25(1)**, [203]
  removal of wires by, **25(1)**, [198], [204]
  recovery of costs, **25(1)**, [205]

overground wires (London)—*contd*
meaning, **25(1)**, [197]
navigation purposes, for, **25(1)**, [215]
notices, service etc, **25(1)**, [217]
owner—
    meaning, **25(1)**, [197]
    notice on, to remove, **25(1)**, [204]
penalties—
    payment, to whom made, **25(1)**, [219]
    recovery of, **25(1)**, [218]
placing—
    consent required, **25(1)**, [198]
    notice of, **25(1)**, [199]
    without consent, penalty, **25(1)**, [198]
Port of London, saving for, **25(1)**, [214]
private rights, saving for, **25(1)**, [208]
proceedings on indictment, **25(1)**, [222]
removal of—
    costs of, **25(1)**, [205]
    court order for, **25(1)**, [204]
    local authority, by, **25(1)**, [198], [204]
safety regulations, **25(1)**, [206]
Secretary of State, inquiries by, **25(1)**, [223]

oversea company
accounts—
    accounting reference period, **8**, 552
    credit and financial institutions to which
        Bank Branches Directive applicable,
        8, 550, 785–91
    delivery of, **8**, 552–3
    financial year, **8**, 552
    penalty for non-compliance, **8**, 553–4
    period allowed for delivery, **8**, 552–3
    preparation, **8**, 551
accounts and reports—
    credit or financial institutions, of,
        8(1), [1128]
    provision for, **8(1)**, [1127]
branch—
    closure, notice of, **8(1)**, [1136]
    registered number, **8(1)**, [1145]
    relocation within UK, **8(1)**, [1137]
branch registration—
    documents to be delivered for, **8**, 546
    duty to register, **8**, 779
    general, **8**, 535, 567
    particulars required, **8**, 779–81
    registered number, allocation of, **8**, 567
    service of documents, **8**, 545
    winding up, **8**, 562–4
charges on property in England and Wales,
    8, 465
charges, registration of, **8(1)**, [1130]
contracts, **8(1)**, [1123]
contracts and execution of documents,
    8, 922–3
documents—
    execution of, **8(1)**, [1123]
    office where to be filed, **8**, 547
    service on, **8**, 545–6
investigation of, **8**, 474–5
liability, regulations providing for, **8(1)**, [1132]
meaning, **8**, 603; **8(1)**, [1122]

oversea company—*contd*
name—
    display of, **8**, 543
    regulation of, **8**, 543–4
offences by, **8**, 548
offences, regulations providing for,
    8(1), [1132]
particulars required of, **8**, 540–3
process, service of, **8**, 545–6
property, situation of, **8**, 560–1
prospectus, country of incorporation,
    statement of, **8**, 543
registered, meaning, **8**, 554
registrar of companies, application of
    provisions relating to, **8(1)**, [1198]
registration—
    altered particulars, of, **8**, 540–5
    change in regime, **8**, 541–2, 783–4
    documents to be delivered for, **8**, 538
    list of directors and officers for, **8**, 538–9
    obligation to state name and other
        particulars, **8**, 542–3
registration of particulars—
    alternative name, **8(1)**, [1126]
    duty of, **8(1)**, [1124]
    name, **8(1)**, [1125]
    registrable presence, notice of cessation of,
        8(1), [1136]
    registrar to whom delivered, **8(1)**, [1135]
    residential addresses, protection from
        disclosure, **8(1)**, [1133]
reports—
    credit and financial institutions to which
        Bank Branches Directive applicable,
        8, 550, 785–91
    delivery of, **8**, 552–3
    preparation of, **8**, 551
returns, **8(1)**, [1131]
service of documents, identification of persons
    authorised to accept, **8(1)**, [1134]
service on, **8**, 545–6
trading disclosures, **8(1)**, [1129]

overseas development
aid, reporting—
    annual reports—
        aid effectiveness, assessment of,
            7(2), [859]
        information in, **7(2)**, [865]
        interpretation, **7(2)**, [862]
        meaning of terms in, **7(2)**, [862]
        Millennium Development Goal 8,
            observations as to, **7(2)**, [860]
        Millennium Development Goals 1 to 7,
            progress towards, **7(2)**, [859]
        policy coherence, observations as to,
            7(2), [860]
        Secretary of State, duty of, **7(2)**, [856]
        United Nations expenditure target,
            progress towards, **7(2)**, [858]
    expenses, **7(2)**, [863]
    statistics, **7(2)**, [857]
    transparency, **7(2)**, [861]
assistance, provision of—
    British overseas territories, for, **7(2)**, [831]

overseas development—*contd*
assistance, provision of—*contd*
development, meaning, **7(2)**, [830]
financial, **7(2)**, [835]; **15(2)**, [330];
19(2), [1061]
humanitarian, **7(2)**, [832]
meaning, **7(2)**, [834]; **15(2)**, [329];
19(2), [1060]
power of, **7(2)**, [830], [833]
terms and conditions, **7(2)**, [836]
terms of, **15(2)**, [331]; **19(2)**, [1062]
third parties, arrangements with,
7(2), [837]
Commonwealth Scholarship Commission. *See*
**Commonwealth Scholarship
Commission**
financial provision, **7(2)**, [840]
general note, **7(2)**, [350]
orders, **7(2)**, [842]
Scottish body, meaning, **7(2)**, [839]
statutory bodies, powers of, **7(2)**, [838], [845]
transitional provisions, **7(2)**, [848]
Welsh body, meaning, **7(2)**, [839]

overseas dividend. *See* **dividend**

overseas investment
summary of provisions, **47**, [1]

overseas leasing
capital allowances, transitional provisions,
43(1), [1224]
change of use of plant or machinery, notice
of, **43(1)**, [679]
connected person, disposal to, **43(1)**, [668]
excess allowances—
connected persons, transactions between,
43(1), [672]
ships, special provision for, **43(1)**, [673]
standard recovery mechanism, **43(1)**, [671]
expenditure, designated period, **43(1)**, [666]
joint lessees—
mitigation of regime, **43(1)**, [676]
notices, **43(1)**, [680]
recovery of allowances, **43(1)**, [677]
meaning, **43(1)**, [665]
normal writing-down allowance, meaning,
43(1), [686]
pool, **43(1)**, [667]
profits chargeable to tax, **43(1)**, [665]
prohibited allowances—
connected persons, transactions between,
43(1), [675]
list of, **43(1)**, [670]
standard recovery mechanism, **43(1)**, [674]
protected, certificate relating to, **43(1)**, [678]
short-term—
meaning, **43(1)**, [681]
qualifying purposes, **43(1)**, [682], [685]
ships and aircraft, **43(1)**, [683]
transport containers, **43(1)**, [684]
writing-down allowances, **43(1)**, [669]

overseas regulatory authority
banking supervisor, as, **19(1)**, [766]

overseas regulatory authority—*contd*
meaning, **19(1)**, [766]
regulatory functions, meaning, **19(1)**, [766]
request for assistance by—
disclosure of information, restrictions on,
19(1), [770]
exceptions, **19(1)**, [771]
information, documents or assistance,
requiring, **19(1)**, [767]
failure to comply, **19(1)**, [769]
Northern Ireland, powers in relation to,
19(1), [772]
offences—
bodies corporate, by, **19(1)**, [774]
jurisdiction, **19(1)**, [775]
partnerships, by, **19(1)**, [774]
procedure, **19(1)**, [775]
prosecutions, **19(1)**, [773]
unincorporated associations by,
19(1), [774]
officer, exercise of powers by, **19(1)**, [768]
powers of Secretary of State, **19(1)**, [766]

overseas securities. *See* **securities**

overseas territories
Air Force Act, application of, **3**, [990]
Army Act, application of, **3**, [718]
Naval Discipline Act, application of, **3**, [1203]

overseers
City of London, **25(1)**, [104]
references to, construction of, **25(1)**, [76],
[147]
transfer of powers from, **25(1)**, [77]

owner
absent and untraced—
compensation, **9**, [23], [27]
notice to treat in case of, **9**, [265], [296]
default in completion by, **9**, [39]
interests when not in occupation, expenses
of, **9**, [226]
meaning, **9**, [4], [136], [207], [416];
17(1), [152], [211]

owner-occupier
displaced, advances to, **21**, [418]
meaning, **21**, [418]; **46**, [414]
planning proposals, interests affected by. *See*
blight notice

Oxford
cathedral. *See under* **cathedral**
Christ Church. *See* **Christ Church, Oxford**
mayor of, liberties of, **15(1)**, [9]
university. *See* **Oxford University**

Oxford, University of. *See also* **universities
and colleges**
advowson, purchase of, **15(1)**, [93]
appointment of constables, **12(1)**, [32], [33]
Bodleian Library, legal deposit library, as,
13, [467]
Chancellor, election of, **15(1)**, [53]

Oxford, University of—*contd*
Christ Church as college of, **15(1)**, [59]
commissioners—
  duties of, **15(1)**, [185]
  election of, **15(1)**, [191]
  establishment of, **15(1)**, [184]
  meetings, notice of, **15(1)**, [191]
  statute applying to, **15(1)**, [186]
  statutes of—
    assessment of college contributions, on, **15(1)**, [187]
    trust, altering, **15(1)**, [187]
  validity of acts, **15(1)**, [191]
Congregation—
  composition of, **15(1)**, [46], [58]
  English, speaking in, **15(1)**, [50]
  Hebdomadal Council, electing members to, **15(1)**, [37], [44]
  provisions, altering, **15(1)**, [58]
  register of members, **15(1)**, [44]
  regulations of, **15(1)**, [47]
  statutes of Hebdomadal Council, promulgating, **15(1)**, [47], [49]–[50]
Convocation—
  powers of, **15(1)**, [52]
  students, receiving at residence of member, **15(1)**, [55]
courts, ceasing jurisdiction, **11(2)**, [381]
Craven Scholarships, status of, **15(1)**, [95]
deeds and obligations, validity of, **15(1)**, [6]
Hebdomadal Council—
  casual vacancies, **15(1)**, [40]
  composition of, **15(1)**, [37]
  non-residence, effect of, **15(1)**, [43]
  professors, eligibility of, **15(1)**, [42]
  provisions, altering, **15(1)**, [58]
  re-election to, **15(1)**, [39]
  regulations on, **15(1)**, [47]
  seats on—
    two, person having, **15(1)**, [37]
    vacating, **15(1)**, [38]
  statutes of, promulgating, **15(1)**, [47], [49]–[50]
  Vice-Chancellor continuing as member, **15(1)**, [41]

Oxford, University of—*contd*
Hebdomadal Council—*contd*
  voting at elections, **15(1)**, [51]
illegal oaths, **15(1)**, [54]
incorporation, **15(1)**, [3]
interpretation of terms, **15(1)**, [62], [106], [146]
land, acquisition of, **15(1)**, [94]
letters patent, **15(1)**, [4]
licensed master, **15(1)**, [56]
matriculation, oath on, **15(1)**, [60]
patents and liberties granted to, **15(1)**, [7]
possessions and privileges, **15(1)**, [5]
private hall, **15(1)**, [56]
professor, meaning, **15(1)**, [106]
professorships—
  election to, mode of, **15(1)**, [97]
  existing, suppression of, **15(1)**, [98]–[99]
  meaning, **15(1)**, [106]
  regulations as to, **15(1)**, [96], [109]
public records in custody of, **18**, [189]
scholarships, variation of trusts of, **15(1)**, [101]
statutes—
  alteration of, **15(1)**, [57], [104]
  Order in Council, approbation by, **15(1)**, [102]
  power to alter, **15(1)**, [103]
  Privy Council, submission to, **15(1)**, [102], [147]
  repeal of, **15(1)**, [104]
  savings, **15(1)**, [105]
  Vinerian Foundation, as to, **15(1)**, [110]
substitution of declaration for oath, by, **18**, [83]
superannuation fund, establishing, **15(1)**, [189]
titles of strangers, etc, saving for, **15(1)**, [8]
trusts. *See* **trusts, university and college**
Vice-Chancellor's Court, regulation of, **15(1)**, [107]

oyster. *See* **shellfish**

P

Pakistan
British ship registered in, **7(2)**, [788]
Commonwealth citizenship, **31**, [186]
Commonwealth, re-admission to, **7(2)**, [786]
existing laws, **7(2)**, [440]
judgments, enforcement of, **7(2)**, [788]
new dominions—
  legislation for, **7(2)**, [437]
  meaning, **7(2)**, [436]
  setting up, effect of, **7(2)**, [438]
Secretary of State, legal proceedings,
  7(2), [439]
visiting forces in, **7(2)**, [788]

palatine court
Public Trustee Act, application of, **48**, 243

Panel on Takeovers and Mergers
amended provisions, **8(1)**, [1042]
annual report, **8(1)**, [1041]
bid documentation rules, failure to comply
  with, **8(1)**, [1031]
Channel Islands, power to extend provisions
  to, **8(1)**, [1043]
co-operation, duty of, **8(1)**, [1028]
directions by, **8(1)**, [1024]
documents, power to require, **8(1)**, [1025]
fees and charges—
  provision for, **8(1)**, [1035]
  recovery of, **8(1)**, [1037]
functions, **8(1)**, [1020]
Hearings Committee, **8(1)**, [1029]
information—
  disclosure, restrictions on, **8(1)**, [1026]
    overseas regulatory bodies, to,
      8(1), [1380]
    specified descriptions, **8(1)**, [1379]
    specified persons, **8(1)**, [1378]
  offence of disclosure, **8(1)**, [1027]
  power to require, **8(1)**, [1025]
  self-incrimination, privilege against,
    8(1), [1040]
Isle of Man, power to extend provisions to,
  8(1), [1043]
levy payable to—
  provision for, **8(1)**, [1036]
  recovery of, **8(1)**, [1037]
liability in damages, exemption from,
  8(1), [1039]
party to proceedings, as, **8(1)**, [1038]
review, decisions subject to, **8(1)**, [1029]
rule-based requirement—
  breach of statutory duty, no action for,
    8(1), [1034]
  enforcement by court, **8(1)**, [1033]

Panel on Takeovers and Mergers—*contd*
rules—
  bid documentation, about, failure to
    comply with, **8(1)**, [1031]
  compensation, requiring payment of,
    8(1), [1032]
  directions, providing for, **8(1)**, [1024]
  enforcement by court, **8(1)**, [1033]
  fees and charges, providing for,
    8(1), [1035]
  interpretation, rulings on, **8(1)**, [1023]
  provisions of, **8(1)**, [1022]
  sanctions, **8(1)**, [1030]
  Takeovers Directive, giving effect to,
    8(1), [1021]
  text, making available, **8(1)**, [1022]
Takeovers Directive, making rules giving effect
  to, **8(1)**, [1021]

Papua New Guinea
British ship registered in, **7(2)**, [740]
Commonwealth citizenship in, **7(2)**, [737]
visiting forces in, **7(2)**, [740]

pardon
warrant, granted by, **12(1)**, [365]

parent
access to child. *See* **child**
adoptive, **6**, [173]
alleged, denial by, **6**, [488]
construction of references to, **6**, [277]
contact with child under care order, **6**, [347]
Crown, saving for persons in service of,
  15(1), [695]
detention by order of court, saving for persons
  in, **15(1)**, [696]
education—
  choices in, local authority's duty to
    increase, **15(2)**, [741]
  duty to secure, **15(1)**, [502]
  wishes on, **15(1)**, [504]
excluded child—
  duty in relation to, **15(2)**, [817]
  notice to parent, **15(2)**, [818]
  reintegration interviews, attendance at,
    15(2), [816]
financial relief order against, **6**, [439]
foster. *See* **foster parents and fostering**
governor, as. *See* **county school**, etc
meaning, **6**, [184], [439]; **15(1)**, [708]
parental responsibilities, rights and duties—
  acquisition by father, **6**, [296], [837]
  agreements between unmarried parents,
    6, [296]
  arrangements between persons, **6**, [294]
  attendance at court, **6**, [24]

parent—*contd*
  parental responsibilities, rights and
      duties—*contd*
    begging by child, for, **6**, [4]
    child employment, furnishing of particulars
        of, **6**, [148]
    construction of references to, **6**, [277]
    division of, **6**, [294]
    education supervision order, superseded
        by, **6**, [445]
    emergency protection order, under,
        6, [362]
    generally, **6**, [278]
    guardian—
      appointment by person having, **6**, [298]
      former powers and duties, **6**, [295]
      vested in, **6**, [298]
    local education authority, power to require
        information, **6**, [148]
    meaning, **6**, [295]
    performance for profit abroad by child, as
        to, **6**, [16]
    residence order, grant of, **6**, [305]
    Scotland, **6**, [571]
    shared, **6**, [294]
    step-parent, acquisition by, **6**, [297]
    unmarried parents, **6**, [294]
  parenting contracts, **15(2)**, [811], [813]
  parenting orders, **15(2)**, [812]–[813]
  step, parental responsibility, acquisition by,
      6, [297]
  unmarried father, as, **6**, [1]

parentage
  blood tests, use in determining—
    consent required for taking, **18**, [213]
    court's power to require, **18**, [212]
    definitions, **18**, [217]
    failure to comply with direction, **18**, [215]
    manner of giving effect to direction,
        18, [214]
    personation, **18**, [216]
    report to court, **18**, [212]
  declaration of—
    application for, **6**, [263], [489]
    Attorney General, powers, **6**, [267]
    child support cases, **6**, [488]
    effect, **6**, [266]
    making of, **6**, [266]
  denial of alleged parent, **6**, [488]
  disputes about, **6**, [488]
  finding of, use in evidence, **18**, [205]
  gamete donors, parental order in favour of,
      6, [488]

parental compensation order
  amount, **6**, [595], [991]
  appeals against, **6**, [597], [991]
  conditions for, **6**, [594], [991]
  subsequent award if damages in civil
      proceedings, effect on, **6**, [598], [991]

parental leave
  employment tribunal, complaint to, **16**, [713]
  entitlement to, **16**, [709]

parental leave—*contd*
  regulations, **16**, [712]
  rights during and after, **16**, [710]
  special cases, **16**, [711]
  unfair dismissal relating to, **16**, [746]

parenting contract
  amended provisions, **6(S)**, 293
  anti-social behaviour, in respect of, **6**, [876]
  criminal conduct, in respect of, **6**, [876]
  exclusion from school, in case of, **6**, [870]
  local authority, entry into by, **6(S)**, 276
  local authority functions, contracting out of,
      6(S), 283
  registered social landlord, entry into by,
      6(S), 276–8
  truancy, in case of, **6**, [870]

parenting order
  amended provisions, **6(S)**, 293
  anti-social behaviour, and, **6**, [1], [877]
  appeals, **6**, [590], [873], [879]
  court, matters taken into account by, **6**, [872],
      [878]
  criminal conduct, in respect of, **6**, [877]
  directions under, **6**, [602]
  discharge, **6**, [589]
  exclusion from school, in case of, **6**, [871]
  generally, **6**, [1]
  implementation, arrangements for, **6**, [588]
  local authority functions, contracting out of,
      6(S), 283
  local authority, application by, **6(S)**, 279–80
    county court proceedings, in, **6(S)**, 281
  making, **6**, [588]–[589]
  meaning, **6**, [588]
  registered social landlord, application by,
      6(S), 280–1
    county court proceedings, in, **6(S)**, 281
  variation, **6**, [589]

parish
  adaptation of references to, **25(1)**, [163]
  alternative styles—
    de-grouping, **25(2)**, [13]
    grouping, **25(2)**, [12]
    groups, **25(2)**, [16]
    meaning, **25(2)**, [22]
    resolution, **25(2)**, [15], [22]
  boundaries, **25(2)**, [238]
  churchwardens—
    references to, **25(1)**, [76]
    transfer of powers from, **25(1)**, [77]
  community governance—
    incidental matters, agreements about,
        26(2), [581]
    interpretation, **26(2)**, [584]
    petition—
      duty to respond to, **26(2)**, [565], [566]
      meaning, **26(2)**, [562]
      power to respond to, **26(2)**, [567]
    regulations, **26(2)**, [579], [580]
    reorganisation, **26(2)**, [568]

parish—*contd*
  community governance—*contd*
    review—
      consequential recommendations,
        26(2), [571], [572], [574]
      duties in undertaking, **26(2)**, [575]
      electoral recommendations, **26(2)**, [577]
      existing parish, recommendations,
        26(2), [570]
      grouping or de-grouping,
        recommendations for, **26(2)**, [573]
      guidance on, **26(2)**, [582]
      meaning, **26(2)**, [561]
      new council, recommendations for,
        26(2), [571]
      new parish, constitution of, **26(2)**, [569]
      outcome, publicising, **26(2)**, [578]
      power of council to undertake,
        26(2), [564]
      recommendation to create parish
        council, **26(2)**, [576]
      recommendations, **26(2)**, [569]–[574]
      retained council, recommendations for,
        26(2), [572]
      terms of reference, **26(2)**, [563]
  divided parishes, list of, **25(2)**, [237]
  existing, review of, **26(2)**, [570]
  grouping of parishes—
    alternative styles, **25(2)**, [12]
    orders, **25(2)**, [11], [14]
    separation from, **25(2)**, [11]
  groups—
    alternative style, **25(2)**, [16]
    de-grouping, alternative style, **25(2)**, [13]
    dissolution of, **25(2)**, [11], [13]
    order, **25(2)**, [14]
  historical summary, **25(1)**, [1]
  insufficient nominations, **15(3)**, [241]
  Local Government Commission for England,
    recommendations of, **26(1)**, [106]
  meaning, **36**, [68]
  name, change of, **25(2)**, [65]
  new—
    amended provisions, **14(S)**, 179–80
    constitution of, **26(2)**, [569]
    postponement, **15(3)**, [238]
  property—
    execution of works, **25(1)**, [154]
    meaning, **25(1)**, [154]
    transfer of, **25(1)**, [162]
  roads, repair or maintenance, **25(1)**, [155]
  small, provisions as to, **25(1)**, [79]
  status of, **25(2)**, [206]
  structure of, **25(1)**, [1]
  town, becoming, **25(2)**, [206]

parish and community council election. *See
also* **local government election**
  insufficient nominations, **15(3)**, [241]
  postponement, **15(3)**, [238]

parish church
  banns of matrimony, publishing, **14**, 1000
  cathedral. *See* **cathedral**
  designation of, **14**, 999–1000

parish church—*contd*
  ecclesiastical offices in, **14**, 1000
  marriage solemnised in, **14**, 1000
  more than one, induction in, **14**, 1063–4
  pastoral order relating to, **14**, 1014
  registers and records, transfer to, **14**, 1000
  sharing agreement, under, **14**, 673–4
  worship and services in, **14**, 1000

parish church cathedral
  Care of Cathedrals Measure 1990, exclusion
    from provisions of, **14**, 1206–7

parish clerk
  appointment and dismissal, **14**, 492

parish council. *See also* **local authority**
  accounts to be kept, **25(2)**, [151]
  acquisition of land by, **25(2)**, [122]
  amenities, public—
    consents and access for, **25(1)**, [519]
    expenses as to, **25(1)**, [520]
    power to provide, **25(1)**, [516]
  appropriation of land by, **25(2)**, [124]
  authentication of instruments, **25(2)**, [18]
  buildings, provision of, **25(2)**, [131]
  byelaws—
    power to make, **25(2)**, [188]
    See further under **local authority**
  capital finance, **26(2)**, [320]
  car-sharing schemes, establishment of,
    26(1), [284]
  chairman, **25(2)**, [19]
    declaration to be made by, **25(2)**, [72]
  clocks, public—
    consents and access for, **25(1)**, [519]
    expenses in connection with, **25(1)**, [520]
    power to provide, **25(1)**, [517]
  community governance review. *See* **parish**
  compulsory acquisition of land on behalf of,
    25(2), [123]
  constitution, **25(2)**, [8], [18], [238]
  councillors—
    appointed, **25(2)**, [21]; **26(2)**, [560]
    casual vacancies, **25(2)**, [78]
    declaration to be made by, **25(2)**, [72]
    election, **25(2)**, [20]
    electoral arrangements, **25(2)**, [246]
    number of, **25(2)**, [20], [240]
    suspension of election, **25(2)**, [240]
  crime prevention, powers, **26(1)**, [287]
  disposal of land by, **25(2)**, [125]
  dissolution—
    alternative style, **25(2)**, [13]
    orders, **25(2)**, [14]
    small parishes, powers as to, **25(2)**, [10]
  documents—
    custody of, **25(2)**, [178]
    deposit of, **25(2)**, [177]
    depositories for, **25(2)**, [179]
    inspection, right of, **25(2)**, [180]
  election of, **25(2)**, [20]
    See councillors *above*
  establishment, **25(2)**, [9]

parish council—*contd*
expenses, **25(2)**, [151]
    contributions by county council,
    25(1), [563]
    defrayment of, **25(1)**, [523]
expenses for traffic calming works,
    contributions to, **36**, [1322]
functions conferred on parish meeting,
    25(2), [109]
grouping parishes under, **25(2)**, [11], [12]
local energy saving measures, powers of,
    17(2), [586]
Local Government Commission for England,
    recommendations of, **26(1)**, [106]
meetings, **25(2)**, [249]
    provisions applied, **25(1)**, [626]
members, temporary appointment, **25(2)**, [80]
minutes, inspection of, **25(2)**, [180]
new, councillors of, **25(2)**, [240]
officers, appointment, **25(2)**, [111]
open space, powers as to, **25(1)**, [522]
parish name, change of, **25(2)**, [65]
parking, provision of. *See* **parking** (places)
powers, **25(2)**, [18]
    additional, **25(1)**, [78]
    transferred to, **25(1)**, [77], [83]
    without reference to county council,
    25(1), [522]
property etc transferred to, **25(1)**, [85]
property, execution of works, **25(1)**, [154]
provisions applied to, **26(2)**, [250]
public health, exercise of powers as to,
    35(1), [118]
public place, lighting of—
    consents and access for, **25(1)**, [519]
    expenses, **25(1)**, [520]
roads, lighting. *See* public place *above*
schoolroom etc, use of, **25(2)**, [132]
seats or shelters in roads—
    consents etc for, **25(1)**, [519]
    expenses, **25(1)**, [520]
    power to provide, **25(1)**, [516]
standards committee for, **26(2)**, [86]
taxi fare concessions, arrangements for,
    26(1), [285]
traffic signs, powers as to, **37**, [245]
transport, investigations concerning,
    26(1), [286]
vice chairman, **25(2)**, [19]
village green, powers as to, **25(2)**, [166]
years of ordinary elections, power to change,
    26(2), [551]

parish (ecclesiastical)
alteration of area—
    burial rights, **14**, 1092–3
    pastoral order, by, **14**, 1013
    pastoral scheme, by, **14**, 982–3
church. *See* **parish church**
churchwardens. *See* **churchwardens**
creation of, **14**, 982–3
dissolution of—
    pastoral scheme, by, **14**, 982–3
    property, vesting of, **14**, 1089–91
    trusts, effect of, **14**, 1089–91

parish (ecclesiastical)—*contd*
electoral roll. *See* **church electoral roll**
enquiry into pastoral situation—
    archdeacon, action by, **14**, 884–5
    breakdown of relationship—
        meaning, **14**, 899
        powers on, **14**, 892–3
    conduct of, **14**, 886
    disability cases, inhibition in, **14**, 891
    incumbent, resignation of, **14**, 886
    institution of, **14**, 885
    provincial tribunal, conducted by, **14**, 886
    report on, **14**, 890
    request for, **14**, 882–3
    Vacation of Benefices Rule Committee,
        14, 898
exercise of ministry outside, **14**, 654
extra-parochial places, incorporation of,
    14, 982–3
funeral, in another, **14**, 1257
library—
    alienable, books not to be, **14**, 58
    catalogue of, **14**, 56
    churchwarden, duty of, **14**, 57
    detained books, action for, **14**, 55–6
    faculty for sale of books, **14**, 639
    incumbent entering into security for,
        14, 55–6
    ordinary, powers of, **14**, 56, 58
    preservation of, **14**, 55
    public business, used for, **14**, 57
    register of books, **14**, 58
    Reigate, proviso for, **14**, 59
    rules and orders, **14**, 58
meaning, **14**, 753, 1073
name, altering—
    pastoral order, by, **14**, 1013
    pastoral scheme, by, **14**, 982–3
new—
    burial rights, **14**, 1092–3
    lands, rights of ownership over, **14**, 170
    parochial church council, representation
        on, **14**, 1091
    parochial scheme, creation by, **14**, 982–3
population, computation of, **14**, 129
public worship, place licensed for, **14**, 1003
reconciliation, code of practice as to, **14**, 881
registers and records. *See* **parochial registers
    and records**
schemes, funded, capital payments, extension
    of period for, **14(S)**, 217

parish meeting. *See also* **parish council**
annual, **25(2)**, [250]
appropriation of land by, **25(2)**, [124]
auditors. *See* **Audit Commission**
authentication of instruments, **25(2)**, [17]
chairman, **25(2)**, [19], [250]
committees of, **25(2)**, [108]
constitution, **25(2)**, [9], [17]
contributions by county council, **25(1)**, [563]
convening, **25(2)**, [250]
documents, deposit of, **25(2)**, [177]
electoral arrangements, **25(2)**, [250]
financial returns by, **25(2)**, [154]

parish meeting—*contd*
functions conferred on, **25(2)**, [109]
minutes—
inspection, **25(2)**, [180]
keeping, **25(2)**, [250]
notice of, **25(2)**, [250]
number of, **25(2)**, [250]
poll, provision for, **25(2)**, [250]
powers of, **25(2)**, [110]
proceedings, **25(2)**, [250]
time for holding, **25(2)**, [250]
trustees of, **25(2)**, [17]
vice-chairman, **25(2)**, [19]
voting at, **25(2)**, [250]

parking
abandoned vehicles. *See* removal *below*
access to premises—
duty of local authority, **37**, [293]
provision of, **37**, [205]
areas. *See* permitted; special *below*
attendants, employment of, **37**, [236]
central reservation, on, by heavy goods
vehicles, prohibition, **37**, [589]
charges—
acceptance of payment, effect of, **37**, [222]
defraud, attempt to, **37**, [221]
designated places. *See under* places
(designated) *below*
devices for payment, **37**, [206], [219], [224]
excess charge—
hired vehicles, in relation to, **37**, [283]
liability for, **37**, [281]
meaning, **37**, [219]
modification of provisions as to,
37, [283]
notice of, **37**, [282]
offence arising from, **37**, [221]
proceedings—
evidence in, **37**, [284]
institution of, **37**, [284]
ownership, presumption and
statements as to, **37**, [281], [331]
statutory statements, **37**, [331], [332]
supplementary provisions, **37**, [285]
failure to pay, **37**, [221]
initial, **37**, [219]
London. *See* London *below*
orders as to, **37**, [206], [219]
parking meters, use of, **37**, [219], [224]
power to make, **37**, [218], [219]
contraventions subject to civil enforcement,
38(2), [377]
cycle tracks, on, **37**, [591]
dangerous, **37**, [270], [592]
designated. *See under* places *below*
devices—
charges, orders as to, **37**, [206]
generally, **37**, [224]
interference with, **37**, [207]
issue, use and surrender of, **37**, [206]
meaning, **37**, [206], [224]
meters, use of, **37**, [219], [223]

parking—*contd*
devices—*contd*
notes, coins or cards—
offences, **37**, [221]
payment by, **37**, [207]
prohibition of use, regulations,
37, [219]
use of, **37**, [221]
offences and proceedings, **37**, [207], [221],
[225]
provision of, **37**, [206], [223]
disabled persons, facilities for, **35(1)**, [288]
documents, mishandling, offences of,
37, [287], [288]
double, prohibition of, **38(2)**, [363]
dropped footways, at, **38(2)**, [364]
facilities generally, local authority duties as
to, **37**, [293]
false statement in obtaining documents,
37, [287]
footways, on, by heavy goods vehicles,
prohibition, **37**, [589]
heavy goods vehicle—
meaning, **37**, [590]
on verge, reservations etc, **37**, [589]
illegal—
immobilisation—
meaning, **37**, [590]
on verge, reservations etc, **37**, [589]
removal of vehicle. *See* removal *below*
immobilisation. *See under* illegal *above*
loading areas—
meaning, **37**, [233]
orders, **37**, [233], [336]
removal of vehicles from, **37**, [276]
London, illegally in, **38(1)**, [279]
London, in—
abandoned vehicles, disposal of,
26(1), [216]
authorisations, false applications for,
26(2), [340]
byelaws as to, **25(2)**, [355]
cabs, **36**, [770]
dropped footways, at, **26(2)**, [341]
footways or verges, on—
offence, as, **25(2)**, [345]
particular vehicles, by, **25(2)**, [345]
permitted, when, **25(2)**, [345]
grass verges, on, **25(2)**, [345]
housing estates, on, **25(2)**, [355]
illegal, immobilisation, **37**, [280]
off-street. *See* off-street (Greater London)
below
release or removal of vehicle—
claim by owner after removal,
26(2), [861]
effect of, **26(2)**, [152]
issue of penalty charge notice on,
26(2), [862]
payment of bond to secure removal,
26(2), [860]
powers of entry, **26(2)**, [157]
unlawful, **26(2)**, [847], [848]
unpaid charges on, **26(2)**, [151]
removal of vehicles, **25(2)**, [510]

parking—*contd*
London, in—*contd*
special areas, meaning, **26(2)**, [150]
street cleansing, removal of vehicles for, **25(2)**, [348]
temporary prohibitions, **26(1)**, [217]
unpaid charges—
appeals, **26(2)**, [154], [868]
charge certificates relating to, **26(2)**, [155]
claim by owner after removal, **26(2)**, [861]
enforcement, **26(2)**, [868]
immobilisation and removal of vehicles, **26(2)**, [857]
interpretation, **26(2)**, [854]
notices, **26(2)**, [156]
ownership details not known, preliminary procedure, **26(2)**, [855]
payment of bond to secure removal, **26(2)**, [860]
preliminary procedure, **26(2)**, [855], [856]
release or removal of vehicle, on, **26(2)**, [151]
removed vehicles and contents, disposal of, **26(2)**, [858]
representations relating to, **26(2)**, [153], [868]
taking possession of vehicle, **26(2)**, [859]
unlawful release of vehicle, on, **26(2)**, [847], [848]
workplace parking levy, **26(1)**, [790]
meters. *See* devices *above*
obstructive, **37**, [270]
offences, **37**, [207]
nuisance—
body corporate, by, **38(2)**, [468]
exposing vehicles for sale on road, **38(2)**, [466]
fixed penalty notices, **38(2)**, [469], [472]
fixed penalty receipts, **38(2)**, [471]
name and address, power to require, **38(2)**, [470]
repairing vehicle on road, **38(2)**, [467]
proceedings, **37**, [207]
off-street—
access to, **37**, [205]
additional powers, **37**, [204]
appeal, rights of, **37**, [323]
buildings, provision of, **37**, [204]
charges for, **37**, [205]
variation, **37**, [209]
control of, **37**, [217], [321]–[325]
controlled areas, designation, **37**, [217]
Greater London—
controlled areas, designation, **37**, [216]
disclosure of information, unlawful, **37**, [216]
licence to operate, **37**, [216]
appeal, right of, **37**, [216], [323]
charges, **37**, [216], [219]
compensation, right to, **37**, [216], [324]

parking—*contd*
off-street—*contd*
Greater London—*contd*
licence to operate—*contd*
revocation or variation, **37**, [216], [322]
public off-street parking place, meaning, **37**, [216]
regulations—
power to make, **37**, [170], [216]
provisions applicable, **37**, [216]
unlicensed operation, **37**, [216], [325]
letting of land for provision by others, **37**, [204]
meaning, **37**, [315]
Orders in Council, by, **37**, [217]
provision and maintenance, **37**, [203], [204]
provisions applicable, **37**, [321], [334]
temporary, **37**, [204]
use of, provisions as to, **37**, [206]
offences, **37**, [207]
proceedings, **37**, [207], [208]
bar to, **37**, [222]
orders as to, power to make, **37**, [204], [206]
places—
See also **lorry area**
acquisition of land for, **37**, [214]
apparatus. *See* devices *above*
bicycle stands and racks—
parish and community councils, provision by, **37**, [229]
provision generally, **37**, [235]
bus or coach station, use as, **37**, [212]
charges for use, **37**, [206], [219]
devices for payment, **37**, [224]
community councils, provision by—
consents to, **37**, [230]–[232]
expenses, **37**, [232]
generally, **37**, [229]
restrictions, **37**, [229]
supplementary provisions, **37**, [232]
designated—
charges—
acceptance as bar to proceedings, **37**, [222]
failure to pay, **37**, [221]
generally, **37**, [219]
method of payment, **37**, [221]
power to make, **37**, [218], [219]
variation, **37**, [220]
classes of persons or vehicles, **37**, [218]
grants towards costs, **37**, [228]
Greater London traffic regulation order inapplicable, **37**, [173]
illegally etc parked vehicles, removal, **37**, [270]
offences relating to, **37**, [221]
parking meters—
inspection, **37**, [219]
use of, **37**, [219], [224]
permits, issue etc, **37**, [218], [219]
regulation of, **37**, [219]
removal of vehicles from, **37**, [223]
revocation, **37**, [223]
suspension of use, temporary, **37**, [223]

parking—*contd*
  places—*contd*
    designation orders—
      charges, power to make, **37**, [218]
      contents, **37**, [219], [226]
      financial provisions, **37**, [227]
      illegally etc parked vehicles, removal,
        37, [270]
      improvement of highway projects,
        37, [227]
      interim, **37**, [218]
      local authorities for purposes of,
        37, [218]
      loss or damage to vehicles, **37**, [218]
      powers, **37**, [218]
    disabled persons, for, misuse by others,
      37, [289]
    exercise of powers, **37**, [213]
    financial provisions, **37**, [215]
    heavy goods vehicles, provision for,
      36, [1134]
    hire, plying for within—
      prohibition, **37**, [207]
        public service vehicles exemption,
          37, [212]
    information, display of, **37**, [208]
    Integrated Transport Executive, provision
      by, **36**, [779]
    London—
      agreements as to provision of,
        25(2), [294]
      charges for use of, **25(1)**, [638]
      off-street, in City, **25(1)**, [880]
      prohibited zones, **26(1)**, [215]
      provision of, **25(1)**, [537]
      regulation of, **25(1)**, [638]
      special, designation, **26(1)**, [215]
    London Regional Transport, by, for cabs,
      36, [770]
    lorry areas, **36**, [1134]
      See also **lorry area**
    meaning, **37**, [203]
    motor cycles, provision for, **37**, [229]
    off-street. *See* off-street *above*
    orders as to—
      matters to be provided for, **37**, [206]
      power to make, **37**, [203]
        See further **traffic regulation**
    parishes, provision by—
      consents to, **37**, [230]–[232]
      expenses, **37**, [232]
      generally, **37**, [229]
      supplementary provisions, **37**, [232]
    Passenger Transport Executive, provision
      by, **36**, [779]
    paying, designation of, **37**, [218]
    provision of, generally, **37**, [203], [206]
    removal of vehicles from. *See* removal *below*
    transitional provisions, **37**, [317], [340]
    underground, nature of, **37**, [203]
    unlicensed, **37**, [325]
  removal of vehicles—
    charges for, **37**, [275]
    disposal after, **37**, [271]

parking—*contd*
  removal of vehicles—*contd*
    owner, right of to recover vehicle or
      proceeds of sale, **37**, [273]
    parking area, from, **37**, [275]
    powers, **37**, [206], [223]
    representations and appeals, **37**, [274]
  roads, use of, for, **37**, [210]
  Royal Parks, in, **37**, [234]
  Secretary of State, reserve powers, **37**, [334]
  special enforcement areas—
    designation, **38(2)**, [362], [386]
    double parking, prohibition, **38(2)**, [363]
    dropped footways, etc, in, **38(2)**, [364]
  unloading areas—
    orders as to, **37**, [233], [336]
    trade or business, for, **37**, [233]
  verges, on, by heavy goods vehicles,
    prohibition, **37**, [589]
  workplace parking levy. *See* **workplace
    parking levy**

parks
  boating pools in, **35(1)**, [266]
  chairs, etc, in, **35(1)**, [68]
  closing, **35(1)**, [56], [265]
  conduct of persons using, regulation of,
    32, [252]
  country. *See* **country park**
  entertainments in, **25(2)**, [147]
  games—
    apparatus for, **35(1)**, [68]
    setting apart for, **35(1)**, [68], [264]
  generally, **32**, [1]
  ice skating in, **35(1)**, [68]
  London. *See* **Greater London**
  management, **35(1)**, [68], [264]
  meaning, **32**, [75]
  National. *See* **National Park**
  offences in, **32**, [11]
  park constable—
    assault on, penalty for, **32**, [12]
    attestation, **32**, [10]
    duties of, **32**, [13]
    meaning, **32**, [9]
    powers and privileges of, **32**, [13]
  pavilions in, **35(1)**, [68]
  pleasure boats in, **35(1)**, [56], [266]
  police constable, powers of, **32**, [14]
  rates, exemption from, **25(2)**, [835]
  reading rooms in, **35(1)**, [68]
  refreshment rooms in, **35(1)**, [68]
  regulations—
    power to make, **32**, [76]
    publication of, **32**, [15]
  rights, saving of, **32**, [16]–[19]
  Royal Botanic Gardens, Kew, provisions
    applying to, **32**, [77]
  Royal Parks—
    trading offences in—
      body corporate, by, **32**, [647]
      meaning, **32**, [645]
      penalties for, **32**, [646]
    property—
      disposal of, **32**, [649]

parks—*contd*
  Royal Parks—*contd*
    trading offences in—*contd*
      property—*contd*
        forfeiture, **32**, [650]
        retention of, **32**, [649]
        seizure of, **32**, [648]
    seats in, **35(1)**, [68]
    skating in, **35(1)**, [68]
    specified, regulation of, **33(2)**, [589]
    sports in, **35(1)**, [68], [99]

Parliament. *See also* **Northern Ireland**
  Act of Union, after, **10**, [56]
  adjournment, **32**, [848]
  armed forces member in, **3**, [1]
  armour, bearing of, **32**, [849]
  assembly, offences relating to, **32**, [895]
  Australia, ending of powers as to, **7(2)**, [768]
  authority of, **32**, [848]
  Bill of Rights, provisions not affecting,
    32(S), Parliament 3
  Bills—
    consolidation, **32**, [848]
    costs, **32**, [848]
    enacting words, **32**, [901]
    local or personal, **32**, [848]
    opposition to, **32**, [848]
    promotion of, **32**, [848]
    provisional orders, confirming—
      power to make, **32**, [848]
      Public Bill not including, **32**, [902]
  Commissioner for Parliamentary Standards—
    annual report, **32(S)**, Parliament 25
    appointment, **32(S)**, Parliament 24
    establishment of office, **32(S)**, Parliament 4
    freedom of information,
      32(S), Parliament 25
    funding, **32(S)**, Parliament 25
    investigations by, **32(S)**, Parliament 9–11
    public records, **32(S)**, Parliament 25
    relevant functions, **32(S)**, Parliament 12
    remuneration, **32(S)**, Parliament 24
    resignation and removal from office,
      32(S), Parliament 24
    status, **32(S)**, Parliament 24
    term of office, **32(S)**, Parliament 24
    terms and conditions, **32(S)**, Parliament 24
  commissions and aids, **10**, [31]–[32]
  courts, jurisdiction of, **32**, [848]
  death of Sovereign, on, **10**, [78]
  delegation of authority, **32**, [848]
  demise of Crown during, **32**, [848], [886]
  demonstration in vicinity of—
    authorisation of, **12(4)**, [129]
    authorisation, without, **12(4)**, [127]
    conditions, **12(4)**, [129]
    designated area, **12(4)**, [133]
    loudspeakers, operation of, **12(4)**, [132]
    notice of, **12(4)**, [128]
    offences, **12(4)**, [127]
    penalties, **12(4)**, [131]
    supplementary directions, **12(4)**, [130]
  dissolution, **32**, [848]
  duration, **32**, [848], [862A]

Parliament—*contd*
  ecclesiastical measures, enactment of,
    32, [848]
  Federation of Malaya, forming part of,
    7(2), [463]
  financial powers, **32**, [848]
  freedom of election, **10**, [40]
  freedom of speech in, **10**, [40]
  frequency of, **10**, [40]
  general note, **32**, [848]
  House of Commons. *See* **House of
    Commons**
  House of Lords. *See* **House of Lords**
  impeachment by, **10**, [50]
  Independent Parliamentary Standards
    Authority—
    accounts, **32(S)**, Parliament 22
    administration and supervision functions,
      separation of, **32(S)**, Parliament 20
    annual report, **32(S)**, Parliament 22
    audit, **32(S)**, Parliament 22
    committees, **32(S)**, Parliament 19
    delegation of functions,
      32(S), Parliament 20–1
    documentary evidence,
      32(S), Parliament 22
    efficiency, **32(S)**, Parliament 19
    establishment of, **32(S)**, Parliament 4
    freedom of information,
      32(S), Parliament 23
    funding, **32(S)**, Parliament 21–2
    members, **32(S)**, Parliament 16–18
    MPs salaries, payment of,
      32(S), Parliament 5
    MPs' allowances scheme—
      claims under, dealing with,
        32(S), Parliament 7
      meaning, **32(S)**, Parliament 5
      payment according to,
        32(S), Parliament 5–6
      preparation or revision of,
        32(S), Parliament 5
    payment functions, contracting out,
      32(S), Parliament 21
    pension functions, contracting out,
      32(S), Parliament 21
    powers, **32(S)**, Parliament 19
    procedure and proceedings,
      32(S), Parliament 19
    public records, **32(S)**, Parliament 23
    registration functions, **32(S)**, Parliament 12
    staff, **32(S)**, Parliament 19–20
    status, **32(S)**, Parliament 19
    summary of provisions, **32(S)**, Parliament 1
    taxation, provision of information and
      guidance as to, **32(S)**, Parliament 7–8
  Independent Parliamentary Standards
    Committee—
    establishment of, **32(S)**, Parliament 4
    members, **32(S)**, Parliament 26
    proceedings, **32(S)**, Parliament 26
    term of office, **32(S)**, Parliament 26
  journals, **32**, [848]
  judicial power, **32**, [848]

Parliament—*contd*
 laying of documents before, **41**, [505]–[508], [516], [721]
   See also **statutory instruments**
 legislation, enactment of, **32**, [848]
 lords and commons, summoning and returning, **31**, [636]
 members—
   allowances claims, providing false or misleading information for, **32(S)**, Parliament 11
   allowances scheme—
     claims under, dealing with, **32(S)**, Parliament 7
     meaning, **32(S)**, Parliament 5
     payment according to, **32(S)**, Parliament 5–6
     preparation or revision of, **32(S)**, Parliament 5
   arrest, freedom from, **32**, [848], [864]
   financial interests, code of conduct, **32(S)**, Parliament 8–9
   generally, **32**, [848]
   jury service, exemption from, **32**, [848]
   privileges, **32**, [848]
   salaries, payment of, **32(S)**, Parliament 5
   speech, freedom of, **32**, [848], [856]–[858]
   taxation, provision of information and guidance as to, **32(S)**, Parliament 7–8
   women, capacity of, **32**, [905]
 Minister, annuity premium, **44(1)**, [432]
 new ordinances, revocation of, **32**, [850]–[854]
 oath, **10**, [433]
   allegiance, of, **32**, [879]
   members, to be taken by, **32**, [879]
   time and manner of taking, **32**, [880]
   voting or sitting without taking, **32**, [881]
 officers and departments, **32**, [848]
 official reports, **32**, [848]
 pension funds, **44(1)**, [428]
   See also **parliamentary pensions**
 printing of proceedings, privilege in, **19(3)**, [268]
 privilege—
   arrest, freedom from, **13**, [2]
   cesser of, **32**, [859]
   Crown debtor, no stay by, process against, **13**, [2]
   individual, **32**, [848]
   limits of, **32**, [848]
   meaning, **32**, [848]
   protection, **19(3)**, [271]
   suits against members, **32**, [863]
 procedure, **32**, [848]
 proceedings—
   evidence concerning, **19(3)**, [337]
   evidence of, **32**, [848]
   petitions, exemption from postage, **34**, [712]
 proclamation, issue of, **32**, [865]–[867]
 prorogation—
   close of session, at, **32**, [884]
   generally, **32**, [848]
   royal proclamation, by, **32**, [883]

Parliament—*contd*
 prorogation—*contd*
   time for summoning during, **32**, [913]
 proroguing by Crown, **10**, [79]–[80]
 retirement annuity premium, **44(1)**, [432]
 returns, **32**, [888]–[889]
 Royal Assent, **32**, [848], [926]
 Scottish members, **10**, [72]–[73], [1396]
 statutory orders, **32**, [848]
 style, **31**, [635]
 style of, **10**, [178]
 subordinate legislation, **32**, [848]
 summoning—
   demise of Crown, effect of, **32**, [964]
   generally, **32**, [848]
   prorogation, during, **32**, [913]
   royal proclamation, by, **32**, [891]
   summons to, obeying, **32**, [855]
   three years, to be held at least once in, **32**, [861]
   William and Mary, Convention, **32**, [860]
   writs, issue once in three years, **32**, [862]

Parliament Square
 byelaws, **26(1)**, [730]
 guidance on, **26(1)**, [731]
 transfer of land and functions, **26(1)**, [729]

Parliamentary Commissioner for Administration
 acting, appointment of, **10**, [544]
 annual report, **10**, [551]
 appointment of, **10**, [541]
 Commission for Local Authorities, as member of, **25(2)**, [307]
 complaints to, **10**, [547]
 Council on Tribunals, member of, **10**, [718]
 Criminal Injuries Compensation Scheme, jurisdiction, **12(2)**, [372]
 ethical standards officer, consultation with, **26(2)**, [107]
 expenses, **10**, [543]
 functions, delegating, **10**, [544]
 generally, **10**, [1]
 Health Service Commissioners, consultations with, **10**, [553]
 Information Commissioner, disclosure of information to, **10**, [554]
 investigations by—
   annual report, **10**, [551]
   Cabinet proceedings, evidence of, **10**, [549]
   contempt, **10**, [550]
   Criminal Injuries Compensation Scheme, of, **10**, [555]
   departmental action, and, **10**, [548]
   departments subject to, **10**, [545], [560]
   disclosure of information, **10**, [549]
   evidence, **10**, [549]
   expenses of complainant, **10**, [548]
   matters not subject to, **10**, [546], [561]
   matters subject to, **10**, [546]
   private, in, **10**, [548]
   procedure, **10**, [548]
   relevant tribunals, **10**, [562]
   report, **10**, [551]

**Parliamentary Commissioner for
Administration**—*contd*
jurisdiction, determining, **10**, [546]
Local Commissioners, collaborative working
with, **25(2)**, [325]
Northern Ireland, application of provisions,
10, [557]
obstruction of, **10**, [550]
officers, appointing, **10**, [544]
Official Secrets Act, proceedings under,
10, [552]
other commissioners, consultation with,
10, [553]; **25(2)**, [324]
pension, **10**, [542], [559]
privileged publication, **10**, [551]
remedy in court of law, priority of, **10**, [546]
salary, **10**, [542]
secrecy of information, **10**, [552]
tenure of office, **10**, [541]
Welsh Administration Ombudsman,
consultations with, **10**, [553], [823], [1178]

parliamentary election
access to documents—
conditions, **15(3)**, [628]
contravention of regulations, **15(3)**, [629]
interpretation, **15(3)**, [630]
relevant officers, **15(3)**, [630]
agent. *See* **election**
ballot box—
provision of, **15(3)**, [204]
sealing, **15(3)**, [204]
ballot paper—
account, **15(3)**, [204]
clear intention on, **15(3)**, [204]
corresponding number list, **15(3)**, [620]
counterfoils, replacement of, **15(3)**, [620]
death of candidate, effect of, **15(3)**, [207]
delivery to voter, dealing with on,
15(3), [204]
design, **15(3)**, [619]
details on, **15(3)**, [204]
directions to voters on, **15(3)**, [207]
form of, **15(3)**, [207]
inspection after poll, order for, **15(3)**, [206]
names on, **15(3)**, [204]
official mark, **15(3)**, [204]
photographs on—
evaluation of pilots, **15(3)**, [622]
pilot schemes, **15(3)**, [621]
revision of electoral provisions,
15(3), [623]
postal—
return of, **15(3)**, [631]
sending out, **15(3)**, [204]
printing, directions on, **15(3)**, [207]
provision of, **15(3)**, [204]
rejected, **15(3)**, [204]
order for inspection of, **15(3)**, [206]
returning officer, decision of, **15(3)**, [204]
review of on election petition, **15(3)**, [204]
sealing up of, **15(3)**, [206]
spoilt, **15(3)**, [204]
tendered, **15(3)**, [204]

parliamentary election—*contd*
candidate—
corrupt or illegal practice, found guilty of,
15(3), [154]
void, election declared, **15(3)**, [155]
death of, **15(3)**, [207], [615]
declaration without consent, **15(3)**, [119]
donations. *See* **election**
employment, absence from, **15(3)**, [119]
home address, withholding from
publication, **15(S)**, Elections 41–3
minimum age, **15(3)**, [608]
more than one constituency, not to stand
in, **15(3)**, [613]
nomination of. *See* nomination *below*
polling and counting agents, appointing,
15(3), [204]
qualifying Commonwealth citizens,
15(3), [609], [655]
withdrawal of, **15(3)**, [203]
Clerk of the Crown—
Crown Office, record of returns in,
15(3), [205]
documents—
delivery to, **15(3)**, [206]
order for production of, **15(3)**, [206]
public inspection of, **15(3)**, [206]
retention of, **15(3)**, [206]
writ—
issuing, **15(3)**, [203]
return to, **15(3)**, [205]
constituencies, **15(3)**, [1],
[254]. *See also* **Boundary Commissions**
contested, declaration of result, **15(3)**, [205]
control of documents after, **15(3)**, [627]
corrupt practices—
avoidance for, **15(3)**, [160]
candidate guilty of. *See* candidate *above*
illegal practice, found guilty on charge of,
15(3), [166]
incapacity—
conviction, on, **15(3)**, [167]
election court, imposed after report of,
15(3), [156]
mitigation, **15(3)**, [169]
remission, **15(3)**, [169]
Scotland, in, **15(3)**, [168]
justice of the peace guilty of, **15(3)**, [157]
legal profession, members guilty of,
15(3), [158]
licensed premises, on, **15(3)**, [159]
persons guilty of, provisions on,
15(3), [155]–[156]
professional person guilty of, **15(3)**, [158]
prosecution and penalties, **15(3)**, [164]
relief, claim for, **15(3)**, [163]
votes struck off for, **15(3)**, [162]
counting, **15(3)**, [204]
deposit—
nomination, on, **15(3)**, [203]
return or forfeit of, **15(3)**, [205]
disclosure of vote, prohibition of, **15(3)**, [204]
disenfranchisement—
mental hospitals, offenders in, **15(3)**, [6]
prison, offenders in, **15(3)**, [5]

parliamentary election—*contd*
  elector—
    convicted person, incapacity of, **15(3)**, [5]
    entitlement to be registered as, **15(3)**, [7]
    one vote only, having, **15(3)**, [3]
    overseas. *See* overseas elector *below*
  Electoral Commission. *See* **Electoral Commission**
  entitlement to vote in, **15(3)**, [3]
  exit polls, prohibitions on publication of, **15(3)**, [66]
  expenses. *See* **election**
  general note, **15(3)**, [1]
  illegal practices—
    avoidance for, **15(3)**, [160]
    candidate guilty of. *See* candidate *above*
    corrupt practice, charge of, **15(3)**, [166]
    incapacity—
      conviction, on, **15(3)**, [167]
      election court, imposed after report of, **15(3)**, [156]
      mitigation, **15(3)**, [169]
      remission, **15(3)**, [169]
    persons guilty of, provisions on, **15(3)**, [155]–[156]
    prosecution and penalties, **15(3)**, [165]
    relief, claim for, **15(3)**, [163]
    votes struck off for, **15(3)**, [162]
  meeting—
    meeting rooms, **15(3)**, [217]
    school premises, in, **15(3)**, [104], [217]
  nomination—
    consent to, **15(3)**, [203]
    deposit on, **15(3)**, [203]
    disqualification of candidate, **15(3)**, [203]
    more than one person standing, **15(3)**, [203]
    one person only standing, **15(3)**, [203]
    paper—
      common names, use of, **15(3)**, [612]
      delivery of, **15(3)**, [203]
      details in, **15(3)**, [203]
      false statements in, **15(3)**, [614]
      form of, **15(3)**, [207]
      place for delivery, **15(3)**, [203]
      registered political party, use of name in, **15(3)**, [203]
      subscription of, **15(3)**, [203]
      validity of, **15(3)**, [203]
    proceedings interrupted by riot, **15(3)**, [203]
    right to attend, **15(3)**, [203]
    statement of, publication of, **15(3)**, [203]
    withdrawal from, **15(3)**, [203]
  Northern Ireland, in. *See* **Northern Ireland**
  notice of, **15(3)**, [203]
  overseas elector—
    declaration, **15(3)**, [232]
    offences, **15(3)**, [236]
    qualification as, **15(3)**, [231]
    registration of, **15(3)**, [232]
  personation, offence of, **15(3)**, [58]
  petition—
    amendment of, **15(3)**, [125]
    appeal, leave for, **15(3)**, [153]

parliamentary election—*contd*
  petition—*contd*
    case, stating, **15(3)**, [148]
    corrupt practice—
      alleging, **15(3)**, [125]
      costs, **15(3)**, [152]
      report on, **15(3)**, [145], [154]
    costs—
      corrupt practice, provisions on, **15(3)**, [152]
      illegal practice, provisions on, **15(3)**, [152]
      neglect or refusal to pay, **15(3)**, [151]
      orders on, **15(3)**, [150]
      security for, **15(3)**, [138]
    election court—
      adjournment, **15(3)**, [126]
      corrupt or illegal practice, finding, **15(3)**, [154]
      meaning, **15(3)**, [126]
      report of, **15(3)**, [145]
    High Court jurisdiction, **15(3)**, [124], [153]
    illegal practice—
      alleging, **15(3)**, [125]
      costs, **15(3)**, [152]
      report on, **15(3)**, [145], [154]
    issue, when at, **15(3)**, [139]
    list of, **15(3)**, [140]
    master as prescribed officer, **15(3)**, [153]
    meaning, **15(3)**, [123], [196]
    no return, complaining of, **15(3)**, [124]
    presentation of, **15(3)**, [124]
    questioning of by, **15(3)**, [123]
    respondent, **15(3)**, [124]
    rules on, **15(3)**, [153]
    security for costs, **15(3)**, [138]
    service of, **15(3)**, [124]
    Speaker of House of Commons, report sent to, **15(3)**, [145]
    special case, hearing of, **15(3)**, [148]
    time for presenting, **15(3)**, [125]
    trial of, **15(3)**, [126]
      corrupt practice, evidence of, **15(3)**, [141]
      determination of, certificate on, **15(3)**, [145]
      equality of votes on, **15(3)**, [141]
      House of Commons shorthand writer attending, **15(3)**, [128]
      judge's expenses, **15(3)**, [127]
      open court, in, **15(3)**, [141]
      place of, **15(3)**, [126]
      proroguing of Parliament, effect of, **15(3)**, [141]
      respondent vacating seat, effect of, **15(3)**, [141]
      undue election, evidence of, **15(3)**, [141]
      witnesses—
        attendance of, **15(3)**, [142]
        examination of, **15(3)**, [142]
        expenses, **15(3)**, [144]
        questions, duty to answer, **15(3)**, [143]

parliamentary election—*contd*
  petition—*contd*
    withdrawal of, **15(3)**, [149]
  political parties. *See* **political parties**
  poll—
    ballot, by, **15(3)**, [204]
    cards—
      details on, **15(3)**, [204]
      imitation, issuing, **15(3)**, [103]
      issue of, **15(3)**, [204]
    close of, procedure on, **15(3)**, [204]
    death of candidate, effect of, **15(3)**, [207]
    notice of, **15(3)**, [204]
    riot, adjournment in case of, **15(3)**, [204]
    schools and public rooms used for,
      15(3), [204]
  polling district—
    alteration of, **15(3)**, [33]
    boundaries of, notice showing, **15(3)**, [33]
    division into, **15(3)**, [33]
    Northern Ireland, in, **15(3)**, [33]
    polling places for, **15(3)**, [33], [607]
    register, adaptation on alteration of,
      15(3), [33]
    review of, **15(3)**, [201], [607]
  polling station, **15(3)**, [204]
  presiding officer, **15(3)**, [204]
  proxy, questions put to, **15(3)**, [204]
  re-count, **15(3)**, [204]
  redistribution of seats. *See* **Boundaries
    Commissions**
  registration, **15(3)**, [208]
  registration officer—
    data controller, as, **15(3)**, [208]
    reference to, construction of, **15(3)**, [220]
    regulations regarding,
      15(3), [208]. *See also* **election**
  regulations, **15(3)**, [195]
  returning officer—
    account, taxation of, **15(3)**, [40]
    England and Wales, in—
      deputy, **15(3)**, [38]
      duties of, **15(3)**, [38]
      person being, **15(3)**, [35]
      sheriff, effect of death of, **15(3)**, [38]
    functions, discharge of, **15(3)**, [38]
    Northern Ireland, in, person being,
      15(3), [36]
    payments by and to, **15(3)**, [39]
    polling station, presiding at, **15(3)**, [204]
    public notice, posting, **15(3)**, [193]
    reference to, construction of, **15(3)**, [220]
    respondent to petition, as, **15(3)**, [124]
    secrecy, declaration of, **15(3)**, [204]
    services and expenses, funding, **15(3)**, [641]
    vote, entitled to, **15(3)**, [37]
    writ, executing, **15(3)**, [37]
  rules for, **15(3)**, [34]
  seats, redistribution of, generally, **15(3)**, [1]
  secrecy—
    notification of requirement of, **15(3)**, [204]
    prohibition of disclosure of vote,
      15(3), [204]
  Speaker's Committee. *See* **Speaker's
    Committee**

parliamentary election—*contd*
  tendered votes, **15(3)**, [626]
  timetable, **15(3)**, [202]
  uncontested, declaration of result,
    15(3), [205]
  vote—
    equality of, procedure on, **15(3)**, [205]
    proxy. *See* **election**
  voter—
    absent. *See* **election**
    blind—
      companion of, declaration by,
        15(3), [207]
      vote for, **15(3)**, [204]
    challenge of, **15(3)**, [204]
    disabilities, with—
      companion of, declaration by,
        15(3), [207]
      vote for, **15(3)**, [204]
    incapacitated, vote for, **15(3)**, [204]
    questions put to, **15(3)**, [204]
  voting procedure, **15(3)**, [204]
  writ—
    certificate endorsed on, **15(3)**, [207]
    Clerk of the Crown, return to,
      15(3), [205]
    direction of, **15(3)**, [207]
    endorsement on, **15(3)**, [207]
    form of, **15(3)**, [207]
    issue of, **15(3)**, [203]
    label of, **15(3)**, [207]
    return of member elected endorsed on,
      15(3), [205]
    returning officer, conveyance to,
      15(3), [203]

parliamentary papers
  absolute privilege,
    19(3), [268]–[271]. *See also* **libel**
  extracts—
    broadcast of, **19(3)**, [314]
    printing of, **19(3)**, [270]

parliamentary pensions
  applicable service, **33(1)**, [194]
  continuation of enactments, **33(1)**, [200]
  financial provisions, **33(1)**, [188]
  Fund—
    continuance of, **33(1)**, [193]
    Exchequer contributions, **33(1)**, [195],
      [209]
    pensions, provision for, **33(1)**, [194]
    Prime Minister and Speaker, participation
      of, **33(1)**, [207]
  increase, provisions for, **33(1)**, [112], [154]
  Lord Chancellor, for, **33(1)**, [153], [206]
  members' contributory scheme, Trustees. *See*
    Fund *above*
  persons ceasing to hold office, grants to,
    33(1), [208]
  Prime Minister, for, **33(1)**, [151], [206]
  regulations—
    power to make, **33(1)**, [194]
    provisions included in, **33(1)**, [199]
  Speaker, for, **33(1)**, [151], [206]

parliamentary pensions—*contd*
summary of provisions, **33**(1), [25]

parliamentary privilege. *See under* **Parliament**

parliamentary proceedings
petitions, exemption from postage, **34**, [712]

parochial church council
accounts of, **14**, 492–3, 706
acts, executing, **14**, 487
advowson, **14**, 1260
allocation of money, powers on, **14**, 492
annual budget, **14**, 492
bishop—
  body corporate, being, **14**, 487
  making representations to, **14**, 492
  rules on measure, making, **14**, 493
casual vacancies, **14**, 748–9
chancel, transfer of liability to repairs to,
  14, 864
church electoral roll—
  acting for, **14**, 1071
  church rate, levying, **14**, 492
  keeping, **14**, 698
  member, as, **14**, 711
  new, informing persons on of, **14**, 701
closed churchyard, maintenance of,
  5(2), [453]
committees, **14**, 766
designated parish church, duties to,
  14, 999–1000
educational schemes, powers on, **14**, 489
enquiry into pastoral situation, notifying,
  14, 889
ex-officio member being elected, **14**, 747
extraordinary meetings of, **14**, 1230
financial statements, **14**(S), 74
functions of, **14**, 486
group ministry, and, **14**, 711
interest in trust, holding, **14**, 633
joint—
  benefice having, **14**, 1170
  generally, **14**, 717, 1091
lay representatives—
  election of, **14**, 706–7
  term of office, **14**, 713
  years of service, limit on, **14**, 714
meaning, **14**, 331
meetings—
  adjournments, **14**, 766
  agenda, **14**, 765
  business of, **14**, 765
  chairman of, **14**, 764–5
  emergency, **14**, 765
  minutes, **14**, 765–6
  notices relating to, **14**, 764
  number of, **14**, 764
  place of, **14**, 765
  power to call, **14**, 764
  quorum, **14**, 765
  requirements as to, **14**, 1141–2
  voting at, **14**, 765
members of, **14**, 711
new parish, representation of, **14**, 1091

parochial church council—*contd*
officers, **14**, 763–4
omission to form, **14**, 751
parish clerk, powers on, **14**, 492
parish with more than one place of worship,
  in, **14**, 714–15
parochial church meeting—
  considering opinion of, **14**, 486
  reporting to, **14**, 706
parsonages board, contributing to expenditure
  of, **14**, 788
patronage—
  duties, **14**, 1141–2, 1146
  information for, **14**, 1140
  joint meeting with bishop, **14**, 1142–3,
    1146
  purchasing. *See* **patronage**
property—
  holding, **14**, 489
  permanent trust, held on, **14**, 490
  power to acquire, **14**, 490
resignation from, **14**, 750
ruins, expenses in connection with, **14**, 1220
service of documents on, **14**, 406
sexton, powers on, **14**, 492
standing committee, **14**, 766
team ministry, and, **14**, 711
term of office, **14**, 713
validity of proceedings, **14**, 766
vesting of powers in, **14**, 487–8

parochial church meeting
annual, to be, **14**, 703–4
auditors to council, appointing, **14**, 706
business of, **14**, 706
chairman of, **14**, 705
clerk in Holy Orders attending, **14**, 703–4
clerk to, **14**, 706
convening, **14**, 704–5
deanery synod, electing representatives to,
  14, 92, 706–7
district church council scheme, voting on,
  14, 714–15
elections—
  churchwardens, of, **14**, 710
  conduct of, **14**, 708–9
  lay representatives, of, **14**, 706–7
  sidesmen, of, **14**, 706–7
  single transferable vote, by, **14**, 709–10
extraordinary, convening, **14**, 721
group council, scheme for, **14**, 720
joint council scheme, to discuss, **14**, 717
notice of, **14**, 757–9
omission to hold, **14**, 751
parochial church council—
  electing laity to, **14**, 706–7
  reports from, **14**, 706
persons entitled to attend, **14**, 703
place of, **14**, 704
postal vote, application for, **14**, 759
procedure, determining, **14**, 706
special—
  convening, **14**, 705, 720–1
  lay representatives, electing, **14**, 706
team council, scheme for, **14**, 718–19

parochial fees. *See* **ecclesiastical fees**

parochial registers and records
  bishop, deputy performing functions of,
    14, 949
  care of, **14**, 939–40
  cupboard to be kept in, **14**, 952–3
  diocesan record office, deposit of in, **14**, 942
    limited period, for, **14**, 944
    order for, **14**, 940–1
    parochial custody, return to, **14**, 942
    requirement of, **14**, 938–9
  dissolution of parish, on, **14**, 946
  guild church, of, **14**, 465–6
  inspection of, **14**, 936–7, 1258
  list of, **14**, 937
  making available for research, etc **14**, 944–5
  meaning, **14**, 950
  notices and orders, service of, **14**, 950
  old register books, closure of, **14**, 937
  parish church, transfer to, **14**, 1000
  report on, **14**, 936
  search in, permitting, **14**, 946–8
  summary of provisions, **36**, [1]
  unauthorised person, in possession of,
    14, 948–9

parsonage. *See also* **house of residence**
  additions and alterations, **14**, 790
  amended provisions, **14(S)**, 79, 99–101
  board. *See* **parsonages board**
  conveyance of house and land for,
    authorisation of, **14**, 199–200
  diocesan surveyor—
    inspection by, **14**, 777
    reports by, **14**, 777–8
  division of, **14**, 383–4
  dwelling-house deemed to be, **14**, 861
  easements over land, vesting of, **14**, 848
  house ceasing to be, **14**, 784
  housing grants, **23**, [608]
  improvements to, **14**, 383–4
  incumbent, obligations and powers of,
    14, 783
  inspection—
    diocesan surveyor, by, **14**, 777
    interim, **14**, 780
    powers of entry, **14**, 781
    scheme for, **14**, 781
  insurance of, **14**, 782
  land—
    diocesan board of finance, transfer to,
      14, 860–1
    meaning, **14**, 866
    sequestrator, let by, **14**, 863
  letting, prohibition of, **14**, 858
  meaning, **14**, 794, 866
  new, erecting or purchasing, **14**, 382–3
  outbuilding, demolishing, **14**, 779
  part let by incumbent—
    particulars, furnishing, **14**, 859
    prohibited, **14**, 858
    rent, paying to diocesan board of finance,
      14, 858–9
  pastoral order relating to, **14**, 1014

parsonage—*contd*
  pastoral scheme providing for, **14**, 1005–6
  power of sale, **14**, 379–81
  power to purchase, **14**, 431
  repair—
    appurtenance, of, **14**, 781
    charity, by, **14**, 791
    diocesan surveyor's report, in, **14**, 777–9
    entry to carry out, **14**, 781
    interim report, after, **14**, 780
    meaning, **14**, 776
    notices, **14**, 792
    party wall, to, **14**, 781
    powers of entry, **14**, 781
    sale or exchange of, **14**, 861
    standard of, **14**, 776
    successor to incumbent, right to have,
      14, 43
    trees, felling, **14**, 789
    vacancy, during, **14**, 792

parsonages board
  annual estimates of expenditure, **14**, 788
  annual report and accounts, **14**, 775
  appointment of, **14**, 774–5
  body corporate, as, **14**, 775
  buildings in diocese, authorisation to repair,
    etc, **14**, 785
  Church Commissioners advising, **14**, 791
  diocesan dilapidations board, transfer of
    functions of, **14**, 793, 798–9
  functions, extending, **14**, 785
  insurance, responsibility for, **14**, 782
  loan, defraying payments on, **14**, 786
  members of, **14**, 755
  parsonages fund, opening. *See* **parsonages
    fund**
  property, being informed of matters
    affecting, **14**, 791
  rates, rents, etc., paying, **14**, 786
  residence not being parsonage house,
    repairing, **14**, 785

parsonages fund
  charge of works on, **14**, 785
  opening of, **14**, 786
  payments into, **14**, 788
  payments out of, **14**, 786
  repair account, etc., payment from, **14**, 787
  reserve, **14**, 787

parties under disability
  sale by agreement by. *See* **acquisition of
    land**

partition of land
  instrument effecting, stamp duty, **41**, [214],
    [262]

partner
  connected person, as, **44(1)**, [621]
  immediate tenant, of, goods not privileged
    from distress for rent, **13**, [1202]
  limited, relief, restriction on **44(1)**, [93]

partnership

accountants, of, **8**, 578–81

accounts, incorrect, **42**, [225], [226]

adjustment income, **44(3)**, [877]

aggregates levy, responsibility for, **43(2)**, [22]

agreement—

  imposed terms, **32**, [1010]

  interests and duties of parties in, **32**, [1033]

anti-avoidance provisions, **43(S)**, 1200–1

assessment, **44(3)**, [865]

associate, meaning, **8(1)**, [1338]

authorised person, as, **19(2)**, [32]

bank administration provisions applying, **19(S)**, Financial 219

bank insolvency provisions applying, **19(S)**, Financial 186

banking—

  accounts and reports provisions, application of, **8(1)**, [548]

  meaning, **8(1)**, [548]

business associates, meaning, **21**, [710]

business name. *See* **business name**

Business Names Act, application of, **48**, 94

business tenancy, holding, **21**, [205]

capital allowances—

  changes—

    application of provisions, **43(1)**, [1194]

    effect of, **43(1)**, [1195]

capital contribution, payments in exchange for, **43(S)**, 1200

capital gains tax on, **42**, [1143]

chargeable gains, information on, **42**, [107]

civil, provision for taxation, **43(2)**, [645]

Class 4 contributions, payment of, **40(1)**, [462]

common law rules, saving for, **32**, [1055]

company auditor, appointment as, **8**, 877

company, involving—

  profits and losses, computing, **44(1)**, [90]

  relief, transfer of, **44(1)**, [92]

company tax return, information in, **43(1)**, [394]

continuance after fixed term, **32**, [1036]

control, meaning, **43(1)**, [1213]

definition, **32**, [1011]

disability discrimination by—

  adjustments, duty to make, **7(1)**, [302]

  harassment, **7(1)**, [301]

  limited liability partnership, **7(1)**, [303]

  limited partnership, **7(1)**, [303]

  proposed partnership, **7(1)**, [303]

  unlawful, **7(1)**, [301]

dissolution—

  application of property after, **32**, [1048]

  bankruptcy, by, **32**, [1042]

  charge of property, on, **32**, [1042]

  court, by, **32**, [1044]

  death of partner on, **32**, [1042]

  debt, outgoing or deceased partner's share as, **32**, [1052]

  distribution of assets on, **32**, [1053]

  expiration of term, by, **32**, [1041]

  fraud or misrepresentation, for, rights on, **32**, [1050]

  generally, **32**, [1010]

partnership—*contd*

dissolution—*contd*

  illegality, on, **32**, [1043]

  notice, by, **32**, [1041]

  notification of, **32**, [1046]

  outgoing partner, rights of, **32**, [1051]

  premium, repayment of, **32**, [1049]

  winding up affairs, authority of partners for, **32**, [1047]

disturbance to business by compulsory acquisition where partners over sixty, **9**, [345]

double taxation agreements, **44(3)**, [875]

equity rules, saving for, **32**, [1055]

estate agency work by, prohibition, **21**, [682]

excise licence for, **13**, [700]

existence of, rules for, **32**, [1012]

failure to make return, penalties for, **43(S)**, 1743

farming and property income, **44(3)**, [876]

film, interest relief, **43(S)**, 67–9

firm—

  acts on behalf of, binding nature of, **32**, [1016]

  change in constitution, dealings after, **32**, [1045]

  guaranty, revocation on change in, **32**, [1028]

  meaning, **32**, [1014]

  name, **32**, [1014]

  partner—

    competing with, **32**, [1039]

    power to bind, **32**, [1015]

    wrongs, liability for, **32**, [1020], [1022]

firms, reference to, **44(3)**, [864]

foreign element, with, **44(3)**, [876]

foreign, UK residents in, **43(S)**, 884

gangmasters, application of provisions on, **1(2)**, [720]

illegality of, **32**, [1043]

insolvent—

  insolvency provisions, application, **4(2)**, [506]

  order against, **4(2)**, [205]

leasing, provisions applying, **43(S)**, 78–80

legality of, **32**, [1010]

limited—

  changes in, registration of, **32**, [1064]

  constitution of, **32**, [1059]

  contribution of partner, restriction on withdrawal, **32**, [1059]

  dissolution of, **32**, [1061]

  Gazette, advertisement of arrangements in, **32**, [1065]

  generally, **32**, [1010]

  law applying to, **32**, [1061]

  liability. *See* limited liability *below*

  partner, powers of, **32**, [1061]

  register, keeping, **32**, [1067]

  registrar, **32**, [1068]

  registration—

    certificate of, **32**, [1066]

    changes, of, **32**, [1064]

    filing of statements, **32**, [1066]

    means of, **32**, [1063]

partnership—*contd*
 limited—*contd*
  registration—*contd*
   particulars, statement containing,
    32, [1063]
   requirement of, **32**, [1060]
   statements, inspection of, **32**, [1069]
  rules, power to make, **32**, [1070]
 limited liability—
  capital gains tax on, **42**, [1144]
  cessation of trade by, **42**, [1285], [1297]
  company law, application of, **32**, [1082]
  ex-members, **32**, [1077]
  generally, **32**, [1010]
  incorporation—
   document, **32**, [1072]
   registration, **32**, [1073]
  inheritance tax, **42**, [810]
  insolvency, **32**, [1081]
  meaning, **32**, [1071]
  members—
   agents, as, **32**, [1076]
   bankrupt, **32**, [1077]
   changes in, registration of, **32**, [1079]
   deceased, **32**, [1077]
   designated, **32**, [1078]
   ex-members, **32**, [1077]
   generally, **32**, [1074]
   relationship of, **32**, [1075]
  names, **32**, [1087]
  profits, taxation of, **32**, [1010]
  registered offices—
   change of, **32**, [1088]
   situation of, **32**, [1088]
  rights of third parties against insurers on
   bankruptcy, **4(2)**, [46]
  stamp duty, **32**, [1080]
  termination, **32**, [1010]
  winding up, **32**, [1081]
 limited liability partnership. *See* **limited
  liability partnership**
 limited, number of members, **8**, 581
 loan to—
  insolvency, effect of, **32**, [1013]
  making of, **32**, [1013]
 meaning, **32**, [1010], [1011]
 medical, **32**, [1010]
 member, bankruptcy of, **4(2)**, [334]
 members—
  limitation of, **8**, 578–81
  more than 20, prohibition, **8**, 578–81
 money—
  misapplication of, **32**, [1021]
  property bought with, **32**, [1031]
 nature of, **32**, [1010]
 non-active, trade loss relief, **43(S)**, 887
 non-resident partners, **43(1)**, [153];
  44(1), [91]
 offences by, **8**, 890
 officer in default, application of provisions,
  8(1), [1201]
 partner—
  accounts, duty to render, **32**, [1037]
  acts, bound by, **32**, [1016]
  admissions made by, **32**, [1025]

partnership—*contd*
 partner—*contd*
  allocation of profits and losses between,
   44(3), [867]
  assignment of share by, **32**, [1040]
  bankruptcy of, **32**, [1042]
  capital gains relief, limit on, **43(S)**, 595–6
   contributions, exclusion of amounts by
    way of, **43(S)**, 596–7
  competition with firm, **32**, [1039]
  credit of firm, using, **32**, [1017]
  death of, **32**, [1042]
  deceased, use of name, **32**, [1024]
  expulsion of, **32**, [1034]
  general, **32**, [1060]
  interests and duties, agreement on,
   32, [1033]
  liability of, **32**, [1010], [1019]
   incoming and outgoing, **32**, [1027]
   joint and several, **32**, [1022]
   person representing himself as,
    32, [1024]
  loss relief—
   chargeable amount, computing,
    43(2), [631]
   excess, recovery of, **43(2)**, [630]
   transitional provision, **43(2)**, [633]
  notice to, effect of, **32**, [1026]
  notional business, carrying on,
   44(3), [871]–[873]
  notional trade, carrying on,
   44(3), [869]–[870]
  power to bind firm, **32**, [1015]
  private profits, accounting for, **32**, [1038]
  relevant loss, meaning, **43(2)**, [632]
  remittance basis applying, **44(3)**, [874]
  restrictions on interest relief, removal of,
   43(2), [629]
  sideways relief, limit on, **43(S)**, 595–6
   contributions, exclusion of amounts by
    way of, **43(S)**, 596–7
 partners' names, display of, **48**, 97
 patent rights, sale of, **44(1)**, [378]
  later cessation of trade, **44(3)**, [879]
  partnership changes, effect of, **44(3)**, [878]
 permanent establishment, **44(1)**, [91]
 professional, **32**, [1010]
 profits, taxation of, **32**, [1010]
 profits or losses—
  allocation between partners, **44(3)**, [867]
  calculation of, **44(3)**, [866]
  other income or losses, firm with,
   44(3), [868]
 property—
  dissolution, application on, **32**, [1048]
  misapplication of, **32**, [1021]
  ownership of, **32**, [1030]
  partner's judgment debt, charge for,
   32, [1032]
 property-investment partnerships, transfer of
  interest in—
   elections in respect of, **43(S)**, 1262
   transitional provision, **43(S)**, 1263

Enquiry Bureau   hsieb@lexisnexis.co.uk

partnership—*contd*
property-investment, stamp duty land tax relief on transfers of interest in, **43(S)**, 929,1260–1
property of partner, using, **43(1)**, [843]
qualifying activities carried out in, **43(1)**, [842]
racial discrimination by, **7(1)**, [137]
registration as company, **8**, 578–9
relationship between, **32**, [1010]
relationships not being, **32**, [1011]
relevant accounting period, **44(1)**, [92]
representations of, **32**, [1025]
restriction of power to bind, **32**, [1018]
retirement, **32**, [1035]
Scottish—
  bank administration provisions applying, **19(S)**, Financial 220
  bank insolvency provisions applying, **19(S)**, Financial 186
  property misdescription offence, **23**, [63]
sex discrimination by, **7(1)**, [49], [116]
shares, change of, **43(S)**, 1201
solicitors, of, **8**, 578–81
stamp duty land tax, amended provisions, **41**, [473]
statement—
  amendment where loss of tax discovered, **42**, [154]
  tax return, in, **42**, [109]
statutory auditor, offences relating to, **8(1)**, [1333]
stockbrokers, of, **8**, 578–81
tax return—
  amendment of, **43(S)**, 571
  commencement of amended provisions, **43(S)**, 573
  company as partner, where, **43(S)**, 570
  contents of, **42**, [108]
  different Cases of Schedule D, choice between, **42**, [114]
  enquiry into—
    amendment by taxpayer during, **42**, [113]
    completion of, **42**, [149]
    notice of, **42**, [112]
    referral of questions during—
      determination, effect of, **42**, [147]
      effect of, **42**, [146]
      notice of, **42**, [143]
      regulations, **42**, [145]
      withdrawal of notice, **42**, [144]
  error in, **43(S)**, 572
  error or mistake in, **42**, [162]
  failure to make, **42**, [223]
    penalty for, **43(S)**, 572
  HM Revenue and Customs, correction by, **42**, [111]
  incorrect, making, **42**, [225], [226]
  partnership statement in, **42**, [109]
  requirement of, **42**, [108]
  taxpayer, amendment by, **42**, [110]
  time for delivery of, **43(S)**, 570
termination, **32**, [1010]

partnership—*contd*
tonnage tax provisions, application of, **43(1)**, [536]
trade profits, **44(3)**, [163]
treatment of, **44(1)**, [89]
trust property, improper employment of, **32**, [1023]
value added tax, registration for, **50**, [64]
variation of terms, **32**, [1029]
winding-up, **32**, [1010]

partnership company
Table G, **8**, 112

party wall or structure
adjacent excavation and construction, **35(2)**, [251]
compensation, **35(2)**, [252]
Crown application, **35(2)**, [264]
disputes, resolution of, appointment of surveyors for, **35(2)**, [255]
easements, **35(2)**, [254]
entry, rights of, **35(2)**, [253]
expenses—
  account for work carried out, **35(2)**, [258]
  defrayment for work carried out, **35(2)**, [256]
  security for, **35(2)**, [257]
  settlement of account, **35(2)**, [259]
held in common, application to court, **20**, [658]
Inns of Court, exception in case of, **35(2)**, [263]
Law of Property Act, transitional provisions, **20**, [812]
meaning, **35(2)**, [265]
new building on line of junction, **35(2)**, [246]
offences, **35(2)**, [261]
party structure notices—
  counter notices, **35(2)**, [249]
  disputes, **35(2)**, [250]
  service of, **35(2)**, [248]
repair of, rights of owner, **35(2)**, [247]
service of notices, **35(2)**, [260]
summary of provisions, **35(1)**, [1]
sums, recovery of, **35(2)**, [262]
surveyors, appointment of, for resolution of disputes, **35(2)**, [255]

passage
access to building, giving, paving and drainage of, **35(1)**, [606]
common, used in, sweeping and cleansing, **35(1)**, [130]

passenger car
meaning, **37**, [583]
seat-belts, wearing by children, **37**, [583]

passenger-carrying vehicles
licensing of drivers. *See* **driving licences**

passenger transport
London, in. *See* **London passenger transport services**

passenger transport—*contd*
road, generally. *See* **passenger transport services**

passenger transport areas
agreements with other areas, **36**, [777]
Authority. *See* **Passenger Transport Authority**
designation of, **36**, [777]
Director General, appointment, **36**, [777]
Executive. *See* **Passenger Transport Executive**
interconnected bodies corporate, disqualification of persons connected with, **36**, [778]
Minister, consents of and directions by, **36**, [789]
railways, interpretation of provisions as to, **36**, [790]
regulations and orders, **36**, [788]
renamed. *See now* **integrated transport area**

Passenger Transport Authority
annual reports, **36**, [786]
approval by, of acts by Executive, **36**, [779], [784]
companies owned by—
bus undertaking, transfer to, **37**, [397]
division of undertakings, **37**, [399]
employee benefits, protection on transfer of undertakings, **37**, [400]
See also **passenger transport services** (public transport companies)
competition, bar on inhibition of, **37**, [417]
duty, **36**, [778]
establishment, **36**, [777]
Executives, incorporation of, in, **37**, [422], [423]
expenditure, when defrayed by Executive, **37**, [464]
functions, **36**, [778], [784]; **37**, [464]
grants to Executive by, **36**, [782]
loans to Executive by, **36**, [781]
order, matters dealt with by, **36**, [880]
policies, formulation of, **36**, [778]
renamed
38(2), [682]. *See now* **Integrated Transport Authority**
stamp duty exemption, **36**, [872]
Strathclyde, **36**, [777]
travel concession scheme, **37**, [430], [475]

Passenger Transport Executive
accounts, **36**, [783]
activities of, tenders for carrying on, **37**, [155], [419]
agency agreements, **36**, [779]; **37**, [419]
agreements, power to enter into, **36**, [778]
annual reports, **36**, [786]
approval by Authority of acts by, **36**, [779], [784]
audit of accounts, **26(1)**, [347]
borrowing powers, **36**, [781]; **37**, [464]

Passenger Transport Executive—*contd*
bus operating powers—
co-operation requirement, exclusion, **37**, [398]
employee benefits, protection on transfer, **37**, [400]
transfer, **37**, [397], [399]
transfer of undertakings, **37**, [397], [460]
bus stations, provision and maintenance, **37**, [418]
capital gains tax liability, **37**, [461]
companies related to, auditors, **26(1)**, [348]
company—
division of undertakings, **37**, [399]
formation for transfer of bus undertakings to, **37**, [397]
shares in, transfer of, **37**, [397]
transfer schemes, **37**, [399], [460]
See also **passenger transport services** (public transport companies)
compulsory purchase of land by, **36**, [779]
consents and directions by Minister, **36**, [789]
constitution, **36**, [879]
control over, **36**, [785]
corporation tax liability, **37**, [461]
duty, **36**, [778]
duty to advise Secretary of State, **38(2)**, [436]
employees, negotiation and consultation machinery, **36**, [865]
estimates of income and expenditure, **36**, [784]
ferries, acquisition of, **36**, [779]
financial duty of, **36**, [780]; **37**, [152]
franchise agreements, **38(2)**, [402]
functions, **36**, [778]
incorporation in Authorities, **37**, [422], [423]
general powers, **36**, [779]
grants by Authority to, **36**, [782]
grants to, **25(2)**, [333]
information, direction to publish, **25(2)**, [430]
land, powers as to, **36**, [779]
loans to, **36**, [781]
management organisation, review of, **37**, [154]
members, **36**, [879]
disqualification, **36**, [778]
order, matters dealt with by, **36**, [880]
orders relating to, power to make, **36**, [879]
organisation of undertaking, review of, **36**, [785]
powers, **36**, [779]
revival of, **38(2)**, [678]
public sector co-operation, exclusion of requirement, **37**, [398]
railway functions, **38(2)**, [402]
railway passenger services—
competent authority for, **38(1)**, [471]
special duties with respect to, **36**, [787]; **37**, [395]
Railways Board, agreements with, **37**, [395]
repeals and savings relating to, **38(2)**, [403]
review of activities of, **36**, [785]
stamp duty exemption, **36**, [872]
Strathcldye, **36**, [777]

Passenger Transport Executive—*contd*
subsidiaries, control over, **36**, [779]
subsidiary activities—
  generally, **36**, [779]
  improper conduct, prevention, **36**, [786]
subsidised services, agreements as to. *See*
  passenger transport services
Town and Country Planning Acts, application
  of, **36**, [866]
travel concession schemes. *See* **passenger
transport services**

passenger transport services. *See also* **bus
services; public service vehicles**
charges. *See* fares and charges *below*
competition, non-inhibition, **37**, [401], [417]
concessionary travel. *See* travel concession
  below
constable's powers, exercise by authorised
  persons, **37**, [781], [785]
consultations as to, requirement, **37**, [402]
co-operation between authorities, **37**, [425]
councils. *See* local authorities *below*
disabled persons—
  Advisory Committee. *See* **Disabled
  Persons Transport Advisory
  Committee**
  meaning, **38(2)**, [136]
  needs of, **36**, [778]; **37**, [401]
  persons providing facilities for, grants for,
    37, [442]
  travel concession, **37**, [430]
driver's hours. *See* **driver's hours**
driver's licences. *See* **driving licence**
elderly persons—
  meaning, **38(2)**, [136]
  needs of, **36**, [778]; **37**, [401]
  travel concession, **37**, [430]; **38(2)**, [229]
expenditure on, generally, **37**, [425]
fares and charges—
  approval of, **36**, [784]; **37**, [153]
  reduction or waiver, **36**, [779], [784]
form of transport, **36**, [779]
goods, carriage of, **36**, [779]
grants to persons providing facilities or
  services, **37**, [442]
information, requirement to display,
  38(2), [681]
interpretation of provisions, **37**, [445]
light passenger vehicle—
  EC certificate of conformity—
    failure to hold, **37**, [644]
    meaning, **37**, [670]
  meaning, **37**, [670]
local authorities, abolition of control over,
  36, [791]
local authorities, certain—
  bus undertakings—
    companies to run—
      formation, **37**, [405]
      orders as to joint undertakings,
        37, [407], [408]
      schemes, **37**, [406], [460]
    exclusion of powers, **37**, [404]
    interpretation of references, **37**, [424]

passenger transport services—*contd*
local authorities, certain—*contd*
  bus undertakings—*contd*
    joint undertakings, **37**, [405], [407]
    small, running of, **37**, [409]
  co-operation in provision of services,
    37, [425]
  functions, **37**, [401]
  Transport for London, co-operation
    between, **37**, [403]
local education authorities, co-operation in
  provision of, **37**, [425]
local services—
  abolition of road service licensing,
    37, [352], [472]
  compensation, **38(2)**, [143]
  information, power to obtain, **38(2)**, [132]
  London. *See* London local service *below*
  meaning, **37**, [353]
  operator, failure or misconduct of,
    37, [375]
  penalties, **38(2)**, [143]
  PSV licence requirement, **37**, [354], [475]
  registration—
    application for, **37**, [354], [475]
      quality contracts scheme, where in
        force, **37**, [356]
      restrictions in force, where, **37**, [355]
    cancellation, **37**, [375]
    not operating in accordance with,
      powers where, **37**, [377], [378]
    records of, **37**, [457]
    regulations as to, **37**, [354]
    requirement, **37**, [354], [475]
  sanctions, **38(2)**, [143]
  taxis, use in provision of, **37**, [362]
  traffic regulation conditions—
    appeals against, **37**, [359]
    application of, to, **37**, [357]
    attachment to licence, **37**, [358]
    enforcement of, **37**, [358]
  transitional provisions, **37**, [475]
London local service—
  appeals arising, **37**, [388], [389]
  excursions or tours, **37**, [385]
  licences—
    abolition of road service licensing,
      37, [352], [472]
    appeals in matters arising, **37**, [388],
      [389]
    application for, **37**, [383]
    conditions attached to, **37**, [384]
    duration, **37**, [387]
    excursions or tours, **37**, [385]
    grant of, **37**, [382], [383]
    record of, **37**, [457]
    revocation, **37**, [386]
    suspension, **37**, [386]
  meaning, **37**, [381]
  PSV licence requirement, **37**, [382]
  repeal of provisions as to, powers, **37**, [392]
  statutory provisions applicable, **37**, [390]
  See also **bus services**
London service undertakings, transfer of,
  36, [611]

passenger transport services—*contd*
  Minister, consents of and directions by,
    36, [789]
  policies, consultation and publicity, **37**, [402]
  powers as to, generally. *See* **Passenger
  Transport Executive**
  provision of—
    co-operation between authorities, **37**, [425]
    generally, **36**, [778]
    integrated transport areas, areas other than
      in, **37**, [401]
    passenger transport areas, **36**, [778]
      areas other than in, **37**, [401]
  public, meaning, **37**, [401]
  public transport companies—
    accounts and audit, **37**, [414]
    activities, control over, **37**, [411]
    compensation for losses, **37**, [421]
    constitution, control over, **37**, [411]
    controlling authorities, **37**, [410]
    directors—
      control over, **37**, [411]
      disabilities, **37**, [412]
      disqualifications, **37**, [412]
    division of undertakings, **37**, [399]
    employee benefits, protection on transfer of
      undertakings, **37**, [400]
    employment, compensation for loss of,
      37, [421]
    financial backing for, **37**, [416]
    formation, **37**, [397], [405]
    interpretation of references, **37**, [424]
    investment powers, **37**, [413]
    loans to, **37**, [416]
    professional and technical services for,
      provision of, **37**, [415]
    shares in, **37**, [413]
    transfer of bus undertakings to, **37**, [397],
      [406]
  Public Transport Users' Committee. *See*
  **Public Transport Users Committee for
  England**
  publicity, **37**, [402]
  railway passenger services, special duty with
    respect to, **36**, [787]
  regulations and orders, **36**, [788]; **38(2)**, [45]
  road service licensing, abolition, **37**, [352],
    [472]
  rural services in Scotland, grants for, **37**, [444]
  stopping place, meaning, **37**, [468]
  subsidies, provision of, **36**, [778]; **37**, [425]
  subsidised—
    agreements providing, **36**, [778]
      by tender, **37**, [426]
      power to enter into, **37**, [401]
    exercise and performance of functions as
      to, **37**, [429]
    securing services in other areas,
      38(2), [679]
    tenders for—
      acceptance, requirements for, **37**, [426]
      exceptions from requirements, **37**, [428]
      issue of invitations, **37**, [426]
      obligation to invite, **37**, [426]
      period to be specified, **37**, [427]

passenger transport services—*contd*
  subsidised—*contd*
    tenders for—*contd*
      regulations as to, **37**, [427]
      supplementary provisions, **37**, [427]
  summary of provisions, **36**, [210]
  Transport for London, co-operation with local
    authorities, **37**, [403]
  travel concessions—
    approval, **36**, [784]
    blind persons, **37**, [430]
    children and young persons, **37**, [430]
    disabled persons, **37**, [430]
    elderly persons, **37**, [430]; **38(2)**, [229]
    mandatory—
      definitions, **38(2)**, [136]
      disabled persons, for, **38(2)**, [134]
      elderly persons, for, **38(2)**, [134]
      enforcement, **38(2)**, [138]
      guidance on, **38(2)**, [134], [135]
      journeys not beginning on London bus
        network, for, **38(2)**, [134]
      reimbursement of operators,
        38(2), [139], [140]
      Wales, in, **38(2)**, [135]
      variation of, **38(2)**, [137]
    meaning, **37**, [445]
    national concession—
      meaning, **38(2)**, [537]
      variation of scope, **38(2)**, [537]
    Passenger Transport Executive, by,
      37, [440]
    provision of—
      Integrated Transport Executives, by,
        36, [784]
      local authorities, by, **37**, [430], [441]
      Passenger Transport Executives, by,
        36, [779], [784]; **37**, [440]
    reciprocal arrangements, **38(2)**, [539]
    schemes—
      administration of, **37**, [431]
      administrative arrangements, variation,
        38(2), [538]
      area covered by, **37**, [430]
      copies, availability of, **37**, [432]
      joint, **37**, [430]
      local authority, establishment by,
        37, [430]
      participation in—
        cancellation of notice, **37**, [435]
        compulsory, **37**, [434]
        enforcement, **37**, [438]
        notices, **37**, [435], [437]
        obligation, **37**, [434], [435]
        regulations, **37**, [437]
        release from, **37**, [436]
        withdrawal by operator, **37**, [434]
      persons eligible, **37**, [430]
      public service vehicles operators,
        participation of, **37**, [433]
      publicity, **37**, [432]
      reimbursement, **37**, [431]; **38(2)**, [538]
      transitional provisions, **37**, [475]
    subsidies for, apart from schemes, **37**, [439]

passenger transport services—*contd*
  undertakings, transfer of. *See* **Passenger Transport Executive**
  vehicles—
    documents, production on request, **37**, [781], [786]
    inspection, when required, **37**, [12]

passenger-carrying vehicles
  licensing of drivers. *See* **driving licences**

passport
  amendment of legislation, **36**, [195]
  application for, verifying information provided with, **36**, [194]
  untrue statement for procuring, **11(2)**, [171]

pastoral committee
  annual report, **14**, 967
  benefices, recommendations on, **14**, 969
  chairman, **14**, 1081
  church buildings closed for regular public worship, functions concerning, **14(S)**, 157
  compensation, determining, **14**, 1095–8
  constitution of, **14**, 966
  conventional districts, supervision of, **14**, 968
  diocesan policy, indication of, **14**, 967
  draft proposals—
    amendment of, **14**, 972–3
    approval by bishop, **14**, 972
    Church Commissioners—
      amending, **14**, 982
      sending to, **14**, 972–3
    formulation of recommendations in, **14**, 968–70
    implementation of, **14**, 972–3
    interested parties, getting view of, **14**, 968–9
  duties of, **14**, 967
  joint, **14**, 960
  loan for church building, requesting, **14**, 478
  members, **14**, 1081–2
  mission and pastoral committee. *See* **mission and pastoral committee**
  period of office, **14**, 1081
  quorum, **14**, 1081
  recommendations affecting another diocese, **14**, 979
  redundancy of church, reporting on, **14**, 969–70
  review of arrangements by, **14**, 967
  sub-committee, **14**, 1082
  voting, **14**, 1082

pastoral order
  amendment of, **14**, 1016
  archdeaconry, affecting, **14**, 1013
  benefice—
    area, altering, **14**, 1013
    name, altering, **14**, 1013
  bishop—
    deanery, affecting, **14**, 1013
    proposals by, **14**, 981
    submitting to, **14**, 975–6
  copies, transmission of, **14(S)**, 151

pastoral order—*contd*
  diocesan registry, filed in, **14**, 978
  draft—
    amendment of, **14**, 975; **14(S)**, 150
    Commissioners—
      consideration by, **14(S)**, 148–9
      supplementary powers of, **14(S)**, 153
    mission and pastoral committees, powers of, **14(S)**, 153
    notice of, **14(S)**, 149
    preparation of, **14**, 972–3
    publication, **14(S)**, 149
    service on interested parties, **14**, 974
  endowments, on income of, **14**, 1014
  making, **14**, 975–6; **14(S)**, 150
  map annexed to, **14**, 1016
  operation of, **14**, 978–9, 1016
  parish—
    area, altering, **14**, 1013
    name, altering, **14**, 1013
  parish church, relating to, **14**, 1014
  parsonage house, on, **14**, 1014
  patronage, on, **14**, 1014
  powers exercisable by, **14**, 1013–14
  presentation pending, **14**, 1060–1
  proposals, power of bishop to formulate and submit, **14(S)**, 151
  provisions in, **14**, 1016
  revocation of, **14**, 1016
  team ministry, relating to, **14**, 1013
  transitional provisions, **14**, 1105–7
  transmission of copies, **14**, 978
  withdrawal, bishop requesting, **14**, 982; **14(S)**, 152

pastoral scheme
  amended provisions, **14(S)**, 146–7
  amendment of, **14**, 1016
  archdeaconry, dealing with, **14**, 985, 997–8
  benefice, dissolving, **14**, 997–8
  bishop, submission to, **14**, 975–6
  burial ground, providing for appropriation of, **14**, 1004
  church buildings closed for regular public worship—
    appropriation or demolition, **14(S)**, 158
    committee and mission, functions of, **14(S)**, 157
    new church, replacement by, **14(S)**, 158
    provision for, **14(S)**, 159
  church buildings disposal—
    contents of, **14(S)**, 161–2
    procedures for, **14(S)**, 160–1
    use seeking period **14(S)**, 159
  churchyard, providing for appropriation of, **14**, 1004
  clergy, dispossessing, **14**, 997–8
  confirmation of, **14**, 976–7
  copies, transmission of, **14(S)**, 151
  deanery, dealing with, **14**, 985, 997–8
  declaration of redundancy in, **14**, 1001–2
  diocesan boundaries—
    altering, **14**, 1012–13
    effect of change in, **14**, 1092–3
  diocesan registry, filed in, **14**, 978

pastoral scheme—*contd*
  draft—
    amendment of, **14**, 975; **14(S)**, 150
    Commissioners—
      consideration by, **14(S)**, 148–9
      supplementary powers of, **14(S)**, 153
    declaration of redundancy in, **14**, 974
    mission and pastoral committees, powers
      of, **14(S)**, 153
    notice of, **14**, 974; **14(S)**, 149
    preparation of, **14**, 972–3; **14(S)**, 147–8
    publication of, **14**, 974; **14(S)**, 149
  draft proposals—
    approval of, **14(S)**, 147–8
    formulation and submission to bishop,
      14(S), 147
  endowments, concerning income of,
    14, 1008–9
  group ministry—
    altering, **14**, 994–5
    establishing, **14**, 992–3, 1086
    terminating, **14**, 994–5
  making of, **14(S)**, 150
  map annexed to, **14**, 1016
  matters providing for, **14**, 982
  new benefice, for—
    incumbent, designation of, **14**, 996–7
    status and duties, **14**, 995–6
  operation of, **14**, 978–9, 1016
  Order in Council—
    confirmation by, **14**, 976–7
    transmission of, **14**, 978
  other diocese, extending to, **14**, 1011–12
  parish church, designating, **14**, 999–1000
  parsonage house, providing for, **14**, 1005–6
  pastoral order, powers exercisable by,
    14(S), 178
  patronage, on, **14**, 1006–7
    special board, **14**, 1007
  plurality, providing for, **14**, 985
  presentation pending, **14**, 1060–1
  Privy Council, appeal to, **14**, 977, 1082–4
  proposals, power of bishop to formulate and
    submit, **14(S)**, 151
  provisions in, **14**, 1016
  reconsideration of, **14**, 977
  rectory, dissolution of, **14**, 995
  redundant buildings, for—
    amended provisions, **14(S)**, 153–4
    amendment of, **14**, 1043–4
    closure for public worship, **14(S)**, 154, 157
    consecration, removal of effects of,
      14, 1048
    contents, care of, **14**, 1050–1
    covenants in, **14**, 1049–50
    draft proposals—
      amendment, **14(S)**, 155
      formulation and submission of,
        14(S), 154
    draft scheme—
      amendment, **14(S)**, 155–6
      copies, transmission of, **14(S)**, 156
      notice of, **14(S)**, 155–6
      preparation of, **14(S)**, 155
      publication, **14(S)**, 155–6

pastoral scheme—*contd*
  redundant buildings, for—*contd*
    easements, giving, **14**, 1047
    guild church, **14**, 1077–8
    human remains, disposal of, **14**, 1052–3,
      1102–3
    provision for, **14**, 1027–8
    restoration, providing for, **14**, 1044
    right of way, **14**, 1047
    trusts for repair, **14**, 1050–1
    vesting of property, **14**, 1045–6
  redundant church, for, **14**, 1025–8
  restoration of building, for, **14**, 1044
  revocation of, **14**, 1016
  sharing agreement, authorising, **14**, 673–4,
    983
  sinecure, on, **14**, 1010
  team ministry—
    altering, **14**, 994–5
    establishing, **14**, 986–9, 1084–7
    terminating, **14**, 994–5, 1085
  transitional provisions, **14**, 1105–7
  union of benefices, providing for, **14**, 995
  validity of, **14**, 978–9
  withdrawal, bishop requesting, **14**, 982;
    14(S), 152

patent
  expenses—
    relief for, **44(1)**, [379]; **44(4)**, [24]
    tax deduction for, **44(3)**, [88]
  fees, deduction of, **44(1)**, [53]
  income, meaning, **44(1)**, [384]
  infringement authorised by Crown, liability
    for, **13**, [12]
  proceedings, state involved in, **10**, [1046]
  rights—
    capital allowance, manner of making,
      44(1), [381]
    Capital Allowances Act 2001, application
      of, **44(1)**, [383]; **44(4)**, [24]
    charge, manner of making, **44(1)**, [381]
    future, right to acquire, **44(1)**, [384]
    licence, **44(1)**, [384]
    meaning, **44(1)**, [384]
    partnership change, effect of, **44(1)**, [378]
    sale—
      proceeds, **44(1)**, [384]
      receipts, taxation of, **44(1)**, [377]
      reference to, **44(1)**, [384]
    winding up, effect of, **44(1)**, [378]
  royalties—
    deduction of tax—
      overview, **44(4)**, [906], [911]
      qualifying, meaning, **44(4)**, [907]
    double taxation arrangements, deduction at
      treaty rate, **44(4)**, [919]–[921]
    gross amount of payment, meaning,
      44(4), [460]
    receipts, spreading, **44(4)**, [469]
    relief for—
      individuals, for, **44(4)**, [456]
      other persons, for, **44(4)**, [457]
      overview, **44(4)**, [455]
      payments ineligible for, **44(4)**, [458]

patent—*contd*
  royalties—*contd*
    relief for—*contd*
      s 733 ICTA, special rule for persons
        affected by, **44(4)**, [459]
      spreading over several years, **44(1)**, [380]
    sale of rights—
      apportionments affecting two or more
        people, **44(3)**, [617]
      body corporate liable for tax, winding up,
        44(3), [604]
      capital sums, meaning, **44(3)**, [618]
      charge to tax, **44(3)**, [597]
      contributions to expenditure,
        44(3), [613]–[614]
      Crown use, sums paid for, **44(3)**, [609]
      death of seller, **44(3)**, [603]
      exchanges, including, **44(3)**, [615]
      expenses, relief for, **44(3)**, [610]–[611]
      future, right to acquire, **44(3)**, [608]
      income charged, **44(3)**, [598]
      licences, **44(3)**, [607]
      partnership—
        changes, effect of, **44(3)**, [878]
        later cessation of trade, **44(3)**, [879]
      payments received after deduction of tax,
        44(3), [612]
      payments to non-UK residents, deduction
        of tax from, **44(3)**, [605]–[606]
      person liable for tax, **44(3)**, [599]
      property sold together, apportionment,
        44(3), [616]
      public bodies not eligible for tax relief,
        contributions by, **44(3)**, [614]
      spreading rules—
        instalments, **44(3)**, [602]
        non-UK resident sellers, **44(3)**, [601]
        UK resident sellers, **44(3)**, [600]
    under-deductions, **44(1)**, [605]

patent agent
  body corporate—
    carrying on business by, **11(1)**, [1138],
      [1141]
    offences by, **11(1)**, [1144]
  comptroller refusing to deal with,
    11(1), [1143]
  European, persons describing themselves as,
    11(1), [1139]
  partnership—
    carrying on business by, **11(1)**, [1138],
      [1141]
    offences by, **11(1)**, [1144]
  patents county court, rights and duties as to
    proceedings in, **11(1)**, [1151]
  persons carrying on business as, **11(1)**, [1136]
  persons describing themselves as,
    11(1), [1138]
  privileged communications with,
    11(1), [1142]
  register, **11(1)**, [1137]

patent allowance
  acquisition of licence, for, **43(1)**, [1101]
  availability of, **43(1)**, [1101]

patent allowance—*contd*
  balancing adjustments—
    amount of, **43(1)**, [1109]
    entitlement or liability, determination of,
      43(1), [1108]
  Crown use, sums paid for, **43(1)**, [1119]
  disposal values—
    generally, **43(1)**, [1113]
    limit on amount of, **43(1)**, [1114]
  entitlement or liability, determination of,
    43(1), [1108]
  future rights, for, **43(1)**, [1102]
  giving effect to—
    non-qualifying trade expenditure, persons
      having, **43(1)**, [1116]–[1117]
    qualifying trade expenditure, persons
      having, **43(1)**, [1115]
  qualifying expenditure—
    available, **43(1)**, [1110]
    limit on, **43(1)**, [1118]
    meaning, **43(1)**, [1104]
    non-trade, **43(1)**, [1106]
    pooling, **43(1)**, [1107]
    pools, allocation to, **43(1)**, [1111]
    trade, **43(1)**, [1105]
    unrelieved, **43(1)**, [1112]
  transitional provisions, **43(1)**, [1230]
  writing-down—
    amount of, **43(1)**, [1109]
    entitlement to, **43(1)**, [1108]

patent attorney
  body corporate—
    carrying on business by, **11(1)**, [1138],
      [1141]
    offences by, **11(1)**, [1144]
  European, persons describing themselves as,
    11(1), [1139]
  partnership—
    carrying on business by, **11(1)**, [1138],
      [1141]
    offences by, **11(1)**, [1144]
  persons describing themselves as,
    11(1), [1138]
  registration of, Secretary of State's functions
    transferred to Institute of Trade Mark
    Attorneys, **11(4)**, [300]
  use of term, **11(1)**, [1140]

Patent Co-operation Treaty
  applications under, treatment of, **11(1)**, [731]
  filing date under, **11(1)**, [733]
  financial provisions, **11(1)**, [739]
  international application, provisions applying
    to, **11(1)**, [732]
  judicial notice of, **11(1)**, [735]

patent court
  business of, **11(2)**, [736]
  constitution, **11(2)**, [673]
  High Court, part of, **11(2)**, [673]
  scientific advisers, **11(2)**, [744]

patent (invention)
Act of 1949—
    appeals under, **11(1)**, [488], [781]
    application of, **11(1)**, [770], [778]
    applications under. *See* application *below*
    priorities in respect of, **11(1)**, [771]
    provisions repealed, **11(1)**, [780]
    transitional provisions, **11(1)**, [781]
addition, of, **11(1)**, [448]
aircraft—
    claims against—
        exemption, **4(1)**, [139]
        when not protected, **4(1)**, [172]
allowances. *See* **patent allowance**
amendment—
    Act of 1949, under, **11(1)**, [442]
    application, of. *See* application *below*
    deceased applicant, in case of, **11(1)**, [442]
    grant, after, **11(1)**, [1195]
    specification, of. *See* specification *below*
application—
    abroad by UK resident—
        authority required for, **11(1)**, [666]
        exception from restrictions, **11(1)**, [666]
        penalties for unauthorised filing,
            11(1), [666]
    Act of 1949, under—
        alteration of, **11(1)**, [429]
        cessation of, **11(1)**, [770]
        convention applications, **11(1)**, [424],
            [483]
        entitlement to make, **11(1)**, [424]
        errors, correction of, **11(1)**, [486]
        examination of, **11(1)**, [429]
        filing of, **11(1)**, [425]
        form, **11(1)**, [425]
        lapsed, restoration of, **11(1)**, [449]
        leave of comptroller, **11(1)**, [450]
        personal representative, by, **11(1)**, [424]
        persons who may make, **11(1)**, [424]
        refusal of, **11(1)**, [433]
        search, **11(1)**, [430]–[431], [434]
        specification for, **11(1)**, [426]
        statement by applicant, **11(1)**, [425]
        substitution of applicant, **11(1)**, [439]
        time for putting in order for
            acceptance, **11(1)**, [435]
    amendment—
        added matter, not to include,
            11(1), [722]
        applicant, by, **11(1)**, [660]
        comptroller, by, **11(1)**, [660]
        general power to make, **11(1)**, [660]
    assignment of, **11(1)**, [674]
    biotechnological inventions, **11(1)**, [723]
    certificate of grant, **11(1)**, [667]
    claim in, **11(1)**, [654]
    co-owners, by, **11(1)**, [678]
    contents, **11(1)**, [654]
    date of filing, **11(1)**, [655]
        meaning, **11(1)**, [773]
    earlier and later—
        disclosure of matter between,
            11(1), [646]

patent (invention)—*contd*
application—*contd*
    earlier and later—*contd*
        relevant intervening acts, meaning,
            11(1), [646]
    errors in, correction of, **11(1)**, [757]
    European patent. *See* European patent *below*
    examination of—
        Act of 1949, under, **11(1)**, [429]
        preliminary—
            matters to be determined,
                11(1), [656]
            reference for, **11(1)**, [656]
            report on, **11(1)**, [656]
        substantive—
            application for, **11(1)**, [659]
            examiner's duty, **11(1)**, [659]
    failure of, **11(1)**, [470]
    form, **11(1)**, [654]
    grant of. *See* grant *below*
    information of, comptroller, by,
        11(1), [760]
    information prejudicial to defence etc—
        direction prohibiting publication,
            11(1), [665]
        penalties for offences, **11(1)**, [665]
    joint applicants—
        Act of 1949, under, **11(1)**, [424]
        disputes between, **11(1)**, [650]
    nature of, **11(1)**, [674]
    pending, provisions as to, **11(1)**, [624]
    procedure, **11(1)**, [654]
    publication of—
        infringement of rights by, **11(1)**, [713]
        omissions, permitted, **11(1)**, [657]
        requirement for, **11(1)**, [657]
    refusal of, **11(1)**, [659]
    requirements not complied with,
        11(1), [659]
    right to make, **11(1)**, [647]
    search—
        application for, **11(1)**, [658]
        purposes of, **11(1)**, [658]
        supplementary, **11(1)**, [659]
    specification of. *See* specification *below*
    time limits, extension by comptroller,
        11(1), [759]
    transfer of—
        effect of, **11(1)**, [651]
        order for, **11(1)**, [648]
    unauthorised claim of, **11(1)**, [753]
    withdrawal of, **11(1)**, [654]
        correction of errors in, **11(1)**, [757]
        resuscitating, **11(1)**, [758]
assignment—
    Act of 1949, under, **11(1)**, [443]
    effect of, **11(1)**, [674]
    registration of, **11(1)**, [676]
biotechnological inventions, **11(1)**, [415],
    [704], [723], [776]–[777]
Board of Trade, proceedings of, **11(1)**, [490]
charters, saving for, **11(1)**, [420]
co-owners—
    directions by comptroller, **11(1)**, [473]
    proceedings by, **11(1)**, [710]

patent (invention)—*contd*
  co-owners—*contd*
    rights of, **11(1)**, [678]
  Community Patent Convention—
    financial provisions, **11(1)**, [739]
    judicial notice of, **11(1)**, [735]
    meaning, **11(1)**, [773]
  competition reference, Competition
    Commission report, **11(1)**, [694]
  comptroller-general—
    agents, certain, refusal to recognise,
      11(1), [1143]
    annual report of, **11(1)**, [763]
    appeal from, **11(1)**, [740]
      Act of 1949, under, **11(1)**, [781]
    appointment, **11(1)**, [422]
    designs, annual report on, **11(1)**, [561]
    discretionary powers, exercise of,
      11(1), [744]
    disputes referred to, **11(1)**, [483]
    information to be given by, **11(1)**, [760]
    infringement references to, **11(1)**, [705]
    leave to amend specification, **11(1)**, [450]
    licence granted by order of, **11(1)**, [750]
    officers and staff, **11(1)**, [422]
    Patent Office, control of, **11(1)**, [421]
    proceedings before—
      audience, right of, **11(1)**, [745]
      costs and expenses, **11(1)**, [749]
      representation in, **11(1)**, [745]
    reference of questions to—
      entitlement, as to. *See* entitlement *below*
      terms of licence, **11(1)**, [651]
    Registrar, as, **48**, 158
    revocation of patent by, **11(1)**, [717]
      Act of 1949, under, **11(1)**, [454], [473]
    trade marks, reports on, **48**, 163
    use of electronic communications,
      directions as to, **11(1)**, [767]
  convention countries—
    British possessions as, **11(1)**, [734]
    orders designating, **11(1)**, [734]
  convention patent—
    application for, **11(1)**, [424]–[426]
    entitlement, determination of, **11(1)**, [652]
    relevant court as to, **11(1)**, [773]
    specification for, **11(1)**, [427]
  conventions—
    community. *See* Community Patent
      Convention *above*
    European. *See* **European Patent
      Convention**
    meaning, **11(1)**, [773]
  Crown—
    application of Act, **11(1)**, [772]
    forfeited articles, right to sell, **11(1)**, [764]
    Royal prerogative, saving for, **11(1)**, [492]
    services of, meaning, **11(1)**, [699]
    use of inventions by—
      Act of 1949, under, **11(1)**, [465]–[468]
      compensation, **11(1)**, [701]
      conditions for, **11(1)**, [698]
      confidentiality of information,
        11(1), [702]

patent (invention)—*contd*
  Crown—*contd*
    use of inventions by—*contd*
      defence purposes, for. *See* defence
        materials, use for *below*
      disputes as to, **11(1)**, [631], [702]
        Act of 1949, under, **11(1)**, [467]
      drugs etc, for production of,
        11(1), [636], [698], [699]
      effects of, **11(1)**, [700]
      emergency, during, **11(1)**, [703]
        Act of 1949, under, **11(1)**, [468]
      foreign defence purposes, for,
        11(1), [699]
      generally, **11(1)**, [698]
      health services, for, **11(1)**, [636]
      interpretation of provisions, **11(1)**, [699]
      notification of proprietor, **11(1)**, [698]
      pharmaceutical services, for, **11(1)**, [636]
      purposes of, **11(1)**, [699], [703]
      rights of third parties, **11(1)**, [466], [700]
      summary of provisions, **11(1)**, [415]
      terms of, **11(1)**, [628], [698]
  date of, **11(1)**, [444]
  defence materials, use for—
    disputes, determination of, **11(1)**, [631]
    technical information—
      authorisation to use, **11(1)**, [629]–[630]
      meaning, **11(1)**, [629]
      payments in respect of, **11(1)**, [631]
  document—
    date of filing, meaning, **11(1)**, [491]
    inspection of, **11(1)**, [760]
    duplicate, issue of, **11(1)**, [487]
  effect, **11(1)**, [443]
  employees' inventions, **11(1)**, [474], [681]
  enemy—
    character, evidence of, **50**, [213]
    grant to, **50**, [210]
    licence of—
      comptroller, grant by, **50**, [207]
      validity of, **50**, [207]
      variation of, **50**, [207], [208]
  entitlement to—
    determination of questions—
      after grant of patent, **11(1)**, [649]
      before granting, **11(1)**, [648]
      comptroller, by, **11(1)**, [648]
      convention patents, **11(1)**, [652]
      court, by, **11(1)**, [652]
      foreign patents, as to, **11(1)**, [652]
      joint applications, as to, **11(1)**, [650]
      orders arising from, **11(1)**, [648]
  errors in, correction of, **11(1)**, [757]
    Act of 1949, under, **11(1)**, [486]
  European patent—
    application—
      language of proceedings for, **11(1)**, [727]
      provisions applied, **11(1)**, [726]
      refusal, effect of, **11(1)**, [659]
    authentic text of, **11(1)**, [727]
    Convention. *See* **European Patent
      Convention**
    decisions of other states, effect,
      11(1), [730]

patent (invention)—*contd*
European patent—*contd*
determination of questions as to,
11(1), [652]
employer-employee question—
determination of, **11(1)**, [729]
meaning, **11(1)**, [729]
jurisdiction as to, **11(1)**, [729]
right to, determination, **11(1)**, [729]
translations, corrections of, **11(1)**, [727]
European patent (UK)—
amendment, effect of, **11(1)**, [724]
application—
conversion of, **11(1)**, [728]
date of filing, **11(1)**, [728]
effect of filing, **11(1)**, [725]
general provisions applied to,
11(1), [725]
effect of, **11(1)**, [724]
meaning, **11(1)**, [773]
revocation, effect of, **11(1)**, [724]
rights in respect of, **11(1)**, [724]
specification—
amendment of, effect, **11(1)**, [724]
English translation for filing,
11(1), [724]
treatment of, **11(1)**, [724]
withdrawn, deemed to be, **11(1)**, [728]
expenses, tax deduction for, **44(3)**, [88]
extension—
grounds of—
inadequate remuneration, **11(1)**, [445]
war loss, **11(1)**, [446]–[447]
opposition to, **11(1)**, [445]
extent of invention, **11(1)**, [768]
fees, renewal, failure to pay, **11(1)**, [668]
food, inventions relating to, **11(1)**, [461]
foreign, determination of entitlement to,
11(1), [652]
forfeited articles, sale of, **11(1)**, [764]
form of, **11(1)**, [443]
grant—
Act of 1949, under, **11(1)**, [441]
amendment of specification after,
11(1), [670]
certification of, **11(1)**, [667]
determination of questions before,
11(1), [648]
determination of rights after, **11(1)**, [679]
effective date, **11(1)**, [668]
eligibility for. *See* patentable inventions
below
entitlement, determination of, **11(1)**, [648]
one invention only, for, **11(1)**, [443]
opposition to, transitional provisions,
11(1), [781]
orders by comptroller as to, **11(1)**, [648]
persons entitled to, **11(1)**, [648]
public notice of, **11(1)**, [667]
revocation. *See* revocation *below*
right to, **11(1)**, [647]
terms of, **11(1)**, [668]
impugned, not to be, **11(1)**, [669]
industrial application, capable of, **11(1)**, [643]

patent (invention)—*contd*
information by comptroller-general of,
11(1), [760]
infringement—
account, order for, **11(1)**, [705]
Act of 1949, under—
aircraft, special provisions, **11(1)**, [485]
damages, restrictions on, **11(1)**, [475]
disputes, reference of, **11(1)**, [483]
exclusive licensee, by, **11(1)**, [479]
groundless threats of proceedings,
11(1), [481]
non-infringement declaration by court,
11(1), [482]
partially valid patent, relief, **11(1)**, [478]
proceedings for, **11(1)**, [475], [479]
revocation, counterclaim for,
11(1), [477]
vessels, special provisions, **11(1)**, [485]
actions held to be, **11(1)**, [704]
amendment of patent, before, **11(1)**, [706]
biotechnological inventions, **11(1)**, [704]
contested validity of patent, **11(1)**, [709]
damages—
claim for, **11(1)**, [705]
exclusive licensee, to, **11(1)**, [711]
restriction on recovery of, **11(1)**, [706]
Act of 1949, under, **11(1)**, [475]
declaration of non-infringement,
11(1), [715]
detention of aircraft, exemption,
4(1), [139]
exceptions from, **11(1)**, [704]
ignorance of existence of patent,
11(1), [706]
lapsed patent, of, **11(1)**, [672]
meaning, **11(1)**, [704]
opinions as to, **11(1)**, [719]–[720]
partial validity—
patent, of, **11(1)**, [707]
relief for, **11(1)**, [1196]
potential, reference in case of, **11(1)**, [432]
proceedings—
amendment of patent in, **11(1)**, [721]
claims in, **11(1)**, [705]
co-owner, by, **11(1)**, [710]
court jurisdiction, **11(1)**, [705]
defence in, **11(1)**, [718]
exclusive licensee, by, **11(1)**, [711]
groundless threats of, **11(1)**, [714]
joint proprietors, by, **11(1)**, [710]
non-registration, effect of, **11(1)**, [712]
part relief given, **11(1)**, [707]
reliefs sought in, **11(1)**, [705]
validity of patent in issue, **11(1)**, [709],
[718]
publication of application, by, **11(1)**, [713]
reference to comptroller, **11(1)**, [705]
transitional provisions, **11(1)**, [781]
use before priority date, effect of,
11(1), [708]
international applications—
adaptation of provisions, **11(1)**, [733]
date of filing, **11(1)**, [731]
English translations, **11(1)**, [732]

patent (invention)—*contd*
  international applications—*contd*
    filing, effect of, **11(1)**, [731]
    meaning, **11(1)**, [773]
    national phases, **11(1)**, [732]
    Patent Co-operation Treaty, provisions of,
      11(1), [732]
  international obligations, amendment of
    provisions, **11(1)**, [1202]
  interpretation of terms, **11(1)**, [773]
  invention. *See* **invention**
  inventor—
    mention of, in patent, **11(1)**, [438], [653]
    statement for Patent Office, **11(1)**, [653]
  Isle of Man, provisions applied, **11(1)**, [494],
    [775]
  journal, rules for, **11(1)**, [765]
  lapsed—
    infringement of, **11(1)**, [672]
    renewal fee not paid, **11(1)**, [668]
    restoration—
      Act of 1949, under, **11(1)**, [449]
      application for, **11(1)**, [671]
      conditions of order for, **11(1)**, [671]
      effect of order, **11(1)**, [672]
  legal proceedings. *See* proceedings *below*
  licence—
    anti-competitive practice situations,
      11(1), [694]
    compulsory—
      Act of 1949, under—
        appeal as to, **11(1)**, [463]
        application, time for, **11(1)**, [457]
        arbitration reference, **11(1)**, [463]
        general provisions, **11(1)**, [458]
        grounds for, **11(1)**, [457]
        powers, exercise of, **11(1)**, [459]
      appeals in respect of, **11(1)**, [695]
      application, time for, **11(1)**, [688]
      arbitration, reference to, **11(1)**, [695]
      exercise of powers as to, **11(1)**, [692]
      general provisions, **11(1)**, [691]
      grant of, **11(1)**, [688], [690]
      grounds for obtaining, **11(1)**, [688]
      invention being worked abroad, where,
        11(1), [697]
      opposition to grant of, **11(1)**, [695]
      purposes of, **11(1)**, [692]
      supplementary provisions, **11(1)**, [696]
      World Trade Organisation proprietors,
        grant of—
          appeals in respect of, **11(1)**, [695]
          generally, **11(1)**, [689]
          opposition to, **11(1)**, [695]
          revocation, **11(1)**, [695]
    exclusive, meaning, **11(1)**, [491], [773]
    forms of, **11(1)**, [686]
    granted by order of comptroller,
      11(1), [750]
    lapse on transfer of party, **11(1)**, [651]
    nature of, **11(1)**, [674]
    of right—
      Act of 1949, under—
        appeal as to, **11(1)**, [463]
        arbitration reference, **11(1)**, [463]

patent (invention)—*contd*
  licence—*contd*
    of right—*contd*
      Act of 1949, under—*contd*
        cancellation of endorsement,
          11(1), [456]
        compulsory endorsement,
          11(1), [457]
        Crown application for,
          11(1), [460]–[462]
        food etc, inventions relating to,
          11(1), [461]
        grounds for endorsement,
          11(1), [457]
        procedure, **11(1)**, [462]
      after transfer of application, **11(1)**, [651]
      availability—
        cancellation, **11(1)**, [687]
        entry in register, **11(1)**, [686]
        endorsement as, **11(1)**, [455]
        entitlement to, **11(1)**, [686]
        terms, settlement of, **11(1)**, [686]
      transitional provisions, **11(1)**, [781]
    licensee—
      infringement—
        duty to prevent, **11(1)**, [686]
        proceedings by, **11(1)**, [710]–[712]
  loss or destruction, replacement, **11(1)**, [487]
  medicine, inventions relating to, **11(1)**, [461]
  merger and market investigations, **11(1)**, [693]
  method of treatment or diagnosis. not granted
    for, **11(1)**, [1194]
  monopolies—
    charters, exception for, **11(1)**, [420]
    existing grants, **11(1)**, [419]
    fourteen years or less, restriction to,
      11(1), [418]
    merger and marketing investigations,
      11(1), [693]
    void, declared, **11(1)**, [417]
  mortgage of, **11(1)**, [674]
  national security—
    information prejudicial to—
      direction as to publication, **11(1)**, [665]
      penalty for publishing, **11(1)**, [665]
  Northern Ireland, provisions applied,
    11(1), [493], [774]
  notices, service of, **11(1)**, [761]
  offences—
    corporations, by, **11(1)**, [755]
    falsification of register, **11(1)**, [751]
    misuse of title "Patent Office", **11(1)**, [754]
    Royal Arms, use of, **11(1)**, [489]
    unauthorised claims, **11(1)**, [752]–[53]
  official acts, immunity for, **11(1)**, [756]
  patentable inventions—
    conditions to be satisfied, **11(1)**, [640]
    exceptions, **11(1)**, [640]
    industrial application, capable of,
      11(1), [643]
    inventive step, involving, **11(1)**, [642]
    methods of treatment or diagnosis not
      qualifying as, **11(1)**, [644]
    new, when taken to be, **11(1)**, [641]
    novelty, necessity for, **11(1)**, [641]

patent (invention)—*contd*
  patentable inventions—*contd*
    third party observations, **11(1)**, [664]
  patented products—
    Crown use of, **11(1)**, [698]
    meaning, **11(1)**, [773]
  personal property, as, **11(1)**, [674]
  post office, transitional provisions relating to, **34**, [590]
  priority date of invention—
    Act of 1949, under, **11(1)**, [472]
    determination of, **11(1)**, [645]
    earlier date accepted, **11(1)**, [645]
    meaning, **11(1)**, [645]
  proceedings—
    agent, communications with, **11(1)**, [747], [1142]
    appeals in, **11(1)**, [740]
    audience, right of, **11(1)**, [745]
    burden of proof in certain cases, **11(1)**, [743]
    comptroller, before, **11(1)**, [740]
    costs and expenses, **11(1)**, [748]–[749]
    infringement, for. *See* infringement *above*
    meaning, **11(1)**, [747]
    privileged communications, **11(1)**, [747], [1142]
    validity of patent, issue as to, **11(1)**, [718]
  proof of, burden of, **11(1)**, [743]
  public safety—
    information prejudicial to—
      direction as to publication, **11(1)**, [665]
      penalty for publishing, **11(1)**, [665]
  publication—
    meaning, **11(1)**, [491]
    national security and public safety, affecting, **11(1)**, [665]
    offences and penalties, **11(1)**, [665]
    previous, under 1949 Act, **11(1)**, [469]
    provisional specification, after, **11(1)**, [471]
  refusal of—
    reinstatement of applications where, **11(1)**, [662]–[663]
    requirements not complied with, where, **11(1)**, [661]
    time for deciding on, **11(1)**, [661]
    without opposition, **11(1)**, [437]
  register—
    certification of entries, **11(1)**, [675]
    copies of entries, right to, **11(1)**, [675]
    correction of errors etc, **11(1)**, [486]
    evidence of, **11(1)**, [675]
    falsification of, **11(1)**, [751]
    form of, **11(1)**, [675]
    licences, entries as to, **11(1)**, [686], [687], [696]
      cancellation of, **11(1)**, [687]
    maintenance of, **11(1)**, [675]
    meaning, **11(1)**, [675]
    non-documentary form, in, **11(1)**, [675]
    public inspection, **11(1)**, [675]
    rectification of, **11(1)**, [677]
    rules, provisions of, **11(1)**, [675]
    variation or deletion of entries, **11(1)**, [677]

patent (invention)—*contd*
  registration—
    assignment etc, of, **11(1)**, [676]
    effect of, **11(1)**, [676]
    renewal, failure to pay fee, **11(1)**, [668]
  revocation—
    Act of 1949, under—
      comptroller, by, **11(1)**, [454]
      counterclaim for, **11(1)**, [477]
      grounds for, **11(1)**, [453]
      patent falsely obtained, **11(1)**, [453]
    amendment of specification to avoid, **11(1)**, [721]
    application for, **11(1)**, [716]
    comptroller, by, **11(1)**, [717]
    grounds for, **11(1)**, [716]
    limited extent, to, **11(1)**, [716]
    powers as to, **11(1)**, [716]
    refusal to grant, **11(1)**, [716]
    transitional provisions, **11(1)**, [781]
  rights—
    assignment, **11(1)**, [674]
    co-ownership, in case of, **11(1)**, [678]
    determination of, **11(1)**, [679]
    employee's invention, **11(1)**, [681]
    registration, effect of, on, **11(1)**, [676]
    unauthorised claim of, **11(1)**, [752]
    vesting of, **11(1)**, [674]
  Royal Arms, unauthorised use, **11(1)**, [489]
  rules—
    power to make, **11(1)**, [765]
    subject matters of, **11(1)**, [765]
  sale of rights. *See* **patent**
  sealing—
    Act of 1949, under, **11(1)**, [441]
    death of applicant before, **11(1)**, [442]
    effect, **11(1)**, [443]
  specification—
    Act of 1949, under—
      acceptance, **11(1)**, [436]
      amendment—
        general provisions, **11(1)**, [452]
        leave of comptroller, **11(1)**, [450]
        leave of court, **11(1)**, [451]
      complete, time for filing, **11(1)**, [426]
      contents of, **11(1)**, [427]
      contested validity, **11(1)**, [480]
      priority date of claims, **11(1)**, [428]
      provisional, **11(1)**, [426]
      publication, **11(1)**, [436]
    amendment—
      added matter, not to include, **11(1)**, [722]
      grant of patent, after, **11(1)**, [670]
      infringement proceedings, in, **11(1)**, [721]
      opposition to, **11(1)**, [721]
      revocation proceedings, in, **11(1)**, [721]
      trade-mark, to acknowledge, **11(1)**, [670]
    biological material, samples of, **11(1)**, [769]
    disclosure of invention in, **11(1)**, [654]
    errors in, correction of, **11(1)**, [757]
  summary of provisions, **11(1)**, [415]
  surrender of, **11(1)**, [673]

patent (invention)—*contd*
  term of—
    Act of 1949, under—
      extension, **11(1)**, [445]–[447]
      sixteen years, **11(1)**, [444]
      effective date, **11(1)**, [668]
      failure to pay renewal fee, **11(1)**, [668]
    time limits, extension in war circumstances,
      50, [212]
  transactions in, **11(1)**, [674]
  transfer of—
    effect of, **11(1)**, [680]
    order of comptroller, on, **11(1)**, [679]
    working invention prior to, **11(1)**, [680]
  validity—
    contested, certificate of, **11(1)**, [709]
    grounds for questioning, **11(1)**, [718]
    issue in proceedings, as, **11(1)**, [718]
    opinions as to, **11(1)**, [719]–[720]
  vesting of, **11(1)**, [674]

Patent Office
  applications filed at, **11(1)**, [425], [655]
  business—
    excluded days, **11(1)**, [558], [762]
    hours of, **11(1)**, [558], [762]
    rules regulating, **11(1)**, [556], [765]
  control of, **11(1)**, [421]
  designs—
    application for registration, filing,
      11(1), [504]
    secrecy in respect of, **11(1)**, [509], [552]
  electronic communications to deliver
    documents to, use of, **11(1)**, [557A]
  hours of business, **48**, 167
  inventor, statement by, filing, **11(1)**, [653]
  misuse of title, **11(1)**, [754]
  register—
    designs, of. *See* **design**
    patents, of. *See* **patent**
  rules, provisions of, **11(1)**, [556]
  seal, judicial notice of, **11(1)**, [423]

patent rights
  allowances. *See* **patent allowances**
  Crown use, sums paid for, **43(1)**, [1119]
  disposal values, **43(1)**, [1113]
  income from, meaning, **43(1)**, [1120]
  meaning, **43(1)**, [1101]

Patents County Court
  patent agents, rights and duties of,
    11(1), [1151]
  pecuniary claim eligible to brought in,
    limitation of costs, **11(1)**, [1149]
  proceedings in, **11(1)**, [1150]
  special jurisdiction—
    exercise of, **11(1)**, [1146]
    financial limits, **11(1)**, [1147]

Patents Court
  appeals to or from, **11(1)**, [740]
  audience, right of, **11(1)**, [745]
  burden of proof in certain cases, **11(1)**, [743]
  business of, **11(2)**, [736]

Patents Court—*contd*
  constitution, **11(2)**, [673]
  costs and expenses, **11(1)**, [748]
  general powers of, **11(1)**, [741]
  High Court, part of, **11(2)**, [673]
  privileged communications, **11(1)**, [747]
  proceedings in, **11(1)**, [740]
  report, power to order, **11(1)**, [742]
  representation in, **11(1)**, [745]
  scientific advisers, **11(2)**, [744]

paternity. *See* **parentage**
pay. *See* **statutory paternity pay**

paternity leave
  additional, rights during and after, **16**, [1020]
  entitlement to—
    adoption, on, **16**, [716], [717]
    birth, on, **16**, [714], [715]
  regulations, **16**, [720]
  rights during and after, **16**, [718]
  special cases, **16**, [719]
  unfair dismissal relating to, **16**, [746]
  unfair employment-related benefit scheme
    provisions, **40(1)**, [205]

Pathogens Access Appeals Commission
  appeal to, **12(3)**, [116]
  constitution and administration, **12(3)**, [163]
  establishment of, **12(3)**, [116]
  procedure, **12(3)**, [163]

pathogens and toxins
  appeals, **12(3)**, [116], [117]
  dangerous substances—
    denial of access—
      appeals, **12(3)**, [116]
      directions requiring, **12(3)**, [110]
    disposal, directions requiring, **12(3)**, [109]
    keeping or using, duty to notify Secretary
      of State, **12(3)**, [105]
    persons with access to, information about,
      12(3), [107]
    powers of entry, **12(3)**, [111]
    search warrants, **12(3)**, [112]
    security, information about, **12(3)**, [106]
    security measures, directions requiring,
      12(3), [108]
  definitions, **12(3)**, [120]
  directions or notices, giving, **12(3)**, [118]
  extension of provisions, **12(3)**, [121]
  offences, **12(3)**, [113]
    body corporate, by, **12(3)**, [114]
    partnerships and unincorporated
      associations, by, **12(3)**, [115]
  orders and regulations, **12(3)**, [119]
  schedule of, **12(3)**, [104], [162]

Patients' Forum
  abolition, **26(2)**, [642]
  advice or recommendations by, **30**, [1043]
  annual reports, **30**, [1046]
  bodies for which established, **30**, [1043]
  duties, **30**, [1043]
  entry and inspection of premises, **30**, [1045]

Patients' Forum—*contd*
establishment of, **30**, [1043]
functions, **30**, [1043]
abolition of, **26(2)**, [641]
further provisions for, **30**, [1047]
PCT, functions of, **30**, [1044]
supplementary provisions, **30**, [632]

patron. *See also* **patronage**
appointment of, **14**, 1259
bishop as, notices, **14**, 390
consent of—
crown, being, **14**, 127–8
dedication of land for highway, to, **14**, 520
giving, **14**, 145
documents, service of, **14**, 406
guild church, of, **14**, 453–4, 511
incapacitated person, as, **14**, 128
Jew as, **14**, 185
meaning, **14**, 1075
minor, being, **14**, 127, 1070
person being, **14**, 127

patronage. *See also* **patron; presentation
(ecclesiastical)**
advowson registration abolished, **14**, 1136
appeals, rules, **14**, 1165–6
augmented cure, of, **14**, 61
benefice—
joint parochial church council, having,
14, 1170
plurality, held in, **14**, 1166–7, 1170
team council, having, **14**, 1170
two or more parishes, comprising,
14, 1168–9
Church Commissioners determining questions
on, **14**, 1068
Crown, **14**, 1157–9
assents, **14**, 127
canonries in St. Pauls in, **14**, 133
dean of old cathedrals, in, **14**, 133
notice of sale of residence to, **14**, 392
provisions applying to, **14**, 1069–70
diocesan board. *See* **diocesan board of
patronage**
documents, provisions as to, **14**, 1159–60
Duchy of Cornwall—
attached to, **14**, 128
provisions applying to, **14**, 1069–70
Duke of Cornwall, **14**, 1157–8
guild church, of—
exercise of rights, **14**, 454–5
lapse, **14**, 455
new benefice, creation of, **14**, 468–9, 471
right of, **14**, 453–4
transfer of right, **14**, 513
incumbent—
patron, bishop acting in place of, **14**, 1149
selection of, **14**, 1144
inhibition, rights during, **14**, 608
lapse, guild church, in case of, **14**, 455
loan of money for parsonages, **14**, 97
new rights, suspension of, **14**, 1062
notices etc, provisions as to, **14**, 1159–60

patronage—*contd*
parochial church council—
duties of, **14**, 1141–2
failure to comply with, **14**, 1146
joint meeting with bishop and patron,
14, 1142–3
pastoral order on, **14**, 1014
pastoral scheme, **14**, 1006–7, 1154
patron—
benefices held in plurality, **14**, 1166–7
death of, **14**, 1135, 1136–7
declaration of membership—
designated officer—
failure to inform, **14**, 1146
information to or by, **14**, 1139–40,
1145
meaning, **14**, 1137
inability to make, **14**, 1137–8
meaning, **14**, 1138
requirement for, **14**, 1137–8
disabilities removed, **14**, 1154
meaning, **14**, 1162
meeting with bishop and parochial church
council, **14**, 1142–3
personal representative of, **14**, 1149–50
pre-emption rights abolished, **14**, 1156–7
registered—
meaning, **14**, 1151
notice to parishes, **14**, 1166
registration—
appeals respecting, **14**, 1165
application for, **14**, 1165
disputes as to, **14**, 1165
generally, **14**, 1132
list for, preparation of, **14**, 1164
representative of—
appointment, **14**, 1138
parochial church council, particulars,
14, 1140
Roman Catholic as, **14**, 1154
Patronage (Appeals) Committee—
constitution of, **14**, 1165–6
establishment, **14**, 1165–6
rules by, **14**, 1165–6
Patronage (Procedure) Committee—
establishment, **14**, 1160–61
members, **14**, 1160–1
register—
duty to keep, **14**, 1132
rectification, **14**, 1134–5
registration—
patronage belonging to office, **14**, 1132
period allowed for, **14**, 1132
requirement, **14**, 1132
rights—
Diocesan Boards, of, **14**, 1152–3
exercise of, **14**, 1135
lapse of, **14**, 1154–5
office, belonging to, **14**, 1167
personal representation, exercise by,
14, 1149
transfer. *See* transfer of rights *below*
sale of, prohibited, **14**, 1133
suspension, rights during, **14**, 608
team ministry, board for, **14**, 1084

patronage—*contd*
  transfer—
    certification by bishop, **14**, 340
    consideration, for, **14**, 1133
    diocesan bishop, by, **14**, 339
    guild church, **14**, 513
    meaning, **14**, 340–1, 1134
    notice of, **14**, 338–40
    patron, duties of, **14**, 338
    proposed, notice of, **14**, 1133
    registration, **14**, 339, 1133
    scheme for, **14**, 925

pawn. *See also* **pledge**
  firearm or ammunition, taking in pawn,
    12(1), [476]
  meaning, **39(1)**, [353]
  minor, article taken from, **39(1)**, [276]
  offences, **39(1)**, [276], [277]
  pawn-receipt—
    giving, **39(1)**, [276]
    loss of, **39(1)**, [280]
  property passing to pawnee, **39(1)**, [282]
  realisation of, **39(1)**, [283]
  redemption—
    failure to redeem, **39(1)**, [282]
    period, **39(1)**, [278]
    procedure, **39(1)**, [279]
  refusal of, **39(1)**, [281]
  sale, information on, **39(1)**, [283]
  theft of, **39(1)**, [281]
  unlawful, return of property, **12(1)**, [41]

pay. *See* **wages**

PAYE
  assessment, additional provision for,
    44(2), [709]
  asset—
    enhancing value of, **44(2)**, [698]
    meaning, **44(2)**, [701]
    readily convertible, **44(2)**, [697], [702]
  cash vouchers taxable under, **44(2)**, [694]
  credit-tokens, application to, **44(2)**, [696]
  debts, recovery of, **43(S)**, 1756–7
  deductions, **43(2)**, [207]
  definitions, **44(2)**, [707], [712]
  employment-related securities, on,
    44(2), [699]
  income—
    cash vouchers, **44(2)**, [694]
    credit-tokens, **44(2)**, [696]
    meaning, **44(2)**, [683]
    non-cash vouchers, **44(2)**, [695]
    readily convertible assets, in, **44(2)**, [697]
    share options, gains from, **44(2)**, [699]
    value of asset, enhancing, **44(2)**, [698]
  mobile UK work force, **44(2)**, [692]
  notional payments, **44(2)**, [710]
  payment—
    agency workers, for, **44(2)**, [688]
    intermediary, by, **44(2)**, [687]
    managed service companies, recovery from
      other persons, **44(2)**, [689]
    meaning, **44(2)**, [686]

PAYE—*contd*
  payment—*contd*
    mobile UK workforce, in respect of,
      44(2), [692]
    non-resident employee, **44(2)**, [691]
    non-UK employer, employee of,
      44(2), [690]
    tip sharing, provision for, **44(2)**, [693]
  regulations—
    past cases under, **43(1)**, [77]
    power to make, **44(2)**, [684]
    provisions in, **44(2)**, [684]
    transitional provisions, **44(2)**, [774]
  repayments, **44(2)**, [708]
  retrospective notional payments, **43(S)**, 90–1
  return, right to make, **44(2)**, [711]
  scope of provisions, **44(2)**, [682]
  settlement agreements, **44(2)**, [703]
    calculation of tax payable, approximations
      in, **44(2)**, [705]
    definitions, **44(2)**, [707]
    general earnings, exclusion from income,
      44(2), [706]
    sums payable by employers under,
      44(2), [704]
  share options etc, gains from, **44(2)**, [699]
  tax tables, **44(2)**, [685]

Paymaster-General
  appointment of, **10**, [297]
  office of, **10**, [296]
  regulations relating to, **10**, [411]–[412]
  salary, **10**, [612]

payment
  making off without, **12(1)**, [693]

payment into court
  amends, offer in libel case, **19(3)**, [280]
  compensation, of. *See under* **compensation**
  exoneration resulting from, **20**, [802]
  fatal accident, claim for damages, **31**, [611]
  life assurance company, **19(1)**, [143]

payroll giving
  agent's expenses, tax deductions for,
    44(3), [71]

pedal cycles. *See* **bicycles**

pedestrian
  directions to, non-compliance with, **37**, [608],
    [787]
  long-distance routes, on, **36**, [633]
  name and address, failure to give, **37**, [787]
  passage of, orders facilitating, **37**, [165]
  planning order, works to give effect to,
    36, [210], [1136]

pedestrian crossings
  local authorities, powers, **37**, [196]
  regulations, power to make, **37**, [198]
  transitional provisions, **37**, [340]
  trunk roads, on, **37**, [197]

pedestrian planning order
works to give effect to, **36**, [1136]

pedigree
falsification, **20**, [784]

pedlar
certificate—
acting without, **27**, [59]
application for, **27**, [60], [63], [72]
assignment, penalty for, **27**, [64]
borrowing, penalty for, **27**, [65]
conditions for grant of, **27**, [60]
convictions endorsed on, **27**, [67]
deprivation of, **27**, [69]
duration of, **27**, [60]
effect of, **27**, [61]
false statement, making, **27**, [66]
fee, **27**, [60], [72]
form of, **27**, [60], [76]
grant, regulations on, **27**, [60]
new, issue of, **27**, [60]
persons not requiring, **27**, [74]
production on demand, **27**, [70]
refusal, appeal against, **27**, [68]
register of, **27**, [62]
requirement of, **27**, [59]
United Kingdom, validity in, **27**, [83]
chief of police, acts of, **27**, [73]
licensed hawker, meaning, **27**, [61]
local authority powers, **27**, [75]
meaning, **27**, [58]
offences, summary proceedings for, **27**, [71]
street trading, London, **25(1)**, [395]

peer
arrest for debt, freedom from, **13**, [2]
disclaimer by. *See* **peerage**
forfeiture of title—
enemy, held by, **33(1)**, [11]
petition for restoration, **33(1)**, [12]
procedure, **33(1)**, [11]
hereditary, restriction of membership of
House of Lords, **33(1)**, [1]
Ireland, provisions contained in the Union,
31, [635]
life, **33(1)**, [17]
Scottish, rights of, **33(1)**, [21]

peerage. *See also* **peer**
adoption, effect on descent of, **6**, [176]
assemblies etc, precedence in, **33(1)**, [10]
creation of, **32**, [848]
disclaimer—
effect of, **33(1)**, [20]
instrument of—
delivery of, **33(1)**, [19]
form of, **33(1)**, [24]
gender recognition certificate, effect of,
7(1), [718]
hereditary—
House of Commons, removal of
disqualifications relating to, **32**, [980]
House of Lords, exclusion from,
32, [978]–[979]

peerage—*contd*
hereditary—*contd*
Weatherill amendment, **32**, [848]
hereditary peerage—
disclaimer, **33(1)**, [19]
House of Lords, restriction of membership
of, **33(1)**, [1]
House of Commons, exclusion from,
32, [848]
House of Lords precedence—
archbishops, **33(1)**, [4]
bishops, **33(1)**, [4]
cloth of estate, right to sit at, **33(1)**, [2]
Constable of England, **33(1)**, [5]
great chamberlain, **33(1)**, [5]
Lord Admiral, **33(1)**, [6]
Lord Chancellor, **33(1)**, [5], [9]
Lord President of the Council, **33(1)**, [5]
Lord Privy Seal, **33(1)**, [5]
Lord Treasurer, **33(1)**, [6]
marshal, **33(1)**, [6]
nobility, **33(1)**, [8]
Queen's chamberlain, **33(1)**, [6]
Queen's chief secretary, **33(1)**, [7]
Queen's children, **33(1)**, [2]
steward, **33(1)**, [6]
meaning, **33(1)**, [1]
Northern Ireland, **33(1)**, [1]
peeresses in own right, **33(1)**, [22]
precedence. *See* House of Lords *above*
privilege of, **32**, [848]
property devolving with, disposition, **6**, [280]
succession to, after artificial insemination,
6, [281]
summary of provisions, **33(1)**, [1]

penal servitude
abolition, **12(1)**, [178], [259]
substitution, **12(1)**, [178]

penalty. *See also* **sentence**
Crown, remitted by, **12(1)**, [58]

penalty points. *See under* **road traffic
offences**

Penang
Federation of Malaya, forming part of,
7(2), [463]

pension. *See also* **retirement pension;
superannuation**
administration, transfer of functions,
40(2), [264]
admissibility of statements, **33(1)**, [882]
alternatively secured—
commencement of provisions, **43(S)**, 706
dependants', maximum, **43(S)**, 700
guaranteed pension and maximum,
43(S), 700
inheritance tax provisions, **43(S)**, 704–6
minimum level of payment, **43(S)**, 702
rights on death, increase in, **43(S)**, 701
unauthorised payment charge, **43(S)**, 703
untraceable members, **43(S)**, 701

pension—*contd*

Appeal Tribunals. *See* **war pensions**

bankruptcy, effect on pension rights—
  approved arrangements regarding,
    33(1), [551]
  unapproved arrangements, **33(1)**, [552]

benefits, orders relating to, **27**, [905]

body corporate and partnership, offences by,
  33(1), [881]

breach of regulations, **33(1)**, [886]

business. *See* **insurance company**

certain categories, modification of provisions
  for, **33(1)**, [879]

Civil Aviation Authority Scheme, **4(1)**, [472]

civil partnership, dissolution or annulment of.
  See **civil partnership**

civil service. *See* **civil service pension**

commencement of provisions, **43(S)**, 716

commutation—
  amount payable, calculation, **33(1)**, [29]
  annuities, repayment by, **33(1)**, [32]
  application of provisions, **33(1)**, [28]
  Board, dissolution of, **33(1)**, [184]
  Consolidated Fund, payments from,
    33(1), [35]
  false declaration, penalty for, **33(1)**, [33]
  meaning of pension, **33(1)**, [27]
  parliamentary pension. *See* **parliamentary
    pensions**
  payment, funds for, **33(1)**, [30]
  pensioner taking office, deduction from
    salary, **33(1)**, [34]
  portion of pension, **33(1)**, [38]
  regulations, **33(1)**, [31], [185]
  summary of provisions, **33(1)**, [25]
  Treasury powers, **33(1)**, [29]

Compensation Board. *See* **Pensions
  Compensation Board**

contributions—
  excessive, recovery on bankruptcy—
    application for, **4(2)**, [421]
    calculation and verification of value,
      4(2), [423]
    estate, part of, **4(2)**, [423]
    information, provision of, **4(2)**, [423]
    orders, **4(2)**, [422]
    pension-sharing, in cases of,
      4(2), [424]–[426]
    regulations, **4(2)**, [423]
  priority in bankruptcy, **4(2)**, [557]
  See also **National Insurance**

contributions deducted from, **40(1)**, [461]

Crown, provisions applying, **33(1)**, [885]

date of commencement of, **33(1)**, [100]

diplomatic, **33(1)**, [112]

disablement—
  constant attendance, requirement of,
    40(1), [348]
  exceptionally severe disablement, increase
    for, **40(1)**, [349]
  industrial injury, in respect of, **40(1)**, [347]

divorce—
  earmarking orders, charges by pension
    arrangements in relation to, **33(1)**, [557]
  generally, **33(1)**, [521]

pension—*contd*

divorce—*contd*
  information, supply of, in connection
    with, **33(1)**, [556]
  sharing on, **43(1)**, [458]
  sharing orders, **33(1)**, [554]–[555]
  splitting on, **27**, [462]
  lump sums, **27**, [463]

documents, unlawful possession, **11(2)**, [172]

employer, meaning, **33(1)**, [837]

employers' contributions, **43(1)**, [18]

exemptions from tax—
  armed forces early departure scheme, lump
    sums provided under, **44(2)**, [637]
  bravery awards, **44(2)**, [634]
  consular employees, foreign pensions of,
    44(2), [645]
  death benefit, **44(2)**, [310]
  disablement, employment ceased due to,
    44(2), [641]
  employer's contributions, **44(2)**, [311]
  former miners' allowances in lieu of coal,
    44(2), [644]
  health and employment insurance
    payments, **44(2)**, [642]
  Malawi, Trinidad and Tobago and Zambia
    government pensions, **44(2)**, [640]
  military or war service, death due to,
    44(2), [635]
    exemption where income withheld,
      44(2), [636]
  National-Socialist persecution,
    compensation for, **44(2)**, [639]
  non-UK resident taxpayers—
    Central African Pension Fund, from,
      44(2), [647]
    Commonwealth government pensions,
      44(2), [648]
    foreign residence condition, **44(2)**, [646]
    Overseas Pensions Act 1973, under,
      44(2), [650]
    Overseas Service Act 1958, under,
      44(2), [651]
    Overseas Service Pension Fund, from,
      44(2), [652]
    Overseas Superannuation Scheme,
      from, **44(2)**, [649]
    Pensions (India, Pakistan and Burma)
      Act 1955, under, **44(2)**, [653]
  overseas scheme, contributions to,
    44(2), [312]
  retirement benefit, **44(2)**, [310]
  social security pension increases in respect
    of children, **44(2)**, [643]
  wounds and disability pensions,
    44(2), [638]

firemen. *See* **firemen's pension scheme**

foreign—
  application of provisions, **44(2)**, [598]
  meaning, **44(2)**, [599]
  person liable for tax, **44(2)**, [601]
  pre-1973, **44(2)**, [623]
    meaning, **44(2)**, [624]
    original pensioner, meaning,
      44(2), [624]

pension—*contd*
  foreign—*contd*
    pre-1973—*contd*
      person liable for tax, **44(2)**, [626]
      taxable income, **44(2)**, [625]
      taxable income, **44(2)**, [600]
  friendly societies' pension business, removal of
    restrictions on, **33(1)**, [381]
  generally, **27**, [462]
  German, pre-1948 insurance affecting
    entitlement, **33(S)**, Pensions 206–7
  House of Commons Member's Fund—
    application of provisions, **44(2)**, [619]
    meaning, **44(2)**, [620]
    person liable for tax, **44(2)**, [622]
    taxable pension income, **44(2)**, [621]
  ill-health conditions, meeting, **43(S)**, 710
  income from—
    structure of provisions, **44(2)**, [590]
    tax on—
      amount of, **44(2)**, [592]
      nature of charge, **44(2)**, [591]
      person liable for, **44(2)**, [593]
      provisions referred to, **44(2)**, [591]
  increase—
    administrative provisions, **33(1)**, [99], [115]
    approved schemes, under, **33(1)**, [106],
      [118]
    basic rate—
      based on, **33(1)**, [94]
      conversions, table of, **33(1)**, [111]
      meaning, **33(1)**, [108]
    benefits of previous Acts, preservation,
      33(1), [98]
    civil service pensions, **33(1)**, [112], [164],
      [174]
    colonial service, **33(1)**, [112]
    conditions for, **33(1)**, [95]
    dependants, for, **33(1)**, [95]
    diplomatic service, **33(1)**, [112]
    European Parliament members,
      33(1), [112]
    expenses of making, **33(1)**, [107]
    extension to other pensions, **33(1)**, [97]
    firemen, **33(1)**, [113]
    gratuities etc, for, **33(1)**, [101]
    Ireland, service in, **33(1)**, [112]
    judicial pensions, **33(1)**, [112]–[113]
    local funds, pensions out of, **33(1)**, [113]
    local government service, **33(1)**, [113],
      [115]
    lump sum payments, **33(1)**, [101]
    meaning of pension, **33(1)**, [100]
    ministerial pensions, **33(1)**, [112]
    miscellaneous pensions, **33(1)**, [113]
    Northern Ireland, provisions applied,
      33(1), [110]
    official pensions—
      base period, meaning of, **33(1)**, [172]
      calculation of, **33(1)**, [169]–[171], [173]
      duty to exercise power, **33(1)**, [165]
      guaranteed minimum, **33(1)**, [172]
      meaning, **33(1)**, [97]
      other pensions deemed to be,
        33(1), [105]

pension—*contd*
  increase—*contd*
    official pensions—*contd*
      overseas, **33(1)**, [105]
      provisions of, **33(1)**, [172]–[173]
      rate for, **33(1)**, [164], [169]–[171]
      transitional provisions, **33(1)**, [176]
    overseas—
      government pensions, **33(1)**, [103],
        [112], [117]
      Indian etc pensions, **33(1)**, [102], [112],
        [116]
      service pension, **33(1)**, [112]
    parliamentary pensions, **33(1)**, [112], [154]
    pension authority for purposes of,
      33(1), [99]
    pensions qualifying for, **33(1)**, [97], [112]
    percentage increases, **33(1)**, [94]
    police pensions, **33(1)**, [112]–[113]
    Post Office pensions, **33(1)**, [115]
    previous, preservation of, **33(1)**, [98]
    probation service, **33(1)**, [113]
    qualifying conditions, **33(1)**, [95]
    Raw Cotton Commission, **33(1)**, [114]
    re-employment, effect, **33(1)**, [96]
    regulations regarding, **33(1)**, [174]–[175]
    school staff, **33(1)**, [113]
    Scottish Parliament and Scottish
      Executive, **33(1)**, [113]
    summary of provisions, **33(1)**, [25]
    teachers, **33(1)**, [113]
    Wales, National Assembly for, **33(1)**, [113]
  interpretation, **33(1)**, [890]
  investment-regulated schemes, taxable
    property held by, **43(S)**, 712
  judicial pension. *See* **judicial pension**
  legislation referring to employers,
    modification of, **33(1)**, [880]
  liability to scheme chargeable payment,
    discharge of, **43(S)**, 703
  lien on documents, **33(1)**, [884]
  life assurance premium contributions—
    amended provisions, commencement,
      43(S), 697–9
    meaning, **43(S)**, 696–7
    relievable pensions contributions, not to
      be, **43(S)**, 696
  lump sums, **27**, [463]
    charity death benefit, **43(S)**, 703
    commencement, **43(S)**, 711
    death benefits, **43(S)**, 711
      inheritance tax, **43(S)**, 715
    transfer death benefit, abolition,
      43(S), 700–1
    winding-up, **43(S)**, 711
  meaning, **33(1)**, [27], [100]
  money purchase contracted-out scheme,
    payments in respect of, **40(2)**, [228]
  non-UK scheme, application of charges,
    43(S), 703
  Northern Ireland, arrangements for,
    31, [1121]
  notifications and other documents—
    electronic form, in, **33(1)**, [876]–[877]
    service of, **33(1)**, [875]

pension—*contd*
  official, adjustment of increase in survivors'
    pensions, **33(S)**, Pensions 203–4
  overseas, **44(1)**, [430]
    assumption by UK of responsibility for—
      agreement for, **33(1)**, [157]
      supplementary provisions, **33(1)**, [159]
    financial provisions, **33(1)**, [160]
    Hong Kong public servants—
      meaning, **33(1)**, [539]
      payments under Orders in Council,
        33(1), [541]
      pension supplements, **33(1)**, [540]
    Overseas Audit Department service,
      33(1), [158]
    schemes, power to make, **33(1)**, [158]
    service, **33(1)**, [158], [162]
    territory, meaning, **33(1)**, [157]
  overseas government, paid in UK—
    application of provisions, **44(2)**, [615]
    person liable for tax, **44(2)**, [618]
    taxable pension income, **44(2)**, [616]
      deduction from, **44(2)**, [617]
  Parliamentary. *See* **parliamentary pensions**
  Pension Protection Fund, **27**, [465]
    compensation, **27**, [906]
    regulations, **43(2)**, [644]
  pensionable age, equalisation of, **33(1)**, [513],
    [534]
  personal. *See* **personal pension scheme**
  police. *See* **police pensions**
  Prime Minister, for dependants of,
    33(1), [523]
  protected items, **33(1)**, [883]
  public service scheme—
    information about, **33(1)**, [524]
    meaning, **33(1)**, [213]
    perpetuities, exemption from rule against,
      33(1), [382]
    special provisions for, **33(1)**, [412]
  registered scheme, persons by whom
    established, **43(S)** 708
  registered scheme, under—
    application of provisions, **44(2)**, [605]
    death benefits, trivial commutation and
      winding-up, **44(2)**, [633]
    definitions, **44(2)**, [608]
    lump sums—
      exemption for, **44(2)**, [631]
      trivial commutation, **44(2)**, [632]
      winding-up, **44(2)**, [632]
    person liable for tax, **44(2)**, [607]
    taxable income, **44(2)**, [606]
  reserve forces, **3**, [1551]
  retirement benefit—
    graduated—
      payment of, **40(1)**, [42]
      regulations, **40(1)**, [311]
      widows, for, **40(1)**, [43]
    See also **retirement benefit schemes**
  sharing—
    activation of, **33(1)**, [561]
    alienation, disapplication of restrictions on,
      33(1), [573]
    benefit sharing, activation of, **40(2)**, [244]

pension—*contd*
  sharing—*contd*
    category A retirement pension—
      entitlement, **40(1)**, [303]
      increase on deferment, **40(1)**, [305],
        [479], [480]
      reduction on, **40(1)**, [290], [304]
      surplus earnings factor, **40(1)**, [471]
      weekly rate of, **40(1)**, [289]
    charges, **33(S)**, Pensions 192
    costs, charges in respect of, **33(1)**, [570]
    Court of Session, extension of time limits
      by, **33(S)**, Pensions 197
    credits—
      adjustment to amount of, **33(1)**, [586]
      cash equivalents, **33(1)**, [563]
      creation of, **33(1)**, [562]
      disqualification as destination for,
        33(1), [586]
      implementation period, **33(1)**, [566]
      liability, discharge of—
        mode of, **33(1)**, [567]
        time for, **33(1)**, [565]
      mode of discharge, **33(1)**, [586]
      rights to, treatment of on winding-up,
        33(1), [568]
    debits—
      cash equivalents, **33(1)**, [563]
      creation of, **33(1)**, [562]
      reduction of benefit, **33(1)**, [564]
    eligible scheme rights becoming subject
      to, **33(1)**, [817]
    information, power to require, **33(1)**, [574]
    interpretation, **33(1)**, [575]
    mechanism for, scope of, **33(1)**, [560]
    order, **40(2)**, [244]
    other pension schemes, **33(1)**, [569]
    regulations and orders, **33(1)**, [576]
    shareable state scheme rights, **40(2)**, [243]
    state scheme pension debts and credits—
      creation of, **40(2)**, [245]
      effect of, **40(2)**, [246]
    statutory schemes, adaptation of—
      judicial pension schemes, power to
        extend, **33(1)**, [572]
      scheme-making powers, extension of,
        33(1), [571]
    winding-up, treatment of pension credit
      rights on, **33(1)**, [568]
  sharing order—
    appeals, **27**, [482]
    court's power to make, **27**, [684]
  simplification of legislation—
    accrued benefits etc, revaluation,
      33(S), Pensions 175, 223–8
    general note, **33(S)**, Pensions 77–8
    safeguarded rights, abolition,
      33(S), Pensions 174
  social security—
    application of provisions, **44(2)**, [602]
    person liable for tax, **44(2)**, [604]
    taxable income, **44(2)**, [603]

pension—*contd*
  social security lump sum—
    income tax on—
      applicable year of assessment,
        43(2), [726]
      charge to, **43(2)**, [725]
      meaning, **43(2)**, [727]
  Speaker, for dependants of, **33(1)**, [523]
  stakeholder pensions. *See* **stakeholder
  pension scheme**
  state pension—
    additional, consolidation of,
      33(S), Pensions 175, 228–34
    credit. *See* **state pension credit**
    information, disclosure of, **40(2)**, [279]
  state second, earnings factor—
    earnings from which derived, **40(2)**, [275]
    revaluation, **40(2)**, [276]
  subordinate legislation, **33(1)**, [887]–[889]
  summary of provisions, **33(1)**, [25]
  surrenders, **43(S)**, 709
  Taxes Act 1988, amendment of, **43(1)**, [505]
  transfer to different employment, **33(1)**, [72],
    [91]
  transitional provisions, **43(1)**, [506]
    enhanced protection, **43(S)**, 712–15
    primary protection, **43(S)**, 712
  unauthorised payments—
    charge, **43(S)**, 703
    scheme sanction charge, reduction by
      amount of, **43(S)**, 709
  United Kingdom—
    application of provisions, **44(2)**, [594]
    person liable for tax, **44(2)**, [597]
    taxable income, **44(2)**, [596]
    voluntary payment, including, **44(2)**, [595]
  unsecured and dependants' unsecured,
    reference periods, **43(S)**, 711
  uprating, report on, **40(2)**, [277]
  voluntary annual payments—
    application of provisions, **44(2)**, [627]
    persons liable for tax, **44(2)**, [630]
    taxable income—
      foreign payments, **44(2)**, [629]
      UK payments, **44(2)**, [628]
  war. *See* **war pensions**
  water authorities, in relation to, **49**, [683]

pension fund
  Indian family, **44(1)**, [429]
  investments or deposits, income from,
    44(1), [429]
  overseas service, **44(1)**, [429]
  overseas territory, **44(1)**, [430]
  parliamentary, **44(1)**, [428]

Pension Protection Fund
  Board. *See* **Pension Protection Fund
  Board**
  compensation paid by—
    amended provisions,
      33(S), Pensions 257–61
    cash equivalents, **33(S)**, Pensions 185
    debits and credits, creation of,
      33(S), Pensions 184

Pension Protection Fund—*contd*
  compensation paid by—*contd*
    discharge of liability, **33(S)**, Pensions 187–8
    time for, **33(S)**, Pensions 186
    divorce, on, **33(S)**, Pensions 244–56
    general note, **33(S)**, Pensions 78–9
    implementation period,
      33(S), Pensions 186
    information, supply of,
      33(S), Pensions 189–90
    interpretation, **33(S)**, Pensions 181
    pension compensation credit, on discharge
      of, **33(S)**, Pensions 235–44
    reduction, **33(S)**, Pensions 185–6
    scope of mechanism, **33(S)**, Pensions 180
    sharing—
      activation of, **33(S)**, Pensions 181–3
      costs, charges, **33(S)**, Pensions 188–9
      information, supply of,
        33(S), Pensions 191
      Scotland, **33(S)**, Pensions 183
  contents of, **33(1)**, [770]
  eligible schemes—
    closed—
      authority to continue as, **33(1)**, [750]
      duty to assume responsibility for,
        33(1), [755]
      further assessment periods, **33(1)**, [756]
      insufficient assets, applications and
        notifications, **33(1)**, [754]
      meaning, **33(1)**, [752]
      reconsideration, **33(1)**, [754]–[756]
      treatment of, **33(1)**, [752]
      valuation, **33(1)**, [753]
    duty of Board to assume responsibility for.
     See **Pensions Protection Fund Board**
  initial levy, **33(1)**, [771]
  pension protection levies—
    amounts raised by, **33(1)**, [774]
    calculation, **33(1)**, [778]
    ceiling, **33(1)**, [775]
    collection, **33(1)**, [778]
    consultations, **33(1)**, [773]
    determinations, **33(1)**, [774]
    imposition of, **33(1)**, [771]
    meaning, **33(1)**, [771]
    recovery of, **33(1)**, [778]
    risk-based, **33(1)**, [772]
    scheme-based, **33(1)**, [772]
    scheme underfunding, valuations to
      determine, **33(1)**, [776]
    transitional period, during, **33(1)**, [777]
  pension sharing, rights becoming subject
    to, **33(1)**, [817]
  protected liabilities, **33(1)**, [728]
  references to, **33(1)**, [723]
  winding up, backdating, **33(1)**, [816]
  employer's insolvency—
    definitions, **33(1)**, [718]
    insolvency events—
      duty to notify, **33(1)**, [717]
      meaning, **33(1)**, [718]
    status of scheme, issue of notice
      confirming—
        approval by Board, **33(1)**, [720]

Pension Protection Fund—*contd*
  employer's insolvency—*contd*
    status of scheme, issue of notice
      confirming—*contd*
        binding, **33(1)**, [722]
        failure to comply, **33(1)**, [721]
      insolvency practitioner, duty of,
        33(1), [719]
    summary of provisions, **33(1)**, [25]

Pension Protection Fund Board
  accounts, **33(1)**, [917]
  administrative levy—
    charge of, **33(1)**, [714]
    late payment, interest on,
      33(S), Pensions 273
  annual reports, **33(1)**, [716]
  borrowing powers, **33(1)**, [712]
  cessation of involvement with scheme—
    circumstances of, **33(1)**, [746]
    consequences of, **33(1)**, [747]
  chairmen, **33(1)**, [914]
  Chief Executive, **33(1)**, [915]
  committees, **33(1)**, [916]
  delegation of functions, **33(1)**, [916]
  disclosure of information for facilitating
    exercise of functions, **33(1)**, [682]
  eligible schemes, assumption of responsibility
    for—
    adjustments on, **33(1)**, [760]
    administration of compensation,
      33(1), [765]
    application or notification, following,
      33(1), [725]–[727]
    assessment date—
      active members over pension age at,
        33(1), [920]
      active members under pension age at,
        33(1), [920]
      deferred members under pension age
        at, **33(1)**, [920]
      definitions, **33(1)**, [920]
      meaning, **33(1)**, [920]
      pension credit members under pension
        age at, **33(1)**, [920]
      pensions benefits postponed at,
        33(1), [920]
      pensions in payment at, **33(1)**, [920]
      pensions in payment before, **33(1)**, [920]
      right to transfer payment or contribution
        refund, compensation for, **33(1)**, [920]
      short periods of service terminating on,
        33(1), [920]
      survivors not meeting condition at,
        33(1), [920]
    assessment period—
      acting as creditor of employer during,
        33(1), [734]
      commencement, **33(1)**, [729]
      contraventions, power to validate,
        33(1), [733]
      contributions, payment during,
        33(1), [730]
      directions during, **33(1)**, [731]

Pension Protection Fund Board—*contd*
  eligible schemes, assumption of responsibility
    for—*contd*
    assessment period—*contd*
      discharge of liabilities during,
        33(1), [732]
      employer, Board to act as creditor of,
        33(1), [734]
      freezing order, effect on, **33(1)**, [631]
      liabilities discharged during, **33(1)**, [764]
      loans to pay scheme benefits,
        33(1), [736]
      new members, admission of,
        33(1), [730]
      postponement of compensation
        entitlement, **33(1)**, [761]
      references to, **33(1)**, [729]
      reviewable ill health pensions,
        33(1), [737]–[739]
      scheme benefits, payment of,
        33(1), [735]
      winding up requirement, **33(1)**, [751]
      winding up, restrictions on, **33(1)**, [732]
    closed schemes, **33(1)**, [750], [755]
    compensation, **33(1)**, [920]
    evaluation and indexation, power to alter
      rates of, **33(1)**, [920]
    effect of, **33(1)**, [758]
    following reconsideration, **33(1)**, [749]
    fraud compensation regime, relationship
      with, **33(1)**, [769]
    guaranteed minimum pensions,
      33(1), [762]
    insolvency events, following, **33(1)**, [724]
    liabilities in respect of compensation,
      discharge of, **33(1)**, [766]
    money purchase benefits, discharge of
      liability in respect of, **33(1)**, [767]
    normal pension age, meaning, **33(1)**, [920]
    pension compensation provisions,
      33(1), [759]
    protected liabilities, **33(1)**, [728]
    reconsideration, application for,
      33(1), [748]
    scheme benefits, duty to pay, **33(1)**, [763]
    transfer notice, **33(1)**, [757]
    valuation of assets and protected liabilities—
      approval of, **33(1)**, [741]
      binding, **33(1)**, [742]
      obligation of, **33(1)**, [740]
  establishment of, **33(1)**, [704]
  expenses, **33(1)**, [917]
  fees charged by, **33(1)**, [715]
  Fraud Compensation Fund—
    contents of, **33(1)**, [785]
    credits to, **33(1)**, [785]
    levy—
      imposition of, **33(1)**, [786]
      late payment, interest on,
        33(S), Pensions 273
    payments out of, **33(1)**, [785]
  fraud compensation payments—
    amount of, **33(1)**, [782]
    applications, duties in respect of,
      33(1), [780]

Pension Protection Fund Board—*contd*
fraud compensation payments—*contd*
cases in which made, **33(1)**, [779]
interim, **33(1)**, [783]
making, **33(1)**, [782]
recovery of value, **33(1)**, [781]
settlement date, **33(1)**, [781]
transfer, **33(1)**, [784]
functions of, **33(1)**, [707]
fund managers, appointment of, **33(1)**, [710]
grant to, **33(1)**, [713]
information relevant to, collection by
Regulator, **33(1)**, [665]
information—
disclosure—
exercise of functions by Board,
facilitating, **33(1)**, [795]
exercise of functions by other
supervisory authorities, facilitating,
33(1), [797], [921]
exercise of functions by Regulator,
facilitating, **33(1)**, [796]
permitted, **33(1)**, [798]
restricted, **33(1)**, [794]
tax, relating to, **33(1)**, [799]
false or misleading, offence of providing,
33(1), [792]
interpretation, **33(1)**, [801]
members of schemes, provision to,
33(1), [800]
notices requiring, **33(1)**, [788]
provision to, **33(1)**, [787]
use of, **33(1)**, [793]
investment of funds, **33(1)**, [710]
investment principles, **33(1)**, [711]
liability in damages, exemption from,
33(1), [918]
maladministration, investigation of complaints
of, **33(1)**, [805]
members—
ordinary, **33(1)**, [914]
remuneration, **33(1)**, [914]
tenure, **33(1)**, [914]
terms of appointment, **33(1)**, [914]
membership, **33(1)**, [705]
non-executive functions, **33(1)**, [709]
Ombudsman for—
annual reports, **33(1)**, [809]
appointment, **33(1)**, [806]
deputy, **33(1)**, [807]
determinations of, **33(1)**, [814]
establishment of, **33(1)**, [806]
maladministration complaints, investigation
of, **33(1)**, [811]
obstruction of, **33(1)**, [815]
payment to, **33(1)**, [806]
questions of law arising, reference to
court, **33(1)**, [812]
reports, **33(1)**, [813]
reviewable matters, reference of,
33(1), [810]
status of, **33(1)**, [808]
payment functions, equal treatment,
33(1), [768]

Pension Protection Fund Board—*contd*
pension protection levies—
amounts raised by, **33(1)**, [774]
calculation, **33(1)**, [778]
ceiling, **33(1)**, [775]
collection, **33(1)**, [778]
consultations, **33(1)**, [773]
determinations, **33(1)**, [774]
imposition of, **33(1)**, [772]
late payment, interest on,
33(S), Pensions 273
meaning, **33(1)**, [772]
recovery of, **33(1)**, [778]
risk-based, **33(1)**, [772]
scheme-based, **33(1)**, [772]
scheme underfunding, valuations to
determine, **33(1)**, [776]
transitional period, during, **33(1)**, [777]
premises, entry on—
penalties relating to, **33(1)**, [790]
powers of, **33(1)**, [789]
warrants, **33(1)**, [791]
procedure, **33(1)**, [916]
property, rights and liabilities transferred to,
33(1), [919]
refusal to assume responsibility for scheme—
new schemes created to replace existing
schemes, **33(1)**, [744]
schemes becoming eligible, **33(1)**, [743]
withdrawal following issue of notice,
33(1), [745]
reports, publication of, **33(1)**, [802]
reviewable matters—
meaning, **33(1)**, [803]
PPF Ombudsman, reference to,
33(1), [810]
review and reconsideration of, **33(1)**, [804]
schedule of, **33(1)**, [922]
seal, **33(1)**, [916]
staff, **33(1)**, [915]
status, **33(1)**, [918]
supplementary powers, **33(1)**, [708]
validity of proceedings, **33(1)**, [918]

pension schemes. *See also* **employers'
associations; trade unions**
abatement, **43(S)**, 453
actuarial guidance, removal of Secretary of
State's role, **33(S)**, Pensions 44–6
alternatively secured, person dying with,
43(S), 442
amended provisions, **43(2)**, [657]
assessments, **43(2)**, [471]
annuities purchase, temporary restriction on,
33(S), Pensions 19
annuity protection lump sum death benefit,
43(S), 452
authorised lump sums, recycling, **43(S)**, 154
authorised member payments, **43(S)**, 1249
benefit crystallisation event, **43(S)**, 1250–3
benefit crystallisation events, **43(S)**, 452
benefit rights, pre-commencement schemes,
43(2), [567]
benefits, taxation of, **43(2)**, [560]

pension schemes—*contd*
  borrowing, unauthorised—
    arrangements, **43(2)**, [398]–[399]
    money purchase arrangements,
      43(2), [396]–[397]
  bridging, **43(S)**, 448–9
  cash balance benefits, **43(2)**, [362]
  commencement lump sums, **43(2)**, [657];
    43(S), 449–51
  commencement of provisions, **43(2)**, [506]
  compulsory membership, ban on, **40(1)**, [205]
  contracting out—
    certificates, **16**, [99]
    protected rights, abolition,
      33(S), Pensions 179–80
  contributions, restriction of employers' relief,
    43(2), [657]
  defined benefits arrangement, meaning,
    43(2), [362]
  defined contribution, abolition of
    contracting-out, **33(S)**, Pensions 13, 31–44
  definitions, **43(2)**, [501]–[502]
  dependant—
    meaning, **43(2)**, [657]
    scheme pensions, **43(2)**, [657]
  dependant's annuities, transfer of, **43(S)**, 1250
  de-registration—
    appeal against decision, **43(2)**, [369]
    charge, **43(2)**, [457]
    grounds for, **43(2)**, [367]
    notification, **43(2)**, [367]
  dispute resolution arrangements,
    33(S), Pensions 14–15
  documents or particulars, notice requiring,
    43(2), [468]
    appeal against, **43(2)**, [469]
    failure to comply, **43(2)**, [477]
  electronic payments, **43(2)**, [657]
  employee benefit contributions, restriction of
    deductions for, **43(2)**, [460]
  enhanced protection, **43(2)**, [657]
  equal treatment, **40(1)**, [205]
  excess contributions lump sum, refund,
    43(S), 452
  exempt approved, employer contributions,
    43(S), 1254
  false statements, penalty for, **43(2)**, [482]
  financial assistance scheme—
    exemptions and reliefs, **43(S)**, 1404
    increased level of payments,
      33(S), Pensions 16–18
    provision for, **43(S)**, 1403–4
    purchase of annuities, restriction on,
      33(S), Pensions 195–6
    qualifying members, payment to,
      33(S), Pensions 79, 194–5
    relevant taxes, **43(S)**, 1403–4
  ill-health insurance contracts,
    pre-commencement schemes, **43(2)**, [568]
  indirect contributions, spreading of relief on,
    43(S), 918–19
  information requirements, **43(2)**, [467], [476],
    [657]
  inheritance of, **43(S)**, 443

pension schemes—*contd*
  inheritance tax—
    amendments, **43(S)**, 441–6
    cash options, **42**, [687]
    liability for, **42**, [747]
    overseas pensions, **42**, [688]
    pension rights, etc, treatment of, **42**, [686]
  insurance company—
    administrator, liable as, **43(2)**, [494], [657]
    meaning, **43(2)**, [497]
  insurance, Financial Services Compensation
    Scheme intervention, **43(S)**, 1405
  insured schemes, transfers to, **43(2)**, [484]
  investment-regulated—
    amended provisions, **43(S)**, 406–39
    definition, **43(S)**, 1250
    non-UK, application of charges, **43(S)**, 433
    taxable property held by, **43(S)**, 407,
      415–33
      income and gains from, **43(S)**, 407–14
      pre and post–commencement holdings,
        43(S), 434–9
  jobholders, membership for—
    agency workers, **33(S)**, Pensions 165–6
    agreements to limit operation of provisions,
      restriction on, **33(S)**, Pensions 141–2
    armed forces, service in,
      33(S), Pensions 167
    automatic enrolment schemes,
      33(S), Pensions 103
    compliance with provisions—
      calculation and payment of
        contributions, **33(S)**, Pensions 121–2
      compliance notice, **33(S)**, Pensions 119,
        134
      employees' payments to personal pension
        schemes, monitoring
        33(S), Pensions 133
      escalating penalty notice,
        33(S), Pensions 125–6
      failure, right of action,
        33(S), Pensions 118
      fixed penalty notice, **33(S)**, Pensions 124
      information, Regulator requiring,
        33(S), Pensions 144–5
      offences, **33(S)**, Pensions 130–2
      penalty notice, **33(S)**, Pensions 135
      Pensions Regulator Tribunal, references
        to, **33(S)**, Pensions 128–9, 135
      premises, entry of Regulator on,
        33(S), Pensions 144–5
      records, requirement to keep,
        33(S), Pensions 143
      recovery of penalties,
        33(S), Pensions 126
      relevant contributions, meaning,
        33(S), Pensions 123
      review of notices, **33(S)**, Pensions 127,
        135
      third party compliance notice,
        33(S), Pensions 120
      unpaid contributions notice,
        33(S), Pensions 121
    contract of employment, meaning,
      33(S), Pensions 165

pension schemes—*contd*
  jobholders, membership for—*contd*
    Crown employment, **33(S)**, Pensions 167
    deduction of contributions,
      33(S), Pensions 117–18
    defined benefits and hybrid schemes,
      transitional period,
      33(S), Pensions 114–15
    definition of worker, extension of,
      33(S), Pensions 172
    definitions, **33(S)**, Pensions 165, 172–4
    directors, position of, **33(S)**, Pensions 166
    employee, meaning, **33(S)**, Pensions 165
    employers' duties—
      automatic enrolment,
        33(S), Pensions 89–90
        postponement, **33(S)**, Pensions 91
      automatic re-enrolment,
        33(S), Pensions 92
        timing, **33(S)**, Pensions 93–4
      continuity of membership,
        33(S), Pensions 89
      introduction of, **33(S)**, Pensions 199
      Pensions Regulator, information to be
        given to, **33(S)**, Pensions 99
      workers, information to be given to,
        33(S), Pensions 98
      workers without qualifying earnings,
        33(S), Pensions 97
    enforcement of rights, **33(S)**, Pensions 138
    freezing order, effect of,
      33(S), Pensions 116
    general note, **33(S)**, Pensions 71–7
    House of Commons staff,
      33(S), Pensions 168
    House of Lords staff, **33(S)**, Pensions 168
    inducements, **33(S)**, Pensions 136
    jobholder, meaning, **33(S)**, Pensions 87
    money purchase and personal pension,
      transitional provisions,
      33(S), Pensions 113–14
    occupational pension schemes,
      33(S), Pensions 104
    offshore employment, persons in,
      33(S), Pensions 171
    orders and regulations,
      33(S), Pensions 208–10
    pension scheme—
      contribution limits, **33(S)**, Pensions 152
      duty to establish, **33(S)**, Pensions 149–50
      enactments, application of,
        33(S), Pensions 154
      members and employers, consultation
        of, **33(S)**, Pensions 151
      orders, **33(S)**, Pensions 151–2
      review of schemes, **33(S)**, Pensions 154
      rules, procedure for, **33(S)**, Pensions 153
      stakeholder, **33(S)**, Pensions 163–4
    Pensions Ombudsman, functions of,
      33(S), Pensions 149
    personal pension schemes,
      33(S), Pensions 104
    police, employment in, **33(S)**, Pensions 169
    private pension and retirement planning,
      information for, **33(S)**, Pensions 147

pension schemes—*contd*
  jobholders, membership for—*contd*
    prohibited recruitment conduct,
      33(S), Pensions 133
    qualifying earnings—
      band, review of, **33(S)**, Pensions 101
      meaning, **33(S)**, Pensions 100–1
      pay reference period,
        33(S), Pensions 102
      workers without, **33(S)**, Pensions 97
    qualifying schemes, **33(S)**, Pensions 102–3
    quality requirement—
      certification of satisfaction of,
        33(S), Pensions 112–13
      non-UK occupational pension scheme
        33(S), Pensions 110
      other personal pension schemes
        33(S), Pensions 111
      test scheme, **33(S)**, Pensions 108
      test scheme standard,
        33(S), Pensions 107
      UK defined benefits schemes,
        33(S), Pensions 106
      UK hybrid schemes ,
        33(S), Pensions 109
      UK money purchase schemes,
        33(S), Pensions 105
      UK personal pension scheme,
        33(S), Pensions 110–11
    Regulator—
      information, requiring,
        33(S), Pensions 144–5
      information to be given to,
        33(S), Pensions 99
      objectives, **33(S)**, Pensions 148
      premises, entry on,
        33(S), Pensions 144–5
    restricted information, penalty for
      disclosure of, **33(S)**, Pensions 148
    right of employee not to be unfairly
      dismissed, **33(S)**, Pensions 139–40
    right of employee not to suffer detriment,
      33(S), Pensions 137
    right to opt-in, **33(S)**, Pensions 94–5
    right to opt-out, **33(S)**, Pensions 96
    tax information, disclosure of,
      33(S), Pensions 145–6
    trustee corporation—
      establishment, **33(S)**, Pensions 155
      financial provisions, **33(S)**, Pensions 220
      functions, **33(S)**, Pensions 151
      members and employees,
        33(S), Pensions 214–16, 221
      name of, **33(S)**, Pensions 155
      pension trustee legislation, application
        of, **33(S)**, Pensions 156
      proceedings, **33(S)**, Pensions 217–18
      property of, **33(S)**, Pensions 155
    trustees, power of to modify scheme,
      33(S), Pensions 117
    vessels, persons working on,
      33(S), Pensions 169–70
    worker, meaning, **33(S)**, Pensions 165, 172
  lifetime allowance, **43(2)**, [657]
    availability of, **43(2)**, [434]; **43(S)**, 452

pension schemes—*contd*
lifetime allowance—*contd*
charge, **43(2)**, [429]
amount of, **43(2)**, [430]
benefit crystallisation events,
43(2), [431], [561]
discharge of liability, **43(2)**, [487], [489]
persons liable to, **43(2)**, [432]
pre-commencement schemes,
43(2), [566]
enhanced protection, benefit accrual,
43(2), [481]
enhanced, regulations, **43(2)**, [474]
documents and information,
43(2), [479]
failure to comply, **43(2)**, [480]
enhancement factor, **43(2)**, [435]
non-residence—
generally, **43(2)**, [436]
money purchase arrangements,
43(2), [437]
other arrangements, **43(2)**, [438]
previously crystallised rights, **43(2)**, [435]
recognised overseas pension scheme,
transfers from—
generally, **43(2)**, [439]
money purchase arrangements,
43(2), [440]
other arrangements, **43(2)**, [441]
standard, **43(2)**, [433]
lifetime annuities, transfer of, **43(S)**, 1250
loans to sponsoring employers,
pre-commencement schemes, **43(2)**, [568]
lump sums, transitional protection of,
43(S), 1253
market value of assets, **43(2)**, [500]
meaning, **8**, 611; **43(2)**, [360]; **48**, 650
member—
arrangement, meaning, **43(2)**, [362]
defined benefits, **43(2)**, [362]
hybrid arrangement, **43(2)**, [362]
meaning, **43(2)**, [361]
money purchase benefits, **43(2)**, [362]
migrant member relief, **43(2)**, [657]
minor amendments, **43(2)**, [503], [564]
modification of rules, power of, **43(2)**, [657]
non-UK—
application of charges to, **43(S)**, 1255
inheritance tax treatment, **43(S)**, 1254
occupational. *See* **occupational pension
scheme**
occupational benefits, limit on increase in,
43(2), [386]
orders and regulations, **43(2)**, [504]
Parliamentary control of, **40(1)**, [58]
power to make, **40(1)**, [57]
other, dependent dying with, **43(S)**, 444
overseas—
annual allowance charge, **43(2)**, [563]
contributions to, **44(2)**, [312]
double tax arrangements, meaning,
43(2), [563]
extension of migrant member relief,
43(S), 453
lifetime allowance charge, **43(2)**, [563]

pension schemes—*contd*
overseas—*contd*
meaning, **43(2)**, [360]
member payment charges, **43(2)**, [563]
migrant member relief, **43(2)**, [562]
overview, **43(2)**, [359]
payments—
cleared, **43(2)**, [473]
electronic means, by, **43(2)**, [472]
lump sums, winding-up to facilitate,
43(2), [483]
pension credit member, **43(S)**, 446
perpetuities, rule against, **40(1)**, [55]
personal. *See* **personal pension scheme**
power to split schemes, **43(2)**, [657]
public service—
abatement, **43(2)**, [657]
perpetuities, rule against, **40(1)**, [55]
recognised transfers, **43(2)**, [657]
registered—
information and inspection powers,
43(S), 1695–6
miscellaneous provisions, **43(S)**, 1253
special annual allowance charge,
43(S), 1635–6
amendment of provisions, **43(S)**, 1645
contributions refund lump sums, taxation
of, **43(S)**, 1645
currently-relieved non-UK pension
schemes, **43(S)**, 1645
increased, **43(S)**, 1645
interpretation, **43(S)**, 1646
pre-22 April 2008 pension input
amount, **43(S)**, 1644
protected pension input amounts,
43(S), 1639–43
relevant income, calculation of,
43(S), 1636–7
relevant refunded amounts,
43(S), 1643–4
tax years to which provisions applicable,
43(S), 1646
total adjusted pension input amount,
43(S), 1638–9
registered, payments by—
authorised, **43(2)**, [370]
authorised employer—
compensation, **43(2)**, [392]
loans, **43(2)**, [393], [559]
nature of, **43(2)**, [389]
public service scheme, **43(2)**, [389]
scheme administration, **43(2)**, [394]
surplus, **43(2)**, [391]
authorised member, **43(2)**, [374]
lump sum death benefit rule,
43(2), [378], [558]
lump sum rule, **43(2)**, [376], [557]
overseas schemes, appeal against decision
to exclude, **43(2)**, [380]
pension death benefit rules, **43(2)**, [377],
[556]
pension rules, **43(2)**, [375], [555]
recognised transfers, **43(2)**, [379]
borrowing, meaning, **43(2)**, [373]

pension schemes—*contd*
registered, payments by—*contd*
connected person, increase of rights on death, **43(2)**, [384]
definitions, **43(2)**, [371]
loan, meaning, **43(2)**, [372]
scheme administration member payments, **43(2)**, [381]
taxation of, **43(2)**, [560]
unallocated employer contributions, **43(2)**, [385]
unauthorised employer—
meaning, **43(2)**, [370]
value shifting, **43(2)**, [395]
unauthorised member—
assignment, **43(2)**, [382]
benefits, **43(2)**, [387]
meaning, **43(2)**, [370]
returned, relief from liability—
member's liability, **43(2)**, [485]
scheme's liability, **43(2)**, [486]
surrender, **43(2)**, [383]
treatment as making, **43(2)**, [387]
value shifting, **43(2)**, [388]
unauthorised, meaning, **43(2)**, [370]
registration—
application for, **43(2)**, [363]
de-registration—
appeal against decision, **43(2)**, [369]
charge, **43(2)**, [457]
grounds for, **43(2)**, [368]
notification, **43(2)**, [367]
deemed, existing schemes, **43(2)**, [565]
definitions, **43(2)**, [365]
eligibility for, **43(2)**, [364]
HM Revenue & Customs decision, **43(2)**, [363]
appeal against, **43(2)**, [366]
pre-commencement schemes, **43(2)**, [565]
withdrawal, **43(2)**, [367]
relevant valuation factor, **43(2)**, [498]
residential interests, **8**, 609, 611–12
return, **43(2)**, [466]
failure to make, **43(2)**, [475]
scheme administrator—
accounting for tax by, **43(2)**, [470]
return, **43(2)**, [478]
insurance company liable as, **43(2)**, [494], [657]
liability of, **43(2)**, [491], [493]
pre-commencement schemes, **43(2)**, [565]
meaning, **43(2)**, [490]
members, liability of, **43(2)**, [493]
pre-commencement schemes, **43(2)**, [565]
trustees, etc, liability of, **43(2)**, [492]
scheme, amendments, **43(2)**, [657]
shares held on trust for, **8**, 610
short service refund lump sum, **43(S)**, 452
splitting, HM Revenue and Customs' powers, **43(2)**, [496]
surrender and allocation of rights, **43(2)**, [657]

pension schemes—*contd*
tax charges—
annual allowance—
amount of, **43(2)**, [443]
cash balance arrangements, **43(2)**, [445]
closing value, adjusting, **43(2)**, [447]
opening value, uprating, **43(2)**, [446]
defined benefits arrangements, **43(2)**, [449]
closing value, adjusting, **43(2)**, [451]
opening value, uprating, **43(2)**, [450]
hybrid arrangements, **43(2)**, [452]
liability to, **43(2)**, [442]
money purchase arrangements, **43(2)**, [448]
pension input period, **43(2)**, [453]
total pension input amount, **43(2)**, [444]
authorised surplus payments, **43(2)**, [422]
de-registration, **43(2)**, [457]
lifetime allowance, **43(2)**, [429]
amount of, **43(2)**, [430]
benefit crystallisation events, **43(2)**, [431]
discharge of liability, **43(2)**, [487], [489]
persons liable to, **43(2)**, [432]
pre-commencement schemes, **43(2)**, [566]
scheme sanction—
amount of, **43(2)**, [455]
discharge of liability, **43(2)**, [488]
liability to, **43(2)**, [454]
scheme chargeable payment, **43(2)**, [456]
short service refund lump sum, on, **43(2)**, [420]
special lump sum death benefits, on, **43(2)**, [421]
unauthorised payments, on, **43(2)**, [423]
crystallised rights, valuation of, **43(2)**, [426]
surcharge, **43(2)**, [424], [488]
surchargeable payments, **43(2)**, [425]
surchargeable unauthorised employer payments, **43(2)**, [428]
uncrystallised rights, valuation of, **43(2)**, [427]
tax reliefs—
capital gains tax, **43(2)**, [401]
employees, for, **43(2)**, [416]
employers' contributions, for—
cessation of business, on, **43(2)**, [413]
deemed, **43(2)**, [414]
no other relief for, **43(2)**, [415]
provision for, **43(2)**, [410]
restriction on, **43(2)**, [411]
spreading, **43(2)**, [412]
income tax, **43(2)**, [400]
inheritance tax exemptions, **43(2)**, [418]
HM Revenue & Customs contributions, **43(2)**, [417]
members' contributions, for—
annual limit, **43(2)**, [404]
claim, making, **43(2)**, [408]
individuals, for, **43(2)**, [402]–[403]
methods of giving, **43(2)**, [405]
net pay arrangements, under, **43(2)**, [407]

pension schemes—*contd*
  tax reliefs—*contd*
    members' contributions, for—*contd*
      source, at, **43(2)**, [406]
      transfer of shares treated as payment of, **43(2)**, [409]
    tax-relieved savings, inheritance of, **43(S)**, 1242–7
    terms of employment, particulars required in, **16**, [99]
    transitional provisions, **40(1)**, [61]; **43(2)**, [505], [565], [657]; **43(S)**, 453–9
    trivial commutation and winding-up lump sums, **43(2)**, [657]
    Trustee Act 2000, application of, **48**, 650
    unauthorised payments, **43(S)**, 446–8
      loans, **43(2)**, [657]
      member's liability, **43(2)**, [657]
      return of, **43(2)**, [657]
    uncrystallised rights, valuation of, **43(2)**, [657]
    unsecured funds, **43(2)**, [657]
    valuation assumptions, **43(2)**, [499]

pensioners
  Christmas bonus—
    decision as to entitlement, **40(2)**, [182]
    determinations, review of, **40(1)**, [569]
    entitlement to, **40(1)**, [400]
    qualifying benefit—
      entitlement to, **40(1)**, [400], [401]
      meaning, **40(1)**, [402]
    United Kingdom, extent of, **40(1)**, [400], [401]

Pensions Appeal Tribunal
  amendment of provisions, **40(1)**, [104]
  President, pension, **11(2)**, [597]

Pensions Compensation Board
  dissolution, **33(1)**, [874]

pensions (ecclesiastical)
  capital, Church Commissioners' power to spend, **14**, 1400
  Church of England Pensions Board—
    audit of accounts, **14**, 541
    Church Commissioners directing, **14**, 535
    church workers pensions augmentation fund—
      dissolution of, **14**, 1398
      establishment of, **14**, 538
    church workers, scheme for, **14**, 537
    clerks, scheme for, **14**, 543
    constitution of, **14**, 533
    deaconesses, provision for, **14**, 957–8
    expenses of, **14**, 534
    functions, **14**, 534–5
    fund, investment in, **14**, 540
    general purposes fund, **14**, 1397–8
    housing association, being, **14**, 538
    investment powers, **14**, 539–40
    lay workers, provision for, **14**, 957–8
    legacy, investment given by, **14**, 540
    loans for residence, making, **14**, 536
    members, **14**, 533

pensions (ecclesiastical)—*contd*
  Church of England Pensions Board—*contd*
    rates of interest, altering, **14**, 806
    residences, providing, **14**, 535–6, 652–3, 963, 1399
    staff of, **14**, 534
    trust corporation, being, **14**, 539
    trustee, power to act as, **14**, 539
  church estates commissioners, of, **14**, 523
  church workers pension fund, **14**, 958
  church workers pensions augmentation fund, dissolution of, **14**, 1398
  clergy, for—
    children, for, **14**, 1188–9
    Church Commissioners, out of fund of, **14**, 531
    clergy pensions augmentation fund, **14**, 532
      dissolution of, **14**, 1398
    clergy (widows and dependants) pension fund, **14**, 532–3
      dissolution of, **14**, 1398
    clergy (widows and dependants) pensions augmentation fund, **14**, 532–3
    determination of questions, **14**, 542
    General Synod, power to make regulations, **14**, 806–7
    lump sum payments, **14**, 651–2
    rates of interest, altering, **14**, 544, 806
    widowers, for, **14**, 1188–9
    widows, for, **14**, 805, 806–7
  clerks, schemes for, **14**, 543
  diocesan widows and dependants committee, **14**, 543
  dispossessed clerks, payments in respect of, **14**, 1399
  ecclesiastical commissioners, to retired officers of, **14**, 521–2
  pensions augmentation funds, dissolution of, **14**, 1398
  Pensions Board, constitution of, **14**, 1318
  Queen Anne's Bounty, to retired officers of, **14**, 521–2
  retirement of dignitary, on, **14**, 435
  schemes—
    Church Commissioners—
      capital, application of, **14**, 1317
      funded scheme, transitional grants for, **14**, 1317
      liability of, **14**, 1316
    funded—
      Church Commissioners, transitional grants from, **14**, 1317
      contributions to, **14**, 1314–15
      establishment of, **14**, 1314
      meaning, **14**, 1312
      rules, **14**, 1313
    past service, meaning, **14**, 1312

Pensions Ombudsman
  advice, obtaining, **33(1)**, [366]
  appointment of, **33(1)**, [360]
  complaints to—
    authorised complainants, death, insolvency or disability of, **33(1)**, [363]
    court proceedings, staying, **33(1)**, [364]

Pensions Ombudsman—*contd*
  complaints to—*contd*
    procedure on investigation,
      33(1), [365]–[366]
    county court rules regulating, **33(1)**, [369]
  Deputy, **33(1)**, [361], [858]
  determinations of, **33(1)**, [367]
  facilities, **33(1)**, [360]
  functions of, **33(1)**, [362]
  late payment of benefit, interest on,
    33(1), [368]
  obstruction of, **33(1)**, [366]
  payments to, **33(1)**, [360], [858]
  pension scheme membership for jobholders,
    functions as to, **33(S)**, Pensions 149
  question of law, referring, **33(1)**, [366]
  reports, **33(1)**, [360]
  staff, **33(1)**, [360]
  summary of provisions, **33(1)**, [25]

Pensions Regulator
  accounts, **33(1)**, [902]
  annual reports to Secretary of State,
    33(1), [423], [614]
  appointment of trustees, **33(1)**, [426]
  breaches of law, duty to report to,
    33(1), [667]
  Chief Executive, **33(1)**, [899]
  civil penalties exercised by, **33(1)**, [429]
  codes of practice—
    evidence, admissible in, **33(1)**, [687]
    issue of, **33(1)**, [687]
    procedure for, **33(1)**, [688]
    publications, **33(1)**, [688]
    revocation, **33(1)**, [689]
    subjects of, **33(1)**, [687]
  committees, **33(1)**, [901]
  contribution notice—
    clearance statements, **33(1)**, [639]
    content and effect of, **33(1)**, [637]
    employer debt—
      avoidance of, **33(1)**, [635]
      relationship with, **33(1)**, [638]
    financial support directions,
      non-compliance with—
        content and effect of, **33(1)**, [646]
        employer debt, relationship with,
          33(1), [647]
        power to issue, **33(1)**, [644]
        sum specified in, **33(1)**, [645]
    issue of, **33(1)**, [635]
    partnerships and limited liability
      partnerships, provisions applying to,
      33(1), [654]
    restoration notice, failure to comply with,
      33(1), [652]–[653]
    sum specified in, **33(1)**, [636]
  delegation of functions, **33(1)**, [901]
  delegation of powers,
    33(S), Pensions 199–200
  Determinations Panel—
    chairman, **33(1)**, [612], [900]
    establishment of, **33(1)**, [612]
    functions of, **33(1)**, [613]

Pensions Regulator—*contd*
  Determinations Panel—*contd*
    members, **33(1)**, [900]
      appointment, **33(1)**, [612]
    reserved regulatory functions,
      33(1), [904]–[908]
  directions where employer fails to comply
    with requirements, **33(1)**, [433]
  duty to notify of certain events, **33(1)**, [666]
  establishment of, **33(1)**, [604]
  expenses, **33(1)**, [902]
  financial support directions—
    clearance statements, **33(1)**, [643]
    financial support, meaning, **33(1)**, [642]
    insufficiently resourced, meaning,
      33(1), [641]
    interpretation, **33(1)**, [648]
    issue of, **33(1)**, [640]
    non-compliance, contribution notice on—
      content and effect of, **33(1)**, [646]
      employer debt, relationship with,
        33(1), [647]
      power to issue, **33(1)**, [644]
      sum specified in, **33(1)**, [645]
    partnerships and limited liability
      partnerships, provisions applying to,
      33(1), [654]
    service company, meaning, **33(1)**, [641]
  functions, **33(1)**, [607]
  funding, **33(1)**, [902]
  improvement notice—
    directions in, **33(1)**, [616]
    issue of, **33(1)**, [616]
  information—
    Board, disclosure for facilitating exercise of
      functions by, **33(1)**, [682]
    corresponding overseas authorities, supplied
      by, **33(1)**, [680]
    disclosure for facilitating exercise of
      functions, **33(1)**, [681]
    other supervisory authorities, disclosure for
      facilitating exercise of functions by,
      33(1), [683], [909]
    permitted disclosures, **33(1)**, [684]
    provision of false or misleading, offence
      of, **33(1)**, [677]
    restricted, **33(1)**, [679]
    tax, relating to, **33(1)**, [685]
    use of, **33(1)**, [678]
  information, education and assistance,
    provision of, **33(1)**, [615]
  information facilitating exercise of functions
    by Board, disclosure of, **33(1)**, [795]
  injunction or interdict, obtaining,
    33(1), [618]
  institutions administered in other member
    state, functions relating to, **33(1)**, [867]
  liability in damages, exemption from,
    33(1), [903]
  members of, **33(1)**, [605], [898]
  modification orders—
    effect of, **33(1)**, [482]
    powers to make, **33(1)**, [480]–[484]
    winding-up, to secure, **33(1)**, [483]
  non-executive functions, **33(1)**, [611]

Pensions Regulator—*contd*
objectives, **33(1)**, [608]
occupational and personal pension scheme, register of—
compilation and maintenance of, **33(1)**, [656]
information, provision of, **33(1)**, [658]
inspection of, **33(1)**, [658]
registrable information, **33(1)**, [657]
reports, **33(1)**, [658]
trustees or managers, duties of, **33(1)**, [659]
Occupational Pensions Regulatory Authority—
employees, transfer of, **33(1)**, [873]
transfer of functions of, **33(1)**, [610]
occupational scheme, freezing order against—
action in contravention of, validation, **33(1)**, [628]
assessment period, effect of, **33(1)**, [631]
ceasing to have effect, power to give direction on, **33(1)**, [632]
consequences of, **33(1)**, [626]
determination to wind up scheme, effect of, **33(1)**, [629]
directions in, **33(1)**, [625]
duration of, **33(1)**, [627]
effect of winding up order on, **33(1)**, [630]
power to make, **33(1)**, [625], [634]
trustees, managers, employers and members, notification of, **33(1)**, [633]
Pension Protection Fund Board, collection of information relevant to, **33(1)**, [665]
pension scheme membership for jobholders—
information, requiring, **33(S)**, Pensions 144–5
information to be given to, **33(S)**, Pensions 99
objectives, **33(S)**, Pensions 148
premises, entry on, **33(S)**, Pensions 144–5
Personal Accounts Delivery Authority, disclosure of information to, **33(S)**, Pensions 160
procedure, **33(1)**, [901]
prohibited trustees, register of, **33(1)**, [663]–[664]
provision of information to, **33(1)**, [669]
prohibition orders by, **33(1)**, [423]
public service schemes—
modification orders, powers to make, **33(1)**, [484]
wind up, powers to, **33(1)**, [431]
regulatory functions—
compulsory review, **33(1)**, [696]
interests of members, duty to have regard to, **33(1)**, [697]
meaning, **33(1)**, [690]
orders, notices or directions, power to vary or revoke, **33(1)**, [698]
procedure, **33(1)**, [690]
publication of procedure, **33(1)**, [691]
special procedure, **33(1)**, [694]–[695]
standard and special procedure, application of, **33(1)**, [692]
standard procedure, **33(1)**, [693]

Pensions Regulator—*contd*
removal or appointment of trustees powers to vest or transfer property, **33(1)**, [428]
report notice—
cost of report, **33(1)**, [668]
failure to comply with, **33(1)**, [668]
issue of, **33(1)**, [668]
requirements in, **33(1)**, [668]
reports, publication of, **33(1)**, [686]
ring-fencing of assets, power to require, **33(1)**, [866]
scheme funding, powers as to, **33(1)**, [828]
scheme returns—
content of, **33(1)**, [662]
definitions, **33(1)**, [662]
notice, issue of, **33(1)**, [660]
trustees or managers, duties of, **33(1)**, [661]
seal, **33(1)**, [901]
staff, **33(1)**, [899]
stakeholder pension schemes, register of, **33(1)**, [546]
status, **33(1)**, [903]
summary of provisions, **33(1)**, [25]
supplementary powers, **33(1)**, [609]
suspension orders by, **33(1)**, [424]
technical provisions improperly determined, intervention, **33(S)**, Pensions 199
third party notice—
directions in, **33(1)**, [617]
issue of, **33(1)**, [617]
transactions at undervalue—
meaning, **33(1)**, [649]
restoration notice—
content and effect of, **33(1)**, [651]
definitions, **33(1)**, [650]
failure to comply with, contribution notice on, **33(1)**, [652]–[653]
partnerships and limited liability partnerships, provisions applying to, **33(1)**, [654]
power to make, **33(1)**, [649]
requirements in, **33(1)**, [650]
transactions defrauding creditors, right to apply for order, **33(1)**, [655]
Tribunal. *See* **Pensions Regulator Tribunal**
unpaid contributions, recovery of, **33(1)**, [620]
validity of proceedings, **33(1)**, [903]
warrant, obtaining, **33(1)**, [675]
winding-up of schemes—
directions by, for facilitating, **33(1)**, [486]
compliance with, **33(1)**, [487]
powers regarding, **33(1)**, [430]
reports to, regarding, **33(1)**, [485]

Pensions Regulator Tribunal
appeal from on point of law, **33(1)**, [701]
constitution, **33(1)**, [911]
costs, **33(1)**, [912]
decisions, **33(1)**, [912]
establishment of, **33(1)**, [699]
evidence, **33(1)**, [912]
expenses, **33(1)**, [910]
functions, **33(1)**, [699]

Pensions Regulator Tribunal—*contd*
legal assistance scheme, provision for,
33(1), [703]
members, **33(1)**, [910]
panels, **33(1)**, [910]
pension scheme membership for jobholders,
references, **33(S)**, Pensions 128–9, 135
practice directions, **33(1)**, [912]
President, **33(1)**, [910]
procedure, **33(1)**, [912]
redetermination by, **33(1)**, [702]
references to, **33(1)**, [700]
staff, **33(1)**, [910]
status, **33(1)**, [913]

performers' rights
consent, **11(1)**, [1044]
Copyright Tribunal—
consent given by, **11(1)**, [1026]
jurisdiction of, **11(1)**, [1059]
county court jurisdiction, **11(1)**, [1059]
definitions, **11(1)**, [1080]–[1081]
duration of, **11(1)**, [1027]
exceptions, **11(1)**, [1025]
generally, **11(1)**, [1011], [1042]
infringement—
breach of statutory duty, actionable as,
11(1), [1045]
illicit recording, importing, possession or
dealing with, **11(1)**, [1020]
summary of provisions, **11(1)**, [415]
use of recording made without consent,
11(1), [1019], [1023]
moral rights—
assignable, not, **11(1)**, [1071]
consent to acts infringing, **11(1)**, [1069]
derogatory treatment of performance,
objection to—
exceptions to, **11(1)**, [1066]
infringing article, possessing or dealing
with, **11(1)**, [1067]
right of, **11(1)**, [1065]
duration of, **11(1)**, [1068]
infringement, remedies for, **11(1)**, [1073]
parts of performances, **11(1)**, [1070]
performer, identification of—
assertion of right, **11(1)**, [1063]
exceptions, **11(1)**, [1064]
rights of, **11(1)**, [1062]
summary of provisions, **11(1)**, [415]
transmission on death, **11(1)**, [1072]
waiver of, **11(1)**, [1069]
offences—
authority to give consent, false
representation of, **11(1)**, [1054]
delivery up, order for, **11(1)**, [1052]
illicit recording, making, dealing with or
using, **11(1)**, [1050]
local weights and measures authority,
enforcement by, **11(1)**, [1051]
search warrants, **11(1)**, [1053]
performance—
meaning, **11(1)**, [1011]
qualifying—
generally, **11(1)**, [1012]

performers' rights—*contd*
performance—*contd*
qualifying—*contd*
recording of—
copying, consent required for,
11(1), [1014]
equitable remuneration for
exploitation of sound recording,
right to, **11(1)**, [1018]
issue of copies to public, consent
required for, **11(1)**, [1015]
lending of copies to public, consent
required for, **11(1)**, [1016]
making available to public by
electronic transmission, **11(1)**, [1017]
rental of copies to public, consent
required for, **11(1)**, [1016]
permitted acts—
broadcast—
archival purposes, recording for,
11(1), [1176]
free public showing, **11(1)**, [1176]
incidental recording, **11(1)**, [1176]
photographs of, **11(1)**, [1176]
reception and re-transmission of wireless
broadcast by cable, **11(1)**, [1176]
sub-titled copies, provision of,
11(1), [1176]
supervision and control, recordings for,
11(1), [1176]
club or society, playing of recordings for,
11(1), [1176]
copy of work as condition of export,
11(1), [1176]
criticism, reviews and news reporting,
11(1), [1176]
educational establishments, **11(1)**, [1176]
electronic form, transfer of copies in,
11(1), [1176]
folksongs, recordings of, **11(1)**, [1176]
incidental inclusion, **11(1)**, [1176]
instruction or examination, things done
for, **11(1)**, [1176]
parliamentary and judicial proceedings,
11(1), [1176]
public records, **11(1)**, [1176]
recordings of performance—
lending of copies by educational
establishments, **11(1)**, [1176]
lending of copies by libraries or
archives, **11(1)**, [1176]
recordings of spoken works, use of,
11(1), [1176]
recordings for time-shifting, **11(1)**, [1176]
Royal Commission, for purposes of,
11(1), [1176]
statutory authority, done under,
11(1), [1176]
statutory inquiries, for purposes of,
11(1), [1176]
time-shifting, recordings for, **11(1)**, [1176]
property rights—
assignment, **11(1)**, [1029]
exclusive licences, **11(1)**, [1031]

performers' rights—*contd*
property rights—*contd*
film production agreement—
transfer of rental right—
equitable remuneration—
Copyright tribunal, reference of
amount to, **11(1)**, [1035]
right to, **11(1)**, [1034]
presumption of, **11(1)**, [1033]
generally, **11(1)**, [1028]
infringement—
actionable by rights owner,
11(1), [1036]
concurrent rights, exercise of,
11(1), [1041]
damages, **11(1)**, [1037]
injunctions against service providers,
11(1), [1038]
licence of right, undertaking to take,
11(1), [1039]
rights and remedies for exclusive
licensee, **11(1)**, [1040]
service providers, injunctions against,
11(1), [1038]
licences, **11(1)**, [1029]
licensing, **11(1)**, [1060]
bodies—
applications, **11(1)**, [1177]
generally, **11(1)**, [1177]
references, **11(1)**, [1177]
competition report, powers exercisable as
result of, **11(1)**, [1177]
royalty or other sum payable for lending,
application to settle, **11(1)**, [1177]
schemes—
applications, **11(1)**, [1177]
certification, **11(1)**, [1177]
generally, **11(1)**, [1177]
references, **11(1)**, [1177]
unreasonable discrimination,
11(1), [1177]
prospective ownership of, **11(1)**, [1030]
summary of provisions, **11(1)**, [415]
will, passing under, **11(1)**, [1032]
qualification for protection—
British ships, aircraft and hovercraft, on,
11(1), [1078]
countries to which extending,
11(1), [1075]
qualifying country, **11(1)**, [1074]
qualifying individual, **11(1)**, [1074]
qualifying person, **11(1)**, [1074]
reciprocal, **11(1)**, [1076]
territorial waters and continental shelf,
11(1), [1077]
recording—
consent required for—
copying of recording, **11(1)**, [1014]
generally, **11(1)**, [1013]
issue of copies to public, **11(1)**, [1015]
lending of copies to public,
11(1), [1016]
making available to public by electronic
transmission, **11(1)**, [1017]
rental of copies to public, **11(1)**, [1016]

performers' rights—*contd*
recording—*contd*
equitable remuneration for exploitation of
sound recording, right to, **11(1)**, [1018]
illicit—
delivery up, order for, **11(1)**, [1046],
[1052], [1056]
disposal, order for, **11(1)**, [1057]
forfeiture of, **11(1)**, [1058]
importing, possession or dealing with,
11(1), [1020]
making, dealing with or using,
11(1), [1050]
local weights and measures authority,
enforcement by, **11(1)**, [1051]
meaning, **11(1)**, [1048]
right to seize, **11(1)**, [1047]
meaning, **11(1)**, [1011]
use without consent, **11(1)**, [1019]
recording rights. *See* **recording rights**
rules, signature of instruments, **11(1)**, [1079]
sheriff court jurisdiction, **11(1)**, [1059]
summary of provisions, **11(1)**, [415]
transmissibility, **11(1)**, [1043]

Performing Right Tribunal
Copyright Tribunal, renamed as, **11(1)**, [971]

periodical payments
stamp duty provisions **41**, [36]

perjury. *See also* **false statement**
aiding and abetting, **12(1)**, [201]
corroboration, **12(1)**, [204]
false written statement as, **12(1)**, [395]
indictment, form of, **12(1)**, [203]
interpreter, by, **12(1)**, [194]
judicial proceeding, in, **12(1)**, [194]
material statement, in, **12(1)**, [194]
offences, **12(1)**, [194]
outside United Kingdom, committed,
12(1), [194], [202]
piracy proceedings, in, **12(1)**, [52]
proof of proceedings, **12(1)**, [205]

perpetuities. *See also* **accumulations;
conveyancing and law of property**
condition subsequent, treatment of,
33(2), [13]
contractual rights, avoidance of, **33(2)**, [11]
disposition—
class, to, **33(2)**, [5]
meaning, **33(2)**, [16]
option, conferring, **33(2)**, [10]
reservations, subject to, **33(2)**, [13]
special power of appointment, under,
33(2), [2]
specified ages, **33(2)**, [5]
expectant interests, saving and acceleration,
33(2), [7]
special power distinguished, **33(2)**, [8]
land—
options relating to, **33(2)**, [10]
religious purposes, used for, **33(2)**, [10]

perpetuities—*contd*
  parenthood—
    future, presumption as to, **33(2)**, [3]
    inability as to, **33(2)**, [3]
  period—
    determination of, **33(2)**, [4]
    option conferred, where, **33(2)**, [10]
    optional, **33(2)**, [2]
    power to specify, **33(2)**, [2]
  power of appointment—
    disposition made under, **33(2)**, [8]
    meaning, **33(2)**, [16]
    special power distinguished, **33(2)**, [8]
    treatment of, **33(2)**, [8]
  pre-emption, rights of, **33(2)**, [10]
  remoteness—
    avoidance—
      exclusion of class members, by,
        33(2), [1], [5]
      reduction of age, by, **33(2)**, [1], [5]
    contractual rights, of, **33(2)**, [11]
    uncertainty as to, **33(2)**, [4]
  rentcharges, right of enforcement, **33(2)**, [12]
  reverter, possibilities of, **33(2)**, [13]
  rule against—
    application of, **33(2)**, [1]
    common law, as, **33(2)**, [1]
    future parenthood, presumption, **33(2)**, [3]
    period of. *See* period *above*
    registered funds, not applying to, **48**, 547
    rentcharges, not applicable to, **33(2)**, [12]
    summary of, **33(2)**, [1]
  special power of appointment—
    disposition under, **33(2)**, [2]
    treatment as, **33(2)**, [8]
  summary of provisions, **33(2)**, [1]
  surviving spouse, condition as to death of,
    33(2), [6]
  trustees, administrative powers, **33(2)**, [9]
  "wait and see" rule, **33(2)**, [1], [4]

perry. *See* **cider**

person
  meaning, **41**, [606]

person of unsound mind
  administration of estate of, **18**, [555]

Personal Accounts Delivery Authority
  accounts, **33(S)**, Pensions 53
  annual report, **33(S)**, Pensions 52
  committees, **33(S)**, Pensions 49–50
  delegation of functions, **33(S)**, Pensions 52
  directions and guidance to,
    33(S), Pensions 159
  disqualification of members from acting,
    33(S), Pensions 50–2
  employees, **33(S)**, Pensions 49
  establishment of, **33(S)**, Pensions 20
  executive members, **33(S)**, Pensions 152
  finance provisions, **33(S)**, Pensions 159
  functions, **33(S)**, Pensions 157
  grants, **33(S)**, Pensions 53

Personal Accounts Delivery Authority—*contd*
  House of Commons disqualification,
    33(S), Pensions 53
  initial function of, **33(S)**, Pensions 20–1
  management of, **33(S)**, Pensions 21–2
  members, **33(S)**, Pensions 46–9
  non-executive committee,
    33(S), Pensions 160–2
  principles, **33(S)**, Pensions 158
  proceedings, **33(S)**, Pensions 49–52
  records of, **33(S)**, Pensions 53
  Regulator, disclosure of information by,
    33(S), Pensions 160
  seal, authentication, **33(S)**, Pensions 52
  summary of provisions, **33(S)**, Pensions 2
  winding up and dissolution,
    33(S), Pensions 22; **33(S)**, Pensions 162–3

personal equity plan
  capital gains tax relief, **42**, [1274]

personal estate
  debts, for payment of, **18**, [535]
  meaning, **18**, [556]; **50**, [485]
  succession to, on intestacy, **18**, [549]
  valuation, mode of, **18**, [501]
  will, disposable by, **50**, [486]

personal injuries scheme. *See* **war pensions**

personal injury
  child at birth. *See* **congenital disabilities**
  common employment, abolition of defence,
    45, [945], [946]
  Crown, liability of, **45**, [949]
  damages for, measure of, **45**, [947]
  defective equipment, **16**, [19]
  employers' liability—
    Crown, application of provisions to,
      16, [19]
    insurance—
      amounts, **16**, [21]
      certificates of insurance, issue, **16**, [24]
      compulsory requirement, **16**, [21]
      diseases arising out of employment,
        inclusion, **16**, [21]
      employees to be covered, **16**, [22]
      employers exempted, **16**, [23]
      excepted employees, **16**, [22]
      failure to insure, **16**, [25]
      nationalized industries exemption,
        16, [23]
      regulations, power to make, **16**, [26]
      requirement, **16**, [21]
  employment, in, **45**, [946]
  hackney carriage driver causing, **36**, [256]
  industrial training, during, **16**, [132]
  limitation of action—
    actions in respect of, **19(3)**, [735]
    discretionary exclusion of time,
      19(3), [764]
    special time limit, **19(3)**, [735]
  loss of services, abolition of actions for,
    45, [983]

personal injury—*contd*
  meaning, **16**, [19]; **19(3)**, [768]; **45**, [948]
  member of armed forces to, liability of Crown
    for, **13**, [14], [45], [46]
  Northern Ireland, exclusion of provisions,
    45, [947]
  public service vehicle, passenger on, **37**, [31]

personal pension scheme
  accrued benefits, revaluation of—
    basis of, **33(1)**, [298]
    scope of provisions, **33(1)**, [297]
    substituted benefit, not applicable to,
      33(1), [299]
    supplementary provisions, **33(1)**, [300]
  advertisements, form and content of,
    33(1), [349]
  advisory bodies, grants to, **33(1)**, [392]
  ages, verification of, **33(1)**, [263]
  alteration of rules of, **33(1)**, [252]
  annual increase in rate of, **33(1)**, [519]–[520]
  appropriate scheme certificate—
    cancellation of, **33(1)**, [248]
    issue of, **33(1)**, [214]
    surrender of, **33(1)**, [248]
    variation of, **33(1)**, [248]
    whistleblowing where requirements not
      met, **33(1)**, [247]
  approved before passing of Finance Act 1989,
    42, [1000]
  bankruptcy, no forfeiture of rights under,
    33(1), [378]
  bodies corporate, offences by, **33(1)**, [388]
  breach of regulations, **33(1)**, [387]
  ceasing to be certified—
    calculation of guaranteed minimum
      pensions preserved under approved
      arrangements, **33(1)**, [269]
    powers of Inland Revenue to approve
      arrangements for scheme, **33(1)**, [268]
    state scheme premiums—
      amount payable, **33(1)**, [276]
      calculations relating to, further provisions
        concerning, **33(1)**, [280]
      no recovery of, from earners etc,
        33(1), [279]
      non-payment of, **33(1)**, [281]–[282]
      payment of, **33(1)**, [273]–[274]
      supervision of schemes, **33(1)**, [270]–[271]
  certification of, **33(1)**, [216]
  choice, schemes restricting to be void,
    33(1), [379]
  Class 1 contributions—
    additional pensions and other benefits,
      33(1), [266]
    alteration of rates and rebates, **33(1)**, [258]
    determination of rates and rebates,
      33(1), [258]
    reduced rates of, **33(1)**, [257]
      social security benefits, effect on,
        33(1), [266]
    women, married women and widows,
      application of provisions to, **33(1)**, [267]
  Crown employment, **33(1)**, [383]

personal pension scheme—*contd*
  employers, regulations for consultations by,
    33(1), [854]–[855]
  employers' payments to, monitoring of,
    33(1), [345]
  enactments, application of, **33(1)**, [371]
  fees for official services, **33(1)**, [394]
  foreign element, application of provisions to
    cases with, **33(1)**, [384]
  guaranteed minimum pension, conversion
    of—
    actuarial equivalence, **33(S)**, Pensions 8
    conditions, **33(S)**, Pensions 7–8
    enforcement of conditions,
      33(S), Pensions 9–11
    interpretation, **33(S)**, Pensions 7
    power to amend schemes,
      33(S), Pensions 9
    procedural requirements, **33(S)**, Pensions 8
    survivors' benefits, **33(S)**, Pensions 8
    transfer out, **33(S)**, Pensions 9
  income withdrawals, **43(1)**, [133]–[134]
  information about, **33(1)**, [372]–[376]
  Inland Revenue, reports by, **33(1)**, [391]
  insurer, meaning, **33(1)**, [399]
  interpretation provisions, **33(1)**, [400]
  levies, general, **33(1)**, [393]
  long-term insurance business, meaning,
    33(1), [399]
  managers, duty to report breaches of law,
    33(1), [667]
  maximum contributions, **43(2)**, [235]
  members, disclosure of information to—
    default powers, **33(1)**, [348]
    regulations, **33(1)**, [346], [594]
    transfers, as to, **33(1)**, [347]
  minimum contributions—
    alteration of rates of, **33(1)**, [262]
    amount of, **33(1)**, [261]
    determination of rates of, **33(1)**, [262]
    earner's chosen scheme, towards,
      33(1), [260]
    payment to, **33(1)**, [259]
  mis-sold, payment for, **43(1)**, [234]
  misuse or misappropriation of assets—
    injunction against, **33(1)**, [618]
    restitution, order for, **33(1)**, [619]
  modification of enactments, **33(1)**, [370]
  money purchase benefits, **33(1)**, [217]
  overriding requirements, **33(1)**, [878]
  payment under—
    earnings including, **40(1)**, [334]
    meaning, **40(1)**, [366]
  pension liberation—
    interpretation, **33(1)**, [621]
    repatriation orders, **33(1)**, [624]
    restitution, power to order, **33(1)**, [622]
    restraining orders, **33(1)**, [623]
  perpetuities, exemption from rule against,
    33(1), [382]
  persons who may establish, **33(1)**, [236]
  prospective and consequential amendments,
    33(1), [408]
  protected rights—
    discharge of, on winding up, **33(1)**, [245]

personal pension scheme—*contd*
  protected rights—*contd*
    effect to, ways of giving, **33(1)**, [238]
    forfeiture of, **33(1)**, [244]
    general, **33(1)**, [217]
    identification of, **33(1)**, [237]
    interim arrangements—
      information about, **33(1)**, [240]
      requirements for, **33(1)**, [239]
    investment and resources, requirements as
      to, **33(1)**, [243]
    liability for, securing of, **33(1)**, [242]
    pension and annuity requirements,
      33(1), [241]
    suspension of, **33(1)**, [244]
    valuation of, **33(1)**, [237]
  rebates, **33(1)**, [515]
  reciprocity with other countries, **33(1)**, [385]
  register of—
    compilation and maintenance of,
      33(1), [656]
    information, provision of, **33(1)**, [658]
    inspection of, **33(1)**, [658]
    registrable information, **33(1)**, [657]
    reports, **33(1)**, [658]
    trustees or managers, duties of, **33(1)**, [659]
  regulations—
    breach of, **33(1)**, [387]
    general power to make, **33(1)**, [253], [526]
    Parliamentary control, **33(1)**, [527]
  repeals, **33(1)**, [406], [416]–[418]
  revaluation, **33(1)**, [297]–[300]
  rules of, alteration of, **33(1)**, [252]
  safeguarded rights—
    generally, **33(1)**, [283]
    liability, power to control transfer or
      discharge of, **33(1)**, [286]
    non-complying schemes, reserve powers
      regarding, **33(1)**, [285]
    requirements relating to, **33(1)**, [284]
  social security benefits, effects of entitlement
    to guaranteed minimum pension on,
    33(1), [264]–[265]
  State scheme contributions, reduced rates of,
    33(1), [515]
  State scheme premiums, information about,
    33(1), [413]
  subordinate legislation regarding,
    33(1), [401]–[405]
  transfer values—
    cash equivalent—
      application, withdrawal of, **33(1)**, [315]
      calculation of, **33(1)**, [312]
      exercise of option, trustees' duties after,
        33(1), [314]
      loss of rights to, **33(1)**, [313]
      right to, **33(1)**, [309]
      variation of rights to, **33(1)**, [313]
      ways of taking right to,
        33(1), [310]–[311]
    scope of provisions, **33(1)**, [307]
    supplementary provisions, **33(1)**, [316]
  transitional provisions and savings,
    33(1), [407], [419]–[420]
  transitory modifications, **33(1)**, [409], [422]

personal pension scheme—*contd*
  trustees, breaches of law, duty to report,
    33(1), [667]
  unpaid contributions—
    payment by Secretary of State of,
      33(1), [350]–[354]
    recovery of, **33(1)**, [620]
  withdrawal of approval, **42**, [1383]

personal reliefs
  adjusted net income, meaning, **44(1)**, [148];
    44(4), [58]
  age allowance, **44(1)**, [150]; **44(4)**, [35]–[37]
  blind person's allowance—
    adjusted net income, meaning, **44(4)**, [58]
    conditions of, **44(4)**, [38]
    entitlement to, **44(4)**, [38]
    indexation of, **44(4)**, [57]
    residence of claimants, **44(4)**, [56]
    transfer to spouse or civil partner,
      44(4), [39]–[40]
  blind persons, for, **44(1)**, [156]
  business expansion scheme. *See* **business
    expansion scheme**
  charities, gift of shares, securities and real
    property to, **44(1)**, [422]–[424]
  civil partners—
    adjusted net income, meaning, **44(4)**, [58]
    allowance, partnerships formed on or after
      5 December 2005, for, **44(4)**, [46]
    entitlement to, **44(4)**, [42]
    indexation of allowances, **44(4)**, [57]
    minimum amount, **44(4)**, [43]
    partial transfer back, elections as to,
      44(4), [49]
      making and withdrawing, **44(4)**, [50]
    transfer of, **44(4)**, [53]
      elections as to, **44(4)**, [47]–[48]
        procedure for making and
          withdrawing, **44(4)**, [50]
    unused—
      transfer back, **44(4)**, [52]
      transfer of, **44(4)**, [51]
    year of entry into civil partnership, in,
      44(4), [54]
  civil partnerships—
    age allowance, **44(1)**, [152]
    allowance, **44(1)**, [152]
    indexation of amounts, **44(1)**, [155]
    transfer—
      election as to, **44(1)**, [153]
      relief exceeding income, where,
        44(1), [154]
  deferred annuity, payments securing,
    44(1), [165], [166]
  entitlement to, **44(1)**, [147], [150]
  individual's, **44(1)**, [147]–[150]
    indexation of amounts, **44(1)**, [155]
  investment plans, **44(1)**, [168]
  life assurance premium. *See* **life assurance
    relief**
  married couples—
    adjusted net income, meaning, **44(4)**, [58]

personal reliefs—*contd*
married couples—*contd*
allowance—
marriages on or after 5 December 2005, for, **44(4)**, [46]
marriages before 5 December 2005, for, **44(4)**, [45]
death in course of year, **44(1)**, [150]
entitlement to, **44(4)**, [42]
indexation of allowances, **44(4)**, [57]
indexation of amounts, **44(1)**, [155]
minimum amount, **44(4)**, [43]
new rules, application of, election for, **44(4)**, [44]
partial transfer back, elections as to, **44(4)**, [49]
making and withdrawing, **44(4)**, [50]
post-December 5th 2005 marriages, age allowance, **44(1)**, [152]
pre-December 5th 2005 marriages—
age allowance, **44(1)**, [151]
allowance, **44(1)**, [151]
transfer—
election as to, **44(1)**, [153]
relief exceeding income, where, **44(1)**, [154]
transfer of, **44(4)**, [53]
elections as to, **44(4)**, [47]–[48]
procedure for making and withdrawing, **44(4)**, [50]
unused—
transfer back, **44(4)**, [52]
transfer of, **44(4)**, [51]
year of marriage, in, **44(4)**, [54]
minimum amount—
indexation of, **44(1)**, [155]
meaning, **44(1)**, [149]
non-residents, claim by, **44(1)**, [167]
overview, **44(4)**, [33]
personal allowances—
adjusted net income, meaning, **44(4)**, [58]
death, in year of, **44(4)**, [41]
indexation of, **44(4)**, [57]
persons aged 65 to 74, for, **44(4)**, [36]
persons aged 75 and over, for, **44(4)**, [37]
persons aged under 65, for, **44(4)**, [35]
residence of claimants, **44(4)**, [56]
transitional provisions and savings, **44(4)**, [1049]

personal representative. *See also*
administrator; executor
actions by and against, **18**, [529]
agent, employing, **48**, 475–6
appropriation, instrument of, stamp duty, **41**, [151]
appropriation, powers of, **18**, [544]
assent or conveyance by, **18**, [539]
assessment on, **42**, [167], [212], [989]
benefits, giving information on, **40(1)**, [633]
conveyance by, implied covenants, **20**, [694]
creditor, as, **18**, [594]
deaths before 1925—
administrative provisions, **20**, [455]
devolution of legal interests, **20**, [454]

personal representative—*contd*
deaths before 1925—*contd*
satisfaction of legacies etc, appropriation of land in, **20**, [457]
transfers to heirs or devisees, **20**, [456]
debts, payment by, **18**, [594]
devolution of property on, **18**, [513]
duty of, **18**, [528]
estate of, liability of, **18**, [532]
executor of, representation by, **18**, [518]
exempt capital gains, **42**, [1084]
expenses, **18**, [537]
family provision, liability respecting, **18**, [624]. *See also* **family provision**
fatal accident, action in case of, **31**, [610]
indemnity—
advertisement, protection by means of, **48**, 483
entitlement, **20**, [601]
notice in regard to, **48**, 485
rents and covenants, liability in respect of, **48**, 481–2
inheritance tax—
liability for, **42**, [738], [742]
payment of, **42**, [768]
law applied to, **18**, [514]
leasehold enfranchisement or extension, rights, **21**, [301]
liabilities, power to compound, **48**, 466–7
meaning, **18**, [559]; **20**, [804]; **42**, [815]; **44(1)**, [443]; **48**, 541
minor's property, appointment of trustees, **18**, [545]
number, **18**, [641]
others, power to concur with, **48**, 477
power of attorney, delegation by, **48**, 478–9
power to remove, **48**, 227
preference, right of, abolition, **18**, [594]
protection of—
adoption of child, **6**, [177]
legitimacy, enquiry as to, **6**, [162]
real estate—
administration, **20**, [455]
appropriation, satisfaction of legacy or share, **20**, [457]
devolution and vesting, **20**, [454]
meaning, **20**, [454]
transfer to heir or devisee, **20**, [456]
removal by High Court, **18**, [661]
residence, **42**, [987]
retainer, right of, abolished, **18**, [594]
rights in another estate, having, **44(1)**, [440]
settled land, disposal, **18**, [527]
special executor, as. *See* **executor**
stock exchange nominee, transfer of securities from, **48**, 596
subsidiary acting as—
employer's right of recovery under pension scheme or employees' share scheme, disregarding, **8(1)**, [218]
residual interest under pension scheme or employees' share scheme, disregarding, **8(1)**, [217]
shares in holding company, holding, **8(1)**, [216]–[218]

personal representative—*contd*
substitute, appointment of, **18**, [661]
summary of provisions, **18**, [447]
sureties by, **18**, [647]
tax liability, **42**, [212]
trust of land, holding on, **20**, [1], [653];
  23, [328]
Trustee Act 2000, application of, **48**, 649
trustee of land, as, **20**, [652]
value added tax, registration for, **50**, [65]

personation
firearm certificate holder, **12(1)**, [476]
holder of certificate of discharge or service,
  3, [266]

pesticides
codes of practice, **1(2)**, [247]
control of—
  due diligence, defence of, **1(2)**, [252]
  enforcement powers, **1(2)**, [249]
  entry on land, **1(2)**, [249]
  expenses, **1(2)**, [253]
  generally, **1(2)**, [246]
  Northern Ireland, **1(2)**, [255]
  offences, **1(2)**, [261]
  officers—
    assistants, **1(2)**, [261]
    enforcement powers, **1(2)**, [249]
  orders and regulations, **1(2)**, [246], [254]
  payments relating to, **1(2)**, [248]
  penalties, **1(2)**, [251]
  vehicle, vessel, etc, entry on, **1(2)**, [249]
crops, etc, seizure, **1(2)**, [246]
Crown land, **1(2)**, [250]
definitions, **1(2)**, [254]
Food and Environment Protection Act 1985
  Pt III, payments for general purposes of,
  1(2), [413]
harmful to wildlife, possession of—
  codes of practice, **32**, [810]
  enforcement powers, **32**, [809]
  offences, **32**, [808]
information, Minister requiring, **1(2)**, [246]
meaning, **1(2)**, [246]
offences, **1(2)**, [246]
regulations, **1(2)**, [246], [254]
residue—
  crop, food or feeding stuff, in, **1(2)**, [246]
  meaning, **1(2)**, [246]
specified prohibitions, **1(2)**, [246]
substances treated as, **1(2)**, [246]

pests
animals deemed to be, **1(1)**, [390]
birds, destruction of, **1(1)**, [390]
brown tail moth, control of, **25(2)**, [421]
chemicals to combat—
  analysis, evidence of, **1(1)**, [686]
  classes of, **1(1)**, [684]
  labelling and marking, **1(1)**, [683]
  penalties for offences, **1(1)**, [685]
  unlabelled, offences of selling, **1(1)**, [685]
Colorado beetle, **1(1)**, [630]

pests—*contd*
compensation for crop, seed, etc destruction,
  1(1), [631]
control—
  advisory committee, **1(2)**, [246], [262]
  competent authorities, **1(1)**, [628]
  equipment and services for, **1(1)**, [393]
  introduction into Great Britain, **1(1)**, [629]
  licences and certificates, charges for,
    1(1), [632]
  ministerial assistance, charges for,
    1(1), [393]
  notices, service of, **1(1)**, [397]
  orders, power to make, **1(1)**, [629]
  regulations and orders, **1(1)**, [398]
  representations, **1(1)**, [394]
  spread of pests, **1(1)**, [630]
  steps to be taken for, **1(1)**, [390]
  transitional provisions, **1(1)**, [636]
coypus, use of poison against, **2**, [363]
crops, treatment or destruction of, **1(1)**, [630]
damage by, prevention of, **1(1)**, [390]
destruction—
  articles landed in Great Britain, **1(1)**, [629]
  cost of, sharing, **1(1)**, [392]
  default respecting, **1(1)**, [392]
  equipment and services for, **1(1)**, [393]
  notice requiring, **1(1)**, [390]
destructive, summary of provisions, **35(1)**, [1]
entry by inspectors, **1(1)**, [396], [631]
government departments, execution of
  provisions by, **1(1)**, [631]
grey squirrels, use of poison against, **2**, [363]
hares, damage by, **1(1)**, [390]
inspectors, powers, **1(1)**, [631]
introduction into Great Britain, control,
  1(1), [630]
local authorities, execution of provisions by,
  1(1), [633], [862]
meaning, **1(2)**, [246]
meaning of reference to, **1(1)**, [628]
ministerial expenses, **1(1)**, [395], [631]
moles, damage by, **1(1)**, [390]
musk rats. *See* **musk rats**
object of provisions, **1(1)**, [628]
offences and proceedings, **1(1)**, [630]
open trapping, **2**, [295]
orders—
  costs involved, payment, **1(1)**, [862]
  power to make, **1(1)**, [630]
  publication of, **1(1)**, [634]
plants and seeds, treatment or destruction,
  1(1), [630]
poisoning—
  grey squirrels and coypus, **2**, [363]
  prohibition or restriction, **2**, [305], [306]
rabbits. *See* **rabbits**
rats. *See* **rats and mice**
spread of, control, **1(1)**, [630]
traps, types of, restriction on, **2**, [294]
vermin, traps for catching, **2**, [294]

pet animals
meaning, **2**, [285]
streets, sale in, prohibited, **2**, [281]

pet shop
accommodation, suitability of, **2**, [280]
disqualification for keeping, **2**, [283]
inspection of, **2**, [282]
interpretation of provisions, **2**, [285]
licence, **2**, [280]
offences and penalties, **2**, [283]
prosecution by local authority, **2**, [284]

Petition of Rights
proceedings against Crown by way of,
abolition, **13**, [10], [43]
text of, **10**, [26]–[30]

petrol substitutes
excise duty on, surcharges or rebates,
13, [898]–[900]
regulations as to, **13**, [851], [857]
use without payment of duty, prohibition on,
13, [852]

petroleum and petroleum spirit. *See also*
energy
abandoned wells, **17(2)**, [296]
application of provisions to other substances,
35(1), [109]
British Coal Corporation—
exploitation rights, **17(2)**, [135]
powers, loss of, **17(2)**, [137]
bulk stocks, maintenance of, **17(1)**, [478]
car consumption, orders as to, **17(1)**, [482]
containers, derelict—
danger from, **35(1)**, [268]
local authority's power as to, **35(1)**, [268]
factors to be taken into account by Secretary
of State, **17(2)**, [299]
forfeiture of, **35(1)**, [108]
fuelling of new and converted power
stations, **17(1)**, [481]
Her Majesty, rights vested in, **17(2)**, [237]
kept, requirements as regards, **35(1)**, [107]
licence to keep—
conditions of, **35(1)**, [103]
exclusion of provisions, **35(1)**, [114]
fees payable for, **35(1)**, [105]
grant—
authorities who may, **35(1)**, [103]
duration of, **35(1)**, [103]
refusal of, appeal against, **35(1)**, [104]
meaning, **35(1)**, [112]
requirement of, **35(1)**, [102]
transfer, **35(1)**, [116]
licences—
model clauses, **17(2)**, [668], [706], [707]
search and bore for, to—
ancillary rights, **17(2)**, [245]
existing, **17(2)**, [240]
further provisions, **17(2)**, [239]
grant of, **17(2)**, [238]
model clauses, **17(2)**, [240], [306]
regulations, **17(2)**, [239]
repayments for development,
17(2), [244]
rights transferred without consent of
Secretary of State, **17(2)**, [241]–[243]

petroleum and petroleum spirit—*contd*
licences—*contd*
See also production licences *below*
loans for development, **17(2)**, [298]
London—
depots—
inspection and samples, **25(1)**, [124]
meaning, **25(1)**, [119]
notice of provisions, **25(1)**, [127]
offences and penalties, **25(1)**, [125]
Port of London exemption, **25(1)**, [126]
register of, **25(1)**, [120]
registration—
application for, **25(1)**, [120]
fees for, **25(1)**, [123]
particulars to be given for,
25(1), [122]
requirement for, **25(1)**, [120]
regulations, **25(1)**, [121]
filling station—
appeal as to, **25(1)**, [194]
conditional consent to, **25(1)**, [194]
control of, **25(1)**, [194]
meaning, **25(1)**, [194]
offences and penalties, **25(1)**, [194]
recovery of penalties, **25(1)**, [195]
meaning, **17(2)**, [236]; **25(1)**, [119];
35(1), [112]
motor vehicles, etc, keeping and use for,
regulations as to, **35(1)**, [107]
offshore activities—
civil law, application of, **17(2)**, [249]
criminal law, application of, **17(2)**, [248]
prosecutions, **17(2)**, [250]
offshore installations. *See* **offshore
installations**
Oil and Pipe Lines Agency. *See* **Oil and Pipe
Lines Agency**
oil processing facilities—
associate, meaning, **17(2)**, [673]
third party access to, **17(2)**, [671], [672]
onshore terminals, security of—
Northern Ireland, provisions, **17(2)**, [58]
preservation, **17(2)**, [57]
pipe lines. *See* **pipe lines**
pipelines, modification of, **17(2)**, [670]
plans of mines near boreholes, power to
inspect, **17(2)**, [246]
Port of London byelaws as to, contravention,
39(2), [356]
Port of London depots, **25(1)**, [126]
price, regulation of, **17(1)**, [473]
production licences (landward areas)—
model clauses—
amendments to, **17(2)**, [708]
development and production
programmes, **17(1)**, [716]
royalty payments—
generally, **17(1)**, [541]
relief from, **17(1)**, [721]
production licences, onshore field,
construction of references to, **17(1)**, [716]
production licences (seaward areas)—
model clauses—
amendments to, **17(2)**, [708]

petroleum and petroleum spirit—*contd*
production licences (seaward areas)—*contd*
model clauses—*contd*
royalty payments—
exemption, new offshore fields,
17(1), [541], [717]
new offshore fields, **17(1)**, [541],
[717]
relief from, **17(1)**, [716], [720]
Southern Basin, royalty payments relief,
17(1), [716]
products, meaning, **17(1)**, [487]
refineries, security of—
preservation, **17(2)**, [57]
Northern Ireland, provisions, **17(2)**, [58]
revenues, Northern Ireland and Isle of Man
shares of, **17(2)**, [297]
royalties—
production licences. *See* production licences
(landward); production licences (seaward)
above
production (seaward areas), exemption,
17(1), [541]
samples, power to take, **25(1)**, [124]
savings, **35(1)**, [113]
search for and seizure, warrant for,
35(1), [108]
security, preservation of, **17(2)**, [57]
Northern Ireland, provisions, **17(2)**, [58]
sent or conveyed, requirements as regards,
35(1), [106]
sold, exposed or offered for sale, requirements
as regards, **35(1)**, [106]
summary of provisions, **17(1)**, [1]
transitional provisions, **17(2)**, [309], [310]
vessels containing, labelling of, **35(1)**, [106]
wells—
abandoned, **17(2)**, [296]
decommissioning of, **17(2)**, [667]

petroleum depot
pipe-line in, **17(1)**, [275]

petroleum revenue tax
abandoned field, allowance of unrelievable loss
from, **43(S)**, 582
abandonment expenditure—
default by participator met by former
participator, **43(S)**, 934–6
reimbursement, **43(S)**, 938
ring fence income, deduction from,
43(S), 937
ring fence trade, after ceasing,
43(S), 942–4
abolition for oil fields with development
consents on or after 16th March, 1993,
43(1), [37]
allowable losses, relief for, **42**, [337]
amount payable, **42**, [339]
appeals, **42**, [346]
areas treated as continuing to be oil fields,
43(S), 1666–8
assessments, **42**, [346]

petroleum revenue tax—*contd*
assets put to other uses—
allowable expenditure, no reduction of,
43(S), 1663–4
chargeable tariff receipts, amounts not
being, **43(S)**, 1663
decommissioning and restoration
expenditure, **43(S)**, 1662–3
blended oil, provisions applying,
43(S), 1651–3
blends of oil from two or more fields, on,
43(S), 1652
British Gas Corporation—
contract for sale of oil to, **43(1)**, [444]
gas sold to, **42**, [341]
charge of, **42**, [329]
corporation tax purposes, deduction for,
44(1), [340]
decommissioning expenditure, allowing,
43(2), [55]
definitions, **42**, [343]
double taxation relief, **43(1)**, [45]
election for oil fields to become non-taxable,
43(S), 940, 1268–73
expenditure supplement—
deferred payment, contracts with, **42**, [428]
net profit period, loss following, **42**, [427]
profit or loss incurred after, **42**, [425]
restriction of, **42**, [425]
transfer of interests, **42**, [426]
fields recommissioned after earlier
decommissioning, abolition for, **43(S)**, 580
former licensees, treatment of, **43(S)**, 1665–6
fractionation, **42**, [404]
gas banking schemes, **42**, [403], [431]
generally, **42**, [1]
incorrect returns, etc, penalty for, **42**, [346]
information and inspection powers,
43(S), 1692–8, 1412–13
information, provision of, **43(1)**, [39], [58]
interest on, **42**, [346]
light gases, alternative valuation of, **42**, [861],
[866]
light gases, valuation of, **43(1)**, [103]
management of, **42**, [346]
offshore fields, oil exported direct from,
42, [1510]
oil field. *See* **oil field**
on-shore/off-shore boundary, **42**, [860]
participator. *See* **oil field**
payment of, **42**, [346]
payments on account of, **42**, [387]
computation of, **42**, [389]
pipe-line usage, with reference to—
allowable expenditure on elected assets,
43(1), [100]
elected assets, transfer of, **43(1)**, [116a]
elections, **43(1)**, [116]–[116a]
excess capacity, **43(1)**, [99]
expenditure incurred between
30 November 1993 and date of election,
43(1), [116a]
more than one taxable field, assets used in
connection with, **43(1)**, [116a]
transfer of interests, **43(1)**, [116a]

petroleum revenue tax—*contd*
  profit and loss, computing, **44(1)**, [332]
  Provisional Collection of Taxes Act,
    application of, **42**, [342]
  provisional expenditure allowance, abolition,
    43(S), 1668–9
  rates, reduction of, **43(1)**, [38]
  relevant sales of oil, returns of, **43(S)**, 939
  reliefs—
    amendments relating to, **42**, [479]
    restriction on, **42**, [500]
  repayment, interest on, **44(1)**, [341]
  subsidised expenditure, disregard of, **42**, [347]
  tax-exempt tariffing receipts, **43(S)**, 581
  time limits for assessments, claims, etc,
    amendment, **43(S)**, 1710–13
  transitional provisions, **42**, [497]
  UK recommissioned field, definition,
    43(S), 581
  unrelievable field losses, **43(2)**, [80]
    allowance of, **42**, [352]

petty sessional court
  appeal to, **35(1)**, [91]

petty sessions
  areas—
    consequential provisions, **11(3)**, [294]
    transitional provisions and savings,
      11(3), [313]

pews
  Church Commissioners, surrender to,
    14, 217–19
  let, not to be, **14**, 240
  rights of ownership, cessation of, **14**, 218

pharmaceutical chemist. *See also* **pharmacist**;
  pharmacy
  certificate—
    offences as to, **28**, [258]
    registration, of, **28**, [258]
  titles and emblems, restriction on use,
    28, [137], [138]

pharmaceutical services
  accommodation, provision of, **30**, [974]
  additional, arrangements for, **30**, [933]
  arrangements for, **30**, [519], [932]
  inadequate provision of, **30**, [939]
  local—
    accommodation, provision of, **30**, [974]
    application of enactments, **30**, [951]
    assistance and support for, **30**, [953]
    charges, regulations for recovery of
      payments and penalties, **30**, [984]
    LPS schemes, **30**, [1103]
    persons performing, **30**, [952]
    pilot schemes—
      contents of, **30**, [940]
      entry regulations, control of, **30**, [949]
      establishment of, **30**, [940]
      initiation of, **30**, [1102]
      making, **30**, [902], [1102]
      NHS contracts, **30**, [945]

pharmaceutical services—*contd*
  local—*contd*
    pilot schemes—*contd*
      preliminary steps, **30**, [1102]
      premises from which provided, **30**, [948]
      preparatory work, funding of, **30**, [946]
      priority neighbourhoods or premises,
        designation of, **30**, [942]
      provision of services, **30**, [945]
      provisions applying, **30**, [947]
      reviews of, **30**, [943]
      termination of, **30**, [944]
      variation of, **30**, [944]
    Local Pharmaceutical Committees, **30**, [973]
    PCT expenditure, **30**, [1105]
    person authorised to provide—
      arrangements for, **30**, [938]
      contingent removal, **30**, [958]
      decisions, regulations as to, **30**, [968]
      disqualification of—
        conditions, **30**, [957]
        regulations, **30**, [968]
        review of decisions, **30**, [963]
        withdrawal from list, **30**, [967]
      fraud and unsuitability, **30**, [959]
      indemnity cover, **30**, [455], [972]
      lists—
        provisional inclusion in, **30**, [954]
        supplementary, regulations, **30**, [456],
          [955]–[956]
        withdrawal from, **30**, [967]
      national disqualification, **30**, [965]
      Northern Ireland, corresponding provisions
        in, **30**, [969]
      remuneration, **30**, [501], [970]–[971];
        30(S), NHS 104, 171–5
      Scotland, corresponding provisions in,
        30, [969]
      suspension, **30**, [960]
        appeals, **30**, [964]
        effect of, **30**, [962]
        notification of decisions, **30**, [966]
        pending appeal, **30**, [961]
        Primary Care Trust, by, **30**, [960]
        regulations, **30**, [968]
        review of, **30**, [963]
        withdrawal from list, **30**, [967]
      Wales. *See* **Wales**
    pilot schemes for, assessing, **30**, [618]
    premises for, provision of, **30**, [827]
    Primary Care Trust—
      additional, arrangements for, **30**, [933]
      arrangements by, **30**, [932]
      fees, power to charge, **30**, [937]
      local scheme. *See* local *above*
    public funding, **30**, [1034]
    regulations—
      appeals, **30**, [936]
      provisions of, **30**, [935]
    remuneration, **30**, [1040]
    terms and conditions for, **30**, [934]

pharmaceutical services—*contd*
Wales. *See* **Wales**

Pharmaceutical Society
certificate, offences relating to, enforcement
of, **28**, [258]
Council for the Regulation of Health Care
Professionals, functions of. *See* **Council for
the Regulation of Health Care
Professionals**
enforcement of provisions by, **28**, [165]
Fellow of, restriction on use of title, **28**, [137]
meaning, **28**, [187]
member, restriction on use of title, **28**, [137]
poisons—
compliance with provisions as to—
inspectors, appointment to secure,
28, [258]
steps to be taken by, to secure, **28**, [258]
proceedings by, **28**, [180]

pharmaceutist
title of, restriction on use, **28**, [137], [138]

pharmacist
bankruptcy of, representative carrying on
business, **28**, [129]
death of, representative carrying on business
after, **28**, [129]
death or disability, representative in case of,
28, [852]
drugs—
controlled—
convicted, prohibition of dealing with,
28, [211]
exemption as regards, **28**, [205]
information, requirement to furnish,
28, [216]
extension or modification of provisions,
28, [132]
information, requirement to furnish, **28**, [216]
meaning, **28**, [187]
medicinal products, exemptions for, **28**, [77]
registration of premises—
certificate of, **28**, [134], [135]
change of ownership, effect of, **28**, [135]
representative—
carrying on business on death or
bankruptcy, **28**, [129]
meaning, **28**, [129]
responsible, **28**, [130], [131], [853]
retail business—
body corporate carrying on, **28**, [126],
[128]
lawfully carrying on, **28**, [126], [127]
partners carrying on, **28**, [126], [127]
sale of poisons by, **28**, [252]
titles and emblems, restriction on use,
28, [137], [138]

pharmacy
certificate of registration, exhibition of,
28, [127]
description, restriction on use, **28**, [137],
[138]

pharmacy—*contd*
disqualification—
grounds for, **28**, [125], [139], [140]
procedure relating to, **28**, [141]
relevant committee, powers of,
28, [139]–[141]
revocation, **28**, [142]
medicinal products, handling in, **28**, [77],
[107]–[109], [117]
offences—
body corporate, by, **28**, [855]
offences—
partnerships, by, **28**, [856]
penalties, **28**, [857]
unincorporated associations, by,
28, [856]
orders and regulations, **28**, [858]
premises—
control of—
body corporate, business carried on by,
28, [851]
death or disability of pharmacist,
representative in case of, **28**, [852]
enforcement, **28**, [854]
individual pharmacist or partners,
business carried on by, **28**, [850]
responsible pharmacist, duty of,
28, [853]
register—
entry in, **28**, [134]
keeping, **28**, [134]
removal from, **28**, [135], [139]
restoration to, **28**, [135], [139]
registered—
meaning, **28**, [133]
power to enter, **28**, [258]
sale of poisons at, **28**, [252]
registration of premises—
application for, **28**, [134]
refusal, **28**, [134]
unsuitable, **28**, [134]
validity of decision as to, **28**, [164]
retail business—
annual return, **28**, [136], [143]
body corporate carrying on, **28**, [126],
[128]
conditions for carrying on, **28**, [126]–[132]
individual pharmacist carrying on,
28, [126], [127]
information, requirement to furnish,
28, [216]
meaning, **28**, [187]
name of pharmacist, display, **28**, [127]
partnership carrying on, **28**, [126], [127]
person lawfully conducting, **28**, [126],
[127]
sale of poisons at, **28**, [252]

photograph
indecent, of children. *See* **child**
items seized by police, of, **12(1)**, [855]

photography
court, prohibition in, **11(2)**, [173]

physical training
    expenses, defrayal, **35(1)**, [221]
    grants towards facilities for, **35(1)**, [221]

picketing
    peaceful, **16**, [422]

picnic area
    acquisition of land for, **36**, [1286]
    byelaws, **32**, [273]
    delegation of management, **36**, [1132]
    facilities, provision of, **36**, [1136]
    lease of, **36**, [1131]
    local authority, provision by, **32**, [261]
    provision of, **36**, [1131]
    title to land, clearance of, **36**, [1306]

pier
    street works near, display of lights,
    38(1), [235]

pier undertakers
    property of, meaning in relation to
    highways, **36**, [1381]

piers. *See under* **ports and harbours**

pig industry
    Aujeszky's disease, costs of eradicating,
    1(2), [206]. *See also* levy *below*
    levy—
        Commission responsible for, meaning,
        1(2), [206]
        general duty of Commission, **1(2)**, [209]
        payments out of—
            directions for, **1(2)**, [207]
            trust, to be held on, **1(2)**, [208]
        purpose of, **1(2)**, [206]
        registration, etc, for purposes of,
        1(2), [206]
        surplus, application of, **1(2)**, [207]
        meaning, **1(2)**, [207]
    pig product, meaning, **1(2)**, [210]

pigeons
    built-up areas in, reduction of numbers,
    35(1), [269]

pigs
    swine-fever—
        meaning, **2**, [548]
        slaughter in case of, **2**, [464], [559]

pigstyes
    street offences, **36**, [229], [385]

pilotage
    authority—
        abolition of, **39(2)**, [559]
        staff, transfer of, **39(2)**, [560]
    certificate, deep sea, **39(2)**, [558]
    charges, competent harbour authority, by,
    39(2), [545]
    competent harbour authority—
        accounts, **39(2)**, [548]

pilotage—*contd*
    competent harbour authority—*contd*
        agent, use of, **39(2)**, [546]
        authorised pilots, employment of,
        39(2), [539]
        charges, **39(2)**, [545]
        compulsory pilotage, provisions on. *See*
        compulsory *below*
        discrimination in favour of ships of,
        39(2), [544]
        disputes between, **39(2)**, [548]
        functions of, **39(2)**, [536]
        joint arrangements, **39(2)**, [546]–[547]
        meaning, **39(2)**, [536]
        pilot, authorising, **39(2)**, [538]
        pilot boats, operating, **39(2)**, [541]
        services, provision of, **39(2)**, [537]
        terms of employment, dispute as to,
        39(2), [540]
    compulsory—
        directions, **39(2)**, [542]
        exemption certificates, **39(2)**, [543]
        liability for ships, **39(2)**, [551]
        requirements, **39(2)**, [550]
    exemption certificates, **39(2)**, [543]
    pilot—
        alcohol and drugs offences. *See* **ship**
        authorised—
            area, not to be taken out of,
            39(2), [554]
            employment of, **39(2)**, [539]
            unauthorised, superseding, **39(2)**, [552]
        boarding and leaving ship, facilities for,
        39(2), [555]
        competent harbour authority, authorised
        by, **39(2)**, [538]
        draught of ship, requiring information on,
        39(2), [553]
        drink or drugs, capability affected by,
        39(2), [1044]
        arrest without warrant, **39(2)**, [1051]
        Crown service, application of provisions
        to, **39(2)**, [1055]
        detention pending arrival of police,
        39(2), [1050]
        drug, meaning, **39(2)**, [1054]
        enforcement, **39(2)**, [1048]
        orders and regulations, **39(2)**, [1053]
        prescribed limit, **39(2)**, [1047]
        right of entry on ship, **39(2)**, [1052]
        specimens, provision of, **39(2)**, [1049]
        territorial application, **39(2)**, [1056]
        EEA qualifications and experience,
        recognition of, **39(2)**, [566]
        limitation of liability, **39(2)**, [557]
        ship or persons on board, endangering,
        39(2), [556]
        terms of employment, dispute as to,
        39(2), [540]
    pilot boat, operation of, **39(2)**, [541]
    reorganisation, funding, **39(2)**, [561]
    summary of provisions, **39(2)**, [1]
    transitional provisions, **39(2)**, [564], [567]
    zero-rating, **50**, [151]

pipe-lines

abandonment, notification of, **17(1)**, [254]

accidents, notification and furnishing of information, **17(1)**, [255]

additional—
  construction of, reducing neccessity for other construction, **17(1)**, [236]
  meaning, **17(1)**, [281]

agricultural land, restoration of, **17(1)**, [261]

amenity, preservation of, **17(1)**, [259]

Associated British Ports, construction and operation of, **39(2)**, [488]

bridge, in or on, etc, **17(1)**, [250]

building or structure imperilling—
  compensation—
    compulsory purchase order, for, **17(1)**, [246], [288]
    compulsory rights order, for, **17(1)**, [249]
    determination of questions as to, **17(1)**, [264]

compulsory purchase order, **9**, [291]
  application for, **17(1)**, [405]
  compensation, determining, **17(1)**, [288]
  map attached to, **17(1)**, [405]
  notice, publication of, **17(1)**, [405]
  obtaining, **17(1)**, [246]
  person aggrieved by, **17(1)**, [405]

compulsory rights order—
  ancillary rights, **17(1)**, [289]
  application for, **17(1)**, [286], [287]
  compensation, **17(1)**, [249]
  conditions attached to, **17(1)**, [248]
  nuisance, saving for, **17(1)**, [283]
  obtaining, **17(1)**, [247]

construction—
  authorisation—
    application for, **17(1)**, [231], [285]
    map attached to, **17(1)**, [253], [285]
    objections, **17(1)**, [285]
  British Waterways Board, by, **36**, [688]
  diversions, **17(1)**, [238]
  map, deposit of, **17(1)**, [253]
  other construction, reducing necessity for, **17(1)**, [235]
  planning permission, provisions as to, **17(1)**, [233]
  unlawful works, removal of, **17(1)**, [232]
  works begun before 1962 Act, provisions applying to, **17(1)**, [278]

continental shelf exploration—
  damage arising, **17(1)**, [293]
  protection in, **17(1)**, [293]

corporations, offences by, **17(1)**, [270]

cross-country—
  authorisation of, **17(1)**, [231]
  meaning, **17(1)**, [281]

customs and excise—
  access to, entry on adjacent land for, **13**, [768]
  approval, **13**, [606]
  deficiency in goods moved by, **13**, [690]
  exportation by—
    notice of goods for, **13**, [645]
    time of, **13**, [594]
  importation by, time of, **13**, [594]

pipe-lines—*contd*

customs and excise—*contd*
  loss or damage to goods in, restriction on compensation for, **13**, [691]
  provisions, application to, **13**, [592]
  uncleared goods, control of movement of, **13**, [606]
  unlawful removal of goods from, restriction on compensation for, **13**, [691]

damage by buildings to, **17(1)**, [272]

diversion—
  authorisation, map, deposit of, **17(1)**, [253]
  compulsory rights order, **17(1)**, [247]
  permitted deviation, **17(1)**, [370]
  planning permission, provision relating to, **17(1)**, [233]

dock, in, exclusion of provisions, **17(1)**, [276]

ecclesiastical property, provision as to, **17(1)**, [267]

expenses and receipts, **17(1)**, [282]

factory, in, exclusion of provisions, **17(1)**, [275]

false documents or information, penalty for, **17(1)**, [262]

gas. *See* **gas**
  additional provisions relating to certain, **17(1)**, [239]–[241]

government oil. *See also* oil *below*
  abandonment, **9**, [175]
  compensation in respect of—
    amount of, **9**, [173]
    condition of payment, **9**, [173]
    damage to crops, **9**, [173]
    diminished value of land, for, **9**, [173]
    interest on, **9**, [173]
    payment of, **9**, [173], [194]
  diversion of, **9**, [172], [174]
  entry on land for purposes of, **9**, [175]
  expenses, **9**, [176]
  highway, passing under, **9**, [175]
  maintenance and use, **9**, [172], [175]
  meaning, **9**, [172], [194]
  minerals, restriction on working, **9**, [175]
  Northern Ireland, application of provisions to, **9**, [178], [207]
  obstruction of use, **9**, [172]
  registration of rights as to, **9**, [174], [194]
  regulations as to, **9**, [177]
  removal, **9**, [172], [174]
  repair, **9**, [175]
  replacement, **9**, [172]
  rights as to, registration as local land charge, **9**, [174]
  tampering with, **9**, [172]

government, provisions applying to, **17(1)**, [277]

length of, **17(1)**, [281]

local—
  authorisation of, **17(1)**, [234]
  exclusion of provisions, **17(1)**, [278]
  meaning, **17(1)**, [281]

meaning, **17(1)**, [280]

mine, in, exclusion of provisions, **17(1)**, [275]

nationally significant infrastructure projects, **46(S)**, 41–2. *See also* **nationally significant**

pipe-lines—*contd*
  infrastructure projects
  navigation, obstruction or danger to,
    17(1), [257]
  nuisance, saving for, **17(1)**, [283]
  oil—
    buildings near, restrictions on, **9**, [198]
    maintenance, **9**, [196], [207]
    meaning, **9**, [207]
    protection, **9**, [198], [212]
    removal, **9**, [196]
    repair, **9**, [197]
    street works or road works provisions,
      modification, **9**, [201]–[202]
    wayleave orders for—
      compensation in respect of, **9**, [200]
      entry on land under, **9**, [197], [212]
      making, **9**, [196]–[197], [210]
      meaning, **9**, [196]
      oil pipe-line, for, **9**, [196], [210]
      procedure for making, **9**, [210]
      protection of pipe-lines and accessory
        works, **9**, [198]–[199]
      registration as local land charge, **9**, [199]
      supplementary provisions as to, **9**, [197]
      Treasury regulations as to, **9**, [197]
    works accessory to—
      construction, **9**, [196]–[197]
      minor, meaning, **9**, [196]
      protection, **9**, [198]
      wayleave order for, **9**, [196]
      See also wayleave orders for *above*
  Oil and Pipe Lines Agency. *See* **Oil and Pipe
    Lines Agency**
  owner, meaning, **13**, [590]
  ownership, change of, notification of,
    17(1), [256]
  particular localities, exclusion of provisions,
    17(1), [279]
  petroleum, depot, in, exclusion of provisions,
    17(1), [275]
  pollution, protection of water against,
    17(1), [260]
  public inquiries, **17(1)**, [263]
  quarry, in, exclusion of provisions,
    17(1), [275]
  railway undertakers, of, provisions not
    applying to, **17(1)**, [274]
  regulations, power to make, **17(1)**, [269]
  removal of—
    planning permission, provisions relating to,
      17(1), [233]
    unauthorised, where, **17(1)**, [232]
  requirements and prohibitions, provisions as
    to, **17(1)**, [266]
  safety requirements, availability of funds for,
    17(1), [252]
  service of documents, **17(1)**, [265]
  small pipes, provisions not applying to,
    17(1), [273]
  statutory bodies, of, provisions not applying
    to, **17(1)**, [271]
  street, in—
    authority, consent of, **17(1)**, [250]
    conditions for consent, **17(1)**, [250]

pipe-lines—*contd*
  street, in—*contd*
    determination of disputes, **17(1)**, [250]
    line crossing street, along, **17(1)**, [250]
    power to place, **17(1)**, [250]
    renewal of, **17(1)**, [250]
    street works code, modification of,
      17(1), [251]
  submarine. *See also* **offshore installations
    and submarine pipelines; submarine
    pipelines**
  telecommunications apparatus, not interfering
    with, **17(1)**, [258]
  transport boards, construction and operation
    by, **36**, [688]
  upstream petroleum—
    compulsory modifications, **17(1)**, [244],
      [245]
    use reducing necessity for construction of
      others, **17(1)**, [242], [243]
  use—
    cesser, notification of, **17(1)**, [254]
    diversions, **17(1)**, [238]
    notification of, **17(1)**, [254]
    other pipe-line, reducing necessity for,
      17(1), [237]
    resumption, notification of, **17(1)**, [254]

pipes and mains
  adoption of—
    agreement to adopt at future date,
      49, [818], [822]
    appeals, **49**, [819], [822]
    compliance, financial conditions of,
      49, [820], [822]
    prohibition on connection without
      adoption, **49**, [821], [822]
  alteration by railway company, etc,
    35(1), [207]
  alteration of, **49**, [1204]
    unauthorised, **49**, [124]
  breaking up streets, powers, **49**, [31]
  cisterns—
    provision of, **49**, [49]
    repair, **49**, [50]
  communication pipe—
    meaning, **49**, [352]
    provision by undertakers—
      duty, **49**, [39]
      failure to provide, **49**, [40]
      purchase by owner, **49**, [42]
      removal, power of, **49**, [41]
  construction, etc—
    conveyance of heat, for, **35(1)**, [311]
    waste—
      collection, for, **35(1)**, [304]
      disposal, for, **35(1)**, [306]
  discharge pipe, meaning, **49**, [1001]
  disposal main, meaning, **49**, [1031]
  Environment Agency, vesting in, **49**, [1224]
  extension or alteration, **49**, [124]
  fittings, meaning, **49**, [352]
  laying and maintenance—
    breaking up streets for, **49**, [31]
    compensation for, **49**, [1054]

pipes and mains—*contd*
  laying and maintenance—*contd*
    entry on land, **49**, [32]
    land apart from streets, in, **49**, [1205]
    land, in, **49**, [968]
    maintenance, **49**, [1001], [1204]
    outside limits of supply, **49**, [363]
    owners or occupiers of houses, by, **49**, [43]
    powers generally, **49**, [362]
    streets, in, **49**, [364], [967], [1204]
  London, in. *See* **Thames Water Authority**
  main, meaning, **49**, [352]
  map of, **35(1)**, [315]
  maps, preparation of, **49**, [355]
  moving, **49**, [994]
  reference to, **49**, [1031], [1267]
  removal or alteration, **49**, [1001]
  requisitions, **49**, [703]
  resource main, meaning, **49**, [1031]
  service pipes—
    laying of, **49**, [364]
    meaning, **49**, [352]
    owner or occupier, laying by—
      bore, **49**, [45]
      breaking up pavements or streets,
        49, [47]
      connection with communication pipe,
        49, [44]
      powers, **49**, [43]
      removal, **49**, [46]
        supply of water after, right to,
          49, [48]
  stopcocks—
    position of, **49**, [966]
    power to fit, **49**, [972]
  supply pipe, meaning, **49**, [352]
  Thames Water Authority, powers. *See*
    Thames Water Authority
  trunk main, meaning, **49**, [352], [1031]
  valves, destroying of, penalty, **49**, [55]

piracy
  aircraft, by or against, **4(1)**, [182]
  condemnation of ships, **12(1)**, [51]
  definition of, **39(2)**, [1035]
  government ship or aircraft whose crew
    mutinied, by, **39(2)**, [1035]
  perjury in proceedings, **12(1)**, [52]
  provisions of United Nations Convention of
    Law of the Sea 1982 to be treated as law of
    nations, **39(2)**, [1028], [1035]
  punishment for, **12(1)**, [36], [51]
  statutory provisions, application to Channel
    Islands etc, **4(1)**, [31]
  trial, **12(1)**, [158]

placard
  removal or obliteration of, **35(2)**, [521]

place of worship. *See also* **chapel; church**
  buildings, care of—
    list specifying—
      compilation of, **14**, 1366
      effect of inclusion in, **14**, 1368–9
      removal from, **14**, 1367–8

place of worship—*contd*
  certified—
    certificate, **14**, 183
    Charities Act, exempt from registration
      under, **14**, 182
    disused, becoming, **14**, 181, 184
    fees, **14**, 180
    list of, **14**, 181
    registrar-general, recorded by, **14**, 180
    requirement of, **14**, 179, 184
  conveyance of land for—
    grant, form of, **14**, 243
    life tenant, by, **14**, 245–6
    person under disability, by, **14**, 242
    powers, **14**, 240–1
    public body, by, **14**, 245
    purchase money, payment of, **14**, 241–2
  exemption from rates, **25(2)**, [835]
  faculty jurisdiction, **14**, 639–40
  leasehold enfranchisement, **14**, 298–301
  licensed, **14**, 1003
  meaning, **14**, 300, 1026; **36**, [1249]
  new, provision of, **14**, 1026
  non-domestic rating relief, **26(2)**, [289]
  private street works expenses, exemption,
    36, [1261]
  redundant—
    transfer of, **14**, 664–6
    trusts for repair of, **14**, 667
  reversionary interests, acquisition of,
    14, 299–300

placement order. *See* **adoption**

plague
  notifiable disease. *See* **notifiable disease**

planning. *See also* **town and country
planning**
  Crossrail, for. *See* **Crossrail**
  housing action trust, role of, **22**, [853], [854]
  nationally significant infrastructure projects.
    See **nationally significant infrastructure
    projects**
  procedure for certain proceedings,
    determination of, **46(S)**, 187–9, 270–5

planning area
  licensing, orders as to, **46**, [610]
  survey of, **46**, [263], [288]

planning authority
  meaning, **7(1)**, [148]
  racial discrimination by, **7(1)**, [148]

planning blight. *See also* **blight notice**
  land affected—
    clearance area, for, **46**, [632]
    general improvement areas, for, **46**, [632]
    highway, required for, **46**, [632]
    new street order, by, **46**, [632]
    new town, order relating to, **46**, [632]
    proposed compulsory purchase order, by,
      46, [632]
    proposed structure plan, by, **46**, [632]

planning blight—*contd*
land affected—*contd*
public authority functions, allocation for,
46, [632]
Secretary of State, acquisition by, **46**, [411]
unitary development plan, in, **46**, [632]
urban development area, provisions
applying to, **46**, [632]
scope of provisions, **46**, [395]

planning board
joint, **46**, [507]–[508]

planning contravention notice
activities on land, power to require
information about, **46**, [420]
meaning, **46**, [420]
non-compliance, penalties for, **46**, [421]

planning contribution
provision for, **46**, [1000]
regulations, **46**, [1001]
Wales, in, **46**, [1002]

planning control
advice and assistance, grants for, **46**, [575]
applications, requirements, **46**, [601]
breach of—
injunction restraining, **46**, [444]
rights of entry—
obstruction, **46**, [456]
requirements, **46**, [456]
warrant, with, **46**, [455]
warrant, without, **46**, [454]
time limits, **46**, [419]
See also **enforcement notice**
continuity of law, **46**, [803], [886]
corporations, offences by, **46**, [607]
decisions, timetable for, **46**, [1057]
generally, **46**, [1]
regulations and orders, **46**, [609]

planning decision
aerodromes, affecting, **4(1)**, [104]
appeal, right of, **46**, [342]
Civil Aviation Authority, recovery of
compensation from, **4(1)**, [104]
compensation. *See* **compensation**
correction of errors in. *See* **development**
decision, default of, **46**, [342]
meaning, **4(1)**, [104]
new development, compensation for
restriction of. *See* **compensation**
procedure, **46**, [597]
purchase notice in respect of, effect of,
4(1), [104]
reference to, **46**, [612]
time for, **46**, [1007]
timetable for, **46**, [1057]
validity of, **46**, [549], [553]

planning inquiry. *See also* **inquiry**
public, attendance at, **46**, [591]

Planning Inquiry Commission
constitution of, **46**, [628]
Joint—
constitution, **46**, [884]
local inquiries, **46**, [884]
reference to, **46**, [879], [884]
local inquiry, holding, **46**, [628]
reference to—
consideration of, **46**, [628]
matters, **46**, [364], [628]
procedure, **46**, [364], [628]
reasons for, stating, **46**, [628]
research, carrying out, **46**, [628]
Scotland, **46**, [877]
responsible Minister or Ministers, **46**, [629]

planning obligations
appeals, **46**, [370]
Crown land, **46**, [569]
deed, **46**, [368]
enforcement, **46**, [368]
entry into, **46**, [368]
local land charge, as, **46**, [368]
meaning, **46**, [368]
modification and discharge, **46**, [369]

planning permission
agricultural housing, suspension of condition
as to occupation, **21**, [483]
appeals—
amended provisions, **46(S)**, 275–7
determination of, **46**, [344]
failure to take decision, against, **46**, [342]
fees, **46(S)**, 194
local planning authority, functions of,
46, [343]
old mining permissions, relating to,
46(S), 191
refusal, against, **46**, [342]
application for—
appeal against enforcement notice, deemed
on, **46**, [432]
certificates accompanying, **46**, [327]
combined, **46**, [608]
conservation area, affecting, **46**, [715]
content of, **46**, [326], [997]
Crown, by or on behalf of, **46**, [567]
Crown land, in anticipation of disposal of,
46, [568]
determination of—
consultations, **46**, [331]
generally, **46**, [329]
form of, **46**, [326], [997]
inquiries, costs of, **46**, [574]
listed building, affecting, **46**, [709]
local planning authority declining,
46, [330], [998]–[999]
fees, **46**, [573]
local planning authority determining,
46, [329]
major infrastructure projects, for, **46**, [339]
inspector, role of, **46**, [340]
manner of dealing with, **46**, [336]
notice of, publication, **46**, [327]

planning permission—*contd*
  application for—*contd*
    previously attached conditions, failure to
      comply with, **46**, [334]
    register of, **46**, [328]
    Secretary of State, reference to, **46**, [341]
    statutory undertakers, by, **46**, [531]
  applications, fees, **46(S)**, 192–3
  assumptions as to, **9**, [229]–[230], [308]
  benefit of land, enuring to, **46**, [337]
  building, specifying purposes for, **46**, [337]
  caravan site, for, **46**, [331]
  coal-mining proposals in application, duties as
    to environment, **17(2)**, [177]
  compensation. *See* **compensation**
  completion notice—
    effect of, **46**, [358]
    service of, **46**, [357], [359]
    validity, **46**, [549]
    withdrawal of, **46**, [357]
  conditional grant of—
    breach of condition notice, **46**, [443]
    compensation, **46**, [372]
    enforcement of conditions, **46**, [443]
    power of, **46**, [333]
    purchase notice. *See* **purchase notice**
  consultation, duty to respond to, **46**, [1006]
  continuance of use, for, **46**, [365]
  Crown land, continuance of use of, **46**, [568]
  decision after acquisition, compensation for
    additional development, **9**, [238]
  deemed—
    advertisement, in respect of, **46**, [486]
    enforcement notice, following compliance
      with, **46**, [427]
    government department, authorisation of,
      46, [318], [353]
  default of decision, appeal in, **46**, [342]
  determination, **9**, [229]
  development already carried out, for,
    46, [335]
  development order, granted by,
    46, [319]–[321]
  development requiring, **46**, [317]
  disabled, provisions for benefit of, **46**, [338]
  disused burial ground, required for use of,
    5(2), [462]
  duration, limit of, **46**, [354], [1004]
  easements and other rights, power to
    override, **46(S)**, 185, 267–9
  effect of, **46**, [337]
  enforcement notice. *See* **enforcement notice**
  Environment Agency, saving in respect of,
    49, [1232]
  environmental effects, assessment of, **46**, [332]
  factors affecting grant of, **9**, [232]
  grant—
    appeal against enforcement notice, on,
      46, [432]
    limited period, for, **46**, [333]
    methods of, **46**, [318]
  highway, in connection with, **9**, [229]
  Highways Act, when obligation to obtain,
    36, [1389]
  land use in 1948, as to, **46**, [622]

planning permission—*contd*
  local development order, granted by,
    46, [322], [324]
  meaning, **9**, [253]
  mineral—
    appeals, **46**, [866]
    ceasing to have effect, **46**, [866]
    compensation, **46**, [866]
    conditions, determination of, **46**, [866]
    development order, **46**, [862]
    directions, **46**, [863]
    first review date, **46**, [866]
      postponement, application for, **46**, [866]
    old—
      appeals, **46**, [865]
      ceasing to have effect, **46**, [865]
      compensation, **46**, [865]
      conditions, approval of, **46**, [865]
      effect of, **46**, [816]
      first list, **46**, [865]
      meaning, **46**, [816]
      Phase I and II sites, **46**, [865]
      registration, **46**, [826]
      review of, **46**, [865]
      second list, **46**, [865]
      Secretary of State, applications referred
        to, **46**, [865]
    periodic review of, **46**, [866]
    second and subsequent reviews, **46**, [866]
    Secretary of State, applications referred to,
      46, [866]
  modification—
    compensation for, **46**, [371]
    operational land, in respect of, **46**, [534]
    opposition to, **46**, [360]
    power of, **46**, [360]
    Secretary of State, by, **46**, [363]
    unopposed, **46**, [361]
    validity of order, **46**, [549]
  non-material changes, power to make,
    46(S), 178–9
  opencast coal working. *See under* **opencast
    coal**
  outline—
    conditions, effect of, **46**, [355]–[356]
    meaning, **46**, [355]
    time limits, **46**, [355], [1004]
  planning-gain, tax on, preparatory
    expenditure, **43(S)**, 503
  refusal, **9**, [228]
  refusal of—
    appeals, **46**, [342]
    compensation, **46**, [372]
    purchase notice. *See* **purchase notice**
  reserved matter—
    final approval of, **46**, [356]
    meaning, **46**, [355]
  retention of buildings or works, for, **46**, [365]
  revocation—
    compensation for, **46**, [371]
    operational land, in respect of, **46**, [534]
    opposition to, **46**, [360]
    power of, **46**, [360]
    Secretary of State, by, **46**, [363]
    unopposed, **46**, [361]

planning permission—*contd*
revocation—*contd*
validity of order, **46**, [549]
simplified planning zone, in, **46**, [345]–[347]
special, **9**, [231]
statutory undertakers, applications and appeals
by, **46(S)**, 186
termination by reference to time limit,
46, [357]
Thames flood barrier, exemptions, **49**, [537],
[551]
town development, for, **46**, [17]
trees, provision for, **46**, [457]
validity of orders, **46**, [551]
walkways, relating to, **25(1)**, [936]
winning and working of minerals, for. *See*
minerals

plans
building—
departure or deviation from, **35(1)**, [551]
deposited—
approved person, by, **35(1)**, [542]
insurance cover in relation to,
35(1), [542]
inspection by approved inspector,
35(1), [568]
lapse of deposit after three years,
35(1), [552]
passing—
appeal provisions, **35(1)**, [562], [563]
certificate by approved person, with,
35(1), [543]
conditions, on, **35(1)**, [542], [544], [557]
local authority, by, **35(1)**, [542]
notice of, **35(1)**, [542]
short-lived materials, building
constructed of, **35(1)**, [544]
summary of provisions, **35(1)**, [1]
unsuitable materials, use of, **35(1)**, [545]
appeal as regards—
High Court, to, **35(1)**, [563]
Secretary of State, to, **35(1)**, [545],
[564]
rejection—
appeal provisions, **35(1)**, [562], [563]
exits and entrances, where
unsatisfactory, **35(1)**, [549]
local authority, by, **35(1)**, [542]
notice of, **35(1)**, [542]
short-lived materials, building
constructed of, **35(1)**, [544]
unsuitable materials, use of, **35(1)**, [545]
water supply to house unsatisfactory,
35(1), [550]
retention, **35(1)**, [658]
certificate. *See* **building**
meaning, **35(1)**, [648]

plant
fixed, removal under emergency powers,
compensation for, **9**, [153]
noise from, regulation of, **35(1)**, [327]

plant and machinery allowances. *See*
machinery and plant allowances

plant breeder's rights
application periods, rights in relation to,
1(2), [591]
body corporate, offences by, **1(2)**, [621]
cancellation, **1(2)**, [608]
compulsory licences, **1(2)**, [603]
proceedings, right to be heard, **1(2)**, [611]
confidential information, disclosure of,
1(2), [619]
Crown, application to, **1(2)**, [624]
definitions, **1(2)**, [623]
dependent varieties, **1(2)**, [593]
duration, **1(2)**, [597]
exceptions—
farm saved seed, **1(2)**, [595]
general, **1(2)**, [594]
exhaustion of, **1(2)**, [596]
existing rights, application of provisions to,
1(2), [625]
false information, **1(2)**, [617]
false representations as to, **1(2)**, [618]
generally, **1(2)**, [587]
grant—
application, on, **1(2)**, [589]
conditions for, **1(2)**, [590]
conditions for, **1(2)**, [639]
harvested material—
proceedings relating to, presumptions in,
1(2), [600]
products made from, presumption in
proceedings relating to, **1(2)**, [601]
holder, duties of—
compulsory licences, **1(2)**, [603]
protected variety, maintenance of,
1(2), [602]
infringement—
presumptions in proceedings relating to
harvested material, **1(2)**, [600]
remedies, **1(2)**, [599]
jurisdiction in relation to offences, **1(2)**, [622]
nullity of, **1(2)**, [607]
priority between applicants, **1(2)**, [640]
protected varieties, **1(2)**, [592]
recent creation, varieties of, **1(2)**, [626]
regulations and orders, **1(2)**, [632]
suspension of, **1(2)**, [609]
transmission, **1(2)**, [598]

plant or machinery. *See* **machinery and
plant**

Plant Varieties and Seeds Tribunal
appeal from, **1(2)**, [630]
appeal to, **1(2)**, [612]
arbitration agreements, jurisdiction under,
1(2), [628]
chairman, **1(2)**, [641]
constitution, **1(2)**, [641]
continuation of, **1(2)**, [627]
costs, **1(2)**, [641]
decisions, **1(2)**, [641]
officers and servants, **1(2)**, [641]

Plant Varieties and Seeds Tribunal—*contd*
remuneration, **1(2)**, [641]
rules, **1(2)**, [641]
sittings, **1(2)**, [641]
statutory jurisdiction, **1(2)**, [629], [631]
two panels, **1(2)**, [641]

Plant Variety Rights Office
authority of officers, **1(2)**, [638]
continuation of, **1(2)**, [588]
Controller—
fees, **1(2)**, [615]
ministerial guidance to, **1(2)**, [613]
outsiders, use of, **1(2)**, [616]
proceedings before—
appeals to tribunal, **1(2)**, [612]
right to be heard, **1(2)**, [610], [611]
reference collections, establishment of,
1(2), [620]
regulations, **1(2)**, [614]
proof of documents, **1(2)**, [638]
remuneration, **1(2)**, [638]
staff, **1(2)**, [638]

plants. *See also* **seeds; wild plants**
breeders' rights. *See* **plant breeder's rights**
Channel Islands, extension of provisions to,
1(1), [584]
departmental expenses and payments,
1(1), [581]
disease spread by seeds, prevention,
1(1), [565]
endangered species, enforcement of
regulations implementing Community
legislation, **12(3)**, [1032]
gazette, publication, **1(1)**, [578]
Isle of Man, extension of provisions to,
1(1), [584]
live or dead—
importation and exportation of certain—
entry of premises, **13**, [566]
forfeiture, **13**, [566]
licence for—
charge for, **13**, [566]
conditions of issue, **13**, [566]
derivatives, **13**, [566]
issue, **13**, [566]
offences as to, **13**, [566]
scientific authorities—
advice on issue, **13**, [566]
establishment and duties, **13**, [567]
voidance on commission of offence,
13, [566]
importation and exportation of certain
restrictions on, **13**, [566], [568], [569]
imported illegally—
body corporate, offences by, **13**, [573]
sale, etc, or display to public—
derivatives, **13**, [569]
licence for, **13**, [569]
offences, **13**, [569]
restricted articles, **13**, [569]
restriction on, **13**, [569]
meaning, **1(2)**, [254]

plants—*contd*
Northern Ireland, application of provisions,
1(1), [583]
notices, publication, **1(1)**, [578]
offences, general provisions, **1(1)**, [579]
pests. *See* **pests**
regulations, **1(1)**, [580]
sale of, restricted, **13**, [583]
Tribunal. *See* **Plant Varieties and Seeds
Tribunal**
varieties—
dependent, **1(2)**, [593]
differing classes or types, regulations,
1(1), [580]
protected—
generally, **1(2)**, [592]
maintenance, **1(2)**, [602]
registered name—
duty to use, **1(2)**, [605]
improper use of, **1(2)**, [606]
selection and registration of names,
1(2), [604]
Rights Office. *See* **Plant Variety Rights
Office**

platform
public occasion, used on, safety of,
35(1), [53]

playgrounds
street—
byelaws, **37**, [202]
prohibition of traffic on roads, **37**, [201]

plays. *See* **theatre**

plea. *See also* **trial**
mute of malice, entry of plea on, **12(1)**, [364]
unfitness to plead. *See* **unfitness to plead**

pleasure boats
byelaws, **25(2)**, [442]
byelaws as to, **35(1)**, [56], [271]
certificates, conditions as to, **38(1)**, [607]
licence for, **35(1)**, [74]
provision in park or pleasure ground,
35(1), [56], [266]
seaside, byelaws as to, **35(1)**, [271], [380]

pleasure fair
byelaws as to, **35(1)**, [270]
meaning, **35(1)**, [270]

pleasure ground. *See also* **open space**
boating pools in, **35(1)**, [266]
byelaws as to, **35(1)**, [24]
chairs, etc in, **35(1)**, [68]
closing, **35(1)**, [56], [265]
contributions by local authority towards,
35(1), [24], [57]
county council powers, **32**, [33]
games—
apparatus for, **35(1)**, [68]
setting apart for, **35(1)**, [68], [264]
ice skating in, **35(1)**, [68]

pleasure ground—*contd*
  lakes in, pleasure boats in, **35(1)**, [56], [380]
  London, Sunday closing, **25(2)**, [397]
  management, **35(1)**, [68], [264]
  pavilions in, **35(1)**, [68]
  pleasure boats in, **35(1)**, [56], [380]
  provision of, **35(1)**, [24]
  reading rooms in, **35(1)**, [68]
  refreshment rooms in, **35(1)**, [68]
  seats in, **35(1)**, [68]
  skating in, **35(1)**, [68]
  sports in, **35(1)**, [68], [99]

pledge. *See also* **pawn**
  acquisition of property subject to, **9**, [133]
  conversion of goods, when, **45**, [973]
  mercantile agent, by. *See* **mercantile agent**

ploughing up land. *See* **agriculture**

plumbago
  metallic mineral, as, **11(2)**, [66]

pluralities
  authorisation of, **14**, 1072
  endowments, aggregation of, **14**, 1008
  incumbent—
    deemed admission of, **14**, 1088
    designation of, **14**, 996–7
    induction of, **14**, 1063–4
    resignation of, **14**, 985
  pastoral order relating to, **14**, 1013
  pastoral scheme providing for, **14**, 984–5
  patronage, rights of, **14**, 1007
  stipend provisions, **14**, 839
  team ministry in one area of, **14**, 988

pneumoconiosis
  compensation, dependant, meaning,
    40(2), [538]
  control of, **40(1)**, [716]
  disablement payments—
    conditions of entitlement, **40(1)**, [90]
    dependants, to, **40(1)**, [91]
    determination of claims, **40(1)**, [92]
    fraudulent statements, **40(1)**, [96]
    lump sum, **40(1)**, [1], [89]
    minors, for benefit of, **40(1)**, [94]
    reconsideration of determinations,
      40(1), [93]
    regulations, **40(1)**, [95]
    relevant employer, definition, **40(1)**, [99]
  industrial injuries benefits, **40(1)**, [354], [488]
  meaning, **40(1)**, [366]

poaching
  deer. *See* **deer**
  game. *See* **game**
  rabbits, **2**, [141]

poison-pen letter
  sending or delivering, offence of,
    12(1), [1078]

poisons. *See also* **drugs**
  book, entry in, **28**, [252]
  compliance with provisions as to, **28**, [258]
  containers, rules as to, **28**, [256]
  enforcement of provisions as to, **28**, [258]
  entry to premises, **28**, [258]
  labelling, rules as to, **28**, [256]
  maliciously administering—
    endangering life or inflicting grievous
      bodily harm, **12(1)**, [79], [81]
    intent to injure, aggrieve or annoy, with,
      12(1), [80]
  non-medicinal—
    meaning, **28**, [260]
    rules as to, **28**, [256]
    sale, **28**, [253]
  offences and penalties, **28**, [257], [262]
  orders regarding, **28**, [259]
  Poisons Board—
    constitution, **28**, [250], [264]
    continuation, **28**, [250]
    directions to, as to making of Poisons
      Rules, **28**, [256]
    procedure, **28**, [250]
  Poisons List—
    amendment or variation, **28**, [251]
    continuation, **28**, [251]
    division into Parts I and II, **28**, [251]
  Poisons Rules—
    compliance with, steps to secure, **28**, [258]
    contravention, penalty for, **28**, [257]
    power to make, **28**, [256], [259]
    scope of, **28**, [256]
  proceedings, institution by inspector,
    28, [258]
  prosecution of offences, time limit for,
    28, [257]
  purchaser, requirements as to, **28**, [252]
  sale—
    container, requirement as to labelling,
      28, [252]
    export, for, **28**, [253]
    hospital purposes, for, **28**, [253]
    local authority's lists—
      entry of names in, **28**, [254], [255]
      fees payable, **28**, [255]
      inspection, **28**, [255]
      keeping, **28**, [254]
      meaning, **28**, [260]
      particulars in, **28**, [255]
      persons on, by, **28**, [252], [254]
      premises of person on, entry to,
        28, [258]
      removal from, **28**, [255]
      title or emblem, wrongful use of,
        28, [255]
    practitioners, to, **28**, [253]
    regulation of, **28**, [252], [253]
    rules as to, **28**, [256]
    wholesale, **28**, [253]
  sample, taking by inspector, **28**, [258]
  seller of, duties of, **28**, [252]
  storage, rules as to, **28**, [256]
  transport, rules as to, **28**, [256]

Poland
accession to European Union, **18**, [54]

police. *See also* **metropolitan police; Ministry of Defence Police**
Advisory Boards, **33(2)**, [242]
airport police, **33(2)**, [17]
See also **airports**
appeals tribunal, **33(2)**, [273]
dismissal, appeals against, **33(2)**, [245]
areas—
alterations—
objections to those proposed by
Secretary of State, **33(2)**, [208]
order, by, **33(2)**, [207], [209]
City of London, summary of provisions,
33(2), [17]
co-operation, **33(2)**, [336]
description of, **33(2)**, [331]
division into, **33(2)**, [156]
list of, **33(2)**, [268]
meaning, **33(2)**, [262]
name, change of, **33(2)**, [331]
summary of provisions, **33(2)**, [17]
arrest. *See* **arrest**
assaults on, **33(2)**, [248]
assistance in enforcement of customs and
excise matters, **13**, [598]
authority. *See* **police authority**
bail. *See* **bail**
British Transport Police. *See* **British
Transport Police**
cadets—
appointment, **33(2)**, [203]
control of, **33(2)**, [203]
employers, police authority as, **33(2)**, [203]
pensions provisions, **33(2)**, [94]
regulations, **33(2)**, [230]
capital expenditure, grants for, **33(2)**, [226]
Central Police Training and Development
Authority. *See* **Central Police Training
and Development Authority**
central services—
common services, **33(2)**, [236]
research, **33(2)**, [237]
chief constable—
appointment, **33(2)**, [183]
assistant, appointment etc, **33(2)**, [185]
deputy—
appointment, **33(2)**, [184]
power to exercise functions of,
33(2), [186]
removal, **33(2)**, [184]
general functions of, **33(2)**, [182]
local government reorganisations, affected
by, **33(2)**, [261]
police area alterations, affected by,
33(2), [261]
removal of, **33(2)**, [183], [220]
reports by, **33(2)**, [197], [223]
chief officer—
codes of practice, **33(2)**, [215], [381]
community safety accreditation schemes.
See community safety accreditation
schemes *below*

police—*contd*
chief officer—*contd*
criminal statistics, return of, **33(2)**, [224]
damages etc awarded against, **33(2)**, [247]
employer, treated as, **33(2)**, [247]
meaning, **33(2)**, [262]
torts, liability for, **33(2)**, [247]
chief officers, reporting to Director of Public
Prosecutions, **12(1)**, [940]
child under protection of. *See* **child**
City of London police fund, expenditure
payable from, **33(2)**, [254]
Civil Nuclear Constabulary. *See* **Civil
Nuclear Constabulary**
civilians. *See* **police civilians**
code of practice—
draft, approval of, **12(1)**, [919]
failure to comply with, **12(1)**, [919]
revision of, **12(1)**, [919]
Secretary of State issuing, **12(1)**, [918]
collaboration agreements, **33(2)**, [198]
Commissioners—
allowances, **33(2)**, [287]
annual report by, **33(2)**, [1534]
appointment of, **33(2)**, [287]
removal of, **33(2)**, [287]
common services—
expenditure, **33(2)**, [146]
financial assistance, **33(S)**, Police 5–6
provision of, **33(2)**, [236]
community safety accreditation schemes—
accreditation under, **33(2)**, [376]
accredited inspector, powers of,
33(2), [409]
accredited persons, powers of, **33(2)**, [408]
generally, **33(2)**, [375]
power to apply accreditation provisions,
33(2), [378]
powers under, **33(2)**, [408]
supplementary provisions, **33(2)**, [379]
weights and measures inspectors,
accreditation of, **33(2)**, [377], [409]
community views, obtaining, **33(2)**, [255]
complaints against—
conduct matters. *See* conduct matters *below*
direction and control matters, **33(2)**, [353]
disciplinary charges—
dismissal, appeals against, **33(2)**, [245]
proceedings, guidance concerning,
33(2), [246]
duties of Commission, **33(2)**, [398]
evidence relating to, duty to preserve,
33(2), [398]
failure to notify or record, **33(2)**, [398]
forces maintained otherwise than by police
authorities, **33(2)**, [365]
handling by appropriate authority,
33(2), [398]
Independent Police Complaints
Commission. *See* **Independent Police
Complaints Commission**
initial handling and recording of,
33(2), [398]
investigation of—
appeals to Commission, **33(2)**, [401]

police—*contd*
  complaints against—*contd*
    investigation of—*contd*
      appropriate authority on its own behalf,
        by, **33(2)**, [401]
      Commission, by, **33(2)**, [401]
      Complainant, duty to keep informed,
        33(2), [360]
      covert human intelligence sources, use
        of, **33(2)**, [359]
      directed or intrusive surveillance, use
        of, **33(2)**, [359]
      disciplinary proceedings, duties with
        respect to, **33(2)**, [401]
      discontinue, power of Commission to,
        33(2), [401]
      final reports, **33(2)**, [401]
      form of, power of Commission to
        determine, **33(2)**, [401]
      managed by Commission, **33(2)**, [401]
      regulations, **33(2)**, [363]–[364]
      relatives, duty to provide information
        for, **33(2)**, [361]
      restriction on proceedings pending
        conclusion of, **33(2)**, [401]
      reviews and re-investigations following
        appeal, **33(2)**, [401]
      special cases, **33(2)**, [401]
      supervision of, **33(2)**, [401]
    local resolution, **33(2)**, [398]
      appeals, **33(2)**, [398]
    reference to Commission, **33(2)**, [398]
  conduct matters, **33(2)**, [351]
    civil proceedings, arising in, **33(2)**, [399]
    evidence relating to, duty to preserve,
      33(2), [399]
    investigation, **33(2)**, [401]
    recording of, in other cases, **33(2)**, [399]
    reference to Commission, **33(2)**, [399]
  constable—
    anti-social behaviour, power to require
      name and address, **33(2)**, [384]
    assaults on, **33(2)**, [248]
    attestation, **33(2)**, [204], [271]
    jurisdiction of, **33(2)**, [205]
    meaning, **33(2)**, [577]
    nationality requirements, **33(2)**, [388]
    powers of, for limited purposes, **33(2)**, [17]
    protection against actions, **33(2)**, [18]
    resumption of service as, **3**, [433]
    rewards for diligence, **33(2)**, [206]
    university, **33(2)**, [17]
    See also **constable**
  corporate manslaughter and homicide
    provisions, application of, **12(4)**, [301]
  criminal records. *See* **criminal records**
  criminal records, certificates relating to,
    33(2), [17]
  criminal statistics, returns of, **33(2)**, [224]
  cross-border aid of one force by another,
    33(2), [259]
  custody officer—
    after charge, duties of, **12(1)**, [882]
    amended provisions, **12(4)**, [120], [121]
    appointment of, **12(1)**, [875]

police—*contd*
  custody officer—*contd*
    arrested juvenile, duties as to, **12(1)**, [882]
    before charge, duties of, **12(1)**, [876]
    detained person, responsibilities relating
      to, **12(1)**, [883]
    functions, carrying out, **12(1)**, [875]
    guidance to, **12(1)**, [877]
    personal effects, seizing, **12(1)**, [900]
    rank of, **12(1)**, [875]
    record of detainee's possessions, making,
      12(1), [900]
    varying directions from higher officer,
      12(1), [883]
  death and serious injury matters, **33(2)**, [400]
    duty to record, **33(2)**, [400]
    evidence relating to, duty to preserve,
      33(2), [400]
    investigation, **33(2)**, [401]
  deer, powers as to, **2**, [663]
  defence regulations, permanent enactment,
    33(2), [84]
  detection, meaning, **33(2)**, [333]
  detention—
    charge, after, **12(1)**, [892]
    charge, before, **12(1)**, [876], [890]
    charge, without, limit on, **12(1)**, [886]
    continued, authorisation of, **12(1)**, [887]
    custody officer. *See* custody officer *above*
    custody record—
      intimate search, details on, **12(1)**, [902]
      keeping, **12(1)**, [876]
      personal possessions, recording on,
        12(1), [900]
    decisions, use of video-conferencing
      facilities for, **12(1)**, [891]
    designated stations, **12(1)**, [874]
    fingerprints—
      checking, **12(1)**, [912]
      destruction of, **12(1)**, [915]
      taking, **12(1)**, [908]; **12(3)**, [51]
      use and destruction, restrictions on,
        12(3), [53]
    footwear, impressions of, **12(1)**, [909]
    further, warrant of—
      extension, **12(1)**, [889]
      information supporting, **12(1)**, [888]
      issuing, **12(1)**, [888]
      refusal, **12(1)**, [888]
    hospital, removal of person to, **12(1)**, [886]
    intimate sample—
      checking, **12(1)**, [912]
      destruction of, **12(1)**, [915]
      meaning, **12(1)**, [917]
      police station, attending for taking of,
        12(1), [912]
      taking, **12(1)**, [910]
    legal advice, access to, **12(1)**, [905]
    limitations on, **12(1)**, [873]
    meaning, **12(1)**, [924]
    non-intimate sample—
      checking, **12(1)**, [912]
      Class A drugs, testing for presence of,
        12(1), [913], [914]

police—*contd*
  detention—*contd*
    non-intimate sample—*contd*
      consent, taking without,
        12(2), [531]–[535]
      destruction of, **12(1)**, [915]
      hair, **12(1)**, [912]
      meaning, **12(1)**, [917]
      pending derogating control order,
        12(4), [67]
      person detained after acquittal on
        grounds of insanity or unfitness to
        plead, from, **12(2)**, [532]
      police station, attending for taking of,
        12(1), [912]
      pre-existing conviction for sexual offence
        etc, taking from person having,
        12(2), [531], [535]
      taking, **12(1)**, [911]
      taking electronically, **12(3)**, [52]
    records of, **12(1)**, [897]
    release from, **12(1)**, [873], [886]
    release on bail—
      breach of, **12(1)**, [879], [880]
      consultation with Director of Public
        Prosecutions, **12(1)**, [878]
      police station, attendance at,
        12(1), [881]
    review of, **12(1)**, [884], [885]
    samples, restrictions on use and
      destruction, **12(3)**, [53]
    telephone, use of, **12(1)**, [885]
    ultrasound scans, **12(1)**, [903]
    x-rays, **12(1)**, [903]
  disability discrimination by, **7(1)**, [440]
  disaffection, inducing, **33(2)**, [250]
  disciplinary charges—
    proceedings, representation in, **33(2)**, [244]
    summary of provisions, **33(2)**, [17]
  disciplinary procedures, **33(S)**, Police 5
  disciplinary proceedings—
    guidance, **33(S)**, Police 16
    representation at, **33(S)**, Police 14–15
  disguises, power to require removal of,
    12(2), [193]
  dismissal, appeals against, **33(2)**, [245]
  disorderly behaviour, powers regarding—
    alcohol related—
      unlicensed premises—
        closure notice, **19(3)**, [476]
        closure order. *See* **intoxicating**
          liquor
      See also **alcohol**
    on the spot penalties for. *See* **disorderly**
      behaviour
  drug traffickers, powers regarding. *See* **drug**
    trafficking
  employment in, **7(1)**, [55]
  employment, provisions applying to, **16**, [848]
  entry and search, powers of—
    arrest, after, **12(1)**, [852]
    authorisation generally, **12(1)**, [842]
    excluded material—
      access to, **12(1)**, [843]
      meaning, **12(1)**, [845]

police—*contd*
  entry and search, powers of—*contd*
    firearms offences, **12(1)**, [530]
    journalistic material—
      excluded material, as, **12(1)**, [845]
      meaning, **12(1)**, [847]
    legal privilege, items subject to,
      12(1), [844]
    offensive weapons, for, **12(1)**, [1100]
    personal records, and, **12(1)**, [845], [846]
    premises, meaning of, **12(1)**, [857]
    search warrant, with—
      execution of, **12(1)**, [850]
      issue of, **12(1)**, [842]
      safeguards, **12(1)**, [849]
    search warrant, without—
      arrest, for, **12(1)**, [851]
      reasons for, **12(1)**, [851]
    special procedure material—
      access to, **12(1)**, [843]
      meaning, **12(1)**, [848]
  equipment, regulations, **33(2)**, [231]
  false information given to, **12(1)**, [363]
  federations. *See* **Defence Police Federation;**
    Police Federation
  firearms, functions relating to, **12(1)**, [539]
  flights and voyages to UK, power to gather
    information relating to, **12(4)**, [259]
  force—
    aid of one to another, **33(2)**, [199]
    civilian employees in, **33(2)**, [189]
    cross-border aid of one force by another,
      33(2), [259]
    maintenance of, **33(2)**, [157]
    meaning, **33(2)**, [262]
    officers engaged in service outside,
      33(2), [258]
    ranks, **33(2)**, [187]
  foreign officers, assaulting, **12(3)**, [611]
  fund—
    accounts, **33(2)**, [188]
    meaning, **33(2)**, [262]
    payments to or from, **33(2)**, [188]
  grants to, **33(2)**, [225]–[227]
  harassment, powers regarding, witnesses. *See*
    witness
  harbour constables, **33(2)**, [17]
  health and safety—
    regulations, breach of, **33(2)**, [281]–[282]
    responsibilities for, **33(2)**, [585]
  health and safety provisions, application of,
    18, [1305]
  health and safety rights, **16**, [673]
  historical survey, **33(2)**, [17]
  impersonation of, **33(2)**, [249]
  Independent Police Complaints Commission.
    See **Independent Police Complaints**
    Commission
  inspectors of constabulary—
    appointment, **33(2)**, [233]
    assistants, **33(2)**, [235]
    Civil Nuclear Constabulary, inspection of,
      33(2), [495]
    co-operation, **33(2)**, [272]
    delegation of functions, **33(2)**, [272]

police—*contd*
 inspectors of constabulary—*contd*
  functions, **33(2)**, [233]; **33(S)**, Police 6
  inspection programmes and frameworks,
   33(2), [272]
  joint action, **33(2)**, [272]
  other inspectors, inspections by,
   33(2), [272]
  public authorities, assistance for,
   33(2), [272]
  remuneration, **33(2)**, [233]
  reports by—
   publication of, **33(2)**, [234]
   requirement for, **33(2)**, [233]
  Serious Organised Crime Agency,
   inspection of, **33(2)**, [533]
  staff officers, **33(2)**, [235]
 international joint investigation teams—
  assaults on members of, **33(2)**, [248]
  wrongful acts of members of, liability for,
   33(2), [247]
 international organisations, provision of advice
  and assistance to, **33(2)**, [201]
 interviews—
  tape-recording, **12(1)**, [906]
  visual recording, **12(1)**, [907]
 metropolitan. *See* **metropolitan police**
 Metropolitan, offices for, **10**, [181]
 Ministry of Defence Police. *See* **Ministry of
  Defence Police**
 misconduct, amended provisions,
  33(S), Police 13–18, 23–31
 misconduct and performance procedures,
  12(4), [585]
 National Crime Squad. *See* **National Crime
  Squad**
 National Criminal Intelligence Service. *See*
  National Criminal Intelligence Service
 national security, grants for safeguarding,
  33(2), [227]
 Northern Ireland. *See* **Northern Ireland**
 offences against—
  assault, **33(2)**, [248]
  disaffection, causing, **33(2)**, [250]
  impersonation, **33(2)**, [249]
 offenders, rehabilitation of, **33(2)**, [332]
 officers, performing duties of higher rank,
  33(2), [122]
 overseas British police force—
  expenses of, **33(2)**, [82]
  maintenance, **33(2)**, [82]
  regulations as to, **33(2)**, [82]
 park constables, **33(2)**, [17]
 pensions. *See* **police pensions**
 photographing of suspects, **12(1)**, [916]
 Police Information Technology Organisation.
  See **Police Information Technology
  Organisation**
 Police Service of Northern Ireland,
  engagement for service in, **33(2)**, [258]
 Port of London Police, **33(2)**, [17]
  See **Port of London Authority**
 power to direct person to leave place,
  12(4), [117]
 powers of, exercise by civilians, **33(2)**, [17]

police—*contd*
 premises—
  inspections on behalf of Independent Police
   Complaints Commission, **33(2)**, [358]
  Serious organised Crime Agency, use by,
   33(2), [543]
 prevention, meaning, **33(2)**, [333]
 prohibited place, interfering with near,
  12(1), [231]
 property—
  authorisations to interfere with—
   absence of authorising officer, given in,
    33(2), [290]
   appeals by authorising officers,
    33(2), [298]–[299]
   approval, requiring, **33(2)**, [293]
   Commissioners—
    appointment, **33(2)**, [287]
    review of performance, **33(2)**, [300]
    supplementary provisions relating to,
     33(2), [300]
   confidential journalistic material,
    33(2), [296]
   confidential personal information,
    33(2), [295]
   duration, **33(2)**, [291]
   form, **33(2)**, [291]
   generally, **33(2)**, [288]–[289]
   legal privilege, matters subject to,
    33(2), [294]
   notification, **33(2)**, [292]
   quashing of, **33(2)**, [297]
  in possession of—
   orders in respect of, **33(2)**, [54]
   perishable articles, **33(2)**, [55]
   return to owner, **33(2)**, [54]
   time for claims, **33(2)**, [55]
   unclaimed, disposal of, **33(2)**, [55]
 protected disclosures, **16**, [657]
 public assembly, powers, **12(1)**, [1005]
 racial discrimination by, **7(1)**, [204], [205]
 rave—
  entry and seizure in relation to,
   12(2), [203]
  power to remove persons attending or
   preparing for, **12(2)**, [202]
  power to stop persons proceeding to,
   12(2), [204]
  sound equipment, forfeiture of,
   12(2), [205]
 reasonable force, using, **12(1)**, [924]
 Registrar General, supply of information by,
  33(2), [618]
 regulations—
  power to make, **33(2)**, [228], [393], [593],
   [620]
  procedures and practices, **33(2)**, [232]
  provisions for, **33(2)**, [228]
 religion or belief, discrimination on grounds
  of, **7(1)**, [819]
 repeals affecting, **41**, [787]
 revenue trader, entry on premises in presence
  of, **13**, [709]
 review officer, **12(1)**, [884]

police—*contd*

Scilly Isles, application of provisions to,
   33(2), [210]
Scotland, **33(2)**, [99]
search by—
   detained person, of, **12(1)**, [900]
   intimate. *See* **search**
   warrant. *See under* entry and search *above*
   without warrant. *See under* entry and search
      above
Secretary of State—
   adverse reports, power to give directions
      after, **33(2)**, [216], [218]
   authority, power to give directions relating
      to, **33(2)**, [217]–[218]
   chief constable—
      removal of, **33(2)**, [220]
      reports by, requirement for, **33(2)**, [223]
   codes of practice—
      chief officers, for, **33(2)**, [215]
      issue of, **33(2)**, [214]
   common services, provision of,
      33(2), [236]
   grants, power to make, **33(2)**, [225]–[227]
   minimum budget, directions as to,
      33(2), [219]
   performance targets, setting of, **33(2)**, [213]
   powers, exercise of, **33(2)**, [211]
   practices, regulation of, **33(2)**, [232]
   procedures, regulation of, **33(2)**, [232]
   regulations, power to make, **33(2)**, [228]
   reports from police authorities to,
      33(2), [222]
   senior officers, removal of, **33(2)**, [221]
seizure, powers of. *See also* **seizure**
   access to seized items, granting,
      12(1), [855]
   charges for property, **12(2)**, [206]
   computer, information in, **12(1)**, [854]
   copies, making, **12(1)**, [855]
   general, **12(1)**, [853]
   motor vehicle used in manner causing
      alarm, distress or annoyance—
      power of, **33(2)**, [386]
      retention of, **33(2)**, [387]
   photograph, request for, **12(1)**, [855]
   premises, meaning of, **12(1)**, [857]
   record of seized items, showing,
      12(1), [855]
   retention of items, **12(1)**, [856];
      12(2), [194], [206]; **12(3)**, [36]
senior officers, removal of, **33(2)**, [221]
service in, **16**, [492]
sex discrimination in, **7(1)**, [55]
special constables—
   appointment, **33(2)**, [202]
      declaration on, **33(2)**, [86]
      nominations for, **33(2)**, [86]
   defence establishments, service at,
      33(2), [63]
   disciplinary proceedings, conduct of,
      33(2), [371]
   pension regulations, **33(2)**, [229]
   regulations, **33(2)**, [229]
   remuneration, **33(2)**, [229]

police—*contd*

special services, provision of, **33(2)**, [200]
station—
   arrested person to be taken to, **12(1)**, [864]
   designated—
      custody officer. *See* custody officer *above*
      detention, for, **12(1)**, [874]
   detainee, search of, **12(1)**, [900]
   fingerprinting at, **12(1)**, [908]
   suspect, photographing, **12(1)**, [916]
   voluntary attendance at, **12(1)**, [863]
station, riotous or indecent behaviour in,
   36, [228]
stop and search powers—
   aerodrome, at, **12(4)**, [258]
   exercise of, **12(1)**, [835]
   firearms, for, **12(1)**, [531]
   garden or yard, in, **12(1)**, [835]
   information, giving, **12(1)**, [836]
   length of detention, **12(1)**, [836]
   no search made, where, **12(1)**, [836]
   persons, of, **12(1)**, [835]
   prohibited article, finding, **12(1)**, [835]
   records, making, **12(1)**, [837], [839]
   reports of, **12(1)**, [839]
   road checks, **12(1)**, [838], [839]
   seizure of articles, **12(1)**, [835]
   unattended vehicle, **12(1)**, [836]
   vehicles, of, **12(1)**, [835]–[837]
   violence, in anticipation of, **12(2)**, [192]
street collections, regulation of, **33(2)**, [60]
teams, liability for members of, **33(2)**, [392]
terrorism, powers, **12(2)**, [936]
three-year strategy plans, **33(2)**, [168]
trade union membership, **33(2)**, [243]
training—
   Central Police Training and Development
      Authority. *See* **Central Police Training
      and Development Authority**
   direction after inspection identifies needs,
      33(2), [341]
   orders and regulations, **33(2)**, [342]
   regulations, **33(2)**, [340]
transitional provisions, **33(2)**, [264],
   [274]–[276]
transport, jurisdiction, **12(3)**, [129]
trespassers, power to remove from land,
   12(2), [195]
   alternative site available, **12(2)**, [197]
   common land, provisions applying,
      12(2), [200]
   failure to comply with direction—
      offences, **12(2)**, [198]
      seizure of articles, **12(2)**, [196], [199]
   interpretation, **12(2)**, [201]
trespassory assembly—
   delegation of functions, **12(1)**, [1009]
   prohibition of, **12(1)**, [1006]
   stopping persons proceeding to,
      12(1), [1008]
unfair dismissal provisions, **16**, [787]
vehicle, excise duty, exemption from,
   13, [1049]
vehicles, speed limit exemption, **37**, [261]

police—*contd*
  war service—
    civil pay, making up, **33(2)**, [66]
    superannuation, reckoning for, **33(2)**, [67]
  warrant, protection where acting under,
    33(2), [18]
  wasteful employment of, causing, **12(1)**, [363]

police authority
  adverse reports, power of Secretary of State to
    give directions after, **33(2)**, [216]
  annual reports by, **33(2)**, [172]
  Association, consultation with, **33(2)**, [615],
    [634]
  audit reports, **26(1)**, [349]
  best value authorities, as, **33(2)**, [613]
  capital expenditure, grants for, **33(2)**, [226]
  chief constable—
    appointment, **33(2)**, [183]
    deputy—
      appointment, **33(2)**, [184]
      removal, **33(2)**, [184]
    removal of, **33(2)**, [183], [220]
    reports by, **33(2)**, [197], [223]
  chief executive, appointment of, **33(2)**, [190],
    [632]
  civilian employees, **33(2)**, [189]
  codes of practice, issue by Secretary of State,
    33(2), [214]
  contracted-out staff, police powers for,
    33(2), [374]
  crime and disorder reduction partnerships,
    33(2), [390]
  delegation of functions, **33(2)**, [612]
  directions to, **33(2)**, [217]–[218]
  employees, police powers for, **33(2)**, [372]
  establishment of, **33(2)**, [158]
  financial administration, **25(2)**, [803]
  financing of new, **33(2)**, [253]
  functions—
    general, **33(2)**, [164], [632]
    particular, power to confer, **33(2)**, [165]
    questions as to, at council meetings,
      33(2), [194]
  gifts, acceptance of, **33(2)**, [252]
  grants to, **33(2)**, [225]–[227], [251]
  information—
    access to. *See* **local authority**
    duty to publish, **25(2)**, [428]
    investigation, subject to, **25(2)**, [310]
    See further **Local Commissioner**
  lay justice members, selection of, **11(3)**, [431]
  loans, acceptance of, **33(2)**, [252]
  local authority provisions applied,
    25(2), [107], [873]
  local policing—
    objectives, **33(2)**, [169]
    plans, **33(2)**, [170]
    summaries, **33(2)**, [171]
  meaning, **33(2)**, [262]; **41**, [605]
  members—
    allowances, **33(2)**, [269]
    appointment of—
      independent, **33(2)**, [269]
      magistrates, **33(2)**, [269]

police authority—*contd*
  members—*contd*
    appointment of—*contd*
      relevant councils, by, **33(2)**, [269]
    chairman, **33(2)**, [269]
    disqualification, **33(2)**, [269]
    eligibility for re-appointment, **33(2)**, [269]
    number of, **33(2)**, [269]
    tenure of office, **33(2)**, [269]
    validity of acts, **33(2)**, [269]
  membership of, **33(2)**, [159]
  minimum budget, directions from Secretary of
    State as to, **33(2)**, [219]
  national security, grants for safeguarding,
    33(2), [227]
  new, financing of, **33(2)**, [253]
  performance targets, setting by Secretary of
    State, **33(2)**, [213]
  persons not employed by, appointment of,
    33(2), [191]
  plans, **33(2)**, [166], [632]
  precepts, approval of decisions about,
    33(2), [193]
  provisions applied to, **33(2)**, [196]
  reports by, **33(2)**, [167], [632]
  reports to Secretary of State, **33(2)**, [222]
  sale of house at discount by, stamp duty,
    41, [145], [167]
  size of, reductions in, **33(2)**, [160]
  strategic priorities, setting, **33(2)**, [212]
  supply of goods and services, **33(2)**, [192]
  three-year strategy plans, **33(2)**, [168]
  traffic offences, payments in relation to
    prevention, detection and enforcement of—
      Scottish Ministers, by, **33(2)**, [584]
      Secretary of State, by, **33(2)**, [583]
  transfer of officers, **25(2)**, [218]
  works contracts. *See* **local authority**

police civilians
  accredited inspectors, powers of, **33(2)**, [409]
  accredited persons—
    offences against, **33(2)**, [382]
    powers of, **33(2)**, [408]
  community safety accreditation schemes—
    accreditation under, **33(2)**, [376]
    generally, **33(2)**, [375]
    offences against designated and accredited
      persons, **33(2)**, [382]
    power to apply accreditation provisions,
      33(2), [378]
    powers under, **33(2)**, [408]
    supplementary provisions, **33(2)**, [379]
    weights and measures inspectors,
      accreditation of, **33(2)**, [377], [409]
  community support officers, powers,
    33(2), [373], [402], [616]
  detention officers, powers, **33(2)**, [404]
  escort officers, powers, **33(2)**, [405]
  exercise of police powers by, **33(2)**, [635]
  investigating officers, powers of **33(2)**, [403]
  police authority employees, powers for,
    33(2), [372]
  relevant police area, **33(2)**, [407]
  staff custody officers, **33(2)**, [406]

police civilians—*contd*
staff, employment of, **33(2)**, [189]
summary of provisions, **33(2)**, [17]

Police Complaints Authority. *See now*
**Independent Police Complaints
Commission**
cessation, **33(2)**, [348]

Police Complaints Board
replaced. *See* **Police Complaints Authority**

Police Federation
constitution of, regulations as to, **33(2)**, [239]
independence of, **33(2)**, [238]
objects of, **33(2)**, [238]
proceedings of, regulations as to, **33(2)**, [239]
representation by, in proceedings, **33(2)**, [238]
summary of provisions, **33(2)**, [17]
tax exemptions, **44(1)**, [315]

police forces
definitions, **3(S)**, 337–8

**Police Information Technology
Organisation**
abolition, **33(2)**, [610]

Police Negotiating Board
chairman and deputy—
appointment, **33(2)**, [240]
remuneration, **33(2)**, [240]
duties, **33(2)**, [240]
expenses, **33(2)**, [240]
regulations, functions as to, **33(2)**, [241]

police pensions
age of retirement, **33(2)**, [103]
appeals—
grounds for, **33(2)**, [107]
regulations as to, **33(2)**, [107]
armed forces, treatment of service in,
33(2), [106]
assignment to be void, **33(2)**, [111]
Association of Chief Police Officers, for staff
of, **33(2)**, [345]
cadets, provisions as to, **33(1)**, [135];
33(2), [95]
contributions—
funds for purposes of, **33(2)**, [108]
transferred service, for, **33(2)**, [105]
conviction of pensioner, effect, **33(2)**, [117]
entitlement, regulations, **33(2)**, [102]
existing members—
application of regulations, **33(2)**, [103]
meaning, **33(2)**, [103]
forfeiture—
appeal against, **33(2)**, [107], [117]
grounds for, **33(2)**, [117]
illegal business, for carrying on,
33(2), [117]
former members, application of regulations,
33(2), [104]
increase, provision for, **33(1)**, [112]–[113]

police pensions—*contd*
information regarding, provision of,
33(2), [110]
merger of schemes, **33(2)**, [633]
metropolitan civil staffs—
meaning, **33(2)**, [96]
pension entitlement, **33(2)**, [96]
national service—
meaning, **33(2)**, [106]
treatment of, **33(2)**, [106]
payment of, funds for, **33(2)**, [108]
regulations—
amending, **33(2)**, [103]
appeals as to, **33(2)**, [107]
application of, **33(2)**, [103]
consolidation of, **33(2)**, [89], [109]
existing members, application to,
33(2), [103]
former members, application to,
33(2), [104]
pensions excluded from, **33(2)**, [117]
provisions made by, **33(2)**, [102]
retrospective effect, having, **33(2)**, [102]
servicemen, as to, **33(2)**, [106]
repealed Acts, under—
excluded from regulations, **33(2)**, [117]
forfeiture of, **33(2)**, [117]
relevant enactments, **33(2)**, [117]
rights—
meaning, **33(2)**, [113]
regulations, **33(2)**, [102]
scale of, regulations as to, **33(2)**, [103]
self-inflicted injury to obtain, **33(2)**, [112]
special constables, regulations, **33(1)**, [135]
summary of provisions, **33(2)**, [17]
transfer value—
calculation, **33(2)**, [94]
payment of, **33(2)**, [105]
war service, reckoning of, **33(2)**, [67]

Polish forces
disablement and death, scheme applying to,
3, [361]
emigration, arrangements for, **3**, [362]
resettlement forces, meaning, **3**, [363]

Polish resettlement
Assistance Board—
accommodation in camps, provision of,
40(1), [3], [6]
allowances from, **40(1)**, [2]
health services, provision of, **30**, [424]
residence in Poland, effect of,
33(S), Pensions 205

political donations and expenditure
application of provisions, **8(1)**, [441]
authorisation, resolution for—
form of, **8(1)**, [445]
period for which having effect, **8(1)**, [446]
requirement of, **8(1)**, [444]
control of, **8(1)**, [440]
definitions, **8(1)**, [457]

political donations and expenditure—*contd*
  donations not amounting to more than
    £5,000 in any twelve month period,
    8(1), [456]
  exemptions by order, **8(1)**, [455]
  organisations to which provisions apply,
    8(1), [441]
    all-party parliamentary group not being,
      8(1), [454]
  political expenditure, meaning, **8(1)**, [443]
  political donation, meaning, **8(1)**, [442]
  political parties to which provisions apply,
    8(1), [441]
  prohibited, **8(1)**, [444]
  shareholders' action, enforcement of directors'
    liability by, **8(1)**, [448]
    application to court by director, **8(1)**, [449]
    costs of, **8(1)**, [450]
    information for purposes of, **8(1)**, [451]
    notice of, **8(1)**, [449]
  trade associations, subscriptions to, **8(1)**, [453]
  trade union, donation to, **8(1)**, [452]
  unauthorised, liability of directors, **8(1)**, [447]

political funds
  trade unions, application of. *See under* **trade
  unions**

political parties
  accounting—
    annual audits, **15(3)**, [344]
    auditors—
      appointment of, **15(3)**, [344]
      supplementary provisions, **15(3)**, [345]
    records, duty to keep, **15(3)**, [342]
    statement of accounts—
      defective, revision of, **15(3)**, [349]
      delivery of, Electoral Commission, to,
        15(3), [346]
      failure to submit, criminal penalty for,
        15(3), [348]
      preparation of, **15(3)**, [343]
      public inspection of, **15(3)**, [347]
      revision of, **15(3)**, [349]
  accounting units, with—
    accounting records, **15(3)**, [490]
    annual audits, **15(3)**, [490]
    annual statements, **15(3)**, [490]
    division of responsibilities, **15(3)**, [350]
  campaign expenditure—
    claims—
      disputed, **15(3)**, [404]
      restrictions, **15(3)**, [403]
    generally, **15(3)**, [398]
    guidance by Commission, **15(3)**, [499]
    incurring, restrictions on, **15(3)**, [401]
    limits on, **15(3)**, [405], [500]–[502]
    meaning, **15(3)**, [398]
    notional, **15(3)**, [399]
    officers with responsibility for, **15(3)**, [400]
    payments, restrictions on, **15(3)**, [402]
    qualifying expenses, **15(3)**, [498]
    returns—
      auditor's report on, **15(3)**, [407]
      declaration by treasurer, **15(3)**, [409]

political parties—*contd*
  campaign expenditure—*contd*
    returns—*contd*
      delivery to Commission, **15(3)**, [408]
      generally, **15(3)**, [406]
      public inspection, **15(3)**, [410]
  conferences, security costs, **12(2)**, [248]
  donations to—
    acceptance of, **15(3)**, [357]
    companies, by, **15(3)**, [459], [517]
    disclosure, **15(3)**, [460], [522]
    exempt trust donations, **15(3)**, [480]
    forfeiture of—
      appeals, **15(3)**, [361]–[362]
      impermissible donors, from, **15(3)**, [360]
      supplementary provisions, **15(3)**, [362]
      unidentifiable donor, from, **15(3)**, [360]
    general note, **15(3)**, [1]
    generally, **15(3)**, [351]
    Gibraltar, **15(3)**, [359]
    holders of elective offices, to, **15(3)**, [636]
      compliance officers,
        15(S), Elections 28–31
    impermissible donor, defence to charge of
      failure to return, **15(S)**, Elections 24
    increased thresholds, **15(S)**, Elections 36
    individuals—
      control of, **15(3)**, [494]
      generally, **15(3)**, [398], [493]
      payments not regarded as donations,
        15(3), [493]
      register of, **15(3)**, [496]
      reporting of donations. regulated donees,
        by, **15(3)**, [495]
      sponsorship, **15(3)**, [493]
      value of, **15(3)**, [493]
    interpretation, **15(3)**, [479]
    meaning, **15(3)**, [351]
    members associations—
      control of, **15(3)**, [494]
      generally, **15(3)**, [398], [493]
      offences, **15(S)**, Elections 27
      payments not regarded as donations,
        15(3), [493]
      register of, **15(3)**, [496]
      reporting of donations, regulated donees,
        by, **15(3)**, [495]
      responsible persons,
        15(S), Elections 25–7
        one third party only, for,
          15(S), Elections 33–2
      sponsorship, **15(3)**, [493]
      value of, **15(3)**, [493]
    non-resident donors,
      15(S), Elections 19–20
    Northern Ireland. *See* **Northern Ireland**
    payments not to be regarded as,
      15(3), [353], [493]
    permissible donors—
      generally, **15(3)**, [355]
      meaning, **15(3)**, [355]
      payments not to be treated as donations
        by, **15(3)**, [356]

political parties—*contd*
  donations to—*contd*
    quarterly reports, **15(3)**, [364], [491]
      exemption from requirement to
        prepare, **15(3)**, [365]
      submission to Electoral Commission,
        15(3), [368]
      treasurer, declaration by, in, **15(3)**, [369]
    register of, **15(3)**, [371]
    reports regarding—
      details to be given, **15(3)**, [491], [635]
      identity of donors, **15(3)**, [491]
      quarterly. *See* quarterly reports *above*,
        15(3), [364], [491]
      submission to Electoral Commission,
        15(3), [368]
      transaction, **15(3)**, [492]
      treasurer, declaration by, in, **15(3)**, [369]
      weekly. *See* weekly reports *below*
    restrictions on, offence of evasion,
      15(3), [363]
    return of—
      generally, **15(3)**, [357]
      unidentifiable donor, where,
        15(3), [358]
    services not to be regarded as, **15(3)**, [353]
    source, declaration as to,
      15(S), Elections 15–18, 85–9
    sponsorship, **15(3)**, [352]
    summary of provisions,
      15(S), Elections 2–3
    unincorporated associations making
      contributions, gifts to,
      15(S), Elections 34–5, 93–8
    value of, **15(3)**, [354]
    weekly reports—
      European Parliament election periods,
        during, **15(3)**, [370]
      general election periods, during,
        15(3), [366]–[367]
      identity of donors, **15(3)**, [491]
      Northern Ireland Assembly election
        periods, during, **15(3)**, [370]
      Scottish Parliament election periods,
        during, **15(3)**, [370]
      submission to Electoral Commission,
        15(3), [368]
      treasurer, declaration by, in, **15(3)**, [369]
      Welsh Assembly election periods,
        during, **15(3)**, [370]
  election material, details appearing on,
    15(3), [640]
  enquiries as to, **15(S)**, Elections 1
  failure to deliver documents, civil penalty
    for, **15(3)**, [464]
  false statements, offence of making,
    15(3), [340]
  financial structure—
    accounting units, **15(3)**, [327]
    adoption of scheme for, **15(3)**, [326]
  gifts to, tax exemption, **42**, [545]
  loans to individuals and member associations,
    control of, controlled transactions,
    15(3), [497], [658]

political parties—*contd*
  loans, regulation of—
    candidates, provision for, **15(3)**, [638]
    holders of elective office, to, compliance
      officers, **15(S)**, Elections 32–3
    members' associations, to—
      responsible persons,
        15(S), Elections 31–2
      residence etc condition, declaration as to
        satisfaction of, **15(S)**, Elections 21–3,
        90–3
    Northern Ireland, **15(3)**, [639]
    referendums, **15(3)**, [638]
    third parties, **15(3)**, [638]
  local constituency association, tax relief on
    reorganisation, **42**, [1413]
  offences—
    convictions, duty of court to report to
      Commission, **15(3)**, [471]
    general, **15(3)**, [465]
    penalties, **15(3)**, [518]
    punishment, **15(3)**, [467]
    reasonable excuse, defence of,
      15(S), Elections 25
    summary proceedings, **15(3)**, [468]
  Parliamentary Parties Panel—
    establishment of, **15(3)**, [295]
    functions, **15(3)**, [295]
  party political broadcasts, **15(3)**, [339]
  referendum material, details appearing on,
    15(3), [640]
  register of—
    changes to, **15(3)**, [332]
    confirmation of particulars, **15(3)**, [334]
    new, **15(3)**, [323]
    party's officers, changes in, **15(3)**, [333]
    Secretary of State, request for copies by,
      15(3), [337]
  registered—
    campaigns officer, as, **15(3)**, [325]
    ceasing to be, **15(3)**, [335]
    existing parties, assistance by Electoral
      Commission for, **15(3)**, [338]
    leader, as, **15(3)**, [324]
    minor parties, **15(3)**, [336]
    nominating officer, as, **15(3)**, [324]
    office-holder, as, **15(3)**, [324]
    party political broadcasts, requirement to
      be, for, **15(3)**, [339]
    requirement to be, **15(3)**, [322]
    treasurer, as, **15(3)**, [324]
    transfer of registration of existing,
      transitional provisions, **15(3)**, [521]
  registration—
    application for—
      additional information, **15(3)**, [486]
      alteration of entry, **15(3)**, [487]
      contents of, **15(3)**, [328]
      declarations regarding, **15(3)**, [328]
      descriptions, **15(3)**, [329], [634]
      emblems, **15(3)**, [331]
      grant of, **15(3)**, [328]
      headquarters, **15(3)**, [486]
      joint descriptions, **15(3)**, [330], [634]
      names, **15(3)**, [486]

political parties—*contd*
registration—*contd*
application for—*contd*
party organisation, **15(3)**, [486]
registered offices, **15(3)**, [486]
removal of entry, **15(3)**, [489]
replacement officer, registration of,
15(3), [488]
generally, **15(3)**, [1]
regulated transactions—
authorised participants, **15(3)**, [380]
credit facility, **15(3)**, [379]
Electoral Commission, submission of
reports to, **15(3)**, [391]
interpretation, **15(3)**, [396]
meaning, **15(3)**, [378]
offences, **15(3)**, [384]
proceedings on applications, **15(3)**, [395]
quarterly reports—
changes recorded in, **15(3)**, [386]
exemption from requirement to
prepare, **15(3)**, [388]
existing transactions, **15(3)**, [387]
preparation of, **15(3)**, [386]
register of, **15(3)**, [394]
treasurer's declaration in reports,
15(3), [392]
unauthorised participants, involving,
15(3), [381]
guarantees and securities, **15(3)**, [382]
transfer to, **15(3)**, [383]
valuation, **15(3)**, [379]
weekly reports—
exemption from requirement to
prepare, **15(3)**, [390]
general election periods, during,
15(3), [389]
other than during general election
periods, **15(3)**, [393]
sponsorship, **15(3)**, [352]
third party national election campaigns—
controlled expenditure—
claims—
disputed, **15(3)**, [419]
restrictions on making, **15(3)**, [418]
generally, **15(3)**, [411]
incurring, restrictions on, **15(3)**, [416]
limits on, **15(3)**, [420], [503]–[505]
notional, **15(3)**, [412]
payments, restrictions on, **15(3)**, [417]
returns—
auditor's report on, **15(3)**, [423]
declarations regarding, **15(3)**, [425]
delivery to Commission, **15(3)**, [424]
generally, **15(3)**, [422]
public inspection of, **15(3)**, [426]
donations to—
controls on, **15(3)**, [507]
general rules, **15(3)**, [506]
payments not regarded as, **15(3)**, [506]
reporting of, **15(3)**, [508]
sponsorship, **15(3)**, [506]
value of, **15(3)**, [506]
not controlled expenditure, **15(3)**, [413]
recognised third parties, **15(3)**, [414]

political parties—*contd*
unincorporated associations making
contributions, gifts to,
15(S), Elections 34–5, 93–8

poll tax. *See* **community charges**

pollution. *See also* **air pollution; dust; noise;
smoke; waste; water**
aircraft, caused by—
byelaws as to, **4(1)**, [302]
minimisation, **4(1)**, [58]
byelaws as to—
continuation of, **49**, [1319]
general provisions, **49**, [327]
power to make, **49**, [326], [1295]
Thames Water Authority, by, **49**, [321]
civil liability for, **35(1)**, [336]
consent for discharge—
appeals, **49**, [1152]
applications for, **49**, [1150]
defence, as, **49**, [1147]
enforcement notice, **49**, [1151]
control—
appeals, power of Secretary of State to
delegate functions of determining or
referring matters involved in,
35(2), [153], [175]
Crown application, **35(2)**, [154]
entry powers of enforcing authorities—
compensation, **35(2)**, [174]
evidence, information obtained
admissible in, **35(2)**, [174]
exercise of powers, manner of,
35(2), [174]
general, **35(2)**, [147]
premises, duty to secure, **35(2)**, [174]
warrants, issue of, **35(2)**, [174]
Environment Agency's general functions
with respect to, **35(2)**, [91]
imminent danger of serious pollution,
powers to deal with articles or substances
which cause, **35(2)**, [148]
information about, **49**, [1252]
Isles of Scilly, application of provisions to,
35(1), [352]; **35(2)**, [157]
obstruction of authorised person, offence
of, **35(2)**, [149]
register, **49**, [1238]
controlled waters, meaning, **49**, [1167]
default powers of Secretary of State,
35(1), [345]
definitions, **49**, [1167]
discharge consents—
application for, **49**, [1278]
conditions, alteration and imposition of,
49, [1278]
consideration and determinations,
49, [1278]
consultation, **49**, [1278]
general review, **49**, [1278]
revocation, **49**, [1278]
Secretary of State, reference to, **49**, [1278]
transfer, **49**, [1278]

pollution—*contd*
  discharge consents—*contd*
    variation and revocation, restrictions on,
      49, [1278]
    variation, application for, **49**, [1278]
    without application, **49**, [1278]
  effluents, sampling of, **49**, [447]
  Environment Agency—
    power of to deal with, **49**, [1211]
    works and operations by, **49**, [1206]
    works notice—
      appeals, **49**, [1209]
      meaning, **49**, [1207]
      non-compliance, consequences of,
        49, [1210]
      power to serve, **49**, [1207]
      requirements of, **49**, [1208]
      rights of entry under, **49**, [1208]
  environment, of, meaning, **35(1)**, [709], [733]
  financial provisions, **35(1)**, [337], [338]
  fish, waters containing, **1(2)**, [4]
  gas manufacture, by—
    ascertainment of source, **49**, [60]
    expenses of undertakers, recovery, **49**, [62]
    generally, **49**, [59]
    penalty, **49**, [59]
    powers of undertakers, **49**, [60]
  good agricultural practice, codes of,
    49, [1160]
  incidents, exchange of information about,
    49, [1253]
  information—
    disclosure, prohibition, **35(1)**, [342]
    power to obtain, **35(1)**, [341]
  international—
    agreements, power to give effect to,
      35(1), [349]
    obligations, giving effect to, **49**, [1165]
  legal proceedings, **35(1)**, [335]
  local inquiries, power to hold, **35(1)**, [344]
  marine—
    Conventions, **39(2)**, [796]
    prevention of, **39(2)**, [796], [797]
    Secretary of State, functions of,
      39(2), [970]
    transfers between ships, regulation of,
      39(2), [798]
    UN Convention on the Law of the Sea,
      giving effect to, **39(2)**, [797]
  mines, abandonment—
    meaning, **49**, [1153]
    requirement to give notice of, **49**, [1154]
  minor and consequential amendments,
    35(1), [353]
  National Rivers Authority, transfer of
    functions to Environment Agency,
    35(2), [88]
  nitrate sensitive areas—
    agreements in, **49**, [1158]
    consents, regulations in relation to,
      49, [1159]
    designation of, **49**, [1157]
    orders—
      application for, **49**, [1280]
      mandatory provisions in, **49**, [1281]

pollution—*contd*
  offences—
    authorised discharges, defences in respect
      of, **49**, [1147]
    consents, applications for, **49**, [1150]
    controlled waters, polluting, **49**, [1144]
    defences, **49**, [1148]
    deposits and vegetation in rivers, as to,
      49, [1149]
    discharges prohibited by notice or
      regulation, **49**, [1145]
    enforcement notices, **49**, [1151]
    evidence in connection with certain,
      35(2), [150]
    fines, **35(S)**, 117
    penalties, **49**, [56]–[59]
    penalties on conviction, **35(2)**, [544]
    public sewers, discharges to and from,
      49, [1146]
  offshore installations, accidents involving,
    35(2), [272]
  oil. *See* **oil pollution**
  penalties, alteration, **35(1)**, [337]
  Port of London, **39(2)**, [397]
  precautions against, requirement to take,
    49, [1155]
  quality of waters—
    classification of, **49**, [1141]
    objectives, **49**, [1141]–[1143]
  radioactive substances, by—
    consents required, **49**, [1162]
    provisions applying, **49**, [1161]
  regulation of activities—
    appeals, **35(2)**, [277]
    charging schemes, **35(2)**, [278]
    consultation, **35(2)**, [271], [277]
    definitions, **35(2)**, [270]
    enforcement, **35(2)**, [277]
    information, **35(2)**, [277]
    meaning, **35(2)**, [270]
    offences, **35(2)**, [277], [278]
    permits, **35(2)**, [277]
    power of, **35(2)**, [271]
    publicity, **35(2)**, [277]
    purpose of, **35(2)**, [271]
    scope of, **35(2)**, [277]
  relevant authority, meaning, **35(1)**, [346]
  rivers. *See* **river pollution**
  savings, **49**, [1163]
  sea, deposit of substances etc in—
    Channel Islands, application of provisions,
      49, [643]
    Conventions, enforcement of, **49**, [633]
    Crown, application of provisions to,
      49, [637]
    dumping at sea, 1974 Act repeal, **49**, [636]
    enforcement officers—
      assistants for, **49**, [646]
      authorisation of, **49**, [632]
      authority, evidence of, **49**, [646]
      containers, powers as to, **49**, [646]
      entry—
        dwellings, into, **49**, [646]
        power of, **49**, [632]
      force, use of, **49**, [646]

pollution—*contd*
  sea, deposit of substances etc in—*contd*
    enforcement officers—*contd*
      offences against, **49**, [646]
      powers, **49**, [632], [646]
      time for performance of duties,
        49, [646]
    financial provision, **49**, [640]
    Isle of Man, application of provisions,
      49, [643]
    licence—
      applicant, information required of,
        49, [629]
      exemptions, **49**, [627]
      fee, **49**, [629]
      matters to be considered, **49**, [629]
      offences generally, **49**, [630]
      provisions to be included in, **49**, [629]
      refusal of, **49**, [647]
      registers—
        contents, **49**, [648]–[649]
        requirement to keep, **49**, [635]
      representations regarding, **49**, [647]
      requirement, **49**, [625]
      revocation and variation, **49**, [629],
        [647]
      vessels and craft to which applicable,
        49, [625]
    licensing authorities, committees,
      appointment and duties, **49**, [647]
    Minister, expenses of, **49**, [640]
    Northern Ireland, application of
      provisions, **49**, [642]
    offences—
      body corporate, by, **49**, [638]
      defence of due diligence, **49**, [639]
      enforcement officers, against, **49**, [646]
      generally, **49**, [630]
      penalties, **49**, [638]
    remedial action, power to take, **49**, [631]
    scuttling of vessels—
      licence requirement, **49**, [625]
      register of licences, **49**, [635],
        [648]–[649]
    sea, meaning, **49**, [641]
  sea, incineration at—
    licence requirements, **49**, [626]
    meaning of incineration, **49**, [626]
    register of licences issued, **49**, [635], [648]
    See generally sea, deposit of substances *above*
  summary of provisions, **39(2)**, [1]
  summary offences, limitation for, **49**, [1164]
  testing, powers as to, **49**, [634]
  Thames. *See* **Thames Water Authority**
  trade effluent, by. *See* **trade effluent**
  transitional provisions, **49**, [1166], [1282]
  undertakers dealing with, **49**, [970]
  waste. *See* **waste**
  water pollution provisions, meaning,
    49, [1267]
  water protection zones—
    consents, regulations in relation to,
      49, [1159]
    designation of, **49**, [1156]
    orders, **49**, [1279]

polygamous marriage
  council tax benefit, effect on, **40(1)**, [381]
  social security benefits, effect on, **40(1)**, [365]

polytechnic
  freedom of speech, **15(1)**, [292]

**Polytechnics and Colleges Funding
Council.** *See also* **Funding Councils and
Assets Board**
  dissolution, **15(1)**, [430]
  persons employed in higher and further
    education, payments for, **15(1)**, [319]
  property, rights and liabilities, transfer of,
    15(1), [430]
  reference to, **15(1)**, [427]

pond
  draining, cleansing, etc, power of parish
    council or local authority as to, **35(1)**, [162]
  foul, statutory nuisance, **35(1)**, [161]

pony
  export of—
    registered ponies, **2**, [492]
    regulation of, **2**, [493]
    restrictions on, **2**, [491]
  meaning, **2**, [548]
  registered, meaning, **2**, [492]
  valuation of, **2**, [491]

pool betting. *See also* **betting; gaming**
  business—
    accounts and records, **5(1)**, [94]
    meaning, **5(1)**, [94]
    permit required, **5(1)**, [94]
  definition, **5(1)**, [56]
  duty—
    accounting period, meaning, **5(1)**, [54]
    amended provisions, **5(1)**, [228], [231]
    bet made for community benefit,
      meaning, **5(1)**, [53]
    bet, meaning, **5(1)**, [55]
    charge of, **5(1)**, [43]
    enforcement, **5(1)**, [94]
    intended bet, no transmission of, **5(1)**, [57]
    losses, relief for, **5(1)**, [45]
    net receipts, on—
      calculating, **5(1)**, [46]
      charge of, **5(1)**, [44]
      dutiable pool bet, meaning, **5(1)**, [47]
      expenses and profits, **5(1)**, [50]
      payment and recovery of, **5(1)**, [52]
      stake money, calculating, **5(1)**, [48]
      stakes falling due, time of, **5(1)**, [49]
      winnings, calculating, **5(1)**, [51]
    Northern Ireland provisions, **5(1)**, [106],
      [108]
    offences and penalties, **5(1)**, [94]
    payment, liability for, **5(1)**, [52]
    persons subject to—
      payments by, **44(3)**, [762]
      trade profits, **44(3)**, [161]
    recovery of, **5(1)**, [52]
    surcharges or rebates, **13**, [898]–[900]

pool betting—*contd*
  horse-race, **5(1)**, [293]
    exclusive licence for—
      effect of, **5(1)**, [241]
      grant of, **5(1)**, [240]
      revocation, **5(1)**, [241]
      Secretary of State, consideration by,
        5(1), [241]
    operating licence, **5(1)**, [375]
    regulation of, **5(1)**, [241]
  meaning, **5(1)**, [293]
  off track, restriction on, **5(1)**, [241]
  operating licence, **5(1)**, [346], [374]
  permit, grant of, **5(1)**, [94]
  premises licence—
    children, exclusion of, **5(1)**, [463]
    dog racing, **5(1)**, [461]
    track, on, **5(1)**, [460]
  stake, deduction by Board from, **5(1)**, [3]
  Totalisator Board, by, **5(1)**, [2], [21]
  track, restriction on, **5(1)**, [241]

pools payments
  football ground improvements, for, **42**, [1029]
  games, to support, **42**, [1066]

poor law
  supersession of, **40(1)**, [7]

poor law officers
  superannuation allowances, **25(1)**, [246]

poor rate
  City of London, in. *See* **London, City of**
  consolidation of, **25(1)**, [20]
  recovery, proceedings for, **25(1)**, [20]

population. *See also* **census**
  statistics—
    annual abstract—
      Registrar General, by, **36**, [150]
      Statistics Board, by, **36**, [136]
    expenses, defrayment, **36**, [45]
    offences and penalties, **36**, [46]
    particulars which may be required,
      36, [44], [49]
    Registrar General, duties, **36**, [45]

pornography
  abuse of child through—
    arranging or facilitating, **12(3)**, [712]
    causing or inciting, **12(3)**, [710]
    controlling, **12(3)**, [711]
    interpretation, **12(3)**, [713]
    sexual services, paying for, **12(3)**, [709]
  extreme images—
    classified films, in, **12(4)**, [497]
    consensual acts, participation in,
      12(4), [499]
    information society services providers, rules
      relating to, **12(4)**, [569]
    meaning, **12(4)**, [496]
    possession of—
      defences, **12(4)**, [498], [499]
      offence, **12(4)**, [496]

pornography—*contd*
  extreme images—*contd*
    possession of—*contd*
      penalties, **12(4)**, [500]
    transitory and transitional provisions,
      12(4), [581]

port
  London, of, port health authority and district
    for, **35(1)**, [448], [449]
  meaning, **35(1)**, [443]
  use of term, **48**, 13, 37, 44

port health authority
  borrowing powers, **35(1)**, [122], [446]
  constitution, **35(1)**, [443], [445]
  default, in, powers of Secretary of State
    where, **35(1)**, [511]
  environmental protection functions of,
    35(1), [712]
  expenses, **35(1)**, [443]
  joint board—
    as, **35(1)**, [443]
    default, in, powers of Secretary of State
      where, **35(1)**, [511]
    expenses, **35(1)**, [446]
  jurisdiction, **35(1)**, [444]
  London—
    Common Council as, **35(1)**, [448]
    functions, rights and liabilities, assignment
      to, **35(1)**, [448]
    international health regulations,
      25(2), [390]
    jurisdiction, **25(2)**, [276]; **35(1)**, [448]
    meaning, **35(1)**, [448]
    provisions applied, **25(1)**, [1014]
    water for consumption in ships,
      25(2), [390]
  members and officers, protection from
    personal liability, **35(1)**, [195], [509], [637]
  powers, **35(1)**, [444]
  riparian authority as, **35(1)**, [443]
  transferred officers of, compensation and
    superannuation rights of, **35(1)**, [203]
  vessels in inland or coastal waters, jurisdiction
    over, **35(1)**, [450]

port health district
  area changes, effect of, **25(2)**, [223]
    Wales, in, **26(1)**, [181]
  constitution, **35(1)**, [443], [445]
  London—
    constitution, **35(1)**, [448]
    meaning, **35(1)**, [448]
  meaning, **25(2)**, [389]
  order constituting, **35(1)**, [121]
  port, meaning, **35(1)**, [443]

Port of London
  access—
    government officers, for, **39(2)**, [378]
    public, to premises, **39(2)**, [229]
  authority. *See* **Port of London Authority**
  bridges—
    maintenance and repair, **39(2)**, [377], [418]

Port of London—*contd*
bridges—*contd*
obstruction of, penalty, **39(2)**, [399]
building on low-lying land, **25(1)**, [178]
bunker fuel, port rates exemption,
39(2), [252]
byelaws—
breach of, **39(2)**, [369]
confirmation, **39(2)**, [370]
fishing, **39(2)**, [368]
increase of penalties, **39(2)**, [497], [501]
petroleum spirit, as to, contravention,
39(2), [356]
port premises, **39(2)**, [366]
power to make, **39(2)**, [366]
proof of, **39(2)**, [371]
Thames, **39(2)**, [367]
charges. *See under* **Port of London
Authority**
costs of Port of London Acts, **39(2)**, [411]
crowds, regulation of, **39(2)**, [327]
Crown rights, **39(2)**, [383]
customs officers, accommodation for,
39(2), [353]
docks—
deemed part of, **39(2)**, [379]
directions to vessels at, **39(2)**, [321]
pollution, **39(2)**, [397]
roads, traffic offences on, **39(2)**, [396]
vessels adrift at, **39(2)**, [317]
draught of vessel, false, **39(2)**, [341]
estuary traffic, port rates exemption,
39(2), [254], [255]
extent of, **35(1)**, [447]
fish, port rates exemption, **39(2)**, [252]
footbridges, maintenance and repair,
39(2), [377], [418]
former seaward limit, meaning, **39(2)**, [225],
[412]
goods traffic—
customs—
entry by authority, **39(2)**, [350]
officers, accommodation for,
39(2), [353]
dangerous goods—
entry of, **39(2)**, [354]
notice concerning, **39(2)**, [355]
imports, account to be given, **39(2)**, [346]
landing places, inspection, **39(2)**, [357]
manifest, supply of copies, **39(2)**, [346]
offensive goods, removal and disposal of,
39(2), [349]
passes for goods, **39(2)**, [352]
petroleum spirit, **39(2)**, [356]
removal of goods to other parts,
39(2), [348]
survey goods, power to, **39(2)**, [347]
warrants for goods, **39(2)**, [351]
weight, under-declaration of, **39(2)**, [358]
goods in transit, port rates exemption,
39(2), [253]
government officers, access for, **39(2)**, [378]
inquiries, **39(2)**, [410]
international health regulations, **25(2)**, [390]
lamps, unlawfully extinguishing, **39(2)**, [400]

Port of London—*contd*
landward limit, meaning, **39(2)**, [225], [412]
legal proceedings, **39(2)**, [402]
lighters—
meaning, **39(2)**, [225]
rates exemption in certain cases,
39(2), [422]
lights, unlawfully extinguishing, **39(2)**, [400]
limits, description of, **39(2)**, [412]
master of ship—
directions, failure to comply with,
39(2), [325]
identification of, **39(2)**, [343]
responsibility of, saving for, **39(2)**, [324]
meaning, **25(1)**, [726]; **39(2)**, [408]
medical officers of health, **25(1)**, [703]
Medway approach, powers not exercised
with, **39(2)**, [384], [419]
Millwall docks, exemption from London
Building Acts, **39(2)**, [376]
moorings, interference with, **39(2)**, [340]
navigation—
general rules, **39(2)**, [316]
hazards to. *See* obstructions *below*
lights detrimental to, **39(2)**, [338]
obstruction or non-compliance with officer's
orders, **39(2)**, [398]
obstructions, removal—
other than vessels, **39(2)**, [329]
projections, **39(2)**, [330]
sunken vessels, **39(2)**, [328]
offences—
bribery, etc, **39(2)**, [401]
increase of penalties, **39(2)**, [497], [500],
[501]
schedule of, **39(2)**, [500]
substituted penalties, **39(2)**, [500]
traffic offences on dock roads, **39(2)**, [396]
overground wires at, **25(1)**, [214]
parking, unlawful, **39(2)**, [374]
petroleum oil depots, **25(1)**, [126]
police. *See* **Port of London Authority**
pollution, prohibition, **39(2)**, [397]
port health authority, and district for,
35(1), [448], [449]
port health district—
authority, application of provisions to,
25(1), [1014]
extension of, **25(1)**, [791]
meaning, **25(1)**, [1013]; **25(2)**, [389]
port rates. *See under* **Port of London
Authority**
public health inspectors, **25(1)**, [703]
rates, exemption from, **39(2)**, [252]–[255],
[375]
registration of craft. *See under* **Port of
London Authority**
river duties of tonnage—
exemption, **39(2)**, [256]
meaning, **39(2)**, [225]
roads—
maintenance and repair, **39(2)**, [377], [418]
traffic offences, **39(2)**, [396]
seaward limit, meaning, **39(2)**, [225], [412]

Port of London—*contd*
Sheerness, powers not exercisable off,
39(2), [384], [419]
Southend-on-Sea, powers not exercisable off,
39(2), [384], [419]
summary of provisions, **39(2)**, [1]
Surrey Canal and commercial docks
discontinuance, **39(2)**, [435]
Thames. *See* **Thames**
traffic offences on dock roads, **39(2)**, [396]
vehicles at port premises, removal,
39(2), [374]
vessels—
adrift, **39(2)**, [317]
boarding of, powers, **39(2)**, [342]
damage caused by, **39(2)**, [339]
docks, at, **39(2)**, [321]
enforcement of directions, **39(2)**, [326]
failure to comply with directions,
39(2), [325]
general directions to, **39(2)**, [319]
master's responsibility, saving for,
39(2), [324]
overcrowding, **39(2)**, [318]
publication of directions, **39(2)**, [322]
special directions to, **39(2)**, [320], [323]
sunken, removal, **39(2)**, [328]
watermen and lightermen, registration,
licences etc. *See under* **Thames**

Port of London Authority
accounts and audit, **39(2)**, [281]
advertising requirements, modification,
39(2), [373]
boats for hire, meaning, **39(2)**, [225]
boats generally, licensing. *See* licensing of
vessels *below*
bonds, regulations as to, **39(2)**, [277]
borrowing powers—
generally, **39(2)**, [270]
lenders not concerned with application,
39(2), [272]
temporary loans, **39(2)**, [271]
Treasury powers, saving for, **39(2)**, [280]
trusts, not recognising, **39(2)**, [273]
bribery offences, **39(2)**, [401]
bridges, obstruction of, **39(2)**, [399]
British Railways Board—
arrangements with, **39(2)**, [239]
protection of, **39(2)**, [436]
byelaws. *See* **Port of London**
capital, power to charge interest to,
39(2), [278]
chairman, **39(2)**, [413]
charges—
assessment, collection and recovery,
39(2), [245]
bunker fuel and fish, port rates exemption,
39(2), [252]
certificate of payment, **39(2)**, [259]
compounding arrangements and rebates,
39(2), [247]
Crown exemption, **39(2)**, [251]
detention of goods, **39(2)**, [261]
enforcement, **39(2)**, [261]

Port of London Authority—*contd*
charges—*contd*
entry on vessels, **39(2)**, [260]
evasion, **39(2)**, [266]
false information, **39(2)**, [266]
landing place, for, refusal to pay,
39(2), [267]
lighters, when exempt from rates,
39(2), [422]
meaning, **39(2)**, [225]
payment of, **39(2)**, [257]
port rates, exemptions, **39(2)**, [252]–[255]
power to make, **39(2)**, [244]
recovery, **39(2)**, [261]
regulations as to, **39(2)**, [245]
Revenue and Customs Commissioners,
arrangements with, **39(2)**, [246]
Richmond footbridge, **39(2)**, [249]
Richmond lock and slipway, exemption,
39(2), [250]
sale of goods or vessels, **39(2)**, [261]
security for, **39(2)**, [258]
City of London, saving as to, **39(2)**, [388]
constables. *See* police *below*
constitution, **39(2)**, [226], [413], [414]
craft, meaning, **39(2)**, [225]
Crossrail, protective provisions, **38(2)**, [644]
customs clearance, refusal of, **39(2)**, [262]
debts, reduction of indebtedness, **39(2)**, [515]
documents—
authentication of, **39(2)**, [380]
publication of, **39(2)**, [382]
service of, **39(2)**, [381]
entry on land in or near Thames, **39(2)**, [312]
entry on vessels, for purposes of charges,
39(2), [260]
Essex and Kent river authorities, protection
of, **39(2)**, [395]
Essex County Council, protection of,
39(2), [390]
financial assistance to, provision, **39(2)**, [467]
fish, area of jurisdiction relating to,
39(2), [308]
flood prevention works, statutory provisions
applicable, **39(2)**, [315]
general duties and powers—
annual reports, **39(2)**, [231]
British Railways Board, arrangements
with, **39(2)**, [239]
City of London, exercise of former
powers, **39(2)**, [238]
Crown, exercise of former powers,
39(2), [238]
donations and subscriptions, **39(2)**, [240]
generally, **39(2)**, [228]
hydrographic surveys, **39(2)**, [230]
legislation, powers relating to, **39(2)**, [235]
money, lending, **39(2)**, [236]
public access to port premises, **39(2)**, [229]
refreshment rooms, provision, **39(2)**, [241]
returns and statistics, **39(2)**, [232]
securities and stock, acquisition,
39(2), [236]
staff—
benefits, **39(2)**, [242]

Port of London Authority—*contd*
  general duties and powers—*contd*
    staff—*contd*
      housing, **39(2)**, [243]
      pensions. *See* pension fund *below*
    undertakings, acquisition, **39(2)**, [233]
    vessels, construction, **39(2)**, [237]
  general reserve, **39(2)**, [279]
  Inner Temple, saving as to, **39(2)**, [389]
  inquiries by Ministers, **39(2)**, [410]
  jurisdiction, **25(1)**, [1]
  Lancaster, Duchy of, sale of land by,
    39(2), [385]
  land—
    powers relating to, **39(2)**, [234]
    sale by Duchy of Lancaster, **39(2)**, [385]
    Town and Country Planning Acts,
      application, **39(2)**, [372]
  landing place. *See under* **Thames**
  legal proceedings—
    institution and defence, **39(2)**, [402]
    jurisdiction of justices, **39(2)**, [404]
    offences triable summarily, **39(2)**, [403]
  licensing of vessels—
    appeals, **39(2)**, [334], [416]
    charges, **39(2)**, [337]
    exemptions, **39(2)**, [332]
    inaccurate or lost licences, reissue,
      39(2), [335]
    mortgages, register of, **39(2)**, [336]
    requirement, **39(2)**, [332]
    revocation or suspension of licence,
      39(2), [333]
    unlicensed vessels not to be navigated,
      39(2), [332]
  loans by, **39(2)**, [236]
  loans to. *See* borrowing powers *above*
  London Regional Transport, saving for,
    39(2), [386], [436]
  master of vessel, identity, right to require
    information as to, **39(2)**, [343]
  See generally under **ports and harbours**
  members—
    appointment, **39(2)**, [413]
    number of, **39(2)**, [226]
    officer as, **39(2)**, [413]
    resignation, **39(2)**, [413]
    salaries and allowances, **39(2)**, [413]
    vacancy, **39(2)**, [413]
  Middle Temple, saving as to, **39(2)**, [389]
  officers. *See* staff *below*
  pension fund rules, **39(2)**, [415]
  police—
    appointment etc of constables, **39(2)**, [359]
    area of authority, **39(2)**, [360]
    declaration on appointment as constable,
      39(2), [359], [417]
    impersonation of constable, **39(2)**, [365]
    port police federation, **39(2)**, [364]
    powers of constables—
      arrest outside area, **39(2)**, [360]
      generally, **39(2)**, [361]
    specified premises, services at, **39(2)**, [363]
    unlawful possession, stop and search of
      suspects, **39(2)**, [362]

Port of London Authority—*contd*
  port fund—
    continuance and maintenance, **39(2)**, [268]
    meaning, **39(2)**, [225]
  Port of Tilbury, disposal of—
    agreements, statutory provisions and
      documents, construction of, **39(2)**, [662]
    division and apportionment of property,
      39(2), [662]
    documents of title, right to production of,
      39(2), [662]
    employment, transfer of rights and liabilities
      relating to, **39(2)**, [662]
    exercise of powers, Secretary of State
      requiring, **39(2)**, [647]
    operating company—
      employee participation, financial
        assistance for, **39(2)**, [648]
      power to form, **39(2)**, [641]
      securities, disposal of, **39(2)**, [646]
      transfer of property. etc., to,
        39(2), [642], [643]
    pension rights, protection of, **39(2)**, [644]
    proof of title by certificate, **39(2)**, [662]
    property, rights and liabilities, identification
      of, **39(2)**, [662]
    transitional hereditaments, rateable values
      of, **39(2)**, [649]
    vesting provisions, third parties affected
      by, **39(2)**, [662]
    works licences, **39(2)**, [645]
  port rates—
    exemptions, **39(2)**, [252]–[255]
    lien for, **39(2)**, [264]
    recovery and enforcement, **39(2)**, [261]
    repayment, claims for, **39(2)**, [263]
    weighing etc of goods, **39(2)**, [265]
  port stock—
    meaning, **39(2)**, [225]
    ranking of, **39(2)**, [274]
    regulations, **39(2)**, [275]
    rights of stockholders, **39(2)**, [276]
  powers and duties. *See* general duties and
    powers *above*
  private street works expenses, exemption
    from, **36**, [1264]
  proceedings, **39(2)**, [414]
  publications, **39(2)**, [382]
  reports, preparation, **39(2)**, [231]
  Revenue and Customs Commissioners,
    arrangements with, **39(2)**, [246]
  revenue, application of, **39(2)**, [269]
  staff—
    benefits, **39(2)**, [242]
    housing, **39(2)**, [243]
    obstruction or non-compliance with orders
      of, **39(2)**, [398]
    pensions. *See* pension fund *above*
  statutory undertakers, saving for, **39(2)**, [392]
  stocks. *See* port stock *above*
  summary of provisions, **39(2)**, [1]
  Surrey Canal and commercial docks,
    discontinuance, **39(2)**, [435]
  surveys—
    entry on land for purposes of, **39(2)**, [312]

Port of London Authority—*contd*
surveys—*contd*
making and publication, **39(2)**, [230]
telecommunications, saving as to, **39(2)**, [387]
Thames. *See* **Thames**
Thames Water Authority, protection for,
39(2), [394]
Trinity House, saving for, **39(2)**, [391]
vessels—
construction of, **39(2)**, [237]
meaning, **39(2)**, [225]

ports and harbours
activities not licensable, **19(3)**, [665]
Admiralty—
authority of, protection, **39(2)**, [119]
powers of, protection, **39(2)**, [122]
rights of, **39(2)**, [90]
aircraft, charges in respect of, **39(2)**, [181]
appointments, power to make orders,
39(2), [168]
arrival of vessel, report by master, **39(2)**, [33]
Associated British Ports. *See* **Associated
British Ports**
ballast, unlawful throwing into harbour or
dock, **39(2)**, [70]
beacons, sanction required for, **39(2)**, [75]
bribery of harbour officers, **39(2)**, [52]
British Transport Docks Board. *See*
Associated British Ports
buoys, undertakers' duty as to, **39(2)**, [74]
byelaws—
application for confirmation, notice,
39(2), [83]
confirmation, **39(2)**, [82]
enforcement, **39(2)**, [81]
inspection of, **39(2)**, [84]
power to make, **39(2)**, [80]
proof of making and publication,
39(2), [86]
publication of, **39(2)**, [85]
cargo, discharge of, **39(2)**, [63]
charges—
aviation, **39(2)**, [181]
combined, power to make, **39(2)**, [175]
discretion as to, **39(2)**, [173]
harbours at which provisions inapplicable,
39(2), [180]
lists to be maintained, **39(2)**, [178]
local light dues, **39(2)**, [177], [220]
mail-bags, **34**, [706]
meaning, **39(2)**, [200]
nationalised transport bodies, by,
39(2), [176]
objection to, **39(2)**, [179]
provisions repealed, **39(2)**, [182]
reasonableness, **39(2)**, [174]
See also rates *below*
charges at, **36**, [715], [747], [748]
Church Commissioners, service of documents
on, **39(2)**, [194]
combustible matter—
guarding at night, **39(2)**, [67]
offences with regard to, **39(2)**, [68]
removal, **39(2)**, [66]

ports and harbours—*contd*
construction—
alterations, authorisation and consents,
39(2), [9]
foreshore, consent to works on, **39(2)**, [13]
intending undertakers, orders conferring
powers on, **39(2)**, [169]
land, taking of, **39(2)**, [7]
Lands Clauses Acts, application, **39(2)**, [7]
plans—
alterations of, **39(2)**, [9], [10]
approval of alterations, **39(2)**, [14]
clerks of the peace, receipt by,
39(2), [10]
correction of errors and omissions,
39(2), [8]
deviation from limits defined,
39(2), [12]
evidence, as, **39(2)**, [11]
inspection, **39(2)**, [10]
See also works *below*
corporations, offences by, **39(2)**, [199]
cranes—
provision of, **39(2)**, [22]
working of, **39(2)**, [23]
Crown—
application of provisions to, **39(2)**, [196]
prerogative of, protection, **39(2)**, [122]
rights of, savings as to, **39(2)**, [90]
customs and excise—
appointment, **13**, [599]
arrival at or departure from, time of,
13, [594]
boarding stations, **13**, [599]
clearance outward of ship from—
boarding, officers' powers of, **13**, [653]
necessity for, **13**, [653]
refusal or cancellation of, **13**, [654]
hovercraft proceeding to or from, control of
movement of, **13**, [605]
meaning, **13**, [590]
procedure on arrival at, **13**, [626]
revocation of appointment, **13**, [599]
uncleared goods—
control of movement, **13**, [613]
licence to move, **13**, [613]
wharves, approval of, **13**, [600]
damage to works—
ascertainment and recovery of amount,
39(2), [72]
liability for, **39(2)**, [71]
damages paid by owner, recovery, **39(2)**, [73]
provisions in Railways Clauses Acts as to,
incorporation, **39(2)**, [87]
dangerous vessels—
Crown, savings for, **39(2)**, [521]
directions—
harbour master, by, **39(2)**, [517]
safety, saving for, **39(2)**, [522]
Secretary of State, by, **39(2)**, [519]
harbour master's powers as to, **39(2)**, [517]
liability arising, **39(2)**, [518]
meaning of vessel, **39(2)**, [523]
offences, **39(2)**, [520]
pleasure boats, savings, **39(2)**, [521]

ports and harbours—*contd*
  dangerous vessels—*contd*
    removal, **39(2)**, [517]
  Defence Reg 56, revocation in part,
    39(2), [156]
  dock master—
    appointment, **39(2)**, [48]
    bribery of, penalty, **39(2)**, [52]
    directions of, penalty for non-compliance
      with, **39(2)**, [50]
    dismantling of vessels, powers as to,
      39(2), [56]
    meaning, **39(2)**, [225]
    misbehaviour by, **39(2)**, [51]
    mooring of vessels, powers as to,
      39(2), [55]
    unserviceable vessels, removal, **39(2)**, [54]
    wreck or obstruction, removal by,
      39(2), [53]
  docks—
    British Transport Docks Board. *See*
      Associated British Ports
    entrance to, placing vessel near, **39(2)**, [60]
    fires within, **39(2)**, [69]
    meaning, **39(2)**, [200], [225]
    owner, limitation of liability of,
      39(2), [868]
    Port of London, deemed part of,
      39(2), [379]
    repairs to, removal of vessels for,
      39(2), [61]
  dockyard. *See* **dockyard ports**
  dockyard services. *See* **dockyard services**
  documents, service of, **39(2)**, [192]
  Duchy interest in land, application of
    provisions, **39(2)**, [196]
  dues. *See* charges *above*
  ecclesiastical property, provisions as to,
    39(2), [194]
  efficiency, orders for securing, **39(2)**, [166],
    [167]
  entrance, placing vessel near, **39(2)**, [60]
  entry in ships in search for fire or lights,
    39(2), [69]
  facilities, provision by Associated British
    Ports, **39(2)**, [473]
  fires—
    docks, in, causing, **39(2)**, [68]
    extinguishing, entry on vessels for,
      39(2), [69]
    vessels, in, causing, **39(2)**, [68]
  fishery. *See* **fishery harbours**
  foreshore, consents for works on, **39(2)**, [13]
  former statutes, protection of acts under,
    39(2), [123]
  goods—
    dues—
      objection to, **39(2)**, [179]
      reasonableness, **39(2)**, [174]
    loading etc, undue preference, **39(2)**, [64]
    meaning, **39(2)**, [200], [225]
    removal from quay, **39(2)**, [65]
    unshipped, account of, **39(2)**, [35]

ports and harbours—*contd*
  harbour authorities. *See* **harbour authorities**
  harbour development, repeal of provisions,
    39(2), [528]
  harbour, dock or pier, meaning, **39(2)**, [4],
    [103]
  harbour master—
    appointment, **39(2)**, [48]
    bribery of, penalty, **39(2)**, [52]
    dangerous vessels, powers as to. *See*
      dangerous vessels *above*
    directions of, penalty for non-compliance
      with, **39(2)**, [50]
    dismantling of vessels, powers as to,
      39(2), [56]
    meaning, **39(2)**, [4], [225]
    misbehaviour by, **39(2)**, [51]
    mooring of vessels, powers as to,
      39(2), [55]
    powers, **39(2)**, [49]
    Queen's. *See under* **dockyard ports**
    removal of vessels by, **39(2)**, [62]
    unserviceable vessels, removal, **39(2)**, [54]
    wreck or obstruction, removal by,
      39(2), [53]
  harbour, meaning, **35(1)**, [112]; **39(2)**, 988]
  harbour reorganisation schemes—
    confirmation, **39(2)**, [171], [209]
    disputes, settlement of, **39(2)**, [219]
    generally, **39(2)**, [217]
    loss of office, compensation, **39(2)**, [172]
    making of, **39(2)**, [171], [209]
    matters covered by, **39(2)**, [171], [217]
    modification of procedure, **39(2)**, [210]
    pensions and benefits, provisions as to,
      39(2), [218]
    procedure, **39(2)**, [209]
    submission of, **39(2)**, [209]
  harbour revision and empowerment orders—
    challenge, right to, **39(2)**, [188]
    conferment of powers, **39(2)**, [169]
    disputes, settlement of, **39(2)**, [219]
    efficiency, for securing, **39(2)**, [166], [167]
    loss of office, compensation, **39(2)**, [172]
    making of, **39(2)**, [169]
    modification of procedure, **39(2)**, [208]
    objects of, provisions as to achievement
      of, **39(2)**, [166], [205]
    port appointments, **39(2)**, [168]
    procedure, **39(2)**, [170], [206]–[208]
    provisional orders, **39(2)**, [170]
    Secretary of State, making of his own
      motion, **39(2)**, [170], [207]
  hawsers, fixing to moorings, **39(2)**, [58]
  herring fisheries, use for, **1(1)**, [125]
  Holyhead harbour, transfer of, **39(2)**, [121]
  improvement by intending undertakers,
    39(2), [169]
  improvement commission, powers, **25(1)**, [84]
  independent harbour undertakings, revision of
    charges, **39(2)**, [155]
  information and forecasts—
    disclosure, restriction on, **39(2)**, [190]
    false, penalty, **39(2)**, [189]
    furnishing of, **39(2)**, [185]

ports and harbours—*contd*
   information and forecasts—*contd*
      power to obtain, **39(2)**, [448]
   inquiries and hearings, provisions as to,
      39(2), [191]
   instruments, execution of, **39(2)**, [111]
   interpretation, **39(2)**, [200]
   land—
      additional, for extraordinary purposes,
         39(2), [21]
      meaning, **39(2)**, [4], [200]
      purchase of, **39(2)**, [113]
      sale of, **39(2)**, [112]
      taking, for construction, **39(2)**, [21]
      vesting of, **39(2)**, [110]
   life-boats and equipment, provision,
      39(2), [17], [18]
   light dues, **39(2)**, [177], [220]
   light vessels, accommodation for, **39(2)**, [63]
   lighthouse authorities, charging of local light
      dues, **39(2)**, [177], [220]
   lighthouses, sanction for erection of,
      39(2), [75]
   limits—
      defined, bar on construction beyond,
         39(2), [12]
      prescribed, meaning, **39(2)**, [4]
   loaded guns, penalty for bringing in,
      39(2), [68]
   loading or unloading goods, undue preference
      in, **39(2)**, [64]
   loans. *See under* **harbour authorities**
   local Acts—
      amendment, powers, **39(2)**, [202]
      powers under, protection, **39(2)**, [118]
   London. *See* **Port of London**
   London, City of, savings as to rights,
      39(2), [92]
   master of vessel—
      certificate of registry, production,
         39(2), [34]
      certificates and documents, production,
         39(2), [34]–[36]
      compliance with harbour master's direction,
         requirement, **39(2)**, [50]
      damage to works, liability, **39(2)**, [71]–[73]
      neglect or refusal to remove vessel,
         39(2), [62]
      offences and penalties, **39(2)**, [36]
      report of arrival by, **39(2)**, [33]
      responsibilities undiminished by orders to,
         39(2), [324]
   meaning, **39(2)**, [988]
   meters and weighers, **39(2)**, [78], [79]
   moorings—
      cutting or destroying, wilful, **39(2)**, [59]
      harbour master's powers, **39(2)**, [55]
      hawsers, use of, **39(2)**, [58]
      without permission, **39(2)**, [60]
   National Ports Council dissolution. *See*
      National Ports Council
   nationally significant infrastructure projects,
      46(S), 45. *See also* **nationally significant
      infrastructure projects**
   offences by corporations, **39(2)**, [199]

ports and harbours—*contd*
   officers of Customs and Revenue,
      accommodation for, **39(2)**, [15]
   operations, meaning, **39(2)**, [200]
   orders, procedure, **39(2)**, [198]
   own account operator, **39(2)**, [536]
   owner, meaning, **39(2)**, [200], [225]
   periods, reckoning of, **39(2)**, [195]
   pier—
      rates. *See* rates *below*
      removal of goods from, undue delay in,
         39(2), [65]
      repairs to, removal of vessels for,
         39(2), [61]
   pier master—
      appointment, **39(2)**, [48]
      bribery of, penalty, **39(2)**, [52]
      directions of, penalty for non-compliance
         with, **39(2)**, [50]
      dismantling of vessels, powers as to,
         39(2), [56]
      misbehaviour by, **39(2)**, [51]
      mooring of vessels, powers as to,
         39(2), [55]
      unserviceable vessels, removal, **39(2)**, [54]
      wreck or obstruction, removal by,
         39(2), [53]
   pilotage. *See* **pilotage**
   pitch etc, boiling or heating, **39(2)**, [68]
   police—
      appointment, **39(2)**, [76]
      dismissal, **39(2)**, [77]
   pollution, summary of provisions, **39(2)**, [1]
   prescribed limits, meaning, **39(2)**, [4]
   private bills, **39(2)**, [202]
   property, vesting of, **39(2)**, [110]
   protection of, generally, **39(2)**, [66]
   provisional orders, meaning, **39(2)**, [200]
   quays, undue delay in removal of goods
      from, **39(2)**, [65]
   Railways Clauses Acts, provisions
      incorporated, **39(2)**, [87], [116]
   rates—
      accounts of goods, production—
         master of vessel, by, **39(2)**, [35]
         shippers, by, **39(2)**, [37]
      accounts of rates, keeping, **39(2)**, [46], [47]
      arrival of vessel, reporting, **39(2)**, [33]
      certificates and documents, production,
         39(2), [34]
      clearance, withholding until payment,
         39(2), [45]
      collection after completion of works,
         39(2), [25]
      collector, power to enter vessels,
         39(2), [32]
      compound for tolls, power to, **39(2)**, [30]
      disputes—
         occasioned by distress, **39(2)**, [44]
         weights and quantities, as to, **39(2)**, [38]
      evasion of payment, penalty, **39(2)**, [41]
      exemption from, **39(2)**, [27]
      freedom of access to public on payment
         of, **39(2)**, [31]

ports and harbours—*contd*
  rates—*contd*
    independent undertakings, revision of
      charges, **39(2)**, [155]
    pier or harbour, opening to public on
      payment, **39(2)**, [31]
    reciprocal provisions, **39(2)**, [29]
    recovery by distraint, **39(2)**, [42]–[44]
    time for payment, **39(2)**, [40]
    tonnage—
      ascertainment, **39(2)**, [26]
      recovery, **39(2)**, [42]
    vessels returning from stress of weather,
      39(2), [28]
    See also charges *above*
  regulations, procedure, **39(2)**, [198]
  reorganisation schemes. *See* harbour
    reorganisation schemes *above*
  Revenue and Customs Commissioners,
    savings for rights of, **39(2)**, [91]
  revenue departments, savings as to, **39(2)**, [91]
  river works, meanings, **39(2)**, [200]
  roads, land for provision of, **39(2)**, [21]
  safety precautions, byelaws, **39(2)**, [80]
  sails, lowering before entering dock,
    39(2), [57]
  sea-marks, sanction required for, **39(2)**, [75]
  services and facilities, use of, **39(2)**, [184]
  ship, passenger and goods dues, meaning,
    39(2), [200]
    See further charges *above*
  shipowner, liability for damage to works,
    39(2), [71]–[73]
  shipping dues, transfer of, **39(2)**, [105]–[108]
  shipping purposes, meaning, **39(2)**, [103]
  special Act—
    access to copies, **39(2)**, [88], [89]
    damages, incorporation of provisions in
      Railways Clauses Acts, **39(2)**, [87]
    incorporation of provisions, **39(2)**, [3]
    interpretation of terms, **39(2)**, [4], [5]
    meaning, **39(2)**, [4]
  special constables—
    appointment, **39(2)**, [76]
    dismissal, **39(2)**, [77]
  statutory duties and powers, meaning,
    39(2), [200]
  statutory undertakers—
    port authority—
      dissolution, **39(2)**, [626]
      exercise of functions, control of,
        39(2), [624]
      holding in successor company, disposal
        of, **39(2)**, [623]
      net proceeds of disposal, treatment of,
        39(2), [627]
      powers of, **39(2)**, [625]
      taxation, **39(2)**, [651]
    schemes—
      annual turnover requirement,
        39(2), [630]
      authority, by, **39(2)**, [628]
      provisions, description of, **39(2)**, [661]
      Secretary of State, by, **39(2)**, [629],
        [631]

ports and harbours—*contd*
  statutory undertakers—*contd*
    successor company—
      definitions, **39(2)**, [657]
      disposal by authority of holding in,
        39(2), [623]
      disposals of land etc., levy on,
        39(2), [637], [638]
      employee participation, financial
        assistance for, **39(2)**, [639]
      formation of, **39(2)**, [620]
      initial disposals of securities, levy on—
        charge of, **39(2)**, [632]
        information for purposes of,
          39(2), [634]
        meaning, **39(2)**, [636]
        notice of assessment, **39(2)**, [635]
        payment of, **39(2)**, [633]
        supplementary provisions, **39(2)**, [636]
      powers of, **39(2)**, [625]
      securities—
        disposal, time of, **39(2)**, [640]
        initial issue of, **39(2)**, [622]
      transfer to, **39(2)**, [621]
    transfer—
      agreements, statutory provisions and
        documents, construction of,
        39(2), [660]
      definitions, **39(2)**, [657]
      employment, transfer of rights and
        liabilities relating to, **39(2)**, [660]
      formation of companies for, **39(2)**, [620]
      procedure, **39(2)**, [621]
      stamp duty exemption, **39(2)**, [652]
      stamp duty land tax exemption,
        39(2), [653]
  street works near, display of lights,
    38(1), [235]
  summary of provisions, **39(2)**, [1]
  telegraphic lines, works involving,
    39(2), [197]
  tidal lands—
    harbour works on, **39(2)**, [115]
    railway works on, **39(2)**, [116]
    works under local Acts on, protection,
      39(2), [118]
  tide gauge, provision, **39(2)**, [19], [20]
  tolls, power to compound for, **39(2)**, [30]
  tonnage of vessels—
    ascertainment, **39(2)**, [26]
    rates on, **39(2)**, [26], [42]
  Trinity House, rights and privileges, savings as
    to, **39(2)**, [93]
  undertakers—
    independent harbour undertakings, revision
      of charges, **39(2)**, [155]
    intending, orders conferring powers on,
      39(2), [169]
    meaning, **39(2)**, [4]
  violence, protection against—
    act of, meaning, **39(2)**, [584]
    authorised persons, offences relating to,
      39(2), [607]
    body corporate, offences by, **39(2)**, [614]
    definitions, **39(2)**, [613]

ports and harbours—*contd*
violence, protection against—*contd*
extension of provisions, **39(2)**, [615]
false statements—
baggage, cargo and stores, in relation
to, **39(2)**, [604]
identity documents, in connection
with, **39(2)**, [605]
general purposes, **39(2)**, [584]
harbour area—
inspection of, **39(2)**, [602]
restricted zones—
designation, **39(2)**, [586]
unauthorised presence in, **39(2)**, [606]
searches, promotion of, **39(2)**, [588],
[589]
maritime security services, approved
providers, **39(2)**, [603]
measures, direction of—
compensation, **39(2)**, [610], [619]
detention of ships, **39(2)**, [601]
enforcement notices—
contents of, **39(2)**, [596]
failure to comply, **39(2)**, [599]
objections, **39(2)**, [598]
offences, **39(2)**, [597]
revocation or variation, **39(2)**, [599]
rights and duties under other laws,
and, **39(2)**, [600]
service of, **39(2)**, [595]
general or urgent, **39(2)**, [593]
general power, **39(2)**, [590]
limitation on scope, **39(2)**, [592]
matters included in, **39(2)**, [591]
objections to, **39(2)**, [594]
reporting requirements, **39(2)**, [609]
sea cargo agents, regulations, **39(2)**, [608]
Secretary of State—
annual report, **39(2)**, [611]
power to require information,
39(2), [585]
service of documents, **39(2)**, [612]
warehouses—
additional land for, **39(2)**, [21]
leasing of, **39(2)**, [24]
provision of, **39(2)**, [22]
waste reception facilities at—
charges for, **39(2)**, [801]
contravention of requirements, **39(2)**, [802]
generally, **39(2)**, [799]
meaning, **39(2)**, [803]
use of, **39(2)**, [801]
waste management plans, **39(2)**, [800]
watch-houses, provision and maintenance,
39(2), [15], [16]
waters, pipe-line over or under, **17(1)**, [257]
weights and measures—
expenses of weighing etc, **39(2)**, [39]
machines, provision, **39(2)**, [22]
materials, provision, **39(2)**, [15]
use in disputes, **39(2)**, [38]
weighers, appointment, **39(2)**, [78]
wharfingers, undue preference in loading or
unloading, **39(2)**, [64]

ports and harbours—*contd*
wharfs—
land for, **39(2)**, [21]
lease of, **39(2)**, [24]
meaning, **39(2)**, [200]
works—
intending undertakers, orders conferring
powers on, **39(2)**, [169]
loans for execution of, **39(2)**, [164]
local Acts, under, protection, **39(2)**, [118]
repairs to harbour or dock, removal of
vessels for, **39(2)**, [61]
tidal lands, harbour works on, **39(2)**, [115]
See also construction *above*
wreck, removal of, **39(2)**, [53]
yards, land for, **39(2)**, [21]

Portugal
accession to European Community, **18**, [28]

possession
enforcement, **9**, [273]
order for. *See* **possession, order for**
refusal to give, **9**, [273]
right to take, **9**, [393]

possession, order for
adjournment, court having discretion,
21, [600]
agricultural employee, against, **21**, [666]
agricultural housing—
alternative accommodation, **21**, [656]
grounds for, **21**, [599]
alternative accommodation—
agricultural workers, for, **21**, [656]
availability of, **21**, [598]; **22**, [917]
suitability of, **21**, [654]; **22**, [918]
assured shorthold tenancy, for, **22**, [819]
assured tenancy. *See* **assured tenancy**
concealment of facts, obtained by, **21**, [602];
22, [805]
court, jurisdiction of, **21**, [671]
Crown, provisions applying to, **21**, [672]
due process of law, requirement of, **21**, [664]
exceptional hardship caused by, **21**, [748]
furnished sub-tenancy, effect on, **21**, [626]
grounds for—
agricultural worker, required for, **21**, [652]
armed forces, owner as member of,
21, [652], [655]
assignment of property, **21**, [651]
death of previous tenant, proceedings
before, **22**, [916]
demolition or reconstruction of premises,
22, [916]
discretionary, **21**, [651]; **22**, [917]
furniture, ill-treatment of, **21**, [651];
22, [917]
general, **21**, [598]; **22**, [798]
holiday, right to occupy for, **21**, [652];
22, [916]
illegal or immoral purpose, premises used
for, **21**, [651]; **22**, [917]
landlord or family, required for occupation
by, **21**, [651], [653]; **22**, [916]

possession, order for—*contd*
  grounds for—*contd*
    landlord's employment, required for person
      in, **21**, [651]; **22**, [917]
    mandatory, **21**, [652]; **22**, [916]
    minister of religion, required for, **21**, [652];
      22, [916]
    mortgagee, sale by, **22**, [916]
    neglect of property, **21**, [651]; **22**, [917]
    notice to quit, contract for sale after,
      21, [651]
    nuisance or annoyance, conduct causing,
      21, [651]; **22**, [917]
    obligation, failure to perform, **21**, [651];
      22, [917]
    owner-occupier requiring, **21**, [652], [655]
    protected shorthold tenancy, let under,
      21, [652]
    rent, failure to pay, **21**, [651]; **22**, [917]
    retirement, property acquired for,
      21, [652], [655]
    student letting, **21**, [652]; **22**, [916]
    sublet part, excessive rent for, **21**, [651]
    subletting, **21**, [651]
  misrepresentation, induced by, **21**, [167],
    [197], [602]; **22**, [805]
  notice to quit, validity of, **21**, [667]
  overcrowding, in case of, **21**, [601]
  postponement of date of, **21**, [747]
  proceedings, discretion of court in, **21**, [600],
    [747]
  protected long tenancy, in case of. *See*
    protected long tenancy
  protected shorthold tenancy, let under,
    21, [652], [726]
  relevant date, reference to, **21**, [653]
  restricted contract, **21**, [608]
  sub-tenancy, effect on, **21**, [625]

post
  ordinary course of post, **41**, [581]
  recorded delivery service, **41**, [530]–[534]
  service by post, construction of reference to,
    41, [581]
  stamps. *See* **stamps**
  Users Councils. *See* **Post Office Users
    Councils**

Post Office
  aircraft, mail-bags, carriage of, **34**, [706]
  Cable and Wireless former employees,
    pensions of, **34**, [581]
  capital gains tax, application, **34**, [582], [600]
  chairman, appointment, **34**, [579]
  Channel Islands—
    application of provisions, **34**, [588], [598]
    privileges as to, surrender of, **34**, [587]
  company—
    accounts and reports, publicity
      requirements, **34**, [689]
    arrangements with government, limit on,
      34, [683]
    assets acquired in 1969, transfer, **34**, [746]
    capital structure, **34**, [686]
    corporation tax, **34**, [746]

Post Office—*contd*
  company—*contd*
    debt, **34**, [746]
    government holdings in, **34**, [675]
    guarantees to, **34**, [681]
    information requirements, **34**, [690]
    liabilities, extinguishment of, **34**, [682]
    loans to, **34**, [680]
      limits on, **34**, [683]
      Secretary of State, accounts of, **34**, [688]
    meaning, **34**, [694]
    nomination, **34**, [674]
    nominees, exercise of functions through,
      34, [691]
    reserves, **34**, [684]
    securities—
      government investment in, **34**, [676]
      issue of, **34**, [746]
    shadow directors, **34**, [692]
    shares—
      approved disposals, **34**, [679]
      issue of, **34**, [746]
      restriction on disposal to third parties,
        34, [678]
      restriction on issue to third parties,
        34, [677]
      rights, meaning, **34**, [694]
    stamp duty, **34**, [746]
    statutory accounts, **34**, [685]
    subsidiaries, **34**, [675]
    tax-free benefits, **34**, [746]
    transfer arrangements, **34**, [746]
    transfer of property to, **34**, [674], [745]
    value added tax, **34**, [746]
  dissolution, **34**, [687]
  employees, preservation of welfare funds on
    transfer to British Telecommunications,
    45, [45]
  enactments relating to—
    adaptation, **34**, [584], [596]
    construction of references, **34**, [592]
    transitional provisions, **34**, [590], [597]
  establishment as public authority, **34**, [579]
  expenses of Secretary of State, **34**, [601]
  Fund, abolition, **34**, [568]
  government holdings in, **34**, [675]
  information, officers of the Crown, duty to
    furnish, **34**, [585]
  instruments, execution and proof, **34**, [594]
  Isle of Man, application of provisions—
    in particular, **34**, [588], [598]
    privileges as to, surrender of, **34**, [587]
  land—
    acquisition, **34**, [580], [747]–[750]
    entry on, **34**, [750]
    meaning, **34**, [586]
  letters—
    conveyance, historical note, **34**, [568]
    meaning, **34**, [736]
  licences issued by, **2**, [339]
  meaning, **34**, [736]
  members—
    disqualifications, **34**, [594]
    number, **34**, [579]
    salaries and allowances, **34**, [594]

Post Office—*contd*
members—*contd*
tenure of office, **34**, [594]
Northern Ireland, application of regulations,
19(2), [888]
officers, appointment, **34**, [594]
patents and inventions, transitional
provisions, **34**, [590]
pensions—
Cable and Wireless Ltd, employees of,
34, [581]
meaning, **34**, [603]
powers to raise money through, **19(2)**, [857]
privileges as to Isle of Man and Channel
Islands, surrender of, **34**, [587]
proceedings, **34**, [594]
property, rights and liabilities, reference to,
34, [694]
public—
provision of, **34**, [654]
subsidy for, **34**, [715]
recorded delivery services, power to make
orders as to, **34**, [578]
register, change of name of, **19(2)**, [884]
registered designs, transitional provisions,
34, [590]
reorganisation—
nominated company. *See* company *above*
provision for, **34**, [568]
rights and liabilities, transfer of, **34**, [580]
seal, authentication, **34**, [594]
secretary, appointment, **34**, [594]
stamp duty, exemptions, **34**, [599]
status of, **34**, [579], [594]
statutes relating to. *See* enactments *above*
statutory undertaker, as, **9**, [417]
See also **statutory undertakers**
summary of provisions, **34**, [568]
taxation of profits and gains, **34**, [582], [600]
telecommunications functions, transfer of,
34, [568], [576]
See further **telecommunications**
telecommunications, transfer of property,
rights, etc, **45**, [40]
trading operations, management of, **34**, [568]
underground works—
British Transport Commission, agreements
with, savings, **34**, [572]
compensation in respect of, **34**, [570]
Prudential Assurance Co, agreement with,
savings, **34**, [573]
superjacent strata, support of, **34**, [571]
vesting of, **34**, [569]
welfare funds, preservation, **34**, [602]
works, execution of, **34**, [580]

Post Office Users Councils
abolition, **34**, [568], [608]
property and employees, transfer of, **34**, [729]

postal packet
removal of adhesive stamp from, **41**, [21]
social security—
redirection, requirement to supply
information about, **40(1)**, [713]

postal packet—*contd*
social security—*contd*
return of, **40(1)**, [712]
stealing, **12(1)**, [567]

postal services
amendment of enactments, **34**, [752]–[753]
blind and partially sighted, free provision for,
34, [653]
Commission. *See* **Postal Services
Commission**
Consumer Council—
abolition, **39(1)**, [697]
directions, **39(1)**, [703]
loss of office, compensation for,
39(1), [701]
transfer of property, rights and
liabilities, **39(1)**, [702], [739]
transitional provision, **39(1)**, [738]
accounts and expenses, **34**, [744]
advice and information, provision of,
34, [664]
annual report, **34**, [667]
Commission—
information, provision of, **34**, [671]
memorandum of understanding,
34, [672]
complaints referred to, **34**, [668]
costs, recovery of, **34**, [651]
creation of, **34**, [568]
delegation by, **34**, [744]
establishment, **34**, [608]
forward work programme, **34**, [673]
functions, **34**, [568]
exercise of, **34**, [666]
information—
Commission, provision to, **34**, [671]
power to require, **34**, [670]
public authorities and licence holders,
provision to, **34**, [664]
users, publication to, **34**, [665]
investigations by, **34**, [669]
members, **34**, [744]
offices, **34**, [666]
Post Office Users' Councils, transfer of
property and employees of, **34**, [729]
powers, **34**, [744]
proceedings, **34**, [744]
property, rights and liabilities of, **34**, [729]
regional committees, **34**, [666], [744]
relevant postal issues and services,
meaning, **34**, [663]
reports, **34**, [667]
staff, **34**, [744]
status, **34**, [608]
definition, **39(1)**, [708]
directions, **34**, [734]
Directive, compliance with, **34**, [714]
financial provisions, **34**, [735]
general note, **34**, [568]
information, disclosure of, **34**, [751]
letter, meaning, **34**, [736]
licences—
application for, **34**, [619]
determination of, **34**, [621]

postal services—*contd*
  licences—*contd*
    conditions, **34**, [622]
    contravention, penalties for—
      appeals, **34**, [648]
      interest on, **34**, [647]
      notice of, **34**, [644]
      payment by instalments, **34**, [647]
      power to impose, **34**, [642]
      procedural requirements, **34**, [644]–[645]
      recovery of, **34**, [649]
      statement of policy, **34**, [643]
      time-limits, **34**, [646]
      variation of, **34**, [645]
    enforcement orders—
      effect of, **34**, [641]
      exceptions from duty as to, **34**, [637]
      final, **34**, [634]
      notices, **34**, [638]
      procedural requirements, **34**, [638]–[639]
      provisional, **34**, [635]
        confirmation of, **34**, [636]
      revocation, **34**, [639]
      validity, **34**, [640]
    general note, **34**, [568]
    grant of, **34**, [619]
      notice of, **34**, [619]
    holders—
      advice and information provided to,
        34, [658], [664]
      directors' remuneration, **34**, [652]
    modification—
      agreement, by, **34**, [623]
      Competition Commission, reference to,
        34, [624]–[632]
      See also **Competition Commission**
      other enactments, by order under,
        34, [633]
      procedural requirements, **34**, [631]
    provisions of, **34**, [622]
    refusal of, **34**, [620]
    register of, **34**, [650]
    requirement of, **34**, [612]
      exceptions, **34**, [613]
      modification, power of, **34**, [615]
      suspension, power of, **34**, [616]–[617]
      transferable, not, **34**, [618]
      validity, **34**, [618]
  local enactments, modifications of, **34**, [739]
  mail-bags—
    carriage by ship or aircraft, **34**, [706]
    control by harbour authorities, not subject
      to, **34**, [710]
    harbour charges, **34**, [709]
    meaning, **34**, [736]
  mails, inviolability of, **34**, [716]
  meaning, **34**, [736]
  money orders—
    exclusion of liability in relation to,
      34, [723]
    foreign, presentation for payment, **34**, [723]
    other countries or territories, special
      arrangements with, **34**, [726]
    schemes, **34**, [724]
    uncrossed, **34**, [723]

postal services—*contd*
  money orders—*contd*
    wrongly paid, recoupment of losses on,
      34, [725]
  non-reservable service, meaning, **34**, [621]
  offences—
    body corporate, of, **34**, [731]
    business of universal service providers,
      obstruction of, **34**, [700]
    general note, **34**, [568]
    letter boxes, affixing advertisements on,
      34, [698]
    mail, interference with, **34**, [695]–[696]
    misleading descriptions, **34**, [699]
    sending certain articles by post, **34**, [697]
  orders and regulations, **34**, [733]
  postage, evidence of amount of, **34**, [719]
  postal orders—
    exclusion of liability in relation to,
      34, [723]
    foreign, presentation for payment, **34**, [723]
    schemes, **34**, [724]
    uncrossed, **34**, [723]
  postal packet—
    contraband, containing, **34**, [718]
    customs and excise enactments, application
      of, **34**, [717]
    delaying or opening, **34**, [695]–[696]
    evidence of thing being, **34**, [721]
    interference with, **34**, [695]–[696]
    inviolability of, **34**, [716]
    meaning, **34**, [736]
    permitted limits, **34**, [610]
    prohibited contents, **34**, [697]
    registered inland, limited liability for,
      34, [703]–[704]
    relevant, **34**, [610]
    transit, conditions of, **34**, [719]
    transmission, in course of, **34**, [736]
  Postcode Address File, **34**, [727]
  relevant, meaning, **34**, [663]
  relevant postal issues, meaning, **34**, [663]
  reservable service, meaning, **34**, [621]
  restriction on provision of, **34**, [612]
    exceptions, **34**, [613]
    modification, power of, **34**, [615]
    suspension, power of, **34**, [616]–[617]
  review and information, **34**, [656]
  service of documents, **34**, [732]
  universal—
    access point, meaning, **34**, [610]
    basic, **34**, [621]
    duty to ensure, **34**, [609]
    entry on land, **34**, [750]
    general note, **34**, [568]
    letter boxes—
      certificates, **34**, [722]
      meaning, **34**, [736]
      prohibition of advertisements on,
        34, [698]
      streets, in, **34**, [750]
    mail-bags, carriage by ship or aircraft,
      34, [706]
    misleading descriptions, **34**, [699]

postal services—*contd*
  universal—*contd*
    postage—
      amount, evidence of, **34**, [720]
      articles exempt from, **34**, [712]
    provider—
      common carrier, not, **34**, [711]
      exclusion of liability, **34**, [702]
      immunity from prosecution, **34**, [708]
      land, acquisition of, **34**, [747]–[750]
      meaning, **34**, [610]
      obstruction of business, **34**, [700]
      registered inland packets, limited liability
        for, **34**, [703]–[704]
    provision, meaning, **34**, [610]
    scope of, **34**, [614]
    terms and conditions, schemes as to,
      34, [701]
  value added tax, exemption from, **50**, [153]

Postal Services Commission
  advice, publication of, **34**, [658]
  annual report, **34**, [657]
  codes of practice, **34**, [662]
  committees, **34**, [743]
  complaints handling—
    standards for—
      compliance, information as to,
        39(1), [712], [740]
      consumers, supply of information to,
        39(1), [713]
      prescription of, **39(1)**, [710]
      regulations, making, **39(1)**, [711]
  constitution, **34**, [607]
  Consumer Council for Postal Services—
    information, provision of, **34**, [671]
    memorandum of understanding, **34**, [672]
  consumer interest, duties in, **34**, [611]
  delegation, **34**, [743]
  entry and seizure, powers of, **34**, [661]
  forward work programme, **34**, [673]
  functions of, **34**, [568], [607], [743]
  general note, **34**, [568]
  information—
    Council, provision by, **34**, [671]
    power to require, **34**, [659]
    enforcement, **34**, [660]
    publication of, **34**, [658]
  licences, grant of. *See* **postal services**
  members, **34**, [743]
  National Consumer Council, reference of
    matters by, **39(1)**, [682]
  national security, directions in interests of,
    34, [713]
  proceedings, **34**, [743]
  public post offices, duties as to, **34**, [654]
  redress schemes—
    approval of—
      application for, **39(1)**, [717]
      considerations, **39(1)**, [716]
      refusal or withdrawal, procedure for,
        39(1), [718]
    interpretation, **39(1)**, [715]
    membership of, **39(1)**, [714], [715]
    qualifying, **39(1)**, [715]

Postal Services Commission—*contd*
  reports, **34**, [657]
  relevant regulator, as, **39(1)**, [709]
  review and information on postal services,
    34, [656]
  social and environmental duties, **34**, [655]
  staff, **34**, [743]
  universal postal service, duty to ensure,
    34, [609]

poster
  removal or obliteration of, **46**, [489]

posthumous child
  citizenship of, **31**, [34], [178]
  nationality, **31**, [178]

Postmaster General
  abolition of office, **34**, [568]
  former department, records of, **34**, [728]
  former functions, adaptation of enactments
    applicable, **34**, [584], [596]
  transfer of functions—
    Commonwealth telegraphs, **34**, [577]
    wireless telegraphy, **34**, [576]

post-mortem examination
  direction of, **11(1)**, [1227]
  inquest, without, **11(1)**, [1226]
  negligence of medical practitioner, where
    death caused by, **11(1)**, [1227]
  removal of body for, **11(1)**, [1229]
  request to specially qualified persons to
    make, **11(1)**, [1227]

post-mortem room
  byelaws as to, **35(1)**, [146]
  provision of, **35(1)**, [146]

post-war credit
  apportioned, **42**, [38]
  building society, repayment to, **42**, [35]
  consolidated fund, payments from, **42**, [36]
  generally, **42**, [1]
  interest on, **42**, [34]
  meaning, **42**, [38]
  regulations on, **42**, [37]
  repayment provisions, **42**, [29], [33], [294]

Posts and Telecommunications, Ministry
  dissolution, **34**, [568]

Potato Marketing Board
  transfer scheme, **1(2)**, [537]

Potato Marketing Scheme
  definitions, **1(2)**, [518]
  revocation—
    Agricultural Marketing Act 1958,
      restrictions of, **1(2)**, [516]
    consequential amendments, **1(2)**, [517]

potatoes. *See also* **agricultural produce**
  guarantee, termination of—
    generally, **1(2)**, [524]

potatoes—*contd*
  guarantee, termination of—*contd*
    Northern Ireland, extension of provisions
      to, **1(2)**, [531]
    repeals, **1(2)**, [532]
  marketing. *See* **Potato Marketing Board;**
    Potato Marketing Scheme
  sale and use, restrictions on, **1(1)**, [480]
  seed—
    entry, powers in connection with,
      1(1), [570]
    inclusion in definition of seeds, **1(1)**, [574]
    provisions applicable, **1(1)**, [574]

poultry
  allotments, right to keep on, **1(1)**, [441]
  damage to, by dogs, **2**, [254], [352]
  diseased—
    inspectors' powers and duties, **2**, [520]
    meaning, **2**, [546]
    separation of, **2**, [445]
    slaughter in case of, **2**, [464], [559]
  dogs injuring, liability, **2**, [254]
  meaning, **2**, [546]
  slaughter of—
    birds to which provisions apply, **1(1)**, [680]
    codes of practice, **1(1)**, [676]
    enforcement of provisions, **1(1)**, [679]
    entry, powers of, **1(1)**, [677]
    extension of provisions to other birds,
      1(1), [680]
    humane conditions, regulations for,
      1(1), [675]
    local authority, enforcement by, **1(1)**, [679]
    offences—
      body corporate, by, **1(1)**, [678]
      obstruction, **1(1)**, [677]
    summary of provisions **1(1)**, [124]

pound
  breach of, penalty, **36**, [383]
  cattle found straying—
    impounding of, **36**, [381]
    sale of, **36**, [382]
  provision of, **36**, [384]

pound-breach
  treble damages for, **13**, [1159]

power
  contract not to exercise, **20**, [765]
  disclaimer, **20**, [766]
  equitable powers—
    conveyance overreaching, **20**, [626]
    operation in equity, **20**, [625]
  legal, meaning, **20**, [804]
  non-compliance with terms of, validation of
    lease granted, **20**, [762]
  release, **20**, [765]

power of appointment
  exclusion of objects, validation, **20**, [768]
  execution, validation, **20**, [769]
  validation of appointments under, **20**, [767]

power of appointment—*contd*
  void appointment, protection of purchaser,
    20, [767]

power of attorney
  donee—
    execution of instrument by, **1(1)**, [24]
    protection on revocation, **1(1)**, [22]
  effect of, in specified form, **1(1)**, [25]
  enduring. *See* **enduring power of attorney**
  execution of, **1(1)**, [19], [24]
  form of, **1(1)**, [27]
  general note, **1(1)**, [1]
  incapable trustee, attorney acting for,
    48, 616–17
  instrument creating—
    certification, **1(1)**, [20]
    contents, **1(1)**, [20]
    execution of, **1(1)**, [19], [24]
    proof of, **1(1)**, [20]; **18**, [178]
    witnesses to, **1(1)**, [19]
  irrevocable, when expressed to be, **1(1)**, [22]
  lasting. *See* **lasting power of attorney**
  letter of, abolition of stamp duty, **41**, [152],
    [157]
  relating to land, filing, **20**, [740]
  revocation—
    knowledge of, effect of, **1(1)**, [22]
    protection of persons on, **1(1)**, [22]
  security, given as, **1(1)**, [21]
  stock exchange transactions, provisions as to,
    1(1), [23]
  trustee, delegation by, **48**, 478–9, 610–11
    beneficial interest, evidence of, **48**, 612–13
    enduring, **48**, 614–15
    land, extent of authority to act in relation
      to, **48**, 617
    specified form, general powers in, **48**, 613
    two-trustee rule, **48**, 616
  trustee, for. *See* **trustee**

Poynings' law
  operation of, **31**, [622]
  statutes adopted by, **31**, [622]
  text, **31**, [622]

preacher
  clerical or ministerial duties, undertaking,
    14, 171
  licensed, to be, **14**, 53

precept
  abolition, **25(2)**, [811]
  City of London, issue in, **25(1)**, [105]
  substituted, **25(2)**, [497]
  supplementary—
    limitation on, **25(2)**, [497]
    transitional provisions, **25(2)**, [503]
  validity, questioning, **25(2)**, [498]

pre-emption
  offers to shareholders, in, **8**, 167–8
  right of—
    Admiralty, **11(2)**, [83]
    deemed capable of release, **20**, [787]

pre-emption—*contd*
right of—*contd*
Defence of the Realm Acts, under,
9, [104], [115]
statutory undertakers, land of, **9**, [85]
equitable interest, as, **20**, [787]
registration as land charge, **20**, [630]
reversion, over, enforcement, **20**, [630]

prefabs
houses, when treated as, **22**, [59]
meaning, **22**, [59]

preferment
cathedral. *See* **cathedral**
lapse, time for, **14**, 607
relinquishment, deed of, *See* **relinquishment,
deed of**

pregnant women
nutrition, benefits under schemes for
improving, **30**, [748]

pregnancy. *See also* **confinement; maternity**
equal pay clauses, exclusion, **16**, [36]
health in pregnancy grant. *See* **health in
pregnancy grant**
medical termination of. *See* **abortion**

premises. *See also* **property**
business. *See* **business premises**
Crown, application of Building Act to,
35(1), [609]
defective. *See* **defective premises**
entry on. *See* **entry on land and premises**;
police
filthy or verminous—
articles in, cleansing or destruction of,
35(1), [136]
cleansing or disinfection of, **35(1)**, [135]
meaning, **1(2)**, [417]
See also under **food and food safety**

premium. *See also* **life assurance relief**
advance payment of rent as, **21**, [618]
allowable—
assignment of tenancy, on, **21**, [658]
Counter-Inflation Act, tenancy regulated by
virtue of, **21**, [613], [659]
long tenancy, in relation to, **21**, [619],
[659]
deductions from, **44(1)**, [25]
lease, meaning, **44(1)**, [17]
meaning, **21**, [620]
protected tenancy, for—
advance payment of rent, prohibited
requirement of, **21**, [618]
assignment, as condition of, **21**, [612]
excessive price for furniture as, **21**, [615],
[616]
prohibition of, **21**, [611]
recovery of, **21**, [617]
regulated tenancy by virtue of
Counter-Inflation Act, on, **21**, [613], [659]
rent or profits, treatment as, **44(1)**, [22], [29]

premium—*contd*
restricted contract, for—
excessive price for furniture as, **21**, [615],
[616]
prohibition of, **21**, [614]
reverse—
life assurance business, rules for,
43(1), [457]
tax treatment, **43(1)**, [427], [457]
Schedule A, sums taxed under, **44(1)**, [17]
Schedule D Case I or II, treatment under,
44(1), [62]
reductions in receipts, **44(1)**, [63]

premium rate services
code for—
absence of, orders by OFCOM in,
45, [540]
approval of, **45**, [539]
conditions regulating, **45**, [538]
enforcement, **45**, [541]
suspension of service provision for
contravention of, **45**, [542]

Premium Savings Bonds
lotteries law not applying to, **19(2)**, [831]
power to issue, **19(2)**, [857]
prize money, increase of, **19(2)**, [880]
regulations, **43(2)**, [530]
series B, transfer to, **19(2)**, [836]
sum repayable on, **19(2)**, [836]
terms of, **19(2)**, [882]

prerogative of mercy
Criminal Cases Review Commission,
assistance of, **12(2)**, [289]
royal, **12(1)**, [365], [463]

presentation (ecclesiastical)
archbishop, by—
benefice vacant 9 months, where,
14, 1146–7
consultations prior to, **14**, 1147
benefice vacant 9 months, where, **14**, 1146–7
bishop refusing—
appeal, **14**, 250–1
grounds, **14**, 250, 251, 801
contract to procure, **14**, 49
Diocesan Board, by, **14**, 1152–3
guild church, to, suspension of, **14**, 512
incumbent, by, **14**, 1149
notice as to, **14**, 1148
presenter, refusal to institute, **14**, 1148
restriction—
notice of vacancy, effect on, **14**, 1062
pastoral scheme or order, pending,
14, 1060–1
right of—
Jew holding, **14**, 185
Roman Catholic holding, **14**, 72
simoniacal, **14**, 49
suspension of—
notice of, **14**, 1057
performance of duties during, **14**, 1057–8
property, dealing with during, **14**, 1104–5

presentation (ecclesiastical)—*contd*
  suspension of—*contd*
    sequestration, and, **14**, 1059
    vacancy, effect of notice of, **14**, 1062
  universities, by, **14**, 252
  vacancy, notification, **14**, 1136–7
  void benefice, in case of, **14**, 1153

preservation
  open spaces, commons, etc, **9**, [432]

President of the Family Division
  appointment of, **11(2)**, [677]
  clerk and secretary to, **11(2)**, [771]
  precedence, **11(2)**, [680]

previous conviction
  evidence of, **12(1)**, [141]; **18**, [104]

prices
  control, summary of provisions, **47**, [1]
  food. *See* **food prices**
  goods and services—
    enforcement of provisions, **47**, [208]
    indication of prices, **47**, [204]
    information, restriction on
      offences, **47**, [208]
    orders as to, **47**, [204]
  misleading indications—
    regulations, power to make, **39(1)**, [614]
    supply, meaning, **39(1)**, [633]
  resale. *See* **resale price maintenance**

priest
  ordination. *See* **ordination**

primary and secondary schools
  acceptable standard of education, failure to
    give. *See* **school**
  baseline assessment scheme—
    adoption of, **15(1)**, [731]
    assessment in accordance with, **15(1)**, [732]
    maintained primary school, for,
      15(1), [731]
    meaning, **15(1)**, [730]
    regulations, **15(1)**, [733]
  boarding hostels, approval of, **15(1)**, [678]
  change in character, reference to, **15(1)**, [706]
  charges—
    boarding schools, board and lodging at,
      15(1), [602]
    civil debt, recovery as, **15(1)**, [605]
    information, provision of, **15(1)**, [603]
    maintained school, meaning, **15(1)**, [593]
    permitted—
      generally, **15(1)**, [599]
      regulations of, **15(1)**, [600]
    policy, **15(1)**, [601]
    prohibition of—
      admission, for, **15(1)**, [594]
      education, for, **15(1)**, [594]–[598]
      examinations, for, **15(1)**, [597]
      incidental, **15(1)**, [598]
    remissions policy, **15(1)**, [601]
    voluntary contributions, **15(1)**, [604]

primary and secondary schools—*contd*
  community school. *See* **community school**
  compulsory school age, **15(1)**, [503]
  corporal punishment, no right to give,
    15(1), [682]
  county school. *See* **county school**
  curriculum. *See* **curriculum**
  definitions, **15(1)**, [500]
  establishment, etc, general note, **15(1)**, [1]
  foundation school. *See* **foundation school**
  general note, **15(1)**, [1]
  governing body—
    distribution of information, **15(1)**, [674]
    individual pupils' performance, provision of
      information about, **15(1)**, [671]
    information, Secretary of State requiring,
      15(1), [670]
    provision of information to Secretary of
      State, **15(1)**, [674]
    school meals, provision of, **15(1)**, [668]
  governors—
    general note, **15(1)**, [1]
    travelling and subsistence allowance,
      15(1), [655]
  high standards in education, duty of local
    education authority to promote,
    15(1), [509]
  inspectorate. *See* **Her Majesty's
    Inspectorate of Schools**
  local education authority—
    board and lodging—
      fees for, **15(1)**, [651]
      providing, **15(1)**, [651]
    cleanliness, power to ensure, **15(1)**, [657]
    maintenance by, **15(1)**, [514]
    meals—
      free, children entitled to, **15(1)**, [720]
      free, providing, **15(1)**, [648]
      power to charge for, **15(1)**, [647]
      providing, **15(1)**, [646]
        governing bodies, functions transferred
        to, **15(1)**, [649]
    medical inspection and treatment,
      arranging, **15(1)**, [656]
    milk—
      free, providing, **15(1)**, [648]
      providing, **15(1)**, [646]
    non-maintained school, **15(1)**, [516]
      payment of fees at, **15(1)**, [653]
      provision of meals at, **15(1)**, [650]
    parental representations, duty to consider,
      15(1), [511]
    political indoctrination, forbidding,
      15(1), [570]
    political issues, securing balanced treatment
      of, **15(1)**, [571]
    provision by, **15(1)**, [510]
    recreational facilities, providing—
      persons aged 13 to 19, for, **15(1)**, [630]
      persons under 13, for, **15(1)**, [629]
    transport—
      arrangements, making,
        15(1), [633]–[635]
      sustainable modes of, promoting,
        15(1), [632]

primary and secondary schools—*contd*
maintained school. *See* **maintained school**
medical treatment and inspection,
 15(1), [656]
premises—
 alteration, reference to, **15(1)**, [706]
 approval of, **15(1)**, [678]
 building byelaws, exemption from,
  15(1), [679]
 nuisance or disturbance on, **15(1)**, [681]
 prescribed standards, **15(1)**, [676]
  relaxation, **15(1)**, [677]
pupil—
 admission of—
  charges, prohibition of, **15(1)**, [594]
  general note, **15(1)**, [1]
  time for, **15(1)**, [575]
 cleanliness—
  arrangements for cleansing, **15(1)**, [659]
  compulsory cleaning, **15(1)**, [658]
  examination for, **15(1)**, [657]
  neglecting, offence of, **15(1)**, [661]
  suspension pending examination or
   cleansing, **15(1)**, [660]
 clothing, provision of, **15(1)**, [644]–[645]
 detention outside school hours,
  15(1), [685]
 junior, meaning, **15(1)**, [498]
 meaning, **15(1)**, [498]
 medical examination, requirement of,
  15(1), [628]
 performance targets, **15(1)**, [734]
 public examinations—
  charge for, **15(1)**, [599]
  obligation to enter for, **15(1)**, [566]
  wasted fees, recovery of, **15(1)**, [597]
 referral unit. *See* **pupil referral unit**
 registration, **15(1)**, [576]
 restraint of, **15(1)**, [683]
 senior, meaning, **15(1)**, [498]
 suspected of carrying weapon, power to
  search, **15(1)**, [684]
 welfare, **15(1)**, [1]
 withdrawal from primary school for
  secondary education, **15(1)**, [577]
voluntary school. *See* **voluntary school**
wasted examination fees, recovery of,
 15(1), [597]
weapons, searching pupils for, **15(1)**, [684]

Primary Care Trust
advice for, **30**, [829]
AIDS and HIV reports, **30**, [505], [509]
births and deaths, notification of, **30**, [1075]
body corporate, to be, **30**, [1087]
Care Trust, designation as, **30**, [883]
charges, pharmaceutical services, for,
 30, [937]
community services, payments towards
 expenditure on, **30**, [1062]
 voluntary organisations, services provided
  by, **30**, [1063]
complaints about health care, **30**, [699], [701]
compulsory acquisition, **30**, [1089]
consultation, reports on, **26(2)**, [645]

Primary Care Trust—*contd*
continuation of, **30**, [824]
dental public health functions, **30**, [917]
dental services. *See* **dental services**
employment in, validity of clearance for,
 30, [750]
exercise of functions, **30**, [813]
expenditure, **30**, [1105]
family health services, duty in relation to,
 30, [446]
financial duties of, **30**, [1035]
functions, exercise of, **30**, [825]
general ophthalmic services. *See* **ophthalmic
 optician; ophthalmic services**
Health Service Commissioner, subject to
 investigation by, **30**, [544]
improvement of health, strategy for, **30**, [830]
instruction, provision of, **30**, [430]
local authorities, payments from, **30**, [882]
Local Dental Committees, **30**, [459], [919]
Local Medical Committees, **30**, [903]
Local Optical Committees, **30**, [457]–[458],
 [931]
Local Pharmaceutical Committees, **30**, [973]
medical services. *See* **medical services**
members, **30**, [1087]
ophthalmic services. *See* **ophthalmic
 services**
Patients' Forum. *See* **Patients' Forum**
PCT orders, **30**, [1088]
pharmaceutical services. *See* **pharmaceutical
 services**
powers and duties, **30**, [1089]
premises, provision of, **30**, [827]
property, transfer of, **30**, [1090]
public funding, **30**, [1034]
public involvement and consultation,
 30, [1048]
quality of health care, arrangements for
 improving, **30(S)**, NHS 103
reallocation of functions of Health Authorities
 to, **30**, [630], [640]
residual liabilities, transfer of, **30**, [876]
resource limits, **30**, [1036]
Secretary of State, powers of, **30**, [824]
services—
 administration and management of,
  30, [828]
 provision of, **30**, [827]
staff, **30**, [1087]
 transfer of, **30**, [1091]
Strategic Health Authority, directions from,
 30, [821], [826]
supplementary lists, **30**, [456]
taxation, **30**, [531]
trust funds and trustees, **30**, [1087]
users, duty to, **26(2)**, [644]

Prime Minister
dependants of, pensions for, **33(1)**, [152]
pension of, **33(1)**, [151], [206]
salary, **10**, [612]

principal councils. *See under* **local authority**

printer
copies of papers printed, preservation, **19(3)**, [283]
imprint—
duty to imprint—
exemptions, **19(3)**, [283]
relaxations, **19(3)**, [322]
requirement, **19(3)**, [261], [283]
failure to print, penalties, **19(3)**, [283]
university presses, in case of, **19(3)**, [283]
limitation of actions, **19(3)**, [283]

priory. *See* **religious houses**

prison. *See also* **imprisonment; prisoner**
administration, **12(1)**, [1], [275A]
annual reports on, **12(1)**, [275D]
articles, unlawful conveyance into, **12(1)**, [275AE]
authorisation, meaning, **12(1)**, [275AJ]
buildings, declaration as prisons, **12(1)**, [275Z]
cells—
certification of, **12(1)**, [275O]
special, for violent prisoner, **12(1)**, [275O]
chaplain—
appointment, **12(1)**, [275G]
assistant, **12(1)**, [275G]
bishop, notice to and licence from, **12(1)**, [275J]
two prisons, officiating in, **12(1)**, [275J]
chief inspector—
annual reports, **12(1)**, [275D]
appointment, **12(1)**, [275E]
co-operation, **12(1)**, [275AU]
delegation of functions, **12(1)**, [275AU]
duty, **12(1)**, [275E]
functions, **12(1)**, [275E]
inspection programmes and frameworks, **12(1)**, [275AU]
joint action, **12(1)**, [275AU]
reference of matters to, **12(1)**, [275E]
summary of provisions, **12(1)**, [1]
closing of, **12(1)**, [275AD]
Commissioners, transfer of functions to Secretary of State, **12(1)**, [328C]
contracted out, functions, **12(2)**, [112], [219]
contracting out—
arrangements for, **12(2)**, [105], [218]
custodial duties at, **12(2)**, [109], [116]
intervention by Secretary of State, **12(2)**, [111]
lease or tenancy for, **12(2)**, [218]
modification of provisions, **12(2)**, [110]
officers, **12(2)**, [106]
prisoner custody officers, powers and duties of, **12(2)**, [107]
suspected offenders, detention of, **12(2)**, [108]
wrongful disclosure of information, **12(2)**, [115]
contractor, provision by, **12(2)**, [214]

prison—*contd*
conveyance to—
expenses, **12(1)**, [275T]
power of constable, **12(1)**, [275V]
coroner, jurisdiction of, **12(1)**, [275AA]
corporal punishment, abolition, **12(1)**, [389]
Crown immunity, extension of, **12(1)**, [275AK]
divisions, abolition of, **12(1)**, [259]
expenses, **12(1)**, [328L]
foreign, goods made in, importation prohibited, **13**, [546]
governor—
appointment, **12(1)**, [275G]
deputy, **12(1)**, [275G]
legal custody of prisoners, **12(1)**, [275N]
writs and instruments addressed to, description of prison in, **12(1)**, [275M]
independent monitoring boards, **12(1)**, [275f]
jurisdiction over, **12(1)**, [275A]
justices, visiting. *See* visiting justices *below*
land for—
acquisition, **12(1)**, [1], [275AC]
compulsory acquisition, **12(1)**, [275AC]
easements, **12(1)**, [1106]
entry in connection with acquisition, **12(1)**, [613]
List A articles, conveyance of into, **12(1)**, [275AF], [275AG]
List B or C articles, conveyance of into, **12(1)**, [275AF], [275AH]
local review committees. *See under* **prisoner**
maintenance of—
expenses incurred, **12(1)**, [275AP]
powers, **12(1)**, [275Z]
management rules, **12(1)**, [275AN]
Millbank, transfer, **12(1)**, [180]
ministers other than Church of England, **12(1)**, [275K]
mutiny, offence of, **12(2)**, [131]
Northern Ireland—
legislative powers, construction of references to, **12(1)**, [328I]
provisions applicable, **12(1)**, [328K]
offences—
generally, **12(1)**, [1]
notice of penalties, display of, **12(1)**, [275AL]
offenders, reports on, **12(1)**, [328F]
officers—
accommodation, vacating of, **12(1)**, [275L]
appointment, **12(1)**, [275B]
contracted out prisons, of, **12(2)**, [106]
ejectment on refusal to quit, **12(1)**, [275L]
generally, **12(1)**, [1]
height, discrimination on, **7(1)**, [56]
inducements to withhold services or to indiscipline, **12(2)**, [231]
power to suspend operation of, provisions, **12(2)**, [323]
industrial action by, **12(4)**, [539]
meaning, **12(2)**, [231]
pay and related conditions, **12(2)**, [233]
powers and privileges, **12(1)**, [275H]
salaries, **12(1)**, [275B]

prison—*contd*
  officers—*contd*
    women, **12(1)**, [275G]
    See also chaplain; governor; medical officer
      above
  orders—
    general provisions, **12(1)**, [328E]
    power to make, exercise of,
      12(1), [275AR]
  Parole Board. *See under* **prisoner**
  Prison Service—
    employment legislation, **12(2)**, [230]
    inducements to withhold services or to
      indiscipline, **12(2)**, [231]
        power to suspend operation of,
          provisions, **12(2)**, [323]
    pay and related conditions, **12(2)**, [233]
  property, vesting of, **12(1)**, [1], [275AB]
  provision of, **12(1)**, [275Z]
  release from. *See* **prisoner**
  rules and regulations, exercise of power to
    make, **12(1)**, [275AR]
  rules (prison)—
    annulment, **12(1)**, [390]
    offences against, **12(1)**, [328B]
    power to make, **12(1)**, [275AN]
  Scotland, provisions applicable, **12(1)**, [328K]
  search, powers of authorised persons,
    12(1), [275I]
  Secretary of State, general duties of,
    12(1), [275C]
  security, offences relating to, **12(1)**, [275AI]
  sentence. *See under* **imprisonment**
  service personnel in—
    absentees etc, **3**, [688]
    governors' duties, **3**, [625], [898], [1184]
    service of sentence in, **3**, [621], [894],
      [1158]
  sheriff, jurisdiction of, **12(1)**, [275AA]
  summary of provisions, **12(1)**, [1]
  tobacco, unlawful conveyance into prison
    etc, **34**, [794]
  visiting justices—
    jurisdiction, **12(1)**, [275AA]
    rights, **12(1)**, [275S]
  visitors' book, inspection of, **12(1)**, [275S]
  See generally **young offenders**

prison, civil. *See* **civil prison**

prison service
  joint working with national health service
    bodies, **30**, [1055], [1304]

prisoner. *See also* **imprisonment; prison**
  alcohol, testing for, **12(1)**, [275R]
  complaints by, hearing, **12(1)**, [275F]
  confinement, legality of, **12(1)**, [275N]
  conveyance to prison—
    expenses, **12(1)**, [275T]
    power of constable, **12(1)**, [275V]
  custody—
    governor, of, deemed to be in,
      12(1), [275N]
    legal, **12(1)**, [275N], [328D], [829]

prisoner—*contd*
  custody officer—
    certification, **12(2)**, [113], [125], [226],
      [252], [253]
    contracted out prisons, at, **12(2)**, [107]
    escorting by, **12(2)**, [101]
    Northern Ireland, **12(2)**, [226]–[229], [253]
    powers and duties of, **12(2)**, [103], [216],
      [224]
    protection of, **12(2)**, [114], [227]
    Scotland, **12(2)**, [220]
    suspected offenders, detention of,
      12(2), [108]
    wrongful disclosure of information,
      12(2), [115], [228]
  detention and release of offender present
    outside country in which required to be
    detained, transfer of responsibility for—
    arrest and detention with view to
      establishing responsibility for,
      12(1), [826], [827]
    designated person, meaning, **12(1)**, [828]
    transfer of responsibility from UK,
      12(1), [824]
    transfer to responsibility to UK,
      12(1), [825]
    warrant, issue of, **12(1)**, [823]
  detention in custody of constable,
    12(1), [710]
  discharge of—
    ill health, on grounds of, **12(1)**, [275X]
    temporary, **12(1)**, [275X]
  discharged, payments to, **12(1)**, [275Y]
  disciplinary offences, additional days for,
    12(2), [86], [1018]; **12(3)**, [993]
  drugs, testing for, **12(1)**, [275Q]
  early removal from United Kingdom,
    12(4), [483]
  earnings, deductions and levies—
    application of amounts, **12(2)**, [499]
    enhanced wages work, meaning,
      12(2), [498]
    net weekly earnings, meaning, **12(2)**, [498]
    power to make, **12(2)**, [498]
    statements of account, **12(2)**, [500]
  escape—
    aiding, **12(1)**, [275AE], [328A]
    conveying articles into prison to assist,
      12(1), [275AE]
    during transfer into or out of UK,
      12(1), [829]
    harbouring after, **12(1)**, [328A]
    permitting, **3**, [511], [784], [1049]
    warrant, issue of, **12(1)**, [394]
  escaped, arrest of, **12(1)**, [394]
  escorts—
    arrangements—
      functions, for, **12(2)**, [101], [215], [222]
      monitoring, **12(2)**, [102], [223]
      prisoner custody officers, powers and
        duties of, **12(2)**, [103], [216], [224]
    breaches of discipline, **12(2)**, [104], [217],
      [225]
    Northern Ireland, **12(2)**, [222]–[225]
    Scotland, **12(2)**, [215]–[217]

prisoner—*contd*
  evidence, giving, **12(1)**, [54]
  extradited, **12(3)**, [974]
  fixed-term—
    disciplinary offences, additional days for,
     12(3), [993]
    early removal from United Kingdom,
     12(3), [997]
      re-entry, **12(3)**, [998]
    extradited, **12(3)**, [974]
    meaning, **12(3)**, [967]
    release on licence—
     compassionate grounds, on, **12(3)**, [979]
     conditions, power to recommend,
      12(3), [968]
     duration, **12(3)**, [980]
     duty as to, **12(3)**, [975]
     intermittent custody prisoners,
      12(3), [976]
     power of, **12(3)**, [977]
      relevant proportion, alteration of,
       12(3), [1005]
  inquest on death of, **11(1)**, [1214]
  intermittent custody—
    consecutive terms, **12(3)**, [1002]
    meaning, **12(3)**, [1006]
    release on licence, **12(3)**, [976]
     power of, **12(3)**, [977]
     recall, **12(3)**, [985]
  liable to removal from United Kingdom,
    12(4), [481], [484]
  life—
    designated, **12(2)**, [594]
    England and Wales, transfer to,
     12(3), [1009]
    mandatory, transitional cases, **12(3)**, [1092]
    meaning, **12(2)**, [577]
    Parole Board, reference of case to,
     12(2), [572]
    preventive sentence—
     meaning, **12(2)**, [575]
     termination of licence, **12(2)**, [575]
    public protection, imprisonment or
     detention for, **12(2)**, [575]
    release—
     compassionate grounds, on, **12(2)**, [573]
     discretionary life prisoners, **12(2)**, [143]
     duty of, **12(2)**, [572]
     licence, on—
      duration and conditions, **12(2)**, [574]
      recall, **12(2)**, [83], [576]
      termination, **12(2)**, [575]
    Scotland, transfer to, **12(2)**, [145]
    supervision, transfer of, **12(2)**, [146]
    transferred, references to, **12(3)**, [1010]
  long-term, release of, **12(4)**, [480]
  maintenance costs, **12(1)**, [275AP]
  measuring, **12(1)**, [275P]
  medical or surgical treatment, removal to
    hospital for, **12(1)**, [275U]
  orders and rules, making, **12(3)**, [1042]
  overseas, transfer to give evidence etc—
    from United Kingdom, **12(2)**, [21]
    to United Kingdom, **12(2)**, [22]

prisoner—*contd*
  Parole Board—
    access to, **12(3)**, [1025]
    accounts and audit, **12(3)**, [1090]
    capacity, **12(3)**, [1090]
    directions to, **12(3)**, [969]
    documents, authenticity of, **12(3)**, [1090]
    duty of, **12(3)**, [969]
    expenses, **12(2)**, [118]
    financial provisions, **12(3)**, [1090]
    life prisoner, reference of case of,
     12(2), [572]
    members, **12(3)**, [1090]
    proceedings, **12(3)**, [1090]
    reference to, **12(3)**, [992]
    reports, **12(3)**, [1090]
    review by, **12(3)**, [991], [992]
    seal, **12(3)**, [1090]
    staff, **12(3)**, [1090]
    status of, **12(3)**, [969], [1090]
    transfer of functions to, **12(2)**, [97]
  period of remand on bail, credit for—
    release, amended provisions **12(4)**, [478]
    terms of imprisonment and detention,
     12(4), [477]
    transitional provisions, **12(4)**, [479], [564]
  photographing, **12(1)**, [275P]
  place of confinement, **12(1)**, [275M]
  recalled, release of, **12(4)**, [482]
  release—
    automatic, **12(3)**, [988]
     prisoners not suitable for, **12(3)**, [989]
    compassionate grounds, on, **12(2)**, [77];
     12(3), [979]
    convictions during currency of original
     sentence, **12(2)**, [150]
    discretionary life prisoners, **12(2)**, [143]
    early—
     amended provisions, **12(3)**, [999]
     contemnors, **12(2)**, [90]; **12(3)**, [994]
     excluded offences, **12(1)**, [782],
      [792]–[794]
     fine defaulters, **12(2)**, [90]; **12(3)**, [994]
     generally, **12(1)**, [1]
     order for, **12(1)**, [782]
     persons extradited to United Kingdom,
      12(2), [95]
     persons eligible for removal from United
      Kingdom, **12(2)**, [92]
     persons liable to removal from United
      Kingdom, **12(2)**, [91], [93], [144]
     powers, **12(1)**, [782]
     recall, **12(3)**, [986]
     re-entry into United Kingdom,
      12(2), [94]
     sexual offenders, **12(2)**, [88], [89]
     special cases, **12(2)**, [74]
     transitional provisions, **12(2)**, [127]
     two or more sentences, **12(2)**, [688]
     violent offenders, **12(2)**, [88], [89]
     young offenders, **12(2)**, [87]
    exercise of powers of, **12(1)**, [393]
    extended sentence prisoners, **12(3)**, [990]

prisoner—*contd*
release—*contd*
  life prisoners. *See* life *above*
  long-term prisoners, **12(2)**, [73], [76]
    recall, **12(2)**, [83]
  on licence—
    conditions, **12(2)**, [78], [79], [147];
      12(3), [981]
      breach by short-term prisoners,
        12(2), [81]
      curfew, **12(2)**, [80], [82]; **12(3)**, [984]
      duty to comply with, **12(3)**, [983]
      failure to comply, recall on,
        12(3), [986]
      meaning, **12(3)**, [981]
      power of court to recommend,
        12(3), [968]
      re-release of prisoner serving sentence
        less than twelve months, on,
        12(3), [982]
    direction as to time on remand, effect
      of, **12(3)**, [972]
    drug-testing requirements, **12(2)**, [998];
      12(3), [1004]
    duration, **12(2)**, [78], [79]; **12(3)**, [980]
    duty as to, **12(3)**, [975]
    extended sentence, prisoner serving,
      12(3), [978]
    fixed-term prisoners. *See* fixed-term
      above
    monitoring, conditions as to,
      12(2), [997]
    power of, **12(3)**, [977]
      relevant proportion, alteration of,
        12(3), [1005]
    preventive detention, transitional
      provisions, **12(1)**, [406]
    recall, **12(2)**, [83], [98]; **12(3)**, [985]
      further release after, **12(3)**, [987]
    return to prison, following, **12(2)**, [84]
    sexual offenders, **12(2)**, [88], [89]
    short-term prisoners, **12(2)**, [75]
    specified offence prisoners, **12(3)**, [989]
    transitional provisions, **12(1)**, [406]
    violent offenders, **12(2)**, [88], [89]
  relevant proportions of sentences, alteration
    of, **12(2)**, [96]
  short-term prisoners, **12(2)**, [73]
    breach of conditions, **12(2)**, [81]
    licence, on, **12(2)**, [75]
    supervision, **12(2)**, [148]
  supervision after—
    elsewhere in UK, **12(1)**, [333C]
    variation of order, **12(2)**, [149]
  temporary—
    remaining at large, **12(2)**, [277]
    rules, **12(1)**, [275AN]
  remand in custody, reference to, **12(3)**, [973]
  remand time counting towards time served,
    12(2), [85]; **12(3)**, [970]
    release on licence, effect of direction on,
      12(3), [972]
    terms of imprisonment and detention,
      12(3), [971]

prisoner—*contd*
removal—
  from one prison to another, **12(1)**, [275M]
  from United Kingdom—
    early, **12(3)**, [997]
    persons eligible for, **12(3)**, [996]
    persons liable to, **12(3)**, [995]
  into or out of the UK. *See* transfer *below*
  judicial purposes, for, **12(1)**, [275U]
  medical or surgical treatment, for,
    12(1), [275U]
  repatriation. *See* transfer *below*; removal *above*
sentence. *See under* **imprisonment**
sufficient accommodation, requirement of,
  12(1), [275O]
summary of provisions, **12(1)**, [1]
transfer—
  British Islands, to, **12(2)**, [590]
  British Islands, within—
    effect of, **12(2)**, [588]
    Isle of Man, application to, **12(2)**, [589]
    powers of, **12(2)**, [587]
    subsequent sentence, **12(2)**, [589]
    unlawfully at large, **12(2)**, [589]
  generally, **12(1)**, [1]
  investigation aboard, to assist, **12(3)**, [605]
  Scotland, from, for security, **12(1)**, [392]
  UK investigation, to assist, **12(3)**, [606]
  warrant for—
    certificates for purposes of, **12(1)**, [832]
    consent of prisoner, **12(1)**, [819]
    escape of prisoner, **12(1)**, [829]
    expenses incurred, **12(1)**, [831]
    international arrangements, **12(1)**, [819]
    into the UK—
      detention of prisoner after,
        12(1), [821]
      operation of statutory provisions on,
        12(1), [821], [834]
      requirements to be met, **12(1)**, [819]
      temporary return, for, **12(1)**, [822]
    issue, **12(1)**, [819]
    new warrant, issue of, **12(1)**, [830]
    Northern Ireland, application of
      provisions, **12(1)**, [833]
    operation of, **12(1)**, [829]
    out of the UK—
      detention order, continuation,
        12(1), [820]
      generally, **12(1)**, [820]
      hospital order, effect of, **12(1)**, [820]
      information, supply to prisoner,
        12(1), [819]
      temporary return, for, **12(1)**, [822]
    persons authorised to conduct prisoner,
      12(1), [829]
    persons to whom provisions apply,
      12(1), [819]
    retaking prisoner, **12(1)**, [829]
    revocation, **12(1)**, [830]
    superseding earlier warrant, **12(1)**, [819]
    when prisoner deemed in legal custody,
      12(1), [829]

prisoner—*contd*
  transfer—*contd*
    See also removal *above*
    transitory and transitional provisions,
      12(4), [578]
  treatment, generally, **12(1)**, [1]
  unlawful release, **3**, [511], [784], [1049]
  unlawfully at large—
    arrest of, **12(1)**, [275AO]; **12(2)**, [19]
    during transfer, **12(1)**, [829]
    generally, **12(1)**, [1]
    transfer, **12(2)**, [589]
  violent, special cell for, **12(1)**, [275O]
  women, detention in remand or youth
    offender institution, **12(1)**, [275AM]
  young offenders. *See* **young offenders**

prisoner of war
  custody, **10**, [949]
  Geneva Conventions, provisions of,
    10, [627]–[659]
  prisoners' representative, **10**, [947]
  protected, meaning, **10**, [952]
  sentence—
    death, appeal against, **10**, [948]
    reduction of, **10**, [949]
  trial of—
    legal representation, **10**, [947]
    notice of, **10**, [946]
    particulars of, **10**, [946]

private company
  accounts—
    elective resolution as to, **8**, 332–3
    shareholder requiring, **8**, 333
  annual general meeting, dispensing with,
    8, 422–3
  auditors. *See* **auditors**
  authority for allotment, election as to, **8**, 160
  certification of, **8**, 821
  director appointed for life, removal, **8**, 827
  elective resolution—
    annual general meeting, dispensing with,
      8, 422–3
    laying of accounts, dispensing with, **8**, 332
    meaning, **8**, 433–4
    notice of, **8**, 433
    registration, **8**, 434–5
    regulations, further provision by, **8**, 921
    re-registration, effect of, **8**, 435
    revocation, **8**, 434
    special resolution, proportion required for,
      8, 432
  extraordinary general meeting, requisition,
    8, 426
  financial assistance for purchase of own
    shares, **8**, 218
    statutory declaration as to, **8**, 220–1
  meaning, **8**, 104
  memorandum, form of, **8**, 106–7
  name of, **8**, 130–1
    omission of "limited" from, **8**, 130–1
  offer of shares or debentures, **8**, 160
  old public company becoming, **8**, 821

private company—*contd*
  own shares, purchase of—
    financing of, **8**, 233–4
    objections to, **8**, 237–8
    payment out of capital, **8**, 234–5
    powers of, **8**, 232–3
    publicity as to payment, **8**, 236–7
    special resolution as to, **8**, 235–6
  public company becoming—
    court powers, **8**, 151–2
    objection to, **8**, 152–3
    procedure, **8**, 151–2
  redeemable shares of, **8**, 232–4
  re-registration as public—
    certificate of, **8**, 146–7
    consideration for recently allotted shares,
      8, 143
    procedure, **8**, 142
    requirements for, **8**, 141–2
    share capital, requirements as to, **8**, 144–5
  striking off on application—
    directors' duties following, **8**, 517–18
    duties, **8**, 515–16
    enforcement, **8**, 519–20
    general, **8**, 515
    offences, **8**, 520
    restoration to register, **8**, 520–1
    supplementary provisions, **8**, 518–19
  written resolutions—
    auditors, rights of, **8**, 437–8
    exceptions, **8**, 765
    procedural requirements, **8**, 765–7
    provisions on, **8**, 436–7
    recording, **8**, 438
    validity, **8**, 438

private hire vehicles
  accident to, notification of, **36**, [933]
  Acts, application of, **36**, [928], [961]
  advance booking, **37**, [361]
  appeals—
    generally, **36**, [960]
    operator, by, **36**, [930], [938]
    refusal of licence, against, **36**, [931]
  authorised officer—
    inspection and testing by, **36**, [951]
    meaning, **36**, [963]
    obstruction of, **36**, [956]
  booking, meaning, **38(2)**, [10]
  code—
    meaning, **37**, [363]
    modifications by Secretary of State,
      37, [363]
  controlled district—
    meaning, **36**, [963]
    resolutions designating, **36**, [928]
  damage to, notification of, **36**, [933]
  district council, adoption of provisions by,
    36, [928]
  driver's badge—
    issue of, **36**, [937]
    return of, **36**, [944]
    wearing of, **36**, [937]
  driver's licence—
    appeals in respect of, **36**, [935], [944]

private hire vehicles—*contd*
  driver's licence—*contd*
    application for, **36**, [934]
    authentication of, **36**, [962]
    conditions attaching to, **36**, [934]
    duration, **36**, [936]
    fee for, **36**, [936], [953]
    fitness to hold, **36**, [934]
    grant of, **36**, [934]
    information required of applicant, **36**, [940]
    necessity for, **36**, [929]
    register of, **36**, [934]
    suspension or revocation, **36**, [944]
  false information in respect of, **36**, [940]
  fitness, inspection and resting for, **36**, [951]
  hackney carriages, used for private hire, **36**, [950]
  inspection and testing—
    fitness, for, **36**, [951]
    presentation for, **36**, [933]
  insurance, necessity for, **36**, [931]
  licence—
    authentication of, **36**, [962]
    conditions attached to, **36**, [930]
    drivers. *See* drivers *above*
    duration of, **36**, [931]
    expiry, return of plate or disc, **36**, [941]
    fees, **36**, [953]
    information required of applicant, **36**, [940]
    matters to be specified in, **36**, [931]
    necessity for, **36**, [929]
    refusal, appeal against, **36**, [931]
    revocation, **36**, [943]
      return of plate or disc, **36**, [941]
    suitability for grant of, **36**, [931]
    transfer, **36**, [932]
  licensed, meaning, **37**, [363]
  limiting number of, bar on, **36**, [931]
  London—
    advertisements, prohibition of, **38(2)**, [40]
    authorised officers, obstruction of, **38(2)**, [36]
    driver's badge—
      issue of, **38(2)**, [23]
      production of, **26(2)**, [814]
    driver's licence—
      appeals, **38(2)**, [22]
      application for, **38(2)**, [22], [24]
      documents, production of, **38(2)**, [30]
      register, **38(2)**, [32]
      requirement for, **38(2)**, [21]
      return of, **38(2)**, [31]
      revocation, **38(2)**, [25], [26]
      suspension, **38(2)**, [25], [26]
    false statements, **38(2)**, [37]
    fixed penalty offences—
      financial provisions, **26(2)**, [842]
      levels of penalty, **26(2)**, [811]
      notice, **26(2)**, [808], [810]
      regulations, power to make, **26(2)**, [813]
      schedule of offences, **26(2)**, [809], [841]
      Secretary of State, reserve powers, **26(2)**, [812]
    funerals and weddings, used for, **38(2)**, [38]
    interpretation, **38(2)**, [45]

private hire vehicles—*contd*
  London—*contd*
    licence—
      appeals, **38(2)**, [16]
      application for, **38(2)**, [16], [24]
      documents, production of, **38(2)**, [30]
      duration, **38(2)**, [16]
      grant of, **38(2)**, [16]
      offences, **38(2)**, [15]
      public register not to include holders' addresses, **26(2)**, [817]
      register, **38(2)**, [32]
      requirement for, **38(2)**, [15]
      return on suspension or revocation, **26(2)**, [815]
      revocation, **38(2)**, [25], [26]
      single vehicle, for, **38(2)**, [16]
      suspension, **38(2)**, [25], [26]
    licensed vehicles—
      change of ownership, **38(2)**, [17]
      disc or plate, display of, **38(2)**, [19]
      fitness of, **38(2)**, [18]
      identification, **38(2)**, [19]
      owners, obligations of, **38(2)**, [17]
      taximeters, prohibition, **38(2)**, [20]
    licensing authority—
      appeals against decisions of, **38(2)**, [34]
        effect of, **38(2)**, [35]
      delegation of functions by, **38(2)**, [33]
    notices, service of, **38(2)**, [43]
    offences due to fault of other person, **38(2)**, [42]
    operator—
      licence. *See* operator's licence *below*
      obligations of, **38(2)**, [13]
      other operator, hirings accepted on behalf of, **38(2)**, [14]
    operator's licence—
      appeals, **38(2)**, [12]
      application for, **38(2)**, [12]
      conditions, **38(2)**, [12]
      display of, **38(2)**, [13]
      documents, production of, **38(2)**, [30]
      fees, **38(2)**, [29]
      grant of, **38(2)**, [12]
      register, **38(2)**, [32]
      requirement for, **38(2)**, [11]
      return of, **38(2)**, [31]
      variation—
        licensing authority, by, **38(2)**, [28]
        operator, at request of, **38(2)**, [27]
    operators, records, **26(2)**, [816]
    owner of vehicle, reference to, **38(2)**, [44]
    regulations, **38(2)**, [41]
    restricted PSV operator's licence, application for, **37**, [364]
    signs and notices, prohibition, **38(2)**, [39]
    transitional provisions, **38(2)**, [46]
  meaning, **38(2)**, [10]
  metropolitan police district, provisions on alteration of, **26(1)**, [644]
  obstruction of authorised officers, **36**, [956]
  offences—
    due to fault of other person, **36**, [955]
    penalties generally, **36**, [959]

private hire vehicles—*contd*
operator—
  appeal by, **36**, [938]
  contract deemed made with, **36**, [939]
  licence—
    duration, **36**, [938]
    fees, **36**, [953]
    information required by applicant,
      36, [940]
    London. *See* London *above*
    production for inspection, **36**, [939]
    suspension or revocation, **36**, [945]
  licensing of, generally, **36**, [938]
  meaning, **38(2)**, [10]
  records to be kept by, **36**, [939]
penalties, generally, **36**, [959]
place of keeping of, notification, **36**, [933]
plate or disc to identify—
  issue of, **36**, [931]
  return on expiry of licence, **36**, [941]
prolongation of journey, unnecessary,
  36, [952]
proprietor—
  general provisions, **36**, [933]
  meaning, **36**, [963]
roof-signs, **36**, [995]
savings—
  certain businesses, **36**, [957]
  certain vehicles, **36**, [958]
sharing use of, **37**, [72], [361]
small PSVs, regulation of, **37**, [61]
suitability for use, **36**, [931]
taximeter—
  inspection and testing, **36**, [951], [954]
  meaning, **36**, [963]
  not compulsory for, **36**, [954]
  tampering with or altering, **36**, [954]
transfer of, notification, **36**, [932]
Transport for London, functions transferred
  to, **26(1)**, [643]
unfitness for use, **36**, [943]
unlicensed vehicle, use of, **36**, [929]
vehicles excluded from regulation, **37**, [60]

private security industry
bodies corporate, offences by, **47**, [661]
contractors, approved—
  approval of—
    appeals relating to, **47**, [656]
    arrangements for grant of, **47**, [653]
    requirements for, imposition of,
      47, [655]
  register of, **47**, [652]
  status of, right to use, **47**, [654]
criminal liability of directors, **47**, [661]
criminal records, access to, **47**, [659]
interpretation of provisions, **47**, [663]
licences for—
  appeals regarding, **47**, [649]
  application for, **47**, [646]
  conditions of, **47**, [647]
  conduct requiring, **47**, [641]
  criteria for, publication by Security
    Industry Authority, **47**, [645]
  door supervisors, **47**, [667]

private security industry—*contd*
licences for—*contd*
  exemptions, **47**, [642]
  grant of, **47**, [646]
  keyholders, **47**, [666]
  licensable conduct, engagement in,
    47, [646]
  local authorities, powers regarding,
    47, [651]
  manned guarding, **47**, [666]
  modification of, **47**, [648]
  offences—
    unlicensed security operative, using,
      47, [643]
    unlicensed wheel-clampers, using,
      47, [644]
  private investigations, **47**, [666]
  register of, **47**, [650]
  revocation of, **47**, [648]
  security consultants, **47**, [666]
  vehicles, immobilisation of, **47**, [666], [667]
  without, conduct prohibited, **47**, [641]
Northern Ireland, in—
  amended provisions,
    31(S), Northern Ireland 104
  appeals, **31(S)**, Northern Ireland 116
  change of personnel,
    31(S), Northern Ireland 116–17
  interim arrangements for regulating,
    31(S), Northern Ireland 103, 112–18
  licences, **31(S)**, Northern Ireland 113–16
  offences, **31(S)**, Northern Ireland 117
  records, **31(S)**, Northern Ireland 117
offences—
  body corporate, by, **47**, [661]
  false information, provision of, **47**, [660]
  unlicensed security operative, using,
    47, [643]
  unlicensed wheel-clampers, use of,
    47, [644]
orders and regulations, **47**, [662]
premises—
  entry, powers of, **47**, [657]–[658]
  inspection, powers of, **47**, [657]
Security Industry Authority—
  annual report, **47**, [665]
  chairman, **47**, [665]
  committees, **47**, [665]
  establishment of, **47**, [639]
  functions—
    delegation to committees, **47**, [665]
    delegation to staff, **47**, [665]
    generally, **47**, [639]
  members, **47**, [665]
  money, **47**, [665]
  proceedings, **47**, [665]
  seal of, **47**, [665]
  Secretary of State, directions from,
    47, [640]
  staff, **47**, [665]
  tenure of office, **47**, [665]
security operative, offence of using
  unlicensed, **47**, [643]
sports grounds, removal from regulation,
  12(4), [249]

private security industry—*contd*
wheel-clampers, offence of using unlicensed,
47, [644]

private street
adoption of—
council, duty of, **36**, [1044]
frontagers requiring, **36**, [1275]
street works, after, **36**, [1274]
built-up, meaning, **36**, [1275]
dedication of use, **36**, [1278]
development plan, land designated by,
36, [1278]
highway—
comprised in, widening, **36**, [1273]
conversion into, **36**, [1038]
land treated as, **36**, [1278]
meaning, **36**, [1249]
safety provisions, **36**, [1070]
works. *See* **private street works**

private street works
adoption of street after, **36**, [1274]
advance payments—
code—
application of, **36**, [1250], [1422]
building frontage, meaning, **36**, [1249]
effect of, **36**, [1250]
meaning, **36**, [1249]
purposes of, **36**, [1250]
determination of sum, **36**, [1266]
division of land after, **36**, [1265], [1266]
interest on, **36**, [1271]
local land charges, matters being,
36, [1270]
new building, by owner of, **36**, [1265]
not required, where, **36**, [1265]
notice requiring, **36**, [1266]
plans not proceeded with, where,
36, [1269]
proceedings for, **36**, [1265]
refund—
authority, work not done at expense of,
36, [1267]
exemption of building, on, **36**, [1265]
highway maintainable at public expense,
street declared, **36**, [1268]
plans not proceeded with, where,
36, [1269]
security, realisation of, **36**, [1266]
sewer works, for, **36**, [1266]
authority—
accounts, keeping, **36**, [1260]
borrowing powers, **36**, [1260]
charging order, granting, **36**, [1283]
expenses, contribution to, **36**, [1282]
incidental works, including, **36**, [1252]
meaning, **36**, [1249]
more than one, where, **36**, [1280]
resolving to execute, **36**, [1251]
specification, etc, approval of, **36**, [1251]
building frontage, **36**, [1249]
code—
designated land, application to, **36**, [1278]
effect of, **36**, [1250]

private street works—*contd*
code—*contd*
meaning, **36**, [1249]
Minister, appeal to, **36**, [1279]
objections, regulating, **36**, [1263]
purposes of, **36**, [1250]
transitional provisions, **36**, [1433]
compensation for damage by, **36**, [1277]
designated land—
code, application of, **36**, [1278]
construction and improvement, **36**, [1278]
regulations relating to, **36**, [1278]
expenses—
amount of payments, **36**, [1266]
annual instalments, paid by, **36**, [1258]
apportionment—
benefit, taking into account, **36**, [1253]
final, **36**, [1257]
frontages, between, **36**, [1251]
objections to, **36**, [1257]
premises not fronting street, including,
36, [1253]
provisional, **36**, [1253]
amendment of, **36**, [1256]
borrowing for, **36**, [1259]
charge on property, as, **36**, [1258]
charging order, grant of, **36**, [1283]
deductions from rent, **36**, [1420]
determination of liability, **36**, [1266]
estimate—
amendment of, **36**, [1256]
preparation, **36**, [1251]
evasion of, **36**, [1281]
exemptions from—
places of religious worship, **36**, [1261]
Port of London Authority, **36**, [1264]
railways and canals, **36**, [1262]
Thames Water Authority, **36**, [1264]
part of street only affected, **36**, [1251]
recovery of, **36**, [1258], [1420]
refunds, **36**, [1267]
security for payment, **36**, [1268]
street works authority, contribution by,
36, [1282]
frontagers—
adoption required by, **36**, [1275]
apportionment of expenses between,
36, [1251]
determination of liability, **36**, [1266]
fronting, meaning, **36**, [1249]
industrial premises, meaning, **36**, [1249]
lighting, **36**, [1251]
meaning, **36**, [1249]
new buildings, payments by owners. *See*
advance payments *above*
notices, particulars to be in, **36**, [1251],
[1256], [1423]
objections to—
costs of proceedings, **36**, [1255]
determination of, **36**, [1255]
grounds for, **36**, [1254]
hearing of, **36**, [1255]
proposed works, **36**, [1254]
provisions of code, to be under, **36**, [1263]

private street works—*contd*
  owners—
    evasion of works expenses by, **36**, [1281]
    limited, borrowing powers, **36**, [1259]
    new buildings, of, payments by, **36**, [1265]
    See further advance payment *above*
  particulars—
    matters comprising, **36**, [1251], [1423]
    notice of, publishing, **36**, [1251], [1256],
      [1423]
  paving, metalling and flagging, meaning,
    36, [1249]
  Port of London Authority, exemption from
    expenses, **36**, [1264]
  railways and canals, certain, exemption from
    expenses, **36**, [1262]
  religious worship, place of, exemption from
    expenses, **36**, [1261]
  sewering, when included, **36**, [1251]
  specification and plans—
    amendment of, **36**, [1256]
    particulars, comprising, **36**, [1251], [1423]
    preparation of, **36**, [1251]
    resolution of approval—
      court, powers of, **36**, [1255]
      passing, **36**, [1251]
  Thames Water Authority, exemption from
    expenses, **36**, [1264]
  urgent repairs, **36**, [1276]
  widening of highway, **36**, [1273]
  width of carriageway and footway, varying,
    36, [1272]

privatisation
  windfall—
    companies benefiting from, **43(1)**, [308]
    quantification of, **43(1)**, [328]
    windfall tax, charge to,
      43(1), 307. *See also* **windfall tax**

privy
  duty to empty, **35(1)**, [304], [306]
  meaning, **35(1)**, [304], [756]
  waste collection authority, emptying by,
    35(1), [756]

Privy Council
  appeals from Australia, **7(2)**, [777]
  appellate jurisdiction of, **14**, 558, 566
  chiropractors—
    default powers, **28**, [718]
    exercise of powers, **28**, [720]
    General Council rules, requirement for
      approval by, **28**, [719]
    members of General Council appointed
      by, **28**, [727], [729]
  clerk—
    absence of, **10**, [418]
    appointment of, **11(2)**, [58]
  committee, rules of, **10**, [460]
  dental matters—
    exercise of powers, **28**, [463]
    inadequacy of courses and examinations,
      powers as to remedying, **28**, [378]

Privy Council—*contd*
  dental matters—*contd*
    particular theories of dentistry, powers as
      regards, **28**, [379]
    rules, approval of, **28**, [461]
    supervision of instruction, directions as to,
      28, [376]
  Great Britain, one for, **10**, [75]
  judicial committee—
    admiralty court, appeal from, **11(2)**, [62]
    appeal—
      colonial court, from, **11(2)**, [57]
      continuing order, **11(2)**, [153]
      courts abroad, decrees on, **11(2)**, [30]
      Crown, to, before, **11(2)**, [15]
      manner of conducting, **11(2)**, [43]
      rules on, **11(2)**, [31]
        practice and procedure, **11(2)**, [50]
      special order of reference, without,
        11(2), [59]
      time for, **11(2)**, [29]
    appearance, compelling, **11(2)**, [44]
    clerk, appointment of, **11(2)**, [58]
    colonial court—
      evidence from, **11(2)**, [60]
      rules binding on, **11(2)**, [61]
    contempt, punishing, **11(2)**, [44], [62]
    costs, **11(2)**, [24], [48]
    Crown referring matters to, **11(2)**, [16]
    decrees—
      enforcing, **11(2)**, [32]
      enrolling, **11(2)**, [25]
    divisions, sitting in, **11(2)**, [166]
    ecclesiastical courts, appeal from,
      11(2), [41]–[51], [62]
    evidence, taking, **11(2)**, [20]
    formation of, **11(2)**, [14]
    generally, **11(2)**, [1]
    immunities and privileges, **11(2)**, [44]
    judge attending, **11(2)**, [19]
    judgment, enforcing, **11(2)**, [44]
    majority concurring in report, **11(2)**, [17]
    members—
      appointment of, **11(2)**, [14]
      colonial judges, **11(2)**, [143]
      Lord Justice of Appeal as, **11(2)**, [110]
      Lord of Appeal as, **11(2)**, [104]
      persons holding high judicial office,
        11(2), [120]
      resignation of, **11(2)**, [152]
    new trial, directing, **11(2)**, [23]
    quorum, **11(2)**, [18]
    registrar, referring matters to, **11(2)**, [26]
    rehearing, remitting case for, **11(2)**, [21]
    witness—
      examination of, **11(2)**, [21]
        oath, on, **11(2)**, [22]
        registrar, by, **11(2)**, [63]
      subpoena, compulsion by, **11(2)**, [28]
  Lord President, salary, **10**, [612]
  meaning, **41**, [605]
  medical matters—
    default powers, **28**, [342]
    examination standards, powers as to,
      28, [283]

Privy Council—*contd*
  medical matters—*contd*
    exercise of powers, **28**, [343], [344]
    instruments, proof of, **28**, [346]
    orders, proof of, **28**, [346]
    training, concerned with, **28**, [281], [283]
  members, eligibility, **10**, [50]
  oath, **10**, [433]
  opticians—
    default powers, **28**, [557]
    documents, **28**, [559]
    membership of General Council, power to
      alter, **28**, [564]
    quorum, **28**, [559]
  osteopaths—
    default powers, **28**, [672]
    exercise of powers, **28**, [674]
    rules of General Council, requirement for
      approval by, **28**, [673]
  pastoral scheme—
    appeal to, on, **14**, 977, 1082–4
    report on, **14**, 977
  Privy Seal—
    impressions of, **10**, [459]
    wafer, **10**, [459]
  public school statutes laid before, **15(1)**, [121]
  registrar—
    appointment of, **11(2)**, [27]
      president, by, **11(2)**, [64]
    witness, examining, **11(2)**, [63]
  Royal College of Veterinary Surgeons—
    appointments to Council of, **28**, [13]
    default powers as to Council of, **28**, [38]
    disciplinary committee, appeal from,
      28, [33]
    exercise of powers, **28**, [39]
  rules—
    engrossing, dispensing with, **10**, [460]
    prescription of documents, **10**, [460]
  Universities Committee—
    constitution of, **15(1)**, [147]
    powers and duties, **15(1)**, [147]
  Welsh Commissioners, appeal from,
    14, 265–6

prize
  Admiralty—
    as droits of, **11(2)**, [84]
    pre-emption, right of, **11(2)**, [83]
  aircraft—
    account required by customs and excise,
      11(2), [90]
    application of provisions, **11(2)**, [182],
      [187]
    custody, when taken as prize, **11(2)**, [76]
    customs duties, liability to, **11(2)**, [88]
    papers—
      bringing in, **11(2)**, [77]
      meaning, **11(2)**, [70]
    recapture from enemy, **11(2)**, [85]–[86]
  awarded abroad, relief from customs and
    excise duties on, **13**, [797]
  captors—
    offences by, **11(2)**, [82]
    proceedings by, **11(2)**, [76]

prize—*contd*
  capture—
    ally, in expedition with, **11(2)**, [81]
    land expedition, in, **11(2)**, [80]
    other than ship of war, **11(2)**, [84]
  cash balance, **3**, [1455]
  Channel Islands, extension of Acts to,
    11(2), [185], [189]
  Commonwealth, parts to which Acts extend,
    11(2), [185], [189]
  Courts. *See* **Prize Court**
  Crown—
    droits of, as, **34**, [1047]
    rights, savings for, **11(2)**, [94]
  customs—
    duties, liability to, **11(2)**, [88]
    regulations, observation of, **11(2)**, [89]
  droits of the Crown or Admiralty, **34**, [1047]
  foreign ship carrying stores to enemy,
    Admiralty rights, **11(2)**, [83]
  generally, **11(2)**, [1]
  goods—
    aircraft, account of goods taken in,
      11(2), [90]
    custody of, **11(2)**, [79]
    customs duty, liability to, **11(2)**, [88]
    meaning, **11(2)**, [70]
    sale of, remission of duty, **11(2)**, [91]
  Her Majesty's ships and aircraft, meanings,
    11(2), [70]
  illegal, restoration of, **12(1)**, [122]
  Isle of Man, extension of Acts to,
    11(2), [185], [189]
  land expedition, capture in, **11(2)**, [80]
  marshal, custody of ships and aircraft,
    11(2), [76]
  meaning, **11(2)**, [1]
  money—
    accrual after World War II, **34**, [1047]
    consolidated fund, transfer to, **3**, [105]
    distribution, **3**, [102]
    investment of, **3**, [109]
  offences, **3**, [480], [481], [753]–[754],
    [1037]–[1038]
    by captors, **11(2)**, [82]
  officers and crew, meaning, **11(2)**, [70]
  Orders in Council, **3**, [112]–[113]
    power to make, **11(2)**, [92]–[93]
  pre-emption, rights of Admiralty, **11(2)**, [83]
  proceedings, oath or affidavit for, **18**, [156]
  recapture of British ship, **11(2)**, [85]
  reservation for Crown, **11(2)**, [82]
  salvage—
    claims, restriction on, **11(2)**, [188]
    recapture from enemy, **11(2)**, [85]
    saving for, **13**, [39]
  salvage and bounty—
    Admiralty directing investment, **3**, [109]
    consolidated fund, transfer of balance to,
      3, [105]
    distribution, **3**, [102]
    Orders in Council, **3**, [112]–[113]
    shares, **3**, [103]
    stamp duty, exemption from, **3**, [104]
    taxation, **3**, [101]

prize—*contd*
  salvage and bounty—*contd*
    See also **salvage**
  shares, **3**, [103]
  ship—
    convoy, under, disobedience of master
      when, **11(2)**, [87]
    custody, when taken as prize, **11(2)**, [76]
    customs duty, liability to, **11(2)**, [88]
    land expedition, taken in, **11(2)**, [80]
    meaning, **11(2)**, [70]
    papers—
      bringing in, **11(2)**, [77]
      meaning, **11(2)**, [70]
    recaptured—
      proceeding on voyage, **11(2)**, [86]
      salvage on, **11(2)**, [85]
    small, several in one adjudication,
      11(2), [78]
  ship's agent—
    appointment of, **3**, [93], [114]
    commanding officer, effect of change of,
      3, [97]
    copies of account, furnished with, **3**, [106]
    disqualified persons, **3**, [95]
    duties of, **3**, [100]
    High Court of Admiralty, under, **3**, [99]
    office of, **3**, [98]
    partnership body as, **3**, [96]
    percentage of prize fund, **3**, [107]
    proctor, etc, acting as, **3**, [111]
    stamp duty, exemption from, **3**, [104]
    summary of provisions, **34**, [1047]
    taxation, **3**, [101]
  treaties, saving for operation of, **11(2)**, [94]
  trust territories, extension of Acts to,
    11(2), [185], [189]

prize competition. *See also* **amusements
with prizes; lottery**
  gambling, participation not being, **5(1)**, [619]
  payment to enter, definition, **5(1)**, [642]

Prize Court
  appeals—
    Her Majesty in Council, to, **11(2)**, [73]
    Judicial Committee of the Privy Council,
      to, **11(2)**, [74]
  British possessions, in, **11(2)**, [1], [140]
  captors, proceedings by, **11(2)**, [76]
  civil salvage services, claims for, **34**, [1047]
  Colonial Court of Admiralty, **11(2)**, [124]
    authorisation to act as, **11(2)**, [140], [184]
    fees, application of, **11(2)**, [141]
  commission, historical note on old form of,
    34, [1047]
  county court jurisdiction excluded,
    11(2), [917]
  decree of condemnation by, **34**, [1047]
  establishment outside dominions, **11(2)**, [183]
  fees, application of, **11(2)**, [141]
  generally, **11(2)**, [1]
  High Court of Admiralty—
    former jurisdiction, **11(2)**, [1]
    jurisdiction, **11(2)**, [72]

Prize Court—*contd*
  High Court of Admiralty—*contd*
    prize court, as, **11(2)**, [71]
    international law, judicial notice of,
      34, [1047]
  Judicial Committee of the Privy Council,
    appeal to, **11(2)**, [74]
  jurisdiction—
    generally, **11(2)**, [1], [71]
    land expedition, capture in, **11(2)**, [80]
  law administered by, **34**, [1047]
  municipal court, as, **34**, [1047]
  orders, enforcement in other courts,
    11(2), [163]
  precedents, binding nature of, **34**, [1047]
  procedure, **11(2)**, [1], [76]–[79], [155]
  proceedings, transfer of, **11(2)**, [162], [168]
  removal of subject matter of proceedings,
    11(2), [164]
  rules of court, **11(2)**, [141]
  status, **34**, [1047]
  summary of provisions, **34**, [1047]
  Vice-Admiralty—
    British possessions, in, **11(2)**, [140]
    costs, rules of court, **11(2)**, [141]
    establishment outside dominions,
      11(2), [183]
    judges and officers, appointment,
      11(2), [183]
    meaning, **11(2)**, [71]
    orders—
      enforcement, **11(2)**, [72]
      other courts, of, enforcement,
        11(2), [75]
    practice and procedure rules, **11(2)**, [142]
    rules of court, **11(2)**, [141]

probate. *See also* **administration of estates**
  action—
    compromise of, powers of High Court,
      18, [660]
    meaning, **18**, [660]
  administration without, **18**, [453]
  affidavit, taking of, **18**, [673]
  assets, title to, **18**, [491]
  British possessions, granted in, **18**, [508]
  colonial—
    Hong Kong, provisions applied, **18**, [506]
    provisions extended to protected states,
      18, [564]
    recognition of, **18**, [505]
    sealing in UK, **18**, [507]
  confirmation, payments made on, **18**, [479]
  disposal without—
    death, on, **18**, [573], [579]–[581]
    nomination, on, **18**, [574], [582]
  evidence of grant of, **8**, 246
  executor. *See* **executor**
  grant of—
    ancillary powers of court, **18**, [649], [650]
    applications for, **18**, [632]
      caveat against, **18**, [635]
      conflicting applications, **18**, [634]
      false or misleading statement in,
        18, [671]

probate—*contd*
  grant of—*contd*
    applications for—*contd*
      reference to High Court, **18**, [633]
    certificate of, **18**, [636]
    copy of, right to, **18**, [652]
    district registrar, by, **18**, [633]
    documents, delivery of, **18**, [637]
    evidence of, **18**, [590]
    foreign country, British court, in, **18**, [508]
    general procedure, **18**, [632]–[638]
    information to IR Commissioners,
      18, [637]
    limited, **18**, [640], [643]
    non-marital birth, provisions as to,
      18, [665]–[667]
    Northern Ireland, recognition in, **18**, [588]
    notices affecting land, service before filing
      of, **18**, [680]
    number of executors, to, **18**, [641]
    part of estate, for, **18**, [640]
    prior claims, passing over, **18**, [643]
    records of, **18**, [638]
    refusal of, where tax unpaid, **18**, [636]
    revocation of, **18**, [648]
      legal proceedings pending on, **18**, [521]
    Scotland, in, recognition in England,
      18, [587]
    Scottish, recognition of, **18**, [587], [588]
    seal, made under, **18**, [633]
    severance by court, **18**, [640]
    trust corporation, to, **18**, [642], [671]
    will annexed, with, **18**, [646]
  oaths, administration, **18**, [673]
  papers, preparation of, unqualified persons, by,
    bar on, **11(2)**, [302]
  payments on—
    indemnification, **18**, [479]
    protection for making, **18**, [538]
  power to increase amount, **18**, [576], [577]
  preparation of papers, **18**, [671],
    [672]. *See further* **probate services**
  protected states, granted in, **18**, [564]
  public trustee, grant to, **48**, 238–9
  refusal of grant where inheritance tax
    unpaid, **43(2)**, [510]
  registry—
    application for grant to, **18**, [632]
    caveat entered in, **18**, [635]
    conflicting applications to, **18**, [634]
    documents, depository for, **18**, [651]
    grants by, **18**, [635]
    records of grants in, **18**, [638]
  renunciation, summons to prove or
    renounce, **18**, [639]
  resealing, cancellation of, **18**, [648]
  rules as to, **18**, [654]
  services. *See* **probate services**
  small payments without representation—
    amount of, **18**, [573]
    disposal on, **18**, [579]–[581]
  trust corporation—
    executor, acting as, **18**, [642]
    grant to, **18**, [642], [671]
    meaning, **18**, [655]

probate—*contd*
  trust territories, granted in, **18**, [564]

probate services
  approved body—
    approval, **18**, [677]
    exemption from restrictions, grant of,
      18, [672]
    meaning, **18**, [672]
    qualifications for provision of services,
      18, [672]
  Consultative Panel, duty and role of,
    18, [677]
  President of the Family Division, advice by,
    18, [677]
  Secretary of State, approval of approved body
    by, **18**, [672], [677]
  unqualified persons, by, **18**, [671], –[672]

probation
  annual plans, **12(4)**, [327]
  approved premises, **12(4)**, [332]
  areas, local probation boards. *See* local boards
    below
  chief officers, transfer, **12(2)**, [988]
  eligible employees—
    meaning, **12(2)**, [985]
    transfer, **12(2)**, [986]
      effect of, **12(2)**, [987]
      scheme, **12(2)**, [989]
  employers, new and old, meaning,
    12(2), [985]
  grants, power to make, **12(4)**, [325]
  hostel or home, discontinuance of, **6**, [130]
  inspectorate—
    chief inspector, **12(2)**, [981]
    continuation of, **12(2)**, [981]
    co-operation, **12(2)**, [1011]
    delegation of functions, **12(2)**, [1011]
    functions, **12(2)**, [982]
    inspection programmes and frameworks,
      12(2), [1011]
    members, **12(2)**, [981]
    renamed, **12(4)**, [331]
  local boards—
    abolition, **12(4)**, [330]
    accounts, **12(2)**, [1010]
    ancillary powers, **12(2)**, [1010]
    annual plan, **12(2)**, [1010]
    areas, **12(2)**, [978]
    chairman's report, **12(2)**, [1010]
    complaints, **12(2)**, [1010]
    constitution, **12(2)**, [1010]
    default powers, **12(2)**, [984]
    delegation of functions, **12(2)**, [1010]
    directions to, **12(2)**, [1010]
    functions, **12(2)**, [979]
    implementation of arrangements by,
      12(2), [979]
    management order, **12(2)**, [984]
    payments to, **12(2)**, [1010]
    procedure, **12(2)**, [1010]
    property and staff, transfers of,
      12(4), [330], [348]
    remuneration, **12(2)**, [1010]

probation—*contd*
  local boards—*contd*
    reports, **12(2)**, [1010]
    secretary and treasurer, **12(2)**, [1010]
    service justice, and, **12(2)**, [980]
    staff, **12(2)**, [1010]
    status, **12(2)**, [1010]
    supervision, **12(2)**, [1010]
    support services, **12(2)**, [983]
    tenure of members, **12(2)**, [1010]
  National Probation Service. *See* **National Probation Service**
  offender management—
    disclosure for purposes of, **12(4)**, [333]
    national standards for, **12(4)**, [326]
  officer—
    abduction of child, report on, **6**, [201]
    custody of child, report on, **6**, [216]
    welfare of child, report on, **6**, [300]
  order—
    combined with driving offence
      conviction, **38(1)**, [55]
    renaming, **12(2)**, [991]
    Scotland, **12(2)**, [349]
      persons residing in England and Wales,
      12(2), [350]
    transfer to or from Northern Ireland,
    12(2), [123]
    See also **community rehabilitation order**
  purposes, meaning, **12(4)**, [320]
  rehabilitation. *See further* **rehabilitation of offenders**
  relevant duty of care, **12(4)**, [295]
  service—
    arrangements for provision of—
      power to make, **12(4)**, [322]
      restriction on, **12(4)**, [323], [334]
    National Probation Service. *See* **National Probation Service**
    officers of providers of—
      authorisation, **12(4)**, [328]
      meaning, **12(4)**, [328]
      qualifications, national framework for,
      12(4), [329]
    responsibility for ensuring provision of,
    12(4), [321]
    voluntary assistants, insurance of,
    25(2), [141]
  staff, transfer of, **12(2)**, [986]
  supervised release orders, **12(2)**, [348]
  trusts—
    accounts and records, **12(4)**, [347]
    annual plans, **12(4)**, [327]
    chief executive, **12(4)**, [347]
    directions, duty to comply with,
    12(4), [347]
    employees, **12(4)**, [347]
    general powers, **12(4)**, [347]
    membership, **12(4)**, [347]
    name and status, **12(4)**, [347]
    power to establish, **12(4)**, [324]
    proceedings and delegation, **12(4)**, [347]
  transitional and transitory provisions,
  12(4), [352]

proceeds of crime
  actions for recovery of property, time limits—
    external order, for purposes of,
    19(3), [756]
    unlawful conduct, obtained through,
    19(3), [755]
  Assets Recovery Agency. *See* **Assets Recovery Agency**
  bankruptcy—
    proceeds of crime, restriction of powers,
    12(3), [496]
    Northern Ireland, **12(3)**, [499]
    property excluded from estate, **12(3)**, [495]
    Northern Ireland, **12(3)**, [498]
    tainted gifts, **12(3)**, [497]
    Northern Ireland, **12(3)**, [500]
  benefit from, what constitutes, **12(3)**, [177]
  civil recovery—
    associated property, meaning, **12(3)**, [335]
    cash of. *See* recovery of cash in summary
      proceedings *below*
    compensation, **12(3)**, [386]
    financial threshold, **12(3)**, [392]
    general purpose of provisions, **12(3)**, [330]
    interim receiving order—
      application for, **12(3)**, [343]
      dealing with property, restrictions on,
      12(3), [349]
    interim receiver—
      functions of, **12(3)**, [344]
      powers of, **12(3)**, [542]
      supervision, **12(3)**, [348]
    proceedings and remedies, restriction
      on, **12(3)**, [350]
    property not recoverable, **12(3)**, [351]
    registration, **12(3)**, [345], [346]
    reporting, **12(3)**, [352]
    respondent, duties of, **12(3)**, [347]
    variation, **12(3)**, [348]
    interpretation, **12(3)**, [421]
    investigation. *See* investigations *below*
    property—
      associated, meaning, **12(3)**, [335]
      ceasing to be recoverable, **12(3)**, [414],
      [415]
      freezing order. *See* **freezing order**
      interests in, grant of, **12(3)**, [416]
      mixing, **12(3)**, [412]
      obtaining and disposing of, **12(3)**, [419]
      profits, accruing, **12(3)**, [413]
      tracing, **12(3)**, [411]
      unlawful conduct, obtained through,
      12(3), [332], [410]
    recovery orders—
      associated and joint property,
      12(3), [373]–[375]
      consent orders, **12(3)**, [379]
      insolvency, in case of, **12(3)**, [417]
      legal expenses, regulations, **12(3)**, [391]
      limit on recovery, **12(3)**, [381]
      making of, **12(3)**, [369]
      original property, recovery of,
      12(3), [382]
      pension schemes—
        consent orders, **12(3)**, [380]

proceeds of crime—*contd*
  civil recovery—*contd*
    recovery orders—*contd*
      pension schemes—*contd*
        consequential adjustments,
          12(3), [377]
        exercise of powers, **12(3)**, [378]
        references to, **12(3)**, [378]
        rights under, payments in respect of,
          12(3), [376]
      pre-emption rights, **12(3)**, [372]
      proceedings for—
        England and Wales, **12(3)**, [333]
        exemptions, **12(3)**, [385]
        Northern Ireland, **12(3)**, [333]
        Scotland, **12(3)**, [334]
      realised proceeds, application of,
        12(3), [383]
      vesting of property, **12(3)**, [369]
      victims of theft, claim by, **12(3)**, [384]
    trustee—
      functions of, **12(3)**, [370]
      payment of, **12(3)**, [387]
      powers of, **12(3)**, [543]
    unlawful conduct—
      meaning, **12(3)**, [331]
      property obtained through, **12(3)**, [332]
  compensation order—
    conditions for, **12(3)**, [233]
    serious default, on, **12(3)**, [233]
    variation or discharge, **12(3)**, [234]
  confiscation—
    absconding defendant—
      convicted or committed, **12(3)**, [196]
      discharge of order, **12(3)**, [199]
      not convicted or acquitted, **12(3)**, [197]
      variation of order, **12(3)**, [198]
    appeal—
      Court of Appeal, to, **12(3)**, [200], [201],
        [250]
      House of Lords, to, **12(3)**, [202], [251]
      powers of court, **12(3)**, [201]
      prosecutor, by, **12(3)**, [200]
    application of sums—
      designated officer, received by,
        12(3), [219]
      enforcement receiver, received by,
        12(3), [218]
    applications, **12(3)**, [247]
    benefit, reconsideration of, **12(3)**, [190]
    court, exercise of powers by, **12(3)**, [230]
    criminal conduct, **12(3)**, [237]
    criminal lifestyle—
      assumptions about, **12(3)**, [179]
      conditions, **12(3)**, [236]
      offences, **12(3)**, [540]
      statement of information, **12(3)**, [185]
    Crown Court Rules, **12(3)**, [252]
    defendant, provision of information by,
      12(3), [187]
    definition of terms used, **12(3)**, [249]
    investigation. *See* investigations *below*
    magistrates' court, committal by,
      12(3), [231]

proceeds of crime—*contd*
  confiscation—*contd*
    no order made—
      reconsideration of benefit, **12(3)**, [189]
      reconsideration of case, **12(3)**, [188]
    Northern Ireland. *See* **Northern Ireland**
    order. *See* confiscation order *below*
    postponement of proceedings, **12(3)**, [183]
      effect of, **12(3)**, [184]
    receiver. *See* receiver *below*
    restraint order. *See* restraint order *below*
    seized money, orders, **12(3)**, [228]
    statement of information—
      court, given to, **12(3)**, [185], [195]
      defendant's response to, **12(3)**, [186]
    tainted gifts, **12(3)**, [238]
      value of, **12(3)**, [242]
    value of property, **12(3)**, [240]
      conduct, obtained from, **12(3)**, [241]
  confiscation order—
    amount payable under—
      available, **12(3)**, [178]
        inadequacy of, **12(3)**, [192], [193]
        reconsideration of, **12(3)**, [191]
      recoverable, **12(3)**, [176]
    conditions, **12(3)**, [175]
    enforcement. *See* enforcement of orders
      below
    external—
      enforcement, **12(1)**, [1086]
      registration of, **12(1)**, [1087]
    magistrates' court, by, **12(4)**, [115]
    making of, **12(3)**, [175]
    other powers of court, effect on,
      12(3), [182]
    satisfaction of, **12(3)**, [248]
    Scotland. *See* **Scotland**
    small amount outstanding, discharge on,
      12(3), [194]
    time for payment, **12(3)**, [180]
    unpaid sums, interest on, **12(3)**, [181]
  criminal conduct, meaning, **12(3)**, [431]
  criminal property, meaning, **12(3)**, [431]
  Crown Court, sentencing by, **12(3)**, [232]
  Crown servants, application of provisions,
    12(3), [528]
  disclosure of information overseas,
    restrictions, **12(3)**, [517]
  enforcement of orders—
    abroad, **12(3)**, [235]
    designated countries, **12(1)**, [1086]
    external confiscation orders—
      meaning, **12(1)**, [1086]
      others, **12(1)**, [1086]
      registration of, **12(1)**, [1087]
    fines, as, **12(3)**, [203]
    imprisonment or detention, **12(3)**, [204]
    receivers. *See* receiver *below*
    reconsideration, variation of term on,
      12(3), [205]
  external requests and orders, **12(3)**, [519],
    [522]
  financial investigators—
    accreditation, **12(3)**, [174]
    applications and appeals by, **12(3)**, [229]

proceeds of crime—*contd*
  financial investigators—*contd*
    offences relating to, **12(3)**, [530]
    reference to, **12(3)**, [409], [529]
  floating charges, **12(3)**, [505]
  gifts, recipients of, **12(3)**, [239]
  inheritance tax functions—
    settlements, **12(3)**, [427]
    transfers of value, **12(3)**, [426]
  insolvency practitioner—
    meaning, **12(3)**, [508]
    seizure or disposal of property by,
      12(3), [507]
  investigations—
    account monitoring order—
      application for, **12(3)**, [481], [484]
      discharge or variation, application for,
        12(3), [486]
      disclosure of information, effect of
        restrictions on, **12(3)**, [485]
      meaning, **12(3)**, [481]
      power to make, **12(3)**, [481]
      practice and procedure, **12(3)**, [486]
      requirements for, **12(3)**, [482]
      statements made under, **12(3)**, [483]
    civil recovery—
      meaning, **12(3)**, [452]
      officers for purpose of, **12(3)**, [489]
      search and seizure warrants, **12(3)**, [467]
    code of practice, **12(3)**, [487], [488]
    confiscation—
      meaning, **12(3)**, [452]
      officers for purpose of, **12(3)**, [489]
      search and seizure warrants, **12(3)**, [466]
    courts, reference to, **12(3)**, [455]
    criminal conduct—
      benefit from, **12(3)**, [491]
      meaning, **12(3)**, [491]
    customer information order—
      application for, **12(3)**, [474], [480]
      customer information, meaning,
        12(3), [475]
      discharge or variation, application for,
        12(3), [480]
      disclosure of information, effect of
        restrictions on, **12(3)**, [479]
      failure to comply with, **12(3)**, [477]
      meaning, **12(3)**, [474]
      offences, **12(3)**, [477]
      power to make, **12(3)**, [474]
      practice and procedure, **12(3)**, [480]
      provision of information under,
        12(3), [474]
      requirements for, **12(3)**, [476]
      statements made under, **12(3)**, [478]
    disclosure order—
      application for, **12(3)**, [473]
      failure to comply with, **12(3)**, [470]
      meaning, **12(3)**, [468]
      offences, **12(3)**, [470]
      power to make, **12(3)**, [468]
      practice and procedure, **12(3)**, [473]
      privileged questions, information and
        material, **12(3)**, [472]
      requirements for, **12(3)**, [469]

proceeds of crime—*contd*
  investigations—*contd*
    disclosure order—*contd*
      statements made under, **12(3)**, [471]
    external, **12(3)**, [520]
    judges, reference to, **12(3)**, [454]
    money laundering—
      meaning, **12(3)**, [452]
      officers for purpose of, **12(3)**, [489]
      search and seizure warrants, **12(3)**, [466]
    officers for purpose of, **12(3)**, [489]
    prejudicing, offences of, **12(3)**, [453]
    production order—
      application for, **12(3)**, [462]
      computer, information on, **12(3)**, [460]
      discharge or variation, application for,
        12(3), [462]
      disclosure of information, restriction
        on, **12(3)**, [459]
      entry on premises, order for,
        12(3), [458]
      government departments, material in
        possession or control of, **12(3)**, [461]
      power to make, **12(3)**, [456]
      privileged material, **12(3)**, [459]
      requirements for, **12(3)**, [457]
      retention of material obtained,
        12(3), [459]
    property, meaning, **12(3)**, [492]
    search and seizure warrants—
      civil recovery investigation, **12(3)**, [467]
      confiscation investigation, **12(3)**, [466]
      detained cash investigation, **12(3)**, [467]
      excluded material, protection of,
        12(3), [465]
      meaning, **12(3)**, [463]
      money laundering investigation,
        12(3), [466]
      power to issue, **12(3)**, [463]
      privileged material, protection of,
        12(3), [465]
      production order not available, where,
        12(3), [464]
  limited liability partnership, winding up,
    12(3), [506]
  money laundering. *See* **money laundering**
  proceedings, institution and conclusion,
    12(3), [246]
  property—
    free, **12(3)**, [243]
    meaning, **12(3)**, [245]
  realisable property, meaning, **12(3)**, [244]
  receiver—
    appeals concerning—
      Court of Appeal, to, **12(3)**, [226]
      House of Lords, to, **12(3)**, [227]
    directions, application for, **12(3)**, [223]
    discharge and variation of orders,
      12(3), [224]
    enforcement—
      application of sums in hands of,
        12(3), [218]
      appointment, **12(3)**, [216]
      powers, exercise of, **12(3)**, [217]
      restrictions, **12(3)**, [221]

proceeds of crime—*contd*
  receiver—*contd*
    exercise of powers, **12(3)**, [230]
    management—
      appointment, **12(3)**, [214]
      discharge, **12(3)**, [225]
      powers, exercise of, **12(3)**, [215]
      protection of, **12(3)**, [222]
  reconsideration of case, **12(3)**, [188]
  recovery of cash in summary proceedings—
    cash, meaning, **12(3)**, [393]
    code of practice, **12(3)**, [396]
    compensation, **12(3)**, [406]
    exercise of powers, report on, **12(3)**, [395]
    forfeiture—
      appeal against, **12(3)**, [403]
      application on, **12(3)**, [404]
      power of, **12(3)**, [402]
      minimum amount, **12(3)**, [408]
      prior approval, **12(3)**, [394]
    prosecutors, appearance in proceedings,
      12(3), [407]
    searches, **12(3)**, [393]
    seizure—
      detention, **12(3)**, [399]
      interest on, **12(3)**, [400]
      power of, **12(3)**, [398]
      release, **12(3)**, [401]
    victims and other owners, claims by,
      12(3), [405]
  restraint order—
    appeals—
      Court of Appeal, to, **12(3)**, [209]
      House of Lords, to, **12(3)**, [210]
    application for, **12(3)**, [208]
    discharge or variation, **12(3)**, [208]
    exercise of powers, **12(3)**, [206]
    hearsay evidence, **12(3)**, [212]
    making of, **12(3)**, [207]
    registered land, **12(3)**, [213]
    restrictions on, **12(3)**, [220]
    seizure of property, **12(3)**, [211]
  Revenue functions—
    appeals, **12(3)**, [425]
    employment, concerning, **12(3)**, [423]
    exercise of, **12(3)**, [429]
    general, **12(3)**, [428]
    meaning, **12(3)**, [428]
    SOCA, of, **12(3)**, [422]
    source of income, inability to identify,
      12(3), [424]
  rules of court, **12(3)**, [521]
  Scotland. *See* **Scotland**
  sums unpaid, interest on, **12(3)**, [181]
  tax provisions, **12(3)**, [548], [549]
  United Kingdom, enforcement of provisions
    in different parts of, **12(3)**, [518]
  winding up—
    order for, **12(3)**, [501]
      Northern Ireland, **12(3)**, [503]
    powers, exercise of, **12(3)**, [501]
    tainted gifts, **12(3)**, [502]
      Northern Ireland, **12(3)**, [504]

process
  armed forces proceedings, relating to,
    3(S), 322
  England and Wales and Scotland, execution
    between, **12(3)**, [1028]
  execution in Scotland, **12(2)**, [830]
  overseas, service in United Kingdom,
    12(3), [562], −[563]
  United Kingdom, service abroad—
    general requirements, **12(3)**, [564]
    other than by post, **12(3)**, [565]
    Scottish citation—
      general requirements, **12(3)**, [568]
      other than by post, **12(3)**, [569]
    written charge or requisition—
      general requirements, **12(3)**, [566]
      other than by post, **12(3)**, [567]

procuration
  deed etc of, abolition of stamp duty,
    41, [152], [157]

product liability
  contributory negligence, **39(1)**, [602]
  Crown, of, **39(1)**, [605]
  damage giving rise to, **39(1)**, [601]
  defective product—
    defect, meaning, **39(1)**, [599]
    liability for, **39(1)**, [598]
  defences, **39(1)**, [600]
  Directive—
    compliance with, **39(1)**, [597]
    modifications, effect of, **39(1)**, [604]
    text of, **39(1)**, [642]
  enactments, application of, **39(1)**, [602]
  exclusion, prohibition on, **39(1)**, [603]
  information, supply of, **39(1)**, [634]
  safety, meaning, **39(1)**, [599]
  supplier, meaning, **39(1)**, [597]
  supply, meaning, **39(1)**, [633]
  tort, in, **39(1)**, [602]

profession
  irrecoverable debts, deduction for, **44(1)**, [66]
  loss relief. *See* **loss relief**
  permanent discontinuance, meaning,
    44(1), [88]
  post-discontinuance receipts, taxation of—
    allowable deductions, **44(1)**, [86]
    conventional basis, **44(1)**, [85]
    earnings basis, **44(1)**, [84]
    right to payment transferred, where,
      44(1), [87]
  profits—
    computation of, **43(1)**, [345]
    conventional basis, **44(1)**, [88]
    earnings basis, **44(1)**, [88]
  Schedule D Case II, charge under, **44(1)**, [13]
  work in progress—
    determination of questions, **44(1)**, [83]
    discontinuance, at, **44(1)**, [82]
    valuation of, **44(1)**, [82]

professional body
subscriptions to, exemption from value added tax on, **50**, [153]

professional premises. *See* **business premises**

professions complementary to dentistry
dental care professionals register—
certificates, **28**, [416]
directions, taking effect, **28**, [434]
erasure from—
deceased persons, **28**, [422]
directions, taking effect, **28**, [434]
fitness to practice grounds, on, **28**, [431]
fraud or error, on grounds of, **28**, [423]
persons ceasing to practice, **28**, [422]
fees, **28**, [420]
insurance, **28**, [426]
interim orders, **28**, [436]
keeping, **28**, [416]
lists, **28**, [416]
publication, **28**, [421]
registration—
appeals, **28**, [476]
conditional—
order for, **28**, [435]
recording, **28**, [438]
directions, taking effect, **28**, [434]
qualification for, **28**, [417]
visiting professionals from relevant European States, **28**, [443], [444]
restoration to, **28**, [432], [442]
rules for, **28**, [419]
suspension—
directions, taking effect, **28**, [434]
immediate, order for, **28**, [435]
recording, **28**, [438]
supplementary provisions, **28**, [437]
education and training, **28**, [418]
fitness to practice—
allegations relating to,
28, [428]–[430]. *See also* **General Dental Council**
appealable decisions, **28**, [433]
guidance, publication of, **28**, [427]
notification and disclosure by Council,
28, [440]
supplementary provisions, **28**, [437]
meaning, **28**, [415]
notifications, service of, **28**, [459]
proceedings before Committees, **28**, [477]
professional conduct, publication of guidance, **28**, [427]
professional training and development requirements, **28**, [441], [442]
regulatory body, **28**, [415]
titles and descriptions, use of, **28**, [425]
visiting professionals from relevant European States, **28**, [443], [444]

profit-related pay
registration, application for, **43(1)**, [424]
relief, phasing out, **43(1)**, [277]
transitional provisions, **43(1)**, [389]
windfall tax, and, **43(1)**, [310]

profit sharing scheme
alteration of, **44(1)**, [637]
appropriate percentage, reference to,
44(1), [641]
approval of, **44(1)**, [637]
approved—
charge to tax, **44(1)**, [107]
meaning, **44(1)**, [57]
phasing out, **43(1)**, [473]
trustees, payments to, **44(1)**, [57]
capital receipts, **44(1)**, [641]
company reconstruction, effect of,
44(1), [641]
contractual obligations of participants,
limitations on, **44(1)**, [641]
costs of establishing, **44(1)**, [56]
definitions, **44(1)**, [108]
excess shares, **44(1)**, [641]
material interest—
person having, **44(1)**, [108]
test, **44(1)**, [485]
PAYE, deduction of tax under, **44(1)**, [641]
payments to trustees of, phasing out of relief for, **43(1)**, [474]
qualifying corporate bonds, acceptance for shares, **43(1)**, [69]
release date, **43(1)**, [226]
requirements, **44(1)**, [638]–[639]
retention period, **44(1)**, [641]
scheme shares, trustees, **44(1)**, [639]
transitional provisions, **44(2)**, [772]
unauthorised shares, **44(1)**, [641]
workers' co-operative, in, **42**, [849]

profits
meaning, **42**, [1]

profits à prendre
general note, **20**, [1]
prescription period for claiming—
infant or other person under disability, in case of, **20**, [67]
interruption to, **20**, [63]
pleadings, **20**, [65]
presumption, restricting, **20**, [66]
sixty years, absolute right after, **20**, [61]
thirty years' enjoyment, **20**, [61]

profits tax
generally, **42**, [1]

prohibited place
approaching or entering, **12(1)**, [210]
meaning, **12(1)**, [211]
police or forces, interfering with near,
12(1), [231]

promenades
byelaws as to, **35(1)**, [73]

promissory note
Bank of England, issue by, **19(1)**, [11]
company, made, accepted or endorsed by,
8(1), [130]
company name in, **8**, 407

promissory note—*contd*

delivery necessary, **19(1)**, [117]

foreign note, **19(1)**, [116]

inland note, **19(1)**, [116]

joint and several, **19(1)**, [118]

liability of maker, **19(1)**, [121]

making, accepting or endorsing, **8**, 138

making etc, by industrial and provident
society, **19(1)**, [352]

meaning, **19(1)**, [116]

payable on demand, **19(1)**, [119]

presentment for payment, **19(1)**, [120]

provisions as to bill, application of,
19(1), [122]

property

adverse occupation, **12(1)**, [678]

business. *See* **property business**

deception, obtaining by, **12(2)**, [162]

destroying or damaging. *See* **criminal
damage**

disposition—

heir and heirs, construction of reference
to, **6**, [280]

meaning, **6**, [280]

relationship between persons, construction
of reference to, **6**, [280]

forcible detainer, **12(1)**, [684]

forcible entry, **12(1)**, [684]

former owner, charge to tax on benefits
received by, **43(S)**, 75–6, 559

aggregate notional values not exceeding
£5,000, exemption for, **43(2)**, [542]

chargeable person resident or domiciled
outside UK, **43(2)**, [542]

chattels, **43(2)**, [542]

connected persons, **43(2)**, [542]

definitions, **43(2)**, [542]

different provisions, persons chargeable
under, **43(2)**, [542]

distribution of estate, changes in,
43(2), [542]

excluded transactions, **43(2)**, [542]

exemption from, **43(2)**, [542]

guarantees, **43(2)**, [542]

inheritance tax provisions, election for
application of, **43(2)**, [542]

intangible property comprised in
settlement, **43(2)**, [542]

land, **43(2)**, [542]

other provisions, relationship with,
43(2), [542]

regulations, **43(2)**, [542]

exemption by, **43(2)**, [542]

valuation, **43(2)**, [542]

home information packs. *See* **home
information packs**

income. *See* **property income**

interest in, severance from, protection,
6, [280]

married woman, of. *See* **married woman**

meaning, **12(1)**, [556], [604]

offences, proceeds of, realisable etc. *See under*
offences

property—*contd*

possession against unauthorised occupiers,
obstruction of enforcement officers,
12(1), [681]

premises, meaning, **12(1)**, [682]

protected intending occupier, **12(1)**, [678],
[683]

purposes of crime, used for—

forfeited, application of proceeds of,
12(2), [822]

police, in possession of, **12(2)**, [821]

power to deprive offender of, **12(2)**, [820]

rental business, meaning, **43(S)**, 103

right to manage. *See* **right to manage**

tort in overseas country, **11(2)**, [824]

trespasser—

deriving title from, **12(1)**, [682]

displaced residential occupier, not being,
12(1), [682]

entering as, **12(1)**, [678]

premises of foreign missions, in,
12(1), [680]

weapon of offence, with, **12(1)**, [679]

valuation, power to inspect for, **42**, [251]

violence for securing entry, **12(1)**, [677]

property business

acquisition, treatment of receipts on,
44(3), [310]

energy-saving items, deductions for
expenditure on, **44(3)**, [312]

regulations, **44(3)**, [314]

restrictions on, **44(3)**, [313]

furnished holiday accommodation, UK
lettings business treated as trade, **44(4)**, [130]

furnished holiday lettings. *See* **furnished
holiday letting**

generating income from land—

activities not for, **44(3)**, [267]

meaning, **44(3)**, [266]

introduction to provisions, **44(3)**, [263]

lease premiums—

additional calculation rule, **44(3)**, [288]

circumstances in which applying,
44(3), [287]

restrictions on expenses,
44(3), [293]–[294]

special cases, **44(3)**, [289]

unreduced amount, meaning,
44(3), [290]

unused amount, meaning, **44(3)**, [290]

corporation tax receipts—

reductions in, **44(3)**, [297]–[298]

treatment of, **44(3)**, [299]

deductions—

expenses, for, **44(3)**, [291]

expenses, tenants treated as incurring,
44(3), [292]

limit on, **44(3)**, [295]

part of premises, lease of, **44(3)**, [294]

restrictions on expenses,
44(3), [293]–[294]

effective duration of lease—

determining, **44(3)**, [303]–[304]

information about, **44(3)**, [305]

property business—*contd*
  lease premiums—*contd*
    introduction to provisions, **44(3)**, [276]
    meaning, **44(3)**, [307]
    payment of tax by instalments, **44(3)**, [299]
    receipts, amounts treated as—
      calculation, **44(3)**, [277]
      profit of lease granted at undervalue,
        assignment for, **44(3)**, [282]–[283]
      sale and leaseback transactions,
        44(3), [285]–[286]
      sales with right to reconveyance,
        44(3), [284], [286]
      sums payable instead of rent,
        44(3), [279]
      surrender, sums payable for, **44(3)**, [280]
      variation or waiver of term, sums paid
        for, **44(3)**, [316]
      work required, where, **44(3)**, [278]
    reductions, limit on, **44(3)**, [295]
    rent, taking account of reductions for,
      44(3), [298]
    repayment of tax, claim for,
      44(3), [301]–[302]
    statement of accuracy, **44(3)**, [300]
    sums paid, presumption as to, **44(3)**, [306]
  losses from—
    corporation tax relief, **44(1)**, [194], [195]
    insurance company, of. *See* **insurance**
    company
    overseas, **44(1)**, [195]
  mineral royalties, relief for, **44(3)**, [319]
  mutual, **44(3)**, [321]
  overseas—
    adaptation of rules, **44(3)**, [363]
    meaning, **44(3)**, [265]
  post-cessation property relief—
    claim for, **44(4)**, [128]
    excess, treating as CGT loss, **44(4)**, [129]
  profits of—
    apportionment, **44(3)**, [275]
    calculation—
      amounts not brought into account,
        44(3), [273]
      deductions, rules prohibiting and
        allowing, **44(3)**, [274]
      trading income rules, application of,
        44(3), [272]
    charge to tax, **44(3)**, [268]
    income charged, **44(3)**, [270]
    person liable, **44(3)**, [271]
    territorial scope, **44(3)**, [269]
  furnished lettings, from, **44(3)**, [308]
  lease premiums. *See* lease premiums *above*
  rent-a-room relief, **44(3)**, [309]
  property loss relief—
    applicable amount of loss, meaning,
      44(4), [125]
    business has relevant agricultural
      connection, meaning, **44(4)**, [126]
    carry forward—
      deductions, how made, **44(4)**, [122]
      subsequent business profits, against,
        44(4), [121]
    claims for, **44(4)**, [123], [127]

property business—*contd*
  property loss relief—*contd*
    deductions, how made, **44(4)**, [124]
    interpretation of terms, **44(4)**, [125]–[126]
    loss having capital allowances connection,
      meaning, **44(4)**, [126]
  reverse premiums, treatment of, **44(3)**, [311]
  sale of estate or interest in land, item
    apportioned on, **44(3)**, [320]
  sea walls, deduction for expenditure on,
    44(3), [315]
    company, transfer involving, **44(3)**, [318]
    interest in premises, transfer of,
      44(3), [316]
    lease of premises, ending, **44(3)**, [317]
  UK, meaning, **44(3)**, [264]

property income
  adjustment income—
    application of provisions, **44(3)**, [329]
    expense—
      meaning, **44(3)**, [330]
      treatment of, **44(3)**, [334]
    income charged, **44(3)**, [331]
    meaning, **44(3)**, [330]
    person liable, **44(3)**, [332]
    treatment of, **44(3)**, [333]
  company starting or ceasing to be within
    charge, **44(3)**, [362]
  furnished holiday lettings. *See* **furnished**
  holiday letting
  lease, meaning, **44(3)**, [364]
  lease premiums—
    break clause, lease with, **43(S)**, 1401–3
    living accommodation, taxable benefit of,
      43(S), 1400–3
  overseas—
    charge to tax, **44(3)**, [357]
    income charged, **44(3)**, [359]
    meaning, **44(3)**, [358]
    person liable, **44(3)**, [360]
  overseas land, adaptation of rules, **44(3)**, [363]
  overview of provisions, **44(3)**, [260]
  partnership, of, **44(3)**, [876]
  personal representatives, changes in,
    44(3), [361]
  post-cessation receipts—
    amounts counting as, **44(3)**, [354]
    charge to tax, **44(3)**, [349]
    extent of charge, **44(3)**, [350]
    income charged, **44(3)**, [351]
    meaning, **44(3)**, [353]
    persons liable, **44(3)**, [352]
    Schedule A business, application to,
      44(3), [356]
    transfer of rights if transferee not carrying
      on UK property business, **44(3)**, [355]
  premises, meaning, **44(3)**, [364]
  priority of provisions, **44(3)**, [261]–[262]
  property business, from. *See* **property**
  business
  rent. *See* **rent**
  transitional provisions, **44(3)**, [906]
  trustees, changes in, **44(3)**, [361]

property insurance
summary of provisions, **19(1)**, [1]

property misdescription
conveyancing services, meaning, **23**, [60]
due diligence defence, **23**, [61]
enforcement authority, **23**, [67]
enforcement officers, **23**, [67]
enforcement provisions, **23**, [62]
false, meaning, **23**, [60]
financial provision, **23**, [65]
offence of—
    bodies corporate, by, **23**, [63]
    generally, **23**, [60]
    prosecution time limit, **23**, [64]
    Scottish partnership, by, **23**, [63]
privilege against self-incrimination, **23**, [67]

Property Services Agency
scheme for transfer of—
    agreements and transactions, construction
      of, **10**, [703]
    certificate of vesting, **10**, [703]
    making, **10**, [697]
    stamp duty exemption, **10**, [703]
staff, transfer of, **10**, [698]
transferee companies, **10**, [699]

prosecution
consents to, **12(1)**, [960], [961]
criminal, instituting, **12(1)**, [937]
Crown. *See* **Crown Prosecution Service**
witnesses, costs and expenses, **12(1)**, [944],
    [949]

prospectus. *See also* **securities**
additional matters included in, **8**, 156
directors, particulars to be given, **8**, 613
mandatory contents, **8**, 613
matters to be stated in, **8**, 613
meaning, **8**, 603
offer of shares to the public—
    deemed to be prospectus, **8**, 156
    exceptions from rule, **8**, 157
    rule governing, **8**, 156
oversea company. *See* **oversea company**
transparency—
    competent authority, power of to call for
      information, **8(1)**, [1345]
    consequential amendments, **8(1)**, [1405]
    corporate governance rules, **8(1)**, [1347]
    false or misleading statements, liability for,
      8(1), [1348]
    infringement of obligation, powers in case
      of, **8(1)**, [1346]
    obligations Directive, **8(1)**, [1343]
    rules, **8(1)**, [1344]
    UK as host member state, exercise of
      powers, **8(1)**, [1349]
unlisted securities, for. *See* **unlisted
securities**

prostitute
brothel, in. *See* **brothel**
living on earnings of, punishment,
    12(1), [308]
loitering for prostitution—
    caution, application to Court on,
      12(1), [307]
    offence, **12(1)**, [306]
premises, tenant permitting use for
    prostitution—
    offence, **12(1)**, [287]
    prosecution and punishment, **12(1)**, [297]
soliciting—
    caution, application to Court on,
      12(1), [307]
    offence, **12(1)**, [306]

prostitution
abuse of child through—
    arranging or facilitating, **12(3)**, [712]
    causing or inciting, **12(3)**, [710]
    controlling, **12(3)**, [711]
    interpretation, **12(3)**, [713]
    sexual services, paying for, **12(3)**, [709]
advertisement relating to, placing, **12(3)**, [28],
    [29]
brothel. *See* **brothel**
causing or inciting for gain, **12(3)**, [714]
controlling for gain, **12(3)**, [715]
gain, meaning, **12(3)**, [716]

protected long tenancy
agreements excluding provisions, **21**, [169]
assessors, summoning of, **21**, [224]
continuation of—
    interim, **21**, [225]
    terms of, **21**, [156]
county court jurisdiction, **21**, [224]
covenants—
    enforcement, relief against, **21**, [168]
    tenant's liability, **21**, [163]
Crown, application of provisions to, **21**, [218]
deemed date of expiry, **21**, [336]
future questions, assumptions on which
    determined, **21**, [172]
information, tenant's duty to give, **21**, [170]
landlord—
    competent, **21**, [239]
    meaning, **21**, [173]
    mesne, **21**, [239]
    superior, **21**, [239]
    termination by, **21**, [157]
long tenancy—
    low rent, at—
      determining, **21**, [155]
      whether protected, **21**, [631]
    meaning, **21**, [155]
    tenancy granted in continuation, provisions
      applying to, **21**, [171], [238]
mortgagee in possession, provisions as to,
    21, [228]
notice—
    form of, **21**, [227]

protected long tenancy—*contd*
notice—*contd*
possession, for. *See* possession *below*
statutory tenancy, proposing. *See* statutory
tenancy following *below*
termination, of—
landlord, by, **21**, [157]
tenant, by, **21**, [158]
possession—
application for, **21**, [165]
election by tenant to retain, **21**, [156]
misrepresentation, obtained by, **21**, [167],
[197]
notice to resume—
meaning, **21**, [157]
service, proceedings after, **21**, [165]
withdrawal of, **21**, [166]
order—
application for, **21**, [165]
court, made by, **21**, [165]
grounds for, **21**, [164], [237]
not made, provisions where, **21**, [166]
postponed date, after, **21**, [165]
redevelopment, for, **21**, [164], [337]
premises qualifying for protection, **21**, [156]
premium for, **21**, [619]
regulated tenancy arising from, rent under,
21, [348]
relevant premises, meaning, **21**, [164]
Rent Acts, application of, **21**, [154], [338]
reversions, provisions as to, **21**, [226]
security of tenure—
entitlement to, **21**, [154]
qualifying condition, **21**, [155]
Rent Acts, protection of, **21**, [154], [338]
separate dwelling, property let as, **21**, [174]
statutory tenancy following—
act or default occurring before, effect of,
21, [163]
covenants in former lease, principles as to,
21, [163]
landlord's notice proposing—
effect, ceasing to have, **21**, [160]
notice to resume possession, following,
21, [164]
proposals, meaning, **21**, [160]
termination by, **21**, [157]
period of, **21**, [160]
Rent Act, application of, **21**, [159]
repairs—
initial, **21**, [161]
expenses, recovery of, **21**, [236]
failure to carry out, **21**, [235], [239]
matters to be agreed on, **21**, [161]
meaning, **21**, [230]
obligations, agreement on, **21**, [161]
principles to be observed, **21**, [162]
record of state of, **21**, [236]
tenant's accrued, **21**, [161]
agreement or determination, variation
of, **21**, [234]
failure to pay for, **21**, [235]
instalments, payment by, **21**, [233]
lump sum payment for, **21**, [232]
repayment of sums for, **21**, [235]

protected long tenancy—*contd*
statutory tenancy following—*contd*
terms—
courts, determination by, **21**, [160]
repairs, principles as to, **21**, [162]
settlement of, **21**, [160]
sub-tenant, protection for, **21**, [170]
superior lease, tenants' covenants in, **21**, [239]
surrender of, **21**, [169]
tenancy—
meaning, **21**, [174]
periodical, application of provisions to,
21, [171], [238]
superior, determination of duration of,
21, [173]
tenancy at low rent, meaning, **21**, [155]
tenant—
covenants in former lease, liability for,
21, [163], [239]
election to retain possession by, **21**, [157]
information, duty to give, **21**, [170]
meaning, **21**, [174]
termination by, **21**, [158]
term date, meaning, **21**, [155]
termination of—
date of, **21**, [158]
landlord, by, **21**, [157]
postponed date of, **21**, [165]
tenant, by, **21**, [158]
transitional provisions, **21**, [242], [348]

protected persons
attacks on, **10**, [1036]
attempt to commit offences,
10, [1036]–[1037]
meaning, **10**, [1036]
proceedings, **10**, [1037]
threats of attack on, **10**, [1036]

protected shorthold tenancy
assignment of, **21**, [725]
conditions for, **21**, [723]
meaning, **21**, [723]; **22**, [827]
possession—
order for, **21**, [652], [726]
proceedings, **21**, [652]
subletting, on, **21**, [725]
tenant, right to terminate by, **21**, [724]
term certain, for, **21**, [723]

protected state
probate granted in, **18**, [564]

protected streets
apparatus, placing in, **38(1)**, [195]
designation as—
criteria for, **38(1)**, [196]
powers, **38(1)**, [195]
special road as, **38(1)**, [195]
street works in, **38(1)**, [195]
traffic-sensitive, designation as, **38(1)**, [198]

protected tenancy
advance payment of rent, avoidance of
requirement for, **21**, [618]

protected tenancy—*contd*
assured tenancy, not being, **22**, [913]
distress for rent, restriction on, **21**, [632]
dwelling-house let as a separate dwelling as,
   21, [520]
excepted tenancies—
   agricultural holdings, **21**, [530]
   assured tenancy, **21**, [537]
   board or attendance, rent including
      payments for, **21**, [527]
   Crown interest, where, **21**, [533]
   holiday lettings, **21**, [529]
   housing association, etc, tenancy, **21**, [535]
   housing co-operative tenancy, **21**, [536]
   licensed premises, **21**, [531]
   local authority interest, where, **21**, [534]
   low rent, let at, **21**, [524]
   other land, dwelling-house let with,
      21, [526]
   rateable value, limit on, **21**, [523]
   resident landlord, where, **21**, [532], [644]
   shared ownership, **21**, [525]
   students, lettings to, **21**, [528]
furnished—
   meaning, **21**, [637]
   sub-tenancy, effect of possession order on,
      21, [626]
   transitional provisions, **21**, [660]
furniture, excessive price for—
   attempt to obtain, punishment of, **21**, [616]
   premium, treated as, **21**, [615]
landlord, reasonable access implied for,
   21, [633]
loan as condition of grant, etc, **21**, [617]
meaning, **21**, [520]
phasing out, **22**, [827]
possession, grounds for. *See* **possession,
  order for**
premium for—
   assignment, as condition for, **21**, [612]
   excessive price for furniture treated as,
      21, [615], [616]
   prohibition of, **21**, [611]
   recovery of, **21**, [617]
rateable values, limit on, **21**, [523]
rent. *See* **rent**
shared accommodation, **21**, [543]
statutory tenancy following, **21**, [521]
sub-tenancy, effect of possession order on,
   21, [625]
subletting—
   effect of, **21**, [544]
   landlord, duty to notify, **21**, [627]
tenancies becoming, **21**, [645]
transitional provisions, **21**, [766]

protected tenant
improvements, making—
   consent for, **21**, [741]–[743]
   county court jurisdiction, **21**, [746]
   meaning, **21**, [741]
   procedure, rules of, **21**, [746]

provident society. *See also* **industrial and
provident society**
periodical statements—
   duty to publish, **8**, 584
   form of, **8**, 794–5

provincial tribunal (ecclesiastical)
constitution of, **14**, 888, 901–2
members of, **14**, 901
objection to member, **14**, 901
pastoral situation, enquiry into—
   bishop, report to, **14**, 890
   enquiries conducted by, **14**, 886
   parochial church council, notifying,
      14, 889
   representation before, **14**, 888
procedure of, **14**, 888

provisional licences. *See under* **driving
licences**

proxies. *See also* **election**
appointment, **8**, 84, 428
audience, right of, **8**, 428
companies clauses. *See* **Companies
  Clauses Acts**
form of, **8**, 68
papers, form of, **8**, 84
poll, right to demand, **8**, 429
power to appoint, **8**, 428
revocation of, **8**, 84
shareholders, deemed to be, **8**, 83
voting by, **8**, 42

Public Accounts Commission
chairman, **19(2)**, [986]
establishment of, **19(2)**, [975]
members of—
   persons being, **19(2)**, [975]
   tenure of office, **19(2)**, [986]
proceedings and business of, **19(2)**, [986]
report, presenting, **19(2)**, [975]

public amenities
summary of provisions, **35(1)**, [1]

public analyst
acting in good faith, protection of, **1(2)**, [458]
analysis by, **1(2)**, [444]
   meaning, **1(2)**, [466]
   regulation of, **1(2)**, [445]
appointment, **1(2)**, [441]
certificates, issue of, **1(2)**, [444]
fees, payment in advance, **1(2)**, [444]
food analyst, meaning, **1(2)**, [444]
qualification, **1(2)**, [441]
remuneration, **1(2)**, [441]
samples, analysis of, **1(2)**, [444]

public assembly
conditions imposed on, **12(1)**, [1005]
meaning, **12(1)**, [1010]
offences and penalties, **12(1)**, [1005]
police powers, **12(1)**, [1005]
   delegation of, **12(1)**, [1009]

public authority

access to information held by, exempt
information, communications with Her
Majesty and honours, **7(1)**, [638]
civil proceedings, disclosure of competition
information in relation to, **8(1)**, [1357]
information held by, access to. *See* **freedom
of information**
meaning, **7(1)**, [149], [796]
racial discrimination by—
  decision not to prosecute, exception for,
  7(1), [153]
  generally, **7(1)**, [149]
  immigration and nationality cases,
  exception for, **7(1)**, [151], [152]
  judicial and legislative acts, exceptions for,
  7(1), [150]
religion or belief, discrimination on grounds
of, **7(1)**, [796]

public bathing

bathing huts, etc, provision by local
authority, **35(1)**, [158]
byelaws as to, **35(1)**, [157], [159], [380]

public baths. *See* washhouses

public benefit corporation

accounts, **30**, [1098]
annual reports, **30**, [1098]
auditor, **30**, [1098]
board of governors, **30**, [1098]
constitution, requirement for, **30**, [1098]
directors, **30**, [1098]
forward plans, **30**, [1098]
initial directors of former NHS trusts,
30, [1098]
membership, eligibility for, **30**, [1098]
NHS foundation trust as, **30**, [836]
register of members, **30**, [1098]

public bill committee

standing Committee, alteration of references
to, **43(S)**, 591

public bodies

accounts regulations, **26(1)**, [344]
area alterations etc affecting, **25(2)**, [58]
audit—
  accounts of officers, of, **26(1)**, [343]
  agreed, **26(1)**, [346]
  bodies subject to, **26(1)**, [383]
  code of practice, **26(1)**, [321]
  extraordinary, **26(1)**, [342]
  fees, **26(1)**, [324]
  inspection of documents, **26(1)**, [334]
  item of account unlawful, declaration of,
  26(1), [336]
  objections, right to make, **26(1)**, [335]
  questions at, **26(1)**, [334]
  regulations, **26(1)**, [344]
  required, **26(1)**, [319]

public bodies—*contd*

auditors—
  advisory notices—
    disposal or acquisition of interest in land,
    effect of contract for, **26(1)**, [340]
    effect of, **26(1)**, [339]
    issue of, **26(1)**, [338]
    meaning, **26(1)**, [338]
  appointment, **26(1)**, [320]
  documents and information, right to,
  26(1), [323]
  general duties of, **26(1)**, [322]
  health service bodies, referral to Secretary
  of State, **26(1)**, [337]
  judicial review, power to apply for,
  26(1), [341]
  meaning, **26(1)**, [379]
  qualifications, **26(1)**, [320]
  reports—
    consideration of, **26(1)**, [328]
    general, **26(1)**, [326]
    inspection of, **26(1)**, [333]
    public interest, in, **26(1)**, [325]
    publicity, **26(1)**, [331], [332]
    transmission and consideration of,
    26(1), [327]
bodies deemed to be, **25(1)**, [628]
contracts etc. *See under* **local authority**
corruption in. *See* **office**
goods and services—
  forms of, **25(1)**, [971]
  provision by local authorities, **25(1)**, [971]
land held by—
  areas in which provisions operate,
  25(2), [432]
  bodies to whom provisions apply,
  25(2), [431]
  direction to dispose of, **25(2)**, [437], [438]
  entry on, powers of, **25(2)**, [439]
  information, Minister's power to require,
  25(2), [436]
  public access to information, **25(2)**, [434]
  registration of holdings, **25(2)**, [433]–[435]
  under-used, register of, **25(2)**, [433]
meaning, **12(1)**, [182]; **12(2)**, [295];
25(1), [971]; **25(2)**, [216], [229]
meetings, admission of public to, **25(1)**, [625]
statements of accounts, inspection of,
26(1), [333]
transfer of powers of, **25(2)**, [216]

public building

obstructions near, **36**, [224]

public charitable collection

certificate—
  appeals against decisions, **5(2)**, [732]
  application for, **5(2)**, [726]
  determination of applications, **5(2)**, [727]
  information and documents, power to call
  for, **5(2)**, [729]
  inquiries, **5(2)**, [727]
  issue of, **5(2)**, [727]
  refusal, grounds for, **5(2)**, [728]

public charitable collection—*contd*
certificate—*contd*
trustees of unincorporated charity, transfer
between, **5(2)**, [730]
withdrawal or variation, **5(2)**, [731]
charitable collections not being, **5(2)**, [721]
door to door, restrictions on, **5(2)**, [724]
interpretation, **5(2)**, [722]
local, short-term, **5(2)**, [725]
meaning, **5(2)**, [720]
offences, **5(2)**, [739]
body corporate, by, **5(2)**, [740]
permits—
appeals against decisions, **5(2)**, [737]
application for, **5(2)**, [733]
determination of applications, **5(2)**, [734]
issue of, **5(2)**, [734]
refusal, grounds for, **5(2)**, [735]
withdrawal or variation, **5(2)**, [736]
public place, restrictions on conducting in,
5(2), [723]
regulation of, **5(2)**, [720]
regulations, **5(2)**, [738]
service of documents, **5(2)**, [741]

public clocks
provision, etc of, **35(1)**, [25]

public conveniences. *See also* **sanitary
conveniences**
acquisition of land for, **36**, [1286]
byelaws as to, **36**, [1133]
delegation of management, **36**, [1132]
land adjoining highway, on, **36**, [1133]
lorry area, in, **36**, [1134]
picnic site, at, **36**, [1131]
provision of, **36**, [210], [1133]

public conveyance
notifiable disease—
disinfection, **35(1)**, [475]
owner, etc, duty of, **35(1)**, [475]
use by person with, **35(1)**, [474]

public departments
application of provisions to, **43(1)**, [22]

public duties
time off for performance of—
amount of, **16**, [674]
employment tribunal, complaint to,
16, [675]
right to, **16**, [674]

public entertainment. *See* **entertainment**

public exhibition. *See* **exhibition**

public expenditure and receipts
fees, increase of, **19(2)**, [877], [879]

public funds
notice of payments from, **42**, [124]

public gas supplier. *See* **gas**

Public Guardian
annual report, **29**, [291]
appointment, **29**, [28]
functions of, **29**, [289]
office of, **29**, [288]
salary, **29**, [288]
summary of provisions, **29**, [1]

Public Guardian Board
duty of, **29**, [290]
establishment of, **29**, [290]
members, appointment, **29**, [290]

public health. *See also appropriate subject matters*
amended provisions,
35(S), Public Health 33–40
bodies corporate, offences by,
35(S), Public Health 36
default powers, **35(S)**, Public Health 38
electronic communications,
35(S), Public Health 35
health measures, order for—
affected persons, **35(S)**, Public Health 19
directions in, **35(S)**, Public Health 17
duration of, **35(S)**, Public Health 18
emergency procedure,
35(S), Public Health 23–4
enforcement, **35(S)**, Public Health 21
interpretation, **35(S)**, Public Health 25
power to make—
groups, in relation to,
35(S), Public Health 16
persons, in relation to,
35(S), Public Health 10–11
premises, in relation to,
35(S), Public Health 14–15
things, in relation to,
35(S), Public Health 12–13
procedure for, **35(S)**, Public Health 18
regulations, **35(S)**, Public Health 19, 22–3
revocation, **35(S)**, Public Health 18–19
scope of, **35(S)**, Public Health 17
territorial sea, application to,
35(S), Public Health 24
variation of, **35(S)**, Public Health 18–19
health protection regulations—
appeal against decisions,
35(S), Public Health 9
domestic, **35(S)**, Public Health 6
functions conferred by,
35(S), Public Health 9
international travel, prevention of danger
from, **35(S)**, Public Health 5
medical treatment, not to require,
35(S), Public Health 8
restrictions on power to make,
35(S), Public Health 8
scope of, **35(S)**, Public Health 9
infection or contamination, protection
against, **35(S)**, Public Health 4
London—
Crown property, provisions applied,
25(1), [252]

public health—*contd*
London—*contd*
dustbins. *See* **refuse**
general application of Acts, **25(1)**, [702]
inspectors, **25(1)**, [703]
medical officers of health, **25(1)**, [703]
modification and re-enactment of Acts,
25(1), [733], [734]
refuse. *See* **refuse**
stagnant water drainage, **25(1)**, [734]
new town, district of, **46**, [165]
notices—
authentication, **35(1)**, [178]
execution of works, requiring—
appeal against, **35(1)**, [183]
enforcement of, **35(1)**, [183]
form of, regulations as to, **35(1)**, [177]
offences—
continuing, **35(1)**, [188], [636]
prosecution of, **35(1)**, [187], [635]
summary proceedings for, **35(1)**, [30],
[187], [190]
printed, **35(1)**, [33]
service, **35(1)**, [34], [179]
writing, in, **35(1)**, [33], [177]
offences—
body corporate, by, **35(2)**, [578]
partnerships, by, **35(2)**, [579]
unincorporated associations, by,
35(2), [579]
orders and regulations, **35(2)**, [580]
personal liability, protection of health
protection agency, **35(S)**, Public Health 38
prosecutions, time limits for,
35(S), Public Health 37
special Act—
copies of, **35(1)**, [9]
incorporation of Acts with, **35(1)**, [2], [8],
[11]
interpretation of terms, **35(1)**, [4], [12],
[13]
meaning, **35(1)**, [3], [12]
unincorporated associations, offences by,
35(S), Public Health 37
urban development area, in, **46**, [79]
wilful obstruction, **35(S)**, Public Health 36
works, execution—
expenses, recovery of, **35(1)**, [184], [185]
local authority, by, **35(1)**, [620]
notice requiring—
appeal against, **35(1)**, [183], [625]
local authority to give effect to,
35(1), [627]
procedure on, **35(1)**, [626]
content and enforcement, **35(1)**, [622]
owner, by, order on occupier to permit,
35(1), [182]
permission of occupier for, power to
require, **35(1)**, [621]
sale of materials, **35(1)**, [623]
streets, breaking open, **35(1)**, [624]

Public Health Laboratory Service Board
abolition of, **30**, [751]

public house. *See also* **innkeeper; intoxicating
liquor (licensed premises)**
application of provisions, **5(1)**, [558]
covenants against use of premises as,
19(3), [351]
exempt gaming in, **5(1)**, [559]–[560]
exemption, removal of, **5(1)**, [564]
gaming machines in, **5(1)**, [562]
exemption, removal of, **5(1)**, [564]
permits—
appeals, **5(1)**, [663]
application for, **5(1)**, [663]
cancellation and forfeiture, **5(1)**, [663]
form of, **5(1)**, [663]
maintenance, **5(1)**, [663]
register of, **5(1)**, [663]
transfer, **5(1)**, [663]
variation, **5(1)**, [663]
high turnover bingo in, **5(1)**, [561]
licensed premises gaming machine permit,
5(1), [563]
Scotland, provision for, **5(1)**, [565]

public lavatories
sexual activity in, **12(3)**, [735]
turnstiles in, abolition of, **35(1)**, [281]

public lending right
annual report to Parliament, **13**, [241]
assignment of, **13**, [239]
books subject to, **13**, [239]
Central Fund—
constitution, **13**, [240]
control and management, **13**, [240]
payments from, **13**, [239], [240]
payments into, **13**, [240]
Registrar—
administrative expenses, **13**, [240]
staff remuneration, etc, payment from,
13, [244]
duration, **13**, [239]
establishment, **13**, [239]
library authorities—
expenditure incurred by, reimbursement,
13, [241]
information required from, **13**, [241]
library, meaning, **13**, [241]
meaning, **13**, [243]
payments to author—
recovery of, **13**, [239]
scales, determination, **13**, [239]
register—
entry in and removal from, **13**, [242]
establishment and maintenance, **13**, [239]
form and contents, **13**, [242]
Registrar—
accounts and audit, **13**, [240]
administrative expenses, **13**, [241]
appointment, **13**, [239]
assistant, **13**, [244]
compensation for loss of office, **13**, [244]
duty of, **13**, [239]
incorporation, **13**, [244]
payments, duty as to, **13**, [239]
remuneration and allowances, **13**, [244]

public lending right—*contd*
  Registrar—*contd*
    staff, **13**, [244]
    status and term of office, **13**, [244]
    tenure, **13**, [244]
  renouncement of, **13**, [239]
  scales of payment, determining, **13**, [239]
  scheme—
    contents, **13**, [241]
    draft, preparation, **13**, [241]
    duty to prepare, **13**, [239]
    provision to be made in, **13**, [239]
    variation, **13**, [241]
  summary of provisions, **13**, [49]

public library. *See also* **libraries**
  Advisory Councils, **13**, [143]
  annual report by Secretary of State, **13**, [157]
  areas, library regions, **13**, [144]
  assets and liabilities—
    meaning, **13**, [162]
    transfer, **13**, [151]
  byelaws, **13**, [158]
  catalogues and indexes, grants to bodies maintaining, **13**, [149]
  charges, **13**, [148]; **25(2)**, [889]
  contributions and grants, **13**, [149]
  default powers of Secretary of State, **13**, [150]
  facilities—
    provision, **13**, [147]
    restriction on charges for, **13**, [148]
  infected books, use of, **13**, [49]
  inspection, **13**, [142]
  inter-library co-operation, **13**, [144]
  Isles of Scilly, application to, **13**, [161]
  joint boards—
    default, on, **13**, [150]
    dissolution, **13**, [146]
    formation, **13**, [146]
  lending right. *See* **public lending right**
  library authorities—
    authorities being, **13**, [204]
    British Library Board, contribution towards expenses, **13**, [196]
    contribution to expenses of another, **13**, [149]
    failure to carry out duties, **13**, [150]
    functions, area of exercise, **13**, [145]
    information and inspection, requirements, **13**, [142]
    joint boards, formation, **13**, [146]
    loan of objects by, indemnity against loss or damage, **13**, [253], [254]
    meaning, **13**, [162]
    provision of services, duty as to, **13**, [147]
    transfer of officers, assets and liabilities, **13**, [151]
  library regions, designation, **13**, [144]
  local Acts, maintained under, **13**, [160]
  local inquiry, order by Secretary of State, **13**, [150], [156]
  London—
    articles provided in, **25(1)**, [577]
    return of books, **25(1)**, [509]
  National Advisory Councils, **13**, [143]

public library—*contd*
  officers—
    meaning, **13**, [162]
    transfer of, **13**, [151], [164]
  premises, use for educational or cultural events, **13**, [159]
  regional councils, **13**, [144]
  service—
    comprehensive and efficient, duty to provide, **13**, [49], [147]
    secretary of State, superintendence by, **13**, [142]
  summary of provisions, **13**, [49]
  transfer of functions, order for, **13**, [150]

public meeting
  endeavouring to break up, **12(1)**, [192]

public office
  corruption in. *See* **office**
  fees payable in, collection of—
    alteration of, **19(2)**, [693]
    application of, **19(2)**, [695]
    application of provisions, **19(2)**, [696]
    debt due to Crown, recovered as, **19(2)**, [722]
    method of, **19(2)**, [691]
    stamping, **19(2)**, [694]
    Treasury regulations, **19(2)**, [692]
  meaning, **12(1)**, [176]; **33(1)**, [81], [90]
  public money, remission of fees paid from, **19(2)**, [714]
  superannuation provisions applied, **33(1)**, [80]–[81]

public order
  anti-social behaviour. *See* **anti-social behaviour**
  enforcement provisions, **12(1)**, [253]
  instruments, construction of, **12(1)**, [1001]
  offences—
    affray, **12(1)**, [993], [997]
    alarm or distress, causing, **12(1)**, [995], [996]
    charging more than one, **12(1)**, [998]
    common law, abolition of, **12(1)**, [1000]
    fear or provocation of violence, causing, **12(1)**, [994], [997]
    generally, **12(1)**, [1]
    harassment, **12(1)**, [995], [996]
    intoxication, effect of, **12(1)**, [997]
    mental element as to, **12(1)**, [997]
    offensive conduct, **12(1)**, [995], [996]
    riot, **12(1)**, [991], [997]
    threatening behaviour, **12(1)**, [994], [997]
    violent disorder, **12(1)**, [992], [997]
  Parliament, demonstration in vicinity of—
    authorisation of, **12(4)**, [129]
    authorisation, without, **12(4)**, [127]
    conditions, **12(4)**, [129]
    designated area, **12(4)**, [133]
    loudspeakers, operation of, **12(4)**, [132]
    notice of, **12(4)**, [128]
    offences, **12(4)**, [127]
    penalties, **12(4)**, [131]

public order—*contd*
Parliament, demonstration in vicinity
of—*contd*
supplementary directions, **12(4)**, [130]
police powers, delegation, **12(1)**, [1009]
processions. *See* **public procession**
punishment, **12(1)**, [253]
quasi-military organisation, prohibition of,
12(1), [252], [253]
racial hatred. *See* **racial hatred**
racially or religiously aggravated offences,
12(2), [671]
riot. *See* **riot**
uniforms, prohibition of, **12(1)**, [251]
violence—
meaning, **12(1)**, [999]
stop and search in anticipation of or after,
12(2), [192]
violent disorder, meaning, **12(1)**, [992]

public passenger vehicles. *See* **public service
vehicles**

public path. *See also* **bridleway; footpath**
creation agreement—
agriculture, forestry and nature
conservation, protection of, **36**, [1033]
making, **36**, [1029]
widening, for, **36**, [1075]
creation order—
agriculture, forestry and nature
conservation, protection of, **36**, [1033]
application for, **38(2)**, [64]
confirmation of, **36**, [1407]
date of operation, **36**, [1408]
determinations, delegation of functions,
36, [1418]
directions under, **36**, [1031]
form of, **36**, [1031]
loss caused by, compensation for,
36, [1032]
making, **36**, [1029]
notices to be given, **36**, [1407]
survey, power of entry for, **36**, [1343]
validity, **36**, [1408]
widening, for, **36**, [1075]
dangerous works, temporary diversion for,
36, [1192], [1193]
diversion order—
agriculture, forestry and nature
conservation, protection of, **36**, [1160]
appeals, **36**, [1164], [1165]
application for, **36**, [1153]
area of more than one council, in,
36, [1160]
compensation for loss, **36**, [1160]
compensation or expenses, payment of,
36, [1152]
confirmation of, **36**, [1152], [1407]
Countryside Agency, consultation with,
36, [1159]
date of operation, **36**, [1152], [1408]
determinations, delegation of functions,
36, [1418]

public path—*contd*
diversion order—*contd*
expedient, diversion to be, **36**, [1152],
[1154]
form of, **36**, [1152]
notices to be given, **36**, [1407]
point of termination, altering, **36**, [1152]
powers of making, exercise of, **36**, [1154]
right of way created by, **36**, [1152]
Secretary of State making, **36**, [1159]
statutory undertakers, extinguishing right of
way of, **36**, [1160]
survey, power of entry for, **36**, [1343]
validity, **36**, [1408]
evidence of, **37**, [89]
extinguishment order—
agriculture, forestry and nature
conservation, protection of, **36**, [1160]
appeals, **36**, [1164], [1165]
application for, **36**, [1148]
area of more than one council, in,
36, [1160]
compensation for loss, **36**, [1160]
confirmation of, **36**, [1152], [1407]
date of operation, **36**, [1152], [1408]
determinations, delegation of functions,
36, [1418]
form of, **36**, [1147]
map, **36**, [1148]
notices to be given, **36**, [1407]
powers of making, exercise of, **36**, [1159]
Secretary of State making, **36**, [1159]
statutory undertakers, extinguishing right of
way of, **36**, [1160]
survey, power of entry for, **36**, [1343]
validity, **36**, [1408]
long-distance route on, **36**, [633]
meaning, **37**, [96]
notice to enforce duty—
application procedure, **36**, [1184]
costs, **36**, [1185]
hearing, **36**, [1184]
orders following, **36**, [1183]
service of, **36**, [1182]

public performance
child taking part in. *See* **child**

public place
alcohol consumed in. *See* **alcohol**
baths, etc deemed, **35(1)**, [151]
disorderly conduct in. *See* **public order**
drinking fountains, provision in, **35(1)**, [93]
drunkenness in, **12(1)**, [396]
apprehension, **19(3)**, [360]
penalty, **19(3)**, [355], [359]
increase, **19(3)**, [370]
extended definition of, **35(1)**, [71]
firearm, carrying in, **12(1)**, [493]
indecent display in. *See* **indecent display**
lighting of—
consents and access for, **25(1)**, [519]
expenses, **25(1)**, [520]
parish council powers, **25(1)**, [518]

public place—*contd*

meaning, **12(1)**, [254], [276], [396], [541], [714]; **19(3)**, [363]; **35(1)**, [98]

offences generally. *See* **street offences**

removal of articles from, **12(1)**, [563]

seats, provision in, **35(1)**, [93]

smoking, prohibition of. *See* **smoking**

soliciting alms in, **12(1)**, [26]

statues and monuments, erection in, **35(1)**, [55]

statues in. *See* **statues**

wires, etc liable to fall on, byelaws as to, **35(1)**, [98]

public processions

advance notice of, **12(1)**, [1002]

conditions imposed on, **12(1)**, [1003]

directions by police, **12(1)**, [1003]

meaning, **12(1)**, [1010]

penalties for offences, **12(1)**, [1003]

prohibition of, **12(1)**, [1004]

regulations and orders, **36**, [224], [379]

public pumps

vesting in local authority, **35(1)**, [141]

Public Record Office

fees, power to charge, **18**, [183]

Keeper, appointment and duties, **18**, [183]

Lord Chancellor, responsibility of, **18**, [182]

records kept in, **18**, [194]

transfer of records from, **18**, [185]

public records

access to, **18**, [186]

See **freedom of information**

advisory council, **18**, [182]

Australian Constitution Act, cessation as, **18**, [277]

categories, **18**, [194]

Chancery of England, records of, **18**, [188], [194]

copies—

making and authentication, **18**, [183], [190]

obtaining, **18**, [183]

validity of, **18**, [190]

court records, **18**, [189], [194]

destruction of, **18**, [184], [187]

establishments under Government departments, **18**, [194]

Government departmental records, **18**, [194]

information from, disclosure prohibited, **18**, [186]

inspection—

facilities for, **18**, [186]

fees, **18**, [183]

legal validity, **18**, [190]

Master of the Rolls, responsibility of, **18**, [188]

meaning, **18**, [191]

Northern Ireland, transmission to, **18**, [192]

Oxford University, in custody of, **18**, [189]

place of deposit of, **18**, [185]

responsibility for, **18**, [183]

selection and preservation, **18**, [184]

public records—*contd*

statutory provisions, amendment, **7(1)**, [694]

tables and lists, departments and organisations, **18**, [194]

transferred, decisions relating to certain, **7(1)**, [667]

tribunals, records of, **18**, [194]

public revenue

cheating, offence of, **12(2)**, [162]

dividends. *See* **dividend**

public school

acquisition of land, **15(1)**, [127]

boys on the foundation, meaning, **15(1)**, [116]

chapels, **15(1)**, [132]

Charterhouse, change of name of governors, **15(1)**, [131]

general note, **15(1)**, [1]

governing body—

body corporate, as, **15(1)**, [117]

existing—

meaning, **15(1)**, [115]

savings for, **15(1)**, [130]

headmaster, consulting, **15(1)**, [125]

new, meaning, **15(1)**, [115]

regulations, making, etc, **15(1)**, [124]

Shrewsbury School, moving, **15(1)**, [128]

statutes and regulations, consolidating, **15(1)**, [119]

statutes—

alteration of, **15(1)**, [123]

approval of, **15(1)**, [122]

disapproval of, **15(1)**, [122]

Privy Council, laid before, **15(1)**, [121]

public inspection of, **15(1)**, [120]

repeal of, **15(1)**, [123]

restrictions on making, **15(1)**, [120]

scholarships, affecting, **15(1)**, [120]

Westminster, for, **15(1)**, [118]

buildings, holding, **15(1)**, [126]

dean and chapter, status of, **15(1)**, [129]

payments made to, **15(1)**, [126]

removal to another site, power of, **15(1)**, [133]

headmaster—

appointment of, **15(1)**, [125]

governing body consulting, **15(1)**, [124]

tenure of office, **15(1)**, [125]

masters, appointment of, **15(1)**, [125]

meaning, **15(1)**, [1], [114]

Westminster, provisions on, **15(1)**, [126]

Winchester, trusts. *See* **trusts, university and college**

public sector authority

Crown treated as, **22**, [389]

disposal of defective dwelling by, **22**, [378]

houses, right to buy. *See* **dwelling-house**

meaning, **22**, [53], [388]

public sector authority—*contd*
  service charges. *See* **service charge**

public sector landlord
  secure tenancy, purchase of interest subject to.
    See **secure tenancy**

public service
  land for, acquisition and disposal, **9**, [382]

public service vehicle. *See also* **motor
vehicle; stage carriage**
  accounts, **36**, [606]
  Acts, construction of references in, **37**, [65]
  agreements as to, **36**, [605]
  alteration—
    examination after, **37**, [128], [137]
    notification of fees payable on, **37**, [137]
  appeals from Secretary of State, **37**, [639]
  appeals to—
    Secretary of State, **37**, [35], [136]
    Transport Tribunal, **37**, [34]
  borrowing powers, **36**, [607]
  buildings, provision, **36**, [603]
  buses. *See* **bus services**
  charges, **36**, [604], [658]
  classification, alternative conditions affecting,
    37, [73]
  community bus services, permits for use as,
    37, [369], [372]
  conductors, regulation of conduct of, **37**, [28]
  damage—
    examination after, **37**, [128]
    reporting of, **37**, [26], [128]
  disabled accessibility regulations—
    appeals, **7(1)**, [408]
    approval certificates, **7(1)**, [406]
    certificates, **7(1)**, [405]
    exemption certificate, appeal against refusal
      of, **7(1)**, [403]
    fees, **7(1)**, [409]
    forgery and false statements, **7(1)**, [425]
    general, **7(1)**, [404]
    offences by bodies corporate, **7(1)**, [424]
    reviews, **7(1)**, [408]
    special authorisations, **7(1)**, [407]
  documents—
    errors in, correction, **37**, [41]
    fees in connection with, **37**, [457]
    forgery and misuse of, **37**, [48], [138],
      [458]
    records of licences, **37**, [40]
  dogs, carriage of, **36**, [604]
  drivers—
    conduct of, regulation of, **37**, [28]
    hours. *See* **drivers' hours**
    identity of—
      information as to, **37**, [54], [781], [782]
      proof of, **37**, [56]
    licence. *See* **driving licence**
    meaning, **37**, [64]
    names and addresses of, power to obtain
      from, **37**, [782]
  educational bodies, permits for use by,
    37, [369]

public service vehicle—*contd*
  European Community, business in another
    State of, **37**, [27]
  examination of—
    failure, damage or alteration, after,
      37, [128]
    generally, **37**, [9], [651]
    private-sector, **37**, [126]
    unfit, found to be. *See* unfit, prohibition of
      driving *below*
    vehicle testing and surveillance, **37**, [127]
    See also **vehicle testing**
  examiners—
    appointment, **37**, [649]
    certificates, issue of. *See* fitness *below*
    powers, **37**, [651], [782]
  expenses, Secretary of State, payment as
    directed by, **37**, [37]
  experimental vehicles, **37**, [13]
  failure—
    examination after, **37**, [128]
    reporting of, **37**, [26], [128]
  false documents, issue of, **37**, [50], [139]
  false statement to obtain licences etc, **37**, [49]
  fares—
    meaning, **36**, [661]
    payments treated as, **37**, [1]
    powers to charge, **36**, [604]
    separate, agreements for paying, **37**, [72]
  fines and fees, application of, **37**, [36], [469]
  fitness of—
    certificate of—
      application for, fees, **37**, [36]
      examination for purpose of, **37**, [128]
      experimental vehicle, **37**, [13]
      initial fitness, **37**, [9], [128]
      requirement, **37**, [9]
      type approval, **37**, [12]
    See also unfit *below*
  foreign, certain prohibitions. *See* **motor
    vehicles** (foreign)
  foreign state, certificate to carry on business
    in, **37**, [27]
  forgery and misuse of documents, **37**, [48],
    [138], [458]
  highway, use of. *See* use *below*
  hire-cars, effect of sharing of, **37**, [72]
  hire or reward, carrying for, criteria, **37**, [1]
  information, duty to furnish, **37**, [26], [128]
  inquiries, power to hold, **37**, [38]
  inspection of—
    constable, by, **37**, [652], [781]
    facilities, **37**, [10]
    powers, **37**, [10], [651]
    prohibition on driving conditional on,
      37, [653]
  inspectors, regulation of conduct of, **37**, [28]
  insurance, production of evidence of,
    37, [782]
  large, prohibition of plying for hire, **37**, [380]
  licence—
    false statement to obtain, **37**, [49]
    forgery and misuse, **37**, [48]
    records of, **37**, [40], [457]
    regulations as to procedure, **37**, [44]

public service vehicle—*contd*
 licence—*contd*
  See also operator's licence *below*
  local Acts, modification or revocation,
   37, [59]
  local authorities—
   acquisition or disposal by, **36**, [793]
   duty and functions, **37**, [293]
   expenses, **36**, [607]
   powers generally, **36**, [602]
  local services, use of taxi in, **37**, [362]
  meaning, **7(1)**, [404]; **36**, [652]; **37**, [1], [28]
  motor vehicles adapted to carry passengers,
   inspection of, **37**, [652]
  national operation, meaning, **37**, [64]
  Northern Ireland, certificate to carry on
   business in, **37**, [27]
  nuisance, saving for law of, **37**, [67]
  offences. *See* **road traffic offences**
  official PSV testing station—
   meaning, **37**, [10]
   provision and maintenance, **37**, [10]
  omnibus shelter. *See* **omnibus**
  omnibuses. *See* **omnibus**
  operation of vehicles, persons in partnership,
   37, [43], [463]
  operator—
   bankruptcy of, **37**, [42]
   death of, **37**, [42]
   disqualification of, **37**, [379]
   information, duty to furnish, **37**, [26],
    [128]
   interpretation of references to, **37**, [63]
   qualifications, **37**, [77]
   travel concession schemes, participation in,
    37, [433]
  operator's licence—
   applicant—
    convictions, duty to notify, **37**, [25]
    qualifications requirements, **37**, [77]
   application for—
    form of, **37**, [14]
    objections to, **37**, [18]
    regulations, **37**, [44]
    taxi licence holder, by, **37**, [362]
   area for use of, **37**, [14]
   classification of, **37**, [16]
   conditions attaching, **37**, [20], [375]
    contravention, **37**, [20], [375]
    matters required to be notified, as to,
     37, [21]
   convictions—
    duty to inform traffic commissioners of,
     37, [25]
    effect on application, **37**, [77]
   decisions, review, **37**, [33]
   detention of certain PSVs used without,
    37, [15], [76]
   disc, exhibition etc of, **37**, [24]
   duration of, **37**, [19]
   exemptions, **37**, [368]
   false statement to obtain, **37**, [49]
   fees, **37**, [36], [457]
   financial standing of holder, **37**, [17], [77]
   forgery and misuse of, **37**, [48]

public service vehicle—*contd*
 operator's licence—*contd*
  good repute of applicant, **37**, [17], [77]
  grant of—
   authority for, **37**, [14]
   engagement before January 1978,
    37, [17], [77]
   fees, **37**, [36]
   objection to, **37**, [18]
   partnerships, **37**, [43]
   qualifications for, **37**, [77]
   requirements, **37**, [17], [77]
  information, duty of holder to furnish,
   37, [26], [128]
  inquiry, request for, **37**, [376]
  local service, provision of, **37**, [354]
  London local service, provision of,
   37, [381]
  maximum number of vehicles, **37**, [20]
  professional competence of holder,
   37, [17], [77]
  refusal, appeal against decision, **37**, [34]
  requirements, **37**, [17]
  restricted—
   maximum number of vehicles, **37**, [20]
   requirements, **37**, [17]
   taxi licence holder, application by, for,
    37, [362]
   use authorised, **37**, [16]
  review of decisions, **37**, [33]
  revocation, **37**, [22], [379]
  Secretary of State to, **37**, [35]
  standard—
   requirements for, **37**, [17]
   use authorised by, **37**, [16]
  suspension, **37**, [22], [379]
  termination by request, **37**, [19]
  transitional provisions, **37**, [475]
  Transport Tribunal, to, **37**, [34]
  two or more, persons holding, **37**, [14]
  undertakings given, **37**, [17], [20]
  variation of, **37**, [20], [22]
  vehicle testing business, holder barred,
   37, [126]
  void, when, **37**, [379]
 parcels, carriage of, **36**, [604]
 partnerships, provisions as to, **37**, [43]
 passengers—
  carrying more than eight as, **37**, [1]
  conduct, regulation of, **37**, [29]
  death or injury to, liability, **37**, [31]
  number of, control, **37**, [30]
  safety and convenience of, **37**, [293]
  See also **passenger transport services**
 permits—
  activities permitted, **37**, [369]
  conditions attaching, **37**, [370]
  designation of bodies, **37**, [369]
  duration, **37**, [370]
  educational use, for, **37**, [369]
  grant of, **37**, [369]
  regulations, **37**, [371]
  religious bodies, use by, **37**, [369]
  social welfare use, for, **37**, [621]
  time limits on, **37**, [374]

public service vehicle—*contd*
  permits—*contd*
    variation or revocation of, **37**, [370]
  proceedings. *See* **road traffic offences**
  public interests, protection of, **37**, [66]
  queue barriers, maintenance of, **36**, [655]
  regulations—
    application for licences, as to, **37**, [44]
    breach of, penalty, **37**, [51]
    exercise of powers, **37**, [46]
    general power to make, **37**, [45], [465]
    procedure for, **37**, [466]
  review of decisions, **37**, [33]
  road, meaning, **37**, [64]
  roof-signs on, **36**, [995]
  school buses—
    fare-paying passengers on, **37**, [32]
    meaning, **37**, [32]
  small, regulation as private hire vehicles,
    37, [61]
  status, alternative conditions affecting, **37**, [73]
  statutory provisions excluded, **37**, [60]
  summary of provisions, **36**, [210]
  taxi—
    effect of sharing of, **37**, [72]
    licence holder, application for PSV licence
      by, **37**, [362]
    use in providing local services, **37**, [362]
  testing. *See* **vehicle testing**
  testing stations, **37**, [10]
  traffic areas, construction of references to,
    37, [62]
  tramcars excluded from meaning, **37**, [1]
  transitional provisions, **37**, [78]
  transport manager—
    meaning, **37**, [64]
    qualifications, **37**, [27]
  type vehicle—
    appeal in matter of, **37**, [136]
    approval of, **37**, [12], [129]
    certificate of conformity, issue of, **37**, [12],
      [128]
    modification of requirements, **37**, [13]
    regulations, power to make, **37**, [128]
    repeal of provisions, power, **37**, [69]
  undertakings, acquisition or disposal by local
    authorities, **36**, [793]
  unfit, prohibition of driving—
    conditional, **37**, [653]
    contravention, penalty, **37**, [655]
    extent of prohibition, **37**, [652]
    imposition, **37**, [652]
    notice of, **37**, [652]
    notice to Commissioners, **37**, [26], [127]
    powers, **37**, [652]
    removal—
      appeal against refusal, **37**, [136], [656]
      fees, **37**, [656]
      foreign vehicle, **37**, [128]
      notice of, **37**, [656], [658]
      when fit, **37**, [656], [658]
    supplementary provisions, **37**, [658]
  use of highways by—
    orders—
      power to make, **37**, [186]

public service vehicle—*contd*
  use of highways by—*contd*
    orders—*contd*
      provisions applicable, **37**, [186], [334]
  "used", meaning, **37**, [1]
  vehicles not treated as, **37**, [1]
  weighing, **37**, [664]
  working agreements as to, **36**, [605]

Public Services Ombudsman for Wales
  accounting officer, **10**, [846]
  accounts, **10**, [846]
  acting, **10**, [846]
  advisers, **10**, [846]
  annual and extraordinary reports, **10**, [846]
  appointment, **10**, [846]
  audit, **10**, [846]
  Commissioner for Older People in Wales—
    working collaboratively with, **10**, [824]
    working jointly with, **10**, [823]
    working with, **35(2)**, [601]
  complaint to—
    alternative resolution, **10**, [800]
    duly made or referred, meaning, **10**, [799]
    existing Ombudsman or Commissioner,
      undetermined by, **10**, [837]
    investigation of. *See* investigation of
      complaints *below*
    made, requirements for, **10**, [802]
    persons entitled to make, **10**, [801]
    procedures, publicity for, **10**, [832]
    referred, requirements for, **10**, [803]
  Comptroller and Auditor General,
    examinations by, **10**, [846]
  defamation claims, protection from, **10**, [831]
  delegation by, **10**, [846]
  disclosure of information, **10**, [825]
  disqualifications, **10**, [846]
  document or information prejudicial to safety
    of state or contrary to public interest,
    disclosure of, **10**, [826]
  establishment of office, **10**, [798]
  estimates, **10**, [846]
  financial provisions, **10**, [846]
  functions of, **26(2)**, [108]
  guidance, power to issue, **10**, [830]
  interpretation, **10**, [[840]
  investigation of complaints—
    compensation for person aggrieved,
      10, [833]
    conduct of, **10**, [810]
    contempt, **10**, [812]
    decisions not to investigate, **10**, [809]
    decisions taken without maladministration,
      exclusion, **10**, [808]
    discontinuation, **10**, [809]
    excluded matters, **10**, [807], [847]
    information, documents, evidence and
      facilities, power to require, **10**, [811]
    listed authorities—
      addition to list, **10**, [827], [829]
      restrictions on power to amend,
        10, [828]
      Schedule of, **10**, [827], [848]

**Public Services Ombudsman for
Wales**—*contd*
　investigation of complaints—*contd*
　　matters not relating to Wales, exclusion of,
　　　10, [805]
　　matters subject to, **10**, [804]
　　obstruction, **10**, [812]
　　other remedies, exclusion in case of,
　　　10, [806]
　　power of, **10**, [799]
　　procedure, **10**, [810]
　　relevant action, **10**, [804]
　　reports—
　　　action following receipt of, **10**, [816]
　　　alternative procedure, **10**, [818]
　　　fee for, **10**, [813]
　　　health care providers, relating to,
　　　　10, [815]
　　　non-action following receipt of,
　　　　10, [817]
　　　persons receiving, **10**, [813]
　　　preparation and publication of, **10**, [813]
　　　publicising, **10**, [814]
　　　special. *See* special reports *below*
　　special reports—
　　　Assembly, relating to, **10**, [821]
　　　fee for, **10**, [820]
　　　permitted period for, **10**, [819]
　　　persons receiving, **10**, [819]
　　　preparation of, **10**, [819]
　　　publication, **10**, [820]
　　investigations by, **26(2)**, [109], [110]
　　monitoring officers, matters referred to,
　　　26(2), [113]
　　other commissioners, consultation with,
　　　25(2), [324]
　　other ombudsmen, consultation and
　　　co-operation with, **10**, [553], [822]
　　privileged statements of, **26(2)**, [114]
　　property, rights and liabilities, transfer of,
　　　10, [849]
　　remuneration, **10**, [846]
　　reports, **26(2)**, [111]
　　　interim, **26(2)**, [112]
　　staff, **10**, [846]
　　　transfer of, **10**, [849]
　　status, **10**, [846]
　　supplementary powers, **10**, [846]
　　term of office, **10**, [846]
　　use of recourses, examinations into, **10**, [846]

public stores
　Act applying to, **12(1)**, [144]
　arrest for offences, **12(1)**, [149]
　boat, suspected of being on, **12(1)**, [147]
　concealment of marks, **12(1)**, [146]
　gathering or searching for, **12(1)**, [148]
　marks applied on, **12(1)**, [145], [151]
　meaning, **12(1)**, [143]
　regimental necessaries from, **12(1)**, [150]
　search warrant, **12(1)**, [149]
　suspected boats and persons, power to stop,
　　12(1), [147]
　sweeping etc near dockyards, prohibiting,
　　12(1), [148]

public transport companies. *See under*
passenger transport services

public transport facilities
　capital expenditure on, **36**, [808]
　grants in respect of, **25(2)**, [333]
　passenger transport areas, in, **25(2)**, [169]
　research and development, grants for,
　　36, [809], [810]

**Public Transport Users' Committee for
England**
　establishment of, **37**, [454]
　functions of, **37**, [455]
　recommendations from, conferring functions
　　on other bodies, **37**, [456]

Public Trustee
　Accountant-General as, **11(3)**, [55]; **48**, 240,
　　597
　appeals, **48**, 242
　appointment of, **48**, 240
　bond or security, not required to give,
　　48, 243
　books of company, entry of name on, **48**, 243
　Consolidated Fund, payment of liabilities
　　from, **48**, 239
　custodian trustee, as, **48**, 235–6
　deputy, **48**, 240
　executor, appointment as, **48**, 237
　fees of, **48**, 220, 241; **48(S)**, Trusts 1–2
　fees order, **48**, 558–9
　functions—
　　Court of Protection, as to, **29**, [215]
　　of, **48**, 597–8
　general deposit fund, **48**, 554–6
　generally, **48**, 221
　legislation, **48**, 216
　liability of Consolidated Fund, repeals,
　　48(S), Trusts 1
　mode of action, **48**, 242–3
　office, establishment of, **48**, 231
　officers, **48**, 240
　offices, **48**, 240
　ordinary trustee, as, **48**, 237
　palatine court, application of provisions to,
　　48, 243
　powers and duties, **48**, 232
　probate, accepting, **48**, 238–9
　proceedings by or against, **13**, [26]
　professional advisers, employment of, **48**, 242
　remuneration, **48**, 240
　rights and immunities, **48**, 232
　rules, **48**, 246
　small estate, administration of, **48**, 233–4
　trust—
　　accounts, investigation and audit of,
　　　48, 244
　　moneys, dealings with, **48**, 554–6
　　not accepting, **48**, 232

public utilities
　privatisation, proposals, power to act in
　　relation to, **49**, [655]

public utility undertaking
drainage work affecting, protection,
19(3), [259]

public vehicles
persons waiting to enter, byelaws as to,
35(1), [100]
railway stations, taken at, **35(1)**, [101]

public walks
byelaws as to, **35(1)**, [24]
contributions by local authority towards,
35(1), [24], [57]
provision of, **35(1)**, [24]

public way
meaning, **37**, [579]
motoring events on, regulation, **37**, [580]

public works
acquisition of land for, powers, **9**, [323]
adverse effect of, mitigation, **9**, [323]
aerodromes as, **9**, [304]
depreciation in value of land by use of—
assessment of extent, **9**, [307]
compensation for—
aerodrome, effect of alterations to,
9, [304], [312]
alterations to works, effect of, **9**, [312]
assessment, general provisions,
9, [307]–[308]
carriageway of highway, effect of
alterations to, **9**, [312], [322]
change of use, effect of, **9**, [312]
claim for—
making, **9**, [304], [306]
notice of, **9**, [306], [312], [379]
out of time, **9**, [379]
time for making, **9**, [306], [315],
[379]
contract of sale, effect of, **9**, [307]
disputes, Lands Tribunal to determine,
9, [319]
ecclesiastical property, **9**, [317]
enfranchisement—
collective, participation in, **9**, [316]
tenant entitled to, **9**, [315]–[316],
[379]
entry on land after notice of claim for,
9, [306]
exclusion of, **9**, [304], [310], [316]
extended lease, tenant entitled to,
9, [315]–[316], [379]
immunity from action for nuisance,
9, [304], [320]
inheritance, interest acquired by,
9, [314], [379]
injurious affection, **9**, [311]
interest on, **9**, [321], [364], [379]
interests qualifying for, **9**, [305], [314],
[379]
limitation of time, **9**, [322], [379]
minimal, exclusion of, **9**, [310]
mortgage, interest subject to, **9**, [307],
[313]

public works—*contd*
depreciation in value of land by use of—*contd*
compensation for—*contd*
planning permission, assumptions as to,
9, [308]
qualifying tenancy, **9**, [315]–[316]
records, keeping of, **9**, [318]
reduction where land benefited, **9**, [309]
relevant date, information for
ascertaining, **9**, [318]
restrictions on, **9**, [304], [307], [311]
right to, **9**, [304]
settled land, interest as, **9**, [314]
sound proofing grants—
effect of making, **9**, [307]
meaning, **9**, [307]
subsequent claim for, treatment of,
9, [311], [379]
tenancy, interest subject to grant of,
9, [307]
trust of land, interest held on, **9**, [313]
two interests in land, where, **9**, [309]
physical factors causing depreciation,
9, [304]
highways as, **9**, [304]
meaning, **9**, [304]
noise caused by construction or use of—
caravans affected by, payments in respect
of, **35(1)**, [299]
insulation of buildings against—
Crown, position of, **35(1)**, [300]
grants towards cost of, **35(1)**, [298]
regulations providing for, **35(1)**, [298]

public works loan
Commissioners. *See* **Public Works Loan
Commissioners**
debtor, bankruptcy of, **19(2)**, [663]
default—
Commissioners, liability of, **19(2)**, [656]
property, possession of, **19(2)**, [653]
rate, powers relating to, **19(2)**, [655]
interest, rate of, **19(2)**, [851], [853], [854]
notices, service of, **19(2)**, [675]
payment before due date, **19(2)**, [661]
payment of instalments, suspension of,
19(2), [668]
priority of, **19(2)**, [650]
re-borrowing powers, **19(2)**, [842]
receipts, **19(2)**, [674]
repayment—
rate for, **19(2)**, [651]
recovery after time for, **19(2)**, [666]
security for, **19(2)**, [649]
term of years for, **19(2)**, [648], [813]
vesting of property on, **19(2)**, [662]
security—
change of, **19(2)**, [669]
completion of works, for, **19(2)**, [667]
discharge of, **19(2)**, [662]
form of, **19(2)**, [664]
mortgaged premises, sale of, **19(2)**, [657]
personal, **19(2)**, [649]
possession etc, money arising on taking of,
19(2), [660]

public works loan—*contd*
　security—*contd*
　　property, charge on, **19(2)**, [650]
　　Secretary of Commissioners, in name of,
　　　19(2), [652]
　　specialty debt, recovery of sums as,
　　　19(2), [665]
　　sufficiency of, **19(2)**, [647], [649]
　　transfer of, **19(2)**, [661]
　　validity of sale, deemed, **19(2)**, [658]
　special Acts—
　　loans under, **19(2)**, [677]
　　meaning, **19(2)**, [678], [683]
　sums payable, recovery of, **19(2)**, [665]
　Treasury warrants, issue of, **19(2)**, [673]

Public Works Loan Commissioners
　accounts, **19(2)**, [672], [851]
　annual report, **19(2)**, [643]
　appointment of, **19(2)**, [821]
　constitution of, **19(2)**, [642]
　conveyances, etc, execution of, **19(2)**, [646],
　　[659]
　declaration, **19(2)**, [681]
　disposition of property, concurrence in,
　　19(2), [670]
　evidence, taking, **19(2)**, [643]
　fees, prescription of, **19(2)**, [812]
　fund or account, moneys carried to,
　　19(2), [814]
　generally, **19(1)**, [1]
　housing purposes, loans for, **22**, [331]
　loans by, **26(2)**, [267]
　　automatic charge, becoming, **19(1)**, [1]
　　National Loans Fund, from, **19(2)**, [851],
　　　[873]
　　repayment of, **19(2)**, [702]
　　security, sufficiency of, **19(2)**, [647], [649]
　　See also **loan, public works loan**
　members, **19(2)**, [821]
　mortgaged property—
　　possession of, **19(2)**, [653]–[655]
　　sale of, **19(2)**, [657], [670]
　notices, service of, **19(2)**, [676]
　officers, **19(2)**, [644]
　possession, liability after taking, **19(2)**, [656]
　powers of, **19(2)**, [643]
　proceedings, evidence of, **19(2)**, [643]
　registered social landlords, loans to, **23**, [368]
　regulations, making, **19(2)**, [671]
　relevant authority, loan to, **19(2)**, [844], [847]
　repayment of loan, extending time for,
　　19(2), [648]
　Secretary—
　　assistant, performance of functions by,
　　　19(2), [810]
　　conveyances, etc, executing, **19(2)**, [646]
　　securities taken in name of, **19(2)**, [652]
　　successor to, property vesting in,
　　　19(2), [645]
　term of office, **19(2)**, [821]
　vacancy in, **19(2)**, [821]

**public-private partnership (PPP)
agreement**
　administration orders—
　　adaptations and savings, **26(1)**, [782]
　　administrator—
　　　appointment, **26(1)**, [780]
　　　duties, **26(1)**, [780]
　　　powers, **26(1)**, [780]
　　applications to court, **26(1)**, [780]
　　charged property, dealing with,
　　　26(1), [780]
　　company, meaning, **26(1)**, [609]
　　discharge of, **26(1)**, [780]
　　effect of, **26(1)**, [605], [780]
　　foreign companies, **26(1)**, [609]
　　　administrator, **26(1)**, [781]
　　　charged property, dealing with,
　　　　26(1), [781]
　　　effect of, **26(1)**, [781]
　　　notice of, **26(1)**, [781]
　　　statement of affairs, **26(1)**, [781]
　　meaning, **26(1)**, [605]
　　modification of provisions,
　　　26(1), [780]–[782]
　　notice of, **26(1)**, [780]
　　relevant activities, transfer of—
　　　application of provisions, **26(1)**, [783]
　　　exercise of functions, **26(1)**, [783]
　　　licences, transfer of, **26(1)**, [783]
　　　transfer schemes, **26(1)**, [783]
　　special petition, made on, **26(1)**, [606]
　　statement of proposals, **26(1)**, [780]
　arbiter—
　　appointment, **26(1)**, [610]
　　consultation, **26(1)**, [617]
　　directions, **26(1)**, [614], [617]
　　disqualifications, **26(1)**, [610]
　　duty of, **26(1)**, [616]
　　expenses of, **26(1)**, [622]
　　functions of, **26(1)**, [610]
　　guidance by, **26(1)**, [615]
　　immunity, **26(1)**, [621]
　　inspections by, **26(1)**, [617]
　　member of Office of Rail Regulation as,
　　　26(1), [613]
　　objective, **26(1)**, [616]
　　provision of information to—
　　　disclosure, restrictions on, **26(1)**, [620]
　　　failure to comply, **26(1)**, [619]
　　　requirement, **26(1)**, [618]
　　staff, **26(1)**, [612]
　　terms of appointment, **26(1)**, [611]
　contract, parties to, **26(1)**, [596]
　definitions, **26(1)**, [624]
　designations, **26(1)**, [598]
　key system assets—
　　meaning, **26(1)**, [599]
　　protection of, **26(1)**, [602]
　　register of, **26(1)**, [600]
　　transfer, schemes for, **26(1)**, [603]
　leases—
　　instrument, certificate on, **26(1)**, [604]
　　meaning, **26(1)**, [604]
　meaning, **26(1)**, [596]
　public sector operators, meaning, **26(1)**, [597]

public-private partnership (PPP)
agreement—*contd*
rate of return incorporated in, **26(1)**, [616]
related third party agreements, **26(1)**, [601]
statutory functions, company exercising,
26(1), [623]
successor bodies, **26(1)**, [602]
taxation provisions—
capital allowances, **26(1)**, [798]
chargeable gains, **26(1)**, [798]
easements, **26(1)**, [798]
interpretation, **26(1)**, [798]
leases, **26(1)**, [798]
machinery and plant, **26(1)**, [798]
payments, revenue nature of, **26(1)**, [798]
sale and leaseback, **26(1)**, [798]
winding-up—
order, restriction on making, **26(1)**, [607]
voluntary, restriction on, **26(1)**, [608]

public-private partnership business
consolidated fund, payments from,
19(2), [1045]
devolved administrations, investment by,
19(2), [1046]
government expenditure, **19(2)**, [1042],
[1045]
investment—
devolved administrations, by, **19(2)**, [1046]
limit for, **19(2)**, [1044]

publications
obscene. *See* **obscene publications**
unsolicited, **12(1)**, [593]
meaning, **12(1)**, [594]

publisher
delivery of publication to, meaning,
19(3), [328]
newspaper, discovery of, **19(3)**, [283]

puffer
auction sale, at. *See* **auction**

pupil referral unit
adaptation of enactments, **15(1)**, [715]
careers education—
advisers, co-operation with, **15(1)**, [755]
extension or modification of provisions,
15(1), [757]
information, provision of, **15(1)**, [756]
provision of, **15(1)**, [754]
charges, **15(1)**, [715]
curriculum, **15(1)**, [715]
Environmental Protection Act, application of,
15(1), [715]
exceptional provision of education,
15(1), [517]
exclusion of pupils, **15(2)**, [383]
information, **15(1)**, [715]
management committees, **15(1)**, [715]
meaning, **15(1)**, [517]
political indoctrination, **15(1)**, [715]
political issues, **15(1)**, [715]
registration, **15(1)**, [715]

pupil referral unit—*contd*
school attendance orders, **15(1)**, [715]
sex education, **15(1)**, [715]

purchase notice
agreement to comply with, **46**, [384]
alteration or removal of buildings or works, in
respect of order requiring, **46**, [381]
compensation, reduction of, **46**, [389]
council, action by, **46**, [384]
Crown land, **46**, [382], [562]
discontinuance of use, in respect of order
requiring, **46**, [381]
listed building. *See* **listed building**
meaning, **46**, [381]
National Parks, provisions applying, **46**, [393]
partially affected agricultural unit,
counter-notice as to, **46**, [390]–[392]
power to refuse to confirm, **46**, [387]
power to serve, **46**, [381]
reasonably beneficial use of land, **46**, [381],
[383]
reference to, **46**, [385]
refusal to comply with, **46**, [384]
repairs notice preceding, **46**, [381]
response notice, **46**, [384]
restricted use, land having, **46**, [387]
Secretary of State—
action by, **46**, [386]
confirmation by, effect of, **46**, [388]
decision by, effect of, **46**, [388]
validity of decision, **46**, [549]

purchase of own shares
authority for—
generally, **8(1)**, [771]
market purchase. *See* market purchase *below*
off-market purchase. *See* off-market
purchase *below*
beneficial interests, interests disregarded in
determining, **8(1)**, [749]
cancellation of shares, **8(1)**, [784]
return to registrar, **8(1)**, [786]
capital redemption reserve, transfer of amounts
to, **8(1)**, [811]
definitions, **8(1)**, [761]
distributable profits, meaning, **8(1)**, [814]
distributable profits, payment to be made
from, **8(1)**, [783]
effect of failure by company, **8(1)**, [813]
employees' share scheme, shares held for—
directors, application of provisions to,
8(1), [754]
residual interest under, **8(1)**, [750]
rights of recovery, **8(1)**, [751]
financial assistance for—
meaning, **8(1)**, [755]
permitted—
conditional, **8(1)**, [760]
unconditional, **8(1)**, [759]
prohibited—
exemptions, **8(1)**, [759]–[760]
offence, as, **8(1)**, [758]

purchase of own shares—*contd*
  financial assistance for—*contd*
    prohibited—*contd*
      private holding company, assistance by
        public company for shares in,
        8(1), [757]
      public company, shares in, **8(1)**, [756]
  financing, **8(1)**, [770]
  general rule against, **8(1)**, [736]
    exceptions to, **8(1)**, [737]
  limited company, power of, **8(1)**, [768]
  market purchase—
    authority for, **8(1)**, [779]
    contract or memorandum of—
      availability for inspection, **8(1)**, [780]
      enforcement of right to inspect,
        8(1), [781]
      meaning, **8(1)**, [771]
    no assignment of right of, **8(1)**, [782]
  nominee—
    failure to make payment, liability in case
      of, **8(1)**, [739]
    shares held by, **8(1)**, [738]
  off-market purchase—
    authority for, **8(1)**, [772]
    contract or memorandum of—
      availability for inspection, **8(1)**, [780]
      enforcement of right to inspect,
        8(1), [781]
      meaning, **8(1)**, [771]
    release of rights under contract, **8(1)**, [778]
    resolution authorising—
      details of contract, disclosure of,
        8(1), [774]
      voting rights, exercise of, **8(1)**, [773]
    variation of contract—
      authorisation, **8(1)**, [775]
      details of variation, disclosure of,
        8(1), [777]
      voting rights, exercise of, **8(1)**, [776]
  payment for, **8(1)**, [769]
  pension scheme, shares held for—
    directors, application of provisions to,
      8(1), [754]
    employer's charges on, **8(1)**, [751]
    pension scheme, meaning, **8(1)**, [753]
    residual interest under, **8(1)**, [750]
    rights of recovery, **8(1)**, [751]
  personal representative or trustee, rights of
    company as, **8(1)**, [752]
  private company, by—
    auditor's report—
      availability for inspection, **8(1)**, [798]
      disclosure of, **8(1)**, [796]
      requirement of, **8(1)**, [792]
    available profits—
      determination of, **8(1)**, [790]
      meaning, **8(1)**, [789]
    capital, out of—
      accounting consequences of, **8(1)**, [812]
      requirements, **8(1)**, [791]
      special resolution, approval by,
        8(1), [794]–[796]
      time of making, **8(1)**, [801]

purchase of own shares—*contd*
  private company, by—*contd*
    directors' statement—
      availability for inspection, **8(1)**, [798]
      disclosure of, **8(1)**, [796]
      made with no reasonable grounds for
        opinion, offence of, **8(1)**, [793]
      requirement of, **8(1)**, [792]
    permissible capital payment, **8(1)**, [788]
    power of, **8(1)**, [787]
    public notice of, **8(1)**, [797]
    special resolution, approval by—
      application to cancel, **8(1)**, [799]
      directors' statement and auditor's report,
        disclosure of, **8(1)**, [796]
      notice of application to cancel,
        8(1), [800]
      passing of, **8(1)**, [794]
      voting rights, exercise of, **8(1)**, [795]
  private company, re-registration of,
    8(1), [746]
  public company, shares held by or for—
    cancellation—
      duty of, **8(1)**, [740]
      failure, offence of, **8(1)**, [745]
      notice of, **8(1)**, [741]
      re-registration as private company in
        consequence of, **8(1)**, [742]
    company re-registering as, **8(1)**, [746]
    lien or charge on, **8(1)**, [748]
    re-registration—
      cancellation of shares, on, **8(1)**, [742]
      certificate of incorporation, issue of,
        8(1), [743]
      failure, effect of, **8(1)**, [744]–[745]
    reserve, transfer to, **8(1)**, [747]
  redeemable shares—
    cancelled, treated as, **8(1)**, [766]
    payment for, **8(1)**, [764]
    power of limited company to issue,
      8(1), [762]
    redemption—
      effect of failure by company, **8(1)**, [813]
      financing, **8(1)**, [765]
      notice to registrar, **8(1)**, [767]
      terms and manner of, **8(1)**, [763]
  regulations, power to make further provision
    by, **8(1)**, [815]
  return of, **8(1)**, [785]
  shares purchased, treatment of, **8(1)**, [784]
  treasury shares—
    application of provisions, **8(1)**, [802]
    cancellation, **8(1)**, [807]
    company holding, reference to, **8(1)**, [802]
    disposal of, **8(1)**, [805]
    exercise of rights in respect of, **8(1)**, [804]
    maximum holdings, **8(1)**, [803]
    notice of cancellation, **8(1)**, [808]
    notice of disposal, **8(1)**, [806]
    offences relating to, **8(1)**, [810]
    proceeds of sale, treatment of, **8(1)**, [809]
    qualifying, meaning, **8(1)**, [802]
    register of members, provisions applying,
      8(1), [202]

purchased life annuity
  meaning, **44(3)**, [423]
  payments—
    charge to tax, **44(3)**, [422]
    deduction of tax, received after,
      44(3), [426]
    immediate needs annuities—
      annual payments under, **44(3)**, [739]
      care provider, meaning, **44(3)**, [740]
    income charged, **44(3)**, [424]
    partial relief for, **44(3)**, [731]
      determinations, **44(3)**, [737]
      duration of life, term dependent on,
        44(3), [734]–[735]
      excluded annuities, **44(3)**, [732]
      extent of, **44(3)**, [733]
      grant, consideration for, **44(3)**, [736]
      regulations, **44(3)**, [738]
    person liable, **44(3)**, [425]

pyramid selling scheme
  advertisements—
    control of, **47**, [186]

pyramid selling scheme—*contd*
  advertisements—*contd*
    offences respecting, **47**, [187]
  description of, **47**, [185]
  elements of, **47**, [185]
  enforcement provisions, **47**, [190]
  nature of, **47**, [185]
  offences—
    defences in proceedings, **47**, [188]
    generally, **47**, [187]
    inducing participation, **47**, [187]
    penalties for, **47**, [189]
    prosecutions, time-limit for, **47**, [191]
  regulations—
    advertisements etc as to, **47**, [186]
    contravention of, **47**, [187]
    prohibitions by, **47**, [186]
    requirements prescribed by, **47**, [186]

pyx
  trial of, **10**, [281]
    attendance of juror, non-payment for,
      19(3), [148]

Q

Quakers
affirmation by, right to, **18**, [75]
burial grounds, discontinuance of use,
5(2), [386]
marriage according to usages of, **27**, [260];
36, [53]
superintendent registrar's certificate, marriage
under, **27**, [232]

Qualifications and Curriculum Authority
accounts, **15(1)**, [765]
bodies awarding qualifications, levy on,
15(1), [748]
chairman and deputy, **15(1)**, [735], [765]
chief officer, **15(1)**, [765]
committees, **15(1)**, [765]
directions, power to give, **15(1)**, [741]
documents, **15(1)**, [765]
establishment of, **15(1)**, [735]
finance, **15(1)**, [765]
functions—
    advice, **15(1)**, [739]
    ancillary activities, **15(1)**, [739]
    curriculum and assessment, in relation to,
      15(1), [737]
    delegation, **15(1)**, [765]
    discharge of, **15(1)**, [740]
    education and training, advancement of,
      15(1), [736]
    England and Northern Ireland, in,
      15(S), Education 281–3
    external vocational and academic
      qualifications, in relation to, **15(1)**, [738]
    vocational qualifications in Northern
      Ireland, as to, **15(S)**, Education 286
members—
    number of, **15(1)**, [735]
    payments to, **15(1)**, [765]
    qualifications, **15(1)**, [735]
    tenure of office, **15(1)**, [765]
powers, **15(1)**, [765]
proceedings, **15(1)**, [765]
staff, **15(1)**, [765]
    transfer to, **15(1)**, [747]
status, **15(1)**, [765]

**Qualifications, Curriculum and Assessment
Authority for Wales.** *See now* **National
Assembly for Wales**

qualifying employee share ownership trust
contributions to, ending of tax relief for,
43(2), [212]

quarry
abandoned, fencing, **17(1)**, [131]
administration of industry, **17(1)**, [2], [3], [6]

quarry—*contd*
advisory committees, appointment, **17(1)**, [3]
disused, fencing, **17(1)**, [131]
fencing, disused and abandoned, **17(1)**, [131]
health and safety. *See* safety etc *below*
information held by Authority, public access
to, **17(2)**, [181]
inquiries, power to hold, **17(1)**, [5]
machinery, compensation for requisition,
9, [123]
meaning, **17(1)**, [151]
nuisance, unfenced as, **17(1)**, [131]
offences, penalty, no express penalty
provided, **17(1)**, [135]
owner, meaning, **17(1)**, [152]
pipe-line in, **17(1)**, [275]
powers as to, transfer, **17(1)**, [2]
railway as part of, **17(1)**, [151]
refuse from, combustion of, **35(2)**, [42]
rents repayable in respect of, **44(1)**, [98]
ropeways, use of, **17(1)**, [151]
summary of provisions, **17(1)**, [1]
tips. *See* **tips**
unfenced, as statutory nuisance, **17(1)**, [131]

quarter sessions
administrative functions, transfer of,
11(2), [263]
transitional provisions, **11(2)**, [264]

quasi-military organisation
generally, **3**, [1]
prohibition of, **12(1)**, [252], [253]

quay
Factories Act, provisions applicable, **18**, [1178]

Queen
saving for proceedings in private capacity,
13, [8]

Queen Anne's Bounty. *See also* **Church
Commissioners**
central authority, meaning, **14**, 327
Church Commissioners, united into, **14**, 418
conveyance, form of, **14**, 95
corporate fund, transfer of, **14**, 424
deed, grant of lands by, **14**, 61
dissolution of, **14**, **18**, 418–19
governors—
    purchase of houses by, **14**, 103
    sale of land by, **14**, 199
incorporation of, **14**, 18
penalties paid to, **14**, 125
pensions, increasing, **14**, 521–2
property, vesting of, **14**, 418–19

Queen Anne's Bounty—*contd*
  residence—
    sale of—
      application of moneys, **14**, 385–6
      rules, making, **14**, 390–1
  Welsh ecclesiastical property vested in,
    14, 258–9

Queen Mother
  civil list allowance, **10**, [202]
  Counsellor of State, to be, **10**, [231]

Queen's Award to Industry
  false representations as to, **39(1)**, [92]

Queen's Printer
  documents printed by, as evidence, **18**, [95],
    [151]

quia emptores
  statutory provisions, **20**, [6]

quoted Eurobond
  meaning, **44(4)**, [995]
  yearly interest excepted from deductions,
    44(4), [890]

quoted option
  abandonment of, **42**, [1250]
  meaning, **42**, [1250]
  new holdings, treated as part of, **42**, [1258]

R

rabbits. *See also* **game**
  allotments, right to keep on, **1(1)**, [441]
  clearance areas, **1(1)**, [464]
  destruction—
    assistance in, **1(1)**, [465]
    authorisation of, **1(1)**, [464]
    expenses, contribution to, **1(1)**, [466]
    firearms, use of, **1(1)**, [464]
  destruction of, rights as to, **2**, [213], [232], [233]
  exempt from hunting provisions, **2**, [749]
  gassing, allowance of, **1(1)**, [390]; **2**, [271]
  myxomatosis, spreading, **2**, [296]
  open trapping, **2**, [295]
  orders, procedure, **1(1)**, [464]
  poaching—
    group of armed persons, by, **2**, [143]
    penalty, **2**, [141]
    poisoning rabbit holes, **2**, [271]
    spring traps, use of, **2**, [272]
    taking etc on public road, **2**, [182]
    traps, type of, restriction on, **2**, [294]
  prevention of damage by, **1(1)**, [390]
  preventive measures—
    contributions to cost, **1(1)**, [466]
    ministerial assistance, **1(1)**, [465]

rabies
  dogs, control orders, **2**, [441]
  entry and search in relation to offences, **2**, [511], [512]
  foxes, destruction of, **2**, [450]
  infected areas, provisions for, **2**, [451]
  notices, form and service, **2**, [542]
  offences, summary, penalty, **2**, [534]
  quarantine of possible carriers, **2**, [455]
  rabid animals, destruction of, **36**, [230]
  virus, control, **2**, [455]

racecourse
  horse. *See* **horse racecourse**
  track. *See* **betting** (track)

Racecourse Betting Control Board
  references to, construction of, **5(1)**, [2]

racial discrimination
  agent, by, **7(1)**, [168]
  amendment of provisions, **7(1)**, [197]
  armed forces, in, **7(1)**, [199]
  assignment of tenancy, **7(1)**, [158]
  association, by, **7(1)**, [159]
    exceptions, **7(1)**, [160]
  barrister or barrister's clerk, by, **7(1)**, [161]
  benefits, indirect access to, **7(1)**, [176]
  charity, by, **7(1)**, [170]

racial discrimination—*contd*
  civil proceedings, **7(1)**, [179]
    burden of proof, **7(1)**, [184]
  claims, **7(1)**, [183]
    immigration cases, in, **7(1)**, [185]
  collective agreements, in terms of, **7(1)**, [195]
    employment tribunal, complaint to, **7(1)**, [196]
  Commission for Racial Equality, replaced. *See now* **Commission for Equality and Human Rights**
  contract term, in, **7(1)**, [194]
  contract worker, against, **7(1)**, [134]
  county court, proceedings in, **7(1)**, [187]
  Crown, application to, **7(1)**, [199]
  damages, **7(1)**, [183]
  discriminatory advertisement—
    meaning, **7(1)**, [207]
    prohibiting, **7(1)**, [165]
  discriminatory practice, **7(1)**, [164]
  education—
    local education authority, **7(1)**, [141], [145]
    person not ordinarily resident in Great Britain, **7(1)**, [172]
    racial groups, special needs, **7(1)**, [173], [174]
  educational establishment, in—
    pupil, meaning, **7(1)**, [144]
    responsible body, **7(1)**, [143]
  employer, by—
    applicant, against, **7(1)**, [130]
    benefits, denying, **7(1)**, [130]
    employee, against, **7(1)**, [130]
    genuine occupational qualification, **7(1)**, [132]
    genuine occupational requirement, **7(1)**, [131]
    liability of, **7(1)**, [168]
    seamen recruited abroad, **7(1)**, [136]
  employment—
    aircraft, on, **7(1)**, [199]
    establishment in Great Britain, in, **7(1)**, [135]
    hovercraft, on, **7(1)**, [199]
    meaning, **7(1)**, [207]
    private household, in, **7(1)**, [130]
    seabed, in connection with, **7(1)**, [135]
    ship, on, **7(1)**, [135], [199]
    training, **7(1)**, [171]–[174]
    training skills used outside Great Britain, **7(1)**, [133]
  employment agency, by—
    generally, **7(1)**, [141]
    meaning, **7(1)**, [207]
  employment tribunal—
    burden of proof, **7(1)**, [181]

racial discrimination—*contd*
employment tribunal—*contd*
collective agreement, complaint as to terms of, **7(1)**, [196]
compensation, awarding, **7(1)**, [182]
jurisdiction, **7(1)**, [180]
remedies, **7(1)**, [182]
rules of undertaking, complaint as to, **7(1)**, [196]
three months, proceedings to be brought in, **7(1)**, [189]
evidence of, **7(1)**, [190]
facilities and services, in provision of—
aircraft, on, **7(1)**, [162]
exceptions, **7(1)**, [157]
generally, **7(1)**, [154]
hovercraft, on, **7(1)**, [162]
indirect access to, **7(1)**, [176]
ship, on, **7(1)**, [162]
travel facilities, **7(1)**, [162]
financial provisions, **7(1)**, [206]
generally, **7(1)**, [1]
goods, in provision of, **7(1)**, [154]
exceptions, **7(1)**, [157]
government appointments, **7(1)**, [202]
harassment, **7(1)**, [129]
inducing, generally, **7(1)**, [167]
instructions to commit unlawful acts, **7(1)**, [166]
local authority, statutory duty of, **7(1)**, [191]–[193]
local education authority, by, **7(1)**, [141], [145]
meaning of, **7(1)**, [126]
national security—
act safeguarding, **7(1)**, [178]
proceedings, restrictions, **7(1)**, [188]
office-holders, in relation to, **7(1)**, [203]
orders and regulations, **7(1)**, [198]
partnership, by, **7(1)**, [137]
persistent, generally, **7(1)**, [186]
planning authority, by, **7(1)**, [148]
police bodies, by, **7(1)**, [205]
police force, in, **7(1)**, [204]
premises, in disposal or management of—
exceptions, **7(1)**, [157]
generally, **7(1)**, [155]
small dwellings, **7(1)**, [156]
pressurising act of, **7(1)**, [167]
principal, liability of, **7(1)**, [168]
proceedings, **7(1)**, [183]
public authorities, by—
additional, **7(1)**, [211], [212]
decision not to prosecute, exception for, **7(1)**, [153]
generally, **7(1)**, [149]
immigration and nationality cases, exception for, **7(1)**, [151], [152]
judicial and legislative acts, exceptions for, **7(1)**, [150]
meaning, **7(1)**, [149]
original categories of, **7(1)**, [210]
qualifying body, by, **7(1)**, [139]
racial grounds, meaning, **7(1)**, [128]

racial discrimination—*contd*
racial group—
meaning, **7(1)**, [128]
special needs of, **7(1)**, [173], [174]
relationships which have come to an end, **7(1)**, [163]
seamen, **7(1)**, [136]
segregation as, **7(1)**, [126]
Sikh, safety helmet, arising from obligation to wear, **7(1)**, [230]
specified bodies, general statutory duty, **7(1)**, [191]–[193]
sports and competitions, in, **7(1)**, [175]
statutory authority, act done under, **7(1)**, [177]
sub-letting, in, **7(1)**, [158]
trade union, by, **7(1)**, [138]
training body, by, **7(1)**, [173], [174]
training, in provision of, **7(1)**, [142]
transitional provisions, **7(1)**, [215]
undertakings, in rules of, **7(1)**, [195]
employment tribunal, complaint to, **7(1)**, [196]
unlawful act, aiding, **7(1)**, [169]
urban development corporation, by, **7(1)**, [148]
victimisation, by, **7(1)**, [127]
vocational training body, by, **7(1)**, [140]

Racial Equality, Commission for. *See under* **Commission for Racial Equality**

racial hatred
chanting at football matches, **13**, [409]
inflammatory material—
entry and search for, **12(1)**, [1018]
forfeiture of, **12(1)**, [1019]
possession of, **12(1)**, [1017]
meaning, **12(1)**, [1011]
offences—
corporations, by, **12(1)**, [1022]
penalties, **12(1)**, [1021]
proceedings for, **12(1)**, [1021]
stirring up—
broadcasting programmes, **12(1)**, [1016]
cable programme service, **12(1)**, [1016]
judicial proceedings, saving for, **12(1)**, [1020]
parliamentary proceedings, saving for, **12(1)**, [1020]
public performance, by, **12(1)**, [1014]
visual or sound recording, by, **12(1)**, [1015]
words or behaviour, by, **12(1)**, [1012]
written material—
displaying, **12(1)**, [1012]
meaning, **12(1)**, [1012]
publishing or distributing, **12(1)**, [1013]

radiation
congenital disability, causing, **45**, [959]

radio. *See* **wireless telegraphy**

Radio Authority
Independent Broadcasting Authority services, transitional arrangements, generally, **45**, [155], [199]
OFCOM, functions transferred to, **45**, [755]

radio services (independent). *See also* **wireless telegraphy**
additional, meaning, **45**, [146]
community radio, **45**, [633]
competition between licensed providers, **45**, [682], [689]
digital. *See* **digital broadcasting** (sound)
equal opportunities and training, promotion of, **45**, [703]
frequencies, assignment of, abolition of function of, **45**, [625]
  See also sound broadcasting frequencies *below*
Independent Broadcasting Authority transitional arrangements, generally, **45**, [155], [199]
  See further under **Independent Broadcasting Authority** (sound broadcasting)
licences—
  abolition of separate licences for certain sound services, **45**, [630]
  duration, **45**, [122]
  enforcement—
    correction or apology, **45**, [141]
    financial penalty, **45**, [142]
    revocation, **45**, [143]
    suspension or shortening, **45**, [142]
  existing, extension and modification of, **45**, [631]
  general conditions, **45**, [123]
  generally, **45**, [122]
    restrictions, **45**, [124]
  holding of—
    disqualification, **45**, [189], [712]
    religious bodies—
      approval required, **45**, [770]
      disqualification, **45**, [189]
    restrictions, **45**, [124], [188]
      relaxation of, **45**, [713]
  local, restrictions on holding, **45**, [768]
  period of, **45**, [122]
  simulcast broadcast, **45**, [130]
  variation, **45**, [122]
licensed services—
  Government requirement for, **45**, [702]
  provision of, **45**, [121]
local and other services licences. *See under* sound broadcasting services *below*
monitoring of programmes, **45**, [700]
national licences. *See under* sound broadcasting services *below*
OFCOM, regulation by, **45**, [624]
party political broadcasts, **45**, [699]
programme and fairness standards, **45**, [693]
  advertisements and sponsorship, objectives for, **45**, [687]

radio services (independent)—*contd*
programme and fairness standards—*contd*
  advertising, supplementary powers relating to, **45**, [688]
  fairness code, duty to observe, **45**, [692]
  OFCOM's standards code, **45**, [685]
    observance of, **45**, [691]
    setting and publication of, **45**, [690]
  special impartiality requirements, **45**, [686]
programme service, meaning, **45**, [184]
proscription orders, **45**, [695]
  effect of, **45**, [696]
  notification, **45**, [697], [698]
providers, OFCOM grants to, **45**, [722]
qualifying revenue, computation, **45**, [153], [193]
radio licensable content services—
  licences—
    abolition of separate licences for certain sound services, **45**, [630]
    application for, **45**, [629]
  meaning, **45**, [626], [628]
  services not being, **45**, [627], [628]
simulcast broadcasts, licence conditions, **45**, [130]
sound broadcasting frequencies—
  additional services on—
    interference with other transmissions, **45**, [151]
    licence—
      additional payments, **45**, [150]
      conditions, **45**, [147], [150]
      enforcement, **45**, [152]
    licensing generally, **45**, [147]
    meaning, **45**, [146]
    provision, **45**, [146]
sound broadcasting services—
  additional—
    licence—
      application for, **45**, [148]
      award, **45**, [149]
      information required for, **45**, [148]
      technical plan requirements, **45**, [148]
  annual report by OFCOM on, **45**, [721]
  change of control—
    meaning, **45**, [720]
    review by OFCOM, **45**, [718]
    variation of licence following, **45**, [719]
  local and other service licences—
    application for, **45**, [135]
    area, **45**, [154]
    character and coverage—
      change of, consultation on, **45**, [140]
      requirements, **45**, [139]
    conditions, **45**, [123]
    duration, **45**, [122]
    enforcement. *See under* licences *above*
    general provisions, **45**, [122]
    grant, **45**, [135]
    holding of—
      disqualifications. *See* licences *above*
      restrictions, **45**, [124]
    renewal, **45**, [136]
    revocation, **45**, [131], [143]
    special application procedure, **45**, [137]

radio services (independent)—*contd*
　sound broadcasting services—*contd*
　　local and other service licences—*contd*
　　　special requirements, **45**, [138]
　　　unlicensed, prohibition, **45**, [126]
　　　variation following change of control,
　　　　45, [140], [718]
　　local, content and character of, **45**, [681]
　　national licence—
　　　additional payments, **45**, [132]
　　　application for, **45**, [127]
　　　　consideration procedure, **45**, [128]
　　　　information required, **45**, [127]
　　　　proposals in, **45**, [127]
　　　　reference to Secretary of State,
　　　　　45, [129]
　　　award—
　　　　highest cash bid, **45**, [129]
　　　　notice of, **45**, [127]
　　　　publication of, **45**, [129]
　　　changes in control over, restriction,
　　　　45, [133]
　　　character and coverage, **45**, [139], [140]
　　　commencement of service, failure in,
　　　　45, [131]
　　　conditions, **45**, [123]
　　　enforcement. *See under* licences *above*
　　　failure to provide service, **45**, [131]
　　　general provisions, **45**, [122]
　　　holder of, changes in control,
　　　　restriction, **45**, [133]
　　　holding of—
　　　　disqualifications. *See* licences *above*
　　　　restrictions, **45**, [124]
　　　period of, **45**, [122]
　　　renewal, **45**, [134]
　　　revocation, **45**, [131], [143]
　　　suspension or shorten period, **45**, [142]
　　　unlicensed, prohibition, **45**, [126]
　　national service—
　　　area, **45**, [127]
　　　character and coverage, requirements,
　　　　45, [139]
　　　differing tastes and interests, provision
　　　　for, **45**, [121]
　　　music and pop music, **45**, [121]
　　　simulcast service, licence conditions as to,
　　　　45, [130]
　　unlicensed, prohibition, **45**, [126]

radioactive substances. *See also* **atomic**
energy
　clocks and watches containing, **17(2)**, [71],
　　[78]
　consents required, **49**, [1162]
　Crown, provisions applied, **17(2)**, [106]
　disregard of radioactivity, **17(2)**, [104], [116]
　documents and records, public access to,
　　17(2), [103]
　enforcement notices, **17(2)**, [86]
　exploration of continental shelf, areas of,
　　17(1), [292]
　interpretation of terms, **17(2)**, [110]
　local authorities, functions of, **17(2)**, [83]
　meaning, **38(1)**, [268]

radioactive substances—*contd*
　mobile apparatus—
　　meaning, **17(2)**, [68]
　　registration of users—
　　　appeals, **17(2)**, [91], [92]
　　　application for, **17(2)**, [73]
　　　cancellation or variation, **17(2)**, [75]
　　　exemptions from, **17(2)**, [74]
　　　requirement for, **17(2)**, [72]
　　waste from. *See* radioactive waste *below*
　offences—
　　another's fault, due to, **17(2)**, [101]
　　bodies corporate, by, **17(2)**, [100]
　　display of documents, relating to,
　　　17(2), [97]
　　false entries, making, **17(2)**, [99]
　　false or misleading statements, making,
　　　17(2), [99]
　　institution of proceedings, **17(2)**, [102]
　　records, relating to, **17(2)**, [97]
　　registration or authorisation, relating to,
　　　17(2), [96]
　　trade secrets, disclosure of, **17(2)**, [98]
　orphan sources, recovery and disposal of,
　　17(2), [95]
　pollution by, **49**, [1161]
　prohibition notices, **17(2)**, [87]
　radioactive material—
　　meaning, **17(2)**, [66]
　　registration of users—
　　　appeals, **17(2)**, [91], [92]
　　　application for—
　　　　matters to be given in, **17(2)**, [70]
　　　　procedure, **17(2)**, [70]
　　　　refusal of, **17(2)**, [70]
　　　exemptions from, **17(2)**, [71]
　　　offences, **17(2)**, [96]
　　　requirement for, **17(2)**, [69]
　　specified elements, **17(2)**, [115]
　　transport, regulation of, **38(2)**, [527]
　radioactive waste—
　　accumulations—
　　　authorisation—
　　　　appeals, **17(2)**, [91], [92]
　　　　meaning, **17(2)**, [79]
　　　　offences, **17(2)**, [96]
　　　　procedure for, **17(2)**, [79]
　　　　public and local authorities, functions
　　　　　of, **17(2)**, [83]
　　　　review of, **17(2)**, [82]
　　　　revocation or variation, **17(2)**, [81]
　　　　transfer of, **17(2)**, [80]
　　disposal. *See* disposal of *below*
　　exemptions, **17(2)**, [78]
　　facilities, provision of, **17(2)**, [93]
　　restrictions as to, **17(2)**, [77]
　　disposal of—
　　　authorisation—
　　　　appeals, **17(2)**, [91], [92]
　　　　meaning, **17(2)**, [79]
　　　　offences, **17(2)**, [96]
　　　　procedure for, **17(2)**, [79]
　　　　public and local authorities, functions
　　　　　of, **17(2)**, [83]
　　　　review of, **17(2)**, [82]

radioactive substances—*contd*
  radioactive waste—*contd*
    disposal of—*contd*
      authorisation—*contd*
        revocation or variation, **17(2)**, [81]
        transfer of, **17(2)**, [80]
      exemptions, **17(2)**, [78]
      facilities, provision of, **17(2)**, [93]
      meaning, **17(2)**, [110]
      means of, **17(2)**, [76]
    documents, display of, **17(2)**, [84]
      offences, **17(2)**, [97]
    meaning, **17(2)**, [67]
    records, retention and production of, **17(2)**, [85]
      offences, **17(2)**, [97]
    Secretary of State, powers of, **17(2)**, [94]
  regulations and orders—
    exercise of power to make, **17(2)**, [107]
    Northern Ireland, **17(2)**, [108]
  Secretary of State—
    applications to be determined by, power to require, **17(2)**, [89]
    directions by, **17(2)**, [88]
    knowledge of applications, restricting, **17(2)**, [90]
  service of documents, **17(2)**, [105]
  transitional provisions, **17(2)**, [118]
  transport by road—
    definitions, **38(1)**, [268]
    enforcement notices, **38(1)**, [271]
    entry, vehicles and premises, powers, **38(1)**, [272]
    examiner—
      entry, power of, **38(1)**, [272]
      meaning, **38(1)**, [268]
      powers, **38(1)**, [270]
    expenses, Secretary of State, **38(1)**, [274]
    inspectors—
      appointment, **38(1)**, [268]
      entry, power of, **38(1)**, [272]
      powers, **38(1)**, [270]
      meaning, **38(1)**, [268]
    Northern Ireland, corresponding provision, **38(1)**, [275]
    offences and penalties, **38(1)**, [273]
    packaging—
      meaning, **38(1)**, [268]
      regulations, **38(1)**, [269]
    prohibitions and directions, **38(1)**, [270]
    regulations, **38(1)**, [269]
    summary of provisions, **36**, [210]

Radiochemical Company
  accounts of, **17(1)**, [437]
  borrowing, Treasury guarantees, **17(1)**, [496]
  employees—
    conditions of employment, **17(1)**, [432]
    contracts of employment, **17(1)**, [433]
    transfer of, to, **17(1)**, [431]
  financial limits, **17(1)**, [497]
  Harwell premises, use of, **17(1)**, [428]
  pension scheme, **17(1)**, [440]
  services for, provision of, **17(1)**, [437]

Radiochemical Company—*contd*
  transfer of undertaking to—
    certification of, **17(1)**, [429]
    directions by Minister, **17(1)**, [429]
    parts transferred, **17(1)**, [426]
    stamp duty exemption, **17(1)**, [442]
    supplementary provisions, **17(1)**, [444]

rag dealer
  inducements offered by, prohibition of, **35(1)**, [496]

Rail Accident Investigation Branch
  aim of, **38(2)**, [235]
  assistance, providing, **38(2)**, [236]
  Chief Inspector—
    annual report, **38(2)**, [237]
    appointment, **38(2)**, [234]
  establishment of, **38(2)**, [234]
  inspectors—
    appointment, **38(2)**, [234]
    functions of, **38(2)**, [234]
    powers of, **38(2)**, [239]
  investigations—
    accidents or incidents, of, **38(2)**, [238]
    regulations, **38(2)**, [240], [244]
    reopening, **38(2)**, [238]

rail crossing
  diversion of footpath—
    bridleway or restricted byway—
      order—
        compensation and expenses, **36**, [1154]
        confirmation, **36**, [1154]
        form of, **36**, [1154]
      right of way—
        created by, **36**, [1154]
  diversion of footpath or bridleway orders, making of, **36**, [1159]
  emergency works affecting, notice of, **38(1)**, [236]
  extinguishment orders, making of, **36**, [1149]
  stopping up, **36**, [1149]
  street works affecting, notice of, **38(1)**, [236]

Rail Passengers' Committees
  abolition, **38(2)**, [408]
  discontinuance of railway services, proposal for, **36**, [717]
  international railway passenger services, **37**, [521]
  services and facilities, recommendations on, **36**, [717]

Rail Passengers' Council
  accounts and audit, **38(2)**, [451]
  annual reports, **38(2)**, [452]
  Central Rail Users' Consultative Committee renamed as, **38(2)**, [190]
  delegation of duties, **38(1)**, [426]
  domestic coach services, functions as to, **38(2)**, [407]
  establishment of, **38(2)**, [406]
  execution of documents, **38(2)**, [454]

Rail Passengers' Council—*contd*
  finance, **38(2)**, [451]
  financial framework, **38(2)**, [452]
  general duties, **38(1)**, [425]
  grants to, **38(2)**, [451]
  information, **38(2)**, [452]
  international railway passenger services,
    37, [521]
  interpretation, **38(2)**, [449]
  local committees, **38(2)**, [454]
  local services, functions as to, **38(2)**, [407]
  meetings, admission of public to, **38(2)**, [454]
  members—
    appointment, **38(2)**, [406]
    remuneration, **38(2)**, [450]
    termination of appointments, **38(2)**, [406]
  non-rail functions conferred on, **38(2)**, [407]
  passenger transport facilities, functions as to,
    38(2), [407]
  procedure, **38(2)**, [454]
  representations by, **38(1)**, [425]
  services and facilities, recommendations on,
    36, [717]
  staff, **38(2)**, [450]
  status, **38(2)**, [453]
  summary of provisions, **36**, [210]
  supplementary powers, **38(2)**, [453]

Rail Regulator
  abolition of office, **38(2)**, [247], [261]–[263]
  Office of Rail Regulation, transfer of
    functions to, **38(2)**, [247]

Rail Users' Consultative Committees. *See
now* **Rail Passengers' Committees**

Railtrack plc
  operational land, entry on, **26(1)**, [221]

railway
  accident—
    compensation—
      arbitrator determining, **36**, [475]
      medical examination, **36**, [476]
    entry on land to prevent, **36**, [239]
    investigation, by industry—
      direction for, **38(2)**, [241]
      requirement, **38(2)**, [241]
    meaning, **38(2)**, [233]
    Rail Accident Investigation Branch. *See*
      Rail Accident Investigation Branch
    referee, matters referred to, **36**, [718]
    regulations, **38(2)**, [242]
  accommodation works—
    additional, owners making, **36**, [322]
    crossing before making of, **36**, [325]
    disputes, determination of, **36**, [320]
    engineer, superintendence by, **36**, [323]
    execution on default, **36**, [321]
    gates, omitting to fasten, **36**, [326]
    prescribed period for, **36**, [324]
    provision and maintenance of, **36**, [319]
  arbitration, service of notices, **36**, [356]

railway—*contd*
  bridge. *See* **bridge**
  bridge over—
    load-bearing capacity, **36**, [856]
    London Regional Transport—
      duties of, **36**, [856]
      works, doing, **36**, [857]
    maintenance, responsibility for, **36**, [855]
    owner, duties of, **36**, [857]
    Railways Board—
      duties of, **36**, [856]
      works, doing, **36**, [857]
    trunk or special road, carrying, **36**, [858]
    undertakers, provisions applied to,
      36, [859]
  bridleway crossing, stopping up, **36**, [1149]
  bridleways over, **38(1)**, [327]
    stopping up and diversion of, **38(1)**, [326]
  byelaws—
    British Railways Board, made by, **36**, [721]
    conduct and accessibility, as to,
      38(2), [432], [457]
    defacement of boards publishing, **36**, [359]
  carriage. *See* **railway carriage**
  cattle-grid, consent for works on, **36**, [1093]
  charge to tax, **44(1)**, [34]
  charges. *See* **British Railways Board**
  closures. *See* **British Railways Board**;
    railway passenger services
  collisions, measures to prevent, **36**, [210]
  common carrier, no person regarded as,
    38(1), [467]
  common form clauses, **36**, [210], [261]
  company. *See* **railway company**
  compliance with condition or requirement,
    orders for, **38(2)**, [222]
    final, **38(1)**, [397]
    information, power to require, **38(1)**, [406]
    penalties—
      imposition of, **38(1)**, [400]
      interest and payment by instalments,
        38(1), [404]
      procedural requirements, **38(1)**, [402]
      statement of policy, **38(1)**, [401]
      time limits, **38(1)**, [403]
      validity and effect of, **38(1)**, [405]
    procedural requirements, **38(1)**, [398]
    provisional, **38(1)**, [397]
    revocation, **38(1)**, [398]
    validity and effect of, **38(1)**, [399]
  construction of—
    accommodation works. *See* accommodation
      works *above*
    arches, marking, **36**, [272]
    compulsory purchase for, **36**, [240]
    compensation, **36**, [265]
    damage, limiting, **36**, [275]
    drains and conduits, making, **36**, [275]
    extension of time for—
      compensation, **36**, [450]
      contracts and notices, not affecting,
        36, [451]
    gas pipes, alteration of, **36**, [277]–[282]
    inclined planes, making, **36**, [275]

railway—*contd*
  construction of—*contd*
    land, temporary use of—
      compensation for, **36**, [284], [297], [298]
      justices' order, **36**, [290], [291]
      materials, for purpose of getting,
        36, [295]
      notice of, **36**, [287], [288]
      objections to, **36**, [285], [289]
      other owners, justices summoning,
        36, [292]
      previous payment, without, **36**, [286]
      private road, of, **36**, [284]
      purchase money or compensation,
        ascertaining, **36**, [298]
      purchase, owners compelling, **36**, [296]
      separation before use, **36**, [294]
      sureties, company giving, **36**, [293]
    obstructing, penalty for, **36**, [283]
    pipes—
      alteration of, **36**, [277]
      culvert, making, **36**, [281]
      damage, making good, **36**, [280]
      regulations to be followed, **36**, [279]
      replacement before removal of, **36**, [278]
      supply, obstruction of, **36**, [282]
      surface road over, **36**, [279]
    plans—
      alterations to, deposit and inspection of,
        36, [268]
      arches, marking, **36**, [272]
      authorised, **36**, [267]
      certified copies as evidence, **36**, [269]
      deposit of, **36**, [267]
      deviation from, **36**, [438]
        curves, as to, **36**, [273]
        datum line, limitation from, **36**, [270]
        gradients, as to, **36**, [273]
        lateral, **36**, [274]
        levels, as to, **36**, [270]
        notice of, **36**, [271]
        tunnels, as to, **36**, [272]
      errors and omissions, correction of,
        36, [266]
      inspection of, **36**, [268]
      tunnels, marking, **36**, [272]
    powers, statutory restrictions on, **36**, [265]
    rivers etc, alteration of course of, **36**, [275]
    road—
      bridge. *See* **bridge**
      bridge over. *See* bridge over *above*
      crossing. *See* **level crossing**
      interference with—
        failure to restore or substitute,
          36, [310]
        penalties, **36**, [308]
        restoration of, **36**, [309]
        special damage, action for, **36**, [308]
        substitution before, **36**, [306], [307]
      modification of construction, **36**, [317]
      private, use of, **36**, [284]
      repair of, **36**, [311]
    tunnels, marking, **36**, [272]
    warehouses, construction of, **36**, [275]
    water pipes, alteration of, **36**, [277]–[282]

railway—*contd*
  construction of—*contd*
    works—
      alteration of, **36**, [275]
      high-water mark, below, **36**, [276]
      power to execute, **36**, [275]
  Convention on International Carriage by,
    giving effect to, **38(2)**, [249], [264]
  crossing. *See* **level crossing**
  crossings, stopping up and diversion of,
    38(1), [326]
  Crossrail. *See* **Crossrail**
  Crown, provisions binding, **38(1)**, [482]
  cutting, running in, **36**, [860]
  damages—
    ascertainment of, **36**, [357]
    proceedings before justices, **36**, [358]
    recovery of, **36**, [360]
  dangerous goods, carriage of, **36**, [343]
  dangerous operations, rules as to. *See* safety
    provisions *below*
  definitions, **43(1)**, [117]
  disabled accessibility regulations—
    Disabled Persons Transport Advisory
      Committee, Secretary of State to consult
      with, **7(1)**, [443]
    exemption from, **7(1)**, [411]
    exemption orders, annual report on,
      7(1), [444]
    general, **7(1)**, [410]
    offences by bodies corporate, **7(1)**, [424]
  disability discrimination provisions, application
    of—
    accessibility compliance certificates,
      7(1), [739]
    accessibility regulations, **7(1)**, [738]
    enforcement and penalties, **7(1)**, [740]
  disclosure of information, restrictions on,
    38(1), [821]
  drink or drugs, offences involving—
    application of provisions, **38(1)**, [310]
    employee, by, **38(1)**, [311]
    evidence—
      documentary, **38(1)**, [320]
      specimens, use of, **38(1)**, [319]
    maintenance worker, by, **38(1)**, [311]
    operator, by, **38(1)**, [312]
    penalties, **38(1)**, [321]
    police, powers of—
      breath tests, **38(1)**, [313]
      entry and arrest, of, **38(1)**, [314]
      hospital patients, protection for,
        38(1), [318]
      persons incapable of consenting,
        specimens of blood from, **38(1)**, [316]
      specimens for analysis, requirement of,
        38(1), [315]
      two specimens of breath, choice of,
        38(1), [317]
    prescribed limit, **38(1)**, [322]
    principal, **38(1)**, [311]
  endangering passengers on—
    firearm, while possessing, **12(1)**, [545]
    offences, **12(1)**, [88]–[90]

railway—*contd*

experimental passenger services. *See* **railway passenger services**

false statements, making, **38(1)**, [477]

flood defence works, protection in relation to, **49**, [1291]

footpath crossing, stopping up, **36**, [1149]

footpaths over, **38(1)**, [327]

stopping up and diversion of, **38(1)**, [326]

goods, carriage of—

dangerous, **36**, [343]

use of equipment for, **36**, [336]

heritage. *See* **railway heritage**

hostilities, control in time of, **38(1)**, [461]

incident—

investigation, by industry—

direction for, **38(2)**, [241]

requirement, **38(2)**, [241]

meaning, **38(2)**, [233]

regulations, **38(2)**, [242]

independent operators, byelaws, **38(1)**, [649]

independent, provisions relating to, **36**, [716]

investment in, encouragement of, **38(1)**, [396]

junction, maintenance of signals and conveniences, **36**, [442]

land—

adjoining, power to enter, **36**, [239]

operator, entry by, **38(1)**, [329]

leases—

conditions in, **36**, [344]

lessees, powers exercised by, **36**, [345]

light railway. *See* **light railway**

London, in—

Public-Private Partnership Agreement Arbiter, provision of information to, **38(2)**, [252]

transfer schemes, **38(2)**, [251]

malicious damage to, **12(1)**, [61]

meaning, **33(2)**, [468]; **36**, [241], [1149]; **38(1)**, [249], [339], [428]; **38(2)**, [232]

milestone—

pulling down, **36**, [340]

setting up and maintaining, **36**, [339]

mines under or near—

agreements, saving for, **36**, [594]

arbitration, provisions as to, **36**, [594]

communications, provision for, **36**, [330]

compensation—

damage, for, **36**, [594]

injury, for, **36**, [331]

leaving unworked, for, **36**, [594]

surface lands, damage to, **36**, [332]

surface owners, **36**, [594]

working, relating to, **36**, [328], [329]

entry and inspection of, **36**, [333]

penalty for refusal to allow, **36**, [334]

existing railway, provisions applying to, **36**, [595]

inspection—

refusal to allow, **36**, [594]

rights of, **36**, [594]

minerals, rights to, **36**, [327]

rights, variation of, **36**, [594]

seam, depth of, **36**, [594]

service of notices, **36**, [594]

railway—*contd*

mines under or near—*contd*

support, agreement as to, **36**, [594]

working—

access, rights of, **36**, [594]

area of protection, **36**, [594]

authorised, liability for, **36**, [594]

compensation, **36**, [328], [329]

conditions for, **36**, [594], [597]–[599]

counter-notice, **36**, [594]

damage done by—

accounts, keeping, **36**, [594]

compensation for, **36**, [594]

notices, **36**, [594]

improper—

damage or obstruction by, **36**, [329]

protection against, **36**, [335], [594]

severance, expenses of, **36**, [594]

national emergency, control in time of, **38(1)**, [461]

nationalisation, **36**, [210]

nationally significant infrastructure projects, **46(S)**, 46–8. *See also* **nationally significant infrastructure projects**

nuisance, statutory authority as defence to actions in, **38(1)**, [466]

obstructing engine or carriage, **12(1)**, [62]

offences—

body corporate, by, **38(1)**, [478]

Scotland, proceedings in, **38(1)**, [479]

Scottish partnerships, by, **38(1)**, [478]

orders—

applications for, **38(1)**, [295]

compulsory purchase, authorisation of, **38(1)**, [302]

consents under enactments, **38(1)**, [305]

Crown land, **38(1)**, [309]

inquiries and hearings, **38(1)**, [301]

made other than on application, **38(1)**, [297]

making, **38(1)**, [303]

model clauses, **38(1)**, [298]

national significance, schemes of, **38(1)**, [299]

objections to, **38(1)**, [300]

other Member States affected, where, **38(1)**, [296]

power to apply for or object to, **38(1)**, [306]

power to make, **38(1)**, [290]

publicity, **38(1)**, [304]

refusal of, **38(1)**, [303]

special parliamentary procedure, **38(1)**, [302]

subject-matter of, **38(1)**, [294], [345]

validity of, **38(1)**, [307]

passenger networks, proposal to close. *See* **railway passenger services**

passenger services, proposal to close. *See* **railway passenger services**

passengers, carriage of—

fare, avoiding, **36**, [568]

penalty fares, **38(1)**, [468]

refusal to quit carriage, **36**, [342]

use of equipment for, **36**, [336]

railway—*contd*
  passengers, carriage of—*contd*
    See also **railway passenger services**
  penalties, recovery of, **36**, [360], [478]
  person killed on, inquest on, **11(1)**, [1217]
  premises—
    disabled persons, provision for, at,
      35(1), [289]
    hackney carriages at, **35(1)**, [101]
    health, safety and welfare—
      See also **health and safety at work**
      agreements, modification, **18**, [1237]
      buildings—
        plurally owned, provisions as to,
          18, [1227]
        single ownership, in, provisions as to,
          18, [1226]
      cleanliness, **18**, [1211]
      clothing, accommodation and drying,
        18, [1219]
      complaint, appeal from order made on,
        18, [1236]
      disclosure of information, restriction of,
        18, [1231]
        public authorities, exception for,
          18, [1232]
      drinking water, supply, **18**, [1218]
      eating facilities, **18**, [1222]
      employment of person, notification,
        18, [1230]
      exemptions, power to grant, **18**, [1229]
      expenses—
        apportionment, **18**, [1237]
        Minister's, **18**, [1242]
      floors and passages, construction and
        maintenance, **18**, [1223]
      fuel storage, **18**, [1228]
      heavy work, prohibitions, **18**, [1225]
      hours worked, limited, exceptions
        where, **18**, [1210]
      lighting, **18**, [1215]
      local Act, exercise of powers under,
        18, [1240]
      machinery, fencing, **18**, [1224]
      meaning, **18**, [1208]
      offences—
        appeal against order, **18**, [1236]
        defence available, **18**, [1234]
        generally, **18**, [1233]
        removal or defacement of
          documents, **18**, [1235]
      overcrowding, **18**, [1212]
      premises to which provisions apply,
        18, [1208]
      sanitary conveniences, **18**, [1216]
      seating facilities, **18**, [1220], [1221]
      stairs and steps, construction and
        maintenance, **18**, [1223]
      temperature, **18**, [1213]
      transitory purposes, exclusion where
        used for, **18**, [1246]
      ventilation, **18**, [1214]
      visiting forces, exclusion of application,
        18, [1244]
      washing facilities, **18**, [1217]

railway—*contd*
  private crossings, signs and barriers at—
    default powers, **38(1)**, [330]
    failure to comply with, **38(1)**, [331]
    meaning, **38(1)**, [332]
    placing of, **38(1)**, [328]
  private, provisions on, **36**, [210]
  property, meaning, **33(2)**, [468]; **38(2)**, [232]
  public sector funding—
    financial assistance—
      Scotland, in, **38(2)**, [397]
      Secretary of State, from, **38(2)**, [395]
      Wales, in, **38(2)**, [399]
    franchising—
      Passenger Transport Executive, functions
        of, **38(2)**, [402]
      Scotland, in, **38(2)**, [397]
      transfer schemes at end of agreements,
        38(2), [401], [446]
      Wales, in, **38(2)**, [399]
    freight services, notification of assistance
      for, **38(2)**, [396]
      Scottish Ministers, from, **38(2)**, [398]
      Welsh Assembly, from, **38(2)**, [400]
  records and artefacts. *See* heritage *above*
  regulations and orders, power to make,
    38(1), [474]
  rent payable in respect of, **44(1)**, [98]
  restricted byway crossing, stopping up,
    36, [1149]
  retention where highway not stopped up or
    diverted, **9**, [141]
  rolling stock—
    appeals, **36**, [543]
    distress, protection from, **36**, [540], [541]
    execution against, restriction on, **36**, [458],
      [459]
    meaning, **36**, [538]
    tenant's interest, protection of, **36**, [542]
    See also **railway carriage; railway engine**
  safety accreditation scheme, **33(2)**, [380]
  safety levy, **18**, [1296]
  safety provisions—
    bodies corporate, offences by, **38(1)**, [335]
    Health and Safety at Work etc Act,
      application of provisions of, **38(1)**, [460]
    insurance, directions requiring, **38(1)**, [325]
    prosecutions, consent to, **38(1)**, [334]
    speeds and loads, directions limiting,
      38(1), [324]
    works, plant and equipment, approval of,
      38(1), [323]
  savings banks, **36**, [720]
  Scotland, **36**, [210]
  Secretary of State—
    requisitions etc to be signed by, **36**, [477]
    transmission of returns to, **36**, [477]
  security—
    approved providers, **38(1)**, [465]
    enforcement notices, **38(1)**, [463]
    inspections, **38(1)**, [464]
    Secretary of State, instructions from,
      38(1), [462]
  service of documents, **38(1)**, [480], [481]
  service of notices, **36**, [356]

railway—*contd*
  service of notices, **38(1)**, [338]
  severe international tension, control in time
    of, **38(1)**, [461]
  site, removal of track from, **36**, [860]
  special Act—
    copies, keeping for inspection, **36**, [361]
    failure to keep copies, **36**, [362]
    interpretation, **36**, [263]
    meaning, **36**, [262]
  station, proposal to close. *See* **railway**
    passenger services
  steam vessels, recovery of tolls and charges
    for, **36**, [452], [453]
  stone etc thrown at, **12(1)**, [89]
  strategy—
    access charges reviews, use of, **38(2)**, [393]
    Scotland, for, **38(2)**, [394]
  streets or bridges controlled by, breaking up
    by water authorities, **49**, [366]
  ticket, failure to produce, **36**, [568]
  tidal lands or water, on, across etc—
    abandoned or decayed work, abatement
      of, **36**, [448]
    bridge—
      construction of, **36**, [444]
      opening, user of, **36**, [445]
    deviation from centre line, **36**, [447]
    shore, access to, **36**, [446]
    survey of works, **36**, [449]
    works, lights on, **36**, [443]
  track, meaning, **38(1)**, [430]
  traffic, having ceased to carry, **36**, [860]
  tramway crossing, **36**, [499]
  transfers—
    capital allowances, **43(1)**, [117]
    chargeable gains—
      agreements and instruments, **43(1)**, [117]
      assets held before 6 April 1965,
        43(1), [117]
      compensation or insurance policies,
        receipt of, **43(1)**, [117]
      debts, disposal of, **43(1)**, [117]
      disposals and acquisitions,
        miscellaneous, **43(1)**, [117]
      gain or loss, transfer without,
        43(1), [117]
      group transactions, **43(1)**, [117]
      roll-over relief, **43(1)**, [117]
      schemes and arrangements, **43(1)**, [117]
    commencement of provisions, **43(1)**, [110]
    employee benefits, **43(1)**, [117]
    group relief, **43(1)**, [117]
    income tax exemption, **43(1)**, [117]
    land, sale with right to reconveyance,
      43(1), [117]
    leased assets, **43(1)**, [117]
    liabilities, of, **43(1)**, [117]
    restructuring scheme, modifications of,
      43(1), [117]
    rights to receipts, of, **43(1)**, [117]
    sale and lease-back, **43(1)**, [117]
    securities issued under Railways Act 1993,
      43(1), [117]
    trading losses, **43(1)**, [117]

railway—*contd*
  transfers—*contd*
    trading stock, of, **43(1)**, [117]
  trees dangerous to, removal of, **36**, [474]
  trespass on, **36**, [210], [236], [473]
  tunnel, carried by, **36**, [860]
  undertakings—
    accounts and returns by, **36**, [659]
    independent, charges of, **36**, [716]
    pipe-lines, provisions as to, **17(1)**, [274]
  Wales-only service, meaning, **38(2)**, [441]
  Welsh service, meaning, **38(2)**, [441]

railway administration order
  charged property, dealing with, **38(1)**, [489]
  company, meaning, **38(1)**, [414]
  court, applications to, **38(1)**, [489]
  discharge, **38(1)**, [489]
  effect of, **38(1)**, [407], [489]
  foreign companies—
    in relation to, **38(1)**, [490]
    provisions on, **38(1)**, [414]
  Government financial assistance, **38(1)**, [411]
  Insolvency Act, modifications of,
    38(1), [489]–[491]
  meaning, **38(1)**, [407], [653]
  notice of making, **38(1)**, [489]
  purposes of, **38(1)**, [407], [653]
  relevant activities, transfer of, **38(1)**, [492]
  Scottish Ministers—
    financial assistance by, **38(1)**, [413]
    functions of, **38(2)**, [434]
  Secretary of State, guarantees by, **38(1)**, [412]
  special petition, made on, **38(1)**, [408], [653]
  special railway administrator, **38(1)**, [489]
    foreign company, for, **38(1)**, [490]
  statement of proposals, **38(1)**, [489]

Railway and Canal Commission
  Northern Ireland, jurisdiction in respect of,
    36, [630]
  transfer of functions, **36**, [628]

railway assets
  meaning, **38(1)**, [350]
  operators—
    licences. *See* operators' licences *below*
    meaning, **38(1)**, [350]
    unauthorised, **38(1)**, [350], [650]
  operators' licences—
    application for, **38(1)**, [352]
    assignment, **38(1)**, [355]
    conditions—
      activities carried on by virtue of
        exemption, **38(1)**, [354]
      general, **38(1)**, [353]
    exemptions, **38(1)**, [351]
    fees, **38(1)**, [352]
    grant of, **38(1)**, [352]
    modification—
      agreement, by, **38(1)**, [356]
      Competition Commission, references
        to, **38(1)**, [357]–[359]
      Enterprise Act, application of provisions
        of, **38(1)**, [359]

railway assets—*contd*
operators' licences—*contd*
modification—*contd*
making of, **38(1)**, [363]
order, by, **38(1)**, [365]
reference, report on, **38(1)**, [360]
report, following, **38(1)**, [361]
veto, power to, **38(1)**, [362]
register of, **38(1)**, [421]
types of, **38(1)**, [352]
standards, setting of, **38(2)**, [194]

railway carriage
construction, regulations as to, **36**, [348], [349]
damage done by, liability for, **36**, [354]
improper, using, **36**, [350]
improperly loaded, removal of, **36**, [353]
non-compliance with regulations, removal on, **36**, [352]
obstruction, causing, **36**, [353]
owner's name and address, particulars of, **36**, [351]
passenger refusing to quit, **36**, [342]
unloading, damage caused by, **36**, [353]
weighing, measuring and gauging, **36**, [351]

railway company
adjoining land, entering on, **36**, [239]
amalgamation of, **36**, [210]
compulsory purchase by, **36**, [240]
culverting of stream or watercourse, saving as to, **35(1)**, [168]
debenture stock, issuing, **36**, [567]
explosives, carriage etc. *See* **explosives**
investment by trustee in, **48**, 457
maintenance of canal by, **36**, [546]
meaning, **35(1)**, [216]; **36**, [241], [457], [471]
obstructing officer of, **36**, [236]
other company, contracting with, **36**, [337]
third parties, not affecting, **36**, [338]
plant, restriction on execution against, **36**, [458], [459]
premises of, access to, **35(1)**, [94]
protected—
foreign, **38(1)**, [414]
insolvency proceedings, restrictions on, **38(1)**, [410]
meaning, **38(1)**, [407], [653]
voluntary winding-up, restrictions on, **38(1)**, [410]
winding-up order, restrictions on, **38(1)**, [409]
protection for works of, **35(1)**, [210]
publicly owned, meaning, **38(1)**, [483]
sea transit, limitation of liability during, **36**, [472]
sewers, etc, vested in local authority, power to alter, **35(1)**, [207]
works, apportionment of expenses, **36**, [552]

railway engine
approval of, **36**, [346]
damage done by, liability for, **36**, [355]

railway engine—*contd*
dark smoke, emission from—
exemption for investigation and research, **35(2)**, [45]
minimising, **35(2)**, [43]
prohibition of, **35(2)**, [43]
emission of smoke by, **36**, [210]
execution against, restriction on, **36**, [458], [459]
fire caused by—
agricultural land, damage to, **36**, [581]
application of provisions, conditions precedent to, **36**, [600]
extinction, powers as to, **36**, [582]
prevention of, **36**, [582]
improper, using, **36**, [347]
report on, **36**, [346]
smoke, emission from—
duty to minimise, **35(2)**, [43]
exemption for investigation and research, **35(2)**, [45]
unfit, removal of, **36**, [346]

railway facilities
access charges, review of, **38(1)**, [488]
access contract—
amendment of agreements, **38(1)**, [381]–[384]
applications for, **38(1)**, [487]
approval of Office of Rail Regulation, requiring, **38(1)**, [376]
directions, **38(1)**, [375], [651]
exemptions, **38(1)**, [379]
installations, **38(1)**, [377]
international, **38(1)**, [375]
meaning, **38(1)**, [375]
model clauses, **38(1)**, [380]
network, use of installations comprised in, **38(1)**, [377]
register of, **38(1)**, [421]
owner—
access contract, entry into, **38(1)**, [375]
meaning, **38(1)**, [375]
permission to use, meaning, **38(1)**, [375]
provision, improvement and development—
applications for, **38(1)**, [368]
code of practice, **38(1)**, [373]
compliance with, **38(1)**, [372]
consideration of, **38(1)**, [369]
decisions on applications, **38(1)**, [370], [371]
directions on, **38(1)**, [366]
exemptions, **38(1)**, [367]
revocation of, **38(1)**, [372]
supplementary provisions, **38(1)**, [374]
variation of, **38(1)**, [372]

railway heritage
bodies to which provisions apply, **38(1)**, [627]
Channel Tunnel. *See* **Channel Tunnel**
Committee, establishment of, **38(1)**, [628]
guidance and information for, **38(1)**, [632]
interpretation, **38(1)**, [633]
records and artefacts—
designation of, **38(1)**, [629]

railway heritage—*contd*
   records and artefacts—*contd*
      disposal of, **38(1)**, [631]
      notice of proposed disposal of, **38(1)**, [630]
   summary of provisions, **36**, [210]

railway passenger services
   closures—
      experimental services, of, **38(1)**, [652]
      guidance—
         consultations, **38(2)**, [428]
         duty to publish, **38(2)**, [428]
         modification, **38(2)**, [429]
         procedure, **38(2)**, [429]
      interpretation, **38(2)**, [431]
      meaning, **38(2)**, [431]
      minor modifications—
         eligibility to be treated as, **38(2)**, [422]
         proposals for, **38(2)**, [421]
      non-ratification notice, issue of,
         38(2), [419]
      proposals for. *See* proposals to close *below*
      railway passenger services, closures, register
         of, **38(1)**, [421]
      ratification notice, issue of, **38(2)**, [419]
      requirements, **38(2)**, [420]
   competent authority, **38(1)**, [471]
   disabled passengers—
      code of practice for interests of,
         38(1), [420]
         Scotland, **38(2)**, [433]
      substitute services to be suitable for,
         38(2), [195]
   experimental, **38(1)**, [652]
      designation of, **38(2)**, [423]
      discontinuance of, **38(2)**, [424]
   franchise agreements—
      absence of, duty of franchising authority
         in, **38(1)**, [393]
      approved discount fare scheme,
         participation in, **38(1)**, [391]
      assets and shares, transfer of, **38(1)**, [390]
      exemptions, **38(1)**, [386]
      fare, provision for, **38(1)**, [391]
      invitations to tender—
         no adequate tenders, **38(1)**, [389]
         procedure, **38(1)**, [388]
      leases in pursuance of, no security of tenure
         for, **38(1)**, [394]
      meaning, **38(1)**, [385]
      provision of services, reference to,
         38(1), [385]
      registers of, **38(1)**, [422], [423]
      subject to, **38(1)**, [385]
      terms and conditions of, **38(1)**, [392]
   franchisee—
      meaning, **38(1)**, [385]
      public service operators not to be,
         38(1), [387]
   grants and subsidies, **38(1)**, [471]
   Integrated Transport Executive, special duty as
      to, **36**, [787]
   passenger licence, meaning, **38(1)**, [430]
   Passenger Transport Executive, special duty as
      to, **36**, [787]

railway passenger services—*contd*
   proposal to close—
      breach of statutory duty, exclusion of
         liability for, **38(2)**, [430]
      consultations, **38(2)**, [455]
      excluded, **38(2)**, [412], [456]
      exclusions, **38(2)**, [425]
      franchised, **38(2)**, [411]
      networks—
         breach of statutory duty, exclusion of
            liability for, **38(2)**, [430]
         consultations, **38(2)**, [455]
         exclusions, **38(2)**, [425]
         funding authority, by, **38(2)**, [414],
            [427]
         operator, by, **38(2)**, [413]
         secured, **38(2)**, [415]
      non-franchised—
         funding authority, by, **38(2)**, [410],
            [427]
         service operator, by, **38(2)**, [409]
      secured, **38(2)**, [411]
      stations—
         breach of statutory duty, exclusion of
            liability for, **38(2)**, [430]
         consultations, **38(2)**, [455]
         exclusions, **38(2)**, [425]
         funding authority, by, **38(2)**, [417],
            [427]
         operator, by, **38(2)**, [416]
         secured, **38(2)**, [418]
   staff, concessionary travel for, **38(1)**, [470]
   substitute services to be suitable for disabled
      passengers, **38(2)**, [195]
   substitution services, road, **38(2)**, [426]
   Wales-only service, meaning, **38(2)**, [441]
   Welsh service, meaning, **38(2)**, [441]

railway services
   consequential modification of enactments,
      38(1), [485]
   grants and subsidies, **38(1)**, [471]
   international, controls on trains engaged on,
      37, [494], [495]
   meaning, **38(1)**, [429]
   network, **38(1)**, [429]
   standards, setting of, **38(2)**, [194]
   station, **38(1)**, [429]

railway station
   cabs, parking of, **36**, [586]
   meaning, **36**, [586]
   privileged cab system, abolition, **36**, [586]

railway undertakers
   drainage work affecting, protection,
      19(3), [259]
   mail, carriage of. *See* **post office**
   meaning, **36**, [1381]
   private street works expenses, exemption
      from, **36**, [1262]
   property of, reference to, **36**, [1381]
   protection of works of, **35(1)**, [650]

railway undertaking
control under emergency powers, exclusion of compensation where, **9**, [131]

railway vehicles
standards, setting of, **38(2)**, [194]

rams. *See* **sheep**

Ramsar sites
generally, **32**, [1]
wetlands, designation of as, **32**, [467]

rape
bail provisions, **12(2)**, [190]
child under 13, of, **12(3)**, [669]
firearm, possessing while committing, **12(1)**, [545]
offence, meaning, **12(1)**, [670]
offence of, **12(3)**, [665]
reasonable belief in consent to penetration, **12(3)**, [665]

rate support grant
increase of, under Children etc Act 1969, **6**, [132]

rateable value
apportionment, determination of, **21**, [546]
appropriate day, **21**, [546]
ascertainment of, **21**, [546]; **22**, [914]
leasehold enfranchisement and extension, and. *See* **leasehold enfranchisement; leasehold extension**
non-domestic rating, **25(2)**, [836]
multipliers, **25(1)**, [1]; **25(2)**, [837], [838]
protected tenancy, limits for, **21**, [523]
restricted contract, limit for, **21**, [540]

rates
abolition, **25(2)**, [811]
agricultural workers housing, **21**, [464], [498]
apportionment, **21**, [577]
borough rate, **25(1)**, [34]
caravan sites. *See* **caravan site**
council tax. *See* **council tax**
county rate, **25(1)**, [35]
demand note, information to accompany, **25(2)**, [428]
drainage. *See* **drainage rate**
former law, **25(1)**, [1]
general rate fund—
borough, of, **25(1)**, [687]
discontinuance of, **25(2)**, [795]
grants in support. *See* **local authority**
judges and justices, liability, not disqualified by, **49**, [346]
liability, **49**, [67], [332]
liability of judge or justice to, no disqualification, **35(1)**, [31], [194], [335], [508], [628]
London—
enactments amended and applied, **25(1)**, [716]

rates—*contd*
London—*contd*
recovery from tenant or lodger, **25(2)**, [296]
unpaid, charge on premises, **25(2)**, [297]
meaning, **21**, [637]
meter, payment by. *See* **water meters**
National Freight Corporation, transfer of liability of, **36**, [999]
non domestic. *See* **non-domestic rates**
occupier, payable by, **49**, [68]
payment of—
advance, in, **49**, [65]
dates for, **49**, [65]
on discontinuance of use, **49**, [66]
power to abolish or modify, **25(2)**, [812]
proceedings—
consolidation of, **25(1)**, [20]
judge, qualification of, **25(1)**, [21]
rate fund revenue accounts. *See* **local authority**
rate support grants—
abolition, **25(2)**, [815]
supplementary grants, **25(2)**, [303]
rating authority. *See* **rating authority**
rating officer, loss of employment, **25(1)**, [409]
recovery by taking control of goods, **25(2)**, [751]
recovery, consolidation of proceedings for, **25(1)**, [20]
recovery of—
generally, **49**, [332]
person using water, from, **49**, [63]
reduction, excess profits, in case of, **49**, [74]
registered rent taking account of, **21**, [572]
rental period, for, amount of, **21**, [646]
revenue support grant. *See* **local authority**
several houses, one pipe to, **49**, [64]
special grants, **25(2)**, [790], [791]
special, power to continue, **25(1)**, [26]
statement of, **20**, [488]
substituted, **25(2)**, [497]
supplementary—
limitation on, **25(2)**, [497]
transitional provisions, **25(2)**, [503]
tenant, recovery from, **49**, [68]
Thames Water Authority. *See* **Thames Water Authority**
validity, questioning, **25(2)**, [498]

rating
statutory references to, **25(2)**, [885]

rating authority
powers, limitation of, **25(2)**, [497]

rating lists
alteration of, **25(2)**, [742]
central—
compiling of, **25(2)**, [739]
contents of, **25(2)**, [740]
liability, **25(2)**, [741]
England and Wales, separate administration in, **25(2)**, [822]

rating lists—*contd*
inspection, **25(2)**, [843]
local—
compiling of, **25(2)**, [722], [723]
contents of, **25(2)**, [724]
Welsh billing authorities, for, **25(2)**, [723]
rural settlement list, **25(2)**, [725], [726]

rats
exempt from hunting provisions, **2**, [749]

rats and mice
destruction—
authentication of documents, **35(1)**, [232]
entry, powers of, **35(1)**, [241]
expenses of local authority, recovery of, **35(1)**, [231]
financial provisions, **35(1)**, [244]
groups of premises, in case of, **35(1)**, [230]
legal proceedings, **35(1)**, [243]
local authorities—
default, in, powers of Minister where, **35(1)**, [233]
expenses, recovery of, **35(1)**, [231]
for purposes of, **35(1)**, [225]
powers and duties as to, **35(1)**, [226]
notice requiring action for—
amendment of Agriculture Act 1947, **35(1)**, [239]
appeal against, **35(1)**, [228]
failure to comply with, remedies for, **35(1)**, [229]
local authority giving, **35(1)**, [228]
service of, **35(1)**, [232]
occupier, obligation to notify local authority of, **35(1)**, [227]
service of notices, **35(1)**, [232]
ships and aircraft—
application to, **35(1)**, [242]
inspection of ships, charges for, **35(1)**, [251]
food, infestation of. *See* **food**
keeping land free from. *See* destruction *above*

rave
entry and seizure, powers of, **12(2)**, [203]
meaning, **12(2)**, [202]
persons attending or preparing for, powers to remove, **12(2)**, [202]
power to stop persons proceeding to, **12(2)**, [204]
sound equipment, forfeiture of, **12(2)**, [205]

raw celluloid
celluloid, meaning, **35(1)**, [81]
premises where kept or stored—
fire in, prevention of, **35(1)**, [76]–[86]
fire-resisting store-rooms, regulations as to, **35(1)**, [76], [84], [86]
general safety provisions at, **35(1)**, [76]
local authorities, duties as regards, **35(1)**, [79]
offences connected with, **35(1)**, [78]

reader
duties performed by, **14**, 803
licence, revocation of, **14**, 1179
licensing for fixed term, **14**, 804

real estate. *See under* **personal representative;** *see also* **conveyancing and law of property**
assets for payment of debts, **18**, [535]
devise without words of limitation, **50**, [509]
escheat of, **18**, [493]
law applied to chattels real, **18**, [514]
meaning, **18**, [515], [556], [559]
personal representative, devolution on, **18**, [513]
succession to, on intestacy, **18**, [549]
valuation, mode of, **18**, [501]
will, disposable by, **50**, [486]

real estate investment trusts
amendment of provisions, **43(S)**, 692–5
asset, reference to, **43(S)**, 133
balance of business, conditions for, **43(S)**, 1633
capital gains—
corporation tax, **43(S)**, 121
movement of assets into ring-fence, **43(S)**, 123
movement of assets out of ring-fence, **43(S)**, 121–2
cessation of business, meaning, **43(S)**, 104
classes of business, **43(S)**, 352
classes of income or profit, **43(S)**, 353
commencement of provisions, **43(S)**, 134
company, conditions for, **43(S)**, 1633
entry notice, **43(S)**, 1633–4
conditions—
balance of business, for, **43(S)**, 107
company, for, **43(S)**, 104–5
tax-exempt business, for, **43(S)**, 105–6
connected persons, **43(S)**, 1635
corporation tax charge, **43(S)**, 116
deemed disposals and acquisitions, **43(S)**, 132
demergers, **43(S)**, 693–4
distributions—
attributions, **43(S)**, 120
deduction of tax, **43(S)**, 119–20
liability to tax, **43(S)**, 117–18
entering regime—
charge, **43(S)**, 109–10
duration, **43(S)**, 108
effects of, **43(S)**, 109
notice, **43(S)**, 108
entry, meaning, **43(S)**, 103
exemptions, benefit from, **43(S)**, 102–3
failure to give notice, penalties for, **43(S)**, 132
funds awaiting re-investment, **43(S)**, 1634
treatment of, **43(S)**, 115
group—
modification of provisions for, **43(S)**, 354–61
principal and subsidiary companies, **43(S)**, 127–8
reliefs, availability of, **43(S)**, 128
transfer within, **43(S)**, 128
indirect holdings in, **43(S)**, 712

real estate investment trusts—*contd*
insurance companies, **43(S)**, 129
interpretation, **43(S)**, 133
joint ventures, **43(S)**, 129–30
key concepts, **43(S)**, 103–4
leaving regime—
  breach of requirement, automatic
   termination by, **43(S)**, 125
  cessation, effect of, **43(S)**, 125
  early exit—
   effect of, **43(S)**, 127
   notice, by, **43(S)**, 126
  termination by notice—
   Commissioners, by, **43(S)**, 124
   company, by, **43(S)**, 124
manufactured dividends, **43(S)**, 130–2
maximum shareholding, **43(S)**, 111–12
meaning, **43(S)**, 103
minor or inadvertent beach of provisions,
  43(S), 113
power to amend provisions, **43(S)**, 354
profit:financing-cost ratio, **43(S)**, 112, 1634
profits, calculation of, **43(S)**, 116–17
property rental business, **43(S)**, 1633
  meaning, **43(S)**, 103
regulations, **43(S)**, 134
summary of provisions, **43(S)**, 4
tax advantage, cancellation of, **43(S)**, 114
tax-exempt business, ring-fencing, **43(S)**, 111

rebuke
censure, as, **14**, 592

receiver
High Court, appointed by, **11(2)**, [707]
income tax, liability to, **42**, [213]
mental patient, for, expenses of council
  officers acting as, **40(1)**, [24]
moneys payable by Crown, payment to,
  13, [30]
mortgagor, appointment by, **20**, [719], [727]
protection for, **42**, [214]
rentcharge, recovery of, **20**, [739]

receiver of wreck
salvage, powers relating to. *See* **salvage**
wreck, powers relating to. *See* **wreck**

receiver or manager
appointment—
  arrears of interest, to enforce, **8**, 34
  generally, **8**, 34–5
disqualification. *See* **disqualification order**
notice of appointment, registration, **8**, 912
powers, extent of, **8**, 87

receivership
Financial Services Authority—
  duty of receiver to report to, **19(2)**, [439]
  participation in proceedings, **19(2)**, [438]

receiving
handling, meaning, **12(1)**, [582]

reckless driving. *See now* **dangerous driving**

recognisance
acknowledging in another's name, **12(1)**, [65]
Director of Public Prosecutions, delivery to,
  12(1), [938]
entering, **12(1)**, [658]
forfeiting—
  enforcement, **12(2)**, [817]
  imprisonment in default, fixing term of,
   12(2), [816]
  search for money, ordering, **12(2)**, [819]
  time for payment, **12(2)**, [818]
land charge, as, **20**, [795]

recognised clearing houses
charges, provisions on, **19(1)**, [795]
Competition Act, exclusion from,
  19(2), [378], [379]
competition scrutiny—
  Competition Commission, consideration or
   report by, **19(2)**, [373]
  definitions, **19(2)**, [369]
  Office of Fair Trading—
   further reports, **19(2)**, [371]
   initial report, **19(2)**, [370]
   investigations by, **19(2)**, [372]
  Treasury—
   directions by, **19(2)**, [375]
   exercise of powers, procedure,
    19(2), [377]
   recognition order, role as to,
    19(2), [374]
   statements by, **19(2)**, [376]
complaints about, **19(2)**, [354]
default proceedings—
  application to determine whether to take,
   19(1), [788]
  assistance for purposes of, **19(1)**, [781]
  completion—
   duty to report on, **19(1)**, [783]
   net sum payable on, **19(1)**, [784]
  disclaimer of property, **19(1)**, [785]
  prior transactions, adjustment of,
   19(1), [786]
  rescission of contracts, **19(1)**, [785]
  supplementary provisions, **19(1)**, [782]
default rules—
  changes in, **19(1)**, [778]
  directions, Secretary of State giving,
   19(1), [787]
  meaning, **19(1)**, [807]
definitions, **19(1)**, [809]–[810]; **19(2)**, [384]
directions to, **19(2)**, [351], [353]
exemption, **19(2)**, [337]
Financial Services and Markets Act, provisions
  applying, **19(1)**, [789]
indemnities, **19(1)**, [803]
insolvency—
  law, modification of, **19(1)**, [779]
  procedures, proceedings taking precedence
   over, **19(1)**, [780]
  proceedings in other jurisdictions,
   19(1), [802]

recognised clearing houses—*contd*
 market abuse, control of. *See* **market abuse**
 market charges—
  administration orders and administrators,
   provisions on, **19(1)**, [794]
  extension of provisions, **19(1)**, [800]
  insolvency law, modification of,
   19(1), [793]
  meaning, **19(1)**, [792]
  priority of—
   subsequent charges, over, **19(1)**, [797]
   unpaid vendor's lien, over, **19(1)**, [798]
 market contracts—
  extension of provisions, **19(1)**, [800]
  meaning, **19(1)**, [777]
  parties, references to, **19(1)**, [806]
 market property—
  margin, application of, **19(1)**, [796]
  unsecured creditors, proceedings by,
   19(1), [799]
 meaning, **19(2)**, [337]
 notification requirements, **19(2)**, [347]
  modification or waiver of rules,
   19(2), [349]
 office-holders, indemnity for, **19(1)**, [803]
 overseas—
  application of default provisions to,
   19(1), [790]
  application for recognition, **19(2)**, [345]
  notification requirements, **19(2)**, [350]
 proceedings before commencement of
  Companies Act, **19(1)**, [801]
 recognition—
  application for, **19(2)**, [340], [341]
  order, **19(2)**, [342]
  qualification for, **19(2)**, [338]
  refusal of, **19(2)**, [343]
  revocation of, **19(2)**, [352], [353]
 regulations, power to make,
  19(1), [804]–[805]
 regulatory functions, liability in relation to,
  19(2), [344]
 regulatory provision—
  consideration by Authority whether to
   disallow, **19(2)**, [359]
  duty to notify proposal to make,
   19(2), [357]
  power of Authority to disallow excessive,
   19(2), [356], [360]
  restriction on making before Authority
   decides whether to act, **19(2)**, [358]
 relevant office-holder, meaning, **19(1)**, [808]
 summary of provisions, **19(1)**, [1]
 supervision of contracts, **19(2)**, [361]
 Tribunal, functions of, **19(2)**, [355]

recognised investment exchange
 charges, provisions on, **19(1)**, [795]
 Competition Act, exclusion from,
  19(2), [378], [379]
 competition scrutiny—
  Competition Commission, consideration or
   report by, **19(2)**, [373]
  definitions, **19(2)**, [369]

recognised investment exchange—*contd*
 competition scrutiny—*contd*
  Office of Fair Trading—
   further reports, **19(2)**, [371]
   initial report, **19(2)**, [370]
   investigations by, **19(2)**, [372]
  Treasury—
   directions by, **19(2)**, [375]
   exercise of powers, procedure,
    19(2), [377]
   recognition order, role as to,
    19(2), [374]
   statements by, **19(2)**, [376]
 complaints about, **19(2)**, [354]
 control over—
  acquisition of or increase in, **19(2)**, [363]
  definitions, **19(2)**, [368]
  improperly acquired shares, **19(2)**, [366]
  obligation to notify Authority,
   19(2), [362]
  offences, **19(2)**, [367]
  procedure, **19(2)**, [364], [365]
 default proceedings—
  application to determine whether to take,
   19(1), [788]
  assistance for purposes of, **19(1)**, [781]
  completion—
   duty to report on, **19(1)**, [783]
   net sum payable on, **19(1)**, [784]
  disclaimer of property, **19(1)**, [785]
  prior transactions, adjustment of,
   19(1), [786]
  rescission of contracts, **19(1)**, [785]
  supplementary provisions, **19(1)**, [782]
 default rules—
  changes in, **19(1)**, [778]
  directions, Secretary of State giving,
   19(1), [787]
  meaning, **19(1)**, [807]
 definitions, **19(1)**, [809]–[810]; **19(2)**, [384]
 directions to, **19(2)**, [351], [353]
 exemption, **19(2)**, [337]
 Financial Services and Markets Act, provisions
  applying, **19(1)**, [789]
 indemnities, **19(1)**, [803]
 information—
  compliance with directly applicable
   Community regulations, **19(2)**, [348]
  publication of, **19(2)**, [346]
 insolvency law, modification of, **19(1)**, [779]
 insolvency procedures, proceedings taking
  precedence over, **19(1)**, [780]
 insolvency proceedings in other jurisdictions,
  19(1), [802]
 market abuse, control of. *See* **market abuse**
 market charges—
  administration orders and administrators,
   provisions on, **19(1)**, [794]
  extension of provisions, **19(1)**, [800]
  insolvency law, modification of,
   19(1), [793]
  meaning, **19(1)**, [792]
  priority of—
   subsequent charges, over, **19(1)**, [797]
   unpaid vendor's lien, over, **19(1)**, [798]

recognised investment exchange—*contd*
market contracts—
  extension of provisions, **19(1)**, [800]
  meaning, **19(1)**, [777]
  parties, references to, **19(1)**, [806]
market property—
  margin, application of, **19(1)**, [796]
  unsecured creditors, proceedings by,
    19(1), [799]
meaning, **19(2)**, [337]
notification requirements, **19(2)**, [347]
  modification or waiver of rules,
    19(2), [349]
office-holders, indemnity for, **19(1)**, [803]
overseas—
  application for recognition, **19(2)**, [345]
  application of default provisions to,
    19(1), [790]
  notification requirements, **19(2)**, [350]
passport rights in EEA States other than UK,
  exercise of, **19(2)**, [382]
proceedings before commencement of
  Companies Act, **19(1)**, [801]
recognition—
  application for, **19(2)**, [339], [341]
  order, **19(2)**, [342]
  qualification for, **19(2)**, [338]
  refusal of, **19(2)**, [343]
  revocation of, **19(2)**, [352], [353]
regulations, power to make,
  19(1), [804]–[805]
regulatory functions, liability in relation to,
  19(2), [344]
regulatory provision—
  consideration by Authority whether to
    disallow, **19(2)**, [359]
  duty to notify proposal to make,
    19(2), [357]
  power of Authority to disallow excessive,
    19(2), [356], [360]
  restriction on making before Authority
    decides whether to act, **19(2)**, [358]
relevant office-holder, meaning, **19(1)**, [808]
summary of provisions, **19(1)**, [1]
supervision of contracts, **19(2)**, [361]
Tribunal, functions of, **19(2)**, [355]

recognizance to keep the peace
coroner, forfeited by, **11(3)**, [63]
Crown Court, appeal to, **11(2)**, [195]
failure to comply, **11(2)**, [536]
forfeiture, **11(2)**, [541]
postponement, **11(2)**, [540]
power of binding over, **11(2)**, [223], [536]
power to order, **11(2)**, [536]
surety, discharge on complaint of,
  11(2), [537]

reconstruction
acquisition of company for, stamp duty relief,
  41, [166], [167]

recorded delivery service
application and interpretation of provisions,
  41, [531]

recorded delivery service—*contd*
enactments, adaptation of, to, **41**, [530], [534]
registered post, alternative to, **41**, [530]

Recorder of London
circuit judge, becoming, **11(2)**, [260]
judicial function, **11(2)**, [209]
remuneration and benefits, **11(2)**, [262]

recording equipment. *See* **driver's hours; vehicle testing**

recording rights
consent, **11(1)**, [1044]
exceptions, **11(1)**, [1025]
exclusive recording contract—
  meaning, **11(1)**, [1021]
  performance subject to, consent required
    for, **11(1)**, [1022]
generally, **11(1)**, [1011]
illicit recording—
  delivery up, order for, **11(1)**, [1046]
  importing, possession or dealing with,
    11(1), [1020], [1024]
  making, dealing with or using,
    11(1), [1050]
    local weights and measures authority,
      enforcement by, **11(1)**, [1051]
  meaning, **11(1)**, [1048]
  presumptions relevant to recordings of
    performances, **11(1)**, [1049]
  summary of provisions, **11(1)**, [415]
person having, **11(1)**, [1021]
transmissibility, **11(1)**, [1043]

records. *See* **documents; public records**

recovery vehicle
vehicle excise duty, **13**, [1045]

recreation
London, in, facilities for, **25(1)**, [842]
trust for. *See* **charitable trust**

recreation ground
management byelaws, **22**, [23]
provision of, in housing development,
  22, [14]

recreational facilities
charges for, **35(1)**, [381]
contributions by local authority towards cost
  of, **35(1)**, [381]
expenses, defraying, **35(1)**, [221]
grants towards, **35(1)**, [221], [381]
income tax exemption, **44(2)**, [262]
  alteration, power of, **44(2)**, [264]
  exclusions, **44(2)**, [263]
list of, **35(1)**, [381]
provision by—
  local authorities, **35(1)**, [381]
  voluntary organisations, **35(1)**, [381]

recruitment officer
air force, **3**, [735]

recruitment officer—*contd*
army, **3**, [462]

rector
cure of souls, not to be discharged from, **14**, 60–1
team ministry, of. *See* **team ministry**

rectory
dissolution of, **14**, 995
sinecure—
  benefice, scheme for merging with, **14**, 1010
  church commissioners, purchase by, **14**, 144
  endowments, vesting of, **14**, 136
  private patronage, in, **14**, 144
  vicarage, held with, **14**, 136
  united benefice as, **14**, 995
  vicarage converted into, **14**, 68–9

Red Crescent
use of emblem, **10**, [950]–[951], [954], [971]

Red Cross
use of emblem, **10**, [950]–[951], [954], [971]

Red Lion and Sun
use of emblem, **10**, [950]–[951], [954], [971]

redemption action
limitation of time, **19(3)**, [743]

Redemption Annuities Account
winding up of, **14**, 1192

re-development
disturbance payment, to person displaced from land in consequence of, **9**, [325]
home loss payment, to person displaced from dwelling in consequence. *See* **home loss payment**
meaning, **9**, [325]

redundancy
adoption leave, during, **16**, [707]
collective agreement, adaptation of provisions in case of, **16**, [397]
dismissal by reason of—
  business, employer ceasing to carry on, **16**, [791]
  circumstances of, **16**, [789]
  renewal of contract or re-engagement not being, **16**, [790], [793]
  summary dismissal, exclusion of, **16**, [792]
  work of particular kind, discontinuance of, **16**, [791]
dismissal, references to, **16**, [394]
employee representatives—
  construction of references to, **16**, [395]
  detriment, right to not suffer, **16**, [664]
  disclosure of information to, **16**, [386]
  duty to consult, **16**, [386]
  election, **16**, [387]
  failure to consult, **16**, [388]

redundancy—*contd*
employee representatives—*contd*
  time off work—
    employment tribunal, complaints to, **16**, [689]
    remuneration, **16**, [688]
    right to, **16**, [687]
    unfair dismissal, **16**, [752]
expiry of employer's notice, anticipation of, **16**, [794]
fund, replacement with National Insurance Fund, **16**, [170]
jobseeker's allowance denied, where, **40(2)**, [67]
lay off. *See* payment *below*
maternity leave period, during, **16**, [703]
notice of extension, **16**, [795], [796]
payment—
  amount of, **16**, [812]
  anticipation of expiry of employer's notice, no right on, **16**, [794]
  claims for, **16**, [814]
  continuous employment, **16**, [861]
  death—
    employee of, effect of, **16**, [826]
    employer of, effect of, **16**, [824]
  deduction, rules allowing, **44(3)**, [75]–[79]
  domestic servants, exclusion of, **16**, [811]
  employment not under contract of employment, **16**, [821]
  employment tribunal, reference of questions to, **16**, [813]
  equivalent, reference to employment tribunal, **16**, [827]
  exemption orders, **16**, [808]
  interpretation of terms, **16**, [831]
  lay-off or short-time working, on—
    counter-notice, **16**, [801]
    death of employer, effect of, **16**, [825]
    dismissal, no entitlement on, **16**, [803]
    eligibility by reason of, **16**, [800]
    likelihood of full employment, effect of, **16**, [804]
    meaning, **16**, [799]
    relevant date, meaning, **16**, [805]
    resignation, no entitlement on, **16**, [802]
    weeks of, **16**, [806]
  maximum amount of week's pay, increase of, **16**, [1023]
  meaning, **44(1)**, [417]
  notices, **16**, [829]
  offences, **16**, [830]
  old statutory compensation schemes, regulations for, **16**, [828]
  overseas government employment, exclusion of, **16**, [810]
  person other than employer, employees paid by, **16**, [823]
  notices, **16**, [829]
  offences, **16**, [830]
  old statutory compensation schemes, regulations for, **16**, [828]
  overseas government employment, exclusion of, **16**, [810]

redundancy—*contd*
  payment—*contd*
    person other than employer, employees paid
      by, **16**, [823]
    Secretary of State, by—
      amount of, **16**, [818]
      applications for, **16**, [816]
      employment tribunal, reference of
        questions to, **16**, [820]
      information relating to applications,
        16, [819]
      making of, **16**, [817]
    statute, termination of employment by,
      16, [822]
    statutory—
      deductions, **44(1)**, [416]
      exemption from income tax liability,
        44(2), [313]
      tax exemption, **44(1)**, [416]
    strike during currency of employer's notice,
      no right on, **16**, [795]
    summary dismissal, no entitlement on,
      16, [792]
    transitional provisions, **16**, [893]
    written particulars of, **16**, [815]
  protected period—
    meaning, **16**, [388]
    termination of employment during,
      16, [390]
  protective award—
    entitlement under, **16**, [389]
    failure to pay under, complaint of,
      16, [391]
    power to make, **16**, [388]
  re-engagement, references to, **16**, [798]
  scheme—
    relief for payments, **44(1)**, [668]
    statutory, **44(1)**, [395]
  Secretary of State, duty to notify, **16**, [392]
    failure to comply, **16**, [393]
  selection for—
    unfair dismissal for reasons of, **16**, [759]
    union membership or activities, on grounds
      related to, **16**, [353]
      continuation of employment, order for,
        16, [361]
      contributory fault, assessment of,
        16, [355]
      failure to comply with order, **16**, [363]
      interim relief, application for, **16**, [358]
      interpretation of terms, **16**, [364]
      minimum basic award, **16**, [356]
      order, making, **16**, [360]
      procedure on hearing of application,
        16, [360]
      prompt determination of applications,
        16, [359]
      qualifying period, disapplication of
        requirement for, **16**, [354]
      third parties, awards against, **16**, [357]
      upper age limit, disapplication of,
        16, [354]
      variation or revocation of order,
        application for, **16**, [362]
    short-term employment, **16**, [493]

redundancy—*contd*
  short-time working. *See* payment *above*
  strike during currency of employer's notice,
    exclusion of, **16**, [795]
  variation of provisions, **16**, [396]

redundant church. *See* **church**

Redundant Churches fund
  annual report, **14**, 1022
  appointment of members, **14**, 1020
  body replacing, **14**, 1023–4
  care and maintenance of historic building by,
    14, 1027–8
  Churches Conservation Trust, renamed as,
    14, 1289
  Commissioners, advice to, **14**, 1022
  contents, care for, **14**, 1050–1
  expenditure of, **14**, 1021
  grants to, **14**, 663
  members, **14**, 1101
  object of, **14**, 1020
  payments to, determining, **14**, 1038
  powers of, **14**, 1020–1
  property vested in—
    dealing with, **14**, 1043
    generally, **14**, 1045
    restoration of, **14**, 1044
  repayment of costs from sale proceeds,
    14, 1034

referees
  panel of, transfer of jurisdiction to Lands
    Tribunal, **9**, [181]

referendum
  assistance for designated organisations—
    application for designation of, **15(3)**, [435]
    assistance available, **15(3)**, [436], [509]
    designation of, **15(3)**, [434]
  campaign broadcasts, **15(3)**, [453]
    assistance available for, **15(3)**, [509]
  conduct of—
    chief counting officers, **15(3)**, [454]
    counting officers, **15(3)**, [454]
    orders regulating, **15(3)**, [455]
  date of poll, **15(3)**, [429]
  declarations and notifications to Commission,
    15(3), [432]–[433]
  expenses—
    claims—
      disputed, **15(3)**, [442]
      restrictions on, **15(3)**, [441]
    general restrictions, **15(3)**, [443]
    generally, **15(3)**, [437]
    guidance by Commission, **15(3)**, [511]
    incurring, restriction on, **15(3)**, [439]
    notional, **15(3)**, [438]
    payments, restrictions on, **15(3)**, [440]
    qualifying, **15(3)**, [510]
    returns—
      auditor's report on, **15(3)**, [447]
      delivery to Commission, **15(3)**, [448]
      generally, **15(3)**, [446]
      public inspection, **15(3)**, [450]

referendum—*contd*
expenses—*contd*
returns—*contd*
responsible person for, declaration of,
15(3), [449]
special restrictions, **15(3)**, [444], [512]
general note, **15(3)**, [1]
meaning, **15(3)**, [427]
offences—
bodies corporate, by, **15(3)**, [469]
convictions, duty of court to report to
Commission, **15(3)**, [471]
general, **15(3)**, [465]
penalties, **15(3)**, [518]
punishment, **15(3)**, [467]
unincorporated associations, by,
15(3), [470]
period, **15(3)**, [428]
permitted participants—
donations to—
controls on, **15(3)**, [514]
general rules, **15(3)**, [513]
payments not regarded as, **15(3)**, [513]
reporting of, **15(3)**, [515]
sponsorship, **15(3)**, [513]
value of, **15(3)**, [513]
meaning, **15(3)**, [431]
publications—
details to appear in, **15(3)**, [452]
restrictions on promotional material by
central and local government,
15(3), [451]
questions, **15(3)**, [430]
summary proceedings, **15(3)**, [468]

refinery
fuel for producing energy for, repayment of
part duty on, **13**, [844], [857], [869]
meaning, **13**, [862]

refreshment house
drunkenness, penalty for permitting,
19(3), [350]
wine sales, restrictive covenants, **19(3)**, [351]

refugee
benefit, back-dating, **31**, [404], [499]
Convention—
Certification, **31**, [577]
construction of, **31**, [576]
exclusion from protection, **31**, [417]
integration loan for, **31**, [500]

refuse. *See also* **rubbish**
abandoned—
motor vehicle. *See* **motor vehicle**
removal—
deposit, **35(1)**, [406]
disposal after, **35(1)**, [406]
duty of local authority as to,
35(1), [406]
entry in connection with, **35(1)**, [408]
expenses, **35(1)**, [406]
colliery spoilbank, from, **35(2)**, [42]
deposit of, places for, **35(1)**, [397]

refuse—*contd*
disposal—
acquisition of land for, **35(1)**, [407]
course of business, in, provision of places
for, **35(1)**, [397]
provision by local authority of places for,
35(1), [397]
dumping—
control of, **35(1)**, [397], [398]
provision of dumps, **35(1)**, [397]
unauthorised, penalty for, **35(1)**, [398]
Isles of Scilly, provisions applying to,
35(1), [409]
London—
collection—
arrangements for, **25(1)**, [651]
use of vehicles for, **25(1)**, [655]
disposal of—
arrangements for, **25(1)**, [651]
facilities for, **25(1)**, [652]
dustbins—
dangerous matter, deposit of,
25(1), [654]
placing for collection, **25(1)**, [651]
power to provide, **25(1)**, [650], [789]
prohibited deposits, **25(1)**, [653], [654]
requirement to provide, **25(1)**, [650]
restrictions on use, **25(1)**, [653]
storage accommodation for, **25(1)**, [622]
incinerators, **25(1)**, [734]
receptacles for, provision of, **25(1)**, [789]
relevant land, cleansing, **26(2)**, [160]
trade refuse, disposal facilities, **25(1)**, [749]
meaning, **35(1)**, [397]
orders and regulations, **35(1)**, [410]
removal—
access to building for, **35(1)**, [548]
mews, stables, etc, from, **35(1)**, [132]
sale, **35(1)**, [397]

Regents Park
Outer Circle, management of, **10**, [186]
Zoo, management of, **10**, [239]

regimental charitable funds
application of, **3**, [337]
transfer to holding trustees, **3**, [336]

regional assemblies
Electoral Commission, advice of,
26(2), [220]–[223]
enactment establishing, **26(2)**, [225]
referendums—
conditions for, **26(2)**, [200]
county area, in, **26(2)**, [201]
Electoral Commission. *See* **Electoral
Commission**
entitlement to vote, **26(2)**, [203]
further, **26(2)**, [205]
legal challenges, **26(2)**, [210]
local government review. *See* **Boundary
Commission for England**
number of votes, determining, **26(2)**, [205]
order for, **26(2)**, [200]
period, **26(2)**, [204]

regional assemblies—*contd*
referendums—*contd*
polls, combination of, **26(2)**, [206]
power to hold, **26(2)**, [200], [211]
questions to be asked in, **26(2)**, [202]
region, meaning, **26(2)**, [228]
regional chambers, funding for, **26(2)**, [224]

regional development agencies
accounts and records, **46**, [910]
annual report, **46**, [913]
audit, **46**, [911]
body corporate, as, **46**, [894]
borrowing by, **46**, [907]
Government guarantees, **46**, [908]
connection notice, service of, **46**, [920]
connection of private street to highway,
46, [920]
constitution, **46**, [895], [946]
delegation of functions to, **46**, [899], [948]
Development Commission, scheme for
transfer of property etc of, **46**, [932], [955]
corporation tax, **46**, [936]
stamp duty, **46**, [937]
directions, power to give, **46**, [939]
establishment, **46**, [894]
financial duties, **46**, [905]
Government loans to, **46**, [909]
grants to, **46**, [906]
housing, provision of, **46**, [898]
land—
acquisition of, **46**, [916], [950]–[951]
acquisition of rights, **46**, [951]
burial grounds, **46**, [952]
consecrated, **46**, [952]
easements, power to override, **46**, [952]
extinguishment of rights over, **46**, [952]
open spaces, **46**, [952]
rights of entry, **46**, [917]
offences, **46**, [918]
vesting by order, **46**, [915], [949]
London. for. *See* **London Development
Agency**
London Olympic Games, purposes relating
to, **13**, [507]
members—
appointment, **46**, [895], [946]
number of, **46**, [895]
qualifications, **46**, [895]
name, change of, **46**, [922]
notices, **46**, [929]
powers, **46**, [898]
property, rights and liabilities, scheme for
transfer to Homes and Communities
Agency, **24**, [590]
taxation, **24**, [865]
purposes of, **46**, [897]
regional accountability, **46**, [914]
regional consultation, **46**, [904]
regional planning bodies, delegation of
functions of, **46(S)**, 168–9
regions—
alteration of, **46**, [921]
list of, **46**, [945]

regional development agencies—*contd*
Secretary of State—
consents by, **46**, [926]
guidance and directions by, **46**, [924]–[925]
provision of information to, **46**, [912]
staff, **46**, [946]
stamp duty land tax, **46**, [938]
status, **46**, [896]
strategy, **46**, [901]
Urban Regeneration Agency, scheme for
transfer of property etc of, **46**, [934], [956]
corporation tax, **46**, [936]
stamp duty, **46**, [937]
stamp duty land tax, **46**, [938]
validity of transactions with, **46**, [927]

regional development grant
investment company, made to, **44(1)**, [73]
meaning, **44(1)**, [73], [336]
oil extraction activities, **44(1)**, [336]
receipt, not being, **44(1)**, [73]

Regional Health Authority
transfer of, **30**, [579]

regional planning bodies
community involvement, policy as to,
46, [962]
direction for recognition of, **46**, [958]
functions of, **46**, [959]
local authorities, assistance from, **46**, [960]
region, meaning, **46**, [968]
regional spatial strategy. *See* **regional spatial
strategy**
regulations, **46**, [967]

regional spatial strategy
climate change policies, **46(S)**, 172
conflict in, **46**, [957]
development plan, as, **46**, [994]
local development documents conforming
with, **46**, [980]
region, meaning, **46**, [968]
regulations, **46**, [967]
report on implementation of, **46**, [959]
requirement of, **46**, [957]
review of, **46**, [959]
revision of—
community involvement in, **46**, [962]
draft, **46**, [961], [966]
examination in public, **46**, [964]
representations on, **46**, [963], [965]
requirement, **46**, [961]
Secretary of State, functions of, **46**, [963],
[965]
simplified planning zone, identification of
need for, **46**, [999]
validity, **46**, [1045]

register. *See also subject matters of registration*
births and deaths, of, false statements as to,
12(1), [198]
copy, destroying or concealing, **12(1)**, [66]
destroying, **12(1)**, [66]
enforcement notices, of, **46**, [445]

register—*contd*
false entries in, **12(1)**, [67]
forging, **12(1)**, [66]
hazardous substances, as to, **46**, [780]
planning applications, of, **46**, [328]
simplified planning zone scheme, information
on, **46**, [328]
stop notices, of, **46**, [445]
trees in conservation areas, notices as to,
46, [475]

registered design
enemy—
character, evidence of, **50**, [213]
grant to, **50**, [210]
licence—
comptroller, grant by, **50**, [208]
validity, **50**, [207]
variation of, **50**, [207], [208]
fees, deduction of, **44(1)**, [53]
time limits, extension in war circumstances,
50, [212]

registered fund
accounts, **48**, 550
Chief Registrar—
meaning, **48**, 552
reports, **48**, 553
defaults, penalties for, **48**, 551
registrar, powers of, **48**, 550
registration—
amendment of rules, effect of, **48**, 548
cancellation of, **48**, 549
certificate of, **48**, 549
fees, **48**, 549
procedure for, **48**, 548–9
provisions for avoiding rule against
perpetuities, deletion of, **48**, 549
qualification for, **48**, 548
reports, **48**, 550
rule against perpetuities not applying to,
48, 547
rules, requirements as to, **48**, 553–4
trustee, breach by, **48**, 550

registered social landlord
accounts and audit, **23**, [549]
acquisitions by, stamp duty land tax relief,
41, [344]
amendments relating to, **24**, [372], [439]
associate, meaning, **23**, [408]
Audit Commission—
advice and assistance from, **26(1)**, [367]
inspections, **26(1)**, [365]
fees, **26(1)**, [366]
reports, **26(1)**, [363], [364]
information, supply of, **26(1)**, [364]
Auditor General for Wales, advice and
assistance from, **26(2)**, [610]
charities, definitions, **23**, [405]
company—
arrangement or reconstruction, **23**, [548]
memorandum or articles, change of,
23, [548]
new director, appointment of, **23**, [548]

registered social landlord—*contd*
complaints. *See* **social landlord**
defective dwelling, repurchase of, **22**, [363]
director, power to remove, **23**, [548]
entry on premises of, **23**, [384]
housing management, financial assistance for,
22, [412]
housing stock as social housing, **24**, [616]
industrial and provident society—
amalgamation and dissolution, **23**, [548]
auditors, **23**, [549]
change of rules, **23**, [548]
definitions, **23**, [404]
new committee member, appointment of,
23, [548]
inquiry into affairs of, **23**, [550]
insolvency—
agreed proposals, effect of, **23**, [392]
assistance by Relevant Authority, **23**, [396]
compliance with proposals, application to
court to secure, **23**, [397]
disposal of land, moratorium on, **23**, [389],
[390]
further notice of, **23**, [388]
initial notice of, **23**, [387]
manager—
appointment of, **23**, [393]
powers of, **23**, [394]
transfer of engagements by, **23**, [395]
ownership and management of land,
23, [391]
scheme of provisions on, **23**, [386]
land—
acquisition by Corporation, **22**, [487]
disposal of—
consent of Relevant Authority required
for, **23**, [348]
first refusal, right of, **23**, [354], [355]
moratorium on, **23**, [389], [390]
not requiring consent, **23**, [349]
power of, **23**, [347]
purchase grant, **23**, [366]
repayment of discount—
charge on house, liability as, **23**, [352]
covenant for, **23**, [350]
deferred resale agreements, treatment
of, **23**, [359]
increase in value attributable to home
improvements disregarded, **23**, [351]
priority of charge, **23**, [353]
disposal proceeds—
application or appropriation of, **23**, [370]
fund, **23**, [369]
information, supply of, **23**, [371]
net, **23**, [369]
landlord authority, as, **22**, [105]
leases, stamp duty exemption of certain. *See*
stamp duty
lettings by, consent not required, **23**, [349]
local authority, assistance from, **23**, [367]
local housing authority, co-operation with,
23, [483]
meaning, **22**, [5], [457]; **26(1)**, [368]
member of person's family, meaning,
23, [409]

registered social landlord—*contd*
objects, **23**, [341]
officer—
  acting while disqualified, **23**, [550]
  disqualification, **23**, [550]
  meaning, **23**, [406]
parenting contract, entry into, **6(S)**, 276–8
parenting order, application for, **6(S)**, 280–1
  county court proceedings, in, **6(S)**, 281
payments to members, control of, **23**, [547]
Public Works Loans Commissioners, loans
  by, **23**, [368]
register—
  appeal against decision, **23**, [345]
    criteria for, **23**, [344]
  Relevant Authority, maintenance by,
    23, [339]
  removal from, **23**, [343]
registered charity—
  accounting and audit, **23**, [549]
  change of objects, **23**, [548]
  director or trustee of—
    appointment, **23**, [548]
    removal of, **23**, [548]
  powers relating to, **23**, [550]
registration—
  application for, **23**, [342]
  criteria for, **23**, [344]
  eligibility for, **23**, [341]
  notice of, **23**, [342]
  Relevant Authority, by, **23**, [342]
  Welsh bodies, **23**, [340]
regulation, **23**, [346]
replacement of system, **24**, [599]
social housing grants—
  conditions, **23**, [363]
  housing management agreement, land
    subject to, **23**, [364]
  power to make, **23**, [363]
  recovery of, **23**, [372]
  reduction, suspension or cancellation of,
    23, [372]
subsidiary, meaning, **23**, [407]
tenant, right of to acquire dwelling,
  23, [360]–[362]
  purchase grant, **23**, [365]
transfer of land, direction for, **23**, [550]
trustee, power to remove, **23**, [548]
Wales, restriction of system to, **24**, [600]
winding up—
  net assets, transfer of, **23**, [548]
  petition for, **23**, [548]

registered tenants' association
managing agents, right to be consulted on,
  22, [543]
meaning, **22**, [540]
service charge, relevant requirements as to,
  22, [525]

registered trade mark
infringement authorised by Crown, liability
  for, **13**, [12]

registers. *See* **parochial registers and records**

registrar (ecclesiastical)
archdeacon's, abolition of office, **14**, 830
baptisms, of. *See* **baptism**
diocese, of, **14**, 827–8
maximum number to be held, **14**, 828
neglect by, **14**, 124
office of, **14**, 827–8
province, of, **14**, 826–7
tenure of office, **14**, 1261
vacation of office, **14**, 828–9

Registrar General
annual abstracts, despatch to Minister,
  36, [150]
appointment, **36**, [1], [121]
census, duties as to. *See* **census**
corporation sole, establishment as, **36**, [203]
documents, transmission to, **36**, [64], [115]
expenses incurred, **36**, [124]
fees received, application of, **36**, [5]
fire-resisting boxes, provision by, **36**, [131]
Fleet, May Fair and Mint records, transfer to,
  36, [17]
forms etc, provision by, **36**, [99]
General Register Office, **36**, [122]
indexes kept by, searches and copies, **36**, [105]
industrial diseases, death from, regulations as
  to, **36**, [152]
marriage register books indexes, searches,
  36, [63]
officers and servants, **36**, [123]
population statistics compilation, duties as to,
  36, [45]
registers—
  Births and Deaths Registration Act 1858,
    deposit under, **36**, [16]
  certified copies, **36**, [3]
  evidence, as, **36**, [4], [11]
  extracts from, **36**, [7]–[11]
  Fleet prison, transfer from, **36**, [17]
  forgery of, **36**, [6]
  legal custody, deemed to be in, **36**, [4]
  offices where deposited, status of, **36**, [2]
  originals, use of, **36**, [10], [12], [15]
  search of, **36**, [3]
  wilful injury, **36**, [6]
regulations, power to make, **36**, [114]
returns to, **36**, [101]
salary, **36**, [124]
Statistics Board, transfers to, **10(S)**, 50, 61–3
sums received by, application, **36**, [5], [124]
tenure of office, **36**, [121]

Registrar General of Shipping and Seamen
births and deaths in ships, returns to,
  39(2), [776]
continuation of, **39(2)**, [972]
death on ship, report on, **39(2)**, [952]
functions of, **39(2)**, [972]
transmission of documents to, **39(2)**, [975]

registrar of companies

administrative restoration to register, decision on, **8(1)**, [1105]

alteration of constitution, notice of—
    enactment, by, **8(1)**, [112]
    order, by, **8(1)**, [113]

amended articles sent to, **8(1)**, [104]
    notice to comply, **8(1)**, [105]

appointment, **8(1)**, [1138]
    duty to notify—
        failure, offence of, **8(1)**, [1233]
        requirement, **8(1)**, [1232]

certificate of incorporation—
    issue, public notice of, **8(1)**, [1142]
    right to, **8(1)**, [1143]

change of company name—
    new certificate of incorporation, issue of, **8(1)**, [158]
    notice of, **8(1)**, [156]–[157]
    registration, **8(1)**, [158]

change of registered office, notice of, **8(1)**, [165]

changes of details of directors, requirement to notify, **8(1)**, [245]

company names, index of—
    amendment of enactments, power of, **8(1)**, [1179]
    maintenance of, **8(1)**, [1177]
    right to inspect, **8(1)**, [1178]

company secretary, notification of changes in, **8(1)**, [354]

contracting out of functions, **8(1)**, [1197]

delivery of documents to—
    accounts, reports and returns, **8(1)**, [1156]
    authentication, **8(1)**, [1146]
    certification or verification, requirements as to, **8(1)**, [1189]
    constitutional, **8(1)**, [1156]
    Directive disclosure requirements, subject to, **8(1)**, [1156]
    document, meaning, **8(1)**, [1192]
    electronic means, by—
        agreement for, **8(1)**, [1148]
        authenticated, **8(1)**, [1193]
        consents to, **8(1)**, [1193]
        power to require, **8(1)**, [1147]
    English, to be in, **8(1)**, [1181]
    false statements, offence, **8(1)**, [1190]
    form, requirements, **8(1)**, [1146]
    informal correction of, **8(1)**, [1153]
    language requirements—
        application of, **8(1)**, [1180]
        certified translations, **8(1)**, [1185]
        English, **8(1)**, [1181]
        other than English, **8(1)**, [1183]
        translations, voluntary filing, **8(1)**, [1184]
        transliteration, **8(1)**, [1186]–[1188]
        Welsh companies, **8(1)**, [1182]
    manner of, **8(1)**, [1146]
    meaning, **8(1)**, [1192]
    other than English, in, **8(1)**, [1183]
    proper—
        power to accept documents not meeting requirements, **8(1)**, [1151]

registrar of companies—*contd*

delivery of documents to—*contd*
    proper—*contd*
        replacement of document not meeting requirements, **8(1)**, [1154]
        requirements for, **8(1)**, [1150]
    public notice of receipt, **8(1)**, [1155]
        failure to give, effect of, **8(1)**, [1157]
    receipt, not delivered until, **8(1)**, [1149]
    translations—
        certified, **8(1)**, [1185]
        voluntary filing, **8(1)**, [1184]
    transliteration—
        certification, **8(1)**, [1188]
        names and addresses, of, **8(1)**, [1186]–[1187]
        permitted characters, **8(1)**, [1186]
        Roman characters, into, **8(1)**, [1187]
    unnecessary material, containing, **8(1)**, [1152]
    Welsh companies, relating to, **8(1)**, [1182]

duty to file accounts and reports with, **8(1)**, [519]

each part of UK, for, **8(1)**, [1138]

fees payable to, **8(1)**, [1141]

filing obligations, enforcement of, **8(1)**, [1191]

functions of, **8(1)**, [1139]

official seal, **8(1)**, [1140]

overseas companies, provisions applying to, **8(1)**, [1198]

payments into Consolidated Fund, **8(1)**, [1196]

production of record kept by, issue of process for, **8(1)**, [1170]

publication of notices, **8(1)**, [1194]

re-registration of public company as private, notice of court application or order, **8(1)**, [177]

register—
    annotation, **8(1)**, [1159]
    copy of material on—
        certification as accurate, **8(1)**, [1169]
        form and manner in which provided, **8(1)**, [1168]
        form of application for, **8(1)**, [1167]
        right to, **8(1)**, [1164]
    dissolved companies, records relating to, **8(1)**, [1162]
    inconsistencies, resolution of, **8(1)**, [1171]
    inspection of—
        application to make address unavailable, **8(1)**, [1166]
        form of application for, **8(1)**, [1167]
        material not available for, **8(1)**, [1165]
        right of, **8(1)**, [1163]
    original documents, preservation of, **8(1)**, [1161]
    records in, **8(1)**, [1158]
    rectification—
        application, on, **8(1)**, [1173]
        court order, under, **8(1)**, [1174]
    removal of material from—
        administrative, **8(1)**, [1172]

registrar of companies—*contd*
register—*contd*
removal of material from—*contd*
powers of court on ordering,
8(1), [1175]
public notice of, **8(1)**, [1176]
unique identifiers, allocation of,
8(1), [1160]
registered number—
allocation of, **8(1)**, [1144]
branch of overseas company, of,
8(1), [1145]
change of, **8(1)**, [1144]
form of, **8(1)**, [1144]
registration by, **8(1)**, [92]
residential address of director—
permitted use or disclosure of, **8(1)**, [321]
public record, putting on,
8(1), [323]–[324]
restriction on use or disclosure of,
8(1), [320]
resolutions and agreements affecting
constitution to be forwarded to, **8(1)**, [108]
restriction on amendment of articles,
notification to, **8(1)**, [101]
rules, **8(1)**, [1195]

Registrar of Criminal Appeals
office, combination with other offices,
11(4), [553]

Registrar of Government Stock
accounting by, **19(2)**, [632]
application of money by, **19(2)**, [631]
meaning, **19(2)**, [624]
second claimant, not responsible to,
19(2), [636]
stocks transferable in books of, provisions
applied to, **19(2)**, [720]
suitably qualified persons, employment of,
19(2), [629]

registration. *See* **birth; death; land
registration; marriage**

registration marks
vehicles, for. *See* **vehicle**

registration of birth
legitimation, on, **6**, [164]
service personnel, **3**, [1]

Registrar of Criminal Appeals
judicial pension, **11(2)**, [600]
office, combination with other offices,
11(3), [131]

registration. *See* **birth; death; land
registration; marriage**

registration marks
vehicles, for. *See* **vehicle**

registration plate suppliers
counterfeit plates, offences relating to,
47, [610]

registration plate suppliers—*contd*
entry and inspection of premises, right of,
47, [608]
interpretation provisions, **47**, [613]
offences, proceedings for, **47**, [612]
records, keeping of, **47**, [606]
registration of—
appeals, **47**, [605]
applications for, **47**, [601]
cancellation of, **47**, [603]
notification requirements, **47**, [609]
register, **47**, [600]
removal or suspension by court, **47**, [602]
representations, right to make, **47**, [604]
requirement for, **47**, [599]
regulation, **38(2)**, [518], [519]
sale of, provision of information on, **47**, [607]
Scotland and Northern Ireland, extension of
provisions to, **38(2)**, [520]
unregistered persons, offence of supplying
plates to, **47**, [611]

regular forces. *See also* **armed forces**
meaning, **3**, [733]

regulated activities
agreements—
approval of arrangements, **19(2)**, [61]
breach of statutory duty, action for,
19(2), [72]
controlled functions, **19(2)**, [60]
determination of applications, **19(2)**, [62]
procedure, **19(2)**, [63]
requirement of, **19(2)**, [60]
Tribunal, reference to, **19(2)**, [63]
unauthorised person—
by, **19(2)**, [26]
through, **19(2)**, [27]
unenforceable, effect of, **19(2)**, [28]
unlawful communications, arising from,
19(2), [30]
withdrawal, **19(2)**, [64]
appointed representatives, exemption of,
19(2), [39]
applicable register, **19(2)**, [39]
authorised person—
acquisition of control over—
approval of, **19(2)**, [234]
conditions of, **19(2)**, [235]
cases of, **19(2)**, [229]
notification of, **19(2)**, [232]
objection to, **19(2)**, [236]
acting without permission, **19(2)**, [20]
authorisation elsewhere in single market,
19(2), [503]
carrying on by, **19(2)**, [19]
conduct, statements and codes as to,
19(2), [65], [66]
control over—
acquisition of. *See* acquisition of control
over *above*
Authority, duty of, **19(2)**, [233]
definition, power to change,
19(2), [242]

regulated activities—*contd*
  authorised person—*contd*
    control over—*contd*
      existing, objection to, **19(2)**, [237]
        notice of, **19(2)**, [238]
      improperly acquired shares, **19(2)**, [239]
      increasing, **19(2)**, [230]
      notification requirement, **19(2)**, [228], [232]
      offences, **19(2)**, [241]
      reducing. *See* reduction of control over *below*
    direction cancelling, **19(2)**, [35]
    EEA firm ceasing to qualify, **19(2)**, [34]
    EEA passport rights—
      defined terms, **19(2)**, [519]
      EEA firms, exercise by, **19(2)**, [520]
      UK firms, exercise by, **19(2)**, [521]
    false claims, **19(2)**, [24]
    partnerships, **19(2)**, [32]
    persons being, **19(2)**, [31]
    record of, **19(2)**, [422]
    reduction of control over—
      cases of, **19(2)**, [231]
      notification, **19(2)**, [240]
    Treaty firms ceasing to qualify, **19(2)**, [35]
    Treaty rights, **19(2)**, [522]
    UK, meaning, **19(2)**, [228]
    unincorporated associations, **19(2)**, [32]
    withdrawal of authorisation, **19(2)**, [33]
  carrying on, **19(2)**, [19]
    business, by way of, **19(2)**, [495]
    cases of, **19(2)**, [494]
  classes of, **19(2)**, [22]
  EEA firms ceasing to qualify for authorisation, **19(2)**, [34]
  EEA rights, exercise by UK firms, **19(2)**, [37], [521]
  exemption orders, **19(2)**, [38]
  financial promotion, **19(2)**, [21], [25]
  general prohibition, **19(2)**, [19]
    acceptance of deposits in breach of, **19(2)**, [29]
    contravention of, **19(2)**, [23]
    false claims, **19(2)**, [24]
  investments, **19(2)**, [517]
  list of, **19(2)**, [516]
  order-making power, **19(2)**, [518]
  permission to carry on—
    additional, **19(2)**, [51]
    applicant, meaning, **19(2)**, [43]
    application for, **19(2)**, [41]
    assets requirement, imposition of, **19(2)**, [49]
    cancellation, **19(2)**, [55]
    connected persons, **19(2)**, [50]
    determination of applications, **19(2)**, [53]
    giving of, **19(2)**, [43]
    procedure, **19(2)**, [52]
    requirements, imposition of, **19(2)**, [44]
    threshold conditions, **19(2)**, [42], [524]–[526]
    Tribunal, matters referred to, **19(2)**, [56]
    variation—
      acquisition of control, on, **19(2)**, [47]

regulated activities—*contd*
  permission to carry on—*contd*
    variation—*contd*
      authorised person, at request of, **19(2)**, [45]
      initiative of Authority, on, **19(2)**, [46], [54]
      overseas regulator, in support of, **19(2)**, [48]
  prohibition orders—
    activities to which relating, **19(2)**, [57]
    applications, **19(2)**, [59]
    breach of statutory duty, action for, **19(2)**, [72]
    meaning, **19(2)**, [57]
    power to make, **19(2)**, [57]
    procedure, **19(2)**, [58]
    Tribunal, reference to, **19(2)**, [58]
    variation or revocation of, **19(2)**, [57]
  tied agents operating outside United Kingdom, exemption of certain, **19(2)**, [40]

regulated market
  EEA market operator—
    meaning, **19(2)**, [384]
    passport rights—
      exercise of, **19(2)**, [380]
      removal of, **19(2)**, [381]
  meaning, **19(2)**, [384]
  recognised investment exchange in EEA States other than UK, passport rights, **19(2)**, [382]

regulated tenancy
  business use, effect of, **21**, [545]
  controlled tenancy converted into, **21**, [539], [610], [735]
  conversion, by, **21**, [554]
  converted, provisions applying to, **21**, [539], [657]
  Counter-Inflation Act—
    ending before, **21**, [660]
    regulation by virtue of, **21**, [548], [613], [647]
  furnished, meaning, **21**, [637]
  housing association tenancy converted to, **21**, [592], [650], [763]
  landlord, service of notices on, **21**, [636]
  meaning, **21**, [538]
  mortgagee, binding on, **21**, [622]
  premium paid for, **21**, [613]
  protected long tenancy, arising from, **21**, [348]
  rates, meaning, **21**, [560]
  rent—
    contractual period, during—
      furniture, increase for use of, **21**, [647]
      limit on, **21**, [548]
      meaning, **21**, [560]
      notice of increase, **21**, [552]
      rates, change in, **21**, [647]
      repairs, adjustment for, **21**, [647]
      service element, adjustment for, **21**, [647]
      special rent limit, **21**, [548], [647]
    contractual rent limit, **21**, [548]

regulated tenancy—*contd*
rent—*contd*
excess, recovery from landlord, **21**, [556]
increase—
notice of—
provisions on, **21**, [552]
registration, effect of, **21**, [573]
phasing of, transitional provisions,
21, [766]
recoverable—
meaning, **21**, [560]
rectification of rent book after
determination of, **21**, [557]
registration of. *See* **rent registration**
regulations, power to make, **21**, [559]
rental periods, adjustment for differences
in, **21**, [558]
security of tenure, agreement with tenant
having—
agreement with tenant having,
meaning, **21**, [553]
conversion of tenancy, following,
21, [554]
protection requirements, failure to
comply with, **21**, [555]
requirements of, **21**, [554]
statutory period, during—
adjustment of—
furniture, use of, **21**, [551]
rates, with respect to, **21**, [550]
rental periods, differences in lengths
of, **21**, [558]
services, provision of, **21**, [551]
limit of, **21**, [549]
meaning, **21**, [560]
notice of increase, **21**, [552]
registered rent, increase to, **21**, [549]
savings, **21**, [660]
security of tenure—
rent agreement with tenant having—
conversion of tenancy, following,
21, [554]
meaning, **21**, [553]
protection requirements, failure to
comply with, **21**, [555]
requirements of, **21**, [554]
statutory tenancy following, **21**, [538]
transitional provisions, **21**, [660]

Regulator of Social Housing
accounts, **24**, [642]
advice, publication of, **24**, [636]
amalgamation of industrial societies,
instrument of, **24**, [794]
annual report, **24**, [631]
body corporate, as, **24**, [620]
borrowing by, **24**, [641]
charging by, **24**, [639]
chief executive, **24**, [623]
committees and sub-committees, **24**, [628]
complaints, guidance on—
consultation, **24**, [755]
contents of, **24**, [754]
publication of, **24**, [754]

Regulator of Social Housing—*contd*
conflict of interest, arrangements for dealing
with, **24**, [627]
delegation of functions, **24**, [629]
determinations by, **23**, [400]
approval, requiring, **23**, [401]
disposal of property by registered provider,
consent to—
exceptions, **24**, [712]
procedure, **24**, [713]
requirement of, **24**, [711]
enforcement notice—
appeal, **24**, [762]
content, **24**, [760]
failure to comply, sanction for, **24**, [764]
grounds for, **24**, [759]
Homes and Communities Agency,
notification to, **24**, [761]
overview, **24**, [758]
withdrawal of, **24**, [763]
enforcement powers, exercise of, **24**, [757]
establishment of, **24**, [620]
failure by registered provider, compensation
for—
appeals, **24**, [784]
enforcement, **24**, [783]
grounds for award, **24**, [776]
housing ombudsman, award by, **24**, [778]
impact, consideration of, **24**, [780]
notice, **24**, [779]
persons to whom made, **24**, [777]
pre-compensation warning, **24**, [781]
representations, **24**, [782]
financial assistance, giving, **24**, [634]
financial year, **24**, [643]
fundamental objectives, **24**, [625]
guidance—
education or training, provision of,
24, [636]
issue of, **23**, [383]
Homes and Communities Agency—
co-operation by, **24**, [576]
co-operation with, **24**, [644]
directions to, **24**, [645]
housing management, financial assistance for,
22, [412]
information—
collection of, **24**, [646]
disclosure, **24**, [647], [648]
disclosure by, **23**, [380]
disclosure to, **23**, [379]
duty of confidentiality, no requirement to
breach, **24**, [647]
enforcement of notice to provide, **23**, [378]
general power to obtain, **23**, [377]
levels of performance, as to, **23**, [382]
publication of, **24**, [636]
insolvency of registered social landlord. *See*
registered social landlord
land, provisions applied, **25(2)**, [450]
Landlord and Tenant Act 1987, exclusion of,
22, [771]
landlord's interest, acquiring, **22**, [828]
management tender—
notice, **24**, [787]

Regulator of Social Housing—*contd*
  management tender—*contd*
    requirement, **24**, [786]
  management transfer—
    notice, **24**, [789]
    requirement, **24**, [788]
  manager of registered provider—
    appointment of, **24**, [790]
    notice of action, **24**, [791]
  meaning, **24**, [617]
  members—
    appointment, **24**, [621]
    number of, **24**, [621]
    remuneration, **24**, [638]
    tenure, **24**, [622]
  monitoring by—
    extraordinary audit, **24**, [749]
    inquiries—
      charity, relating to, **24**, [748]
      evidence, **24**, [747]
      holding, **24**, [745]
      procedure, **24**, [746]
      removal or suspension of officers
        following, **24**, [799], [800]
      reports, **24**, [746]
      restrictions on dealings during,
        24, [795], [797]
      restrictions on dealings following,
        24, [796], [797]
      suspension of officers during, **24**, [798],
        [800]
    inspections—
      fees, **24**, [741]
      power to arrange, **24**, [740]
      powers of inspectors, **24**, [742]
      purpose of, **24**, [740]
      report, **24**, [741]
    performance information—
      annual report, **24**, [743]
      publication of, **24**, [744]
      requirement, **24**, [743]
    survey—
      entry on premises, **24**, [739]
      notice of, **24**, [738]
      power to arrange, **24**, [738]
      report, **24**, [738]
  officers of registered societies—
    disqualified persons, register of, **24**, [802]
    new, appointment of, **24**, [808]
    non-profit registered provider, of, removal,
      24, [805], [806]
    removal or suspension of officers
      following, **24**, [799], [800]
    suspension during inquiry, **24**, [798], [800]
  penalties imposed on registered providers—
    amount of, **24**, [768]
    appeals, **24**, [774]
    destination of money, **24**, [772]
    enforcement, **24**, [773]
    grounds for, **24**, [766]
    Homes and Communities Agency,
      notification to, **24**, [771]
    penalty notice, **24**, [767]
    pre-penalty warning, **24**, [769]
    representations, **24**, [770]

Regulator of Social Housing—*contd*
  petition to wind up regulated provider,
    presentation of, **24**, [705]
  powers—
    considering exercise of, evidence as to,
      24, [635]
    financial assistance, giving, **24**, [634]
    general, **24**, [632]
    guidance, education or training, provision
      of, **24**, [636]
    information and advice, publication of,
      24, [636]
    research, undertaking, **24**, [636]
    studies, as to, **24**, [633]
  powers of entry, **23**, [384]
  procedure, **24**, [626]
  property, rights and liabilities, transfer to—
    Housing Corporation, of—
      interim arrangements, **24**, [605]
      scheme for, **24**, [604], [864]
      taxation, **24**, [865]
      transitional arrangements, **24**, [606]
  providers of social housing, register of—
    de-registration—
      appeals, **24**, [660]
      compulsory, **24**, [657]
      notice of, **24**, [659]
      voluntary, **24**, [658]
    entry on, **24**, [655]
    fees for registration, **24**, [656]
    maintenance of, **24**, [650]
    registration—
      appeals, **24**, [660]
      eligibility for, **24**, [651]
      fees, **24**, [656]
      local authorities, of, **24**, [653]
      local authority non-registrable bodies,
        24, [652]
      notice of, **24**, [659]
      overview, **24**, [649]
      profit-making or non-profit making
        organisation, as, **24**, [654]
      removal from, **24**, [657], [658]
      transitional provisions, **24**, [817]
  provision of services between other
    regulators, **22**, [461]
  register of social landlords. *See* **registered
    social landlord**
  relevant authority, as, **22**, [7]
  Relevant Authority, meaning, **23**, [403]
  research, undertaking, **24**, [636]
  seal, **24**, [630]
  Secretary of State, assistance by, **24**, [640]
  social housing grants by. *See* **registered
    social landlord**
  staff, **24**, [624]
  standards—
    code of practice—
      charities, applying to, **24**, [735]
      consultation, **24**, [735]
      issue of, **24**, [734]
      revision, **24**, [734], [737]
      withdrawal, **24**, [734], [737]
    failure to meet, **24**, [737]
    management, **24**, [733]

Regulator of Social Housing—*contd*
standards—*contd*
  Secretary of State, direction by, **24**, [736]
  setting, **24**, [732]
  specified rules, **24**, [732]
standards of performance, determining,
  23, [381]
studies by, **24**, [633]
tenant involvement, requirement, **24**, [637]
transfer of land of registered provider—
  inquiry or audit, after, **24**, [792]
  price, **24**, [793]
  terms of, **24**, [793]

regulatory enforcement
civil sanctions—
  appeals, **10(S)**, 94
  combination of, **10(S)**, 92
  consequential provisions, **10(S)**, 94–5
  Consolidated Fund, payment of penalties
    into, **10(S)**, 104
  consultation and consent—
    generally, **10(S)**, 97
    Scotland, **10(S)**, 96
    Wales, **10(S)**, 96
  costs recovery, **10(S)**, 93
  discretionary requirements—
    criminal proceedings and conviction,
      exclusion of, **10(S)**, 85–6
    enforcement, **10(S)**, 86
    final notice, **10(S)**, 84–5
    meaning, **10(S)**, 83
    non-monetary, **10(S)**, 83
    notice of intent, **10(S)**, 84
    power to impose, **10(S)**, 83
    procedure, **10(S)**, 84–5
    variable monetary penalty, **10(S)**, 83
  early payment discount, **10(S)**, 92
  enforcement action, publication of,
    10(S), 100–1
  enforcement undertakings, **10(S)**, 90–1
  excluded provisions—
    Northern Ireland, **10(S)**, 96
    Scotland, **10(S)**, 95
  fixed monetary penalties—
    Consolidated Fund, payment into,
      10(S), 104
    criminal proceedings and conviction,
      exclusion of, **10(S)**, 82
    early payment discount, **10(S)**, 92
    final notice, **10(S)**, 81
    meaning, **10(S)**, 80
    notice of intent, **10(S)**, 81
    power to impose, **10(S)**, 80
    procedure, **10(S)**, 81
  general note, **10(S)**, 73–5
  guidance as to use of, **10(S)**, 99
  interpretation, **10(S)**, 105
  orders for—
    consultation and consent, **10(S)**, 96–7
    excluded provisions, **10(S)**, 95–6
    Parliamentary and Assembly procedure,
      10(S), 98
    power to make, **10(S)**, 78
    specified enactments, **10(S)**, 113–16

regulatory enforcement—*contd*
civil sanctions—*contd*
  regulator—
    designated, list of, **10(S)**, 111
    meaning, **10(S)**, 79
  relevant offence—
    guidance as to enforcement, **10(S)**, 100
    meaning, **10(S)**, 79
  stop notice—
    compensation, provision for, **10(S)**, 89
    enforcement, **10(S)**, 89–90
    meaning, **10(S)**, 87
    power to serve, **10(S)**, 87
    procedure, **10(S)**, 88
  subordinate legislation, offences under,
    10(S), 98, 119–20
  suspension of powers, **10(S)**, 102–3
information, disclosure of, **10(S)**, 104–5
regulatory principles, compliance with,
  10(S), 101
review of provisions, **10(S)**, 102

regulatory functions
burdens—
  general—
    general note, **10(S)**, 75
    unnecessary, duty not to impose or
      maintain, **10(S)**, 106–8
code of practice—
  issue and revision of, **10**, [907]
  procedure for, **10**, [908]
interpretation, **10**, [910]
principles for exercise of, **10**, [906]
Scotland, Wales or Northern Ireland,
  exercisable in, **10**, [909]
specification of, **10**, [909]

regulatory reform orders
summary of provisions, **41**, [480]

rehabilitation of land. *See* **clearance area**

rehabilitation of offenders
absolute discharge, effect of, **12(1)**, [630],
  [634]
binding over to keep the peace, effect on,
  12(1), [634]
child, orders relating to, **12(1)**, [634]
children's hearings, disposal by, **12(1)**, [632],
  [634]
conditional discharge, effect of, **12(1)**, [630],
  [634]
conviction—
  circumstances ancillary to, **12(1)**, [633],
    [636]
  meaning, **12(1)**, [630]
  previous, effect, **12(1)**, [636]
defamation action, effect on, **12(1)**, [637]
detention and training order, effect on,
  12(1), [634]
effect of, **12(1)**, [633]
gambling offences, **5(1)**, [406]
hospital order, where made, **12(1)**, [634]
limitations on, **12(1)**, [636]
National Lottery, restrictions relating to,
  5(1), [149]

rehabilitation of offenders—*contd*
orders, exercise of power, **12(1)**, [641]
proceedings before judicial authority—
disclosure of convictions in, **12(1)**, [636]
meaning, **12(1)**, [633]
rehabilitated person, being, **12(1)**, [630]
rehabilitation period—
breach of discharge or order, sentence on,
12(1), [635]
conviction, applicable to, **12(1)**, [635]
further offence during, **12(1)**, [635]
length of, **12(1)**, [634]
more than one sentence, where,
12(1), [635]
particular sentences, for, **12(1)**, [634]
sentence—
meaning, **12(1)**, [630]
provisions, excluded from, **12(1)**, [634]
service disciplinary proceedings, finding of
guilt in, **12(1)**, [631], [643]
spent caution—
protection afforded to, **12(1)**, [638], [644];
12(4), [490], [567]
unauthorised disclosure of, **12(1)**, [640]
spent conviction—
conditions, **12(1)**, [630]
disclosing, **12(1)**, [633]
questions as to, **12(1)**, [633]
unauthorised disclosure of, **12(1)**, [639]
summary of provisions, **12(1)**, [1]
transitory and transitional provisions,
12(4), [580]
youth offender contract, where made,
12(1), [634]

reinstatement grant
amount of, **22**, [358]
conditions for, **22**, [353]
breach of, effect of, **22**, [361]
contributions by Minister, **22**, [384]
determination as to, **22**, [352]
notice of, **22**, [355]
entitlement to, **22**, [356]
notice of, **22**, [355]
instalments, payable by, **22**, [360]
payment—
conditions of, **22**, [357]
methods of, **22**, [360]
repayment for breach of conditions, **22**, [361]
repurchase in lieu of. *See* **defective housing**
shared ownership lease—
application of provisions to, **22**, [382]
meaning, **22**, [382]
work required—
associated arrangement, **22**, [354]
changes in, **22**, [359]
condition for payment, **22**, [357]
effective result of, **22**, [353]
meaning, **22**, [354]
more extensive than stated, **22**, [359]
period allowed for, **22**, [357]
qualifying work, **22**, [356]

reinstatement in civil employment
application for—
cessation of effect, **3**, [1466]
delay in making, **3**, [1466]
generally, **3**, [1464]
mode of, **3**, [1466]
regulation of, **3**, [1481]
time for, **3**, [1466]
to whom made, **3**, [1466]
waiver of requirement, **3**, [1469]
availability, notification, **3**, [1467]
compensation—
amount of, **3**, [1471], [1473]
court order for, **3**, [1473]
former employer, liability of, **3**, [1488]
proceedings for, **3**, [1475]
summary recovery, **3**, [1474]
termination of employment, for, **3**, [1480]
continuous employment, computing period
of, **3**, [1470]
discharge of another, requiring, **3**, [1468]
dismissal prior to service—
compensation, **3**, [1479]
prohibition of, **3**, [1479]
employment made available, **3**, [1464]
enforcement of orders, **3**, [1473]
evidence—
committee orders, of, **3**, [1476]
identity, of, **3**, [1476]
whole-time service, of, **3**, [1476]
former employer—
additional provisions, **3**, [1486]
change of employer, **3**, [1486]
compensation order against, **3**, [1488]
default by, **3**, [1471]
meaning, **3**, [1465]
notice to, of availability, **3**, [1467]
obligation on—
discharge of, **3**, [1464]
extent of, **3**, [1470]
generally, **3**, [1464]
waiver of requirements by, **3**, [1470]
identity, proof of, **3**, [1478]
inability to take up employment, **3**, [1488]
Isle of Man, application to, **3**, [1484]
obligation after, **3**, [1470]
period of re-employment, **3**, [1470]
persons entitled, **3**, [1464]
priorities as to, **3**, [1468]
proceedings—
evidence in, **3**, [1476]–[1478]
institution of, **3**, [1475]
proof of identity in, **3**, [1478]
restrictions on, **3**, [1475]
reasonable and practical, **3**, [1468]
Reinstatement Committee—
appeal to umpire from, **3**, [1472]
application to, right to make, **3**, [1471]
appointment of, **3**, [1487]
assessors to assist, **3**, [1487]
constitution of, **3**, [1487]
determinations, evidence of, **3**, [1477]
orders—
compensation, for, **3**, [1471], [1488]
enforcement, **3**, [1473]

reinstatement in civil employment—*contd*
Reinstatement Committee—*contd*
orders—*contd*
evidence, as, **3**, [1477]
former employer, against, **3**, [1488]
kinds of, **3**, [1471]
reinstatement, for, **3**, [1471], [1488]
remuneration, **3**, [1487]
reserve forces, **3**, [1441]
service, certification of, **3**, [1476]
terms and conditions, **3**, [1464]
time limit, **3**, [1464]
umpire—
appeal to, **3**, [1472]
appointment, **3**, [1487]
powers of, **3**, [1472]
remuneration, **3**, [1487]
whole-time service—
evidence of, **3**, [1476]
meaning, **3**, [1482]

relapsing fever
notifiable disease. *See* **notifiable disease**

relative
connected person, as, **44(1)**, [621]
meaning, **44(1)**, [621]

release
stamp duty on, **41**, [214]

religious educational trusts
endowments, orders as to use of—
content of, **15(1)**, [690]
power to make, **15(1)**, [688]
procedure, **15(1)**, [689]
statutory trusts, adoption of, **15(1)**, [691],
[722]

religious hatred
inflammatory material—
entry and search for, **12(1)**, [1032]
forfeiture of, **12(1)**, [1033]
possession of, **12(1)**, [1031]
meaning, **12(1)**, [1024]
offences, **12(4)**, [167]
corporations, by, **12(1)**, [1038]
penalties, **12(1)**, [1037]
proceedings for, **12(1)**, [1037]
stirring up—
broadcasting programmes, **12(1)**, [1030]
cable programme service, **12(1)**, [1030]
judicial proceedings, saving for,
12(1), [1036]
parliamentary proceedings, saving for,
12(1), [1036]
public performance, by, **12(1)**, [1028]
recording, distributing, showing or
playing, **12(1)**, [1029]
words or behaviour, by, **12(1)**, [1026]
written material—
displaying, **12(1)**, [1026]
meaning, **12(1)**, [1039]
publishing or distributing, **12(1)**, [1027]

religious houses
grants from Rome, validity of, **14**, 37
pension to See of Rome, not paying, **14**, 37
privileges, saving for, **14**, 38
visitation of, **14**, 36

religious worship
place for. *See* **place of worship**

relinquishment, deed of
consequences of, **14**, 221–2
copy of record as evidence, **14**, 223
enrolment, **14**, 221
execution of, **14**, 221
form of, **14**, 224
pecuniary liability, saving for, **14**, 223
proceedings, where pending, **14**, 222
recording of, **14**, 221–2
service of notices, **14**, 222
vacation of enrolment—
clerk, position of after, **14**, 356
copy of record as evidence, **14**, 357
procedure, **14**, 355–6

remainderman
barring of entail, rights, **20**, [75]

remand
young persons, **12(1)**, [260]

remand centres. *See under* **young offenders**

remand home
absence from, **6**, [128]
discontinuance of, **6**, [130]
expenses, payment of, **6**, [52]
home for children in care, use as, **6**, [139]
provision by councils, **6**, [41]
use of premises for, **12(1)**, [265]

remuneration of teachers. *See* **teachers' pay
and conditions**

renewables obligation. *See under* **electricity**

renewal area
declaration—
generally, **23**, [28]
representations, **23**, [28]
steps to be taken after, **23**, [29]
directions and guidance, **23**, [37]
entry, powers of—
obstruction, **23**, [35]
survey and examination, for, **23**, [35]
extension, steps to be taken after, **23**, [29]
highway, extinguishment of right to use
vehicles on, **23**, [32]
housing conditions, consideration of,
22, [395]
information, publication of, **23**, [30]
interpretation of terms, **23**, [38]
land excluded from, **23**, [33]
land not included in, **23**, [28]
local housing authority—
general powers of, **23**, [31]

renewal area—*contd*
  local housing authority—*contd*
    housing association, agreements with,
      23, [31]
    objectives, **23**, [31]
  report on, **23**, [28]
  resolution—
    cessation of area, declaring, **23**, [33]
    exclusion of land by, **23**, [33]
    local land charge, as, **23**, [28]
  Secretary of State, contributions of, **23**, [34]
  termination of, **23**, [33]

renovation grant. *See also* **housing grants**
  means testing of owner-occupier or tenant,
    23, [584]

rent. *See also* **rent registration**
  advance payment, avoidance of requirement
    for, **21**, [618]
  agricultural holdings. *See* **agricultural
    holdings**
  agricultural housing. *See* **agricultural
    workers**
  allowance subsidy, rent officers, functions of,
    23, [426]
  apportionment of—
    application for order, **21**, [66]
    compulsory purchase, on, **9**, [76], [216],
      [279]
    disclaimer of requisitioned land, after,
      21,]131]
    equitable, **20**, [791]
    part of land acquired, **9**, [279]
    payable, becoming, **20**, [394]
    policy of assurance, provisions not applying
      to, **20**, [397]
    recovery, remedies for, **20**, [395]
    time, in respect of, **20**, [393]
    war damage, following, **21**, [121]
  arrears—
    commercial recovery, **20**, [233]
      See also commercial rent arrears recovery
        (CRAR) *below*
    determination of lease, recovery after,
      20, [27]
    distraint, abolition of common law right,
      24, [517]
    ejectment, proceedings for, **20**, [232]
    execution of judgment, payment on,
      20, [25]
    tenant for life, recovery from, **20**, [26]
  assize, of, recovery of, **20**, [31]
  assured tenancy, under. *See* **assured tenancy**
  bankrupt, due from, **4(2)**, [419]
  chief, recovery of, **20**, [31]
  commercial, **44(1)**, [523]
  commercial rent arrears recovery (CRAR)—
    agricultural holdings, application to,
      24, [526]
    amended provisions, **24**, [539]
    commercial premises, lease of, **24**, [521]
    contracts for similar rights, void, **24**, [531]
    court, intervention of, **24**, [524]
    end of lease, use after, **24**, [525]

rent—*contd*
  commercial rent arrears recovery
    (CRAR)—*contd*
    landlord, meaning, **24**, [519]
    lease, meaning, **24**, [520]
    procedure, **24**, [518]
    recoverable rent, **24**, [523]
    regulations, **24**, [535]
    rent, meaning, **24**, [522]
    sub-tenant—
      offsetting payments, **24**, [528]
      overpayments, **24**, [530]
      recovery of sums due, **24**, [530]
      right to rent from, **24**, [527]
      withdrawal and replacement of notices,
        24, [529]
  deductions from, recovery of highway
    expenses by, **36**, [1420]
  deductions where premium paid, **44(1)**, [25]
  demand—
    contravention of provisions, penalty for,
      20, [490]
    landlord's name and address to be in,
      22, [762]
    meaning, **20**, [489]
    statement of rates in, **20**, [488]
  distress for, restriction on, **21**, [632]
    See also **distress**
  electric line wayleaves, in respect of,
    44(1), [99]
  factoring, **44(1)**, [532]
  failure to pay as ground for possession,
    21, [651]
  growing crops, seizure and sale under
    execution, **20**, [229]
  holding over, double value on, **20**, [30]
  housing association tenancy. *See* **housing
    association**
  increase—
    tenancy not secure, where, **22**, [25]
    tenant's improvements, for, **22**, [91]
  indemnities against, **20**, [790]
  interim, on continuation of business
    tenancy—
    application for determination of, **21**, [177]
    date from which payable, **21**, [178]
    new tenancy of whole premises granted,
      where, **21**, [179]
    reasonable, **21**, [180]
  landlord's lien restricted, **19(3)**, [5]
  limit, power to order—
    business tenancy, exclusion of, **22**, [545]
    Secretary of State, by, **22**, [544]
  limitation of action—
    part payment, effect, **19(3)**, [759]
    recovery, action for, **19(3)**, [746]
  meaning, **20**, [396], [436], [804]; **22**, [544];
    44(1), [17]
  mine, quarry, etc, in connection with,
    44(1), [98]
  non-payment—
    ejectment for, **20**, [232], [233]
    remedies, **20**, [791]
  notices, regulations as to, **21**, [559]

rent—*contd*
  payment—
    natural days and times for, **45**, [924], [926]
    premium as, **44(1)**, [22]
  person demanding, offences by, **22**, [511]
  power to charge, **22**, [24]
  rack rent, meaning, **36**, [1381]
  receipt—
    meaning, **20**, [489]
    statement of rates in, **20**, [488]
  recovery of, **20**, [26], [27]
  references to, **44(1)**, [523]
  regulated tenancy, under. *See* **regulated
   tenancy**
  regulation, release from, **21**, [629]
  rendering of certain, by corporation of
   London, **13**, [5]
  renewal of business tenancy, paid on,
   21, [177], [193]
  rental period, meaning, **22**, [108]
  restricted contract, under. *See* **restricted
   contract**
  reviews of, **22**, [24]
  Schedule A, under, **44(1)**, [12]
  seck, recovery of, **20**, [31]
  sublet part of dwelling, excessive amount for,
   21, [651]
  taxation of, **43(1)**, [343], [387]
  UK s 12(4) concern, receivable in connection
   with—
    charge to tax, **44(3)**, [335]
    income charged, **44(3)**, [337]
    meaning, **44(3)**, [336]
    mineral lease or agreement, meaning,
     44(3), [341]
    mineral rights, deduction for management
     expense of, **44(3)**, [339]
    mineral royalties—
     Commissioners determining,
      44(3), [343]
     meaning, **44(3)**, [341]
     relief for, **44(3)**, [340]
    person liable, **44(3)**, [338]
  wayleaves, receivable for—
    charge to tax, **44(3)**, [344]
    extent of charge, **44(3)**, [346]
    income charged, **44(3)**, [347]
    meaning, **44(3)**, [345]
    person liable, **44(3)**, [348]

rent-a-room
  property income relief, **44(3)**, [309]
  receipts, meaning, **44(3)**, [803]
  relief—
    adjustment of assessment, time limit,
     44(3), [818]
    alternative calculation of profits—
     application of provisions, **44(3)**, [812]
     election for, **44(3)**, [817]
     income not otherwise charged,
      44(3), [815]
     property income, **44(3)**, [814]
     trading income, **44(3)**, [813]
    exclusive receipts condition, **44(3)**, [807]

rent-a-room—*contd*
  relief—*contd*
    full—
     application of provisions, **44(3)**, [808]
     election not to apply, **44(3)**, [816]
     income not otherwise charged,
      44(3), [811]
     property income, **44(3)**, [810]
     trading income, **44(3)**, [809]
    individual's limit, **44(3)**, [806]
    overview of provisions, **44(3)**, [801]
    qualification for, **44(3)**, [802]
    residence, meaning, **44(3)**, [804]
    total amount, meaning, **44(3)**, [805]
    trade profits, income taxed as, **44(3)**, [23]

rent allowance subsidy
  rent officers, functions of, **22**, [903]

rent assessment committee
  assured shorthold tenancy, reference of
   excessive rents to, **22**, [820]
  assured tenancy—
    determination of rent under, **22**, [807]
    interim determination of rent where
     landlord liable to council tax, **22**, [809]
  constitution of, **21**, [566], [648]
  determination of rents—
    amounts attributable to services, **22**, [835]
    information as to, **22**, [837]
  exemption from council tax, provision of
   information, **22**, [836]
  fair rent, determining, **21**, [649]
  functions of, **21**, [737]
  information, requiring, **22**, [834]
  leasehold valuation tribunal, treated as,
   21, [750]
  objections to rent heard by, **21**, [649]
  procedure, **22**, [834]
  rent tribunal functions, carrying out,
   21, [737]
  statutory periodic tenancy, determining terms
   of, **22**, [796]
  termination of functions, **22**, [821]

rent book
  arrears, false entry of, **21**, [556], [594]
  board, rent including payment for, **22**, [508]
  determination of recoverable rent, rectification
   after, **21**, [557]
  duty to provide, **22**, [508]
  failure to provide, **22**, [511]
  information in, **22**, [509]
  inspection by housing authority, **22**, [289]
  irrecoverable rent, entry as to, **21**, [618]
  obligation to provide, **22**, [508]
  permitted number in house to be shown in,
   22, [285]

rent officer
  administration, basis for, **21**, [565]
  application to, procedure, **21**, [649]
  appointment, **22**, [902]
  chief, designation of, **21**, [562]
  dismissal, restriction on, **21**, [562]

rent officer—*contd*
  duties, allocation of, **21**, [562]
  exemption from council tax, provision of
    information, **22**, [836]
  expenditure, grants for, **21**, [562]
  fair rent, determining, **21**, [570]
  housing benefit and rent allowances subsidy,
    functions relating to, **22**, [903]
  local authority—
    function, not being, **21**, [565]
    in employment of, **21**, [562]
  number of, determining, **21**, [562]
  office accommodation, **21**, [562]
  register of rents, keeping, **21**, [567]
  remuneration and allowances, **21**, [562]
  rent, registering, **21**, [759]
  schemes for appointment of—
    incidental and transitional provisions in,
      21, [563]
    provisions in, **21**, [562]
    Secretary of State, default powers of,
      21, [563]
    variation or revocation, **21**, [562], [563]

rent registration
  amalgamation of areas, **21**, [564]
  amount to be registered, **21**, [572]
  application for—
    certificate of fair rent, unsupported by,
      21, [649]
    form of, **21**, [568]
    particulars in, **21**, [568]
    person making, **21**, [568]
    procedure, **21**, [568]
    regulations, **21**, [576]
    rent officer, registration by, **21**, [649], [759]
    two years from relevant date, after,
      21, [568]
  areas of, **21**, [561], [564]
  cancellation of, **21**, [575]
  date for taking effect, **21**, [573]
  effect of, **21**, [573]
  fair rent—
    circumstances, change in, **21**, [568]
    council tax liability of landlord to be taken
      into account, **21**, [570]
    determination of—
      disregarded matters, **21**, [570]
      matters taken into account, **21**, [570]
      rent assessment committee, by, **21**, [649]
  furniture and services, rent including,
    21, [588]
  hereditament, where dwelling-house forms
    part of, **21**, [568]
  housing association tenancy, **21**, [589], [590]
  interim increase in rent where landlord liable
    for council tax—
    application for, **21**, [569]
    determination of fair rent, **21**, [571]
  local authority, meaning, **21**, [586]
  maintenance works, taking account of,
    21, [572]
  notice of increase, effect of, **21**, [573]
  notification of, **21**, [649]
  objections, **21**, [649]

rent registration—*contd*
  reconsideration after, **21**, [581]
  register—
    contents of, **21**, [567]
    copies of entries in, **21**, [567]
    rates, burden to be noted, **21**, [572]
    responsibility for, **21**, [567]
  regulations, power to make, **21**, [576], [587]
  rent officer, by, **21**, [649]
  repair, taking account of, **21**, [570], [647]
  restricted contract, under—
    cancellation of, **21**, [584]
    effect of, **21**, [583]
    excess, recovery of, **21**, [583]
    interim increase of rent where lessor liable
      for council tax, reference to rent tribunal
      for, **21**, [582]
    reconsideration, **21**, [581]
    register, maintenance of, **21**, [580]
  savings, **21**, [660]
  services, taking account of, **21**, [572], [574],
    [647]
  transitional provisions, **21**, [660]

rent tribunal
  abolition of, **21**, [737]
  rent assessment committee known as,
    21, [737]
  restricted contract referred to—
    information, notice requiring, **21**, [578]
    jurisdiction, **21**, [585]
    notice to quit after, **21**, [604]
    period of notice to quit, reducing,
      21, [607]
    powers of, **21**, [579]
    security of tenure, application for,
      21, [605]

rental compensation
  income tax on, **9**, [121]
  land, taking possession of, **9**, [121], [168]
  maxima, **9**, [169]

rental purchase agreement
  eviction, protection from, **21**, [765]
  proceedings for possession following,
    21, [747]

rentcharge. *See also* **tithe**
  See also redemption *below*
  apportionment—
    appeals, **21**, [506]
    application for—
      expenses, **21**, [515]
      form, **21**, [504]
      matters to be specified, **21**, [504]
      objections to, **21**, [505]
      order for, **21**, [504]
    custody of documents, **14**, 365, 444
    documents, production of, **21**, [504]
    draft order for, **21**, [505]
    equitable, meaning, **21**, [513]
    expenses, **21**, [515]
    financial hardship, causing, **21**, [507]
    generally, **21**, [505]

rentcharge—*contd*
apportionment—*contd*
Lands Tribunal to determine, **9**, [181], [278]
legal, meaning, **21**, [513]
meaning, **21**, [513]
order for—
application, **21**, [504]
draft, **21**, [505]
effect, **21**, [507]
making of, **21**, [505]
meaning, **21**, [513]
rentcharges excepted from, **21**, [504]
transcript of, **14**, 88
arrears, recovery of, **14**, 1218
breach of covenant, remedies, **20**, [791]
cessation of power to create, **14**, 443
charged on another rentcharge, **20**, [739]
Church Commissioners, held by, **14**, 846
covenants enforceable, **21**, [502]
creation, **20**, [13]
before 1977 Act, **21**, [517]
new, prohibition of, **21**, [502]
permitted, **21**, [502]
Crown, application of provisions, **21**, [514]
Crown lands, application of provisions to, **14**, 365
demise of land charged, **20**, [738]
distress, **20**, [738]
documents—
delivery to Secretary of State, **21**, [504]
mortgagee, in possession of, **21**, [504], [508]
service of, **21**, [516]
drainage of land, on. *See* **drainage and improvement of land (private works)**
enforcement, **20**, [632], [738]
entry, enforcement by right of, **20**, [738]
estate rentcharge—
creation, **21**, [502]
extinguishment, excepted from, **21**, [503]
meaning, **21**, [502]
extinction—
exceptions from, **21**, [503]
expenses, **21**, [515]
time for, **21**, [503]
See also redemption *below*
extinguishment of—
date of, **14**, 358
past dealings, confirmation of, **14**, 441–2
generally, **20**, [1]
implied covenants to pay, **21**, [511]
improvement, application of capital money, **1(1)**, [664]
improvement works, creation, **21**, [502]
information, furnishing to Secretary of State, **21**, [504]
land, merger in, charges thereon, **14**, 130
land subject to compulsory purchase, on—
apportionment, **9**, [73], [278]
compensation for release of, **9**, [72], [278]
continuance on land not taken, **9**, [75], [278]
deed poll extinguishing, **9**, [74], [278]

rentcharge—*contd*
land subject to compulsory purchase, on—*contd*
refusal, deposit of compensation on, **9**, [74], [278]
release—
compensation for, **9**, [72], [278]
consideration for, **9**, [72]
part of land, **9**, [72], [278]
payment of compensation into court, **9**, [74], [278]
land subject to—
Crown disclaimer of bona vacantia, **8(1)**, [1097]
implied covenants in conveyance, **20**, [695]
lay impropriator, liability of, **14**, 278
lease, part of land under, **9**, [76]
liability for on land of dissolved company, **8(1)**, [1101]
meaning, **9**, [278]; **20**, [804]; **21**, [78], [501]
mistaken payment, recovery, **9**, [398]
non-payment, remedies, **20**, [791]
notices, service of, **21**, [516]
owner in relation to land, meaning, **21**, [513]
owner of land, vesting in, **14**, 360–1
perpetual—
Law of Property Act, application, **20**, [800]
legal estate, as, **20**, [625]
property subject to, implied covenants, **23**, [224]
purchase by agreement, in case of. *See* **acquisition of land**
Queen Anne's Bounty, vested in. *See* **Queen Anne's Bounty**
rate assessed on, information on, **14**, 364
receiver, appointment, **20**, [739]
recovery, by distress, **14**, 1218
recovery, remedies, **20**, [738], [739]
redemption—
certificate—
application for—
documents to accompany, **21**, [508]
form, **21**, [508]
notice, **21**, [509]
effect of, **21**, [510]
issue of, **21**, [509]
consideration, annuity, discharged by, **14**, 302
exceptions from, **21**, [508]
expenses, **21**, [515]
false statements respecting, **21**, [510]
generally, **20**, [791]
instructions for redemption notice, **21**, [509]
payments into court, **21**, [510]
price, calculation of, **21**, [510]
rent-owner, notification to, **21**, [509]
references to, adaptation, **14**, 366
regulations, power to make, **21**, [512]
release of part of land charged, **20**, [688], [689]
rent, equitable apportionment, **20**, [791]
rent-owner—
appeal against apportionment order, **21**, [506]

rentcharge—*contd*
rent-owner—*contd*
meaning, **21**, [513]
notice to, of application, **21**, [509]
repeals affecting, **41**, [545]
sale in consideration of, **14**, 304
sale of—
augmentation of benefice, for, **14**, 199
power of, **14**, 376
sale of land or right in consideration of,
20, [492]
Schedule A, under, **44(1)**, [12]
tithe, instead of, **14**, 146
trust of land, respecting, **21**, [502]
trustees, liability of, **14**, 364
variable rentcharges, **21**, [503]
vesting declaration, provisions relating to,
9, [398], [404]
Welsh Church, transfer on disestablishment
of, **14**, 261, 268–9

renunciation
letter of, abolition of stamp duty, **41**, [152],
[157]
letters of allotment—
stamp duty exemption, **41**, [148]
stamp duty reserve tax exemption,
41, [178]
stamp duty on, **41**, [214]

repairing covenant
breach of—
action for—
counter-notice, **21**, [80]
expenses of survey, etc, recovery of,
21, [81]
jurisdiction, **21**, [84]
notice before, **21**, [80]
past breaches, provisions on, **21**, [83]
possession, repairs on taking, **21**, [82]
provisions relating to, **21**, [85]
restriction on, **21**, [80]
damages, amount of, **21**, [64]
forfeiture, enforcement of right, **21**, [64]
opposition to business tenancy renewal,
ground for, **21**, [188]
proposed demolition, etc, effect of, **21**, [64]
re-entry, enforcement of right, **21**, [64]
extension of provisions, **21**, [215]
landlord, specific performance of obligations,
22, [521]
requisitioned land, on. *See* **requisitioned
land**
short lease, in—
age and character of property, regard to,
22, [515]
contracting out, restriction on, **22**, [516]
county court, jurisdiction of, **22**, [519]
excepted leases, **22**, [518]
lease, meaning of, **22**, [520]
leases to which provisions applicable,
22, [517]
lessee, duties of, **22**, [515]
lessor—
implied by, **22**, [515]

repairing covenant—*contd*
short lease, in—*contd*
lessor—*contd*
power of entry to view, **22**, [515]
locality of property, regard to, **22**, [515]
war damage. *See* **war damage**

repairs
demoted tenancy, **23**, [461]
introductory tenancy, **23**, [441]
mortgaged property, **22**, [317]
secure tenant, by—
recovery of cost, **22**, [84]
regulations for, **22**, [84]

repayment of tax
interest on overpaid tax, **44(1)**, [609]
investment income, tax deducted from,
43(1), [52]
supplement—
companies, to, **44(1)**, [608]
individuals, to, **44(1)**, [607]

repayment supplement
repayments attracting, **43(1)**, [423]

replevy. *See* **distress**

repo
cases in which deeming rules apply,
44(4), [609]
deemed manufactured payments, **44(4)**, [610]
interim holder under, no tax credits for,
44(4), [601]
non-standard cases, power to modify
provisions for, **44(4)**, [620], [622]
original owner, no tax credits for,
44(4), [602]
price differences under, **44(4)**, [612]
additional tax treatment, **44(4)**, [617]
main tax treatment of, **44(4)**, [615]–[616]
non-arm's length case, modification of
provisions for, **44(4)**, [619]
redemption arrangements, cases involving,
power to modify provisions for,
44(4), [621]–[622]
repurchase price, deemed increase in,
44(4), [612]–[613]
transitional provisions and savings,
44(4), [1057]

reptiles
importation and exportation, restriction on.
See **animals**
sale, etc, restriction on. *See* **animals**

Republic of Ireland
veterinary surgeons, reciprocal arrangements,
28, [37]

repurchase arrangements
insolvency, stamp taxes in event of—
application of provisions,
41(S), Stamp Duties 6–7
replacement stock, **41(S)**, Stamp Duties 9

repurchase arrangements—*contd*
  insolvency, stamp taxes in event of—*contd*
    stamp duty, **41(S)**, Stamp Duties 9
    stamp duty reserve tax,
      41(S), Stamp Duties 10–12

requisitioned land
  authority taking possession, references to,
    21, [138]
  buildings and fixtures, adjustment of rights
    to, **21**, [132]
  certificates, evidence of, **21**, [134], [145]
  compensation for damage—
    evidence of right to, **21**, [145]
    references to, construction of, **21**, [145]
    tenant, expenditure by, **21**, [144]
  county court jurisdiction, **21**, [135]
  Crown land, application of provisions to,
    21, [137], [146]
  disclaimer—
    abroad, tenant being, **21**, [130]
    agricultural holding of, **21**, [127]
    compensation following surrender,
      21, [131]
    conditions for, **21**, [126]
    lease, adaptations and modifications of,
      21, [127]
    leases to which provisions applicable,
      21, [136]
    mortgage or charge, notice to person
      having, **21**, [127]
    multiple leases, effect on, **21**, [128]
    notice of—
      effect of, **21**, [127]
      service of, **21**, [126]
    rent, apportionment of, **21**, [131]
    stages, land taken in, **21**, [129]
    subsequent occasion, land possessed on,
      21, [138]
  interpretation of terms, **21**, [138], [147]
  Northern Ireland, application of provisions
    to, **21**, [139]
  notices, service of, **21**, [134]
  rent, reduction of, **21**, [133]
  repairing covenant—
    enforcement, proceedings for, **21**, [145]
    meaning, **21**, [147]
    modification of obligations under,
      21, [143]
  services, provision by landlord, **21**, [133]

requisitioning
  emergency powers, under, compensation for.
    See **emergency powers**
  forage and stores, **3**, [672]
  horses and mules, **3**, [672]
  meaning, **9**, [136]
  vehicles. *See* **vehicles**

research. *See also* **National Research**
Development Corporation
  atomic energy, **17(1)**, [579]
  funds for promotion of, **47**, [45]
  grants for, **46**, [575]
  Secretary of State, powers, **16**, [67], [119]

research and development
  allowances. *See* **research and development**
  allowance
  claims for relief—
    return, included in, **43(S)**, 175–6
    tax credit, substitution of provisions,
      43(S), 176–7
  clinical trials, payments to subjects of,
    43(S), 17, 174–5
  expenditure on, **43(1)**, [1074]
    externally provided workers, on,
      43(1), [521]
    tax relief for—
      artificially inflated claims, **43(1)**, [523];
        43(2), [142]
      company and sub-contractor connected,
        where, **43(1)**, [521]
      connected person treatment, election
        for, **43(1)**, [521]
      consortium relief, restriction on,
        43(1), [523]
      consumable items, on, **43(1)**, [521]
      deemed trading loss, treatment of,
        43(1), [523]
      definitions, **43(2)**, [143]
      entitlement to, **43(1)**, [521]
      giving effect to, **43(1)**, [522]
      group companies, **43(2)**, [142]
      independent, refund of contributions,
        43(2), [142]
      insurance companies, special provision
        for, **43(2)**, [141]
      intellectual property, meaning,
        43(1), [521]
      large companies, **43(2)**, [137]
      profits, deduction from, **43(2)**, [140]
      provision for, **43(2)**, [99]
      qualifying expenditure, **43(1)**, [521]
      relevant research and development,
        43(1), [521]
      small and medium-sized enterprises,
        for, **43(1)**, [521]; **43(S)**, 545–6
        large companies additional relief,
          entitlement to, **43(2)**, [139]
        work subcontracted to, **43(2)**, [138]
      software, on, **43(1)**, [521]
      staffing costs, **43(1)**, [521]
      sub-contracted research and
        development, on, **43(1)**, [521]
      subsidised, **43(1)**, [521]
      tax credit, **43(1)**, [522]
      transitional provision, **43(2)**, [143]
      vaccine research, **43(2)**, [144]
    treatment of, **43(2)**, [290]
  expenditure on—
    deductions for, **44(1)**, [51]
    relief for, **43(2)**, [229]
  expenses of, tax deduction for, **44(3)**, [86]
  meaning, **43(1)**, [480], [519]; **44(1)**, [617]
  research institution spin-out companies. *See*
    research institution spin-out companies
  scientific research organisation. *See* **scientific**
    research organisation
  software or consumable items, expenditure
    on, **43(2)**, [354]

research and development—*contd*
tax credit, **43(1)**, [522]
claims for, **43(1)**, [402]

research and development allowance
additional VAT liabilities—
additional expenditure, treated as,
43(1), [1084]
meaning, **43(1)**, [1083]
additional VAT rebates—
balancing charges, effect on, **43(1)**, [1086]
disposal value, generating, **43(1)**, [1085]
meaning, **43(1)**, [1083]
amended provisions, **43(S)**, 856
availability of, **43(1)**, [1074]
balancing charges—
additional VAT rebate generating,
43(1), [1085]
liability to, **43(1)**, [1079]
cap on, **43(S)**, 858, 1120–2
cessation of ownership, time of, **43(1)**, [1088]
companies in difficulty, for, **43(S)**, 1117–18
disposal values—
additional VAT rebate generating,
43(1), [1085]
bringing into account, **43(1)**, [1080]
demolition costs, **43(1)**, [1082]
disposal events, **43(1)**, [1080]
period for which brought into account,
43(1), [1081]
table of, **43(1)**, [1080]
entitlement to, **43(1)**, [1078]
expenditure on, **43(2)**, [229]
fixture on which claimed, **43(1)**, [754]
insurance company, for, **43(S)**, 1161
giving effect to, **43(1)**, [1087]
qualifying expenditure—
excluded, **43(1)**, [1077]
land, exclusion of expenditure on,
43(1), [1077]
meaning, **43(1)**, [1076]
rates of—
large companies, **43(S)**, 1116
small and medium-sized enterprises,
43(S), 1116
total aid, calculation of, **43(S)**, 1120–1
transitional provisions, **43(1)**, [1229]
writing off, **43(1)**, [914]

research councils. *See also* **Medical Research Council, etc**
accounts of, **10**, [533]
charters, **10**, [537]
Council for Scientific and Industrial Research,
taking over, **10**, [534]
establishment of, **10**, [532]
expenses of, **10**, [533]
land occupied by, **10**, [533]
report and accounts, **10**, [533], [539]
transfer of activities, **10**, [534], [540]

research institution spin-out companies
employment–related securities in—
application of provisions, **43(2)**, [581]
pre-2nd December 2004 cases, **43(2)**, [582]

research institution spin-out companies—*contd*
employment–related securities in—*contd*
shares, date of acquisition, **43(2)**, [581]

Reserve and Auxiliary Forces
service in, protection as to agricultural
holdings, **22**, [673]

reserve associations
accounts, **3**, [1658]
compensation for displaced employees,
3, [1661]
constitution of—
generally, **3**, [1654]
schemes for, provision of, **3**, [1678]
displacement of employees, compensation
for, **3**, [1661]
establishment of, for areas in UK, **3**, [1653]
expenses, **3**, [1657]
general duties of, **3**, [1655]
joint committees, **3**, [1659]
powers and duties, **3**, [1656]
regulations, **3**, [1660]
winding-up, **3**, [1662]

Reserve Bank of India
capital gains tax exemption, **42**, [1420]
no income tax liability for issue department,
44(4), [847]
tax exemption, **44(1)**, [373]

reserve forces. *See also* **Air Force Reserve, etc**
absence for voting, **3**, [1667]
absence without leave. *See* **absence without leave**
additional duties commitments, **3**, [1568]
Air Force Act, application to, **3**, [986]
allowances, **3**, [1550]
appeals tribunals—
chairmen, appointment of panel of,
3, [1633]
constitution, **3**, [1631]
jurisdiction, **3**, [1632]
membership, **3**, [1635]
offences in connection with appeals,
3, [1637]
ordinary members, appointment of panel
of, **3**, [1634]
powers, **3**, [1632]
practice and procedure, Secretary of State's
power to make rules with respect to,
3, [1636]
Army—
Act, application to, **3**, [714]
postponement of transfer to reserve or
discharge from, **3**, [1683]
associations. *See* **reserve associations**
attack on UK—
call out for—
maximum duration of service on,
3, [1596]
powers to authorise, **3**, [1595]

reserve forces—*contd*
  attack on UK—*contd*
    recall for service for—
      maximum duration of service on,
        3, [1612]
      powers to authorise, **3**, [1611]
  billeting, **3**, [1665]
  bounty, **3**, [1550]
  call out—
    acceptance into service, **3**, [1602]
    alteration of authority for, **3**, [1604]
    attack on UK—
      maximum duration of service on, call
        out for, **3**, [1595]
      powers to authorise, where, **3**, [1595]
    certain operations—
      maximum duration of service on,
        3, [1600]
      powers to authorise, **3**, [1599]
    differing service liabilities, **3**, [1402], [1464]
    exemptions from—
      effect of, **3**, [1623]
      individual, **3**, [1621]
      offences, **3**, [1625]
      supplementary provisions, **3**, [1624]
    great emergency, where—
      maximum duration of service on,
        3, [1596]
      powers to authorise, **3**, [1595]
      suspension of payments due to, powers
        of, **3**, [1629]
    interpretation provisions, **3**, [1607]
    liability—
      exempt persons from or relax, power
        to, **3**, [1605]
      general, **3**, [1593]
      geographical extent of, **3**, [1594]
    national danger—
      for, **3**, [1386]
      where—
        maximum duration of service on,
          3, [1596]
        powers to authorise, **3**, [1595]
        suspension of payments due to, powers
          of, **3**, [1629]
    notices, **3**, [1401]
    service of, **3**, [1601]
    payments for—
      employers, to, **3**, [1627]
      individuals, to, **3**, [1626]
      offences in connection with claims for,
        3, [1630]
      supplementary provisions, **3**, [1628]
      suspension of, powers of, **3**, [1629]
    release from service, **3**, [1403], [1603]
    warlike operations, for, **3**, [1387]
      maximum duration of service on,
        3, [1598]
      powers to authorise, **3**, [1597]
  charitable property on disbanding of units—
    preliminary, **3**, [1679]
    succession to—
      England and Wales, **3**, [1680]
      Northern Ireland, **3**, [1682]
      Scotland, **3**, [1681]

reserve forces—*contd*
  civil interests, preserving. *See* **civil interests
    of servicemen**
  command of men in permanent service,
    3, [1563]
  commitments—
    additional duties, **3**, [1568]
    full-time service, to period of, **3**, [1567]
    parliamentary control of, **3**, [1569]
  control of numbers, **3**, [1546]
  desertion. *See* **desertion**
  disbanding of units, charitable property on—
    preliminary, **3**, [1679]
    succession to—
      England and Wales, **3**, [1680]
      Northern Ireland, **3**, [1682]
      Scotland, **3**, [1681]
  discharge—
    commanding officer, by, **3**, [1558]
    entitlement to, **3**, [1558]
    general powers, **3**, [1558]
    postponement of, **3**, [1560]
    rights upon, **3**, [1561]
  employee agreements, **3**, [1581]–[1582],
    [1591]
  employment, safeguards for members,
    3, [1664]
  enlistment—
    appropriate minimum age, meaning of,
      3, [1675]
    attestation—
      papers—
        evidence as to, **3**, [1675]
        false answers in, **3**, [1675]
      procedure on, **3**, [1675]
      validity of, **3**, [1675]
    conditions, **3**, [1552], [1675]
    enlistment officer, meaning of, **3**, [1552]
    foreign nationals and residents, **3**, [1553]
  full-time service commitments, **3**, [1567]
  great emergency—
    call out for—
      maximum duration of service on,
        3, [1596]
      powers to authorise, **3**, [1595]
      suspension of payments due to, powers
        of, **3**, [1629]
    recall for service for—
      maximum duration of service on,
        3, [1612]
      powers to authorise, **3**, [1611]
      suspension of payments due to, powers
        of, **3**, [1629]
  interpretation provisions, **3**, [1669]
  land and air forces, service in, on enlistment,
    3, [1555]
  liability to be called out for permanent
    service—
    general, **3**, [1593]
    geographical extent of liability, **3**, [1594]
  maintain, power to, **3**, [1544]
  marines, service of in Royal Fleet Reserve,
    3, [1564]
  meaning, **3**, [1]
  membership, **3**, [1545]

reserve forces—*contd*
  minor and consequential amendments,
    3, [1687]
  national danger—
    call out for—
      maximum duration of service on,
        3, [1596]
      powers to authorise, **3**, [1595]
      suspension of payments due to, powers
        of, **3**, [1629]
    recall for service for—
      maximum duration of service on,
        3, [1612]
      powers to authorise, **3**, [1611]
      suspension of payments due to, powers
        of, **3**, [1629]
  numbers, control of, **3**, [1546], [1590]
  offences—
    absence without leave, punishment of,
      3, [1641]
    civil court—
      court-martial—
        evidence, **3**, [1651], [1677]
        time for institution of proceedings,
          3, [1650]
        triable by, **3**, [1649]
      evidence, **3**, [1651], [1677]
      jurisdiction of, **3**, [1647]
      meaning, **3**, [1652]
      time for institution of proceedings,
        3, [1650]
      triable by, **3**, [1649]
      trial by, **3**, [1646]
    deserters—
      punishment of, **3**, [1641]
      treatment of, **3**, [1643]
    duty or training, failure to attend for,
      3, [1640]
    false pretence of illegal absence, **3**, [1641],
      [1642]
    good order and discipline, against,
      3, [1638]
    inducing a person to desert or absent
      himself, **3**, [1644]
    service, failure to attend for, **3**, [1639]
    trial of, under service law, **3**, [1646]
  orders and regulations, **3**, [1547]
  organisation of, **3**, [1548]
  pay, **3**, [1550]
  pensions, **3**, [1549]
  permanent service, command and posting of
    men in, **3**, [1563]
  permanent staff, **3**, [1549]
  posting of men in permanent service,
    3, [1563]
  power to maintain, **3**, [1544]
  re-engagement for service, **3**, [1554]
  recall for service—
    acceptance into service, **3**, [1614]
    attack on UK—
      authorisation by Secretary of State,
        3, [1617]
      discharge from, **3**, [1615]
      exemptions from—
        effect of, **3**, [1623]

reserve forces—*contd*
  recall for service—*contd*
    attack on UK—*contd*
      exemptions from—*contd*
        individual, **3**, [1622]
        offences, **3**, [1625]
        supplementary provisions, **3**, [1624]
      maximum duration of service on, call
        out for, **3**, [1612]
      powers to authorise, where, **3**, [1611]
    great emergency, where—
      maximum duration of service on,
        3, [1612]
      powers to authorise, **3**, [1611]
      suspension of payments due to, powers
        of, **3**, [1629]
    information, power to require, **3**, [1618]
    interpretation provisions, **3**, [1620]
    liability—
      exempt persons from or relax, power
        to, **3**, [1616]
      general, **3**, [1608]
      geographical extent of, **3**, [1610]
      persons subject to, **3**, [1609]
    national danger, where—
      maximum duration of service on,
        3, [1612]
      powers to authorise, **3**, [1611]
      suspension of payments due to, powers
        of, **3**, [1629]
    notice, service of, **3**, [1613]
    payments for—
      employers, to, **3**, [1627]
      individuals, to, **3**, [1626]
      offences in connection with claims for,
        3, [1630]
      supplementary provisions, **3**, [1628]
      suspension of, powers of, **3**, [1629]
    pensions, not to affect, **3**, [1619]
    release from, **3**, [1615]
  repeals, **3**, [1688]
  Royal Air Force, postponement of transfer to
    reserve or discharge from, **3**, [1683]
  Royal Fleet Reserve. *See* **Royal Fleet**
    Reserve
  Royal Marines, postponement of transfer to
    reserve or discharge from, **3**, [1683]
  Royal Navy, postponement of transfer to
    reserve or discharge from, **3**, [1683]
  safeguard of employment for members,
    3, [1664]
  special agreements—
    acceptance into service, **3**, [1576]
    call out of persons entered into, **3**, [1575]
    employers' consent before entering,
      3, [1572]
    interpretation provisions, **3**, [1580]
    nature of, **3**, [1571]
    new employers' consent to continuation
      of, **3**, [1573]
    parliamentary control of numbers,
      3, [1579]
    release from service, **3**, [1577]
    report by Secretary of State relating to,
      3, [1579]

reserve forces—*contd*
special agreements—*contd*
termination of, **3**, [1574]
special members—
acceptance into service, **3**, [1587]
call out, **3**, [1586]
liabilities—
called out, to be, **3**, [1583]
cessation of, **3**, [1584]
discharge of, **3**, [1585]
train, to, **3**, [1583]
parliamentary control of numbers,
3, [1590]
release from service, **3**, [1588]
report by Secretary of State relating to,
3, [1590]
staff, permanent, **3**, [1549]
summary of provisions, **3**, [1]
tolls, exemptions from, **3**, [1666]
training obligations, **3**, [1565]
transfer between forces, **3**, [1556]
transitional class of members—
application of 1996 Act to, **3**, [1671],
[1686]
meaning, **3**, [1685]
transitory and transitional provisions, **3**, [1684]
voluntary training and other duties, **3**, [1570]
voting, absence for, **3**, [1667]
warlike operations, call out for—
maximum duration of service on, **3**, [1598]
powers to authorise, **3**, [1595]

reserve or auxiliary force
reinstatement in employment. *See*
reinstatement in civil employment

reserve tax. *See under* **stamp duty**

reservoirs
abandoned—
emergency powers, **49**, [594]
entry, power of, **49**, [595], [607]
notification of, **49**, [217]
report on, **49**, [592]
restoration of, **49**, [582]
re-use of—
inspection required, **49**, [585]
new reservoir, treated as, **49**, [582]
safety measures, report on, **49**, [585]
abandonment, **49**, [592]
alteration—
in course of, before 1975 Act, **49**, [604]
provisions as to, **49**, [582]
application of statutory provisions, **49**, [577]
authorities for purposes of, **49**, [577]
civil engineer—
appointment, notice requiring, **49**, [584],
[585]
certificate of—
final, **49**, [583]
general provisions, **49**, [598]
interim, **49**, [583]
particulars required in, **49**, [583]
preliminary, **49**, [583]
re-use, as to, **49**, [1], [585]

reservoirs—*contd*
civil engineer—*contd*
design and supervision, by, **49**, [582]
failure to appoint, **49**, [584]
independent, meaning, **49**, [586]
panels of—
application for place on, **49**, [580]
formation, **49**, [580]
removal from, **49**, [580]
construction or enlargement—
before commencement of 1930 Act,
49, [605]
before commencement of 1975 Act—
civil engineer not employed, where,
49, [606]
newly constructed or altered, **49**, [604]
notices etc concerning, **49**, [603]
provisions applied, **49**, [604]
transitional provisions, **49**, [602]
certification for use, **49**, [583]
civil engineer, requirements as to. *See* civil
engineer *above*
continuity with 1930 Act, **49**, [602]
design and supervision, **49**, [582]
inspection and report on, **49**, [583]
recreation facilities, provision during,
49, [568]
reports on—
appointed engineer, by, **49**, [584]
general provisions, **49**, [598]
covering, provision for, Thames Water
Authority, **49**, [85]
Crown, application of provisions to, **49**, [607]
damages, claims for, excluded, **49**, [577]
dangerous, inquiry into, **49**, [108]
definitions generally, index of, **49**, [611]
disputes, reference of recommendations to
referee, **49**, [597]
emergency powers, **49**, [594]
enforcement authority—
emergency powers, **49**, [594]
meaning, **49**, [578]
notices by—
appointment of engineer, as to,
49, [584]
failure as to safety measures, **49**, [592]
safety measures, as to, **49**, [586], [592]
reserve powers, **49**, [593]
entry on land—
compensation for damage or disturbance,
49, [596]
powers of, **49**, [595], [607]
escape of water from, liability for, **49**, [612]
expressions defined, index, **49**, [577], [611]
Lands Tribunal, reference of disputes to,
49, [596]
large raised—
abandoned. *See* abandoned *above*
alteration—
inspection and report, **49**, [583]
supervision of, **49**, [582]
capacity, **49**, [582]
construction etc. *See* construction *above*
depth of water, record of, **49**, [587]
discontinuance, **49**, [591]

reservoirs—*contd*

large raised—*contd*

flood plans, **49**, [589]–[590]

inspection—

default in making, **49**, [586]

periodical, **49**, [586]

report on, **49**, [586]

meaning, **49**, [577]

registration, **49**, [578]

safety measures—

abandonment, on, **49**, [592]

inspecting engineer, report, **49**, [586]

recommendations, failure to comply with, **49**, [593]

re-use of abandoned reservoir, **49**, [585]

supervising engineer—

appointment, **49**, [588]

duties, **49**, [588]

supervision generally, **49**, [588]

water levels—

record of, **49**, [587]

specification of, **49**, [583]

leakages, record of, **49**, [587]

local authorities—

areas, two or more, in, **49**, [578]

default by, inquiry into, **49**, [579]

enforcement of provisions by, **49**, [578]

notice to, as to existing reservoirs, **49**, [603]

registers, keeping etc, **49**, [578]

reports by, **49**, [579]

London, in, covering of, **49**, [85]

meaning, **49**, [577]

raised, meaning, **49**, [577]

regulations, power to make, **49**, [581]

repair of—

appeal against order, **49**, [114]

consequences of order, protection of undertakers, **49**, [115]

costs and expenses of order, **49**, [113]

failure, **49**, [110]

form of order, **49**, [111], [126]

order for, **49**, [109]

persons acting under order, protection, **49**, [112]

reports, general provisions, **49**, [598]

safety measures, notices as to, **49**, [586], [592]

saving as to, **35(1)**, [208]

Staines, transfer of, **49**, [204]

undertakers—

criminal liability, **49**, [600]

default of duties, **49**, [593]

information, duty to furnish, **49**, [599]

meaning, **49**, [577]

offences and penalties, **49**, [600]

vesting in local authority, **35(1)**, [141]

Wales, in, provision of recreational facilities, **49**, [1000], [1233]

water authority as undertakers for purposes of, **49**, [577]

resettlement places

grants for, **40(2)**, [78]

meaning, **40(2)**, [78]

residence. *See also* **domicile**

controlled foreign company, of, **44(1)**, [462], [463]

dispute as to, determination of, **44(2)**, [42]

appeal, **44(2)**, [43]

qualifying hospital patient, in relation to, **40(2)**, [452]

double taxation relief, requirements for, **44(1)**, [546]

employment income of individuals in UK for temporary purpose, **44(4)**, [840]

foreign income of individuals in UK for temporary purpose, **44(4)**, [839]

National Assistance Act provisions, for purposes of, **40(2)**, [599]

periods of, **43(S)**, 854

personal representatives, of, **42**, [987]; **44(4)**, [842]

staff of designated allied headquarters, **44(4)**, [841]

temporarily abroad, **44(4)**, [837]

trustees and companies, **44(4)**, [843]

trustees, of, **42**, [986]

visiting forces, **44(4)**, [841]

working abroad, **44(4)**, [838]

residential accommodation

displaced occupiers. *See* **displaced persons**

energy efficiency, **24**, [371]

final management orders. *See under* **local housing authority**

interim management orders. *See under* **local housing authority**

selective licensing areas—

designation of, **24**, [261]

confirmation of, **24**, [263]

duration of, **24**, [265]

general approval of, **24**, [263]

local housing authority's powers, **24**, [262]

notification requirements, **24**, [264]

proof of, **24**, [395]

review of, **24**, [265]

revocation of, **24**, [265]

residential care home

meaning, **35(2)**, [282]

residential conversions

reduced rate VAT, **50**, [149]

residential family centre

meaning, **35(2)**, [283]

notice restricting accommodation at, **6(S)**, 464

appeals, **6(S)**, 465

persons carrying on or managing, notification of matters relating to, **6(S)**, 466–7

residential property loan

land for residential use, specification of, **11(3)**, [136]; **11(4)**, [558]

meaning, **11(3)**, [135]; **11(4)**, [557]

tying-in arrangements—

conditions for, **11(3)**, [135]; **11(4)**, [557]

residential property loan—*contd*
  tying-in arrangements—*contd*
    controlled services—
      meaning, **11(3)**, [136]; **11(4)**, [558]
      provision of, **11(3)**, [135]; **11(4)**, [557]
      enforcement, **11(3)**, [138]; **11(4)**, [560]
      institution of proceedings, **11(3)**, [138]
      offences, **11(3)**, [137]; **11(4)**, [559]

residential property tribunals
  appeals from, **24**, [377], [440]
  jurisdiction of, **24**, [375]
  powers, **24**, [376]
  procedure of, **24**, [376], [440]

residuary bodies. *See* **Greater London;
  metropolitan counties**
  Wales, for. *See* **Wales**

resignation
  abolition of stamp duty on, **41**, [152], [157]

resolutions
  adjourned meeting, passed at, **8(1)**, [410]
  meetings, at. *See* **general meetings**
  ordinary, **8(1)**, [360]
  private company—
    passed by, **8(1)**, [359]
    written. *See* written *below*
  public company, passed by, **8(1)**, [359]
  records of—
    class of members, of, **8(1)**, [437]
    evidence, as, **8(1)**, [434]
    inspection of, **8(1)**, [436]
    preservation, time for, **8(1)**, [433]
    requirement to keep, **8(1)**, [433]
  special, **8(1)**, [361]
  special notice, requiring, **8(1)**, [390]
  voting on—
    articles, provisions in, **8(1)**, [365]
    general rules, **8(1)**, [362]
    joint holders of shares, by, **8(1)**, [364]
    specific requirements, **8(1)**, [363]
  written—
    agreement to—
      period for, **8(1)**, [375]
      procedure for signifying, **8(1)**, [374]
    articles, relationship of provisions with,
      8(1), [378]
    circulation of—
      application not to circulate statement,
        8(1), [373]
      date, **8(1)**, [368]
      directors, resolution proposed by,
        8(1), [369]
      expenses of, **8(1)**, [372]
      members, resolution proposed by,
        8(1), [371]
      power of members to require,
        8(1), [370]
      statement with, **8(1)**, [369]
    documents relating to, sending by
      electronic means, **8(1)**, [376]
    majority of not less than 75%, passed by,
      8(1), [361]

resolutions—*contd*
  written—*contd*
    meaning, **8(1)**, [366]
    members eligible to vote on, **8(1)**, [367]
    private companies, of, **8(1)**, [366]
    subject matter of, **8(1)**, [366]
    votes on, **8(1)**, [362]
    website, publication on, **8(1)**, [377]

restitution
  Financial Services Authority, powers of. *See*
    Financial Services Authority

restitution order
  annulment or variation, **12(1)**, [445]
  application, no need for, **12(2)**, [826]
  powers, exercise of, **12(2)**, [825]
  suspension, **12(1)**, [445]; **12(2)**, [826]
  theft offences, **12(2)**, [825]

restraint of trade
  employers' associations, purposes of, **16**, [322]
  trade union, purposes of, **16**, [184]

restricted contract
  assured tenancy, exclusion of, **21**, [540]
  board, payments for rent including, **21**, [540]
  Crown interest, where, **21**, [540]
  exceptions, **21**, [540]
  holiday letting, exclusion of, **21**, [540]
  housing association, etc, as landlord, **21**, [540]
  local authority interest, where, **21**, [540]
  meaning, **21**, [540]
  notice to quit—
    application of provisions, **21**, [603]
    owner-occupier, by, **21**, [606]
    period of, reduction by tribunal, **21**, [607]
    rent tribunal, after reference to, **21**, [604]
    security of tenure, application for,
      21, [605]
    order for possession, provisions on, **21**, [608]
  part of house, dwelling being, **21**, [540]
  phasing out, **22**, [829]
  premium for—
    excessive price for furniture treated as,
      21, [615], [616]
    prohibition of, **21**, [614]
    recovery of, **21**, [617]
  protected occupancy, exclusion of, **21**, [540]
  rateable value, limitation, **21**, [540]
  regulated tenancy, creating, exclusion of,
    21, [540]
  release from provisions, **21**, [630]
    rent, registration of, cancellation of,
      21, [584]
  rent, registration of—
    cancellation of, **21**, [584]
    effect of, **21**, [583]
    excess, recovery of, **21**, [583]
    reconsideration after, **21**, [581]
    register, maintenance of, **21**, [580]
  rent tribunal, reference to—
    information, notice requiring, **21**, [578]
    jurisdiction, **21**, [585]
    notice to quit after, **21**, [604]

restricted contract—*contd*
 rent tribunal, reference to—*contd*
  period of notice to quit, reducing,
   21, [607]
  powers of, **21**, [579]
  security of tenure, application for,
   21, [605]
 shared ownership lease, exclusion of,
  21, [540]
 tenant sharing accommodation with
  landlord, **21**, [542]
 unfurnished tenancies treated as, **21**, [541]
 variation of, **22**, [829]

restrictive covenant
 affecting land. *See under* **covenant; land
  registration**
 breach, compensation for, **9**, [103]
 discharge and modification, Lands Tribunal
  jurisdiction, **9**, [181]
 disposal of land, free from, **9**, [114]
 leasehold enfranchisement, conveyed on,
  21, [307]
 war damage, effect of, **21**, [102]

Restrictive Practices Court. *See also*
 restrictive trade agreement
 administration, **47**, [270]
 appeals from, **47**, [274]
 audience, right of, **47**, [272]
 constitution, **47**, [285]
 contempt of court, **47**, [273]
 decisions of—
  appeal from, **47**, [274]
  questions of fact, on, finality, **47**, [274]
 divisions, sitting in, **47**, [270]
 fees, determination of, **47**, [273]
 hearings, constitution of court for, **47**, [271]
 judges—
  additional, **47**, [268]
  nomination of, **47**, [266]
  number of, **47**, [285]
  temporary absence of, **47**, [266]
 judgment—
  delivery of, **47**, [271]
  majority, **47**, [271]
 members—
  appointment, **47**, [267]
  increase of number, **47**, [268]
  judges. *See* judges *above*
  non-judicial, **47**, [267]
  pay and pensions, **47**, [269]
 officers and servants, **47**, [270]
 official seal of, **47**, [285]
 pension scheme, **47**, [269]
 president of, **47**, [266]
 procedure of, **47**, [273]
 rules of procedure, **47**, [273]
 sittings, venues, **47**, [270]
 status of, **47**, [285]
 witnesses, examination etc, **47**, [273]

Restrictive Practices Court—*contd*
 See also decisions of *above*

restrictive trade agreement
 court proceedings. *See* **Restrictive Practices
  Court**
 Director's duties. *See* **Director General of
  Fair Trading**
 excepted agreements, provisions not applying
  to, **47**, [202]
 meaning, **47**, [195]
 registrar, abolition of office, **47**, [184], [202]
  See now **Director General of Fair
   Trading**
 registration, exceptions. *See* excepted
  agreements *above*

restructuring
 mining industry—
  generally. *See* **British Coal Corporation**
  licensing. *See* **coal mining operations**

retail prices index
 fundamental change in, **10(S)**, 22–3
 Statistics Board, compilation, maintenance and
  publication by, **10(S)**, 22–3

retirement annuity
 Ministers, of, **44(1)**, [432]

retirement benefit
 graduated—
  payment of, **40(1)**, [42]
  preliminary note, **40(1)**, [1]
  regulations, **40(1)**, [311]
  widows, for, **40(1)**, [43]

retirement benefits scheme
 administrator, **43(1)**, [71]
 amendment of provisions, **42**, [997]
 approved—
  accelerated accrual, **42**, [998]
  additional voluntary contributions,
   42, [999]
  associated employments, **42**, [998]
  augmentation, **42**, [998]
  centralised schemes, **42**, [998]
  cessation of, **42**, [1382]
  commutation of pension, **42**, [998]
  connected schemes, **42**, [998]
  election to join, **42**, [998]
  modification, **43(1)**, [391]
  regulations, **42**, [998]
  remuneration—
   calculation of, **42**, [998]
   relevant annual, meaning, **42**, [998]
 employer-financed—
  benefits under—
   employment income treated as—
    application of provisions, **44(2)**, [397]
    charge to tax, **44(2)**, [400]
    employee contributions, reduction
     for, **44(2)**, [401]
    relevant benefits, **44(2)**, [399]

retirement benefits scheme—*contd*
  employer-financed—*contd*
    benefits under—*contd*
      employment-related loans, treatment of
        interest on, **44(2)**, [403]
      termination of employment,
        contributions made on, **44(2)**, [414]
      valuation of, **44(2)**, [402]
    employee contributing to, **43(2)**, [465]
    employer payments, abolition of income tax
      charge, **43(2)**, [463]
    employer's contributions, restriction of
      deduction for, **43(2)**, [460]
    meaning, **43(2)**, [465]; **44(2)**, [398]
    no relief, cases where, **43(2)**, [462]
    non-contributory provision, restriction of
      deduction for, **43(2)**, [461]
    non-payment of benefit, cost of insuring
      against, **43(2)**, [464]
    non-pension benefits, taxation of,
      43(2), [465]
    relevant benefits, **43(2)**, [465]
    responsible person, **43(2)**, [465]
      meaning, **44(2)**, [404]
  non-approved, **42**, [962]
    taxation of benefits, **43(1)**, [72]

retirement pension
  additional—
    accrual rates, simplified, **40(2)**, [575]
    upper accrual point, **40(2)**, [562]
  age addition—
    entitlement to, **40(1)**, [326]
    rate of, **40(1)**, [467]
  basic, removal of link with lower earnings
    limit, **40(2)**, [561]
  Category A—
    additional pension—
      amount of, **40(1)**, [470], [474]
      contracted-out employment,
        40(1), [472], [476]
      interpretation, **40(1)**, [478]
      non-contracted-out employment,
        40(1), [475]
      pension sharing—
        entitlement, **40(1)**, [303]
        increase on deferment, **40(1)**, [305],
          [479], [480]
        reduction on, **40(1)**, [290], [304]
      preservation of rights, **40(2)**, [248]
      surplus earnings factor, **40(1)**, [471]
      weekly rate of, **40(1)**, [289]
    adult dependency increases, abolition,
      40(2), [558], [573]
    calculation, modification of, **40(1)**, [291]
    components of, **40(1)**, [285]
    contribution conditions, **40(1)**, [463]
      failure to satisfy—
        entitlement on, **40(1)**, [307]
        increase of benefit, exclusion of,
          40(1), [308]
    contributions credits, **40(1)**, [263]
    earnings factor, **40(1)**, [285]
    elections as to, **40(1)**, [301]
    entitlement to, **40(1)**, [285]

retirement pension—*contd*
  Category A—*contd*
    former civil partner's contributions, use of,
      40(1), [293]
    former spouse's contributions, use of,
      40(1), [293]
    husband, increase for, **40(1)**, [329]
    invalidity, increase for, **40(1)**, [292]
    married person, for, **40(1)**, [299]
    person with care of children, increase for,
      40(1), [330]
    rate of, **40(1)**, [285]
    regulations, **40(1)**, [301]
    up-rating of, **40(1)**, [674], [679], [680]
    wife, increase for, **40(1)**, [328]
  Category B—
    civil partner, for, **40(1)**, [294]
    contribution conditions, **40(1)**, [463]
      failure to satisfy—
        entitlement on, **40(1)**, [307]
        increase of benefit, exclusion of,
          40(1), [308]
    contributions credits, **40(1)**, [263]
    elections as to, **40(1)**, [301]
    entitlement—
      bereavement allowance, by reference to,
        40(1), [296]
      commencement of, **40(1)**, [297]
      widowed parent's allowance, by reference
        to, **40(1)**, [296]
    married person, for, **40(1)**, [294], [299]
    rate of, **40(1)**, [465]
    regulations, **40(1)**, [301]
    restriction on entitlement, removal of,
      40(2), [557], [572]
    spouse, increase for, **40(2)**, [98]
    up-rating of, **40(1)**, [674], [679], [680]
    widowers, for, **40(1)**, [295], [298]
    widows, for, **40(1)**, [295]
  Category C—
    abolition of adult dependency increases,
      40(2), [558], [573]
    entitlement to, **40(1)**, [325]
    person with care of children, increase for,
      40(1), [330]
    rate of, **40(1)**, [467]
    wife, increase for, **40(1)**, [328]
  Category D—
    entitlement to, **40(1)**, [325]
    rate of, **40(1)**, [325], [467]
  Christmas bonus, for purposes of,
    40(1), [402]
  contribution conditions, **40(1)**, [260]
  contributions paid in error, **40(1)**, [310]
  contributory, being, **40(1)**, [259]
  deferred entitlement, increase in case of,
    40(1), [302], [474]
  earnings factor—
    credits, **40(1)**, [288]
    deemed, **40(1)**, [286], [287]
  home responsibilities protection, **40(2)**, [98]
  increments, **40(2)**, [98]
  lump sum, increase in case of deferred
    entitlement, **40(1)**, [302], [479], [480]

retirement pension—*contd*
more than one employment, earner in, **40(2)**, [91]
more than one, person entitled to, **40(1)**, [284]
Northern Ireland, provision for, **40(2)**, [94]
operation of provisions, review of, **40(2)**, [564]
pensionable age—
  equalisation of, **40(2)**, [89], [97]
  increase in, **40(2)**, [563], [576]
prices, preservation of link with, **40(2)**, [560]
surpluses, calculation of, **40(2)**, [90]
surviving spouses, for, **40(1)**, [300]
up-rating by reference to earnings, **40(2)**, [559]
up-rating order, power to anticipate, **40(1)**, [679]

retirement planning
combined pension forecasts, provision of, **33(1)**, [835]
employees, information and advice to, **33(1)**, [836]
facilitating, **33(1)**, [832]
information—
  supply of, **33(1)**, [833], [923]
  use of, **33(1)**, [923]
promotion of, **33(1)**, [832]
summary of provisions, **33(1)**, [25]

revenue trader. *See* **customs and excise**

reversion
acquisition at under value, voidable, **20**, [777]
assured tenancy, **22**, [813]
base fee, enlargement by union with, **20**, [93]
compensation arising from, application of, **9**, [37]
competing interests, priority of, **20**, [747]
continuation of business tenancy, on, **21**, [226]
covenants to run with—
  lessee's, rent and benefit of, **20**, [751]
  lessor, obligation of, **20**, [752]
extinguishment, effect, **20**, [749]
merger with satisfied term, **20**, [629]
pre-emption right, **20**, [630]
protected long tenancy, under, **21**, [226]
title to, period, **20**, [662]

reversionary interest
acquisition under Defence Acts, **9**, [148]

reverter
sites, of. *See* **land**

revocation
use or trust of property, of, abolition of stamp duty on, **41**, [152], [157]

reward
apprehension of offenders, for, **12(1)**, [34]
stolen goods, for, advertising, **12(1)**, [574]

Rhodesia and Nyasaland
Federation, dissolution of, **7(2)**, [526]

Richmond
river works etc. *See under* **Thames**

Richmond Green
management of, **10**, [170]

riding establishment
inspection, **2**, [316]
interpretation of provisions, **2**, [320]
licensing—
  appeals respecting, **2**, [315]
  conditions for, **2**, [315]
  disqualification, **2**, [318]
  provisional, **2**, [343]
  requirement for, **2**, [315]
offences, **2**, [317]
  penalties, **2**, [318]
  prosecution of, **2**, [318]
veterinary practitioner's report, **2**, [315]

rifle club
air weapon, use in, **12(1)**, [498]
approval, **12(1)**, [1127]
approved, **12(2)**, [523]
firearms certificate, exemption, **12(1)**, [485], [1127]

right of way. *See also* **public path**
alleged, proceedings on, **36**, [1181]
body corporate, offences by, **37**, [99]; **38(2)**, [389]
bridleways, orders creating, extinguishing or diverting, **37**, [95], [108]
bulls, prohibition on keeping on, **37**, [93]
clearance area, in, extinguishment, **22**, [253]
Crown land, application of provisions to, **37**, [97]
cycle, use of, **37**, [344]
definitive map and statement—
  appeal against decision as to, **37**, [106]
  byway open to all traffic not to be shown on, **37**, [87]
  consolidation, **37**, [91]
  continuous review of, **37**, [84]
  copy, preparation of, **37**, [90]
  effect of, **37**, [89]
  inspection of, **37**, [90]
  local inquiries, **37**, [107]
  London, application to, **37**, [92]
  meaning, **37**, [84]
  modifications to, **37**, [84]
  orders—
    application for, **37**, [84], [106]
    confirmation, restriction on, **37**, [107]
    consultation before making, **37**, [107]
    effect, taking, **37**, [107]
    final decision, notice of, **37**, [107]
    form of, **37**, [90]
    inspectors, appointment of, **37**, [107]
    modifications, for, **37**, [84]–[86], [107]
    notice of application for, **37**, [106]
    opposed, **37**, [107]

right of way—*contd*
  definitive map and statement—*contd*
    orders—*contd*
      procedure for, **37**, [107]
      publicity for, **37**, [107]
      regulations on, **37**, [107]
      relevant date for purposes of, **37**, [89]
      representations and objections, **37**, [107]
      severance of, **37**, [107]
      unopposed, **37**, [107]
      validity, questioning, **37**, [107]
    supplementary provisions, **37**, [90]
  disturbance by ploughing, **36**, [1190], [1419]
  diversion, Thames flood barrier, **49**, [549]
  evidence of, **37**, [89]
  extinction, Thames flood barrier, **49**, [504]
  extinguishment, **9**, [444], [454]
    acquisition, **9**, [444]
    certificates, **9**, [452]–[453]
    commons and open spaces, **9**, [453]
  extinguishment in interests of civil aviation,
    4(1), [97]
  financial provisions, **37**, [100]
  footpaths, orders affecting, **37**, [95], [108]
  functions, reports on, **38(2)**, [69]
  gas underground storage, **17(1)**, [306]
  highway ceasing to be such, **37**, [84]
  Homes and Communities Agency land, power
    to extinguish on, **24**, [856]
  horseback, on, **37**, [89]
  housing action trust, extinguishment by,
    22, [930]
  improvement plans—
    consultation on, **38(2)**, [67]
    draft, publication of, **38(2)**, [67]
    Inner London, in, **38(2)**, [68]
    local rights of way, meaning, **38(2)**, [66]
    meaning, **38(2)**, [66]
    preparation of, **38(2)**, [66]
  Isles of Scilly, provisions relating to, **36**, [644];
    37, [98]
  long-distance route—
    accommodation, provision of, **36**, [636]
    approval of proposals, **36**, [634]
    Crown land, over, **36**, [641]
    estimate of cost, **36**, [633]
    ferry, provision of, **36**, [635]
    Isles of Scilly, application to, **36**, [644]
    local authorities, contributions by,
      36, [639]
    local inquiries, **36**, [642]
    meals and refreshments, provision of,
      36, [636]
    regulations and orders, **36**, [643]
    report by Countryside Agency on,
      36, [633], [637]
    service of notices, **36**, [642]
    traffic, restriction of, **36**, [633]
    variation of proposals, **36**, [637]
    Wales, application of provisions, **36**, [632]
  notice deterring public use, penalty for,
    36, [638]
  notices, service of, **36**, [642]; **37**, [101]
  obstruction by fencing, **36**, [1083]

right of way—*contd*
  opencast coal working. *See* **opencast coal**
  orders affecting footpaths, **37**, [95], [108]
  pedal cycle, on, **36**, [774]; **37**, [344]
  ploughing up of footpaths and bridleways,
    effect of, **36**, [1190], [1191]
  prescription period for claiming—
    forty years—
      absolute right after, **20**, [62]
      time excluded in computing, **20**, [68]
    infant or other person under disability, in
      case of, **20**, [67]
    interruption to, **20**, [61], [64]
    nature of right, **20**, [61]
    pleadings, **20**, [65]
    presumption, restricting, **20**, [66]
    twenty years' enjoyment, **20**, [62]
  private, extinguishment for waterworks
    purposes, **49**, [353]
  proceedings by a council, **36**, [1181]
  public, new, restriction on creation of,
    38(2), [493]
  public path creation order, created by,
    36, [1030]
  public path diversion order, created by,
    36, [1152]
  rail crossing diversion order, created by,
    36, [1154]
  reversioner, protection of rights of, **36**, [1039]
  special diversion order, created by, **36**, [1155]
  SSSI diversion order, created by, **36**, [1157]
  survey or review, ceasing, **37**, [88], [107]
  surveying authority, meaning, **37**, [96]
  unrecorded, extinguishment of, **38(2)**, [59],
    [494]
    date, **38(2)**, [62]
  wardens, appointment of, **37**, [94]

right to buy. *See* **dwelling-house**

right to manage. *See* **collective
  enfranchisement (leasehold reform)**

rights over land
  acquisition, **9**, [440], [452]
  commons and open spaces, **9**, [453]
  compulsory acquisition—
    gas, underground storage for, **9**, [442]
    new rights—
      acquisition of, **9**, [452]
      creation of, **9**, [440]
    Opencast Coal Act, application of
      provisions, **9**, [441]
    special kinds of land, **9**, [453]
  compulsory rights orders, **9**, [441]
  fuel or field garden allotments, **9**, [453]
  land, **9**, [452]–[453]
  local authority, by, **9**, [371]
  National Trust land, **9**, [453]
  special parliamentary procedure, orders subject
    to, **9**, [453]
  statutory undertakers' land, **9**, [453]

riot
  common law offence abolished, **12(1)**, [1000]

riot—*contd*
  compensation for damage—
    amount, fixing, **33(2)**, [42]
    authority responsible for, action against,
      33(2), [44]
    churches and chapels, **33(2)**, [47]
    claims for, **33(2)**, [44]
    insurance payment, reduction for,
      33(2), [42]
    machinery, to, **33(2)**, [46]
    mode of awarding, **33(2)**, [43]
    nature of riot for purposes of, **33(2)**, [42]
    payment of, **33(2)**, [45]
    person aggrieved, action by, **33(2)**, [44]
    police fund, payable from, **33(2)**, [42], [45]
    public buildings, **33(2)**, [47]
    regulations, **33(2)**, [43]
  elements of, **33(2)**, [42]
  intention element, **12(1)**, [997]
  justice of the peace, jurisdiction of,
    11(2), [1A]
  meaning, **12(1)**, [991]
  nature of, **12(1)**, [991]
  penalty for, **12(1)**, [991]
  prosecution of offenders, **12(1)**, [998]

riotous behaviour
  street offences, **36**, [228], [386]

riparian authority
  meaning, **35(1)**, [443]
  port health authority, as, **35(1)**, [443]
  transferred officers of, compensation and
    superannuation rights of, **35(1)**, [203]

river
  drainage works affecting, **20**, [300], [319],
    [326], [351]
  flood defence. *See* **flood**
  Lee, flood works on, **49**, [173]
  main—
    maps of—
      amendment of, **49**, [1244]
      evidence, as, **49**, [1243]
      keeping, **49**, [1243]
      meaning, **49**, [1243]
    meaning, **49**, [1267]
  pollution. *See* **river pollution**
  protection for, **35(1)**, [208]
  Thames. *See* **Thames river**

river authority
  discharge of water by or by agreement with,
    49, [468]
  engineering or building operations,
    compulsory powers for, **49**, [457]
  expenses, payment of, **1(1)**, [624]
  land control, exemption from, **1(1)**, [652]
  London—
    excavations near highway, by, **25(1)**, [813]
    meaning, **25(1)**, [813]
    sludge mains affecting, **25(1)**, [932]
  officers and servants, compensation, **49**, [459]
  staff superannuation, **33(1)**, [136]

river pollution. *See also* **pollution**
  byelaws, power to make, **49**, [430]
  control—
    generally. *See* **pollution**
    note, **49**, [1]
  effluent, sampling of, **49**, [447]
  information, disclosure of, restriction,
    49, [448]
  prevention generally. *See* **pollution**
  samples of effluent, **49**, [447]

River Thames. *See* **Thames**

road. *See also* **highway; street**
  bridge. *See* **bridge**
  boundary, **37**, [299]
  charging schemes—
    appeals, **38(2)**, [184]
    authority making, **38(2)**, [148]
      powers of, **38(2)**, [181]
    charges—
      different, for different cases, **38(2)**, [158]
      payment of, **38(2)**, [148]
      penalty, **38(2)**, [161]
      use of motor vehicle on road, as to,
        38(2), [158]
    confirmation, **38(2)**, [156]
    consultation and inquiries, **38(2)**, [157]
    Crown roads, application to, **38(2)**, [185]
    definitions, **38(2)**, [187]
    disputes, determination of, **38(2)**, [184]
    enforcement, **38(2)**, [161]
    entry, seizure and search, powers of,
      38(2), [162]
    equipment, installation and maintenance
      of, **38(2)**, [164]
    examination of vehicles, **38(2)**, [162]
    exemptions, **38(2)**, [159]
    financial provisions, **38(2)**, [213]
    guidance, issue of, **38(2)**, [182]
    immobilisation devices, use of, **38(2)**, [163]
    information—
      disclosure of, **38(2)**, [183]
      requirements, **38(2)**, [166]
    Integrated Transport Authority, duty to
      provide information as to, **38(2)**, [166]
    local, **38(2)**, [149]
      joint, **38(2)**, [150]
      ITA, **38(2)**, [150]
      ITA-London, **38(2)**, [153]
      local-London, **38(2)**, [152]
    making of, **38(2)**, [155]
    matters to be dealt with, **38(2)**, [158]
    meaning, **38(2)**, [148]
    regulations and orders, **38(2)**, [186]
    supplementary provisions as to contents,
      38(2), [159]
    suspension of, **38(2)**, [160]
    traffic signs, **38(2)**, [165]
    trunk road, **38(2)**, [154]
  classified—
    classification of, **36**, [1015]
    meaning, **36**, [210]
    property and liabilities, transfer of,
      36, [1316]

road—*contd*
  classified—*contd*
    references to, **36**, [1016]
    road being, **36**, [1015]
    road crossing or joining, **36**, [1017]
  concession agreements. *See* **special road**
    (new roads)
  GLA—
    certification, **36**, [1020]
    designation, **36**, [1018]
    highway authority for, **36**, [1005], [1019]
    highway becoming or ceasing to be—
      employees, transfer of, **36**, [1314]
      property and liabilities, transfer of,
        36, [1313]
    orders changing, **36**, [1019]
    provisions relating to, construction of,
      36, [1021]
    records of, **36**, [1020]
  GLA side roads—
    certification and records, **37**, [298]
    designation of, **37**, [296]
    nature of, **37**, [296]
    orders changing, **37**, [297]
  home zones, designation of, **38(2)**, [201]
  industrial estate, on, **43(1)**, [863]
  interference during construction of railway.
    See **railway**
  level crossing. *See* **level crossing**
  lighting—
    consents and access for, **25(1)**, [519]
    expenses, **25(1)**, [520]
    parish council powers, **25(1)**, [518]
  meaning, **6**, [458]; **25(1)**, [518], [521];
    36, [210], [905]; **37**, [64], [315], [808]
  new roads. *See* **special road** (new roads)
  principal—
    designation, changing, **36**, [1016]
    road being, **36**, [1015]
  prospective exercise of powers, **37**, [294]
  provision in housing development, **22**, [15]
  public path, used as, restricted byway, now
    shown as, **38(2)**, [817]
  quiet lanes, designation of, **38(2)**, [201]
  regulation order, preservation of amenities,
    37, [165]
  seats and shelters in—
    consents and access, **25(1)**, [519]
    expenses relating to, **25(1)**, [520]
    power to provide, **25(1)**, [516]
  special. *See* **special road**
  tramway on. *See* **tramway**
  trunk. *See* **trunk road**
  urban, district council maintaining,
    36, [1046], [1409]
  width, exercise of powers in relation to,
    37, [300]
  works for road purposes, **36**, [1065]

road accident
  casualties, payments for hospital or emergency
    treatment, **37**, [772]–[774]
    See also **National Health Service**
  driver of vehicle, duty in case of, **37**, [788]
  Greater London, inquiries in, **37**, [798]

road accident—*contd*
  inquiry into, powers, **37**, [797]

road checks
  conduct of, **12(1)**, [838]
  records of, **12(1)**, [839]

road fuel gas. *See* **hydrocarbon oil**

road fund
  winding up, **36**, [664]

road haulage
  nationalisation, **36**, [210]

road humps
  construction of, **36**, [1065], [1094], [1098]
  consultation on, **36**, [1096]
  local inquiry on, **36**, [1096]
  London, in, **36**, [1097]
  maintenance, **36**, [1065], [1098]
  meaning, **36**, [1100]
  part of highway, as, **36**, [1099]
  regulations, **36**, [1098]
  removal of, **36**, [1065], [1094]
  Secretary of State, powers of, **36**, [1095]
  speed limit, where road subject to, **36**, [1094]
  status of, **36**, [1099]

road passenger transport. *See* **passenger
  transport service**

road roller
  vehicle excise duty, **13**, [1044]

road safety
  grants from national transport authority,
    37, [611]
  information and training, provision of,
    37, [610]
  safety camera enforcement, application of
    surplus income from, **38(2)**, [500]
  summary of provisions, **36**, [210]

road traffic. *See also* **motor vehicle**
  airports, at—
    control of, **4(1)**, [304]
    enactments applied, **4(1)**, [304]
    regulation of, **4(1)**, [226], [302]
    transitional provisions, **4(1)**, [326]
  bridges, on, de-control of, **25(2)**, [449]
  councils responsible for, **25(2)**, [583]
  London—
    authorised officer—
      meaning, **26(2)**, [347]
      obstruction of, **26(2)**, [348]
      provision of information to, **26(2)**, [349]
    contraventions, penalty charges for—
      charge certificate, **26(2)**, [353]
      claim by owner after removal,
        26(2), [861]
      enforcement, **26(2)**, [868]
      financial provisions, **26(2)**, [354]
      immobilisation and removal of vehicles,
        26(2), [857]

road traffic—*contd*
  London—*contd*
    contraventions, penalty charges for—*contd*
      interpretation, **26(2)**, [854]
      limitation on, **26(2)**, [334]
      notices, **26(2)**, [332], [353]
      ownership details not known,
        preliminary procedure, **26(2)**, [855]
      payment of bond to secure removal,
        26(2), [860]
      preliminary procedure, **26(2)**, [855],
        [856]
      provisions applying, **26(2)**, [332]
      release or recovery of vehicle, issue of
        penalty charge notice on, **26(2)**, [862]
      removed vehicles and contents, disposal
        of, **26(2)**, [858]
      representation and appeals, **26(2)**, [868],
        [353]
      scheduled traffic signs, **26(2)**, [355]
      taking possession of vehicle, **26(2)**, [859]
    disapplication of offences, **26(2)**, [335]
    financial provisions, **25(1)**, [824]–[831];
      26(2), [864]
    fixed penalties—
      financial provisions, **26(2)**, [354]
      levels of, **26(2)**, [338]
      notices, **26(2)**, [337]
      offences, **26(2)**, [336], [356]
      Secretary of State, reserve powers of,
        26(2), [339]
    guidance, **26(2)**, [865]
    level of charges, **26(2)**, [864]
    London Traffic Control System, transfer
      of, **26(1)**, [648]
    lorry ban order, contraventions of,
      26(2), [333]
    offences—
      directors, liability of, **26(2)**, [351]
      due diligence defence, **26(2)**, [350]
      information, duty to give, **25(2)**, [267]
    regulations, **26(2)**, [352]
    repeal of enactments, **26(1)**, [649]
    street trading interfering with, **25(1)**, [390]
  management. *See* **traffic management**
  offences. *See* **road traffic offences**
  officers. *See* **traffic officers**
  regulation, provisions as to concession
    agreements, **38(1)**, [161]
  transfer of functions, **25(2)**, [583]

Road Traffic Acts
  Crown, application to. *See under* **Crown**
  meaning, **38(1)**, [119], [127]
  old and new law, construction of references,
    38(1), [128]

road traffic calming. *See also* **road humps;
speed limit**
  regulations, **36**, [1103]
  works—
    authorisation of, **36**, [1101]
    construction, **36**, [1101]–[1104]
    contribution towards expenses by parish or
      community councils, **36**, [1322]

road traffic calming—*contd*
  works—*contd*
    London, in, **36**, [1102]
    part of highway, as, **36**, [1104]
    prescribing of, **36**, [1103]
    removal, **36**, [1101]
    status of, **36**, [1104]

road traffic offences. *See also* **street offences**
  accidents, failure to report etc, **37**, [788]
  aggravated vehicle-taking, **12(1)**, [565]
  alcohol concentration—
    above prescribed limit, **37**, [564], [566]
    arrest without warrant, **37**, [571]
    assumption as to proportion, **38(1)**, [14]
    attempting to drive, **37**, [566]
    being in charge of a vehicle, **37**, [566]
    blood and urine tests, provision of
      specimens, **37**, [573]
    detention of persons affected, **37**, [577]
    power of entry, **37**, [572]
    preliminary tests, power to administer,
      37, [567]
      breath test, **37**, [568]
      drug test, **37**, [570]
      impairment test, **37**, [569]
    prescribed limit, **37**, [578]
    provision of specimens, **37**, [573]
    testing, protection of hospital patients,
      37, [576]
    See also blood test; breath test; drink *below*
  armed forces, application of provisions,
    37, [800]
  arrest without warrant, **37**, [571]
  birth date and sex, information as to—
    after conviction, **38(1)**, [21]
    guilty plea, inclusion, **38(1)**, [8]
  blood test—
    assumption as to proportion, **38(1)**, [14]
    specimens—
      documentary evidence, **38(1)**, [15]
      person incapable of consenting, from,
        37, [574]
      provision of, **37**, [573]
      use in proceedings, **38(1)**, [14]
  body corporate, by, **38(2)**, [203]
  breath test—
    assumption as to proportion, **38(1)**, [14]
    detention of person in police station,
      37, [577]
    meaning, **37**, [578]
    preliminary, **37**, [568]
    protection of hospital patients, **37**, [576]
    specimen—
      analysis, **37**, [573]
      choice of, **37**, [575]
      documentary evidence, **38(1)**, [15]
      failure to provide, **37**, [573]
      provision of, **37**, [573], [575]
      use in proceedings, **38(1)**, [14]
  bridleway—
    driving on, **37**, [301], [605]
    motor vehicle trials on, **37**, [604]
  bus lane contraventions, **38(2)**, [133]
  cabman, defrauding, **36**, [570]

road traffic offences—*contd*
careless driving, **37**, [561], [786]
  death, caused by, **37**, [560]; **38(2)**, [509]
  meaning, **37**, [562]
civil enforcement—
  areas, **38(2)**, [352], [381], [382]
  bus lane contraventions, **38(2)**, [378]
  contraventions subject to, **38(2)**, [351]
  Crown, application of provisions to,
    38(2), [368]
  definitions, **38(2)**, [370], [371]
  financial provisions, **38(2)**, [366]
  London lorry ban contraventions,
    38(2), [379]
  moving traffic contraventions, **38(2)**, [380]
  officers, **38(2)**, [354]
  parking contraventions, **38(2)**, [377]
  penalties, **38(2)**, [350]
  penalty charges—
    adjudicators, **38(2)**, [359]
    certificated bailiffs, **38(2)**, [361]
    enforcement, **38(2)**, [360]
    guidance, **38(2)**, [365]
    immobilisation of vehicle where
      payable, **38(2)**, [357]
    level, setting, **38(2)**, [355], [383]–[385]
    notification, **38(2)**, [356]
    representations and appeals, **38(2)**, [358]
  powers, power to require authority to apply
    for, **38(2)**, [353]
  regulations and orders, **38(2)**, [367]
  special enforcement areas. *See* **parking**
  visiting forces, application of provisions to,
    38(2), [368]
companies, offences by, **37**, [58], [748]
construction and use of vehicles, as to,
  38(1), [16]
Convention, notice under, **38(2)**, [283]
conviction, requirements before, **38(1)**, [1]
counterpart of licence, production of,
  38(1), [7], [23]
Crown, provisions applicable to persons and
  vehicles, **38(1)**, [115]
cycle—
  carriage of persons on, **37**, [595]
  equipment on, as to, **37**, [666]
  pedal, electrically assisted, under age using
    of, **37**, [603]
  racing on public ways, **37**, [602]
  tracks, driving or parking on, **37**, [591]
cycling, careless and inconsiderate, **37**, [600],
  [786]
cyclist—
  identification of, **37**, [286]
  under influence of drink or drugs,
    37, [601]
danger to road-users, causing, **37**, [593]
dangerous driving—
  aggravated vehicle taking, arising from,
    12(1), [565]
  causing death by, **37**, [557]; **38(1)**, [33]
  cyclist, by, **37**, [599]
  meaning, **37**, [559]
  offence of, **37**, [558]

road traffic offences—*contd*
dangerous position, leaving vehicle in,
  37, [592]
death caused by dangerous driving, **37**, [557]
defective eyesight, driving with, **37**, [683]
defences available, **36**, [975]; **37**, [52]
detection, equipment for, **36**, [1110]
devices, power to make orders as to,
  38(1), [18]
disability—
  non-disclosure, **37**, [679]
  notification of, in proceedings, **38(1)**, [19]
disabled person's badge, wrongful use of,
  37, [289]
disqualification—
  aiding, abetting etc offence, application,
    38(1), [41]
  alcohol ignition interlock programme—
    approval of, **38(1)**, [39]
    failing fully to participate, certificates
      of, **38(1)**, [38]
    guidance to programme providers,
      38(1), [40]
    orders for, **38(1)**, [37]
  appeal against, **38(1)**, [44]
  attendance on course, reduction for,
    38(2), [513]
  certain offences, **38(1)**, [33]
  Community licence holder, **38(1)**, [111]
  counterpart of licence, production of,
    38(1), [7]
  course, attendance on—
    certificate of completion, **38(1)**, [35]
    guidance for course organisers,
      38(1), [36]
    reduction of period after, **38(1)**, [34]
    suspension pending determination,
      38(1), [47]
  determination of end of, rule for,
    38(1), [50]
  discharge order, combined with,
    38(1), [55]
  discretionary, when, **38(1)**, [7], [33], [117],
    [122], [123]
  driving test, until passing, **38(2)**, [514]
  effect of order, **38(1)**, [43], [55]
  exemption, construction and use offences,
    38(1), [57]
  foreign, recognition of, **38(2)**, [270]
  interim, on committal for sentence,
    38(1), [22]
  licence, production of, **38(1)**, [7], [23]
  non-UK resident—
    application of provisions, **38(2)**, [267]
    definitions, **38(2)**, [287]
    driving disqualification condition,
      38(2), [267]
    duty to give notice to foreign
      authority, **38(2)**, [268]
    notices, **38(2)**, [284]
    order for minimum period necessary,
      38(2), [294]
    order for minimum period unnecessary,
      38(2), [293]
    regulations, **38(2)**, [285], [286]

road traffic offences—*contd*
disqualification—*contd*
Northern Ireland, etc, in, **37**, [699]
obligatory, when—
meaning of offence involving,
38(1), [117]
schedule, **38(1)**, [122], [123]
obtaining licence whilst disqualified,
37, [700]
offences outside UK, in respect of—
appeals, **38(2)**, [272]
application of provisions, **38(2)**, [269]
Crown vehicles, **38(2)**, [288]
definitions, **38(2)**, [287]
driving disqualification condition,
38(2), [269]
effect of, **38(2)**, [279]
end of period of, **38(2)**, [280]
England and Wales, suspension in,
38(2), [273]
Northern Ireland, suspension in,
38(2), [275]
notice, **38(2)**, [271], [284]
production of licence,
38(2), [276]–[278]
recognition of foreign disqualification,
38(2), [270]
regulations, **38(2)**, [285], [286]
Scotland, suspension in, **38(2)**, [274]
period, **38(1)**, [33], [56]
reduction, **38(1)**, [34]
alcohol ignition interlock programme
orders, **38(1)**, [37]
repeated offences, on, **38(1)**, [41]
previous, effect of, **38(1)**, [41]
probation order, combined with,
38(1), [55]
provision of licence, **38(1)**, [7]
removal of, **38(1)**, [49]
repeated offences, **38(1)**, [41]
supplementary provisions, **38(1)**, [56]
suspension—
appellate courts, powers, **38(1)**, [46]
pending appeal, **38(1)**, [45], [47]
pending completion of course,
38(1), [47]
test of competence, **38(1)**, [42]
disqualified drivers causing death by driving,
37, [563]; **38(2)**, [510]
documents—
false, issue of, **37**, [50], [139], [793]
forgery and misuse of, **37**, [48], [138],
[791]
inspection, arising from, **36**, [823]
dogs—
control of, on roads, **37**, [598]
ferocious and unmuzzled, **36**, [226]
drink or drugs, under influence of—
alcohol ignition interlock programme
orders, experimental period, **38(2)**, [505]
arrest without warrant, **37**, [571]
attempting to drive, **37**, [565]
being in charge of a vehicle, **37**, [565]
cyclist, **37**, [601]
detention of persons, **37**, [577]

road traffic offences—*contd*
drink or drugs, under influence of—*contd*
driving etc, **37**, [564], [565]
high risk offenders, medical enquiries,
38(2), [503]
in charge of vehicle, **37**, [565]
Licensing Act offence, exemption,
38(1), [5]
meaning of drug, **37**, [578]
power of entry, **37**, [572]
preliminary tests, power to administer,
37, [567]
breath test, **37**, [568]
drug test, **37**, [570]
impairment test, **37**, [569]
prescribed limits, meaning, **37**, [578]
sentence, **38(1)**, [33]
specimen—
documentary evidence, **38(1)**, [15]
use in proceedings, **38(1)**, [14]
tramcars and guided vehicles, **37**, [809]
See also alcohol *above*
driver—
disabilities, failure as to notification of,
37, [678], [679]
evidence as to, **38(1)**, [10]
identification of, **36**, [674]; **37**, [54], [56],
[286]; **38(1)**, [11]
information to be given of, **36**, [672];
37, [54], [286]
meaning, **38(1)**, [100]
offences applicable, **38(1)**, [121]
physical fitness requirement, involving,
37, [678], [679]
under age, **37**, [714]
unlicensed, **37**, [672]
driver information system, as to, **38(1)**, [144],
[146], [154]
driving elsewhere than on roads, **37**, [605]
driving instructors and instruction. *See under*
driving instruction
driving licence—
driving without, **37**, [672]
failure to produce, **37**, [781]
driving record, endorsement, all drivers,
38(2), [501], [533]
driving while disqualified, **37**, [700]
drugs. *See* drink or drugs *above*
endorsement—
consequences of, escaping by deception,
38(1), [58]
counterpart of licence—
Community licence, **38(1)**, [112]
court order, **38(1)**, [51]
effect of, **38(1)**, [53]
exemption, construction and use
offences, **38(1)**, [57]
existing endorsement, taking into
consideration, **38(1)**, [31]
fixed penalty, payment of conditional
offer, **38(1)**, [86]
penalty points, **38(1)**, [65]
supplementary provisions, **38(1)**, [56]
without court order, **38(1)**, [65]

road traffic offences—*contd*
  endorsement—*contd*
    driving record—
      court order, **38(1)**, [51]
      effect of, **38(1)**, [54]
      exemption, construction and use
        offences, **38(1)**, [57]
      existing endorsement, taking into
        consideration, **38(1)**, [31]
      fixed penalty, payment of conditional
        offer, **38(1)**, [87]
      meaning, **38(1)**, [118]
      penalty points, **38(1)**, [66]
      supplementary provisions, **38(1)**, [56]
      without court order, **38(1)**, [66]
    licence, supplementary provisions,
      38(1), [56]
    Northern Ireland, licence holders,
      38(1), [110]
    obligatory—
      meaning of offence involving,
        38(1), [116]
      schedule of, **38(1)**, [122], [123]
    probation order, combined with,
      38(1), [55]
  endorsement of licence—
    all drivers, **38(2)**, [501]
    hackney carriage driver, **36**, [252]
    large goods vehicle, **37**, [720]
    offences outside UK, in respect of,
      38(2), [281], [282]
    passenger-carrying vehicles, **37**, [720]
  enforcement generally, **36**, [959]
  evidence—
    certificate, by, **36**, [673]
      driver, user or owner, as to, **38(1)**, [10]
      driving instruction, as to, **38(1)**, [17]
      offences applicable, **38(1)**, [10], [121]
      public service vehicles, involving,
        37, [55]
    records as, **38(1)**, [12]
    specimens of blood or urine, **38(1)**, [14],
      [15]
  examiner, obstruction of, **37**, [652]
  experimental traffic order, as to, **37**, [174]
  false documents, issue or use of, **37**, [50],
    [139], [793]
  false statements—
    generally, **37**, [792]
    obtaining licence etc, **37**, [49], [458]
  financial penalty deposits—
    interpretation provisions, **38(1)**, [107]
    orders about, **38(1)**, [106]
    requirement, **38(1)**, [103]
      making of payment in compliance with,
        38(1), [104]
        prohibition on driving on failure of,
          38(1), [105]
    power to impose, **38(1)**, [102]
  fines—
    maximum, schedule of, **38(1)**, [32], [122],
      [123]
    standard level of, schedule of, **38(1)**, [122],
      [123]

road traffic offences—*contd*
  fixed penalties—
    accounting for, **38(1)**, [92]
    amount, **38(1)**, [61]
    conditional offer—
      conditions, setting out of, **38(1)**, [84]
      contents, **38(1)**, [84]
      dishonoured cheque in payment,
        38(1), [86], [87]
      effect of, **38(1)**, [85]
      endorsement when paid, **38(1)**, [86],
        [87]
      issue of, **38(1)**, [84]
      meaning, **38(1)**, [84]
      payment of penalty, **38(1)**, [85]
    deception, powers of court in cases of,
      38(1), [93]
    endorsement—
      counterpart of licence, without hearing,
        38(1), [65], [67]
      driving record—
        meaning, **38(1)**, [118]
        without hearing, **38(1)**, [66], [68]
      when invalid, **38(1)**, [81]
    exclusion of procedures, **38(1)**, [69]
    facts, statutory statement of, **38(1)**, [126]
    guidance to chief officers of police,
      38(1), [98]
    hired vehicle—
      in case of, **38(1)**, [75]
      statutory statement—
        meaning, **38(1)**, [77]
        as to, **38(1)**, [75], [125]
    meaning, **38(1)**, [59]
    newly qualified driver, **38(1)**, [508]
    notices—
      constable, given by, **38(1)**, [62]
      contents, **38(1)**, [60]
      effect of, **38(1)**, [63]
      fixing to vehicle—
        provisions as to, **38(1)**, [71]
        registration invalid, **38(1)**, [82], [83]
        time of offence, **38(1)**, [83]
      meaning, **38(1)**, [60]
      mistakenly given, **38(1)**, [69], [70]
      on-the-spot—
        generally, **38(1)**, [62]
        registration invalid, **38(1)**, [81]
        time of offence, **38(1)**, [83]
      Secretary of State, to, **38(1)**, [95]
      surrender of licence, **38(1)**, [62], [64]
      vehicle examiner, given by, **38(1)**, [62]
    offences involving, schedule of,
      38(1), [124]
    official form, meaning, **38(1)**, [77]
    orders, procedure for, **38(1)**, [99]
    owner—
      enforcement against, **38(1)**, [73]
      false statements by, **38(1)**, [76]
      meaning, **38(1)**, [77]
      notice, when unpaid, **38(1)**, [72]
      proceedings against, **38(1)**, [73]
      restriction of proceedings, **38(1)**, [74]
    ownership, statutory statements as to,
      38(1), [74], [125]

road traffic offences—*contd*
fixed penalties—*contd*
paying authorities, accounting between,
38(1), [92]
payment of penalty, **38(1)**, [78]
penalty points—
attendance on course, reduction for,
38(2), [513]
modification, **38(1)**, [26]
range of numbers, used in connection
with, **38(1)**, [24]
proceedings—
certificates about payment, **38(1)**, [90]
documents signed by accused,
38(1), [91]
general restrictions, **38(1)**, [88]
statements by constables, **38(1)**, [89]
registration—
certificate, issue of, **38(1)**, [79]
fine as, **38(1)**, [79]
invalid, when, **38(1)**, [82], [83]
sums payable in default, **38(1)**, [80]
regulations, power to make, **38(1)**, [94],
[99]
repeated offences, for **12(4)**, [10]
schedule of offences involving, **38(1)**, [124]
service of documents, **38(1)**, [96]
statutory declarations, **38(1)**, [81]
statutory statements—
facts, of, **38(1)**, [126]
meaning, **38(1)**, [77], [125], [126]
ownership, as to, **38(1)**, [74], [125]
traffic wardens, functions of, **38(1)**, [97]
unpaid, service of notice on owner,
38(1), [72]
footpaths—
driving on, **37**, [301], [605]
motor vehicle trials on, **37**, [604]
footways, parking of heavy goods vehicles
on, **37**, [589]
foreign vehicles, driving of, **36**, [903]
forgery of documents, **37**, [48], [138], [458],
[791]
goods vehicles—
breach of requirements, **37**, [615]
inspection, refusal to permit, **37**, [652]
overloaded, in connection with, **37**, [655]
unauthorised weights, using, **37**, [644]
unfit, in connection with, **37**, [655]
guilty plea, inclusion of date of birth and
sex, **38(1)**, [8]
hackney carriage—
driver unlicensed, **36**, [246], [395]
due to fault of other person, **36**, [955]
furious driving, **36**, [256], [410]
misconduct of driver, **36**, [257], [429]
penalties generally, **36**, [959]
penalties under London Hackney Carriage
Acts, **36**, [246], [256], [257], [431]
See also **hackney carriage**
heavy goods vehicle, parking on verges,
reservations etc, **37**, [589]
identification of driver. *See* driver *above*
impersonation, **37**, [140], [795]; **38(2)**, [304]

road traffic offences—*contd*
imprisonment—
maximum term, schedule, **38(1)**, [32],
[122], [123]
period of, schedule, **38(1)**, [122], [123]
inconsiderate driving, **37**, [561], [562], [786]
causing death by, **38(2)**, [509]
increase in penalties for, **12(3)**, [1020], [1021]
information, withholding, **37**, [792]
inquiry, failure to comply with provisions,
37, [797]
insurance, failure to give information as to,
37, [790]
large goods vehicles, **37**, [714], [720]
licence, production of, **38(1)**, [7], [23]
Licensing Act offence, exemption from charge
as to, **38(1)**, [5]
London. *See* **London**
motor cycles—
carriage of persons on, restrictions,
37, [594]
noise from exhausts, **37**, [480]
motor cyclists, wearing of protective
headgear—
armed forces, application of provisions,
38(1), [114]
contravention, **37**, [586]
proceedings, **37**, [587], [815]
motor vehicle—
construction and use regulations,
contravention, **37**, [614]–[618];
38(1), [16]
dangerous position, leaving in, **37**, [592]
insurance requirements, not meeting—
immobilisation of vehicles, **38(2)**, [511]
offence, **38(2)**, [511]
penalties, **38(2)**, [511]
parts, defective or unsuitable, fitting and
supply, **37**, [661]
seizure of—
alarm, distress or annoyance, used in
manner causing, **33(2)**, [386]
retention of, **33(2)**, [387]
trials on footpaths etc, **37**, [604]
type, contravention of requirements,
37, [640], [644]
weighing, refusal to allow, **37**, [663]
motor vehicle, taking without authority,
12(1), [564], [1084]
motoring events, authorised, disapplication of
certain provisions, **37**, [581]
overloaded goods vehicle, driving of,
37, [655]
owner—
evidence as to, **38(1)**, [10]
meaning, **38(1)**, [77]
service of notice to, **38(1)**, [72]
statutory statement of ownership,
38(1), [74], [77], [125]
parking. *See also* **parking**
dangerously parked vehicles, **37**, [270],
[592]
documents, mishandling, **37**, [287], [288]
excess charges. *See* **parking** (charges)
places, as to, **37**, [221], [225]

road traffic offences—*contd*

passenger-carrying vehicles, **37**, [714], [720]

payments to police authorities in relation to prevention, detection and enforcement of—

Scottish Ministers, by, **33(2)**, [584]

Secretary of State, by, **33(2)**, [583]

pedestrians, non-compliance with directions to, **37**, [608], [787]

penalties, fixed. *See* fixed penalties *above*

penalty points—

attribution to offence, **38(1)**, [24], [26]

connected offences, **38(1)**, [26]

course—

approval of, **38(1)**, [29]

certificates of completion, **38(1)**, [28]

providers, guidance to, **38(1)**, [30]

reduced penalty points for attendance on, **38(1)**, [27]

supplementary provisions, **38(1)**, [30]

modification where fixed penalty in question, **38(1)**, [26]

number, explanation, **38(1)**, [24]

range of numbers, alteration, **38(1)**, [24]

schedule of, **38(1)**, [122], [123]

taking into account, **38(1)**, [25]

two or more offences, **38(1)**, [24]

See also under fixed penalties *above*

penalty, where none expressly provided, **36**, [959]

private hire vehicles, **36**, [952], [959]; **38(2)**, [15], [42]

probation order combined with disqualification, **38(1)**, [55]

proceedings—

committal by magistrate, **38(1)**, [22]

conduct of, **37**, [701]

construction and use of vehicles and equipment, **38(1)**, [16]

driver, identification. *See* driver *above*

evidence in. *See* evidence *above*

institution of—

fixed penalty proceedings, **38(1)**, [74]

local authorities, by, **38(1)**, [4]

restriction on, **37**, [53], [458]; **38(1)**, [3]

time for, **37**, [57], [284], [458]

interim disqualification during, **38(1)**, [22]

meaning, **38(1)**, [100]

summary—

identity of driver, proof, **37**, [56]; **38(1)**, [11]

offences applicable, **38(1)**, [6]

time for commencement, **37**, [57]; **38(1)**, [6]

prosecution—

mode of, **38(1)**, [122], [123]

notice of, **38(1)**, [1]

warning of—

requirement, **38(1)**, [1], [2]

schedule of offences applicable, **38(1)**, [121]

punishments, schedule of, **38(1)**, [9], [122], [123]

radioactive material transport, **38(1)**, [273]

road traffic offences—*contd*

reckless driving, failure to give name and address, **37**, [786]

See now dangerous driving *above*

recording equipment, in use of, **36**, [812], [813], [814]

records as evidence, **38(1)**, [12], [13]

reflectors and tail lamps, as to, **37**, [668]

refusal of licence, driving after, **37**, [681]

regulations—

breach of, penalties, **36**, [486]; **37**, [51], [458]; **38(1)**, [108]

generally, power to make, **37**, [702]

repeated, disqualification for, **38(1)**, [41]

Road Traffic Acts—

continuity, old and new law, **38(1)**, [128]

meaning, **38(1)**, [119], [127]

road user charging schemes, as to, **38(2)**, [163]

safety equipment in motor vehicles, **38(1)**, [4]

seat belts, as to, **37**, [582], [583]; **38(1)**, [4]

sentence, committal for, **38(1)**, [22]

service of notices, **38(1)**, [1]

speed assessment equipment detection devices, use of, **38(2)**, [507]

speeding, **37**, [263]

devices, use in evidence, **38(1)**, [18]

penalty points, **38(2)**, [506]

street. *See* **street offences**

summary of provisions, **36**, [210]

summary proceedings. *See* proceedings *above*

summons, requirement to serve, **38(1)**, [1]

tampering with motor vehicles, **37**, [596]

test certificate, use of vehicle without, **37**, [625]

test of competence, on disqualification. *See under* disqualification *above*

tests, goods vehicles, **37**, [630], [631]

third party risk insurance, driving without, **37**, [754]

towed or carried, holding on etc, to vehicle in order to be, **37**, [597]

traffic—

directions, non-compliance with, **37**, [606]

officer, in relation to, **38(2)**, [304]

regulation order, contravention, **37**, [169], [172]

signs, non-compliance with, **37**, [607]

uninsured drivers causing death by driving, **37**, [563]; **38(2)**, [510]

unlicensed drivers, causing death, **38(2)**, [510]

unroadworthy vehicles, sale of, **37**, [660]

urine tests—

assumption as to proportion, **38(1)**, [14]

specimens—

documentary evidence, **38(1)**, [15]

provision of, **37**, [573]

use in proceedings, **38(1)**, [14]

user, evidence as to, **38(1)**, [10]

vehicle, failure to stop, **37**, [780]

verdicts, alternative, **38(1)**, [20]

warning—

at time of offence, **38(1)**, [1]

road traffic offences—*contd*
  warning—*contd*
    prosecution, of. *See* prosecution *above*
  weight of vehicles, proceedings as to,
    38(1), [16]

road traffic reduction
  interpretation, **38(2)**, [1]
  Northern Ireland, in, **38(2)**, [8]
  principal councils, reports by, **38(2)**, [2]
  road traffic, meaning, **38(2)**, [5]
  targets, **38(2)**, [2], [6]

road-ferries
  acquisition of land for, **36**, [1290]
  improvement of, **36**, [1120]
  provision and maintenance, **36**, [1028]

roadside sales
  body corporate, offence by, **36**, [927]
  control order, **36**, [926]
  documents, service of, **36**, [927]
  exemptions, **36**, [926]
  offences and penalties, **36**, [926], [1202]
  provisions on, **36**, [1212]

roadside tests. *See under* **vehicle testing**

robbery
  imprisonment, **12(1)**, [560]
  mail bag, taking, **12(1)**, [567]
  meaning, **12(1)**, [560]
  postal packet, taking, **12(1)**, [567]

Rochester Bridge
  provisions not applying to, **36**, [1312]

Rockall, Island of
  United Kingdom, incorporation into, **10**, [87]

rogues and vagabonds
  appeal, **12(1)**, [30]
  imprisonment, **12(1)**, [27]
  incorrigible. *See* **incorrigible rogue**
  persons being, **12(1)**, [27]
  proof of being, **12(1)**, [249]
  wounds, exposing, **12(1)**, [784]

roller skating rink
  byelaws as to, **35(1)**, [270]
  meaning, **35(1)**, [270]

Roman Catholic
  benefice, presentation to, right to, holding,
    14, 72
  church appointment, not advising on, **14**, 72
  civil office, holding, **14**, 70
  Crown, barred from succession to, **10**, [40],
    [49]
  disabilities from office, **14**, 71
  ecclesiastical appointment, not voting on,
    14, 71
  franchise, exercising, **14**, 70
  lay corporation, member of, **14**, 71
  Lord Chancellor as, **10**, [578]–[579]

Roman Catholic—*contd*
  military office, holding, **14**, 70
  offices in Church of England or Scotland,
    holding, **14**, 72
  penalties, recovery of, **14**, 73
  place of worship, certifying, **14**, 179
  regent, not to be, **14**, 71

Romania
  accession to European Union, **18**, [57]

Romney Marsh
  corporation of, saving for, **25(1)**, [52]

room. *See also* **underground room**
  construction below subsoil water level—
    consent of local authority to, **35(1)**, [596],
      [597]
    notice requiring alteration or filling in
      where, **35(1)**, [596], [625]
    prohibition, **35(1)**, [596]

Roosevelt Memorial. *See* **Grosvenor Square**

Roumania
  peace treaty, **10**, [916]

Royal Air Force
  absence without leave. *See* **absence without
    leave**
  active service, **3**, [994], [1278]
  age, evidence of, **3**, [972]
  aircraft, inaccurate certification, **3**, [781]
  alcohol, testing for, **3**, [1]
  aliens serving in, **3**, [747]
  annoyance by flying, **3**, [783]
  arrest—
    absentees, of, **3**, [957], [960]
    commanding officer, under warrant of,
      3, [962]
    deserters, **3**, [957]
    entry to premises for, **3**, [1717]
    generally, **3**, [1]
    persons unlawfully at large, **3**, [963]
    power of, **3**, [807]
    proceedings, during, **3**, [818]
    resisting, **3**, [785]
    search upon, **3**, [1718]
  billeting. *See* **billeting**
  board of inquiry—
    absence, into, **3**, [906]
    generally, **3**, [905]
  charge—
    court-martial trial, right to opt for,
      3, [824]
    higher authority, reference to, **3**, [823],
      [825]
    investigation of, **3**, [822]
    summary dealings—
      findings, review of, **3**, [875]
      generally, **3**, [825]
      punishments available on, **3**, [826]
      regulations as to, **3**, [829]
      summary appeal court. *See* summary
        appeal court *below*

Royal Air Force—*contd*
children of personnel, caring for, **3**, [294]
civil court, trial by, **3**, [1279]
civil custody, reception in, **3**, [976]
civil offence, committing, **3**, [799]
commanding officer—
  officer acting as, **3**, [828]
  powers of command, **3**, [950]
complaints, **3**, [953]
confinement, escape from, **3**, [786]
constitution, **3**, [1]
court-martial. *See* **court-martial**
custody—
  after charge—
    generally, **3**, [814]
    release from, **3**, [817]
    review of, **3**, [815]
  court-martial proceedings, during, **3**, [816]
  release from, **3**, [817]
  review of, **3**, [810]
    after charge, **3**, [815]
  rules, **3**, [821]
  Standing Civilian Court, in case of trial
    by, **3**, [820], [998]
  without charge—
    authorisation of, **3**, [809]
    extension of, **3**, [811]
    illegal absence, in case of, **3**, [812]
    limitations on, **3**, [808]
    supplementary provisions, **3**, [813]
dangerous flying, **3**, [780]
decorations—
  offences relating to, **3**, [776]
  unauthorised use and dealing, **3**, [970]
desertion. *See* **desertion**
discharge—
  generally, **3**, [740]
  postponement of, **3**, [738]
    proceedings, pending, **3**, [742]
  reserve, from, **3**, [1683]
discipline—
  conduct to prejudice of, **3**, [798]
  disgraceful conduct, **3**, [795]
  generally, **3**, [1], [287]
drugs, testing for—
  generally, **3**, [1]
  sample, failure to provide, **3**, [762], [763]
drunkenness, **3**, [770]
enlistment. *See* **enlistment**
equipment, interference with, **3**, [774]
establishment, meaning, **3**, [913]
execution of orders, **3**, [993]
execution of property, exemption from,
  3, [956]
failure to attend for duty, **3**, [756]
false air signal, giving, **3**, [752]
false document, making, **3**, [790]
fighting, unlawful, **3**, [771]
financial penalty enforcement orders, **3**, [903]
fines, colonies, in, **3**, [992]
forfeiture of service, **3**, [1250]
formation into units, **3**, [287]
government of, **3**, [287]
ill-treatment of men, **3**, [794]

Royal Air Force—*contd*
information, unauthorised disclosure of,
  3, [788]
insubordinate behaviour, **3**, [760]
issues, offences relating to, **3**, [776]
judicial officers, appointment of, **3**, [819]
law—
  auxiliary forces, applying to, **3**, [986]
  Channel Islands, applying to, **3**, [989]
  Isle of Man, applying to, **3**, [989]
  military forces, applying to, **3**, [1003]
  naval forces, applying to, **3**, [1003]
  Northern Ireland, applying to, **3**, [988]
  overseas territories, applying to, **3**, [990]
  persons subject to—
    attached forces, members of, **3**, [983]
    civilians, **3**, [985], [1001]
    colonial forces, **3**, [982]
    Commonwealth forces, **3**, [981]
    generally, **3**, [980]
    passengers in ships and aircraft, **3**, [984]
  reserve forces, applying to, **3**, [986]
  women, applying to, **3**, [987]
lawful commands, disobedience to, **3**, [761]
looting, **3**, [757]
low flying, **3**, [782]
malingering—
  aiding, **3**, [967]
  generally, **3**, [769]
mental disorder, treatment for, **3**, [1452]
military forces, attachment to, **3**, [952]
mobilisation documents, illegal dealing in,
  3, [969]
mutiny—
  failure to suppress, **3**, [759]
  generally, **3**, [758]
naval forces, attachment to, **3**, [952]
neglect of duty, **3**, [756]
negligence, loss occasioned by, **3**, [1252]
non-commissioned officer—
  obstruction in execution of duty, **3**, [966]
  reduction in rank, **3**, [975]
offences—
  aiding and abetting, **3**, [797]
  assisting the enemy, **3**, [751]
  attempt to commit, **3**, [796]
  civilian population, against, **3**, [791]
  decorations, relating to, **3**, [776]
  disposal by civil court, **3**, [904]
  equipment, messages or signals, interference
    with, **3**, [774]
  generally, **3**, [1]
  issues, relating to, **3**, [776]
  limitation of time for trial, **3**, [901]
  misconduct in action, **3**, [750]
  morale, against, **3**, [792]
  persons on watch, **3**, [755]
  persons subject to air-force law, **3**, [900]
  prosecuting authority. *See* prosecuting
    authority *below*
  required custodial sentences, **3**, [1726],
    [1742]
  sentries, **3**, [755]
  standing civilian court, custody in case of
    trial by, **3**, [1743]

Royal Air Force—*contd*
offences—*contd*
  summary appeal court, eligibility of warrant
    officers for membership, **3**, [1725]
officer—
  affidavits and declarations, taking, **3**, [978]
  ill-treatment of, **3**, [794]
  rights of, **3**, [289]
  scandalous conduct by, **3**, [793]
  sheriff, not to be, **3**, [954]
operations, obstructing, **3**, [752]
overseas authority, person arrested by,
  3, [1274]
pay and pensions. *See* **armed forces**
pensioner—
  meaning, **3**, [1406]
  recall, **3**, [1406]
    exemption, **3**, [1449]
    occasion for, **3**, [1407]
    period of, **3**, [1407]
powers of command, **3**, [950]
  co-operating naval or military forces, of,
    3, [951]
prison, meaning, **3**, [913]
prisoner, assisting escape and harbouring
  after, **12(1)**, [328A]
  permitting escape of, **3**, [784]
  unlawful release of, **3**, [784]
prize offences, **3**, [753]–[754]
property—
  damage to, **3**, [772]
  loss of, **3**, [772]
  meaning, **3**, [995]
  misapplication and waste, **3**, [775]
prosecuting authority—
  appointment of, **3**, [841]
  commanding officer, power to refer cases
    back to, **3**, [843]
  functions of, **3**, [842]
  police forces, advising, **3**, [844]
  prosecuting officers, **3**, [845]
  qualification as, **3**, [841]
provost officer, obstructing, **3**, [764]
raising and maintaining, **3**, [286]
recruiting officers, **3**, [735]
reserve. *See* **Air Force Reserve**
resisting arrest, **3**, [785]
sentence. *See* **sentence**
Service Acts, continuation of, **3**, [1709]
ship—
  inaccurate certification, **3**, [781]
  loss or hazarding, **3**, [779]
signals, interference with, **3**, [774]
standing orders, disobeying, **3**, [765]
stores, unlawful purchase of, **3**, [968]
summary appeal court—
  appeal—
    constitution for, **3**, [833]
    hearing of, **3**, [835]
    right of, **3**, [834]
  decisions, **3**, [837]
  generally, **3**, [1]
  Judge advocates, appointment of, **3**, [831]
  members, **3**, [830]
    administration of oaths to, **3**, [839]

Royal Air Force—*contd*
summary appeal court—*contd*
  members—*contd*
    officers qualifying as, **3**, [832]
  powers, **3**, [836]
  purpose, **3**, [830]
  rules, **3**, [838]
  witnesses, privileges of, **3**, [840]
summary finding, review of, **3**, [875]
theft—
  compensation, **3**, [908], [1376]
  restitution, **3**, [908], [1376]
threatening words, using, **3**, [771]
tolls, exemption from, **3**, [955]
transfer from other forces, **3**, [288]
transfer to reserve—
  generally, **3**, [741]
  national danger, during, **3**, [739]
  postponement of, **3**, [738], [1683]
    proceedings, pending, **3**, [742]
unit inquiries, **3**, [907]
vehicles, requisitioning. *See* **vehicles**
warrant officer—
  reduction in rank, **3**, [975]
  reduction to ranks, **3**, [743]
women—
  application of Act to, **3**, [987]
  including, **3**, [368]
wrongful act, loss occasioned by, **3**, [1252]
young offenders, amendment of law as to,
  6, [551]

royal approval
false representations as to, **39(1)**, [92]

Royal Arms
trade mark registration, protection from,
  48, 112–3
unauthorised use of, **48**, 12, 179

Royal Auxiliary Air Force. *See also* **reserve
forces**
Air Force Act, application to, **3**, [986]
call out—
  generally, **3**, [1388]
  home defence service, for, **3**, [1397]
  notices, **3**, [1401]
discharge, postponement of, **3**, [1431]
home service only, **3**, [1386]
service of notices, **3**, [1433]
training—
  annual, **3**, [1415]
  cancellation of, **3**, [1416]
  preliminary, **3**, [1414]
  variation of, **3**, [1416]

Royal Botanic Gardens, Kew
admission, hours and payment, **13**, [284]
Board of Trustees—
  accounts and audit, **13**, [300]
  advice, instruction and education,
    provision, **13**, [284]
  allowances, **13**, [300]
  appointment, **13**, [300]
  committees, **13**, [300]

Royal Botanic Gardens, Kew—*contd*
Board of Trustees—*contd*
companies, power to form, **13**, [285]
contracts and agreements, entry into, **13**, [284]
establishment, **13**, [283]
general functions, **13**, [284]
incorporation, **13**, [300]
information, supply by, **13**, [300]
investigation and research, **13**, [284]
land, acquisition and disposal, **13**, [284]
membership, **13**, [300]
ministerial function, exercise of, **13**, [284]
proceedings, **13**, [300]
reports, **13**, [300]
sealing of instruments, **13**, [300]
status, **13**, [300]
vesting of property, rights and liabilities in, **13**, [286]
collections, care and duty as to, **13**, [284]
director, **13**, [300]
finance, **13**, [289]
history, **13**, [49]
Kew, activities elsewhere, **13**, [284]
objects—
acquisition and disposal of, **13**, [287]
lending and borrowing, **13**, [288]
provisions applying to, **32**, [77]
staff, **13**, [300]

Royal College of Physicians of England
new charter in name of, **28**, [3], [5]

Royal College of Physicians of London
censors of, **28**, [8]
elects of, repeal of provisions as to, **28**, [8]
new charter—
grant of, provision for, **28**, [3], [5]
name, change of, **28**, [3], [5], [7]
new restrictions, not to contain, **28**, [4]
saving for rights, **28**, [6]
president, election of, **28**, [9]

Royal College of Veterinary Surgeons
Council of—
casual vacancies, **28**, [45]
constitution, **28**, [13]
continuation, **28**, [13]
default powers of Privy Council, **28**, [38]
elections to, **28**, [45]
members, **28**, [13], [45]
preliminary investigation and disciplinary
committees, setting up by, **28**, [32],
[47]. *See also* **veterinary surgeon**
president and vice-presidents, **28**, [13], [45]
registration appeals committee, **28**, [21]
regulations, making by, **28**, [22], [27], [35],
[40]
rules of procedure before disciplinary
committee, **28**, [48]
supervisory functions, **28**, [17]
temporary registration, direction for,
28, [23]
tenure of office, **28**, [45]

Royal College of Veterinary Surgeons—*contd*
disciplinary cases. *See* **veterinary surgeon**
examination of students by, **28**, [16]
member of, **28**, [15], [16], [18], [22]
transitional provisions as to, **28**, [43]

Royal Commission
superannuation provisions, **33(1)**, [89]

Royal Fleet Reserve. *See also* **reserve forces**
call out—
generally, **3**, [1388]
permanent service, for, **3**, [1389], [1450]
notices, **3**, [1401]
cessation of maintenance as division of Royal
Naval Reserve, **3**, [1684]
enlistment—
false answers on, **3**, [1419]
Greenwich Hospital, admission to,
3, [1422]
regular forces, in, void, **3**, [1420]
special class of, **3**, [1423]
transfer to, **3**, [1424]
generally, **3**, [14]–[15]
service of marines in, **3**, [1564]
special class of, **3**, [1684]

Royal Hospital School
girls and boys, power to admit regardless of
seafaring family connection, **3**, [1519]

Royal Household
members, salaries of, **10**, [609], [613]
retired allowances, **10**, [205], [219]

Royal Marines
Army Act, application to, **3**, [713]
discharge, **3**, [732], [1251], [1272]
enlistment, **3**, [732], [1251]
forfeiture of service, **3**, [1451]
generally, **3**, [1]
naval law, subject to, **3**, [1189]
pensioners, recall of, **3**, [1401], [1405]
property of deceased. *See* **navy**
re-engagement, **3**, [732]
reserve, transfer to, **3**, [1272]
Royal Fleet Reserve, transfer to, **3**, [732]
service, **3**, [732], [1251]
transfer to other corps, **3**, [734]
transfer to reserve or discharge from,
postponement of, **3**, [1683]

Royal Marines Reserve. *See also* **reserve forces**
call out, **3**, [1390]
enlistment—
false answers on, **3**, [1419]
regular forces, in, void, **3**, [1420]
Greenwich Hospital, admission to, **3**, [1422]

Royal Naval Reserves. *See also* **reserve forces**
call out, **3**, [1390], [1401]
discharge from, **3**, [1421]
enlistment—
false answers on, **3**, [1419]

Royal Naval Reserves—*contd*
  enlistment—*contd*
    regular forces in, void, **3**, [1420]
    Greenwich Hospital, admission to, **3**, [1422]
  property of deceased. *See* **Royal Navy**
  transfer to reserve or discharge from,
    postponement of, **3**, [1683]

Royal Navy. *See* **navy**

Royal Navy College
  site, grants for preservation of, **13**, [292]

Royal Ordnance factories. *See* **ordnance factories**

Royal Parks
  Commissioners of Works—
    duties of, **10**, [121], [147]–[148]
    powers of, **10**, [122], [149]
  Constabulary, abolition of, **33(2)**, [588]
    Amendment of provisions, **33(2)**, [607]
    Metropolitan Police Authority, transfers to, **33(2)**, [606]
  exchange of houses, **10**, [180]
  management of roads or traffic in, **36**, [1353]; **37**, [305]
  meaning, **36**, [1353]
  parking in, **37**, [234]
  trading offences in—
    body corporate, by, **32**, [647]
    meaning, **32**, [645]
    penalties for, **32**, [646]
    property—
      disposal of, **32**, [649]
      forfeiture, **32**, [650]
      retention of, **32**, [649]
      seizure of, **32**, [648]

Royal Patriotic Fund
  air force, extension to, **3**, [376]
  business premises, of, serviceman. *See* **civil interests of servicemen**
  Corporation—
    constitution of, **3**, [263]
    objects of, **3**, [260]
    property, rights and liabilities transferred to registered charity, **3**, [1758]
    provisions as to, **3**, [279]
    staff, transfer of, **3**, [1766]
  incorporation of, **3**, [259]
  representation of Ministry of Pensions, **3**, [293]
  residence of servicemen. *See* **civil interests of servicemen**
  soldier's effect fund, extension of, **3**, [376]

Royal Ulster Constabulary. *See* **Northern Ireland**

royalty
  discretion to make payments gross—
    EU companies, **44(4)**, [922]–[923]
    payee's duty to notify if payment not exempt., **44(4)**, [924]

royalty—*contd*
  discretion to make payments gross—*contd*
    supplementary provisions, **44(4)**, [925]
  double taxation arrangements, deduction at treaty rate, **44(4)**, [919]–[921]
  double taxation relief, special relationship provision, **44(1)**, [591]
  exempt payments between associated companies of different Member states—
    anti-avoidance, **44(3)**, [780]
    companies being 25% associated, **44(3)**, [776]
    conditions for, **44(3)**, [773]
    exemption notices, **44(3)**, [777]
    interpretation, **44(3)**, [781]
    person beneficially entitled, **44(3)**, [775]
    person making, **44(3)**, [774]
    power to amend Directive, **44(3)**, [782]
    provision for, **44(3)**, [772]
    special relationships, **44(3)**, [778]–[779]
  exemption of payments from tax, payment without deduction at source, **43(2)**, [325]
  further provision, **44(4)**, [917]
  patent. *See under* **patent**
  "relevant intellectual property right", meaning, **44(4)**, [915]
  several years, spreading over, **44(1)**, [380]
  UK resident agents, made through, **44(4)**, [916]
  under-deductions, **44(1)**, [605]
  where usual place of owner's abode is abroad, **44(4)**, [914]

RTE company
  constitutional documents, access to, **8(1)**, [1259]

RTM company. *See also* **collective enfranchisement (leasehold reform)**
  constitutional documents, access to, **8(1)**, [1259]

rubbish. *See also* **refuse**
  accumulations of, steps for removing, **35(1)**, [260]
  meaning, **35(1)**, [260]
  nuisances from, byelaws for prevention of, **35(1)**, [133]
  removal of, resulting from demolition, **35(1)**, [599], [601], [604]

Rule Committee (ecclesiastical)
  constitution, **14**, 1233
  functions of, **14**, 1235–6
  members, **14**, 1233–4

rules of court
  civil proceedings by or against Crown—
    institution in accordance with, **13**, [17]
    meaning, **13**, [17]
    prize court rules, **13**, [17]
    scope of, **13**, [36]
  discovery and production of documents by Crown, **13**, [31]

rules of court—*contd*
High Court application by Crown in accordance with, **13**, [18]
interrogatories to and by Crown, **13**, [31]

rural area
houses, restriction on disposal, **22**, [44]

Rural Development Boards
accounts, **1(1)**, [655]
acquisition of land by, **1(1)**, [648]
afforestation—
control of, **1(1)**, [654]
licensing, **1(1)**, [654]
amalgamation of agricultural land—
co-ordinated schemes for, **1(1)**, [653]
promotion of, **1(1)**, [650]
amenities, consideration of, **1(1)**, [647]
annual report, **1(1)**, [655]
area—
specification, **1(1)**, [672]
variation of, **1(1)**, [672]
boundary adjustments, powers as to, **1(1)**, [650]
composition of, **1(1)**, [673]
co-ordinated schemes, **1(1)**, [653]
directions by minister to, **1(1)**, [656]
dissolution, **1(1)**, [672]
entry, powers of, **1(1)**, [657]
establishment—
objections to, **1(1)**, [672]
objects of, **1(1)**, [647]
procedure, **1(1)**, [672]
public inquiry as to, **1(1)**, [672]
expenses, defrayment, **1(1)**, [647]
financial assistance by, **1(1)**, [649]
forestry—
camping etc sites, financial aid, **1(1)**, [649]

Rural Development Boards—*contd*
forestry—*contd*
control of, **1(1)**, [654]
Forestry Commission, consultation with, **1(1)**, [648]
functions generally, **1(1)**, [648]
information—
power to require, **1(1)**, [657]
wrongful disclosure, penalty, **1(1)**, [657]
land—
acquisition, **1(1)**, [648]
compulsory purchase—
compensation, assessment, **1(1)**, [652]
outstanding land, of, **1(1)**, [653]
provision for, **1(1)**, [651]
provisions applied, **1(1)**, [672]
purchase notice, withdrawal, **1(1)**, [651]
sale. *See* sale of land *below*
loans or grants by, **1(1)**, [649]
members, **1(1)**, [673]
obstruction of officers, **1(1)**, [657]
officers and servants, **1(1)**, [673]
proceedings, validity of, **1(1)**, [673]
proposals, submission to minister, **1(1)**, [648]
public inquiry as to schemes, **1(1)**, [653]
public services, financial aid, **1(1)**, [649]
reports by, **1(1)**, [655]
sale of land—
application for consent, **1(1)**, [651]
consent required, **1(1)**, [651]
control of, **1(1)**, [651]
exceptions from control, **1(1)**, [652]
members of family, to, **1(1)**, [652]
status of, **1(1)**, [673]
tenancies granted by, **1(1)**, [650]

ruri-decanal conference
deanery synod taking place of, **14**, 689

S

sacrament. *See also* **Holy Communion**
administration of, **14**, 44–5, 52
receiving, **14**, 44–5

safety in the home
promotion of, **25(1)**, [643]

safety of goods. *See also* **consumer protection**
body corporate, offence by, **39(1)**, [627]
Commissioners of Customs and Excise, detention of goods by, **39(1)**, [619]
Commissioners for Her Majesty's Revenue and Customs, disclosure of information by, **39(1)**, [625]
defences—
  act or default of another, **39(1)**, [627]
  due diligence, of, **39(1)**, [626]
enforcement—
  authorities—
    bodies being, **39(1)**, [615]
    container or machine, opening, **39(1)**, [617]
    disclosure of information, **39(1)**, [625]
    entry and inspection, powers of, **39(1)**, [617], [618]
    information, giving, **39(1)**, [618]
    obstruction of officer, **39(1)**, [620]
    procedure for production of goods, inspection of, **39(1)**, [617]
    records, requiring, **39(1)**, [617]
    reports by, **39(1)**, [629]
    search, powers of, **39(1)**, [617], [618]
    test on goods by, **39(1)**, [616], [618]
    test purchases by, **39(1)**, [616]
  detention of goods, **39(1)**, [617]
    appeal against, **39(1)**, [621]
    compensation for, **39(1)**, [622]
    customs officer, by, **39(1)**, [619]
  duties, transfer of, **39(1)**, [615]
  expenses, recovery of, **39(1)**, [623]
  false information, giving, **39(1)**, [620]
  seizure of goods, **39(1)**, [617]
    compensation for, **39(1)**, [622]
  tests, **39(1)**, [616], [618]
forfeiture of goods—
  appeals, **39(1)**, [611]
  application for, **39(1)**, [611]
  destruction of goods, **39(1)**, [611]
health and safety at work provisions, amendment, **39(1)**, [624]
information, disclosure of—
  Her Majesty's Revenue and Customs, by, **39(1)**, [625]
  privilege, saving for, **39(1)**, [634]
  information, Secretary of State requiring, **39(1)**, [612]

safety of goods—*contd*
marine. *See* **ship**
Northern Ireland, application of provisions to, **39(1)**, [636]
notice to warn—
  contravention of, **39(1)**, [608]
  information, Secretary of State requiring, **39(1)**, [612]
  notification of, **39(1)**, [639], [640]
  power to serve, **39(1)**, [608]
  relevant goods, **39(1)**, [608]
  representations as to, **39(1)**, [639]
  revocation of, **39(1)**, [639]
product liability. *See* **product liability**
prohibition notice—
  consent of Secretary of State to, **39(1)**, [608]
  content of, **39(1)**, [638]
  contravention of, **39(1)**, [608]
  information, Secretary of State requiring, **39(1)**, [612]
  notification of, **39(1)**, [638], [640]
  power to serve, **39(1)**, [608]
  relevant goods, **39(1)**, [608]
  representations as to, **39(1)**, [638]
  revocation of, **39(1)**, [638]
  variation of, **39(1)**, [638]
provisions, contravention of, **39(1)**, [632]
regulations—
  breach, action for, **39(1)**, [628]
  civil liability, **39(1)**, [628]
  consultations on, **39(1)**, [606]
  contravention of, **39(1)**, [606]
  information, Secretary of State requiring, **39(1)**, [612]
  making, **39(1)**, [606]
  offences against, **39(1)**, [607]
  power to make, **39(1)**, [606]
  provisions in, **39(1)**, [606]
safe, meaning, **39(1)**, [613]
Secretary of State, reports by, **39(1)**, [629]
service of documents, **39(1)**, [631]
supply of goods, meaning, **39(1)**, [633]
suspension notice—
  appeal against, **39(1)**, [610]
  compensation following, **39(1)**, [609]
  consent of enforcement authority to, **39(1)**, [609]
  contravention of, **39(1)**, [609]
  power to serve, **39(1)**, [609]

St Christopher, Nevis and Anguilla. *See* **Anguilla**
Commonwealth citizenship, **31**, [186]

Saint Helena
crown, vesting in, **7(2)**, [351]

Saint Lucia
Commonwealth citizenship, **31**, [186]

St Margaret's Island
Tenby, part of, **25(2)**, [903]

Saint Paul's Cathedral
canonries, patronage of, **14**, 133
charges on income, **14**, 161–2

Saint Peter, Westminster
canonry, annexation to, **14**, 134

Saint Vincent and the Grenadines
Commonwealth citizenship, **31**, [186]

sale
food, of. *See* **food and food safety**

sale of goods
acceptance, **39(1)**, [410]
auction, at, **39(1)**, [438]
bailee, by. *See* **bailment**
bankruptcy rules, saving for, **39(1)**, [442]
buyer—
  acceptance by, **39(1)**, [410]
  consumer cases, rights in—
    application of provisions, **39(1)**, [424]
    conformity with contract, **39(1)**, [429]
    court, powers of, **39(1)**, [428]
    other remedies, relation to, **39(1)**, [427]
    purchase price, reduction of,
      39(1), [426]
    repair or replacement of goods,
      39(1), [425]
    rescission of contract, **39(1)**, [426]
  deterioration, taking risk of, **39(1)**, [408]
  duties of, **39(1)**, [402]
  examination, right of, **39(1)**, [409]
  failure to take delivery, liability for,
    39(1), [413]
  partial rejection, right of, **39(1)**, [411]
  possession after sale by, **39(1)**, [400]
  rejected goods, return of, **39(1)**, [412]
  remedies—
    breach of warranty, for, **39(1)**, [434]
    non-delivery, damages for, **39(1)**, [432]
    specific performance, **39(1)**, [433]
competitive bidding, by, London—
  application of 1936 provisions,
    25(2), [555], [562]
  interpretation and application, **25(2)**, [544]
  meaning, **25(2)**, [544]
  offences—
    directors, liability of, **25(2)**, [553]
    obstruction of authorised person,
      25(2), [554]
    penalties for, **25(2)**, [547]
    prosecution of, **25(2)**, [552]
  premises, entry and inspection, **25(2)**, [551]
  registration of premises—
    appeals, **25(2)**, [549]
    application for, **25(2)**, [546]
    conditions, imposition of, **25(2)**, [548]
    exemptions, **25(2)**, [550]

sale of goods—*contd*
competitive bidding, by, London—*contd*
  registration of premises—*contd*
    refusal of, **25(2)**, [548]
    revocation, **25(2)**, [548]
    suitability for, **25(2)**, [548]
  unregistered premises, prohibition,
    25(2), [545]
contract—
  absolute or conditional, being, **39(1)**, [374]
  Act, application of, **39(1)**, [373]
  agreement to sell, **39(1)**, [374]
  auction, sale at, **39(1)**, [438]
  capacity, **39(1)**, [375]
  common law rules, application of,
    39(1), [442]
  condition—
    implied. *See* implied terms *below*
    warranty, treated as, **39(1)**, [383]
  conflict of laws, **39(1)**, [437]
  existing or future goods, for, **39(1)**, [377]
  formalities of, **39(1)**, [376]
  implied terms—
    exclusion of, **39(1)**, [436]
    fitness for purpose, as to, **39(1)**, [386]
    quiet possession, of, **39(1)**, [384]
    sale by description, on, **39(1)**, [385]
    satisfactory quality, as to, **39(1)**, [386]
    title, about, **39(1)**, [384]
  meaning, **39(1)**, [374]
  part owners, between, **39(1)**, [374]
  perished goods, for, **39(1)**, [378]
    perishing before sale but after agreement
      to sell, **39(1)**, [379]
  price—
    ascertainment of, **39(1)**, [380]
    consumer cases, reduction in,
      39(1), [426]
    valuation, agreement to sell at,
      39(1), [381]
  rescission, **39(1)**, [423], [426]
  sale by sample, for, **39(1)**, [387]
  security, operating as, **39(1)**, [442]
  subject matter of, **39(1)**, [377]
  summary of provisions, **39(1)**, [1]
  terms—
    breach, remedy for, **39(1)**, [434]
    delivery, about, **39(1)**, [404]
  time, stipulations about, **39(1)**, [382]
  warranty—
    breach of, **39(1)**, [434]
    condition treated as, **39(1)**, [383]
    implied. *See* **implied terms** *above*
delivery—
  buyer failing to take, **39(1)**, [413]
  carrier, to, **39(1)**, [407]
  contract term, as, **39(1)**, [404]
  distant place, at, **39(1)**, [408]
  examination by buyer, **39(1)**, [409]
  expenses of, **39(1)**, [404]
  instalments, by, **39(1)**, [406]
  meaning, **39(1)**, [441]
  part, unpaid seller making, **39(1)**, [417]
  payment of price, concurrent with,
    39(1), [403]

sale of goods—*contd*
  delivery—*contd*
    place of, **39(1)**, [404]
    reasonable hour, at, **39(1)**, [404]
    rules as to, **39(1)**, [404]
    sea transit, insurance during, **39(1)**, [407]
    third party, goods in possession of,
      39(1), [404]
    time for, **39(1)**, [404]
    wrong quantity, of, **39(1)**, [405]
  description, by, **39(1)**, [385]
  disposal, reservation of right of, **39(1)**, [392]
  enforcement of rights, etc, **39(1)**, [440]
  exclusion clause—
    guarantee, in, **11(1)**, [312]
    undertakings, implied, of, **11(1)**, [313]
  interest, recovery of, **39(1)**, [435]
  interpretation of terms, **39(1)**, [441]
  market overt, in, **39(1)**, [397]
  mercantile agent—
    meaning, **39(1)**, [401]
    possession of goods after sale by,
      39(1), [399]
  money paid, recovery of, **39(1)**, [435]
  non-consumer, breach of condition in,
    39(1), [388]
  partial rejection, right of, **39(1)**, [411]
  person not the owner, by, **39(1)**, [396]
  price—
    action for, **39(1)**, [430]
    payment concurrent with delivery,
      39(1), [403]
  property, transfer of—
    ascertained, goods to be, **39(1)**, [389]
    dealings in bulk goods, deemed consent by
      co-owner to, **39(1)**, [395]
    goods forming part of bulk, undivided
      shares in, **39(1)**, [394]
    intended time of, **39(1)**, [390], [391]
    risk passing with, **39(1)**, [393]
  reasonable time, references to, **39(1)**, [439]
  rejected goods, return of, **39(1)**, [431]
  risk, passing of, **39(1)**, [393]
  sample, by, **39(1)**, [387]
  savings, **39(1)**, [442], [447]
  seeds, regulation of, **1(1)**, [566]
  seller—
    duties of, **39(1)**, [402]
    possession after sale by, **39(1)**, [399]
    remedies—
      non-acceptance, damages for,
        39(1), [431]
      price, action for, **39(1)**, [430]
      unpaid—
        lien, having, **39(1)**, [416]
        meaning, **39(1)**, [414]
        part delivery, having made, **39(1)**, [417]
        re-sale, right of, **39(1)**, [423]
        rights of, **39(1)**, [415]
        stoppage in transit, right of, **39(1)**, [419]
        sub-sale by buyer, effect of, **39(1)**, [422]
        termination of lien, **39(1)**, [418]
  special damages, recovery of, **39(1)**, [435]
  stoppage in transit—
    duration of transit, **39(1)**, [420]

sale of goods—*contd*
  stoppage in transit—*contd*
    effecting, **39(1)**, [421]
    right of, **39(1)**, [419]
  street trading. *See* **street trading**
  summary of provisions, **39(1)**, [1]
  title, transfer of—
    implied term as to, **39(1)**, [384]
    market overt, sale in, **39(1)**, [397]
    person not the owner, sale by, **39(1)**, [396]
    possession after sale—
      buyer in, **39(1)**, [400]
      seller in, **39(1)**, [399]
    voidable, seller having, **39(1)**, [398]
  transitional provisions, **39(1)**, [445]
  Uniform Law—
    application of, **39(1)**, [75], [80]
    buyer, obligations of, **39(1)**, [83]
    Channel Islands, application to, **39(1)**, [78]
    communications, **39(1)**, [81]
    conformity of goods, **39(1)**, [82]
    contract of sale—
      avoidance of, **39(1)**, [84]
      concurrent conditions, **39(1)**, [84]
      damages, **39(1)**, [84]
      evidence of, **39(1)**, [81]
      exemptions, **39(1)**, [84]
      expenses, **39(1)**, [84]
      fundamental breach, **39(1)**, [81]
      non-performance of, **39(1)**, [84]
      specific performance, **39(1)**, [81]
    current price, meaning, **39(1)**, [81]
    delivery, **39(1)**, [82]
    documents, handing over, **39(1)**, [82]
    formation, on—
      acceptance, **39(1)**, [86]
      application of, **39(1)**, [76], [86]
      communication, **39(1)**, [86]
      offer, **39(1)**, [86]
      usage, **39(1)**, [86]
    fundamental breach of contract, **39(1)**, [81]
    Isle of Man, application to, **39(1)**, [78]
    meaning, **39(1)**, [75]
    preservation of goods, **39(1)**, [84]
    price, payment of, **39(1)**, [83]
    promptly, act performed, **39(1)**, [81]
    property, transfer of, **39(1)**, [82]
    reasonable person, knowledge of,
      39(1), [81]
    revision of, **39(1)**, [77]
    risk, passing, **39(1)**, [85]
    seller, obligations of, **39(1)**, [82]
    summary of provisions, **39(1)**, [1]
    taking delivery, **39(1)**, [83]
    usages and practices, parties bound by,
      39(1), [81]
    voidable title, under, **39(1)**, [398]

sale of land. *See also* **land**
  auction, by. *See* **auction**
  conditions—
    implied, exclusion, **20**, [677]
    prescribed forms, **20**, [664]
    statutory, **20**, [662], [663]

sale of land—*contd*
  contract for. *See* **land**
  court—
    applications by vendor and purchaser,
      20, [667]
    incumbrances, discharge by, **20**, [668]
    equitable interests, subject to, **20**, [660], [661]
    expenses, borne by purchaser, **20**, [663]
    incumbrances, discharge by court, **20**, [668]
    insurance money, application on completion,
      20, [665]
    lease, held by, **20**, [663]
    limitation of action for recovery of proceeds,
      19(3), [748]
    lots in, **20**, [663]
    recitals in instruments, validity, **20**, [663]
    registered land. *See* **land registration**
    services, apportionment, **20**, [7]
    solicitor, void restriction on employment,
      20, [666]

sale of occupation income
  charge to tax, **44(4)**, [784]
    applicable conditions, **44(4)**, [785]
    apportionments, **44(4)**, [791]
    capital amount obtained, income arising
      where, **44(4)**, [786]
    derivative property or right obtained,
      income arising where, **44(4)**, [787]
    exemptions—
      going concerns, for sales of, **44(4)**, [792]
      sales of future earnings, restriction on,
        44(4), [793]
    information, power to obtain, **44(4)**, [796]
    "other person", meaning, **44(4)**, [790]
    relevant transactions, sales and realisations,
      44(4), [788]
    tracing value, **44(4)**, [789]
    valuations, **44(4)**, [791]
  "occupation", meaning, **44(4)**, [782]
  overview, **44(4)**, [781]
  priority of other tax provisions, **44(4)**, [783]
  recovery of tax—
    certificates of tax paid, **44(4)**, [795]
    person not assessed, where consideration
      receivable by, **44(4)**, [794]

salmon. *See under* **freshwater fisheries**

salt
  springs or works, charge to tax, **44(1)**, [34]

salvage. *See also* **prize**
  aircraft, application of law to, **4(1)**, [137]
  apportionment—
    Admiralty court, by, **39(2)**, [907]
    receiver, by, **39(2)**, [906]
  Convention—
    force of law, having, **39(2)**, [902]
    provisions having effect with, **39(2)**, [1007]
    text of, **39(2)**, [1006]
  Crown—
    claims against, **39(2)**, [908]
    rights, **39(2)**, [908]
  disputes, valuation of property, **39(2)**, [903]

salvage—*contd*
  prize, saving for, **13**, [39]
  receiver of wreck—
    apportionment by, **39(2)**, [906]
    detained property—
      powers relating to, **39(2)**, [904]
      sale of, **39(2)**, [905]
    valuation of property by, **39(2)**, [903]
  summary of provisions, **39(2)**, [1]
  wreck, of, **39(2)**, [921]
  zero rating, **50**, [151]

samples
  fertilisers and feeding stuffs. *See under*
    fertilisers and feeding stuffs
  food, of. *See under* **food and food safety**
  hydrocarbon oil, **13**, [857], [870]
  intimate, taking as evidence. *See* **search**
  seeds. *See* **seeds**
  trade, relief from customs and excise duties
    for, **13**, [796]

sampling
  seeds. *See* **seeds**

sand
  sea-sand, Devon and Cornwall, right to take,
    49, [2]–[3]

sand pit
  charge to tax, **44(1)**, [34]

sanitary appliance
  maintenance, **35(1)**, [382]
  meaning, **35(1)**, [382]
  provision at place of entertainment—
    notice requiring—
      appeal against, **35(1)**, [383]
      betting office, at, **35(1)**, [382]
      building regulations, where, **35(1)**, [382]
      compliance with—
        entry to ascertain, **35(1)**, [382]
        expenses of, **35(1)**, [383]
        failure of, **35(1)**, [382]
      entry, powers of, **35(1)**, [382]
      modification on appeal, **35(1)**, [383]
      occasional, **35(1)**, [382]
      quashing on appeal, **35(1)**, [383]
      scope of, **35(1)**, [382]
      service of, **35(1)**, [382]
      specified occasions, on, **35(1)**, [382]
    water, etc, provision in connection with,
      35(1), [382]

sanitary authority
  public health provisions, for, **35(1)**, [293]
  urban and rural, **35(1)**, [19]

sanitary conveniences. *See also* **privy; public
convenience; water closet**
  byelaws as to persons using, **35(1)**, [139]
  charges for use of, **35(1)**, [139]
  disabled persons, for—
    notices as to, **35(1)**, [288]
    provision of, **35(1)**, [286], [287]

sanitary conveniences—*contd*
  disconnection, loan of temporary convenience
    on, **35(1)**, [591]
  examination and testing of suspected
    defective, **35(1)**, [125]
  lavatories, including, **35(1)**, [139]
  meaning, **35(1)**, [140], [648]
  provision of, **35(1)**, [139], [589]
  public—
    disabled persons, for—
      provision of, **35(1)**, [286], [287]
      removal or closure, notice requiring,
        35(1), [592]
      sign-posting of, **35(1)**, [288]
    street, erection in—
      consent to, **35(1)**, [592]
        appeal against refusal of, **35(1)**, [592]
  soil from, **35(1)**, [584]
  used in common, care of, **35(1)**, [129]

Sarawak
  Malaysia, forming part of, **7(2)**, [529]

satellite television services
  domestic licences, grant of, **45**, [198]
  foreign—
    meaning, **45**, [169]
    unacceptable, **45**, [169]
      supporting, offence of, **45**, [170]
  IBA transitional arrangements. *See under*
    Independent Broadcasting Authority
    (services)
  Licence, duration, **45**, [122]

Save As You Earn
  certified savings arrangements—
    certification, **44(3)**, [719]
    certifications and connected requirements,
      withdrawal and variation of, **44(3)**, [720]
    exempt income, **44(3)**, [716]
    meaning, **44(3)**, [717]
    providers, authorisation of, **44(3)**, [721]
      withdrawal and variation of, **44(3)**, [722]
    types of, **44(3)**, [718]
  savings arrangements, certification,
    43(S), 1607–8
  supplements, **19(2)**, [971]

saving certificates
  income arising from, **44(1)**, [31]
  meaning, **44(1)**, [32]

savings and investment income
  corporate strips—
    acquisitions and disposals, **44(3)**, [458]
    application of provisions, **44(3)**, [453]
    interest-bearing corporate security—
      conversion to strips, **44(3)**, [455]–[456]
      meaning, **44(3)**, [454]
    manipulation of payments, **44(3)**, [459]
    meaning, **44(3)**, [457]
  deeply discounted securities, profits from—
    calculation of, **44(3)**, [438]–[442]
    charge to tax, **44(3)**, [427]
    definitions, **44(3)**, [467]

savings and investment income—*contd*
  deeply discounted securities, profits
    from—*contd*
    disposals, transactions being, **44(3)**, [437]
    excluded indexed security, meaning,
      44(3), [433]
    excluded occasions of redemption,
      44(3), [431]
    income charged, **44(3)**, [428]
    listed securities held since 26th March
      2003—
      application of provisions, **44(3)**, [460]
      connected persons, issue to at excessive
        price, **44(3)**, [463]
      loss relief, **44(3)**, [461]
      profit or loss on disposals, calculation
        of, **44(3)**, [462]
    market value acquisitions, **44(3)**, [441]
    market value disposals, **44(3)**, [440]
    meaning, **44(3)**, [430]
    person liable, **44(3)**, [429]
    qualifying earn-out right, issue in
      accordance with, **44(3)**, [442]
    securities not being, **44(3)**, [432]
    separate tranches, issued in—
      basic rule, **44(3)**, [435]
      nominal value rule, **44(3)**, [436]
      rules for, **44(3)**, [434]
    strips of government securities—
      acquisitions and disposals, **44(3)**, [445]
      application of provisions, **44(3)**, [443]
      foreign stock exchange lists, quoted in,
        44(3), [451]
      loss relief, **44(3)**, [446]
      manipulation of payments, **44(3)**, [449]
      market value, **44(3)**, [450]
      meaning, **44(3)**, [444]
      modification of provisions, **44(3)**, [452]
      original acquisition cost—
        restriction by reference to,
          44(3), [447]
        restriction of losses by reference to,
          44(3), [448]
    transfer of assets abroad, **44(3)**, [466]
    transfers and acquisitions, timing,
      44(3), [438]
    trustees—
      disposal by, **44(3)**, [464]
      non-UK resident, **44(3)**, [465]
  deposits, transactions in—
    charge to tax, **44(3)**, [561]
    deposit rights, meaning, **44(3)**, [562]
    income charged, **44(3)**, [563]
    person liable, **44(3)**, [564]
  disposals of futures and options involving
    guaranteed returns—
    charge to tax, **44(3)**, [565]
    deemed disposal, **44(3)**, [574]
    definitions, **44(3)**, [568]
    income charged, **44(3)**, [566]
    losses, **44(3)**, [577]
    one or more disposals, returns from,
      44(3), [571]
    person liable, **44(3)**, [567]

savings and investment income—*contd*
disposals of futures and options involving
guaranteed returns—*contd*
production of guaranteed returns,
44(3), [570]
related disposals, **44(3)**, [573]
related transactions, **44(3)**, [576]
running of future to delivery, meaning,
44(3), [575]
transfer of assets abroad, **44(3)**, [579]
trustees, income of, **44(3)**, [578]
underlying subject matter, **44(3)**, [575]
when occurring, **44(3)**, [569], [572]
dividends. *See* **dividends**
foreign dividend coupons, sales of,
44(3), [580]–[583]
interest. *See* **interest**
life insurance contracts, gains from. *See* **life
assurance**
loan to participator in close company, release
of,
44(3), [415]–[421]. *See also* **close company**
overview of provisions, **44(3)**, [365]
priority of provisions, **44(3)**, [366]–[367]
purchased life annuity payments,
44(3), [422]–[426]
territorial scope of charges, **44(3)**, [368]
transitional provisions, **44(3)**, [907]–[909]
unauthorised unit trust, distributions from. *See*
unit trust

savings bank
annuity—
certification of amounts payable,
19(2), [773]
executors and administrators, validity of
payments to, **19(2)**, [774]
false declaration as to, **19(2)**, [780]
forgery of documents, **19(2)**, [781]
fraudulent receipt of, **19(2)**, [779]
incapacitated person, payment to,
19(2), [769]
insurance commuted to, **19(2)**, [838]
National Loans Fund, charged on,
19(2), [761], [855]
nominees, death of, **19(2)**, [762]
payment—
mode of, **19(2)**, [763]
time of, **19(2)**, [762]
regulations, power to make, **19(2)**, [771],
[887]
Savings Banks Acts, application of,
19(2), [767]
small sums, payment of, **19(2)**, [775]
transfer of, **19(2)**, [764]
transitional provisions, **19(2)**, [782], [786]
trusts relating to, **19(2)**, [778]
two or more people, granted to,
19(2), [769]
unclaimed, account of, **19(2)**, [770]
warrants, provisions as to, **19(2)**, [777]
insurance—
annuity, commuted to, **19(2)**, [765], [838]
county court, recovery of money in,
19(2), [768]

savings bank—*contd*
insurance—*contd*
false declaration as to, **19(2)**, [780]
forgery of documents, **19(2)**, [781]
fraudulent receipt of, **19(2)**, [779]
incapacitated person, payment to,
19(2), [769]
investment of sums for, **19(2)**, [772]
payment, mode of, **19(2)**, [763]
premium, default in paying, **19(2)**, [766],
[838]
regulations, power to make, **19(2)**, [771]
Savings Banks Acts, application of,
19(2), [767]
security for, **19(2)**, [761]
stamp duty, exemption of documents
from, **19(2)**, [776]
surrender of, **19(2)**, [766], [838]
transfer of, **19(2)**, [764]
trusts relating to, **19(2)**, [778]
two or more people, granted to,
19(2), [769]
National. *See* **National Savings Bank**
naval, abolition of, **19(2)**, [823]

savings committees
stamp duty exemption, **41**, [91]

Savings Gateway accounts
account ceasing to be, **40(S)**, 11
transfer of funds on, **40(S)**, 14
alternative finance arrangements, **40(S)**, 14
appeals, **40(S)**, 20–2
approvals, **40(S)**, 8
approved account provider, held with,
40(S), 7
death payments, **40(S)**, 7
eligible persons, **40(S)**, 5–6
HMRC—
decisions and notices, **40(S)**, 19
appeals, **40(S)**, 20–2
recovery of payments by, **40(S)**, 12
returns of information to, **40(S)**, 11
income and capital gains tax relief, **40(S)**, 13
information—
disclosure of, **40(S)**, 16
incorrect, penalties for, **40(S)**, 16
relevant persons, supply by, **40(S)**, 15
interest payable, **40(S)**, 13
maturity payment—
calculation, **40(S)**, 9–10
meaning, **40(S)**, 7
maturity period, **40(S)**, 7
meaning, **40(S)**, 4
Northern Ireland, **40(S)**, 23
notices of eligibility, **40(S)**, 5
opening, **40(S)**, 8
orders and regulations, **40(S)**, 24
penalties—
account provider, non-compliance by,
40(S), 18
failure to submit return etc, for, **40(S)**, 17
incorrect information, for, **40(S)**, 16
requirements, **40(S)**, 7
review and report to Parliament, **40(S)**, 23

Savings Gateway accounts—*contd*
  statements, **40(S)**, 10
  summary of provisions, **40(S)**, 1–2
  transfers, **40(S)**, 9

savings income
  Community obligations, **43(2)**, [246]
  highest part of total income, treated as, **44(4)**, [16]
  income tax on, rate for, **44(4)**, [7], [12]
  international arrangements, **43(2)**, [246]
  meaning, **44(4)**, [18]

scaffolding
  London—
    licence to erect, **25(1)**, [1004]
      access, measures to prevent, **25(2)**, [973]
      security, measures to protect, **25(2)**, [973]
    lighting at night, **25(1)**, [1004]
    unlicensed, fines for, **25(2)**, [527]

SCE. *See* **European Cooperative Society**

Schedule A
  business, meaning, **44(1)**, [615]
  charge to tax, **44(1)**, [12]
  computation of amounts payable, **44(1)**, [14]
  deductions—
    energy-saving items, expenditure on, **44(1)**, [19]–[21]
    rent, from. *See* **rent**
    sea walls, expenditure on, **44(1)**, [18]
  determinations, appeal against, **44(1)**, [30]
  exceptions, **44(1)**, [12]
  ITTOIA receipt, reductions in, **44(1)**, [26]
  loss relief, **44(1)**, [194]
  mutual business, application of charge to, **44(1)**, [16]
  premium, sum paid by way of, **44(1)**, [17]
  provisions applying, **44(1)**, [15]
  rent. *See* **rent**

Schedule D
  Case I and II—
    aggregation of profits, etc, **44(1)**, [40]
    apportionment of profits etc, **44(1)**, [40]
    charge to tax under, **44(1)**, [13]
    deductions—
      approved profit sharing scheme, payments to trustees of, **44(1)**, [57]
      cemetery, carrying on, **44(1)**, [68]
      charitable donations, agent's expenses, **44(1)**, [61]
      debt—
        incurred and released, **44(1)**, [75]
        restrictions in case of, **44(1)**, [65]
      educational establishments, gifts to, **44(1)**, [55]
      employee share ownership trust, costs of establishing, **44(1)**, [58]
      expenses of management. *See* **corporation tax**
      Export Credit Guarantee Department, payments to, **44(1)**, [64]

Schedule D—*contd*
  Case I and II—*contd*
    deductions—*contd*
      irrecoverable debts, for, **44(1)**, [66]
      local enterprise company, contribution to, **44(1)**, [49]
      not allowable, **44(1)**, [41]
      patent fees, **44(1)**, [53]
      profit sharing schemes, costs of establishing, **44(1)**, [56]
      registered design fees, **44(1)**, [53]
      research and development, **44(1)**, [51]
      seconded employees, for, **44(1)**, [60]
      share option scheme, costs of establishing, **44(1)**, [56]
      trade mark fees, **44(1)**, [53]
      training and enterprise councils, contributions to, **44(1)**, [49]
      urban regeneration company, contribution to, **44(1)**, [50]
      waste disposal—
        preparation expenditure, **44(1)**, [70]
        restoration payments, **44(1)**, [69]
    distributions, dealer's receipt of, **44(1)**, [76]
    insurance company expenses, **44(1)**, [570]–[572]
    land, commercial occupation of, **44(1)**, [33]
    life assurance business, profits charged to tax, **44(1)**, [248], [249], [269], [270]
    life assurance company expenses, **44(1)**, [571]
    mines, quarries and other concerns, **44(1)**, [34]
    redundant employees, additional payments to, **44(1)**, [67]
    taxable premiums, etc, treatment of, **44(1)**, [62], [63]
  Case III, charge to tax under, **44(1)**, [13]
  Case IV, charge to tax under, **44(1)**, [13]
  Case V—
    charge to tax under, **44(1)**, [13]
    land outside UK, corporation tax, **44(1)**, [39]
  Case VI—
    aggregation of profits, etc, **44(1)**, [40]
    apportionment of profits, etc, **44(1)**, [40]
    charge to tax under, **44(1)**, [13]
    deposits, disposal or exercise of rights in pursuance of, **44(1)**, [36]
    losses, **44(1)**, [200]
    patent rights, receipts from sale of, **44(1)**, [377]
    post-discontinuance receipts, taxation of—
      allowable deductions, **44(1)**, [86]
      conventional basis, **44(1)**, [85]
      earnings basis, **44(1)**, [84]
      right to payment transferred, where, **44(1)**, [87]
      right to receive interest, disposal of, **44(1)**, [35]
  Cases. *See* Case I, etc *above*
  charge to tax under, **44(1)**, [13]
  chargeable persons, **44(1)**, [37]
  charities, gifts in kind to, **44(1)**, [54]

Schedule D—*contd*
corporation tax. *See* **corporation tax**

Schedule E
benefits in kind. *See* **benefits in kind**
emoluments—
  living accommodation. *See* **living accommodation**
  transitional provisions, **44(1)**, [691]
pay as you earn. *See* **PAYE**

scheduled monument
cathedral church, application for consent relating to, **14**, 1205–6

scholarship
arrangements entered into by employer or connected person, under, **44(2)**, [213]
cost of, **44(2)**, [215]
exemption of income, limitation of, **44(2)**, [216]
special rules for, **44(2)**, [212]
trusts or schemes, under, **44(2)**, [214]

school. *See also* **primary and secondary schools**
admissions—
  ability, restriction on selection by, **15(2)**, [774]
  appeals—
    arrangements, **15(2)**, [90]
    child permanently excluded from two or more schools, **15(2)**, [91]–[92]
  arrangements—
    adjudicator, reference of objections to, **15(S)**, Education 264
    alteration following—
      adjudicator's decision, restriction on, **15(2)**, [87]
      establishment or expansion, power to restrict, **15(2)**, [85]; **15(S)**, Education 263
    changes to, **15(S)**, Education 265–6
    child looked after by local authority, **15(S)**, Education 260
    co-ordination of, **15(2)**, [83]–[84]
    co-ordination schemes, **15(S)**, Education 268–9
    decisions of adjudicator, **15(S)**, Education 266–7
    functions of adjudicator, **15(S)**, Education 265
    grammar schools, **15(2)**, [105]–[110]
    meaning, **15(2)**, [79]
    number, determination of, **15(S)**, Education 260–1
    objections, reference of, **15(2)**, [86]
    procedure for determining, **15(2)**, [81]; **15(S)**, Education 260
    regulations, **15(S)**, Education 262
    reports by local education Authority to adjudicator, **15(S)**, Education 270–1
    restriction on alteration following adjudicator's decision, **15(S)**, Education 267

school—*contd*
admissions—*contd*
  arrangements—*contd*
    sharing of information, **15(S)**, Education 270
    variation of, **15(S)**, Education 261
  authority, meaning, **15(2)**, [79]
  child permanently excluded from two or more schools, **15(2)**, [78]
  code for, **15(2)**, [775]
    issue and revision of, **15(2)**, [73]
    making and approval, **15(2)**, [74]
  forums—
    establishment of, **15(2)**, [75]
    functions, **15(2)**, [75]
      Academies, in relation to, **15(2)**, [76]
    reports, preparation by, **15(2)**, [75]
  information, publication of, **15(2)**, [88]
  interviews, prohibition on, **15(2)**, [80]
  looked after children—
    appeals, child permanently excluded from two or more schools, **15(2)**, [92]
    power to direct, **15(2)**, [95]–[97]
  numbers—
    determination of, **15(2)**, [82]
    fixing, **15(2)**, [89], [169]–[171]
  nursery education, to, **15(2)**, [99]
  parental preference, **15(2)**, [77]
  power to direct, **15(2)**, [93]–[97]
  publication of information about, **15(2)**, [88]
  pupil banding, **15(2)**, [776]
  special educational needs, child with, **15(2)**, [99]
  special school, to, **15(2)**, [99]
alterations, **15(2)**, [754]–[755]
  restrictions on, **15(2)**, [764]
army. *See* **army school**
attendance—
  choice of school—
    child with statement of special educational needs, **15(1)**, [583]
    child without statement of special educational needs, **15(1)**, [580]
    opportunities for, local authority to increase, **15(2)**, [741]
  education supervision orders, **15(1)**, [592]
  failure to secure, **15(1)**, [586]; **15(2)**, [823]–[824]
  general note, **15(1)**, [1]
  National Assembly for Wales, powers, **15(2)**, [882]
  order—
    alternative education provision, applied to, **15(1)**, [587]
    amendment, child without statement of special educational needs, **15(1)**, [582]
    excluded pupils, applicable to, **15(1)**, [587]
    non-compliance with, **15(1)**, [585]
      penalty notices, **15(1)**, [588]–[589]
    revocation, **15(1)**, [579], [584]
    service of, **15(1)**, [579]
    specification of school in, **15(1)**, [581]
  proceedings, institution of, **15(1)**, [591]

school—*contd*
  attendance—*contd*
    targets, **15(2)**, [56]
  boarding, as children's home—
    entry by authorised person, **6**, [415]
    suspension of duty, **6**, [416]
    inspection—
      authorised inspector—
        appointment, **6**, [416]
        duties of, **6**, [417]
      welfare of children, **6**, [415]
  building byelaws, exemption of plans from, **15(1)**, [679]
  building regulations, exemption from, **35(1)**, [530]
  careers education—
    advisers, co-operation with, **15(1)**, [755]
    extension or modification of provisions, **15(1)**, [757]
    information, provision of, **15(1)**, [756]
    provision of, **15(1)**, [754]
  changes not amounting to discontinuance, **15(1)**, [707]
  children's home, as, **35(2)**, [280]
    inspection, **6**, [409]
  Church of England, financial assistance, **14**, 629–30
  collective worship—
    exceptions and special arrangements, **15(2)**, [59]
    requirements, **15(2)**, [58], [159]
  community cohesion, contribution to, **15(2)**, [868]
  community school. *See* **community school**
  concern, causing—
    closure of school, **15(2)**, [788]
    governing body—
      additional governors, appointment of, **15(2)**, [787]
      interim executive members, consisting of, **15(2)**, [790], [905]
    intervention—
      eligible for, **15(2)**, [780]–[782]
      LEA, by, **15(2)**, [783]–[786]
      Secretary of State, by, **15(2)**, [787]–[789]
  day, duration of, **15(1)**, [686]
  denominational character, institutions of, **15(2)**, [688]
  denominational education, meaning, **15(2)**, [642]–[643]
  disabled person, access of to, **15(1)**, [265]
  discipline—
    behaviour policy, head teacher to determine, **15(2)**, [803]
    breakdown, LEA's power to prevent, **15(2)**, [55]
    disciplinary penalty—
      confiscation from pupils, **15(2)**, [808]
      enforcement—
        detention outside school sessions, **15(2)**, [806]
        generally, **15(2)**, [805]
      meaning, **15(2)**, [804]

school—*contd*
  discipline—*contd*
    excluded pupils—
      attendance, failure to secure, **15(2)**, [823]–[824]
      governing body, duty in relation to, **15(2)**, [814]
      LEA, duty in relation to, **15(2)**, [815]
      parents—
        duty in relation to, **15(2)**, [817]
        notice to, **15(2)**, [818]
      present in public place, penalty notices when, **15(2)**, [819]–[821]
      proprietor, duty in relation to, **15(2)**, [814]
      reintegration interviews, **15(2)**, [816]
      removal of, to designated premises, **15(2)**, [822]
    governing body and head teacher, responsibility of, **15(2)**, [54], [802]
    National Assembly for Wales, powers, **15(2)**, [882]
    reasonable force, use of, **15(2)**, [807]
  discontinuance—
    consultation on, **15(2)**, [752]
    disposal of land on, **15(2)**, [64], [163]–[167]
    proposals for, **15(2)**, [144]–[148], [751]
    restrictions on, **15(2)**, [764]
  Endowed Schools Acts, schemes under, **15(1)**, [687]
  establishment or alteration, proposals for, **15(2)**, [144]–[148]
  exclusion from, of child liable to convey notifiable disease, **35(1)**, [462]
  exits, etc, **35(1)**, [549]
  extra-parochial services at, **14**, 655
  federated, proposals for establishment of, **15(2)**, [661]
  food and drink provided on premises, **15(2)**, [114], [801]
  foundation. *See* **foundation school**
  governing body, general duties of, **15(2)**, [773]
  grammar—
    ballot—
      eligibility of parents to request or vote, **15(2)**, [107]
      publication of material relating to, restriction on, **15(2)**, [108]
      selective admission arrangements, decision on retaining, **15(2)**, [106]
    designation of, **15(2)**, [105]
    selective admission arrangements—
      decision on retaining, **15(2)**, [106]
      implementation of decision, **15(2)**, [109]
      proposal to end, **15(2)**, [110]
  grant-maintained. *See* **grant-maintained schools**
  having case of notifiable disease, list of day pupils at, **35(1)**, [463]
  health and fitness, **15(2)**, [454]
  highway crossing land, of—
    special diversion order—
      power to make, **36**, [1155]

school—*contd*
  highway crossing land, of—*contd*
    special diversion order—*contd*
      proprietor, application by, **36**, [1156]
    special extinguishment order—
      power to make, **36**, [1150]
      proprietor, application by, **36**, [1151]
  home-school agreements, **15(2)**, [111]–[112]
  improvement partner, appointment of,
    15(2), [742]
  independent. *See* **independent schools**
  infant class sizes—
    duty to set limit on, **15(2)**, [1]
    reduction, grant, payment of, **15(2)**, [2]
  inspections—
    combined reports, **15(2)**, [655]
    computer records, inspection of,
      15(2), [654]
    concern, schools causing, **15(2)**, [641]
    general note, **15(1)**, [1]
    LEA, power of, **15(2)**, [647]
    maintained schools, destination of report
      on, **15(2)**, [611]
    non-maintained schools, destination of
      report on, **15(2)**, [613]
    Office for Standards in Education,
      Children's Services and Skills. *See* **Office
      for Standards in Education,
      Children's Services and Skills**
    proprietor, statement on report,
      15(2), [614]
    religious education, of, **15(2)**, [644]–[645]
    special measures, report requiring,
      15(2), [612]
    Wales, in. *See* **Wales**
  inspectorate. *See* **Her Majesty's Chief
    Inspector of Education, Children's
    Services and Skills; Her Majesty's Chief
    Inspector of Education and Training in
    Wales; Office for Standards in
    Education, Children's Services and
    Skills**
  intervention—
    LEA, by—
      additional governors, power to appoint,
        15(2), [13]
      cases for, **15(2)**, [12]
      delegated budget, suspension of right
        to, **15(2)**, [15]
      interim executive members for governing
        body, power to provide for, **15(2)**, [14],
        [19], [137]
      power of, **15(2)**, [11]
    Secretary of State, by—
      additional governors, power to appoint,
        15(2), [16]
      closure, power to direct, **15(2)**, [18]
      interim executive members for governing
        body, power to provide for, **15(2)**, [17],
        [19], [137]
  land, stamp duty on transfer of, **41**, [475]
  London, non-teaching staff, superannuation,
    25(1), [258], [543]
  maintained. *See* **maintained school**
  marriage at, **14**, 654–5

school—*contd*
  meals, **15(1)**, [646]–[649], [668]
  meaning, **15(1)**, [499]; **35(1)**, [514], [648]
  music tuition at, charges for, **15(2)**, [778]
  new—
    establishment of—
      consultation on, **15(2)**, [745]
      federated school, as, **15(2)**, [748]
      notices as to, **15(2)**, [745]
      proposals for, **15(2)**, [897]
        adjudicator, consideration by,
          15(2), [898]
        implementation of, **15(2)**, [899]
        invitations for, **15(2)**, [743], [897]
        local authority, consideration by,
          15(2), [898]
        publication of, **15(2)**, [746]
        relevant LEA, outside area of,
          15(2), [749]
        restrictions on, **15(2)**, [764]
        in Wales, not by English LEA,
          15(2), [750]
    land, transfer of—
      appointed day, on, **15(2)**, [62],
        [160]–[162]
      governing body to trustees, by,
        15(2), [63]
      regulations providing for, **15(2)**, [60]
      staff, transfer of, **15(2)**, [61]
  new secondary, proposals for, **15(2)**, [659]
  non-maintained, financial assistance to,
    15(2), [124]
  opposite side of Welsh border, restrictions on
    establishment, **15(2)**, [662]
  places, rationalisation of, **15(2)**, [660]
    proposals—
      directions to bring forward, **15(2)**, [726]
      procedure for dealing with, **15(2)**, [728]
      Secretary of State, by, **15(2)**, [727]
      sex discrimination, transitional
        exemption orders, **15(2)**, [729]
  playing fields, disposal or changes in use,
    15(2), [65]
  potentially harmful materials and apparatus,
    control of, **15(1)**, [680]
  premises, having article with blade or point or
    offensive weapon on, **12(1)**, [1096]
  public. *See* **public school**
  pupils—
    disabled. *See* disabled pupils *above*
    Key Stage 4, extended work experience
      for, **15(2)**, [113]
    selection—
      ability or aptitude, by, **15(2)**, [100]
      banding, **15(2)**, [102]
      grammar schools, **15(2)**, [105]–[110]
      introduction, variation or abandonment
        of provision, **15(2)**, [104]
      particular subjects, aptitude for,
        15(2), [103]
      pre-existing arrangements, **15(2)**, [101]
  religious education—
    duty to secure provision of, **15(2)**, [57]
    exceptions and special arrangements,
      15(2), [59]

school—*contd*
  religious education—*contd*
    required provision, **15(2)**, [158]
  reorganisation, further education corporations,
    involving establishment of, **15(1)**, [426]
  secondary, proposals for establishment of—
    approval of, **15(2)**, [722]
    implementation, **15(2)**, [724]
    LEA, determination of implementation,
      15(2), [723]
    significant improvement, requiring,
      15(2), [781]
  sites. *See* **school sites**
  special. *See* **special school**
  special measures, requiring, **15(2)**, [782]
  staffing—
    religious character, schools with,
      15(2), [51]
    religious opinions, **15(2)**, [52]
  training, references to, **15(2)**, [687]
  travel schemes—
    child with irregular attendance, and,
      15(2), [798]
    National Assembly for Wales, powers,
      15(2), [882]
    piloting, **15(2)**, [796]
    power to repeal provisions, **15(2)**, [797]
    sixth formers, for, **15(2)**, [799]
  truancy. *See* **truancy**
  trust deeds, modification of, **15(2)**, [71]
  use of swimming baths and bathing places
    by, **35(1)**, [152]
  voluntary. *See* **voluntary school**
  Wales—
    Admissions, looked after children,
      Assembly's power to make regulations
      about, **15(2)**, [98]
    discontinuance, proposals for,
      15(2), [145]–[148]
    establishment or alteration, proposals for,
      15(2), [145]–[148]
    places, rationalisation of—
      dealing with proposals, **15(2)**, [152]
      directions to bring forward proposals,
        15(2), [149]–[150]
      National Assembly, proposals by,
        15(2), [151]
      transitional exemption orders,
        15(2), [153]
  walking distance to, **15(1)**, [586]
  workforce—
    information about, **15(2)**, [700]–[701]
    training—
      amended provisions, **15(2)**, [732]
      provision of, **15(2)**, [686]
  year, duration of, **15(1)**, [686]

school bus
  fare-paying passengers on, **36**, [974]; **37**, [32]
  free, provision, **37**, [32]
  meaning, **37**, [32]

school crossings
  patrolling of, **37**, [199]
  patrols, training and uniform, **37**, [199]

school crossings—*contd*
  provision, **37**, [32]
  stopping of vehicles at, **37**, [200]

School Curriculum and Assessment
Authority
  transfer of staff from, **15(1)**, [747]

school forums
  establishment of, **15(2)**, [42], [75]
  functions, **15(2)**, [75]
    Academies, in relation to, **15(2)**, [76]
  reports, preparation by, **15(2)**, [75]

school sites
  conveyance of land for—
    corporation, by, **20**, [121]
    Duchy of Lancaster, by, **20**, [118]
    equitable owner, by, **20**, [119]
    form of, **20**, [124]
    landlord, by, **20**, [117]
    minister and churchwardens, to, **20**, [133]
    part only—
      rents and fines, apportionment, **20**, [218]
      unconveyed land, liabilities on, **20**, [219]
    persons under disability, by, **20**, [119]
    school purposes, held for, **20**, [121]
    schools to which applying, **20**, [231]
    trustees, corporation as, **20**, [222]
  corporation, grant of land to, **20**, [121]
  ecclesiastical corporation—
    certificate as to extent of land conveyed,
      20, [126]
    grant by, **20**, [120]
    purchase money, applying, **20**, [125]
    restrictions on grant, **20**, [268]
    sale or exchange of land, consent to,
      20, [127]
  ecclesiastical district, grant to, **15(1)**, [8]
  exchange of, **20**, [127]
  forms of grant, **20**, [124]
  general note, **15(1)**, [1]
  glebe, grant of part of, **20**, [134]
  land, use arising from right of reverter,
    22, [694]
  parish—
    meaning, **20**, [129], [227]
    quantity of land in, **20**, [220]
  parliamentary aid, conditions on, **20**, [131]
  reversion on cessation of use, **20**, [118]
  sale of—
    parliamentary grant, purchase made from,
      20, [268]
    purchasers for value without notice, to,
      20, [269]
    trustees, by, **20**, [127]
  schoolmaster not acquiring interest, **20**, [128]
  separate schools, for, **20**, [123]
  summary of provisions, **20**, [1]
  teachers, for instruction of, **20**, [221]
  trustees—
    grant of land to, **20**, [121]
    minister and churchwardens, conveyance
      to, **20**, [122]
    rebuilding, applying for aid for, **20**, [132]

school sites—*contd*
  trustees—*contd*
    sale or exchange by, **20**, [127]

School Teachers' Review Body
  allowances, **15(2)**, [527]
  chairman, **15(2)**, [433], [527]
  consultation by, **15(2)**, [435]
  deputy chairman, **15(2)**, [527]
  functions, **15(2)**, [434]
  membership, **15(2)**, [433], [527]
  proceedings, **15(2)**, [527]
  reference to, **15(2)**, [439]
  remuneration, **15(2)**, [527]
  transitional provisions, **15(2)**, [527]

Schools Examinations and Assessment Council. *See* **Curriculum and Assessment Councils**

Science Museum
  admission, payments for, **13**, [270]
  Board of Trustees—
    allowances, **13**, [298]
    committees, **13**, [298]
    companies, formation by, **13**, [271]
    establishment, **13**, [269]
    general functions, **13**, [270]
    incorporation, **13**, [298]
    land, acquisition and disposal, **13**, [270]
    membership, **13**, [298]
    ministerial function, exercise of, **13**, [270]
    proceedings, **13**, [298]
    reports, **13**, [298]
    research and services, **13**, [270]
    sealing of instruments, **13**, [298]
    status, **13**, [298]
    vesting of property, rights and liabilities in, **13**, [272]
  collections, care and preservation, **13**, [270]
  director, **13**, [298]
  gifts, vesting of, **13**, [273]
  grants, **13**, [431], [432]
  history, **13**, [49]
  land, transfer of, **13**, [430]
  loans by, **13**, [275]
  objects—
    acquisition and disposal of, **13**, [274]
    lending and borrowing, **13**, [275]
  premises, use of, **13**, [270]
  staff, **13**, [298]

Science Research Council
  establishment of, **10**, [532]
  National Institute for Research in Nuclear Science, taking over, **10**, [534], [540]

scientific institutions. *See* **literary and scientific institutions**

scientific research
  expenses incurred in, **10**, [536]
  meaning, **10**, [537]

scientific research association
  payments to, deductions for, **44(1)**, [52]

scientific research organisation
  corporation tax—
    deduction for payments to, **43(2)**, [732]
    exemption for, **43(2)**, [730]
  income tax deduction for payments to, **43(2)**, [731]
  tax exemption, **44(1)**, [367]

Scilly Isles. *See* **Isles of Scilly**

scire facias
  writ of, abolition, **13**, [43]

scold
  common, abolition of offence, **12(1)**, [369]

Scotch whisky
  meaning, **19(3)**, [464]
  production, safeguarding, **19(3)**, [462]
  sale of spirits as, **19(3)**, [463]

Scotland
  abuse of position of trust, acts in, **12(3)**, [684]
  Advocate General—
    salary, **10**, [614]
    vacancy in office, **10**, [1397]
  aliment, action for—
    decree for payment, enforcement of, **27**, [290]
    service of process, **27**, [289]
  asylum-seekers, exclusion from homelessness provisions, **31**, [308]
  Auditor General—
    financial control, **10**, [1381]
    office of, **10**, [1380]
  bank notes, issue of. *See* **bank note**
  bankruptcy and insolvency—
    claim, submission of—
      effect of, **4(2)**, [56]
      trustee, to, **4(2)**, [58]
    creditors—
      meeting of, voting at, **4(2)**, [56]
      voluntary trust deeds for, **4(2)**, [61], [66]
    debtor—
      attendance at examination, **4(2)**, [57]
      discharge of, **4(2)**, [59], [60], [65]
      examination of, **4(2)**, [57]
      meaning, **4(2)**, [62]
  banns of marriage published in, **27**, [219]
  British Waterways Board—
    accounts, **36**, [702]
    annual report, **36**, [704]
    application of provisions to, **38(1)**, [620]
    Bills, promoting or opposing, **36**, [694]
    borrowing powers—
      Exchequer loans, **36**, [697]
      limits, **36**, [696]
    compulsory purchase of land, **36**, [682]
    duties of, enforcement, **36**, [842]
    employees, negotiation and consultation machinery, **36**, [865]

Scotland—*contd*
British Waterways Board—*contd*
land—
acquisition, power of, **36**, [802]
development, power of, **36**, [802]
development, powers of, **36**, [687]
disposal, power of, **36**, [802]
maintenance of waterways, **36**, [841]
members, appointment of, **36**, [682], [738]
pipe-lines, construction and operation of, **36**, [688]
powers of, **36**, [690], [803]–[805]
Scottish Ministers—
consent of, powers subject to, **36**, [705]
directions of, **36**, [731]
guarantees by, **36**, [699]
local enactments, repeal of, **36**, [732]
powers of, **36**, [704]
subsidiaries—
control over, **36**, [703]
functions carried out by, **36**, [804]
joint, **36**, [804]
capital gains tax on death, **42**, [1148]
child offender, detention of, **12(2)**, [318], [346]
churches in, **14**, 5
citation, effecting, **11(2)**, [399]
citation, service abroad—
general requirements, **12(3)**, [568]
other than by post, **12(3)**, [569]
civil protection. *See* **civil protection**
civil recovery of proceeds of unlawful conduct—
cash, code of practice for recovery of, **12(3)**, [397]
constables, performance of functions by, **12(3)**, [418]
interim administration order—
application for, **12(3)**, [359]
arrestment of property, **12(3)**, [368]
dealing with property, restrictions on, **12(3)**, [364]
inhibition of property affected by, **12(3)**, [361]
interim administrator—
functions of, **12(3)**, [360]
payment of, **12(3)**, [387]
powers of, **12(3)**, [542]
supervision, **12(3)**, [363]
proceedings and remedies, restriction on, **12(3)**, [365]
property not recoverable, **12(3)**, [366]
reporting, **12(3)**, [367]
respondent, duties of, **12(3)**, [362]
variation, **12(3)**, [363]
Lord Advocate and Scottish Ministers, disclosure to and by, **12(3)**, [514]–[516]
order—
diligence, effect on, **12(3)**, [388]
proceedings for, **12(3)**, [334]
recording, **12(3)**, [371]
scope of powers, **12(3)**, [389]
See also **proceeds of crime**
prohibitory property order—
application for, **12(3)**, [353]

Scotland—*contd*
civil recovery of proceeds of unlawful conduct—*contd*
prohibitory property order—*contd*
arrestment of property affected by, **12(3)**, [357]
conditions for, **12(3)**, [353]
exclusions, **12(3)**, [355]
inhibition of property affected by, **12(3)**, [358]
meaning, **12(3)**, [353]
proceedings and remedies, restrictions on, **12(3)**, [356]
recall, **12(3)**, [354]
variation, **12(3)**, [354]
See also **proceeds of crime**
community patients, responsibilities for, transferred to, **29**, [133]
community service orders, **12(2)**, [351]
England and Wales, persons residing in, **12(2)**, [352], [353]
Northern Ireland, persons residing in, **12(2)**, [353]
compensation orders, enforcement of, **12(2)**, [354]
Consolidated Fund, **10**, [1375]
payments out of, **10**, [1376]
Scottish functions, **10**, [1429]
continuity of law, **12(2)**, [312]; **46**, [886]
criminal law, references to, **10**, [1436]
cross-border public authorities—
initial status, **10**, [1398]
modification of functions, **10**, [1399]
property, transfer of, **10**, [1400]
provision for, **10**, [1399]
designated site, trespass on, **12(2)**, [1482]; **12(4)**, [124]
devolution, **30**, [610]
general note, **10**, [1]
referendums—
advertisements, **10**, [1258]
application of enactments, **10**, [1258]
ballot papers, **10**, [1255]–[1256], [1258]
Chief Counting Officer, **10**, [1249]
conduct of, **10**, [1258]
counting, **10**, [1258]
counting officers, **10**, [1258]
expenditure, **10**, [1253]
holding, **10**, [1249]
hours of polling, **10**, [1258]
legal proceedings, exclusion of, **10**, [1252]
premises, **10**, [1258]
returning officers, **10**, [1258]
drug trafficking. *See* **drug trafficking**
emergency regulations, consultation with ministers regarding, **50**, [321]
England, union with—
Acts of Parliament, **10**, [71]
Court of Session, **10**, [62]
ensigns armorial, **10**, [54]
heritable offices, **10**, [63]
inconsistent laws, **10**, [67]
monarchy, succession to, **10**, [55]
ratification of, **10**, [68]

Scotland—*contd*

England, union with—*contd*
religion, maintenance of, **10**, [68]
royal burghs, privileges of, **10**, [64], [77]
writers to the signet, **10**, [62]
English court, maintenance order registered in, **27**, [313]
English probates, recognition of, **18**, [589]
execution of process between England and Wales and Scotland, **12(2)**, [830]; **12(3)**, [1028]
execution of warrant in, **11(2)**, [554]
extradition jurisdiction, **18**, [751]
fixed penalties—
conditional offer of, **12(2)**, [355]
enforcement, **12(2)**, [356]
funds attached rule, abolition for cheques, **19(S)**, Financial 281
foreign disqualification, power to suspend, **38(2)**, [274]
Gaelic television programmes. *See* **Gaelic television**
Gun Barrel Proof Acts, extension of, **48**, 90
heraldry regalia, **10**, [66]
heritable property, disposition **41**, [262]
HM Revenue and Customs, amendment of provisions, **43(S)**, 719–20
human rights action, legislative competence, **7(1)**, [752]
inquiries, **10**, [879]
International Criminal Court, provisions relating to, **10**, [1215]
Island of Rockall, incorporation of, **10**, [87]
Joint Planning Inquiry Commission, reference of questions to, **46**, [879], [884]
judges, appointment and removal of, **10**, [1405]
justices of the peace, **10**, [76]
lease of agricultural property, accounting for, **42**, [712]
legitim, claim of, **42**, [684]
lieutenants—
appointment of, **26(1)**, [271]
areas, **26(1)**, [280]
clerks, **26(1)**, [275]
functions, **26(1)**, [276]
lord-lieutenant—
absence of, **26(1)**, [274]
appointment of, **26(1)**, [271]
deputies, **26(1)**, [272]
vice, **26(1)**, [273]
transitional provisions, **26(1)**, [281]
local acts, repeal of **41**, [696], [711]
Lord Advocate, investigatory powers. *See* **criminal investigations**
maintenance order registered in—
arrears, enforcement of, **27**, [294]
court to which sent, **27**, [291]
variation or discharge, evidence supporting, **27**, [295]
marriage—
parent of party residing in, **27**, [307]
party residing in, **27**, [307]
members of Parliament, **10**, [72]–[73]

Scotland—*contd*

mentally disordered patients—
application of Act to, **29**, [201]
compulsion in the community—
England and Wales, removal to, **29**, [136]
conditionally discharged—
England and Wales, transfer to, **29**, [137]
responsibilities for, transferred to, **29**, [134]
hospital—
meaning, **29**, [212]
visiting patients in, **29**, [211]
mental disorder, meaning, **29**, [210]
removal to, authorisation of, **29**, [132]
welfare, **29**, [211]
offences, proceeds of—
administrator of property, **12(2)**, [344]
civil recovery. *See* civil recovery of proceeds of unlawful conduct *above*
confiscation orders—
administration of property. *See* administrator *above*
enforcement—
designated country, in, **12(2)**, [337]
external orders, **12(2)**, [334], [335]
family home, disposal of, **12(2)**, [339]
property, meaning, **12(2)**, [320]
disclosure of information, **12(2)**, [815]–[817]
enforcement of orders **12(2)**, [318]
designated country, action in, **12(2)**, [337]
England and Wales, Scottish orders in, **12(2)**, [336]
external orders, registration of, **12(2)**, [335]
made outside United Kingdom, **12(2)**, [334]
realisable property—
administrator. *See* administrator of property *above*
compensation for, **12(2)**, [344]
diligence, effect of appointment on, **12(2)**, [344]
persons holding, sequestration of, **12(2)**, [338], [345]
sequestration, **12(2)**, [338], [345]
restraint order—
action in designated country, **12(2)**, [337]
administrator. *See* administrator of property *above*
cases for making, **12(2)**, [328]
enforcement in designated country, **12(2)**, [337]
forfeitable property, in relation to, **12(2)**, [329]
power to make, **12(2)**, [328]
property affected by—
arrestment, **12(2)**, [332]
inhibition, **12(2)**, [331]
variation or recall, **12(2)**, [330]
sequestration, **12(2)**, [338], [345]

Scotland—*contd*
Parliamentary Under Secretary for Health for, **10**, [496]
passenger services in rural areas, grants for, **37**, [444]
peers of, **10**, [65], [72]–[73]
planning authorities, **46**, [877]
Planning Inquiry Commission, reference of questions to, **46**, [878]
Presbyterian Church, securing, **10**, [68]
Principal Secretary of State for, **10**, [496]
private law, references to, **10**, [1436]
probate—
  estate may include estate in UK, **18**, [592]
  recognition of, **18**, [587], [588]
  trust property in England or Wales, **18**, [591]
probation orders, **12(2)**, [349]
  persons residing in England and Wales, **12(2)**, [350]
proceedings involving children, restriction on reporting, **12(2)**, [347]
process, service in, **11(2)**, [114], [271]
property used in crime, forfeiture—
  appeals, **12(2)**, [327]
  death of accused, on, **12(2)**, [340]
  district court, order of, **12(2)**, [322]
  restraint order, **12(2)**, [329]
  suspended order, **12(2)**, [321]
    property subject to, **12(2)**, [324]
    recall or variation of, **12(2)**, [325]
  warrant for search and seizure, **12(2)**, [323]
  wrongful, return of or compensation for, **12(2)**, [326]
Protestant Episcopal Church—
  meaning, **14**, 197
  person admitted in, restriction on, **14**, 197
Queen's Printer, **10**, [1402]
railways—
  disabled rail users, code of practice for, **38(2)**, [433]
  proceedings for offences, **38(1)**, [479]
  Scottish Ministers—
    breach of statutory duty, exclusion of liability for, **38(1)**, [395]
    duty to furnish information to, **38(1)**, [427]
    financial assistance by, **38(1)**, [413]
    franchise agreements—
      assets and shares, transfer of, **38(1)**, [390]
      conditions, **38(1)**, [392]
      invitations to tender—
        no adequate tenders, **38(1)**, [389]
        procedure, **38(1)**, [388]
      investment, encouragement of, **38(1)**, [396]
      penalties, statement of policy as to, **38(1)**, [401]
      register, keeping, **38(1)**, [423]
Scottish taxpayer—
  meaning, **10**, [1386]
  social security purposes, for, **10**, [1420]
Secretary for, **10**, [496]
seizure of property, **12(3)**, [48]

Scotland—*contd*
sequestration, effect of petition for, **4(2)**, [55]
serious or complex fraud, investigation—
  attendance for purposes of, **12(2)**, [308]
  documents, production of, **12(2)**, [308]
  entry and search powers, **12(2)**, [308]
  Lord Advocate's direction, **12(2)**, [307]
  nominated officers for, **12(2)**, [307]
  offences in relation to, **12(2)**, [309]
  powers of, **12(2)**, [308]
  warrant, issue of, **12(2)**, [308]
sheriff. *See* **sheriff**
sheriff court, recovery of tax in, **42**, [785]
sheriffs, offices and titles of **41**, [549]
solicitors admitted in—
  evidence of, **11(2)**, [309]; **11(4)**, [400]
  meaning, **11(2)**, [367]; **11(4)**, [462]
statutory nuisance, new provision in relation to, **35(2)**, [146]
succession, inheritance tax liability on, **42**, [746]
summary warrant, enforcement under, **43(S)**, 962–3, 1346–7
supervised release orders, **12(2)**, [348]
terrorism, forfeiture orders, **12(2)**, [961]
trade mark jurisdiction, **48**, 183
transfer of fines to or from, **11(2)**, [510]–[511]
trusts, **43(1)**, [19]
Tweed and Esk fisheries, regulation of, **10**, [1421]
universities, continuation of, **10**, [68]
unregistered company—
  inability to pay debts, **4(2)**, [260]
  meaning, **4(2)**, [256]
warrant to obtain evidence for use abroad, issue of, **12(3)**, [581]
winding up—
  application for leave to proceed, **4(2)**, [236]
  diligence, effect of, **4(2)**, [223]
  examination of persons, **4(2)**, [235]
  unregistered company, **4(2)**, [260]
  voluntary, **4(2)**, [154]

Scottish Administration
Civil Service, **10**, [1362]
Crown, rights and liabilities of, **10**, [1409]
Law Officers, **10**, [1359]
Ministers. *See* **Scottish Parliament**
non-ministerial offices, **10**, [1436]
office-holders, **10**, [1436]
references to, **10**, [1436]

Scottish Agricultural Securities Corporation
repeals, **1(2)**, [479], [483]

Scottish Environment Protection Agency
accounts, **35(2)**, [117]
air quality, reserve powers in relation to, **35(2)**, [134]
annual report, **35(2)**, [124]
audit, **35(2)**, [118]
borrowing—
  government guarantees, **35(2)**, [122]

Scottish Environment Protection Agency—*contd*

borrowing—*contd*
government loans, **35(2)**, [121]
powers, **35(2)**, [120]
charges, incidental power to impose, **35(2)**, [115]
charging schemes—
approval of, **35(2)**, [114]
greenhouse gas emissions permits, in respect of, **35(2)**, [113]
power to make, **35(2)**, [112]
transitional provisions, **35(2)**, [178]
costs and benefits in exercising powers, general duty to have regard to, **35(2)**, [110]
directions to, **35(2)**, [161]
financial duties, **35(2)**, [116]
functions—
continuity of exercise of, **35(2)**, [127]
delegation of, by Ministers, **35(2)**, [109]
discharge of, **35(1)**, [712]
incidental, **35(2)**, [108]
scope of, **35(1)**, [712]
government loans to, **35(2)**, [121]
grants to, **35(2)**, [119]
harm, power to remedy, **35(1)**, [731]
information—
disclosure of, **35(2)**, [152]
provision of, **35(2)**, [123]
inquiries and other hearings, **35(2)**, [125]
interpretation provisions, **35(2)**, [128]
Ministerial directions to, **35(2)**, [111]
records, **35(2)**, [117]
service of documents, **35(2)**, [162]
summary of provisions, **35(1)**, [1]
waste regulation, **35(1)**, [734]

Scottish Executive

accounts and audit, **10**, [1381]
Crown land, references to, **10**, [1432]
existing debt, **10**, [1382]
financial control, **10**, [1381]
Judicial Committee, decisions of, **10**, [1413]
members of, **10**, [1355]
oath, **10**, [424]
pensions, **43(1)**, [456]
remuneration, **10**, [1392]
information, publication of, **10**, [1394]
retrospective decisions, power of courts or tribunals to vary, **10**, [1412]
statutory bodies, borrowing by, **10**, [1379]

Scottish Homes

provision of services between other regulators, **22**, [461]
relevant authority, as, **22**, [7]
sale of houses at discount, stamp duty, **41**, [138], [145]

Scottish Law Commission

functions, **41**, [625]

Scottish National Heritage

traffic regulation in special areas, **37**, [189]

Scottish Parliament

accommodation, expenditure by members on, **43(1)**, [585]
Acts of—
interpretation, **10**, [1411]; **41**, [599]
legislative competence, outside, **10**, [1340]
making, **10**, [1339]
private legislation, **10**, [1404]
retrospective decisions, power of courts or tribunals to vary, **10**, [1412]
Royal Assent, **10**, [1339]
validity, **10**, [1339]
Acts of Union, effect of, **10**, [1348]
Bills, **10**, [1339]
ECJ, references to, **10**, [1345]
Judicial Committee, scrutiny by, **10**, [1344]
Royal Assent, submission for, **10**, [1343]
scrutiny, **10**, [1342]
Secretary of State, intervention by, **10**, [1346]
stages of, **10**, [1347]
Boundary Committee for Scotland—
reports, **10**, [1465]
review and recommendations by, **10**, [1464]
transfer of functions, **10**, [1460], [1464]
Clerk, **10**, [1331]
committees, **10**, [1445]
constituencies, substitution of provisions, **10**, [1460]
contempt of court, strict liability rule, **10**, [1353]
copyright in Bills of, **11(1)**, [994]
Corporate Body—
Crown status, **10**, [1444]
delegation of functions, **10**, [1444]
establishment, **10**, [1332]
membership, **10**, [1332], [1444]
powers, **10**, [1444]
proceedings and business of, **10**, [1444]
property, holding, **10**, [1444]
staff, **10**, [1444]
creation of, **32**, [848]
devolution issues—
England and Wales, proceedings in, **10**, [1454]
expenses, **10**, [1456]
House of Lords, proceedings in, **10**, [1456]
Judicial Committee, references to, **10**, [1456]
meaning, **10**, [1452]
Northern Ireland, proceedings in, **10**, [1455]
procedure, **10**, [1456]
references for decisions, **10**, [1456]
Scotland, proceedings in, **10**, [1453]
elections—
candidates, **10**, [1316]
electors, **10**, [1322]
extraordinary general, **10**, [1314]
ordinary general, **10**, [1313]
provision, power to make, **10**, [1323]
vacancies, filling, **10**, [1320]
establishment of, **10**, [1], [1312]

Scottish Parliament—*contd*
First Minister—
  appointment, **10**, [1356]
  choice of, **10**, [1357]
  office of, **10**, [1356]
  property and liabilities of, **10**, [1372]
human rights, compatibility of legislation
  with, **10**, [1368], [1410]
legislative competence, **10**, [1340]–[1341]
  enactments protected from modification,
    10, [1446]
  consequential modification, **10**, [1448]
  exceptions, **10**, [1447]
  financial assistance to industry, **10**, [1451]
  interpretation, **10**, [1451]
  reserved bodies, **10**, [1451]
  reserved matters, **10**, [1450]
    general reservations, **10**, [1449]
  Scottish public authorities, **10**, [1451]
Letters Patent, recording of, **10**, [1349]
maladministration, investigation of, **10**, [1401]
members—
  accommodation expenses, **44(2)**, [370]
  constituencies, for, **10**, [1312], [1443]
  disqualification, **10**, [1326]
    effect of, **10**, [1328]
    exceptions and relief from, **10**, [1327]
    judicial proceedings, **10**, [1329]
  European travel expenses, **44(2)**, [296]
  interests, register of, **10**, [1350]
  oath of allegiance, **10**, [1395]
  overnight expenses, **44(2)**, [295]
  regional, **10**, [1316], [1443]
    allocation of seats to, **10**, [1319]
    poll for, **10**, [1317]
    regional figures, calculation of,
      10, [1318]
    vacancies, filling, **10**, [1321]
  remuneration, **10**, [1392]
  resignation, **10**, [1325]
  return of, **10**, [1312]
  salaries—
    information, publication of, **10**, [1394]
    limits on, **10**, [1393]
    payment of, **10**, [1392]
    tax treatment, **43(1)**, [425]
  term of office, **10**, [1324]
Ministers—
  agency arrangements, **10**, [1403]
  appointment, **10**, [1358]
  borrowing by, **10**, [1377]
  functions—
    additional power to transfer, **10**, [1374]
    agreement, exercisable with, **10**, [1366]
    Community law, relating to, **10**, [1368]
    devolved competence, **10**, [1365]
    general transfer of, **10**, [1364]
    redistribution, agreed, **10**, [1418]
    shared powers, **10**, [1367]
    statutory, exercise of, **10**, [1363]
  junior, **10**, [1360]
  loans to, accounts of, **10**, [1383]
  modification of enactments, **10**, [1427]
  property and liabilities of, **10**, [1370]
  redistribution, agreed, **10**, [1419]

Scottish Parliament—*contd*
Ministers—*contd*
  stamp duty exemption, **10**, [1433]
  transfer of property to, **10**, [1371]
  Treasury, provision of information to,
    10, [1406]
  validity of acts of, **10**, [1361]
modification of enactments, **10**, [1458]
opposition parties, assistance for, **10**, [1407]
petitions, exemption from postage, **34**, [712]
Presiding Officer, **10**, [1330], [1445]
privileged statements in, **10**, [1352]
proceedings by or against, **10**, [1351]
proclamations, recording of, **10**, [1349]
public body, as, **10**, [1354]
regions, **10**, [1443]
  substitution of provisions, **10**, [1460]
reports before, **10**, [1431]
Scottish law officers, participation of,
  10, [1338]
Secretary of State—
  lending by, **10**, [1378]
  power to prevent or require action,
    10, [1369]
staff, **10**, [1362]
standing orders—
  committees, provision for, **10**, [1445]
  Crown interests, Bills concerning,
    10, [1445]
  preservation of order, for, **10**, [1445]
  Presiding officer and deputies, political
    parties of, **10**, [1445]
  public proceedings, provision for,
    10, [1445]
  regulation by, **10**, [1333]
  reporting and publication of proceedings,
    for, **10**, [1445]
  withdrawal of rights and privileges,
    provision for, **10**, [1445]
subordinate legislation—
  functions, adaptation of, **10**, [1416]
  member of Executive, exercise of functions
    by, **10**, [1428]
  modification of enactments by, **10**, [1415],
    [1424], [1434]
  power to make, **10**, [1422]
  pre-commencement enactments, provisions
    of, **10**, [1428]
  procedure for, **10**, [1425], [1457]
  property, transfer of, **10**, [1426]
  provision for, **10**, [1414]
  scope of powers, **10**, [1423]
  ultra vires acts, remedying, **10**, [1417]
tax-varying power—
  additional tax, accounting for, **10**, [1388]
  basic rate, fixing, **10**, [1384]
  expenses, reimbursement of, **10**, [1391]
  income tax structure, changes to,
    10, [1387]
  modification of enactments, **10**, [1390]
  reduction, effect of, **10**, [1389]
  resolutions, **10**, [1384]–[1385]
  Scottish taxpayer, meaning, **10**, [1386]
time for meeting, calculation of, **10**, [1315]

Scottish Parliament—*contd*
　witnesses and documents—
　　generally, **10**, [1337]
　　notice, **10**, [1335]
　　oaths, **10**, [1337]
　　offences, **10**, [1336]
　　power to call for, **10**, [1334]

Scottish Public Services Ombudsman
　other commissioners, consultation with,
　25(2), [324]

scrap metal
　dealer—
　　books to be kept by, **47**, [57]
　　convicted, requirements imposed on,
　　　47, [59]
　　destruction of motor vehicles, notification
　　　of, **47**, [60]
　　partnerships, provisions as to, **47**, [63]
　　place of business, **47**, [56]
　　records of dealings, **47**, [57]
　　　special provisions, **47**, [58]
　　registration. *See* registration *below*
　　unregistered, penalty, **47**, [56]
　entry of stores—
　　inspection of scrap etc, **47**, [62]
　　obstruction of, **47**, [62]
　　police or authorised officer, by, **47**, [62]
　　warrant for, **47**, [62]
　itinerant collector—
　　meaning, **47**, [64]
　　offences and penalties, **47**, [58]
　　records to be kept, **47**, [58]
　　requirements, subject to, **47**, [58]
　motor vehicles, notification of destruction of,
　　47, [60]
　offences relating to, **47**, [61]
　processing, meaning, **47**, [57]
　registration of dealers—
　　application for, **47**, [56]
　　meaning, **47**, [64]
　　particulars required for, **47**, [56]
　　period of, **47**, [56]
　　register—
　　　amendment of, **47**, [56]
　　　local authority to keep, **47**, [56]
　　seller, false name given by, **47**, [61]
　summary of provisions, **47**, [1]

scrip certificate
　stamp duty, abolition, **41**, [152], [157]

SE. *See* **European Company/SE**

sea. *See also* **coast preservation works**
　accretions from, annexation of, **25(2)**, [62]
　bed, deposit of substances under, licensing,
　　49, [625]
　defence commissioners—
　　coast protection—
　　　board, representation on, **49**, [381]
　　　failure to carry out work, **49**, [393]
　　meaning, **49**, [422]

sea—*contd*
　dumping at. *See* **pollution** (sea)
　meaning, **49**, [484], [641]
　offences committed at, **12(1)**, [12]
　pollution. *See* **oil pollution**
　Royal Hospital School, admission of girls and
　　boys regardless of family connection,
　　3, [1519]
　sand, Devon and Cornwall, right to take,
　　49, [2]–[3]

Sea Fish Industry Authority
　accounts, **1(2)**, [165]
　annual report, **1(2)**, [165]
　body corporate, as, **1(2)**, [187]
　borrowing powers, **1(2)**, [160]
　chairman, **1(2)**, [155]
　committees of, **1(2)**, [187]
　constitution of, **1(2)**, [155]
　contract, member having interest in,
　　1(2), [187]
　Crown, not acting for, **1(2)**, [187]
　disclosure of information, **1(2)**, [166]
　documents, execution of, **1(2)**, [187]
　duties of, **1(2)**, [156]
　fees, charging, **1(2)**, [157]
　financial assistance—
　　giving, **1(2)**, [157]
　　scheme, administering, **1(2)**, [170]
　financial provisions, **1(2)**, [184]
　government loans to, **1(2)**, [161]
　grants to, **1(2)**, [162]
　guarantee of borrowings, **1(2)**, [163]
　Herring Industry Board, transfer of rights etc
　　from, **1(2)**, [189]
　industry outside UK, assisting, **1(2)**, [157]
　levy—
　　notice of, **1(2)**, [188]
　　rates of, **1(2)**, [158]
　　records and information on, **1(2)**, [159]
　　regulations on, **1(2)**, [158]
　meetings, **1(2)**, [187]
　members of, **1(2)**, [155], [187]
　Minister directing, **1(2)**, [156]
　officers and servants, **1(2)**, [187]
　powers of, **1(2)**, [157]
　procedure, **1(2)**, [187]
　property, dealing with, **1(2)**, [157]
　reserve funds, investment of, **1(2)**, [164]
　training, providing, **1(2)**, [157]
　validation of charges by, **1(2)**, [695]
　White Fish Authority, transfer of rights etc
　　from, **1(2)**, [189]

Sea Fish Licence Tribunal
　appeals to, **1(1)**, [720]

sea fisheries
　byelaws. *See under* local fisheries committee
　　below
　Channel Islands, provisions applying to,
　　1(1), [743], [772]; **1(2)**, [136], [220]
　conservation, **1(2)**, [486], [488]
　disclosure of information—
　　penalty for, **1(1)**, [778]

sea fisheries—*contd*
  disclosure of information—*contd*
    restriction on, **1(1)**, [777]
  districts. *See under* sea fisheries districts *below*
  financial provisions, **1(1)**, [739]
  fishery limits—
    British—
      access to, **1(2)**, [129]
      extent of, **1(2)**, [128]
    Channel Islands, provisions extending to,
      1(2), [136]
    Isle of Man, provisions extending to,
      1(2), [136]
    median line for, **1(2)**, [128]
    Northern Ireland, provisions extending to,
      1(2), [135]
    offences, **1(2)**, [130]
    orders as to, **1(2)**, [131]
    transitional provisions, **1(2)**, [138]
  fishery officer—
    British—
      appointment of, **1(1)**, [449], [561], [760]
        local fisheries committee, by,
          1(1), [615]
      assaulting, **1(2)**, [214]
      collision regulations, enforcing,
        1(1), [761]
      conventions, enforcing, **1(1)**, [762]
      entry on land, powers of, **1(2)**, [213]
      evidence of, **1(1)**, [764]
      examination and inquiry by, **1(1)**, [761]
      fishing boat—
        boarding, **1(1)**, [761]
        powers relating to, **1(1)**, [735]
        restricted area, in, powers on,
          1(2), [212]
      food emergency, as investigating officer
        during, **1(2)**, [244]
      investigating and enforcement officer,
        as, **1(2)**, [244]
      local byelaws, enforcing, **1(1)**, [615]
      meaning, **1(2)**, [254]
      obstructing, **1(2)**, [214]
      offences relating to, **1(1)**, [763]
      persons being, **1(1)**, [146], [760]
      port, detaining boat in, **1(1)**, [761]
      powers of, **1(1)**, [735], [761]; **1(2)**, [214]
      proceedings, liability in, **1(1)**, [763];
        1(2), [214]
      requiring boat to move, **1(1)**, [761]
      trans-shipment, powers relating to,
        1(2), [174]
    foreign—
      meaning, **1(1)**, [760]
      persons being, **1(1)**, [146]
      proceedings, liability in, **1(1)**, [763]
      obstructing, **1(1)**, [616]
      powers of, **1(1)**, [615]
  fishing boat—
    arrestment of, **1(1)**, [765]
    British—
      meaning, **1(1)**, [719]; **1(2)**, [219]
      size limits for fish, offences as to,
        1(1), [716]
    charterer, liability for offences, **1(1)**, [719]

sea fisheries—*contd*
  fishing boat—*contd*
    Community rules, enforcement of,
      1(2), [175]
    detention of, powers, **1(1)**, [131]
    distress for penalties, **1(1)**, [765]
    fishery officer, powers of. *See* fishery officer
      above
    fishing operations, regulation of,
      1(1), [759]
    foreign—
      British fishery limits, in, **1(2)**, [129]
      meaning, **1(1)**, [131], [771]; **1(2)**, [133]
      official papers, possession when in British
        waters, **1(1)**, [131]
      provisions applying to, **1(1)**, [759]
      size limits for fish, offences as to,
        1(1), [716]
    identification and marking, **1(1)**, [759]
    jurisdiction as to, **1(1)**, [133]
    licensing—
      conditions, differing, **1(1)**, [719]
      information, giving, **1(1)**, [719]
      provisions on, **1(1)**, [719]
      receiving of trans-shipped fish,
        1(1), [721]
      regulations, power to make, **1(1)**, [722]
      time spent at sea, appeals to Sea Fish
        Licence Tribunal as to restrictions, [720]
    master—
      liability of, **1(1)**, [151], [719]
      meaning, **1(1)**, [131]; **1(2)**, [175], [219]
      official papers, possession of, **1(1)**, [131]
    meaning, **1(1)**, [130], [155], [741];
      1(2), [175], [219]
    official papers, requiring, **1(1)**, [131]
      offences, **1(1)**, [131]
    registration, **1(1)**, [131]
    restrictions on fishing, **1(1)**, [724];
      1(2), [211]
    service of summons on, **1(1)**, [134]
    wreck, treated as, **1(1)**, [769]
  fishing gear—
    construction, etc, requirements on,
      1(1), [718]
    identification and marking, **1(1)**, [759]
    regulation of, **1(1)**, [718]
    restrictions on, **1(1)**, [718]
    wreck, treated as, **1(1)**, [769]
  fishing implements, byelaws on use of,
    1(1), [609]
  fishing operations—
    marine environmental purposes—
      meaning, **1(1)**, [725]
      power to restrict, for, **1(1)**, [725]
    power to restrict, **1(1)**, [724]
    regulation of conduct of, **1(1)**, [759]
  industry—
    Authority. *See* **Sea Fish Industry
      Authority**
    financial assistance schemes—
      administration by Authority, **1(2)**, [170]
      making, **1(2)**, [169]
      offences relating to, **1(2)**, [171]

sea fisheries—*contd*
  Isle of Man, provisions applying to,
    1(1), [743], [772]; **1(2)**, [220]
  landing of fish—
    declaration, requiring of, **1(1)**, [727]
    foreign-caught, regulation of, **1(1)**, [728]
    limitations, subject to, **1(1)**, [726]
    prohibition on, **1(1)**, [726]
    restrictions on, **1(2)**, [211]
    salmon or migratory trout, restriction on,
      1(1), [738]
    scientific operations, for, **1(1)**, [729]
  limits. *See* fishery limits *above*
  local fisheries committee—
    accounts of, **1(1)**, [622]
    byelaws, making of, **1(1)**, [609]
      confirmation of, **1(1)**, [612]
      contravention of, **1(1)**, [616]
      copies, supplying, **1(1)**, [614]
      evidence of, **1(1)**, [614]
      fishery officers, enforcement by,
        1(1), [615]
      marine environmental purposes, for,
        1(1), [610]
      power of, **1(1)**, [609]
      premises on which offence committed,
        entry on, **1(1)**, [617]
      restrictions on, **1(1)**, [611]
      revocation by Minister, **1(1)**, [613]
      salmon, as to, **1(2)**, [405]
    constitution of, **1(1)**, [606]
    enforcement of Acts by, **1(1)**, [618]
    establishment, **1(1)**, [605]
    expenses, payment of, **1(1)**, [622]
    fishery officers, appointing, **1(1)**, [615]
    fishing interests, members having,
      1(1), [606]
    harbour authority—
      committee, as, **1(1)**, [623]
      contributing to expenses of, **1(1)**, [618]
    harbour, contributing to works on,
      1(1), [618]
    institution of proceedings by, **1(1)**, [733]
    members of, **1(1)**, [606]
    predators, destroying, **1(1)**, [618]
    public fishery, restocking, **1(1)**, [618]
    representatives of, annual meeting of,
      1(1), [620]
    returns by, **1(1)**, [619]
    term of office, **1(1)**, [606]
    travelling expenses, payment of, **1(1)**, [621]
  marine environmental purposes—
    byelaws, for, **1(1)**, [610]
    fishing operations, power to restrict for,
      1(1), [725]
    meaning, **1(1)**, [610], [725]
  marine resources, measures to improve,
    1(1), [730]
  minor and consequential amendments relating
    to, **1(2)**, [585]
  nets—
    enforcement of orders, **1(1)**, [737]
    evasion of restrictions, **1(1)**, [718]
    mesh—
      measuring, **1(1)**, [718]

sea fisheries—*contd*
  nets—*contd*
    mesh—*contd*
      minimum size of, **1(1)**, [718]
    regulation of, **1(1)**, [718]
  North Sea. *See* **North Sea fisheries**
  Northern Ireland, protection in waters
    adjoining, **1(2)**, [181]
  offences—
    body corporate, by, **1(1)**, [732];
      1(2), [183], [216]
    compensation for damage caused by,
      1(1), [766]
    documents, evidence of, **1(1)**, [148]
    evidence of, **1(1)**, [764]
    fines—
      amounts, **1(1)**, [731]
      application of, **1(1)**, [135], [152]
      master, liability of, **1(1)**, [151], [719]
      recovery of, **1(1)**, [147], [765];
        1(2), [215]
      scale of, **1(1)**, [731]; **19(2)**, [25]
    fish farming, exemptions for, **1(2)**, [190],
      [191]
    forfeiture of fish, **1(1)**, [731]
    institution of proceedings, **1(1)**, [733]
    jurisdiction of courts, **1(1)**, [133], [149],
      [734], [767]; **1(2)**, [217]
    master, liability of, **1(1)**, [151], [719]
    penalties, **1(1)**, [132], [731]
    service in legal proceedings, **1(1)**, [150]
    summary prosecution, **1(1)**, [147]
  officers. *See* fishery officers *above*
  orders, making, **1(1)**, [740]
  publication of information, penalty for,
    1(1), [778]
  restriction on—
    power to order, **1(1)**, [724]
    salmon and migratory trout, relating to,
      1(1), [738]
  river authority, expenses of, **1(1)**, [624]
  Sea Fish Licence Tribunal, appeals to,
    1(1), [720]
  scientific operations, exemption for,
    1(1), [560]
  sea fish—
    meaning, **1(1)**, [130]
    salmon, not including, **1(1)**, [130]
  Sea Fish Licence Tribunal. *See* **Sea Fish
    Licence Tribunal**
  sea fisheries district—
    creation of, **1(1)**, [605]
    harbour authority, area under jurisdiction
      of, **1(1)**, [623]
    local inquiry, **1(1)**, [608]
    publication of draft order, **1(1)**, [608]
    ratepayers applying for order for,
      1(1), [607]
    river authority, adjoining area of,
      1(1), [623]
    uniting or dissolving, **1(1)**, [605]
  sea-fishing boat. *See* fishing boat *above*
  shellfish. *See* **shellfish**
  size limits—
    contravention of, **1(1)**, [716]

sea fisheries—*contd*
  size limits—*contd*
    course of business, for use in, **1(1)**, [717]
    enforcement of orders, **1(1)**, [736];
      1(2), [173]
  summary of provisions, **1(1)**, [124]
  trans-shipment of fish—
    declarations, requirement of, **1(1)**, [727]
    fishery officer, powers of, **1(2)**, [174]
    licensing—
      charge for, **1(1)**, [721]
      generally, **1(1)**, [721]
      offences, **1(1)**, [721]
        automatic recording equipment for,
          use of in proceedings for, **1(1)**, [723]
      regulations, power to make, **1(1)**, [722]
    offences, **1(1)**, [726]
    prohibition on, **1(1)**, [726]
    restrictions on, **1(2)**, [211]

sea freight
  financial assistance, **38(2)**, [202]

sea otter
  North Pacific, in, **1(1)**, [227]

sea wall
  expenditure on, treatment of, **44(1)**, [18]
  property income, deduction from for
    expenditure on, **44(3)**, [315]
    company, transfer involving, **44(3)**, [318]
    interest in premises, transfer of,
      44(3), [316]
    lease of premises, ending, **44(3)**, [317]

seabed
  exploitation activities—
    meaning, **44(1)**, [613]
    profits or gains, **44(1)**, [613]
  exploitation rights—
    meaning, **44(1)**, [613]
    profits or gains, **44(1)**, [613]
  exploration or exploitation activities,
    meaning, **42**, [305]
  exploration or exploitation rights—
    disposal of, **42**, [305]
    meaning, **42**, [305]

seafarer
  deduction from earnings—
    calculation, **44(2)**, [390]
    eligibility, **44(2)**, [389]
    incidental duties, place of performance,
      44(2), [394]
    limit on where UK duties make amount
      unreasonable, **44(2)**, [391]
    other deductions, taking account of,
      44(2), [392]
    ship, duties on board, **44(2)**, [393]
  employment as, meaning, **44(2)**, [395]
  ship, meaning, **44(2)**, [396]
  travel costs and expenses, **44(2)**, [383]

seal
  evidence of, **18**, [93]

seal fisheries
  Behring Sea, in—
    arbitration award—
      enactment of articles, **1(1)**, [177]
      forfeitures, provisions on, **1(1)**, [186]
      provisions of, **1(1)**, [185]
    close time in, **1(1)**, [187]
    distress, sums leviable by, **1(1)**, [186]
    document, proof of, **1(1)**, [186]
    duration of provisions, **1(1)**, [184]
    enforcement of provisions, **1(1)**, [180]
    equipment, meaning of, **1(1)**, [181]
    foreign ship, arrest of, **1(1)**, [186]
    master, liability of, **1(1)**, [180]
    offences—
      committed, where deemed to be,
        1(1), [186]
      institution of proceedings, time for,
        1(1), [186]
      penalties—
        application of, **1(1)**, [186]
        recovery of, **1(1)**, [186]
        punishment of, **1(1)**, [186]
    Orders in Council, **1(1)**, [179]
    seizure on reasonable grounds, liability for,
      1(1), [186]
    service of summons, **1(1)**, [186]
    ship—
      coast, lying off, jurisdiction over,
        1(1), [186]
      detention of, **1(1)**, [186]
    ship's papers, seizure of, **1(1)**, [178]
  close time—
    Behring Sea, **1(1)**, [187]
    Greenland coast, **1(1)**, [138]
    grey seals, for, **1(1)**, [781]
    offences and penalties, **1(1)**, [139]
  entry on land, power to authorise, **1(1)**, [790]
  foreign states, application of provisions to,
    1(1), [137]
  grey seal, close season, **1(1)**, [781]
  killing of seals—
    damage, to prevent, **1(1)**, [788]
    disabled seal, of, **1(1)**, [788]
    entry on land for, **1(1)**, [790]
    lawful action, as result of, **1(1)**, [788]
    offences—
      attempt to commit, **1(1)**, [787]
      exceptions, **1(1)**, [788]
      forfeiture, **1(1)**, [785]
      jurisdiction of courts, **1(1)**, [786]
      penalties, **1(1)**, [784]
      stop and search powers, **1(1)**, [783]
    order prohibiting, **1(1)**, [782]
    prohibited methods, **1(1)**, [780]
  licence, grant of, **1(1)**, [789]
  National Environmental Research Council,
    duty of, **1(1)**, [792]
  North Pacific, in—
    enforcement of provisions, **1(1)**, [189]
    evidence of statement, **1(1)**, [191]
    extension of provisions, **1(1)**, [230]
    Orders in Council, **1(1)**, [192]
    ports, prohibition on using, **1(1)**, [228]
    prohibited area, **1(1)**, [226]

seal fisheries—*contd*

North Pacific, in—*contd*

prohibition on hunting in, **1(1)**, [187]

regulations, power to make, **1(1)**, [188]

ship's papers, seizure of, **1(1)**, [190]

skins illegally captured, prohibition on importation, **1(1)**, [229]

notice, giving of, **1(1)**, [791]

offences—

Behring Sea. *See* Behring Sea *above*

distress of ship, **1(1)**, [141]

master and owner, liability of, **1(1)**, [140]

prosecution of, **1(1)**, [139]

prohibited methods of killing, **1(1)**, [780]

scientific or educational purposes, taking seal for, **1(1)**, [789]

sea otter, protection of, **1(1)**, [227]

seal, meaning, **1(1)**, [142]

summary of provisions, **1(1)**, [124]

zoological gardens, taking seal for, **1(1)**, [789]

seamen. *See also* **crew**

application of provisions, **39(2)**, [691]

assignments by, exemption from stamp duty, **41**, [77]

British, offences by, **39(2)**, [959]

British seamen's cards, issue of, **39(2)**, [745]

burial or cremation, expenses of, **39(2)**, [712]

canteens. *See* **intoxicating liquor**

certificates, production of, **39(2)**, [717]

civil liability—

absence without leave, for, **39(2)**, [736]

immigration laws, fines imposed under, **39(2)**, [738]

smuggling, for, **39(2)**, [737]

code of conduct, breach of, **39(2)**, [727]

concerted disobedience, **39(2)**, [726]

conduct, inquiry into—

holding, **39(2)**, [730]

re-hearing and appeal, **39(2)**, [731]

rules, **39(2)**, [732]

witness, summoning, **39(2)**, [735]

death, inquiry into, **39(2)**, [950]

discharge—

books, **39(2)**, [746]

meaning, **39(2)**, [750]

regulations on, **39(2)**, [694]

UK, ship ceasing to be registered in, **39(2)**, [696]

drink or drugs, capability affected by—

arrest without warrant, **39(2)**, [1051]

Crown service, application of provisions to, **39(2)**, [1055]

detention pending arrival of police, **39(2)**, [1050]

drug, meaning, **39(2)**, [1054]

enforcement, **39(2)**, [1048]

off duty, **39(2)**, [1045]

on duty, **39(2)**, [1044]

orders and regulations, **39(2)**, [1053]

prescribed limit, **39(2)**, [1047]

right of entry on ship, **39(2)**, [1052]

specimens, provision of, **39(2)**, [1049]

territorial application, **39(2)**, [1056]

employment, provisions applying to, **16**, [847]

seamen—*contd*

fitness, inquiry into, **39(2)**, [730]

left behind abroad—

employer's liability, limit of, **39(2)**, [740]

expenses, recovery of, **39(2)**, [741]

regulations, **39(2)**, [695], [739]

relief and maintenance of, **39(2)**, [739]

return of, **39(2)**, [739]

meaning, **39(2)**, [988]

medical etc treatment, expenses of, **39(2)**, [712]

national minimum wage, **16**, [947]

neglect of duty, **39(2)**, [726]

offenders, return of, **39(2)**, [960]

professional, **39(2)**, [1045]

provisions and water—

complaints, **39(2)**, [711]

regulations on, **39(2)**, [711]

qualification, production of documents, **39(2)**, [717]

ships, structures or individuals, conduct endangering, **39(2)**, [725]

unqualified person acting as qualified, **39(2)**, [719]

wage claims, jurisdiction, **11(2)**, [917]

wages—

account of, **39(2)**, [698]

allotment of, **39(2)**, [703]

assignment of, **39(2)**, [701]

attachment of earnings, **39(2)**, [701]

charges on, **39(2)**, [701]

dependants, claim for maintenance of, **39(2)**, [707]

disputes, **39(2)**, [700]

interest on, **39(2)**, [702]

payment of, **39(2)**, [697]

person named in allotment, action by, **39(2)**, [704]

regulations, **39(2)**, [699]

rights and remedies, **39(2)**, [706]

termination of employment, rights on, **39(2)**, [705]

wills by. *See* **will**

seaplane

byelaws as to, **4(1)**, [146]

vessels, when deemed, **4(1)**, [146]

search

arrest, on, **12(1)**, [872]

arrestable offences outside United Kingdom, as to, **12(3)**, [579]

article with blade or point, for, **12(1)**, [1097]

child in need of protection, for, **6**, [365]

children for, constable's powers, **6**, [432]

common law rules, abolition, **12(1)**, [899]

counterfeit currency, for, **12(1)**, [740]

cross-border arrest, after, **12(2)**, [237]

crossbows, for, **12(1)**, [1051]

detained person, of, **12(1)**, [900]

entry and seizure. *See* **police; search warrant**

explosives, **12(1)**, [167]

identity, to ascertain, **12(1)**, [901]

indecent display offences, **12(1)**, [715]

search—*contd*
intimate—
annual report, information in, **12(1)**, [902]
authorisation for, **12(1)**, [902]
custody record, details on, **12(1)**, [902]
drugs, for, **12(1)**, [902]
meaning, **12(1)**, [917]
place for carrying out, **12(1)**, [902]
reasons for authorising, **12(1)**, [902]
same sex, to be carried out by,
12(1), [902]
samples—
destruction of, **12(1)**, [915]
meaning, **12(1)**, [917]
taking, **12(1)**, [910]
use and destruction, restrictions on,
12(3), [53]
seizure of articles, **12(1)**, [902]
suitably qualified person, by, **12(1)**, [902]
offensive weapons, for, **12(1)**, [1097], [1100]
samples, non-intimate—
Class A drugs, testing for presence of,
12(1), [913], [914]; **12(4)**, [151]
consent, taking without, **12(2)**, [531]–[535]
destruction of, **12(1)**, [915]
meaning, **12(1)**, [917]
person detained after acquittal on grounds
of insanity or unfitness to plead, from,
12(2), [532]
pre-existing conviction for sexual etc
offence, taking from person having,
12(2), [531], [535]
taking, **12(1)**, [911]
taking electronically, **12(3)**, [52]
stop and search. *See* **police**
ultrasound scans, **12(1)**, [903]
x-rays, use of, **12(1)**, [903]

search warrant
amended provisions, **12(2)**, [1473]–[1474];
12(4), [118]
biological weapons, for, **12(1)**, [627]
child—
in need of protection, **6**, [365]
in search for, generally, **6**, [432]
computer, unauthorised access to, **12(2)**, [47],
[49]
counterfeit notes and coins, for, **12(1)**, [740]
criminal damage, thing intended for,
12(1), [601]
dangerous substances, search for,
12(1), [2391]
disclosure notice, following—
conditions for, **12(4)**, [86]
meaning, **12(4)**, [87]
offences, **12(4)**, [87]
documents constituting incitement to
disaffection, for, **12(1)**, [246]
drug trafficking, **12(2)**, [259]
execution of, **12(1)**, [850]
false instrument, for, **12(1)**, [726]
firearms offences, on, **12(1)**, [530]
harmful publications supplied to children,
for, **12(1)**, [280]

search warrant—*contd*
indecent photographs of children, for,
12(1), [703]
issue of, justices' powers, **12(1)**, [842]
landmines, in relation to, **12(2)**, [634]
nuclear material, for, **12(2)**, [611]
obscene publications, for, **12(1)**, [312], [386]
official secrets offences, on, **12(1)**, [214];
12(2), [11]
petroleum-spirit, for, **35(1)**, [108]
premises, entry and search of, **12(2)**, [1473]
proceeds of crime, investigation of. *See*
proceeds of crime
public stores offences, on, **12(1)**, [149]
quasi-military organisation, suspicion of,
12(1), [252]
racial hatred material, for, **12(1)**, [1018]
religious hatred material, for, **12(1)**, [1032]
safeguards, **12(1)**, [849]
serious or complex fraud investigation in case
of, **12(1)**, [1057]
ship employed by foreign state, for,
12(1), [133]
special procedure—
access to material, **12(1)**, [843]
application for order, **12(1)**, [930]
circuit judge, orders made by, **12(1)**, [930]
costs, **12(1)**, [930]
issue of, **12(1)**, [930]
stolen goods, for, **12(1)**, [578]
terrorism offences, on, **12(2)**, [909], [964]

seashore
byelaws for regulating use of, **35(1)**, [72]
excavation. *See* **coast protection work**
materials, removal or deposit of, **49**, [412]
meaning, **49**, [422]
rivers and waters excluded, **49**, [429]

seat belts
adults, **37**, [582]
bus passengers wearing, notification
requirements as to, **37**, [585]
children—
age and height, **37**, [583]
below age of fourteen, **37**, [583]
equipment, **37**, [584]
not wearing belts, restrictions on carrying,
37, [583]
offences arising, **38(1)**, [4]
proceedings for, **37**, [815]
passenger car—
meaning, **37**, [583]
travelling in, **37**, [583]
rear seat belts, wearing of, **37**, [583]
Northern Ireland, corresponding
provisions, **37**, [555]
regulations, **37**, [583], [587]
warning of prosecution for offences,
38(1), [1], [2]
exceptions to requirements, **37**, [582]
exemption from wearing, payments in respect
of applicants for, **37**, [142]
meaning, **37**, [583]

seat belts—*contd*
    Member states other than UK, authorised
      by, **37**, [582]

seats
    streets or public places, provision in,
      35(1), [93]

secondary schools. *See* **primary and
secondary schools**

Secret Intelligence Service. *See* **Intelligence
Service**

Secretary of State. *See also under name of
department*
    advertisements, dispensing with publication,
      22, [415]
    airports, transfer of, **25(2)**, [600]
    annual report by, **8**, 590
    annual report, repeal of requirement,
      8(1), [1257]
    atomic energy, powers and duties, **17(1)**, [76]
    Audit Commission studies. *See* **Audit
      Commission for Local Authorities**
    British Shipbuilders—
      directions to, **47**, [282]
      information to be furnished by, **47**, [287]
      loans to, **47**, [291]
    British Steel successor company, loans to,
      47, [420]
    byelaws, saving for, **25(1)**, [69]
    civil proceedings on behalf of company, repeal
      of power to bring, **8(1)**, [1254]
    company name, direction to change,
      8, 127–8, 131–2
    consent to disposal of housing land, **22**, [37]
    contributions—
      housing action areas, for, **22**, [215]
      improvement areas, for, **22**, [229]
      improvement of dwellings, for, **22**, [445]
      local housing authorities, to, **23**, [605]
        recovery of, **23**, [606]
      superseded housing provisions, under,
        22, [450]
    Corporation—
      delegation of functions to, **22**, [845]
      directions to, **22**, [477]
    corporation sole, becoming, **10**, [596]
    defective housing designation, **22**, [343]
      control over, **22**, [376]
    departments of office, changes in, **10**, [595]
    determinations by, **23**, [400]
    designs, rules as to, **11(1)**, [556]
    development area reports etc, **47**, [383]
    directions by—
      disposal of land, for, **25(2)**, [437], [438]
      Welsh Boundary Commission, to,
        25(2), [53]
    drainage works—
      foreshore, on, consent to, **20**, [319]
      saving of rights, **20**, [318]
      survey expenses, **20**, [320]
    electricity transfer schemes, powers as to,
      17(1), [834]

Secretary of State—*contd*
    energy conservation report, functions as to,
      17(2), [213]
    Export Credit Guarantee Department and
      Export Guarantees Advisory Council,
      performance of functions by, **47**, [463]
    finance for companies transferred to, **47**, [355]
    fines, power to up-rate level of, **24**, [398]
    forms, prescription of, **22**, [414]
    general duties and objective of, **17(1)**, [728]
      exceptions, **17(1)**, [731]
    generally, **10**, [1]
    grant, consents as to, **23**, [607]
    grants—
      ethnic minorities, as to, **25(1)**, [797]
      special social need, **25(1)**, [913]
    grants for drainage purposes, **19(3)**, [228]
    guidance, **23**, [482]
    health and safety, consultation on,
      17(1), [730]
    homeless persons—
      guidance as to, **23**, [495]
      information as to, provision of, **23**, [500]
    housing—
      contributions under superseded provisions,
        22, [450]
      defective, contributions in respect of,
        22, [384], [385]
      first-time buyers, assistance for, **22**, [322]
      local inquiries, power to require, **22**, [416]
    housing action area—
      contributions in respect of, **22**, [215]
      direction not to extend duration of,
        22, [221]
      functions as to, **22**, [211]
    housing action trust—
      area, designation of, **22**, [847]
      establishment of, **22**, [849]
      functions of. *See* **housing action trust**
    housing association, contributions to,
      22, [500]
    housing finance—
      consultations as to, **23**, [25]
      determination or direction as to, **23**, [25]
      statements by, **23**, [27]
    housing management, financial assistance for,
      22, [307]
    housing orders, **23**, [399]
    improvement area notification, **22**, [223]
    insurance companies, intervention in affairs.
      See **insurance company**
    land drainage provisions—
      officers, powers of, **20**, [288]
      rights, saving for, **20**, [315]
      service of notices, **20**, [289], [290]
    land, transfer of, **10**, [596]
    liability for damages, exemption from,
      11(3), [123]
    local authority—
      codes of practice, **25(2)**, [428], [429]
      control of, relaxation, **25(2)**, [427], [447]
      information, direction to publish,
        25(2), [430]
    local byelaws, confirming, **25(2)**, [188]

Secretary of State—*contd*
local government—
  areas, reviews of, **25(2)**, [50]
  Boundary Commission, directions to,
    25(2), [53]
  orders relating to, **25(2)**, [200]
  powers transferred from Treasury,
    25(2), [204]
local housing authority, supply of information
  by, **23**, [23]
local social services, guidance as to,
  25(1), [977]
London housing, powers as to, **25(2)**, [624]
London passenger transport services,
  consultations etc. *See* **London Regional
  Passengers' Committee**
market investigation references. *See*
  Competition Commission
new techniques, promotion of, **17(1)**, [853]
notices, dispensing with, **22**, [415]
orders and regulations, power to make,
  24, [396]
patent—
  grant of, immunity as to, **11(1)**, [756]
  rules, power to make, **11(1)**, [765]
police, powers and duties. *See* **police;
  Serious Organised Crime Agency**
privately let accommodation, consent for
  financial assistance, **22**, [780], [781]
professional, etc, services, contributions to,
  23, [42]
properties transferred to, **47**, [354]
prosecution of offences by, **8**, 592
provision of services between other
  regulators, **22**, [461]
public statues, powers,
  25(1), [12]–[17]. *See also* **statues**
radioactive substances—
  applications to be determined by, power to
    require, **17(2)**, [89]
  directions by, **17(2)**, [88]
  knowledge of applications, restricting,
    17(2), [90]
  waste, disposal of, **17(2)**, [94]
reasons for decisions, publication of,
  17(1), [810]
relevant authority, as, **22**, [7], [475]
  guidance, issue of, **23**, [383]
  information—
    disclosure by, **23**, [380]
    disclosure to, **23**, [379]
    enforcement of notice to provide,
      23, [378]
    general power to obtain, **23**, [377]
    levels of performance, as to, **23**, [382]
  insolvency of registered social landlord. *See*
    registered social landlord
  meaning, **23**, [403]
  powers of entry, **23**, [384]
  register of social landlords. *See* **registered
    social landlord**
  social housing grants by. *See* **registered
    social landlord**
  standards of performance, determining,
    23, [381]

Secretary of State—*contd*
renewal area, contributions to, **23**, [34]
salary, **10**, [612]
Scotland, for, **10**, [496]
second audit, power to require, **8(1)**, [1326]
social and environmental issues, guidance on,
  17(1), [729]
social housing. *See* **social housing**
statistical information, provision of,
  17(1), [852]
statutory auditors—
  delegation of functions—
    existing body, to, **8(1)**, [1331]
    order, **8(1)**, [1330], [1403]
  international obligations, directions to
    comply with, **8(1)**, [1332]
  matters to be notified, **8(1)**, [1301]
  power to call for information, **8(1)**, [1302]
  register of, **8(1)**, [1317]
  registered third country—
    matters to be notified, **8(1)**, [1321]
    power to call for information,
      8(1), [1322]
street trading, powers, **25(1)**, [390]
tenants' right to buy—
  legal proceedings, assistance in, **22**, [183]
  powers as to, **22**, [177]–[182]
traffic control, reserve powers, **25(2)**, [638]
United Kingdom Atomic Energy Authority,
  transfer schemes. *See* **United Kingdom
  Atomic Energy Authority**
water supply, charge relating to, **20**, [450],
  [451]
weights and measures, duties. *See* **weights
  and measures** (packaged goods)
Welsh Boundary Commission, directions to,
  25(2), [53]

Secretary of State for Education and Skills
allowances for eligible persons, paying—
  delegation of functions relating to,
    15(2), [495]–[496]
  education and training, in respect of,
    15(2), [492]
  learning agreements, **15(2)**, [493]
  transfer of functions relating to,
    15(2), [494]
awards, making—
  provision for, **15(1)**, [250]–[251]
  regulations on, **15(1)**, [250]–[251]
communication with schools, **15(2)**, [379]
default powers, **15(1)**, [622]
disputes, determination of, **15(1)**, [620]
duties of, **15(1)**, [1]
education support grant. *See* **education
  support grant**
educational institutions, powers as to,
  15(1), [358]
fees and expenses, assisting with, **15(1)**, [617]
financial assistance to education and child
  care—
    delegation of arrangements, **15(2)**, [355]
    forms of, **15(2)**, [353]
    power to give, **15(2)**, [352]
    terms, **15(2)**, [354]

Secretary of State for Education and Skills—*contd*
  further education institution, intervention in affairs, **15(1)**, [377]
  general duty of, **15(1)**, [505]
  governors, appointment of, **15(1)**, [626]
  grant-maintained schools. *See* **grant-maintained schools**
  grants—
    displaced persons, for education of, **15(1)**, [351], [615]
    education standards, for, **15(1)**, [611]
    educational services or research, for, **15(1)**, [612]
    Fellowship of Engineering, to, **15(1)**, [289]
    Further Education Unit, to, **15(1)**, [289]
    immigrants, special provision for, **15(1)**, [352]
    mandatory awards, **15(1)**, [350]
    nursery education, for. *See* **nursery education**
    payment of, **15(1)**, [616]
    promotion of learning or research, for, **15(1)**, [613]
    travellers, for education of, **15(1)**, [351], [615]
    Welsh, for teaching in, **15(1)**, [614]
  guidance, publication of, **15(1)**, [704]
  Higher Education Funding Councils—
    directions to, **15(1)**, [444]
    grants to, **15(1)**, [434]
    information and advice from, **15(1)**, [435]
    property, exercise of functions in relation to, **15(1)**, [435]
  information, power to require, **15(1)**, [670]
  local education authority—
    advisory services, power to require LEA to obtain, **15(2)**, [384]–[386]
    supplementary awards, **15(1)**, [269]
  medical examination of pupil, power to require, **15(1)**, [628]
  members of education committees, power to direct appointment, **15(1)**, [627]
  orders and regulations by, **15(1)**, [701]–[703]
  primary, secondary and further education, duty in respect of, **15(1)**, [506]
  proper performance of local education authority's functions, power to secure, **15(1)**, [623]–[625]
  regulations, power to make, **15(1)**, [364]–[365], [702]
  revocation and variation of orders and directions, **15(1)**, [703]
  student loans, powers as to, **15(1)**, [380]. *See also* **student loans**
  support for 13 to 19 year olds—
    consultation and coordination, **15(2)**, [281]
    provision of, **15(2)**, [280]
    social security information, supply of, **15(2)**, [285]
  teacher training, general duty as to, **15(1)**, [468]
  unreasonable exercise of functions, power to prevent, **15(1)**, [621]

Secretary of State for Employment. *Now* **Secretary of State for Work and Pensions**
  incorporation of, **16**, [164]

Secretary of State for Environment, Food and Rural Affairs
  co-operation between water regulators, **49**, [1365]
  forms, prescription of, **49**, [1027]
  regulations, power to make, **49**, [1026]
  water industry, general duties in respect of, **49**, [1359]

Secretary of State for the Environment, Transport and the Regions. *Now* **Secretary of State for Environment, Food and Rural Affairs; Secretary of State for Transport**

Secretary of State for Trade and Industry
  Codes of Practice—
    failure to comply with, **16**, [406], [407]
    later Code superseding, **16**, [408]
    power to issue, **16**, [402]
    procedure for issue, **16**, [403]
    revision, **16**, [404]
    revocation, **16**, [405]
    subject-matter of, **16**, [402]
  redundancies, notification of, **16**, [392]
    failure to comply, **16**, [393]

Secretary of State for Transport
  British Railways Board—
    subsidiaries, directions on, **38(1)**, [435]
    transfer of property from, **38(2)**, [191], [214]
  certificates, authentication of, **36**, [318]
  construction of works, powers to modify, **36**, [317]
  consultations by, **38(1)**, [333]
  directions, giving, **36**, [731]
  discount fare scheme, approval of, **38(1)**, [391]
  duty to furnish information to, **38(1)**, [427]
  expenses of, **36**, [735]
  franchise agreements—
    assets and shares, transfer of, **38(1)**, [390]
    conditions, **38(1)**, [392]
    invitations to tender—
      no adequate tenders, **38(1)**, [389]
      procedure, **38(1)**, [388]
  highway authority, as, **36**, [210]. *See also* **highway authority**
  inquiries, holding, **36**, [548], [1354]
  local enactments, repeal of, **36**, [732]
  network, use of installations comprised in, **38(1)**, [377]
  Office of Rail Regulation, provision of information by, **38(1)**, [418]
  orders—
    guided transport system, as to, **38(1)**, [291]
    inland waterways, as to, **38(1)**, [292]
  prosecutions, consent to, **38(1)**, [334]
  railway companies, not regarded as shadow director of, **38(1)**, [458]

Secretary of State for Transport—*contd*
railways—
  duties in relation to, **38(1)**, [349]
  financial status regulations, **38(1)**, [471]
register, keeping, **38(1)**, [422]
road humps, authorising, **36**, [1095]
security of railways—
  enforcement notices, **38(1)**, [463]
  inspections, **38(1)**, [464]
  instructions on, **38(1)**, [462]
transfer schemes—
  functions as to, **38(1)**, [443]
  information, power to require, **38(1)**, [442]
  power to make, **38(1)**, [434]
transport systems, orders for—
  applications for, **38(1)**, [295]
  appointed person, exercise of functions by,
    38(1), [308]
  compulsory purchase, authorisation of,
    38(1), [302]
  consents under enactments, **38(1)**, [305]
  Crown land, **38(1)**, [309]
  inquiries and hearings, **38(1)**, [301]
  made other than on application,
    38(1), [297]
  making, **38(1)**, [303]
  model clauses, **38(1)**, [298]
  national significance, schemes of,
    38(1), [299]
  objections to, **38(1)**, [300]
  other Member States affected, where,
    38(1), [296]
  power to apply for or object to,
    38(1), [306]
  power to make, **38(1)**, [290]
  publicity, **38(1)**, [304]
  refusal of, **38(1)**, [303]
  special parliamentary procedure,
    38(1), [302]
  subject-matter of, **38(1)**, [294], [345]
  validity of, **38(1)**, [307]

Secretary of State for Work and Pensions
employment agencies and businesses, licensing
  of, **16**, [90]
functions as to employment and training—
  advice, power to obtain, **16**, [67]
  careers services—
    arrangement for, **16**, [69]
    duty to ensure provision of, **16**, [68]
    inspection, **16**, [72]
    provision of, **16**, [70]
  disabled persons, **16**, [65], [74]
  education authorities providing services,
    control of, **16**, [70]
  financial provisions, **16**, [73]
  generally, **16**, [65]
  grants and loans, **16**, [65]
  inspection, **16**, [72]
  meaning of functions, **16**, [75]
  payments by, **16**, [65]
  research, as to, **16**, [67], [119]
  status of trainees etc, orders as to, **16**, [142]
  women and girls, **16**, [65]
grants and loans by, **16**, [65]

**Secretary of State for Work and
Pensions**—*contd*
  health and safety responsibilities, **16**, [79]
  industrial training, powers, **16**, [65]
  research, payments in aid, **16**, [67], [119]
  temporary employment, provision, **16**, [65]

secure tenancy
anti-social behaviour—
  demotion due to, **22**, [68]
  orders, disclosure of information as to,
    24, [362]
  right to buy, suspension of, **24**, [361]
assignment—
  exceptions from prohibition, **22**, [79]
  exchange, by way of, **22**, [80]
  matrimonial causes, as to, **22**, [76]
  prohibition of, **22**, [79]
  tenant condition not satisfied, **22**, [83]
  withholding consent, grounds for,
    22, [433]
  written consent required, **22**, [80]
assured tenancy, not being, **22**, [913]
conditions for, **22**, [65], [66]
death of tenant, effect, **22**, [75]
demoted tenancy becoming, **23**, [451]
exceptions from—
  agricultural holdings, **22**, [427]
  almshouses, **22**, [427]
  asylum-seekers, **22**, [427]
  business premises, **22**, [427]
  employees, accommodation for, **22**, [427]
  homeless persons, accommodation for,
    22, [427]
  introductory tenant, **22**, [427]
  land acquired for development, **22**, [427]
  licensed premises, **22**, [427]
  long tenancy, **22**, [427]
  short-term lease, **22**, [427]
  student accommodation, **22**, [427]
  temporary accommodation, **22**, [427]
exchange of—
  assignment by way of, **22**, [80]
  withholding consent to, **22**, [433]
forfeiture, restriction on, **22**, [67]
heating charges, **22**, [98]
housing action trust, disposal of dwelling
  subject to, **22**, [869]
  order, transfer by, **22**, [870]
information—
  allocation of housing, as to, **22**, [96]
  provision of, **22**, [94]
interest of landlord, requirement as to
  possession of, **22**, [828]
jurisdiction of county court, **22**, [101]
landlord condition, **22**, [65]
licensed occupation as, **22**, [64]
lodgers, power to take, **22**, [81]
long tenancy, meaning, **22**, [106]
management—
  arrangements for, publication of, **22**, [95]
  consultation on, **22**, [95]
  matters concerning, **22**, [95]
meaning, **22**, [64], [205]
member of family, meaning, **22**, [104], [206]

secure tenancy—*contd*
notification of tenancy becoming, **22**, [65]
periodic tenancy—
  fixed term, following, **22**, [74]
  succession to, **22**, [77]
  variation, notice of, **22**, [93]
possession—
  alternative accommodation—
    availability of, **22**, [429]
    suitability of, **22**, [431]
  anti-social behaviour, **22**, [73]
  grounds for, **22**, [69]–[71], [428]
    alternative accommodation available,
      22, [430]
    statement of, **22**, [70]
  order for, **22**, [67]
    postponement of, **22**, [72]
    stay or suspension, **22**, [72]
  proceedings for—
    adjournment, **22**, [72]
    discretion of court in, **22**, [72]
    notice required, **22**, [69], [70]
    periodic tenancy, in case of, **22**, [69]
  redevelopment schemes, approval of,
    22, [432]
  tenant's spouse, rights of, **22**, [72]
private sector landlord, consultation before
  disposal to, **22**, [97], [434]
public sector landlord, acquisition of interest
  of—
    applicant—
      approval of, **22**, [880]
      consultations by, **22**, [888]
      duty to complete, **22**, [890]
      notice of intention to proceed, **22**, [889]
      revocation of approval, **22**, [880], [896]
    application for, **22**, [882]
      approved persons, **22**, [880]
    completion, consequences of, **22**, [890]
    county court jurisdiction, **22**, [899]
    excluded houses, sum referable to,
      22, [886]
    excluded property, **22**, [881]
    forms, prescription of, **22**, [897]
    houses, amount attributable to, **22**, [886]
    information—
      advice and assistance, provision of,
        22, [892]
      service on applicant, **22**, [883]
    meaning, **22**, [879]
    orders and regulations, **22**, [898]
    property included, determination of,
      22, [884]
    public open spaces, inclusion of, **22**, [895]
    purchase price, determination of, **22**, [885]
    qualifying tenant, **22**, [879]
    relevant date, **22**, [879]
      tenancy granted after, **22**, [887]
    relevant period—
      extension of, **22**, [896]
      meaning, **22**, [896]
    right, generally, **22**, [879]
    subsequent disposals—
      consent for, **22**, [891]
      exempt, **22**, [891]

secure tenancy—*contd*
public sector landlord, acquisition of interest
  of—*contd*
    tenants—
      continuation of tenancy, **22**, [886]
      legal assistance for, **22**, [893]
    title, registration of, **22**, [894], [933]
repairing covenant—
  landlords' obligations under, **22**, [84]
  meaning, **22**, [84]
repairs, carrying out, **22**, [84]
requirements for, **22**, [828]
residence of servicemen. *See* **civil interests
  of servicemen**
right to buy. *See* **dwelling-house**
security of tenure, **22**, [67]
shared ownership lease. *See* **dwelling-house**
statutory tenancy, acquisition of
  dwelling-house subject to, **22**, [100]
subletting—
  consent to, **22**, [82]
  tenant condition not satisfied, **22**, [83]
succession to—
  assignment giving, **22**, [76]
  death of tenant, on, **22**, [75]
  periodic tenancy, **22**, [77]
  tenant himself as successor, **22**, [76]
  term certain, **22**, [78]
tenancies ceasing to be, **22**, [78]
tenant—
  improvements by—
    compensation for—
      persons qualifying for, **22**, [89]
      regulations, **22**, [88]
      right to, **22**, [88]
    conditional consent to, **22**, [87]
    consent required, **22**, [86]
    meaning, **22**, [85]
    refusal of consent, **22**, [86]
    reimbursement of cost, **22**, [90]
    rent not to be increased, **22**, [91]
    withholding consent to, **22**, [85], [86]
  meaning, **22**, [205]
  relationship with, **22**, [104]
  repairs, right to have carried out, **22**, [84]
tenant condition, **22**, [66]
term certain, for—
  assignment of, **22**, [79]
  devolution of, **22**, [78]
termination of—
  grounds for, **22**, [69], [71], [428]–[430]
  periodic tenancy arising on, **22**, [74]
  proceedings for possession on, **22**, [69],
    [70]
terms of, variation of, **22**, [92]

secure training centres
inspection of, by Chief Inspector,
  15(2), [860]

securities
acquired under emergency powers, no
  compensation for, **9**, [131]
ad valorem duty on, **41**, [35]
bearer, investment in, **48**, 458, 637

securities—*contd*
"buying back", meaning, **44(4)**, [578]
capital gains tax. *See* **capital gains tax**
chargeable. *See under* **clearance services;
depository receipts**
Commonwealth government, unstamped,
  issue of, **41**, [42]
competent authority. *See* official listing *below*
corporate governance rules, **8(1)**, [1347],
  [1351]; **19(2)**, [75], [124]
  breach of—
    investigations, **19(2)**, [137]
    penalties, **19(2)**, [128]–[131]
  competition scrutiny, **19(2)**, [132]
dealer in, trade profits. *See* **trade profits**
dealing in—
  borrowed money, exclusion of interest on,
    44(1), [322]
  circulating capital, held as, conversion of,
    44(1), [321]
  reserves, taxation of amount taken to,
    44(1), [320]
  tax-free Treasury securities, interest on,
    44(1), [322]
debenture. *See* **debenture**
debt, meaning, **19(2)**, [143]
disclosure rules, **19(2)**, [75]
  breach of—
    competent authority's powers where UK
      is host member state, **19(2)**, [140]
    investigations, **19(2)**, [137]
    penalties, **19(2)**, [128]–[131], [139]
  compliance, persons responsible for,
    19(2), [135]
  continued admission of financial
    instruments to trading, fees for., [138]
  general provisions, **19(2)**, [141]
  information requirements, disclosure of,
    19(2), [134]
  liability in damages, exemption from,
    19(2), [142]
  persons responsible for compliance with,
    19(2), [135]
  suspension of trading, **19(2)**, [136]
  trading, suspension of, **19(2)**, [136]
earn-outs treated as, **43(2)**, [224]
employee, **43(2)**, [253]
employment-related. *See also*
  employment-related securities
employment-related—
  anti-avoidance, and, **43(2)**, [762]
  deductible amounts, **43(S)**, 877–8
  obsolete provisions, repeal of, **43(S)**, 879
  taxable specific income, effect of remittance
    basis, **43(S)**, 1072, 1077
employment-related, research institution
  spin-out companies, in. *See* **research
  institution spin-out companies**
employment, relating to. *See* **employment**
enemy, transfer by or to, **50**, [191]
equity, meaning, **8**, 170
false or misleading statements, liability for,
  8(1), [1348]

securities—*contd*
FOTRA—
  income from—
    deductions, restrictions on, **44(3)**, [730]
    exemption of profits, **44(3)**, [728]
    introduction to provisions, **44(3)**, [727]
    trust, held on, **44(3)**, [729]
  modification of provisions, **43(1)**, [237]
  references to, **43(1)**, [237]
gift to charities, **44(1)**, [422]
gilt-edged, interest paid gross, **43(1)**, [320]
"gilt-edged", meaning, **44(4)**, [1031]
gilt stripping, **43(1)**, [250]
government. *See* **government stock**
government securities held by non-UK
  resident central banks, no income tax
  liability for, **44(4)**, [848]
holding, **44(4)**, [683]
income from, information on, **42**, [138]
insider dealings—
  applicable securities, **8**, 963–4, 973–4
  dealing, meaning, **8**, 964
  defences, **8**, 963, 971–3
  definition of offence, **8**, 962
  general note, **8**, 9–10
  information, made public, **8**, 966
  inside information, meaning, **8**, 965
  insiders, meaning, **8**, 965
  investigations into, **8**, 861–2
  issuer, meaning, **8**, 967
  penalties and prosecution, **8**, 968
  powers of entry, **8**, 866–7
  professional intermediary, meaning,
    8, 966–7
  regulated market, meaning, **8**, 967
  territorial scope of offence, **8**, 969
interest—
  accrued, transfer with or without. *See*
    transfer *below*
  exemptions relating to, **44(4)**, [686]–[689]
  meaning, **44(4)**, [679]
  payment day, meaning, **44(4)**, [680]
  period, meaning, **44(4)**, [681]
issuers—
  meaning, **19(2)**, [143]
  obligations of, **19(2)**, [133]
  published information, liability for,
    19(2), [127]
listed—
  issuers, body for supervision of periodic
    accounts and reports of—
    appointment of, **8(1)**, [15]
    disclosure of information to auditors,
      statement as to, **8(1)**, [16]
    documents, information and
      explanations, power of authorised
      person to require, **8(1)**, [16]
listing. *See* official listing *below*
listing particulars—
  competent authority, submission to,
    19(2), [82]
  disclosure—
    competition scrutiny, **19(2)**, [132]
    exemption from, **19(2)**, [85]
    general duty of, **19(2)**, [83]

securities—*contd*
listing particulars—*contd*
false or misleading, compensation for, **19(2)**, [125], [529]
meaning, **19(2)**, [82]
supplementary, **19(2)**, [84]
loan relationships. *See* **loan relationships**
manufactured interest on UK securities—
administrative provisions, powers about, **44(4)**, [594]
allowable deductions—
double counting, restriction on, **44(4)**, [588]
matching, **44(4)**, [587]
foreign payers, reverse charge, **44(4)**, [928]
generally, **44(4)**, [586]
payments by UK residents, **44(4)**, [927]
power to deal with, **44(4)**, [593]
relief, eligibility for, **44(4)**, [595]
underlying payments—
exceeded by, **44(4)**, [591]
greater than, **44(4)**, [592]
underlying securities paid gross, cases where, **44(4)**, [929]
marketable. *See* **marketable security**
meaning, **8(1)**, [861]; **19(1)**, [314]; **19(2)**, [143]; **20**, [436], [804]; **44(4)**, [627]
nominal value of—
foreign currency securities, **44(4)**, [685]
generally, **44(4)**, [684]
non-FOTRA, treatment of, **43(1)**, [381]
official listing—
application for, **19(2)**, [77]
decisions on, **19(2)**, [78]
fees, **19(2)**, [137]
competent authority, **19(2)**, [73], [527]
competition scrutiny, **19(2)**, [132]
discontinuance, **19(2)**, [79]
procedure, **19(2)**, [80], [81]
duty of competent authority, **19(2)**, [74]
fees, **19(2)**, [137]
list, maintenance of, **19(2)**, [76]
listing rules, **19(2)**, [75]
breach of, investigations, **19(2)**, [137]
general provisions, **19(2)**, [141]
liability in damages, exemption from, **19(2)**, [142]
penalties, **19(2)**, [128]–[131], [139]
particulars. *See* listing particulars *above*
rules—
general provisions, **19(2)**, [159]
liability in damages, exemption from, **19(2)**, [142]
sponsors—
arrangements with, **19(2)**, [108]
meaning, **19(2)**, [108]
public censure, **19(2)**, [109]
refusal or cancellation of approval, **19(2)**, [108]
rules, **19(2)**, [108]
suspension of, **19(2)**, [79]
procedure, **19(2)**, [80], [81]
overseas, meaning, **44(4)**, [575]

securities—*contd*
Part 6 rules—
breach of—
investigations, **19(2)**, [137]
penalties, **19(2)**, [128]
policy statement—
issue of, **19(2)**, [130]
procedure, **19(2)**, [131]
procedure, **19(2)**, [129]
definition, **19(2)**, [75]
general provisions, **19(2)**, [141]
liability in damages, exemption from, **19(2)**, [142]
publications, compensation for false or misleading statements in, **19(2)**, [126]
registers, power to obtain copies, **42**, [137]
relevant discounted, transfer of, **43(1)**, [430]
"repo", meaning, **44(4)**, [577]
restricted—
approved plans and schemes, through, **43(2)**, [320]
artificially depressed market value, with, **43(2)**, [319]
right to receive distributions, transfer of, **44(1)**, [454]
sale and repurchase of, **44(4)**, [877]
borrower—
effect on, **43(S)**, 665
finance charges, relief for, **43(S)**, 665–6
creditor quasi-repo—
meaning, **43(S)**, 667
sale of securities, effect on lender, **43(S)**, 667–8
creditor repo—
chargeable gains, ignored for, **43(S)**, 668–9
lender, change for finance return, **43(S)**, 668
manufactured payments, requirement to deduct tax from, **43(S)**, 669–70
meaning, **43(S)**, 666–7
sale of securities, effect on lender, **43(S)**, 667–8
debtor quasi-repo, meaning, **43(S)**, 664
debtor repo—
chargeable gains, ignored for, **43(S)**, 666
manufactured payments, requirement to deduct tax from, **43(S)**, 669–70
meaning, **43(S)**, 664
interpretation, **43(S)**, 670–1
manufactured payments, requirement to deduct tax from, **43(S)**, 669–70
minor and consequential amendments, **43(S)**, 673–7
nature of transaction, **43(S)**, 663
quasi-interest, arrangement designed to produce, **43(S)**, 669
Schedule D Cases III and IV, income charged under, **44(1)**, [13]
services. *See* **clearance services**
shares. *See* **shares**
stamp duty—
See also **stamp duty**
Commonwealth or foreign, issued unstamped, **41**, [42]

securities—*contd*
  stamp duty—*contd*
    exempt, **41**, [198]
    offences, fines, **41**, [42]
    transfer of, on, **41**, [159], [186], [187]
      abolition, **41**, [210]
      members of electronic transfer systems,
        to, **41**, [239]
    warrant to purchase, **41**, [198]
  stock lending—
    cash collateral under—
      deemed interest, and, **44(1)**, [457]
      quasi, meaning, **44(1)**, [458]
    manufactured payments, deemed, in case
      of, **44(1)**, [456]
    quasi, meaning, **44(1)**, [458]
  take-over offer. *See* **companies**
  tax advantages, transactions in, **43(1)**, [244]
  title to—
    evidencing and transferring—
      arrangements for, enabling, **8(1)**, [864]
      duty to consult on regulations,
        8(1), [867]
      order-making powers, **8(1)**, [865]
      procedures for, enabling, **8(1)**, [863]
      provisions included in regulations,
        8(1), [866]
      regulations, power to make, **8(1)**, [862]
      resolutions, forwarding to registrar,
        8(1), [868]
    meaning, **8(1)**, [861]
  transactions in. *See* **transactions in
    securities**
  transactions, information on, **42**, [135]
  transfer of—
    accrued interest, with **44(4)**, [631]
      calculation of, **44(4)**, [667]
      default, interest in, **44(4)**, [667]
      double taxation relief, **44(1)**, [587]
      excluded transferors and transferees,
        44(4), [647]–[649]
      payment, treatment of, **44(4)**, [640]
    accrued interest, without **44(4)**, [632]
      calculation of, **44(4)**, [667]
      default, interest in, **44(4)**, [667]
      double taxation relief, **44(1)**, [587]
      excluded transferors and transferees,
        44(4), [647]–[649]
      payment, treatment of, **44(4)**, [641]
    accrued profits and losses, calculation of,
      44(4), [636]–[639], [667]–[673]
    applicable transactions, **44(4)**, [628]
    charitable trusts, securities ceasing to be
      held on, **44(4)**, [660]
    different kinds, **44(4)**, [630]
    excluded transferors and transferees—
      charitable trusts, **44(4)**, [653]
      disregard of certain payments and
        transfers, **44(4)**, [646]
      individuals to whom remittance basis
        applies, **44(4)**, [652]
      manufactured payments, makers of,
        44(4), [655], [671]
      non-residents, **44(4)**, [651]
      pension scheme trustees, **44(4)**, [654]

securities—*contd*
  transfer of—*contd*
    excluded transferors and transferees—*contd*
      small holdings—
        individuals, **44(4)**, [647]
        personal representatives, **44(4)**, [648]
        trustees of disabled person's trusts,
          44(4), [649]
      traders, **44(4)**, [650]
    excluded transfers—
      sale and repurchase agreements,
        44(4), [662]
      non-standard, power to modify
        regulations for, **44(4)**, [664], [666]
      redemption arrangements, power to
        modify regulations for,
        44(4), [665]–[666]
      transfer under, **44(4)**, [663]
    stock lending, **44(4)**, [661]
  foreign currency securities—
    sterling equivalents of payments on
      transfers, **44(4)**, [672]
    unrealised interest payable in foreign
      currency, **44(4)**, [673]
  information, power to obtain, **44(1)**, [453]
  interest on—
    foreign trustees, **44(4)**, [688]
    generally, **44(4)**, [687]
  legatee, exception where transfer to,
    44(4), [644]
  new securities with extra return,
    44(4), [657], [670]
  nominees and trustees, **44(4)**, [674]–[675]
  owner becoming entitled to securities as
    trustee, **44(4)**, [659]
  "settlement day", meaning, **44(4)**, [682]
  strips of gilt-edge securities, **44(4)**, [656]
  trading stock, appropriations, **44(4)**, [658]
  transferees, **44(4)**, [629]
  transferors, **44(4)**, [629]
  unrealised interest, **44(4)**, [633]
    calculation of, **44(4)**, [668]–[669]
    default, interest in, **44(4)**, [668]–[669]
    payment, treatment of, **44(4)**, [642]
    received by transferee after, **44(4)**, [689]
  variable rate securities, **44(4)**, [634]
    meaning, **44(4)**, [635]
    payment, treatment of, **44(4)**, [643]
  transfer, simplified. *See* **stock transfer**
  transferable—
    admission to trading on regulated market,
      competent authority's power to suspend or
      prohibit, **19(2)**, [101], [104]
    home State, meaning, **19(2)**, [145]
    issuers—
      provision of information by, **19(2)**, [112]
      public censure of, **19(2)**, [102], [103]
      meaning, **19(2)**, [143]
    offer to public—
      competent authority's power to suspend
        or prohibit, **19(2)**, [100], [104]
      meaning, **19(2)**, [144]

securities—*contd*
  transferable—*contd*
    prospectus—
      approval by competent authority—
        application for, **19(2)**, [92]–[95]
        fees, **19(2)**, [138]
        criteria for, **19(2)**, [90]
        requirements imposed as condition
          of, **19(2)**, [99]
      competition scrutiny, **19(2)**, [132]
      disclosure, exemptions from, **19(2)**, [91]
      election to have, **19(2)**, [89]
      exempt offers to public, **19(2)**, [88]
      false or misleading statements in,
        compensation for, **19(2)**, [125]
      investor's right to withdraw where no
        final offer price in prospectus,
        19(2), [106]
      passporting—
        approval in another EEA State,
          19(2), [97]
        host Member State, provision of
          information to, **19(2)**, [98]
      prohibition of dealing without
        approved, **19(2)**, [87], [530], [531]
      rules, **19(2)**, [75]
        breach of—
          investigations, **19(2)**, [137]
          penalties, **19(2)**, [128]–[131], [139]
        general provisions, **19(2)**, [141]
        liability in damages, exemption from,
          19(2), [142]
      rules for, **19(2)**, [86]
      supplementary, **19(2)**, [96]
    register of investors, **19(2)**, [107]
  transitional provisions, **44(1)**, [691]
  transparency rules, **19(2)**, [75], [110]
    breach of—
      competent authority's powers where UK
        is host member state, **19(2)**, [140]
      penalties, **19(2)**, [128]–[131], [139]
    competition scrutiny, **19(2)**, [132]
    continued admission of financial
      instruments to trading, fees for,
      19(2), [138]
    general provisions, **19(2)**, [141]
    information, competent authority's power
      to call for, **19(2)**, [117]–[119]
    infringement of—
      public censure of issuer, **19(2)**, [120]
      suspension or prohibition of trading,
        power of, **19(2)**, [121], [122]
      Tribunal, referral to, **19(2)**, [123]
    interpretation provisions, **19(2)**, [115]
    liability in damages, exemption from,
      19(2), [142]
    proposed amendment of issuer's
      constitution, notification of, **19(2)**, [114]
    supplementary provisions, **19(2)**, [116]
    voteholder information, provision of,
      19(2), [111]
    voting rights held by issuer, notification
      of, **19(2)**, [113]
  Treasury, **43(1)**, [379]
    power to issue, **19(2)**, [735]

securities—*contd*
  UK gilts—
    administration, **43(2)**, [130]
    Bank of England, discharge of functions in
      place of Bank of Ireland, **43(2)**, [128]
    registers kept in Ireland, closure of,
      43(2), [129]
  unlisted. *See* **unlisted securities**

securities options
  acquisition, no charge on, **44(2)**, [511]
  application of provisions, **44(2)**, [507]
  associated persons, meaning, **44(2)**, [508]
  cases in which provisions not applying,
    44(2), [510]
  definitions, **44(2)**, [520]
  exchange of, **44(2)**, [519]
  introduction to taxation, **44(2)**, [509]
  PAYE on, **44(2)**, [700]
  post-acquisition chargeable events—
    amount of charge, **44(2)**, [514]
    charge on occurrence of, **44(2)**, [512]
    deductible amounts, **44(2)**, [516]
    events being, **44(2)**, [513]
    gain realised on, amount of, **44(2)**, [515]
    secondary Class 1 contributions, relief for,
      44(2), [517]
    special contribution, relief for, **44(2)**, [518]

securitisation company
  accounting standards, application of,
    43(2), [636]; **43(S)**, 101
  asset-holding, **43(2)**, [636]
  commercial paper funded, **43(2)**, [636]
  connected persons, **43(2)**, [636]
  intermediate borrowing, **43(2)**, [636];
    43(S), 101
  meaning, **43(2)**, [636]
  note-issuing, **43(2)**, [636]; **43(S)**, 101
  old UK GAAP, application of, **43(S)**, 555–6
  taxation of, **43(2)**, [637]
  warehouse, **43(2)**, [636]

security
  entry on land on giving, **9**, [48]–[49], [297]
  power of attorney given as, **1(1)**, [21]
  private. *See* **private security industry**

security assets and services
  benefits in kind, as. *See* **income tax**
  costs and expenses of, **44(2)**, [388]

security goods
  reduced rate VAT, **50**, [149]

security of tenure
  assured agricultural occupancy, **22**, [823]
  assured tenancy. *See* **assured tenancy**
  business premises, of. *See* **business premises**
  ground lease, tenants under, **21**, [154]
  long residential tenancy, on ending of,
    23, [44], [55]
  regulated tenancy, under. *See* **regulated
    tenancy**

security of tenure—*contd*
rent agreement with tenant having. *See*
 regulated tenancy
residential tenant on long lease, of. *See*
 protected long tenancy
restricted covenant, under, **21**, [605]
secure tenancy, **22**, [67]
statutory tenancy, under, **21**, [522]

Security Service
continuation of, **10**, [693]
Director-General, duties of, **10**, [694]
disclosure of information, **10**, [694]
function of, **10**, [693]

sedition
alien, acts by, likely to cause, **31**, [6]

seduction
action for, abolition, **45**, [954], [983]

See **(ecclesiastical)**
change of name of, **14**, 1178; **14(S)**, 135
suffragan—
 creation of, **14(S)**, 142
 filling of, **14(S)**, 141

seeds. *See also* **plants**
allium, maintenance of purity of, **1(1)**, [577]
beta, maintenance of purity of, **1(1)**, [577]
brassica, maintenance of purity of, **1(1)**, [577]
Channel Islands, extension of provisions to,
 1(1), [584]
controlled crops or plants—
 injurious cross-pollination, prevention,
  1(1), [577]
  notices, **1(1)**, [577], [587]
 meaning, **1(1)**, [577]
corporation, offences by, **1(1)**, [579]
criminal proceedings—
 institution of, **1(1)**, [573]
 samples, use in, **1(1)**, [571]
dealers—
 civil liabilities, **1(1)**, [566]
 information and records, **1(1)**, [565]
deleterious, prevention of sale, **1(1)**, [565]
description, regulation of, **1(1)**, [565]
disease, prevention of spread of, **1(1)**, [565]
entry, powers of, **1(1)**, [570], [577]
export, regulation of, **1(1)**, [565]
gazette, publication, **1(1)**, [578]
import, regulation of, **1(1)**, [565]
injurious cross-pollination, prevention,
 1(1), [577], [587]
Isle of Man, extension of provisions to,
 1(1), [584]
marketing, regulation of, **1(1)**, [565]
meaning, **1(1)**, [575]
Northern Ireland, application of provisions,
 1(1), [583]
notices, publication, **1(1)**, [578]
offences—
 contravention of provisions, interpretation,
  1(1), [575]
 corporation, by, **1(1)**, [579]

seeds—*contd*
offences—*contd*
 defences in proceedings, **1(1)**, [567]
 general provisions, **1(1)**, [579]
 obstruction of officers, **1(1)**, [570], [577]
 regulations, contravention, **1(1)**, [565]
 samples, use in proceedings, **1(1)**, [571]
 tampering with samples, **1(1)**, [572]
packaging, regulations as to, **1(1)**, [565]
potatoes, application of provisions to,
 1(1), [574]
protected crops—
 injurious cross-pollination, prevention,
  1(1), [577]
  notices, **1(1)**, [577], [587]
 meaning, **1(1)**, [577]
purity of, maintenance, **1(1)**, [577]
regulations as to—
 exemptions, **1(1)**, [565]
 offences, defences in proceedings,
  1(1), [567]
 power to make, **1(1)**, [565], [580]
 samples, taking of, **1(1)**, [571]
sale—
 contract for, **1(1)**, [566]
 particulars, delivery or display, **1(1)**, [565]
 reliable information, **1(1)**, [565]
 weed seeds, containing, **1(1)**, [565]
samples—
 criminal proceedings, use in, **1(1)**, [571]
 method of taking, **1(1)**, [571]
 person authorised to take, **1(1)**, [565]
 taking of, **1(1)**, [565]
 tampering with, **1(1)**, [572]
 testing, for purposes of, **1(1)**, [566], [569]
statutory statement—
 false, **1(1)**, [571]
 particulars in, **1(1)**, [566]
 presumption as to, **1(1)**, [568]
 warranty, as, **1(1)**, [566]
testing—
 certificate of test, **1(1)**, [569]
 sale without, prevention, **1(1)**, [565]
 sample for purposes of, **1(1)**, [571]
 stations—
  licensing, **1(1)**, [565]
  official, **1(1)**, [569]
  procedure at, **1(1)**, [565]
warranty as to, **1(1)**, [566]

Seirbheis nam Meadhanan Gàidhlig. *See*
Gaelic Media Service

seisin
abolition of stamp duty on, **41**, [152], [157]

seizure
appropriate judicial authority—
 application to, **12(3)**, [39]
 meaning, **12(3)**, [44]
copies, taking, **12(3)**, [43]
definitions and interpretation, **12(3)**, [46]
documents, of, **12(2)**, [1438]; **12(4)**, [86]
duty to secure property, **12(3)**, [40], [41]

seizure—*contd*

examination and return of property, **12(3)**, [33]

excluded material, return of, **12(3)**, [35], [64]

HM Revenue and Customs officers, powers of, **12(3)**, [47]

inextricably linked property, use of, **12(3)**, [42]

items subject to legal privilege, return of, **12(3)**, [34]

meaning, **12(3)**, [45]

person to whom property returned, **12(3)**, [38]

powers of—

   application of, **12(3)**, [62]–[64]

   designated by order, **12(3)**, [49]

   judicial authority, application to, **12(3)**, [39]

   notice of exercise of, **12(3)**, [32]

   persons, from, **12(3)**, [31], [63]

   police. *See* **police**

   premises, from, **12(3)**, [30], [62]

   Revenue and Customs, officers of, **12(3)**, [47]

retention of items, **12(3)**, [37]

police, by, **12(3)**, [36]

Scotland, **12(3)**, [48]

special procedure material, return of, **12(3)**, [35], [64]

self-assessment

corporation tax—

   amendment during enquiry, **43(1)**, [396]

   appointed day, **43(1)**, [406]

   Inland Revenue determination taking effect as, **43(1)**, [397]

double taxation relief, **43(1)**, [115]

exploitation of provisions, prevention of—

   interpretation, **43(1)**, [176]

   procedural provisions, **43(1)**, [175]

   Schedule D Cases I and II, **43(1)**, [173]

   Schedule D Cases III, IV and V, **43(1)**, [174]

loss relief, **43(1)**, [84]

machinery of, amendments, **43(2)**, [52]

overdue tax, **43(1)**, [264]

payment after amendment or correction, due date, **42**, [266]

return, gift aid through, **43(2)**, [316]

returns including, **42**, [101]

transitional provisions, **43(1)**, [115], [172]

trustees, liability of, **43(1)**, [146]

self-build society. *See also* **housing association**

claim, provisions on, **44(1)**, [328]

land, acquisition by Corporation, **22**, [487]

loans to—

   power to make, **22**, [480]

   security for, **22**, [480]

meaning, **22**, [5], [455]; **44(1)**, [328]

semen

taking as sample. *See* **search (intimate)**

sentence. *See also* **imprisonment**

absolute and conditional discharge. *See* **absolute discharge; conditional discharge**

Air Force—

   Army Act, application of, **3**, [626]

   civil prison, served in, **3**, [894]

   commencement of, **3**, [884]

   commanding officer, awarded by, **3**, [885]

   consecutive terms, **3**, [886]

   country in which served, **3**, [896]

   defect in warrant, **3**, [912]

   detention—

      restrictions on, **3**, [893]

      total period of, **3**, [888]

   duration, **3**, [887]

   Imprisonment and Detention Rules, **3**, [891]

   military establishment, application to, **3**, [899]

   postponement, **3**, [890]

   promulgation, **3**, [909]

   suspended, **3**, [884], [889]

   UK, served outside, **3**, [895]

appeal against. *See* **criminal appeal**

appeal to Crown Court, **11(2)**, [721]

armed forces, offence by. *See* **armed forces**

army—

   civil offence, for, **3**, [613]

   civil prison, served in, **3**, [621]

   commencement of, **3**, [611]–[612]

   compassionate grounds, release on, **3**, [614]

   consecutive terms, **3**, [613]

   country to be served in, **3**, [623]

   detention, of, prison, serving in, **3**, [620]

   duration of, **3**, [614]

   Imprisonment and Detention Rules, **3**, [618]–[619]

   imprisonment, outside UK, served, **3**, [622]

   postponement of, **3**, [617]

   promulgation, **3**, [636]

   recall, **3**, [614]

   suspended—

      commencement of, **3**, [611]

      generally, **3**, [616]

attendance centre orders. *See* **attendance centre order**

Borstal training. *See* **Borstal training**

committal for—

   another offence, offender committed in respect of, **12(2)**, [721], [722]

   child or young person, indication of guilty plea by, **12(2)**, [715]

      powers of Crown Court, **12(2)**, [720]

      related offences, with, **12(2)**, [718]

   Crown Court, powers of, **12(2)**, [719], [720], [722]

   dangerous adult offenders, of, **12(2)**, [714], [720]

sentence—*contd*
  committal for—*contd*
    dangerous young offenders, of,
      12(2), [716], [720]
    indication of guilty plea to offence triable
      either way, on, **12(2)**, [717], [719]
    summary trial of offence triable either way,
      of, **12(2)**, [713], [719]
  community, meaning, **12(2)**, [41]
  community order. *See* **community orders**
  offender aged under 16—
    action plan orders. *See* **action plan
      order**
    supervision orders. *See* **supervision
      order**
  compensation orders. *See* **compensation
    order**
  conditional caution—
    conditions, **12(4)**, [260]
    failure to comply, arrest for, **12(4)**, [261]
    financial penalties, **12(4)**, [260]
  Crown Court, of—
    alteration, **12(2)**, [829]
    commencement of, **12(2)**, [828]
  custodial. *See* **custodial sentence**
  death, of. *See* **death sentence**
  deferment of, **12(2)**, [708], [712]
    conviction of offence during period of,
      12(2), [711]
    undertakings, **12(2)**, [708], [709]
      breach, **12(2)**, [710]
  duty of court to explain, **12(3)**, [906]
  financial reporting order. *See* **financial
    reporting order**
  guilty plea, reduction for, **12(3)**, [875]
  imprisonment. *See* **imprisonment**
  increase in—
    disability, for aggravation related to,
      12(3), [877]
    racial or religious aggravation, for,
      12(3), [876]
    sexual orientation, for aggravation related
      to, **12(3)**, [877]
  indeterminate, determination of tariffs,
    12(4), [475]
  lenient, unduly. *See* **criminal procedure
    and practice** (sentencing)
  life—
    determination of tariff, **12(2)**, [777]
    minimum term, determination of,
      12(3), [1007], [1091]
    reasons for deciding on order, court
      giving, **12(3)**, [1008]
  meaning, **12(1)**, [464], [1081]
  mentally disordered offender, dealing with,
    12(3), [898]
  mitigation of, **12(3)**, [898]
  navy—
    commencement of, **3**, [1160]
    compassionate release, periods of, **3**, [1163]
    detention—
      consecutive, **3**, [1162]
      country served in, **3**, [1157]
      Naval Detention Quarters Rules,
        3, [1156]

sentence—*contd*
  navy—*contd*
    detention—*contd*
      place of, **3**, [1155]
      summary trial, awarded on, **3**, [1161]
      total period, limitation on, **3**, [1165]
    guilty pleas, reduction of minimum for,
      3, [1065]
    imprisonment—
      civil prison, in, **3**, [1158]
      consecutive terms, **3**, [1162]
      country served in, **3**, [1157]
      place of, **3**, [1155]
    postponement of, **3**, [1166]
    prison officers, indemnity for, **3**, [1218]
    reconsideration, **3**, [1169]
    remission, **3**, [1169]
    removal of prisoners, **3**, [1159]
    summary trial, detention awarded on,
      3, [1161]
    suspension, **3**, [1167]
      committal or re-committal, **3**, [1168]
    unlawful absence, periods of, **3**, [1164]
  Northern Ireland. *See* **Northern Ireland**
  offender, assistance by—
    exclusion of public from proceedings,
      12(4), [94]
    reduction for, **12(4)**, [92]
    review on, **12(4)**, [93]
  period of remand on bail, credit for—
    release, amended provisions **12(4)**, [478]
    terms of imprisonment and detention,
      12(4), [477]
    transitional provisions, **12(4)**, [479], [564]
  quashing orders, variation on application for,
    11(2), [714]
  racial or religious aggravation, increase for,
    12(3), [876]
  remission for—
    magistrates' court, to—
      another magistrates' court, by,
        12(2), [725]
      youth court, by, **12(2)**, [724]
    youth court, to, **12(2)**, [723]
  restitution orders. *See* **restitution order**
  review of. *See under* **criminal procedure
    and practice**
  review on reference by Attorney General,
    12(4), [488]
  sexual offenders. *See* **sexual offences**
  summary of provisions, **12(1)**, [1]
  suspended. *See* **suspended sentence**
  transitional provisions, **12(2)**, [852]–[855]
  transitory modifications, **12(2)**, [851]
  young offender, on. *See* **young offenders**

sentencing
  amended provisions, **12(3)**, [1096], [1097]
  guidelines—
    compliance with, **12(3)**, [906]
    Council. *See* **Sentencing Guidelines
      Council**
    court, duty of, **12(3)**, [904]
    meaning, **12(3)**, [902]

sentencing—*contd*
purposes of, **12(3)**, [872]
offenders under 18, **12(3)**, [873];
12(4), [472]
seriousness of offence, determining,
12(3), [874]
surcharge—
amount of, **12(3)**, [893]
conviction, payable on, **12(4)**, [8]
power to order payment of, **12(3)**, [892]
transitional provisions, **12(3)**, [1114]
transitory and transitional provisions,
12(4), [578]

Sentencing Advisory Panel
continuation of, **12(3)**, [901]

Sentencing Guidelines Council
allocation guidelines—
framing or revision, **12(3)**, [902]
functions relating to, **12(3)**, [903]
annual report, **12(3)**, [905]
establishment of, **12(3)**, [899]
members of—
appointment, **12(3)**, [899]
eligibility, **12(3)**, [899]
remuneration and expenses, **12(3)**, [900]
resignation, **12(3)**, [900]
term of office, **12(3)**, [900]
vacancy among, **12(3)**, [900]
sentencing guidelines—
framing or revision, **12(3)**, [902]
functions relating to, **12(3)**, [903]

separation
adjournment of proceedings, **27**, [635]
arrangements for future—
court orders and agreements, **27**, [683]
declarations, **27**, [683]
exemptions, **27**, [683]
financial arrangements, **27**, [683]
negotiated agreements, **27**, [683]
requirements as to, **27**, [630]
children, provision for separate
representation, **27**, [679]
connected proceedings, **27**, [644]
financial provision—
arrangements, **27**, [636]
orders—
grounds for, in magistrates' court,
27, [637]
meaning, **27**, [684]
secured and unsecured payments orders,
27, [684]
general principles underlying provisions,
27, [622]
information meetings, requirements about
attendance at, **27**, [629]
intestacy, effect of, on, **27**, [640]
judicial—
adultery, parties to proceedings alleging,
27, [486]
agreement or arrangement, consideration
of, **27**, [447]
divorce following, **27**, [433]

separation—*contd*
judicial—*contd*
effect of decree, **27**, [448]
facts, proof of, **27**, [447]
grounds for, **27**, [447]
intestacy, succession on, **27**, [492]
parties to proceedings, **27**, [486]
recognition of decree—
British Isles, granted in, **27**, [582]
commencement of Act, grant before,
27, [589]
cross-proceedings, in, **27**, [584]
different systems of law, countries
having, **27**, [586]
generally, **27**, [127]
grounds for, **27**, [583]
proof of facts, **27**, [585]
refusal of, **27**, [588]
United Kingdom, in, **27**, [582]
reconciliation of parties, **27**, [447]
jurisdiction of court, **27**, [638]
marital breakdown—
requirements to be met, **27**, [626]
statement, **27**, [627]
mediation, directions with respect to,
27, [634]
minor and consequential amendments,
27, [691]
orders—
children, welfare of, **27**, [632]
circumstances in which made, **27**, [624]
power of court to make, **27**, [624]
procedure, rules as to, **27**, [633]
property adjustment orders, meaning,
27, [684]
reflection and consideration, requirement for
period of, **27**, [628]
separate representation for children, provision
for, **27**, [679]
stay of proceedings—
ancillary matters, **27**, [685]
concurrent proceedings, duty to furnish
particulars of, **27**, [685]
discharge of orders, **27**, [685]
discretionary stays, **27**, [685]
interpretation provisions, **27**, [685]
time when proceedings begin, **27**, [639]
transfer of certain tenancies on—
assured agricultural occupancy, **27**, [689]
assured tenancy, **27**, [689]
cases in which court may make order,
27, [688]
compensation, **27**, [690]
date when order made between spouses to
take effect, **27**, [690]
entitlement to occupy, references to,
27, [689]
interpretation provisions, **27**, [688]
liabilities and obligations in respect of
dwelling-house, **27**, [690]
matters to which court must have regard,
27, [688]
protected tenancy, **27**, [689]
remarriage of either spouse, **27**, [690]
rules of court, **27**, [690]

separation—*contd*
transfer of certain tenancies on—*contd*
secure tenancy, **27**, [689]
statutory tenancy, **27**, [689]

sepulture
rights for purposes of, **14**, 641

sequestration
debtor's property, **4(2)**, [9]
drug trafficking, property arising from,
Scotland, **12(2)**, [338], [345]
moneys payable by Crown, payment to,
13, [30]
petition for, effect of, **4(2)**, [55]

serious crime prevention order
appeal—
Court of Appeal, to, **12(4)**, [380], [381]
Crown Court, from, **12(4)**, [381]
decision of High Court, on, **12(4)**, [380]
applicant authorities, functions of,
12(4), [444]
authorised monitors—
compliance, enforcing, **12(4)**, [396]
costs, **12(4)**, [397]
meaning, **12(4)**, [396]
body corporate, against, **12(4)**, [387]
compliance with, authorised monitors,
12(4), [396]
Crown Court, jurisdiction of—
breach, variation on, **12(4)**, [378]
conviction, on, **12(4)**, [376]
variation on, **12(4)**, [377]
inter-relationship of orders, **12(4)**, [379]
proceedings in, **12(4)**, [393]
defined expressions, **12(4)**, [400]
discharge of, **12(4)**, [375]
duration of, **12(4)**, [373]
failure to comply with—
forfeiture, power of, **12(4)**, [383]
offence, **12(4)**, [382]
penalty for, **12(4)**, [382]
winding up petition, presentation of,
12(4), [384]–[386]
High Court—
appeal from, **12(4)**, [380]
power of to make, **12(4)**, [358]
proceedings in, **12(4)**, [392]
information, disclosure of, **12(4)**, [395]
information society services, effect on
provider of, **12(4)**, [391]
law enforcement officer—
documents, powers to retain, **12(4)**, [398]
meaning, **12(4)**, [362]
meaning, **12(4)**, [358]
notice requirements, **12(4)**, [367]
body corporate, **12(4)**, [387]
overseas body, against, **12(4)**, [390]
partnership, against, **12(4)**, [388]
prohibitions, restrictions or requirements in,
12(4), [362]
provision made by, **12(4)**, [362]
safeguards—
applicants, class of, **12(4)**, [365]

serious crime prevention order—*contd*
safeguards—*contd*
information—
banking information, **12(4)**, [370]
excluded material, **12(4)**, [370]
legal professional privilege, restrictions
for, **12(4)**, [369]
oral answers, restrictions on, **12(4)**, [368]
other enactments, relating to,
12(4), [371]
us, restrictions on, **12(4)**, [372]
minimum age limit, **12(4)**, [363]
notice requirements, **12(4)**, [367]
specified description, person failing
within, **12(4)**, [364]
third parties, representations by,
12(4), [366]
serious crime, involvement in—
commission by another person,
facilitating, **12(4)**, [361]
consideration by court, **12(4)**, [361]
England and Wales, **12(4)**, [359]
Northern Ireland, **12(4)**, [360], [443]
schedule of offence, **12(4)**, [442], [443]
third parties, representations by, **12(4)**, [366]
transitional and transitory provisions and
savings, **12(4)**, [462]
unincorporated association, against,
12(4), [389]
variation of, **12(4)**, [374]
breach, powers of Crown Court on,
12(4), [378]
conviction in Crown Court, on,
12(4), [377]
inter-relationship of orders, **12(4)**, [379]

Serious Fraud Office
constitution, **12(1)**, [1056]
Director—
annual reports by, **12(1)**, [1077]
application for serious crime prevention
order, **12(4)**, [365]
See also **serious crime prevention
order**
appointment, **12(1)**, [1056]
attendance before, **12(1)**, [1057]
Attorney General, superintendence of,
12(1), [1056]
bribery and corruption, pre-investigation
powers, **12(1)**, [1058]
delegation of powers by, **12(1)**, [1056]
documents, request for production,
12(1), [1057]
information, disclosure of, **12(1)**, [1059]
investigation, powers of, **12(1)**, [1056],
[1057]
See also **serious or complex fraud**
powers and duties, **12(1)**, [1056]
proceedings, conduct of, **12(1)**, [1056],
[1077]
prosecutions by, **12(1)**, [1077]
remuneration, **12(1)**, [1077]
Director of Prosecutions—
crime reduction, contribution to,
12(3), [171]

Serious Fraud Office—*contd*
  Director of Prosecutions—*contd*
    information—
      disclosure by, **12(3)**, [513]
      disclosure to, **12(3)**, [511], [512]
      Lord Advocate and Scottish Ministers,
        disclosure to and by, **12(3)**, [514]–[516]
      use of, **12(3)**, [510]
    staff, activities authorised to be done by,
      12(3), [173]
  establishment, **12(1)**, [1056]
  members—
    audience, right of, **12(1)**, [1056]
    powers, **12(1)**, [1056]
    qualification, **12(1)**, [1056]
  procedure, **12(1)**, [1077]
  staff, **12(1)**, [1077]

serious or complex fraud
  arraignment, **12(1)**, [1064]
  Attorney-General—
    regulations, power to make, **12(1)**, [1077]
    superintendence of, **12(1)**, [1056]
  broadcast reports of proceedings,
    12(1), [1068]
  committal proceedings, cessation,
    12(1), [1061]
  dismissal, application for, **12(1)**, [1062]
  information—
    agreements as to, **12(1)**, [1059]
    disclosure of—
      competent authorities, to, **12(1)**, [1059]
      generally, **12(1)**, [1059]
      HM Revenue and Customs, by,
        12(1), [1059]
  investigation—
    Channel Islands, **12(1)**, [1057]
    documents—
      concealment etc, **12(1)**, [1057]
      meaning, **12(1)**, [1057]
      production, **12(1)**, [1057]
      search warrant, issue of, **12(1)**, [1057]
    Isle of Man, **12(1)**, [1057]
    persons not members of Office, by,
      12(1), [1057]
    powers, **12(1)**, [1056], [1057]
  Northern Ireland, application of provisions,
    12(1), [1057], [1071]
  Office. *See* **Serious Fraud Office**
  person under investigation—
    attendance of, requirement, **12(1)**, [1057]
    meaning, **12(1)**, [1057]
    offences by, **12(1)**, [1057]
    protection, **12(1)**, [1057]
    statement by, use of, **12(1)**, [1057]
  preparatory hearing—
    appeal from ruling, **12(1)**, [1065]
    case statement, supply of, **12(1)**, [1065]
    conduct of, **12(1)**, [1065]
    defendant, judge's order to, **12(1)**, [1065]
    judge's powers, **12(1)**, [1065]
    meaning, **12(1)**, [1065]
    order before, **12(1)**, [1066]
    order for, **12(1)**, [1063]
    prosecution, order by judge, **12(1)**, [1065]

serious or complex fraud—*contd*
  preparatory hearing—*contd*
    purposes of, **12(1)**, [1065]
    reporting restrictions, **12(1)**, [1068], [1069]
    ruling etc, appeal from, **12(1)**, [1065]
  proceedings—
    conduct of, **12(1)**, [1056], [1077]
    justice of the peace, delivery of documents
      by, **12(1)**, [1077]
  prosecutions—
    conduct of, **12(1)**, [1077]
    evidence in, **12(1)**, [1059]
    reportable matters, **12(1)**, [1068]
    reporting restrictions, **12(1)**, [1068]
    offences, **12(1)**, [1069]
  regulations, power to make, **12(1)**, [1077]
  reporting restrictions, **12(1)**, [1068]
    offences, **12(1)**, [1069]
  Scotland. *See under* **Scotland**
  transfer of cases to Crown Court—
    appearance, ensuring, **12(1)**, [1061]
    designated authorities for purpose of,
      12(1), [1060]
    dismissal of transferred charge,
      12(1), [1062]
    notices, **12(1)**, [1060]; **12(2)**, [468]
    procedure, **12(1)**, [1061]
  trial—
    commencement, **12(1)**, [1064]
    later stages of, **12(1)**, [1067]
  trial on indictment without jury, application
    for, **12(3)**, [825]

Serious Organised Crime Agency
  accounts, **33(2)**, [537]
  action plan—
    inadequate, revision of, **33(2)**, [530]
    meaning, **33(2)**, [529]
    power to direct submission of, **33(2)**, [529]
    procedure, **33(2)**, [531]
    reports, **33(2)**, [532]
  annual plans, **33(2)**, [523]
  annual reports, **33(2)**, [524]
  Assets Recovery Agency, transfers from,
    12(4), [458]
  assistance from, **33(2)**, [522]
  Board, **33(2)**, [600]
  charges by, **33(2)**, [536]
  Civil Nuclear Constabulary member serving
    with, **33(2)**, [492]
  committees, **33(2)**, [602]
  constable, staff having powers of—
    conduct of, **33(2)**, [567]
    designation of, **33(2)**, [560]
    employment provisions, **33(2)**, [570]
    evidence of designation, **33(2)**, [567]
    exercise of, **33(2)**, [563]
    Scotland and Northern Ireland, in,
      33(2), [564]
  crime reduction, contribution to, **12(3)**, [171]
  customs officer, staff having powers of—
    conduct of, **33(2)**, [567]
    designation of, **33(2)**, [560]
    evidence of designation, **33(2)**, [567]
    exercise of, **33(2)**, [565]

Serious Organised Crime Agency—*contd*
designated staff—
  assaults, obstruction or deception relating
    to, **33(2)**, [568]
  conduct of, **33(2)**, [567]
  delegation of power to designate,
    33(2), [561]
  employment provisions, **33(2)**, [570]
  evidence of designation, **33(2)**, [567]
  interpretation, **33(2)**, [571]
  modification of enactments, **33(2)**, [569]
  modification or withdrawal of designation
    33(2), [562]
  powers of constable or other officer,
    designation as having, **33(2)**, [560]
Director General—
  appointment, **33(2)**, [601]
  delegation of functions, **33(2)**, [601]
  operational responsibility, **33(2)**, [538]
  powers of constable or other officer,
    designation of staff as having, **33(2)**, [560]
    delegation of power, **33(2)**, [561]
    modification or withdrawal of,
      33(2), [562]
  termination or suspension of appointment,
    33(2), [601]
disclosure to, **12(3)**, [449]
duty of police to assist, **33(2)**, [554]
equipment, regulations, **33(2)**, [544]
establishment, **33(2)**, [518]
functions of—
  codes of practice, **33(2)**, [527]
  exercise of, general considerations,
    33(2), [521]
  information relating to crime, as to,
    33(2), [520]
  serious organised crime, as to, **33(2)**, [519]
  strategic priorities, determining,
    33(2), [526]
general powers, **33(2)**, [522]
grants to, **33(2)**, [534]
  determinations, **33(2)**, [535]
immigration officer, staff having powers of—
  conduct of, **33(2)**, [567]
  designation of, **33(2)**, [560]
  evidence of designation, **33(2)**, [567]
  exercise of, **33(2)**, [566]
incidental powers, **33(2)**, [603]
Independent Police Complaints Commission,
  agreement for corresponding staff
  procedures, **33(2)**, [366]
information—
  disclosure by, **33(2)**, [550]
  disclosure to, **33(2)**, [551]
  duty of police to pass on, **33(2)**, [553]
  further disclosure, restrictions on,
    33(2), [552]
  use of, **33(2)**, [549]
inheritance tax functions—
  settlements, **12(3)**, [427]
  transfers of value, **12(3)**, [426]
inspections of, **33(2)**, [533]
interpretation, **33(2)**, [559]
joint investigation teams—
  assaults or obstruction, **33(2)**, [574]

Serious Organised Crime Agency—*contd*
joint investigation teams—*contd*
  unlawful conduct of members, liability
    for, **33(2)**, [547]
law enforcement agencies, mutual assistance—
  directed arrangements, **33(2)**, [541]
    Scotland, **33(2)**, [542]
  voluntary arrangements, **33(2)**, [540]
Ministry of Defence Police constables serving
  with, **33(2)**, [134]
police premises, use of, **33(2)**, [543]
property in possession of, disposal of,
  33(2), [56]
prosecutions—
  instigation of, **33(2)**, [555]
  reference of cases and proceedings to
    appropriate prosecutor, **33(2)**, [556]
Revenue functions—
  appeals, **12(3)**, [425]
  employment, concerning, **12(3)**, [423]
  exercise of, **12(3)**, [429]
  general, **12(3)**, [422]
  meaning, **12(3)**, [428]
  source of income, inability to identify,
    12(3), [424]
Scotland, activities in, **33(2)**, [539]
Scottish Ministers—
  annual report, laying before Scottish
    Parliament, **33(2)**, [524]
  compliance with directions by, **33(2)**, [558]
  general duty of, **33(2)**, [525]
seconded staff—
  discrimination legislation, application of,
    33(2), [573]
  liability for acts of, **33(2)**, [545]
    joint investigation teams, members of,
      33(2), [547]
    payment of amounts in relation to,
      33(2), [546]
Secretary of State—
  amounts paid to, **33(2)**, [536]
  annual report, laying before Parliament,
    33(2), [524]
  compliance with directions by, **33(2)**, [558]
  general duty of, **33(2)**, [525]
  grants by, **33(2)**, [534]
    determinations, **33(2)**, [535]
  reports to, **33(2)**, [528]
  strategic priorities, determining,
    33(2), [526]
  submission of action plan, directions for,
    33(2), [529]
    procedure, **33(2)**, [531]
    reports, **33(2)**, [532]
staff, **12(3)**, [172]; **33(2)**, [601]
  declaration, **12(3)**, [430], [544]
  pseudonyms, use of, **12(3)**, [524]–[526]
  transfers, **33(2)**, [604]
status, **33(2)**, [603]
transfers to, **33(2)**, [604]
unlawful conduct, liability for—
  designated staff, **33(2)**, [567]
  joint investigation teams, members of,
    33(2), [547]

Serious Organised Crime Agency—*contd*
  unlawful conduct, liability for—*contd*
    payment of amounts in relation to,
      33(2), [546]
    seconded staff, acts of, **33(2)**, [545]
    special police forces and law enforcement
      agencies, of, **33(2)**, [548]

servant
  accomplices, identifying, **12(1)**, [21]
  Crown, liability for torts of, **13**, [11]
  discharge, asserting time of, **12(1)**, [18]
  harm to, causing, **12(1)**, [82]
  hire of, falsely asserting, **12(1)**, [17]
  master of, personating, **12(1)**, [16]
  neglect by master, **12(1)**, [172]
  service, pretence of, **12(1)**, [20]
  services of, abolition of action for loss of,
    45, [983]

service charge
  amendment of provisions, **24**, [152], [153]
  codes of management practice, approval by
    Secretary of State, **23**, [163]
  demands, notice accompanying, **22**, [530]
  designated account, contributions to be held
    in, **22**, [758]
    failure to comply, **22**, [759]
  designated accounts, **24**, [871]
  disposal of house, after—
    provisions applied to, **22**, [53]
    relevant disposals, **22**, [53]
  equitable interest, purchase for purpose of
    financial assistance, **22**, [330]
  failure to pay, restriction on termination of
    tenancy for, **23**, [413]
  Housing Revenue Account and Housing
    Repairs Account, treatment for, **23**, [13]
  information, provision of, **24**, [871]
  insurance cover, summary of, **22**, [554]
  landlord, meaning, **22**, [541]
  limitation of, **22**, [54]
    court proceedings, costs of, **22**, [528]
    demands, time limit on, **22**, [527]
    estimates and consultation, requirements
      of, **22**, [524], [525]
    grant-aided works, **22**, [526]
    public authorities, exception for tenants
      of, **22**, [536]
    reasonableness, **22**, [523]
    registered and unvariable, rent being,
      22, [537]
  loan for, tenant having right to, **22**, [327]
  meaning, **22**, [422], [522]; **23**, [163]
  offences connected with, **22**, [56]
  qualifying works, **22**, [525]
  recognised tenants' association—
    meaning, **22**, [540]
    relevant requirements relating to, **22**, [525]
  regulation of, **22**, [756]
  relevant costs—
    based on, **22**, [54]
    change of landlord, effect of, **22**, [533]
    determination as to reasonableness,
      22, [523]

service charge—*contd*
  relevant costs—*contd*
    information as to—
      application for, **22**, [55]
      offences, **22**, [56]
      time for supplying, **22**, [55]
    inspection of documents, **24**, [121]
    liability to pay, jurisdiction, **22**, [538]
    meaning, **22**, [522]
    payment before costs incurred, **22**, [54],
      [522]
    qualified accountant—
      certification by, **22**, [55]
      meaning, **22**, [57]
    reasonably incurred, to be, **22**, [523]
    summary of, **22**, [55]
      accounts supporting, request to inspect,
        22, [531]
      assignment of tenancy, effect on
        request, **22**, [534]
      failure to supply information, **22**, [535]
      public authorities, exception for tenants
        of, **22**, [536]
      qualified accountant, certified by,
        22, [529], [539]
      rent registered and unvariable, exception
        for, **22**, [537]
      request for, **22**, [529]
      superior landlord, information held by,
        22, [532]
  right to buy, information in notice, **22**, [121]
  social landlords, charges by, **23**, [532], [533]
  statements of account, **24**, [120]
  surveyor to advise on, right to appoint,
    23, [414], [552]
  tenant, meaning, **22**, [541]
  trust, contributions held in, **22**, [757]
  variation of lease, application for, **22**, [750]
  withholding, **24**, [120]

Service Civilian Court
  appeal from—
    findings and sentence on, **3(S)**, 262
    hearing, **3(S)**, 261
    right of, **3(S)**, 260–1
  charges allocated for, **3(S)**, 129
    powers of DSP, **3(S)**, 130
  constitution, **3(S)**, 257
  court administration officer, **3(S)**, 326
  Court Martial—
    decision as to appropriateness of trial by,
      3(S), 257
    reference of cases to, **12(2)**, [285]
    right to elect trial by, **3(S)**, 258
  Criminal Cases Review Commission, powers
    of, **3(S)**, 381
  custody during proceedings of, **3(S)**, 116
  establishment of, **3(S)**, 256
  fines and compensation orders imposed,
    maximum amounts, **3(S)**, 260
  fitness to stand trial, question of, **3(S)**, 379
  imprisonment, maximum term imposed by,
    3(S), 259
  insanity, question of, **3(S)**, 379
  jurisdiction of, **3(S)**, 66

Service Civilian Court—*contd*
offences other than charged, conviction of, **3(S)**, 258
proceedings, **3(S)**, 257
public, sitting in, **3(S)**, 379
punishments available to, **3(S)**, 259
rules, **3(S)**, 263
sentences—
  commencement of, **3(S)**, 264
  explanation, duty to give, **3(S)**, 235–7
  individual, for each offence, **3(S)**, 238
  pre-sentence reports, **3(S)**, 238–40
  reasons, duty to give, **3(S)**, 235–7
service parent or guardian, recognizance and fines by—
  amount of, **3(S)**, 219
  appeals, **3(S)**, 220
  duration, **3(S)**, 219
  forfeiture of recognizance, **3(S)**, 221–2
  order for, **3(S)**, 219
  variation and revocation, **3(S)**, 220
service restraining order—
  appeals, **3(S)**, 218
  power to make, **3(S)**, 216
sitting, place of, **3(S)**, 256
witnesses and others, privilege of, **3(S)**, 379

Service Complaints Commissioner
appointment of, **3(S)**, 328
referral of allegations to, **3(S)**, 306–7
reports by, **3(S)**, 307–8

service contract
stamp duty, exempt from **41**, [234]

service court
meaning, **10**, [1210]
witness anonymity order, decision as to, **18**, [439]

service mark
meaning, **48**, 3
registration of, **48**, 3

service of documents
provision relating to, **17(2)**, [187]

service qualification
persons having, **15(3)**, [29]
service declaration—
  attested, when, **15(3)**, [31]
  contents of, **15(3)**, [31]
  effect of, **15(3)**, [32]
  making, **15(3)**, [30]
  offences, **15(3)**, [60]

services
charges for. *See* **prices**
contracts as to—
  refusal to deal on grounds of union exclusion, prohibition, **16**, [385]
  trade union membership, void provisions on, **16**, [338]
  union recognition requirement, void, **16**, [384]

services—*contd*
intermediary, provision through, **43(2)**, [208]
restrictive practices. *See* **restrictive trade agreement**
supply, contract for—
  exceptions, **39(1)**, [467]
  implied terms—
    care and skill, **39(1)**, [468]
    consideration, as to, **39(1)**, [470]
    exclusion of, **39(1)**, [471]
    performance, time for, **39(1)**, [469]
  meaning, **39(1)**, [467]
  orders relating to, **39(1)**, [467]
supply of, monopoly situations. *See* **Competition Commission**
unsolicited—
  directory entries. *See* **directory**
  offences, prosecution of, **47**, [209]

servitude
creation over land for civil aviation, **4(1)**, [95], [165]

settled land
additional development after acquisition, compensation, **9**, [260]
advance payment of compensation for compulsory acquisition, **9**, [350]
capital money, application of, **46**, [602], [736]
charitable trust, of, **20**, [531]
conveyance of—
  change of ownership, on, **20**, [511]
  conditions, **20**, [512]
  costs of, **20**, [512]
  mode of, **20**, [512]
  reservation of rights, **20**, [512]
compensation for depreciation in case of, **9**, [313]
disposition where trustee not discharged, **20**, [521]
ecclesiastical trust of, **20**, [531]
equitable charge as land charge, **21**, [392]
equitable interests, enforcement of, **20**, [519]
estate owner, powers against, **20**, [519]
hill farming, improvements, **1(1)**, [368]
improvements—
  farm capital grants, **1(1)**, [799]
  rentcharges, application of capital money, **1(1)**, [664]
incumbrance—
  charging, **20**, [572]
  meaning, **20**, [572]
  shifting, **20**, [571]
  variation of, **20**, [572]
limitation of action, **19(3)**, [745], [772]
meaning, **18**, [525]; **20**, [497], [506], [618]
ownership, change of, **20**, [511]
proceedings for protection or recovery of, **20**, [595]
public trust, of, **20**, [531]
purchaser, rights of, **20**, [611]
registered. *See* **land registration**
released charges, substituted security for, **20**, [585]
resettlement, limitation on, **20**, [525]

settled land—*contd*
restoration of interest in, **20**, [525]
sale, etc, of. *See* **tenant for life**
special executors as respects, **18**, [525]
special personal representatives, power of disposal, **18**, [527]
surface and minerals, dealing with, **20**, [552]
tenant for life, powers of. *See* **tenant for life**
undivided shares, held in, **20**, [538]
vesting—
breach of covenant, etc, as, **20**, [518]
disposition subject to, **20**, [517]
stamp duty, exemption from, **20**, [518]
vesting order, power to make, **20**, [516]
war damage, raising money for making good, **21**, [89]

settlement. *See also* **trustees**
absolute owner subject to interests, powers of, **20**, [524]
acquisition of land for, **20**, [514]
aggregate estates, **20**, [594]
beneficiaries, attribution of gains to, **43(2)**, [226]
beneficiary, payments to, **43(S)**, 341
breach of covenant, damages for, **20**, [583]
capital gains tax. *See* **capital gains tax**
capital money—
arising otherwise than under Act, **20**, [584]
breach of covenant, as damages for, **20**, [583]
improvements, for. *See* improvements *below*
in court, application of, **20**, [579]
incumbrances, use to redeem, **20**, [576]
investment or application of—
modes of, **20**, [575]
purchase of land, **20**, [575]
regulations, **20**, [577]
tenant for life, direction of, **20**, [577]
trustees, by, **20**, [577]
lease or reversion, paid for, **20**, [582]
money held on trust by reference to, **20**, [581]
payment into court, **20**, [577]
personal estate settled by reference to, **20**, [581]
trustees, paid to, **20**, [598]
application of, **20**, [580]
commencement date, no postponement of, **43(S)**, 398
compound—
disposition, provisions on, **20**, [535]
references, **20**, [505]
trustees of, **20**, [533]
contract for, **20**, [515]
costs, etc, payment of, **20**, [615]
court—
jurisdiction of, **20**, [614]
procedure, **20**, [614]
references of questions to, **20**, [596]
deeds effecting, **20**, [508]
different estates on same limitations, of, **20**, [594]
disposal of interest in, **43(S)**, 314–15
disposition, requirements for, **20**, [517]

settlement—*contd*
dower, rights of, **20**, [505]
duration of, **20**, [507]
estate owner—
bankrupt, becoming, **20**, [604]
equitable interests and powers, enforcement of, **20**, [519]
vesting of land in, **20**, [604]
fine and recovery, **48**, 224
general provision, overview, **44(4)**, [473]
goods comprised in, not privileged from distress for rent, **13**, [1202]
grandchildren, for, **43(1)**, [370], [407]
heritage maintenance settlements—
income from—
double taxation, prevention of, **44(4)**, [519]
elections by trustees, **44(4)**, [516]
change of circumstances affecting, **44(4)**, [517]
non-heritage purposes, used for—
rate of tax, **44(4)**, [523]
tax charged on, **44(4)**, [520]–[521]
transfer of property between settlements, **44(4)**, [524]
property maintenance, sums applied for, **44(4)**, [518]
meaning, **44(4)**, [515]
non-heritage purposes, application of property for—
rate of tax, **44(4)**, [523]
tax charged on, **44(4)**, [520]–[521]
exemptions, **44(4)**, [525]
transfer of property between settlements, **44(4)**, [524]
historical development, **48**, 224
improvements—
authorised, **20**, [586]
capital money—
mode of application, **20**, [587]
rentcharge to discharge instalments of, **20**, [588]
repayment of, **20**, [587]
costs—
not liable to be replaced by instalments, **20**, [622]
required to be replaced by instalments, **20**, [623], [624]
insurance of, **20**, [591]
maintenance and repair, **20**, [591]
payment, court ordering, **20**, [590]
tenant for life concurring in, **20**, [589]
Secretary of State—
certificates, filing, **20**, [617]
powers of, **20**, [616]
reports, **20**, [617]
income arising under, references to, **44(3)**, [660]
income, calculation of, **43(S)**, 340
inheritance tax amendments, **43(S)**, 390–401
interests in, **43(S)**, 313–14
interests in possession—
beneficiary's life, ending during, **43(S)**, 394
close company, of, **43(S)**, 400
conditional exemption, relief, **43(S)**, 405–6

settlement—*contd*
  interests in possession—*contd*
    estate not including, **43(S)**, 391–2
    extension of transitional period, **43(S)**, 978
    maintenance fund, property entering after
      death of person entitled, **43(S)**, 396
    participator in close company, trustee as,
      43(S), 399
    qualifying, **43(S)**, 397–8
    rate of tax on ending of, **43(S)**, 396
    termination, gifts with reservation,
      43(S), 403–4
  land subject to incumbrances, acquisition of,
    20, [576]
  legislation, **48**, 224–6
  life assurance policies entered into before 22nd
    March 2006, **43(S)**, 392–4
  maintenance funds for historic buildings. *See*
    historic buildings
  meaning, **20**, [505]; **41**, [563]; **44(3)**, [631]
  minor and consequential amendments,
    43(S), 319–27, 337–41
  minor, conveyance of estate to, **20**, [530]
  more than one, settlor making, **43(S)**, 335
  non-aggregation with estate, conditions for,
    43(S), 395–6
  omission to exercise right, deemed
    disposition, **43(S)**, 390
  particulars, notice of, **42**, [141]
  personalty, implied trust for sale, **20**, [651]
  potentially exempt transfers, **43(S)**, 391
  power of appointment, exercise of, **41**, [563]
  property settled by will, distributions within
    two years of death, **43(S)**, 400–1
  protector of. *See* **entail**
  provisions in conflict with Act, where,
    20, [609]
  referential, trustee of, **20**, [534]
  remainderman, surrender of estate to,
    20, [606]
  settled land. *See* **settled land**
    advance payment of compensation for
      compulsory acquisition, **9**, [350]
    capital money, application of, **46**, [602],
      [736]
    improvements. *See* improvements *above*
    registered. *See* **land registration**
    sale, etc, of. *See* **tenant for life**
    tenant for life, powers of. *See* **tenant for**
      life
    war damage, raising money for making
      good, **21**, [89]
  settled property—
    capital gains tax. *See* **capital gains tax**
    inheritance tax. *See* **inheritance tax**
    meaning, **43(S)**, 309–12, 329; **44(4)**, [474]
    references to, **44(4)**, [486]
  settlor—
    amounts treated as income of—
      calculation of, **44(3)**, [634]
      capital sums, **44(3)**, [644]–[648]
      charge to tax, **44(3)**, [629]
      connected bodies, capital sums paid by,
        44(3), [652]–[654]
      excepted income, **44(3)**, [638]

settlement—*contd*
  settlor—*contd*
    amounts treated as income of—*contd*
      gifts to charities, **44(3)**, [639]
      grossing-up, **44(3)**, [651]
      highest part of total income,
        44(3), [630]
      income charged, **44(3)**, [632]
      information, power to obtain,
        44(3), [659]
      interest, retention of, **44(3)**, [635]
      loan or repayment of loan, sums paid by
        way of, **44(3)**, [649]
      outright gifts between spouses or civil
        partners, **44(3)**, [637]
      participants in close companies, loans
        to, **44(3)**, [650]
      person liable for tax, **44(3)**, [633]
      property or income originating from
        settlor, **44(3)**, [656]
      relevant children, income paid to,
        44(3), [640]–[643]
      retained interest, **44(3)**, [636]
      trustee—
        adjustments with, **44(3)**, [657]
        expenses of, to be rateably
          apportioned, **44(3)**, [658]
      two or more settlors, settlements by,
        44(3), [655]
    charge on, **43(1)**, [370]–[371], [408]
    disposable property, meaning, **44(4)**, [476]
    gains treated as accruing to, deduction of
      personal losses from, **43(2)**, [136]
    identification of, following transfer,
      44(4), [479]
    meaning, **44(3)**, [631]; **44(4)**, [475]
    meaning and identification, **43(S)**, 309–12,
      329–31
    non-resident, charge on beneficiaries,
      43(1), [369]
    person ceasing to be, **44(4)**, [477]
    residence of, **44(4)**, [484]
    variation of will—
      deceased person as, where, **44(4)**, [481]
      property settled because of, **44(4)**, [480]
  settlor-interested, **43(S)**, 336
    income of beneficiaries, **43(S)**, 895
  special rules, transitional provisions and
    savings, **44(4)**, [1055]
  statutory owner. *See* **statutory owner**
  sub-fund, **43(S)**, 315–19, 325–6, 333
    Sch 4ZA to TCGA 1992, elections under,
      44(4), [485]
  substituted security, land as, **20**, [585]
  summary of provisions, **20**, [1]
  tenant for life. *See* **tenant for life**
  tenant in tail, powers of, **20**, [523]
  termination, deed of discharge on, **20**, [520]
  transfer between, **43(S)**, 310–11; **44(4)**, [478]
  transitional provisions, **20**, [539], [621]
  trust for sale, by, **20**, [1]
  trust instrument—
    effect of, **20**, [508]
    instruments deemed to be, **20**, [513]
    will as, **20**, [510]

settlement—*contd*
trust of land in place of, **23**, [311], [335]
trustee—
appointment of, **20**, [513]
court, by, **20**, [536]
new, procedure on appointment of,
20, [537]
companies, discretionary payments to,
44(1), [435]
compound settlement, of, **20**, [533]
connected person, as, **44(1)**, [621]
contingency, management of land
pending, **20**, [603]
continuation in office, **20**, [535]
dispositions where not discharged,
20, [521]
indemnities, **20**, [601]
minority, management of land during,
20, [603]
money in hands of, application of,
20, [580]
notice to, **20**, [602]
number of, **20**, [597]
persons being, **20**, [532]
powers—
exercise of, **20**, [613]
no tenant for life, where, **20**, [526]
protection of—
generally, **20**, [599]
particular cases, in, **20**, [600]
receipts, **20**, [598]
referential settlement, of, **20**, [534]
Settled Land Act, under, application of
provisions to, **48**, 538–9
statutory owner as, **20**, [608]
tenant for life as, **20**, [608]
trustees of, **43(S)**, 332
income, receipts treated as, **43(S)**, 334–5
vesting deed—
contents of, **20**, [509]
effect of, **20**, [508]
principal, **20**, [509]
execution of, **20**, [513]
subsidiary, contents, **20**, [514]
vesting orders, **20**, [614]
where constituted, **20**, [505]
will, by, **20**, [510]

severance
additional development after acquisition,
compensation, **9**, [260]
bridge, culvert etc, division of land by, effect
of, **9**, [55]
compensation for—
apportionment of rent, **9**, [279]
assessment, **9**, [26], [267]
ecclesiastical property, **9**, [289]
provisions to be observed, **9**, [268]
tenancy at will, in case of, **9**, [280]
effect of, **9**, [54]–[55]
part of house or building, requirements as to,
9, [53], [403]
vesting declaration, objection to—
notice of—
effect, **9**, [403]

severance—*contd*
vesting declaration, objection to—*contd*
notice of—*contd*
Lands Tribunal, reference to, **9**, [403]
meaning, **9**, [403]
service, **9**, [403]
response by acquiring authority, **9**, [403]

severe disablement allowance
disablement, assessment of extent of,
40(1), [481]
disablement questions—
determination of, **40(1)**, [547]
meaning, **40(1)**, [547]
medical appeals and references, **40(1)**, [548]
medical decisions, review of, **40(1)**, [549]
question of law, appeal on, **40(1)**, [550]
rate of, **40(1)**, [467]

sewage disposal
London—
enactments applied, **25(1)**, [700]
modifications of Public Health Act,
25(1), [733], [734]
vesting of land used for, **25(1)**, [700]

sewer. *See also* **drain**
adoption of—
agreements for, **49**, [903]
appeals, **49**, [904]
cross-border, **49**, [902]
generally, **49**, [901]
schemes for, **49**, [905]–[907]
alteration by railway company, etc,
35(1), [207]
alteration, power of undertakers, **49**, [993]
amendment of provisions, **49**, [698]
available for water closet, **35(1)**, [588], [590],
[647]
channel tunnel—
protection from, **37**, [549]
sewer diversions, **38(1)**, [688]
collegiate and corporate bodies, of,
35(1), [212]
Commissioners of, **49**, [1319]
compensation on removal of, **36**, [1026],
[1027]
construction, reference to, **35(1)**, [647]
cross boundary—
adoption of, **49**, [902]
allocation of, **49**, [664]
disputes, determination of, **49**, [912]
defective, investigation of, **49**, [917]
disposal works, adoption of—
agreements for, **49**, [903]
appeals, **49**, [904]
generally, **49**, [901]
diversion by navigation authority,
19(3), [243]
domestic purposes, use for—
conditions to be satisfied, **49**, [567]
meaning, **49**, [567]
payment in respect of, **49**, [567]
requisition for, **49**, [567]
drain, connection with, **35(1)**, [546], [586]

sewer—*contd*
general system, constructed as part of,
  49, [915]
highway drains, use of, **49**, [918]
London—
  application of enactments, **25(1)**, [701]
  notices relating to, **25(1)**, [930]
  sludge mains—
    construction etc—
      proposed, notice of, **25(1)**, [930]
      stopping up streets for, **25(1)**, [931]
    maintenance, **25(1)**, [929]
    meaning, **25(1)**, [928]
    provision of, **25(1)**, [929]
    river authorities, protection, **25(1)**, [932]
  vesting of land, **25(1)**, [700]
maps of—
  generally, **49**, [706]
  local authorities, provision to, **49**, [1012]
  requirement to keep, **49**, [1011]
meaning, **35(1)**, [216], [648]; **49**, [1031]
private—
  defective, **35(1)**, [583]
  examination and testing of suspected
    defective, **35(1)**, [125]
  insufficiency of, **35(1)**, [583]
  meaning, **35(1)**, [216], [648]
  removal of obstructions from, **35(1)**, [390]
public—
  communication of private sewers with—
    notice of, **49**, [908]
    right of, **49**, [908]
    sewerage undertakers, made by,
      49, [909]
    unlawful, **49**, [911]
    works by person entitled to, **49**, [910]
  connections between, **49**, [913]
  discharges to and from, offences, **49**, [1146]
  meaning, **35(1)**, [216], [648]; **49**, [1031],
    [1267]
  power to close or restrict use of, **49**, [919]
  provision other than by requisition,
    49, [899]
    lateral drains, power to construct,
      49, [900]
  requisition of—
    completion date, determination of,
      49, [898]
    discounted aggregate deficit, calculation
      of, **49**, [897]
    duty to comply with, **49**, [894]
    financial conditions, **49**, [895]
    persons requiring, **49**, [894]
    relevant deficit, calculation of, **49**, [896]
    route, determination of, **49**, [898]
  requisitions, transitional provisions,
    49, [1319]
  substances not permitted in, **49**, [914]
  trade effluents, consent for discharge of—
    appeals, **49**, [926]
    appeals as to variation, **49**, [930]
    application for, **49**, [923], [1388]
    conditions of, **49**, [925]
    special category, **49**, [924], [927]

sewer—*contd*
public—*contd*
  trade effluents, consent for discharge
    of—*contd*
    time for, application for variation,
      49, [932]
    time limits, variation within, **49**, [929]
    use, restriction on, **49**, [914]
    variation of, **49**, [928]
  removal of, **36**, [1026]
  saving for, **35(1)**, [43]
  soil washed into, **36**, [1216]
  street works affecting. *See* **street works**
  summary of provisions as to, **35(1)**, [1]
  Thames flood barrier, work involving,
    49, [518]
  tramway interfering with, **36**, [504]
  vesting of, **36**, [1310]
  works, power of local authority to execute,
    35(1), [173]

sewerage
agricultural land, supply of sewage to,
  35(1), [123]
domestic purposes, meaning, **49**, [921]
entry on land for purposes of, **49**, [980]
forms, prescription of, **49**, [1027]
functions—
  conferment on joint board, **35(1)**, [294]
  meaning, **35(1)**, [294]
levels of performance, information as to,
  49, [889]
local authority for purposes of, **35(1)**, [294]
local inquiries, **49**, [1028]
offences, limitation on right to prosecute,
  49, [1024]
Public Health Act, under, **49**, [703]
services, VAT zero-rating, **50**, [151]
standards of performance, **49**, [888]
  customers, information for, **49**, [892]
  levels, information as to, **49**, [889]
  regulations, **49**, [891], [1361]
system—
  drain or sewer constructed as part of,
    49, [915]
  duty to provide, **49**, [887]
  protection of, **49**, [914]–[917]
transitional provisions, **49**, [703]
undertaker, service of documents on,
  35(1), [343]
works—
  obstruction of, **49**, [987]
  protective provisions, **49**, [1056]
  purposes of, for, **49**, [969]
  vesting of, **49**, [988]

sewerage authority
meaning, **38(1)**, [232]
street works, and. *See* **street works**

sewerage undertaker
drainage works affecting, protection,
  19(3), [259]
meaning, **41**, [689]

sewerage undertaker—*contd*
mineral working, application for restriction
on, **17(1)**, [372]

sewerage undertaking
mergers, **47**, [762]

sex discrimination
actuarial data, based on, **7(1)**, [90]
agent, by, **7(1)**, [85]
armed forces, **7(1)**, [119]
assignment of tenancy, in—
generally, **7(1)**, [73]
small dwelling, **7(1)**, [74]
associated employers, **7(1)**, [116]
barrister or clerk, by, **7(1)**, [78], [79]
benefits, indirect access to, **7(1)**, [95]
charity, by, **7(1)**, [88]
civil proceedings, **7(1)**, [104]
claims, **7(1)**, [104]
communal accommodation, in use of,
7(1), [91]
contract term, in, **7(1)**, [112]
contract worker, against, **7(1)**, [45]
county court, proceedings in, **7(1)**, [104]
burden of proof, **7(1)**, [105]
national security, **7(1)**, [106]
damages, **7(1)**, [104]
discriminatory advertisement—
meaning, **7(1)**, [116]
prohibiting, **7(1)**, [82]
discriminatory practices, **7(1)**, [81]
duty to eliminate, **7(1)**, [81]
education—
further, in, **7(1)**, [61]
general duty, **7(1)**, [67]
higher, in, **7(1)**, [61]
public authorities, by, **7(1)**, [60]
educational charities, and, **7(1)**, [113]
educational establishment, in—
boarding school, **7(1)**, [69]
co-educational, becoming, **7(1)**, [70]
exemption for discrimination, **7(1)**, [226]
Northern Ireland, corresponding
provision for, **7(1)**, [231]
orders, power to make, **7(1)**, [232]
generally, **7(1)**, [61]
head teachers or principals, exemptions,
7(1), [226]
meaning, **7(1)**, [226]
post-16 education and training, **7(1)**, [68]
religious order, exemption for appointment
of member, **7(1)**, [226]
single-sex, **7(1)**, [69]
transitional orders, **7(1)**, [123]
types of, **7(1)**, [61]
university appointments, exemptions,
7(1), [226]
election candidates, selection of, **7(1)**, [87],
[698]
employer, by—
applicant, against, **7(1)**, [39]
benefits, denying, **7(1)**, [39]
employee, against, **7(1)**, [39]

sex discrimination—*contd*
employer, by—*contd*
gender assignment, on grounds of,
7(1), [42], [43]
genuine occupational qualification,
7(1), [41]
harassment, **7(1)**, [39]
maternity leave, exception relating to terms
and conditions during, **7(1)**, [40]
employment—
aircraft, on, **7(1)**, [46], [119]
civil partner, **7(1)**, [34]
collective agreements, **7(1)**, [217]
conflicting statutory requirements—
exemptions, **7(1)**, [225]
Northern Ireland, corresponding
provision for, **7(1)**, [231]
orders, power to make, **7(1)**, [232]
overriding of, **7(1)**, [223]
repeal of provisions, **7(1)**, [224]
contract of—
terms, unlawful, **7(1)**, [112], [217]
validity and revision, **7(1)**, [112], [217]
void, when unlawful, **7(1)**, [217]
hovercraft, on, **7(1)**, [46], [119]
married person, **7(1)**, [34]
maternity leave, on ground of, **7(1)**, [35]
meaning, **7(1)**, [46]
organisations to which provisions apply,
7(1), [217]
pregnancy, on ground of, **7(1)**, [35]
rules of undertakings, **7(1)**, [217]
seabed, concerned with, **7(1)**, [46]
ship, on, **7(1)**, [46], [119]
termination, **7(1)**, [116]
training, **7(1)**, [92], [93]
employment agency, by—
generally, **7(1)**, [53]
meaning, **7(1)**, [116]
employment tribunal—
burden of proof, **7(1)**, [102], [105]
compensation, awarding, **7(1)**, [103]
jurisdiction of, **7(1)**, [101]
remedies, **7(1)**, [103]
three months, proceedings to be brought
in, **7(1)**, [108]
Equal Opportunities Commission, replaced.
See now **Commission for Equality and
Human Rights**
equal pay, **7(1)**, [44], [217]
See also **equal pay**
facilities and services, in provision of—
aircraft, on, **7(1)**, [80]
generally, **7(1)**, [71]
Highlands and Islands Enterprise, by,
7(1), [54]
hospital premises, in, **7(1)**, [77]
hovercraft, on, **7(1)**, [80]
indirect access to, **7(1)**, [95]
outside Great Britain, **7(1)**, [80]
physical contact, likelihood of, **7(1)**, [77]
religion, for purpose of, **7(1)**, [77]
Scottish Enterprise, by, **7(1)**, [54]
Secretary of State, by, **7(1)**, [54]
ship, on, **7(1)**, [80]

sex discrimination—*contd*
　facilities and services, in provision of—*contd*
　　travel facilities, **7(1)**, [80]
　　user in state of undress in, **7(1)**, [77]
　financial provisions, **7(1)**, [118]
　forces, in, **7(1)**, [119]
　Further Education Councils, by, **7(1)**, [64],
　　[146]
　gender assignment, on grounds of—
　　employer, treatment by, **7(1)**, [42], [43]
　　genuine occupational qualification,
　　　7(1), [43]
　　less favourable treatment, **7(1)**, [33]
　generally, **7(1)**, [1]
　goods, in provision of—
　　aircraft, on, **7(1)**, [80]
　　generally, **7(1)**, [71]
　　hovercraft, on, **7(1)**, [80]
　　outside Great Britain, **7(1)**, [80]
　　ship, on, **7(1)**, [80]
　government appointments, **7(1)**, [47], [48]
　harassment, **7(1)**, [37]
　Higher Education Funding Councils, by,
　　7(1), [64], [146]
　House of Commons staff, **7(1)**, [120]
　House of Lords staff, **7(1)**, [121]
　inducing, **7(1)**, [84]
　instructions to procure, **7(1)**, [83]
　insurance, in, **7(1)**, [90]
　　local education authority, duties of,
　　　7(1), [67]
　lone parent, exemption in favour of,
　　7(1), [228]
　man, meaning, **7(1)**, [38]
　married person, against, **7(1)**, [34]
　meaning of, **7(1)**, [31]
　men, against, **7(1)**, [32]
　midwives, **7(1)**, [58], [124]
　ministers of religion, **7(1)**, [57]
　national security—
　　act safeguarding, **7(1)**, [98]
　　court proceedings, and, **7(1)**, [106]
　office-holders, against, **7(1)**, [47], [48]
　orders, **7(1)**, [115]
　partnership, by, **7(1)**, [49], [116]
　　expulsion from, **7(1)**, [116]
　　termination of, **7(1)**, [116]
　person aggrieved, information, obtaining,
　　7(1), [107]
　police force, in, **7(1)**, [55]
　political party, by, **7(1)**, [75]
　premises, in disposal or management of,
　　7(1), [72]
　pressuring act of, **7(1)**, [84]
　principal, liability of, **7(1)**, [85]
　prison officers, height of, **7(1)**, [56]
　proceedings, **7(1)**, [100], [104]
　　time limit for bringing, **7(1)**, [108]
　public authorities—
　　duties—
　　　general statutory, **7(1)**, [109]
　　　Scottish, **7(1)**, [111]
　　　specific, **7(1)**, [110]
　qualifying body, by, **7(1)**, [51]

sex discrimination—*contd*
　relationships which have ended, in relation
　　to, **7(1)**, [59]
　employment agencies and businesses, licensing
　　of, **16**, [90]
　functions as to employment and training—
　　advice, power to obtain, **16**, [67]
　　careers services—
　　　arrangement for, **16**, [69]
　　　duty to ensure provision of, **16**, [68]
　　　inspection, **16**, [72]
　　　provision of, **16**, [70]
　　disabled persons, **16**, [65], [74]
　　education authorities providing services,
　　　control of, **16**, [70]
　　financial provisions, **16**, [73]
　　generally, **16**, [65]
　　grants and loans, **16**, [65]
　　inspection, **16**, [72]
　　meaning of functions, **16**, [75]
　　payments by, **16**, [65]
　　research, as to, **16**, [67], [119]
　　status of trainees etc, orders as to, **16**, [142]
　　women and girls, **16**, [65]
　grants and loans by, **16**, [65]
　health and safety responsibilities, **16**, [79]
　industrial training, powers, **16**, [65]
　redundancies, notification of, **16**, [392]
　　failure to comply, **16**, [393]
　research, payments in aid, **16**, [67], [119]
　temporary employment, provision, **16**, [65]
　Scottish Administration, appointments made
　　by, **7(1)**, [47], [48]
　sexual harassment, **7(1)**, [37]
　skill, in exercise of, **7(1)**, [71]
　sport, in, **7(1)**, [89]
　statutory authority, acts under—
　　exemptions, **7(1)**, [97], [225], [227]
　　Northern Ireland, corresponding provision
　　　for, **7(1)**, [231]
　　orders, power to make, **7(1)**, [232]
　　overriding of provisions, **7(1)**, [223]
　　protection of women at work, certain
　　　exemptions, **7(1)**, [225]
　　repeal of provisions, **7(1)**, [224]
　　Secretary of State's powers, **7(1)**, [224],
　　　[227]
　student complaints scheme, **15(2)**, [552]
　sub-letting, in—
　　generally, **7(1)**, [73]
　　small dwelling, **7(1)**, [74]
　summary of provisions, **16**, [1]
　Teacher Training Agency, by, **7(1)**, [65]
　trade union, by—
　　election arrangements, **7(1)**, [94]
　　generally, **7(1)**, [50]
　training, **7(1)**, [92], [93]
　Training and Development Agency for
　　Schools, by, **7(1)**, [147]
　unlawful acts, aiding, **7(1)**, [86]
　　conflicting statutory requirements,
　　　overriding, **7(1)**, [223]
　victimisation, by, **7(1)**, [36]
　vocational training—
　　body giving, by, **7(1)**, [52]

sex discrimination—*contd*
  vocational training—*contd*
    conflicting statutory requirements—
      exemptions, **7(1)**, [225]
      Northern Ireland, corresponding
        provision for, **7(1)**, [231]
      overriding of, **7(1)**, [223]
      repeal of provisions, **7(1)**, [224]
    guidance included in references to,
      7(1), [233]
    voluntary body, by, **7(1)**, [76]
    Welsh ministers, appointments made by,
      7(1), [47], [48]
    women, against—
      direct and indirect, **7(1)**, [31]
      meaning, **7(1)**, [38]
      protection of—
        acts done for, **7(1)**, [96]
        employment field, in, generally,
          7(1), [39], [96]
        statutory authority, acts under—
          exemptions, **7(1)**, [227]
          provisions concerned with,
            7(1), [235]
      requirement or condition, imposing,
        7(1), [31]
      vocational training, in, **7(1)**, [52], [96]

sex establishments
  control of—
    application of provisions, resolution as to
      area, **13**, [259]
    generally, **13**, [259]
    saving for existing law, **13**, [261]
  licences—
    appeals, **13**, [261]
    application for, **13**, [261]
    cancellation, **13**, [261]
    copies, display and transmission, **13**, [261]
    death of holder, **13**, [261]
    enforcement of provisions, **13**, [261]
    fees, **13**, [261]
    grant, **13**, [261]
    notices, **13**, [261]
    objections to grant, **13**, [261]
    refusal, **13**, [261]
    renewal, **13**, [261]
    requirements, **13**, [261]
    revocation, **13**, [261]
    standard conditions, power to prescribe,
      13, [261]
    terms, conditions or restrictions, **13**, [261]
    transfer, **13**, [261]
    transmission, **13**, [261]
    variation of, **13**, [261]
  local authority—
    meaning, **13**, [259]
    officers' powers, **13**, [261]
    resolutions by, **13**, [259]
  London, amendments as to, **25(2)**, [670],
    [673]
  meaning, **13**, [261]
  offences—
    bar on certain defences, **13**, [261]
    bodies corporate, by, **13**, [261]

sex establishments—*contd*
  offences—*contd*
    penalties, **13**, [261]
    persons under 18, relating to, **13**, [261]
    police, powers of constables, **13**, [261]
    premises—
      existing, savings, **13**, [261]
      licensing. *See* licences *above*
    sex article, meaning, **13**, [261]
    sex cinemas—
      commencement of provisions, **13**, [261]
      licensing. *See* licences *above*
      meaning, **13**, [261]
    sex shop—
      meaning, **13**, [261]
      video, supply of, to, **13**, [311], [316]
    vessels—
      application of provisions, **13**, [261]
      meaning, **13**, [261]
    video recordings, display of certain,
      26(2), [735]
    young persons, admission to or employment
      in, **13**, [261]

sex offender. *See also* **sexual offences**
  polygraph condition—
    application of, **12(4)**, [335]
    effect of, **12(4)**, [336]
    rules, **12(4)**, [336]
  sentences. *See* **sentence**

sexton
  appointment and dismissal, **14**, 492

sexual harassment. *See* **harassment**

sexual intercourse
  boy, abolition of presumption of incapacity,
    12(2), [160]

sexual offences. *See also* **sexual intercourse**
  abduction. *See* **abduction**
  administering substance with intent,
    12(3), [725]
  adult relative, sex with—
    consent to penetration, **12(3)**, [729]
    penetration, **12(3)**, [728]
  animal, intercourse with, **12(3)**, [733]
  anonymity of victims—
    contravention of provisions, **12(2)**, [139]
    courts martial, application of provisions to,
      12(2), [141]
    displacement of provisions, powers,
      12(2), [137]
    offences in contravention, **12(2)**, [139],
      [141]
    offences to which applicable, **12(2)**, [136]
    preservation, **12(2)**, [135]
    special rules, **12(2)**, [138]
  buggery. *See* **buggery**
  certificates, **12(3)**, [756]
  child sex offence—
    aiding, abetting and counselling, exception
      to, **12(3)**, [737]

sexual offences—*contd*
child sex offence—*contd*
arranging or facilitating commission of,
12(3), [678]
children or young persons, committed by,
12(3), [677]
schedule of, **12(3)**, [1098]
children, against—
bill of indictment, **12(1)**, [242]
place of trial, transfer—
delay, avoidance, **12(2)**, [124]
generally, **12(2)**, [100]
notice of, **12(2)**, [100], [124]
procedure in lieu of committal,
12(2), [124]
regulations, power to make, **12(2)**, [124]
remand, person on, **12(2)**, [124]
reporting restriction, **12(2)**, [124]
witness, child as, **12(2)**, [100]
committing offence with intent to commit,
12(3), [726]
conditional discharge, provisions not
applying, **12(3)**, [792]
conduct punishable outside United
Kingdom, **12(2)**, [493]
consent—
conclusive presumptions, **12(3)**, [740]
evidential presumptions, **12(3)**, [739]
meaning, **12(3)**, [738]
relevant acts, **12(3)**, [741]
continuity of law, **12(4)**, [244]
corpse, penetration of, **12(3)**, [734]
cross-border provisions, **12(4)**, [245]
custodial sentence for, committed before
30 September 1998, **12(2)**, [779]
engaging in sexual activity in presence of
child, **12(3)**, [675]
abuse of position of trust, **12(3)**, [682]
exposure, **12(3)**, [730]
extended sentence for, **12(3)**, [958]
persons under 18, **12(3)**, [959]
familial—
family relationships, interpretation,
12(3), [691]
inciting engagement in sexual activity,
12(3), [690]
marriage or civil partnership exception,
12(3), [692]
relationships pre-dating family relationship,
12(3), [693]
sexual activity with child, **12(3)**, [689]
foreign, reference to, 12(3), [790]
foreign travel order—
appeal against, **12(3)**, [779]
application for, **12(3)**, [774]
breach of, **12(3)**, [780]
discharge, **12(3)**, [778]
effect of, **12(3)**, [777]
grounds, **12(3)**, [774]
interpretation, **12(3)**, [775]
meaning, **12(3)**, [774]
qualifying offenders, **12(3)**, [776]
renewal, **12(3)**, [778]
variation, **12(3)**, [778]
generally, **12(1)**, [1]

sexual offences—*contd*
grooming—
amended provisions, **12(4)**, [503]
meeting child following, **12(2)**, [973];
12(3), [679]
incest. *See* **incest**
incitement to commit outside United
Kingdom, **12(2)**, [492], [493]
indecency with children. *See* **child**
indecent assault. *See* **assault**
interpretation, **12(2)**, [1081]; **12(3)**, [791]
kerb-crawling, **12(1)**, [969]
listed, **12(2)**, [497]
meaning, **12(2)**, [832]
mentally disordered offenders, interpretation,
12(2), [1083]; **12(3)**, [793]
Northern Ireland, application of provisions,
12(2), [1084]; **12(3)**, [794]
notification—
abolished homosexual offences, procedure
for ending in relation to, **12(3)**, [804]
changes, of, **12(3)**, [748]
initial, **12(3)**, [747]
interpretation, **12(3)**, [752]
method of, **12(3)**, [751]
offences, **12(3)**, [755]
orders—
appeal against, **12(3)**, [766]
application for, **12(3)**, [762]
effect of, **12(3)**, [763]
grounds, **12(3)**, [762]
interim, **12(3)**, [765]
meaning, **12(3)**, [762]
relevant offences, **12(3)**, [764]
period, **12(3)**, [746]
periodic, **12(3)**, [749]
persons becoming subject to, **12(3)**, [744],
[803]
previous provisions, under, **12(3)**, [745]
travel outside United Kingdom, as to,
12(3), [750]
observation, reference to, **12(2)**, [1034];
12(3), [743]
offender—
evidence from polygraph sessions, use in
proceedings, **12(4)**, [337]
polygraph condition—
application of, **12(4)**, [335]
effect of, **12(4)**, [336]
rules, **12(4)**, [336]
orders and regulations, **12(2)**, [1086];
12(3), [796]
outside United Kingdom, jurisdiction,
12(2), [1027], [1092]; **12(3)**, [736], [802]
part of the body, reference to, **12(2)**, [1034];
12(3), [743]
penalties, **12(1)**, [369]
penetration, assault by, **12(2)**, [960];
12(3), [666]
child under 13, of, **12(3)**, [670]
penetration, meaning, **12(2)**, [1034];
12(3), [743]

sexual offences—*contd*
person with mental disorder impeding choice, against—
care worker, by—
causing or inciting to engage in sexual activity, **12(3)**, [703]
interpretation, **12(3)**, [706]
marriage or civil partnership exception, **12(3)**, [707]
relationships pre-dating care relationship, **12(3)**, [708]
sexual act, causing to watch, **12(3)**, [705]
sexual act in presence of, **12(3)**, [704]
sexual activity with, **12(3)**, [702]
causing or inciting to engage in sexual activity, **12(3)**, [695]
care worker, by, **12(3)**, [703]
inducement, threat or deception, procured by, **12(3)**, [699]
engaging in sexual activity in presence of, **12(3)**, [696]
inducement, threat or deception, procured by, **12(3)**, [700]
mental disorder, meaning, **12(3)**, [743]
sexual act, causing to watch, **12(3)**, [697]
care worker, by, **12(3)**, [705]
inducement, threat or deception, procured by, **12(3)**, [701]
sexual act in presence of, by care worker, **12(3)**, [704]
sexual activity with, **12(3)**, [694]
care worker, by, **12(3)**, [702]
inducement, threat or deception, procured by, **12(3)**, [698]
penalties, **12(1)**, [390]
power to amend provisions, **12(2)**, [1078]; **12(3)**, [788]
preparatory—
administering substance with intent, **12(3)**, [725]
committing offence with intent to commit, **12(3)**, [726]
trespass with intent to commit, **12(3)**, [727]
prevention order—
appeal against, **12(3)**, [772]
application for, **12(3)**, [767]
breach of, **12(3)**, [773]
discharge, **12(3)**, [770]
effect of, **12(3)**, [769]
grounds, **12(3)**, [767]
interim, **12(3)**, [771]
listed offences, **12(3)**, [805]
meaning, **12(3)**, [768]
qualifying offenders, **12(3)**, [768]
renewal, **12(3)**, [770]
variation, **12(3)**, [770]
probation order, provisions not applying, **12(2)**, [1082]; **12(3)**, [792]
proceedings for—
interpretation of terms, **12(2)**, [548]
protected material—
applicable offences, **12(2)**, [558]

sexual offences—*contd*
proceedings for—*contd*
protected material—*contd*
Criminal Cases Review Commission, regulation of disclosures by, **12(2)**, [553]
defendant's legal representative, disclosure to, **12(2)**, [550], [552]
disclosure, offences, **12(2)**, [554]
meaning, **12(2)**, [547]
modification of enactments, **12(2)**, [555]
prosecutor, regulation of disclosures by, **12(2)**, [549], [552]
unrepresented defendant, disclosure to, **12(2)**, [551]
prosecution and punishment, **12(1)**, [288], [297]
prostitution and pornography, abuse of child through—
arranging or facilitating, **12(3)**, [712]
causing or inciting, **12(3)**, [710]
controlling, **12(3)**, [711]
interpretation, **12(3)**, [713]
sexual services, paying for, **12(3)**, [709]
public lavatory, sexual activity in, **12(2)**, [1026]; **12(3)**, [735]
rape. *See* **rape**
reporting restrictions, **12(2)**, [137]
reports, supply of information for, **12(2)**, [1050]; **12(3)**, [759]
risk of sexual harm order—
appeal against, **12(3)**, [785]
application for, **12(3)**, [781]
breach of, **12(3)**, [786]
effect of conviction, **12(3)**, [787]
discharge, **12(3)**, [783]
effect of, **12(3)**, [781]
grounds, **12(3)**, [781]
interim, **12(3)**, [784]
interpretation, **12(3)**, [782]
meaning, **12(3)**, [781]
renewal, **12(3)**, [783]
variation, **12(3)**, [783]
serious—
life sentence for, **12(3)**, [956]
persons under 18, **12(3)**, [957]
meaning, **12(3)**, [955]
public protection, imprisonment for, **12(3)**, [956]
persons under 18, **12(3)**, [957]
specified, **12(3)**, [1081]–[1087]
service court, findings of, **12(2)**, [1085]; **12(3)**, [795]
sex offender—
child, disclosure of information relating to, **12(3)**, [1038], [1039]
home address, power of entry and search, **12(3)**, [761]
release or transfer, information about, **12(3)**, [760]
risk posed by, assessment of—
arrangements for, **12(3)**, [1035]
interpretation, **12(3)**, [1037]
review of arrangements, **12(3)**, [1036]

sexual offences—*contd*
  sex offender—*contd*
    verification, supply of information for,
      12(3), [758]
  sexual act, causing child to watch,
    12(2), [970]; **12(3)**, [676]
    abuse of position of trust, **12(3)**, [683]
  sexual activity, causing person to engage in—
    child under 13, **12(3)**, [672]
    consent, without, **12(3)**, [668]
  sexual activity, interpretation, **12(2)**, [1033];
    12(3), [742]
  sexual activity with child—
    abuse of position of trust, **12(3)**, [680]
    causing or inciting engagement in,
      12(3), [674]
      abuse of position of trust, **12(3)**, [681]
      family member, **12(3)**, [690]
    family member, **12(3)**, [689]
    offence of, **12(3)**, [673]
  sexual assault, **12(2)**, [961]; **12(3)**, [667]
    child under 13, of, **12(3)**, [671]
  sexual exploitation, trafficking for—
    interpretation, **12(3)**, [721]
    into UK, **12(3)**, [718]
    jurisdiction, **12(3)**, [721]
    out of UK, **12(3)**, [720]
    vehicle, ship or aircraft—
      detention of, **12(3)**, [723]
      forfeiture of, **12(3)**, [722]
      interpretation, **12(3)**, [724]
    within UK, **12(3)**, [719]
  soliciting by man, motor vehicle, from,
    12(1), [969]
  thresholds, with, **12(2)**, [1080]; **12(3)**, [790]
  trespass with intent to commit, **12(2)**, [1018];
    12(3), [727]
  victim—
    hospital direction, where made,
      12(4), [27]–[30]
    hospital order, where made,
      12(4), [20]–[25]
    information, right to receive, **12(4)**, [19]
      hospital direction, where made,
        12(4), [29]
      hospital order, where made, **12(4)**, [24]
      no restriction direction given,
        12(4), [34]
      transfer direction, where made,
        12(4), [35]
    representations, right to make, **12(4)**, [19]
      hospital direction, where made,
        12(4), [28]
      hospital order, where made, **12(4)**, [22]
      no restriction direction given,
        12(4), [34]
      transfer direction, where made,
        12(4), [33]
    transfer direction, where made,
      12(4), [31]–[37]
      no restriction direction given,
        12(4), [34], [36]
      no restriction order made, **12(4)**, [32]
      removal of restriction, **12(4)**, [37]

sexual offences—*contd*
  voyeurism, **12(2)**, [1022]–[1023];
    12(3), [731], [732]
  young offenders—
    application of provisions, **12(3)**, [789]
    parental directions in relation to—
      discharge, **12(3)**, [754]
      effect of, **12(3)**, [753]
      renewal, **12(3)**, [754]
      table of, **12(3)**, [753]
      variation, **12(3)**, [754]
    periods of detention, **12(3)**, [789]

sexual orientation
  hatred on grounds of, **12(4)**, [504], [571]
  freedom of expression, protection of,
    12(1), [1035]
  meaning, **12(1)**, [1025]

Seychelles
  British ship registered in, **7(2)**, [678]
  Commonwealth citizenship, **31**, [186]
  Constitution, provision for, **7(2)**, [673]
  existing law, operation of, **7(2)**, [674]
  fully responsible status of, **7(2)**, [672]
  visiting forces in, **7(2)**, [678]

Shakespeare Memorial Trust
  National Theatre, **13**, [112]
  trustees, appointment, **13**, [112]

share acquisition scheme. *See* **shares in company**

share capital
  allotted, meaning, **8(1)**, [624]
  alteration of—
    consolidation of shares, **8(1)**, [696]
      notice to registrar, **8(1)**, [697]
    limited company, **8(1)**, [695]
    methods of, **8**, 192
    notice to registrar, **8**, 192–3
    redenomination. *See* redenomination *below*
    stock, reconversion to shares, **8(1)**, [698]
      notice to registrar, **8(1)**, [699]
    sub-division of shares, **8(1)**, [696]
      notice to registrar, **8(1)**, [697]
  annual return as to, **8**, 764–5
  authorised minimum—
    meaning, **8**, 190
    orders increasing, **8**, 190
    public companies, **8**, 114
    reduction below, **8**, 207
  bonus, meaning, **44(1)**, [143]
  called up, meaning, **8**, 599; **8(1)**, [625]
  cancellation of shares, **8**, 192
    notice to registrar, **8**, 192
  certification of, **8**, 189
  company with—
    class rights, variation of, **8(1)**, [708]
    guarantee, limited by, **8(1)**, [83]
    initial shareholdings, **8(1)**, [88]
    meaning, **8(1)**, [623]
    statement of capital, **8(1)**, [88]
      members, provided to, **8(1)**, [110]

share capital—*contd*
  consolidation of, **8**, 192
  conversion of shares into stock, **8**, 192
  differing amounts, provision for, **8**, 191
  Directive disclosure requirements, documents
    subject to, **8(1)**, [1156]
  due date of issue, meaning, **44(1)**, [143]
  employees' shares excluded, **8**, 189
  equity, meaning, **8**, 604; **8(1)**, [626]
  general provisions, **8**, 189
  increase of—
    new shares, by, **8**, 192
    notice to registrar, **8**, 193
  interests in, disclosure of, **8**, 252–3
  issued, meaning, **8(1)**, [624]
  memorandum, statement in, **8**, 105, 114
  new consideration, **44(1)**, [146]
  ordinary, meaning, **44(1)**, [615]
  private company becoming public, **8**, 144–5
  public companies, minimum for—
    authorised, **8(1)**, [841]
      different currencies, shares denominated
        in, **8(1)**, [844]
      initial requirement, application of,
        8(1), [843]
      power to alter, **8(1)**, [842]
    requirement, **8(1)**, [839]
    trading certificate—
      doing business without, **8(1)**, [845]
      issue of, **8(1)**, [839]
      procedure for obtaining, **8(1)**, [840]
  public company, requirements, **8**, 189
  redenomination—
    effect of, **8(1)**, [702]
    meaning, **8(1)**, [700]
    new nominal values, calculation of,
      8(1), [701]
    notice to registrar, **8(1)**, [703]
    rate of exchange, **8(1)**, [700]
    reduction of capital—
      notice to registrar, **8(1)**, [705]
      resolution, **8(1)**, [704]
    reserve, **8(1)**, [706]
    resolution for, **8(1)**, [700]
  reduction of—
    "and reduced", adding to name, **8**, 204–5
    authorised minimum below, **8**, 207
    cancellation of shares, by, **8**, 192
    circumstances for, **8(1)**, [719]
    court, confirmation by—
      application for, **8(1)**, [723]
      objection by creditors, **8(1)**, [724]–[725]
      order, **8(1)**, [726]
      registration of order and statement of
        capital, **8(1)**, [727]
    creditors—
      concealing names of, **8**, 208
      consent, dispensing with, **8**, 203–4
      objections by, **8**, 203–4
      settlement of list of, **8**, 203–4
    liability of members after, **8**, 207–8;
      8(1), [730]
    methods, **8**, 202–3
    minute of, **8**, 206
    notice to registrar, **8**, 192

share capital—*contd*
  reduction of—*contd*
    objection by creditors—
      entitlement, **8(1)**, [724]
      omission from list of—
        liability to creditor, **8(1)**, [731]
        offences, **8(1)**, [725]
    order confirming—
      application to court for, **8**, 203
      court's power to make, **8**, 204–5
    private company, resolution supported by
      solvency statement—
      conditions for, **8(1)**, [720]
      registration, **8(1)**, [722]
      solvency statement, meaning, **8(1)**, [721]
    public company reducing below authorised
      minimum, **8(1)**, [728]
      re-registration as private company,
        expedited procedure, **8(1)**, [729]
    public notice of, **8**, 206
    registration of order for, **8**, 206
    reserve arising from, treatment of,
      8(1), [732]
    special resolution for, **8**, 202–3
  regulations, power to make provision by,
    8(1), [735]
  repayment—
    bonus issue following, **44(1)**, [113]
    matters treated as, **44(1)**, [114]
  re-registration of private company as public,
    requirements, **8(1)**, [169]
  reserve—
    liability of limited company, **8**, 191
    unlimited company, of, **8**, 193–4
  serious loss of, duty of directors to call
    meeting, **8(1)**, [734]
  share premium account as part of, **8**, 198
  statutory declaration as to, **8**, 189
  stock dividend—
    distributions, **44(1)**, [134]
    income, treated as, **44(1)**, [141]
    returns, **44(1)**, [142]

share fishermen
  employment provisions applying to, **16**, [494]
  national minimum wage, exclusion from
    provisions, **16**, [950]

share incentive plan. *See* **approved share
incentive plan**
  approval—
    application for, **44(2)**, [737]
    application of provisions, **44(2)**, [728]
    general requirements, **44(2)**, [729]
    individuals, eligibility of, **44(2)**, [730]
    refusal, appeal against, **44(2)**, [737]
    types of shares to be awarded, **44(2)**, [731]
    withdrawal, **44(2)**, [737]
  approved—
    application of provisions, **44(2)**, [521]
    associated company, meaning, **44(2)**, [738]
    award of shares, meaning, **44(2)**, [728]
    cash dividends, **44(2)**, [735]
      reinvestment, retained for, **44(2)**, [526]
    company reconstructions, **44(2)**, [738]

share incentive plan—*contd*
approved—*contd*
definitions, **44(2)**, [738]
dividend shares, **44(2)**, [735]
no charge on acquisition of, **44(2)**, [525]
free shares, **44(2)**, [728], [732]
ceasing to be subject to plan,
44(2), [535]
group plans, **44(2)**, [728]
information, officer of Revenue and
Customs requiring, **44(2)**, [738]
jointly owned companies, **44(2)**, [738]
market value, determination of,
44(2), [738]
matching shares, **44(2)**, [728], [734]
ceasing to be subject to plan,
44(2), [535]
partnership shares, **44(2)**, [728], [733]
ceasing to be subject to plan,
44(2), [536]
money deducted from salary, no charge
on, **44(2)**, [524]
relevant employment, participant ceasing to
be in, **44(2)**, [738]
rights issue, shares acquired under,
44(2), [738]
shares ceasing to be subject to plan,
44(2), [738]
employer company, payments by trustees
to, **44(2)**, [540]
free or matching, **44(2)**, [535]
identification of, **44(2)**, [538]
partnership, **44(2)**, [536]
PAYE—
deductions, **44(2)**, [541]
modification of provisions,
44(2), [539]
shares withdrawn from plan, **44(2)**, [738]
specified retirement age, meaning,
44(2), [738]
tax advantages—
award of shares, connected with,
44(2), [523]
holding of shares, connected with,
44(2), [526]
incidental expenditure, **44(2)**, [529]
other Acts, under, **44(2)**, [545]
scope of, **44(2)**, [522]
shares ceasing to be subject to plan,
connected with, **44(2)**, [527]–[528]
tax charges—
beneficial interest, disposal of,
44(2), [537], [542]
capital receipts, on, **44(2)**, [531], [543]
meaning, **44(2)**, [532]
PAYE deductions, **44(2)**, [544]
operation of, **44(2)**, [530]
other Acts, under, **44(2)**, [545]
partnership money paid over to
employee, no liability on, **44(2)**, [533]
partnership share agreement, cancellation
payments in respect of, **44(2)**, [534]
PAYE, **44(2)**, [539]–[541]
shares ceasing to be subject to plan,
connected with, **44(2)**, [535]–[538]

share incentive plan—*contd*
approved—*contd*
termination of plan, **44(2)**, [738]
trustees, **44(2)**, [736]
distributions, exemption from tax,
44(3), [785]
shares in—
cash dividends, payment of, **44(3)**, [393]
dividend shares ceasing to be subject to,
44(3), [394]
interpretation, **44(3)**, [396]
introduction to provisions, **44(3)**, [392]
non-UK resident companies—
cash dividends, payment of, **44(3)**, [406]
dividend shares ceasing to be subject to,
44(3), [407]
introduction to provisions, **44(3)**, [405]
reduction in tax, **44(3)**, [408]
reduction in tax, **44(3)**, [395]

share option
contributions, effect on. *See* **contributions**
right to control shares, as, **44(1)**, [640]
scheme. *See* **share option scheme**

share option scheme
approved, **44(1)**, [637]
approved CSOP schemes—
application of provisions, **44(2)**, [549]
approval, **44(2)**, [749], [754]
associated company, meaning, **44(2)**, [755]
definitions, **44(2)**, [755]
discount, option granted at, **44(2)**, [552]
eligibility to participate, **44(2)**, [750]
exchange of options, **44(2)**, [753]
exercise, no charge on, **44(2)**, [551]
group, **44(2)**, [748]
information, officer of Revenue and
Customs requiring, **44(2)**, [755]
jointly owned companies, **44(2)**, [755]
meaning, **44(2)**, [748]
scope of provisions, **44(2)**, [550]
share options, requirements, **44(2)**, [752]
shares to which schemes apply,
44(2), [751]
tax charge, **44(2)**, [552]
approved SAYE schemes—
application of provisions, **44(2)**, [546]
approval of, **44(2)**, [739]–[740], [746]
associated company, meaning, **44(2)**, [747]
definitions, **44(2)**, [747]
eligibility to participate, **44(2)**, [741]
exchange of options, **44(2)**, [745]
exercise of option, no charge on,
44(2), [548]
group, **44(2)**, [739]
information, officer of Revenue and
Customs requiring, **44(2)**, [747]
jointly owned companies, **44(2)**, [747]
linked savings arrangement, requirements
for, **44(2)**, [743]
meaning, **44(2)**, [739]
scope of provisions, **44(2)**, [547]
share options, requirements, **44(2)**, [744]

share option scheme—*contd*
　approved SAYE schemes—*contd*
　　shares to which scheme applying,
　　　44(2), [742]
　costs of establishing, **44(1)**, [56]
　definitions, **44(1)**, [108]
　enterprise management incentives—
　　amendment of provisions, **44(2)**, [763]
　　annual returns, **44(2)**, [763]
　　company reorganisations, **44(2)**, [761]
　　definitions, **44(2)**, [763]
　　disqualifying events, tax advantages—
　　　employee, relating to, **44(2)**, [560]
　　　events being disqualifying, **44(2)**, [558],
　　　　[561]
　　　modified tax consequences, **44(2)**, [557]
　　　relevant company, relating to,
　　　　44(2), [559]
　　　relevant share options, **44(2)**, [564]
　　　share capital, alteration of, **44(2)**, [562]
　　　share conversions, excluded, **44(2)**, [563]
　　eligible employees, **44(2)**, [759]
　　employer company, meaning, **44(2)**, [756]
　　excluded activities, **44(2)**, [758]
　　exercise of option, tax advantage on,
　　　44(2), [554]–[556]
　　general requirements, **44(2)**, [757]
　　information, power to require, **44(2)**, [763]
　　market value of shares, **44(2)**, [763]
　　maximum entitlement, **44(2)**, [757]
　　maximum value, **44(2)**, [757]
　　officer of Revenue and Customs,
　　　notification to, **44(2)**, [762]
　　options, requirements for, **44(2)**, [760]
　　other income tax charges, effects on,
　　　44(2), [566]
　　purpose of grant, **44(2)**, [757]
　　qualifying companies, **44(2)**, [758]
　　qualifying option, meaning, **44(2)**, [553]
　　relevant company, meaning, **44(2)**, [756]
　　share capital, alterations of, **44(2)**, [562]
　　share conversions, **44(2)**, [563]
　　taxable events, tax advantages, **44(2)**, [565]
　　time limits, compliance with, **44(2)**, [763]
　material interest in company, person having,
　　44(1), [108], [640]
　requirements, **44(1)**, [638]

share premium
　account—
　　meaning, **8(1)**, [688]
　　transfer of sums to, **8(1)**, [688]
　application of, **8(1)**, [688]
　definitions, **8(1)**, [694]
　issue at, **8(1)**, [688]
　relief from requirements—
　　balance sheet, reflected in, **8(1)**, [693]
　　further provision, power to make,
　　　8(1), [692]
　　group reconstruction, **8(1)**, [689]
　　merger, **8(1)**, [690]
　　　90% equity holding, meaning,
　　　　8(1), [691]

share warrant
　issue and effect of, **8**, 247
　meaning, **8**, 247
　register entries respecting, **8**, 412

shareholders
　accounts—
　　right to copy of, **8**, 302–3
　　right to inspect, **8**, 56
　addresses, register of, **8**, 17
　annual return, details in, **8**, 420–1
　class rights. *See* **shares in company**
　companies clauses. *See* **Companies
　　Clauses Acts**
　execution against, **8**, 28
　meaning, **8**, 15
　minority, right to buy out or takeover. *See*
　　companies
　nominee, notice by, **42**, [140]
　offers to, pre-emption rights, **8**, 167–8
　persons deemed to be, **8**, 16
　register, contents, **8**, 16–17
　subsequent, liability of, **8**, 185–6

shares
　acquired under EMI option, corporation tax
　　relief for, **43(S)**, 89
　acquisition of own by limited company. *See*
　　purchase of own shares
　acquisition, stamp duty relief, **41**, [168]
　allotment—
　　certificate, issue of, **8(1)**, [847]
　　commissions, discount or allowances, not to
　　　be applied for payment of, **8(1)**, [630]
　　directors' power of—
　　　authorisation by company, **8(1)**, [629]
　　　exercise of, **8(1)**, [627]
　　　private company with one class of
　　　　shares, **8(1)**, [628]
　　discount, prohibition, **8(1)**, [658]
　　equity securities, meaning, **8(1)**, [638]
　　formation, shares not taken on, **8(1)**, [637]
　　payment. *See* payment for *below*
　　permitted commission, **8(1)**, [631]
　　pre-emption right. *See* pre-emption right
　　　below
　　public companies, non-cash consideration.
　　　See public company *below*
　　public company issue not fully subscribed,
　　　where—
　　　irregular, effect of, **8(1)**, [657]
　　　prohibition of allotment, **8(1)**, [656]
　　　repayment of money subscribed,
　　　　8(1), [656]
　　registration, **8(1)**, [632]
　　return of—
　　　failure to make, offence of, **8(1)**, [635]
　　　limited company, by, **8(1)**, [633]
　　　unlimited company, new class of shares
　　　　allotted by, **8(1)**, [634]
　　time of, **8(1)**, [636]
　　bonus, exception to pre-emption right,
　　　8(1), [642]
　　certificate—
　　　allotment, issue on, **8(1)**, [847]

shares—*contd*
  certificate—*contd*
    default, court making good, **8(1)**, [860]
    evidence of title, as, **8(1)**, [846]
    issue of, **8(1)**, [847]
    official seal, **8(1)**, [128]
    surrender of warrant, issue on, **8(1)**, [858]
    transfer, issue on—
      duty of company, **8(1)**, [854]
      financial institution, allotment or transfer
        to, **8(1)**, [856]
      Stock Transfer Act, cases within,
        8(1), [855]
  class rights—
    uniform, **8(1)**, [707]
    variation of—
      court order, forwarding to registrar,
        8(1), [713]
      particulars, notification to registrar,
        8(1), [718]
      powers of court under other provisions,
        saving for, **8(1)**, [710]
      right to object to—
        share capital, company with,
          8(1), [711]
        share capital, company without,
          8(1), [712]
      share capital, company with, **8(1)**, [708]
      share capital, company without,
        8(1), [709]
  classes of, **8(1)**, [707]
    matters notified to registrar—
      name or designation of class of members,
        notice of, **8(1)**, [717]
      name or designation of class of shares,
        notice of, **8(1)**, [714]
      new class, notice of, **8(1)**, [716]
      variation of class rights, particulars of,
        8(1), [718]
      variation of rights attached to shares,
        particulars of, **8(1)**, [715]
    new, notice of, **8(1)**, [716]
  consolidation, **8(1)**, [696]
    notice to registrar, **8(1)**, [697]
  disposal of, losses on—
    qualifying trading companies—
      control requirement, **44(4)**, [142]
      gross assets requirement, **44(4)**, [145]
      independence requirement, **44(4)**, [142]
      meaning, **44(4)**, [137]
      property managing subsidiaries
        requirement, **44(4)**, [144]
      qualifying subsidiaries requirement,
        44(4), [143]
      trading requirement, **44(4)**, [140]
        administration or receivership, ceasing
          to meet because of, **44(4)**, [141]
      unquoted status requirement,
        44(4), [146]
    relief—
      deductions, how made, **44(4)**, [136]
      eligibility for, **44(4)**, [134]
      entitlement to claim, **44(4)**, [135]
      limits on, **44(4)**, [150]
      mixed holdings, **44(4)**, [151]–[152]

shares—*contd*
  disposal of, losses on—*contd*
    relief—*contd*
      qualifying shares, **44(4)**, [134]
  distributions. *See* **distributions**
  EIS relief not attributable to—
    disposal of—
      new, **44(4)**, [139]
      qualifying trading companies,
        44(4), [137]
      exchange of shares for shares in
        another company, **44(4)**, [148]
      new shares substituted for old shares,
        44(4), [149]
    subscriptions for, **44(4)**, [138]
  equity securities—
    allotment, meaning, **8(1)**, [638]
    meaning, **8(1)**, [638]
    pre-emption right. *See* pre-emption right
      below
  holding of as no bar to damages against
    company, **8(1)**, [733]
  institutional investors, exercise of voting rights
    by—
    power to require information, **8(1)**, [1353]
    provision of information, **8(1)**, [1356]
    relevant institutions, **8(1)**, [1354]
    relevant shares, **8(1)**, [1355]
  interests in—
    connected persons, **8(1)**, [1377]
    corporate, **8(1)**, [901]
    family, **8(1)**, [900]
    information protected from wider
      disclosure, **8(1)**, [904]
    investigation of—
      power of members to require company
        to act, **8(1)**, [881]–[882]
      report to members, **8(1)**, [883]–[885]
    issued shares, in relation to, **8(1)**, [870]
    meaning, **8(1)**, [898]
    notice by company requiring information
      on—
      compliance, persons exempted from,
        8(1), [874]
      details required, **8(1)**, [871]
      offences, **8(1)**, [873]
      power of members to require company
        to act, **8(1)**, [881]–[882]
      restrictions on shares, order imposing,
        8(1), [872]
    periods for fulfilling obligations, reckoning
      of, **8(1)**, [905]
    public companies, provision applying to,
      8(1), [869]
    register of. *See* register of interests *below*
    regulations, power to make further
      provision by, **8(1)**, [906]
    right to subscribe, **8(1)**, [899]
    share acquisition agreement—
      arising from, **8(1)**, [902]
      extent of obligation, **8(1)**, [903]
    voting rights, temporary suspension of,
      8(1), [870]
  issue of, deemed time of, **44(4)**, [153]
  meaning, **8(1)**, [618]

shares—*contd*
nature of, **8(1)**, [619]
nominal value, **8(1)**, [620]
numbering, **8(1)**, [621]
ordinary, meaning, **8(1)**, [638]
payment for—
  cash, in, **8(1)**, [661]
  contravention of provisions—
    penalty for, **8(1)**, [668]
    relief, power of court to grant,
      8(1), [667]
    subsequent holders, liability of,
      8(1), [666]
  different amounts, provision for, **8(1)**, [659]
  discount, allotment at, **8(1)**, [658]
  interest, appropriate rate of, **8(1)**, [670]
  means of, general rule, **8(1)**, [660]
  public company—
    long-term undertaking, payment by,
      8(1), [665]
    one-quarter paid up, minimum of,
      8(1), [664]
    subscribers of memorandum, by,
      8(1), [662]
    undertaking to do work or perform
      services, no acceptance of, **8(1)**, [663]
  subscribers of memorandum, by,
    8(1), [662]
  undertakings, enforceability, **8(1)**, [669]
pre-emption right—
  communication of offers, **8(1)**, [640]
  contravention of provision, liability for,
    8(1), [641]
  disapplication of—
    directors' statement, liability for false
      statement in, **8(1)**, [650]
    general authorisation, directors acting
      under, **8(1)**, [648]
    private companies, with one class of
      shares, **8(1)**, [647]
    special resolution, by, **8(1)**, [649]
    treasury shares, sale of, **8(1)**, [651]
  exceptions—
    bonus shares, **8(1)**, [642]
    employees' share scheme, shares held
      under, **8(1)**, [644]
    non-cash consideration, issue for,
      8(1), [643]
  exclusion of—
    articles, corresponding right in,
      8(1), [646]
    private companies, by, **8(1)**, [645]
  existing shareholders, of, **8(1)**, [639]
  formation, shares not taken on, **8(1)**, [655]
  holder of shares, reference to, **8(1)**, [652]
  older requirements, saving for, **8(1)**, [654]
  other resolutions, saving for, **8(1)**, [653]
premium. *See* **share premium**
public company—
  non-cash asset, valuation of agreement for
    transfer of—
    re-registered company, adaptation of
      provisions to, **8(1)**, [681]
    approval by members, requirement,
      8(1), [679]

shares—*contd*
public company—*contd*
  non-cash asset, valuation of agreement for
    transfer of—*contd*
    contravention of provisions, **8(1)**, [682]
      penalty for, **8(1)**, [685]
    relief, power to grant, **8(1)**, [684]
    subsequent holder of shares, liability
      of, **8(1)**, [683]
    independent, requirement, **8(1)**, [677]
    initial period, in, **8(1)**, [676]
    interest, appropriate rate of, **8(1)**, [687]
    resolution, delivery to registrar,
      8(1), [680]
    valuation and report, requirement,
      8(1), [678]
    valuation requirements,
      8(1), [1227]–[1231]
  non-cash consideration for, independent
    valuation—
    arrangement with other company,
      exception for, **8(1)**, [672]
    contravention—
      penalty for, **8(1)**, [685]
      relief, power to grant, **8(1)**, [684]
      subsequent holder of shares, liability
        of, **8(1)**, [683]
    copy of report, delivery to registrar,
      8(1), [675]
    interest, appropriate rate of, **8(1)**, [687]
    merger, exception on, **8(1)**, [673]
    report, requirement for, **8(1)**, [674]
    requirement, **8(1)**, [671], [674]
    undertakings to do work, enforceability,
      8(1), [686]
  payment for shares—
    long-term undertaking, payment by,
      8(1), [665]
    one-quarter paid up, minimum of,
      8(1), [664]
    subscribers of memorandum, by,
      8(1), [662]
    undertaking to do work or perform
      services, no acceptance of, **8(1)**, [663]
purchase by company of own, stamp duty
  on, **41**, [158]
purchase of own. *See* **purchase of own
shares**
reconversion of stock to, **8(1)**, [698]
  notice to registrar, **8(1)**, [699]
redeemable—
  cancelled, treated as, **8(1)**, [766]
  payment for, **8(1)**, [764]
  power of limited company to issue,
    8(1), [762]
  redemption—
    financing, **8(1)**, [765]
    notice to registrar, **8(1)**, [767]
    terms and manner of, **8(1)**, [763]
register of interests—
  copies—
    default in providing, **8(1)**, [891]
    right to require, **8(1)**, [889]
  index, **8(1)**, [888]
  information in, **8(1)**, [886]

shares—*contd*
  register of interests—*contd*
    inspection—
      availability for, **8(1)**, [887]
      exercise of rights, court supervision,
        8(1), [890]
      offences, **8(1)**, [892]
      refusal of, **8(1)**, [891]
      right of, **8(1)**, [889]
    public, company ceasing to be, **8(1)**, [897]
    removal of entries from—
      old entries, **8(1)**, [894]
      prohibition, **8(1)**, [893]
      third party, incorrect entry relating to,
        8(1), [895]
    requirement to keep, **8(1)**, [886]
    share acquisition agreement, adjustment of
      entry relating to, **8(1)**, [896]
  renounceable letter of allotment, **41**, [148]
  restrictions on—
    attempted evasion, penalty for, **8(1)**, [876]
    effect of, **8(1)**, [875]
    order imposing—
      application for, **8(1)**, [872]
      consequences of, **8(1)**, [875]
    relaxation of, **8(1)**, [877]
    removal of, **8(1)**, [878]
    sale of shares subject to—
      application of proceeds, **8(1)**, [880]
      order for, **8(1)**, [879]
  right to subscribe for, **8(1)**, [899]
  stock, not convertible to, **8(1)**, [618]
  sub-division, **8(1)**, [696]
    notice to registrar, **8(1)**, [697]
  takeover offer. *See* **takeover offer**
  title to. *See* **securities**
  transfer—
    application of transferor, on, **8(1)**, [850]
    certificate issued on—
      duty of company, **8(1)**, [854]
      financial institution, allotment or transfer
        to, **8(1)**, [856]
      Stock Transfer Act, cases within,
        8(1), [855]
    certification of instrument of, **8(1)**, [853]
    grant of probate, evidence of, **8(1)**, [852]
    personal representative, execution by,
      8(1), [851]
    procedure on lodging, **8(1)**, [849]
    registration of, **8(1)**, [848]
  transferability, **8(1)**, [622]
  treasury—
    application of provisions, **8(1)**, [802]
    cancellation, **8(1)**, [807]
    company holding, reference to, **8(1)**, [802]
    disposal of, **8(1)**, [805]
    exercise of rights in respect of, **8(1)**, [804]
    maximum holdings, **8(1)**, [803]
    notice of cancellation, **8(1)**, [808]
    notice of disposal, **8(1)**, [806]
    offences relating to, **8(1)**, [810]
    proceeds of sale, treatment of, **8(1)**, [809]
    qualifying, meaning, **8(1)**, [802]

shares—*contd*
  voteholder information, transparency—
    competent authority, power of to call for
      information, **8(1)**, [1345]
    infringement of obligation, powers in case
      of, **8(1)**, [1346]
    obligations Directive, **8(1)**, [1343]
    rules, **8(1)**, [1344]
  warrant—
    bearer, issue to, **8(1)**, [857]
    issue of certificate on surrender of,
      8(1), [858]
    register of members, entry of details in,
      8(1), [200]

shares in company. *See also* **securities**
  acquisition of—
    company's nominee, by, **8**, 210
    dissenting minority, of. *See* **companies**
  acquisition, stamp duty relief **41**, [293]
  allotment. *See* **allotment (shares and
    debentures)**
  calls on. *See* **Companies Clauses Acts**
  cancellation of—
    general meeting necessary, **8**, 192
    notice to registrar, **8**, 192
    public company, by, **8**, 211–14
    reduction of capital by, **8**, 192
  capital to be divided into, **8**, 16
  certificate. *See* **Companies Clauses Acts**
  charges on company's own shares, **8**, 214–15
  chartered company. *See* **chartered company**
  class rights—
    court's powers, saving for, **8**, 195
    memorandum etc, not stated in, **8**, 196
    newly created, registration of, **8**, 197–8
    special, registration of, **8**, 197
    variation of—
      abrogation, included, **8**, 196
      meetings for purposes of, **8**, 195
      objections to, **8**, 196
      requirements for, **8**, 194–5
  companies acquiring own, treatment of,
    43(2), [242]
    bonus shares, **43(2)**, [242]
  companies clauses. *See* **Companies
    Clauses Acts**
  company having beneficial interest in—
    references to, interpretation, **8**, 609
    residual interests, **8**, 609
    treatment of, **8**, 211–12
  company's own shares—
    acquisition of—
      company limited by shares, **8**, 209–10
      general rule against, **8**, 209–10
      nominee, by, **8**, 210
      offence as to, penalty, **8**, 210
    charges on, **8**, 214–15
    lien on, **8**, 214
    non-compliance, sanctions, **8**, 214
    public company, treatment of, **8**, 211–14
    purchase of—
      contingent purchase contract—
        approval of, **8**, 228
        meaning, **8**, 228

shares in company—*contd*
  company's own shares—*contd*
    purchase of—*contd*
      disclosure of, **8**, 230–1
      failure as to, effect of, **8**, 239
      market purchase—
        authority for, **8**, 228
        meaning, **8**, 226
        procedure, **8**, 228
      off-market—
        authority for, **8**, 226–7
        meaning, **8**, 226
      payments from distributable profits,
        8, 229–30
      private company, by—
        financing of, **8**, 233–4
        objections, to, **8**, 237–8
        payment out of capital, **8**, 234–5
        powers of, **8**, 232–3
        publicity for payment, **8**, 236–7
        special resolution as to, **8**, 235–6
      redeemable shares, **8**, 225
      returns as to, **8**, 230
      right to, assignment of, **8**, 229
      special resolution for, **8**, 226–7
      transitional cases, **8**, 241
    redeemable shares. *See* **companies**
  consideration for, valuation—
    full disclosure to valuer, **8**, 184
    person qualified for, **8**, 181
    report on, contents, **8**, 182–3
    requirement for, before allotment, **8**, 177–8
  controlled foreign company, in, gains from,
    44(1), [675]
  conversion into stock, **8**, 192
    notice to registrar, **8**, 192
  dealings, investigation of, **8**, 492–3
  dissenting minority, of, acquisition of. *See*
    companies
  employee share acquisition, corporation tax
    relief—
    award of shares, on, **43(2)**, [255]
    convertible, provisions applying to,
      43(2), [258]
    death of employee or recipient, exercise of
      option after, **43(2)**, [259]
    definitions, **43(2)**, [259]
    grant of option, on, **43(2)**, [256]
    other deductions, relationship with,
      43(2), [259]
    provision for, **43(2)**, [254]
    requirements for, **43(2)**, [254]
    restricted, provisions applying to,
      43(2), [257]
    transfer of business within group,
      43(2), [259]
    transitional provisions, **43(2)**, [260]
  employment-related securities. *See*
    employment-related securities
  exchanges on reconstructions, **43(2)**, [134]
  financial assistance for purchase of—
    companies affected by restrictions, **8**, 215
    contravention of provisions, **8**, 215
    general prohibition, **8**, 215
    meaning, **8**, 216

shares in company—*contd*
  financial assistance for purchase of—*contd*
    methods of giving, **8**, 216
    private company, relaxation for, **8**, 218
    public companies, special restrictions,
      8, 219
    requirements for giving, **8**, 218
    special resolution for—
      cancellation by court, **8**, 222
      general provisions for, **8**, 222
      requirement for, **8**, 222
    statutory declaration respecting, **8**, 220–1
    time for giving, **8**, 222–3
    transactions not prohibited, **8**, 217–18
  forfeiture. *See* **Companies Clauses Acts**
  gift to charities, **44(1)**, [422]
  insider dealings. *See* **securities**
  interest in—
    agreement to acquire, **8**, 258–9
      obligation of disclosure, **8**, 259–60
      persons acting together, duty of,
        8, 260–1
    attribution, by, **8**, 262–3
    company investigations, **8**, 271–2
      inspection of report on, **8**, 277
      report to members of, **8**, 274
      requisition by members, on, **8**, 273
    director, by. *See* **director**
    exemptions from disclosure, **8**, 264–6
    information—
      failure to provide, **8**, 275
      notice requiring, **8**, 271
    interests disregarded, **8**, 264–6
    joint interest, **8**, 263
    matters for disclosure, **8**, 253–4
    meaning, **8**, 263
    notifiable interests, **8**, 263
    notification of—
      corporate interests, **8**, 257–8
      default in giving, **8**, 268
      family interests, **8**, 257–8
      general provisions, **8**, 268
      particulars to be given in, **8**, 256–7
      time for giving, **8**, 256
    obligation of disclosure, **8**, 252–3
      when arising, **8**, 253–4
    percentage level of, **8**, 255–6
    references to, interpretation, **8**, 757
    register of, **8**, 270–1
      inspection, open to, **8**, 277
      removal of entries, **8**, 276
    registration, **8**, 272–3
    regulations, power to make, **8**, 269
  issue of—
    at premium, retrospective relief, **8**, 825
    restrictions, in contravention of, **8**, 505
    subscribers to memorandum, to, **8**, 181
    See also **allotment of shares and
      debentures**
  liabilities—
    relief in respect of, **8**, 186–7
    subsequent holder, of, **8**, 185–6
  lien on company's own shares, **8**, 214
  meaning, **8**, 604; **19(2)**, [499]
  nature of, **8**, 242

shares in company—*contd*
new consideration not derived from,
44(1), [114]
non-cash assets, valuation of—
agreements contravening, **8**, 180–1
full disclosure to valuer, **8**, 184
requirement for, **8**, 179
valuers' report, **8**, 182–3
numbering of, **8**, 242
offer to the public—
exceptions from rule, **8**, 157
pre-emption rights, **8**, 167–8
private limited company, by, **8**, 160
prospectus, as, **8**, 156
rule governing, **8**, 156
See also **prospectus**
option. *See* **share option**
options, directors dealing in, **8**, 387–8
ownership, information as to, **8**, 491
paid up, meaning, **8**, 600
payment for—
cash, other than by, **8**, 176
differentials, provision for, **8**, 191
discount, prohibition of, **8**, 175
general rules, **8**, 174–5
interest—
appropriate rate, meaning, **8**, 181
liability to pay, **8**, 174–5
liability, relief from, **8**, 186–7
long-term undertaking, by, **8**, 176–7
quarter paid up, to be, **8**, 176
undertaking to do work etc, enforcement,
8, 188
pre-1982 restrictions, **8**, 829
preference, meaning, **44(1)**, [113]
priority allocation to employees—
definitions, **44(2)**, [573]
different offer to public, **44(2)**, [569]
discount not covered, **44(2)**, [570]
public, offer also made to, **44(2)**, [567]
discount not covered, **44(2)**, [568]
registrant discount, meaning and amount,
44(2), [572]
similar terms, entitlement on, **44(2)**, [571]
public, beneficially held by, **44(1)**, [229]
public company, of, treatment of, **8**, 211–14
public offer, acquired on, **43(2)**, [321]
purchase by company of own, stamp duty on
41, [283]
purchase of own—
advance clearance of payments,
44(1), [129]
associated persons, **44(1)**, [131]
conditions for, **44(1)**, [127]
dealer's receipts, taxation of, **44(1)**, [76]
information, power to require, **44(1)**, [130]
ownership, period of, **44(1)**, [124]
purchasing company member of group,
where, **44(1)**, [126]
relaxation of conditions, **44(1)**, [128]
residence conditions, **44(1)**, [124]
returns, **44(1)**, [130]
unquoted trading company, by,
44(1), [123]

shares in company—*contd*
purchase of own—*contd*
vendor's interest as shareholder, reduction
of, **44(1)**, [125]
qualification of directors, **8**, 367–8
redemption. *See* **companies**
renounceable letter of allotment **41**, [273]
research institution spin-out companies, in—
application of provisions, **44(2)**, [497]
artificially enhanced market value,
disapplication of provisions, **44(2)**, [501]
controlled company, transfer of intellectual
property by, **44(2)**, [505]
definitions, **44(2)**, [506]
intellectual property, meaning, **44(2)**, [502]
involved in research, meaning, **44(2)**, [504]
market value on acquisition, **44(2)**, [498]
research institution, meaning, **44(2)**, [503]
restricted securities, election for
disapplication of provisions, **44(2)**, [500]
tax relief following acquisition, **44(2)**, [499]
residual interest, meaning, **8**, 609
restrictions as to—
application to court to remove, **8**, 505–6
evasion of, penalty, **8**, 505
imposed pre-1982, **8**, 829
order imposing, effect of, **8**, 504, 924–5
relaxation or removal of, **8**, 505–6
sale of shares subject to, **8**, 507
subscribers, commission to. *See* **companies**
subsequent holder, liability of, **8**, 185–6
title to, evidence of, **8**, 246
transfer—
articles, regulation by, **8**, 242
certificates—
duty to issue, **8**, 244–5
evidence of title, as, **8**, 246
certification of, **8**, 243–4
companies clauses. *See* **Companies**
Clauses Acts
delivery of warrant, by, **8**, 247
instrument of, delivery of, **8**, 242–3
meaning, **8**, 244
personal representative, by, **8**, 242
registration of, **8**, 242–3
winding-up, after, **8**, 549
unquoted—
loss relief—
companies, for, **44(1)**, [396]
exclusion of, **44(1)**, [397]
qualifying shares, disposal of, **44(1)**, [398]
qualifying trading companies, **44(1)**, [399]
exchange of shares for shares in another
company, relief after, **44(1)**, [408]
new for old shares, substitution of,
44(1), [409]
requirements—
amendment by Treasury order, power
of, **44(1)**, [407]
control and independence,
44(1), [402]
gross assets, **44(1)**, [405]
property managing subsidiaries,
44(1), [404]
qualifying subsidiaries, **44(1)**, [403]

shares in company—*contd*
  unquoted—*contd*
    qualifying trading companies—*contd*
      requirements—*contd*
        trading, **44(1)**, [400], [401]
        unquoted status, **44(1)**, [406]
  warrant. *See* **share warrant**

shed
  abatement notice to occupier of, **35(1)**, [170]
  byelaws as to, **35(1)**, [170]
  human habitation, used for—
    control over, **35(1)**, [497]
    order prohibiting, **35(1)**, [170]
  public health provisions applicable to, **35(1)**, [170]
  statutory nuisance, when, **35(1)**, [170]

sheep
  dipping, facilities for, **2**, [506]
  diseases. *See* **diseases of animals**
  distress, no taking against, **13**, [1156]
  hill farming. *See* **hill farming**
  quality, improving, **1(1)**, [370]
  rams—
    castration or slaughter, **1(1)**, [370], [445]
    control of, **1(1)**, [370], [445]
    inspection, marking etc, **1(1)**, [370], [445]
    licence to keep, **1(1)**, [370]
    offences and penalties, **1(1)**, [371], [445]
    regulations, provisions of, **1(1)**, [445]
    requisitions to slaughtering, **1(1)**, [445]
  regulations and orders, **1(1)**, [377]
  scab, prevention, **2**, [442]
  subsidies. *See* **hill farming**

Sheerness
  Port of London powers not exercisable off, **39(2)**, [384], [419]

Sheffield
  assay office, **48**, 14
  assay town, as, **48**, 13
  mark. *See* **Sheffield mark**
  wrought plate—
    assaying and marking of, **48**, 13
    guardian of standard, **48**, 14

Sheffield mark
  transitional provisions, **48**, 195

Shelley's case
  rule in, abolition, **20**, [742]

shellfish
  bed, meaning, **1(1)**, [710]
  Channel Islands, provisions applying to, **1(1)**, [711]
  cleansing of, provision of facilities for, **1(2)**, [439]
  crab—
    byelaws on taking, **1(1)**, [609]
    illegally in possession, seizure of, **1(1)**, [706]
    shell, having cast, protection of, **1(1)**, [705]

shellfish—*contd*
  crab—*contd*
    spawn-carrying, protection of, **1(1)**, [705]
  cultivation, structure for, **1(2)**, [179]
  deposit of—
    inspection of waters, **1(1)**, [702]
    offences, **1(1)**, [702]
    power to prohibit, **1(1)**, [700]
  diseases—
    public fishery, in, **1(1)**, [703]
    spread, measures to prevent, **1(1)**, [700]
  farming—
    information, power to require, **1(2)**, [223]
    meaning, **1(2)**, [223]
  financial provisions, **1(1)**, [709]
  fishery—
    byelaws, provisions in, **1(1)**, [609]
    cultivation, structure for, in, **1(2)**, [179]
    documents, service of, **1(1)**, [699]
    establishment etc, power as to, **1(1)**, [689]
    inspection of, **1(1)**, [702]
    jurisdiction in respect of, **1(1)**, [698]
    orders as to—
      annual report on, **1(1)**, [694]
      application for, **1(1)**, [689]
      Crown and Duchy rights, saving for, **1(1)**, [689]
      inquiry on making, **1(1)**, [714]
      making, provisions on, **1(1)**, [714]
      power to make, **1(1)**, [689]
      proof of requirements, **1(1)**, [696]
      rights conferred by, **1(1)**, [689]
      savings, **1(1)**, [689]
      specified description of shellfish, for, **1(1)**, [689], [768]
      tolls or royalties, imposing, **1(1)**, [768]
      variation of, **1(1)**, [689]
    propagation, structure for, in, **1(2)**, [179]
    protection of, **1(1)**, [695], [705]
    regulating, right of—
      cesser, **1(1)**, [693]
      effect of grant, **1(1)**, [691]
      inquiry and examination into, **1(1)**, [693]
      licensing powers, **1(1)**, [692]
      order conferring, **1(1)**, [689]
      restrictions under, **1(1)**, [691]
    restoration of, grant or loan for, **1(1)**, [697]
    samples, taking from, **1(1)**, [702]
    several fishery, right of—
      cesser, **1(1)**, [693]
      effect of grant, **1(1)**, [690]
      grantee, absolute property of, **1(1)**, [695]
      inquiry and examination into, **1(1)**, [693]
      order conferring, **1(1)**, [689]
      protection of, **1(1)**, [695]
      types of shellfish in, **1(1)**, [689]
  gangmasters. *See* **agriculture**
  importation of—
    offences, **1(1)**, [702]
    power to prohibit, **1(1)**, [701]
  Isle of Man, provisions applying to, **1(1)**, [711]

shellfish—*contd*
  lobster—
    byelaws on taking, **1(1)**, [609]
    illegally in possession, seizure of,
      1(1), [706]
    spawn-carrying, protection of, **1(1)**, [705]
  meaning, **1(1)**, [710]; **1(2)**, [701]
  offences—
    fines, application of, **1(1)**, [707]
    place of committal, deemed, **1(1)**, [707]
  orders and regulations, making, **1(1)**, [708]
  oysters—
    bed—
      close season, having dredge on board
        during, **1(1)**, [695]
      owner, absolute property of, **1(1)**, [695]
      protection of, **1(1)**, [695]
      sale, for, **1(1)**, [704]
    cultivation, byelaws on, **1(1)**, [609]
    illegally in possession, seizure of,
      1(1), [706]
    not to be sold between certain dates,
      1(1), [704]
  propagation of, structure for, **1(2)**, [179]
  size limits, byelaws on, **1(1)**, [609]

sheriff. *See also* **distress**
  appointment of—
    annual, to be, **39(1)**, [746]
    City of London, for, **39(1)**, [743], [764]
    duration of, **39(1)**, [746]
    formalities of, **39(1)**, [749]
    generally, **39(1)**, [743]
    twice in three years, limit on, **39(1)**, [748]
    warrant, **39(1)**, [749], [768]
  Cinque Ports, in, **39(1)**, [743]
  county, meaning, **39(1)**, [770]
  death of, **39(1)**, [759]
  declaration of office, **39(1)**, [750], [763]
  deputy resident in London, appointment of,
    39(1), [758]
  disqualification for service, **39(1)**, [743]
  Duchy of Cornwall, saving for rights of,
    39(1), [765]
  escape from custody of, **39(1)**, [754]
  fees and poundage, **39(1)**, [743], [756]
  Greater London, appointment, **25(1)**, [759]
  high sheriff, to be known as, **25(2)**, [173]
  judicial functions, **39(1)**, [743]
  justice of the peace, not acting as,
    39(1), [755]
  liability to serve, exemption from,
    39(1), [743]
  meaning, **9**, [273]
  misconduct of, **39(1)**, [762]
  nomination of, **39(1)**, [749]
  officers—
    declaration of office, **39(1)**, [760], [769]
    misconduct by, **39(1)**, [762]
  posse comitatus, powers for, **39(1)**, [751]
  prisons, jurisdiction as to, **12(1)**, [275AA]
  qualification of, **39(1)**, [747]
  returning officer, as, **39(1)**, [743]
  sale of offices, **39(1)**, [761]
  selection of, **39(1)**, [743]

sheriff—*contd*
  under sheriff—
    appointment of, **39(1)**, [757]
    areas for, **25(2)**, [173]
    declaration of office, **39(1)**, [757], [763],
      [769]
    execution of office by, **39(1)**, [743]
    misconduct by, **39(1)**, [762]
    sale of offices, **39(1)**, [761]
  writ—
    receipt for, **39(1)**, [752]
    resistance in execution of, powers on,
      39(1), [751]
  wrongful imprisonment by, **39(1)**, [753]

sheriff court
  delivery up or disposal of infringing goods,
    jurisdiction to order, **48**, **128**
  jurisdiction—
    copyright, **11(1)**, [930]
    performers' rights, in respect of,
      11(1), [1059]

ship. *See also* **vessel**
  aircraft in distress, duty to assist, **39(2)**, [757]
  alcohol and drugs offences. *See* **master (of
    ship); pilotage; seamen**
  appropriate non-ship pool, allocation of
    expenditure to, **43(1)**, [688]
  assessments, adjustment of, **43(1)**, [717]
  balancing charge, deferment of—
    attribution—
      amounts ceasing to be subject to,
        43(1), [704]
      earlier expenditure first, **43(1)**, [701]
      effect of, **43(1)**, [703]
      new expenditure, to, **43(1)**, [700]
      variation of, **43(1)**, [702]
    claim for, **43(1)**, [695]
    conditions for, **43(1)**, [695]–[696]
    connected persons, transactions between,
      43(1), [716]
    effect of, **43(1)**, [697]
    limit on amount, **43(1)**, [698]
    new shipping, expenditure on—
      deferment, object of securing,
        43(1), [708]
      later events, **43(1)**, [709]
      meaning, **43(1)**, [706]
      ship previously owned, **43(1)**, [707]
      shipowner, not incurred by, **43(1)**, [710]
    no entitlement, requirement to notify,
      43(1), [705]
    old ship, amount taken into account for,
      43(1), [699]
    persons carrying on qualifying activity,
      change in, **43(1)**, [715]
    qualifying ship—
      meaning, **43(1)**, [711]
      registration requirement, **43(1)**, [714]
      ships not being, **43(1)**, [713]
      under 100 tons, **43(1)**, [712]
    rules, **43(1)**, [694]
  bareboat charter by British charterers,
    39(2), [685]

ship—*contd*
  births and deaths, return of, **39(2)**, [776]
  British—
    aliens, disqualification for ownership,
      31, [2]
    bareboat charter by British charterers,
      39(2), [685]
    British connection, offences relating to,
      39(2), [682]
    central register, maintenance of,
      39(2), [676]
    character—
      assuming, **39(2)**, [671]
      concealing, **39(2)**, [671]
    flag—
      duty to show, **39(2)**, [673]
      red ensign, **39(2)**, [670]
    foreign character, assuming, **39(2)**, [671]
    improper colours, carrying, **39(2)**, [672]
    meaning, **39(2)**, [669]
    national colours, failure to show,
      39(2), [672]
    registration. *See* registration *below*
  broadcasting from—
    facilitating, **45**, [856]
      enforcement powers, **45**, [864]
      territorial scope, **45**, [860]
    prohibition, **45**, [851]
  capital allowances, transitional provisions,
    43(1), [1224]
  charge on, registration, **8**, 456
  charges, **39(2)**, [1008]
  chartered by demise to Crown, application of
    provisions to, **39(2)**, [986]
  coast, off, jurisdiction over, **39(2)**, [957]
  collision at sea. *See* **collision**
  construction credits, **39(2)**, [452]
  construction grants, **39(2)**, [454], [459]
  convoy, under, **3**, [1219]
  crew. *See* **crew**
  customs and excise—
    access, powers of, **13**, [611], [919]
    arrival or departure, time of, **13**, [594]
    boarding, powers of, **13**, [610], [919]
    cargo—
      jettisoning, forfeiture, **13**, [683]
      manifest, **13**, [655]
      missing, inability to account for,
        13, [684]
    clearance outward of ships. *See*
      exportation
    coasting ship—
      boarding and searching, **13**, [663]
      cargo records, **13**, [664]
      clearance, **13**, [662]
      documents, production, **13**, [663]
      examination of goods, **13**, [663]
      explosives, carriage in, **13**, [666]
    coastwise trade—
      control of, **13**, [660]–[665]
      directions as to, **13**, [660]
      exceptional provisions as to, **13**, [661]
      permission for, **13**, [661]
    concealed goods, forfeiture, **13**, [611],
      [633], [682]

ship—*contd*
  customs and excise—*contd*
    condemnation, **13**, [748], [785]
    detention, powers of, **13**, [612], [749],
      [919]
    entry outwards, **13**, [652]
    explosives, carriage in, **13**, [666]
    exportation etc, **13**, [645], [655]
    failure to bring to, **13**, [685]
    foreign, rules for, **13**, [536]
      information as to goods, **13**, [667],
        [670]–[673]
      offences—
        deviation from voyage, **13**, [665]
        loading or unloading outside UK,
          13, [665]
        prohibition or restriction, carriage
          contrary to, **13**, [665]
        touching at place outside UK,
          13, [665]
      prohibited or restricted goods, forfeiture
        of, **13**, [665]
      transire, general, grant and revocation,
        13, [662]
      unauthorised unloading in UK,
        13, [665]
    forfeiture of—
      concealing goods, constructed for,
        13, [682]
      failure to bring to, **13**, [685]
      jettisoning, etc, cargo, **13**, [683]
      missing cargo, inability to account for,
        13, [684]
    fuel, certificate of, **13**, [655]
    HM ships, etc, account of goods before
      unloading, **13**, [618]
    loading, control of, **13**, [655]
    minimum tonnage for export goods,
      13, [649]
    naval, goods supplied to, relief from duties
      for, **13**, [590], [801]
    report inwards, **13**, [617]
    responsible officer—
      implication in offence, **13**, [748]
      meaning, **13**, [748]
    stationing officers in, **13**, [610]
    stores—
      duty and drawback on, **13**, [650]
      entry outwards of goods shipped as,
        13, [637]
      failure to reach destination, **13**, [650]
      landing or unloading in UK, **13**, [650]
      port, goods consumed in, **13**, [913]
      quantity, control of, **13**, [650]
    unauthorised unloading, **13**, [656]
  dangerous goods on, search for, **12(1)**, [167]
  dangerously unsafe—
    detention notice—
      arbitration, reference to, **39(2)**, [760]
      contents of, **39(2)**, [759]
      invalid detention, compensation for,
        39(2), [761]
    meaning, **39(2)**, [758]
    owner and master, liability of, **39(2)**, [762]
    power to detain, **39(2)**, [759]

ship—*contd*
  dangers to navigation, report of, **39(2)**, [755]
  death on—
    returns of, **39(2)**, [776]
    transmission of particulars of, **39(2)**, [952]
  destroying, **39(2)**, [577]
  detention of, enforcement, **39(2)**, [961]
  detention, enforcement of, **39(2)**, [1034]
  distress, levy of, **39(2)**, [962]
  documents, powers to required production of, **39(2)**, [936]
  drug trafficking on board. *See under* **drug trafficking**
  dues levied on, sale or charge of, **39(2)**, [95]
  equipment, inspection of, **39(2)**, [937]
  exemption from requirements, **39(2)**, [971]
  explosives, provisions as to. *See* **explosives**
  Factories Acts, provisions applicable, **18**, [1179]
  fees, **39(2)**, [979]
  food safety provisions. *See* **food and food safety**
  foreign—
    building, **12(1)**, [116]
    civil jurisdiction, **10**, [994]
    commissioned, **12(1)**, [139]
    criminal jurisdiction, **10**, [995]
    disciplinary offences, detention for, **10**, [996]
    warlike equipment, penalty on aiding, **12(1)**, [118]
  foreign state, aiding—
    appeals, **12(1)**, [135]
    detention of—
      chief executive authority, by, **12(1)**, [131], [134]
      local authority, by, **12(1)**, [132]
      Secretary of State, by, **12(1)**, [131], [134]
    forfeiture, **12(1)**, [127]
    indemnities, **12(1)**, [136], [137]
    proceedings against, **12(1)**, [128]
    search warrant, **12(1)**, [133]
    seizure of, **12(1)**, [129]
      powers of officers, **12(1)**, [130]
  forfeiture of, **39(2)**, [675], [688]
  goods, carriage of. *See* **carriage of goods by sea**
  Government, registration of, **39(2)**, [985]
  hazarding, **3**, [506], [779], [1033]
  hazardous and noxious substances, carriage of—
    International Convention—
      power to give effect to, **39(2)**, [858]
      text of, **39(2)**, [999]
    introductory, **39(2)**, [857]
    Secretary of State's power to make order, **39(2)**, [859]
  hijacking, **39(2)**, [575]
  Her Majesty's, meaning of, **3**, [1220]
  HM—
    account of goods before unloading, **13**, [618]
    arrest, etc, exclusion of proceedings for, **13**, [32]

ship—*contd*
  HM—*contd*
    duty-free goods on, **13**, [801]
    meaning, **13**, [38]
  home port, meaning of, **11(1)**, [299]
  hovercraft included in term, **31**, [180]
  illegally enlisted persons on, **12(1)**, [115]
  importation and exportation, control of, **50**, [181]
  improvement notice—
    arbitration, reference to, **39(2)**, [943]
    directions in, **39(2)**, [940], [942]
    extension of, **39(2)**, [942]
    requirements, contravention of, **39(2)**, [945]
    service of, **39(2)**, [940]
    withdrawal of, **39(2)**, [942]
  inaccurate certification, **3**, [508], [781], [1039]
  injury to person on, **39(2)**, [951]
  inquiry, casualty, into. *See* casualty *above*
  inspection, power of, **39(2)**, [937]
  insurance. *See* **marine insurance**
  interest grants, **39(2)**, [453]
  lessors, restrictions on capital allowances, **43(2)**, [265]
  light dues—
    application of, **39(2)**, [887]
    collection of, **39(2)**, [882]
    distress for, **39(2)**, [885]
    local, **39(2)**, [887]
    payment of, **39(2)**, [887]
    receipt for, **39(2)**, [886]
    recovery of, **39(2)**, [884]
    regulations, copies of, **39(2)**, [882]
  mail-bags, carriage of, **34**, [706]
  manning—
    application of provisions, **39(2)**, [713]
    exemption, power of, **39(2)**, [715]
    regulations, **39(2)**, [714]
    undermanning, **39(2)**, [716]
  master—
    alcohol and drugs offences. *See* alcohol and drugs offences *above*
    duties in harbour. *See under* **ports and harbours**
    See **master**
  meaning, **1(2)**, [466]; **3**, [723]; **9**, [136]; **35(1)**, [112]; **39(2)**, [1054]
  medical treatment on, **39(2)**, [720]
  national character, declaration of, **39(2)**, [674]
  national colours—
    failure to show, **39(2)**, [671]
    improper, use of, **39(2)**, [672]
  new, expenditure on—
    exclusions—
      deferment, object of securing, **43(1)**, [708]
      later events, **43(1)**, [709]
      ship previously owned, **43(1)**, [707]
      shipowner, not incurred by, **43(1)**, [710]
    meaning, **43(1)**, [706]
  non-professional on, ability to exercise function impaired by drink or drugs, **39(2)**, [1046]
    arrest without warrant, **39(2)**, [1051]

ship—*contd*
  non-professional on, ability to exercise
    function impaired by drink or drugs—*contd*
    Crown service, application of provisions
      to, **39(2)**, [1055]
    detention pending arrival of police,
      39(2), [1050]
    drug, meaning, **39(2)**, [1054]
    enforcement, **39(2)**, [1048]
    orders and regulations, **39(2)**, [1053]
    prescribed limit, **39(2)**, [1047]
    right of entry on ship, **39(2)**, [1052]
    specimens, provision of, **39(2)**, [1049]
    territorial application, **39(2)**, [1056]
  non-United Kingdom, application of
    provisions to, **39(2)**, [984]
  officer. *See* **ship's officer**
  official log book, **39(2)**, [743]
  overseas leasing, **43(1)**, [673]
  owner—
    dangerously unsafe ship, liability for,
      39(2), [762]
    exclusion of liability, **39(2)**, [863]
    limitation of liability, **39(2)**, [862]
    unsafe operation, liability for, **39(2)**, [764]
  passenger—
    application of service acts to, **3**, [711],
      [984]
    drunken passengers, power to exclude,
      39(2), [770]
    offences in connection with, **39(2)**, [769]
    returns, **39(2)**, [775]
  person under eighteen, employment of,
    39(2), [722]
  police entering on board, **12(1)**, [37]
  pollution from, prevention of, **39(2)**, [796],
    [797]
  postponement of allowances, notice of,
    43(1), [690]
    effect of, **43(1)**, [691]
  prize, as. *See* **prize**
  prohibition notice—
    arbitration, reference to, **39(2)**, [943]
    directions in, **39(2)**, [941], [942]
    extension of, **39(2)**, [942]
    invalid, compensation in respect of,
      39(2), [944]
    requirement, contravention of, **39(2)**, [945]
    service of, **39(2)**, [941]
    withdrawal of, **39(2)**, [942]
  public health provisions applicable to certain,
    35(1), [169]
  qualifying foreign ship, **39(2)**, [989]
  registered—
    mortgages, **39(2)**, [993]
    private law provisions, **39(2)**, [684], [993]
    transfer of, **39(2)**, [993]
  registration—
    bareboat charter, **39(2)**, [685]
    British connection, offences relating to,
      39(2), [682]
    British possessions, in, **39(2)**, [686]
    certificate, status of, **39(2)**, [681]
    entitlement, **39(2)**, [677]
    false statements, **39(2)**, [682]

ship—*contd*
  registration—*contd*
    government departments, disclosure of
      information by, **39(2)**, [689]
    law of another country, under, **39(2)**, [677]
    regulations, **39(2)**, [678]
    termination, **39(2)**, [684]
    tonnage ascertained for, **39(2)**, [679]
  requisition of—
    compensation for, **9**, [123]
    space and accommodation in, compensation
      for, **9**, [120], [124]
  safe navigation, action endangering,
    39(2), [578]
  safety and health on—
    assistance at sea, **39(2)**, [756], [757]
    dangerous goods, carriage of, **39(2)**, [753]
    dangers to navigation, report of,
      39(2), [755]
    regulations, **39(2)**, [751], [752]
    submersible and supporting apparatus, safety
      of, **39(2)**, [754], [994]
    unauthorised persons, offences,
      39(2), [774]
    unsafe lighters or barges, use of,
      39(2), [763]
    unsafe operation, liability for, **39(2)**, [764]
  safety directions, **39(2)**, [777], [995]
  safety, endangering, **39(2)**, [577]
  same group, members of, **43(1)**, [718]
  Scottish officers, **39(2)**, [935]
  seamen. *See* **seamen**
  search by immigration officers, **31**, [128]
  seaworthiness, duty to ensure, **39(2)**, [709]
  security—
    bodies corporate, offences by, **39(2)**, [614]
    extension of provisions, **39(2)**, [615]
    offences outside United Kingdom,
      39(2), [580]
    prosecution of offences, **39(2)**, [582]
    safe navigation, action endangering,
      39(2), [578]
  seizure of petroleum-spirit in, **35(1)**, [108]
  service offences—
    prize—
      officer in command, by, **3(S)**, 53–4
      person subject to service law, by,
        3(S), 54–5
    ship, hazarding, **3(S)**, 48
    stop and search powers, **3(S)**, 92
  short-term overseas leasing, **43(1)**, [683]
  single ship pool—
    allocation of expenditure to, **43(1)**, [687]
    disposal events, **43(1)**, [692]
    expenditure not allocated to, **43(1)**, [688]
  smoking on, prohibition, **35(2)**, [569]
  smuggling. *See* **smuggling**
  state immunity, and, **10**, [1049]
  stores, duty and drawback on, **13**, [1075]
  stowaways, **39(2)**, [771]
  structures, application of legislation to,
    39(2), [1057]
  submersible and supporting apparatus, safety
    of, **39(2)**, [754], [994]
  surveyor, appointment of, **39(2)**, [934]

ship—*contd*
  terrorism offences, **18**, [752], [757]
  threats, offences involving, **39(2)**, [579]
  tonnage—
    fees for measurement of, **39(2)**, [979]
    foreign countries, regulations adopted by,
      39(2), [680]
    registration, ascertained for, **39(2)**, [679]
    regulations, **39(2)**, [687]
    tax. *See* **tonnage tax**
  trans-shipped fish, receiving, **39(2)**, [767],
    [768]
  unauthorised presence on, **39(2)**, [772]
  United Kingdom, meaning, **39(2)**, [669]
  unsafe lighters or barges, use of, **39(2)**, [763]
  unsafe operation, liability for, **39(2)**, [764]
  unused, **43(1)**, [693]
  violence, protection against. *See* **ports and**
    harbours
  war risks. *See* **war risks insurance**
  will executed on, **50**, [534]
  wireless telegraphy, offences, **45**, [879]
  wreck. *See* **wreck**
  young person employed on, **39(2)**, [722]
  zero-rating, **50**, [151]

shipbuilders
  open market value—
    determination of, **13**, [557]
    reductions in, **13**, [558]
  reliefs—
    ending of, **13**, [1120]
    hydrocarbon oil duty, from, **13**, [555],
      [557]
    vehicle excise duty, from, **13**, [555], [557]

shipbuilding. *See also* **British Shipbuilders**
  corporate venturing scheme, exclusion for,
    43(S), 1123
  enterprise investment scheme, exclusion for,
    43(S), 1123
  enterprise management incentives, exclusion,
    43(S), 861
  generally, **47**, [1]
  illegal—
    evidence, presumption as to, **12(1)**, [117]
    penalty, **12(1)**, [116]
  venture capital trusts, exclusion for,
    43(S), 1124

Shipping Claims Tribunal
  constitution, **9**, [127]
  powers, **9**, [128]

shipping services
  coastal—
    legal proceedings, **39(2)**, [1018]
    non British-based, power to prohibit
      provision of, **39(2)**, [1016], [1017]
  foreign action, power to regulate in event
    of—
      charging order, **39(2)**, [1013]
      conditions for, **39(2)**, [1012]
      enforcement of orders, **39(2)**, [1014]
      legal proceedings, **39(2)**, [1018]

shipping services—*contd*
  foreign action, power to regulate in event
    of—*contd*
      Parliamentary control of orders,
        39(2), [1015]
      protective order, **39(2)**, [1012]

ship's officer
  certificate of competency. *See* **merchant**
    shipping (certificate of competency)
  conduct, inquiry into, **39(2)**, [728]
  fitness, inquiry into, **39(2)**, [728]
  unqualified person acting as qualified,
    39(2), [719]

shipwreck. *See* **wreck**

shop
  Christmas Day trading—
    enforcement, **18**, [1344]
    large shops, prohibition, **18**, [1342]
    loading and unloading, **18**, [1343]
  clearance area, in, compensation for, **22**, [400]
  definitions, **16**, [879]
  disorderly persons, harbouring in, **12(1)**, [64]
  health, safety and welfare—
    See also **health and safety at work**
    agreements, modification, **18**, [1237]
    buildings—
      plurally owned, provisions as to,
        18, [1227]
      single ownership, in, provisions as to,
        18, [1226]
    cleanliness, **18**, [1211]
    clothing, accommodation and drying,
      18, [1219]
    complaint, appeal from order made on,
      18, [1236]
    Crown, application to, **18**, [1243]
    disclosure of information, restriction of,
      18, [1231]
      public authorities, exception for,
        18, [1232]
    drinking water, supply, **18**, [1218]
    eating facilities, **18**, [1222]
    employer's relatives, exception from
      provisions, **18**, [1209]
    employment of persons, notification,
      18, [1230]
    exemptions, power to grant, **18**, [1229]
    expenses—
      apportionment, **18**, [1237]
      Minister's, **18**, [1242]
    fish salerooms, limited application to,
      18, [1245]
    floors and passages, construction and
      maintenance, **18**, [1223]
    fuel storage, **18**, [1228]
    heavy work, prohibitions, **18**, [1225]
    hours worked, limited, exceptions where,
      18, [1210]
    lighting, **18**, [1215]
    local Act, exercise of powers under,
      18, [1240]
    machinery, fencing, **18**, [1224]

shop—*contd*
  health, safety and welfare—*contd*
    offences—
      appeal against orders, **18**, [1236]
      defence available, **18**, [1234]
      generally, **18**, [1233]
      removal or defacement of documents,
        18, [1235]
    outworkers, exceptions for, **18**, [1209]
    overcrowding, **18**, [1212]
    premises to which provisions apply,
      18, [1208]
    regulations and orders, making of,
      18, [1241]
    sanitary conveniences, **18**, [1216]
    seating facilities, **18**, [1220], [1221]
    stairs and steps, construction and
      maintenance, **18**, [1223]
    temperature, **18**, [1213]
    transitory purposes, exclusion where
      premises used for, **18**, [1246]
    ventilation, **18**, [1214]
    visiting forces, exclusion of application,
      18, [1244]
    washing facilities, **18**, [1217]
  large, prohibition on Christmas Day
    opening, **18**, [1342]
  premises—
    disabled persons, provision for, **35(1)**, [289]
    meaning, **18**, [1208]
  provision of, in housing development,
    22, [14]
  retail trade or business, meaning, **18**, [1208]
  shop workers, refusing Sunday working, unfair
    dismissal on, **16**, [748]
  subways, London, in, **25(1)**, [750]
  Sunday trading—
    enforcement of provisions, **18**, [1335]
    Jewish Sabbath, persons observing,
      18, [1336]
    large shops—
      loading and unloading at, **18**, [1327],
        [1337]
      notice of, **18**, [1334]
      offences, **18**, [1334]
      restrictions on, **18**, [1334]
    leases and agreements, construction of,
      18, [1328]
    local Acts, repeal or amendment of,
      18, [1330]
    local authority, meaning, **18**, [1332]
    reform of law, **18**, [1326]
  unitary authority, meaning, **18**, [1332]
  workers—
    meaning, **16**, [879]
    protected—
      meaning, **16**, [639]
      reduction of pay, **16**, [642]
      Sunday working, as to, **16**, [639]
    Sunday working—
      contractual requirements, **16**, [640],
        [646]
      detriment, right to not suffer, **16**, [661]
      explanatory statement, **16**, [645]

shop—*contd*
  workers—*contd*
    Sunday working—*contd*
      guaranteed hours, contracts with,
        16, [641]
      notice of objection to, **16**, [643]
      opting-in notice, **16**, [640]
      opting-out of, **16**, [644]
      protection against, **16**, [630]
      refusing, unfair dismissal on, **16**, [748]
    transitional provisions, **16**, [893]

shopping trolleys
  abandoned, **32**, [573], [590]
    transitional provision, **35(2)**, [542]

short-life assets
  connected person, disposal to, **43(1)**, [649]
  leasing, provided for, **43(1)**, [647]
  meaning, **43(1)**, [643]
  pool, **43(1)**, [646]
  treatment of plant or machinery as—
    election for, **43(1)**, [645]
    ruled out, where, **43(1)**, [644]
    table of, **43(1)**, [644]
  under-value, sales at, **43(1)**, [648]
  VAT liabilities, additional, **43(1)**, [819]

short-time working
  redundancy payment. *See under* **redundancy**

shot gun
  artificial targets, shooting at, **12(1)**, [485]
  borrowing on private premises, **12(1)**, [485]
  certificate—
    application for, **12(1)**, [503]
    false statement concerning, **12(1)**, [506]
    fees, **12(1)**, [513], [527]
    form of, **12(1)**, [505]
    grant of, **12(1)**, [505]
    period in force, **12(1)**, [506]
    production, demanding, **12(1)**, [532]
    purposes for use of weapon, **12(1)**, [505]
    reasons for grant, **12(1)**, [505]
    refusal, appeal against, **12(1)**, [506]
    register of holders, **12(2)**, [521]
    renewal of, **12(1)**, [506]
    requirement of, **12(1)**, [475]
    revocation, **12(1)**, [510], [511]
  components, trade in, **12(1)**, [525]
  European firearms pass, **12(1)**, [514]
  loaded—
    carrying in public place, **12(1)**, [493]
    when deemed, **12(1)**, [541]
  meaning, **12(1)**, [541]
  Northern Irish certificate, **12(1)**, [488]
  person under fifteen or eighteen—
    having, **12(1)**, [497], [498]
    supplying to, **12(1)**, [499]
    unauthorised use by, **12(1)**, [497], [505]
  prosecution and punishment of offences,
    table, **12(1)**, [550]
  shortening barrel, **12(1)**, [477]
  unlawful possession, penalties, **12(1)**, [550]
  vermin, shooting of, **12(1)**, [505], [541]

shot gun—*contd*
  visitors' permits, **12(1)**, [1131]
    transactions under, **12(1)**, [526]

Si Quis
  procedure for reading, **14**, 821–2

Sianel Pedwar Cymru. *See* **Welsh Authority**

sickness benefit
  remuneration, payment treated as,
    40(1), [461]

sidesmen
  guild church, in, **14**, 463
  parochial church meeting, elected at,
    14, 706–7

Sierra Leone
  area included in, **7(2)**, [485]
  British ship registered in, **7(2)**, [487]
  Commonwealth citizenship, **31**, [186]
  existing law, operation of, **7(2)**, [654]
  fully responsible status of, **7(2)**, [482]
  legislative powers in, **7(2)**, [486]
  republic, becoming, **7(2)**, [654]
  visiting forces in, **7(2)**, [487]

sight testing
  duties to be performed on, **28**, [548]
  meaning, **28**, [560]
  provided by employer, exemption for,
    44(2), [329]
  rules as to, **28**, [546]

Significant Market Power conditions. *See*
SMP conditions

signpost
  destruction or defacement, **36**, [773]
  footpaths and bridleways, erection, **36**, [773]

Sikhs
  safety helmets, wearing of—
    construction or building site, working on,
      7(1), [229]
    exemption from obligation, **7(1)**, [229]
    injury, loss or damage resulting from
      omission, **7(1)**, [229]
    racial discrimination arising form,
      7(1), [230]

silver
  Britannia, use of, **48**, 74
  sterling, use of, **48**, 74

simony
  contract, where not prejudicial, **14**, 54
  corrupt resignation, **14**, 50–1
  declaration against, **14**, 831–2
  lease, validity of, **14**, 54
  presentation—
    devolution to Crown, **14**, 49
    penalty, **14**, 50

simony—*contd*
  presentation—*contd*
    voidance, **14**, 49

simplified planning zone
  excluded descriptions of land, **46**, [350]
  meaning, **46**, [345]
  notification of proposals, **46**, [627]
  scheme—
    alteration of, **46**, [349]
    consultation, **46**, [627]
    content, **46**, [627]
    duration of, **46**, [438]
    local inquiry, **46**, [627]
    making, **46**, [346], [999]
    objections to, **46**, [627]
    planning permission—
      conditions and limitations, **46**, [347]
      grant of, **46**, [345]
    proposals, adoption and approval of,
      46, [627]
    publicity, **46**, [627]
    register of information on, **46**, [328]
    regulations, **46**, [627]
    Secretary of State—
      default powers, **46**, [627]
      directions by, **46**, [627]
      power to direct making etc, **46**, [627]
      proposals, calling in, **46**, [627]

Singapore
  independent sovereign state, becoming,
    7(2), [601]
  Commonwealth citizenship, **31**, [186]
  Judicial Committee of Privy Council, appeal
    to, **7(2)**, [602]
  Malaysia, forming part of, **7(2)**, [529]
  visiting forces in, **7(2)**, [605]

site notice
  display of, **46**, [439]

sites of special interest
  undertakings, holding by, **49**, [965]
  water undertakers, notification to, **49**, [715]

sites of special scientific interest
  drainage board, duty of, **19(3)**, [233]
  meaning, **36**, [1158]
  SSSI diversion order—
    appeals, **36**, [1164], [1165]
    application for, **36**, [1158], [1161]
    compensation for, **36**, [1160]
    confirmation, **36**, [1157]
    contribution to, **36**, [1157], [1160]
    council declining to determine
      applications, **36**, [1163]
    determinations, delegation of functions,
      36, [1418]
    form, **36**, [1158]
    notice of intention to make, **36**, [1158]
    notices to be given, **36**, [1407]
    power to make, **36**, [1157], [1159]
    procedure for making, **36**, [1407]
    provisions applying to, **36**, [1158]

sites of special scientific interest—*contd*
SSSI diversion order—*contd*
register of applications, **36**, [1162]
statutory undertakers, agreement of,
36, [1160]
validity and operation of, **36**, [1408]

sittings (church). *See also* **pews**
Church Commissioners, surrender to,
14, 217–19
rights of ownership, cessation of, **14**, 218
Westminster churches, in, to be free, **14**, 204

sketching
court, prohibition in, **11(2)**, [173]

skin-colouring
regulation of business, **26(2)**, [323]

slander. *See also* **defamation**
action for, defence of justification,
19(3), [312]
amends, offer of, **19(3)**, [311], [329]
acceptance of, **19(3)**, [330]
failure to accept, **19(3)**, [331]
apology for, **19(3)**, [311]
broadcasting, **19(3)**, [324]
business reputation, affecting, **19(3)**, [309]
civil proceedings, **19(3)**, [261]
claim, summary disposal of—
Northern Ireland, **19(3)**, [336]
power of, **19(3)**, [333]
rules of court, **19(3)**, [335]
summary relief, meaning, **19(3)**, [334]
damages—
actions for same slander, in case of,
19(3), [317]
evidence in mitigation, **19(3)**, [317]
evidence, **19(3)**, [261]
fair comment, defence of, **19(3)**, [313]
goods, of, proof of special damage
unnecessary, **19(3)**, [310]
justification, defence of, **19(3)**, [312]
libel distinguished, **19(3)**, [261]
limitation of actions—
discretionary exclusion of, **19(3)**, [763]
generally, **19(3)**, [261]
period, **19(3)**, [728]
malicious falsehood, proof of special damage
unnecessary, **19(3)**, [310]
meaning of statement, ruling on, **19(3)**, [332]
official reputation, affecting, **19(3)**, [309]
proceedings in Parliament, evidence
concerning, **19(3)**, [337]
professional reputation, affecting, **19(3)**, [309]
rehabilitation of offenders, effect on action,
12(1), [637]
special damage, where proof unnecessary,
19(3), [310]
statutes, summary of, **19(3)**, [261]
title, of, proof of special damage unnecessary,
19(3), [310]
unintentional defamation, **19(3)**, [311]
women, of, **19(3)**, [307]

slaughterhouse
acquisition by local authority, **1(1)**, [868]
animals awaiting slaughter, conditions for,
1(1), [880]
Community livestock carcase grading
procedures at, recovery of cost of
supervising, **1(2)**, [480]
compulsory purchase of land, **1(1)**, [875]
construction of, regulations as to, **1(1)**, [880]
discontinuance of use, agreement on,
1(1), [868]
enforcement of provisions, **1(1)**, [881];
1(2), [539], [542]
entry, powers of, **1(1)**, [883]
horse, premises for slaughter of. *See* **horse**
licence, cancellation for offence, **1(1)**, [880]
licensee, offence under Food Safety Act by,
1(2), [449]
local authority—
acquisition by, **1(1)**, [868]
meaning, **1(1)**, [873]
provision of by, **1(1)**, [869]
local inquiry, **1(1)**, [876]
management, **1(1)**, [870]
market, in—
nuisance, indictment for, **27**, [20]
power to erect, **27**, [19]
slaughtering other than in, **27**, [21]
tolls, etc, demand for, **27**, [25], [27]
meaning, **1(1)**, [878], [886]; **1(2)**, [466], [480]
offences—
prosecution and punishment, **1(1)**, [884]
regulations, against, **1(1)**, [880]
premises, regulations on, **1(1)**, [880]
private, restriction of, **1(1)**, [868]
public—
acquisition of land or facilities for,
1(1), [869]
charges for use, **1(1)**, [871]
cold store, provision of, **1(1)**, [872]
local authority providing, **1(1)**, [869]
management of, **1(1)**, [870]
refrigerator, provision of, **1(1)**, [872]
religious community, requirements on
slaughter, **1(1)**, [870]
public health provisions, incorporation of,
1(1), [877]
regulations, making, **1(1)**, [880], [885]
restriction of, by agreement, **1(1)**, [868]
slaughter—
humane conditions of, regulations for,
1(1), [880]
religious communities, requirements of,
1(1), [870]
summary of provisions, **1(1)**, [124]
transitional provisions, **1(1)**, [888], [890]

slave trade
contracts, illegality, **47**, [2]
court, jurisdiction, **47**, [11]
dealing in slaves, penalty, **47**, [3]
illegality, declaration of, **47**, [2]
interpretation of terms, **47**, [7]
slave ships—
forfeiture, **47**, [8]

slave trade—*contd*
slave ships—*contd*
seamen on, liability of, **47**, [4]
seizure, authorised, protection of, **47**, [9]
suspected, seizure of, **47**, [8]
summary of provisions, **47**, [1]
trafficking people for exploitation,
31, [493]–[494]
world-wide application of provisions, **47**, [5]

sleeping accommodation
London—
appointed day for provisions, **25(2)**, [532]
buildings excepted from provisions,
25(2), [534]
Development of Tourism Act, application
of, **25(2)**, [542]
Kensington and Chelsea—
registered, deemed to be, **25(2)**, [538]
repeal of 1972 provisions, **25(2)**, [531]
register, obligation to compile, **25(2)**, [535]
registration—
appeals, **25(2)**, [540]
applications for, **25(2)**, [537]
exemptions from, **25(2)**, [534]
period of, **25(2)**, [536]
refusal of, **25(2)**, [539]
specified purpose, meaning, **25(2)**, [533]
temporary accommodation, **25(2)**, [295]
unregistered, penalty, **25(2)**, [541]
using before appointed day, **25(2)**, [541]

Slovak Republic
accession to European Union, **18**, [54]

Slovenia
accession to European Union, **18**, [54]

slum clearance. *See also* **clearance area;
demolition order**
subsidy, calculation, **23**, [39]

small dwellings
acquisition in London, expenses, **25(1)**, [401]
advances for purchase—
accounts to be kept, **22**, [449]
date of, determining, **22**, [449]
former provisions, **22**, [334]
interest, rate of, **22**, [449]
list of advances to be kept, **22**, [449]
proprietor—
bankruptcy of, **22**, [449]
personal liability, **22**, [449]
recovery of possession, **22**, [449]
repayment, period for, **22**, [449]
residence condition, dispensing with,
22, [449]
sale by local authority, **22**, [449]
statutory conditions, **22**, [449]

smallholding. *See also* **allotments
(agricultural)**
allotments provisions repealed in respect of,
1(1), [384], [401]

smallholding—*contd*
amalgamations—
grants in respect of, **1(1)**, [815]
reorganisation involving, **1(1)**, [805]
arbitrations and valuations, **1(1)**, [219], [222]
authorities—
accounts, **1(1)**, [822]
acquisition of land by, **1(1)**, [813]
annual reports, **1(1)**, [823]
contributions by Minister to, **1(1)**, [817]
councils deemed to be, **1(1)**, [803]
default of, **1(1)**, [821]
financial aid to, **1(1)**, [124]
functions of, **1(1)**, [804]
generally, **1(1)**, [124]
grants to, **1(1)**, [815]
loans and guarantees by, **1(1)**, [818]
management powers, **1(1)**, [812]
meaning, **1(1)**, [803]
records to be kept by, **1(1)**, [822]
reviews to be made by, **1(1)**, [805]
surplus land held by, **1(1)**, [814]
breach of conditions, **1(1)**, [279]
building on, **1(1)**, [279]
compensation—
arbitration on, **1(1)**, [222]
improvements, for, **1(1)**, [214]
compulsorily hired land, **1(1)**, [288]
conditions affecting, **1(1)**, [279]
co-operative schemes, promoting, **1(1)**, [812]
cottage holding. *See* **cottage holding**
creation of, references to, **1(1)**, [802]
cropping, **22**, [647]
Crown land for, **1(1)**, [825]
cultivation, condition for, **1(1)**, [279]
delegation of council's powers, **1(1)**, [282]
disposal of, by local authority, **1(1)**, [280]
disposal of produce, **22**, [647]
employment, providing for, **1(1)**, [804]
enlargement of, **1(1)**, [805]
equipment, fixed—
assistance in providing, **1(1)**, [285]
meaning, **1(1)**, [399]
provision of, **1(1)**, [811]
estate—
meaning, **1(1)**, [802]
reorganisation. *See* reorganisation *below*
existing, meaning, **1(1)**, [802]
glebe land, use of, **1(1)**, [825]
grants, capital, increase of, **1(1)**, [816]
grazing rights, **1(1)**, [209]
improvements—
compensation, **1(1)**, [214]
matters treated as, **1(1)**, [224], [225]
land—
acquired, powers as to, **1(1)**, [234]
acquisition—
amendments as to, **1(1)**, [287]
entry, powers of, **1(1)**, [232]
Minister, by, **1(1)**, [820]
Minister's consent not required,
1(1), [235]
smallholdings authority, by, **1(1)**, [813]
annuity for sale or acquisition, **1(1)**, [233]
appropriated, letting of, **1(1)**, [262]

smallholding—*contd*
  land—*contd*
    appropriation, restrictions on, **1(1)**, [244]
    compulsory hiring, **1(1)**, [288]
    compulsory purchase—
      amendments as to, **1(1)**, [237]
      notice to treat, **1(1)**, [261]
      orders, **1(1)**, [222]
      procedure, **1(1)**, [206]
    entry to inspect, **1(1)**, [239]
    interchange of, **1(1)**, [212]
    lease of, by local authority, **1(1)**, [234]
    letting to parish council, **1(1)**, [238]
    limited owners, sale by, **1(1)**, [207]
    Minister, held by, **1(1)**, [819]
    surplus, held for, **1(1)**, [814]
  letting of, special provisions as to, **1(1)**, [809]
  loans for, **1(1)**, [284], [818]
  local authority—
    borrowing powers, **1(1)**, [216], [217]
    expenses of, **1(1)**, [217]
    loans to, **1(1)**, [236]
  local inquiries, **1(1)**, [218]
  management of—
    general powers of, **1(1)**, [812]
    summary of provisions, **1(1)**, [124]
  meaning, **1(1)**, [124], [220]
  Minister—
    acquisition of land by, **1(1)**, [820]
    default powers, **1(1)**, [821]
    grants by, **1(1)**, [815]
    land held by, powers as to, **1(1)**, [819]
    loans by, **1(1)**, [818], [819]
  Ministers responsible for, **1(1)**, [802]
  notice to quit, **22**, [670], [671]
  owners etc, lists of, **1(1)**, [283]
  possession, recovery of, **1(1)**, [280]
  produce, disposal of, **1(1)**, [812]
  provision of, **1(1)**, [124]
  purchase of, loans for, **1(1)**, [284]
  qualifications for renting, **1(1)**, [809]
  records of, **1(1)**, [822]
  regulations, power to make, **1(1)**, [827]
  rent—
    arbitration as to, **1(1)**, [810]
    determination of, **1(1)**, [810]
  reorganisation—
    aim of, **1(1)**, [805]
    exemption from, **1(1)**, [805]
    grants in respect of, **1(1)**, [815]
    letting holdings after, **1(1)**, [809]
    proposals—
      amending or superseding, **1(1)**, [806]
      approval by Minister, **1(1)**, [806]
      formulation, **1(1)**, [805]
      further reorganisation, for, **1(1)**, [807]
      reviews, without, **1(1)**, [808]
    review for purposes of, **1(1)**, [805]
    subsequent reviews for, **1(1)**, [807]
    summary of provisions, **1(1)**, [124]
  sale of—
    annuity, by, **1(1)**, [278]
    conditions attaching to, **1(1)**, [279]
    Minister's consent, without, **1(1)**, [289]
    procedure, **1(1)**, [281]

smallholding—*contd*
  societies—
    formation etc, **1(1)**, [215]
    grants and loans to, **1(1)**, [215]
  special classes of land, **1(1)**, [825]
  statutory, aim of, **1(1)**, [804]
  summary of provisions, **1(1)**, [124]
  supplementary provisions, **1(1)**, [124]
  tenant—
    loans to, **1(1)**, [284], [818]
    removal of improvements by, **1(1)**, [214]
  Wales and Monmouthshire, in, **1(1)**, [826]

smallpox
  notifiable disease. *See* **notifiable disease**

smart meters
  electricity. *See under* **electricity**
  gas. *See under* **gas**
  licences—
    activities requiring, **17(2)**, [682]
    conditions, power to amend,
      17(2), [679]–[681]

smell
  public works, from, compensation for,
    9, [304]
  See also **public works**

smoke
  chimney from—
    smoke control area, in, **35(2)**, [19]
      exemption for investigation and
        research, **35(2)**, [45]
  colliery spoilbank—
    combustion of refuse from, prevention of,
      35(2), [42]
    prevention of emission of, from,
      35(2), [42]
  control area—
    creation, powers of Secretary of State to
      require, **35(2)**, [18]
    Crown premises in, emission of smoke
      from, **35(2)**, [46]
    declaration of districts as, **35(2)**, [17]
    emission of smoke from chimney in,
      offence, as, **35(2)**, [19]
    exemptions, **35(2)**, [21], [22]
    fireplaces—
      adaptation—
        avoiding contraventions of provisions,
          for, **35(2)**, [26]
        church, chapel, etc, in, grants
          towards, **35(2)**, [25]
        private dwellings, in—
          expenses of carrying out,
            35(2), [24], [27]
          new dwellings excluded,
            35(2), [24]
          requirement to carry out,
            35(2), [23]
          towards, **35(2)**, [69]
      exemptions, **35(2)**, [21], [22]
    investigation and research, exemption
      from, **35(2)**, [45]

smoke—*contd*
  control area—*contd*
    orders as to—
      coming into operation, **35(2)**, [68], [73]
      making, **35(2)**, [17]
      scope of, **35(2)**, [17]
    unauthorised fuel, acquisition and sale in,
      35(2), [22]
  Crown premises, application of control
    provisions to, **35(2)**, [46]
  dark—
    chimney, emission from—
      Crown premises, **35(2)**, [46]
      offence of—
        defence, **35(2)**, [1]
        exemption for investigations and
          research, **35(2)**, [45]
        prohibition of, **35(2)**, [1]
    Crown premises, from, **35(2)**, [46]
    enforcement of provisions, **35(2)**, [55]
    entry and inspection, rights of, **35(2)**, [56],
      [57]
    industrial or trade premises, emission from,
      Crown premises, **35(2)**, [46]
    meaning, **35(2)**, [3]
    offences—
      act or default of another, due to,
        35(2), [53]
      bodies corporate, by, **35(2)**, [52]
      cumulative penalties, **35(2)**, [50]
      occupiers, notification of, **35(2)**, [51]
      prohibition of, **35(2)**, [1]
    railway engines, emission from, **35(2)**, [43]
    vessel, emission from, **35(2)**, [44]
    visiting forces, from premises of,
      35(2), [46]
  emission of—
    Crown premises, provisions as to,
      35(2), [46]
    furnace, from, **35(2)**, [1]
    smoke control area, in. *See* control area
      above
    visiting forces, provisions as to, **35(2)**, [46]
  interrelationship of provisions, **35(2)**, [40],
    [41]
  investigation and research, exemption from
    provisions for, **35(2)**, [45]
  new furnace, smokeless, to be, **35(2)**, [4]
  public works, from, compensation for,
    9, [304]
  See also **public works**
  railway engine, emission from—
    duty to minimise, **35(2)**, [43]
    exemption for investigation and research,
      35(2), [45]
    prohibition of, **35(2)**, [43]

smoke-free premises
  summary of provisions, **35(1)**, [1]

smoking
  authorised officers—
    obstruction of, **35(2)**, [575]
    powers of entry, **35(2)**, [585]
  enforcement regulations, **35(2)**, [574]

smoking—*contd*
  meaning, **35(2)**, [565]
  no smoking signs, display of, **35(2)**, [570]
  offences—
    failing to prevent smoking in smoke-free
      place, **35(2)**, [572]
    fixed penalties, **35(2)**, [573], [584]
    obstruction, etc of officers, **35(2)**, [575]
    smoke-free place, smoking in, **35(2)**, [571]
  public place, prohibition in, smoking,
    meaning, **35(2)**, [565]
  smoke-free places—
    designation of, **35(2)**, [568]
    failing to prevent smoking in, offence,
      35(2), [572]
    meaning, **35(2)**, [571]
    offence of smoking in, **35(2)**, [571]
  smoke-free premises—
    exemptions, **35(2)**, [567]
    public, open to, **35(2)**, [566]
  smoke-free vehicles, **35(2)**, [569]

SMP conditions
  apparatus supply, **45**, [511]
  carrier selection and pre-selection, **45**, [508]
  circumstance required for setting of, **45**, [496]
  contravention—
    apparatus supply, suspension of, **45**, [519],
      [520]
    civil liability for, **45**, [522]
    directions, enforcement of, **45**, [521]
    enforcement notification, **45**, [513]
    notification of, **45**, [512]
    penalties, **45**, [514], [515]
    service provision, suspension of, **45**, [518],
      [520]
    urgent cases, power to deal with, **45**, [516],
      [517]
  end users, regulation of services for, **45**, [509]
  European Commission's powers in respect of
    proposals, **45**, [500]
  leased lines, **45**, [510]
  market power determinations, **45**, [497]–[500]
  meaning, **45**, [568]
  network access, **45**, [505]–[507], [523]
  review of identifications and determinations,
    45, [502]–[504]
  transnational markets, special rules for,
    45, [501]

smuggling
  firing on service vessels, etc, **13**, [680]
  interfering with revenue vessels, etc, **13**, [680]
  patrolling coasts, etc, **13**, [678]
  prevention, **13**, [677]–[681]
  revenue vessel—
    hauling up and mooring, **13**, [678]
    interfering with, **13**, [680]
  seal, lock or mark, removal of, **13**, [679]
  small ship, **13**, [677]
  smuggled goods, offering for sale, **13**, [681]
  tobacco products—
    manufacturer's duty not to facilitate,
      13, [878]
    penalty for facilitating, **13**, [879]–[881]

snow
nuisances from, byelaws for prevention of, **35(1)**, [133]

socage
free and common, conversion of tenures into, **20**, [15]

social care
Councils. *See* **Care Council for Wales; General Social Care Council**
day centre, meaning, **35(2)**, [320]
definitions, **35(2)**, [360]
direct payments in lieu of provision of services, **40(2)**, [597]
establishments and agencies. *See* **care establishments and agencies**
maintenance liability of relatives, abolition, **40(2)**, [598], [609]
Minister, default powers of, **35(2)**, [352]
National Assembly for Wales, powers of, **40(2)**, [326]
nursing care, **40(2)**, [313]
orders and regulations, **35(2)**, [357]
preserved rights—
accommodation, transfer of responsibilities for, **40(2)**, [314]
disclosure of information, **40(2)**, [315]
social security benefits, alignment of, **40(2)**, [316]
public function for human rights purposes, provision as, **40(2)**, [596]
qualifying bodies—
financial assistance to—
company, power to form, **30(S)**, NHS 114
forms of, **30(S)**, NHS 112
interpretation, **30(S)**, NHS 115
power to give, **30(S)**, NHS 110–11
terms of, **30(S)**, NHS 113
third parties, arrangements with, **30(S)**, NHS 114
meaning, **30(S)**, NHS 111–12
regulations and orders, **40(2)**, [322]
residential accommodation. *See* **local authority**
summary of provisions, **35(1)**, [1]
transfer of staff, schemes for—
date of transfer, meaning, **35(2)**, [355]
effect of, **35(2)**, [354]
power to make, **35(2)**, [354]
transferee, meaning, **35(2)**, [355]
vulnerable adults, protection of—
care position, meaning, **35(2)**, [338]
care worker—
duty to refer, **35(2)**, [340]
meaning, **35(2)**, [338]
registration authority, reference by, **35(2)**, [342]
employment, meaning, **35(2)**, [338]
inquiries, reference of individuals named in findings of, **35(2)**, [343]
meaning, **35(2)**, [338]
persons providing care for, **35(2)**, [338]

social care—*contd*
vulnerable adults, protection of—*contd*
persons unsuitable to work with, list of—
access, before commencement of provisions, **35(2)**, [348]
appeals, **35(2)**, [344]
applications for removal from, **35(2)**, [345], [346]
care workers, duty to refer, **35(2)**, [340]
effect of inclusion, **35(2)**, [347]
employment agencies and businesses, duty to refer, **35(2)**, [341]
extension of provisions, power of, **35(2)**, [350]
inquiries, reference of individuals named in findings of, **35(2)**, [343]
Protection of Children Act, persons referred under, **35(2)**, [349]
registration authority, reference by, **35(2)**, [342]
Secretary of State keeping, **35(2)**, [339]
supply worker, duty to refer, **35(2)**, [341]
regulations, **35(2)**, [338]
supply worker—
duty to refer, **35(2)**, [341]
meaning, **35(2)**, [338]
Wales, provisions in, **35(2)**, [359]
workers. *See* **social care workers**

social care workers
meaning, **35(2)**, [320], [338]
persons treated as, **35(2)**, [320]
registration—
application for, **35(2)**, [322]
conditions, **35(2)**, [323]
grant of, **35(2)**, [323]
refusal of, **35(2)**, [323]
register of, **35(2)**, [321]
publication of, **35(2)**, [335]
removal from, **35(2)**, [324]
rules, **35(2)**, [325]
standard of proof in proceedings, **28(S)**, 38
use of title without, **35(2)**, [326]
regulation of, **28(S)**, 37–8, 74–5
relevant social work, meaning, **35(2)**, [320]
training—
courses, approval of, **35(2)**, [328]
examinations, conduct of, **35(2)**, [328]
Minister, functions of, **35(2)**, [332]
post-registration, **35(2)**, [330]
qualifications gained outside area of Council, **35(2)**, [329]
Special Health Authority, grants from, towards, **35(2)**, [333]
Tribunal, appeals to, **35(2)**, [334]
visitors, appointment of, **35(2)**, [331]

social fund
accounts, **40(1)**, [696]
allocations from, **40(1)**, [697]
annual report, **40(1)**, [696]
application for payments, **40(1)**, [512]
awards, recovery of, **40(1)**, [582]
Commissioner, **40(1)**, [567]; **40(2)**, [186]

social fund—*contd*
  continuation of, **40(1)**, [696]
  general note, **40(1)**, [1]
  inspectors, **40(1)**, [567]; **40(2)**, [186]
  officers—
    appointment of, **40(1)**, [566]
    appropriate officers, **40(2)**, [185]
    awards by, **40(1)**, [388]
    determinations—
      principles of, **40(1)**, [389]
      review of, **40(1)**, [568]; **40(2)**, [187],
        [210]
    general guidance, issuing, **40(1)**, [566]
  other sources of finance, adjustments
    between, **40(1)**, [698]
  overpayments out of, **40(1)**, [574];
    40(2), [194], [210]
  payments into, **40(1)**, [696]
  payments out of, **40(1)**, [387]

social housing
  accommodation becoming, **24**, [607]
  basic principle, **24**, [607]
  community land trust, meaning, **24**, [618]
  disposal of property, meaning, **24**, [812]
  enforcement powers, exercise of, **24**, [757]
  English bodies, meaning, **24**, [618]
  family, members of, **24**, [811]
  Homes and Communities Agency, powers of.
    See Homes and Communities Agency
  interpretation, **24**, [814], [815]
  low cost home ownership—
    equity percentage arrangements, meaning,
      24, [609]
    meaning, **24**, [609]
    shared ownership arrangements, meaning,
      24, [609]
  low cost rental accommodation, meaning,
    24, [608]
  managers, accreditation, **24**, [756]
  meaning, **24**, [607]
  National Assembly for Wales, references to,
    24, [602]
  provider of—
    construction of reference to, **24**, [619]
    de-registration—
      compulsory, **24**, [657]
      notice of, **24**, [659]
      voluntary, **24**, [658]
    register—
      entry on, **24**, [655]
      maintenance of, **24**, [650]
      removal from, **24**, [657], [658]
      transitional provisions, **24**, [817]
    registered. *See* registered providers *below*
    registration—
      appeals, **24**, [660]
      eligibility for, **24**, [651]
      fees, **24**, [656]
      local authorities, of, **24**, [653]
      local authority non-registrable bodies,
        24, [652]
      notice of, **24**, [659]
      overview, **24**, [649]

social housing—*contd*
  provider of—*contd*
    registration—*contd*
      profit-making or non-profit making
        organisation, as, **24**, [654]
  registered providers—
    accounts—
      charity, of. *See* **charity**
      directions, **24**, [666]
      disclosure of information, **24**, [682]
      failure to comply with direction,
        provision or requirement, **24**, [681]
      non-audited industrial and provident
        society, of, **24**, [673]
      offences, **24**, [680]
      submission to regulator, **24**, [667]
    acquisitions by, stamp duty land tax,
      41(S), Stamp Duties 3–4
    associate of, **24**, [810]
    audit, companies exempt from—
      accountant's report, **24**, [668], [669]
      Companies Act provisions, application
        of, **24**, [671]
      extraordinary audit, **24**, [672]
      reporting accountant, **24**, [670]
    charity. *See* **charity**
    company—
      arrangements and reconstructions,
        24, [699]
      articles, change of, **24**, [753]
      industrial and provident society,
        conversion to, **24**, [700]
      subsidiary, **24**, [810]
      winding up, **24**, [701]
    complaints, guidance on—
      consultation, **24**, [755]
      contents of, **24**, [754]
      publication of, **24**, [754]
    complaints, investigation of, **24**, [663]
    disposal of property—
      amended provisions, **24**, [730]
      change of use, **24**, [726]
      charity, powers of, **24**, [728]
      consents under other legislation,
        24, [729]
      former providers, provisions applying,
        24, [725]
      meaning, **24**, [812]
      notification where consent not
        required, **24**, [715]
      power of, **24**, [710]
      proceeds—
        disposal proceeds fund, **24**, [716]
        separate accounting, **24**, [716]
        use of, **24**, [717]
      regulator, consent of—
        exceptions, **24**, [712]
        procedure, **24**, [713]
        requirement, **24**, [711]
      tenant, to. *See* tenant's right to acquire
        below
      tenants' rights and duties, **24**, [718]
      trustees, provisions applying to, **24**, [727]
      without consent, void, **24**, [714]

social housing—*contd*
registered providers—*contd*
enforcement notice—
appeal, **24**, [762]
content, **24**, [760]
failure to comply, sanction for, **24**, [764]
grounds for, **24**, [759]
Homes and Communities Agency,
notification to, **24**, [761]
overview, **24**, [758]
withdrawal of, **24**, [763]
extraordinary audit of, **24**, [749]
failure by, compensation for—
appeals, **24**, [784]
enforcement, **24**, [783]
grounds for award, **24**, [776]
housing ombudsman, award by,
24, [778]
impact, consideration of, **24**, [780]
notice, **24**, [779]
persons to whom made, **24**, [777]
pre-compensation warning, **24**, [781]
representations, **24**, [782]
industrial and provident society—
amalgamation, instrument of, **24**, [794]
change of rules, **24**, [751]
company, conversion of, **24**, [700]
dissolution, **24**, [704]
restructuring, **24**, [702]
winding up, **24**, [703]
inquiries—
charity, relating to, **24**, [748]
evidence, **24**, [747]
holding, **24**, [745]
procedure, **24**, [746]
removal or suspension of officers
following, **24**, [799], [800]
reports, **24**, [746]
restrictions on dealings during,
24, [795], [797]
restrictions on dealings following,
24, [796], [797]
suspension of officers during, **24**, [798],
[800]
insolvency. *See* **insolvency**
inspections—
fees, **24**, [741]
purpose of, **24**, [740]
report, **24**, [741]
management tender—
notice, **24**, [787]
requirement, **24**, [786]
management transfer—
notice, **24**, [789]
requirement, **24**, [788]
manager—
appointment of, **24**, [790]
notice of action, **24**, [791]
members, payments to, **24**, [661]
non-profit, provisions applying to,
24, [750]
officers—
acting while disqualified—
offence, **24**, [803]
repayment of sums, **24**, [804]

social housing—*contd*
registered providers—*contd*
officers—*contd*
appeal against removal or suspension,
24, [807]
disqualified persons, register of, **24**, [802]
meaning, **24**, [809]
new, appointment of, **24**, [808]
non-profit registered provider, of,
removal, **24**, [805], [806]
removal or suspension following
inquiry, **24**, [799], [800]
removed person, disqualification of,
24, [801]
suspension during inquiry, **24**, [798],
[800]
penalties imposed on—
amount of, **24**, [768]
appeals, **24**, [774]
destination of money, **24**, [772]
enforcement, **24**, [773]
grounds for, **24**, [766]
Homes and Communities Agency,
notification to, **24**, [771]
penalty notice, **24**, [767]
pre-penalty warning, **24**, [769]
representations, **24**, [770]
performance information—
annual report, **24**, [743]
publication of, **24**, [744]
requirement, **24**, [743]
regulator—
accounts—
directions as to, **24**, [666]
submission of, **24**, [667]
voluntary undertakings to, **24**, [664]
standards. *See* standards *below*
survey—
entry on premises, **24**, [739]
notice of, **24**, [738]
power to arrange, **24**, [738]
report, **24**, [738]
sustainable community strategies,
co-operation in preparing, **24**, [665]
transfer of land—
inquiry or audit, after, **24**, [792]
price, **24**, [793]
terms of, **24**, [793]
winding up—
company, **24**, [701]
industrial and provident society,
24, [703]
regulator, petition by, **24**, [705]
transfer of property, **24**, [706]–[708]
regulation of—
purpose of provisions, **24**, [598]
structural overview, **24**, [599]
regulations, **24**, [611]
regulatory powers, overview, **24**, [731]
shared ownership low cost rental, **24**, [610]
standards—
code of practice—
charities, applying to, **24**, [735]
consultation, **24**, [735]
issue of, **24**, [734]

social housing—*contd*
  standards—*contd*
    code of practice—*contd*
      revision, **24**, [734], [737]
      withdrawal, **24**, [734], [737]
    failure to meet, **24**, [737]
    management, **24**, [733]
    Secretary of State, direction by, **24**, [736]
    setting, **24**, [732]
    specified rules, **24**, [732]
  stock—
    Housing Act 1996, under, **24**, [616]
    leaving—
      disposal with consent, on, **24**, [614]
      expiry of lease, on, **24**, [613]
      regulator, by direction of, **24**, [615]
      sale, on, **24**, [612]
  tenant's right to acquire—
    amended provisions, **24**, [724]
    conditions for, **24**, [719]
    dwelling remaining in social rented sector,
      meaning, **24**, [721]
    interpretation, **24**, [722]
    publicly funded provision, meaning,
      24, [720]
    Secretary of State, orders by, **24**, [723]
  Welsh Ministers, reference to, **24**, [601]

Social Housing Ombudsman for Wales
  abolition of office, **10**, [835]

social landlord
  charges by, **23**, [532], [533]
  complaints against—
    communications, privileged, **23**, [551]
    housing ombudsman, determination by,
      23, [551]
    investigation, scheme for, **23**, [398]
      amendment, **23**, [551]
      approval, **23**, [551]
      matters provided for, **23**, [551]
      membership of, **23**, [551]
      notice of membership, **23**, [551]
      register of, **23**, [551]
      subscriptions, **23**, [551]
      withdrawal from, **23**, [551]
    publication of determinations, **23**, [551]
  meaning, **23**, [398]
  registered. *See* **registered social landlord**
  service charge income, special trust rate not
    applying to, **43(S)**, 87

social security
  administration—
    persons employed in, **40(1)**, [729]
    preliminary note, **40(1)**, [1]
  age, determining, **40(1)**, [456]
  armed forces personnel, and, **3**, [1]
  authorised officer—
    authorisations, **40(1)**, [589]
    information, power to require, **40(1)**, [590]
    local authority authorisations, **40(1)**, [594]
    powers of entry, **40(1)**, [592]
  authorities, obtaining information from,
    43(1), [289]

social security—*contd*
  awards by employment tribunals, recoupment
    of benefits on, **16**, [562], [563]
  benefits chargeable to tax, **44(1)**, [431]
  benefits, regulations as to forfeiture rule,
    12(1), [777]
  body corporate, offences by, **40(1)**, [176],
    [604]
  civil partnership, relationship arising through,
    27, [880], [964]–[966]
  commissioner—
    pension, **11(2)**, [599]
    relevant service, **11(2)**, [603]
  contributions—
    enforcement of payment, **4(2)**, [48], [51]
    non-deductible, **44(1)**, [431]
    See also **National Insurance**
  documents—
    illegal possession of, **40(1)**, [711]
    stamp duty exemption, **40(1)**, [720]
  emergency payments, **40(1)**, [518]
  enforcement, definitions, **40(1)**, [618]
  financial provisions, **3**, [1514]
  financial review and report, **40(1)**, [695]
  friendly society benefit, provision of
    information, **19(1)**, [911]
  Government pilot schemes, **43(1)**, [235]
  income support, fines deducted from,
    11(3), [169]
  Independent Living Funds, cessation of,
    40(2), [539]
  information—
    authorised officer, power of to require,
      40(1), [590]
    authorities administering, supply to,
      40(2), [534]
    benefits, relating to, **40(2)**, [532]
    electronic access, power to require—
      local authority, of, **40(1)**, [595]
      Secretary of State, of, **40(1)**, [591]
    payments, arrangements for, **40(2)**, [301]
    supply of, **40(2)**, [251]
    unlawful disclosure, **40(2)**, [533]
    use of, **40(2)**, [152], [532]
    use of powers, code of practice,
      40(2), [300]
  inspectors—
    delaying, **40(1)**, [596]
    obstructing, **40(1)**, [596]
  investigators, authorisations for, **40(1)**, [589]
  legal proceedings—
    conduct of, **40(1)**, [607]
    issues arising in, **40(1)**, [609], [610]
    local authority, prosecution powers,
      40(1), [608]
  legislation—
    consequential amendments, **40(2)**, [4]
    consolidation of, **40(1)**, [65]
    continuity, **40(2)**, [2]
    repeals, **40(1)**, [68]; **40(2)**, [8]
    transitional provisions, **40(1)**, [69], [75];
      40(2), [5], [9], [10]
    transitory modifications, **40(2)**, [6], [11],
      [12]

social security—*contd*
local tribunals, exercise of functions of,
40(1), [136]
medical boards, **40(1)**, [137]
Northern Ireland, arrangements for,
31, [1121]
offences, loss for commission of, **40(2)**, [535]
officers, impersonation of, **40(1)**, [710]
old cases, payment administration,
40(1), [735]
old people, provision of meals and recreation
for, **40(1)**, [138]
orders—
parliamentary control of, **40(1)**, [459]
power to make, **40(1)**, [458]
overseas authorities, exchange of information
with, **40(1)**, [707]
person employed in administration,
unauthorised disclosure of information by,
40(1), [629]
post—
redirection, requirement to supply
information about, **40(1)**, [713]
return of, **40(1)**, [712]
regulations and orders—
breach of, **40(1)**, [174]
parliamentary control of, **40(1)**, [459],
[722]
power to make, **40(1)**, [179], [192], [201],
[458], [721]
war pensions committees, **3**, [1515]
schemes, **40(1)**, [458]
system, preliminary note, **40(1)**, [1]
systems outside Great Britain—
information, exchange of, **40(1)**, [707]
reciprocal arrangements, **40(1)**, [706]
territorial waters, application of provisions
to, **40(1)**, [455]
travelling expenses, payment of, **40(1)**, [708],
[709]

social security adjudication
adjudicating medical practitioner—
appointment of, **40(1)**, [552]
procedure, regulations as to, **40(1)**, [727]
adjudication officer—
appointment of, **40(1)**, [540]
Chief—
annual report, **40(1)**, [541]
appointment of, **40(1)**, [541]
duty of, **40(1)**, [541]
claims and questions submitted to,
40(1), [522]
decision of, **40(1)**, [523]
certificate of, **40(1)**, [726]
review of—
appeals following, **40(1)**, [530], [535]
attendance allowance, on,
40(1), [532]–[537]
claimant appeals, after, **40(1)**, [531]
conditions for, **40(1)**, [537]
decision subject to, **40(1)**, [527]
disability living allowance, on,
40(1), [532]–[537]

social security adjudication—*contd*
adjudication officer—*contd*
decision of—*contd*
review of—*contd*
disability working allowance, on,
40(1), [532]–[537]
procedure for, **40(1)**, [528]
regulations, **40(1)**, [529]
right of, **40(1)**, [527]
functions of, **40(1)**, [136]
amendments, **40(1)**, [128]
appeals. *See* **social security appeal
tribunal; tribunals**
assessors, appointment of, **40(1)**, [558]
decisions—
certificate of, **40(2)**, [188]
finality of, **40(1)**, [563]
use of computers, **40(2)**, [151]
experts, matters referred to, **40(1)**, [555]
general note, **40(1)**, [1]
industrial diseases, as to, **40(1)**, [565]
insurance officers, exercise of functions of,
40(1), [136]
medical practitioners, by, **40(1)**, [137]
persons employed in, **40(1)**, [729]
question of law, appeal on, **40(1)**, [520]
procedure, regulations as to, **40(2)**, [163],
[209]
regional chairmen, appointment of,
40(1), [553]
regulations—
determination of questions, as to,
40(1), [561]
Parliamentary control of, **40(2)**, [198]
power to make, **40(2)**, [197]
procedure, **40(1)**, [562]
reviews and appeals, as to, **40(1)**, [561]
supplementary matters relating to
determinations, **40(1)**, [564]
Secretary of State—
appeal from on question of law,
40(1), [520]
decisions by, **40(2)**, [153]
earlier decisions, superseding,
40(2), [155]
First-tier tribunal, appeal to, **40(2)**, [158]
issues arising on appeal in other cases,
involving, **40(2)**, [174]
regulations, **40(2)**, [157]
revision of, **40(2)**, [154]
decisions, review of, **40(1)**, [521]
HM Revenue and Customs, reference of
issues to, **40(2)**, [156], [173]
inquiry, appointment of person to hold,
40(1), [519]
medical examination, requiring,
40(2), [166]
questions for, **40(1)**, [519]
reports by, **40(2)**, [199]
transfer of functions to, **40(2)**, [150]
expenditure for facilitating, **40(2)**, [196]
special difficulty, assistance of assessors in
questions of, **40(1)**, [558]
travelling and other expenses, payment of,
40(2), [168]

social security adjudication—*contd*
 work-focused interview—
  decisions, **40(1)**, [500]
  entitlement conditional on, **40(1)**, [498]
  meaning, **40(1)**, [498]
  optional, **40(1)**, [501]
  partner, for, **40(1)**, [499]
  regulations, **40(1)**, [498]
  relevant decisions, **40(1)**, [500]

Social Security Advisory Committee
 constitution, **40(1)**, [731]
 continuation of, **40(1)**, [699]
 members, **40(1)**, [731]
 regulations—
  consultation not required, where,
   40(1), [702], [733]
  consultation on, **40(1)**, [701]
  report, **40(1)**, [703]

social security appeal tribunal
 appeal from, **40(1)**, [525], [536]
 appeal to, **40(1)**, [524]; **40(2)**, [210]
 chairmen—
  nomination of, **40(1)**, [543]
  remuneration, **40(1)**, [726]
  tenure of office, **40(1)**, [726]
 clerks to, **40(1)**, [726]
 constitution, **40(1)**, [543]; **40(2)**, [210]
 decisions—
  certificate of, **40(1)**, [726]
  review of—
   appeals following, **40(1)**, [530]
   claimant appeals, after, **40(1)**, [531]
   decision subject to, **40(1)**, [527]
   procedure for, **40(1)**, [528]
   regulations, **40(1)**, [529]
   right of, **40(1)**, [527]
 decisions of—
  finality of, **40(2)**, [164]
  issues arising on appeal in other cases,
   involving, **40(2)**, [174]
  matters arising, **40(2)**, [165]
 finality of decisions, **40(2)**, [164]
 First-tier—
  appeal from—
   issues arising on appeal in other cases,
    involving, **40(2)**, [175]
   leave for, **40(2)**, [160]
   redetermination, **40(2)**, [159]
   trade union, at instance of, **40(2)**, [160]
   Upper Tribunal, to, **40(2)**, [160], [294]
  appeal to, **40(2)**, [161]
   benefit decisions, as to, **40(2)**, [207]
   child support, relating to, **40(2)**, [210]
   contributions decisions, as to,
    40(2), [208]
   council tax benefit, as to, **40(2)**, [294]
   housing benefit, as to, **40(2)**, [294]
   issues arising on appeal in other cases,
    involving, **40(2)**, [175]
   mesothelioma lump sum payments, as
    to, **40(2)**, [587]
   not lying, where, **40(2)**, [206]

social security appeal tribunal—*contd*
 First-tier—*contd*
  certificate of recoverable benefit, reference
   of, **40(2)**, [117]
  medical examination, requiring,
   40(2), [167]
 functions of, **40(1)**, [136]
 HM Revenue and Customs, issues falling to
  be decided by, **40(2)**, [173]
 members—
  appointment of, **40(1)**, [542]
  period of office, **40(1)**, [542]
  same sex as claimant, one to be,
   40(1), [543]
 officers and staff, **40(1)**, [726]
 panels for appointment to, **40(1)**, [542]
 President—
  administrative duties, **40(1)**, [726]
  appointment of, **40(1)**, [553]
  remuneration, **40(1)**, [726]
  tenure of office, **40(1)**, [726]
 procedure, regulations as to, **40(1)**, [727];
  40(2), [163], [209]
 questions first arising on appeal, **40(1)**, [538]
 Senior President, functions of, **40(2)**, [162]
 special questions, reference of, **40(1)**, [539]
 Upper—
  appeal from, application for permission,
   40(2), [161]
  appeal to—
   certificate of recoverable benefit,
    concerning, **40(2)**, [118]
   council tax benefit, as to, **40(2)**, [294]
   First-tier tribunal, from, **40(2)**, [160]
   housing benefit, as to, **40(2)**, [294]

social security benefits
 adult dependants, for—
  husband, pension increase for, **40(1)**, [329]
  incapacity benefit, **40(1)**, [331]
  one only, for, **40(1)**, [333]
  person with care of children, increase for,
   40(1), [330]
  reduced contributions, where, **40(1)**, [332]
  short-term benefit, increase in, **40(1)**, [327]
  wife, pension increase for, **40(1)**, [328]
 age-related—
  disqualifications, **40(2)**, [474]
  entitlement to—
   basic cases, **40(2)**, [472]
   special cases, **40(2)**, [473]
  interpretation, **40(2)**, [478]
  power to provide for, **40(2)**, [477]
  procedure for claiming, **40(2)**, [475]
  qualifying individuals, **40(2)**, [471]
  relevant week, meaning, **40(2)**, [471]
  tax and social security, disregarded for,
   40(2), [476]
 airmen, for, **40(1)**, [361]
 alignment, **40(2)**, [316]
 armed forces, members of, **40(1)**, [359], [360]
 benefits offences—
  loss of benefit on commission of,
   40(2), [302]
  meaning, **40(2)**, [302]

social security benefits—*contd*
  benefits offences—*contd*
    members of offender's family, effect on,
      40(2), [304]
  breach of community order, loss on,
    40(2), [280]
  children, in respect of, **40(1)**, [677]
  claim—
    duties of employer, **40(1)**, [637]
    made before 1 October 1990, **40(1)**, [725]
    necessity of, **40(1)**, [496]
    regulations, **40(1)**, [504]
    retrospective provisions, **40(1)**, [497]
    sharing of functions, **40(1)**, [507]
  computation, effect of alteration of rates,
    40(1), [678]
  continental shelf operations, modifications in
    respect of, **40(1)**, [364]
  contributory—
    contribution conditions, **40(1)**, [260]
    contributions credits, **40(1)**, [263]
    descriptions of, **40(1)**, [259]
    general note, **40(1)**, [1]
    See also **invalidity benefits, etc**
  Crown employment, application of
    provisions, **40(1)**, [359]
  definitions, **40(1)**, [366]
  dependants, persons maintaining, **40(1)**, [358]
  dependency increases—
    adults, for, **40(1)**, [327]–[333]
    amount of, **40(1)**, [334]
    fluctuating earnings, continuation of
      awards, **40(1)**, [337]
    pensions, earnings including, **40(1)**, [334]
    rates of, **40(1)**, [468]
    termination of employment after
      entitlement to disability working
      allowance, **40(1)**, [338]
    trade disputes, effect of, **40(1)**, [336]
  dishonest representation to obtain,
    40(1), [597]
  disqualification and suspension, **40(1)**, [357]
  earnings factor. *See* **contributions**
  employment and support allowance—
    attainment of certain age, implementation
      due to, **40(1)**, [689]
    effect of alteration of rates of, **40(1)**, [686]
  errors—
    correction of, **40(1)**, [572]; **40(2)**, [177]
    decisions, setting aside, **40(2)**, [177]
    determinations, review of, **40(1)**, [571]
    restrictions on entitlement in cases of,
      40(1), [570]; **40(2)**, [176], [210]
  exempt from tax, **43(S)**, 875
  exemption from tax on—
    children, increases in respect of,
      44(2), [675]
    foreign benefits, **44(2)**, [680]
    income support—
      amounts in excess of taxable maximum,
        44(2), [666]
      child maintenance bonus, **44(2)**, [665]
      exemption unless paid to member of
        couple involved in trade dispute,
        44(2), [664]

social security benefits—*contd*
  exemption from tax on—*contd*
    income support—*contd*
      interpretation, **44(2)**, [668]
      amounts in excess of taxable maximum,
        44(2), [666]
      child maintenance bonus, **44(2)**, [665]
      exemption unless paid to member of
        couple involved in trade dispute,
        44(2), [664]
      interpretation, **44(2)**, [668]
    jobseeker's allowance—
      amounts in excess of taxable maximum,
        44(2), [670]
      child maintenance bonus, **44(2)**, [669]
      contribution-based, **44(2)**, [673]
      income-based, **44(2)**, [672]
      interpretation, **44(2)**, [674]
      taxable maximum, **44(2)**, [671]–[673]
    long-term incapacity benefit, **44(2)**, [662]
    short-term incapacity benefit, **44(2)**, [663]
    table of, **44(2)**, [676]
  false representation to obtain, **40(1)**, [598]
  foreign, taxable—
    application of provisions, **44(2)**, [677]
    consular employees, benefits of,
      44(2), [681]
    exemptions, **44(2)**, [680]
    income, **44(2)**, [678]
    person liable for tax, **44(2)**, [679]
  inalienable, **40(1)**, [719]
  incapacity for work—
    application of provisions, **40(1)**, [454]
    disqualification for receiving benefit,
      40(1), [452]
    existing enactments, saving for, **40(2)**, [37]
    Northern Ireland, provision for, **40(2)**, [38]
    own occupation test, **40(1)**, [449]
    personal capability assessments, **40(1)**, [450]
    persons treated as incapable or capable,
      40(1), [451]
    regulations, **40(2)**, [180]
    remunerative work, meaning, **40(1)**, [449]
    test of, **40(1)**, [448]; **40(2)**, [32]
      new, transition to, **40(2)**, [33]
    work as councillor, disregard of,
      40(1), [453]
  income—
    meaning, **44(2)**, [656]
    structure of provisions, **44(2)**, [654]
    tax charge on—
      amount of, **44(2)**, [657]
      nature of, **44(2)**, [655]
      person liable for, **44(2)**, [658]
    taxable benefits, meaning, **44(2)**, [656]
    transitional provisions, **44(2)**, [773]
  income-related—
    applicable amount, **40(1)**, [383]
    definitions, **40(1)**, [386]
    description of, **40(1)**, [367]
    exclusions from, **40(1)**, [382]
    general note, **40(1)**, [1]
    income and capital of family member,
      treatment of, **40(1)**, [384]
    meaning, **40(1)**, [723]

social security benefits—*contd*
income-related—*contd*
prescribed schemes, **40(1)**, [367]
regulations, **40(1)**, [384]
state pension credit, attaining qualifying age
for, **40(1)**, [385]
See also **income support, etc**
increases, effect of trade disputes on,
40(1), [336]
industrial injuries, for. *See* **industrial injuries
benefits**
information, use of, **40(1)**, [508]
legal proceedings, **40(1)**, [175]
long-term, **40(1)**, [259]
loss of—
benefits offences, on commission of,
40(2), [302]
breach of community order, on,
40(2), [280]
information provision, **40(2)**, [282]
joint-claim jobseeker's allowance,
40(2), [281], [303]
regulations, **40(2)**, [283], [306]
supplementation and mitigation of
provisions, **40(2)**, [305]
maintenance payments collected by Secretary
of State, payment where, **40(1)**, [578]
mariners, for, **40(1)**, [361]
married women, for, **40(1)**, [362]
meaning, **40(1)**, [366]
descriptions of, **40(1)**, [312]
general note, **40(1)**, [1]
See also **attendance allowance**, etc
Northern Ireland, recovery of, **40(1)**, [583]
occupational and personal pension payments,
earnings including, **40(1)**, [334]
overlapping, **40(1)**, [576]
overpayments—
housing benefit, **40(1)**, [579]
misrepresentation, **40(1)**, [573]
not recoverable, **40(2)**, [250]
penalty as alternative to prosecution,
40(1), [605], [606]
recovery of, **40(1)**, [573]; **40(2)**, [103]
persons outside Great Britain, modification of
provisions for, **40(1)**, [363]
pilot schemes, **40(2)**, [195]
polygamous marriage, effect of, **40(1)**, [365]
questions relating to, **40(2)**, [9]
rates of, **40(1)**, [465]–[469]
recovery of—
cases to which provisions applying,
40(2), [105]
certificate of recoverable benefit—
appeals, **40(2)**, [116]
application for, **40(2)**, [109]
First-tier tribunal, reference of questions
to, **40(2)**, [117]
fresh, **40(2)**, [109], [119]
information in, **40(2)**, [110]
review of, **40(2)**, [115], [119]
Upper Tribunal, appeal to, **40(2)**, [118]
compensation payments—
application of provisions, **40(2)**, [107]

social security benefits—*contd*
recovery of—*contd*
compensation payments—*contd*
calculation, **40(2)**, [142]
power to amend provisions,
40(2), [129]
calculation of, information as to,
40(2), [114]
court order for, **40(2)**, [120]
disregarded, **40(2)**, [126]
exempted, **40(2)**, [140]
gross amount, **40(2)**, [114]
insurers, liability of, **40(2)**, [127]
nil, **40(2)**, [114]
payments into court, **40(2)**, [121]
reduction of, **40(2)**, [113]
lump sum and periodical payments,
40(2), [123]
more than one person, payments by,
40(2), [124]
small, disregard of, **40(2)**, [141]
courts, jurisdiction of, **40(2)**, [132]
damages, benefits irrelevant to, **40(2)**, [122]
definitions, **40(2)**, [134]
financial arrangements, **40(2)**, [136]
information, provision of, **40(2)**, [128]
lump sum payments, regulation-making
power, **40(2)**, [106]
Northern Ireland, **40(2)**, [130]–[132]
person paying compensation—
recovery of payments due, **40(2)**, [112]
overpayments, **40(2)**, [125]
Secretary of State, liability to pay
amount to, **40(2)**, [111]
regulations and orders, **40(2)**, [135], [255]
relevant period, meaning, **40(2)**, [108]
residence of injured person, **40(2)**, [131]
transitional and consequential provisions,
40(2), [137]
regulations, breach of, **40(1)**, [599]
short-term, **40(1)**, [259]
suspension—
information, for failure to furnish,
40(2), [170]
medical examination, for failure to submit
to, **40(2)**, [172]
prescribed circumstances, in, **40(2)**, [169]
regulations, **40(2)**, [169]
transitory provisions, **40(2)**, [210]
taxable—
application of provisions, **44(2)**, [660]
exemption. *See* exemption from tax on
above
foreign. *See* foreign, taxable *above*
persons liable for tax, **44(2)**, [661]
table of, **44(2)**, [659]
termination—
information, for failure to furnish,
40(2), [171]
medical examination, for failure to submit
to, **40(2)**, [172]
up-rating of—
annual, **40(1)**, [672]
basic pension, **40(1)**, [673]
directions, **40(1)**, [674]

social security benefits—*contd*
up-rating of—*contd*
mistakes in orders, rectification of,
40(1), [675]
regulations, **40(1)**, [114], [189]
standard minimum guarantee, **40(1)**, [673]
voidable marriage, effect of, **40(1)**, [365]
widows, for, **40(1)**, [362]

Social Security Commissioners
appeals from, **33(1)**, [60]
appeal from on point of law, **40(1)**, [526]
appeal to, **40(1)**, [525], [536]
transitory provisions, **40(2)**, [210]
appointment of, **40(1)**, [554]
Chief, appointment of, **40(1)**, [554]
decisions, review of—
appeals following, **40(1)**, [530]
claimant appeals, after, **40(1)**, [531]
decision subject to, **40(1)**, [527]
procedure for, **40(1)**, [528]
regulations, **40(1)**, [529]
right of, **40(1)**, [527]
Deputy, **40(1)**, [554]
medical appeal tribunal, appeal from,
40(1), [550]
National Insurance Commissioners, change of
name, **40(1)**, [103]
Pensions Appeal Tribunal, appeals from,
33(1), [58]
procedure in appeals, **33(1)**, [61]
procedure, regulations as to, **40(1)**, [727]
questions first arising on appeal, **40(1)**, [538]
remuneration, **40(1)**, [726]
special difficulty, questions of, **40(1)**, [558]
special questions, reference of, **40(1)**, [539]
Tribunal of, **40(1)**, [559]

social security contributions
deduction from earnings, disallowed,
44(2), [371]
profits, restriction of deduction from,
44(3), [52]
transfer of functions from Contributions
Agency to Commissioners of Inland
Revenue. *See under* **Commissioners of
Inland Revenue**

social services
general note, **40(1)**, [1]
local involvement networks—
annual reports, **26(2)**, [638]
contractual arrangements for, **26(2)**, [632],
[633]
further provision, power to make,
26(2), [634]
local authority, meaning, **26(2)**, [640]
meaning, **26(2)**, [633]
service-providers, duties of—
entry, to allow, **26(2)**, [636]
respond, to, **26(2)**, [635]
social care matters, referrals of, **26(2)**, [637]
transitional arrangements, **26(2)**, [639]

Social Welfare Organisation. *See* **Coal
Industry Social Welfare Organisation**

Societas Europaea. *See* **European
Company/SE**

society
lottery. *See* **lottery**
non-commercial, meaning, **5(1)**, [300]

Society of Friends. *See* **Quakers**

Sodor and Man
augmentation grants in, **14**, 337
bishop of, stipend, **14**, 819
York, within province of, **14**, 5

soil pipes
execution of works, notice requiring—
appeal provisions, **35(1)**, [583]
contents, **35(1)**, [583]
enforcement, **35(1)**, [583]
giving by local authority, **35(1)**, [583]
insufficiency, **35(1)**, [583]
use, **35(1)**, [584]
ventilation, **35(1)**, [584]

soliciting. *See also* **prostitute**
murder, to commit, **12(1)**, [69]
offence of, **12(1)**, [306]
references to, interpretation of, **12(1)**, [971]
woman, by—
application to court by, after caution,
12(1), [307]
offence, **12(1)**, [306]
women, of—
motor vehicle, from, **12(1)**, [969]
persistent, for purposes of prostitution,
12(1), [970]

solicitor
accountants' reports, **11(2)**, [314];
11(4), [405]
accounts—
bank or building society, keeping in,
11(2), [366]; **11(4)**, [460]
client account, **11(2)**, [311]; **11(4)**, [402]
duty to keep, **11(2)**, [311]; **11(4)**, [402]
investigation of, **11(2)**, [311]; **11(4)**, [402]
practice, inspection of, **11(2)**, [313];
11(4), [404]
rules, **11(2)**, [311]; **11(4)**, [402]
administration of oaths by, **18**, [75], [280]
admission of—
application for, **11(2)**, [280]
justices' clerk, assistant to, of, **11(2)**, [280]
qualifications, **11(2)**, [277]; **11(4)**, [370]
regulations, **11(2)**, [307]; **11(4)**, [398]
requirements as to, **11(2)**, [268];
11(4), [374]
training regulations, compliance with,
11(4), [374]
affidavit—
fee for taking, **11(2)**, [363]
power to take, **11(2)**, [362]

solicitor—*contd*
 alien as, **11(2)**, [308]
 articles—
  meaning, **11(2)**, [367]
  training under, **11(2)**, [279]
 assessment of costs—
  application for—
   party chargeable, by, **11(4)**, [450]
   solicitor, by, **11(4)**, [450]
   third parties, by, **11(4)**, [451]
  costs officer, county court district judge
   as, **11(4)**, [454]
  supplementary provisions, **11(4)**, [452]
 audience, right of **12(1)**, [1056]
  generally, **11(2)**, [297]
  Law Society, granted by, **11(3)**, [89]
  specification of courts etc, **11(2)**, [297]
 bank account, rights of bank respecting
  11(2), [366]; **11(4)**, [460]
  See also client account *below*
 bankruptcy of—
  file, inspection by Society, **11(2)**, [364];
   11(4), [458]
  intervention by Society, on, **11(2)**, [372];
   11(4), [466]
  suspension of certificate on, **11(2)**, [293]
 bill of costs—
  contentious business, **11(2)**, [345];
   11(4), [444]
  delivery, methods of, **11(2)**, [350];
   11(4), [449]
  disbursements included in, **11(2)**, [348];
   11(4), [447]
  gross sum bill, **11(2)**, [345]; **11(4)**, [444]
  order to deliver, **11(2)**, [349]; **11(4)**, [448]
  signature to, **11(2)**, [350]; **11(4)**, [449]
  taxation of, payment before, **11(2)**, [347]
 building society account, **11(2)**, [366];
  11(4), [460]
 charging order for costs, **11(2)**, [354];
  11(4), [453]
 child, interest of, in certain proceedings,
  6, [356]
 Church Commissioners, to, **11(2)**, [369];
  11(4), [308], [463]
 City of London, to, saving for, **11(2)**, [369];
  11(4), [308], [463]
 civil liability, indemnity, **11(2)**, [317];
  11(4), [411]
 client, meaning **11(2)**, [367]; **11(4)**, [462]
 client account—
  meaning, **11(2)**, [367]; **11(4)**, [462]
  opening and keeping, **11(2)**, [311];
   11(4), [402]
  specification of banks for, **11(2)**, [311]
 client's money—
  control by Society, **11(2)**, [373];
   11(4), [467]
  deposit account, in, **11(2)**, [311]
  interest on, **11(2)**, [312]; **11(4)**, [403]
  meaning, **11(2)**, [311]
  rules relating to, **11(2)**, [311]; **11(4)**, [402]
 commissioner for oaths, as, **11(2)**, [362]
  powers, **18**, [153]

solicitor—*contd*
 compensation fund. *See* **Law Society**
 conduct of, Law Society's power in relation
  to, **11(3)**, [284], [306]
 contentious business—
  county court, in, **11(2)**, [355]; **11(4)**, [454]
  meaning, **11(2)**, [367]; **11(4)**, [462]
  remuneration. *See* remuneration *below*
 costs—
  See also remuneration *below*
  action to recover—
   county court, in, **11(2)**, [349], [350];
    11(4), [449]
   High Court, in, **11(2)**, [350];
    11(4), [449]
   requirements for, **11(2)**, [350];
    11(4), [449]
   time for, **11(2)**, [350]; **11(4)**, [449]
  assessment of, **11(4)**, [446]
  bill of. *See* bill of costs *above*
  charging order for, **11(2)**, [353];
   11(4), [453]
  contentious business. *See* remuneration
   below
  county court, in, **11(2)**, [355]; **11(4)**, [454]
  incorporated practice, **11(3)**, [44];
   11(4), [518]
  meaning, **11(2)**, [367]; **11(4)**, [462]
  security for, **11(2)**, [346]; **11(4)**, [445]
  See also remuneration *below*
  taxation. *See* taxation *below*
  unqualified person, non-recoverable,
   11(2), [304]
 county court—
  bill of costs, order to deliver, **11(2)**, [349];
   11(4), [448]
  contentious business, special provisions,
   11(2), [355]; **11(4)**, [454]
  right of audience, **11(2)**, [297]
 Crown Court centres, existing rights in
  certain, **11(3)**, [311]
 disciplinary proceedings—
  allegations, requirement to answer,
   11(2), [336]; **11(4)**, [435]
  appeals, **11(2)**, [330], [331]; **11(4)**, [428],
   [429]
   High Court, to, **11(4)**, [428]
   Tribunal, to, **11(4)**, [429]
  costs of, **11(2)**, [332]
  High Court, in, **11(2)**, [331]
  jurisdiction, courts having, **11(2)**, [331]
  order of court—
   drawing up, **11(2)**, [333]; **11(4)**, [432]
   production to Society, **11(2)**, [334];
    11(4), [433]
  restrictions on powers, **11(2)**, [335];
   11(4), [434]
  Supreme Court, before, **11(2)**, [331]
  Tribunal. *See* **Solicitors Disciplinary
   Tribunal**
 Disciplinary Tribunal. *See* **Solicitors
  Disciplinary Tribunal**
 dishonesty, suspected, **11(2)**, [372];
  11(3), [44]; **11(4)**, [466]

solicitor—*contd*
documents—
delivery up to Society, **11(2)**, [373]; **11(4)**, [467]
production for investigation, **11(2)**, [325]; **11(4)**, [417]–[420]
service of, **11(2)**, [365]; **11(4)**, [459]
unqualified person, drawing by. *See* unqualified persons *below*
Duchy of Cornwall, for, saving for, **11(2)**, [369]; **11(4)**, [308], [463]
employed, practising certificate, **11(2)**, [278]; **11(4)**, [371]
employees and consultants—
criminal offence, conviction of, **11(2)**, [323]; **11(4)**, [415]
employment, control of, **11(2)**, [323]; **11(4)**, [415]
offences, **11(2)**, [324]; **11(4)**, [416]
employment by—
employees and consultants, control of, **11(2)**, [323]; **11(4)**, [415]
person struck off or suspended, of, **11(2)**, [321]; **11(4)**, [412]
estate agency work by, **21**, [678]
foreign. *See* **Law Society (foreign lawyers)**
former—
employment of, **11(2)**, [321]
restoration of, **11(2)**, [283]
fraud, conviction for, **11(2)**, [291]; **11(4)**, [386]
generally, **11(2)**, [1]
High Court, jurisdiction of over, **11(2)**, [328], [331]; **11(4)**, [426]
inadequate professional services—
compensation, **11(2)**, [374]
costs incurred by solicitor, **11(2)**, [374]
taxation of, **11(2)**, [374]
directions, **11(2)**, [374]
failure to comply with, **11(2)**, [374]
fees, **11(2)**, [374]
Law Society Council—
costs incurred, **11(2)**, [374]
directions by, **11(2)**, [374]
powers, **11(2)**, [374]; **11(3)**, [44]
redress, **11(2)**, [318]
transitional provisions, **11(3)**, [54]
Tribunal, duty of, **11(2)**, [374]
incorporated practice—
accountant's reports, **11(3)**, [44]; **11(4)**, [518]
accounts rules, **11(3)**, [44]; **11(4)**, [518]
bank accounts, inspection, **11(3)**, [44]; **11(4)**, [518]
client's money, interest on, **11(3)**, [44]; **11(4)**, [518]
compensation fund contribution, **11(3)**, [44]; **11(4)**, [518]
complaints as to, **11(3)**, [44]; **11(4)**, [518]
costs of investigation, payment of, **11(3)**, [44]; **11(4)**, [518]
director, default by, **11(3)**, [44]; **11(4)**, [518]

solicitor—*contd*
incorporated practice—*contd*
foreign solicitors. *See under* **Law Society**
intervention by Society, **11(3)**, [44]; **11(4)**, [518]
legal aid complaints, **11(3)**, [44]; **11(4)**, [518]
legal service bodies, rules, **11(4)**, [470]
management and control, **11(3)**, [2]; **11(4)**, [470]
multi-national partnerships, rules, **11(3)**, [2]
Northern Ireland, provision for, **11(3)**, [42]
offences, **11(3)**, [3]; **11(4)**, [472]
provisions applied to, **11(3)**, [44]; **11(4)**, [518]
recognised body—
bank account, **11(3)**, [44]; **11(4)**, [518]
bill of costs etc, **11(3)**, [44]; **11(4)**, [518]
clients' money, payment over, **11(3)**, [44]; **11(4)**, [518]
complaints to Tribunal, **11(3)**, [44]; **11(4)**, [518]
contentious business agreements, **11(3)**, [44]; **11(4)**, [518]
conveyancing enactments, modification, **11(3)**, [44]; **11(4)**, [518]
costs, action to recover, **11(3)**, [44]; **11(4)**, [518]
documents—
examination of, **11(3)**, [44], [54]; **11(4)**, [518]
provision of, **11(4)**, [518]
employee convicted of offence, **11(3)**, [44]
failure to disclose suspension etc, **11(3)**, [44]; **11(4)**, [518]
inadequate service by, **11(3)**, [44]
information, provision of, **11(4)**, [518]
Justice of the Peace, restriction on, **11(3)**, [44]; **11(4)**, [518]
meaning, **11(3)**, [2]
person struck off etc, restriction on, **11(3)**, [44]; **11(4)**, [518]
pretending to be, **11(3)**, [3]; **11(4)**, [472]
privilege of, **11(3)**, [44]; **11(4)**, [518]
provisions applied to, **11(3)**, [2]
remuneration, **11(3)**, [44]; **11(4)**, [518]
rules applicable, **11(3)**, [2]; **11(4)**, [470]
Tribunal, powers, **11(3)**, [44]; **11(4)**, [518]
recognition—
application for, **11(3)**, [2]
refusal, appeal against, **11(3)**, [44]; **11(4)**, [518]
revocation of, **11(3)**, [44]; **11(4)**, [518]
registered foreign lawyers, rules, **11(3)**, [2]
rules for, **11(3)**, [2]; **11(4)**, [470]
transitional provisions, **11(3)**, [54]
indemnity—
civil liability, as to, **11(2)**, [317]; **11(4)**, [411]
fund, establishment etc, **11(2)**, [316]

solicitor—*contd*
  indemnity—*contd*
    rules—
      failure to comply with, **11(2)**, [317];
        11(4), [411]
      provisions of, **11(2)**, [317]; **11(4)**, [411]
      purposes of, **11(2)**, [317]; **11(4)**, [411]
  information—
    offences, **11(4)**, [420]
    provision for investigation,
      11(4), [417]–[420]
  instrument—
    meaning **11(2)**, [300]
    unqualified person drawing up. *See*
      unqualified person *below*
  intervention in practice. *See* **Law Society**
  jurisdiction over, **11(2)**, [331]
  justices' clerk—
    as, **11(2)**, [193]
    assistant to, admission of, **11(2)**, [280]
  legal aid work—
    complaints, **11(3)**, [33], [36], [44];
      11(4), [507], [518]
      against, jurisdiction and powers,
        11(4), [510]
    order for exclusion from, **11(2)**, [328]
  legal service bodies—
    incorporated practices, rules, **11(4)**, [470]
    meaning, **11(4)**, [471]
  lessee, right to employ, **20**, [666]
  letters of administration, preparation,
    11(2), [302]
  magistrates' court, representing party before,
    11(2), [543]
  Master of the Rolls, jurisdiction of. *See*
    Master of the Rolls
  meaning, **11(2)**, [367]; **11(4)**, [462]
  mortgagee, when, remuneration, **11(2)**, [339];
    11(4), [438]
  multi-disciplinary practices, rules,
    11(3), [122]; **11(4)**, [546]
  multi-national partnerships—
    foreign lawyers, application of provisions,
      11(3), [134]; **11(4)**, [556]
    incorporated practices, rules, **11(3)**, [2]
    meaning, **11(3)**, [2]
    rules as to, power to make, **11(3)**, [2]
    unincorporated association with, rules,
      power to make, **11(3)**, [122]; **11(4)**, [546]
    unqualified persons provisions, when
      inapplicable, **11(3)**, [2]
  name struck off, restoration of, **11(4)**, [376]
  non-British subject as, **11(2)**, [308];
    11(4), [399]
  non-contentious business—
    meaning **11(2)**, [367]; **11(4)**, [462]
    remuneration for. *See* remuneration *below*
  non-practising, membership of Law Society,
    11(2), [357]
  oaths—
    commissioner for, as, **11(2)**, [362]
    fee for administering, **11(2)**, [363]
    power to administer, **11(2)**, [362]
  offences—
    arrestable, conviction for, **11(2)**, [291]

solicitor—*contd*
  offences—*contd*
    body corporate, by, **11(2)**, [303]
    employment of convicted employee, as to,
      11(2), [324]; **11(4)**, [416]
    fraud or serious crime, by, **11(2)**, [291];
      11(4), [386]
    incorporated practice, as to, **11(3)**, [3];
      11(4), [472]
    unqualified person, by, **11(2)**, [298], [302];
      11(4), [393], [394]
  Officer of the Supreme Court, as,
    11(2), [331]
  partnership of, **8**, 578–81
  place of business, notification of, **11(2)**, [365];
    11(4), [393], [394]
  power of attorney, certificate as to, **1(1)**, [20]
  practice rules—
    failure to comply, **11(2)**, [311];
      11(4), [401]
    making of, **11(2)**, [311]; **11(4)**, [401]
  practising as—
    justice of the peace, **11(2)**, [319];
      11(4), [412]
    rights, **11(2)**, [297]
    specified courts, **11(2)**, [297]
    suspension from. *See* suspension *below*
    unqualified persons. *See* unqualified persons
      below
  practising certificate—
    appeal—
      costs of, **11(2)**, [289]
      postponement pending, **11(2)**, [287]
      powers of Master of the Rolls in,
        11(2), [289]
      refusal to issue, as to, **11(2)**, [287]
    application for, **11(4)**, [378]
      additional fee, when required,
        11(2), [288]
      appropriate fee, **11(4)**, [378]
      false statement, making, **11(2)**, [284]
      former solicitor, by, **11(2)**, [283]
      previous notice of, **11(2)**, [287]
      procedure, **11(2)**, [284]
    conditions, imposition of—
      appeal respecting, **11(2)**, [290];
        11(4), [385]
      purposes of, **11(2)**, [287]
      when certificate is in force, **11(2)**, [290];
        11(4), [385]
    dating of, **11(2)**, [292]
    employed solicitors, **11(2)**, [278];
      11(4), [371]
    entitlement to, **11(2)**, [285]
    evidence of holding, **11(2)**, [296]
    expiry, **11(2)**, [292]
    false statement to obtain, **11(2)**, [284]
    fees for, **11(3)**, [283]
    fees payable, **11(2)**, [286], [288]
    issue—
      appeals in connection with, **11(2)**, [289];
        11(4), [382]
      conditions, subject to, **11(2)**, [290]
      discretion as to, **11(2)**, [287]
      fee payable, **11(4)**, [381]

solicitor—*contd*
  practising certificate—*contd*
    issue—*contd*
      generally, **11(2)**, [285]; **11(4)**, [379]
      qualifying conditions, **11(2)**, [285];
        11(4), [379]
      refusal of, **11(2)**, [289]
      requirements in certain cases,
        11(2), [287]
      special cases, in, **11(2)**, [287]
      training, subject to, **11(2)**, [289]
    register—
      entries in, **11(2)**, [284]
      inspection, **11(2)**, [284]
    register of holders, **11(4)**, [380]
      extracts from, as evidence, **11(4)**, [392]
    regulations, **11(4)**, [398]
    regulations as to, **11(2)**, [307]
    replacement, **11(2)**, [292]
    requirement for, **11(2)**, [278]
    sole practitioner, application to practise as,
      11(4), [383]
    sole solicitor endorsement, **11(4)**, [372]
    suspension—
      duration, **11(2)**, [287], [294];
        11(4), [388]
      effect of, **11(2)**, [293]
      expiration, **11(2)**, [294]
      fraud or serious crime, for, **11(2)**, [291];
        11(4), [386]
      Gazette notice of, **11(2)**, [295]
      intervention, exercise of powers as to,
        11(2), [293]
      procedure for, **11(4)**, [387]
      publicity, **11(4)**, [389]
      publicity in relation to, **11(2)**, [295]
      reasons for, **11(2)**, [291], [293];
        11(4), [291]
      termination of, **11(2)**, [287], [294];
        11(4), [388]
    transitional provisions, **11(3)**, [54]
    withdrawal, **11(2)**, [292]
  practising—
    certificates, fees for, **11(3)**, [283]
    meaning, **21**, [678]
  prison, in, effect of, **11(2)**, [320]
  probate papers, preparing, **11(2)**, [302]
  professional conduct, rules regulating,
    11(2), [310]
  professional misconduct—
    compensation fund. *See under* **Law Society**
    disciplinary action, **11(4)**, [422]
      appeals against, **11(4)**, [423]
    files, inspection, **11(2)**, [325]
    investigation, **11(2)**, [325]
      costs of, **11(2)**, [326]
    investigations—
      costs, power to charge for, **11(4)**, [421]
      provision of information and documents
        for, **11(4)**, [417]–[420]
  professional practice, conduct and discipline,
    rules regulating, **11(4)**, [401]
  protection, under Law of Property Act 1925,
    20, [783]

solicitor—*contd*
  public departments, to, **11(2)**, [369];
    11(4), [463]
  purchaser's right to employ, **20**, [666]
  qualifications, generally, **11(2)**, [277];
    11(4), [370]
  register, practising certificates, as to
    11(2), [284]
    See also roll *below*
  regulations—
    Master of the Rolls, by, **11(2)**, [307]
    training, for, **11(2)**, [279]; **11(4)**, [373]
  regulations and rules, **11(3)**, [311]
  remuneration—
    agreement as to, **11(2)**, [338]; **11(4)**, [437]
      costs, objection to, **11(2)**, [338], [342];
        11(4), [437]
      disbursements, inclusion of, **11(2)**, [338];
        11(4), [437]
      hourly rate, **11(2)**, [340]–[342];
        11(4), [439], [441]
    bill of costs. *See* bill of costs *above*
    charging order for, **11(2)**, [353];
      11(4), [453]
    committee—
      composition of, **11(2)**, [337];
        11(4), [436]
      orders made by, **11(2)**, [337];
        11(4), [436]
    contentious business—
      agreement—
        action on, **11(2)**, [342]; **11(4)**, [441]
        assessment of costs, **11(4)**, [441]
        costs excluded from taxation,
          11(2), [341]
        effect of, **11(2)**, [341]; **11(4)**, [440]
        enforcement, **11(2)**, [342];
          11(4), [441]
        examination by taxing officer,
          11(2), [342]–[343]
        mode of payment, **11(2)**, [340];
          11(4), [439]
        power to make, **11(2)**, [340];
          11(4), [439]
        representative, made by, **11(2)**, [343];
          11(4), [442]
        scope of, **11(2)**, [342]
        set aside by court, **11(2)**, [342];
          11(4), [441]
        taxation of costs order, **11(2)**, [342]
      assessments of costs, **11(4)**, [446]
      bill of costs, **11(2)**, [345]; **11(4)**, [444]
      county court, in, **11(2)**, [355];
        11(4), [454]
      death etc of solicitor, effect,
        11(2), [344]; **11(4)**, [443]
      gross sum bill, **11(2)**, [345]; **11(4)**, [444]
      negligence, liability, **11(2)**, [341]
      order for taxation, **11(2)**, [344]
      security for costs, **11(2)**, [346];
        11(4), [445]
      taxation with respect to, **11(2)**, [347]
      termination of retainer, **11(2)**, [346];
        11(4), [445]

solicitor—*contd*
  remuneration—*contd*
    incorporated practice, **11(3)**, [44];
      11(4), [518]
    mortgage, in respect of, **11(2)**, [339];
      11(4), [438]
    non-contentious business—
      agreement for, **11(2)**, [338]; **11(4)**, [437]
      mode of paying, **11(2)**, [337];
        11(4), [436]
      orders prescribing, **11(2)**, [337];
        11(4), [436]
    regulation of, **11(2)**, [337]; **11(4)**, [436]
    retainer, termination, **11(2)**, [346];
      11(4), [445]
  revenue solicitors, **11(2)**, [13]
  right of audience. *See* audience, right of *above*
  right of detained person to consult,
    12(1), [905]
  roll—
    computerised, **11(2)**, [281]
    entry on, **11(2)**, [282]; **11(4)**, [376]
    extracts from, as evidence, **11(4)**, [392]
    keeping of, **11(2)**, [281]; **11(4)**, [375]
    person struck off—
      failure to disclose fact, **11(2)**, [322];
        11(4), [414]
      restriction on employing, **11(2)**, [321];
        11(4), [412]
    regulations, **11(4)**, [398]
    regulations as to, **11(2)**, [322]
    removal from—
      application by solicitor, **11(2)**, [283];
        11(4), [377]
      conditions for, **11(2)**, [307]
    restoration to—
      former solicitor, of, **11(2)**, [283];
        11(4), [377]
      order for, **11(2)**, [282], [328];
        11(4), [376], [426]
    striking off. *See* striking off *below*
  Scotland, admitted in—
    evidence of, **11(2)**, [309]; **11(4)**, [400]
    meaning, **11(4)**, [462]
  serious crime, conviction for, **11(2)**, [291];
    11(4), [386]
  service on, **11(2)**, [365]; **11(4)**, [459]
  sole—
    application to practise as, while practising
      certificate in force, **11(4)**, [383]
    death of, effect, **11(2)**, [372]; **11(4)**, [466]
    employees of—
      rules relating to, **11(4)**, [406]
      accounts, **11(4)**, [407]
    endorsement—
      fees payable, **11(4)**, [384]
      meaning, **11(4)**, [462]
      regulations, **11(4)**, [398]
      suspension, **11(4)**, [390]
        duration of, **11(4)**, [391]
        publicity, **11(4)**, [391]
      meaning, **11(2)**, [367]; **11(4)**, [462]
    restriction on practice as, **11(4)**, [372]

solicitor—*contd*
  striking off—
    application to High Court, **11(2)**, [332];
      11(4), [431]
    cessation of Law Society membership,
      11(2), [359]
    court procedure, **11(2)**, [332]; **11(4)**, [431]
    employment after, restriction on,
      11(2), [321]; **11(4)**, [412]
    expiry of certificate on, **11(2)**, [292]
    failure to disclose fact, **11(2)**, [322];
      11(4), [414]
    order by Tribunal, **11(2)**, [328];
      11(4), [426]
    order of court, **11(2)**, [332]; **11(4)**, [432]
    proceedings for. *See* disciplinary
      proceedings *above*
    restrictions on powers, **11(2)**, [335];
      11(4), [434]
  Supreme Court—
    jurisdiction over, **11(2)**, [328], [331];
      11(4), [426], [430]
    officers of, as, **11(2)**, [331]; **11(4)**, [430]
    right of audience in, **11(2)**, [297]
  suspension—
    employment of person under, **11(2)**, [321];
      11(4), [412]
    failure to disclose fact, **11(2)**, [322];
      11(4), [414]
    order by Tribunal for, **11(2)**, [328];
      11(4), [426]
    See also under practising certificate *above*
  taxation of costs—
    application for—
      party chargeable, by, **11(2)**, [351]
      procedure, **11(2)**, [353]
      solicitor, by, **11(2)**, [351]
      third parties, by, **11(2)**, [352]
    certificate, finality of, **11(2)**, [353]
    contentious business, in respect of,
      11(2), [347]
    costs of taxation, inclusion of, **11(2)**, [351]
    exclusions from, **11(2)**, [340]
    inadequate professional services,
      11(2), [374]
    order of court for, **11(2)**, [342]–[344]
    saving for certain provisions, **11(2)**, [356]
    supplementary provisions, **11(2)**, [353]
    taxing master—
      county court registrar as, **11(2)**, [355]
      powers and duties, **11(2)**, [353]
  training—
    conditions, power to specify, **11(2)**, [307]
    regulations, **11(4)**, [373]
      matters prescribed by, **11(2)**, [279]
  trust accounts—
    accounts, rules, **11(2)**, [311]; **11(4)**, [402]
    meaning, **11(2)**, [367]; **11(4)**, [462]
  unqualified person—
    acting as solicitor—
      costs not recoverable, **11(2)**, [304]
      penalties, **11(2)**, [298]; **11(4)**, [393],
        [394]
      prohibition, **11(2)**, [298]; **11(4)**, [393]
    body corporate, **11(2)**, [303]; **11(4)**, [395]

solicitor—*contd*
unqualified person—*contd*
contempt of court by, **11(2)**, [298]
costs recoverable, **11(4)**, [396]
documents, preparation of, by, **11(2)**, [300]
entry on premises, suspected unlawful
preparation of instruments, **11(2)**, [301]
evidence as to, **11(2)**, [297]
instruments—
meaning, **11(2)**, [300]
preparation, bar on, **11(2)**, [300]
excepted persons, **11(2)**, [300]
suspected, right of entry, **11(2)**, [301]
weights and measures authorities
powers, **11(2)**, [301]
letters of administration, preparation, bar
on, **11(2)**, [302]
meaning, **11(2)**, [367]; **11(4)**, [462]
offences and penalties, **11(2)**, [298], [302]
pretending to be qualified, **11(2)**, [299];
11(4), [299]
probate papers, preparing, **11(2)**, [302]
proceedings—
limitation of time, **11(2)**, [305]
power to conduct, **11(2)**, [300], [306]
time limit for commencement,
11(4), [397]
supervision, acting under, **11(2)**, [300]

Solicitor General
Attorney General, exercising functions of,
10, [791]
Attorney General for Northern Ireland,
exercising functions of, **10**, [792]
fees, **10**, [440]
salary, **10**, [614]

Solicitors Act 1974
amendments to, **11(4)**, [357]

Solicitors Disciplinary Tribunal
appeal from—
High Court, to, **11(2)**, [330]; **11(4)**, [428]
Master of the Rolls, to, **11(2)**, [330]
appeals to, **11(4)**, [429]
applications to, **11(4)**, [426]
grounds for, **11(2)**, [328]
legal aid work exclusion, **11(2)**, [328]
making, **11(2)**, [327], [328]
number of members to hear, **11(2)**, [327]
chairman, appointment, **11(2)**, [327]
complaints to—
accounts, relating to, **11(2)**, [311], [314];
11(4), [402], [405]
incorporated practice, as to, **11(3)**, [44];
11(4), [518]
indemnity rules, as to, **11(2)**, [317]
making, **11(2)**, [327]; **11(4)**, [424]
matters subject to, **11(2)**, [328];
11(4), [426]
members to hear, **11(2)**, [327]
more than one allegation, **11(2)**, [328]
non-compliance with rules, of,
11(2), [310]; **11(4)**, [401]
constitution, **11(2)**, [327]; **11(4)**, [424]

Solicitors Disciplinary Tribunal—*contd*
costs of proceedings, order as to, **11(2)**, [328]
decisions, announcement of, **11(2)**, [327]
employing person struck off, **11(2)**, [321];
11(4), [412]
findings, statement of, **11(2)**, [329]
functions, **11(4)**, [295]
funding, **11(4)**, [425]
inadequate professional services, consideration
by **11(2)**, [374]
See further under **solicitor**
incorporated practice, recognised body, powers
as to, **11(3)**, [44]; **11(4)**, [518]
jurisdiction, **11(2)**, [328]; **11(4)**, [426]
lay members, **11(2)**, [327]; **11(4)**, [424]
legal aid complaints, jurisdiction and powers,
11(3), [36]; **11(4)**, [510]
legal aid work, order for exclusion from,
11(2), [328]
Legal Services Board, directions from,
11(4), [294]
members—
appointment, **11(2)**, [327]; **11(4)**, [424]
terms of office, **11(2)**, [327]
oaths, power to administer, **11(2)**, [327];
11(4), [424]
orders, **11(4)**, [427]
filing of, **11(2)**, [329]
Gazette notice of, **11(2)**, [329]
power to make, **11(2)**, [328]
restoration to roll, for, **11(2)**, [328]
striking off, for, **11(2)**, [328]
suspension from practice, for, **11(2)**, [328]
powers of, **11(2)**, [328]; **11(4)**, [426]
president, election of, **11(2)**, [327]
procedure, rules of, **11(2)**, [327]
punishments, award of, **11(2)**, [328];
11(4), [328]
rules, **11(2)**, [327]; **11(4)**, [424]
approval of alterations to, **11(4)**, [293]
writs, issue of, **11(2)**, [327]; **11(4)**, [424]

solid fuel
carriage of—
rail, by, **39(1)**, [577]
road, by, **39(1)**, [576]
damping of, offence of, **39(1)**, [574]
meaning, **39(1)**, [574]
vending machines, sale from, **39(1)**, [574]
weighing at buyer's request, **39(1)**, [575]
weights and measures provisions—
byelaws under, **39(1)**, [574]
containers—
indication of quantity, **39(1)**, [574]
quantities in, **39(1)**, [574]
exemptions from, **39(1)**, [574]
net weight, to be sold by, **39(1)**, [574]
sale from vehicles, **39(1)**, [574]

Solomon Islands
British protected persons, **7(2)**, [691]–[692]
British ship registered in, **7(2)**, [697]
connection with, meaning, **7(2)**, [690]
Commonwealth citizenship, **31**, [186]
independent, becoming, **7(2)**, [688]

Solomon Islands—*contd*
meaning, **7(2)**, [695]
nationality—
  construction of provisions, **7(2)**, [693]
  effect of independence, **7(2)**, [689]
  visiting forces in, **7(2)**, [697]

sound broadcasting. *See* **digital broadcasting (sound); radio services**

sound recording
commencement of provisions, **43(S)**, 35
expenditure—
  allocation of, **43(S)**, 32
  revenue nature of, **43(S)**, 31
intangible fixed assets, as, **43(S)**, 33–4
meaning, **43(S)**, 32
non-trade business—
  calculation of income, **44(3)**, [622]
  charge to tax, **44(3)**, [619]
  income charged, **44(3)**, [620]
  person liable for tax, **44(3)**, [621]
  trading income rules, application of, **44(3)**, [623]
original master version, meaning, **44(3)**, [130]
production or acquisition expenditure, **44(3)**, [133]
relief from customs duty, **13**, [790]
revenue, expenditure treated as, **44(3)**, [132]
trade profits—
  definitions, **44(3)**, [130]–[131]
  expenditure to which provisions apply, **44(3)**, [129]

sound-proofing grants
compensation for depreciation, effect on assessment of, **9**, [307]
meaning, **9**, [307]

South Africa
colonial probates in, **7(2)**, [504]
Commonwealth citizenship, **31**, [186]
companies registers, **7(2)**, [504]
existing law, provision, **7(2)**, [501]
re-admission to Commonwealth, **7(2)**, [795]
visiting forces in, **7(2)**, [797]

South Essex Waterworks Company
saving for, **49**, [228]

South West Suburban Water Company
saving for, **49**, [225]

South Yorkshire
statutes repealed, **41**, [655]

south-eastern and metropolitan traffic area
exclusion of certain enactments respecting, **37**, [47]

Southend-on-Sea
Port of London powers not exercisable off, **39(2)**, [384], [419]

Southern Rhodesia
amnesty for acts done in, **7(2)**, [730]
powers relating to, **7(2)**, [713]
Zimbabwe, becoming, **7(2)**, [711]

Southwark Bridge
trunk road, not being, **36**, [1013]

Southwell, collegiate church
provisions for, **14**, 142

Sovereign
offences against. *See* **treason**

sovereign immunity. *See* **state immunity**

space
outer. *See* **outer space**

Spain
accession to European Community, **18**, [28]

sparrows
built-up areas, in, reduction of numbers, **35(1)**, [269]

Speaker of the House of Commons
ecclesiastical committee members, nominating, **14**, 296
salary, **10**, [605]
  alteration of, **10**, [606]–[607]

Speaker's Committee
establishment of, **15(3)**, [293]
members—
  generally, **15(3)**, [293]
  term of office, **15(3)**, [483]
proceedings, **15(3)**, [483]
reports, **15(3)**, [483]

special charge
generally, **42**, [1]

Special Commissioners
appeal from, **42**, [188]
appeal to, **42**, [158], [159], [175]
  corporation tax, **43(1)**, [406]
appointment of, **42**, [94]
change of name, **42**, [1511]
claims, jurisdiction over, **42**, [178]
company tax return enquiry, referral of questions during, **43(1)**, [396]
costs, order for, **42**, [190]
declaration on taking office, **42**, [97], [261], [272]
deputy, **42**, [95]
generally, **42**, [1]
inheritance tax appeal—
  determination, against, **42**, [763]
  High Court, to, **42**, [766]
  procedure before, **42**, [765]
interest in proceedings, having, **42**, [96]
jurisdiction, **43(1)**, [406]
regulations, **42**, [176]

Special Commissioners—*contd*
penalty awarded by, recovery of, **42**, [794]
penalty proceedings before, **42**, [238]
presiding, **42**, [94]
proceedings, transfer of, **42**, [173]
qualifications, **42**, [94]
questions to be determined by, **42**, [177]
quorum, **42**, [174]
removal from office, **42**, [94]
reports of decisions, publishing, **42**, [191]
salary etc, **42**, [94]

special contribution
assessment, terminal date for, **42**, [39]
generally, **42**, [1]

special educational needs. *See* **child**

**Special Educational Needs and Disability
Tribunal**
admissions decision, claim relating to,
7(1), [369]
constitution, **15(1)**, [545]
exclusion decision, claim relating to,
7(1), [370]
jurisdiction and powers of, **7(1)**, [367]
lay panel, appointment to, **15(2)**, [324]
orders by, compliance of local education
authority with, **15(1)**, [550]
panels—
appointment, **15(1)**, [546]
qualification, **15(1)**, [546]
resignation, **15(1)**, [546]
tenure, **15(1)**, [546]
President—
appointment, **15(1)**, [546]
qualification, **15(1)**, [546]
resignation, **15(1)**, [546]
revocation of appointment, **15(1)**, [546]
procedure, **7(1)**, [368]; **15(1)**, [548]
remuneration and expenses, **15(1)**, [547]
Special Educational Needs Tribunal, change of
name, **7(1)**, [366]
Wales, in. *See* **Special Educational Needs
Tribunal for Wales**

Special Educational Needs Tribunal
renamed. *See* **Special Educational Needs
and Disability Tribunal**

**Special Educational Needs Tribunal for
Wales**
constitution, **15(1)**, [545]
establishment of, **15(1)**, [549]
panels, **15(1)**, [546]
President of, **15(1)**, [546]
remuneration and expenses, **15(1)**, [547]

Special Health Authority. *See also* **District
Health Authority; Family Health Services
Authority; health authority; Regional
Health Authority**
AIDS and HIV reports, **30**, [505], [509]
body corporate, to be, **30**, [1097]
complaints about health care, **30**, [699], [701]

Special Health Authority—*contd*
employment in, validity of clearance for,
30, [750]
establishment of, **30**, [834]
exercise of functions, **30**, [813]
financial duties of, **30**, [1032]
functions, exercise of, **30**, [835]
Health Service Commissioner, subject to
investigation by, **30**, [544]
instruction, provision of, **30**, [430]
meetings, provisions applied to, **25(1)**, [628]
members, **30**, [1097]
public funds, means of meeting expenditure
from, **30**, [1031]
quality in health care—
duty to attain, **30**, [661]
standards set by—
Assembly, **30**, [663]
Secretary of State, **30**, [662]
redress scheme, as authority for, **30**, [1373]
regulations, **30**, [1097]
repeals and revocations, **30**, [572]
residual liabilities, transfer of, **30**, [876]
resource limits, **30**, [1033]
staff, **30**, [1097]
transitional provisions and savings, **30**, [571],
[579]
Wales. *See* **Wales**

Special Immigration Appeals Commission
appeals—
appellant, appointment of representative
for, **31**, [232]
application for leave to appeal, **31**, [234]
from, **31**, [233]
chairman, **31**, [236]
establishment of, **31**, [227]
jurisdiction—
bail, **31**, [230], [237]
deprivation of citizenship, appeal as to,
31, [229]
procedure as to, **31**, [231]
generally, **31**, [228]
members, **31**, [236]
proceedings, **31**, [236]
staff, **31**, [236]
suspected international terrorist, Refugee
Convention not applying, **12(2)**, [380];
12(3), [91]

special parliamentary procedure
compulsory purchase order subject to—
common lands, **9**, [432], [453]
fuel or field garden allotment, **9**, [432],
[453]
local authority land, **9**, [430], [453]
National Trust land, **9**, [431], [453]
open spaces, **9**, [432], [453]
statutory undertakers' land, **9**, [430], [453]
urban development corporation land,
9, [430], [453]
compulsory rights order subject to, **9**, [441]
new rights, compulsory purchase order subject
to, **9**, [452]
orders subject to, **46**, [556]

special reception centre
absence from, **6**, [128]

special resolution regime
bank, meaning, **19(S)**, Financial 66
Banking Liaison Panel, **19(S)**, Financial 73
bridge bank—
  property, transfer of—
    compensation scheme order,
      19(S), Financial 111
    resolution fund order,
      19(S), Financial 111
    third party compensation order,
      19(S), Financial 111
  report on transfer to, **19(S)**, Financial 137
  reverse share transfer, **19(S)**, Financial 91–2
  share transfer instrument,
    19(S), Financial 90–1
  share transfers, **19(S)**, Financial 90–1
    reverse, **19(S)**, Financial 91–2
  stabilisation options, **19(S)**, Financial 75
  stabilisation powers, exercise of,
    19(S), Financial 71
    international obligation notice,
      19(S), Financial 135
    public funds, **19(S)**, Financial 137
building societies—
  consequential provisions,
    19(S), Financial 145
  dissolution or winding up, distribution of
    assets on, **19(S)**, Financial 144–5
  interpretation, **19(S)**, Financial 145
  provisions applied to,
    19(S), Financial 141–3
  temporary public ownership,
    19(S), Financial 143–4
code of practice—
  contents of, **19(S)**, Financial 68
  issue of, **19(S)**, Financial 68
  procedure, **19(S)**, Financial 69
credit unions, application of provisions to,
  19(S), Financial 146
Financial Services Compensation Scheme,
  contribution to costs, **19(S)**, Financial 224–6
general note, **19(S)**, Financial 41–7
holding companies—
  references to, **19(S)**, Financial 139–41
  temporary public ownership,
    19(S), Financial 138
objectives, **19(S)**, Financial 67
overview, **19(S)**, Financial 64–5
power to change law, **19(S)**, Financial 133
property, transfer of—
  compensation scheme order—
    bridge bank, transfer to,
      19(S), Financial 111
    independent valuer,
      19(S), Financial 112–15
    meaning, **19(S)**, Financial 108–9
    onward transfer, **19(S)**, Financial 112
    private sector purchaser, sale to,
      19(S), Financial 110
    procedure, **19(S)**, Financial 120
    reverse transfers, **19(S)**, Financial 112

special resolution regime—*contd*
property, transfer of—*contd*
  compensation scheme order—*contd*
    sources of compensation,
      19(S), Financial 120
    valuation principles,
      19(S), Financial 115–16
  continuity, **19(S)**, Financial 95–6
  continuity obligations—
    consideration and terms,
      19(S), Financial 127–8
    general, **19(S)**, Financial 121
    onward transfers, **19(S)**, Financial 123–4
    special, **19(S)**, Financial 122
    termination, **19(S)**, Financial 128
  disputes, **19(S)**, Financial 131
  effect of, **19(S)**, Financial 93–4
  enforcement of obligations,
    19(S), Financial 130
  foreign property, **19(S)**, Financial 98–9
  licence, continuation of,
    19(S), Financial 96
  partial, restriction of, **19(S)**, Financial 106
  pension provision, **19(S)**, Financial 129
  procedure, **19(S)**, Financial 100
  property transfer instrument—
    continuity, **19(S)**, Financial 95–6
    effect of, **19(S)**, Financial 93–4
    incidental provision, **19(S)**, Financial 99
    meaning, **19(S)**, Financial 93
    onward transfer, **19(S)**, Financial 102
    procedure, **19(S)**, Financial 100
    reverse, **19(S)**, Financial 103
    supplementary, **19(S)**, Financial 101
    transferable property,
      19(S), Financial 94–5
  protection of interests,
    19(S), Financial 107–8
  resolution fund order—
    bridge bank, transfer to,
      19(S), Financial 111
    meaning, **19(S)**, Financial 109
    procedure, **19(S)**, Financial 120
    provisions of, **19(S)**, Financial 116–17
    sources of compensation,
      19(S), Financial 120
  reverse, **19(S)**, Financial 103
  temporary public ownership,
    19(S), Financial 105
  tax consequences, **19(S)**, Financial 132
  temporary public ownership—
    property transfer, **19(S)**, Financial 104
    reverse property transfer,
      19(S), Financial 105
  termination rights, **19(S)**, Financial 97–8
  third party compensation order—
    bridge bank, transfer to,
      19(S), Financial 111
    discretionary provision,
      19(S), Financial 117
    independent valuer,
      19(S), Financial 112–15
    mandatory provision,
      19(S), Financial 118–19
    meaning, **19(S)**, Financial 109

special resolution regime—*contd*
　property, transfer of—*contd*
　　third party compensation order—*contd*
　　　private sector purchaser, sale to,
　　　　19(S), Financial 110
　　　procedure, **19(S)**, Financial 120
　　　reverse transfers, **19(S)**, Financial 112
　　　sources of compensation,
　　　　19(S), Financial 120
　　transferable property, **19(S)**, Financial 94–5
　　Type 1 default event, **19(S)**, Financial 97
　　Type 2 default event, **19(S)**, Financial 97
　purpose of, **19(S)**, Financial 64
　securities, transfer of—
　　ancillary instruments, **19(S)**, Financial 82
　　bridge bank—
　　　reverse share transfer,
　　　　19(S), Financial 91–2
　　　share transfers, **19(S)**, Financial 90–1
　　compensation scheme order—
　　　independent valuer,
　　　　19(S), Financial 112–15
　　　meaning, **19(S)**, Financial 108–9
　　　onward transfer, **19(S)**, Financial 112
　　　private sector purchaser, sale to,
　　　　19(S), Financial 110
　　　procedure, **19(S)**, Financial 120
　　　reverse transfers, **19(S)**, Financial 112
　　　sources of compensation,
　　　　19(S), Financial 120
　　　temporary public ownership, transfer to,
　　　　19(S), Financial 110
　　　valuation principles,
　　　　19(S), Financial 115–16
　　continuity obligations—
　　　consideration and terms,
　　　　19(S), Financial 127–8
　　　general, **19(S)**, Financial 124–5
　　　onward transfers, **19(S)**, Financial 126–7
　　　special, **19(S)**, Financial 125–6
　　　termination, **19(S)**, Financial 128
　　conversion on, **19(S)**, Financial 80
　　delisting on, **19(S)**, Financial 80
　　directors, removal etc of,
　　　19(S), Financial 81
　　disputes, **19(S)**, Financial 131
　　effect of, **19(S)**, Financial 79
　　enforcement of obligations,
　　　19(S), Financial 130
　　incidental provision, **19(S)**, Financial 84
　　meaning of securities, **19(S)**, Financial 77
　　meaning, **19(S)**, Financial 79
　　onward transfer, **19(S)**, Financial 88
　　pension provision, **19(S)**, Financial 129
　　resolution fund order—
　　　meaning, **19(S)**, Financial 109
　　　procedure, **19(S)**, Financial 120
　　　provisions of, **19(S)**, Financial 116–17
　　　sources of compensation,
　　　　19(S), Financial 120
　　　temporary public ownership, transfer to,
　　　　19(S), Financial 110
　　reverse, **19(S)**, Financial 89–90
　　　bridge bank, **19(S)**, Financial 91–2

special resolution regime—*contd*
　securities, transfer of—*contd*
　　share transfer instrument—
　　　ancillary instruments, **19(S)**, Financial 82
　　　bridge bank, **19(S)**, Financial 90–1
　　　continuity, **19(S)**, Financial 80
　　　incidental provision, **19(S)**, Financial 84
　　　meaning, **19(S)**, Financial 78
　　　procedure, **19(S)**, Financial 85
　　　supplementary, **19(S)**, Financial 86
　　share transfer order—
　　　ancillary instruments, **19(S)**, Financial 82
　　　continuity, **19(S)**, Financial 80
　　　incidental provision, **19(S)**, Financial 84
　　　meaning, **19(S)**, Financial 78
　　　onward transfer, **19(S)**, Financial 88
　　　procedure, **19(S)**, Financial 85
　　　reverse, **19(S)**, Financial 89–90
　　　supplementary, **19(S)**, Financial 87
　　tax consequences, **19(S)**, Financial 132
　　termination rights, **19(S)**, Financial 83
　　third party compensation order—
　　　discretionary provision,
　　　　19(S), Financial 117
　　　independent valuer,
　　　　19(S), Financial 112–15
　　　mandatory provision,
　　　　19(S), Financial 118–19
　　　meaning, **19(S)**, Financial 109
　　　onward transfer, **19(S)**, Financial 112
　　　private sector purchaser, sale to,
　　　　19(S), Financial 110
　　　procedure, **19(S)**, Financial 120
　　　sources of compensation,
　　　　19(S), Financial 120
　　　temporary public ownership, transfer to,
　　　　19(S), Financial 110
　　Type 1 default event, **19(S)**, Financial 83
　　Type 2 default event, **19(S)**, Financial 83
　stabilisation options, **19(S)**, Financial 64
　　bridge bank, **19(S)**, Financial 75
　　private sector purchaser,
　　　19(S), Financial 74
　　temporary public ownership,
　　　19(S), Financial 76
　stabilisation powers, exercise of—
　　bridge bank, **19(S)**, Financial 71
　　general conditions, **19(S)**, Financial 70
　　international obligation notice—
　　　bridge bank, **19(S)**, Financial 135
　　　general, **19(S)**, Financial 135
　　private sector purchaser,
　　　19(S), Financial 71
　　public funds—
　　　bridge bank, **19(S)**, Financial 137
　　　general, **19(S)**, Financial 136
　　temporary public ownership,
　　　19(S), Financial 72
　temporary public ownership—
　　building society, **19(S)**, Financial 143–4
　　holding company, **19(S)**, Financial 138–41
　　property, transfer of—
　　　property transfer, **19(S)**, Financial 104
　　　reverse, **19(S)**, Financial 105
　　report on transfer to, **19(S)**, Financial 137

special resolution regime—*contd*
  temporary public ownership—*contd*
    securities, transfer of—
      compensation scheme order,
        19(S), Financial 110
      resolution fund order,
        19(S), Financial 110
      third party compensation order,
        19(S), Financial 110
    stabilisation options, **19(S)**, Financial 76
    stabilisation powers, exercise of,
      19(S), Financial 72
  costs, contribution to, **19(S)**, Financial 224–5

special road
  acquisition of land for, **36**, [1285]
  appropriation of highway as, **36**, [1005],
    [1022], [1024]
  authority—
    highway authority being, **36**, [1022]
    land of, extinguishment of undertakers'
      rights over, **36**, [1026]
    orders authorising functions of, **36**, [1024]
    payment of contributions by, **36**, [1024]
    transfer of highway to, **36**, [1022], [1024]
    works executed by, compensation for
      damage, **36**, [1026], [1027]
  bridge in—
    liability to maintain, extinguishment,
      36, [1059]
    transfer of, **36**, [1315]
  centre line, indication on map, **36**, [1376]
  classification of traffic for purposes of,
    36, [1023], [1404]
  construction or improvement—
    environmental impact assessment,
      36, [1122]
    powers, **36**, [1028], [1065]
  contributions, payment of, **36**, [1024]
  further provisions, **37**, [184]
  general provision as to, **36**, [1022]
  highway included in, improvement of,
    36, [1285]
  meaning, **36**, [1381]; **37**, [315]
  new roads—
    concession agreement—
      annual reports, **38(1)**, [176]
      generally, **38(1)**, [159]
      highway authority powers, savings,
        38(1), [177]
      Highways Act, application, **38(1)**, [177]
      interpretation and meanings,
        38(1), [178]
      joint, by two or more authorities,
        38(1), [178]
      leasing of land to concessionaire,
        38(1), [162]
      long-term damage, cost of making
        good, **38(1)**, [220]
      matters to be provided for, **38(1)**, [159]
      meaning, **38(1)**, [159]
      monopolies, application of enactments,
        38(1), [168]
      navigable waters, major crossing of,
        38(1), [166]

special road—*contd*
  new roads—*contd*
    concession agreement—*contd*
      remedial works, costs, **38(1)**, [220]
      restriction or prohibition of traffic,
        temporary, **38(1)**, [161]
      roads, protection of status of,
        38(1), [177]
      termination, **38(1)**, [257]
      toll orders. *See* toll order *below*
      toll period, **38(1)**, [165]
      toll roads, restriction of access to,
        38(1), [175]
      tolls. *See* tolls *below*
      traffic—
        authority, powers under, **38(1)**, [161]
        regulation, **38(1)**, [219], [220]
        signs, **38(1)**, [161]
      transfer of, **38(1)**, [163], [257]
      transfer of land to highway authority,
        38(1), [159]
    concessionaire—
      compensation, payment by or to,
        38(1), [159]
      functions, exercise of, **38(1)**, [160]
      highway functions, **38(1)**, [160]
      land, leasing of, to, **38(1)**, [162]
      new, appointment on termination of
        former agreement, **38(1)**, [163]
      obligations, **38(1)**, [159]
      rights—
        assignment of, **38(1)**, [163]
        enjoyed by, **38(1)**, [159]
      toll charges by, authorisation,
        38(1), [164]
      withdrawal of authority, **38(1)**, [160]
    highway functions, exercise of—
      concessionaire, by, **38(1)**, [160]
      emergency or expediency, in,
        38(1), [160]
    Highways Act 1980, application of
      provisions, **38(1)**, [159], [177]
    relationship to other roads, **38(1)**, [159]
    road subject to a concession—
      use of term, **38(1)**, [159]
      See also concession agreement *above*
    toll orders—
      annual reports, **38(1)**, [176]
      certificates, **38(1)**, [258]
      confirmation, **38(1)**, [164], [258]
      exemptions from toll, **38(1)**, [171]
      existing highway or tolls, procedure,
        38(1), [258]
      extension, **38(1)**, [170]
      local inquiry after objection,
        38(1), [258]
      making of, **38(1)**, [164], [258]
      notices, **38(1)**, [258]
      objections to, **38(1)**, [258]
      procedure, **38(1)**, [164], [258]
      proposals, publicity for, **38(1)**, [258]
      revocation, **38(1)**, [169]
      suspension of operation, **38(1)**, [258]
      validity of, challenge to, **38(1)**, [258]
      variation, **38(1)**, [169]

special road—_contd_
  new roads—_contd_
    tolls—
      chargeable amount, maximum,
        38(1), [166]
      charging of, authorisation, **38(1)**, [164]
      collection of, **38(1)**, [172], [174]
      different rates of, **38(1)**, [172]
      exemptions from, **38(1)**, [171]
      failure to pay, **38(1)**, [173]
      highway authority, amount charged by,
        38(1), [167]
      major crossing of navigable waters,
        38(1), [166]
      power to charge, **38(1)**, [159]
      refusal to pay, **38(1)**, [173]
      vehicles exempted, **38(1)**, [171]
      traffic regulation, concession agreement,
        38(1), [161], [218]
  opening for use, **37**, [183]
  order—
    concurrent proceedings, **36**, [1399]
    confirmation of, **36**, [1397]
    date of operation, **36**, [1400]
    draft, publication of, **36**, [1397]
    inquiry, **36**, [1397], [1399]
    modifications, **36**, [1397]
    objections to, **36**, [1397], [1399]
    provisions in, **36**, [1024]
    supplementary, **36**, [1024]
    validity, **36**, [1400]
  property and liabilities, transfer of, **36**, [1316]
  protected streets as, **38(1)**, [195]
  provision of, **36**, [1022]
  roads being, **36**, [1022]
  scheme for—
    authorisation by, **36**, [1022]
    concurrent proceedings, **36**, [1399]
    confirmation of, **36**, [1022], [1398]
    date of operation, **36**, [1400]
    inquiry, **36**, [1398]
    meaning, **38(1)**, [171]
    modifications, **36**, [1398]
    objections to, **36**, [1022], [1398]
    procedure for making, **36**, [1376], [1377]
    proposed, publication of, **36**, [1398]
    publicity for, **36**, [1399]
    regulations for confirming, **36**, [1377]
    revocation and variation, **36**, [1378]
    validity, **36**, [1400]
  service area. _See under_ **highway**
  speed limit—
    when applicable, **37**, [259]
    when inapplicable, **37**, [258]
  statutory undertakers—
    removal of apparatus, compensation for,
      36, [1026], [1027]
    rights, extinguishment, **36**, [1026]
  toll orders. _See under_ new roads _above_
  traffic, classes of, **36**, [1023], [1404]
  traffic regulation on, **37**, [183], [187]
  transitional provisions, **36**, [1433]
  trunk road, becoming, **36**, [1025]
  use, meaning, **37**, [183]
  vesting of, **36**, [1309]

special school
  acceptable standard of education, failure to
    give. _See_ **school**
  discontinuance—
    direction requiring, **15(2)**, [34]
    disposal of land on, **15(2)**, [64]
    further provisions, **15(2)**, [35]
    proposals for, **15(2)**, [33]
  establishment or alteration, proposals for,
    15(2), [33]
  funding, **15(2)**, [139], [141]
  general note, **15(S)**, Education 108
  governing body—
    individual pupils' performance, provision of
      information about, **15(1)**, [671]
    provision of information to Secretary of
      State, **15(1)**, [673]
    Secretary of State requiring information
      from, **15(1)**, [670]
  governors, access to papers, **15(1)**, [294]
  independent—
    approval requirement—
      abolition, **15(S)**, Education 253
      consequential amendments,
        15(S), Education 254
      transitional provision,
        15(S), Education 255
  interpretation, **15(S)**, Education 249
  maintained, meaning, **15(1)**, [551]
  meaning, **15(1)**, [501]; **15(S)**, Education 249
  non-maintained—
    approval of, **15(1)**, [552]
    decisions of Secretary of State, appeal
      against, **15(S)**, Education 252
    meaning, **15(1)**, [552]
    order of justice of the peace, appeal
      against, **15(S)**, Education 252
    pupils, emergency, protection in,
      15(S), Education 251
  proprietor—
    exemption order from education legislation
      requirements—
        application for, **15(2)**, [342]
        generally, **15(2)**, [340]
        revocation of, **15(2)**, [341]
        variation of, **15(2)**, [341]
  religious education, requirements for,
    15(2), [59]
  religious opinions of staff, **15(2)**, [52]
  religious worship, right to opt out of,
    15(S), Education 250

special withholding tax
  capital gains tax credit for, **43(2)**, [329]
  certificate to avoid levy of—
    appeals, **43(2)**, [333]
    issue of, **43(2)**, [332]
    refusal to issue, **43(2)**, [333]
  double taxation relief—
    definitions, **43(2)**, [327]
    means of giving, **43(2)**, [327]
    order of credits, **43(2)**, [330]
  income only subject to, computation,
    43(2), [331]

special withholding tax—*contd*
income subject to foreign tax and,
computation, **43(2)**, [331]
income tax credit for, **43(2)**, [328]
meaning, **43(2)**, [327]

speciality
action on, limitation, **19(3)**, [732]

specially authorised societies. *See* **friendly society**

specific performance
Crown, order against, declaratory order
instead of, **13**, [24]
limitation of action, **19(3)**, [766]

speed limit
ambulances, **37**, [261]
armed forces, variation of provisions in case
of, **37**, [302]
cameras, unified power for Secretary of State
to fund, **47**, [615]
Crown, vehicles in service of, **37**, [302]
devices, record produced by as evidence,
38(1), [18]
exceeding, **37**, [260], [263]
evidence of, **38(1)**, [18]
exemptions, **37**, [261]; **38(2)**, [508]
fire and rescue vehicles, **37**, [261]
imposition of, power of district councils,
36, [1046]
marine salvage vehicles, variation in case of,
37, [306]
offences generally, **37**, [263]; **38(1)**, [18]
devices, use in evidence, **38(1)**, [18]
orders, making of, **37**, [258]
particular classes of vehicles, for, **37**, [260]
police vehicles, **37**, [261]
regulations, power to make, **37**, [258]
restricted roads—
directions, provisions as to, **37**, [257]
general limit for, **37**, [255]
roads being, **37**, [256]
road humps, in connection with, **36**, [1094]
roads other than restricted, **37**, [258]
Secretary of State's powers, extent and
limitation, **37**, [260]
signs for indicating, **37**, [259]
special roads—
when applicable, **37**, [259]
when inapplicable, **37**, [258]
statutory, meaning, **36**, [1100]
street lighting as indication, **37**, [256], [259]
temporary, **37**, [177], [262]
transitional provisions, **37**, [340]
variation of, **37**, [260]
vehicles of particular classes—
application of provisions, **37**, [330]
generally, **37**, [260]
pneumatic tyres—
with, **37**, [327]
without, **37**, [328]
schedule of limits, **37**, [327]–[330]
track-laying vehicles, **37**, [329]

spirits. *See also* **intoxicating liquor**
alcohol contained in, computation,
19(3), [373]
angostura bitters—
deemed not to be spirit, **19(3)**, [372]
duty, power to exempt, **19(3)**, [378]
art, used in, **19(3)**, [381]
British compounded—
drawback on, **19(3)**, [391]
meaning, **19(3)**, [375]
compounder—
drawback on, **19(3)**, [391]
meaning, **19(3)**, [375]
distiller's warehouse—
approval, **19(3)**, [385]
deposit of spirit in, **19(3)**, [385]
meaning, **19(3)**, [375]
regulations, **19(3)**, [385]
revocation of approval, **19(3)**, [385]
distillery—
meaning, **19(3)**, [375]
racking of duty-paid spirits at, **19(3)**, [386]
removal of spirits from, offences,
19(3), [391]
drawback—
British compounds, on, **19(3)**, [391]
spirits of wine, on, **19(3)**, [391]
excise duty—
art, remission where used in, **19(3)**, [381]
charge of, **19(3)**, [376]
exemption from, for spirits in flavourings,
19(3), [377]
goods relieved from, restrictions on use,
19(3), [393]
imported goods not for human
consumption, relief, **19(3)**, [382]
manufacture, remission where used in,
19(3), [381]
medical purposes, for, **19(3)**, [379], [380]
scientific purposes, remission where used
for, **19(3)**, [380]
summary of provisions, **19(3)**, [349]
excise duty, surcharges or rebates,
13, [898]–[900]
flavourings, in, exemption from duty,
19(3), [377]
forfeiture—
excess in rectifier's stock, **19(3)**, [390]
regulations, offences against, **19(3)**, [385]
removal of spirits, for, **19(3)**, [387]
unlawful manufacture, in case of,
19(3), [392]
gravity, ascertaining, **19(3)**, [374]
grogging, prohibition, **19(3)**, [394]
imported, duty on, **19(3)**, [376]
manufacture of—
licence for, **19(3)**, [383]
regulations, **19(3)**, [384]
unlawful, penalty, **19(3)**, [392]
use in, remission of duty, **19(3)**, [381]
meaning, **19(3)**, [372]
medical purposes, remission and exemption
from duty, **19(3)**, [379], [380]
methyl alcohol—
deemed not to be spirit, **19(3)**, [372]

spirits—*contd*
  methyl alcohol—*contd*
    prohibited uses, **19(3)**, [430]
  naphtha deemed not to be, **19(3)**, [372]
  North Sea, liquor traffic in—
    convention as to, **1(1)**, [165]
    See also under **North Sea fisheries**
  rectifier—
    excess or deficiency in stock, **19(3)**, [390]
    licence, **19(3)**, [388]
    meaning, **19(3)**, [375]
    warehousing on drawback, **19(3)**, [391]
  rectifying, regulations, **19(3)**, [389]
  sale by retail, meaning, **19(3)**, [375]
  scientific purposes, remission of duty on use
    for, **19(3)**, [380]
  scotch whisky, sale as, **19(3)**, [463]
  search of premises for, **13**, [767]
  spirituous liquors, meaning, **1(1)**, [173]
  still—
    forfeiture, **19(3)**, [392]
    unlawful use, **19(3)**, [392]
  strength, ascertainment, **19(3)**, [373]
  tinctures, **19(3)**, [391]
  volume, ascertainment, **19(3)**, [373]
  warehouse, distillers'. *See* distiller's warehouse
    above
  weight, ascertainment, **19(3)**, [373]
  wholesale, meaning, **19(3)**, [375]
  wholesaler, meaning, **19(3)**, [375]
  wine, of. *See* **spirits of wine**
  wort, unlawful brewing, **19(3)**, [392]

spirits of wine
  British, drawback on, **19(3)**, [391]
  meaning, **19(3)**, [375]

spiritual persons. *See* **clergy**

sport. *See also* **entertainment; football
matches**
  community amateur sports clubs, relief for.
    See **community amateur sports clubs**
  gender recognition certificate, effect of,
    7(1), [721]
  racial discrimination in, **7(1)**, [175]
  sex discrimination in, **7(1)**, [89]

sporting events
  alcohol—
    enforcement of provisions, **12(1)**, [985]
    penalties for offences, **12(1)**, [986]
    possession of, **12(1)**, [982]
    vehicles, found on, **12(1)**, [981]
  bars, closing of, **12(1)**, [965]
  coaches etc going to—
    alcoholic drinks on, **12(1)**, [980]
    drunkenness on, **12(1)**, [982]
    penalties for offences, **12(1)**, [986]
  dangerous articles, carrying, **12(1)**, [982]
  exclusion orders affecting, **12(1)**, [1041]
  fireworks etc, possession of, **12(1)**, [983]
  flares etc, offence of possessing, **12(1)**, [983]
  football. *See* **football match**
  meaning, **12(1)**, [987]

sporting events—*contd*
  motor vehicle going to—
    alcohol, carrying on, **12(1)**, [981]
    meaning, **12(1)**, [981]
  period of, calculation of, **12(1)**, [987]
  private facilities, restricted period in relation
    to, **12(1)**, [984]
  Sundays, on, **12(1)**, [1277]
  trains etc carrying persons to—
    alcoholic drinks on, **12(1)**, [980]
    penalties for offences, **12(1)**, [986]

sports broadcasting. *See* **broadcasting**

sports ground
  accommodation in, estimate of capacity,
    13, [211]
  alterations or extensions to, **13**, [219]
  application for, by qualified person, **13**, [213]
  capacity of, estimation of, **13**, [211]
  classes of, modification of provisions for,
    13, [228]
  designated—
    regulated stands, safety at, **43(1)**, [582]
    safety precautions at, expenditure on,
      43(1), [581]
  designation—
    order—
      making, **13**, [211]
      meaning, **13**, [211]
    safety certificate, as requiring, **13**, [211]
  documents, service of, **13**, [227]
  enforcement provisions, **13**, [223]
  entry and inspection, **13**, [224]
  meaning, **13**, [230]
  not designated, safety measures at,
    43(1), [583]
  notices, service of, **13**, [227]
  private security industry regulation, removal
    from, **12(4)**, [249]
  prohibition notice—
    appeals, **13**, [222]
    procedure, **13**, [221]
  records to be kept, **13**, [212], [217]
  regulations as to, **13**, [217]
  risk to spectators at, restriction on admission
    where, **13**, [221]
  safety at—
    regulations for securing, **13**, [217]
    summary of provisions, **13**, [49]
  safety certificate for—
    amendment, **13**, [214]
    appeals as regards, **13**, [216], [218]
    application for—
      duties of local authority where,
        13, [213]
      fees in respect of, **13**, [217]
      information and plans, furnishing by
        applicant, **13**, [213]
      withdrawal, **13**, [214]
    civil liability, position as to, **13**, [226]
    contents, **13**, [212]
    Crown premises, application to, **13**, [229]
    fire safety, and, **13**, [215], [353]

sports ground—*contd*
  safety certificate for—*contd*
    general—
      alterations and extensions by holder of, **13**, [219]
      amendment, **13**, [214]
      exclusion of certain statutory requirements, **13**, [220]
      issue, **13**, [213]
      meaning, **13**, [211]
      plan of stadium, attachment to, **13**, [213]
    meaning, **13**, [211]
    offences and penalties, **13**, [225]
    procedure, regulations governing, **13**, [217]
    qualified person for holding, **13**, [213]
    replacement, **13**, [214]
    special—
      issue, **13**, [213]
      meaning, **13**, [211]
    stands, for—
      alteration or extension of stand, **13**, [356]
      amendment of, **13**, [352]
      appeals, **13**, [354]
      application for, **13**, [351]
      cancellation of, **13**, [352]
      civil liability, **13**, [361]
      classes of, modification for, **13**, [363]
      contents of, **13**, [350]
      Crown, application to, **13**, [364]
      enforcement, **13**, [358]
      entry and inspection, **13**, [359]
      false statements, **13**, [360]
      issue of, **13**, [351]
      offences, **13**, [360]
      other statutory requirements, exclusion of, **13**, [357]
      plan, **13**, [350]
      regulated, **13**, [349]
      regulations, **13**, [355]
      requirement of, **13**, [349]
      service of documents, **13**, [362]
      transitional provisions, **13**, [369]
    surrender, **13**, [214]
    terms and conditions of, **13**, [212]
    transfer, **13**, [214]
  spectators at, **13**, [211], [217], [230]

sports pavilion
  industrial buildings allowance, qualification for, **43(1)**, [859]

sportsman
  income, attribution of, **44(1)**, [389]
  payment of tax, **44(1)**, [390]
  trade, activity treated as, **44(1)**, [389]
  valuation, **44(1)**, [390]

spray irrigation
  water resources charges, **49**, [1184]–[1186]

spring gun
  offences, **12(1)**, [87]

springs
  utilising by parish council for water supply, **35(1)**, [142]

spying. *See also* **official secrets**
  abolition of death penalty, **3**, [1453]
  generally, **3**, [1170]
  harbouring spies, **12(1)**, [212]
  penalties, **12(1)**, [210]

squirrels
  grey, use of poison against, **2**, [363]

Sri Lanka
  British ship registered in, **7(2)**, [448]
  Commonwealth citizenship, **31**, [186]
  existing law, operations of, **7(2)**, [656]
  fully responsible status of, **7(2)**, [444]
  legislative powers of, **7(2)**, [447]
  republic, becoming, **7(2)**, [656]
  visiting forces in, **7(2)**, [448]

stables
  removal of manure, etc, from, **35(1)**, [132]

stage carriages. *See also* **public service vehicles**
  driver—
    badge, wearing of, **36**, [249]
    unlicensed, penalty, **36**, [246]
  licences—
    acting without, **36**, [246]
    delivery up of, **36**, [250]
    false representation relating to, **36**, [247]
    forgery of, **37**, [138]
  meaning, **36**, [481], [587]
  metropolitan—
    certificate, production of, **36**, [245]
    driver—
      abstract of laws, issues of, to, **36**, [245]
      badge—
        delivery up of, **36**, [250]
        issue of, to, **36**, [245]
        lost or defaced, **36**, [251]
      unauthorised person acting as, **36**, [246]
    licence—
      application for, **36**, [247]
      grant of, **36**, [245]
      particulars, recording of, **36**, [248]
      retention by proprietor, **36**, [252]
  passengers or property endangered, **36**, [217]
  regulations, **36**, [485]
  route, deviation from, **36**, [225], [380]

Staines reservoir
  transfer of undertaking of, **49**, [204]

stakeholder pension scheme
  access to, employer's duty to facilitate, **33(1)**, [547]
  Employment Rights Act 1996, provisions applying, **33(1)**, [548]
  interpretation provisions, **33(1)**, [550]
  meaning, **33(1)**, [545]
  provisions applying to, **33(1)**, [585]

stakeholder pension scheme—*contd*
  reduced rate of contributions, power to
    specify different percentages, **33(1)**, [549]
  registration of, **33(1)**, [546]
  summary of provisions, **33(1)**, [25]

stamp duty
  abolition on—
    appointments, **41**, [152], [157]
    bearer instrument, **41**, [208]
    charter of resignation, **41**, [152], [157]
    covenant, **41**, [152], [157]
    deed, **41**, [152], [157]
    gifts inter vivos, **41**, [149]
    Highway Acts, agreements under,
      41, [152], [157]
    letter of—
      allotment, **41**, [152], [157]
      power of attorney, **41**, [152], [157]
      renunciation, **41**, [152], [157]
    notarial instrument, **41**, [152], [157]
    partition or division, **41**, [214]
    precept of clare constat, **41**, [152], [157]
    procuration, deed or instrument of,
      41, [152], [157]
    renunciation or release, **41**, [214]
    reserve tax, **41**, [211]
    resignation, charter of, **41**, [152], [157]
    revocation of use of trust property,
      41, [152], [157]
    scrip certificate, scrip, **41**, [152], [157]
    seisin, **41**, [152], [157]
    separate deed of covenant, **41**, [152], [157]
    transfer of securities, **41**, [210]
    trustee, new, appointment of, **41**, [152],
      [157]
    warrant of attorney, **41**, [152], [157]
    writ, **41**, [152], [157]
  accountability for, **41**, [4]
  Act of Parliament, property vested by,
    41, [49], [84], [218]
  ad valorem duty, calculation in certain cases,
    41, [20], [250]
  ad valorem, relief for low value transactions,
    43(S), 930
  adjudication—
    appeal, **41**, [25]
      High Court, to, **41**, [27]
      Special Commissioners, to, **41**, [26]
      time for, **41**, [25]
    Commissioners, by, **41**, [23]
    stamping, **41**, [23], [24]
    statutory declaration, **41**, [24]
  administration, regulations, **41**, [255]
  agreements—
    lease or tack, for. *See* **lease**
    sale of property, for, **41**, [260]
    voidance of, **41**, [44]
  allied headquarters, **41**, [99]
  alternative finance investment bonds, on,
    43(S), 988–9
  annuity, **41**, [36], [39]
    not before in existence, **41**, [39]
  apportionment of consideration, **41**, [38],
    [216]

stamp duty—*contd*
  appropriation by personal representative,
    instrument of, **41**, [151]
  approved share incentive plans, **43(2)**, [53]
  assessment, **41**, [23]
  bearer instruments, **41**, [251], [265]–[267]
    abolition, **41**, [208]
    exemptions, **41**, [266]
    paired shares, **41**, [202]
  bill of exchange, **41**, [75]
  bill of sale, **41**, [134]
  blank transfers, prohibition on circulation,
    41, [108]
  certificates—
    cancellation, **41**, [210]
    unstamped, issued, penalty, **41**, [43]
  certification of certain instruments, **41**, [153],
    [217]
  chargeable gains, renounceable letters of
    allotment, **41**, [148]
  charities, **41**, [141], [183]
  civil partnership, exemption of property
    transfer in connection with, **41**, [150]
  clearance services. *See* **clearance services**
  clearing houses, exemption, **41**, [219]
  Commission for New Towns—
    sale of house at discount, **41**, [138], [145]
    shared ownership lease, **41**, [134], [139]
  company—
    acquisition—
      relief for—
        restriction of, **41**, [299]
        withdrawal of, **41**, [300], [306], [411]
      share capital, of, **41**, [168]
      undertaking, of, **41**, [166]
    associated, transfers between, **41**, [68],
      [114]
    connected—
      grant of lease to, **41**, [279]
      transfer of land to, **41**, [277], [278]
    loan capital, transfer of, **41**, [169]
    notifications, when required, **41**, [160],
      [210]
    paired shares, **41**, [202]
    purchase of own shares, **41**, [158]
    reconstruction, **41**, [166], [167]
    renounceable letters of administration,
      41, [148]
    securities, transfer of, **41**, [159], [186]
    share capital, on, relief, **41**, [168]
  composition, financial institutions, by,
    41, [210]
  conditions as to, voidance of, **41**, [44]
  consideration—
    apportionment of, **41**, [38], [216]
    transfer etc, market value, **41**, [228]
    where not ascertainable, **41**, [229]
  conveyance—
    composition in respect of, **41**, [124]
    contracts chargeable as, **41**, [301],
      [307]–[309]
    debt, in consideration of, **41**, [37], [136]
    dissolution or annulment of civil
      partnership, in connection with, **41**, [150]
    divorce etc, in connection with, **41**, [150]

stamp duty—*contd*
  conveyance—*contd*
    right to buy under Housing Act, **41**, [138]
  conveyance on sale—
    abolition, **41**, [214]
    charities, to, exemption, **41**, [141], [183]
    consideration of debts etc, **41**, [37], [136]
    foreclosure decrees, **41**, [51]
    improvement, payment for, **41**, [60]
    reduction of duty, **41**, [114], [215]
  corporations, associated, relief for transfers
    between, **41**, [68], [235]
  counterpart, on, **41**, [262]
  covenants, on—
    abolition, **41**, [152], [157]
    sale of right secured by, **41**, [39]
  Crown—
    exemption, **41**, [200]
    property, on instrument relating to,
      41, [45]
  death, varying disposition arising, exemption,
    41, [151]
  debentures, issue of, **8**, 250–1
  debt, conveyance in consideration of,
    41, [37], [136]
  declaration of use or trust, on, **41**, [214]
  denoting, method of, **41**, [224]
  depository receipts. *See* **depository receipts**
  development corporation—
    sale of house at discount, **41**, [138], [145]
    shared ownership lease, **41**, [134], [139]
  die—
    discontinuance of use, **41**, [11], [55]
    offences as to, **41**, [8], [9]
  disadvantaged areas, exemptions for—
    land in, **41**, [290], [296], [297]
    residential property, in, **41**, [291]
      meaning, **41**, [292]
  disposition, **41**, [151]
    Scotland, in, **41**, [262]
  dissolution or annulment of civil partnership,
    conveyance in connection with, **41**, [150]
  division of property, instrument effecting,
    41, [262]
  divorce, conveyance in connection with,
    41, [150]
  double, relief from, **41**, [247]
  duplicate of instrument, **41**, [262]
  duplicates and counterparts, abolition on,
    41(S), Stamp Duties 41
  education, exemptions for, **15(1)**, [758]
  electricity, provisions on, **17(1)**, [855]
  European Communities and Investment Bank,
    exemptions, **42**, [835]
  exchange—
    partition, etc, payment on, **41**, [228]
    rates applicable, **41**, [20], [154]
  excluded transfers, **15(1)**, [363]
  exemption—
    airport company formation, **4(1)**, [312]
    Atomic Energy Authority, **17(1)**, [463]
    bankruptcy documents, **4(2)**, [461]
    Civil Aviation Authority transfer schemes,
      4(1), [497]
    civil aviation conveyances, **4(1)**, [109]

stamp duty—*contd*
  exemption—*contd*
    Nuclear Fuels Company, **17(1)**, [442]
    Radiochemical Company, **17(1)**, [442]
    Welsh Development Agency, **47**, [258],
      [354]
    winding up documents, **4(2)**, [228]
  exemption from—
    acquisition—
      share capital, **41**, [168]
      undertaking of company, **41**, [166],
        [167]
    allied headquarters, **41**, [99]
    appropriation by personal representative,
      41, [151]
    assignments by seamen, **41**, [77]
    associated companies, transfers between,
      41, [68]
    building society, **19(1)**, [713]
    charities, **41**, [141], [183]
    church buildings, property for, **14**, 69, 404
    churchyard, gift for enlarging, **14**, 207
    civil partnership, transfers in connection
      with, **41**, [150]
    clearing houses, **41**, [219]
    Commission for the New Towns, **46**, [189]
    conveyances on sale, **41**, [60], [68]
    Crown, for, **41**, [200]
    death, varying dispositions arising,
      41, [151]
    disadvantaged areas—
      land in, **41**, [290], [296], [297]
      residential property, in, **41**, [291]
        meaning, **41**, [292]
    dissolution or annulment of civil
      partnership, transfers in connection with,
      41, [150]
    district councils, **46**, [189]
    divorce etc, transfers in connection with,
      41, [150]
    friendly society documents, **19(1)**, [542],
      [900]
    hire-purchase agreement, **41**, [62]
    Historic Buildings and Monuments
      Commission, **41**, [183]
    historic buildings, maintenance funds for,
      41, [135]
    house of residence, in respect of, **14**, 62
    Inter-American Development Bank,
      41, [132]
    intermediaries, sales to, **41**, [171], [172]
    International Bank etc, transfer of stock,
      41, [86]
    investment exchange, **41**, [219]
    joint boards etc, **41**, [88]
    local authorities, joint bodies, transfers,
      41, [88]
    marriage, transfers in connection with,
      41, [150]
    National Debt, gifts for reduction of,
      41, [66]
    National Endowment for Science,
      Technology and the Arts, **41**, [141], [183]
    National Heritage Memorial Fund,
      41, [141], [183]

stamp duty—*contd*
  exemption from—*contd*
    national ownership, undertakings under, **41**, [81]
    nationalisation schemes, documents, **41**, [79]
    new town development corporation, **46**, [189]
    Passenger Transport Executive instruments, **36**, [872]; **37**, [462]
    regional development agencies, transfers to, **46**, [937]
    renounceable letters of allotment, **41**, [148]
    savings committees, as to, **41**, [91]
    seamen, assignments by, **41**, [77]
    service contracts, **41**, [198]
    stock exchange transfer, **41**, [131], [174]
    stock lending, **41**, [173]
    transfer of—
      loan capital, **41**, [169], [170]
      stock, **41**, [86], [171], [173]
    transfers to—
      clearance house, **41**, [174]
      investment exchange, **41**, [174]
      joint bodies, local authorities, **41**, [88]
    varying dispositions after death, **41**, [151]
    visiting forces, **41**, [99]
  fixed, abolition on certain instruments, **43(S)**, 931, 1264–7
  foreign company, paired shares, **41**, [202]
  foreign currency, expressed in, **41**, [20], [154]
  foreign security, issue unstamped, penalty, **41**, [42]
  frauds in relation to, **41**, [10], [21]
  further or higher education corporation, exempted transfers to, **15(1)**, [453]
  gifts inter vivos, adjudication on, **43(S)**, 931
  goodwill, abolition of duty on instruments relating to, **41**, [302]
  group relief, withdrawal of, **41**, [298], [305], [410]
  harbour reorganisation schemes, **41**, [112]
  High Court, summary application by Crown to, in matters of, **13**, [18]
  hire purchase agreement, exemption, **41**, [62]
  Historic Buildings and Monuments Commission, exemption, **41**, [183]
  historic buildings maintenance fund, **41**, [135]
  House of Commons resolutions affecting, **41**, [126], [129], [219]
  instrument—
    ad valorem duty, **41**, [20]
    adhesive stamp on, fraud as to, **41**, [21]
    assessment, **41**, [23]
    certification, **41**, [153], [217]
    charge of duty, **41**, [260]
    counterpart, **41**, [262]
    duplicate, **41**, [262]
    executed before coming into effect of Finance Act 2000, **41**, [284]
    goodwill, abolition of duty, **41**, [302], [310]
    group relief, withdrawal of, **41**, [298], [410]

stamp duty—*contd*
  instrument—*contd*
    intellectual property, abolition on, **41**, [282], [289]
    late stamping—
      interest on, **41**, [30]
      penalties, **41**, [31]
    lost or spoilt, allowance for, **41**, [7]
    not duly stamped, production in evidence, **41**, [28]
    principal, **41**, [38]
    production to Commissioners, **41**, [70], [74], [155]
    regulations for payment, **41**, [16]
    rent, increasing, **41**, [262]
    rolls—
      entry of unstamped in, **41**, [33]
      inspection, **41**, [32]
    schedule, **41**, [260]–[263]
    separate charging of, **41**, [18]
    several instruments, where, **41**, [38]
    stamped, meaning, **41**, [46]
    stamping after execution, **41**, [29]
    stock or marketable securities, chargeable on, **41**, [409], [456]
    transfer of securities, abolition when applicable, **41**, [209]
    transferring land, production to Commissioners, **41**, [70]
    writing and stamping, **41**, [117], [202]
  insurance company, demutualisation, **41**, [242]
  insurance policy, marine, references to, **41**, [93]
  intellectual property, abolition on instruments relating to, **41**, [282], [289]
  Inter-American Development Bank, exemption for, **41**, [132]
  International Bank, exemption, **41**, [86]
  investment companies, open-ended, **41**, [236]
  investment exchanges, exemption, **41**, [219]
  land transfer and leases, **41**, [70], [74], [155]
  land transferred for other property, on, **41**, [276]
  lease. *See* **lease**
  lease, on, **20**, [500]
  leases, provisions relating to, **41(S)**, Stamp Duties 18
  legal aid application, exemption **41**, [231]
  loan capital, on, **43(S)**, 932
  loan capital, on transfer, **41**, [169], [170]
    meaning, **41**, [209]
    when abolished, **41**, [209]
  local authorities, **41**, [88], [138]
    joint bodies, transfers, exemption, **41**, [88]
  local constituency associations, **41**, [143]
  lost or spoilt instruments, allowance for, **41**, [7]
  management by Commissioners of HMRC, **41**, [2]
  market value, on exchange, partition etc, **41**, [228]
  marketable security. *See* **marketable security**
  marriage, exemption of property transfer in connection with, **41**, [150]
  money received for, recovery of, **41**, [3]

stamp duty—*contd*

National Debt, exemption of gifts for reduction of, **41**, [66]

National Endowment for Science, Technology and the Arts, exemption, **41**, [141], [183]

National Heritage Memorial Fund, exemption, **41**, [141], [183]

national ownership, undertakings under, exemption, **41**, [81]

nationalisation schemes, **41**, [79]

Northern Ireland. *See* **Northern Ireland**

open-ended investment companies, **41**, [236]

overpaid, interest on repayment, **41**, [249]

paired shares, **41**, [202]

partition, instrument effecting, **41**, [214], [228], [262]

abolition, when applicable, **41**, [214]

payment, regulations for, **41**, [16]

penalties—

amendments, **41**, [269]

appeals, **41**, [270]

application of provisions, **41**, [252]

collection and recovery, **41**, [271]

determination of, **41**, [271]

periodical payments, **41**, [36]

port successor companies, exemptions, **39(2)**, [652]

post office instruments, exemptions, **34**, [599], [746]

power of attorney, letter of, **41**, [152], [157]

power to vary, **41**, [288]

property—

in lieu of capital transfer tax, exemption, **42**, [393]

other than land, dealings in, **41**, [214]

vested by statute, conveyance, **41**, [49], [84], [218]

reduction, avoidance devices, **41**, [110]

registered social landlords—

exemption for leases granted by, **41**, [412]

granted before section 128 takes effect, **41**, [413]

granted between 1 January 1990 and 27 March 2000, **41**, [414]

transfers to, **41**, [283]

release, on, **41**, [214]

renounceable letters of allotment, exemption, **41**, [148]

rent to mortgage terms, acquisition on, **41**, [223]

renunciation, on, **41**, [214]

repurchase and stock lending arrangements in event of insolvency—

application of provisions, **41(S)**, Stamp Duties 6–7

replacement stock, **41(S)**, Stamp Duties 9

reserve tax. *See* **stamp duty reserve tax**

roll—

entry of unstamped instrument, **41**, [33]

inspection of, **41**, [32]

sale of local authority house at discount, **41**, [138], [145]

savings committees, as to, exemption, **41**, [91]

school land, transfers of, **41**, [475]

stamp duty—*contd*

seamen, exemption of assignments by, **41**, [77]

securities—

ad valorem duty, calculation, **41**, [35]

foreign or Commonwealth, issue unstamped, penalty, **41**, [42]

transfer of, **41**, [159], [186], [187]

abolition of, **41**, [209]

members of electronic transfer system, to, **41**, [239]

warrant to purchase, **41**, [198]

See also **securities**

shared ownership lease, **41**, [134], [139], [199]

shares—

acquisition of, relief for, **41**, [168]

ordinary share capital, meaning, **41**, [68]

purchase by company of own, **41**, [158]

transfer of, abolition of duty, **41**, [209]

social security documents, exemption of, **40(1)**, [720]

stamps. *See* **stamps**

statutory conveyances, **41**, [49], [84], [88], [218]

statutory declaration, how made, **41**, [13], [53]

stock—

ad valorem duty, calculation, **41**, [35]

blank transfers, prohibition of circulation, **41**, [108], [210]

certificate to bearer, cancellation, **41**, [43]

unstamped, penalty, **41**, [43], [210]

government, warrant to purchase, **41**, [198]

guaranteed by Treasury, exemption on transfer of certain, **41**, [81]

intermediaries, sales to, **41**, [171], [172]

lending, **41**, [173]

on instruments relating to, **41**, [409], [456]

repurchases, **41**, [173]

transfer—

abolition of duty, **41**, [209]

exemption, **41**, [86]

stock exchange, nominee, transfers to and from, **41**, [131], [174], [204]

See also **stock exchange**

sub-purchaser, conveyance to, **41**, [38]

substitute instruments, exemptions, **41**, [266]

summary of provisions, **41**, [1]

surrender of leases, on, **41**, [281]

tack, on. *See* **lease**

transfer of school land, on, **15(2)**, [67]

transfer on sale—

charge, **41**, [260]

provisions applicable, **41**, [260]

unit trust. *See* **unit trust**

visiting forces, **41**, [99]

warrant of attorney, abolition, **41**, [152], [182]

stamp duty land tax

acquisition of major interests in land, exceptions for, **43(S)**, 922–3

acquisition relief, **41**, [335]

administration of, **41**, [311]

allied headquarters, **41**, [100]

stamp duty land tax—*contd*

  amendment of provisions before
    implementation, **41**, [396]

  amount of, **41**, [326]
    rent, on, **41**, [419]

  anti-avoidance—
    incidental transactions, **41**, [353]
    provisions generally, **41**, [472]
    scheme transactions, **41**, [352], [354]

  appeals, **41**, [399], [435], [453]

  assessment, **41**, [367]

  bare trust, meaning, **41**, [452]

  bare trustee, **41**, [452]

  building society demutualisation, exemption,
    41, [337]

  charge to, **41**, [311]

  chargeable consideration, **41**, [321]
    annuities, **41**, [323]
    capital gains tax liability, purchaser
      bearing, **41**, [418]
    contingent, **41**, [322]
      application to defer payment, **41**, [374]
      cessation, adjustment on, **41**, [361]
    costs of enfranchisement, **41**, [418]
    debt as, **41**, [418]
    employment, transaction by reason of,
      41, [418]
    exchanges, for, **41**, [418]
    foreign currency, in, **41**, [418]
    indemnity by purchaser, **41**, [418]
    inheritance tax liability, purchaser bearing,
      41, [418]
    just and reasonable apportionment,
      41, [418]
    money or money's worth, **41**, [418]
    non-monetary, valuation of, **41**, [418]
    partition or division, on, **41**, [418]
    postponed, **41**, [418]
    public or educational bodies, arrangements
      involving, **41**, [418]
    rent, including, **41**, [327]
    twelve years' payments, limited to,
      41, [323]
    uncertain or unascertained, **41**, [322]
      application to defer payment, **41**, [374]
      ascertainment, adjustment on, **41**, [361]
    value added tax, including, **41**, [418]
    works, carrying out, **41**, [418]

  chargeable interest—
    creation of, **41**, [312]
    exempt, **41**, [319]
    lease, variation of, **41**, [312]
    meaning, **41**, [319]
    release of, **41**, [312]
    surrender of, **41**, [312]
    variation of, **41**, [312]

  chargeable rent, amount of, **43(S)**, 924–6

  charities, relief for, **41**, [341]

  Chequers Estate, exemption of transactions,
    10, [483]

  Chevening Estate, exemption of transactions,
    10, [525]

  collection and recovery of, **41**, [375]

  collective enfranchisement by leaseholders,
    on, **41**, [350]

stamp duty land tax—*contd*

  company, provisions applied to, **41**, [384]

  compulsory purchase facilitating development,
    exemption, **41**, [333]

  criminal proceedings, effect of offer of
    settlement, **41**, [382]

  crofting community right to buy, on,
    41, [351]

  Crown, application to, **41**, [391]

  declarations, **41**, [364]

  disadvantaged areas—
    annual rent, meaning, **41**, [423]
    land partly in, **41**, [422]
    land wholly in, **41**, [421]
    meaning, **41**, [420]
    notification of transactions, **41**, [423]
    relevant consideration, **41**, [423]
    relevant rental value, **41**, [423]
    relief for, **41**, [328]
    rent, meaning, **41**, [423]

  documents, delivery and service of, **41**, [368]

  e-convenyancing, **41**, [458]

  education, exemptions for, **15(1)**, [759]

  exemptions—
    acquisition relief, **41**, [426]
    airport company formation, **4(1)**, [313]
    allied headquarters, **41**, [100]
    alternative property finance,
      41, [345]–[348]
    bodies established for national purposes,
      acquisition by, **41**, [342]
    building society, **19(1)**, [714]
    building society demutualisation, **41**, [337]
    charities—
      acquisitions by, **41**, [341]
      relief, **41**, [427]
    compulsory purchase facilitating
      development, **41**, [333]
    dissolution of civil partnership, transactions
      in connection with, **41**, [417]
    divorce, transactions in connection with,
      41, [417]
    group relief. *See* group relief *below*
    insurance company demutualisation,
      41, [336]
    limited liability partnership, incorporation,
      41, [338]
    planning obligations, compliance with,
      41, [334]
    public bodies, transfers involving, **41**, [339]
    reconstruction relief, **41**, [426]
    regional development agencies, transfers
      to, **46**, [938]
    registered social landlord—
      acquisitions by, **41**, [344]
      leases granted by, **41**, [417]
    reorganisation of parliamentary
      constituencies, transfer in consequence
      of, **41**, [340]
    right to buy transactions, **41**, [343], [428]
    sale and leaseback arrangements, **41**, [329]
    shared ownership leases, **41**, [343], [428]
    summary of provisions, **41**, [1]
    testamentary dispositions, variation of,
      41, [417]

stamp duty land tax—*contd*
  exemptions—*contd*
    visiting forces, **41**, [100]
    Welsh Development Agency, **47**, [258],
      [354]
  exercise of collective enfranchisement,
    provisions on, **41(S)**, Stamp Duties 2–3
  falsification of documents, offences, **41**, [447]
  fraudulent evasion, offence of, **41**, [379]
  further or higher education corporation,
    exempted transfers, **15(1)**, [454]
  further time for doing anything required,
    power to allow, **41**, [381]
  General and Special Commissioners,
    41, [399], [453]
  group relief, **41**, [335]
    exemption from charge, **41**, [425]
    recovery from another group company or
      controlling director, **41**, [425]
    restrictions on, **41**, [425]
    withdrawal of, **41**, [425]; **43(S)**, 927
      vendor leaving group, exclusion on,
        43(S), 927–8
  HMRC—
    administration by, **41**, [311]
      functions conferred on, **41**, [397]
      information powers, **41**, [377]
        copies of documents, taking, **41**, [444]
        delivery of documents or information,
          notice requiring, **41**, [444]
        entry on premises, powers of,
          41, [446]
        falsification of documents, offences,
          41, [447]
        journalistic material, exclusion of,
          41, [444]
        judicial authority for delivery of
          documents, **41**, [445]
        restrictions on, **41**, [443]
        tax accountant, papers of, **41**, [442]
        taxpayer, obtaining from, **41**, [440]
        third party, documents of, **41**, [441]
      premises, power to inspect, **41**, [378]
      regulations by, **41**, [398]
    assessments—
      excessive, relief in case of, **41**, [434]
      loss of tax discovered, where, **41**, [433]
    cheque to, **41**, [376]
    further time, power to allow, **41**, [381]
    land transaction returns—
      enquiries into, **41**, [431]
      not delivered, determination of tax
        chargeable in cases where, **41**, [432]
    loss of tax discovered, assessments where,
      41, [433]
    penalty determinations, **41**, [448]
    regulations—
      approval of, **41**, [394]
      claim for repayment in default of
        approval, **41**, [395]
      power to vary provisions by, **41**, [393]
    information and inspection powers,
      43(S), 1412–13, 1692–8
  insurance companies demutualisation,
    exemption **41**, [336]

stamp duty land tax—*contd*
  interest—
    overpaid tax, on, **41**, [373]
    penalties, on, **41**, [372]
    unpaid tax, on, **41**, [371]
  land transaction returns, **41**, [358]
    agent, declaration by, **41**, [429]
    amendment by purchaser, **41**, [429]
    claims not included in, **41**, [366], [437]
    contents of, **41**, [429]
    correction by HMRC, **41**, [429]
    delivery of, **41**, [429]
    disclosure of information in, **41**, [359],
      [459]
    duty to deliver, **41**, [355]
    enquiry into, **41**, [431]
    filing date, meaning, **41**, [429]
    incorrect—
      assisting in preparation of, **41**, [380]
      penalty for, **41**, [429]
    loss, damage or destruction of, **41**, [365]
    not delivered, HMRC's determination of
      tax chargeable in cases where, **41**, [432]
    Official Solicitor, declaration by, **41**, [429]
    records, purchaser's duty to keep and
      preserve, **41**, [430]
    uncorrected, penalty for, **41**, [429]
  land transactions—
    application of provisions, **41**, [312]
    chargeable, **41**, [320]
    compliance with planning obligations,
      41, [334]
    connected party, deemed market value in
      case of, **41**, [324], [325]
    contract and conveyance for, **41**, [313]
      secondary contract, **41**, [315]
      third party, **41**, [314]
      transfer of rights, effect of, **41**, [315],
        [316]
    effective date of, **41**, [403]
    exchanges, **41**, [318]
    joint purchasers, involving, **41**, [387]
    linked, **41**, [392]
    meaning, **41**, [312]
    not notifiable, record-keeping where,
      41, [436]
    notifiable, **41**, [356]
      exceptions, **41**, [357]
    options, **41**, [317]
    pre-emption rights, **41**, [317]
    purchaser and vendor, **41**, [312]
    registration, **41**, [360]
    return. *See* land transaction returns *above*
    subject-matter of, **41**, [312]
  later linked transactions, returns in
    consequence of, **41**, [363]
  leases, **41**, [404], [454]
  major interest in land, meaning, **41**, [401]
  market value, meaning, **41**, [402]
  notifiable transactions, **43(S)**, 922
  notification, consequential provisions,
    43(S), 1259
  open-ended investment schemes, provisions
    applied to, **41**, [386]
  overpaid, interest on, **41**, [373]

stamp duty land tax—*contd*
parliamentary constituencies, exemptions for
transfers in case of reorganisation, **41**, [340]
partnerships, **41**, [388], [449]
amended provisions, **41**, [473]
meaning, **41**, [449]
ordinary transactions, **41**, [450]
transactions to which special provisions
apply, **41**, [451]
payment of, **41**, [370]
cheque, by, **41**, [376]
liability for, **41**, [369]
penalties—
determinations, **41**, [367], [448]
general provisions, **41**, [383]
incorrect returns, assisting in preparation
of, **41**, [380]
interest on, **41**, [372]
port successor companies, exemptions,
39(2), [653]
property in lieu of capital transfer tax,
exemption, **42**, [394]
property-investment partnerships, transfer of
interest in, **43(S)**, 929, 1260–1
elections in respect of, **43(S)**, 1262
transitional provision, **43(S)**, 1263
public bodies, exemptions for transfers
involving, **41**, [339]
reconstruction relief, **41**, [335]
record-keeping, **43(S)**, 1703–5
recovery of—
county court proceedings, **41**, [439]
Court of Session proceedings, **41**, [439]
court of summary jurisdiction, proceedings
in, **41**, [439]
diligence, **41**, [438]
distraint, **41**, [438]
High Court proceedings, **41**, [439]
magistrates' court proceedings, **41**, [439]
sheriff court proceedings, **41**, [439]
tax demands and receipts, issue of,
41, [438]
unpaid tax, evidence of, **41**, [439]
registered providers of social housing,
acquisitions by, **41(S)**, Stamp Duties 3–4
regulations by Treasury or HMRC, **41**, [398]
rent to shared ownership trust, charge on,
41(S), Stamp Duties 5–6
representative capacity, persons acting in,
41, [390]
residential property—
acquisitions, relief for, **41**, [330]
eaning, **41**, [400]
relief for certain acquisitions, **41**, [424]
thresholds for, **41(S)**, Stamp Duties 2
zero-carbon homes, relief on first
acquisition of, **41**, [331], [332]
sale and leaseback arrangements, exemptions
for, **41**, [329]
school land, transfers of, **41**, [475]
settlement, meaning, **41**, [452]
shared ownership lease, grant not linked with
staircasing transactions, **43(S)**, 926
shared ownership trust, declaration not linked
with staircasing transactions, **43(S)**, 926

stamp duty land tax—*contd*
summary of provisions, **41**, [1]
time limits for assessments, claims, etc,
amendment, **43(S)**, 1709–10
transfer of school land, on, **15(2)**, [68]
transitional provisions, **41**, [455]
trust property, reallocation as between
beneficiaries, **41**, [452]
trustees, **41**, [389], [452]
unit trust schemes—
application of provisions to, **41**, [385]
transactions relating to, **41**, [467]
unpaid, interest on, **41**, [371]
visiting forces, **41**, [100]
withdrawal of relief, further relief on,
41, [362]
zero-carbon homes, relief on first acquisition
of, **43(S)**, 921
0% band, **43(S)**, 924–6

stamp duty reserve tax
abolition of duty, **41**, [211]
administration, **41**, [195]
alternative finance investment bonds, on,
43(S), 988–9
care and management, **41**, [176]
charge to—
clearance services,
41, [190]. *See also* **clearance services**
depository receipts,
41, [186]–[189]. *See also* **depository receipts**
exemptions, **41**, [178]
depositary receipt system and clearance
system, transfer between, **41**, [194]
individual pension accounts, **41**, [293]
information, **41**, [206]
information and inspection powers,
43(S), 1412–13, 1692–8
intermediaries—
connected persons, **41**, [180]
definitions, **41**, [180]
transfers to, **41**, [179]
introduction, **41**, [176]
liability to, **41**, [184], [190]
open-ended investment companies, **41**, [293]
principal charge to—
application of, **41**, [177]
cancellation of tax, **41**, [185]
excepted transfers—
authorised unit trusts—
direction to hold property on other
trusts, **41**, [244]
mergers of, **41**, [243]
charities, **41**, [183]
intermediaries, to, **41**, [179], [180]
public issues, **41**, [181]
repurchases, **41**, [182]
stock exchange nominee, **41**, [178],
[205]
stock lending, **41**, [182]
unit trust schemes, **41**, [183], [256],
[274]
various agreements, **41**, [183]
repayment of tax, **41**, [185]

stamp duty reserve tax—*contd*
    repurchase and stock lending arrangements in
        event of insolvency—
        agreement to transfer,
            41(S), Stamp Duties 10–12
        application of provisions,
            41(S), Stamp Duties 6–7
    special cases, **41**, [178]
    summary of provisions, **41**, [1]

stamps
    adhesive, frauds in relation to, **41**, [21]
    adjudication, **41**, [23]
    allowances for spoiled or misused, **41**, [4]
    denoting, **41**, [22]
    dies—
        discontinuance of use, **41**, [11], [55]
        forged, detection of, **41**, [9]
        fraudulent printing from, **41**, [8]
        meaning, **41**, [14]
        new, use of, **41**, [11]
        offences in relation to, **41**, [8]
    excise labels, offences in relation to, **41**, [12]
    meaning, **41**, [14], [46]
    misused, allowances for, **41**, [5]
    mutilation of, **41**, [8]
    offences relating to, generally, **41**, [8]
    postage. *See* **post office**
    spoiled, allowances for, **41**, [4]
    stamped, meaning, **41**, [14]

Standards Board for England
    accounts, **26(2)**, [145]
    allegations referred to, **26(2)**, [94]
    annual report, **26(2)**, [145]
    chairman and deputy, **26(2)**, [145]
    documents, evidence of, **26(2)**, [145]
    employees, **26(2)**, [145]
    establishment of, **26(2)**, [89]
    ethical standards officers—
        advice, obtaining, **26(2)**, [98]
        appointment of, **26(2)**, [89]
        conduct of investigations by,
            26(2), [96]–[98]
            procedure, **26(2)**, [97]
        disclosure of information, restrictions on,
            26(2), [99]
        documents, access to, **26(2)**, [98]
        functions of, **26(2)**, [95]
        information provided to, **26(2)**, [98]
        monitoring officers—
            disclosure of reports by, **26(2)**, [102]
            matters referred to, **26(2)**, [103]
        ombudsmen, consultation with,
            26(2), [107]
        reports, **26(2)**, [100]
            interim, **26(2)**, [101]
            monitoring, **26(2)**, [102]
    financial provisions, **26(2)**, [145]
    functions, **26(2)**, [89]
    general powers, **26(2)**, [145]
    guidance, issue of, **26(2)**, [89]
    information requests, **26(2)**, [106]
    members, **26(2)**, [89]
        disqualifications, **26(2)**, [145]

Standards Board for England—*contd*
    members—*contd*
        interests of, **26(2)**, [145]
        remuneration, **26(2)**, [145]
        tenure of office, **26(2)**, [145]
    periodic returns, **26(2)**, [105]
    privileged statements, **26(2)**, [145]
    procedure, **26(2)**, [145]
    seal, **26(2)**, [145]
    status, **26(2)**, [145]
    written allegations referred to, **26(2)**, [94]

Standing Civilian Court. *See* **civilians**

stannaries
    courts—
        abolition, **17(1)**, [1]
        summary of provisions, **17(1)**, [1]
    legislation, summary of provisions, **17(1)**, [1]
    local rights and customs, **17(1)**, [1]
    obsolete provisions, repeal of, **8**, 830
    redeemable stock, issue of, **8**, 85–6

Stannaries Court
    arbitration, reference of disputes to,
        11(2), [148]
    consolidation into one, **11(2)**, [35]
    generally, **11(2)**, [1]
    jurisdiction—
        extension, **11(2)**, [66]
        non-metallic mining, over, **11(2)**, [66]
    vice-warden—
        abolition of court, **11(2)**, [146]
        common law jurisdiction, **11(2)**, [34]–[36]

starlings
    built-up areas, in, reduction of numbers,
        35(1), [269]

State Bank of Pakistan
    capital gains tax exemption, **42**, [1420]
    no income tax liability for issue department,
        44(4), [847]
    tax exemption, **44(1)**, [373]

state immunity
    convention, **10**, [1061]
    diplomatic privileges, and, **10**, [1054]
    document, failure to disclose, **10**, [1052]
    entities entitled to, **10**, [1053]
    evidence by certificate, **10**, [1060]
    exceptions—
        arbitration, relating to, **10**, [1048]
        body corporate, membership of, **10**, [1047]
        commercial transactions, for, **10**, [1042]
        customs duties, liability for, **10**, [1050]
        damage to property, liability for, **10**, [1044]
        design proceedings, **10**, [1046]
        employment, contracts of, **10**, [1043]
        partnership, membership of, **10**, [1047]
        patents, proceedings on, **10**, [1046]
        personal injury, liability for, **10**, [1044]
        plant breeders' rights proceedings,
            10, [1046]

state immunity—*contd*
  exceptions—*contd*
    property, proceedings relating to,
      10, [1045]
    ships used for commercial purposes, and,
      10, [1049]
    submission to jurisdiction, **10**, [1041]
    trade-mark proceedings, **10**, [1046]
    unincorporated body, membership of,
      10, [1047]
    value added tax, liability to, **10**, [1050]
  excluded matters, **10**, [1055]
  extension of, **10**, [1054]
  generally, **10**, [1]
  heads of state, **10**, [1059]
  International Criminal Court, in relation to,
    10, [1161]
  judgment in default of appearance, **10**, [1051]
  jurisdiction, general immunity from,
    10, [1040]
  procedural privileges, **10**, [1052]
  property, relief relating to, **10**, [1052]
  recognition of judgments—
    exceptions, **10**, [1058]
    proceedings, in, **10**, [1057]
  relief against state, **10**, [1052]
  restriction of, **10**, [1054]
  service of process, **10**, [1051]
  states entitled to, **10**, [1053]

state pension credit
  assessed income period, extension of,
    33(S), Pensions 178–9
  capital, meaning, **40(2)**, [350]
  entitlement to—
    amount payable for periods less than a
      week, **40(2)**, [357]
    conditions of, **40(2)**, [336]
    exclusions, **40(2)**, [339]
    polygamous marriages, persons in,
      40(2), [347]
  guarantee credit, entitlement to, **40(2)**, [337]
  income, meaning, **40(2)**, [350]
  polygamous marriages, **40(2)**, [347]
  qualifying age, **40(2)**, [336]
  recipient, disclosure of information relating
    to, **33(S)**, Pensions 207–8
  retirement pension income, **40(2)**, [351]
  retirement provision—
    assessed income period—
      assessed amount, variation of,
        40(2), [342], [345]
      duration of, **40(2)**, [344]
      fixing of, for, **40(2)**, [342]
      fresh determinations increasing claimant's
        entitlement, **40(2)**, [343]
      specification of, **40(2)**, [341]
      termination of, **40(2)**, [344]
    meaning, **40(2)**, [342]
  savings credit, entitlement to, **40(2)**, [338]
  social security rules, amended to apply to,
    40(2), [346]
  spouse's income, treated as income of
    claimant, **40(2)**, [340]

state pensions
  deferral, **33(1)**, [924]
  reciprocal arrangements with Australia, claims
    for benefits following, **33(1)**, [871]
  summary of provisions, **33(1)**, [25]

stateless persons
  birth—
    after commencement of Act, **31**, [185]
    before commencement of Act, **31**, [185]
    late registration of, former avoidance in
      case of, **31**, [62]
    special circumstances, **31**, [185]
  children of British subject, former provisions,
    31, [70]
  statelessness, reduction of, provisions
    applicable, **31**, [163], [185]

statement
  evidence, as, rules of court, **18**, [279]
  oral evidence by witness, of, **18**, [279]

Statistics Board
  ancillary powers, **10(S)**, 25
  annual abstracts, despatch to Minister,
    36, [136]
  census, functions relating to, **10(S)**, 25
  Code of Practice—
    assessment, **10(S)**, 16
      programme for, **10(S)**, 19
      requests for, **10(S)**, 19
    duty to comply with, **10(S)**, 17
    interim period, **10(S)**, 21
    preparation and publication of, **10(S)**, 14
    re-assessment, **10(S)**, 18
      programme for, **10(S)**, 19
    revision, **10(S)**, 21
  committees, **10(S)**, 32
  data protection provisions, **10(S)**, 48
  delegation of functions, **10(S)**, 32
  directions to, **10(S)**, 27–8
  duties, **36**, [1], [26]
  efficiency, **10(S)**, 26
  establishment, **10(S)**, 7
  expenditure, **10(S)**, 53
  functions delegated to, **10(S)**, 24
  Head of Assessment—
    advisor, as, **10(S)**, 31
    member, as, **10(S)**, 10
    separation of functions, **10(S)**, 31
  human rights provisions, **10(S)**, 48
  information—
    births and deaths, relating to, **10(S)**, 37–8
    disclosure by, authorisation, **10(S)**, 45–6
      Northern Ireland **10(S)**, 47
    disclosure to, authorisation, **10(S)**, 41–2
      Northern Ireland **10(S)**, 43–4
    freedom of, application of provisions,
      10(S), 36
    HMRC, held by, **10(S)**, 40
    NHS registration, relating to, **10(S)**, 38–9
      Wales, **10(S)**, 39
    personal, confidentiality of, **10(S)**, 34–5
    service providers, disclosure to, **10(S)**, 37
    sharing, amended provisions, **10(S)**, 63–5

Statistics Board—*contd*
  information—*contd*
    use of, **10(S)**, 33
  interpretation. **10(S)**, 58
  members—
    executive, **10(S)**, 8, 10
    Head of Assessment, **10(S)**, 10
    House of Commons disqualification,
      10(S), 55
    National Statistician, **10(S)**, 10
    non-executive, **10(S)**, 8
      appointment, **10(S)**, 9
      dismissal, **10(S)**, 9
  Ministers, transfers from, **10(S)**, 51
  National Statistician—
    advisory functions, **10(S)**, 28–9
    executive functions, **10(S)**, 29
    executive office, establishment of, **10(S)**, 30
    member, as, **10(S)**, 10
    separation of functions, **10(S)**, 31
  National Statistics—
    designation, **10(S)**, 16
    list of, **10(S)**, 21
    re-assessment, **10(S)**, 18
  objective, **10(S)**, 12
  Office for National Statistics, transfers from,
    10(S), 49–50, 65–7
  official statistics—
    definitions, **10(S)**, 13
    monitoring and reporting, **10(S)**, 13
  orders and regulations, **10(S)**, 55–6
  Parliamentary Commissioner, investigations
    by, **10(S)**, 54
  principles and procedure, statement of,
    10(S), 20
  proceedings, regulation of, **10(S)**, 33
  production of statistics, **10(S)**, 22
  Registrar General, transfers from, **10(S)**, 50,
    61–3
  reports, **10(S)**, 26
  retail price index—
    compilation, maintenance and publication,
      10(S), 22–3
    fundamental change in, **10(S)**, 22–3
  seal, authentication, **10(S)**, 54
  services and facilities, provision of, **10(S)**, 52
  staff, **10(S)**, 10
  statistical research by, **10(S)**, 24
  statistical services, provision of, **10(S)**, 23
  status, **10(S)**, 8
  summary of provisions, **10(S)**, 2–3

Statistics Commission
  cessation of, **10(S)**, 48

statistics of trade. *See* **trade statistics**

statues
  erection and maintenance in streets,
    35(1), [55]
  London, list of, **25(1)**, [17]
  public, meaning, **25(1)**, [11]
  public place—
    erection in, **25(1)**, [12]
    meaning, **25(1)**, [11]

statues—*contd*
  repair of, **25(1)**, [12]
  Secretary of State—
    consent to erection, **25(1)**, [14]
    power to erect or repair, **25(1)**, [14]
  transfer to Minister, **25(1)**, [16]

statutes
  Act, meaning, **41**, [480], [596]
  adaptation, recorded delivery service, to,
    41, [534]
  amendment—
    alteration of penalties, for, **41**, [382]
    deregulation, for purposes of—
      appeals, model provisions with respect
        to, **41**, [685]
      enforcement procedures, **41**, [685]
      removal of statutory burdens, **41**, [684]
      repeals, **41**, [690]
    extent of, **41**, [480]
    implied powers of, **41**, [588]
    mode of, **41**, [480]
    same session in which passed, in, **41**, [576]
    statutory instrument, by, **41**, [480]
  appointed day, **41**, [480]
  burdens, imposing—
    meaning of burden, **41**, [717]
    provisions reforming—
      enforcement, codes of practice as to,
        41, [724]
      Ministers of Crown, by, **41**, [725]
      National Assembly for Wales, by,
        41, [726]
    power to make, **41**, [716]
      limitations on, **41**, [718]
      Parliament—
        consideration of proposals,
          41, [723]
        laying of documents before,
          41, [721]
        preliminary consultation, **41**, [720]
        representations as to—
          damaging information, containing,
            41, [722]
          made in confidence, **41**, [722]
        statutory instrument procedure,
          41, [718]
    reduction of, **41**, [716]
      powers as to, **41**, [751]
    reformation of law, **41**, [716]
    removal of, **41**, [684], [716]
      deregulation for purpose of, **41**, [684]
      powers as to, **41**, [751]
  Channel Islands, when applicable to,
    41, [628], [645], [692], [731], [780]
  chapter numbers, style of, **41**, [480]
  Church of England Measures. *See* Measures
    below
  citation—
    See also short titles *below*
    another Act, of, **41**, [593]
    calendar year and number, **41**, [535]
    methods of, **41**, [480], [487]
    repeals, **41**, [697]
  classification of, **41**, [480]

statutes—*contd*
  collective titles, **41**, [489]
  colonies, repeals affecting, **41**, [628]
  commencement—
    anticipatory exercise of powers, **41**, [480]
    date, endorsement of, **41**, [481]
    meaning, **41**, [480], [605]
    time of, **41**, [578]
  Commonwealth—
    certain countries of, jurisdiction, omission
      of references to, **41**, [524]
    UK legislation affecting, by consent,
      41, [480]
  Community instruments, references to,
    41, [595]
  consolidation—
    amendments included in, **41**, [480]
    corrections and improvements, making,
      41, [521]
      meaning, **41**, [522]
    procedure, **41**, [521]
  constituent parts, **41**, [480]
  construction—
    definitions, **41**, [579]
    inconsistent provisions, **41**, [480]
    sheriff (Scotland), references to, **41**, [549],
      [551]
    subordinate legislation, **41**, [585]
    United Kingdom Parliament, Act of,
      41, [480]
    See also interpretation *below*
  continuance of, **41**, [483]
  contradiction between two sections, **41**, [480]
  definitions—
    construction, **41**, [579]
    generally. *See* meanings *below*
  duration of, **41**, [480]
  endorsement on, on receipt of Royal Assent,
    41, [481]
  Enfield Chase, affecting, **41**, [664]
  expiry of, continuance after, **41**, [483]
  framework, **41**, [480]
  headings, parts etc—
    insertion of, **41**, [480]
    use in interpretation, **41**, [480]
  inconsistency between Acts, **41**, [480]
  inconsistent provisions, **41**, [480]
  internet, published on, **41**, [480]
  interpretation—
    Acts—
      application to existing enactments,
        41, [606]
      United Kingdom, application to whole
        of, **41**, [480]
    brackets, **41**, [480]
    common law rules, **41**, [480]
    courts, by, **41**, [480]
    distance, references to, **41**, [582]
    expressions, **41**, [579]
    gender, references to, **41**, [580]
    General Synod, Church of England,
      Measures, **41**, [480], [597]
    generally, **41**, [480]
    headings, assistance by, **41**, [480]
    Heydon's case, rule in, **41**, [480]

statutes—*contd*
  interpretation—*contd*
    judges, duty of, **41**, [480]
    meanings. *See* meanings *below*
    Measures, **41**, [480], [597]
    National Assembly for Wales, of, **41**, [600]
    Northern Ireland, application to, **41**, [601]
    number, references to, **41**, [580]
    offences, expressions relating to, **41**, [605]
    Parliamentary bills or debates, reference
      to, **41**, [480]
    preamble, use of, in, **41**, [480]
    provisos, **41**, [480]
    punctuation, **41**, [480]
    relationships, references to, **41**, [605]
    repealed Acts, **41**, [680]
    saving clauses, **41**, [480]
    schedules, **41**, [480]
    Scottish Parliament, of, **41**, [599]
    sections, **41**, [480]
    service by post, reference to, **41**, [581]
    sidenotes, use of, in, **41**, [480]
    Sovereign, references to, **41**, [584]
    statutory provisions for, **41**, [480]
    subordinate legislation as aid to, **41**, [480]
    time of day, references to, **41**, [583]
    words employed—
      meaning of. *See* meanings *below*
      unnecessary, **41**, [519]
    year or date, **41**, [606]
  Ireland—
    extension to, **41**, [480]
    GB Acts as evidence in, **41**, [482]
    references to, **41**, [480], [482], [524]
  Irish, evidence in GB courts, **41**, [482]
  irreconcilable contradiction between sections,
    41, [480]
  Isle of Man—
    repealing Acts, lists, **41**, [659], [661], [662]
    revision, generally, **41**, [659]
    when applicable to, **41**, [560], [628], [645],
      [692], [731], [780]
  judicial notice of, **41**, [577]
  Law Commission. *See* **Law Commission**
  legislative reform. *See* **legislative reform**
  local and personal Acts—
    classification, **41**, [480]
    proof of, **41**, [480]
  long title, **41**, [480]
  marginal notes, **41**, [480]
  meanings—
    Act, **41**, [480], [596], [605]
    Bank of England, **41**, [605]
    Bank of Ireland, **41**, [605]
    British Islands, **41**, [605], [606]
    British possessions, **41**, [605]
    British subject, **41**, [480]
    building regulations, **41**, [605]
    central funds, **41**, [605]
    Charity Commission, **41**, [605]
    Church Commissioners, **41**, [605]
    colonial legislature, **41**, [605]
    colony, **41**, [605], [606]
    commencement, **41**, [605]
    committed for trial, **41**, [605]

statutes—*contd*
  meanings—*contd*
    Commonwealth citizen, **41**, [480]
    Comptroller and Auditor General,
      41, [605]
    consular officer, **41**, [605]
    Corporation Tax Acts, **41**, [605]
    county court, **41**, [605]
    Court of Appeal, **41**, [605]
    court of summary jurisdiction, **41**, [605]
    Crown Court, **41**, [605]
    Crown Estate Commissioners, **41**, [605]
    enactment, **41**, [605]
    England, **41**, [605]
    financial year, **41**, [605]
    Governor-General, **41**, [605]
    High Court, **41**, [605]
    Income Tax Acts, **41**, [605]
    indictable offence, **41**, [605]
    land, **41**, [605]
    Lands Clauses Acts, **41**, [605]
    local land charges register, **41**, [605], [607]
    London borough, **41**, [605]
    Lord Chancellor, **41**, [605], [606]
    magistrates' court, **41**, [605]
    month, **41**, [605]
    National Debt Commissioners, **41**, [605]
    Northern Ireland legislation, **41**, [605]
    offence triable either way, **41**, [605]
    offences, expressions relating to, **41**, [605]
    ordnance map, **41**, [605]
    Parliamentary election, **41**, [605]
    person, **41**, [606]
    police area etc, **41**, [605]
    Privy Council, **41**, [605]
    registered medical practitioner, **41**, [605]
    registered (nurses etc) **41**, [605]
    relationships, references to, **41**, [605]
    Rules of Court, **41**, [605]
    Secretary of State, **41**, [605]
    sewerage undertaker, **41**, [605]
    standard scale, **41**, [605]
    statutory declaration, **41**, [605]
    statutory maximum, **41**, [605]
    summary offence, **41**, [605]
    Supreme Court, **41**, [605]
    Tax Acts, **41**, [605]
    Treasury, **41**, [605]
    trust and trustees of land, **41**, [605]
    United Kingdom, **41**, [480]
    Wales, **41**, [605]
    water undertaker, **41**, [605]
    writing, **41**, [605]
  Measures (General Synod)—
    force and effect, **41**, [480]
    interpretation, **41**, [480], [597]
  National Savings Stock Register, repeal
    affecting, **41**, [666]
  Northern Ireland—
    interpretation, application generally,
      41, [601]
    repeals affecting, **41**, [547], [554], [560],
      [613], [628], [645], [703], [731]
    revised editions, provisions affecting,
      41, [526]

statutes—*contd*
  numbering of, **41**, [535]
  obsolete or unnecessary words, repeal,
    41, [519]
  offences—
    references to, construction, **41**, [605]
    under two or more Acts, **41**, [592]
  official copies, **41**, [480]
  omissions permitted from revised editions,
    41, [519], [524]
  operation of—
    anticipatory, **41**, [480]
    "appointed day", from, **41**, [480]
    commencement, **41**, [480]
    Commonwealth countries, in, **41**, [480]
    law relating to, **41**, [480]
    territorial, **41**, [480]
  orders, rules, etc, powers as to, Minister on
    whom conferred, **41**, [510], [512]
  overseas territories, repeals affecting,
    41, [554], [731]
  powers and duties under, continuity of,
    41, [586]
  powers, anticipatory exercise of, **41**, [587]
  preamble, **41**, [480]
  preservation of copies, **41**, [480]
  proof of, **41**, [480]
  property vested by, acquisition, **41**, [49], [84],
    [218]
  provisos, **41**, [480]
  public general, classification, **41**, [480]
  re-enactment—
    effect of, **41**, [591]
    Government War Obligations Act,
      41, [528]
    summary as to, **41**, [480]
    with or without modification, **41**, [591]
  repeal—
    agriculture, **41**, [631], [668], [734]
    allotments, **41**, [669], [735]
    amending Acts, of, **41**, [480]
    animals, **41**, [749]
    armed forces, **41**, [737], [782]
    aviation, **41**, [736]
    banking, **41**, [616]
    banks, **41**, [749]
    Bedfordshire, **41**, [694]
    betting, **41**, [749]
    broadcasting, **41**, [737]
    building societies, **41**, [749]
    Channel Islands etc, affecting, **41**, [554],
      [560], [731]
    charities, **41**, [617], [749]
    children, **41**, [737]
    civil rights and liberties, **41**, [737]
    commons, **41**, [670]
    companies, **41**, [671], [749]
    constitutional provisions, **41**, [618], [639],
      [677]
    county gaols, **41**, [783]
    criminal law, **41**, [784]
    debt, **41**, [749]
    defunct bodies, **41**, [737]
    Derwent Valley, **41**, [694]
    East India Company, **41**, [785]

statutes—*contd*
  repeal—*contd*
    ecclesiastical law, **41**, [556], [564], [672], [706], [738]
    education, **41**, [707], [737], [739]
    effect of, **41**, [480], [589]
    electricity, **41**, [737]
    employment, **41**, [740]
    explosives, **41**, [673]
    exports, **41**, [633]
    family law, **41**, [674]
    films, **41**, [737]
    finance, **41**, [619], [632], [648], [675], [708], [741]
    fisheries, **41**, [640], [668], [737]
    food, **41**, [668]
    gaming, **41**, [749]
    gas, **41**, [737]
    harbours, **41**, [640], [737]
    health services, **41**, [637]
    Hereford, **41**, [709]
    highway law, **41**, [557], [624]
    housing, **41**, [620]
    implication, by, **41**, [480]
    imports, **41**, [633]
    inclosure, **41**, [710]
    industrial relations, **41**, [634]
    insolvency, **41**, [749]
    intellectual property, **41**, [635]
    Ireland, **41**, [649]
    justice, administration of, **41**, [615], [630], [647], [667], [705], [733]
    land, **41**, [653]
    local government, **41**, [621], [636], [650], [676], [742]
    London, **41**, [786]
    lotteries, **41**, [749]
    marriage, evidence of, savings, **41**, [571]
    medicine, **41**, [637], [651], [749]
    mental health, **41**, [749]
    minerals, **41**, [737]
    mines, **41**, [737]
    mode of, **41**, [480]
    National Heritage, **41**, [737]
    National Trust, **41**, [749]
    navigation, **41**, [737]
    NHS, **41**, [737]
    Northern Ireland, affecting, **41**, [554], [560]
    Nottingham, **41**, [694]
    oaths and affirmations, **41**, [622]
    open spaces, **41**, [670]
    overseas jurisdiction, **41**, [638], [652], [695]
    parliamentary provisions, **41**, [639], [677]
    pensions, **41**, [623], [737], [743]
    pharmacy, **41**, [678]
    planning, **41**, [653]
    police, **41**, [787]
    ports, **41**, [737]
    property, **41**, [744]
    property law, **41**, [679]
    public health, **41**, [745]
    public school enactments, **41**, [558]
    quarries, **41**, [737]
    railways, **41**, [737]

statutes—*contd*
  repeal—*contd*
    rating, **41**, [788]
    re-enactment after, **41**, [480], [589]
    registration concerning individuals, **41**, [749]
    religious disabilities, **41**, [654]
    repealing Act, of, **41**, [589]
    road traffic, **41**, [624], [737], [746]
    saving clauses, **41**, [480]
    savings banks, **41**, [737]
    Scottish local acts, **41**, [696], [711], [747]
    shipping, **41**, [640], [737]
    slave trade acts, **41**, [712]
    smallholdings, **41**, [735]
    South Yorkshire, **41**, [655]
    statutory instrument, effect of, **41**, [480]
    subordinate legislation, **41**, [641]
    tax and duties, **41**, [789]
    taxation, **41**, [737]
    telecommunications, **41**, [737]
    town and country planning, **41**, [790]
    trade and industry, **41**, [748]
    traffic law, **41**, [557]
    transport, **41**, [656], [681], [698]
    transport enactments, **41**, [563]
    turnpikes, **41**, [791]
    war and emergency, **41**, [625]
    Warwickshire, **41**, [694]
    weights and measures, **41**, [737]
    Worcester, **41**, [709]
  revised—
    Church Measures, **41**, [525]
    Northern Ireland, affecting, **41**, [526]
    obsolete words, repeal of, **41**, [519]
    omissions from—
      enacting words, **41**, [519]
      general, **41**, [519]
      references to certain territories, **41**, [524]
      unnecessary words, **41**, [519]
    substitution of short titles in, **41**, [484]
  revival, **41**, [480]
  Royal assent, endorsement of date, **41**, [481]
  saving clauses, **41**, [480]
  schedules, **41**, [480]
  sections—
    contradiction between two, **41**, [480]
    effect of, **41**, [480]
    interpretation of, **41**, [480]
    substantive enactment, as, **41**, [575]
  sheriff (Scotland) references to, **41**, [549], [551]
  short titles—
    assignment of, **41**, [487]
    citation by, **41**, [480], [487]
    substitution of, in revised edition, **41**, [484]
    weight to be given to, **41**, [480]
  sidenotes, **41**, [480]
  statutory instrument—
    amendment or repeal of Act by, **41**, [480]
    See also **statutory instruments**
  statutory powers—
    anticipatory exercise of, **41**, [587]
    continuity of, **41**, [586]

statutes—*contd*
  subordinate legislation. *See* **subordinate legislation**
  summary of provisions, **41**, [480]
  suspension of, **41**, [480]
  United Kingdom Parliament, application to whole Kingdom, **41**, [480]
  volumes of, **41**, [480]

statutory adoption pay
  adoption cases not involving placement, application to, **40(1)**, [447]
  conditions, **40(1)**, [439]
  contracting out, restrictions on, **40(1)**, [442]
  Crown employment, in relation to, **40(1)**, [444]
  definitions, **40(1)**, [446]
  employment and support allowance, relationship with, **40(2)**, [515]
  entitlement to, **40(1)**, [439]
  fraud, penalties for, **40(2)**, [435]
    appeals, **40(2)**, [444]
    procedure, **40(2)**, [444]
  funding of employers' liabilities, **40(2)**, [431]
  information—
    HM Revenue and Customs—
      supplied by, **40(2)**, [436]
      used by, **40(2)**, [438]
    requirements, **40(2)**, [433]
      non-compliance with, penalties for, **40(2)**, [434]
        appeals, **40(2)**, [444]
        procedure, **40(2)**, [444]
    Secretary of State, supplied by, **40(2)**, [437]
  liability to pay, **40(1)**, [440]
  more than one contract of employment, treatment of, **40(1)**, [446]
  other benefits, relationship with, **40(1)**, [443]
  payment of, regulations about, **40(2)**, [432]
  period of, **40(1)**, [441]
  rate of, **40(1)**, [441]
  special classes of person, for, **40(1)**, [445]

statutory auditor
  associate, meaning, **8(1)**, [1338]
  audited person, meaning, **8(1)**, [1288]
  Auditors General—
    compliance orders, **8(1)**, [1314]
    conduct of audit on behalf of, **8(1)**, [1305]
    eligibility for appointment, **8(1)**, [1304]
    Independent Supervisor—
      appointment of, **8(1)**, [1306]
      compliance order, issue of, **8(1)**, [1314]
      grants to, **8(1)**, [1316]
      information, power to call for, **8(1)**, [1311]
      matters to be notified to, **8(1)**, [1310]
      proceedings involving, **8(1)**, [1315]
      reports by, **8(1)**, [1309]
      supervision by, **8(1)**, [1307]
      suspension notice, issue of, **8(1)**, [1312]
    supervision—
      duties relating to, **8(1)**, [1308]
      Independent Supervisor, by, **8(1)**, [1307]

statutory auditor—*contd*
  Auditors General—*contd*
    suspension notice—
      effect of, **8(1)**, [1313]
      issue of, **8(1)**, [1312]
  changes affecting accountancy bodies, power to make provision for, **8(1)**, [1341]
  consequential amendments, **8(1)**, [1404]
  continuing to act while not appropriate, **8(1)**, [1327]
  electronic form, notices in, **8(1)**, [1337]
  eligibility for appointment—
    individuals and firms. *See* individuals and firms *below*
    overview, **8(1)**, [1289]
  individuals and firms—
    compliance orders, **8(1)**, [1303]
    eligibility for appointment, **8(1)**, [1290]
    independence requirement, **8(1)**, [1292]
    ineligibility, effect of, **8(1)**, [1291]
    lack of independence, effect of, **8(1)**, [1293]
    matters to be notified to Secretary of State, **8(1)**, [1301]
    partnership, appointment of, **8(1)**, [1294]
    power of Secretary of State to call for information, **8(1)**, [1302]
    professional qualifications, **8(1)**, [1297]–[1300]
    supervisory bodies, **8(1)**, [1295]–[1296]
      arrangements in which participating, **8(1)**, [1399]
      grant and revocation of recognition order, **8(1)**, [1397]
      requirements for recognition, **8(1)**, [1398]
  international obligations, directions to comply with, **8(1)**, [1332]
  interpretation of terms, **8(1)**, [1339]–[1340]
  interpretation, **8(1)**, [1288]
  meaning, **8(1)**, [1288]
  misleading, false and deceptive statement by, **8(1)**, [1328]
  offences—
    body corporate, by, **8(1)**, [1333]
    jurisdiction and procedure, **8(1)**, [1335]
    misleading, false and deceptive statements, **8(1)**, [1328]
    partnership, by, **8(1)**, [1333]
    time limits for prosecution, **8(1)**, [1334]
    unincorporated association, by, **8(1)**, [1333]
  partnership, appointment of, **8(1)**, [1294]
  professional qualifications—
    appropriate, **8(1)**, [1297]
    individuals retaining only 1967 Act authorisation, **8(1)**, [1300]
    overseas, approval of, **8(1)**, [1299]
    qualifying bodies, **8(1)**, [1298]
    recognised, **8(1)**, [1298]
      grant and revocation of recognition order, **8(1)**, [1400]
      requirements for recognition, **8(1)**, [1401]

statutory auditor—*contd*
public, information to be made available to, **8(1)**, [1318]
purpose of provisions, **8(1)**, [1287]
recognition order, fee for, **8(1)**, [1329]
register of, **8(1)**, [1317]
registered third country—
arrangements in which participating, **8(1)**, [1402]
compliance orders, **8(1)**, [1323]
duties of, **8(1)**, [1320]
grants, **8(1)**, [1325]
interpretation, **8(1)**, [1319]
matters to be notified to Secretary of State, **8(1)**, [1321]
meaning, **8(1)**, [1319]
power of Secretary of State to call for information, **8(1)**, [1322]
register, removal from, **8(1)**, [1324]
Secretary of State's functions, delegation of—
existing body, to, **8(1)**, [1331]
order, **8(1)**, [1330]
senior statutory, **8(1)**, [582]
service of notices, **8(1)**, [1336]

statutory corporation
borrowing powers, extension of, **19(2)**, [934]; **36**, [909]

statutory declaration
acceptance by courts, **18**, [84], [86]
affidavit, in lieu of, **18**, [79]
Bank of England, required by, **18**, [85]
Crown debts proved by, **18**, [88]
execution of will, to prove, **18**, [87]
false, **12(1)**, [199]
fees payable, **18**, [90]
financial assistance in purchase of shares, as to, **8**, 220–1
form of, **18**, [91], [92]
making, procedure for, **41**, [13], [53]
oath etc, substituted for, **18**, [79], [86]
publication, **18**, [80]
re-registration as limited company, for, **8**, 148
solvency, of, in winding-up, **8**, 827

statutory instrument
amendment of, **41**, [480]
annulment by either House, **41**, [506]
burdens, imposing—
reduction of, powers as to, **41**, [751]
removal of, powers as to, **41**, [751]
citation of, **41**, [480], [503]
commencement of, **41**, [480]
construction, **41**, [480]
expiry of, **41**, [480]
extension of provisions to other orders, **41**, [510]
Gazette notices of, **41**, [514]
laying before Parliament—
coming into operation before, **41**, [505], [516]
drafts, **41**, [505]–[507], [762]
instruments requiring, **41**, [505], [507]
meaning, **41**, [516]

statutory instrument—*contd*
laying before Parliament—*contd*
notification during vacancy in offices, **41**, [517]
operation before, **41**, [505]
statement to appear on, **41**, [505]
making, procedure, **41**, [480]
meaning, **41**, [502]
modification of provisions, **41**, [510]
numbering of, **41**, [503]
powers granted by, extent, **41**, [480]
printing of, **41**, [503]
proof of, **41**, [480]
publication of, **41**, [480], [503], [504]
questions as to, determination of, **41**, [509]
regulations as to, **41**, [509]
revocation, **41**, [480]
special Parliamentary procedure, subject to, exception for, **41**, [508]
time limits, reckoning, **41**, [507]
validity, **41**, [480]
Wales, application of provisions to, **41**, [513]

statutory maternity pay
adjudication officer—
decision of, **40(1)**, [522]
questions submitted to, **40(1)**, [522]
conditions, **40(1)**, [415]
Crown employment, in relation to, **40(1)**, [420]
definitions, **40(1)**, [422]
employer—
duties of, **40(1)**, [639]
former, liability of, **40(1)**, [415]
funding of liabilities, **40(1)**, [418]
records, maintenance of, **40(1)**, [639]
recovery of amounts by, **40(1)**, [418]
employment and support allowance, relationship with, **40(2)**, [515]
entitlement to, **40(1)**, [415]
information, disclosure of, **40(1)**, [638]
fraud, **40(1)**, [601]
general note, **40(1)**, [1]
information, claimant providing, **40(1)**, [516]
meaning, **40(1)**, [415]
more than one contract of employment, treatment of, **40(1)**, [422]
negligence, **40(1)**, [601]
normal weekly earnings, meaning, **40(1)**, [422]
notice of absence, giving, **40(1)**, [415]
other benefits, relationship with, **40(1)**, [419], [495]
pay period, **40(1)**, [416]
rates of, **40(1)**, [417]
regulations, **40(1)**, [415]
breach of, **40(1)**, [600]
Social Security Commissioner, appeal to, **40(1)**, [525]
special classes of persons, for, **40(1)**, [421]

statutory nuisance
abandoned etc, mine or quarry, unfenced, **17(1)**, [131]
abatement, **35(1)**, [815]

statutory nuisance—*contd*
  act or default outside local authority area,
    caused by, **35(1)**, [816]
  appeals, **35(1)**, [863]
  default powers, **35(1)**, [863]
  definitions, **35(1)**, [813]
  High Court proceedings, **35(1)**, [816]
  inspection of premises, **35(1)**, [813]
  matters constituting, **35(1)**, [813]
  more than one person responsible for,
    35(1), [816]
  noise in street—
    abatement notice for, **35(1)**, [815]
    audible intruder alarms, **35(2)**, [77], [83]
    expenses recoverable from owner to be
      charge on premises, **35(1)**, [817], [818]
    loudspeakers—
      local authority's consent, **35(2)**, [76],
        [82]
      operation of, **35(2)**, [76]
  person aggrieved, summary proceedings by,
    35(1), [819]
  personal liability, protection from,
    35(1), [863]
  powers of entry, **35(1)**, [863]
  right of appeal, statement of, **35(1)**, [863]
  Scotland, new provision in relation to,
    35(2), [146]
  summary of provisions, **35(1)**, [1]
  summary proceedings, **35(1)**, [814]

statutory order
  burdens, imposing—
    reduction of, powers as to, **41**, [751]
    removal of, powers as to, **41**, [751]
  opposed orders, **41**, [494]
  petition against—
    joint committee, reference to, **41**, [494]
    proceedings following report on, **41**, [493]
    report on, **41**, [492]
    time for presenting, **41**, [492]
    Transport and Works Act 1992, order
      under **41**, [492]
  special procedure—
    amendment, **41**, [543]
    costs, **41**, [496]
    existing Acts, made under, **41**, [497]
    future enactments, made under, **41**, [490]
    local inquiry, **41**, [501]
    notice before making, **41**, [501]
    objections to order, **41**, [501]
    operation of order, **41**, [495]
    preliminary proceedings, **41**, [491], [501]
    standing orders for, **41**, [498]

statutory owner
  charge, power to accept as security for part
    payment for land, **20**, [578]
  conveyance of land to, **20**, [511]
  death of, **20**, [511]
  meaning, **20**, [618]
  notice of intention, giving, **20**, [602]
  power of attorney, delegation by, **48**, 478–9
  powers—
    exercise of, **20**, [613]

statutory owner—*contd*
  powers—*contd*
    limitation of exercise of, **20**, [607]
    purchaser dealing with, protection of,
      20, [570]
    trustee for other parties, as, **20**, [608]

statutory paternity pay
  additional—
    conditions—
      adoption, on, **40(1)**, [429]
      birth, on, **40(1)**, [428]
    entitlement to—
      adoption, on, **40(1)**, [429]
      birth, on, **40(1)**, [428]
    generally, **40(1)**, [430]
    payment of—
      commencement of, notice as to,
        40(1), [430]
      liability to make, **40(1)**, [431]
    period of, **40(1)**, [432]
    rate of, **40(1)**, [432]
  adoption cases not involving placement,
    application to, **40(1)**, [438]
  conditions—
    adoption, on, **40(1)**, [424]
    birth, on, **40(1)**, [423]
  contracting out, restrictions on, **40(1)**, [433]
  contractual remuneration, relationship with,
    40(1), [434]
  Crown employment, in relation to,
    40(1), [435]
  definitions, **40(1)**, [437]
  employment and support allowance,
    relationship with, **40(2)**, [515]
  entitlement to—
    adoption, on, **40(1)**, [424]
    birth, on, **40(1)**, [423]
    generally, **40(1)**, [425]
  fraud, penalties for, **40(2)**, [435]
    appeals, **40(2)**, [444]
    procedure, **40(2)**, [444]
  funding of employers' liabilities, **40(2)**, [431]
  information—
    HM Revenue and Customs—
      supplied by, **40(2)**, [436]
      used by, **40(2)**, [438]
    requirements, **40(2)**, [433]
      non-compliance with, penalties for,
        40(2), [434]
        appeals, **40(2)**, [444]
        procedure, **40(2)**, [444]
    Secretary of State, supplied by, **40(2)**, [437]
  more than one contract of employment,
    treatment of, **40(1)**, [437]
  ordinary, references to, **16**, [1021], [1030]
  payment of—
    commencement of, notice as to,
      40(1), [425], [430]
    liability to make, **40(1)**, [426]
    regulations about, **40(2)**, [432]
  period of, **40(1)**, [427]
  rate of, **40(1)**, [427]
  special classes of persons, for, **40(1)**, [436]

statutory sick pay
adjudication officer—
  decision of, **40(1)**, [523]
  questions submitted to, **40(1)**, [522]
Crown employment, in relation to,
  40(1), [412]
definitions, **40(1)**, [414]
employees, duties of, **40(1)**, [515]
employment and support allowance,
  relationship with, **40(2)**, [515]
employer—
  duties of, **40(1)**, [637]
  information, disclosure to, **40(1)**, [636]
  liability of, **40(1)**, [403]
  meaning, **40(1)**, [414]
  records, maintenance of, **40(1)**, [637]
  recovery of sums by, **40(1)**, [410]
  written statement, providing, **40(1)**, [516]
entitlement—
  first three days, after, **40(1)**, [407]
  information, disclosure of, **40(1)**, [636]
  limitations on, **40(1)**, [407]
  maximum, **40(1)**, [407]
  period of, **40(1)**, [405]
  periods not arising, where, **40(1)**, [493]
fraud, **40(1)**, [601]
general note, **40(1)**, [1]
incapacity for work—
  notification of, **40(1)**, [408]
  period of, **40(1)**, [404]
meaning, **40(1)**, [403]
more than one contract of service, where,
  40(1), [414]
negligence, **40(1)**, [601]
normal weekly earnings, meaning,
  40(1), [414]
other benefits, relationship with, **40(1)**, [112],
  [411], [494]
qualifying days, **40(1)**, [406]
rate of payment, **40(1)**, [409]; **40(2)**, [34]
recovery of, **40(2)**, [27]
regulations, breach of, **40(1)**, [600]
Social Security Commissioner, appeal to,
  40(1), [525]
special classes of persons, for, **40(1)**, [413]
termination of pregnancy, exclusion of,
  40(1), [405]
transitional provisions, **40(2)**, [26]

statutory tenancy
agricultural. *See* **agricultural workers**
  (housing)
assured tenancy, as. *See* **assured tenancy**
conditions of, **21**, [522]
distress for rent, restriction on, **21**, [632]
excluded tenancies, **21**, [533]
furnished—
  meaning, **21**, [637]
  transitional provisions, **21**, [660]
furnished sub-tenancy, effect of possession
  order on, **21**, [626]
landlord's right of access, **21**, [522]
licensed premises, exclusion of, **21**, [531]
meaning, **21**, [521]

statutory tenancy—*contd*
possession—
  grounds for. *See* **possession, order for**
  notice of giving up, **21**, [522]
  payment of sum for, **21**, [643]
protected long tenancy, following. *See*
  protected long tenancy
protected tenancy, on termination of,
  21, [521]
regulated tenancy, following, **21**, [538]
repair, right of access for, **21**, [522]
security of tenure, **21**, [522]
shared accommodation, **21**, [543]
subletting—
  effect of, **21**, [544]
  landlord, duty to notify, **21**, [627]
sub-tenancy, effect of possession order on,
  21, [625]
succession, by—
  meaning, **21**, [521]
  person entitled to, **21**, [642]
  provisions applying to, **22**, [832]
terms of, **21**, [522]
transitional provisions, **21**, [660], [766]
works, consent of tenant to, **21**, [610]

statutory tenant
change of—
  agreement, by, **21**, [522], [643]
  pecuniary consideration for agreeing,
    21, [643]
displaced, home loss payment to, **9**, [325]
improvements, making—
  consent for, **21**, [741]–[743]
  county court jurisdiction, **21**, [746]
  meaning, **21**, [741]
  rules of procedure, **21**, [746]
notices, exclusion from receipt of, **21**, [151]
payment for giving up possession, **21**, [643]
person being, **21**, [521]
successor, person being, **21**, [642]

statutory undertakers. *See also* **river**
authority; water undertakers
access to premises of, **35(1)**, [94]
acquisition of land by, **46**, [540]
aerodromes, protection in matter of
  obstructions, **4(1)**, [98]
air traffic services licence holders as,
  4(1), [495]
apparatus in clearance area—
  meaning, **22**, [255]
  notice of intent to remove etc, **22**, [256]
  removal or alteration, **22**, [255], [411]
  requirements by undertakers, **22**, [256]
apparatus, vesting on compulsory acquisition,
  46, [693]
appropriate Minister, meaning, **46**, [530]
civil aviation—
  compensation for compulsory acquisition of
    land of, **4(1)**, [102]
  land acquired for, adjustment of functions
    after, **4(1)**, [170], [171]
  rights over land, **4(1)**, [95], [163]

statutory undertakers—*contd*
  civil aviation—*contd*
    safety requirements by Secretary of State,
      4(1), [98]
  coal, working of, transitional provisions,
    17(2), [206]
  compensation—
    ascertainment, election as to, **46**, [546]
    assessment of, **46**, [547]
    measure of, **46**, [545]
    proceedings giving rise to, **46**, [545]
    right to, **46**, [544]
  compulsorily acquired land, rights over—
    developing authority, notice to, **46**, [538]
    notices, **46**, [526]–[538]
    orders, **46**, [539]
  contributions to expenses by, **46**, [578]
  countryside, consultations on, **32**, [284]
  decision relating to, **46**, [555]
  drainage of buildings of, **35(1)**, [583]
  exemption from building regulations,
    35(1), [530]
  functions, extension or modification of—
    objections, **46**, [543]
    orders, **46**, [541]
    powers, **46**, [540]
  Green Belt land, savings for, **32**, [100], [102]
  Homes and Communities Agency land—
    extension or modification or functions,
      24, [860]
    extinguishment or removal powers,
      24, [858]
    notice to carry out works, **24**, [859]
    obligations, relieving of, **24**, [861]
    orders and directions, **24**, [862]
  housing action trust, rights on land vested in,
    22, [930]
  impracticable obligations, relief from—
    objections, **46**, [543]
    orders, **46**, [542]
  land of—
    compulsory purchase—
      certificate, without, **9**, [443]
      compensation, **9**, [227]
      exclusion from, **9**, [429], [454]
      joint ministerial orders, **9**, [443]
      special parliamentary procedure,
        9, [430], [453]
    conveyance on sale, **9**, [87]
    new rights over, **9**, [453]
    offer to original or adjoining owner,
      9, [84]
    pre-emption, right of, **9**, [85]
    price, arbitration as to, **9**, [86]
    sale of, **9**, [83], [291]
    vesting in adjoining owners, **9**, [83]
  local planning authorities as, **46**, [587]
  meaning, **4(1)**, [153]; **9**, [417], [429], [430];
    17(2), [46]; **22**, [255]; **32**, [91]; **35(1)**, [216],
    [648]; **46**, [92], [527], [880]
  new town development corporation, transfer
    of undertaking by, **46**, [170]

statutory undertakers—*contd*
  new town, in. *See* **new town**
  opencast coal working—
    entry for purposes of on land of,
      17(1), [201]
    protection of undertakers' apparatus and
      rights, **17(1)**, [166], [172]
  operational land—
    advertisements, display of, **46**, [548]
    buildings or works, alteration etc, **46**, [535]
    determination of, **46**, [612]
    development—
      government department, authorisation
        of, **46**, [533]
      planning permission, **46**, [531]
    discontinuance of use, order requiring,
      46, [535]
    land not treated as, **46**, [529]
    meaning, **46**, [528]
    new towns, acquisition in. *See* **new town**
  planning permission, application for, **46**, [531]
  Port of London Act, saving in, **39(2)**, [392]
  regional development agencies, vesting of land
    in, **46**, [952]
  rights, extinguishment of—
    developing authority, notice given to,
      46, [538]
    orders, **46**, [539]
    preliminary notices, **46**, [536]–[537]
    telecommunications code system
      operators, **46**, [537]
  urban development corporation—
    rights over land acquired by, **46**, [107]
    transfer of undertaking of, **46**, [85]
  Urban Regeneration Agency, land of,
    46, [859]

statutory water companies. *See* **water
companies**

stay of execution
  Crown proceedings, in, **13**, [25]

stay of proceedings
  child custody application, **6**, [236]
  Northern Ireland, **6**, [242]

steel
  production—
    corporate venturing scheme, exclusion for,
      43(S), 1123
    enterprise investment scheme, exclusion
      for, **43(S)**, 1123
    enterprise management incentives,
      exclusion from, **43(S)**, 861
    venture capital trusts, exclusion for,
      43(S), 1124

step-parent
  parental responsibility, acquisition by, **6**, [297]

still
  search of premises for, **13**, [767]

still born child
  birth—
    certificate as to registration, **36**, [83]
    custody of registers, **36**, [102]
    quarterly returns, **36**, [100], [101]
    registers, **36**, [1], [102]
    registration, **36**, [70], [72]
  burial, **36**, [18], [38]
  exposed, particulars required by registrar, **36**, [72]
  meaning, **36**, [42], [116]
  Northern Ireland, provision for, **36**, [154]

stipend (ecclesiastical)
  annuity, church commissioners paying, **14**, 837–8, 841
  archdeacon, of, **14**, 841
  benefices held in plurality, provisions, **14**, 839
  benefits under private Acts, scheme on, **14**, 841, 869–70
  Church Commissioners paying, **14**, 411
  curate, of, **14**, 843
  diocesan board of finance, transfer of administration to, **14**, 416–17
  diocesan fund. *See* **diocesan stipends fund**
  lay worker, of, **14**, 843
  property held for augmenting, **14**, 842
  revocation of schemes for, **14**, 846–7

stipendiary magistrate
  pension, **11(2)**, [593], [625]
  relevant service, **11(2)**, [603]
  salary, **11(2)**, [274]
  transitory provisions, **11(2)**, [638]

stock. *See also* **stamp duty**
  ad valorem duty, **41**, [35]
  borrowing, stamp duty, **41**, [173]
  certificate, bearer, to, cancellation, **41**, [43]
  companies clauses. *See* **Companies Clauses Acts**
  conversion of shares into, **8**, 192
    notice to registrar, **8**, 192
  distraining. *See* **distress**
  farming, taken in execution. *See* **distress**
  government. *See* **government stock**
  government etc, warrant to purchase, **41**, [198]
  intermediaries, sales to, **41**, [171], [172]
  International Bank, stamp duty exemption, **41**, [86]
  lending, **41**, [173]
  marketable security, including, **41**, [175]
  meaning, **41**, [46]
  national debt, part of. *See* **national debt**
  reconversion to shares, **8(1)**, [698]
    notice to registrar, **8(1)**, [699]
  renounceable letter of allotment, **41**, [148]
  repurchases, **41**, [173]
  shares not convertible to, **8(1)**, [618]
  transfer of—
    blank, in, circulation of, **41**, [108]
    clearing house, to, stamp duty, **41**, [174]
    investment exchange, to, stamp duty, **41**, [174], [210]

stock—*contd*
  transfer of—*contd*
    stamp duty exemption, **41**, [86]
    stock exchange nominee, to, **41**, [131], [174]
    Treasury—
      guaranteed by, duty on, **41**, [81]
      in name of, **44(1)**, [32]

stock dividend
  capital gains tax, **42**, [1248]
  UK resident companies, from——
    cash equivalent of share capital, **44(3)**, [412]
    charge to tax, **44(3)**, [409]
    income arising, time of, **44(3)**, [410]
    income charged, **44(3)**, [411]
    income tax treated as paid, **44(3)**, [414]
    person liable, **44(3)**, [413]

stock exchange
  allotments to be dealt in on, **8**, 164–5
  composition agreements, **41**, [210]
  directors' interests, notification of, **8**, 393
  intermediaries—
    connected persons, **41**, [180]
    definitions, **41**, [180]
    meaning, **41**, [180]
    sales to, **41**, [171], [172]
    transfers to, **41**, [179], [180]
  meaning, **19(1)**, [314]
  nominee—
    meaning, **41**, [131], [204]
    reserve tax, **41**, [178], [205]
    transfer to, **41**, [131], [174]
    See **stamp duty**
  recognised—
    composition in respect of transfer duty, **41**, [124]
    foreign, **41**, [172]
    meaning **41**, [124], [172]; **43(S)**, 589, 733; **44(1)**, [625]; **44(4)**, [1013]
    minor and consequential amendments, **43(S)**, 734–5
    valuation of shares listed on, **43(S)**, 733–4
  references to, construction, **41**, [127]
  reforms, day of, **41**, [175]
  reforms, transactions on, **42**, [858], [859], [863]
  transfers, stamp duty on, **41**, [131]
    exemption, **41**, [131], [174]

stock lending
  arrangement—
    cash collateral under—
      deemed interest, **44(4)**, [605]
      quasi, **44(4)**, [607]–[608]
      supplementary, **44(4)**, [606]
    deemed manufactured payments, **44(4)**, [604]
    excluded transfer, **44(4)**, [661]
    manufactured dividends, gains accruing, **42**, [1412]
    meaning, **42**, [1410]; **44(4)**, [576]

stock lending—*contd*
  arrangement—*contd*
    no tax credits for borrower under,
      44(4), [600]
    quasi, **44(4)**, [607]–[608]
  capital gains tax exemption, **42**, [1410]
  chargeable gains, effect of insolvency of
    borrower, **43(S)**, 1481–3
  fees, **44(1)**, [104]
  insolvency, stamp taxes in event of—
    application of provisions,
      41(S), Stamp Duties 6–7
    replacement stock, **41(S)**, Stamp Duties 9
    stamp duty, **41(S)**, Stamp Duties 9
    stamp duty reserve tax,
      41(S), Stamp Duties 10–12
  manufactured overseas dividends, **43(S)**, 1614
  redemption, involving, **42**, [1411]

stock transfer
  brokers transfer, including, **19(1)**, [312]
  computerised system, through—
    exempt transfer, being, **19(1)**, [603]
    regulations, power to make, **19(1)**, [605]
    specified securities, **19(1)**, [604], [607]
  forged—
    compensation for loss, **19(1)**, [132]
    harbour and conservancy authorities,
      provisions applying to, **19(1)**, [135]
    industrial society, etc, provisions applying
      to, **19(1)**, [134]
    take-over, effect of, **19(1)**, [138]
  forms, **19(1)**, [313], [317], [318]
  references to, **19(1)**, [312]
  securities applied to, **19(1)**, [311]
  simplified, **19(1)**, [311], [312]

stockbroker
  chargeable gains, return of, **42**, [139]
  meaning, **1(1)**, [20]
  partnership, number of partners, **8**, 578–81
  power of attorney, certificate as to, **1(1)**, [20]

stockjobber
  transactions, information on, **42**, [135]

stolen goods
  broker or dealer, recovery from, **12(1)**, [40]
  handling—
    evidence, **12(1)**, [579]
    indictment, **12(1)**, [579]
    offence, **12(1)**, [573]; **12(2)**, [162]
    meaning, **12(1)**, [575]
  offences, scope of, **12(1)**, [575]
  receiving, construction of references to,
    12(1), [582]
  restitution, order for, **12(2)**, [825]
  rewards, advertising, **12(1)**, [574]
  search for, **12(1)**, [578]

stop notice
  ceasing to have effect, where, **46**, [439]
  compensation for loss, **46**, [441]
  contravention of, **46**, [442]
  effective date, **46**, [439]

stop notice—*contd*
  matters not prohibited by, **46**, [438]
  meaning, **46**, [438]
  person having interest in land, service on,
    46, [438]
  register of, **46**, [445]
  Secretary of State, issue by, **46**, [440]
  service of, **46**, [438]
  temporary—
    compensation for issue, **46**, [425]
    offences, **46**, [424]
    power to issue, **46**, [422]
    restrictions, **46**, [423]
    withdrawal of, **46**, [422]
  withdrawal of, **46**, [438]

stoppage in transit
  vendor's right, defeat of, **1(1)**, [11]

Strategic Health Authority
  abolition, relevant transferee, **30**, [819]
  advice for, **30**, [823]
  body corporate, to be, **30**, [1086]
  complaints about health care, **30**, [699], [701]
  consultation, reports on, **26(2)**, [645]
  continuation of, **30**, [819]
  directions by and to, **30**, [821]
  employment in, validity of clearance for,
    30, [750]
  exercise of functions, **30**, [813]
  financial duties of, **30**, [1032]
  functions, exercise of, **30**, [820], [822]
  Health Service Commissioner, subject to
    investigation by, **30**, [544]
  local authorities, payments from, **30**, [882]
  members—
    appointment of, **30**, [1086]
    pay and allowances, **30**, [1086]
  name of, **30**, [819]
  Primary Care Trust, directions to, **30**, [821],
    [826]
  primary dental services. *See* **dental services**
  primary medical services. *See* **medical
    services**
  public funds, means of meeting expenditure
    from, **30**, [1030]
  public involvement and consultation,
    30, [1048]
  residual liabilities, transfer of, **30**, [876]
  resource limits, **30**, [1033]
  Secretary of State, powers of, **30**, [819]
  staff, **30**, [1086]
  users, duty to, **26(2)**, [644]

Strategic Rail Authority
  abolition, **38(2)**, [391]
  carriage by, **36**, [210]
  Franchising Director, transfer of functions of,
    38(2), [189]
  franchising, securing of services by,
    38(2), [222]
  Office of Rail Regulation, licences, consumer
    protection conditions, **38(2)**, [222]
  pensions indexation, duty to continue Board's
    practice of, **38(2)**, [193]

Strategic Rail Authority—*contd*
  railway services, securing of, by franchising,
    38(2), [222]
  transfer scheme, **38(2)**, [391], [446]
    consumer protection and licensing,
      38(2), [445]
    franchise assets, transfers of, **38(2)**, [220]
    safety functions, **38(2)**, [392], [447]
    taxation provisions, **38(2)**, [215]–[221],
      [458]–[462]
  transitional provisions and savings,
    38(2), [222]

straw
  burning, **35(1)**, [847]

stream
  culvert—
    approved plans, in accordance with,
      35(1), [164]
    repair and cleansing, urban authority
      requiring, **35(1)**, [166]
    saving as to railway company and dock
      undertaker, **35(1)**, [168]
  land drainage authorities, saving for,
    35(1), [168]
  meaning, **49**, [5], [431]
  pollution. *See* **river pollution**
  protection for, **35(1)**, [208]
  reservation of rights of owners to use,
    49, [18]
  utilising by parish council for water supply,
    35(1), [142]
  water undertakers, powers as to, **49**, [15]

street. *See also* **highway; road**
  animals, leading or driving in, **35(1)**, [70]
  arch under, control of, **36**, [1246]
  barrier erected in, **36**, [1337]
  breaking open, **35(1)**, [624]
    See also **waterworks**
    water pipes, laying of, **49**, [31], [306],
      [365]
  cabmen's shelter in, **35(1)**, [54]
  cattle passing along, to or from market,
    35(1), [70]
  cellar—
    construction, control of, **36**, [1245]
    openings, control of, **36**, [1246]
  cleaning—
    highway or local authority, duty as to,
      35(1), [312]
    prohibition of parking to facilitate,
      35(1), [313]
  damage by negligence to lamp, etc, in,
    recovery of damages for, **35(1)**, [273]
  dangerous land adjoining, **36**, [1227]
  door opening outwards on, **36**, [1218]
  drinking fountains, provision in, **35(1)**, [93]
  engineering difficulties, with, works in. *See*
    under **street works**
  extinguishing light, unlawful, **36**, [226]
  footway, damage to, **36**, [1189]
  illuminations and public processions,
    regulations, **36**, [224], [379]

street—*contd*
  lamps, etc, attachment to buildings—
    appropriate authority as regards,
      35(1), [263], [280]
    compensation to owner for damage,
      35(1), [263]
    conditions for, **35(1)**, [263]
    consent of owner to, **35(1)**, [263]
    street lighting authority, by, **35(1)**, [263]
  lands adjoining, fencing of, **35(1)**, [67]
  lighting—
    meaning, **35(1)**, [263]
    provision for,
      35(1), [23]. *See also* lamps etc *above*
  London. *See* **London streets**
  loudspeakers in, restriction on operation of,
    35(1), [321]
  major highway works—
    affecting undertakers' apparatus,
      38(1), [227]
    meaning, **38(1)**, [229]
  managers, meaning, **38(1)**, [180]
  materials in, disposal of, **36**, [1345]
  meaning, **35(1)**, [18], [216], [514], [648];
    36, [377], [1381]; **37**, [170]; **38(1)**, [179];
    49, [347]
    extension of, **35(1)**, [71]
  monuments, erection and maintenance in,
    35(1), [55]
  name—
    alteration, **35(1)**, [66], [96]
    assignment of, **35(1)**, [97]
    indication of, **35(1)**, [97]
    notices as to, **35(1)**, [95]
    painting on building, etc, **35(1)**, [6], [22],
      [66], [97]
    pulling down, offence of, **35(1)**, [97]
    requirements as to, **35(1)**, [6], [66], [95]
  obstruction—
    bollards etc as traffic regulation, **37**, [264]
    prevention, **36**, [379]
    regulations as to, **36**, [224]
  obstruction and nuisance in, **35(1)**, [26]
  pavement lights, control of, **36**, [1246]
  pipe-lines in. *See* **pipe-lines**
  private. *See* **private street**
  refuse bins, provision of, **36**, [1248]
  retaining walls near, powers on, **36**, [1229]
  seats, provision in, **35(1)**, [93]
  special controls, subject to, works. *See under*
    street works
  statues, erection and maintenance in,
    35(1), [55]
  statutory right, meaning, **38(1)**, [249]
  stopping up, Thames flood barrier, for,
    49, [519], [524], [565]
  storage bins, provision of, **36**, [1248]
  traffic-sensitive, designation as, **38(1)**, [198]
  tramway, breaking up for, **36**, [499], [505]
  users, danger or annoyance to. *See* **highway**
  vaults, control of, **36**, [1246]
  ventilators in, control of, **36**, [1246]
  wires, etc, liable to fall on, byelaws as to,
    35(1), [98]

street—*contd*
wires over. *See* **overground wires**
works. *See* **street works**
works, consents for execution of certain,
35(1), [279]

street collections
regulation of, **33(2)**, [60]

street offences
advertisements, carriage of, **36**, [464]
animals—
    exposure for sale, **36**, [226], [385]
    feeding or foddering, **36**, [226]
    obstruction by, **36**, [385]
    sale in streets, **36**, [226], [385]
    treatment of, **36**, [226], [385]
    turning loose, **36**, [226]
annoyance, causing, **36**, [226], [385]
bill posting, **36**, [226]
bonfires, **36**, [226], [385]
carpet or mat, cleaning or beating, **36**, [229],
    [385]
cart or carriage, control over, **36**, [226], [385]
cattle, involving, **36**, [226], [381]
cellars, **36**, [229], [385]
deposits on streets, **36**, [385], [462], [468]
dogs, involving, **36**, [226], [230], [385]
doors, wilful ringing of bells or knocking
    on, **36**, [226], [385]
driving, furious, **36**, [226], [385]
drunkenness, **36**, [228], [386]
firearms, wanton discharge, **36**, [226], [385]
fireworks, setting off, **36**, [226], [385]
footway, involving, **36**, [226], [385], [462]
games, playing of, **36**, [226]
goods, obstruction by deposit of, **36**, [385]
hawking, **36**, [226]
indecent—
    behaviour, **36**, [228], [386]
    exposure, **36**, [385]
kite flying, **36**, [226]
lights, extinguishing, **36**, [226]
loading and unloading, **36**, [226], [385]
musicians, **36**, [454]
noise, **36**, [226]
obscene publications, sale or distribution,
    36, [226], [385]
obstruction by goods, merchandise, etc,
    36, [226], [385]
penalties—
    generally, **36**, [226], [229]
    payment of—
        boats detained as security for, **36**, [231]
        carriages detained as security for,
            36, [231]
        horses detained as security for, **36**, [231]
    penalties generally, **36**, [385]
pigs, keeping of, **36**, [229], [385]
placards as to, attachment to lamp posts,
    36, [465], [490]
projections, **36**, [385]
public processions, **36**, [224], [379]
regulations or directions, wilful disregard of,
    36, [226]

street offences—*contd*
riding, furious, **36**, [226]
riotous behaviour, **36**, [228], [386]
rubbish, involving, **36**, [229], [385]
sale, exposure for, **36**, [226], [229], [385]
show or entertainment, **36**, [226], [385]
slides, ice or snow, **36**, [226]
stone throwing, **36**, [226], [385]
straying cattle, impounding of, **36**, [381]
summary conviction for, **36**, [233]
tree, timber, beams etc, on vehicles, safety of,
    36, [385]
underground rooms, entrance, **36**, [229],
    [385]
upper windows, articles in, **36**, [385]
vaults, **36**, [229], [385]
window cleaning etc, **36**, [385]

street playground
byelaws, **37**, [202]
prohibition of traffic on roads, orders,
    37, [201]

street trading
charges, appeals as to, **25(2)**, [396]
child, involvement in, **6**, [12]
City of London, in—
    appeals respecting, **25(1)**, [780]
        suspension of proceedings pending,
            25(2), [687]
    byelaws for, **25(1)**, [782]; **25(2)**, [684]
    evidence in proceedings, **25(1)**, [784];
        25(2), [688]
    existing licensees, **25(2)**, [692]
    itinerant traders, **25(1)**, [785]; **25(2)**, [689]
    licence, refusal etc of, **25(1)**, [780];
        25(2), [694]
    markets or fairs, **25(1)**, [787]; **25(2)**, [691]
    Middlesex Street market, **25(2)**, [677],
        [678]
    newsvendors etc, saving for, **25(1)**, [785];
        25(2), [689]
    obstruction of traffic by, **25(1)**, [786]
    offences and penalties, **25(1)**, [783];
        25(2), [686]
    photographing, **25(2)**, [694]
    refuse, containers for, **25(1)**, [781];
        25(2), [683]
    registered traders, **25(1)**, [779]; **25(2)**, [693]
    Sunday, on, **25(1)**, [779]
    unauthorised, prohibition, **25(1)**, [779];
        25(2), [685]
consents to, **47**, [372]
designation of streets for, **47**, [372]
district council powers as to, **47**, [370]
exceptions from, **47**, [372]
interpretation of provisions, **47**, [372]
licences, **47**, [372]
London, in—
    annual licence—
        appeals, **25(1)**, [391]
        application for, **25(1)**, [387]
        charges to holders, **25(1)**, [392]
        fees, **25(1)**, [389]
        grounds for refusing etc, **25(1)**, [387]

street trading—*contd*
London, in—*contd*
annual licence—*contd*
meaning, **25(1)**, [381]
period of, **25(1)**, [387]
refusal to grant or renew, **25(1)**, [387]
renewal, **25(1)**, [387], [549]
revocation, **25(1)**, [387]
surrender of, **25(1)**, [550]
transfer on death, **25(1)**, [387]
appeal—
designation of streets, as to, **25(1)**, [382]
refusal of licence etc, **25(1)**, [391]
right of, notice of, **25(1)**, [578]
time for bringing, **25(1)**, [554]
authority, production of, **25(1)**, [551]
bridges, on, **26(2)**, [724]
buildings for, erection, **25(1)**, [99]
byelaws, **25(1)**, [99], [553]
certificate, issue of, **25(1)**, [385]
cleansing streets, charges for, **25(1)**, [392]
considerations by local authorities,
25(1), [382]
Crown rights, saving for, **25(1)**, [562]
days and times, prescription of,
25(1), [553]
definition of terms, **25(1)**, [381];
25(2), [910]
designation of streets for—
application for, **25(1)**, [382]
preliminaries to, **25(1)**, [545]
representations as to, **25(1)**, [545]
enactments—
repealed, **25(2)**, [402]
replaced in relation to, **25(2)**, [400],
[401]
evidence of, **25(1)**, [555]; **25(2)**, [347]
existing street trader—
meaning, **25(1)**, [381]
position of, **25(1)**, [384]
fairs, sales in, **25(1)**, [398]
fines and penalties, **25(2)**, [471]
ice cream trading, **25(2)**, [927]
inquiries, power to hold, **25(1)**, [579]
licence—
annual. *See* annual *above*
appeals as to, **25(1)**, [391]; **25(2)**, [681],
[920]
application for, **25(2)**, [914]
charges for, **25(2)**, [396], [682], [922]
conditions, **25(2)**, [916]
existing traders entitled to, **25(1)**, [384]
fees, **25(1)**, [389]; **25(2)**, [680], [922]
former Act, granted under, **25(1)**, [399]
lapse, **25(2)**, [919]
Middlesex Street, for, **25(2)**, [677], [678]
modification of provisions, **25(2)**, [511],
[514]
notices, **25(2)**, [918]
preferences in granting, **25(2)**, [914]
prescriptions attached to, **25(2)**, [679]
qualification for, **25(2)**, [914]
refusal of, **25(2)**, [914]
requirement for, **25(1)**, [383];
25(2), [912]

street trading—*contd*
London, in—*contd*
licence—*contd*
revocation, **25(2)**, [917]
streets, designation of, **25(2)**, [913]
succession to, **25(2)**, [915]
surrender, **25(2)**, [914]
temporary, **25(1)**, [388]; **25(2)**, [921]
variation, **25(2)**, [917]
licensee—
employment of persons by, **25(1)**, [385],
[393]; **25(2)**, [926]
relatives of, meaning, **25(1)**, [387], [548]
residence, **25(2)**, [918]
local enactments, repeal, **25(2)**, [933], [937]
markets, sales in, **25(1)**, [398]; **25(2)**, [934]
meaning, **25(1)**, [381]; **25(2)**, [676]
misrepresentation by trader, **25(1)**, [394]
newsvendors, rights of, **25(1)**, [395]
notices by local authority, **25(1)**, [382]
occasional sales—
application of provisions, **26(1)**, [254]
licence—
appeals, **26(1)**, [258]
application for, **26(1)**, [256]
conditions, **26(1)**, [257]
fee for, **26(1)**, [256]
grant of, **26(1)**, [257]
requirement of, **26(1)**, [255]
meaning, **26(1)**, [253]
offences and penalties, **26(1)**, [260]
powers of entry, **26(1)**, [259]
prosecutions, restriction on, **26(1)**, [261]
resolution, notice of, **26(1)**, [254]
offences and penalties, **25(1)**, [394];
25(2), [464], [924]
pedlars, rights of, **25(1)**, [395]
places for, provision of, **25(1)**, [99]
proceedings, evidence in, **25(1)**, [555]
public inquiry respecting, **25(1)**, [382]
refuse—
containers for, **25(1)**, [552];
25(2), [683], [923]
removal, charge for, **25(1)**, [392];
25(2), [925]
registered trader—
conviction, effect of, **25(1)**, [386]
conditions to be satisfied, **25(1)**, [385]
notice to be given by, **25(1)**, [385]
rights of, **25(1)**, [385]
registration of traders—
alteration of particulars, **25(1)**, [546]
appeals, **25(1)**, [391]
cancellation, **25(1)**, [386]
certificate of, **25(1)**, [385]
particulars to be included in,
25(1), [385]
refusal of, **25(1)**, [385]
restoration of, **25(1)**, [547]
suspension, **25(1)**, [547]
temporary licence, **25(1)**, [388];
25(2), [921]
trader's family, meaning, **25(1)**, [387], [548]
trading deemed to be, **25(1)**, [383]
trading not amounting to, **25(2)**, [910]

Enquiry Bureau   hsieb@lexisnexis.co.uk

street trading—*contd*
London, in—*contd*
traffic, interference with, **25(1)**, [390]
transitional provisions, **26(2)**, [725]
two or more places, in, **25(1)**, [546]
unlicensed—
disposal orders, **25(2)**, [931]
motor vehicles, seizure of, **25(2)**, [930]
offence, **25(2)**, [928]
perishable items, seizure of, **25(2)**, [929]
Woolwich borough council, rights etc,
25(1), [397]
See also **London**
London Olympic Games, in vicinity of—
arrest of offenders, **13**, [510]
effect of regulations, authorities giving
information as to, **13**, [501]
enforcement of regulations, powers of
entry, **13**, [499]
offences, **13**, [498]
Olympic Delivery Authority, role of,
13, [500]
regulations, **13**, [496]
meaning, **6**, [21]
offences, **47**, [372]
retail trade, **6**, [80]
street, meaning, **6**, [55]
trading deemed not to be, **47**, [372]

street works
advance notice of, **38(1)**, [186]
agreements inconsistent with statutory
provisions, **38(1)**, [244]
apparatus—
abandonment, notice of, **38(1)**, [259]
affected by—
major works—
measures necessary, **38(1)**, [227]
sharing of costs, **38(1)**, [228]
works for road purposes, **38(1)**, [226]
engineering difficulties, special, streets
with, **38(1)**, [197]
inspection of, **38(1)**, [181]
licence—
decision by highway authority, appeal
against, **38(1)**, [259]
requirements under as to, **38(1)**, [181],
[259]
location of—
duty to inform undertakers of,
38(1), [223]
records of, **38(1)**, [222], [246];
38(2), [336]
maintenance of, **38(1)**, [181], [224]
meaning, **36**, [1381]; **38(1)**, [249]
other undertakers' works, affected by,
38(1), [203]
protected streets, placing in, **38(1)**, [195]
removal of—
land ceasing to be controlled, from,
38(1), [247]
termination of licence, on, **38(1)**, [259]
unexpected, location of, **38(2)**, [337]
arbitration, reference to, **38(1)**, [243]

street works—*contd*
authority. *See* street authority *below*
barriers and traffic signs, erection of,
36, [1239]
blind persons, regard to needs of, **36**, [1241]
bridge—
affecting, undertakers' obligations,
38(1), [231]
major works affecting undertakers'
apparatus, **38(1)**, [227]
building adjoining, shoring up, **36**, [1239]
charges by highway, work prolonged,
38(1), [214]–[216]
code—
co-ordination of street works, **38(1)**, [193]
purposes of, **36**, [210]
timing of works, guidance on, **38(1)**, [188]
completion within reasonable period,
38(1), [214]
consents for, **36**, [1411]; **38(1)**, [245], [247]
controlled land, former, cessation of powers
and rights as to, **38(1)**, [247]
co-ordination of, **38(1)**, [193]; **38(2)**, [334]
costs, recovery of, generally, **38(1)**, [240]
Crown, application of provisions generally,
38(1), [252]
damage—
arising, liability for, **38(1)**, [225]
long-term, costs of making good,
38(1), [220]
date of commencement, notice of,
38(1), [187]
delay in—
unnecessary, avoidance of, **38(1)**, [200]
works unreasonably prolonged,
38(1), [214]–[216]
disabled persons, regard to needs of,
36, [1241]; **38(1)**, [199], [204]
district council, power to undertake works,
38(1), [237]
documents, service of, **38(1)**, [241]
duration of, exceeding prescribed period,
38(1), [214]
emergency works—
meaning, **38(1)**, [183]
need for, **38(1)**, [183]
notice of, **38(1)**, [190]
enactments—
existing, effect of 1991 Act on—
existing, effect of 1991 Act on—
orders amending etc—
power to make, **38(1)**, [246]
procedure for making, **38(1)**, [264]
instruments, inconsistent, **38(1)**, [245]
meaning, **38(1)**, [249]
special—
inconsistent with provisions—
effect of, **38(1)**, [245]
orders, **38(1)**, [245]
meaning, **38(1)**, [249]
engineering difficulties, special, streets with—
apparatus in, **38(1)**, [197]
designation as, **38(1)**, [197]
meaning, **38(1)**, [261]
plan and section, **38(1)**, [261]

street works—*contd*
excavations by undertakers, **36**, [1076], [1077]
execution of works, interpretation of term, **38(1)**, [249]
expenses, recovery of, generally, **38(1)**, [240]
gas explosion, etc, liability for, **38(1)**, [225]
guarded, to be, **36**, [1239]; **38(1)**, [199]
hoardings, setting up during building, **36**, [1237]
housing action trust, powers of, **22**, [856]
improvement line. *See under* **highway**
inspection—
    fees, **38(1)**, [217]; **38(2)**, [342]
    guidance, **38(1)**, [213]
licence—
    apparatus—
        abandonment etc, **38(1)**, [259]
        removal on termination, **38(1)**, [259]
    appeal as to line of street decision, **38(1)**, [259]
    conditions attaching, **38(1)**, [259]
    expiration, removal of apparatus on, **38(1)**, [259]
    grant—
        fees, **38(1)**, [259]
        notice of, **38(1)**, [259]
        persons to whom given, **38(1)**, [181]
        work permitted under, **38(1)**, [181], [259]
    ownership, change of, notice of, **38(1)**, [259]
    transfer of, **38(1)**, [259]
    withdrawal of, **38(1)**, [259]
    works under, **38(1)**, [181]
        notice required as to, **38(1)**, [259]
licensee—
    indemnification of street authority by, **38(1)**, [259]
    interest in land, parting with, **38(1)**, [259]
    other licences, permission, etc, obtaining of, **38(1)**, [181]
lighting of, **36**, [1239]; **38(1)**, [199]
lights, displaying of, special precautions, **38(1)**, [235]
meaning, **38(1)**, [179]
    index of defined expressions, **38(1)**, [250]
notices—
    apparatus, of abandonment, **38(1)**, [259]
    certain works, in advance, **38(1)**, [186]
    change of ownership, of, **38(1)**, [259]
    emergency works, as to, **38(1)**, [190]
    proposed works, **38(1)**, [246]
    service of, **38(1)**, [241]
    starting date of works, **38(1)**, [187]
    works following substantial work, **38(1)**, [191], [260]
obstruction, unnecessary, avoidance of, **38(1)**, [200]
offences—
    bodies corporate, by, **38(1)**, [251]
    fixed penalties, **38(1)**, [239], [262], [263]
    proceedings, **38(1)**, [238]
    Scottish partnership, by, **38(1)**, [251]
    summary penalties, increase, **38(2)**, [333]

street works—*contd*
operatives, qualifications of, **38(1)**, [201]; **38(2)**, [338]
period for completion—
    duration of works exceeding, **38(1)**, [214]
    reckoning of, **38(1)**, [242]
private. *See* **private street works**
prolongation, unreasonable, charge for, **38(1)**, [214]–[216]
protected streets—
    apparatus, placing of, **38(1)**, [195]
    designation as, **38(1)**, [196]
railway, near, display of lights, **38(1)**, [235]
railway undertakers—
    works involving, **38(1)**, [234]
    See also transport authority *below*
re-surfacing—
    code of practice, **38(1)**, [212]
    costs, contribution to, **38(1)**, [221]; **38(2)**, [341]
    materials, for, **38(1)**, [210]
    power to require, **38(1)**, [208]; **38(2)**, [340]
    regulations, **38(1)**, [211]
    standard of, **38(1)**, [210]
    timing, specifying, **38(1)**, [209]
    workmanship, **38(1)**, [210]
register, maintenance of, **38(1)**, [184]; **38(2)**, [335]
regulations generally, **38(1)**, [248]
reinstatement after—
    failure to carry out, **38(1)**, [206]
    materials used in, **38(1)**, [205]
    meaning, **38(1)**, [249]
    notice requiring remedial works, **38(2)**, [339]
    sewer, of, **38(1)**, [232]
    standard of, **38(1)**, [205]
    street authority, by, **38(1)**, [206]
    subsequent works, affected by, **38(1)**, [207]
    tunnel, of, **38(1)**, [233]
    undertakers, by, **38(1)**, [204]
    workmanship, standard of, **38(1)**, [205]
remedial works, costs, **38(1)**, [220]
safety precautions and measures, **36**, [1239]; **38(1)**, [199]
sewer authority—
    construction of references, **38(1)**, [232]
    consultation with, as to works, **38(1)**, [232]
    meaning, **38(1)**, [232]
sewer, involving—
    Crown, application of provisions, **38(1)**, [252]
    notice of, **38(1)**, [232]
    reinstatement, **38(1)**, [233]
special controls, streets subject to—
    engineering difficulties, with, **38(1)**, [197]
    protected streets—
        criteria, **38(1)**, [196]
        designation, **38(1)**, [196]
        special roads as, **38(1)**, [195]
        streets being, **38(1)**, [195]
        supplementary provisions, **38(1)**, [196]
    traffic-sensitive streets, **38(1)**, [198]
street authority—
    facilities to be afforded to, **38(1)**, [202]

street works—*contd*

  street authority—*contd*

    inspections by, **38(1)**, [213]

    meaning, **38(1)**, [180]

    power to undertake works, **38(1)**, [237]

  street managers, meaning, **38(1)**, [180]

  street, meaning, **36**, [1381]; **38(1)**, [179]

  substantial, restriction on works following, **38(1)**, [191], [260]

  supervisors, qualifications of, **38(1)**, [201]; **38(2)**, [338]

  timing of, directions as to, **38(1)**, [188]

  traffic—

    meaning, **38(1)**, [249]

    signs, placing and maintenance, **38(1)**, [199]

      concession agreements, placing under, **38(1)**, [161]

  traffic-sensitive streets, **38(1)**, [198]

  tramway—

    display of lights near, **38(1)**, [235]

    meaning, **38(1)**, [249]

  transplant undertaking—

    major works, **38(1)**, [234]

    meaning, **38(1)**, [234]

  transport authority, meaning, **38(1)**, [234]

  transport works, major, affecting undertakers' apparatus, **38(1)**, [227]

  unauthorised, prohibition, **38(1)**, [182]

  undertakers—

    agreements to undertake works on behalf of, **36**, [654]

    alternative route, liability for cost of, **38(1)**, [219]

    apparatus—

      affected by major works, **38(1)**, [227]

      directions as to placing, **38(1)**, [189]

      location of—

        others to supply information, **38(1)**, [223]

        records, keeping of, **38(1)**, [222], [246]; **38(2)**, [336]

      maintenance of, duty as to, **38(1)**, [224]

      unexpected, location of, **38(2)**, [337]

    co-ordination of works, duty as to, **38(1)**, [194]

    compensation, paying to street authority, **38(1)**, [225]

    costs, payment of—

      long-term damage, **38(1)**, [220]

      prolongation of work, **38(1)**, [214]–[216]

      remedial works, **38(1)**, [220]

      re-surfacing, **38(1)**, [221]; **38(2)**, [341]

      traffic regulation, **38(1)**, [218]

    damage or loss, liability for, **38(1)**, [220], [225]

    duty to co-operate, **38(1)**, [194]

    inspection fees, payment of, **38(1)**, [217]; **38(2)**, [342]

    liability of, **38(1)**, [225]

    long-term damage, making good, costs of, **38(1)**, [220]

    meaning, **36**, [1381]; **38(1)**, [179]

street works—*contd*

  undertakers—*contd*

    other undertakers' apparatus, affecting, **38(1)**, [203]

    prolongation of work, unreasonable, payment of charges, **38(1)**, [214]–[216]

    records, duty to inspect, **38(1)**, [185]

    reinstatement after, duty as to, **38(1)**, [204]

    re-surfacing by—

      code of practice, **38(1)**, [212]

      costs, contribution to, **38(1)**, [221]; **38(2)**, [341]

      materials, for, **38(1)**, [210]

      power to require, **38(1)**, [208]; **38(2)**, [340]

      regulations, **38(1)**, [211]

      standard of, **38(1)**, [210]

      timing, specifying, **38(1)**, [209]

      workmanship, **38(1)**, [210]

    safety requirements, **36**, [1239]; **38(1)**, [199]

    traffic regulation, temporary, liability for cost, **38(1)**, [218]

strike. *See* **trade unions**

structure plan

  adoption of, **46**, [293]

  alteration of, **46**, [290]

  authorities responsible for local plans, notification of, **46**, [296]

  continuity, **46**, [289]

  enterprise zone, in, **46**, [311]

  examination in public, **46**, [295]

  form of, **46**, [289]

  joint, **46**, [308]

  local plan, conflict with, **46**, [306]

  other enactments, development authorised by, **46**, [307]

  policy and general proposals, **46**, [289]

  preparation of, **46**, [289]

  public participation, **46**, [291]

  regulations as to, **46**, [312]

  replacement of, **46**, [290]

  revocation, **46**, [616]

  Secretary of State—

    calling in of proposals for approval, **46**, [294]

    default powers, **46**, [309]

  transitional provisions, **46**, [616]–[619], [1063]

  urban development area, in, **46**, [310]

  validity, **46**, [549], [552]

  withdrawal of, **46**, [292]

  written statement, as, **46**, [289]

structured finance arrangement

  disregard of intended effects of—

    change in relation to partnership, where involving, **44(1)**, [515], [516], [517]

    disposals of assets, where involving, **44(1)**, [513], [516], [517]

    meaning, **44(1)**, [512], [514]

structured settlement. *See* **damages**

stubble
burning, **35(1)**, [847]

student loans
administration, **15(1)**, [386]
   public sector, **15(1)**, [776]
agreements, regulations to prescribe certain
   terms of, **15(1)**, [775]
arrangements for, **15(1)**, [800]
certificates, **15(1)**, [386]
consequential amendments, **15(1)**, [779]
consumer credit regulation, exclusion from,
   15(S), Education 54
courses of higher education, **15(1)**, [385]
financial provisions, **15(1)**, [383], [778]
general note, **15(1)**, [1]
information—
   disclosure of, **15(1)**, [386]
   supply by HMRC, **15(S)**, Education 53
   supply of, **15(1)**, [802]
insolvency, provisions on, **15(1)**, [386]
minors, circulars to, **15(1)**, [386]
Northern Ireland, **15(1)**, [382], [482], [777]
power to make, **15(1)**, [380]
principal, interest and payments, **15(1)**, [386]
private sector, **15(1)**, [380]
public sector loans, transfer to private sector,
   15(1), [381]
regulations, **15(2)**, [497];
   15(S), Education 51–2
repayment, **15(S)**, Education 51–2
repeals, **15(1)**, [779], [781]
sale of—
   purchaser, lender as, **15(S)**, Education 51
   summary of provisions,
      15(S), Education 45–6
   transfer arrangements, repayment, provision
      for, **15(S)**, Education 51–2
transfer arrangements—
   entry into, **15(S)**, Education 47–8
   onward, **15(S)**, Education 50
   provisions in, **15(S)**, Education 47–9
   report on, **15(S)**, Education 51
   Wales, in, **15(S)**, Education 55
transitional provisions, **15(2)**, [322]

students' union
meaning, **15(1)**, [473]
references to, **15(1)**, [473]
relevant establishments, **15(1)**, [474]
requirements to be observed, **15(1)**, [475]

sturgeon
Crown right to, **1(1)**, [124]

sub-contractor
construction contract—
   contractor, body being, **43(2)**, [295]
   deduction of sums, provision for,
      43(2), [293]
   meaning, **43(2)**, [293]
construction industry scheme, consequential
   amendments, **43(2)**, [541]

sub-contractor—*contd*
construction operations, meaning,
   43(2), [310]
contract payments—
   collection and recovery of sums deducted,
      43(2), [298], [307]
   deductions on account of tax from,
      43(2), [297]
   gross, **43(2)**, [296]
   meaning, **43(2)**, [296]
   periodic returns, **43(2)**, [306]
   regulations, **43(2)**, [309]
deductions from payments—
   exemption certificates, **43(1)**, [426]
   relevant percentage, **43(1)**, [161], [191]
deductions, interest on late payment or
   repayment, **43(2)**, [214]
HM Revenue & Customs, meaning,
   43(2), [311]
meaning, **43(2)**, [294]
receipts of trade, transitional provisions,
   43(1), [348], [388]
registration—
   commencement and transitional provision,
      43(2), [313]
   false or reckless statements, penalties for,
      43(2), [308]
   gross payment, for, **43(2)**, [299]
      appeals, **43(2)**, [303]
      cancellation, **43(2)**, [302]
      change in control of company,
         43(2), [301]
      conditions, **43(2)**, [537]–[540]
      requirement, **43(2)**, [300]
   payment under deduction, for, **43(2)**, [299]
      appeals, **43(2)**, [304]
      cancellation, **43(2)**, [304]
   verification of status, **43(2)**, [305]

subject
liberty of—
   Bill of Rights, **10**, [40]–[42]
   confirmation of, **10**, [4], [18], [21]
   statutes ensuring, **10**, [1]
rights of, **10**, [1]

subletting. *See also* **underletting**
secure tenancy, in case of, **22**, [81]

submarine cables
continental shelf, exploration, protection in,
   17(1), [293]
convention—
   application, **45**, [16]
   Art 2, violation, **45**, [7]
   Arts 5 & 6, carrying into effect, **45**, [8]
   belligerents, freedom of action of, **45**, [16]
   confirmation, **45**, [6]
   offences against, **45**, [7], [16]
   officers, British and foreign, powers, **45**, [9]
   parties to, **45**, [16]
   text, **45**, [16]
   tribunals, **45**, [16]
   vessels, obligations of, **45**, [16]
damage to, **45**, [7]

submarine cables—*contd*
evidence, **45**, [11]
extension of Act relating to, **45**, [14]
interruption of communication, **45**, [7]
masters of vessels, liability, **45**, [12]
Merchant Shipping Act, incorporation of
  Part X, **45**, [10]
obstruction of officers, **45**, [9]
officers, British and foreign, powers, **45**, [9]
savings relating to, **45**, [13]
telecommunications, interruption of, **45**, [7]
Thames flood barrier, dredging affecting,
  49, [515]

submarine pipelines
application of provisions, **17(2)**, [272]
authorisations—
  generally, **17(2)**, [253]
  other than works, **17(2)**, [308]
  termination, **17(2)**, [266], [267]
  works authorisations, **17(2)**, [307]
breach of duty, civil liability for, **17(2)**, [271]
compulsory modifications, **17(2)**, [254]
construction, **17(2)**, [252]
controlled petroleum—
  acquisition of rights to use, **17(2)**, [261],
  [262]
  meaning, **17(2)**, [276]
  Norwegian access system, subject to,
  17(2), [263], [264]
criminal proceedings, **17(2)**, [270]
downstream gas—
  meaning, **17(2)**, [276]
  provisions relating to, **17(2)**, [256], [257]
enforcement provisions, **17(2)**, [265], [269]
inspectors, **17(2)**, [268]
interpretation, **17(2)**, [276]
meaning, **17(2)**, [274]
offshore gas storage facilities,
  17(2), [258]–[260]
orders and regulations, **17(2)**, [273]
owner, meaning, **17(2)**, [275]
rights to use, acquisition of, **17(2)**, [255]
use, **17(2)**, [252]

submersible apparatus
meaning, **39(2)**, [754]
offences, **39(2)**, [994]
registration of, **39(2)**, [994]
regulations, **39(2)**, [994]
safety of, **39(2)**, [754]
supporting, safety of, **39(2)**, [754]

subordinate legislation. *See also* **statutory
instrument**
construction of, **41**, [585]
interpretation provisions applied, **41**, [598],
  [607]
powers as to, Minister on whom conferred,
  41, [510], [512]
publication etc of, **41**, [480]
purposes of, **41**, [480]
repeals, **41**, [641]
Scottish, **41**, [480]
summary of provisions, **41**, [480]

subordinate legislation—*contd*
Welsh, **41**, [480]

subornation
perjury, of, **12(1)**, [201]

subpoena
disobedience to, **18**, [115]
issue and enforcement, **18**, [76]
territorial currency, **18**, [113]
witness attendance, for, expenses to be
  tendered, **18**, [77], [116]
witness summons, replaced by, **12(1)**, [356]
writ, statement at foot of, **18**, [114]

subpoena ad respondendum
writ of, abolition, **13**, [43]

subpoena ad testificandum
writ, issue by Solicitors Disciplinary
  Tribunal, **11(2)**, [327]; **11(4)**, [424]

subpoena duces tecum
writ, issue by Solicitors Disciplinary
  Tribunal, **11(2)**, [327]; **11(4)**, [424]

subscriptions
relief for, Schedule E, **44(2)**, [353]

subsidence
mining, due to. *See* **coal mining subsidence**

subsidiary company
amendment of definitions, **8**, 599
directors, power to appoint or remove,
  8, 597–8
holding company, as member of—
  authorised dealer in securities, acting as—
    prohibition not applying, **8(1)**, [219]
    third parties, protection of, **8(1)**, [220]
  companies not limited by shares, provisions
    applying to, **8(1)**, [221]
  employer's right of recovery under pension
    scheme or employees' share scheme,
    disregarding, **8(1)**, [218]
  nominees, provisions applying to,
    8(1), [222]
  personal representative or trustee, acting
    as, **8(1)**, [216]–[218]
  prohibition, **8(1)**, [214]
  residual interest under pension scheme or
    employees' share scheme, disregarding,
    8(1), [217]
  shares acquired before prohibition
    applicable, **8(1)**, [215]
majority of directors, right to appoint or
  remove, **8**, 754
meaning, **8**, 595–7; **8(1)**, [1237], [1392]
power to amend definition, **8(1)**, [1238]
reference to, **8**, 926–7
trustee, acting as—
  employer's right of recovery under pension
    scheme or employees' share scheme,
    disregarding, **8(1)**, [218]

subsidiary company—*contd*
  trustee, acting as—*contd*
    residual interest under pension scheme or
      employees' share scheme, disregarding,
      8(1), [217]
    shares in holding company, holding,
      8(1), [216]–[218]
  undertakings, **8(1)**, [1240], [1393]
  voting rights, **8**, 597–8, 754; **8(1)**, [1392]
  wholly owned, meaning, **8**, 595–7

subsidies
  housing. *See* **housing subsidy**
  imported goods, on, customs duties to offset,
    ECSC products, in relation to, **13**, [588]
  slum clearance. *See* **slum clearance**
  superseded, **22**, [444]
  town development. *See* **town development
    subsidy**

succession
  agricultural tenancies. *See* **agricultural
    tenancy; agricultural workers** (housing)

succession duty
  generally, **42**, [1]

successor companies
  borrowings—
    financial limits on, **17(1)**, [843]
    temporary restrictions on, **17(1)**, [840]
  flotation—
    composite listing particulars, responsibility
      for, **17(1)**, [844]
    Trustee Investments Act, application of,
      17(1), [845]
  Government lending to, **17(1)**, [841]
  nominees of Treasury or Secretary of State,
    17(1), [837]
  statutory accounts, **17(1)**, [839]
  statutory reserves, **17(1)**, [838]
  Treasury guarantees, **17(1)**, [842]

sugar beet
  amendments to enactment relating to,
    1(2), [465]
  crop price, determining, **1(2)**, [229]
  home-grown, meaning, **1(2)**, [229]
  information—
    disclosure of, **1(2)**, [230]
    provision by processor, **1(2)**, [230]

sugar trade
  summary of provisions, **47**, [1]

suicide
  another's, aiding and abetting—
    child or young person, **12(1)**, [332]
    criminal liability, **12(1)**, [330]
    institution of proceedings, **12(1)**, [330]
    murder or manslaughter trial, verdict in,
      12(1), [330]
  crime, ceasing to be, **12(1)**, [329]
  pact, **12(1)**, [301]

summary jurisdiction, court of. *See*
magistrates' court

summary trial. *See also* **magistrates' court**
  accused ignorant of, validity, **11(2)**, [429]
  accused, in absence of—
    amended provisions, **11(S)**, Courts 9–10
    guilty, plea of, **11(2)**, [426]–[427]
    powers of court, **11(2)**, [425]–[426]
    warrant for arrest, issue of, **11(2)**, [428]
  adjournment, **11(2)**, [424]
  child or young person, indictable offence by,
    11(2), [444]
  conviction, adjournment after, **11(2)**, [424]
  offences triable either way—
    absence of accused, in, **11(2)**, [443]
    accused—
      absence of, in, **11(2)**, [434]
      explanation to, **11(2)**, [440]
      plea, intention as to, **11(2)**, [433]
      proceedings, adjournment of,
        11(2), [435]
    adjournment, **11(2)**, [438]
    committal proceedings, change to,
      11(2), [441], [449]
    consent to, **11(2)**, [440]
    dismissal of information, **11(2)**, [451]
    maximum penalties for certain,
      11(2), [436]
    penalties on conviction, **11(2)**, [454]
    remand of accused, **11(2)**, [438]
    single justice, functions exercised by,
      11(2), [437]
    suitable mode of trial—
      consideration of, **11(2)**, [439]
      procedure, **11(2)**, [440]
    summons to accused, issue of, **11(2)**, [450]
    trial on indictment, application for,
      11(2), [439]
    value involved not exceeding relevant
      sum, **11(2)**, [442], [580]
      penalties, maximum, **11(2)**, [455]
    young person—
      plea, intention as to, **11(2)**, [445]
      absence during, **11(2)**, [446]
      proceedings, adjournment of,
        11(2), [447]
      single justice, functions exercisable
        by, **11(2)**, [448]
  parties, non-appearance by, **11(2)**, [431]
  penalties—
    mitigation of, **11(2)**, [456]
    offence triable either way, on conviction,
      11(2), [454]
  pre-trial hearing—
    reporting restrictions, **11(2)**, [421]
    offences, **11(2)**, [422]
    rulings from magistrates' court—
      effect of, **11(2)**, [420]
      power to make, **11(2)**, [419]
  procedure, **11(2)**, [423]
  prosecutor, non-appearance of, **11(2)**, [430]

summer time
  advance of time, **45**, [940]

summer time—*contd*
Northern Ireland, application of provisions,
45, [942]

summons
complaint, issue on, **11(2)**, [468]
information, issue on laying of, **11(2)**, [405]
presence of accused before court, requiring,
11(2), [450]
service out of time, **11(2)**, [465]
United Kingdom, service throughout,
11(2), [399]
witness, issue of, **11(2)**, [519]–[520]

Sunday
elections due to be held on, **45**, [929]
parks etc, London, closing of, **25(2)**, [397]
street trading, City of London, **25(1)**, [779]
trading on. *See under* **shop**
two services on, **14**, 117

superannuation. *See also* **pension**
approved school officers, **33(1)**, [73]
British Council staff, **33(1)**, [190]
civil service. *See* **civil service pensions**
Commonwealth Institute staff, **33(1)**, [190]
Comptroller and Auditor General,
33(1), [134]
compulsory national service, treatment of,
33(1), [71]
diplomatic service, **33(1)**, [112]
distribution without probate, **33(1)**, [39], [41]
employees at voluntary schools, **25(1)**, [543]
Groundwork Foundation, employment with,
35(1), [849]
health service staff. *See* **national health
service**
judicial offices, **33(1)**, [82]
local Act schemes—
meaning, **33(1)**, [129]
winding up etc, **33(1)**, [129]
local government. *See* **local government
officers and staff**
London authorities and agencies, employment
with, **26(1)**, [732], [733]
museum employees, **33(1)**, [89]
overseas service—
enactments as to, **33(1)**, [162]
schemes for, power of Minister to make,
33(1), [158]
supplementary provisions, **33(1)**, [159]
payment out without probate, **33(1)**, [39],
[41]
payments for, relief for—
family members, for benefit of,
44(4), [467]
police organisations, to, **44(4)**, [466]
residence of claimants, **44(4)**, [468]
trade unions, to, **44(4)**, [465]
polytechnics etc staffs, **25(1)**, [166]
repealed provisions, continuation of
application, **33(1)**, [138], [148]
river authority staff, **33(1)**, [136]
Royal Commissioners, **33(1)**, [89]
Rules, **33(1)**, [74]

superannuation—*contd*
statutory bodies, **33(1)**, [137], [147]
summary of provisions, **33(1)**, [25]
teachers. *See* **teachers' superannuation**
transfer of employment, **33(1)**, [72], [91]
transferred officers of authorities, right as to,
35(1), [203]
war service—
benefits, continuance of, **33(1)**, [47]
contributions during, **33(1)**, [47]
pensions. *See* **war pensions**
persons excepted from provisions,
33(1), [49]

superfluous land
conveyance on sale, **9**, [87]
offer to original or adjoining owner, **9**, [84]
pre-emption, right of, **9**, [85]
price, arbitration as to, **9**, [86]
sale of, **9**, [83], [291]
vesting in adjoining owners, **9**, [83]

supervision order. *See further* **community
orders**
age limitation, **6**, [343]
amendment, **12(1)**, [347]; **12(2)**, [849]
appeal against—
disposal of, **12(1)**, [434]
right of, **12(1)**, [433]
appeal, on, **12(1)**, [430]
appeals, **12(2)**, [849]
application for—
attendance of child at, **6**, [426]
evidence, giving of, **6**, [429]
generally, **6**, [343]
local authority, by, **6**, [343]
National Society for the Prevention of
Cruelty to Children, by, **6**, [343]
period for disposal of, **6**, [345]
self-incrimination in evidence, **6**, [429]
application on behalf of young person,
12(2), [849]
authorised person—
application by, **6**, [343]
meaning, **6**, [343]
breach—
attendance centre order, imposition of,
12(2), [849]
curfew order, imposition of, **12(2)**, [849]
relevant court, meaning, **12(2)**, [849]
requirement, of, **12(2)**, [849]
cessation of, effect, **6**, [237]
copies, provision of, **12(2)**, [760]
curfew order in addition to, **12(2)**, [762]
definitions, **12(2)**, [765]
discharge of, **6**, [354], [422]
duration of, **6**, [444]; **12(2)**, [760]
earlier order, effect on, **6**, [444]
education. *See* **education supervision order**
electronic monitoring of requirements,
12(2), [751]
generally, **6**, [1], [343]
Hague Convention on Child Abduction,
effect, **6**, [204]

supervision order—*contd*
  harm—
    child suffering form, **6**, [343]
    meaning, **6**, [343]
  implementation, facilities for, **12(2)**, [764]
  interim—
    examination or assessment of child,
      6, [351]
    exclusion requirement in, **6**, [352]
    making of, **6**, [351]
    period of, **6**, [351]
    residence order with, **6**, [351]
  investigation into child's circumstances,
    6, [350]
  local authority—
    application by, **6**, [343]
    functions and expenditure, **6**, [444]
    supervisor, as, **12(2)**, [761]
  making and effect of, **12(1)**, [346]
  making of, **6**, [204], [215], [343];
    12(2), [1290]–[1291]
  meaning, **6**, [100], [343]; **12(1)**, [345]
  medical examinations and treatment,
    requirements, **6**, [443]
  medical treatment requirement, **12(1)**, [346]
  National Society for the Prevention of
    Cruelty to Children, application by, **6**, [343]
  power to make, **12(1)**, [341], [422];
    12(2), [760]
  presence of offender in court, **12(2)**, [849]
  psychiatric examination and treatment,
    requirements, **6**, [443]
  requirements, **12(1)**, [345]; **12(2)**, [848]
  residence requirement, **12(1)**, [346]
  responsible person—
    meaning, **6**, [443]
    obligations, **6**, [443]
  revocation, **6**, [204], [215]; **12(1)**, [347];
    12(2), [849]
  statutory amendments, **6**, [454]
  substitution order, **6**, [354]
  supervisor—
    directions by, **6**, [443]
    duty of, **6**, [348]
    information, furnishing to, **6**, [444]
    role of, **12(2)**, [761]
    selection of, **6**, [444]
  variation of, **6**, [215], [354]

supplementary benefit
  adjudication, **40(1)**, [736]
  amendment of enactments, **40(1)**, [101],
    [102]
  claims and payments, **40(1)**, [736]
  inspection, **40(1)**, [736]
  legal proceedings, **40(1)**, [736]
  overpayments, **40(1)**, [736]
  personal representatives, information from,
    40(1), [633]
  transitional provisions and savings, **40(1)**, [76],
    [78]–[79]; **40(2)**, [10]

supply of goods
  guarantee, exclusion in, **11(1)**, [312]

supply powers
  articles required for public service, **10**, [587]
  disclosure of information, **10**, [585]
  offences, **10**, [586]
  reserves, creation of, **10**, [583]
  Secretary of State—
    land, holding, **10**, [582], [590]
    powers, **10**, [581]–[582]
  stocks—
    creation of, **10**, [583]
    return of, **10**, [584]

support
  mines, in. *See under* **mines and mining**
  right of, protection against opencast coal
    working, **17(1)**, [166]

Supreme Court. *See also* **Court of Appeal;
  Crown Court; High Court**
  accommodation and resources, **11(3)**, [504]
  Accountant General—
    accounts, **11(2)**, [884]
    charity commissioners, funds transferred
      to, **11(2)**, [880]
    church commissioners, funds transferred
      to, **11(2)**, [880]
    default of, **11(2)**, [882]
    funds, managing, **11(2)**, [877]
    office of, **11(2)**, [770]; **11(3)**, [55]
    official custodian for charities, funds
      transferred to, **11(2)**, [880]
    Public Trustee, as, **48**, 240, 597
    statutory deposits, **11(2)**, [879]
  advisers, **11(3)**, [498]
  annual report, **11(3)**, [508]
  appeal to, **11(3)**, [494]
  carrying on business, system supporting,
    11(3), [505]
  central office, **11(2)**, [769]
  chief executive, **11(3)**, [502]
  composition, **11(3)**, [496]
    changes in, **11(3)**, [497]
  constitution of, **11(2)**, [668]; **11(3)**, [477]
  conveyancing counsel, **11(2)**, [777]
  Court-Martial Appeal Court, reference of
    point of law from, **3(S)**, 253–4
  definitions, **11(3)**, [514]
  documents—
    filed, production of, **11(2)**, [782]
    seal, bearing, proof of, **11(2)**, [778]
  fees, **11(3)**, [506]–[507]
  first members of, **11(3)**, [478]
  funds, **11(2)**, [211]
    charity commissioners, transfer to,
      11(2), [880]
    church commissioners, transfer to,
      11(2), [880]
    common investment schemes. *See*
      Common investment schemes
    default of Accountant General, **11(2)**, [882]
    National Debt Commissioners, transfer to,
      11(2), [878]
    generally, **11(2)**, [1]
  instruments, enrolment and engrossment of,
    11(2), [779]

Supreme Court—*contd*
judge of—
  allowances, **11(2)**, [679]
  appointment of, **11(2)**, [677]
  clerks and secretaries, **11(2)**, [771]
  competent, where, **11(2)**, [676]
  incapacity of, **11(2)**, [678]
  pension. *See* **judicial pension**
  precedence, **11(2)**, [680]
  rates case, acting in, **11(2)**, [681]
  relevant service, **11(2)**, [588], [603]
  retiring age, **11(2)**, [678]
  salary, **11(2)**, [679]
  tax case, acting in, **11(2)**, [681]
  tenure of office, **11(2)**, [678]
judges of—
  acting, **11(3)**, [492]
  first, **11(3)**, [478]
  judicial oath, **11(3)**, [486]
  medical retirement, **11(3)**, [490]
  number of, **11(3)**, [477]
  oath of allegiance, **11(3)**, [486]
  pensions, **11(3)**, [491]
  qualifications for appointment, **11(3)**, [479]
  resignation, **11(3)**, [489]
  retirement, **11(3)**, [489]
  salaries and allowances, **11(3)**, [488]
  selection of—
    commission for—
      chairing, **11(3)**, [603]
      convening, **11(3)**, [480]
      Deputy President, for office of,
        11(3), [605]
      dissolution of, **11(3)**, [604]
      duty to convene, **11(3)**, [605]
      interpretation, **11(3)**, [603]
      judge, for office of, **11(3)**, [605]
      membership, **11(3)**, [603]
      non-judicial members, **11(3)**, [603]
      report, **11(3)**, [482]
    Lord Chancellor, options of,
      11(3), [483]
    process, **11(3)**, [481]
    recommendations, **11(3)**, [480]
    reconsideration, **11(3)**, [485]
    report, **11(3)**, [482]
  supplementary panel, **11(3)**, [493]
  tenure, **11(3)**, [487]
judicial business, assistance for transaction of,
  11(2), [676]
jurisdiction, **11(3)**, [494]
  devolution, **11(3)**, [607]
  House of Lords, transferred from,
    11(3), [606]
  transferred, proceedings under, **11(3)**, [608]
Lord Chancellor's advisory committees,
  11(2), [250]
masters, **11(2)**, [763]
meaning, **41**, [605]
Northern Ireland. *See* **Northern Ireland**
officers—
  civil service pension scheme, in,
    11(2), [631]
  deputy, **11(2)**, [765]

Supreme Court—*contd*
officers—*contd*
  injury during discharge of duties,
    11(2), [633]
  pensions, **11(2)**, [632]–[633]
    abolished offices, **11(2)**, [638]
  property held by, **11(2)**, [768]
  qualifications, **11(2)**, [762]
  relevant service, **11(2)**, [631]
  removal of, **11(2)**, [766]
  salaries, **11(2)**, [763], [767]
  status of, **11(2)**, [767]
  temporary appointments, **11(2)**, [765]
  tenure of office, **11(2)**, [766]
  transitional provisions, **11(2)**, [796]
officers and staff, **11(3)**, [503]
offices in, **11(2)**, [792]–[794]
official solicitor, **11(2)**, [764]
payment of money into, **11(2)**, [783]
photography in, **11(3)**, [501]
power of attorney deposited in, **11(2)**, [780]
Public Trustee—
  office of, **11(3)**, [55]
  qualification, meaning, **11(3)**, [125];
    11(4), [547]
Queen's Remembrancer, **11(2)**, [763]
records, **11(3)**, [510]
  preservation, **18**, [189], [194]
relation to other courts, **11(3)**, [495]
renaming, **11(3)**, [513]
  acts and rules, citation of, **11(3)**, [609]
  England and Wales, of, **11(3)**, [610]
  Northern Ireland, miscellaneous
    amendments, **11(3)**, [611]
  specific amendments, **11(3)**, [612]
rules—
  Lord Chancellor, submission to,
    11(3), [500]
  making, **11(3)**, [499]
  power to make, **11(2)**, [757]
  special, **11(2)**, [757]
seal, **11(3)**, [509]
solicitors—
  jurisdiction over, **11(2)**, [331]; **11(4)**, [430]
  officers of court, as, **11(2)**, [331];
    11(4), [430]
  right of audience, **11(2)**, [297]
superior court of record, as, **11(3)**, [494]

Surrey
references to, in enactments, **25(1)**, [64]

Surrey Canal
discontinuance, rights and obligations on,
  39(2), [435]

Surrey commercial docks
discontinuance, rights and obligations on,
  39(2), [435]

surrogacy
arrangements—
  advertisements of, **12(1)**, [977]
  amended provisions, **28(S)**, 174
  body of persons, by, **12(1)**, [976]

surrogacy—*contd*
  arrangements—*contd*
    commercial basis, on, **12(1)**, [976]
    meaning, **12(1)**, [974]
    negotiating, **12(1)**, [976]
    payment, involving, **12(1)**, [976]
    unenforceable, **12(1)**, [975]
  interpretation of expressions, **12(1)**, [974]
  lawful, when, **12(1)**, [976]
  offences—
    body corporate, by, **12(1)**, [978]
    evidence of, **12(1)**, [978]
    generally, **12(1)**, [1], [976]
    penalties, **12(1)**, [978]
    proceedings for, **12(1)**, [978]
  surrogate mother, meaning, **12(1)**, [974]

surtax
  additional particulars for, **42**, [136]
  generally, **42**, [1]

surveillance
  codes of practice—
    effect of, **45**, [400]
    issue and revision of, **45**, [399]
  Commissioners—
    appeals, **45**, [366], [367]
    assistant, **45**, [391]
    Chief, functions of, **45**, [390]
    delegation of functions, **45**, [392]
    information provided to, **45**, [368]
  conduct, **45**, [354]
  covert—
    authorisation of, **45**, [357]
    meaning, **45**, [354]
    persons granting, **45**, [358]
  directed—
    authorisation of, **45**, [356]
    persons granting, **45**, [358]
  directors, criminal liability of, **45**, [405]
  foreign operations, **45**, [402]
  grant of authorisations—
    appeals, **45**, [366], [367]
    approval, **45**, [364]
    cancellation, **45**, [373]
    duration, rules for, **45**, [371]
    extension or modification of provisions, **45**, [375]
    intelligence services, by, **45**, [370], [372]
    intrusive—
      conduct authorised, **45**, [360]
      notification of, **45**, [363]
    Northern Ireland, **45**, [359]
    persons giving, **45**, [358]
    quashing, **45**, [365]
    renewal, rules for, **45**, [371]
    rules for, **45**, [361], [371], [372]
    Scotland, **45**, [374]
    Secretary of State, by, **45**, [369]
    senior officers—
      absence, in, **45**, [362]
      powers as to, **45**, [360]
  interception of communications. *See*
    telecommunications

surveillance—*contd*
  intrusive—
    authorisation of, **45**, [360]
    notification, **45**, [363]
  lawful, **45**, [355]
  lawful conduct, **45**, [406]
  ministerial expenditure, **45**, [403]
  orders, **45**, [404]
  regulations, **45**, [404]
  relevant authorities, **45**, [410], [411]
  rules, **45**, [404]
  Scotland, operations beginning in, **45**, [401]
  summary of provisions, **45**, [1]
  Tribunal—
    allocation of proceedings, **45**, [394]
    complaints jurisdiction, abolished, **45**, [398]
    establishment of, **45**, [393]
    exercise of jurisdiction, **45**, [395]
    jurisdiction, **45**, [393]
    members—
      expenses, **45**, [413]
      President, **45**, [413]
      salaries, **45**, [413]
      special responsibilities, with, **45**, [413]
      Vice-President, **45**, [413]
    membership, **45**, [413]
    officers, **45**, [413]
    procedure, **45**, [396]
    rules, **45**, [397]
    summary of provisions, **45**, [1]

survey
  entry on land for. *See under* **entry on land**
  geological—
    entry onto land, **10**, [304]
    land, meaning of, **10**, [306]
    marks, fixing, **10**, [304]
    penalties, **10**, [305]
  local authority, by, of land to be compulsorily acquired, **9**, [373]
  ordnance. *See* **ordnance survey**

surveyor
  compensation, determination by—
    absent parties, in case of, **9**, [23], [234]
    certificate, application for, **9**, [233]
    committee not appointed, where, **9**, [63]
    valuation by, **9**, [24], [234]
  Lands Tribunal, selected by, **9**, [181]

survivorship
  presumption as to, **20**, [785]

suspended sentence
  less than 12 months, sentence for—
    amendment of, **12(3)**, [1074]
    breach of, **12(3)**, [1072], [1073]
    Northern Ireland, transfer to, **12(3)**, [1076]–[1078]
    order—
      activity requirement, **12(3)**, [932]
      alcohol treatment requirement, **12(3)**, [943]
      attendance centre requirement, **12(3)**, [945]

suspended sentence—*contd*
  less than 12 months, sentence for—*contd*
    order—*contd*
      curfew requirement, **12(3)**, [935]
      drug rehabilitation requirement,
        12(3), [940]–[942]
      electronic monitoring requirement,
        12(3), [946]
      exclusion requirement, **12(3)**, [936]
      imposition of requirements by,
        12(3), [921]
      limits of requirements, amendment of,
        12(3), [954]
      local justice area, specification of,
        12(3), [947]
      mental health treatment requirement,
        12(3), [938], [939]
      periodic review, **12(3)**, [923]
      prohibited activity requirement,
        12(3), [934]
      provision of copies of, **12(3)**, [950],
        [1079]
      religious beliefs, avoidance of conflict
        with, **12(3)**, [948]
      residence requirement, **12(3)**, [937]
      responsible officer—
        duties of, **12(3)**, [929]
        duty of offender to keep in touch
          with, **12(3)**, [951]
        meaning, **12(3)**, [928]
      review of, **12(3)**, [922]
      supervision requirement, **12(3)**, [944]
      unpaid work requirement, **12(3)**, [930],
        [949]
      work or education times, avoidance of
        conflict with, **12(3)**, [948]
    rules, **12(3)**, [953]
    Scotland, transfer to, **12(3)**, [1075], [1077],
      [1078]
    supervision period, **12(3)**, [920]

suspended sentence—*contd*
  pre-sentence drug testing, **12(2)**, [1175];
    12(3), [891]

suspension
  clergy—
    performance of duties during, **14**, 605–6
    presentation, of. *See* **presentation
      (ecclesiastical)**
    readmission to benefice after, **14**, 592
    restrictions during, **14**, 607
    rights of patronage during, **14**, 608

Sutton District Water Company
  saving for, **49**, [226]

swan eggs
  taking, destroying etc, **2**, [166]

swans
  royal right to, **10**, [84]

Swaziland
  Commonwealth citizenship, **31**, [186]
  existing law, operation of, **7(2)**, [627]
  fully responsible status of, **7(2)**, [626]
  visiting forces in, **7(2)**, [630]

Sweden
  accession to European Union, **18**, [47]

swimming baths
  London, provision of, **25(1)**, [842]

swine fever. *See* **diseases of animals**

Swiss Confederation
  heraldic emblem, use of, **10**, [950]–[951],
    [954], [971]

T

Takeover Appeal Board
decisions of Hearings Committee, appeals
against, **8(1)**, [1029]

takeover offer
associate, meaning, **8(1)**, [1066]
conditions, **8(1)**, [1052]
convertible securities, treatment of,
8(1), [1067]
debentures carrying voting rights, treatment
of, **8(1)**, [1068]
definitions, **8(1)**, [1069]
directors' report, disclosure in, **8(1)**, [1070]
impossibility of accepting, **8(1)**, [1056]
impossibility of communicating, **8(1)**, [1056]
meaning, **8(1)**, [1052]
minority shareholder, right of to be bought
out—
all shares in company, offer relating to,
8(1), [1061]
applications to court, **8(1)**, [1064]
communication of, **8(1)**, [1062]
consideration, choice of, **8(1)**, [1063]
joint offers, **8(1)**, [1065]
non-voting shares, **8(1)**, [1061]
notice of, **8(1)**, [1062]
minority shareholder, right to buy out—
applications to court, **8(1)**, [1064]
conditions for, **8(1)**, [1057]
consideration held on trust—
entitlement to, **8(1)**, [1060]
requirement, **8(1)**, [1059]
separate bank account, **8(1)**, [1060]
joint offers, **8(1)**, [1065]
notices—
effect of, **8(1)**, [1059]
entitlement to, **8(1)**, [1057]
manner of giving, **8(1)**, [1058]
offences, **8(1)**, [1058]
same terms, treated as being on, **8(1)**, [1054]
sell-out, **8(1)**, [1061]–[1063]
See also minority shareholder, right of to be
bought out *above*
shares already held by offeror, meaning,
8(1), [1053]
shares to which relating, **8(1)**, [1055]
squeeze-out, **8(1)**, [1057]–[1060]
See also minority shareholder, right to buy
out *above*

takeovers
offer. *See* **takeover offer**
opting-in resolution—
Channel Islands, power to extend
provisions to, **8(1)**, [1051]
communication of decisions, **8(1)**, [1048]
conditions, **8(1)**, [1044]

takeovers—*contd*
opting-in resolution—*contd*
consequences of—
contractual restrictions, effect on,
8(1), [1046]
general meeting, power of offeror to
call, **8(1)**, [1047]
definitions, **8(1)**, [1049]
effect of, **8(1)**, [1044]
effective date, **8(1)**, [1045]
Isle of Man, power to extend provisions
to, **8(1)**, [1051]
revocation, **8(1)**, [1044]
transitory provision, **8(1)**, [1050]
opting-out resolution—
Channel Islands, power to extend
provisions to, **8(1)**, [1051]
communication of decisions, **8(1)**, [1048]
definitions, **8(1)**, [1049]
effect of, **8(1)**, [1044]
effective date, **8(1)**, [1045]
Isle of Man, power to extend provisions
to, **8(1)**, [1051]
transitory provision, **8(1)**, [1050]
Panel. *See* **Panel on Takeovers and
Mergers**

tallage
assent of Parliament for, **10**, [10]

Tanganyika. *See also* **Tanzania**
British ship registered in, **7(2)**, [492]
existing law, operation of, **7(2)**, [524]
fully responsible status of, **7(2)**, [488]
legislative powers of, **7(2)**, [491]
repeal of enactments, **7(2)**, [634]
republic, becoming, **7(2)**, [524]
Tanzania, becoming, **7(2)**, [632]
visiting forces in, **7(2)**, [492]

tankers
oil pollution, liability for, **39(2)**, [822], [827]

Tanzania. *See also* **Tanganyika; Zanzibar**
British ship registered in, **7(2)**, [632]
Commonwealth citizenship, **31**, [186]
republic, becoming, **7(2)**, [632]
statutory provisions applying to, **7(2)**, [633]

tape recorder
court, used in, **11(2)**, [654]

Tate Gallery
Board of Trustees, new—
accounts and audit, **13**, [422]
agreements, party to, **13**, [413]
allowances, **13**, [425]

Tate Gallery—*contd*
  Board of Trustees, new—*contd*
    British works, maintenance of collection
      of, **13**, [414]
    companies, power to form, **13**, [415]
    establishment, **13**, [413]
    general functions, **13**, [414]
    land, transfer of, **13**, [421], [430]
      stamp duty exemption, **13**, [421]
      stamp duty land tax exemption,
        13, [421]
    membership, **13**, [425]
    pictures and relevant objects—
      acquisition and disposal of, **13**, [416]
      lending and borrowing, **13**, [417]
      transfer between institutions, **13**, [418],
        [428], [429]
    predecessor, meaning, **13**, [413]
    proceedings, **13**, [425]
    reports, **13**, [425]
    sealing of instruments, **13**, [425]
    status, **13**, [425]
    vesting of property, rights and liabilities in,
      13, [413]
  companies, objects of, **13**, [415]
  director, **13**, [425]
  finances, **13**, [422]
  grants, **13**, [422], [431], [432]
  history, **13**, [49]
  National Gallery—
    separation from, **13**, [49]
    transfer of responsibility from, **13**, [49]
  staff, **13**, [425]
  will, gifts by, **13**, [419]

tattooing
  business of—
    byelaws as to, **35(1)**, [434]
    entry on premises, powers of, **35(1)**, [436]
    local application of provisions as to,
      35(1), [432]
    medical practitioner, under supervision of,
      35(1), [434]
    person or premises for carrying on—
      offences by, **35(1)**, [436]
      registration of—
        certificate of—
          display on premises, **35(1)**, [435]
          issue of, **35(1)**, [434]
        charge for, **35(1)**, [434]
        requirement of, **35(1)**, [434], [435]
        suspension or cancellation,
          35(1), [435]
  minors, of, **6**, [106]

tattooists
  amendment of enactments, **26(2)**, [163]
  application of provisions, **26(2)**, [164]
  entry, powers of, **25(2)**, [969]
  existing, application of provisions to,
    25(2), [970]
  licence—
    appeals, **25(2)**, [967]; **26(2)**, [163]
    application for, **25(2)**, [961]
    cancellation, **25(2)**, [963]

tattooists—*contd*
  licence—*contd*
    conditions, **25(2)**, [960]
    enforcement, **25(2)**, [968]
    provisional grant, **25(2)**, [965]
    refusal of, **25(2)**, [962]
    renewal and transfer, **26(2)**, [163]
    requirement of, **25(2)**, [960]
    standard terms, conditions and restrictions,
      25(2), [964]
    transmission, **25(2)**, [963]
    variation, **25(2)**, [966]
  registration of, **25(2)**, [466]
  special treatment premises, as, **25(2)**, [958]
  termination of registration, **26(1)**, [238]

tax
  arrears, evidence of, **42**, [207]
  community investment tax relief. *See*
    community investment tax relief
  computer records, production of, **42**, [924]
  demand, **42**, [200]
  disclosure of information, **42**, [991]
  extra-statutory concessions, **42**, [1]
  international exchange of information,
    43(1), [496]
  non-payment, distraint for, **42**, [201]
  overdue, interest on. *See* **interest**
  overpayment, recovery of, **42**, [152]
  payment—
    account of income tax, on, **42**, [194]
    amendment or correction of
      self-assessment, after, **42**, [266]
    cheque, by, **42**, [208]
  priority of claim for, **42**, [202]
  recovery of—
    appeal, pending, **42**, [186]
    county court, in, **42**, [204]
    High Court, in, **42**, [205]
    magistrates' court, in, **42**, [203]
    overpayment, of, **42**, [152]
  restructuring of coal industry, arising from. *See*
    under **British Coal Corporation**
    (restructuring)
  temporary—
    House of Commons resolution, **42**, [63]
    meaning, **42**, [64]
    payment or deduction on account of,
      42, [64]
  unpaid—
    certificate of debt, **43(S)**, 973, 1347–8
    disaster or emergency, in case of, interest
      relief, **43(S)**, 970–1

tax accountant
  documents—
    appropriate judicial authority, meaning,
      42, [134]
    entry with warrant to obtain, **42**, [132]
    falsification of, **42**, [131]
    notice requiring, **42**, [129]
    opportunity to deliver, **42**, [129]
    order for delivery, **42**, [130], [262]
    power to call for, **42**, [128]
    removal, procedure on, **42**, [133]

tax accountant—*contd*
person standing as, **42**, [134]

tax avoidance
alternative property finance, transfer of control of financial institution, **43(S)**, 990
annual payments, transfers of rights to receive, **44(1)**, [519]
associated persons, transactions between—
dealing and associated companies, **44(1)**, [511]
meaning, **44(1)**, [689]
provision not at arm's length, **44(1)**, [689]
transfer pricing, basic rule on, **44(1)**, [689]
benefit derived by connected person, **43(S)**, 208–9
capital redemption policy, removal of exclusion from loan relationships computations, **43(2)**, [770]
change in ownership of company. *See* **companies**
charitable companies, by, **44(1)**, [361]
controlled foreign company. *See* **controlled foreign company**
creditor relationships, **43(S)**, 208–9
deductible payments made pursuant to arrangements, **43(S)**, 1397
deemed manufactured payments, **43(S)**, 196
derivative contracts——
fair value, meaning, **43(S)**, 212
generally accepted accounting practice, computation in accordance with, **43(S)**, 211
transactions within groups, **43(S)**, 211–12
dividend stripping, **43(S)**, 193
double taxation relief, and, **44(1)**, [596]
finance arrangements, involving—
collective investment schemes, holdings in, **43(S)**, 603–4
derivative contracts—
connected companies, transfers of value to, **43(S)**, 605
financial asset or liability, treated as, **43(S)**, 605
exchange gains and losses where loan not on arm's length terms, **43(S)**, 602–3
groups of companies, **43(S)**, 601
income, amounts not forming part of, **43(S)**, 598
lease and finance leaseback, plant or machinery subject to, **43(S)**, 604
loan relationships, **43(S)**, 601–2
manufactured payments, **43(S)**, 601
options, **43(S)**, 601
structured arrangements, **43(S)**, 599–601
losses or gains, restrictions on companies buying, **43(S)**, 530–1
financial arrangements avoidance—
interest arrangements appearing very likely to produce post-tax advantage, **43(S)**, 1615–17
manufactured interest, credits and debits, **43(S)**, 1620

tax avoidance—*contd*
financial arrangements, involving, **43(2)**, [748], [770]; **43(S)**, 193–212
commercial rate of interest, meaning, **43(S)**, 1202
connected debtor and creditor, loan relationships treated differently by, **43(S)**, 1201–2
continuity of treatment provisions, relying on, **43(S)**, 1197–8
depreciatory transactions, **43(S)**, 1198–9
derivative contracts, **43(S)**, 1202
disposals for consideration not recognised by accounting practice, **43(S)**, 1196–7
distributions arising from tax arrangements, **43(S)**, 1196
distributions from shares treated as loan relationships, **43(S)**, 1198
exit arrangements, **43(S)**, 1200
falsifying transactions, **43(S)**, 1199
income producing assets, **43(S)**, 1199
interest, credit allowable in relation to, **43(S)**, 1196
interest payments, restrictions on relief for, **43(S)**, 1202
interest-like returns, schemes designed to reproduce, **43(S)**, 1200
lease of plant or machinery. rent factoring, **43(S)**, 1195
non-qualifying shares, **43(S)**, 1199
partnerships, **43(S)**, 1200–1
manufactured payments, **43(S)**, 1207–10
generally, **42**, [1]
income receipts, factoring, **43(S)**, 197–203
information, power to obtain, **44(1)**, [522]
intention of person, ascertaining, **44(1)**, [521]
interest relief, restriction of, **44(1)**, [538]
international leasing, involving, **43(S)**, 232
leased assets. *See* **leasing**
loan relationships—
amounts not fully recognised for accounting purposes, **43(S)**, 205–6
fair value, meaning, **43(S)**, 209
generally accepted accounting practice, computation in accordance with, **43(S)**, 205
groups, continuity of treatment of, **43(S)**, 210
mandatory convertibles, **43(S)**, 205
money debts not arising from lending of money, **43(S)**, 209
repo and stock-lending arrangements, **43(S)**, 211
shares treated as, **43(S)**, 206–8
loans or credit transactions, **43(S)**, 204
loans or credit, transactions associated with, **44(1)**, [537]
migration of company, **44(1)**, [495]
obsolete provisions, repeal of, **43(S)**, 893
options, using, **43(S)**, 88
plant and machinery allowances, **43(S)**, 1185–7
plant or machinery leases, rent factoring, **43(S)**, 203
property or right, transfer etc of, **44(1)**, [521]

tax avoidance—*contd*
  quasi-cash collateral, **43(S)**, 195–6
  quasi-stock lending arrangements,
    43(S), 195–6
  remittance basis, transfers from mixed funds,
    43(S), 1063
  rent factoring, **43(2)**, [770]
    provisions, repeal of, **43(S)**, 193
  sale and leaseback—
    consideration, taxation of, **44(1)**, [524]
    limitation on tax reliefs, **44(1)**, [523]
  sale of occupation income—
    charge to tax, **44(4)**, [784]
      applicable conditions, **44(4)**, [785]
      apportionments, **44(4)**, [791]
      capital amount obtained, income arising
        where, **44(4)**, [786]
      derivative property or right obtained,
        income arising where, **44(4)**, [787]
      exemptions—
        going concerns, for sales of,
          44(4), [792]
        sales of future earnings, restriction
          on, **44(4)**, [793]
      information, power to obtain,
        44(4), [796]
      "other person", meaning, **44(4)**, [790]
      relevant transactions, sales and
        realisations, **44(4)**, [788]
      tracing value, **44(4)**, [789]
      valuations, **44(4)**, [791]
    "occupation", meaning, **44(4)**, [782]
    overview, **44(4)**, [781]
    priority of other tax provisions,
      44(4), [783]
    recovery of tax—
      certificates of tax paid, **44(4)**, [795]
      person not assessed, where consideration
        receivable by, **44(4)**, [794]
  scheme, disclosure of—
    amendment of provisions, **43(S)**, 584–8
    notifiability, doubt as to, **43(S)**, 584–5
    order for, **43(S)**, 586
    pre-disclosure enquiry, **43(S)**, 586
    reasons for non-disclosure, supporting
      information, **43(S)**, 586
    Special Commissioners, procedure of,
      43(S), 587
    supplemental information, **43(S)**, 585
  schemes—
    commencement and savings, **43(2)**, [525]
    disclosure of, **43(S)**, 1309–12
    information, form and manner of
      providing, **43(2)**, [522]
    notifiable arrangements—
      definitions, **43(2)**, [524]
      duty to notify Board of number,
        43(2), [520]
      legal professional privilege, **43(2)**, [521]
      meaning, **43(2)**, [513]
      not involving promoter, duties of parties
        to, **43(2)**, [517]
      reference number, **43(2)**, [518]
      regulations, **43(2)**, [523]

tax avoidance—*contd*
  schemes—*contd*
    notifiable proposal—
      definitions, **43(2)**, [524]
      meaning, **43(2)**, [513]
      reference number, **43(2)**, [518]
      regulations, **43(2)**, [523]
    promoter, **43(2)**, [514]
      dealing with outside UK, **43(2)**, [516]
      duties of, **43(2)**, [515]
      notification of number to client,
        43(2), [519]
  securities, transactions in. *See* **transactions in
    securities**
  stock lending arrangements, cash collateral
    under, **43(S)**, 193–5
  stock lending, involving, **43(2)**, [770]
  structured finance arrangements—
    chargeable gains treatment of acquisitions
      and disposals, **43(S)**, 204
    income receipts, factoring, **43(S)**, 197–203
  tax arbitrage, involving—
    deduction cases, **43(2)**, [736]
      commencement of provisions,
        43(2), [742]
      notices as to, **43(2)**, [740]
      rules as to, **43(2)**, [737]
    notices as to, **43(2)**, [736]
    qualifying schemes—
      hybrid effect, involving, **43(2)**, [765]
        connected persons, and, **43(2)**, [766]
      hybrid entities, involving, **43(2)**, [764]
    receipts cases, **43(2)**, [738]
      commencement of provisions,
        43(2), [742]
      notices as to, **43(2)**, [740]
      qualifying payments, rules as to,
        43(2), [739]
  trading losses, involving—
    excess sideways or capital gains relief,
      partners claiming, **44(4)**, [800]
    income receivable under—
      calculating amount of, **44(4)**, [801]
      charge to tax on, **44(4)**, [799]
      "post-December 2004 loss",
        meaning, **44(4)**, [803]
      "total amount of trade losses claimed",
        meaning, **44(4)**, [802]
    film-related trading losses, individuals
      claiming sideways or capital gains relief
      for, **44(4)**, [805]
      capital contribution by a partner,
        exclusion of amounts in calculating,
        44(4), [810]
      "capital contribution", meaning,
        44(4), [809]
      charge to tax on income receivable
        under, **44(4)**, [804]
      "disposal of right of individual to
        profits", meaning, **44(4)**, [807]
      double counting, prohibition against,
        44(4), [811]
      "film-related losses", meaning,
        44(4), [808]

tax avoidance—*contd*
  trading losses, involving—*contd*
    film-related trading losses, individuals
      claiming sideways or capital gains relief
      for—*contd*
        "non-taxable consideration", meaning,
          44(4), [806]
    licence-related trading losses, partners
      claiming relief for, **44(4)**, [813]
      "disposal of licence", meaning,
        44(4), [816]
      income receivable under—
        calculation of amount of,
          44(4), [814]–[815]
        charge to tax on, **44(4)**, [812]
    overview, **44(4)**, [798]
  transactions in land—
    disposing of land, meaning, **44(4)**, [761]
    gains from, charge to tax on, **44(4)**, [763]
      "another person", meaning, **44(4)**, [771]
    apportionments, **44(4)**, [772]
    clearance procedure, **44(4)**, [778]
    exemptions—
      disposals of shares in companies
        holding land as trading stock,
        44(4), [774]
      gain attributable to period before
        intention to develop formed,
        44(4), [773]
      private residences, **44(4)**, [775]
    income charged, **44(4)**, [766]
    information, power to obtain,
      44(4), [779]
    method of calculating gain, **44(4)**, [768]
    person liable, **44(4)**, [767]
    relevant transactions, sales and
      realisations, **44(4)**, [769]
    tracing value, **44(4)**, [770]
    valuations, **44(4)**, [772]
    land disposals, income treated as arising
      when gains obtained from some,
      44(4), [764]–[765]
    overview, **44(4)**, [760]
    priority of other income tax provisions,
      44(4), [762]
    recovery of tax—
      certificates of tax paid, **44(4)**, [777]
      person not assessed, where consideration
        receivable by, **44(4)**, [776]
    taxation of capital gains on, **44(1)**, [520],
      [521]
  transactions in securities—
    clearance of—
      application for, **44(4)**, [709]
      clearance notification, effect of,
        44(4), [710]
    income tax advantage—
      abnormal dividends—
        accrual condition, excessive,
          44(4), [702]
        exemptions or reliefs, used for,
          44(4), [694]
        return condition, excessive,
          44(4), [701]

tax avoidance—*contd*
  transactions in securities—*contd*
    income tax advantage—*contd*
      counteraction of—
        appeals from High Court or Court of
          Session, **44(4)**, [718]
        cases before High Court or Court of
          Session, **44(4)**, [716]
        information, power to obtain,
          44(4), [711]
        limit on the amount assessed,
          44(4), [707]
        Northern Ireland, proceedings in,
          44(4), [719]
        notices, **44(4)**, [706]
          appeals against, **44(4)**, [713]
          rehearing by tribunal of appeal
            against, **44(4)**, [714], [717]
        opposed notifications—
          determinations by tribunal,
            44(4), [705]
          statutory declarations, **44(4)**, [704]
        person liable to, **44(4)**, [692]–[693]
          death of, **44(4)**, [720]
        preliminary notification, **44(4)**, [703]
        statement of case by tribunal for
          opinion of High Court or Court of
          Session, **44(4)**, [715]
        timing of assessments, **44(4)**, [708]
      deductions from profits obtained
        following distributions of dealings,
        44(4), [695]
      meaning, **44(4)**, [691]
      overview, **44(4)**, [690]
      receipt of consideration—
        company's assets, future receipts or
          trading stock, representing,
          44(4), [696]
        relevant company distribution, in
          connection with, **44(4)**, [697]
      relevant company—
        meaning, **44(4)**, [699]
        receipt of assets of, **44(4)**, [698]
    "transactions in securities", meaning,
      44(4), [721]
    transitional provisions and savings,
      44(4), [1059]
    tribunal, **44(4)**, [712]
  transfer of assets abroad—
    accrued income profits and related interest,
      amounts corresponding to, **44(4)**, [755]
    "assets", meaning, **44(4)**, [725]
    associated operation, meaning, **44(4)**, [727]
    benefit received, charge where,
      44(4), [739]–[743]
      income charged, **44(4)**, [741]
      non-domiciled individuals, **44(4)**, [743]
      non-transferors receiving benefit as result
        of relevant transaction, **44(4)**, [740]
      reduction amount charged, **44(4)**, [742]
    capital sums received, charge where,
      44(4), [735]–[738]
      capital receipt conditions, **44(4)**, [737]
      deductions and reliefs, **44(4)**, [754]
      non-domiciled individuals, **44(4)**, [738]

tax avoidance—*contd*
transfer of assets abroad—*contd*
capital sums received, charge where—*contd*
rates of tax applicable, **44(4)**, [753]
definitions, **44(4)**, [724]–[727]
duplication of charge, no, **44(4)**, [751]
exemptions—
all relevant transactions—
both pre-5 December 2005 and
post-4 December 2005, **44(4)**, [748]
post-4 December 2005, **44(4)**, [745]
pre-5 December 2005, **44(4)**, [747]
"commercial transaction", meaning,
44(4), [746]
generally, **44(4)**, [744]
partial, **44(4)**, [749]–[750]
information, power to obtain, **44(4)**, [756]
overview, **44(4)**, [722]
"person abroad", meaning, **44(4)**, [726]
power to enjoy income, charge where,
44(4), [728]–[734]
controlled foreign company involvement,
reduction in amount charged where,
44(4), [733]
deductions and reliefs, **44(4)**, [754]
enjoyment conditions, **44(4)**, [731]
non-domiciled individuals, **44(4)**, [734]
rates of tax applicable, **44(4)**, [753]
special rules where benefit provided out
of income of person abroad,
44(4), [732]
restrictions on particulars—
banks, provided by, **44(4)**, [758]
solicitors, provided by, **44(4)**, [757]
Special Commissioners' jurisdiction on
appeals, **44(4)**, [759]
transitional provisions and savings,
44(4), [1059]
transfer of securities. *See* **securities**

tax claim
amendment, **42**, [263]
appeals, **42**, [263]
consequential, **42**, [172]
corporation tax. *See* **corporation tax**
enquiry into—
amendment of claims, **42**, [263]
completion of, **42**, [263]
documents, power to call for, **42**, [263]
power of, **42**, [263]
further assessment, in relation to, **42**, [170],
[171]
giving effect to, **42**, [263]
incapacitated person, on behalf of, **42**, [168]
income tax purposes, for, **43(1)**, [363]
making, **42**, [263]
time limit for, **42**, [169]
meaning, **42**, [263]
potential claimants, notice to, **43(1)**, [360]
procedure for making, **42**, [168], [263]
records, keeping and preserving, **42**, [263]
relief involving two or more years, for,
42, [264]
Special Commissioners, jurisdiction of,
42, [178]

tax claim—*contd*
time limit for, **42**, [169]

tax credit
amendment of provisions, **43(1)**, [316]
annual review by Treasury, **40(2)**, [401]
awards, period of, **40(2)**, [365]
changes of circumstances, notifications of,
40(2), [366]
charities, transitional relief for, **43(1)**, [318],
[331]
child. *See* **child tax credit**
civil partnership, relationship arising through,
27, [880], [969]
claims—
generally, **40(2)**, [363]
initial decisions, **40(2)**, [374]
other revised decisions, **40(2)**, [376]
regulations, **40(2)**, [364]
revised decisions after notifications,
40(2), [375]
Crown employment, **40(2)**, [404]
decisions after final notice, **40(2)**, [378]
disabled person's, abolition of, **40(2)**, [361]
documents, powers as to, **40(2)**, [396]
final notice, **40(2)**, [377]
foreign distributions, for, **43(S)**, 1125–30
fraud, **40(2)**, [395]
free school lunches, supply of information
on, **15(2)**, [698]–[699]
friendly society, distributions to, **43(1)**, [356]
HM Revenue and Customs—
annual reports to Treasury, **40(2)**, [400]
decisions by—
after final notice, **40(2)**, [378]
appeals against, **40(2)**, [398], [399]
temporary modifications, **40(2)**, [420]
initial, **40(2)**, [374]
notice of, **40(2)**, [383]
official error, subject to, **40(2)**, [381]
revisions—
after notifications, **40(2)**, [375]
on discovery, **40(2)**, [380]
other, **40(2)**, [376]
enquire, power to, **40(2)**, [379]
information—
provision of, **40(2)**, [429]
requirements, **40(2)**, [382]
notices, giving of, **40(2)**, [406]
overpayment by, **40(2)**, [388], [389]
interest on, **40(2)**, [397]
payment and management by, **40(2)**, [362],
[384]
penalties, determined by, **40(2)**, [428]
underpayment by, **40(2)**, [390]
immigration control, persons subject to,
40(2), [402]
inalienability, **40(2)**, [405]
income test, **40(2)**, [367]
individual savings accounts, for, **43(1)**, [354]
information—
administrative arrangements, **40(2)**, [415]
exchange of, **40(2)**, [429]
powers to use, **40(2)**, [429]

tax credit—contd
information—contd
provision by HM Revenue and Customs,
40(2), [429]
overpayments, 40(2), [388], [389]
interest on, 40(2), [397]
parliamentary control of instruments,
40(2), [423]
payments, 40(2), [384]
penalties—
determination of, by HM Revenue and
Customs, 40(2), [428]
failure to comply with requirements,
40(2), [392]
incorrect statements, for, 40(2), [391]
mitigation of, 40(2), [428]
proceedings, 40(2), [428]
recovery of, HM Revenue and Customs,
40(2), [428]
time limits for, 40(2), [428]
polygamous marriages, 40(2), [403]
provisional repayment regime, end of,
43(2), [51]
rate, 40(2), [373]
regulations, orders and schemes, power to
make, 40(2), [422]
remediation of land, expenditure on. See
contaminated land
Schedule 13 to Finance Act 2002, claims
under, 43(1), [404]
tax exempt payments, 43(S), 875
unauthorised disclosure of information,
15(2), [697]
underpayments, 40(2), [390]
working families', abolition, 40(2), [361]
working tax credit. See working tax credit

tax deposit
certificate of, 19(2), [1022]

tax penalty. See also customs duties
additional provision for, 43(S), 957
agent, failure by, 43(S), 1337
amended provisions, 43(S), 1321–6
appeals, 43(S), 1336
appeals against, 42, [184]
assessment, 43(S), 1336
certificate of non-liability to income tax,
giving of, 42, [234]
Commissioners, proceedings before, 42, [238]
company officers, liability of, 43(S), 1337
company records, failure to keep and
preserve, 43(1), [395]
company tax return—
failure to deliver, 43(1), [394]
incorrect or uncorrected, 43(1), [394]
consequential repeals, 43(S), 1338
court, proceedings before, 42, [239]
criminal proceedings, saving for, 42, [244]
deduction of income tax, refusal to allow,
42, [246]
degrees of culpability, 43(S), 1332
determination of—
appeals, 42, [237]
death of person incurring, 42, [236]

tax penalty—contd
determination of—contd
officer of board, by, 42, [235], [236]
time limit, 42, [242]
disclosure of information, 42, [991], [992]
disclosure, reduction for, 43(S), 1334–5
double jeopardy, 43(S), 1338
errors, for, 43(S), 1321–6
European Economic Interest Grouping, on,
43(1), [406]
evasion of tax or duty, for. See customs
duties
evidence in proceedings, 42, [240]
admissibility not affected by offer of
settlement, 42, [245]
failure to notify, for, 43(S), 1328–39
Finance Act 2004, Pt 7, failure to notify
under, 42, [232]
fraudulent conduct, admissibility of evidence
not affected by offer of settlement, 42, [245]
incorrect accounts, for, 42, [224], [225]
interaction, 43(S), 1335
interest on, 42, [243]
interpretation, 43(S), 1338
late payment surcharge, and, 43(S), 1335
mitigation of, 42, [241]
multiple, in respect of same accounting
period, 43(1), [406]
potential lost revenue, meaning,
43(S), 1333–4
power to obtain information and documents,
as to, 43(S), 1291–4
reasonable excuse, effect of, 43(S), 1337
recovery of—
procedure for, 42, [206], [238]
time limit for, 42, [242]
return—
failure to make, 42, [222]
incorrect, assisting in making, 42, [233]
special penalties, 42, [230]
special reduction, 43(S), 1335
special return, failure to make, 42, [229]
standard amount, 43(S), 1333
transitory provisions, 42, [272]
two or more, incurring, 42, [228]
VAT and excise wrongdoing, for,
43(S), 1328–39
windfall tax, relating to, 43(1), [329]

tax relief
agreement to forgo, 43(S), 1373–4
meaning, 43(S), 1374

tax reserve certificates
income arising from, 44(1), [31]

tax return
agency workers, remuneration, 42, [121]
claims for capital allowances in, 43(1), [554]
commencement of amended provisions,
43(S), 573
company, 43(1), [362]
accounts required, 43(1), [394]
amendment by company, 43(1), [394]

tax return—*contd*
  company—*contd*
    chargeable gains, information about,
      43(1), [394]
    claims. *See* **corporation tax**
    conclusiveness of amounts stated in,
      43(1), [406]
    delivery, meaning, **43(1)**, [394]
    different Cases of Schedule D, choice
      between, **43(1)**, [405]
    enquiry into, **43(1)**, [396]
    failure to deliver, penalty for, **43(1)**, [394]
    filing date, **43(1)**, [394]
    fraud or negligence, penalty for,
      43(1), [406]
    further, **43(1)**, [396]
    incorrect or uncorrected, penalty for,
      43(1), [394]
    Inland Revenue, correction by,
      43(1), [394]
    late delivery, excuse for, **43(1)**, [394]
    mistake in, **43(1)**, [398]
    notice requiring, **43(1)**, [394]
    partnership, including amount for share in,
      43(1), [394]
    period beginning before appointed day,
      notice relating to, **43(1)**, [394]
    period for which required, **43(1)**, [394]
    records, keeping and preservation of,
      43(1), [395]
    self-assessment, including, **43(1)**, [394]
  correction and amendment, **43(S)**, 952–3
  determination of tax where none delivered,
    43(S), 572
  electronic filing, mandatory, **43(S)**, 574
  electronic lodgment of—
    conditions, **42**, [269]
    documents supporting, **42**, [268]
    hard copies of information, **42**, [270]
    status of information, **42**, [271]
  employees' earnings, of, **42**, [119], [314]
  enquiry—
    amendment by—
      officer during, **42**, [106]
      taxpayer during, **42**, [105]
    completion of, **42**, [148]
    into, **43(S)**, 578
    notice of, **42**, [104]
    referral of questions during—
      determination, effect of, **42**, [147]
      effect of, **42**, [146]
      notice of, **42**, [143]
      regulations, **42**, [145]
      withdrawal of notice, **42**, [144]
  ethane, alternative valuation of, as to,
    42, [450]
  European Economic Interest Grouping, of,
    42, [115], [231]
  failure to make, **42**, [222], [223]
  failure to make, penalties for—
    amount of, **43(S)**, 1738–40
    appeals, **43(S)**, 1742
    application of provisions, **43(S)**, 1419–20
    assessment, **43(S)**, 1741–2
    disclosure, reductions for, **43(S)**, 1740–1

tax return—*contd*
  failure to make, penalties for—*contd*
    double jeopardy, **43(S)**, 1744
    other penalties and surcharges, interaction
      with, **43(S)**, 1741
    partnerships, **43(S)**, 1743
    reasonable excuse, **43(S)**, 1743
    special disclosure, **43(S)**, 1741
    table of, **43(S)**, 1737–8
    tax liability, determination geared to,
      43(S), 1743
  fees and commissions, of, **42**, [120]
  form of, **42**, [253]
  incorrect—
    assisting in making, **42**, [233]
    error, failure to remedy, **42**, [226]
    making, **42**, [224], [226]
  lodgers and inmates, of, **42**, [118]
  loss or destruction of, **42**, [252]
  meaning, **42**, [258]
  none made, determination of tax on,
    42, [150]
  oil field participator, by, **42**, [346], [487],
    [882]
  partnership—
    amendment of, **43(S)**, 571
    company as partner, where, **43(S)**, 570
    contents of, **42**, [108]
    different Cases of Schedule D, choice
      between, **42**, [114]
    enquiry into—
      amendment of return during, **42**, [113]
      completion of, **42**, [149]
      notice of, **42**, [112]
    error in, **43(S)**, 572
    error or mistake in, **42**, [162]
    failure to make, penalty for, **43(S)**, 572
    HM Revenue and Customs, correction
      by, **42**, [111]
    incorrect, **42**, [225], [226]
    partnership statement in, **42**, [109]
    requirement of, **42**, [108]
    taxpayer, amendment by, **42**, [110]
    time for delivery of, **43(S)**, 570
  person responsible for oil field, by, **42**, [346]
  personal, **42**, [99]
    amended provisions, **43(S)**, 567–8
    amendment by taxpayer, **42**, [102]
    amendment of, **43(S)**, 571
    enquiry into. *See* enquiry *above*
    failure to make, penalty for, **43(S)**, 572
    HM Revenue and Customs, correction
      by, **42**, [103]
    time for delivery of, **43(S)**, 568
  persons treated as employees, of, **42**, [314]
  records kept for purposes of, **42**, [116]
  self-assessment, including, **42**, [101];
    43(S), 571
  special, failure to make, **42**, [229]
  special penalties, **42**, [230]
  taxable income belonging to another, persons
    having, **42**, [117]
  trustee's, **42**, [100]
    amended provisions, **43(S)**, 569
    amendment by taxpayer, **42**, [102]

tax return—*contd*
trustee's—*contd*
amendment of, **43(S)**, 571
enquiry into. *See* enquiry *above*
failure to make, penalty for, **43(S)**, 572
HM Revenue and Customs, correction
by, **42**, [103]
time for delivery of, **43(S)**, 569
windfall tax, for, **43(1)**, [329]

taxation
criminal investigation—
Revenue and Customs, powers of,
43(S), 562–4
restriction on exercise of functions,
43(S), 565
enforcement, international arrangements,
43(S), 157–8
double taxation agreements, procedure,
43(S), 160
information powers, **43(S)**, 158–9
recovery of debts, **43(S)**, 159
error or mistake—
limitation period, **43(2)**, [526]
prescriptive period, **43(2)**, [527]
foot-and-mouth disease, deferment due to,
10, [796]
information, exchange of, **43(2)**, [244]
mutual legal assistance, transfer of functions,
12(4), [511], [582]
Parliament, consent of to, **10**, [26]
payment—
cheque, by, **43(S)**, 576–7
mandatory electronic payment,
43(S), 575–6
penalties—
agency provisions, **43(S)**, 728–9
amended provisions, **43(S)**, 1753–5
appeal against determination, **43(S)**, 727–8
assessment, **43(S)**, 726–7
commencement of provisions, **43(S)**, 579
company officers, liability of, **43(S)**, 729
culpability, degrees of, **43(S)**, 722
currency of agreement for deferred
payment, suspension during,
43(S), 1421–2
deliberate tax defaulters, publication of
details of, **43(S)**, 1410–11
disclosure, reductions for, **43(S)**, 725
double jeopardy, **43(S)**, 729
failure to make returns, for—
amount of, **43(S)**, 1738–40
appeals, **43(S)**, 1742
application of provisions,
43(S), 1419–20
assessment, **43(S)**, 1741–2
disclosure, reductions for, **43(S)**, 1740–1
double jeopardy, **43(S)**, 1744
other penalties and surcharges,
interaction with, **43(S)**, 1741
partnerships, **43(S)**, 1743
reasonable excuse, **43(S)**, 1743
special disclosure, **43(S)**, 1741
table of, **43(S)**, 1737–8

taxation—*contd*
penalties—*contd*
failure to make returns, for—*contd*
tax liability, determination geared to,
43(S), 1743
failure to pay tax, for—
agreement for deferred payment,
suspension during currency of,
43(S), 1750
amount of, **43(S)**, 1749
appeals, **43(S)**, 1751
application of provisions, **43(S)**, 1420
assessment, **43(S)**, 1750–1
assessments and determinations in default
of return, **43(S)**, 1748
double jeopardy, **43(S)**, 1752
reasonable excuse, **43(S)**, 1752
partnerships, **43(S)**, 1750
table of, **43(S)**, 1745–8
inaccurate information and documents,
for, **43(S)**, 1689
interaction with other penalties, **43(S)**, 726
partnerships, liability of, **43(S)**, 729
potential lost revenue—
delayed tax, **43(S)**, 725
losses, **43(S)**, 724
meaning, **43(S)**, 1410
multiple errors, **43(S)**, 724
normal rule, **43(S)**, 723
relevant, meaning, **43(S)**, 1410
special reduction, **43(S)**, 726
standard amount, **43(S)**, 723
suspension, **43(S)**, 727
table of, **43(S)**, 721–2
underassessment, for, **43(S)**, 722
restructuring of coal industry, arising from. *See
under* **British Coal Corporation**
(restructuring)
Scottish Parliament, tax-varying power of. *See*
Scottish Parliament

taxation appeals
agreement, settled by, **42**, [185]
assessment, against—
General Commissioners, to, **42**, [157]
notice of, **42**, [156]
right of, **42**, [155]
Special Commissioners, to, **42**, [158],
[159], [175]
chargeable gains, regulations about, **42**, [192]
Court of Appeal, to, **42**, [187], [188]
High Court, to, **42**, [187], [188]
House of Lords, to, **42**, [187], [188]
inheritance tax. *See* **inheritance tax**
meaning, **42**, [181]
out of time, brought, **42**, [182]
penalty, appeal against, **42**, [184]
petroleum revenue tax—
allowable expenditure for, **42**, [349]
in connection with, **42**, [346]
procedure for, **42**, [183]
recovery of tax pending, **42**, [186]
regulations, **42**, [189]
Special Commissioners, from, **42**, [188]
statement of case following, **42**, [187]

taxis and taxicabs. *See also* **hackney carriage**
  advance booking, **37**, [361]
  areas for hire, designation of, **37**, [360]
  authorised place, operation from, **37**, [360]
  cab, meaning, **36**, [571], [587]
  cabman, penalty for defrauding, **36**, [570]
  code—
    meaning, **37**, [363]
    modifications by Secretary of State,
      37, [363]
  disabled persons—
    accessibility regulations—
      exemptions from, **7(1)**, [399]
      forgery and false statements, **7(1)**, [425]
      general, **7(1)**, [396]
      new licences conditional on compliance
        with, **7(1)**, [398]
    guide dogs, carrying of, **7(1)**, [401]
    hearing dogs, carrying of, **7(1)**, [401]
    wheelchairs, carrying of passengers in,
      7(1), [400]; **38(2)**, [675], [676]
  fares, power to make byelaws as to, **36**, [416]
  fares, provisions regarding, **37**, [360]
  immediate hiring at separate fares, **37**, [360]
  licence holder, application for PSV operator's
    licence by, **37**, [362]
  licence, meaning, **37**, [363]
  licensed, meaning, **37**, [363]
  licensing—
    appeals, **37**, [367]
    authorities, **37**, [360]
    charges, **37**, [80]
    control of numbers, **37**, [366]
    extension of, **37**, [365]
    generally. *See* **hackney carriage**
  local transport services, use in providing,
    37, [362]
  London taxis—
    appeals, **37**, [367]
    licence holder, application for PSV
      operator's licence by, **37**, [364]
  meaning, **36**, [995]
  non-obligatory journeys, regulation of fares,
    36, [768]
  obligatory journeys, increase of length,
    36, [769]
  parking of, **36**, [770]
  plate, mark or sign, display of, **37**, [360]
  privilege system, abolition, **36**, [586]
  public service vehicle operator's licence,
    application by taxi licence holder, **37**, [362]
    London, in, **37**, [364]
  railway station, at, **36**, [586]
  schemes for hire at separate fares, **37**, [361]
  Secretary of State, powers of, **37**, [363]
  sharing use of, **37**, [361]
  taximeter—
    fares to be paid by, **36**, [585]
    inspection and testing, **36**, [951]
    meaning, **36**, [587], [963]
    private hire vehicles, **36**, [951], [954]
    tampering with or altering, **36**, [954]
  touting for services, **12(2)**, [245]
  use of words as roof-signs, **36**, [995]

taxpayer
  documents—
    appropriate judicial authority, meaning,
      42, [134]
    entry with warrant to obtain, **42**, [132]
    falsification of, **42**, [131]
    notice requiring, **42**, [129]
    opportunity to deliver, **42**, [129]
    order for delivery of, **42**, [130], [262]
    power to call for, **42**, [127]
    removal, procedure on, **42**, [133]
  persons treated as, **42**, [127]

teacher
  aided schools, in, dismissal of, **16**, [786]
  General Teaching Council. *See* **General
    Teaching Council; General Teaching
    Council for Wales**
  governor, as. *See* **county school, etc**
  head—
    discipline, responsibility for, **15(2)**, [54]
    qualifications, **15(1)**, [798]; **15(2)**, [448]
  loss of office, compensation for, **33(1)**, [139]
  misconduct, prohibition from teaching for,
    15(2), [455]–[457]
  pay and conditions. *See* **teachers' pay and
    conditions**
  performance, appraisal of, **15(2)**, [444]
  primary and secondary school. *See* **primary
    and secondary schools**
  qualified—
    head teacher to be, **15(2)**, [448]
    meaning, **15(2)**, [445]
    registered, requirement to be, **15(2)**, [447]
    requirement to be, **15(2)**, [446]
    specification of qualification or course,
      15(2), [458]
  registered, code of practice, **15(1)**, [787]
  registration. *See* **General Teaching Council**
  regulations, **15(1)**, [357]
  remuneration. *See* **teachers' pay and
    conditions**
  superannuation. *See* **superannuation of
    teachers**
  training—
    former employees, payments to,
      15(1), [469]
    induction period, requirement to serve,
      15(1), [799]
    inspection of, **15(1)**, [470];
      15(S), Education 286

Teacher Training Agency
  Training and Development Agency for
    Schools, becoming, **15(2)**, [665]

teachers
  General Teaching Council. *See* **General
    Teaching Council; General Teaching
    Council for Wales**

teachers' pay and conditions
  contractual terms, avoidance of certain,
    15(1), [417]

teachers' pay and conditions—*contd*
  pay and conditions orders—
    consultation by Secretary of State,
      15(2), [440]
    education action zones, in relation to
      schools in, **15(2)**, [442]
    guidance regarding, **15(2)**, [441]
    making, **15(2)**, [436]
    scope, **15(2)**, [437]
    supplementary provisions, **15(2)**, [439]
    transfer of employment, teachers on,
      15(2), [443]
  pay-scale, application of, **15(2)**, [460]
  review body—
    allowances, **15(2)**, [527]
    chairman, **15(2)**, [433], [527]
    consultation by, **15(2)**, [435]
    deputy chairman, **15(2)**, [527]
    functions, **15(2)**, [434]
    membership, **15(2)**, [433], [527]
    proceedings, **15(2)**, [527]
    reference to, **15(2)**, [439]
    remuneration, **15(2)**, [527]
    transitional provisions, **15(2)**, [527]

teachers' superannuation
  administrative expenses, **33(1)**, [130]
  allowances—
    assignment of, **15(1)**, [168]
    payment of, **15(1)**, [168]
  annuity—
    assignment of, **15(1)**, [168]
    payment of, **15(1)**, [168]
  contributions, collection of, **15(1)**, [164]
  deferred annuity fund—
    annuity from, **15(1)**, [162]
    payment into, **15(1)**, [162]
  disablement allowance—
    provisions on, **15(1)**, [163]
    reconsideration of, **15(1)**, [163], [177]
    sixty-five years, grantee attaining,
      15(1), [163], [177]
  elementary school teacher, certificated,
    provisions on, **15(1)**, [162]
  general note, **15(1)**, [1]
  Isle of Man, application of provisions,
    15(1), [178]
  Jersey, in, **15(1)**, [172]–[176]
  misconduct, effect of, **15(1)**, [167]
  pension increase, provision for,
    33(1), [112]–[113], [115]
  provision for, **33(1)**, [130]
  questions as to, determination of, **33(1)**, [132]
  recorded service, meaning, **15(1)**, [162]
  regulations—
    provisions included in, **33(1)**, [130], [146]
    retrospective effect, **33(1)**, [133]
  rules on, **15(1)**, [165]
  transitional provisions, **33(1)**, [149]
  Treasury and Education department deciding
    questions on, **15(1)**, [166]

team ministry
  1968 Measure, established under, **14**, 991–2
  amended provisions, **14(S)**, 179–80

team ministry—*contd*
  benefice, held in plurality, in, **14**, 988
  meetings, **14**, 988
  office held for term of years, compensation,
    14, 1095
  parochial church council, members of,
    14, 711
  parochial church meeting, attending,
    14, 703–4
  pastoral order relating to, **14**, 1013
  pastoral scheme—
    altering, **14**, 994–5
    benefice, dissolving, **14**, 995
    establishing, **14**, 986–9, 1084–7
    terminating, **14**, 994–5, 1085
  patronage board, **14**, 1085
  rector—
    admission, deemed, **14**, 1087
    office of, **14**, 986
  team chapter, **14**, 986
  team council—
    amended provisions, **14(S)**, 179–80
    scheme for, **14**, 718–19
  vicar—
    abolition of office, **14**, 997
    house, provisions applying to, **14**, 794–5
    office of, **14**, 986
    rent free house on glebe land for, **14**, 858

technical and industrial institution
  conveyance of land for—
    agreement, by, **15(1)**, [156]
    governing body, to, **15(1)**, [156]
    limited owners, by, **15(1)**, [158]
    sale, exchange or gift, by, **15(1)**, [157]
  governing body, **15(1)**, [154]
  Land Clauses Acts applying to, **15(1)**, [155]
  meaning, **15(1)**, [153]
  public, to be, **15(1)**, [159]
  sale or exchange of land, **15(1)**, [160]

telecommunications. *See also* **British**
Telecommunications plc; post office;
wireless telegraphy
  Airports Authority, application of code to,
    4(1), [303]
  apparatus—
    conduits, installed in, **45**, [62], [72]
    on or under highway, **36**, [1231]
    saving as to, **35(1)**, [92]
    sharing, effect of agreements concerning,
      45, [72]
    See also **telecommunications code**
  Cable & Wireless Ltd—
    associated companies, consequential
      provisions, **45**, [22]
    Commonwealth telegraphs—
      agreement, **45**, [25]
      operating company, **45**, [25], [26]
      pensions, **45**, [26]
      referees, **45**, [27]
    compensation, **45**, [20]
    employees, rights of, **45**, [26]
    Imperial telegraphs, **45**, [17], [18]

telecommunications—*contd*
  Cable & Wireless Ltd—*contd*
    operating company, consequential
      provisions, **45**, [21]
    regulations, **45**, [26]
    shares, disposal or transfer of, **45**, [20], [41]
    summary of provisions, **45**, [1]
    Treasury—
      arrangements with, **45**, [18]
      disposal of shares by, **45**, [41]
      instruments, exemption from stamp
        duty, **45**, [42]
      transfer of shares to, **45**, [20]
  cable programme service. *See* **cable services**
  call boxes, amendment of enactments relating
    to, **45**, [73]
  Channel Islands, extension of provisions to,
    45, [4], [68]
  civil aviation, safety requirements by Secretary
    of State, **4(1)**, [99]
  code, **45**, [72]
  Commonwealth. *See* Cable and Wireless Ltd
    above
  Commonwealth Telecommunications Bureau,
    45, [38]
  competition legislation, application, **45**, [177]
  conduits, use of, **45**, [62], [72]
  designs, transitional provisions as to, **45**, [69]
  directions by Secretary of State, **45**, [67]
  Director General—
    annual report by, **45**, [58]
    appointment, **45**, [57]
    directions by Secretary of State, **45**, [67]
    remuneration and allowances, **45**, [71]
    reports by, **45**, [58]
    seal, authentication of, **45**, [71]
  documents as evidence, **45**, [71]
  financial provisions generally, **45**, [181]
  fly lines, installation, **45**, [72]
  highways, amendment of 1980 Act, **45**, [73]
  housing action trust, on land acquired by,
    22, [930]
  housing, Northern Ireland, amendment of
    provisions, **45**, [73]
  information and advice, general restrictions on
    disclosure, **45**, [63]
  interception. *See under* **communications;
    post office**
  interpretation, general, **45**, [67]
  Isle of Man, extension of provisions to,
    45, [4], [68]
  local Acts, general adaptations, **45**, [73]
  London Building Acts, amendments, **45**, [73]
  messages, interception generally. *See*
    communications
  national security, directions as to interests of,
    45, [61], [67]
  new towns, Northern Ireland, orders, **45**, [73]
  non-trading income—
    charge to tax, **44(3)**, [624]
    deductions in calculating income charged,
      44(3), [627]
    income charged, **44(3)**, [625]
    payments received after deduction of tax,
      44(3), [628]

telecommunications—*contd*
  non-trading income—*contd*
    person liable for tax, **44(3)**, [626]
  Northern Ireland, application of provisions,
    45, [70]
  offences—
    bodies corporate, by, **45**, [179]
    summary proceedings, **45**, [64]
  opencast coal mining, protection against
    interference by, **17(1)**, [207]
  operators, meaning, **45**, [73]
  orders, power to make, **45**, [65]
  patents for inventions, transitional provisions as
    to, **45**, [49]
  Port of London Act, saving in, **39(2)**, [387]
  post office, functions, transfer of, **34**, [568],
    [576]
  Postmaster General, transfer of functions of—
    Commonwealth telegraphs, **34**, [577]
    wireless telegraphy, **34**, [576]
  priority of, **10**, [1015]
  providers, relaxation of licence restrictions,
    45, [713]
    See also telephone call box *below*
  public systems. *See* systems *below*
  registered designs, transitional provisions,
    45, [49]
  rights as to, savings, **36**, [1386]
  rights of, in clearance area, **22**, [257]
  schemes, power to make, **45**, [65]
  seal, **45**, [71]
  Secretary of State, annual report on
    functions, **45**, [734]
  sewer, use as conduit, **45**, [62]
  signals—
    meaning, **45**, [102]
    transmission of additional services. *See*
      independent television (additional
      services)
    wireless telegraphy, by, use for television
      broadcasts, **45**, [102]
  street works, **45**, [72]
  system—
    interception of messages. *See*
      communications
    local delivery services. *See under*
      independent television
  telephone call box—
    enactments relating to, **45**, [73]
    substitution of references to, **45**, [73]
  telephone numbers. *See* **telephone numbers**
  television broadcasting frequencies, additional
    services on. *See* **independent television**
    (additional services)
  trade profits—
    professions and vocations, rules applying,
      44(3), [834]
    relevant rights, meaning, **44(3)**, [835]
    revaluation, credit or debts arising from,
      44(3), [837]
    revenue, expenditure treated as,
      44(3), [836]
  transitional provisions and savings—
    generally, **45**, [69]
    patents for inventions, **45**, [49]

telecommunications—*contd*
  transitional provisions and savings—*contd*
    registered designs, **45**, [49]
    transfer date, in force on, **45**, [74]
  water main conduit, use of, **45**, [62]
  waterworks involving, **49**, [347]

telecommunications code
  telecommunications code **45**, [72]

telegraphic line
  stopping up of highway, saving for, **9**, [145]

telegraphs and telephones. *See*
telecommunications

telephone claims
  income tax purposes, **43(1)**, [363]

telephone numbers
  access to, conditions to secure, **45**, [475]
  adoption of, **45**, [476]
  allocation—
    conditions about, **45**, [476]
    OFCOM's withdrawal of, **45**, [479]
  conditions to secure access to, **45**, [475]
  modification of documents referred to in
    numbering conditions, **45**, [478]
  National Telephone Numbering Plan,
    45, [474]
  non-providers, conditions binding, **45**, [477]
  numbering reorganisations, **45**, [480]
  OFCOM's duty as to, **45**, [481]

telephones
  mobile. *See* **mobile telephones**

teletext services
  co-operation with provider, **45**, [647]
  DBS contracts, replacement, **45**, [198]
  interference with other services, conditions
    prohibiting, **45**, [668]
  international obligations, compliance with,
    45, [701]
  licence—
    applications for, **45**, [105], [760]
    award of, revocation of, **45**, [760]
    enforcement, **45**, [761]
    grant of, notices regarding, **45**, [760]
    new licensing round, report in anticipation
      of, **45**, [609]
    payments required under, **45**, [761]
    period—
      meaning, **45**, [762]
      shortening of, **45**, [761]
    renewal of, **45**, [602], [603]
    replacement of existing, **45**, [601]
    reviews relating to, **45**, [605]–[608]
    revocation, **45**, [761]
  licensing of, **45**, [599]
  news provision, **45**, [655]
  providers, corrections and statements of
    findings by, **45**, [761]
  provision of, **45**, [103], [105], [197], [598]
    delegation of, **45**, [600]

teletext services—*contd*
  regional matters, **45**, [660]
  service policy—
    changes of, **45**, [640]
    statements by provider, **45**, [639]
  visually impaired, assistance for, **45**, [677]

television. *See also* **broadcasting**
  apparatus. *See* sets *below*
  archive, national, maintenance and funding,
    45, [175]
  Channels. *See* **independent television**
  closed-circuit, provision of, **12(2)**, [242]
  dealers. *See* sets *below*
  evidence in criminal proceedings. *See under*
    evidence
  foreign, proscription orders, **45**, [695]
    effect of, **45**, [696]
    notification, **45**, [697], [698]
  Gaelic, programmes in. *See* **Gaelic television**
  indecent display, provisions excluded,
    12(1), [714]
  independent. *See* **independent television**
  legislative amendments, minor and
    consequential, **45**, [202]
  licences—
    conditions of, **45**, [726]
    enforcement, **45**, [728]
    fees, **45**, [727]
    functions connected with, transfer to
      BBC, **45**, [171]
    information—
      disclosure of, **45**, [322]
      offences—
        directors, liability of, **45**, [325]
        generally, **45**, [324]
        unlawful disclosure, **45**, [324]
      use of, **45**, [323]
    OFCOM, licensing functions transferred
      to, **45**, [755]
    receiver, for, **45**, [725]
    restrictions on, **45**, [726]
    revocation, **45**, [726]
    social security information—
      provision to BBC, **45**, [322]
      unlawful disclosure, **45**, [324]
      use of, **45**, [323]
  multiplex services—
    frequencies reserved for qualifying services,
      powers where, **45**, [622]
    generally, **45**, [621]
    reservation of spectrum for, **45**, [781]
  programme services, meaning, **45**, [184]
  receivers. *See* sets *below*
  satellite. *See* **satellite television**
  services—
    independent. *See generally* **independent**
      television
    meaning, **45**, [184]
  sets—
    auction, sale by, **45**, [32]
    BBC, powers, **45**, [29]
    credit-sale contracts, **45**, [30]
    dealers—
      meaning, **45**, [32]

television—*contd*
  sets—*contd*
    dealers—*contd*
      particulars, recording and notification,
        45, [29], [35]–[37]
      transactions, notification to BBC,
        45, [29]
    enforcement of provisions, **45**, [31]
    false information, **45**, [31]
    forms, prescribed, **45**, [29]
    hire, information as to, **45**, [29]
    information required—
      additional, **45**, [30]
      generally, **45**, [29]
    meaning, **45**, [32]
    notices, service of, **45**, [31]
    offences, **45**, [31]
    particulars, noting and recording, **45**, [29],
      [35]–[37]
    receiver—
      licence required for use of, **45**, [725]
      meaning, **45**, [729]
    records, keeping of, **45**, [29], [35]–[37]
    sale, information as to, **45**, [29]
    See also dealers *above*
    transactions, notification and recording,
      45, [29], [35]–[37]
  Welsh. *See* **Welsh Authority**

temporary employment
  provision by Secretary of State, **16**, [65]

tenancy. *See also* **lease**
  agricultural. *See* **agricultural tenancy;**
    agricultural workers
  assignment of—
    racial discrimination in, **7(1)**, [158]
    sex discrimination in, **7(1)**, [73]
  assured. *See* **assured tenancy**
  beginning of, meaning, **22**, [839]
  collective, **9**, [316]
  co-ownership—
    meaning, **21**, [589]
    rent. *See* **housing association**
  defective house. *See* **defective housing**
  defective premises, **21**, [387]
  demoted. *See* **demoted tenancy**
  enfranchisement or extended lease,
    compensation for depreciation where,
    9, [315], [379]
  eviction. *See* **eviction**
  family intervention, termination, **24**, [833]
  fitness for human habitation—
    agricultural workers, houses for, **22**, [513]
    implied terms, **22**, [512]
    matters taken into consideration, **22**, [514]
    rent limit, **22**, [512]
    tenant required to effect, where, **22**, [512]
  inferior, continuation beyond term of
    superior, **21**, [226]
  interest subject to contract for grant of,
    compensation for depreciation where,
    9, [307]

tenancy—*contd*
  introductory. *See* **introductory tenancy**
  long—
    exceptions from, **22**, [106]
    meaning, **22**, [106], [207]
    security of tenure on ending of, **23**, [44],
      [55]
  long, protected. *See* **protected long tenancy**
  meaning, **21**, [389]; **22**, [421]; **23**, [542]
  possession orders, **24**, [869]
  private sector, transfer to, **22**, [831]
  protected. *See* **protected tenancy**
  protected shorthold. *See* **protected**
    shorthold tenancy
  public body, landlord's interest held by—
    meaning, **22**, [831]
    private sector, transfer to, **22**, [831]
    status of, **22**, [828]
  public to private sector, transferred, **22**, [831]
  regulated. *See* **regulated tenancy**
  secure. *See* **secure tenancy**
  shared ownership, enfranchisement or
    extension of lease, **21**, [334], [347]
  statutorily protected, meaning, **21**, [670]
  statutory. *See* **agricultural tenancy;**
    agricultural workers (housing);
    statutory tenancy
  summary of provisions, **20**, [1]
  terminated, replacement of, **24**, [870]
  vesting declaration, mistaken payment after,
    9, [398]

tenancy by the courtesy
  abolition, **20**, [9]
  entailed interest, devolution of, **20**, [741]
  qualification, former provisions, **20**, [9]

tenancy deposit
  information provided, **24**, [367]
  non-compliance, sanctions for, **24**, [369]
  proceedings, **24**, [368]
  requirements, **24**, [367]
  scheme—
    arrangements for, **24**, [366]
    custodial, **24**, [438]
    insurance, **24**, [438]
    provisions applying, **24**, [438]

tenant
  agricultural employee, provisions applying to,
    21, [666]
  audit of management by landlord—
    details of, **23**, [156]
    notice of—
      procedure following—
        details of, **23**, [159]
        superior landlord, obtaining
          information held by, **23**, [160]
      requirement for, **23**, [158]
    qualifying tenants, **23**, [155]
    right to, **23**, [154]
    rights exercisable in connection with,
      23, [157]
    supplementary provisions, **tit**, [161]

tenant—*contd*
   collective enfranchisement. *See* **collective
   enfranchisement (leasehold reform)**
   compensation on compulsory acquisition—
      agricultural holding, of, **9**, [347]
      business premises, of, **9**, [346]
      entitlement to, **9**, [77], [280]
   distress for rent owing. *See* **distress**
   information given to—
      assignment of landlord's interest, notice of,
         22, [506]
      business tenancies, exclusion of, **22**, [545]
      corporate landlord, request for details of,
         22, [505], [510]
      name and address of landlord, request for,
         22, [504]
      possible right to acquire landlord's interest,
         notice of, **22**, [507]
   insurance, rights relating to, **22**, [542], [554]
   landlord's interest, compulsory acquisition of.
      See **flats**
   lease, acquisition of new. *See* **lease
   (acquisition of new)**
   leasehold enfranchisement or extension,
      provisions on. *See* **leasehold
   enfranchisement, lease-hold extension**
   manager, application for appointment of,
      22, [736]
   meaning, **21**, [70], [637]
   protected. *See* **protected tenant**
   protected long tenancy, in. *See* **protected
   long tenancy**
   protected, mining subsidence damage to
      property of, **17(2)**, [21], [51]
   rehoused, compensation for compulsory
      acquisition where, **9**, [349]
   right of first refusal. *See* **flats**
   statutory. *See* **statutory tenant**

tenant for life
   absent, presumption of death, **20**, [17],
      [20]–[24]
   absolute owner having powers of, **20**, [524]
   consideration paid by, **20**, [563]
   conveyance, completion of transactions by,
      20, [574]
   conveyance of land to, **20**, [511]
   dealings with, **20**, [570]
   death of, **20**, [511]
      presumption of, **20**, [17], [20]–[24]
   exchange by—
      power of, **20**, [540]
      regulations, **20**, [542]
   improvements—
      concurrence in, **20**, [589]
      insurance of, **20**, [591]
      maintenance and repair of, **20**, [591]
      waste, protection as regards, **20**, [592]
   incumbrance—
      charging, **20**, [572]
      shifting, **20**, [571]
      varying, **20**, [572]
   interest, having parted with, **20**, [527]
   joint, **20**, [522]
   lease, accepting, **20**, [555]

tenant for life—*contd*
   lease of land by—
      building lease—
         duration of, **20**, [543]
         regulations, **20**, [546]
         variation of, **20**, [548]
      covenant of renewal, **20**, [545]
      duration of term, **20**, [543]
      forestry lease—
         duration of, **20**, [543]
         meaning, **20**, [618]
         regulations, **20**, [550]
      long term, conversion into, **20**, [564]
      mining lease—
         capitalisation, **20**, [549]
         duration of, **20**, [543]
         regulations, **20**, [547]
         variation of, **20**, [548]
      power of, **20**, [543]
      previous lease, confirming, **20**, [545]
      regrant, **20**, [554]
      regulations, **20**, [544]
      surrender of, **20**, [554]
      variation of, **20**, [561]
   limited owners having powers of, **20**, [523]
   married woman as, **20**, [528]
   meaning, **20**, [618]
   mines, working facilities grants, protection,
      17(1), [376]
   minor as, **20**, [529]
   notice of intention, giving, **20**, [602]
   notices served on, **20**, [614]
   person being, **20**, [522]
   power of attorney, delegation by, **48**, 478–9
   powers of—
      additional, grant of, **20**, [610]
      approval, giving, **20**, [561]
      assignment, not capable of, **20**, [605]
      claims, compromising, **20**, [560]
      consent, giving, **20**, [561]
      contract not to exercise, **20**, [605]
      contracts, entering into, **20**, [593]
      dwellings, provision of land for, **20**, [559]
      exercise of, **20**, [613]
      heirloom, sale of, **20**, [569]
      larger than in Act, grant of, **20**, [610]
      lease, to, **20**, [543]
      leasehold enfranchisement or extension,
         21, [301]
      licence, giving, **20**, [561]
      limitation of exercise of, **20**, [607]
      mansion, disposal of, **20**, [567]
      mortgage, raising money by, **20**, [573]
      options, to grant, **20**, [553]
      order of court, effecting transactions
         under, **20**, [566]; **21**, [141]
      person having, **20**, [526]
      predecessor's contracts, completion of,
         20, [565]
      public and charitable purposes, grant of
         land for, **20**, [557]
      public purposes, dedication of land for,
         20, [558]
      release, not capable of, **20**, [605]
      rent, apportionment of, **20**, [562]

tenant for life—*contd*

powers of—*contd*

reservations, making, **20**, [551]

restrictions—

imposition of, **20**, [551]

releasing, **20**, [560]

sale and exchange, of, **20**, [540]

saving for, **20**, [609]

small holdings, provision of land for, **20**, [559]

stipulations, making, **20**, [551]

streets, etc, dedication of, **20**, [558]

surface and minerals, dealing with, **20**, [552]

timber, cutting and sale of, **20**, [568]

water rights, grant of, **20**, [556]

purchaser dealing with—

beneficial interest vested in, **20**, [612]

protection of, **20**, [611]

sale by—

charge, power to accept as security, **20**, [578]

powers, **20**, [540]

regulations, **20**, [541]

rent, in consideration of, **20**, [541]

surrender of life estate by, **20**, [606]

trustee for other parties, as, **20**, [608]

tenant in common

future dispositions to, effect, **20**, [653]

tenant in tail. *See* **entail**

tenant management organisation

management agreements, **22**, [28]

meaning, **22**, [28]

tenement

London—

common staircase, lighting, **25(1)**, [515]

meaning, **25(1)**, [515]

tent

abatement notice to occupier of, **35(1)**, [170]

byelaws as to, **35(1)**, [170]

human habitation, use for—

control over, **35(1)**, [497]

order prohibiting, **35(1)**, [170]

public health provisions applicable to, **35(1)**, [170]

statutory nuisance, when, **35(1)**, [170]

tenure. *See* **land**

termination of employment. *See also* **dismissal**

compensation, provision for, **3**, [1480]

death of employer or employee, effect of, **16**, [785]

national service, by reason of, **3**, [1479]

notice—

absence from work during, **16**, [730]

breach of contract of employment during, **16**, [730]

conduct, effect of, **16**, [725]

termination of employment—*contd*

notice—*contd*

contributory employment and support allowance, payment of, **16**, [729]

failure to give, **16**, [730]

industrial injury benefit, payment of, **16**, [729]

minimum period of, **16**, [725]

normal working hours—

employments with, **16**, [727]

employments without, **16**, [728]

rights of employee in period of, **16**, [726]

short-term incapacity benefit, payment of, **16**, [729]

payments and other benefits on—

application of provisions, **44(2)**, [406]

benefit, meaning, **44(2)**, [407]

death or disability, for, **44(2)**, [412]

earnings, exception for payments exempted when received as, **44(2)**, [411]

employee liabilities and indemnity insurance, in respect of, **44(2)**, [415]

deceased individual, **44(2)**, [416]

employment income, treated as, **44(2)**, [408]–[410]

forces, for, **44(2)**, [417]

foreign governments, provided by, **44(2)**, [418]

foreign service, relating to, **44(2)**, [419]–[420]

notional interest, treatment of, **44(2)**, [422]

registered pension schemes, under, **44(2)**, [413]

contributions to, **44(2)**, [414]

tax-exempt pension schemes, under, **44(2)**, [413]

valuation, **44(2)**, [421]

terms and conditions of employment

changes in, **16**, [102]

contract for fixed term, statement, **16**, [100]

disciplinary rules, **16**, [101]

documents referred to, access to, **16**, [100]

exclusion—

employees becoming or ceasing to be excluded, **16**, [104]

requirements, from, **16**, [101], [103]

holidays and holiday pay, statement of, **16**, [99]

statement of—

changes, **16**, [102]

contracts excluded from requirement, **16**, [103]

failure to give, **16**, [995], [1005]

further particulars, powers of Secretary of State, **16**, [105]

not required, where, **16**, [101]

particulars required in, **16**, [99]

written particulars of. *See* statement *above*

Territorial Army. *See also* **reserve forces**

Army Act, application of, **3**, [714]

call-out—

generally, **3**, [1386]

Territorial Army—*contd*
  call-out—*contd*
    home defence service, for, **3**, [1397]
      notices, **3**, [1401]
      training, **3**, [1450]
  discharge, postponement of, **3**, [1431]–[1432]
  service of notices, **3**, [1433]
  training—
    call out, **3**, [1450]
    generally, **3**, [1412]–[1413]

Territorial Reserve. *See* **reserve associations**

territorial sea
  on-shore/off-shore boundary, **42**, [860]
  UK, part of, **44(1)**, [613]

territorial waters
  British Coal Corporation, exploitation
    rights, **17(2)**, [134]
  Civil Aviation Act, application, **4(1)**, [154]
  extension of breadth of—
    effect on enactments, **49**, [651]
    United Kingdom, **49**, [1], [650]
  food safety, in relation to, **1(2)**, [470]
  meaning of "territorial sea", **12(2)**, [28]
  nautical mile, meaning, **49**, [650]
  offence committed in—
    drug trafficking on British ship,
      12(2), [25], [26]
    institution of proceedings, **12(1)**, [155]
    jurisdiction, **12(1)**, [154], [157]
    procedure for trial, **12(1)**, [156]
  oil pollution of. *See* **oil pollution**
  part of the UK, as, **4(1)**, [236]

terrorism
  account monitoring order, **12(2)**, [966]
  action being, **12(2)**, [863]
  acts of—
    arrest for, **12(2)**, [908]
    information, duty to give, **12(2)**, [905]
  airports. *See further* ports and harbour control
    below
  annual report under Criminal Justice
    (Terrorism and Conspiracy) Act, cessation of
    requirement for, **12(4)**, [495]
  arrest of suspects, powers of, **12(2)**, [908]
  bombing, **12(2)**, [928]
  control order—
    appeals, **12(4)**, [73]
    contravention of obligations, **12(4)**, [71]
    controlled person—
      anonymity, application for, **12(S)**, 86
      representation by, time for, **12(S)**, 85
    convictions, effect of decisions on,
      12(4), [74]
    criminal investigations after making of,
      12(4), [70]
    decisions and derogation matters not to be
      questioned in legal proceedings,
      12(4), [73]
    derogating—
      arrest and detention pending, **12(4)**, [67]
      duration, **12(4)**, [68]

terrorism—*contd*
  control order—*contd*
    derogating—*contd*
      modification, **12(4)**, [69]
      power to make, **12(4)**, [66]
      revocation, **12(4)**, [69]
    duration of provisions, **12(4)**, [75]
    entry and search, powers of—
      absconding, **12(S)**, 83
      access to premises, failure to grant,
        12(S), 83
      compliance with order, monitoring,
        12(S), 84
    interpretation, **12(4)**, [77]
    involvement in terrorism-related activity,
      meaning, **12(S)**, 85
    jurisdiction, **12(4)**, [73]
    meaning, **12(4)**, [63]
    non-derogating—
      appeals, **12(4)**, [72]
      modification, **12(4)**, [69]
      power to make, **12(4)**, [64]
      revocation, **12(4)**, [69]
    obligations imposed by, **12(4)**, [63]
    offences, **12(4)**, [71]
    power to make, **12(4)**, [63]
    proceedings, **12(4)**, [73], [79]
    proof of, **12(4)**, [69]
    reporting and review of powers, **12(4)**, [76]
    rules of court, **12(4)**, [79]
    supervision by court, **12(4)**, [65]
  Convention offences, **12(4)**, [192]
  counter-terrorist powers. *See* **terrorism**
  definitions, **12(2)**, [944], [945]
    amendment, **12(S)**, 80
  detention of suspects—
    continued, grounds for, **12(2)**, [969]
    extension of period, **12(2)**, [970]
      amended provisions, **12(4)**, [184]
      grounds for, **12(4)**, [185]
      maximum, expiry or renewal of,
        12(4), [186]
    identification, **12(2)**, [968]
    interviews, audio and visual recording,
      12(2), [968]
    place of, **12(2)**, [968]
    powers, **12(2)**, [908]
    pre-charge, **12(S)**, 86-7
    representations as to, **12(2)**, [969], [970]
    review of, **12(2)**, [969]
    rights of detainees, **12(2)**, [968]
    status, **12(2)**, [968]
  directions, **12(2)**, [947]
  employment, meaning, **12(S)**, 82
  encouragement of—
    internet activity, **12(4)**, [171]
      notices, giving, **12(4)**, [172]
    offence, **12(4)**, [169]
    penalty for, **12(4)**, [169]
    statement, publication of, **12(4)**, [169]
  evidence, **12(2)**, [942]
  extra-territorial jurisdiction—
    attacks abroad on UK nationals, residents or
      diplomatic staff, **12(2)**, [932]
    proceedings, **12(2)**, [934]

terrorism—*contd*
  extra-territorial jurisdiction—*contd*
    UK diplomatic premises, attacks or threats
      in connection with, **12(2)**, [933]
    UK national or resident, acts outside UK,
      12(2), [930], [931]
  financial information, **12(2)**, [965]
  financial restriction proceedings—
    duty to give reasons, qualification of,
      12(S), 77
    financial restriction decision, application to
      set aside, **12(S)**, 70–1
    general note, **12(S)**, 5
    intercept evidence, **12(S)**, 76
    Lord Chancellor, initial exercise of powers
      by, **12(S)**, 77–8
    meaning, **12(S)**, 72
    Queen's Bench Division, allocation of
      proceedings to, **12(S)**, 77
    rules of court—
      disclosure, as to, **12(S)**, 73–4
      general provisions, **12(S)**, 73
      meaning, **12(S)**, 79
    special advocate, appointment of, **12(S)**, 75
    UN terrorism orders, meaning,
      12(S), 71–2
  financing—
    general note, **12(S)**, 4–5
    money laundering. *See* **money laundering**
  fingerprints and samples—
    power to take—
      England and Wales, in, **12(S)**, 20–1
      transitional provision, **12(S)**, 22
    retention and use of—
      existing statutory restrictions, material
        not subject to, **12(S)**, 25–6
      Police and Criminal Evidence Act,
        material subject to, **12(S)**, 22
      Terrorism Act 2000, material subject to,
        12(S), 23–4
  forfeiture orders—
    British Islands, made in parts of,
      12(2), [960]
    compensation, provision for, **12(2)**, [960]
    designated countries, made in, **12(2)**, [960]
    implementation of, **12(2)**, [960]
    insolvency, **12(2)**, [963]
    interpretation, **12(2)**, [960]
    Northern Ireland, **12(2)**, [962]
    powers of court, **12(2)**, [943]
    proceedings for offence, timing,
      12(2), [960]
    restraint orders, **12(2)**, [960]
    Scotland, **12(2)**, [961]
  freezing order. *See* **freezing order**
  gas facility, cost of policing at—
    consultation, **12(S)**, 92–3
    costs incurred before commencement,
      12(S), 93
    England and Wales, **12(S)**, 89
    gas transporters, designated, **12(S)**, 91
    recovery of, **12(S)**, 91–2
    Scotland, **12(S)**, 90
  inciting overseas, **12(2)**, [926], [927]

terrorism—*contd*
  information—
    disclosure of—
      definitions, **12(3)**, [90]
      extension of powers, **12(3)**, [87], [160],
        [161]
      investigation, for, **12(3)**, [87], [160],
        [161]
      overseas purposes, restriction for,
        12(3), [88]
      revenue departments, held by,
        12(3), [89]
    intelligence services, disclosure to—
      consequential amendments,
        12(S), 99–101
      duties not affected, **12(S)**, 28
      interpretation, **12(S)**, 29
      prohibited disclosures, **12(S)**, 28
      purposes of, **12(S)**, 27
      use of, **12(S)**, 27
    powers to gather and share, general note,
      12(S), 1–2
    removal of documents for examination—
      access to documents, request for,
        12(S), 17
      authorised officer, by, **12(S)**, 20
      documents, meaning, **12(S)**, 19
      legal privilege, items subject to,
        12(S), 14
      obstruction, offence of, **12(S)**, 13
      photographing and copying documents,
        12(S), 18
      power of, **12(S)**, 12
      record of, **12(S)**, 15–16
      retention, **12(S)**, 16
      return, **12(S)**, 19
  inquiries, intercept evidence in, **12(S)**, 79
  interpretation of provisions, **12(4)**, [183]
  investigations—
    cordoned areas—
      designation, **12(2)**, [899]
        duration of, **12(2)**, [900]
      excepted material, **12(2)**, [964]
      explanations, **12(2)**, [964]
      meaning, **12(2)**, [898]
      Northern Ireland, **12(2)**, [964]
      police powers, **12(2)**, [901]
      searches, **12(2)**, [964]
      special procedure material, **12(2)**, [964]
      urgent cases, **12(2)**, [964]
    meaning, **12(2)**, [897]
  legislation, review of, **12(4)**, [188]
  meaning, **12(2)**, [863]; **12(S)**, 94
  Northern Ireland emergency provisions,
    extension of, **12(2)**, [954]
  nuclear facilities—
    damaging, **12(4)**, [178]
    threats relating to, **12(4)**, [179]
  offences—
    ancillary, meaning, **12(S)**, 95
    armed forces, eliciting, publishing or
      communicating evidence as to members
      of, **12(S)**, 80–1, 142–4
    bombing, **12(2)**, [928]
    commission abroad, **12(4)**, [180]

terrorism—*contd*
  offences—*contd*
    company directors, liability of, **12(4)**, [181]
    defences, **12(2)**, [940]
    extension to Crown servants, **12(2)**, [941]
    finance, **12(2)**, [929]
    information—
      collection of, **12(2)**, [925]
      notification to police—
        absence abroad, effect of, **12(S)**, 63–4
        acknowledgement, **12(S)**, 58
        changes, notification of, **12(S)**, 55–6
        definitions, **12(S)**, 67
        foreign travel restriction orders,
          12(S), 108–12
        general note, **12(S)**, 3–4
        initial, **12(S)**, 53–4
        local police area, meaning, **12(S)**, 58
        method of, **12(S)**, 57–8
        offences dealt with before
          commencement, **12(S)**, 49
        offences in relation to, **12(S)**, 62
        orders, **12(S)**, 105–7
        period for which requirements
          applying, **12(S)**, 60–1
        periodic re-notification, **12(S)**, 57
        periods of imprisonment or detention,
          power to amend, **12(S)**, 53
        person being dealt with for offence,
          reference to, **12(S)**, 68–9
        persons to whom requirements
          applying, **12(S)**, 50
        return to UK, on, **12(S)**, 65
        scheme of provisions, **12(S)**, 46–7
        sentences or orders triggering
          requirements, **12(S)**, 50–2
        service offences, application to,
          12(S), 113–17
        specified terms, power to amend,
          12(S), 53
        terrorism connection, offences with,
          12(S), 48
        terrorism offences to which applying,
          12(S), 47–8
        travel outside UK, as to, **12(S)**, 59
      meaning, **12(S)**, 34
    possession for terrorist purposes,
      12(2), [924]
    possible, disclosure of information as to,
      12(S), 82
    prosecution—
      consent to, **12(2)**, [939]
      general note, **12(S)**, 2–3
      jurisdiction, **12(S)**, 35
      offences committed in UK, **12(S)**, 35
      offences committed outside UK, consent
        to prosecution, **12(S)**, 36
    punishment—
      armed forces, sentences, **12(S)**, 38
      general note, **12(S)**, 2–3
      sentencing, **12(S)**, 37–8
      terrorist connection, consideration of,
        12(S), 37–8
    terrorist connection, with—
      consideration of, **12(S)**, 101–2

terrorism—*contd*
  offences—*contd*
    terrorist connection, with—*contd*
      meaning, **12(S)**, 94
    terrorist organisation, directing,
      12(2), [923]
    weapons training, **12(2)**, [921]
  officers' powers, **12(2)**, [971]
  orders and regulations, **12(2)**, [946]
  parking restrictions, power to impose,
    12(2), [915]–[919]
  police powers, **12(2)**, [936]
  port and border controls, **12(2)**, [967]
  preparation of acts, offence, **12(4)**, [173]
  property—
    cash, forfeiture of—
      appeals, **12(S)**, 88–9
      period for which detained, **12(S)**, 87
    possible offences, disclosure of information
      as to, **12(S)**, 82
    forfeiture—
      amendments, **12(S)**, 44–6
      application of proceeds to compensate
        victims, **12(S)**, 42–4
      consequential amendments,
        12(S), 103–5
      devices, materials or facilities, of,
        12(S), 45–6
      offences, for, **12(S)**, 39–42
  proscribed organisations—
    deproscription—
      appeal, **12(2)**, [867]–[869]
      application, **12(2)**, [866]
      conviction, effect on, **12(2)**, [869]
      Northern Ireland, **12(2)**, [870]
      Scotland, **12(2)**, [870]
    human rights provisions, application of,
      12(2), [871]
    immunity in proceedings, **12(2)**, [872]
    list of, **12(2)**, [955]
    meaning, **12(2)**, [865]
    membership of, **12(2)**, [873]
    supporting, **12(2)**, [874]
    uniform, wearing, **12(2)**, [875]
  Proscribed Organisations Appeal
    Commission—
    appeal from, **12(2)**, [868]
    appeal to, **12(2)**, [867]
    constitution and administration,
      12(2), [956]
    establishment of, **12(2)**, [867]
    human rights provisions, application of,
      12(2), [871]
    procedure, **12(2)**, [956]
  prosecution of offences, **12(2)**, [939]
  prosecutions, consent to, **12(4)**, [182]
  publications—
    dissemination of—
      internet activity, **12(4)**, [171]
      notices, giving, **12(4)**, [172]
      offence, **12(4)**, [170]
      penalty for, **12(4)**, [170]
      search, seizure and forfeiture of,
        12(4), [187]
      seizure and forfeiture of, **12(4)**, [193]

terrorism—*contd*
  radioactive devices and materials—
    definition, **12(4)**, [177]
    making and possession of, **12(4)**, [177]
    misuse, **12(4)**, [178]
    threats relating to, **12(4)**, [179]
  regulated sector, **12(2)**, [957]
  supervisory authorities, **12(2)**, [958]
  suspected persons—
    arrest of, **12(2)**, [908]
    detention of. *See* detention *above*
    premises, search of, **12(2)**, [909]
    searching, **12(2)**, [910]
    stopping and searching—
      authorisations, **12(2)**, [911], [913]
      container, of, **12(2)**, [938]
      offences, **12(2)**, [914]
      power of, **12(2)**, [910], [912]
  suspects—
    post-charge questioning—
      code of practice, **12(S)**, 32–3
      detention for, **12(S)**, 30
      England and Wales, in, **12(S)**, 29–30
      general note, **12(S)**, 2
      interviews, recording, **12(S)**, 32
      Northern Ireland, in, **12(S)**, 31–2
  temporary legislation ceasing to have effect,
    12(2), [864]
  terrorist cash—
    forfeiture, **12(3)**, [73], [155]
    compensation for, **12(3)**, [156]
    meaning, **12(3)**, [153]
    release, application for, **12(3)**, [156]
    seizure of, **12(3)**, [154]
  terrorist funds—
    cash, seizure of, **12(2)**, [896]
    forfeiture of, **12(2)**, [896]
    fund-raising, offence of, **12(2)**, [877]
    funding arrangements, **12(2)**, [879]
  terrorist, meaning, **12(2)**, [907]
  terrorist property—
    cash, seizure of, **12(2)**, [896]
    cooperation with police, **12(2)**, [883]
    disclosure of information—
      arrangements, after entering into,
        12(2), [885]
      constable, to, **12(2)**, [882]
      duty as to, **12(2)**, [881]
      failure of, **12(2)**, [886], [887]
      institutions, between, **12(2)**, [892]
      interpretation, **12(2)**, [894]
      permitted, **12(2)**, [892], [893]
      protected disclosures, **12(2)**, [888]
      SOCA, to, **12(2)**, [889]
      tipping off, regulated sector, **12(2)**, [890]
      undertaking or group, within,
        12(2), [891]
    earmarking of, **12(3)**, [157]
    forfeiture, **12(2)**, [896]
    freezing order. *See* **freezing order**
    meaning, **12(2)**, [876]; **12(3)**, [158]
    money laundering, **12(2)**, [880]
    obtaining and disposing of, **12(3)**, [158]
    offences, penalties for, **12(2)**, [895]

terrorism—*contd*
  terrorist property—*contd*
    prior consent, arrangements with,
      12(2), [884]
    use and possession of, **12(2)**, [878]
    traffic regulation for purposes related to,
      37, [194]
    restrictions, **37**, [195]
  training—
    attendance at place used for, **12(4)**, [176]
    forfeiture, powers of, **12(4)**, [175]
    offence, **12(4)**, [174]
    penalty for, **12(4)**, [174]
  transitional provisions, **12(2)**, [935], [951]
  weapons training—
    meaning, **12(2)**, [922]
    offences, **12(2)**, [921]

terrorism suppression
  aircraft, offences on, **18**, [752], [757]
  Channel Islands, terrorism provisions applied,
    18, [754]
  convention country, meaning, **18**, [755]
  Isle of Man, provisions applied, **18**, [754]
  non-convention countries, in, **18**, [753]
  offences—
    abduction, **18**, [757]
    aircraft, on, **18**, [752], [757]
    attempts to commit, **18**, [752], [757]
    Channel Tunnel, relating to, **18**, [757]
    committed outside UK, jurisdiction,
      18, [752]
    common law, **18**, [757]
    conspiracy, **18**, [757]
    explosives, **18**, [757]
    financing of, **18**, [757]
    firearms, **18**, [757]
    hostage-taking, **18**, [757]
    hovercraft, on, **18**, [752]
    nuclear material, involving, **18**, [757]
    person, against, **18**, [757]
    property, against, **18**, [757]
    ship, on, **18**, [752], [757]
  repeals, **18**, [757]

testamentary power. *See also* **will**
  historical development, **50**, [484]

tests. *See* **driving instruction; driving
  licence; vehicle testing**

Thames Conservators
  pension provisions, **33(1)**, [136]

Thames flood barrier. *See also* **Thames river**
  acquisition of land—
    agreement with adjoining owner, **49**, [502]
    extension of time for, **25(2)**, [354]
    general powers, **49**, [495]
    owner, power to reinstate, **49**, [501]
    part of property only, **49**, [497]
      counter-notice, **49**, [497]
      reference to tribunal, **49**, [497]
    provisions applied to, **49**, [494]
    purposes of, **49**, [495]

Thames flood barrier—*contd*
appropriation of land for, **49**, [500]
arbitration of differences, **49**, [563]
book of reference, errors in, correction,
  49, [496]
byelaws—
  penalties under, **49**, [531]
  power to make, **49**, [531]
  sea defence, **49**, [552]
closing of. *See* operation *below*
compensation—
  access, loss of, for, **49**, [515]
  certain occupiers, to, **49**, [506]
  damage to works, for, **49**, [515]
  existing jetties, as to, **49**, [534]
  improvements disregarded, **49**, [507]
  land injuriously affected, **49**, [506]
  rights of way, for, **49**, [504]
  undefended lands, respecting, **49**, [534]
compulsory acquisition—
  easements, of, **49**, [498]–[499]
  land. *See* acquisition *above*
Crown rights, saving for, **49**, [543]
dams, closing of, **49**, [557]–[558]
defence works—
  adjoining areas, in, **49**, [556]
  agreements for carrying out, **49**, [553]
  byelaws, contravention of, **49**, [552]
  expenditure incurred in, **49**, [533]
  highways, affecting, **49**, [546]
  meaning, **49**, [533]
  orders for carrying out, **49**, [545]
deposited plans—
  deviation from, limits of, **49**, [509]
  errors in, correction of, **49**, [496]
easements—
  acquisition of, **49**, [498]
  grant by person under disability, **49**, [499]
enactments applied to—
  Land Drainage Acts, **49**, [547]
  Public Utilities Street Works Act, **49**, [523]
  Water Resources Act, **49**, [550]
Exchequer grants for, **49**, [532]
execution of works—
  cables etc, laying or placing, **49**, [513]
  closing of river for, **49**, [517]
  deviation from lines and levels, **49**, [509]
  discharge of water, **49**, [516]
  dredging, provisions as to, **49**, [515]
  general powers, **49**, [508]
  materials, disposal of, **49**, [522]
  moorings, removal of, **49**, [514]
  pipes, placing of, **49**, [513]
  pumping water, **49**, [516]
  sewers, dealing with, **49**, [518]
  specified works, **49**, [508]
  spoil, deposit of, **49**, [495]
  streets, stopping up, **49**, [519]–[521], [565]
    temporary, notice of, **49**, [524]
  subsidiary works, **49**, [510]
  tidal works, **49**, [508]
  tugs, provision of, **49**, [511]
highways—
  stopping up, **49**, [549]
  works affecting, **49**, [546]

Thames flood barrier—*contd*
land—
  acquisition. *See* acquisition *above*
  adjoining owner, agreement with, **49**, [502]
  appropriation, powers of, **49**, [500]
  ascertained value of, **49**, [500]
  inaccurate description of, **49**, [496]
  owner, power to reinstate, **49**, [501]
  reclaimed, vesting of, **49**, [512]
landing places, existing—
  extinction of, **49**, [504]
  meaning, **49**, [505]
Lee Board, contributions by, **49**, [535]
local inquiries, power to hold, **49**, [562]
meaning, **49**, [493]
misuse of, penalty, **49**, [530]
moorings, removal of, **49**, [514]
navigation—
  closure of river to, **49**, [517], [525]
  protection of, **49**, [515], [526]
  tugs to assist vessels, **49**, [511]
offences respecting—
  corporation, by, **49**, [561]
  interference or misuse, **49**, [530]
operation of—
  closing, references to, **49**, [493]
  general provisions, **49**, [525]
  interests affected by, **49**, [525]
  notice of closing, **49**, [525]
  offences respecting, **49**, [530]
planning provisions, exemption, **49**, [537],
  [551]
protection of—
  British Railways Board, **49**, [540]
  navigation, **49**, [515], [526]
  Port Authority, **49**, [539]
  river users, **49**, [539]
  statutory undertakers, **49**, [541]
public, admission and facilities, **49**, [529]
rating, exemption from, **49**, [536]
reclaimed land, ownership of, **49**, [512]
rights of way—
  diversion of, **49**, [549]
  extinction of, **49**, [504]
river users, protection of, **49**, [539]
sea defence works. *See* defence works *above*
site of, admission of public to, **49**, [529]
streets—
  power to stop up, **49**, [519], [565]
  stopped up, vesting of sites of, **49**, [520]
  temporary closure, **49**, [521], [524]
submarine cables, dredging affecting,
  49, [515]
subsidiary works, power to make, **49**, [510]
subsoil of streets, power to use, **49**, [503]
summary of provisions, **49**, [1]
tidal works—
  execution of, **49**, [508]
  marking of, **49**, [526]
  survey of, **49**, [528]
vessels, powers to remove, **49**, [527]
water authority—
  borrowing powers, **49**, [555]
  defence works. *See* defence works *above*
  entry on land, right of, **49**, [550]

Thames flood barrier—*contd*
  water authority—*contd*
    Exchequer grants, to, **49**, [554]
    expenditure on works by, **49**, [533]
    highways, power to stop up, **49**, [549]
    payments to, **49**, [533]
    works in adjoining areas, **49**, [556]
  watercourses, stopping up, **49**, [549]
  wireless apparatus, provisions as to, **49**, [542]
  wrecks etc, removal of, **49**, [527]

Thames river. *See also* **Port of London**
  banks—
    alteration without consent, **49**, [176]
    damaged, temporary repair, **49**, [438]
    inspection of, **49**, [293]
    interference with, **49**, [265]
    maintenance, liability for, **49**, [175], [181]
    repair of—
      liability for, **49**, [175], [181]
      notice requiring, **49**, [177]
      temporary, **49**, [438]
    supervision of, **49**, [293]
    survey of, **49**, [177]
  barrier. *See* **Thames flood barrier**
  bed of—
    dredging etc, licensing, **39(2)**, [295]
    meaning, **39(2)**, [225]
    surveys of, **39(2)**, [230]
    works in or upon, **39(2)**, [287]
      temporary, **49**, [438]
      supervision of, **49**, [293]
      survey of, **49**, [177]
  boat race, restricted use during, **39(2)**, [313]
  bridges—
    maintenance and repair, **39(2)**, [377], [418]
    management of, **49**, [186]
    obstruction of, penalty, **39(2)**, [399]
  buoys, beacons and lights—
    approval required, **39(2)**, [284]
    Merchant Shipping Acts, provisions
      applicable, **39(2)**, [393]
  byelaws—
    powers to make, **39(2)**, [367]; **49**, [186]
    waste of water, to prevent, **49**, [311]
  Canal Tolls and Charges No 6 Order
    Confirmation Act, inapplicability,
    39(2), [248]
  creeks, etc, reclamation, **39(2)**, [287]
  crowds, regulation of, **39(2)**, [327]
  dam—
    closing of, **49**, [557]–[558]
    installations below river level to protect,
      49, [453]
    temporary or movable—
      authorisation of, **49**, [164]
      breach of regulations as to, **49**, [165]
      continuance of, authorisation, **49**, [187]
      order as to, **49**, [437]
        cessation of, **49**, [439]
        service of, **49**, [440]
      permanent replacement, **49**, [439]
      requirement to provide, **49**, [266]
  drainage authority, dredging etc by,
    39(2), [295]

Thames river—*contd*
  dredging and improvement—
    Crown property, **39(2)**, [296]
    licensing of, **39(2)**, [295]
    powers, **39(2)**, [282]
    protection in relation to, **39(2)**, [283]
  embanked land, vesting of, **39(2)**, [294]
  embankment, repair of, **39(2)**, [331]
  estuary traffic, port rates exemption,
    39(2), [254], [255]
  fish, jurisdiction as to, **39(2)**, [308]
  fishing, byelaws as to, **39(2)**, [368]
  fishing vessel, entry on, **39(2)**, [309]
  flood prevention—
    banks. *See* banks *above*
    barrier. *See* **Thames flood barrier**
    dam. *See* dam *above*
    emergency measures, **49**, [437]
    expenses—
      landowner, of, **49**, [180]
      recovery of, **49**, [179], [182]
    flood defence level—
      installations deemed below, **49**, [453]
      works to prevent overflow, **49**, [453]
    high tide warning system, **49**, [298]
    limits of provisions, **49**, [159]
    railway premises, **49**, [443]
    statutory provisions applicable, **39(2)**, [315]
    statutory undertakers premises, **49**, [444]
    water circulation plant, **49**, [453]
    works. *See* flood works *below*
  flood works—
    barrier. *See* **Thames flood barrier**
    bed of river, on, **49**, [170]
    commencement date, notice of, **49**, [456]
    compensation for damage, **49**, [178], [437]
    dock companies, affecting, **49**, [171], [268]
    emergency measures, **49**, [437]
      compensation for damage, **49**, [437]
      obstruction of, **49**, [437]
    entry for purposes of, **49**, [441]
    execution of—
      default of owner etc, on, **49**, [167]
      entry to effect, **49**, [441]
      expenses, recovery of, **49**, [179], [182]
      notice as to, **49**, [263]
      objection by owner as to, **49**, [166]
      persons etc liable for, **49**, [161]
      plans, in accordance with, **49**, [160]
      powers for, **49**, [168]
    expenses—
      Authority, of, **49**, [179]
      landowner, of, **49**, [180]
      recovery of, **49**, [179], [182]
    land for—
      inspection of, **49**, [172]
      power to take, **49**, [169]
    landlord and tenant agreements, **49**, [183]
    liability for, no exemption from, **49**, [181]
    limitation of powers, **49**, [163]
    meaning, **49**, [158]
    notice of intention to commence,
      49, [263], [456]
    objection to—
      owner, by, **49**, [162], [166]

Thames river—*contd*
 flood works—*contd*
  objection to—*contd*
   period for notice of, **49**, [267]
  obstruction of, **49**, [441]
  plans—
   amendment of, **49**, [162]
   duty to make, **49**, [162]
   execution without, penalty, **49**, [264]
   inspection of, **49**, [162]
   notice of making, **49**, [162]
   objection to, **49**, [162], [166]
   transmission of copies of, **49**, [188]
  Port of London Authority, by, **49**, [171]
  protection for, **49**, [442], [453]
  rentcharge in respect of, **49**, [180]
  River Lee, on, **49**, [173]
  shores, construction on, **49**, [170]
  supervision of, **49**, [293]
  temporary—
   authorisation of, **49**, [164]
   breach of regulations as to, **49**, [165]
   continuance of, authorisation, **49**, [187]
   damaged banks, at, **49**, [438]
   permanent replacement, **49**, [439]
 footbridges, maintenance and repair,
  39(2), [377], [418]
 goods traffic. *See under* **Port of London**
 high tides, warnings of, **49**, [298]
 hydrographic surveys of bed, **39(2)**, [230]
 land drainage affecting, **20**, [323]
 land in or near, entry on, **39(2)**, [312]
 landing places—
  access, improving etc, **25(2)**, [284]
  acquisition by water authority, **25(2)**, [281]
   agreements binding after, **25(2)**, [291]
   continuance of byelaws etc on,
    25(2), [290]
  Acts repealed or modified, **25(2)**, [292]
  agreements as to calling at, **39(2)**, [307]
  assaults etc on officers, **25(2)**, [289]
  byelaws for use of, **25(2)**, [283]
  charges for use of, **25(2)**, [285]
   default in paying, **25(2)**, [287]
   list to be displayed, **25(2)**, [285]
  control of use, **25(2)**, [287]
  dangerous materials, search for,
   25(2), [288]
  disposal, **39(2)**, [303]
  dredging, powers of, **25(2)**, [284]
  explosives, search for, **25(2)**, [288]
  inspection of, **39(2)**, [357]
  land for, compulsory purchase, **25(2)**, [282]
  marked, replacement of, **39(2)**, [306]
  meaning, **25(2)**, [280]; **39(2)**, [225]
  offences under byelaws, **25(2)**, [283]
  Port of London Authority, belonging to,
   39(2), [303]
  powers of water authority as to,
   25(2), [281]
  provision of, **25(2)**, [281]
  public access, **25(2)**, [287]; **39(2)**, [305]
  repair of, **39(2)**, [331]
  transfer of, by Thames Water Authority,
   39(2), [304]

Thames river—*contd*
 landing places—*contd*
  use of—
   control of, **25(2)**, [287]
   permission for, grant of, **25(2)**, [286]
   regulation of, **25(2)**, [283], [286]
 mean high water level—
  lands above, works on, **39(2)**, [297]
  meaning, **39(2)**, [297]
 meaning, **39(2)**, [225]; **49**, [158]
 moorings—
  interference with, **39(2)**, [340]
  private, removal of, **39(2)**, [285]
 navigation—
  general rules, **39(2)**, [316]
  hazards to. *See* obstructions *below*
  lights detrimental to, **39(2)**, [338]
  tidal works dangerous to, **39(2)**, [299]
 nuisance on, abatement, **39(2)**, [314]
 obstructions, removal—
  other than vessels, **39(2)**, [329]
  projections, **39(2)**, [330]
  sunken vessels, **39(2)**, [328]
 pollution, prohibition, **39(2)**, [397]
 public use, permitted restrictions, **39(2)**, [313]
 reclamation of creeks, mud flats, etc,
  39(2), [287]
 registration of craft. *See under* **Port of
  London Authority**
 Richmond—
  footbridge, charges for, **39(2)**, [249]
  lock and slipway, exemption from charges,
   39(2), [250]
  maintenance of works, **39(2)**, [310]
  sluices, working of, **39(2)**, [310]
  works, meaning, **39(2)**, [225]
 river authority, dredging etc by, **39(2)**, [295]
 summary of provisions, **39(2)**, [1]
 surveys, entry on land in or near, **39(2)**, [312]
 tidal works—
  abandoned or decayed, abatement of,
   39(2), [300]
  approval of, **39(2)**, [298]
  danger to navigation, provision against,
   39(2), [299]
  permanent lights on, **39(2)**, [302]
  survey of, **39(2)**, [301]
 Trinity High Water or Standard, construction
  of references to, **39(2)**, [311]
 vessels—
  adrift in, **39(2)**, [317]
  areas, special directions for designation,
   39(2), [319]
  boarding of, powers, **39(2)**, [342]
  damage caused by, **39(2)**, [339]
  docks, at, **39(2)**, [321]
  enforcement of directions, **39(2)**, [326]
  failure to comply with directions,
   39(2), [325]
  false draught, giving, **39(2)**, [341]
  general directions to, **39(2)**, [319]
  master's responsibility, saving for,
   39(2), [324]
  meaning, **39(2)**, [225]
  overcrowding, **39(2)**, [318]

Thames river—*contd*
  vessels—*contd*
    publication of directions, **39(2)**, [322]
    special directions to, **39(2)**, [320], [323]
    sunken, removal, **39(2)**, [328]
  water from, use of, **39(2)**, [286]
  watermen and lightermen—
    fares, list of, **39(2)**, [345]
    licences, fees for, **39(2)**, [345]
    meaning, **39(2)**, [225]
    register, **39(2)**, [344]
  works—
    control of, **39(2)**, [288]–[297]
    Crown property, **39(2)**, [296]
    laying down, maintenance and operation,
      39(2), [284]
    licensing—
      appeal against refusal, **39(2)**, [291], [416]
      application for licence, **39(2)**, [288]
      consideration, **39(2)**, [289]
      exemptions, **39(2)**, [290]
      generally, **39(2)**, [288]
      works without licence, prohibition,
        39(2), [292]
    mean high water level, lands above,
      39(2), [297]
    meaning, **39(2)**, [225]
    parish, within, **39(2)**, [293]
    tidal. *See* tidal works *above*
  Yantlet line—
    area of jurisdiction relating to fish,
      39(2), [308]
    meaning, **39(2)**, [225]

Thames Water Authority. *See also* **water
authorities**
  accounts and audit, **49**, [213]
  annual report by, **49**, [221]
  aqueducts, open, restriction of, **49**, [86]
  area of, **49**, [1], [104]
    adaptation of Acts to, **49**, [193]
  assets transferred to, **49**, [197]
  bills, power to promote etc, **49**, [217], [223]
  borrowing powers, **49**, [210]
    discharge of loans etc, **49**, [212]
    flood barrier, purposes of, **49**, [555]
    issue of water stock, by, **49**, [211]
    returns to Minister as to, **49**, [315]
  breaking up streets—
    communication pipes, to lay, **49**, [306]
    powers of, **49**, [304]
  bridges, management of, **49**, [186]
  buildings, powers respecting, **49**, [217]
  byelaws—
    pollution, to prevent, **49**, [321]
    waste, to prevent, **49**, [311]
  cables, electric, power to lay, **49**, [374]
  committee members, allowances to, **49**, [378]
  companies transferred to. *See* transfer etc *below*
  contributions by, to associations, **49**, [286]
  disputes, arbitration in, **49**, [148], [323], [379]
  domestic supply. *See* supply of water *below*
  electric cables, power to lay, **49**, [374]
  establishment, **49**, [196]

Thames Water Authority—*contd*
  expenses of—
    ceremonies, in connection with, **49**, [377]
    generally, **49**, [209]
  filtration of water, **49**, [87]
  financial provisions, **49**, [214]
  fittings. *See* water fittings *below*
  flood works. *See* **Thames flood barrier;
    Thames river**
  Hertfordshire, special provisions, **49**, [208],
    [258], [277]
  instruments, form and service of, **49**, [151]
  insurance fund—
    deficiency or surplus in, **49**, [290]
    establishment, **49**, [290]
    payments into, **49**, [290]
    purposes of, **49**, [290]
    risks covered by, **49**, [290]
    statutory securities—
      investment in, **49**, [290]
      meaning, **49**, [290], [316]
  land, powers as to, **49**, [217]
  landing places, transfer of, **39(2)**, [304]
  legal proceedings by or against, **49**, [217]
  members travelling etc allowances, **49**, [378]
  ministry inspectors—
    appointment, notice of, **49**, [89]
    new sources, report on, **49**, [88]
  New River Company—
    provisions not applicable to, **49**, [152]
    special provisions, **49**, [203]
  offences by, recovery etc of penalties,
    49, [149]
  pipes and mains. *See* water fittings; water pipes
    below
  Port of London Act, protection under,
    39(2), [394]
  precepts, issue of, **49**, [209]
  private street works expenses, exemption
    from, **36**, [1264]
  provisional orders relating to, **49**, [219]
  provisions repealed, **49**, [240]
  reservoirs—
    covering, provision for, **49**, [85]
    Staines, transfer of, **49**, [204]
  Secretary of State, inquiries, power to hold,
    49, [220]
  sluices, interfering with, **49**, [284]
  status of, **49**, [196]
  streets—
    boundary of supply, forming, **49**, [285]
    breaking up, powers, **49**, [304]
  summary of provisions, **49**, [1]
  supply of water—
    agreement, by, **49**, [250]
    appeal relating to, **49**, [134]
    application for, **49**, [133]
    areas partly supplied by other bodies,
      49, [249]
    building purposes, for, **49**, [245]
    bulk, in—
      certain boroughs, to, **49**, [207]
      outside limit of supply, **49**, [281]

Thames Water Authority—*contd*
supply of water—*contd*
charges scheme, **49**, [209]
See also water rate *below*
constant, provision of, **49**, [132],
[136]–[137]
consumers—
local authority aid to, **49**, [192]
meaning, **49**, [194], [229], [300]
courts, passages etc, to, **49**, [139]
cutting off—
actions warranting, **49**, [102]
expenses, recovery of, **49**, [283]
discontinuance, notice by consumer,
49, [253]
disputes, arbitration of, **49**, [148]
domestic supply—
charges for, **49**, [242]
exceptions from, **49**, [251]
failure to provide, **49**, [243]
filtration of water for, **49**, [87]
meaning, **49**, [251]
exceptions from, **49**, [251]
failure to provide, **49**, [243]
filtration of water for, **49**, [87]
meaning, **49**, [251]
duty to provide—
drought, exception for, **49**, [140], [243]
exception, **49**, [135], [248]–[249]
frost preventing, **49**, [140], [243]
extension of time for, **49**, [138]
filtration of, **49**, [87]
Government buildings, to, **49**, [252]
height at which furnished, **49**, [132], [248]
hospitals, to, **49**, [276]
houses used partly for trade, **49**, [246]
hydraulic power, for, **49**, [247]
limits of, **49**, [234]
boundary, streets and roads, forming,
49, [285]
meaning, **49**, [373]
powers exercisable within, **49**, [375]
market garden, to, **49**, [254]
measure, by—
application for, **49**, [275]
building sites, to, **49**, [245]
Government premises, to, **49**, [252]
maximum quantity, **49**, [275]
meter, provision of, **49**, [275]
premises partly trade, **49**, [246], [276]
railway premises, to, **49**, [275]
rates of charge, **49**, [398]
uniformity of charges, **49**, [275]
meters—
See also measure, by *above*
provision of, **49**, [275]
test, **49**, [282]
Minister may require, **49**, [136]
new sources of, **49**, [88]
non-domestic—
notice of, **49**, [317]
railway premises, to, **49**, [275]
restriction on, **49**, [254]
notices—
form and service of, **49**, [151]

Thames Water Authority—*contd*
supply of water—*contd*
notices—*contd*
Gazette publication of, **49**, [143]
requiring supply, **49**, [137]
offences—
fittings, failure to repair, **49**, [146]
penalties, **49**, [141]
pollution, byelaws to prevent—
compensation, provision for, **49**, [321]
procedure for making, **49**, [321]
provisions, made by, **49**, [321]
public purposes, for, **49**, [276]
pure and wholesome—
examination and report, **49**, [218]
provisions for securing, **49**, [218]
quality etc—
complaints as to, **49**, [92]
inquiry and report, **49**, [92], [147]
well-founded complaints, **49**, [95]
regulations—
binding on all parties, **49**, [142]
saving for, **49**, [256]
sanitorium, to, **49**, [276]
sluices, interference with, **49**, [284]
sources—
disapproval of, **49**, [90]–[91]
ministerial approval, **49**, [90]
new, report on, **49**, [88]
stand-pipe, by means of, **49**, [139]
Sundays, on, **49**, [131]
test meters, power to affix, **49**, [282]
transfer of undertakings to—
Barnet Water Company, saving for,
49, [227]
byelaws, existing, saving for, **49**, [232]
capital receipts, application of, **49**, [216]
Cheshunt, special provisions, **49**, [206]
Colne Valley Water Company, saving for,
49, [224]
compensation, provision for, **49**, [197]
contracts existing on, **49**, [231]
Croydon, special provisions, **49**, [206]
debenture stock—
cancellation of, **49**, [201]
meaning, **49**, [229]
redeemable, provisions as to, **49**, [202]
substitution of water stock for, **49**, [201]
debts—
security for, **49**, [199]
transfer of, **49**, [198]
substitution of water stock for, **49**, [201]
debts—
security for, **49**, [199]
transfer of, **49**, [198]
meaning of undertaking, **49**, [229]
mortgage debt—
meaning, **49**, [229]
redemption of, **49**, [202]
security for, **49**, [199]
New River Company, special provisions,
49, [203]
payments by local authorities, **49**, [215]
Richmond, special provisions, **49**, [206]
sinking funds, application of, **49**, [200]

Thames Water Authority—*contd*
transfer of undertakings to—*contd*
South Essex Waterworks, saving for,
49, [228]
South West Suburban Company, saving
for, **49**, [225]
Staines reservoir, **49**, [204]
Sutton Water Company, saving for,
49, [226]
Tottenham district's undertaking, **49**, [205]
Ware, special provisions, **49**, [206]
Water Board, former—
abolition, **49**, [1]
constitution of, **49**, [235]
water stock—
discharge of, **49**, [212]
extinguishment, **49**, [201]
issue of, **49**, [211]
redemption, time for, **49**, [202], [212]
substitution for debenture stock,
49, [201]
waste of water—
byelaws to prevent, **49**, [311]
constructions to prevent, **49**, [100]
water fittings—
disrepair, penalty, **49**, [146]
faulty, requirement to remedy, **49**, [135]
meaning, **49**, [129]
prescribed, notice requiring, **49**, [144]
sufficiency, disputes as to, **49**, [145]
water fund—
deficiency in, **49**, [209], [274]
establishment, **49**, [209]
insurance fund contributions from,
49, [290]
payments to and from, **49**, [209], [322]
stock charged on, **49**, [211]
surplus, carrying forward, **49**, [274]
water pipes—
communication pipes—
breaking up streets to lay, **49**, [306]
connections with, **49**, [309]
enactments relating to, **49**, [310]
maintenance of, **49**, [307]
meaning, **49**, [300]
stopcocks on, **49**, [308]
supplies after transfer date, for, **49**, [302]
transfer to water authority, **49**, [301]
laying of—
breaking up streets for, **49**, [306]
obligation as to, **49**, [241]
mains, connections with, **49**, [309]
map of—
matters to be marked on, **49**, [154]
provisions for, **49**, [98]
particulars of, furnishing, **49**, [99]
separate, substituted for single, **49**, [303]
service pipes—
Clauses Act, application of, **49**, [305]
connecting up, **49**, [309]
meaning, **49**, [300]
payments to be made, **49**, [309]
stopcock—
effect of fitting, **49**, [301]
marking of, **49**, [154]

Thames Water Authority—*contd*
water pipes—*contd*
stopcock—*contd*
meaning, **49**, [300]
position of, **49**, [308]
supply pipes—
breaking up streets for, **49**, [306]
maintenance of, **49**, [307]
meaning, **49**, [300]
transfer of, date of, **49**, [300]
water rate—
action to recover, **49**, [255]
arrears, incoming tenant not liable for,
49, [153]
Government buildings—
arbitration as to, **49**, [252]
contributions in lieu of, **49**, [244]
occupiers, list, owner to provide, **49**, [376]
owner, information to be given by,
49, [376]
rateable value, meaning, **49**, [189]
recovery of, **49**, [255]
water stock, discharge of, **49**, [212]
Waterworks Clauses Act—
amendments of, **49**, [272]
incorporation of, **49**, [238], [271]

theatre
bodies corporate, offences by, **13**, [192]
censorship, abolition, **13**, [181]
entry and inspection of premises, **13**, [191]
exits, etc, **35(1)**, [549]
Isles of Scilly, application of provisions,
13, [195]
plays—
broadcast programme, performance for
making of, **13**, [186]
domestic occasion, **13**, [186]
films or records, for making of, **13**, [186]
licences. *See under* performance *below*
nature of, restriction on, prohibition on
licensing authority, **13**, [182]
obscene—
defence of public good, **13**, [183]
private gain, presentation for, **13**, [182]
prohibition on presentation, **13**, [182]
performance—
presenter or director, person regarded
as, **13**, [193]
public, meaning, **13**, [193]
police powers as to scripts, **13**, [189]
private dwelling, performance in, **13**, [186]
private gain, presentation of obscene plays
for, **13**, [182]
proceedings, institution of, **13**, [187]
rehearsals, **13**, [186]
scripts—
British Museum, delivery to, **13**, [190]
copies, power to make, **13**, [189]
evidence, as, **13**, [188]
meaning, **13**, [188]
transitional provisions, **13**, [194]

Theatres Trust
accounts and audit, **13**, [238]

Theatres Trust—*contd*
borrowing powers, **13**, [234]
establishment, **13**, [233]
executive committee, **13**, [238]
incorporation, **13**, [233]
land, dealings in, **13**, [234]
objects of, **13**, [234]
staff, employment of, **13**, [235]
theatres, acquisition, maintenance, etc,
13, [234]
trustees—
appointment, **13**, [238]
chairman and deputy, **13**, [238]
constitution, **13**, [238]
executive committee, appointment,
13, [238]
financial or other interests, **13**, [238]
management and administration by,
13, [234]
number, **13**, [238]
powers generally, **13**, [234]
term of office, **13**, [238]

theft
abolition of certain offences, **12(1)**, [582]
airports, at, prevention, **4(1)**, [224]
appropriation—
dishonesty, **12(1)**, [554]
meaning, **12(1)**, [555]
payment, willingness to make, **12(1)**, [554]
purpose of, **12(1)**, [553]
rights of owner, assuming, **12(1)**, [555]
assumption of owner's rights, **12(1)**, [555]
civil proceedings, and, **12(1)**, [581]
common law offences, abolition of,
12(1), [582]
creature, wild, of, **12(1)**, [556]
deception. *See* **deception**
definition of, **12(1)**, [553]
dishonestly, meaning, **12(1)**, [554]
flowers, fruit and foliage, of, **12(1)**, [556]
generally, **12(1)**, [1]
going equipped for, **12(1)**, [577]
imprisonment, **12(1)**, [559]
indictment, **12(1)**, [559], [579]
land, of, **12(1)**, [556]
limitation of action, **19(3)**, [727]
mail bag, of, **12(1)**, [567]
making off without payment, **12(1)**, [693]
meaning, **19(3)**, [727]
motor vehicle, taking without authority,
12(1), [1084]
mushrooms, wild, of, **12(1)**, [556]
offences, group A, list of, **12(2)**, [162]
permanent deprivation, intention of,
12(1), [558]
places open to the public, removal of articles
from, **12(1)**, [563]
postal packet, of, **12(1)**, [567]
property—
another person, received for, **12(1)**, [557]
belonging to another, **12(1)**, [557]
corporation sole, belonging to,
12(1), [557]
meaning, **12(1)**, [556]

theft—*contd*
property—*contd*
mistake, got by, **12(1)**, [557]
trust, belonging to, **12(1)**, [557]
restitution order, **12(2)**, [825], [826]
stolen goods. *See* **stolen goods**
transmission, in course of, **12(1)**, [579]
trigger offences, **12(2)**, [1012]

theological college
loans for, **14**, 629–30

thermal insulation
capital allowances, **43(S)**, 897–8
grants for, **40(1)**, [1], [214]

third parties
mining rights, protection, **17(1)**, [1]

third party insurance. *See* **insurance**

tickets
internet, sale and disposal on, **12(2)**, [244]
unauthorised persons, sale by, **12(2)**, [243]

tidal lands
Crown and Duchies, savings, **19(3)**, [249]
high-water mark, works below, **35(1)**, [214]
levy of drainage rates in respect of,
19(3), [249]
meaning, **19(3)**, [249]

tidal waters
meaning, **18**, [718]
pollution generally. *See* **pollution**
telecommunications works in, **45**, [72]

tied premises
profits or gains, computing, **44(1)**, [79]
receipts and expenses treated as those of
trade, **43(1)**, [344]; **44(1)**, [79]
trading income, **44(3)**, [19]

timber
transfer of rights as to, **17(1)**, [170]

time
calendar. *See* **calendar**
Channel Islands, summer time provisions,
45, [943]
computation generally, **45**, [918]
day, **45**, [918]
divisions of, **45**, [918]
Manx time, **45**, [943]
month, **45**, [918]
summer time, **45**, [940]
week, **45**, [918]
year, **45**, [918]

time off work
ante-natal care, for—
employment tribunal, complaints to,
16, [681]
remuneration, **16**, [680]

time off work—*contd*
ante-natal care, for—*contd*
right to, **16**, [679]
dependants, in relation to—
employment tribunal, complaint to, **16**, [683]
meaning, **16**, [682]
right to, **16**, [682]
employee representatives, for—
employment tribunal, complaints to, **16**, [689]
remuneration, **16**, [688]
right to, **16**, [687]
pension scheme trustees, for—
employment tribunal, complaints to, **16**, [686]
remuneration, **16**, [685]
right to, **16**, [684]
public duties, for—
amount of, **16**, [674]
employment tribunal, complaints to, **16**, [675]
right to, **16**, [674]
study or training, for—
detriment, right not to suffer, **16**, [665]
employment tribunal, complaint to, **16**, [692]
remuneration, **16**, [691]
young person, right of, **16**, [690]
trade union duties and activities, for. *See* **trade unions**
training, to arrange—
employment tribunal, complaints to, **16**, [678]
remuneration, **16**, [677]
right to, **16**, [676]
union learning representatives, for, **16**, [366]
work, to look for—
employment tribunal, complaints to, **16**, [678]
remuneration, **16**, [677]
right to, **16**, [676]

timeshare
accommodation—
information, obligation to provide, **11(1)**, [345]
meaning, **11(1)**, [344]
advertisement of rights, **11(1)**, [346]
agreement—
cancellation—
automatic, **11(1)**, [357]
credit and interest, repayment of, **11(1)**, [358]
right of, **11(1)**, [358]
advance payments before expiry of period of, **11(1)**, [355]
obligation to give notice, **11(1)**, [350], [352]
civil proceedings, **11(1)**, [362]
due diligence, defence of, **11(1)**, [359]
enforcement, **11(1)**, [367]
form, **11(1)**, [348]
information, obligation to provide, **11(1)**, [345]

timeshare—*contd*
agreement—*contd*
items for inclusion in, **11(1)**, [366]
language, **11(1)**, [348]
liability of persons, principal offender, other than, **11(1)**, [360]
meaning, **11(1)**, [344]
obligatory terms, **11(1)**, [347], [366]
prosecution, time limit for, **11(1)**, [363]
summary of provisions, **11(1)**, [293]
translation, **11(1)**, [349]
brochure—
form, **11(1)**, [348]
language, **11(1)**, [348]
credit agreement—
cancellation—
automatic, **11(1)**, [357]
credit and interest, repayment of, **11(1)**, [358]
right of, **11(1)**, [356]
obligation to contain information on, **11(1)**, [351]–[352]
meaning, **11(1)**, [344]

tin
mining for. *See* **stannaries**

tipping-off. *See under* **money laundering**

tips (mines and quarries)
association with mine or quarry, determination, **17(1)**, [391]
closed—
as part of mine or quarry, **17(1)**, [419]
plans and sections, **17(1)**, [389]
disused, prevention of danger from—
appeal against notice, **17(1)**, [397]
contribution orders, **17(1)**, [401]
court, meaning for purposes of, **17(1)**, [410]
damage or disturbance, compensation—
entitlement, **17(1)**, [402]
schedule of provisions, **17(1)**, [421]
ecclesiastical property, **17(1)**, [413]
entry, right of, **17(1)**, [395], [400]
expenses—
appeal against demand—
contributory, by, **17(1)**, [404], [406], [422]
owner, by, **17(1)**, [406]
contribution orders, **17(1)**, [401]
grants to local authorities, **17(1)**, [407]
raising of money in special cases, **17(1)**, [414]
recovery—
local authority, by, **17(1)**, [405]
owner, by, **17(1)**, [403]
where notice cancelled, **17(1)**, [403], [422]
exploratory tests, **17(1)**, [395]
information relating to, **17(1)**, [394]
local authorities, functions, **17(1)**, [393], [420]
offences, prosecution of, **17(1)**, [409]
owner, meaning, **17(1)**, [416]

tips (mines and quarries)—*contd*
disused, prevention of danger from—*contd*
Public Health Act, application, **17(1)**, [415]
regulations and orders, **17(1)**, [411]
remedial operations—
damaging completed works, penalty,
17(1), [408]
entry for, **17(1)**, [396], [400]
expenses. *See* expenses *above*
local authority, by—
carrying out of operations,
17(1), [399], [420]
reinstatement, **17(1)**, [399]
meaning, **17(1)**, [396]
notice requiring, **17(1)**, [396]
appeal against, **17(1)**, [397]
cancellation of, **17(1)**, [398]
obstruction of, penalty, **17(1)**, [408]
reinstatement after, **17(1)**, [399], [400]
right of entry, **17(1)**, [400]
service of documents, **17(1)**, [412]
geological map of district, regulations in
force, **17(1)**, [391]
meaning, **17(1)**, [385]
plans, **17(1)**, [389]
right of entry, **17(1)**, [395], [400]
security of—
abandoned mines and quarries,
17(1), [390]
generally, **17(1)**, [1]
inspectors, powers of, **17(1)**, [386]
owners and managers, duties of,
17(1), [386]
plans and sections, **17(1)**, [389]
requirement, **17(1)**, [384]
tipping—
operations—
beginning and ending, notification,
17(1), [387]
meaning, **17(1)**, [392]
rules, **17(1)**, [387]

tithe
commissioners. *See* **tithe commissioners**
redemption commission. *See* **tithe
redemption commission**
rentcharge. *See* **tithe rentcharge**

tithe commissioners
apportionments, instruments, sealing, **14**, 88

tithe redemption commission
arbitration provisions, **14**, 366–7
documents—
placed at disposal of, **14**, 360
possession of, in, **14**, 444
duties of, **14**, 359
entry and inspection of land, **14**, 368
establishment of, **14**, 359
exercise of powers, **14**, 367–8
liability to repair chancels, apportioning,
14, 373–4
procedure, **14**, 371–2
records, keeping, **14**, 442
redemption annuities account, audit, **14**, 361

tithe redemption commission—*contd*
reports of proceedings, **14**, 443
transfer of functions, **14**, 445–6

tithe rentcharge. *See also* **rentcharge; tithe**
Queen Anne's Bounty, vested in. *See* **Queen
Anne's Bounty**
redemption, apportionment of charges
payable, **20**, [792]

tithes. *See also* **rentcharge**
annuities—
extinguishment, **14**, 879
register, **14**, 440–1
apportionment, transcript of, **14**, 88
Church Commissioners, held by, **14**, 846
composition for, validity, **14**, 78
corn rents replacing, **14**, 20
discharge from, validity, **14**, 77–8
exemption from, validity, **14**, 77–8
generally, **14**, 20
land, merging with, charges thereon, **14**, 130
meaning, **14**, 146
payment of by house, **14**, 45
rectorial, surrender, **14**, 68–9
rentcharge. *See* **rentcharge**
sale for augmentation of benefice, **14**, 199
term of years, devised for, **14**, 79
vacancy, accruing during, **14**, 42

title
abstract of. *See* **abstract of title**
commencement, **20**, [662]; **21**, [368]
computation of time, **45**, [927]
conversion of perpetually renewable lease,
acquired on, **20**, [500]
covenants for. *See* **covenant**
documents of, general vesting declaration,
production and delivery, **9**, [399]
See also under **documents**
failure to make, **9**, [269]
registration. *See* **land registration**
safe custody, **9**, [399]

title of honour
property devolving with, disposition, **6**, [280]
succession to, after artificial insemination,
6, [281]

title to goods
conversions and extinction, after time limit,
19(3), [726]
extinction, **45**, [965]
slander of, **19(3)**, [310], [318]

title to land
extinction after expiration of time limit,
19(3), [744]
slander of, **19(3)**, [310], [318]

tobacco
advertisement—
broadcasting, **47**, [679]
developments in technology, effect of,
47, [674]

tobacco—*contd*
advertisement—*contd*
display as, **47**, [675]
meaning, **47**, [668]
offences—
burden of proof, **47**, [684]
defences, **47**, [672]
exclusions, **47**, [671]
generally, **47**, [669]
newspapers and periodicals, publication in, **47**, [670]
prohibition, **47**, [669]
specialist tobacconists, at premises of, **47**, [673]
age for sale of, power to amend, **35(2)**, [577]
brandsharing, **47**, [678]
child or young person, sale to—
body corporate, offence by, **6**, [462]
cigarette papers, **6**, [6]
commencement of legislation, **6**, [231], [465]
enforcement action, **6**, [463]
meaning of 'tobacco', **6**, [6], [462]
offence, **6**, [6]
prohibition, **6**, [6]
unpackaged cigarettes, prohibition, **6**, [461]
vending machines, warning notices, **6**, [462]
warning statements, display of, **6**, [462]
coupons, distribution of, **47**, [676]
enforcement of provisions—
authority, **47**, [680]
entry on premises, **47**, [681]
obstruction of officers, **47**, [682]
interpretation of provisions, **47**, [688]
offences—
bodies corporate, by, **47**, [685]
burden of proof, **47**, [684]
meaning, **6(S)**, 296
obstruction of officers, **47**, [682]
penalties, **47**, [683]
Scottish partnership, by, **47**, [685]
product—
displays, **47**, [675]
free distributions, prohibited, **47**, [676]
meaning, **47**, [668]
regulations, **47**, [686]
restricted premises order, **6(S)**, 295
restricted sale order, **6(S)**, 295–6
sale to persons under 18, persistent, **6(S)**, 294–7
sponsorship, prohibited, **47**, [677]
transitional provisions, **47**, [687]
summary of provisions, **47**, [1]

tobacco products
advertising. *See* **tobacco**
dealer in—
cigars, rate of, **13**, [896]
default, charge in case of, **13**, [882]
excise duty—
alteration of rates, **13**, [876]
charge of, **13**, [873]
cigarettes—
long, calculation of duty on, **13**, [874]

tobacco products—*contd*
dealer in—*contd*
excise duty—*contd*
cigarettes—*contd*
rate of, **13**, [896]
retail price for purposes of, **13**, [875]
security for payment, **13**, [875]
excise licence trade, deemed carrying on, **13**, [590]
hand-rolling tobacco—
meaning, **13**, [872]
rate of duty, **13**, [896]
management of, **13**, [877]
rates of, **13**, [896]
remission, **13**, [873]
repayment, **13**, [873]
replacement of other tobacco duties by, **13**, [876]
revenue trader, as, **13**, [590]
fiscal marks—
failure to comply with regulations and public notices, **13**, [887]
interfering with, penalties for, **13**, [891]
introductory, **13**, [883]
possession and sale of unmarked tobacco, offences, **13**, [889]
power to alter range of products to which applicable, **13**, [884]
public notices, **13**, [886]
regulations, **13**, [885]
sale of marked tobacco when not permitted, penalties for, **13**, [888]
use of premises for sale of unmarked tobacco, offences, **13**, [890]
herbal smoking products excluded from, **13**, [872]
meaning, **13**, [872]
records and returns, **13**, [877]
registration of premises—
manufacture, for, **13**, [877]
storage, for, **13**, [877]
smuggling—
duty not to facilitate, **13**, [878]
penalty for facilitating, **13**, [879]–[881]

tobacco products duty
rates of, **13(S)**, Customs 3; **43(S)**, 843
wrongdoing, penalties, **43(S)**, 1328–39. *See also* **tax penalty**

Tokyo Convention
aircraft, registration of, application of provisions to, **4(1)**, [147]
convention country, meaning, **4(1)**, [153]

toll
canal—
determination of lease, **36**, [373]
lease of, **36**, [370]
lessee—
collectors, as, **36**, [371]
default by, **36**, [372]
reletting, **36**, [373]
canal company, agreement by, **36**, [556]
charge to tax, **44(1)**, [34]

toll—*contd*
Defence Regulation 56, revocation of,
  36, [658]
exemption—
  air force, **3**, [955]
  armed forces, **3**, [1], [682]
ferry, for—
  exemptions, **36**, [592]
  local authority, power of, **36**, [589]
payment, default in, **36**, [341]
railway company, contracts between, **36**, [338]
  third parties, not affecting, **36**, [338]
rent payable in respect of, **44(1)**, [98]
special road. *See* **special roads**
steam vessels, for, recovery of, **36**, [452],
  [453]
tramway—
  account of, **36**, [510], [511]
  dispute as to amount of, **36**, [512]
  licences, specified in, **36**, [508]
  licensee's failure to pay, **36**, [509]
  power to charge, **36**, [516]
  recovery of, **36**, [526]

toll roads. *See* **special roads (new roads)**

Tonga
Commonwealth citizenship, **31**, [186]
existing law, operation of, **7(2)**, [640]
fully responsible statutes of, **7(2)**, [640]
Orders in Council, **7(2)**, [641]
visiting forces in, **7(2)**, [643]

tonnage tax
allowable losses, **43(1)**, [531]
appeals, **43(1)**, [528]
associate, meaning, **43(1)**, [538]
bareboat charter terms, meaning, **43(1)**, [538]
capital allowances—
  industrial buildings, **43(1)**, [532]
  interpretation, **43(1)**, [532]
  plant and machinery—
    assets beginning to be used for tonnage
      tax trade, **43(1)**, [532]
    assets used partly for tonnage tax trade,
      43(1), [532]
    assets used wholly for tonnage tax
      trade, **43(1)**, [532]
    balancing charges, **43(1)**, [532]
    change of use, **43(1)**, [532]
    disposals, **43(1)**, [532]
    exit, **43(1)**, [532]
    new expenditure, **43(1)**, [532]
    unrelieved qualifying expenditure,
      surrender of, **43(1)**, [532]
ship leasing, **43(1)**, [533]; **43(2)**, [265];
  43(S), 270–3
ships—
  acquired and disposed of within twelve
    months, **43(1)**, [532]
  disposal, deferred balancing charge,
    43(1), [532]
chargeable gains, **43(1)**, [531]
commencement of provisions, **43(2)**, [656]

tonnage tax—*contd*
company—
  control, meaning, **43(1)**, [535]
  controlled by individual, treated as,
    43(1), [535]
  demerger, **43(1)**, [535]
  leaving regime, withdrawal of relief on,
    43(1), [533]
  meaning, **43(1)**, [524]
  profits of, **43(1)**, [524]
  qualifying, **43(1)**, [526]
controlled foreign companies, profits of,
  43(1), [530]
election for—
  application of regime, **43(1)**, [524]
  ceasing to be in force, **43(1)**, [525]
  company or group, **43(1)**, [525]
  further opportunity for, **43(1)**, [525]
  method of making, **43(1)**, [525]
  period of, **43(1)**, [525]
  person making, **43(1)**, [525]
  renewal, **43(1)**, [525]
  taking effect, **43(1)**, [525]
  time of, **43(1)**, [525]
finance costs—
  meaning, **43(S)**, 269
  treatment of, **43(1)**, [530]
fleet tonnage, percentage chartered in,
  43(1), [528]
group—
  arrangements for dealing with matters of,
    43(1), [535]
  changes, notifying Inland Revenue of,
    43(1), [535]
  company as member of one only,
    43(1), [535]
  demerger—
    effect of, **43(1)**, [535]
    meaning, **43(1)**, [535]
  meaning, **43(1)**, [524], [535]
  member, meaning, **43(1)**, [535]
  merger—
    dominant party, **43(1)**, [535]
    meaning, **43(1)**, [535]
    tonnage tax groups or companies,
      between, **43(1)**, [535]
    tonnage tax and non-qualifying groups
      or companies, between, **43(1)**, [535]
    tonnage tax and non-tonnage tax groups
      or companies, between, **43(1)**, [535]
  qualifying, **43(1)**, [526]
interpretation, **43(1)**, [538]
measurement of tonnage, **43(1)**, [524]
no tax avoidance requirement, **43(1)**, [528]
offshore activities, rules for, **43(1)**, [534]
partnerships, application of provisions to,
  43(1), [536]
profits, calculation, **43(1)**, [524]
qualifying—
  dredgers and tugs, **43(1)**, [526]
  ships, **43(1)**, [526]
regime, **43(1)**, [524]
relevant shipping profits, **43(1)**, [529]
reliefs and set-offs, exclusion of, **43(1)**, [530]
ring fence provisions, **43(1)**, [530]

tonnage tax—*contd*
 ship, meaning, **43(1)**, [538]
 trade, **43(1)**, [530]
 training requirement, **43(1)**, [527]
 transactions not at arm's length, **43(1)**, [530]
 transitional provisions, **43(2)**, [656]

tort
 acts in contemplation or furtherance of trade
  dispute, protection in relation to, **16**, [421]
 champerty, civil rights in respect of,
  abolition, **45**, [945], [952]
 child, abolition of actions as to, **45**, [954],
  [983]
 civil remedies, **45**, [945]
 common employment, abolition of defence,
  45, [945], [946]
 congenital injury. *See* **congenital disabilities**
 contribution towards damages for. *See*
  damage
 criminal offence, when, **45**, [945]
 Crown, extent binding on, **45**, [978]
 damages—
  action for, **45**, [945]
  exclusion of right to, **45**, [945]
 enticement actions, abolition, **45**, [954]
 foreign element involved, where—
  choice of applicable law—
   abolition of certain common law rules,
    45, [989]
   Crown application, **45**, [994]
   defamation claims, exclusion from
    provisions, **45**, [992]
   displacement of general rule, **45**, [991]
   general rule, **45**, [990]
   purpose of provisions, **45**, [988]
   summary of provisions, **45**, [945]
   transitional provisions and savings,
    45, [993]
 goods, as to. *See* **wrongful interference
  with goods**
 harbouring, spouse or child, abolition of
  actions, **45**, [954]
 liability in—
  acts giving rise to, **16**, [19]
  generally, **45**, [945]
  restriction, **45**, [945]
 liability of Crown in, **13**, [11],
  [44]–[48]. *See also* **Crown**
 limitation of action, **19(3)**, [725]
 maintenance, civil rights in respect of,
  abolition, **45**, [945], [952]
 married woman, committed by, **27**, [197]
 meaning, **45**, [945]
 rape, loss of services in case of, **45**, [954],
  [983]
 remedy, **45**, [945]
 seduction, abolition of action for, **45**, [954],
  [983]
 spouse, abolition of actions as to, **45**, [954]
 trade unions—
  liability of, **16**, [193]
  limit on damages in, **16**, [195]
  repudiation of acts, **16**, [194]

torture
 application of provisions, **12(1)**, [1094]
 defence to charge, **12(1)**, [1092]
 nationality of offender immaterial,
  12(1), [1092]
 nature of, **12(1)**, [1092]
 Northern Ireland, consent to prosecution in,
  12(1), [1093]
 penalty on conviction, **12(1)**, [1092]
 person acting in an official capacity,
  commission by, **12(1)**, [1092]
 prosecution, consent to, **12(1)**, [1093]
 public official, commission of offence by,
  12(1), [1092]
 United Kingdom—
  outside, **12(1)**, [1092]
  within, **12(1)**, [1092]

total loss
 meaning, **9**, [123]
 requisitioned property, compensation for,
  9, [123]

totalisator
 financing of facilities, **5(1)**, [23]

Totalisator Board
 abolition, **5(1)**, [1]
 additional powers, **5(1)**, [4]
 betting, exclusive right respecting, **5(1)**, [3]
 betting office licence, application for,
  5(1), [22]
  See also **betting** (licensed betting office)
 borrowing powers, **5(1)**, [4]
 composition of, **5(1)**, [2]
 dissolution—
  preparatory work for, **5(1)**, [243]
  provision for, **5(1)**, [233]
  reference to following, **5(1)**, [235]
 establishment, **5(1)**, [2]
 financial provisions, **5(1)**, [4]
 functions, **5(1)**, [3]
 levy contributions by—
  amount, determination, **5(1)**, [18]
  liability for, **5(1)**, [5]
  objections to, **5(1)**, [17]
  remission of, **5(1)**, [26]
 members, **5(1)**, [2]
 moneys available to, application of, **5(1)**, [4]
 National Lottery, powers as to, **5(1)**, [149]
 new corporate powers, **5(1)**, [21]
 pool betting, promotion of, **5(1)**, [3], [21]
 powers of, **5(1)**, [21]
 sale, consequential amendments, **5(1)**, [275]
 stakes, deduction from, **5(1)**, [3]
 status of, **5(1)**, [2]
 successor company—
  accounts, **5(1)**, [238]
  contract of employment, transfer of
   liabilities under, **5(1)**, [235]
  exclusive licence for pool betting—
   effect of, **5(1)**, [241]
   grant to, **5(1)**, [240]
   revocation, **5(1)**, [241]

Totalisator Board—*contd*
　successor company—*contd*
　　exclusive licence for pool betting—*contd*
　　　Secretary of State, consideration by,
　　　　5(1), [241]
　　information, provision of, **5(1)**, [235]
　　matters treated as done by, **5(1)**, [235]
　　meaning, **5(1)**, [234]
　　property, rights and liabilities, transfer of,
　　　5(1), [234]
　　shadow directors, **5(1)**, [239]
　　shares, etc, issue to government, **5(1)**, [237]
　　tax provisions, **5(1)**, [236]

tour operator
　value added tax on supplies by, **50**, [75]

tourism
　accommodation. *See* tourist accommodation
　　below
　amenities and facilities—
　　meaning, **26(1)**, [727]; **47**, [103]
　　provision etc of, **47**, [103]
　　See also tourist accommodation *below*
　British Tourist Authority—
　　constitution of, **47**, [102]
　　establishment, **47**, [102]
　　functions, **47**, [103]
　　miscellaneous duties, **47**, [106]
　Channel Isles, promotion of, **47**, [106]
　Greater London Authority—
　　advice, provision of, **26(1)**, [724]
　　delegation of functions, **26(1)**, [725]
　　functions, meaning, **26(1)**, [727]
　　grants for, **26(1)**, [726]
　　promotion by, **26(1)**, [723]
　hotel development. *See* **hotel**
　Isle of Man, in, **47**, [106]
　Northern Ireland, **47**, [106]
　projects—
　　execution of, **47**, [105]
　　financial assistance for, **47**, [104]
　publicity outside UK, **47**, [103]
　Scotland, in, overseas promotion, **47**, [400]
　summary of provisions, **47**, [1]
　tourist accommodation—
　　classification or grading, **47**, [108]
　　inspection of, **47**, [108]
　　prices of, requirement to display, **47**, [109]
　　register—
　　　contents and form, **47**, [108]
　　　publication of, **47**, [108]
　　registration, **47**, [108]
　Tourist Boards—
　　accounts, **47**, [107]
　　activities, reports on, **47**, [107]
　　borrowing powers, **47**, [104]
　　charges for services, **47**, [103]
　　constitution of, **47**, [102]
　　directions by Minister to, **47**, [110]
　　establishment, **47**, [102]
　　financial provisions, **47**, [111]
　　functions, **47**, [103]

tourism—*contd*
　Tourist Boards—*contd*
　　grants or loans by—
　　　hotels, for. *See* **hotel**
　　　projects eligible for, **47**, [104]
　　information, power to require, **47**, [114]
　　meaning, **47**, [102]
　　members—
　　　remuneration, **47**, [113]
　　　terms of office, **47**, [113]
　　names of, **47**, [102]
　　officers and servants, **47**, [113]
　　proceedings of, **47**, [113]
　　status of, **47**, [113]
　Wales, in, overseas promotion, **47**, [467]

towage
　Admiralty jurisdiction, **11(2)**, [917]
　zero-rating, **50**, [151]

Tower Bridge
　byelaws, **25(1)**, [189]
　trunk road, not being, **36**, [1013]

town
　new. *See* **new town**

town and country planning. *See also*
planning
　development, appropriate alternative—
　　assumptions as to permission, **9**, [230]
　　certificate of—
　　　appeal against, **9**, [233]
　　　extension of provisions, **9**, [234]
　　　interpretation of provisions, **9**, [237]
　　　issue of, **9**, [232], [235]
　　　special cases, **9**, [234]
　errors in decisions, correction of, **46(S)**, 173
　London—
　　joint planning committee, abolition,
　　　26(1), [691]
　　Mayor, functions of, **26(1)**, [690]
　regional planning bodies. *See* **regional
　　planning bodies**
　Regional Spatial Strategy. *See* **regional
　　spatial strategy**
　strategies, plans and documents, right of High
　　Court to remit, **46(S)**, 174
　sustainable development, **46(S)**, 173
　Wales. *See* **Wales**

town development
　adjustments following, **46**, [12]
　definition, **46**, [2]
　expenses of, **46**, [18]
　functions, **46**, [57]
　land drainage works, contributions to,
　　46, [14]
　legislation, **46**, [1]
　orders, making, **46**, [16]
　participation in—
　　agreement, by, **46**, [9]
　　authorities eligible, **46**, [8]
　　contributions to authorities, **46**, [11]
　　minister, by order of, **46**, [10]

town development—*contd*
payments, making and receipt of, **46**, [11]
planning permission for, **46**, [17]
planning purposes, appropriation of land for, **46**, [15]
provisions applicable to, **46**, [26]
receiving district—
  agreement, participation by, **46**, [9]
  compulsory acquisition of land by, **46**, [7]
  council, exercise of powers for other area, **46**, [6]
  exchequer contributions to—
    conditions of payment, **46**, [4]
    expenses, for, **46**, [3]
  land drainage works, expenses of, **46**, [14]
  local authorities, contributions of, **46**, [5]
  meaning, **46**, [2]
repeal of provisions, **46**, [247]
re-transfer of land following, **46**, [12]
transfer of land following, **46**, [12]–[13]

town development subsidy
payments to receiving authority, **22**, [446]
reduction or discontinuance, **22**, [446]
transitional subsidy, **22**, [446]

Town Police Clauses Act 1847
incorporation with other Acts, **35(1)**, [11], [26]

town scheme
agreement, **46**, [721]
buildings in, grants for repair of, **46**, [722]
list, **46**, [721]
map, **46**, [721]

Towns Improvement Clauses Act 1847
incorporation with other Acts, **35(1)**, [2], [8], [22]

toxins. *See* **pathogens and toxins**

trade
Act of Union, rights after, **10**, [57]
company, of. *See* **company**
farming as, **44(1)**, [33]
irrecoverable debts, deduction for, **44(1)**, [66]
loss relief. *See* **loss relief**
market gardening as, **44(1)**, [33]
meaning, **44(1)**, [1], [615]
permanent discontinuance, meaning, **44(1)**, [88]
post-discontinuance receipts, taxation of—
  allowable deductions, **44(1)**, [186]
  conventional basis, **44(1)**, [85]
  earnings basis, **44(1)**, [84]
  right to payment transferred, where, **44(1)**, [87]
profits—
  computation of, **43(1)**, [345]
  conventional basis, **44(1)**, [88]
  earnings basis, **44(1)**, [88]
Schedule D Case I, charge under, **44(1)**, [13]
tied premises, receipts and expenses of, **43(1)**, [344]

trade and industry
anti-competitive practice. *See* **fair trading**
careers, grants for promoting, **47**, [379]
common ownership enterprises, nature of, **47**, [278]
development of. *See* **industrial development**
enforcement procedures, appeals, model provisions, **47**, [471]
information—
  offences, **47**, [935]
  permitted disclosure—
    Community obligations, **47**, [930]
    consent to, **47**, [929]
    criminal proceedings, in relation to, **47**, [932]
    overseas, **47**, [933]
    specified information, considerations, **47**, [934], [960]
    statutory functions, exercise of, **47**, [931], [961]
  restriction on disclosure—
    general, **47**, [927]
    specified, **47**, [928], [960]
statistics. *See* **trade statistics**
statutory burdens—
  law imposing, reformation of—
    enforcement, codes of practice for—
      generally, **47**, [633]
      making, **47**, [634]
      National Assembly for Wales, making by, **47**, [635]
    limitations on, **47**, [627]
    orders for, **47**, [625]
    Parliament—
      documents to be laid before, **47**, [630]
      proposals, consideration of, **47**, [632]
    preliminary consultation for, **47**, [629]
    representations, **47**, [631]
    statutory instrument procedure for, **47**, [628]
  meaning, **47**, [626]
statutory burdens, power to remove or reduce, **47**, [570]
summary of provisions, **47**, [1]

trade description
advertisement—
  meaning, **39(1)**, [112]
  use in, **39(1)**, [91]
broadcast, **39(1)**, [112]
civil rights, saving for, **39(1)**, [109]
country of origin, deemed, **39(1)**, [110]
enforcement of provisions—
  authorised officers, obstruction of, **39(1)**, [104]
  goods and documents, seizure of, **39(1)**, [103], [107]
  notice of test and intended prosecution, **39(1)**, [105]
  test purchases, **39(1)**, [102]
  weights and measures authority, by, **39(1)**, [101]
false—
  indication of origin, as to, **39(1)**, [93]

trade description—*contd*
> false—*contd*
>> meaning, **39(1)**, [89]
>> prohibition of, **39(1)**, [87]
>
> fineness of precious metal, indicating, **48**, 52
> goods, applied to, **39(1)**, [90]
> mark not being, **39(1)**, [88]
> meaning, **39(1)**, [88]
> misleading, **39(1)**, [89]
> Northern Ireland, provisions applying to, **39(1)**, [113]
> offences—
>> abroad, committed, accessories to, **39(1)**, [97]
>> authorised officer, obstruction of, **39(1)**, [104]
>> corporation, by, **39(1)**, [96]
>> defence—
>>> accident, of, **39(1)**, [99]
>>> advertisement, innocent publication of, **39(1)**, [100]
>>> due diligence, of, **39(1)**, [100]
>>> mistake, of, **39(1)**, [99]
>>> other person, due to fault of, **39(1)**, [98]
>>
>> penalties, **39(1)**, [94]
>> prosecution, time limit for, **39(1)**, [95]
>
> oral statement as, **39(1)**, [90]
> orders, **39(1)**, [111]
> proceedings—
>> evidence by certificate, **39(1)**, [106]
>> notice of, **39(1)**, [105]
>
> published, **39(1)**, [112]
> statement not being, **39(1)**, [88]
> trade mark containing, **39(1)**, [108]

trade disputes. *See also* **industrial action; trade unions**
> acts in contemplation or furtherance of—
>> offence of conspiracy, restriction of, **16**, [456]
>> peaceful picketing, **16**, [422]
>> tort liabilities, protection from, **16**, [421]
>>> exclusions, **16**, [424]–[427]
>
> arbitration and conciliation. *See* **Advisory, Conciliation and Arbitration Service**
> Courts of Inquiry. *See* **Courts of Inquiry**
> income support during—
>> calculation of, **40(1)**, [369]
>> return to work, effect of, **40(1)**, [370]
>
> increases in benefit, effect of entitlement to, **40(1)**, [336]
> injunctions and interdicts, restrictions on grant of, **16**, [423]
> jobseeker's allowance, effect on, **40(2)**, [62]
>> joint-claim couples, **40(2)**, [64]
>> other claimants, **40(2)**, [62]
>
> meaning, **16**, [420], [457]

trade effluent
> appeals, statement of case, **49**, [942]
> application of provisions, **49**, [944], [1387]
> charges, fixing, **49**, [939]
> discharge, duty as to, **49**, [887]
> discharge into public sewer, adaptation of local Acts, **35(1)**, [219]

trade effluent—*contd*
> disposal etc, agreements with respect to, **49**, [933]–[935]
> information as to, provision of, **49**, [1016]
> meaning, **35(1)**, [351]; **49**, [946], [1267]
> meters, evidence from, **49**, [941]
> new rights, modification of compensation requirements, **49**, [1051]
> pre-1989 Act authority for, **49**, [945], [1050]
> protection of public health, compensation in respect of, **49**, [938]
> public sewer, consent for discharge into—
>> appeals, **49**, [926]
>>> variation, as to, **49**, [930]
>>
>> application for, **49**, [923], [1388]
>> conditions of, **49**, [925]
>> requirement of, **49**, [922]
>> special category, **49**, [924], [927], [931]
>> time for, application for variation, **49**, [932]
>> time limits, variation within, **49**, [929]
>> variation of, **49**, [928]
>
> references and reviews—
>> determination, effect of, **49**, [937]
>> powers and procedure on, **49**, [936]
>
> register of, **49**, [1008]
> special category—
>> agreements relating to, reference to Environment Agency, **49**, [934]
>>> meaning, **49**, [943]
>>> review of, **49**, [935]–[938]
>>
>> application for discharge of, **49**, [924]
>> appeals, **49**, [927]
>>> Environment Agency, review by, **49**, [931]
>>
>> functions of Environment Agency, power to obtain information relating to, **49**, [940]

trade losses
> capital gains relief—
>> early tax year, meaning, **44(4)**, [115]
>> limited partners, restrictions on, for, **44(4)**, [108]
>> limits on amount of, **44(4)**, [106]
>> LLP members—
>>> non-active partners—
>>>> contribution to the firm—
>>>>> amounts excluded when calculating, **44(4)**, [117]–[118]
>>>>> meaning, **44(4)**, [114]
>>>>
>>>> restrictions on relief for in early tax years, **44(4)**, [113]
>>>> unrelieved losses brought forward, **44(4)**, [116]
>>>
>>> restrictions on, for, **44(4)**, [110]
>>> unrelieved losses brought forward, **44(4)**, [112]
>>
>> meaning, **44(4)**, [103]
>> restrictions on—
>>> films, exploitation of, **44(4)**, [119]
>
> capital gains tax losses, treating as, **44(4)**, [71]
> double counting, prohibition against, **44(4)**, [63], [100]
> foreign trades, reliefs against foreign income, **44(4)**, [95]

trade losses—*contd*
limited liability partnerships—
contribution to—
amounts excluded when calculating,
44(4), [117]–[18]
meaning, **44(4)**, [111]
restrictions on reliefs for members of,
44(4), [110]
non-partners, made by, **44(4)**, [61]
partners—
film trades, in, restrictions on reliefs for,
44(4), [119]
limited—
contribution to firm—
amounts excluded when calculating,
44(4), [117]–[118]
meaning, **44(4)**, [109]
meaning, **44(4)**, [104]
restriction on reliefs for, **44(4)**, [108]
made by, **44(4)**, [62]
non-active—
meaning, **44(4)**, [105]
restriction on reliefs in early tax years,
44(4), [113]
relief—
capital gains. *See* capital gains relief *above*
carry-forward—
deductions, how made, **44(4)**, [84]
insufficient trade profits, use of
trade-related interest or dividends
where, **44(4)**, [8]
interest as loss, **44(4)**, [88]
ring fence trades, **44(4)**, [87]
subsequent trade profits, against,
44(4), [83]
trade transferred to company, **44(4)**, [86]
early—
deductions, how made, **44(4)**, [73]
first 4 years of trade, relief for losses in,
44(4), [72]
non-commercial trade, restrictions on
relief, **44(4)**, [74]
farming—
losses in previous tax years,
determining, **44(4)**, [70]
reasonable expectation of profit test,
44(4), [68]
restrictions on, **44(4)**, [67]
trade treated as same, whether,
44(4), [69]
general income, against—
claim for, **44(4)**, [64]
deduction of losses, **44(4)**, [64]
method for making, **44(4)**, [65]
rules as to, **44(4)**, [65]
uncommercial trades, restrictions on,
44(4), [66]
market gardening—
losses in previous tax years,
determining, **44(4)**, [70]
reasonable expectation of profit test,
44(4), [68]
restrictions on, **44(4)**, [67]
trade treated as same, whether,
44(4), [69]

trade losses—*contd*
relief—*contd*
overview, **44(4)**, [60]
post-cessation—
CGT loss, excess treated as, **44(4)**, [101]
claim for, **44(4)**, [96]
qualifying event, meaning, **44(4)**, [98]
qualifying payment, meaning,
44(4), [97]
double counting, prohibition against,
44(4), [100]
unpaid expenses, reduction for,
44(4), [99]
restrictions on, generally, **44(4)**, [102]
sideways. *See* sideways relief *below*
terminal—
claim for, **44(4)**, [89]
deductions, how made, **44(4)**, [91]
insufficient trade profits, use of
trade-related interest or dividends
where, **44(4)**, [92]
losses—
carried back on permanent cessation
of trade, **44(4)**, [89]
meaning, **44(4)**, [90]
mineral extraction trade and balancing
allowances, **44(4)**, [93]
transitional provisions and savings,
44(4), [1050]
reliefs—
restrictions on—
limited partners, for, **44(4)**, [108]
LLPs, for members of, **44(4)**, [110]
sideways relief—
early tax year, meaning, **44(4)**, [115]
limited partners, restrictions on, for,
44(4), [108]
limits on amount of, **44(4)**, [106]
LLP members—
non-active partners—
contribution to the firm—
amounts excluded when
calculating, **44(4)**, [117]–[118]
meaning, **44(4)**, [114]
restrictions on relief for in early tax
years, **44(4)**, [113]
unrelieved losses brought forward,
44(4), [116]
restrictions on, for, **44(4)**, [110]
unrelieved losses brought forward,
44(4), [112]
meaning, **44(4)**, [103]
restrictions on—
capital allowances restrictions,
44(4), [79]
commodity futures, dealings in,
44(4), [81]
films, exploitation of, **44(4)**, [82], [119]
first-year allowances—
partnerships with companies,
44(4), [76]–[77]
reduction of tax liabilities,
arrangements for, **44(4)**, [76], [78]
ring fence income, **44(4)**, [80]

trade losses—*contd*
  sideways relief—*contd*
    restrictions on—*contd*
      trade leasing allowances given to
        individuals, **44(4)**, [75]
  tax avoidance, involving—
    excess sideways or capital gains relief,
      partners claiming, **44(4)**, [800]
      income receivable under—
        calculating amount of, **44(4)**, [801]
        charge to tax on, **44(4)**, [799]
        "post-December 2004 loss",
          meaning, **44(4)**, [803]
        "total amount of trade losses claimed",
          meaning, **44(4)**, [802]
    film-related trading losses, individuals
      claiming sideways or capital gains relief
      for, **44(4)**, [805]
      capital contribution by a partner,
        exclusion of amounts in calculating,
        44(4), [810]
      "capital contribution", meaning,
        44(4), [809]
      charge to tax on income receivable
        under, **44(4)**, [804]
      "disposal of right of individual to
        profits", meaning, **44(4)**, [807]
      double counting, prohibition against,
        44(4), [811]
      "film-related losses", meaning,
        44(4), [808]
      "non-taxable consideration", meaning,
        44(4), [806]
    licence-related trading losses, partners
      claiming relief for, **44(4)**, [813]
      "disposal of licence", meaning,
        44(4), [816]
      income receivable under—
        calculation of amount of,
          44(4), [814]–[815]
        charge to tax on, **44(4)**, [812]
  overview, **44(4)**, [798]

trade mark
  certification marks. *See* **certification marks**
  classification, **48**, 137
  collective marks. *See* **collective marks**
  Community—
    generally, **48**, 7
    meaning, **48**, 150
    Regulation—
      meaning, **48**, 150
      provision in connection with, power to
        make, **48**, 150
  compulsory, **48**, 10–12
  consequential amendments, **48**, 196–7
  Convention application—
    meaning, **48**, 138
    priority, claim to, **48**, 138
  counterfeit goods, forfeiture of, **48**, 178
  defined expressions, index of, **48**, 181–2
  earlier—
    acquiescence by proprietor, **48**, 148
    honest concurrent use, **48**, 117

trade mark—*contd*
  earlier—*contd*
    identical mark to, refusal of registration,
      48, 114
    meaning, **48**, 116
    opposition proceedings, relative grounds
      raised in, **48**, 118
  emergencies, meeting, **48**, 3
  enemy—
    grant to, **50**, [210]
    suspension of rights of, **50**, [209]
  expenses, tax deduction for, **44(3)**, [89]
  fees, deduction of, **44(1)**, [53]
  forms, **48**, 160
  High Court, proceedings in, **48**, 164
  infringement—
    action for, **48**, 124
    acts of, **48**, 120
    erasure, etc, of offending sign, order for,
      48, 124
    groundless threat of proceedings, remedy
      for, **48**, 128
    infringing goods, materials or articles—
      delivery up of, **48**, 125–7
      disposal, order for, **48**, 127–8
      information, disclosure by
        Commissioners of Customs and
        Excise, **48**, 174
      meaning, **48**, 125–6
      Northern Ireland county court,
        jurisdiction of, **48**, 128
      prohibited goods, treated as, **48**, 172
      regulations, **48**, 173
      sheriff court, jurisdiction of, **48**, 128
    licensee, rights of, **48**, 134
    particular locality, use in, **48**, 122
    proceedings, meaning, **48**, 181
    transitional provisions, **48**, 192
    use without consent as, **48**, 119
  International Bureau, meaning, **48**, 151
  international, meaning, **48**, 151
  journal, **48**, 168
  legislation, **48**, 1–10
  Madrid Protocol—
    meaning, **48**, 151
    provision giving effect to, power to make,
      48, 152
  mark, meaning, **48**, 2
  meaning, **48**, 2, 108
  new classification, adaptation of entries to,
    48, 160
  offences—
    body corporate, by, **48**, 180
    counterfeit goods, forfeiture of, **48**, 178
    false representation of trade mark as
      registered, **48**, 177
    generally, **48**, 9
    partnership, by, **48**, 180
    penalties, **48**, 175
    register, falsification of, **48**, 177
    unauthorised use, **48**, 174–5
    weights and measures authority,
      enforcement function, **48**, 176
  Olympics association right. *See* **Olympics**
    association right

trade mark—*contd*
Olympic Symbol. *See* **Olympic Symbol**
opposition—
  notice of, **48**, 141
  relative grounds, raising, **48**, 118
Paris Convention—
  agent or representatives, acts of, **48**, 156
  Convention country, meaning, **48**, 153
  flags and emblems, protection of,
    48, 154–6
  meaning, **48**, 153
  well-known trade marks, protection of,
    48, 153–4
Patent Office, hours of business and business
  days, **48**, 167
priority—
  Convention application, of, **48**, 138
  overseas application, claim from, **48**, 139,
    193–4
proceedings, state involved in, **10**, [1046]
register—
  classification, adaptation of entries on
    change in, **48**, 160
  correction of, **48**, 159
  enemy character, evidence of, **50**, [213]
  entry on, **48**, 142, 158
  falsification of, **48**, 177
  keeping of, **48**, 158
  proceedings involving, appearance of
    registrar in, **48**, 164
  rectification of, **48**, 159
registered—
  alteration of, **48**, 144
  assignment of, **48**, 140
  co-ownership of, **48**, 129
  equities, enforcement of, **48**, 132
  exhaustion of rights, **48**, 123
  false representation of, **48**, 177
  generally, **48**, 2, 4–7
  information about, provision of, **48**, 161
  infringement. *See* infringement *above*
  licence—
    exclusive, **48**, 134
    general, **48**, 133
    generally, **48**, 6
    limited, **48**, 133
    sub-licence, **48**, 133
  licensee—
    exclusive, rights of, **48**, 135–6
    infringement, rights in respect of,
      48, 134
  limits on effect of, **48**, 121–2
  meaning, **48**, 2, 110
  nature of, **48**, 129
  register. *See* register *above*
  rights conferred by, **48**, 119
  surrender, **48**, 145
  transactions affecting, registration of,
    48, 131
  transitional provisions, **48**, 191–4
  trust affecting, **48**, 132
Registrar—
  annual reports, **48**, 163
  appeals from—
    court, reference to, **48**, 165

trade mark—*contd*
Registrar—*contd*
  appeals from—*contd*
    generally, **48**, 165
    persons appointed to hear and
      determine, **48**, 165–6
  Comptroller-General as, **48**, 158
  costs, award of, **48**, 161
  court, submission of statement to, **48**, 164
  evidence before, **48**, 162
  examination of application, **48**, 140
  forms, requiring use of, **48**, 160
  generally, **48**, 3, 8
  information, provision of, **48**, 161
  meaning, **48**, 8, 158
  official acts, exclusion of liability for,
    48, 162
  proceedings involving register, appearance
    in, **48**, 164
  registration by, **48**, 142
  security for costs, requiring, **48**, 161
registration—
  application for—
    amendment, **48**, 141
    contents of, **48**, 136–7
    date of filing, **48**, 137
    division, **48**, 143
    examination of, **48**, 140
    fees, **48**, 167
    generally, **48**, 6
    information about, provision of, **48**, 161
    observations, **48**, 140–1
    pending, **48**, 193
    priority, **48**, 138–9
    publication, **48**, 140–1
    registrar, made to, **48**, 136
    restriction, **48**, 141
    withdrawal, **48**, 141
  certificate of, **48**, 142
  contested, certificate of validity, **48**, 163–4
  disclaimer, subject to, **48**, 123
  duration of, **48**, 143
  effect of, **48**, 142
  fees, **48**, 167
  invalidity, grounds for, **48**, 147
  limitation, subject to, **48**, 123
  object of property, as, **48**, 133
  opposition to, **48**, 140–1
  process of, **48**, 142
  publication, **48**, 142
  refusal of—
    absolute grounds for, **48**, 110–11
    emblems, specially protected, **48**, 112–3
    relative grounds for, **48**, 114, 117
  renewal of, **48**, 144
  revocation, **48**, 145–6
  rules, **48**, 143
  series, of, **48**, 143
  transitional provisions, **48**, 191–4
  validity, prima facie evidence of, **48**, 163
rules, power to make, **48**, 166
Scotland, jurisdiction in, **48**, 183
sign—
  graphical representation, **48**, 108
  shape of goods as, **48**, 111

trade mark—*contd*
time limit, extension in war circumstances,
50, [212]
trade description containing, **39(1)**, [108]
transitional provisions, **48**, 191–5
unauthorised use of, **48**, 174–5
search warrants issued in case of,
11(1), [1191]
United Kingdom, territorial waters and
continental shelf, **48**, 183
use, burden of proving, **48**, 180
well-known, protection of, **48**, 153–4

trade mark agent
generally, **48**, 9
recognition of, **48**, 168
register of, **48**, 168
registered—
body corporate as, **48**, 169–70
communications with, privileged, **48**, 171
generally, **48**, 3
partnership as, **48**, 169–70
unregistered persons not to be described
as, **48**, 169
registrar refusing to deal with, **48**, 172
transitional provisions, **48**, 195

trade mark attorney
registration of, Secretary of State's functions
transferred to Institute of Trade Mark
Attorneys, **11(4)**, [299]
use of term, **48**, 171

trade name
generally, **48**, 12–13

trade plates
foreign vehicles, **36**, [905]
international road haulage, use in case of,
36, [919]

trade premises
goods on, certain not privileged from distress
for rent, **13**, [1202]

trade profits
animals kept for trade purposes, treatment of,
44(3), [30]
authorised persons, levies and repayments,
44(3), [154]
barristers and advocates, of, **44(3)**, [159]
cemeteries of. *See* **cemetery**
charity, gifts to—
benefit attributable to, receipt of,
44(3), [108]
designated educational establishment,
meaning, **44(3)**, [109]
professions and vocations, **44(3)**, [106]
trading stock, of, **44(3)**, [107]
crematoria, of. *See* **crematorium**
deductions—
deemed employment payment, for,
44(3), [132], [164]
employee benefit contributions—
interpretation, **44(3)**, [44]

trade profits—*contd*
deductions—*contd*
employee benefit contributions—*contd*
meaning, **44(3)**, [39]
profits calculated before end of 9 month
period, **44(3)**, [43]
provision or payment out of, **44(3)**, [42]
qualifying, provision of, **44(3)**, [40]
restriction of, **44(3)**, [38]–[44]
timing and amount of benefits,
44(3), [41]
rules allowing—
approved contractual payments,
44(3), [75]
ceasing to carry on trade, payments to
employee on, **44(3)**, [78]
convertible loans, **44(3)**, [58]
counselling and other outplacement
services, **44(3)**, [72]
designs, expenses connected with,
44(3), [89]
employment in more than one capacity,
payments in respect of, **44(3)**, [77]
employment wholly within employer's
trade, payments in respect of,
44(3), [76]
Export Credit Guarantee Department,
payments to, **44(3)**, [90]
family expenses, **44(3)**, [93]
finance, incidental costs of obtaining,
44(3), [57]
foreign trade, expenses connected with,
44(3), [91]–[92]
government redundancy payments,
44(3), [79]
loan stock, obtaining, **44(3)**, [58]
local enterprise organisations, payments
to, **44(3)**, [81]
patents, expenses of, **44(3)**, [88]
payroll deduction scheme, agents'
expenses, **44(3)**, [71]
personal security expenses, **44(3)**, [80]
pre-trading expenses, **44(3)**, [56]
professions and vocations, **44(3)**, [55]
redundancy payments, **44(3)**, [75]
research associations, payments to,
44(3), [87]
research and development expenses,
44(3), [86]
restrictive undertakings, payments for,
44(3), [68]
retraining courses, **44(3)**, [73]–[74]
seconded employees, **44(3)**, [69]
taxed leases, tenants under,
44(3), [59]–[66]. *See also* **lease**
trade marks, expenses connected with,
44(3), [89]
trade tools, replacement and alteration
of, **44(3)**, [67]
universities, payments to, **44(3)**, [87]
urban regeneration companies,
contributions to, **44(3)**, [81]
rules prohibiting and allowing, relationship
between, **44(3)**, [31]

trade profits—*contd*
deductions—*contd*
rules restricting—
bad and doubtful debts, **44(3)**, [35]
business entertaining and gifts,
44(3), [45]–[47]
capital expenditure, **44(3)**, [33]
car or motor cycle hire, **44(3)**, [48]–[50]
crime-related payments, **44(3)**, [54]
employee benefit contributions,
44(3), [38]–[44]
expenses not wholly and exclusively for
trade, **44(3)**, [34]
interest, double relief for, **44(3)**, [51]
penalties, interest and VAT surcharges,
44(3), [53]
professions and vocations, **44(3)**, [32]
social security contributions, **44(3)**, [52]
unconnected losses, **44(3)**, [34]
unpaid remuneration, **44(3)**, [36]–[37]
unremittable amounts—
application of provisions, **44(3)**, [188]
professions and vocations, rules
applying, **44(3)**, [187]
relief for, **44(3)**, [189]
restrictions on relief, **44(3)**, [190]
withdrawal of relief, **44(3)**, [191]
films. *See* **films**
generally accepted accounting practice,
calculation according to, **44(3)**, [25]
herd basis rules. *See* **herd basis**
income taxed as—
becoming or ceasing to be UK resident,
effect of, **44(3)**, [17]
caravan sites, of, **44(3)**, [20]
charge to income tax, **44(3)**, [5]
company starting or ceasing to be within
charge, **44(3)**, [18]
foster-care relief, **44(3)**, [23]
full amount of, **44(3)**, [7]
person liable, **44(3)**, [8]
rent-a-room, **44(3)**, [23]
surplus business accommodation, from,
44(3), [21]
territorial scope, **44(3)**, [6]
tied premises, of, **44(3)**, [19]
trades—
commercial occupation of land,
44(3), [20]
divers and diving supervisors, **44(3)**, [25]
farming, **44(3)**, [9]
market gardening, **44(3)**, [9]
mines, quarries and other concerns,
44(3), [12]
oil extraction, **44(3)**, [16]
visiting performers, **44(3)**, [13]–[14]
woodlands, commercial occupation of,
44(3), [11]
wayleaves, from, **44(3)**, [22]
interest, **44(3)**, [29]
know-how. *See* **know-how**
land, dealers in—
lease premiums, reduction of receipts,
44(3), [157]
mineral royalties, **44(3)**, [156]

trade profits—*contd*
land, dealers in—*contd*
woodlands, purchase or sale of,
44(3), [155]
mineral exploitation and access, **44(3)**, [160]
ministers of religion, of, **44(3)**, [158]
partnership, of, **44(3)**, [163]
pool betting tax, persons liable to,
44(3), [161]
professions and vocations, from, **44(3)**, [24]
receipts—
acquisition of trade, on, **44(3)**, [97]
capital, **44(3)**, [95]
debt incurred and later released, **44(3)**, [96]
industrial development grants, **44(3)**, [104]
insurance policies, sums recovered under,
44(3), [105]
mutual concern, distribution of assets of,
44(3), [103]
professions and vocations, **44(3)**, [94]
reverse premiums, **44(3)**, [98]–[102]
receipts and expenses—
capital allowances provisions, treated as
under, **44(3)**, [28]
reference to, **44(3)**, [27]
securities, dealers in—
amount taken to reserves, taxation of,
44(3), [148]
circulating capital, conversion of,
44(3), [149]
gilt strips—
consolidation, **44(3)**, [151]
exchange of gilts for, **44(3)**, [150]
market value, regulations for
determining, **44(3)**, [153]
meaning, **44(3)**, [152]
market value of securities or strips,
regulations for determining, **44(3)**, [153]
sound recordings. *See* **sound recordings**
telecommunication rights. *See*
telecommunications
trading stock. *See* **trading stock**
waste disposal. *See* **waste disposal**
work in progress. *See* **work in progress**

trade refuse
London, disposal facilities, **25(1)**, [749]

trade secret
disclosure—
fertilisers and feeding stuffs, as to,
1(1), [849]
penalty for, **9**, [373]

trade statistics. *See also* **census of production**
competent authorities for purposes of—
delegation of functions, **47**, [24]
expenses of, **47**, [33]
meaning, **47**, [34]
information—
false, penalty, **47**, [24]
improper disclosure, **47**, [27]
offences relating to, **47**, [22]
bodies corporate, by, **47**, [32]
power to obtain, **47**, [19]

trade statistics—*contd*
  information—*contd*
    Secretary of States, authorised disclosure
      by, **47**, [28]
    Northern Ireland, in respect of, **47**, [35]
    notices, service of, **47**, [31]
    orders, power to make, **47**, [30]
    report to Parliament, **47**, [25]
    returns—
      falsification, **47**, [24]
      Gazette notice requiring, **47**, [24]
    subjects of, **47**, [20], [36]

trade unions. *See also* **trade disputes**
  accounting records—
    duty to keep, **16**, [202]
    duty to keep available for inspection,
      16, [203]
    failure to comply with request, **16**, [205]
    right of access to, **16**, [204]
  activities—
    blacklists, prohibition, **16**, [969]
    detriment on grounds of—
      consideration of complaint, **16**, [348]
      interpretation of terms, **16**, [351]
      prohibition of, **16**, [346]
      remedies, **16**, [349]
      third parties, awards against, **16**, [350]
      time limit for proceedings, **16**, [347]
    dismissal of employee on grounds related
      to, **16**, [352]
      continuation of employment, order for,
        16, [361]
      contributory fault, assessment of,
        16, [355]
      failure to comply with order, **16**, [363]
      interim relief, application for, **16**, [358]
      interpretation of terms, **16**, [364]
      minimum basic award, **16**, [356]
      order, making, **16**, [360]
      procedure on hearing of application,
        16, [360]
      prompt determination of applications,
        16, [359]
      qualifying period, disapplication of
        requirement for, **16**, [354]
      third parties, awards against, **16**, [357]
      upper age limit, disapplication of,
        16, [354]
      variation or revocation of order,
        application for, **16**, [362]
    inducements relating to, **16**, [340]
      consideration of complaint, **16**, [343]
      interpretation of terms, **16**, [345]
      remedies, **16**, [344]
      time limit for proceedings, **16**, [342]
    selection for redundancy on grounds related
      to, **16**, [353]
      continuation of employment, order for,
        16, [361]
      contributory fault, assessment of,
        16, [355]
      failure to comply with order, **16**, [363]
      interim relief, application for, **16**, [358]
      interpretation of terms, **16**, [364]

trade unions—*contd*
  activities—*contd*
    selection for redundancy on grounds related
      to—*contd*
      minimum basic award, **16**, [356]
      order, making, **16**, [360]
      procedure on hearing of application,
        16, [360]
      prompt determination of applications,
        16, [359]
      qualifying period, disapplication of
        requirement for, **16**, [354]
      third parties, awards against, **16**, [357]
      upper age limit, disapplication of,
        16, [354]
      variation or revocation of order,
        application for, **16**, [362]
    time off for carrying out—
      complaints to industrial tribunal,
        16, [368]
      interpretation of terms, **16**, [371]
      permitting, **16**, [368]
      remedies, **16**, [370]
      time limit for proceedings, **16**, [369]
  amalgamation—
    appeals, **16**, [302]
    ballot—
      counting of votes, **16**, [295]
      entitlement to vote, **16**, [293]
      independent scrutineer, appointment of,
        16, [292]
      requirement of, **16**, [291]
      scrutineer's report, **16**, [296]
      voting, method of, **16**, [294]
    complaints as to passing of resolution,
      16, [301]
    generally, **16**, [1]
    information, supply of, **16**, [299]
    instrument of—
      approval of, **16**, [289]
      registration of, **16**, [297]
    listing and certification after, **16**, [298]
    Northern Ireland, involving, **16**, [304]
    notice to members, **16**, [290]
    political resolution on, **16**, [284]
    regulations, power to make, **16**, [306]
    requirements for, **16**, [288]
    transfer of property on, **16**, [303]
  annual return—
    Certification Officer, sending to, **16**, [206]
    contents of, **16**, [206]
    form of, **16**, [206]
    inspection of, **16**, [206]
    statement to members following, **16**, [207]
  auditors—
    appointment, **16**, [210]
    duty to appoint, **16**, [208]
    eligibility for appointment as, **16**, [209]
    removal, **16**, [211]
    report, **16**, [211]
    rights of, **16**, [212]
  ballots—
    conduct of, **16**, [235]
    confidentiality of register, securing,
      16, [198]

trade unions—*contd*

  ballots—*contd*

    counting of votes, **16**, [236]

    employers' premises, use of, **16**, [525]

    financial assistance towards, repeal of provisions, **16**, [525]

    industrial action, before, right to, **16**, [248]

    See also **industrial action**

    instrument of amalgamation or transfer, approving—

      counting of votes, **16**, [295]

      entitlement to vote, **16**, [293]

      independent scrutineer, appointment of, **16**, [292]

      requirement of, **16**, [291]

      scrutineer's report, **16**, [296]

      voting, method of, **16**, [294]

    means of voting in, **16**, [1014]

    political resolution, for—

      Certification Officer, application to, **16**, [272]

      counting of votes, **16**, [269]

      court, application to, **16**, [273]

      date of ballot, **16**, [287]

      entitlement to vote, **16**, [267]

      failure to comply with rules, remedy for, **16**, [271]

      independent scrutineer, appointment of, **16**, [266]

      passing and effect of, **16**, [264]

      political ballot rules, approval of, **16**, [265]

      scrutineer's report, **16**, [270]

      voting, **16**, [268]

    use of employers' premises for, repeal of provisions, **16**, [525]

  branch or sections, with, discharge of duties, **16**, [224]

  British Transport Police Force, prohibition of membership by constable or cadet of, **33(2)**, [424]

  Certification Officer—

    Amalgamated union, listing, **16**, [298]

    annual return, receipt of, **16**, [206]

    appeal against decisions, **16**, [182], [229], [242], [286], [302]

    ballot on political resolution, application on, **16**, [272]

    breach of rules—

      appeals, **16**, [309]

      application as to, **16**, [307]

      declarations and orders, **16**, [308]

    documents, etc, power to require production of, **16**, [213]

    election requirement, application for remedy for failure to comply with, **16**, [240]

    employers' associations. *See* **employers' associations**

    inspectors—

      appointment of, **16**, [214]

      investigations by, **16**, [214]

      reports, **16**, [215]

    list kept by, **16**, [175]

trade unions—*contd*

  Certification Officer—*contd*

    remedy for failure to comply with requirements for register, application for, **16**, [199], [200]

    superannuation scheme, powers relating to, **16**, [221]

  Civil Nuclear Constabulary members, exclusion from right to join, **33(2)**, [500]

  collective bargaining. *See* **collective bargaining**

  disciplinary or grievance hearings, worker accompanied to—

    detriment and dismissal, protection from, **16**, [972]

    employment tribunal, complaint to, **16**, [971]

    national security employees, provisions not applicable to, **16**, [975]

    right of, **16**, [970]

    worker, meaning, **16**, [973]

  dissolution, payment of annuity on, **42**, [31]

  dockyard services transfer, consultations as to, **39(2)**, [531], [532]

  duties—

    time off for carrying out—

      complaints to industrial tribunal, **16**, [365], [369]

      interpretation of terms, **16**, [371]

      learning representatives, **16**, [366]

      payment for, **16**, [367]

      permitting, **16**, [365]

      remedies, **16**, [370]

  elections—

    addresses, **16**, [232]

    candidates, **16**, [231]

    counting of votes, **16**, [236]

    date of, **16**, [247]

    duty to hold, **16**, [230]

    entitlement to vote, **16**, [234]

    general secretary, for, **16**, [230]

    independent scrutineer—

      appointment of, **16**, [233]

      notices, **16**, [233]

      report, **16**, [237]

    means of voting in, **16**, [1014]

    members of the executive, as, **16**, [230]

    newly formed trade unions, exemption of, **16**, [243]

    overseas members, position of, **16**, [246]

    period for giving effect to, **16**, [245]

    persons nearing retirement, exemption from provisions, **16**, [244]

    president, for, **16**, [230]

    remedy for failure to comply with requirements—

      appeals, **16**, [242]

      Certification Officer, application to, **16**, [240]

      court, application to, **16**, [241]

      generally, **16**, [239]

      uncontested, **16**, [238]

      voting, method of, **16**, [235]

    federated—

      meaning, **16**, [312]

trade unions—*contd*
  federated—*contd*
    provisions applying to, **16**, [312]
  financial affairs, investigation of—
    disclosure of information, **16**, [217]
    documents, etc, power of Certification
      Officer to require production of,
      16, [213]
    exercise of powers, **16**, [217]
    expenses of, **16**, [216]
    inspectors—
      investigations by, **16**, [214]
      reports, **16**, [215]
  friendly society, application of provisions,
    16, [192]
  funds—
    death of member, payment out on,
      16, [191]
    political. *See* political fund *below*
    political objects, use for—
      application in breach, **16**, [263]
      independent scrutineer, appointment of,
        16, [266]
      meaning, **16**, [262]
      political ballot rules, approval of,
        16, [265]
      political resolution, passing, **16**, [264]
      restriction on, **16**, [261]
    political. *See* political fund *below*
    use to indemnify unlawful conduct,
      prohibition of, **16**, [188]
  general secretary—
    election for, **16**, [230]
    meaning, **16**, [313]
  independent—
    certificate of independence—
      application for, **16**, [179]
      cancellation, **16**, [180]
      evidence of independence, as, **16**, [181]
      record of, **16**, [179]
      withdrawal of, **16**, [180]
    meaning, **16**, [178], [882]
  industrial assurance, application of provisions,
    16, [192]
  interpretation of terms, **16**, [313]
  learning representatives, time off for,
    16, [366]
  library or reading room maintained by,
    offences in, **13**, [80]–[83]
  list of—
    appeal against decisions, **16**, [182]
    application to enter name on, **16**, [176]
    certificate of inclusion, **16**, [175]
    Certification Officer, kept by, **16**, [175]
    inclusion of name in, **16**, [175]
    removal from, **16**, [177]
  meaning, **16**, [174]; **44(1)**, [315]
  members—
    constituent or affiliated organisation, of,
      16, [257]
    death, payment out of funds on, **16**, [191]
    meaning, **16**, [188]
    names and addresses, register of—
      ballots, confidentiality during, **16**, [198]
      computer, kept on, **16**, [197]

trade unions—*contd*
  members—*contd*
    names and addresses, register of—*contd*
      duty to maintain, **16**, [197]
      failure to comply with requirements,
        remedy for, **16**, [199], [200]
      inspection of, **16**, [197]
    nomination by, **16**, [190]
    rights of—
      access to courts, not to be denied,
        16, [249]
      ballot before industrial action, to,
        16, [248]
      deduction of unauthorised or excessive
        subscriptions, not to suffer, **16**, [254],
        [255]
      infringement, complaint of, **16**, [252],
        [255]
      membership, to terminate, **16**, [256]
      unjustifiably disciplined, not to be,
        16, [250]–[253]
    superannuation scheme—
      appropriately qualified actuary,
        meaning, **16**, [222]
      Certification Officer, powers of,
        16, [221]
      new, examination of proposals for,
        16, [219]
      periodic re-examination of, **16**, [220]
      separate fund, maintenance of, **16**, [218]
  membership—
    action to enforce, **16**, [424]
    detriment on grounds of—
      consideration of complaint, **16**, [348]
      interpretation of terms, **16**, [351]
      prohibition of, **16**, [346]
      remedies, **16**, [349]
      third parties, awards against, **16**, [350]
      time limit for proceedings, **16**, [347]
    dismissal of employee on grounds related
      to, **16**, [352]
      continuation of employment, order for,
        16, [361]
      contributory fault, assessment of,
        16, [355]
      failure to comply with order, **16**, [363]
      interim relief, application for, **16**, [358]
      interpretation of terms, **16**, [364]
      minimum basic award, **16**, [356]
      order, making, **16**, [360]
      procedure on hearing of application,
        16, [360]
      prompt determination of applications,
        16, [359]
      qualifying period, disapplication of
        requirement for, **16**, [354]
      third parties, awards against, **16**, [357]
      upper age limit, disapplication of,
        16, [354]
      variation or revocation of order,
        application for, **16**, [362]
    employment agency, refusal of service on
      grounds of—
        complaint, **16**, [332]

trade unions—*contd*

  membership—*contd*

    employment agency, refusal of service on grounds of—*contd*

      employer and employment agency, complaints against, **16**, [335]

      interpretation of terms, **16**, [337]

      remedies, **16**, [334]

      third parties, awards against, **16**, [336]

      time limit for proceedings, **16**, [333]

    goods and services contracts, void provisions in, **16**, [338]

    inducements relating to, **16**, [340]

      consideration of complaint, **16**, [343]

      interpretation of terms, **16**, [345]

      remedies, **16**, [344]

      time limit for proceedings, **16**, [342]

    interpretation of terms, **16**, [375]

    refusal of employment on grounds related to—

      complaint, **16**, [331]

      employer and employment agency, complaints against, **16**, [335]

      interpretation of terms, **16**, [337]

      remedies, **16**, [334]

      third parties, awards against, **16**, [336]

      time limit for proceedings, **16**, [333]

    refusal to deal on grounds of, prohibition, **16**, [339]

    right to—

      remedies, **16**, [374]

      requirements, **16**, [372]

      time limit for proceedings, **16**, [373]

    selection for redundancy on grounds related to, **16**, [353]

      continuation of employment, order for, **16**, [361]

      contributory fault, assessment of, **16**, [355]

      failure to comply with order, **16**, [363]

      interim relief, application for, **16**, [358]

      interpretation of terms, **16**, [364]

      minimum basic award, **16**, [356]

      order, making, **16**, [360]

      procedure on hearing of application, **16**, [360]

      prompt determination of applications, **16**, [359]

      qualifying period, disapplication of requirement for, **16**, [354]

      third parties, awards against, **16**, [357]

      upper age limit, disapplication of, **16**, [354]

      variation or revocation of order, application for, **16**, [362]

  modernisation, provision of money for, **16**, [310]

  name, change of, **16**, [305]

  newly formed, application of provisions to, **16**, [223], [243]

  Northern Ireland—

    amalgamation or transfer, **16**, [304]

    meaning, **16**, [314]

  offences—

    documents, alteration of, **16**, [225]

trade unions—*contd*

  offences—*contd*

    duties, refusal or wilful neglect to perform, **16**, [225]

    false statements, **16**, [225]

    penalties, **16**, [226]

    prosecution time limits, **16**, [226]

    remedies and enforcement, **16**, [228]

  offenders, positions not to be held by, **16**, [227]

  officer, meaning, **16**, [313]

  official, meaning, **16**, [313]

  payments to, relief for, **44(1)**, [157]

  political fund—

    administration where no political resolution in force, **16**, [280]

    appeals, **16**, [286]

    assets and liabilities, **16**, [275]

    discontinuance of contributions, **16**, [281]

    exemptions, giving effect to, **16**, [277]

    notice of objection to contributing to, **16**, [276]

    political resolution—

      amalgamation of unions, **16**, [284]

      ballot. *See* ballots *above*

      independent scrutineer, appointment of, **16**, [266]

      overseas members, effect on, **16**, [285]

      passing, **16**, [264]

      political ballot rules, approval of, **16**, [265]

    rules ceasing to have effect, **16**, [282]

    rules relating to, **16**, [274]

    union contributions, deduction by employer—

      certificate of exemption or objection, **16**, [278]

      complaint, **16**, [279]

  president—

    election for, **16**, [230]

    meaning, **16**, [313]

  property—

    amalgamation or transfer, transfer on, **16**, [303]

    enforcement of awards against, restriction on, **16**, [196]

    protected, **16**, [196]

    trustees, vested in, **16**, [185]

      new, **16**, [186]

    unlawful use, remedy against trustees for, **16**, [189]

    use to indemnify unlawful conduct, prohibition of, **16**, [188]

  provident benefits, **44(1)**, [315]

  quasi-corporate status of, **16**, [183]

  racial discrimination by, **7(1)**, [138]

  recognition—

    agreement for, **16**, [513]

    collective bargaining, for purposes of, **16**, [512]

      unit, changes affecting, **16**, [514]

      voluntary, **16**, [513]

    competing applications, **16**, [512]

    consequences of, **16**, [512]

trade unions—*contd*
  recognition—*contd*
    contract for goods and services, void
      requirement in, **16**, [384]
    derecognition—
      ballot, **16**, [515]–[517]
      fewer than 21 workers, where, **16**, [515]
      recognition automatic, where, **16**, [516]
      request of employer, **16**, [515], [516]
      union not independent, where, **16**, [517]
      workers' application, **16**, [515], [516]
    detriment, worker's right not to suffer,
      16, [519]
    independence, loss of, **16**, [518]
    meaning, **16**, [376]
    request for, **16**, [512]
    requirement, action pressing to impose,
      16, [427]
    settlement of disputes, information required
      for, **16**, [411]
  regulation of, **16**, [1]
  repudiation of acts by, **16**, [194]
  restraint of trade, exclusion of common law
    rules, **16**, [184]
  rules—
    breach of—
      appeals, **16**, [309]
      Certification Officer, right to apply to,
        16, [307]
      declarations and orders, **16**, [308]
    copy, duty to supply, **16**, [201]
    making, **16**, [283]
    meaning, **16**, [193], [313]
    political fund, as to, **16**, [274], [283]
  securities held in trust for, transfer of,
    16, [187]
  sex discrimination by—
    election arrangements, in, **7(1)**, [94]
    unlawful, **7(1)**, [50]
  special register bodies—
    meaning, **16**, [311]
    provisions applying to, **16**, [311]
  subscriptions to, exemption from VAT,
    50, [153]
  tax exemption, **44(1)**, [315]
  tort—
    liability in, **16**, [193]
    limit on damages in, **16**, [195]
    repudiation of acts, **16**, [194]
  transfer of engagements—
    appeals, **16**, [302]
    ballot—
      counting of votes, **16**, [295]
      entitlement to vote, **16**, [293]
      independent scrutineer, appointment of,
        16, [292]
      requirement of, **16**, [291]
      scrutineer's report, **16**, [296]
      voting, method of, **16**, [294]
    complaints as to passing of resolution,
      16, [301]
    instrument of—
      approval of, **16**, [289]
      registration of, **16**, [297]
    Northern Ireland, involving, **16**, [304]

trade unions—*contd*
  transfer of engagements—*contd*
    notice to members, **16**, [290]
    regulations, power to make, **16**, [306]
    requirements for, **16**, [288]
    transfer of property on, **16**, [303]
    transferee union, power to alter rules of,
      16, [300]
  trustees—
    appointment or discharge, **16**, [186]
    new, vesting in, **16**, [186]
    removal, order for, **16**, [189]
    unlawful use of property, remedy for,
      16, [189]
    vesting of property in, **16**, [185]

trading fund
  accounts, **10**, [572]
  assets and liabilities, determining, **10**, [566]
  borrowing by—
    maximum, **10**, [570]
    power of, **10**, [569]
    rate of interest, **10**, [569]
  Crown services, for, **10**, [565]
  Crown Suppliers, winding up, **10**, [700]
  establishment of, **10**, [565]
  excess of revenues, **10**, [572]–[573]
  initial reserves, **10**, [567]
  investment, **10**, [572]
  issues to, **10**, [565]
  management by Minister, **10**, [572]
  mint, for, **10**, [574]
  National Loans Fund, issued from, **10**, [565]
  operations ceasing to be funded, **10**, [573]
  orders, **10**, [575]
  payments into and out of, **10**, [571]
  public dividend capital, as, **10**, [568]
  reserves, **10**, [572]
  Royal Ordnance factories, liability,
    extinguishing on transfer, **10**, [671]

trading income
  accounting date—
    basis period ending on, **44(3)**, [209]
    change of—
      commercial reasons for, **44(3)**, [218]
      ineffective, **44(3)**, [219]
      later tax year, in, **44(3)**, [216]
      occurrence of, **44(3)**, [214]
      overlap profit, deduction for,
        44(3), [220]
      third tax year, in, **44(3)**, [215]
      late, rules for, **44(3)**, [208]
      meaning, **44(3)**, [197]
      middle date, treatment of,
        44(3), [211]–[213]
      new, period ending with, **44(3)**, [217]
      no, rule for, **44(3)**, [210]
      tax year without, **44(3)**, [201]
  adjustment income—
    assets realised or written off, **44(3)**, [235]
    change of basis, on—
      application of provisions, **44(3)**, [227]
      calculation, **44(3)**, [231]
      income charged, **44(3)**, [229]

trading income—*contd*
  adjustment income—*contd*
    change of basis, on—*contd*
      person liable, **44(3)**, [230]
    expense—
      calculation, **44(3)**, [228]
      treatment of, **44(3)**, [233]
    expenses previously brought into account,
      44(3), [234]
    mark to market, change from realisation,
      44(3), [236]–[237]
    personal representative, liability of,
      44(3), [240]
    professions and vocations, rules applying,
      44(3), [226]
    spreading—
      exemption for barristers and advocates,
        on ending of, **44(3)**, [238]–[236]
      mark to market, change from
        realisation, **44(3)**, [236]
      treatment of, **44(3)**, [232]
  basis periods—
    accounting date. *See* accounting date *above*
    final tax year, in, **44(3)**, [202]
    first tax year, in, **44(3)**, [199]
    general rule, **44(3)**, [198]
    overlap period—
      business start-up payments, treatment
        of, **44(3)**, [207]
      losses brought into account twice,
        restriction on, **44(3)**, [206]
      meaning, **44(3)**, [204]
    overlap profit—
      change of accounting date, on,
        44(3), [220]
      final year, deduction in, **44(3)**, [205]
      meaning, **44(3)**, [204]
    professions and vocations, rules applying,
      44(3), [196]
    profits, apportionment of, **44(3)**, [203]
    second tax year, in, **44(3)**, [200]
  farmers and creative artists, averaging—
    adjustment, **44(3)**, [223]–[225]
    claim for—
      circumstances for, **44(3)**, [222]
      making, **44(3)**, [221]
  overview of provisions, **44(3)**, [3]
  personal representatives, changes in,
    44(3), [258]
  post-cessation receipts—
    allowable deductions, **44(3)**, [254]–[255]
    amounts counting as, **44(3)**, [247]
    charge to tax, **44(3)**, [242]
    debts—
      paid, **44(3)**, [248]
      released, **44(3)**, [249]
    election to carry back, **44(3)**, [257]
    expenditure, relating to, **44(3)**, [250]
    extent of charge, **44(3)**, [243]
    income charged, **44(3)**, [244]
    meaning, **44(3)**, [246]
    personal representatives, lump sums paid
      to, **44(3)**, [253]
    persons liable, **44(3)**, [245]

trading income—*contd*
  post-cessation receipts—*contd*
    professions and vocations, rules applying,
      44(3), [241]
    trading stock, transfer of, **44(3)**, [252]
    transfer of rights if transferee not carrying
      on trade, **44(3)**, [251]
    treatment of, **44(3)**, [256]
    work in progress, transfer of, **44(3)**, [252]
  priority, provisions given, **44(3)**, [4]
  statutory insolvency arrangement, meaning,
    44(3), [259]
  trade profits, taxed as. *See* **trade profits**
  transitional provisions, **44(3)**, [905]
  trustees, changes in, **44(3)**, [258]

trading interests
  foreign action, power to regulate in event
    of—
    charging order, **39(2)**, [1013]
    conditions for, **39(2)**, [1012]
    enforcement of orders, **39(2)**, [1014]
    Parliamentary control of orders,
      39(2), [1015]
    protective order, **39(2)**, [1012]

trading interests, protection of
  documents required by overseas court—
    directions as to, scope of, **47**, [325]
    inadmissible, when, **47**, [325]
      offences respecting, **47**, [326]
    prohibition on supplying, **47**, [325]
  orders, power to make, **47**, [324]
  overseas court—
    judgments—
      overseas, enforcement, **47**, [329]
      restriction on enforcement, **47**, [327]
    multiple damages, recovery of, **47**, [328]
  overseas measures affecting—
    compliance with, power to prohibit,
      47, [324]
    offences as to, **47**, [326]
    powers of Secretary of State, **47**, [324]

trading losses
  carry-back of, **43(1)**, [321]
  group relief, amounts eligible for,
    44(1), [208]

trading scheme. *See also* **pyramid selling
scheme**
  meaning, **47**, [185]

trading stamps
  advertisements—
    misleading, **47**, [74]
    value, of, **47**, [74]
  business, unlawfully conducting, **47**, [69]
  meaning, **47**, [77]
  offences—
    corporations, by, **47**, [76]
    generally, **47**, [70], [73]–[75]
  promoter—
    name etc to appear on catalogues and
      books, **47**, [73]

trading stamps—*contd*
  promoter—*contd*
    restrictions as to, **47**, [69]
  redemption for cash—
    agreement against, void, **47**, [71]
    minimum holding for, **47**, [71]
    procedure for, **47**, [71]
    redeemable stamps, meaning, **47**, [71]
    right of, **47**, [71]
    statement of value of stamps, **47**, [75]
  redemption for goods—
    catalogues—
      availability of, **47**, [75]
      particulars to appear on, **47**, [73]
    meaning of goods, **47**, [77]
    terms implied on, **47**, [72]
  scheme—
    meaning, **47**, [77]
    promoter of, restrictions, **47**, [69]
  schemes, value of, for VAT purposes, **50**, [74]
  shop operating scheme—
    catalogue to be available, **47**, [75]
    information to be displayed, **47**, [75]
  stamp books, particulars to appear on, **47**, [73]
  statements required on, **47**, [70]
  value—
    advertisements referring to, **47**, [74]
    meaning, **47**, [77]
    notice in shops as to, **47**, [75]
    stamps to show, **47**, [70]

trading stock
  cessation of trade, transfer on, **44(3)**, [252]
  changes in, effect on trade profits, **43(S)**, 864
    corporation tax, **43(S)**, 1140–1
    income tax, **43(S)**, 1138–40
  meaning, **44(1)**, [81]; **44(3)**, [174]
  valuation of—
    basis of, **44(3)**, [175]
    cessation, on, **44(3)**, [173]
    Commissioners, determination of questions by, **44(3)**, [186]
    connected persons, meaning, **44(3)**, [179]
    determination of questions, **44(1)**, [83]
    discontinuance of trade, at, **44(1)**, [81]
    sale basis—
      buyer, cost to, **44(3)**, [180]
      connected person, sale to, **44(3)**, [177]
      election by connected person, **44(3)**, [178]
      unconnected person, sale to, **44(3)**, [176]
    sale, meaning, **44(3)**, [181]

Trafalgar Square
  byelaws, **26(1)**, [730]
  guidance on, **26(1)**, [731]
  transfer of functions, **26(1)**, [728]

traffic areas
  construction of references to, **37**, [62]
  division of Great Britain into, **37**, [2]
  variation of, **37**, [2]

traffic authority
  City of London, **37**, [290]
  Greater London, **37**, [290]
    Authority, functions of, **37**, [292]
    outside, **37**, [290]
  local—
    exercise of functions by, **37**, [293]
    meaning, **37**, [290]
    network management—
      arrangements for, **38(2)**, [310]
      definitions, **38(2)**, [324]
      duty, **38(2)**, [309]
      guidance on, **38(2)**, [311]
      information, power to require, **38(2)**, [312]
      intervention notice, **38(2)**, [313]
      intervention order, **38(2)**, [314]–[320]
      joint exercise of functions, **38(2)**, [319]
    traffic director—
      appointment, **38(2)**, [314]
      costs, recovery of, **38(2)**, [323]
      functions of, **38(2)**, [314]
      guidance to, **38(2)**, [321]
      intervention order, provision in, **38(2)**, [314], [317]
      London, in, **38(2)**, [322]
      powers of, **38(2)**, [317]
  Secretary of State, as, **37**, [290]

traffic calming works. *See* **road traffic calming**

Traffic Commissioners
  acting, appointment of, during vacancy, **38(2)**, [648]
  annual reports, **37**, [39]
  appeal from decision of, **37**, [34]
  appointment of, **37**, [3], [75], [475]
  areas, licences issued before variation of, **37**, [2]
  assessors to assist, **37**, [23]
  decisions, review of, **38(1)**, [558]
  declaration of interests, **37**, [3], [75]
  deputies—
    appointment, **37**, [75]; **38(2)**, [648]
    terms of office, **37**, [75]
  existing, transitional provisions, **38(2)**, [649]
  expenses, **37**, [37]
  fees received by, **37**, [36], [469]
  goods vehicles operator's licence—
    assessors, assistance by, **38(1)**, [566]
    functions as to, **38(1)**, [522]
  information—
    publication of, **37**, [8]
    required by, duty to give, **37**, [26]
  inquiries, power to hold, **37**, [38]; **38(1)**, [557]
  large goods vehicles, licensing of drivers. *See* **driving licences**
  licences. *See* **public service vehicles**
  local services, application of traffic regulation conditions to, **37**, [357]
  meaning, **37**, [64]
  misbehaving, **38(2)**, [648]
  number of, **38(2)**, [646]

Traffic Commissioners—*contd*
passenger-carrying vehicles, licensing of
drivers. See **driving licences**
remuneration and pensions, **37**, [75]
retirement, **37**, [3]
Scottish, **38(2)**, [646]
senior, **38(2)**, [647]
appointment of, **37**, [4]
deployment of other commissioners, **37**, [5]
guidance and directions from, **37**, [6]
guidance to, by Secretary of State, **37**, [7]
staff, **37**, [75]
terms of service, **37**, [75]
traffic regulation orders, consultation with,
before making, **37**, [336], [338]
transitional provisions, **37**, [475]

traffic lights
lights mistaken for, precautions, **38(1)**, [235]

traffic management
network. See **traffic authorities**
officers. See **traffic officers**

traffic officers
definitions, **38(2)**, [308]
designation, **38(2)**, [296]
direction from constable or national
authority, **38(2)**, [298]
duties of, **38(2)**, [295]
failure to comply with directions of,
38(2), [304]
financial assistance in relation to, **38(2)**, [307]
impersonation, **38(2)**, [304]
jurisdiction, **38(2)**, [297]
offences against, **38(2)**, [304]
powers—
further, power to confer, **38(2)**, [302]
special, **38(2)**, [299]
temporary traffic signs, to place,
38(2), [301]
traffic, to stop or direct, **38(2)**, [300]
vehicles, removal of, **38(2)**, [303]
relevant road network, meaning, **38(2)**, [295]
services, power to charge for, **38(2)**, [306]
uniform, **38(2)**, [305]

traffic regulation
alternative routes, following restrictions,
37, [177]
amenities, preservation of, **37**, [165]
bollards on roads, powers and duties,
37, [264]–[266]
compliance with directions, **37**, [606]
conservation of natural beauty, for purpose
of, **37**, [190]
control, general scheme of, **37**, [211]
countryside, special areas in, **37**, [189]
Crown, application of provisions to, **37**, [302]
experimental traffic schemes—
Greater London—
discretionary exemptions, **37**, [173];
38(1), [503]
orders, **37**, [173]
temporary suspension, **37**, [176]

traffic regulation—*contd*
experimental traffic schemes—*contd*
Greater London—*contd*
regulations, **37**, [173], [321]
illegally etc parked vehicles, removal,
37, [270]
orders—
contravention, **37**, [175]
power to make, **37**, [173]
provisions, applicable, **37**, [173], [334]
supplementary provisions, **37**, [174]
suspension, temporary, **37**, [176]
traffic signs, London, **37**, [173]
flares, use of, **36**, [915]
foot passengers, construction of references to,
37, [340]
general scheme of traffic control, **37**, [211]
Greater London. See London *below*
local authorities, exercise of functions,
37, [293]
local transport service, application of
conditions to, **37**, [357]
London—
bollards on roads, **37**, [266]
experimental traffic schemes. See
experimental *above*
Greater London Authority, exercise of
functions of, **37**, [292]
powers affecting another authority's
roads, exercising, **37**, [292]
lorries, controls on, **38(1)**, [503]
Olympic Delivery Authority, powers of,
13, [485]
enforcement, **13**, [486]
orders—
consultation with police, **37**, [171]
contravention, **37**, [172]
deregulatory, **38(1)**, [503]
heavy commercial vehicles, **38(1)**, [503]
matters to be covered by, **37**, [320]
power to make, **37**, [170]
provisions, application, **37**, [170], [334]
supplementary provisions, **37**, [171]
suspension, temporary, **37**, [176]
parking. See **parking**
priority routes, Royal Parks, **37**, [305]
long-distance routes, on, **37**, [191]
orders—
authorised authorities, **37**, [334]
consent to, **37**, [295], [335]
consultation, **37**, [336], [338]
contravention of, **37**, [169], [172]
directions by Secretary of State, **37**, [334]
experimental traffic schemes, **37**, [173]
extension of powers, **37**, [211]
Greater London. See London *above*
matters to be included, **37**, [166], [168]
power to make, **37**, [165]
reserve powers, **37**, [334]
procedure, **37**, [295], [336]
public inquiry, **37**, [334]
reserve powers, **37**, [334]
restricting use of roads, **37**, [335]
exemptions, **37**, [167]
restrictions on, **37**, [167]

traffic regulation—*contd*
  orders—*contd*
    suspension, temporary, **37**, [176]
    validity of, **37**, [295], [339]
    variation or revocation, **37**, [295], [334], [337]
  pedestrians, directions to, **37**, [608], [787]
  processions etc, routes to be observed during, **36**, [224]
  prohibition in use of roads—
    certain classes, **37**, [187]
    temporary. *See* temporary *below*
  public service vehicles, use of highways by, **37**, [186]
  restrictions—
    certain classes of roads, **37**, [187]
    notification of, **37**, [177]
    temporary. *See* temporary prohibition or restrictions *below*
  school crossings. *See* **school crossings**
  special events, **37**, [180]–[182]
  special roads, **37**, [183], [187]
    notice, **37**, [184]
    opening for use, **37**, [183]
  summary of provisions, **36**, [210]
  temporary prohibition or restrictions—
    alternative routes, **37**, [177]
    certain events—
      alternative routes for traffic, **37**, [180]
      annual, **37**, [181]
      consent to restrictions, **37**, [180], [181]
      contravention of order, **37**, [182]
      events barred, **37**, [180]
      length of road involved, **37**, [181]
      orders, power to make, **37**, [180]
        restrictions on, **37**, [174]
      pedestrians, involving, **37**, [180]
      sporting or social, or entertainment, **37**, [180]
      statutory provisions, suspension of, **37**, [180]
      supplementary provisions, **37**, [182]
    orders and notices—
      continuation, **37**, [178]
      contravention, **37**, [179]
      duration, **37**, [178]
      powers, **37**, [177]
      procedure, regulations as to, **37**, [179], [182]
    Secretary of State's powers, **37**, [178]
    special cases, **37**, [177]
    supplementary provisions, **37**, [179]
  terrorism, for purposes related to, **37**, [194]
    restrictions, **37**, [195]
  time of arrival and departure of vehicles, devices indicating, **37**, [168]
  transitional provisions, **37**, [317], [340]
  use of vehicles in contravention, **37**, [169]

traffic sign
  advances by Secretary of State, **37**, [253]
  bollards, **37**, [264]–[266]
  buildings, affixing to in London, **37**, [247], [326]
  City of London, in, **37**, [251]

traffic sign—*contd*
  community councils, powers, **37**, [245]
  compliance with, **37**, [237], [239], [607]
  concession agreements, placing under, **38(1)**, [161]
  default power of Secretary of State, **37**, [243]
  directions by Secretary of State, **37**, [238]
  display of, **37**, [237]
  emergency, **37**, [240]
  entry on land in connection with, **37**, [244]
  experimental traffic schemes, **37**, [173]
  general provisions, **37**, [237]
  Greater London, in—
    borough councils, powers of, **37**, [248]
    London traffic control system, in relation to, **37**, [248]
    powers and duties, **37**, [246]
    traffic authority, **37**, [250]
    transfer of traffic control systems, **37**, [249]
    Transport for London, work by, **37**, [248]
    walls, affixing to, **37**, [247]
  local traffic regulations, giving effect to, **37**, [239]
  London—
    City of, in, **37**, [251]
    overhanging trees obstructing view of, **26(2)**, [850]
  meaning, **37**, [237]
  non-compliance with, **37**, [607]
  obstructions, temporary, **37**, [240], [264]
  orders, provisions included in, **37**, [166]
    restrictions on, **37**, [167]
  parish councils, powers, **37**, [245]
  placing and maintenance, **38(1)**, [199]
  placing of—
    connected with exercise of other powers, **37**, [241]
    powers and duties, **37**, [238]
    restrictions, **37**, [237]
  pulling down or obliterating, **36**, [1048]
  regulations, power to make, **37**, [237]
  removal of, **37**, [242]
  road user charging schemes, as to, **38(2)**, [165]
  school crossings, **37**, [200]
  size, type and colour, regulations as to, **37**, [237]
  speed restrictions, **37**, [259]
  summary of provisions, **36**, [210]
  temporary, power of traffic officer to place, **38(2)**, [301]
  traffic authorities—
    construction of references to, **37**, [254]
    powers and duties, **37**, [238]
    tramways, relating to, **37**, [237]
  walls, affixing to, in London, **37**, [247]

traffic wardens
  appointment, **37**, [267]
  constable, assistance to, **37**, [267]
  control and regulation of traffic by, **37**, [267]
  functions, **37**, [268]; **38(1)**, [97]
  powers, **37**, [268]
  stationary vehicles, functions limited to, **38(1)**, [97]

traffic wardens—*contd*
supplementary provisions, **37**, [269]
trunk roads, on, **37**, [252]

traffic-sensitive street
designation as, **38(1)**, [198]

trailer
articulated vehicle, as, **37**, [311]
brakes, breach of requirement as to, **37**, [614]
carriage, when deemed, **37**, [807]
construction and use, regulation of—
    contravention, **37**, [614]–[616], [618]
    powers, **37**, [613]
    temporary exemption, **37**, [619]
dangerous condition, in, using, **37**, [612]
foreign vehicles with, **36**, [903], [905]
international carriage of goods, use in,
    36, [919]
locomotive, permitted weight where drawn
    by, **37**, [188]
meaning, **36**, [677], [919]; **37**, [309], [311]
partial superimposition on vehicle, **37**, [310],
    [802]
small, meaning, **38(1)**, [583]
special types, authorisation of, **37**, [620]
speed assessment detection devices, breach of
    requirement as to, **37**, [616]
steering-gear, breach of requirement as to,
    37, [614]
tyres, breach of requirement as to, **37**, [614]
unroadworthy, sale prohibited, **37**, [660]
use of, **36**, [677]
weighing of, when required, **37**, [663]
weight—
    calculation, method of, **37**, [806]
    excess, permit to carry, **37**, [188]

train. *See also* **railway engine**
controls on trains engaged on international
    services, **37**, [494], [495]
level crossing, on. *See* **level crossing**
power to prohibit of sale of alcohol on,
    19(3), [647]

training. *See also* **industrial training**
adult skills—
    general note, **15(S)**, Education 105
    information—
        benefit and training, use of,
            15(S), Education 202
        disclosure of, **15(S)**, Education 205
        Revenue and Custom, disclosure of,
            15(S), Education 203
        use of, **15(S)**, Education 204
        wrongful onward disclosure,
            15(S), Education 204
    persons aged 19 or over, learning aims—
        facilities, provision of,
            15(S), Education 197–8
        qualification to which applying,
            15(S), Education 200
        regulations, **15(S)**, Education 199
        specified qualifications,
            15(S), Education 200–1

training—*contd*
adult skills—*contd*
    persons aged 19 or over, learning
        aims—*contd*
        tuition fees, payment of,
            15(S), Education 198–9
    attendance notice—
        appeal arrangements, **15(S)**, Education 160
        attendance panel, **15(S)**, Education 159–60
        contents of, **15(S)**, Education 157
        education or training, description of,
            15(S), Education 158–9
        failure to comply with—
            offence, **15(S)**, Education 162
            penalty notice—
                appeal arrangements,
                    15(S), Education 165–6
                issue of, **15(S)**, Education 164–5
                regulations, **15(S)**, Education 164–5
            proceedings restrictions on,
                15(S), Education 163
        initial operation of provisions, review of,
            15(S), Education 172
        issue of, **15(S)**, Education 157
        variation and revocation,
            15(S), Education 161
    children's services authorities, co-operation
        by, **15(S)**, Education 196
    duty to participate in—
        alternative ways of working,
            15(S), Education 173
        contract of employment, relevant,
            15(S), Education 134
        Crown employment,
            15(S), Education 173–4
        employers enabling. *See* employers *below*
        financial penalties, payment of,
            15(S), Education 176
        general note, **15(S)**, Education 101–4
        House of Commons staff,
            15(S), Education 175
        House of Lords staff, **15(S)**, Education 175
        interpretation, **15(S)**, Education 177
        local education authority—
            fulfilment of duty, promotion of,
                15(S), Education 124
            guidance, issue of, **15(S)**, Education 133
            parenting contract, power to enter into,
                15(S), Education 151
            parenting order, power to apply for,
                15(S), Education 152
            public bodies, supply of information by,
                15(S), Education 131
            sharing and use of information
                supplied, **15(S)**, Education 132–3
            social security information supplied to,
                15(S), Education 129–30
            young persons not complying,
                notification of, **15(S)**, Education 126–8
            young persons not fulfilling duty,
                identification of, **15(S)**, Education 126
        non-participation fines. *See*
            non-participation fines *below*

training—*contd*
  duty to participate in—*contd*
    parenting contract—
      power to enter into,
        15(S), Education 151
      regulations, **15(S)**, Education 154
    parenting order—
      appeal against, **15(S)**, Education 153
      making of, **15(S)**, Education 152
      matters taken into account in making,
        15(S), Education 153
      meaning, **15(S)**, Education 152
      regulations, **15(S)**, Education 154
    Wales, provision for, **15(S)**, Education 178
    young persons—
      appropriate full-time training,
        15(S), Education 119
      attendance notice. *See* attendance notice
        above
      failure to fulfil duty—
        identification, **15(S)**, Education 126
        initial steps, **15(S)**, Education 155–6
      full-time occupation, person in,
        15(S), Education 120–1
      hours of guided learning to external
        qualification, assignment of,
        15(S), Education 124
      level 3 qualification,
        15(S), Education 118
      non-compliance, notification of,
        15(S), Education 126–8
      persons to whom provisions applying,
        15(S), Education 117
      relevant period, **15(S)**, Education 122
      relevant training, **15(S)**, Education 121
      scope of, **15(S)**, Education 117–18
      sufficient relevant training,
        15(S), Education 123
  employers—
    appropriate arrangements by,
      15(S), Education 135
    commencement of employment, before,
      15(S), Education 135–40
    penalty notices,
      15(S), Education 136–40
    duty to enable participation in—
      arrangements subsequently notified,
        15(S), Education 141–2
      enforcement notice—
        contravention of provisions, service
          on, **15(S)**, Education 143–4
        non-compliance with,
          15(S), Education 145–6
        withdrawal of, **15(S)**, Education 146
      initial arrangements,
        15(S), Education 140–1
      penalty notice—
        appeal against,
          15(S), Education 148–9
        non-compliance with enforcement
          notice, issue on,
          15(S), Education 145–6
        power to withdraw,
          15(S), Education 149

training—*contd*
  employers—*contd*
    duty to enable participation in—*contd*
      penalty notice—*contd*
        withdrawal or variation of,
          15(S), Education 147–50
      persons reaching 18, extension for,
        15(S), Education 143
  individual learning account—
    contributions to, exemption from income
      tax liability, **44(2)**, [256]
    excluded purposes, for, **44(2)**, [259]
    meaning, **44(2)**, [257]
    non-deductible travel expenses, treatment
      of, **44(2)**, [258]
    staff, not generally available to, **44(2)**, [261]
    unrelated assets, provision of, **44(2)**, [260]
  non-participation fines—
    enforcement—
      normal powers, **15(S)**, Education 170
      normal provisions, **15(S)**, Education 170
      person aged 18 or over,
        15(S), Education 169
      person reaching 18,
        15(S), Education 167–8
    meaning, **15(S)**, Education 166
    sums recovered, application of,
      15(S), Education 171
  retraining courses, payment of expenses of,
    44(2), [315]–[316]
  support for participation in—
    conditional basis, provision on,
      15(S), Education 182
    educational institutions—
      access and facilities,
        15(S), Education 184–5
      information, provision of,
        15(S), Education 183–4
    existing functions ceasing to have effect,
      15(S), Education 190
    general note, **15(S)**, Education 104–5
    interpretation, **15(S)**, Education 189
    learning and support agreements,
      15(S), Education 182–3
    learning difficulties, assessments relating
      to, **15(S)**, Education 190–2
    public bodies, supply of information by,
      15(S), Education 188
    services—
      directions, **15(S)**, Education 180
      inspection of, **15(S)**, Education 186
      internet and telephone,
        15(S), Education 185
      local education authorities, provision
        by, **15(S)**, Education 179
      supplementary powers of authorities,
        15(S), Education 181
    social security information, provision to
      young persons, **15(S)**, Education 187
  time off work to arrange—
    employment tribunals, complaints to,
      16, [678]
    remuneration, **16**, [677]
    right to, **16**, [676]

training—*contd*
  work-related—
    excluded purposes, for, **44(2)**, [254]
    exemption from income tax liability,
      44(2), [251]
    meaning, **44(2)**, [252]
    non-deductible travel expenses, treatment
      of, **44(2)**, [253]
    unrelated assets, provision of, **44(2)**, [255]
  young person, time off for—
    employment tribunal, complaint to,
      16, [692]
    remuneration, **16**, [691]
    right of, **16**, [690]

**Training and Development Agency for
Schools**
  accounts, **15(2)**, [731]
  annual reports, **15(2)**, [731]
  chief officer, **15(2)**, [731]
  committees, **15(2)**, [731]
  delegation of functions, **15(2)**, [731]
  directions to, **15(2)**, [675]
  efficiency studies, **15(2)**, [684]
  financial support—
    forms of, **15(2)**, [670]
    provision of, **15(2)**, [669], [671]
  functions of, **15(2)**, [666]
  grants to, **15(2)**, [672]–[673]
  information, provision of, **15(2)**, [685]
  joint exercise of functions, **15(2)**, [683]
  members—
    salaries, allowances and pensions,
      15(2), [731]
    tenure, **15(2)**, [731]
  membership, **15(2)**, [668]
  non-funding functions, **15(2)**, [674]
  proceedings, **15(2)**, [731]
  seal, **15(2)**, [731]
  staff, **15(2)**, [731]
  status, **15(2)**, [731]
  supplementary powers, **15(2)**, [731]
  Teacher Training Agency, change of name of,
    15(2), [665]

training and enterprise councils
  contributions to, **44(1)**, [49]

Training Commission
  dissolution, **16**, [157]
  effect on 1982 Act provisions, **16**, [164]
  information, obtaining and disclosure,
    16, [66]
  property, rights and liabilities, transfer of,
    16, [157], [164]

training school
  absence from, **6**, [128]
  meaning, **6**, [124]
  transfer to local authority care, **6**, [124]

Training Services Agency
  abolition, **16**, [109]

tramcar
  drink and drugs offences, **37**, [809]
  meaning, **37**, [64], [314]
  passengers, regulation of conduct, **37**, [29]
  public service vehicle, exclusion from
    meaning of, **37**, [1]
  regulations, **37**, [314]
  road traffic provisions inapplicable to,
    36, [836]; **37**, [314], [810]
  vehicle excise duty, exemption from,
    13, [1049]

tramway
  abandonment, protection for gas and water
    undertakers, **36**, [612]
  assets, disposal of, **36**, [898]
  bridleways over, **38(1)**, [327]
    stopping up and diversion of, **38(1)**, [326]
  byelaws—
    notice of, **36**, [517], [537]
    penalties imposed by, **36**, [518]
    power to make, **36**, [517]
    Secretary of State, sent to, **36**, [517]
  carriage—
    extension over wheels, **36**, [507]
    flange wheels, to have, **36**, [507]
    power for moving, **36**, [507]
    sale in default of payment of tolls,
      36, [509]
  construction—
    gas and water pipes, alteration of, **36**, [503]
    gauge of, **36**, [498]
    provisional orders for. *See* provisional orders
      below
    road. *See* road *below*
    streets, power to break up, **36**, [499]
  crossings, stopping up and diversion of,
    38(1), [326]
  damages, responsibility for, **36**, [525]
  dangerous goods, bringing on to, **36**, [523]
  display of lights near, **38(1)**, [235]
  drink or drugs, offences involving—
    application of provisions, **38(1)**, [310]
    employee, by, **38(1)**, [311]
    evidence—
      documentary, **38(1)**, [320]
      specimens, use of, **38(1)**, [319]
    maintenance worker, by, **38(1)**, [311]
    operator, by, **38(1)**, [312]
    penalties, **38(1)**, [321]
    police, powers of—
      breath tests, **38(1)**, [313]
      entry and arrest, of, **38(1)**, [314]
      hospital patients, protection for,
        38(1), [318]
      persons incapable of consenting,
        specimens of blood from, **38(1)**, [316]
      specimens for analysis, requirement of,
        38(1), [315]
      two specimens of breath, choice of,
        38(1), [317]
    prescribed limit, **38(1)**, [322]
    principal, **38(1)**, [311]
  fare, avoiding, **36**, [521]

tramway—*contd*
footpaths over, **38(1)**, [327]
stopping up and diversion of, **38(1)**, [326]
formation, mode of, **36**, [498]
inquiries, holding, **36**, [532]
land, entry by operator, **38(1)**, [329]
lease—
deposit of, **36**, [536]
notice of, **36**, [536]
leasing, **38(1)**, [336]
licences to use—
grant of, **36**, [508]
tolls, payment of. *See* **toll**
trespass or damage, liability for, **36**, [513]
local authority—
meaning, **36**, [494], [534]
promoters, disputes with, **36**, [506]
sale of undertaking to, **36**, [514]
local rate, meaning, **36**, [494], [534]
London, provisions applying, **36**, [613]
meaning, **33(2)**, [468]; **38(1)**, [249], [339]
mines under or near, rights of owners, **36**, [528]
obstructing, **36**, [520]
orders—
applications for, **38(1)**, [295]
compulsory purchase, authorisation of, **38(1)**, [302]
consents under enactments, **38(1)**, [305]
Crown land, **38(1)**, [309]
inquiries and hearings, **38(1)**, [301]
made other than on application, **38(1)**, [297]
making, **38(1)**, [303]
model clauses, **38(1)**, [298]
national significance, schemes of, **38(1)**, [299]
objections to, **38(1)**, [300]
other Member States affected, where, **38(1)**, [296]
power to apply for or object to, **38(1)**, [306]
power to make, **38(1)**, [290]
publicity, **38(1)**, [304]
refusal of, **38(1)**, [303]
special parliamentary procedure, **38(1)**, [302]
subject-matter of, **38(1)**, [294], [345]
validity of, **38(1)**, [307]
other tramway, crossing, **36**, [499]
private crossings, signs and barriers at—
default powers, **38(1)**, [330]
failure to comply with, **38(1)**, [331]
meaning, **38(1)**, [332]
placing of, **38(1)**, [328]
promoters—
damages, responsibility for, **36**, [525]
local authority—
disputes with, **36**, [506]
sale of undertaking to, **36**, [514]
meaning, **36**, [497]
obstructing, penalty for, **36**, [519]
power of sale of, **36**, [515]
regulations, power to make, **36**, [517]
right of user, having, **36**, [527]

tramway—*contd*
promoters—*contd*
road authority, disputes with, **36**, [506]
streets, power to break up, **36**, [499]
provisional order, incorporation of provisions into, **36**, [495]
railway—
crossing, **36**, [499]
not treated as, **38(2)**, [238]
retention where highway not stopped up or diverted, **9**, [141]
road—
authority—
meaning, **36**, [494], [535]
promoters, disputes with, **36**, [506]
maintenance and repair, **36**, [501]
opening and breaking up, **36**, [499], [505]
paving, contract for, **36**, [502]
power of authorities to alter, **36**, [529]
public right to use, **36**, [531]
regulation of traffic in, **36**, [530]
reinstatement of, **36**, [500]
rules, power to make, **36**, [533]
safety—
bodies corporate, offences by, **38(1)**, [335]
insurance, directions requiring, **38(1)**, [325]
prosecutions, consent to, **38(1)**, [334]
speeds and loads, directions limiting, **38(1)**, [324]
works, plant and equipment, approval of, **38(1)**, [323]
service of notices, **38(1)**, [338]
sewers and drains, protection of, **36**, [504]
special Act, meaning, **36**, [496]
street works affecting, notice of, **38(1)**, [236]
tolls. *See* **toll**
traffic signs, provisions as to, **37**, [237]
transient offenders, **36**, [522]
using without a licence, **36**, [524]
watercourse, protection of, **36**, [504]
wilful injury to, **36**, [520]

tramway undertakers
streets or bridges controlled by, breaking up by water authorities, **49**, [366]
underground strata, references to water contained in, **49**, [1267]

transactions in securities
clearance of—
application for, **44(4)**, [709]
clearance notification, effect of, **44(4)**, [710]
corporation tax advantage—
abnormal dividend, receiving, **44(1)**, [445], [452]
advance clearance, **44(1)**, [450]
cancellation of—
appeals, **44(1)**, [446]
application of provisions, **44(1)**, [444]
Northern Ireland, proceedings in, **44(1)**, [448]
prescribed circumstances, **44(1)**, [445]
tribunal—
constitution, **44(1)**, [449]

transactions in securities—*contd*
  corporation tax advantage—*contd*
    cancellation of—*contd*
      tribunal—*contd*
        statement of case by, **44(1)**, [447]
    counteraction of, **44(1)**, [444]
    information, power to obtain, **44(1)**, [451]
    meaning, **44(1)**, [452]
    statutory declaration, **44(1)**, [444]
  income tax advantage—
    abnormal dividends—
      accrual condition, excessive, **44(4)**, [702]
      exemptions or reliefs, used for,
        44(4), [694]
      return condition, excessive, **44(4)**, [701]
    counteraction of—
      appeals from High Court or Court of
        Session, **44(4)**, [718]
      cases before High Court or Court of
        Session, **44(4)**, [716]
      information, power to obtain,
        44(4), [711]
      limit on the amount assessed,
        44(4), [707]
      Northern Ireland, proceedings in,
        44(4), [719]
      notices, **44(4)**, [706]
        appeals against, **44(4)**, [713]
        rehearing by tribunal of appeal
          against, **44(4)**, [714], [717]
      opposed notifications—
        determinations by tribunal,
          44(4), [705]
        statutory declarations, **44(4)**, [704]
      person liable to, **44(4)**, [692]–[693]
        death of, **44(4)**, [720]
      preliminary notification, **44(4)**, [703]
      statement of case by tribunal for opinion
        of High Court or Court of Session,
        44(4), [715]
      timing of assessments, **44(4)**, [708]
    deductions from profits obtained following
      distributions of dealings, **44(4)**, [695]
    meaning, **44(4)**, [691]
    overview, **44(4)**, [690]
    receipt of consideration—
      company's assets, future receipts or
        trading stock, representing, **44(4)**, [696]
      relevant company distribution, in
        connection with, **44(4)**, [697]
    relevant company—
      meaning, **44(4)**, [699]
      receipt of assets of, **44(4)**, [698]
  meaning, **44(1)**, [452]; **44(4)**, [721]
  return of information, **44(1)**, [453]
  tribunal, **44(4)**, [712]

transfer of undertakings
  amendment of regulations, **16**, [984]

transfer pricing
  new regime for, **43(1)**, [358]

transparency
  competent authority, power of to call for
    information, **8(1)**, [1345]
  consequential amendments, **8(1)**, [1405]
  corporate governance rules, **8(1)**, [1347],
    [1351]
  false or misleading statements, liability for,
    8(1), [1348]
  infringement of obligation, powers in case
    of, **8(1)**, [1346]
  obligations Directive, **8(1)**, [1343]
  rules, **8(1)**, [1344]
  UK as host member state, exercise of powers,
    8(1), [1349]

transplants. *See* **human organs**

transport
  advisory committees, representation of
    disabled on, **16**, [45]
  arrangements, local authority's duties as to,
    15(1), [633]–[635]
  persons of sixth form age—
    disabled persons, for, **15(1)**, [640]
    learning difficulties, for persons with,
      15(1), [640]
    local authority's duty to provide,
      15(1), [639]–[640]
    meaning, **15(1)**, [641]
    providing for, **15(1)**, [639]–[640]
  schemes for—
    amendment of, **15(1)**, [721]
    charges, **15(1)**, [721]
    commencement of, **15(1)**, [721]
    duties as to, **15(1)**, [636]
    power to make, **15(1)**, [721]
  sustainable modes of, local education
    authority to promote, **15(1)**, [632]
  zero-rating, **50**, [151]

transport authority
  meaning, **38(1)**, [234], [236]
  street works involving. *See under* **street works**

Transport for London
  agent, agreements with, **26(1)**, [555]
  agreements with, **37**, [475]
  agricultural land, notice to quit, **22**, [683]
  annual report, **26(1)**, [560]
  anti-social behaviour orders, application for,
    26(2), [819]
  authorised officer—
    meaning, **26(2)**, [347]
    obstruction of, **26(2)**, [348]
    provision of information to, **26(2)**, [349]
  Bills—
    opposition to, **26(1)**, [565]
    promotion of, **26(1)**, [565], [779]
  capacity, **26(1)**, [776]
  chairman, **26(1)**, [776]
  chief finance officer, **26(1)**, [502]
  committees and sub-committees, **26(1)**, [776]
  common carrier, not, **26(1)**, [777]
  company—
    exercise of powers through, **26(1)**, [556]

Transport for London—*contd*
 company—*contd*
  formation, promotion or assisting,
   26(1), [555]
 contractor, agreements with, **26(1)**, [555]
 contractual restrictions, relaxation of,
  38(2), [404]
 co-operation with certain local authorities,
  37, [403]
 delegation by, **26(1)**, [776]
 delegation of functions to, **26(1)**, [470]
 deputy chairman, **26(1)**, [776]
 disposal of land, restriction on, **26(1)**, [562]
 establishment, **26(1)**, [553]
 financial assistance by, **26(1)**, [558]
 financial obligations, guaranteeing,
  26(1), [559]
 fixed penalties—
  financial provisions, **26(2)**, [354]
  levels of, **26(2)**, [338]
  notices, **26(2)**, [337], [353]
  offences, **26(2)**, [336], [356]
  Secretary of State, reserve powers of,
   26(2), [339]
 functional body, as, **26(1)**, [762]
 functions of, **26(1)**, [553]
 highway authority, as,
  36, [1005]. *See also* **London streets**
 highway, removal of things deposited on—
  notice—
   appeals, **26(2)**, [344]
   power to serve, **26(2)**, [343]
   service of, **26(2)**, [345]
 information, provision of, **26(1)**, [561]
 local authorities, joint committees with,
  26(1), [776]
 local authority, treatment for tax purposes,
  26(1), [757]
 local enactments, application of, **26(1)**, [777]
 London Regional Transport, transition from—
  capital allowances, **26(1)**, [797]
  chargeable gains, **26(1)**, [797]
  continuity, **26(1)**, [655]
  fares, **26(1)**, [654]
  former functions, transfer of, **26(1)**, [656]
  group transactions, **26(1)**, [797]
  preparatory transfers, **26(1)**, [797]
  property, rights and liabilities, transfers of,
   26(1), [652]
  records and relics, transfer of, **26(1)**, [656]
  repealed or revoked functions, **26(1)**, [655]
  taxation provisions, **26(1)**, [797]
  transitional period, functions during,
   26(1), [653]
 London Traffic Control System, transfer of,
  26(1), [648]
 lost property—
  charges for redelivery etc, **25(2)**, [519]
  meaning, **25(2)**, [519]
  official documents etc, **25(2)**, [522]
  opening for examination, **25(2)**, [522]
  packing and carriage, cost of, **25(2)**, [522]
  perishable nature, of, **25(2)**, [522]
  record of, **25(2)**, [522]

Transport for London—*contd*
 lost property—*contd*
  return of, on payment of charge,
   25(2), [522]
  safe custody, **25(2)**, [522]
  unclaimed etc, vesting of, **25(2)**, [522]
 Mayor of London—
  directions from, **26(1)**, [554]
  transfer of functions, **26(1)**, [557]
 members—
  appointment, **26(1)**, [776]
  disqualification, **26(1)**, [776]
  interests of, **26(1)**, [776]
 membership of, **38(2)**, [405]
 minutes of proceedings, **26(1)**, [776]
 owner of vehicle, disclosure of information as
  to, **26(2)**, [346]
 police powers of search and arrest,
  25(2), [520]
 powers affecting authority's roads, proposal to
  exercise, **36**, [1352]
 powers of—
  carriage and storage, **26(1)**, [777]
  commercial opportunities, exploitation of,
   26(1), [777]
  company, exercise through, **26(1)**, [556]
  discharge of functions, for, **26(1)**, [777]
  employees, welfare and efficiency of,
   26(1), [777]
  general, **26(1)**, [555]
  incidental amenities and facilities, provision
   of, **26(1)**, [777]
  intermodal freight facilities, provision of,
   26(1), [777]
  land, acquisition, disposal and development
   of, **26(1)**, [777]
  landing place, byelaws for, **26(1)**, [777]
  machinery and components, manufacture
   etc, **26(1)**, [777]
  museum, provision of, **26(1)**, [777]
  policies, development of, **26(1)**, [777]
  railways, byelaws for, **26(1)**, [777]
  research, **26(1)**, [777]
  services and facilities, charges for,
   26(1), [777]
  supplementary, **26(1)**, [777]
  technical advice and assistance, providing,
   26(1), [777]
  undertakings, acquisition of, **26(1)**, [777]
 private hire vehicles—
  functions transferred, **26(1)**, [643]
  PSV operator's licence, application for,
   37, [364]
 proceedings, **26(1)**, [776]
 proof of documents, **26(1)**, [776]
 property, rights and liabilities—
  distribution of, **26(1)**, [564]
  transfer of—
   contracts of employment, **26(1)**, [749]
   foreign, **26(1)**, [753]
   modification of instruments, **26(1)**, [752]
   pensions, **26(1)**, [750]
   provision for, **26(1)**, [747]

Transport for London—*contd*
property, rights and liabilities—*contd*
transfer of—*contd*
schemes. *See* transfer schemes *below*
stamp duty and stamp duty reserve tax
exemptions, **26(1)**, [756]
transfer or pension instruments, common
provisions, **26(1)**, [751]
public passenger transport. *See* **London
passenger transport services**
risk mitigation, arrangements for,
26(2), [839], [843]
road traffic. *See* **road traffic**
road user charges, imposition of. *See* **London
streets**
seal, **26(1)**, [776]
service on or by, **26(1)**, [776]
staff, **26(1)**, [776]
status, **26(1)**, [776]
subsidiaries, control of, **26(1)**, [563]
superannuation provisions, **26(1)**, [732], [733]
traffic director, appointment of, **38(2)**, [322]
traffic light installations, provision of,
37, [248]
transfer of traffic control systems, **37**, [249]
transfer schemes—
apportionment and division, **26(1)**, [778]
approval of, **26(1)**, [795]
contents of, **26(1)**, [778]
continuity, **26(1)**, [778]
effect of, **26(1)**, [778], [795]
employees, transfer of, **26(1)**, [778]
information, provision of, **26(1)**, [778]
local Acts, functions under, **26(1)**, [778]
making of, **26(1)**, [748], [795]
meaning, **26(1)**, [778]
modification of, **26(1)**, [778]
property, rights and liabilities transferred,
definition, **26(1)**, [778]
provision made by, **26(1)**, [778], [795]
supplementary provisions, power to make,
26(1), [778]
Transport and Works Act orders, functions
under, **26(1)**, [778]
transport subsidiary's agreement, meaning,
26(1), [566]
transport systems, application or objection to
orders for, **38(1)**, [306]
waterways, provision of facilities to benefit
users of, **26(1)**, [645]
Woolwich Ferry, functions transferred,
26(1), [646]
workplace parking levy, **26(1)**, [790]

Transport Holding Company
dissolution, powers of, **36**, [806]
employment, compensation for loss of,
36, [863], [899]
liabilities, transfer of, **36**, [898]
pension scheme—
orders, **36**, [725]
powers, **36**, [724]
rights, safeguarding, **36**, [899]
Secretary of State, powers of, **36**, [725],
[899]

Transport Holding Company—*contd*
pension scheme—*contd*
transfer of, **36**, [864], [899]
transitional provisions, **36**, [745]
property, rights and liabilities, transfer of,
36, [878]

Transport, Minister of. *See also* **Minister of
Transport**
advances, power to make, **10**, [487]
local authority expenditure, consent for,
10, [488]
war risks insurance, generally, **19(1)**, [289],
[290]

transport police. *See* **British Transport
Police**

Transport Stock
liability for, **36**, [711]
transitional provisions, **36**, [743]

Transport Tribunal
annual reports, **37**, [473]
appeals—
from, **37**, [473]
goods vehicles operators licensing matters,
38(1), [559]
to, **37**, [34]
constitution, **37**, [473]
court of record, as, **37**, [473]
Lord Chancellor, exercise of powers by,
37, [473]
members—
number, **37**, [446], [473]
remuneration and expenses, **37**, [473]
tenure of office, **37**, [473]
powers and proceedings, **37**, [473]
president, **37**, [473]
pension, **11(2)**, [601], [631]
relevant service, **11(2)**, [631]
reconstitution of, **37**, [446]
staff, **37**, [473]
transitional provisions, **37**, [475]

transport undertaking. *See also* name of *relevant
undertaking*
meaning, **38(1)**, [234]

transport works
major, affecting street works undertakers'
apparatus, **38(1)**, [227]

transportation
construction of references to, **12(1)**, [57]
sentence of, abolition, **12(1)**, [56]

travel concession. *See* under **passenger
transport services**

travelling expenses
disallowance, **44(2)**, [369]
foreign travel—
civil partner, **44(2)**, [382]

travelling expenses—*contd*
  foreign travel—*contd*
    duties performed wholly outside UK,
      44(2), [352]
    employee, of, **44(2)**, [381]
    non-domiciled persons, **44(2)**, [384]–[386]
    seafarer, duties of, **44(2)**, [383]
    spouse or child, **44(2)**, [382]
  relief for—
    group employments, travel between,
      44(2), [350]
    necessarily incurred in performance of
      duties of employment, **44(2)**, [347]
    necessary attendance, travel for,
      44(2), [348]
    overseas employment, start or finish of,
      44(2), [351]
    workplace, definitions, **44(2)**, [349]

treason
  disqualification for offices, **12(1)**, [108]
  felonies, **12(1)**, [45]
  high—
    form of sentence, **12(1)**, [25]
    punishment for, **12(1)**, [44]
  indictment—
    felony, for, **12(1)**, [47]
    limitation on, **12(1)**, [10]
  offences being, **12(1)**, [2]
  procedure on trials, **12(1)**, [368]
  punishment, **12(1)**, [44]
  Royal Family, compassing death of, **12(1)**, [2]
  sentence, form of, **12(1)**, [25]
  Sovereign—
    assassination of, designing, **12(1)**, [11]
    compassing death of, **12(1)**, [2]
    firearms, discharging near, **12(1)**, [43]
    offensive weapon near, **12(1)**, [43]
    service to in war, **12(1)**, [4]–[6]
    war, levying against, **12(1)**, [2]
  succession to Crown, hindering, **10**, [52]

treasure
  Act, report on operation of, **32**, [637]
  code of practice, **32**, [636]
  coin, meaning, **32**, [628]
  coroners—
    duty of finder to notify, **32**, [633]
    inquests, procedure for, **32**, [634]
    jurisdiction of, **32**, [632]
  Crown, vesting in, **32**, [631]
  finding—
    coroner, duty to notify, **32**, [633]
    ownership, **32**, [629]
  franchisee, meaning, **32**, [630]
  generally, **32**, [1]
  meaning, **32**, [626]
  power to alter, **32**, [627]
  precinct of cathedral, found within, **14(S)**, 53
  rewards, **32**, [635]

treasure trove
  jurisdiction of coroners, **11(1)**, [1238]

Treasury
  accounts, preparation of, **19(2)**, [1035]
  alteration of amounts, **44(2)**, [716]
  annual budget documents, **43(1)**, [377]
  appropriation in aid, directions regarding,
    19(2), [1030]
  Bank of England, borrowing from,
    19(2), [857]
  borrowing powers, **19(2)**, [857], [885]
  British Gas plc, functions as to. *See under*
    British Gas plc
  Chief Secretary, salary of, **10**, [612]
  commissioners—
    lord lieutenant, function of, **19(2)**, [596]
    meaning, **19(2)**, [594]
    powers of, **19(2)**, [593]
    quarter days, ordering payments on,
      19(2), [601]
  Commissioners of signing instruments,
    10, [413]
  Comptroller and Auditor General, accounts
    rendered to. *See* **Comptroller and Auditor
    General**
  Crown agents, guarantees to—
    Holding and Realisation Board, **10**, [658]
    loans, **10**, [640]
  Debt Management Account, **19(2)**, [874]
  Exchange Equalisation Account, controlling,
    19(2), [962]
  fees, payable in public offices, collection of.
    See **public office**
  financial dealings, power to suspend,
    19(1), [440]
  fiscal stability, code for, **43(1)**, [376]
  guaranteed loans, loan to redeem,
    19(2), [795]
  Junior Lord—
    numbers of, **10**, [616]
    salary, **10**, [615]
  money issuable by, **19(2)**, [630]
  National Loans Act, raising of money under,
    19(2), [885]
  orders, **19(1)**, [1028]
  orders and regulations, **44(1)**, [612];
    44(3), [890]
  Parliamentary Secretary, salary of, **10**, [615]
  payment by voucher, proof of, **19(2)**, [708]
  public accounts—
    consolidating, **19(2)**, [617]
    determining, **19(2)**, [616]
  public works loans. *See* **public works loans**
  retrospective non-charging provision, power
    to make, **43(S)**, 1406
  securities—
    issue of, **19(2)**, [805], [806]; **42**, [7], [16]
    powers, **43(1)**, [379]
  solicitor to, savings for privileges,
    11(2), [369]; **11(4)**, [308], [463]
  stock and dividends in name of, **44(1)**, [32]
  stock guaranteed by, transfer, duty on,
    41, [81]
  war, obligations arising out of, **19(2)**, [818]

Treasury bill
  interest, **19(2)**, [686]

Treasury bill—*contd*
issue of, **19(2)**, [688]
length of, **19(2)**, [686]
National Loans Fund, payable out of,
    19(2), [687]
prescribed form, to be in, **19(2)**, [686]
regulations, **19(2)**, [689]
signature on, **19(2)**, [712]

Treasury Solicitor
assistant, powers of, **10**, [452]
corporation sole, as, **10**, [450]
disposal of property, **10**, [453]
grant of administration, **10**, [451]
rules, **10**, [454]
service of documents on, **13**, [22]

treaties. *See* **European Community; EU
Treaty**
ratifying, **10**, [1]

tree felling
committee of reference, appointment of,
    18, [1118]
Crown or Duchy land, application of
    provisions to, **18**, [1124]
diameter of trees, measuring, **18**, [1097]
felling directions—
    considerations, **18**, [1109]
    enforcement of, **18**, [1115]
    identification of trees, **18**, [1119]
    meaning, **18**, [1126]
    notice requiring acquisition of land after,
        18, [1112]
    notice requiring compliance with—
        appeal against, **18**, [1116]
        Commissioners giving, **18**, [1115]
        expenses, **18**, [1117]
        failure to carry out, **18**, [1115]
    person adversely affected, courses open to,
        18, [1112], [1113]
    power of Forestry Commission to give,
        18, [1109]
    proceedings in respect of, **18**, [1114]
    restrictions on, **18**, [1110]
felling licence—
    application for, **18**, [1098]
    approved working plan, in accordance
        with, **18**, [1102]
    compensation on refusal of, **18**, [1099]
    conditions, subject to, **18**, [1100]
    deferred decisions on, **18**, [1101]
    duration of, **18**, [1098]
    enforcement of conditions, **18**, [1115]
    exceptions to requirement of, **18**, [1097]
    felling without, penalty, **18**, [1105]
    grant of, **18**, [1098]
    identification of trees, **18**, [1119]
    meaning, **18**, [1126]
    notice requiring compliance with—
        appeal against, **18**, [1116]
        Commissioners giving, **18**, [1115]
        expenses, **18**, [1117]
        failure to carry out, **18**, [1115]
    refusal of, **18**, [1098]

tree felling—*contd*
felling licence—*contd*
    regulations on, **18**, [1097]
    requirement of, **18**, [1097]
    review of refusal or conditions, **18**, [1104]
    tree preservation order, tree subject to,
        18, [1103]
Lands Tribunal, determination of matters by,
    18, [1122]
London, application of provisions to,
    18, [1127]
meaning, **18**, [1126]
owner, meaning, **18**, [1125]
regulations as to, making, **18**, [1123]
restocking after, **18**, [1106]
restocking notice—
    appeal against, **18**, [1107]
    Commissioners' powers, **18**, [1106]
    enforcement of, **18**, [1108]
    issue of, **18**, [1106]
    review of, **18**, [1111]
    tree preservation order, on tree subject to,
        18, [1106]
    unauthorised, restocking after, **18**, [1106]
service of documents, **18**, [1121]
working plan, in accordance with, **18**, [1102]

tree preservation order
amended provisions, **46(S)**, 264–6
existing, transitional provisions, **46(S)**, 185
felling directions on tree subject to,
    18, [1109]
felling licence where tree subject to,
    18, [1103]
meaning, **18**, [1126]
regulations—
    compensation, payment of, **46(S)**, 183
    making of order, provision for, **46(S)**, 181
    power to make, **46(S)**, 181
    prohibited activities—
        consent for, **46(S)**, 182
        provision for, **46(S)**, 181
    registers, **46(S)**, 183
    supplementary, **46(S)**, 183–4
restocking after unauthorised felling,
    provisions unapplicable, **18**, [1106]
special controls, **46(S)**, 180
Town and Country Planning Acts,
    proceedings under, **18**, [1103], [1144]

trees. *See also* **forestry**
aerodromes, near, control over, **4(1)**, [97]
conservation area, in, **46**, [471]–[474], [1038]
dangerous—
    entry on land in connection with,
        35(1), [385], [386]
    powers as to, **35(1)**, [385], [386]
depreciation in value on refusal of felling
    licence, **18**, [1099]
diameter of, measuring, **18**, [1097]
dying, dead or dangerous, dealing with,
    46, [458]
felling. *See* **tree felling**
heritable security, interest of owner subject
    to, **18**, [1120]

trees—*contd*
highway, adjoining etc. *See under* **highway**
identification of, **18**, [1119]
injunctions, **46**, [475]
lopping, telecommunications works, **45**, [72]
mortgage, interest of owner subject to,
  18, [1120]
pests. *See* **pests**
planning permission, provision for in,
  46, [457]
preservation order—
  compensation, **46**, [463], [465], [614]
  Crown land, in anticipation of disposal of,
    46, [570]
  decisions, validity of, **46**, [549], [553]
  Forestry Commission land, in respect of,
    46, [460], [1037]
  form of, **46**, [459]
  making, **46**, [458]
  non-compliance with, **46**, [470]
  procedure for, **46**, [459]
  provisional, **46**, [461]
  provisions in, **46**, [458]
  replacement of tree subject to, **46**, [466]
  rights of entry, **46**, [476]–[478]
  Secretary of State, power of, **46**, [462]
  validity of, **46**, [549], [553]
replacement—
  appeals, **46**, [468]
  duty of, **46**, [466]
  enforcement of duties, **46**, [467]
  execution and cost of works, **46**, [469]
replanting, compensation for, **46**, [464]
rights of entry, **46**, [476]–[478]
settled land, provisions relating to, **18**, [1120]

trespass
aerodromes, on, **4(1)**, [90]; **12(3)**, [127]
aggravated—
  offence of, **12(2)**, [207]
  persons committing or participating in,
    removal of, **12(2)**, [208]
aircraft, by, liability, **4(1)**, [125]
assemblies. *See* **assembly**
burglary, in connection with, **12(1)**, [561]
conspiracy, **12(1)**, [676]
designated site, on—
  access provisions not applying, **12(4)**, [126]
  arrest, power of, **12(4)**, [125]
  meaning, **12(4)**, [123]
  notices, **12(4)**, [126]
  offence, **12(4)**, [123]
  Scotland, **12(4)**, [124]
entering premises, **12(1)**, [678]
firearm, with, **12(1)**, [494]
intent to commit sexual offence, with,
  12(3), [727]
interim possession order—
  false or misleading statements, **12(2)**, [209]
  meaning, **12(2)**, [209]
  trespass during currency of, **12(2)**, [210]
meaning, **12(2)**, [195]
persons and vehicles unlawfully on land, order
  for removal of, **12(2)**, [212], [213]
premises of foreign missions, on, **12(1)**, [680]

trespass—*contd*
property in overseas country, **11(2)**, [824]
seizure, power of, **12(2)**, [196]
title to property deriving from, **12(1)**, [682]
trespasser—
  deriving title from, **12(1)**, [682]
  displaced residential occupier, **12(1)**, [678]
  interpretation, **12(2)**, [195]
  power to remove from land, **12(2)**, [195]
    alternative site available, **12(2)**, [197]
    common land, provisions applying,
      12(2), [200]
    failure to comply with direction,
      12(2), [198]–[199]
    interpretation, **12(2)**, [201]
    offences, **12(2)**, [198]
    seizure of articles, **12(2)**, [196], [199]
unauthorised campers, power to direct
  removal of, **12(2)**, [211], [213]
weapon of offence, with, **12(1)**, [679]

trespass to goods. *See also* **wrongful
interference with goods**
co-ownership no defence, **45**, [972]
contributory negligence, **45**, [973]

trespass to the person
civil proceedings, offender bringing,
  12(3), [1041]

trial
allocation guidelines, meaning, **12(3)**, [902]
allocation of cases triable either way,
  11(S), Courts 30
attendance at, expenses, **12(1)**, [944], [949]
child, presence of, **6**, [25]
derogatory assertions at—
  orders, **12(2)**, [474]
  reporting—
    application of provisions, **12(2)**, [477]
    offences, **12(2)**, [476], [477]
    restrictions on, **12(2)**, [475]
hospital order ceasing, on, **12(1)**, [424]
indictment—
  committal for either way offence on,
    12(1), [1085]
  person arraigned on, plea, **12(1)**, [364]
jury, without—
  certain counts, of—
    application for, **12(4)**, [11]
    conditions for, **12(4)**, [11]
    effect of order, **12(4)**, [13]
    Northern Ireland, **12(4)**, [15], [56]
  conviction, reasons for, **12(3)**, [830]
  effect of order for, **12(3)**, [830]
  fraud cases, application in, **12(3)**, [825]
  Northern Ireland, in, **12(3)**, [832]
  powers of court, **12(3)**, [830]
  procedure on application for, **12(3)**, [827];
    12(4), [12]
  rules of court, **12(3)**, [831]; **12(4)**, [14]
  tampering, danger of, **12(3)**, [826]
lesser offence—
  finding of guilty, **12(1)**, [364]
  plea of guilty to, **12(1)**, [364]

trial—*contd*
mute of malice, defendant being, **12(1)**, [364]
not guilty plea, **12(1)**, [364]
not guilty verdict ordered by judge,
12(1), [384]
order of speeches, **12(1)**, [264]
postponement of, **12(1)**, [223]
preparatory hearings—
appeals, **12(2)**, [459], [460]
application of provisions, **12(2)**, [452]
arraignment, **12(2)**, [454]
Criminal Procedure rules, **12(2)**, [457]
judge, powers of, **12(2)**, [455]
orders before, **12(2)**, [456]
power to order, **12(2)**, [453]
reporting restrictions, **12(2)**, [461], [462]
serious or complex fraud cases. *See* **serious
or complex fraud**
trial, start of, **12(2)**, [454]
pre-trial hearing—
application of provisions, **12(2)**, [467]
meaning, **12(2)**, [463]
reporting restrictions, **12(2)**, [465], [466]
rulings, power to make, **12(2)**, [464]
retrial—
depositions, **12(1)**, [470]
fresh indictment, referral of, **12(1)**, [424]
orders on, **12(1)**, [424]
power to order, **12(1)**, [423]
procedural provisions, **12(1)**, [470]
sentence on conviction at, **12(1)**, [470]
retrial after acquittal—
armed forces, provisions applying,
12(3), [868]
arrest and charge, **12(3)**, [861]
bail and custody—
application, before, **12(3)**, [862]
before hearing, **12(3)**, [863]
during and after hearing, **12(3)**, [864]
revocation of bail, **12(3)**, [865]
Court of Appeal—
application to, **12(3)**, [850]
determination by, **12(3)**, [851]
Criminal Appeal Acts, application of,
12(3), [871]
Director of Public Prosecutions, functions
of, **12(3)**, [866]
evidence, **12(3)**, [854]
indictment, on, **12(3)**, [857]
interests of justice, in, **12(3)**, [853]
interpretation, **12(3)**, [869]
investigation—
authorisation of, **12(3)**, [858]
urgent steps, **12(3)**, [859]
new and compelling evidence, requirement
of, **12(3)**, [852]
Northern Ireland, **12(3)**, [870]
Police Ombudsman, investigations by,
12(3), [860]
procedure, **12(3)**, [854]
publication, restriction of inclusion of
matters in, **12(3)**, [855]
offences, **12(3)**, [856]
qualifying offences, **12(3)**, [849],
[1054]–[1056]

trial—*contd*
retrial after acquittal—*contd*
rules of court, **12(3)**, [867]
separate, ordering, **12(1)**, [223]
serious or complex fraud cases. *See* **serious
or complex fraud**
special verdict, insanity, acquittal on grounds
of, **12(1)**, [338]
unfitness to plead. *See* **unfitness to plead**
unsworn statement, **12(1)**, [785]
young persons, remand for, **12(1)**, [260]

tribunal. *See also* **Employment Appeal
Tribunal; employment tribunal; industrial
tribunal; Lands Tribunal; Shipping Claims
Tribunal**
accommodation, provision of, **11(4)**, [42];
11(S), Courts 55
additional, applying Act to, **10**, [729]
Administrative Council. *See* **Administrative
Justice and Tribunals Council**
appeals, **10**, [727]
chairman, appointment, **10**, [722]
constitution of, **9**, [127]
contempt of, **11(2)**, [663]
council on. *See* **Council on Tribunals**
decision, reasons for, **10**, [726]
determination of claims by, **9**, [126]
efficient and effective system, general duty as
to, **11(4)**, [40]; **11(S)**, Courts 53
fees, **11(4)**, [43]; **11(S)**, Courts 55–6
First-tier Tribunal—
assessors, **11(4)**, [29]; **11(S)**, Courts 40
chambers—
Acting President, **11(4)**, [82];
11(S), Courts 134
Deputy President, **11(4)**, [82];
11(S), Courts 133
judges and members of, **11(4)**, [83];
11(S), Courts 135–8
organisation into, **11(4)**, [8];
11(S), Courts 15
president of, **11(S)**, Courts 15–16
President, **11(4)**, [8], [82];
11(S), Courts 131–5
costs or expenses in, **11(4)**, [30];
11(S), Courts 40–1
decision, review of, **11(4)**, [10];
11(S), Courts 17–18
establishment of, **11(4)**, [4];
11(S), Courts 10
judges of, **11(4)**, [5], [7]; **11(S)**, Courts 12,
14
appointment of, **11(4)**, [80];
11(S), Courts 124
neither appointed nor transferred in,
11(4), [80]; **11(S)**, Courts 125–6
oaths, **11(4)**, [80]; **11(S)**, Courts 126–7
removal from office, **11(4)**, [80];
11(S), Courts 124
remuneration, allowances and expenses,
11(4), [80]; **11(S)**, Courts 125
terms of appointment, **11(4)**, [80];
11(S), Courts 124–5
training, **11(4)**, [80]; **11(S)**, Courts 126

tribunal—*contd*
First-tier Tribunal—*contd*
members of, **11(4)**, [4], [5];
11(S), Courts 10, 12
appointment of, **11(4)**, [80];
11(S), Courts 124
neither appointed nor transferred in,
11(4), [80]; **11(S)**, Courts 126
oaths, **11(4)**, [80]; **11(S)**, Courts 126–7
removal from office, **11(4)**, [80];
11(S), Courts 124
remuneration, allowances and expenses,
11(4), [80]; **11(S)**, Courts 125
terms of appointment, **11(4)**, [80];
11(S), Courts 124–5
training, **11(4)**, [80]; **11(S)**, Courts 126
point of law, right of appeal on,
11(4), [12]; **11(S)**, Courts 20–1
practice directions, **11(4)**, [24];
11(S), Courts 36
Senior President presiding over, **11(4)**, [4];
11(S), Courts 10
sittings, location of, **11(4)**, [27];
11(S), Courts 38
sums payable in pursuance of decision,
recovery of, **11(4)**, [28]; **11(S)**, Courts 39
judicial review, **10**, [728]
judiciary, independence, **11(4)**, [2];
11(S), Courts 8
meditation, provision for, **11(4)**, [25];
11(S), Courts 37
members—
Council on Tribunals recommending,
10, [721]
removal of, **10**, [723]
panels, **10**, [721]
orders and regulations, **11(4)**, [50];
11(S), Courts 61–2
Parliamentary Commissioner, investigations
by, **10**, [562]
powers, **9**, [128]
procedural rules, **10**, [724]
records, preservation of, **18**, [189], [194]
reform of system, **11(S)**, Courts 1–2
restricted application of provisions, **10**, [730]
rules and orders, **10**, [731]
Senior President—
appointment, **11(4)**, [3]; **11(S)**, Courts 9
delegation of functions, **11(4)**, [9];
11(S), Courts 16–17
First-tier Tribunal, presiding over,
11(4), [4]; **11(S)**, Courts 10
functions of, **11(4)**, [79]; **11(S)**, Courts 123
Judicial Appointments Commission,
selection by, **11(4)**, [77];
11(S), Courts 117–20
oath, **11(4)**, [78]; **11(S)**, Courts 122
recommendations for appointment,
11(4), [76]; **11(S)**, Courts 116–17
removal from office, **11(4)**, [78];
11(S), Courts 121–2
remuneration, allowances and expenses,
11(4), [78]; **11(S)**, Courts 122
report, **11(4)**, [44]; **11(S)**, Courts 57

tribunal—*contd*
Senior President—*contd*
resignation, **11(4)**, [78];
11(S), Courts 121–2
tenure, **11(4)**, [78]; **11(S)**, Courts 121–2
terms of office, **11(4)**, [78];
11(S), Courts 121–2
Upper Tribunal, presiding over, **11(4)**, [4];
11(S), Courts 10
services, **11(4)**, [41]; **11(S)**, Courts 54
staff, **11(4)**, [41]; **11(S)**, Courts 54
special case, stating, **10**, [727]
statutory—
meaning, **9**, [184]
transfer of powers to Lands Tribunal,
9, [184]
transfer of functions—
abolition of tribunals, **11(4)**, [32];
11(S), Courts 43
amendment of lists of tribunals, **11(4)**, [38];
11(S), Courts 52
authorised decision-maker, meaning,
11(4), [32]; **11(S)**, Courts 44
Ministerial responsibilities, transfer of,
11(4), [36]; **11(S)**, Courts 48–50
office holders, **11(4)**, [32];
11(S), Courts 43–4
order for, **11(4)**, [31]; **11(S)**, Courts 41–2
orders, form of, **11(4)**, [39];
11(S), Courts 53
procedural rules, **11(4)**, [32], [37];
11(S), Courts 44–5
procedural rules, power to make,
11(S), Courts 50–1
relevant tribunals, **11(4)**, [88]–[94];
11(S), Courts 146–52
Scotland or Wales, in, **11(4)**, [31];
11(S), Courts 42
transitional provisions, **11(4)**, [100]–[104];
11(S), Courts 183–92
Tribunal Procedure Committee—
expenses, **11(4)**, [85]; **11(S)**, Courts 144
Lord Chancellor's appointees, **11(4)**, [85];
11(S), Courts 142
Lord Chief Justice's appointees, **11(4)**, [85];
11(S), Courts 143
Lord President's appointees, **11(4)**, [85];
11(S), Courts 143
membership, **11(4)**, [85];
11(S), Courts 142
rules, making, **11(4)**, [86];
11(S), Courts 144–5
Senior President's appointees, **11(4)**, [85];
11(S), Courts 143
Tribunal Procedure Rules—
amendment of legislation in connection
with, **11(4)**, [87]; **11(S)**, Courts 146
ancillary powers, **11(4)**, [84];
11(S), Courts 141
arbitration, **11(4)**, [84]; **11(S)**, Courts 141
Committee, making by, **11(4)**, [86];
11(S), Courts 144–5
concurrent functions, **11(4)**, [84];
11(S), Courts 139

tribunal—*contd*
  Tribunal Procedure Rules—*contd*
    content of, **11(4)**, [23], [84];
      11(S), Courts 35, 139
    costs and expenses, **11(4)**, [84];
      11(S), Courts 141
    differential provisions, **11(4)**, [84];
      11(S), Courts 142
    errors, correction of, **11(4)**, [84];
      11(S), Courts 141
    evidence, witnesses and attendance,
      11(4), [84]; **11(S)**, Courts 140
    hearings, **11(4)**, [84]; **11(S)**, Courts 140
    information, use of, **11(4)**, [84];
      11(S), Courts 140
    meditation, provision for, **11(4)**, [25];
      11(S), Courts 37
    own initiative, tribunal acting of,
      11(4), [84]; **11(S)**, Courts 140
    power to make, exercise of, **11(4)**, [23];
      11(S), Courts 35
    practice directions, reference to,
      11(4), [84]; **11(S)**, Courts 142
    presumptions, **11(4)**, [84];
      11(S), Courts 142
    procedural grounds, setting-aside of
      decisions on, **11(4)**, [84];
      11(S), Courts 141
    proceedings without notice, **11(4)**, [84];
      11(S), Courts 140
    repeat applications, **11(4)**, [84];
      11(S), Courts 140
    representation, **11(4)**, [84];
      11(S), Courts 140
    set-off and interest, **11(4)**, [84];
      11(S), Courts 141
    staff, delegation of functions to,
      11(4), [84]; **11(S)**, Courts 139
    time limits, **11(4)**, [84]; **11(S)**, Courts 139
  Upper Tribunal—
    appeal from—
      proceedings, **11(4)**, [15];
        11(S), Courts 24–5
      right of, **11(4)**, [14]; **11(S)**, Courts 22–4
    appeal to—
      point of law, on, **11(4)**, [12];
        11(S), Courts 20–1
      proceedings, **11(4)**, [13];
        11(S), Courts 21–2
      right of, **11(4)**, [12]; **11(S)**, Courts 20–1
      tribunals in Northern Ireland, from,
        11(4), [35]; **11(S)**, Courts 47–8
      tribunals in Scotland, from, **11(4)**, [34];
        11(S), Courts 47
      tribunals in Wales, from, **11(4)**, [33];
        11(S), Courts 46
    assessors, **11(4)**, [29]; **11(S)**, Courts 40
    chambers—
      Acting President, **11(4)**, [82];
        11(S), Courts 134
      Deputy President, **11(4)**, [82];
        11(S), Courts 133
      judges and members of, **11(4)**, [83];
        11(S), Courts 135–8

tribunal—*contd*
  Upper Tribunal—*contd*
    chambers—*contd*
      organisation into, **11(4)**, [8];
        11(S), Courts 15
      president of, **11(4)**, [8], [82];
        11(S), Courts 15–16
      President, **11(S)**, Courts 131–5
    costs or expenses in, **11(4)**, [30];
      11(S), Courts 40–1
    decision, review of, **11(4)**, [11];
      11(S), Courts 18–19
    establishment of, **11(4)**, [4];
      11(S), Courts 10
    judges of, **11(4)**, [6], [7];
      11(S), Courts 13–15
      appointment of, **11(4)**, [81];
        11(S), Courts 127–8
      deputy, **11(4)**, [81]; **11(S)**, Courts 129
      neither appointed nor transferred in,
        11(4), [81]; **11(S)**, Courts 129
      oaths, **11(4)**, [81]; **11(S)**, Courts 130
      removal from office, **11(4)**, [81];
        11(S), Courts 128
      remuneration, allowances and expenses,
        11(4), [81]; **11(S)**, Courts 128
      terms of appointment, **11(4)**, [81];
        11(S), Courts 128
      training, **11(4)**, [81]; **11(S)**, Courts 130
    judicial review—
      application for relief, **11(4)**, [17];
        11(S), Courts 27
      Court of Session, transfer of applications
        from, **11(4)**, [21]; **11(S)**, Courts 33–4
      High Court, transfer of application—
        from, **11(4)**, [20]; **11(S)**, Courts 30–2
        to, **11(4)**, [19]; **11(S)**, Courts 29
      jurisdiction, **11(4)**, [16];
        11(S), Courts 25–6
        limits of **11(4)**, [19]; **11(S)**, Courts 29
      quashing orders, **11(4)**, [18];
        11(S), Courts 28
      Scotland, jurisdiction relating to,
        11(4), [22]; **11(S)**, Courts 34
    members of, **11(4)**, [4], [6];
      11(S), Courts 10, 13
      appointment of, **11(4)**, [81];
        11(S), Courts 128
      neither appointed nor transferred in,
        11(4), [81]; **11(S)**, Courts 130
      oaths, **11(4)**, [81]; **11(S)**, Courts 130
      removal from office, **11(4)**, [81];
        11(S), Courts 128
      remuneration, allowances and expenses,
        11(4), [81]; **11(S)**, Courts 128
      terms of appointment, **11(4)**, [81];
        11(S), Courts 128
      training, **11(4)**, [81]; **11(S)**, Courts 130
    practice directions, **11(4)**, [24];
      11(S), Courts 36
    Senior President presiding over, **11(4)**, [4];
      11(S), Courts 10
    sittings, location of, **11(4)**, [27];
      11(S), Courts 38

tribunal—*contd*
Upper Tribunal—*contd*
sums payable in pursuance of decision,
recovery of, **11(4)**, [28]; **11(S)**, Courts 39
supplementary powers, **11(4)**, [26];
11(S), Courts 38

tricycle
local regulations, **25(1)**, [63]

Trinidad and Tobago
British ship registered in, **7(2)**, [516]
Commonwealth citizenship, **31**, [186]
existing law, operation of, **7(2)**, [679]
fully responsible status of, **7(2)**, [511]
Judicial Committee of Privy Council, appeal
to, **7(2)**, [680]
legislative powers of, **7(2)**, [515]
meaning, **7(2)**, [513]
republic, becoming, **7(2)**, [679]
visiting forces in, **7(2)**, [516]

Trinity College, Dublin
legal deposit library, as, **13**, [467]
regulations, **13**, [466]

Trinity House
lighthouses, beacons etc, sanction for
erection, **39(2)**, [75]
Port of London Act, saving in, **39(2)**, [391]
rates, property exempt from, **25(2)**, [835]
rights and privileges as to harbours etc,
39(2), [93]

Trinity Masters
Admiralty appeals, assistance, **11(2)**, [960]

trolley vehicle
legislation, **36**, [210]
meaning, **37**, [315]
new town, service in, **46**, [164]
regulations, **37**, [314]
road traffic provisions inapplicable to,
36, [836]; **37**, [314], [810]

trolley vehicle system
meaning, **38(1)**, [339]
orders—
applications for, **38(1)**, [295]
compulsory purchase, authorisation of,
38(1), [302]
consents under enactments, **38(1)**, [305]
Crown land, **38(1)**, [309]
inquiries and hearings, **38(1)**, [301]
made other than on application,
38(1), [297]
making, **38(1)**, [303]
model clauses, **38(1)**, [298]
national significance, schemes of,
38(1), [299]
objections to, **38(1)**, [300]
other Member States affected, where,
38(1), [296]
power to apply for or object to,
38(1), [306]

trolley vehicle system—*contd*
orders—*contd*
power to make, **38(1)**, [290]
publicity, **38(1)**, [304]
refusal of, **38(1)**, [303]
special parliamentary procedure,
38(1), [302]
subject-matter of, **38(1)**, [294], [345]
validity of, **38(1)**, [307]
safety—
bodies corporate, offences by, **38(1)**, [335]
insurance, directions requiring, **38(1)**, [325]
prosecutions, consent to, **38(1)**, [334]
speeds and loads, directions limiting,
38(1), [324]
works, plant and equipment, approval of,
38(1), [323]
service of notices, **38(1)**, [338]

trover. *See also* **wrongful interference with
goods**
conversion of goods, as, **45**, [963]

truancy
designated premises, removal of truants to,
6, [601]
parenting contract in cases of, **6**, [870]
penalty notices for parents in cases of, **6**, [874]

trunk road. *See also* **highway**
acquisition of land for, **36**, [1285]
authority—
on cessation of status as, **36**, [1006]
delegation of functions, **36**, [1010]
Minister as, **36**, [1005]
centre line, indication on map, **36**, [1376]
cessation as. *See* road ceasing to be *below*
charging schemes, **38(2)**, [154]
Wales, in—
information, disclosure of, **38(2)**, [710]
National Assembly, powers of,
38(2), [709]
City, highways within, **36**, [1013]
construction of, **36**, [1028]
creation of, **36**, [210]
cycle tracks, construction of, **36**, [1013]
delegation of functions, **36**, [1433]
designation of substituted road as, **9**, [140]
general provision as to, **36**, [1013]
highway authority. *See* **highway authority**
highway becoming—
bridge carrying, transfer of, **36**, [1312]
documents and information, authority
furnishing, **36**, [1311]
property or liabilities, agreement on,
36, [1311]
rights and liabilities not transferred,
36, [1311]
transitional matters, **36**, [1429]
vesting of, **36**, [1311]
land drainage works benefiting, contribution
to, **36**, [1324]
local Act, functions under, **36**, [1014]
London bridges exclusion, **36**, [1013]

trunk road—*contd*
London traffic, local plans. *See* **traffic regulation**
main carriageway, relieving, **36**, [1013], [1066]
maintenance of. *See* **highway**
meaning, **36**, [1381]
one-way traffic, **37**, [185]
orders—
date of operation, **36**, [1400]
making of, **36**, [1017]
procedure, **36**, [1397]
validity, **36**, [1400]
pedestrian crossings on, **37**, [197]
picnic area on. *See* **picnic area**
private Act, functions under, **36**, [1014]
privately maintainable part, powers on, **36**, [1333]
property and liabilities, transfer of, **36**, [1311], [1316]
public conveniences on. *See* **public conveniences**
road ceasing to be—
highway authority for, **36**, [1006]
orders, **36**, [1013]
property and liabilities, transfer of, **36**, [1311]
transitional matters, **36**, [1429]
road crossing or joining, provisions on, **36**, [1017]
roads being or becoming, **36**, [1013], [1311]
Secretary of State, miscellaneous functions, **36**, [1334]
special road becoming, **36**, [1025]
stamp duty, exemption from, **36**, [1329]
stamp duty land tax, exemption from, **36**, [1330]
system, review of, **36**, [1013]
traffic signs, **37**, [252]
transitional provisions, **36**, [1433]

trunk road picnic area
byelaws, **32**, [273]
stopping up, **9**, [140]

trust
accounts—
auditor, **48**, 244
beneficiary, rights of, **48**, 244
investigation and audit of, **48**, 244
accumulation and maintenance, **43(S)**, 377–84
age 18–25, **43(S)**, 377–84
applicable law, **48**, 601–2
bare, meaning **41**, [452]
beneficial owner, acquisition by bare trustee attributed to, **41**, [452]
beneficiaries, interests of, **41**, [452]
beneficiary's estate, settled property as art of, **43(S)**, 385–90
bereaved minors, for, **43(S)**, 377–84, 396
charitable, becoming, **43(S)**, 398
breach of, loans and investments not being, **48**, 458–9
business tenancy held on, **21**, [204]

trust—*contd*
capital money—
advancement, payment for, **48**, 493
calls on shares, payment of, **48**, 463
insurance money as, **48**, 471–2
power to raise, **48**, 469
rights in securities, used for, **48**, 461
charity, gifts to, **43(1)**, [470]
civil jurisdiction, allocation of, **11(2)**, [809]
company, for, taxation of profits, **44(1)**, [2]
corporation, nomination to receive notices, **20**, [748]
costs of order, charging on estate, **48**, 532
county court, jurisdiction of, **48**, 537–8
court—
jurisdiction of, **48**, 540
powers of, **48**, 218–19
disabled person, for, **42**, [605], [621]
discretionary—
companies, payments to, **44(1)**, [435]
double taxation relief, **44(1)**, [592]
payments under, companies, to, **44(1)**, [435]
domicile of, **11(2)**, [837], [848]
dual resident, gift into. *See* **capital gains tax**
employee. *See* **employee**
foreign, purchase of interests in, **43(S)**, 152–3
fund—
division of, **48**, 572, 579
National Debt, for reduction of, **41**, [66]
valuation of, **48**, 572
implied, when arising, **20**, [671]
income, receipts treated as, **43(S)**, 552
income tax rate, **44(4)**, [9]
income charged on, **44(4)**, [15]
inheritance tax. *See* **inheritance tax**
international recognition of—
Convention, **48**, 599, 601–3
generally, **48**, 221
land held on, limitation of action, **19(3)**, [745]
land, of. *See* **trust of land**
legislation, **48**, 216–24
management expenses, setting against income, order of, **44(1)**, [436]
meaning, **48**, 541
National Debt, for reduction of, **48**, 552
newspaper, relevant property, **43(S)**, 397
newspapers, inheritance tax, **42**, [603], [619]
non-resident—
notice of particulars, **42**, [142]
remittance basis—
accrued income profits, **43(S)**, 1110–11
beneficiaries, attribution of gains to, **43(S)**, 1095–1106
commencement and amendments, **43(S)**, 1099–1105
existing Schedule 4C pools, **43(S)**, 1109–10
transfers of value, cases involving, **43(S)**, 1105–9
market value of assets, **43(S)**, 1112
offshore income gains, **43(S)**, 1091–4
transfer of assets abroad, **43(S)**, 1111–13
order, persons applying for, **48**, 531

trust—*contd*
  property dealings, court authorising, **48**, 528
  property, limitation of action, **19(3)**, [749]
  protective, **43(S)**, 399
    generally, **48**, 496
    variation of, **48**, 561
    inheritance tax, **42**, [604], [620]
    relationship between persons, **6**, [280]
  register of members, not to be entered on, **8(1)**, [204]
  registered fund. *See* **registered fund**
  registered trade mark, affecting, **48**, 132
  religious, public trustee not accepting, **48**, 232
  repayment supplement, **44(1)**, [607]
  Scottish, **43(1)**, [19]
  service charge contributions, of, **22**, [757]
  share option scheme, interests under, **44(1)**, [640]
  shared ownership, rent to, charge to tax, **41(S)**, Stamp Duties 5–6
  special rates of tax not to apply to social landlords' service charge income, **43(S)**, 87
  statutory, **20**, [654]
  Trustee Act 1925, application of, **48**, 544–5
  trustee investment powers, persons having, **48**, 574
  trustee, residence, **43(S)**, 312–13, 323–5
  unit. *See* **unit trusts**
  variation of, jurisdiction of court, **48**, 561–2
  vesting order—
    beneficial interest of infant, as to, **48**, 525
    charity property, **48**, 524
    court, powers of, **48**, 515
    effect of, **48**, 520–1
    evidence of allegations, as, **48**, 527
    infant mortgagee, in respect of, **48**, 518
    judgment for specific performance, consequential on, **48**, 519–20
    mortgage, consequential on, **48**, 519
    order for sale, consequential on, **48**, 519
    person to convey land, appointment of, **48**, 521
    property out of England, application to, **48**, 528
    stock, as to, **48**, 522–3
    thing in action, as to, **48**, 522–3
    unborn persons, contingent rights of, **48**, 518
  vulnerable beneficiary, with—
    actual gains and actual losses, meaning, **43(2)**, [649]
    actual income, meaning, **43(2)**, [649]
    assumed gains and assumed losses, meaning, **43(2)**, [649]
    capital gains tax—
      deemed taxable amount, **43(2)**, [649]
      non-UK vulnerable persons, treatment of, **43(2)**, [592]
      special treatment, **43(2)**, [590]
      UK resident vulnerable persons, treatment of, **43(2)**, [591]
      vulnerable person's liability, **43(2)**, [593]
    commencement of provisions, **43(2)**, [603]

trust—*contd*
  vulnerable beneficiary, with—*contd*
    disabled persons, for, **43(2)**, [594]
      meaning, **43(2)**, [598]
    enquiries, power to make, **43(2)**, [600]
    income tax—
      relief, amount of, **43(2)**, [586]
      special treatment, **43(2)**, [585]
      trustees' liability, **43(2)**, [587]
      vulnerable person—
        liability of, **43(2)**, [588]
        part years, election for, **43(2)**, [589]
    interpretation, **43(2)**, [601]
    introduction of provisions, **43(2)**, [583]
    notional section 77 gains, meaning, **43(2)**, [649]
    part of assets held on, **43(2)**, [596]
    relevant assumptions, **43(2)**, [649]
    relevant minors, for, **43(2)**, [595]
      meaning, **43(2)**, [599]
    Scotland, application of provisions in, **43(2)**, [602]
    special tax treatment—
      capital gains tax, **43(2)**, [590]–[593]
      entitlement to make claim for, **43(2)**, [584]
      income tax, **43(2)**, [585]–[588]
    trustees' specially taxed income, meaning, **43(2)**, [649]
    vulnerable person—
      election, **43(2)**, [597]
      meaning, **43(2)**, [583], [601]

trust corporation
  meaning, **18**, [559], [655]; **21**, [48]
  officers, powers of, **18**, [642]
  probate, grant of, to, **18**, [642], [671]

trust for sale
  beneficiaries, consultation with, **20**, [645]
  capital money arising on sale, **20**, [647]
  consents to execution—
    beneficiaries, consultation with, **20**, [645]
    generally, **20**, [645]
    inability to obtain, **20**, [649]
    requirement, **20**, [645]
  doctrine of conversion, abolition, **23**, [312]
  duration, **20**, [642]
  equitable interests—
    giving effect to, **20**, [627]
    overreaching, **20**, [626], [647]
  execution of, consent to, **20**, [645]
  general note, **20**, [1]
  implied—
    duration of, **20**, [642]
    personalty settlements, **20**, [651]
  intestacy, arising on, **18**, [536]
  jurisdiction as to, **20**, [649]
  meaning, **20**, [497], [804]
  mortgage by way of, **20**, [703]
  partition of unsold land, **20**, [647]
  postponement, **20**, [644]
  proceeds of sale—
    application, **20**, [627], [646]
    trusts affecting, **20**, [646]

trust for sale—*contd*
proceeds of sale—*contd*
undivided shares, held in trust as, **20**, [627]
whether purchaser concerned with, **20**, [646]
purchaser, protection of, **20**, [642]
rents and profits, **20**, [647]
restraining order, **20**, [642]
settlement by, **20**, [1]
statutory trusts, **20**, [654]
trustees—
management powers, **20**, [647]
mental disorder, replacement for, **20**, [641]
powers of—
consent to exercise, **20**, [647]
delegation, **20**, [648]
generally, **20**, [647]
refusal to exercise, **20**, [649]
refusal or neglect by, **20**, [627]
undivided shares—
transitional provisions, **20**, [811]
vesting of proceeds, **20**, [647]
vesting order, court's power, **20**, [649]

trust of land
bankruptcy jurisdiction, **4(2)**, [413]
beneficiaries—
direction by, **48**, 607
meaning, **48**, 608
beneficiary—
consultation with, **23**, [321]
meaning, **23**, [329]
right to occupy land—
exclusion and restriction of, **23**, [323]
existence of, **23**, [322]
charitable, ecclesiastical and public trusts, **23**, [335]
consequential provisions, **48**, 609
Crown, provisions applying to, **23**, [331]
disposition creating, consent to, **23**, [320]
entailed interests, **23**, [335]
express trust for sale as, **23**, [313]
family charges, **23**, [335]
general note, **20**, [1]
generally, **48**, 221, 222, 225, 226
implied trust for sale as, **23**, [314]
interest, failure to register as local land charge, **21**, [441]
interest subject to, compensation for depreciation where, **9**, [313]
joint tenants, legal estate held in trust for, **20**, [655]
meaning, **20**, [1]; **23**, [310]
mentally disordered person, land vested in, **20**, [641]
minor, conveyance to, **23**, [335]
mortgaged property, redemption barred, **20**, [650]
orders, application to court for—
matters relevant in determining, **23**, [325]
power of, **23**, [324]
personal representative holding on, **20**, [1], [652]; **23**, [328]
proceeds of sale, application of provisions to, **23**, [327]

trust of land—*contd*
purchaser, meaning, **48**, 608
purchasers, protection of, **23**, [326]
rentcharge, creation, **21**, [502]
reverter of land—
arising from, **22**, [689]
right of, replacement by, **22**, [689]
settlements, in place of, **23**, [311], [335]
trustees—
appointment, **20**, [643]
beneficiaries, consultation with, **23**, [321]
delegation by—
duties as to, **23**, [319]
generally, **23**, [318]
exclusion and restriction of powers, **23**, [317]
general powers of, **23**, [315]
intervention, power of, **23**, [319]
meaning, **23**, [310]
orders, application to court for—
matters relevant in determining, **23**, [325]
power of, **23**, [324]
partition by, **23**, [316]
personal representative as, **20**, [1], [652]
purchasers, protection of, **23**, [326]

trust territory
enactments, application to, **7(2)**, [449]

trustee. *See also* **settlement**
absence of, judgment in, **48**, 531
acquisition of land, power of—
existing trusts, **48**, 629
freehold and leasehold, **48**, 628
restrictions or exclusion of provisions, **48**, 629
advancement, power of, **48**, 493
agent—
asset management, restrictions on, **48**, 634
duty of care, **48**, 654
employing, power of, **48**, 475–6, 630
liability for, **48**, 639, 641
linked functions, **48**, 633
persons acting as, **48**, 632
powers, trustees exceeding, **48**, 641
remuneration, **48**, 647
restriction or exclusion of powers, **48**, 642
review of, **48**, 639–40
sole trustee, of, **48**, 641
terms of agency, **48**, 633
appointment of—
additional, **48**, 500–2
beneficiaries, at instance of, **48**, 604–5
court, by, **48**, 511, 515
generally, **48**, 218
new, **48**, 499–502
retirement without, **48**, 508
separate parts of property, for, **48**, 506
substitute for incapable trustee, for, **48**, 606
vacancy, evidence of, **48**, 507
appointment of new, abolition of stamp duty, **41**, [152], [157]

trustee—*contd*
approved share incentive plans, of—
"applicable period" in relation to shares,
determining, **44(4)**, [497]
income from, special rates for, **44(4)**, [496]
assessment on, **42**, [989]
audit, carrying out, **48**, 474
authorised unit trust, of, **48**, 651
breach of trust, **48**, 534
capital gains tax. *See* **capital gains tax**
charity, of. *See* **charitable trust**
Class 4 contributions, payment of,
40(1), [462]
common investment scheme for charities, of,
48, 651
company securities—
concurrence in scheme or arrangement
for, **48**, 461
rights, dealing with, **48**, 461
compensation, payment to, **9**, [34]–[36],
[295], [313]
conveyance by, implied covenants, **20**, [694]
court, powers of—
appointment, of, **48**, 511
dealings with property, authorising, **48**, 528
personal liability, relief from, **48**, 532
remuneration, authorisation of, **48**, 514
custodian—
bearer securities, of, **48**, 637
duty of care, **48**, 645
liability for, **48**, 639, 641
persons eligible to be, **48**, 637–8
power to appoint, **48**, 636
powers, trustees exceeding, **48**, 641
public trustee as, **48**, 235–6
remuneration, **48**, 647
restriction or exclusion of powers, **48**, 642
review of, **48**, 639–40
rules relating to, **48**, 235–6
sole trustee, powers of, **48**, 641
terms of appointment, **48**, 638–9
delegation by—
generally, **48**, 222
power of attorney, by, **48**, 478–9, 610–11
beneficial interest, evidence of,
48, 612–13
enduring, **48**, 614–15
land, extent of attorney's authority to act
in relation to, **48**, 617
specified form, general powers in,
48, 613
period not exceeding twelve months, for,
48, 478, 615
two-trustee rules, **48**, 616
deposit at bank by, **48**, 463
discharge of, **48**, 218
discretion of, **48**, 455
discretionary payments by—
conditions applicable to, **44(4)**, [501]
grossing up, **44(4)**, [502]
income tax—
charged on, **44(4)**, [504]
payment of, **44(4)**, [502]
statement about deduction of,
44(4), [503]

trustee—*contd*
discretionary payments by—*contd*
tax pool, calculation of, **44(4)**, [505]
types of income, **44(4)**, [506]
documents, deposit of, **48**, 473
duty of care—
application of, **48**, 622, 654–5
meaning, **48**, 621
skill and care, exercise of, **48**, 621
employee share ownership trusts, of—
functions, **42**, [996]
securities acquired by, **42**, [996]
sums received by, **42**, [996]
trust deed, provision of, **42**, [996]
expenses—
beneficiary's income, use of, to reduce—
non-UK resident beneficiaries,
44(4), [509]
untaxed income, meaning,
44(4), [510]
reduction, steps to achieve, **44(4)**, [511]
restrictions on, **44(4)**, [508]
entitlement to, **48**, 646
trust rate income, set against, **44(4)**, [492],
[494]
unused, carry forward of, **44(4)**, [493]
friendly society. *See* **friendly society**
general provision, overview, **44(4)**, [473]
heritage maintenance settlements, **44(4)**, [515]
income from—
double taxation, prevention of,
44(4), [519]
elections as to, **44(4)**, [516]
change of circumstances affecting,
44(4), [517]
non-heritage purposes, used for—
rate of tax, **44(4)**, [523]
tax charged on, **44(4)**, [520]–[521]
property maintenance, sums applied for,
44(4), [518]
non-heritage purposes, application of
property for—
rate of tax, **44(4)**, [523]
tax charged on, **44(4)**, [520]–[521]
exemptions, **44(4)**, [525]
transfer of property between
settlements, **44(4)**, [524]
incapable—
appointment of substitute for, **48**, 606
attorney acting for, **48**, 616–17
incapacitated person, liability to tax for,
42, [210]
income, special rates for—
accumulated or discretionary income—
charged at, **44(4)**, [487]
meaning, **44(4)**, [488]
other amounts charged at, **44(4)**, [489]
personal representatives, sums paid by,
44(4), [491]
types of amounts charged at, **44(4)**, [490]
indemnity—
advertisement, protection by means of,
48, 483
implied, **48**, 485
notice, in regard to, **48**, 485

trustee—*contd*
 indemnity—*contd*
  rents and covenants, liability in respect of,
   48, 481–2
 inheritance tax. *See* **inheritance tax**
 insurance money, use of, **48**, 471–2
 insure, power to, **48**, 470, 648, 655
 investment—
  advice, consideration of, **48**, 625
  bearer securities, in, **48**, 458, 637
  charge, in, **48**, 457
  choosing, duty as to, **48**, 572–3
  discretion in, **48**, 455
  drainage charge, land subject to, **48**, 457
  duty of care, **48**, 654
  existing trusts, **48**, 627
  improper, liability for, **48**, 460
  land sold, charge on, **48**, 461
  loan, period of, **48**, 461
  mortgage, in, **48**, 457
  narrower range, **48**, 568, 581–5, 591, 595
  persons having powers of, provisions
   relating to, **48**, 574
  powers, **48**, 568, 587–9
   additional, **48**, 578
   court, powers of, **48**, 528, 579
   existing trusts, for, **48**, 627
   general, **48**, 622
   restriction or exclusion of provisions,
    48, 626
   special, **48**, 570–1
  property, meaning, **48**, 571
  railway company, in, **48**, 457
  redeemable stocks, in, **48**, 454
  securities, retention of, **48**, 575
  special cases, application of provisions in,
   48, 575
  special powers, **48**, 570–1
  special-range property, **48**, 570–1, 590–1
  standard criteria, **48**, 624
  trust fund, division of, **48**, 572, 579
  unauthorised, continuing to hold, **48**, 456
  wider range—
   compensating transfer, **48**, 569
   meaning, **48**, 568
   restrictions on, **48**, 569–70
   Schedule of, **48**, 587
   special powers, **48**, 570–1
 judicial—
  administration, inquiry into, **48**, 227
  directions, in, **48**, 227
  jurisdiction as to, **48**, 228
  legislation, **48**, 216
  powers to appoint, **48**, 227
  remuneration, **48**, 227
  rules, **48**, 229
 land, of, appointment and retirement at
  instance of beneficiaries, **48**, 604–5
 liabilities, power to compound, **48**, 466–7
 liability of, **43(1)**, [146]
 mental disorder, having, **48**, 502
 minor, appointment void, **20**, [639]
 minority, application of income during,
  48, 487–9

trustee—*contd*
 new—
  appointment of, **48**, 499–502
  court, appointment by, **48**, 511, 515
  vesting of property in, **48**, 509
 nominees—
  duty of care, **48**, 654
  liability for, **48**, 639, 641
  persons eligible to be, **48**, 637–8
  power to appoint, **48**, 635
  powers, trustees exceeding, **48**, 641
  remuneration, **48**, 647
  restriction or exclusion of powers, **48**, 642
  review of, **48**, 639–40
  sole trustee, **48**, 641
  terms of appointment, **48**, 638–9
 non-UK resident, **44(4)**, [495]
 number—
  increase in, **48**, 506
  limitation on, **48**, 498–9
 others, power to concur with, **48**, 477
 patient, being, **48**, 526
 payment into court by, **48**, 535–6
 pension fund, of, **48**, 650
 personal liability, relief from, **48**, 532
 personal representatives, sums paid by,
  44(4), [491]
 powers, exceeding, **48**, 641
 protection—
  acting with or without, **20**, [783]
  Law of Property Act 1925, **20**, [783]
 protection of, **42**, [214]
  adoption of child, **6**, [177]
  legitimacy, enquiry as to, **6**, [162]
 protection of persons dealing with, **48**, 469
 Public. *See* **Public Trustee**
 receipt—
  power to give, **48**, 465
  unable to give, **48**, 506
 references to, **44(4)**, [486]
 reimbursement, **48**, 223, 485
 relevant, **42**, [247]
 remuneration—
  agent, nominee or custodian, of, **48**, 647
  application of provisions, **48**, 647
  charitable trustees, of, **48**, 645
  court, powers of, **48**, 514
  entitlement to under trust instrument,
   48, 642–3
  generally, **48**, 222
  reasonable, trustees entitled to, **48**, 644
 residence, **42**, [986]
  of, **44(4)**, [483]
 retirement, **48**, 508
  beneficiaries, at instance of, **48**, 604–5
 reversionary interests, valuation of, **48**, 474
 sale, power of—
  auction, by, **48**, 464
  capital money, to raise, **48**, 468
  contract, by, **48**, 464
  depreciatory conditions, subject to, **48**, 465
  part, of, **48**, 464
 Scottish trusts, **44(4)**, [472]
 security, loan of money on, **48**, 458–9
 "settled property", meaning, **44(4)**, [474]

trustee—*contd*
settlement, of. *See* **settlement**
shares, payment of calls on, **48**, 463
single and distinct person, treatment as,
44(4), [482]
sole, powers of, **48**, 641
special rules, transitional provisions and
savings, **44(4)**, [1055]
statutory powers, **48**, 217
stock exchange nominee, transfer of securities
from, **48**, 596
subsidiary acting as—
employer's right of recovery under pension
scheme or employees' share scheme,
disregarding, **8(1)**, [218]
residual interest under pension scheme or
employees' share scheme, disregarding,
8(1), [217]
shares in holding company, holding,
8(1), [216]–[218]
surviving, devolution of powers on, **48**, 469
tax pool, calculation of, **44(4)**, [505]
types of income, **44(4)**, [506]
tax return, **42**, [100]
amended provisions, **43(S)**, 569
amendment by taxpayer, **42**, [102]
amendment of, **43(S)**, 571
commencement of amended provisions,
43(S), 573
correction and amendment, **43(S)**, 952–2
enquiry into. *See* **return**
failure to make, penalty for, **43(S)**, 572
HM Revenue and Customs, correction
by, **42**, [103]
time for delivery of, **43(S)**, 569
trust of land, as. *See* **trust of land**
trust rate income—
expenses set against, **44(4)**, [492], [494]
first slice of—
more than one settlement, where,
44(4), [500]
special rates not applicable to,
44(4), [499]
Trustee Act 1925, application of, **48**, 544–5
unauthorised unit trust—
affected by s.733 ICTA, special rules for,
44(4), [514]
relief for, **44(4)**, [513]
treatment of income from, **44(4)**, [512]
valuation by, **48**, 474
vesting instruments by, as conveyance,
20, [633]
vesting of property in, **48**, 509

trustee in bankruptcy. *See* **bankruptcy**

trustee savings bank
summary of provisions, **19(1)**, [1]

trusts, university and college
administration of, schemes for, **15(1)**, [239]
contributions charged on, **15(1)**, [241]

trusts, university and college—*contd*
students' union. *See* **students' union**

TSB group
capital allowances, **19(2)**, [1002]
existing banks—
dissolution of, **19(2)**, [996]
meaning, **19(2)**, [994]
property, rights, liabilities and obligations
of, **19(2)**, [995]
new holding company—
dividends, deemed to have paid,
19(2), [1001]
meaning, **19(2)**, [994]
vesting of assets in, **19(2)**, [995]
See also transfer provisions *below*
new, meaning, **19(2)**, [994]
reorganisation, provisions on, **19(2)**, [995],
[996]
taxation, provisions on, **19(2)**, [1002]
transfer provisions—
accounting, relating to, **19(2)**, [1001]
agreements and documents, construction
of, **19(2)**, [1000]
authorised institution, status as,
19(2), [1001]
chargeable gains, no accrual of,
19(2), [1002]
distribution, profits available for,
19(2), [1001]
effect of, **19(2)**, [999]
remedies, **19(2)**, [1000]
vesting of assets, **19(2)**, [995]

tunnel
explosives, conveyance of in, **25(1)**, [95]
highway, part of, **36**, [1380]
navigable waters, under—
construction, order or scheme for,
36, [1125]
diversion of watercourse, order for,
36, [1127]
navigation, reasonable needs of, **36**, [1126]
objection to, **36**, [1126]
plans and specifications of, **36**, [1126]
schemes, **36**, [1398]
street works, reinstatement after, **38(1)**, [233]

turkeys
slaughter. *See* **poultry**

turnstiles
public lavatories, in, abolition of, **35(1)**, [281]

Tuvalu
British ship registered in, **7(2)**, [703]
Commonwealth citizenship, **31**, [186]
independence of, **7(2)**, [698]
legislative powers of, **7(2)**, [702]
meaning, **7(2)**, [700]
visiting forces in, **7(2)**, [703]

typhus
public disease. *See* **notifiable disease**

U

Uganda
agreements, **7(2)**, [522]
British ship registered in, **7(2)**, [523]
Commonwealth citizenship, **31**, [186]
existing law, operation of, **7(2)**, [547]
fully responsible status of, **7(2)**, [517]
legislative powers in, **7(2)**, [521]
visiting forces in, **7(2)**, [523]

UK Border Agency
Chief Inspector, inspections by,
13(S), Customs 47–8
functions transferred to, summary of
provisions, **13(S)**, Customs 15–17
information—
onward disclosure of, **13(S)**, Customs 39
supply to, **13(S)**, Customs 39
property, rights and liabilities, transfer to,
13(S), Customs 45–6

Ulster Defence Regiment
absence without leave, **3**, [1440]
acceptance of members, **3**, [1436]
call out—
emergency service, for, **3**, [1399]
generally, **3**, [1386]
permanent service, for, **3**, [1398]
notices, **3**, [1399]
desertion, **3**, [1440]
enactments relating to, **3**, [1540]
enrolment, **3**, [1435]
failure to attend, **3**, [1439]
members of armed forces, to be, **3**, [1437]
membership, cessation of, **3**, [1]
military law applying to, **3**, [1437]
orders and regulations, **3**, [1436]
re-engagement, **3**, [1435]
resignation, **3**, [1435]
service, **3**, [1436]
serving members, transfer of, **3**, [1538]
summary of provisions, **3**, [1]
training, **3**, [1418]

Ulster savings certificates
exempt income from, **44(3)**, [707]
taxation of, **44(1)**, [31]

umpire. *See also* **arbitration; arbitrator**
appointment of, **8**, 60

under tenant
goods of, protection from distress, **13**, [1199],
[1200], [1205]
rent, payable direct to superior landlord,
13, [1201], [1205]

underground
air-raid shelters, **50**, [241]
See also **air-raid shelter**

underground room
London—
appeals relating to, **25(2)**, [667]
infilling, **25(2)**, [665]
street offences involving, **36**, [229], [385]

underground water
information about, **49**, [1247]
confidentiality of, **49**, [1255]

underlease
meaning, **20**, [498]
perpetually renewable. *See* **lease**

underletting
application for consent, passing on, **22**, [785]
assured tenancy, of, **22**, [810]
breach of duty, **22**, [787]
consent of another, approval of, **22**, [786]
county court jurisdiction, **21**, [216]
covenants against, **21**, [65]

undertakers. *See types of undertakers*

undertaking
another, rights held for, **8**, 754
certain circumstances, rights exercisable in,
8, 754
directors, right to appoint or remove majority
of, **8**, 754
disregarded rights, **8**, 755
disturbance payment, to person displaced from
land in consequence of, **9**, [341]
dominant influence, right to exercise, **8**, 754
home loss payment to person displace from
dwelling, **9**, [325]
meaning, **8**, 341–2
parent, **8**, 340–1
rights attributed to, **8**, 755
participating interest in, **8**, 342–3
security, rights attached to shares by way of,
8, 754–5
subsidiary, **8**, 340–1
voting rights in, **8**, 754

underwriter
ancillary trust funds—
corporate members, of, **43(1)**, [92]
entitlement to, **43(1)**, [29]
meaning, **43(1)**, [36]
assessment and collection of tax, **43(1)**, [90],
[97]

underwriter—*contd*
  corporate—
    accounting period in which profits or losses
      arising, **43(1)**, [89]
    ancillary trust funds, **43(1)**, [92]
    assessment and collection of tax,
      43(1), [90]
    cessation of business, **43(1)**, [95]
    inheritance tax, property not relevant for,
      43(1), [106]
    loan relationships, **43(1)**, [260]
    meaning, **43(1)**, [98]
    premium trust funds, **43(1)**, [91], [94]
    profits and losses, **43(1)**, [98]
    quota share insurance, **43(1)**, [93]
    stop-loss insurance, **43(1)**, [93]
    taxation of profits, **43(1)**, [88]
  death of, **43(1)**, [32]
  definitions, **43(1)**, [36], [98]
  final year of assessment, **43(1)**, [31]
  individuals, **43(1)**, [96]
  investment income, repayment of tax
    deducted from, **43(1)**, [52]
  limited liability underwriting, conversion to,
    43(1), [33]
    resignation notice, withdrawal of,
      43(1), [57]
    successor companies, through, **43(1)**, [55]
    successor partnerships, through, **43(1)**, [56]
  Lloyd's. *See* **Lloyd's**
  losses—
    accounting period in which arising,
      43(1), [89]
    allowance of, **43(1)**, [24]
    syndicate's, determination of, **43(1)**, [51]
    year of assessment in which arising,
      43(1), [25]
  premiums trust fund—
    assets, entitlement to, **43(1)**, [27]
    corporate members, of, **43(1)**, [91]
    meaning, **43(1)**, [36]
    pooling, **42**, [1452]
  profits—
    accounting period in which arising,
      43(1), [89]
    earned income, as, **43(1)**, [34]
    syndicate's, determination of, **43(1)**, [51]
    taxation of, **43(1)**, [24], [88]
    year of assessment in which arising,
      43(1), [25]
  quota share insurance, **43(1)**, [30], [93]
  regulations, **43(1)**, [35], [97]
  special reserve funds—
    assets of, profits arising from, **43(1)**, [53]
    cessation of business, tax consequences of,
      43(1), [53]
    definitions, **43(1)**, [53]
    entitlement of members, **43(1)**, [53]
    excess amounts, valuation and payments
      out, **43(1)**, [53]
    general requirements, **43(1)**, [53]
    meaning, **43(1)**, [36]
    new-style, **43(1)**, [53]
    old-style, winding up, **43(1)**, [54]
    payments into, **43(1)**, [53]

underwriter—*contd*
  special reserve funds—*contd*
    payments out of, **43(1)**, [53]
    taxation provisions, **43(1)**, [28]
  stop-loss insurance, **43(1)**, [30], [93]
  syndicate—
    meaning, **43(1)**, [36]
    profit or loss, determining, **43(1)**, [51]

unfair dismissal
  arbitration scheme, **16**, [414]
  compensation for—
    adjustments, **16**, [778]
    basic award—
      amount of, **16**, [772]
      minimum, **16**, [773]
      two weeks' pay, of, **16**, [774]
    compensatory award—
      amount of, **16**, [776]
      contribution, reduction for, **16**, [776]
      limit of, **16**, [777]
    discriminatory, act also being, **16**, [779]
    indexation, **16**, [982]
  education or training, participation in,
    16, [750]
  employee representatives, of, **16**, [752]
  fairness—
    determining, **16**, [736]
    reason, showing, **16**, [736]
    retirement dismissals, **16**, [743]
  family reasons, leave for, **16**, [746]
  flexible working, reasons relating to, **16**, [757]
  health and safety cases, in, **16**, [747]
  industrial action, loss of rights on,
    16, [449]–[453]
  interim relief—
    continuation of contract of employment,
      order for, **16**, [782]
    determination of complaint, pending,
      16, [780]
    order—
      failure to comply with, **16**, [784]
      making, **16**, [781]
      variation or revocation, application for,
        16, [783]
    procedure on hearing, **16**, [781]
  jury service, on summoning for, **16**, [745]
  national minimum wage, for reasons
    connected to, **16**, [755]
  occupational pension scheme trustees, of,
    16, [751]
  pension enrolment, **16**, [758]
  police, provisions applying to, **16**, [787]
  pregnancy and childbirth, for reasons of,
    16, [746]
  pressure on employer for, **16**, [761]
  protected disclosure, for reasons of, **16**, [753]
  redundancy, for reasons of, **16**, [759]
  refusal of Sunday working, for, **16**, [748]
  remedies—
    choice and terms of order, **16**, [769]
    compensation, award of—
      adjustments, **16**, [778]
      basic, **16**, [773]–[775]
      compensatory, **16**, [776], [777]

unfair dismissal—*contd*
remedies—*contd*
compensation, award of—*contd*
components of, **16**, [771]
discriminatory, act also being, **16**, [779]
employment tribunal, complaint to,
16, [764]
enforcement, **16**, [770]
interim relief—
continuation of contract of employment,
order for, **16**, [782]
determination of complaint, pending,
16, [780]
failure to comply with order, **16**, [784]
order, making, **16**, [781]
procedure on hearing, **16**, [781]
variation or revocation of order,
application for, **16**, [783]
orders and compensation, **16**, [765]
re-engagement, order for, **16**, [766], [768]
reinstatement, order for, **16**, [766], [767]
replacements, of, **16**, [760]
retirement—
fairness, **16**, [743]
no normal retirement age—
dismissal at or after 65, **16**, [738]
dismissal before 65, **16**, [737]
normal retirement age—
dismissal at or after, **16**, [740], [741]
dismissal before, **16**, [739]
meaning, **16**, [744]
notification of reason for dismissal,
16, [742]
right not to be unfairly dismissed—
assertion of, **16**, [754]
dismissal, circumstances of, **16**, [734]
effective date of termination, **16**, [735]
exclusion of—
dismissal procedures agreement, existence
of, **16**, [763]
qualifying period of employment,
16, [762]
statement of, **16**, [733]
tax credit, for reasons relating to, **16**, [756]
transitional provisions, **16**, [893]
working time cases, in, **16**, [749]

unfair prejudice
orders respecting, **8**, 531–3

unfit house. *See also* **defective housing**
amendment of provisions, **23**, [40]
breach of covenant, rights arising from,
22, [265]
condemned. *See* **clearance area**
demolition order. *See* **demolition order**
order to occupier etc to permit works,
22, [269]
re-development by owner—
proposals for, acceptance of, **22**, [266]
recovery of possession for, **22**, [267]
subsidy. *See* **slum clearance**
works of improvement, authorisation by
tribunal, **22**, [272]

unfitness to plead
finding of—
accused did the act or made omission,
that, **12(1)**, [340]
appeal against, **12(1)**, [431], [432]
substitution, **12(1)**, [422], [430]
supervision order. *See* supervision order
below
verdict of acquittal on, **12(1)**, [340]
hospital order, making, **12(1)**, [341], [342],
[422], [430]
disposal of appeal, **12(1)**, [434]
power to make, **12(1)**, [422]
right of appeal against, **12(1)**, [433]
persons not guilty by reason of, powers as to,
12(1), [341], [422]
proof of, **12(1)**, [343]
question of—
determination, **12(1)**, [339]
jury's functions, **12(1)**, [339], [340]
special verdict where, **12(1)**, [338]
supervision and treatment order—
amendment, **12(1)**, [347]
appeal, on, **12(1)**, [430]
disposal of appeal, **12(1)**, [434]
making and effect of, **12(1)**, [346]
medical treatment requirement,
12(1), [346]
meaning, **12(1)**, [345]
power to make, **12(1)**, [341], [422]
requirements, **12(1)**, [345]
residence requirement, **12(1)**, [346]
revocation, **12(1)**, [347]
right of appeal against, **12(1)**, [433]

uniform
authority, worn without, **3**, [249]
contempt, bringing on, **3**, [250]
political object, wearing in connection with,
12(1), [251]
proscribed organisation, of, **12(2)**, [875]
stage play, use in, **3**, [249]
unauthorised use of, **12(1)**, [229]
wearing illegally, **3**, [1]

unincorporated association
gangmasters, application of provisions on,
1(2), [719]
offences by, **8**, 890
statutory auditor, offences relating to,
8(1), [1333]

unincorporated bodies
authorised person, as, **19(2)**, [32]
officer in default, application of provisions,
8(1), [1201]
proceedings against, **8(1)**, [1208]

unincorporated companies
general note, **8**, 8–9

unit trust
authorised—
court common investment funds treated
as, **44(1)**, [319]

unit trust—*contd*
  authorised—*contd*
    dividend distributions, **44(3)**, [389]–[391]
    income, treatment of, **44(1)**, [316]
    interest distributions, **44(3)**, [376]–[378]
    loan relationships, **43(1)**, [258]
    management expenses, **44(1)**, [335]
    meaning, **44(1)**, [316]; **48**, 651
    Trustee Act 2000, application of, **48**, 651
  authorised, mergers of—
    direction to hold trust property on other
      trusts, **41**, [244]
    stamp duty relief, **41**, [241]
    stamp duty reserve tax relief, **41**, [243]
  authorised investment fund, as, **43(2)**, [733]
  insurance companies, deemed disposal by,
    43(1), [7]
  scheme—
    authorisation—
      applications for, **19(2)**, [295]
      determination of applications,
        19(2), [297]
      orders, **19(2)**, [296]
      refusal of application, procedure,
        19(2), [298]
      revocation—
        other than by consent, **19(2)**, [307]
        procedure, **19(2)**, [308]
        requests for, **19(2)**, [309]
    authorised—
      alteration, **19(2)**, [304]
      certificates, **19(2)**, [299]
      exclusion clauses, avoidance,
        19(2), [306]
      intervention, powers of—
        application to court, **19(2)**, [311]
        directions, **19(2)**, [310]–[314]
        investigations, **19(2)**, [336]
      manager or trustee, change of,
        19(2), [304]
        refusal of approval of, **19(2)**, [305]
      meaning, **19(2)**, [290]
      modification or waiver of rules,
        19(2), [303]
      scheme particulars rules, **19(2)**, [301]
      trust scheme rules, **19(2)**, [300]
        breach, disqualification of auditor for,
        19(2), [302]
    capital gains tax. *See* **capital gains tax**
    exclusion clauses in trust deed, avoidance
      of, **19(2)**, [306]
    manager—
      activities, restriction on, **19(2)**, [190]
      change of, **19(2)**, [304], [305]
      meaning, **19(2)**, [500]
    meaning, **19(2)**, [290]; **41**, [275];
      42, [1191]; **43(2)**, [733]; **44(4)**, [1015]
    repealed provisions, **42**, [1021]
    schemes not treated as, **41**, [275]
    stamp duty, abolition, **41**, [273]
    stamp duty land tax provisions applied,
      41, [385]
    transactions, stamp duty land tax
      provisions, **41**, [467]

unit trust—*contd*
  scheme—*contd*
    transfer under, reserve tax, **41**, [183], [256],
      [274]
    trustee—
      change of, **19(2)**, [304], [305]
      meaning, **19(2)**, [290]
    umbrella, **43(1)**, [74]
  umbrella scheme, **41**, [275]; **44(1)**, [315]
  unauthorised—
    calculation of trustees' income pool,
      44(4), [951]
    collection of tax from trustees, **44(4)**, [950]
    deemed deductions, **44(4)**, [949]
    deemed payments to unit holders,
      44(4), [949]
    distributions from—
      charge to tax, **44(3)**, [557]
      income charged, **44(3)**, [558]
      income tax treated as paid, **44(3)**, [560]
      person liable, **44(3)**, [559]
    foreign income dividends, **43(1)**, [315]
    qualifying distributions, **43(1)**, [315]
    treatment of income, **44(1)**, [318];
      44(4), [512]
    trustees of—
      affected by s 733 ICTA, special rules
        for, **44(4)**, [514]
      relief for, **44(4)**, [513]
  unit transfer, stamp duty reserve tax
    exemption **41**, [178]

unitary development plan
  transitional provisions, **46**, [1063]

unitary state
  non-resident company connected with,
    44(1), [594]
  qualifying presence in, **44(1)**, [594]
  transitional provisions, **44(1)**, [691]

united district
  constitution, **35(1)**, [119]
  discharge of functions by local authority in,
    restriction on, **35(1)**, [120]
  joint board for, **35(1)**, [119]
  orders constituting, **35(1)**, [121]

United Kingdom
  Acts of Parliament, application to whole
    Kingdom, **41**, [480]
  meaning, **41**, [480]
  merger of Parliaments, **41**, [480]
  Northern Ireland as part of, **31**, 634

United Kingdom Atomic Energy Authority
  accounts of, **17(1)**, [77]
  additional functions, **17(2)**, [430]
  borrowing—
    limits on, **17(1)**, [575]
    loans by Minister, **17(1)**, [576]
    methods of, **17(1)**, [574]
    subsidiaries, by, **17(1)**, [574]
    Treasury guarantees, **17(1)**, [577]

**United Kingdom Atomic Energy
Authority**—*contd*
building regulations, application to,
  35(1), [566]
cessation of certain enactments, **43(2)**, [754]
commercial exploitation by, **17(1)**, [579]
companies, disposal of shares in, **17(1)**, [509]
compulsory purchase powers, **17(1)**, [78]
constabulary, nuclear transfer scheme,
  33(2), [503]
constitution of, **17(1)**, [74]
disposal of waste by, **35(1)**, [348]
employees—
  remuneration of, **17(1)**, [84]
  safety, health and welfare, **17(1)**, [80]
  terms of employment, settling, **17(1)**, [80]
  transferred from, **17(1)**, [431]
enactments adapted to, **17(1)**, [86]
establishment, **17(1)**, [74]
exemption from building regulations,
  35(1), [530]
expenses, defrayment, **17(1)**, [77]
financial provisions—
  borrowing powers. *See* borrowing *above*
  commencing capital debt, **17(1)**, [573]
  generally, **17(1)**, [77]
functions of—
  generally, **17(1)**, [75]
  restriction on, **17(1)**, [75]
general provisions for, **17(1)**, [84]
land—
  Crown land, deemed to be, **17(1)**, [79]
  exclusive occupation rights, **17(1)**, [428]
  powers as to, **17(1)**, [78]
loans from Secretary of State, **17(1)**, [576]
members—
  appointment, **17(1)**, [74]
  interest in contracts, **17(1)**, [84]
  remuneration, **17(1)**, [74]
  terms of office, **17(1)**, [74]
Northern Ireland, provisions applied,
  17(1), [82]
nuclear installations—
  duty as to, **17(1)**, [338]
  See **nuclear installations**
nuclear transfer schemes, powers regarding,
  17(2), [424]
officers and staff, **17(1)**, [84]
patent rights reserved to, **17(1)**, [467]
pension scheme—
  designated BNFL companies, for employees
    of, **17(2)**, [551]
  public sector transfers of members,
    17(2), [549]
  scope of, **17(1)**, [228]
premises—
  continued use of, **17(1)**, [428]
  Official Secrets Act applied, **17(1)**, [79]
property transferred to, **17(1)**, [85]
reports by, **17(1)**, [77]
research functions, **10**, [535]
research, powers respecting, **17(1)**, [579]
sale of houses at discount, stamp duty,
  41, [138], [145]

**United Kingdom Atomic Energy
Authority**—*contd*
Secretary of State—
  directions, power to give, **17(1)**, [76]
  duties generally, **17(1)**, [76]
  information to be given to, **17(1)**, [77]
  supervision by, **17(1)**, [578]
services, provision of, **17(1)**, [437]
shares, power to dispose of, **17(1)**, [509]
status of, **17(1)**, [84]
subsidiaries, borrowing by, **17(1)**, [574]
summary of provisions, **17(1)**, [1]
supervision by Secretary of State, **17(1)**, [578]
transfer of part of undertaking—
  directions by Minister, **17(1)**, [429]
  exclusions from, **17(1)**, [427], [430]
  Nuclear Fuels Company, to, **17(1)**, [425]
  Radiochemical Company, to, **17(1)**, [426]
transfer of property to, **17(1)**, [85]
weapon production, prohibition of,
  17(1), [462]
Weapons Group—
  employees—
    pension rights, **17(1)**, [458]
    transfer to civil service, **17(1)**, [458]
  technical information by, **17(1)**, [461]
  transfer to Secretary of State—
    appointed day for, **17(1)**, [465]
    certificate of, **17(1)**, [459]
    financial provisions, **17(1)**, [464]
    order for, **17(1)**, [457]
    powers in relation to, **17(1)**, [459]
    properties etc affected by, **17(1)**, [457]
    stamp duty, **17(1)**, [463]
    transitional provisions, **17(1)**, [460]

United Nations
offences, proceedings for, **10**, [1134]
operation, meaning, **10**, [1133]
Orders in Council, **10**, [914]
personnel, amended provisions, **10(S)**, 125
premises, attacks on, **10**, [1131]
priority of telecommunications, **10**, [1015]
Security Council, complying with decisions
  of, **10**, [1]
specialised agencies of, **10**, [1008]
vehicles, attacks on, **10**, [1131]
workers—
  attacks on, **10**, [1130]
  threats of, **10**, [1132]
  meaning, **10**, [1133]

United States of America
municipal securities issued in, exemption from
  taxation, **42**, [2]

universal postal service
providers, land drainage affecting, **19(3)**, [259]

universal services
conditions, obligations secured by, **45**, [483]
  sharing of burden of, **45**, [489]
    report on, **45**, [490]
  subject-matter of, **45**, [485]

universal services—*contd*
directories and directory enquiry facilities, **45**, [487]
providers, designation of, **45**, [484]
review of compliance costs, **45**, [488]
tariffs for, **45**, [486]

universities and colleges. *See also names of universities etc*
benefice, presentation to, rights of, **14**, 252
capital moneys, application of, **46**, [602]
Commissioners. *See* **University Commissioners**
constables, appointing, **12(1)**, [32], [33]
Durham, of, trusts for, **14**, 143
estates. *See* **estates, universities and college**
exempt charity, as, **5(2)**, [691]
extra-parochial services at, **14**, 654–5
loan of objects by, indemnity against loss or damage, **13**, [253], [254]
marriage at, **14**, 654–5
payments to, deductions for, **44(1)**, [52]
privileges etc, **25(1)**, [45]
Scottish, continuation of, **10**, [68]
tests. *See* **universities tests**
trusts. *See* **trusts, university and college**

Universities Funding Council. *See also* **Funding Councils and Asset Board**
dissolution, **15(1)**, [430]
property, rights and liabilities, transfer of, **15(1)**, [430]
reference to, **15(1)**, [427]
Scottish Committee, **15(1)**, [374]
Welsh Committee, **15(1)**, [374]

universities tests
chapel services, **15(1)**, [139]
college, meaning, **15(1)**, [135]
formulary of faith, subscription to, **15(1)**, [136]
lecture, objection on religious grounds, **15(1)**, [140]
office, meaning, **15(1)**, [135]
religious instruction, **15(1)**, [138]
theological offices, applying to, **15(1)**, [148]

university. *See also* **Cambridge, University of; Oxford, University of**
charter, laying before Parliament, **15(1)**, [143]
college, meaning, **15(1)**, [135], [144]
Commissioners. *See* **University Commissioners**
disabled persons, access of to, **15(1)**, [265]
estates. *See* **estates, universities and college**
fees, regulations on, **15(1)**, [279]
freedom of speech, **15(1)**, [292]
general note, **15(1)**, [1]
higher education institutions, use of title by, **15(1)**, [441]
tests. *See* **universities tests**
trusts. *See* **trusts, university and college**
use of 'university' in title, unauthorised, **15(1)**, [806]

university—*contd*
women, admitting to membership, **15(1)**, [182]

University Commissioners
appointment, **15(1)**, [377]
constitution, **15(1)**, [344]
duration of powers, **15(1)**, [377]
duties of, **15(1)**, [345]
expenses, **15(1)**, [377]
functions, exercise of, **15(1)**, [344]
powers—
generally, **15(1)**, [377]
modification of statutes, **15(1)**, [346]
Northern Ireland, **15(1)**, [349]
Orders in Council, **15(1)**, [348]
procedure for exercise of, **15(1)**, [347]
proceedings, **15(1)**, [377]
qualifying institutions, **15(1)**, [344]
remuneration, **15(1)**, [377]
staff, **15(1)**, [377]
tenure of office, **15(1)**, [377]

university land
summary of provisions., **20**, [1]

unlawful assembly
common law offence of, abolition, **12(1)**, [1000]

unlawful conduct
meaning, **12(3)**, [331]
proceeds, civil recovery of. *See* **proceeds of crime**
property obtained through, **12(3)**, [332], [410]

unlimited company
accounts and reports, exemption from requirement to deliver, **8**, 334–5
limited company re-registering as—
certificate of, **8**, 149
procedure, **8**, 147–8
statutory declaration for, **8**, 148
limited, re-registering as—
certificate of, **8**, 151
modification of provisions, **8**, 147
procedure, **8**, 150
special resolution, **8**, 150
meaning, **8**, 104
reserve capital, **8**, 193–4

unlisted securities
listing. *See* **securities**

unregistered company
doctrine of deemed notice, abolition, **8**, 926
inability to pay debts—
action brought, after, **4(2)**, [259]
generally, **4(2)**, [260]
grounds for winding up, **4(2)**, [257]
Northern Ireland company, **4(2)**, [260]
Scottish company, **4(2)**, [260]
when deemed to be, **4(2)**, [258]
meaning, **4(2)**, [256]

unregistered company—*contd*
provisions applicable to—
  exceptions from, **8**, 582
  generally, **8**, 582
  list of, **8**, 792–3
winding up—
  ceasing business in GB, on, **4(2)**, [261]
  circumstances for, **4(2)**, [257]
  contributories in, **4(2)**, [262]
  cumulative provisions, **4(2)**, [265]
  debt qualifying for, **4(2)**, [258], [502]
  jurisdiction, determination, **4(2)**, [257]
  order, actions stayed on, **4(2)**, [264]
  oversea company, **4(2)**, [261]
  provisions applied to, **4(2)**, [257]
  stay of proceedings, **4(2)**, [263]

unsolicited goods and services
directory entries. *See* **directory**
goods. *See* **goods**

unsworn statement
right to make, abolition, **12(1)**, [785]

Upper Tribunal
compensation disputes, settlement by,
  36, [1359]

uranium. *See* **radioactive substances**

urban development area
compulsory acquisition, compensation,
  9, [259]
designation of, **46**, [58], [844]
ecclesiastical property in, **46**, [91]
generally, **46**, [1]
highway authority—
  acquisition of land by, **46**, [67]
  burial grounds, use of, **46**, [107]
  consecrated land, use of, **46**, [107]
  displacement of persons, **46**, [107]
  easements, power to override, **46**, [107]
  open spaces, use of, **46**, [107]
  public rights of way, extinguishment of,
    46, [107]
    rights over land, extinguishment of,
      46, [107]
  telegraphic lines, provisions on, **46**, [107]
land, power to survey, **46**, [89]
local planning authority, **46**, [845]
notices, **46**, [850]
private streets—
  adoption of, **46**, [76], [846]
  highway, connection to, **46**, [77], [839]
  traffic regulation orders, **46**, [78], [847]
structure and local plans, **46**, [310]
unitary development plan for, **46**, [265]
urban development corporation—
  accounts, **46**, [113]
  acquisition of land by, **46**, [66]
    agreement, by, **46**, [106]
  annual reports, **46**, [113]
  assumption of debts by, **46**, [112]
  audit, **46**, [113]
  borrowing powers, **46**, [112]

urban development area—*contd*
urban development corporation—*contd*
  building agreement, loan in pursuance of,
    46, [81]
  building control functions, **46**, [72]
  building, loans for, **46**, [80]
  burial ground, use of, **46**, [107]
  compulsory acquisition of land by,
    46, [105]
  consecrated land, use of, **46**, [107]
  displacement of persons, **46**, [107]
  disposal of land by, **46**, [69]
  dissolution of, **46**, [88]
  easements, power to override, **46**, [107]
  establishment of, **46**, [59]
  exclusion of functions, **46**, [61]
  extinguishment of rights over land,
    46, [107]
  financial duties, **46**, [112]
  financial limits, **46**, [112]
  financial year, **46**, [111]
  fire and rescue authority, as, **46**, [73]
  functions, allocation or transfer of, **46**, [63]
  general powers of, **46**, [60]
  government grants to, **46**, [112]
  grants and loans, accounts of, **46**, [112]
  home insulation, grants for, **46**, [73]
  housing authority, as, **46**, [74]
  information, provision of, **46**, [113]
  instruments of, **46**, [103]
  land vested in, **46**, [65], [104]
  local authorities, code of practice on
    consultation, **46**, [64]
  local development provisions not applying
    in area of, **46**, [989], [1026]
  meetings, **46**, [103]
  members, **46**, [103]
  modification of enactments, **46**, [71],
    [104]–[105], [109]–[110]
  notices, service of, **46**, [90]
  objects, **46**, [60]
  open spaces, use of, **46**, [107]
  orders subject to special parliamentary
    procedure, **9**, [430], [453]
  planning authority, as, **46**, [71], [257]
  planning control by, **46**, [70]
  planning functions, **46**, [71], [109]–[110]
  proceedings, **46**, [103]
  property, rights and liabilities, transfer of,
    46, [86]–[87]
  public health functions, **46**, [79]
  public rights of way, extinguishment of,
    46, [107]
  relevant land in designated district, powers
    as to, **46**, [82]
    rent rebates by, **46**, [75]
  restrictions on powers, **46**, [62]
  rights, acquisition of, **46**, [108]
  Secretary of State, directions of, **46**, [62]
  staff, **46**, [103]
  status of, **46**, [59]
  statutory undertakers, rights of, **46**, [107]
  supply of goods and services to, **46**, [83]
  surplus funds of, **46**, [112]
  telegraphic lines, provisions as to, **46**, [107]

urban development area—*contd*
  urban development corporation—*contd*
    transfer of undertakings, **46**, [85]
    Treasury guarantees, **46**, [112]
    Urban Regeneration Agency, as agent of,
      46, [849]
    vesting of land in, **9**, [405]; **46**, [65], [104]
  valuation of land, **46**, [89]

urban development corporation
  Homes and Communities Agency, agency
    arrangements with, **24**, [581]
  housing action trust, supply of goods and
    services, **22**, [875]
  landlord authority, as, **22**, [105]
  meaning, **22**, [4]; **24**, [581]
  orders subject to special parliamentary
    procedure, **9**, [430], [453]
  racial discrimination by, **7(1)**, [148]
  vesting of land in, **9**, [405]

urban district council
  development of, **25(1)**, [1]

Urban Regeneration Agency
  abolition, **24**, [588]
  accounts, **46**, [856]
  agents of, **46**, [849]
  annual reports, **46**, [856]
  audit, **46**, [856]
  borrowing, **46**, [856]
  burial grounds, use of, **46**, [859]
  connection notice, service of, **46**, [839]
  consecrated land, use of, **46**, [859]
  constitution, **46**, [855]
  delegation of powers, **46**, [855]
  displacement of persons, **46**, [859]
  establishment of, **46**, [832]
  finances, **46**, [856]
  financial assistance by, **46**, [838]
  functions, powers of Secretary of State,
    46, [935]
  hazardous substances authority, as, **46**, [752]
  land—
    acquisition of, **46**, [836], [858]
    easements, power to override, **46**, [859]
    power to enter and survey, **46**, [837]
    public rights of way, extinguishment of,
      46, [859]
    rights, acquisition of, **46**, [860]
    rights over, extinguishment of, **46**, [859]
    statutory undertakers, of, **46**, [859]
    telegraphic lines on, **46**, [859]
    vesting in, **46**, [835], [857]
  local planning authority, as, **46**, [259], [845]

Urban Regeneration Agency—*contd*
  members' interests, **46**, [855]
  membership, **46**, [855]
  objects of, **46**, [833]
  open spaces, use of, **46**, [859]
  powers of, **46**, [834]
  proceedings, **46**, [855]
  property, rights and liabilities, transfer to
    Homes and Communities Agency—
      interim arrangements, **24**, [592]
      scheme for, **24**, [590], [864]
      taxation, **24**, [865]
  regional development agencies, scheme for
    transfer of property etc to, **46**, [934], [956]
      corporation tax, **46**, [936]
      stamp duty, **46**, [937]
      stamp duty land tax, **46**, [938]
  seal, **46**, [855]
  Secretary of State—
    agent of, as, **46**, [848]
    consents, **46**, [840]
    guidance, **46**, [841]
  staff, **46**, [855]
  status, **46**, [832]
  Treasury guarantees, **46**, [856]
  validity of transactions, **46**, [842]

urban regeneration companies
  contributions to, **44(1)**, [50]
  meaning, **44(3)**, [82]
  payments to, tax deduction for, **44(3)**, [81]

urinal. *See also* **sanitary convenience**
  improper construction or repair, penalty for,
    35(1), [587]

urine test. *See under* **road traffic offences**

user
  alteration of, **21**, [65]

uses
  conveyances and devises, **20**, [10]
  easements, transfer by, **20**, [12]
  historical note, **20**, [1]
  persons entitled, seisin of, **20**, [11]
  rentcharge, creation by, **20**, [13]
    historical note, **20**, [1]
    repeal, **20**, [10]
    text, **20**, [10]–[13]

usufructuary
  consent to sale of chattels, **20**, [741]

V

Vacation of Benefices Rule Committee
powers, **14**, 898

vaccination
severe disablement resulting from—
payment for—
amount of, **35(1)**, [415]
civil proceedings, saving for, **35(1)**, [421]
claim for, determination of—
appeals, **35(1)**, [419], [427]
reconsideration, **35(1)**, [420]
reversal of earlier decisions,
35(1), [418]
Secretary of State, by, **35(1)**, [417]
disablement—
entitlement to, conditions of,
35(1), [416]
errors, correction of, **35(1)**, [423]
extra-statutory, **35(1)**, [422]
false statements and documents to
obtain, **35(1)**, [426]
finality of decisions, **35(1)**, [424]
financial provisions, **35(1)**, [428]
HM forces abroad and families,
35(1), [416]
making by Secretary of State,
35(1), [415]
misrepresentation, recovery where,
35(1), [420]
non-disclosure, recovery where,
35(1), [420]
person to whom made, **35(1)**, [421]
regulations as to, **35(1)**, [425]
resulting from vaccination, whether,
35(1), [417]
setting aside decisions, **35(1)**, [423]
severely disabled, person being,
35(1), [415]

vaccine damage payments
Northern Ireland, appeals to appeal tribunals
in, **40(2)**, [537]
overseas vaccinations, **40(2)**, [536]
summary of provisions, **35(1)**, [1]

vaccine research
tax relief—
amended provisions, **43(S)**, 856
artificially inflated claims, **43(2)**, [148]
companies in difficulty, for, **43(S)**, 1117–19
definitions, **43(2)**, [144], [148]
effect of, **43(S)**, 859
entitlement to, **43(2)**, [144]
independent—
qualifying expenditure, **43(2)**, [144]
refund of contributions, **43(2)**, [148]

vaccine research—*contd*
tax relief—*contd*
insurance companies, special provision for,
43(2), [147]
large companies, **43(2)**, [146]
qualifying expenditure, **43(2)**, [144]
qualifying R & D activity, **43(2)**, [144]
rates of, **43(S)**, 1116–17
small and medium-sized companies,
43(2), [145]
small and medium-sized enterprises,
deduction for, **43(S)**, 543–4
sub-contracted, **43(2)**, [144]
transitional provision, **43(2)**, [148]
tax relief for expenditure on, claims for tax
credits, **43(1)**, [404]

vaccinium
burning, regulation of, **1(1)**, [372]

vagabond
justice of the peace, jurisdiction over,
11(2), [1A]

vagrancy
appeal, **12(1)**, [30]
fines, **12(1)**, [784]; **12(2)**, [71]
house of correction, removal to, **12(1)**, [26]
idle and disorderly, persons being, **12(1)**, [26]
loitering with intent, abolition, **12(1)**, [758]
offences, **12(1)**, [27], [784]

valuable security
suppression, etc, **12(1)**, [571]

valuation
surveyor, by, **9**, [24], [234]

valuation list. *See also* **rating lists**
caravan site, treatment of, **25(2)**, [359]
current, alteration of, **25(2)**, [814]
introduction of, **25(1)**, [1]

valuation office
rights of entry, **46**, [598]

valuation officer
billing authority, for, **25(2)**, [749]
caravan site, information on, **25(2)**, [360]
central, appointment of, **25(2)**, [749]
information, giving access to, **25(2)**, [843]
rating lists, compiling, **25(2)**, [722], [723]
valuation list, duties as to. *See* **valuation list**

Valuation Tribunal for England
appeals, **25(2)**, [846]
constitution, **25(2)**, [844]

Valuation Tribunal for England—*contd*
orders, **25(2)**, [846]
procedure, **25(2)**, [846]
rules, **25(2)**, [846]

Valuation Tribunal Service
accounts, **26(2)**, [321]
amended provisions, **26(2)**, [669]
chairman and deputy, **26(2)**, [321]
committees, **26(2)**, [321]
delegation of functions, **26(2)**, [321]
establishment of, **26(2)**, [307], [630]
functions, **26(2)**, [307]
grants and loans, **26(2)**, [321]
members, **26(2)**, [321]
minutes, **26(2)**, [321]
proceedings, **26(2)**, [321]
property, rights and liabilities transferred to,
26(2), [308], [322]
staff, **26(2)**, [321]
transitional provisions, **26(2)**, [631]

valuation tribunals
abolition, **26(2)**, [630]
appeal to—
annual value determination, against,
19(3), [215]
grounds for, **26(1)**, [19]
notice of, **26(1)**, [19]
jurisdiction, **26(1)**, [18]
valuation and community charge tribunal,
change of name from, **26(1)**, [18]
Wales, for—
appeals, **25(2)**, [846]
constitution, **25(2)**, [845]
finance, **25(2)**, [847]
orders, **25(2)**, [846]
procedure, **25(2)**, [846]
rules, **25(2)**, [847]

value added tax
accounting for, **50**, [157]
acquisition of goods from another member
State, on—
liability for, **50**, [4]
meaning, **50**, [16]
non-taxable persons, by, assessments,
50, [101]
persons belonging in other member States,
from, **50**, [19]
place of, **50**, [18]
registration. *See* registration *below*
scope of, **50**, [15]
taxable, where, **50**, [15]
time of, **50**, [17]
valuation of, **50**, [31], [147]
additional liabilities and rebates—
apportionment, **43(1)**, [1187]
chargeable period, **43(1)**, [1186]
administration, **50**, [1]
agent, liability of, **50**, [66]
appeal—
agreement, settled by, **50**, [115]
Court of Appeal, **50**, [116]
generally, **50**, [1]

value added tax—*contd*
appeal—*contd*
requirements, **50**, [114]
tribunal, to, **50**, [112]
where lying, **50**, [114]
application of, **50**, [157]
assessment—
acquisitions of goods by non-taxable
persons, **50**, [101]
interest, **50**, [100]
interest overpayments, for, **50**, [106]
penalty, interest or surcharge, of, **50**, [102]
supplementary, **50**, [103]
time limits, **50**, [103], [167]
avoidance and fraud, **50(S)**, VAT 1
avoidance schemes—
Commissioners for HM Revenue and
Customs, duty to notify, **50**, [158]
designation by order, **50**, [158]
disclosure of, **50**, [158]
penalty for failure to notify, **50**, [158]
tax advantage, obtaining, **50**, [158]
buildings—
non-residential, developers of, **50**, [155]
residential and charitable—
change of use, **50**, [155]
election to waiver exemption, **50**, [155]
buildings and land, amendment of provisions,
50(S), VAT 1, 3–4
business property, non-business use of,
50, [175]
business, meaning, **50**, [124]
capital goods, relief for, **50**, [47]
capital items legislation, meaning,
43(1), [1188]
charge of, **50**, [1], [4]
claims, time limits, **43(S)**, 1314–20
collection, **50**, [1]
Commissioners of Customs and Excise—
certificate, evidence by, **50**, [157]
documents, producing to, **50**, [157]
evidence, requiring, **50**, [157]
information, furnishing to, **50**, [157]
penalty, assessing, **50**, [85]
security, requiring, **50**, [157]
credit vouchers, treatment of,
50(S), VAT 13–14
credits, set-off, **43(S)**, 966
Crown, application to, **50**, [55]
default surcharge, **50**, [82]–[84]
dishonesty, conduct involving, **50**, [85]
documents, removal of, **50**, [157]
EC sales statements—
failure to submit, **50**, [91]
inaccuracies in, **50**, [90]
EC Second VAT Simplification Directive,
50, [164]
enforcement, **50**, [3]–[4]
evasion—
named officer of company, by, **50**, [86]
penalties, **50**, [85]
exemption—
betting, gaming and lotteries, **50**, [153]
burial, **50**, [153]
cremation, **50**, [153]

value added tax—*contd*
  exemption—*contd*
    cultural services, **50**, [153]
    education, **50**, [153]
    finance, **50**, [153]
    fund-raising events, **50**, [153]
    generally, **50**, [44]
    health services, **50**, [153]
    insurance, **50**, [153]
    investment gold, **50**, [153]
    land, **50**, [153]
    physical education, **50**, [153]
    postal services, **50**, [153]
    professional body, subscriptions to,
      50, [153]
    sport, **50**, [153]
    sports competitions, **50**, [153]
    supplies of goods where input tax cannot
      be recovered, **50**, [153]
    trade union, subscriptions to, **50**, [153]
    welfare services, **50**, [153]
    works of art, **50**, [153]
  false statements and documents, **50**, [98]
  farmers, regime for, **50**, [76]
  fiscal warehousing. *See under* warehousing
    below
  fraudulent evasion of, **50**, [98]
  free zone regulations, **50**, [22]
  fuel for private use—
    accounting for, **50**, [78]
    consideration, determination of, **50**, [79],
      [177]
    meaning, **50**, [78]
    provision of, **50**, [78]
    supply, acquisition or importation, tax on,
      50, [78]
  galleries, refund to, **50**, [46]
  gaming machine provisions, **50(S)**, VAT 1–3
  gaming machines—
    charge on, **50**, [33]
    opening, power to require, **50**, [157]
  gaming participation fees, exemption for,
    50(S), VAT 30
  gold—
    accounting for tax on, **50**, [77]
    record-keeping requirements for
      transactions, breach of, **50**, [95]
  groups of companies—
    anti-avoidance provisions—
      directions—
        assessment in consequence of,
          50, [154]
        form of, **50**, [154]
        manner of giving, **50**, [154]
        power to give, **50**, [154]
        restrictions on giving, **50**, [154]
        time limit on, **50**, [154]
    applications, **50**, [60]
    duplication, **50**, [62]
    eligibility, **50**, [58]
      power to alter, **50**, [59]
    liabilities of, **50**, [57]
    members of, **50**, [57]
    supplies to, **50**, [63]
    termination of membership, **50**, [61]

value added tax—*contd*
  groups of companies—*contd*
    transitional provisions, **50**, [172]
  High Court, summary application by Crown
    to, in matters of, **13**, [18]
  importation of goods—
    charged on, **50**, [4]
    customs enactments, application of,
      50, [21]
    outside member States, from, **50**, [20]
    private purposes, for, **50**, [39]
    relief on, **50**, [50]–[51]
    taxable person, by, **50**, [52]
  imported goods—
    antiques, as, value of, **50**, [32]
    value of, **50**, [32]
    works of art, as—
      meaning, **50**, [32]
      value of, **50**, [32]
    zero-rating, **50**, [151]
  imported works of art, auctioneer's
    commission on, **50(S)**, VAT 1, 5
  industrial buildings allowance. *See* **industrial
    buildings allowance**
  input tax—
    allowable credit, **50**, [36]
    credit against output tax, **50**, [35], [36]
    meaning, **50**, [34]
  interest—
    assessment of, **50**, [100]
    credit, by, **50**, [111]
    official error, in case of, **50**, [105]
    overpayments, assessment of, **50**, [106]
    set-off of credits, by, **50**, [111], [168]
  invoices—
    electronic communication and storage of,
      50, [157]
    regulations, **50**, [157]
    self-billed, **50**, [157]
  legislation, **50**, [1]
  liability to, **50**, [4]
  local authority—
    refund to, **50**, [45]
    registration of, **50**, [56]
  meaning, **43(1)**, [1184]
  misdeclaration—
    penalties for, **50**, [88]
    repeated, **50**, [89]
  missing trader intra-community fraud—
    output tax adjustment, **50(S)**, VAT 8–9
    supplies of goods, accounting for tax on,
      50(S), VAT 6–8
  museums, refund to, **50**, [46]
  new means of transport supplied to other
    member States—
    meaning, **50**, [125]
    refunds in relation to, **50**, [54]
  non-business use of business goods, treatment
    of, **50(S)**, VAT 19
  Northern Ireland, refund to, **50**, [130]
  notices, service of, **50**, [129]
  offences, **50**, [98]
  official error, **50**, [105]
  orders, **50**, [127]

value added tax—*contd*
  other member States—
    laws of, taxation under, **50**, [122]
    territories of, **50**, [123]
  output tax—
    input tax, credit against, **50**, [35], [36]
    meaning, **50**, [34]
  overpaid—
    arrangements for reimbursing customers, **50**, [109]
    assessments of amounts due, **50**, [110]
    credit for, **50**, [108]
    recovery of, **50**, [108]
  overstated—
    credit for, **50**, [108]
    recovery of, **50**, [108]
  partnership, registration of, **50**, [64]
  payment by cheque, **43(S)**, 577
  payment of, **50**, [157]
  payments on account, **50**, [40]
  penalties, etc, treatment of, **44(1)**, [611]
  penalty—
    assessment, **50**, [102]
    dishonesty, conduct involving, **50**, [85]
    EC sales statements—
      failure to submit, **50**, [91]
      inaccuracies in, **50**, [90]
    evasion, for, **50**, [85]
    failure to notify, **50**, [92]
    generally, **50**, [98]
    incorrect certificate as to zero-rating, **50**, [87]
    invoice, unauthorised issue of, **50**, [92]
    misdeclaration or neglect, for, **50**, [88]
    mitigation, **50**, [96]
    reasonable excuse, **50**, [97]
    record-keeping requirements for gold transactions, breach of, **50**, [95]
    regulatory provisions, breach of, **50**, [94]
    repeated misdeclarations, for, **50**, [89]
    walking possession agreement, breach of, **50**, [93]
  persons in business in other States, repayment to, **50(S)**, VAT 27–8
  persons not registered, due from, **43(S)**, 1731
  persons, search of, **50**, [157]
  place of supply orders, transitional provisions, **50**, [128]
  plant and machinery allowances. *See*
  machinery and plant allowances
  power to inspect goods, **50(S)**, VAT 10
  premises, entry and search of, **50**, [157]
  Provisional Collection of Taxes Act, failure of resolution under, **50**, [120]
  rate—
    change—
      contract, adjustments to, **50**, [119]
      supplies spanning, **50**, [118]
    generally, **50**, [5]
  reasonable excuse for conduct, **50**, [97]
  recipient of services, place of, **50**, [13]
  record-keeping requirements, **43(S)**, 1305–8
  record-keeping requirements for gold transactions, breach of, **50**, [95]

value added tax—*contd*
  recorded information, order for access to, **50**, [157]
  records, direction to keep, **50(S)**, VAT 11–13
  recovery of, **50**, [157]
  reduced rate, supplies charged at, **50**, [42]
    children's car seats, **50**, [149]
    domestic fuel or power, **50**, [149]
    energy-saving materials, installation of, **50**, [149]
    gas supply, connection to, **50**, [149]
    heating equipment, grant-funded installation of, **50**, [149]
    re-enactment of provisions, **50**, [173]
    residential—
      conversion, **50**, [149]
      renovations and alterations, **50**, [149]
    security goods, **50**, [149]
    women's sanitary products, **50**, [149]
  reduced standard rate, extension of, **50(S)**, VAT 26
  refund of—
    bad debts, in cases of, **50**, [49]
    bodies entitled to, **50**, [45]–[46]
    certain buildings, on construction of, **50**, [48]
    new means of transport supplied to other member States, for, **50**, [54]
  registration—
    acquisitions from other member States, in respect of—
      cancellation, **50**, [136]
      continuance, notification of matters affecting, **50**, [136]
      entitlement, **50**, [136]
      exemption, **50**, [136]
      liability, **50**, [136]
      notification of liability, **50**, [136]
    appeals, **50**, [113]
    cancellation, **50**, [134]
    direction by Commissioners, **50**, [134]
    disposals of assets for which VAT repayment claimed, in respect of—
      cancellation, **50**, [137]
      exemption, **50**, [137]
      liability, **50**, [137]
      notification of liability, **50**, [137]
    divisions, business carried out in, **50**, [65]
    entitlement to, **50**, [134]
    exemption, **50**, [134]
    liability for—
      end, notification of, **50**, [134]
      notification of, **50**, [134]
      value of supplies, **50**, [134]
    local authority, of, **50**, [56]
    partnership, of, **50**, [64]
    personal representatives, **50**, [65]
    register, in, **50**, [6]
    requirement of, **50**, [6]
    supplies from other member States, in respect of—
      cancellation, **50**, [135]
      continuance, notification of matters affecting, **50**, [135]
      liability, **50**, [135]

value added tax—*contd*
  registration—*contd*
    supplies from other member States, in
      respect of—*contd*
        notification of liability, **50**, [135]
        request for, **50**, [135]
    supply of electronic services in member
      States, special accounting scheme for—
        cancellation, **50**, [138]
        changes, obligation to notify, **50**, [138]
        date on which registration takes effect,
          50, [138]
        number, **50**, [138]
        obligations following, **50**, [139]
        qualifying supplies, **50**, [138]
        register, **50**, [138]
        registrable persons, **50**, [138]
        registration request, **50**, [138]
    terminal markets, dealings on, **50**, [69]
    time of, **50**, [134]
    transfer of business as going concern,
      50, [68]
    unincorporated body, **50**, [65]
  regulations, **50**, [127]
  regulatory provisions, breach of, **50**, [94]
  reliefs—
    capital goods, for, **50**, [47]
    generally, **50**, [1]
    immunities and privileges, persons
      enjoying, **13**, [803]–[805]
    imported legacies, **13**, [795]
    persons entering UK, **13**, [802]
  rent for agricultural holdings, effect of changes
    on, **50(S)**, VAT 29
  repayment claims, applications for forwarding
    to, **50(S)**, VAT 28
  repayments—
    business overseas, to, **50**, [53]
    generally, **50**, [1]
    supplement, **50**, [107]
    time limits, **50**, [167]
  representatives, **50**, [67]
  research and development, on. *See* **research
    and development allowances**
  return, default in making, **50**, [99]
  samples, power to take, **50**, [157]
  scope of, **50**, [8]
  services, place of supply—
    amended provisions, **50(S)**, VAT 41–7
    cross-border supplies to taxable recipients,
      50(S), VAT 28
    cultural, educational and entertainment,
      50(S), VAT 45, 50
    determining, **50(S)**, VAT 41–2
    electronic, **50(S)**, VAT 48
    electronically-supplied services,
      50(S), VAT 47
    hiring means of transport, **50(S)**, VAT 45,
      51
    hiring of goods, **50(S)**, VAT 46
    land, relating to, **50(S)**, VAT 44
    passenger transport, **50(S)**, VAT 44–5
    relevant business person, not made to,
      50(S), VAT 48–9

value added tax—*contd*
  services, place of supply—*contd*
    relevant business person, supplies to,
      50(S), VAT 47
    restaurant and catering, **50(S)**, VAT 45–6
    telecommunications and broadcasting,
      50(S), VAT 46–7
    transitional provisions, **50(S)**, VAT 51
    transport, **50(S)**, VAT 45, 48
    valuation, **50(S)**, VAT 48
  set-off, **50**, [111]
  simplification of, EC Second VAT
    Simplification Directive on, **50**, [164]
  Sixth Directive, **43(1)**, [1188]
  statistical purposes, disclosure of information
    for, **50**, [121]
  supplementary charge, **50(S)**, VAT 32–5
    administration, **50(S)**, VAT 39–40
    amended provisions, **50(S)**, VAT 40–1
    exceptions, **50(S)**, VAT 36
    interpretation, **50(S)**, VAT 40
    liability and amount, **50(S)**, VAT 37
    listed supplies, **50(S)**, VAT 38–9
  supplier or recipient, place where belonging,
    50(S), VAT 43
  supplier of services, place of, **50**, [13]
    outside UK, **50**, [14]
  supplies received from abroad, reverse charge
    on, **50(S)**, VAT 42
  supply—
    co-owners of buildings and land, by,
      50, [72], [162]
    disallowance of input tax where
      consideration not paid, **50**, [37]
    electronic services in member States, special
      accounting scheme for—
        appeals, **50**, [141]
        de-registration, **50**, [141]
        generally, **50**, [7]
        non-UK VAT to other member States,
          payment of, **50**, [141]
        obligations following registration—
          liability for VAT, **50**, [139]
          payment of VAT, **50**, [139]
          records, keeping and production of,
            50, [139]
          special accounting returns, submission
            of, **50**, [139]
        refund of UK VAT, **50**, [141]
        registration—
          cancellation, **50**, [138]
          changes, obligation to notify,
            50, [138]
          date on which takes effect, **50**, [138]
          number, **50**, [138]
          qualifying supplies, **50**, [138]
          register, **50**, [138]
          registrable persons, **50**, [138]
          request, **50**, [138]
        supplementary provisions, **50**, [142]
        understatements and overstatements of
          UK VAT, **50**, [140]
        VAT representatives, **50**, [141]
    employees, to, **50**, [146]
    exempt, **50**, [44]

value added tax—*contd*
  supply—*contd*
    face-value vouchers—
      credit vouchers, treatment of, **50**, [156]
      goods or services, supplied free with, **50**, [156]
      meaning, **50**, [156]
      nature of supply, **50**, [156]
      postage stamps, treatment of, **50**, [156]
      retailer vouchers, treatment of, **50**, [156]
    farmers, by, **50**, [76]
    flat-rate scheme, **50**, [38]
    gas and electricity, received from abroad, reverse charge on, **50**, [14]
    gold, of, **50**, [77], [170]
    groups of companies, to, **50**, [63]
    input tax allowed, **50**, [36]
    margin schemes, under, **50**, [70]
    matters treated as, **50**, [143]
    meaning, **50**, [9]
    place of, **50**, [11]
    rate change, spanning, **50**, [118]
    received from abroad, reverse charge on, **50**, [12], [14]
    services, where received, **50**, [144]
    tax invoice, time of, **50**, [10]
    time of, **50**, [10]
    tour operators, by, **50**, [75]
    trading stamp schemes, under, **50**, [74]
    Treasury order alteration of meaning by, **50**, [9]
    value. *See* value *below*
    warehouse, dutiable goods in, **50**, [23]
    zero-rated, **50**, [43]
  supply of goods and services, on, **50**, [4]
  tax invoice—
    meaning, **50**, [10]
    provision of, **50**, [10]
    recipients of goods or services, provided by, **50**, [41]
    unauthorised issue of, **50**, [92]
  taxable person—
    default in making return, **50**, [99]
    importation by, **50**, [52]
    meaning, **50**, [6]
    private purposes, importation for, **50**, [39]
    records, keeping, **50**, [157]
  taxable supply, charged on, **50**, [8]
  time limits—
    excess credits, assessment of, **43(S)**, 954
    old claims, for, **43(S)**, 955
  time of, **43(1)**, [1185]
  traders in supply chain, joint and several liability for unpaid tax, **50(S)**, VAT 17–18
  transfer of going concern, on, **50(S)**, VAT 20–1
  transitional provisions, **50**, [160]
  tribunal—
    appeals. *See* appeal *above*
    appointments to, **50**, [159]
    composition, **50**, [159]
    enforcement of decisions, **50**, [117]
    establishment of, **50**, [159]
    jury service, exemption from, **50**, [159]
    membership, **50**, [159]

value added tax—*contd*
  tribunal—*contd*
    President, **50**, [159]
    procedure, rules of, **50**, [159]
    sittings, **50**, [159]
  unauthorised invoices, **43(S)**, 1731
  unauthorised person, invoice showing VAT by, **43(S)**, 1331
  unpaid, joint and several liability in supply chain where, **50**, [104]
  value—
    acquisitions from other member States, of, **50**, [31], [147]
    determination of, **50**, [30]
    discount, effect of, **50**, [146]
    foreign currency, conversion of, **50**, [146]
    imported goods, of, **50**, [32]
    special cases, **50**, [146]
    supply of goods or services, of, **50**, [30]
    trading stamp schemes, **50**, [74]
  VAT and duties tribunals—
    appeals to—
      burden of proof, **13**, [937]
      decisions, types of, **13**, [937]
      exclusions, **13**, [937]
      power of tribunal, **13**, [937]
      security, certificate as to, **13**, [937]
      settling of, by agreement, **13**, [925]
    costs against appellant, recovery of, **13**, [925]
    enforcement of decisions of, **13**, [925]
  vehicles for export becoming liable to, **13**, [970]
  walking possession agreement, breach of, **50**, [93]
  warehousing—
    fiscal—
      generally, **50**, [165]
      goods subject to—
        deficiency in, **50**, [28]
        eligibility, **50**, [145]
        relief for, **50**, [25]
      services under, **50**, [26]
      supplementary provisions, **50**, [29]
      warehouse, meaning, **50**, [24]
      warehousekeeper—
        application to be, **50**, [24]
        approval of, **50**, [24]
    generally, **50**, [165]
    goods subject to—
      acquisition or supply, place and time of, **50**, [23]
      dutiable goods, meaning, **50**, [23]
      duty point, meaning, **50**, [23]
      removal from, accountability for, **50**, [27]
      services under, **50**, [26]
  wrongdoing, penalties, **43(S)**, 1328–39. *See also* **tax penalty**
  zero-rating—
    bank notes, **50**, [151]
    blind, aids for, **50**, [151]
    books, **50**, [151]
    buildings, construction of, **50**, [151]
    caravans, **50**, [151]
    charities, **50**, [151]

value added tax—*contd*
  zero-rating—*contd*
    clothing, **50**, [151]
    exported goods, **50**, [151]
    food, **50**, [151]
    footwear, **50**, [151]
    generally, **50**, [43]
    gold, **50**, [151]
    handicapped, goods for, **50**, [151]
    imported goods, **50**, [151]
    incorrect certificates, **50**, [87]
    international services, **50**, [151]
    newspapers, **50**, [151]
    protected building, **50**, [151]
    sewerage services, **50**, [151]
    terminal markets, dealings on, **50**, [69]
    transport, **50**, [151]
    water, **50**, [151]

van
  abatement notice to occupier of, **35(1)**, [170]
  alternative, offer of, **44(2)**, [130]
  available to employee, meaning, **44(2)**, [127]
  byelaws as to, **35(1)**, [170]
  cash equivalent—
    calculating, **44(2)**, [166]
    payments for private use, reduction for, **44(2)**, [169]
    reduction where unavailable, **44(2)**, [167]
    shared, reduction for, **44(2)**, [168]
  company, fuel benefit, **43(S)**, 877
  earnings, benefit treated as, **44(2)**, [165]
  fuel—
    cash equivalent, **44(2)**, [172]
    earnings, benefit treated as, **44(2)**, [171]
    proportionate reduction of cash equivalent, **44(2)**, [174]
    reduction of cash equivalent, **44(2)**, [175]
  human habitation, used for—
    control over, **35(1)**, [497]
    order prohibiting, **35(1)**, [170]
  lower-emission, vehicle excise duty rate, **43(S)**, 983
  made available by reason of employment, **44(2)**, [128]
  meaning, **44(2)**, [126]
  more than one member of family or household employed by same employer, available to, **44(2)**, [179]
  payments for private use, **44(2)**, [169]
  pooled, **44(2)**, [176]
  private use, available for, **44(2)**, [129]
  public health provisions applicable to, **35(1)**, [170]
  shared, meaning, **44(2)**, [168]
  statutory nuisance, when, **35(1)**, [170]
  temporary replacement, **44(2)**, [170]

Vanuatu
  Commonwealth citizenship, **31**, [186]
  independence of, **7(2)**, [741]

vaults
  burial. *See* **burial**
  London. *See* **Greater London**
  street offences as to, **36**, [229], [385]

VCT. *See* **venture capital trusts**

vegetables. *See* **horticultural produce**

vehicle. *See also* **mechanically propelled vehicle; motor vehicle**
  activities not licensable, **19(3)**, [665]
  air force—
    billeting, **3**, [928], [931]
    record and inspection, **3**, [943]
    requisitioning, **3**, [938]
      avoidance of hardship, **3**, [942]
      bringing into operation, **3**, [947]
      Crown, liability of for damage, **3**, [946]
      enforcement of provisions, **3**, [944]
      offences, **3**, [778]
      payment for, **3**, [941], [1000]
      period of, **3**, [940]
      provision of, **3**, [939]
  army—
    billeting, **3**, [655], [658]
    inspection of, **3**, [670]
    records of, **3**, [670]
    requisitioning, **3**, [654]
      damage, **3**, [673]
      enforcement of provisions, **3**, [671]
      hardships, avoidance of, **3**, [669]
      offences, **3**, [505]
      operation of, **3**, [674]
      orders, **3**, [665]
      payment, **3**, [668], [728]
      period of, **3**, [667]
      provision, **3**, [666]
  axle, meaning of, **13**, [1032]
  bodily harm, causing with, **12(1)**, [91]
  body corporate, offences by, **47**, [616]
  class of vehicles, interpretation of references to, **37**, [808]
  excise duty. *See also* **vehicle excise duty**
  excise licence. *See* licences *below*
  export, becoming liable to VAT, **13**, [970]
  foreign-registered—
    information—
      disclosure of, **38(2)**, [524]
      use of, **38(2)**, [525]
  incorrectly registered, offence of using, **13**, [1010]
  inhabited, burglary of, **12(1)**, [561]
  insurance status, disclosure of information as to, **33(2)**, [582]
  interpretation provisions, **13**, [1032]
  licences—
    appropriately covered—
      ceasing to be—
        notices as to, **13**, [959]
        supplement payable upon, **13**, [958], [959]
      meaning, **13**, [958]
    combined road-rail transport of goods, rebate for, **13**, [975]

vehicle—*contd*
  licences—*contd*
    consequential amendments, **13**, [1033]
    disabled persons, nil licences for vehicles
      for, **13**, [978]
    duration of, **13**, [953]
    excise licence, conditions for grant of,
      37, [648]
    general, **13**, [951]
    interpretation provisions, **13**, [1032]
    issue of, **13**, [957]
    nil licence for exempt vehicle, failure to
      have, **13**, [1008]
    offences relating to—
      dishonoured cheques, **13**, [999]
      failure to return, **13**, [998]
      false or misleading declarations and
        information, **13**, [1012]
      fraud, **13**, [1011]
      not exhibiting, **13**, [996]
      penalties and fines, **13**, [1023]
      vehicle identity checks, impersonation of
        authorised examiners, **13**, [1009]
    orders, **13**, [1027]
    payment for—
      by cheque, **13**, [972]
      by credit card, fee for, **13**, [974]
      issue of, before, **13**, [973]
    regulations, **13**, [1024]
      fees prescribed by, **13**, [1025]
      offences, **13**, [1026]
    repeals, **13**, [1035], [1052]
    revocations, **13**, [1035], [1053]
    surrender of, **13**, [962], [971]
    temporary, **13**, [961]
    trade—
      amount of duty, **13**, [965], [1051]
      duration of, **13**, [965], [1051]
      issue of, **13**, [963]
      legal proceedings—
        authorised persons to conduct and
          appear in, **13**, [1016]
        evidence—
          admissions, **13**, [1018]
          burden of proof, **13**, [1021]
          records, **13**, [1020]
        institution of, **13**, [1015]
        overpayments, time-limit for recovery
          of, **13**, [1017]
        underpayments, time-limit for
          recovery of, **13**, [1017]
      offences relating to—
        dishonoured cheques, **13**, [1000]
        false or misleading declarations and
          information, **13**, [1012]
        forgery, **13**, [1011]
        fraud, **13**, [1011]
        information, duty to give, **13**, [1013]
        penalties, **13**, [997]
      supplementary, **13**, [966]
      use of vehicles by holders of, **13**, [964]
    transfer of, **13**, [962]
    transitional provisions, **13**, [1034], [1051]
    unlicensed. *See* unlicensed *below*
    vehicles removed into UK, **13**, [960]

vehicle—*contd*
  Licensing Act 2003, application of,
    19(3), [681]
  moving, prohibition of sale of alcohol on,
    19(3), [646]
  navy, requisitioning, **3**, [1048]
  obscene article, search for on, **12(1)**, [312]
  pedestrians, controlled by, **37**, [313]
  reduced pollution, certificates as to,
    13, [1031]
  registration—
    documents, power of constable to require,
      13, [987]
    foreign authorities, disclosure of
      information to, **38(2)**, [523]
    general, **13**, [976]
    marks—
      assignment of, by motor dealers,
        13, [981]
      engines and bodies, marking of,
        13, [986]
      false or misleading declarations and
        information, **13**, [1012]
      forgery, **13**, [1011]
      fraud, **13**, [1011]
      general, **13**, [980]
      not fixing, **13**, [1006]
      obscured, **13**, [1007]
      penalties and fines for offences,
        13, [1023]
      registration plates, **13**, [985]
      request for, charge on, **13**, [982]
      retention of, pending transfer, **13**, [983]
      sale of rights to particular, **13**, [984]
    plates, suppliers. *See* **registration plate
      suppliers**
    register, information in, **38(2)**, [521]
    regulations, **13**, [977], [1024]
      fees prescribed by, **13**, [1025]
      offences, **13**, [1026]
    vehicle identity checks, **13**, [979], [1009]
  registration documents, power of constable to
    require, **33(2)**, [581]
  requisition of, compensation for, **9**, [123]
  revenue weights, meaning of, **13**, [1028]
  smoking on, prohibition, **35(2)**, [569]
  stop and search powers, **12(1)**, [835]
  taking. *See under* **motor vehicle**
  tester, definition of, **13**, [1032]
  traffic contraventions, exemption from, **3**, [1]
  unlicensed—
    additional liability for keeper of, **13**, [989],
      [990]
    disposal of vehicle, **13**, [995], [1050]
    disputes, **13**, [1050]
    immobilisation of vehicle, **13**, [995], [1050]
    information, duty to give, **13**, [1013]
    legal proceedings—
      authorised persons to conduct and
        appear in, **13**, [1016]
      evidence—
        admissions, **13**, [1019]
        burden of proof, **13**, [1021]
        guilty plea by absent accused,
          13, [1022]

vehicle—*contd*
  unlicensed—*contd*
    legal proceedings—*contd*
      evidence—*contd*
        records, **13**, [1020]
        institution of, **13**, [1015]
        overpayments, time-limit for recovery
          of, **13**, [1017]
        underpayments, time-limit for recovery
          of, **13**, [1017]
      offence by registered keeper where,
        13, [991]
        exceptions, **13**, [992]
        penalties for, **13**, [993]
      orders, **13**, [1027]
      penalty for using or keeping, **13**, [988]
      possession of, securing, **13**, [1050]
      regulations, **13**, [1024]
        fees prescribed by, **13**, [1025]
        offences, **13**, [1026]
      removal of vehicle, **13**, [995], [1050]
      sum where licence not produced—
        authorised persons, **13**, [1050]
        payment of, **13**, [1050]
        vouchers in respect of—
          authorised persons, **13**, [1050]
          general, **13**, [1050]
          offences relating to, **13**, [1050]
      supplementary, **13**, [994]
    weights—
      certificates etc as to, **13**, [1030]
      meaning, **13**, [1029]

vehicle excise duty
  amount of, **13**, [954]
  collection etc of, **13**, [956]
  consequential amendments, **13**, [1033]
  conveying loads, vehicles capable of,
    13, [1061]
  cylinder capacity, calculating, **13**, [1099]
  exempt vehicles—
    agricultural, **13**, [955], [1049]
    ambulances, **13**, [1049]
    disabled people, vehicles for, **13**, [1049],
      [1051]
    electrically assisted pedal cycles, **13**, [1049]
    electrically propelled vehicles, **13**, [1049]
    export, for, **13**, [1049]
    fire engines, **13**, [1049]
    general, **13**, [955]
    health service vehicles, **13**, [1049]
    imported by members of foreign armed
      forces, **13**, [1049]
    lifeboat vehicles, **13**, [1049]
    light agricultural vehicles, **13**, [1049],
      [1089]
    mine rescue vehicles, **13**, [1049]
    mowing machines, **13**, [1049]
    old vehicles, **13**, [1049]
    relief where exemption abolished,
      13, [1060]
    snow ploughs, **13**, [1049]
    steam powered vehicles, **13**, [1049]
    testing, **13**, [1049]
    tractors, **13**, [955], [1049]

vehicle excise duty—*contd*
  exempt vehicles—*contd*
    trams, **13**, [1049]
    vehicles not for carriage, **13**, [1049]
    vehicles used between different parts of
      land, **13**, [1049]
  general, **13**, [951]
  higher rate—
    legal proceedings—
      authorised persons to conduct and
        appear in, **13**, [1016]
      evidence—
        burden of proof, **13**, [1021]
        records, **13**, [1020]
      institution of, **13**, [1015]
      overpayments, time-limit for recovery
        of, **13**, [1017]
      underpayments, time-limit for recovery
        of, **13**, [1017]
    offence of not paying—
      additional liability for keeper of,
        13, [1002]–[1005]
      information, duty to give, **13**, [1014]
      penalty for, **13**, [1001]
      supplementary provisions, **13**, [1005]
    other exceptions, **13**, [969]
    tractive units excepted from, **13**, [968]
    vehicles becoming chargeable at, **13**, [967]
  interpretation provisions, **13**, [1032]
  licence—
    failure to exhibit, period of grace,
      43(S), 984
    surrender, rebates, **43(S)**, 980–1
  lower-emission vans, rates for, **43(S)**, 983
  orders, **13**, [1027]
  rates of, **13(S)**, Customs 12–13; **43(S)**, 847–8
    annual, **13**, [952], [1039]
    April 2010, from, **13(S)**, Customs 5–6
    buses, **13**, [1043]
    digging machine, **13**, [1044]
    exceptional loads, vehicles used for,
      13, [1046]
    goods vehicles—
      conveying machines, for, **13**, [1048]
      exceptions, **13**, [1048]
      island goods vehicle, meaning of,
        13, [1048]
      reduced plated weights, with, **13**, [1048]
      rigid, exceeding 7,500 kilos plated gross
        weight or relevant maximum weight,
        13, [1048], [1082]
      tractive units exceeding 7,500 kilos train
        weight, **13**, [1048]
      trailer, meaning of, **13**, [1048]
    graduated, enforcement provisions,
      13, [1086]
    haulage vehicles, **13**, [1047]
    light goods vehicle, **13**, [1041]
    light passenger vehicle, **13**, [1040]
    mobile crane, **13**, [1044]
    mobile pumping vehicles, **13**, [1088]
    motorcycles, **13**, [1042]
    recovery vehicles, **13**, [1045]
    road roller, **13**, [1044]
    special vehicles, **13**, [1044]

vehicle excise duty—*contd*
  rates of—*contd*
    threshold for reduced general rate,
      13, [1083], [1087]
    works truck, **13**, [1044]
    2009–10, for, **13(S)**, Customs 4
  reduced pollution certificate, **43(S)**, 984–5
  registered vehicles, **13**, [1098]
  regulations, **13**, [1024]
    fees prescribed by, **13**, [1025]
    offences, **13**, [1026]
  relief—
    shipbuilders, **13**, [555]
      ending of, **13**, [1120]
    where vehicle changes category, **13**, [1060]
  repeals, **13**, [1035], [1052]
  replaced registration documents, requirement
    to destroy, **13(S)**, Customs 9
  revocations, **13**, [1035], [1053]
  surrender of licence, rebates, **43(S)**, 980–1
  trade licences, rate of duty for, **13**, [965],
    [1051]
  transitional provisions, **13**, [1034], [1051]
  unlicensed vehicle, using or keeping,
    43(S), 1349–51
  wrongdoing, penalties,
    43(S), 1328–39. *See also* **tax penalty**

vehicle licence. *See* **vehicle**

vehicle testing
  ADR Convention, inspections, **37**, [130]
  alterations—
    examination after, **37**, [137], [630]
    notification, fees payable on, **37**, [137]
  appeals as to, **37**, [136], [621], [629]
  approved testing authority—
    authorisation of—
      conditions, regulations as to, **37**, [126]
      limitation on, **37**, [126], [403]
      powers, **37**, [126]
      proposals, notice of, **37**, [126]
      withdrawal of, **37**, [126]
    conditions to be complied with, **37**, [403]
    meaning, **37**, [126]
  business of—
    authorisation—
      persons barred, **37**, [126]
      powers, **37**, [126]
      proposals, notice of, **37**, [126]
    security of tenure of premises, exclusion
      of, **37**, [132]
    vehicle testing business, meaning, **37**, [126]
  certificates—
    duplicates, **37**, [622]
    forgery, **37**, [791]
    functions as to, exercise of, **37**, [127]
    issue, **37**, [127], [621], [627]
    obligatory, **37**, [625]
    plating, **37**, [139], [627]
    production to police when required,
      37, [782]
    record of, **37**, [128], [622]
      evidence, as, **37**, [624]
      use of, **37**, [623]

vehicle testing—*contd*
  certificates—*contd*
    refusal, **37**, [128], [621]
    register of, **37**, [128]
    supplementary provisions, **37**, [128], [626]
    vehicle excise licence, required for grant
      of, **37**, [648]
  Community Recording Equipment—
    installation, **37**, [621], [627]
    regulation, meaning, **37**, [670]
  condition, satisfactory, tests of, **37**, [621]
  consultations by Secretary of State, **37**, [133]
  documents—
    falsification of, **37**, [139]
    forgery and misuse of, **37**, [48], [138],
      [791]
  examinations—
    alterations, after, **37**, [136]–[138], [630]
    conduct of, **37**, [621]
    fees, **37**, [133]
    private sector, in. *See* private sector *below*
    records—
      evidence from, **37**, [624]
      use of, **37**, [623]
    standards of, maintenance of, **37**, [133]
    testing and surveillance functions, **37**, [127]
  examiners—
    appointment
    identity of drivers and others etc,
      37, [781], [782]; **38(1)**, [278]
    impersonation of, **37**, [795]
    inspector, as, **37**, [128]
    powers, **37**, [651], [781], [782]
    sale rooms, powers as to used vehicles in,
      37, [662]
  examiners, authorisation of—
    foreign vehicles, **37**, [149]
    generally, **37**, [621]
    regulations, **37**, [622]
  fees—
    examination, **37**, [133]
    notification of alterations, on, **37**, [137]
  foreign vehicles, **37**, [128], [149]
  forgery and misuse of documents, **37**, [48],
    [138], [791]
  functions, surveillance, **37**, [126], [127]
  goods vehicles—
    determination of plated particulars—
      alteration of plated weights, **37**, [643]
      appeals against, **37**, [629]
      plating certificates, **37**, [627]
      regulations as to, **37**, [627], [630]
    examination stations, **37**, [631], [641]
    examinations, **37**, [627]
    forgery of documents, **37**, [791]
    obligatory, **37**, [632]
    periodic intervals, **37**, [630]
    records, use of, **37**, [628]
  Government testing stations, former,
    investment in company interested in,
    37, [131]
  individuals, authorisation of, **37**, [126]
  inspections in connection with international
    conventions, **37**, [130]

vehicle testing—*contd*
  inspector—
    approved assistant, authorisation of,
      37, [126]
    authorised, **37**, [126], [149]
      conditions, regulations as to, **37**, [126]
      meaning, **37**, [126]
    examiner, as, **37**, [128]
    foreign vehicles, **37**, [149]
    impersonation of, **37**, [140], [795]
    international conventions, powers in
      connection with, **37**, [130]
    period after which required, **37**, [625], [626]
    persons barred from, **37**, [126]
    plating, **37**, [627]
    premises used for, security of tenure,
      37, [132]
    private-sector—
      examination, supervision or review of,
        37, [126], [128]
      functions—
        exercise of, **37**, [127]
        new, addition of, **37**, [126]
      testing and surveillance functions, **37**, [127]
    public-service vehicle—
      as type vehicle—
        appeal in matter of, **37**, [136]
        approval of, **37**, [12], [129]
      temporary exemption, **37**, [626]
    recording equipment, **37**, [621], [627]
    regulations and orders, **37**, [128], [145], [621],
      [630]
    requirement, **37**, [621]
    road, testing on—
      accident, after, **37**, [650]
      construction and use requirements,
        compliance with, **37**, [650]
      defects discovered, test after remedy,
        37, [650], [816]
      deferred, **37**, [816]
      powers, **37**, [650]
    sale rooms, used vehicles in, **37**, [662]
    testing stations—
      company interests—
        interests in land, transfer or grant of,
          37, [131]
        investment in, **37**, [131]
      former Government investment in
        company, **37**, [131]
      premises, consultations as to, **37**, [133]
      provision of, **37**, [621], [631], [641]
      PSV—
        meaning, **37**, [10]
        provision and maintenance, **37**, [10]
      representative bodies, consultation with,
        37, [133]
    TIR Convention, inspections, **37**, [130]

vending machine
  information to be displayed on, **39(1)**, [499],
    [500]
  inspectors' powers, **39(1)**, [514]
  sales from—
    exceptions as to, **39(1)**, [504]
    offences, **39(1)**, [502]

vending machine—*contd*
  sales from—*contd*
    solid fuel, **39(1)**, [574]

venison. *See* **deer**

venture capital trust
  administration or receivership, company in—
    meaning, **44(4)**, [339]
    qualifying activity requirements, ceasing to
      meet, **44(4)**, [298]
  amended provisions, **43(S)**, 1122–4, 1453
  approval—
    15% holding limit condition, **44(4)**, [282]
    effective, time from which, **44(4)**, [289]
    eligible shares, conditions relating to,
      44(4), [285]
    income—
      nature of, **44(4)**, [281]
      retention condition, **44(4)**, [281]
    procedure, power to make regulations as
      to, **44(4)**, [290]
    qualifying holdings—
      70% disposal of, **44(4)**, [286]
      conditions relating to, **44(4)**, [285]
    requirements for, **44(4)**, [279]–[280]
    value of investments—
      15% holding limit condition,
        44(4), [282]
      conditions relating to, **44(4)**, [283]–[284]
      eligible shares—
        30% condition, **44(4)**, [283]
        meaning, **44(4)**, [291]
      qualifying holdings condition,
        44(4), [283]–[284]
    withdrawal of, **44(4)**, [287]–[288]
      loss of relief where, **44(4)**, [273]
  capital gains tax relief, **42**, [1275]
  company reorganisations involving exchange
    of shares, **44(4)**, [338]
  deferral relief, abolition, **43(2)**, [548]
  dividends—
    exempt income, **44(3)**, [723]
    meaning, **44(3)**, [723]
  excluded activities—
    coal production, **43(S)**, 1123
    shipbuilding, **43(S)**, 1123
    steel production, **43(S)**, 1123
  gross assets of issuers of shares or securities,
    limits on, **43(S)**, 343
  in liquidation—
    conditions for VCT approval, power to
      treat as met, **44(4)**, [323]
    disposal to VCT, facilitating, **44(4)**, [325]
    distributions by, **44(4)**, [324]
    meaning, **43(2)**, [197]; **44(4)**, [328]
    periods before and after winding up,
      powers in respect of, **44(4)**, [326]
    provisions regarding, **43(2)**, [197]
    regulations, **44(4)**, [332]
    supplementary provisions, **44(4)**, [327]
    treatment as VCT, powers as to,
      44(4), [322]
  income tax relief, rate of, **43(2)**, [324]
  investment of money, time for, **43(2)**, [199]

venture capital trust—*contd*
  investments—
    meaning, **43(S)**, 345
    rate of relief for, **43(S)**, 344
  lengthening of periods applicable to,
    43(S), 344
  loan relationships, **43(1)**, [258]
  meaning, **44(4)**, [264]
  merger, **43(2)**, [198]
    facilitating, powers as to,
      44(4), [329]–[330]
    meaning, **44(4)**, [331]
    regulations, **44(4)**, [332]
    successor company, meaning, **44(4)**, [331]
  overview, **44(4)**, [263]
  qualifying holdings, **44(4)**, [292]
    70% condition, disposal of holding,
      44(4), [286]
    conditions, governing approval,
      44(4), [285]
    excluded activities—
      facilities for another business, providing,
        44(4), [318]
      licence fees, receipt of, **44(4)**, [314]
      meaning, **44(4)**, [311]
      nursing homes, **44(4)**, [317]
      property development, **44(4)**, [315]
      residential care homes, **44(4)**, [317]
      royalties, receipt of, **44(4)**, [314]
      services for another business, providing,
        44(4), [318]
      ships, leasing of, **44(4)**, [313]
      wholesale and retail distribution,
        44(4), [312]
    meaning, **43(2)**, [69]
    "qualifying 90% subsidiary", meaning,
      44(4), [309]
    "qualifying subsidiary", meaning,
      44(4), [310]
    "qualifying trade", meaning, **44(4)**, [308]
    requirements—
      administration or receivership, ceasing to
        meet because of, **44(4)**, [298]
      control, **44(4)**, [303]
      eligible shares, proportion of,
        44(4), [295]
      employees, number of, **44(4)**, [305]
      gross assets, **44(4)**, [304]
      independence, **44(4)**, [303]
      maximum qualifying investment,
        44(4), [293]
      no guaranteed loan, **44(4)**, [294]
      property managing subsidiaries,
        44(4), [307]
      qualifying activity, carrying on,
        44(4), [297]
      qualifying subsidiaries, **44(4)**, [306]
      relevant qualifying activity to be carried
        on by relevant company, **44(4)**, [301]
      risk capital schemes, maximum amount
        raised annually through, **44(4)**, [299]
      trading, **44(4)**, [296]
      unquoted status, **44(4)**, [302]
      use of money raised, **44(4)**, [300]
    winding-up of company, **44(4)**, [320]

venture capital trust—*contd*
  qualifying trade, **43(1)**, [351]
  relief—
    amount of, **44(4)**, [268]
    eligibility for, **44(4)**, [266]
    entitlement to—
      claim, **44(4)**, [267]
      linked loan, none where, **44(4)**, [269]
      none—
        linked loan, where, **44(4)**, [269]
        where relief would have been lost if
          already obtained, **44(4)**, [270]
    form of, **44(4)**, [268]
    linked loan, no entitlement where,
      44(4), [269]
    loss of—
      approval withdrawn, if, **44(4)**, [273]
      shares—
        civil partners, transfers between,
          44(4), [272]
        disposed of within 5 years,
          44(4), [271]
        spouses, transfers between,
          44(4), [272]
      subsequently found not to have been
        due, where, **44(4)**, [274]
    other than income tax relief, **44(4)**, [265]
    procedure, rules as to, **44(4)**, [277]
    which would have been lost if already
      obtained, no entitlement to, **44(4)**, [270]
    withdrawal or reduction of—
      assessment on, **44(4)**, [275]
      information requirements, **44(4)**, [276]
  repayment supplements, **43(2)**, [69]
  restructuring, acquisitions for purposes of,
    44(4), [334]–[336]
  securities, conversion of, **44(4)**, [337]
  shares—
    annual acquisition limit exceeded, treatment
      where, **44(3)**, [724]
    company reorganisations involving
      exchange of, **44(4)**, [338]
    conversion of, **44(4)**, [337]
    disposals, identification after, **44(3)**, [725]
    loss of relief. *See* relief *above*
    reorganisations, identification after,
      44(3), [726]
  transitional provisions and savings,
    44(4), [1053]
  winding up, **43(2)**, [197]

vermin. *See also* **rats and mice**
  destruction, **35(1)**, [135]
  use of gas for destroying—
    local authority, by, **35(1)**, [135]
    vacation of premises during, **35(1)**, [261]

verminous articles
  cleansing or destruction, **35(1)**, [136]
  disinfection or destruction, **35(1)**, [262]
  sale, etc, prohibition of, **35(1)**, [262]

verminous persons
  cleansing of persons and clothing,
    35(1), [137]

verminous persons—*contd*
  removal to cleansing station, **35(1)**, [137]

vessel. *See also* **ship**
  Antarctica, entering, **10**, [1093]
  certificates, conditions as to, **38(1)**, [607]
  dark smoke, emission from, **35(2)**, [44]
  designated, meaning, **38(1)**, [607]
  dumping at sea by. *See* **pollution** (sea)
  emissions from—
    enforcement of provisions, **35(2)**, [55]
    entry and inspection, rights of, **35(2)**, [56],
      [57]
  infectious diseases in, **35(1)**, [454]
  inhabited, burglary of, **12(1)**, [561]
  insurance policies for, **38(1)**, [607], [624]
  licences, conditions as to, **38(1)**, [607]
  Licensing Act 2003, application of,
    19(3), [681]
  meaning, **9**, [136]; **38(1)**, [593]
  obstruction of inland waterways by,
    38(1), [608]
  pollution by. *See* **oil pollution; pollution**
  removal to permit works, **38(1)**, [609]
  requisition of—
    compensation for, **9**, [123]
    space and accommodation in, compensation
      for, **9**, [120], [124]
  scuttling—
    licensing requirement, **49**, [625]
    register of licences issued, **49**, [635], [649]
  standards of construction and equipment of,
    compliance with, **38(1)**, [607], [625]

vesting
  deed poll, by. *See* **deed poll**

vesting declaration, general. *See* **general
  vesting declaration**

vestry
  church rate, voting on at, **14**, 215
  meaning, **25(1)**, [86]
  notice of, church door, fixed to, **14**, 94
  powers, transfer of—
    parish council, to, **25(1)**, [77]
    property included in, **25(1)**, [85]

veterinary inspector
  animal diseases. *See* **diseases of animals**
  dog breeding establishments, inspection,
    2, [367]
  pet shops, inspection, **2**, [282]

veterinary practitioner
  controlled drugs—
    directions as regards, **28**, [211]–[215]
    exemptions as regards, **28**, [205]
  entitlement to practise, **28**, [23]
  exemptions for, **28**, [205]
  meaning, **28**, [24], [187]
  medicinal products on prescription only,
    28, [114], [115]
  riding establishment, report on, **2**, [315]
  sale of poisons to, **28**, [253]

veterinary practitioner—*contd*
  supplementary register, registration in,
    28, [24]
  zoos, for. *See* **zoo**

veterinary surgeon
  controlled drugs—
    directions as regards, **28**, [211]–[215]
    exemption as regards, **28**, [205]
  disciplinary proceedings—
    disciplinary committee—
      assessor to advise, **28**, [48]
      constitution, **28**, [31], [47]
      duty, **28**, [31]
      evidence, rules as to, **28**, [48]
      procedure, **28**, [31], [48]
      reference of disciplinary cases to,
        28, [31]
      removal or suspension from register—
        appeal from, **28**, [33]
        direction for, **28**, [32]
    preliminary investigation committee—
      constitution, **28**, [47]
      duty, **28**, [31]
      setting up, **28**, 783
  drugs, misuse of. *See* **drugs**
  examinations, **28**, [15]–[17], [22]
  exemptions for, **28**, [205]
  general note, **28**, [1]
  meaning, **28**, [187]
  medicinal products on prescription only,
    28, [114], [115]
  Privy Council, powers of, **28**, [38]
  qualifications—
    abroad, abbreviation of, **28**, [28]
    Commonwealth or foreign, **28**, [22]
    European, **28**, [18], [19], [46]
    meaning, **28**, [42]
    wrongfully claiming, **28**, [36]
  register—
    contents, **28**, [14]
    copy as evidence, **28**, [25]
    entitlement to registration—
      Commonwealth practitioners, **28**, [22]
      examination, after, **28**, [16]
      foreign practitioners, **28**, [22]
      graduates from UK university, **28**, [15]
      recognition orders giving, **28**, [15]
    European qualifications—
      knowledge and skill of, **28**, [19]
      meaning, **28**, [18], [46]
      refusal to register, appeals, **28**, [20]
      registration by virtue of, **28**, [18]
    fees on entry etc, **28**, [27]
    incorrect and fraudulent entries in, **28**, [30]
    keeping, **28**, [25]
    lists, division into four, **28**, [14]
    printing and publication, **28**, [25]
    registration in—
      application for, **28**, [26]
      entitlement to. *See* entitlement to
        registration *above*
      suspension, **28**, [32]
      temporary, **28**, [23]
    regulations as to, **28**, [27]

veterinary surgeon—*contd*
  register—*contd*
    removal from, **28**, [29], [32]
    restoration to, **28**, [27], [29], [34]
    supplementary—
      application for registration in, **28**, [26]
      contents, **28**, [24]
      entitlement to registration in, **28**, [24]
      regulations as to, **28**, [27]
      removal from, **28**, [29], [32]
      restoration to, **28**, [27], [29], [34]
      suspension of registration in, **28**, [32]
  Republic of Ireland, agreements with,
    28, [37]
  Royal College. *See* **Royal College of
    Veterinary Surgeons**
  sale of poisons to, **28**, [253]
  transitional provisions, **28**, [43]
  unqualified—
    restrictions on practice, **28**, [35]
      exemptions from, **28**, [35], [49], [50]
    students, exemptions from restrictions on
      practice, **28**, [35]
    treatment and operations which may be
      given or carried out by, **28**, [35], [49]
    use of title by, prohibition of, **28**, [36]
  veterinary surgery, meaning, **28**, [42]

vibration
  public works, from, compensation for,
    9, [304]

vicar. *See also* **incumbent**
  cure of souls, not to be discharged from,
    14, 60–1
  guild church, of—
    licensing, **14**, 453–4
    rights and duties, **14**, 456–7
    vacancy in office, **14**, 457
  team ministry, of, **14**, 986

vicarage. *See also* **benefice**
  new benefice as, **14**, 996
  rectory, conversion into, **14**, 68–9
  sinecure rectory, annexation of, **14**, 136

Vice-Admiralty Courts. *See* **Prize Courts**

Vice-Chancellor
  clerk and secretary to, **11(2)**, [771]

victim of crime
  code of practice—
    issue of, **12(4)**, [16]
    non-compliance with, **12(4)**, [18]
    procedure, **12(4)**, [17]
    services, as to, **12(4)**, [16]
  Commissioner for Victims and Witnesses. *See*
    **Commissioner for Victims and
    Witnesses**
  grants for assisting, **12(4)**, [48]
  meaning, **12(4)**, [44]
  Northern Ireland, **12(4)**, [39]
  relevant authority, disclosure of information
    to, **12(4)**, [46]

victim of crime—*contd*
  sexual or violent offence, of—
    hospital direction, where made,
      12(4), [27]–[30]
      removal of restriction, **12(4)**, [30]
    hospital order, where made,
      12(4), [20]–[25]
      no restriction order made, where,
        12(4), [21], [23], [25]
      removal of restriction, **12(4)**, [26]
      representations, **12(4)**, [22], [23]
    information, right to receive, **12(4)**, [19]
      hospital direction, where made,
        12(4), [29]
      hospital order, where made, **12(4)**, [24]
      no restriction direction given,
        12(4), [36]
      no restriction order made, where,
        12(4), [25]
      transfer direction, where made,
        12(4), [35]
    representations, right to make, **12(4)**, [19]
      hospital direction, where made,
        12(4), [28]
      hospital order, where made, **12(4)**, [22]
      no restriction direction given,
        12(4), [34]
      no restriction order made, where,
        12(4), [23]
      transfer direction, where made,
        12(4), [33]
    transfer direction, where made,
      12(4), [31]–[37]
      no restriction direction given,
        12(4), [34], [36]
      no restriction order made, **12(4)**, [32]
      removal of restriction, **12(4)**, [37]
  Victim's Advisory Panel, **12(4)**, [47]

Victoria and Albert Museum
  admission, payments for, **13**, [263]
  Board of Trustees—
    allowances, **13**, [297]
    appointment, **13**, [297]
    committees, **13**, [297]
    companies, formation by, **13**, [264]
  admission, payments for, **13**, [263]
  Board of Trustees—
    allowances, **13**, [297]
    appointment, **13**, [297]
    committees, **13**, [297]
    companies, formation by, **13**, [264]
    proceedings, **13**, [297]
    reports, **13**, [297]
    research and services, **13**, [263]
    status, **13**, [297]
    vesting of property, rights and liabilities in,
      13, [265]
  collections, care and preservation, **13**, [263]
  director, **13**, [297]
  gifts, vesting of, **13**, [266]
  grants, **13**, [431], [432]
  history, **13**, [49]
  land, transfer of, **13**, [430]
  loans by, **13**, [268]

Victoria and Albert Museum—*contd*
objects—
  acquisition, **13**, [267]
  disposal, **13**, [267]
  lending and borrowing, **13**, [268]
premises, use of, **13**, [263]
staff, **13**, [297]

video recordings
admissibility in evidence, **18**, [413], [414]
animals, violence towards, works depicting,
  13, [304]
broadcasting, exempted supply for, **13**, [305]
children, viewing by, advice as to, **13**, [311]
classification certificate—
  appeals, **13**, [306]
  breach of, supply in, **13**, [315]
  contents, **13**, [311]
  determination—
    authority for purposes of, **13**, [306]
    record of, **13**, [306]
    title assigned, **13**, [306]
  exempted supply on submission for,
    13, [305]
  false indication as to, **13**, [318]
  fee, **13**, [306]
  issue, **13**, [311]
  labelling, **13**, [312]
  meaning, **13**, [311]
  requirements, **13**, [311]
  suitability, **13**, [306]
  supply for purposes of, **13**, [305]
  title of work, requirement, **13**, [306]
criminal proceedings, meaning in, **18**, [359]
designated authority—
  annual reports by, **13**, [310]
  purposes and functions, **13**, [306]
  Secretary of State, powers, **13**, [306]
designation—
  designated authority, by, **13**, [306]
  parliamentary procedure, **13**, [309]
enforcement of provisions, **13**, [322]
entry and search of premises, **13**, [325]
forfeiture, on conviction, **13**, [328]
general viewing, statement as to, on
  certificate, **13**, [311]
human organs or functions, works depicting,
  13, [304]
labelling etc, requirements—
  generally, **13**, [312]
  non-compliance with, **13**, [317]
meaning, **13**, [303]; **18**, [416]
medical or related occupation, supply in
  connection with, **13**, [305]
national health service, supply for purposes
  of, **13**, [305]
offences—
  arrest, powers of, **13**, [326]
  bodies corporate, by, **13**, [321]
  classification, supply in breach of, **13**, [315]
  evidence by certificate, **13**, [327]
  forfeiture of recordings, **13**, [328]
  general defences to, **13**, [319]
  magistrates' courts, extension of jurisdiction
    in linked cases, **13**, [323], [324]

video recordings—*contd*
offences—*contd*
  penalties, **13**, [313]
  prosecutions, time limits for, **13**, [320]
  unclassified works, supply of, **13**, [313]
seizure, power of, **13**, [325]
sex shops, supply to—
  classification certificate requirement,
    13, [311]
  offences and defences, **13**, [316]
  recordings limited to, **13**, [316]
sexual activity, works depicting, **13**, [304]
suitability—
  determination as to—
    criteria for, **13**, [307]
    review of, **13**, [308]
  meaning, **13**, [307]
  potential viewer, meaning, **13**, [307]
  violent behaviour, **13**, [307]
supply—
  breach of classification, in, **13**, [315]
  broadcasting, for purposes of, **13**, [305]
  business, in course of, **13**, [305]
  children, suitability for, **13**, [311]
  classification certificate, in breach of,
    13, [315]
  exempted, **13**, [305]
  exhibition, for purpose of, **13**, [305]
  false indication of classification, recordings
    containing, **13**, [318]
  labelling, non-compliance with, **13**, [317]
  meaning, **13**, [303]
  otherwise than for reward, **13**, [305]
  sex shops, to, recordings limited to,
    13, [316]
  unclassified, possession for purposes of,
    13, [314]
  unclassified work, **13**, [313]
  what constitutes, **13**, [305]
title, assignment of, **13**, [306]
trade descriptions, application of provisions,
  13, [322]
unclassified works, supply of, **13**, [313]
violence, works depicting, **13**, [304]
weights and measures authority, enforcement
  of provisions by, **13**, [322]
works—
  exempted, **13**, [305]
  meaning, **13**, [303]

Vienna Convention on Consular Relations
application of, **10**, [991], [1005]

**Vienna Convention on Diplomatic
Relations**
application of, **10**, [984], [990]

village green
nuisances, prevention of, **25(2)**, [166]

Vintners Company
privileges and exemptions, removal of,
  19(3), [688]

violent offender
sentences. *See* **sentence**

violent offender order
appeals, **12(4)**, [520]
application for, **12(4)**, [514]
  notice of, **12(4)**, [519]
discharge, **12(4)**, [517]
failure to comply, **12(4)**, [527]
information, supply of, **12(4)**, [528], [529]
interim, **12(4)**, [518]
interpretation, **12(4)**, [531]
making of, **12(4)**, [515]
meaning, **12(4)**, [512]
notification requirements—
  acknowledgement, **12(4)**, [526]
  changes, relating to, **12(4)**, [523]
  initial notification, **12(4)**, [522]
  method of notification, **12(4)**, [526]
  notifiable events, **12(4)**, [523]
  offenders subject to, **12(4)**, [521]
  periodic notification, **12(4)**, [524]
  required information, **12(4)**, [522]
    new, **12(4)**, [523]
  travel outside United Kingdom,
    12(4), [525]
offences, **12(4)**, [527]
provisions in, **12(4)**, [516]
qualifying offenders, **12(4)**, [513]
release of transfer, information as to,
  12(4), [530]
renewal, **12(4)**, [517]
service sentences, **12(4)**, [531]
specified offences, **12(4)**, [512]
transitory and transitional provisions,
  12(4), [583]
variation, **12(4)**, [517]

Virgin Islands
Court, powers of, **7(2)**, [613]

visiting forces
Abortion Act applying to, **12(1)**, [411]
absence without leave, **3**, [452]
arrest of member, **3**, [441], [444]
Bahamas, in, **7(2)**, [665]
Bangladesh, in, **7(2)**, [669]
Barbados, in, **7(2)**, [611]
Belize, in, **7(2)**, [755]
Botswana, in, **7(2)**, [594]
Brunei and Maldives, in, **7(2)**, [763]
Cameroon, in, **7(2)**, [854]
capital gains tax, residence for purposes of,
  42, [1093]
Channel Islands, in, **3**, [454]
civilian component of, **3**, [449]
colonies, application to, **3**, [331]
countries to which provisions apply, **3**, [440]
Cyprus, in, **7(2)**, [475]
desertion, **3**, [452]
evidence of membership, **3**, [450]
extension of Act, **3**, [454]
Fiji, in, **7(2)**, [653]
Gambia, in, **7(2)**, [573]
generally, **3**, [1]

visiting forces—*contd*
Ghana, in, **7(2)**, [462]
Guyana, in, **7(2)**, [588]
home forces law, application of, **3**, [447]
income tax exemption, **44(2)**, [306]
inheritance tax provisions, **42**, [690]
international headquarters, **10**, [982]
Isle of Man, in, **3**, [454]
Jamaica, in, **7(2)**, [510]
Kenya, in, **7(2)**, [539]
Kiribati, in, **7(2)**, [710]
Lesotho, in, **7(2)**, [599]
Malawi, in, **7(2)**, [555]
Malaya, in, **7(2)**, [466]
Malta, in, **7(2)**, [567]
mandated territories, application to, **3**, [332]
Mauritius, in, **7(2)**, [625]
meaning, **3**, [334], [456]; **41**, [99], [100]
Mozambique, in, **7(2)**, [854]
mutual powers of command, **3**, [330]
Namibia, in, **7(2)**, [791]
Nauru, in, **7(2)**, [740]
New Hebrides, in, **7(2)**, [743]
Nigeria, in, **7(2)**, [481]
Pakistan, in, **7(2)**, [788]
Papua New Guinea, in, **7(2)**, [740]
personnel, attachment of, **3**, [330]
presence in UK, proving, **3**, [455]
service authorities—
  meaning, **3**, [451]
  powers of, **3**, [441]
service courts—
  meaning, **3**, [451]
  powers of, **3**, [441]
  trial by, **3**, [443]
settlement of claim against, **3**, [448]
Seychelles, in, **7(2)**, [678]
Shops, Offices and Railway Premises
  Act 1963, exclusion of application,
  18, [1244]
Sierra Leone, in, **7(2)**, [487]
Singapore, in, **7(2)**, [605]
smoke control provisions, application to,
  35(2), [46]
stamp duty exemption, **41**, [99]
stamp duty land tax exemption, **41**, [100]
Solomon Islands, in, **7(2)**, [697]
South Africa, in, **7(2)**, [797]
Sri Lanka, in, **7(2)**, [448]
Swaziland, in, **7(2)**, [630]
Tanganyika, in, **7(2)**, [492]
territories, application to, **3**, [332]
Tonga, in, **7(2)**, [643]
Trinidad and Tobago, in, **7(2)**, [516]
Tuvalu, in, **7(2)**, [703]
Uganda, in, **7(2)**, [523]
United Kingdom court—
  offences—
    person, against, **3**, [458]
    property, against, **3**, [458]
  trial by, **3**, [441]–[443]
Western Samoa, in, **7(2)**, [740]
Zambia, in, **7(2)**, [560]
Zanzibar, in, **7(2)**, [542]

vocation
irrecoverable debts, deduction for, **44(1)**, [66]
loss relief. *See* **loss relief**
permanent discontinuance, meaning,
44(1), [88]
post-discontinuance receipts, taxation of—
allowable deductions, **44(1)**, [86]
conventional basis, **44(1)**, [85]
earnings basis, **44(1)**, [84]
right to payment transferred, where,
44(1), [87]
profits—
computation of, **43(1)**, [345]
conventional basis, **44(1)**, [88]
earnings basis, **44(1)**, [88]
registration, false declaration to obtain,
12(1), [200]
Schedule D Case II, charge under, **44(1)**, [13]
trade including, **44(1)**, [1]
work in progress—
determination of questions, **44(1)**, [83]
discontinuance, at, **44(1)**, [82]
valuation of, **44(1)**, [82]

vocational training
construction of references to, **7(1)**, [99]
person undergoing, discrimination against,
7(1), [140]
protection of women, **7(1)**, [52], [96]

void marriage
abroad, celebrated, **27**, [444]
Church of England rites, defect in, **27**, [231]
foreign law, governed by, **27**, [444]
grounds for, **27**, [441]
nullity proceedings, provisions applying to,
27, [445]
persons under age, between, **27**, [206]
procedural defects, **27**, [262]
Registrar General's licence, where solemnised
by, **27**, [363]
rites, defect in, **27**, [231]
sexual capacity, evidence on, **27**, [485]
transitional provisions, **27**, [492]

voidable marriage
bars to relief, **27**, [443]
decree of nullity, effect of, **27**, [446]
foreign law, governed by, **27**, [444]
grounds for, **27**, [442]
nullity proceedings, provisions applying to,
27, [445]
proceedings to be instituted within three
years, where, **27**, [443]
sexual capacity, evidence on, **27**, [485]
social security benefits, effect on, **40(1)**, [365]
transitional provisions, **27**, [492]

voluntary arrangement
Financial Services Authority, participation
by—
company, **19(2)**, [431]
individual, **19(2)**, [432]

voluntary home. *See also* **voluntary**
organisation
accommodation in, child requiring advice and
assistance, **6**, [329]
controlled or assisted home, designated as,
40(1), [121]
generally, **6**, [1]
grants to, **6**, [410]
maintenance of children in, **6**, [375]
meaning of, **6**, [376]
refuge for children at risk, as, **6**, [368]

voluntary organisation. *See also* **children's**
home; community home; voluntary home
accommodation—
information, transmission to Secretary of
State, **6**, [411]
provided by, nature of, **6**, [375]
computer used by, inspection, **6**, [378]
disabled, welfare arrangements for, **40(1)**, [14]
duties of, **6**, [377]
expenses in providing physical training and
recreation, grants towards, **35(1)**, [221],
[381]
financial assistance by local authority,
25(2), [135]
grants to, schemes for, **25(2)**, [607]
financial support, **6**, [410]
generally, **6**, [1]
grants to, **6**, [131], [410]
homeless persons functions, assistance,
23, [493], [494]
inspection—
by local authority, **6**, [378]
Secretary of State's powers, **6**, [409]
local authority, duties as to, **6**, [378]
meaning, **6**, [100], [184], [435]; **25(2)**, [607];
35(1), [223]
premises—
maintained by, provision of local authority
accommodation in, **40(1)**, [12]
powers of entry, **6**, [378]
records, production of, **6**, [378]
regulations, Secretary of State making,
6, [375]
visitation of homes, local authority's duty,
6, [378]

voluntary school
acceptable standard of education, failure to
give. *See* **school**
admissions—
ability, restriction on selection by,
15(2), [774]
code for, **15(2)**, [775]
pupil banding, **15(2)**, [775]
aided school—
capital expenditure, meaning, **15(2)**, [770]
funding, **15(2)**, [140]
generally, **15(2)**, [377]
staffing, **15(2)**, [377], [526]
delegated budget, suspension of,
15(2), [526]

voluntary school—*contd*
alterations to, **15(2)**, [754]–[755]
foundation proposals, governing body to
determine, **15(2)**, [758]
proposals—
implementation of, **15(2)**, [760]
interested bodies, rights of, **15(2)**, [759]
restriction on publication of,
15(2), [756]–[757]
restrictions on, **15(2)**, [764]
collective worship—
exceptions and special arrangements,
15(2), [59]
requirements, **15(2)**, [58], [159]
curriculum. *See* **curriculum**
discontinuance—
disposal of land on, **15(2)**, [64],
[163]–[167], [771], [902]–[903]
further provisions, **15(2)**, [35]
notice by governing body, **15(2)**, [32]
proposals for, **15(2)**, [31], [144]–[148]
restrictions on, **15(2)**, [764]
establishment or alteration, proposals for,
15(2), [29], [30], [35], [144]–[148]
financial delegation, local education authority
scheme for financing. *See* **local education
authority**
foundation, requirements as to, **15(2)**, [769]
funding, **15(2)**, [139], [141]
governing body—
exemption order from education legislation
requirements—
application for, **15(2)**, [342]
generally, **15(2)**, [340]
revocation of, **15(2)**, [341]
variation of, **15(2)**, [341]
general duties of, **15(2)**, [773]
individual pupils' performance, provision of
information about, **15(1)**, [671]
information, power of Secretary of State to
require, **15(1)**, [670]
provision of information to Secretary of
State, **15(1)**, [673]
teaching services for day nurseries,
provision of, **15(1)**, [669]
governors, ex officio trustees, as, **15(2)**, [72]
new—
premises, provision of, **15(2)**, [900]
restrictions on, **15(2)**, [764]
pupils, admissions. *See* admissions *above*
religious character, teachers at schools with,
15(2), [53], [772]
religious education, duty to secure provision
of, **15(2)**, [57], [158]
religious opinions of staff, **15(2)**, [52]
religious worship, sixth form pupils excused
from attendance at, **15(2)**, [777]
types of, **15(2)**, [21]

voluntary winding-up
Financial Services Authority, participation by,
19(2), [440]
insurers, of, **19(2)**, [441]
protected railway company, restrictions as to,
38(1), [410]

Volunteer Reserve. *See* **reserve associations**

voucher
cash—
application of provisions to, **44(2)**, [83]
approved scheme, issued under, **44(2)**, [89]
earnings, benefit treated as, **44(2)**, [91]
meaning, **44(2)**, [85]
member of employee's family, provision for
or receipt by, **44(2)**, [84]
PAYE treatment, **44(2)**, [694]
payment of sums exempt from tax,
44(2), [90]
public, made available to, **44(2)**, [88]
childcare, qualifying, **44(2)**, [272]
cost of provision, apportionment, **44(2)**, [87]
credit-tokens—
application of provisions to, **44(2)**, [100]
dispensations, **44(2)**, [106]
earnings, benefit treated as, **44(2)**, [104],
[374]
exempt benefits, for, **44(2)**, [268]
exemption of use to obtain benefits,
44(2), [107]
incidental overnight expenses, for,
44(2), [269]
meaning, **44(2)**, [102]
member of employee's family, provision for
or receipt by, **44(2)**, [101]
PAYE, application of, **44(2)**, [696]
public generally, made available to,
44(2), [103]
third parties, small gifts from, **44(2)**, [271]
vehicle, benefits or money obtained in
connection with, **44(2)**, [270]
credit, treatment of, **50(S)**, VAT 13–14
dispensation from tax charge, **44(2)**, [106]
exemption of use to obtain exempt benefits,
44(2), [107]
money, goods or services obtained, disregard,
44(2), [105]
non-cash—
application of provisions to, **44(2)**, [92]
earnings, benefit treated as, **44(2)**, [97],
[373]
exempt benefits, for, **44(2)**, [267]
exemption of use to obtain benefits,
44(2), [107]
incidental overnight expenses, for,
44(2), [269]
meal, for, **44(2)**, [99]
meaning, **44(2)**, [94]
member of employee's family, provision for
or receipt by, **44(2)**, [93]
PAYE treatment, **44(2)**, [695]
public generally, made available to,
44(2), [95]
third parties, small gifts from, **44(2)**, [271]
vehicle, benefits or money obtained in
connection with, **44(2)**, [270]
year in which treated as received,
44(2), [98]
sickness benefits-related, **44(2)**, [86]
transport, under pre-26th March 1982
arrangements, **44(2)**, [96]

vulnerable adult
assistance in conduct of affairs, requiring,
  6(S), 229
controlled activity relating to—
  reference to, **6(S)**, 196–7
  regulations, **6(S)**, 197–8
death of, causing or allowing—
  evidence and procedure, **12(4)**, [3]
    court-martial, **12(4)**, [5]
    Northern Ireland, **12(4)**, [4]
  offence of, **12(4)**, [2]
evidence, live link directions, **12(4)**, [274]
health care, **6(S)**, 229
lawful custody, in, **6(S)**, 229
meaning, **6(S)**, 228–30
regulated activity relating to—
  appropriate verification—
    default provision, **6(S)**, 255–6
    definitions, **6(S)**, 259
    prescribed, **6(S)**, 256–8
  barred person engaging in—
    monitoring, subject to, **6(S)**, 181–2
    offences, **6(S)**, 180
    use of person not subject to monitoring,
      offence, **6(S)**, 183–4
    use of, offence, **6(S)**, 182–3
  code of practice, **6(S)**, 203
  companies or partnerships, offences by,
    6(S), 191
  Crown, provisions applying to, **6(S)**, 222
  damages, claim for, **6(S)**, 227
  devolution, alignment of provisions,
    6(S), 224
  educational establishments—
    checks, making, **6(S)**, 187–8
    members of governing body, check on,
      6(S), 186
  family and personal relationships, in course
    of, **6(S)**, 227
  meaning, **6(S)**, 178, 252–4
  monitoring—
    application, **6(S)**, 198–9
    ceasing, **6(S)**, 200
    cessation of registration **6(S)**, 206
    false declaration, offence of making,
      6(S), 206
    fees, **6(S)**, 200
    identification requirements, **6(S)**, 199
    independent monitor, **6(S)**, 201–2
    individual subject to, **6(S)**, 198
    notification of cessation of, **6(S)**, 205
    register, **6(S)**, 205
  Northern Ireland, provisions applying,
    6(S), 225
  offences, **6(S)**, 191–2
    exclusions and defences, **6(S)**, 192–3
  office holders—
    checks, making, **6(S)**, 187–8
    offences, **6(S)**, 187
  orders and regulations, **6(S)**, 231
  period condition, **6(S)**, 255
  personnel suppliers—
    barred person, supply of, **6(S)**, 182–3

vulnerable adult—*contd*
regulated activity relating to—*contd*
  personnel suppliers—*contd*
    employment business, failure to check,
      6(S), 260–1
    exclusions and defences, **6(S)**, 192–3
    failure to check on person engaging in,
      6(S), 186
    offences, **6(S)**, 191–2
    prescribed information, duty to refer,
      6(S), 208
  providers—
    duty to provide information on request,
      6(S), 209
    failure to check on person engaging in,
      6(S), 185
    meaning, **6(S)**, 179
    NHS employment, **6(S)**, 190
    prescribed information, duty to refer,
      6(S), 207
    private arrangements, **6(S)**, 179
    use of person not subject to monitoring,
      offence, **6(S)**, 183–4
  registers—
    barring and cessation of monitoring,
      notice of, **6(S)**, 214–15
    cessation of registration **6(S)**, 206
    duty to provide information on request,
      6(S), 214
    establishment and maintenance of,
      6(S), 205
    prescribed information, duty of keeper
      to refer, **6(S)**, 212–13
    vetting information, power to apply for,
      6(S), 215–16
  relevant records, prohibition of requirement
    to produce, **6(S)**, 201
  requirement to make monitoring check,
    exceptions to, **6(S)**, 188–9
  supervisory authorities—
    barring, notification of, **6(S)**, 221
    duty to provide information on request,
      6(S), 218
    meaning, **6(S)**, 217
    prescribed information, duty to refer,
      6(S), 216–18
    provision of information to, **6(S)**, 222
    vetting information, power to apply for,
      6(S), 218–19
  transitional provisions, **6(S)**, 264–5
  vetting information—
    provision of, **6(S)**, 203–4
    relevant, meaning, **6(S)**, 204
    table of, **6(S)**, 261–3
  Wales, provisions applying, **6(S)**, 225–6
residential accommodation, in, **6(S)**, 228
residential special school, in, **6(S)**, 228
vetting and barring scheme—
  Independent Barring Board. *See*
    Independent Barring Board
  summary of provisions, **6(S)**, 173
welfare service, reference to, **6(S)**, 229

W

wages
  agricultural. *See* **agricultural wages**
  deductions—
    employment tribunal, complaint to—
      determination of, **16**, [627], [628]
      presentation of, **16**, [626]
      remedies, **16**, [629]
    permitted, **16**, [617]
    reimbursements, as, **16**, [619]
    unauthorised, right not to suffer, **16**, [616]
  equal pay. *See* **equal pay**
  guarantee payments—
    amount and entitlement, limits on,
      16, [634]
    calculation of, **16**, [633]
    contractual remuneration, and, **16**, [635]
    employment tribunal, complaint to,
      16, [637]
    entitlement to, **16**, [631]
    exclusions from right to, **16**, [632]
    exemption orders, **16**, [638]
    indexation, **16**, [982]
    meaning, **16**, [631]
    power to modify provisions, **16**, [636]
  itemised pay statement—
    contents of, **16**, [611]
    employment tribunals, reference to—
      determination of, **16**, [615]
      requirement of, **16**, [614]
    fixed deductions, standing statement of,
      16, [612]
    power to amend provisions, **16**, [613]
    right to, **16**, [611]
  meaning, **16**, [630]
  national minimum—
    agency workers, **16**, [940]
    agricultural wages legislation—
      non-compliance, arrears payable in case
        of, **16**, [1032]
      relationship with, **16**, [956], [957]
    agricultural wages officers, information
      obtained by, **16**, [921]
    armed forces, **16**, [943]
    asylum seekers detained in removal centres,
      exclusion, **16**, [955]
    Cadet Force Adult Volunteers, **16**, [944]
    contracting-out, restriction on, **16**, [959]
    Crown employees, **16**, [942]
    definitions, **16**, [964], [965]
    detriment, right not to suffer, **16**, [934],
      [935]
    enforcement—
      burden of proof, reversal of, **16**, [936]
      notice of underpayment, **16**, [1033]
        appeals, **16**, [928]
        arrears, served in cases of, **16**, [925]
        contents of, **16**, [925]

wages—*contd*
  national minimum—*contd*
    enforcement—*contd*
      notice of underpayment—*contd*
        financial penalties—
          suspension of, **16**, [927]
          under, **16**, [926]
        non-compliance with—
          arrears, recovery of, **16**, [929]
          penalty, recovery of, **16**, [930]
        replacement notices, **16**, [932], [933]
        withdrawal of, **16**, [931]
      special classes of workers, **16**, [924]
    exclusions, **16**, [908], [909]
    first six months of employment, in,
      16, [908]
    general note, **16**, [1]
    home workers, **16**, [941]
    hourly rate of remuneration, determining,
      16, [907]
    House of Commons staff, **16**, [945]
    House of Lords staff, **16**, [945]
    individuals not otherwise workers,
      application of provisions to, **16**, [948]
    information, exchange of, **16**, [985]
    Low Pay Commission. *See* **Low Pay
      Commission**
    mariners, **16**, [947]
    non-compliance—
      additional remuneration—
        entitlement to, **16**, [923]
        formula for calculating, **16**, [923]
    offences, **16**, [937], [1035]
      body corporate, by, **16**, [938]
      proceedings, **16**, [939], [1035]
    officers—
      appointment of, **16**, [918]
      disclosure of information, **16**, [922]
      information obtained by, **16**, [920]
      powers of, **16**, [919], [1034]
    offshore employment, application of
      provisions to, **16**, [949]
    pay reference period, meaning, **16**, [906]
    persons discharging fines by unpaid work,
      exclusion, **16**, [954]
    persons under 26, **16**, [908]
    prisoners, exclusion, **16**, [953]
    publicity for provisions, **16**, [960]
    records—
      copies of, power to take, **16**, [1034]
      failure to allow access to, **16**, [916]
      production notice, **16**, [915]
      requirement to keep, **16**, [914]
      worker's right of access to, **16**, [915]
    regulations and orders, **16**, [961]
    religious communities, exclusion, **16**, [952]
    requirement to be paid, **16**, [906]

wages—*contd*
national minimum—*contd*
resident workers, exclusion, **16**, [952]
schemes, persons participating in, **16**, [908]
share fishermen, exclusion of, **16**, [950]
statement, provision of, **16**, [917]
superior employers, **16**, [958]
unfair dismissal, reason for, **16**, [755]
voluntary workers, exclusion of, **16**, [951]
work experience, persons in, **16**, [908]
payments to employer—
permitted, **16**, [618], [619]
right not to have to make, **16**, [618]
regulation, summary of provisions, **16**, [1]
retail employment, cash shortages and stock
deficits in—
cash shortage, meaning, **16**, [620]
deductions—
amount and time, limits on, **16**, [621]
references to, **16**, [620]
determination of wages, **16**, [622]
final instalment of wages, **16**, [625]
payments—
amount of, limits on, **16**, [624]
method and time of, limits on, **16**, [623]
retail employment, meaning, **16**, [620]
seamen's, **11(2)**, [917], [920]
stannaries. *See* **stannaries**
stock deficiency, meaning, **16**, [620]
week's pay—
average hourly rate, **16**, [870], [876]
calculation date—
rights during employment, **16**, [872]
termination, rights on, **16**, [873]
calculation of amount, **16**, [867]
maximum amount of, **16**, [874]
new employments, **16**, [875]
no normal working hours, employments
with, **16**, [871]
normal working hours, employments
with—
average hourly rate, **16**, [870]
remuneration for, **16**, [868]
time of work, remuneration varying
according to, **16**, [869]
special cases, **16**, [875], [876]

Wages Councils
transitional provisions, **16**, [535]

waggon
highway, driving on, **36**, [222]

Wales *See also* **National Assembly for Wales**
administrative areas, **25(2)**, [25]
air transport services, financial assistance for,
4(1), [519]
Auditor General. *See* **Auditor General for
Wales**
best value authorities, **26(1)**, [423]
code of practice, **26(1)**, [400], [401]
extension or disapplication of provisions,
26(1), [393]
fees, **26(1)**, [400]
grants, **26(2)**, [266]

Wales —*contd*
best value authorities—*contd*
inspections, **26(1)**, [404]
fees, **26(1)**, [407]
reports, **26(1)**, [409]
modification of enactments, **26(1)**, [413],
[414]
new powers, conferring, **26(1)**, [413],
[414]
performance indicators and standards,
26(1), [396]
performance plans—
audit, **26(1)**, [399]
code of practice, **26(1)**, [400], [401]
fees, **26(1)**, [400]
response to, **26(1)**, [402]
orders relating to, **26(1)**, [398]
preparation of, **26(1)**, [398]
reviews, **26(1)**, [397]
biodiversity lists and action, **32**, [807]
blighted land, transitional provisions,
46(S), 198
Boundary Commission. *See* **Local
Government Boundary Commission**
business improvement districts, provisions
applying, **26(2)**, [287]
careers services, inspection of,
15(2), [650]–[653]
Centre for Health—
accounts, **30**, [654]
Assembly directions, **30**, [654]
audit, **30**, [654]
chief executive, **30**, [654]
constitution, **30**, [645]
establishment of, **30**, [413], [645]
evidence, **30**, [654]
fees, charging of, **30**, [654]
functions, **30**, [646], [654]
general powers, **30**, [654]
members, **30**, [654]
regulations, **30**, [654]
reports, **30**, [654]
staff, **30**, [654]
Chief Inspector of Education and Training—
accounting officer, **10**, [1300]
accounts, **10**, [1300]
audit, **10**, [1300]
funding, **10**, [1266]
receipts, **10**, [1300]
status, **10**, [1300]
use of resources, examination into,
10, [1300]
child day-care providers—
inspection of, **6**, [404]
National Assembly's functions regarding,
6, [403]
child minders—
inspection of, **6**, [404]
National Assembly's functions regarding,
6, [403]
childcare, provision of. *See* **child care**
Children's Commissioner. *See* **Children's
Commissioner for Wales**
children's services authorities—
children and young people's plans, **6**, [939]

Wales —*contd*
  children's services authorities—*contd*
    functions—
      inspection of, **6**, [943]
      responsibility for, **6**, [940]
    information databases, **6**, [942]
    lead director for children and young
      people's services, appointment of, **6**, [940]
    Local Safeguarding Children Boards,
      functions relating to, **6**, [947]
    welfare, arrangements to safeguard and
      promote, **6**, [941]
    well-being, co-operation to improve,
      6, [938]
  climate change, report on, **35(S)**, 113–14
  Commissioner for Local Administration,
    abolition of office, **10**, [835]
  Commissioner for Older People. *See*
    Commissioner for Older People in
    Wales
  communities—
    applications concerning, **25(2)**, [37], [38]
    establishment of, **25(2)**, [25]
    grouping of, **25(2)**, [35]
    groups of—
      dissolution of, **25(2)**, [36]; **26(1)**, [170]
      separation of, **26(1)**, [170]
    names, change of, **25(2)**, [66]
    review of areas, **25(2)**, [49]
    schoolrooms, use of, **25(2)**, [132]
    status, **25(2)**, [206]
    town, having status of, **25(2)**, [208]
  community councils—
    accounts to be kept, **25(2)**, [151]
    acquisition of land by, **25(2)**, [122]
    annual meetings, **25(2)**, [251]
    applications concerning, **25(2)**, [37], [38]
    appropriation of land by, **25(2)**, [124]
    authentication of instruments, **25(2)**, [41]
    buildings, power to provide, **25(2)**, [131]
    byelaws—
      power to make, **25(2)**, [188]
      See further under **local authority**
    capital finance, **26(2)**, [320]
    car-sharing schemes, **26(1)**, [284]
    casual vacancies, **25(2)**, [78]
    chairman, **25(2)**, [43], [252]
      declaration by, **25(2)**, [72]
    compulsory acquisition of land on behalf
      of, **25(2)**, [123]
    constitution, **25(2)**, [41]
    consultation with, **25(2)**, [42]
    continuation, **25(2)**, [33]
    councillors—
      election of, **25(2)**, [44]
      electoral arrangements, **25(2)**, [246]
    crime prevention, **26(1)**, [287]
    disposal of land by, **25(2)**, [125]
    dissolution, application for, **25(2)**, [34]
    documents—
      custody of, **25(2)**, [178]
      deposit of, **25(2)**, [177]
      depositories for, **25(2)**, [179]
      inspection, right of, **25(2)**, [180]
    election of, **25(2)**, [44]

Wales —*contd*
  community councils—*contd*
    electoral arrangements, **25(2)**, [246]
    establishment, **25(2)**, [34]
    expenses of, **25(2)**, [151]
    grouping of communities under,
      25(2), [35]
    local energy saving measures, powers of,
      17(2), [586]
    meetings, **25(2)**, [251]
      provisions applied, **25(1)**, [626]
    members, temporary appointment,
      25(2), [80]
    minutes, right to inspect, **25(2)**, [180]
    officers, appointment, **25(2)**, [111]
    powers of, **25(2)**, [41]
    provisions applied to, **26(2)**, [250]
    public places, lighting of, **25(1)**, [518]
    roads, lighting of, **25(1)**, [518]
    standards committee, **26(2)**, [87]
    taxi fare concessions, arrangements for,
      26(1), [285]
    transport, investigations as to, **26(1)**, [286]
    vice-chairman, **25(2)**, [43]
    See further under **local authority**
  Community Health Councils—
    continuity of, **30**, [1298]
    duties of, **30**, [1340]
    regulations, **30**, [1340]
    Welsh Ministers, powers of, **30**, [1298]
  community meeting—
    authentication of instruments, **25(2)**, [40]
    constitution, **25(2)**, [40]
    convening, **25(2)**, [33], [252]
    council chairman may attend, **25(2)**, [252]
    minutes of proceedings, **25(2)**, [252]
    notice of, **25(2)**, [252]
    poll at, **25(2)**, [252]
    powers of, **25(2)**, [110]
    time and place of, **25(2)**, [252]
    voting at, **25(2)**, [252]
  community planning—
    community involvement, **25(S)**, 87–8
    guidance, issue of, **25(S)**, 88, 90
    interpretation, **25(S)**, 89
    local authority area, for, **25(S)**, 81
    partners—
      meaning, **25(S)**, 82–3
      participation by, **25(S)**, 81
    summary of provisions, **25(S)**, 47
    Welsh Ministers, role of, **25(S)**, 89
  community school, development work and
    experiments, **15(2)**, [425]
  community strategies—
    duty to review, **25(S)**, 84–5
    implementation, **25(S)**, 87
    interpretation, **25(S)**, 89
    monitoring, **25(S)**, 86
    production of, **25(S)**, 83–4
    review of, **25(S)**, 85–6
    summary of provisions, **25(S)**, 47
  Consolidated Fund. *See* **National Assembly**
    for Wales
  constituencies in, **15(3)**, [265]
  contracts, competitive tendering, **26(1)**, [174]

Wales —*contd*
coroners' districts, **11(1)**, [1210]
council tax discounts, **26(1)**, [13]
See also **council tax**
counties—
areas comprising, **25(2)**, [25]
county borough, change of status to,
25(2), [207]
preserved—
areas of, **25(2)**, [243]
lieutenancies, **26(1)**, [183]
sheriffs, **26(1)**, [184]
schedule of, **25(2)**, [241]
Countryside Council for—
advice from, **32**, [800]
areas of natural beauty—
advice on, **32**, [180]
designation of—
generally, **32**, [700]
orders, procedure for, **32**, [701]
area of special scientific interest,
compulsory acquisition of land for,
32, [266]
committees, **32**, [591]
constitution, **32**, [591]
countryside functions of, **32**, [576]
delegation of powers, **32**, [591]
directions to, **32**, [803]
documents, **32**, [591]
establishment of, **32**, [140]
functions. *See* **Nature Conservancy
Council**
functions of—
general, **32**, [254], [578]
national or international importance of,
32, [799]
purpose of, **32**, [798]
wildlife, as to, **32**, [801]
generally, **32**, [1]
grants and loans by, **32**, [579]
grants to, **32**, [475], [575]
incidental powers, **32**, [802]
information services, **32**, [182], [255]
Joint Nature Conservation Committee. *See*
**Joint Nature Conservation
Committee**
land, **32**, [591]
limestone pavements, **32**, [439]
maps—
conclusive form, in—
generally, **32**, [661]
review of, **32**, [662]
confirmed—
appeals against—
generally, **32**, [658]
National Assembly, delegation of
functions, **32**, [660], [723]
procedure, **32**, [659]
draft form, publication in, **32**, [657]
duty to prepare, **32**, [656]
regulations, **32**, [663]
membership of, **32**, [574], [591]
Minister giving directions to, **32**, [141]
National Assembly, creation of, **32**, [848]
national nature reserve, declaring, **32**, [464]

Wales —*contd*
Countryside Council for—*contd*
nature conservation functions, **32**, [577]
new functions of, **32**, [255]
proceedings, **32**, [591]
remuneration and allowances, **32**, [591]
reports and accounts, **32**, [591]
sites of special scientific interest, **32**, [439]
staff, **32**, [591]
transitional provisions, **32**, [592]
See also **Nature Conservancy Council**
county borough council—
chairman, **25(2)**, [27]
election, **25(2)**, [28]
title, **25(2)**, [31]
constitution, **25(2)**, [26]
vice-chairman, title, **25(2)**, [31]
county boroughs—
counties, change of status, **25(2)**, [207]
electoral arrangements, **25(2)**, [246]
list of, **25(2)**, [242]
county council—
constitution, **25(2)**, [26]
grants, transport matters, **25(2)**, [303]
See also principal councils *below*
curriculum—
assessment arrangements, meaning,
15(2), [411]
attainment targets, meaning, **15(2)**, [411]
basic, **15(2)**, [415]
general requirements, **15(2)**, [413]
duty to implement, **15(2)**, [414]
National—
establishment by order, **15(2)**, [422]
exceptions—
development work and experiments,
15(2), [425]
regulations, by, **15(2)**, [426]
special educational needs, pupils
with, **15(2)**, [427]
temporary, for individual pupils,
15(2), [428]–[430]
foundation stage, **15(2)**, [416], [418]
implementation of, **15(2)**, [423]
individual pupils, directions for
temporary exceptions—
appeals, **15(2)**, [430]
conditions, **15(2)**, [428]
information concerning, **15(2)**, [429]
regulations, **15(2)**, [428]
key stages, **15(2)**, [417]
first, **15(2)**, [419]
second, **15(2)**, [419]
third, **15(2)**, [419]
fourth, **15(2)**, [420]–[421]
nursery schools, implementation in
respect of, **15(2)**, [424]
order, establishment by, **15(2)**, [422]
orders and regulations, procedure for
making, **15(2)**, [431]
programmes of research in relation to,
15(2), [432]
National Assembly, powers as to,
15(2), [882]
school year, meaning, **15(2)**, [411]

Wales —*contd*
dental services—
 charges, **30**, [1241]
  exemptions, **30**, [1242]
 dental public health functions, **30**, [1183]
 general, contracts—
  disputes, **30**, [1178]
  enforcement, **30**, [1178]
  entry into, **30**, [1173]
  payments, **30**, [1176]
  persons eligible to enter into, **30**, [1175]
  primary services, requirement to
   provide, **30**, [1174]
  required terms, **30**, [1177]
  requirements, **30**, [1173]
 Local Dental Committees, **30**, [1185]
 primary—
  accommodation, provision of, **30**, [1186]
  arrangements for provision of, **30**, [1180]
  assistance and support for, **30**, [1184]
  Local Health Boards—
   duty of, **30**, [1172]
   functions of, **30**, [1130]
  persons performing, lists of, **30**, [1179]
  persons with whom agreements made,
   30, [1181]
  regulations as to arrangements,
   30, [1182]
  remuneration, arrangements for payment
   of, **30**, [1296]
development plan—
 joint unitary, **46**, [277]
 National Parks, for, **46**, [279]
 meaning, **46**, [284]
 transitional provisions, **46**, [286], [617]
devolution, **30**, [610]
 general note, **10**, [1]
 referendums—
  advertisements, **10**, [1258]
  application of enactments, **10**, [1258]
  ballot papers, **10**, [1257]–[1258]
  Chief Counting Officer, **10**, [1250]
  conduct of, **10**, [1258]
  counting, **10**, [1258]
  counting officers, **10**, [1258]
  expenditure, **10**, [1253]
  holding, **10**, [1250]
  hours of polling, **10**, [1258]
  legal proceedings, exclusion of,
   10, [1252]
  premises, **10**, [1258]
  returning officers, **10**, [1258]
district council. *See* principal councils *below*
education and training, duty to participate
 in, **15(S)**, Education 178
education, local curriculum. *See* local
 curriculum *below*
education, training and skills services—
 curriculum information, provision of,
  15(S), Education 370–1
 further education institutions, provision
  by, **15(S)**, Education 366–7
 governing bodies, duties of,
  15(S), Education 367

Wales —*contd*
education, training and skills services—*contd*
 learning pathways—
  document, **15(S)**, Education 368–9
  interpretation, **15(S)**, Education 369–70
 maintained schools, provision by,
  15(S), Education 366–7
 services, summary of provisions,
  15(S), Education 329–30
educational support for 11 to 25 year olds,
 15(2), [288]–[294]
electoral arrangements, **25(2)**, [246]
family proceedings—
 advisory and support services for, **6**, [979]
 Children and Family Court Advisory and
  Support Service—
  property transferred to Assembly,
   6, [955]
  sharing information with Assembly,
   6, [954]
  staff transferred to Assembly, **6**, [956]
 National Assembly—
  ancillary powers, **6**, [949]
  functions regarding, **6**, [948]
  property transferred from CAFCASS,
   6, [955]
  sharing information with CAFCASS,
   6, [954]
  staff transferred from CAFCASS,
   6, [956]
  officers, **6**, [950]
   adoption agency records, right of access
    to, **6**, [829]
   rules of appointment, **6**, [828]
fire services, **26(1)**, [151]
Forestry Commissioners—
 accounting officer, **10**, [1301]
 accounts, **10**, [1301]
 audit, **10**, [1301]
 exercise of functions, **10**, [1301]
 funding, **10**, [1267]
 receipts, **10**, [1301]
 reports, **10**, [1301]
 status, **10**, [1301]
 use of resources, examination into,
  10, [1301]
former health care providers and social
 landlords, modification of provisions,
 10, [841]
foster parents and fostering, registration
 scheme, power to establish, **6**, [958]–[959]
fraud and unlawful activities, protection of
 NHS from—
 compulsory disclosure of documents,
  30, [1259]
 disclosure notice—
  contents of, **30**, [1261]
  delegation of functions,
   30, [1263]–[1264]
  disclosure of information obtained,
   30, [1265]
  manner of service, **30**, [1267]
  personal information, protection of,
   30, [1266]
  power to serve, **30**, [1261]

Wales —*contd*
fraud and unlawful activities, protection of
NHS from—*contd*
disclosure notice—*contd*
production of documents, **30**, [1262]
interpretation, **30**, [1274]
offences—
bodies corporate, by, **30**, [1270]
disclosure or use of information,
30, [1269]
partnership, by, **30**, [1271]
penalties, **30**, [1272]
production of documents, relating to,
30, [1268]
unincorporated association, by,
30, [1271]
orders and regulations, **30**, [1273]
persons and bodies, provisions applying to,
30, [1260]
further education—
governors, appointment by National
Assembly, **15(2)**, [219]
institutions, training in provision of,
15(2), [451]
gamekeepers, appointment, **2**, [159]
General Teaching Council for. *See* **General
Teaching Council for Wales**
grant-aided institutions, transfer of property
to, **15(1)**, [362]
health and well-being strategies, **30**, [1156]
health authorities, abolition, **30**, [791]
Health Professions Wales—
establishment of, **30**, [647]
functions, **30**, [647]
further provisions about, **30**, [648]
health service bodies—
directed partnership arrangements—
directions, **30**, [1152]–[1153]
Welsh Ministers, direction by, **30**, [1152]
directions and regulations, **30**, [1147]
goods and services, supply of—
local authorities, by, **30**, [1148]
Welsh Ministers, by, **30**, [1154]–[1155]
local authorities, arrangements with,
30, [1149], [1344]
Local Health Boards. *See* Local Health
Boards *below*
losses and liabilities, scheme for meeting,
30, [1146]
meaning, **30**, [1123]
members—
allowances, **30**, [1295]
NHS Trust. *See* NHS Trust *below*
Northern Ireland, in, **30**, [1124]
remuneration, arrangements for payment
of, **30**, [1294]
residual liabilities, transfer of, **30**, [1145]
Special Health Authority. *See* Special
Health Authority *below*
Health Service Commissioner for. *See* **Health
Service Commissioners**
health services in—
advisory committees, **30**, [1306], [1346]
births, notification of, **30**, [1316]

Wales —*contd*
health services in—*contd*
charges—
dental services, for, **30**, [1241]–[1242]
designated services or facilities, for,
30, [1251]
drugs, medicines and appliances, for,
30, [1237]
employed patients, **30**, [1254]
general, exemption from, **30**, [1238]
goods and services, recovery for,
30, [1256]
more expensive supplies for, **30**, [1249]
non-residents, in respect of, **30**, [1240]
offences, **30**, [1258]
optical appliances, for, **30**, [1244]–[1245]
part payment, hospital accommodations
on, **30**, [1253]
penalties for non-payment, **30**, [1257]
pharmaceutical services, for, **30**, [1201],
[1237], [1243]
pre-payment certificates, **30**, [1239]
recovery of, **30**, [1255]–[1256]
remission and repayment of, **30**, [1246]
repairs and replacements, for, **30**, [1250]
sums otherwise payable to persons
providing services, **30**, [1252]
travelling expenses, **30**, [1247]–[1248]
complaints, independent advocacy services
for, **30**, [1303]
contraceptive services, **30**, [1326]
deaths, notification of, **30**, [1316]
development, persons displaced by,
30, [1315]
disabled persons, provision of vehicles for,
30, [1326]
exempt information—
descriptions of, **30**, [1341]
interpretation, **30**, [1343]
qualifications, **30**, [1342]
fraud and unlawful activities, protection
from. *See* fraud and unlawful activities,
protection of NHS from *above*
high security psychiatric services, provision
of, **30**, [1120]
interpretation, **30**, [1322]–[1323]
intervention orders—
effect of, **30**, [1143]
power to make, **30**, [1142]
suspension of members under,
30, [1143]
money, raising, **30**, [1285]
NHS contracts—
arrangements treated as, **30**, [1125]
commissioners, **30**, [1123]
meaning, **30**, [1123]
providers, **30**, [1123]
orders, regulations and directions,
30, [1319]–[1321]
performance outside Wales, **30**, [1122]
prison service, joint working with,
30, [1304]
private practice, permissions for use of
facilities in, **30**, [1314]

Wales —*contd*
  health services in—*contd*
    property, acquisition, use and maintenance
      of, **30**, [1275]
    property transferred under 1946 Act—
      free of trusts, **30**, [1282]
      general hospital purposes, previously held
        for, **30**, [1283]
      voluntary hospitals, **30**, [1284]
    public-private partnerships, **30**, [1286]
    pupils, medical examination of, **30**, [1326]
    special trustees, transfer of functions or
      property to and from, **30**, [1278]–[1279]
    transfer of functions, **30**, [1351]
    trust property—
      application of, **30**, [1280]
      special trustees, transfer of functions or
        property to and from,
        30, [1278]–[1279]
      supplementary provisions, **30**, [1281]
      transfers of, **30**, [1277]
    voluntary organisations—
      provision of services, arrangements for,
        30, [1126]
    Welsh Ministers—
      default powers, **30**, [1144]
      duty of to promote, **30**, [1117]
      emergency powers, **30**, [1307]
      expenditure on community services,
        payments towards, **30**, [1312]
      general power of, **30**, [1118]
      goods and services, supply of,
        30, [1154]–[1155]
      high security psychiatric services,
        provision of, **30**, [1120]
      NHS trusts, directions to, **30**, [1135]
      other bodies, arrangements with,
        30, [1126]
      particular services, provision of,
        30, [1119]
      performance of functions outside Wales,
        30, [1122]
      research, powers as to, **30**, [1326]
      services provided by, **30**, [1326]
      standing advisory committees,
        30, [1305], [1345]
      supplies not readily obtainable,
        arrangement for, **30**, [1309]
      territorial limit of exercise of functions,
        30, [1318]
  higher education, provision of, **15(2)**, [452]
  Housing for. *See* **Housing for Wales**
  housing functions, devolution, **24**, [413]
  independent schools, inspection,
    15(2), [473]–[474]
  inquiries, **10**, [880]
  inspection of schools. *See* **Her Majesty's
    Chief Inspector of Education and
    Training in Wales; Office for Standards
    in Education, Children's Services and
    Skills**
  joint authorities, **26(1)**, [159]
  joint boards and committees, **26(1)**, [181]
  Land Authority for—
    ceasing to exist, **10**, [1275]

Wales —*contd*
  Land Authority for—*contd*
    functions ceasing to exist, **10**, [1272]
    transitional provisions, **10**, [1274]
    Welsh Development Agency, transfer of
      property and staff etc to, **10**, [1273]
  learner travel—
    arrangements—
      certain types of education or training,
        not to favour, **15(S)**, Education 77–8
      charge for, **15(S)**, Education 89
      co-operation with, **15(S)**, Education 85
      compulsory school age, for child of,
        15(S), Education 72–3
      general note, **15(S)**, Education 63–5
      information, publication of,
        15(S), Education 84
      learners in post-16 education and
        training, for, **15(S)**, Education 75–6
      local authorities, powers of,
        15(S), Education 74–5
      meaning, **15(S)**, Education 66
      nursery education, to and from,
        15(S), Education 76
      school attendance, **15(S)**, Education 87
      suitable, **15(S)**, Education 73
      transport, **15(S)**, Education 69–72
      withdrawal, **15(S)**, Education 81–2
    behaviour code—
      enforcement, **15(S)**, Education 80–2
      general note, **15(S)**, Education 64
      making, **15(S)**, Education 79
      meaning, **15(S)**, Education 79
      withdrawal of travel arrangements,
        enforcement by, **15(S)**, Education 81–2
    costs, payment by local authority looking
      after child, **15(S)**, Education 85
    duties, limits of, **15(S)**, Education 74
    guidance and directions,
      15(S), Education 83
    interpretation, **15(S)**, Education 91–2
    learners, meaning, **15(S)**, Education 67
    needs—
      duty to assess, **15(S)**, Education 67–8
      meaning, **15(S)**, Education 68
    ordinary residence, determination of,
      15(S), Education 86
    relevant places, **15(S)**, Education 67
    sustainable modes of, **15(S)**, Education 64,
      79
  legislation, interpretation provisions applied,
    41, [600]
  lieutenancies, **26(1)**, [183]
  lieutenants—
    appointment of, **26(1)**, [271]
    areas, **26(1)**, [280]
    clerks, **26(1)**, [275]
    functions, **26(1)**, [276]
    lord-lieutenant—
      absence of, **26(1)**, [274]
      appointment of, **26(1)**, [271]
      deputies, **26(1)**, [272]
      vice, **26(1)**, [273]
    transitional provisions, **26(1)**, [281]

Wales —*contd*
local Acts and instruments—
application of, **26(1)**, [179]
modification of, **26(1)**, [180]
local authorities, representations to,
consideration of, **6**, [337]
local authority—
acquisition of land by, **9**, [430]
area alterations etc affecting, **25(2)**, [58]
charitable purposes, property held for,
26(1), [171]
continuity of exercise of functions,
26(1), [175]
disposals and contracts, control of,
26(1), [173]
employees—
continuity of employment in case of
voluntary transfer, **26(1)**, [163]
diminution of emoluments,
compensation for, **26(1)**, [165]
loss of office, compensation for,
26(1), [165]
redundancy payments, **26(1)**, [166]
termination of employment,
compensation for, **26(1)**, [167]
transfers, **26(1)**, [164]
existing, committees of, **26(1)**, [168]
for, **15(S)**, Education 90
goods and services, supply of, **30**, [1148]
members. *See* **local authority**
name, change of, **25(2)**, [64]
NHS bodies—
arrangements with, **30**, [1149], [1344]
payments to, **30**, [1150]
overview and scrutiny committees—
exempt information, **30**, [1302]
functions of, **30**, [1300]
joint, **30**, [1301]
savings, **26(1)**, [191]
transitional provisions, **26(1)**, [192]
Welsh Church funds, **26(1)**, [172]
local curriculum—
operation of, regulations,
15(S), Education 371–2
pupils in Key Stage 4—
alteration or removal of requirements,
15(S), Education 348
children being registered pupils of special
schools, application of provisions to,
15(S), Education 347
children not being registered pupils,
application of provisions to,
15(S), Education 346
courses, pupils' choice of,
15(S), Education 338
directions, **15(S)**, Education 348
duty to implement,
15(S), Education 334
entitlements—
delivery of, **15(S)**, Education 341,
344
head teacher's decision as to,
15(S), Education 340
head teacher's decision to remove,
15(S), Education 341–2

Wales —*contd*
local curriculum—*contd*
pupils in Key Stage 4—*contd*
entitlements—*contd*
pupils, of, **15(S)**, Education 339
formation of, **15(S)**, Education 335
interpretation, **15(S)**, Education 332–3
joint-working—
delivery of entitlements,
15(S), Education 344
guidance and directions,
15(S), Education 345
planning, **15(S)**, Education 343
learning domain, power to amend,
15(S), Education 346
maintained schools, for,
15(S), Education 334
more than one, authorities with,
15(S), Education 337
planning, **15(S)**, Education 343
regulations and orders,
15(S), Education 349
summary of provisions,
15(S), Education 327–8
Welsh language, taught in,
15(S), Education 336–7
students aged 16–18—
children being registered pupils of special
schools or having learning difficulties,
application of provisions to,
15(S), Education 364
courses, pupils' choice of,
15(S), Education 353–4
directions, **15(S)**, Education 363–4
education and training,
15(S), Education 349
entitlements—
delivery of, **15(S)**, Education 357,
359–60
head teacher's or principal's decision as
to, **15(S)**, Education 355–6
head teacher's or principal's decision
to remove, **15(S)**, Education 357–8
students, of, **15(S)**, Education 355
formation of, **15(S)**, Education 350
institutions within higher education
sector, application of
provisions to, **15(S)**, Education 365
interpretation, **15(S)**, Education 362–3
joint-working—
delivery of entitlements,
15(S), Education 359–60
guidance and directions,
15(S), Education 361
planning, **15(S)**, Education 358–9
learning domain, power to amend,
15(S), Education 362
more than one, areas with,
15(S), Education 351
planning, **15(S)**, Education 358–9
regulations and orders,
15(S), Education 366
relevant school or institution,
determination of, **15(S)**, Education 352

Wales —*contd*
  local curriculum—*contd*
    students aged 16–18—*contd*
      summary of provisions,
        15(S), Education 328–9
      Welsh language, taught in,
        15(S), Education 351
  Local Dental Committees, **30**, [1185]
  local development plan—
    adoption of, **46**, [1019]
    Assembly, intervention by, **46**, [1017]
    community involvement scheme, in
      accordance with, **46**, [1015]
    contents of, **46**, [1014]
    default power, **46**, [1023]
    independent examination of, **46**, [1016],
      [1046]
    joint, **46**, [1024]
    preparation requirements, **46**, [1015]
    regulations, **46**, [1029]
    requirement to prepare, **46**, [1014]
    review, **46**, [1021]
    revision, **46**, [1022]
    revocation, **46**, [1020]
    withdrawal, **46**, [1018]
  local education authority—
    partnership agreements and statements,
      15(2), [506]
    publication and provision of material by,
      15(2), [505]
    recreational facilities, providing,
      15(1), [631]
    social and physical training facilities,
      providing, **15(1)**, [631]
  local government areas—
    name, change of, **25(2)**, [64]
    administration commissions. *See*
      **Commissions for Local
      Administration**
    alteration, watercourse forming boundary,
      25(2), [63]
    counties, list of, **25(2)**, [241]
    divisions of, **25(2)**, [25]
    electoral divisions, **25(2)**, [30]
    former, replacement of, **25(2)**, [25]
  local government bodies—
    advisory notice—
      effect of, **26(2)**, [379]
      issue by auditor, **26(2)**, [378]
      legal actions, **26(2)**, [380]
      meaning, **26(2)**, [378]
      withdrawal, **26(2)**, [378]
    audit of accounts—
      auditors. *See* auditors *below*
      code of audit practice, **26(2)**, [361]
      documents, inspection of, **26(2)**, [375]
      extraordinary, **26(2)**, [382]
      immediate reports, publicity for,
        26(2), [372]
      meetings, publicity for, **26(2)**, [371]
      non-immediate reports, publicity for,
        26(2), [373]
      objections, right to make, **26(2)**, [376]
      officers, of, **26(2)**, [383]

Wales —*contd*
  local government bodies—*contd*
    audit of accounts—*contd*
      police authorities, documents relating
        to, **26(2)**, [385]
      questions at, **26(2)**, [375]
      regulations, **26(2)**, [384]
      reports and recommendations, procedure
        for consideration of, **26(2)**, [370]
      requirement, **26(2)**, [358]
      statements of accounts, inspection of,
        26(2), [374]
    auditors—
      advisory notice, issue of, **26(2)**, [378]
      appointment of, **26(2)**, [359], [423]
      disclosure of information, **26(2)**, [399],
        [400]
      documents and information, rights to,
        26(2), [363], [364]
      fees, **26(2)**, [365], [366]
      general duties, **26(2)**, [362]
      general reports, **26(2)**, [368]
      inspection of reports, **26(2)**, [374]
      judicial review, claim for, **26(2)**, [381]
      meaning, **26(2)**, [405]
      persons assisting, arrangements for,
        26(2), [360]
      public interest reports, **26(2)**, [367],
        [369]
      unlawful item of account, declaration as
        to, **26(2)**, [377]
      meaning, **26(2)**, [357]
    performance standards—
      information, publication of,
        26(2), [391]–[394]
      relevant body for, **26(2)**, [391]
      studies by Auditor General, request for,
        26(2), [389]
    local government finance reports, **26(2)**, [269]
    local government functions—
      general provision for transfer of,
        26(1), [147]
      specific, transfer of, **26(1)**, [150]
    local government improvement—
      annual improvement reports, **25(S)**, 70
      aspects of, **25(S)**, 52–4
        amendment, **25(S)**, 55
        interpretation, **25(S)**, 53
      assessments, **25(S)**, 64
      audit and assessment reports—
        Auditor General, issue by, **25(S)**, 64–5
        each authority, for, **25(S)**, 64–5
        response to, **25(S)**, 66
      Auditor General—
        annual improvement reports, **25(S)**, 70
        audit and assessment reports,
          25(S), 64–6
        co-ordination of regulatory functions,
          25(S), 69–70
        improvement assessments, **25(S)**, 64
        information and planning audit,
          25(S), 63
        information sharing, **25(S)**, 79
        scales of fees, prescription of,
          25(S), 73–4

Wales —*contd*
  local government improvement—*contd*
    Auditor General—*contd*
      special inspections, **25(S)**, 67–9
      statement of practice, **25(S)**, 71
    authority—
      collaboration, powers of, **25(S)**, 57–9
      fire and rescue, delegation by, **25(S)**, 57
      general duty, **25(S)**, 51
      information related to performance,
        collection of, **25(S)**, 59
      information, publication of, **25(S)**, 60–1
      meaning, **25(S)**, 50
      objectives, **25(S)**, 51–2
      performance indicators, use of,
        25(S), 60
      planning, **25(S)**, 60–1
    consultation, **25(S)**, 54
    guidance, **25(S)**, 54, 90
    information and planning—
      arrangements for, **25(S)**, 60–1
      audit, **25(S)**, 63
    inspectors, powers and duties, **25(S)**, 72–3
    interpretation, **25(S)**, 80
    objectives, **25(S)**, 51–2
    performance indicators and standards,
      25(S), 55–6
    relevant functions—
      co-ordination, **25(S)**, 69–70
      meaning, **25(S)**, 62
    relevant regulators—
      co-ordination of regulatory functions,
        25(S), 69–70
      information sharing, **25(S)**, 79
      meaning, **25(S)**, 62
      use of information by, **25(S)**, 80
    special inspections—
      Auditor General, by, **25(S)**, 67–8
      report of, **25(S)**, 68
    summary of provisions, **25(S)**, 45–7
    Welsh Ministers—
      authorities, supporting, **25(S)**, 74–5
      enactments, power to modify,
        25(S), 77–9
      new powers, conferring, **25(S)**, 77–9
      orders, procedure for, **25(S)**, 78–9
      powers of direction, etc, **25(S)**, 75–7
  local government provisions applied to,
    26(2), [255]
  local health board—
    accommodation or services, making
      available, **30**, [1329]
    accounts and audit, **30**, [1339]
    administration and management of
      services, **30**, [1131]
    advice for, **30**, [1132]
    body corporate, as, **30**, [1327]
    compulsory acquisition, **30**, [1329]
    consultation requirements, **30**, [1127]
    dental public health functions, **30**, [1183]
    dissolution, **30**, [1329]
    duties, regulations, **30**, [1329]
    establishment of, **30**, [1127]
    expenditure, **30**, [1338]

Wales —*contd*
  local health board—*contd*
    expenditure on community services,
      payments towards—
        conditions, **30**, [1310]
        scope of, **30**, [1310]
        voluntary organisations, in respect of,
          30, [1311]
    externally financed development
      agreements, entry into, **30**, [1329]
    financial duties, **30**, [1291]
    functions of—
      directions, **30**, [1128]–[1129]
      exercise of, **30**, [1129]
      primary dental services, as to, **30**, [1130]
      primary medical services, as to,
        30, [1130]
    general power of, **30**, [1329]
    health and well-being strategies, **30**, [1156]
    improvement of health, strategy for,
      30, [1133]
    LHB orders, **30**, [1328]
    local authorities, payments from, **30**, [1150]
    membership, **30**, [1327]
    ophthalmic services, provision of,
      30, [1187]. See also ophthalmic services *below*
    pharmaceutical services, provision of,
      30, [1196]. See also pharmaceutical services *below*
    primary dental services, duty as to,
      30, [1172]. See also dental services *above*
    primary medical services, duty as to,
      30, [1157]. See also medical services *below*
    property, transfer of, **30**, [1329]
    public funding, **30**, [1290]
    public involvement and consultation,
      30, [1299]
    research by, **30**, [1329]
    residual liabilities, transfer of, **30**, [1145]
    resource limits, **30**, [1292]
    rights and liabilities, **30**, [1329]
    staff, **30**, [1327]
      transfer of, **30**, [1329]
    status, **30**, [1327]
    training, **30**, [1329]
  Local Medical Committees, **30**, [459], [1170]
  local non-domestic rating lists, **25(2)**, [723]
  Local Optical Committees, **30**, [457]–[458],
    [1194]
  Local Pharmaceutical Committees, **30**, [1206]
  local planning authorities—
    principal councils as, **26(1)**, [148]
    unitary development plans, transitional
      provisions, **26(1)**, [189]
  local planning authority in, **46**, [262]
    annual monitoring report, **46**, [1028]
    guidance to, **46**, [1027]
    matters kept under review, **46**, [1013]
    meaning, **46**, [1030]
    plan. See local development plan *above*
  Local Safeguarding Children Boards—
    children's services authority, functions of,
      6, [947]
    establishment of, **6**, [944]
    functions of, **6**, [945]
    funding, **6**, [946]

Wales —*contd*
  Local Safeguarding Children Boards—*contd*
    objective, **6**, [945]
    procedure, **6**, [945]
  local social services authority—
    care and after-care by, **30**, [1347]
    functions of, **30**, [1308]
    mothers and young children, care of,
      30, [1347]
    prevention of illness, arrangements for,
      30, [1347]
    Primary Care Trust, payments by,
      30, [1062]
    research by, **30**, [1347]
    residential accommodation, provision of,
      30, [1308]
  magistrates' courts, areas of, **26(1)**, [177]
  maintained school—
    admission, prohibition on interviews,
      15(S), Education 306
    code of practice for securing effective
      relationship with LEA, **15(2)**, [123]
    committees or adjudicators for, **15(2)**, [28]
    curriculum—
      basic, **15(2)**, [415]
      general requirements, **15(2)**, [413]–[414]
      National. *See* curriculum *above*
    financing—
      financial statements, certification by
        Auditor General, **15(2)**, [50]
      minimum schools budget for LEA,
        Assembly's power to set,
        15(2), [40D]–[40F]
      school funding provisions, Assembly's
        power to repeal, **15(2)**, [40F]
      schools budget, LEAs to determine,
        15(2), [40B]–[40C]
    governing bodies—
      annual parents' meeting, **15(2)**, [374]
      reports, **15(2)**, [49]
    school terms and holidays, fixing dates of,
      15(S), Education 87–9
  meaning, **25(2)**, [228]; **41**, [605]
  medical examinations, payments for,
    30, [1297]
  medical services—
    general, contracts—
      disputes, **30**, [1164]
      drugs, prescription of, **30**, [1162]
      enforcement, **30**, [1164]
      entry into, **30**, [1158]
      payments, **30**, [1161]
      persons eligible to enter into, **30**, [1160]
      primary services, requirement to
        provide, **30**, [1159]
      required terms, **30**, [1163]
      requirements, **30**, [1158]
    Local Medical Committees, **30**, [1170]
    primary—
      accommodation, provision of, **30**, [1171]
      arrangements for provision of, **30**, [1166]
      assistance and support for, **30**, [1169]
      Local Health Boards, duty of, **30**, [1157]
      Local Health Boards, functions of,
        30, [1130]

Wales —*contd*
  medical services—*contd*
    primary—*contd*
      persons performing, lists of, **30**, [1165]
      persons with whom agreements made,
        30, [1167]
      regulations as to arrangements,
        30, [1168]
      remuneration, arrangements for payment
        of, **30**, [1296]
  National Assembly. *See* **National Assembly
    for Wales**
  National Council for Education and Training.
    See **National Council for Education and
    Training for Wales**
  National Health Service. *See* **National
    Health Service**
  National Park—
    authorities, **32**, [601]
    provisions applying to, **32**, [142], [470]
    unitary development plans for, **46**, [278]
      joint, **46**, [278]
  NHS bodies. *See* **National Health Service**
  NHS trusts—
    accommodation or services, payment for,
      30, [1331]
    accounts and audit, **30**, [1339]
    additional income, **30**, [1331]
    board of directors, **30**, [1330]
    body corporate, as, **30**, [1330]
    borrowing by, **30**, [1334]
    Care Trusts, designation as, **30**, [1151]
    compulsory acquisition, **30**, [1331]
    consecrated land and burial grounds, use
      and development of, **30**, [1333]
    directions to, **30**, [1135]
    dissolution, **30**, [1332]
    establishment of, **30**, [1134]
    establishment prior to operational date,
      30, [1330]
    externally financed development
      agreements, entry into, **30**, [1331]
    financial obligations, **30**, [1334]
    first NHS trust order, **30**, [1330]
    further powers, conferral of, **30**, [1331]
    general duty of, **30**, [1136]
    investment by, **30**, [1334]
    joint exercise of functions, **30**, [1331]
    NHS contracts, entry into, **30**, [1331]
    originating capital, **30**, [1334]
    pay and allowances, **30**, [1330]
    pensions, provision of, **30**, [1331]
    powers and duties, **30**, [1331]
    property and liabilities, transfer of,
      30, [1330]
    public dividend capital, **30**, [1334]
    regulations, **30**, [1330]
    reports and information, **30**, [1330]
    research by, **30**, [1331]
    residual liabilities, transfer of, **30**, [1145]
    staff, **30**, [1330]–[1331]
    status, **30**, [1330]
    supplementary payments to, **30**, [1334]
    surplus funds, **30**, [1334]
    training, **30**, [1331]

Wales —*contd*
 NHS trusts—*contd*
  trust funds and trustees, **30**, [1330]
 nursery education, funded, **15(2)**, [412]
 nursery school—
  maintained—
   curriculum—
    basic, **15(2)**, [415]
    general requirements,
     15(2), [413]–[414]
    National, *See under* curriculum *above*
 offshore generating station, development of,
  46(S), 55
 ophthalmic services—
  charges, **30**, [1244]–[1245]
  disqualification of practitioners—
   conditions, **30**, [1223]
   national, **30**, [1231]
   regulations, **30**, [1234]
   withdrawal from list, **30**, [1233]
  general—
   accommodation, provision of, **30**, [1195]
   arrangements for, **30**, [1187]
   choice of practitioners, **30**, [1190]
   expenditure on, **30**, [1338]
   inadequate provision of, **30**, [1191]
   medical practitioners, qualifications of,
    30, [1189]
   regulations, **30**, [1188]
   remuneration, **30**, [1192]–[1193]
    arrangements for payment of,
     30, [1296]
  Local Optical Committees, **30**, [1194]
  practitioners—
   contingent removal of, **30**, [1224]
   disqualification. *See* disqualification of
    practitioners *above*
   fraud and unsuitability, **30**, [1225]
   indemnity cover, **30**, [1236]
   national disqualification, **30**, [1231]
   notification of decisions, **30**, [1232]
   Scotland and Northern Ireland,
    corresponding provisions in, **30**, [1235]
   suspension. *See* suspension of
    practitioners *below*
   withdrawal from list, **30**, [1233]
  qualifications to practice—
   conditional inclusion in lists, **30**, [1220]
   supplementary lists, **30**, [1221]–[1222]
  suspension of practitioners, **30**, [1226]
   appeals, **30**, [1230]
   effect of, **30**, [1228]
   notification of decisions, **30**, [1232]
   pending appeal, **30**, [1227]
   regulations, **30**, [1234]
   review of, **30**, [1229]
 Partnership Council for, **10**, [1537]
 pharmaceutical services—
  accommodation, provision of, **30**, [1207]
  additional, arrangements for, **30**, [1197]
  application of enactments, **30**, [1219]
  arrangements for, **30**, [1196]
  charges, **30**, [1237], [1243]
  disqualification of practitioners—
   conditions, **30**, [1223]

Wales —*contd*
 pharmaceutical services—*contd*
  disqualification of practitioners—*contd*
   national, **30**, [1231]
   regulations, **30**, [1234]
   withdrawal from list, **30**, [1233]
  expenditure on, **30**, [1338]
  fees, power to charge, **30**, [1201]
  inadequate provision of, **30**, [1203]
  Local Pharmaceutical Committees,
   30, [1206]
  local, pilot schemes—
   application of provisions, **30**, [1215]
   contents of, **30**, [1208]
   control of entry regulations, **30**, [1217]
   establishment of, **30**, [1208]
   making, **30**, [1209], [1336]
   NHS contracts, **30**, [1213]
   premises from which service provided,
    30, [1216]
   preparatory work, funding, **30**, [1214]
   priority neighbourhoods or premises,
    designation of, **30**, [1210]
   provision of services, **30**, [1213]
   reviews, **30**, [1211]
   termination, **30**, [1212]
   variation, **30**, [1212]
  LPS schemes, **30**, [1218], [1337]
  persons authorised to provide, **30**, [1202]
  practitioners—
   contingent removal of, **30**, [1224]
   disqualification. *See* disqualification of
    practitioners *above*
   fraud and unsuitability, **30**, [1225]
   indemnity cover, **30**, [1236]
   national disqualification, **30**, [1231]
   notification of decisions, **30**, [1232]
   Scotland and Northern Ireland,
    corresponding provisions in, **30**, [1235]
   suspension. *See* suspension of
    practitioners *below*
   withdrawal from list, **30**, [1233]
  qualifications to practice—
   conditional inclusion in lists, **30**, [1220]
   supplementary lists, **30**, [1221]–[1222]
  regulations—
   appeals, **30**, [1200]
   provisions of, **30**, [1199]
  remuneration, **30**, [1204]–[1205]
   arrangements for payment of, **30**, [1296]
  suspension of practitioners, **30**, [1226]
   appeals, **30**, [1230]
   effect of, **30**, [1228]
   notification of decisions, **30**, [1232]
   pending appeal, **30**, [1227]
   regulations, **30**, [1234]
   review of, **30**, [1229]
  terms and conditions for, **30**, [1198]
 planning contribution in, **46**, [1002]
 planning functions, exercise of, **46**, [615]
 planning inquiries, **46**, [593]
 planning provisions for, **46(S)**, 196–7
 port health districts, **26(1)**, [181]
 Primary Care Trust, local authorities,
  payments from, **30**, [1150]

Wales —*contd*
primary to secondary school, transition,
  15(2), [507]
principal councils—
  area review by, **25(2)**, [50]
  billing authorities, as, **26(1)**, [160]
  chairmen, **25(2)**, [27]
    election of, **25(2)**, [28]
  community council, consultation with,
    25(2), [42]
  constitution of, **25(2)**, [26]
  council funds, **25(2)**, [150]; **26(1)**, [161]
  councillors—
    election of, **25(2)**, [32], [244]
    retirement of, **25(2)**, [30]
    terms of office, **25(2)**, [30]
  decentralisation scheme—
    approval of, **26(1)**, [154]
    area committee—
      meaning, **26(1)**, [153]
      membership, **26(1)**, [156]
      safeguards, **26(1)**, [155]
      sub-committees, **26(1)**, [157]
    guidance on, **26(1)**, [153]
    implementation, **26(1)**, [154]
    preparation of, **26(1)**, [153]
    suspending resolution, **26(1)**, [155]
  electoral arrangements, **25(2)**, [246]
  electoral divisions, **25(2)**, [244]
  establishment of, **25(2)**, [45], [244]
  joint working arrangements, **26(1)**, [158],
    [159]
  local planning authorities, as, **26(1)**, [148]
  orders by, **25(2)**, [39]
  provision of services by one for another,
    26(1), [152]
  records, **26(1)**, [182]
  same name, old and new areas with,
    26(1), [169]
  transitional provisions, **26(1)**, [192]
  vice-chairmen, **25(2)**, [29]
  Welsh Church funds, **26(1)**, [172]
province of, **14**, 5
public bodies—
  accountability, **10**, [1280]
  property and finance of, **26(1)**, [178]
  provision of information by, **15(2)**, [298]
public records—
  audit, **10**, [1302]–[1304]
  meaning, **10**, [1613]
  status of, **10**, [1611]
  transfer of responsibility for, **10**, [1612]
Public Services Ombudsman. *See* **Public
Services Ombudsman for Wales**
Public Transport Users' Committee for
Wales—
  establishment of, **38(2)**, [484]
  functions of, **38(2)**, [485]
  guidance and directions to, **38(2)**, [486]
Qualifications, Curriculum and Assessment
  Authority. *See* **Qualifications, Curriculum
and Assessment Authority for Wales**
registered social landlord system, **24**, [600]
regulated services in, **35(2)**, [611]
representations, exclusion of, **46**, [1025]

Wales —*contd*
Residuary Body (Corff Dweddilliol Cymru)—
  appointment of, **26(1)**, [162]
  constitution, **26(1)**, [190]
revenue support grant—
  additional grant—
    distribution of, **25(2)**, [786]
    provision for, **25(2)**, [785]
  amount, calculation of, **25(2)**, [776]
    amending report, following, **25(2)**, [779]
  determinations as to, **25(2)**, [773]
  information deadlines, **25(2)**, [781]
  instalments, payment in, **25(2)**, [777]
  payment of, **25(2)**, [777]
    amending report, following, **25(2)**, [780]
  power to pay, **25(2)**, [772]
  provisions applying, **25(2)**, [771]
  report, **25(2)**, [774]
    amending, **25(2)**, [778]–[780]
    effect of publication, **25(2)**, [775]
rural, development of, Development Board.
  See **Development Board for Rural Wales**
school—
  admissions, looked after children, Assembly's
    power to make regulations about,
    15(2), [98]
  discontinuance, **15(2)**, [145]–[148]
  establishment or alteration,
    15(2), [145]–[148]
  inspection of—
    denominational education, of,
      15(2), [718]
    duty to report, **15(2)**, [630]
    framework, power of Assembly to
      change, **15(2)**, [657]
    LEA, power of, **15(2)**, [648]
    maintained schools—
      appropriate authority, statement to be
        prepared by, **15(2)**, [636]
      causing concern, notification,
        15(2), [634]
      destination of report on, **15(2)**, [635]
      LEA, statement to be prepared by,
        15(2), [637]
    members of inspectorate, inspections
      by, **15(2)**, [629]
    non-maintained schools—
      destination of report on, **15(2)**, [638]
      proprietor, statement to be prepared
        by, **15(2)**, [639]
    religious education, of, **15(2)**, [646]
    reports on, **15(2)**, [632]
    special measures, report requiring,
      15(2), [631]
    timing, **15(2)**, [633]
  local curriculum. *See* local curriculum *above*
  places, rationalisation of—
    dealing with proposals, **15(2)**, [152]
    directions to bring forward proposals,
      15(2), [149]–[150]
    National Assembly, proposals by,
      15(2), [151]
    transitional exemption orders,
      15(2), [153]
seaward boundaries, review of, **25(2)**, [61]

Wales —*contd*

separate provision for, **46**, [249]

services related to careers services, inspection of, **15(2)**, [652]

sheriffs, **26(1)**, [184]

smallholdings, provision as to, **1(1)**, [826]

social development, financial assistance for, **46**, [34]

Social Housing Ombudsman for. *See* **Social Housing Ombudsman for Wales**

Spatial Plan—

meaning, **46**, [1012]

preparation and publication of, **46**, [1012]

revision, **46**, [1012]

validity, **46**, [1045]

special educational needs, regional provision for—

Assembly's powers to make proposals to secure, **15(2)**, [503]

generally, **15(2)**, [501]

proposals to secure, directions to bring forward, **15(2)**, [502]

Special Educational Needs Tribunal. *See* Special Educational Needs Tribunal for Wales

special grants, **25(2)**, [791]

Special Health Authority—

accounts and audit, **30**, [1339]

body corporate, as, **30**, [1335]

directions to, **30**, [1139]

establishment of, **30**, [1138]

financial duties, **30**, [1288]

functions, exercise of, **30**, [1141]

health service functions, exercise of, **30**, [1140]

local authorities, payments from, **30**, [1150]

pay and allowances, **30**, [1335]

public funds, means of meeting expenditure from, **30**, [1287]

regulations, **30**, [1335]

residual liabilities, transfer of, **30**, [1145]

resource limits, **30**, [1289]

staff, **30**, [1335]

status, **30**, [1335]

statutes, interpretation, **41**, [600]

repeal, ecclesiastical enactments, **41**, [738]

statutory instruments, application of provisions to, **41**, [513]

survey, **46**, [1013]

teacher training, inspection of, **15(1)**, [471]

teaching hospital, special trustees, **30**, [1276]

transfer of functions or property to and from, **30**, [1278]–[1279]

tourism, overseas promotion of, **47**, [467]

town and country planning, powers, **46(S)**, 14

Training and Development Agency for Schools—

functions of, **15(2)**, [667]

grants to, **15(2)**, [673]

transport—

joint authority, establishment of, **38(2)**, [481]

local functions, financial assistance for, **38(2)**, [482]

Wales —*contd*

transport—*contd*

National Assembly, functions of. *See* **National Assembly for Wales**

Wales Transport Strategy, preparation and publication of, **38(2)**, [478]

trunk road charging schemes in—

information, disclosure of, **38(2)**, [710]

National Assembly, powers of, **38(2)**, [709]

unitary development plans, power of High Court to remit, **46(S)**, 175

universities—

clinical teaching and research, **30**, [1313]

hospital, special trustees, **30**, [1276]

transfer of functions or property to and from, **30**, [1278]–[1279]

urban development corporations, provisions not applying in area of, **46**, [1026]

valuation tribunals—

appeals, **25(2)**, [846]

constitution, **25(2)**, [845]

finance, **25(2)**, [847]

orders, **25(2)**, [846]

procedure, **25(2)**, [846]

rules, **25(2)**, [847]

vocational training. *See* **vocational training**

water functions, intervention by Secretary of State, **10**, [1617]

Wales, Church in

buildings, charges on, **14**, 281

burial ground—

closed, maintaining, **14**, 276

maintenance of, **14**, 415

parish burial authority, **14**, 275

registration of burial, **14**, 415

representative body, vesting in, **14**, 413

rights of burial, **14**, 274–5, 415

rights of way, **14**, 275

untransferred, provisions on, **14**, 413

use of, **14**, 274–5

chancel, liability to repair, **14**, 18

church buildings, sharing, **14**, 674–5

Church Commissioners—

appointment of property by, **14**, 258–9

powers and liabilities, **14**, 1107–259–60

Church of England law binding on, **14**, 256

churchwardens, transfer of powers, **14**, 276

clergy, titles and precedence of, **14**, 256

disestablishment—

arbitration, **14**, 283

bishops, provision as to, **14**, 256

books and documents, provisions as to, **14**, 278–9

border parishes, **14**, 263

cathedrals, **14**, 256

commutation, provisions as to, **14**, 270–1, 287–8, 291

data of, **14**, 290

debts and liabilities, adjustment of, **14**, 282

divided parishes, **14**, 294

ecclesiastical corporations, **14**, 256

first fruits and tenths, **14**, 273–4

local authorities, differences between, **14**, 282

Wales, Church in—*contd*
  disestablishment—*contd*
    private benefactions, **14**, 260
    property—
      distribution of, **14**, 261–2
      exchange and adjustments, **14**, 285
      existing interests, saving for, **14**, 266–8,
        289
      incumbent, existing interest of,
        14, 276–7
      management and sale, powers of,
        14, 277–8
      postponement of transfer, **14**, 291–2
      residue, application of, **14**, 272–3
      trusts, **14**, 274
      vesting of, **14**, 257–8
      Welsh ecclesiastical, meaning, **14**, 285
    tithe rentcharge, provisions as to,
      14, 268–9, 278, 292
  ecclesiastical courts, cesser of jurisdiction,
    14, 256
  ecclesiastical office, provisions on income,
    14, 266–7
  freehold offices, compensation to holders of,
    14, 270
  funds, vesting of, **25(2)**, [171]; **26(1)**, [172]
  future appointments, prohibition of, **14**, 255
  glebe, transfer of, **14**, 261, 278
  lay patrons, compensation to, **14**, 269
  marriage in, **14**, 293
  representative body—
    burial grounds, vesting of, **14**, 413
    capital sum paid to, **14**, 292–3
    charities administered by, **14**, 293
    constitution of, **14**, 266
    grant to, amount of, **14**, 287
    property transferred to, **14**, 259, 286,
      291–2
  synods, power to hold, **14**, 266
  vestries, transfer of powers, **14**, 276

walkway
  agreement, creation by, **36**, [1040]
  amenities, provision. *See* **highway** (services
    etc)
  byelaws, **36**, [1040]
  City of London—
    acquisition of land for, **25(1)**, [874]
    area scheduled as, **25(1)**, [881]
    breaking open etc, **25(1)**, [866]
    bridges and subways for, **25(1)**, [866]
    byelaws, **25(1)**, [870]
    compensation respecting, **25(1)**, [873]
    condition in planning permission for,
      25(1), [864]
    construction etc, responsibility for,
      25(1), [866]
    costs in respect of, **25(1)**, [877];
      25(2), [944]
    Crown rights, protection of, **25(1)**, [874]
    declaration of, **25(1)**, [863]
      confirmation by Minister, **25(1)**, [863]
    development, provision for, in, **25(1)**, [865]
    drainage apparatus, fixing of, **25(1)**, [872]

walkway—*contd*
  City of London—*contd*
    enactments applied to—
      general, **25(1)**, [878], [882]
      local, **25(1)**, [883]
    exhibitions on, **25(1)**, [875]
    financial provisions, **25(1)**, [810]
    free literature, etc, distribution containers
      for, **25(2)**, [943]
    generally, **25(1)**, [862]
    highway etc, deemed not to be,
      25(1), [862]
    improvement of, **25(1)**, [868]
    interpretation of expressions, **25(1)**, [861]
    land development, affecting, **25(1)**, [865]
    local inquiry as to, **25(1)**, [863]
    maintenance, responsibility for,
      25(1), [866]
    material deposited near, removal of,
      25(2), [942]
    meaning, **25(1)**, [861], [862]
    owner of land—
      appeals by, **25(1)**, [868]
      consent to drainage apparatus,
        25(1), [872]
      notice to, requiring works, **25(1)**, [868]
    paving of, **25(1)**, [866]
    pedestrian access, temporary restriction or
      prohibition of, **25(1)**, [869]
    placing of things in, **25(1)**, [875]
    planning permission relating to,
      25(1), [864]
    policing of, **25(1)**, [871]
    protection of, **25(1)**, [868]
    representations against, **25(1)**, [863]
    statutory undertakers' works, **25(1)**, [876]
    support for, **25(1)**, [867]
    user of, effect of, **25(1)**, [862]
  consent—
    council obtaining, **36**, [1136]
    meaning, **36**, [1135]
    permission for carrying out works, etc,
      before, **36**, [1139]
    recreation or refreshment facilities, for,
      36, [1137]
  different classes of, **36**, [1040]
  footpath becoming, **36**, [1040]
  Greater London—
    acquisition of land for, **25(1)**, [947]
    agreements as to, **25(1)**, [955]
    amendments respecting, **25(1)**, [1002]
    appeals relating to, **25(1)**, [941]
    breaking up, tunnelling etc, **25(1)**, [939]
    byelaws, **25(1)**, [942]
    cleaning, lighting etc, **25(1)**, [939]
    compensation provisions, **25(1)**, [946]
    consultations as to, **25(1)**, [956]
    declaration of, **25(1)**, [935]
    development of land affecting, **25(1)**, [938]
    drainage of, **25(1)**, [945]
    enactments applied to, **25(1)**, [957], [969],
      [970], [1002]
    entertainments on, **25(1)**, [948]
    exercise of powers as to, **25(1)**, [937]
    highway, deemed not to be, **25(1)**, [934]

walkway—*contd*
Greater London—*contd*
improvement of, **25(1)**, [941]
interpretation of expressions, **25(1)**, [933]
invalid carriages on, **25(1)**, [943]
lighting of, **25(1)**, [939]
London Building Acts, effect, **25(1)**, [954]
modification of provisions by agreement,
25(1), [952]
notice requiring works, **25(1)**, [941]
notices relating to, **25(1)**, [937]
offences, increased fines, **25(2)**, [527], [560]
paving etc, **25(1)**, [939]
placing of things on, **25(1)**, [948]
planning permission relating to,
25(1), [936]
policing, **25(1)**, [944]
protection of, **25(1)**, [941]
provision of, **25(1)**, [935]
representations as to, **25(1)**, [935]
resolution by borough council for,
25(1), [935]
rights in land, acquisition of, **25(1)**, [947]
rights of way, power to acquire,
25(1), [1001]
statutory undertakers—
apparatus, removal of, **25(1)**, [951]
liability of, **25(1)**, [953]
notices to be given to, **25(1)**, [950]
particular provisions as to, **25(1)**, [950]
works, execution of, **25(1)**, [949]
support for, **25(1)**, [940]
user by public, effect of, **25(1)**, [934]
vehicles on, authorised use of, **25(1)**, [943]
local Act—
consent, **36**, [1135]
meaning, **36**, [1135]
maintenance of, **36**, [1040]
meaning, **25(1)**, [934]
regulations, **36**, [1040]
services and amenities on. *See* **highway**
statutory undertakers, rights of, **36**, [1040]

Wallace Collection
Board of Trustees, new—
accounts and audit, **13**, [422]
agreements, party to, **13**, [413]
allowances, **13**, [427]
British works, maintenance of collection
of, **13**, [414]
companies, power to form, **13**, [415]
establishment, **13**, [413]
general functions, **13**, [414]
land, transfer of, **13**, [421], [430]
stamp duty exemption, **13**, [421]
stamp duty land tax exemption,
13, [421]
membership, **13**, [427]
pictures and relevant objects, acquisition
and disposal of, **13**, [416]
predecessor, meaning, **13**, [413]
proceedings, **13**, [427]
reports, **13**, [427]
sealing of instruments, **13**, [427]
status, **13**, [427]

Wallace Collection—*contd*
Board of Trustees, new—*contd*
vesting of property, rights and liabilities in,
13, [413]
company, objects of, **13**, [415]
director, **13**, [427]
grants, **13**, [431], [432]
maintenance of objects in, **13**, [414]
staff, **13**, [427]
will, gifts by, **13**, [419]

war
essential commodities. *See* **essential commodities**

war crimes
ancillary offence—
investigation, rights during, **10**, [1224]
meaning, **10**, [1193]
application of provisions, **10**, [1188]
commanders and other superiors,
responsibility of, **10**, [1203]
committed outside the jurisdiction, conduct
ancillary to, **10**, [1190]
elements of, **10**, [1231]
England and Wales, offence in, **10**, [1189]
extradition request in respect of, **18**, [956]
general principles of liability, application of,
10, [1194]
International Criminal Court, offences in
relation to, **10**, [1192]
investigations, expenses involved, **12(2)**, [60]
jurisdiction over, **12(2)**, [59]
meaning, **10**, [1188], [1231]
mental element, **10**, [1204]
Northern Ireland. *See* **Northern Ireland**
omission, act including, **10**, [1207]
person subject to UK service jurisdiction,
meaning, **10**, [1205]
persons becoming resident in the jurisdiction,
proceedings against, **10**, [1206]
proceedings, limitation on, **12(2)**, [59]
trial and punishment of, **10**, [1191]
UK national, meaning, **10**, [1205]
UK resident, meaning, **10**, [1205]
victims and witnesses, protection of,
10, [1195]

war damage
agricultural lease—
court, powers of, **21**, [103]
exclusion of, **21**, [101]
meaning, **21**, [108]
apportionment of rent following, **21**, [121]
assessor, summoning of, **21**, [107]
bailment, liability in respect of, **50**, [202]
common law, right to compensation at,
50, [276]
contracting out, **21**, [105]
county court jurisdiction, **21**, [107]
Crown, application of provisions to, **21**, [106]
customs and excise duties, liability in respect
of, **50**, [205]
disclaimer of lease, **21**, [90]

war damage—*contd*

dwelling house, application of provisions to, **21**, [116]

entry, power of—

  landlord, **21**, [88], [120]

  tenant, **21**, [120]

generally, **50**, [180]

goods on approval or sale or return, liability in respect of, **50**, [203]

ground lease—

  meaning, **21**, [108]

  provisions applicable to, **21**, [118]

  restrictive covenants, discharge or modification of, **21**, [102]

  whole property, recovery of possession of, **21**, [100]

innkeeper, liability of, **50**, [204]

insurance against, relief from obligation, **21**, [119]

meaning, **21**, [124]

mining lease—

  court, powers of, **21**, [103]

  exclusion of, **21**, [101]

  meaning, **21**, [108]

mortgage, provisions implied in, **21**, [88]

multiple lease—

  meaning, **21**, [108]

  provisions applying to, **21**, [99]

  restrictive covenants, discharge or modification of, **21**, [102]

  whole property, recovery of possession of, **21**, [100]

notice—

  damage, informing landlord of, **21**, [88]

  disclaimer, of—

    effect of, **21**, [94]

    modification by court, **21**, [95]

    multiple lease, application to, **21**, [99]

    other interested parties, service on, **21**, [92]

    particulars included in, **21**, [93]

    service of, **21**, [90]

    unfitness of premises, disputes as to, **21**, [92]

  elect, to—

    counter-notice, **21**, [92]

    failure to comply, **21**, [90]

    multiple lease, application to, **21**, [99]

    period for compliance, **21**, [91]

    service of, **21**, [90]

  recurrence after service, **21**, [98]

  retention, of—

    effect of, **21**, [96]

    service of, **21**, [90]

  service of, **21**, [104]

  to avoid disclaimer—

    effect of, **21**, [97]

    period allowed for, **21**, [91], [93]

    service of, **21**, [90]

obligation to repair, relief from, **21**, [87]

premises rendered fit, disputes as to, **21**, [122]

reinstatement, other damage, increase of cost due to, **21**, [123]

restrictive covenants, discharge or modification of, **21**, [102]

war damage—*contd*

settled land, on, raising money for, **21**, [89]

short tenancies, application of provisions to, **21**, [116]

War Graves Commission

protection of, **25(2)**, [271]

War Graves Endowment Fund

accumulation of, **3**, [324]

incorporation of trustees, **3**, [323]

war injuries

disallowance of payments for, **44(1)**, [421]

meaning, **44(1)**, [421]

war insurance premium

disallowance of deductions, **44(1)**, [420]

meaning, **44(1)**, [166]

War Loan

National Loans Fund, charged on, **19(2)**, [927]

war memorial

alteration for subsequent war, **25(1)**, [408]

maintenance etc, expenditure in, **25(1)**, [143], [144]

war pensions

alteration of, effect on state pension credit, **40(1)**, [685]

Appeal Tribunals—

  appeal from decisions of, **33(1)**, [58]

  appeal to—

    assessments, against, **33(1)**, [54]

    award withheld etc, where, **33(1)**, [53]

    civil defence volunteers, by, **33(1)**, [52]

    civilians, by, **33(1)**, [52]

    disablement, as to extent of, **33(1)**, [54]

    fees, exemption from, **33(1)**, [70]

    grounds of, **33(1)**, [51]

    matters relevant on, **33(1)**, [56]

    Minister's decision, from, **33(1)**, [50], [55]

    notice to be given, **33(1)**, [64]

    rehearing, **33(1)**, [57]

    redetermination of, **33(1)**, [59]

    rules for, **33(1)**, [70]

    service members, by, **33(1)**, [51]

    time limit for, **33(1)**, [63], [596]

  constitution, **33(1)**, [70]

  expenses of, **33(1)**, [70]

  members—

    appointment, **33(1)**, [70]

    qualifications, **33(1)**, [70]

    remuneration, **33(1)**, [70]

  procedure of, **33(1)**, [70]

  summary of provisions, **33(1)**, [25]

awards of, **40(1)**, [115]

civil defence volunteers—

  appeals by, **33(1)**, [52]

  meaning, **33(1)**, [45]

  personal injuries payments, **33(1)**, [42]

civilians, appeals by, **33(1)**, [52]

war pensions—*contd*
committee—
  establishment, **3**, [1513]
  financial provisions, **3**, [1514]
  functions, **3**, [1513]
  orders, **3**, [1515]
  regulations, **3**, [1515]
council tax benefit, disregard for, **40(1)**, [644]
disablement—
  alteration of, affect on state pension credit, **40(1)**, [685]
  assessment of, **33(1)**, [54]
  entitlement to, **40(1)**, [401]
  meaning, **40(1)**, [402]
grounds for refusing, **33(1)**, [50]–[51]
information, use of, **40(2)**, [152]
injuries for which payable, **33(1)**, [42]
later marriage or civil partnership, effect of, **33(S)**, Pensions 204–4
meaning, **3**, [1513]; **40(1)**, [115]
Minister, meaning, **33(1)**, [45]
notices by Minister, form etc, **33(1)**, [64]
past decisions and assessments, **33(1)**, [62]
personal injuries scheme—
  civil defence volunteers—
    inclusion of, **33(1)**, [42]
    meaning, **33(1)**, [45]
  injuries covered by, **33(1)**, [42]
  parliamentary control, **33(1)**, [43]
  payments under—
    assignment etc void, **33(1)**, [44]
    decisions as to, **33(1)**, [42]
    procedure as to, **33(1)**, [43]
    provisions of, **33(1)**, [42]
provisions, power to modify, **33(1)**, [65]
regulations, **33(1)**, [67]
rejection of claims—
  armed forces members, **33(1)**, [50]
  civil defence volunteers, **33(1)**, [52]
  civilians, **33(1)**, [52]
  mariners, pilots etc, **33(1)**, [51]
  serious negligence or misconduct, on ground of, **33(1)**, [53]
  specification of grounds for, **33(1)**, [55]
relevant service, meaning, **33(1)**, [68]
Social Security Commissioners—
  appeals from, **33(1)**, [60]
  appeals to, **33(1)**, [58]
  procedure in appeals, **33(1)**, [61]
statutory right to, **33(1)**, [66]
war pensioner, meaning, **3**, [1513]
war service injury, meaning, **33(1)**, [45]
widows, effect of remarriage of, on, **33(1)**, [522]

war, prisoner of. *See* **prisoner of war**

war risks insurance
advertisements—
  Advisory Committee on, **19(1)**, [268]
  exceptions from restriction, **19(1)**, [266]
  offences and penalties, **19(1)**, [269]
  permitted, requirements where, **19(1)**, [267]
  restriction, **19(1)**, [266]

war risks insurance—*contd*
aircraft—
  compensation respecting, **19(1)**, [291]
  insolvency of insurer, **19(1)**, [292]
  Minister's powers, **19(1)**, [289], [290]
  re-insurance agreements, **19(1)**, [289]
business, requirements as to, **19(1)**, [267]
circulars inviting, **19(1)**, [266]
insolvency of insurer, **19(1)**, [292]
marine and aviation fund, establishment of, **19(1)**, [293]
meaning of war risks, **19(1)**, [270], [296]
re-insurance—
  agreements for, **19(1)**, [289]
  liability of re-insurer, **19(1)**, [292]
ships or cargoes—
  advertisements for, **19(1)**, [266]
  compensation as to, **19(1)**, [291]
  insolvency of insurer, **19(1)**, [292]
  Minister's powers, **19(1)**, [289], [290]
  re-insurance agreements, **19(1)**, [289]
summary of provisions, **19(1)**, [1]

war savings certificates
continuation of, **19(2)**, [923]
meaning, **19(2)**, [923]

War, Secretary of State for
ordnance department—
  sale, exercise of powers of, **10**, [416]
  transfer of, **10**, [414]
  vesting of lands of, **10**, [415]
  style and title of, **10**, [417]

war work
government—
  compensation for. *See under* **emergency powers**
  evidence, certificate of Minister as, **9**, [158]
  extension of provisions, **9**, [194]
  maintenance and use, **9**, [146], [172]
  meaning, **9**, [159], [194]
  possession, continuance of, **9**, [146]

ward church
alteration of, **14**, 514–15
designation and establishment, **14**, 467–8

ward of court
child subject to care order, protection from wardship, **6**, [430]
continuance of order, **6**, [116]
end of wardship, **6**, [422], [454]
High Court order, **11(2)**, [712]
removal out of jurisdiction, automatic restriction, **6**, [257]

wardens. *See* **traffic wardens**

Wards and Liveries, Court of
abolition, **20**, [14], [15]

wardship
cessation, **6**, [422], [454]
jurisdiction, restriction on use of, **6**, [430]

warehouse. *See* **customs and excise**

warehouseman
firearms, possession of, **12(1)**, [483], [1126]

warrant
approved enforcement agency—
  execution by, **11(2)**, [548]
  powers, **11(2)**, [549], [583]
arrest, of—
  bail, endorsed for, **11(2)**, [538]
  defendant to complaint, for, **11(2)**, [472]
  England and Wales, executed outside, **11(2)**, [554]
  execution of, **11(2)**, [546]
  failure to answer information or complaint, on, **11(2)**, [114]
  hearing on default, securing offender's presence at, **11(2)**, [505]
  indictable offence, for, **11(2)**, [405]
  information, on laying of, **11(2)**, [405]
  non-appearance of accused, issue on, **11(2)**, [428]
  person under 18, for, **11(2)**, [405]
  presence of accused in court, where required, **11(2)**, [450]
  validity, **11(2)**, [545]
  witness, to procure attendance of, **11(2)**, [519]–[520]
arrest without. *See* **arrest**
Channel Islands—
  backed in, **12(1)**, [48]
  endorsed in, **12(1)**, [53]
child, in respect of, arrest, execution of, **6**, [145]
civilian enforcement officer—
  execution by, **11(2)**, [547]
  powers, **11(2)**, [549], [583]
commitment, of—
  application for cancellation of, **27**, [321]
  default in payment of sum by order, on, **11(2)**, [512]
  England and Wales, executed outside, **11(2)**, [554]
  execution of, **11(2)**, [546]
    approved enforcement agency, execution by, **11(2)**, [548]
    civilian enforcement officer, by, **11(2)**, [547]
    person not in possession of, by, **11(2)**, [553]
  information, disclosure of, for enforcing, **11(2)**, [550]
  maintenance order, enforcing, **27**, [185]
  postponement of issue, **11(2)**, [495]
  restriction on, **11(2)**, [500]
  review of, **27**, [321]
  sums adjudged to be paid on conviction, for, **11(2)**, [494], [500]
  United Kingdom, execution throughout, **11(2)**, [398]
disclosure orders—
  information supplied under, use of, **11(2)**, [551]

warrant—*contd*
disclosure orders—*contd*
  magistrates' court's power to make, **11(2)**, [551]
  meaning, **11(2)**, [551]
distress, of—
  case stated as to, **11(2)**, [575]
  defect in, **11(2)**, [496]
  execution of, **11(2)**, [546]
    approved enforcement agency, execution by, **11(2)**, [548]
    civilian enforcement officer, by, **11(2)**, [547]
    person not in possession of, by, **11(2)**, [553]
  information, disclosure of, for enforcing, **11(2)**, [550]
  irregularity in execution, **11(2)**, [496]
  maintenance order, enforcing, **27**, [185]
  postponement of issue, **11(2)**, [495]
  rates, for, **11(2)**, [575]
  Scotland, executed in, **11(2)**, [115]
  sums adjudged to be paid on conviction, for, **11(2)**, [494]
execution, cross-border, **12(2)**, [234]
imprisonment for non-payment of fine, execution throughout United Kingdom, **11(2)**, [397]
indorsement in backing, **12(1)**, [50]
Isle of Man, backed in, **12(1)**, [48]
search—
  execution of, **11(2)**, [546]
    approved enforcement agency, execution by, **11(2)**, [548]
    civilian enforcement officer, by, **11(2)**, [547]
    person not in possession of, by, **11(2)**, [553]
  information, disclosure of, for enforcing, **11(2)**, [550]
  See **search warrant**
search for child, application for, **6**, [432]

warrant of attorney
stamp duty, abolition, **41**, [152], [157]

warranty
fertilisers and feeding stuffs, sale of—
  fitness, as to, **1(1)**, [836]
  implied, **1(1)**, [834]
marine insurance, arising in. *See* **marine insurance**
seeds, sale of, **1(1)**, [566]

Warsaw Convention. *See* **carriage by air**

Warwickshire
statutes repealed, **41**, [694]

washhouses
charges for, **35(1)**, [149]
provision of, **35(1)**, [148]
public—
  infected articles, restriction on sending to, **35(1)**, [465]

washhouses—*contd*
public—*contd*
place, deemed, **35(1)**, [151]
regulation of, byelaws for, **35(1)**, [150]
sale etc, trustees to local authority,
35(1), [155]
water, or electricity, supply on favourable
terms to, **35(1)**, [156]
water to or from, laying of pipes for
conducting, **35(1)**, [154]

waste. *See also* **refuse**
acceptance, treatment, disposal or delivery,
requirement of, **35(1)**, [769]
appeals, **35(1)**, [780]
biodegradable, meaning, **35(2)**, [403]
categories of, **35(1)**, [862]
cesspool, emptying, **35(1)**, [304], [306]
charges for collecting, **35(1)**, [304]
collection and disposal of, **26(2)**, [161]
collection authorities—
collection of waste, **35(1)**, [756]
disposal, duties as to, **35(1)**, [764]
fixed penalty receipts, use of, **35(1)**, [781]
public registers—
confidential information, exclusion of,
35(1), [778]
information affecting national security,
exclusion of, **35(1)**, [777]
maintenance of, **35(1)**, [776]
receptacles, provision of—
commercial or industrial waste, for,
35(1), [760]
household waste, for, **35(1)**, [759]
recycling powers, **35(1)**, [768]
summary of provisions, **35(1)**, [1]
commercial—
meaning, **35(1)**, [783]
receptacles for, **35(1)**, [760]
composting, Parliament, duty of authorities to
report to, **35(1)**, [763]
contracts, information about—
confidentiality, **26(1)**, [703]
existing, **26(1)**, [701]
interpretation, **26(1)**, [704]
new, **26(1)**, [702]
controlled—
authority to transport, requirement to
produce, **35(1)**, [698]
fixed penalties—
notices for, **35(1)**, [700]
use of, **35(1)**, [701]
vehicles, seizure of, **35(1)**, [699]
collection, duty of collection authority as
to, **35(1)**, [304], [756]
disposal—
cost of, **35(1)**, [306]
dangerous, **35(1)**, [308]
duty as to, **35(1)**, [306]
generation, minimising, **35(1)**, [775]
meaning, **35(1)**, [317], [783]
deposit of—
unauthorised or harmful, prohibition of,
35(1), [735]

waste—*contd*
deposit of—*contd*
unlawful—
clean-up costs, **35(1)**, [737]
fixed penalty notices, **35(1)**, [740]
forfeiture of vehicles, **35(1)**, [738]
investigation and enforcement costs,
35(1), [736]
penalties, **35(2)**, [522]
search and seizure of vehicles,
35(1), [741], [742]; **35(2)**, [523]
unlawful, power to require removal of,
35(1), [770]–[772]
development scheme, **46**, [972]
disposal. *See also* **waste disposal**
illegal, seizure and disposal of vehicles used
for, **35(1)**, [702]
licence, time-limited, **35(2)**, [273]
payments for, **35(1)**, [766]; **35(2)**, [524]
provisions, meaning, **35(1)**, [317]
UK Atomic Energy Authority, by,
35(1), [348]
unauthorised or harmful, prohibition of,
35(1), [735]
unlawful—
clean-up costs, **35(1)**, [737]
fixed penalty notices, **35(1)**, [740]
forfeiture of vehicles, **35(1)**, [738]
search and seizure of vehicles,
35(2), [523]
disposal authorities—
functions of, **35(1)**, [765]
land occupied by, **35(1)**, [303]
meaning, **35(1)**, [317]
recycling powers, **35(1)**, [768]
unlawful, investigation and enforcement
costs, **35(1)**, [736]
duty of care, **35(1)**, [739]
fixed penalty notices, **35(1)**, [740]
search and seizure of vehicles, **35(1)**, [741],
[742]
duty of care as respects, amendment of,
35(2), [84]
enactments, enforcement of, **26(2)**, [159]
exportation, power to prohibit or restrict,
35(1), [844]
hazardous, lists of, **35(1)**, [774]
heat and electricity, production from,
35(1), [311]
household—
collection of, **35(S)**, 111
meaning, **35(1)**, [783]
receptacles for, **35(1)**, [759]
illegal disposal, seizure and disposal of vehicles
used for, **35(1)**, [702]
importation, power to prohibit or restrict,
35(1), [844]
industrial, meaning, **35(1)**, [783]
joint authorities—
amended provisions, **26(2)**, [667]
consultations, **26(2)**, [617]
implementation of proposals by order,
26(2), [618]
membership, **26(2)**, [619]
proposals for, **26(2)**, [616]

waste—*contd*

joint authorities—*contd*
Wales, in, **26(2)**, [621]
joint municipal management strategies—
disapplication of duties, **35(2)**, [414]
two-tier area, for, **35(2)**, [413], [415]
land, on—
disposal, meaning, **35(1)**, [733]
environment, meaning, **35(1)**, [733]
landfill, biodegradeable municipal waste sent
to—
allocating authority—
allocation of allowances by, **35(2)**, [387]
disclosure of information by,
35(2), [397]
landfill operators, powers as to,
35(2), [396]
meaning, **35(2)**, [406]
monitoring authority, appointment,
35(2), [393]
scheme regulations, **35(2)**, [394]
waste disposal authorities, powers relating
to, **35(2)**, [395]
allowances—
allocation of, **35(2)**, [387]
alteration of allocations, **35(2)**, [388]
banking, **35(2)**, [389]
borrowing, **35(2)**, [389]
duty not to exceed, **35(2)**, [392]
meaning, **35(2)**, [406]
monitoring authorities, **35(2)**, [393]
offences, **35(2)**, [391]
scheme regulations, **35(2)**, [394]
trading, **35(2)**, [390]
transfer, **35(2)**, [390]
excluded activities, **35(2)**, [407]
monitoring authority—
appointment, **35(2)**, [393]
disclosure of information by,
35(2), [397]
landfill operators, powers as to,
35(2), [396]
registers, **35(2)**, [398]
non-target years—
default rules, **35(2)**, [386]
maximum weight of material in,
35(2), [385]
penalties, **35(2)**, [408]
registers—
maintenance of, **35(2)**, [399]
public access to, **35(2)**, [399]
regulations—
consultation on, **35(2)**, [409]
power to make, **35(2)**, [417]
procedural provisions, **35(2)**, [410]
scheme year, meaning, **35(2)**, [405]
strategies for reducing—
England, **35(2)**, [400]
Northern Ireland, **35(2)**, [402]
Wales, **35(2)**, [401]
target years, **35(2)**, [384], [405]
landfill, meaning, **35(2)**, [404]
landfills, sent to, summary of provisions,
35(1), [1]

waste—*contd*

London Waste and Recycling Board—
Constitution, **26(1)**, [700]
establishment of, **26(1)**, [699]
objectives, **26(1)**, [699]
payments to, **26(1)**, [700]
management licences—
application for, **35(1)**, [745]
compensation, **35(1)**, [744]
conditions, **35(1)**, [743]
consultation before grant of certain,
35(1), [746]
false statement, making, **35(1)**, [754]
fit and proper person, meaning,
35(1), [782]
grant of, **35(1)**, [743], [745]
holder, requirement to accept, treat, dispose
of or deliver waste, **35(1)**, [769]
licensed activities, supervision of,
35(1), [752]
meaning, **35(1)**, [743]
revocation, **35(1)**, [749]
Secretary of State, appeals to, **35(1)**, [753]
surrender, **35(1)**, [751]
suspension, **35(1)**, [749]
time-limited, **35(2)**, [273]
transfer, **35(1)**, [751]
variation, **35(1)**, [747], [748]
Mayor of London, plan by—
consultations, **26(1)**, [695]
implementation, directions for, **26(1)**, [698]
preparation and publication of, **26(1)**, [695]
Secretary of State, directions by,
26(1), [696]
waste collection and disposal authorities
having regard to, **26(1)**, [697]
meaning, **35(1)**, [317], [783]; **35(2)**, [418]
municipal, meaning, **35(2)**, [403]
national strategy, **35(1)**, [755], [861]
nationally significant infrastructure projects,
46(S), 50–1. *See also* **nationally significant
infrastructure projects**
offences, **35(1)**, [780]
pipes, construction, etc, for, **35(1)**, [304],
[315]
other than, provisions as to, **35(1)**, [309]
places for, **35(1)**, [306]
plant and equipment for, **35(1)**, [306]
recycling, **35(1)**, [306], [310]
registration of carriers—
appeals, **35(1)**, [697]
application, refusal of, **35(1)**, [696]
partnership, **35(1)**, [696]
regulations, **35(1)**, [695]
revocation of, **35(1)**, [696]
transporting without, **35(1)**, [694]
removal, where deposited in breach of
licensing provisions, **35(1)**, [307]
special waste, regulations for, **35(1)**, [308]
summary of provisions, **35(1)**, [1]
unauthorised or harmful deposit or
disposal, prohibition of, **35(1)**, [735]
waste paper, **35(1)**, [306]
pre-separated, payments for delivering,
35(1), [767]

waste—*contd*
 privies—
  emptying, **35(1)**, [304], [306]
  meaning, **35(1)**, [304]
 producer responsibility—
  general, **35(2)**, [143]
  offences, **35(2)**, [145]
  supplementary provisions, **35(2)**, [144]
 prohibition of, **20**, [3]
 purchase, **35(1)**, [311]
 radioactive, provisions applying to,
  35(1), [786]
  See also **radioactive substances**
 receptacles for—
  commercial or industrial, **35(1)**, [760]
  fixed penalty notices, **35(1)**, [761], [762]
  household, **35(1)**, [305], [759]
  interference with, **35(1)**, [773]
 reclamation, **35(1)**, [310]
 recyclable, separate collection of—
  arrangements for, **35(1)**, [757]
  Wales, in, **35(1)**, [758]
 recycling, **35(1)**, [310]
  duty to prepare plans, repeal, **35(2)**, [416]
  Parliament, duty of authorities to report
   to, **35(1)**, [763]
  payments for, **35(1)**, [766]; **35(2)**, [524]
  powers, **35(1)**, [768]
 reduction schemes—
  amended provisions, **35(S)**, 155
  charging, **35(S)**, 151
  interim report, **35(S)**, 109
  making of, **35(S)**, 150–5
  piloting of provisions, **35(S)**, 108
  report and review, **35(S)**, 109
  roll-out or repeal of provisions, **35(S)**, 110
 regulation authorities—
  licences. *See* management licences *above*
  London Waste Regulation Authority,
   replaced. *See now* **Environment Agency**
  management licences, time-limited,
   35(2), [273]
  meaning, **35(2)**, [128]
  public registers—
   confidential information, exclusion of,
    35(1), [778]
   information affecting national security,
    exclusion of, **35(1)**, [777]
   maintenance of, **35(1)**, [776]
  transfer of functions to Environment
   Agency. *See* **Environment Agency**
 regulations, power to make, **35(2)**, [417]
 relevant land, cleansing, **26(2)**, [160]
 sale, **35(1)**, [311]
 Secretary of State, information, obtaining,
  35(1), [779]
 site, management plans, **35(2)**, [525]
 sites, interference with, **35(1)**, [773]
 transitional provisions, **35(1)**, [785]
 treatment of, summary of provisions,
  35(1), [1]
 unlawful, search and seizure of vehicles,
  35(1), [741], [742]
 unlawfully deposited, **35(2)**, [439]

waste—*contd*
 Wales—
  biodegradable municipal waste sent to
   landfill, strategy for reducing, **35(2)**, [401]
  local authorities, provision of information
   by, **35(2)**, [412]
  municipal waste management strategies,
   35(2), [411]

waste disposal
 allowances, entitlement of successor to,
  44(1), [71]
 joint arrangements for, **25(2)**, [585]
 licence, meaning, **44(3)**, [167]
 preparation expenditure, **44(1)**, [70]
 restoration payments, **44(1)**, [69]
 site preparation expenditure—
  allocation of, **44(3)**, [166]
  deduction from trade profits, **44(3)**, [165]
  meaning, **44(3)**, [167]
 site restoration payments, **44(3)**, [168]
 transfer of functions, **25(2)**, [584]

waste land
 access to, public right, **20**, [793]
 opencast coal compulsory rights order, effect,
  17(1), [192]

water
 authorities. *See* **water authority**
 company. *See* **water companies**
 consequential amendments, **49**, [1315], [1318]
 Crown land, application of provisions to,
  49, [694]
 efficient use, promotion of—
  compliance with requirements, information
   as to, **49**, [886]
  duty as to, **49**, [883]
  publicity, **49**, [885]
  requirements, imposition of, **49**, [884]
 Environment Agency's duty in relation to—
  augmentation, **35(2)**, [92]
  conservation, **35(2)**, [92]
  redistribution, **35(2)**, [92]
 gas washing, pollution by, penalty for,
  35(1), [20]
 Isles of Scilly, provisions apply to, **49**, [695]
 local authority for provisions as to,
  35(1), [294]
 local statutory provisions—
  consequential amendments, **49**, [692]
  meaning, **49**, [691], [1310], [1314]
  National Rivers Authority, effect on,
   49, [680]
  savings for, **49**, [1319]
  Secretary of State, amendment by,
   49, [1310]
  transitional provisions, **49**, [707]
 nationally significant infrastructure projects,
  46(S), 48–50. *See also* **nationally significant
  infrastructure projects**
 periods of time, specification of, **49**, [707]

water—*contd*
  pipe-lines. *See* **pipe-line**
  pipes—
    construction of railway, works due to,
      36, [277]–[282]
    tramway, alteration for purpose of,
      36, [503]
  pipes etc, removal, **35(1)**, [21], [176]
  railway across. *See* **railway**
  right to take, **9**, [146], [180]
  rights, injurious affection, **35(1)**, [209]
  supply—
    baths, etc to, favourable terms for,
      35(1), [156]
    insanitary cistern, etc, from, **35(1)**, [144]
    polluted source of, **35(1)**, [143]
    sanitary appliances, in connection with,
      35(1), [382]
    utilisation of wells, etc, by parish council
      for, **35(1)**, [142]
    water-closet, for, **35(1)**, [588], [590], [647]
    works for, vesting in local authority,
      35(1), [141]
    See **water supply**
  transitional provisions and savings, **49**, [1315],
    [1319]–[1320]
  zero-rating, **50**, [151]

water authority. *See also* **drainage board;
Environment Agency; water resources;
water supply**
  amendment of provisions, **49**, [699]
  Building Act notice, transitional provisions,
    49, [703]
  byelaws, **49**, [707]
  charges—
    Equalisation Act 1977, repeal, **49**, [616]
    metering trials schemes, **49**, [656]
    transitional provisions, **49**, [703]
  criminal liability, **49**, [707]
  engineering operations, telecommunications
    system, protection, **49**, [457]
  financial provisions, loans and grants,
    49, [574]
  former provisions—
    borrowing powers, **19(3)**, [163]
    expenses, **19(3)**, [163]
  goods and services, supply of, **49**, [566]
  grants to, **49**, [574]
    See further **Local Commissioner**
  joint water board or committee, transitional
    provisions, **49**, [703]
  land drainage etc functions, **25(2)**, [586]
  London. *See* **Thames Water Authority**
  members—
    appointment of, **49**, [573]
    compensation on cessation of office,
      49, [573]
    generally, **49**, [702]
    remuneration and allowances, **49**, [573]
    superannuation, **49**, [573]
  National Rivers Authority, transfer of
    functions to, **49**, [660]
  notices etc—
    service of, **49**, [344]

water authority—*contd*
  notices etc—*contd*
    writing, in, **49**, [342]
  orders, Minister's power to make, **49**, [571]
  pension funds, payments into, **49**, [683]
  pensions, **49**, [702]
  public utility, as, **49**, [655]
  recreation facilities, provision of, **49**, [568]
  regulations, Minister's power to make,
    49, [571]
  supply, duty as to—
    domestic use, for, **49**, [33], [48]
    generally. *See* **supply**
  Thames. *See* **Thames flood barrier;
    Thames Water Authority**
  transfer of powers and duties to Environment
    Agency, **19(3)**, [161]; **20**, [1]
  transfer schemes—
    duties after coming into effect, **49**, [697]
    making, **49**, [697]
    supplementary provisions, **49**, [697]
    transfers by, **49**, [697]
  transitional provisions, **49**, [575], [702]
  Treasury guarantees, **49**, [707]

water bailiff. *See under* **freshwater fisheries**

water butt
  insanitary, **35(1)**, [144]

water closet
  care of, **35(1)**, [128]
  improper construction or repair, penalty for,
    35(1), [587]
  meaning, **35(1)**, [140], [648]
  provision in building, notice by local
    authority requiring, **35(1)**, [588]
  replacing other closets, notice by local
    authority requiring, **35(1)**, [590]
  sewer available, **35(1)**, [588], [647]
  soil pipe from, ventilation of, **35(1)**, [584]
  sufficient water supply for, **35(1)**, [588], [647]

water companies. *See also* **water undertakers**
  bodies corporate, offences by, **49**, [686]
  costs, **49**, [1357]
  Crown, wholly owned by, **49**, [691]
  directors, power to appoint officers as,
    49, [1306]
  disclosure of information, general restrictions
    on, **49**, [684]
  dividends, maximum rates of, **49**, [369]
  documents, service of, **49**, [690]
  false statements, making, **49**, [685]
  financial provisions, **49**, [687]
  protected land, meaning, **49**, [1031]
  regulations, power to make, **49**, [689]
  statutory—
    act or omission, liability for, **49**, [1297]
    arrangements and reconstructions,
      49, [1305]
    borrowing, relaxation of limits on,
      49, [1300]–[1301]
    capital, relaxation of limits on,
      49, [1300]–[1301]

water companies—*contd*
statutory—*contd*
dividends, relaxation of limits on,
  49, [1300]–[1301]
general powers of, **49**, [1297]
information, provision of, **49**, [1312]
interest, relaxation of restrictions on
  payment of, **49**, [1302]
local statutory provisions, amendment by
  Secretary of State, **49**, [1310]
memorandum and articles—
  adoption of, **49**, [1308]
  meaning, **49**, [1311]
  resolution substituting, review by High
    Court, **49**, [1309]
profits, relaxation of restrictions on
  application of, **49**, [1303]
redeemable stock—
  power to issue, **49**, [1298]
  terms and conditions of, **49**, [1299]
registration of, **49**, [1307]
sale of shares or stock, relaxation of
  restrictions on, **49**, [1304]
undertakers, appointment as. *See* **water
  undertakers**
water fittings, not to manufacture,
  49, [1297]
successor—
  capital allowances, **49**, [678]
  Government guarantees, **49**, [688]
  group borrowings, temporary restrictions
    on, **49**, [675]
  holdings companies—
    financial assistance for, **49**, [667]
    Government investment in, **49**, [670]
    Government shareholding, target
      investment limit for, **49**, [672]
    investments, application of Trustee
      Investments Act 1961 to, **49**, [677]
    liabilities, transfer to, **49**, [668]
    listing particulars, responsibility for,
      49, [673]
    nominees, exercise of functions
      through, **49**, [671]
    statutory accounts, **49**, [674]
  initial Government holdings, **49**, [666]
  loans, conversion of, **49**, [669]
  reserves, **49**, [676]
  statutory accounts, **49**, [674]
  tax provisions, **49**, [678]

water conservation
duty to encourage, **49**, [1382]
public authorities, by, **49**, [1383]

water industry
Crown, application of provisions to,
  49, [1034]
Director General of Water Services. *See*
  Director General of Water Services
Environment Agency, general duties of,
  49, [680]–[681]
  See also **Environment Agency**
international obligations, giving effect to,
  49, [881]

water industry—*contd*
Isles of Scilly, application of provisions to,
  49, [1035]
local Acts, effect of, **49**, [1033]
Secretary of State—
  environmental and recreational duties—
    codes of practice, **49**, [716]
    general, **49**, [714]
  general duties of, **49**, [712]

water meters
consent for use of, **49**, [985]
hire of, **49**, [119]
inspection and examination, **49**, [120]
installation, **49**, [657]
interference with, financial obligations,
  49, [986]
metering. *See* **water undertakers**
regulations, **49**, [657]
removal, **49**, [120]
supply of, **49**, [119]
tampering with, **49**, [984]
Thames Water Authority, **49**, [275]

water protection zones
consents, regulations in relation to, **49**, [1159]
designation of, **49**, [1156]
orders, **49**, [1279]

water rates
appeals, **25(1)**, [405]
valuation, determination of, **25(1)**, [151],
  [407]

water regulators
co-operation between, **49**, [1365]

water resources
abstraction of water—
  borings, notices not requiring licences,
    49, [1079]
  British Waterways Board, by, **49**, [1125]
  claims arising, **49**, [1348]
  curtailment of rights, **49**, [1061]
  damage, civil remedies for, **49**, [1103]
  drainage purposes, for, **49**, [1078],
    [1335]–[1336]
  emergency, **49**, [1335]
  enforcement notices, **49**, [1071]
    appeals, **49**, [1072]
    non-compliance with, **49**, [1073]
    rights of entry, **49**, [1072]
  Environment Agency, by, **49**, [1123]
  evidence of, **49**, [1259]
  exception orders, **49**, [1337]
  information as to, power to require,
    49, [1251], [1375]
  licence for—
    appeals, **49**, [1096]
    determination of, **49**, [1097]
    regulations, **49**, [1098]
  application for—
    call in, **49**, [1094], [1340]
    called-in, consideration of, **49**, [1095]
    determination, **49**, [1089]

water resources—*contd*
  abstraction of water—*contd*
    licence for—*contd*
      application for—*contd*
        publication of, **49**, [1087]–[1088], [1341]
        regulations, **49**, [1083]
        who may apply, **49**, [1084], [1338]
      apportionment of, **49**, [1116]–[1117], [1347]
      breach of conditions, **49**, [1071]
      death of holder, **49**, [1104]–[1105], [1115]
      effect, **49**, [1102], [1348]
      Environment Agency, by, **49**, [1123]
      existing rights and privileges, having regard to, **49**, [1090], [1342]
      form and contents of, **49**, [1099], [1344]
      full licence, **49**, [1069], [1086], [1329]
      holders, **49**, [1101], [1347]
      impounding, combined with, **49**, [1085]
        abolition of, **49**, [1339]
      matters to be specified in, **49**, [1099]
      modification—
        application of licence holder, on, **49**, [1106], [1345]
        applications, regulations as to, **49**, [1113]
        compensation for, **49**, [1119]–[1120], [1275], [1349]
        Environment Agency—
          at instance of, **49**, [1107], [1346]
          indemnity for, **49**, [1122]
        owner of fishing rights, application by, **49**, [1110]–[1111], [1121]
        proposals—
          in pursuance of, **49**, [1108]
          reference to Secretary of State, **49**, [1109]
        Secretary of State, at instance of, **49**, [1107], [1346]
        spray irrigation purposes, for, **49**, [1112]
      necessity for, **49**, [1068]
      protected rights—
        compulsory registration, **49**, [1274]
        infringed by, **49**, [1090]
        meaning, **49**, [1091]
        register of, **49**, [1092]
      register of, **49**, [1237]
      regulations as to, **49**, [1083], [1099]
      requirement, **49**, [1068]
      revocation of, **49**, [1350]
      right, of. *See* licence of right *below*
      river flow, taking into account, **49**, [1093]
      succession to, **49**, [1104]–[1105]
      temporary licence, **49**, [1069], [1086], [1329]
      transfer licence, **49**, [1069], [1086], [1329]
      transfer of, **49**, [1114], [1347]
      types of, **49**, [1069], [1086]
      validity, extension of, **49**, [1100]
      variation of, **49**, [1350]

water resources—*contd*
  abstraction of water—*contd*
    licence of right, **49**, [1275]
      generally, **49**, [1124]
      references to, **49**, [1275]
    loss, civil remedies for, **49**, [1103], [1348]
    meaning, **49**, [1267]
    minor and consequential amendments, **49**, [1405]
    miscellaneous rights, **49**, [1081]
    navigation, harbour or conservancy authority, rights of, **49**, [1074], [1333]
    protected rights, derogation from, **49**, [1118], [1275]
    repeals and revocation, **49**, [1409]
    restrictions—
      exemptions from, **49**, [1081]–[1082]
      general, **49**, [1068]
    right, licence of. *See* licence of right *above*
    small quantities, of, **49**, [1075], [1334]
      curtailment of rights, **49**, [1077]
      orders, **49**, [1274]
      threshold, variation of, **49**, [1076]
    summary of provisions, **49**, [1]
    underground strata, **49**, [1075]
  British Waterways Board, inland waters owned by, **49**, [1125]
  byelaws as to. *See under* **water supply**
  charges—
    British Waterways Board, for abstraction of water from, **49**, [1187]
    specific exemptions from, **49**, [1182]–[1183]
    spray irrigation, in respect of—
      appeals, **49**, [1186]
      application for agreement, **49**, [1184]
      apportionment of, **49**, [1184]
      directions, **49**, [1186]
      duration of agreement, **49**, [1185]
      payment of, **49**, [1184]
  Church Commissioners, provisions as to, **49**, [1126]
  civil liability, **49**, [1128]
  compulsory purchase, transitional provisions, **49**, [706]
  conservation notices—
    appeal against, **49**, [1080]
    measures specified in, **49**, [1079]
  Crown, application of provisions to, **49**, [1268]
  documents, service of, **49**, [1266]
  ecclesiastical property, provisions as to, **49**, [1136]
  false statements, making, **49**, [1256]
  impounding works—
    enforcement notices, **49**, [1071]
      appeals, **49**, [1072]
      non-compliance with, **49**, [1073]
      rights of entry, **49**, [1072]
    existing, **49**, [1331]
    works notices, **49**, [1332]
    licence for—
      abstraction, combined with, **49**, [1085]
        abolition of, **49**, [1339]
      breach of conditions, **49**, [1071]

water resources—*contd*
impounding works—*contd*
licence for—*contd*
register of, **49**, [1237]
requirement, **49**, [1070]
meaning, **49**, [1070]
minor and consequential amendments,
49, [1405]
navigation, harbour or conservancy
authorities, rights of, **49**, [1074]
repeals and revocation, **49**, [1409]
restrictions on, **49**, [1070], [1330]
summary of provisions, **49**, [1]
Isles of Scilly, application of provisions to,
49, [1270]
legislation relating to, summary, **19(3)**, [161];
20, [1]
local enactments, repeal, amendment, etc,
49, [1129]
management schemes, **49**, [1061]
other abstractors, **49**, [1062]
Secretary of State, referral to, **49**, [1063]
minimum acceptable flow—
consideration of, **49**, [1066]
inland waters, of, **49**, [1067]
statement on, **49**, [1065], [1273]
offences—
body corporate, liability of, **49**, [1264]
enforcement provisions, **49**, [1263]
pollution. *See* **pollution**
regulations, power to make, **49**, [1265]
samples and abstractions, evidence of,
49, [1259]
Secretary of State, validity of decisions of,
49, [1127]
transitional provisions, **49**, [704]
visiting forces, exemption for, **49**, [1269],
[1352]
watercourse, references to, **49**, [1130]
works agreements, **49**, [1203]

Water Services Regulation Authority
annual report, **49**, [1003]
co-operation between water regulators,
49, [1365]
code of practice, **49**, [1038]
committees, **49**, [1038]
complaints handling, enforcement of
requirements, **39(1)**, [718]
constitution, **49**, [1038]
Consumer Council for Water—
copies of notices, requirement to send to,
49, [783]
duty to consult, **49**, [782]
Director General of Water Services, functions
transferred from, **49**, [1356], [1401]
establishment of, **49**, [711], [1354]
forward work programmes, **49**, [1002]
functions, performance of, **49**, [1038]
members—
appointment, **49**, [1038]
pensions, **49**, [1038]
remuneration, **49**, [1038]
membership, **49**, [1038]
payments to, **49**, [1038]

Water Services Regulation Authority—*contd*
proceedings, **49**, [1038]
relevant regulator, as, **39(1)**, [709]
reports, **49**, [1003]
social and environmental matters, guidance
on, **49**, [713]
staff, **49**, [1038]
supplementary powers, **49**, [1038]
water industry, general duties in respect of,
49, [1359]

Water Space Amenity Commission
dissolution provisions—
expenses of Secretary of State, **49**, [615]
final reports, **49**, [621]
functions—
completion, continuance of Commission
until, **49**, [621]
determination of, **49**, [614]
orders, power to make, **49**, [614], [617]

water suppliers. *See* **licensed water suppliers**

water supply. *See also* **water resources**
abstraction of water. *See* **water resources**
boreholes, sinking of. *See* **borehole**
bulk, in—
agreement, by, **49**, [703]
arrangements for, **49**, [1064], [1351]
requirement to make, **49**, [804]
Thames Water Authority, by, **49**, [207],
[281]
variation and termination of agreements,
49, [805]
charge on land for, **20**, [448]–[451]
cisterns, provision, repair etc, **49**, [51]
Coal Authority, acquisition of rights,
17(1), [177]
competition, functions respecting, **49**, [785]
complaints, procedure for dealing with,
49, [874]
constancy, duty as to, **49**, [33], [840]
consumer, meaning, **49**, [959]
contaminating—
offence of, **49**, [860]
regulations preventing, **49**, [861]
steps to prevent, **49**, [862]
cutting off—
meaning, **49**, [347]
on failure to pay rate, **49**, [332]
premises excepted from, **49**, [1045]
restoration by borough council,
25(1), [835]
undertakers' powers, **49**, [121]
damage, power to prevent, **49**, [862]
disconnections—
necessary works, for, **49**, [831]
non-payment of charges, for, **49**, [832]
request of customer, at, **49**, [833]
domestic purposes—
See also **Thames Water Authority**
connections—
ancillary works, carrying out, **49**, [812]
conditions of—
disputes as to, **49**, [815]

water supply—*contd*
  domestic purposes—*contd*
    connections—*contd*
      conditions of—*contd*
        metering, **49**, [815]
        requirements, **49**, [813]
        separate service pipes, requirement
         of, **49**, [816]
        sums deposited, interest on, **49**, [814]
      duty to make, **49**, [811]
    constancy and pressure, **49**, [33], [840],
      [1046]
    demand for, **49**, [823]
    duty to supply, **49**, [33], [48]
      compliance, conditions of, **49**, [824]
      enforcement of, **49**, [825]
      generally, **49**, [823]
      requirements, **49**, [823]
    licensed water suppliers, by, **49**, [835]
    meaning, **49**, [352]
    notices, **49**, [811]
    performance of duties, time for, **49**, [817]
    purposes excluded from, **49**, [117]
    purposes, meaning, **49**, [1031]
    rights to, **49**, [48]
  drought. *See* **drought**
  duty to provide for public purposes, **49**, [35]
  expenses—
    City of London, **49**, [341]
    Minister's, **49**, [340]
  fire fighting, taking for, **49**, [36]–[38], [828]
  fire plugs, placing of, **49**, [36]
  firefighting, for. *See under* **fire authority**
  fittings—
    meaning, **49**, [347]
    regulations as to, **49**, [861]
  flow. *See* **water resources**
  fluoridation—
    concentration, **49**, [875], [1370]
      target, power to vary, **49**, [877]
    consultation as to, **49**, [878]
    indemnities, **49**, [879]
    permitted agents, power to vary, **49**, [876]
    pre-1985 schemes, **49**, [880], [1049]
    publicity, **49**, [878]
    request of relevant authorities, at,
      49, [875], [1370]
  food safety, in relation to, **1(2)**, [468]
  fouling of. *See* **pollution**
  hosepipes, restriction or prohibition of use,
    49, [863]
  inquiries and hearings, **49**, [337]
  insufficient or unwholesome, local authority
    functions where, **49**, [463]
  level. *See* **water resources**
  levels of performance, information as to,
    49, [798], [801]
  limiting devices, prohibition of use, **49**, [838]
  limits of, meaning, **49**, [347], [352]
  London—
    City of, expenses of Common Council,
      49, [341]

water supply—*contd*
  London—*contd*
    See generally **Thames Water Authority**
  meters. *See* **water meters**
  misusing water—
    offence of, **49**, [860]
    regulations preventing, **49**, [861]
  non-domestic purposes, for—
    charges for, **49**, [827]
    duty as to, **49**, [826]
    licensed water suppliers, by, **49**, [836]
    requests for, determinations, **49**, [827]
    transitional provisions, **49**, [703]
  notices etc—
    service of, **49**, [344]
    writing, in, **49**, [342]
  offences—
    misusing, contaminating and wasting
      water, **49**, [860]
    penalties generally, **49**, [335]
    pollution, **49**, [56]–[59]
    prosecutions, restriction on, **49**, [334]
  opencast coal working—
    acquisition of rights for, **17(1)**, [177]
    cessation of powers, **17(2)**, [176]
    protection of drainage board's rights,
      17(1), [166]
  orders, revocation and variation, **49**, [338]
  pollution. *See* **pollution**
  pressure—
    duty as to, **49**, [840], [1046]
    high, when not required at, **49**, [49]
    requirements for maintaining, **49**, [841]
  private, meaning, **49**, [882]
  public purposes, for, duty to provide,
    49, [35], [830]
  reduction in, for necessary works, **49**, [831]
  regulations, power to make, **49**, [339]
  reservoirs. *See* **reservoirs**
  resolutions as to, proof of, **49**, [345]
  restoration or continuance of, **25(2)**, [369]
  separate service pipes, by, **49**, [839]
  service pipes, assistance to provide, **22**, [338]
  shortage orders. *See* **drought**
  source of, **49**, [1267]
  standards of performance, **49**, [797]
    information as to, **49**, [798], [801]
    regulations, **49**, [800], [1360]
    statistical information about complaints,
      publication of, **49**, [799]–[800]
  Thames water. *See* **Thames Water
    Authority**
  unauthorised, **49**, [123]
  undertaker, application for restriction on
    working minerals, **17(1)**, [372]
  undertakers. *See* **water undertakers**
  use, unlawful, **49**, [53]
  waste, prevention of—
    apparatus—
      byelaws as to, **49**, [325]
      non-repair, penalty, **49**, [122]
    byelaws as to—
      general provisions, **49**, [327]
      power to make, **49**, [325]
      Thames Water Authority, by, **49**, [311]

water supply—*contd*
waste, prevention of—*contd*
cisterns—
provisions of, **49**, [50]
repair of, **49**, [51], [122]
fittings, byelaws as to, **49**, [325]
mis-use of water, penalties, **49**, [325], [860]
pipes, extension or alteration, penalty,
49, [124]
offence of, **49**, [860]
regulations preventing, **49**, [861]
unauthorised use, **49**, [53]
wrongful taking of water, **49**, [54], [125]
water main requisition—
completion date, determination of,
49, [810]
discounted aggregate deficit, calculation
of, **49**, [809]
duty to comply with, **49**, [806]
financial conditions, **49**, [807]
meaning, **49**, [808]
relevant deficit, calculation of, **49**, [808]
route, determination of, **49**, [810]
water quality—
assessors for enforcement of, **49**, [873]
duties regarding, **49**, [855]
local authority, general functions of,
49, [864]
regulations for preserving, **49**, [856]
water sources—
contamination of, **49**, [859]
waste from, **49**, [858]
works, agreements for, **49**, [973]
water supply licence—
combine licence, **49**, [733]
conditions, **49**, [739]–[740]
determinations by Authority, **49**, [737]
household premises, meaning of, **49**, [735]
modification of—
agreement, by, **49**, [741]
by order under other enactments,
49, [750]
following report, **49**, [747]
references to Competition Commission,
49, [743]–[746]
standard conditions, **49**, [742]
veto following report, Commission's
power of, **49**, [748]
procedure for granting, **49**, [738]
requirements, **49**, [733]
retail licence, **49**, [733]
supplementary, **49**, [734]
threshold requirement, **49**, [736]
water supply system, duty to maintain,
49, [792]
water unfit for human consumption, offence
of supplying, **49**, [857]
wholesomeness of, **49**, [854], [866]

water undertakers. *See also* **water authority;
water companies**
accounts, annual, **49**, [77]
advice, publication of, **49**, [1013]
amalgamation of—
application for, **49**, [324]

water undertakers—*contd*
amalgamation of—*contd*
orders for, **49**, [324]
appointment—
companies eligible for, **49**, [717]
conditions—
agreement, modification by, **49**, [724]
Competition Commission, modification
references to, **49**, [725]–[727]
determinations under, **49**, [723], [1367]
financial penalties for contravention of—
appeals, **49**, [760]
generally, **49**, [756]
interest and payment of instalments,
49, [759]
recovery of, **49**, [761]
statement of policy with respect to,
49, [757]
time limits on imposition, **49**, [758]
order, modification by, **49**, [732]
power to impose, **49**, [722]
report, modification following,
49, [729], [1368]
continuity of, **49**, [718]
duties affecting making of, **49**, [720]
environmental and recreational duties,
codes of practice, **49**, [716]
generally, **49**, [717]
instrument making, **49**, [717]
procedure, **49**, [719]
references to, **49**, [791]
replacement, **49**, [718]
transitional provisions, **49**, [721]
termination of—
generally, **49**, [718]
provisions, application of, **49**, [1039]
transfer of appointment, **49**, [1039]
transfer schemes, **49**, [1039]
transitional provisions, **49**, [1039]
transfer of, **49**, [1039]
body corporate, offences by, **49**, [1023]
books, production of, **49**, [76]
byelaws, power to make, **49**, [325], [703]
charges—
billing disputes, **49**, [958]
connection, **49**, [953]
emergency use of water, for, **49**, [954]
highway drainage, for, **49**, [953]
metering—
entry on land for, **49**, [981]
information, exchange of, **49**, [1017]
tenants, rights of, **49**, [1022]
works, charging for, **49**, [955]
works in connection with, **49**, [971]
meters—
consent for use of, **49**, [985]
interference with, financial obligations,
49, [986]
tampering with, **49**, [984]
methods of calculation etc, **49**, [947]
non-payment, premises excepted from
disconnection for, **49**, [1045]
occupiers, liability of, **49**, [950]
power to make, **49**, [947]
references to, **49**, [712]

water undertakers—*contd*
  charges—*contd*
    schemes—
      making, **49**, [948]
      provisions to be included in,
        regulations, **49**, [949]
      requirements of, **49**, [948]
      service, for, **49**, [957], [1371]
    volume—
      regulations, **49**, [1050]
      revocation of notice, **49**, [951]
      right of consumer to elect for, **49**, [951]
      undertakers' power to require, restriction
        on, **49**, [952]
  combination of—
    application for, **49**, [324]
    orders for, **49**, [324]
  complaints, procedure for dealing with,
    49, [874]
  compliance with provisions, **49**, [751]
  compulsory works orders, **49**, [976], [1053]
  constancy and pressure, duties as to, **49**, [840],
    [1046]
  consumer, meaning, **49**, [882]
  customer service committees—
    chairman, **49**, [1043]
    complaints by, **49**, [781]
    consumer complaints, **49**, [1362]
    duties of, **49**, [779], [1362]
    establishment of, **49**, [778]
    financial provisions, **49**, [1043]
    maintenance of, **49**, [778]
    members of, **49**, [778]
      expenses of, **49**, [1043]
    reports, **49**, [1005]
    staff, **49**, [1043]
    sub-committees, **49**, [1043]
  customers—
    disputes, determination of, **49**, [784]
    review, Director's duty as to, **49**, [766]
  damage, power to prevent, **49**, [862]
  discharges—
    consents for, **49**, [975]
    works purposes, for, **49**, [974]
  disconnections—
    general duties as to, **49**, [834]
    necessary works, **49**, [831]
    non-payment of charges, for, **49**, [832]
    offences, **49**, [834]
    request of customer, at, **49**, [833]
  dividends, maximum rates of, **49**, [369]
  dock, meaning, **49**, [921]
  documents, authentication of, **49**, [343]
  domestic connections—
    ancillary works, carrying out, **49**, [812]
    conditions of—
      disputes as to, **49**, [815]
      metering, **49**, [815]
      requirements, **49**, [813]
      separate service pipes, requirement of,
        49, [816]
      sums deposited, interest on, **49**, [814]
    duty to make, **49**, [811]
    notices, **49**, [811]
    performance of duties, time for, **49**, [817]

water undertakers—*contd*
  domestic supplies—
    demand for, **49**, [823]
    duty as to—
      compliance, conditions of, **49**, [824]
      enforcement of, **49**, [825]
      generally, **49**, [823]
      requirements, **49**, [823]
  drainage works affecting, protection,
    19(3), [259]
  enforcement orders—
    effect of, **49**, [755]
    final, power to make, **49**, [751]
    meaning, **49**, [751]
    obligation to comply with, **49**, [755]
    procedure for, **49**, [753]
    provisional, making, **49**, [751]
    revocation of, **49**, [753]
    validity, **49**, [754]
  entry on premises—
    notice, **49**, [336]
    obstruction of, **49**, [336]
    powers generally, **49**, [52], [336], [369a]
  escape of water, civil liability for, **49**, [1021]
  false information by, **49**, [1019]
  financial provisions applicable to water
    companies as, **49**, [369]
  fire-fighting, duty to provide water for,
    49, [828]
  flood prevention works affecting, **49**, [444]
  foul water, dealing with, **49**, [970]
  functions—
    powers conferred by reference to,
      49, [1030]
    transfer of, **49**, [663]
  guarantees, **49**, [963]
  information—
    disclosure, restriction on, **49**, [1018],
      [1058]
    enforcement purposes, acquisition for,
      49, [1015]
    false, provision of, **49**, [1019]
    metering, exchange of, **49**, [1017]
    publication of, **49**, [1013]
    Secretary of State, furnishing to, **49**, [1014]
    trade effluent discharges, with respect to,
      49, [1016]
  insolvency proceedings, restrictions on,
    49, [765]
  judicial disqualification, **49**, [1025]
  land—
    byelaws, **49**, [966], [1052]
    compulsory acquisition, **49**, [964]
    entry on—
      compensation, **49**, [1048]
      confidentiality, maintaining, **49**, [1047]
      designated persons, **49**, [979]
      metering purposes, for, **49**, [981]
      notice of, **49**, [1047], [1048]
      obstruction, **49**, [1047], [1048]
      person making, supplementary power,
        49, [1047], [1048]
      persons entitled to, impersonation of,
        49, [982]
      premises, securing, **49**, [1048]

water undertakers—*contd*
  land—*contd*
    entry on—*contd*
      purposes of, **49**, [979]
      sewerage purposes, for, **49**, [980]
      surveys, carrying out, **49**, [978]
      warrants, **49**, [1047], [1048]
      water, to search for, **49**, [978]
      works purposes, for, **49**, [977]
    holdings, restriction on, **49**, [965]
    protection, **49**, [965]
  licensed water supplier—
    duty to supply—
      collective strategic supply, designation
        of, **49**, [849]
      determinations and agreements,
        49, [845]–[847]
      introduction of water into undertaker's
        supply system, **49**, [843]
      strategic supply, designation of, **49**, [848]
      wholesale supply by—
        primary water undertaker, **49**, [842]
        secondary water undertaker, **49**, [844]
  limiting devices, prohibition of use, **49**, [838]
  local authority, functions of. *See* **local
    authority**
  London Passenger Transport Act, protection
    under, **36**, [612]
  meaning, **41**, [605]
  merger reference—
    duty to make, **49**, [786]
    interpretation of provisions, **49**, [791]
    provisions applying to, **49**, [788], [1044]
    small mergers, exclusion of, **49**, [787]
  metering information, exchange of,
    49, [1017]
  metering trials schemes, **49**, [656]
  mineral rights, acquisition of, **49**, [997],
    [1057]
  national security purposes, grants for,
    49, [961]
  non-domestic purposes, supplies for—
    charges for, **49**, [827]
    duty as to, **49**, [826]
    fire-fighting, for, **49**, [828]
    public purposes, for, **49**, [830]
    requests for, determinations, **49**, [827]
  notices etc—
    service of, **49**, [344]
    writing, in, **49**, [342]
  officers, compensation for loss of
    employment, **49**, [445]
  pipes and mains, laying etc. *See* **pipes and
    mains**
  pollution—
    avoidance of, **32**, [272]
    dealing with, **49**, [970]
  powers—
    orders conferring, **49**, [328]
    water supply, as to, **49**, [328]
  premises served by, **49**, [791]
  pressure, requirements for maintaining,
    49, [841]
  private supply, meaning, **49**, [882]

water undertakers—*contd*
  profits—
    deficiency, making good, **49**, [73]
    excess, **49**, [69]
      limitation on, **49**, [69]
      reduction in rates where, **49**, [74]
  public purposes, supply for, **49**, [830]
  records, false information in, **49**, [333]
  recreation facilities, provision, **49**, [568]
  reserve funds, provisions as to, **49**, [70]
  reservoirs—
    repair, orders to effect, **49**, [109]–[110]
    See also **reservoirs**
  rights of way, extinguishment for water works
    purposes, **49**, [353]
  rural water supplies and sewerage, expenses,
    government contributions, **49**, [960]
  security deposits, interest on, **49**, [665]
  separate service pipes, supply by, **49**, [839]
  service of documents on, **35(1)**, [343]
  sewerage—
    alterations by, **49**, [993]
    complaints, procedures for dealing with,
      49, [920]
    local authorities, performance of functions
      by, **49**, [893]
    minerals, power to sell, **49**, [998]
    public sewer, duty to provide, **49**, [894],
      [899]
    sewer maps, keeping, **49**, [1011]
    system, general duty to provide,
      49, [481]. *See also* **sewerage**
    trade effluent—
      discharges, provision of information as
        to, **49**, [1016]
      registers, **49**, [1008]
    works, power to carry out, **49**, [969]
  special administration orders, Government
    assistance where, **49**, [962]
    court, applications to, **49**, [1040]
    discharge of, **49**, [1040]
    effect of, **49**, [762], [1040]
    meaning, **49**, [762]
    modifications of 1986 Act, **49**, [1040]
    notice of making, **49**, [1040]
    special administrator, appointment and
      powers, **49**, [1040]
    special petitions, made on, **49**, [763]
    statement of proposals, **49**, [1040]
    winding-up petition, made on, **49**, [764]
  specially requested fire hydrants, fixing,
    49, [829]
  stopcocks, power to fit, **49**, [972]
  supply, duty to—
    See also **water supply**
    cleansing sewers, drains, etc, for, **49**, [35]
    domestic use, for, **49**, [33], [48]
    non-domestic purposes, for,
      49, [826]–[830]
    public purposes, for, **49**, [35]
    purposes excluded, **49**, [118]
  supply for fire fighting. *See under* **fire
    authority**
  surveys, carrying out, **49**, [978]
  temporary hosepipe bans, imposing, **49**, [863]

water undertakers—*contd*
  transfer of undertakings—
    application for, **49**, [324]
    orders for, **49**, [324]
  water—
    directors' remuneration and standards of
      performance, **49**, [790]
    drought plans, duty to prepare and review,
      49, [802]
    efficient use, promotion of—
      compliance with requirements,
        information as to, **49**, [886]
      duty as to, **49**, [883]
      publicity, **49**, [885]
      requirements, imposition of, **49**, [884]
    information as to water flow, provision of,
      49, [1246]
    maps of waterworks, keeping, **49**, [1010]
    overall performance, duty to inform
      customers about, **49**, [801]
    pollution incidents, exchange of
      information about, **49**, [1253]
    quality—
      assessors, **49**, [873]
      duties regarding, **49**, [855]
      local authority, general functions of,
        49, [864]
      publication of information about,
        49, [856]
      regulations for preserving, **49**, [856]
    resource management plans—
      duty to prepare and review, **49**, [793]
      information, provision of, **49**, [795]
      publication and representations,
        49, [794]
      supplementary, **49**, [796]
    searching for, **49**, [978]
    sources, agreements as to works with
      respect to, **49**, [973]
    supply by. *See* **water supply**
    unfit for human consumption, offence of
      supplying, **49**, [857]
    water supply system, duty to maintain,
      49, [792]
  water main requisition—
    completion date, determination of,
      49, [810]
    discounted aggregate deficit, calculation
      of, **49**, [809]
    duty to comply with, **49**, [806]
    financial conditions, **49**, [807], [1389]
    meaning, **49**, [808]
    payments, calculation of, **49**, [1390]
    relevant deficit, calculation of, **49**, [808]
    route, determination of, **49**, [810]
  waterways—
    byelaws, **49**, [966], [1052]
    meaning, **49**, [966]
  waterworks, construction. *See* **waterworks**
  works—
    another person, for, recovery of cost of,
      49, [811]
    damage caused by, compensation for,
      49, [989], [1055]
    discharges, register of, **49**, [1009]

water undertakers—*contd*
  works—*contd*
    interference with, **49**, [983]
    particular undertakings, protection for,
      49, [992]
    planning controls, saving for, **49**, [999]
    private land, on—
      codes of practice, **49**, [991]
      exercise of powers, **49**, [990]
    tidal lands, in, **49**, [996]
    vesting of, **49**, [988]

water undertakings
  Environment Agency, protection provisions,
    49, [1291]
  mergers, **47**, [762]

watercourse. *See also* **navigable waters**
  alterations affecting boundaries, **25(2)**, [63]
  byelaws protecting, **19(3)**, [241]
  culvert for—
    approved plans, in accordance with,
      35(1), [165]
    repair and cleansing, urban authority
      requiring, **35(1)**, [166]
    saving as to railway company and dock
      undertaker, **35(1)**, [168]
    where building operations in prospect,
      35(1), [164]
  culverting of, **36**, [1116]
  diversion of, nationally significant
    infrastructure project, grant of development
    consent for, **46(S)**, 143
  drainage authorities, saving for works of,
    36, [1391]
  duty to keep open, **20**, [346]
  flow, maintenance of—
    competing jurisdictions, **19(3)**, [195]
    notice—
      appeal against, **19(3)**, [196]
      remedy, requiring, **19(3)**, [194]
    power to require, **19(3)**, [194]
  foul and offensive, near or forming boundary
    of district, order for cleansing, **35(1)**, [163]
  foul, statutory nuisance, **35(1)**, [161]
  impeded flow, remedying, **19(3)**, [194]
  land drainage authority—
    saving for, **35(1)**, [168]
    vested in, alteration of, **35(1)**, [207]
  level, alteration etc, **19(3)**, [243]
  local authority powers, **19(3)**, [194]
  maintenance of, **19(3)**, [183]
  meaning, **19(3)**, [171], [247]; **36**, [844];
    49, [347], [352], [1267]
  metropolitan, **19(3)**, [171]
  navigable—
    diversion of—
      compensation for damage, **36**, [1128]
      order for, **36**, [1127]
    meaning, **36**, [1130]
    new length of, **36**, [1128]
    works carried out on, **36**, [1129]
  navigation authorities, diversion by,
    49, [1229]
  non-navigable, diversion of, **36**, [1129]

watercourse—*contd*
  obstructions—
    consent required for, **19(3)**, [192]
    penalties for offences, **19(3)**, [193]
    prohibition on, **19(3)**, [192]
  ordinary, meaning, **19(3)**, [247]
  protection for, **35(1)**, [208]
  protective provisions, **49**, [995], [1228]
  repair, enforcement of obligation, **19(3)**, [190]
  scheme with respect to, **49**, [1191]
  silted up, statutory nuisance, **35(1)**, [161]
  stopping up, **49**, [549]
  towing path, diversion of, **36**, [1127]
  tramway interfering with, **36**, [504]
  works for—
    defrayal by local authority of cost,
      35(1), [167]
    execution by local authority, **35(1)**, [167]

waterways *See also* **inland waterways**
  access order, work specified in, **32**, [173]
  byelaws, **32**, [184], [192]
  country park, in, **32**, [259]
  landing places—
    byelaws, **26(1)**, [777]
    transfer of rights and obligations,
      26(1), [647]
  meaning, **32**, [201]
  National Park, in, access to, **32**, [172]
  National Trust property, on, admission to,
    32, [63]
  open-air recreation, improvement for,
    32, [149]
  restrictions as to use, general, **32**, [205]
  Transport for London, provision of facilities to
    benefit users, **26(1)**, [645]
  wardens, **32**, [186]

waterworks
  breaking up streets—
    failure to comply with requirements,
      49, [367]
    powers generally, **49**, [31], [365]
    protection for railways, navigation
      authorities etc, **49**, [366]
    verges, application of provisions, **49**, [368]
  charge to tax, **44(1)**, [34]
  Clauses Acts—
    application of, **49**, [107]
    incorporation in other Acts, **49**, [8]
  code. *See* **waterworks code**
  construction of—
    accommodation works, **49**, [19]
    damage, compensation for, **49**, [15]
    diversion of water, illegal, **49**, [17]
    failure to execute works, **49**, [20]
    obstruction of, penalty, **49**, [16]
    plans—
      certified copies as evidence, **49**, [13]
      correction of errors and omissions,
        49, [10]
      deposit, **49**, [11]
      deviation from, bar on, **49**, [14]
    streams, owners' rights to use, **49**, [18]

waterworks—*contd*
  construction of—*contd*
    underground works—
      maps and plans—
        deposit, **49**, [23]
        preparation, **49**, [22], [355]
        preservation and inspection, **49**, [24]
  magistrates, acts by, **49**, [79]
  maps of, **49**, [1010], [1245]
  minerals underlying, undertakers'
    non-entitlement to, **49**, [354]
  mines near—
    communications, **49**, [27], [358]
    compensation to owners etc, **49**, [26]
    damage to, liability for, **49**, [30]
    disputes, settlement, **49**, [28]
    entry and inspection of, powers, **49**, [29],
      [360]
    injury to, liability for, **49**, [361]
    map and plan of, **49**, [22]–[23]
    purchase by undertakers, **49**, [21]
    severance, **49**, [28], [359]
    working by owners—
      communication, power to make,
        49, [358]
      compensation, payment of, **49**, [26],
        [357]
      inspection by water undertakers,
        49, [360]
      notice of, **49**, [356]
    working of, generally, **49**, [25]
  pollution of water in, **49**, [859]
  rent payable, in respect of, **44(1)**, [98]
  telecommunications apparatus, work
    involving, **49**, [347]
  underground. *See* construction *above*

waterworks code
  application of provisions—
    orders as to, **49**, [330]
    procedure, **49**, [330]
  incorporation of, **49**, [330]
  local enactments, repeal and amendment of,
    49, [331]
  modification, **49**, [330]
  special Act—
    access to, provisions as to, **49**, [81]–[84]
    accounts under, **49**, [77]
    interpretation, **49**, [5]
    land, taking of, **49**, [9]
    meaning, **49**, [352]
    penalties, etc, Metropolitan police district,
      49, [80]
    Railways Clauses Acts, incorporation in,
      49, [78]

waybill
  air, requirements, **4(1)**, [17], [19], [21], [37]

wayleave
  electricity supply licence holders, and,
    17(1), [869]
  order. *See* **pipe-lines**
  rent in respect of, **44(1)**, [99]

wayleave—*contd*
  rent receivable for—
    charge to tax, **44(3)**, [344]
    extent of charge, **44(3)**, [346]
    income charged, **44(3)**, [347]
    meaning, **44(3)**, [345]
    person liable, **44(3)**, [348]
  temporary continuation, **17(1)**, [869]
  trading income, payments as, **44(3)**, [22]

weapons. *See also* **firearms**
  air. *See* **air weapons**
  ammunition for—
    expanding, **12(1)**, [478], [479]
    prohibition, **12(1)**, [478]
  armour piercing missiles, **12(1)**, [478]
  attendance centres, power to search persons
    in, **12(4)**, [239]
  biological, **12(1)**, [622]–[627]
  chemical. *See* **chemical weapons**
  collections, cultural or historical, **12(1)**, [479]
  dangerous—
    meaning, **12(4)**, [228]
    minding, using person for—
      offence, **12(4)**, [228]
      penalties, **12(4)**, [229]
  European weapons directive—
    expanding ammunition, as to, **12(1)**, [479]
    use under, **12(1)**, [541]
  exemptions from, **12(1)**, [479]
  exportation of, controls on, **50**, [279]–[294]
  general prohibition, subject to, **12(1)**, [478]
  further education institutions, searching
    students of, for, **15(1)**, [450]
  knives. *See* **knives**
  military use, for—
    unlawful possession, **12(1)**, [478]
    what deemed to be for, **12(1)**, [478]
  missiles, unlawful possession, **12(1)**, [478]
  Northern Ireland, provisions applying,
    12(4), [254]
  nuclear. *See* **nuclear weapons**
  offensive. *See* **offensive weapon**
  primary schools, searching pupils of, for,
    15(1), [684]
  rockets and launchers, unlawful possession,
    12(1), [478]
  secondary schools, searching pupils of, for,
    15(1), [684]
  slaughter of animals, for, **12(1)**, [479], [484],
    [541]

weapons (explosive). *See also* **firearms**
  chemical. *See* **chemical weapons**

weeds
  chemicals to control—
    analysis, evidence of, **1(1)**, [686]
    classes of, **1(1)**, [684]
    labelling and marking, **1(1)**, [683]
    penalties for offences, **1(1)**, [685]
    unlabelled, offences of selling, **1(1)**, [685]
  default powers of minister, **1(1)**, [544]
  entry on land, powers of, **1(1)**, [545]
  injurious, what are, **1(1)**, [541]

weeds—*contd*
  local authority, powers of, **1(1)**, [546]
  minister's expenses, **1(1)**, [549]
  occupier of land—
    failure to comply with requirements,
      1(1), [543]
    meaning, **1(1)**, [551]
    notice requiring action by, **1(1)**, [541]
    service of notices on, **1(1)**, [547]
  offences and penalties, **1(1)**, [543]
  ragwort—
    code of practice, **1(1)**, [542]
    control of, **1(2)**, [697]
  regulations for control of, **1(1)**, [548]
  spread, prevention of, **1(1)**, [541]

week
  period represented by, **45**, [918]

weighbridges
  provision and maintenance, **37**, [813]

weights and measures
  adjustment of—
    fees for, **39(1)**, [527]
    supervision by inspector, **39(1)**, [527]
  agricultural liming, etc, materials for,
    39(1), [580]
  approved verifiers—
    duties, **39(1)**, [571]
    offences by, **39(1)**, [528]
    quality system—
      maintenance of, **39(1)**, [571]
      manual for, preparation of, **39(1)**, [571]
    records, **39(1)**, [571]
  area, of—
    supplementary indication, use as,
      39(1), [558]
    units of measurement, **39(1)**, [554]
  authorities. *See* **weights and measures
    authority**
  ballast—
    carriage by road, **39(1)**, [573]
    meaning, **39(1)**, [572]
    measures for, **39(1)**, [572]
    volume, to be sold by, **39(1)**, [572]
      exceptions, **39(1)**, [572]
  byelaws, continuation of, **39(1)**, [594]
  capacity—
    goods sold by, **39(1)**, [587], [588]
    liquids, statement of quantity, **39(1)**, [503]
    meaning, **39(1)**, [547]
    units of measurement—
      definition of, **39(1)**, [556]
      supplementary indication, use as,
        39(1), [558]
      trade, use for, **39(1)**, [568]
  cement, ready-mixed, **39(1)**, [579]
  check-weighing of vehicles—
    meaning, **39(1)**, [547]
    power to require, **39(1)**, [517]
  coal. *See* **solid fuel**
  coinage standards—
    maintenance of, **39(1)**, [477]
    meaning, **39(1)**, [477]

weights and measures—*contd*
  collections of articles, for, **39(1)**, [591]
  composite goods, for, **39(1)**, [591]
  containers—
    indication of quantity—
      meaning, **39(1)**, [547]
      requirement for, **39(1)**, [499]
    information to be given on, **39(1)**, [499],
      [500]
    inspectors' powers to open, **39(1)**, [514]
    marking of, **39(1)**, [499]
    meaning, **39(1)**, [547]
    orders relating to, **39(1)**, [499]
    quantity less than stated, **39(1)**, [506]
    solid fuel, for, **39(1)**, [574]
  cosmetic products, for, **39(1)**, [582]
  Crown, application of provisions to,
    39(1), [541]
  cubic measures, **39(1)**, [567]
  drugs, units of measurement, **39(1)**, [484]
  electricity, units of measurement, **39(1)**, [559]
  enforcement of fair trading orders, **47**, [141]
  equipment. *See* weighing, etc, equipment
    below
  food—
    bread, retail sales, **39(1)**, [504]
    marking of, **39(1)**, [546]
    packaged. *See* packaged goods *below*
  fuel—
    liquid, provisions as to, **39(1)**, [574]
    solid. *See* **solid fuel**
    wood, provisions for, **39(1)**, [581]
  goods—
    armed forces, for, **39(1)**, [501]
    carriage for reward, **39(1)**, [499]
    containers. *See* containers *above*
    documents as to—
      alleged inaccuracy in, **39(1)**, [515]
      incorrect statements, **39(1)**, [507]
      power to inspect, **39(1)**, [515]
      inspection of, **39(1)**, [514]
      See also inspectors *below*
    liquid, quantity, statement of, **39(1)**, [503]
    offences as to—
      defences, **39(1)**, [509]–[513]
      due to another's default, **39(1)**, [508]
    packaged. *See* packaged goods *below*
    quantity—
      buyer, to be made known to,
        39(1), [503]
      correct, precautions to ensure,
        39(1), [510]
      deficiency—
        due diligence to avoid, **39(1)**, [510]
        evaporation, etc, due to, **39(1)**, [511]
        subsequent, **39(1)**, [511]
      excess, reason for, **39(1)**, [512]
      exemption from requirements,
        39(1), [504]
      expression of, manner of, **39(1)**, [499]
      liquid goods, statement as to,
        39(1), [503]
      pre-packed goods. *See* packaged goods
        below

weights and measures—*contd*
  goods—*contd*
    quantity—*contd*
      sale by—
        compliance with requirements,
          39(1), [519]
        intoxicating liquor, **39(1)**, [504]
        making quantity known, **39(1)**, [520]
        offences relating to, **39(1)**, [502]
        orders as to, **39(1)**, [499]
        weighing in presence, **39(1)**, [521]
      short weight, offence of giving,
        39(1), [505]
      statement of, in writing, **39(1)**, [503]
      tests of, **39(1)**, [513]
      warranty as to, **39(1)**, [509]
    sale of—
      capacity, by, **39(1)**, [587], [588]
      net weight, by, **39(1)**, [585], [589]
    summary of provisions, **39(1)**, [1]
    test purchases, **39(1)**, [518]
    transactions in—
      exemptions from requirements,
        39(1), [501]
      offences relating to, **39(1)**, [502]
      orders relating to, **39(1)**, [499]
      regulation of, **39(1)**, [1]
    vehicles, carried on—
      check-weighing, of, **39(1)**, [517]
      meaning, **39(1)**, [547]
      exceptions as to, **39(1)**, [504]
      inspectors' powers, **39(1)**, [516]
    warranty, defence, as, in proceedings,
      39(1), [509]
    See also miscellaneous goods *below*
  gram, etc, spelling of, **39(1)**, [545]
  harbours, provision etc. *See under* **ports and
    harbours**
  inspectors—
    adjustment of weights, etc—
      fee for, **39(1)**, [527]
      supervision of, **39(1)**, [527]
    appointment, **39(1)**, [525]
    assistance to—
      failure to provide, **39(1)**, [534]
      reduction of fees for, **39(1)**, [530]
    certain goods, special powers, **39(1)**, [514]
    certification of, **39(1)**, [526]
    chief, functions of, **39(1)**, [525]
    containers, power to open, **39(1)**, [514]
    documents, inspection, **39(1)**, [515]
    entry, powers of, **39(1)**, [532]
    fees, accounting for, **39(1)**, [531]
    functions of, additional, **39(1)**, [527]
    goods—
      liability to examination, **39(1)**, [514]
      power to inspect, **39(1)**, [514]
      weight, etc, checking, **39(1)**, [514]
    information to, default in giving,
      39(1), [534]
    inspections—
      general powers as to, **39(1)**, [532]
      scope of, **39(1)**, [524]
    intoxicating liquor, provisions as to,
      39(1), [504]

weights and measures—*contd*
  inspectors—*contd*
    kilogram, standards. *See* standards *below*
    obstruction of, **39(1)**, [533]
    offences by, **39(1)**, [528]
    purchase of goods by, **39(1)**, [514]
    qualifications, examination of, **39(1)**, [526]
    seizure of goods, **39(1)**, [532]
    special powers, **39(1)**, [514]
    tenure of office, **39(1)**, [525]
    test purchases by, **39(1)**, [518]
    transitional provisions, **39(1)**, [594]
    UK primary standard, **39(1)**, [560]–[564]
    unit of measurement, **39(1)**, [475]
    vehicles, powers as to goods carried on,
      39(1), [516]
    working standards for, **39(1)**, [479]
  kilogram, standards. *See* standards *below*
  legislation, shortages, orders for alleviating,
    39(1), [368]
  length—
    goods sold by, **39(1)**, [584]
    trade, use for, **39(1)**, [553], [558]
  liquid fuel, provisions for, **39(1)**, [574]
  local standards—
    certification of, **39(1)**, [478]
    custody, etc of, **39(1)**, [525]
    form of, **39(1)**, [478]
    general provisions, **39(1)**, [478]
    maintenance of, **39(1)**, [478]
    tertiary standards, comparison with,
      39(1), [477]
    See also standards *below*
  London, gaugable liquors imported into,
    39(1), [543]
  lubricating oil, provisions for, **39(1)**, [574]
  metre—
    standards. *See* standards *below*
    UK primary standard, **39(1)**, [562]
    unit of measurement, **39(1)**, [475]
  metric units—
    conversion charts, **39(1)**, [483]
    dual marking, **39(1)**, [483]
    meaning, **39(1)**, [483]
    schedule of, **39(1)**, [553]–[557],
      [565]–[569]
  miscellaneous goods—
    capacity, marked with, **39(1)**, [587], [588]
    composite goods, **39(1)**, [591]
    length, sold by or marked with,
      39(1), [584]
    net weight, sale by, **39(1)**, [585]
    number, marked by, **39(1)**, [590]
    pre-packed goods, **39(1)**, [586]–[590]
  nails, for, **39(1)**, [585]
  Northern Ireland provisions, **39(1)**, [592]
  number, goods sold by, **39(1)**, [590]
  offences—
    approved patterns, respecting, **39(1)**, [489]
    corporations, by, **39(1)**, [535]
    default of another, due to, **39(1)**, [508]
    defences in proceedings, **39(1)**, [509]
    due diligence, defence of, **39(1)**, [510]
    false or unjust equipment, **39(1)**, [494]
    obstruction of inspector, **39(1)**, [533]

weights and measures—*contd*
  offences—*contd*
    penalties, **39(1)**, [537]
    prosecution of, **39(1)**, [536]
    short weight, giving, **39(1)**, [505]
    stamping, as to, **39(1)**, [493], [528]
    use of equipment, in, **39(1)**, [485]
  ounce troy—
    restriction on use, **39(1)**, [482]
    weights of, **39(1)**, [482]
  packaged goods—
    containers—
      meaning, **39(1)**, [547]
      See also containers *above*
    inspectors. *See* inspectors *above*
    packer—
      identification of, **39(1)**, [500]
      name, etc, to be shown, **39(1)**, [500]
    quantity—
      less than stated, **39(1)**, [506]
      subsequent deficiency, **39(1)**, [511]
      tests of, **39(1)**, [513]
    quantity control, offences. *See* offences
      above
    Secretary of State—
      determination of questions by,
        39(1), [538]
      report to Parliament by, **39(1)**, [540]
    short weight, etc, **39(1)**, [505]
  paints, etc, for, **39(1)**, [585]
  pound—
    primary standard, authorised copies,
      39(1), [561]
    standards. *See* standards *below*
    UK primary standard, **39(1)**, [561]
    unit of measurement, **39(1)**, [475]
  regulations and orders, **39(1)**, [539]
  safety—
    provisions, enforcement of, **39(1)**, [615]
    reports on, **39(1)**, [629]
  sand. *See* ballast *above*
  soap, for, **39(1)**, [583]
  solid fuel. *See* **solid fuel**
  stamp (stamping)—
    equipment for, provision of, **39(1)**, [479]
    fees for, **39(1)**, [530]
    meaning, **39(1)**, [547]
    offences in respect of, **39(1)**, [528]
    responsibility for, **39(1)**, [525]
    transitional provisions, **39(1)**, [594]
    validity of, **39(1)**, [485]
    weighing, etc, equipment—
      Channel Islands, in, **39(1)**, [485]
      forgery, etc, **39(1)**, [493]
      Isle of Man, in, **39(1)**, [485]
      offences in connection with,
        39(1), [493]
      procedure, **39(1)**, [485]
      reinstallation, after, **39(1)**, [485]
      requirements, **39(1)**, [485]
  standards of measurement—
    coinage standards—
      maintenance of, **39(1)**, [477]
      meaning, **39(1)**, [477]

weights and measures—*contd*
standards of measurement—*contd*
Department for Innovation, Universities
and Skills standards, **39(1)**, [477]
meaning, **39(1)**, [547]
divisions, marking of, **39(1)**, [477]
local. *See* local standards *above*
meaning, **39(1)**, [477]
Northern Ireland, for, **39(1)**, [593]
primary—
copies, authorised, **39(1)**, [476],
[560]–[564]
definition of, **39(1)**, [476]
description of, **39(1)**, [560]–[564]
maintenance of, **39(1)**, [476]
redetermining, **39(1)**, [476]
replacement, **39(1)**, [477]
secondary—
maintenance of, **39(1)**, [477]
meaning, **39(1)**, [477]
summary of provisions, **39(1)**, [1]
tertiary—
maintenance of, **39(1)**, [477]
meaning, **39(1)**, [477]
testing of, **39(1)**, [480]
working. *See* working standards *below*
testing—
equipment. *See* weighing, etc, equipment
below
fees for, **39(1)**, [530]
standards, of, **39(1)**, [480]
toiletries, for, **39(1)**, [582], [583]
trade descriptions provisions, enforcing—
authorities, **39(1)**, [101]
notice of test and intended prosecution,
39(1), [105]
officers, obstruction of, **39(1)**, [104]
premises, entry into, **39(1)**, [103]
seizure of goods and documents,
39(1), [103], [107]
test purchases, making, **39(1)**, [102]
trade, use for—
capacity measures, **39(1)**, [569]
cubic measures, **39(1)**, [567]
divisions of units, **39(1)**, [484]
drugs, dispensing, **39(1)**, [482], [484]
equipment in, **39(1)**, [481]
exceptions from, **39(1)**, [481]
linear measures, **39(1)**, [565]
meaning, **39(1)**, [481]
metric units—
conversion charts, **39(1)**, [483]
dual marking, **39(1)**, [483]
multiples of units, **39(1)**, [484]
square measures, **39(1)**, [566]
summary of provisions, **39(1)**, [1]
supplementary indications, except as for,
39(1), [558]
units of measurement—
lawful, **39(1)**, [565]–[569]
restriction on, **39(1)**, [482]
transitional provisions, **39(1)**, [594]
units of measurement—
area, of—
definitions, **39(1)**, [554]

weights and measures—*contd*
units of measurement—*contd*
area, of—*contd*
supplementary indication, use as,
39(1), [558]
capacity, of—
definition, **39(1)**, [556]
trade, use for, **39(1)**, [568]
electricity, for, **39(1)**, [559]
fractions of, marking, **39(1)**, [484]
length, **39(1)**, [475], [553]
trade use, supplementary indications,
except as for, **39(1)**, [558]
meaning, **39(1)**, [482]
summary of provisions, **39(1)**, [1]
use for trade. *See* trade, use for *above*
volume, of, **39(1)**, [555]
weight, **39(1)**, [475], [557]
wholesale transactions, use in, **39(1)**, [542]
yard or metre, **39(1)**, [475]
vending machines—
information to be displayed on,
39(1), [499], [500]
inspectors' powers, **39(1)**, [514]
sales from—
exceptions as to, **39(1)**, [504]
offences as to, **39(1)**, [502]
solid fuel, **39(1)**, [574]
volume, units of measurement—
definition, **39(1)**, [555]
supplementary indication, use as,
39(1), [558]
warranty, quantity, as to, **39(1)**, [509]
weighing and measuring equipment—
approval of manufacturers to test—
conditions of, **39(1)**, [570]
effect of, **39(1)**, [570]
fees for, **39(1)**, [570]
form of, **39(1)**, [570]
further approval, application for,
39(1), [570]
generally, **39(1)**, [486]
grant of new approval, **39(1)**, [570]
suspension of, **39(1)**, [570]
withdrawal of, **39(1)**, [570]
false, use of, **39(1)**, [494]
forfeiture of, **39(1)**, [491], [493]
general specifications of, **39(1)**, [490]
exemption from, **39(1)**, [490]
variation or revocation, **39(1)**, [490]
inspection of, **39(1)**, [532]
manufacturers, pre-test stamping by,
39(1), [492]
meaning, **39(1)**, [547]
offences in use of, **39(1)**, [485]
passing as fit for use, **39(1)**, [485]
patterns—
approval of—
certificate of, **39(1)**, [488]
procedure, **39(1)**, [488]
approved—
marking of, **39(1)**, [488]
meaning, **39(1)**, [488]
offences respecting, **39(1)**, [489]

weights and measures—*contd*
  weighing and measuring equipment—*contd*
    patterns—*contd*
      certificate of approval—
        meaning, **39(1)**, [489]
        offences relating to, **39(1)**, [489]
        renewal of, **39(1)**, [489]
        revocation of, **39(1)**, [488]
      model or drawings of, **39(1)**, [488]
      public equipment—
        charges for use of, **39(1)**, [496]
        keepers of—
          certificate, to hold, **39(1)**, [495]
          offences by, **39(1)**, [495]
        offences in connection with,
          39(1), [497]
        provision of, **39(1)**, [496]
        records of use, **39(1)**, [497]
      refusal to pass, **39(1)**, [485]
      regulations for, **39(1)**, [491]
      stamping. *See* stamp *above*
      testing—
        assistance to be given in, **39(1)**, [485]
        equipment for, **39(1)**, [479], [480]
        fees for, **39(1)**, [485]
        official EEA tester, by, **39(1)**, [487]
        procedure, **39(1)**, [485]
        records of, **39(1)**, [485]
        regulations for, **39(1)**, [491]
        submission for, **39(1)**, [485]
      trade, in use for—
        possession, evidence of, **39(1)**, [481]
        when deemed to be, **39(1)**, [481]
      unjust, use of, **39(1)**, [494]
    weight, units of measurement—
      definition, **39(1)**, [557]
      supplementary indication, use as,
        39(1), [558]
      use for trade, **39(1)**, [569]
    wood fuel, for, **39(1)**, [581]
    working standards—
      custody, etc, of, **39(1)**, [525]
      material and form, **39(1)**, [479]
      provision of, **39(1)**, [479]
      testing of, **39(1)**, [479]
    yard—
      primary standards, authorised copies,
        39(1), [560]
      standards. *See* standards *above*
      UK primary standard, **39(1)**, [560]
      unit of measurement, **39(1)**, [475]

weights and measures authority
  annual report by, **39(1)**, [523]
  fees—
    EEC obligations, under, **39(1)**, [529]
    inspectors, paid to, **39(1)**, [531]
    reduction of, **39(1)**, [530]
  Hallmarking Act, enforcing, **48**, 61
  inspections, duties as to, **39(1)**, [524]
  inspectors. *See* **weights and measures**
  joint authorities, Greater London,
    39(1), [594]
  meaning, **39(1)**, [522]

weights and measures authority—*contd*
  trade mark offences, enforcement function,
    48, 176

weirs
  watercourse, causing obstruction of,
    19(3), [192]

welfare food
  distribution, schemes for, **40(1)**, [190]

welfare food schemes
  replacement of, Northern Ireland, **30**, [748]

welfare services
  meaning, **22**, [13]; **50**, [153]
  power to repeal provisions, **23**, [182]
  provision by local housing authority, **22**, [13]
  value added tax, exemption from, **50**, [153]

well
  insanitary, **35(1)**, [144]
  polluted water from, protection from,
    35(1), [143]
  utilising by parish council for water supply,
    35(1), [142]
  vesting in local authority, **35(1)**, [141]

Wellington Museum
  Apsley House—
    destruction or damage to, **13**, [105]
    Dukes of Wellington—
      access by, **13**, [102], [110]
      maintenance, duty as to, **13**, [104]
      occupation of part, **13**, [102]
    establishment, **13**, [49], [100]
    expenses, **13**, [107]
    heirlooms, transfer of, **13**, [100]
    history, **13**, [49]
    maintenance, **13**, [104]
    rates and taxes, **13**, [103]
    transfer, **13**, [100]
    use of—
      government entertainment, for,
        13, [101]
      museum, part as, **13**, [101], [109]
      occupation of part by Dukes of
        Wellington, **13**, [102]
      public purposes, **13**, [101]
    variation of provisions, power as to,
      13, [106]

Welsh
  election forms, **15(3)**, [242]
  grants for education in, **15(1)**, [614]

Welsh Administration Ombudsman
  abolition of office, **10**, [835]

Welsh Assembly
  copyright in Measures and Bills of,
    11(1), [996]–[997]

Welsh Authority (Sianel Pedwar Cymru)
television—
  accounts and audit, **45**, [191]
  advertisements—
    control, **45**, [197]
    rules as to, **45**, [112]
  advertising, directions with respect to,
    45, [765]
  advisory committees, **45**, [191]
  annual reports, **45**, [191]
  audience research, **45**, [116]
  continuance as body corporate, **45**, [110]
  deaf, services for, **45**, [765]
  documents, presumption of authenticity,
    45, [191]
  employees, **45**, [191]
  equality of opportunity, **45**, [765]
  fairness standards, **45**, [765]
  finances, **45**, [589]
  Fourth Channel Authority, use as name,
    45, [110]
  funding, **45**, [113]
  government control, **45**, [115]
  independent productions—
    programme quotas for, **45**, [764]
    programming quotas for, **45**, [765]
  information, provision of, **45**, [708]
  international obligations—
    compliance with, **45**, [765]
    directions by Secretary of State as to,
      45, [176]
  licence fees, statement of charging
    principles, **45**, [711]
  members—
    appointment, **45**, [110], [191]
    remuneration and pensions, **45**, [191]
    tenure of office, **45**, [191]
  monitoring of programmes, **45**, [765]
  must-offer obligations in relation to
    networks and satellite services, **45**, [765]
  news and current affairs programmes,
    45, [765]
  OFCOM's function in relation to,
    45, [585]
  other activities, **45**, [588]
  other services, powers to provide, **45**, [587]
  party political broadcasts, **45**, [765]
  penalties, imposition of, **45**, [707]
  proceedings, **45**, [191]
  programme commissioning, code relating
    to, **45**, [765]
  programme policy, statement of, **45**, [765]
  programme quotas for independent
    productions, **45**, [764], [765]
  programme standards, **45**, [765]
  public service fund, **45**, [114]
  public service remits—
    generally, **45**, [765]
    remedial action, directions to take,
      45, [706]
    review of fulfilment of, **45**, [705]
  public services, meaning, **45**, [765]
  public teletext provider, co-operation
    with, **45**, [765]
  S4C, provision of, **45**, [586]

**Welsh Authority (Sianel Pedwar
Cymru)**—*contd*
television—*contd*
  status and capacity, **45**, [191]
  supply of services by satellite in certain
    areas, **45**, [765]
  transitional arrangements, **45**, [157]
  visually impaired, services for, **45**, [765]

Welsh (Church) Commissioners
accounts and audit, **14**, 280
annual report, **14**, 265
appointment of, **14**, 263–4
books and documents, delivery to, **14**, 278–9
borrowing powers, **14**, 279–80
compensation, paying—
  freehold offices, holders of, **14**, 270
  lay patrons, **14**, 269
continuation of, **14**, 290
copyhold land vested in, conveying,
  14, 280–1
final, orders being, **14**, 265
local authorities, settling differences between,
  14, 282
management and sale, powers of, **14**, 277–8
powers of, **14**, 264–5
Privy Council, appeal to, **14**, 265–6
procedure, **14**, 264–5
property, transfer to representative body,
  14, 261
residue of property, application of, **14**, 272–3
stock vested in, dealing with, **14**, 280–1

Welsh company
cyfyngedig, improper use of, **8**, 134
documents relating to, **8**, 573–4
name of, **8**, 125
  general requirements, **8**, 533
  use of "limited" in, **8**, 131–2, 533

Welsh Development Agency
accounts of, **47**, [260]
acquisition of share capital—
  consent, requirement for, **47**, [248]
  publishing business, in, **47**, [247]
  television company, in, **47**, [247]
Advisory Board, establishment, **47**, [241]
agents, power to appoint, **47**, [234]
assistance by local authorities etc, **47**, [234]
borrowing—
  aggregate amount, **47**, [246]
  general external, meaning, **47**, [246]
  methods of, **47**, [260]
  subsidiaries, by, **47**, [260]
  Treasury guarantees, **47**, [260]
business premises, provisions on, **21**, [223]
chairman and deputy, **47**, [232], [258]
charges for services of, **47**, [233]
chief executive—
  appointment, **47**, [232]
  removal from office, **47**, [258]
committees, power to form, **47**, [235]
constitution of, **47**, [232]
derelict land, powers respecting, **47**, [244]

Welsh Development Agency—contd
Development Board for Rural Wales, transfer
of property etc of, **10**, [1269]
directions to, **47**, [231]
documents—
authentication of, **47**, [258]
service of, **47**, [254]
establishment, **47**, [231]
financial provisions—
accounting year, meaning, **47**, [255]
capital debt, **47**, [260]
duties as to, **47**, [245]
generally, **47**, [246]
Government loans, **47**, [260]
financing of, **47**, [260]
functions generally, **47**, [231]
Government loan debt—
meaning, **47**, [362]
reduction of, **47**, [362]
grants for land improvement, **47**, [244]
incorporation of, **47**, [258]
industry—
premises for, provision of, **47**, [238]
services for, provision of, **47**, [239]
sites, provision of, **47**, [238]
information, disclosure of, **47**, [253]
land—
acquisition of—
agreement, by, **47**, [262]
cleansing provisions, **47**, [263]
compulsory, **47**, [261]
Crown land, **47**, [264]
documents, regulations as to form of,
47, [264]
entry, rights of, **47**, [264]
generally, **47**, [250]
information, **47**, [264]
local inquiries, **47**, [264]
offences by corporations, **47**, [264]
possession, displacement of legislation
preventing, **47**, [264]
register of land holdings, **47**, [264]
disposal, powers of, **47**, [251]
improvement grants, **47**, [244]
matters, powers to advise on, **47**, [252]
meaning, **47**, [255]
reclamation etc, **47**, [244]
transfer to, **47**, [237]
Land Authority for Wales, transfer of property
etc of, **10**, [1273]
members—
appointment, **47**, [232], [258]
financial etc interests of, **47**, [258]
pensions, provision for, **47**, [258]
qualifications, **47**, [232]
remuneration etc, **47**, [258]
terms of office, **47**, [258]
newspapers, restriction on publishing,
47, [247]
orders and regulations, **47**, [256]
powers—
ancillary, **47**, [233]
derelict land, as to, **47**, [244]
generally, **47**, [231]
information, to obtain, **47**, [253]

Welsh Development Agency—contd
powers—contd
land, as to, **47**, [250]–[252]
restrictions on, **47**, [248]
proceedings of, **47**, [258]
public dividend capital—
meaning, **47**, [361]
reduction of, **47**, [361]
publicly-owned property—
meaning, **47**, [255]
transfer to Agency, **47**, [242]
purposes of, **47**, [231]
regeneration and development, financial
assistance for, **47**, [240]
regulations, **47**, [256]
reports—
annual, **47**, [260]
contents, **47**, [231]
schemes—
duty to prepare, **47**, [231]
environmental improvement etc, for,
47, [243]
services of—
charges for, **47**, [233]
industrial development, for, **47**, [239]
staff—
appointment, **47**, [258]
transfer from Estates Corporation, **47**, [259]
stamp duty exemption, **47**, [258], [354]
stamp duty land tax exemption, **47**, [258],
[355]
status of, **47**, [232], [258]
taxes etc, liability for, **47**, [232]
television programmes, restriction as to,
47, [248]
transfer of property to Minister, **47**, [354]

**Welsh Industrial Development Advisory
Board**
constitution of, **47**, [241]
establishment, **47**, [241]
recommendations by, **47**, [241]

Welsh Industrial Estates Corporation
dissolution of, **47**, [236]
staff—
compensation for, **47**, [259]
transfer of, **47**, [259]

Welsh language
affirmations, use of in, **7(1)**, [271]
Board—
accounts, **7(1)**, [280]
annual reports, **7(1)**, [280]
chairman, **7(1)**, [280]
directions to, **7(1)**, [252]
establishment of, **7(1)**, [249]
evidence, **7(1)**, [280]
expenses, **7(1)**, [280]
functions, **7(1)**, [251]
members, **7(1)**, [280]
membership, **7(1)**, [250]
notices to, **7(1)**, [276]
procedure, **7(1)**, [280]
remuneration, **7(1)**, [280]

Welsh language—*contd*
Board—*contd*
staff, **7(1)**, [280]
status, **7(1)**, [280]
summary of provisions, **7(1)**, [1]
supplementary provisions, **7(1)**, [252]
forms, Welsh, power to prescribe, **7(1)**, [274], [275]
knowledge of, in mine operations, **17(1)**, [145]
legal proceedings—
interpreters, provision of, for, **7(1)**, [272]
use in, **7(1)**, [270]
marriage in, **27**, [265]
oaths, use of in, **7(1)**, [271]
repeals, **7(1)**, [277], [281]
schemes—
amendment of, **7(1)**, [264]
approval of, **7(1)**, [262]
compliance with—
directions by Secretary of State, **7(1)**, [268]
investigations, **7(1)**, [265]
non-compliance, complaints of, **7(1)**, [266]
reports on investigations, **7(1)**, [267]
guidelines on—
approval of, **7(1)**, [258]
Board's duty to issue, **7(1)**, [257]
revision of, **7(1)**, [259]
imposition of, **7(1)**, [262]
persons acting on behalf of Crown, **7(1)**, [269]
public bodies—
duty of to prepare, **7(1)**, [253]
meaning of, **7(1)**, [254]
notices to, **7(1)**, [255], [276]
preparation by—
consultation on, **7(1)**, [261]
general, **7(1)**, [260]
revision of, periodic, **7(1)**, [263]
summary of provisions, **7(1)**, [1]
time limits for submitting, objections to, **7(1)**, [256]
statutory bodies, power to give Welsh names to, **7(1)**, [273], [275]

Welsh Ministers
housing legislation, reference in, **24**, [601]

Welsh television
advertising on, **45**, [197]
rules as to, **45**, [112]
Authority. *See* **Welsh Authority**
Programmes, sources of, **45**, [111]

West Indies
associated state—
common courts, establishment of, **7(2)**, [613]
persons in public service, provisions for, **7(2)**, [614]
colonies—
government of, **7(2)**, [495]–[496]
grants for, **7(2)**, [498]

West Indies—*contd*
common courts, **7(2)**, [494]
Federal public service officers, compensation, **7(2)**, [493]
government of, **7(2)**, [496]
Orders in Council, **7(2)**, [497], [615]

Western Samoa
British ship registered in, **7(2)**, [740]
Commonwealth—
citizenship, **31**, [186]
entry into, **7(2)**, [737]
visiting forces in, **7(2)**, [740]

Westminster
canonries, annexation of rectories to, **14**, 134
capitular revenues, charges on, **14**, 161–2
free seats in churches, **14**, 204

Westminster Hospital
site, development of, **10**, [505]–[513]. *See also* **Works, Minister of**

Westminster School. *See* **public school**

Westminster Technical Institute
hotel as part of, **25(1)**, [253]

wetlands
designation of, **32**, [1]
Ramsar sites, **32**, [467]

Wey Navigation
management of, **32**, [309]
meaning, **32**, [308]

whales and whaling
blue whales, names of, **1(1)**, [344]
Board of Trade, exercise of powers of, **1(1)**, [338]
British possessions, exempted operations in coastal waters of, **1(1)**, [336]
catching, prohibition of, **1(1)**, [326]
classification of whales, **1(1)**, [327], [343]–[346]
coastal waters—
British possessions, of, operations in, **1(1)**, [336]
local law, protected by, **1(1)**, [336]; **1(2)**, [180]
meaning, **1(1)**, [340]
UK, of, prohibition of taking and treating in, **1(1)**, [326]
colonies, application of provisions to, **1(1)**, [335]
Crown right to, **1(1)**, [124]
Crown right to, **1(1)**, [124]; **10**, [11], [84]
expenses, application of fees and fines to, **1(1)**, [339]
female with calf, protection of, **1(1)**, [327]
fin whales, names of, **1(1)**, [345]
fishery inspectors, **1(1)**, [332]
grey—
names of, **1(1)**, [346]
protection of, **1(1)**, [327]

whales and whaling—*contd*
immature whale, protection of, **1(1)**, [327]
legal proceedings, provisions on, **1(1)**, [334]
length of, regulations on, **1(1)**, [327], [341]
licence—
conditions attached to, **1(1)**, [330]
document presumed to be, **1(1)**, [334]
duration of, **1(1)**, [364]
exercise of powers, **1(1)**, [338]
fee, **1(1)**, [329], [364]
forgery of, **1(1)**, [333]
grant of, **1(1)**, [329]
ship, for, **1(1)**, [328]
whale-oil factory, for, **1(1)**, [328]
non-British ship, application of provisions to, **1(1)**, [335]
protected whales, **1(1)**, [327], [363]
regulation of, **1(2)**, [180]
right whale—
meaning, **1(1)**, [327]
names of, **1(1)**, [343]
protection of, **1(1)**, [327]
scientific purposes, permits for, **1(1)**, [331]
summary of provisions, **1(1)**, [124]
treating, prohibition, **1(1)**, [326]
UK waters, prohibition on taking or treating in, **1(1)**, [326]
whales to which restrictions apply, **1(1)**, [325]

wharves
customs and excise purposes, for, approval of, **13**, [600], [601]
Factories Acts, provisions applicable, **18**, [1178]

wheat. *See also* **cereals**
weights for basis of payment, **1(1)**, [248]

whisky
defined, **13**, [560], [563]
meaning, **19(3)**, [464]
Scotch. *See* **Scotch whisky**

White Fish Authority
abolition of, **1(2)**, [167]
Sea Fish Industry Authority, transfer to, **1(2)**, [189]

widow
provision for. *See* **family provision**

widowed parent's allowance
application of provisions, **40(1)**, [274]
Category B retirement pension, entitlement to, **40(1)**, [296]
contribution conditions, **40(1)**, [463]
contributions credits, **40(1)**, [263]
entitlement to, **40(1)**, [278]

widower's benefits
bereavement allowance—
application of provisions, **40(1)**, [274]
Category B retirement pension, entitlement to, **40(1)**, [296]
contribution conditions, **40(1)**, [463]

widower's benefits—*contd*
bereavement allowance—*contd*
entitlement to, **40(1)**, [279]
rate of, **40(1)**, [280], [466]
bereavement payment, **40(1)**, [273]
long-term incapacity benefit—
application of provisions, **40(1)**, [274]
entitlement to, **40(1)**, [282]
period of employment or training for work, after, **40(1)**, [283]
retirement pension, Category B, **40(1)**, [295], [298]

widow's benefits
bereavement allowance—
application of provisions, **40(1)**, [274]
Category B retirement pension, entitlement to, **40(1)**, [296]
contribution conditions, **40(1)**, [463]
entitlement to, **40(1)**, [279]
rate of, **40(1)**, [280], [465]
bereavement payment, **40(1)**, [273]
contribution conditions, **40(1)**, [260]
contributory, being, **40(1)**, [259]
death difficult to establish, where, **40(1)**, [502]
graduated retirement, **40(1)**, [43]
long-term incapacity benefit—
application of provisions, **40(1)**, [274]
entitlement to, **40(1)**, [281]
period of employment or training for work, after, **40(1)**, [283]
payments, treatment of, **40(1)**, [503]
pension—
application of provisions, **40(1)**, [274]
contribution conditions, **40(1)**, [463]
failure to satisfy—
entitlement on, **40(1)**, [307]
increase of benefit, exclusion of, **40(1)**, [309]
proportion, entitlement to, **40(1)**, [308]
entitlement to, **40(1)**, [276]
rate of, **40(1)**, [277]
regulations, **40(1)**, [362]
retirement pension, Category B, **40(1)**, [295]
war widow's pension, meaning, **40(1)**, [402]
widowed mother's allowance—
application of provisions, **40(1)**, [274]
contribution conditions, **40(1)**, [463]
failure to satisfy—
entitlement on, **40(1)**, [307]
increase of benefit, exclusion of, **40(1)**, [309]
proportion, entitlement to, **40(1)**, [308]
entitlement to, **40(1)**, [275]
rate of, **40(1)**, [277]
women widowed before 11 April 1988, for, **40(1)**, [199], [220], [277]

wife. *See also* **married woman**
enticement and harbouring etc, actions for, abolition, **45**, [954], [983]

wife—*contd*
  evidence of. *See* **evidence**
  tenant, of, goods of, not privileged from
    distress for rent, **13**, [1202]

wild animals
  advertisement—
    meaning, **32**, [438]
    offence of publishing, **32**, [410]
  advisory body, **32**, [434]
  badgers. *See* **badgers**
  bats, protection of, **32**, [411]
  conditions for keeping, **2**, [408]
  dangerous—
    breach of conditions for keeping, **2**, [409]
    circus animals, **2**, [412]
    insurance against liability, **2**, [408]
    keepers—
      existing, protection of, **2**, [416]
      meaning, **2**, [414]
    licence to keep—
      cancellation on conviction of offence,
        2, [413]
      conditions for granting, **2**, [408]
      death of holder, **2**, [409]
      duration, **2**, [409]
      exemptions, **2**, [412]
      refused, appeal as to, **2**, [409]
      requirement for, **2**, [408]
      variation or revocation, **2**, [408]
    offences and penalties, **2**, [409], [413]
    premises where kept—
      inspection, **2**, [408], [410]
      specified in licence, **2**, [408]
    schedule of, **2**, [418]
      power to modify, **2**, [415]
    seizure and disposal, **2**, [411]
  destruction to control diseases, **2**, [452], [453]
  disabled, tending, **32**, [411]
  dolphin, protection of, **32**, [410]
  endangered species, **32**, [418]
  GB conservation bodies, functions of,
    32, [435]
  killing, injuring or taking—
    disabled, where, **32**, [411]
    illegal methods, **32**, [412], [502]
    licences for, **32**, [419]
    livestock or foodstuffs, preventing damage
      to, **32**, [411]
    offences, **32**, [410]
    public health purposes, for, **32**, [412]
  licences concerning—
    false statements, **32**, [420]
    licensing authority, **32**, [419]
    poison, use of, **32**, [419]
    purposes of, **32**, [419]
  local authorities, functions of, **32**, [436]
  mammals, protection of, **32**, [503]
  meaning, **32**, [438]
  new species, introduction of, **32**, [415], [419]
  offences—
    attempt to commit, **32**, [421]
    body corporate, by, **32**, [484]
    enforcement—
      offences, **32**, [430]

wild animals—*contd*
  offences—*contd*
    enforcement—*contd*
      powers, **32**, [428]–[431]
      samples, power to take, **32**, [429]
    exceptions, **32**, [411]
    false statement, making, **32**, [420]
    forfeiture, powers of, **32**, [432]
    killing or taking, illegal methods of,
      32, [412]
    penalties, **32**, [432]
    protection, relating to, **32**, [410]
    summary prosecution, **32**, [431]
  official requirement, act in pursuance of,
    32, [411]
  order, making of, **32**, [437]
  possessing, offences, **32**, [410]
  protected, list of, **32**, [501]
  protection of—
    defences, **32**, [410]
    dwelling-house, acts done in, **32**, [411]
    exceptions, **32**, [411]
    generally, **32**, [1]
    offences, **32**, [410]
  sale of—
    licensing, **32**, [419]
    meaning, **32**, [438]
    offence, as, **32**, [410]
  schedules, variation of, **32**, [433]
  shark, protection of, **32**, [410]
  shelter or protection, offences relating to,
    32, [410]
  theft of, **12(1)**, [556]
  whale, protection of, **32**, [410]
  wild, established in, **32**, [505]
  wildlife inspectors—
    examination of specimens and taking
      samples—
        group 1 offences and licences, **32**, [424]
        group 2 offences and licences, **32**, [426]
    live specimens, restrictions on taking
      samples from, **32**, [427]
    meaning, **32**, [422]
    power to enter premises—
      group 1 offences and licences, **32**, [423]
      group 2 offences and licences, **32**, [425]

wild birds
  advertisement—
    licensed, **32**, [419]
    meaning, **32**, [438]
    offence of publishing, **32**, [407]
  advisory body, **32**, [434]
  area of special protection, **32**, [404]
  aviculture, meaning, **32**, [438]
  bred in captivity, where, **32**, [402]
  captive birds—
    cage, size of, **32**, [409]
    liberation for shooting, **32**, [410]
    licensing, **32**, [419]
    registration of, **32**, [408], [500]
      fee for, **32**, [408]
    ringing or marking, **32**, [407], [500]
  close season—
    meaning, **32**, [403]

wild birds—*contd*
  close season—*contd*
    prescription of, **32**, [433]
  competition—
    licensing, **32**, [419]
    showing in, **32**, [407]
  dependent young, disturbing, **32**, [402], [404]
  disabled, tending, **32**, [405]
  egg, protection of—
    destroying, meaning, **32**, [438]
    exceptions, **32**, [403]
    human consumption, food for, **32**, [419]
    offences relating to, **32**, [402]
    sale of, **32**, [407]
    special, areas of, **32**, [404]
  GB conservation bodies, functions of,
    32, [435]
  human consumption, food for, **32**, [419]
  illegal possession of—
    defences, **32**, [402]
    offence, as, **32**, [402]
  keeping of, fee for registration for, **32**, [642]
  killing or taking—
    area of special protection, in, **32**, [404]
    cage-trap, use of, **32**, [406]
    close season, outside, **32**, [403]
    defences, **32**, [402]
    disabled, where, **32**, [405]
    illegal methods, **32**, [406]
    licences, **32**, [419]
    net, use of, **32**, [406]
    offence, as, **32**, [402]
    permitted, **32**, [495]–[496]
    public health purposes, for, **32**, [405]
  licences concerning—
    false statements, **32**, [420]
    licensing authority, **32**, [419]
    matters covered by, **32**, [419]
  local authorities, functions of, **32**, [436]
  meaning, **32**, [438]
  nesting—
    area of special protection, in, **32**, [404]
    disturbing, **32**, [402]
    protection of—
      exceptions, **32**, [403]
      offences relating to, **32**, [402]
      special, areas of, **32**, [404]
  nests, re-using, **32**, [492]
  offences—
    areas of special protection, in, **32**, [404]
    attempt to commit, **32**, [421]
    body corporate, by, **32**, [484]
    captive birds, relating to, **32**, [408]–[409]
    competition, showing in, **32**, [407]
    enforcement—
      offences, **32**, [430]
      powers, **32**, [428]–[431]
      samples, power to take, **32**, [429]
    exceptions, **32**, [403]
    false statement, making, **32**, [420]
    forfeiture, powers of, **32**, [432]
    killing or taking, illegal methods of,
      32, [406]
    penalties, **32**, [432]
    previous offence, following, **32**, [408]

wild birds—*contd*
  offences—*contd*
    protection, relating to, **32**, [402]
    sale, relating to, **32**, [407]
    summary prosecution, **32**, [431]
  official requirements, acts in pursuance of,
    32, [405]
  order, making of, **32**, [437]
  protection of—
    exceptions, **32**, [403]
    excluded purposes, **32**, [419]
    generally, **32**, [1]
    offences, **32**, [402]
  registration—
    captive birds, of, **32**, [408]
    conviction, following, **32**, [408]
    false statements, **32**, [420]
    fees, **32**, [642]
  sale of—
    fee for registration for, **32**, [642]
    licensing, **32**, [419]
    meaning, **32**, [438]
    offences, **32**, [407]
    permitted, **32**, [497]–[499]
  schedules, variation of, **32**, [433]
  special penalties, protected by, **32**, [493]–[494]
  special protection—
    areas of, **32**, [404]
    period of, **32**, [403]
  wildlife inspectors—
    examination of specimens and taking
    samples—
      group 1 offences and licences, **32**, [424]
      group 2 offences and licences, **32**, [426]
    live specimens, restrictions on taking
    samples from, **32**, [427]
    meaning, **32**, [422]
    power to enter premises—
      group 1 offences and licences, **32**, [423]
      group 2 offences and licences, **32**, [425]

wild flora and fauna
  Antarctica, in. *See* **Antarctica**

wild fowl
  eggs, taking or destroying, **2**, [166]

wild mammals
  falconry, exempt from hunting provisions,
    2, [749]
  meaning, **2**, [708], [742]
  offences—
    confiscation, court powers of, **2**, [711]
    constable, powers of, **2**, [709]
    exceptions from, **2**, [707]
    generally, **2**, [706]
    hare coursing. *See* **hares** (coursing)
    hunting with dogs—
      assistance, **2**, [735]
      body corporate, by, **2**, [741]
      Crown application, **2**, [743]
      defences, **2**, [736]
      exemptions, **2**, [734], [749]
      forfeiture, **2**, [740]
      generally, **2**, [733]

wild mammals—*contd*
  offences—*contd*
    hunting with dogs—*contd*
      meaning, **2**, [742]
      penalties, **2**, [739]
      search and seizure, power of, **2**, [739]
    penalties for, **2**, [710]
    rabbits, exempt from hunting provisions,
      2, [749]
    rats, exempt from hunting provisions, **2**, [749]
    recapture of, exempt from hunting
      provisions, **2**, [749]
    rescue of, exempt from hunting provisions,
      2, [749]
    research and observation, exempt from
      hunting provisions, **2**, [749]
    stalking and flushing out, exempt from
      hunting provisions, **2**, [749]

wild plants
  advertisement—
    meaning, **32**, [438]
    offence, as, **32**, [414]
  advisory body, **32**, [434]
  destruction of, **32**, [414]
  GB conservation bodies, functions of,
    32, [435]
  invasive non-native species—
    codes of practice, **32**, [417]
    sale etc of, **32**, [416]
  licences concerning—
    false statements, **32**, [420]
    licensing authority, **32**, [419]
    matters covered by, **32**, [419]
  meaning, **32**, [438]
  new species, introduction of, **32**, [415], [419]
  offences—
    attempt to commit, **32**, [421]
    body corporate, by, **32**, [484]
    enforcement—
      offences, **32**, [430]
      powers, **32**, [428]–[431]
      samples, power to take, **32**, 429]
    false statement, making, **32**, [420]
    forfeiture, powers of, **32**, [432]
    invasive non-native species, sale etc of,
      32, [416]
    new species, relating to, **32**, [415]
    penalties, **32**, [432]
    protection, relating to, **32**, [414]
    summary prosecution, **32**, [431]
  order, making of, **32**, [437]
  picking—
    meaning, **32**, [438]
    offences, **32**, [414]
  protected, list of, **32**, [504]
  protection of, **32**, [414]
  sale of—
    licensing, **32**, [419]
    meaning, **32**, [438]
    offence, as, **32**, [414]
  schedules, variation of, **32**, [433]
  uprooting—
    meaning, **32**, [438]
    offences, **32**, [414]

wild plants—*contd*
  wild, established in, **32**, [506]
  wildlife inspectors—
    examination of specimens and taking
      samples—
        group 1 offences and licences, **32**, [424]
        group 2 offences and licences, **32**, [426]
      meaning, **32**, [422]
    power to enter premises—
        group 1 offences and licences, **32**, [423]
        group 2 offences and licences, **32**, [425]

wildlife
  biodiversity—
    duty to conserve, **32**, [805]
    lists and action, **32**, [806]–[807]
  codes of practice, **32**, [841]
  conservation functions as to, **32**, [801]
  inspectors, other Acts, powers extended to,
    32, [840]
  offences, time limit for proceedings, **32**, [843]
  pesticides harmful to, possession of—
    codes of practice, **32**, [810]
    enforcement powers, **32**, [808]
    offences, **32**, [808]
  search warrants, **32**, [842]

will
  accumulations, restrictions on, **20**, [773],
    [774]
  administration without proving, penalty,
    18, [453]
  adoption, effect of, **6**, [174]
  age, minimum for making, **50**, [487]
  aircraft, executed on, **50**, [534]
  airmen, by. *See* servicemen *below*
  alteration—
    after execution, **50**, [502]
    court order for, **50**, [543]
  annexed with administration grant, **18**, [646]
  appointments by, execution of, **50**, [489]
  armed forces personnel, made by, **3**, [1]
  attestation—
    creditor, by, **50**, [494]
    incompetency of witness, **50**, [492]
    requirements, **50**, [488]
  child—
    age for executing will, **50**, [487]
    illegitimate. *See* illegitimate person *below*
    under 18, made by, **50**, [541]
  civil partnership, **27**, [898]
    dissolution, effect of, **50**, [499]
    revocation by, **50**, [498]
  clerical errors in, **50**, [543]
  codicil—
    date of, effect in disposition by, **6**, [280]
    included in term, **20**, [436], [804]
    revival of will by, **50**, [503]
    revocation, **50**, [501]
  construction—
    rules of, **50**, [484], [536]
    uniform law Convention, **50**, [555]
  contingent and future gifts, intermediate
    income, **20**, [778]
  contract to leave property by, **18**, [610]

will—*contd*

copy of, right to obtain, **18**, [652]

copyhold land, devise of, **50**, [507]

copyright passing under—

  generally, **11(1)**, [599], [620]

  transitional provisions, **11(1)**, [1175]

  unpublished work, **11(1)**, [901]

death of testator, deemed to speak from, **50**, [505]

deposit, rules as to, **50**, [548]

deposit of, place for, **18**, [651]

depositories—

  deposit in, fee for, **50**, [546]

  international wills, deposit of, **50**, [550]

  provision of, **50**, [546]

destruction, revocation by, **50**, [501]

devise—

  "die without issue", meaning, **50**, [510]

  domicile, change of, after execution, **50**, [533]

  errors, correction of, **50**, [543]

  estate tail, of, **50**, [513]

  evidence as to, **50**, [484]

  executor, to, **50**, [511]

  without words of limitation, property passing on, **50**, [509]

devise in fee or in tail, **18**, [485]

devisee raising money charged on land, **18**, [481]

disposition or devolution of property under, effect of gender recognition certificate, **7(1)**, [720]

evidence, general rules, **50**, [544]

examination, in court, **18**, [649]

execution, proof of, **18**, [87]

executor—

  devise to, property passing on, **50**, [511]

  witness, as, **50**, [495]

foreign country, executed in—

  formal requirements, **50**, [535]

  internal law, conforming to, **50**, [533]

  summary of provisions, **50**, [484]

  validity, rules as to, **50**, [533]

form—

  generally, **50**, [484]

  international law, **50**, [555]

  prescribed, **20**, [780]

gift—

  attesting witness, to, **50**, [493], [539]

  general, property included in, **50**, [508]

  issue of children, to, **50**, [514]

  spouse, to, effect of, **50**, [545]

gift by, intermediate income, **20**, [778]

Hague Convention, provisions of, **50**, [533]–[538]

illegitimate person, deceased, inheritance by issue of, **50**, [514]

international will—

  certification of, **50**, [555]

  convention on, **50**, [555]

  deposit of, **50**, [550]

  evidence of, **50**, [555]

  form of, will, **50**, [555]

  meaning, **50**, [549]

  procedure in respect of, **50**, [550]

will—*contd*

interpretation of, rules, **50**, [544]

issue, deceased, taking by issue of, **50**, [514]

land, general devise of, **50**, [507]

leasehold land, devise of, **50**, [507]

legitimation, effect of, **6**, [160]

living person, of, depositaries for, **18**, [653]

made before 1838, **50**, [515]

marriage—

  dissolution, effect of, **50**, [497]

  made in contemplation of, **50**, [496]

  revocation by, **50**, [496]

married woman, of, **27**, [160]

meaning, **18**, [559], [662]; **50**, [485]

performer's property rights passing under, **11(1)**, [1032]

personal estate—

  disposable, **50**, [486]

  meaning, **50**, [485]

persons lacking mental capacity, for, **29**, [320]

presumption, not to be revoked by, **50**, [500]

prisoner of war, of, **50**, [520]

probate of. *See* **probate**

property disposable by—

  generally, **50**, [486]

  summary of, **50**, [484]

property settled by, distributions within two years of death, **43(S)**, 400–1

publication not required, **50**, [491]

real estate—

  devise without words of limitation, **50**, [509]

  disposable, **50**, [486]

  disposition by servicemen, **50**, [523]

  meaning, **50**, [485]

rectification of, **50**, [543]

registration of—

  authorities responsible for, **50**, [546]

  Principal Registry, functions, **50**, [547]

  regulations, **50**, [548]

residual devise, lapsed, etc, devise included in, **50**, [506]

revival of, **50**, [503]

revocation—

  another will, by, **50**, [501]

  civil partnership, by, **50**, [498]

  exceptions as to, **50**, [503]

  international will, **50**, [555]

  marriage, by, **50**, [496]

  methods of, **50**, [501]

  person under 18, by, **50**, [541]

  revival after, **50**, [503]

seamen and mariners—

  age for capacity to make, **50**, [521]

  form, exemption as to, **50**, [528]

  prisoners of war, in case of, **50**, [520]

  privilege as to, **50**, [490]

  real property, validity of disposition, **50**, [523]

  repeal of certain provisions, **50**, [530]

  testamentary guardian, power to appoint, **50**, [524]

  wages, prize money, etc, provisions as to, **50**, [519]

will—*contd*
  servicemen—
      age for capacity to make, **50**, [521]
      privilege as to, **50**, [490]
      real property, validity of disposition,
        50, [523]
      summary of provisions, **50**, [484]
      testamentary guardian, power to appoint,
        50, [524]
  settlement by, **20**, [510]
  ship, executed on, **50**, [534]
  signature—
      international will, on, **50**, [555]
      requirements, **50**, [488]
  soldier, by. *See* servicemen *above*
  spouses, gifts to, presumption as to, **50**, [545]
  subsequent conveyance or act, not revoked
    by, **50**, [504]
  summary of provisions, **50**, [484]
  suppression, etc, **12(1)**, [571]
  tenant in tail in possession, powers, **20**, [779]
  testamentary power, development of,
    50, [484]
  trustees—
      devise to, property passing on, **50**, [511]
      unlimited devise to, **50**, [512]
  validity—
      additional rules, **50**, [534]
      general rule, **50**, [533]
  variation, identification of settlor,
    43(S), 311–12, 331–2
  witness—
      creditor attesting as, **50**, [494]
      executor admitted as, **50**, [495]
      gift to, avoidance, **50**, [493], [539]
      incompetency, not void for, **50**, [492]
  writing, to be in, **50**, [488]

Winchelsea
  ancient town, status as, **25(1)**, [51]

Winchester College. *See* **public school**

windfall tax
  administration, **43(1)**, [309], [329]
  appeals, **43(1)**, [329]
  assessment, power to make, **43(1)**, [329]
  charge to, **43(1)**, [307]
  companies benefiting from windfalls,
    43(1), [308]
  information—
      collection of, **43(1)**, [329]
      false, providing, **43(1)**, [329]
  interest on, **43(1)**, [329]
  interpretation, **43(1)**, [311], [329]
  liability, notification of, **43(1)**, [329]
  payment of, **43(1)**, [329]
  penalties, **43(1)**, [329]
  profit-related pay, and, **43(1)**, [310]
  provisions applied, **43(1)**, [329]
  quantification of windfall, **43(1)**, [328]
  recovery of, **43(1)**, [329]
  returns, **43(1)**, [329]

winding-up
  building society. *See* **building society**
  charitable company, **5(2)**, [620]
  charitable incorporated organisation,
    5(2), [642]
  credit union, **19(1)**, [585]
  expenses, payment of, **8(1)**, [1358]
  friendly society. *See* **friendly society**
  industrial and provident society—
      Financial Services Authority's petition, on,
        19(1), [383]
      liability of members in, **19(1)**, [384]
      payment of debts etc, **19(1)**, [384]
  licensed coal mining operating company,
    17(2), [161]
  protected railway company, restrictions as to,
    38(1), [409]
  serviceman, stay of proceedings against,
    3, [388]
  venture capital trust, of, **43(2)**, [197]

winding up by court. *See also* **winding up
(generally)**
  absconding—
      contributory, arrest, **4(2)**, [197]
      officer, arrest of, **4(2)**, [176]
  affidavits, swearing, **4(2)**, [237]
  application for, **4(2)**, [163]
  assets—
      application of, **4(2)**, [188]
      attachment etc, void, **4(2)**, [170]
      expenses payable from, **4(2)**, [196]
      making over to employees, **4(2)**, [225]
  attachment, avoidance of, **4(2)**, [170]
  books—
      falsification, **4(2)**, [245]
      inspection by creditors, **4(2)**, [195]
      lien on, unenforceable, **4(2)**, [280]
  calls, power to make, **4(2)**, [190]
  circumstances for, **4(2)**, [161]
  commencement of, **4(2)**, [171]
  company—
      dealings, inquiry into, **4(2)**, [272], [273]
      registered office, meaning, **4(2)**, [158]
  connected with company, meaning,
    4(2), [283]
  contributories—
      absconding, arrest of, **4(2)**, [197]
      calls on, **4(2)**, [190]
      debts due to company, **4(2)**, [189]
      list, settlement of, **4(2)**, [188]
      nomination of liquidator by, **4(2)**, [180]
      order on—
          conclusive evidence, **4(2)**, [192]
          debts to company, to pay, **4(2)**, [189]
          payment into bank for, **4(2)**, [191]
      rights, adjustment of, **4(2)**, [194]
      wishes of, ascertainment of, **4(2)**, [232]
  court—
      case stated by, **4(2)**, [160]
      cumulative powers, **4(2)**, [198]
      jurisdiction, **4(2)**, [158]
      powers, delegation to liquidator,
        4(2), [199]
      wrong, proceedings taken in, **4(2)**, [159]

winding up by court—*contd*
  creditors—
    books, power to inspect, **4(2)**, [195]
    failure to prove in time, **4(2)**, [193]
    meeting—
      choice of liquidator by, **4(2)**, [189]
      final, duty to summon, **4(2)**, [186]
    secured, meaning, **4(2)**, [282]
    transactions in fraud of, **4(2)**, [243], [249]
  debts, interest on, **4(2)**, [227]
  directors—
    delinquent—
      penalisation of, **4(2)**, [248]
      prosecution of, **4(2)**, [254]
  dissolution of company, **4(2)**, [239]
  documents—
    judicial notice of, **4(2)**, [233]
    stamp duty exemption, **4(2)**, [228]
  early dissolution—
    application for, **4(2)**, [239]
    consequences as to, **4(2)**, [240]
  extortionate credit transactions, **4(2)**, [278]
  Financial Services Authority—
    participation by, **19(2)**, [446]
    petition by, **19(2)**, [442], [443]
      EEA and Treaty firms, in relation to, **19(2)**, [443]
    report to, **19(2)**, [445]
  floating charge—
    avoidance of, **4(2)**, [279]
    meaning, **4(2)**, [285]
  fraud—
    creditors, of, **4(2)**, [243], [249]
    in anticipation of, **4(2)**, [242]
  High Court—
    case stated for, **4(2)**, [160]
    jurisdiction, **4(2)**, [158]
  inability to pay debts—
    grounds for winding up, **4(2)**, [161]
    meaning, **4(2)**, [162]
  insurers, of, **19(2)**, [444]
  investigation of company—
    malpractice etc, of, **4(2)**, [254]
    obligation in respect of, **4(2)**, [255]
    official receiver, by, **4(2)**, [174]
  jurisdiction in, **4(2)**, [158]
  liquidation—
    committee—
      disposals notified to, **4(2)**, [204]
      establishment, **4(2)**, [182]
      functions, exercise of, **4(2)**, [182]
    company in, notice of, **4(2)**, [226]
    go into, meaning, **4(2)**, [281]
    malpractice in respect of, **4(2)**, [242]
  liquidator—
    actions by or against, **4(2)**, [185]
    application for directions, **4(2)**, [205]
    appointment—
      administration order, following, **4(2)**, [181]
      court, by, **4(2)**, [181]
      Minister, by, **4(2)**, [179]
      notice of, **4(2)**, [179]
      voluntary arrangement, following, **4(2)**, [181]

winding up by court—*contd*
  liquidator—*contd*
    custody of property by, **4(2)**, [184]
    delegation of powers to, **4(2)**, [199]
    disposal of property by, **4(2)**, [204]
    duties, **4(2)**, [183]
    final meeting, duty to summon, **4(2)**, [186]
    functions, general, **4(2)**, [183]
    meetings, summoning, **4(2)**, [182], [186], [204]
    nomination of, **4(2)**, [180]
    official receiver as, **4(2)**, [178]
    powers—
      control by court, **4(2)**, [204]
      exercisable with sanction, **4(2)**, [547]
      exercise of, **4(2)**, [204]
    provisional, appointment and powers of, **4(2)**, [177]
    questioning actions of, **4(2)**, [205]
    release of, **4(2)**, [210]
    removal etc, **4(2)**, [208]
    replacement, procedure for, **4(2)**, [208]
    supplementary powers, **4(2)**, [205]
    vacation of office, time for, **4(2)**, [208]
    vesting of property in, **4(2)**, [185]
  member of company—
    meaning, **4(2)**, [284]
    offences, prosecution of, **4(2)**, [254]
    register, rectification of, **4(2)**, [188]
  misconduct in course of, **4(2)**, [244]
  money due to company—
    contributory, from, **4(2)**, [189]
    order to pay, **4(2)**, [189]
    payment into bank, **4(2)**, [191]
  offences—
    investigations respecting, **4(2)**, [255]
    prosecution of, **4(2)**, [254]
    summary proceedings, **4(2)**, [521]
  office-holder—
    duty to co-operate with, **4(2)**, [271]
    meaning, **4(2)**, [266]
  officers of company—
    examination of. *See* public examination *below*
    false representations by, **4(2)**, [247]
    fraud etc by, **4(2)**, [242]
    material omissions by, **4(2)**, [246]
    meaning, **4(2)**, [242]
    misconduct by, **4(2)**, [244]
  order for—
    consequences of, **4(2)**, [172]
    power to make, **4(2)**, [167]
    proceedings stayed by, **4(2)**, [172]
  petition for—
    grounds for, **4(2)**, [161]
    persons qualified to present, **4(2)**, [163]
    powers of court on hearing, **4(2)**, [167]
    public interest, on ground of, **4(2)**, [164]
  preferences given, order as to, **4(2)**, [275]
  proceedings—
    case stated in, **4(2)**, [160]
    stay or restraint of, **4(2)**, [168], [187]
    time of commencement, **4(2)**, [171]
    wrong court, taken in, **4(2)**, [159]

winding up by court—*contd*
property—
 attachment, avoidance of, **4(2)**, [170]
 custody of, **4(2)**, [184]
 disposal etc—
  avoidance of, **4(2)**, [169]
  notice to liquidation committee,
   4(2), [204]
 getting in, **4(2)**, [270]
 malpractice as to, **4(2)**, [242]
 vesting in liquidator, **4(2)**, [185]
public examination of officers—
 absconding to avoid, **4(2)**, [176]
 application for, **4(2)**, [175]
 attendance, enforcement of, **4(2)**, [176]
 persons taking part in, **4(2)**, [175]
 powers as to, **4(2)**, [175]
public interest, on ground of, **4(2)**, [164]
public-private partnership (PPP), order
 relating to—
  order, restriction on making, **26(1)**, [607]
  voluntary, restriction on, **26(1)**, [608]
reasons for, **4(2)**, [161]
resolution for, **4(2)**, [161]
secured creditor, meaning, **4(2)**, [282]
serious crime prevention order, failure to
 comply with, **12(4)**, [384]–[386]
statement of affairs—
 affidavit, verification by, **4(2)**, [173]
 contents, **4(2)**, [173]
 default as to, **4(2)**, [173]
 material omissions from, **4(2)**, [246]
 official receiver may require, **4(2)**, [173]
 persons liable to make, **4(2)**, [173]
stay of, **4(2)**, [168], [187]
transactions at undervalue—
 order to negative, **4(2)**, [274]
 relevant time for, **4(2)**, [276]
 requirements under orders, **4(2)**, [277]
unregistered company. *See* **unregistered
company**

winding up (generally). *See also* **winding up
by court; winding up, voluntary**
accounting periods, effect on, **44(1)**, [7]
action against company—
 control of, by court, **8**, 827
 leave to proceed, **8**, 828
Acts controlling, **8**, 828
affidavits, swearing, **4(2)**, [237]
air traffic licence company, protection of. *See*
 air traffic services
alternative modes of, **4(2)**, [114]
assets, making over to employees, **4(2)**, [225]
associate of person, meaning, **4(2)**, [528]
attachment, effect of, **4(2)**, [221]
banks, formerly authorised, **4(2)**, [509]
books, evidence, as, **4(2)**, [229]
building society. *See* **building society**
charitable company, **5(2)**, [620]
commission for receiving evidence,
 4(2), [234]
company name, re-use of—
 contravention, personal liability, **4(2)**, [253]
 restriction on, **4(2)**, [252]

winding up (generally)—*contd*
contracts, rescission of, **4(2)**, [224]
contributories—
 bankruptcy, effect of, **4(2)**, [123]
 company limited by guarantee, **4(2)**, [115]
 death of member, on, **4(2)**, [122]
 directors, unlimited liability, **4(2)**, [116]
 liability—
  calls for enforcing, **4(2)**, [121]
  extent of, **4(2)**, [115]
  nature of, **4(2)**, [121]
 manager of company, **4(2)**, [116]
 meaning, **4(2)**, [120]
 past and present members as, **4(2)**, [117]
 personal representative as, **4(2)**, [122]
 registered companies, **4(2)**, [124]
 shareholders, past, as, **4(2)**, [117]
 trustee in bankruptcy as, **4(2)**, [123]
creditors—
 false representations to, **4(2)**, [247]
 interest on, **4(2)**, [227]
 personal liability for, **4(2)**, [253]
 transactions in fraud of, **4(2)**, [243], [249]
 unsecured, share of assets for, **4(2)**, [214]
 wishes of, ascertaining, **4(2)**, [232]
defunct company—
 restoration to register, **8**, 520
 striking off, **8**, 513
diligence (Scotland), effect of, **4(2)**, [223]
directors—
 delinquent, penalisation of, **4(2)**, [248]
 past, liability of, **4(2)**, [117]
 unlimited liability of, **4(2)**, [116]
 wrongful trading by, **4(2)**, [250]
dissolution of company, **4(2)**, [238]–[241]
documents—
 judicial notice of, **4(2)**, [233]
 stamp duty exemption, **4(2)**, [228]
employees, payments to, **4(2)**, [225]
evidence, commission for receiving,
 4(2), [234]
examination of persons (Scotland), **4(2)**, [235]
execution—
 completed, meaning, **4(2)**, [221]
 effect of, **4(2)**, [221]
 officer charged with execution of writs and
  processes, duties of, **4(2)**, [222]
floating charge, effect of, **8**, 828
fraudulent trading in course of, **4(2)**, [249]
leaseholds—
 disclaimer of, **4(2)**, [217]
 vesting order, **4(2)**, [220]
limited company—
 formerly unlimited, **4(2)**, [118]
 unlimited company formerly, **4(2)**, [119]
liquidation, pending, information as to,
 4(2), [230]
liquidator—
 appointment, corruption in, **4(2)**, [201]
 default by, **4(2)**, [206]
 delinquent, remedies against, **4(2)**, [248]
 duties, enforcement of, **4(2)**, [206]
 offences by, **4(2)**, [248]
 powers, exercise of, **4(2)**, [547]
 style and title, **4(2)**, [200]

winding up (generally)—*contd*
  manager, liability of, **4(2)**, [116]
  monetary limits, **4(2)**, [501]
    company moratorium, **4(2)**, [503]
  offences—
    schedule of, **4(2)**, [561]
    summary proceedings, **4(2)**, [521]
  officer charged with execution of writs and
    processes, duties of, **4(2)**, [222]
  old debts, priority, **8**, 828
  old liquidations, saving as to, **8**, 828
  onerous property, disclaimer of—
    effect of, **4(2)**, [216]
    land subject to rentcharge, **4(2)**, [218]
    leaseholds, **4(2)**, [217], [220]
    loss or damage by, **4(2)**, [216]
    meaning, **4(2)**, [216]
    notice required, **4(2)**, [216]
    powers of court on, **4(2)**, [219]
    vesting order after, **4(2)**, [219]
  oversea company, of, **4(2)**, [261]
  oversea company with branch registered in
    Great Britain—
    insolvency proceedings, **8**, 563–4
    particulars to be delivered to registrar,
      8, 562–3
    penalty for non-compliance, **8**, 564
  petition for—
    European Cooperative Society, **4(2)**, [166]
    Societas Europaea, **4(2)**, [165]
  preferential debts—
    charge on distrained goods, **4(2)**, [212]
    payment of expenses of winding up,
      4(2), [213]
    priority for, **4(2)**, [211]
    ranking of, **4(2)**, [211]
  private company—
    striking off on application—
      directors' duties following, **8**, 517–18
      duties, **8**, 515–16
      enforcement, **8**, 519–20
      general, **8**, 515
      offences, **8**, 520
      restoration to register, **8**, 520–1
      supplementary provisions, **8**, 518–19
  proceeds of crime. *See* **proceeds of crime**
  property—
    execution against, effect, **4(2)**, [221]
    vesting order, **4(2)**, [219]
  provisions applicable to, **4(2)**, [114]
  registered provider of social housing, of—
    company, **24**, [701]
    industrial and provident society, **24**, [703]
    regulator, petition by, **24**, [705]
    transfer of property, **24**, [706]–[708]
  registered social landlord—
    net assets, transfer of, **23**, [548]
    petition for, **23**, [548]
  residuary bodies, **25(2)**, [617]
  resolution for—
    adjourned meeting, at, **4(2)**, [231]
    consequences of, **4(2)**, [128]
  Scotland. *See* **Scotland**
  shareholders, past, liability of, **4(2)**, [117]

winding up (generally)—*contd*
  special manager—
    accounting by, **4(2)**, [215]
    appointment, **4(2)**, [215]
    powers, **4(2)**, [215]
  stay of, **4(2)**, [74]
  taxation on, **44(1)**, [174]
  transitional provisions, **4(2)**, [562]
  unlimited company—
    becoming limited, **4(2)**, [118]
    formerly limited, **4(2)**, [119]
  unregistered company. *See* **unregistered
    company**
  unsecured creditors, share of assets for,
    4(2), [214]
  wrongful trading in course of—
    evidence of, **4(2)**, [251]
    persons liable for, **4(2)**, [250]
    proceedings for, **4(2)**, [251]

winding up under supervision. *See also*
  winding up (generally)
  transitional provisions, **4(2)**, [562]

winding up, voluntary. *See also* **winding up
  (generally)**
  account of, presentation of, **4(2)**, [134]
  affidavits, swearing, **4(2)**, [237]
  assets, making over to employees, **4(2)**, [225]
  books—
    falsification of, **4(2)**, [245]
    lien on, unenforceable, **4(2)**, [280]
  business to cease on, **4(2)**, [128]
  circumstances for, **4(2)**, [125]
  commencement of, **4(2)**, [127]
  company—
    insolvency, effect of, **4(2)**, [136]
    meeting—
      account to be presented to, **4(2)**, [134]
      advertisement of, **4(2)**, [136]
      final, before dissolution, **4(2)**, [135],
        [147]
      quorum, lack of, **4(2)**, [135]
      year's end, at, **4(2)**, [146]
    registered in Scotland, **4(2)**, [154]
  connected with company, meaning,
    4(2), [283]
  contributories' rights, saving for, **4(2)**, [157]
  creditors—
    fraud of, **4(2)**, [243], [249]
    list of, inspection of, **4(2)**, [139]
    meeting—
      business at, **4(2)**, [136]
      company to call, **4(2)**, [139]
      converted winding up, where,
        4(2), [143]
      insolvency, in case of, **4(2)**, [136]
      liquidator to attend, **4(2)**, [203]
      notices of, **4(2)**, [136]
        matters to be given in, **4(2)**, [130]
        time for giving, **4(2)**, [139]
    statement of affairs for—
      contents, **4(2)**, [140]
      directors, by, **4(2)**, [140]
      evidence, admissible in, **4(2)**, [523]

winding up, voluntary—*contd*
  creditors—*contd*
    meeting—*contd*
      statement of affairs for—*contd*
        liquidator, by, **4(2)**, [136]
        verification by affidavit, **4(2)**, [140]
      summoning by liquidator, **4(2)**, [136]
      year's end, at, **4(2)**, [146]
    rights, saving for, **4(2)**, [157]
    secured, meaning, **4(2)**, [282]
    transactions in fraud of, **4(2)**, [243], [249]
    winding up—
      application of provisions, **4(2)**, [138]
      conversion to, **4(2)**, [137]
      documents, stamp duty exemption,
        4(2), [228]
      final meeting prior to dissolution,
        4(2), [147]
      liquidation committee in, **4(2)**, [142]
      liquidator—
        appointment, **4(2)**, [141]
        replacement, **4(2)**, [141]
        vacancy in office of, **4(2)**, [145]
      members' distinguished, **4(2)**, [131]
      powers and duties, **4(2)**, [202]
  debts, interest on, **4(2)**, [227]
  dissolution of company—
    final meeting prior to, **4(2)**, [135], [147]
    time of, **4(2)**, [238]
  documents—
    judicial notice of, **4(2)**, [233]
    stamp duty exemption, **4(2)**, [228]
  expenses of, **4(2)**, [156]
  extortionate credit transactions, **4(2)**, [278]
  floating charges—
    avoidance of, **4(2)**, [279]
    meaning, **4(2)**, [285]
  fraud in anticipation of, **4(2)**, [242]
  general meeting—
    appointment of liquidator, **4(2)**, [132]
    year's end, at, **4(2)**, [134]
  liquidation—
    committee—
      appointment, **4(2)**, [142]
      members, number of, **4(2)**, [142]
      property disposal, notice of, **4(2)**, [202]
    company in, notice of, **4(2)**, [226]
    go into, meaning, **4(2)**, [281]
    malpractice in respect of, **4(2)**, [242]
  liquidator—
    account by, **4(2)**, [134]
    appointment—
      cesser of directors' powers on,
        4(2), [132], [144]
      court, by, **4(2)**, [149]
      general meeting, by, **4(2)**, [132]
      notice of, **4(2)**, [150]
    death, resignation etc, **4(2)**, [133]
    meetings—
      attendance at, **4(2)**, [203]
      to be called by, **4(2)**, [135]
    nomination by creditors, **4(2)**, [141]
    not appointed, position where, **4(2)**, [155]
    notice by, of his appointment, **4(2)**, [150]

winding up, voluntary—*contd*
  liquidator—*contd*
    officer of company, deemed to be,
      4(2), [126]
    powers and duties, **4(2)**, [132]
      exercisable without sanction, **4(2)**, [548],
        [549]
      exercise of, **4(2)**, [202]
    reference of questions by, **4(2)**, [153]
    notice by, of his appointment, **4(2)**, [150]
    officer of company, deemed to be,
      4(2), [126]
    powers and duties, **4(2)**, [132]
      exercisable without sanction, **4(2)**, [548],
        [549]
      exercise of, **4(2)**, [202]
    reference of questions by, **4(2)**, [153]
  members winding up—
    creditors'—
      conversion to, **4(2)**, [137]
      distinguished, **4(2)**, [131]
    final meeting before dissolution, **4(2)**, [135]
    general meeting, calling, **4(2)**, [134]
  misconduct in course of, **4(2)**, [244]
  offences, summary proceedings, **4(2)**, [521]
  officer of company—
    false representations by, **4(2)**, [247]
    fraud by, **4(2)**, [242]
    material omissions by, **4(2)**, [246]
    meaning, **4(2)**, [242]
    misconduct by, **4(2)**, [244]
  petition for winding up by court, **4(2)**, [163]
  preferences given, order as to, **4(2)**, [275]
  property—
    disposal, notice to liquidation committee,
      4(2), [202]
    distribution of, **4(2)**, [148]
    malpractice as to, **4(2)**, [242]
    sale of, acceptance of shares for, **4(2)**, [151]
    transfer to another company, **4(2)**, [151],
      [152]
  questions referred to court, **4(2)**, [153]
  resolution for—
    adjourned meeting, passed at, **4(2)**, [231]
    consequences of, **4(2)**, [128]
    default in notifying, **4(2)**, [126]
    notice in Gazette of, **4(2)**, [126]
    passing of, **4(2)**, [125]
  share transfers, avoidance of, **4(2)**, [129]
  solvency, declaration of—
    conditions for making, **4(2)**, [130]
    delivery to registrar, **4(2)**, [130]
    no reasonable grounds for, **4(2)**, [130]
    time for making, **4(2)**, [130]
  statement of affairs—
    creditors' meeting, for, **4(2)**, [136]
    directors to lay, **4(2)**, [140]
    material omissions from, **4(2)**, [246]
  status of company, effect on, **4(2)**, [128]
  time of commencement of, **4(2)**, [127]
  transactions at undervalue—
    order to negative, **4(2)**, [274]
    relevant time, **4(2)**, [276]
    requirements under orders, **4(2)**, [277]

winding up, voluntary—*contd*
unregistered company. *See* **unregistered
company**

Windsor Estate
houses, dealing with, **10**, [237]
management of, **10**, [237]
meaning, **10**, [237]
sale or exchange of land, **10**, [237]

wine
blending, **19(3)**, [412]
constituent wines, **19(3)**, [412]
excise duty—
charge of, **19(3)**, [412]
made-wine, **19(3)**, [413]
rates of, **19(3)**, [412], [435]
spoilt, remission on, **19(3)**, [419]
summary of provisions, **19(3)**, [349]
surcharges or rebates, **13**, [898]–[900]
excise licence, **19(3)**, [412]
gravity, **19(3)**, [374]
London, imported into, gauging of,
39(1), [543]
made-wine—
cider labelled as, **19(3)**, [414]
excise duty—
charge of, **19(3)**, [413]
rates of, **19(3)**, [435]
repayment or remission, **19(3)**, [419]
summary of provisions, **19(3)**, [349]
surcharges or rebates, **13**, [898]–[900]
making, regulation of, **19(3)**, [415]
meaning, **19(3)**, [372]
producer's licence, abolition of duty,
19(3), [461]
sale by retail, meaning, **19(3)**, [375]
sparkling, **19(3)**, [418], [435]
licence exemption, **19(3)**, [413]
spirits, mixing with in warehouse,
19(3), [416]
spoilt, remission of duty, **19(3)**, [419]
making, power to regulate, **19(3)**, [415]
meaning, **19(3)**, [372]
producer, meaning, **19(3)**, [375]
producer's licence, **19(3)**, [412]
duty, abolition, **19(3)**, [461]
production, what constitutes, **19(3)**, [412]
refreshment houses, restrictive covenants,
19(3), [351]
retailer, meaning, **19(3)**, [375]
sale by retail, meaning, **19(3)**, [375]
sparkling, rendering, **19(3)**, [412], [418],
[435]
spirit, mixing with in warehouse, **19(3)**, [417]
spirits of. *See* **spirits of wine**
spoilt, remission of duty, **19(3)**, [419]
strength, ascertainment, **19(3)**, [373]
volume, ascertainment, **19(3)**, [373]
weight, ascertainment, **19(3)**, [373]
wholesale, meaning, **19(3)**, [375]
wholesaler, meaning, **19(3)**, [375]

wireless installations
wires, etc, connected with, byelaws as to,
35(1), [98]

wireless telegraphy. *See also* **broadcasting;
telecommunications; radio services**
acts connected with broadcasting, offences,
45, [854]
aircraft, unauthorised broadcasting from,
generally. *See* **broadcasting**
apparatus—
approval of—
application for, **45**, [843]
exercise of functions, **45**, [844]
fees, **45**, [844]
instrument, for purposes of, **45**, [843]
relevant authority, **45**, [845]
requirements, **45**, [843]
authority to operate, **45**, [837]
deliberate interference with, **45**, [842]
enforcement provisions—
appeal against notices, **45**, [831]
contravention of notice, **45**, [832]
entry and search of premises, **45**, [833]
notice prohibiting use, **45**, [829]
obstruction and failure to assist,
45, [834]
sale, requirement, **45**, [830]
use of apparatus, **45**, [829]
importation, powers of HM Revenue and
Customs, **45**, [839]
international obligations, compatibility
with, **45**, [838]
interpretation, **45**, [889]
maintaining or repairing, offences,
45, [858]
marking of—
advertisements, information in, **45**, [847]
information, provision of, **45**, [846]
offences, **45**, [848]
third persons, default of, **45**, [849]
meaning, **45**, [835], [891]
OFCOM, functions of and grant of
licences. *See* **Office of
Communications**
offences, **45**, [840]
restricted—
forfeiture of, **45**, [878]
seizure and forfeiture of, **45**, [906]
restriction orders, **45**, [836]
use and sale, regulations, **45**, [828]
broadcast—
licence, under, **45**, [868]
meaning, **45**, [869]
digital switchover, disclosure of information—
directors, liability of, **45**, [915]
interpretation, **45**, [913], [916]
offences, **45**, [914]
pensions information, **45**, [912], [913]
social security information, **45**, [912], [913]
switchover help functions, meaning,
45, [912]
disclosure of information, general
restrictions, **45**, [885]

wireless telegraphy—*contd*
electronic communications networks, time
  and location of things done by, **45**, [888]
enforcement officers, **45**, [862]
  assaulting, **45**, [866]
  obstructing, **45**, [866]
enforcement powers—
  conditions, **45**, [863]
  entry and search, **45**, [871]
  exercise of, **45**, [865]
  facilitation offences, **45**, [864]
  failure to comply, **45**, [866], [872]
  obstructing, **45**, [872]
  seizure, **45**, [873]
    detention and disposal of property,
      45, [875], [876]
    obstruction, **45**, [874]
frequencies—
  assignment of, **45**, [102]
  television broadcasting, additional services
    provided on, **45**, [102]
high seas, prohibition from broadcasting from
  prescribed area of, **45**, [853]
interception. *See* **communications**
licences—
  application for, **45**, [901]
  bidding for, **45**, [788]
  charge for grant of, **45**, [786]
  contravention of terms, **45**, [813]
  duration, **45**, [901]
  exemptions, **45**, [782]
  grant, procedure for, **45**, [901]
  meaning, **45**, [782]
  power to charge, matters taken into
    account, **45**, [787]
  recognised spectrum access, conversion to
    and from, **45**, [801]
  recovery of sums, **45**, [789]
  refusal, proposed, **45**, [901]
  regulations, **45**, [790]
  renewal, **45**, [791]
  repeated contravention of terms, **45**, [814]
  requirement, **45**, [782]
  revocation or variation, **45**, [901]
  surrender, **45**, [785]
  terms, provisions and limitations, **45**, [783]
  transfer of, **45**, [804]
meaning, **45**, [890]
Northern Ireland, application of provisions,
  45, [34]
OFCOM. *See* **Office of Communications**
offences—
  acts relating to broadcast material, **45**, [859]
  broadcasting station, related to management
    of, **45**, [855]
  civil proceedings, **45**, [882]
  committal abroad, procuring, **45**, [861]
  company directors, liability of, **45**, [884]
  continuing, **45**, [880]
  conviction, forfeiture on, **45**, [905]
  fixed penalties, **45**, [904]
  maintaining or repairing apparatus,
    45, [858]
  obstruction and failure to assist, **45**, [872]
  penalties and proceedings, **45**, [867]

wireless telegraphy—*contd*
offences—*contd*
  proceedings and enforcement, **45**, [881]
  Scotland, fines in, **45**, [883]
  ships or aircraft, relating to, **45**, [879]
orders and regulations, **45**, [33]
  OFCOM, by, **45**, [896]
  Secretary of State, by, **45**, [895]
radio spectrum—
  competence of personnel, **45**, [826]
  foreign-registered ships or aircraft, apparatus
    on, **45**, [824]
  interception and disclosure of messages,
    45, [822]
  interception authorities, **45**, [823]
  misleading messages, sending, **45**, [821]
  multiplex licence holders, offences by—
    amount of penalty, **45**, [817]
    gross revenue, relevant amount of,
      45, [818]
    special procedure, **45**, [816]
  OFCOM, functions of and grant of
    licences. *See* **Office of**
    Communications
  offences—
    contravention of terms of licence,
      45, [813]
    interception and disclosure of messages,
      45, [822]
    misleading messages, sending, **45**, [821]
    multiplex licence holders, by,
      45, [816]–[818]
    prosecutions, procedure for, **45**, [815]
    regulations, contravention of, **45**, [820]
    repeated contravention of terms of
      licence, **45**, [814]
    station or apparatus kept for
      unauthorised use, **45**, [810]
    unauthorised use of station or
      apparatus, **45**, [809]
    unlawful broadcasting—
      allowing premises to be used for,
        45, [811]
      facilitating, **45**, [812]
  personnel, written authorities—
    advisory committee, references to,
      45, [903]
    issue of, **45**, [826]
    revocation, **45**, [903]
    surrender of, **45**, [827]
    suspension, **45**, [903]
  register of relevant information, **45**, [805]
  regulations, **45**, [819]
  vehicles, apparatus in, **45**, [825]
service of documents, **45**, [886]
  electronic form, in, **45**, [887]
ships and aircraft, broadcasting from—
  facilitating, **45**, [856]
    enforcement powers, **45**, [864]
    territorial scope, **45**, [860]
  prohibition, **45**, [851]
stations, meaning, **45**, [891]
structure, broadcasting from—
  facilitating, **45**, [857]
    enforcement powers, **45**, [864]

wireless telegraphy—*contd*
  structure, broadcasting from—*contd*
    facilitating—*contd*
      prohibition, **45**, [852]
      territorial scope, **45**, [860]
  summary of provisions, **45**, [1]
  transitional provisions, **45**, [908], [909]

withholding tax
  special. *See* **special withholding tax**

witness. *See also* **evidence**
  accused person as, **18**, [165], [166]
  adverse, contradictory statements of, **18**, [127]
  anonymity—
    interpretation, **18**, [443]
    new rules for, **18**, [432]
    order—
      application for, **18**, [434]
      conditions for making, **18**, [435]
      discharge, **18**, [437]
      expiry of power to make, **18**, [445]
      jury, warning to, **18**, [438]
      meaning, **18**, [433]
      pre-commencement—
        appeals, **18**, [442]
        existing proceedings, **18**, [441]
      proceedings to which applying, **18**, [440]
      relevant considerations, **18**, [436]
      service courts, special provision for, **18**, [439]
      variation, **18**, [437]
  anti-social behaviour order, on application for, **12(2)**, [658]
  appeal hearing, at, **12(1)**, [442]
  appearance—
    another jurisdiction, in, **18**, [76], [228]
    expenses to be tendered, **18**, [77], [116]
  arrest of, **12(1)**, [355]
  assistance to—
    child, eligibility for, **18**, [312]
    court, exclusion of individuals from, **18**, [321]
    distress, on grounds of, **18**, [313]
    eligibility for, **18**, [312]
    fear, on grounds of, **18**, [313]
    intermediary, examination through, **18**, [325]
    mentally handicapped person, eligibility for, **18**, [312]
    screening from accused, **18**, [319]
    special measures—
      aids to communication, **18**, [326]
      availability, **18**, [314]
      court, exclusion of individuals from, **18**, [321]
      directions, **18**, [315], [316]
      evidence given under, status of, **18**, [327]
      intermediary, examination through, **18**, [325]
      screening from accused, **18**, [319]
      television link, **18**, [320]
      transitional provisions and savings, **18**, [369]

witness—*contd*
  assistance to—*contd*
    special measures—*contd*
      video recording, **18**, [323], [324]
      wigs and gowns, removal of, **18**, [322]
    television link, **18**, [320]
  attendance—
    default in, **18**, [115]
    enforcing, **18**, [75]
    warrant, territorial extent, **18**, [228]
  attendance of—
    arrest to ensure, **12(1)**, [355]
    securing, **12(1)**, [1]
  child as, **6**, [427]; **12(2)**, [100], [124]
    assistance, eligibility for, **18**, [312]
    cross-examination by accused—
      direction prohibiting, **18**, [335], [336]
      protection from, **18**, [334]
      transitional provisions and savings, **18**, [369]
    evidence—
      coherence of, meaning, **18**, [312]
      giving of, measures to assist in, **18**, [75]
    identity, concealment of, **18**, [75]
    reporting of—
      defences to, **18**, [348]
      offence of, **18**, [347], [349]
      penalties for, **18**, [347]
      power to restrict, **18**, [343]
      public interest, in, **18**, [343]
      restrictions on, **18**, [342]
    sexual offences, **11(2)**, [525]
    special provisions relating to, **18**, [317], [318]
  civil partner as, **18**, [256], [257]
  commission to examine, issue of, **18**, [119]
  Commissioner for Victims and Witnesses. *See* **Commissioner for Victims and Witnesses**
  compellability, spouse, **18**, [111], [256]
  competency—
    civil partner, of, **18**, [256], [257]
    criminal cases, in, **18**, [165], [351]
    determination of, **18**, [352]
    parties to action, **18**, [97]
    spouses, **18**, [98], [110], [256], [257]
    summary of provisions, **18**, [75]
    transitional provisions and savings, **18**, [369]
  conviction, proof of, **18**, [129], [248]
  cross-examination—
    accused, by—
      child complainants and witnesses, protection of, **18**, [334]
      definitions, **18**, [358]
      direction prohibiting, **18**, [335], [336]
      sexual offences, complainants in proceedings for, **18**, [333]
      service courts, application of provisions to, **18**, [357]
    defence representation for, **18**, [337]
    warning to jury against prejudice, **18**, [338]
    previous written statement, as to, **18**, [128]
    video recording, **18**, [324]

witness—*contd*
  defence—
    notification of intention to call,
      12(2), [428]
    police interviews, code of practice,
      12(2), [445]
  documents, use to refresh memory, **18**, [415]
  expenses, **12(1)**, [944], [949]; **18**, [77], [116]
  expert, rules of court, **18**, [220]
  grants for assisting, **12(4)**, [48], [113]
  harming, **12(3)**, [23]
    relevant proceedings, **12(3)**, [24]
  identity, protection of, **18**, [75]
  impeaching credit of, **18**, [126]
  incompetency, **18**, [165]
  inconsistent statements, **18**, [397]
  incriminating questions, **18**, [98], [207]
  intimidation, **12(2)**, [191]; **12(3)**, [22]
    relevant proceedings, **12(3)**, [24]
  liability to answer questions, **18**, [75]
  live link, evidence given by—
    criminal proceedings, in, **18**, [330]
    definitions, **18**, [375]
    direction for, **18**, [330], [332], [370]
    effect of direction, **18**, [371]
    jury, warning to, **18**, [373]
    magistrates' court, removal to other
      location, **18**, [372]
    meaning, **18**, [331]
    rescission of direction, **18**, [371]
    rules of court, **18**, [374]
  meaning, **12(4)**, [44]
  mentally handicapped person as—
    assistance, eligibility for, **18**, [312]
    evidence, coherence of, meaning, **18**, [312]
  Northern Ireland, corresponding provisions
    for, **18**, [362]
  oral evidence by, statement of, **18**, [279]
  outside UK, television, evidence by, **18**, [272]
  parties admissible as, **18**, [97]
  person charged as, **18**, [166], [167]
  prisoner as, **7(1)**, [15]
  privilege—
    abolition of, **18**, [208]
    amendments relating to, **18**, [209]
    evidence for other jurisdictions, **18**, [227]
    incrimination of self or spouse, as to,
      18, [207]
  protection of—
    disclosure of information about
      arrangements, defences to liability,
      12(4), [106]
      national security, on grounds of,
        12(4), [106]
      offence, **12(4)**, [105]
    interpretation, **12(4)**, [113]
    persons assuming new identity, disclosure of
      information about—
        defences to liability, **12(4)**, [108]
        offence, **12(4)**, [107]
    protected person, representation relating
      to, **12(4)**, [109]
    protection provider—
      arrangements by, **12(4)**, [101]
      duty to assist, **12(4)**, [104]

witness—*contd*
  protection of—*contd*
    protection provider—*contd*
      information, provision of, **12(4)**, [112]
      joint arrangements by, **12(4)**, [102]
      meaning, **12(4)**, [101]
      transfer of responsibility, **12(4)**, [103]
    specified persons, **12(4)**, [145]
    transitional provisions, **12(4)**, [110], [111]
  public inquiry, at, **12(1)**, [183], [184]
  questions to—
    incriminating, **18**, [98], [207]
    refusing to answer, **18**, [78]
  re-examination, video recording, in, **18**, [324]
  refusal to give evidence, **11(2)**, [519]–[520]
  regulations and orders, **18**, [360]
  remand by court, **12(1)**, [355]
  reporting restrictions, **18**, [344]
    amendments, **18**, [346], [365]
    offences, **18**, [347], [349]
      defences as to, **18**, [348]
      penalties for, **18**, [347]
    public interest, in, **18**, [350]
    transitional provisions and savings, **18**, [369]
  spouse as, **18**, [98], [110], [256]
    failure to give evidence, **18**, [257]
  subpoena—
    disobedience to, **18**, [115]
    runs throughout UK, **18**, [113]
    writ, statement at foot of, **18**, [114]
  summons—
    failure to attend following,
      11(2), [519]–[520]
    issue of, **11(2)**, [519]–[520]
  supplementary provisions, **18**, [361]
  sworn, whether to be, **18**, [353]
  telephone, hearing by, **12(3)**, [594], [620]
  television links, hearing through—
    abroad, **12(3)**, [592]
    attendance, securing, **12(3)**, [619]
    conduct of hearing, **12(3)**, [619]
    in UK, **12(3)**, [593]
    privilege, **12(3)**, [619]
    procedure, **12(3)**, [619]
    record of hearing, **12(3)**, [619]
  transitional provisions and savings, **18**, [363],
    [369]
  video recording—
    account of events in, **18**, [413]
    cross-examination, **18**, [324]
    evidence in chief, as, **18**, [323], [414]
    meaning, **18**, [416]
    re-examination, **18**, [324]

witness summons
  advance production, **12(1)**, [349]
  application to make ineffective, **12(1)**, [353]
  Crown Court—
    application to, **12(1)**, [348]
    own motion of, **12(1)**, [352]
    proceedings before, **12(1)**, [355]
  disobedience to, **12(1)**, [354]
  ineffective, **12(1)**, [351]
  issue of, **12(1)**, [348]
  not required, **12(1)**, [350]

witness summons—*contd*
subpoena, replacing, **12(1)**, [356]

women
Air Force law, application to, **3**, [987]
Army Act, application to, **3**, [715]
citizenship. *See* **citizenship** (marriage)
Commissions, holding, **3**, [369]
discrimination against, generally. *See* **sex discrimination**
discrimination, removal, **16**, [2]
equal pay. *See* **equal pay**
equality clause in contracts, **16**, [28]
forces including, **3**, [368]
industrial training, **16**, [65]
service law, application to, **3**, [1454], [1461]
meaning, **7(1)**, [38]
miscrimination against, generally. *See* **sex discrimination**
ordination. *See* **ordination**
protection of, acts done for, **7(1)**, [96]
    See also **sex discrimination**
slander of, **19(3)**, [307]

Women's Royal Air Force
generally, **3**, [1]

Women's Royal Army Corps
generally, **3**, [1]

Women's Royal Naval Service
generally, **3**, [1]

women's sanitary products
reduced rate VAT, **50**, [149]

woodland. *See also* **forestry**
chargeable gains, **42**, [1395]
commercial—
    meaning, **42**, [979]
    Schedule B charge, abolition of, **42**, [920], [937]
    Schedule D election, abolition of, **42**, [979]
    transitional provisions, **42**, [979]
commercial basis, managed on, **44(1)**, [33]
commercial occupation of, **44(3)**, [11]
    exempt income, **44(3)**, [783]
conversion of land for, grants, **1(2)**, [411]
dealers in land, computation of profits or gains, **44(1)**, [80]
drainage charges, partial exemption from, **49**, [1284]
EEA land, inheritance tax relief, **43(S)**, 1425–6
inheritance tax. *See* **inheritance tax**
meaning, **1(1)**, [658]
opencast coal mining in, compensation, **17(1)**, [220]
planting, licensing, **1(1)**, [654]
purchase or sale, trade profits, **44(3)**, [155]

wool
British Wool Marketing Board, power to grant relief, **1(2)**, [526]

wool—*contd*
guarantee, termination of—
    generally, **1(2)**, [523]
    repeals consequential on, **1(2)**, [532]

Woolwich Ferry
Transport for London, functions transferred to, **26(1)**, [646]

Worcester
statutes repealed, **41**, [709]

work
suspension from—
    employment tribunal, complaints to, **16**, [699]
    maternity grounds, on—
        alternative work, right to offer of, **16**, [696]
        meaning, **16**, [695]
        remuneration, right to, **16**, [697]
    medical grounds, on—
        exclusions from right to remuneration, **16**, [694]
        meaning, **16**, [693]
        remuneration, right to, **16**, [693]
        remuneration, calculation of, **16**, [698]
time off during. *See* **time off work**

work in progress
cessation of trade, transfer on, **44(3)**, [252]
meaning, **44(3)**, [183]
valuation—
    basis of, **44(3)**, [184]
    cessation, on, **44(3)**, [182]
    Commissioners, determination of questions by, **44(3)**, [186]
    cost, at, election for, **44(3)**, [185]

worker. *See also* **employee**
annual leave, right to, **16**, [1022]
meaning, **16**, [504], [656], [877], [964], [973]
protected disclosures. *See* **employee**

workers. *See also* **employee**
agricultural. *See* **agricultural workers**
forestry. *See* **forestry workers**
free movement of, **18**, [55], [58]

workers' co-operative
meaning, **44(1)**, [108]

working families' tax credit. *See also* **tax credits**
abolition of, **40(2)**, [361]

working hours
normal, meaning, **16**, [881]
time off during. *See* **time off work**

working tax credit
child care element, **40(2)**, [372]
entitlement, **40(2)**, [370]
immigration control, persons subject to, **40(2)**, [402]

working tax credit—*contd*
  introduction of, **40(2)**, [361]
  liability of officers for sums paid to
    employers, **40(2)**, [386]
  maximum rate, **40(2)**, [371]
  payment by employer, **40(2)**, [385]
    failure to make correct payments,
      40(2), [393]

workman. *See* **employee**

workmen's compensation
  administration of, **40(1)**, [717]
  continuation of, **40(1)**, [355], [488]
  dependant, meaning, **40(2)**, [538]
  meaning, **40(1)**, [490]
  regulations, **40(1)**, [489]
  schemes for supplementing, **40(1)**, [488]

workplace
  meaning, **35(1)**, [648]
  sanitary conveniences in—
    notice as to, local authority, by,
      35(1), [589]
    provision of, **35(1)**, [589]

workplace parking levy
  licensing schemes—
    appeals, **38(2)**, [184]
    authorities making, **38(2)**, [167]
      powers of, **38(2)**, [181]
    charges—
      different, for different cases, **38(2)**, [175]
      payment of, **38(2)**, [167]
      penalty, **38(2)**, [178]
    confirmation, **38(2)**, [173]
    consultation and inquiries, **38(2)**, [174]
    definitions, **38(2)**, [187]
    disputes, determination of, **38(2)**, [184]
    enforcement, **38(2)**, [178]
    exemptions, **38(2)**, [176]
    financial provisions, **38(2)**, [213]
    guidance, issue of, **38(2)**, [182]
    information, disclosure of, **38(2)**, [183]
    licence—
      contents of, **38(2)**, [177]
      provision for, **38(2)**, [175]
      scope of, **38(2)**, [167]
    local, **38(2)**, [168]
      joint, **38(2)**, [169]
      joint local–London, **38(2)**, [170]
    making of, **38(2)**, [172]
    matters to be dealt with, **38(2)**, [175]
    meaning, **38(2)**, [167]
    regulations and orders, **38(2)**, [186]
    rights of entry, **38(2)**, [179]
  parking places, provision of, **38(2)**, [171]

workshops. *See also* **factories and workshops**
  employment of women in, soon after birth,
    prohibition of, **35(1)**, [147]

Works, Commissioners of. *See* **Crown lands**

Works, Minister of
  corporation sole, as, **10**, [498]
  documents, proof of, **10**, [498]
  Orders in Council, **10**, [499]
  seal of, **10**, [498]
  Westminster Hospital site—
    buildings, power to erect, **10**, [510]
    compensation for alterations, **10**, [508]
    district railway, not interfering with,
      10, [511]
    Land Clauses Act, incorporation of,
      10, [507]
    London Passenger Transport Board, and,
      10, [511]
    obstruction, **10**, [512]
    power to acquire, **10**, [506]
    surveying, entry on land for, **10**, [509]

works of art. *See also names of art galleries and*
museums
  capital gains tax exemption, **42**, [1401]
  imported, auctioneer's commission on,
    50(S), VAT 1, 5
  inheritance tax. *See* **inheritance tax**
  value added tax, **50**, [32]
    exemption from, **50**, [153]

works truck
  vehicle excise duty, **13**, [1044]

World Health Organisation
  International Health Regulations,
    implementation of, **35(S)**, Public Health 1

worship, place of. *See* **place of worship**
  sites, reverter of. *See* **land**

wreck
  adjoining lands, power to pass over,
    39(2), [912]
  aircraft, application of law to, **4(1)**, [137]
  application of provisions, **39(2)**, [909]
  cargo from, **39(2)**, [915]
  coastguard, remuneration for services by,
    39(2), [928]
  Commissioner, **39(2)**, [974]
  concealment of, **39(2)**, [924]
  dangerous, approaching, **39(2)**, [463]
  delivery of, **39(2)**, [922]
  discharge of functions, **39(2)**, [909]
  finding, action on, **39(2)**, [914]
  fishing boat and gear, when treated as,
    1(1), [769]
  foreign port, taking to, **39(2)**, [923]
  historic, protection of sites, **39(2)**, [462]
  impeding lifesaving, **12(1)**, [74]
  interference with, **39(2)**, [924]
  magistrate preserving, assault on, **12(1)**, [93]
  meaning, **39(2)**, [933]
  offences, **39(2)**, [464], [923]–[925]
  oil pollution consequent on removal,
    49, [474]
  owners, claim of, **39(2)**, [917]

wreck—*contd*

plunder, liability for damage, **39(2)**, [913]

protected, function of Historic Buildings and Monuments Commission, **32**, [542]

protection of, implementation of international agreements relating to, **39(2)**, [1026]

receiver—

direction of, disobeying, **39(2)**, [910]

discharge from liability, **39(2)**, [922]

expenses and fees of, **39(2)**, [927]

immediate sale by, **39(2)**, [918]

notice, giving, **39(2)**, [916]

powers of, **39(2)**, [925]

vessel in distress, powers and duties where, **39(2)**, [910], [911]

removal of—

authorities, resolution of questions between, **39(2)**, [932]

conservancy authority, powers of, **39(2)**, [930]

harbour authority, powers of, **39(2)**, [930]

harbour master, by, **39(2)**, [53]

lighthouse authority, powers of, **39(2)**, [931]

Queen's harbour master, by, **39(2)**, [140]

Revenue and Customs control, release of goods from, **39(2)**, [929]

salvage, **39(2)**, [921]

Secretary of State, functions of, **39(2)**, [926]

summary of provisions, **39(2)**, [1]

taking possession of, action on, **39(2)**, [914]

temporary exclusion zones—

offences, **39(2)**, [766]

power to establish, **39(2)**, [765]

Thames, removal from, **49**, [527]

unclaimed—

Crown right to, **39(2)**, [919]

disposal of, **39(2)**, [921]

persons entitled, notice given to, **39(2)**, [920]

writing

meaning, **41**, [605]

print, included in term, **20**, [436]

writs

abolition of—

appraisement, **13**, [43]

capias ad respondendum, **13**, [43]

diem clausit extremum, **13**, [35], [43]

extent, **13**, [35], [43]

scire facias, **13**, [43]

stamp duty on, **41**, [152], [157]

subpoena ad respondendum, **13**, [43]

summons under Crown Suits Act 1865, **13**, [43]

wrongful interference with goods. *See also* **bailment**

co-ownership, **45**, [972]

competing rights to goods, **45**, [970]

concurrent actions, **45**, [971]

contributing negligence, **45**, [965], [973]

conversion—

action in, **45**, [964]

wrongful interference with goods—*contd*

conversion—*contd*

co-ownership no defence, **45**, [972]

denial of title not of itself being, **45**, [973]

Crown, provisions binding on, **45**, [978]

damages—

additional to return of goods, **45**, [965]

claim for, **45**, [965]

claimant's liability to third party, **45**, [967]

order for payment, **45**, [965]

reduction for contributory negligence, **45**, [965]

two or more claimants, **45**, [969]

delivery up of goods—

bailor, payment to bailee, **45**, [965]

damages in addition, **45**, [965]

interlocutory order for, **45**, [966]

order for, **45**, [965]

detention of goods—

improvement allowance, **45**, [965], [968]

interlocutory relief, **45**, [966]

judgment in respect of, form, **45**, [965]

orders, **45**, [965]

relief—

court's discretion as to, **45**, [965]

form of, **45**, [965]

interlocutory, **45**, [966]

detinue, abolition, **45**, [945], [964]

double liability, **45**, [969]

goods, meaning, **45**, [976]

improvement of goods, allowance for, **45**, [965], [968]

jus tertii rule, abolition, **45**, [970]

meaning, **45**, [963]

Northern Ireland, application of provisions, **45**, [976]

pledge, goods received by way of, **45**, [973]

possessory title, claimant having, **45**, [969]

proceedings—

concurrent actions, **45**, [971]

consumer protection, including, **45**, [963]

county court, transfer to High Court, **45**, [971]

detention of goods, for, **45**, [965]

meaning, **45**, [966]

rules of court, **45**, [966], [970]

purchaser in good faith, position of, **45**, [968]

sale of goods—

authorised by Court, **45**, [975]

in good faith, **45**, [972]

summary of provisions, **45**, [945]

third party, claimant accounting over to, **45**, [967]

title—

competing rights, **45**, [970]

denial of, not necessarily conversion, **45**, [973]

extinction, **45**, [967]

particulars by plaintiff, **45**, [970]

transitional provisions, **45**, [982]

trespass to goods—

co-ownership no defence, **45**, [972]

contributory negligence, **45**, [973]

trover, **45**, [963]

Y

yards
  appurtenant to building, paving and
    drainage, **35(1)**, [606]
  common, used in, sweeping and cleansing,
    35(1), [130]
  entrance to, circulation of air through,
    35(1), [607]

year
  commencement, **45**, [918]
  common, **45**, [920]
  leap, **45**, [920]

Yelverton's Act
  Northern Ireland—
    application to, **31**, [622]
    text, **31**, [632]–[634]

York
  Chancery Court. *See* **Chancery Court of**
    York
  registrar, office of, **14**, 836–7
  senior bishop, **14**, 1109

Yorkshire Deeds Registries
  charges registered in, transfer of, **21**, [363]
  closed registers, disposal of, **21**, [364]
  closing, indemnity for loss by, **21**, [366]
  registrars, provisions as to, **21**, [365]
  registration in, proof of, **21**, [367]

young offenders
  accommodation for. *See* **local authority**
  adult, charged jointly with, **11(2)**, [444],
    [453]
  age, determining, **12(2)**, [834]
  anti-social behaviour, and. *See* **anti-social**
    behaviour
  armed forces, service law in, amendment,
    6, [551]
  arrest of, **6**, [126]
    See also under **child**
  attendance centre, meaning, **12(1)**, [275AS]
  bail, grant of, **6**, [34]
  committal—
    alternative periods, **6**, [606]
    local authority accommodation, to,
      6, [545]
  contempt, detention for, **12(2)**, [800]
  conviction while subject to referral order,
    12(2), [745]
  court proceedings—
    absence, in, **6**, [29]
    particulars, prohibition on publication,
      6, [428]
    See also **child**
  crime, provisions as to, **6**, [1]

young offenders—*contd*
  custodial sentence—
    general restriction, **12(1)**, [781]
    limitation on, **12(1)**, [1114]
  custody—
    for life, **12(2)**, [784]–[786]
    legal, **12(1)**, [328D]
  dangerous, committal for sentence,
    12(2), [716]
  default, detention for, **12(2)**, [800]
  deposition of, power to take, **6**, [30]
  detention—
    contempt, for, **12(2)**, [800]
    custody of constable, in, **12(1)**, [710]
    default, for, **12(2)**, [800]
    detention and training order, interaction
      with, **12(2)**, [798]
    eighteen years, offender under, **12(2)**, [781]
    Her Majesty's pleasure, at, **12(2)**, [781]
    meaning, **12(1)**, [328G]
    place of, **12(2)**, [783]
    specified period, for, **12(2)**, [782], [783]
    transitional provisions, **12(1)**, [797]
    young offender institution, in—
      consecutive sentences, **12(2)**, [788]
      detention and training order, interaction
        with, **12(2)**, [797]
      offender between 18 and 21,
        12(2), [787]
      place of, **12(2)**, [789]
      sentence of imprisonment, conversion
        to, **12(2)**, [790]
      term of, **12(2)**, [788]
    youth detention accommodation,
      meaning, **12(2)**, [799]
  detention and training orders—
    consecutive terms, **12(2)**, [792]
    detention in young offender institution,
      interaction with sentence of, **12(2)**, [797]
    early release from, **12(4)**, [339]
    meaning, **12(2)**, [791]
    offences during currency of, **12(2)**, [796]
    period of, **12(2)**, [793]
    power to make, **12(2)**, [791]
    remands, taking account of, **12(2)**, [792]
    sentence of detention, interaction with,
      12(2), [798]
    supervision—
      breach of requirements, **12(2)**, [795]
      period of, **12(2)**, [794]
      supervisor, **12(2)**, [794]
    term of, **12(2)**, [792], [793]; **12(3)**, [1026]
    youth detention accommodation,
      meaning, **12(2)**, [799]
  detention centre, change in reference to,
    12(1), [1114]

young offenders—*contd*
detention of—
accommodation for, **6**, [321]
community home, in, **6**, [127]
release, **6**, [126]
escape—
aiding, **12(1)**, [275AE]
harbouring after, **12(1)**, [328A]
mentally disordered persons, arrest of,
12(1), [394]
financial penalties—
magistrates' courts, limit on power of,
12(2), [812]
parent or guardian—
financial circumstances, power to order
statement as to, **12(2)**, [813]
fixing of amount, **12(2)**, [815]
responsibility of for payment,
12(2), [814]
fine on—
enforcement of, **11(2)**, [499], [518]
maximum, **11(2)**, [444]
guilty plea, committal for sentence on
indication of, **12(2)**, [715]
powers of Crown Court, **12(2)**, [720]
related offences, with, **12(2)**, [718]
imprisonable offence, convicted of, **6**, [120]
imprisonment—
application of provisions, **12(2)**, [87]
restriction on, **12(2)**, [780]
sentence of detention, conversion of,
12(2), [790]
institution, detention in, **12(1)**, [260]
abolition of sentence, **12(2)**, [996]
parent or guardian, binding over,
12(2), [827]
regulations, **12(2)**, [747]
investigations by local authority, **6**, [119]
oath by, form of, **6**, [78]
offences committed by, restriction on
proceedings, **6**, [117]
See further **child**
offences triable on indictment or summarily—
plea, intention as to, **11(2)**, [445]
absence during, **11(2)**, [446]
proceedings, adjournment of,
11(2), [447]
single justice, functions exercisable by,
11(2), [448]
persons under 17 as, **6**, [549], [555]
prison, detention in. *See* imprisonment *above*
prosecution, alternatives to, **6(S)**, 292, 304–8
referral conditions, **12(4)**, [485]
referral order, power to revoke, **12(4)**, [486]
release—
on licence—
transitional provisions, **12(1)**, [406]
after, **6**, [548]
remand centre—
committal to, **12(1)**, [260]
jurisdiction over, **12(1)**, [275AM]
management rules, **12(1)**, [275AN]
provision, **12(1)**, [275AM]
provisions applicable, **12(1)**, [275AM]
provisions ceasing to exist, **12(2)**, [994]

young offenders—*contd*
remand centre—*contd*
release, temporary, rules as to,
12(1), [275AN]
women prisoners, detention in,
12(1), [275AM]
remand of, **6**, [321]
alternative periods, **6**, [606]
bail, on, **6**, [123]
conditions, breaking, **6**, [122]
reparation orders—
amendment, **12(2)**, [850]
appeals, **12(2)**, [850]
appropriate court, meaning, **12(2)**, [850]
breach of requirement, **12(2)**, [850]
obligations of person subject to,
12(2), [772]
power to make, **12(2)**, [771]
presence of offender in court, **12(2)**, [850]
provisions of, **12(2)**, [772]
report before, **12(2)**, [771]
requirements of, **12(2)**, [772]
revocation, **12(2)**, [850]
reports on, **12(1)**, [328F]
reprimands and warnings, **6**, [1], [604]–[605]
rules of court, **12(2)**, [748]
rules, offences against, **12(1)**, [328B]
secure accommodation, remand and committal
to, **12(3)**, [57]
secure training centres—
contracted out—
custody officers, powers and duties of,
12(2), [182]
management, intervention by Secretary
of State, **12(2)**, [184]
officers of, **12(2)**, [181]
contracted out functions, **12(2)**, [185]
contracting out, **12(2)**, [180]
custody officers—
certification, **12(2)**, [186], [252]
contracted out centres, at, **12(2)**, [182]
meaning, **12(2)**, [186]
protection of, **12(2)**, [187]
suspected offenders, power to detain,
12(2), [183]
escort arrangement, **12(2)**, [186], [251]
lease or tenancy of land, **12(2)**, [180]
summary of provisions, **12(1)**, [1]
summary trial of indictable offence,
11(2), [444]
supervisor, directions by, **6**, [443]
transitional provisions, **12(1)**, [797]
transitory and transitional provisions,
12(4), [577]
treatment of, alteration in, **6**, [118]
unlawfully at large, **12(1)**, [275AO];
12(2), [19]
violent or sexual offence, convicted of,
6, [120]
young offender institutions—
management rules, **12(1)**, [275AN]
provision, **12(1)**, [275AM]
release, temporary, rules as to,
12(1), [275AN]

young offenders—*contd*

youth conditional caution—
  code of practice, **6(S)**, 306–7
  failure to comply with conditions,
    6(S), 306
  financial penalties, **6(S)**, 305
  five requirements, **6(S)**, 305
  power to give, **6(S)**, 304–5
  sentencing powers, restriction on,
    6(S), 306
  variation of conditions, **6(S)**, 306
youth court. *See* **youth court**
youth custody centres, change in reference
  to, **12(1)**, [1114]
youth default orders, **11(S)**, Courts 5, 36–8
youth detention accommodation, wrongful
  disclosure of information, **12(2)**, [188]
youth offender contract—
  agreement with offender, **12(2)**, [738]
  duration of, **12(2)**, [739]
  extension of period. **12(2)**, [744], [840]
  failure to agree, **12(2)**, [740]
youth offender panel—
  duty and power to refer to, **12(2)**, [731]
  establishment of, **12(2)**, [736]
  further offences during referral,
    12(2), [842]
  meetings—
    attendance at, **12(2)**, [737]
    final, **12(2)**, [742]
    first, **12(2)**, [738]–[740]
    progress, **12(2)**, [741]
    reference to, **12(2)**, [736]
  members, **12(2)**, [736]
  other court's sentencing powers, effect on,
    12(2), [734]
  parent or guardian, referral for breach of
    order, **12(2)**, [841]
  parents, attendance of, **12(2)**, [735]
  referral back to court, **12(2)**, [745], [839],
    [840]
  referral conditions, **12(2)**, [732]
  referral order—
    conviction while subject to, **12(2)**, [745]
    making, **12(2)**, [733]
    revocation where offender making good
      progress, **12(2)**, [743]
youth offending team—
  functions of, **12(2)**, [746]
  referral order, implementation of,
    12(2), [733]

young person. *See also* **child; children and
young persons; local authority (children
etc); minor**
age for employment, **16**, [9]
arrest of. *See* **young offenders**
arrested—
  after charge, dealing with, **12(1)**, [882]
  before charge, dealing with, **12(1)**, [876]
  juvenile, duty of custody officer,
    12(1), [882]
  local authority, transferred to care of,
    12(1), [882]
coal mines, employment in, **16**, [5]

young person—*contd*

Convention on employment, **16**, [9]
court proceedings, in, particulars, prohibition
  on publishing, **6**, [428]
criminal proceedings, in. *See* **child; young
offenders**
deposition of, power to take, **6**, [30]
detention of. *See* **young offenders**
dog, owning, **2**, [684]
employment in mine or quarry—
  medical examination, regulations as to,
    savings, **17(1)**, [121]
  unlawful, parent's responsibility,
    17(1), [139], [143]
employment of. *See also* **employment**
  factories, ascertainment of age, **18**, [1201]
  fitness for work, certificates as to,
    18, [1173]
  holidays, removal of restrictions as to,
    16, [156]
  hours, removal of restrictions as to,
    16, [156]
  restrictions on, removal of, **16**, [156]
  school-leaving age—
    meaning, **16**, [156]
    provisions as to, **16**, [156]
employment, regulation of, **16**, [1]
factories and workshops, employment in,
  16, [5]
financial relief, persons over eighteen, **6**, [439]
gambling, protection from. *See* **gambling**
harmful publications supplied to—
  corrupt, tending to, **12(1)**, [278]
  defences, **12(1)**, [279]
  importation, prohibition, **12(1)**, [281]
  meaning, **12(1)**, [278]
  plate for making, having, **12(1)**, [280]
  printing, publishing and selling,
    12(1), [279]
  prosecution, **12(1)**, [279]
  search warrant, **12(1)**, [280]
  seizure of, **12(1)**, [280]
horse riding, protective headgear—
  definitions, **6**, [458]
  Northern Ireland provisions, **6**, [459]
  regulations, **6**, [457]
  requirement, **6**, [456]
industrial undertakings, in, **16**, [5]
intoxicating liquor, sale to. *See* **intoxicating
liquor**
intoxicating substances, supply to,
  12(1), [967]
meaning, **6**, [1], [120]; **12(1)**, [282]; **16**, [7];
  17(1), [153]
mines, employment in, **16**, [5]
oath by, form of, **6**, [78]
offence by. *See* **child; young offenders**
offences against, special provisions, **6**, [58]
parent or guardian as security for,
  12(1), [647]
place of safety for. *See* **child**
quarries, employment in, **16**, [5]
registers of, maintenance, **16**, [5], [9]
remand, on—
  accommodation for, **6**, [120], [321]

young person—*contd*
　remand, on—*contd*
　　conditions, breaking, **6**, [122]
　　electronic monitoring conditions, **6**, [121]
　restriction, **16**, [5]
　sexual offences with. *See* **sexual offences**
　ship, employed on, **39(2)**, [722]
　social services functions, **6(S)**, 439
　social work services, provision of—
　　discharge of care functions, arrangements
　　　for—
　　　effect of, **6(S)**, 437
　　　piloting and expiry of, **6(S)**, 439
　　　power to enter into, **6(S)**, 434
　　　restrictions on, **6(S)**, 436
　　piloting and expiry of arrangements,
　　　6(S), 439
　　providers, regulation of, **6(S)**, 438
　　summary of provisions, **6(S)**, 427
　study or training, time off work for—
　　employment tribunal, complaint to,
　　　16, [692]
　　remuneration, **16**, [691]
　　right of, **16**, [690]
　suicide of, aiding, **12(1)**, [332]
　unruly character, with, committal,
　　12(4), [248]
　tattooing, **6**, [106]
　well-being of, **6(S)**, 440

youth community orders. *See also*
attendance centre order, etc
　electronic monitoring of requirements,
　　12(2), [751]
　Isles of Scilly, provisions applying to,
　　12(2), [766]
　meaning, **12(2)**, [750]

youth court
　application of provisions, **11(2)**, [576]
　assignment of matters to, **6**, [34]
　care proceedings—
　　execution of process, **6**, [145]
　　local authority, investigations by, **6**, [119]
　composition, London, **25(1)**, [758]
　day for sitting, **6**, [36]
　joint charge, hearing, **6**, [34]
　justice of the peace, authorisation to sit as
　　member, **6**, [33]
　juvenile court, change of name, **6**, [1], [550]
　magistrates' court, remission to on offender
　　reaching 18, **12(2)**, [724]
　matters assigned to, **6**, [34]
　meaning, **6**, [1], [33]
　medical evidence, **6**, [77]
　oath, form of, **6**, [78]
　offence committed by child, jurisdiction on,
　　6, [76]
　panel, **6**, [1]
　person between 17 and 18, before, **6**, [79]
　person over 17, before, **6**, [36]
　powers, **6**, [36], [603]
　procedure in, **6**, [33], [35]
　remission of young offenders for sentence,
　　12(2), [723]

youth court—*contd*
　remission to, **11(2)**, [453]
　restrictions on newspaper reporting, **6**, [37],
　　[89]
　rules, **11(2)**, [576]
　saving for, **11(2)**, [572]
　sittings, **6**, [36]
　transitional provisions and savings,
　　11(3), [313]

youth custody centre
　change of name, **12(1)**, [1114]
　See now **young offenders**

youth employment service
　disabled persons, representation of, **16**, [44]

youth justice
　Board. *See* **Youth Justice Board**
　definitions, **12(2)**, [679]
　local provision of services, **12(2)**, [675]
　plans, **12(2)**, [677]
　system—
　　aim of, **12(2)**, [674]
　　Northern Ireland. *See* **Northern Ireland**
　youth offending teams, **12(2)**, [676]

Youth Justice Board
　annual reports and accounts, **12(2)**, [696]
　constitution, **12(2)**, [678]
　directions to, **12(2)**, [678]
　expenses, **12(2)**, [696]
　functions, **12(2)**, [678]
　members, **12(2)**, [678], [696]
　procedure, **12(2)**, [696]

youth offending teams
　functions of, **12(2)**, [745]

youth rehabilitation order
　activity requirement, **12(4)**, [551]
　adjournment of proceedings, **12(4)**, [559]
　amendment, **12(4)**, [554], [557]
　appearance of offender in court, **12(4)**, [559]
　attendance centre requirement, **12(4)**, [551]
　breach of, **12(4)**, [554], [555]
　compliance with requirements, date for,
　　12(4), [553]
　consequential amendments, **12(4)**, [562]
　curfew requirement, **12(4)**, [551]
　drug treatment requirement, **12(4)**, [551]
　drug testing requirement, **12(4)**, [551]
　education requirement, **12(4)**, [551]
　electronic monitoring requirement,
　　12(4), [550], [551]
　exclusion requirement, **12(4)**, [551]
　fostering, with, **12(4)**, [550], [551]
　further proceedings, **12(4)**, [553]
　intensive supervision and surveillance, with,
　　12(4), [550]
　interpretation, **12(4)**, [470]
　intoxicating substance treatment requirement,
　　12(4), [551]
　Isles of Scilly, provisions applying,
　　12(4), [471]

youth rehabilitation order—*contd*
local authority residence requirement,
12(4), [551]
meaning, **12(4)**, [464]
mental health treatment requirement,
12(4), [551]
Northern Ireland, transfer to, **12(4)**, [560],
[561]
power to make, **12(4)**, [464]
programme requirement, **12(4)**, [551]
prohibited activity requirement, **12(4)**, [551]
proposal to make, considerations, **12(4)**, [552]
provisions in, **12(4)**, [553]
qualifying officer, meaning, **12(4)**, [467]

youth rehabilitation order—*contd*
related amendments, **12(4)**, [563]
requirements in, **12(4)**, [464], [550], [551]
residence requirement, **12(4)**, [551]
responsible officer—
meaning, **12(4)**, [467]
offender, duties to and by, **12(4)**, [468]
revocation, **12(4)**, [554], [556]
subsequent conviction, powers of court,
12(4), [558]
supervision requirement, **12(4)**, [551]
unpaid work requirement, **12(4)**, [551]
warrants, **12(4)**, [559]

Enquiry Bureau hsieb@lexisnexis.co.uk

Z

Zambia, Republic of
Barotseland, agreements relating to,
  7(2), [558]
Commonwealth citizenship, **31**, [186]
establishment of, **7(2)**, [556]
existing law, operation of, **7(2)**, [557]
visiting forces in, **7(2)**, [560]

Zanzibar. *See also* **Tanzania**
British ship registered in, **7(2)**, [542]
existing law, operation of, **7(2)**, [540]
foreign jurisdiction, **7(2)**, [543]
independent state, becoming, **7(2)**, [540]
repeal of enactments, **7(2)**, [634]
Tanzania, becoming, **7(2)**, [632]
visiting forces in, **7(2)**, [542]

Zimbabwe
amnesty for certain acts, **7(2)**, [730]
colonial probates in, **7(2)**, [735]
Commonwealth citizenship, **31**, [186]
constitution of, **7(2)**, [711]–[712]
dentist, registration of, **7(2)**, [735]
independence for, **7(2)**, [729]
maintenance orders, enforcement in,
  7(2), [735]
member of Commonwealth, provisions for
  becoming, **7(2)**, [732]
powers exercisable on independence,
  7(2), [731]
veterinary surgeon, registration of, **7(2)**, [735]

zoo
animals—
  care and wellbeing, **2**, [566]
  closure, welfare following, **2**, [584], [585]
  disposal of, **2**, [586]
  inspection, **2**, [573]
  meaning, **2**, [591]
closed—
  disposal of animals, **2**, [586]
  inspection of, **2**, [575]
closure—
  animals, welfare of, **2**, [584], [585]
  direction—
    appeals, **2**, [588]
    licence, revocation of, **2**, [582]
    notification, **2**, [590]
    power to make, **2**, [582]
    zoos without licences, on, **2**, [583]
  offences and penalties, **2**, [589]

zoo—*contd*
closure—*contd*
  section, of, **2**, [562]
conservation measures, **2**, [563]
damage liability, insurance against, **2**, [567]
dangerous animals kept in, **2**, [412]
directions, notification of, **2**, [590]
enforcement of provisions, **2**, [580]–[589]
inspection—
  closed zoo, of, **2**, [575]
  grant, etc of licence, before, **2**, [572]
  informal, **2**, [576]
  objection to inspector, **2**, [573]
  periods for, **2**, [573]
  persons competent for, **2**, [570]
  provisions applicable to, **2**, [573], [574]
  special, **2**, [574]
licence—
  alteration, **2**, [580]
  appeals respecting, **2**, [588]
  application—
    matters to be specified, **2**, [564]
    notices to be given, **2**, [564]
    representations as to, **2**, [565]
  conditions attached to, **2**, [567]
    enforcement, **2**, [581]
  considerations for granting, **2**, [565]
  dispensation for certain zoos, **2**, [578]
  fees and charges, **2**, [579]
  grant of, **2**, [566]
  inspections before grant etc of, **2**, [572]
  local authorities for issuing, **2**, [562]
  periods of, **2**, [567]
  refusal of, **2**, [566]
  renewal, **2**, [568]
  requirement for, **2**, [562]
  revocation, zoo closure direction, on
    making, **2**, [582]
  surrender, **2**, [569]
  transfer or transmission, **2**, [569]
local authority—
  fees and charges by, **2**, [579]
  owned by, licensing, **2**, [577]
meaning, **2**, [562]
offences and penalties, **2**, [589]
powers of entry, **2**, [587]
section, meaning, **2**, [562]
small, modification of provisions for, **2**, [578]
standards of practice, **2**, [571]
veterinary practitioners—
  charges for services, **2**, [570]
  Minister's list of, **2**, [570]